Mitchell Repair™
Information Company

D0514712

ELECTRICAL SERVICE & REPAIR

1999 Domestic Vehicles

FORD MOTOR CO.

Accessories & Equipment

Latest Changes & Corrections

HOW TO FIND
THE INFORMATION

3 Quick Steps

1 On facing page, you'll find the Contents of this manual arranged according to manufacturer. Locate the manufacturer of the vehicle you're working on...notice it has a Black square next to it.

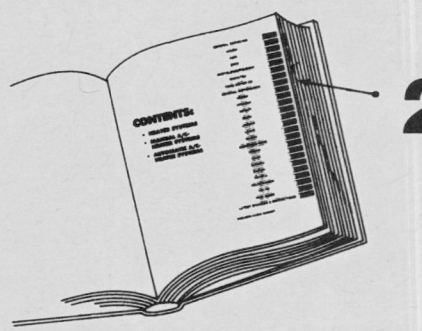

2 **THUMB INDEX RECTANGLE**

Looking along the right-hand edge of the manual, you'll notice additional Black squares. Match the Black square of the appropriate manufacturer with the Black squares in line with it on the manual's edge. Turn directly to the first page (Contents Page) of that manufacturer's "section".

3 Scan the Subjects listed in the Contents page: then turn to the page indicated for the Specific Information you desire.

Information Company

ELECTRICAL SERVICE & REPAIR

1999 Domestic Vehicles

FORD MOTOR CO.

Accessories & Equipment

Latest Changes & Corrections

Mitchell Repair™
Information Company

| ACKNOWLEDGMENT | Mitchell Repair Information Company thanks the domestic and import automobile and light truck manufacturers, distributors, and dealers for their generous cooperation and assistance which make this manual possible. |

MARKETING

Senior Vice President
David Peterson

Directors
David R. Koontz
Daniel Ramirez

Product Managers
Catherine Smith
Victor Addison
Nick DiVerde
Robert Gardner
Brian Warfield

TECHNICAL LIBRARIAN
Debbie Hickman

EDITORIAL

Director, Annual Data Editorial
Mike Mancini

Director, Special Product Editorial
Ronald E. Garrett

Senior Editors
Chuck Vedra (ASE-Quadruple Master)
Ramiro Gutierrez
John M. Fisher (ASE)
Tom L. Hall (ASE-Quadruple Master)
James A. Hawes (ASE-Quadruple Master)
Eddie Santangelo (ASE)

Technical Editors
Thomas L. Landis
Scott A. Olsen (ASE)
Bob Reel
David W. Himes (ASE)
Alex A. Solis (ASE)
James R. Warren (ASE)
Bobby R. Gifford (ASE)
Linda M. Murphy (ASE)
Donald Lawler (ASE)
Wayne D. Charbonneau (ASE-World Class)
Sal Caloca (ASE)
Bud Gardner (ASE)
Robert L. Eller (ASE-Quadruple Master)
John Schartz (ASE)
Richard C. Hamilton (ASE-Quadruple Master)
Leonid A. Shneyder (ASE)
Brian Yockey (ASE)
John Howard (ASE)
Todd Mercer (ASE)
James Barrow (ASE)
Demian Hurst (ASE)
Jeff Wyatt (ASE)
Patrick Bolton (ASE)
David Steckling (ASE)
Tim Flannery (ASE)
Robert Therieau
Susan Schalk (ASE)
Andrew Smith (ASE)

WIRING DIAGRAMS
Manager
Matthew M. Krimple

PRINT COMPOSITION
Brian Henderson
Julia Gillis (ASE)

TECHNICAL SUPPORT
Bob Pilz

PRODUCT SUPPORT
Product Specialists
James A. Wafford (ASE)
Jeff Hicks
David Block (ASE)
Carol Menickelly
Matt Mathews (ASE)
Bill Belliston (ASE)

GRAPHICS
Manager
Judith A. La Pierre
Supervisor
Ann Klimetz
Graphic Specialists
Sally Muhlbaier
Lynn Plummer
Percella Kuhns
Carmen Rusnak
Deb Eaton
Edder Naguit
Jordan Butcher
Cheryl Griffin
Jean Petaja
Robert Taylor

ISBN 0-8470-2215-3

Published By

MITCHELL REPAIR INFORMATION COMPANY
9889 Willow Creek Road
P.O. Box 26260
San Diego, California 92196-0260

© 1999 Mitchell Repair Information Company, LLC
All Rights Reserved

Printed in U.S.A.

Customer Service Numbers
For Subscription, Billing or Technical Information call:
1-888-724-6742 Toll Free or 858-549-7809
Or Write: P.O. Box 26260, San Diego, CA 92196-0260

ACCESSORIES & EQUIPMENT

ACCESSORIES & EQUIPMENT (Cont.)

1999 FORD MOTOR CO.
Contents (Cont.)

ACCESSORIES & EQUIPMENT (Cont.)

ACCESSORIES & EQUIPMENT (Cont.)

ACCESSORIES & EQUIPMENT (Cont.)

ACCESSORIES & EQUIPMENT (Cont.)

1999 FORD MOTOR CO.
Contents (Cont.)

ACCESSORIES & EQUIPMENT (Cont.)

ANALOG INSTRUMENT PANELS

ACCESSORIES & EQUIPMENT (Cont.)

ANALOG INSTRUMENT PANELS (Cont.)

1999 FORD MOTOR CO.
Contents (Cont.)

ACCESSORIES & EQUIPMENT (Cont.)

ACCESSORIES & EQUIPMENT (Cont.)

ACCESSORIES & EQUIPMENT (Cont.)

ACCESSORIES & EQUIPMENT (Cont.)

ACCESSORIES & EQUIPMENT (Cont.)

ACCESSORIES & EQUIPMENT (Cont.)

Adjustable Pedal Assembly Systems

WIRING DIAGRAMS

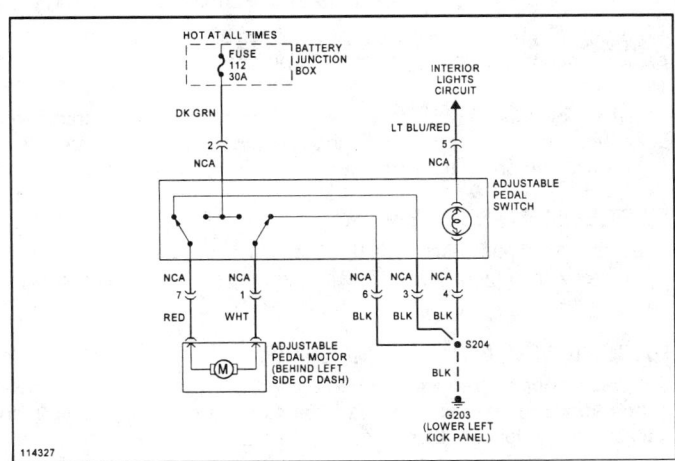

**Fig. 1: Adjustable Pedal Assembly System Wiring Diagram
(Expedition & Navigator – Without Memory)**

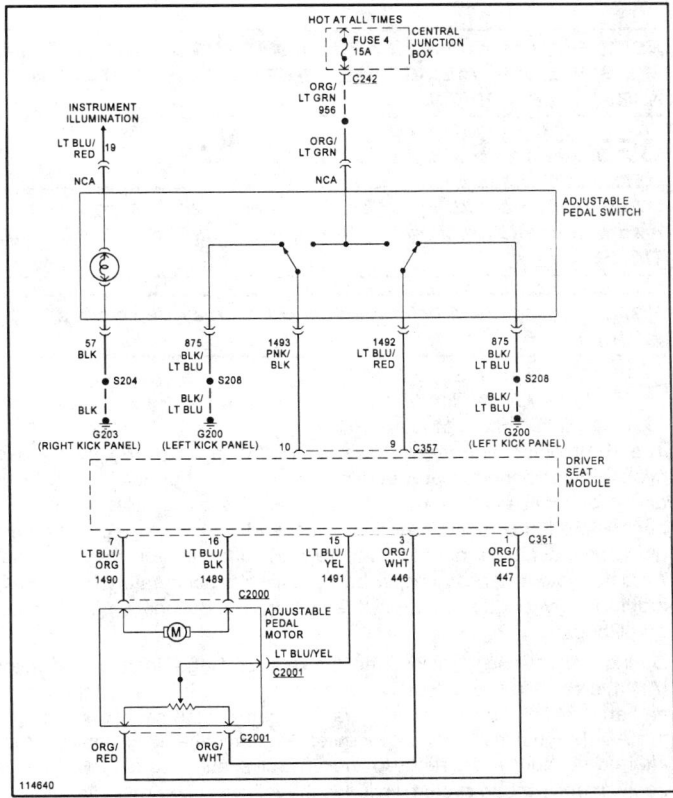

**Fig. 2: Adjustable Pedal Assembly System Wiring Diagram
(Navigator – With Memory)**

FORD
4-2

1999 ACCESSORIES & EQUIPMENT
Air Bag Restraint Systems – Continental, Contour, Cougar, Escort, Mustang, Mystique, Sable, Taurus & Tracer

NOTE: For information on air bag DIAGNOSIS & TESTING, see MITCHELL® AIR BAG SERVICE & REPAIR MANUAL, DOMESTIC & IMPORTED MODELS.

DESCRIPTION & OPERATION

WARNING: To avoid injury from accidental air bag deployment, read and carefully follow all WARNINGS and SERVICE PRECAUTIONS.

NOTE: Air Bag Diagnostic Monitor (ADM) may be referred to by other names:

- Electronic Crash Sensor (ECS).
- Electronic Crash Unit (ECU).
- Restraints Control Module (RCM).

The Supplemental Restraint System (SRS), also known as air bag system, is designed to provide increased accident protection for driver and passenger by deploying air bags in a front-end collision. The air bags, stored in center of steering wheel and in instrument panel above glove box, deploy in about 40 milliseconds after impact sensors close. Air bag system is designed to be used with 3-point safety belts. Seat mounted driver and passenger side air bags are optional on Continental and Cougar.

During a front-end collision, the air bag Air Bag Diagnostic Monitor (ADM) discriminates between an event that warrants air bag deployment and an event that does not. In a crash of sufficient force, two sensors in the ADM signal the air bag modules to simultaneously deploy. Both internal sensors must react to the impact simultaneously for air bag deployment. Air bag system includes the following components: Air Bag Diagnostic Monitor (ADM), two sensors (located inside the ADM), a back-up power supply (also located inside the ADM), driver air bag module, passenger air bag module, AIR BAG warning light, ignitor assemblies (located in air bag modules), clockspring, associated wiring harnesses and connectors.

AIR BAG DIAGNOSTIC MONITOR (ADM)

The ADM contains a microcomputer, (which monitors electrical system components and connections), two internal sensors, and a back-up power supply. ADM performs a system self-check of air bag system internal circuits every time ignition switch is turned to RUN position. ADM also energizes AIR BAG warning light during initial system self-check and whenever a fault is detected. Faults are stored in ADM memory and translated into flash codes which are displayed through AIR BAG warning light. ADM also communicates through Data Link Connector (DLC) current and historical Diagnostic Trouble Codes (DTCs). Fort location of ADM, see COMPONENT LOCATIONS table.

If a system fault exists and AIR BAG warning light is malfunctioning, ADM activates chime module, indicating need for service.

BACK-UP POWER SUPPLY

Back-up power supply is located inside ADM. If battery or battery cables are damaged in a collision before sensor circuit closes, back-up power supply will supply energy to deploy air bags. Back-up power supply will hold a deployment charge for approximately one minute after battery or cable is disconnected.

CLOCKSPRING

The steering column contains a clockspring contact assembly to transfer electrical signals from steering column wiring harness to driver air bag module. Clockspring is mounted on steering column between steering wheel and combination switch assembly.

DRIVER AIR BAG MODULE

The driver air bag module is mounted on front face of steering wheel, covered by steering wheel trim cover. When impact sensors close,

signaling an impact, ignitor triggers inflator. During ignition, sodium azide reacts with copper oxide, producing nitrogen gas, which inflates air bag.

When air bag deploys, tear-seams molded into steering wheel trim cover separate, allowing inflation of air bag assembly. Driver air bag module is not serviceable and must be replaced as a complete assembly.

ELECTRICAL SYSTEM

The main functions performed by electrical subsystem are switching electric power to ignitors for air bags, and monitoring readiness of air bag system.

PASSENGER AIR BAG MODULE

The passenger air bag module is mounted in right side of instrument panel, above glove box. When a impact sensors close, signaling an impact, air bag ignitors trigger inflator.

Since passenger air bag is larger than driver air bag, inflator contains more gas generant in a different configuration to produce more gas. When air bag is activated, instrument panel trim cover tears at seams and hinges, allowing inflation. Passenger air bag module is only serviced as a complete assembly.

SIDE AIR BAG MODULES (CONTINENTAL & COUGAR)

Side air bags are optional on Continental and Cougar. Air bag modules are mounted in seat backs. If ADM determines driver and passenger air bag deployment is necessary, side air bag sensors, mounted under each front seat, may also indicate the need for side air bag deployment. Because side air bags are controlled by separate sensors, they can be deployed individually or not at all, as determined by ADM.

When either side air bag is activated, seat bolster tears at seams to allow for inflation. Side air bag modules are not serviceable, and must be replaced as a complete assembly

SIDE AIR BAG IMPACT SENSORS (CONTINENTAL & COUGAR)

Side air bag impact sensors are located under each front seat. If ADM determines driver and passenger air bag deployment is necessary, side air bag sensors may also indicate the need for side air bag deployment by determining both severity and direction of impact. Because each sensor only controls one side air bag, ADM may deploy one, both or neither side air bag.

TONE GENERATOR

AIR BAG warning light is the primary means of determining air bag system condition; however, a series of audible tones, indicating that system requires servicing, will sound if AIR BAG warning light is not functioning, and a fault occurs in system. Unless serviced, air bag system may not function properly in an accident.

POST-COLLISION INSPECTION

If vehicle has been in a collision and air bags deployed, perform the following:

- Replace Air Bag Diagnostic Monitor (ADM).
- Inspect area near ADM for damage. ADM orientation is critical to proper operation. Repair as necessary.
- Replace air bag modules, (including deployed side air bag modules, if equipped).
- Replace Air Bag Diagnostic Monitor (ADM).
- Inspect undeployed side air bag modules, if equipped.
- Check side air bag crash sensors, if equipped.
- Inspect areas near air bag modules. If interfering with deployment, replace as necessary.
- Inspect steering wheel, clockspring and column for damage. Replace as necessary.

Air Bag Restraint Systems – Continental, Contour, Cougar, Escort, Mustang, Mystique, Sable, Taurus & Tracer (Cont.)

- Inspect wiring and harness connectors. Replace as necessary.
- Inspect seat belt assemblies for damage. Replace as necessary.
- Perform SYSTEM OPERATION CHECK.

If a collision has occurred and air bags did not deploy, perform the following:

- Remove both air bag modules and inspect wiring and connectors for damage.
- Check area near ADM for damage, check ADM for fit. ADM orientation is critical to proper operation. Repair as necessary.
- Inspect steering wheel, clockspring and column for damage. Replace as necessary.
- Inspect areas near air bag modules. If interfering with deployment, replace as necessary.
- Inspect side air bag sensors and nearby area (if equipped). Sensor orientation is critical to proper operation. Repair as necessary.

SYSTEM OPERATION CHECK

1) When checking air bag system operation (also known as prove out system), and upon completion of each diagnostic test, check for faults in air bag system. To check system, turn ignition switch to RUN position. If AIR BAG warning light illuminates for 4-8 seconds and then goes out, air bag system is functioning properly and no fault codes exist.

2) If a fault is detected in air bag system during initial system check, AIR BAG warning light will either fail to light, stay on continuously, or flash a code sequence. If AIR BAG warning light flashes, indicating a fault in system, count number of flashes after fault code has cycled twice. Number of flashes represents a code number used to diagnose air bag system. See MITCHELL® AIR BAG SERVICE & REPAIR MANUAL, DOMESTIC & IMPORTED MODELS.

3) If a system fault exists and AIR BAG warning light fails to light, an audible tone will be heard, indicating AIR BAG warning light is out and service is required.

SERVICE PRECAUTIONS

These precautions should be observed when working with air bag system:

- Disable air bag system before servicing any air bag system or steering column components. Failure to do so may result in accidental air bag deployment and personal injury. See DISABLING & ACTIVATING AIR BAG SYSTEM.
- Wait one minute after disabling air bag system before working on vehicle. Back-up power supply holds a deployment charge for approximately one minute after positive battery cable is disconnected. Servicing air bag system before one minute may cause accidental air bag deployment and possible personal injury.
- Because of critical system operating requirements, DO NOT service impact sensors, clockspring, ADM or air bag modules. Repairs are made by replacement only.
- Always wear safety glasses whenever servicing an air bag equipped vehicle or handling an air bag.
- When carrying a live air bag module, ensure air bag module and trim cover are pointed away from your body. This minimizes chance of injury in event of an accidental deployment.
- When placing a live air bag module on a bench or other surface, always face air bag module and trim cover facing up and away from surface. This will reduce motion of module if it is accidentally deployed.
- After deployment, air bag surface may contain deposits of sodium hydroxide, which may irritate skin. Sodium hydroxide is a product of gas generant combustion. Always wear gloves and safety glasses when handling a deployed air bag. Wash your hands using mild soap and water. Follow correct disposal procedures. See DISPOSAL PROCEDURES.
- If scrapping a vehicle with an undeployed air bag module, air bag must be deployed. See DISPOSAL PROCEDURES.

- If a part is replaced and new part does not correct condition, reinstall original part and perform diagnostic procedure again.
- Never probe connectors on air bag module. Doing so may cause air bag deployment and/or personal injury.
- Instruction to disconnect always refers to connector. DO NOT remove component from vehicle if instructed to disconnect.
- After any servicing, ensure AIR BAG warning light does not indicate any fault codes. See SYSTEM OPERATION CHECK.
- Replace air bag module if trim cover (deployment door) is marred or damaged. DO NOT repaint trim cover. Paint may degrade cover material. Replace air bag module as necessary. Ensure damaged air bag is deployed. See DISPOSAL PROCEDURES.

DISABLING & ACTIVATING AIR BAG SYSTEM

WARNING: Wait one minute after disabling air bag system before working on vehicle. Back-up power supply holds a deployment charge for approximately one minute after positive battery cable is disconnected. Servicing air bag system before one minute may cause accidental air bag deployment and possible personal injury.

CAUTION: When battery is disconnected, vehicle computer and memory systems may lose memory data. Driveability problems may exist until computer systems have completed a relearn cycle. See COMPUTER RELEARN PROCEDURES in GENERAL INFORMATION.

DISABLING SYSTEM

1) Record USER 1 and USER 2 preset radio frequencies for reprogramming (if equipped). Disconnect negative battery cable. Wait at least one minute for back-up power supply to deplete stored energy.

2) Remove driver air bag module. See DRIVER AIR BAG MODULE under REMOVAL & INSTALLATION. Connect appropriate air bag simulator to clockspring connector at top of steering column (in place of air bag). See AIR BAG SIMULATOR.

3) Remove passenger air bag module. See PASSENGER AIR BAG MODULE under REMOVAL & INSTALLATION. Connect appropriate air bag simulator to passenger air bag vehicle harness connector (in place of air bag).

4) If equipped with side air bags, remove both side air bag modules. See SIDE AIR BAG MODULE under REMOVAL & INSTALLATION. Connect appropriate air bag simulator to both side air bag connectors (in place of side air bags).

5) Connect negative battery cable. To reactivate SRS, see ACTIVATING SYSTEM under DISABLING & ACTIVATING AIR BAG SYSTEM.

AIR BAG SIMULATOR

An Air Bag Simulator (105-00012) or equivalent is required to perform diagnosis and testing of the air bag system. *See Fig. 1.* An air bag simulator is an approximately 2-ohm resistor, with appropriate connector, used to simulate an air bag module. DO NOT short-circuit air bag module connections with a zero-ohm jumper wire. If zero-ohm jumper is used, a Light Flash Code (LFC) will be displayed.

ACTIVATING SYSTEM

1) Disconnect negative battery cable. Wait at least one minute for back-up power supply to deplete stored energy. Remove air bag simulator from clockspring connector. Remove air bag simulator from passenger air bag vehicle harness connector. Install driver air bag module. See DRIVER AIR BAG MODULE under REMOVAL & INSTALLATION.

2) Install passenger air bag module. See PASSENGER AIR BAG MODULE under REMOVAL & INSTALLATION. Reconnect negative

FORD
4-4

1999 ACCESSORIES & EQUIPMENT
Air Bag Restraint Systems -- Continental, Contour, Cougar, Escort, Mustang, Mystique, Sable, Taurus & Tracer (Cont.)

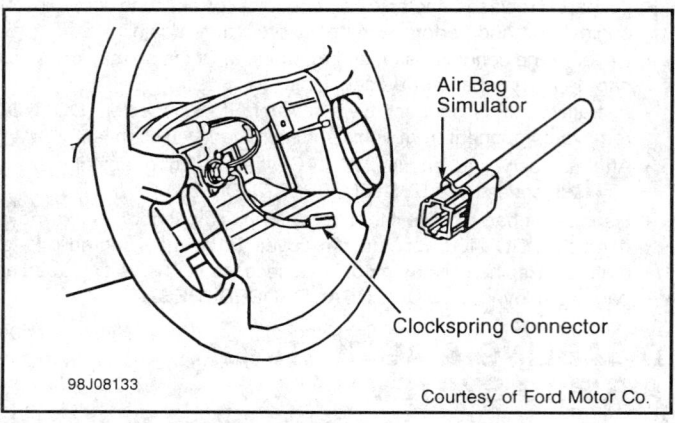

98J08133

Courtesy of Ford Motor Co.

Fig. 1: Identifying Air Bag Simulator

battery cable. Recheck system operation. See SYSTEM OPERATION CHECK. Reprogram USER 1 and USER 2 preset radio frequencies and set clock.

DISPOSAL PROCEDURES

WARNING: Refer to SERVICE PRECAUTIONS before proceeding.

Air bag disposal may be necessary in following situations:
- Scrapping vehicle with deployed air bag.
- Scrapping vehicle with live air bag.
- Disposal of a live but electrically faulty air bag module.
- Disposal of a deployed air bag module.

DEPLOYED AIR BAG

Dispose of deployed air bag module as any other part. Air bag module components are not reusable.

UNDEPLOYED AIR BAG – FAULTY UNIT

If an undeployed air bag module is diagnosed as faulty, remove air bag module and return intact to Ford Motor Company for proper disposal. Return carton for warranty claim credit. Air bag must be packaged and shipped according to U.S. Department of Transportation procedures. Retain replacement packaging including label. DO NOT deploy air bag.

SCRAPPED VEHICLE

CAUTION: DO NOT dispose of undeployed air bag module without first deploying air bag. If this is not possible through procedures outlined, contact vehicle manufacturer for further instructions.

If vehicle is to be scrapped, undeployed air bag module must first be deployed. Use the following procedure for deployment of air bag.

WARNING: Perform remote deployment outdoors. Keep all personnel at least 20 feet away to ensure physical and hearing safety from projected objects and loud noise of air bag deployment.

Remote Deployment Of Air Bag – This procedure is to be used when a vehicle with a live driver air bag is to be scrapped, but a problem in air bag electrical system prevents deployment with air bag still installed in vehicle.
1) Before proceeding, see SERVICE PRECAUTIONS. Deactivate air bag system. See DISABLING SYSTEM under DISABLING & ACTIVATING AIR BAG SYSTEM. Remove driver and/or passenger air bag module. See DRIVER AIR BAG MODULE and PASSENGER AIR BAG MODULE under REMOVAL & INSTALLATION.
2) With air bag module removed, cut air bag connector from wiring harness near air bag module. Strip 1" of insulation from wire ends.

Obtain 2 wires at least 20 feet long. Connect one end of each 20 foot wire to one end of each air bag module wire.

WARNING: When placing a live air bag on a bench or other surface, always face air bag and trim cover up and away from surface. This will reduce motion of air bag module if it is accidentally deployed.

3) Place air bag module with trim cover facing upward on a flat surface, in remote area such as parking lot or field. Remain at least 20 feet away from air bag module. Deploy air bag by touching loose ends of both wires to 12-volt battery terminals.
4) If successful, a loud noise will be heard and bag material will be visible. Allow at least 10 minutes for cooling and dissipation of air bag effluents before approaching air bag. Air bag is now inoperative. If air bag does not deploy, air bag module is faulty. Contact vehicle manufacturer for further instructions on disposal procedures.

REMOVAL & INSTALLATION

WARNING: Failure to follow service precautions may result in air bag deployment and personal injury. See SERVICE PRECAUTIONS. After component replacement, check system operation. See SYSTEM OPERATION CHECK.

CAUTION: When battery is disconnected, vehicle computer and memory systems may lose memory data. Driveability problems may exist until computer systems have completed a relearn cycle. See COMPUTER RELEARN PROCEDURES in GENERAL INFORMATION.

AIR BAG DIAGNOSTIC MONITOR

Removal & Installation (Continental) – 1) Before proceeding, see SERVICE PRECAUTIONS. The Air Bag Diagnostic Monitor (ADM) is mounted on the center tunnel. Disable air bag system. See DISABLING SYSTEM under DISABLING & ACTIVATING AIR BAG SYSTEM. Leave negative battery cable disconnected. If equipped with bench seats, go to next step. If equipped with bucket seats, go to step 3).
2) Remove driver bench seat. Disconnect 2 ADM electrical connector locking clips and 2 electrical connectors. Pull carpet back and remove 3 ADM bracket bolts. Remove ADM with bracket.
3) Remove floor console. See FLOOR CONSOLE. Remove rear seat ventilation duct. Pull carpet back and remove 3 center console mounting bracket nuts. Remove center console mounting bracket. Disconnect electrical connectors. Pull carpet back and remove 3 ADM bracket bolts. Remove ADM with bracket.
4) To install, reverse removal procedure. Tighten ADM bracket bolts to specification. See TORQUE SPECIFICATIONS. Activate air bag system.
5) New ADM must be programmed differently for vehicles with and without side air bag option. Verify all air bag system components and battery are connected. Use New Generation Star (NGS) scan tester. Insert Ford Service Function (FSF) card into NGS. Connect NGS to vehicle data link connector.
6) Turn igniton to run. Select SERVICE BAY FUNCTIONS. Select RCM – RESTRAINTS CONTROL MODULE. For vehicles with side air bag option, select AIR BAG CONFIGURATION 12. For vehicles without side air bag option, select AIR BAG CONFIGURATION 13.
7) Wait for MODULE CONFIGURATION COMPLETE message. Press trigger to exit. Turn ignition off. Ensure system is functioning properly. See SYSTEM OPERATION CHECK.
Removal & Installation (Contour & Mystique) – 1) Before proceeding, see SERVICE PRECAUTIONS. Disable air bag system. See DISABLING SYSTEM under DISABLING & ACTIVATING AIR BAG SYSTEM. Leave negative battery cable disconnected.
2) Remove floor console. See FLOOR CONSOLE. Disconnect ADM electrical connectors. Remove 3 bolts and remove ADM from vehicle.

Air Bag Restraint Systems – Continental, Contour, Cougar, Escort, Mustang, Mystique, Sable, Taurus & Tracer (Cont.)

3) To install, reverse removal procedure. Ensure ADM mounting surfaces are clean, to allow for proper ADM grounding through mounting bolts. Tighten ADM bolts to specification. See TORQUE SPECIFICATIONS. Activate air bag system. See ACTIVATING SYSTEM under DISABLING & ACTIVATING AIR BAG SYSTEM. Check AIR BAG warning light to ensure system is functioning properly. See SYSTEM OPERATION CHECK.

Removal & Installation (Cougar) – 1) Before proceeding, see SERVICE PRECAUTIONS. Disable air bag system. See DISABLING SYSTEM under DISABLING & ACTIVATING AIR BAG SYSTEM. Leave negative battery cable disconnected.

2) Remove 2 steering column lower panel bolt trim plugs. Remove 4 steering column lower panel bolts. Depress ADM electrical connector retaining tab in 2 steps. Remove 3 bolts and remove ADM.

3) To install, reverse removal procedure. Tighten ADM bolts to specification. See TORQUE SPECIFICATIONS. Activate air bag system. See ACTIVATING SYSTEM under DISABLING & ACTIVATING AIR BAG SYSTEM. Ensure system is functioning properly. See SYSTEM OPERATION CHECK.

Removal & Installation (Escort & Tracer) – 1) Before proceeding, see SERVICE PRECAUTIONS. Disable air bag system. See DISABLING SYSTEM under DISABLING & ACTIVATING AIR BAG SYSTEM. Leave negative battery cable disconnected.

2) Remove floor console. See FLOOR CONSOLE. Disconnect ADM electrical connectors. Remove 3 bolts and remove ADM from vehicle.

3) To install, reverse removal procedure. Tighten ADM bolts to specification. See TORQUE SPECIFICATIONS. Activate air bag system. See ACTIVATING SYSTEM under DISABLING & ACTIVATING AIR BAG SYSTEM. Ensure system is functioning properly. See SYSTEM OPERATION CHECK.

Removal & Installation (Mustang) – 1) Before proceeding, see SERVICE PRECAUTIONS. Disable air bag system. See DISABLING SYSTEM under DISABLING & ACTIVATING AIR BAG SYSTEM. Leave negative battery cable disconnected.

2) Pull carpet back from right side of instrument panel center support bracket and remove ADM bracket bolt. Pull carpet back from left side of instrument panel and disconnect electrical connector locking clip and connector. Remove 2 bracket bolts and remove ADM with bracket.

3) To install, reverse removal procedure. Tighten ADM bracket bolts to specification. See TORQUE SPECIFICATIONS. Activate air bag system. See ACTIVATING SYSTEM under DISABLING & ACTIVATING AIR BAG SYSTEM. Check AIR BAG warning light to ensure system is functioning properly. See SYSTEM OPERATION CHECK.

Removal & Installation (Taurus & Sable) – 1) Before proceeding, see SERVICE PRECAUTIONS. The Air Bag Diagnostic Monitor (ADM) is mounted on the center tunnel under instrument panel. Disable air bag system. See DISABLING SYSTEM under DISABLING & ACTIVATING AIR BAG SYSTEM. Leave negative battery cable disconnected.

2) Remove floor console, if equipped. See FLOOR CONSOLE. Pull back carpet to reveal ADM. Disconnect ADM module electrical connector locking clip and disconnect connector. Remove ADM module retaining nuts and remove ADM module.

3) To install, reverse removal procedure. Tighten fasteners to specification. See TORQUE SPECIFICATIONS. Activate air bag system. See ACTIVATING SYSTEM under DISABLING & ACTIVATING AIR BAG SYSTEM. Check AIR BAG warning light to ensure system is functioning properly. See SYSTEM OPERATION CHECK.

CLOCKSPRING

Removal (Continental) – 1) Before proceeding, see SERVICE PRECAUTIONS. Clockspring is located on steering column between steering wheel and combination switch. Disable air bag system. See DISABLING SYSTEM under DISABLING & ACTIVATING AIR BAG SYSTEM. Leave negative battery cable disconnected.

2) Ensure front wheels are in straight-ahead position and steering column shaft alignment mark is at 12 o'clock position. Remove steering wheel. See STEERING WHEEL. Place two strips off tape across

clockspring to prevent rotation during removal. Remove 3 screws and lower instrument panel cover. Remove hood release and emergency brake release handles and position out of the way. Remove 5 screws and lower instrument panel reinforcement.

3) Place tilt wheel in lowest position. Unscrew and remove tilt wheel lever. Remove 4 screws and lower steering column cover. Position ignition lock cylinder in RUN position. Using small drift, push upward on cylinder release tab through hole in lower shroud while pulling cylinder outward. Remove 1 screw near steering column and carefully pull instrument panel center panel to access temperature control assembly. Push side tabs to release temperature controls from panel, and remove panel.

4) Remove 2 push pins and light socket from panel below steering column. Remove panel. Loosen 4 steering column nuts, and remove upper steering column cover. Remove Passive Anti-Theft System (PATS) transmitter.

5) Remove key-in warning switch. Press release tab and remove cellular phone microphone (if equipped), from clockspring. Disconnect lower clockspring electrical connector and separate connector from bracket. Pry clockspring retaining clips loose. Separate wiring from 2 retaining clips holding wire to steering column. Remove clockspring.

Installation – 1) To install, reverse removal procedure. Tighten fasteners to specification. See TORQUE SPECIFICATIONS.

2) Press clockspring at 12, 3 and 6 o'clock positions to seat on steering column. Remove service lock before installing steering wheel. Activate air bag system. See ACTIVATING SYSTEM under DISABLING & ACTIVATING AIR BAG SYSTEM. Check AIR BAG warning light for proper system function. See SYSTEM OPERATION CHECK.

Removal (Contour & Mystique) – 1) Before proceeding, see SERVICE PRECAUTIONS. Clockspring is located on steering column between steering wheel and combination switch. Disable air bag system. See DISABLING SYSTEM under DISABLING & ACTIVATING AIR BAG SYSTEM. Leave negative battery cable disconnected. Disconnect positive battery cable.

2) Ensure front tires are pointing straight ahead. Center steering wheel and remove key from ignition. Remove 3 screws from steering column lower shroud, and remove lower shroud. Remove 2 screws from steering column upper shroud, and remove upper shroud.

3) Remove steering wheel. See STEERING WHEEL.

4) Disconnect clockspring electrical connectors. Disengage connectors from bracket on column. Using thin screwdriver, release 3 retaining tabs and remove clockspring from vehicle.

Installation – On new clockspring, rotate inner rotor against outer rotor until limit is reached. Rotate back 2.75 turns and line up inner and outer rotor alignment marks at 6 o'clock position. To complete installation, reverse removal procedure. Install steering wheel. See STEERING WHEEL. Activate air bag system. See ACTIVATING SYSTEM under DISABLING & ACTIVATING AIR BAG SYSTEM. Check AIR BAG warning light for proper system function. See SYSTEM OPERATION CHECK.

Removal (Cougar) – 1) Before proceeding, see SERVICE PRECAUTIONS. Clockspring is located on steering column between steering wheel and combination switch. Disable air bag system. See DISABLING SYSTEM under DISABLING & ACTIVATING AIR BAG SYSTEM. Leave negative battery cable disconnected.

2) Ensure front wheels are in straight-ahead position and steering column shaft alignment mark is at 12 o'clock position. Remove 3 steering column lower shroud screws and remove shroud. Remove 2 screws and steering column upper shroud. Remove steering wheel. See STEERING WHEEL.

3) Disconnect clockspring electrical connectors and detach connector from steering column. Press multifunction switch release tabs on top of steering column and remove switch. Using thin screwdriver, release 3 clockspring retaining tabs. Remove clockspring.

Installation – To install, reverse removal procedure. Adjust clockspring before installation. Rotate inner rotor fully counterclockwise against outer rotor. Rotate inner rotor clockwise 2.75 turns. Align markings, and

FORD
4-6

1999 ACCESSORIES & EQUIPMENT
Air Bag Restraint Systems – Continental, Contour, Cougar, Escort, Mustang, Mystique, Sable, Taurus & Tracer (Cont.)

verify locking tabs align. Ensure 3 clockspring tabs engage properly. Install multifunction switch. Ensure 2 retaining tabs lock into position. Reconnect electrical connectors and attach to steering column. Install steering wheel. See STEERING WHEEL. Install upper and lower steering column covers. Activate air bag system. See ACTIVATING SYSTEM under DISABLING & ACTIVATING AIR BAG SYSTEM. Check AIR BAG warning light for proper system function. See SYSTEM OPERATION CHECK.

Removal (Escort & Tracer) – 1) Before proceeding, see SERVICE PRECAUTIONS. Clockspring is located on steering column between steering wheel and combination switch. Disable air bag system. See DISABLING SYSTEM under DISABLING & ACTIVATING AIR BAG SYSTEM. Leave negative battery cable disconnected.

2) Remove steering wheel. See STEERING WHEEL.

3) Remove 3 screws from lower steering column shroud and remove upper and lower steering column shrouds. Place tape across inner and outer clockspring rotors to prevent movement if clockspring is to be reused.

4) Disconnect clockspring electrical connectors. Remove clockspring retaining screws and remove front clockspring from vehicle.

Installation – 1) Ensure front wheels are in straight ahead position. To align clockspring, turn inner portion fully one direction. For clocksprings with yellow instruction label, turn back 3.5 turns and align arrows. For clocksprings with orange instruction labels, turn back 2.5 turns and align arrows. Install steering wheel. See STEERING WHEEL. To complete installation, reverse removal procedure.

2) Activate air bag system. See ACTIVATING SYSTEM under DISABLING & ACTIVATING AIR BAG SYSTEM. Check AIR BAG warning light for proper system function. See SYSTEM OPERATION CHECK.

Removal (Mustang) – 1) Before proceeding, see SERVICE PRECAUTIONS. Clockspring is located on steering column between steering wheel and combination switch. Disable air bag system. See DISABLING SYSTEM under DISABLING & ACTIVATING AIR BAG SYSTEM. Leave negative battery cable disconnected.

2) Ensure front wheels are in straight-ahead position and steering column shaft alignment mark is at 12 o'clock position. Remove steering wheel. See STEERING WHEEL. Apply 2 strips of masking tape across clockspring to prevent accidental rotation. Place steering column in full down position. Twist tilt wheel handle and shank and remove.

3) Remove headlight knob. Remove 2 instrument cluster trim panel screws. Remove instrument cluster trim panel. Remove 2 lower steering column panel bolts and remove panel. Remove 2 lower steering column reinforcement panel bolts and remove panel. Remove 4 screws and lower steering column shroud. Position ignition lock cylinder in RUN position. Using small drift, push upward on cylinder release tab while pulling cylinder outward. Remove steering column upper shroud.

4) Remove Passive Anti-Theft System (PATS) transmitter retaining screw, and position out of the way. Remove key-in warning switch from ignition switch housing. Disconnect clockspring connectors, and remove connectors from bracket. Remove harness from holders. Pry clockspring retaining clips loose, and remove clockspring.

Installation – To install, reverse removal procedure. Press clockspring to seat on steering column. Remove masking tape, if installed, before installing steering wheel. Activate air bag system. See ACTIVATING SYSTEM under DISABLING & ACTIVATING AIR BAG SYSTEM. Check AIR BAG warning light for proper system function. See SYSTEM OPERATION CHECK.

Removal (Sable & Taurus) – 1) Record radio preset stations for reprogramming following procedure. Before proceeding, see SERVICE PRECAUTIONS. Disable air bag system. See DISABLING SYSTEM under DISABLING & ACTIVATING AIR BAG SYSTEM.

2) Remove driver air bag module. See DRIVER AIR BAG MODULE. Ensure front wheels are in straight-ahead position and steering column shaft alignment mark is at 12 o'clock position. Remove steering wheel. See STEERING WHEEL.

3) Turn ignition switch lock cylinder to RUN position. Place 1/8" (3.17 mm) diameter wire pin or small drift punch in hole in lower steering column shroud under ignition switch. Press retaining pin while pulling out on ignition switch lock cylinder and remove it from steering column lock cylinder housing.

4) Remove instrument panel steering column panel and upper and lower steering column shroud. Disconnect clockspring harness connectors. Clockspring harness runs down steering column with connectors at top and base of steering column. Apply 2 strips of tape across clockspring stator and rotor to prevent accidental rotation. Remove 3 clockspring retaining screws and pull clockspring off steering column shaft.

Installation – 1) Ensure front wheels are in straight-ahead position, and steering column shaft alignment mark is at 12 o'clock position. Rotate ring in clockspring counterclockwise until tight, then rotate clockspring ring clockwise 2.5 turns. Align Yellow arrows on clockspring and ring.

2) Install clockspring to steering column lock cylinder housing with 3 retaining screws and tighten to specification. See TORQUE SPECIFICATIONS. Route clockspring assembly wiring down column assembly and connect harness connectors.

3) Remove tape strips. If new clockspring is being installed, remove locking mechanism. Install steering column lower shroud and lower instrument panel cover. Install ignition switch lock cylinder and steering wheel. Reactivate air bag system. See ACTIVATING SYSTEM under DISABLING & ACTIVATING AIR BAG SYSTEM. Check AIR BAG warning light for proper system function. See SYSTEM OPERATION CHECK.

DRIVER AIR BAG MODULE

Removal & Installation – 1) Before proceeding, see SERVICE PRECAUTIONS. Disconnect negative battery cable. Remove module retaining screw trim plugs, (if equipped), from back of steering wheel. Remove driver air bag retaining screws. Disconnect air bag module wiring connector from clockspring connector. Disconnect horn switch connector. Remove air bag module.

2) To install, reverse removal procedure. Tighten air bag module bolts to specification. See TORQUE SPECIFICATIONS. Connect negative battery cable. Ensure system is functioning properly. See SYSTEM OPERATION CHECK.

FLOOR CONSOLE

Removal & Installation (Continental With Bucket Seats) – Before proceeding, see SERVICE PRECAUTIONS. Disable air bag system. See DISABLING SYSTEM under DISABLING & ACTIVATING AIR BAG SYSTEM. Leave negative battery cable disconnected. Remove console glove compartment. Disconnect cellular phone electrical connectors (if equipped). If equipped with compact disc changer, remove 4 screws, disconnect electrical connector and remove compact disc changer. Place gear selector in position "1". Remove top console cover. Disconnect lighter electrical connector. Remove 2 floor console-to-floor bracket screws. Remove 2 floor console-to- gearshift bracket screws. Slide floor console rearward and remove console. To install, reverse removal procedure.

Removal & Installation (Contour & Mystique – Automatic Transmission) – Disconnect negative battery cable. Position seats forward and remove 2 floor console screws. Apply parking brake. Carefully pry shift indicator bezel from floor console. Raise rear of floor console and pull back to disengage front retaining clips. To install, reverse removal procedure.

Removal & Installation (Contour & Mystique – Manual Transmission) – Disconnect negative battery cable. Unscrew shift knob, and remove reverse selector spring and spacer. Remove shift lever boot. Position seats forward and remove 2 floor console screws. Disengage floor console locating pegs, accessible through shift lever boot opening. Apply parking brake. Raise rear of floor console and pull back to remove. To install, reverse removal procedure.

Removal & Installation (Escort & Tracer) – Move front seats forward. Remove 2 screws from sides of parking brake console. Engage parking brake. Lift rear of parking brake console and remove. Remove 2 revealed shift panel console screws. Remove 4 pushpins from side of

1999 ACCESSORIES & EQUIPMENT

FORD
4-7

Air Bag Restraint Systems – Continental, Contour, Cougar, Escort, Mustang, Mystique, Sable, Taurus & Tracer (Cont.)

console. Place gear selector lever in "L" position on vehicle equipped with automatic transmission. Unscrew and remove gearshift knob on vehicles equipped with manual transmission. On all vehicles, lift out cup holder assembly. Lift rear of console and remove. To install, reverse removal procedure.

Removal (Sable & Taurus) – Remove beverage holder by carefully unsnapping front portion using a flat-blade screwdriver. Grasp beverage holder and unsnap from console panel. Open ash tray and move gearshift lever to "1" position. Grasp console top panel and pull rearward to unsnap from console center finish panel. Remove electrical connectors from cigarette lighter socket, retainer and light assembly. Remove 2 screws retaining console finish panel (armrest) to console panel and remove console finish panel. Remove 2 screws retaining front of console to instrument panel. Pull 2 carpet-covered kick panels at lower front of console to disengage clips from bracket. Remove 4 bolts retaining console side to floor mounting bracket. Remove 2 bolts retaining console to rear bracket and remove console from vehicle. To install, reverse removal procedure.

PASSENGER AIR BAG MODULE

Removal & Installation (Continental, Escort & Tracer) – **1)** Before proceeding, see SERVICE PRECAUTIONS. The passenger air bag module is mounted in right side of instrument panel, above glove box. Disable air bag system. See DISABLING SYSTEM under DISABLING & ACTIVATING AIR BAG SYSTEM. Leave negative battery cable disconnected.

2) Open glove box. Push in on glove box door tabs and position glove box door downward. Remove passenger air bag module retaining bolts and pull module from instrument panel. Disconnect passenger air bag module electrical connector and remove module from vehicle.

3) To install, reverse removal procedure. Tighten passenger air bag module bolts to specification. See TORQUE SPECIFICATIONS. Activate air bag system. See ACTIVATING SYSTEM under DISABLING & ACTIVATING AIR BAG SYSTEM. Check AIR BAG warning light to ensure system is functioning properly. See SYSTEM OPERATION CHECK.

Removal & Installation (Contour & Mystique) – **1)** Before proceeding, see SERVICE PRECAUTIONS. The passenger air bag module is mounted in right side of instrument panel, above glove box. Disable air bag system. See DISABLING SYSTEM under DISABLING & ACTIVATING AIR BAG SYSTEM. Leave negative battery cable disconnected.

2) Open glove box. Push in on glove box door tabs and position glove box door downward. Remove 4 screws from glove box upper finish panel, and remove panel. Disengage air duct from heater case and instrument panel vent, and remove from vehicle. Disconnect air bag module connector. Remove 2 module retaining bolts from cross beam. Remove 2 remaining nuts while supporting module. Remove module from vehicle by rolling it down and over the cross beam.

3) To install, reverse removal procedure. Tighten passenger air bag module bolts to specification. See TORQUE SPECIFICATIONS. Activate air bag system. See ACTIVATING SYSTEM under DISABLING & ACTIVATING AIR BAG SYSTEM. Check AIR BAG warning light to ensure system is functioning properly. See SYSTEM OPERATION CHECK.

Removal & Installation (Cougar) – **1)** Before proceeding, see SERVICE PRECAUTIONS. The passenger air bag module is mounted in right side of instrument panel, above glove box. Disable air bag system. See DISABLING SYSTEM under DISABLING & ACTIVATING AIR BAG SYSTEM. Leave negative battery cable disconnected.

2) Remove 3 Torx screws at base of glove box. Open glove box. Push in on glove box door tabs and remove glove box. Remove 4 Torx screws and remove panel from behind glove box. Pull passenger air duct from heater box and passenger register, and remove. Disconnect passenger air bag module electrical connector. Remove 2 nuts and 2 bolts from passenger air bag module and remove module.

3) To install, reverse removal procedure. Tighten passenger air bag module fasteners to specification. See TORQUE SPECIFICATIONS.

Activate air bag system. See ACTIVATING SYSTEM under DISABLING & ACTIVATING AIR BAG SYSTEM. Check AIR BAG warning light to ensure system is functioning properly. See SYSTEM OPERATION CHECK.

Removal & Installation (Mustang) – **1)** Before proceeding, see SERVICE PRECAUTIONS. The passenger air bag module is mounted in right side of instrument panel, above glove box. Disable air bag system. See DISABLING SYSTEM under DISABLING & ACTIVATING AIR BAG SYSTEM. Leave negative battery cable disconnected.

2) Open glove box. Push in on glove box door tabs and position glove box door downward. Remove 2 screws and A/C evaporator duct. Disconnect passenger air bag module electrical connector and disengage connector from instrument panel reinforcement. Remove 2 passenger air bag module retaining bolts and remove module.

3) To install, reverse removal procedure. Tighten passenger air bag module bolts to specification. See TORQUE SPECIFICATIONS. Activate air bag system. See ACTIVATING SYSTEM under DISABLING & ACTIVATING AIR BAG SYSTEM. Check AIR BAG warning light to ensure system is functioning properly. See SYSTEM OPERATION CHECK.

Removal & Installation (Taurus & Sable) – **1)** Before proceeding, see SERVICE PRECAUTIONS. The passenger air bag module is mounted in right side of instrument panel, above glove box. Disable air bag system. See DISABLING SYSTEM under DISABLING & ACTIVATING AIR BAG SYSTEM. Leave negative battery cable disconnected.

2) Lift passenger air bag trim cover from instrument panel to disengage retaining tabs. Open glove box. Push in on glove box door tabs and position glove box door downward. Disconnect passenger air bag module electrical connector. Remove 2 passenger air bag module retaining bolts and remove module.

3) To install, reverse removal procedure. Tighten passenger air bag module fasteners to specification. See TORQUE SPECIFICATIONS. Activate air bag system. See ACTIVATING SYSTEM under DISABLING & ACTIVATING AIR BAG SYSTEM. Check AIR BAG warning light to ensure system is functioning properly. See SYSTEM OPERATION CHECK. Reprogram radio presets and reset clock. Repeat SYSTEM OPERATION CHECK.

SIDE AIR BAG IMPACT SENSOR

Removal & Installation (Continental) – **1)** Before proceeding, see SERVICE PRECAUTIONS. Move driver's seat to farthest forward position. Disable air bag system. See DISABLING SYSTEM under DISABLING & ACTIVATING AIR BAG SYSTEM. Leave negative battery cable disconnected.

2) Side impact sensor can be seen through opening in carpet, under seat. Remove harness pin from sensor bracket. Remove 2 sensor bracket bolts. Pull sensor and bracket assembly free to access electrical connector. Disconnect electrical connector and remove sensor with bracket.

3) To install, reverse removal procedure. Torque sensor bracket bolts to specification. See TORQUE SPECIFICATIONS.

Removal & Installation (Cougar) – **1)** Before proceeding, see SERVICE PRECAUTIONS. Disable air bag system. See DISABLING SYSTEM under DISABLING & ACTIVATING AIR BAG SYSTEM. Leave negative battery cable disconnected.

2) Remove front seat and driver's door sill trim. Lift hood release handle and pull driver's kick panel back to disengage retaining clips. Remove kick panel. Fold back carpet and padding. Remove 3 sensor bolts and remove sensor. Disconnect electrical connector.

3) To install, reverse removal procedure. Use new sensor mounting bolts. Torque to specification. See TORQUE SPECIFICATIONS.

SIDE AIR BAG MODULE

Removal & Installation (Continental) – **1)** Before proceeding, see SERVICE PRECAUTIONS. Disable air bag system. See DISABLING SYSTEM under DISABLING & ACTIVATING AIR BAG SYSTEM. Leave negative battery cable disconnected.

FORD
4-8

1999 ACCESSORIES & EQUIPMENT
Air Bag Restraint Systems -- Continental, Contour, Cougar, Escort, Mustang, Mystique, Sable, Taurus & Tracer (Cont.)

2) Remove appropriate seat. Push up on seat back rear trim panel. Pull at bottom corners of panel to disengage hooks. Push panel down to remove. Inspect all 4 hooks on panel, and replace panel if damaged.

3) Release 4 seat trim clips. Unzip side air bag module deployment chute. Remove 2 module retaining nuts. Pull seat cover forward and free side air bag module from seat frame. Slide electrical connector clip and press tabs in to disconnect electrical connector.

4) To install, reverse removal procedure. Position side air bag module in bracket, noting inboard and outboard sides. Use new mounting nuts if installing new side air bag module. Torque to specification. See TORQUE SPECIFICATIONS. Verify deployment chute completely covers sides of module before zipping. Deployment chute should not cover top or bottom of module. Zip deployment chute, and tuck zipper pull tab into seat back opening.

Removal & Installation (Cougar) – 1) Before proceeding, see SERVICE PRECAUTIONS. Disable air bag system. See DISABLING SYSTEM under DISABLING & ACTIVATING AIR BAG SYSTEM. Leave negative battery cable disconnected.

2) Remove appropriate seat. Remove headrest. Using a screwdriver, release headrest tube tabs and pull tube from seat back assembly. Fold seat back forward and release plastic strips at base and sides of seat back. Disconnect hog-rings from bottom corners of seat back.

3) Pull seat back release handle and disconnect 2 release cables. Remove handle. Remove seat covering and pad assembly. Disconnect side air bag module electrical connector. Remove 2 side air bag module retaining nuts, and remove module.

4) To install, reverse removal procedure. Torque side air bag module retaining nuts to specification. See TORQUE SPECIFICATIONS. Use hog-ring pliers to reinstall hog-rings.

STEERING WHEEL

CAUTION: When removing steering wheel, DO NOT use a knock-off type steering wheel puller, or strike steering wheel or shaft with a hammer. A sudden impact could damage bearing or collapse steering column.

Removal – 1) Before proceeding, see SERVICE PRECAUTIONS. Disable air bag system. See DISABLING SYSTEM under DISABLING & ACTIVATING AIR BAG SYSTEM. Leave negative battery cable disconnected. Ensure front wheels are in straight-ahead position. Disconnect cruise control wiring harness connector (if equipped) from steering wheel.

2) Remove steering wheel retaining bolt. Reference mark steering wheel hub to steering wheel shaft to ensure proper alignment during installation. On all models except Contour and Mystique, remove steering wheel using Puller (T67L-3600-A. On Contour and Mystique, turn ignition switch to ACC position and pull steering wheel from column by hand. Route clockspring wiring harness through steering wheel as wheel is lifted off shaft.

Installation – 1) To install, reverse removal procedure. Route clockspring wiring harness through opening. Ensure clockspring wire is not pinched when positioning steering wheel.

2) Install steering wheel retaining bolt and tighten to specification. On Mustang, Taurus and Sable, use new bolt. See TORQUE SPECIFICATIONS. Activate air bag system. See ACTIVATING SYSTEM under DISABLING & ACTIVATING AIR BAG SYSTEM. Check AIR BAG warning light to ensure system is functioning properly. See SYSTEM OPERATION CHECK.

WIRE REPAIR

To repair damage to sensor wiring and wiring harnesses, note following conditions and proceed to REPAIR PROCEDURE.

- All wire splice connections must be staggered at least 2" (51 mm) apart.
- Use proper size, waterproof butt-splice connectors on any exposed wiring. Use only connectors lined with sealer that melts when heat is applied, to completely seal repairs.
- Use heat shrink nylon splice to prevent water, salt, condensation and heat from affecting the wiring repair. Tubing should extend at least 1" (25 mm) to each side of splice.

REPAIR PROCEDURE

Insert pre-stripped wire ends into proper size waterproof butt-splice connector, and crimp connector using appropriate crimping pliers. *See Fig. 2.* Using heat gun, hair dryer or match, heat splice until it shrinks and adhesive oozes from each end of tubing. Connection is now waterproofed.

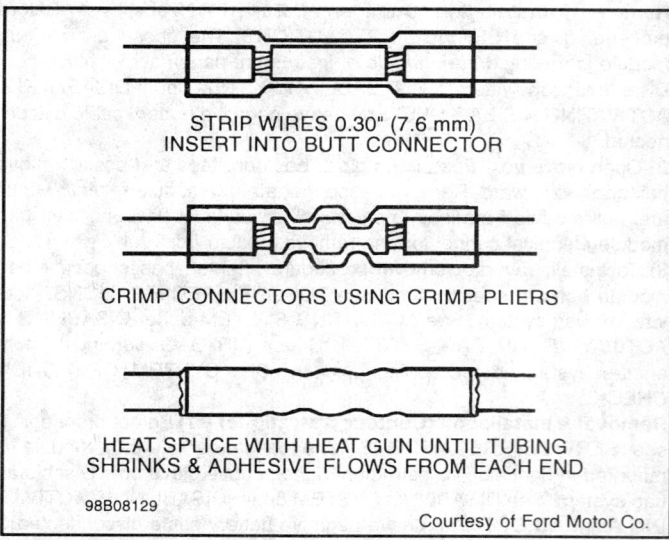

STRIP WIRES 0.30" (7.6 mm)
INSERT INTO BUTT CONNECTOR

CRIMP CONNECTORS USING CRIMP PLIERS

HEAT SPLICE WITH HEAT GUN UNTIL TUBING
SHRINKS & ADHESIVE FLOWS FROM EACH END

98B08129   Courtesy of Ford Motor Co.

Fig. 2: Repairing & Waterproofing Wiring Connections

COMPONENT LOCATIONS

COMPONENT LOCATIONS

Component	Location
Air Bag Diagnostic Monitor	
Continental	
With Bench Seats	Under Driver's Seat, Near Center Of Vehicle
With Bucket Seats	Under Floor Console
Contour & Mystique	Under Floor Console
Cougar	Behind LH Side Of Instrument Panel On Steering Column
Escort & Tracer	Under Floor Console
Mustang, Sable & Taurus	Behind Center Of Instrument Panel
Clockspring	Between Steering Wheel & Steering Column
Driver's Air Bag Module	On Steering Wheel
Passenger's Air Bag Module	On RH Side Of Instrument Panel, Above Glove Box
Side Air Bag Modules	In Driver's & Passenger's Seat Backs
Side Air Bag Impact Sensors	Under Each Front Seat

1999 ACCESSORIES & EQUIPMENT

FORD
4-9

Air Bag Restraint Systems – Continental, Contour, Cougar, Escort, Mustang, Mystique, Sable, Taurus & Tracer (Cont.)

TORQUE SPECIFICATIONS

TORQUE SPECIFICATIONS (CONTINENTAL)

Application	Ft. Lbs. (N.m)
Driver Air Bag Module Bolts	9 (12)
Air Bag Diagnostic Module Bracket Bolts	17 (23)
Side Air Bag Impact Sensor	9 (12)
Side Air Bag Module Nuts	5 (7)
Steering Column Mounting Nuts/Bolts	11 (15)
Steering Wheel Bolt	25 (33)

	INCH Lbs. (N.m)
Hood Release Handle Screws	18-26 (2-3)
Lower Steering Column Shroud Screws	6-8 (0.7-0.9)
Parking Brake Handle Screws	18-26 (2-3)
Passenger Air Bag Module Bolts	80 (9)
Side Air Bag Impact Sensor Bolts	80 (9)

TORQUE SPECIFICATIONS (CONTOUR & MYSTIQUE)

Application	Ft. Lbs. (N.m)
Air Bag Diagnostic Monitor Bolts	8 (11)
Passenger Air Bag Module Nuts/Bolts	12 (16)
Steering Wheel Bolt	38 (50)

	INCH Lbs. (N.m)
Driver Air Bag Module Bolts	44 (5)

TORQUE SPECIFICATIONS (COUGAR)

Application	Ft. Lbs. (N.m)
Passenger Air Bag Module Nuts/Bolts	12 (16)
Side Air Bag Module Nuts	12 (16)
Steering Column Mounting Nuts	18 (24)
Steering Wheel Bolt	37 (50)

	INCH Lbs. (N.m)
Driver Air Bag Module Bolts	44 (5)
Air Bag Diagnostic Module Mounting Bolts	53 (6)
Side Air Bag Impact Sensor Bolts	80 (9)

TORQUE SPECIFICATIONS (ESCORT & TRACER)

Application	Ft. Lbs. (N.m)
Air Bag Diagnostic Monitor Bolts	8-10 (11-13)
Driver Air Bag Module Bolts	5.8-8.6 (7.9-11.7)
Passenger Air Bag Module Bolts	5.8-8.6 (7.9-11.7)
Steering Wheel Bolt	34-46 (46-63)

TORQUE SPECIFICATIONS (MUSTANG)

Application	Ft. Lbs. (N.m)
Air Bag Diagnostic Module Bracket Bolts	9 (12)
Steering Column Mounting Nuts	12 (15)
Steering Wheel Bolt	23-32 (31-44)

	INCH Lbs. (N.m)
Driver Air Bag Module Bolts	80 (9)
Passenger Air Bag Module Bolts	80 (9)

TORQUE SPECIFICATIONS (TAURUS & SABLE)

Application	Ft. Lbs. (N.m)
Side Air Bag Module Nuts/Bolts	12 (16)
Steering Column Mounting Nuts	10-13 (13-17)
Steering Column-To-Steering Gear Bolt	17-20 (22-28)
Steering Wheel Bolt	25-34 (34-46)

	INCH Lbs. (N.m)
Clockspring Mounting Screws	18-26 (2-3)
Driver Air Bag Module Bolts	90-122 (10.2-13.8)
Air Bag Diagnostic Module Nuts	90-122 (10.2-13.8)
Lower Steering Column Shroud Screws	7-8 (0.8-0.9)
Passenger Air Bag Module Nuts/Bolts	67-92 (7.6-10.4)

WIRING DIAGRAMS

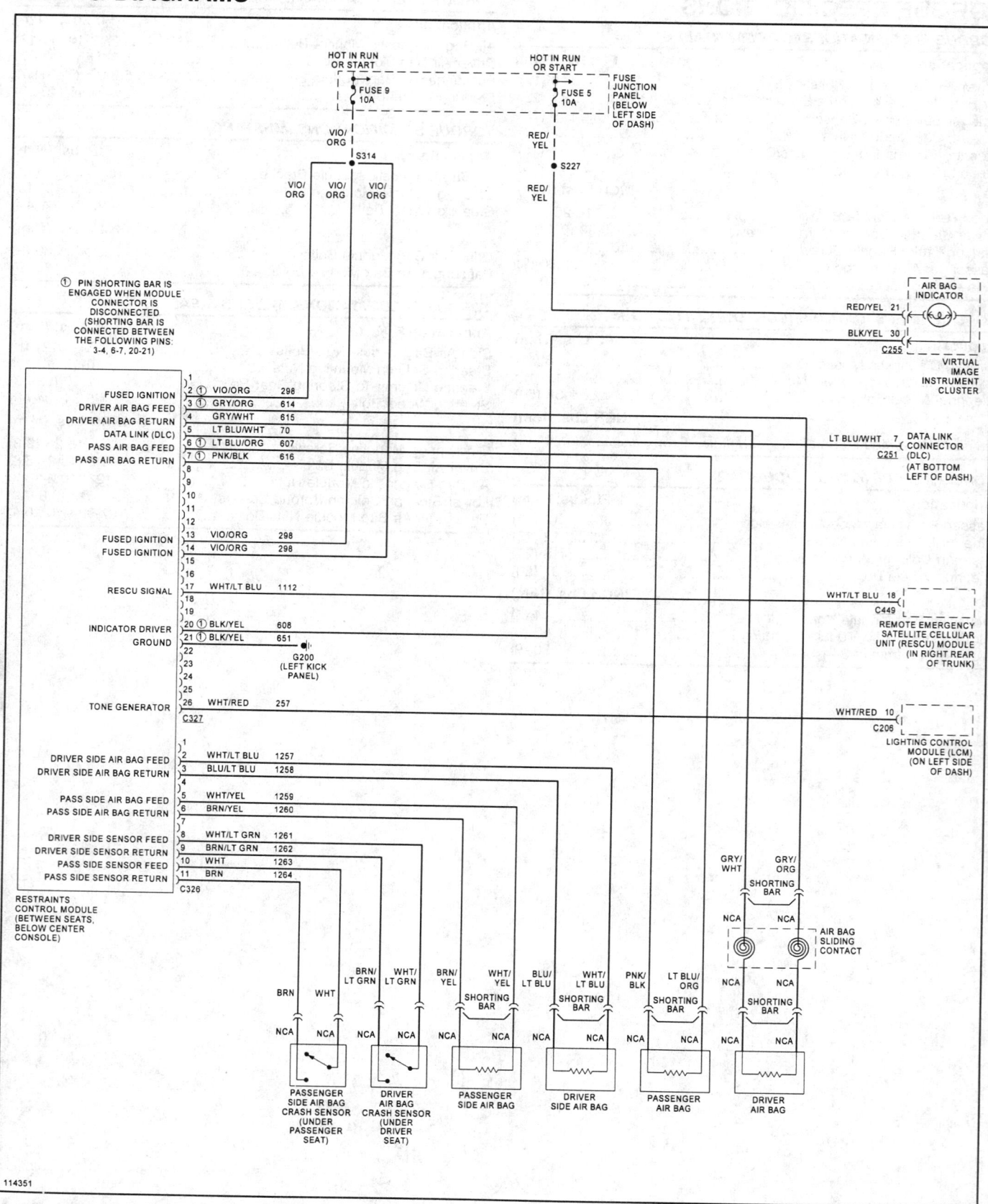

Fig. 3: Air Bag System Wiring Diagram (Continental)

114351

1999 ACCESSORIES & EQUIPMENT

Air Bag Restraint Systems – Continental, Contour, Cougar, Escort, Mustang, Mystique, Sable, Taurus & Tracer (Cont.)

FORD
4-11

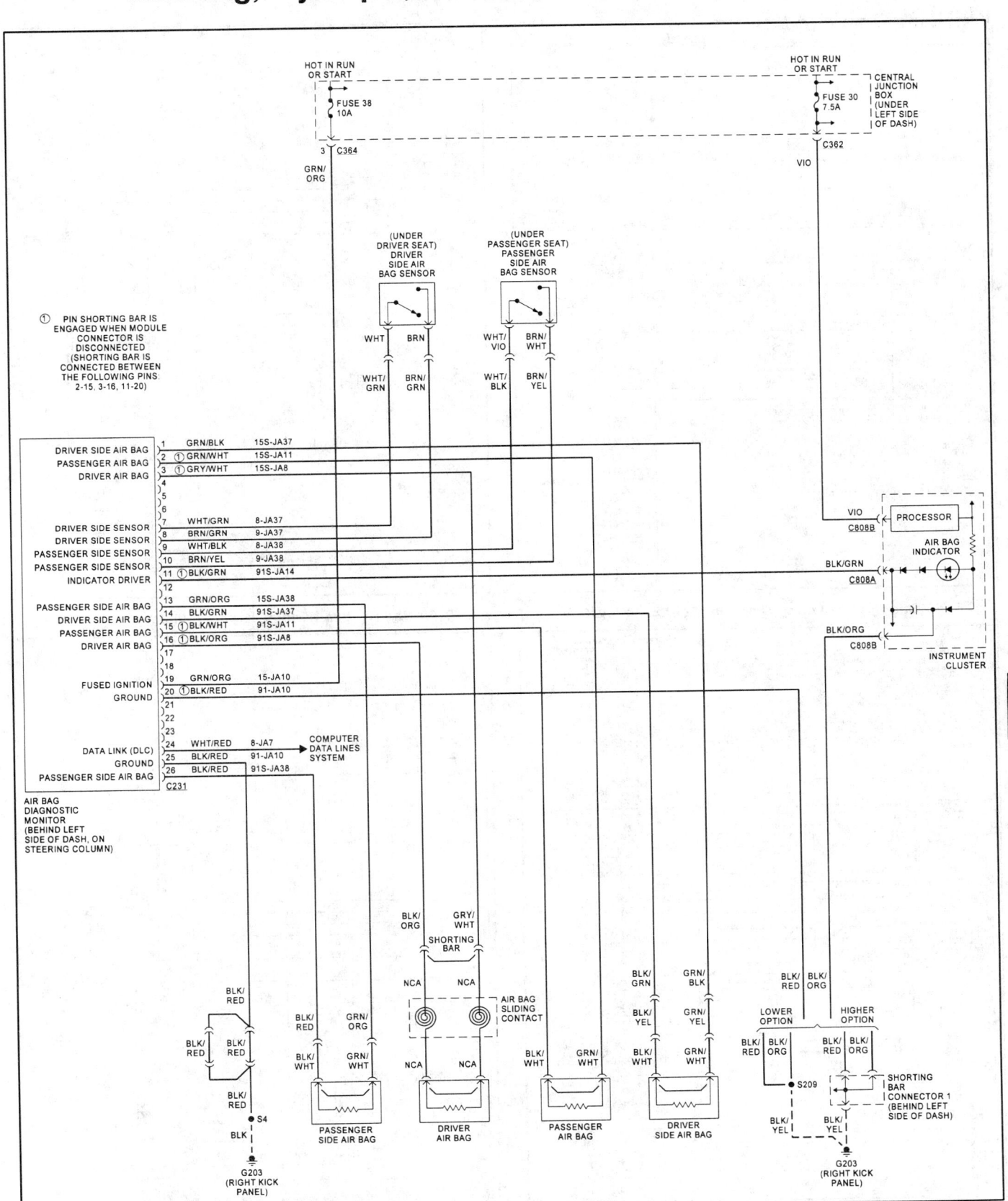

Fig. 4: Air Bag System Wiring Diagram (Cougar)

114501

FORD
4-12

1999 ACCESSORIES & EQUIPMENT
Air Bag Restraint Systems – Continental, Contour, Cougar, Escort, Mustang, Mystique, Sable, Taurus & Tracer (Cont.)

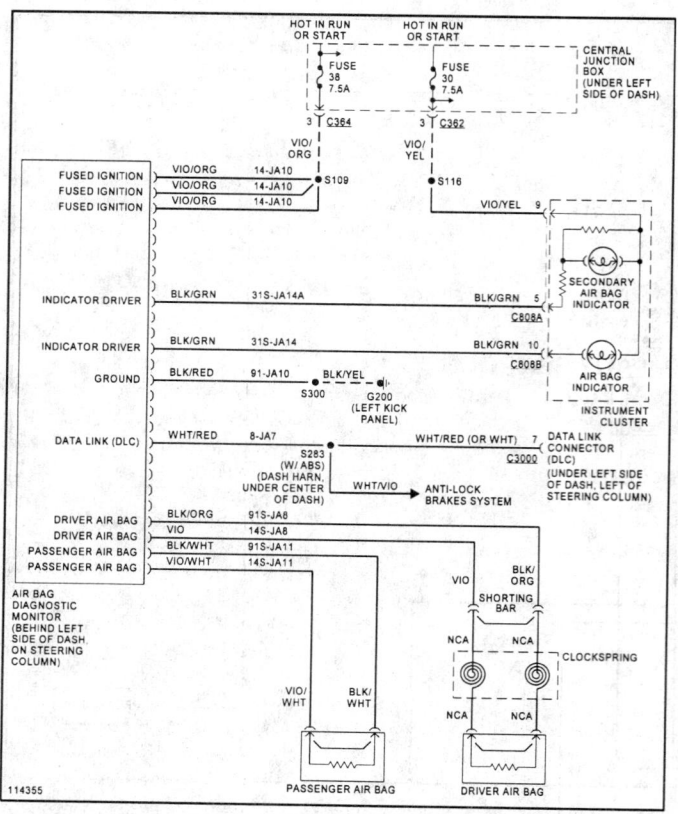

Fig. 5: Air Bag System Wiring Diagram (Contour & Mystique)

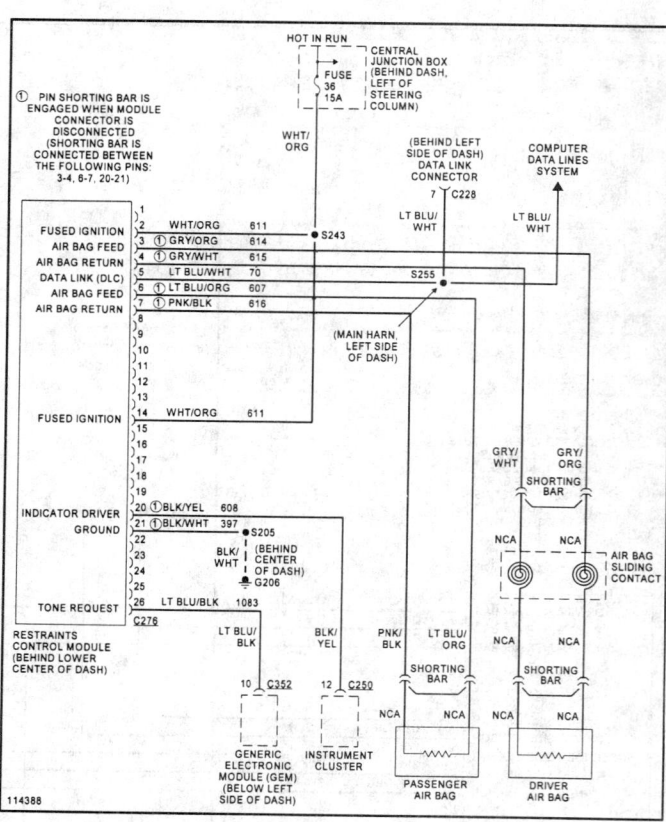

Fig. 7: Air Bag System Wiring Diagram (Mustang)

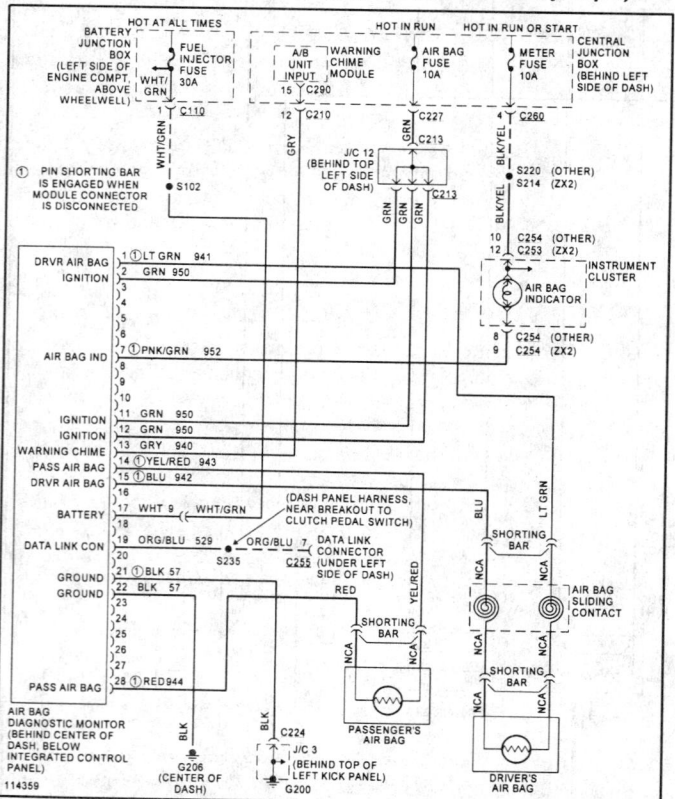

Fig. 6: Air Bag System Wiring Diagram (Escort & Tracer)

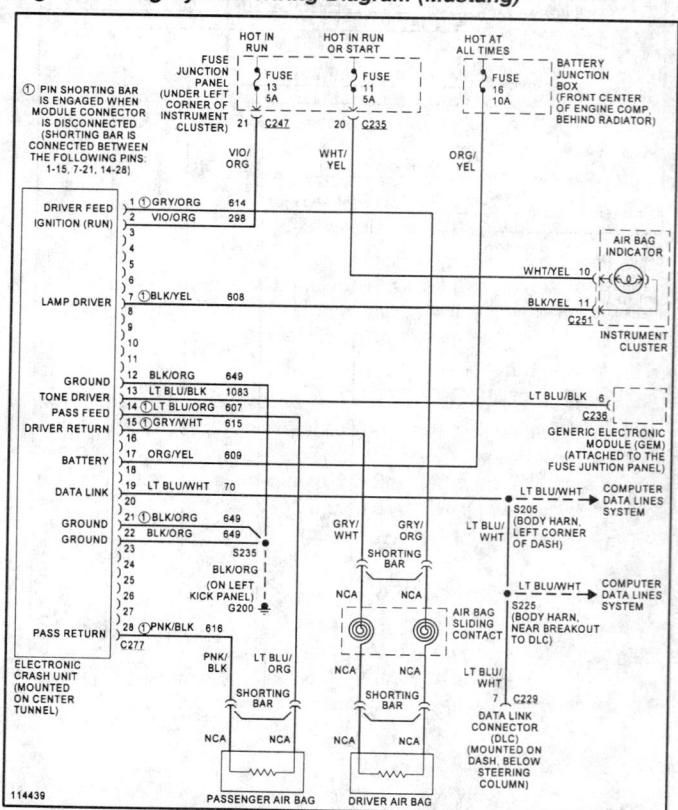

Fig. 8: Air Bag System Wiring Diagram (Sable & Taurus)

NOTE: For information on air bag DIAGNOSIS & TESTING, see MITCHELL® AIR BAG SERVICE & REPAIR MANUAL, DOMESTIC & IMPORTED MODELS.

DESCRIPTION

WARNING: To avoid injury from accidental air bag deployment, read and carefully follow all WARNINGS and SERVICE PRECAUTIONS.

NOTE: Air Bag Diagnostic Monitor (ADM) may be referred to by other names:

- Electronic Crash Sensor (ECS).
- Electronic Crash Unit (ECU).
- Restraints Control Module (RCM).

The Supplemental Restraint System (SRS), also known as air bag system, is designed to provide increased accident protection for driver and passenger by deploying air bags in the event of a serious impact. Air bags are mounted in steering wheel, instrument panel above glove box and in outboard seatback bolsters, (if equipped). Air bag modules deploy in about 40 milliseconds after impact sensors close. Air bag system is designed to be used with 3-point safety belts.

Air bag system includes the following components: Air Bag Diagnostic Monitor (ADM), driver's air bag module, passenger air bag module, AIR BAG warning light, side air bag modules, (if equipped), side impact sensors, (if equipped), ignitor assemblies (in air bag modules), clockspring (also known as sliding contact) and associated wiring harnesses.

OPERATION

AIR BAG DIAGNOSTIC MONITOR

The Air Bag Diagnostic Monitor (ADM) contains a microcomputer, which monitors electrical system components and connections, and a safing sensor. Diagnostic monitor performs a system self-check of air bag system internal circuits every time ignition switch is turned to RUN position. Monitor also energizes air bag system AIR BAG warning light during initial system self-check and whenever a fault is detected. Diagnostic monitor can disarm air bag system if certain faults occur.

The ADM also receives input from side impact sensors, and determines the need for side air bag deployment. Driver's and passenger's air bags will always deploy simultaneously. Side air bags modules are deployed independently as determined by individual side impact sensors.

BACK-UP POWER SUPPLY

A back-up power supply is located inside diagnostic monitor. If battery or battery cables are damaged in a collision before sensor circuits close, back-up power supply will supply sufficient electrical power to deploy air bags. Back-up power supply will hold a deployment charge for approximately one minute after battery is disconnected.

CLOCKSPRING

The steering column contains a clockspring (also called sliding contact) assembly to transfer electrical signals between air bag diagnostic monitor and driver air bag module. Clockspring is mounted to steering column switch mounting bracket behind steering wheel.

DRIVER AIR BAG MODULE

The driver air bag module is mounted on center of steering wheel, covered by steering wheel trim cover. When a front impact sensor and safing sensor close, signaling an impact, air bag ignitor triggers inflator. During ignition, sodium azide reacts with copper oxide to produce nitrogen gas, which inflates air bag.

When air bag deploys, tear-seams molded into steering wheel trim cover separate, allowing inflation of air bag assembly. Driver air bag module is not serviceable and must be replaced as a complete assembly.

ELECTRICAL SYSTEM

Air bag system is powered directly from battery and can function with ignition switch in any position, including OFF and LOCK. System can also function when driver and passenger seats are unoccupied. The 3 main functions performed by electrical subsystem are: detecting an impact, switching electric power to ignitor for air bags, and monitoring readiness of air bag system. The air bag sections of wiring harness are identified by Yellow insulation to aid identification.

IMPACT SENSORS

Front Impact Sensor – Front impact sensor contain a sensor mass, bias magnet, cylindrical tube, and electrical connector. Upon sufficient frontal impact, the sensing mass breaks away from bias magnet and rolls along a cylinder towards electrical contacts. If deceleration is above predetermined limit, the sensing mass will bridge the electrical contacts and complete the air bag system primary deployment circuit.

Safing Sensor – Safing sensor consists of a sensor mass, bias magnet, cylindrical tube, and electrical connector. Design and operation of safing sensor is similar to front impact sensors, except for the sensor calibration. Front impact sensor and safing sensor must both complete circuits for air bag deployment. This ensures that air bag modules do not deploy in the event of an electrical short circuit in the system.

Side Impact Sensors – Side air bag impact sensors are located near the base of each "B" pillar. If ADM determines driver and passenger air bag deployment is necessary, side air bag sensors may also indicate the need for side air bag deployment by determining both severity and direction of impact. Because each sensor only controls one side air bag, ADM may deploy one, both or neither side air bag.

PASSENGER AIR BAG MODULE

The passenger air bag module is mounted in right side of instrument panel, above glove box. When a front impact sensor and safing sensor close, signaling an impact, air bag ignitor trigger inflator.

Since passenger air bag is larger than driver air bag, inflator contains more gas generant in a different configuration to produce more gas. When air bag is activated, instrument panel trim cover tears at seams and hinges, allowing inflation. Passenger air bag module is only serviced as a complete assembly.

SYSTEM OPERATION CHECK

1) When checking air bag system operation (also called prove out system), and upon completion of each diagnostic test, check for faults in air bag system. To check system, turn ignition switch to RUN position. If AIR BAG warning light illuminates for approximately 6 seconds and then goes out, air bag system is functioning properly and no fault codes exist.
2) If a fault is detected in air bag system during initial system check, AIR BAG warning light will either fail to light, stay on continuously, or flash. Flashing may not begin for up to 30 seconds after initial bulb-check. If AIR BAG warning light flashes, indicating a fault in system, see MITCHELL® AIR BAG SERVICE & REPAIR MANUAL, DOMESTIC & IMPORTED MODELS.

SERVICE PRECAUTIONS

These precautions should be observed when working with air bag system:

- Disable air bag system before servicing any air bag system or steering column components. Failure to do so may result in accidental air bag deployment and personal injury. See DISABLING & ACTIVATING AIR BAG SYSTEM.
- Wait one minute after disabling air bag system before working on vehicle. Back-up power supply holds a deployment charge for

FORD
4-14

1999 ACCESSORIES & EQUIPMENT
Air Bag Restraint Systems
Crown Victoria, Grand Marquis & Town Car (Cont.)

approximately one minute after positive battery cable is disconnected. Servicing air bag system before one minute may cause accidental air bag deployment and possible personal injury.

- Because of critical system operating requirements, DO NOT service impact sensors, clockspring, diagnostic monitor or air bag modules. Repairs are made by replacement only.
- Always wear safety glasses whenever servicing an air bag equipped vehicle or handling an air bag.
- When carrying a live air bag module, ensure air bag module and trim cover are pointed away from your body. This minimizes chance of injury in event of an accidental deployment.
- When placing a live air bag module on a bench or other surface, always face air bag module and trim cover facing up and away from surface. This will reduce motion of module if it is accidentally deployed.
- After deployment, air bag surface may contain chemical deposits which may irritate skin. Always wear gloves and safety glasses when handling a deployed air bag. Wash your hands using mild soap and water. Follow correct disposal procedures. See DISPOSAL PROCEDURES.
- If scrapping a vehicle with an undeployed air bag module, air bag must be deployed. See DISPOSAL PROCEDURES.
- If a part is replaced and new part does not correct condition, reinstall original part and perform diagnostic procedure again.
- Never probe connectors on air bag module. Doing so may cause air bag deployment and/or personal injury.
- Instruction to disconnect always refers to connector. DO NOT remove component from vehicle if instructed to disconnect.
- After any servicing, ensure AIR BAG warning light does not indicate any system faults. See SYSTEM OPERATION CHECK.
- Replace air bag module if trim cover (deployment doors) is marred or damaged. DO NOT repaint trim cover. Paint may degrade cover material. Replace air bag module as necessary. Ensure damaged air bag is deployed. See DISPOSAL PROCEDURES.

DISABLING & ACTIVATING AIR BAG SYSTEM

WARNING: Wait one minute after disabling air bag system before working on vehicle. Back-up power supply holds a deployment charge for approximately one minute after negative battery cable is disconnected. Servicing air bag system before one minute may cause accidental air bag deployment and possible personal injury.

CAUTION: When battery is disconnected, vehicle computer and memory systems may lose memory data. Driveability problems may exist until computer systems have completed a relearn cycle. See COMPUTER RELEARN PROCEDURES in GENERAL INFORMATION.

DISABLING SYSTEM

1) Record USER 1 and USER 2 preset radio frequencies for reprogramming (if equipped). Disconnect negative battery cable. Wait at least one minute for back-up power supply to deplete stored energy.
2) Remove driver air bag module. See DRIVER AIR BAG MODULE under REMOVAL & INSTALLATION. Connect appropriate air bag simulator to clockspring connector at top of steering column (in place of air bag). See AIR BAG SIMULATOR.
3) Disconnect passenger air bag module electrical connector. Connect appropriate air bag simulator to passenger air bag vehicle harness connector (in place of air bag).
4) Disconnect driver's side air bag electrical connector, if equipped. Side air bag connectors are located under front seats. Connect an air bag simulator to connector. Repeat for passenger's side air bag. Connect negative battery cable. To reactivate SRS, see ACTIVATING SYSTEM.

AIR BAG SIMULATOR

An Air Bag Simulator (105-R0012) is required to perform diagnosis and testing of the air bag system. *See Fig. 1.* An air bag simulator is a 2-ohm resistor, with appropriate connector, used to simulate an air bag module. DO NOT short-circuit air bag module connections with a zero-ohm jumper wire. If zero-ohm jumper wire is used, an appropriate Diagnostic Trouble Code (DTC) will be set.

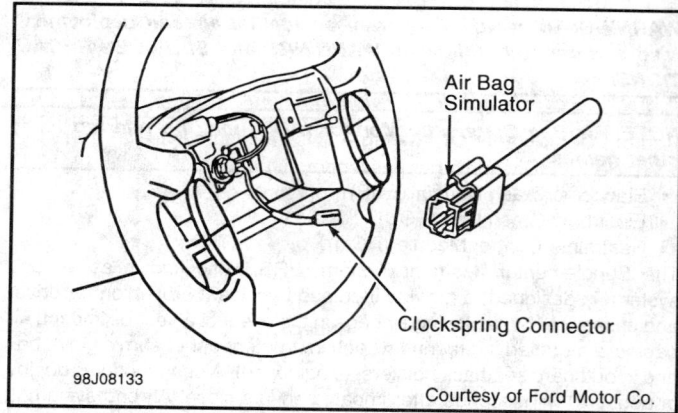

98J08133
Courtesy of Ford Motor Co.

Fig. 1: Identifying Air Bag Simulator

ACTIVATING SYSTEM

1) Disconnect negative battery cable. Wait at least one minute for back-up power supply to deplete stored energy. Remove air bag simulator from clockspring connector. Remove air bag simulator from passenger air bag vehicle harness connector. Install driver air bag module. See DRIVER AIR BAG MODULE under REMOVAL & INSTALLATION.
2) Install passenger air bag module. See PASSENGER AIR BAG MODULE under REMOVAL & INSTALLATION. Remove air bag simulators from side air bag connectors under front seats. Reconnect side air bags. Reconnect negative battery cable. Recheck system operation. See SYSTEM OPERATION CHECK. Reprogram USER 1 and USER 2 preset radio frequencies and set clock.

DISPOSAL PROCEDURES

WARNING: Refer to SERVICE PRECAUTIONS before proceeding.

Air bag disposal may be necessary in the following situations:
- Scrapping vehicle with deployed air bag.
- Scrapping vehicle with live air bag.
- Disposal of a live but electrically faulty air bag module.
- Disposal of a deployed air bag module.

DEPLOYED AIR BAG

Dispose of deployed air bag module as any other part. Air bag module components are not reusable.

UNDEPLOYED AIR BAG – FAULTY UNIT

If an undeployed air bag module is diagnosed as faulty, contact vehicle manufacturer for proper disposal instructions.

1999 ACCESSORIES & EQUIPMENT
Air Bag Restraint Systems
Crown Victoria, Grand Marquis & Town Car (Cont.)

FORD
4-15

SCRAPPED VEHICLE

CAUTION: DO NOT dispose of undeployed air bag module without first deploying air bag. If this is not possible through the following procedures, contact vehicle manufacturer for further instructions.

If vehicle is to be scrapped, undeployed air bag module must first be deployed. Use the following procedures for deployment of air bag.

WARNING: Perform remote deployment outdoors. Keep all personnel at least 20 feet away to ensure physical and hearing safety from projected objects and loud noise of air bag deployment.

Remote Deployment Of Air Bag – This procedure is to be used when a vehicle with a live driver or passenger air bag is to be scrapped, but a problem in air bag electrical system prevents deployment with air bag still installed in vehicle.

1) Before proceeding, see SERVICE PRECAUTIONS. Deactivate air bag system. See DISABLING & ACTIVATING AIR BAG SYSTEM.

2) Remove air bag modules. See DRIVER AIR BAG MODULE and PASSENGER AIR BAG MODULE under REMOVAL & INSTALLATION. With air bag modules removed, cut air bag connector from wiring harness near air bag module. Strip 1" of insulation from wire ends. Obtain 2 wires at least 20 feet long. Connect one end of each 20-foot wire to one end of each air bag module wire.

WARNING: When placing a live air bag on a bench or other surface, always face air bag and trim cover up and away from surface. This will reduce motion of air bag module if it is accidentally deployed.

3) Place air bag module with trim cover facing upward on a flat surface, in a remote area such as a parking lot or field. Remain at least 20 feet away from air bag module. Deploy air bag by touching loose ends of both wires to 12-volt battery terminals.

4) If successful, a loud noise will be heard and bag material will be visible. Allow at least 10 minutes for cooling and dissipation of air bag effluents before approaching air bag. Air bag is now inoperative. If air bag does not deploy, air bag module is faulty. Contact vehicle manufacturer for further instructions on disposal procedures.

POST-COLLISION INSPECTION

If vehicle has been in a collision and air bags deployed, perform the following:

- Replace deployed air bag modules.
- Replace Air Bag Diagnostic Monitor (ADM).
- Check crash sensor on front of vehicle, and side impact sensors, if equipped.
- Inspect areas near air bag modules. If interfering with deployment, replace as necessary.
- Inspect steering column for load damage. Replace as necessary.
- Inspect wiring and harness connectors. Replace as necessary.
- Perform SYSTEM OPERATION CHECK.

If a collision has occurred and air bags did not deploy, perform the following:

- Verify proper sensor and ADM orientation. Inspect mounting brackets.
- Remove air bag modules and inspect wiring and connectors for damage.
- Check area near modules for damage. Check modules for fit. Repair as necessary.
- Inspect steering column for load damage. Replace as necessary.
- Inspect areas near air bag modules. If interfering with deployment, replace as necessary.

REMOVAL & INSTALLATION

WARNING: Failure to follow service precautions may result in air bag deployment and personal injury. See SERVICE PRECAUTIONS. After component replacement, ensure proper system operation. See SYSTEM OPERATION CHECK.

CAUTION: When battery is disconnected, vehicle computer and memory systems may lose memory data. Driveability problems may exist until computer systems have completed a relearn cycle. See COMPUTER RELEARN PROCEDURES in GENERAL INFORMATION.

AIR BAG DIAGNOSTIC MONITOR (ADM)

Removal & Installation – **1)** Before proceeding, see SERVICE PRECAUTIONS. Record USER 1 and USER 2 preset radio frequencies for reprogramming. Disable air bag system. See DISABLING & ACTIVATING AIR BAG SYSTEM. Leave negative battery cable disconnected.

2) Remove right side sill plate. Pull carpet back to reveal ADM. Disengage ADM electrical connector locking clips. Disconnect electrical connectors. Remove 3 ADM retaining bolts. Remove ADM from vehicle.

3) To install, reverse removal procedure. Tighten fasteners to specification. See TORQUE SPECIFICATIONS. Activate air bag system. See DISABLING & ACTIVATING AIR BAG SYSTEM. Check AIR BAG warning light to ensure system is functioning properly. See SYSTEM OPERATION CHECK.

CLOCKSPRING

CAUTION: When removing steering wheel, DO NOT use a knock-off type steering wheel puller, or strike steering wheel or shaft with a hammer. A sudden impact could damage bearing or collapse steering column.

Removal & Installation – **1)** Before proceeding, see SERVICE PRECAUTIONS. Record USER 1 and USER 2 preset radio frequencies for reprogramming. Disable air bag system. See DISABLING & ACTIVATING AIR BAG SYSTEM. Leave negative battery cable disconnected. Ensure front wheels are in straight-ahead position and steering column shaft alignment mark is at 12 o'clock position. Turn key to LOCK position.

2) Remove driver air bag module. See DRIVER AIR BAG MODULE under REMOVAL & INSTALLATION. Remove steering wheel. See STEERING WHEEL.

3) If clockspring is to be reused, apply tape across clockspring to prevent accidental rotation. Position tilt column in full down position. Unscrew tilt wheel lever. Remove 2 parking brake release lever bolts and position lever to one side. Remove lower steering column cover. Remove 5 bolts and remove lower steering column reinforcement. Remove 4 screws and remove lower steering column shroud.

4) Turn ignition switch to RUN position. Using suitable punch, depress tab through hole in ignition housing and pull ignition switch lock cylinder from housing. Remove instrument panel lower insulator. Loosen forward steering column mounting nuts. Disconnect transmission range indicator cable. Loosen rear steering column nuts to allow column to drop for upper steering column shroud removal. Remove upper steering column shroud.

5) Depress tab and remove voice-activated cellular microphone, (if equipped). Remove screw from Passive Anti-Theft System (PATS) transmitter and remove transmitter. Remove key-in warning indicator switch from ignition switch lock cylinder housing. Cut air bag harness tie strap. Disengage harness from retainer. Remove connectors from bracket and disconnect connectors. Pry clockspring tabs loose and remove clockspring from column.

6) To install, reverse removal procedure. Ensure clockspring tabs fully engage during installation. Install new harness tie strap. Tighten fasten-

FORD
4-16

1999 ACCESSORIES & EQUIPMENT
Air Bag Restraint Systems
Crown Victoria, Grand Marquis & Town Car (Cont.)

ers to specification. See TORQUE SPECIFICATIONS. Activate air bag system. See DISABLING & ACTIVATING AIR BAG SYSTEM. Ensure proper system function. See SYSTEM OPERATION CHECK.

DRIVER AIR BAG MODULE

Removal & Installation – 1) Before proceeding, see SERVICE PRECAUTIONS. Record USER 1 and USER 2 preset radio frequencies for reprogramming. Disconnect negative battery cable.
2) Remove 2 bolts from sides of steering wheel. Disconnect air bag module and horn wiring connectors from clockspring connector, and remove driver air bag module.
3) To install, connect air bag module wiring connector to clockspring connector. Position air bag module on steering wheel and install bolts. Tighten fasteners to specification. See TORQUE SPECIFICATIONS. Connect negative battery cable. Ensure system is functioning properly. See SYSTEM OPERATION CHECK.

FRONT IMPACT SENSOR

NOTE: Vehicle sensor orientation is critical for proper system operation. If a vehicle equipped with air bag system is involved in a crash, and fenders or grille area have been damaged, inspect sensor mounting brackets for deformation. If damaged, system should be deactivated to ensure air bag does not deploy. See DISABLING & ACTIVATING AIR BAG SYSTEM. Damaged sensor(s) should be replaced, whether or not air bag has been deployed. In addition, ensure body structure in area of sensor mounting is restored to its original construction.

Removal & Installation – Before proceeding, see SERVICE PRECAUTIONS. Disable air bag system. See DISABLING & ACTIVATING AIR BAG SYSTEM. Leave negative battery cable disconnected. Remove radiator upper shield. Disconnect front impact sensor electrical connector. Remove 3 retaining screws and remove sensor from vehicle. To install, reverse removal procedure. Tighten sensor bolts to specification. See TORQUE SPECIFICATIONS. Activate air bag system. See DISABLING & ACTIVATING AIR BAG SYSTEM. Ensure proper system function. See SYSTEM OPERATION CHECK.

PASSENGER AIR BAG MODULE

Removal & Installation – Before proceeding, see SERVICE PRECAUTIONS. Disable air bag system. See DISABLING & ACTIVATING AIR BAG SYSTEM. Open glove box door. Press door side tabs inward and lower glove box toward floor. Disconnect air bag module electrical connector. Remove two bolts retaining air bag module to cross vehicle beam. Pull down to release upper module retaining clips. Remove passenger air bag module from vehicle. To install, reverse removal procedure. Tighten air bag module bolts to specification. See TORQUE SPECIFICATIONS. Activate air bag system. See DISABLING & ACTIVATING AIR BAG SYSTEM. Check AIR BAG warning light to ensure system is functioning properly. See SYSTEM OPERATION CHECK.

SIDE AIR BAG MODULES

Removal & Installation – 1) Before proceeding, see SERVICE PRECAUTIONS. Record USER 1 and USER 2 preset radio frequencies for reprogramming. Disable air bag system. See DISABLING & ACTIVATING AIR BAG SYSTEM. Leave negative battery cable disconnected.
2) Move appropriate seat forward. Remove rear track covers. Remove track mounting nuts. Move seat rearward and remove front track covers. Remove front track bolts. Disconnect seat electrical connectors and remove seat from vehicle.
3) Carefully slide seat back trim panel up. Pull out bottom corners of panel to disengage "J" hooks. Slide panel down and remove from seat. Inspect panel "J" hooks for damage. replace as necessary. Release 4 seat back cover "J" couplings. Pull seat cover aside to reveal side air bag deployment chute. Unzip deployment chute. Remove and discard side air bag retaining nuts. Remove side air bag module from seat frame

while pulling seat cover and pad aside. Disconnect electrical connector and complete removal. Inspect mounting surfaces for damage or debris and repair as necessary.
4) To install, reverse removal procedure. Install new side air bag module nuts and torque to specification. See TORQUE SPECIFICATIONS. Ensure module fit is okay and deployment chute zipper operates properly. Chute should cover length of module, but not ends. If Improperly installed air bag may not deploy properly. Activate air bag system. See DISABLING & ACTIVATING AIR BAG SYSTEM. Check AIR BAG warning light to ensure system is functioning properly. See SYSTEM OPERATION CHECK.

SIDE IMPACT SENSORS

Removal & Installation – 1) Before proceeding, see SERVICE PRECAUTIONS. Record USER 1 and USER 2 preset radio frequencies for reprogramming. Disable air bag system. See DISABLING & ACTIVATING AIR BAG SYSTEM. Leave negative battery cable disconnected.
2) Move appropriate seat forward. Remove rear track covers. Remove track mounting nuts. Move seat rearward and remove front track covers. Remove front track bolts. Disconnect seat electrical connectors and remove seat from vehicle. Remove carpet to gain access to side impact sensor. Remove 2 sensor bolts. Disconnect electrical connector and remove sensor from vehicle.
3) To install, reverse removal procedure. Tighten air bag module bolts to specification. See TORQUE SPECIFICATIONS. Activate air bag system. See DISABLING & ACTIVATING AIR BAG SYSTEM. Check AIR BAG warning light to ensure system is functioning properly. See SYSTEM OPERATION CHECK.

STEERING WHEEL

Removal & Installation – 1) Before proceeding, see SERVICE PRECAUTIONS. Record USER 1 and USER 2 preset radio frequencies for reprogramming. Disable air bag system. See DISABLING & ACTIVATING AIR BAG SYSTEM. Leave negative battery cable disconnected.
2) Ensure front wheels are in straight-ahead position. Remove driver air bag module. See DRIVER AIR BAG MODULE. Disconnect horn and cruise control wiring harness connector (if equipped) from steering wheel.

NOTE: Ensure air bag clockspring harness does not get caught on steering wheel when lifting steering wheel from steering column.

3) Remove and discard steering wheel retaining bolt. Reference mark steering wheel hub to steering wheel shaft to ensure proper alignment during installation. Using Steering Wheel Puller (T77F-4220-B1), remove steering wheel. Route clockspring wiring harness through steering wheel as wheel is lifted off steering shaft. To install, reverse removal procedures. Install new steering wheel retaining bolt and tighten to specification. See TORQUE SPECIFICATIONS.

COMPONENT LOCATIONS

COMPONENT LOCATIONS

Component	Location
Air Bag Diagnostic Monitor	Behind Right Side Of Instrument Panel
Clockspring	On Steering Column, Behind Steering Wheel
Driver Air Bag Module	On Center Of Steering Wheel
Front Impact Sensor	Center Front Of Engine Compartment
Passenger Air Bag Module	Above Glove Box
Side Air Bag Modules	In Outboard Side Of Front Seats
Side Impact Sensors	Under Front Seats

1999 ACCESSORIES & EQUIPMENT
Air Bag Restraint Systems
Crown Victoria, Grand Marquis & Town Car (Cont.)

FORD
4-17

WIRE REPAIR

To repair damage to sensor wiring and wiring harnesses, note following conditions before proceeding:

- All wire splice connections must be staggered at least 2" (50 mm) apart.
- Use proper size, waterproof butt-splice connectors on any exposed wiring.
- Use heat shrink nylon splice to prevent water, salt, condensation and heat from affecting the wiring repair. Insert pre-stripped wire ends into proper size waterproof butt-splice connector, and crimp connector using appropriate crimping pliers. *See Fig. 2.* Using heat gun, hair dryer or match, heat splice until it shrinks and adhesive oozes from each end of tubing. Connection is now waterproofed.

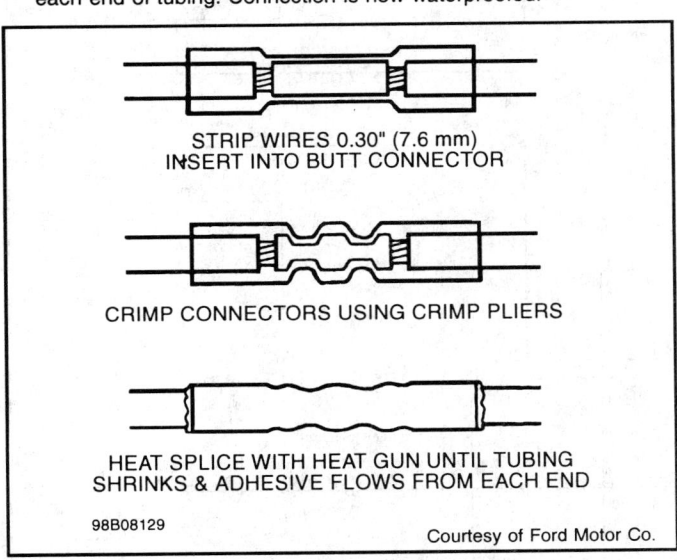

STRIP WIRES 0.30" (7.6 mm)
INSERT INTO BUTT CONNECTOR

CRIMP CONNECTORS USING CRIMP PLIERS

HEAT SPLICE WITH HEAT GUN UNTIL TUBING
SHRINKS & ADHESIVE FLOWS FROM EACH END

98B08129   Courtesy of Ford Motor Co.

Fig. 2: Repairing & Waterproofing Wiring Connections

TORQUE SPECIFICATIONS

TORQUE SPECIFICATIONS

Application	Ft. Lbs. (N.m)
Air Bag Diagnostic Module	9 (12)
Driver Air Bag Bolts	9 (12)
Side Impact Sensor Bolts	9 (12)
Steering Column Nuts	11 (15)
Steering Wheel Bolt	30 (40)
	INCH Lbs. (N.m)
Side Air Bag Nuts	62 (7)
Passenger Air Bag Bracket Bolts	80 (9)

1999 ACCESSORIES & EQUIPMENT
Air Bag Restraint Systems
Crown Victoria, Grand Marquis & Town Car (Cont.)

WIRING DIAGRAMS

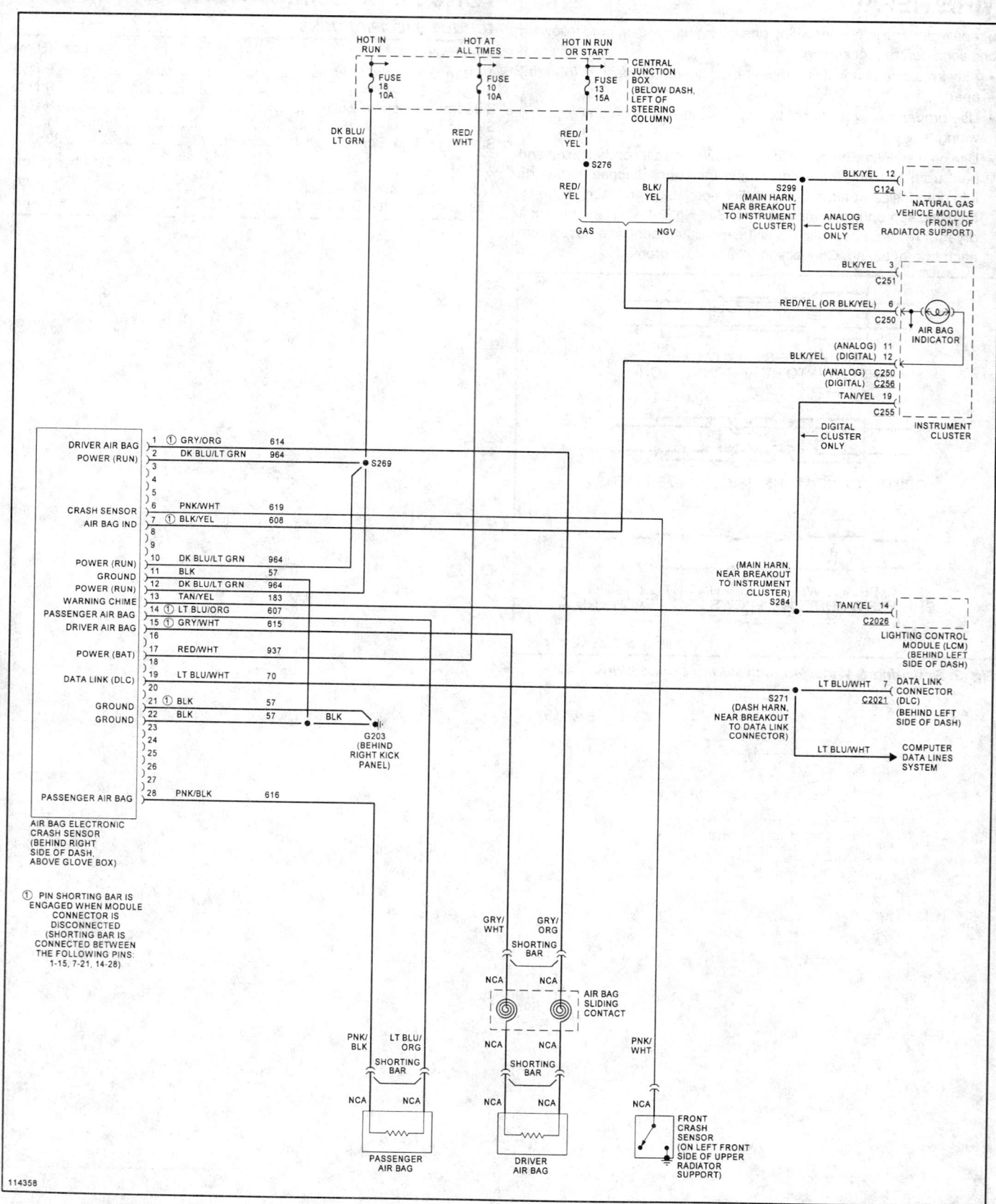

Fig. 3: Air Bag System Wiring Diagram (Crown Victoria & Grand Marquis)

1999 ACCESSORIES & EQUIPMENT
Air Bag Restraint Systems
Crown Victoria, Grand Marquis & Town Car (Cont.)

FORD
4-19

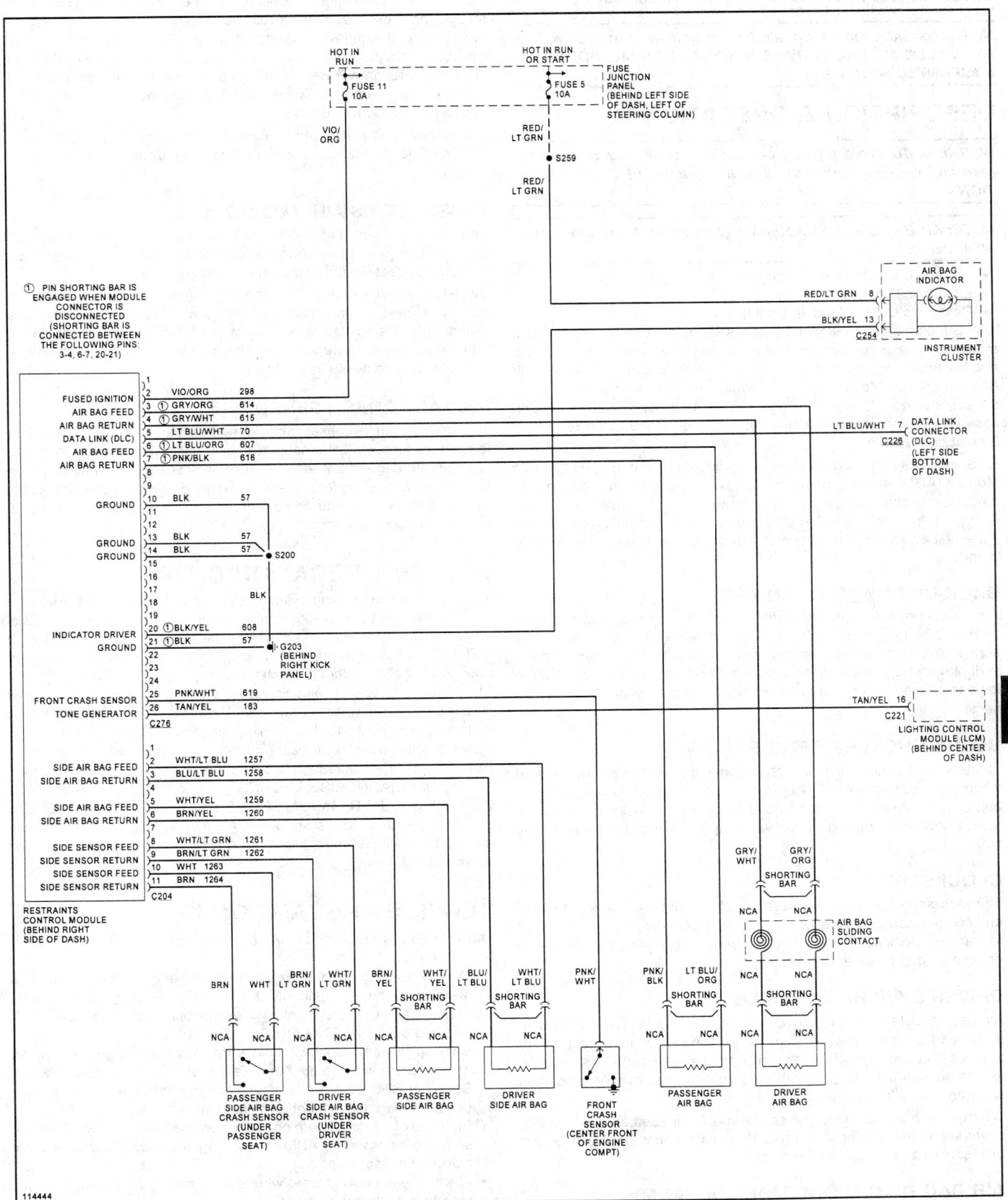

Fig. 4: Air Bag System Wiring Diagram (Town Car)

NOTE: This article includes Cutaway and RV Cutaway.

NOTE: For information on air bag diagnosis and testing, see MITCHELL® AIR BAG SERVICE & REPAIR MANUAL, DOMESTIC & IMPORTED MODELS.

DESCRIPTION & OPERATION

WARNING: To avoid injury from accidental air bag deployment, read and carefully follow all WARNINGS and SERVICE PRECAUTIONS.

NOTE: Air Bag Diagnostic Monitor (ADM) may be referred to by other names:

- Electronic Crash Sensor (ECS).
- Electronic Crash Unit (ECU).
- Restraints Control Module (RCM).

The Supplemental Restraint System (SRS), also known as air bag system, is designed to provide increased accident protection for driver and front passenger by deploying air bag in a front-end collision. The Air Bag Diagnostic Monitor (ADM) module, together with primary crash sensor, determines when to deployed air bags and belt and buckle assembly pretensioners. Air bag system is designed to be used with 3-point safety belts.

SRS includes the following major components: Air Bag Diagnostic Monitor (ADM) module, primary crash sensor, driver's air bag module, passenger's side air bag module, inflator (in air bag module), clockspring, air bag indicator (AIR BAG warning light), driver's and passenger's belt and buckle assembly pretensioners, and associated wiring harnesses.

BACK-UP POWER SUPPLY

A back-up power supply is located inside Air Bag Diagnostic Monitor (ADM). If battery or battery cables are damaged in a collision before sensor circuits close, back-up power supply will provide electrical power to deploy air bags. Back-up power supply will hold a deployment charge for approximately one minute after negative battery cable is disconnected.

BELT & BUCKLE PRETENSIONER

The belt and buckle assembly pretensioner is a pyrotechnic device that when signaled by the ADM module, removes excess webbing from seat belt system. When the belt and buckle assembly deploys, the buckle moves downward, pulling excess webbing from lap and shoulder safety belts.

CLOCKSPRING

The clockspring, located on steering column between steering wheel and combination switch assembly, is a contact and wire assembly used to transfer electrical signals from steering column wiring harness to driver's air bag module and horn.

DRIVER'S AIR BAG MODULE

Air bag module is located in center of steering wheel, encased in steering wheel trim cover. When primary crash sensor and safing sensor signal an impact, ignitor ignites inflator gas generant. This reaction ignites sodium azide/copper oxide gas generant in inflator, producing nitrogen gas which inflates air bag.

When air bag is activated, tear seams molded into steering wheel trim cover separate, allowing inflation of air bag assembly. Air bag module is only serviced as a complete assembly.

AIR BAG DIAGNOSTIC MONITOR (ADM)

The Air Bag Diagnostic Monitor (ADM) module is located behind passenger's side kick panel. The ADM module contains a microcomputer, which monitors electrical system components and connections.

ADM module performs a system self-check of air bag system internal circuits every time ignition switch is turned to RUN position. ADM module also energizes AIR BAG warning light during initial system self-check and whenever a fault is detected. Faults are stored in ADM module memory and translated into Light Flash Codes (LFC) which are displayed through AIR BAG warning light. ADM module also communicates through Data Link Connector (DLC) current and historical Diagnostic Trouble Codes (DTCs).

If a system fault exists and AIR BAG warning light is malfunctioning, ADM module will activate an audible chime or buzzer, indicating need for service.

PASSENGER'S AIR BAG MODULE

The passenger's air bag module is located in right side of instrument panel, above glove box. When primary crash sensor and safing sensor signal an impact, ignitor ignites inflator gas generant.

Since passenger's air bag is larger than driver's air bag, inflator contains more gas generant in a different configuration to produce more gas. When air bag is activated, instrument panel trim cover tears at seams and hinges, allowing deployment. Passenger's air bag module is only serviced as a complete assembly.

PRIMARY CRASH SENSOR

The primary crash sensor, also known as center air bag sensor, is located on center radiator support behind grill. When an impact occurs requiring air bag deployment, sensor contacts close, completing electrical circuit necessary for system operation. Both safing sensor (located inside ADM module) and primary crash sensor must activate simultaneously to deploy air bags.

SYSTEM OPERATION CHECK

1) When checking air bag system operation (also known as prove out system), and upon completion of each diagnostic test, check for faults in air bag system. To check system, turn ignition switch to RUN position. If AIR BAG warning light illuminates for approximately 6 seconds and then goes out, air bag system is functioning properly and no fault exist.
2) If a fault is detected in air bag system during initial system check, AIR BAG warning light will either fail to light, stay on continuously, or flash a code sequence. If AIR BAG warning light flashes, indicating a fault in system, count number of flashes after fault code has cycled twice. Number of flashes represents a code number used to diagnose air bag system. See DIAGNOSIS & TESTING article in MITCHELL® AIR BAG SERVICE & REPAIR MANUAL, DOMESTIC & IMPORTED MODELS.
3) If a system fault exists and AIR BAG warning light fails to light, an audible tone will be heard, indicating AIR BAG warning light is out and service is required.

SERVICE PRECAUTIONS

The following precautions should be observed when working with air bag systems:

- Disable air bag system before servicing any air bag system or steering column components. Failure to do so may result in accidental air bag deployment and cause personal injury. See DISABLING & ACTIVATING AIR BAG SYSTEM.
- Back-up power supply will hold a deployment charge for approximately one minute after negative battery cable is disconnected. Servicing SRS before one-minute waiting period may cause accidental air bag deployment and possible personal injury.
- Because of critical system operating requirements, DO NOT service sensors, clockspring, ADM, or air bag modules. Corrections are made by replacement only.
- Always wear safety glasses whenever servicing an air bag-equipped vehicle or handling an air bag.
- When carrying a live air bag module, ensure air bag module and trim cover are pointed away from your body. This minimizes chance of injury in event of an accidental deployment.

- When placing a live air bag module on a bench or other surface, always face air bag module and trim cover up and away from surface. This will reduce module motion if it is accidentally deployed.
- After deployment, air bag surface may contain deposits of sodium hydroxide, which may irritate skin. Sodium hydroxide is a product of gas generant combustion. Always wear gloves and safety glasses when handling a deployed air bag. Wash your hands using mild soap and water. Follow correct disposal procedures. See DISPOSAL PROCEDURES.
- If a part is replaced and new part does not correct condition, reinstall original part and perform diagnostic procedure again.
- Never probe connectors on air bag module. Doing so may cause air bag deployment and/or personal injury.
- The instruction to disconnect always refers to a connector. DO NOT remove a component from vehicle when instructed to disconnect.
- After repairs, ensure AIR BAG warning light does not indicate any other faults. See SYSTEM OPERATION CHECK.

DISABLING & ACTIVATING AIR BAG SYSTEM

WARNING: Wait one minute after disabling air bag system before working on vehicle. Back-up power supply holds a deployment charge for approximately one minute after positive battery cable is disconnected. Servicing air bag system before one minute may cause accidental air bag deployment and possible personal injury.

CAUTION: When battery is disconnected, vehicle computer and memory systems may lose memory data. Driveability problems may exist until computer systems have completed a relearn cycle. See COMPUTER RELEARN PROCEDURES in GENERAL INFORMATION.

DISABLING SYSTEM

1) Record USER 1 and USER 2 preset radio frequencies for reprogramming (if equipped). Disconnect battery(s). Follow appropriate procedure. See SINGLE BATTERY, DUAL BATTERY (DIESEL) or DUAL BATTERY (GASOLINE). Wait at least one minute for back-up power supply to deplete stored energy.
2) Remove driver's air bag. See DRIVER'S AIR BAG MODULE under REMOVAL & INSTALLATION. Connect appropriate air bag simulator to clockspring connector at top of steering column (in place of air bag). See AIR BAG SIMULATOR.
3) Remove passenger's air bag module. See PASSENGER'S AIR BAG MODULE under REMOVAL & INSTALLATION. Connect appropriate air bag simulator to passenger's air bag vehicle harness connector (in place of air bag). Connect battery. To reactivate SRS, see ACTIVATING SYSTEM.
Single Battery – Disconnect negative battery cable in usual manner.
Dual Battery (Diesel) – Disconnect secondary battery positive battery cable from primary battery positive terminal. Insulate secondary positive battery cable with non-conductive material. Disconnect primary battery negative cable.
Dual Battery (Gasoline) – Disconnect primary battery negative cable. Remove ground bolt and pull secondary battery negative cable away from frame. Insulate secondary negative battery cable with non-conductive material.

AIR BAG SIMULATOR

An Air Bag Simulator (418-F088 or 105-R0012) or equivalent is required to perform diagnosis and testing of the air bag system. *See Fig. 1.* An air bag simulator is a 2-ohm resistor, with appropriate connector, used to simulate an air bag module. DO NOT short-circuit air bag module connections with a zero-ohm jumper wire. If zero-ohm jumper is used, a Diagnostic Trouble Code (DTC) will be set.

ACTIVATING SYSTEM

1) Disconnect battery(s). Follow appropriate procedure. See SINGLE BATTERY, DUAL BATTERY (DIESEL) or DUAL BATTERY (GASO-

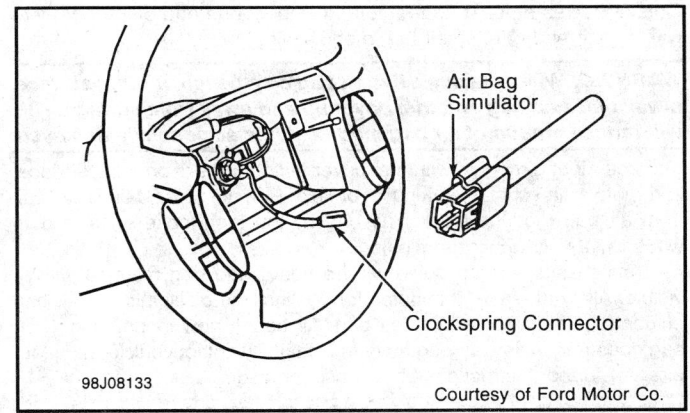

Fig. 1: Identifying Air Bag Simulator

LINE). Wait at least one minute for back-up power supply to deplete stored energy. Remove air bag simulator from clockspring connector. Remove air bag simulator from passenger's side air bag vehicle harness connector. Install driver's air bag module. See DRIVER'S AIR BAG MODULE under REMOVAL & INSTALLATION.
2) Install passenger's side air bag module. See PASSENGER'S SIDE AIR BAG MODULE under REMOVAL & INSTALLATION. Reconnect battery. Recheck system operation. See SYSTEM OPERATION CHECK. Reprogram USER 1 and USER 2 preset radio frequencies and set clock.

DISPOSAL PROCEDURES

WARNING: Refer to SERVICE PRECAUTIONS before proceeding.

Air bag disposal may be necessary in following situation:
- Scrapping vehicle with deployed air bag.
- Scrapping vehicle with live air bag.
- Disposal of a live but electrically faulty air bag module.
- Disposal of a deployed air bag module.

DEPLOYED AIR BAG

Dispose of deployed air bag module as any other part. Air bag module components are not reusable.

UNDEPLOYED AIR BAG – FAULTY UNIT

If an undeployed air bag module is diagnosed as faulty, contact vehicle manufacturer for proper disposal instructions.

SCRAPPED VEHICLE

CAUTION: DO NOT dispose of undeployed air bag modules without first deploying air bag. If this is not possible through procedure outlined, contact vehicle manufacturer for further instructions.

If vehicle is to be scrapped, undeployed air bag module must first be deployed. Use the following procedure for deployment of air bag.
Remote Deployment Of Air Bag – This procedure is to be used when a vehicle with a live driver's or passenger's air bag is to be scrapped, but a problem in air bag electrical system prevents deployment with air bag still installed in vehicle.

WARNING: Perform remote deployment outdoors. Keep all personnel at least 20 feet away to ensure physical and hearing safety from projected objects and loud noise of air bag deployment.

1) Before proceeding, see SERVICE PRECAUTIONS. Deactivate system. See DISABLING & ACTIVATING AIR BAG SYSTEM.
2) Remove air bag modules. See DRIVER'S AIR BAG MODULE and PASSENGER'S AIR BAG MODULE under REMOVAL & INSTALLATION. With air bag modules removed, cut air bag connector from wiring harness near air bag module. Strip 1" of insulation from wire ends.

Obtain 2 wires at least 20 feet long. Connect one end of each 20-foot wire to one end of each air bag module wire.

WARNING: When placing a live air bag on a bench or other surface, always face air bag and trim cover up and away from surface. This will reduce motion of air bag module if it is accidentally deployed.

3) Place air bag module with trim cover facing upward on a flat surface, in remote area such as parking lot or field. Remain at least 20 feet away from air bag module. Deploy air bag by touching loose ends of both wires to 12-volt battery terminals.

4) If successful, a loud noise will be heard and bag material will be visible. Allow at least 10 minutes for cooling and dissipation of air bag effluents before approaching air bag. Air bag is now inoperative. If air bag does not deploy, air bag module is faulty. Contact vehicle manufacturer for further instructions on disposal procedures.

POST-COLLISION INSPECTION

If vehicle has been in a collision and air bags deployed, perform the following:

- Replace air bag modules.
- Replace Air Bag Diagnostic Monitor (ADM).
- Check crash sensors on front of vehicle.
- Inspect areas near air bag modules. If interfering with deployment, replace as necessary.
- Inspect steering column for load damage. Replace as necessary.
- Inspect wiring and harness connectors. Replace as necessary.
- Perform SYSTEM OPERATION CHECK.

If a collision has occurred and air bags did not deploy, perform the following:

- Remove both air bag modules and inspect wiring and connectors for damage.
- Check area near modules for damage, check modules for fit. Repair as necessary.
- Inspect steering column for load damage. Replace as necessary.
- Inspect areas near air bag modules. If interfering with deployment, replace as necessary.

REMOVAL & INSTALLATION

WARNING: Failure to follow service precautions may result in air bag deployment and personal injury. See SERVICE PRECAUTIONS. After component replacement, ensure proper system operation. See SYSTEM OPERATION CHECK.

CAUTION: When battery is disconnected, vehicle computer and memory systems may lose memory data. Driveability problems may exist until computer systems have completed a relearn cycle. See COMPUTER RELEARN PROCEDURES in GENERAL INFORMATION.

AIR BAG DIAGNOSTIC MONITOR

Removal – 1) Electronic Crash Sensor (ADM) is located behind passenger's side kick panel. Before proceeding, see SERVICE PRECAUTIONS. Disable air bag system. See DISABLING & ACTIVATING AIR BAG SYSTEM. Leave battery(s) disconnected.

2) Remove passenger's side kick panel. Disconnect ADM module connector locking clip and disconnect ADM connector. Remove 3 retaining bolts and remove ADM from vehicle.

Installation – To install ADM, reverse removal procedure. Tighten fasteners to specification. See TORQUE SPECIFICATIONS. Activate air bag system. See DISABLING & ACTIVATING AIR BAG SYSTEM. Check AIR BAG warning light to ensure system is functioning properly. See SYSTEM OPERATION CHECK.

BELT & BUCKLE PRETENSIONER

Removal – 1) Belt and buckle assembly pretensioners are located at lower outboard sides of front seats. Before proceeding, see SERVICE PRECAUTIONS. Disable air bag system. See DISABLING & ACTIVATING AIR BAG SYSTEM. Leave battery(s) disconnected.

2) On driver's side remove front seat back latch lower cover. On passenger's side, remove front seat back pivot side outer cover. Disconnect belt and buckle assembly pretensioner harness connector. Using Safety Belt Bolt Bit (501-010 or T77L-2100-A) or T-50 Torx tool, remove belt and buckle pretensioner retaining bolt and remove belt and buckle pretensioner.

Installation – To install, reverse removal procedure. Align both anti-rotation tabs on belt and buckle pretensioner into seat track prior to tightening bolt to specifications. See TORQUE SPECIFICATIONS. Check AIR BAG warning light to ensure system functions properly. See SYSTEM OPERATION CHECK.

CLOCKSPRING

Removal – 1) Clockspring is located on steering column between steering wheel and combination switch. Before proceeding, see SERVICE PRECAUTIONS. Disable air bag system. See DISABLING & ACTIVATING AIR BAG SYSTEM. Leave battery(s) disconnected.

2) Remove driver's side air bag module. See DRIVER'S AIR BAG MODULE. Ensure front wheels are in straight-ahead position. Remove steering wheel. See STEERING WHEEL.

3) Twist tilt wheel handle and remove (if equipped). Remove 3 screws and lower steering column shroud. Turn ignition switch to RUN position. Using suitable tool, push upward on cylinder release tab through hole in lower shroud while pulling cylinder outward to remove ignition switch lock cylinder.

4) Carefully pry to release clips and remove lower steering column opening cover. Remove upper steering column shroud. Install service lock on clockspring. If service lock is missing, apply 2 strips of tape across clockspring to prevent accidental rotation. See Fig. 2.

5) Remove key-in ignition warning indicator switch, disconnect clockspring connector and separate air bag electrical connector from bracket. Pry 3 clockspring retaining clips loose. Separate wire from 2 retaining clips and remove clockspring.

NOTE: Service replacement clockspring will contain a plastic locking insert to prevent rotation. DO NOT remove insert until clockspring is securely installed on column.

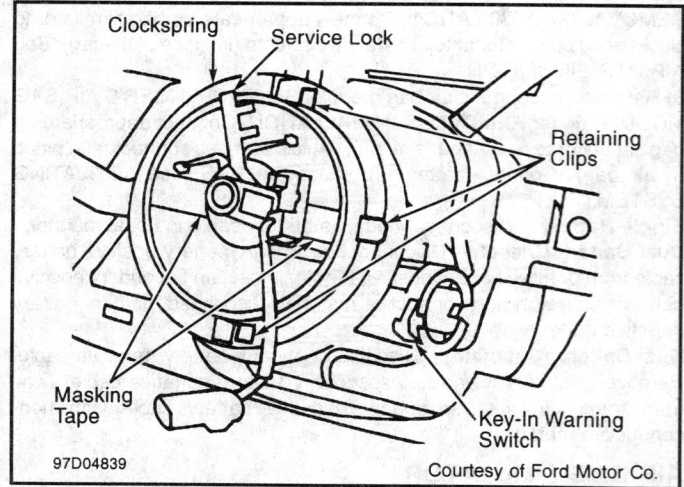

Courtesy of Ford Motor Co.

Fig. 2: Removing Clockspring

Installation – To install, reverse removal procedure. Properly orientate clockspring assembly. Align air bag pigtail to 3 o'clock position. Align dot on steering shaft to 9 o'clock position. Press clockspring into place at 6, 12, and 3 o'clock positions. If new clockspring is being installed, remove locking mechanism. Tighten fasteners to specification. See TORQUE SPECIFICATIONS. Activate air bag system. See DISABLING & ACTIVATING AIR BAG SYSTEM. Check AIR BAG warning light for proper system function. See SYSTEM OPERATION CHECK.

DRIVER'S AIR BAG MODULE

Removal – 1) Driver's air bag module is located in center of steering wheel. Before proceeding, see SERVICE PRECAUTIONS. Disconnect .battery(s). On vehicles with a single battery, disconnect negative battery cable. On vehicles with diesel engines and dual batteries, disconnect secondary battery positive battery cable from primary battery positive terminal. Insulate secondary positive battery cable with non-conductive material. Disconnect primary battery negative battery cable. On vehicles with gasoline engines and dual batteries, disconnect primary battery negative cable. Remove ground bolt and pull secondary battery negative cable away from frame. Insulate secondary negative battery cable with non-conductive material.

2) Ensure front wheels are in straight-ahead position. Remove 2 back cover plugs from rear of steering wheel. Remove 2 air bag module retaining screws and disconnect electrical connectors. Remove air bag module.

Installation – Connect air bag module to clockspring connector. Connect horn connector. Position air bag module on steering wheel. Tighten fasteners to specification. See TORQUE SPECIFICATIONS. Activate air bag system. See DISABLING & ACTIVATING AIR BAG SYSTEM. Check AIR BAG warning light to ensure system is functioning properly. See SYSTEM OPERATION CHECK.

PASSENGER'S AIR BAG MODULE

Removal – 1) Passenger's air bag module is located in right side of instrument cluster above glove box. Before proceeding, see SERVICE PRECAUTIONS. Disable air bag system. See DISABLING & ACTIVATING AIR BAG SYSTEM. Leave battery(s) disconnected.

2) Remove passenger's side lower instrument panel finish panel (knee bolster) and reinforcement. Remove passenger's air bag module retaining nuts. *See Fig. 3.* Using a 3/8 inch x 4 inch flat screwdriver (or equivalent), carefully slide head of screwdriver under right bottom edge of air bag door and lift upward, separating door from clip. Separate rest of door from clips by lifting door with hands.

3) Disconnect passenger's side air bag module connector and remove passenger's side air bag module. Remove 6 offset fasteners used for retaining air bag module door from instrument panel.

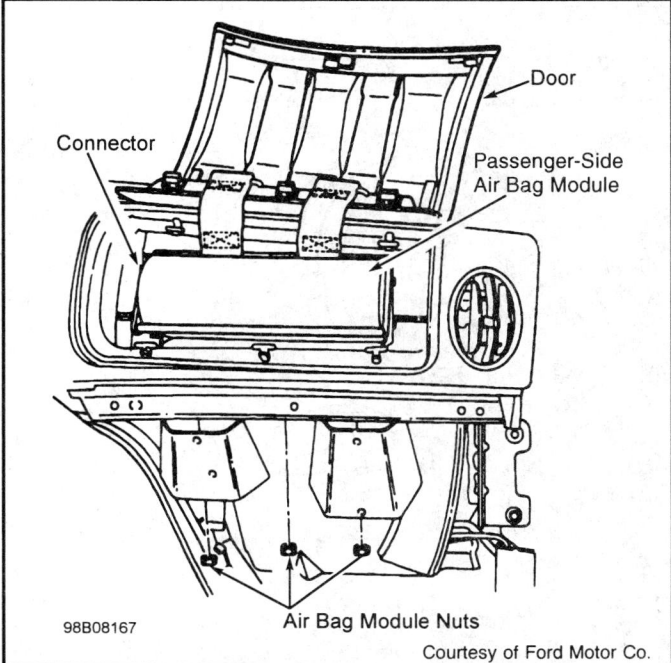

Fig. 3: Removing Passenger's Side Air Bag Module

Installation – To install, reverse removal procedure. Use 6 NEW offset fasteners on air bag module door. Tighten fasteners to specification. See TORQUE SPECIFICATIONS. Activate air bag system. See DISABLING

& ACTIVATING AIR BAG SYSTEM. Check AIR BAG warning light to ensure system is functioning properly. See SYSTEM OPERATION CHECK.

PRIMARY CRASH SENSOR

NOTE: Vehicle sensor orientation is critical for proper system operation. If vehicle is involved in a collision where fenders or grille area have been damaged, inspect primary sensor mounting brackets for deformation. Damaged sensor(s) should be replaced whether or not air bag has been deployed. In addition, ensure body structure in area of sensor mounting is restored to its original construction.

Removal – Primary crash sensor is located on center radiator support behind grill. Before proceeding, see SERVICE PRECAUTIONS. Disable air bag system. See DISABLING & ACTIVATING AIR BAG SYSTEM. Leave battery(s) disconnected. Remove radiator grill. Disconnect primary crash sensor connector, remove screws and remove primary crash sensor.

Installation – To install, reverse removal procedure. Tighten fasteners to specification. See TORQUE SPECIFICATIONS. Activate air bag system. See DISABLING & ACTIVATING AIR BAG SYSTEM. Check AIR BAG warning light to ensure system is functioning properly. See SYSTEM OPERATION CHECK.

STEERING WHEEL

Removal – 1) Ensure front wheels are in straight-ahead position. Before proceeding, see SERVICE PRECAUTIONS. Disable air bag system. See DISABLING & ACTIVATING AIR BAG SYSTEM. Remove air bag module from steering wheel. See DRIVER'S AIR BAG MODULE. Disconnect speed control wiring harness (if equipped) from steering wheel.

2) Loosen steering wheel retaining bolt several turns. Mark steering wheel hub and steering shaft for installation reference. Using 2-Jaw Puller (205-116 or T77F-4220-B1) or equivalent, pull steering wheel from steering shaft. Remove and discard steering wheel retaining bolt. Route clockspring (contact assembly) wiring harness through steering wheel as wheel is lifted from steering shaft.

Installation – 1) Ensure front wheels are straight. Route clockspring wiring harness through steering wheel opening at 3 o'clock position. Position steering wheel on steering shaft. Align marks made during removal procedure.

2) Ensure air bag clockspring wire is not pinched when positioning steering wheel. Install NEW steering wheel retaining bolt and tighten to specification. See TORQUE SPECIFICATIONS. Connect speed control wiring harness (if equipped) to steering wheel and snap connector assembly into steering wheel clip.

3) Install air bag module. Activate air bag system. See DISABLING & ACTIVATING AIR BAG SYSTEM. Check AIR BAG warning light to ensure system functions properly. See SYSTEM OPERATION CHECK.

WIRE REPAIR

Note following conditions when repairing damage to sensor wiring and wiring harnesses:

- All wire splice connections must be staggered at least 2" (50 mm) apart.
- Use proper size, waterproof butt-splice connectors on any exposed wiring.
- Use heat shrink nylon splice to prevent water, salt, condensation and heat from affecting the wiring repair. Insert pre-stripped wire ends into proper size waterproof butt-splice connector, and crimp connector using appropriate crimping pliers. *See Fig. 4.* Using heat gun, hair dryer or match, heat splice until it shrinks and adhesive oozes from each end of tubing. Connection is now waterproofed.

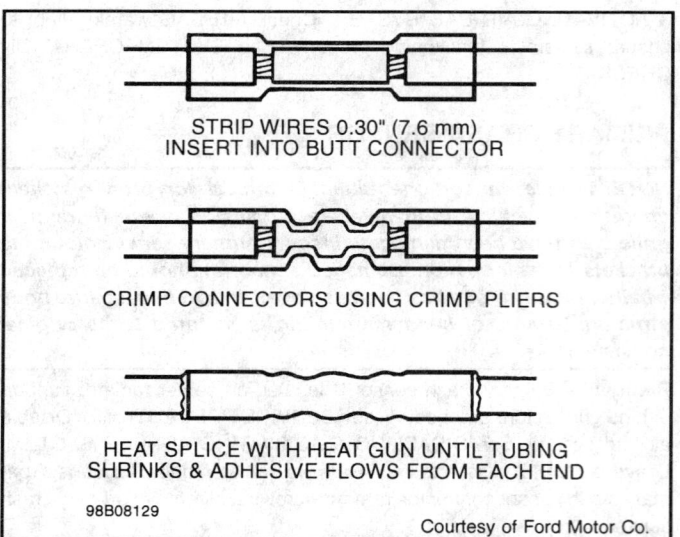

STRIP WIRES 0.30" (7.6 mm)
INSERT INTO BUTT CONNECTOR

CRIMP CONNECTORS USING CRIMP PLIERS

HEAT SPLICE WITH HEAT GUN UNTIL TUBING
SHRINKS & ADHESIVE FLOWS FROM EACH END

98B08129

Courtesy of Ford Motor Co.

Fig. 4: Repairing & Waterproofing Wiring Connections

TORQUE SPECIFICATIONS

TORQUE SPECIFICATIONS

Application	Ft. Lbs. (N.m)
Belt & Buckle Assembly Pretensioner Bolt	25-34 (34-46)
Passenger-Side Air Bag Module Nuts	14-19 (19-26)
Driver-Side Air Bag Module Screws	7-10 (10.0-14.0)
Steering Wheel Retaining Bolt	23-32 (31-44)
	INCH Lbs. (N.m)
Electronic Crash Sensor (ECS) Bolts	97-115 (11.0-13.0)
Primary Crash Sensor Screws	97-115 (11.0-13.0)
Steering Column Shroud Screws	7-10 (0.7-1.1)
Tilt Wheel & Handle	27-44 (3.0-5.0)

WIRING DIAGRAMS

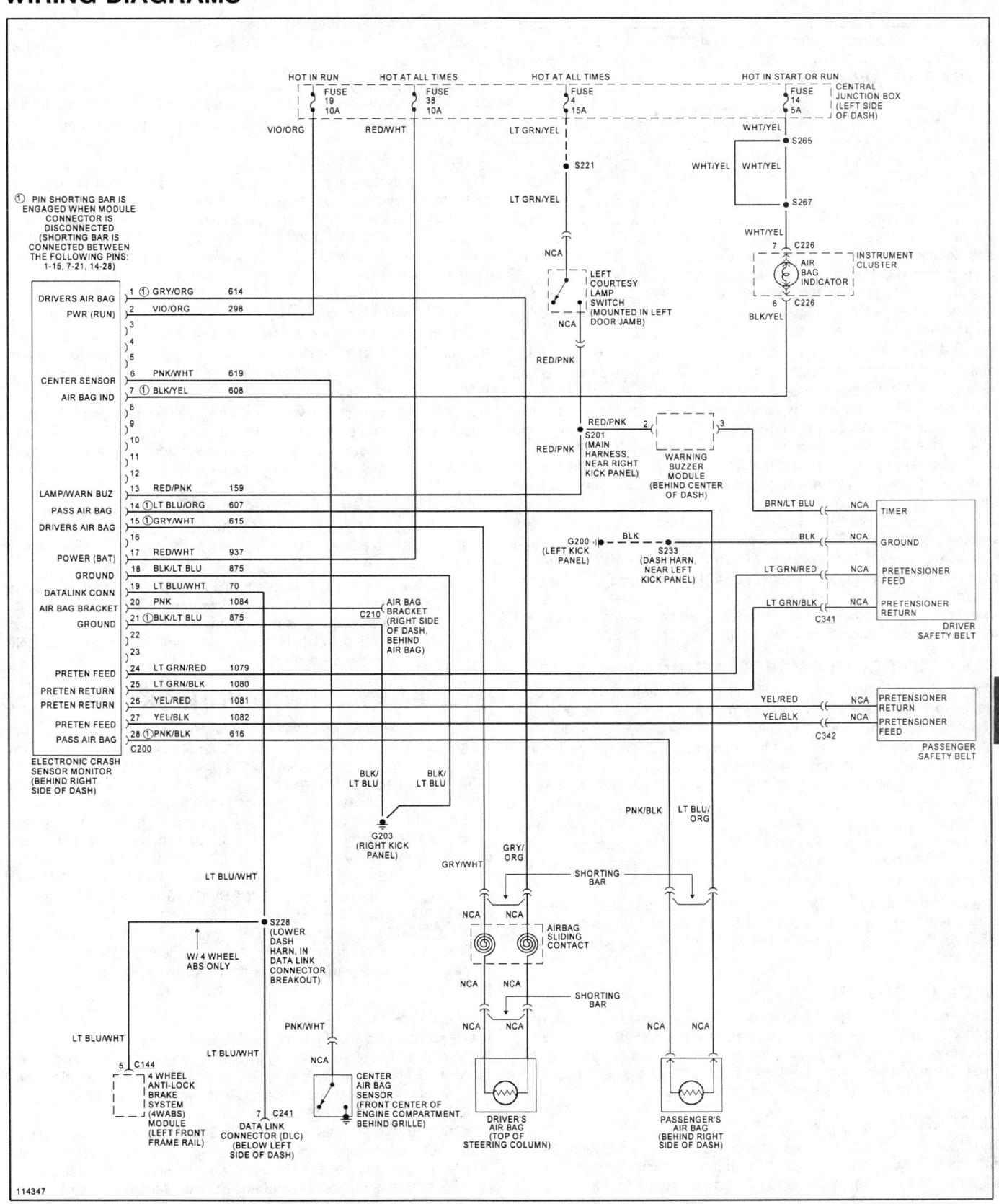

Fig. 5: Air Bag System Wiring Diagram (Econoline)

114347

NOTE: For information on air bag DIAGNOSIS & TESTING, see MITCHELL® AIR BAG SERVICE & REPAIR MANUAL, DOMESTIC & IMPORTED MODELS.

DESCRIPTION & OPERATION

WARNING: To avoid injury from accidental air bag deployment, read and carefully follow all WARNINGS and SERVICE PRECAUTIONS.

The Supplemental Restraint System (SRS), also known as air bag system, is designed to provide increased accident protection for driver and passenger by deploying air bags in a front-end collision. The air bags, stored in center of steering wheel, in instrument panel above glove box and in outboard front seat bolsters (if equipped), deploy in about 40 milliseconds after impact sensors close. Air bag system is designed to be used with 3-point safety belts.

During a front-end collision of sufficient force, either front impact sensor and a safing sensor will activate simultaneously to inflate air bag. When at least one front impact sensor and safing sensor are closed at same time, electrical current will flow, igniting the driver's and passenger's air bag module. Optional seat-mounted side air bags on Explorer and Mountaineer use side impact sensors, located on each "B" pillar. Side impact sensors operation is similar to front impact sensors. Side air bags may be deployed together, independently or not at all, depending on direction and severity of impact.

Air bag system includes the following components: Restraint Control Module (RCM), driver's air bag module, passenger air bag module and deactivation switch, (if equipped), AIR BAG warning light, side air bag modules (if equipped), side impact sensors (if equipped), front impact sensors, safing sensor (integral with RCM), ignitor assemblies (in air bag modules), clockspring (also known as sliding contact) and associated wiring harnesses. See COMPONENT LOCATIONS.

RESTRAINT CONTROL MODULE (RCM)

The Restraint Control Module (RCM), located behind right side of instrument panel, contains a microcomputer, which monitors electrical system components and connections. Diagnostic monitor performs a system self-check of air bag system internal circuits every time ignition switch is turned to RUN position. Monitor also energizes air bag system AIR BAG warning light during initial system self-check and whenever a fault is detected.

If a system fault exists and/or AIR BAG warning light is malfunctioning, RCM will signal Generic Electronic Module (GEM) to emit an audible tone indicating need for service. Diagnostic monitor can also disarm air bag system if certain faults occur.

The RCM does not deploy air bags in the event of a collision. The right and/or left front impact sensors and safing sensor determine air bag deployment. The safing sensor is internal to RCM and is not replaced separately.

BACK-UP POWER SUPPLY

A back-up power supply is located inside diagnostic monitor. If battery or battery cables are damaged in a collision before sensor circuits close, back-up power supply will supply sufficient electrical power to deploy air bags. Back-up power supply will hold a deployment charge for approximately one minute after battery is disconnected.

CLOCKSPRING

The clockspring, located on the steering column between steering wheel and combination switch, is used to transfer electrical signals from steering column wiring harness to driver's air bag module.

DRIVER'S AIR BAG MODULE

The driver's air bag module is mounted on center of steering wheel, covered by steering wheel trim cover. When a front impact sensor and

safing sensor close, signaling an impact, ignitor triggers inflator. During ignition, sodium azide reacts with copper oxide, producing nitrogen gas, which inflates air bag.

When air bag deploys, tear-seams molded into steering wheel trim cover separate, allowing inflation of air bag assembly. Driver's air bag module is not serviceable and must be replaced as a complete assembly.

ELECTRICAL SYSTEM

The air bag system is powered directly from battery and can function with ignition switch in any position, including OFF and LOCK. System can also function when driver's side seat is unoccupied. The 3 main functions performed by electrical subsystem are: detecting an impact, switching electric power to ignitors for air bag deployment, and monitoring readiness of air bag system.

FRONT IMPACT SENSORS

Front impact sensors are located at right and left sides of radiator support. Each impact sensor reacts to impacts according to direction and force. It discriminates between impacts that require air bag deployment and impacts that do not.

When an impact occurs requiring air bag deployment, impact sensor contacts close, completing electrical circuit necessary for system operation. At least 2 sensors, safing sensor and one front impact sensor, must be activated simultaneously to deploy air bags.

PASSENGER'S AIR BAG MODULE

The passenger's air bag module is mounted in right side of instrument panel, above glove box. When a front impact sensor and safing sensor close, signaling an impact, air bag ignitors trigger inflator.

Since passenger's air bag is larger than driver's air bag, inflator contains more gas generant in a different configuration to produce more gas. When air bag is activated, instrument panel trim cover tears at seams and hinges, allowing inflation. Passenger's air bag module is only serviced as a complete assembly.

SYSTEM OPERATION CHECK

1) When checking air bag system operation (also known as prove out system), and upon completion of each diagnostic test, check for faults in air bag system. To check system, turn ignition switch to RUN position. If AIR BAG warning light illuminates for approximately 6 seconds and then goes out, air bag system is functioning properly and no fault codes exist.
2) If a fault code is detected in air bag system during initial system check, AIR BAG warning light will either fail to light, stay on continuously, or flash. Flashing may be delayed up to 30 seconds. If AIR BAG warning light flashes, indicating a fault in system, see DIAGNOSIS & TESTING article in MITCHELL® AIR BAG SERVICE & REPAIR MANUAL, DOMESTIC & IMPORTED MODELS.
3) If a system fault exists and AIR BAG warning light fails to light, an audible tone will be generated by Generic Electronic Module (GEM), indicating AIR BAG warning light is out and service is required.

SERVICE PRECAUTIONS

These precautions should be observed when working with SRS:
- Disable SRS before servicing any SRS or steering column components. Failure to do so may result in accidental air bag deployment and personal injury. See procedures under DISABLING & ACTIVATING AIR BAG SYSTEM.
- Wait one minute after disabling SRS before working on vehicle. Back-up power supply holds a deployment charge for approximately one minute after negative battery cable is disconnected. Servicing SRS before one minute may cause accidental air bag deployment and possible personal injury.
- Because of critical system operating requirements, DO NOT service impact sensors, clockspring, diagnostic monitor or air bag module. Repairs are made by replacement only.

1999 ACCESSORIES & EQUIPMENT
Air Bag Restraint Systems
Expedition, Explorer, Mountaineer & Navigator (Cont.)

FORD
4-27

- Always wear safety glasses whenever servicing an air bag equipped vehicle or handling an air bag.
- When carrying a live air bag module, ensure air bag module and trim cover are pointed away from your body. This minimizes chance of injury in event of an accidental deployment.
- When placing a live air bag module on a bench or other surface, always face air bag module and trim cover facing up and away from surface. This will reduce motion of module if it is accidentally deployed.
- After deployment, air bag surface may contain deposits of sodium hydroxide, which may irritate skin. Sodium hydroxide is a product of gas generant combustion. Always wear gloves and safety glasses when handling a deployed air bag. Wash your hands using mild soap and water. Follow correct disposal procedures. See DISPOSAL PROCEDURES.
- If scrapping a vehicle with an undeployed air bag module, air bag must be deployed. See DISPOSAL PROCEDURES.
- If a part is replaced and new part does not correct condition, reinstall original part and perform diagnostic procedure again.
- Never probe connectors on air bag module. Doing so may cause air bag deployment and/or personal injury.
- Instruction to disconnect always refers to connector. DO NOT remove component from vehicle if instructed to disconnect.
- After any servicing, ensure AIR BAG warning light does not indicate any fault codes. See SYSTEM OPERATION CHECK.
- Replace air bag module if trim cover (deployment doors) is marred or damaged. DO NOT repaint trim cover. Paint may degrade cover material. Replace air bag module as necessary. Ensure damaged air bag is deployed. See DISPOSAL PROCEDURES.

DISABLING & ACTIVATING AIR BAG SYSTEM

WARNING: Wait one minute after disabling air bag system before working on vehicle. Back-up power supply holds a deployment charge for approximately one minute after negative battery cable is disconnected. Servicing air bag system before one minute may cause accidental air bag deployment and possible personal injury.

CAUTION: When battery is disconnected, vehicle computer and memory systems may lose memory data. Driveability problems may exist until computer systems have completed a relearn cycle. See COMPUTER RELEARN PROCEDURES in GENERAL INFORMATION.

DISABLING SYSTEM

1) Record USER 1 and USER 2 preset radio frequencies for reprogramming (if equipped). Disconnect negative battery cable. Wait at least one minute for back-up power supply to deplete stored energy.
2) Remove driver's air bag module. See DRIVER'S AIR BAG MODULE under REMOVAL & INSTALLATION. Connect appropriate air bag simulator to clockspring connector at top of steering column (in place of air bag). See AIR BAG SIMULATOR.
3) Remove passenger's air bag module. See PASSENGER'S AIR BAG MODULE under REMOVAL & INSTALLATION. Connect appropriate air bag simulator to passenger's air bag vehicle harness connector (in place of air bag). For Explorer and Mountaineer models equipped with optional side air bags, go to next step. For all others, go to step **5)**.
4) Disconnect driver's side air bag connector, located under driver's seat. Connect side air bag simulator. *See Fig. 2.* Repeat for passenger side air bag, and go to next step.
5) Connect negative battery cable. To reactivate SRS, see ACTIVATING SYSTEM.

AIR BAG SIMULATORS

An Air Bag Simulator (418-F088 or 105-R0012) or equivalent is required to perform diagnosis and testing of the air bag system. *See Figs. 1 and*

2. An air bag simulator is a 2-ohm resistor, with appropriate connector, used to simulate an air bag module. DO NOT short-circuit air bag module connections with a zero-ohm jumper wire. If zero-ohm jumper is used, a Diagnostic Trouble Code (DTC) will be set.

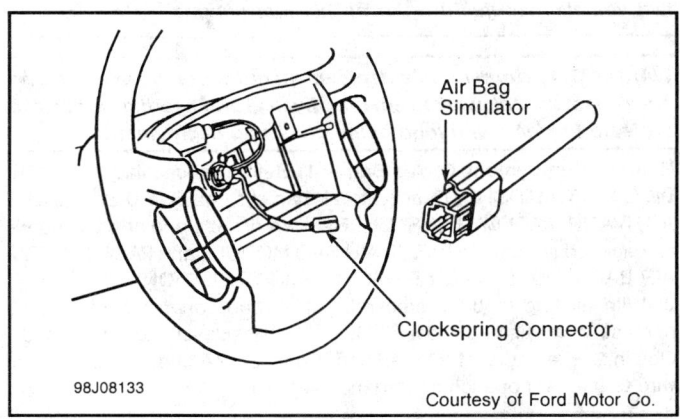

98J08133

Courtesy of Ford Motor Co.

Fig. 1: Identifying Air Bag Simulator

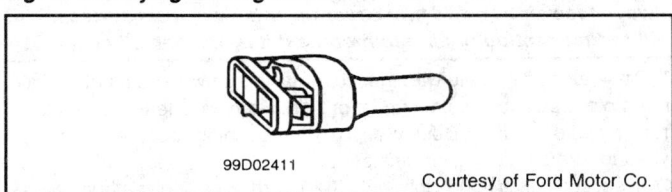

99D02411

Courtesy of Ford Motor Co.

Fig. 2: Identifying Side Air Bag Simulator (Explorer & Mountaineer)

ACTIVATING SYSTEM

1) Disconnect negative battery cable. Wait at least one minute for back-up power supply to deplete stored energy. Remove air bag simulator from clockspring connector. Remove air bag simulator from passenger's air bag vehicle harness connector. Install driver's air bag module. See DRIVER'S AIR BAG MODULE under REMOVAL & INSTALLATION.
2) Install passenger's air bag module. See PASSENGER'S AIR BAG MODULE under REMOVAL & INSTALLATION. Reconnect negative battery cable. Recheck system operation. Perform SYSTEM OPERATION CHECK. Reprogram USER 1 and USER 2 preset radio frequencies and set clock.

DISPOSAL PROCEDURES

WARNING: Refer to SERVICE PRECAUTIONS before proceeding.

Air bag disposal may be necessary in following situations:

- Scrapping vehicle with deployed air bag.
- Scrapping vehicle with live air bag.
- Disposal of a live but electrically faulty air bag module.
- Disposal of a deployed air bag module.

DEPLOYED AIR BAG

Dispose of deployed air bag module as any other part. Air bag module components are not reusable.

UNDEPLOYED AIR BAG – FAULTY UNIT

If an undeployed air bag module is diagnosed as faulty, remove air bag module and return intact to Ford Motor Company for proper disposal. Return carton for warranty claim credit. Air bag must be packaged and shipped according to U.S. Department of Transportation procedures. Retain replacement packaging including label. DO NOT deploy air bag.

FORD
4-28

1999 ACCESSORIES & EQUIPMENT
Air Bag Restraint Systems
Expedition, Explorer, Mountaineer & Navigator (Cont.)

SCRAPPED VEHICLE

CAUTION: DO NOT dispose of undeployed air bag module. If this is not possible to deploy air bag through procedures outlined, contact vehicle manufacturer for further instructions.

WARNING: Perform remote deployment outdoors. Keep all personnel at least 20 feet away to ensure physical and hearing safety from projected objects and loud noise of air bag deployment.

Remote Deployment Of Air Bag – 1) Before proceeding, see SERVICE PRECAUTIONS. Deactivate air bag system. See DISABLING & ACTIVATING AIR BAG SYSTEM. Remove driver's and/or passenger's air bag module. See DRIVER'S AIR BAG MODULE and PASSENGER'S AIR BAG MODULE under REMOVAL & INSTALLATION.
2) With air bag module removed, cut air bag connector from wiring harness near air bag module. Strip 1" of insulation from wire ends. Obtain 2 wires at least 20 feet long. Connect one end of each 20-foot wire to one end of each air bag module wire.

WARNING: When placing a live air bag on a bench or other surface, always face air bag and trim cover up and away from surface. This will reduce motion of air bag module if it is accidentally deployed.

3) Place air bag module with trim cover facing upward on a flat surface, in remote area such as parking lot or field. Remain at least 20 feet away from air bag module. Deploy air bag by touching loose ends of both wires to 12-volt battery terminals.
4) If successful, a loud noise will be heard and bag material will be visible. Allow at least 10 minutes for cooling and dissipation of air bag effluents before approaching air bag. Air bag is now inoperative. If air bag does not deploy, air bag module is faulty. Contact vehicle manufacturer for further instructions on disposal procedures.

POST-COLLISION INSPECTION

If vehicle has been in a collision and air bags deployed, perform the following:
- Replace air bag modules.
- Replace Restraint Control Module (RCM).
- Check crash sensors on front of vehicle.
- Inspect areas near air bag modules. If interfering with deployment, replace as necessary.
- Inspect steering column for load damage. Replace as necessary.
- Inspect wiring and harness connectors. Replace as necessary.
- Perform SYSTEM OPERATION CHECK.

If a collision has occurred and air bags did not deploy, perform the following:
- Remove both air bag modules and inspect wiring and connectors for damage.
- Check area near modules for damage, check modules for fit. Repair as necessary.
- Inspect steering column for load damage. Replace as necessary.
- Inspect areas near air bag modules. If interfering with deployment, replace as necessary.

REMOVAL & INSTALLATION

WARNING: Failure to follow service precautions may result in air bag deployment and personal injury. See SERVICE PRECAUTIONS. After component replacement, ensure proper system operation. See SYSTEM OPERATION CHECK.

CAUTION: When battery is disconnected, vehicle computer and memory systems may lose memory data. Driveability problems may exist until computer systems have completed a relearn cycle. See COMPUTER RELEARN PROCEDURES in GENERAL INFORMATION.

RESTRAINT CONTROL MODULE (RCM)

Removal (Expedition & Navigator) – 1) Before proceeding, see SERVICE PRECAUTIONS. Diagnostic monitor is located behind passenger's kick panel. Disable air bag system. See DISABLING & ACTIVATING AIR BAG SYSTEM. Leave negative battery cable disconnected.
2) Remove right front door opening sill panel. Remove right kick panel. Open glove box past stop to access 3 hinge mounting screws. Remove screws, and remove glove box from vehicle. Disconnect RCM electrical connector. Remove 4 RCM bracket bolts. Remove RCM and bracket as an assembly.
Installation – To install RCM, reverse removal procedure. Tighten fasteners to specification. See TORQUE SPECIFICATIONS. Activate air bag system. See DISABLING & ACTIVATING AIR BAG SYSTEM. Check AIR BAG warning light for proper system function. See SYSTEM OPERATION CHECK.
Removal (Explorer & Mountaineer) – 1) Before proceeding, see SERVICE PRECAUTIONS. Diagnostic monitor is located behind passenger's kick panel. Disable air bag system. See DISABLING & ACTIVATING AIR BAG SYSTEM. Leave negative battery cable disconnected.
2) Remove passenger's kick panel. Disconnect RCM electrical connectors. Remove 3 RCM bracket retaining bolts. Remove RCM with bracket.
Installation – To install RCM, reverse removal procedure. Tighten fasteners to specification. See TORQUE SPECIFICATIONS. Activate air bag system. See DISABLING & ACTIVATING AIR BAG SYSTEM. Check AIR BAG warning light for proper system function. See SYSTEM OPERATION CHECK.

CLOCKSPRING

Removal (Expedition & Navigator) – 1) Before proceeding, see SERVICE PRECAUTIONS. Clockspring is located on steering column between steering wheel and combination switch. Disable air bag system. See DISABLING & ACTIVATING AIR BAG SYSTEM. Leave negative battery cable disconnected. Ensure front wheels are in straight-ahead position. Remove steering wheel. See STEERING WHEEL.
2) If clockspring is to be reused, apply tape or service lock, (if available), across clockspring face to prevent accidental rotation. *See Fig. 3.* Twist tilt wheel handle and shank and remove. Remove upper instrument panel steering column cover. Remove junction box fuse/relay panel cover. Remove 2 parking brake release lever bolts and position lever aside. Remove 2 hood release lever bolts and position lever aside. Remove 6 lower instrument panel steering column cover bolts and remove cover. Remove 3 lower steering column shroud screws and remove shroud.
3) Turn ignition lock cylinder to RUN position. Using suitable tool, push upward on cylinder release tab through hole in lock cylinder housing while pulling cylinder outward. Remove steering column upper shroud. Remove passive anti-theft transmitter screw and remove transmitter. Remove key-in warning switch from ignition lock cylinder housing. *See Fig. 3.* Disengage clockspring electrical connectors from bracket. Dis-

1999 ACCESSORIES & EQUIPMENT
Air Bag Restraint Systems
Expedition, Explorer, Mountaineer & Navigator (Cont.)

FORD
4-29

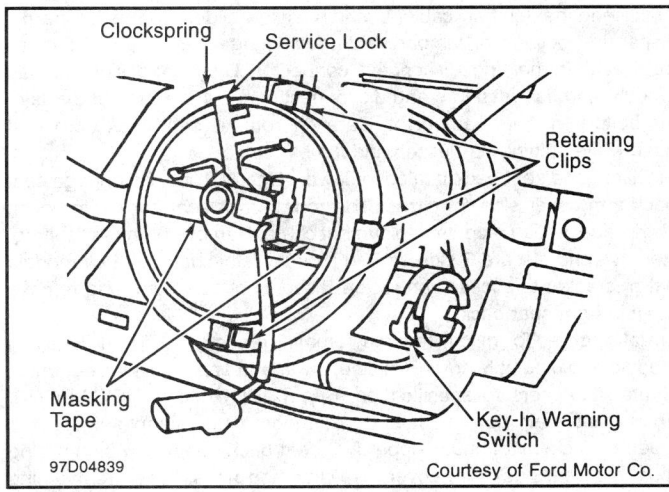

Fig. 3: Removing Clockspring

connect connectors and remove harness from retaining clips. Pry 2 clockspring retaining clips loose and remove clockspring.

NOTE: Service replacement clockspring will contain a Red plastic locking insert to prevent rotation. DO NOT remove insert until clockspring is securely installed on column.

Installation – To install, reverse removal procedure. Ensure front wheels are not turned, and clockspring is centered. Tighten fasteners to specification. See TORQUE SPECIFICATIONS. If new clockspring is being installed, remove locking mechanism. Activate air bag system. See DISABLING & ACTIVATING AIR BAG SYSTEM. Check AIR BAG warning light for proper system function. See SYSTEM OPERATION CHECK.

Removal (Explorer & Mountaineer) – 1) Before proceeding, see SERVICE PRECAUTIONS. Clockspring is located on steering column between steering wheel and combination switch. Disable air bag system. See DISABLING & ACTIVATING AIR BAG SYSTEM. Leave negative battery cable disconnected. Ensure front wheels are in straight-ahead position. Remove steering wheel. See STEERING WHEEL.

2) If clockspring is to be reused, apply tape or service lock, (if available), across clockspring face to prevent accidental rotation. See Fig. 3. Remove 2 hood release handle screws and position handle to one side. Remove 2 lower steering column opening finish panel retaining screws and pull panel out to disengage retaining clips. Remove panel. Remove 4 bolts and remove lower steering column opening finish panel reinforcement.

3) Loosen 4 steering column fasteners. Lower column slightly. Unscrew tilt wheel handle, if equipped. Remove 3 lower steering column shroud screws and remove lower shroud. Position ignition lock cylinder in RUN position. Using suitable tool, push upward on cylinder release tab through hole in lower shroud while pulling cylinder outward. Remove upper steering column shroud.

4) Remove passive anti-theft system transmitter screw and remove transmitter from vehicle. Remove key-in warning switch from ignition lock cylinder housing. Disconnect clockspring electrical connector and separate connector from bracket. Pry retaining clips loose and separate wire from two retaining clips holding wire to column. Disengage lower clockspring retaining clip. Disengage 2 upper clockspring retaining clips and remove clockspring from vehicle.

NOTE: Service replacement clockspring will contain a Red plastic locking insert to prevent rotation. DO NOT remove insert until clockspring is securely installed on column.

Installation – To install, reverse removal procedure. Ensure front wheels are not turned, and clockspring is centered. Tighten fasteners to specification. See TORQUE SPECIFICATIONS. If new clockspring is

being installed, remove locking mechanism. Activate air bag system. See DISABLING & ACTIVATING AIR BAG SYSTEM. Check AIR BAG warning light for proper system function. See SYSTEM OPERATION CHECK.

DRIVER'S AIR BAG MODULE

Removal – Before proceeding, see SERVICE PRECAUTIONS. Disconnect negative battery cable. Remove 2 back cover plugs from rear of steering wheel. Remove bolts retaining air bag module to steering wheel. See Fig. 4. Disconnect electrical connector(s) from air bag module. Remove air bag module from steering wheel.

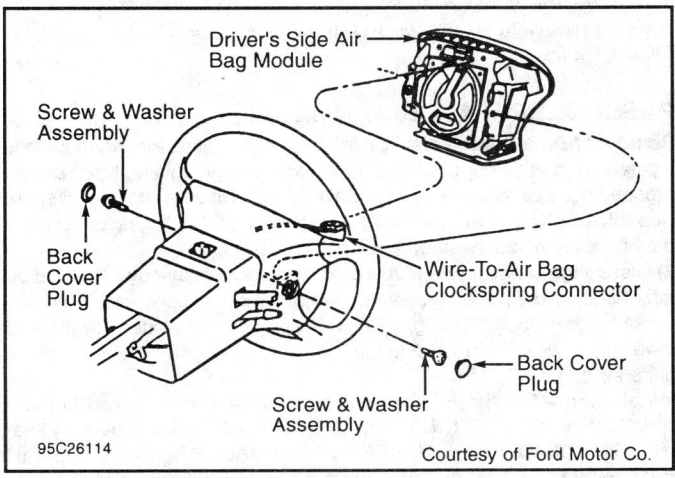

Fig. 4: Removing Driver's Air Bag Module

Installation – To install, reverse removal procedure. Tighten bolts to specification. See TORQUE SPECIFICATIONS. Connect negative battery cable. Check AIR BAG warning light for proper system function. See SYSTEM OPERATION CHECK.

FRONT IMPACT SENSORS

NOTE: Vehicle sensor orientation is critical for proper system operation. If a vehicle equipped with air bag system is involved in a crash, and fenders or grille area have been damaged, inspect sensor mounting brackets for deformation. If damaged, system should be deactivated to ensure air bag does not deploy. See DISABLING & ACTIVATING AIR BAG SYSTEM. Damaged sensor(s) should be replaced, whether or not air bag has been deployed. In addition, ensure body structure in area of sensor mounting is restored to its original construction.

Removal (Expedition & Navigator) – 1) Before proceeding, see SERVICE PRECAUTIONS. Front impact sensors (also known as primary crash sensors) are located on right and left of radiator support. Disable air bag system. See DISABLING & ACTIVATING AIR BAG SYSTEM. Leave negative battery cable disconnected.

2) Remove eight push clips and remove radiator air deflector. Disconnect right and/or left front impact sensor electrical connector(s). Remove sensor retaining screws from bracket. Remove right and/or left front impact sensor.

Installation – To install, reverse removal procedure. Tighten screws to specification. See TORQUE SPECIFICATIONS. Activate air bag system. See DISABLING & ACTIVATING AIR BAG SYSTEM. Check AIR BAG warning light for proper system function. See SYSTEM OPERATION CHECK.

Removal (Explorer & Mountaineer) – 1) Before proceeding, see SERVICE PRECAUTIONS. Front impact sensors (also known as primary crash sensors) are located on right and left of radiator support. Disable air bag system. See DISABLING & ACTIVATING AIR BAG SYSTEM. Leave negative battery cable disconnected.

FORD
4-30

1999 ACCESSORIES & EQUIPMENT
Air Bag Restraint Systems
Expedition, Explorer, Mountaineer & Navigator (Cont.)

2) Raise and support hood. Remove 4 upper radiator shield bolts and disengage pin retainers. Remove upper radiator shield. Disconnect upper parking lamp screws and pull parking lamps forward. Disconnect electrical connectors and remove parking lamps. Remove 6 radiator grill screws and release 4 lower clips. Remove grill from vehicle. It may also be necessary to remove radiator opening panel. Disconnect right and/or left front impact sensor electrical connector(s). Remove 3 sensor retaining screws from bracket. Remove right and/or left front impact sensor.

Installation – To install, reverse removal procedure. Tighten screws to specification. See TORQUE SPECIFICATIONS. Activate air bag system. See DISABLING & ACTIVATING AIR BAG SYSTEM. Check AIR BAG warning light for proper system function. See SYSTEM OPERATION CHECK.

PASSENGER'S AIR BAG MODULE

Removal (Expedition & Navigator) – 1) Passenger's air bag module is located in right side of instrument panel above glove box. Before proceeding, see SERVICE PRECAUTIONS. Disable air bag system. See DISABLING & ACTIVATING AIR BAG SYSTEM. Leave negative battery cable disconnected.

2) Disengage clips and remove instrument panel relay cover located on top of instrument panel. Disconnect air bag module connector. Remove upper retaining bolt. Open glove box. Press glove box sides inward, and lower glove box. Remove 2 lower retaining bolts and remove passenger's air bag module.

Installation – To install, reverse removal procedure. Tighten bolts to specification. See TORQUE SPECIFICATIONS. Activate air bag system. See DISABLING & ACTIVATING AIR BAG SYSTEM. Check AIR BAG warning light for proper system function. See SYSTEM OPERATION CHECK.

Removal (Explorer & Mountaineer) – 1) Passenger's air bag module is located in right side of instrument panel above glove box. Before proceeding, see SERVICE PRECAUTIONS. Disable air bag system. See DISABLING & ACTIVATING AIR BAG SYSTEM. Leave negative battery cable disconnected.

2) Open glove box. Remove 2 passenger air bag module mounting screws through glove box opening. Remove passenger air bag module by pushing module out of instrument panel from back. Do not pull on deployment door. Disconnect air bag module connectors. Remove passenger's air bag module.

Installation – To install, reverse removal procedure. Tighten screws to specification. See TORQUE SPECIFICATIONS. Activate air bag system. See DISABLING & ACTIVATING AIR BAG SYSTEM. Check AIR BAG warning light for proper system function. See SYSTEM OPERATION CHECK.

SIDE AIR BAG MODULES (EXPLORER & MOUNTAINEER)

Removal – 1) Side air bag modules are located in front seats, in outboard side of each seat back. Before proceeding, see SERVICE PRECAUTIONS. Disable air bag system. See DISABLING & ACTIVATING AIR BAG SYSTEM. Leave negative battery cable disconnected.

2) On models with 6-way power seats, move appropriate seat to full up position. On all models, remove rear track mounting covers. Remove rear mounting bolts. Remove slide bar bolt cover plug. Using tool No. T77L-2100–A, or equivalent Torx T50 bit, remove slide bar bolt at rear of track. (Slide bar bolt retains inboard safety belt anchor.) Remove front track mounting bolts. Tilt seat to disconnect electrical connectors. Remove seat from vehicle.

3) Disconnect seat motor electrical connector, if equipped. Remove 4 seat bolts and separate seat track from seat. Disconnect power seat switch electrical connector, if equipped. Rotate lumbar support knob fully to release cable tension. Remove knob. Remove seat switch trim cover screw. Press tabs on 2 retaining clips and pull cover from seat. Disconnect switch(es) and remove seat switch cover.

4) Disengage lumbar cable pushpin style holder from seat frame. Separate sections of lumbar cable. Disengage heated seat harness from seat frame and disconnect connector. Disengage side air bag module harness retainers and disconnect connector. Remove 3 retaining bolts from seat back pivot. Carefully remove seat back from seat base while guiding harnesses and lumbar cable.

5) Disengage seat back trim cover lower edge "J" clips. Disengage seat back trim cover side "J" clips. Slide rods out of seat back trim cover. Unzip side air bag module deployment chute. Remove harness tie strap. Remove and discard 3 side air bag module retaining nuts. Pull module out of bracket to access connector. Disconnect connector and remove module from seat back.

Installation – To install, reverse removal procedure. When installing module retaining nuts, torque middle, lower and upper nuts in sequence. Tighten fasteners to specification. See TORQUE SPECIFICATIONS. Ensure side air bag module deployment chute completely covers module. Tuck tail of chute zipper into seat back opening. When sliding rods into seat back trim cover, use new hog rings. When reattaching seat back to seat base, be careful to properly route harnesses and cable. Activate air bag system. See DISABLING & ACTIVATING AIR BAG SYSTEM. Check AIR BAG warning light for proper system function. See SYSTEM OPERATION CHECK.

SIDE IMPACT SENSORS (EXPLORER & MOUNTAINEER)

NOTE: Vehicle sensor orientation is critical for proper system operation. If a vehicle equipped with air bag system is involved in a crash, and "B" pillar areas have been damaged, inspect sensor mounting brackets for deformation. If damaged, system should be deactivated to ensure air bag does not deploy. See DISABLING & ACTIVATING AIR BAG SYSTEM. Damaged sensor(s) should be replaced, whether or not air bag has been deployed. In addition, ensure body structure in area of sensor mounting is restored to its original construction.

Removal – 1) Side impact sensors are located on each "B" pillar. Before proceeding, see SERVICE PRECAUTIONS. Disable air bag system. See DISABLING & ACTIVATING AIR BAG SYSTEM. Leave negative battery cable disconnected.

2) Remove appropriate "B" pillar lower trim cover with scuff plates. Disconnect side impact sensor electrical connector. Remove 2 retaining bolts. Remove sensor and bracket as an assembly.

Installation – To install, reverse removal procedure. Tighten bolts to specification. See TORQUE SPECIFICATIONS. Activate air bag system. See DISABLING & ACTIVATING AIR BAG SYSTEM. Check AIR BAG warning light for proper system function. See SYSTEM OPERATION CHECK.

STEERING WHEEL

Removal – 1) Before proceeding, see SERVICE PRECAUTIONS. Ensure front wheels are in straight-ahead position. Disable air bag system. See DISABLING & ACTIVATING AIR BAG SYSTEM. Leave negative battery cable disconnected.

2) Ensure front wheels are in straight-ahead position. Remove steering wheel retaining bolt and discard. Use a 2-jaw puller to unseat steering wheel from steering shaft. Match mark steering shaft and steering wheel for reassembly. Route clockspring wiring harness through steering wheel as wheel is lifted from steering shaft.

Installation – To install, reverse removal procedure. Tighten steering wheel bolt to specification. See TORQUE SPECIFICATIONS. Activate air bag system. See DISABLING & ACTIVATING AIR BAG SYSTEM. Check AIR BAG warning light for proper system function. See SYSTEM OPERATION CHECK.

1999 ACCESSORIES & EQUIPMENT
Air Bag Restraint Systems
Expedition, Explorer, Mountaineer & Navigator (Cont.)

FORD
4-31

COMPONENT LOCATIONS

COMPONENT LOCATIONS

Component	Location
Restraint Control Module	Behind Right Kick Panel
Clockspring	On Steering Column, Behind Steering Wheel
Driver's Air Bag Module	Steering Wheel
Left Impact Sensor	Left Side Of Radiator Support
Passenger Air Bag Module	Right Side Of Instrument Panel, Above Glove Box
Right Impact Sensor	Right Side Of Radiator Support

WIRE REPAIR

To repair damage to sensor wiring and wiring harnesses, note following conditions:

- All wire splice connections must be staggered at least 2" (50 mm) apart.
- Use proper size, waterproof butt-splice connectors on any exposed wiring.
- Use heat shrink nylon splice to prevent water, salt, condensation and heat from affecting the wiring repair. Insert pre-stripped wire ends into proper size waterproof butt-splice connector, and crimp connector using appropriate crimping pliers. See Fig. 5. Using heat gun, hair dryer or match, heat splice until it shrinks and adhesive oozes from each end of tubing. Connection is now waterproofed.

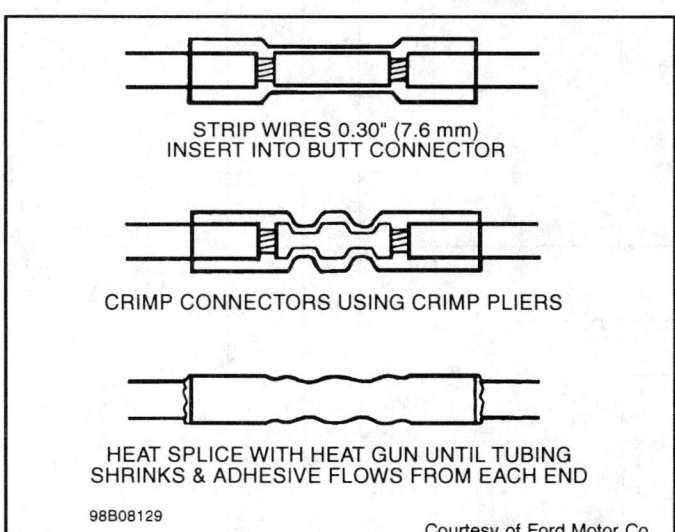

STRIP WIRES 0.30" (7.6 mm)
INSERT INTO BUTT CONNECTOR

CRIMP CONNECTORS USING CRIMP PLIERS

HEAT SPLICE WITH HEAT GUN UNTIL TUBING
SHRINKS & ADHESIVE FLOWS FROM EACH END

98B08129

Courtesy of Ford Motor Co.

Fig. 5: Repairing & Waterproofing Wiring Connections

TORQUE SPECIFICATIONS

TORQUE SPECIFICATIONS (EXPEDITION & NAVIGATOR)

Application	Ft. Lbs. (N.m)
Restraint Control Module Bolts	9 (12)
Driver's Air Bag Module Bolts	8 (11)
Steering Wheel Bolt	25-32 (34-44)
	INCH Lbs. (N.m)
Front Impact Sensors Screws	90-122 (10.2-13.8)
Passenger's Air Bag Module Screws	80 (9)

TORQUE SPECIFICATIONS (EXPLORER & MOUNTAINEER)

Application	Ft. Lbs. (N.m)
Restraint Control Module Bolts	9 (12)
Front Seat Track Bolt	15-21 (21-28)
Front Seat Slide Bar Bolt	30 (40)
Side Impact Sensors	9 (12)

TORQUE SPECIFICATIONS (EXPLORER & MOUNTAINEER) (Cont.)

Application	Ft. Lbs. (N.m)
Steering Wheel Bolt	25-32 (34-44)
	INCH Lbs. (N.m)
Driver's Air Bag Module Bolts	80 (9)
Front Impact Sensors Screws	90-122 (10.2-13.8)
Passenger's Air Bag Module Screws	80 (9)
Side Air Bag Modules	71 (8)

WIRING DIAGRAMS

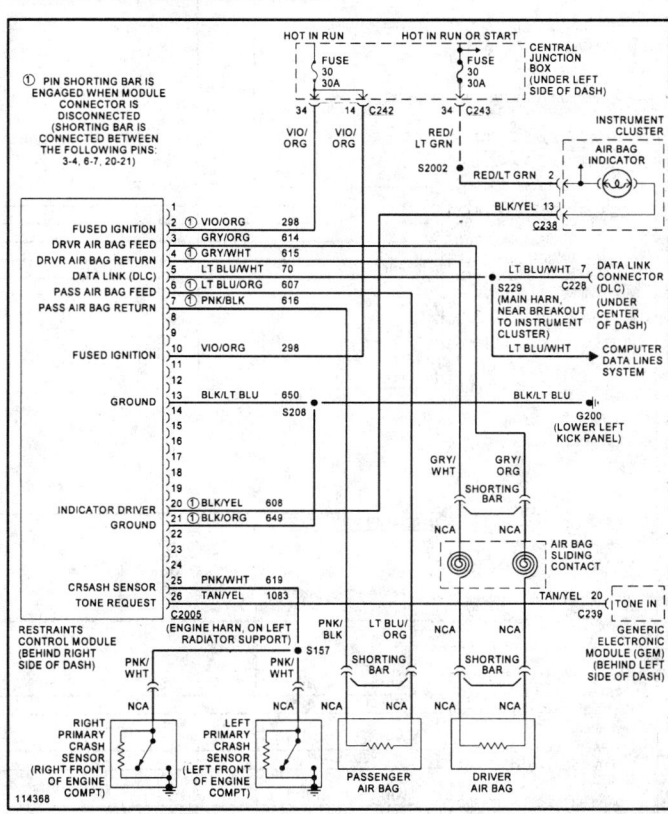

Fig. 6: Air Bag System Wiring Diagram (Expedition & Navigator)

FORD
4-32

1999 ACCESSORIES & EQUIPMENT
Air Bag Restraint Systems
Expedition, Explorer, Mountaineer & Navigator (Cont.)

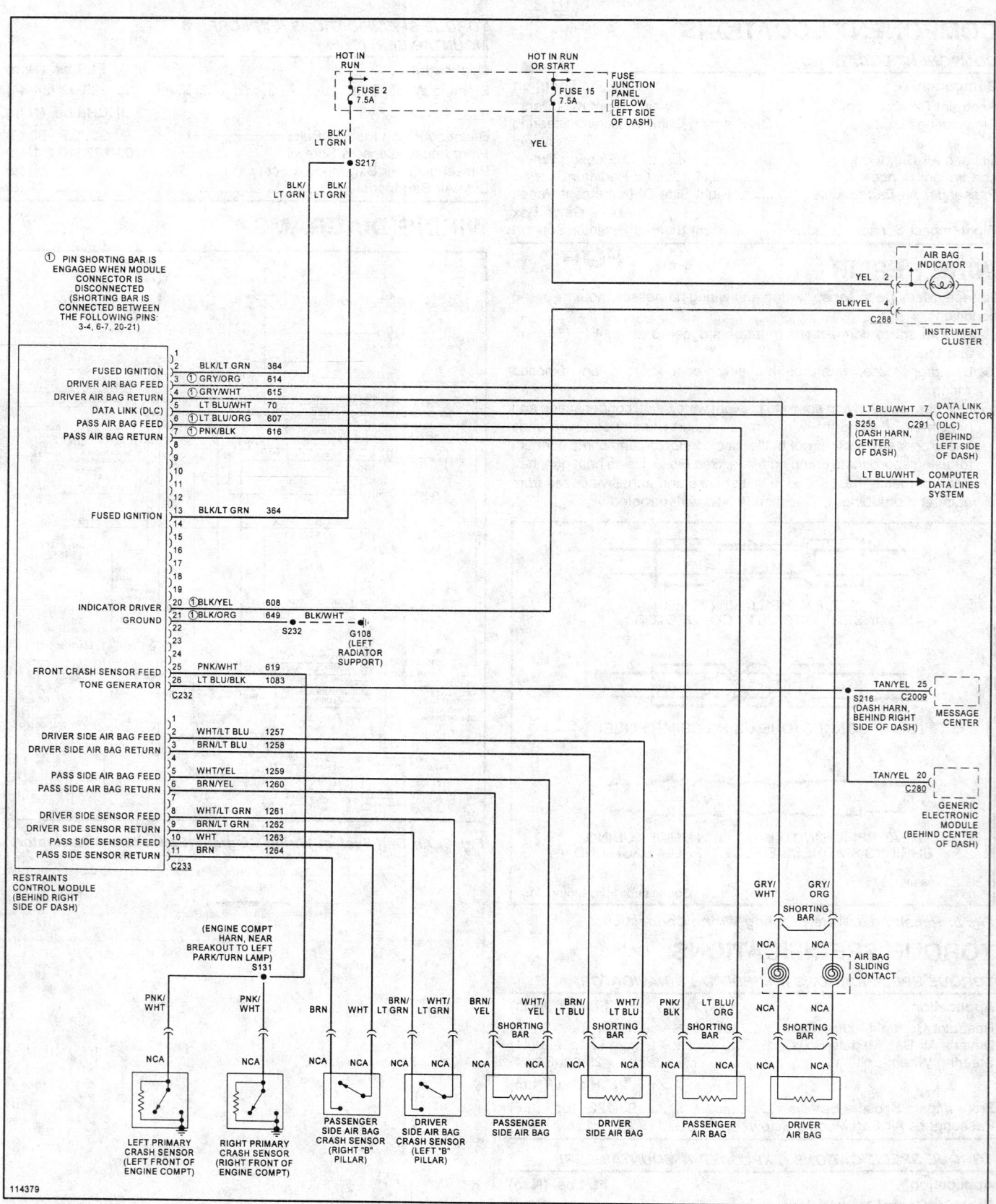

Fig. 7: Air Bag System Wiring Diagram (Explorer & Mountaineer)

NOTE: This article includes Cab & Chassis.

NOTE: For information on air bag DIAGNOSIS & TESTING, see MITCHELL® AIR BAG SERVICE & REPAIR MANUAL, DOMESTIC & IMPORTED MODELS.

DESCRIPTION & OPERATION

WARNING: To avoid injury from accidental air bag deployment, read and carefully follow all WARNINGS and SERVICE PRECAUTIONS.

The Supplemental Restraint System (SRS), also known as air bag system, is designed to provide increased accident protection for driver and passenger by deploying air bags in a front-end collision. The air bags, stored in center of steering wheel and in instrument panel above glove box, deploy in about 40 milliseconds after impact sensors close. Air bag system is designed to be used with 3-point safety belts.

During a front-end collision of sufficient force, impact sensor and safing sensor must activate simultaneously to inflate air bag modules. When impact sensor and safing sensor are closed, electrical current will flow, igniting the driver and passenger air bag modules.

Air bag system includes the following components: Air Bag Diagnostic Monitor (ADM), driver air bag module, passenger air bag module and deactivation (PAD) switch, AIR BAG warning light, impact sensor and safing sensor (both integral with ADM), ignitor assemblies (in air bag modules), clockspring (also known as sliding contact) and associated wiring harnesses. See COMPONENT LOCATIONS.

AIR BAG DIAGNOSTIC MONITOR (ADM)

The Air Bag Diagnostic Monitor (ADM), located behind instrument panel lower center console, contains a microcomputer, which monitors electrical system components and connections. Diagnostic monitor performs a system self-check of air bag system internal circuits every time ignition switch is turned to RUN position. Monitor also energizes air bag system AIR BAG warning light during initial system self-check and whenever a fault is detected. Faults are translated into Light Flash Codes (LFC) and are displayed through AIR BAG warning light.

If a system fault exists and/or AIR BAG warning light is malfunctioning, ADM will signal Generic Electronic Module (GEM) to emit an audible tone indicating need for service. Diagnostic monitor can also disarm air bag system if certain faults occur.

Impact sensor and safing sensor are part of ADM, and cannot be serviced separately.

BACK-UP POWER SUPPLY

A back-up power supply is located inside diagnostic monitor. If battery or battery cables are damaged in a collision before sensor circuits close, back-up power supply will supply sufficient electrical power to deploy air bags. Back-up power supply will hold a deployment charge for approximately one minute after battery is disconnected.

CLOCKSPRING

The clockspring, located on the steering column between steering wheel and combination switch, is used to transfer electrical signals from steering column wiring harness to driver air bag module.

DRIVER AIR BAG MODULE

The driver air bag module is mounted on center of steering wheel, covered by steering wheel trim cover. When impact sensor and safing sensor close, signaling an impact, ignitor triggers inflator. During ignition, sodium azide reacts with copper oxide, producing nitrogen gas, which inflates air bag.

When air bag deploys, tear-seams molded into steering wheel trim cover separate, allowing inflation of air bag assembly. Driver air bag module is not serviceable and must be replaced as a complete assembly.

ELECTRICAL SYSTEM

The air bag system is powered by ignition switch, and is only functional with ignition in RUN position. The 3 main functions performed by electrical subsystem are: detecting an impact, switching electric power to ignitors for air bag, and monitoring readiness of air bag system.

PASSENGER AIR BAG MODULE

The passenger air bag module is mounted in right side of instrument panel, above glove box. When a impact sensor and safing sensor close, signaling an impact, air bag ignitors trigger inflator.

Since passenger air bag is larger than driver air bag, inflator contains more gas generant in a different configuration to produce more gas. When air bag is activated, instrument panel trim cover tears at seams and hinges, allowing inflation. Passenger air bag module is only serviced as a complete assembly.

PASSENGER AIR BAG DEACTIVATION SWITCH

The Passenger Air bag Deactivation (PAD) switch is located on center of instrument panel, below climate control vent. It contains a Light Emitting Diode (LED) that indicates when PAD switch is activated. This switch allows the passenger air bag deployment circuit to be disabled by inserting ignition key into PAD switch lock cylinder and turning key. It should be used whenever child safety seat is being used in front passenger seating position.

SYSTEM OPERATION CHECK

1) When checking air bag system operation (also known as prove out system), and upon completion of each diagnostic test, check for faults in air bag system. To check system, turn ignition switch to RUN position. If AIR BAG warning light illuminates for approximately 6 seconds and then goes out, air bag system is functioning properly and no fault codes exist.
2) If a fault code is detected in air bag system during initial system check, AIR BAG warning light will either fail to light, stay on continuously, or flash a code sequence. If AIR BAG warning light flashes, indicating a fault in system, count number of flashes after fault code has cycled twice. Number of flashes represents a code number used to diagnose air bag system. See DIAGNOSIS & TESTING article in MITCHELL® AIR BAG SERVICE & REPAIR MANUAL, DOMESTIC & IMPORTED MODELS.
3) If a system fault exists and AIR BAG warning light fails to light, an audible tone will be heard, indicating AIR BAG warning light is out and service is required.

SERVICE PRECAUTIONS

These precautions should be observed when working with SRS:
- Disable SRS before servicing any SRS or steering column components. Failure to do so may result in accidental air bag deployment and personal injury. See procedures under DISABLING & ACTIVATING AIR BAG SYSTEM.
- Wait one minute after disabling SRS before working on vehicle. Back-up power supply holds a deployment charge for approximately one minute after negative battery cable is disconnected. Servicing SRS before one minute may cause accidental air bag deployment and possible personal injury.
- Because of critical system operating requirements, DO NOT service impact sensors, clockspring, diagnostic monitor or air bag module. Repairs are made by replacement only.
- Always wear safety glasses whenever servicing an air bag equipped vehicle or handling an air bag.
- When carrying a live air bag module, ensure air bag module and trim cover are pointed away from your body. This minimizes chance of injury in event of an accidental deployment.
- When placing a live air bag module on a bench or other surface, always face air bag module and trim cover facing up and away from surface. This will reduce motion of module if it is accidentally deployed.

- After deployment, air bag surface may contain deposits of sodium hydroxide, which may irritate skin. Sodium hydroxide is a product of gas generant combustion. Always wear gloves and safety glasses when handling a deployed air bag. Wash your hands using mild soap and water. Follow correct disposal procedures. See DISPOSAL PROCEDURES.
- If scrapping a vehicle with an undeployed air bag module, air bag must be deployed. See DISPOSAL PROCEDURES.
- If a part is replaced and new part does not correct condition, reinstall original part and perform diagnostic procedure again.
- Never probe connectors on air bag module. Doing so may cause air bag deployment and/or personal injury.
- Instruction to disconnect always refers to connector. DO NOT remove component from vehicle if instructed to disconnect.
- After any servicing, ensure AIR BAG warning light does not indicate any fault codes. See SYSTEM OPERATION CHECK.
- Replace air bag module if trim cover (deployment doors) is marred or damaged. DO NOT repaint trim cover. Paint may degrade cover material. Replace air bag module as necessary. Ensure damaged air bag is deployed. See DISPOSAL PROCEDURES.

DISABLING & ACTIVATING AIR BAG SYSTEM

WARNING: Wait one minute after disabling air bag system before working on vehicle. Back-up power supply holds a deployment charge for approximately one minute after negative battery cable is disconnected. Servicing air bag system before one minute may cause accidental air bag deployment and possible personal injury.

CAUTION: When battery is disconnected, vehicle computer and memory systems may lose memory data. Driveability problems may exist until computer systems have completed a relearn cycle. See COMPUTER RELEARN PROCEDURES in GENERAL INFORMATION.

DISABLING SYSTEM

1) Record USER 1 and USER 2 preset radio frequencies for reprogramming (if equipped). Disconnect negative battery cable. Wait at least one minute for back-up power supply to deplete stored energy.
2) Remove driver air bag module. See DRIVER AIR BAG MODULE under REMOVAL & INSTALLATION. Connect appropriate air bag simulator to clockspring connector at top of steering column (in place of air bag). See AIR BAG SIMULATOR.
3) Disconnect passenger air bag module. Connect appropriate air bag simulator to passenger air bag vehicle harness connector (in place of air bag). Connect negative battery cable. To reactivate SRS, see ACTIVATING SYSTEM.

AIR BAG SIMULATOR

An Air Bag Simulator (105-00012) or equivalent is required to perform diagnosis and testing of the air bag system. *See Fig. 1.* An air bag simulator is a 2-ohm resistor, with appropriate connector, used to simulate an air bag module. DO NOT short-circuit air bag module connections with a zero-ohm jumper wire. If zero-ohm jumper is used, a Diagnostic Trouble Code (DTC) will be set.

ACTIVATING SYSTEM

1) Disconnect negative battery cable. Wait at least one minute for back-up power supply to deplete stored energy. Remove air bag simulator from clockspring connector. Remove air bag simulator from passenger air bag vehicle harness connector. Install driver air bag module. See DRIVER AIR BAG MODULE under REMOVAL & INSTALLATION.
2) Reconnect passenger air bag module connector. Reconnect negative battery cable. Recheck system operation. Perform SYSTEM OPERATION CHECK. Reprogram USER 1 and USER 2 preset radio frequencies and set clock.

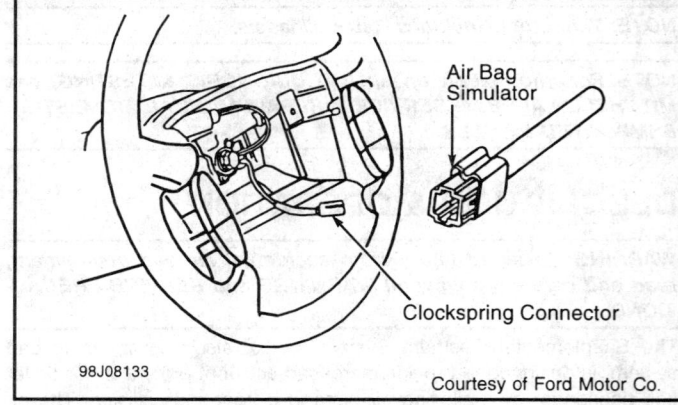

98J08133

Air Bag Simulator

Clockspring Connector

Courtesy of Ford Motor Co.

Fig. 1: Identifying Air Bag Simulator

DISPOSAL PROCEDURES

WARNING: Refer to SERVICE PRECAUTIONS before proceeding.

Air bag disposal may be necessary in following situations:
- Scrapping vehicle with deployed air bag.
- Scrapping vehicle with live air bag.
- Disposal of a live but electrically faulty air bag module.
- Disposal of a deployed air bag module.

DEPLOYED AIR BAG

Dispose of deployed air bag module as any other part. Air bag module components are not reusable.

UNDEPLOYED AIR BAG – FAULTY UNIT

If an undeployed air bag module is diagnosed as faulty, remove air bag module and return intact to Ford Motor Company for proper disposal. Return carton for warranty claim credit. Air bag must be packaged and shipped according to U.S. Department of Transportation procedures. Retain replacement packaging including label. DO NOT deploy air bag.

SCRAPPED VEHICLE

CAUTION: DO NOT dispose of undeployed air bag module. If this is not possible to deploy air bag through procedures outlined, contact vehicle manufacturer for further instructions.

WARNING: Perform remote deployment outdoors. Keep all personnel at least 20 feet away to ensure physical and hearing safety from projected objects and loud noise of air bag deployment.

Remote Deployment Of Air Bag – 1) Before proceeding, see SERVICE PRECAUTIONS. Deactivate air bag system. See DISABLING & ACTIVATING AIR BAG SYSTEM. Remove driver and/or passenger air bag module. See DRIVER AIR BAG MODULE and PASSENGER AIR BAG MODULE under REMOVAL & INSTALLATION.
2) With air bag module removed, cut air bag connector from wiring harness near air bag module. Strip 1" of insulation from wire ends. Obtain 2 wires at least 20 feet long. Connect one end of each 20-foot wire to one end of each air bag module wire.

WARNING: When placing a live air bag on a bench or other surface, always face air bag and trim cover up and away from surface. This will reduce motion of air bag module if it is accidentally deployed.

3) Place air bag module with trim cover facing upward on a flat surface, in remote area such as parking lot or field. Remain at least 20 feet away from air bag module. Deploy air bag by touching loose ends of both wires to 12-volt battery terminals.
4) If successful, a loud noise will be heard and bag material will be visible. Allow at least 10 minutes for cooling and dissipation of air bag effluents before approaching air bag. Air bag is now inoperative. If air

bag does not deploy, air bag module is faulty. Contact vehicle manufacturer for further instructions on disposal procedures.

POST-COLLISION INSPECTION

If vehicle has been in a collision and air bags deployed, perform the following:

- Replace air bag modules.
- Replace Air Bag Diagnostic Monitor (ADM).
- Inspect areas near air bag modules. If interfering with deployment, replace as necessary.
- Inspect steering column for load damage. Replace as necessary.
- Inspect wiring and harness connectors. Replace as necessary.
- Perform SYSTEM OPERATION CHECK.

If a collision has occurred and air bags did not deploy, perform the following:

- Remove both air bag modules and inspect wiring and connectors for damage.
- Check area near modules for damage, check modules for fit. Repair as necessary.
- Inspect steering column for load damage. Replace as necessary.
- Inspect areas near air bag modules. If interfering with deployment, replace as necessary.

REMOVAL & INSTALLATION

WARNING: Failure to follow service precautions may result in air bag deployment and personal injury. See SERVICE PRECAUTIONS. After component replacement, ensure proper system operation. See SYSTEM OPERATION CHECK.

CAUTION: When battery is disconnected, vehicle computer and memory systems may lose memory data. Driveability problems may exist until computer systems have completed a relearn cycle. See COMPUTER RELEARN PROCEDURES in GENERAL INFORMATION.

AIR BAG DIAGNOSTIC MONITOR (ADM)

Removal (F150 & F250 Light-Duty Pickup) – 1) Before proceeding, see SERVICE PRECAUTIONS. ADM is located behind instrument panel lower center console. Disable air bag system. See DISABLING & ACTIVATING AIR BAG SYSTEM. Leave negative battery cable disconnected.

2) Remove 2 instrument panel lower center console retaining pins and remove panel. Disconnect ADM electrical connectors. Remove 3 retaining bolts retaining ADM bracket to vehicle. Remove ADM and bracket as an assembly.

Installation (F150 & F250 Light-Duty Pickup) – To install diagnostic monitor, reverse removal procedure. ADM bracket bolt torque is critical for proper system operation. Tighten fasteners to specification. See TORQUE SPECIFICATIONS. Activate air bag system. See DISABLING & ACTIVATING AIR BAG SYSTEM. Check AIR BAG warning light for proper system function. See SYSTEM OPERATION CHECK.

Removal (F250 Super-Duty & F350 Pickup) – 1) Before proceeding, see SERVICE PRECAUTIONS. ADM is located under center of instrument panel. Disable air bag system. See DISABLING & ACTIVATING AIR BAG SYSTEM. Leave negative battery cable disconnected.

2) Remove ADM protective cover. Disconnect ADM electrical connector locking clip and disconnect connector. Remove retaining screws and remove ADM from vehicle.

Installation (F250 Super-Duty & F350 Pickup) – To install, reverse removal procedure. ADM fastener torque is critical for proper system operation. Tighten fasteners to specification. See TORQUE SPECIFICATIONS. Activate air bag system. Activate air bag system. See DISABLING & ACTIVATING AIR BAG SYSTEM. Check AIR BAG warning light to ensure system is functioning properly. See SYSTEM OPERATION CHECK.

CLOCKSPRING

Removal (F150 & F250 Light-Duty Pickup) – 1) Before proceeding, see SERVICE PRECAUTIONS. Clockspring is located on steering column between steering wheel and combination switch. Disable air bag system. See DISABLING & ACTIVATING AIR BAG SYSTEM. Leave negative battery cable disconnected. Ensure front wheels are in straight-ahead position. Remove steering wheel. See STEERING WHEEL. Apply two tape strips across clockspring and housing to prevent rotation.

2) Twist tilt wheel handle and shank and remove. Remove upper instrument panel steering column cover. Remove junction box fuse/relay panel cover. Remove 6 lower instrument panel steering column cover bolts, parking brake release lever bolts and hood release lever bolts. Remove cover. Remove 3 lower steering column shroud screws and remove shroud. Turn ignition switch to RUN position. Using suitable tool, push upward on cylinder release tab through hole in lower shroud while pulling cylinder outward.

3) Remove upper steering column shroud. Remove screw and Passive Anti-Theft System (PATS) transmitter. Remove key-in-ignition warning switch. Disconnect clockspring electrical connector and separate connector from bracket. Pry retaining clips loose and separate wire from two retaining clips holding wire to column. Remove clockspring, feeding wiring harness through column.

Installation (F150 & F250 Light-Duty Pickup) – To install, reverse removal procedure. Tighten fasteners to specification. See TORQUE SPECIFICATIONS. Properly orient clockspring assembly. Ensure harness is routed properly during reassembly. Activate air bag system. See DISABLING & ACTIVATING AIR BAG SYSTEM. Check AIR BAG warning light for proper system function. See SYSTEM OPERATION CHECK.

Removal (F250 Super-Duty & F350 Pickup) – 1) Before proceeding, see SERVICE PRECAUTIONS. Clockspring is located on steering column between steering wheel and combination switch. Disable air bag system. See DISABLING & ACTIVATING AIR BAG SYSTEM. Leave negative battery cable disconnected. Ensure front wheels are in straight-ahead position. Remove steering wheel. See STEERING WHEEL. Apply two tape strips across clockspring and housing to prevent rotation.

2) Twist tilt wheel handle and shank and remove. Remove 3 lower steering column shroud screws and remove shroud. Turn ignition switch to RUN position. Using suitable tool, push upward on cylinder release tab through hole in lower shroud while pulling cylinder outward. Remove steering column upper shroud.

3) Remove key-in-ignition warning switch. Release lower steering column opening cover by turning 4 retaining clips counterclockwise. Disconnect clockspring electrical connector and separate connector from bracket. Pry retaining clips loose and separate wire from two retaining clips holding wire to column. Pry upper right clockspring retaining clips loose and remove clockspring from column, feeding wiring harness through column.

Installation (F250 Super-Duty & F350 Pickup) – To install, reverse removal procedure. Tighten fasteners to specification. See TORQUE SPECIFICATIONS. Properly orient clockspring assembly. If new clockspring is installed, remove anti-rotation tab. Ensure harness is routed properly during reassembly. Activate air bag system. See DISABLING & ACTIVATING AIR BAG SYSTEM. Check AIR BAG warning light for proper system function. See SYSTEM OPERATION CHECK.

DRIVER AIR BAG MODULE

Removal – Before proceeding, see SERVICE PRECAUTIONS. Disconnect negative battery cable. Wait at least one minute for depletion of back-up power source. Remove 2 back cover plugs from rear of steering wheel. Remove 2 fasteners retaining air bag module to steering wheel. Pull module out and disconnect horn and clockspring electrical connectors. Remove air bag module from steering wheel.

Installation – To install, reverse removal procedure. Tighten fasteners to specification. See TORQUE SPECIFICATIONS. Activate air bag system. Connect negative battery cable. Check AIR BAG warning light for proper system function. See SYSTEM OPERATION CHECK.

PASSENGER AIR BAG MODULE

Removal (F150 & F250 Light-Duty Pickup) – 1) Passenger air bag module is located in right side of instrument panel above glove box. Before proceeding, see SERVICE PRECAUTIONS. Disable air bag system. See DISABLING & ACTIVATING AIR BAG SYSTEM. Leave negative battery cable disconnected.

2) Remove instrument panel relay cover located on top of instrument panel. Disconnect air bag module electrical connector. Remove air bag module upper mounting bolt. Open glove box and push in door tabs to lower door beyond stops. Lower door towards floor. Remove 2 lower air bag module mounting bolts and remove passenger air bag module.

Installation (F150 & F250 Light-Duty Pickup) – To install, reverse removal procedure. Tighten bolts to specification. See TORQUE SPECIFICATIONS. Activate air bag system. Activate air bag system. See DISABLING & ACTIVATING AIR BAG SYSTEM. Check AIR BAG warning light to ensure system is functioning properly. See SYSTEM OPERATION CHECK.

Removal (F250 Super-Duty & F350 Pickup) – 1) Passenger air bag module is located in right side of instrument panel above glove box. Before proceeding, see SERVICE PRECAUTIONS. Disable air bag system. See DISABLING & ACTIVATING AIR BAG SYSTEM. Leave negative battery cable disconnected.

2) Open glove box and push in door tabs to lower door beyond stops. Lower door towards floor. Disengage air bag module electrical connector from bracket. Disconnect air bag module electrical connector. Remove 4 air bag module mounting screws.

3) Insert 3/8″ flathead screwdriver carefully under right bottom of air bag deployment door. Lift upward to disengage clip. Disengage remaining clips by pulling up on door by hand. Remove air bag module from behind deployment door.

Installation (F250 Super-Duty & F350 Pickup) – To install, reverse removal procedure. Fastener torque is critical for proper system operation. Tighten fasteners to specification. See TORQUE SPECIFICATIONS. Activate air bag system. Activate air bag system. See DISABLING & ACTIVATING AIR BAG SYSTEM. Check AIR BAG warning light to ensure system is functioning properly. See SYSTEM OPERATION CHECK.

PASSENGER AIR BAG MODULE DEACTIVATION (PAD) SWITCH

Removal (F150 & F250 Light-Duty Pickup) – 1) Before proceeding, see SERVICE PRECAUTIONS. Passenger Air bag Deactivation (PAD) switch is located on center of instrument panel, below climate control vent. Disable air bag system. See DISABLING & ACTIVATING AIR BAG SYSTEM. Leave negative battery cable disconnected.

2) Remove center instrument panel finish panel from around radio and HVAC controls. Disconnect PAD switch electrical connector. Remove 3 retaining bolts and remove PAD switch from vehicle.

Installation (F150 & F250 Light-Duty Pickup) – To install, reverse removal procedure. Activate air bag system. See DISABLING & ACTIVATING AIR BAG SYSTEM. Check AIR BAG warning light for proper system function. See SYSTEM OPERATION CHECK.

Removal (F250 Super-Duty & F350 Pickup) – 1) Before proceeding, see SERVICE PRECAUTIONS. Passenger Air bag Deactivation (PAD) switch is located on center of instrument panel. Disable air bag system. See DISABLING & ACTIVATING AIR BAG SYSTEM. Leave negative battery cable disconnected.

2) Remove ash tray, screws and ash tray bracket. Open beverage holder. Remove 4 screws and remove beverage holder. Remove 4 screws and remove instrument panel center finish panel. Disconnect PAD switch electrical connector. Remove 3 retaining screws and remove PAD switch from vehicle.

Installation (F250 Super-Duty & F350 Pickup) – To install, reverse removal procedure. Activate air bag system. See DISABLING & ACTIVATING AIR BAG SYSTEM. Check AIR BAG warning light for proper system function. See SYSTEM OPERATION CHECK.

STEERING WHEEL

Removal – 1) Before proceeding, see SERVICE PRECAUTIONS. Ensure front wheels are in straight-ahead position. Disable air bag system. See DISABLING & ACTIVATING AIR BAG SYSTEM. Leave negative battery cable disconnected.

2) Ensure front wheels are in straight-ahead position. Loosen steering wheel retaining bolt. Use a 2-jaw puller (Tool No. T77F-4220–B1) to unseat steering wheel from steering shaft. Remove and discard steering wheel retaining bolt. Route clockspring wiring harness through steering wheel as wheel is lifted from steering shaft.

Installation – 1) Ensure front wheels are in straight-ahead position. Route clockspring wiring harness properly during installation. Use new steering wheel retaining bolt. Tighten fasteners to specification. See TORQUE SPECIFICATIONS.

2) Activate air bag system. See DISABLING & ACTIVATING AIR BAG SYSTEM. Check AIR BAG warning light for proper system function. See SYSTEM OPERATION CHECK.

COMPONENT LOCATIONS

COMPONENT LOCATIONS

Component	Location
Air Bag Diagnostic Monitor (ADM)	
F150 & F250 Light-Duty Pickup	Behind Instrument Panel Lower Center Console
F250 Super-Duty & F350 Pickup	Below Center Of Instrument Panel
Clockspring	On Column, Under Steering Wheel
Driver Air Bag Module	Center Of Steering Wheel
Impact And Safing Sensors	Inside ADM
Passenger Air Bag Deactivation Switch	On Center Of Instrument Panel
Passenger Air Bag Module	Right Side Of Instrument Panel

WIRE REPAIR

To repair damage to sensor wiring and wiring harnesses, note following conditions:

- All wire splice connections must be staggered at least 2″ (50 mm) apart.
- Use proper size, waterproof butt-splice connectors on any exposed wiring.
- Use heat shrink nylon splice to prevent water, salt, condensation and heat from affecting the wiring repair. Insert pre-stripped wire ends into proper size waterproof butt-splice connector, and crimp connector using appropriate crimping pliers. See Fig. 2. Using heat gun, hair dryer or match, heat splice until it shrinks and adhesive oozes from each end of tubing. Connection is now waterproofed.

TORQUE SPECIFICATIONS

TORQUE SPECIFICATIONS

Application	Ft. Lbs. (N.m)
Air Bag Diagnostic Monitor (ADM)	9 (12)
Steering Wheel Bolt	23-32 (31-44)

	INCH Lbs. (N.m)
Driver's Air Bag Module	98 (11)
Passenger Air Bag Module Screws	80 (9)

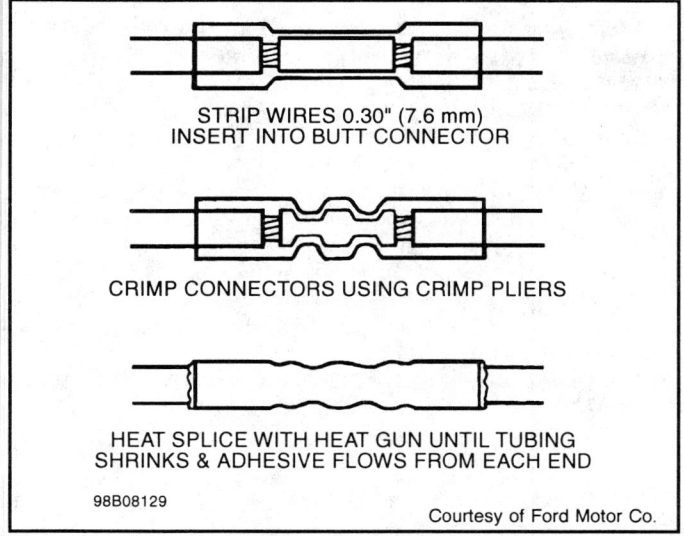

Fig. 2: *Repairing & Waterproofing Wiring Connections*

WIRING DIAGRAMS

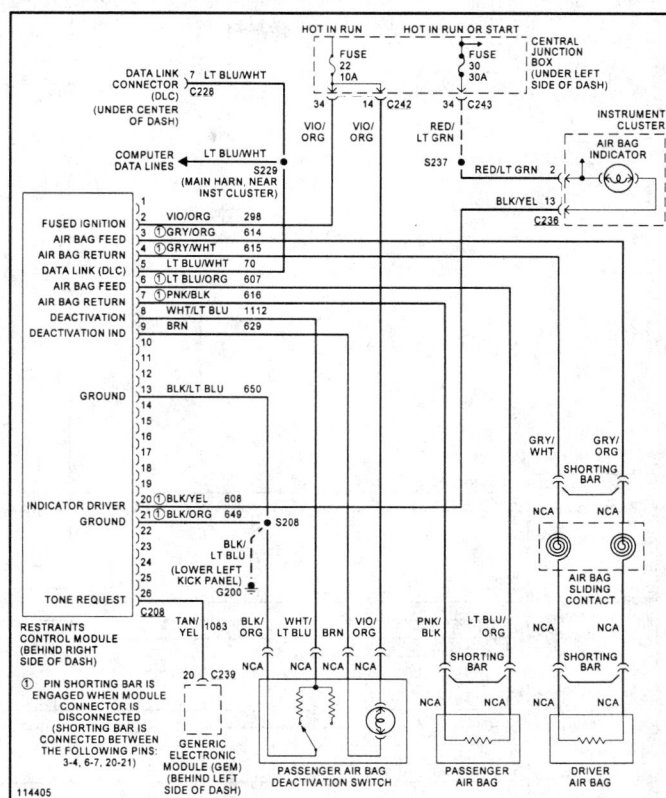

Fig. 3: *Air Bag System Wiring Diagram (F150 & F250 Light-Duty Pickup)*

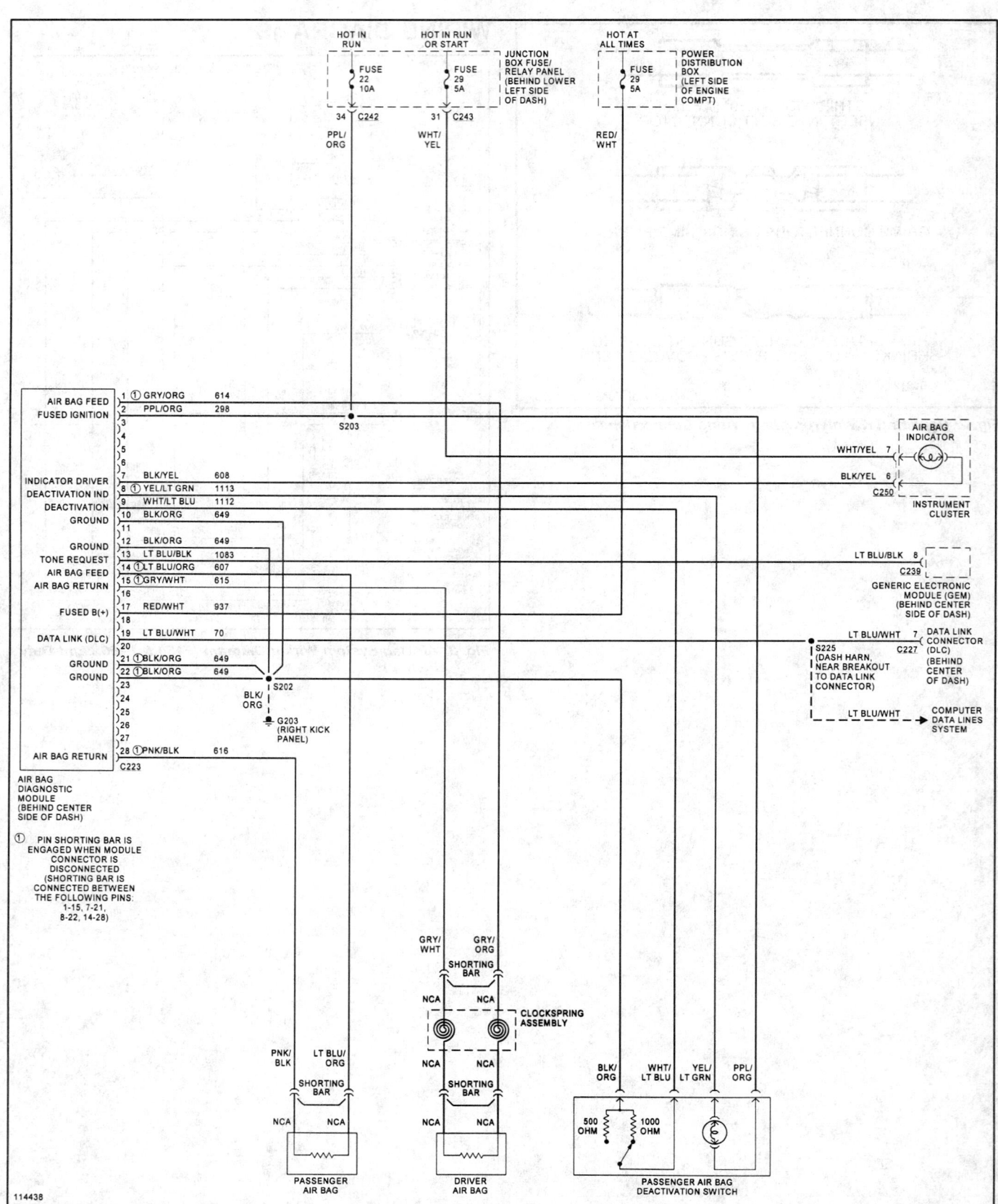

Fig. 4: Air Bag System Wiring Diagram (F250 Super-Duty & F350 Pickup)

NOTE: For information on air bag diagnosis and testing, see MITCHELL® AIR BAG SERVICE & REPAIR MANUAL, DOMESTIC & IMPORTED MODELS.

DESCRIPTION & OPERATION

WARNING: To avoid injury from accidental air bag deployment, read and carefully follow all WARNINGS and SERVICE PRECAUTIONS.

NOTE: Restraints Control Module (RCM) may also be referred to as Electronic Crash Sensor (ECS) or Air Bag Diagnostic Monitor (ABDM).

The Supplemental Restraint System (SRS), also known as air bag system, is designed to provide increased accident protection for driver and passenger by deploying air bags in a front-end collision. The air bags, stored in center of steering wheel and in instrument panel above glove box, deploy about 40 milliseconds after impact sensors close. SRS is designed to be used with 3-point safety belts.

During a front-end collision, the air bag Restraints Control Module (RCM) discriminates between an event that warrants air bag deployment and an event that does not. In a crash of sufficient force, the RCM signals the air bag modules to simultaneously inflate.

SRS includes following components: Restraints Control Module (RCM), a safing sensor (located inside the RCM), a back-up power supply (also located inside the RCM), right and left front impact sensors, driver's side air bag module, passenger's side air bag module, Passenger's Side Air Bag Deactivation (PAD) switch, AIR BAG warning light, ignitor assemblies (located in air bag modules), clockspring and associated wiring harnesses. *See Fig. 1.*

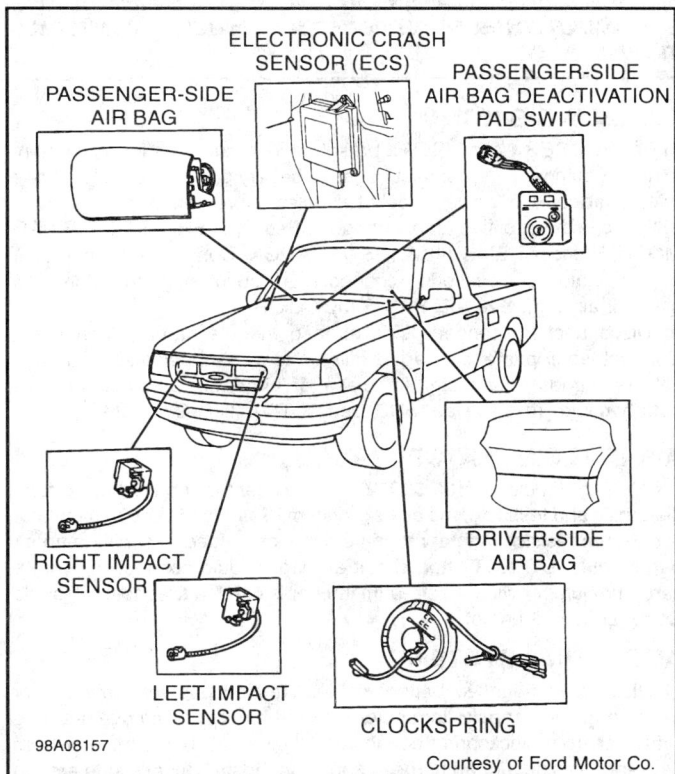

ELECTRONIC CRASH
SENSOR (ECS)

PASSENGER-SIDE
AIR BAG

PASSENGER-SIDE
AIR BAG DEACTIVATION
PAD SWITCH

RIGHT IMPACT
SENSOR

DRIVER-SIDE
AIR BAG

LEFT IMPACT
SENSOR

CLOCKSPRING

98A08157

Courtesy of Ford Motor Co.

Fig. 1: Locating Supplemental Restraint System Components

BACK-UP POWER SUPPLY

A back-up power supply is located inside Restraints Control Module (RCM). If battery or battery cables are damaged in a collision before sensor circuits close, back-up power supply will provide electrical power

to deploy air bags. Back-up power supply will hold a deployment charge for approximately one minute after negative battery cable is disconnected.

CLOCKSPRING

The clockspring, located on the steering column between steering wheel and combination switch assembly, is a contact and wire assembly used to transfer electrical signals from steering column wiring harness to driver's side air bag module. *See Fig. 1.*

DRIVER'S SIDE AIR BAG MODULE

The driver's side air bag module is mounted on front face of steering wheel, covered by steering wheel trim cover. *See Fig. 1.* When front impact sensors and safing sensor close, signaling an impact, ignitor triggers inflator. During ignition, sodium oxide reacts with copper oxide, producing nitrogen gas, which inflates air bag.

When air bag deploys, tear-seams molded into steering wheel trim cover separate, allowing deployment of air bag assembly. Driver's side air bag module is not serviceable and must be replaced as a complete assembly.

ELECTRICAL SYSTEM

SRS is powered directly from battery and can function with ignition switch in any position, including OFF and LOCK. System can also function when driver's side and passenger's side seats are unoccupied. The 3 main functions performed by electrical subsystem are: detecting an impact, switching electric power to ignitors for air bags, and monitoring system readiness.

RESTRAINTS CONTROL MODULE (RCM)

NOTE: Restraints Control Module (RCM) may also be referred to as Electronic Crash Sensor (ECS) or Air Bag Diagnostic Monitor (DM).

The Restraints Control Module (RCM) module is located on center tunnel under instrument panel. *See Fig. 1.* The RCM contains a microcomputer, which monitors electrical system components and connections. RCM performs a system self-check of air bag system internal circuits every time ignition switch is turned to RUN position. RCM also energizes AIR BAG warning light during initial system self-check and whenever a fault is detected. Faults are stored in RCM memory and translated into flash codes, which are displayed through AIR BAG warning light. RCM also communicates through Data Link Connector (DLC) current and historical Diagnostic Trouble Codes (DTCs).

If a system fault exists and AIR BAG warning light is malfunctioning, RCM signals Generic Electronic Module (GEM) to activate a chime. The chime is a series of 5 sets of 5 tone burst, indicating need for service.

IMPACT SENSORS

Impact sensors are located at left and right sides of radiator support. Impact sensor reacts to impacts according to direction and force. They discriminate between impacts that require air bag deployment and impacts that do not.

When an impact occurs requiring air bag deployment, impact sensor contacts close, completing electrical circuit necessary for system operation. *See Fig. 1.* At least 2 sensors, safing sensor and one front impact sensor, must be activated simultaneously to deploy air bags. Safing sensor is integral with Restraints Control Module (RCM).

PASSENGER'S SIDE AIR BAG DEACTIVATE SWITCH

The Passenger's Side Air Bag Deactivate (PAD) switch is located at the center of the instrument panel. *See Fig. 1.* PAD allows the vehicle operator to deactivate the passenger's side air bag when a rear facing infant seat is in the passenger's seat.

PASSENGER'S SIDE AIR BAG MODULE

The passenger's side air bag module is mounted in right side of instrument panel, above glove box. *See Fig. 1.* When a at least one front impact sensor and safing sensor close, signaling an impact, air bag ignitors trigger inflator.

Since passenger's side air bag is larger than driver's side air bag, inflator contains more gas generant in a different configuration to produce more gas. When air bag is activated, instrument panel trim cover tears at seams and hinges, allowing deployment. Passenger's side air bag module is only serviced as a complete assembly.

SYSTEM OPERATION CHECK

1) When checking air bag system operation (also known as prove out system), and upon completion of each diagnostic test, check for faults in air bag system. To check system, turn ignition switch to RUN position. If AIR BAG warning light illuminates for 4-8 seconds and then goes out, air bag system is functioning properly and no fault exist.

2) If a fault is detected in air bag system during initial system check, AIR BAG warning light will either fail to light, stay on continuously, or flash a code sequence. If AIR BAG warning light flashes, indicating a fault in system, count number of flashes after fault code has cycled twice. Number of flashes represents a code number used to diagnose air bag system. See DIAGNOSIS & TESTING article in MITCHELL® AIR BAG SERVICE & REPAIR MANUAL, DOMESTIC & IMPORTED MODELS.

3) If a system fault exists and AIR BAG warning light fails to light, a chime (a series of 5 sets of 5 tone burst) will be heard, indicating AIR BAG warning light is malfunctioning and service is required.

POST-COLLISION INSPECTION

If vehicle has been in a collision and air bags deployed, perform the following:

- Replace air bag modules.
- Check crash sensors at front of vehicle.
- Inspect areas near air bag modules. If interfering with deployment, replace as necessary.
- Inspect steering column for load damage. Replace as necessary.
- Inspect wiring and harness connectors. Replace as necessary.
- Perform SYSTEM OPERATION CHECK.

If a collision has occurred and air bags did not deploy, perform the following:

- Remove both air bag modules and inspect wiring and connectors for damage.
- Check area near modules for damage, check modules for fit. Repair as necessary.
- Inspect steering column for load damage. Replace as necessary.
- Inspect areas near air bag modules. If interfering with deployment, replace as necessary.

SERVICE PRECAUTIONS

These precautions should be observed when working with air bag system:

- Disable air bag system before servicing any air bag system or steering column components. Failure to do so may result in accidental air bag deployment and personal injury. See DISABLING & ACTIVATING AIR BAG SYSTEM.
- Wait one minute after disabling air bag system before working on vehicle. Back-up power supply holds a deployment charge for approximately one minute after negative battery cable is disconnected. Servicing air bag system before one minute may cause accidental air bag deployment and possible personal injury.
- Because of critical system operating requirements, DO NOT service impact sensors, clockspring, restraints control module or air bag modules. Repairs are made by replacement only.
- Always wear safety glasses whenever servicing an air bag equipped vehicle or handling an air bag.
- When carrying a live air bag module, ensure air bag module and trim cover are pointed away from your body. This minimizes chance of injury in event of an accidental deployment.
- When placing a live air bag module on a bench or other surface, always face air bag module and trim cover facing up and away from surface. This will reduce motion of module if it is accidentally deployed.

- After deployment, air bag surface may contain deposits of sodium hydroxide, which may irritate skin. Sodium hydroxide is a product of gas generant combustion. Always wear gloves and safety glasses when handling a deployed air bag. Wash your hands using mild soap and water. Follow correct disposal procedures. See DISPOSAL PROCEDURES.
- If scrapping a vehicle with an undeployed air bag module, air bag must be deployed. See DISPOSAL PROCEDURES.
- If a part is replaced and new part does not correct condition, reinstall original part and perform diagnostic procedure again.
- Never probe connectors on air bag module. Doing so may cause air bag deployment and/or personal injury.
- Instruction to disconnect always refers to connector. DO NOT remove component from vehicle if instructed to disconnect.
- After any servicing, ensure AIR BAG warning light does not indicate any fault codes. See SYSTEM OPERATION CHECK.
- Replace air bag module if trim cover (deployment doors) is marred or damaged. DO NOT repaint trim cover. Paint may degrade cover material. Replace air bag module as necessary. Ensure damaged air bag is deployed. See DISPOSAL PROCEDURES.

DISABLING & ACTIVATING AIR BAG SYSTEM

WARNING: Wait one minute after disabling air bag system before working on vehicle. Back-up power supply holds a deployment charge for approximately one minute after positive battery cable is disconnected. Servicing air bag system before one minute may cause accidental air bag deployment and possible personal injury.

CAUTION: When battery is disconnected, vehicle computer and memory systems may lose memory data. Driveability problems may exist until computer systems have completed a relearn cycle. See COMPUTER RELEARN PROCEDURES in GENERAL INFORMATION.

DISABLING SYSTEM

1) Record USER 1 and USER 2 preset radio frequencies for reprogramming (if equipped). Disconnect negative battery cable. Wait at least one minute for back-up power supply to deplete stored energy.

2) Remove driver's side air bag module. See DRIVER'S SIDE AIR BAG MODULE under REMOVAL & INSTALLATION. Connect appropriate air bag simulator to clockspring connector at top of steering column (in place of air bag). See AIR BAG SIMULATOR.

3) Disconnect passenger's side air bag module harness connector. Connect appropriate air bag simulator to passenger's side air bag vehicle harness connector (in place of air bag). Connect negative battery cable. To reactivate SRS, see ACTIVATING SYSTEM.

AIR BAG SIMULATOR

An Air Bag Simulator (105-00012) or equivalent is required to perform diagnosis and testing of the air bag system. *See Fig. 2.* Air bag simulator is a 2-ohm resistor, with appropriate connector, used to simulate an air bag module. DO NOT short-circuit air bag module connections with a zero-ohm jumper wire. If zero-ohm jumper is used, a Diagnostic Trouble Code (DTC) will be set.

ACTIVATING SYSTEM

1) Disconnect negative battery cable. Wait at least one minute for back-up power supply to deplete stored energy. Remove air bag simulator from clockspring connector. Remove air bag simulator from passenger's side air bag harness connector. Install driver's side air bag module. See DRIVER'S SIDE AIR BAG MODULE under REMOVAL & INSTALLATION.

2) Connect passenger's side air bag module harness connector. Connect negative battery cable. Check system operation. See SYSTEM OPERATION CHECK. Reprogram USER 1 and USER 2 preset radio frequencies and set clock.

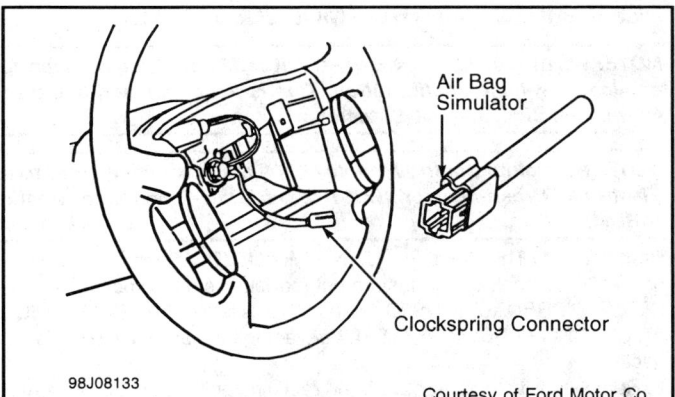

98J08133 Courtesy of Ford Motor Co.

Fig. 2: Identifying Air Bag Simulator

DISPOSAL PROCEDURES

WARNING: Refer to SERVICE PRECAUTIONS before proceeding.

Air bag disposal may be necessary in following situations:
- Scrapping vehicle with deployed air bag.
- Scrapping vehicle with live air bag.
- Disposal of a live but electrically faulty air bag module.
- Disposal of a deployed air bag module. To determine how air bag should be disposed, see AIR BAG DISPOSAL PROCEDURES table.

AIR BAG DISPOSAL PROCEDURES

Condition	Instructions
Module Replacement	
Deployed Air Bag	[1] Dispose Of In Usual Manner
Faulty But Live Air Bag Module	[2] Return For Disposal
Vehicle To Be Scrapped	
Deployed Air Bag	[1] Dispose Of In Usual Manner
Live Air Bag	[3] Deploy Air Bag

[1] – See DEPLOYED AIR BAG.
[2] – See UNDEPLOYED AIR BAG – FAULTY UNIT.
[3] – See SCRAPPED VEHICLE.

DEPLOYED AIR BAG

Dispose of deployed air bag module as any other part. Air bag module components are not reusable.

UNDEPLOYED AIR BAG – FAULTY UNIT

NOTE: All inoperative air bag modules have been placed on mandatory return list. All discolored or damaged air bag modules should be treated as inoperative live air bag modules.

If an undeployed air bag module is diagnosed as faulty, contact vehicle manufacturer for proper disposal instructions.

SCRAPPED VEHICLE

CAUTION: DO NOT dispose of undeployed air bag modules without first deploying air bag. If this is not possible through procedure outlined, contact vehicle manufacturer for further instructions.

If vehicle is to be scrapped, undeployed air bag module must first be deployed. Use the following procedure for deployment of air bag.
Remote Deployment Of Air Bag – This procedure is to be used when a vehicle with a live driver's side or passenger's side air bag is to be scrapped, but a problem in air bag electrical system prevents deployment with air bag still installed in vehicle.

WARNING: Perform remote deployment outdoors. Keep all personnel at least 20 feet away to ensure physical and hearing safety from projected objects and loud noise of air bag deployment.

1) Before proceeding, see SERVICE PRECAUTIONS. Deactivate system. See DISABLING & ACTIVATING AIR BAG SYSTEM.

2) Remove air bag modules. See DRIVER'S SIDE AIR BAG MODULE and PASSENGER'S SIDE AIR BAG MODULE under REMOVAL & INSTALLATION. With air bag modules removed, cut air bag connector from wiring harness near air bag module. Strip 1" (25.4 mm) of insulation from wire ends. Obtain 2 wires at least 20 feet long. Connect one end of each 20-foot wire to one end of each air bag module wire.

WARNING: When placing a live air bag on a bench or other surface, always face air bag and trim cover up and away from surface. This will reduce motion of air bag module if it is accidentally deployed.

3) Place air bag module with trim cover facing upward on a flat surface, in remote area such as parking lot or field. Remain at least 20 feet away from air bag module. Deploy air bag by touching loose ends of both wires to 12-volt battery terminals.

4) If successful, a loud noise will be heard and bag material will be visible. Allow at least 10 minutes for cooling and dissipation of air bag effluents before approaching air bag. Air bag is now inoperative. If air bag does not deploy, air bag module is faulty. Contact vehicle manufacturer for further instructions on disposal procedures.

REMOVAL & INSTALLATION

WARNING: Failure to follow service precautions may result in air bag deployment and personal injury. See SERVICE PRECAUTIONS. After component replacement, ensure proper system operation. See SYSTEM OPERATION CHECK.

CAUTION: When battery is disconnected, vehicle computer and memory systems may lose memory data. Driveability problems may exist until computer systems have completed a relearn cycle. See COMPUTER RELEARN PROCEDURES in GENERAL INFORMATION.

CLOCKSPRING

1) Before proceeding, see SERVICE PRECAUTIONS. Disable air bag system. See DISABLING & ACTIVATING AIR BAG SYSTEM. Leave negative battery cable disconnected.

CAUTION: When removing steering wheel, DO NOT use a knock-off type steering wheel puller, or strike steering wheel or shaft with a hammer. A sudden impact could damage bearing or collapse steering column.

2) Remove driver's side air bag module. See DRIVER'S SIDE AIR BAG MODULE. Ensure vehicle front wheels are in straight-ahead position and steering column shaft alignment mark is at 12 o'clock position. Remove steering wheel. See STEERING WHEEL.

3) Remove upper and lower steering column shrouds. Unscrew tilt wheel lever (if equipped). Remove ignition switch lock cylinder by turning key to RUN position, removing lower shroud and using a 1/8" (3.17 mm) wire pin inserted into hole in steering column under lock cylinder to depress retaining pin. Pull out on lock cylinder to remove from steering column

4) Remove key warning chime contact from lock cylinder. Remove ground wire eyelet bolt. Remove clockspring down lead harness hanger clips from steering column. Disconnect clockspring wire harness. Remove connectors from bracket.

5) Install service lock on clockspring. If service lock is missing, apply 2 strips of tape across clockspring hub and rotor to maintain alignment. *See Fig. 3.* Pry 3 retaining snaps to release clockspring from steering column. Remove clockspring from steering column shaft.

NOTE: Service replacement clockspring will contain a plastic locking insert to prevent rotation. DO NOT remove insert until clockspring is securely installed on column.

Installation – To install, reverse removal procedure. Adjust clockspring (if necessary), see CLOCKSPRING under ADJUSTMENTS. Properly orientate clockspring assembly. Align air bag pigtail to 3 o'clock position.

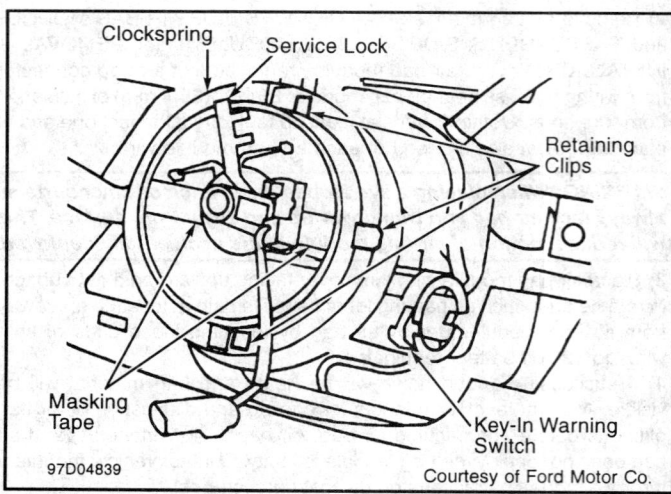

Fig. 3: Removing Clockspring

Align dot on steering shaft to 9 o'clock position. If new clockspring is being installed, remove locking mechanism. Activate air bag system. See DISABLING & ACTIVATING AIR BAG SYSTEM. Check AIR BAG warning light for proper system function. See SYSTEM OPERATION CHECK.

DRIVER'S SIDE AIR BAG MODULE

Removal – 1) Before proceeding, see SERVICE PRECAUTIONS. Disable air bag system. See DISABLING & ACTIVATING AIR BAG SYSTEM. Leave negative battery cable disconnected.
2) Remove 2 back cover plugs from rear of steering wheel. Remove screws and washers that retain air bag module to steering wheel. *See Fig. 4.* Disconnect air bag electrical connector from clockspring assembly. Remove air bag module from vehicle.

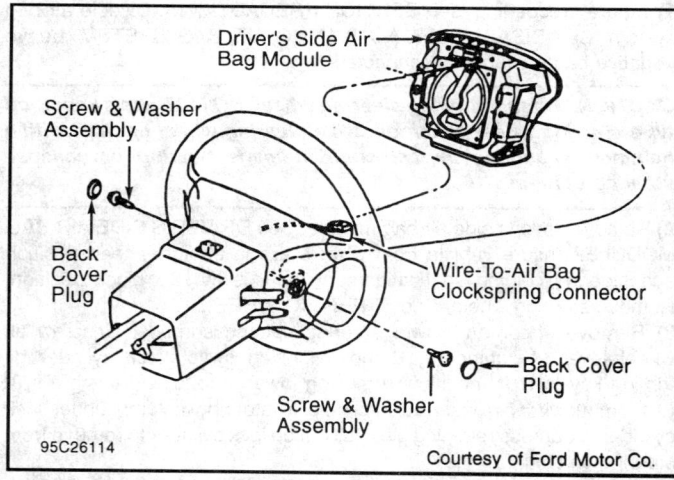

Fig. 4: Removing Driver's Side Air Bag Module

Installation – Connect air bag module to clockspring connector. Position air bag module onto steering wheel. Install air bag module retaining screws and washers and tighten to specification. See TORQUE SPECIFICATIONS. Activate air bag system. See DISABLING & ACTIVATING AIR BAG SYSTEM. Check AIR BAG warning light to ensure system is functioning properly. See SYSTEM OPERATION CHECK.

RESTRAINTS CONTROL MODULE (RCM)

NOTE: When installing a NEW RCM it MUST BE programmed for applicable vehicle configuration. This is accomplished using the New Generation Star (NGS) tester.

NOTE: Restraints Control Module (RCM) may also be referred to as Electronic Crash Sensor (ECS) or Air Bag Diagnostic Monitor (ABDM).

Removal – 1) The Restraints Control Module (RCM) module is located on center tunnel under instrument panel. Before proceeding, see SERVICE PRECAUTIONS. Disable air bag system. See DISABLING & ACTIVATING AIR BAG SYSTEM. Leave negative battery cable disconnected.
2) Remove utility tray. Remove RCM retaining bolts. Slide RCM harness connector locking clip away from RCM. Disconnect harness connector from RCM. Remove RCM.
Installation – To install, reverse removal procedure. Tighten fasteners to specification. See TORQUE SPECIFICATIONS. Activate air bag system. Check AIR BAG warning light to ensure system is functioning properly. See SYSTEM OPERATION CHECK.

PASSENGER'S SIDE AIR BAG MODULE

Removal – 1) Before proceeding, see SERVICE PRECAUTIONS. Disable air bag system. See DISABLING & ACTIVATING AIR BAG SYSTEM. Leave negative battery cable disconnected.
2) Open glove box door to access air bag mounting screws. From upper-inside glove box, remove 2 passenger's side air bag module retaining screws. Pull each corner of air bag module to disengage air bag module from instrument panel. Disconnect harness connector and remove air bag module from vehicle.
Installation – Position air bag module into instrument panel opening. Connect air bag module harness connector. Install air bag module retaining screws, and tighten to specification. See TORQUE SPECIFICATIONS. Close glove box. Activate air bag system. See DISABLING & ACTIVATING AIR BAG SYSTEM. Check AIR BAG warning light to ensure system is functioning properly. See SYSTEM OPERATION CHECK.

PASSENGER'S SIDE AIR BAG DEACTIVATE SWITCH

Removal – Before proceeding, see SERVICE PRECAUTIONS. Disable air bag system. See DISABLING & ACTIVATING AIR BAG SYSTEM. Leave negative battery cable disconnected. Remove ash tray. Remove 4 ash tray bracket retaining bolts and lower bracket. Disconnect Passenger's Side Air Bag Deactivate Switch (PAD) harness connector.
Installation – To install, reverse removal procedure. Tighten bracket bolts to specifications. See TORQUE SPECIFICATIONS. Activate air bag system. See DISABLING & ACTIVATING AIR BAG SYSTEM. Check AIR BAG warning light to ensure system is functioning properly. See SYSTEM OPERATION CHECK.

FRONT IMPACT SENSORS

NOTE: Front impact sensor orientation is critical for proper system operation. If a vehicle equipped with air bag system is involved in a crash, and fenders or grille area have been damaged, inspect sensor mounting brackets for deformation. Damaged sensor(s) should be replaced, whether or not air bag has been deployed. In addition, ensure body structure in area of sensor mounting is restored to its original construction.

Removal – Front impact sensors are attached to left and right sides of radiator support. Before proceeding, see SERVICE PRECAUTIONS. Disable air bag system. See DISABLING & ACTIVATING AIR BAG SYSTEM. Leave negative battery cable disconnected. Remove radiator grill and radiator opening cover. Remove screws, disconnect connectors and remove sensor and bracket.

Installation – To install, reverse removal procedure. Tighten retaining screws to specification. See TORQUE SPECIFICATIONS. If proper torque cannot be achieved, replace stripped mounting bracket and screw with Bracket (14B191), Screw (N806327-S190), and Screw (W620397-S36). Check AIR BAG warning light to ensure system is functioning properly. See SYSTEM OPERATION CHECK.

STEERING WHEEL

Removal – **1)** Before proceeding, see SERVICE PRECAUTIONS. Disable air bag system. See DISABLING & ACTIVATING AIR BAG SYSTEM. Leave negative battery cable disconnected.

2) Disconnect speed control wiring harness (if equipped) from steering wheel. Loosen steering wheel retaining bolt 2-3 turns. Install Differential Side Bearing Puller (T77F-4220-B1), at position marked PULL. Unseat steering wheel and remove puller.

3) Remove and discard steering wheel retaining bolt. Remove steering wheel. Route clockspring wiring harness through steering wheel as wheel is lifted from steering shaft.

Installation – **1)** Ensure front wheels are in straight-ahead position. Route clockspring wiring harness through steering wheel opening at 3 o'clock position. Position steering wheel on steering shaft and align installation marks.

2) Ensure air bag clockspring wire is not pinched when positioning steering wheel. Install new steering wheel retaining bolt, and tighten to specification. See TORQUE SPECIFICATIONS. Connect speed control wiring harness (if equipped) to steering wheel, and snap connector assembly into steering wheel clip.

3) Install driver's side air bag module. See DRIVER'S SIDE AIR BAG MODULE. Activate air bag system. See DISABLING & ACTIVATING AIR BAG SYSTEM. Check AIR BAG warning light to ensure system is functioning properly. See SYSTEM OPERATION CHECK.

ADJUSTMENTS

CLOCKSPRING

If clockspring becomes misaligned, turn clockspring rotor counterclockwise until tight. Back off 2 revolutions. Install service lock and install clockspring assembly.

WIRE REPAIR

To repair damage to sensor wiring and wiring harnesses, note following conditions and proceed to REPAIR PROCEDURE.

- All wire splice connections must be staggered at least 2" (50 mm) apart.
- Use proper size, waterproof butt-splice connectors on any exposed wiring.
- Use heat shrink nylon splice to prevent water, salt, condensation and heat from affecting the wiring repair.

REPAIR PROCEDURE

Insert pre-stripped wire ends into proper size waterproof butt-splice connector, and crimp connector using appropriate crimping pliers. *See Fig. 5.* Using heat gun, hair dryer or match, heat splice until it shrinks and adhesive oozes from each end of tubing. Connection is now waterproofed.

TORQUE SPECIFICATIONS

TORQUE SPECIFICATIONS

Application	Ft. Lbs. (N.m)
Impact Sensor Mounting Screws	8-10 (10-14)
Steering Wheel Bolt	25-34 (34-46)

	INCH Lbs. (N.m)
Ash Tray Bracket Bolts	18-27 (2.0-3.0)
Electronic Crash Sensor Bracket Screws	97-115 (11.0-13.0)
Electronic Crash Sensor Mounting Screws	97-115 (11.0-13.0)

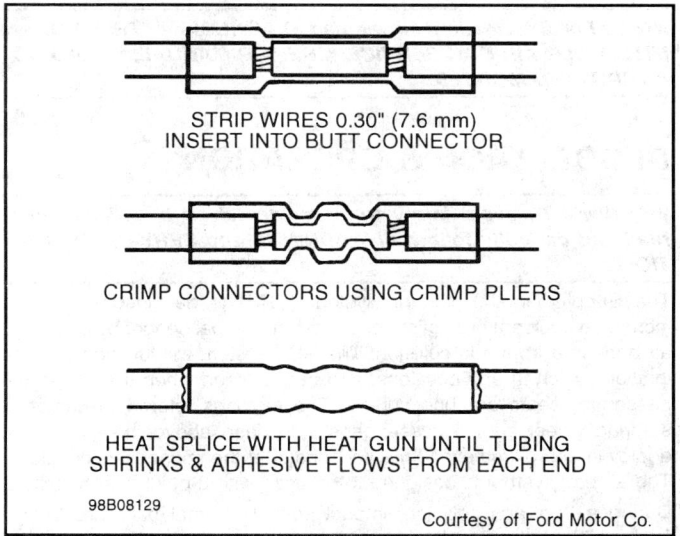

STRIP WIRES 0.30" (7.6 mm)
INSERT INTO BUTT CONNECTOR

CRIMP CONNECTORS USING CRIMP PLIERS

HEAT SPLICE WITH HEAT GUN UNTIL TUBING SHRINKS & ADHESIVE FLOWS FROM EACH END

98B08129

Courtesy of Ford Motor Co.

Fig. 5: Repairing & Waterproofing Wiring Connections

TORQUE SPECIFICATIONS (Cont.)

Application	INCH Lbs. (N.m)
Driver's Side Air Bag Module Retaining Screws	80 (9)
Lower Steering Column Shroud Screws	7-10 (0.7-1.1)
Passenger's Side Air Bag Module Retaining Bolts	67-92 (7.6-10.4)
Tilt Wheel Handle & Shank	27-44 (3.0-5.0)

WIRING DIAGRAMS

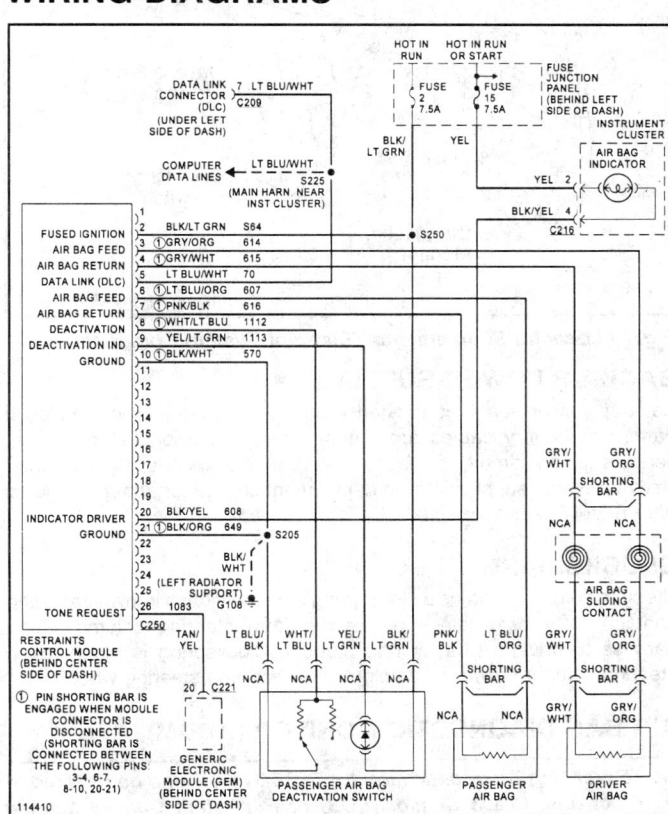

Fig. 6: Air Bag System Wiring Diagram (Ranger)

NOTE: For information on air bag DIAGNOSIS & TESTING, see MITCHELL® AIR BAG SERVICE & REPAIR MANUAL, DOMESTIC & IMPORTED MODELS.

DESCRIPTION & OPERATION

WARNING: To avoid injury from accidental air bag deployment, read and carefully follow all WARNINGS and SERVICE PRECAUTIONS.

The Supplemental Restraint System (SRS) is designed to provide increased accident protection for the driver and passenger by deploying air bags in a front-end collision. The SRS system will function with the ignition switch in any positions, and can function when the driver and passenger seats are unoccupied. The air bags, stored in center of steering wheel and in passenger's side dash above the glove box, deploy in approximately 40 milliseconds after the impact sensors close. The air bag system is designed to be used with 3-point seat belts.

During a front-end collision, impact sensor internal balls are thrown forward. The balls complete an electrical circuit to ignite the inflators and deploy air bags. The safing sensor and the impact sensor must activate simultaneously to inflate air bags.

The SRS includes the following major components: air bag diagnostic monitor (incorporating an impact and a safing sensor), driver's side air bag module, AIR BAG warning light, air bag clockspring (sliding contact), and associated wiring harnesses. *See Fig. 1.*

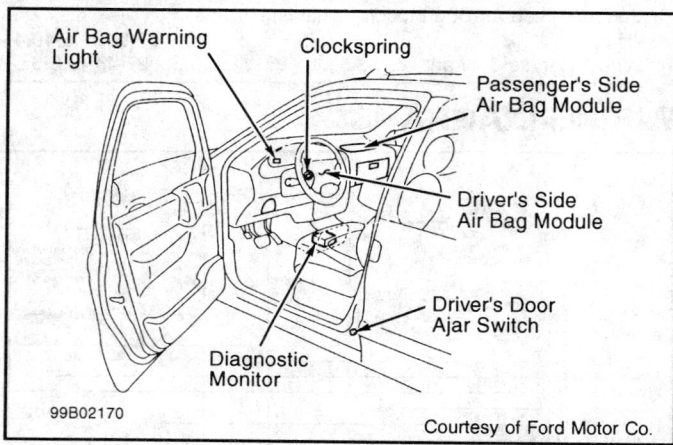

Air Bag Warning Light
Clockspring
Passenger's Side Air Bag Module
Driver's Side Air Bag Module
Driver's Door Ajar Switch
Diagnostic Monitor

99B02170

Courtesy of Ford Motor Co.

Fig. 1: Locating Supplemental Restraint System Components

BACK-UP POWER SUPPLY

Back-up power supply is located inside air bag diagnostic monitor. If battery or battery cables are damaged in a collision before impact sensors close circuit, back-up power supply will deploy air bags. Back-up power supply will hold deployment charge for about 3 minutes after battery is disconnected.

CLOCKSPRING

Steering column contains a clockspring assembly (also known as sliding contact) to transfer electrical signals from steering column wiring harness to driver's side air bag module. Clockspring is mounted on steering column between combination switch and steering wheel.

AIR BAG DIAGNOSTIC MONITOR (ABDM)

NOTE: Air Bag Diagnostic Monitor (ABDM) may also be referred to as Electronic Crash Sensor (ECS) or Restraints Control Module (RCM).

ABDM is located under instrument panel, right of steering column. ABDM contains a microcomputer that monitors electrical system components and wiring. ABDM performs a system self-check of internal circuits every time ignition switch is turned to RUN position. ABDM energizes AIR BAG warning light during initial system self-check and when a fault is detected. Faults are translated into flash codes and displayed through AIR BAG warning light. ABDM incorporates a primary impact sensor and a safing sensor. The sensors are not serviceable components.

DRIVER'S SIDE AIR BAG MODULE

Driver's side air bag module is mounted in center of steering wheel, under steering wheel trim cover. When impact sensor and safing sensor close, signaling an impact, the ignitor activates inflator gas generator. In the ensuing chemical reaction, sodium nitrate/boron potassium nitrate gas generant in the inflator, produces nitrogen gas, which inflates air bag.

When air bag is activated, tear seams molded into steering wheel trim cover separate, allowing inflation of the air bag assembly. Air bag module is only serviced as a complete assembly.

PASSENGER'S SIDE AIR BAG MODULE

Passenger's side air bag module is mounted in right side of instrument panel, above glove box. When an impact sensor and the safing sensor close, signaling an impact, the ignitor activates inflator gas generator. In the ensuing chemical reaction, sodium nitrate/boron potassium nitrate gas generant in the inflator produces nitrogen gas, which inflates air bag.

When air bag is activated, tear seams molded into trim cover separate, allowing inflation of the air bag assembly. Air bag module is only serviced as a complete assembly.

ELECTRICAL SYSTEM

Air bag system is powered directly from battery and can function with ignition switch in any position, including OFF and LOCK. System can also function when driver's and passenger's seats are unoccupied. The 3 main functions performed by electrical subsystem are detecting an impact, switching electric power to air bag ignitor, and monitoring status of air bag system.

When an impact occurs requiring air bag inflation, sensor contacts close, completing electrical circuit necessary for system operation. Safing sensor and impact sensor must close simultaneously to inflate air bag. The 2 sensors are incorporated into the air bag diagnostic monitor.

IMPACT SENSORS

The sensors (incorporated into the air bag diagnostic monitor) react to impacts according to direction and force. It discriminates between impacts that require air bag inflation and impacts that do not require air bag inflation. The sensors are not serviceable components.

SYSTEM OPERATION CHECK

1) When checking air bag system operation, and at completion of each diagnostic test, check for faults in air bag system. To check system, turn ignition switch to ON position. If AIR BAG warning light illuminates for 7 seconds and then goes out, air bag system is functioning properly, and no fault codes exist.
2) If AIR BAG warning light does not illuminate, stays on continuously, or flashes continuously, the SRS system is not functioning properly and requires service. See MITCHELL® AIR BAG SERVICE & REPAIR MANUAL, DOMESTIC & IMPORTED MODELS.

POST-COLLISION INSPECTION

If vehicle has been in a collision and air bags deployed, perform the following:
- Replace air bag modules.
- Check crash sensors on front of vehicle.
- Inspect areas near air bag modules. If interfering with deployment, replace as necessary.
- Inspect steering column for load damage. Replace as necessary.

- Inspect wiring and harness connectors. Replace as necessary.
- Perform SYSTEM OPERATION CHECK.

If a collision has occurred and air bags did not deploy, perform the following:

- Remove both air bag modules and inspect wiring and connectors for damage.
- Check area near modules for damage, check modules for fit. Repair as necessary.
- Inspect steering column for load damage. Replace as necessary.
- Inspect areas near air bag modules. If interfering with deployment, replace as necessary.

SERVICE PRECAUTIONS

The following precautions should be observed when working with air bag systems:

- Disable air bag system before servicing any air bag system or steering column components. Failure to do so may result in accidental air bag deployment and possible personal injury. See DISABLING & ACTIVATING AIR BAG SYSTEM.
- Back-up power supply holds a deployment charge for approximately 3 minutes after positive battery cable is disconnected. Servicing SRS before 3-minute period may cause accidental air bag deployment and possible personal injury.
- Because of critical system operating requirements, DO NOT service sensors, clockspring, air bag diagnostic monitor, or air bag module. Repair is made by replacement only.
- Always wear safety glasses when servicing an air bag equipped vehicle or handling an air bag.
- When carrying a live air bag module, ensure air bag module and trim cover are pointed away from your body. This minimizes chance of injury in event of an accidental deployment.
- When placing a live air bag module on a bench or other surface, always face air bag module and trim cover up and away from surface. This will reduce motion of module if it is accidentally deployed.
- After deployment, air bag surface may contain deposits of sodium hydroxide, which is a skin irritant. Sodium hydroxide is a product of the gas generant combustion. Always wear gloves and safety glasses when handling a deployed air bag. Wash your hands using mild soap and water. Follow correct disposal procedures. See DISPOSAL PROCEDURES.
- If a part is replaced and new part does not correct condition, reinstall original part and perform diagnostic procedure again.
- Never probe connectors on air bag module. Doing so may cause air bag deployment and/or personal injury.
- The instruction to disconnect always refers to a connector. DO NOT remove a component from vehicle when instructed to disconnect.
- After any servicing, ensure AIR BAG warning light does not indicate any faults still exist. See SYSTEM OPERATION CHECK.

DISABLING & ACTIVATING AIR BAG SYSTEM

WARNING: Back-up power supply holds a deployment charge for approximately 3 minutes after battery cable is disconnected. Servicing SRS before 3-minute period may cause accidental air bag deployment and possible personal injury.

CAUTION: When battery is disconnected, vehicle computer and memory systems may lose memory data. Driveability problem symptoms may exist until computer systems have completed a relearn cycle. See COMPUTER RELEARN PROCEDURES in GENERAL INFORMATION.

DISABLING SYSTEM

1) Disconnect negative battery cable. Wait at least 3 minutes to deplete charge in back-up power supply. Remove cover panel on lower portion of steering wheel to access air bag module connector. Disconnect air bag connector and install Air Bag Simulator (T94P-50-A) to vehicle harness connector. *See Fig. 2.*

2) Disconnect passenger's side air bag module connector located behind glove box. Connect Air Bag Simulator (T96P-50-A) to vehicle connector. *See Fig. 2.* To perform necessary tests, reconnect negative battery cable. To reactivate SRS system, see ACTIVATING SYSTEM.

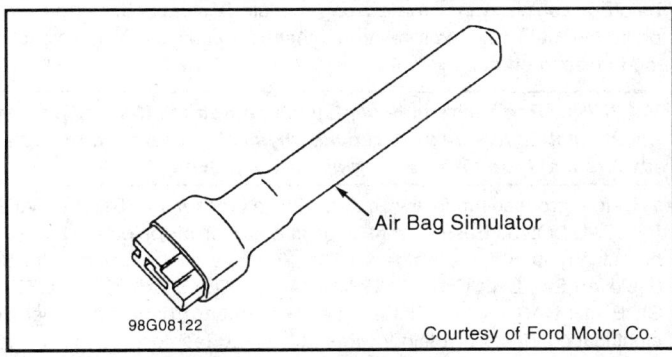

Air Bag Simulator

98G08122

Courtesy of Ford Motor Co.

Fig. 2: Identifying Typical Air Bag Simulator

ACTIVATING SYSTEM

Disconnect negative battery cable. Wait at least 3 minutes to deplete charge in back-up power supply. Disconnect and remove air bag simulators from vehicle. Reconnect driver's side and passenger's side air bag module connectors. Reconnect negative battery cable. Perform SYSTEM OPERATION CHECK.

DISPOSAL PROCEDURES

WARNING: Refer to SERVICE PRECAUTIONS before proceeding.

Air bag disposal may be necessary in the following situations:

- Scrapping vehicle with deployed air bag.
- Scrapping vehicle with live air bag.
- Disposal of a live but electrically faulty air bag module.
- Disposal of a deployed air bag module. To determine how air bag should be disposed, see AIR BAG DISPOSAL PROCEDURES table.

AIR BAG DISPOSAL PROCEDURES

Condition	Instructions
Module Replacement	
Deployed Air Bag	[1] Dispose Of In Usual Manner
Faulty But Live Air Bag Module	[2] Return For Disposal
Vehicle To Be Scrapped	
Deployed Air Bag	[1] Dispose Of In Usual Manner
Live Air Bag	[3] Deploy Air Bag

[1] – See DEPLOYED AIR BAG.
[2] – See UNDEPLOYED AIR BAG – FAULTY UNIT.
[3] – See SCRAPPED VEHICLE.

DEPLOYED AIR BAG

Dispose of deployed air bag in same manner as you would any part. Air bag module components are not reusable. To service vehicle with deployed air bag, replace air bag module with a new module.

UNDEPLOYED AIR BAG – FAULTY UNIT

If an undeployed air bag module is diagnosed as faulty, contact vehicle manufacturer for proper disposal instructions. Air bag module cannot be disposed of in usual manner.

SCRAPPED VEHICLE

CAUTION: DO NOT dispose of undeployed air bag module without first deploying air bag. If this is not possible through the following procedures, contact vehicle manufacturer for further instructions.

Remote Deployment of Air Bag – This procedure must be performed before a vehicle with a live air bag module is scrapped. Perform this procedure outdoors and away from other personnel, as air bag makes a loud noise upon deployment.

WARNING: Perform remote deployment outdoors. Keep all personnel at least 20 feet away to reduce physical hazard from projected objects and loud noise during air bag deployment.

1) Before proceeding, follow air bag service precautions. See SERVICE PRECAUTIONS. Ensure front seat is clear of all objects. DO NOT permit any occupants inside vehicle. Remove air bag module to be deployed See DRIVER'S SIDE AIR BAG MODULE or PASSENGER'S SIDE AIR BAG MODULE. Remove shorting bar from air bag module electrical connector. Obtain 2 wires at least 20 feet long.

2) Connect one end of each 20-foot wire to each pin in air bag module connector. Remain at least 20 feet away from air bag module. Deploy air bag by touching loose ends of wires to 12-volt battery terminals. If successful, a loud noise will be heard, and air bag material will be visible.

3) Allow at least 30 minutes for cooling and dissipation of air bag material before approaching air bag. Air bag is now inoperative and vehicle may be scrapped in usual manner. If air bag does not deploy, air bag module is faulty. Contact vehicle manufacturer for proper disposal instructions. Repeat procedure for other air bag.

REMOVAL & INSTALLATION

WARNING: Failure to follow service precautions may result in air bag deployment and personal injury. See SERVICE PRECAUTIONS. After component replacement, ensure proper system operation. See SYSTEM OPERATION CHECK.

CAUTION: When battery is disconnected, vehicle computer and memory systems may lose memory data. Driveability problems may exist until computer systems have completed a relearn cycle. See COMPUTER RELEARN PROCEDURES in GENERAL INFORMATION.

CLOCKSPRING

NOTE: New clockspring will contain a Red locking insert to prevent rotation. DO NOT remove insert until clockspring is installed onto steering column.

Removal & Installation – 1) Before proceeding, see SERVICE PRECAUTIONS. Disable air bag system. See DISABLING & ACTIVATING AIR BAG SYSTEM. Position front wheels in straight-ahead position. Remove driver's side air bag module. See DRIVER'S SIDE AIR BAG MODULE. Remove steering wheel. See STEERING WHEEL.

2) Remove lower steering column shroud. Match mark and apply 2 strips of tape across clockspring hub and rotor elements to prevent accidental rotation. *See Fig. 3.* Loosen shifter boot and position upper steering column shroud out of the way. Remove 3 clockspring screws.

3) Pull clockspring off upper steering column shaft and position aside. Disconnect air bag module and ignition key reminder switch connectors. Remove clockspring from vehicle. To install, reverse removal procedure.

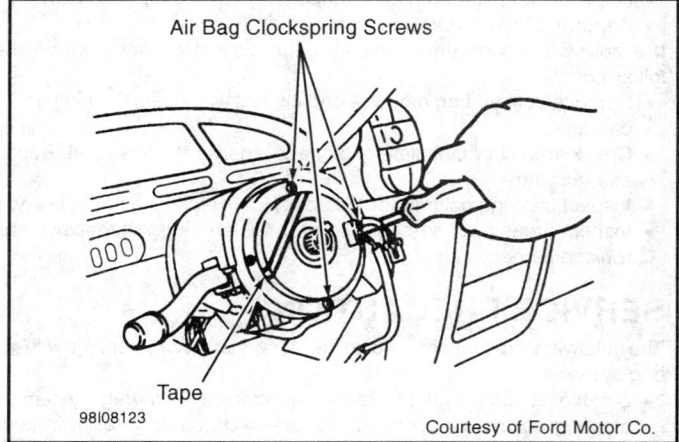

Fig. 3: Installing Tape Strips On Clockspring Before Removal

AIR BAG DIAGNOSTIC MONITOR

NOTE: Air Bag Diagnostic Monitor (ABDM) may also be referred to as Electronic Crash Sensor (ECS) or Restraints Control Module (RCM).

Removal – 1) Air bag diagnostic monitor is located under center of instrument panel, to the right of the steering column. Before proceeding, see SERVICE PRECAUTIONS. Disable air bag system. See DISABLING & ACTIVATING AIR BAG SYSTEM.

2) Remove 4 plastic screws from console compartment or CD changer cover (if equipped). Remove console compartment door or CD cover. *See Fig. 4.* Remove 2 screws, plastic nut and driver's side inner instrument panel lower cover. *See Fig. 5.* Disconnect footwell light connector. Remove passenger's side inner instrument panel lower cover and disconnect footwell light connector.

3) Using No. 50 Torx bit, remove 4 bolts and air bag diagnostic monitor. *See Fig. 6.* Disconnect air bag diagnostic monitor connector. Remove air bag diagnostic monitor from vehicle.

Installation – To install, reverse removal procedure. Ensure arrow on air bag diagnostic monitor points toward front of vehicle. Tighten air bag diagnostic monitor retaining bolts to specification. See TORQUE SPECIFICATIONS. Activate air bag system. See DISABLING & ACTIVATING AIR BAG SYSTEM. Check AIR BAG warning light to ensure system is functioning properly. See SYSTEM OPERATION CHECK.

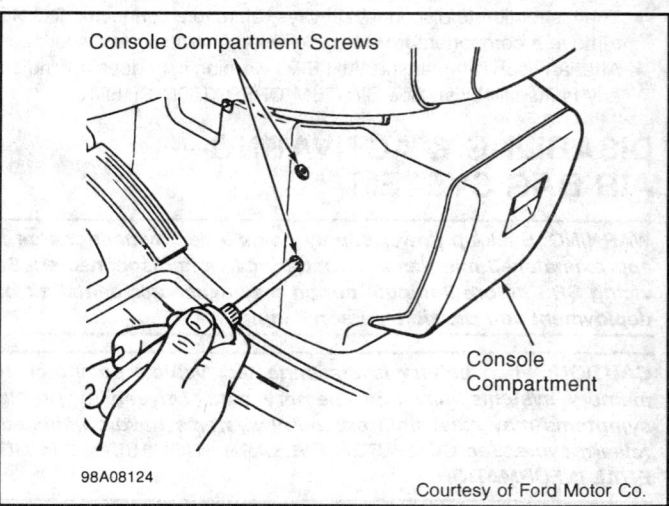

Fig. 4: Removing Driver's Side Console Compartment

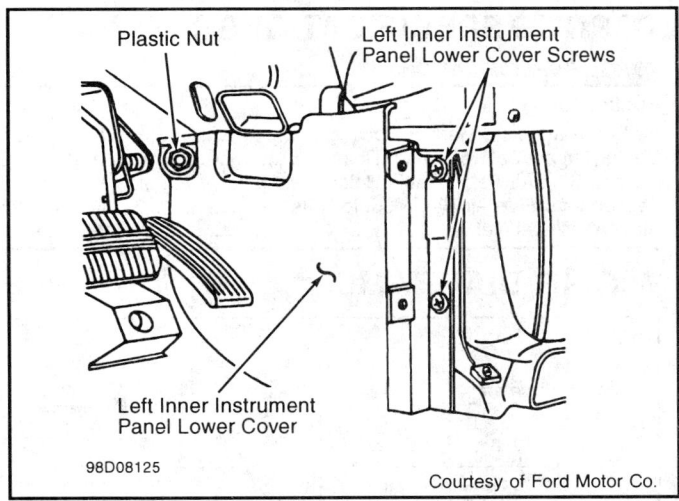

98D08125   Courtesy of Ford Motor Co.

Fig. 5: Removing Driver's Side Instrument Panel Lower Cover

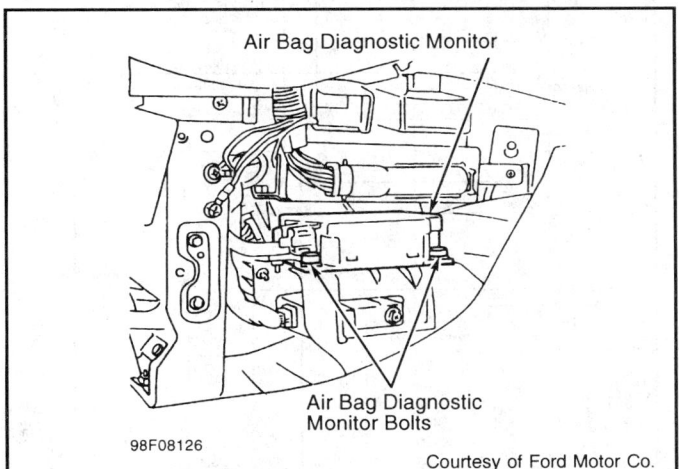

98F08126   Courtesy of Ford Motor Co.

Fig. 6: Identifying Air Bag Diagnostic Monitor

DRIVER'S SIDE AIR BAG MODULE

Removal – 1) Before proceeding, see SERVICE PRECAUTIONS. Disable air bag system. See DISABLING & ACTIVATING AIR BAG SYSTEM. Ensure that front wheels are in straight-ahead position.

2) Remove left and right air bag module bolt access covers from rear of steering wheel. Remove steering wheel bottom access cover and disconnect air bag module connector. Remove and discard 2 air bag module retaining bolts. *See Fig. 7.* Remove air bag module.

Installation – To install, align splines and reverse removal procedure. Tighten 2 NEW air bag module retaining bolts to specification. See TORQUE SPECIFICATIONS. Activate air bag system. See DISABLING & ACTIVATING AIR BAG SYSTEM. Check AIR BAG warning light to ensure system is functioning properly. See SYSTEM OPERATION CHECK.

PASSENGER'S SIDE AIR BAG MODULE

Removal – 1) Before proceeding, see SERVICE PRECAUTIONS. Passenger's side air bag module is located in instrument panel above glove box. Disable air bag system. See DISABLING & ACTIVATING AIR BAG SYSTEM.

2) Remove 4 plastic screws from console compartment or CD changer cover (if equipped). Remove console compartment door or CD cover. *See Fig. 4.* Remove 2 screws, plastic nut and driver's side inner instrument panel lower cover. *See Fig. 5.* Disconnect footwell light connector. Remove passenger's side inner instrument panel lower cover and disconnect footwell light connector.

3) Remove glove box screws/bolts. *See Fig. 8.* Separate glove box from instrument panel. Disconnect glove compartment striker plate catch

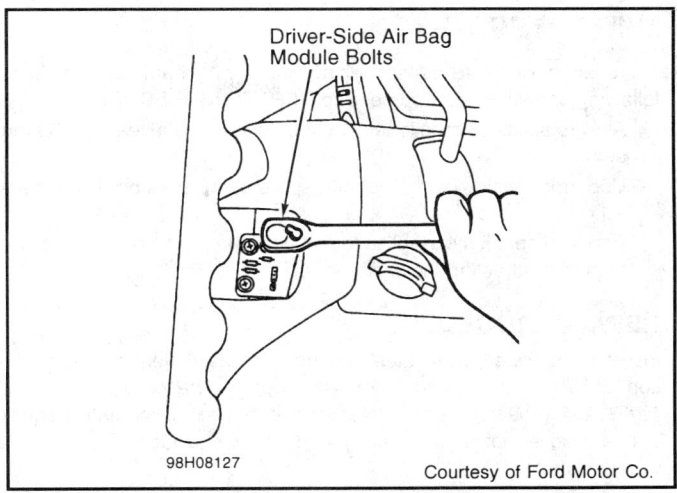

98H08127   Courtesy of Ford Motor Co.

Fig. 7: Removing Driver's Side Air Bag Module

electrical connector. Disconnect passenger's side air bag module electrical connector. Remove 4 air bag module nuts and air bag module.

Installation – To install, reverse removal procedure. Tighten passenger's side air bag module retaining nuts to specification. See TORQUE SPECIFICATIONS. Activate air bag system. See DISABLING & ACTIVATING AIR BAG SYSTEM. Check AIR BAG warning light to ensure system is functioning properly. See SYSTEM OPERATION CHECK.

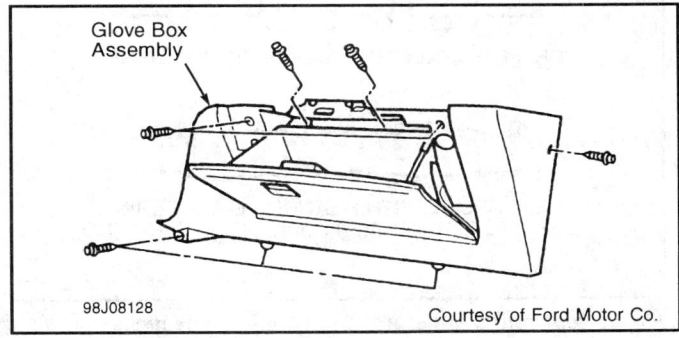

98J08128   Courtesy of Ford Motor Co.

Fig. 8: Removing Glove Box Assembly

STEERING WHEEL

Removal & Installation – 1) Position front wheels in straight-ahead position. Before proceeding, see SERVICE PRECAUTIONS. Disable air bag system. See DISABLING & ACTIVATING AIR BAG SYSTEM. Remove air bag module from steering wheel. See DRIVER'S SIDE AIR BAG MODULE. Disconnect cruise control (if equipped) and horn connectors.

2) Remove steering wheel nut. Match mark steering wheel hub and steering shaft for installation reference. Using appropriate steering wheel remover, remove steering wheel. Route clockspring wiring harness through steering wheel while steering wheel is lifted from steering shaft.

3) To install, reverse removal procedure. Tighten steering wheel nut to specification. See TORQUE SPECIFICATIONS. Activate air bag system. See DISABLING & ACTIVATING AIR BAG SYSTEM. Check AIR BAG warning light to ensure system is operating properly. See SYSTEM OPERATION CHECK.

ADJUSTMENTS

CLOCKSPRING CENTERING

If clockspring has been misaligned, ensure front wheels are in straight-ahead position. Rotate inner element of clockspring counterclockwise until tight. Place alignment marks on clockspring. Rotate inner element clockwise 2 1/2 turns and align alignment marks. Tape inner and outer elements in place.

WIRE REPAIR

To repair damage to sensor wiring and wiring harnesses, note the following conditions and proceed to REPAIR PROCEDURE:

- All wire splice connections should be staggered at least 2" (50 mm) apart.
- Use proper size, waterproof butt-splice connectors on any exposed wiring.
- Use heat shrink nylon splice to prevent water, salt, condensation and heat from affecting the wiring repair.

REPAIR PROCEDURE

Insert pre-stripped wire ends into proper size waterproof butt-splice connector and crimp connector using appropriate crimping tool. *See Fig. 9*. Using heat gun, hair dryer, or match, heat splice until it shrinks and adhesive oozes from each end of tubing. Connection is now waterproofed.

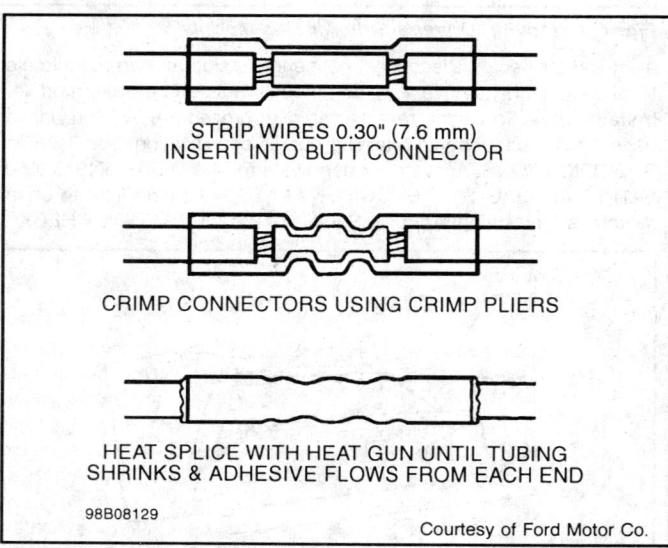

STRIP WIRES 0.30" (7.6 mm)
INSERT INTO BUTT CONNECTOR

CRIMP CONNECTORS USING CRIMP PLIERS

HEAT SPLICE WITH HEAT GUN UNTIL TUBING
SHRINKS & ADHESIVE FLOWS FROM EACH END

98B08129

Courtesy of Ford Motor Co.

Fig. 9: Repairing & Waterproofing Wiring Connections

TORQUE SPECIFICATIONS

TORQUE SPECIFICATIONS

Application	Ft. Lbs. (N.m)
Air Bag Diagnostic Monitor Bolts	11-18 (15-25)
Center Impact/Safing Sensor Bolts	11-18 (15-25)
Driver's Side Air Bag Module Bolts	11-18 (15-25)
Passenger's Side Air Bag Module Nuts	11-18 (15-25)
Steering Wheel Nut	22-29 (29-39)

WIRING DIAGRAMS

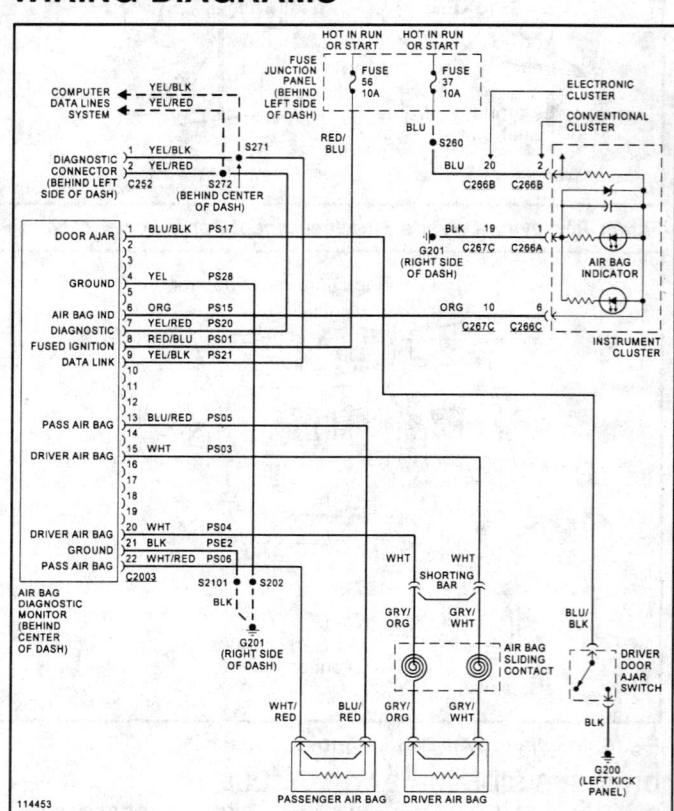

Fig. 10: Air Bag System Wiring Diagram (Villager)

NOTE: *For information on air bag DIAGNOSIS & TESTING, see MITCHELL® AIR BAG SERVICE & REPAIR MANUAL, DOMESTIC & IMPORTED MODELS.*

DESCRIPTION & OPERATION

WARNING: *To avoid injury from accidental air bag deployment, read and carefully follow all WARNINGS and SERVICE PRECAUTIONS.*

The Supplemental Restraint System (SRS), also known as air bag system, is designed to provide increased accident protection for driver and passenger by deploying air bags in a front-end collision. The air bags, stored in center of steering wheel and in instrument panel above glove box, deploy in about 40 milliseconds after impact sensors close. Air bag system is designed to be used with 3-point safety belts.

During a front-end collision of sufficient force, impact sensor and safing sensor will activate simultaneously to inflate air bag. When impact sensor and safing sensor are closed at same time, electrical current will flow, igniting the driver and passenger air bag module.

Air bag system includes the following components: Air Bag Diagnostic Monitor (ADM), driver air bag module, passenger air bag module, side air bag modules, AIR BAG warning light, impact sensor and safing sensor (both integral with ADM), side impact sensors, ignitor assemblies (in air bag modules), clockspring (also known as sliding contact) and associated wiring harnesses. See COMPONENT LOCATIONS.

AIR BAG DIAGNOSTIC MONITOR

The Air Bag Diagnostic Monitor (ADM) contains a microcomputer which monitors electrical system components and connections. Diagnostic monitor performs a system self-check of air bag system internal circuits every time ignition switch is turned to RUN position. Monitor also energizes air bag system AIR BAG warning light during initial system self-check and whenever a fault is detected. Faults are translated into Light Flash Codes (LFC) and are displayed through AIR BAG warning light.

If a system fault exists and/or AIR BAG warning light is malfunctioning, ADM will signal Generic Electronic Module (GEM) to emit an audible tone indicating need for service. Diagnostic monitor can also disarm air bag system if certain faults occur. Impact sensor and safing sensor are part of ADM, and cannot be serviced separately.

BACK-UP POWER SUPPLY

A back-up power supply is located inside diagnostic monitor. If battery or battery cables are damaged in a collision before sensor circuits close, back-up power supply will supply sufficient electrical power to deploy air bags. Back-up power supply will hold a deployment charge for approximately one minute after battery is disconnected.

CLOCKSPRING

The clockspring, located on the steering column between steering wheel and combination switch, is used to transfer electrical signals from steering column wiring harness to driver air bag module.

DRIVER'S AIR BAG MODULE

The driver air bag module is mounted on center of steering wheel, covered by steering wheel trim cover. When impact sensor and safing sensor close, signaling an impact, ignitor triggers inflator. During ignition, sodium azide reacts with copper oxide, producing nitrogen gas, which inflates air bag.

When air bag deploys, tear-seams molded into steering wheel trim cover separate, allowing inflation of air bag assembly. Driver's air bag module is not serviceable and must be replaced as a complete assembly.

ELECTRICAL SYSTEM

The air bag system is powered by ignition switch, and is only functional with ignition in RUN position. The 3 main functions performed by electrical subsystem are: detecting an impact, switching electric power to ignitors for air bag, and monitoring readiness of air bag system.

PASSENGER'S AIR BAG MODULE

The passenger air bag module is mounted in right side of instrument panel, above glove box. When impact sensor and safing sensor close, signaling an impact, air bag ignitors trigger inflator.

Since passenger air bag is larger than driver air bag, inflator contains more gas generant in a different configuration to produce more gas. When air bag is activated, instrument panel trim cover tears at seams and hinges, allowing inflation. Passenger's air bag module is only serviced as a complete assembly.

SIDE AIR BAG MODULES

Air bag modules are mounted in seat backs. If ADM determines driver and passenger air bag deployment is necessary, side air bag sensors, mounted under each front seat, may also indicate the need for side air bag deployment. Because side air bags are controlled by separate sensors, they can be deployed individually or not at all, as determined by ADM.

When either side air bag is activated, seat bolster tears at seams to allow for inflation. Side air bag modules are not serviceable, and must be replaced as a complete assembly

SIDE IMPACT SENSORS

Side impact sensors consist of a sensor mass, bias magnet, cylindrical tube, and electrical connector. In the event of a side impact of sufficient force, movement of sensor mass completes an electrical circuit signalling deployment of side air bag module. Sensors operate independently, so one, both or neither side air bag module may deploy in a collision.

SYSTEM OPERATION CHECK

1) When checking air bag system operation (also known as prove out system), and upon completion of each diagnostic test, check for faults in air bag system. To check system, turn ignition switch to RUN position. If AIR BAG warning light illuminates for approximately 6 seconds and then goes out, air bag system is functioning properly and no fault codes exist.
2) If a fault code is detected in air bag system during initial system check, AIR BAG warning light will either fail to light, stay on continuously, or flash a code sequence. If AIR BAG warning light flashes, indicating a fault in system, count number of flashes after fault code has cycled twice. Number of flashes represents a code number used to diagnose air bag system. See DIAGNOSIS & TESTING article in MITCHELL® AIR BAG SERVICE & REPAIR MANUAL, DOMESTIC & IMPORTED MODELS.
3) If a system fault exists and AIR BAG warning light fails to light, an audible tone will be heard, indicating AIR BAG warning light is out and service is required.

SERVICE PRECAUTIONS

These precautions should be observed when working with SRS:
- Disable SRS before servicing any SRS or steering column components. Failure to do so may result in accidental air bag deployment and personal injury. See procedures under DISABLING & ACTIVATING AIR BAG SYSTEM.
- Wait one minute after disabling SRS before working on vehicle. Back-up power supply holds a deployment charge for approximately one minute after negative battery cable is disconnected. Servicing SRS before one minute may cause accidental air bag deployment and possible personal injury.
- Because of critical system operating requirements, DO NOT service impact sensors, clockspring, diagnostic monitor or air bag module. Repairs are made by replacement only.
- Always wear safety glasses whenever servicing an air bag equipped vehicle or handling an air bag.
- When carrying a live air bag module, ensure air bag module and trim cover are pointed away from your body. This minimizes chance of injury in event of an accidental deployment.

- When placing a live air bag module on a bench or other surface, always face air bag module and trim cover facing up and away from surface. This will reduce motion of module if it is accidentally deployed.
- After deployment, air bag surface may contain deposits of sodium hydroxide, which may irritate skin. Sodium hydroxide is a product of gas generant combustion. Always wear gloves and safety glasses when handling a deployed air bag. Wash your hands using mild soap and water. Follow correct disposal procedures. See DISPOSAL PROCEDURES.
- If scrapping a vehicle with an undeployed air bag module, air bag must be deployed. See DISPOSAL PROCEDURES.
- If a part is replaced and new part does not correct condition, reinstall original part and perform diagnostic procedure again.
- Never probe connectors on air bag module. Doing so may cause air bag deployment and/or personal injury.
- Instruction to disconnect always refers to connector. DO NOT remove component from vehicle if instructed to disconnect.
- After any servicing, ensure AIR BAG warning light does not indicate any fault codes. See SYSTEM OPERATION CHECK.
- Replace air bag module if trim cover (deployment doors) is marred or damaged. DO NOT repaint trim cover. Paint may degrade cover material. Replace air bag module as necessary. Ensure damaged air bag is deployed. See DISPOSAL PROCEDURES.

DISABLING & ACTIVATING AIR BAG SYSTEM

WARNING: Wait one minute after disabling air bag system before working on vehicle. Back-up power supply holds a deployment charge for approximately one minute after negative battery cable is disconnected. Servicing air bag system before one minute may cause accidental air bag deployment and possible personal injury.

CAUTION: When battery is disconnected, vehicle computer and memory systems may lose memory data. Driveability problems may exist until computer systems have completed a relearn cycle. See COMPUTER RELEARN PROCEDURES in GENERAL INFORMATION.

DISABLING SYSTEM

1) Record USER 1 and USER 2 preset radio frequencies for reprogramming (if equipped). Disconnect negative battery cable. Wait at least one minute for back-up power supply to deplete stored energy.
2) Remove access panel on rear of steering wheel. Disconnect air bag module connector. Connect appropriate air bag simulator to clockspring connector at top of steering column (in place of air bag). See AIR BAG SIMULATOR.
3) Open glove box. Press in on sides to release stops and lower glove box. Disconnect passenger air bag module electrical connector. Connect appropriate air bag simulator to passenger air bag vehicle harness connector (in place of air bag).
4) Disconnect side air bag module connector under driver seat. Connect appropriate air bag simulator to vehicle harness connector. See AIR BAG SIMULATOR. Repeat for passenger side.
5) Connect negative battery cable. To reactivate SRS, see ACTIVATING SYSTEM.

AIR BAG SIMULATOR

An Air Bag Simulator (418-F088 or 105-R0012) is required to perform diagnosis and testing of the air bag system. *See Fig. 1 or 2.* An air bag simulator is a 2-ohm resistor, with appropriate connector, used to simulate an air bag module. DO NOT short-circuit air bag module connections with a zero-ohm jumper wire. If zero-ohm jumper is used, a Diagnostic Trouble Code (DTC) will be set.

ACTIVATING SYSTEM

1) Disconnect negative battery cable. Wait at least one minute for back-up power supply to deplete stored energy. Remove air bag

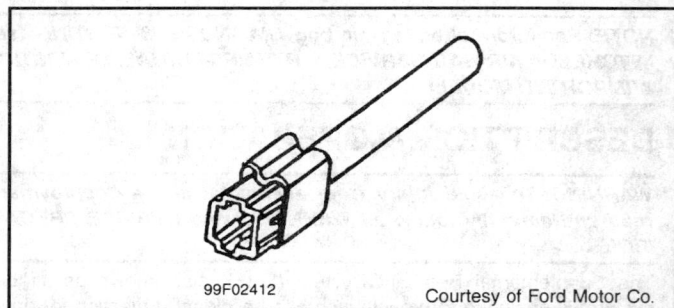

99F02412　　　　　　　　　Courtesy of Ford Motor Co.

Fig. 1: Identifying Air Bag Simulator

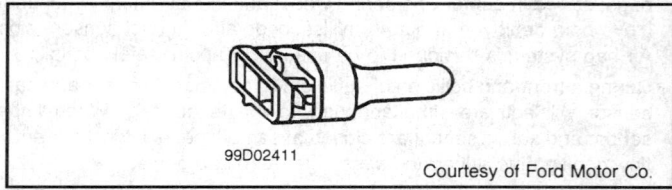

99D02411　　　　　　　　　Courtesy of Ford Motor Co.

Fig. 2: Identifying Side Air Bag Simulator

simulator from clockspring connector. Reconnect air bag module connector and install steering wheel access panel. Remove air bag simulator from passenger air bag vehicle harness connector. Restore glove box to original position.
2) Disconnect side air bag simulators. Reconnect side air bag module connectors. Reconnect negative battery cable. Recheck system operation. Perform SYSTEM OPERATION CHECK. Reprogram USER 1 and USER 2 preset radio frequencies and set clock.

DISPOSAL PROCEDURES

WARNING: Refer to SERVICE PRECAUTIONS before proceeding.

Air bag disposal may be necessary in following situations:
- Scrapping vehicle with deployed air bag.
- Scrapping vehicle with live air bag.
- Disposal of a live but electrically faulty air bag module.
- Disposal of a deployed air bag module.

DEPLOYED AIR BAG

Dispose of deployed air bag module as any other part. Air bag module components are not reusable.

UNDEPLOYED AIR BAG – FAULTY UNIT

If an undeployed air bag module is diagnosed as faulty, remove air bag module and return intact to Ford Motor Company for proper disposal. Return carton for warranty claim credit. Air bag must be packaged and shipped according to U.S. Department of Transportation procedures. Retain replacement packaging including label. DO NOT deploy air bag.

SCRAPPED VEHICLE

CAUTION: DO NOT dispose of undeployed air bag module. If this is not possible to deploy air bag through procedures outlined, contact vehicle manufacturer for further instructions.

WARNING: Perform remote deployment outdoors. Keep all personnel at least 20 feet away to ensure physical and hearing safety from projected objects and loud noise of air bag deployment.

Remote Deployment Of Air Bag – 1) Before proceeding, see SERVICE PRECAUTIONS. Deactivate air bag system. See DISABLING & ACTIVATING AIR BAG SYSTEM. Remove driver and/or passenger air bag module. See DRIVER'S AIR BAG MODULE and PASSENGER'S AIR BAG MODULE under REMOVAL & INSTALLATION.

2) With air bag module removed, cut air bag connector from wiring harness near air bag module. Strip 1" of insulation from wire ends. Obtain 2 wires at least 20 feet long. Connect one end of each 20-foot wire to one end of each air bag module wire.

WARNING: When placing a live air bag on a bench or other surface, always face air bag and trim cover up and away from surface. This will reduce motion of air bag module if it is accidentally deployed.

---

3) Place air bag module with trim cover facing upward on a flat surface, in remote area such as parking lot or field. Remain at least 20 feet away from air bag module. Deploy air bag by touching loose ends of both wires to 12-volt battery terminals.

4) If successful, a loud noise will be heard and bag material will be visible. Allow at least 10 minutes for cooling and dissipation of air bag effluents before approaching air bag. Air bag is now inoperative. If air bag does not deploy, air bag module is faulty. Contact vehicle manufacturer for further instructions on disposal procedures.

POST-COLLISION INSPECTION

If vehicle has been in a collision and air bags deployed, perform the following:

- Replace air bag modules.
- Replace Air Bag Diagnostic Monitor (ADM).
- Inspect areas near air bag modules. If interfering with deployment, repair as necessary.
- Inspect steering column for load damage. Repair or replace as necessary.
- Inspect wiring and harness connectors. Repair or replace as necessary.
- Perform SYSTEM OPERATION CHECK.

If a collision has occurred and air bags did not deploy, perform the following:

- Remove air bag modules and inspect wiring and connectors for damage.
- Check area near modules for damage, check modules for fit. Repair as necessary.
- Inspect steering column for load damage. Replace as necessary.
- Inspect areas near air bag modules. If interfering with deployment, replace as necessary.

REMOVAL & INSTALLATION

WARNING: Failure to follow service precautions may result in air bag deployment and personal injury. See SERVICE PRECAUTIONS. After component replacement, ensure proper system operation. See SYSTEM OPERATION CHECK.

CAUTION: When battery is disconnected, vehicle computer and memory systems may lose memory data. Driveability problems may exist until computer systems have completed a relearn cycle. See COMPUTER RELEARN PROCEDURES in GENERAL INFORMATION.

AIR BAG DIAGNOSTIC MONITOR

Removal – 1) Diagnostic monitor is located behind utility compartment at lower center of instrument panel. Before proceeding, see SERVICE PRECAUTIONS. Disable air bag system. See DISABLING & ACTIVATING AIR BAG SYSTEM. Leave negative battery cable disconnected.

2) Remove 4 rivets retaining utility compartment to metal support. Pull utility compartment toward rear of vehicle to disengage 4 retaining clips, and remove utility compartment. Pull carpet back and remove 2 ADM bracket bolts. Disconnect ADM connectors. Remove 2 remaining ADM bracket bolts. Remove diagnostic monitor with bracket.

Installation – To install, reverse removal procedure. Tighten fasteners to specification. See TORQUE SPECIFICATIONS. Activate air bag system. See DISABLING & ACTIVATING AIR BAG SYSTEM. Check AIR BAG warning light to ensure system is functioning properly. See SYSTEM OPERATION CHECK.

CLOCKSPRING

Removal – 1) Clockspring is located on steering column between steering wheel and combination switch. Before proceeding, see SERVICE PRECAUTIONS. Disable air bag system. See DISABLING & ACTIVATING AIR BAG SYSTEM. Leave negative battery cable disconnected.

2) Remove steering wheel. See STEERING WHEEL. Remove driver air bag module. See DRIVER AIR BAG MODULE. Place tape across face of clockspring to prevent accidental rotation.

3) Remove 2 lower steering column opening panel screws. Remove panel by pulling out on lower edge. Remove 3 bolts and remove lower steering column opening reinforcement panel. Loosen 4 steering column retaining nuts and lower column slightly. Do not bend or stretch shift indicator cable. Pull 2 finish panels from instrument panel, on either side of steering column. Disconnect headlight switch electrical connector.

4) Remove 4 lower steering column shroud screws and remove shroud. Turn ignition switch to RUN position. Insert suitable tool in hole at bottom of ignition lock cylinder housing. Depress tab and remove ignition lock cylinder from housing.

5) Place transmission range selector lever in lowest position. Remove 4 instrument cluster finish panel screws and remove panel. Place transmission range selector lever in highest position. Remove upper steering column shroud. Remove Passive Anti-Theft System (PATS) transmitter screw and remove transmitter from ignition lock cylinder housing. Remove key-in switch from ignition lock cylinder housing.

6) Disconnect clockspring electrical connectors and disengage connectors from bracket. Remove clockspring by disengaging 3 tabs from back of clockspring. Remove clockspring from steering shaft.

Installation – To install, reverse removal procedure. Tighten fasteners to specification. See TORQUE SPECIFICATIONS. Activate air bag system. See DISABLING & ACTIVATING AIR BAG SYSTEM. Check AIR BAG warning light to ensure system is functioning properly. See SYSTEM OPERATION CHECK.

DRIVER'S AIR BAG MODULE

Removal – Before proceeding, see SERVICE PRECAUTIONS. Disconnect negative battery cable. Wait at least one minute for back-up power supply to deplete. Remove steering wheel. See STEERING WHEEL. Remove 2 cover screws from rear of steering wheel and remove cover. Remove steering wheel harness from shield and disconnect connectors. Remove and discard 3 allen screws retaining air bag module to steering wheel. Remove air bag module and wire shield as an assembly.

Installation – To install, reverse removal procedure. Use NEW allen screws to fasten air bag module to steering wheel. Gently install wiring harness and connectors into wire shield on air bag module. Tighten fasteners to specification. See TORQUE SPECIFICATIONS. Activate air bag system. Connect negative battery cable. Check AIR BAG warning light for proper system function. See SYSTEM OPERATION CHECK.

PASSENGER'S AIR BAG MODULE

Removal – 1) Passenger's air bag module is located in right side of instrument panel above glove box. Before proceeding, see SERVICE PRECAUTIONS. Disable air bag system. See DISABLING & ACTIVATING AIR BAG SYSTEM. Leave negative battery cable disconnected.

2) Press glove box sides inward, and lower glove box to floor. Disengage air bag module connector from instrument panel frame. Disconnect air bag module connectors. Remove 3 air bag module mounting bolts. Push air bag module out and remove from vehicle.

Installation – To install, reverse removal procedure. Ensure proper routing of harness during installation. Tighten fasteners to specification. See TORQUE SPECIFICATIONS. Activate air bag system. See DISABLING & ACTIVATING AIR BAG SYSTEM. Check AIR BAG warning light to ensure system is functioning properly. See SYSTEM OPERATION CHECK.

SIDE AIR BAG MODULES

Removal – 1) Side air bag module are located in each front seatback, on outboard side of each seat. Before proceeding, see SERVICE PRECAUTIONS. Disable air bag system. See DISABLING & ACTIVATING AIR BAG SYSTEM. Leave negative battery cable disconnected.

2) Remove 4 seat retaining nuts from underside of vehicle. Disconnect electrical connectors and remove seat from vehicle. Remove retaining screws from back of lower seat trim panels. Carefully pry out retaining clips at front of panels and remove panels from lower seat.

3) Remove armrest by depressing release tab located on armrest pivot. Remove armrest stop and retainer from seatback. Remove pushpins retaining side air bag module wiring harness to seat and pull harness free. Remove 1 seatback pivot bolt on one side, and 2 seatback ratchet assembly pivot bolts from other side. Remove seatback.

4) Disengage seatback cover retaining strips. Peel seat cover upward until side air bag module access is obtained. Release pin retaining side air bag module harness to seatback. Do not disconnect connector at air bag module. Module and harness are remove as an assembly. Remove 2 side air bag module retaining bolts and remove module from seatback.

Installation – To install, reverse removal procedure. Ensure proper routing of harness during installation. Tighten fasteners to specification. See TORQUE SPECIFICATIONS. Activate air bag system. See DISABLING & ACTIVATING AIR BAG SYSTEM. Check AIR BAG warning light to ensure system is functioning properly. See SYSTEM OPERATION CHECK.

SIDE IMPACT SENSORS

Removal – 1) Side impact sensors are located under each front seat. Before proceeding, see SERVICE PRECAUTIONS. Disable air bag system. See DISABLING & ACTIVATING AIR BAG SYSTEM. Leave negative battery cable disconnected.

2) Remove 4 seat retaining nuts from underside of vehicle. Disconnect electrical connectors and remove seat from vehicle. Pull carpet back to reveal sensor. Disengage wiring harness retaining pin from sensor. Disconnect electrical connector. Remove 2 retaining bolts and remove sensor and bracket as an assembly.

Installation – To install, reverse removal procedure. Ensure proper routing of harness during installation. Tighten fasteners to specification. See TORQUE SPECIFICATIONS. Activate air bag system. See DISABLING & ACTIVATING AIR BAG SYSTEM. Check AIR BAG warning light to ensure system is functioning properly. See SYSTEM OPERATION CHECK.

STEERING WHEEL

Removal – Before proceeding, see SERVICE PRECAUTIONS. Ensure front wheels are in straight-ahead position. Disable air bag system. See DISABLING & ACTIVATING AIR BAG SYSTEM. Leave negative battery cable disconnected and steering wheel access cover removed. Using Tool No. 501–052, turn pinion shaft through steering wheel access panel to release steering wheel from column.

Installation – To install, reverse removal procedure. Ensure proper routing of harness during installation. Tighten fasteners to specification. See TORQUE SPECIFICATIONS. Activate air bag system. See DISABLING & ACTIVATING AIR BAG SYSTEM. Check AIR BAG warning light to ensure system is functioning properly. See SYSTEM OPERATION CHECK.

COMPONENT LOCATIONS

COMPONENT LOCATIONS

Component	Location
Air Bag Diagnostic Monitor	Center Of Instrument Panel, In Front Of Utility Compartment
Driver's Air Bag Module	Center Of Steering Wheel
Passenger's Air Bag Module	Top Right Side Of Instrument Panel
Safing Sensor	Within Diagnostic Monitor
Side Air Bag Modules	In Each Front Seatback
Side Impact Sensor	Under Each Front Seat

WIRE REPAIR

To repair damage to wiring harnesses, note following conditions:

- All wire splice connections must be staggered at least 2" (50 mm) apart.
- Use proper size, waterproof butt-splice connectors on any exposed wiring.
- Use heat shrink nylon splice to prevent water, salt, condensation and heat from affecting the wiring repair. Insert pre-stripped wire ends into proper size waterproof butt-splice connector, and crimp connector using appropriate crimping pliers. *See Fig. 3.* Using heat gun, hair dryer or match, heat splice until it shrinks and adhesive oozes from each end of tubing. Connection is now waterproofed.

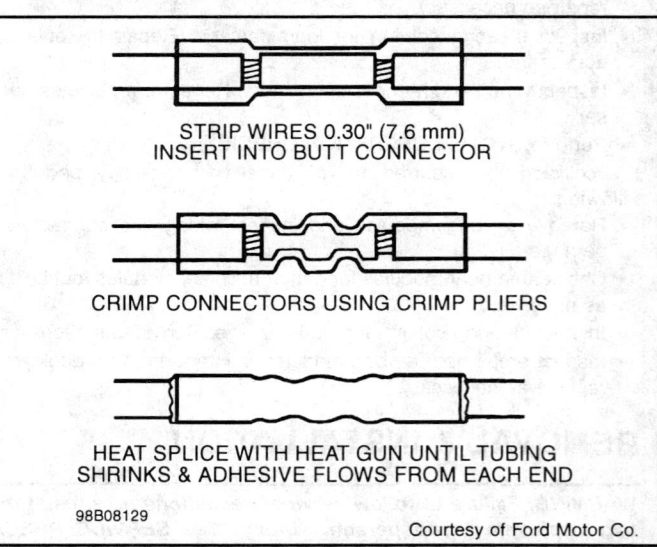

STRIP WIRES 0.30" (7.6 mm)
INSERT INTO BUTT CONNECTOR

CRIMP CONNECTORS USING CRIMP PLIERS

HEAT SPLICE WITH HEAT GUN UNTIL TUBING
SHRINKS & ADHESIVE FLOWS FROM EACH END

98B08129   Courtesy of Ford Motor Co.

Fig. 3: Repairing & Waterproofing Wiring Connections

TORQUE SPECIFICATIONS

TORQUE SPECIFICATIONS

Application	Ft. Lbs. (N.m)
Air Bag Diagnostic Monitor Bolts	9 (12)
Arm Rest Mount And Stop Bolts	30 (40)
Front Seat Retaining Nuts	59 (80)
Passenger's Air Bag Module	9 (12)
Seatback Pivot Bolt	17 (23)
Seatback Ratchet Assembly Pivot Bolts	33 (45)
Side Air Bag Modules	10 (14)
Side Impact Sensors	9 (12)
Steering Column Retaining Nuts	12 (15)
Steering Column Opening Reinforcement Panel Bolts	9 (12)
Steering Wheel Pinion Shaft	13 (18)

	INCH Lbs. (N.m)
Driver's Air Bag Module Screws	71 (8)

WIRING DIAGRAMS

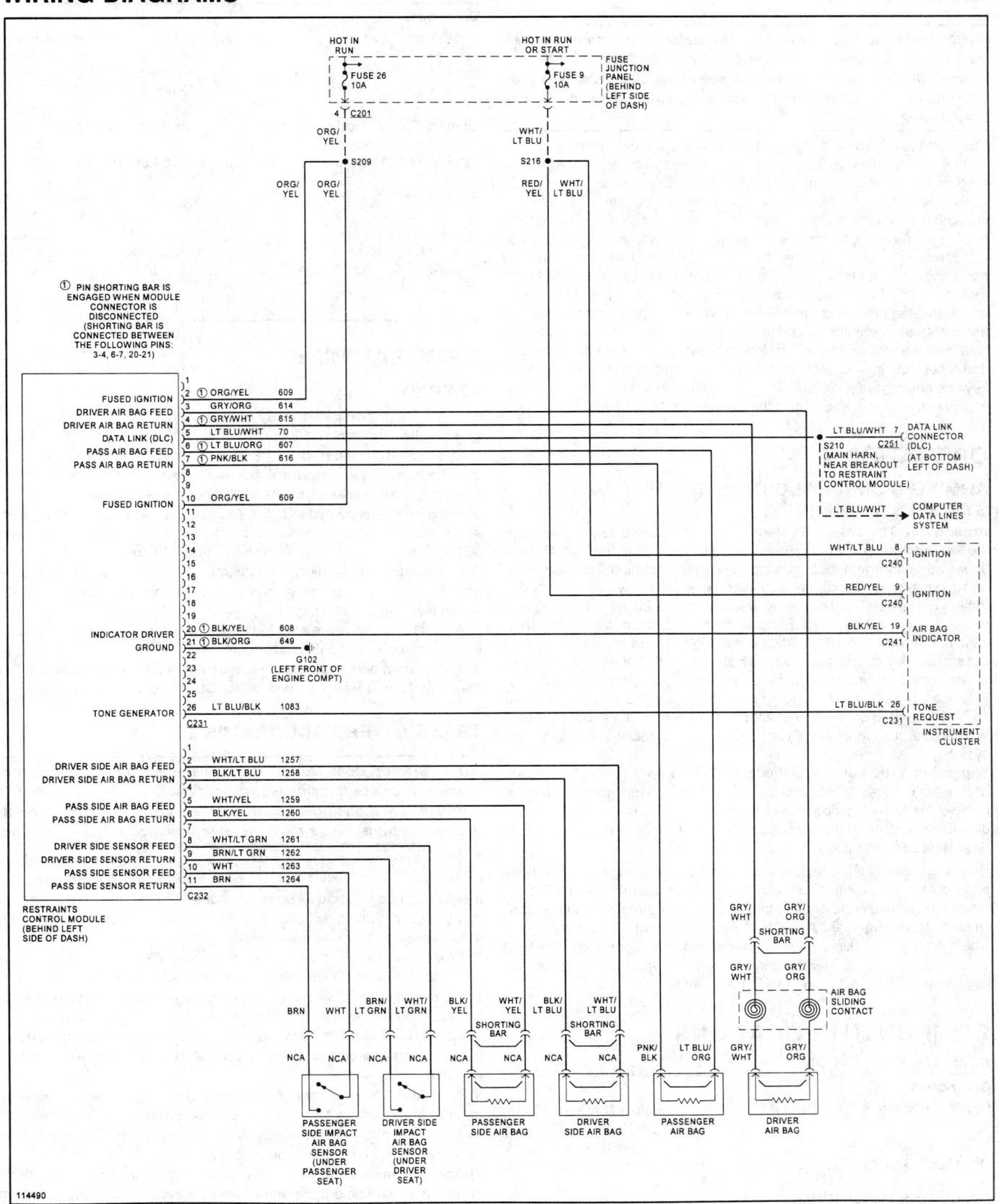

Fig. 4: Air Bag System Wiring Diagram (Windstar)

DESCRIPTION

WARNING: Deactivate air bag system before performing any service operation. See appropriate AIR BAG RESTRAINT SYSTEMS article. DO NOT apply electrical power to any component on steering column without first deactivating air bag system. Air bag may deploy.

The anti-theft system is designed to prevent unauthorized entry into engine compartment, passenger doors or luggage compartment. When triggered, horn sounds and headlights and taillights flash. This system does not enable/disable engine from starting but may be used in conjunction with the passive anti-theft system. Some system functions may also tie in with remote keyless entry system. When armed, unauthorized entry is detected by the door disarm switches located in each door, a lock tamper detection switch in the luggage compartment lock cylinder and a hood tamper switch on left fender panel. An alarm light is located in the instrument cluster. When triggered, system flashes the low beam headlights, parking lights, taillights and alarm indicator light. Models with an electronic door lock system have a PANIC feature that operates in conjunction with the anti-theft system and remote keyless entry system. When the PANIC button on the remote transmitter is pushed, horn will sound and the exterior lights will flash.

OPERATION

ARMING & DISARMING OF ANTI-THEFT ALARM SYSTEM

Arming Anti-Theft Alarm System – Use the following sequence to arm the anti-theft alarm system. Remove ignition key from ignition. Open a door and ensure anti-theft indicator light starts flashing. Lock all doors using power door locks, keyless entry keypad, or by pressing LOCK button on remote keyless entry transmitter. Close all doors. Ensure doors are fully closed. Wait approximately 30 seconds for anti-theft indicator light to turn off to indicate anti-theft system is armed.

Disarming An Untriggered Anti-Theft Alarm System – System may be disarmed by unlocking driver's or passenger's door with the key, unlocking driver's door using keyless entry keypad or using remote keyless entry transmitter to unlock the driver's door. If remaining inside the vehicle, turn ignition switch to ON or ACC position to disarm the system.

Triggering Anti-Theft Alarm System – The horn will sound, headlights, park lights, courtesy lights and anti-theft indicator light will start flashing if any of the following trigger the system: any door is opened without first disarming anti-theft alarm system or hood is opened without first disarming anti-theft alarm system.

Within approximately 3 minutes after the system is triggered, the horn and lights will shut off automatically. Anti-theft alarm system will then reset to an armed state and will trigger again if another intrusion occurs.

Disarming A Triggered Anti-Theft Alarm System – System may be disarmed by unlocking driver's or passenger's door with the key, unlocking driver's door using keyless entry keypad or using remote keyless entry transmitter to unlock the driver's door.

COMPONENT LOCATIONS

COMPONENT LOCATIONS

Component	Location
Data Link Connector (DLC)	Below Driver's Side Of Instrument Panel, To Right Of Steering Column
Door Lock Switch	Appropriate Door Panel Arm Rest
Driver's Door Module (DDM)	Behind Driver's Door Panel, Lower Front Corner
Driver's Seat Module (DSM)	Under Driver's Seat
Heated Seat Module	Under Appropriate Seat

COMPONENT LOCATIONS (Cont.)

Component	Location
Heated Seat Switch	Center Of Instrument Panel, Under Heater Controls
Instrument Panel Fuse Box	Below Left Instrument Panel
Keyless Entry Keypad	Driver's Door Below Exterior Door Handle
Lighting Control Module (LCM)	On Instrument Panel, Behind Headlight Switch
Light Sensor Amplifier	Top Left Side Of Instrument Panel
Power Distribution Box	Left Side Of Engine Compartment, Above Wheelwell
Power Mirror Switch	Driver's Door Panel Arm Rest
Powertrain Control Module (PCM)	In Passenger's Side Of Engine Compartment, On Firewall

PROGRAMMING

KEYPAD

1) Enter 5-digit permanent entry code at keypad. Within 5 seconds of pressing last digit, press 1/2 button on keypad to activate programming mode. Hold 1/2 button for more than 2 seconds to erase all stored customer codes. Door locks will lock and unlock to confirm all codes are erased. Existing codes do not need to be erased to program new codes.

2) Enter new 5-digit keypad code. To associate new code with personality position No. 1 or 2, press 1/2 button within 7.5 seconds of entering last digit of new code for position No. 1 or 3/4 button for position No. 2. Doors will lock and unlock to confirm new code is programmed. If another code is to be programmed, begin entering code within 7.5 seconds of pressing last button.

3) After all new codes are programmed, a new remote transmitter can be programmed within 7.5 seconds of pressing last digit in keypad code. To exit program mode, press keyless entry keypad buttons 7/8 and 9/0 at the same time or wait 7.5 seconds for DDM to exit automatically.

TRANSMITTER PROGRAMMING

NOTE: Driver's Door Module (DDM) will erase all previously programmed remote transmitters when a new remote transmitter is programmed. If adding an additional remote transmitter, all existing remote transmitters must be reprogrammed at the same time.

1) Enter 5-digit permanent entry code at keypad. Within 5 seconds of pressing last digit, press 1/2 button on keypad. Hold 1/2 button for more than 2 seconds to erase all stored customer codes. Door locks will lock and unlock to confirm all codes are erased. Existing codes do not need to be erased to program new codes.

2) Press and hold any button on remote transmitter within 5 seconds of pressing 1/2 button. Doors will lock and unlock to confirm programming. Driver's door module will automatically associate remote transmitters to a personality setting. The first remote transmitter to be programmed will be position No. 1, and the second remote transmitter will be position No. 2. Remaining remote transmitters if programmed, will not be associated to a personality setting.

3) If additional remote transmitters are to be programmed, press any button on next remote transmitter to be programmed within 7.5 seconds of pressing button on last transmitter. If programming is successful, doors will signal by locking and unlocking.

4) After all remote transmitters are programmed, a new keyless entry keypad code can be programmed within 7.5 seconds of pressing button on last remote transmitter. To exit program mode, press keyless entry keypad buttons 7/8 and 9/0 at the same time or wait 7.5 seconds for DDM to exit automatically.

COMPONENT TESTS

DOOR LOCK SWITCH

Using an ohmmeter, check for continuity between indicated switch terminals when switch is operated as specified. See POWER DOOR LOCK SWITCH CONTINUITY TEST table. *See Fig. 1.* Replace switch if it does not test as specified.

POWER DOOR LOCK SWITCH CONTINUITY TEST

Switch Position	Continuity Between Pins
Lock	1 & 6
Unlock	5 & 6

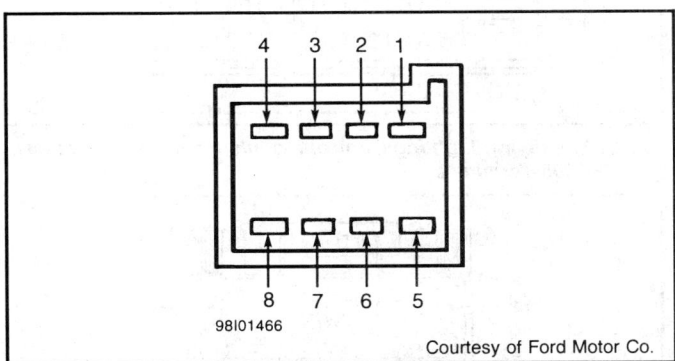

98I01466   Courtesy of Ford Motor Co.

Fig. 1: Identifying Power Door Lock Switch & Mirror Control Switch Terminals

MIRROR CONTROL SWITCH

Using an ohmmeter, check for continuity between indicated switch terminals when switch is activated as specified. See POWER MIRROR SWITCH CONTINUITY TEST table. *See Fig. 1.* Replace switch if it does not test as specified.

POWER MIRROR SWITCH CONTINUITY TEST

Switch Position	Continuity Between Pins
Left Mirror	
Up	1 & 6; 3 & 5
Down	1 & 3; 5 & 6
Left	1 & 6; 4 & 5
Right	1 & 4; 5 & 6
Right Mirror	
Up	1 & 6; 5 & 7
Down	1 & 7; 5 & 6
Left	1 & 6; 5 & 8
Right	1 & 8; 5 & 6

SELF-DIAGNOSTIC SYSTEM

Verify customers complaint. Check for loose or corroded connectors, damaged wiring harness, damaged ignition switch or door ajar switches. Repair or replace components as necessary.

If all components are okay, connect New Generation Star (NGS) tester to Data Link Connector (DLC), located beneath instrument panel. Using NGS tester, perform data link diagnostics test. See DATA LINK DIAGNOSTIC TEST under COMMUNICATION NETWORK DIAGNOSTICS in MODULE COMMUNICATIONS NETWORK – CONTINENTAL article. If NGS tester responds with CKT914, CKT915 or CKT70=ALL ECUS NO RESP/NOT EQUIP, repair module communications concern. See MODULE COMMUNICATIONS NETWORK – CONTINENTAL article. If NGS tester displays NO RESP/NOT EQUIP for Lighting Control Module (LCM), perform TEST A: NO COMMUNICATION WITH LIGHTING CONTROL MODULE under SYSTEM TESTS. If NGS tester displays NO RESP/NOT EQUIP for Driver's Door Module (DDM), perform TEST B: NO COMMUNICATION WITH DRIVER'S DOOR MODULE under SYSTEM TESTS.

If NGS tester responds with SYSTEM PASSED, retrieve and record continuous DTCs. Erase continuous DTCs. Using NGS tester, perform DDM and LCM self-test. Perform appropriate test in accordance with DTC retrieved. See LIGHTING CONTROL MODULE DTC INDEX and/or DRIVER'S DOOR MODULE DTC INDEX table. Codes listed in these tables are only for testing covered in this article. For complete DTC listing, see MODULE COMMUNICATIONS NETWORK – CONTINENTAL article. If no DTCs are retrieved, repair by symptom. See SYMPTOM CHART table under SYSTEM TESTS.

LIGHTING CONTROL MODULE DTC INDEX

DTC [1]	Description	Test
B1342	ECU Defective	[2]
B1495	Decklid Punch Out Sensor Circuit Failure	G
B1498	Decklid Punch Out Sensor Short To Ground	G
B1522	Hood Switch Circuit Short To Ground	G

[1] – Codes listed in this table are only for testing covered in this article. For complete DTC listing, see MODULE COMMUNICATIONS NETWORK – CONTINENTAL article.

[2] – Using NGS tester, retrieve and document continuous DTCs. Clear all DTCs. Perform Lighting Control Module (LCM) self-test. If DTC B1342 is retrieved again, replace LCM.

DRIVER'S DOOR MODULE DTC INDEX

DTC [1]	Description	Test
B1342	ECU Defective	[2]

[1] – Codes listed in this table are only for testing covered in this article. For complete DTC listing, see MODULE COMMUNICATIONS NETWORK – CONTINENTAL article.

[2] – Using NGS tester, retrieve and document all continuous. Perform DDM self-test. If DTC B1342 is retrieved again, replace DDM.

SYSTEM TESTS

NOTE: *Before performing any system test, perform self-diagnostics. See SELF-DIAGNOSTIC SYSTEM.*

CAUTION: *When battery is disconnected or modules are replaced, vehicle computer and memory systems may lose memory data. Driveability problems may exist until computer systems have completed a relearn cycle. See COMPUTER RELEARN PROCEDURES article in GENERAL INFORMATION before disconnecting battery.*

SYMPTOM CHART

Symptom	Test
No Communication With Lighting Control Module	A
No Communication With Driver's Door Module	B
Anti-Theft Indicator Light Is Always/Never On	C
Alarm System Does Not Arm Or Disarm Using Remote Keyless Entry Transmitter Or Keyless Entry Keypad	D
Alarm System Does Not Arm Using Door Lock Switch	E
Alarm System Does Not Disarm Using Door Lock Cylinder	F
Alarm Sound Without Violation	G
Alarm System Does Not Operate Properly	H

TEST A: NO COMMUNICATION WITH LIGHTING CONTROL MODULE

1) Turn ignition switch to LOCK position. Connect New Generation Star (NGS) tester to Data Link Connector (DLC). Monitor Lighting Control Module (LCM) PID IGN_LC. If NGS tester does not display UNABLE TO PERFORM TEST/FUNCTION or MODULE NOT RESPONDING: LCM or CHECK IGNITION STATUS/VERIFY CABLE REQUIREMENTS or CHECK CABLE CONNECTIONS, go to next step. If NGS tester displays UNABLE TO PERFORM TEST/FUNCTION or MODULE NOT RESPONDING: LCM or CHECK IGNITION STATUS/VERIFY CABLE REQUIREMENTS or CHECK CABLE CONNECTIONS, go to step **16)**.
2) Turn ignition switch to RUN position. Monitor LCM PID IGN_LC while turning key to each position. If PID IGN_LC shows ACCY while in

ACCESSORY position and OFF in all other positions, replace LCM. If PID IGN_LC shows ACCY while in RUN position, go to next step. If PID IGN_LC shows OFF in all positions, go to step 7).

3) Turn ignition switch to RUN position. Measure voltage at output side of fuse No. 5 (10-amp) in instrument panel fuse box. If battery voltage does not exist, go to next step. If battery voltage exists, repair open in Red/Yellow wire between instrument panel fuse box and LCM.

4) Check fuse No. 5 in instrument panel fuse box. If fuse is blown, go to next step. If fuse is okay, repair open in Brown/Pink wire between instrument panel fuse box and ignition switch.

5) Turn ignition switch to LOCK position. Disconnect LCM harness connector C206. Disconnect light sensor amplifier harness connector C243. Measure resistance between ground and terminal No. 17 (Red/Yellow wire) at LCM harness connector C206. See Fig. 2. If resistance is 20 ohms or less, go to next step. If resistance is greater than 20 ohms, repair short to ground in Red/Yellow wire.

6) Turn ignition switch to LOCK position. Connect LCM harness connector C206. Remove fuse No. 5 (10-amp) in instrument panel fuse box. Measure resistance between ground and output side of fuse No. 5 in instrument panel fuse box. If resistance is 20 ohms or less, repair autolamp concern. See AUTOLAMP SYSTEMS – CONTINENTAL article. If resistance is greater than 20 ohms, replace LCM.

7) Turn ignition switch to RUN position. Measure voltage at output side of fuse No. 4 (10-amp) in instrument panel fuse box. If battery voltage exists, go to next step. If battery voltage does not exist, go to step 9).

8) Turn ignition switch to LOCK position. Disconnect LCM harness connector C208. Turn ignition switch to RUN position. Measure voltage at terminal No. 2 (Black/Pink wire) at LCM harness connector C208. See Fig. 3. If battery voltage exists, replace LCM. If battery voltage does not exist, repair open in Black/Pink wire.

9) Turn ignition switch to LOCK position. Check fuse No. 4 (10-amp) in instrument panel fuse box. If fuse is blown, go to next step. If fuse is okay, repair open in Black/Light Green wire between instrument panel fuse box and ignition switch.

10) Disconnect driver's door lock switch harness connector C505. Measure resistance between ground and terminal No. 2 (Black/Pink wire) at LCM harness connector C208. If resistance is 10 k/ohms or less, go to next step. If resistance is greater than 10 k/ohms, replace driver's door lock switch.

11) Disconnect passenger's door lock switch harness connector C602. Measure resistance between ground and terminal No. 2 (Black/Pink wire) at LCM harness connector C208. If resistance is 10 k/ohms or less, go to next step. If resistance is greater than 10 k/ohms, replace passenger's door lock switch.

12) Disconnect passenger's power window switch harness connector C600. Measure resistance between ground and terminal No. 2 (Black/Pink wire) at LCM harness connector C208. If resistance is 10 k/ohms or less, go to next step. If resistance is greater than 10 k/ohms, replace passenger's power window switch.

13) Disconnect left rear power window switch harness connector C709. Measure resistance between ground and terminal No. 2 (Black/Pink wire) at LCM harness connector C208. If resistance is 10 k/ohms or less, go to next step. If resistance is greater than 10 k/ohms, replace left rear power window switch.

14) Disconnect right rear power window switch harness connector C809. Measure resistance between ground and terminal No. 2 (Black/Pink wire) at LCM harness connector C208. If resistance is 10 k/ohms or less, go to next step. If resistance is greater than 10 k/ohms, replace right rear power window switch.

15) Ensure ignition switch is in LOCK position. Connect LCM harness connector C208. Using and ohmmeter, measure resistance by back-probing between ground and terminal No. 2 (Black/Pink wire) at LCM harness connector C208. If resistance is greater than 2 k/ohms, replace LCM. If resistance is 2 k/ohms or less, repair Black/Pink wire.

16) Turn ignition switch to LOCK position. Disconnect LCM harness connectors. Measure resistance between ground and terminal No. 13 (Black wire) at LCM harness connector C206. See Fig. 2. Measure resistance between ground and terminal No. 1 (Black wire) at LCM harness connector C207. See Fig. 4. Measure resistance between

ground and terminal No. 9 (Black wire) at LCM harness connector C211. See Fig. 5. If all resistance readings are 5 ohms or less, go to next step. If any resistance reading is greater than 5 ohms, repair appropriate Black wire.

17) Measure resistance between ground and terminal No. 15 (Black/Light Blue wire) at LCM harness connector C207. If resistance is 5 ohms or less, repair module communication concern. See MODULE COMMUNICATIONS NETWORK – CONTINENTAL article. If resistance is greater than 5 ohms, repair open in Black/Light Blue wire.

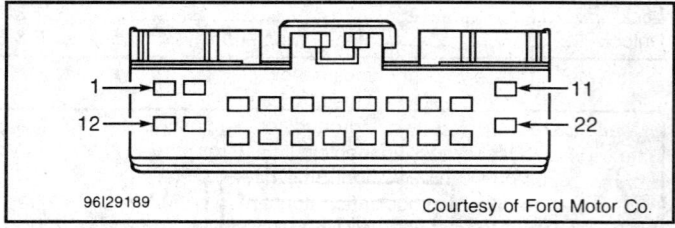

Fig. 2: Identifying Lighting Control Module Harness Connector C206 Terminals

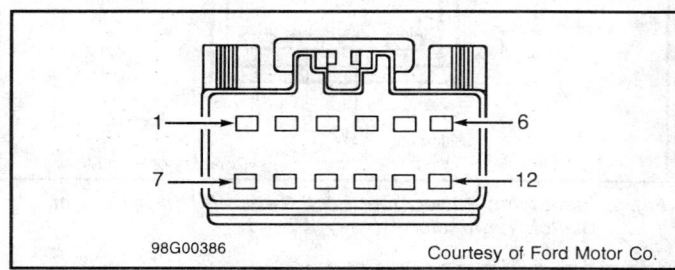

Fig. 3: Identifying Lighting Control Module Harness Connector C208 Terminals

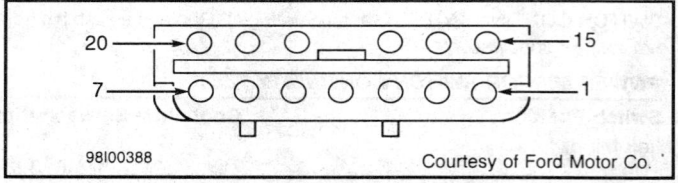

Fig. 4: Identifying Lighting Control Module Harness Connector C207 Terminals

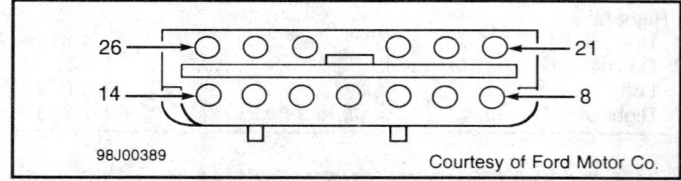

Fig. 5: Identifying Lighting Control Module Harness Connector C211 Terminals

TEST B: NO COMMUNICATION WITH DRIVER'S DOOR MODULE

NOTE: After any repairs are complete, ensure all component are properly installed and all harness connectors are connected properly and repeat data link diagnostic test.

1) Connect NGS tester to Data Link Connector (DLC). Turn ignition switch to RUN position. Monitor Driver's Door Module (DDM) PIDs SFWD_SW, SREAR_SW, SFNT_SW and SRCL_SW while activating power seat control switch. If UNABLE TO PERFORM TEST FUCTION MODULE NOT RESPONDING: DDM CHECK IGNITION STATUS/ VERIFY CABLE REQUIREMENTS CHEK CABLE CONNECTIONS? is not displayed, go to next step. If UNABLE TO PERFORM TEST FUCTION MODULE NOT RESPONDING: DDM CHECK IGNITION

STATUS/VERIFY CABLE REQUIREMENTS CHEK CABLE CONNECTIONS? is displayed, perform TEST A: NO COMMUNICATION WITH LIGHTING CONTROL MODULE.

2) Turn ignition switch to LOCK position. Remove fuse No. 39 (10-amp) in instrument panel fuse box. Check fuse. If fuse is okay, go to next step. If fuse is blown, go to step **6)**.

3) Measure voltage at input side of fuse No. 39 in instrument panel fuse box. If battery voltage exists, go to next step. If battery voltage does not exist, go to step **24)**.

4) Install fuse No. 39. Disconnect Driver's Door Module (DDM) harness connector C524. Measure voltage at terminal No. 6 (Black/White wire) at DDM harness connector C524. *See Fig. 6*. If battery voltage exists, go to next step. If battery voltage does not exist, repair open in Black/White wire between instrument panel fuse box and DDM.

5) Measure resistance between ground and terminal No. 14 (Black/Light Blue wire) at DDM harness connector C524. If resistance is greater than 5 ohms, repair open in Black/Light Blue wire. If resistance is 5 ohms or less, repair module communication concern. See MODULE COMMUNICATIONS NETWORK – CONTINENTAL article.

6) Replace fuse No. 39. DO NOT operate any switches. If fuse blows, go to next step. If fuse does not blow, go to step **14)**.

7) Remove fuse No. 39. Disconnect DDM harness connector C524, Driver's Seat Module (DSM) harness connector C342, keyless entry keypad harness connector C525, driver's seat control switch harness connector C520, driver's door lock switch harness connector C505, passenger's door lock switch harness connector C602 and power mirror control switch harness connector C550. Measure resistance between ground and terminal No. 6 (Black/White wire) at DDM harness connector C524. If resistance is greater than 10 k/ohms, go to next step. If resistance is 10 k/ohms or less, repair short to ground in Black/White wire.

8) Connect keyless entry keypad harness connector C525. Measure resistance between ground and terminal No. 6 (Black/White wire) at DDM harness connector C524. If resistance is greater than 10 k/ohms, go to next step. If resistance is 10 k/ohms or less, replace keyless entry keypad.

9) Connect driver's seat control switch harness connector C520. Measure resistance between ground and terminal No. 6 (Black/White wire) at DDM harness connector C524. If resistance is greater than 10 k/ohms, go to next step. If resistance is 10 k/ohms or less, replace driver's seat control switch.

10) Connect DSM harness connector C342. Measure resistance between ground and terminal No. 6 (Black/White wire) at DDM harness connector C524. If resistance is greater than 10 k/ohms, go to next step. If resistance is 10 k/ohms or less, replace driver's seat module.

11) Connect DDM harness connector C524. Measure resistance between ground and terminal No. 6 (Black/White wire) at driver's door lock switch harness connector C505. *See Fig. 7*. If resistance is greater than 10 k/ohms, go to next step. If resistance is 10 k/ohms or less, replace driver's door module.

12) Connect passenger's door lock switch harness connector C602. Measure resistance between ground and terminal No. 6 (Black/White wire) at driver's door lock switch harness connector C505. If resistance is greater than 10 k/ohms, go to next step. If resistance is 10 k/ohms or less, replace passenger's door lock switch.

13) Connect power mirror control switch harness connector C550. Measure resistance between ground and terminal No. 6 (Black/White wire) at driver's door lock switch harness connector C505. If resistance is greater than 10 k/ohms, replace driver's door lock switch. If resistance is 10 k/ohms or less, replace power mirror control switch.

14) Lock and unlock doors at all door lock switches. If fuse No. 39 blows, go to next step. If fuse No. 39 does not blow, go to step **17)**.

15) Remove driver's and passenger's door lock switches. Test both door lock switches. See DOOR LOCK SWITCH under COMPONENT TESTS. If both door lock switches are okay, go to next step. If either door lock switch is defective, replace appropriate door lock switch.

16) Disconnect Driver's Door Module (DDM) harness connector C506. Measure resistance between ground and terminal No. 1 (Pink/Yellow wire) at driver's door lock switch harness connector C505. Also,

measure resistance between ground and terminal No. 5 (Pink/Light Green wire) at driver's door lock switch harness connector C505. *See Fig. 7*. If either resistance reading is 10 k/ohms or less, repair short to ground in appropriate wire(s). If both resistance readings are greater than 10 k/ohms, replace driver's door module.

17) Press each number on keyless entry pad one at a time. If fuse No. 39 blows, go to next step. If fuse No. 39 does not blow, go to step **19)**.

18) Disconnect Driver's Door Module (DDM) harness connector C523. Disconnect keyless entry keypad harness connector C525. Measure resistance between ground and appropriate terminals at remote keyless entry keypad harness connector C525. See REMOTE KEYLESS ENTRY TERMINAL IDENTIFICATION table. *See Fig. 8*. If all resistance readings are greater than 10 k/ohms, replace driver's door module. If any resistance readings are 10 k/ohms or less, repair short to ground in appropriate wire.

REMOTE KEYLESS ENTRY TERMINAL IDENTIFICATION

Terminal	Wire Color
1	Red
2	Yellow
3	Yellow/Black
4	Light Green/Red
5	Light Blue/Yellow
9	Light Blue

19) Activate mirrors in all directions. If fuse No. 39 blows, go to next step. If fuse No. 39 does not blow, go to step **22)**.

20) Remove mirror control switch. Test mirror control switch. See MIRROR CONTROL SWITCH under COMPONENT TESTS. If mirror control switch is okay, go to next step. If mirror control switch is defective, replace mirror control switch.

21) Disconnect Driver's Door Module (DDM) harness connector C506. Disconnect mirror control switch harness connector C550. Measure resistance between ground and appropriate terminals at mirror control switch harness connector C550. See MIRROR CONTROL SWITCH TERMINAL IDENTIFICATION table. *See Fig. 9*. If all resistance readings are greater than 10 k/ohms, replace driver's door module. If any resistance reading are 10 k/ohms or less, repair short to ground in appropriate wire.

MIRROR CONTROL SWITCH TERMINAL IDENTIFICATION

Terminal	Wire Color
3	Dark Blue/Orange
4	Red/Orange
6	Yellow/Black
7	Violet/Orange
8	Dark Green/Orange

22) Activate driver's seat control switch in all directions. If fuse No. 39 blows, go to next step. If fuse No. 39 does not blow, system is operating properly at this time.

23) Disconnect Driver's Door Module (DDM) harness connector C506. Disconnect driver's seat control switch harness connector C520. Measure resistance between ground and appropriate terminals at driver's seat control switch harness connector C520. See DRIVER'S SEAT CONTROL SWITCH TERMINAL IDENTIFICATION table. *See Fig. 10*. If all resistance readings are greater than 10 k/ohms, replace driver's door module. If any resistance readings are 10 k/ohms or less, repair short to ground in appropriate wire.

DRIVER'S SEAT CONTROL SWITCH TERMINAL IDENTIFICATION

Terminal	Wire Color
2	Red/White
3	Red/Light Green
4	Red/Light Blue
5	Gray
7	Yellow/White
8	Yellow/Light Green
9	Yellow/Light Blue
10	Gray/Black

24) Turn ignition switch to LOCK position. Remove fuse No. 1 (30-amp) in power distribution box. Check fuse. If fuse is okay, go to next step. If fuse is blown, go to step **26**.

25) Measure voltage at input side of fuse No. 1 in power distribution box. If battery voltage exists, repair open in Red wire between power distribution box and instrument panel fuse box. If battery voltage does not exist, repair or replace power distribution box as necessary.

26) Ensure fuse No. 1 in power distribution box is still removed. Disconnect Driver's Seat Module (DSM) harness connector C362. Disconnect driver's heated seat module harness connector C352. Disconnect driver's lumbar switch harness connector C348. Measure resistance between ground and terminal No. 1 (Red wire) at DSM harness connector C362. If resistance is greater than 10 k/ohms, go to next step. If resistance is 10 k/ohms or less, repair short to ground in Red wire.

27) Connect DSM harness connector C362. Measure resistance between ground and output side of fuse No. 1 in power distribution box. If resistance is greater than 10 k/ohms, go to next step. If resistance is 10 k/ohms or less, replace driver's seat module.

28) Replace fuse No. 1 (30-amp) in power distribution box. Connect driver's lumbar switch harness connector C348. Operate driver's lumbar switch in both directions. If fuse No. 1 blows, go to next step. If fuse No. 1 does not blow, go to step **32**.

29) Remove fuse No. 1 (30-amp) from power distribution box. Measure resistance between ground and output side of fuse No. 1 in power distribution box. If resistance is greater than 10 k/ohms, go to next step. If resistance is 10 k/ohms or less, replace driver's lumbar switch.

30) Disconnect driver's lumbar switch harness connector C348. Measure resistance between ground and terminal No. 4 (Pink wire) at driver's lumbar switch harness connector C348. Also, measure resistance between ground and terminal No. 2 (Brown wire) at driver's lumbar switch harness connector C348. See Fig. 11. If both resistance readings are greater than 10 k/ohms, go to next step. If either resistance reading is 10 k/ohms or less, replace driver's lumbar switch.

31) Disconnect driver's lumbar motor harness connector C315. Measure resistance between ground and terminal No. 4 (Pink wire) at driver's lumbar switch harness connector C348. Also, measure resistance between ground and terminal No. 2 (Brown wire) at driver's lumbar switch harness connector C348. If both resistance readings are greater than 10 k/ohms, replace power lumbar motor. If either resistance reading is 10 k/ohms or less, repair short to ground in appropriate wire.

32) Disconnect driver's heated seat module harness connector C352. Measure resistance between ground and appropriate terminals at driver's heated seat module harness connector C352. See HEATED SEAT MODULE CONNECTOR TERMINAL IDENTIFICATION table. See Fig. 6. If all resistance readings are greater than 10 k/ohms, replace driver's heated seat module. If any resistance readings are 10 k/ohms or less, repair short to ground in appropriate wire.

HEATED SEAT MODULE CONNECTOR TERMINAL IDENTIFICATION

Terminal	Wire Color
5	Black/Light Blue
6	Brown/Light Blue
8	Yellow/Light Blue
9	Gray/Light Blue
10	Red/Light Blue
11	Orange/Light Blue
12	Violet/Light Blue
13	White/Light Blue

TEST C: ANTI-THEFT INDICATOR LIGHT IS ALWAYS/NEVER ON

1) Turn ignition switch to RUN position. If THEFT indicator does not illuminate, go to next step. If THEFT indicator illuminates, go to step **9**.

2) Turn ignition switch to LOCK position. Using NGS tester, trigger LCM active command WARNING LAMPS AND CHIME ANTI-THEFT to ON. If

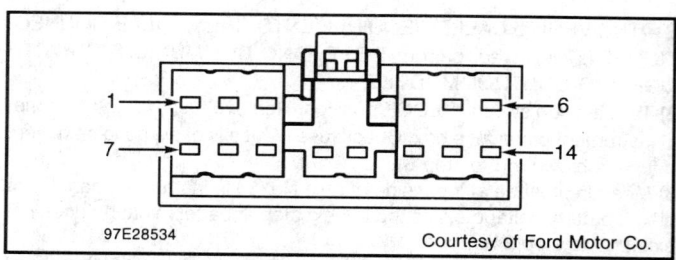

97E28534   Courtesy of Ford Motor Co.

Fig. 6: Identifying Driver's Door Module Harness Connector C524 & Driver's Heated Seat Module Harness Connector C352 Terminals

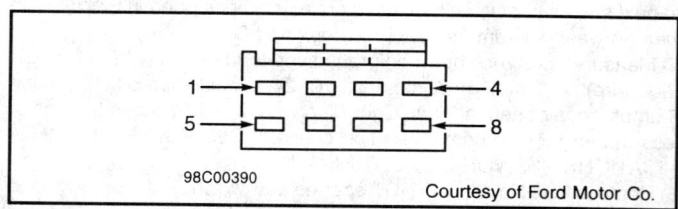

98C00390   Courtesy of Ford Motor Co.

Fig. 7: Identifying Driver's Door Lock Switch Harness Connector C505 Terminals

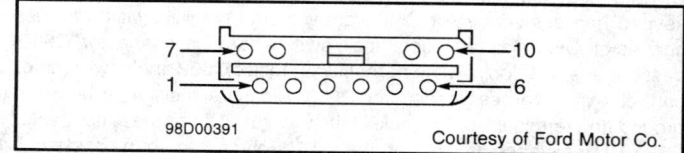

98D00391   Courtesy of Ford Motor Co.

Fig. 8: Identifying Remote Keyless Entry Keypad Harness Connector C525 Terminals

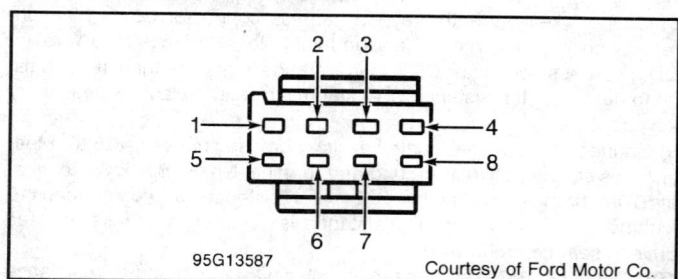

95G13587   Courtesy of Ford Motor Co.

Fig. 9: Identifying Mirror Control Switch Harness Connector C550 Terminals

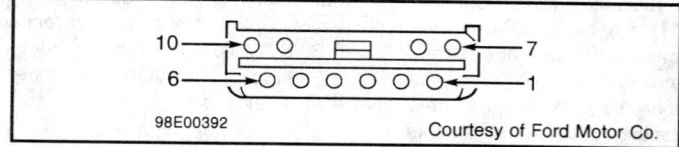

98E00392   Courtesy of Ford Motor Co.

Fig. 10: Identifying Driver's Seat Control Switch Harness Connector C520 Terminals

THEFT indicator does not illuminate, go to next step. If THEFT indicator illuminates, system is okay at this time.

3) Turn ignition switch to LOCK position. Disconnect light sensor amplifier harness connector C243. Turn ignition switch to RUN position. Measure voltage at terminal No. 2 (Dark Blue/Light Green wire) at light sensor amplifier harness connector C243 while triggering LCM active command WARNING LAMPS AND CHIME ANTI-THEFT to ON. See Fig. 12. If battery voltage does not exist, go to next step. If battery voltage exists, go to step **5**.

4) Turn ignition switch to LOCK position. Disconnect LCM harness connector C208. Measure resistance in Dark Blue/Light Green wire between terminal No. 8 at LCM harness connector C208 and terminal No. 2 at light sensor amplifier harness connector C243. See Figs. 3 and 12. If resistance is 5 ohms or less, replace LCM. If resistance is greater than 5 ohms, repair open in Dark Blue/Light Green wire between LCM and light sensor amplifier.

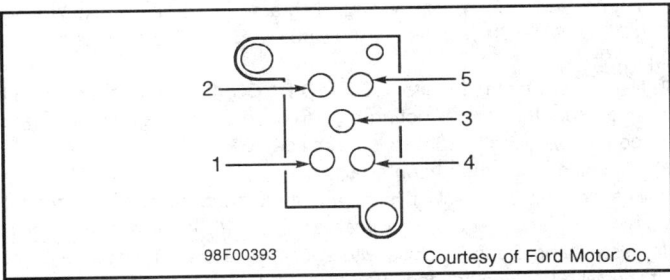

98F00393   Courtesy of Ford Motor Co.

Fig. 11: Identifying Driver's Lumbar Switch Harness Connector C348 Terminals

5) Turn ignition switch to LOCK position. Measure resistance between ground and terminal No. 1 (Black wire) at light sensor amplifier C243. If resistance is 5 ohms or less, go to next step. If resistance is greater than 5 ohms, repair open in Black wire between light sensor amplifier and ground.

6) Remove anti-theft LED. Measure resistance between anti-theft LED terminals in both directions. Resistance should be greater than 10 k/ohms in one direction and 10-20 ohms in the other. If resistance is as specified, go to next step. If resistance is not as specified, replace anti-theft LED and return to step **2)**.

7) Disconnect LCM harness connector C208. Turn ignition switch to RUN position. Measure voltage at terminal No. 3 (Pink wire) at light sensor amplifier harness connector C243. If battery voltage exists, go to next step. If battery voltage does not exist, repair open in Pink wire between instrument panel fuse box and light sensor amplifier.

8) Turn ignition switch to RUN position. Measure voltage at terminal No. 6 (Red/Yellow wire) at light sensor amplifier harness connector C243. If battery voltage exists, replace light sensor amplifier. If battery voltage does not exist, repair open in Red/Yellow wire between instrument panel fuse box and light sensor amplifier.

9) Turn ignition switch to LOCK position. Disconnect light sensor amplifier harness connector C243. Turn ignition switch to RUN position. If THEFT indicator does not illuminate, go to next step. If THEFT indicator illuminates, replace light sensor amplifier.

10) Turn ignition switch to LOCK position. Disconnect LCM harness connector C208. Turn ignition switch to RUN position. Measure voltage at terminal No. 2 (Dark Blue/Light Green wire) at light sensor amplifier harness connector C243. *See Fig. 12.* If voltage exists, repair short to voltage in Dark Blue/Light Green wire between LCM and light sensor amplifier. If no voltage exists, replace LCM.

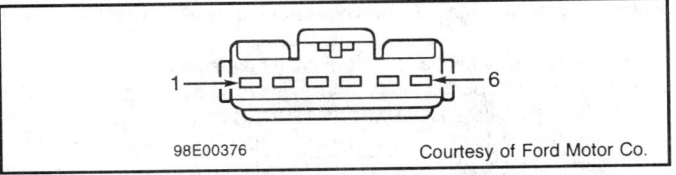

98E00376   Courtesy of Ford Motor Co.

Fig. 12: Identifying Light Sensor Amplifier Harness Connector C243 Terminals

TEST D: ALARM SYSTEM DOES NOT ARM OR DISARM USING REMOTE KEYLESS ENTRY TRANSMITTER OR KEYLESS ENTRY KEYPAD

1) Ensure all doors are locked. Press UNLOCK button on remote transmitter. If courtesy lights illuminate, go to next step. If courtesy lights do not illuminate, repair courtesy lights. See AUTOLAMP SYSTEMS – CONTINENTAL article.

2) Lock and unlock all doors using keyless entry keypad and remote transmitter. If door locks operate properly, go to next step. If door locks do not operate properly, repair power door locks. See appropriate wiring diagram in REMOTE KEYLESS ENTRY SYSTEMS article.

3) Turn ignition switch to RUN position. Ensure all doors are fully closed. Turn ignition switch to LOCK position. Open and close the driver's door. Remove key from ignition switch. Press LOCK button on remote transmitter and note operation of THEFT indicator. If THEFT indicator

illuminates for 30 seconds and then goes off, go to next step. If THEFT indicator does not illuminate for 30 seconds and then go off, replace Driver's Door Module (DDM) and retest system operation. If system is still inoperative, replace LCM.

4) Turn ignition switch to RUN position. Ensure all doors are fully closed. Turn ignition switch to LOCK position. Open and close the driver's door. Remove key from ignition switch. Lock doors using keyless entry keypad and note operation of THEFT indicator. If THEFT indicator illuminates for 30 seconds and then goes off, system is okay at this time. If THEFT indicator does not illuminate for 30 seconds and then goes off, replace DDM and retest system operation. If system is still inoperative, replace LCM.

TEST E: ALARM SYSTEM DOES NOT ARM USING DOOR LOCK SWITCH

1) Ensure all doors are locked. Press UNLOCK button on remote transmitter. If courtesy lights illuminate, go to next step. If courtesy lights do not illuminate, repair courtesy lights. See AUTOLAMP SYSTEMS – CONTINENTAL article.

2) Lock and unlock all doors using door lock switch on driver's door. If door locks operate properly, go to next step. If door locks do not operate properly, repair power door locks. See appropriate wiring diagram in REMOTE KEYLESS ENTRY SYSTEMS article.

3) Ensure all doors are fully closed. Turn ignition switch to RUN position and then to LOCK position. Open driver's door. Lock doors by using door lock switch on driver's door. Close driver's door and note operation of THEFT indicator. If THEFT indicator illuminates for 30 seconds and then goes off, system is okay at this time. If THEFT indicator does not illuminate for 30 seconds and then goes off, replace Driver's Door Module (DDM) and retest system operation. If system is still inoperative, replace LCM.

TEST F: ALARM SYSTEM DOES NOT DISARM USING DOOR LOCK CYLINDER

1) Turn ignition switch to LOCK position. Using NGS tester, retrieve and record continuous DTCs. Clear DTCs and perform Driver's Door Module (DDM) self-test. If DTC B1562 is not retrieved, go to next step. If DTC B1562 is retrieved, go to step **10)**.

2) Using NGS tester, monitor DDM PID DRLKCYL while using key to rotate driver's door lock cylinder to UNLOCK position. If DDM PID DRLKCYL does not indicate ON in the UNLOCK position, go to next step. If DDM PID DRLKCYL indicates ON in the unlock position, go to step **5)**.

3) Using NGS tester, monitor DDM PID DRLKCYL while using key to rotate passenger's door lock cylinder to UNLOCK position. If DDM PID DRLKCYL does not indicate ON in the UNLOCK position, go to next step. If DDM PID DRLKCYL indicates ON in the UNLOCK position, go to step **7)**.

4) Ensure ignition is off. Disconnect DDM harness connector C523. Measure resistance between ground and terminal No. 18 (Dark Green/Violet wire) at DDM harness connector C523 while using key to rotate driver's door lock cylinder to UNLOCK position. *See Fig. 13.* If resistance is 5 ohms or less, replace DDM. If resistance is greater than 5 ohms, repair open in Dark Green/Violet wire between DDM and disarm switch on driver's door.

5) Disconnect driver's door disarm switch harness connector C510. Measure resistance between ground and Black/Light Blue wire terminal at driver's door disarm switch harness connector C510. If resistance is 5 ohms or less, go to next step. If resistance is greater than 5 ohms, repair open in Black/Light Blue wire between driver's door disarm switch and ground.

6) Turn ignition switch to RUN position. Connect jumper wire between Dark Green/Violet wire terminal and Black/Light Blue wire terminal at driver's door disarm switch harness connector C510. Using NGS tester, monitor DDM PID DRLKCYL. If DDM PID DRLKCYL indicates ON, replace driver's door disarm switch. If DDM PID DRLKCYL does not indicate ON, repair open in Dark Green/Violet wire between DDM and driver's door disarm switch.

7) Using NGS tester, monitor DDM PID DRLKCYL while using key to rotate passenger's door lock cylinder to UNLOCK position. If DDM PID DRLKCYL does not indicate ON in the UNLOCK position, go to next step. If DDM PID DRLKCYL indicates ON in the UNLOCK position, replace DDM.

8) Disconnect passenger's door disarm switch harness connector C610. Measure resistance between ground and Black/Light Blue wire terminal at passenger's door disarm switch harness connector C610. If resistance is 5 ohms or less, go to next step. If resistance is greater than 5 ohms, repair open in Black/Light Blue wire between passenger's door disarm switch and ground.

9) Connect jumper wire between Dark Green/Violet wire terminal and Black/Light Blue wire terminal at passenger's door disarm switch harness connector C610. Using NGS tester, monitor DDM PID DRLK-CYL. If DDM PID DRLKCYL indicates ON, replace passenger's door disarm switch. If DDM PID DRLKCYL does not indicate ON, repair open in Dark Green/Violet wire between DDM and passenger's door disarm switch.

10) Using NGS tester, monitor DDM PID DRLKCYL. Using key, lock driver's door, unlock driver's door and return key to NEUTRAL position while monitoring the DDM PID DRLKCYL in all 3 positions. If DDM PID DRLKCYL does not indicate ON in the UNLOCK position and OFF in the LOCK and NEUTRAL positions, go to next step. If DDM PID DRLKCYL indicates ON in the UNLOCK position and OFF in the LOCK and NEUTRAL positions, repair or replace driver's door lock cylinder for binding or sticking.

11) Using NGS tester, monitor DDM PID DRLKCYL. Using key, lock passenger's door, unlock passenger's door and return key to NEUTRAL position while monitoring the DDM PID DRLKCYL in all 3 positions. If DDM PID DRLKCYL does not indicate ON in the UNLOCK position and OFF in the LOCK and NEUTRAL positions, go to next step. If DDM PID DRLKCYL indicates ON in the UNLOCK position and OFF in the LOCK and NEUTRAL positions, repair or replace passenger's door lock cylinder for binding or sticking.

12) Disconnect driver's door disarm switch harness connector C510. Using NGS tester, monitor DDM PID DRLKCYL. If DDM PID DRLKCYL does not indicate OFF, go to next step. If DDM PID DRLKCYL indicates OFF, replace driver's door disarm switch.

13) Disconnect passenger's door disarm switch harness connector C610. Using NGS tester, monitor DDM PID DRLKCYL. If DDM PID DRLKCYL does not indicate OFF, go to next step. If DDM PID DRLKCYL indicates OFF, replace passenger's door disarm switch.

14) Ensure ignition switch is in LOCK position. Disconnect DDM harness connector C523. Using NGS tester, monitor DDM PID DRLKCYL. If DDM PID DRLKCYL does not indicate OFF, replace DDM. If DDM PID DRLKCYL indicates OFF, repair short to ground in Dark Green/Violet wire between DDM and driver's door disarm switch.

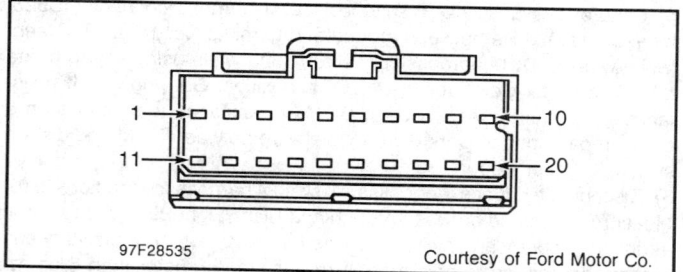

97F28535   Courtesy of Ford Motor Co.

Fig. 13: Identifying Driver's Door Module Harness Connector C523 Terminals

TEST G: ALARM SOUND WITHOUT VIOLATION

1) Turn ignition switch to LOCK position. Connect NGS tester to Data Link Connector (DLC). Turn ignition switch to RUN position. Using NGS tester, monitor LCM PID AL_EVT#. If PID indicates HOODTR, go to next step. If PID indicates DROPEN, go to step 4). If PID indicates T_AJAR, go to step 5). If PID indicates PANIC, repair keyless entry system

concern. See appropriate wiring diagram in REMOTE KEYLESS ENTRY SYSTEMS article. If PID indicates NOEVENT, system is okay at this time.

2) Using NGS tester, monitor LCM PID HOOD_SW while opening and closing hood. If PID does not agree with hood position, go to next step. If hood agrees with hood position, replace LCM.

3) Disconnect anti-theft hood switch harness connect C149. Measure resistance between terminals at anti-theft hood switch (component side). Resistance should be greater than 10 k/ohms with switch depressed and 5 ohms or less with switch released. If resistance is not as specified, replace anti-theft hood switch. If resistance is as specified, repair open in Yellow/Red wire between anti-theft hood switch and LCM.

4) Open and close each door while observing courtesy light operation. If courtesy lights operate properly, replace LCM. If courtesy light do not operate properly, repair courtesy light concern. See AUTOLAMP SYSTEMS – CONTINENTAL article.

5) Using NGS tester, monitor LCM PID DECKLID while opening and closing trunk. PID should indicate AJAR when trunk is open and CLOSED when trunk lid is closed. If PID does not agree with trunk lid position, go to next step. If PID agrees with trunk lid position, replace LCM.

6) Disconnect trunk lid lock cylinder anti-theft switch harness connector C429. Measure resistance between terminals at trunk lid lock cylinder anti-theft switch (component side). Resistance should be greater than 10 k/ohms with switch depressed and 5 ohms or less with switch released. If resistance is not as specified, replace trunk lid lock cylinder anti-theft switch. If resistance is as specified, repair open in White/Violet wire between trunk lid lock cylinder anti-theft switch and LCM.

TEST H: ALARM SYSTEM DOES NOT OPERATE PROPERLY

1) Using NGS tester, retrieve and record continuous DTCs. Clear continuous DTCs and perform Lighting Control Module (LCM) self-test. If no DTCs are retrieved, go to next step. If DTC B1522 is retrieved, go to step 9). If DTC B1498 is retrieved, go to step 15).

2) Ensure both windows are opened. Arm anti-theft system. Trigger alarm by opening driver's and passenger's doors from inside vehicle. Trigger alarm by opening hood. If alarm operates, anti-theft system is okay at this time. If horn does not sound when alarm is triggered, go to next step. If parking lights do not illuminate when alarm is triggered, go to step 6). If high beams do not illuminate when alarm is triggered, go to step 7). If alarm does not trigger when driver's or passenger door is opened, go to step 8). If courtesy lights do not illuminate when alarm is triggered, go to next step. If alarm does not trigger when hood is opened, go to step 12).

3) Press steering wheel pad horn switch. If horn sounds, go to next step. If horn does not sound, repair horn system. See appropriate wiring diagram in STEERING COLUMN SWITCHES article.

4) Turn ignition switch to LOCK position. Using NGS tester, trigger LCM active command HORN CONTROL to ON. If horn does not sound, go to next step. If horn sounds, anti-theft system is okay at this time.

5) Turn ignition switch to LOCK position. Disconnect LCM harness connector C208. Remove horn relay from power distribution box. Measure resistance in Dark Blue wire between terminal No. 2 at horn relay socket and terminal No. 9 at LCM 12-pin connector C208. *See Figs. 3 and 14.* Resistance should be 5 ohms or less. Check resistance between ground and terminal No. 9 (Dark Blue wire) at LCM harness connector C208. Resistance should be greater than 10 k/ohms If both resistance readings are as specified, replace LCM. If either resistance reading is not as specified, repair open or short to ground in Dark Blue wire between horn relay and LCM.

6) Turn headlight switch to parking light position. If parking lights illuminate, replace LCM. If parking lights do not illuminate, repair parking lights. See AUTOLAMP SYSTEMS – CONTINENTAL article.

7) Turn headlight switch to headlight position. Place multifunction switch in high beam position. If high beams illuminate, replace LCM. If high beams do not illuminate, repair high beams. See AUTOLAMP SYSTEMS – CONTINENTAL article.

8) Open driver's door. If courtesy lights illuminate, replace LCM. If courtesy lights do not illuminate, repair courtesy lights, See AUTOLAMP SYSTEMS – CONTINENTAL article.

9) Using NGS tester, monitor LCM PID HOOD_SW while opening and closing hood. LCM PID HOOD_SW should indicate AJAR with hood open and CLOSED with hood closed If PID does not agree with hood position, go to next step. If PID agrees with hood position, check anti-theft hood switch for proper mounting. If anti-theft hood switch is properly mounted, lubricate anti-theft hood switch if necessary. If necessary, adjust hood so hood closes properly.

10) Turn ignition switch to LOCK position. Disconnect anti-theft hood switch harness connector C149. Using NGS tester, monitor LCM PID HOOD_SW. If LCM PID HOOD_SW does not indicate CLOSED with connector disconnected, go to next step. If LCM PID HOOD_SW indicates CLOSED with connector disconnected, replace anti-theft hood switch.

11) Turn ignition switch to LOCK position. Disconnect LCM harness connector C206. Turn ignition switch to RUN position. Using NGS tester, monitor LCM PID HOOD_SW. If LCM PID HOOD_SW does not indicate CLOSED with connector disconnected, replace LCM. If LCM PID HOOD_SW indicates CLOSED with connector disconnected, repair short to ground in Yellow/Red wire between anti-theft hood switch and LCM.

12) Turn ignition switch to LOCK position. Disconnect anti-theft hood switch harness connector C149. Measure resistance between terminals at anti-theft hood switch (component side). If resistance is 5 ohms or less, go to next step. If resistance is greater than 5 ohms, replace anti-theft hood switch.

13) Measure resistance between ground and Black wire terminal at anti-theft hood switch harness connector C149. If resistance is 5 ohms or less, go to next step. If resistance is greater than 5 ohms, repair open in Black wire between anti-theft hood switch and ground.

14) Turn ignition switch to LOCK position. Disconnect LCM harness connector C206. Measure resistance in Yellow/Red wire between anti-theft hood switch and terminal No. 11 at LCM harness connector C206. *See Fig. 2.* If resistance is 5 ohms or less, replace LCM. If resistance is greater than 5 ohms, repair open in Yellow/Red wire between anti-theft hood switch and LCM.

15) Using NGS tester, monitor LCM DLIDPCH while placing key in and out of trunk lock cylinder. If PID does not agree with key position, go to next step. If PID agrees with key position, replace LCM.

16) Turn ignition switch to LOCK position. Disconnect LCM harness connector C206. Disconnect trunk lid anti-theft switch harness connector C429. Measure resistance in White/Violet wire between terminal No. 22 at LCM harness connector C206 and trunk lid anti-theft switch connector C429. If resistance is greater than 10 k/ohms, replace trunk lid anti-theft switch. If resistance is 10 k/ohms or less, repair short to ground in White/Violet wire between LCM and trunk lid anti-theft switch.

REMOVAL & INSTALLATION

CAUTION: When battery is disconnected or modules are replaced, vehicle computer and memory systems may lose memory data. Driveability problems may exist until computer systems have completed a relearn cycle. See COMPUTER RELEARN PROCEDURES article in GENERAL INFORMATION before disconnecting battery.

ANTI-THEFT HOOD SWITCH

Removal & Installation – Anti-theft hood switch is located below the hood on left fender, just above fenderwell. Disconnect connector and remove fasteners securing it to fender. To install, reverse removal procedure.

DOOR DISARM SWITCH

NOTE: Door disarm switch can be installed in more than one position. Mark position of disarm switch in relation to lock cylinder before removing disarm switch from lock cylinder.

Removal & Installation – Disconnect negative battery cable. Remove door trim panel. Remove protective watershield. Remove clip and disconnect latch lever from door lock cylinder. Remove door disarm switch and disconnect connector. To install, reverse removal procedure.

DRIVER'S DOOR MODULE (DDM)

Removal & Installation – Disconnect negative battery cable. Remove door trim panel. Remove protective watershield. Disconnect electrical connectors from DDM. Release module retaining clips and remove DDM. To install, reverse removal procedure.

DRIVER'S SEAT MODULE (DSM)

Removal & Installation – Disconnect negative battery cable. Remove driver's seat. Disconnect electrical connectors from DSM. Remove 2 DSM retaining screws and remove DSM. To install, reverse removal procedure.

LIGHTING CONTROL MODULE (LCM)

Removal & Installation – Disconnect negative battery cable. Remove lower instrument panel steering column cover. Remove 3 LCM retaining screws. Remove LCM from instrument panel and disconnect connectors. To install, reverse removal procedure.

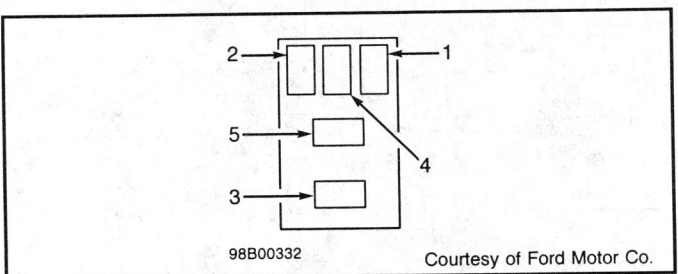

98B00332   Courtesy of Ford Motor Co.

Fig. 14: Identifying Horn Relay Socket Terminals

1999 ACCESSORIES & EQUIPMENT
Active Anti-Theft Systems – Continental (Cont.)

WIRING DIAGRAMS

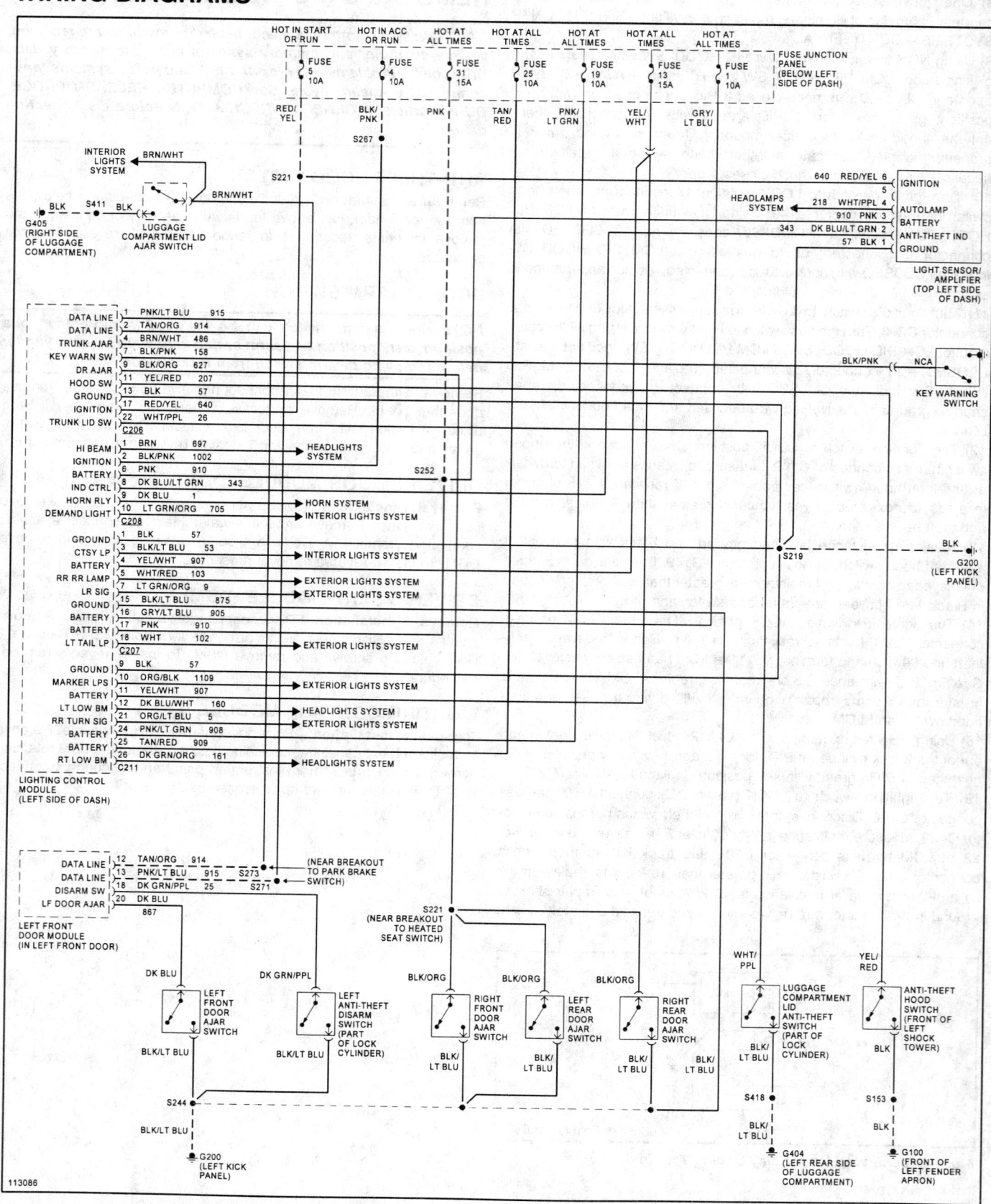

Fig. 15: Active Anti-Theft Alarm System Wiring Diagram (Continental)

DESCRIPTION

WARNING: Deactivate air bag system before performing any service operation. See appropriate AIR BAG RESTRAINT SYSTEMS article. DO NOT apply electrical power to any component on steering column without first deactivating air bag system. Air bag may deploy.

The anti-theft system is designed to prevent unauthorized entry into passenger compartment, luggage compartment, or engine compartment. When alarm is triggered, horn sounds, headlights and parking lights flash. This system also disables engine from starting. Some system functions may tie in with remote keyless entry system.

When armed, unauthorized entry is detected by ajar switches located in each door. An alarm light LED is located on the clock. Models with an electronic door lock system have a PANIC feature that operates in conjunction with the anti-theft system and remote keyless entry system. When the PANIC button on the remote transmitter is pushed, horn will sound and the exterior lights will flash.

OPERATION

ARMING SYSTEM

NOTE: System can be armed in one of following 2 ways.

1) Turn ignition switch to LOCK position and remove key. Close all doors. Press LOCK button on transmitter to lock doors. Alarm warning light will turn on. Wait for anti-theft warning light to turn off.

2) System can also be armed by turning ignition switch to LOCK position and removing key. Open a door. Alarm warning will flash. Lock doors with power door switches. Alarm warning light will turn on. Close all doors. Wait for anti-theft warning light to turn off.

DISARMING AN UNTRIGGERED SYSTEM

Unlock driver's or passenger's door using vehicle key or remote transmitter. Turn ignition switch to RUN or ACC position.

TRIGGERING SYSTEM

Alarm will sound when any door is opened without first using key or remote transmitter to unlock door first.

DISARMING A TRIGGERED SYSTEM

Unlock driver's or passenger's door with key, or unlock driver's door using remote transmitter.

COMPONENT LOCATIONS

COMPONENT LOCATIONS

Component	Location
Anti-Theft/Central Locking Control Module	Behind Passenger's Kick Panel
Anti-Theft Indicator	Center Of Instrument Panel
Door Lock Arm/Disarm Switch	Behind Door Panel, On Door Lock Cylinder
Panic Alarm Brakelight Relay	Behind Passenger's Kick Panel
Panic Alarm Headlight Relay	Behind Passenger's Kick Panel
Powertrain Control Module	Right Side Of Engine Compartment, On Firewall

PROGRAMMING

TRANSMITTER

NOTE: Once programming mode has been enter and transmitter button is pressed for the first time, all previously stored transmitter codes will be erased. All transmitters to be used with this system must be programmed at the same time (maximum of 4 transmitters).

1) Turn ignition switch to RUN position. Access programming connector. Programming connector is next to anti-theft/central locking control module (behind glove box). Using jumper wire, momentarily short the 2 terminals of programming connector together. Horn will sound to confirm program mode has been entered.

2) Press any button on keyless entry remote transmitter. Horn will sound to confirm that transmitter has been programmed.

3) Repeat step 2) to program all other transmitter (maximum of 4 transmitters) to be used with this system before exiting programming. To exit programming, turn ignition switch to LOCK position. To confirm programming mode has been exited, horn will sound.

TROUBLE SHOOTING

Before performing any tests on anti-theft system, check the following items to eliminate common problems:
- Damaged door lock cylinder.
- Blown fuse(s).
- Loose or corroded connections.
- Damaged wiring harness.
- Damaged relay(s).
- Damaged anti-theft/central locking control module.
- Horn, headlights, hazard flashers, power door locks and remote keyless entry system operation.

COMPONENT TESTS

DOOR LOCK ARM/DISARM SWITCH

1) Disconnect door lock arm/disarm switch harness connector to be tested. Measure resistance between terminals No. 1 and 2, between terminals No. 1 and 3 and between terminals No. 2 and 3 at door lock arm/disarm switch (component side). *See Fig. 1.* If all resistance readings are approximately 1000 ohms, go to next step. If any resistance readings is not approximately 1000 ohms, replace door lock arm/disarm switch.

2) Measure resistance between terminals No. 2 and 3 while turning key to LOCK position. Also, measure resistance between terminals No. 1 and 3 while turning key to UNLOCK position. If both resistance readings are 10 k/ohms or less, door lock arm/disarm switch is okay at this time. If either resistance reading is greater than 10 k/ohms, replace door lock arm/disarm switch.

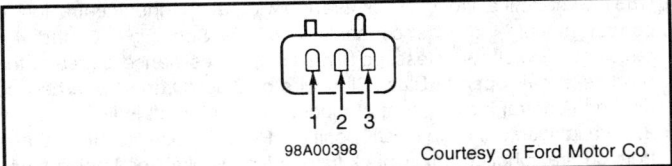

98A00398　　　Courtesy of Ford Motor Co.

Fig. 1: Identifying Door Lock Arm/Disarm Switch Terminals

RELAYS

Panic Alarm Headlight Relay & Panic Alarm Brakelight Relay – 1) Remove relay to be tested. Measure resistance between terminal No. 5 and all other terminals. Resistance should be greater than 5 ohms. Measure resistance between terminals No. 3 and 4. Resistance should be less than 5 ohms. *See Fig. 2.* If resistance is as specified, go to next step. If resistance is not as specified, replace relay.

2) Using a fused jumper wires, connect positive battery voltage to terminal No. 1 and ground terminal No. 2. With voltage applied, resistance between terminals No. 3 and 5 should be 5 ohms or less and

FORD
4-64

1999 ACCESSORIES & EQUIPMENT
Active Anti-Theft Systems – Contour & Mystique (Cont.)

resistance between terminals No. 3 and 4 should be greater than 5 ohms. If resistance is as specified, relay is okay at this time. If resistance is not as specified, replace relay.

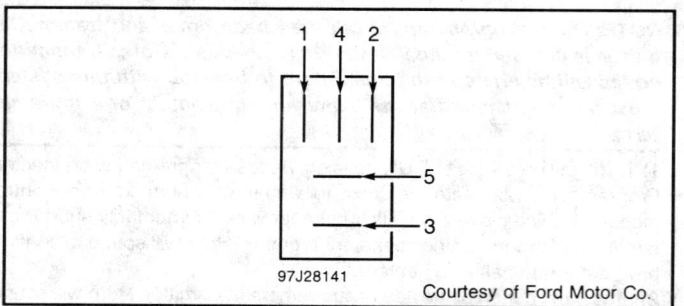

Fig. 2: Panic Alarm Headlight Relay & Panic Alarm Brakelight Relay Terminals

SYSTEM TESTS

SYMPTOM CHART

Symptom	Test
Anti-Theft Indicator Always On	A
Anti-Theft Indicator Never On	B
Alarm System Does Not Operate Correctly	C
Alarm System Does Not Arm	D
Alarm System Does Not Disarm	E

TEST A: ANTI-THEFT INDICATOR ALWAYS ON

1) Turn ignition switch to LOCK position. Disconnect anti-theft/central locking control module harness connector C451B. If anti-theft indicator does not turn off and vehicle is equipped with passive anti-theft system, go to next step. If anti-theft indicator does not turn off and vehicle is not equipped with passive anti-theft system, repair short to ground in Black/Blue wire or Black/Orange wire between anti-theft/central locking control module and anti-theft indicator. If anti-theft indicator turns off, replace anti-theft/central locking control module.
2) Ensure ignition switch is in LOCK position. Disconnect PCM harness connector C421. If anti-theft indicator does not turn off, repair short to ground in Black/Blue wire or Black/Orange wire between anti-theft/central locking control module, PCM and anti-theft indicator. If anti-theft indicator turns off, repair passive anti-theft system. See PASSIVE ANTI-THEFT SYSTEMS – CONTOUR & MYSTIQUE article.

TEST B: ANTI-THEFT INDICATOR NEVER ON

1) Turn ignition switch to LOCK position. Disconnect anti-theft indicator harness connector C831. Disconnect anti-theft/central locking control module harness connector C451B. Measure resistance between terminals No. 6 (Black/Blue wire) at anti-theft indicator harness connector C831 and terminal No. 9 (Black/Orange wire) at anti-theft/central locking control module harness connector C451B. *See Figs. 3 and 4.* If resistance is 5 ohms or less, go to next step. If resistance is greater than 5 ohms, repair open in Black/Blue wire or Black/Orange wire between anti-theft/central locking control module and anti-theft indicator.
2) Turn ignition switch to LOCK position. Remove fuse No. 34 (7.5-amp) from central junction box. Check fuse. If fuse is okay, go to next step. If fuse is blown, repair short to ground in power distribution circuit. See appropriate wiring diagram in POWER DISTRIBUTION article in WIRING DIAGRAMS.
3) Install fuse No. 34. Measure voltage at terminal No. 4 (Orange wire) at anti-theft indicator harness connector C831. If battery voltage exists, go to next step. If battery voltage does not exist, repair open in Orange/Black or Orange/Black wire between central junction box and anti-theft indicator.
4) Measure resistance between ground and terminal No. 9 (Black/Orange wire) at anti-theft/central locking control module harness connector C451B. If resistance is greater than 10 k/ohms, replace anti-theft/central locking control module. If resistance is 10 k/ohms or less, repair

short to ground in Black/Blue wire or Black/Orange wire between anti-theft/central locking control module and anti-theft indicator.

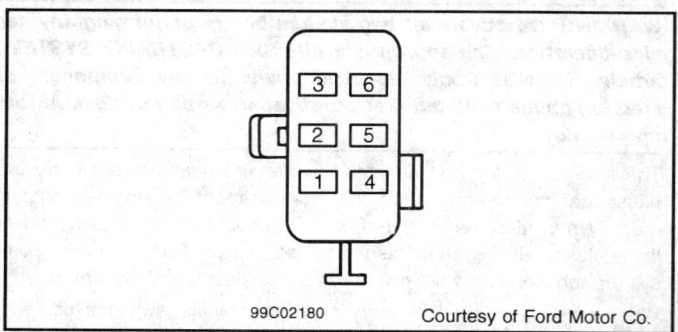

Fig. 3: Identifying Anti-Theft Indicator Harness Connector C831 Terminals

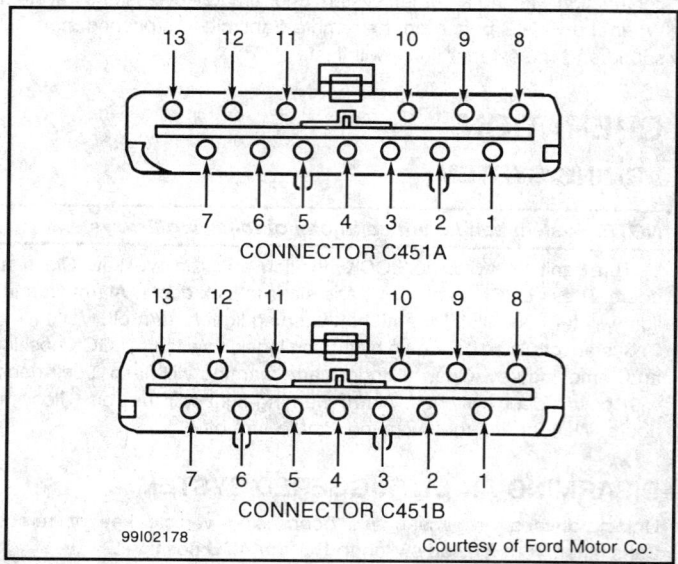

Fig. 4: Identifying Anti-Theft/Central Locking Control Module Harness Connector C451A & C451B Terminals

TEST C: SYSTEM DOES NOT OPERATE PROPERLY

1) Turn ignition switch to LOCK position. Remove fuse No. 25 (20-amp) from central junction box. Check fuse. If fuse is okay, go to next step. If fuse is blown, replace fuse. If fuse blows again, repair short to ground in power distribution circuit. See appropriate wiring diagram in POWER DISTRIBUTION article in WIRING DIAGRAMS.
2) Open left front door window. Arm anti-theft system. Open left front door without using key or Remote Keyless Entry (RKE) transmitter. Repeat test for each door. If alarm system operates correctly, go to next step. If alarm does not activate for left front door, go to step 16). If alarm does not activate for right front door, go to step 18). If alarm does not activate for left rear door, go to step 20). If alarm does not activate for right rear door, go to step 22). If horn does not operate, go to step 8). If headlights and brakelights do not operate, go to step 10). If headlights do not operate but brakelights do, go to step 11). If brakelights do not operate but headlights do, go to step 13).
3) Arm anti-theft system. Open luggage compartment. If alarm does not activate, go to next step. If alarm activates, go to step 5).
4) Disconnect anti-theft/central locking control module harness connector C451A. Disconnect luggage compartment light switch harness connector C798. Measure resistance in Black/Red wire between terminal No. 2 at luggage compartment switch harness connector C798 and terminal No. 12 at anti-theft/central locking control module harness connector C451A. *See Fig. 4.* If resistance is 5 ohms or less, replace anti-theft/central locking control module. If resistance is greater than 5 ohms, repair open in Black/Red wire.

1999 ACCESSORIES & EQUIPMENT
Active Anti-Theft Systems – Contour & Mystique (Cont.)

FORD
4-65

5) Disconnect engine compartment switch harness connector C897. Measure resistance between engine compartment switch terminals (component side) while depressing and releasing button on engine compartment switch. Resistance should be 5 ohms or less with button depressed and greater than 10 k/ohms with button released. If resistance is as specified, go to next step. If resistance is not as specified, replace switch.

6) Measure resistance between ground and terminal No. 2 (Black wire) at engine compartment switch harness connector C897. If resistance is 5 ohms or less, go to next step. If resistance is greater than 5 ohms, repair open in Black wire.

7) Disconnect anti-theft/central locking control module harness connector C451B. Measure resistance in Black/Yellow wire between terminal No. 1 at engine compartment switch harness connector C897 and terminal No. 6 at anti-theft/central locking control module harness connector C451B. *See Fig. 4.* If resistance is 5 ohms or less, replace anti-theft/central locking control module. If resistance is greater than 5 ohms, repair open in Black/Yellow wire.

8) Press horn pad on steering wheel. If horn operates, go to next step. If horn does not operate, repair horn as necessary. See STEERING COLUMN SWITCHES – CONTOUR & MYSTIQUE article.

9) Disconnect anti-theft/central locking control module harness connector C451A. Using a fused jumper wire, ground terminal No. 8 (Black/White wire) at anti-theft/central locking control module harness connector C451A. If horn operates, replace anti-theft/central locking control module. If horn does not operate, repair open in Black/White wire.

10) Disconnect anti-theft/central locking control module harness connector C451B. Using a fused jumper wire, ground terminal No. 10 (Black/Red wire) at anti-theft/central locking control module harness connector C451B. If headlights and brakelights turn on, replace anti-theft/central locking control module. If headlights and brakelights do not turn on, repair open in Black/Red wire.

11) Disconnect panic alarm headlight relay harness connector C1904 located behind right side of glove box. Measure voltage at terminals No. 3 (Orange/White wire) and No. 1 (Orange/Green wire) at panic alarm headlight relay harness connector C1904. *See Fig. 5.* If battery voltage exists at both terminals, go to next step. If battery voltage does not exist and either terminal, repair open in Orange/White and/or Orange/Green wire(s).

12) Test panic alarm headlight relay. See RELAYS under COMPONENT TESTS. If relay is defective, replace panic alarm headlight relay. If relay is okay, repair open in Orange/White wire.

13) Disconnect panic alarm brakelight relay harness connector C1910 located behind right side of glove box. Measure voltage at terminals No. 1 (Orange/Yellow wire) and No. 3 (Orange wire) at panic alarm brakelight relay harness connector C1910. *See Fig. 5.* If battery voltage exists at both terminals, go to next step. If battery voltage does not exist and either terminal, repair open in Orange and/or Orange/Yellow wire(s).

14) Ensure panic alarm brakelight relay and panic alarm headlight relay are still disconnected. Measure resistance in Black/Yellow wire between terminal No. 2 at panic alarm headlight relay connector C1904 and terminal No. 2 at panic alarm brakelight relay connector C1910. If resistance is 5 ohms or less, go to next step. If resistance is greater than 5 ohms, repair open in Black/Yellow wire.

15) Test panic alarm brakelight relay. See RELAYS under COMPONENT TESTS. If relay is defective, replace panic alarm brakelight relay. If relay is okay, repair open in Orange/Yellow wire.

16) Turn ignition switch to LOCK position. Disconnect anti-theft/central locking control module harness connector C451A. Open left front door. Measure resistance between ground and terminal No. 3 (Black/Yellow wire) at anti-theft/central locking control module harness connector C451A. *See Fig. 4.* If resistance is 5 ohms or less, go to next step. If resistance is greater than 5 ohms, replace anti-theft/central locking control module.

17) Disconnect left front door ajar switch harness connector C818. Measure resistance between ground and terminal No. 3 (Black/Yellow wire) at anti-theft/central locking control module harness connector

C451A. If resistance is greater than 10 k/ohms, replace left front door ajar switch. If resistance is 10 k/ohms or less, repair short to ground in Black/Yellow wire.

18) Turn ignition switch to LOCK position. Disconnect anti-theft/central locking control module harness connector C451B. Open right front door. Measure resistance between ground and terminal No. 3 (Black/Blue wire) at anti-theft/central locking control module harness connector C451B. *See Fig. 4.* If resistance is 5 ohms or less, go to next step. If resistance is greater than 5 ohms, replace anti-theft/central locking control module.

19) Disconnect right front door ajar switch harness connector C819. Measure resistance between ground and terminal No. 3 (Black/Blue wire) at anti-theft/central locking control module harness connector C451B. If resistance is greater than 10 k/ohms, replace right front door ajar switch. If resistance is 10 k/ohms or less, repair short to ground in Black/Blue wire.

20) Turn ignition switch to LOCK position. Disconnect anti-theft/central locking control module harness connector C451A. Open left rear door. Measure resistance between ground and terminal No. 5 (Black/Orange wire) at anti-theft/central locking control module harness connector C451A. *See Fig. 4.* If resistance is 5 ohms or less, go to next step. If resistance is greater than 5 ohms, replace anti-theft/central locking control module.

21) Disconnect left rear door ajar switch. Measure resistance between ground and terminal No. 5 (Black/Orange wire) at anti-theft/central locking control module harness connector C451A. If resistance is greater than 10 k/ohms, replace left rear door ajar switch. If resistance is 10 k/ohms or less, repair short to ground in Black/Orange wire.

22) Turn ignition switch to LOCK position. Disconnect anti-theft/central locking control module harness connector C451B. Open right rear door. Measure resistance between ground and terminal No. 5 (Black/Green wire) at anti-theft/central locking control module harness connector C451B. *See Fig. 4.* If resistance is 5 ohms or less, go to next step. If resistance is greater than 5 ohms, replace anti-theft/central locking control module.

23) Disconnect right rear door ajar switch. Measure resistance between ground and terminal No. 9 (Black/Green wire) at anti-theft/central locking control module harness connector C451B. If resistance is greater than 10 k/ohms, replace right rear door ajar switch. If resistance is 10 k/ohms or less, repair short to ground in Black/Green wire.

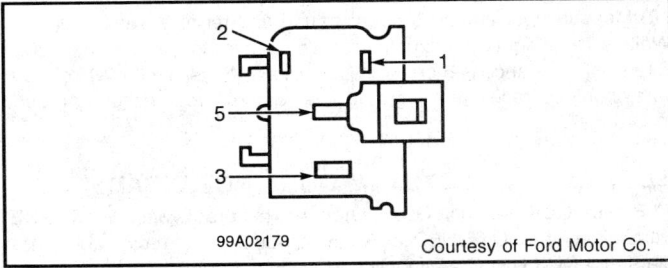

99A02179   Courtesy of Ford Motor Co.

Fig. 5: Identifying Panic Alarm Headlight Relay Harness Connector C1904 & Panic Alarm Brakelight Relay Harness Connector C1910 Terminals

TEST D: ALARM SYSTEM DOES NOT ARM

1) Press LOCK and UNLOCK buttons on Remote Keyless Entry (RKE) transmitter. If LOCK/UNLOCK function operates, go to next step. If LOCK/UNLOCK function does not operate, repair remote keyless entry system as necessary. See appropriate wiring diagram in REMOTE KEYLESS ENTRY SYSTEMS article.

2) Press UNLOCK button on RKE transmitter. Ensure all doors are closed and unlocked. While watching anti-theft indicator LED, press LOCK button on RKE transmitter. If anti-theft indicator comes on and vehicle is not equipped with door unlock arm/disarm switches, then goes off after 30 seconds, system is okay. If anti-theft indicator comes on and vehicle is equipped with door unlock arm/disarm switches, go to next step. If anti-theft indicator stays on, go to TEST A: ANTI-THEFT

INDICATOR ALWAYS ON. If anti-theft indicator does not come on, go to TEST B: ANTI-THEFT INDICATOR NEVER ON.

3) Insert door key into left front door and turn to UNLOCK position. Ensure all doors are closed and unlocked. While watching anti-theft indicator, turn door key to LOCK position to arm anti-theft system. If anti-theft indicator does not come on, then go off after 30 seconds, go to next step. If anti-theft indicator comes on, then goes off after 30 seconds, go to step **7)**.

4) Turn ignition switch to LOCK position. Disconnect anti-theft/central locking control module harness connector C451B. Ensure door key is in LOCK position. Measure resistance between terminals No. 1 (White/Red wire) and No. 2 (Orange/Blue wire) at anti-theft/central locking control module harness connector C451B. *See Fig. 4.* If resistance is greater than 5 ohms, go to next step. If resistance is 5 ohms or less, replace anti-theft/central locking control module.

5) Disconnect left door lock arm/disarm switch harness connector C708. Check switch. See DOOR LOCK ARM/DISARM SWITCH under COMPONENT TESTS. If switch is okay, go to next step. If switch is defective, replace left door lock arm/disarm switch.

6) Measure resistance between terminal No. 2 (Orange/Blue wire) at anti-theft/central locking control module harness connector C451B and terminal No. 3 (Orange/White wire) at left front door lock arm/disarm switch harness connector C708. If resistance is 5 ohms or less, repair open in White/Red or White/Violet wire. If resistance is greater than 5 ohms, repair open in Orange/White or Orange/Blue wire.

7) Insert door key into right front door and turn to UNLOCK position. Ensure all doors are closed and unlocked. While watching anti-theft indicator, turn door key to LOCK position to arm anti-theft system. If anti-theft indicator does not come on, then go off after 30 seconds, go to next step. If anti-theft indicator comes on, then goes off after 30 seconds, system is okay.

8) Turn ignition switch to LOCK position. Disconnect anti-theft/central locking control module harness connector C451B. Ensure door key is in LOCK position. Measure resistance between ground and terminal No. 1 (White/Red wire) at anti-theft/central locking control module harness connector C451B. *See Fig. 4.* If resistance is greater than 5 ohms, go to next step. If resistance is 5 ohms or less, replace anti-theft/central locking control module.

9) Disconnect right front door lock arm/disarm switch harness connector C1895. Test switch. See DOOR LOCK ARM/DISARM SWITCH under COMPONENT TESTS. If switch is okay, go to next step. If switch is defective, replace right door lock arm/disarm switch.

10) Measure resistance between ground and terminal No. 3 (Orange/White wire) at right front door lock arm/disarm switch harness connector C1895. If resistance is 5 ohms or less, repair White/Red or White/Violet wire circuits. If resistance is greater than 5 ohms, repair short to ground in Orange/White wire.

TEST E: ALARM SYSTEM DOES NOT DISARM

1) Press LOCK and UNLOCK button on Remote Keyless Entry (RKE) transmitter. If LOCK/UNLOCK function operates correctly, go to next step. If LOCK/UNLOCK function does not operate correctly, repair remote keyless entry system as necessary. See appropriate wiring diagram in REMOTE KEYLESS ENTRY SYSTEMS article.

2) Open left front window. Arm anti-theft system. Reach inside window and unlock door. Open left front door to trigger anti-theft system. Press UNLOCK button on RKE transmitter to disarm system. If anti-theft system disarms and vehicle is not equipped with door lock/disarm switches, system is okay. If anti-theft system disarms and vehicle is equipped with door lock/disarm switches, go to next step. If anti-theft system does not disarm, disconnect negative battery cable to disable alarm and replace anti-theft/central locking control module.

3) Arm anti-theft system. Reach inside window and manually unlock door. Open left front door to trigger anti-theft system. Insert door key into left front door and turn to UNLOCK position. If anti-theft system disarms, go to step **7)**. If anti-theft system does not disarm, disconnect negative battery cable to disable alarm. Reconnect negative battery cable, then go to next step.

4) Turn ignition switch to LOCK position. Disconnect both anti-theft/central locking control module harness connectors. Ensure door key is in UNLOCK position. Measure resistance between terminal No. 1 (Yellow/Red wire) at anti-theft/central locking control module harness connector C451A and terminal No. 7 (Orange/Blue wire) at anti-theft/central locking control module harness connector C451B. *See Fig. 4.* If resistance is greater than 5 ohms, go to next step. If resistance is 5 ohms or less, replace anti-theft/central locking control module.

5) Disconnect left door lock arm/disarm switch harness connector C708. Test switch. See DOOR LOCK ARM/DISARM SWITCH under COMPONENT TESTS. If switch is okay, go to next step. If switch is defective, replace left door lock arm/disarm switch.

6) Measure resistance between terminal No. 2 (Orange/Blue wire) at anti-theft/central locking control module harness connector C451B and terminal No. 3 (Orange/White wire) at left front door lock arm/disarm switch harness connector C708. If resistance is 5 ohms or less, repair open Yellow/Violet or White/Violet wire. If resistance is greater than 5 ohms, repair open in Orange/White or Orange/Blue wire.

7) Open right front door window. Arm anti-theft system. Reach inside window and unlock door. Open right front door to trigger anti-theft system. Insert door key into right front door and turn to UNLOCK position. If anti-theft system disarms, system is okay. If anti-theft system does not disarm, disconnect negative battery cable to deactivate alarm. Reconnect negative battery cable, then go to next step.

8) Turn ignition switch to LOCK position. Disconnect anti-theft/central locking control module harness connector C451A. Ensure door key is in UNLOCK position. Measure resistance between ground and terminal No. 7 (Yellow/Red wire) at anti-theft/central locking control module harness connector C451A. *See Fig. 4.* If resistance is greater than 5 ohms, go to next step. If resistance is 5 ohms or less, replace anti-theft/central locking control module.

9) Disconnect right front door lock arm/disarm switch harness connector C1895. Test switch. See DOOR LOCK ARM/DISARM SWITCH under COMPONENT TESTS. If switch is okay, go to next step. If switch is defective, replace right front door lock arm/disarm switch.

10) Measure resistance between ground and terminal No. 3 (Orange/White wire) at right front door lock arm/disarm switch harness connector C1895. If resistance is 5 ohms or less, repair White/Violet or Yellow/Violet wire circuits. If resistance is greater than 5 ohms, repair Orange/White wire circuit.

REMOVAL & INSTALLATION

ANTI-THEFT/CENTRAL LOCKING CONTROL MODULE

Removal & Installation – Disconnect negative battery cable. Open glove box. Depress sides of glove box, and remove glove box to access module. Unplug antenna connector. Remove module from bracket. Unplug remaining wiring connectors. To install, reverse removal procedure.

ANTENNA

Removal & Installation – Disconnect negative battery cable. Lower glove box. Remove "A" pillar trim panel. Unplug antenna connector from electronic door lock control module. Detach antenna from retaining clip. Pull antenna downward to remove. To install, reverse removal procedure.

Active Anti-Theft Systems – Contour & Mystique (Cont.)

WIRING DIAGRAMS

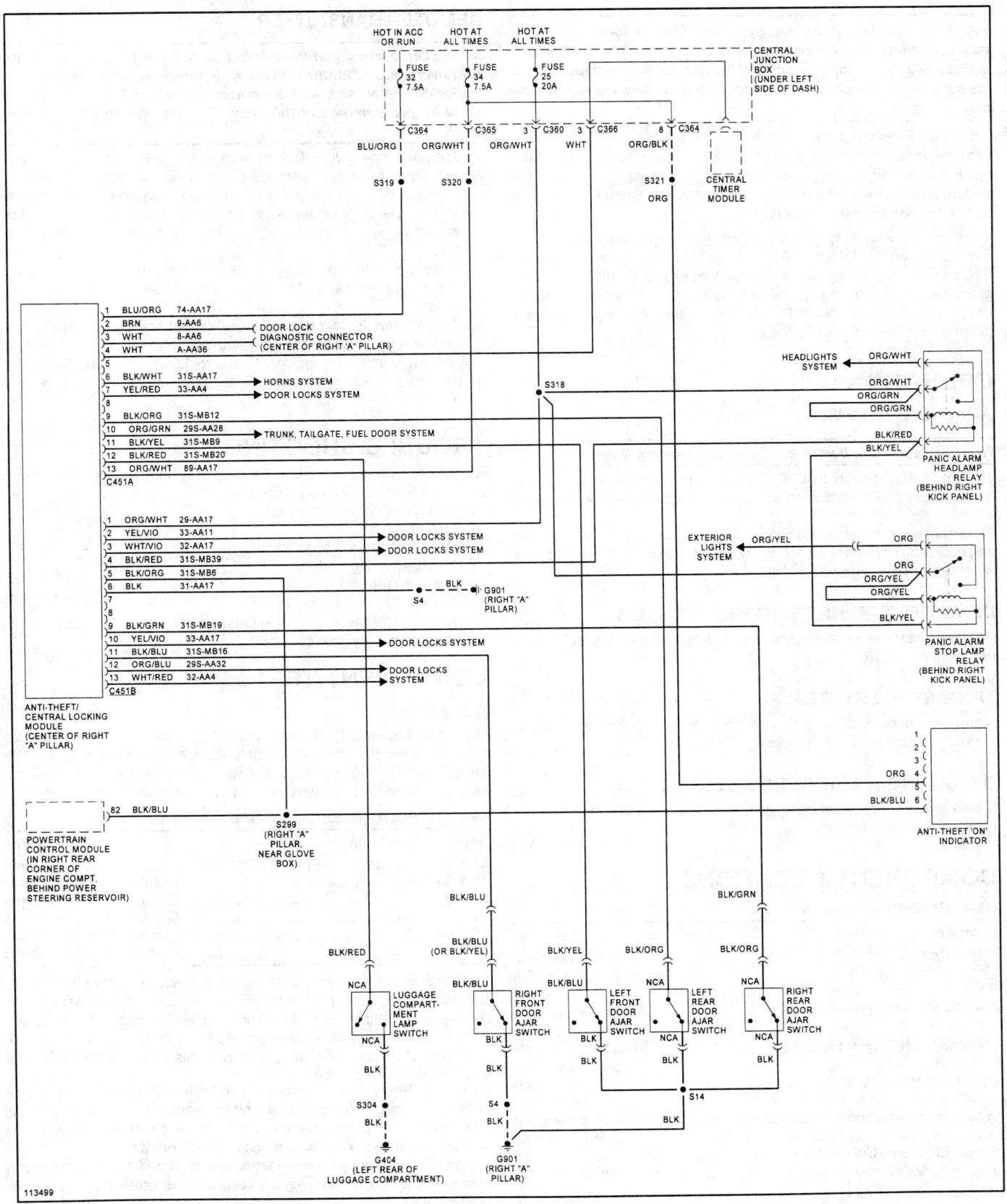

Fig. 6: Active Anti-Theft System Wiring Diagram (Contour & Mystique)

DESCRIPTION

WARNING: Deactivate air bag system before performing any service operation. See appropriate AIR BAG RESTRAINT SYSTEMS article. DO NOT apply electrical power to any component on steering column without first deactivating air bag system. Air bag may deploy.

The active anti-theft system is designed to prevent unauthorized entry into passenger compartment, luggage compartment, or engine compartment. When alarm is triggered, horn sounds, parking lights flash. This system also disables engine from starting. Some system functions may tie in with remote keyless entry system.

When armed, unauthorized entry is detected by ajar switches located in each door. An alarm light LED is located on the instrument panel. Models with an electronic door lock system have a PANIC feature that operates in conjunction with the anti-theft system and remote keyless entry system. When the PANIC button on the remote transmitter is pushed, horn will sound and the parking lights will flash.

OPERATION
ARMING SYSTEM

NOTE: System can be armed in one of following 2 ways.

1) Turn ignition switch to LOCK position and remove key. Close all doors. Press LOCK button on transmitter to lock doors. Parking lights will flash if system armed.
2) System can also be armed by turning ignition switch to LOCK position and removing key. Close all doors. Lock vehicle using key. Parking lights will flash if system armed.

DISARMING AN UNTRIGGERED SYSTEM

Unlock driver's or passenger's door using vehicle key or remote transmitter.

TRIGGERING SYSTEM

Alarm will sound when any door is opened without first using key or remote transmitter to unlock door first.

DISARMING A TRIGGERED SYSTEM

Unlock driver's or passenger's door with key or unlock driver's door using remote transmitter.

COMPONENT LOCATIONS

COMPONENT LOCATIONS

Component	Location
Alarm System Horn	Behind Passenger's Side Rear Quarter Trim Panel
Anti-Theft/Central Locking Module [1]	Above Passenger's Side Kick Panel
Anti-Theft Turn Signal Light Relay	Above Passenger's Side Kick Panel
Door Lock Motor	Part Of Door Latch Assembly
In-Line Harness Connector C2109	Behind Passenger's Side Kick Panel
Hybrid Electronic Cluster Module	[2]
Interior Scan Sensor	Top Of Pillar "B"

[1] – Anti-theft/central locking module may also be referred to as Central Security Module (CSM).
[2] – Hybrid Electronic Cluster (HEC) module is built into instrument cluster.

PROGRAMMING
REMOTE TRANSMITTER

NOTE: Once programming mode has been enter and transmitter button is pressed for the first time, all previously stored transmitter codes will be erased. All transmitters to be used with this system must be programmed at the same time (maximum of 4 transmitters).

1) Open driver's window. Turn ignition switch to RUN or ACC position. Access programming connector. Programming connector is behind left trunk trim panel, attached to relay panel. Using jumper wire, momentarily short the 2 terminals of programming connector together. Both doors should lock then unlock to confirm program mode has been entered.
2) Press any button on keyless entry remote transmitter. Both doors should lock then unlock to confirm that transmitter has been programmed.
3) Repeat step **2)** to program all other transmitter (maximum of 4 transmitters) to be used with this system before exiting programming. To exit programming, turn ignition switch to LOCK position. To confirm programming mode has been exited, both doors should lock then unlock.

TROUBLE SHOOTING

Before performing any tests on anti-theft system, check the following items to eliminate common problems:
- Damaged door lock cylinder.
- Blown fuse(s).
- Loose or corroded connections.
- Damaged wiring harness.
- Damaged relay(s).
- Damaged central security module.
- Horn, headlights, hazard flashers, power door locks and remote keyless entry system operation.

COMPONENT TESTS
RELAYS

Mini ISO Relay – 1) Remove mini ISO relay. Measure resistance between appropriate relay terminals. See MINI ISO RELAY RESISTANCE SPECIFICATIONS table. *See Fig. 1.* If resistance is as specified, go to next step. If resistance is not as specified, replace relay.

MINI ISO RELAY RESISTANCE SPECIFICATIONS

Between Terminals	Resistance
85 & 86	50-100 Ohms
30 & 87a	5 Ohms Or Less
30 & 87	Greater Than 10 K/Ohms
30 & 86	Greater Than 10 K/Ohms
86 & 87a	Greater Than 10 K/Ohms
86 & 87	Greater Than 10 K/Ohms

2) Using a fused jumper wire, connect positive battery voltage to terminal No. 85. Using another jumper wire, ground terminal No. 86. Resistance should now be 5 ohms or less between terminals No. 30 and 87 and greater than 10 k/ohms between terminals No. 30 and 87a. If resistance is as specified, relay is okay at this time. If resistance is not as specified, replace relay.
Micro ISO Relay – 1) Remove relay to be tested. Measure resistance between terminal No. 5 and all other terminals. *See Fig. 2.* If all resistance reading are greater than 5 ohms, go to next step. If any resistance reading is 5 ohms or less, replace relay.
2) Measure resistance between terminals No. 3 and 4. If resistance is 5 ohms or less, go to next step. If resistance is greater than 5 ohms, replace relay.
3) Apply battery voltage and ground between terminals No. 1 and 2. Measure resistance between terminals No. 3 and 5. Resistance should be 5 ohms or less. Measure resistance between terminals No. 3 and 4.

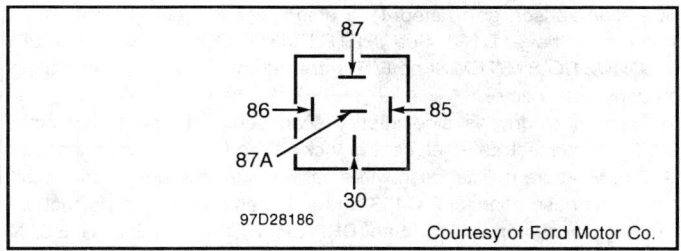

97D28186

Courtesy of Ford Motor Co.

Fig. 1: Identifying Mini ISO Relay Terminals

Resistance should be greater than 10 k/ohms. If resistance is not as specified, replace relay. If resistance is as specified, relay is okay at this time.

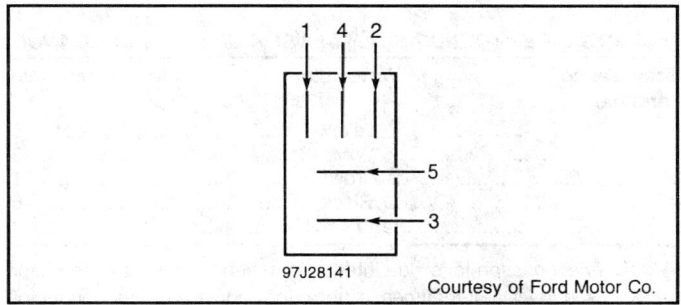

97J28141

Courtesy of Ford Motor Co.

Fig. 2: Identifying Micro ISO Relay Terminals

SELF-DIAGNOSTIC SYSTEM

RETRIEVING CODES

NOTE: *Anti-theft/central locking module may also be referred to as Central Security Module (CSM).*

Connect New Generation Star (NGS) tester to Data Link Connector (DLC), located beneath instrument panel. Using NGS tester, perform data link diagnostics test. See DATA LINK DIAGNOSTIC TEST under COMMUNICATION NETWORK DIAGNOSTICS in MODULE COMMUNICATIONS NETWORK – COUGAR article. If NGS tester responds with CKT914, CKT915 or CKT70=ALL ECUS NO RESP/NOT EQUIP, repair module communications concern. See MODULE COMMUNICATIONS NETWORK – COUGAR article. If NGS tester displays NO RESP/NOT EQUIP for anti-theft/central locking module, perform TEST B: NO COMMUNICATION WITH ANTI-THEFT/CENTRAL LOCKING MODULE under SYSTEM TESTS. If NGS tester displays NO RESP/NOT EQUIP for Hybrid Electronic Cluster (HEC), perform TEST C: NO COMMUNICATION WITH HYBRID ELECTRONIC CLUSTER MODULE under SYSTEM TESTS.

If NGS tester responds with SYSTEM PASSED, retrieve and record continuous DTCs. Erase continuous DTCs. Using NGS tester, perform HEC and anti-theft/central locking module self-test. Perform appropriate test in accordance with DTC retrieved. See ANTI-THEFT/CENTRAL LOCKING MODULE DTC INDEX and/or HYBRID ELECTRONIC CLUSTER MODULE DTC INDEX table. Codes listed in these table are only for testing covered in this article. For complete DTC listing, see MODULE COMMUNICATIONS NETWORK – COUGAR article. If no DTCs are retrieved, repair by symptom. See SYMPTOM CHART table under SYSTEM TESTS.

ANTI-THEFT/CENTRAL LOCKING MODULE DTC INDEX

DTC [1]	Description	Test
B1298	Interior Sensor Power Short To Voltage	A
B1299	Interior Sensor Power Short To Ground	A
B1309	Power Door Lock Circuit Short To Ground	2
B1341	Power Door Unlock Circuit Short To Ground	2
B1342	ECU Defective	3
B1520	Hood Switch Circuit Open	A
B1755	Hazard Flash Output Circuit Short To Voltage	A
B1756	Hazard Flash Output Circuit Short To Ground	A
B2108	Trunk Key Cylinder Switch Failure	A
B2112	Driver's Door Set Switch Stuck Failure	A
B2150	Power Supply Circuit Short To Ground (1)	A
B2151	Power Supply Circuit Short To Ground (2)	A
B2153	Rear Echo Sensor Circuit Failure	A
B2154	Front Echo Sensor Circuit Failure	A
B2156	Rear Doppler Sensor Circuit Failure	A
B2157	Rear Doppler Sensor Circuit Failure	A
B2478	Anti-Theft Input Signal Stuck Failure	A
B2477	Module Configuration Failure	4

[1] – Codes listed in this table are only for testing covered in this article. For complete DTC listing, see MODULE COMMUNICATIONS NETWORK – COUGAR article.

[2] – This DTC can be set because of many different reasons. If this DTC is set, repair appropriate system by symptom.

[3] – Using NGS tester, retrieve and document all continuous DTCs. Perform anti-theft/central locking module self-test. If DTC B1342 is retrieved again, replace anti-theft/central locking module.

[4] – Anti-theft/central locking module requires programming. See COMPUTER RELEARN PROCEDURES article in GENERAL INFORMATION. If DTC B2477 still exists after programming, replace anti-theft/central locking module.

HYBRID ELECTRONIC CLUSTER MODULE DTC INDEX

DTC [1]	Description	Test
B1342 .... ECU Defective		2

[1] – Codes listed in this table are only for testing covered in this article. For complete DTC listing, see MODULE COMMUNICATIONS NETWORK – COUGAR article.

[2] – Using NGS tester, retrieve and document all continuous DTCs. Perform Hybrid Electronic Cluster (HEC) module self-test. If DTC B1342 is retrieved again, replace HEC module.

SELF-TEST

NOTE: *Anti-theft/central locking module is equipped with a manually activated self-test. When activated, anti-theft/central locking module will give a visual and audible every time an input is received.*

1) To activate self-test mode, turn ignition switch to RUN position, open hood and press and release hood ajar switch 7 times within 6 seconds. Turn signals will flash and horn will sound once to confirm self-test mode has been entered.

2) The following inputs can be tested: remote transmitter, hood ajar switch, driver's door ajar switch, passenger's door ajar switch, driver's door lock motor set/reset switch, passenger's door lock motor set/reset switch, liftgate ajar switch, liftgate anti-theft inhibit switch, driver's door lock cylinder switch and passenger's door lock cylinder switch.

3) When an input is received by anti-theft/central locking module, turn signals will flash and horn will sound once to confirm signal was received. To exit self-test mode, turn ignition switch to LOCK position.

SYSTEM TESTS

SYMPTOM CHART

Symptom	Test
System Does Not Operate Properly	A
No Communication With Anti-Theft/Central Locking Module	B
No Communication With Hybrid Electronic Cluster Module	C

TEST A: SYSTEM DOES NOT OPERATE PROPERLY

NOTE: *Anti-theft/central locking module may also be referred to as Central Security Module (CSM).*

1) Perform self-test. See SELF-TEST under SELF-DIAGNOSTIC SYSTEM. If anti-theft/central locking module does not receive an input from all switches, go to appropriate step. See TEST STEP table. If anti-theft/central locking module receives an input from all switches and vehicle is equipped with interior scanning, go to next step. If anti-theft/central locking module receives an input from all switches and vehicle is not equipped with interior scanning, retrieve DTC. See RETRIEVING CODES under SELF-DIAGNOSTIC SYSTEM. If no DTCs are retrieved, system is operating properly at this time.

TEST STEP

Symptom	Step
Does Not Enter Self-Test Mode	**5)**
Horn Does Not Sound	**8)**
Turn Signals Do Not Flash	**9)**
No Response From Remote Transmitter	1
No Response From Door Lock Motor	**16)**
No Response From Door Ajar Switch	**21)**
No Response From Liftgate Key Switch	**22)**
No Response From Liftgate Ajar Switch	**24)**

[1] – Repair remote keyless entry system as necessary. See appropriate wiring diagram in REMOTE KEYLESS ENTRY SYSTEMS article.

2) Partially lower driver's and passenger's window. Arm anti-theft system. Wait approximately one minute. Wave hand by driver's side and passenger's side scan sensor. If alarm was not triggered at driver's side scan sensor, go to next step. If alarm was not triggered at passenger's

side scan sensor, go to step **4)**. If alarm was triggered at both scan sensors, retrieve DTC. See RETRIEVING CODES under SELF-DIAGNOSTIC SYSTEM. If no DTCs are retrieved, system is operating properly at this time.

3) Disconnect driver's side interior scan sensor harness connector C453. Disconnect anti-theft/central locking module harness connector C451c. Measure resistance in wires between driver's side interior scan sensor harness connector C453 and anti-theft/central locking module harness connector C451c. See DRIVER'S SIDE INTERIOR SCAN SENSOR CIRCUIT RESISTANCE table. *See Figs. 3 and 4.* If any resistance reading is greater than 5 ohms, repair open in appropriate wire. If all resistance readings are 5 ohms or less, retrieve DTC. See RETRIEVING CODES under SELF-DIAGNOSTIC SYSTEM. If no DTCs are retrieved and problem persist, replace driver's side interior scan sensor.

DRIVER'S SIDE INTERIOR SCAN SENSOR CIRCUIT RESISTANCE

Scan Sensor Terminal	Wire Color	Module Terminal
1	Yellow	5
2	White	9
3	Brown	1
4	Black	6
5	Orange/Yellow	2

4) Disconnect passenger's side interior scan sensor harness connector C452. Disconnect anti-theft/central locking module harness connector C451c. Measure resistance in wires between passenger's side interior scan sensor harness connector C452 and anti-theft/central locking module harness connector C451c. See PASSENGER'S SIDE INTERIOR SCAN SENSOR CIRCUIT RESISTANCE table. *See Figs. 3 and 4.* If any resistance reading is greater than 5 ohms, repair open in appropriate wire. If all resistance readings are 5 ohms or less, retrieve DTC. See RETRIEVING CODES under SELF-DIAGNOSTIC SYSTEM. If no DTCs are retrieved and problem persist, replace driver's side interior scan sensor.

PASSENGER'S SIDE INTERIOR SCAN SENSOR CIRCUIT RESISTANCE

Scan Sensor Terminal	Wire Color	Module Terminal
1	Yellow/Red	4
2	White/Red	8
3	Brown/Red	10
4	Black	6
5	Orange/Blue	3

5) Turn ignition switch to LOCK position. Disconnect anti-theft/central locking module harness connector C451b. Measure resistance between ground and terminal No. 3 (Black/Yellow wire) at anti-theft/central locking module harness connector C451b while opening and closing hood. *See Fig. 5.* Resistance should be 5 ohms or less with hood closed and greater than 10 k/ohms with hood open. If resistance is not as specified, go to next step. If resistance is as specified, retrieve DTC. See RETRIEVING CODES under SELF-DIAGNOSTIC SYSTEM. If no DTCs are retrieved and problem persist, replace anti-theft/central locking module.

6) Disconnect hood ajar switch harness connector C897. Measure resistance between terminals at hood ajar switch (component side). Resistance should be 5 ohms or less with switch in hood closed position and greater than 10 k/ohms with switch in hood open position. If resistance is as specified, go to next step. If resistance is not as specified, replace hood ajar switch.

7) Measure resistance between ground and Black wire terminal at hood ajar switch harness connector C897. If resistance is greater than 5 ohms, repair open in Black wire. If resistance is 5 ohms or less, repair open in Black/Yellow wire between hood ajar switch and anti-theft/central locking module.

8) Disconnect alarm system horn harness connector. Measure resistance between ground and horn terminal (component side). If resistance is 5 ohms or less, repair open in Blue/Yellow wire between alarm system horn and anti-theft/central locking module. If resistance is greater than 5 ohms, check alarm system horn ground point and clean as necessary. If alarm system horn ground point is okay, replace alarm system horn.

9) Remove right anti-theft turn signal light relay. Remove left anti-theft turn signal light relay. Test relays. See RELAYS under COMPONENT TESTS. If relays are okay, go to next step. If either relay is defective, replace relay.

10) Measure voltage at terminal No. 5 (Orange wire) at right anti-theft turn signal light relay harness connector C2107. *See Fig. 6.* If battery voltage exists, go to next step. If battery voltage does not exist, repair power distribution circuit as necessary. See appropriate wiring diagram in POWER DISTRIBUTION article in WIRING DIAGRAMS.

11) Measure voltage at terminal No. 5 (Orange/White and Orange/Green wires) at left anti-theft turn signal light relay harness connector C2108. If battery voltage exists, go to next step. If battery voltage does not exist, repair open in Orange/White wire between right anti-theft turn signal light relay and left anti-theft turn signal light relay.

12) Measure voltage at terminal No. 1 (Orange/Green and Orange/Yellow wires) at left anti-theft turn signal light relay harness connector C2108. If battery voltage exists, go to next step. If battery voltage does not exist, repair open in Orange/Green wire between terminals No. 1 and 5 at left anti-theft turn signal light relay.

13) Measure voltage at terminal No. 1 (Orange/Yellow wire) at right anti-theft turn signal light relay harness connector C2107. If battery voltage exists, go to next step. If battery voltage does not exist, repair open in Orange/Yellow wire between right anti-theft turn signal light relay and left anti-theft turn signal light relay.

14) Measure resistance between ground and terminal No. 3 (Blue/White wire) at right anti-theft turn signal light relay harness connector C2107. Also, measure resistance between ground and terminal No. 3 (Blue/Orange wire) at left anti-theft turn signal light relay harness connector C2108. If both resistance readings are 0.5-5.0 ohms, go to next step. If either resistance readings is not 0.5-5.0 ohms, repair appropriate turn signal circuit. See appropriate wiring diagram in EXTERIOR LIGHTS article.

15) Measure resistance between terminal No. 2 (Black/Red wire) at left anti-theft turn signal light relay harness connector C2108 and terminal No. 2 (Black/Red wire and Black/Yellow wire) at right anti-theft turn signal light relay harness connector C2107. If resistance is 5 ohms or less, repair open in Black/Yellow wire between right anti-theft turn signal light relay and anti-theft/central locking module. If resistance is greater than 5 ohms, repair open in Black/Red wire.

16) Operate power door locks. If power door lock operate properly, go to next step. If power door locks do not operate properly, repair power door locks as necessary. See appropriate wiring diagram in POWER DOOR LOCKS & TRUNK RELEASE article.

17) Turn ignition switch to LOCK position. Disconnect anti-theft/central locking module harness connector C451b. Measure resistance between ground and terminal No. 11 (Black/Blue wire) at anti-theft/central locking module harness connector C451b while locking doors at driver's and passenger's with key. *See Fig. 5.* If resistance is greater than 5 ohms, go to next step. If resistance is 5 ohms or less, go to step 19).

18) Measure resistance between ground and terminal No. 15 (Black/White wire) at anti-theft/central locking module harness connector C451b while unlocking doors at driver's and passenger's with key. If resistance is greater than 5 ohms, go to step 20). If resistance is 5 ohms or less, connect all disconnect components and retest system. If problem still exists, replace anti-theft/central locking module.

19) Disconnect inoperative door lock motor harness connector. Measure resistance in Black/Blue wire between terminal No. 11 at anti-theft/central locking module harness connector C451b and terminal No. 5 at appropriate door lock motor harness connector. *See Figs. 5 and 7.* Resistance should be 5 ohms or less. Also, measure resistance between ground and terminal No. 11 (Black/Blue wire) at anti-theft/central locking module harness connector C451b. Resistance should be greater than 10 k/ohms. If resistance readings are as specified, replace appropriate door lock motor. If resistance readings are not as specified, repair open or short to ground in Black/Blue wire.

20) Disconnect inoperative door lock motor harness connector. Measure resistance in Black/White wire between terminal No. 15 at anti-theft/central locking module harness connector C451b and terminal No. 7 at appropriate door lock motor harness connector. *See Figs. 5 and 7.* Resistance should be 5 ohms or less. Also, measure resistance between ground and terminal No. 15 (Black/White wire) at anti-theft/central locking module harness connector C451b. Resistance should be greater than 10 k/ohms. If resistance readings are as specified, replace appropriate door lock motor. If resistance readings are not as specified, repair open or short to ground in Black/White wire.

21) Check courtesy light operation. If courtesy lights do not operate, repair courtesy lights as necessary. See appropriate wiring diagram in ILLUMINATION/INTERIOR LIGHTS article. If courtesy lights operate, repair open in Black/Yellow wire if passenger's door did not respond during self-test or Black/Blue wire if driver's door did not respond during self-test.

22) Disconnect liftgate key switch harness connector C632. Measure resistance in Black/Orange wire between terminal No. 1 at liftgate key switch harness connector C632 and terminal No. 1 at anti-theft/central locking module harness connector C451b. *See Fig. 5.* If resistance is 5 ohms or less, go to next step. If resistance is greater than 5 ohms, repair open in Black/Orange wire.

23) Measure resistance between terminals at liftgate key switch (component side). Resistance should be 5 ohms or less when unlocking liftgate with key and greater than 10 k/ohms otherwise. If resistance is as specified, repair open in Black wire. If resistance is not as specified, replace liftgate key switch.

24) Place courtesy lights in 12 second position. Open liftgate. If courtesy lights do not operate, repair courtesy lights as necessary. See appropriate wiring diagram in ILLUMINATION/INTERIOR LIGHTS article. If courtesy lights operate, repair open in Black/Red wire between liftgate ajar switch and in-line harness connector C2109.

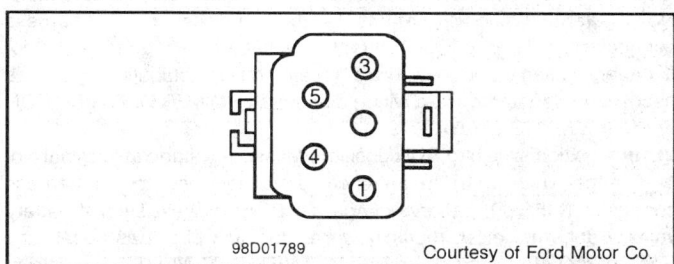

98D01789   Courtesy of Ford Motor Co.

Fig. 3: Identifying Driver's Side & Passenger's Interior Scan Sensor Harness Connector Terminals

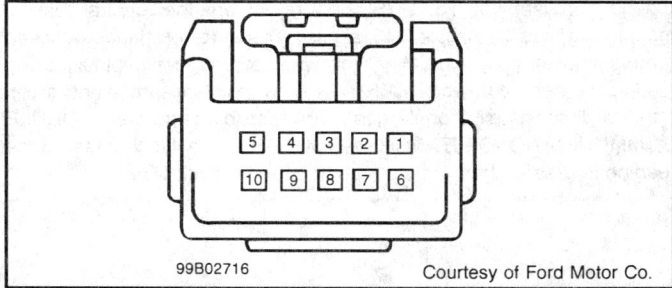

99B02716   Courtesy of Ford Motor Co.

Fig. 4: Identifying Anti-Theft/Central Locking Module Harness Connector C451c Terminals

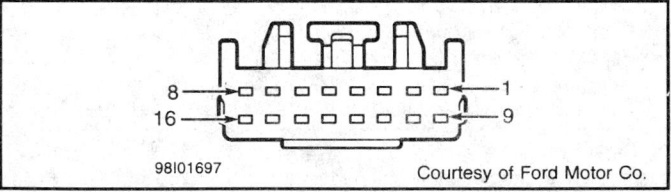

98I01697   Courtesy of Ford Motor Co.

Fig. 5: Identifying Anti-Theft/Central Locking Module Harness Connector C451a & C451b Terminals

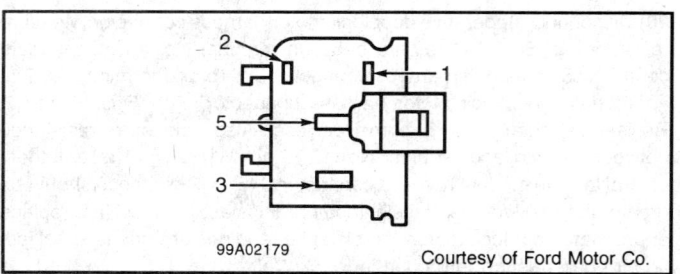

99A02179   Courtesy of Ford Motor Co.

Fig. 6: Identifying Right & Left Anti-Theft Turn Signal Light Relay Harness Connector Terminals

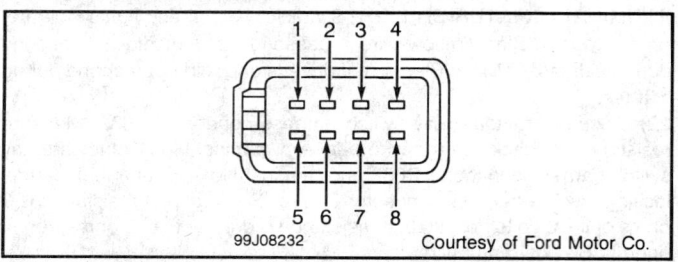

99J08232   Courtesy of Ford Motor Co.

Fig. 7: Identifying Driver's & Passenger's Side Door Lock Motor Harness Connector Terminals

TEST B: NO COMMUNICATION WITH ANTI-THEFT/CENTRAL LOCKING MODULE

NOTE: Anti-theft/central locking module may also be referred to as Central Security Module (CSM).

1) Turn ignition switch to LOCK position. Disconnect anti-theft/central locking module harness connector C451a. Measure voltage at terminal No. 1 (Orange/White wire) at anti-theft/central locking module harness connector C451a. *See Fig. 5.* If battery voltage exists, go to next step. If battery voltage does not exist, repair power distribution circuit as necessary. See appropriate wiring diagram in POWER DISTRIBUTION article in WIRING DIAGRAMS.

2) Turn ignition switch to RUN position. Measure voltage at terminal No. 1 (Orange/White wire) at anti-theft/central locking module harness connector C451a. If battery voltage exists, go to next step. If battery voltage does not exist, repair power distribution circuit as necessary. See appropriate wiring diagram in POWER DISTRIBUTION article in WIRING DIAGRAMS.

3) Turn ignition switch to LOCK position. Measure resistance between ground and terminal No. 5 (Black wire) at anti-theft/central locking module harness connector C451a. Also, measure resistance between ground and terminal No. 11 (Black wire) at anti-theft/central locking module harness connector C451a. If both resistance readings are 5 ohms or less, repair module communication concern. See MODULE COMMUNICATIONS NETWORK – COUGAR article. If either resistance reading is greater than 5 ohms, repair open in Black wire.

TEST C: NO COMMUNICATION WITH HYBRID ELECTRONIC CLUSTER MODULE

1) Turn ignition switch to LOCK position. Disconnect Hybrid Electronic Cluster (HEC) module harness connector C808b. Measure voltage at terminal No. 14 (Orange wire) at HEC module harness connector C808b. *See Fig. 8.* If battery voltage exists, go to next step. If battery voltage does not exist, repair power distribution circuit as necessary. See appropriate wiring diagram in POWER DISTRIBUTION article in WIRING DIAGRAMS.

2) Turn ignition switch to RUN position. Measure voltage at terminal No. 15 (Violet wire) at HEC module harness connector C808b. If battery voltage exists, go to next step. If battery voltage does not exist, repair power distribution circuit as necessary. See appropriate wiring diagram in POWER DISTRIBUTION article in WIRING DIAGRAMS.

3) Turn ignition switch to LOCK position. Measure resistance between ground and terminal No. 2 (Black/Orange wire) at HEC module harness connector C808b. Also, measure resistance between ground and terminal No. 16 (Black/Orange wire) at HEC module harness connector C808b. If both resistance readings are 5 ohms or less, repair module communication concern. See MODULE COMMUNICATIONS NETWORK – COUGAR article. If either resistance reading is greater than 5 ohms, repair open in Black/Orange wire.

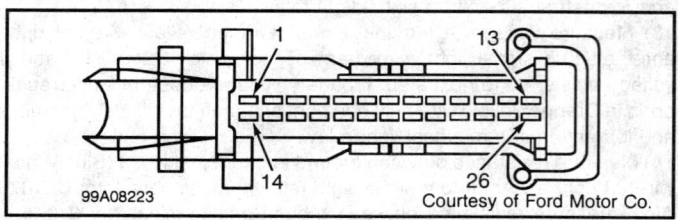

99A08223   Courtesy of Ford Motor Co.

Fig. 8: Identifying HEC Module Harness Connector C808b Terminals

REMOVAL & INSTALLATION

ANTI-THEFT/CENTRAL LOCKING CONTROL MODULE

NOTE: It may be necessary to remove passenger's side kick panel to access module

Removal & Installation – Disconnect negative battery cable. Open glove box. Depress sides of glove box, and remove glove box to access module on pillar "A". Drill out rivets holding relay bracket in place. Remove module retaining screws. Disconnect module harness connectors and remove. To install, reverse removal procedure.

WIRING DIAGRAMS

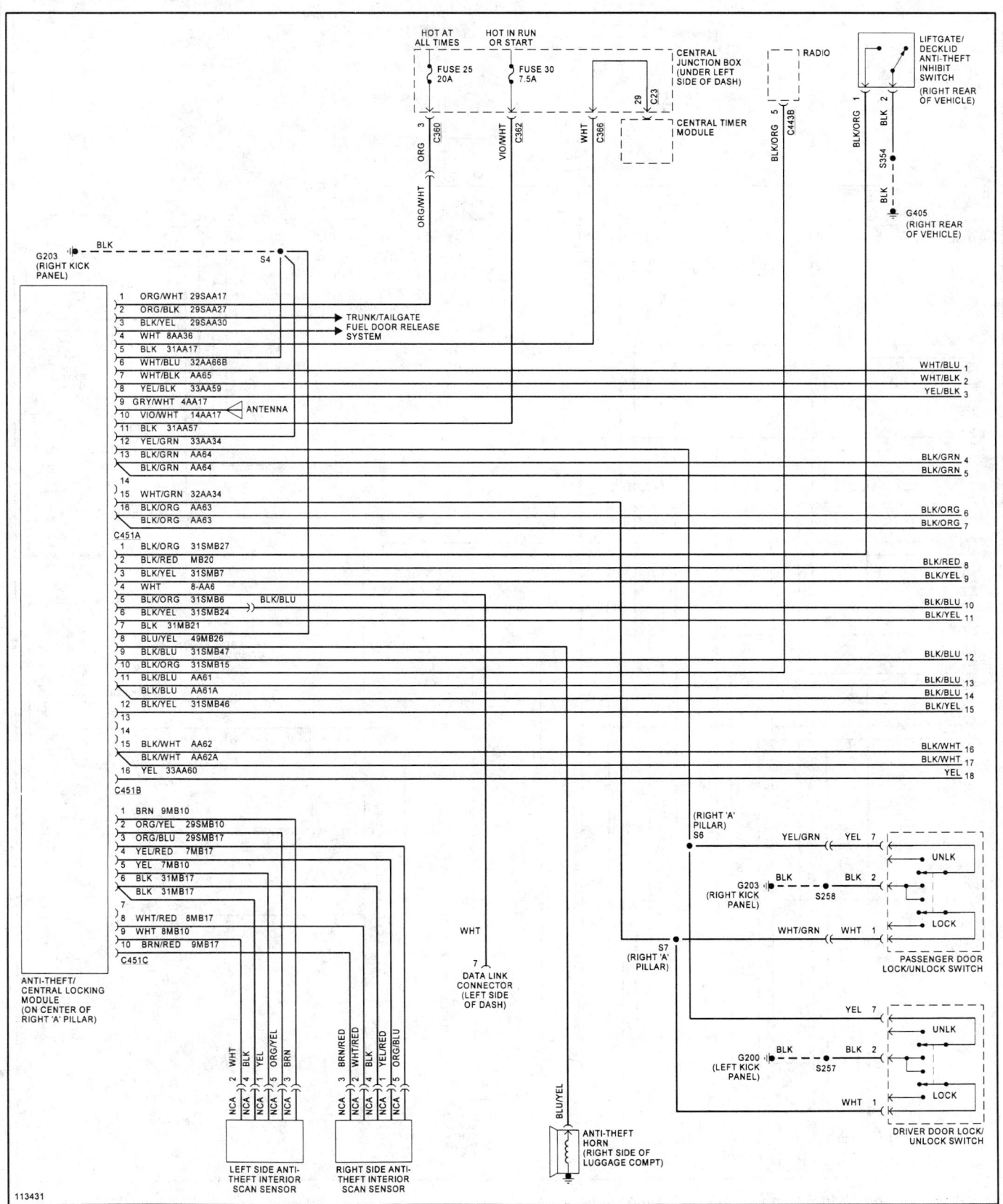

Fig. 9: Active Anti-Theft System Wiring Diagram (Cougar – 1 Of 2)

113431

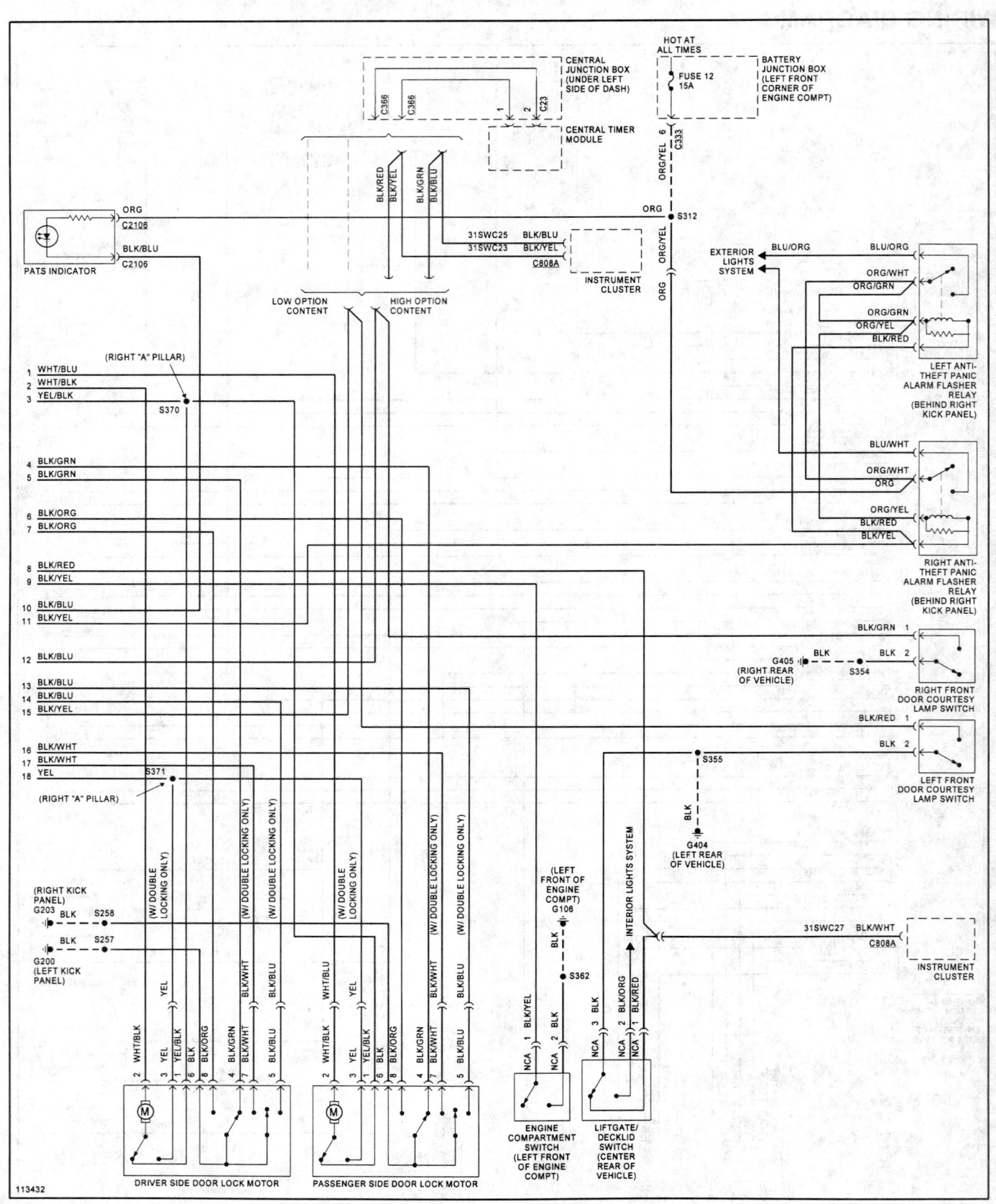

Fig. 10: Active Anti-Theft System Wiring Diagram (Cougar – 2 Of 2)

Active Anti-Theft Systems – Escort & Tracer

DESCRIPTION & OPERATION

WARNING: Deactivate air bag system before performing any service operation. See appropriate AIR BAG RESTRAINT SYSTEMS article. Do not apply electrical power to any component on steering column without first deactivating air bag system. Air bag may deploy.

The anti-theft system is designed to prevent unauthorized entry into the passenger compartment, engine compartment, trunk lid (sedan), or luggage compartment (coupe and wagon). When triggered, the system will provide audible and visual alarms. The horn will sound, parking lights will flash and THEFT indicator on right side of instrument cluster will flash. The remote entry transmitter can also activate a PANIC alarm which is similar to the anti-theft alarm, but does not cause the THEFT indicator to flash.

The system is controlled by a Remote Anti-Theft Personality (RAP) module. Whenever the system is armed, unauthorized entry will be detected by switches located at each door including, trunk (sedan), liftgate (coupe and wagon), and hood.

To arm the system, the ignition switch must be in the OFF position and the PANIC alarm must be off. If system is armed with door open, THEFT light will remain illuminated until 30 seconds after door is closed. The system is armed by pressing the lock button on the remote entry transmitter. The system will arm after 30 seconds has elapsed. The THEFT warning light will flash quickly every 2 seconds until the system is triggered or disarmed.

To disarm untriggered system, press the unlock button on the remote entry transmitter. If the driver arms the system and remains inside the vehicle, the system may be disarmed by turning the ignition switch to the ON position. To disarm triggered system, press the unlock or panic button on the remote entry transmitter or turn the ignition switch to the ACC or ON position.

The Anti-Theft System (ATS) utilizes a self-diagnostic system which stores a Diagnostic Trouble Code (DTC) in the Remote Anti-Theft Personality (RAP) module if a problem exists in the system. DTCs may be retrieved from RAP module by using a New Generation Star (NGS) tester and Data Link Connector (DLC) for diagnosis of system. Before performing system tests, a preliminary procedure should be performed. See SELF-DIAGNOSTIC SYSTEM.

COMPONENT LOCATIONS

COMPONENT LOCATIONS

Component	Location
Data Link Connector (DLC)	Below Driver's Side Of Instrument Panel, To Right Of Steering Column
Door Lock Switch	Appropriate Door Panel Arm Rest
Instrument Cluster [1]	Behind Left Side Of Instrument Panel
Central Junction Box	Below Left Instrument Panel
Power Distribution Box	Left Side Of Engine Compartment, Above Wheelwell
Powertrain Control Module (PCM)	In Center Console Below Shifter
Remote Anti-Theft Personality Module	
Coupe & Sedan	In Luggage Compartment Behind Right Trim Panel
Wagon	In Luggage Compartment Behind Left Trim Panel

[1] – Instrument cluster may also be referred to as Virtual Instrument Cluster (VIC).

PROGRAMMING

REMOTE TRANSMITTER REPROGRAMMING

To reprogram all transmitters, cycle ignition switch from OFF to ON position 8 times within 10 seconds, ending in ON position or OFF to START position 4 times in 10 seconds, ending in ON position. After doors lock and unlock, press any button on all remote transmitters (up to limit of 4). With each button press on remote transmitter, door locks should cycle (lock/unlock) to confirm programming. Once completed, turn ignition switch to OFF position. Door locks should cycle (lock/unlock) one last time to confirm completion of programming. All transmitters must be reprogrammed at the same time.

TROUBLE SHOOTING

Verify customer's complaint by operating anti-theft system. Check for damaged door lock cylinder or ignition cylinder. Check for open fuse(s). Check for loose or corroded connectors, damaged wiring harness, damaged switch(es) or faulty relay(s). Repair or replace components as necessary. If no problem is found, go to SELF-DIAGNOSTIC SYSTEM.

SELF-DIAGNOSTIC SYSTEM

1) Verify customer's complaint by operating anti-theft system. Check for damaged door lock cylinder or ignition cylinder. Check for loose or corroded connectors, damaged wiring harness or components. If all components are okay, connect New Generation Star (NGS) tester to DLC located below instrument panel. Using NGS tester, perform DATA LINK DIAGNOSTIC TEST.

2) If NGS tester displays CKT914, CKT915 or CKT70=ALL ECUS NO RESP/NOT EQUIP, see appropriate MODULE COMMUNICATIONS NETWORK article to continue diagnosis. If NGS tester displays NO RESP/NOT EQUIP for RAP module, go to TEST A: NO COMMUNICATION WITH RAP MODULE under SYSTEM TESTS.

3) If NGS tester displays SYSTEM PASSED, retrieve and record continuous DTCs. Erase continuous DTCs and perform self-test diagnostics for RAP module. Perform appropriate system test in accordance with DTC retrieved. See RAP MODULE SELF-TEST DTC INDEX table. If no DTCs are retrieved, go to SYSTEM TESTS.

FORD
4-76

1999 ACCESSORIES & EQUIPMENT
Active Anti-Theft Systems – Escort & Tracer (Cont.)

RAP MODULE SELF-TEST DTC INDEX

DTC [1]	Description	Test
B1334	Luggage Compartment/Trunk Lid Door Ajar Circuit Short To Ground	B
B1341	Power Door Unlock Circuit Short To Ground	[2]
B1522	Hood Switch Circuit Short To Ground	D
B2425	Keyless Entry Out Of Synchronization	[3]

[1] – Codes listed in this table are only for testing covered in this article. For complete DTC listing, see MODULE COMMUNICATIONS NETWORK – ESCORT & TRACER article.

[2] – See appropriate REMOTE KEYLESS ENTRY SYSTEMS article for wiring diagram.

[3] – Perform DTC B2425: REMOTE KEYLESS ENTRY OUT OF SYNCHRONIZATION under DIAGNOSTIC TROUBLE CODE TESTS.

DIAGNOSTIC TROUBLE CODE TESTS

DTC B2425: REMOTE KEYLESS ENTRY OUT OF SYNCHRONIZATION

1) Press any button on inoperative remote entry transmitter 4 times consecutively. If remote transmitter still does not operate properly, go to next step. If remote transmitter now operates properly, system is okay at this time. Clear DTCs and retest system operation.

2) Check to see if all other remote transmitters operate properly. If all other remote transmitters operate properly, go to next step. If all other remote transmitters do not operate properly, go to step 4).

3) Press any button on any operating remote transmitters. Within 30 seconds of pressing any button on any operating remote transmitter, press a button on inoperative remote transmitter. Check to see if inoperative remote transmitter now operates properly. If inoperative remote transmitter still does not operate properly, go to next step. if inoperative remote transmitter now operates properly, clear DTCs and retest system operation.

4) Reprogram inoperative remote transmitter(s). See PROGRAMMING. If inoperative remote transmitter(s) still does not operate properly, repair power door lock system. See appropriate wiring diagram in POWER DOOR LOCKS & TRUNK RELEASE article. If inoperative remote transmitter(s) now operate properly, inform customer that any additional remote transmitters not available during reprogram will not operate with vehicle. All remote transmitters must be programmed at the same time. Clear DTCs and retest system operation.

SYSTEM TESTS

CAUTION: When battery is disconnected or modules are replaced, vehicle computer and memory systems may lose memory data. Driveability problems may exist until computer systems have completed a relearn cycle. See COMPUTER RELEARN PROCEDURES article in GENERAL INFORMATION before disconnecting battery.

NOTE: Before beginning system tests, perform TROUBLE SHOOTING.

NOTE: After repairs are complete, ensure all component are properly installed and all harness connectors are connected properly and repeat data link diagnostic test. See DATA LINK DIAGNOSTIC TEST under COMMUNICATIONS NETWORK DIAGNOSTICS in MODULE COMMUNICATIONS NETWORK – ESCORT & TRACER article.

SYSTEM TEST INDEX

Symptom	Test
No Communication With RAP Module	A
Alarm System Does Not Arm	B
Alarm System Does Not Disarm	C
Alarm System Does Not Operate Properly	D
Anti-Theft Indicator Is Never On	[1]
Anti-Theft Indicator Is Always On	[2]

SYSTEM TEST INDEX (Cont.)

[1] – See appropriate ANALOG INSTRUMENT PANELS article for testing procedures.

[2] – Disconnect RAP module. If THEFT indicator is still illuminated, ensure all doors are closed. If THEFT indicator only remains illuminated when attempting to arm system, perform TEST B: ALARM SYSTEM DOES NOT ARM. If THEFT indicator does not illuminate, replace RAP module and retest system operation.

NOTE: A New Generation Star (NGS) tester is required for system testing.

TEST A: NO COMMUNICATION WITH RAP MODULE

1) Turn ignition off. Check condition of central junction box ROOM fuse (10-amp) and RADIO fuse (5-amp). If fuses are okay, reinstall fuses and go to step 4). If ROOM fuse is not okay, go to next step. If RADIO fuse is not okay, go to step 3).

2) Disconnect RAP module Gray, 22-pin connector C404 (located in luggage compartment, behind right trim panel on coupe and sedan, or located behind left rear quarter trim panel on wagon). Replace central junction box ROOM fuse (10-amp). Check condition of replaced ROOM fuse. If fuse is okay, replace RAP module and retest system operation. If fuse is not okay, repair short to ground in Blue/Red wire between central junction box ROOM fuse and RAP module connector C404 terminal No. 12. Retest system operation.

3) Disconnect RAP module Gray, 26-pin connector C405 (located in luggage compartment, behind right trim panel on coupe and sedan, or located behind left rear quarter trim panel on wagon). Replace central junction box RADIO fuse (5-amp). Check condition of replaced fuse. If fuse is okay, replace RAP module and retest system operation. If fuses are not okay, repair short to ground in Blue/Black wire between central junction box and RAP module connector C405 terminal No. 25. Retest system operation.

4) Disconnect RAP module Gray, 22-pin connector C404 (located in luggage compartment, behind right trim panel on coupe and sedan, or located behind left rear quarter trim panel on wagon). Using an ohmmeter, check resistance between ground and RAP module 22-pin connector C404 terminal No. 14 (Black wire). See Fig. 1. If resistance is less than 5 ohms, go to next step. If resistance is 5 ohms or more, repair open in Black wire between RAP module and ground. Retest system operation.

5) Using a voltmeter, check voltage between ground and RAP module 22-pin connector C404 terminal No. 12 (Blue/Red wire). See Fig. 1. If voltage is more than 10 volts, go to next step. If voltage is 10 volts or less, repair Blue/Red wire between central junction box and RAP module. Retest system operation.

6) Disconnect RAP module Gray, 26-pin connector C405. Turn ignition on. Using a voltmeter, check voltage between ground and RAP module 26-pin connector C405 terminal No. 25 (Blue/Black wire). See Fig. 2. If voltage is more than 10 volts, go to appropriate MODULE COMMUNICATIONS NETWORK article to continue diagnosis. If voltage is 10 volts or less, repair Blue/Black wire between central junction box and RAP module. Retest system operation.

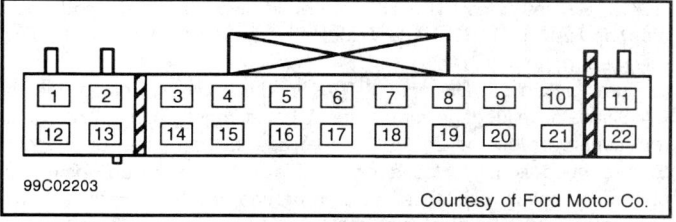

99C02203

Courtesy of Ford Motor Co.

Fig. 1: Identifying RAP Module 22-Pin Connector C404

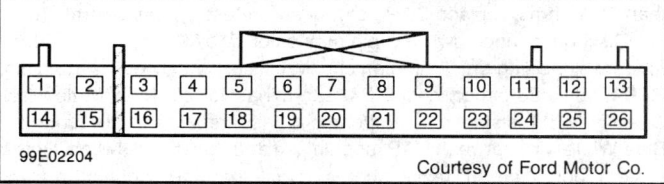

99E02204

Courtesy of Ford Motor Co.

Fig. 2: Identifying RAP Module 26-Pin Connector C405

TEST B: ALARM SYSTEM DOES NOT ARM

1) Turn ignition off. Using NGS tester, retrieve and record continuous DTCs. Clear continuous DTCs and perform RAP module On-Demand Self-Test. If no DTCs are retrieved, go to next step. If DTC B1334 is retrieved, go to step **8)** .

2) Turn ignition off. Operate driver door lock switch from lock to unlock position. Using key, lock and unlock door. If door locks operate correctly, go to next step. If door locks do not operate correctly, repair door lock system.

3) Press lock and unlock buttons on keyless entry transmitter. If door locks operate correctly, go to next step. If door locks do not operate correctly, repair or replace remote transmitter.

4) Open driver door window. Perform arming sequence using remote transmitter. If THEFT indicator does not illuminate, wait 30 seconds after all doors are closed and locked. Reach through window and open door with front inside door handle to trigger armed system. If system arms and triggers, see appropriate INSTRUMENT PANELS article for repair of THEFT indicator. If system does not arm and trigger, go to next step.

5) Using NGS tester, monitor RAP PID DOORRAP. Close all doors. RAP PID DOORRAP should indicate CLOSED. Open any door. The RAP PID DOORRAP should indicate AJAR. If RAP PID changes as specified, go to step **8)**. If RAP PID DOORRAP is not as specified, go to next step.

6) Open and close any door. If interior courtesy lights operate properly, go to next step. If interior courtesy lights do not operate properly, see appropriate wiring diagram in ILLUMINATION/INTERIOR LIGHTS article to continue diagnosis.

7) Turn ignition off. Disconnect RAP module Gray, 26-pin connector C405 (located in luggage compartment, behind right trim panel on coupe and sedan, or located behind left rear quarter trim panel on wagon). Disconnect driver door courtesy light switch connector C324 (located in driver door jamb). Using an ohmmeter, check resistance of Red/White wire between RAP module 26-pin connector C405 terminal No. 11 and driver door courtesy light switch connector C324. If resistance is less than 5 ohms, replace RAP module and retest system operation. If resistance is 5 ohms or more, repair open in Red/White wire between RAP module and driver door courtesy light switch. Retest system operation.

8) Using NGS tester, monitor RAP PID DECKLD while opening and closing luggage compartment. If RAP PID DECKLD does not indicate AJAR when luggage compartment is opened and CLOSED when luggage compartment is closed, go to next step. If RAP PID DECKLD indicates AJAR when luggage compartment is opened and CLOSED when luggage compartment is closed, go to step **12)**.

9) Open and close luggage compartment. If luggage compartment courtesy light illuminates, go to next step. If luggage compartment courtesy light does not illuminate, see appropriate wiring diagram in ILLUMINATION/INTERIOR LIGHTS article to continue diagnosis.

10) Turn ignition off. Disconnect RAP module Gray, 26-pin connector C405 (located in luggage compartment, behind right trim panel on coupe and sedan, or located behind left rear quarter trim panel on wagon). Disconnect luggage compartment switch connector C418. Using an ohmmeter, check resistance in Orange/White wire between RAP module 26-pin connector C405 terminal No. 21 and luggage compartment switch connector C418. *See Fig. 2.* Check resistance between ground and RAP module 26-pin connector C405 terminal No. 21. If resistance is less than 5 ohms between connectors and more than 10 k/ohms between ground and RAP module, go to next step. If resistance is 5 ohms or more between connectors and 10 k/ohms or less between ground and RAP module, repair Orange/White wire and retest system operation.

11) Using an ohmmeter, check resistance between luggage compartment switch terminals while opening and closing luggage compartment switch. Resistance should be less than 5 ohms with luggage compartment switch opened. Resistance should be more than 10 k/ohms with luggage compartment switch closed. If resistance is as specified, replace RAP module and retest system operation. If resistance is not as specified, replace luggage compartment switch and retest system operation.

12) Using NGS tester, select RAP PID IGN_RAP. With ignition off, RAP PID IGN_RAP should indicate OFF. With the ignition switch in RUN position, RAP PID IGN_RAP should indicate RUN. If RAP PID changes as specified, replace RAP module and retest system operation. If RAP PID IGN_RAP only indicates RUN, go to next step. If RAP PID IGN_RAP only indicates OFF, go to step **14)**.

13) Turn ignition off. Disconnect RAP module Gray, 26-pin connector C405. Using a voltmeter, check voltage between ground and RAP module 26-pin connector C405 terminal No. 25 (Blue/Black wire). *See Fig. 2.* If voltage is 10 volts or less, replace RAP module and retest system operation. If voltage is more than 10 volts, repair Blue/Black wire between RAP module and central junction box. Retest system operation.

14) Turn ignition off. Disconnect RAP module Gray, 26-pin connector C405. Turn ignition switch to RUN position. Using a voltmeter, check voltage between ground and RAP module 26-pin connector C405 terminal No. 25 (Blue/Black wire). *See Fig. 2.* If voltage is more than 10 volts, replace RAP module and retest system operation. If voltage is 10 volts or less, repair Blue/Black wire between RAP module and central junction box. Retest system operation.

TEST C: ALARM SYSTEM DOES NOT DISARM

1) Arm system. Perform disarming sequence, using remote transmitter, by pressing unlock button. If system does not disarm, go to next step. If system disarms, go to step **3)**.

2) Press unlock button on remote transmitter. If driver door unlocks, replace RAP module and retest system operation. If driver door does not unlock, repair or replace remote transmitter.

3) Arm system. Perform disarming sequence by turning ignition switch to ON position. If system does not disarm, go to next step. If system disarms, system is operating properly. Verify concern with customer. Return to SYSTEM TEST INDEX table if necessary.

4) Turn ignition off. Using NGS tester, select RAP PID IGN_RAP. With ignition off, RAP PID IGN_RAP should indicate OFF. With the ignition in the ON position, RAP PID IGN_RAP should indicate RUN. If RAP PID changes as specified, system is disarming properly. Verify concern with customer. Return to SYSTEM TEST DIRECTORY table if necessary. If RAP PID IGN_RAP only indicates RUN, go to next step. If RAP PID IGN_RAP only indicates OFF, go to step **6)**.

5) Turn ignition off. Disconnect RAP module Gray, 26-pin connector C405 (located in luggage compartment behind right trim panel on coupe and sedan, or located behind left rear quarter trim panel on wagon). Using a voltmeter, check voltage between ground and RAP module 26-pin connector C405 terminal No. 25 (Blue/Black wire). *See Fig. 2.* If voltage is more than 10 volts, repair Blue/Black wire between RAP module and central junction box. Retest system operation. If voltage is 10 volts or less, replace RAP module and retest system operation.

6) Turn ignition off. Disconnect RAP module Gray, 26-pin connector C405 (located in luggage compartment, behind right trim panel on coupe and sedan, or located behind left rear quarter trim panel on wagon). Turn

FORD
4-78

1999 ACCESSORIES & EQUIPMENT
Active Anti-Theft Systems – Escort & Tracer (Cont.)

ignition switch to RUN position. Using a voltmeter, check voltage between ground and RAP module 26-pin connector C405 terminal No. 25 (Blue/Black wire). *See Fig. 2*. If voltage is more than 10 volts, replace RAP module and retest system operation. If voltage is 10 volts or less, repair Blue/Black wire between RAP module and central junction box. Retest system operation.

TEST D: ALARM SYSTEM DOES NOT OPERATE PROPERLY

1) Turn ignition off. Using NGS tester, retrieve and record continuous DTCs. Clear continuous DTCs and perform RAP module On-Demand Self-Test. If RAP module DTC B1522 is not retrieved, go to next step. If RAP module DTC B1522 is retrieved, go to step **8)**.

2) Arm system. Trigger alarm. If alarm operates properly, RAP system is operating properly. Verify concern with customer. If horn does not sound, go to next step. If parking lights do not illuminate, go to step **6)**. If concern is false system activation, go to step **14)**.

3) Press steering wheel horn pad switch. If vehicle was manufactured in Mexico and horn operates properly when alarm is triggered but does not chirp when activating or deactivating alarm, go to next step. If horn operates properly, go to step **5)**. On all other models, if horn does not operate properly, repair horn system. See WIRING DIAGRAMS in appropriate STEERING COLUMN SWITCHES article to continue diagnosis.

4) Using NGS tester, monitor RAP CONFIGURATION HORNCHIRP. If RAP CONFIGURATION HORNCHIRP indicates ENABLED, go to next step. If RAP CONFIGURATION HORNCHIRP does not indicate ENABLED, ENABLE horn chirp feature by triggering RAP configuration command HORNCHIRP CONFIGURATION to ENABLED. Retest system operation.

5) Turn ignition off. Disconnect RAP module Gray, 22-pin connector C404 (located in luggage compartment, behind right trim panel on coupe and sedan, or located behind left rear quarter trim panel on wagon). Remove horn relay (located behind left side of instrument panel). Using an ohmmeter, check resistance in Green/Orange wire between RAP module 22-pin connector C404 terminal No. 20 and horn relay connector terminal No. 85. *See Figs. 1 and 3*. Check resistance between ground and horn relay connector terminal No. 85. If resistance is less than 5 ohms between RAP module 22-pin connector C404 and horn relay and more than 10 k/ohms between horn relay and ground, replace RAP module and retest system operation. If resistance is 5 ohms or more between RAP module 22-pin connector C404 and horn relay and 10 k/ohms or less between horn relay and ground, repair open or short to ground in Green/Orange wire. Retest system operation.

6) Turn headlight switch to parking lights position. If parking lights operate properly, go to next step. If parking lights do not operate properly, see appropriate wiring diagram in EXTERIOR LIGHTS article to continue diagnosis.

7) Turn ignition off. Disconnect RAP module Gray, 22-pin connector C404 (located in luggage compartment, behind right trim panel on coupe and sedan, or located behind left rear quarter trim panel on wagon). Remove parking light relay (located behind left side of instrument panel. Using an ohmmeter, check resistance in White wire between RAP module 22-pin connector C404 terminal No. 19 and parking light relay connector terminal No. 85. *See Figs. 1 and 3*. Check resistance between ground and parking light relay connector terminal No. 85. If resistance is less than 5 ohms between RAP module 22-pin connector C404 and parking light relay and more than 10 k/ohms between horn relay and ground, replace RAP module and retest system operation. If resistance is 5 ohms or more between RAP module 22-pin connector C404 and parking light relay and 10 k/ohms or less between parking light relay and ground, repair open or short to ground in White wire. Retest system operation.

8) Open hood. Using NGS tester, monitor RAP PID HOOD_SW while pressing and releasing hood switch plunger. If RAP PID HOOD_SW indicates PUNCHD with hood switch released and notPUN with hood switch pressed, verify hood switch is mounted correctly. If necessary, correct condition. If hood switch is mounted correctly, replace RAP module. Clear DTCs and retest system operation. If RAP PID HOOD_SW indicates PUNCHD with hood switch pressed, go to next step. If RAP PID HOOD_SW indicates notPUN with hood switch released, go to step **11)**.

9) Turn ignition off. Disconnect RAP module Gray, 26-pin connector C405 (located in luggage compartment, behind right trim panel on coupe and sedan, or located behind left rear quarter trim panel on wagon). Ensure hood is fully closed or hood switch is pressed. Using an ohmmeter, check resistance between ground and RAP module 26-pin connector C405 terminal No. 23 (Blue/White wire). *See Fig. 2*. If resistance is 10 k/ohms or less, go to next step. If resistance is more than 10 k/ohms, replace RAP module and retest system operation.

10) Disconnect hood switch 2-pin connector C107 (located on left front fenderwell). Using an ohmmeter, check resistance between ground and RAP module 26-pin connector C405 terminal No. 23 (Blue/White wire). *See Fig. 2*. If resistance is 10 k/ohms or less, repair short to ground in Blue/White wire between RAP module and anti-theft hood switch. Retest system operation. If resistance is more than 10 k/ohms, replace anti-theft hood switch and retest system operation.

11) Turn ignition off. Disconnect RAP module Gray, 26-pin connector C405 (located in luggage compartment, behind right trim panel on coupe and sedan, located behind left rear quarter trim panel on wagon). Open hood. Using an ohmmeter, check resistance between ground and RAP module 26-pin connector C405 terminal No. 23 (Blue/White wire). *See Fig. 2*. If resistance is 5 ohms or more, go to next step. If resistance is less than 5 ohms, replace RAP module and retest system operation.

12) Disconnect hood switch 2-pin connector C107 (located on left front fenderwell). Using an ohmmeter, check resistance between ground and anti-theft hood switch connector Black wire terminal. If resistance is less than 5 ohms, go to next step. If resistance is 5 ohms or more, repair open in Black wire between anti-theft hood switch and ground. Retest system operation.

13) Using an ohmmeter, check resistance in Blue/White wire between RAP module 26-pin connector C405 terminal No. 23 and anti-theft hood switch 2-pin connector C107. *See Fig. 2*. If resistance is less than 5 ohms, replace anti-theft hood switch and retest system operation. If resistance is 5 ohms or more, repair open in Blue/White wire. Retest system operation.

14) Using NGS tester, monitor RAP PID AL_EVT1 through AL_EVT8 to monitor last 8 events that caused alarm to trigger. Record all alarm events in case display is changed by triggering alarm. If RAP PID AL_EVT1 through AL_EVT8 indicates DROPEN triggers, go to next step. If RAP PID AL_EVT1 through AL_EVT8 does not indicate DROPEN triggers, go to step **18)**.

15) Using NGS tester, monitor RAP PID DOORRAP while opening and closing both doors. If RAP PID DOORRAP does not indicate AJAR when any door is opened and CLOSED when all doors are closed, go to next step. If RAP PID DOORRAP indicates AJAR when any door is opened and CLOSED when all doors are closed, check for possible intermittent door open warning light switch by opening doors and monitoring PIDs. If door open warning light switches are okay, clarify concern with customer.

16) Open and close any door. If interior lights operate properly, go to next step. If interior lights do not operate properly, see appropriate wiring diagram in ILLUMINATION/INTERIOR LIGHTS article to continue diagnosis.

17) Turn ignition off. Disconnect RAP module Gray 26-pin connector C405 (located in luggage compartment, behind right trim panel on coupe and sedan, located behind left rear quarter trim panel on wagon). Disconnect driver door courtesy light switch 2-pin connector C324 (located in driver door jamb). Using an ohmmeter, check resistance between RAP module 26-pin connector C405 terminal No. 11 (Red/White wire) and driver door courtesy light switch connector C324 (Red/White wire). Check resistance between ground and RAP module 26-pin connector C405 terminal No. 11 (Red/White wire). If resistance is less than 5 ohms between connectors and more than 10 k/ohms between RAP connector and ground, replace RAP module and retest system operation. If resistances are not as specified, repair Red/White wire. Retest system operation.

1999 ACCESSORIES & EQUIPMENT
Active Anti-Theft Systems – Escort & Tracer (Cont.)

FORD
4-79

18) Check the record of alarm events (RAP PID AL_EVT1 through AL_EVT8). If RAP PID AL_EVT1 through AL_EVT8 indicate PANIC, go to next step. If RAP PID AL_EVT1 through AL_EVT8 do not indicate PANIC, go to step **20)**.

NOTE: Remote entry transmitter PANIC alarm is not an anti-theft alarm trigger event. On occasion a customer accidentally presses the PANIC button. If several PANIC codes appear in alarm history, this is more than likely the cause. Customer may need to step closer to vehicle from where alarm was started to stop the alarm.

19) If false alarms are caused by accidental triggering by customer, system is okay. Clarify concern with customer. If necessary, return to SYSTEM TEST INDEX table. If false alarms are not caused by accidental triggering by customer, return to SYSTEM TEST INDEX table.

20) Check the record of alarm events (RAP PID AL_EVT1 through AL_EVT8). If RAP PID AL_EVT1 through AL_EVT8 do not indicate HOODTR, go to next step. If RAP PID AL_EVT1 through AL_EVT8 indicate HOODTR, return to step **8)**.

21) Check the record of alarm events (RAP PID AL_EVT1 through AL_EVT8). If RAP PID AL_EVT1 through AL_EVT8 indicate TRAJAR, go to step **8)** in TEST B: ALARM SYSTEM DOES NOT ARM. If RAP PID AL_EVT1 through AL_EVT8 do not indicate TRAJAR, AL_EVT1 through AL_EVT8 are past history. System is operating properly at this time.

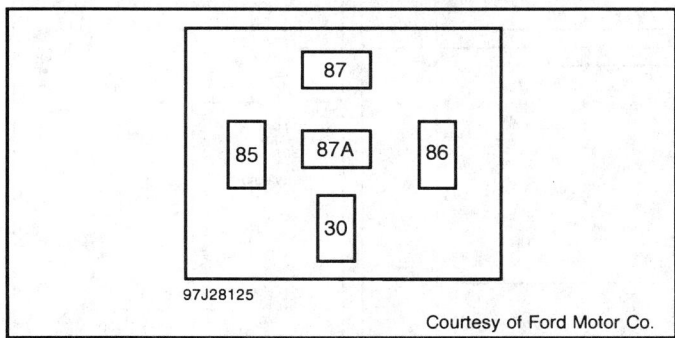

97J28125

Courtesy of Ford Motor Co.

Fig. 3: Identifying Horn Relay & Parking Light Relay Connector Terminals

REMOVAL & INSTALLATION

WARNING: Deactivate air bag system before performing any service operation. See appropriate AIR BAG RESTRAINT SYSTEMS article. Do not apply electrical power to any component on steering column without first deactivating air bag system. Air bag may deploy.

CAUTION: When battery is disconnected, vehicle computer and memory systems may lose memory data. Driveability problems may exist until computer systems have completed a relearn cycle. See COMPUTER RELEARN PROCEDURES article in GENERAL INFORMATION before disconnecting battery.

RAP MODULE

Removal & Installation – Disconnect negative battery cable. On coupe and sedan, remove right rear quarter trim panel. On wagon, remove left rear quarter trim panel. On all models, disconnect 2 RAP module electrical connectors. Disconnect ground strap and RAP module antenna. Remove 2 RAP module mounting nuts and remove RAP module. Lift 2 tabs and remove RAP module from bracket. To install, reverse removal procedure. Tighten RAP module mounting nuts to 6.8-8.5 INCH lbs. (9-11.5 N.m).

HOOD SWITCH

Removal & Installation – Disconnect negative battery cable. Disconnect hood switch electrical connector. Remove hood switch fasteners and remove switch. To install, reverse removal procedure.

FORD
4-80

1999 ACCESSORIES & EQUIPMENT
Active Anti-Theft Systems – Escort & Tracer (Cont.)

WIRING DIAGRAMS

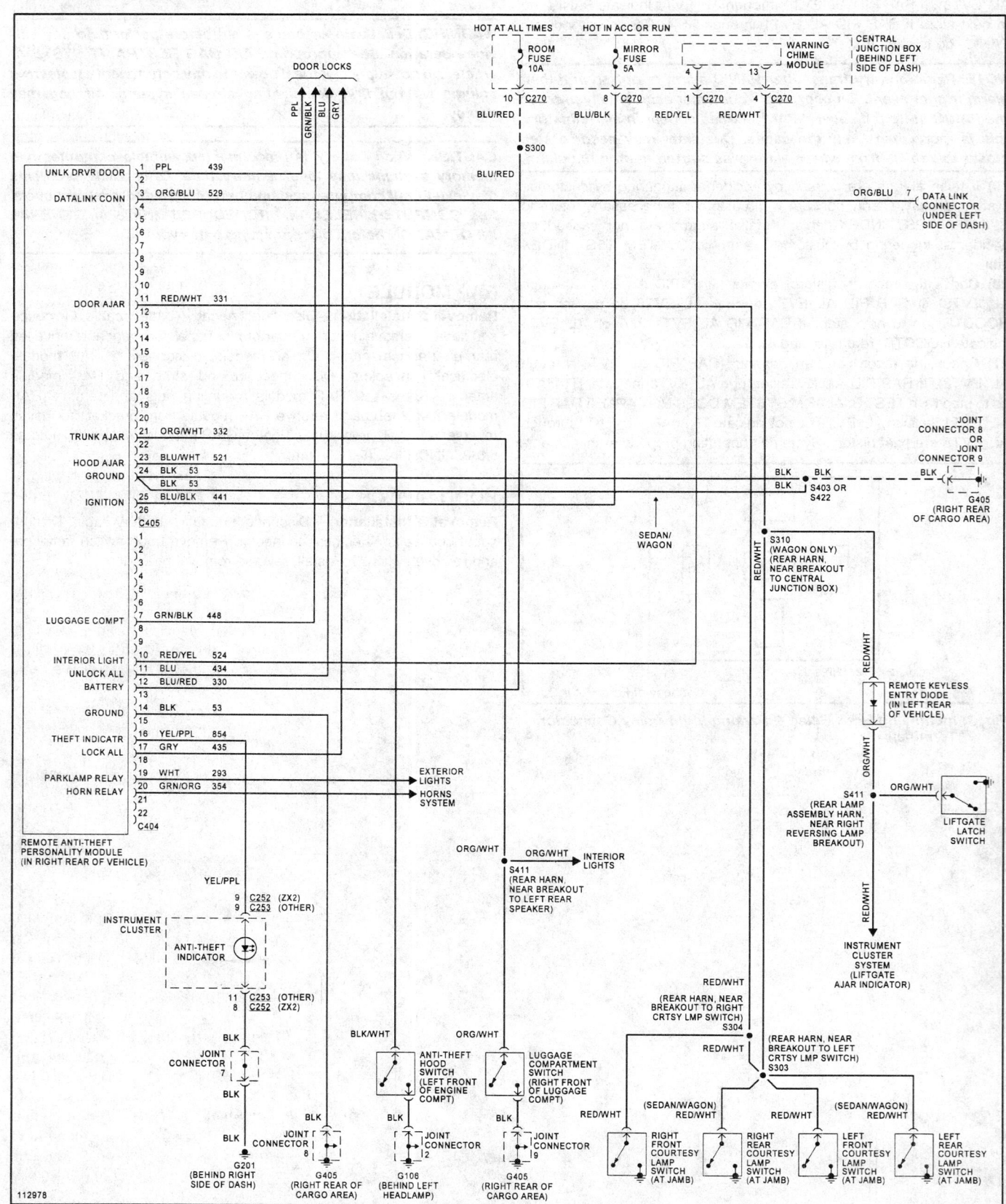

Fig. 4: Active Anti-Theft System Wiring Diagram (Escort & Tracer)

WIRING DIAGRAMS

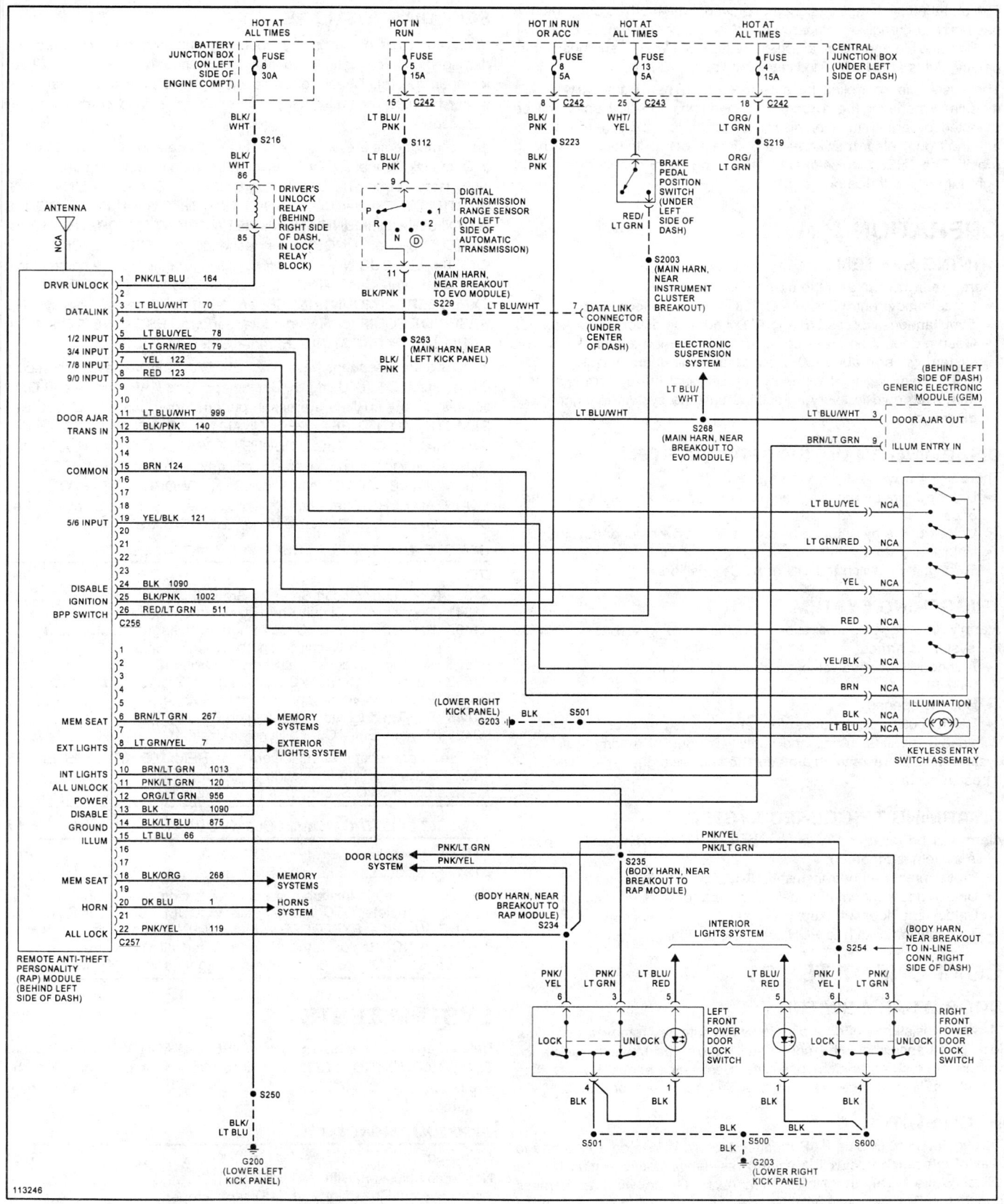

Fig. 1: Active Anti-Theft System Wiring Diagram (Expedition & Navigator)

113246

DESCRIPTION

The anti-theft system is designed to prevent unauthorized entry into the passenger or engine compartment. When triggered, the system will provide audible and visual alarms. The horn will sound, and headlights, parking lights and THEFT indicator will flash.

The system is controlled by a Remote Anti-Theft Personality (RAP) module. Whenever the system is armed, unauthorized entry will be detected by anti-theft door disarm switches located in each door, a anti-theft door disarm switch at the liftgate lock cylinder, or the hood switch. The THEFT indicator is located in the instrument cluster right of right turn signal indicator.

OPERATION

ARMING SYSTEM

There are 3 ways to arm the system:
- Press remote entry transmitter LOCK button to lock doors.
- Simultaneously press 7/8 and 9/0 buttons on driver's door keypad.
- Open a door, then press power door lock button to lock doors. The system will arm about 30 seconds after all doors are closed. The THEFT warning light will glow steadily until the system is armed, then flash quickly every 2 seconds until the system is triggered or disarmed.

DISARMING AN UNTRIGGERED SYSTEM

There are 4 ways to disarm the system:
- Unlock doors by pressing remote entry transmitter UNLOCK button once.
- Unlock doors by entering unlock code at driver's door keypad.
- Unlock any door with key.
- Turn ignition switch to RUN or ACCY position.

TRIGGERING SYSTEM

Alarm will be triggered whenever any of the following actions occur while the system is armed:
- Any door is opened without first using key or remote entry transmitter.
- Hood is opened.
- PANIC button on remote entry transmitter is pressed.

Within 2-3 minutes, horns and lights will shut off automatically. The system will then reset to an armed state and will trigger again if another intrusion occurs.

DISARMING TRIGGERED SYSTEM

Alarm will be disarmed whenever any of the following actions occur while system is triggered:
- Press remote entry transmitter UNLOCK or PANIC button.
- Unlock doors by entering unlock code at driver's door keypad.
- Unlock any door with key.
- Turn ignition switch to RUN or ACCY position.

COMPONENT TESTS

DOOR DISARM SWITCH

Measure resistance of door disarm switch with key removed from door lock. Resistance should be more than 25,000 ohms. Measure resistance with key in lock and unlock positions. Resistance should be less than 200 ohms. If resistance is not as specified, replace door switch.

HOOD SWITCH

Turn ignition off. Unplug RAP module. Module is located above and to rear of left rear wheelwell. Measure resistance between pins No. 14 (Black/White wire) and No. 23 (Tan/Light Green wire) at harness connector. Resistance should be more than 25,000 ohms with hood closed, and less than 200 ohms with hood open. If resistance is not as specified, replace hood switch and/or repair Black/White and/or Tan/Light Green wire. See WIRING DIAGRAMS.

SELF-DIAGNOSTIC SYSTEM

SELF-DIAGNOSTIC TEST

Verify customer complaint by operating anti-theft system. Check for damaged door lock cylinder, ignition lock cylinder or hood switch. Check for open fuse(s). Check for loose or corroded connectors, damaged wiring harness, or faulty relay(s). Repair or replace components as necessary.

If all components are okay, connect New Generation Star (NGS) tester to Data Link Connector (DLC), located beneath instrument panel. Using NGS tester, preform data link diagnostic test. See DATA LINK DIAGNOSTIC TEST under COMMUNICATION NETWORK DIAGNOSTICS in MODULE COMMUNICATIONS NETWORK – EXPLORER & MOUNTAINEER article. If NGS tester responds with CKT914, CKT915 or CKT70=ALL ECUS NO RESP/NOT EQUIP, repair module communications concern. See MODULE COMMUNICATIONS NETWORK – EXPLORER & MOUNTAINEER article. If NGS tester displays NO RESP/NOT EQUIP for RAP module, perform TEST A: NO COMMUNICATION WITH RAP MODULE under SYSTEM TESTS.

If NGS tester responds with SYSTEM PASSED, retrieve and record DTCs. Erase DTCs. Using NGS tester, perform RAP module and GEM self-test. If any DTCs are present, perform appropriate DTC test. See REMOTE ANTI-THEFT PERSONALITY MODULE DTCS and/or GENERIC ELECTRONIC MODULE DTCS tables. Codes listed in this table are only for testing covered in this article. For complete DTC listing, see MODULE COMMUNICATIONS NETWORK – EXPLORER & MOUNTAINEER article. If no DTCs are present, repair by symptom. See SYMPTOM DIAGNOSIS table under SYSTEM TESTS.

REMOTE ANTI-THEFT PERSONALITY MODULE DTCS

DTC	Test
B1309 (Door Lock Circuit Short To Ground)	[1]
B1341 (Door Unlock Circuit Short To Ground)	[1]
B1485 (Brake Pedal Input Circuit Short To Voltage)	[1]
B1522 (Hood Switch Circuit Short To Ground)	C
B1526 (Keypad Switch Circuit Short To Ground)	[1]
B1562 (Door Lock Cylinder Circuit Short To Ground)	B
B1629 (PRNDL Reverse Input Short To Voltage)	[1]
B1845 (Anti-Theft Ignition Lock Switch Failure)	[2]
B2425 (Keyless Entry Out Of Synchronization)	[1]

[1] – See appropriate wiring diagram in REMOTE KEYLESS ENTRY SYSTEMS article for testing procedure.
[2] – Disregard DTC B1845. This is an invalid DTC.

GENERIC ELECTRONIC MODULE DTCS

DTC [1]	Description	Test
B1342	GEM Failure	[2]

[1] – Codes listed in this table are only for testing covered in this article. For complete DTC listing, see MODULE COMMUNICATIONS NETWORK – EXPLORER & MOUNTAINEER article.
[2] – Using NGS tester, retrieve and recored all DTCs. Perform GEM self-test. If DTC B1342 is retrieved again, replace GEM.

SYSTEM TESTS

Before beginning any testing, perform SELF-DIAGNOSTIC TEST under SELF-DIAGNOSTIC SYSTEM. If no DTCs are present, diagnose by symptom. See SYMPTOM DIAGNOSIS table. Perform appropriate system test.

SYMPTOM DIAGNOSIS

Symptom	Test
No Communication With RAP Module	A
Alarm System Does Not Arm Or Disarm Properly	B
Alarm System Does Not Operate Properly	C
THEFT Indicator Is Always/Never On	D
No Communication With GEM	E

1999 ACCESSORIES & EQUIPMENT
Active Anti-Theft Systems – Explorer & Mountaineer (Cont.)

FORD
4-83

TEST A: NO COMMUNICATION WITH RAP MODULE

1) Turn ignition off. Check condition of instrument panel fuse block fuse No. 20 (7.5-amp) and engine compartment fuse block fuse No. 9 (20-amp). If fuses are okay, go to next step. If fuse(s) are not okay, replace fuse(s). Retest system operation. If fuse(s) fail again, check for short to ground in appropriate circuit and repair as necessary. See WIRING DIAGRAMS.

2) Disconnect RAP module 22-pin connector C338. RAP module is located behind left rear quarter panel. Using a voltmeter, measure voltage between ground and RAP module 22-pin connector C338, terminal No. 12 (White/Light Blue wire). *See Fig. 1.* If voltage is more than 10 volts, go to next step. If voltage is 10 volts or less, repair open in White/Light Blue wire between RAP module and engine compartment fuse block. Retest system operation.

3) Disconnect RAP module 26-pin connector C336. Turn ignition on. Measure voltage between ground and RAP module 26-pin connector C336, terminal No. 25 (Black/Pink wire). *See Fig. 2.* If voltage is more than 10 volts, go to next step. If voltage is 10 volts or less, repair open in Black/Pink wire between RAP module and instrument panel fuse block. Retest system operation.

4) Turn ignition off. Measure resistance between ground and RAP module 22-pin connector C338, terminal No. 14 (Black/White wire). *See Fig. 1.* If resistance is less than 5 ohms, go to MODULE COMMUNICATIONS NETWORK – EXPLORER & MOUNTAINEER article to continue diagnosis. If resistance is 5 ohms or more, repair open in Black/White wire between RAP module and ground. Retest system operation.

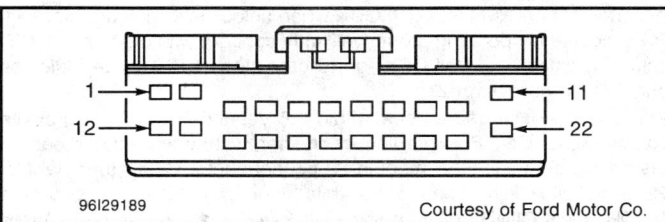

96I29189   Courtesy of Ford Motor Co.

Fig. 1: Identifying RAP Module C338 22-Pin Connector Terminals

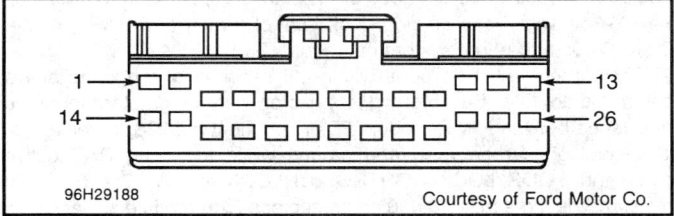

96H29188   Courtesy of Ford Motor Co.

Fig. 2: Identifying RAP Module C336 & GEM C280 26-Pin Connector Terminals

TEST B: ALARM SYSTEM DOES NOT ARM OR DISARM PROPERLY

1) Turn ignition off. Using NGS tester, retrieve and record continuous DTCs. Clear DTCs. Perform RAP module self-test and GEM self-test. If RAP module DTC B1562 is retrieved, go to next step. If GEM DTCs B1833, B1834, or B1836 is retrieved, repair door unlock switch circuit. See wiring diagram in appropriate POWER DOOR LOCKS article. If no DTCs are retrieved, go to step **7**).

2) Using NGS tester, select RAP PID DR_DARM from PID/DATA monitor menu. If PID value indicates ACTIVE, go to next step. If PID value does not indicate ACTIVE, repeat RAP module self-test.

3) Turn ignition off. Disconnect RAP module 26-pin connector C336. RAP module is located behind left rear quarter panel. Disconnect GEM 26-pin connector C280. GEM is located behind center of instrument panel. Using an ohmmeter, measure resistance between ground and RAP module 26-pin connector C336, terminal No. 9 (Dark Green/Purple wire). *See Fig. 2.* If resistance is 10,000 ohms or less, go to next step. If resistance is more than 10,000 ohms, replace RAP module. Clear DTCs and retest system operation.

4) Ensure key is not in driver's door lock cylinder. Disconnect driver's door disarm switch connector C510. Driver door disarm switch is located in rear of driver door. Using an ohmmeter, measure resistance between driver door disarm switch connector C510 Dark Green/Purple wire terminal and Black wire terminal. If resistance is 200 ohms or more, go to next step. If resistance is less than 200 ohms, replace driver door disarm switch. Clear DTCs and retest system operation.

5) Ensure key is not in passenger's door lock cylinder. Disconnect passenger door disarm switch connector C607. Passenger door disarm switch is located in rear of passenger door. Using an ohmmeter, measure resistance between passenger door disarm switch connector C607 Dark Green/Purple wire terminal and Black wire terminal. If resistance is 200 ohms or more, go to next step. If resistance is less than 200 ohms, replace passenger door disarm switch. Clear DTCs and retest system operation.

6) Ensure key is not in liftgate lock cylinder. Disconnect liftgate disarm switch connector C426. Liftgate disarm switch is located near liftgate lock cylinder. Using an ohmmeter, measure resistance between liftgate disarm switch connector C426 Dark Green/Purple wire terminal and Black wire terminal. If resistance is less than 200 ohms, replace liftgate disarm switch. Clear DTCs and retest system operation. If resistance is 200 ohms or more, repair Dark Green/Purple wire between liftgate disarm switch and RAP module. Clear DTCs and retest system operation.

7) Turn ignition off. Press driver's side door lock switch to LOCK and UNLOCK position. Use key to lock and unlock driver's door. If door locks operate properly, go to next step. If door locks do not operate properly, repair power door locks as necessary. See wiring diagram in appropriate POWER DOOR LOCKS & TRUNK RELEASE article.

8) Press LOCK and UNLOCK button on keyless entry remote transmitter. If door locks operate properly, go to next step. If door locks do not operate properly, repair remote keyless entry system as necessary. See wiring diagram in REMOTE KEYLESS ENTRY SYSTEMS article.

9) Press 7/8 and 9/0 buttons on keyless entry keypad to lock doors. Enter 5-digit unlock code on keyless entry keypad to unlock driver's door. If door locks operate properly, go to next step. If door locks do not operate properly, repair remote keyless entry system as necessary. See wiring diagram in REMOTE KEYLESS ENTRY SYSTEMS article.

10) Open driver's door window. Arm system by pressing LOCK button on keyless entry remote transmitter. Wait at least 30 seconds after all doors are closed and locked. Reach through window and open door to trigger alarm system. If system does not trigger, go to next step. If system triggers, system is operating properly. Clarify concern with customer.

11) Using NGS tester, select RAP PID DOORRAP from PID/DATA monitor menu. Monitor PID while opening and closing driver's door. If PID value indicates AJAR when door is opened and CLOSED when door is closed, go to step **17**). If PID value only indicates AJAR, go to next step. If PID value only indicates CLOSED, go to step **14**).

12) Turn ignition on. Using NGS tester, perform GEM self-test. If no DTCs are retrieved, go to next step. If GEM DTC B1322, B1330, B1334, B1338, or B1574 is retrieved, repair appropriate circuit. See MODULE COMMUNICATIONS NETWORK – EXPLORER & MOUNTAINEER article for description of codes.

13) Turn ignition off. Disconnect RAP module 26-pin connector C336. RAP module is located behind left rear quarter panel. Disconnect GEM 16-pin connector C281. GEM is located behind center of instrument panel. Using an ohmmeter, measure resistance between ground and RAP module 26-pin connector C336, terminal No. 11 (Light Blue/White wire). *See Fig. 2.* If resistance is 10,000 ohms or less, repair short to ground in Light Blue/White wire between RAP module and GEM. Clear DTCs and retest system operation. If resistance is more than 10,000 ohms, replace RAP module. Clear DTCs and retest system operation.

14) Using NGS tester, monitor D_DR_SW GEM PID while opening and closing driver's door. Monitor P_DR_SW GEM PID while opening and closing passenger's door. Monitor LRDR_SW GEM PID while opening and closing left rear door. Monitor RRDR_SW GEM PID while opening and closing right rear door. Monitor LGATE_SW GEM PID while opening and closing liftgate. If all GEM PID values indicate OPEN when doors are opened and CLOSED when doors are closed, go to next step. If any

FORD
4-84

1999 ACCESSORIES & EQUIPMENT
Active Anti-Theft Systems – Explorer & Mountaineer (Cont.)

GEM PID value does not indicate OPEN when doors are opened and CLOSED when doors are closed, repair appropriate open or shorted door ajar circuit. See appropriate wiring diagram in ILLUMINATION/ INTERIOR LIGHTS article.

15) Turn ignition off. Disconnect RAP module 26-pin connector C336. RAP module is located behind left rear quarter panel. Open driver's door. Measure resistance between ground and RAP module 26-pin connector C336, terminal No. 11 (Light Blue/White wire). *See Fig. 2.* If resistance is 5 ohms or more, go to next step. If resistance is less than 5 ohms, replace RAP module. Clear DTCs and retest system operation.

16) Disconnect GEM 16-pin connector C281. GEM is located behind center of instrument panel. Measure resistance in Light Blue/White wire between RAP module 26-pin connector C336, terminal No. 11 and GEM 16-pin connector C281 terminal No. 3. *See Figs. 2 and 3.* If resistance is less than 5 ohms, replace GEM. Clear DTCs and retest system operation. If resistance is 5 ohms or more, repair open Light Blue/White wire between RAP module and GEM. Clear DTCs and retest system operation.

17) Using NGS tester, select RAP PID IGN_RAP from PID/DATA monitor menu. Monitor PID value while turning ignition switch from off to on. If PID value indicates RUN with ignition on and OFF with ignition off, go to step **20)**. If PID value indicates OFF only, go to step **19)**. If PID value indicates RUN only, go to next step.

18) Turn ignition off. Disconnect RAP module 26-pin connector C336. RAP module is located behind left rear quarter panel. Remove instrument panel fuse block fuse No. 20 (7.5-amp). Turn ignition on. Using a voltmeter, measure voltage between ground and RAP module 26-pin connector C336, terminal No. 25 (Black/Pink wire). If any voltage is present, repair short to power in Black/Pink wire between instrument panel fuse block fuse No. 20 and RAP module. Clear DTCs and retest system operation. If no voltage is present, replace RAP module. Clear DTCs and retest system operation.

19) Turn ignition off. Disconnect RAP module 26-pin connector C336. Turn ignition on. Using a voltmeter, measure voltage between ground and RAP module 26-pin connector C336, terminal No. 25 (Black/Pink wire). *See Fig. 2.* If voltage is more than 10 volts, replace RAP module. Clear DTCs and retest system operation. If voltage is 10 volts or less, repair Black/Pink wire between instrument panel fuse block fuse No. 20 (7.5-amp) and RAP module. Retest system operation.

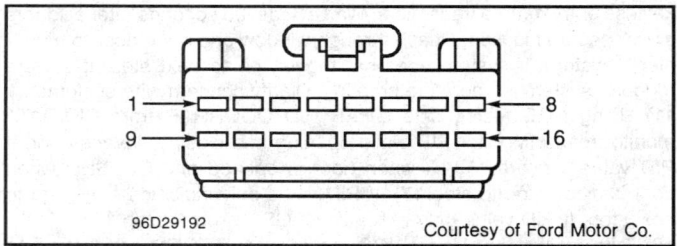

96D29192   Courtesy of Ford Motor Co.

Fig. 3: Identifying GEM C281 16-Pin Connector Terminals

NOTE: If RAP module receives a shorted door disarm switch signal, module will react by disarming anti-theft system. Even when valid arming sequence has been entered, anti-theft system will disarm as soon as system is armed.

20) Using NGS tester, select RAP PID DR_DARM from PID/DATA monitor menu. Monitor PID value while locking and unlocking doors. If PID value indicates notACT when doors are unlocked and ACTIVE when doors are locked, go to step **25)**. If PID value only indicates ACTIVE, go to step **2)**. If PID value only indicates notACT, go to next step.

21) Disconnect RAP module 26-pin connector C336. RAP module is located behind left rear quarter panel. Using an ohmmeter, measure resistance between ground and RAP module 26-pin connector C336, terminal No. 9 (Dark Green/Purple wire) while turning driver's door lock cylinder to UNLOCK position. *See Fig. 2.* If resistance is less than 200 ohms, go to next step. If resistance is 200 ohms or more, replace driver's door disarm switch. Clear DTCs and retest system operation.

22) Measure resistance between ground and RAP module 26-pin connector C336, terminal No. 9 (Dark Green/Purple wire) while turning passenger's door lock cylinder to UNLOCK position. If resistance is less than 200 ohms, go to next step. If resistance is 200 ohms or more, replace passenger's door disarm switch. Clear DTCs and retest system operation.

23) Measure resistance between ground and RAP module 26-pin connector C336, terminal No. 9 (Dark Green/Purple wire) while turning liftgate door lock cylinder to UNLOCK position. If resistance is less than 200 ohms, go to next step. If resistance is 200 ohms or more, replace liftgate disarm switch. Clear DTCs and retest system operation.

24) Disconnect driver's door disarm switch connector C510. Driver's door disarm switch is located in rear of driver's door. Using an ohmmeter, measure resistance of Dark Green/Purple wire between RAP module 26-pin connector C336, terminal No. 9 and driver's door disarm switch connector C510. If resistance is less than 5 ohms, replace RAP module. Clear DTCs and retest system operation. If resistance is 5 ohms or more, repair open in Dark Green/Purple wire between driver's door disarm switch and RAP module. Clear DTCs and retest system operation.

NOTE: If RAP system module received an all door unlock signal shorted, RAP module will react by disarming anti-theft system. Even when valid arming sequence has been entered, anti-theft system will immediately disarm.

25) Using NGS tester, RAP PID select DD_LOCK from PID/DATA monitor menu. Monitor PID while pressing lock and unlock switches on driver and passenger doors. If PID value indicates LOCK when lock switches are pressed and UNLOCK when unlock switches are pressed, RAP module is operating properly. Clarify concern with customer. If PID value indicates only UNLOCK, go to next step. If PID value indicates only LOCK, go to step **27)**.

26) This check must be done within 2.5 seconds of triggering active command to ON. Backprobing connector with ohmmeter, measure resistance between RAP module 22-pin connector C338, terminal No. 22 (Pink/Yellow wire) and ground while triggering RAP active command DOOR LOCK CONTROL LOCK to ON. *See Fig. 1.* If resistance is more than 10,000 ohms, replace RAP module. Clear DTCs and retest system operation. If resistance is 10,000 ohms or less, repair short to ground in Pink/Yellow wire between door lock control switch and RAP module. Clear DTCs and retest system operation.

27) This check must be done within 2.5 seconds of triggering active command to ON. Backprobing connector with ohmmeter, measure resistance between RAP module 22-pin connector C338, terminal No. 11 (Pink/Light Green wire) and ground while triggering RAP active command DOOR LOCK CONTROL UNLOCK to ON. *See Fig. 1.* If resistance is more than 10,000 ohms, replace RAP module. Clear DTCs and retest system operation. If resistance is 10,000 ohms or less, repair short to ground in Pink/Light Green wire between door lock control switch and RAP module. Clear DTCs and retest system operation.

TEST C: ALARM SYSTEM DOES NOT OPERATE PROPERLY

1) Turn ignition off. Using NGS tester, retrieve and document continuous DTCs. Clear DTCs. Perform RAP module self-test. If DTC B1522 is retrieved, go to next step. If DTC B1522 is not retrieved, go to step **5)**. If DTC B1845 is retrieved, disregard this DTC. This is an invalid DTC.

NOTE: DTC B1522 will be stored during operational mode if hood is open for 5 consecutive arming cycles. DTC B1522 is stored during RAP module self-test if hood is open at that time.

2) Using NGS tester, select RAP PID HOOD_SW from PID/DATA monitor menu. Monitor PID value with hood closed. If PID value indicates PUNCHD, go to next step. If PID value does not indicate PUNCHD, repeat RAP module self-test.

3) Turn ignition off. Disconnect RAP module 26-pin connector C336. RAP module is located behind left rear quarter panel. Using an ohmmeter, measure resistance between ground and RAP module 26-pin connector C336, terminal No. 23 (Tan/Light Green wire). *See*

Fig. 2. If resistance is 10,000 ohms or less, go to next step. If resistance is more than 10,000 ohms, replace RAP module. Clear DTCs and retest system operation.

4) Disconnect anti-theft hood switch connector C191. Connector C191 is located on upper right fender apron. Using an ohmmeter, measure resistance between anti-theft hood switch Tan/Light Green wire terminal and Black wire terminal while depressing anti-theft hood switch plunger. If resistance is 10,000 ohms or less, replace anti-theft hood switch. Clear DTCs and retest system operation. If resistance is more than 10,000 ohms, verify anti-theft hood switch is mounted correctly so plunger is depressed when hood is closed. If hood switch is mounted correctly, repair Tan/Light Green wire between RAP module and anti-theft hood switch. Clear DTCs and retest system operation.

5) Arm anti-theft system by pressing lock button on remote entry transmitter. Trigger alarm. If alarm operates properly, RAP system is operating properly. Verify concern with customer. If horn does not sound, go to next step. If parking lights do not illuminate, go to step **8)**. If concern is false system activation, go to step **10)**.

6) Press steering wheel horn pad switch. If horn operates properly, go to next step. If horn does not operate properly, repair horn system. See WIRING DIAGRAMS in STEERING COLUMN SWITCHES – EXPLORER & MOUNTAINEER article to continue diagnosis.

7) Turn ignition off. Disconnect RAP module 22-pin connector C338. Remove horn relay. Horn relay is located in engine compartment fuse block. Using an ohmmeter, measure resistance of Yellow/Light Green wire between RAP module 22-pin connector C338, terminal No. 20 and horn relay connector terminal No. 2. *See Figs. 1 and 4*. Also measure resistance between ground and at horn relay connector terminal No. 2 (Yellow/Light Green wire). If resistance of Yellow/Light Green wire is less than 5 ohms between RAP module 22-pin connector C338 and horn relay and more than 10, 000 ohms between horn relay and ground, replace RAP module and retest system operation. If resistance in Yellow/Light Green wire is 5 ohms or more between RAP module 22-pin connector C338 and horn relay, or 10,000 ohms or less between horn relay and ground, repair open or short to ground in Yellow/Light Green wire between RAP module and horn relay. Retest system operation.

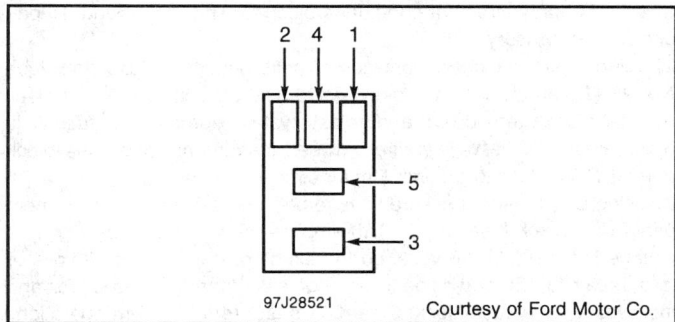

2 4 1

5

3

97J28521   Courtesy of Ford Motor Co.

Fig. 4: Identifying Horn Relay & Parking Light Relay Connector Terminals

8) Turn headlight switch to PARKING LIGHTS position. If parking lights operate properly, go to next step. If parking lights do not operate properly, see appropriate wiring diagram in EXTERIOR LIGHTS article to continue diagnosis.

9) Turn ignition off. Disconnect RAP module 22-pin connector C338. Remove parking light relay. Parking light relay is located behind lower instrument panel on right of steering column. Using an ohmmeter, measure resistance in White/Purple wire between RAP module 22-pin connector C338, terminal No. 8 and parking light relay connector terminal No. 2. *See Figs. 1 and 4*. Also measure resistance between ground and at parking light relay connector terminal No. 2 (White/Purple wire). If resistance in White/Purple wire is less than 5 ohms between RAP module 22-pin connector C338 and parking light relay and more than 10,000 ohms between horn relay and ground, replace RAP module and retest system operation. If resistance in White/Purple wire is 5 ohms or more between RAP module 22-pin connector C338 and parking light relay, or 10,000 ohms or less between parking light relay and ground,

repair open or short to ground in White/Purple wire between RAP module and parking light relay. Retest system operation.

10) Using NGS tester, monitor RAP PID AL_EVT1 through AL_EVT8 to monitor last 8 events that caused alarm to trigger. Record all alarm events in case display is changed by triggering alarm. If RAP PID AL_EVT1 through AL_EVT8 indicates 2 door open triggers (DROPEN), go to next step. If RAP PID AL_EVT1 through AL_EVT8 does not indicate 2 door open triggers (DROPEN), go to step **17)**.

11) Using NGS tester, select RAP PID DOORRAP from PID/DATA monitor menu. Monitor PID value while opening and closing both doors individually. If PID value indicates AJAR when doors are opened and CLOSED when doors are closed, check for possible intermittent door open warning light switch by opening doors and monitoring PIDs. If door open warning light switches are okay, verify concern with customer. If PID value only indicates AJAR, go to next step. If PID value only indicates CLOSED, go to step **14)**.

12) Close all doors. Using NGS tester, perform GEM self-test. If no DTCs are retrieved, go to next step. If DTC B1322, B1330, B1334, B1338, or B1574 is retrieved, repair appropriate circuit. See MODULE COMMUNICATIONS NETWORK – EXPLORER & MOUNTAINEER article for description of codes.

13) Turn ignition off. Disconnect RAP module 26-pin connector C336. RAP module is located behind left rear quarter panel. Disconnect GEM 16-pin connector C281. GEM/CTM is located behind center of instrument panel. Using an ohmmeter, measure resistance between ground and RAP module 26-pin connector C336, terminal No. 11 (Light Blue/White wire). *See Fig. 2*. If resistance is 10,000 ohms or less, repair short to ground in Light Blue/White wire between RAP module and GEM. Clear DTCs and retest system operation. If resistance is more than 10,000 ohms, replace RAP module. Clear DTCs and retest system operation.

14) Using NGS tester, select GEM PID D_DR_SW from PID/DATA monitor menu. Monitor PID value while opening and closing driver's door. Monitor GEM PID P_DR_SW while opening and closing passenger's door. Monitor GEM PID LRDR_SW while opening and closing left rear door. Monitor GEM PID RRDR_SW while opening and closing right rear door. If all PID values indicate OPEN when doors are opened and CLOSED when doors are closed, go to next step. If any PID value does not indicate OPEN when doors are opened and CLOSED when doors are closed, repair appropriate open or shorted door ajar circuit. See appropriate wiring diagram in ILLUMINATION/INTERIOR LIGHTS article.

15) Turn ignition off. Disconnect RAP module 26-pin connector C336. Disconnect GEM 16-pin connector C281. GEM is located behind center of instrument panel. Using an ohmmeter, measure resistance of Light Blue/White wire between RAP module 26-pin connector C336, terminal No. 11 and GEM16-pin connector C281 terminal No. 3. *See Figs. 2 and 3*. If resistance is less than 5 ohms, go to next step. Clear DTCs and retest system operation. If resistance is 5 ohms or more, repair open in Light Blue/White wire between RAP module and GEM. Clear DTCs and retest system operation.

16) Reconnect GEM 16-pin connector C281. Open driver's door. Using an ohmmeter, measure resistance between ground and RAP module 26-pin connector C336, terminal No. 11 (Light Blue/White wire). *See Fig. 1*. If resistance is more than 10,000 ohms, replace GEM. Clear DTCs and retest system operation. If resistance is 10,000 ohms or less, replace RAP module. Clear DTCs and retest system operation.

17) Check record of alarm events (RAP PIDs AL_EVT1 through AL_EVT8) recorded in step **10)**. If RAP PID AL_EVT1 through AL_EVT8 indicate 2 PANIC triggers, go to next step. If RAP PID AL_EVT1 through AL_EVT8 do not indicate 2 PANIC triggers, go to step **19)**.

NOTE: Remote entry transmitter PANIC alarm is not an anti-theft alarm trigger event. On occasion, a customer accidentally presses the PANIC button. If several PANIC codes appear in alarm history, this is more than likely the case. Customer may need to step closer to vehicle (from where alarm was started) to stop alarm.

18) If false alarms are caused by accidental triggering by customer, system is okay. Clarify concern with customer. If necessary, return to

FORD
4-86

1999 ACCESSORIES & EQUIPMENT
Active Anti-Theft Systems – Explorer & Mountaineer (Cont.)

SYMPTOM DIAGNOSIS. If false alarms are not caused by accidental triggering by customer, return to SYMPTOM DIAGNOSIS.

19) Check record of alarm events (RAP PIDs AL_EVT1 through AL_EVT8) recorded in step **10)**. If RAP PID AL_EVT1 through AL_EVT8 indicate 2 HOODTR triggers, go to next step. If RAP PID AL_EVT1 through AL_EVT8 do not indicate 2 HOODTR triggers, system is okay. Verify concern with customer. If necessary, return to SYMPTOM DIAGNOSIS.

20) Using NGS tester, select RAP PID HOOD_SW from PID/DATA monitor menu. Monitor PID value while depressing hood switch plunger. If PID value does not indicate notPUN, go to next step. If PID value indicates notPUN, verify anti-theft hood switch is mounted correctly so plunger is depressed when hood is closed. If necessary, correct condition. If hood switch is mounted correctly, clarify concern with customer. If necessary, return to SYMPTOM DIAGNOSIS.

21) Turn ignition off. Disconnect RAP module 26-pin connector C336. RAP module is located behind left rear quarter panel. Using an ohmmeter, measure resistance between ground and RAP module 26-pin connector C336, terminal No. 23 (Tan/Light Green wire). *See Fig. 2.* If resistance is 10,000 ohms or less, go to next step. If resistance is more than 10,000 ohms, replace RAP module. Clear DTCs and retest system operation.

22) Disconnect anti-theft hood switch connector C191. Connector C191 is located on upper right fender apron. Using an ohmmeter, measure resistance between anti-theft hood switch Tan/Light Green wire terminal and Black wire terminal while depressing anti-theft hood switch plunger. If resistance is 10,000 ohms or less, replace anti-theft hood switch. Clear DTCs and retest system operation. If resistance is more than 10,000 ohms, repair Tan/Light Green wire between RAP module and anti-theft hood switch. Clear DTCs and retest system operation.

TEST D: THEFT INDICATOR IS ALWAYS/NEVER ON

NOTE: DO NOT treat THEFT indicator LED like a bulb. If battery voltage is supplied directly to THEFT indicator LED, THEFT indicator LED will burn out.

1) Turn ignition off. Using NGS tester, command RAP module active command THEFT LED to ON. If THEFT indicator does not illuminate, go to next step. If THEFT indicator illuminates, RAP module is operating properly. Review alarm setting procedure and operation with customer.

2) Turn ignition off. Disconnect instrument cluster 16-pin connector C286. Turn ignition on. Using NGS tester, command RAP Module active command THEFT LED to ON. Using a voltmeter, measure voltage between ground and instrument cluster 16-pin connector C286, terminal No. 6 (Dark Blue/Light Green wire). *See Fig. 5.* If voltage is 3 volts or less, go to next step. If voltage is more than 3 volts, go to step **4)**.

3) Turn ignition off. Disconnect RAP module 22-pin connector C338. RAP module is located behind left rear quarter panel. Using an ohmmeter, measure resistance of Dark Blue/Light Green wire between RAP module 22-pin connector C338, terminal No. 16 and instrument cluster 16-pin connector C286 terminal No. 6. *See Figs. 1 and 5.* Also measure resistance between ground and RAP module 22-pin connector C338, terminal No. 16 (Dark Blue/Light Green wire). If resistance in Dark Blue/Light Green wire is less than 5 ohms between RAP module 22-pin connector C338 and instrument cluster connector C286 and more than 10,000 ohms between RAP module 22-pin connector C338 and ground, replace RAP module. Clear DTCs and retest system operation. If resistance is 5 ohms or more between RAP module 22-pin connector C338 and instrument cluster connector C286, or 10,000 ohms or less between RAP module 22-pin connector C338 and ground, repair open or short to ground in Dark Blue/Light Green wire between RAP module and instrument cluster. Clear DTCs and retest system operation.

4) Remove anti-theft indicator LED. Using an ohmmeter, measure resistance between instrument cluster C286 terminal No. 6 (printed circuit) and lower contact pad of anti-theft LED. *See Fig. 6.* If resistance is less than 5 ohms, go to next step. If resistance is 5 ohms or more, replace instrument cluster printed circuit. Clear DTCs and retest system operation.

5) Using an ohmmeter, measure resistance between instrument cluster connector C286 terminal No. 7 (printed circuit) and upper contact pad of anti-theft LED. *See Fig. 6.* If resistance is less than 5 ohms, replace anti-theft LED. Clear DTCs and retest system operation. If resistance is 5 ohms or more, replace instrument cluster printed circuit. Clear DTCs and retest system operation

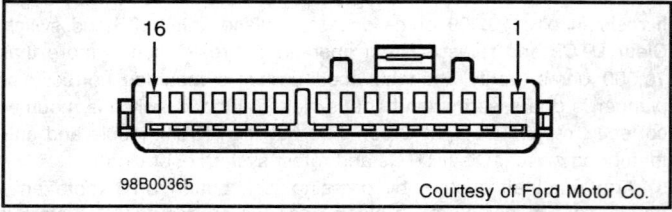

Fig. 5: Identifying Instrument Cluster Connector C286

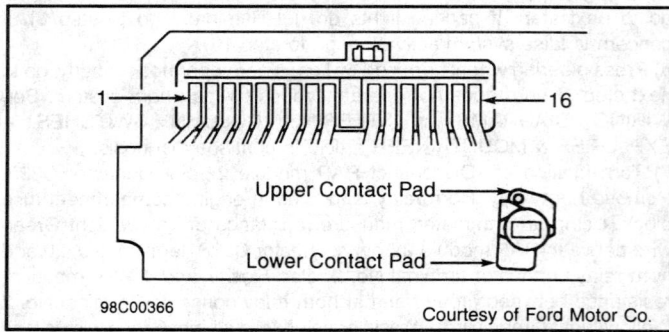

Fig. 6: Identifying Instrument Cluster Printed Circuit

TEST E: NO COMMUNICATION WITH GEM

1) Using ohmmeter, check condition of maxi-fuse No. 1 (60-amp) in engine compartment fuse block. If fuse is okay, go to next step. If fuse is not okay, replace fuse. Clear DTCs and retest system operation. If fuse fails again, check Tan/Black wire between engine compartment fuse block and instrument panel fuse block for short to ground. Repair circuit as necessary.

2) Using ohmmeter, check condition of instrument panel fuse block fuse No. 25 (7.5-amp). If fuse is okay, go to next step. If fuse is not okay, replace fuse. Clear DTCs and retest system operation. If fuse fails again, check White/Yellow wire between instrument panel fuse block and GEM for short to ground. Repair circuit as necessary.

3) Using a voltmeter, measure voltage between ground and instrument panel fuse block fuse No. 25 (7.5-amp) terminal No. 2. *See Fig. 7.* If voltage is more than 10 volts, go to next step. If voltage is 10 volts or less, repair Tan/Black wire between engine compartment fuse block and instrument panel fuse block. Clear DTCs and retest system operation.

4) Turn ignition off. Disconnect GEM 18-pin connector C283. GEM is located behind center of instrument panel. Using a voltmeter, measure voltage between ground and GEM 18-pin connector C283, terminal No. 11 (White/Yellow wire). *See Fig. 8.* If voltage is more than 10 volts, go to next step. If voltage is 10 volts or less, repair White/Yellow wire between instrument panel fuse block and GEM/CTM. Clear DTCs and retest system operation.

5) Disconnect GEM 26-pin connector C280. Using an ohmmeter, measure resistance between ground and GEM 26-pin connector C280, terminal No. 14 (Black/White wire). *See Fig. 2.* Also measure resistance between ground and GEM 26-pin connector C280, terminal No. 26 (Black/White wire). If any resistance reading is 5 ohms or more, repair appropriate open circuit. Clear DTCs and retest system operation. If both resistance readings are less than 5 ohms, repair module communication concern. See MODULE COMMUNICATIONS NETWORK – EXPLORER & MOUNTAINEER article.

1999 ACCESSORIES & EQUIPMENT
Active Anti-Theft Systems – Explorer & Mountaineer (Cont.)

FORD
4-87

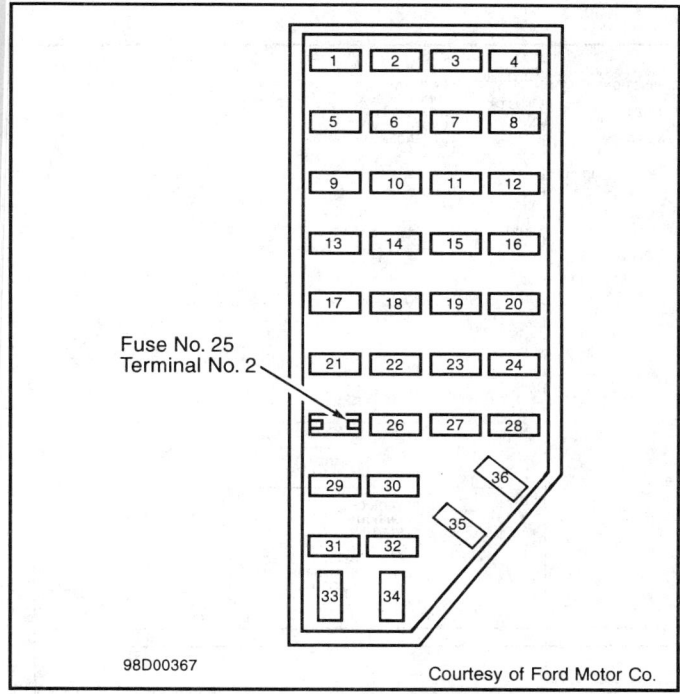

Fuse No. 25
Terminal No. 2

98D00367

Courtesy of Ford Motor Co.

Fig. 7: Identifying Instrument Panel Fuse Block Fuse No. 25 Terminals

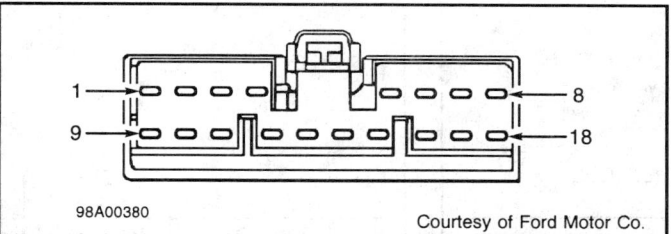

98A00380

Courtesy of Ford Motor Co.

Fig. 8: Identifying GEM C283 18-Pin Connector Terminals

REMOVAL & INSTALLATION

WARNING: Disable air bag system before working around steering column or removing any air bag system component. See appropriate AIR BAG RESTRAINT SYSTEMS article.

CAUTION: When battery is disconnected, vehicle computer and memory systems may lose memory data. Driveability problems may exist until computer systems have completed a relearn cycle. See COMPUTER RELEARN PROCEDURES article in GENERAL INFORMATION before disconnecting battery.

DOOR DISARM SWITCH

Removal & Installation – 1) Remove door trim and position water shield away from access holes. Remove door lock cylinder retainer. Disconnect door latch control cylinder rod at door lock cylinder. Disconnect door lock cylinder switch connector. Remove door lock cylinder from door. Before disassembling switch assembly, place reference mark on operating lever and door lock cylinder for installation reference.
2) Remove clip and operating lever from door lock cylinder. Note direction of disarm switch installation on door lock cylinder by noting location of switch wiring. Switch must be installed on door lock cylinder so switch wiring is in proper direction. Remove switch from door lock cylinder. To install, reverse removal procedure.

HOOD SWITCH

Removal & Installation – Disconnect negative battery cable. Locate hood switch on right side of fender apron. Remove switch bracket retainers. Unplug electrical connector. Remove switch. To install, reverse removal procedure.

RAP MODULE

Removal & Installation – Module is located above and to rear of left rear wheelwell. Disconnect negative battery cable. Remove trim panel. Remove control module bracket screws. Unplug 22-pin connector, then 26-pin connector. Separate control module from retaining bracket. To install, reverse removal procedure.

FORD
4-88

1999 ACCESSORIES & EQUIPMENT
Active Anti-Theft Systems – Explorer & Mountaineer (Cont.)

WIRING DIAGRAMS

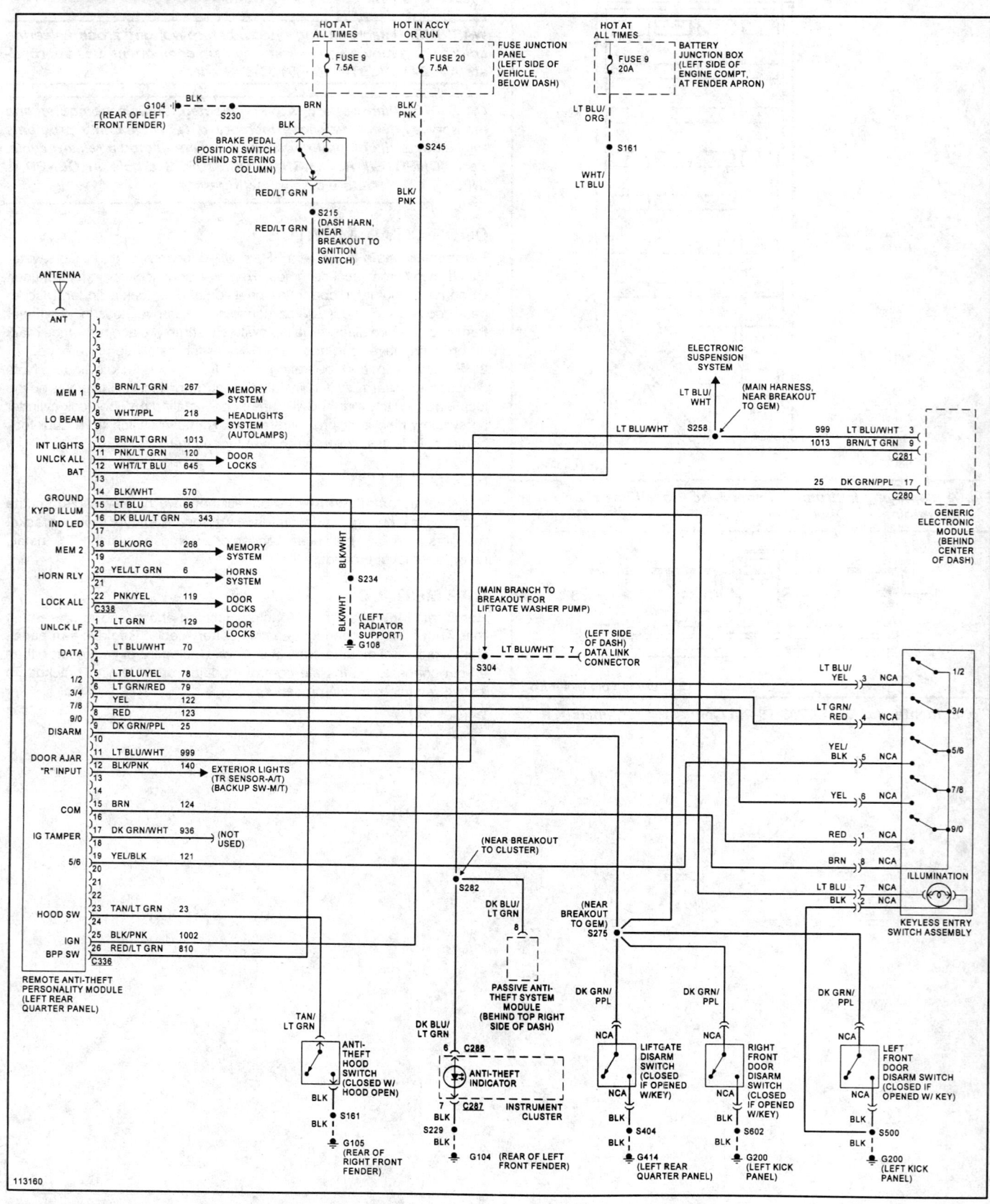

Fig. 9: Anti-Theft System Wiring Diagram (Explorer & Mountaineer)

WIRING DIAGRAMS

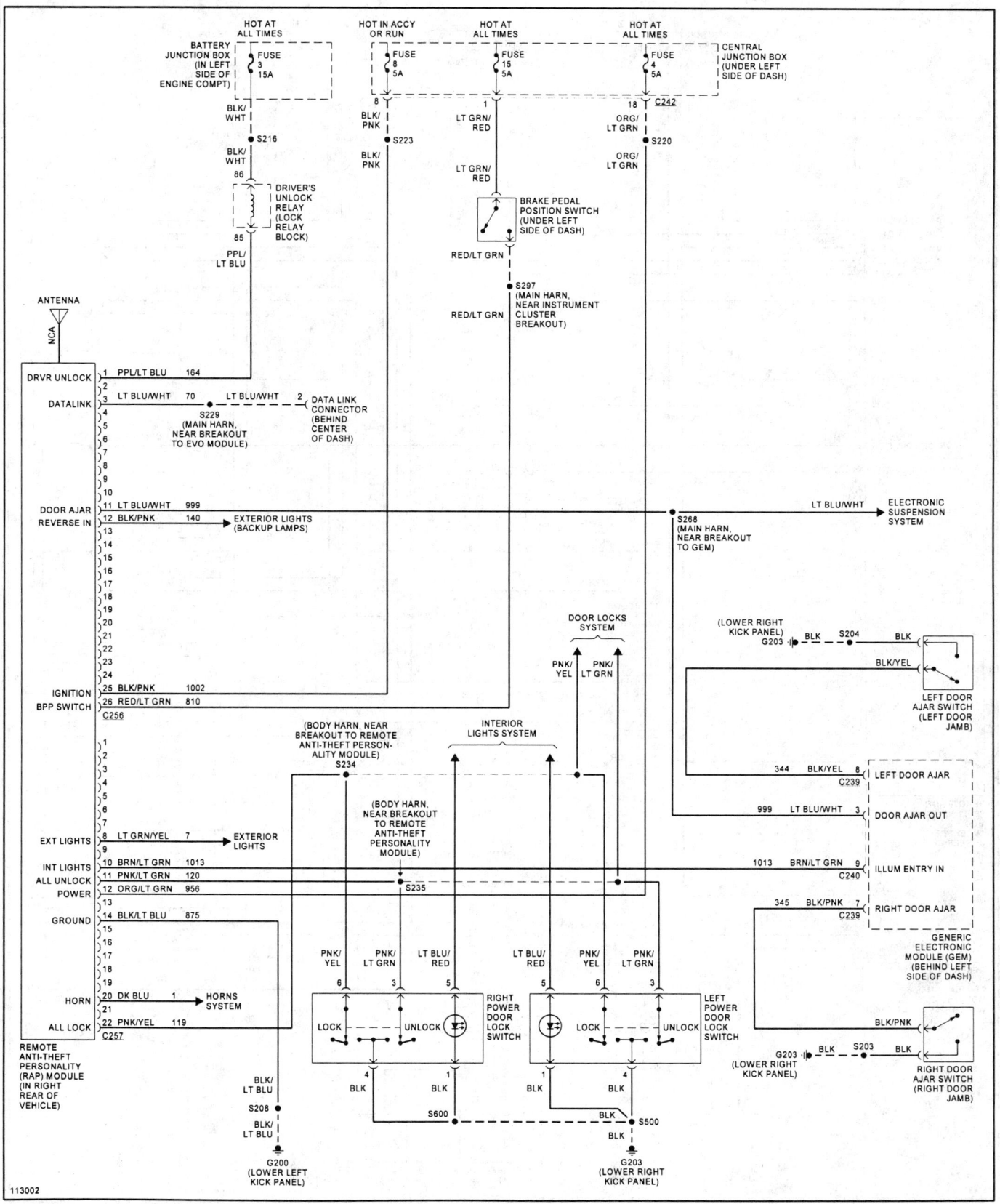

Fig. 1: Active Anti-Theft System Wiring Diagram (F150 & F250 Light-Duty Pickup)

113002

WIRING DIAGRAMS

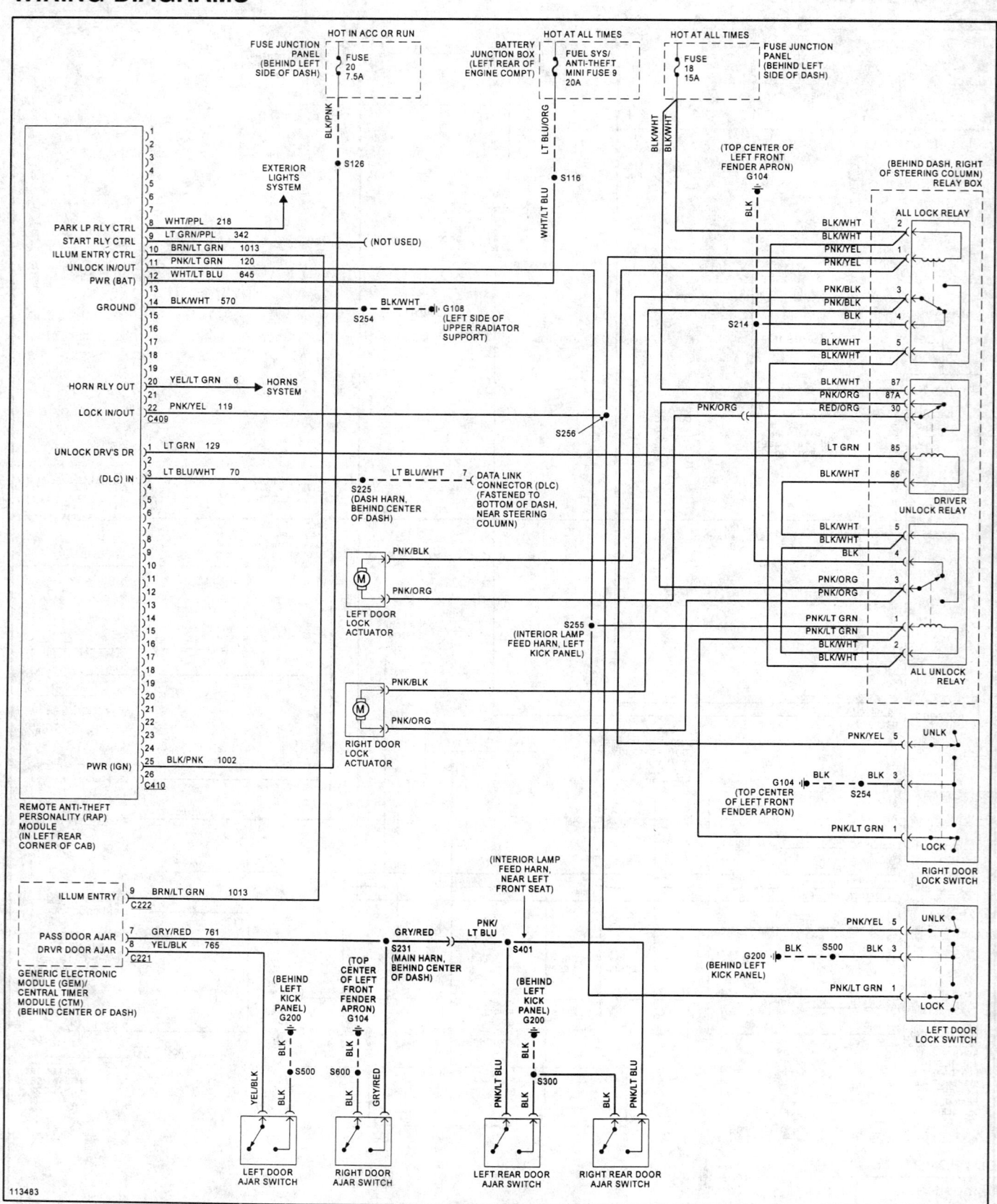

Fig. 1: Active Anti-Theft System Wiring Diagram (Ranger)

Active Anti-Theft Systems – Sable & Taurus

DESCRIPTION

WARNING: Deactivate air bag system before performing any service operation. See appropriate AIR BAG RESTRAINT SYSTEMS article. DO NOT apply electrical power to any component on steering column without first deactivating air bag system. Air bag may deploy.

The anti-theft system is designed to prevent unauthorized entry into engine compartment, passenger doors or luggage compartment. When alarm is triggered, horn sounds and headlights and taillights flash. This system does not enable/disable engine from starting but may be used in conjunction with the passive anti-theft system. Some system functions may also tie in with remote keyless entry system.

When armed, unauthorized entry is detected by the door ajar switches located in each door, a lock tamper detection switch in the trunk lid lock cylinder and a hood tamper switch on left fender panel. An alarm light is located on the instrument panel.

When triggered, system flashes the low beam headlights, parking lights, taillights and alarm indicator light. Models with an electronic door lock system have a PANIC feature that operates in conjunction with the anti-theft system and remote keyless entry system. When the PANIC button on the remote transmitter is pushed, horn will sound and the exterior lights will flash.

OPERATION

ARMING SYSTEM

There are 4 ways to arm the system once the ignition switch is turned to LOCK position:

- Press remote transmitter once to lock doors.
- Press 7/8 and 9/0 buttons on keyless entry keypad at the same time to lock doors.
- Open a door and press power door lock button to lock doors.
- Turn key to LOCK position in driver's or passenger's door to activate central lock feature.

DISARMING AN UNTRIGGERED SYSTEM

Unlock driver's or passenger's door using key, enter keyless entry code, press unlock button on remote transmitter or turn ignition switch to RUN or ACC position.

TRIGGERING SYSTEM

Alarm will sound when any of the following actions occur with alarm armed:

- Any door is opened without first using key, keyless entry code or remote transmitter.
- Trunk lid or liftgate lock cylinder is tampered or removed.
- Hood is opened.

Within 2-4 minutes, horns and lights will shut off automatically. System will then reset to an armed state and will trigger again if another intrusion occurs.

DISARMING A TRIGGERED SYSTEM

Unlock driver, passenger door or luggage compartment with key, or unlock driver's door using keyless entry code or remote transmitter. Turn ignition switch to RUN or ACC position. Press PANIC button on remote transmitter.

COMPONENT LOCATIONS

COMPONENT LOCATIONS

Component	Location
Data Link Connector	Under Instrument Panel, Below Steering Column
Generic Electronic Module	Attached To Under Side Of Instrument Panel Fuse Box

COMPONENT LOCATIONS (Cont.)

Component	Location
Liftgate Interface Module	Left Side Of Cargo Area, On Anti-Theft Disarm Switch
Passive Anti-Theft System Module	Behind Center Of Instrument Panel, Behind Integrated Control Panel
Powertrain Control Module	On Right Side Of Firewall In Engine Compartment
Remote Anti-Theft Personality Module	Above Accelerator Pedal

PROGRAMMING

ENABLING & DISABLING FEATURES ON REMOTE ANTI-THEFT PERSONALITY MODULE

Enable/disable mode allows technician to set alarm configuration to match the laws for alarm operation in the country where vehicle is to be driven. Enable/disable mode will also enable/disable autolock. Alarm configurations are set by assembly plant for regulations in expected destination and should not be modified for use in other countries. Remote keyless entry transmitter PANIC will share exterior lights and horn characteristics. PANIC alarm will also turn on interior lights in all cases for 25 seconds.

NOTE: Step 2) must be completed within 30 seconds of turning ignition switch to RUN position in step 1). While in enable/disable mode, RAP module will not have any other functionality except enabling/disabling features. Enabling a new alarm configuration will automatically disable previous alarm configuration.

1) Ensure anti-theft system is not armed or triggered. Turn ignition switch to LOCK position. Close all doors. Turn ignition switch from LOCK to RUN position.

2) Press power door UNLOCK button 3 times. Turn ignition switch from RUN to LOCK position. Press power door UNLOCK button 3 times. Turn ignition switch back to RUN position. If enable/disable mode has been entered successfully, horn will chirp.

3) Press power door UNLOCK button number of times associated with function you would like to enable or disable as shown in table. See ENABLE/DISABLE FUNCTIONS table. Press power door LOCK button once after last UNLOCK button press in order to enter enable/disable code. System will confirm altered function by chirping horn same number of times as number of unlock presses registered. If function has been enabled, a long horn sound will follow sequence of horn chirps. If function has been disabled, no horn sound will follow sequence of horn chirps.

4) After horn chirp sequence has occurred in enable/disable mode, another function may be enabled or disabled. To exit enable/disable mode, turn ignition switch to LOCK position or allow 5 minutes to pass after entering enable mode. After exiting, system will confirm exit with horn chirp if a function has been changed.

ENABLE/DISABLE FUNCTIONS

Function	Press Unlock Button
Autolock/Relock	1 Time
North America/Gulf Coast/Korea Alarm [1]	5 Times
Europe/Australia Alarm [1]	6 Times

[1] – Locations not listed use North America standards.

TROUBLE SHOOTING

Before performing any tests on anti-theft system, check the following items to eliminate common problems:

- Damaged trunk or door lock cylinder.
- Blown fuse(s).
- Loose or corroded connections.
- Damaged wiring harness.
- Damaged relay(s).

FORD
4-92

1999 ACCESSORIES & EQUIPMENT
Active Anti-Theft Systems – Sable & Taurus (Cont.)

- Damaged anti-theft control module.
- Horn, headlights, hazard flashers, interior lights, trunk lights, power door locks and remote keyless entry system operation.

COMPONENT TESTS

DOOR LOCK SWITCH TEST

Remove door lock switch. Measure resistance between switch terminals. With switch in neutral position, resistance should be 25 k/ohms or greater. With switch in unlock position, resistance should be less than 200 ohms. Replace switch if resistance is not within specification.

SELF-DIAGNOSTIC SYSTEM

Connect New Generation Star (NGS) tester to Data Link Connector (DLC), located beneath instrument panel. Using NGS tester, perform data link diagnostics test. See DATA LINK DIAGNOSTIC TEST under COMMUNICATION NETWORK DIAGNOSTICS in MODULE COMMUNICATIONS NETWORK – SABLE & TAURUS article. If NGS tester responds with CKT914, CKT915 or CKT70=ALL ECUS NO RESP/NOT EQUIP, repair module communications concern. See MODULE COMMUNICATIONS NETWORK – SABLE & TAURUS article. If NGS tester displays NO RESP/NOT EQUIP for Generic Electronic Module (GEM), perform TEST G: NO COMMUNICATION WITH GENERIC ELECTRONIC MODULE under SYSTEM TESTS. If NGS tester displays NO RESP/NOT EQUIP for Remote Anti-Theft Personality (RAP), perform TEST A: NO COMMUNICATION WITH REMOTE ANTI-THEFT PERSONALITY MODULE under SYSTEM TESTS.

If NGS tester responds with SYSTEM PASSED, retrieve and record continuous DTCs. Erase continuous DTCs. Using NGS tester, perform GEM and RAP module self-test. Perform appropriate test in accordance with DTC retrieved. See GENERIC ELECTRONIC MODULE DTC INDEX and/or REMOTE ANTI-THEFT PERSONALITY MODULE DTC INDEX table. Codes listed in these table are only for testing covered in this article. For complete DTC listing, see MODULE COMMUNICATIONS NETWORK – SABLE & TAURUS article. If no DTCs are retrieved, repair by symptom. See SYMPTOM CHART table under SYSTEM TESTS.

REMOTE ANTI-THEFT PERSONALITY MODULE DTC INDEX

DTC [1]	Description	Test
B1522	Hood Switch Circuit Short To Ground	DTC B1522
B1562	Door Lock Cylinder Circuit Short To Ground	DTC B1562

[1] – Codes listed in this table are only for testing covered in this article. For complete DTC listing, see MODULE COMMUNICATIONS NETWORK – SABLE & TAURUS article.

GENERIC ELECTRONIC MODULE DTC INDEX

DTC [1]	Description	Test
B1342	ECU Failure	[2]

[1] – Codes listed in this table are only for testing covered in this article. For complete DTC listing, see MODULE COMMUNICATIONS NETWORK – SABLE & TAURUS article.

[2] – Using NGS tester, retrieve and document all continuous. Perform Generic Electronic Module (GEM) self-test. If DTC B1342 is retrieved again, replace GEM.

DIAGNOSTIC TESTS

DTC B1522: HOOD SWITCH CIRCUIT SHORT TO GROUND

1) Turn ignition switch to LOCK position. Connect New Generation Star (NGS) tester to Data Link Connector (DLC). On sedans, close trunk lid. On all models, turn ignition switch to RUN position. Using NGS tester, monitor RAP module PID HOOD_SW. Ensure hood is closed. Read PID while opening and closing hood. If PID always indicates PUNCHED, go to step **4)**. If PID does not always indicate PUNCHED, go to step **4)**.

2) Disconnect Remote Anti-Theft Personality (RAP) module harness connector C253. Measure resistance between ground and terminal No. 23 (Tan/Light Green wire) at RAP module harness connector C253. See Fig. 1. If resistance is 5 ohms or less, go to next step. If resistance is greater than 5 ohms, replace RAP module.

3) Disconnect hood tamper switch harness connector C111. On sedans, disconnect trunk lid anti-theft switch harness connector C473. On all models, measure resistance between ground and terminal No. 23 (Tan/Light Green wire) at RAP module harness connector C253. On all models if resistance is 10 k/ohms or less, repair short to ground in Tan/Light Green wire and/or White/Violet wire. See WIRING DIAGRAMS. On station wagons if resistance is greater than 10 k/ohms, replace hood tamper switch. On sedans if resistance is greater than 10 k/ohms, go to step **7)**.

4) Disconnect hood tamper switch harness connector C111. Disconnect RAP module harness connector C253. Measure resistance in Tan/Light Green wire between terminal No. 23 at RAP module harness connector C253 and hood tamper switch connector C111. See Fig. 1. If resistance is 5 ohms or less, go to next step. If resistance is greater than 5 ohms, repair open in Tan/Light Green wire.

5) Measure resistance between ground and Black wire terminal at hood tamper switch harness connector C111. If resistance is 5 ohms or less, go to next step. If resistance is greater than 5 ohms, repair open in Black wire.

6) Ensure hood is opened. Measure resistance between hood tamper switch terminals (component side). If resistance is 5 ohms or less, replace RAP module. If resistance is greater than 5 ohms, replace hood tamper switch.

7) Measure resistance between trunk lid anti-theft switch terminals (component side) with switch plunger fully pressed. If resistance is greater than 10 k/ohms, replace hood tamper switch. If resistance is 10 k/ohms or less, replace trunk lid anti-theft switch.

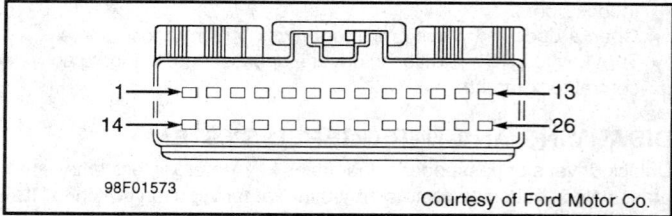

98F01573 Courtesy of Ford Motor Co.

Fig. 1: Identifying RAP Module Harness Connector C253 & GEM Harness Connector C248 Terminals

DTC B1562: DOOR LOCK CYLINDER CIRCUIT SHORT TO GROUND

NOTE: If RAP module receives a shorted door switch signal, module will disarm system. Even when valid arming sequence is entered, system will immediately disarm as soon as system is armed.

1) Turn ignition switch to LOCK position. Connect New Generation Star (NGS) tester to Data Link Connector (DLC). Using NGS tester, monitor RAP module PID DR_DARM while turning key in driver's door lock to UNLOCK and LOCK positions. If PID always indicates ACTIVE, go to next step. If PID always indicates NOTACT, go to step **3)**. If PID indicates ACTIVE when key is turned and NOTACT when key is not turned, go to step **4)**.

2) Using NGS tester, monitor Generic Electronic Module (GEM) PID CDR_ULK. Turn key in each door lock cylinder and liftgate to UNLOCK position. Read PID after each lock cylinder is turned. Each turn to UNLOCK position should change state of PID to ACTIVE. If PID responds as specified, replace RAP module. If PID does not respond as specified, repair appropriate door lock circuit. See appropriate wiring diagram in POWER DOOR LOCKS & TRUNK RELEASE article.

3) Using NGS tester, monitor GEM PID CDR_ULK while turning each door lock cylinder to LOCK and UNLOCK positions. If PID always indicates ACTIVE, go to next step. If PID always indicates NOTACT,

1999 ACCESSORIES & EQUIPMENT
Active Anti-Theft Systems – Sable & Taurus (Cont.)

**FORD
4-93**

repair appropriate door lock circuit. See appropriate wiring diagram in POWER DOOR LOCKS & TRUNK RELEASE article.

4) Disconnect Remote Anti-Theft Personality (RAP) module harness connector C253. Measure resistance between ground and terminal No. 9 (Pink/White wire) at RAP module harness connector C253 while turning door lock cylinders to UNLOCK position. If resistance is 5 ohms or less, replace RAP module. If resistance is greater than 5 ohms, repair open in Pink/White wire(s).

SYSTEM TESTS

SYMPTOM CHART

Symptom	Test
No Communication With Remote Anti-Theft Personality Module	A
Alarm System Does Not Arm Or Disarm Properly	B
Alarm System Does Not Disarm After Activation	C
Alarm Indicator Does Not Turn On To Indicate Arming	D
Horn, Headlights/Exterior Lights Always On	E
System Activates Falsely	F
No Communication With Generic Electronic Module	G

TEST A: NO COMMUNICATION WITH REMOTE ANTI-THEFT PERSONALITY MODULE

1) Remove fuse No. 23 (5-amp) from instrument panel fuse box. Measure resistance between ground and output side of fuse No. 23. If resistance does not start at greater than one megohm and drop steadily to less than 3 k/ohms, go next step. If resistance starts at greater than one megohm and drops steadily to less than 3 k/ohms, go to step **7)**.

2) Using same setup as in step **1)**, recheck resistance. If resistance is 10 ohms or less, go to next step. If resistance is greater than 10 ohms, go to step **7)**.

3) Disconnect Generic Electronic Module (GEM) from back of instrument panel fuse box (connector C201). Disconnect then reconnect ohmmeter as in step **1)**. If resistance does not start at greater than one megohm (it may drop steadily to less than 3 k/ohms), go to next step. If resistance starts at greater than one megohm (it may drop steadily to less than 3 k/ohms), replace GEM.

4) Disconnect instrument panel fuse box harness connector C247. Measure resistance between ground and output side of fuse No. 23. If resistance is 10 k/ohms or less, replace instrument panel fuse box. If resistance is greater than 10 k/ohms and equipped with Passive Anti-Theft System (PATS), connect GEM and instrument panel fuse harness connector C247 and go to next step. If resistance is greater than 10 k/ohms and not equipped with Passive Anti-Theft System (PATS), go to step **6)**.

5) Disconnect Passive Anti-Theft System (PATS) module harness connector C242. Disconnect and reconnect ohmmeter as in step **1)**. If resistance does not start at greater than one megohm and drop steadily to less than 3 k/ohms, go next step. If resistance starts at greater than one megohm and drops steadily to less than 3 k/ohms, replace PATS module.

6) Disconnect Remote Anti-Theft Personality (RAP) module harness connector C254. Disconnect and reconnect ohmmeter as in step **1)**. If resistance is greater than one megohm, replace RAP module. Is resistance is one megohm or less, repair short to ground in White/Yellow wire.

7) Disconnect Remote Anti-Theft Personality (RAP) module harness connector C254. Measure resistance between ground and terminal No. 14 (Black/White wire) at RAP module harness connector C254. *See Fig. 2*. If resistance is 5 ohms or less, go to next step. If resistance is greater than 5 ohms, repair open in Black/White wire.

8) Disconnect RAP module harness connector C253. Turn ignition switch to RUN position. Measure voltage at terminal No. 25 (Black/Pink wire) at RAP module harness connector C253. *See Fig. 1*. If battery voltage does not exist, go to next step. If battery voltage exists, repair module communications concern. See MODULE COMMUNICATIONS NETWORK – SABLE & TAURUS article.

9) Remove fuse No. 20 (5-amp) from instrument panel fuse box. Inspect fuse. If fuse is okay, repair open in Black/Pink wire. If fuse is blown, repair short to ground in Black/Pink wire.

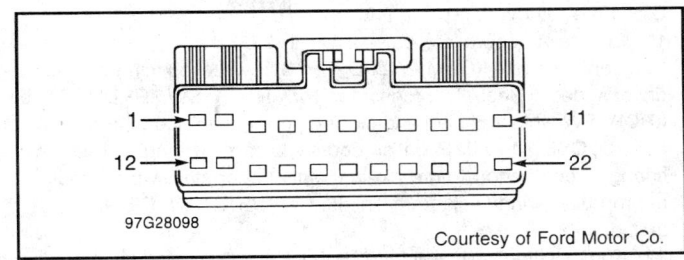

97G28098   Courtesy of Ford Motor Co.

Fig. 2: Identifying RAP Module Harness Connector C254 & GEM Harness Connector C223 Terminals

TEST B: ALARM SYSTEM DOES NOT ARM OR DISARM PROPERLY

1) Lock and unlock doors using the driver's door lock switch and key in door lock cylinder. If door locks operate properly, go to next step. If door locks do not operate properly, repair power door locks as necessary. See appropriate wiring diagram in POWER DOOR LOCKS & TRUNK RELEASE article.

2) Lock and unlock doors using remote transmitter and keyless entry keypad. If door locks operate properly, go to next step. If door locks do not operate properly, repair remote keyless entry system as necessary. See appropriate wiring diagram in REMOTE KEYLESS ENTRY SYSTEMS article.

3) Open driver's door window. Arm system by pressing LOCK button on remote transmitter. If THEFT indicator does not light, wait 45 seconds after all doors are closed and locked. System may still arm, but indicator may not be working. Reaching through open window, open door to trigger alarm. If the system armed and triggered, go to next step. If system did not arm and trigger, go to step **8)**.

4) Confirm system is disarmed by pressing UNLOCK button on remote transmitter. Arm system by pressing LOCK on door lock switch and closing door. Observe THEFT indicator. If system armed, go to next step. If system does not arm, go to step **8)**.

5) Confirm system is disarmed by pressing UNLOCK button on remote transmitter. Ensure all doors, liftgate, trunk and hood are closed. Using key, turn driver's door lock cylinder to LOCK position. Observe THEFT indicator. If system armed and equipped with keypad, go to next step. If system armed and not equipped with keypad, go to step **7)** . On all models if system did not arm, go to step **8)**.

6) Confirm system is disarmed by pressing UNLOCK button on remote transmitter. Arm system by pressing 7/8 and 9/0 buttons on keypad at same time. Observe THEFT indicator. If system armed, go to next step. If system did not arm, go to step **8)**.

7) If THEFT indicator illuminated when system armed and flashed when system triggered during steps 3)- 6), system is operating properly. If THEFT indicator did not illuminate when system armed or flash when system triggered during steps 3)-6), perform TEST D: ALARM INDICATOR DOES NOT TURN ON TO INDICATE ARMING.

8) Turn ignition switch to LOCK position. Connect New Generation Star (NGS) tester to Data Link Connector (DLC). Using NGS tester, monitor Remote Anti-Theft Personality (RAP) module PID DOORRAP. Close all doors and liftgate. PID should indicate CLOSED. Open any door. PID should indicate AJAR. If PID always indicates AJAR, go to next step. If PID always indicates CLOSED, go to step **11)**. If PID is as specified, go to step **14)**.

9) Ensure all doors and liftgate are closed and ignition switch is in LOCK position. Disconnect RAP module harness connector C253. Disconnect Generic Electronic Module (GEM) harness connector C248. Measure resistance between ground and terminal No. 11 (Light Blue/White wire) at RAP module harness connector C253. *See Fig. 1*. If resistance is greater than 10 k/ohms, go to next step. If resistance is 10 k/ohms or less, repair short to ground in Light Blue/White wire.

10) Connect GEM harness connector C248. Turn ignition switch to RUN position. Ensure all doors are closed. Using NGS tester, perform GEM

FORD
4-94

1999 ACCESSORIES & EQUIPMENT
Active Anti-Theft Systems – Sable & Taurus (Cont.)

self-test. If DTC B1322, B1330, B1334, B1338 and/or B1574 is retrieved, repair appropriate circuit. See MODULE COMMUNICATIONS NETWORK – SABLE & TAURUS article for description of codes. If no DTCs are retrieved, replace RAP module.

11) Ensure all doors are closed. Using NGS tester, monitor Generic Electronic Module (GEM) PID D_DR_SW while opening and closing driver's door. Repeat process for PID R_DR_SW, RRDR_SW and LRDR_SW while opening and closing appropriate door. If PID changed from CLOSED to AJAR on all doors, go to next step. If PID did not change, repair short to ground in suspect door ajar switch circuit. See appropriate wiring diagram in ILLUMINATION/INTERIOR LIGHTS article.

12) Turn ignition switch to LOCK position. Disconnect RAP module harness connector C253. Disconnect GEM harness connector C248. Measure resistance in Light Blue/White wire between terminal No. 11 at RAP module harness connector C253 and terminal No. 2 at GEM harness connector C248. See Fig. 1. If resistance is 25 ohms or less, go to next step. If resistance is greater than 25 ohms, repair open in Light Blue/White wire.

13) Connect GEM harness connector C248. Open driver's door. Measure resistance between ground and terminal No. 11 (Light Blue/White wire) at RAP module harness connector C253. If resistance is 10 k/ohms or less, replace RAP module. If resistance is greater than 10 k/ohms, replace GEM.

14) Using NGS tester, monitor RAP PID IGN_RAP. With ignition switch in LOCK position, PID should indicate OFF. With ignition switch in RUN position, PID should indicate RUN/ACC. If PID always indicates RUN/ACC, go to next step. If PID always indicates OFF, go to step 16). If PID is as specified, go to step 17).

15) Turn ignition switch to LOCK position. Disconnect RAP module harness connector C253. Measure voltage at terminal No. 25 (Black/Pink wire) at RAP module harness connector C253. See Fig. 1. If voltage exists, repair short to voltage in Black/Pink wire. If no voltage exists, replace RAP module.

16) Turn ignition switch to RUN position. Measure voltage at terminal No. 25 (Black/Pink wire) at RAP module harness connector C253. If battery voltage exists, replace RAP module. If battery voltage does not exist, repair open in Black/Pink wire.

NOTE: *If RAP module receives a shorted door switch signal, module will disarm system. Even when valid arming sequence is entered, system will immediately disarm as soon as system is armed.*

17) Using NGS tester, monitor RAP module PID DR_DARM. PID should indicate NOTACT. Turn key in each door lock cylinder and liftgate to UNLOCK position. PID should indicate ACTIVE on each turn. If PID is as specified, go to next step. If PID is not as specified, perform DTC B1562: DOOR LOCK CYLINDER CIRCUIT SHORT TO GROUND under DIAGNOSTIC TESTS.

18) Using NGS tester, monitor RAP module PID DD_LOCK. Press front door lock switches to LOCK position. PID should indicate LOCK for each door lock switch. If PID is as specified, go to step 21). If PID is as specified, go to step 21).

19) Using NGS tester, monitor GEM PID DDLCK. Press front door lock switches to LOCK position. PID should indicate LOCK for each door lock switch. If PID is as specified, go to next step. If PID is not as specified, repair suspect power door lock circuit. See appropriate wiring diagram in POWER DOOR LOCKS & TRUNK RELEASE article.

20) Using NGS tester, select RAP active command DOOR LOCK CONTROL. Using a ohmmeter connected to ground, backprobe at terminal No. 22 (Pink/Yellow wire) at RAP module connector C254 while triggering DOOR LOCK CONTROL to ON. See Fig. 2. If resistance is greater than 10 k/ohms, replace RAP module. If resistance is 10 k/ohms or less, repair Pink/Yellow wire.

21) Using NGS tester, monitor RAP module PID DD_LOCK. Press front door lock switches to UNLOCK position. PID should indicate UNLOCK for each door lock switch. If PID is not as specified, go to next step. If PID is as specified, system operating properly.

22) Using NGS tester, select GEM PID DR_UNLK. Press front door lock switches to UNLOCK position. PID should indicate UNLOCK for each door lock switch. If PID is as specified, go to next step. If PID is not as specified, repair suspect power door lock circuit. See appropriate wiring diagram in POWER DOOR LOCKS & TRUNK RELEASE article.

23) Disconnect RAP module harness connector C254. Using NGS tester, select RAP active command DOOR LOCK CONTROL. Measure resistance between ground and terminal No. 11 (Pink/Light Green wire) at RAP module harness connector C254 while triggering DOOR LOCK CONTROL active command UNLOCK to ON. If resistance is 10 k/ohms or less, repair Pink/Light Green wire. If resistance is greater than 10 k/ohms, replace RAP module.

TEST C: ALARM SYSTEM DOES NOT DISARM AFTER ACTIVATION

1) Arm system using any method. Disarm system using UNLOCK button on keyless entry remote transmitter. If system did not disarm and/or THEFT indicator did not turn off, go to next step. If system disarmed and THEFT indicator turned off, go to step 3).

2) If door unlocked when disarming with keyless entry remote transmitter, replace RAP module. If door did not unlock when disarming with remote transmitter, repair remote keyless entry system as necessary. See appropriate wiring diagram in REMOTE KEYLESS ENTRY SYSTEMS article.

3) Arm system using any method. Disarm system by turning driver's door lock cylinder to UNLOCK position. Repeat disarm at each door, trunk and liftgate. If system did not disarmed and/or THEFT indicator did not turn off, go to next step. If system disarmed and THEFT indicator turned off, go to step 5).

4) Verify doors unlock when disarming alarm with door lock key. If doors unlocked when disarming with door lock key (all doors and liftgate), go to step 12). If doors did not unlock when disarming with door lock key, repair suspect power door lock circuit. See appropriate wiring diagram in POWER DOOR LOCKS & TRUNK RELEASE article.

5) If vehicle is not equipped with keyless entry keypad, go to step 7). Arm system using any method. Disarm system using keyless entry keypad. If system did not disarmed and/or THEFT indicator did not turn off, go to next step. If system disarmed and THEFT indicator turned off, go to step 7).

6) Attempt to unlock doors by entering keypad code. If doors unlocked when entering keypad code, replace RAP module. If doors did not unlock when entering keypad code, repair keyless entry system as necessary. See appropriate wiring diagram in REMOTE KEYLESS ENTRY SYSTEMS article.

7) Arm system using any available method. Disarm system by turning ignition switch to ACC or RUN position. If system did not disarm and/or THEFT indicator did not turn off, go to next step. If system disarmed and THEFT indicator turned off, go to step 11).

8) Using NGS tester, monitor RAP module PID IGN_RAP. With ignition switch in LOCK position, PID should indicates OFF. With ignition switch in RUN position, PID should indicate RUN/ACC. If PID always indicates RUN/ACC, go to next step. If PID always indicates OFF, go to step 10). If PID is as specified, system disarming is functioning properly.

9) Turn ignition switch to LOCK position. Disconnect RAP module harness connector C253. Measure voltage at terminal No. 25 (Black/Pink wire) at RAP module harness connector C253. See Fig. 1. If voltage exists, repair short to voltage in Black/Pink wire. If no voltage exists, replace RAP module.

10) Turn ignition switch to LOCK position. Disconnect RAP module harness connector C253. Turn ignition switch to RUN position. Measure voltage at terminal No. 25 (Black/Pink wire) at RAP module harness connector C253. See Fig. 1. If battery voltage exists, replace RAP module. If battery voltage does not exist, repair open in Black/Pink wire.

11) Using NGS tester, monitor RAP module PID DR_DARM. PID should indicate NOTACT. Turn key in each door lock cylinder and liftgate to UNLOCK position. PID should indicate ACTIVE on each turn. If PID always indicates ACTIVE, go to next step. If PID always indicates NOTACT, go to step 14). If PID is as specified, replace RAP module.

12) Turn ignition switch to LOCK position. Disconnect RAP module harness connector C253. Measure resistance between ground and terminal No. 9 (Pink/White wire) at RAP module connector C253. *See Fig. 1.* On station wagons if resistance is 10 k/ohms or less, go to next step. On sedans if resistance is 10 k/ohms or less, repair power door locks as necessary. See appropriate wiring diagram in POWER DOOR LOCKS & TRUNK RELEASE article. On all models if resistance is greater than 10 k/ohms, replace RAP module.

13) Disconnect liftgate interface module harness connector C498. Measure resistance between ground and terminal No. 9 (Pink/White wire) at RAP module harness connector C253. If resistance is 10 k/ohms or less, repair power door lock circuit as necessary. See appropriate wiring diagram in POWER DOOR LOCKS & TRUNK RELEASE article. If resistance is greater than 10 k/ohms, replace liftgate interface module.

14) Turn ignition switch to LOCK position. Disconnect RAP module harness connector C253. Measure resistance between ground and terminal No. 9 (Pink/White wire) at RAP module harness connector C253 as each door lock cylinder is turned to UNLOCK position. *See Fig. 1.* On all models if resistance is 5 ohms or less when each door lock cylinder is turned to UNLOCK position, replace RAP module. On station wagons if resistance is greater than 5 ohms when each door lock cylinder is turned to UNLOCK position, go to next step. On sedans if resistance is greater than 5 ohms when each door lock cylinder is turned to UNLOCK position, repair appropriate door lock switch circuit as necessary. See appropriate wiring diagram in POWER DOOR LOCKS & TRUNK RELEASE article.

15) Measure resistance between ground and terminal No. 9 (Pink/White wire) at RAP module harness connector C253 as liftgate lock cylinder is turned to UNLOCK position. If resistance is greater than 5 ohms when liftgate lock cylinder is turned to UNLOCK position, go to next step. If resistance is 5 ohms or less when liftgate lock cylinder is turned to UNLOCK position, replace RAP module.

16) Disconnect liftgate interface module harness connector C498. Measure resistance in Pink/White wire between terminal No. 9 at RAP module harness connector C253 and liftgate interface module harness connector C498. If resistance is 5 ohms or less, go to next step. If resistance is greater than 5 ohms, repair open in Pink/White wire.

17) Measure voltage at Dark Green wire terminal at liftgate interface module harness connector C498. If battery voltage exists, go to next step. If battery voltage does not exist, repair power distribution circuit as necessary. See appropriate wiring diagram in POWER DISTRIBUTION article in WIRING DIAGRAMS.

18) Measure resistance between ground and Black wire terminal at liftgate interface module harness connector C498. If resistance is 5 ohms or less, replace liftgate interface module. If resistance is greater than 5 ohms, repair open in Black wire.

TEST D: ALARM INDICATOR DOES NOT TURN ON TO INDICATE ARMING

CAUTION: DO NOT jumper battery voltage to THEFT indicator directly. THEFT indicator is an LED, not a bulb.

1) Connect New Generation Star (NGS) tester to Data Link Connector (DLC). Select Remote Anti-Theft Personality (RAP) module ACTIVE COMMAND mode. Trigger THEFT LED ALARM to ON. If THEFT indicator does not illuminate, go to next step. If THEFT indicator illuminates, system is operating properly.

2) Turn ignition switch to LOCK position. Disconnect instrument cluster harness connector C250. Measure voltage at terminal No. 6 (Dark Blue/Light Green wire) at instrument cluster harness connector C250 while triggering THEFT LED ALARM to ON. *See Fig. 3.* If voltage is 3 volts or less, go to next step. If voltage is greater than 3 volts, go to step **4)**.

3) Turn ignition switch to LOCK position. Disconnect RAP module harness connector C254. Measure resistance in Dark Blue/Light Green wire between terminal No. 16 at RAP module harness connector C254 and terminal No. 6 at instrument cluster harness connector C250. *See*

Figs. 2 and 3. If resistance is 3 ohms or less, replace RAP module. If resistance is greater than 3 ohms, repair open in Dark Blue/Light Green wire.

4) Remove THEFT indicator LED from instrument cluster. Measure resistance between THEFT indicator LED terminals. If resistance is 10-12 ohms, replace instrument cluster printed circuit. If resistance is not 10-12 ohms, replace THEFT indicator LED.

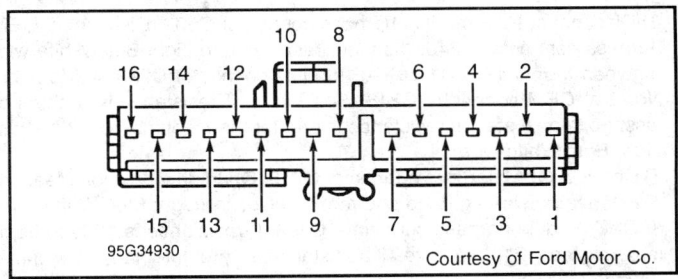

Fig. 3: Identifying Instrument Cluster Harness Connector C250 Terminals

TEST E: HORN, HEADLIGHTS/EXTERIOR LIGHTS ALWAYS ON

1) Disarm system by turning driver's door lock cylinder to UNLOCK position. If horn, headlights or exterior lights are still activated, go to next step. If horn, headlights or exterior lights are deactivated, system is functioning properly.

2) Disarm system using remote transmitter, keyless entry keypad and ignition switch. If horn is cycling or staying on constantly, go to next step. If horn is not cycling or staying on constantly, go to step **4)**.

3) Disconnect Remote Anti-Theft Personality (RAP) module harness connector C254. If horn is cycling or staying on constantly, repair horn circuit. See WIRING DIAGRAMS in STEERING COLUMN SWITCHES – SABLE & TAURUS article. If horn is not cycling or staying on constantly, replace RAP module.

4) Disarm system using remote transmitter, keyless entry keypad and ignition switch. If horn and headlights/exterior lights are cycling or staying on constantly, go to next step. If horn and headlights/exterior lights are not cycling or staying on constantly, system is operating properly.

5) Turn ignition switch to LOCK position. Disconnect Remote Anti-Theft Personality (RAP) module harness connector C254. If horn and headlights/exterior lights are cycling or staying on constantly, repair White/Violet and/or Dark Blue wire(s). If horn and headlights/exterior lights are not cycling or staying on constantly, system is operating properly.

TEST F: SYSTEM ACTIVATES FALSELY

1) Connect New Generation Star (NGS) tester to Data Link Connector (DLC). Enter Remote Anti-Theft Personality (RAP) module PID/DATA monitor and record mode. Select PID AL_EVT1 through AL_EVT8 to monitor last 8 events. Record all alarm events. If PID AL_EVT1 through AL_EVT8 show 2 door open (DROPEN) triggers, go to next step. If PID AL_EVT1 through AL_EVT8 does not show 2 door open (DROPEN) triggers, go to step **8)**.

2) Using NGS, monitor Generic Electronic Module (GEM) PID DOOR-RAP. Close all doors, liftgate and liftgate glass. PID should indicate CLOSED. Open each door, liftgate and liftgate glass separately. PID should indicate AJAR. If PID always indicates AJAR, go to next step. If PID always indicates CLOSED, go to step **5)**. If PID is as specified, check for intermittent problems.

3) Disconnect RAP module harness connector C253. Measure resistance between ground and terminal No. 11 (Light Blue/White wire) at RAP module harness connector C253. *See Fig. 1.* If resistance is greater than 10 k/ohms, go to next step. If resistance is 10 k/ohms or less, repair short to ground in Light Blue/White wire.

4) Close all doors. Using NGS tester, perform GEM self-test. If DTC B1322, B1330, B1334, B1338 and/or B1574 is retrieved, repair appropriate door ajar circuit short to ground. See MODULE COMMUNICA-

FORD
4-96

1999 ACCESSORIES & EQUIPMENT
Active Anti-Theft Systems – Sable & Taurus (Cont.)

TIONS NETWORK – SABLE & TAURUS article for description of codes. If no DTCs are retrieved, replace RAP module.

5) Using NGS tester, monitor GEM PID D_DR_SW while opening and closing driver's door. If PID state changed from CLOSED to AJAR, go to next step. If PID did not change, repair driver's door ajar switch circuit. See appropriate wiring diagram in ILLUMINATION/INTERIOR LIGHTS article.

6) Disconnect RAP module harness connector C253. Disconnect GEM harness connector C248. Measure resistance in Light Blue/White wire between terminal No. 11 at RAP module connector C253 and terminal No. 2 at GEM connector C248. See Fig. 1. If resistance is 5 ohms or less, go to next step. If resistance is greater than 5 ohms, repair open in Light Blue/White wire.

7) Connect GEM harness connector C248. Open driver's door. Measure resistance between ground and terminal No. 11 (Light Blue/White wire) at RAP module harness connector C253. If resistance is 10 k/ohms or less, replace RAP module. If resistance is greater than 10 k/ohms, replace GEM.

8) Check recorded alarm events. If PID AL_EVT1 through AL_EVT8 shows 2 hood tamper switch (HOODTR) triggers, go to next step. If PID AL_EVT1 through AL_EVT8 does not show 2 hood tamper switch (HOODTR) triggers, go to step **21)**.

NOTE: If front end cover (bra) is installed on vehicle, hood may not close far enough to fully depress hood tamper switch plunger.

9) Ensure hood is closed. On sedans, close trunk lid. On all models, monitor RAP module PID HOOD_SW using NGS tester while opening and closing hood. PID state should change from NOTPUN to PUNCHD. Attempt to move hood up and down while it is fully latched while observing PID. PID state should not change from NOTPUN. If PID always indicates NOTPUN, go to next step. If PID always indicates PUNCHD, go to step **18)**. On sedans if PID is as specified, go to step **14)**. On station wagons if PID is as specified, hood tamper switch is operating properly.

10) Disconnect RAP module harness connector C253. Disconnect hood tamper switch harness connector C111. Measure resistance in Tan/Light Green wire between terminal No. 23 at RAP module harness connector C253 and hood tamper switch harness connector C111. See Fig. 1. If resistance is 5 ohms or less, go to next step. If resistance is greater than 5 ohms, repair open in Tan/Light Green wire.

11) Measure resistance between hood tamper switch terminals (component side) with switch plunger fully extended. If resistance is 5 ohms or less, go to next step. If resistance is greater than 5 ohms, replace hood tamper switch.

12) Measure resistance between ground and Black wire terminal at hood tamper switch harness connector C111. If resistance is 5 ohms or less, go to next step. If resistance is greater than 5 ohms, repair open in Black wire.

13) Ensure hood is opened. Measure resistance between hood tamper switch terminals (component side). If resistance is 5 ohms or less, replace RAP module. If resistance is greater than 5 ohms, replace hood tamper switch.

14) Ensure hood and trunk are closed. Using NGS tester, monitor RAP module PID HOOD_SW. PID should indicate NOTPUN. Open trunk lid. PID should indicate PUNCHD. If PID always indicates NOTPUN, go to next step. If PID always indicates PUNCHD, go to step **18)**. If PID is as specified, hood tamper switch is operating properly.

15) Disconnect RAP module harness connector C253. Measure resistance between ground and terminal No. 23 (Tan/Light Green wire) at RAP module harness connector C253. See Fig. 1. If resistance is greater than 5 ohms, go to next step. If resistance is 5 ohms or less, replace RAP module.

16) Disconnect trunk lid anti-theft switch harness connector C473. Measure resistance between ground and Black wire terminal at trunk lid anti-theft switch harness connector C473. If resistance is 5 ohms or less, go to next step. If resistance is greater than 5 ohms, repair open in Black wire.

17) Ensure trunk lid is open. Measure resistance between trunk lid anti-theft switch terminals (component side). If resistance is 5 ohms or

less, repair White/Purple wire between trunk lid anti-theft switch and splice S421 (located in main wiring harness, near brake pedal position switch). If resistance is greater than 5 ohms, replace trunk lid anti-theft switch.

18) Turn ignition switch to LOCK position. Disconnect RAP module harness connector C253. On sedans, disconnect trunk lid anti-theft switch harness connector C473. On all models, disconnect hood tamper switch harness connector C111. Measure resistance between ground and Tan/Light Green wire terminal at hood tamper switch harness connector C111. If resistance is 10 k/ohms or less, go to next step. If resistance is greater than 10 k/ohms, repair short to ground in Tan/Light Green wire.

19) Measure resistance between hood tamper switch terminals (component side) with hood tamper switch plunger fully pressed. On sedans if resistance is greater than 10 k/ohms, go to next step. On station wagons if resistance is greater than 10 k/ohms, replace RAP module. On all models if resistance is 10 k/ohms or less, replace hood tamper switch.

20) Measure resistance between trunk lid anti-theft switch terminals (component side) with trunk lid anti-theft switch plunger fully pressed. If resistance is greater than 10 k/ohms, replace RAP module. If resistance is 10 k/ohms or less, replace trunk lid anti-theft switch.

NOTE: Remote entry transmitter PANIC alarm is not an anti-theft alarm trigger event. On occasion, a customer accidentally presses the PANIC button. If several PANIC codes appear in alarm history, this is more than likely the case. Customer may need to step closer to vehicle from where alarm was started to stop the alarm.

21) If false alarms are caused by accidental triggering by customer, system is okay. Clarify concern with customer. If necessary, return to SYMPTOM CHART. If false alarms are not caused by accidental triggering by customer, return to SYMPTOM CHART.

TEST G: NO COMMUNICATION WITH GENERIC ELECTRONIC MODULE

1) Remove fuse No. 23 from instrument panel fuse box. Measure resistance between ground and output side of fuse No. 23 in instrument panel fuse box. Resistance should start at greater than one m/ohm and drop steadily to less than 3 k/ohms. If resistance is not as specified, go to next step. If resistance is as specified, go to step **7)**.

2) If resistance in step **1)** read greater than 10 ohms, go to next step. If resistance in step **1)** read 10 ohms or less, go to step **4)**.

3) Remove Generic Electronic Module (GEM) from instrument panel fuse box. Disconnect and reconnect ohmmeter as in step **1)**. If resistance is not greater than one m/ohm (may drop steadily to less than 3 k/ohms), go to next step. If resistance is greater than one m/ohm (may drop steadily to less than 3 k/ohms), replace GEM.

4) Disconnect instrument panel fuse box harness connector C247. Measure resistance between ground and output side of fuse No. 23. If resistance is 10 k/ohms or less, replace instrument panel fuse box. If resistance is greater than 10 k/ohms and equipped with anti-theft system, connect instrument panel fuse box harness connector C247 and go to next step. If resistance is greater than 10 k/ohms and not equipped with anti-theft system, connect instrument panel fuse box harness connector C247 and go to step **7)**.

5) Disconnect Passive Anti-Theft System (PATS) module harness connector C242. Disconnect and reconnect ohmmeter as in step **1)**. If resistance does not read greater than one m/ohm and drops steadily to less than 3 k/ohms, go to next step. If resistance reads greater than one m/ohm and drops steadily to less than 3 k/ohms, replace PATS module.

6) Disconnect Remote Anti-Theft Personality (RAP) module harness connector C254. Disconnect and reconnect ohmmeter as in step **1)**. If resistance reads greater than one m/ohm, replace RAP module. If resistance reads one m/ohm or less, repair short to ground in White/Yellow wire between fuse No. 23 and RAP module.

7) Disconnect Generic Electronic Module (GEM) harness connector C248. Measure resistance between ground and terminals No. 14 and 25 (both Black wires) at GEM harness connector C248. See Fig. 1. If both

1999 ACCESSORIES & EQUIPMENT
Active Anti-Theft Systems – Sable & Taurus (Cont.)

FORD
4-97

resistance readings are 5 ohms or less, go to next step. If either resistance reading is greater than 5 ohms, repair open in appropriate wire(s).

8) Disconnect GEM harness connector C223. Measure resistance between ground and terminal No. 12 (Black/White wire) at GEM harness connector C223. *See Fig. 2*. If resistance is 5 ohms or less, go to next step. If resistance is greater than 5 ohms, repair open in Black/White wire.

9) Disconnect GEM harness connector C236. Turn ignition switch to RUN position. Measure voltage at terminal No. 14 (Red/Yellow wire) at GEM harness connector C236. *See Fig. 4*. If battery voltage does not exist, go to next step. If battery voltage exists, go to step **11)**.

10) Remove fuse No. 12 (5-amp) from instrument panel fuse box. Inspect fuse. If fuse tests okay, repair open in Red/Yellow wire between instrument panel fuse box and GEM. If fuse is blown, repair short to ground in Red/Yellow wire between instrument panel fuse box and GEM.

11) Measure resistance between ground and terminal No. 22 (Black/Light Green wire) at GEM harness connector C223. If resistance is 5 ohms or less, repair module communication concern. See MODULE COMMUNICATIONS NETWORK – SABLE & TAURUS article. If resistance is greater than 5 ohms, repair open in Black/Light Green wire.

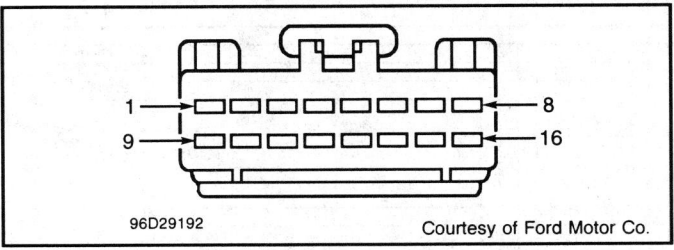

96D29192   Courtesy of Ford Motor Co.

Fig. 4: Identifying GEM Harness Connector C236 Terminals

REMOVAL & INSTALLATION

CAUTION: When battery is disconnected, vehicle computer and memory systems may lose memory data. Driveability problems may exist until computer systems have completed a relearn cycle. See COMPUTER RELEARN PROCEDURES article in GENERAL INFORMATION before disconnecting battery.

REMOTE ANTI-THEFT PERSONALITY (RAP) MODULE

Removal & Installation – Disconnect negative battery cable. Locate RAP module under left side of instrument panel, above brake pedal. Disengage clip retaining wiring harness to RAP module/relay box bracket. Remove screws securing relay box bracket-to-RAP module bracket. Remove relay box bracket. Remove 2 nuts, RAP module and bracket from dash panel. Insert small screwdriver or pick into RAP module mounting tab hole, pull up on mounting tab and remove RAP module from bracket. Unplug harness connectors. To install, reverse removal procedure.

ANTI-THEFT HOOD SWITCH

Removal & Installation – Disconnect negative battery cable. Locate anti-theft hood switch on left fenderwell. Disconnect switch connector. Remove retaining screws. Remove switch. To install, reverse removal procedure.

ANTI-THEFT DOOR LOCK SWITCH

Removal & Installation – Remove door trim and position water shield away from access holes. Disconnect and remove outside door handle. Disconnect door lock cylinder switch and remove 2 harness retaining clips from inner door. Remove door lock cylinder retainer. Disconnect door latch control cylinder rod at door lock cylinder. Remove door lock cylinder from door. Before disassembling switch assembly, place reference mark on operating lever and door lock cylinder for installation reference. Remove clip and operating lever from door lock cylinder. Note direction of disarm switch installation on door lock cylinder by noting location of switch wiring. Switch must be installed on door lock cylinder so switch wiring is in proper direction. Remove switch from door lock cylinder. To install, reverse removal procedure.

FORD
4-98

1999 ACCESSORIES & EQUIPMENT
Active Anti-Theft Systems – Sable & Taurus (Cont.)

WIRING DIAGRAMS

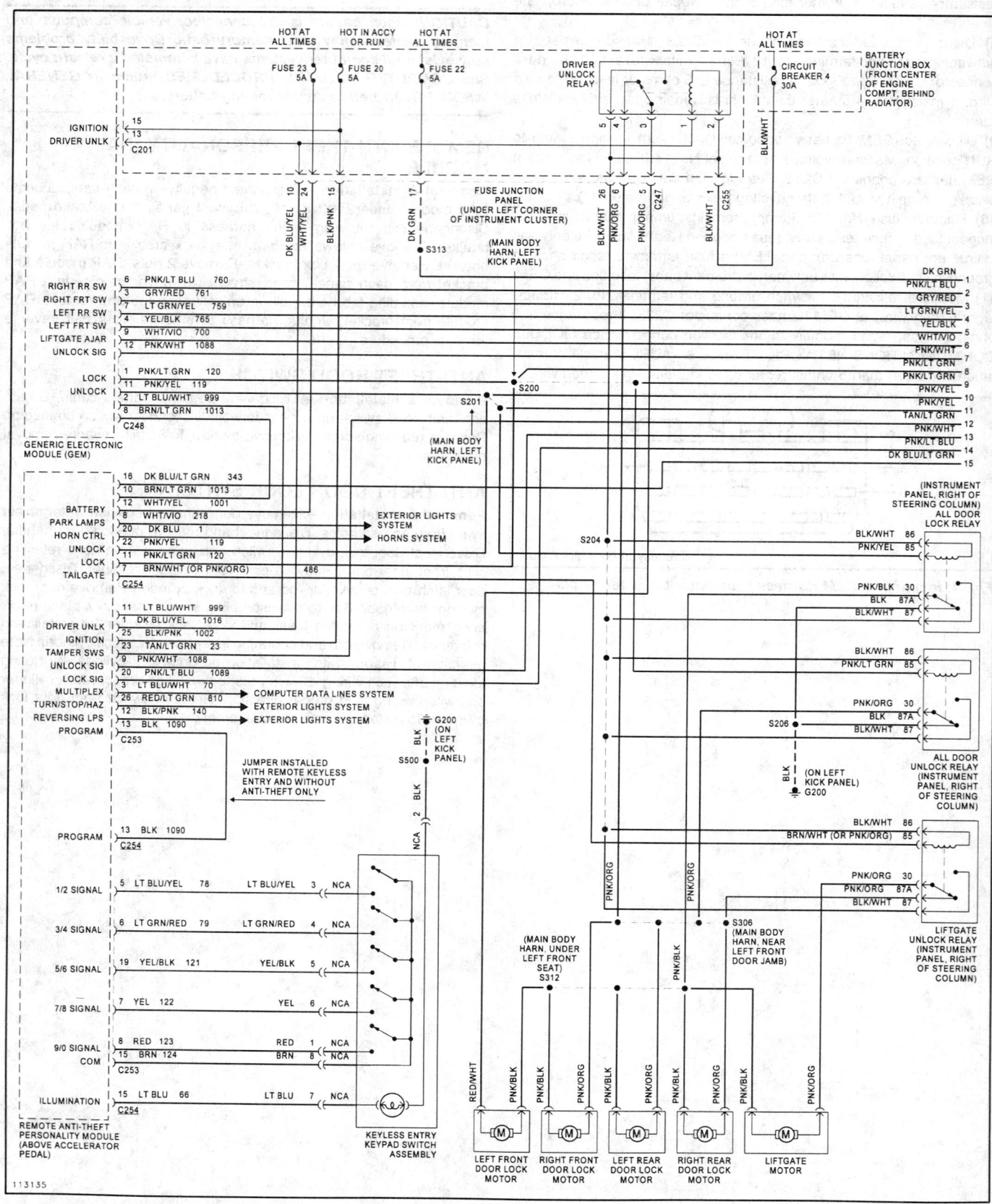

Fig. 5: Active Anti-Theft System Wiring Diagram (Sable & Taurus – 1 Of 2)

1999 ACCESSORIES & EQUIPMENT
Active Anti-Theft Systems – Sable & Taurus (Cont.)

FORD
4-99

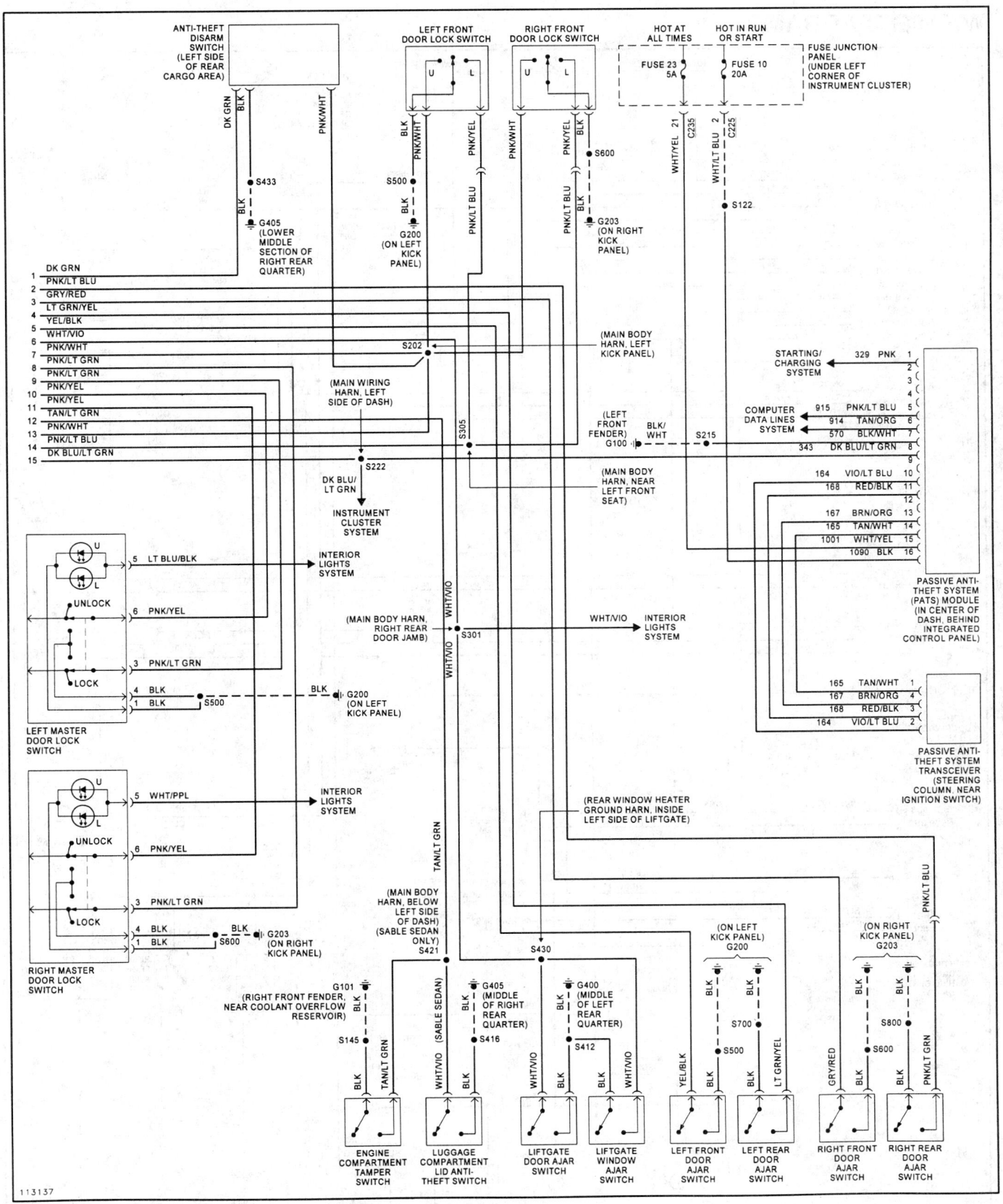

Fig. 6: Active Anti-Theft System Wiring Diagram (Sable & Taurus – 2 Of 2)

WIRING DIAGRAMS

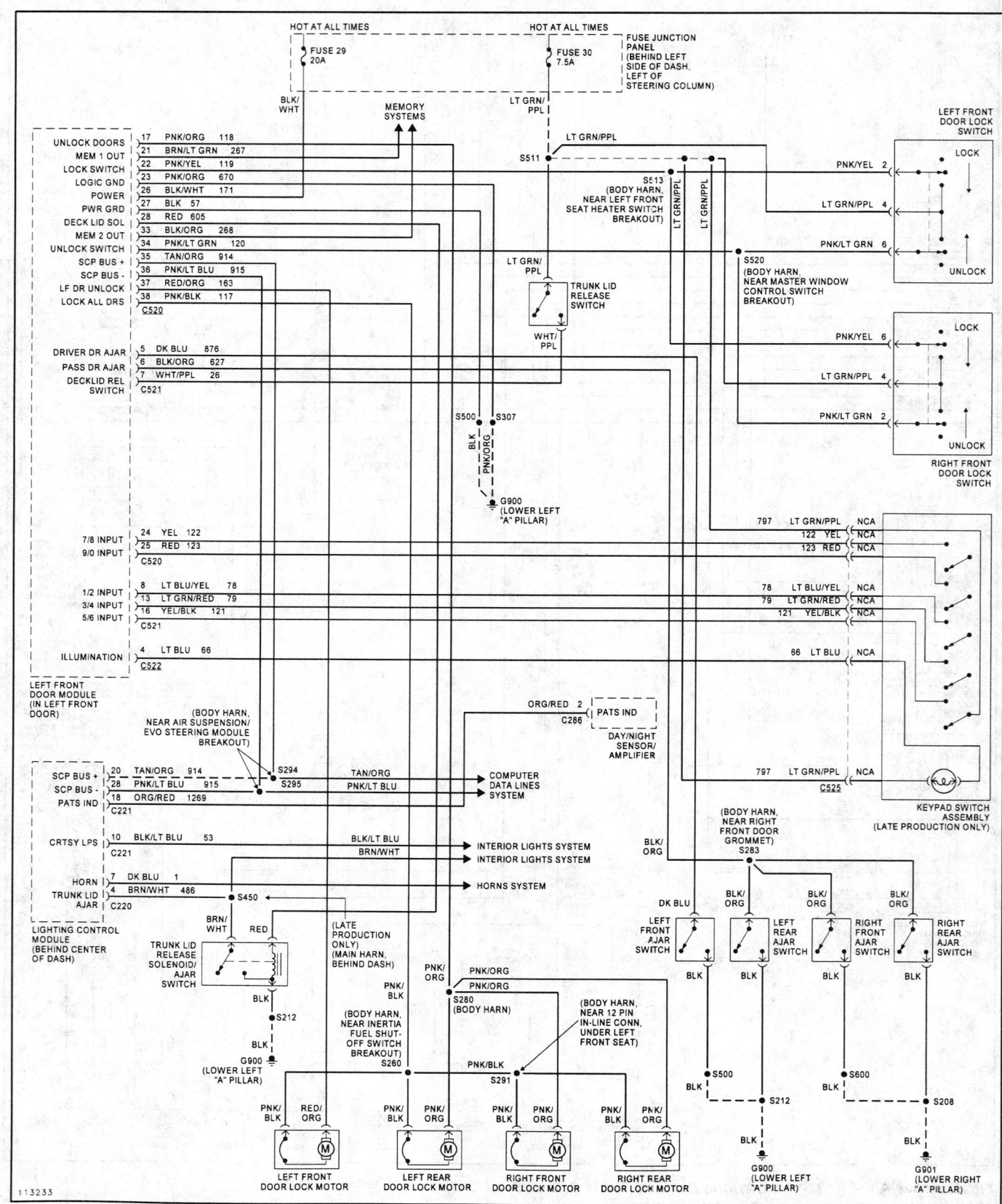

Fig. 1: Active Anti-Theft System Wiring Diagram (Town Car)

DESCRIPTION

When triggered, the anti-theft system horn sounds, headlights and taillights flash and starter is disabled. When armed, unauthorized entry is detected by the door ajar switches located in each door, a lock tamper detection switch in the liftgate lock cylinder, a hood switch on right front fenderwell, or the ignition lock cylinder tamper switch. A THEFT indicator light is located on left side of instrument panel.

Anti-theft components include Smart Entry Control (SEC) timer/module, body side door control module, power door lock switches, door ajar switches, ignition lock cylinder tamper switch, anti-theft relay, horn relay, starter relay and remote keyless entry transmitter.

Models with remote keyless entry and electronic door lock system have a PANIC feature that operates in conjunction with the anti-theft system and remote keyless entry system. When the PANIC button on the remote transmitter is pushed, the horns will sound and the exterior lights will flash.

OPERATION

ARMING SYSTEM

Use the following sequence to arm system. Turn ignition switch to OFF position. Remove key from ignition. Lock doors using vehicle key, power door lock switch or remote keyless entry transmitter. THEFT indicator will illuminate constantly for 30 seconds. After 30 seconds has passed, THEFT indicator will flash. System is now armed.

DISARMING SYSTEM

Unlock driver or passenger door using vehicle key or remote keyless entry transmitter. THEFT indicator will stop flashing and stay off.

TRIGGERING SYSTEM

Alarm will be activated if vehicle is entered without first using key or remote keyless entry transmitter. Within 2-3 minutes, horns and lights will shut off automatically. System will then reset to an armed state and will trigger again if another intrusion occurs. Vehicle starting system will remain disabled until system is disarmed.

DISARMING A TRIGGERED SYSTEM

Unlock any door or liftgate using vehicle key or remote keyless entry transmitter. Enter vehicle and use vehicle key to turn ignition switch to RUN position.

COMPONENT LOCATIONS

COMPONENT LOCATIONS

Component	Location
Anti-Theft Relay	Engine Compartment Relay Box
Data Link Connector (DLC)	Below Driver's Side Of Instrument Panel, To Right Of Steering Column
Engine Compartment Relay Box	Left Front Side Of Engine Compartment
Fuse Junction Panel	Below Left Side Of Instrument Panel
Inhibit Relay	Engine Compartment Relay Box
Horn Relay	Engine Compartment Relay Box
Power Distribution Box	In Engine Compartment, Next To Battery
Powertrain Control Module (PCM)	Behind Glove Box
Smart Entry Control (SEC) Timer/Module	Behind Center Top Of Dash Panel

TROUBLE SHOOTING

Verify customers complaint by operating anti-theft system. Check for damaged door lock cylinder or ignition cylinder. Check for open fuse(s). Check for loose anti-theft hood switch. Check door and trunk courtesy light switches. Check for loose or corroded connectors, damaged wiring harness, damaged switch(es) or faulty relay(s). Repair or replace components as necessary. If no problem is found, go to SYSTEM TESTS.

SYSTEM TESTS

CAUTION: When battery is disconnected or modules are replaced, vehicle computer and memory systems may lose memory data. Driveability problems may exist until computer systems have completed a relearn cycle. See COMPUTER RELEARN PROCEDURES article in GENERAL INFORMATION before disconnecting battery.

Before performing any tests on anti-theft system, perform TROUBLE SHOOTING. See SYMPTOM TEST DIRECTORY table to determine appropriate test according to symptom.

SYMPTOM TEST DIRECTORY

Symptom	Test
System Does Not Arm Or Disarm Properly	A
Engine Will Not Crank	B
THEFT Indicator Is Always On	C
THEFT Indicator Does Not Illuminate To Indicate Arming	D
System Does Not Disarm	E

TEST A: SYSTEM DOES NOT ARM OR DISARM PROPERLY

1) Use the door lock switch at each door to lock and unlock doors. If all door locks operate correctly, go to next step. If all door locks do not operate correctly, repair power door locks as necessary. See appropriate wiring diagram in POWER DOOR LOCKS article.

2) Remove key from ignition switch and close all doors. Press LOCK button on keyless entry remote transmitter. If system is arming correctly, doors will lock, horn will sound once, hazard lights will flash 2 times and THEFT indicator will illuminate for 30 seconds. If system is arming correctly, unlock doors and go to step **5)**. If system is not arming correctly, proceed as follows:

- If THEFT indicator does not illuminate, go to TEST D: THEFT INDICATOR DOES NOT ILLUMINATE TO INDICATE ARMING.
- If doors do not lock, see appropriate wiring diagram in REMOTE KEYLESS ENTRY SYSTEMS article.
- If horn does not sound, go to next step.

3) Sound horn by pressing horn button. If horn sounds, go to next step. If horn does not sound, see appropriate wiring diagram in STEERING COLUMN SWITCHES – VILLAGER article to continue diagnosis.

4) Turn ignition off. Remove horn relay (located in engine compartment relay box, next to battery). Disconnect Smart Entry Control (SEC) Timer/Module 12-pin connector C2032B (located behind center top of dash). Using an ohmmeter, check resistance between SEC timer/module 26-pin connector C2032B, terminal No. 6 (Yellow wire) and horn relay socket Yellow wire terminal. *See Fig. 1.* If resistance is less than 5 ohms, replace SEC timer/module. See SMART ENTRY CONTROL (SEC) TIMER/MODULE under REMOVAL & INSTALLATION. If resistance is 5 ohms or more, repair open in Yellow wire between SEC timer/module and horn relay. Retest system operation.

5) Close all doors. If courtesy lights dim out completely, go to next step. If courtesy lights do not dim out completely, fault is in courtesy light system. See appropriate wiring diagram in ILLUMINATION/INTERIOR LIGHTS article to continue diagnosis.

6) Attempt to arm, and then disarm the alarm using left door key lock switch, right door key lock switch, and the liftgate key lock switch. If any key lock switches do not arm and disarm system, go to next step. If any key lock switch arms and disarms system, go to step **9)**.

7) Disconnect left door key lock switch 4-pin connector C515 (located in center of left door). Check resistance of Red wire between left door key lock switch 4-pin connector C515 and SEC timer/module connector C2032B terminal No. 8. If resistance is less than 5 ohms, go to next step. If resistance is 5 ohms or more, repair open in Red wire between left door key lock switch and SEC timer/module.

8) Using a voltmeter, check voltage between ground and left door key lock switch 4-pin connector C515 Red/Black wire terminal. If voltage is more than 10 volts, replace SEC timer/module. Retest system operation. If voltage is 10 volts or less, repair Red/Black wire between left door key lock switch and SEC timer/module. Retest system operation.

9) Disconnect inoperative door key lock switch connector. Using a voltmeter, check voltage between ground and inoperative door key lock switch connector Red wire terminal. If voltage is more than 10 volts, go to next step. If voltage is 10 volts or less, repair Red wire between inoperative door key lock switch and SEC timer/module. Retest system operation.

10) Using a voltmeter, check voltage between ground and inoperative door key lock switch connector Red/Black wire terminal. If voltage is more than 10 volts, go to next step. If voltage is 10 volts or less, repair Red/Black wire between inoperative door key lock switch and SEC timer/module. Retest system operation.

11) Using an ohmmeter, check resistance between ground and inoperative door key lock switch connector Black wire terminal. If resistance is less than 5 ohms, replace inoperative door key lock switch and retest system operation. If resistance is 5 ohms or more, repair open in Black wire between inoperative door key lock switch and ground. Retest system operation.

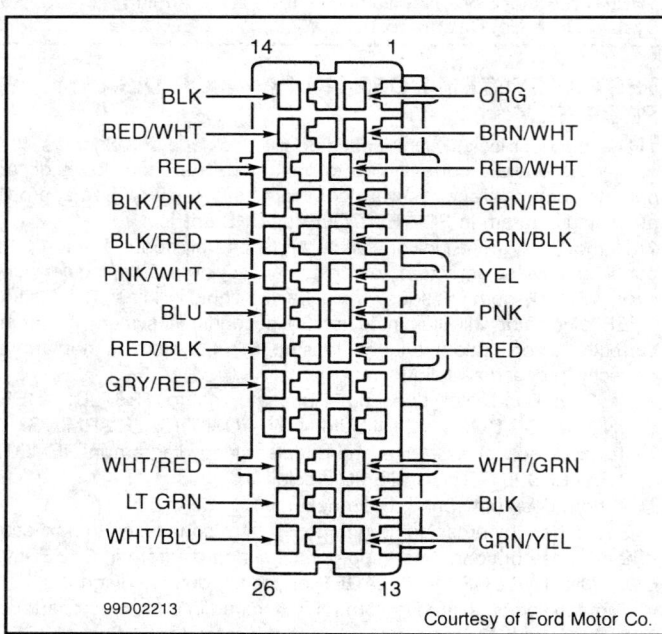

Fig. 1: Identifying Timer Module Connector C2032B Terminals

TEST B: ENGINE WILL NOT CRANK

1) Turn ignition off. Disconnect transmission range switch connector C161. Using an ohmmeter, check resistance between transmission range switch component C161 pins No. 2 (Light Green/Black wire) and No. 3 (Light Green wire) with gearshift lever in the following positions: See Fig. 2.

- In Park, resistance should be less than 5 ohms.
- In Neutral, resistance should be less than 5 ohms.
- In all other positions, resistance should be more than 10 k/ohms.

If resistance is not as specified, replace transmission range switch. If resistance is as specified, go to next step.

2) Remove anti-theft relay (located in engine compartment relay box, next to battery). Using an ohmmeter, check resistance between ground and anti-theft relay socket terminal No. 4 (center terminal, Light Green/

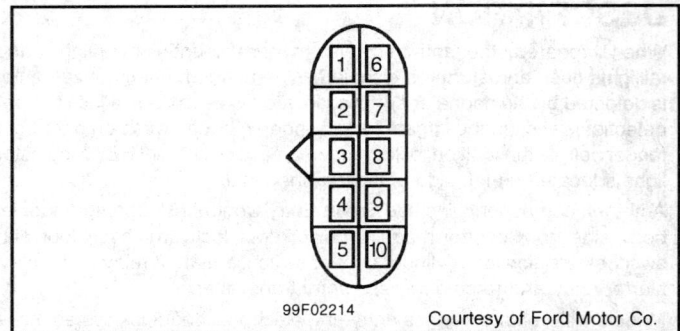

Fig. 2: Identifying Transmission Range Switch Component Pins

Black wire). Resistance should be more than 10 k/ohms. Check resistance of Light Green/Black wire between anti-theft relay connector terminal No. 4 (center terminal) and transmission range switch connector terminal No. 2. See Figs. 3 and 4. Resistance should be less than 5 ohms. If resistance is as specified, go to next step. If resistance is not as specified, repair short to ground or open in Light Green/Black wire between anti-theft relay and transmission range switch connector.

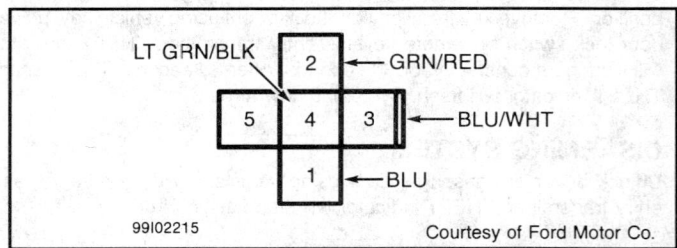

Fig. 3: Identifying Anti-Theft Relay Socket Terminals

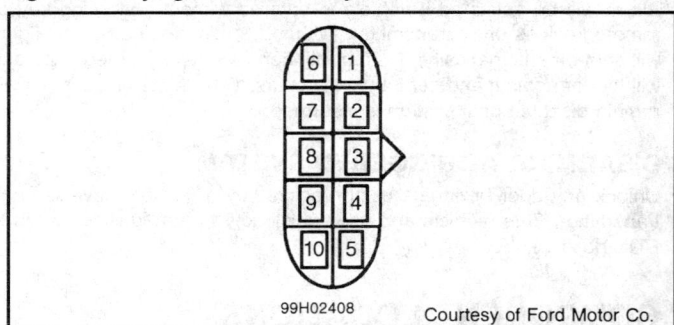

Fig. 4: Identifying Transmission Range Switch Connector Terminals

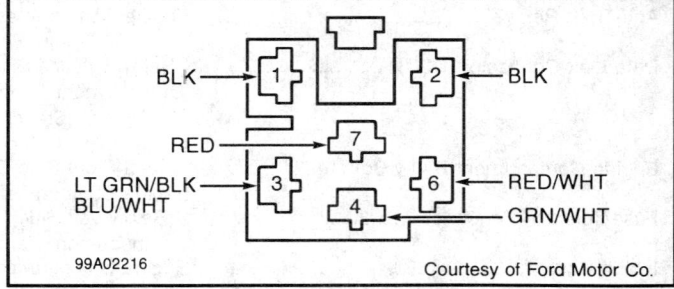

Fig. 5: Identifying Inhibit Relay Socket Terminals

3) Remove inhibit relay (located in engine compartment relay box, next to battery). Turn ignition on. Using a voltmeter, check voltage between ground and inhibit relay socket terminal No. 1 (Blue/White wire). See Fig. 5. If voltage is 10 volts or less, go to next step. If voltage is more than 10 volts, go to step **8)**.

4) Check voltage between ground and anti-theft relay terminal No. 2 (Green/Red wire). *See Fig. 3.* If voltage is more than 10 volts, go to next step. If voltage is 10 volts or less, repair open Green/Red wire.

5) Leave ignition off and relays disconnected. Using an ohmmeter, check resistance in Blue/White wire between anti-theft relay socket terminal No. 3 and inhibit relay socket terminal No. 1. Resistance should be less than 5 ohms. Check resistance between ground and anti-theft relay socket terminal No. 3 (Blue/White wire). Resistance should be more than 10 k/ohms. If resistance is as specified, go to next step. If resistance is not as specified, repair open or short to ground in Blue/White wire and retest system operation.

6) Using jumper wire, connect anti-theft relay terminal No. 2 to positive battery terminal. *See Fig. 6.* Check relay resistance as follows:

- Between terminals No. 3 and 4, resistance should be less than 5 ohms.
- Between terminals No. 3 and 5, resistance should be more than 10 k/ohms.

Using another jumper wire, connect anti-theft relay terminal No. 1 to negative battery terminal. Check relay resistance as follows:

- Between terminals No. 3 and 5, resistance should be less than 5 ohms.
- Between terminals No. 3 and 4, resistance should be more than 10 k/ohms.

If resistance is as specified, go to next step. If resistance is not as specified, replace anti-theft relay and retest system operation.

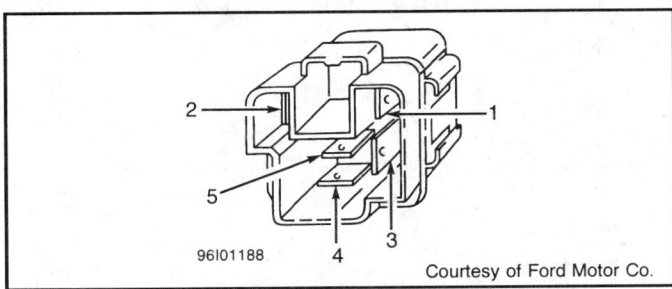

Fig. 6: Identifying Anti-Theft Relay Terminals

7) Leave ignition off and anti-theft relay disconnected. Disconnect SEC timer/module connector C2032B (located behind center top of dash panel). Using an ohmmeter, check resistance in Blue wire between anti-theft relay socket terminal No. 1 and SEC timer/module connector C2032B terminal No. 20. *See Figs. 2 and 3.* Resistance should be less than 5 ohms. Check resistance between ground and anti-theft relay socket terminal No. 1 (Blue wire). Resistance should be more than 10 k/ohms. If resistance is as specified, replace SEC timer/module. If resistance is not as specified, repair Blue wire and retest system operation.

8) Leave ignition off and inhibit relay disconnected. Using an ohmmeter, check resistance in Black wire between ground and inhibit relay socket terminal No. 2. If resistance is less than 5 ohms, go to next step. If resistance is 5 ohms or more, repair open in Black wire between inhibit relay and ground. Retest system operation.

9) Turn ignition on. Check voltage between ground and inhibit relay socket terminal No. 7 (Red wire). If voltage is more than 10 volts, go to next step. If voltage is 10 volts or less, fault is in starting system. See STARTERS – VILLAGER article in STARTING & CHARGING SYSTEMS to continue diagnosis.

10) Leave ignition off and relays disconnected. Disconnect Red/White wire to starter motor. Check resistance in Red/White wire between starter motor connector and inhibit relay socket terminal No. 6. *See Fig. 5.* Resistance should be less than 5 ohms. Check resistance between ground and inhibit relay socket terminal No. 6 (Red/White wire). Resistance should be more than 10 k/ohms. If resistance is as specified, replace inhibit relay and retest system. If resistance is not as specified, see STARTERS – VILLAGER article in STARTING & CHARGING SYSTEMS to continue diagnosis.

TEST C: THEFT INDICATOR IS ALWAYS ON

Turn ignition off. Disconnect THEFT indicator connector C2020 (located behind right side of instrument cluster). Disconnect Smart Entry Control (SEC) timer/module connector C2032B (located behind center top of dash panel). Using an ohmmeter, check resistance in Gray wire between ground and THEFT indicator connector C2020. If resistance is more than 10 k/ohms, replace SEC timer/module and retest system operation. If resistance is 10 k/ohms or less, repair Gray wire and retest system operation.

TEST D: THEFT INDICATOR DOES NOT ILLUMINATE TO INDICATE ARMING

1) Turn ignition off. Disconnect THEFT indicator connector C2020 (located behind right side of instrument cluster). Using a voltmeter, check voltage between ground and THEFT indicator connector C2020 Gray/Yellow wire terminal. If voltage is more than 10 volts, go to next step. If voltage is 10 volts or less, repair open in Gray/Yellow wire and retest system operation.

2) Leave THEFT indicator disconnected. Using a fused jumper wire, connect THEFT indicator connector C2020 Gray/Yellow wire terminal to positive battery terminal. Using a fused jumper wire, connect Gray wire circuit at THEFT indicator connector C2020 to negative battery terminal. If THEFT indicator illuminates, go to next step. If THEFT indicator does not illuminate, replace THEFT indicator and retest system operation.

3) Leave THEFT indicator disconnected. Disconnect Smart Entry Control (SEC) timer/module connector C2032A (located behind center top of dash panel). Using an ohmmeter, check resistance in Gray wire between THEFT indicator connector C2020 and SEC timer/module connector C2032B terminal No. 17. *See Fig. 7.* If resistance is less than 5 ohms, replace SEC timer/module and retest system operation. If resistance is 5 ohms or more, repair open in Gray wire and retest system operation.

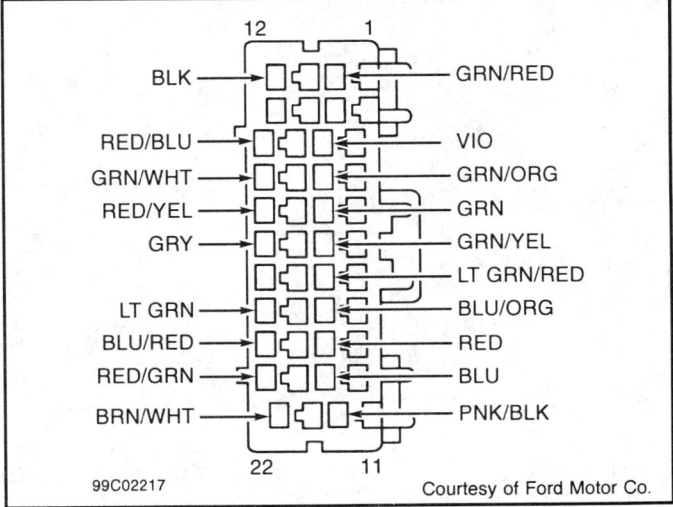

Fig. 7: Identifying Timer Module Connector C2032A Terminals

TEST E: SYSTEM DOES NOT DISARM

1) Disarm anti-theft system. If horn, headlights and parking lights turn off, system is operating properly. If horn, headlights and parking lights do not turn off, proceed as follows:

- If headlights are always on, go to step **3)**.
- If horn is always on, go to next step.
- If exterior lights are always on, fault is not in anti-theft system. See appropriate wiring diagram in EXTERIOR LIGHTS article to continue diagnosis.

2) Disconnect Smart Entry Control (SEC) timer/module connector C2030B (located behind center top of dash panel). If horn still does not turn off, fault is in horn system. See appropriate wiring diagram in STEERING COLUMN SWITCHES – VILLAGER article to continue diagnosis. If horn turns off, reprogram SEC timer/module. If fault is still present, replace SEC timer/module and retest system operation.

3) Disconnect Smart Entry Control (SEC) timer/module connector C2030B (located behind center top of dash panel). If headlights still do not turn off, fault is not in anti-theft system. See appropriate wiring diagram in HEADLIGHT SYSTEMS article to continue diagnosis. If headlights turn off, reprogram SEC timer/module. If fault is still present, replace SEC timer/module and retest system operation.

REMOVAL & INSTALLATION

WARNING: *Disable air bag system before working around steering column or removing any air bag system component. See appropriate AIR BAG RESTRAINT SYSTEMS article.*

CAUTION: *When battery is disconnected, vehicle computer and memory systems may lose memory data. Driveability problems may exist until computer systems have completed a relearn cycle. See COMPUTER RELEARN PROCEDURES article in GENERAL INFORMATION before disconnecting battery.*

HOOD SWITCH

Removal & Installation – Disconnect negative battery cable. Disconnect hood switch wiring harness connector. Remove bolt retaining hood switch. Remove hood switch. To install, reverse removal procedure.

SMART ENTRY CONTROL (SEC) TIMER/MODULE

Removal & Installation – Disconnect negative battery cable. Remove Transmission Control Module (TCM) from bracket and position to side. Remove TCM bracket. *See Fig. 8.* Remove SEC timer/module wiring harness connector. Remove 3 mounting screws. Remove SEC timer/module. To install, reverse removal procedure.

99E02218   Courtesy of Ford Motor Co.

Fig. 8: Removing Smart Entry Control/Timer Module

WIRING DIAGRAMS

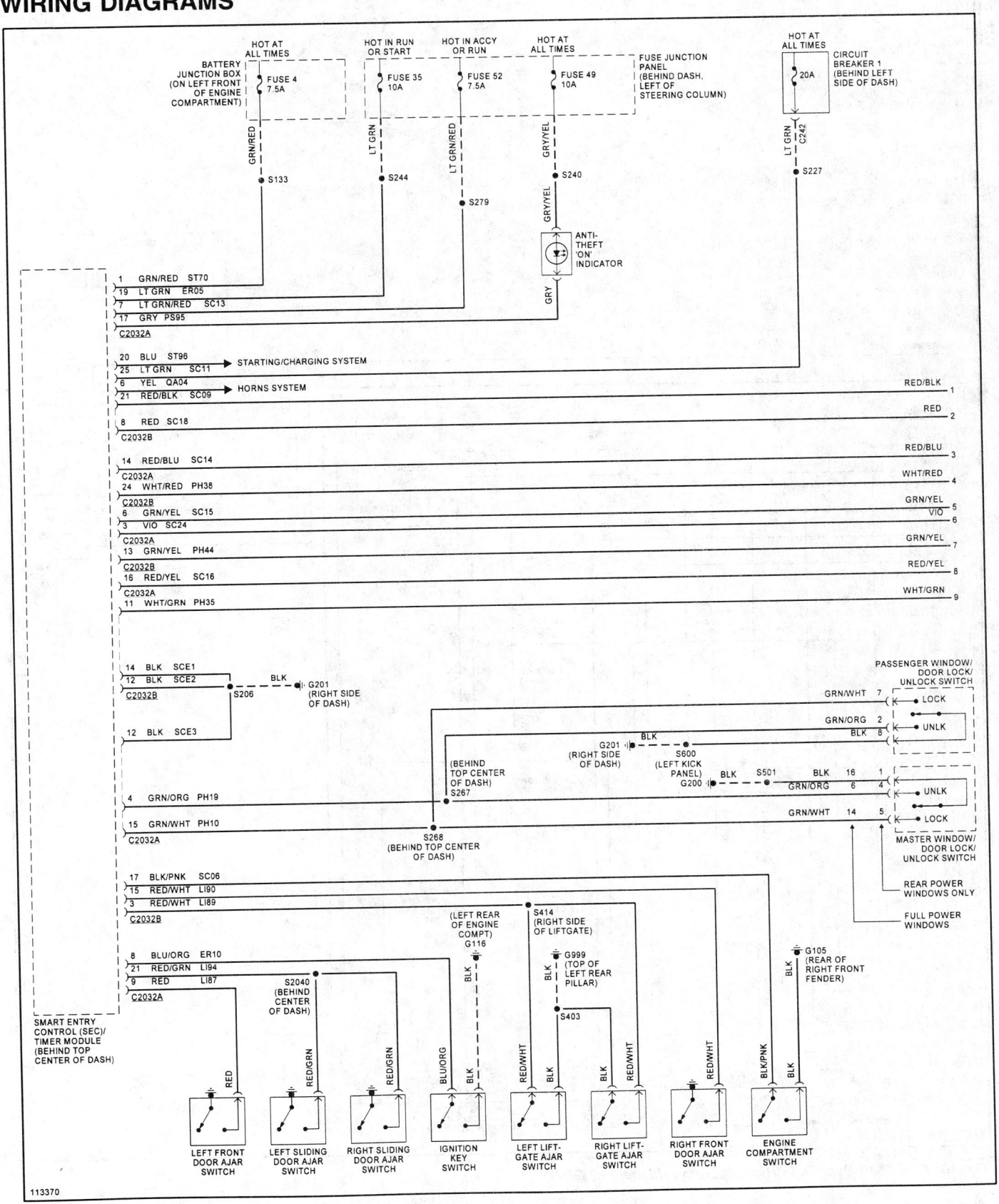

Fig. 9: Anti-Theft System Wiring Diagram (Villager – 1 Of 2)

113370

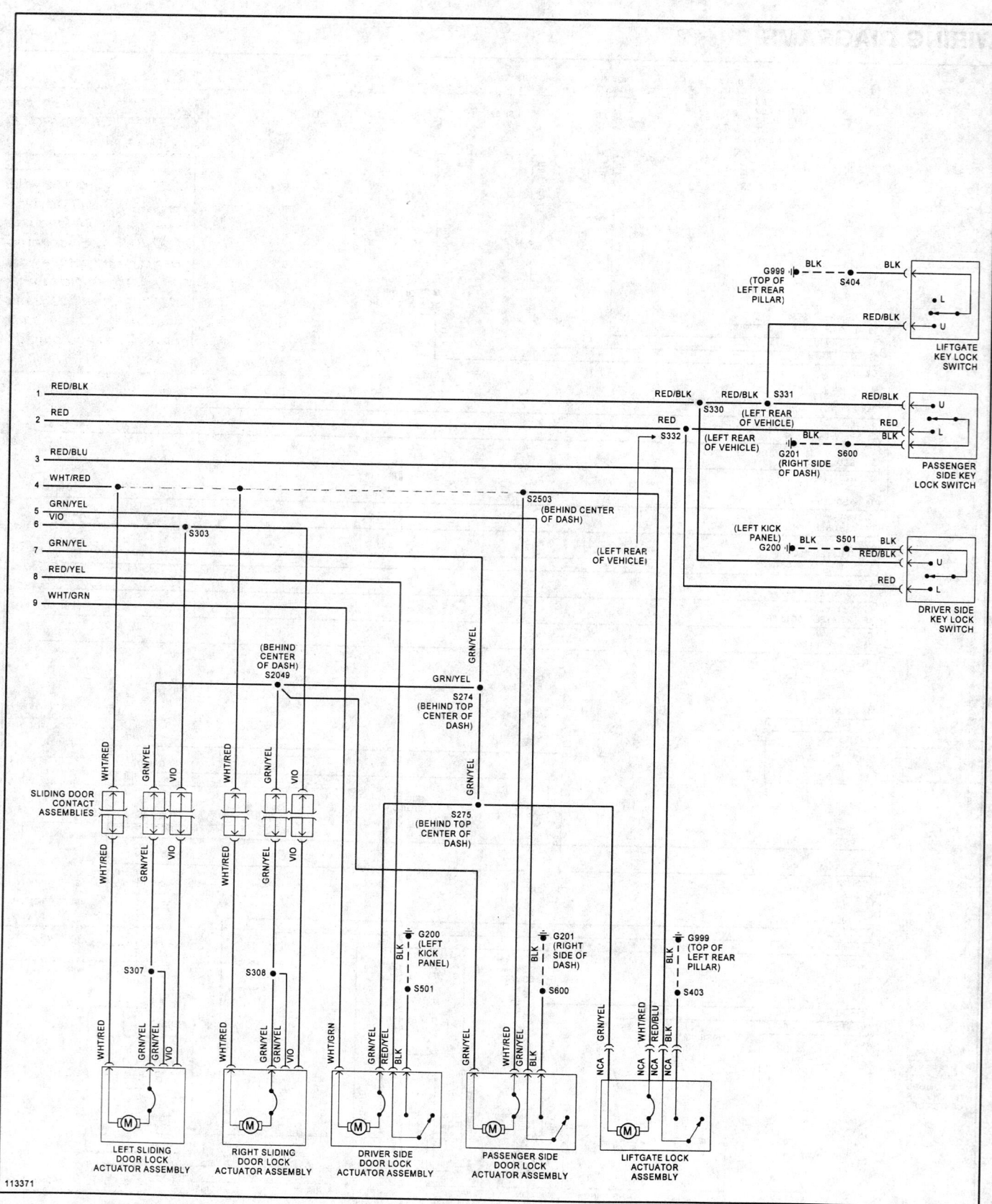

Fig. 10: Anti-Theft System Wiring Diagram (Villager – 2 Of 2)

DESCRIPTION & OPERATION

Anti-theft perimeter protection feature is controlled by Front Electronic Module (FEM), Rear Electronic Module (REM) and Remote Keyless Entry (RKE) module. This feature is configurable to FEM and REM. Alarm can be armed using remote transmitter to RKE module or by using driver's door lock switch. FEM and REM will also monitor radio, ignition switch and anti-theft switches. Diagnostics are accessed through Standard Corporate Protocol (SCP) network. Once alarm has been armed, if any of previous mentioned features receive activation, alarm will activate visual and audible alerts.

COMPONENT LOCATIONS

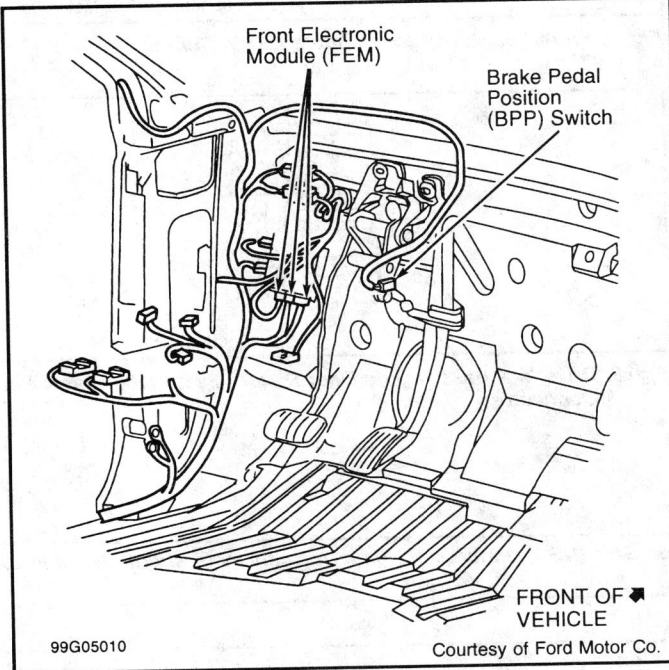

99G05010   Courtesy of Ford Motor Co.

Fig. 1: Locating Front Electronic Module (FEM)

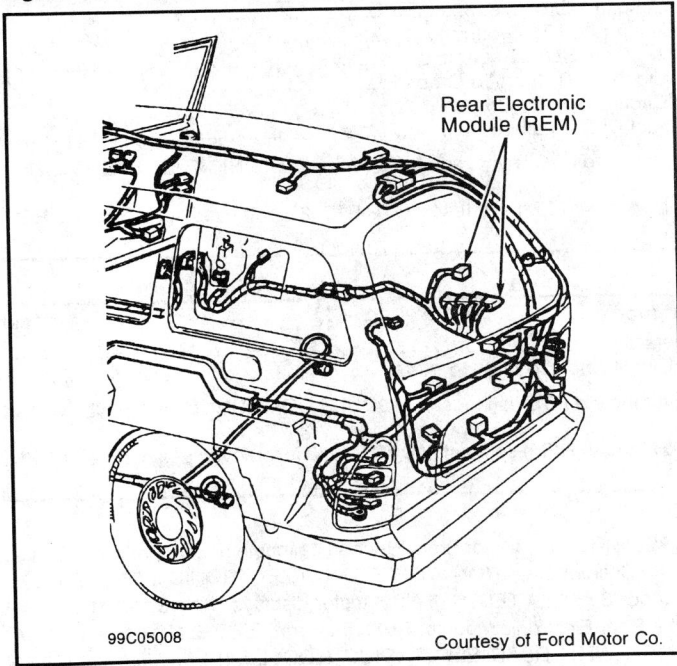

99C05008   Courtesy of Ford Motor Co.

Fig. 2: Locating Rear Electronic Module (REM)

PROGRAMMING

MODULE CONFIGURATION

NOTE: Powertrain Control Module (PCM) has to be flash programmed using a flash cable. See COMPUTER RELEARN PROCEDURES article in GENERAL INFORMATION.

NOTE: Newly released modules will require configuration after being installed on vehicle. All configurable modules will be packaged in a kit which contains a warning label and multi-language sheet reemphasizing requirements to configure replacement modules. A New Generation Star (NGS) tester or Ford compatible scan tool MUST be used to retrieve configuration data from old module before it is removed from vehicle. This information will be transferred into new module so that new module will contain same settings as old module. NGS tester will not retain stored configuration information for longer than 24 hours.

Following manufacturer's instructions, upload old information from old module using Ford Service Function (FSF) card and NGS tester. Install new module and download stored information into new module using FSF card and NGS tester.

TROUBLE SHOOTING

Verify customer concern. Check all fuses for appropriate system. Check Fuse Junction Box/Panel (FJB) fuses No. 14 and 16 (both 10-amp). Check Battery Junction Box (BJB) fuse No. 2 (10-amp) and fuse No. 23 (15-amp). Check for damaged wiring harness and/or loose, corroded connections. Check for damage to Front Electronic Module (FEM), Rear Electronic Module (REM), door disarm switches, liftgate disarm switch, ignition switch and anti-theft horn.

CONNECTOR IDENTIFICATION

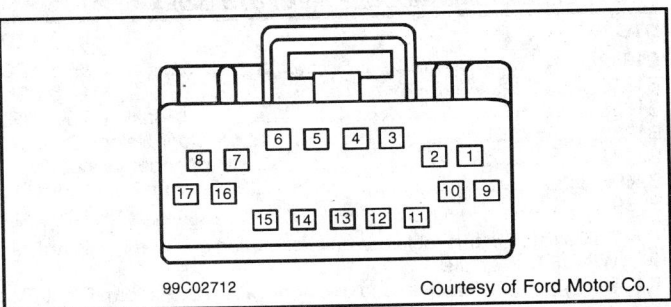

99C02712   Courtesy of Ford Motor Co.

Fig. 3: Front/Rear Electronic Module 17-Pin Connector

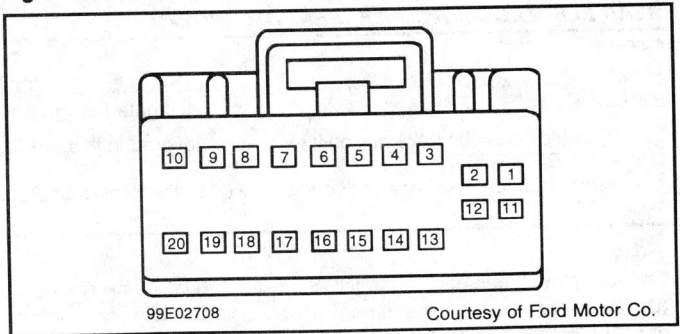

99E02708   Courtesy of Ford Motor Co.

Fig. 4: Front/Rear Electronic Module 20-Pin Connector

1999 ACCESSORIES & EQUIPMENT
Active Anti-Theft Systems – Windstar (Cont.)

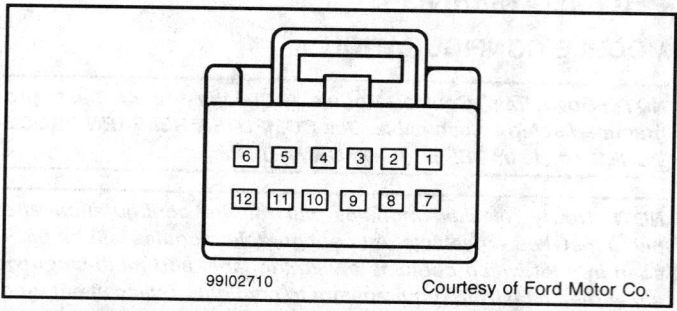

Fig. 5: Front/Rear Electronic Module 12-Pin Connector

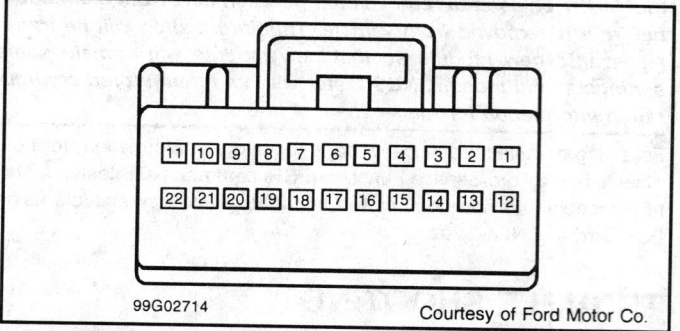

Fig. 6: Front/Rear Electronic Module 22-Pin Connector

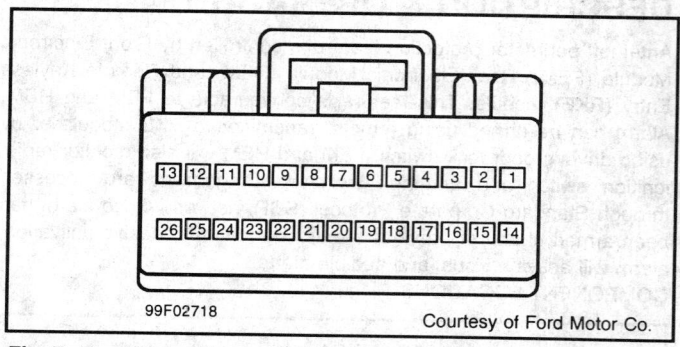

Fig. 7: Front/Rear Electronic Module 26-Pin Connector

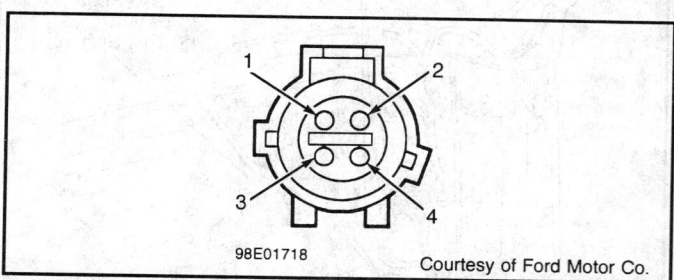

Fig. 8: Driver's & Passenger's Door Disarm Switch Harness 4-Pin Connector

SELF-DIAGNOSTIC SYSTEM

NOTE: All diagnostic tests are written specifically for New Generation Star (NGS) tester. Most generic scan tools should be able to perform all test procedures.

FRONT ELECTRONIC MODULE (FEM) DTC INDEX

DTC [1]	Description	Test
B1342	ECU Defective	[2]
B1519	Hood Switch Circuit Failure	H
B1558	Ignition START/RUN Circuit Short To Ground	F
B1833	Door Unlock Disarm Switch Circuit Short To Ground	C
B2473	Passenger's Door Disarm Switch Circuit Short To Ground	D
B2496	Anti-Theft Horn Output Circuit Short To Ground	F
B2595	Anti-Theft Input Signal Circuit Failure	H

[1] – DTCs listed in this table are only for testing covered in this article. For complete DTC listing, see MODULE COMMUNICATIONS NETWORK – WINDSTAR article.

[2] – Using NGS tester, clear and document all DTC. Perform Front Electronic Module (FEM) self-test. If DTC B1342 is retrieved again, replace FEM.

REAR ELECTRONIC MODULE (REM) DTC INDEX

DTC [1]	Description	Test
B1342	ECU Defective	[2]
B2569	Liftgate Disarm Switch Circuit Short To Ground	E

[1] – DTCs listed in this table are only for testing covered in this article. For complete DTC listing, see MODULE COMMUNICATIONS NETWORK – WINDSTAR article.

[2] – Using NGS tester, clear and document all DTC. Perform Rear Electronic Module (REM) self-test. If DTC B1342 is retrieved again, replace REM.

Connect New Generation Star (NGS) tester to Data Link Connector (DLC), located beneath instrument panel. Using NGS tester, perform data link diagnostics test. See DATA LINK DIAGNOSTIC TEST under COMMUNICATION NETWORK DIAGNOSTICS in MODULE COMMUNICATIONS NETWORK – WINDSTAR article. If NGS tester responds with CKT914, CKT915 or CKT70=ALL ECUS NO RESP/NOT EQUIP, repair module communications concern. See MODULE COMMUNICATIONS NETWORK – WINDSTAR article. If NGS tester displays NO RESP/NOT EQUIP for Front Electronic Module (FEM), perform TEST A: NO COMMUNICATION WITH FRONT ELECTRONIC MODULE (FEM) under SYSTEM TESTS. If NGS tester displays NO RESP/NOT EQUIP for Rear Electronic Module (REM), perform TEST B: NO COMMUNICATION WITH REAR ELECTRONIC MODULE (REM) under SYSTEM TESTS.

If NGS tester responds with SYSTEM PASSED, retrieve and record continuous DTCs. Erase continuous DTCs. Using NGS tester, perform FEM and REM self-test. Perform appropriate test in accordance with DTC retrieved. See FRONT ELECTRONIC MODULE (FEM) DTC INDEX and/or REAR ELECTRONIC MODULE (REM) DTC INDEX table. Codes listed in these tables are only for testing covered in this article. For complete DTC listing, see MODULE COMMUNICATIONS NETWORK – WINDSTAR article. If no DTCs are retrieved, repair by symptom. See SYMPTOM CHART table under SYSTEM TESTS.

SYSTEM TESTS

NOTE: *Many steps in the following tests refer to various connectors. These connectors are identified in illustrations. See Figs. 3-8 under CONNECTOR IDENTIFICATION.*

SYMPTOM CHART

Symptom	Test
No Communication With Front Electronic Module (FEM)	A
No Communication With Rear Electronic Module (REM)	B
Driver's Door Lock Does Not Disarm	C
Passenger's Door Lock Does Not Disarm	D
Liftgate Lock Does Not Disarm	E
Anti-Theft Horn Inoperative	F
Anti-Theft Horn Always On	G
Turn Signals Do Not Flash When Arming	H

TEST A: NO COMMUNICATION WITH FRONT ELECTRONIC MODULE (FEM)

NOTE: *Turn ignition switch from OFF to ON position to enable system power feature.*

1) Turn ignition switch to OFF position. Remove fuses No. 2 (10-amp) and No. 23 (15-amp) from Battery Junction Box (BJB). Turn ignition switch to ON position. Measure voltage between input side of fuses No. 2 and 23 and ground. If voltages are more than 10 volts, install fuses No. 2 and 23 and go to next step. If voltages are 10 volts or less, repair power supply circuit(s) as necessary. See WIRING DIAGRAMS.

2) Turn ignition switch to OFF position. Disconnect FEM connectors C190, C192 and C346. Measure voltage between FEM connector C346 terminal No. 1 (Light Blue/Red wire) and ground. Also, measure voltage between FEM connector C190 terminal No. 6 (Red wire) and ground. If voltages are more than 10 volts, go to next step. If voltages are 10 volts or less, repair open in appropriate wire(s). See WIRING DIAGRAMS.

3) Measure resistance between ground and FEM connector C190 terminal No. 12 (Black wire), FEM connector C192 terminals No. 11, 13, 14 and 15 (all Black wires). If resistance is less than 5 ohms at every terminal, repair module communication concern. See MODULE COMMUNICATIONS NETWORK – WINDSTAR article. If resistance is 5 ohms or more at any terminal, repair open in appropriate wire. See WIRING DIAGRAMS.

TEST B: NO COMMUNICATION WITH REAR ELECTRONIC MODULE (REM)

NOTE: *Turn ignition switch from OFF to ON position to enable system power feature.*

1) Turn ignition switch to OFF position. Remove fuse No. 16 (10-amp) from Fuse Junction Box/Panel (FJB). Turn ignition switch to ON position. Measure voltage between FJB fuse No. 16 input terminal and ground. If voltage is more than 10 volts, reinstall fuse No. 16 and go to next step. If voltage is 10 volts or less, repair FJB power supply circuit. See WIRING DIAGRAMS.

2) Turn ignition switch to OFF position. Disconnect REM connector C343. Turn ignition switch to ON position. Measure voltage between REM connector C343 terminal No. 3 (White/Yellow wire) and ground. If voltage is more than 10 volts, go to next step. If voltage is 10 volts or less, repair open in White/Yellow wire. See WIRING DIAGRAMS.

3) Turn ignition switch to OFF position. Disconnect REM 22-pin connector C341 and 26-pin connector C342 . Measure resistances between REM connector C341 terminal No. 12 (Black wire), REM connector C342 terminals No. 11, 12, 25 and 26 (all Black wires) and ground. If all resistances are less than 5 ohms, repair module communication concern. See MODULE COMMUNICATIONS NETWORK – WINDSTAR article. If any resistance is 5 ohms or more, repair open in appropriate wire. See WIRING DIAGRAMS.

TEST C: DRIVER'S DOOR LOCK DOES NOT DISARM

1) Using NGS tester, reform Front Electronic Module (FEM) self-test. If DTC B1833 is retrieved, go to next step. If no DTCs are retrieved, go to step 4). If any other DTCs are retrieved, perform appropriate test. See FRONT ELECTRONIC MODULE (FEM) DTC INDEX table under SELF-DIAGNOSTIC SYSTEM.

2) Turn ignition switch to OFF position. Disconnect driver's door disarm switch 4-pin connector C504. Measure resistance between driver's door disarm switch terminals No. 1 and 3 (component side) while turning driver's door lock cylinder from LOCK to UNLOCK position. Resistance should be less than 5 ohms when key is in one position and more than 10 k/ohms when key is in other position. If resistance is as specified, go to next step. If resistance is not as specified, replace driver's door disarm switch. See FRONT DOOR DISARM SWITCH under REMOVAL & INSTALLATION.

3) Turn ignition switch to OFF position. Disconnect FEM 26-pin connector C347. Measure resistance between driver's door disarm switch connector C504 terminal No. 3 (Light Blue/Black wire) and ground. If resistance is more than 10 k/ohms, replace FEM. See FRONT ELECTRONIC MODULE (FEM) under REMOVAL & INSTALLATION. If resistance is 10 k/ohms or less, repair short to ground in Light Blue/Black wire. See WIRING DIAGRAMS.

4) Turn ignition switch to OFF position. Disconnect driver's door disarm switch 4-pin connector C504. Measure resistance between driver's door disarm switch terminals No. 1 and 3 (component side) while turning driver's door lock cylinder from LOCK to UNLOCK position. Resistance should be less than 5 ohms when key is in one position and more than 10 k/ohms when key is in other position. If resistance is as specified, go to next step. If resistance is not as specified, replace driver's door disarm switch. See FRONT DOOR DISARM SWITCH under REMOVAL & INSTALLATION.

5) Measure voltage between driver's door disarm switch connector C504 terminal No. 3 (Light Blue/Black wire) and ground. If voltage is more than 10 volts, go to next step. If voltage is 10 volts or less, go to step 7).

6) Turn ignition switch to OFF position. Disconnect FEM 26-pin connector C347. Measure voltage between driver's door disarm switch connector C504 terminal No. 3 (Light Blue/Black wire) and ground. If voltage is more than 10 volts, repair short to voltage in Light Blue/Black wire. See WIRING DIAGRAMS. If voltage is 10 volts or less, replace FEM. See FRONT ELECTRONIC MODULE (FEM) under REMOVAL & INSTALLATION.

7) Turn ignition switch to OFF position. Measure resistance between driver's door disarm switch connector C504 terminal No. 3 (Light Blue/Black wire) and FEM connector C347 terminal No. 14 (Light Blue/Black wire). If resistance is less than 5 ohms, go to next step. If resistance is 5 ohms or more, repair open in Light Blue/Black wire. See WIRING DIAGRAMS.

8) Measure resistance between driver's door disarm switch connector C504 terminal No. 1 (Black wire) and ground. If resistance is less than 5 ohms, replace FEM. See FRONT ELECTRONIC MODULE (FEM) under REMOVAL & INSTALLATION. If resistance is 5 ohms or more, repair open in Black wire. See WIRING DIAGRAMS.

TEST D: PASSENGER'S DOOR LOCK DOES NOT DISARM

1) Using NGS tester, perform Front Electronic Module (FEM) self-test. If DTC B2473 is retrieved, go to next step. If no DTCs are retrieved, go to step **4)**. If any other DTCs are retrieved, perform appropriate test. See FRONT ELECTRONIC MODULE (FEM) DTC INDEX table under SELF-DIAGNOSTIC SYSTEM.

2) Turn ignition switch to OFF position. Disconnect passenger's door disarm switch 4-pin connector C604. Measure resistance between passenger's door disarm switch terminals No. 1 and 3 (component side) while turning passenger's door lock cylinder from LOCK to UNLOCK position. Resistance should be less than 5 ohms when key is in one position and more than 10 k/ohms when key is in other position. If resistance is as specified, go to next step. If resistance is not as specified, replace passenger's door disarm switch. See FRONT DOOR DISARM SWITCH under REMOVAL & INSTALLATION.

3) Turn ignition switch to OFF position. Disconnect FEM 26-pin connector C347. Measure resistance between passenger's door disarm switch connector C604 terminal No. 3 (Light Blue/Pink wire) and ground. If resistance is more than 10 k/ohms, replace FEM. See FRONT ELECTRONIC MODULE (FEM) under REMOVAL & INSTALLATION. If resistance is 10 k/ohms or less, repair short to ground in Light Blue/Pink wire. See WIRING DIAGRAMS.

4) Turn ignition switch to OFF position. Disconnect passenger's door disarm switch 4-pin connector C604. Measure resistance between passenger's door disarm switch terminals No. 1 and 3 (component side) while turning passenger's door lock cylinder from LOCK to UNLOCK position. Resistance should be less than 5 ohms when key is in one position and more than 10 k/ohms when key is in other position. If resistance is as specified, go to next step. If resistance is not as specified, replace passenger's door disarm switch. See FRONT DOOR DISARM SWITCH under REMOVAL & INSTALLATION.

5) Measure voltage between passenger's door disarm switch connector C604 terminal No. 3 (Light Blue/Pink wire) and ground. If voltage is more than 10 volts, go to next step. If voltage is 10 volts or less, go to step **7)**.

6) Turn ignition switch to OFF position. Disconnect FEM 26-pin connector C347. Measure voltage between passenger's door disarm switch connector C604 terminal No. 3 (Light Blue/Pink wire) and ground. If voltage is more than 10 volts, repair short to voltage in Light Blue/Pink wire. See WIRING DIAGRAMS. If voltage is 10 volts or less, replace FEM. See FRONT ELECTRONIC MODULE (FEM) under REMOVAL & INSTALLATION.

7) Turn ignition switch to OFF position. Measure resistance between passenger's door disarm switch connector C604 terminal No. 3 (Light Blue/Pink wire) and FEM connector C347 terminal No. 14 (Light Blue/Pink wire). If resistance is less than 5 ohms, go to next step. If resistance is 5 ohms or more, repair open in Light Blue/Pink wire. See WIRING DIAGRAMS.

8) Measure resistance between passenger's door disarm switch connector C604 terminal No. 1 (Black wire) and ground. If resistance is less than 5 ohms, replace FEM. See FRONT ELECTRONIC MODULE (FEM) under REMOVAL & INSTALLATION. If resistance is 5 ohms or more, repair open in Black wire. See WIRING DIAGRAMS.

TEST E: LIFTGATE LOCK DOES NOT DISARM

1) Using NGS tester, perform Rear Electronic Module (REM) self-test. If no DTCs are retrieved, go to next step. If DTC B2569 is retrieved, go to step **3)**. If any other DTCs are retrieved, perform appropriate test. See REAR ELECTRONIC MODULE (REM) DTC INDEX table under SELF-DIAGNOSTIC SYSTEM.

2) Turn ignition switch to OFF position. Turn ignition switch to ON position. Using NGS tester, monitor REM PID DL_DSRM while turning liftgate lock key cylinder from LOCK to UNLOCK position. If PID does not agree with liftgate key lock cylinder position, go to next step. If PID agrees with key lock cylinder position, replace REM. See REAR ELECTRONIC MODULE (REM) under REMOVAL & INSTALLATION.

3) Turn ignition switch to OFF position. Disconnect liftgate disarm switch 2-pin connector C906. Measure resistance between liftgate disarm switch terminals No. 1 and 2 (component side) while turning liftgate lock

cylinder from LOCK to UNLOCK position. Resistance should be less than 5 ohms when key is in one position and more than 10 k/ohms when key is in other position. If resistance is as specified and DTC B2569 was retrieved, go to step **7)**. If resistance is as specified and any other DTC was retrieved, repair other DTCs and go to next step. See REAR ELECTRONIC MODULE (REM) DTC INDEX table under SELF-DIAGNOSTIC SYSTEM. If resistance is not as specified, replace liftgate disarm switch. See LIFTGATE DISARM SWITCH under REMOVAL & INSTALLATION.

4) Measure resistance between liftgate disarm switch connector C906 terminal No. 2 (Black wire) and ground. If resistance is less than 5 ohms, go to next step. If resistance is 5 ohms or more, repair open in Black wire. See WIRING DIAGRAMS.

5) Measure voltage between liftgate disarm switch connector C906 terminal No. 1 (White/Pink wire) and ground. If voltage is 10 volts or less, go to next step. If voltage is more than 10 volts, go to step **8)**.

6) Disconnect REM 22-pin connector C341. Measure resistance between liftgate disarm switch connector C906 terminal No. 1 (White/Pink wire) and REM connector C341 terminal No. 15 (White/Pink wire). If resistance is less than 5 ohms, go to next step. If resistance is 5 ohms or more, repair open in White/Pink wire. See WIRING DIAGRAMS.

7) Measure resistance between liftgate disarm switch connector C906 terminal No. 1 (White/Pink wire) and ground. If resistance is more than 10 k/ohms, replace REM. See REAR ELECTRONIC MODULE (REM) under REMOVAL & INSTALLATION. If resistance is 10 k/ohms or less, repair short to ground in White/Pink wire. See WIRING DIAGRAMS.

8) Measure voltage between liftgate disarm switch connector C906 terminal No. 1 (White/Pink wire) and ground. If voltage is present, repair short to voltage in White/Pink wire. See WIRING DIAGRAMS. If no voltage is present, replace REM. See REAR ELECTRONIC MODULE (REM) under REMOVAL & INSTALLATION.

TEST F: ANTI-THEFT HORN INOPERATIVE

1) Using NGS tester, perform Front Electronic Module (FEM) self-test. If DTC B1558 is retrieved, go to next step. If DTC B2496 is retrieved, go to step **3)**. If no DTCs are retrieved, go to step **5)**.

2) Disconnect FEM 20-pin connector C346. Measure resistance between FEM connector C346 terminal No. 3 (Red/Yellow wire) and ground. If resistance is more than 10 k/ohms, replace FEM. See FRONT ELECTRONIC MODULE (FEM) under REMOVAL & INSTALLATION. If resistance is 10 k/ohms or less, repair short to ground in Red/Yellow wire. See WIRING DIAGRAMS.

3) Turn ignition switch to OFF position. Disconnect FEM 17-pin connector C192. Connect 10-amp fused jumper wire between FEM connector C192 terminal No. 16 (Black/Light Green wire) and No. 1 (Brown/Orange wire). If anti-theft horn does not sound, go to next step. If anti-theft horn sounds, replace FEM. See FRONT ELECTRONIC MODULE (FEM) under REMOVAL & INSTALLATION.

4) Turn ignition switch to OFF position. Measure resistance between FEM connector C192 terminal No. 16 (Black/Light Green wire) and ground. If resistance is more than 10 k/ohms, replace anti-theft horn. See ANTI-THEFT HORN under REMOVAL & INSTALLATION. If resistance 10 k/ohms or less, repair short to ground in Black/Light Green wire. See WIRING DIAGRAMS.

5) Turn ignition switch to OFF position. Disconnect FEM 20-pin connector C346. Turn ignition switch to ON position. Measure voltage between FEM connector C346 terminal No. 3 (Red/Yellow wire) and ground. If voltage is more than 10 volts, reconnect FEM connector C346 and go to next step. If voltage is 10 volts or less, repair open in Red/Yellow wire. See WIRING DIAGRAMS.

6) Turn ignition switch to OFF position. Connect NGS tester. Turn ignition switch to ON position. Using NGS tester, trigger FEM active command HORN to ON. If anti-theft horn does not sound, go to next step. If anti-theft horn sounds, replace FEM. See FRONT ELECTRONIC MODULE (FEM) under REMOVAL & INSTALLATION.

7) Turn ignition switch to OFF position. Disconnect FEM 17-pin connector C192 and anti-theft horn single-pin connector C339. Measure resistance between FEM connector C192 terminal No. 16 (Black/Light Green wire) and anti-theft horn connector C339 (Black/Light Green wire). If resistance is less than 5 ohms, replace anti-theft horn. See ANTI-THEFT HORN under REMOVAL & INSTALLATION. If resistance is 5 ohms or more, repair open in Black/Light Green wire. See WIRING DIAGRAMS.

TEST G: ANTI-THEFT HORN ALWAYS ON

1) Using NGS tester, perform Front Electronic Module (FEM) self-test. If no DTCs were retrieved, go to next step. If any DTCs are retrieved, perform appropriate test. See FRONT ELECTRONIC MODULE (FEM) DTC INDEX table under SELF-DIAGNOSTIC SYSTEM.

2) Turn ignition switch to ON position. Remove fuse No. 14 (10-amp) from Fuse Junction Box/Panel (FJB). Disconnect FEM 20-pin connector C346. Measure voltage output side of fuse No. 14 (Red/Yellow wire) and ground. If no voltage is present, go to next step. If voltage is present, repair short to voltage in Red/Yellow wire. See WIRING DIAGRAMS.

3) Turn ignition switch to OFF position. Disconnect FEM 17-pin connector C192. If anti-theft horn does not stop sounding, go to next step. If anti-theft horn stops sounding, replace FEM. See FRONT ELECTRONIC MODULE (FEM) under REMOVAL & INSTALLATION.

4) Turn ignition switch to RUN position. Measure voltage between FEM connector C192 terminal No. 16 (Black/Light Green wire) and ground. If voltage is more than 10 volts, repair short to voltage in Black/Light Green wire. See WIRING DIAGRAMS. If voltage is 10 volts or less, replace anti-theft horn. See ANTI-THEFT HORN under REMOVAL & INSTALLATION.

TEST H: TURN SIGNALS DO NOT FLASH WHEN ARMING

1) Using NGS tester, perform Front Electronic Module (FEM) self-test. If DTC B1519 is retrieved, go to next step. If DTC B2595 is retrieved or if no DTC are retrieved, go to step **7**).

2) Disconnect hood ajar switch 2-pin connector C189. Measure resistance between hood ajar switch terminals No. 1 and 2 (component side). Resistance should be less than 5 ohms with hood ajar switch not depressed and more than 10 k/ohms with hood ajar switch depressed. If resistance is as specified, go to next step. If resistance is not as specified, replace hood ajar switch.

3) Measure resistance between hood ajar switch connector C189 terminal No. 2 (Black wire) and ground. If resistance is less than 5 ohms, go to next step. If resistance is 5 ohms or more, repair open in Black wire. See WIRING DIAGRAMS.

4) Measure resistance between hood ajar switch connector C189 terminal No. 1 (Violet/Orange wire) and ground. If voltage is not present, go to next step. If voltage is present, go to step **6**).

5) Turn ignition switch to OFF position. Disconnect FEM 12-pin connector C190. Measure resistance between hood ajar switch connector C189 terminal No. 1 (Violet/Orange wire) and FEM connector C190 terminal No. 3 (Violet/Orange wire). If resistance is less than 5 ohms, replace FEM. See FRONT ELECTRONIC MODULE (FEM) under REMOVAL & INSTALLATION. If resistance is 5 ohms or more, repair open in Violet/Orange wire. See WIRING DIAGRAMS.

6) Turn ignition switch to OFF position. Measure voltage between FEM connector C190 terminal No. 3 (Violet/Orange wire) and ground. If voltage is present, repair short to voltage in Violet/Orange wire. See WIRING DIAGRAMS. If voltage is not present, replace FEM. See FRONT ELECTRONIC MODULE (FEM) under REMOVAL & INSTALLATION.

7) Turn ignition switch to OFF position. Disconnect FEM 20-pin connector C346. Measure voltage between FEM connector C346 terminal No. 5 (Pink/White wire) and ground. If voltage is more than 10 volts, go to next step. If voltage is 10 volts or less, go to step **9**).

8) Turn ignition switch to OFF position. Disconnect REM 20-pin connector C343. Measure voltage between FEM connector C346 terminal No. 5 (Pink/White wire) and ground. If voltage is more than 10 volts, repair short to voltage in Pink/White wire. See WIRING DIAGRAMS. If voltage is 10 volts or less, replace REM. See REAR ELECTRONIC MODULE (REM) under REMOVAL & INSTALLATION.

9) Turn ignition switch to OFF position. Connect FEM 20-pin connector C346. Measure voltage between REM connector C343 terminal No. 5 (Pink/White wire) and ground. If voltage is 10 volts or less, go to next step. If voltage is more than 10 volts, replace FEM. See FRONT ELECTRONIC MODULE (FEM) under REMOVAL & INSTALLATION.

10) Turn ignition switch to OFF position. Disconnect FEM 20-pin connector C346. Measure resistance between FEM connector C346 terminal No. 5 (Pink/White wire) and REM connector C343 terminal No. 5 (Pink/White wire). If resistance is less than 5 ohms, replace REM. See REAR ELECTRONIC MODULE (REM) under REMOVAL & INSTALLATION. If DTC B2595 is still present, replace FEM. See FRONT ELECTRONIC MODULE (FEM) under REMOVAL & INSTALLATION. If resistance is 5 ohms or more, repair open in Pink/White wire. See WIRING DIAGRAMS.

REMOVAL & INSTALLATION

ANTI-THEFT HORN

Removal & Installation – Remove right side interior quarter trim panel. See QUARTER TRIM PANEL. Disconnect anti-theft horn electrical connector. Remove bolt retaining anti-theft horn and remove anti-theft horn. To install, reverse removal procedure.

FRONT DOOR DISARM SWITCH

Removal & Installation – Disconnect negative battery cable. Remove window regulator control switch and door handle escutcheon. Remove mirror access cover and disconnect electrical connectors. Remove 5 door trim panel screws and remove door trim panel. Remove courtesy lamp if equipped. Position watershield aside. Remove door disarm switch "E" clip and lock rod actuator. Disconnect electrical connector and remove door disarm switch.

FRONT ELECTRONIC MODULE (FEM)

CAUTION: Electronic modules are sensitive to static electrical charges. Proper grounding of technician and workplace is essential to prevent damage.

CAUTION: Prior to removal of module, it is necessary to upload module configuration information to New Generation Star (NGS) tester. This information needs to be downloaded into new module once installed. See PROGRAMMING.

NOTE: When battery is disconnected and reconnected, some abnormal drive symptoms may occur while vehicle relearns it's adaptive strategy. Vehicle may need to be driven 10 miles or more to learn strategy.

Removal & Installation – Disconnect battery ground cable. Remove 2 bolts holding instrument panel lower steering column opening cover. Remove cover. Remove 3 bolts holding instrument panel opening cover reinforcement. Remove reinforcement. Disconnect 6 electrical connectors to FEM, remove 3 bolts holding FEM and remove FEM. To install, reverse removal procedures.

LIFTGATE DISARM SWITCH

Removal & Installation – Remove upper liftgate trim panel. Remove liftgate garnish molding. Remove 2 interior liftgate pull handle screw covers and remove handle screws. Remove liftgate inside trim panel screw and liftgate trim panel. Position watershield aside. Remove liftgate lock cylinder disarm switch "E" clip and lock rod actuator. Disconnect liftgate disarm switch electrical connector and remove liftgate lock cylinder disarm switch. To install, reverse removal procedure.

QUARTER TRIM PANEL

NOTE: Liftgate lock cylinder disarm switch locator mark must be positioned towards harness side of switch prior to installation.

Removal & Installation – Remove sliding door and liftgate scuff plates. Remove upper "C" and "D" pillar safety belt guide covers and remove safety belt guide nut from "C" pillar side and safety belt guide bolt from "D" pillar side. Remove "C" pillar trim panel and "D" pillar trim panels. Remove 2 quarter trim panel screws, 3 pin-type retainers and remove quarter trim panel. To install, reverse removal procedures.

REAR ELECTRONIC MODULE (REM)

CAUTION: Electronic modules are sensitive to static electrical charges. Proper grounding of technician and workplace is essential to prevent damage.

CAUTION: Prior to removal of module, it is necessary to upload module configuration information to New Generation Star (NGS) tester. This information needs to be downloaded into new module once installed. See PROGRAMMING.

NOTE: When battery is disconnected and reconnected, some abnormal drive symptoms may occur while vehicle relearns it's adaptive strategy. Vehicle may need to be driven 10 miles or more to learn strategy.

Removal & Installation – Disconnect battery ground cable. Remove right quarter trim panel. Remove 3 bolts holding service jack mounting bracket and remove bracket. Disconnect 5 electrical connectors to REM, remove 3 nuts holding REM and remove REM. To install REM, reverse removal procedure.

WIRING DIAGRAMS

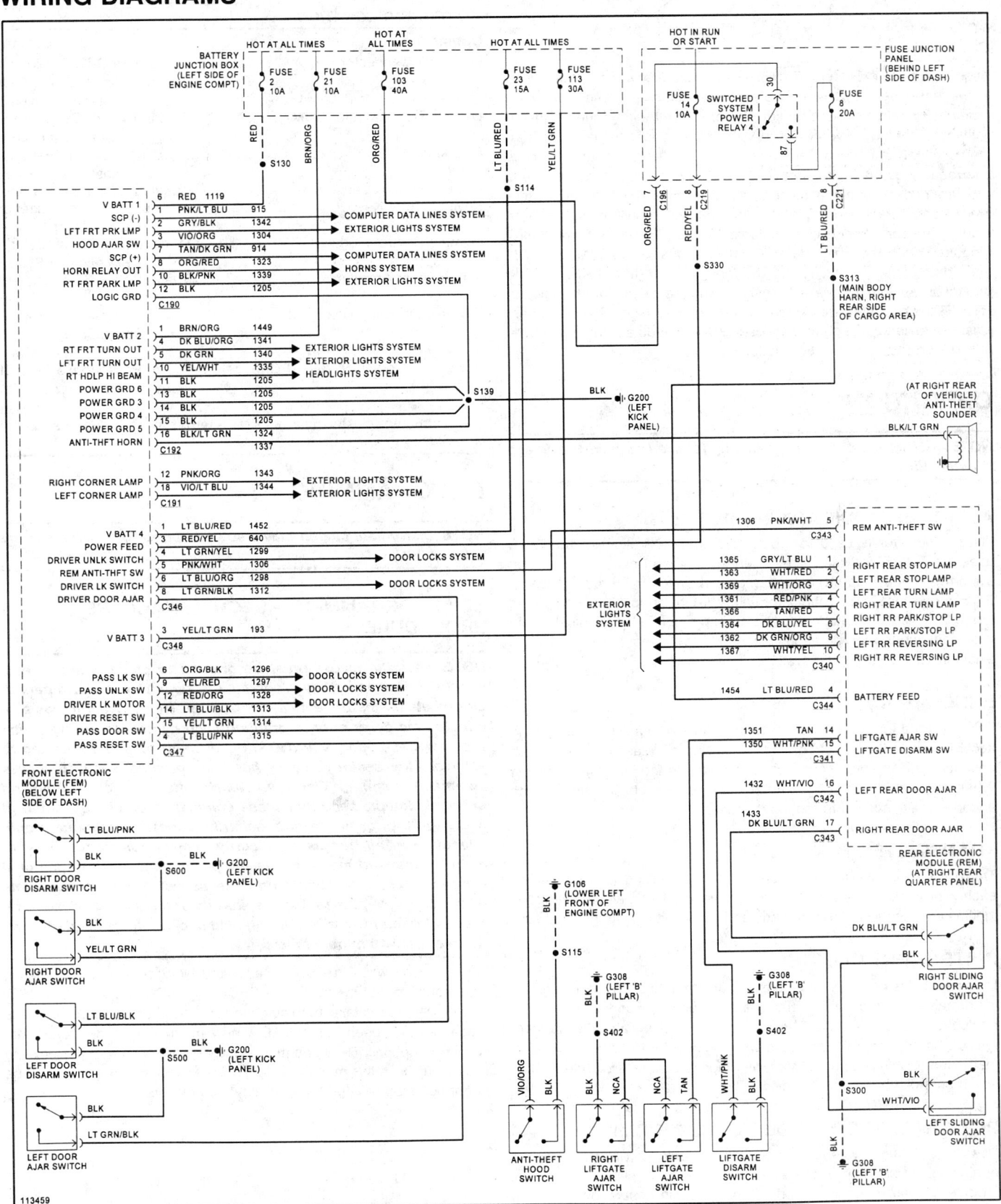

Fig. 9: Active Anti-Theft System Wiring Diagram (Windstar)

1999 ACCESSORIES & EQUIPMENT
Passive Anti-Theft Systems – Continental

DESCRIPTION

NOTE: *Instrument cluster may also be referred to as Virtual Image Cluster (VIC).*

Passive Anti-Theft System (PATS) vehicle protection system is designed to prevent driveaway thefts. The system is passive in that it does not require any activity from the user. System uses radio frequency identification technology to verify if proper key is being used to attempt to start the vehicle. During each starting sequence, the encoded ignition key is interrogated by the instrument cluster. If the key's identification code is programmed into anti-theft system, vehicle is capable of starting. If key's identification code is incorrect or missing, vehicle is prevented from starting. Instrument cluster communicates with the Powertrain Control Module (PCM) through Module Communications Network (MCN). PCM then determines if engine will be enabled to start. PATS vehicle protection system consists of these components: anti-theft indicator (THEFT) light, transceiver module, encoded ignition key, instrument cluster, Powertrain Control Module (PCM), module communications network and Lighting Control Module (LCM).

OPERATION

NOTE: *Instrument cluster may also be referred to as Virtual Image Cluster (VIC).*

ANTI-THEFT INDICATOR (THEFT) LIGHT

THEFT indicator is used to proveout system operation status. PATS uses the THEFT indicator light when ignition is in start or run. When system is functioning properly and ignition switch is turned to RUN or START position, THEFT indicator light will turn on for 3 seconds, then turn off. Vehicle will be enabled to start and run. If THEFT indicator light is on continuously for more than 3 seconds or flashes rapidly, a problem exists in passive anti-theft system.

ENCODED IGNITION KEY

This encoded ignition key is much larger in size than a regular key to accommodate the electronics located inside plastic cover. Each encoded ignition key must be programmed into the instrument cluster. When ignition is in start or run, the instrument cluster initiates the encoded ignition key interrogation process.

TRANSCEIVER MODULE

Transceiver module communicates with encoded ignition key. During each vehicle start sequence, the transceiver module reads the encoded ignition key identification code and sends data to the instrument cluster.

INSTRUMENT CLUSTER

Instrument cluster performs all passive anti-theft system functions. The instrument cluster receives identification code from encoded ignition key and controls engine enable. The instrument cluster initiates the encoded ignition key interrogation process when ignition is in start or run. The instrument cluster communicates with Lighting Control Module (LCM), which controls the anti-theft indicator light.

POWERTRAIN CONTROL MODULE (PCM)

Passive anti-theft system uses PCM to enable or disable vehicle's engine. The instrument cluster communicates with PCM over the module communications network to enable engine operation.

COMPONENT LOCATIONS

COMPONENT LOCATIONS

Component	Location
Data Link Connector (DLC)	Below Driver's Side Of Instrument Panel, To Right Of Steering Column
Driver's Door Module (DDM)	Behind Driver's Door Panel, Lower Front Corner
Instrument Cluster [1]	Behind Left Side Of Instrument Panel
Instrument Panel Fuse Box	Below Left Instrument Panel
Keyless Entry Keypad	Driver's Door Below Exterior Door Handle
Lighting Control Module (LCM)	On Instrument Panel, Behind Headlight Switch
Light Sensor Amplifier	Top Left Side Of Instrument Panel
Power Distribution Box	Left Side Of Engine Compartment, Above Wheelwell
Powertrain Control Module (PCM)	In Passenger's Side Of Engine Compartment, On Firewall

[1] – Instrument cluster may also be referred to as Virtual Instrument Cluster (VIC).

PROGRAMMING

NOTE: *Instrument cluster may also be referred to as Virtual Image Cluster (VIC).*

KEY PROGRAMMING – SECURITY ACCESS PROCEDURE

NOTE: *Security access must be granted to erase ignition keys, enable/disable spare key programming switch, or perform parameter resets for instrument cluster or PCM. This procedure has a 10 minute time delay prior to granting security access during which the New Generation Star (NGS) tester must remain connected to vehicle. After security access has been granted, security access command menu is displayed which offers various command options. Multiple security access commands can be executed (if necessary) prior to exiting security access command menu. Execution of all necessary security access commands prior to exiting command menu avoids the performance of an additional security access procedure and the associated 10 minute time delay. Security access for the instrument cluster and security access for the PCM must be obtained separately as needed (each will require a 10 minute time delay.*

With ignition switch in RUN position and NGS connected to vehicle, enter function test menu. Select SECURITY ACCESS PROCEDURE. This procedure will take 10 minutes to perform. After the security access procedure has been completed, a new menu will be displayed with command options. Select as many functions as required before exiting this menu. Once this menu is exited, security access procedure must be performed again to perform additional commands.

KEY PROGRAMMING – WITH PROGRAMMED KEYS

NOTE: *This procedure will only work if 2 or more programmed ignition keys are available and there is a need to program additional keys. If 2 keys are not available, perform KEY PROGRAMMING – WITHOUT PROGRAMMED KEYS. PID SPARE_KY must be enabled for this procedure to operate. To enable this PID, perform KEY PROGRAMMING – SECURITY ACCESS PROCEDURE and enable spare key programming switch. If programming procedure is successful, new key(s) will start vehicle and THEFT indicator will illuminate for 3 seconds. If programming procedure is not successful, new key(s) will not start vehicle and THEFT indicator will flash for one minute (after flashing for one minute, THEFT indicator will flash fault code). If necessary, repeat programming procedure. If programming of key(s) is still unsuccessful, perform self-diagnostics. See SELF-DIAGNOSTIC SYSTEM. Maximum of 8 keys can be programmed into system. If procedure is not performed as outlined, programming procedure will end. Ignition keys must have correct mechanical key cut for vehicle and must be an encoded key.*

1) Insert the first programmed ignition key into ignition lock cylinder. Turn ignition switch from OFF to RUN position (ignition switch must stay in RUN position for one second). Turn ignition switch to OFF position and remove ignition key from ignition lock cylinder.

2) Within 5 seconds of turning ignition switch to OFF position, insert second programmed ignition key into ignition lock cylinder. Turn ignition switch from OFF to RUN position (ignition switch must stay in RUN position for one second). Turn ignition switch to OFF position and remove second ignition key from ignition lock cylinder.

3) Within 10 seconds of turning ignition switch to OFF position, insert a NEW unprogrammed ignition key into ignition lock cylinder. Turn ignition switch from OFF to RUN position (ignition switch must stay in RUN position for one second). Turn ignition switch to OFF position and remove ignition key from ignition lock cylinder. The NEW ignition key should now be programmed. To program additional key(s), repeat key programming procedure from step **1**).

KEY PROGRAMMING – WITHOUT PROGRAMMED KEYS

NOTE: *This procedure is used when a customer needs keys programmed into system and does not have 2 programmed ignition keys available, or when programmed ignition keys have been lost and/or ignition switch assembly has been replaced. This procedure will erase all programmed ignition keys from memory and prevent vehicle from starting until 2 keys have been programmed. Ignition keys must have correct mechanical key cut for vehicle and must be an encoded key. If additional key(s) are to be programmed, perform KEY PROGRAMMING – WITH PROGRAMMED KEYS. If remaining keys are with customer and not with vehicle, instruct customer to see owner's manual to program spare key(s).*

1) Turn ignition switch from OFF to RUN position. With NGS tester connected to vehicle, enter function test menu. Select SECURITY ACCESS PROCEDURE. This procedure will take 10 minutes to perform. After the security access procedure has been completed, a new menu will be displayed with command options. Select IGNITION KEY CODE ERASE.

2) Turn ignition switch to OFF position and disconnect NGS tester. Insert first encoded ignition key into ignition lock cylinder. Turn ignition switch to RUN position for 30 seconds. Turn ignition switch to OFF position and remove first encoded key.

3) Insert second encoded ignition key into ignition lock cylinder. Turn ignition switch to RUN position for 30 seconds. Turn ignition switch to OFF position and remove second encoded key. Both encoded ignition keys should now start vehicle.

KEY PROGRAMMING – SPARE KEY PROGRAMMING SWITCH

NOTE: *The spare key programming switch is a programmable switch which provides the capability to enable/disable the normal customer spare key programming procedure detailed in the owner's manual. This programmable switch is provided as a convenience for rental company fleets or other fleet purchasers who may not want the spare key programming procedure available to the vehicle driver. The spare key programming switch state can be viewed using VIC PID SPARE_KY.*

Insert a programmed ignition key into the ignition lock cylinder. Turn ignition switch from OFF to RUN position. With NGS tester connected to vehicle, enter function test menu. Select SECURITY ACCESS PROCEDURE. This procedure will take 10 minutes to perform. After the security access procedure has been completed, a new menu will be displayed with command options. The default setting on all new vehicles is ENABLE. Select SPARE KEY PROGRAMMING SWITCH. Set SPARE KEY PROGRAMMING SWITCH to ENABLE or DISABLE.

SELF-DIAGNOSTIC SYSTEM

NOTE: *Instrument cluster may also be referred to as Virtual Image Cluster (VIC).*

Verify customers complaint. Ensure electronically coded ignition key is being used. Check for damaged ignition lock cylinder switch, damaged encoded ignition key or blown fuses. Check for loose or corroded connectors, damaged wiring harness, damaged ignition switch or damaged transceiver module. Repair or replace components as necessary.

If all components are okay, connect New Generation Star (NGS) tester to Data Link Connector (DLC). Using NGS tester, perform data link diagnostics test. See DATA LINK DIAGNOSTIC TEST under COMMUNICATION NETWORK DIAGNOSTICS in MODULE COMMUNICATIONS NETWORK – CONTINENTAL article. If NGS tester responds with CKT914, CKT915 or CKT70=ALL ECUS NO RESP/NOT EQUIP, repair module communications concern. See MODULE COMMUNICATIONS NETWORK – CONTINENTAL article. If NGS tester displays NO RESP/NOT EQUIP for instrument cluster, perform TEST A: NO COMMUNICATION WITH INSTRUMENT CLUSTER under SYSTEM TESTS. If NGS tester displays NO RESP/NOT EQUIP for Lighting Control Module (LCM), perform TEST B: NO COMMUNICATION WITH LIGHTING CONTROL MODULE under SYSTEM TESTS.

If NGS tester responds with SYSTEM PASSED, retrieve and record continuous DTCs. Erase continuous DTCs. Using NGS tester, perform instrument cluster and LCM self-test. Perform appropriate test in accordance with DTC retrieved. See INSTRUMENT CLUSTER DTC INDEX and/or LIGHTING CONTROL MODULE DTC INDEX table. Codes listed in these tables are only for testing covered in this article. For complete DTC listing, see MODULE COMMUNICATIONS NETWORK – CONTINENTAL article. If no DTCs are retrieved, repair by symptom. See SYMPTOM CHART table under SYSTEM TESTS.

INSTRUMENT CLUSTER DTC INDEX

DTC [1]	Description	Test
B1213	Anti-Theft Number Of Programmed Ignition Keys Is Below Minimum	[2] DTC B1213
B1232 Or B2103	Defective Transceiver	DTC B1232
B1342	ECU Defective	[3]
B1600	PATS Ignition Key Transponder Signal Not Received	DTC B1600
B1601	PATS Received Incorrect Key Code From Transponder	DTC B1601
B1602	PATS Received Invalid Key Code Format From Transponder	DTC B1602
B1681	PATS Transceiver Signal Not Received	DTC B1681
B2139	Security Identification Does Not Match Between Instrument Cluster & PCM	DTC B2139
B2141	NVM Configuration Failure	DTC B2141
U1147	SCP Invalid Or Missing Data For Vehicle Security	DTC U1147

[1] – Codes listed in this table are only for testing covered in this article. For complete DTC listing, see MODULE COMMUNICATIONS NETWORK – CONTINENTAL article.
[2] – If DTCs B1232, B1600, B1601, B1602 OR B1681 are also present, service these DTCs frist then recheck codes.
[3] – Using NGS tester, retrieve and record DTCs. Perform instrument cluster self-test. If DTC B1342 still exists, replace instrument cluster.

LIGHTING CONTROL MODULE DTC INDEX

DTC [1]	Decsription	Test
B1342	ECU Defective	[2]

[1] – Codes listed in this table are only for testing covered in this article. For complete DTC listing, see MODULE COMMUNICATIONS NETWORK – CONTINENTAL article.
[2] – Using NGS tester, retrieve and document continuous DTCs. Clear all DTCs. Perform Lighting Contol Module (LCM) self-test. If DTC B1342 is retrieved again, replace LCM.

DIAGNOSTIC TESTS

NOTE: Instrument cluster may also be referred to as Virtual Image Cluster (VIC).

CAUTION: When battery is disconnected or modules are replaced, vehicle computer and memory systems may lose memory data. Driveability problems may exist until computer systems have completed a relearn cycle. See COMPUTER RELEARN PROCEDURES article in GENERAL INFORMATION before disconnecting battery.

DTC B1213: ANTI-THEFT NUMBER OF PROGRAMMED IGNITION KEYS IS BELOW MINIMUM

NOTE: If DTCs B1232, B1600, B1601, B1602 OR B1681 are also present, service these DTCs frist then recheck codes.

1) Using NGS tester, retrieve and record continuous DTCs. Clear continuous DTCs and perform instrument cluster self-test. If only DTC B1213 is retrieved, go to next step. If DTC B1213 is not the only code retrieved, repair other DTCs irst. See INSTRUMENT CLUSTER DTC INDEX table under SELF-DIAGNOSTIC SYSTEM. After all other DTCs are repair, clear DTCs. Repeat instrument cluster self-test.
2) Using NGS tester, monitor VIC PID NUMKEYS. If PID indicates less than 2 encoded ignition keys programmed, go to next step. If PID indicates more than 2 encoded ignition keys programmed, system is okay at this time.
3) Obtain NEW encoded ignition key(s). Insert NEW key into ignition lock cylinder. Turn ignition switch to RUN position. Program key. See KEY PROGRAMMING – WITHOUT PROGRAMMED KEYS under PROGRAMMING. If THEFT indicator illuminates for 3 seconds and then goes out, clear DTCs and perform instrument cluster self-test to ensure all codes have been cleared. If THEFT indicator illuminates continuously, repeat this step with a second NEW encoded ignition key. If THEFT indicator flashes, retrieve DTC for new fault. Perform appropriate test. See INSTRUMENT CLUSTER DTC INDEX table under SELF-DIAGNOSTIC SYSTEM.

DTC B1232: DEFECTIVE TRANSCEIVER

Turn ignition switch to LOCK position. Verify transceiver module is installed properly. Using NGS tester, retrieve and record continuous DTCs. Clear continuous DTCs and perform instrument cluster self-test. If DTC B1232 or B2103 is not retrieved, system is okay at this time. If DTC B1232 or B2103 is retrieved again, replace transceiver module. Clear DTCs and repeat instrument cluster self-test.

DTC B1600: PATS IGNITION KEY TRANSPONDER SIGNAL NOT RECEIVED

NOTE: Large metallic objects, a second PATS ignition key, or devices such as electronic credit cards on the same key ring may cause vehicle starting problem and possibly set this code. Ensure customers encoded ignition key is an approved Ford encoded ignition key. Encoded keys from Rotunda, Ilco, and Strattec are also approved keys.

1) Using NGS tester, retrieve and record continuous DTCs. Clear continuous DTCs. Perform instrument cluster self-test. If DTC B1600 is retrieved, go to next step. If any other DTCs are retrieved, perform appropriate test. See INSTRUMENT CLUSTER DTC INDEX table under SELF-DIAGNOSTIC SYSTEM. If no DTCs are retrieved, system is okay at this time.
2) Obtain NEW encoded ignition key(s). Insert NEW key into ignition. Turn ignition switch to RUN position. Program key. See KEY PROGRAMMING – WITHOUT PROGRAMMED KEYS under PROGRAMMING. Using NGS tester, perform instrument cluster self-test. If DTC B1600 is still present, go to next step. If any other DTCs are present, perform appropriate test. See INSTRUMENT CLUSTER DTC INDEX table under SELF-DIAGNOSTIC SYSTEM. If no DTCs are present, system is okay at this time.
3) Ensure ignition switch is in LOCK position. Replace transceiver module. Using customers original encoded ignition key, turn ignition switch to RUN position. Using NGS tester, perform instrument cluster self-test. If DTC B1600 is retrieved, replace instrument cluster. If DTC B1600 is not retrieved, system is okay at this time.

DTC B1601: PATS RECEIVED INCORRECT KEY CODE FROM TRANSPONDER

NOTE: Large metallic objects, a second PATS ignition key, or devices such as electronic credit cards on the same key ring may cause vehicle starting problem and possibly set this code. Ensure customers encoded ignition key is an approved Ford encoded ignition key. Encoded keys from Rotunda, Ilco, and Strattec are also approved keys.

1) Using NGS tester, retrieve and record continuous DTCs. Clear continuous DTCs and perform instrument cluster self-test. If DTC B1601 is retrieved, go to next step. If DTC B1601 is not present, system is okay at this time. Check all existing encoded ignition keys with instrument cluster self-test to verify all other encoded ignition keys are programmed.

2) Using NGS tester, monitor VIC PID NUMKEYS. If PID NUMKEYS does not indicate 8 encoded ignition keys programmed, go to next step. If PID indicates 8 encoded ignition keys programmed, erase and reprogram key codes. See KEY PROGRAMMING – WITHOUT PROGRAMMED KEYS under PROGRAMMING.

3) Verify there are at least 2 currently programmed encoded ignition keys available with vehicle. If 2 currently programmed encoded ignition keys are available with vehicle, go to next step. If 2 currently programmed encoded ignition keys are not available with vehicle, obtain 2 NEW encoded ignition keys. Program NEW encoded ignition keys. See KEY PROGRAMMING – WITHOUT PROGRAMMED KEYS under PROGRAMMING. After new encoded ignition keys are programmed, go to next step.

4) Using NGS tester, monitor VIC PID SPAREKY. If PID indicates ENABLE, perform KEY PROGRAMMING – WITHOUT PROGRAMMED KEYS under PROGRAMMING then go to next step. If PID does not indicate ENABLE, see KEY PROGRAMMING – SPARE KEY PROGRAMMING SWITCH under PROGRAMMING then go to next step.

5) Turn ignition switch to LOCK position. Using first encoded ignition key, turn ignition switch to RUN position for 30 seconds and remove first encoded ignition key. Using second encoded ignition key, turn ignition switch to RUN position for 30 seconds and remove second encoded ignition key. Attempt to start vehicle with both encoded ignition keys. If both encoded ignition keys do not start vehicle, go to next step. If both encoded ignition keys start vehicle, system is okay at this time. If there is a need to program additional encoded ignition keys, perform KEY PROGRAMMING – SPARE KEY PROGRAMMING SWITCH under PROGRAMMING.

6) Using NGS tester, retrieve and record continuous DTCs. Clear continuous DTCs and perform instrument cluster self-test. If DTC B1601 is retrieved, replace instrument cluster. If DTC B1601 is not retrieved, system is okay at this time. If any other DTCs are retrieved, perform appropriate test. See INSTRUMENT CLUSTER DTC INDEX table under SELF-DIAGNOSTIC SYSTEM.

DTC B1602: PATS RECEIVED INVALID KEY CODE FORMAT FROM TRANSPONDER

NOTE: Large metallic objects, a second PATS ignition key, or devices such as electronic credit cards on the same key ring may cause vehicle starting problem and possibly set this code. Ensure customers encoded ignition key is an approved Ford encoded ignition key. Encoded keys from Rotunda, Ilco, and Strattec are also approved keys.

1) Turn ignition switch to LOCK position. Using NGS tester, retrieve and record continuous DTCs. Clear continuous DTCs and perform instrument cluster self-test. If DTC B1602 is retrieved, go to next step. If DTC B1602 is not retrieved, system is okay at this time. Check all customer encoded ignition keys with instrument cluster self-test to verify all other keys are programmed.

2) Turn ignition switch to LOCK position. Obtain a NEW encoded ignition key. Using new encoded ignition key, turn ignition switch to RUN position. Program new encoded ignition key. See KEY PROGRAM-

MING – WITHOUT PROGRAMMED KEYS under PROGRAMMING. Using NGS tester, perform instrument cluster self-test. If DTC B1602 is retrieved, go to next step. If any DTCs are retrieved, perform appropriate test. See INSTRUMENT CLUSTER DTC INDEX table under SELF-DIAGNOSTIC SYSTEM. If no DTCs are retrieved, system is okay at this time.

3) Ensure ignition switch is in LOCK position. Replace transceiver module. Turn ignition switch to RUN position. Using NGS tester, perform instrument cluster self-test. If DTC B1602 is retrieved, replace instrument cluster. If any other DTCs are retrieved, perform appropriate test. See INSTRUMENT CLUSTER DTC INDEX table under SELF-DIAGNOSTIC SYSTEM. If DTC B1602 is not retrieved, system is okay at this time.

DTC B1681: PATS TRANSCEIVER SIGNAL IS NOT RECEIVED

1) Turn ignition switch to LOCK position. Using NGS tester, retrieve and record continuous DTCs. Clear continuous DTCs and perform instrument cluster self-test. If DTC B1681 is retrieved, go to next step. If DTC B1681 is not retrieved, system is okay at this time.

2) Ensure ignition switch is in LOCK position. Disconnect transceiver module harness connector C228. Turn ignition switch to RUN position. Measure voltage at terminal No. 2 (Red/Yellow wire) at transceiver module harness connector C228. *See Fig. 1.* If voltage is greater than 9 volts, go to next step. If voltage is 9 volts or less, repair open in Red/Yellow wire between instrument panel fuse box and transceiver module.

3) Turn ignition switch to LOCK position. Measure resistance between ground and terminal No. 1 (Black/Light Blue wire) at transceiver module harness connector C228. If resistance is 5 ohms or less, go to next step. If resistance is greater than 5 ohms, repair open in Black/Light Blue wire between transceiver module and ground.

4) Connect transceiver module harness connector C228. Turn ignition switch to RUN position. Using a voltmeter, backprobe at terminal No. 3 (Gray/Orange wire) at transceiver module harness connector C228. If voltage is 9 volts or less, go to next step. If voltage is greater than 9 volts, go to step 7).

5) Turn ignition switch to LOCK position. Disconnect transceiver module harness connector C228. Measure resistance between ground and terminal No. 3 (Gray/Orange wire) at transceiver module harness connector C228. If resistance is greater than 100 ohms, go to next step. If resistance is 100 ohms or less, check Gray/Orange wire for short to ground and repair as necessary. If circuit is okay, replace instrument cluster.

6) Ensure ignition switch is in LOCK position. Disconnect instrument cluster harness connector C256. Measure resistance in Gray/Orange wire between terminal No. 6 at instrument cluster harness connector C256 and terminal No. 3 at transceiver module harness connector C228. *See Figs. 1 and 2.* If resistance is 5 ohms or less, go to next step. If resistance is greater than 5 ohms, repair open in Gray/Orange wire.

7) Ensure ignition switch is in LOCK position. Connect transceiver module harness connector C228. Connect instrument cluster harness connector C256. Turn ignition switch to RUN position. Using a voltmeter, backprobe at terminal No. 4 (White/Light Green wire) at transceiver module harness connector C228. If voltage is 9 volts or less, go to next step. If voltage is greater than 9 volts, go to step 9).

8) Turn ignition switch to LOCK position. Disconnect transceiver module harness connector C228. Measure resistance between ground and terminal No. 4 (White/Light Green wire) at transceiver module harness connector C228. If resistance is greater than 100 ohms, go to next step. If resistance is 100 ohms or less, check White/Light Green wire for short to ground and repair as necessary. If circuit is okay, replace instrument cluster.

9) Connect transceiver module harness connector C228. Turn ignition switch to RUN position. Using NGS tester, trigger instrument cluster active command TRANSMIT SIGNAL COMMAND to ON. Using a voltmeter, backprobe at terminal No. 4 (White/Light Green wire) at transceiver module harness connector C228 and ground while triggering active command from ON to OFF. Voltage should be greater than 9 volts

in OFF position and less than one volt in ON position. If voltage is as specified, go to next step. If voltage is not as specified, check for open in White/Light Green wire between transceiver module and instrument cluster and repair as necessary. If circuit is okay, replace instrument cluster.

10) Turn ignition switch to LOCK position. Replace transceiver module. Turn ignition switch to RUN position. Using NGS tester, perform instrument cluster self-test. If DTC B1681 is retrieved, go to next step. If DTC B1681 is not retrieved, system is okay at this time.

11) Turn ignition switch to LOCK position. Replace instrument cluster. Turn ignition switch to RUN position. Using NGS tester, perform instrument cluster self-test. If DTC B1681 is retrieved, repair White/Light Green or Gray/Orange wire(s) between transceiver module and instrument cluster. If no DTCs are retrieved, system is okay at this time. If any other DTCs are retrieved, perform appropriate test. See INSTRUMENT CLUSTER DTC INDEX table under SELF-DIAGNOSTIC SYSTEM.

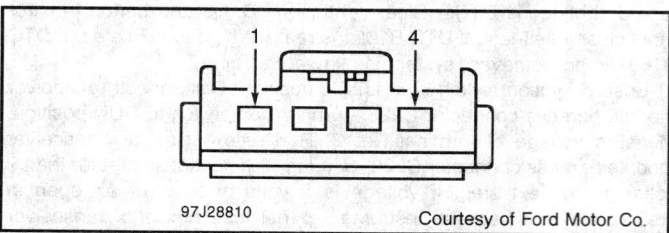

97J28810   Courtesy of Ford Motor Co.

Fig. 1: Identifying Transceiver Module Harness Connector C228 Terminals

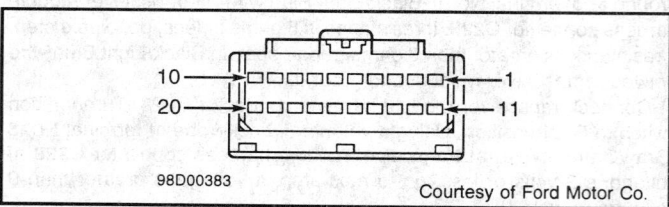

98D00383   Courtesy of Ford Motor Co.

Fig. 2: Identifying Instrument Cluster Harness Connector C256 Terminals

DTC B2139: SECURITY IDENTIFICATION DOES NOT MATCH BETWEEN INSTRUMENT CLUSTER & PCM

1) Turn ignition switch to LOCK position. Using NGS tester, retrieve and record continuous DTCs. Clear continuous DTCs and perform instrument cluster self-test. If DTC B2139 is retrieved, go to next step. If DTC B2139 is not retrieved, system is okay at this time.

2) Perform security access for instrument cluster. See KEY PROGRAMMING – SECURITY ACCESS PROCEDURE under PROGRAMMING. Using NGS tester, select PARAMETER RESET command for instrument cluster. Using NGS tester, select PARAMETER RESET command for PCM. Turn ignition switch to RUN position for 30 seconds. Turn ignition switch to LOCK position. Using NGS tester, perform instrument cluster self-test. If DTC B2139 is not retrieved, system is okay at this time. If DTC B2139 is retrieved, verify PCM calibration is correct for vehicle. If calibration is okay, replace instrument cluster. If DTC B2139 still exists, replace PCM.

DTC B2141: NVM CONFIGURATION FAILURE

1) Turn ignition switch to LOCK position. Using NGS tester, retrieve and record continuous DTCs. Clear continuous DTCs and perform instrument cluster self-test. If no DTCs or only DTC B2141 is retrieved, go to next step. If DTC B2141 and DTC U1147 are retrieved together, perform DTC U1147: SCP INVALID OR MISSING DATA FOR VEHICLE SECURITY.

2) Perform security access for PCM. See KEY PROGRAMMING – SECURITY ACCESS PROCEDURE under PROGRAMMING. Using NGS tester, select PCM active command KEEP ALIVE MEMORY RESET. Turn ignition switch to LOCK position. Turn ignition switch to

RUN position for 30 seconds. Turn ignition switch to LOCK position. Start vehicle. If vehicle does not start, go to next step. If vehicle starts, system is okay at this time.

3) Turn ignition switch to LOCK position. Using NGS tester, clear all continuous DTCs. Turn ignition switch to LOCK position. Turn ignition switch to RUN position for 30 seconds. Turn ignition switch to LOCK position. Using NGS tester, perform instrument cluster self-test. If no DTCs are not retrieved, system is okay at this time. If DTC B2141 is retrieved, verify PCM calibration is correct for vehicle. If calibration is okay, replace instrument cluster. If DTC B2141 still exists, replace PCM. If any other DTCs are retrieved, perform appropriate test. See INSTRUMENT CLUSTER DTC INDEX table under SELF-DIAGNOSTIC SYSTEM.

DTC U1147: SCP INVALID OR MISSING DATA FOR VEHICLE SECURITY

1) Start engine. If vehicle does not start with THEFT indicator flashing, go to next step. If vehicle starts with THEFT indicator flashing, problem is in PCM. See appropriate SELF-DIAGNOSTICS article in ENGINE PERFORMANCE in appropriate MITCHELL® manual.

2) Using NGS tester, retrieve and record continuous DTCs. Clear continuous DTCs and perform PCM self-test. If NGS tester communicates with PCM, go to next step. If NGS tester does not communicate with NGS tester, repair network communication concern. See MODULE COMMUNICATIONS NETWORK – CONTINENTAL article.

3) Using NGS tester, retrieve and record continuous DTCs. If DTC P1260 is retrieved, go to next step. If DTC P1260 is not retrieved, check PCM power and ground circuits. See appropriate SELF-DIAGNOSTICS article in ENGINE PERFORMANCE in appropriate MITCHELL® manual.

4) Repeat self-diagnostics. See SELF-DIAGNOSTIC SYSTEM. Turn ignition switch to LOCK position. Using NGS tester, retrieve and record continuous DTCs. Clear continuous DTCs and perform instrument cluster self-test. If DTC U1147 is not retrieved, system is okay at this time. If DTC U1147 is retrieved, replace instrument cluster. If DTC U1147 still exists, replace PCM.

SYSTEM TESTS

NOTE: Instrument cluster may also be referred to as Virtual Image Cluster (VIC).

CAUTION: When battery is disconnected or modules are replaced, vehicle computer and memory systems may lose memory data. Driveability problems may exist until computer systems have completed a relearn cycle. See COMPUTER RELEARN PROCEDURES article in GENERAL INFORMATION before disconnecting battery.

SYMPTOM CHART

Symptom	Test
No Communication With Instrument Cluster	A
No Communication With Lighting Control Module	B
THEFT Indicator Is Always/Never On Or THEFT Indicator Will Not Proveout	C
Alarm System Does Not Operate Properly – Vehicle Starts But THEFT Indicator Flashes Fault Code When Key Is In RUN Position	1
Vehicle Does Not Start	2

¹ – Perform DTC U1147: SCP INVALID OR MISSING DATA FOR VEHICLE SECURITY under DIAGNOSTIC TROUBLE CODE TESTS.

² – Using NGS tester, perform instrument cluster self-test. Retrieve DTCs. If DTCs are present, perform appropriate test. See INSTRUMENT CLUSTER DTC INDEX table under SELF-DIAGNOSTIC SYSTEM. If no DTCs are present, system is okay at this time.

TEST A: NO COMMUNICATION INSTRUMENT CLUSTER

NOTE: Perform data link diagnostic test after any repairs are complete. See DATA LINK DIAGNOSTIC TEST under COMMUNICATION NETWORK DIAGNOSTICS in MODULE COMMUNICATIONS NETWORK – CONTINENTAL article.

1) Turn ignition switch to LOCK position. Disconnect instrument cluster harness connector C256. Measure voltage at terminal No. 9 (Violet wire) at instrument cluster harness connector C256. *See Fig. 2.* If battery voltage exists, go to next step. If battery voltage does not exist, go to step **6)**.

2) Turn ignition switch to RUN position. Measure voltage at terminal No. 20 (Light Green/Violet wire) at instrument cluster harness connector C256. If battery voltage exists, go to next step. If batter voltage does not exist, go to step **9)**.

3) Turn ignition switch to LOCK position. Disconnect instrument cluster harness connector C255. Measure voltage at terminal No. 21 (Red/Yellow wire) at instrument cluster harness connector C255. *See Fig. 3.* If battery voltage exists, go to next step. If battery voltage does not exist, go to step **12)**.

4) Ensure ignition switch is in LOCK position. Measure resistance between ground and terminal No. 10 (Black/Light Blue wire) at instrument cluster harness connector C256. If resistance is 5 ohms or less, go to next step. If resistance is greater than 5 ohms, repair open in Black/Light Blue wire between instrument cluster and ground then go to next step.

5) Ensure ignition switch is in LOCK position. Measure resistance between ground and terminal No. 26 (Black wire) at instrument cluster harness connector C255. Measure resistance between ground and terminal No. 27 (Black/Light Blue wire) at instrument cluster harness connector C255. If both resistance readings are 5 ohms or less, repair network communication concern. See MODULE COMMUNICATIONS NETWORK – CONTINENTAL article. If either resistance reading is greater than 5 ohms, repair open in Black wire or Black/Light Blue wire between instrument cluster and ground.

6) Turn ignition switch to LOCK position. Remove fuse No. 26 (10-amp) in instrument panel fuse box. Check fuse. If fuse is okay, go to next step. If fuse is blown, go to step **8)**.

7) Turn ignition switch to RUN position. Measure voltage at input side of fuse No. 26 (10-amp) in instrument panel fuse box. If battery voltage exists, repair open in Violet wire between instrument panel fuse box and instrument cluster. If battery voltage does not exist, repair open in Tan/Black wire between instrument panel fuse box and power distribution box.

8) Ensure fuse No. 26 is still removed. Turn ignition switch to LOCK position. Measure resistance between ground and terminal No. 9 (Violet wire) at instrument cluster harness connector C256. If resistance is 10 k/ohms or less, repair short to ground in Violet wire between instrument panel fuse box and instrument cluster. If resistance is greater than 10 k/ohms, replace fuse No. 26. If fuse fails again, replace instrument cluster.

9) Turn ignition switch to LOCK position. Remove fuse No. 28 (10-amp) in instrument panel fuse box. Check fuse. If fuse is okay, go to next step. If fuse is blown, go to step **11)**.

10) Turn ignition switch to RUN position. Measure voltage at input side of fuse No. 28 in instrument panel fuse box. If battery voltage exists, repair open in Light Green/Violet wire between instrument panel fuse box and instrument cluster. If battery voltage does not exist, repair open in Gray/Yellow wire between instrument panel fuse box and ignition switch.

11) Turn ignition switch to LOCK position. Measure resistance between ground and terminal No. 20 (Light Green/Violet wire) at instrument cluster harness connector C256. If resistance is 10 k/ohms or less, repair short to ground in Light Green/Violet wire between instrument panel fuse box and instrument cluster. If resistance is greater than 10 k/ohms, replace fuse No. 28. If fuse fails again, replace instrument cluster.

12) Turn ignition switch to LOCK position. Remove fuse No. 5 (10-amp) in instrument panel fuse box. If fuse is okay, go to next step. If fuse is blown, go to step **14)**.

13) Turn ignition switch to RUN position. Measure voltage between at input side of fuse No. 5 in instrument panel fuse box. If battery voltage exists, repair open in Red/Yellow wire between instrument panel fuse box and instrument cluster. If battery voltage does not exist, repair open in Brown/Pink wire between instrument panel fuse box and ignition switch.

14) Ensure fuse No. 5 is still removed. Turn ignition switch to LOCK position. Measure resistance between ground and terminal No. 21 (Red/Yellow wire) at instrument cluster harness connector C255. If resistance is 10 k/ohms or less, repair short to ground in Red/Yellow wire between instrument panel fuse box and instrument cluster. If resistance is greater than 10 k/ohms, replace fuse No. 5. If fuse fails again, replace instrument cluster.

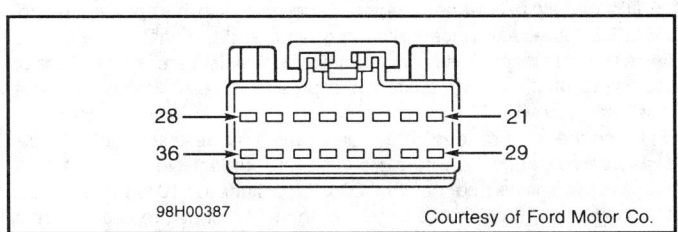

98H00387   Courtesy of Ford Motor Co.

Fig. 3: Identifying Instrument Cluster Harness Connector C255 Terminals

TEST B: NO COMMUNICATION WITH LIGHTING CONTROL MODULE

1) Turn ignition switch to LOCK position. Connect New Generation Star (NGS) tester to Data Link Connector (DLC). Monitor Lighting Control Module (LCM) PID IGN_LC. If NGS tester does not display UNABLE TO PERFORM TEST/FUNCTION or MODULE NOT RESPONDING: LCM or CHECK IGNITION STATUS/VERIFY CABLE REQUIREMENTS or CHECK CABLE CONNECTIONS, go to next step. If NGS tester displays UNABLE TO PERFORM TEST/FUNCTION or MODULE NOT RESPONDING: LCM or CHECK IGNITION STATUS/VERIFY CABLE REQUIREMENTS or CHECK CABLE CONNECTIONS, go to step **16)**.

2) Turn ignition switch to RUN position. Monitor LCM PID IGN_LC while turning key to each position. If PID IGN_LC shows ACCY while in ACCESSORY position and OFF in all other positions, replace LCM. If PID IGN_LC shows ACCY while in RUN position, go to next step. If PID IGN_LC shows OFF in all positions, go to step **7)**.

3) Turn ignition switch to RUN position. Measure voltage at output side of fuse No. 5 (10-amp) in instrument panel fuse box. If battery voltage does not exist, go to next step. If battery voltage exists, repair open in Red/Yellow wire between instrument panel fuse box and LCM.

4) Check fuse No. 5 in instrument panel fuse box. If fuse is blown, go to next step. If fuse is okay, repair open in Brown/Pink wire between instrument panel fuse box and ignition switch.

5) Turn ignition switch to LOCK position. Disconnect LCM harness connector C206. Disconnect light sensor amplifier harness connector C243. Measure resistance between ground and terminal No. 17 (Red/Yellow wire) at LCM harness connector C206. *See Fig. 4.* If resistance is 20 ohms or less, go to next step. If resistance is greater than 20 ohms, repair short to ground in Red/Yellow wire.

6) Turn ignition switch to LOCK position. Connect LCM harness connector C206. Remove fuse No. 5 (10-amp) in instrument panel fuse box. Measure resistance between ground and output side of fuse No. 5 in instrument panel fuse box. If resistance is 20 ohms or less, repair autolamps. See AUTOLAMP SYSTEMS – CONTINENTAL article. If resistance is greater than 20 ohms, replace LCM.

7) Turn ignition switch to RUN position. Measure voltage at output side of fuse No. 4 (10-amp) in instrument panel fuse box. If battery voltage exists, go to next step. If battery voltage does not exist, go to step **9)**.

8) Turn ignition switch to LOCK position. Disconnect LCM harness connector C208. Turn ignition switch to RUN position. Measure voltage at terminal No. 2 (Black/Pink wire) at LCM harness connector C208. *See*

Fig. 5. If battery voltage exists, replace LCM. If battery voltage does not exist, repair open in Black/Pink wire.

9) Turn ignition switch to LOCK position. Check fuse No. 4 (10-amp) in instrument panel fuse box. If fuse is blown, go to next step. If fuse is okay, repair open in Black/Light Green wire between instrument panel fuse box and ignition switch.

10) Disconnect driver's door lock switch harness connector C505. Measure resistance between ground and terminal No. 2 (Black/Pink wire) at LCM harness connector C208. If resistance is 10 k/ohms or less, go to next step. If resistance is greater than 10 k/ohms, replace driver's door lock switch.

11) Disconnect passenger's door lock switch harness connector C602. Measure resistance between ground and terminal No. 2 (Black/Pink wire) at LCM harness connector C208. If resistance is 10 k/ohms or less, go to next step. If resistance is greater than 10 k/ohms, replace passenger's door lock switch.

12) Disconnect passenger's power window switch harness connector C600. Measure resistance between ground and terminal No. 2 (Black/Pink wire) at LCM harness connector C208. If resistance is 10 k/ohms or less, go to next step. If resistance is greater than 10 k/ohms, replace passenger's power window switch.

13) Disconnect left rear power window switch harness connector C709. Measure resistance between ground and terminal No. 2 (Black/Pink wire) at LCM harness connector C208. If resistance is 10 k/ohms or less, go to next step. If resistance is greater than 10 k/ohms, replace left rear power window switch.

14) Disconnect right rear power window switch harness connector C809. Measure resistance between ground and terminal No. 2 (Black/Pink wire) at LCM harness connector C208. If resistance is 10 k/ohms or less, go to next step. If resistance is greater than 10 k/ohms, replace right rear power window switch.

15) Ensure ignition switch is in LOCK position. Connect LCM harness connector C208. Using and ohmmeter, measure resistance by back-probing between ground and terminal No. 2 (Black/Pink wire) at LCM harness connector C208. If resistance is greater than 2 k/ohms, replace LCM. If resistance is 2 k/ohms or less, repair Black/Pink wire.

16) Turn ignition switch to LOCK position. Disconnect LCM harness connectors. Measure resistance between ground and terminal No. 13 (Black wire) at LCM harness connector C206. *See Fig. 4.* Measure resistance between ground and terminal No. 1 (Black wire) at LCM harness connector C207. *See Fig. 6.* Measure resistance between ground and terminal No. 9 (Black wire) at LCM harness connector C211. *See Fig. 7.* If all resistance readings are 5 ohms or less, go to next step. If any resistance reading is greater than 5 ohms, repair appropriate Black wire.

17) Measure resistance between ground and terminal No. 15 (Black/Light Blue wire) at LCM harness connector C207. If resistance is 5 ohms or less, repair module communication concern. See MODULE COMMUNICATIONS NETWORK – CONTINENTAL article. If resistance is greater than 5 ohms, repair open in Black/Light Blue wire.

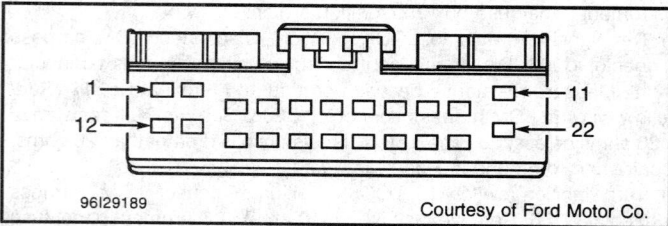

Fig. 4: Identifying Lighting Control Module Harness Connector C206 Terminals

TEST C: THEFT INDICATOR IS ALWAYS/NEVER ON OR THEFT INDICATOR WILL NOT PROVEOUT

1) Turn ignition switch to LOCK position. Using NGS tester, select instrument cluster active command mode. If active command mode can be entered, go to next step. If active command mode can not be entered, perform TEST A: NO COMMUNICATION WITH INSTRUMENT CLUSTER.

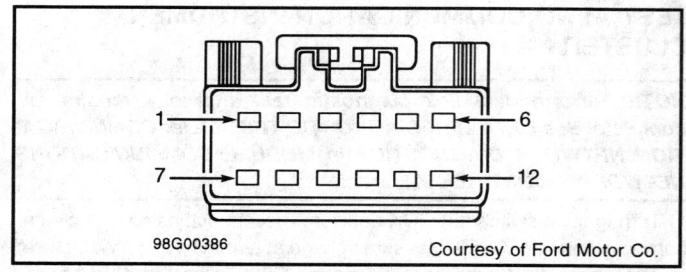

Fig. 5: Identifying Lighting Control Module Harness Connector C208 Terminals

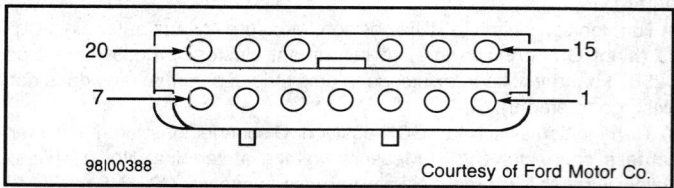

Fig. 6: Identifying Lighting Control Module Harness Connector C207 Terminals

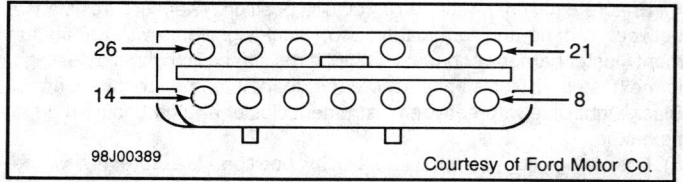

Fig. 7: Identifying Lighting Control Module Harness Connector C211 Terminals

2) Using NGS tester, trigger LCM active command WARNING LAMPS AND CHIME ANTI-THEFT to ON. If THEFT indicator does not illuminate, go to next step. If THEFT indicator illuminates, system is okay at this time. Verify concern with customer.

3) Turn ignition switch to LOCK position. Disconnect light sensor amplifier harness connector C243. Turn ignition switch to RUN position. Measure at terminal No. 2 (Dark Blue/Light Green wire) at light sensor amplifier harness connector C243 while triggering LCM active command WARNING LAMPS AND CHIME ANTI-THEFT to ON. *See Fig. 8.* If battery voltage does not exist, go to next step. If battery voltage exists, go to step 5).

4) Turn ignition switch to LOCK position. Disconnect LCM harness connector C208. Measure resistance in Dark Blue/Light Green wire between terminal No. 8 at LCM harness connector C208 and terminal No. 2 at light sensor amplifier harness connector C243. *See Figs. 5 and 8.* If resistance is 5 ohms or less, replace LCM. If resistance is greater than 5 ohms, repair open in Dark Blue/Light Green wire between LCM and light sensor amplifier.

5) Turn ignition switch to LOCK position. Measure resistance between ground and terminal No. 1 (Black wire) at light sensor amplifier C243. If resistance is 5 ohms or less, go to next step. If resistance is greater than 5 ohms, repair open in Black wire between light sensor amplifier and ground.

6) Remove anti-theft LED. Measure resistance between anti-theft LED terminals in both directions. Resistance should be greater than 10 k/ohms in one direction and 10-20 ohms in the other. If resistance is as specified, go to next step. If resistance is not as specified, replace anti-theft LED and return to step 2).

7) Check LCM and light sensor amplifier connectors for damaged pins or corroded wires. If connectors and wires are okay, go to next step. If connectors and wires are not okay, repair or replace connectors and wires as necessary.

8) Turn ignition switch to RUN position. Measure voltage at terminal No. 3 (Pink wire) at light sensor amplifier harness connector C243. If battery voltage exists, go to next step. If battery voltage does not exist, repair open in Pink wire between instrument panel fuse box and light sensor amplifier.

9) Turn ignition switch to RUN position. Measure voltage at terminal No. 6 (Red/Yellow wire) at light sensor amplifier harness connector C243. If battery voltage exists, replace light sensor amplifier. If battery voltage does not exist, repair open in Red/Yellow wire between instrument panel fuse box and light sensor amplifier.

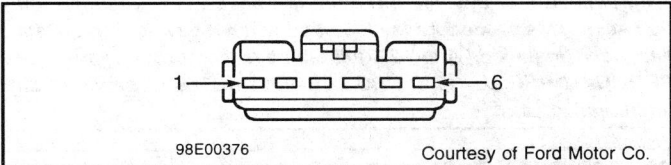

98E00376   Courtesy of Ford Motor Co.

Fig. 8: Identifying Light Sensor Amplifier Harness Connector C243 Terminals

REMOVAL & INSTALLATION

CAUTION: When battery is disconnected or modules are replaced, vehicle computer and memory systems may lose memory data. Driveability problems may exist until computer systems have completed a relearn cycle. See COMPUTER RELEARN PROCEDURES article in GENERAL INFORMATION before disconnecting battery.

TRANSCEIVER MODULE

NOTE: If transceiver module is replaced, all existing ignition keys must be reprogrammed. See PROGRAMMING.

Removal & Installation – 1) Disconnect negative battery cable. Transceiver module is located on ignition switch lock cylinder. Insert ignition key into ignition switch lock cylinder. Turn ignition switch lock cylinder to RUN position. Insert a punch in steering column cover hole and press ignition switch lock cylinder release tab while removing ignition switch lock cylinder. Remove tilt wheel lever.

2) Remove lower steering column opening cover. Remove upper and lower steering column covers. Remove hood release handle screw and position hood release handle aside. Remove parking brake release handle screw and position parking brake release handle aside. Remove instrument panel steering column opening cover reinforcement.

3) Remove transceiver module retaining screw from steering column. Carefully pry transceiver over rib on ignition switch lock cylinder housing. Remove transceiver module harness retainers. Disconnect transceiver module harness connector and remove transceiver module. To install, reverse removal procedure.

LIGHTING CONTROL MODULE (LCM)

NOTE: Lighting Control Module (LCM) must be reconfigured if replaced. Refer to NGS tester help screen on configuration card to program Daytime Running Lamps (DRL).

Removal & Installation – Lighting Control Module (LCM) is located on left side of steering column. Disconnect negative battery cable. Remove lower steering column opening cover. Remove 3 LCM retaining screws. Disconnect LCM harness connectors and remove LCM. To install, reverse removal procedure.

WIRING DIAGRAMS

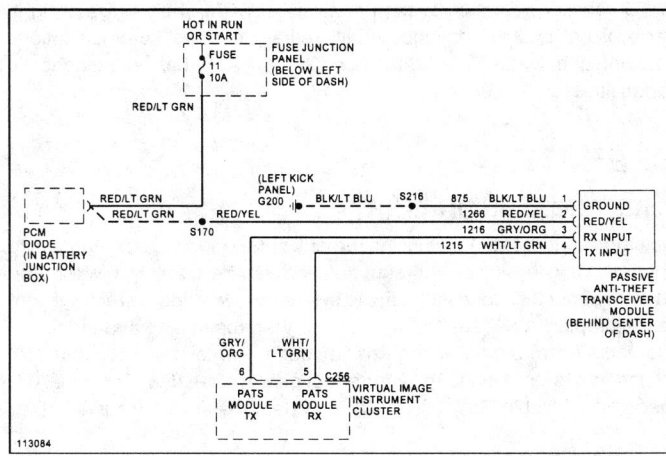

Fig. 9: Passive Anti-Theft System (PATS) Wiring Diagram (Continental)

DESCRIPTION

Passive Anti-Theft System (PATS) is available on some vehicles. The system is passive in that it does not require any activity from the user. System uses radio frequency identification technology to verify if proper key is being used to attempt to start the vehicle.

During each starting sequence, the transceiver module reads the encoded ignition key identification code and sends the data to the Powertrain Control Module (PCM). If the key's identification code is programmed into anti-theft system, vehicle is capable of starting. If key's identification code is incorrect or missing, vehicle is prevented from starting.

PATS vehicle protection system consists of PCM, theft indicator light, transceiver module, encoded ignition key, module communications network and Data Link Connector (DLC). PATS has self-diagnostic capabilities.

OPERATION

THEFT INDICATOR LIGHT

Indicator light located in the instrument panel digital clock is used to determine system operation status. Upon vehicle start, light will illuminate for about 3 seconds to indicate system is operating correctly. If light flashes rapidly for about one minute and then repeatedly at an irregular interval, system did not recognize key code. Remove and reinsert key. If light comes on continuously for about one minute, then flashes PATS Diagnostic Trouble Code(s) (DTC), a system malfunction is indicated.

ENCODED IGNITION KEY

When ignition is in START or RUN position, PCM initiates the encoded ignition key interrogation process. Each encoded ignition key must be programmed into PCM before it can be used to start the vehicle.

TRANSCEIVER MODULE

Transceiver module communicates with encoded ignition key. During each starting sequence, the transceiver module reads the encoded ignition key identification code and sends the data to the PCM.

COMPONENT LOCATIONS

COMPONENT LOCATIONS

Component	Location
Anti-Theft Indicator	Center Of Instrument Panel
Data Link Connector	Below Driver's Side Of Instrument Panel, To Right Of Steering Column
Powertrain Control Module	Right Side Of Engine Compartment, On Firewall
Passive Anti-Theft System Module	1
Passive Anti-Theft System Transceiver Module	On Steering Column

1 – Passive Anti-Theft System (PATS) module is built into Powertrain Control Module (PCM).

PROGRAMMING

ERASE ALL KEYS & PROGRAM 2 KEYS

NOTE: This procedure is to be used when a customer needs keys programmed into system and does not have 2 programmed ignition keys. This procedure is also used when a new ignition switch has been installed. After 2 ignition keys are programmed, see PROGRAMMING USING 2 PROGRAMMED KEYS to program any additional keys.

CAUTION: This procedure will erase all programmed ignition keys from vehicles memory and vehicle will not start until at least 2 ignition keys have been programmed.

1) Ensure 2 PATS key are available and both operate ignition switch. Turn ignition switch to START position. Connect NGS tester to Data Link Connector (DLC). Install Ford Service Function (FSF) card in NGS tester. Follow service access procedure to obtain security access. See SECURITY ACCESS.

2) Select IGNITION KEY CODE ERASE on NGS tester. Place ignition switch in RUN position and disconnect NGS tester. Turn ignition switch to LOCK position. Install first key to be programmed in ignition switch. Turn ignition switch to RUN position for 3 seconds then back to LOCK position and remove key. Within 5 seconds insert second ignition key to be programmed into ignition switch and turn ignition switch to RUN position for 3 second. Turn igniton switch to LOCK position and remove key. Vehicle should now start with both these keys. If any additional key are to be programmed, see PROGRAMMING USING 2 PRO-GRAMMED KEYS.

PROGRAMMING USING 2 PROGRAMMED KEYS

NOTE: This procedure only works if 2 or more keys are already programmed, 2 of the programmed keys are available and PCM PID SPARE_KEY is enabled. See SPARE KEY PROGRAMMING SWITCH. A maximum of 8 keys can be programmed.

Insert a programmed key into ignition switch. Turn ignition switch to START position for one second. Turn ignition switch to LOCK position and remove key. Within 5 seconds insert another programmed ignition key into ignition switch and turn ignition switch to START position for one second. Turn igniton switch to LOCK position and remove key. Within 5 seconds insert ignition key to be programmed into ignition switch and turn ignition switch to START position for one second. Turn igniton switch to LOCK position and remove key. Vehicle should now start with new ignition key.

PROGRAMMING WITHOUT USING 2 PROGRAMMED KEYS

NOTE: This procedure is used when customer needs extra keys programmed and 2 programmed keys are not available but system has 2 ignition keys programmed. A maximum of 8 keys can be programmed. If 8 keys are already programmed, this procedure will not allow any more to be programmed. The number of programmed key can be determined by accessing PCM PID NUMKEYS with NGS tester.

Insert unprogrammed key in ignition and turn ignition switch to START position. Connect New Generation Star (NGS) tester to Data Link Connector (DLC). Insert Ford Service Function (FSF) card in NGS tester. Perform security access procedure. See SECURITY ACCESS. Select IGNITION KEY CODE PROGRAM. Turn ignition switch to LOCK position. Disconnect NGS tester. Key should now be programmed and be able to start vehicle.

1999 ACCESSORIES & EQUIPMENT
Passive Anti-Theft Systems – Contour & Mystique (Cont.)

FORD
4-123

SECURITY ACCESS

NOTE: DO NOT disconnect NGS tester during this procedure or procedure will have to be started over from beginning.

Connect NGS tester to Data Link Connector (DLC). Insert Ford Service Function (FSF) card in NGS tester. Turn ignition switch to RUN position. Enter PCM. Select SECURITY ACCESS. Wait 10 minutes. After 10 minutes, a new menu will be displayed with command options (IGNITION KEY CODE ERASE or SPARE KEY PROGRAMMING SWITCH). Select desired function. Once NGS tester exists this menu, security access procedure must be carried out again to carry out additional commands.

SPARE KEY PROGRAMMING SWITCH

NOTE: Spare key programming switch is not a visible mechanical switch. A NGS tester is necessary to enable and disable this switch. The state of this switch can be viewed by accessing PCM PID SPARE_KY with NGS tester.

Insert a programmed ignition key into ignition switch. Turn ignition switch to RUN position. Connect NGS tester to Data Link Connector (DLC). Insert Ford Service Function (FSF) card into NGS tester. Obtain security access. See SECURITY ACCESS. Using NGS tester, toggle SPARE KEY PROGRAMMING SWITCH to desired position.

SELF-DIAGNOSTIC SYSTEM

Verify customers complaint. Ensure electronically coded ignition key is being used. Check for damaged ignition lock cylinder switch, damaged encoded ignition key or open fuses. Check for loose or corroded connectors, damaged wiring harness, damaged ignition switch or damaged transceiver module. Repair or replace components as necessary.

If all components are okay, connect New Generation Star (NGS) tester to Data Link Connector (DLC), located beneath instrument panel. Using NGS tester, perform data link diagnostics test. See DATA LINK DIAGNOSTIC TEST under COMMUNICATION NETWORK DIAGNOSTICS in MODULE COMMUNICATIONS NETWORK – CONTOUR & MYSTIQUE article. If NGS tester responds with CKT914, CKT915 or CKT70=ALL ECUS NO RESP/NOT EQUIP, repair module communications concern. See MODULE COMMUNICATIONS NETWORK – CONTOUR & MYSTIQUE article. If NGS tester displays NO RESP/NOT EQUIP for Powertrain Control Module (PCM), perform TEST A: NO COMMUNICATION WITH INSTRUMENT CLUSTER under SYSTEM TESTS.

If NGS tester responds with SYSTEM PASSED, retrieve and record continuous DTCs. Erase continuous DTCs. Using NGS tester, perform PCM. Perform appropriate test in accordance with DTC retrieved. See PCM DTC INDEX table. Codes listed in this table are only for testing covered in this article. For complete DTC listing, see appropriate SELF-DIAGNOSTICS article in ENGINE PERFORMANCE in appropriate MITCHELL® manual. Codes listed in this table are only for testing covered in this article. For complete DTC listing, see appropriate

SELF-DIAGNOSTICS article in ENGINE PERFORMANCE in appropriate MITCHELL® manual. If no DTCs are retrieved, repair by symptom. See SYMPTOM CHART table under SYSTEM TESTS.

SYSTEM TESTS

SYMPTOM CHART

Symptom	Test
Pats Transceiver Antenna Not Connected	A
No Key Code Received/Damaged Encoded Ignition Key Or Use Of Non-Pats Key	B
Incorrect Key Code From Ignition Key Transponder	C
Invalid Key Code Format From Ignition Key Transponder	D
Transceiver Defective Or Not Connected	E
Anti-Theft Number Of Keys Is Below Minimum	F
Anti-Theft Indicator Always/Never On (No Indicator Prove Out)	G
Engine Does Not Crank But Anti-Theft Indicator Proves Out	H

TEST A: PATS TRANSCEIVER ANTENNA NOT CONNECTED

Turn ignition switch to RUN position. Ensure PATS transceiver module is correctly installed. Connect NGS tester to Data Link Connector (DLC). Using NGS tester, clear continuous DTCs. Turn ignition switch to LOCK position. Turn ignition switch to RUN position. Retrieve continuous PCM DTCs. If DTC B1232 is retrieved, replace PATS transceiver module. If DTC B1232 is not retrieved, system is okay at this time.

TEST B: NO KEY CODE RECEIVED/DAMAGED ENCODED IGNITION KEY OR USE OF NON-PATS KEY

NOTE: If PCM is replace, PCM MUST be reprogrammed and all ignition keys MUST be programmed into PCM.

1) Ensure ignition switch is in LOCK position. Connect NGS tester to Data Link Connector (DLC). Turn ignition switch to RUN position. Using NGS tester, retrieve and record continuous DTCs. Clear continuous DTCs and perform PCM self-test. If DTC B1600 is retrieved, go to next step. If no DTCs are retrieved, system is okay at this time. If any other DTCs are retrieved, perform appropriate test. See PCM DTC INDEX table under SELF-DIAGNOSTIC SYSTEM.

2) Turn ignition switch to LOCK position. Cut a NEW encoded ignition key. Using NEW key, turn ignition switch to RUN position. Program NEW key. See PROGRAMMING WITHOUT USING 2 PROGRAMMED KEYS under PROGRAMMING. Clear continuous PCM DTCs. Turn ignition switch to LOCK position. Turn ignition switch to RUN position. Retrieve PCM continuous DTCs. If DTC B1600 is retrieved, go to next step. If no DTCs are retrieved, system is okay at this time. If any other DTCs are retrieved, perform appropriate test. See PCM DTC INDEX table under SELF-DIAGNOSTIC SYSTEM.

PCM DTC INDEX

DTC [1]	Description	Test
B1213	Anti-Theft Number Of Programmed Keys Is Below Minimum	[2] F
B1600	No Key Code Received/Damaged Encoded Ignition Key Or Use Of Non-PATS Key	B
B1601	Incorrect Key Code From Ignition Key Transponder	C
B1602	Invalid Key Code Format From Ignition Key Transponder	D
B1681	Transceiver Defective Or Not Connected	E
B2103	PATS Antenna Not Connected	A

[1] – For a listing of all "P" code, see appropriate SELF-DIAGNOSTICS article in ENGINE PERFORMANCE in appropriate MITCHELL® manual.
[2] – If DTCs B1232, B1600, B1601, B1602 OR B1681 are also present, service these DTCs frist then recheck codes.

FORD
4-124

1999 ACCESSORIES & EQUIPMENT
Passive Anti-Theft Systems – Contour & Mystique (Cont.)

3) Turn ignition switch to LOCK position. Install a new PATS transceiver. Turn ignition switch to RUN position. Clear continuous DTCs. Turn ignition switch to LOCK position. Remove NEW key from ignition. Using customers old key, turn ignition switch to RUN position. Retrieve continuous PCM DTCs. If DTC B1600 exists, replace PCM. If no DTCs are retrieved, system is okay at this time. If any other DTCs are retrieved, perform appropriate test. See PCM DTC INDEX table under SELF-DIAGNOSTIC SYSTEM.

TEST C: INCORRECT KEY CODE FROM IGNITION KEY TRANSPONDER

NOTE: If PCM is replace, PCM MUST be reprogrammed and all ignition keys MUST be programmed into PCM.

NOTE: PCM disables engine for 20 seconds every time DTC B1601 is set. Ignition switch must remain in RUN position for at least 20 seconds before attempting to start vehicle. Using NGS tester, check PCM PID ANTISCAN for unprogrammed key timeout status.

1) Connect NGS tester at Data Link Connector (DLC). Using NGS tester, clear continuous DTCs. Turn ignition switch to LOCK position. Turn ignition switch to RUN position. Retrieve continuous PCM DTCs. If DTC B1601 is retrieved, go to next step. If no DTCs are retrieved, system is okay at this time. If any other DTCs are retrieved, perform appropriate test. See PCM DTC INDEX table under SELF-DIAGNOSTIC SYSTEM.

2) Using NGS tester, monitor PCM PID NUMKEYS. If PID indicates less than 8, go to next step. If PID indicates 8, erase any reprogram all keys to be used with system. See ERASE ALL KEYS & PROGRAM 2 KEYS under PROGRAMMING. Repeat PCM self-test.

3) If PCM NUMKEYS indicates at least 2, go to next step. If PID NUMKEYS indicates less than 2, cut and program a NEW encoded ignition key then go to step **5)**. See PROGRAMMING WITHOUT USING 2 PROGRAMMED KEYS under PROGRAMMING.

4) Using NGS tester, monitor PCM PID SPARE_KEY. If PID indicates YES, program key. See PROGRAMMING USING 2 PROGRAMMED KEYS. If PID does not indicate YES, perform SPARE KEY PROGRAMMING SWITCH.

5) Turn ignition switch to LOCK position. Insert programmed key in ignition switch and turn ignition switch to RUN position for 3 second. Turn ignition switch to LOCK position. Using another programmed ignition key, turn ignition switch to RUN position for 3 seconds. Start vehicle using second ignition key. If vehicle does not start, go to next step. If vehicle starts, see PROGRAMMING USING 2 PROGRAMMED KEYS.

6) Using NGS tester, clear continuous DTCs. Turn igniton switch to LOCK position. Turn ignition switch to RUN position. Retrieve continuous PCM DTCs. If DTC B1601 is retrieved, replace PCM. If DTC B1601 is not retrieved, system is okay at this time.

TEST D: INVALID KEY CODE FORMAT FROM IGNITION KEY TRANSPONDER

NOTE: Large metallic objects, a second PATS ignition key, or devices such as electronic credit cards on the same key ring may cause vehicle starting problem and possibly set this code. Ensure customers encoded ignition key is an approved Ford encoded ignition key. Encoded keys from Rotunda, Ilco, and Strattec are also approved keys.

1) Connect NGS tester to Data Link Connector (DLC). Using NGS tester, clear continuous DTCs. Turn ignition switch to LOCK position. Turn ignition switch to RUN position. Retrieve continuous PCM DTCs. If DTC B1602 is retrieved, go to next step. Id DTC B1602 is not retrieved, system is okay at this time.

2) Turn ignition switch to LOCK position. Obtain NEW encoded ignition key and insert into ignition lock cylinder. Using NEW key, turn ignition switch to RUN position. Program NEW encoded ignition key. See PROGRAMMING WITHOUT USING 2 PROGRAMMED KEYS under PROGRAMMING. Turn ignition switch to LOCK position. Turn ignition

switch to RUN position. Using NGS tester, retrieve continuous PCM DTCs. If DTC B1602 is retrieved, go to next step. If DTC B1602 is not retrieved, system is okay at this time.

3) Turn ignition switch to LOCK position. Install a new PATS transceiver. Turn ignition switch to RUN position. Using NGS tester, clear continuous DTCs. Turn ignition switch to LOCK position. Retrieve continuous PCM DTCs. If any DTCs are retrieved, perform appropriate test. See PCM DTC INDEX table under SELF-DIAGNOSTIC SYSTEM. If no DTCs are retrieved, system is okay at this time.

TEST E: TRANSCEIVER DEFECTIVE OR NOT CONNECTED

NOTE: If PCM is replace, PCM MUST be reprogrammed and all ignition keys MUST be programmed into PCM.

1) Connect NGS tester to Data Link Connector (DLC). Using NGS tester, clear continuous DTCs. Turn ignition switch to LOCK position. Turn ignition switch to RUN position. Retrieve continuous PCM DTCs. If DTC B1681 is retrieved, go to next step. Id DTC B1681 is not retrieved, system is okay at this time.

2) Turn ignition off. Disconnect PATS transceiver module harness connector C1945. Turn ignition switch to RUN position. Measure voltage at terminal No. 1 (Green/Black wire) at PATS transceiver module harness connector C1945. *See Fig. 1.* If battery voltage exists, go to next step. If battery voltage does not exist, repair open in Green/Black wire.

3) Turn ignition switch to LOCK position. Measure resistance between ground and terminal No. 2 (Black/Green wire) at PATS transceiver module harness connector C1945. If resistance is 5 ohms or less, go to next step. If resistance is greater than 5 ohms, repair open in Black/Green wire.

4) Connect PATS transceiver module harness connector C1945. Turn ignition switch to RUN position. Using a voltmeter, backprobe at terminal No. 4 (White/Green wire) at PATS transceiver module harness connector C1945. If voltage is 8 volts or less, go to next step. If voltage is greater than 8 volts, go to step **6)**.

5) Turn ignition switch to LOCK position. Disconnect PCM harness connector C421 and PATS transceiver module harness connector C1945. Measure resistance between ground and terminal No. 4 (White/Green wire) at PATS transceiver module harness connector C1945. If resistance is greater than 10 k/ohms, go to next step. If resistance is 10 k/ohms or less, repair short to ground in White/Green wire. Using NGS tester, repeat PCM self-test. If system fails again, replace PCM.

6) Turn ignition switch to LOCK position. Connect PCM harness connector C421 and PATS transceiver module harness connector C1945. Turn ignition switch to RUN position. Using a voltmeter, backprobe at terminal No. 3 (Gray/Orange wire) at PATS transceiver module harness connector C1945. If voltage is 8 volts or less, go to next step. If voltage is greater than 8 volts, go to step **10)**.

7) Turn ignition switch to LOCK position. Disconnect PCM harness connector C421. Connect breakout box to PCM harness connector. Measure resistance between ground and terminal No. 17 at breakout box. If resistance is 10 k/ohms or less, go to next step. If resistance is greater than 10 k/ohms, go to step **9)**.

8) Ensure ignition switch is in LOCK position. Disconnect PATS transceiver module harness connector C1945. Measure resistance between ground and terminal No. 3 (Gray/Orange wire) at PATS transceiver module harness connector C1945. If resistance is 10 k/ohms or less, repair short to ground in Gray/Orange wire. If resistance is greater than 10 k/ohms, replace PATS transceiver module.

9) Disconnect PATS transceiver module harness connector C1945. Measure resistance in Gray/Orange wire between terminal No. 3 at PATS transceiver module harness connector and terminal No. 17 at breakout box. If resistance is 5 ohms or less, replace PCM. If resistance is greater than 5 ohms, repair open in Gray/Orange wire.

10) Using NGS tester, trigger PCM active command TRANSMIT SIGNAL to on. Using a voltmeter, backprobe at terminal No. 3 (Gray/Orange wire at PATS transceiver module harness connector C1945. If greater than 5 volts exists, go to next step. If 5 volts or less exists, replace PATS transceiver module.

11) Turn ignition switch to LOCK position. Disconnect PCM harness connector C421. Disconnect PATS transceiver module harness connector C1945. Turn ignition switch to RUN position. Measure voltage at terminal No. 3 (Gray/Orange wire) at PATS transceiver module harness connector C1945. Is voltage exists, repair short to voltage in Gray/Orange wire. If voltage does not exist, replace PCM.

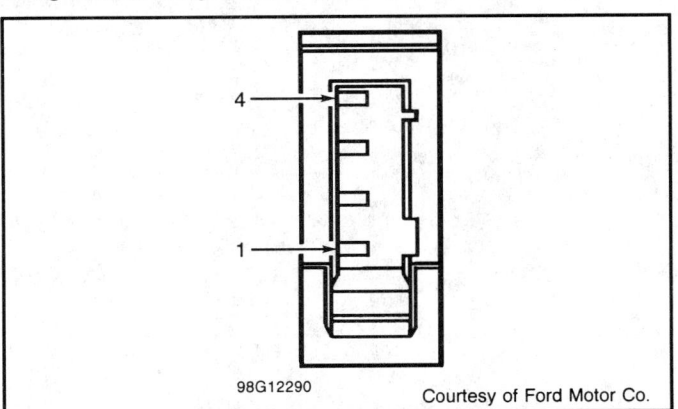

98G12290   Courtesy of Ford Motor Co.

Fig. 1: Identifying PATS Transceiver Module Harness Connector C1945 Terminals

TEST F: ANTI-THEFT NUMBER OF KEYS IS BELOW MINIMUM

1) Turn ignition switch to LOCK position. Connect NGS tester to Data Link Connector (DLC). Turn ignition switch to RUN position. Using NGS tester, retrieve continuous PCM DTCs. Clear continuous DTCs. Turn ignition switch to LOCK position. Turn ignition switch to RUN position. Retrieve continuous PCM DTCs. If DTC B1213 is the only DTC retrieved, go to next step. If any other DTCs are retrieved, perform appropriate test. See PCM DTC INDEX table under SELF-DIAGNOSTIC SYSTEM.

2) Using NGS tester, monitor and record check PCM PID NUMKEYS. If PID indicates less than 2 keys, go to next step. If PID does not indicate less than 2 keys, system is okay at this time.

3) Obtain NEW encoded ignition key and insert into ignition lock cylinder. Using NEW key, turn ignition switch to RUN position. Program NEW encoded ignition key. See PROGRAMMING WITHOUT USING 2 PROGRAMMED KEYS under PROGRAMMING. If theft indicator does not illuminates for 3 seconds and then go out, go to next step. If theft indicator illuminates for 3 seconds and then goes out, clear DTCs and perform PCM self-test. Verify no DTCs are present.

4) Using NGS tester, monitor PCM PID SERV_MOD. If PID indicates YES, reprogram all keys and then repeat PCM self-test. If PID does not indicate YES and LED is continuously illuminated, repeat step **3)**. If PID does not indicate YES and LED is flashing, retrieve PCM DTCs and perform appropriate test. See PCM DTC INDEX table under SELF-DIAGNOSTIC SYSTEM.

TEST G: ANTI-THEFT INDICATOR ALWAYS/NEVER ON (NO INDICATOR PROVE OUT)

NOTE: If PCM is replace, PCM MUST be reprogrammed and all ignition keys MUST be programmed into PCM.

1) Turn ignition switch to LOCK position. Disconnect PCM harness connector C421. Connect breakout box to PCM harness connector C421. Using a fused jumper wire, ground terminal No. 82 at breakout box. If anti-theft indicator does not illuminate, go to next step. If anti-theft indicator illuminates, replace PCM.

2) Disconnect anti-theft indicator harness connector C831. Measure voltage at terminal No. 4 (Orange wire) at anti-theft indicator harness connector C831. *See Fig. 2.* If battery voltage exists, go to next step. If battery voltage does not exist, repair open in Orange wire.

3) Measure resistance in Black/Blue wire between terminal No. 6 at anti-theft indicator harness connector C831 and terminal No. 82 at breakout box. If resistance is greater than 5 ohms, repair open in Black/Blue wire. If resistance is 5 ohms or less, replace anti-theft indicator.

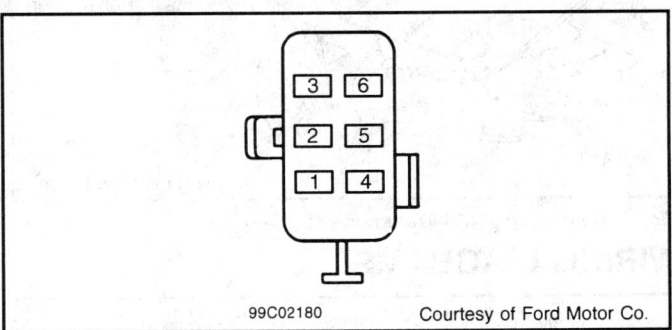

99C02180   Courtesy of Ford Motor Co.

Fig. 2: Identifying Anti-Theft Indicator Harness Connector C831 Terminals

TEST H: ENGINE DOES NOT CRANK BUT ANTI-THEFT INDICATOR PROVES OUT

1) Turn ignition switch to LOCK position. Disconnect PCM harness connector. Connect breakout box to PCM harness connector. Turn ignition switch to RUN position. Measure voltage at terminal No. 18 at breakout box. If voltage is greater than 8 volts, go to next step. If voltage is 8 volts or less, repair starting system. See appropriate STARTERS article in STARTING & CHARGING SYSTEMS.

2) Turn ignition switch to LOCK position. Turn ignition switch to RUN position. Measure voltage at terminal No. 18 at breakout box. If voltage is greater than 2 volts, replace PCM. If voltage is 2 volts or less, repair starting system. See appropriate STARTERS article in STARTING & CHARGING SYSTEMS.

REMOVAL & INSTALLATION

PATS MODULE

NOTE: PATS module is built into PCM. If PCM is replace, PCM MUST be reprogrammed and all ignition keys MUST be programmed into PCM.

PATS TRANSCEIVER

WARNING: To avoid injury from accidental air bag deployment, read and carefully follow all WARNINGS and SERVICE PRECAUTIONS in appropriate AIR BAG RESTRAINT SYSTEMS article.

Removal & Installation – Disconnect negative battery cable. Remove lower steering column cover. Disconnect wiring harness connector. Remove PATS transceiver. *See Fig. 3.* To install, reverse removal procedure.

FORD
4-126

1999 ACCESSORIES & EQUIPMENT
Passive Anti-Theft Systems – Contour & Mystique (Cont.)

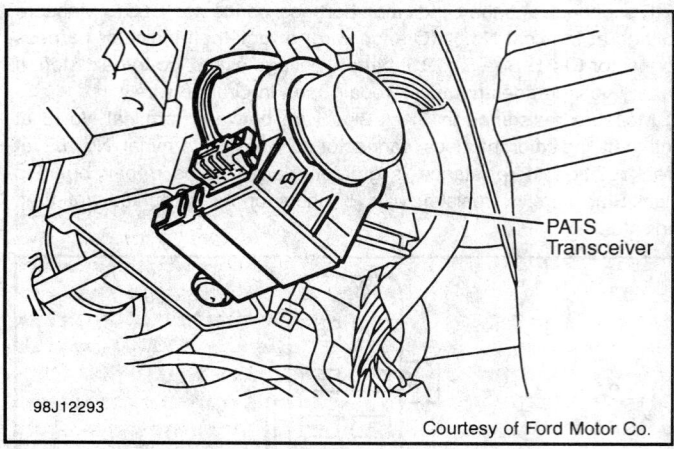

Fig. 3: Removing PATS Transceiver

WIRING DIAGRAMS

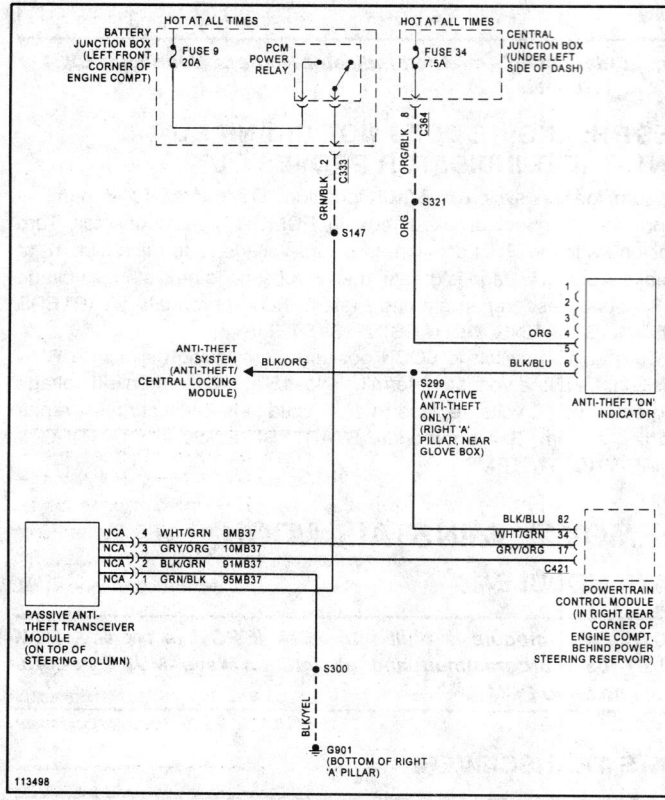

Fig. 4: Passive Anti-Theft System Wiring Diagram
(Contour & Mystique)

DESCRIPTION

Passive Anti-Theft System (PATS) is available on some vehicles. The system is passive in that it does not require any activity from the user. System uses radio frequency identification technology to verify if proper key is being used to attempt to start the vehicle.

During each starting sequence, the transceiver module reads the encoded ignition key identification code and sends the data to the Powertrain Control Module (PCM). If the key's identification code is programmed into anti-theft system, vehicle is capable of starting. If key's identification code is incorrect or missing, vehicle is prevented from starting.

PATS vehicle protection system consists of PCM, theft indicator light, transceiver module, encoded ignition key, module communications network and Data Link Connector (DLC). PATS has self-diagnostic capabilities.

OPERATION

THEFT INDICATOR LIGHT

Indicator light located in the instrument panel digital clock is used to determine system operation status. Upon vehicle start, light will illuminate for about 3 seconds to indicate system is operating correctly. If light flashes rapidly for about one minute and then repeatedly at an irregular interval, system did not recognize key code. Remove and reinsert key. If light comes on continuously for about one minute, then flashes PATS Diagnostic Trouble Codes (DTCs), a system malfunction is indicated.

ENCODED IGNITION KEY

When ignition is in START or RUN position, PCM initiates the encoded ignition key interrogation process. Each encoded ignition key must be programmed into PCM before it can be used to start the vehicle.

TRANSCEIVER MODULE

Transceiver module communicates with encoded ignition key. During each starting sequence, the transceiver module reads the encoded ignition key identification code and sends the data to the PCM.

COMPONENT LOCATIONS

COMPONENT LOCATIONS

Component	Location
Anti-Theft Indicator	Center Of Instrument Panel
Data Link Connector	Below Driver's Side Of Instrument Panel, To Right Of Steering Column
Powertrain Control Module	Right Side Of Engine Compartment, On Firewall [1]
Passive Anti-Theft System Module	
Passive Anti-Theft System Transceiver Module	On Steering Column

[1] – Passive Anti-Theft System (PATS) module is built into Powertrain Control Module (PCM).

PROGRAMMING

KEY PROGRAMMING – ERASE ALL KEYS & PROGRAM 2 KEYS

NOTE: This procedure is used when a customer needs keys programmed into system and does not have 2 programmed ignition keys available, or when programmed ignition keys have been lost and/or ignition switch assembly has been replaced. This procedure will erase all programmed ignition keys from memory and prevent vehicle from starting until 2 keys have been programmed. Ignition keys must have correct mechanical key cut for vehicle and must be an encoded key. If additional key(s) are to be programmed, perform KEY PROGRAMMING – USING 2 PROGRAMMED KEYS. If remaining keys are with customer and not with vehicle, instruct customer to see owner's manual to program spare key(s).

1) Insert Ford Service Function (FSF) card into NGS tester. Turn ignition switch from LOCK to RUN position. With NGS tester connected to vehicle, enter PCM then select SECURITY ACCESS PROCEDURE. This procedure will take 10 minutes to perform. After the security access procedure has been completed, a new menu will be displayed with command options. Select IGNITION KEY CODE ERASE.

2) Turn ignition switch to LOCK position and disconnect NGS tester. Insert first encoded ignition key into ignition lock cylinder. Turn ignition switch to RUN position for 3 seconds. Turn ignition switch to LOCK position and remove first encoded key.

3) Within 5 seconds, insert second encoded ignition key into ignition lock cylinder. Turn ignition switch to RUN position for 3 seconds. Turn ignition switch to LOCK position and remove second encoded key. Both encoded ignition keys should now start vehicle.

KEY PROGRAMMING – SECURITY ACCESS PROCEDURE

NOTE: Security access must be granted to erase ignition keys, enable/disable spare key programming switch, or perform parameter resets for PCM. This procedure has a 10-minute time delay prior to granting security access during which the New Generation Star (NGS) tester must remain connected to vehicle. After security access has been granted, security access command menu is displayed which offers various command options. Multiple security access commands can be executed (if necessary) prior to exiting security access command menu. Execution of all necessary security access commands prior to exiting command menu avoids the performance of an additional security access procedure and the associated 10-minute time delay.

Insert Ford Service Function (FSF) card into NGS tester. Turn ignition switch from LOCK to RUN position. With NGS tester connected to vehicle, enter PCM then select SECURITY ACCESS PROCEDURE. This procedure will take 10 minutes to perform. After the security access procedure has been completed, a new menu will be displayed with command options. Select as many functions as required before exiting this menu. Once this menu is exited, security access procedure must be performed again to perform additional commands.

KEY PROGRAMMING – SPARE KEY PROGRAMMING SWITCH

NOTE: The spare key programming switch is a programmable switch which provides the capability to enable/disable the normal customer spare key programming procedure detailed in the owner's manual. This programmable switch is provided as a convenience for rental company fleets or other fleet purchasers who may not want the spare key programming procedure available to the vehicle driver. The spare key programming switch state can be viewed using PCM PID SPARE_KY.

Insert a programmed ignition key into the ignition lock cylinder. Insert Ford Service Function (FSF) card into NGS tester. Turn ignition switch from LOCK to RUN position. With NGS tester connected to vehicle, enter PCM then select SECURITY ACCESS PROCEDURE. This procedure will take 10 minutes to perform. After the security access procedure has been completed, a new menu will be displayed with command options. The default setting on all new vehicles is ENABLE. Select SPARE KEY PROGRAMMING SWITCH. Set SPARE KEY PROGRAMMING SWITCH to ENABLE to allow keys to be programmed or DISABLE to make key programming not accessible.

KEY PROGRAMMING – USING 2 PROGRAMMED KEYS

NOTE: This procedure will only work if 2 or more programmed ignition keys are available and there is a need to program additional keys. If 2 keys are not available, perform KEY PROGRAMMING – ERASE ALL KEYS & PROGRAM 2 KEYS. PID SPARE_KY must be enabled for this procedure to operate. To enable this PID, perform KEY PROGRAMMING – SPARE KEY PROGRAMMING SWITCH and enable spare key programming switch. If programming procedure is successful, new key(s) will start vehicle and THEFT indicator will illuminate for 3 seconds. If programming procedure is not successful, new key(s) will not start vehicle and THEFT indicator will flash for one minute (after flashing for one minute, THEFT indicator will flash fault code). If necessary, repeat programming procedure. If programming of key(s) is still unsuccessful, perform self-diagnostics. See SELF-DIAGNOSTIC SYSTEM. Maximum of 8 keys can be programmed into system. If procedure is not performed as outlined, programming procedure will end. Ignition keys must have correct mechanical key cut for vehicle and must be an encoded key.

1) Insert the first programmed ignition key into ignition lock cylinder. Turn ignition switch from LOCK to RUN position (ignition switch must stay in RUN position for one second). Turn ignition switch to LOCK position and remove ignition key from ignition lock cylinder.
2) Within 5 seconds of turning ignition switch to LOCK position, insert second programmed ignition key into ignition lock cylinder. Turn ignition switch from LOCK to RUN position (ignition switch must stay in RUN position for one second). Turn ignition switch to LOCK position and remove second ignition key from ignition lock cylinder.
3) Within 5 seconds of turning ignition switch to LOCK position, insert a NEW unprogrammed ignition key into ignition lock cylinder. Turn ignition switch from LOCK to RUN position (ignition switch must stay in RUN

position for one second). Turn ignition switch to LOCK position and remove ignition key from ignition lock cylinder. The NEW ignition key should now be programmed. To program additional key(s), repeat key programming procedure from step 1).

KEY PROGRAMMING – WITHOUT USING 2 PROGRAMMED KEYS

NOTE: This procedure is used when customer needs extra keys programmed and 2 programmed keys are not available but system has 2 ignition keys programmed. A maximum of 8 keys can be programmed. If 8 keys are already programmed, this procedure will not allow any more to be programmed. The number of programmed keys can be determined by accessing PCM PID NUMKEYS with NGS tester.

Insert unprogrammed key in ignition and turn ignition switch to RUN position. Connect New Generation Star (NGS) tester to Data Link Connector (DLC). Insert Ford Service Function (FSF) card in NGS tester. Perform security access procedure. See KEY PROGRAMMING – SECURITY ACCESS PROCEDURE. Select IGNITION KEY CODE PROGRAM. Turn ignition switch to LOCK position. Disconnect NGS tester. Key should now be programmed and be able to start vehicle.

TROUBLE SHOOTING

Verify customers complaint. Ensure electronically coded ignition key is being used. Check for damaged ignition lock cylinder switch, damaged encoded ignition key, more than one PATS key on key chain or blown fuses. Check for loose or corroded connectors, damaged wiring harness, damaged ignition switch or damaged transceiver module. If problem exists, repair or replace components as necessary. If problem does not exist, perform self-diagnostics. See SELF-DIAGNOSTIC SYSTEM.

SELF-DIAGNOSTIC SYSTEM

Connect New Generation Star (NGS) tester to Data Link Connector (DLC), located beneath instrument panel. Using NGS tester, perform data link diagnostics test. See DATA LINK DIAGNOSTIC TEST under COMMUNICATION NETWORK DIAGNOSTICS in MODULE COMMUNICATIONS NETWORK – COUGAR article. If NGS tester responds with CKT914, CKT915 or CKT70=ALL ECUS NO RESP/NOT EQUIP, repair module communications concern. See MODULE COMMUNICATIONS NETWORK – COUGAR article. If NGS tester displays NO RESP/NOT EQUIP for Powertrain Control Module (PCM), perform TEST I: NO COMMUNICATION WITH POWERTRAIN CONTROL MODULE under SYSTEM TESTS.

If NGS tester responds with SYSTEM PASSED, retrieve and record continuous DTCs. Erase continuous DTCs. Using NGS tester, perform PCM self-test. Perform appropriate test in accordance with DTC retrieved. See POWERTRAIN CONTROL MODULE DTC INDEX table. Codes listed in these table are only for testing of PCM body codes. For testing of "P" codes, see appropriate SELF-DIAGNOSTICS article in ENGINE PERFORMANCE in appropriate MITCHELL® manual. If no DTCs are retrieved, repair by symptom. See SYMPTOM CHART table under SYSTEM TESTS.

POWERTRAIN CONTROL MODULE DTC INDEX

DTC [1]	Description	Test
B1213	Anti-Theft Number Of Programmed Keys Is Below Minimum	F
B1232 Or B2103	Pats Transceiver Antenna Not Connected	A
B1600	No Key Code Received, Damaged Encoded Ignition Key Or Use Of Non-PATS Key	B
B1601	Unprogrammed Encoded Ignition Key (Unprogrammed Ignition Key)	D
B1602	Invalid Key Code Format From Ignition Key Transponder (Partial Key Read)	C
B1681	Transceiver Defective Or Not Connected	E

[1] – Codes list in this table are only Powertrain Control Module (PCM) body codes. For a list of all "P" codes, see appropriate SELF-DIAGNOSTICS article in ENGINE PERFORMANCE in appropriate MITCHELL® manual.

SYSTEM TESTS

SYMPTOM CHART

Symptom	Test
Pats Transceiver Antenna Not Connected	A
No Key Code Received/Damaged Encoded Ignition Key Or Use Of Non-Pats Key	B
Incorrect Key Code From Ignition Key Transponder	C
Invalid Key Code Format From Ignition Key Transponder	D
Transceiver Defective Or Not Connected	E
Anti-Theft Number Of Keys Is Below Minimum	F
Anti-Theft Indicator Always/Never On (No Indicator Prove Out)	G
Engine Does Not Crank But Anti-Theft Indicator Proves Out	H
No Communication With Powertrain Control Module	I

TEST A: PATS TRANSCEIVER ANTENNA NOT CONNECTED

Turn ignition switch to RUN position. Ensure PATS transceiver module is correctly installed. Connect New Generation Star (NGS) tester to Data Link Connector (DLC). Using NGS tester, clear continuous DTCs. Turn ignition switch to LOCK position. Turn ignition switch to RUN position. Retrieve continuous PCM DTCs. If DTC B1232 is retrieved, replace PATS transceiver module. If DTC B1232 is not retrieved, system is okay at this time.

TEST B: NO KEY CODE RECEIVED/DAMAGED ENCODED IGNITION KEY OR USE OF NON-PATS KEY

NOTE: If PCM is replace, PCM MUST be reprogrammed and all ignition keys MUST be programmed into PCM. See COMPUTER RELEARN PROCEDURES article in GENERAL INFORMATION.

1) Ensure ignition switch is in LOCK position. Connect New Generation Star (NGS) tester to Data Link Connector (DLC). Turn ignition switch to RUN position. Using NGS tester, retrieve and record continuous DTCs. Clear continuous DTCs and perform PCM self-test. If DTC B1600 is retrieved, go to next step. If no DTCs are retrieved, system is okay at this time. If any other DTCs are retrieved, perform appropriate test. See POWERTRAIN CONTROL MODULE DTC INDEX table under SELF-DIAGNOSTIC SYSTEM.

2) Turn ignition switch to LOCK position. Cut a NEW encoded ignition key. Using NEW key, turn ignition switch to RUN position. Program NEW key. See KEY PROGRAMMING – WITHOUT USING 2 PROGRAMMED KEYS under PROGRAMMING. Clear continuous PCM DTCs. Turn ignition switch to LOCK position. Turn ignition switch to RUN position. Using NGS tester, retrieve PCM continuous DTCs. If DTC B1600 is retrieved, go to next step. If no DTCs are retrieved, system is okay at this time. If any other DTCs are retrieved, perform appropriate test. See POWERTRAIN CONTROL MODULE DTC INDEX table under SELF-DIAGNOSTIC SYSTEM.

3) Turn ignition switch to LOCK position. Install a new PATS transceiver. Turn ignition switch to RUN position. Clear continuous DTCs. Turn ignition switch to LOCK position. Remove NEW key from ignition. Using customers old key, turn ignition switch to RUN position. Retrieve continuous PCM DTCs. If DTC B1600 exists, replace PCM. If no DTCs are retrieved, system is okay at this time. If any other DTCs are retrieved, perform appropriate test. See POWERTRAIN CONTROL MODULE DTC INDEX table under SELF-DIAGNOSTIC SYSTEM.

TEST C: INCORRECT KEY CODE FROM IGNITION KEY TRANSPONDER

NOTE: If PCM is replace, PCM MUST be reprogrammed and all ignition keys MUST be programmed into PCM. See COMPUTER RELEARN PROCEDURES article in GENERAL INFORMATION.

NOTE: PCM disables engine for 20 seconds every time DTC B1601 is set. Ignition switch must remain in RUN position for at least 20 seconds before attempting to start vehicle. Using NGS tester, check PCM PID ANTISCAN for unprogrammed key timeout status.

1) Connect New Generation Star (NGS) tester at Data Link Connector (DLC). Using NGS tester, clear continuous DTCs. Turn ignition switch to LOCK position. Turn ignition switch to RUN position. Retrieve continuous PCM DTCs. If DTC B1601 is retrieved, go to next step. If no DTCs are retrieved, system is okay at this time. If any other DTCs are retrieved, perform appropriate test. See POWERTRAIN CONTROL MODULE DTC INDEX table under SELF-DIAGNOSTIC SYSTEM.

2) Using NGS tester, monitor PCM PID NUMKEYS. If PID indicates less than 8, go to next step. If PID indicates 8, erase an reprogram all keys to be used with system. See KEY PROGRAMMING – ERASE ALL KEYS & PROGRAM 2 KEYS under PROGRAMMING. Repeat PCM self-test.

3) If PCM NUMKEYS indicates at least 2, go to next step. If PID NUMKEYS indicates less than 2, cut and program a NEW encoded ignition key then go to step 5). See KEY PROGRAMMING – WITHOUT USING 2 PROGRAMMED KEYS under PROGRAMMING.

4) Using NGS tester, monitor PCM PID SPARE_KEY. If PID indicates YES, program key. See KEY PROGRAMMING – USING 2 PROGRAMMED KEYS. If PID does not indicate YES, perform KEY PROGRAMMING – SPARE KEY PROGRAMMING SWITCH.

5) Turn ignition switch to LOCK position. Insert programmed key in ignition switch and turn ignition switch to RUN position for 3 second. Turn ignition switch to LOCK position. Using another programmed ignition key, turn ignition switch to RUN position for 3 seconds. Start vehicle using second ignition key. If vehicle does not start, go to next step. If vehicle starts, see KEY PROGRAMMING – USING 2 PROGRAMMED KEYS.

6) Using NGS tester, clear continuous DTCs. Turn ignition switch to LOCK position. Turn ignition switch to RUN position. Retrieve continuous PCM DTCs. If DTC B1601 is retrieved, replace PCM. If DTC B1601 is not retrieved, system is okay at this time.

TEST D: INVALID KEY CODE FORMAT FROM IGNITION KEY TRANSPONDER

NOTE: Large metallic objects, a second PATS ignition key, or devices such as electronic credit cards on the same key ring may cause vehicle starting problem and possibly set this code. Ensure customers encoded ignition key is an approved Ford encoded ignition key. Encoded keys from Rotunda, Ilco, and Strattec are also approved keys.

1) Connect New Generation Star (NGS) tester to Data Link Connector (DLC). Using NGS tester, clear continuous DTCs. Turn ignition switch to LOCK position. Turn ignition switch to RUN position. Retrieve continuous PCM DTCs. If DTC B1602 is retrieved, go to next step. If DTC B1602 is not retrieved, system is okay at this time.

2) Turn ignition switch to LOCK position. Obtain NEW encoded ignition key and insert into ignition lock cylinder. Using NEW key, turn ignition

switch to RUN position. Program NEW encoded ignition key. See KEY PROGRAMMING – WITHOUT USING 2 PROGRAMMED KEYS under PROGRAMMING. Turn ignition switch to LOCK position. Turn ignition switch to RUN position. Using NGS tester, retrieve continuous PCM DTCs. If DTC B1602 is retrieved, go to next step. If DTC B1602 is not retrieved, system is okay at this time.

3) Turn ignition switch to LOCK position. Install a new PATS transceiver. Turn ignition switch to RUN position. Using NGS tester, clear continuous DTCs. Turn ignition switch to LOCK position. Retrieve continuous PCM DTCs. If any DTCs are retrieved, perform appropriate test. See POWERTRAIN CONTROL MODULE DTC INDEX table under SELF-DIAGNOSTIC SYSTEM. If no DTCs are retrieved, system is okay at this time.

TEST E: TRANSCEIVER DEFECTIVE OR NOT CONNECTED

NOTE: If Powertrain Control Module (PCM) is replace, PCM MUST be reprogrammed and all ignition keys MUST be programmed into PCM. See COMPUTER RELEARN PROCEDURES article in GENERAL INFORMATION.

1) Connect New Generation Star (NGS) tester to Data Link Connector (DLC). Using NGS tester, clear continuous DTCs. Turn ignition switch to LOCK position. Turn ignition switch to RUN position. Retrieve continuous PCM DTCs. If DTC B1681 is retrieved, go to next step. If DTC B1681 is not retrieved, system is okay at this time.

2) Turn ignition switch to LOCK position. Disconnect Passive Anti-Theft System (PATS) transceiver module harness connector C1945. Turn ignition switch to RUN position. Measure voltage at terminal No. 1 (Green/Black wire) at PATS transceiver module harness connector C1945. *See Fig. 1.* If battery voltage exists, go to next step. If battery voltage does not exist, repair open in Green/Black wire.

3) Turn ignition switch to LOCK position. Measure resistance between ground and terminal No. 2 (Black/Green wire) at PATS transceiver module harness connector C1945. If resistance s 5 ohms or less, go to next step. If resistance is greater than 5 ohms, repair open in Black/Green wire.

4) Connect PATS transceiver module harness connector C1945. Turn ignition switch to RUN position. Using a voltmeter, backprobe at terminal No. 4 (White/Green wire) at PATS transceiver module harness connector C1945. If voltage is 8 volts or less, go to next step. If voltage is greater than 8 volts, go to step **7)**.

5) Turn ignition switch to LOCK position. Disconnect PCM harness connector C421 and PATS transceiver module harness connector C1945. Measure resistance between ground and terminal No. 4 (White/Green wire) at PATS transceiver module harness connector C1945. If resistance is greater than 10 k/ohms, go to next step. If resistance is 10 k/ohms or less, repair short to ground in White/Green wire. Using NGS tester, repeat PCM self-test. If system fails again, replace PCM.

6) Measure resistance in White/Green wire between terminal No. 4 at PATS transceiver module harness connector C1945 and terminal No. 34 at PCM harness connector C421. *See Figs. 1 and 2.* If resistance is 5 ohms or less, go to next step. If resistance is greater than 5 ohms, repair open in White/Green wire.

7) Turn ignition switch to LOCK position. Connect PCM harness connector C421 and PATS transceiver modu e harness connector C1945. Turn ignition switch to RUN position. Using a voltmeter, backprobe at terminal No. 3 (Gray/Orange wire) at PATS transceiver module harness connector C1945. If voltage is 8 volts or less, go to next step. If voltage is greater than 8 volts, go to step **11)**.

8) Turn ignition switch to LOCK position. Disconnect PCM harness connector C421. Connect breakout box to PCM harness connector. Measure resistance between ground and terminal No. 17 at breakout box. If resistance is 10 k/ohms or less, go to next step. If resistance is greater than 10 k/ohms, go to step **10)**.

9) Ensure ignition switch is in LOCK position. Disconnect PATS transceiver module harness connector C1945. Measure resistance between ground and terminal No. 3 (Gray/Orange wire) at PATS transceiver module harness connector C1945. If resistance is 10 k/ohms or less,

repair short to ground in Gray/Orange wire. If resistance is greater than 10 k/ohms, replace PATS transceiver module.

10) Disconnect PATS transceiver module harness connector C1945. Measure resistance in Gray/Orange wire between terminal No. 3 at PATS transceiver module harness connector and terminal No. 17 at breakout box. If resistance is 5 ohms or less, replace PCM. If resistance is greater than 5 ohms, repair open in Gray/Orange wire.

11) Using NGS tester, trigger PCM active command TRANSMIT SIGNAL to on. Using a voltmeter, backprobe at terminal No. 3 (Gray/Orange wire) at PATS transceiver module harness connector C1945. If greater than 5 volts exists, go to next step. If 5 volts or less exists, replace PATS transceiver module.

12) Turn ignition switch to LOCK position. Disconnect PCM harness connector C421. Disconnect PATS transceiver module harness connector C1945. Turn ignition switch to RUN position. Measure voltage at terminal No. 3 (Gray/Orange wire) at PATS transceiver module harness connector C1945. If voltage exists, repair short to voltage in Gray/Orange wire. If voltage does not exist, replace PCM.

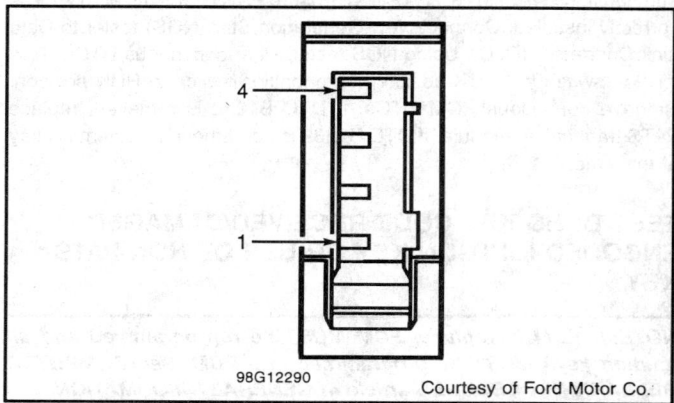

98G12290   Courtesy of Ford Motor Co.

Fig. 1: Identifying PATS Transceiver Module Harness Connector C1945 Terminals

TEST F: ANTI-THEFT NUMBER OF KEYS IS BELOW MINIMUM

1) Turn ignition switch to LOCK position. Connect New Generation Star (NGS) tester to Data Link Connector (DLC). Turn ignition switch to RUN position. Using NGS tester, retrieve continuous PCM DTCs. Clear continuous DTCs. Turn ignition switch to LOCK position. Turn ignition switch to RUN position. Retrieve continuous PCM DTCs. If DTC B1213 is the only DTC retrieved, go to next step. If any other DTCs are retrieved, perform appropriate test. See POWERTRAIN CONTROL MODULE DTC INDEX table under SELF-DIAGNOSTIC SYSTEM.

2) Using NGS tester, check PCM PID NUMKEYS. If PID indicates less than 2 keys, go to next step. If PID does not indicate more than 2 keys, system is okay at this time.

3) Obtain NEW encoded ignition key and insert into ignition lock cylinder. Using NEW key, turn ignition switch to RUN position. Program NEW encoded ignition key. See KEY PROGRAMMING – WITHOUT USING 2 PROGRAMMED KEYS under PROGRAMMING. If theft indicator does not illuminates for 3 seconds and then go out, go to next step. If theft indicator illuminates for 3 seconds and then goes out, clear DTCs and perform PCM self-test. Verify no DTCs are present.

4) Using NGS tester, monitor PCM PID SERV_MOD. If PID indicates YES, reprogram all keys and then repeat PCM self-test. If PID does not indicate YES and LED is continuously illuminated, repeat step **3)**. If PID does not indicate YES and LED is flashing, retrieve PCM DTCs and perform appropriate test. See POWERTRAIN CONTROL MODULE DTC INDEX table under SELF-DIAGNOSTIC SYSTEM.

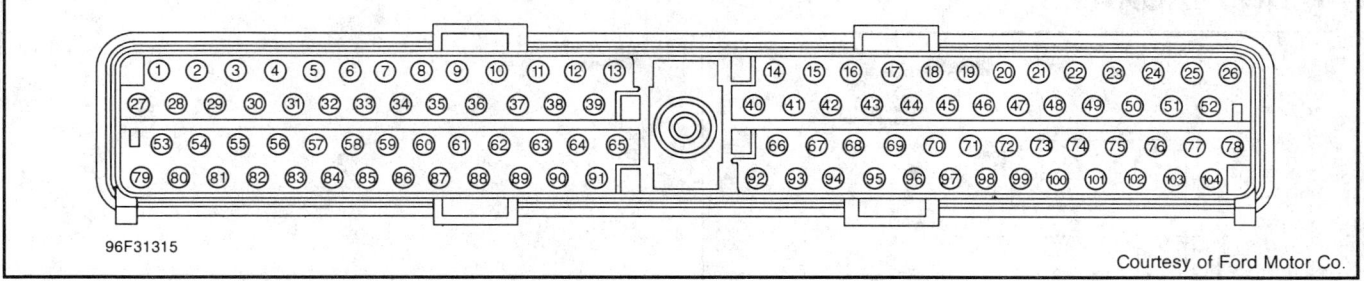

96F31315

Courtesy of Ford Motor Co.

Fig. 2: Identifying PCM Harness Connector C421 Terminals

TEST G: ANTI-THEFT INDICATOR ALWAYS/NEVER ON (NO INDICATOR PROVE OUT)

NOTE: If PCM is replace, PCM MUST be reprogrammed and all ignition keys MUST be programmed into PCM. See COMPUTER RELEARN PROCEDURES article in GENERAL INFORMATION.

1) Turn ignition switch to LOCK position. Disconnect PCM harness connector C421. Connect breakout box to PCM harness connector C421. Using a fused jumper wire, ground terminal No. 82 at breakout box. If anti-theft indicator does not illuminate, go to next step. If anti-theft indicator illuminates, replace PCM.

2) Disconnect anti-theft indicator harness connector C2106. Measure voltage at terminal No. 4 (Orange wire) at anti-theft indicator harness connector C2106. *See Fig. 3.* If battery voltage exists, go to next step. If battery voltage does not exist, repair open in Orange wire.

3) Measure resistance in Black/Blue wire between terminal No. 6 at anti-theft indicator harness connector C2106 and terminal No. 82 at breakout box. If resistance is greater than 5 ohms, repair open in Black/Blue wire. If resistance is 5 ohms or less, replace anti-theft indicator.

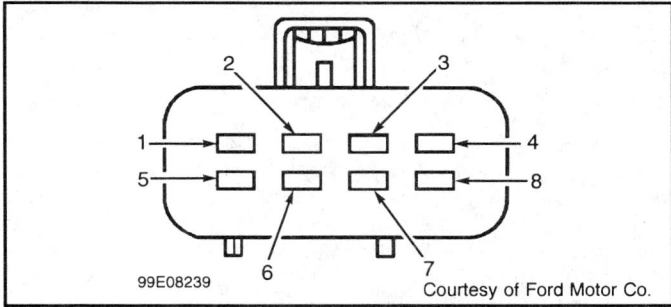

99E08239

Courtesy of Ford Motor Co.

Fig. 3: Identifying Anti-Theft Indicator Harness Connector C2106 Terminals

TEST H: ENGINE DOES NOT CRANK BUT ANTI-THEFT INDICATOR PROVES OUT

1) Turn ignition switch to LOCK position. Disconnect PCM harness connector C421. Connect breakout box to PCM harness connector C421. Turn ignition switch to RUN position. Measure voltage at terminal No. 18 at breakout box. If voltage is greater than 8 volts, go to next step. If voltage is 8 volts or less, repair starting system. See appropriate STARTERS article in STARTING & CHARGING SYSTEMS.

2) Turn ignition switch to LOCK position. Turn ignition switch to RUN position. Measure voltage at terminal No. 18 at breakout box. If voltage is greater than 2 volts, replace PCM. If voltage is 2 volts or less, repair starting system. See appropriate STARTERS article in STARTING & CHARGING SYSTEMS.

TEST I: NO COMMUNICATION WITH POWERTRAIN CONTROL MODULE

1) Turn ignition switch to LOCK position. Disconnect Powertrain Control Module (PCM) harness connector C421. Measure voltage at terminal No. 55 (Orange/Yellow wire) at PCM harness connector C421. *See Fig. 2.* If battery voltage exists, go to next step. If battery voltage does

not exist, repair power distribution circuit as necessary. See appropriate wiring diagram in POWER DISTRIBUTION article in WIRING DIAGRAMS.

2) Turn ignition switch to RUN position. Measure voltage at terminals No. 71 an 97 (both Green/Yellow wires) at PCM harness connector C421. If battery voltage exists at both terminals, go to next step. If battery voltage does not exist at both terminals, repair PCM power relay power distribution circuit.

3) Turn ignition switch to LOCK position. Measure resistance between ground and terminals No. 24, 51, 77 and 103 (all Black/Yellow wires) at PCM harness connector C421. Also, measure resistance between ground and terminal No. 25 (Black/Red wire) at PCM harness connector C421. If all resistance readings are 5 ohms or less, repair module communication concern. See MODULE COMMUNICATIONS NETWORK – COUGAR article. If any resistance reading is greater than 5 ohms, repair open in appropriate wire.

REMOVAL & INSTALLATION

PATS MODULE

NOTE: If PCM is replace, PCM MUST be reprogrammed and all ignition keys MUST be programmed into PCM. See COMPUTER RELEARN PROCEDURES article in GENERAL INFORMATION.

PATS TRANSCEIVER

WARNING: To avoid injury from accidental air bag deployment, read and carefully follow all WARNINGS and SERVICE PRECAUTIONS in appropriate AIR BAG RESTRAINT SYSTEMS article.

Removal & Installation – Disconnect negative battery cable. Remove lower steering column cover. Disconnect harness connector. Remove PATS transceiver. *See Fig. 4.* To install, reverse removal procedure.

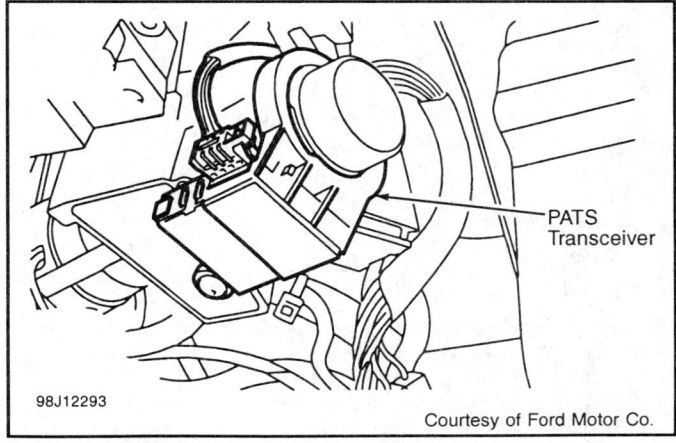

98J12293

Courtesy of Ford Motor Co.

Fig. 4: Removing PATS Transceiver

WIRING DIAGRAMS

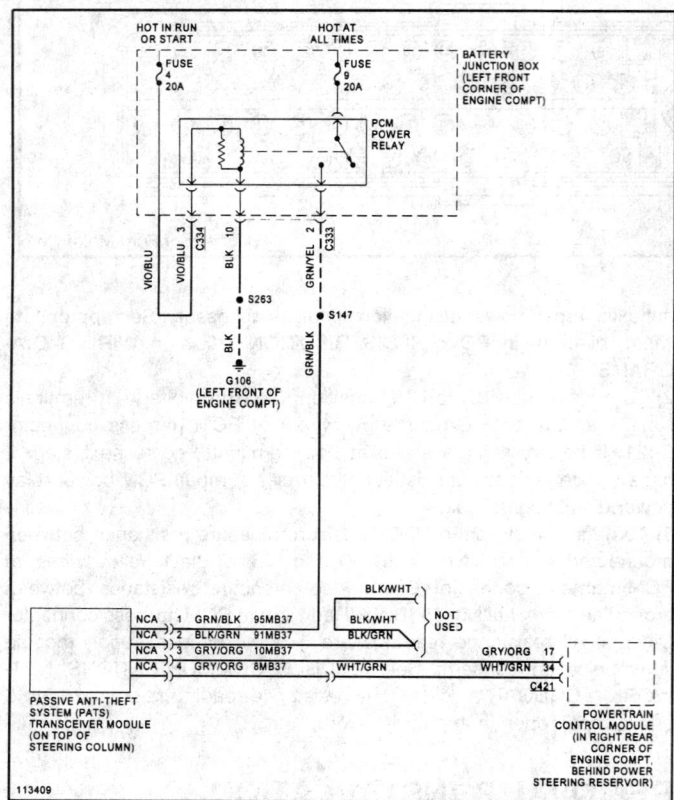

Fig. 5: Passive Anti-Theft System Wiring Diagram (Cougar)

Passive Anti-Theft Systems
Crown Victoria & Grand Marquis

DESCRIPTION

Passive Anti-Theft System (PATS) vehicle protection system consists of these components: PATS module, THEFT indicator light, transceiver module, encoded ignition key, module communications network and Data Link Connector (DLC).

PATS vehicle protection system is designed to prevent driveaway thefts. The system is passive in that it does not require any activity from the user. System uses radio frequency identification technology to verify proper key is being used to attempt to start the vehicle.

During each starting sequence, the transceiver module reads the encoded ignition key identification code and sends the data to the PATS module. If the key's identification code is programmed into anti-theft system, vehicle is allowed to start. If key's identification code is incorrect or missing, vehicle is prevented from starting.

PATS module communicates with the Powertrain Control Module (PCM) through Module Communications Network. PCM then determines if engine will be enabled to start. If the PCM prevents vehicle from starting because of PATS system, a Diagnostic Trouble Code (DTC) will be stored in memory.

OPERATION

THEFT INDICATOR LIGHT

THEFT indicator, located in the instrument cluster, is used to proveout system operation status. PATS uses the THEFT indicator light when ignition switch is in START or RUN positions. For more information, see POWERTRAIN CONTROL MODULE (PCM).

ENCODED IGNITION KEY

When ignition switch is in START or RUN position, PATS module initiates the encoded ignition key interrogation process. Each encoded ignition key must be programmed into PATS module before it can be used to start the vehicle. This encoded ignition key is much larger in size than a standard key to accommodate the electronics located inside plastic cover.

TRANSCEIVER MODULE

Transceiver module communicates with encoded ignition key. During each starting sequence, the transceiver module reads the encoded ignition key identification code and sends the data to the PATS module.

PASSIVE ANTI-THEFT SYSTEM (PATS) MODULE

Anti-theft alarm system control functions are contained in the PATS module. PATS module receives identification code from encoded ignition key and control engine enable. PATS module initiates encoded ignition key interrogation sequence when ignition switch is in RUN or START positions. PATS module can be diagnosed through NGS tester connected to Data Link Connector (DLC).

POWERTRAIN CONTROL MODULE (PCM)

Passive anti-theft system uses PCM to enable or disable vehicle's engine. When system is functioning properly and ignition switch is turned to RUN or START position, THEFT indicator light will turn on for 3 seconds, then turn off. Vehicle will be enabled to start and run. If there is a problem with PATS, THEFT indicator light will flash rapidly or glow constantly for more than 3 seconds when ignition switch is turned to RUN or START position.

COMPONENT LOCATIONS

COMPONENT LOCATIONS

Component	Location
Data Link Connector	Behind Left Side Of Instrument Panel
Driver's Door Module	Behind Driver's Door Panel
Ignition Switch	On Steering Column
Instrument Panel Fuse Box	Behind Left Side Of Instrument Panel
Lighting Control Module	Behind Instrument Panel, Right Of Steering Column
Light Sensor Amplifier	Behind Instrument Panel, Above Instrument Cluster
Passive Anti-Theft System Module	Behind Instrument Panel, Near Parking Brake
PATS Transceiver Module	On Top Of Steering Column
Power Distribution Box	Right Front Of Engine Compartment Next To Battery
Powertrain Control Module	Left Rear Corner Of Engine Compartment, In Firewall

PROGRAMMING

KEY PROGRAMMING – SECURITY ACCESS PROCEDURE

NOTE: Security access must be granted to erase ignition keys, enable/disable spare key programming switch, or perform parameter resets for PATS or PCM. This procedure has a 10 minute time delay prior to granting security access during which the New Generation Star (NGS) tester must remain connected to vehicle. After security access has been granted, security access command menu is displayed which offers various command options. Multiple security access commands can be executed (if necessary) prior to exiting security access command menu. Execution of all necessary security access commands prior to exiting command menu avoids the performance of an additional security access procedure and the associated 10 minute time delay. Security access for the PATS and security access for the PCM must be obtained separately as needed (each will require a 10 minute time delay).

With ignition switch in RUN position and NGS tester connected to vehicle, enter function test menu. Select SECURITY ACCESS PROCEDURE. This procedure will take 10 minutes to perform. After the security access procedure has been completed, a new menu will be displayed with command options. Select as many functions as required before exiting this menu. Once this menu is exited, security access procedure must be performed again to perform additional commands.

FORD
4-134

1999 ACCESSORIES & EQUIPMENT
Passive Anti-Theft Systems
Crown Victoria & Grand Marquis (Cont.)

KEY PROGRAMMING – WITH PROGRAMMED KEYS

NOTE: *This procedure will only work if 2 or more programmed ignition keys are available and there is a need to program additional keys. If 2 keys are not available, perform KEY PROGRAMMING – WITHOUT PROGRAMMED KEYS. PID SPAREKY must be enabled for this procedure to operate. To enable this PID, perform KEY PROGRAMMING – SECURITY ACCESS PROCEDURE and enable spare key programming switch. If programming procedure is successful, new key(s) will start vehicle and THEFT indicator will illuminate for 3 seconds. If programming procedure is not successful, new key(s) will not start vehicle and THEFT indicator will flash for one minute (after flashing for one minute, THEFT indicator will flash fault code). If necessary, repeat programming procedure. If programming of key(s) is still unsuccessful, perform self-diagnostics. See SELF-DIAGNOSTIC SYSTEM. Maximum of eight keys can be programmed into system. If procedure is not performed as outlined, programming procedure will end. Ignition keys must have correct mechanical key cut for vehicle and must be an encoded key.*

1) Insert the first programmed ignition key into ignition lock cylinder. Turn ignition switch from OFF to RUN position (ignition switch must stay in RUN position for one second). Turn ignition switch to OFF position and remove ignition key from ignition lock cylinder.

2) Within 5 seconds of turning ignition switch to OFF position, insert second programmed ignition key into ignition lock cylinder. Turn ignition switch from OFF to RUN position (ignition switch must stay in RUN position for one second). Turn ignition switch to OFF position and remove second ignition key from ignition lock cylinder.

3) Within 10 seconds of turning ignition switch to OFF position, insert a NEW unprogrammed ignition key into ignition lock cylinder. Turn ignition switch from OFF to RUN position (ignition switch must stay in RUN position for one second). Turn ignition switch to OFF position and remove ignition key from ignition lock cylinder. New ignition key should now be programmed. To program additional key(s), repeat key programming procedure from step 1).

KEY PROGRAMMING – WITHOUT PROGRAMMED KEYS

NOTE: *This procedure is used when a customer needs keys programmed into system and does not have 2 programmed ignition keys available, or when programmed ignition keys have been lost and/or ignition switch assembly has been replaced. This procedure will erase all programmed ignition keys from memory and prevent vehicle from starting until 2 keys have been programmed. Ignition keys must have correct mechanical key cut for vehicle and must be an encoded key. If additional key(s) are to be programmed, perform KEY PROGRAMMING – WITH PROGRAMMED KEYS. If remaining keys are with customer and not with vehicle, instruct customer to see owner's manual to program spare key(s).*

1) Turn ignition switch from OFF to RUN position. With NGS tester connected to vehicle, enter function test menu. Select SECURITY ACCESS PROCEDURE. This procedure will take 10 minutes to perform. After the security access procedure has been completed, a new menu will be displayed with command options. Select IGNITION KEY CODE ERASE.

2) Turn ignition switch to OFF position and disconnect NGS tester. Insert first encoded ignition key into ignition lock cylinder. Turn ignition switch to RUN position for 3 seconds. Turn ignition switch to OFF position and remove first encoded key.

3) Insert second encoded ignition key into ignition lock cylinder. Turn ignition switch to RUN position for 3 seconds. Turn ignition switch to OFF position and remove second encoded key. Both encoded ignition keys should now start vehicle.

KEY PROGRAMMING – SPARE KEY PROGRAMMING SWITCH

NOTE: *The spare key programming switch is a programmable switch which provides the capability to enable/disable the normal customer spare key programming procedure detailed in the owner's manual. This programmable switch is provided as a convenience for rental company fleets or other fleet purchasers who may not want the spare key programming procedure available to the vehicle driver. The spare key programming switch state can be viewed using PATS PID SPAREKY.*

Insert a programmed ignition key into ignition lock cylinder. Turn ignition switch from OFF to RUN position. With NGS tester connected to vehicle, enter function test menu. Select SECURITY ACCESS PROCEDURE. This procedure will take 10 minutes to perform. After security access procedure has been completed, a new menu will be displayed with command options. Default setting on all new vehicles is ENABLE. Select SPARE KEY PROGRAMMING SWITCH. Set SPARE KEY PROGRAMMING SWITCH to ENABLE or DISABLE.

SELF-DIAGNOSTIC SYSTEM

Verify customers complaint by operating PATS. Ensure electronically coded ignition key is being used. Check for damaged ignition lock cylinder switch, damaged encoded ignition key or open fuses. Check for loose or corroded connectors, damaged wiring harness, damaged ignition switch or damaged transceiver module. Repair or replace components as necessary.

Connect New Generation Star (NGS) tester to Data Link Connector (DLC), located beneath instrument panel. Using NGS tester, perform data link diagnostics test. See DATA LINK DIAGNOSTIC TEST under COMMUNICATION NETWORK DIAGNOSTICS in MODULE COMMUNICATIONS NETWORK – CROWN VICTORIA & GRAND MARQUIS article. If NGS tester responds with CKT914, CKT915 or CKT70=ALL ECUS NO RESP/NOT EQUIP, repair module communications concern. See MODULE COMMUNICATIONS NETWORK – CROWN VICTORIA & GRAND MARQUIS article. If NGS tester displays NO RESP/NOT EQUIP for Passive Anti-Theft System (PATS) module, perform TEST A: NO COMMUNICATION WITH PASSIVE ANTI-THEFT SYSTEM MODULE under SYSTEM TESTS. If NGS tester displays NO RESP/NOT EQUIP for Driver's Door Module (DDM), perform TEST C: NO COMMUNICATION WITH DRIVER'S DOOR MODULE under SYSTEM TESTS.

If NGS tester responds with SYSTEM PASSED, retrieve and record continuous DTCs. Erase continuous DTCs. Using NGS tester, perform PATS module and DDM self-test. Perform appropriate test in accordance with DTC retrieved. See DRIVER'S DOOR MODULE DTC INDEX and/or PASSIVE ANTI-THEFT SYSTEM MODULE DTC INDEX table. If no DTCs are retrieved, repair by symptom. See SYMPTOM CHART table under SYSTEM TESTS.

DRIVER'S DOOR MODULE DTC INDEX

DTC [1]	Description	Test
B1322	Driver's Door Ajar Circuit Short To Ground	B1322
B1342	ECU Defective	[2]

[1] – Codes listed in this table are only for testing covered in this article. For complete DTC listing, see MODULE COMMUNICATIONS NETWORK – CROWN VICTORIA & GRAND MARQUIS article.

[2] – Using NGS tester, retrieve and document all continuous DTCs. Perform Driver's Door Module (DDM) self-test. If DTC B1342 is retrieved again, replace DDM.

PASSIVE ANTI-THEFT SYSTEM MODULE DTC INDEX

DTC	Description	Test
B1213	Anti-Theft Number Of Programmed Keys Is Below Minimum	[1] B1213
B1232/B2103	PATS Transceiver Antenna Not Connected	B1232
B1600	PATS Ignition Key Transponder Signal Not Received/Damaged Encoded Ignition Key Or Use Of Non-PATS Key	B1600
B1601	PATS Received Incorrect Key Code From Ignition Key Transponder	B1601
B1602	Invalid Key Code Format From Ignition Key Transponder	B1602
B1681	PATS Transceiver Signal Is Not Received	B1681
B2139	Security Identification Does Not Match Between PATS & PCM	B2139
B2141	No Security Identification Exchange Between PATS & PCM	B2141
U1147	Invalid Or Missing Data For Vehicle Security	U1147
U1262	SCP Bus Communication Fault	[2]

[1] – If DTCs B1232, B1600, B1601, B1602 OR B1681 are also present, service these DTCs first then recheck codes.
[2] – Repair SCP bus communications concern. See MODULE COMMUNICATIONS NETWORK – CROWN VICTORIA & GRAND MARQUIS article.

DIAGNOSTIC TESTS

NOTE: Before performing any testing procedures, self-diagnosics must be performed. See SELF-DIAGNOSTIC SYSTEM.

DTC B1213: ANTI-THEFT NUMBER OF PROGRAMMED KEYS IS BELOW MINIMUM

1) Using NGS tester, perform PATS module self-test. If DTC B1213 is the only code retrieved, go to next step. If any other DTCs are retrieved, perform appropriate test. See PASSIVE ANTI-THEFT SYSTEM MODULE DTC INDEX table under SELF-DIAGNOSTIC SYSTEM.

2) Using NGS tester, monitor Passive Anti-Theft System (PATS) PID NUMKEYS. If PID indicates less than 2 keys, go to next step. If PATS PID NUMKEYS indicates 2 keys or more, clear DTCs and perform PATS module self-test. Verify no DTCs are present.

3) Obtain NEW encoded ignition key and insert into ignition. Program NEW encoded ignition key. See KEY PROGRAMMING – WITHOUT PROGRAMMED KEYS under PROGRAMMING. If THEFT indicator illuminates for 3 seconds and then goes out, clear DTCs and perform PATS module self-test. Verify no DTCs are present. If THEFT indicator illuminates continuously, repeat this step with the other NEW encoded ignition key. If THEFT indicator is flashing, retrieve DTC for new fault. See SELF-DIAGNOSTIC SYSTEM.

DTC B1232: PATS TRANSCEIVER ANTENNA NOT CONNECTED

Ensure ignition is switch is in LOCK position. Verify PATS transceiver module antenna is properly connected, and transceiver module is properly installed. See TRANSCEIVER MODULE under REMOVAL & INSTALLATION. Using NGS tester, perform PATS module self-test. Retrieve and record continuous DTCs. Clear continuous DTCs. If DTC B1232 is retrieved, replace PATS transceiver module. Clear DTCs and repeat PATS module self-test. If DTC B1232 is not retrieved, system is okay at this time.

DTC B1322: DRIVER'S DOOR AJAR CIRCUIT SHORT TO GROUND

1) Turn ignition switch to LOCK position. Disconnect Driver's Door Module (DDM) harness connector C518. Ensure all doors are closed. Measure resistance between ground and terminal No. 9 (Black/Yellow wire) at DDM harness connector C518. See Fig. 1. If resistance is 5 ohms or less, go to next step. If resistance is greater than 5 ohms, replace DDM.

2) Disconnect Lighting Control Module (LCM) harness connector C2026. Measure resistance between ground and terminal No. 10 (Black/Yellow wire) at LCM harness connector C2026. See Fig. 2. If resistance is greater than 10 k/ohms, replace LCM. If resistance is 10 k/ohms or less, repair short to ground in Black/Yellow wire.

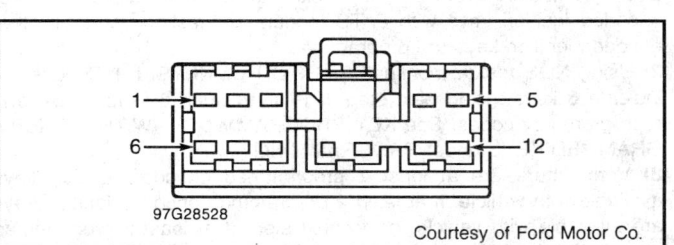

Fig. 1: Identifying Driver's Door Module Harness Connector C518 Terminals

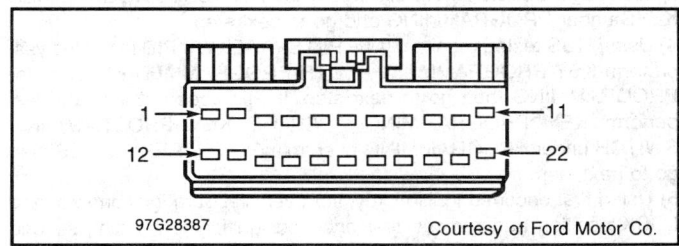

Fig. 2: Identifying Lighting Control Module Harness Connector C2026 Terminals

DTC B1600: PATS IGNITION KEY TRANSPONDER SIGNAL NOT RECEIVED/DAMAGED ENCODED IGNITION KEY OR USE OF NON-PATS KEY

NOTE: Large metallic objects, a second PATS ignition key, or devices such as electronic credit cards on the same key ring may cause vehicle starting problem and possibly set this code. Ensure customers encoded ignition key is an approved Ford encoded ignition key. Encoded keys from Rotunda, Ilco, and Strattec are also approved keys.

1) Turn ignition switch to LOCK position. Using NGS tester, retrieve and record continuous DTCs. Clear continuous DTCs and perform PATS module self-test. If DTC B1600 is retrieved, go to next step. If any other DTCs are retrieved, perform appropriate test. If no DTCs are retrieved, system is okay at this time.

2) Obtain NEW encoded ignition key and insert into ignition. Turn ignition switch to RUN position. Program NEW encoded ignition key. See KEY PROGRAMMING – WITHOUT PROGRAMMED KEYS under PROGRAMMING. Using NGS tester, perform PATS module self-test. If DTC B1600 is retrieved, go to next step. If any other DTCs are retrieved, perform appropriate test. If no DTCs are retrieved, system is okay at this time.

3) Turn ignition switch to LOCK position. Replace PATS transceiver module. See TRANSCEIVER MODULE under REMOVAL & INSTALLATION. Using NEW encoded ignition key from previous step, turn ignition switch to RUN position. Using NGS tester, perform PATS module

FORD
4-136

1999 ACCESSORIES & EQUIPMENT
Passive Anti-Theft Systems
Crown Victoria & Grand Marquis (Cont.)

self-test. If DTC B1600 is retrieved, replace PATS module. If no DTCs are retrieved, system is okay at this time.

DTC B1601: PATS RECEIVED INCORRECT KEY CODE FROM IGNITION KEY TRANSPONDER

NOTE: Large metallic objects, a second PATS ignition key, or devices such as electronic credit cards on the same key ring may cause vehicle starting problem and possibly set this code. Ensure customers encoded ignition key is an approved Ford encoded ignition key. Encoded keys from Rotunda, Ilco, and Strattec are also approved keys.

1) Turn ignition switch to LOCK position. Using NGS tester, retrieve and record continuous DTCs. Clear continuous DTCs and perform PATS module self-test. If DTC B1601 is retrieved, go to next step. If DTC B1601 is not retrieved, system is okay at this time. Check all other encoded ignition keys with PATS module self-test to verify all other encoded ignition keys are programmed.
2) Using NGS tester, monitor PATS PID NUMKEYS. If PID does not indicate 8 keys, go to next step. If PID indicates 8 keys, erase and reprogram key codes. See KEY PROGRAMMING – WITHOUT PROGRAMMED KEYS under PROGRAMMING.
3) Verify there are at least 2 programmed encoded ignition keys available with vehicle. If at least 2 programmed encoded ignition keys are available with vehicle, go to next step. If at least 2 programmed encoded ignition keys are not available with vehicle, obtain a NEW encoded ignition key so at least 2 keys are available. Program encoded ignition keys. See KEY PROGRAMMING – WITHOUT PROGRAMMED KEYS under PROGRAMMING and go to next step.
4) Using NGS tester, monitor PATS PID SPAREKY. If PID indicates yes, preform KEY PROGRAMMING – WITH PROGRAMMED KEYS under PROGRAMMING then go to next step. If PID does not indicate yes, perform KEY PROGRAMMING – SPARE KEY PROGRAMMING SWITCH under PROGRAMMING to enable PID SPAREKY to YES then go to next step.
5) Using first encoded ignition key, start vehicle. Turn ignition switch to LOCK position and remove first encoded ignition key. Using second encoded ignition key, start vehicle. If vehicle does not start using both encoded ignition keys, go to next step. If vehicle starts using both encoded ignition keys, system is okay at this time. If additional encoded ignition keys are needed, see KEY PROGRAMMING – SPARE KEY PROGRAMMING SWITCH under PROGRAMMING.
6) Using NGS tester, retrieve and record continuous DTCs. Clear continuous DTCs and perform PATS module self-test. If DTC B1601 is retrieved, replace PATS module. If DTC B1601 is not retrieved, system is okay at this time. If any other DTCs are retrieved, perform appropriate test.

DTC B1602: INVALID KEY CODE FORMAT FROM IGNITION KEY TRANSPONDER

NOTE: Large metallic objects, a second PATS ignition key, or devices such as electronic credit cards on the same key ring may cause vehicle starting problem and possibly set this code. Ensure customers encoded ignition key is an approved Ford encoded ignition key. Encoded keys from Rotunda, Ilco, and Strattec are also approved keys.

1) Turn ignition switch to LOCK position. Connect NGS tester to Data Link Connector (DLC). Using NGS tester, retrieve and record continuous DTCs. Clear continuous DTCs and perform PATS self-test. If DTC B1602 is retrieved, go to next step. If DTC B1602 is not retrieved, system is okay at this time. Check all customer encoded ignition keys with PATS self-test to verify all other keys are programmed.
2) Turn ignition switch to LOCK position. Obtain a NEW encoded ignition key. Using encoded ignition key, turn ignition switch to RUN position. Program encoded ignition key. See KEY PROGRAMMING – WITHOUT

PROGRAMMED KEYS under PROGRAMMING. Using NGS tester, perform PATS self-test. If DTC B1602 is retrieved, go to next step. If no DTCs are retrieved, system is okay at this time.
3) Ensure ignition switch is in LOCK position. Replace transceiver module. Turn ignition switch to RUN position. Using NGS tester, perform PATS self-test. If no DTCs are retrieved, system is okay at this time. If any other DTCs are retrieved, perform appropriate test.

DTC B1681: PATS TRANSCEIVER MODULE SIGNAL IS NOT RECEIVED

1) Turn ignition switch to LOCK position. Using NGS tester, retrieve and record continuous DTCs. Clear continuous DTCs and perform PATS module self-test. If DTC B1681 is retrieved, go to next step. If DTC B1681 is not retrieved, system is okay at this time.
2) Turn ignition switch to LOCK position. Disconnect PATS transceiver module harness connector C221. Turn ignition switch to RUN position. Measure voltage at terminal No. 2 (Red/Yellow wire) at PATS transceiver module harness connector C221. *See Fig. 3.* If greater than 9 volts exists, go to next step. If 9 volts or less exists, repair Red/Yellow wire between PATS module and PATS transceiver module.
3) Turn ignition switch to LOCK position. Measure resistance between ground and terminal No. 1 (Black/Yellow wire) at PATS transceiver module harness connector C221. If resistance is 5 ohms or less, go to next step. If resistance is greater than 5 ohms, repair Black/Yellow wire between PATS module and PATS transceiver module.
4) Connect PATS transceiver module harness connector C221. Turn ignition switch to RUN position. Using a voltmeter, backprobe at terminal No. 3 (Gray/Orange wire) at PATS transceiver module harness connector C221. If voltage is 9 volts or less, go to next step. If voltage is greater than 9 volts, go to step **7)**.
5) Turn ignition switch to LOCK position. Disconnect PATS transceiver module harness connector C221. Measure resistance between ground and terminal No. 3 (Gray/Orange wire) at PATS transceiver module harness connector C221. If resistance is greater than 100 ohms, go to next step. If resistance is 100 ohms or less, check for short to ground in Gray/Orange wire between PATS module and PATS transceiver module. If Gray/Orange wire is shorted to ground, repair or replace as necessary. If wire is okay, replace PATS module.
6) Turn ignition switch to LOCK position. Disconnect PATS transceiver module harness connector C221. Disconnect PATS module harness connector C229. Measure resistance in Gray/Orange wire between terminal No. 3 at PATS transceiver module harness connector C221 and terminal No. 11 at PATS module harness connector C229. *See Figs. 3 and 4.* If resistance is 5 ohms or less, go to next step. If resistance is greater than 5 ohms, repair open in Gray/Orange wire.
7) Connect PATS transceiver module harness connector C221. Connect PATS module harness connector C229. Turn ignition switch to RUN position. Using a voltmeter, backprobe at terminal No. 4 (White/Light Green wire) at PATS transceiver module harness connector C221. If 9 volts or less exists, go to next step. If greater than 9 volts exists, go to step **9)**.
8) Turn ignition switch to LOCK position. Disconnect PATS transceiver module harness connector C221. Measure resistance between ground and terminal No. 4 (White/Light Green wire) PATS transceiver module harness connector C221. If resistance is greater than 100 ohms, go to next step. If resistance is 100 ohms or less, check for short to ground in White/Light Green wire between PATS module and PATS transceiver module. If White/Light Green wire is shorted to ground, repair or replace as necessary. If wire is okay, replace PATS module.
9) Turn ignition switch to LOCK position. Connect PATS transceiver module harness connector C221. Turn ignition switch to RUN position. Using NGS tester, select PATS module ACTIVE COMMAND. Trigger TRANSMIT SIGNAL COMMAND to ON. Transmit signal produces a 2 seconds on, 2 seconds off voltage cycle. Using a voltmeter, backprobe at terminal No. 4 (White/Light Green wire) at PATS transceiver module harness connector C221. If voltage drops from greater than 9 volts to less than one volt when active command is triggered on, go to next step.

If voltage does not drop from greater than 9 volts to less than one volt when active command is triggered on, check for open in Gray/Orange wire between PATS module and PATS transceiver module. Repair or replace Gray/Orange wire as necessary. If Gray/Orange wire is okay, replace PATS module.

10) Turn ignition switch to LOCK position. Replace PATS transceiver module. See TRANSCEIVER MODULE under REMOVAL & INSTALLATION. Turn ignition switch to RUN position. Using NGS tester, perform PATS module self-test. If DTC B1681 is retrieved, go to next step. If DTC B1681 is not retrieved, system is okay at this time. If any other DTCs are retrieved, perform appropriate test.

11) Turn ignition switch to LOCK position. Replace PATS module. See PATS MODULE under REMOVAL & INSTALLATION. Turn ignition switch to RUN position. Using NGS tester, perform PATS module self-test. If DTC B1681 is retrieved, repair appropriate faulty circuit between PATS module and PATS transceiver module. If no DTCs are retrieved, system is okay at this time. If any other DTCs are retrieved, perform appropriate test.

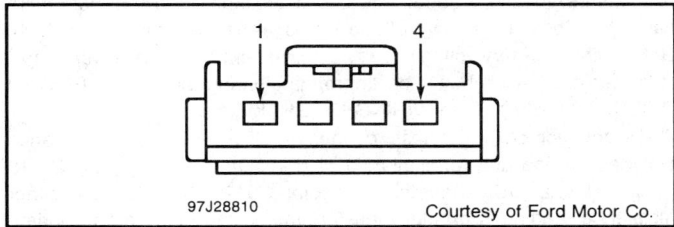

97J28810   Courtesy of Ford Motor Co.

Fig. 3: Identifying PATS Transceiver Module Connector C221 Terminals

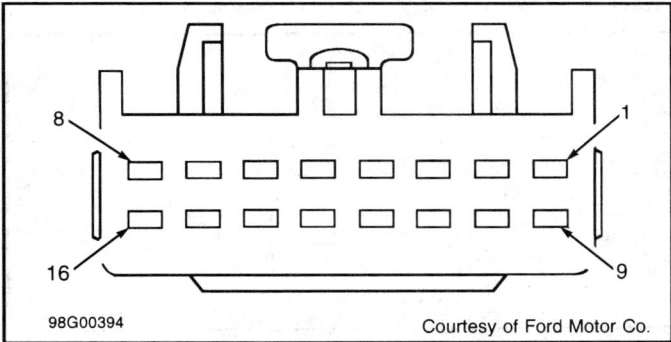

98G00394   Courtesy of Ford Motor Co.

Fig. 4: Identifying PATS Module Harness Connector C229 Terminals

DTC B2139: SECURITY IDENTIFICATION DOES NOT MATCH BETWEEN PATS & PCM

1) Turn ignition switch to LOCK position. Using NGS tester, retrieve and record continuous DTCs. Clear continuous DTCs and perform PATS module self-test. If DTC B2139 is retrieved, go to next step. If DTC B2139 is not retrieved, system is okay at this time.

2) Perform security access for PATS module. See KEY PROGRAMMING – SECURITY ACCESS PROCEDURE under PROGRAMMING. Using NGS tester, select PARAMETER RESET command for PATS module. Perform PCM active command ACTIVE COMMAND KEEP ALIVE MEMORY RESET. Turn ignition switch to LOCK position. Turn ignition switch to RUN position for 30 seconds then using NGS tester, clear continuous DTCs. Turn ignition switch to LOCK position. Using NGS tester, perform PATS self-test. If DTC B2139 is not retrieved, system is okay at this time. If DTC B2139 is retrieved, verify PCM calibration is correct for vehicle. If calibration is okay, replace PATS module. Clear DTCs and retest system operation. If DTC B2139 still exists, replace PCM and retest system operation.

DTC B2141: NO SECURITY IDENTIFICATION EXCHANGE BETWEEN PATS & PCM

1) Turn ignition switch to LOCK position. Using NGS tester, retrieve and record continuous DTCs. Clear continuous DTCs and perform PATS module self-test. If DTC B2141 and DTC U1147 are retrieved together, perform DTC U1147: INVALID OR MISSING DATA FOR VEHICLE SECURITY. If DTC B2141 is retrieved, go to next step. If no DTCs are retrieved, system is okay at this time.

2) Using NGS tester, perform PCM active command KEEP ALIVE MEMORY RESET. Turn ignition switch to LOCK position. Turn ignition switch to RUN position for 30 seconds. Turn ignition switch to LOCK position. Start vehicle. If vehicle does not start, go to next step. If vehicle starts, system is okay at this time.

3) Using NGS tester, perform PATS module self-test. If DTC B2141 is not retrieved, system is okay at this time. If DTC B2141 is retrieved, verify PCM calibration is correct for vehicle. If calibration is okay, replace PATS module. Clear TCs and retest system operation. If DTC B2141 still exists, replace PCM and retest system operation.

DTC U1147: INVALID OR MISSING DATA FOR VEHICLE SECURITY

1) Start vehicle. If vehicle does not start and THEFT indicator is flashing, go to next step. If vehicle starts with THEFT indicator flashing, problem is in PCM. See appropriate SELF-DIAGNOSTICS article in ENGINE PERFORMANCE in appropriate MITCHELL® manual.

2) Using NGS tester, retrieve and record continuous DTCs. Clear continuous DTCs and perform PCM self-test. If NGS tester communicates with PCM, go to next step. If NGS tester does not communicate with NGS tester, repair communications concern. See MODULE COMMUNICATIONS NETWORK – CROWN VICTORIA & GRAND MARQUIS article.

3) If DTC P1260 was retrieved during PCM self-test, go to next step. If DTC P1260 was not retrieved during PCM self-test, check PCM power and ground circuits. See appropriate SELF-DIAGNOSTICS article in ENGINE PERFORMANCE in appropriate MITCHELL® manual.

4) Perform self-diagnostics. See SELF-DIAGNOSTIC SYSTEM. If DTC U1147 is not retrieved, system is okay at this time. If DTC U1147 is retrieved, replace PATS module. If DTC U1147 still exists, replace PCM.

SYSTEM TESTS

SYMPTOM CHART

Symptom	Test
No Communication With Passive Anti-Theft System Module	A
No THEFT Indicator Proveout	B
No Communication With Driver's Door Module	C

TEST A: NO COMMUNICATION WITH PASSIVE ANTI-THEFT SYSTEM MODULE

1) Turn ignition switch to LOCK position. Disconnect PATS module harness connector C229. Turn ignition switch to RUN position. Measure voltage at terminals No. 15 (Light Green/Yellow wire) and No. 16 (Red/Light Green wire) at PATS module harness connector C229. *See Fig. 4.* If battery voltage does not exist, go to next step. If battery voltage exists at both terminals, go to step **3)**.

2) Turn ignition switch to LOCK position. Remove fuses No. 7 (25-amp) and No. 8 (15-amp) from instrument panel fuse box. Measure resistance in Light Green/Yellow wire between output side of fuse No. 8 in instrument panel fuse box and terminal No. 15 at PATS module harness connector C229. Also, measure resistance in Red/Light Green wire between output side of fuse No. 7 in instrument panel fuse box and terminal No. 16 at PATS module harness connector C229. If both resistance readings are 5 ohms or less, repair power distribution to appropriate fuse. See appropriate wiring diagram in POWER DISTRIBUTION article in WIRING DIAGRAMS. If either resistance reading is greater than 5 ohms, repair open in appropriate wire.

FORD
4-138

1999 ACCESSORIES & EQUIPMENT
Passive Anti-Theft Systems
Crown Victoria & Grand Marquis (Cont.)

3) Measure resistance between ground and terminal No. 7 (Pink/Orange wire) at PATS module harness connector C229. If resistance is 5 ohms or less, repair module communications concern. See MODULE COMMUNICATIONS NETWORK – CROWN VICTORIA & GRAND MARQUIS article. If resistance is greater than 5 ohms, repair open in Pink/Orange wire between PATS module and ground.

TEST B: NO THEFT INDICATOR PROVEOUT

1) Turn ignition switch to LOCK position. Using NGS tester, enter PATS module ACTIVE COMMAND MODE. If ACTIVE COMMAND MODE can be entered, go to next step. If ACTIVE COMMAND MODE cannot be entered, perform TEST A: NO COMMUNICATION WITH PATS MODULE.

2) Using NGS tester, trigger active command PATS ANTI-THEFT INDICATOR to ON. If anti-theft indicator light does not illuminate, go to next step. If anti-theft indicator illuminates, system is okay at this time.

3) Turn ignition switch to LOCK position. Disconnect light sensor amplifier harness connector C286. Turn ignition switch to RUN position. Measure voltage at terminal No. 2 (Orange/Red wire) at light sensor amplifier harness connector C286 while triggering PATS ANTI-THEFT INDICATOR to ON. *See Fig. 5.* If battery voltage does not exist, go to next step. If battery voltage exists, go to step 5).

4) Turn ignition switch to LOCK position. Disconnect PATS module harness connector C229. Measure resistance in Orange/Red wire between terminal No. 2 at PATS module harness connector C229 and terminal No. 2 at light sensor amplifier connector C286. *See Figs. 4 and 5.* If resistance is 5 ohms or less, replace PATS module. If resistance is greater than 5 ohms, repair open in Orange/Red wire between PATS module and light sensor amplifier.

5) Turn ignition switch to LOCK position. Measure resistance between ground and terminal No. 1 (Pink/Orange wire) at light sensor amplifier connector C286. If resistance is 5 ohms or less, go to next step. If resistance is greater than 5 ohms, repair open in Pink/Orange wire between light sensor amplifier and ground.

6) Remove anti-theft LED. Measure resistance between anti-theft LED terminals. Reverse ohmmeter leads. Resistance should be greater than 10 k/ohms in one direction and 10-20 ohms in the other. If resistance is as specified, go to next step. If resistance is not as specified, replace anti-theft LED.

7) Check PATS module and light sensor amplifier connectors for damaged pins or corroded wires. If connectors and wires are okay, go to next step. If connectors and wires are not okay, repair or replace connectors and wires as necessary.

8) Turn ignition switch to RUN position. Measure voltage at terminal No. 3 (Tan/White wire) at light sensor amplifier connector C286. If battery voltage exists, go to next step. If battery voltage does not exist, repair Tan/White wire between fuse No. 4 (15-amp) in instrument panel fuse box and light sensor amplifier.

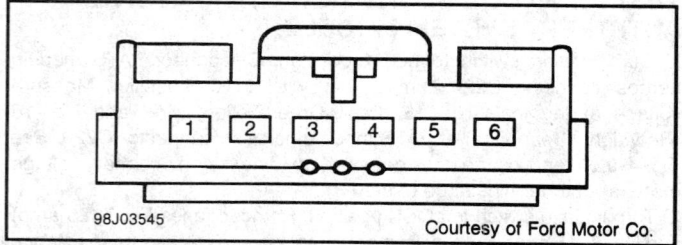

Fig. 5: Identifying Light Sensor Amplifier Connector C286

TEST C: NO COMMUNICATIONS WITH DRIVER'S DOOR MODULE

1) Turn ignition switch to LOCK position. Disconnect Driver's Door Module (DDM) harness connector C520. Measure voltage at terminal No. 4 (Black/White wire) at DDM harness connector C520. *See Fig. 6.* If battery voltage does not exist, go to next step. If battery voltage exists, go to step 4).

2) Remove circuit breaker No. 7 (20-amp) from power distribution box. Measure resistance between ground at terminal No. 4 (Black/White wire) at DDM harness C520. If resistance is greater than 10 k/ohms, go to next step. If resistance is 10 k/ohms or less, repair short to ground in Black/White wire.

3) Measure voltage between ground and input side circuit breaker No. 7 in power distribution box. If battery voltage exists, repair open in Black/White wire. If battery voltage does not exist, repair open in power supply to power distribution box. See appropriate wiring diagram in POWER DISTRIBUTION article in WIRING DIAGRAMS.

4) Measure voltage at terminal No. 3 (Yellow/Light Green wire) at DDM harness connector C520. If battery voltage does not exist, go to next step. If battery voltage exists, go to step 7).

5) Remove circuit breaker No. 14 (20-amp) from instrument panel fuse box. Measure resistance between ground and terminal No. 3 (Yellow/Light Green wire) at DDM harness connector C520. If resistance is greater than 10 k/ohms, go to next step. If resistance is 10 k/ohms or less, repair short to ground in Yellow/Light Green wire.

6) Measure voltage at input side circuit breaker No. 14 in instrument panel fuse box. If battery voltage exists, repair open in Yellow/Light Green wire. If battery voltage does not exist, repair open in power supply to power distribution box. See appropriate wiring diagram in POWER DISTRIBUTION article in WIRING DIAGRAMS.

7) Disconnect DDM harness connector C519. Measure resistance between ground and terminals No. 4 (Pink/Orange wire) and No. 15 (Black wire) at DDM harness connector C519. *See Fig. 7.* If either resistance reading is greater than 5 ohms, repair open in appropriate wire. If both resistance readings are 5 ohms or less, repair module communications concern. See MODULE COMMUNICATIONS NETWORK – CROWN VICTORIA & GRAND MARQUIS article.

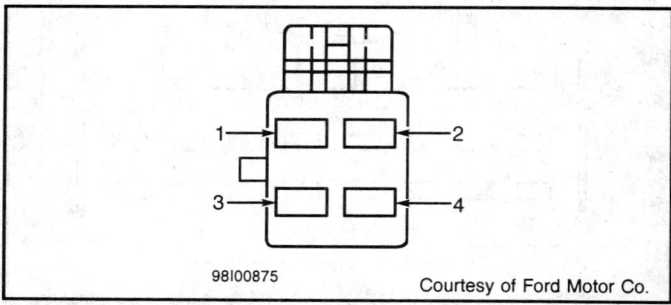

Fig. 6: Identifying Driver's Door Module Harness Connector C520 Terminals

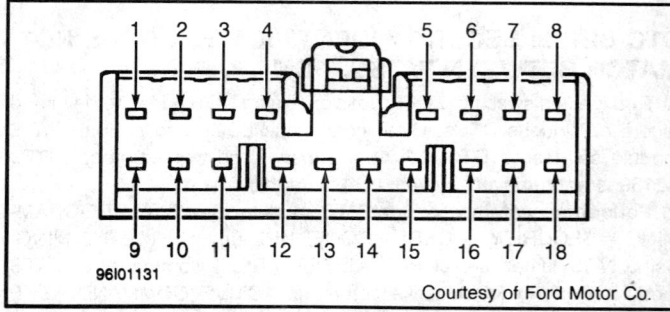

Fig. 7: Identifying Driver's Door Module Harness Connector C519 Terminals

Passive Anti-Theft Systems
Crown Victoria & Grand Marquis (Cont.)

REMOVAL & INSTALLATION

CAUTION: When battery is disconnected, vehicle computer and memory systems may lose memory data. Driveability problems may exist until computer systems have completed a relearn cycle. See COMPUTER RELEARN PROCEDURES article in GENERAL INFORMATION before disconnecting battery.

PATS MODULE

NOTE: Before replacing PATS module, it is necessary to upload module configuration to NGS tester. For reprogramming assistance, refer to help screen on NGS tester configuration card.

Removal & Installation – Disconnect negative battery cable. PATS module is located behind instrument panel, to right of fuse box. Remove steering column opening cover assembly and reinforcement. Remove 2 screws retaining PATS module to bracket. Disconnect wiring harness connector and remove PATS module. To install, reverse removal procedure.

TRANSCEIVER MODULE

NOTE: If transceiver module is replaced, all existing ignition keys must be reprogrammed. See PROGRAMMING.

Removal & Installation – 1) Disconnect negative battery cable. Transceiver module is located on ignition switch lock cylinder. Insert ignition key into ignition switch lock cylinder. Turn ignition switch lock cylinder to RUN position. Insert a punch in steering column cover hole and press ignition switch lock cylinder release tab while removing ignition switch lock cylinder.

2) Remove upper and lower steering column covers. Remove transceiver module retaining screw from steering column. Carefully pry transceiver over rib on ignition switch lock cylinder housing. Remove transceiver module harness retainers. Disconnect transceiver module harness connector and remove transceiver module. To install, reverse removal procedure.

WIRING DIAGRAMS

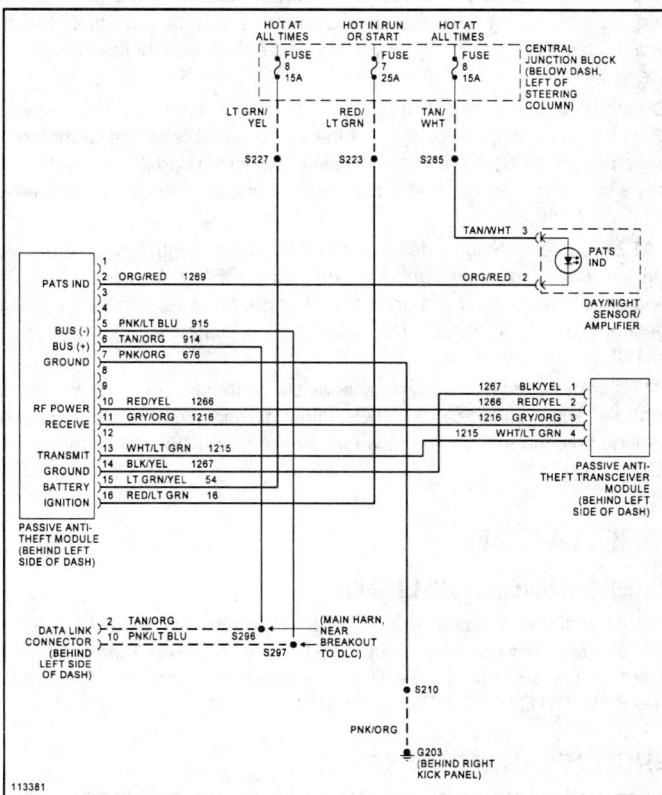

Fig. 8: Passive Anti-Theft System (PATS) Wiring Diagram (Crown Victoria & Grand Marquis)

DESCRIPTION

Passive Anti-Theft System (PATS) vehicle protection system is designed to prevent driveaway thefts. The system is passive in that it does not require any activity from the user. System uses radio frequency identification technology to verify if proper key is being used to attempt to start the vehicle.

During each starting sequence. the encoded ignition key is interrogated by vehicle anti-theft electronics. If the key's identification code matches code programmed into anti-theft system, vehicle is capable of starting. If key's identification code is incorrect or missing, vehicle is prevented from starting.

PATS module communicates with the Powertrain Control Module (PCM) via Module Communications Network (MCN). PCM then determines if engine will be enabled to start. If the PCM prevents vehicle from starting because of PATS system, PCM will store a Diagnostic Trouble Code (DTC) in memory.

PATS vehicle protection system consists of these components: PATS module, anti-theft indicator (THEFT) light, transceiver module, encoded ignition key, module communications network and Data Link Connector (DLC).

OPERATION

THEFT INDICATOR LIGHT

THEFT indicator located on right side of instrument cluster is used to prove out system operation status. PATS uses the THEFT indicator light when ignition switch is in START or RUN position. For more information, see POWERTRAIN CONTROL MODULE (PCM).

ENCODED IGNITION KEY

When ignition switch is in START or RUN position, PATS module initiates the encoded ignition key interrogation process. PATS module supplies both power and carrier signal to transceiver module to momentarily energize ignition key. After energize period has expired, key transmits its identification code to transceiver module. This encoded ignition key is much larger in size than a non-encoded key to accommodate the electronics located inside plastic cover.

PASSIVE ANTI-THEFT SYSTEM (PATS) MODULE

PATS module contains circuitry to interface to vehicle electrical system, transceiver module, Module Communications Network (MCN) system and THEFT indicator light. PATS module stores ignition key codes in non-volatile memory. PATS module can be diagnosed through Data Link Connector (DLC). After receiving key code during a start sequence, PATS module sends this data to instrument cluster.

POWERTRAIN CONTROL MODULE (PCM)

Passive anti-theft system communicates PCM through the instrument cluster to enable or disable vehicle's engine. Within one second after engine start, PCM must receive an enable signal from instrument cluster or the engine will be disabled. Along with enable signals, instrument cluster and PCM share messages that confirm the security codes shared during initial installation. This shared security data makes the instrument cluster and PCM a matched pair, so neither will operate in another vehicle.

When system is functioning properly and ignition switch is turned to RUN or START position, THEFT indicator light will turn on for 3 seconds, then turn off. Vehicle will be enabled to start and run.

If there is a problem in the system, THEFT indicator light will stay on or flash continuously. Go to SELF-DIAGNOSTIC SYSTEM.

COMPONENT LOCATION

PATS COMPONENT LOCATION

Component	Location
PATS Transceiver Module	Behind Steering Column Shroud
Powertrain Control Module (PCM)	Right Side Of Engine Compartment
THEFT Indicator Light	On Instrument Cluster

PROGRAMMING

ERASE ALL KEYS & PROGRAM 2 KEYS

NOTE: This procedure is used when a customer needs keys programmed into system and does not have 2 programmed ignition keys available, or when programmed ignition keys have been lost and/or ignition switch assembly has been replaced. This procedure will erase all programmed ignition keys from memory and prevent vehicle from starting until 2 keys have been programmed. Ignition keys must have correct mechanical key cut for vehicle and must be an encoded key. If additional key(s) are to be programmed, perform KEY PROGRAMMING USING 2 PROGRAMMED KEYS. If remaining keys are with customer and not with vehicle, instruct customer to see owner's manual to program spare key(s).

1) Insert Ford Service Function (FSF) card into NGS tester. Turn ignition switch from LOCK to RUN position. Perform SECURITY ACCESS PROCEDURE. After the security access procedure has been completed, a new menu will be displayed with command options. Select IGNITION KEY CODE ERASE.

2) Turn ignition switch to LOCK position and disconnect NGS tester. Insert first encoded ignition key into ignition lock cylinder. Turn ignition switch to RUN position for 3 seconds. Turn ignition switch to LOCK position and remove first encoded key.

3) Within 5 seconds, insert second encoded ignition key into ignition lock cylinder. Turn ignition switch to RUN position for 3 seconds. Turn ignition switch to LOCK position and remove second encoded key. Both encoded ignition keys should now start vehicle.

SECURITY ACCESS PROCEDURE

NOTE: Security access must be granted to erase ignition keys, enable/disable spare key programming switch, or perform parameter resets for PATS module and PCM. This procedure has a 10 minute time delay prior to granting security access during which the New Generation Star (NGS) tester must remain connected to vehicle. After security access has been granted, security access command menu is displayed which offers various command options. Multiple security access commands can be executed (if necessary) prior to exiting security access command menu. Execution of all necessary security access commands prior to exiting command menu avoids the performance of an additional security access procedure and the associated 10 minute time delay.

Insert Ford Service Function (FSF) card into NGS tester. Turn ignition switch from LOCK to RUN position. With NGS tester connected to vehicle, enter PATS then select SECURITY ACCESS PROCEDURE. This procedure will take 10 minutes to perform. After the security access procedure has been completed, a new menu will be displayed with command options. Select as many functions as required before exiting this menu. Once this menu is exited, security access procedure must be performed again to perform additional commands.

SPARE KEY PROGRAMMING SWITCH

NOTE: The spare key programming switch is a programmable switch which provides the capability to enable/disable the normal customer spare key programming procedure detailed in the owner's manual. This programmable switch is provided as a convenience for rental company fleets or other fleet purchasers who may not want the spare key programming procedure available to the vehicle driver. The spare key programming switch state can be viewed using PATS PID SPARE_KY.

Insert a programmed ignition key into the ignition lock cylinder. Insert Ford Service Function (FSF) card into NGS tester. Turn ignition switch from LOCK to RUN position. With NGS tester connected to vehicle, enter PATS then select SECURITY ACCESS PROCEDURE. This procedure will take 10 minutes to perform. After the security access procedure has been completed, a new menu will be displayed with command options. The default setting on all new vehicles is ENABLE. Select SPARE KEY PROGRAMMING SWITCH. Set SPARE KEY PROGRAMMING SWITCH to ENABLE to allow keys to be programmed or DISABLE to make key programming not accessible.

KEY PROGRAMMING USING 2 PROGRAMMED KEYS

NOTE: This procedure will only work if 2 or more programmed ignition keys are available and there is a need to program additional keys. If 2 keys are not available, perform ERASE ALL KEYS & PROGRAM 2 KEYS. PID SPARE_KY must be enabled for this procedure to operate. To enable this PID, perform SPARE KEY PROGRAMMING SWITCH and enable spare key programming switch. If programming procedure is successful, new key(s) will start vehicle and THEFT indicator will illuminate for 3 seconds. If programming procedure is not successful, new key(s) will not start vehicle and THEFT indicator will flash for one minute (after flashing for one minute, THEFT indicator will flash fault code). If necessary, repeat programming procedure. If programming of key(s) is still unsuccessful, perform procedures in SELF-DIAGNOSTIC SYSTEM. Maximum of 8 keys can be programmed into system. If procedure is not performed as outlined, programming procedure will end. Ignition keys must have correct mechanical key cut for vehicle and must be an encoded key.

1) Insert the first programmed ignition key into ignition lock cylinder. Turn ignition switch from LOCK to RUN position (ignition switch must stay in RUN position for one second). Turn ignition switch to LOCK position and remove ignition key from ignition lock cylinder.

2) Within 5 seconds of turning ignition switch to LOCK position, insert second programmed ignition key into ignition lock cylinder. Turn ignition switch from LOCK to RUN position (ignition switch must stay in RUN position for one second). Turn ignition switch to LOCK position and remove second ignition key from ignition lock cylinder.

3) Within 5 seconds of turning ignition switch to LOCK position, insert a NEW unprogrammed ignition key into ignition lock cylinder. Turn ignition switch from LOCK to RUN position (ignition switch must stay in RUN position for one second). Turn ignition switch to LOCK position and remove ignition key from ignition lock cylinder. The NEW ignition key should now be programmed. To program additional key(s), repeat key programming procedure from step **1)**.

KEY PROGRAMMING WITHOUT USING 2 PROGRAMMED KEYS

NOTE: This procedure is used when customer needs extra keys programmed and 2 programmed keys are not available but system has 2 ignition keys programmed. A maximum of 8 keys can be programmed. If 8 keys are already programmed, this procedure will not allow any more to be programmed. The number of programmed key can be determined by accessing PATS PID NUMKEYS with NGS tester.

Insert unprogrammed key in ignition and turn ignition switch to RUN position. Connect New Generation Star (NGS) tester to Data Link Connector (DLC). Insert Ford Service Function (FSF) card in NGS tester. Perform security access procedure. See SECURITY ACCESS PROCEDURE. Select IGNITION KEY CODE PROGRAM. Turn ignition switch to LOCK position. Disconnect NGS tester. Key should now be programmed and be able to start vehicle.

SELF-DIAGNOSTIC SYSTEM

NOTE: Metallic objects and encoded devices on key ring may interfere with PATS system, causing a no-start condition and setting DTCs. If fault cannot be identified, remove encoded key from key ring and attempt to start vehicle.

SELF-DIAGNOSTICS

The Passive Anti-Theft System (PATS) utilizes a self-diagnostic system which stores a Diagnostic Trouble Code (DTC) in the Powertrain Control Module (PCM) if a problem exists in the PATS. DTCs may be retrieved from PCM by using a NGS tester and Data Link Connector (DLC). Before retrieving DTCs, a preliminary procedure should be performed. See PRELIMINARY PROCEDURE.

PRELIMINARY PROCEDURE

1) Verify customers complaint by operating PATS. Ensure electronically coded ignition key is being used. Check for damaged ignition lock cylinder switch, damaged encoded ignition key or open fuses. Check for loose or corroded connectors, damaged wiring harness, damaged ignition switch or damaged transceiver module. Repair or replace components as necessary. If all components are okay, connect NGS tester to DLC located below instrument panel. Perform DATA LINK DIAGNOSTIC TEST.

2) If NGS tester displays CKT914, CKT915 or CKT70=ALL ECUS NO RESP/NOT EQUIP, see appropriate MODULE COMMUNICATIONS NETWORK article to continue diagnosis. If NGS tester displays NO RESP/NOT EQUIP for PATS, go to TEST A: NO COMMUNICATION WITH MODULE test under SYSTEM TESTS. If NGS tester displays SYSTEM PASSED, retrieve DTCs and perform appropriate DTC test. See RETRIEVING DIAGNOSTIC TROUBLE CODES.

RETRIEVING DIAGNOSTIC TROUBLE CODES

NOTE: A New Generation Star (NGS) Tester (007-00500) is required for retrieving DTCs and testing the passive ant-theft control system.

1) Observe THEFT indicator light on instrument cluster and turn ignition on. If THEFT indicator light illuminates for 3 seconds and then turns off, system is functioning properly at this time. If THEFT indicator light operates abnormally, go to next step. If THEFT indicator light does not illuminate, go to TEST B: THEFT INDICATOR LIGHT DOES NOT ILLUMINATE/NO THEFT INDICATOR LIGHT PROVE OUT test under SYSTEM TESTS.

2) Turn ignition off. Connect NGS tester to DLC located below instrument panel. Retrieve and record stored DTCs. Using NGS tester, perform On-Demand Self-Test. Once on-demand self-test has been completed, retrieve DTCs. If any DTCs are retrieved, perform appropriate test under SYSTEM TESTS. If NGS tester cannot communicate with

PATS module, go to TEST A: NO COMMUNICATION WITH MODULE test under SYSTEM TESTS. See DTC INDEX table. If no DTCs are retrieved, system is functioning properly at this time.

DTC INDEX

DTC	Description	Test
B1213	Anti-Theft Number Of Programmed Keys Is Below Minimum	C
B1232	Antenna Not Connected Or Defective Tranciever	D
B1600	No Key Code Received/Damaged Encoded Ignition Key Or Use Of Non-PATS Key	E
B1601	Incorrect Key Code From Ignition Key Transponder	F
B1602	Invalid Key Code Format From Ignition Key Transponder	G
B1681	Transceiver Defective Or Not Connected	H
B2103	PATS Antenna Not Connected	D
B2139	PCM ID Does Not Match Between Instrument Cluster and PCM	I
B2141	No PCM ID Exchange Between Instrument Cluster And PCM	J
U1147	Invalid Or Missing Vehicle Security Data	K

SYSTEM TESTS

NOTE: Metallic objects and encoded devices on key ring may interfere with PATS system, causing a no-start condition and setting DTCs. If fault cannot be identified, remove encoded key from key ring and attempt to start vehicle.

SYMPTOM CHART

Symptom	Test
No Communication With Module, (Instrument Cluster)	A
No THEFT Indicator Prove Out	B
Vehicle Starts, THEFT Indicator Flashes DTC With KOEO	K
Vehicle Does Not Start, THEFT Indicator Operated Normally	L

TEST A: NO COMMUNICATION WITH MODULE

1) Turn ignition off. Disconnect Black 20-pin instrument cluster connector. Turn ignition switch to RUN position. Measure voltage between terminal No. 2 (Red/Light Green wire) and ground, terminal No. 3 (Light Green/Red wire) and ground, and terminal No. 11 (Gray/Yellow wire) and ground. *See Fig. 1.* If voltage is greater than 10 volts at all 3 terminals, go to next step. If voltage at any terminal is 10 volts or less, repair appropriate wire or fuse. See WIRING DIAGRAMS. Repeat self test and clear DTCs.

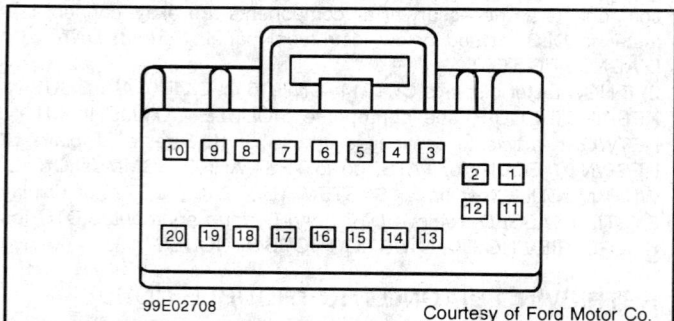

99E02708   Courtesy of Ford Motor Co.

Fig. 1: Identifying Instrument Cluster Black 20-Pin Connector Terminals

2) Turn ignition off. Measure resistance between Black 20-pin instrument cluster connector terminal No. 1 (Black wire) and ground. *See Fig. 1.* If resistance is greater than 5 ohms, repair open or high resistance in Black wire or connections. See WIRING DIAGRAMS. If resistance is 5 ohms or less, diagnose problem in module communications network. See appropriate MODULE COMMUNICATIONS NETWORK article.

TEST B: THEFT INDICATOR LIGHT DOES NOT ILLUMINATE/NO THEFT INDICATOR LIGHT PROVE OUT

Remove instrument cluster and access THEFT indicator LED. See appropriate INSTRUMENT PANELS article. Measure resistance

between LED terminals in both directions. Resistance should be greater than 10 k/ohms in one direction, and between 10 and 20 ohms with test leads reversed. If resistance is as specified, install new instrument cluster, repeat self test and clear DTCs. If resistance is not as specified, install new LED, repeat self test and clear DTCs.

TEST C: ANTI-THEFT NUMBER OF PROGRAMMED KEYS IS BELOW MINIMUM

1) Turn ignition switch to LOCK position. Connect NGS tester to Data Link Connector (DLC). Turn ignition switch to RUN position. Using NGS tester, retrieve continuous PCM DTCs. Clear continuous DTCs. Turn ignition switch to LOCK position. Turn ignition switch to RUN position. Retrieve continuous PCM DTCs. If DTC B1213 is the only DTC retrieved, go to next step. If any other DTCs are retrieved, perform appropriate test before diagnosing DTC B1213.

2) Using NGS tester, monitor and record check PCM PID NUMKEYS. If PID indicates less than 2 keys, go to next step. If PID does not indicate less than 2 keys, system is okay at this time.

3) Obtain NEW encoded ignition key and insert into ignition lock cylinder. Using NEW key, turn ignition switch to RUN position. Program NEW encoded ignition key. See PROGRAMMING WITHOUT USING 2 PROGRAMMED KEYS under PROGRAMMING. If theft indicator does not illuminates for 3 seconds and then go out, go to next step. If theft indicator illuminates for 3 seconds and then goes out, clear DTCs and perform PCM self-test. Verify no DTCs are present.

4) Repeat step **3)** with a different encoded key. If theft indicator is flashing, retrieve DTCs and perform appropriate test.

TEST D: ANTENNA NOT CONNECTED

Verify transceiver module is correctly installed. See PATS TRANSCEIVER MODULE under REMOVAL & INSTALLATION. Connect NGS tester and clear DTCs. Perform instrument cluster on-demand self test. If DTCs B1232 or B2103 are retrieved, install new PATS transceiver module. Repeat self test and clear DTCs. If DTCs B1232 or B2103 are not retrieved, system is okay at this time.

TEST E: IGNITION KEY TRANSPONDER SIGNAL NOT RECEIVED

1) If any other DTCs were retrieved, repair those DTCs before diagnosing B1600. If only DTC B1600 was retrieved, go to next step.

2) Cut a new encoded ignition key. Program key. See ERASE ALL KEYS & PROGRAM 2 KEYS under PROGRAMMING. Using NGS tester clear DTCs and perform instrument cluster on-demand self test. If DTC B1600 is still retrieved, go to next step. If other DTCs are retrieved, perform appropriate code test. See DTC INDEX table. If no DTC's are retrieved, system is okay.

3) Turn ignition off. Install new PATS transceiver module. See PATS TRANSCEIVER MODULE under REMOVAL & INSTALLATION. Turn ignition switch to RUN position using an original key, (not the key programmed in step **2)**. Using NGS tester perform instrument cluster on-demand self test. If DTC B1600 is not retrieved, system is okay. If

DTC B1600 is retrieved, Replace instrument cluster. See appropriate INSTRUMENT PANELS article. Cycle ignition using 2 encoded keys. Repeat self test and clear DTCs.

TEST F: INCORRECT KEY CODE FROM IGNITION KEY TRANSPONDER

NOTE: DTC B1601 is stored when a key that is not programmed into PATS module memory has been used. This indicates key needs to be programmed into PATS module memory. See SPARE KEY PROGRAMMING under PROGRAMMING. Maximum of 8 keys can be stored into PATS module memory.

1) Connect NGS tester to DLC and monitor PID NUMKEYS. If PID NUMKEYS displays any number other than "8", go to next step. If PID NUMKEYS display is "8", erase and reprogram all keys. See ERASE ALL KEYS & PROGRAM 2 KEYS under PROGRAMMING. Using NGS tester and perform instrument cluster on-demand self test. Clear DTCs.

2) If there are at least 2 programmed encoded keys available, go to next step. If there are not at least 2 keys available, cut and program new key(s). See ERASE ALL KEYS & PROGRAM 2 KEYS under PROGRAMMING, then proceed to next step.

3) Start vehicle using an encoded key. Repeat with a second encoded key. If vehicle starts with both keys, system is okay. If vehicle does not start with both keys, go to next step.

4) Turn ignition switch to RUN position. Using NGS tester, retrieve instrument cluster continuous DTCs. Clear continuous DTCs. Perform instrument cluster on-demand self test using both keys used in step 3). If DTC B1601 is not retrieved, system is okay. If other DTCs are retrieved perform appropriate test. See DTC INDEX table. If DTC B1601 is retrieved, replace instrument cluster. See appropriate INSTRUMENT PANELS article. Cycle ignition using 2 encoded keys. Repeat self test and clear DTCs. Test system for proper operation.

TEST G: INVALID FORMAT KEY CODE FROM IGNITION KEY TRANSPONDER

1) Cut and program new encoded key. See ERASE ALL KEYS & PROGRAM 2 KEYS under PROGRAMMING. Perform instrument cluster on-demand self test. If DTC B1602 is retrieved, go to next step. If DTC B1602 is not retrieved, system is okay.

2) Turn ignition off. Replace PATS transceiver module. See PATS TRANSCEIVER MODULE under REMOVAL & INSTALLATION. Turn ignition switch to RUN position and perform instrument cluster on-demand self test. If any DTCs are retrieved, perform appropriate test. See DTC INDEX table. If no DTCs are retrieved, system is okay.

TEST H: TRANSCEIVER MODULE SIGNAL NOT RECEIVED

1) Turn ignition off. Disconnect PATS transceiver module 4-pin connector. Turn ignition switch to RUN position. Measure voltage between connector terminal No. 2 (Red/Light Green wire) and ground. *See Fig. 2.* If voltage is greater than 9 volts, go to next step. If voltage is 9 volts or less, repair Red/Light Green wire, repeat self test and clear DTCs. See WIRING DIAGRAMS.

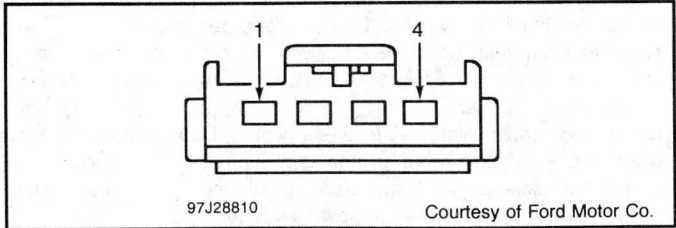

97J28810   Courtesy of Ford Motor Co.

Fig. 2: Identifying Transceiver Module Connector Terminals

2) Turn ignition off. Measure resistance between PATS transceiver module connector terminal No. 1 (Black/Light Blue wire) and ground. *See Fig. 2.* If resistance is less than 5 ohms, go to next step. If resistance is 5 ohms or greater, repair Black/Light Blue wire, repeat self test and clear DTCs. See WIRING DIAGRAMS.

3) Reconnect PATS transceiver module connector. Turn ignition switch to RUN position. Backprobe PATS transceiver module connector terminal No. 3 (Gray/Orange wire) with positive voltmeter probe. Measure voltage between terminal No. 3 and ground. If voltage is greater than 9 volts, go to step 5). If voltage is 9 volts or less, go to next step.

4) Turn ignition off. Disconnect PATS transceiver module 4-pin connector. Measure resistance between connector terminal No. 3 (Gray/Orange wire) and ground. *See Fig. 2.* If resistance is greater than 100 ohms, go to next step. If resistance is 100 ohms or less, inspect Gray/Orange wire for short to ground. Repair as necessary. See WIRING DIAGRAMS. If wire is okay, replace instrument cluster. See appropriate INSTRUMENT PANELS article. Cycle 2 encoded ignition keys to RUN position. Go to DTC B2139: PCM ID DOES NOT MATCH INSTRUMENT CLUSTER ID to match new instrument cluster ID to PCM. Repeat self test and clear DTCs.

5) Measure resistance of Gray/Orange wire between PATS transceiver module connector terminal No. 3 and White instrument cluster 22-pin connector terminal No. 14. *See Figs. 2 and 3.* If resistance is less than 5 ohms, go to next step. If resistance is 5 ohms or greater, repair Gray/Orange wire. See WIRING DIAGRAMS. Repeat self test and clear DTCs.

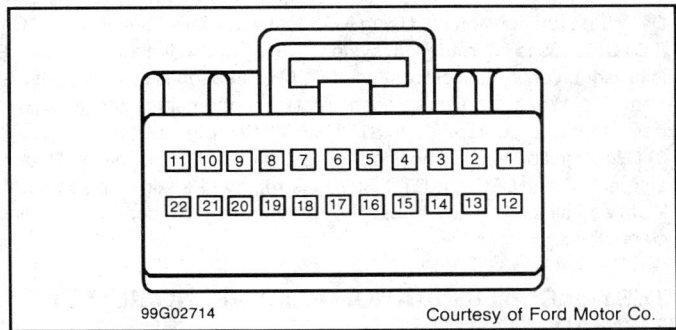

99G02714   Courtesy of Ford Motor Co.

Fig. 3: Identifying Instrument Cluster White 22-Pin Connector Terminals

6) Turn ignition off. Reconnect PATS transceiver module. Turn ignition switch to RUN position. Backprobe PATS transceiver module connector terminal No. 4 (White/Light Green wire) with voltmeter positive lead. Measure voltage between connector terminal No. 4 and ground. If voltage is greater than 9 volts, go to step 8). If voltage is 9 volts or less, go to next step.

7) Turn ignition off. Disconnect PATS transceiver module 4-pin connector. Measure resistance between connector terminal No. 4 (White/Light Green wire) and ground. *See Fig. 2.* If resistance is greater than 100 ohms, go to next step. If resistance is 100 ohms or less, inspect White/Light Green wire for short to ground. Repair as necessary. See WIRING DIAGRAMS. If wire is okay, replace instrument cluster. See appropriate INSTRUMENT PANELS article. Cycle two encoded ignition keys to RUN position. Go to TEST I: PCM ID DOES NOT MATCH INSTRUMENT CLUSTER ID to match new instrument cluster ID to PCM. Repeat self test and clear DTCs.

8) Reconnect PATS transceiver module and instrument cluster connectors. Turn ignition switch to RUN position. Backprobe PATS transceiver module connector terminal No. 4 (White/Light Green wire) with positive voltmeter probe. Measure voltage between terminal No. 4 and ground. Using NGS tester, trigger the instrument cluster active command TRANSMIT SIGNAL COMMAND to ON. Voltage should drop from greater than 9 volts to less than one volt when instrument cluster active command is triggered on. If voltage is as specified, go to next step. If voltage is not as specified, inspect White/Light Green wire for short to ground. Repair as necessary. See WIRING DIAGRAMS. If wire is okay, replace instrument cluster. See appropriate INSTRUMENT PANELS article. Cycle two encoded ignition keys to RUN position. Go to TEST I: PCM ID DOES NOT MATCH INSTRUMENT CLUSTER ID to match new instrument cluster ID to PCM. Repeat self test and clear DTCs.

9) Turn ignition off. Replace PATS transceiver module. See PATS TRANSCEIVER MODULE under REMOVAL & INSTALLATION. Using

FORD
4-144

1999 ACCESSORIES & EQUIPMENT
Passive Anti-Theft Systems – Expedition & Navigator (Cont.)

NGS tester, perform instrument cluster on cemand self test. If DTC B1681 is retrieved, go to next step. If DTC B1681 is not retrieved, system is okay.

10) Turn ignition off. Replace instrument cluster. See appropriate INSTRUMENT PANELS article. Cycle ignition to RUN position using 2 encoded keys. Using NGS tester, perform instrument cluster on demand self test. If DTC B1681 is retrieved, repair PATS system wiring, repeat self test and clear DTCs. See WIRING DIAGRAMS. If DTC B1681 is not retrieved, system is okay.

TEST I: PCM ID DOES NOT MATCH INSTRUMENT CLUSTER ID

1) Turn ignition off. Connect New Generation Star (NGS) tester to DLC. Turn ignition switch to RUN position. PerfcrmSECURITY ACCESS PROCEDURE. From NGS menu, select PARAMETER RESET command for instrument cluster. Do not make any other selections in this menu. Use diagnostic card for PCM Active Command Keep Alive Memory Reset. Turn ignition off and selec: PARAMETER RESET command for PCM.

2) Turn ignition switch to RUN position for 3 seconds. Clear continuous DTCs and turn ignition off. Using NGS tester, retrieve continuous DTCs. If DTC B2139 is not retrieved, system is okay at this time. If DTC B2139 is present, verify PCM calibration. If PCM calibration is okay, repeat test from step 1). If code is still present, replace instrument cluster and go to next step. See appropriate INSTRUMENT PANELS article.

3) Cycle ignition to RUN position using 2 encoded ignition keys. Repeat self test. Clear DTCs. If DTC B2139 is retrieved again, replace PCM. PCM and all ignition keys must be reprogrammed. Repeat self-test and clear DTCs.

TEST J: CONFIGURATION FAILURE, NO PCM ID EXCHANGED

1) If DTC U1147 is also retrieved, go to TEST K: INVALID OR MISSING VEHICLE SECURITY DATA. If only DTC B2141 is retrieved, go to next step.

2) With NGS tester connected to DLC, use diagnostic card for PCM Active Command Keep Alive Memory Reset. Turn ignition off. Turn ignition switch to RUN position for 30 seconds. Turn ignition off. Attempt to start vehicle. If vehicle starts, system is okay. If vehicle does not start, go to next step.

3) Turn ignition switch to RUN position. Using NGS tester, retrieve and record instrument cluster continuous DTCs. Clear continuous DTCs. Retrieve and record instrument cluster on demand DTCs. If no DTCs are retrieved, system is okay. If DTC B2141 is retr eved, repeat step 2). If fault persists, verify PCM calibration. If PCM calibration is okay, replace instrument cluster. See appropriate INSTRUMENT PANELS article. Cycle ignition to RUN position using 2 encoded keys. Go to TEST I: PCM ID DOES NOT MATCH INSTRUMENT CLUSTER ID to match new instrument cluster ID to PCM. Repeat self test and clear DTCs.

TEST K: INVALID OR MISSING VEHICLE SECURITY DATA

1) Turn ignition switch to RUN position and observe THEFT indicator. Indicator should illuminate, then goes out within 3 seconds. Attempt to start vehicle. If THEFT indicator does not operate as specified or vehicle will not start, go to next step. If THEFT indicator operates as specified and vehicle starts, verify proper PCM calibration.

2) Turn ignition off. Connect New Generation Start (NGS) tester to vehicle DLC. Turn ignition switch to RUN position. Using NGS tester, perform PCM continuous self test. Record any DTCs present. Clear continuous DTCs. Perform PCM KOEO self test. Record any DTCs and go to next step. If NGS tester does not communicate with PCM, see appropriate SELF-DIAGNOSTICS article in ENGINE PERFORMANCE in appropriate MITCHELL® manual.

3) If DTC P1260 was retrieved in previous step, go to next step. If DTC P1260 was not retrieved during previous step, check PCM for power and ground. See PIN VOLTAGE/PID VALUE CHARTS article in ENGINE PERFORMANCE in appropriate MITCHELL® manual.

4) Perform PRELIMINARY PROCEDURE under SELF-DIAGNOSTIC SYSTEM. Turn ignition off. If continuous or on demand DTC U1147 is not retrieved, system is okay. If continuous or on demand DTC U1147 is retrieved, replace instrument cluster. See appropriate INSTRUMENT PANELS article. Cycle ignition to RUN position using 2 encoded keys. Go to TEST I: PCM ID DOES NOT MATCH INSTRUMENT CLUSTER ID to match new instrument cluster ID to PCM. Clear DTCs. Check system for normal operation. If DTC U1147 is still present, replace PCM. PCM and all ignition keys must be reprogrammed. Repeat self test and clear DTCs.

TEST L: VEHICLE DOES NOT START, THEFT INDICATOR OPERATES NORMALLY

Using NGS tester, perform instrument cluster on demand self test. Record any DTCs. Cycle ignition switch and retrieve and continuous DTCs. If any DTCs were present, perform appropriate testing procedure. See DTC INDEX. If no DTCs were retrieved, investigate the following possible causes:

- Less than 2 keys programmed to the system.
- PATS transceiver module not connected or defective.
- Faulty system wiring or connections.
- Damaged PATS transceiver module internal antenna.
- Damaged, unprogrammed or non-PATS key used.
- No PCM ID stored in PATS transceiver module, or ID does not match.
- Problem with Standard Corporate Protocol (SCP) network.
- Partial PATS key read.

REMOVAL & INSTALLATION

CAUTION: When battery is disconnected, vehicle computer and memory systems may lose memory data. Driveability problems may exist until computer systems have completed a relearn cycle. See COMPUTER RELEARN PROCEDURES article in GENERAL INFORMATION before disconnecting battery.

PATS TRANSCEIVER MODULE

NOTE: If transceiver module is replaced, all existing ignition keys must be reprogrammed. See PROGRAMMING.

Removal & Installation – Disconnect negative battery cable. Transceiver module is located on steering column, attached to ignition lock cylinder housing. Turn ignition switch lock cylinder to RUN position. Push ignition switch lock cylinder release tab with punch while removing ignition switch lock cylinder. Unscrew and remove tilt wheel lever. Remove instrument panel steering column cover to access column shroud screws. Remove 3 screws and remove upper and lower steering column shrouds. Remove PATS transceiver module retaining screw. Disconnect transceiver electrical connector. Locate rib on steering column lock cylinder housing, and gently pry transceiver over rib to remove transceiver (apply pressure or leverage below key cylinder lower rib). To install, reverse removal procedure.

Passive Anti-Theft Systems – Expedition & Navigator (Cont.)

WIRING DIAGRAMS

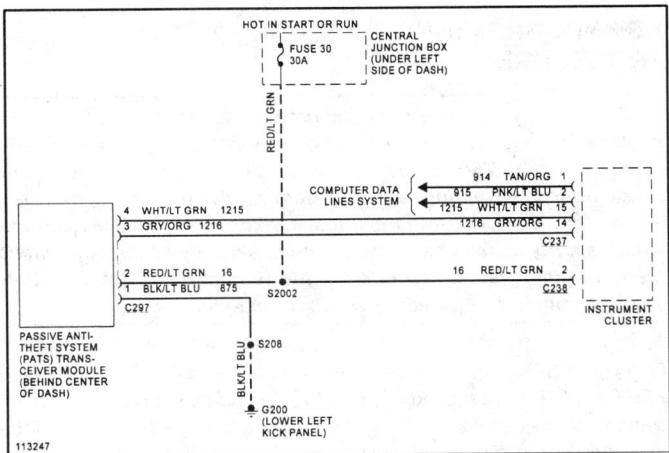

Fig. 4: Passive Anti-Theft System (PATS) Wiring Diagram (Expedition & Navigator)

DESCRIPTION

Passive Anti-Theft System (PATS) vehicle protection system is designed to prevent driveaway thefts. The system is passive in that it does not require any activity from the user. System uses radio frequency identification technology to verify if proper key is being used to attempt to start the vehicle.

During each starting sequence, the encoded ignition key is interrogated by vehicle anti-theft electronics. If the key's identification code is programmed into anti-theft system, vehicle is capable of starting. If key's identification code is incorrect or missing, vehicle is prevented from starting.

PATS module communicates with the Powertrain Control Module (PCM) via Module Communications Network (MCN). PCM then determines if engine will be enabled to start. If the PCM prevents vehicle from starting because of PATS system, PCM will store a Diagnostic Trouble Code (DTC) in memory.

PATS vehicle protection system consists of these components: PATS module, anti-theft indicator (THEFT) light, transceiver module, encoded ignition key, module communications network and Data Link Connector (DLC).

OPERATION

ANTI-THEFT INDICATOR (THEFT) LIGHT

THEFT indicator light located on right side of instrument cluster is used to proveout system operation status. Under normal operation THEFT indicator light will illuminate for 3 seconds when ignition switch is in RUN or START position, and then turn off. If a problem exists in PATS, THEFT indicator light will flash rapidly or illuminate constantly with ignition switch in RUN or START position.

ENCODED IGNITION KEY

When ignition switch is in RUN or START position, PATS module initiates the encoded ignition key interrogation process. PATS module supplies both power and carrier signal to transceiver module to momentarily energize ignition key. After energize period has expired, key transmits its identification code to transceiver module. This encoded ignition key is much larger in size to accommodate the electronics located inside plastic cover.

TRANSCEIVER MODULE

Transceiver module receives ignition key identification code and interfaces with PATS module.

PASSIVE ANTI-THEFT SYSTEM (PATS) MODULE

PATS module contains circuitry to interface to vehicle electrical system, transceiver module, Module Communications Network (MCN) system and THEFT indicator light. PATS module stores ignition key codes in non-volatile memory. PATS module can be diagnosed through Data Link Connector (DLC).

POWERTRAIN CONTROL MODULE (PCM)

Passive anti-theft system uses PCM to enable or disable vehicle's engine. Within one second after engine starts, PCM must receive an enable signal or the engine will be disabled.

COMPONENT LOCATION

PATS COMPONENT LOCATION

Component	Location
PATS Module	Behind Right Side Of Instrument Panel
THEFT Indicator Light	Right Side Of Instrument Cluster
Transceiver Module	Bottom Right Side Of Steering Column

PROGRAMMING

KEY PROGRAMMING – SECURITY ACCESS PROCEDURE

NOTE: Security access must be granted to erase ignition keys, enable/disable spare key programming switch, or perform parameter reset for PATS module. This procedure has a 10 minute time delay prior to granting security access during which the New Generation Star (NGS) tester must remain connected to vehicle. After security access has been granted, security access command menu is displayed which offers various command options. Only select command required by appropriate system test.

Turn ignition switch to RUN position. Using NGS tester and Ford Service Function (FSF) card, select PATS module. Select SECURITY ACCESS PROCEDURE. This procedure will take 10 minutes to perform. After the security access procedure has been completed, a new menu will be displayed with command options. Select as many functions as required before exiting this menu. Once this menu is exited, security access procedure must be performed again to perform additional commands.

KEY PROGRAMMING – WITH PROGRAMMED KEYS

NOTE: This procedure will only work if 2 or more programmed ignition keys are available and there is a need to program additional keys. If 2 keys are not available, perform KEY PROGRAMMING – WITHOUT PROGRAMMED KEYS under PROGRAMMING. PID SPARE_KY must be enabled for this procedure to operate. To enable this PID, perform KEY PROGRAMMING – SECURITY ACCESS PROCEDURE and enable spare key programming switch. If programming procedure is successful, new key(s) will start vehicle and THEFT indicator light will illuminate for 3 seconds. If programming procedure is not successful, new key(s) will not start vehicle and THEFT indicator light will flash for one minute (after flashing for one minute, THEFT indicator light will flash fault code). If necessary, repeat programming procedure. If programming of key(s) is still unsuccessful, check for Diagnostic Trouble Codes (DTCs) and repair as necessary. See SELF-DIAGNOSTIC SYSTEM. Maximum of eight keys can be programmed into system. If procedure is not performed as outlined, programming procedure will end. Ignition keys must have correct mechanical key cut for vehicle and must be an encoded key.

1) Insert the first programmed ignition key into ignition lock cylinder. Turn ignition switch from OFF to RUN position (ignition switch must stay in RUN position for one second). Turn ignition switch to OFF position and remove ignition key from ignition lock cylinder.

2) Within 5 seconds of turning ignition switch to OFF position, insert second programmed ignition key into ignition lock cylinder. Turn ignition switch from OFF to RUN position (ignition switch must stay in RUN position for one second). Turn ignition switch to OFF position and remove second ignition key from ignition lock cylinder.

3) Within 10 seconds of turning ignition switch to OFF position, insert a NEW unprogrammed ignition key into ignition lock cylinder. Turn ignition switch from OFF to RUN position (ignition switch must stay in RUN position for one second). Turn ignition switch to OFF position and remove ignition key from ignition lock cylinder. The NEW ignition key should now be programmed. To program additional key(s), repeat key programming procedure from step **1)**.

1999 ACCESSORIES & EQUIPMENT
Passive Anti-Theft Systems – Explorer & Mountaineer (Cont.)

FORD
4-147

KEY PROGRAMMING – WITHOUT PROGRAMMED KEYS

NOTE: This procedure is used when a customer needs keys programmed into system and does not have 2 programmed ignition keys available, or when programmed ignition keys have been lost and/or ignition switch assembly has been replaced. This procedure will erase all programmed ignition keys from memory and prevent vehicle from starting until 2 keys have been programmed. Ignition keys must have correct mechanical key cut for vehicle and must be an encoded key. If additional key(s) are to be programmed, perform KEY PROGRAMMING – WITH PROGRAMMED KEYS. If remaining keys are with customer and not with vehicle, instruct customer to see owner's manual to program spare key(s).

1) Turn ignition switch from OFF to RUN position. With NGS tester connected to vehicle, enter function test menu. Select SECURITY ACCESS PROCEDURE. This procedure will take 10 minutes to perform. After the security access procedure has been completed, a new menu will be displayed with command options. Select IGNITION KEY CODE ERASE.

2) Turn ignition switch to OFF position and disconnect NGS tester. Insert first encoded ignition key into ignition lock cylinder. Turn ignition switch to RUN position for 3 seconds. Turn ignition switch to OFF position and remove first encoded key.

3) Insert second encoded ignition key into ignition lock cylinder. Turn ignition switch to RUN position for 3 seconds. Turn ignition switch to OFF position and remove second encoded key. Both encoded ignition keys should now start vehicle.

KEY PROGRAMMING – SPARE KEY PROGRAMMING SWITCH

NOTE: The spare key programming switch is a programmable switch which provides the capability to enable/disable the normal customer spare key programming procedure detailed in the owner's manual. This programmable switch is provided as a convenience for rental company fleets or other fleet purchasers who may not want the spare key programming procedure available to the vehicle driver. The spare key programming switch state can be viewed using PATS module SPARE_KY PID.

Insert a programmed ignition key into the ignition lock cylinder. Turn ignition switch from OFF to RUN position. Using NGS tester and Ford Service Function (FSF) card, select PATS module. Select SECURITY ACCESS PROCEDURE. This procedure will take 10 minutes to perform. After the security access procedure has been completed, a new menu will be displayed with command options. The default setting on all new vehicles is ENABLE. Select SPARE KEY PROGRAMMING SWITCH. Set SPARE KEY PROGRAMMING SWITCH to ENABLE or DISABLE.

SELF-DIAGNOSTIC SYSTEM

SELF-DIAGNOSTIC TEST

Verify customers complaint. Ensure electronically coded ignition key is being used. Check for damaged ignition lock cylinder switch, damaged encoded ignition key or open fuses. Check for loose or corroded connectors, damaged wiring harness, damaged ignition switch or damaged transceiver module. Repair or replace components as necessary.

If all components are okay, connect New Generation Star (NGS) tester to Data Link Connector (DLC), located beneath instrument panel. Using NGS tester, preform data link diagnostic test. See DATA LINK DIAGNOSTIC TEST under COMMUNICATION NETWORK DIAGNOSTICS in MODULE COMMUNICATIONS NETWORK – EXPLORER & MOUNTAINEER article. If NGS tester responds with CKT914, CKT915 or CKT70=ALL ECUS NO RESP/NOT EQUIP, repair module communications concern. See MODULE COMMUNICATIONS NETWORK – EXPLORER & MOUNTAINEER article. If NGS tester displays NO RESP/NOT EQUIP for PATS module, perform TEST A: NO COMMUNICATION WITH PATS MODULE under SYSTEM TESTS.

If NGS tester responds with SYSTEM PASSED, retrieve and record continuous DTCs. Erase continuous DTCs. Using NGS tester, perform PATS module self-test. If any DTCs are present, perform appropriate DTC test. See PATS MODULE DTCS table. Codes listed in this table are only for testing covered in this article. For complete DTC listing, see MODULE COMMUNICATIONS NETWORK – EXPLORER & MOUNTAINEER article. If no DTCs are present, repair by symptom. See SYMPTOM DIAGNOSIS table under SYSTEM TESTS.

PATS MODULE DTCS

DTC	Test
B1213 (Number Of Programmed Ignition Keys Below Minimum)	DTC B1213
B1232 (Defective Transceiver Module	DTC B1232 Or B2103
B1600 (PATS Ignition Key Transponder Signal Not Received)	DTC B1600
B1601 (PATS Received Incorrect Key Code From Ignition Key Transponder)	DTC B1601
B1602 (PATS Received Invalid Key Code Format From Ignition Key Transponder)	DTC B1602
B1681 (PATS Transceiver Signal Is Not Received)	DTC B1681
B2103 (Antenna Not Connected)	DTC B1232 Or B2103
B2139 (Security Identification Does Not Match Between PATS Module & PCM)	DTC B2139
B2141 (No Security Identification Exchange Between PATS Module & PCM)	DTC B2141
U1147 (Faulty SCP Link Or Incorrect PCM Calibration)	DTC U1147
U1262 (Missing SCP Message)	[1]

[1] – Go to PASSIVE ANTI-THEFT SYSTEM (PATS) MODULE DOES NOT RESPOND TO NGS TESTER under TESTING in MODULE COMMUNICATIONS NETWORK – EXPLORER & MOUNTAINEER article.

DIAGNOSTIC TROUBLE CODE TESTS

DTC B1213: NUMBER OF PROGRAMMED IGNITION KEYS BELOW MINIMUM

1) Using NGS tester, retrieve and record continuous DTCs. Clear DTCs and perform PATS module self-test to check for DTCs. If DTC B1213 is present, go to next step. If other DTCs are present, go to appropriate DTC test and repair as necessary. If no DTCs are present, system is operating properly. Check system for normal operation.

2) Using NGS tester, select NUMKEYS PID from PID/DATA monitor menu. If PID value indicates less than 2 encoded ignition keys programmed, go to next step. If PID value indicates 2 or more encoded ignition keys programmed, system is operating properly. Clear DTCs and check system for normal operation.

3) Obtain NEW encoded ignition key and insert into ignition lock cylinder. Turn ignition switch to RUN position. Program NEW encoded key. See KEY PROGRAMMING – WITHOUT PROGRAMMED KEYS under PROGRAMMING. If THEFT indicator light illuminates for 3 seconds and goes out, system is operating properly. If THEFT indicator light illuminates at all times, repeat this step with a second NEW encoded ignition key. If THEFT indicator light is flashing, perform appropriate DTC test for trouble code received.

DTC B1232 OR B2103: DEFECTIVE TRANSCEIVER MODULE OR ANTENNA NOT CONNECTED

1) Turn ignition switch to OFF position. Verify transceiver module is installed properly. See TRANSCEIVER MODULE under REMOVAL & INSTALLATION. Repair as necessary. Clear DTCs and check system for normal operation. If transceiver module is installed properly, go to next step.

FORD
4-148

1999 ACCESSORIES & EQUIPMENT
Passive Anti-Theft Systems – Explorer & Mountaineer (Cont.)

2) Using NGS tester, retrieve and record continuous DTCs. Clear DTCs and perform PATS module self-test to check for DTCs. If DTC B1232 is present, replace transceiver module. Clear DTCs and repeat PATS module self-test. If DTC B1232 or B2103 is not present, system is operating properly.

DTC B1600: PATS IGNITION KEY TRANSPONDER SIGNAL NOT RECEIVED

NOTE: Large metallic objects, a second PATS ignition key, or devices such as electronic credit cards on the same key ring may cause vehicle starting problem and possibly set this code. Ensure customers encoded ignition key is an approved Ford encoded ignition key. Encoded keys from Rotunda, Ilco, and Strattec are also approved keys.

1) Using NGS tester, retrieve and record continuous DTCs. Clear DTCs and perform PATS module self-test to check for DTCs. If DTC B1600 is present, go to next step. If other DTCs are present, go to appropriate DTC test and repair as necessary. If no DTCs are present, system is operating properly.

2) Obtain NEW encoded ignition key and insert into ignition lock cylinder. Turn ignition switch to RUN position. Program NEW encoded ignition key. See KEY PROGRAMMING – WITHOUT PROGRAMMED KEYS under PROGRAMMING. Using NGS tester, clear DTCs and repeat PATS module self-test. If DTC B1600 is still present, go to next step. If any other DTCs are present, perform appropriate DTC test and repair as necessary. If no DTCs are present, system is operating properly.

3) Turn ignition switch to OFF position. Replace PATS transceiver module. See TRANSCEIVER MODULE under REMOVAL & INSTALLATION. Using customers original encoded ignition key, repeat PATS module self-test. If DTC B1600 is not present, system is operating properly. If DTC B1600 is present, replace PATS MODULE. See PATS MODULE under REMOVAL & INSTALLATION. Cycle igniton switch using newly encoded ignition keys. Using NGS tester, repeat PATS module self-test. If no DTCs are present, testing is complete. If DTC B2139 is present, go to DTC B2139: SECURITY IDENTIFICATION DOES NOT MATCH BETWEEN PATS MODULE & PCM test under DIAGNOSTIC TROUBLE CODE TESTS. Repair as necessary and check system for normal operation.

DTC B1601: PATS RECEIVED INCORRECT KEY CODE FROM IGNITION KEY TRANSPONDER

NOTE: Large metallic objects, a second PATS ignition key, or devices such as electronic credit cards on the same key ring may cause vehicle starting problem and possibly set this code. Ensure customers encoded ignition key is an approved Ford encoded ignition key. Encoded keys from Rotunda, Ilco, and Strattec are also approved keys.

1) Using NGS tester, retrieve and record continuous DTCs. Clear DTCs and repeat PATS module self-test to check for DTCs. If DTC B1601 is present, go to next step. If other DTCs are present, go to appropriate DTC test and repair as necessary. If no DTCs are present, system is operating properly. Check all other customer encoded ignition keys to ensure they are programmed.

2) Using NGS tester, select NUMKEYS PID from PID/DATA monitor menu. If PID value does not indicate 8 encoded ignition keys programmed, go to next step. If PID value indicates 8 encoded ignition keys programmed, erase and reprogram key codes. See KEY PROGRAMMING – WITHOUT PROGRAMMED KEYS under PROGRAMMING.

3) Verify that at least 2 programmed encoded ignition keys are available with vehicle. If 2 programmed encoded ignition keys are available with vehicle, go to next step. If 2 programmed encoded ignition keys are not available with vehicle, obtain 2 NEW encoded ignition keys. Program NEW encoded ignition keys. See KEY PROGRAMMING – WITHOUT PROGRAMMED KEY under PROGRAMMING. After keys are programmed, go to next step.

4) Using NGS tester, select SPARE_KY PID from PID/DATA monitor menu. If PID value indicates YES, perform KEY PROGRAMMING –

WITH PROGRAMMED KEY under PROGRAMMING. Retest system operation. If PID value indicates NO, perform KEY PROGRAMMING – SPARE KEY PROGRAMMING SWITCH under PROGRAMMING to enable PATS SPARE_KY PID to YES.

5) Turn ignition switch to OFF position. Attempt to start vehicle with first encoded ignition key. Turn ignition switch to OFF position and remove first encoded ignition key. Attempt to start vehicle with second encoded ignition key. Turn ignition switch to OFF position. If vehicle does not start using both encoded ignition keys, go to next step. If vehicle starts using both encoded ignition keys, system is operating properly. If additional spare encoded ignition keys need to be programmed, perform KEY PROGRAMMING – SPARE KEY PROGRAMMING SWITCH under PROGRAMMING.

6) Using NGS tester, retrieve and record continuous DTCs. Clear DTCs and repeat PATS module self-test. If no DTCs are present, system is operating properly. If DTC B1601 is present, replace PATS module. See PATS MODULE under REMOVAL & INSTALLATION. Cycle igniton switch using newly encoded ignition keys. Using NGS tester, repeat PATS module self-test. If no DTCs are present, testing is complete. If DTC B2139 is present, go to DTC B2139: SECURITY IDENTIFICATION DOES NOT MATCH BETWEEN PATS MODULE & PCM test under DIAGNOSTIC TROUBLE CODE TESTS. Repair as necessary and check system for normal operation.

DTC 1602: PATS RECEIVED INVALID KEY CODE FORMAT FROM IGNITION KEY TRANSPONDER

NOTE: Large metallic objects, a second PATS ignition key, or devices such as electronic credit cards on the same key ring may cause vehicle starting problem and possibly set this code. Ensure customers encoded ignition key is an approved Ford encoded ignition key. Encoded keys from Rotunda, Ilco, and Strattec are also approved keys.

1) Using NGS tester, retrieve and record continuous DTCs. Clear DTCs and repeat PATS module self-test to check for DTCs. If DTC B1602 is present, go to next step. If DTC B1602 is not present, system is operating properly.

2) Obtain a NEW encoded ignition key. Program NEW key. Perform KEY PROGRAMMING – WITHOUT PROGRAMMED KEYS under PROGRAMMING. Retrieve DTCs. If DTC B1602 is present, go to next step. If no DTCs are present, system is operating properly. If customer has any other encoded ignition keys at home, instruct customer to see owner's manual to program spare key(s).

3) Turn ignition switch to OFF position. Replace PATS transceiver module. See TRANSCEIVER MODULE under REMOVAL & INSTALLATION. Using NGS tester, repeat PATS module self-test. If DTC B1602 is present, replace PATS module. If DTC B1602 is not present, system is operating properly.

DTC B1681: PATS TRANSCEIVER SIGNAL NOT RECEIVED

1) Using NGS tester, retrieve and record continuous DTCs. Clear and then repeat PATS module self-test to check for DTCs. If DTC B1681 is present, go to next step. If DTC B1681 is not present, system is operating properly.

2) Turn ignition switch to OFF position. Disconnect transceiver module 4-pin connector C221 located at bottom right side of steering column. Turn ignition switch to RUN position. Using voltmeter, measure voltage between ground and transceiver module 4-pin connector C221 terminal No. 2 (Dark Green/White wire). *See Fig. 1.* If voltage is more than 9 volts, go to next step. If voltage is 9 volts or less, repair Dark Green/White wire between transceiver module and PATS module. Clear DTCs and retest system operation.

3) Turn ignition switch to OFF position. Using an ohmmeter, measure resistance between ground and transceiver module 4-pin connector C221 terminal No. 1 (Black/Yellow wire). If resistance is less than 5 ohms, go to next step. If resistance is 5 ohms or more, repair Black/Yellow wire between transceiver module and PATS module. Clear DTCs and retest system operation.

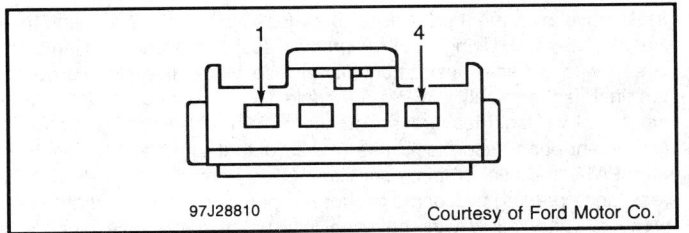

97J28810   Courtesy of Ford Motor Co.

Fig. 1: Identifying Transceiver Module Connector C221 Terminals

4) Turn ignition switch to OFF position. Connect transceiver module 4-pin connector C221. Turn ignition switch to RUN position. Using a voltmeter, measure voltage by backprobing between transceiver module 4-pin connector C221 terminal No. 3 (Gray/Orange wire) and ground. If voltage is 9 volts or less, go to next step. If voltage is more than 9 volts, go to step **7)**.

5) Turn ignition switch to OFF position. Disconnect transceiver module 4-pin connector C221 located at bottom right side of steering column. Using an ohmmeter, measure resistance between ground and transceiver module 4-pin connector C221 terminal No. 3 (Gray/Orange wire). If resistance is more than 100 ohms, go to next step. If resistance is 100 ohms or less, check Gray/Orange wire for short to ground. Repair circuit as necessary. Clear DTCs and retest system operation. If wire is okay, replace PATS module. See PATS MODULE under REMOVAL & INSTALLATION. Cycle igniton switch using newly encoded ignition keys. Using NGS tester, repeat PATS module self-test. If no DTCs are present, testing is complete. If DTC B2139 is present, go to DTC B2139: SECURITY IDENTIFICATION DOES NOT MATCH BETWEEN PATS MODULE & PCM test under DIAGNOSTIC TROUBLE CODE TESTS. Repair as necessary and check system for normal operation.

6) Measure resistance of Gray/Orange wire between transceiver module 4-pin connector C221 terminal No. 3 and PATS module 16-pin connector C222 terminal No. 11. *See Figs. 1 and 2.* If resistance is less than 5 ohms, go to next step. If resistance is 5 ohms or more, repair open Gray/Orange wire. Clear DTCs and retest system operation.

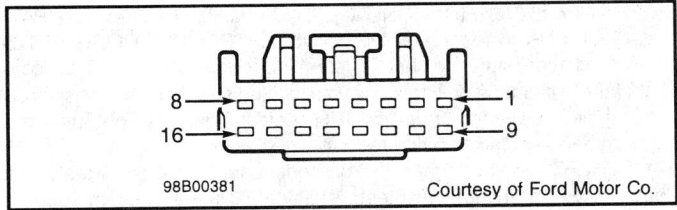

98B00381   Courtesy of Ford Motor Co.

Fig. 2: Identifying PATS Module 16-Pin Connector C222 Terminals

7) Turn ignition switch to OFF position. Connect transceiver module 4-pin connector C221. Turn ignition switch to RUN position. Using a voltmeter, measure voltage by backprobing between transceiver module 4-pin connector C221 terminal No. 4 (White/Light Green wire) and ground. If voltage is 9 volts or less, go to next step. If voltage is more than 9 volts, go to step **9)**.

8) Turn ignition switch to OFF position. Disconnect transceiver module 4-pin connector C221 located at bottom right side of steering column. Using an ohmmeter, measure resistance between ground and transceiver module 4-pin connector C221 terminal No. 4 (White/Light Green wire). If resistance is more than 100 ohms, go to next step. If resistance is 100 ohms or less, check White/Light Green wire for short to ground. Repair circuit as necessary. Clear DTCs and retest system operation. If wire is okay, replace PATS module. See PATS MODULE under REMOVAL & INSTALLATION. Cycle igniton switch using newly encoded ignition keys. Using NGS tester, repeat PATS module self-test. If no DTCs are present, testing is complete. If DTC B2139 is present, go to DTC B2139: SECURITY IDENTIFICATION DOES NOT MATCH BETWEEN PATS MODULE & PCM test under DIAGNOSTIC TROUBLE CODE TESTS. Repair as necessary and check system for normal operation.

9) Turn ignition switch to OFF position. Connect transceiver module 4-pin connector C221. Turn ignition switch to RUN position. Using NGS

tester, trigger PATS active command TRANSMIT SIGNAL COMMAND to ON. Using a voltmeter, measure voltage by backprobing between transceiver module 4-pin connector C221 terminal No. 4 (White/Light Green wire) and ground while triggering active command on. If voltage drops from more than 9 volts to less than one volt when active command is triggered on, go to next step. If voltage does not drop from more than 9 volts to less than one volt when active command is triggered on, check White/Light Green wire between transceiver module and PATS module. Repair circuit as necessary. Clear DTCs and retest system operation. If wire is okay, replace PATS module. See PATS MODULE under REMOVAL & INSTALLATION. Cycle igniton switch using newly encoded ignition keys. Using NGS tester, repeat PATS module self-test. If no DTCs are present, testing is complete. If DTC B2139 is present, go to DTC B2139: SECURITY IDENTIFICATION DOES NOT MATCH BETWEEN PATS MODULE & PCM test under DIAGNOSTIC TROUBLE CODE TESTS. Repair as necessary and check system for normal operation.

10) Turn ignition switch to OFF position. Replace PATS transceiver module. See TRANSCEIVER MODULE under REMOVAL & INSTALLATION. Turn ignition switch to RUN position. Perform PATS module self-test. If DTC B1681 is present, go to next step. If DTC B1681 is not present, system is operating properly.

11) Turn ignition switch to OFF position. Replace PATS module. See PATS MODULE under REMOVAL & INSTALLATION. Ensure ignition keys are programmed to new PATS module. See KEY PROGRAMMING – WITHOUT PROGRAMMED KEYS under PROGRAMMING. Turn ignition switch to RUN position. Perform PATS module self-test. If DTC B1681 is present, check circuits between PATS module and transceiver module. See WIRING DIAGRAMS. Repair circuits as necessary. Clear DTCs and retest system operation. If no DTCs are present, system is operating properly. If any other DTCs are present, perform appropriate DTC test and repair as necessary.

DTC B2139: SECURITY IDENTIFICATION DOES NOT MATCH BETWEEN PATS MODULE & PCM

1) Turn ignition switch to OFF position. Using NGS tester, retrieve and record continuous DTCs. Clear continuous DTCs and perform PATS module self-test. If DTC B2139 is present, go to next step. If DTC B2139 is not present, system is operating properly.

2) Perform security access for PATS Module. See KEY PROGRAMMING – SECURITY ACCESS PROCEDURE under PROGRAMMING. Using NGS tester, select PARAMETER RESET command for PATS module. Using NGS tester, clear PCM Keep Alive Memory (KAM). Turn ignition switch to RUN position for 30 seconds. Using NGS tester, perform PATS module self-test. If DTC B2139 is not present, system is operating properly. If DTC B2139 is present, verify PCM calibration is correct for vehicle. If calibration is okay, replace PATS module. Clear DTCs and retest system operation. If DTC B2139 still exists, replace PCM and retest system operation.

DTC B2141: NO SECURITY IDENTIFICATION EXCHANGE BETWEEN PATS MODULE & PCM

1) Turn ignition switch to OFF position. Using NGS tester, retrieve and record continuous DTCs. Clear continuous DTCs and perform PATS module self-test. If DTC B2141 and DTC U1147 are retrieved together, perform DTC U1147: FAULTY SCP LINK OR INCORRECT PCM CALIBRATION test. If only DTC B2141 is present, go to next step.

2) Using NGS tester, clear PCM Keep Alive Memory (KAM). Turn ignition switch to RUN position for 30 seconds. Turn ignition switch to OFF position. Attempt to start engine. If engine does not start, go to next step. If engine starts, system is operating properly. Clear DTCs and retest system operation.

3) Clear continuous DTCs. Turn ignition on and perform PATS module self-test. If DTC B2141 is not present, system is operating properly. If any other DTCs are present, perform appropriate DTC test and repair as necessary. If DTC B2141 is present, verify PCM calibration is correct for vehicle. If calibration is okay, replace PATS module. See PATS MODULE under REMOVAL & INSTALLATION. Cycle igniton switch using newly encoded ignition keys. Using NGS tester, repeat PATS module

FORD
4-150

1999 ACCESSORIES & EQUIPMENT
Passive Anti-Theft Systems – Explorer & Mountaineer (Cont.)

self-test. If no DTCs are present, testing is complete. If DTC B2139 is present, go to DTC B2139: SECURITY IDENTIFICATION DOES NOT MATCH BETWEEN PATS MODULE & PCM test under DIAGNOSTIC TROUBLE CODE TESTS. Repair as necessary and check system for normal operation.

DTC U1147: FAULTY SCP LINK OR INCORRECT PCM CALIBRATION

1) Start engine. If vehicle does not start with THEFT indicator light flashing, go to next step. If vehicle starts with THEFT indicator light flashing, problem is in PCM. See SELF-DIAGNOSTICS – EEC-V article in ENGINE PERFORMANCE in appropriate MITCHELL® manual.

2) Using NGS tester, retrieve and record continuous DTCs. Clear DTCs and perform PCM self-test. If NGS tester communicates with PCM, go to next step. If NGS tester does not communicate with NGS tester, problem is in communications network. See MODULE COMMUNICATIONS NETWORK – EXPLORER & MOUNTAINEER article.

3) Using NGS tester, retrieve and record continuous DTCs. If DTC P1260 is present, go to next step. If DTC P1260 is not present, check PCM power and ground circuits. See SELF-DIAGNOSTICS – ECC-V article in ENGINE PERFORMANCE in appropriate MITCHELL® manual.

4) Repeat SELF-DIAGNOSTIC TEST under SELF-DIAGNOSTIC SYSTEM. Turn ignition off. Using NGS tester, retrieve and record continuous DTCs. Clear DTCs and perform PATS self-test. If DTC U1147 is not present, system is operating properly. If DTC U1147 is present, replace PATS module. See PATS MODULE under REMOVAL & INSTALLATION. Cycle igniton switch using newly encoded ignition keys. Using NGS tester, repeat PATS module self-test. If no DTCs are present, testing is complete. If DTC B2139 is present, go to DTC B2139: SECURITY IDENTIFICATION DOES NOT MATCH BETWEEN PATS MODULE & PCM test under DIAGNOSTIC TROUBLE CODE TESTS. Repair as necessary and check system for normal operation.

SYSTEM TESTS

NOTE: See SYSTEM DIAGNOSIS table to determine testing according to symptom.

SYMPTOM DIAGNOSIS

Symptom	Test
No Communication With PATS Module	A
THEFT Indicator Never/Always Illuminates Or THEFT Indicator Does Not Proveout	B
Vehicle Does Not Start	1
Vehicle Starts Although THEFT Indicator Light Flashes Fault Code With Key In RUN	2

[1] – Using NGS tester, perform PATS self-test. Retrieve DTCs. If DTCs are present, perform appropriate DTC test. See PATS MODULE DTCs table under DIAGNOSTIC TROUBLE CODE TESTS. If no DTCs are retrieved, PATS system is operating properly.

[2] – Perform DTC U1147: FAULTY SCP LINK OR INCORRECT PCM CALIBRATION under DIAGNOSTIC TROUBLE CODE TESTS.

TEST A: NO COMMUNICATION WITH PATS MODULE

1) Remove instrument panel fuse block fuse No. 19 (25-amp), and fuse No. 25 (7.5-amp). Using an ohmmeter, check condition of removed fuses. If fuses are okay, go to next step. If fuse(s) are not okay, replace fuse(s). Retest system operation. If fuse(s) fail again, check for short(s) to ground in White/Yellow wire or Red/Light Green wire between instrument panel fuse block and PATS module. Retest system operation.

2) Turn ignition switch to OFF position. Disconnect PATS module 16-pin connector C222 located behind right side of instrument panel. Turn ignition switch to RUN position. Using a voltmeter, measure voltage between ground and PATS module 16-pin connector C22 terminal No. 15 (White/Yellow wire). *See Fig. 2.* Also measure voltage between ground and PATS module 16-pin connector C222 terminal No. 16 (Red/Light Green wire). If any voltage reading is 10 volts or less, go to next step. If both voltage readings are more than 10 volts, go to step **4)**.

3) Remove instrument panel fuse block fuse No. 19 (25-amp), and fuse No. 25 (7.5-amp). Using an ohmmeter, measure resistance or Red/Light Green wire between instrument panel fuse block fuse No. 19 output terminal (left terminal) and PATS module 16-pin connector C222 terminal No. 16. Also measure resistance of White/Yellow wire between instrument panel fuse block fuse No. 25 output terminal (left terminal) and PATS module 16-pin connector C222 terminal No. 15. If any resistance reading is 5 ohms or more, repair open in Red/Light Green wire or White/Yellow wire between instrument panel fuse block and PATS module. Clear DTCs and retest system operation. If both resistance readings are less than 5 ohms, repair Tan/Black wire between instrument panel fuse block and engine compartment power distribution box, or Light Green/Purple wire between instrument panel fuse block and ignition switch. Clear DTCs and retest system operation.

4) Using an ohmmeter, measure resistance between ground and PATS module 16-pin connector C222 terminal No. 7 (Black/White wire). If resistance is less than 5 ohms, problem is in communications network. See MODULE COMMUNICATIONS NETWORK – EXPLORER & MOUNTAINEER article to continue diagnosis. If resistance is 5 ohms or more, repair open in Black/White wire between PATS module and ground. Clear DTCs and retest system operation.

TEST B: THEFT INDICATOR LIGHT NEVER/ALWAYS ILLUMINATES OR THEFT INDICATOR DOES NOT PROVEOUT

1) Observe THEFT indicator light with ignition switch in OFF position. Turn ignition switch to RUN position and observe THEFT indicator light. If indicator light fails to flash every 2 seconds with ignition switch in OFF position but after ignition switch is turned to RUN position light remains on for 3 seconds then turns off, repair White/Yellow wire between instrument panel fuse block and PATS module. Clear DTCs and retest system operation. If THEFT indicator light still does not flash properly, replace PATS module. See PATS MODULE under REMOVAL & INSTALLATION. Cycle igniton switch using newly encoded ignition keys. Using NGS tester, repeat PATS module self-test. If no DTCs are present, testing is complete. If DTC B2139 is present, go to DTC B2139: SECURITY IDENTIFICATION DOES NOT MATCH BETWEEN PATS MODULE & PCM test under DIAGNOSTIC TROUBLE CODE TESTS. Repair as necessary and check system for normal operation. If indicator light fails to flash every 2 seconds with ignition switch in OFF position, or after ignition switch is turned to RUN position light does not turn on or light remains on, go to next step.

2) If THEFT indicator light stays on continuously, use NGS tester and perform PATS module self-test. If any DTCs are present, perform appropriate DTC test and repair as necessary. If no DTCs are present, go to next step. If THEFT indicator light does not stay on continuously, go to step **5)**.

3) Turn ignition switch to OFF position. Disconnect PATS module 16-pin connector C222 located behind right side of instrument panel. Turn ignition switch to RUN position. Observe THEFT indicator light. If THEFT indicator light is still on continuously, check for short to power in Dark Blue/Light Green wire between PATS module and THEFT indicator light. See WIRING DIAGRAMS. Check system for normal operation. If THEFT indicator light is off, go to next step.

4) Turn ignition switch to OFF position. Reconnect PATS module 16-pin connector C222. Turn ignition switch to RUN position. Using NGS tester, enter PATS ACTIVE COMMAND MODE. Trigger THEFT LMP ON and OFF. If THEFT indicator light functions properly, perform PATS module self-test. If any DTCs are present, perform appropriate DTC test and repair as necessary. If no DTCs are present, replace PATS module. See PATS MODULE under REMOVAL & INSTALLATION. Retest system for normal operation. If THEFT indicator light does not function properly, replace PATS module. See PATS MODULE under REMOVAL & INSTALLATION. Cycle igniton switch using newly encoded ignition keys. Using NGS tester, repeat PATS module self-test. If no DTCs are present, testing is complete. If DTC B2139 is present, go to DTC B2139: SECURITY IDENTIFICATION DOES NOT MATCH BETWEEN PATS MODULE & PCM test under DIAGNOSTIC TROUBLE CODE TESTS. Repair as necessary and check system for normal operation.

5) Using NGS tester, enter PATS ACTIVE COMMAND MODE. If PATS ACTIVE COMMAND MODE cannot be entered, go to TEST A: NO COMMUNICATION WITH PATS MODULE. If PATS ACTIVE COMMAND MODE can be entered, go to next step.

6) Using NGS tester, trigger PATS ANTI-THEFT INDICATOR THEFT LMP to ON. If THEFT indicator light illuminates, system is functioning properly. If THEFT indicator light does not illuminate, go to next step.

7) Turn ignition switch to OFF position. Disconnect instrument cluster Gray 16-pin connector C286 located behind instrument cluster. Turn ignition switch to RUN position. Using NGS tester, trigger PATS ANTI-THEFT INDICATOR THEFT LMP to ON. Using a voltmeter, measure voltage between ground and instrument cluster 16-pin connector C286 terminal No. 6 (Dark Blue/Light Green wire). See Fig. 2. If voltage is more than 9 volts, go to step **11)**. If voltage is 9 volts or less, go to next step.

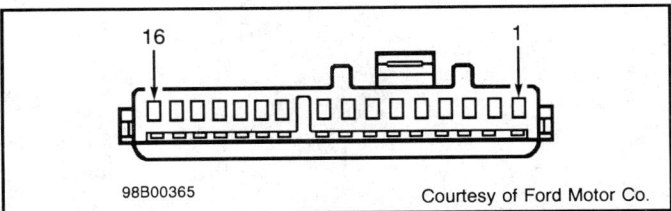

98B00365   Courtesy of Ford Motor Co.

Fig. 3: Identifying Instrument Cluster 16-Pin Connector C286 Terminals

8) Turn ignition switch to OFF position. Disconnect PATS module 16-pin connector C222 located behind right side of instrument panel. Measure resistance of Dark Blue/Light Green wire between instrument cluster 16-pin connector C286 terminal No. 6 and PATS module 16-pin connector C222 terminal No. 8. If resistance is less than 5 ohms, go to next step. If resistance is 5 ohms or more, repair open in Dark Blue/Light Green wire. Check system for normal operation.

9) Using an ohmmeter, measure resistance between ground and PATS module 16-pin connector C222 terminal No. 8 (Dark Blue/Light Green wire). If resistance is more than 10,000 ohms, go to next step. If resistance is 10,000 ohms or less, repair short in Dark Blue/Light Green wire. Check system for normal operation.

10) Reconnect PATS module 16-pin connector C222. Turn ignition switch to RUN position. Using NGS tester, trigger PATS ANTI-THEFT INDICATOR THEFT LMP to ON. Measure voltage between ground and instrument cluster 16-pin connector C286 terminal No. 6 (Dark Blue/Light Green wire). If voltage is more than 9 volts, go to next step. If voltage is 9 volts or less, replace PATS module.

11) Turn ignition switch to OFF position. Using an ohmmeter, measure resistance between ground and instrument cluster 16-pin connector C286 terminal No. 7 (Black wire). If resistance is 5 ohms or more, repair open in Black wire between instrument cluster and ground. Clear DTCs and retest system operation. If resistance is less than 5 ohms, replace THEFT indicator LED or repair instrument cluster as necessary. Clear DTCs and retest system operation.

REMOVAL & INSTALLATION

CAUTION: When battery is disconnected, vehicle computer and memory systems may lose memory data. Driveability problems may exist until computer systems have completed a relearn cycle. See COMPUTER RELEARN PROCEDURES article in GENERAL INFORMATION before disconnecting battery.

PATS MODULE

NOTE: If PATS module is replaced, all existing ignition keys must be reprogrammed. See PROGRAMMING.

Removal & Installation – Disconnect negative battery cable. PATS module is located behind right side of instrument panel. Remove passenger-side air bag module. See appropriate AIR BAG RESTRAINT SYSTEMS article. Remove 2 bolts securing PATS module bracket. Disconnect wiring harness connector and remove PATS module and bracket assembly. Release retainer tabs and remove PATS module from bracket. To install, reverse removal procedure.

TRANSCEIVER MODULE

Removal & Installation – 1) Disconnect negative battery cable. Insert ignition key into ignition switch lock cylinder. Turn ignition switch lock cylinder to RUN position. Push ignition switch lock cylinder release tab with punch (through small hole in bottom steering column cover) while removing ignition switch lock cylinder. Remove tilt wheel lever.

2) Remove screws and upper/lower steering column covers. Remove hood latch release handle retaining screws and position assembly aside. Remove lower instrument panel steering column cover. Remove lower instrument panel steering column opening cover reinforcement. Remove transceiver assembly retaining screw.

3) Disconnect transceiver electrical connector. Locate rib on steering column lock cylinder housing, and gently pry transceiver over rib to remove transceiver (apply pressure or leverage below key cylinder lower rib). To install, reverse removal procedure.

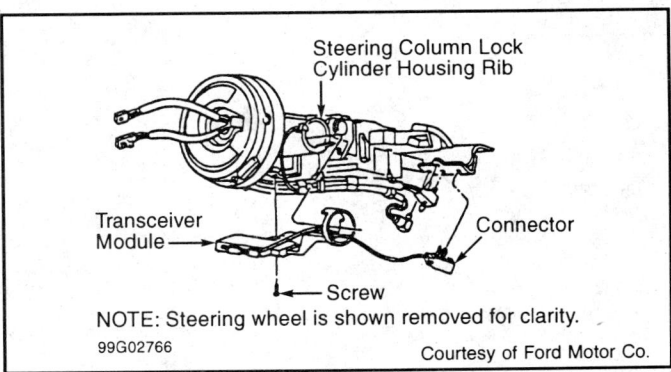

NOTE: Steering wheel is shown removed for clarity.
99G02766   Courtesy of Ford Motor Co.

Fig. 4: Removing Transceiver Module

FORD
4-152

1999 ACCESSORIES & EQUIPMENT
Passive Anti-Theft Systems – Explorer & Mountaineer (Cont.)

WIRING DIAGRAMS

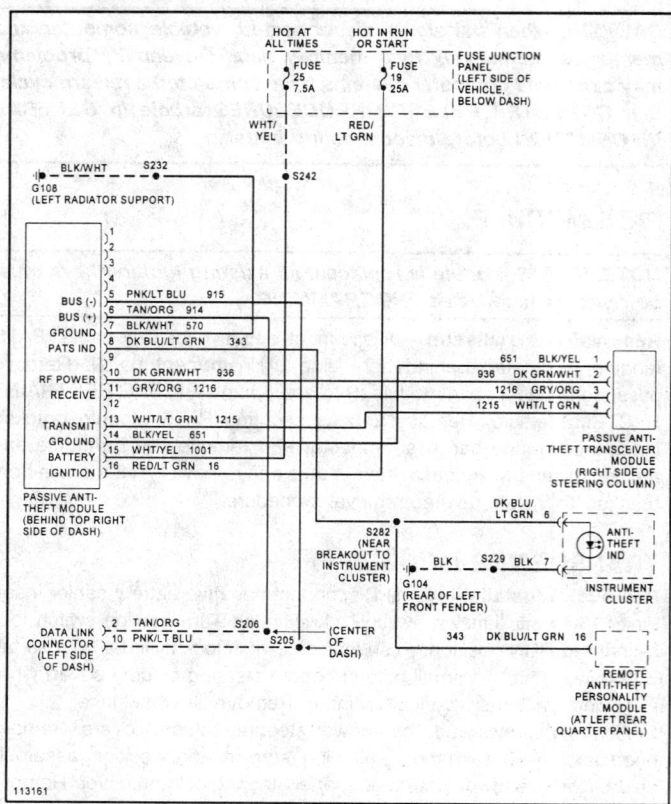

*Fig. 5: Passive Anti-Theft System (PATS) Wiring Diagram
(Explorer & Mountaineer)*

DESCRIPTION

Passive Anti-Theft System (PATS) vehicle protection system is designed to prevent driveaway thefts. The system is passive in that it does not require any activity from the user. System uses radio frequency identification technology to verify if proper key is being used to attempt to start the vehicle.

During each starting sequence, the encoded ignition key is interrogated by vehicle anti-theft electronics. If the key's identification code matches code programmed into anti-theft system, vehicle is capable of starting. If key's identification code is incorrect or missing, vehicle is prevented from starting.

PATS module communicates with the Powertrain Control Module (PCM) via Module Communications Network (MCN). PCM then determines if engine will be enabled to start. If the PCM prevents vehicle from starting because of PATS system, PCM will store a Diagnostic Trouble Code (DTC) in memory.

PATS vehicle protection system consists of these components: PATS module, anti-theft indicator (THEFT) light, transceiver module, encoded ignition key, module communications network and Data Link Connector (DLC).

OPERATION

THEFT INDICATOR LIGHT

THEFT indicator located on right side of instrument cluster is used to prove out system operation status. PATS uses the THEFT indicator light when ignition switch is in START or RUN position. For more information, see POWERTRAIN CONTROL MODULE (PCM).

ENCODED IGNITION KEY

When ignition switch is in START or RUN position, PATS module initiates the encoded ignition key interrogation process. PATS module supplies both power and carrier signal to transceiver module to momentarily energize ignition key. After energize period has expired, key transmits its identification code to transceiver module. This encoded ignition key is much larger in size than a non-encoded key to accommodate the electronics located inside plastic cover.

PASSIVE ANTI-THEFT SYSTEM (PATS) MODULE

PATS module contains circuitry to interface to vehicle electrical system, transceiver module, Module Communications Network (MCN) system and THEFT indicator light. PATS module stores ignition key codes in non-volatile memory. PATS module can be diagnosed through Data Link Connector (DLC). After receiving key code during a start sequence, PATS module sends this data to instrument cluster.

POWERTRAIN CONTROL MODULE (PCM)

Passive anti-theft system communicates PCM through the instrument cluster to enable or disable vehicle's engine. Within one second after engine start, PCM must receive an enable signal from instrument cluster or the engine will be disabled. Along with enable signals, instrument cluster and PCM share messages that confirm the security codes shared during initial installation. This shared security data makes the instrument cluster and PCM a matched pair, so neither will operate in another vehicle.

When system is functioning properly and ignition switch is turned to RUN or START position, THEFT indicator light will turn on for 3 seconds, then turn off. Vehicle will be enabled to start and run.

If there is a problem in the system, THEFT indicator light will stay on or flash continuously. Go to SELF-DIAGNOSTIC SYSTEM.

COMPONENT LOCATION

PATS COMPONENT LOCATION

Component	Location
PATS Transceiver Module	Behind Steering Column Shroud
Powertrain Control Module (PCM)	Right Side Of Engine Compartment
THEFT Indicator Light	On Instrument Cluster

PROGRAMMING

ERASE ALL KEYS & PROGRAM 2 KEYS

NOTE: This procedure is used when a customer needs keys programmed into system and does not have 2 programmed ignition keys available, or when programmed ignition keys have been lost and/or ignition switch assembly has been replaced. This procedure will erase all programmed ignition keys from memory and prevent vehicle from starting until 2 keys have been programmed. Ignition keys must have correct mechanical key cut for vehicle and must be an encoded key. If additional key(s) are to be programmed, perform KEY PROGRAMMING USING 2 PROGRAMMED KEYS. If remaining keys are with customer and not with vehicle, instruct customer to see owner's manual to program spare key(s).

1) Insert Ford Service Function (FSF) card into NGS tester. Turn ignition switch from LOCK to RUN position. Perform SECURITY ACCESS PROCEDURE. After the security access procedure has been completed, a new menu will be displayed with command options. Select IGNITION KEY CODE ERASE.

2) Turn ignition switch to LOCK position and disconnect NGS tester. Insert first encoded ignition key into ignition lock cylinder. Turn ignition switch to RUN position for 3 seconds. Turn ignition switch to LOCK position and remove first encoded key.

3) Within 5 seconds, insert second encoded ignition key into ignition lock cylinder. Turn ignition switch to RUN position for 3 seconds. Turn ignition switch to LOCK position and remove second encoded key. Both encoded ignition keys should now start vehicle.

SECURITY ACCESS PROCEDURE

NOTE: Security access must be granted to erase ignition keys, enable/disable spare key programming switch, or perform parameter resets for PATS module and PCM. This procedure has a 10 minute time delay prior to granting security access during which the New Generation Star (NGS) tester must remain connected to vehicle. After security access has been granted, security access command menu is displayed which offers various command options. Multiple security access commands can be executed (if necessary) prior to exiting security access command menu. Execution of all necessary security access commands prior to exiting command menu avoids the performance of an additional security access procedure and the associated 10 minute time delay.

Insert Ford Service Function (FSF) card into NGS tester. Turn ignition switch from LOCK to RUN position. With NGS tester connected to vehicle, enter PATS then select SECURITY ACCESS PROCEDURE. This procedure will take 10 minutes to perform. After the security access procedure has been completed, a new menu will be displayed with command options. Select as many functions as required before exiting this menu. Once this menu is exited, security access procedure must be performed again to perform additional commands.

FORD
4-154

1999 ACCESSORIES & EQUIPMENT
Passive Anti-Theft Systems
F150 & F250 Light-Duty Pickup (Cont.)

SPARE KEY PROGRAMMING SWITCH

NOTE: The spare key programming switch is a programmable switch which provides the capability to enable/disable the normal customer spare key programming procedure detailed in the owner's manual. This programmable switch is provided as a convenience for rental company fleets or other fleet purchasers who may not want the spare key programming procedure available to the vehicle driver. The spare key programming switch state can be viewed using PATS PID SPARE_KY.

Insert a programmed ignition key into the ignition lock cylinder. Insert Ford Service Function (FSF) card into NGS tester. Turn ignition switch from LOCK to RUN position. With NGS tester connected to vehicle, enter PATS then select SECURITY ACCESS PROCEDURE. This procedure will take 10 minutes to perform. After the security access procedure has been completed, a new menu will be displayed with command options. The default setting on all new vehicles is ENABLE. Select SPARE KEY PROGRAMMING SWITCH. Set SPARE KEY PROGRAMMING SWITCH to ENABLE to allow keys to be programmed or DISABLE to make key programming not accessible.

KEY PROGRAMMING USING 2 PROGRAMMED KEYS

NOTE: This procedure will only work if 2 or more programmed ignition keys are available and there is a need to program additional keys. If 2 keys are not available, perform ERASE ALL KEYS & PROGRAM 2 KEYS. PID SPARE_KY must be enabled for this procedure to operate. To enable this PID, perform SPARE KEY PROGRAMMING SWITCH and enable spare key programming switch. If programming procedure is successful, new key(s) will start vehicle and THEFT indicator will illuminate for 3 seconds. If programming procedure is not successful, new key(s) will not start vehicle and THEFT indicator will flash for one minute (after flashing for one minute, THEFT indicator will flash fault code). If necessary, repeat programming procedure. If programming of key(s) is still unsuccessful, perform procedures in SELF-DIAGNOSTIC SYSTEM. Maximum of 8 keys can be programmed into system. If procedure is not performed as outlined, programming procedure will end. Ignition keys must have correct mechanical key cut for vehicle and must be an encoded key.

1) Insert the first programmed ignition key into ignition lock cylinder. Turn ignition switch from LOCK to RUN position (ignition switch must stay in RUN position for one second). Turn ignition switch to LOCK position and remove ignition key from ignition lock cylinder.

2) Within 5 seconds of turning ignition switch to LOCK position, insert second programmed ignition key into ignition lock cylinder. Turn ignition switch from LOCK to RUN position (ignition switch must stay in RUN position for one second). Turn ignition switch to LOCK position and remove second ignition key from ignition lock cylinder.

3) Within 5 seconds of turning ignition switch to LOCK position, insert a NEW unprogrammed ignition key into ignition lock cylinder. Turn ignition switch from LOCK to RUN position (ignition switch must stay in RUN position for one second). Turn ignition switch to LOCK position and remove ignition key from ignition lock cylinder. The NEW ignition key should now be programmed. To program additional key(s), repeat key programming procedure from step **1)**.

KEY PROGRAMMING WITHOUT USING 2 PROGRAMMED KEYS

NOTE: This procedure is used when customer needs extra keys programmed and 2 programmed keys are not available but system has 2 ignition keys programmed. A maximum of 8 keys can be programmed. If 8 keys are already programmed, this procedure will not allow any more to be programmed. The number of programmed key can be determined by accessing PATS PID NUMKEYS with NGS tester.

Insert unprogrammed key in ignition and turn ignition switch to RUN position. Connect New Generation Star (NGS) tester to Data Link Connector (DLC). Insert Ford Service Function (FSF) card in NGS tester. Perform security access procedure. See SECURITY ACCESS PROCEDURE. Select IGNITION KEY CODE PROGRAM. Turn ignition switch to LOCK position. Disconnect NGS tester. Key should now be programmed and be able to start vehicle.

SELF-DIAGNOSTIC SYSTEM

NOTE: Metallic objects and encoded devices on key ring may interfere with PATS system, causing a no-start condition and setting DTCs. If fault cannot be identified, remove encoded key from key ring and attempt to start vehicle.

SELF-DIAGNOSTICS

The Passive Anti-Theft System (PATS) utilizes a self-diagnostic system which stores a Diagnostic Trouble Code (DTC) in the Powertrain Control Module (PCM) if a problem exists in the PATS. DTCs may be retrieved from PCM by using a NGS tester and Data Link Connector (DLC). Before retrieving DTCs, a preliminary procedure should be performed. See PRELIMINARY PROCEDURE.

PRELIMINARY PROCEDURE

1) Verify customers complaint by operating PATS. Ensure electronically coded ignition key is being used. Check for damaged ignition lock cylinder switch, damaged encoded ignition key or open fuses. Check for loose or corroded connectors, damaged wiring harness, damaged ignition switch or damaged transceiver module. Repair or replace components as necessary. If all components are okay, connect NGS tester to DLC located below instrument panel. Perform DATA LINK DIAGNOSTIC TEST.

2) If NGS tester displays CKT914, CKT915 or CKT70=ALL ECUS NO RESP/NOT EQUIP, see appropriate MODULE COMMUNICATIONS NETWORK article to continue diagnosis. If NGS tester displays NO RESP/NOT EQUIP for PATS, go to TEST A: NO COMMUNICATION WITH MODULE test under SYSTEM TESTS. If NGS tester displays SYSTEM PASSED, retrieve DTCs and perform appropriate DTC test. See RETRIEVING DIAGNOSTIC TROUBLE CODES.

RETRIEVING DIAGNOSTIC TROUBLE CODES

NOTE: A New Generation Star (NGS) Tester (007-00500) is required for retrieving DTCs and testing the passive ant-theft control system.

1) Observe THEFT indicator light on instrument cluster and turn ignition on. If THEFT indicator light illuminates for 3 seconds and then turns off, system is functioning properly at this time. If THEFT indicator light operates abnormally, go to next step. If THEFT indicator light does not illuminate, go to TEST B: THEFT INDICATOR LIGHT DOES NOT ILLUMINATE/NO THEFT INDICATOR LIGHT PROVE OUT test under SYSTEM TESTS.

2) Turn ignition off. Connect NGS tester to DLC located below instrument panel. Retrieve and record stored DTCs. Using NGS tester, perform ON-DEMAND SELF-TEST. Once on-demand self-test has been

1999 ACCESSORIES & EQUIPMENT
Passive Anti-Theft Systems
F150 & F250 Light-Duty Pickup (Cont.)

FORD
4-155

completed, retrieve DTCs. If any DTCs are retrieved, perform appropriate test under SYSTEM TESTS. If NGS tester cannot communicate with PATS module, go to TEST A: NO COMMUNICATION WITH MODULE test under SYSTEM TESTS. See DTC INDEX table. If no DTCs are retrieved, system is functioning properly at this time.

DTC INDEX

DTC	Description	Test
B1213	Anti-Theft Number Of Programmed Keys Is Below Minimum	C
B1232	Antenna Not Connected Or Defective Tranceiver	D
B1600	No Key Code Received/Damaged Encoded Ignition Key Or Use Of Non-PATS Key	E
B1601	Incorrect Key Code From Ignition Key Transponder	F
B1602	Invalid Key Code Format From Ignition Key Transponder	G
B1681	Transceiver Defective Or Not Connected	H
B2103	PATS Antenna Not Connected	D
B2139	PCM ID Does Not Match Between Instrument Cluster & PCM	I
B2141	No PCM ID Exchange Between Instrument Cluster & PCM	J
U1147	Invalid Or Missing Vehicle Security Data	C

SYSTEM TESTS

NOTE: Metallic objects and encoded devices on key ring may interfere with PATS system, causing a no-start condition and setting DTCs. If fault cannot be identified, remove encoded key from key ring and attempt to start vehicle.

SYMPTOM CHART

Symptom	Test
No Communication With Module, (Instrument Cluster)	A
No THEFT Indicator Prove Out	B
Vehicle Starts, THEFT Indicator Flashes DTC With KOEO	C
Vehicle Does Not Start, THEFT Indicator Operated Normally	K

TEST A: NO COMMUNICATION WITH MODULE

1) Turn ignition off. Disconnect Black 20-pin instrument cluster connector. Turn ignition switch to RUN position. Measure voltage between terminal No. 2 (Red/Light Green wire) and ground, terminal No. 3 (Light Green/Red wire) and ground, and terminal No. 11 (Gray/Yellow wire) and ground. See Fig. 1. If voltage is greater than 10 volts at all 3 terminals, go to next step. If voltage at any terminal is 10 volts or less, repair appropriate wire or fuse. See WIRING DIAGRAMS. Repeat self test and clear DTCs.

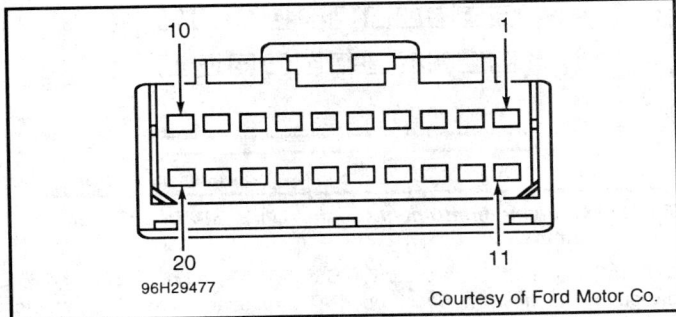

Fig. 1: Identifying Instrument Cluster Black 20-Pin Connector Terminals

96H29477
Courtesy of Ford Motor Co.

2) Turn ignition off. Measure resistance between Black 20-pin instrument cluster connector terminal No. 1 (Black wire) and ground. See Fig. 1. If resistance is greater than 5 ohms, repair open or high resistance in Black wire or connections. See WIRING DIAGRAMS. If resistance is 5 ohms or less, diagnose problem in module communications network. See appropriate MODULE COMMUNICATIONS NETWORK article.

TEST B: THEFT INDICATOR LIGHT DOES NOT ILLUMINATE/NO THEFT INDICATOR LIGHT PROVE OUT

Remove instrument cluster and access THEFT indicator LED. See appropriate INSTRUMENT PANELS article. Measure resistance between LED terminals in both directions. Resistance should be greater than 10 k/ohms in one direction, and between 10 and 20 ohms with test leads reversed. If resistance is as specified, install new instrument cluster, repeat self test and clear DTCs. If resistance is not as specified, install new LED, repeat self test and clear DTCs.

TEST C: ANTI-THEFT NUMBER OF PROGRAMMED KEYS IS BELOW MINIMUM

1) Turn ignition switch to LOCK position. Connect NGS tester to Data Link Connector (DLC). Turn ignition switch to RUN position. Using NGS tester, retrieve continuous PCM DTCs. Clear continuous DTCs. Turn ignition switch to LOCK position. Turn ignition switch to RUN position. Retrieve continuous PCM DTCs. If DTC B1213 is the only DTC retrieved, go to next step. If any other DTCs are retrieved, perform appropriate test before diagnosing DTC B1213.

2) Using NGS tester, monitor and record check PCM PID NUMKEYS. If PID indicates less than 2 keys, go to next step. If PID does not indicate less than 2 keys, system is okay at this step.

3) Obtain NEW encoded ignition key and insert into ignition lock cylinder. Using NEW key, turn ignition switch to RUN position. Program NEW encoded ignition key. See PROGRAMMING WITHOUT USING 2 PROGRAMMED KEYS under PROGRAMMING. If theft indicator does not illuminates for 3 seconds and then go out, go to next step. If theft indicator illuminates for 3 seconds and then goes out, clear DTCs and perform PCM self-test. Verify no DTCs are present.

4) Repeat step **3)** with a different encoded key. If theft indicator is flashing, retrieve DTCs and perform appropriate test.

TEST D: ANTENNA NOT CONNECTED

Verify transceiver module is correctly installed. See PATS TRANSCEIVER MODULE under REMOVAL & INSTALLATION. Connect NGS tester and clear DTCs. Perform instrument cluster on-demand self test. If DTCs B1232 or B2103 are retrieved, install new PATS transceiver module. Repeat self test and clear DTCs. If DTCs B1232 or B2103 are not retrieved, system is okay at this time.

TEST E: IGNITION KEY TRANSPONDER SIGNAL NOT RECEIVED

1) If any other DTCs were retrieved, repair those DTCs before diagnosing B1600. If only DTC B1600 was retrieved, go to next step.

2) Cut a new encoded ignition key. Program key. See ERASE ALL KEYS & PROGRAM 2 KEYS under PROGRAMMING. Using NGS tester clear DTCs and perform instrument cluster on-demand self test. If DTC B1600

FORD
4-156

1999 ACCESSORIES & EQUIPMENT
Passive Anti-Theft Systems
F150 & F250 Light-Duty Pickup (Cont.)

is still retrieved, go to next step. If other DTCs are retrieved, perform appropriate code test. See DTC INDEX table. If no DTC's are retrieved, system is okay.

3) Turn ignition off. Install new PATS transceiver module. See PATS TRANSCEIVER MODULE under REMOVAL & INSTALLATION. Turn ignition switch to RUN position using an original key, (not the key programmed in step **2**). Using NGS tester perform instrument cluster on-demand self test. If DTC B1600 is not retrieved, system is okay. If DTC B1600 is retrieved, Replace instrument cluster. See appropriate INSTRUMENT PANELS article. Cycle ignition using 2 encoded keys. Repeat self test and clear DTCs.

TEST F: INCORRECT KEY CODE FROM IGNITION KEY TRANSPONDER

NOTE: DTC B1601 is stored when a key that is not programmed into PATS module memory has been used. This indicates key needs to be programmed into PATS module memory. See SPARE KEY PROGRAMMING under PROGRAMMING. Maximum of 8 keys can be stored into PATS module memory.

1) Connect NGS tester to DLC and monitor PID NUMKEYS. If PID NUMKEYS displays any number other than "8", go to next step. If PID NUMKEYS display is "8", erase and reprogram all keys. See ERASE ALL KEYS & PROGRAM 2 KEYS under PROGRAMMING. Using NGS tester and perform instrument cluster on-demand self test. Clear DTCs.

2) If there are at least 2 programmed encoded keys available, go to next step. If there are not at least 2 keys available, cut and program new key(s). See ERASE ALL KEYS & PROGRAM 2 KEYS under PROGRAMMING, then proceed to next step.

3) Start vehicle using an encoded key. Repeat with a second encoded key. If vehicle starts with both keys, system is okay. If vehicle does not start with both keys, go to next step.

4) Using NGS tester, monitor instrument cluster PID SPARE_KY. If PID SPARE_KY is enabled, perform ERASE ALL KEYS & PROGRAM 2 KEYS under PROGRAMMING. Repeat self test, clear DTCs and go to next step. If PID SPARE_KY is disabled, enable using procedure in SPARE KEY PROGRAMMING SWITCH under PROGRAMMING. Repeat self test, clear DTCs and go to next step.

5) Turn ignition switch to RUN position. Using NGS tester, retrieve instrument cluster continuous DTCs. Clear continuous DTCs. Perform instrument cluster on-demand self test using both keys used in step **3**). If DTC B1601 is not retrieved, system is okay. If other DTCs are retrieved perform appropriate test. See DTC INDEX table. If DTC B1601 is retrieved, replace instrument cluster. See appropriate INSTRUMENT PANELS article. Cycle ignition using 2 encoded keys. Repeat self test and clear DTCs. Test system for proper operation.

TEST G: INVALID FORMAT KEY CODE FROM IGNITION KEY TRANSPONDER

1) Cut and program new encoded key. See ERASE ALL KEYS & PROGRAM 2 KEYS under PROGRAMMING. Perform instrument cluster on-demand self test. If DTC B1602 is retrieved, go to next step. If DTC B1602 is not retrieved, system is okay.

2) Turn ignition off. Replace PATS transceiver module. See PATS TRANSCEIVER MODULE under REMOVAL & INSTALLATION. Turn ignition switch to RUN position and perform instrument cluster on-demand self test. If any DTCs are retrieved, perform appropriate test. See DTC INDEX table. If no DTCs are retrieved, system is okay.

TEST H: TRANSCEIVER MODULE SIGNAL NOT RECEIVED

1) Turn ignition off. Disconnect PATS transceiver module 4-pin connector. Turn ignition switch to RUN position. Measure voltage between connector terminal No. 2 (Red/Light Green wire) and ground. *See Fig. 2.* If voltage is greater than 9 volts, go to next step. If voltage is 9 volts or less, repair Red/Light Green wire, repeat self test and clear DTCs. See WIRING DIAGRAMS.

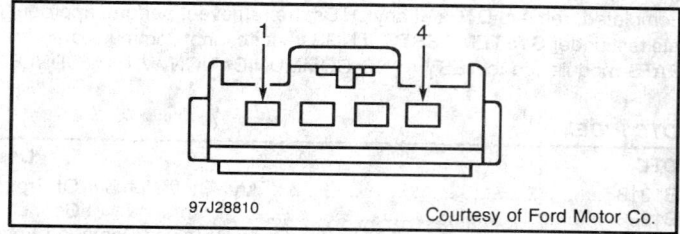

97J28810   Courtesy of Ford Motor Co.

Fig. 2: Identifying Transceiver Module Connector Terminals

2) Turn ignition off. Measure resistance between PATS transceiver module connector terminal No. 1 (Black/Light Blue wire) and ground. *See Fig. 2.* If resistance is less than 5 ohms, go to next step. If resistance is 5 ohms or greater, repair Black/Light Blue wire, repeat self test and clear DTCs. See WIRING DIAGRAMS.

3) Reconnect PATS transceiver module connector. Turn ignition switch to RUN position. Backprobe PATS transceiver module connector terminal No. 3 (Gray/Orange wire) with positive voltmeter probe. Measure voltage between terminal No. 3 and ground. If voltage is greater than 9 volts, go to step **5**). If voltage is 9 volts or less, go to next step.

4) Turn ignition off. Disconnect PATS transceiver module 4-pin connector. Measure resistance between connector terminal No. 3 (Gray/Orange wire) and ground. *See Fig. 2.* If resistance is greater than 100 ohms, go to next step. If resistance is 100 ohms or less, inspect Gray/Orange wire for short to ground. Repair as necessary. See WIRING DIAGRAMS. If wire is okay, replace instrument cluster. See appropriate INSTRUMENT PANELS article. Cycle two encoded ignition keys to RUN position. Go to DTC B2139: PCM ID DOES NOT MATCH INSTRUMENT CLUSTER ID to match new instrument cluster ID to PCM. Repeat self test and clear DTCs.

5) Measure resistance of Gray/Orange wire between PATS transceiver module connector terminal No. 3 and White instrument cluster 22-pin connector terminal No. 14. *See Figs. 2 and 3.* If resistance is less than 5 ohms, go to next step. If resistance is 5 ohms or greater, repair Gray/Orange wire. See WIRING DIAGRAMS. Repeat self test and clear DTCs.

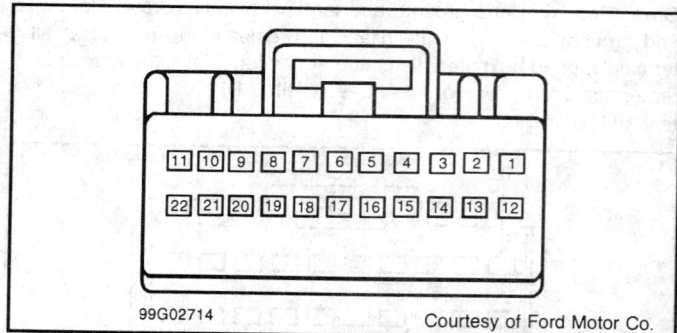

99G02714   Courtesy of Ford Motor Co.

Fig. 3: Identifying Instrument Cluster White 22-Pin Connector Terminals

6) Turn ignition off. Reconnect PATS transceiver module. Turn ignition switch to RUN position. Backprobe PATS transceiver module connector terminal No. 4 (White/Light Green wire) with voltmeter positive lead. Measure voltage between connector terminal No. 4 and ground. If voltage is greater than 9 volts, go to step **8**). If voltage is 9 volts or less, go to next step.

7) Turn ignition off. Disconnect PATS transceiver module 4-pin connector. Measure resistance between connector terminal No. 4 (White/Light Green wire) and ground. *See Fig. 2.* If resistance is greater than 100 ohms, go to next step. If resistance is 100 ohms or less, inspect White/Light Green wire for short to ground. Repair as necessary. See WIRING DIAGRAMS. If wire is okay, replace instrument cluster. See appropriate INSTRUMENT PANELS article. Cycle two encoded ignition keys to RUN position. Go to TEST I: PCM ID DOES NOT MATCH

Passive Anti-Theft Systems
F150 & F250 Light-Duty Pickup (Cont.)

INSTRUMENT CLUSTER ID to match new instrument cluster ID to PCM. Repeat self test and clear DTCs.

8) Reconnect PATS transceiver module and instrument cluster connectors. Turn ignition switch to RUN position. Backprobe PATS transceiver module connector terminal No. 4 (White/Light Green wire) with positive voltmeter probe. Measure voltage between terminal No. 4 and ground. Using NGS tester, trigger the instrument cluster active command TRANSMIT SIGNAL COMMAND to ON. Voltage should drop from greater than 9 volts to less than one volt when instrument cluster active command is triggered on. If voltage is as specified, go to next step. If voltage is not as specified, inspect White/Light Green wire for short to ground. Repair as necessary. See WIRING DIAGRAMS. If wire is okay, replace instrument cluster. See appropriate INSTRUMENT PANELS article. Cycle two encoded ignition keys to RUN position. Go to TEST I: PCM ID DOES NOT MATCH INSTRUMENT CLUSTER ID to match new instrument cluster ID to PCM. Repeat self test and clear DTCs.

9) Turn ignition off. Replace PATS transceiver module. See PATS TRANSCEIVER MODULE under REMOVAL & INSTALLATION. Using NGS tester, perform instrument cluster on demand self test. If DTC B1681 is retrieved, go to next step. If DTC B1681 is not retrieved, system is okay.

10) Turn ignition off. Replace instrument cluster. See appropriate INSTRUMENT PANELS article. Cycle ignition to RUN position using 2 encoded keys. Using NGS tester, perform instrument cluster on demand self test. If DTC B1681 is retrieved, repair PATS system wiring, repeat self test and clear DTCs. See WIRING DIAGRAMS. If DTC B1681 is not retrieved, system is okay.

TEST I: PCM ID DOES NOT MATCH INSTRUMENT CLUSTER ID

1) Turn ignition off. Connect New Generation Star (NGS) tester to DLC. Turn ignition switch to RUN position. Perform SECURITY ACCESS PROCEDURE. From NGS menu, select PARAMETER RESET command for instrument cluster. Do not make any other selections in this menu. Use diagnostic card for PCM Active Command Keep Alive Memory Reset. Turn ignition off and select PARAMETER RESET command for PCM.

2) Turn ignition switch to RUN position for 3 seconds. Clear continuous DTCs and turn ignition off. Using NGS tester, retrieve continuous DTCs. If DTC B2139 is not retrieved, system is okay at this time. If DTC B2139 is present, verify PCM calibration. If PCM calibration is okay, repeat test from step **1)**. If code is still present, replace instrument cluster and go to next step. See appropriate INSTRUMENT PANELS article.

3) Cycle ignition to RUN position using 2 encoded ignition keys. Repeat self test. Clear DTCs. If DTC B2139 is retrieved again, replace PCM. PCM and all ignition keys must be reprogrammed. Repeat self-test and clear DTCs.

TEST J: CONFIGURATION FAILURE, NO PCM ID EXCHANGED

1) If DTC U1147 is also retrieved, go to TEST C: ANTI-THEFT NUMBER OF PROGRAMMED KEYS IS BELOW MINIMUM. If only DTC B2141 is retrieved, go to next step.

2) With NGS tester connected to DLC, use diagnostic card for PCM Active Command Keep Alive Memory Reset. Turn ignition off. Turn ignition switch to RUN position for 30 seconds. Turn ignition off. Attempt to start vehicle. If vehicle starts, system is okay. If vehicle does not start, go to next step.

3) Turn ignition switch to RUN position. Using NGS tester, retrieve and record instrument cluster continuous DTCs. Clear continuous DTCs. Retrieve and record instrument cluster on demand DTCs. If no DTCs are retrieved, system is okay. If DTC B2141 is retrieved, repeat step **2)**. If fault persists, verify PCM calibration. If PCM calibration is okay, replace instrument cluster. See appropriate INSTRUMENT PANELS article. Cycle ignition to RUN position using 2 encoded keys. Go to TEST I: PCM ID DOES NOT MATCH INSTRUMENT CLUSTER ID to match new instrument cluster ID to PCM. Repeat self test and clear DTCs.

TEST K: VEHICLE DOES NOT START, THEFT INDICATOR OPERATES NORMALLY

Using NGS tester, perform instrument cluster on demand self test. Record any DTCs. Cycle ignition switch and retrieve and continuous DTCs. If any DTCs were present, perform appropriate testing procedure. See DTC INDEX. If no DTCs were retrieved, investigate the following possible causes:

- Less than 2 keys programmed to the system.
- PATS transceiver module not connected or defective.
- Faulty system wiring or connections.
- Damaged PATS transceiver module internal antenna.
- Damaged, unprogrammed or non-PATS key used.
- No PCM ID stored in PATS transceiver module, or ID does not match.
- Problem with Standard Corporate Protocol (SCP) network.
- Partial PATS key read.

REMOVAL & INSTALLATION

CAUTION: When battery is disconnected, vehicle computer and memory systems may lose memory data. Driveability problems may exist until computer systems have completed a relearn cycle. See COMPUTER RELEARN PROCEDURES article in GENERAL INFORMATION before disconnecting battery.

PATS TRANSCEIVER MODULE

NOTE: If transceiver module is replaced, all existing ignition keys must be reprogrammed. See PROGRAMMING.

Removal & Installation – Disconnect negative battery cable. Transceiver module is located on steering column, attached to ignition lock cylinder housing. Turn ignition switch lock cylinder to RUN position. Push ignition switch lock cylinder release tab with punch while removing ignition switch lock cylinder. Unscrew and remove tilt wheel lever. Remove instrument panel steering column cover to access column shroud screws. Remove 3 screws and remove upper and lower steering column shrouds. Remove PATS transceiver module retaining screw. Disconnect transceiver electrical connector. Locate rib on steering column lock cylinder housing, and gently pry transceiver over rib to remove transceiver (apply pressure or leverage below key cylinder lower rib). To install, reverse removal procedure.

WIRING DIAGRAMS

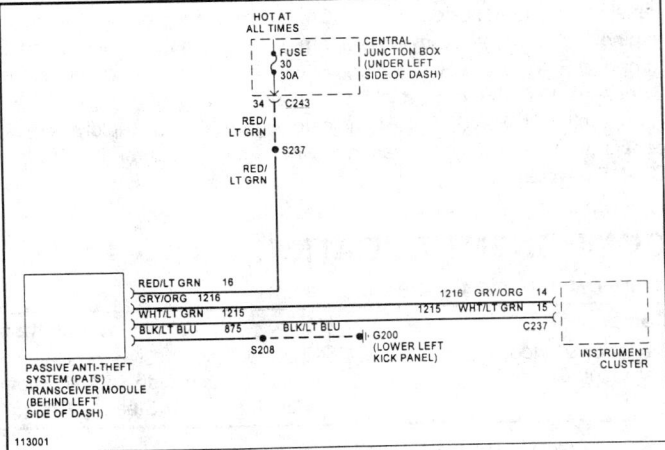

Fig. 4: Passive Anti-Theft System (PATS) Wiring Diagram (F150 & F250 Light-Duty Pickup)

DESCRIPTION

The Passive Anti-Theft System (PATS) is designed to prevent driveaway thefts. The system is passive in that it does not require any activity from the user. System uses radio frequency identification technology to verify proper key is being used to attempt to start the vehicle.

During each starting sequence, the transceiver module reads the encoded ignition key identification code and sends the data to the instrument cluster. If the key's identification code is programmed into anti-theft system, vehicle is capable of starting. If key's identification code is incorrect or missing, vehicle is prevented from starting.

Instrument cluster communicates with the Powertrain Control Module (PCM) through Module Communications Network. PCM then determines if engine will be enabled to start. If the PCM prevents vehicle from starting because of PATS system, a Diagnostic Trouble Code (DTC) will be stored in instrument cluster memory.

PATS vehicle protection system consists of these components: instrument cluster, THEFT indicator light, transceiver module, encoded ignition key, module communications network, PCM and Data Link Connector (DLC).

OPERATION

THEFT INDICATOR LIGHT

THEFT indicator, located in the instrument cluster, is used to proveout system operation status. PATS uses the THEFT indicator light when ignition switch is in START or RUN position. For more information, see POWERTRAIN CONTROL MODULE (PCM).

ENCODED IGNITION KEY

When ignition switch is in START or RUN position, instrument cluster initiates the encoded ignition key interrogation process. Each encoded ignition key must be programmed into instrument cluster before it can be used to start the vehicle. This encoded ignition key is much larger in size to accommodate the electronics located inside plastic cover.

TRANSCEIVER MODULE

Transceiver module communicates with encoded ignition key. During each starting sequence, the transceiver module reads the encoded ignition key identification code and sends the data to the instrument cluster.

POWERTRAIN CONTROL MODULE (PCM)

Passive anti-theft system uses PCM to enable or disable vehicle's engine. When system is functioning properly and ignition switch is turned to RUN or START position, THEFT indicator light will turn on for 3 seconds, then turn off. Vehicle will be enabled to start and run. If there is a problem in PATS, THEFT indicator light will flash rapidly or glow constantly for more than 3 seconds when ignition is turned to RUN or START position.

COMPONENT LOCATIONS

COMPONENT LOCATIONS

Component	Location
Transceiver Module	On Top Of Steering Column
Data Link Connector	Behind Driver's Side Of Instrument Panel, Right Of Steering Column

PROGRAMMING

KEY PROGRAMMING – ERASE ALL KEYS & PROGRAM 2 KEYS

NOTE: This procedure is used when a customer needs keys programmed into system and does not have 2 programmed ignition keys available, or when programmed ignition keys have been lost and/or ignition switch assembly has been replaced. This procedure will erase all programmed ignition keys from memory and prevent vehicle from starting until 2 keys have been programmed. Ignition keys must have correct mechanical key cut for vehicle and must be an encoded key. If additional key(s) are to be programmed, perform KEY PROGRAMMING – USING 2 PROGRAMMED KEYS. If remaining keys are with customer and not with vehicle, instruct customer to see owner's manual to program spare key(s).

1) Turn ignition switch from LOCK to RUN position. With NGS tester connected to vehicle, enter function test menu. Select SECURITY ACCESS PROCEDURE. This procedure will take 10 minutes to perform. After the security access procedure has been completed, a new menu will be displayed with command options. Select IGNITION KEY CODE ERASE.

2) Turn ignition switch to LOCK position and disconnect NGS tester. Insert first encoded ignition key into ignition lock cylinder. Turn ignition switch to RUN position for 3 seconds. Turn ignition switch to LOCK position and remove first encoded key.

3) Within 5 seconds, insert second encoded ignition key into ignition lock cylinder. Turn ignition switch to RUN position for 3 seconds. Turn ignition switch to LOCK position and remove second encoded key. Both encoded ignition keys should now start vehicle.

KEY PROGRAMMING – SECURITY ACCESS PROCEDURE

NOTE: Security access must be granted to erase ignition keys, enable/disable spare key programming switch, or perform parameter resets for instrument cluster and PCM. This procedure has a 10 minute time delay prior to granting security access during which the New Generation Star (NGS) tester must remain connected to vehicle. After security access has been granted, security access command menu is displayed which offers various command options. Multiple security access commands can be executed (if necessary) prior to exiting security access command menu. Execution of all necessary security access commands prior to exiting command menu avoids the performance of an additional security access procedure and the associated 10 minute time delay.

With ignition switch in RUN position and NGS connected to vehicle, enter function test menu. Select SECURITY ACCESS PROCEDURE. This procedure will take 10 minutes to perform. After the security access procedure has been completed, a new menu will be displayed with command options. Select as many functions as required before exiting this menu. Once this menu is exited, security access procedure must be performed again to perform additional commands.

KEY PROGRAMMING – SPARE KEY PROGRAMMING SWITCH

NOTE: The spare key programming switch is a programmable switch which provides the capability to enable/disable the normal customer spare key programming procedure detailed in the owner's manual. This programmable switch is provided as a convenience for rental company fleets or other fleet purchasers who may not want the spare key programming procedure available to the vehicle driver. The spare key programming switch state can be viewed using instrument cluster PID SPARE_KY.

Insert a programmed ignition key into the ignition lock cylinder. Turn ignition switch from LOCK to RUN position. With NGS tester connected to vehicle, enter function test menu. Select SECURITY ACCESS PROCEDURE. This procedure will take 10 minutes to perform. After the security access procedure has been completed, a new menu will be displayed with command options. The default setting on all new vehicles is ENABLE. Select SPARE KEY PROGRAMMING SWITCH. Set SPARE KEY PROGRAMMING SWITCH to ENABLE to allow keys to be programmed or DISABLE to make key programming not accessible.

KEY PROGRAMMING – USING 2 PROGRAMMED KEYS

NOTE: This procedure will only work if 2 or more programmed ignition keys are available and there is a need to program additional keys. If 2 keys are not available, perform KEY PROGRAMMING – ERASE ALL KEYS & PROGRAM 2 KEYS. PID SPARE_KY must be enabled for this procedure to operate. To enable this PID, perform KEY PROGRAMMING – SPARE KEY PROGRAMMING SWITCH and enable spare key programming switch. If programming procedure is successful, new key(s) will start vehicle and THEFT indicator will illuminate for 3 seconds. If programming procedure is not successful, new key(s) will not start vehicle and THEFT indicator will flash for one minute (after flashing for one minute, THEFT indicator will flash fault code). If necessary, repeat programming procedure. If programming of key(s) is still unsuccessful, perform self-diagnostics. See SELF-DIAGNOSTIC SYSTEM. Maximum of 8 keys can be programmed into system. If procedure is not performed as outlined, programming procedure will end. Ignition keys must have correct mechanical key cut for vehicle and must be an encoded key.

1) Insert the first programmed ignition key into ignition lock cylinder. Turn ignition switch from LOCK to RUN position (ignition switch must stay in RUN position for one second). Turn ignition switch to LOCK position and remove ignition key from ignition lock cylinder.
2) Within 5 seconds of turning ignition switch to LOCK position, insert second programmed ignition key into ignition lock cylinder. Turn ignition switch from LOCK to RUN position (ignition switch must stay in RUN position for one second). Turn ignition switch to LOCK position and remove second ignition key from ignition lock cylinder.
3) Within 5 seconds of turning ignition switch to LOCK position, insert a NEW unprogrammed ignition key into ignition lock cylinder. Turn ignition switch from LOCK to RUN position (ignition switch must stay in RUN position for one second). Turn ignition switch to LOCK position and remove ignition key from ignition lock cylinder. The NEW ignition key should now be programmed. To program additional key(s), repeat key programming procedure from step 1).

KEY PROGRAMMING – WITHOUT USING 2 PROGRAMMED KEYS

NOTE: This procedure is used when customer needs extra keys programmed and 2 programmed keys are not available but system has 2 ignition keys programmed. A maximum of 8 keys can be programmed. If 8 keys are already programmed, this procedure will not allow any more to be programmed. The number of programmed key can be determined by accessing instrument cluster PID NUMKEYS with NGS tester.

Insert unprogrammed key in ignition and turn ignition switch to RUN position. Connect New Generation Star (NGS) tester to Data Link Connector (DLC). Insert Ford Service Function (FSF) card in NGS tester. Perform security access procedure. See KEY PROGRAMMING – SECURITY ACCESS PROCEDURE. Select IGNITION KEY CODE PROGRAM. Turn ignition switch to LOCK position. Disconnect NGS tester. Key should now be programmed and be able to start vehicle.

TROUBLE SHOOTING

Verify customers complaint. Ensure electronically coded ignition key is being used. Check for damaged ignition lock cylinder switch, damaged encoded ignition key or blown fuses. Check for loose or corroded connectors, damaged wiring harness, damaged ignition switch or damaged transceiver module. Repair or replace components as necessary. If problem still exists, perform self-diagnostics. See SELF-DIAGNOSTIC SYSTEM.

SELF-DIAGNOSTIC SYSTEM

NOTE: It is also possible to retrieve instrument cluster DTCs using instrument cluster. See ANALOG INSTRUMENT PANELS – MUSTANG article.

Connect New Generation Star (NGS) tester to Data Link Connector (DLC), located beneath instrument panel. Using NGS tester, perform data link diagnostics test. See DATA LINK DIAGNOSTIC TEST under COMMUNICATION NETWORK DIAGNOSTICS in MODULE COMMUNICATIONS NETWORK – MUSTANG article. If NGS tester responds with CKT914, CKT915 or CKT70=ALL ECUS NO RESP/NOT EQUIP, repair module communications concern. See MODULE COMMUNICATIONS NETWORK – MUSTANG article. If NGS tester displays NO RESP/NOT EQUIP for instrument cluster, perform TEST A: NO COMMUNICATION WITH INSTRUMENT CLUSTER under SYSTEM TESTS.

If NGS tester responds with SYSTEM PASSED, retrieve and record continuous DTCs. Erase continuous DTCs. Using NGS tester, perform instrument cluster self-test. Perform appropriate test in accordance with DTC retrieved. See INSTRUMENT CLUSTER DTC INDEX table. Codes listed in this table is only for testing covered in this article. For complete DTC listing, see MODULE COMMUNICATIONS NETWORK – MUSTANG article. If no DTCs are retrieved, repair by symptom. See SYMPTOM CHART table under SYSTEM TESTS.

INSTRUMENT CLUSTER DTC INDEX

Scan Tool DTC [1]	Dealer Test Mode DTC [1]	Description	Test
B1213	9213	Anti-Theft Number Of Programmed Ignition Keys Is Below Minimum	D
B1232 Or B2103	A103 Or 9232	Defective Transceiver	E
B1342	9342	ECU Defective	2
B1600	9600	PATS Ignition Key Transponder Signal Not Received	F
B1601	9601	PATS Received Incorrect Key-Code From Transponder	G
B1602	9602	PATS Received Invalid Key-Code Format From Transponder	H
B1681	9681	PATS Transceiver Signal Not Received	I
B2139	A139	Security Identification Does Not Match Between Instrument Cluster & PCM	J
B2141	A141	NVM Configuration Failure	K
B2143	A143	NVM Memory Failure	3
U1147	D147	Invalid/Missing Data For Vehicle Security	C

[1] – Codes listed in this table are only for testing covered in this article. For complete DTC listing, see MODULE COMMUNICATIONS NETWORK – MUSTANG article.

[2] – Using NGS tester, retrieve and document continuous DTCs. Clear all DTCs. Perform instrument cluster self-test. If DTC B1342 is retrieved again, replace instrument cluster.

[3] – Replace instrument cluster.

SYSTEM TESTS

SYMPTOM CHART

Symptom	Test
No Communication With Instrument Cluster	A
Theft Indicator Is Always/Never On Or Theft Indicator Will Not Proveout	B
Vehicle Does Not Start	1
Anti-Theft System Does Not Operate Properly (Vehicle Starts)	C

[1] – Using NGS tester, perform instrument cluster self-test. If any DTCs exist, perform appropriate test in accordance with DTC(s) received. See INSTRUMENT CLUSTER DTC INDEX table under SELF-DIAGNOSTIC SYSTEM. If no DTCs exist, check for other possible causes of vehicle not starting.

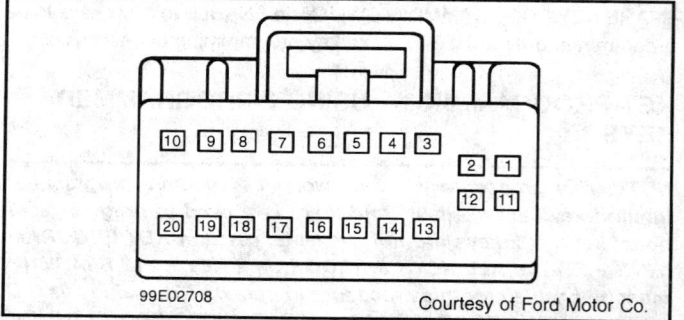

99E02708   Courtesy of Ford Motor Co.

Fig. 1: Identifying Instrument Cluster Harness Connector C251 Terminals

TEST A: NO COMMUNICATION WITH INSTRUMENT CLUSTER

1) Turn ignition switch to LOCK position. Disconnect instrument cluster harness connector C251. Measure voltage at terminal No. 10 (Red/White wire) at instrument cluster harness connector C251. *See Fig. 1.* If battery voltage exists, go to next step. If battery voltage does not exist, repair power distribution circuit. See appropriate wiring diagram in POWER DISTRIBUTION article in WIRING DIAGRAMS.

2) Turn ignition switch to RUN position. Measure voltage at terminal No. 11 (Pink/Black wire) at instrument cluster harness connector C251. If battery voltage exists, go to next step. If battery voltage does not exist, repair power distribution circuit. See appropriate wiring diagram in POWER DISTRIBUTION article in WIRING DIAGRAMS.

3) Measure voltage at terminal No. 12 (White/Light Blue wire) at instrument cluster harness connector C251. If battery voltage exists, go to next step. If battery voltage does not exist, repair power distribution circuit. See appropriate wiring diagram in POWER DISTRIBUTION article in WIRING DIAGRAMS.

4) Turn ignition switch to LOCK position. Measure resistance between ground and terminal No. 20 (Black/White wire) at instrument cluster harness connector C251. If resistance is 5 ohms or less, go to next step. If resistance is greater than 5 ohms, repair open in Black/White wire.

5) Measure resistance between ground and terminal No. 1 (Black wire) at instrument cluster harness connector C251. If resistance is 5 ohms or less, repair module communication concern. See MODULE COMMUNICATIONS NETWORK – MUSTANG article. If resistance is greater than 5 ohms, repair open in Black wire.

TEST B: THEFT INDICATOR IS ALWAYS/NEVER ON OR THEFT INDICATOR WILL NOT PROVEOUT

1) Turn ignition switch to LOCK position. Connect New Generation Star (NGS) tester to Data Link Connector (DLC). Using NGS tester, enter instrument cluster active command mode. If active command mode can

be entered, go to next step. If active command mode can not be entered, perform TEST A: NO COMMUNICATION WITH INSTRUMENT CLUSTER.

2) Using NGS tester, trigger instrument cluster active command WARNING LAMPS AND CHIME to ON. If THEFT indicator does not illuminate, go to next step. If THEFT indicator illuminates, system is okay at this time. Verify concern with customer.

3) Remove anti-theft LED. Measure resistance between anti-theft LED terminals in both directions. Resistance should be greater than 10 k/ohms in one direction and 10-20 ohms in the other. If resistance is as specified, replace instrument cluster. If resistance is not as specified, replace anti-theft LED.

TEST C: INVALID/MISSING DATA FOR VEHICLE SECURITY

1) Start engine. If vehicle does not start with THEFT indicator flashing, go to next step. If vehicle starts with THEFT indicator flashing, problem is in PCM. See appropriate SELF-DIAGNOSTICS article in ENGINE PERFORMANCE in appropriate MITCHELL® manual.

2) Using NGS tester, retrieve and record continuous DTCs. Clear continuous DTCs and perform PCM self-test. If NGS tester communicates with PCM, go to next step. If NGS tester does not communicate with NGS tester, repair network communication concern. See MODULE COMMUNICATIONS NETWORK – MUSTANG article.

3) Using NGS tester, retrieve and record continuous DTCs. If DTC P1260 is retrieved, go to next step. If DTC P1260 is not retrieved, check PCM power and ground circuits. See appropriate SELF-DIAGNOSTICS article in ENGINE PERFORMANCE in appropriate MITCHELL® manual.

4) Repeat self-diagnostics. See SELF-DIAGNOSTIC SYSTEM. Turn ignition switch to LOCK position. Using NGS tester, retrieve and record continuous DTCs. Clear continuous DTCs and perform instrument cluster self-test. If DTC U1147 is not retrieved, system is okay at this time. If DTC U1147 is retrieved, replace instrument cluster then perform

TEST J: SECURITY IDENTIFICATION DOES NOT MATCH BETWEEN INSTRUMENT CLUSTER & PCM. If DTC U1147 still exists after instrument cluster has been replaced, replace PCM.

TEST D: ANTI-THEFT NUMBER OF PROGRAMMED IGNITION KEYS IS BELOW MINIMUM

1) Using NGS tester, perform instrument cluster self-test. If DTC B1213 is retrieved, go to next step. If DTC B1213 is not retrieved, repair other DTCs. See INSTRUMENT CLUSTER DTC INDEX table under SELF-DIAGNOSTIC SYSTEM.

2) Using NGS tester, monitor instrument cluster PID NUMKEYS. If PID indicates less than 2 encoded ignition keys programmed, go to next step. If PID indicates more than 2 encoded ignition keys programmed, system is okay at this time.

3) Obtain NEW encoded ignition key(s). Insert NEW key into ignition lock cylinder. Turn ignition switch to RUN position. Program key. See KEY PROGRAMMING – ERASE ALL KEYS & PROGRAM 2 KEYS under PROGRAMMING. If THEFT indicator illuminates for 3 seconds and then goes out, clear DTCs and perform instrument cluster self-test to ensure all codes have been cleared. If THEFT indicator illuminates continuously, repeat this step with a second NEW encoded ignition key. If THEFT indicator flashes, retrieve DTCs for new fault. Perform appropriate test. See INSTRUMENT CLUSTER DTC INDEX table under SELF-DIAGNOSTIC SYSTEM.

TEST E: DEFECTIVE TRANSCEIVER

Turn ignition switch to LOCK position. Verify transceiver module is installed properly. Using NGS tester, retrieve and record continuous DTCs. Clear continuous DTCs and perform instrument cluster self-test. If DTC B1232 or B2103 is not retrieved, system is okay at this time. If DTC B1232 or B2103 is retrieved again, replace transceiver module.

TEST F: PATS IGNITION KEY TRANSPONDER SIGNAL NOT RECEIVED

NOTE: Large metallic objects, a second PATS ignition key, or devices such as electronic credit cards on the same key ring may cause vehicle starting problem and possibly set this code. Ensure customers encoded ignition key is an approved Ford encoded ignition key. Encoded keys from Rotunda, Ilco, and Strattec are also approved keys.

1) Using NGS tester, perform instrument cluster self-test. If DTC B1600 is retrieved, go to next step. If any other DTCs are retrieved, perform appropriate test. See INSTRUMENT CLUSTER DTC INDEX table under SELF-DIAGNOSTIC SYSTEM. If no DTCs are retrieved, system is okay at this time.

2) Turn ignition switch to LOCK position. Obtain NEW encoded ignition key(s). Insert NEW key into ignition. Turn ignition switch to RUN position. Program key. See KEY PROGRAMMING – ERASE ALL KEYS & PROGRAM 2 KEYS under PROGRAMMING. Using NGS tester, perform instrument cluster self-test. If DTC B1600 is still present, go to next step. If any other DTCs are present, perform appropriate test. See INSTRUMENT CLUSTER DTC INDEX table under SELF-DIAGNOSTIC SYSTEM. If no DTCs are present, system is okay at this time.

3) Turn ignition switch to LOCK position. Replace transceiver module. Using customers original encoded ignition key, turn ignition switch to RUN position. Using NGS tester, perform instrument cluster self-test. If DTC B1600 is retrieved, replace instrument cluster then perform TEST J: SECURITY IDENTIFICATION DOES NOT MATCH BETWEEN INSTRUMENT CLUSTER & PCM. If DTC B1600 is not retrieved, system is okay at this time.

TEST G: PATS RECEIVED INCORRECT KEY – CODE FROM TRANSPONDER

NOTE: Large metallic objects, a second PATS ignition key, or devices such as electronic credit cards on the same key ring may cause vehicle starting problem and possibly set this code. Ensure customers encoded ignition key is an approved Ford encoded ignition key. Encoded keys from Rotunda, Ilco, and Strattec are also approved keys.

1) Using NGS tester, perform instrument cluster self-test. If DTC B1601 is retrieved, go to next step. If DTC B1601 is not present, system is okay at this time. Check all existing encoded ignition keys with instrument cluster self-test to verify all other encoded ignition keys are programmed.

2) Using NGS tester, monitor instrument cluster PID NUMKEYS. If PID NUMKEYS does not indicate 8, go to next step. If PID indicates 8, erase and reprogram key codes. See KEY PROGRAMMING – ERASE ALL KEYS & PROGRAM 2 KEYS under PROGRAMMING.

3) Verify there are at least 2 currently programmed encoded ignition keys available with vehicle. If 2 currently programmed encoded ignition keys are available with vehicle, go to next step. If 2 currently programmed encoded ignition keys are not available with vehicle, obtain 2 NEW encoded ignition keys. Program NEW encoded ignition keys. See KEY PROGRAMMING – ERASE ALL KEYS & PROGRAM 2 KEYS under PROGRAMMING. After new encoded ignition keys are programmed, go to next step.

4) Using NGS tester, monitor instrument cluster PID SPARE_KY. If PID indicates ENABLE, perform KEY PROGRAMMING – ERASE ALL KEYS & PROGRAM 2 KEYS under PROGRAMMING then go to next step. If PID does not indicate ENABLE, perform KEY PROGRAMMING – SPARE KEY PROGRAMMING SWITCH under PROGRAMMING then go to next step.

5) Turn ignition switch to LOCK position. Using first encoded ignition key, start vehicle. Using second encoded ignition key, start vehicle. If both encoded ignition keys do not start vehicle, go to next step. If both encoded ignition keys start vehicle, system is okay at this time. If there is a need to program additional encoded ignition keys, perform KEY PROGRAMMING – USING 2 PROGRAMMED KEYS under PROGRAMMING.

6) Using NGS tester, retrieve and record continuous DTCs. Clear continuous DTCs and perform instrument cluster self-test. If DTC B1601 is retrieved, replace instrument cluster then perform TEST J: SECURITY IDENTIFICATION DOES NOT MATCH BETWEEN INSTRUMENT CLUSTER & PCM. If DTC B1601 is not retrieved, system is okay at this time. If any other DTCs are retrieved, perform appropriate test. See INSTRUMENT CLUSTER DTC INDEX table under SELF-DIAGNOSTIC SYSTEM.

TEST H: PATS RECEIVED INVALID KEY – CODE FORMAT FROM TRANSPONDER

NOTE: Large metallic objects, a second PATS ignition key, or devices such as electronic credit cards on the same key ring may cause vehicle starting problem and possibly set this code. Ensure customers encoded ignition key is an approved Ford encoded ignition key. Encoded keys from Rotunda, Ilco, and Strattec are also approved keys.

1) Using NGS tester, perform instrument cluster self-test. If DTC B1602 is retrieved, go to next step. If DTC B1602 is not retrieved, system is okay at this time. Check all customer encoded ignition keys with instrument cluster self-test to verify all other keys are programmed.

2) Turn ignition switch to LOCK position. Obtain a NEW encoded ignition key. Using new encoded ignition key, turn ignition switch to RUN position. Program new encoded ignition key. Perform KEY PROGRAMMING – ERASE ALL KEYS & PROGRAM 2 KEYS under PROGRAMMING. Using NGS tester, perform instrument cluster self-test. If DTC B1602 is retrieved, go to next step. If any DTCs are retrieved, perform appropriate test. See INSTRUMENT CLUSTER DTC INDEX table under SELF-DIAGNOSTIC SYSTEM. If no DTCs are retrieved, system is okay at this time.

3) Ensure ignition switch is in LOCK position. Replace transceiver module. Turn ignition switch to RUN position. Using NGS tester, perform instrument cluster self-test. If any DTCs are retrieved, perform appropriate test. See INSTRUMENT CLUSTER DTC INDEX table under SELF-DIAGNOSTIC SYSTEM. If no DTCs are retrieved, system is okay at this time.

TEST I: PATS TRANSCEIVER SIGNAL IS NOT RECEIVED

1) Using NGS tester, perform instrument cluster self-test. If DTC B1681 is retrieved, go to next step. If DTC B1681 is not retrieved, system is okay at this time.

2) Turn ignition switch to LOCK position. Disconnect transceiver module harness connector C221. Turn ignition switch to RUN position. Measure voltage at terminal No. 2 (White/Light Blue wire) at transceiver module harness connector C221. See Fig. 2. If voltage is greater than 9 volts, go to next step. If voltage is 9 volts or less, repair open in White/Light Blue wire between instrument panel fuse box and transceiver module.

3) Turn ignition switch to LOCK position. Measure resistance between ground and terminal No. 1 (Black/White wire) at transceiver module harness connector C221. If resistance is 5 ohms or less, go to next step. If resistance is greater than 5 ohms, repair open in Black/White wire between transceiver module and ground.

4) Connect transceiver module harness connector C228. Turn ignition switch to RUN position. Using a voltmeter, backprobe at terminal No. 3 (Gray/Orange wire) at transceiver module harness connector C221. If voltage is 9 volts or less, go to next step. If voltage is greater than 9 volts, go to step 6).

5) Turn ignition switch to LOCK position. Disconnect transceiver module harness connector C221. Measure resistance between ground and terminal No. 3 (Gray/Orange wire) at transceiver module harness connector C221. If resistance is greater than 100 ohms, go to next step. If resistance is 100 ohms or less, check Gray/Orange wire for short to ground and repair as necessary. If circuit is okay, replace instrument cluster then perform TEST J: SECURITY IDENTIFICATION DOES NOT MATCH BETWEEN INSTRUMENT CLUSTER & PCM.

6) Turn ignition switch to LOCK position. Disconnect transceiver module harness connector C221. Disconnect instrument cluster harness connector C250. Measure resistance in Gray/Orange wire between terminal No. 7 at instrument cluster harness connector C250 and terminal No. 3 at transceiver module harness connector C221. See Figs. 2 and 3. If resistance is 5 ohms or less, go to next step. If resistance is greater than 5 ohms, repair open in Gray/Orange wire.

7) Ensure ignition switch is in LOCK position. Connect transceiver module harness connector C221. Connect instrument cluster harness connector C250. Turn ignition switch to RUN position. Using a voltmeter, backprobe at terminal No. 4 (White/Light Green wire) at transceiver module harness connector C221. If voltage is 9 volts or less, go to next step. If voltage is greater than 9 volts, go to step 9).

8) Turn ignition switch to LOCK position. Disconnect transceiver module harness connector C221. Measure resistance between ground and terminal No. 4 (White/Light Green wire) at transceiver module harness connector C221. If resistance is greater than 100 ohms, go to next step. If resistance is 100 ohms or less, check White/Light Green wire for short to ground and repair as necessary. If circuit is okay, replace instrument cluster then perform TEST J: SECURITY IDENTIFICATION DOES NOT MATCH BETWEEN INSTRUMENT CLUSTER & PCM.

9) Connect transceiver module harness connector C221. Turn ignition switch to RUN position. Using NGS tester, trigger instrument cluster active command RF SIGNAL to ON. Using a voltmeter, backprobe at terminal No. 4 (White/Light Green wire) at transceiver module harness connector C221 and ground while triggering active command from ON to OFF. Voltage should be greater than 9 volts in OFF position and less than one volt in ON position. If voltage is as specified, go to next step. If voltage is not as specified, check for open in White/Light Green wire between transceiver module and instrument cluster and repair as

necessary. If circuit is okay, replace instrument cluster then perform TEST J: SECURITY IDENTIFICATION DOES NOT MATCH BETWEEN INSTRUMENT CLUSTER & PCM.

10) Turn ignition switch to LOCK position. Replace transceiver module. Turn ignition switch to RUN position. Using NGS tester, perform instrument cluster self-test. If DTC B1681 is retrieved, go to next step. If DTC B1681 is not retrieved, system is okay at this time.

11) Turn ignition switch to LOCK position. Replace instrument cluster then perform TEST J: SECURITY IDENTIFICATION DOES NOT MATCH BETWEEN INSTRUMENT CLUSTER & PCM and return to finish this procedure. Turn ignition switch to RUN position. Using NGS tester, perform instrument cluster self-test. If DTC B1681 is retrieved, repair White/Light Green or Gray/Orange wire(s) between transceiver module and instrument cluster. If no DTCs are retrieved, system is okay at this time. If any other DTCs are retrieved, perform appropriate test. See INSTRUMENT CLUSTER DTC INDEX table under SELF-DIAGNOSTIC SYSTEM.

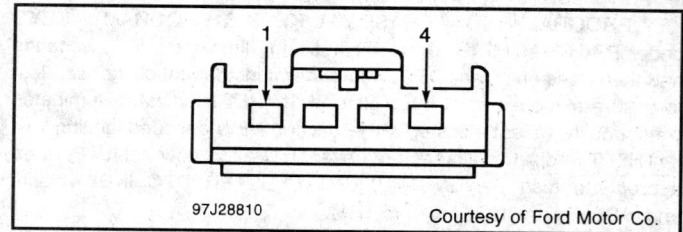

Fig. 2: Identifying Transceiver Module Harness Connector C221 Terminals

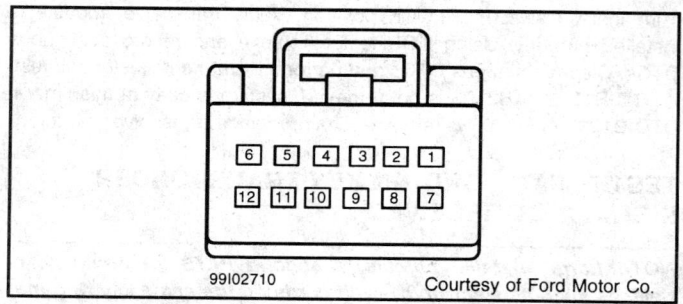

Fig. 3: Identifying Instrument Cluster Harness Connector C250 Terminals

TEST J: SECURITY IDENTIFICATION DOES NOT MATCH BETWEEN INSTRUMENT CLUSTER & PCM

1) Using NGS tester, perform instrument cluster self-test. If DTC B2139 is retrieved, go to next step. If DTC B2139 is not retrieved, system is okay at this time.

2) Perform security access for instrument cluster. See KEY PROGRAMMING – SECURITY ACCESS PROCEDURE under PROGRAMMING. Using NGS tester, select PARAMETER RESET command for instrument cluster. Using NGS tester, select PARAMETER RESET command for PCM. Turn ignition switch to RUN position for 3 seconds. Turn ignition switch to LOCK position. Using NGS tester, perform instrument cluster self-test. If DTC B2139 is not retrieved, system is okay at this time. If DTC B2139 is retrieved, verify PCM calibration is correct for vehicle. If calibration is okay, replace instrument cluster and repeat this test. If DTC B2139 still exists, replace PCM.

TEST K: NVM CONFIGURATION FAILURE

1) Turn ignition switch to LOCK position. Using NGS tester, perform instrument cluster self-test. If no DTCs or only DTC B2141 is retrieved, go to next step. If DTC B2141 and DTC U1147 are retrieved together, perform TEST C: INVALID/MISSING DATA FOR VEHICLE SECURITY.

2) Perform security access for PCM. See KEY PROGRAMMING – SECURITY ACCESS PROCEDURE under PROGRAMMING. Using NGS tester, select PCM active command KEEP ALIVE MEMORY RESET. Turn ignition switch to LOCK position. Turn ignition switch to

RUN position for 30 seconds. Turn ignition switch to LOCK position. Start vehicle. If vehicle does not start, go to next step. If vehicle starts, system is okay at this time.

3) Turn ignition switch to LOCK position. Using NGS tester, clear all continuous DTCs. Turn ignition switch to LOCK position. Turn ignition switch to RUN position for 30 seconds. Turn ignition switch to LOCK position. Using NGS tester, perform instrument cluster self-test. If no DTCs are not retrieved, system is okay at this time. If DTC B2141 is retrieved, verify PCM calibration is correct for vehicle. If calibration is okay, replace instrument cluster then perform TEST J: SECURITY IDENTIFICATION DOES NOT MATCH BETWEEN INSTRUMENT CLUSTER & PCM. If any other DTCs are retrieved, perform appropriate test. See INSTRUMENT CLUSTER DTC INDEX table under SELF-DIAGNOSTIC SYSTEM.

REMOVAL & INSTALLATION

TRANSCEIVER MODULE

WARNING: To avoid injury from accidental air bag deployment, read and carefully follow all WARNINGS and SERVICE PRECAUTIONS in appropriate AIR BAG RESTRAINT SYSTEMS article.

Removal & Installation – Remove ignition lock cylinder. See STEERING COLUMN SWITCHES – MUSTANG article. Remove upper and lower steering column covers. Remove screw attaching transceiver to underside of steering column. Using a small screwdriver, gently pry transceiver over key cylinder lower rib. Disconnect harness connector and remove transceiver module. To install, reverse removal procedure.

WIRING DIAGRAMS

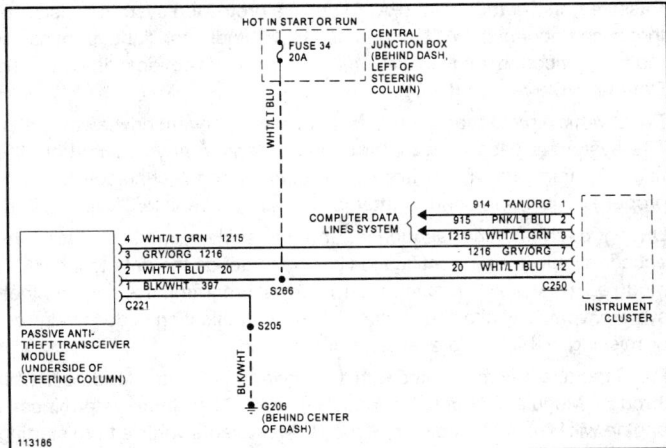

Fig. 4: Passive Anti-Theft System Wiring Diagram (Mustang)

DESCRIPTION

Passive Anti-Theft System (PATS) vehicle protection system consists of these components: PATS module, THEFT indicator light, transceiver module, encoded ignition key, module communications network and Data Link Connector (DLC) .

PATS vehicle protection system is designed to prevent driveaway thefts. The system is passive in that it does not require any activity from the user. System uses radio frequency identification technology to verify proper key is being used to attempt to start the vehicle.

During each starting sequence, the transceiver module reads the encoded ignition key identification code and sends the data to the PATS module. If the key's identification code is programmed into anti-theft system, vehicle is allowed to start. If key's identification code is incorrect or missing, vehicle is prevented from starting.

PATS module communicates with the Powertrain Control Module (PCM) through Module Communications Network. PCM then determines if engine will be enabled to start. If the PCM prevents vehicle from starting because of PATS system, a Diagnostic Trouble Code (DTC) will be stored in memory.

OPERATION

THEFT INDICATOR LIGHT

THEFT indicator, located in the instrument cluster, is used to prove out system operation status. PATS uses the THEFT indicator light when ignition switch is in START or RUN positions. For more information, see POWERTRAIN CONTROL MODULE (PCM).

ENCODED IGNITION KEY

When ignition switch is in START or RUN position, PATS module initiates the encoded ignition key interrogation process. Each encoded ignition key must be programmed into PATS module before it can be used to start the vehicle. This encoded ignition key is much larger in size than a standard key to accommodate the electronics located inside plastic cover.

TRANSCEIVER MODULE

Transceiver module communicates with encoded ignition key. During each starting sequence, the transceiver module reads the encoded ignition key identification code and sends the data to the PATS module.

PASSIVE ANTI-THEFT SYSTEM (PATS) MODULE

Anti-theft alarm system control functions are contained in the PATS module. PATS module receives identification code from encoded ignition key and control engine enable. PATS module initiates encoded ignition key interrogation sequence when ignition switch is in RUN or START positions. PATS module can be diagnosed through NGS tester connected to Data Link Connector (DLC).

POWERTRAIN CONTROL MODULE (PCM)

Passive anti-theft system uses PCM to enable or disable vehicle's engine. When system is functioning properly and ignition switch is turned to RUN or START position, THEFT indicator light will turn on for 3 seconds, then turn off. Vehicle will be enabled to start and run. If there is a problem with PATS, THEFT indicator light will flash rapidly or glow constantly for more than 3 seconds when ignition switch is turned to RUN or START position.

COMPONENT LOCATIONS

COMPONENT LOCATIONS

Component	Location
Air Bag Diagnostic Monitor [1]	Behind Right Kick Panel
Data Link Connector (DLC)	Below Driver's Side Of Instrument Panel, To Right Of Steering Column
Generic Electronic Module (GEM)	Behind Center Of Instrument Panel
Passive Anti-Theft System (PATS) Module	Behind Passenger Air Bag Module
Powertrain Control Module (PCM)	Mounted Through Firewall, On Passenger's Side
THEFT Indicator Light	On Right Side Of Instrument Cluster
Transceiver Module	On Ignition Switch Lock Cylinder

[1] – Air bag diagnostic monitor may also be known as Electronic Crash Sensor (ECS) module.

PROGRAMMING

KEY PROGRAMMING – SECURITY ACCESS PROCEDURE

NOTE: Security access must be granted to erase ignition keys, enable/disable spare key programming switch, or perform parameter resets for PATS or PCM. This procedure has a 10 minute time delay prior to granting security access during which the New Generation Star (NGS) tester must remain connected to vehicle. After security access has been granted, security access command menu is displayed which offers various command options. Multiple security access commands can be executed (if necessary) prior to exiting security access command menu. Execution of all necessary security access commands prior to exiting command menu avoids the performance of an additional security access procedure and the associated 10 minute time delay. Security access for the PATS and security access for the PCM must be obtained separately as needed (each will require a 10 minute time delay).

With ignition switch in RUN position and NGS tester connected to vehicle, enter function test menu. Select SECURITY ACCESS PROCEDURE. This procedure will take 10 minutes to perform. After the security access procedure has been completed, a new menu will be displayed with command options. Select as many functions as required before exiting this menu. Once this menu is exited, security access procedure must be performed again to perform additional commands.

KEY PROGRAMMING – WITH PROGRAMMED KEYS

NOTE: This procedure will only work if 2 or more programmed ignition keys are available and there is a need to program additional keys. If 2 keys are not available, perform KEY PROGRAMMING – WITHOUT PROGRAMMED KEYS. PID SPARE_KY must be enabled for this procedure to operate. To enable this PID, perform KEY PROGRAMMING – SECURITY ACCESS PROCEDURE and enable spare key programming switch. If programming procedure is successful, new key(s) will start vehicle and THEFT indicator will illuminate for 3 seconds. If programming procedure is not successful, new key(s) will not start vehicle and THEFT indicator will flash for one minute (after flashing for one minute, THEFT indicator will flash fault code). If necessary, repeat programming procedure. If programming of key(s) is still unsuccessful, perform self-diagnostics. See SELF-DIAGNOSTIC SYSTEM. Maximum of eight keys can be programmed into system. If procedure is not performed as outlined, programming procedure will end. Ignition keys must have correct mechanical key cut for vehicle and must be an encoded key.

1) Insert the first programmed ignition key into ignition lock cylinder. Turn ignition switch from OFF to RUN position (ignition switch must stay in RUN position for one second). Turn ignition switch to OFF position and remove ignition key from ignition lock cylinder.

2) Within 5 seconds of turning ignition switch to OFF position, insert second programmed ignition key into ignition lock cylinder. Turn ignition switch from OFF to RUN position (ignition switch must stay in RUN position for one second). Turn ignition switch to OFF position and remove second ignition key from ignition lock cylinder.

3) Within 10 seconds of turning ignition switch to OFF position, insert a NEW unprogrammed ignition key into ignition lock cylinder. Turn ignition switch from OFF to RUN position (ignition switch must stay in RUN position for one second). Turn ignition switch to OFF position and remove ignition key from ignition lock cylinder. New ignition key should now be programmed. To program additional key(s), repeat key programming procedure from step **1)**.

KEY PROGRAMMING – WITHOUT PROGRAMMED KEYS

NOTE: This procedure is used when a customer needs keys programmed into system and does not have 2 programmed ignition keys available, or when programmed ignition keys have been lost and/or ignition switch assembly has been replaced. This procedure will erase all programmed ignition keys from memory and prevent vehicle from starting until 2 keys have been programmed. Ignition keys must have correct mechanical key cut for vehicle and must be an encoded key. If additional key(s) are to be programmed, perform KEY PROGRAMMING – WITH PROGRAMMED KEYS. If remaining keys are with customer and not with vehicle, instruct customer to see owner's manual to program spare key(s).

1) Turn ignition switch from OFF to RUN position. With NGS tester connected to vehicle, enter function test menu. Select SECURITY ACCESS PROCEDURE. This procedure will take 10 minutes to perform. After the security access procedure has been completed, a new menu will be displayed with command options. Select IGNITION KEY CODE ERASE.

2) Turn ignition switch to OFF position and disconnect NGS tester. Insert first encoded ignition key into ignition lock cylinder. Turn ignition switch to RUN position for 3 seconds. Turn ignition switch to OFF position and remove first encoded key.

3) Insert second encoded ignition key into ignition lock cylinder. Turn ignition switch to RUN position for 3 seconds. Turn ignition switch to OFF position and remove second encoded key. Both encoded ignition keys should now start vehicle.

KEY PROGRAMMING – SPARE KEY PROGRAMMING SWITCH

NOTE: The spare key programming switch is a programmable switch which provides the capability to enable/disable the normal customer spare key programming procedure detailed in the owner's manual. This programmable switch is provided as a convenience for rental company fleets or other fleet purchasers who may not want the spare key programming procedure available to the vehicle driver. The spare key programming switch state can be viewed using PATS PID SPARE_KY.

Insert a programmed ignition key into ignition lock cylinder. Turn ignition switch from OFF to RUN position. With NGS tester connected to vehicle, enter function test menu. Select SECURITY ACCESS PROCEDURE. This procedure will take 10 minutes to perform. After security access procedure has been completed, a new menu will be displayed with command options. Default setting on all new vehicles is ENABLE. Select SPARE KEY PROGRAMMING SWITCH. Set SPARE KEY PROGRAMMING SWITCH to ENABLE or DISABLE.

TROUBLE SHOOTING

Before performing any tests on anti-theft system, check the following to eliminate common problems. Correct any obvious defects before proceeding.

- Damaged ignition cylinder.
- Use of non-encoded ignition key.
- Use of non-programmed encoded ignition key.
- Blown fuse(s).
- Damaged wiring.
- Loose or corroded connections.
- Faulty ignition switch.

SELF-DIAGNOSTIC SYSTEM

Verify customers complaint by operating PATS. Ensure electronically coded ignition key is being used. Check for damaged ignition lock cylinder switch, damaged encoded ignition key or open fuses. Check for loose or corroded connectors, damaged wiring harness, damaged ignition switch or damaged transceiver module. Repair or replace components as necessary.

Connect New Generation Star (NGS) tester to Data Link Connector (DLC), located beneath instrument panel. Using NGS tester, preform data link diagnostics test. See DATA LINK DIAGNOSTIC TEST under COMMUNICATION NETWORK DIAGNOSTICS in MODULE COMMUNICATIONS NETWORK – RANGER article. If NGS tester responds with CKT914, CKT915 or CKT70=ALL ECUS NO RESP/NOT EQUIP, repair module communications concern. See MODULE COMMUNICATIONS NETWORK – RANGER article. If NGS tester displays NO RESP/NOT EQUIP for Passive Anti-Theft System (PATS) module, perform TEST A: NO COMMUNICATION WITH PASSIVE ANTI-THEFT SYSTEM MODULE under SYSTEM TESTS.

If NGS tester responds with SYSTEM PASSED, retrieve and record continuous DTCs. Erase continuous DTCs. Using NGS tester, perform PATS self-test. Perform appropriate test in accordance with DTC retrieved. See PASSIVE ANTI-THEFT SYSTEM MODULE DTC INDEX table. If no DTCs are retrieved, repair by symptom. See SYMPTOM CHART table under SYSTEM TESTS.

PASSIVE ANTI-THEFT SYSTEM MODULE DTC INDEX

DTC	Description	Test
B1213	Anti-Theft Number Of Programmed Keys Is Below Minimum	[1] B1213
B1232/B2103	PATS Transceiver Antenna Not Connected	B1232
B1600	PATS Ignition Key Transponder Signal Not Received/Damaged Encoded Ignition Key Or Use Of Non-PATS Key	B1600
B1601	PATS Received Incorrect Key Code From Ignition Key Transponder	B1601
B1602	Invalid Key Code Format From Ignition Key Transponder	B1602
B1681	PATS Transceiver Signal Is Not Received	B1681
B2139	Security Identification Does Not Match Between PATS & PCM	B2139
B2141	No Security Identification Exchange Between PATS & PCM	B2141
U1147	Invalid Or Missing Data For Vehicle Security	U1147
U1262	SCP Bus Communication Fault	[2]

[1] – If DTCs B1232, B1600, B1601, B1602 OR B1681 are also present, service these DTCs first then recheck codes.
[2] – Repair SCP bus communications concern. See MODULE COMMUNICATIONS NETWORK – RANGER article.

DIAGNOSTIC TESTS

DTC B1213: ANTI-THEFT NUMBER OF PROGRAMMED KEYS IS BELOW MINIMUM

1) Using NGS tester, perform PATS module self-test. If DTC B1213 is the only code retrieved, go to next step. If any other DTCs are retrieved, perform appropriate test. See PASSIVE ANTI-THEFT SYSTEM MODULE DTC INDEX table under SELF-DIAGNOSTIC SYSTEM.
2) Using NGS tester, monitor Passive Anti-Theft System (PATS) PID NUMKEYS. If PID indicates less than 2 keys, go to next step. If PATS PID NUMKEYS indicates 2 keys or more, clear DTCs and perform PATS module self-test. Verify no DTCs are present.
3) Obtain NEW encoded ignition key and insert into ignition. Program NEW encoded ignition key. See KEY PROGRAMMING – WITHOUT PROGRAMMED KEYS under PROGRAMMING. If THEFT indicator illuminates for 3 seconds and then goes out, clear DTCs and perform PATS module self-test. Verify no DTCs are present. If THEFT indicator illuminates continuously, repeat this step with the other NEW encoded ignition key. If THEFT indicator is flashing, retrieve DTC for new fault. See SELF-DIAGNOSTIC SYSTEM.

DTC B1232: PATS TRANSCEIVER ANTENNA NOT CONNECTED

Ensure ignition is switch is in LOCK position. Verify PATS transceiver module antenna is properly connected, and transceiver module is properly installed. See TRANSCEIVER MODULE under REMOVAL & INSTALLATION. Using NGS tester, perform PATS module self-test. Retrieve and record continuous DTCs. Clear continuous DTCs. If DTC B1232/B2103 is retrieved, replace PATS transceiver module. Clear DTCs and repeat PATS module self-test. If DTC B1232/B2103 is not retrieved, system is okay at this time.

DTC B1600: PATS IGNITION KEY TRANSPONDER SIGNAL NOT RECEIVED/DAMAGED ENCODED IGNITION KEY OR USE OF NON-PATS KEY

NOTE: Large metallic objects, a second PATS ignition key, or devices such as electronic credit cards on the same key ring may cause vehicle starting problem and possibly set this code. Ensure customers encoded ignition key is an approved Ford encoded ignition key. Encoded keys from Rotunda, Ilco, Curtis and Strattec are also approved keys.

1) Turn ignition switch to LOCK position. Using NGS tester, retrieve and record continuous DTCs. Clear continuous DTCs and perform PATS module self-test. If DTC B1600 is retrieved, go to next step. If any other DTCs are retrieved, perform appropriate test. If no DTCs are retrieved, system is okay at this time.
2) Obtain NEW encoded ignition key and insert into ignition. Turn ignition switch to RUN position. Program NEW encoded ignition key. See KEY PROGRAMMING – WITHOUT PROGRAMMED KEYS under PROGRAMMING. Using NGS tester, perform PATS module self-test. If DTC

B1600 is retrieved, go to next step. If any other DTCs are retrieved, perform appropriate test. If no DTCs are retrieved, system is okay at this time.
3) Turn ignition switch to LOCK position. Replace PATS transceiver module. See TRANSCEIVER MODULE under REMOVAL & INSTALLATION. Using original ignition key, turn ignition switch to RUN position. Using NGS tester, perform PATS module self-test. If DTC B1600 is retrieved, replace PATS module. Cycle ignition off and on with 2 NEW encoded ignition keys. Go to test DTC B2139: SECURITY IDENTIFICATION DOES NOT MATCH BETWEEN PATS & PCM. Clear DTCs and repeat PATS module self-test. If no DTCs are retrieved, system is okay at this time.

DTC B1601: PATS RECEIVED INCORRECT KEY CODE FROM IGNITION KEY TRANSPONDER

NOTE: Large metallic objects, a second PATS ignition key, or devices such as electronic credit cards on the same key ring may cause vehicle starting problem and possibly set this code. Ensure customers encoded ignition key is an approved Ford encoded ignition key. Encoded keys from Rotunda, Ilco, Curtis and Strattec are also approved keys.

1) Turn ignition switch to LOCK position. Using NGS tester, retrieve and record continuous DTCs. Clear continuous DTCs and perform PATS module self-test. If DTC B1601 is retrieved, go to next step. If DTC B1601 is not retrieved, system is okay at this time. Check all other encoded ignition keys with PATS module self-test to verify all other encoded ignition keys are programmed.
2) Using NGS tester, monitor PATS PID NUMKEYS. If PID does not indicate 8 keys, go to next step. If PID indicates 8 keys, erase and reprogram key codes. See KEY PROGRAMMING – WITHOUT PROGRAMMED KEYS under PROGRAMMING.
3) Verify there are at least 2 programmed encoded ignition keys available with vehicle. If at least 2 programmed encoded ignition keys are available with vehicle, go to next step. If at least 2 programmed encoded ignition keys are not available with vehicle, obtain a NEW encoded ignition key so at least 2 keys are available. Program encoded ignition keys. See KEY PROGRAMMING – WITHOUT PROGRAMMED KEYS under PROGRAMMING and go to next step.
4) Using NGS tester, monitor PATS PID SPARE_KY. If PID indicates YES, preform KEY PROGRAMMING – WITH PROGRAMMED KEYS under PROGRAMMING then go to next step. If PID does not indicate YES, perform KEY PROGRAMMING – SPARE KEY PROGRAMMING SWITCH under PROGRAMMING to enable PID SPARE_KY to YES then go to next step.
5) Using first encoded ignition key, start vehicle. Turn ignition switch to LOCK position and remove first encoded ignition key. Using second encoded ignition key, start vehicle. If vehicle does not start using both encoded ignition keys, go to next step. If vehicle starts using both encoded ignition keys, system is okay at this time. If additional encoded ignition keys are needed, see KEY PROGRAMMING – SPARE KEY PROGRAMMING SWITCH under PROGRAMMING.

6) Using NGS tester, retrieve and record continuous DTCs. Clear continuous DTCs and perform PATS module self-test. If DTC B1601 is retrieved, replace PATS module. Cycle ignition off and on with 2 NEW encoded ignition keys. Go to test DTC B2139: SECURITY IDENTIFICATION DOES NOT MATCH BETWEEN PATS & PCM. Clear DTCs and repeat PATS module self-test. If DTC B1601 is not retrieved, system is okay at this time. If any other DTCs are retrieved, perform appropriate test.

DTC B1602: INVALID KEY CODE FORMAT FROM IGNITION KEY TRANSPONDER

NOTE: Large metallic objects, a second PATS ignition key, or devices such as electronic credit cards on the same key ring may cause vehicle starting problem and possibly set this code. Ensure customers encoded ignition key is an approved Ford encoded ignition key. Encoded keys from Rotunda, Ilco, Curtis and Strattec are also approved keys.

1) Turn ignition switch to LOCK position. Connect NGS tester to Data Link Connector (DLC). Using NGS tester, retrieve and record continuous DTCs. Clear continuous DTCs and perform PATS self-test. If DTC B1602 is retrieved, go to next step. If DTC B1602 is not retrieved, system is okay at this time. Check all customer encoded ignition keys with PATS self-test to verify all other keys are programmed.

2) Turn ignition switch to LOCK position. Obtain a NEW encoded ignition key. Using encoded ignition key, turn ignition switch to RUN position. Program encoded ignition key. See KEY PROGRAMMING – WITHOUT PROGRAMMED KEYS under PROGRAMMING. Using NGS tester, perform PATS self-test. If DTC B1602 is retrieved, go to next step. If no DTCs are retrieved, system is okay at this time.

3) Ensure ignition switch is in LOCK position. Replace transceiver module. Turn ignition switch to RUN position. Using NGS tester, perform PATS self-test. If no DTCs are retrieved, system is okay at this time. If any other DTCs are retrieved, perform appropriate test.

DTC B1681: PATS TRANSCEIVER MODULE SIGNAL IS NOT RECEIVED

1) Turn ignition switch to LOCK position. Using NGS tester, retrieve and record continuous DTCs. Clear continuous DTCs and perform PATS module self-test. If DTC B1681 is retrieved, go to next step. If DTC B1681 is not retrieved, system is okay at this time.

2) Turn ignition switch to LOCK position. Disconnect PATS transceiver module harness connector C245. Turn ignition switch to RUN position. Measure voltage at terminal No. 2 (Dark Green/White wire) at PATS transceiver module harness connector C245. *See Fig. 1.* If greater than 9 volts exists, go to next step. If 9 volts or less exists, repair Red/Yellow wire between PATS module and PATS transceiver module.

3) Turn ignition switch to LOCK position. Measure resistance between ground and terminal No. 1 (Black/Yellow wire) at PATS transceiver module harness connector C245. If resistance is 5 ohms or less, go to next step. If resistance is greater than 5 ohms, repair Black/Yellow wire between PATS module and PATS transceiver module.

4) Connect PATS transceiver module harness connector C245. Turn ignition switch to RUN position. Using a voltmeter, backprobe at terminal No. 3 (Gray/Orange wire) at PATS transceiver module harness connector C245. If voltage is 9 volts or less, go to next step. If voltage is greater than 9 volts, go to step 7).

5) Turn ignition switch to LOCK position. Disconnect PATS transceiver module harness connector C245. Measure resistance between ground and terminal No. 3 (Gray/Orange wire) at PATS transceiver module harness connector C245. If resistance is greater than 100 ohms, go to next step. If resistance is 100 ohms or less, check for short to ground in Gray/Orange wire between PATS module and PATS transceiver module. If Gray/Orange wire is shorted to ground, repair or replace as necessary. If wire is okay, replace PATS module.

6) Turn ignition switch to LOCK position. Disconnect PATS transceiver module harness connector C245. Disconnect PATS module harness connector C255. Measure resistance in Gray/Orange wire between terminal No. 3 at PATS transceiver module harness connector C245 and terminal No. 11 at PATS module harness connector C255. *See Figs. 1 and 2.* If resistance is 5 ohms or less, go to next step. If resistance is greater than 5 ohms, repair open in Gray/Orange wire.

7) Connect PATS transceiver module harness connector C245. Connect PATS module harness connector C255. Turn ignition switch to RUN position. Using a voltmeter, backprobe at terminal No. 4 (White/Light Green wire) at PATS transceiver module harness connector C245. If 9 volts or less exists, go to next step. If greater than 9 volts exists, go to step 9).

8) Turn ignition switch to LOCK position. Disconnect PATS transceiver module harness connector C245. Measure resistance between ground and terminal No. 4 (White/Light Green wire) PATS transceiver module harness connector C245. If resistance is greater than 100 ohms, go to next step. If resistance is 100 ohms or less, check for short to ground in White/Light Green wire between PATS module and PATS transceiver module. If White/Light Green wire is shorted to ground, repair or replace as necessary. If wire is okay, replace PATS module.

9) Turn ignition switch to LOCK position. Connect PATS transceiver module harness connector C245. Turn ignition switch to RUN position. Using NGS tester, select PATS module ACTIVE COMMAND. Trigger TRANSMIT SIGNAL COMMAND to ON. Transmit signal produces a 2 seconds on, 2 seconds off voltage cycle. Using a voltmeter, backprobe at terminal No. 4 (White/Light Green wire) at PATS transceiver module harness connector C245. If voltage drops from greater than 9 volts to less than one volt when active command is triggered on, go to next step. If voltage does not drop from greater than 9 volts to less than one volt when active command is triggered on, check for open in White/Light Green wire between PATS module connector terminal No. 13 and PATS transceiver module connector terminal No. 4. Repair or replace White/Light Green wire as necessary. If White/Light Green wire is okay, replace PATS module.

10) Turn ignition switch to LOCK position. Replace PATS transceiver module. See TRANSCEIVER MODULE under REMOVAL & INSTALLATION. Turn ignition switch to RUN position. Using NGS tester, perform PATS module self-test. If DTC B1681 is retrieved, go to next step. If DTC B1681 is not retrieved, system is okay at this time. If any other DTCs are retrieved, perform appropriate test.

11) Turn ignition switch to LOCK position. Replace PATS module. See PATS MODULE under REMOVAL & INSTALLATION. Turn ignition switch to RUN position. Using NGS tester, perform PATS module self-test. If DTC B1681 is retrieved, repair appropriate faulty circuit between PATS module and PATS transceiver module. See WIRING DIAGRAMS. If no DTCs are retrieved, system is okay at this time. If any other DTCs are retrieved, perform appropriate test.

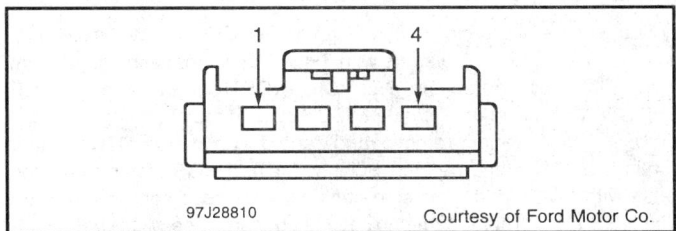

97J28810   Courtesy of Ford Motor Co.

Fig. 1: Identifying PATS Transceiver Module Connector C245 Terminals

DTC B2139: SECURITY IDENTIFICATION DOES NOT MATCH BETWEEN PATS & PCM

1) Turn ignition switch to LOCK position. Using NGS tester, retrieve and record continuous DTCs. Clear continuous DTCs and perform PATS module self-test. If DTC B2139 is retrieved, go to next step. If DTC B2139 is not retrieved, system is okay at this time.

2) Perform security access for PATS module. See KEY PROGRAMMING – SECURITY ACCESS PROCEDURE under PROGRAMMING. Using NGS tester, select PARAMETER RESET command for PATS module. Perform PCM active command ACTIVE COMMAND KEEP ALIVE MEMORY RESET. Turn ignition switch to LOCK position. Turn

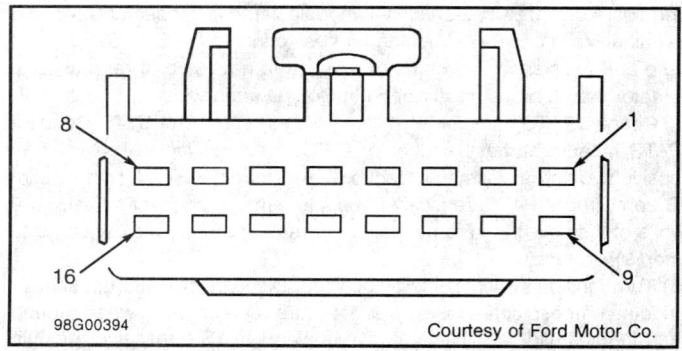

Fig. 2: Identifying PATS Module Connector C255 Terminals

ignition switch to RUN position for 30 seconds then using NGS tester, clear continuous DTCs. Turn ignition switch to LOCK position. Using NGS tester, perform PATS self-test. If DTC B2139 is not retrieved, system is okay at this time. If DTC B2139 is retrieved, verify PCM calibration is correct for vehicle. If calibration is okay, replace PATS module. Clear DTCs and retest system operation. If DTC B2139 still exists, replace PCM and retest system operation.

DTC B2141: NO SECURITY IDENTIFICATION EXCHANGE BETWEEN PATS & PCM

1) Turn ignition switch to LOCK position. Using NGS tester, retrieve and record continuous DTCs. Clear continuous DTCs and perform PATS module self-test. If DTC B2141 and DTC U1147 are retrieved together, perform DTC U1147: INVALID OR MISSING DATA FOR VEHICLE SECURITY. If DTC B2141 is retrieved, go to next step. If no DTCs are retrieved, system is okay at this time.

2) Using NGS tester, perform PCM active command KEEP ALIVE MEMORY RESET. Turn ignition switch to LOCK position. Turn ignition switch to RUN position for 30 seconds. Turn ignition switch to LOCK position. Start vehicle. If vehicle does not start, go to next step. If vehicle starts, system is okay at this time.

3) Using NGS tester, perform PATS module self-test. If DTC B2141 is not retrieved, system is okay at this time. If DTC B2141 is retrieved, verify PCM calibration is correct for vehicle. If calibration is okay, replace PATS module. Clear DTCs and retest system operation. If DTC B2141 still exists, replace PCM and retest system operation.

DTC U1147: INVALID OR MISSING DATA FOR VEHICLE SECURITY

1) Start vehicle. If vehicle does not start and THEFT indicator is flashing, go to next step. If vehicle starts with THEFT indicator flashing, problem is in PCM. See appropriate SELF-DIAGNOSTICS article in ENGINE PERFORMANCE in appropriate MITCHELL® manual.

2) Using NGS tester, retrieve and record continuous DTCs. Clear continuous DTCs and perform PCM self-test. If NGS tester communicates with PCM, go to next step. If NGS tester does not communicate with NGS tester, repair communications concern. See MODULE COMMUNICATIONS NETWORK – RANGER article.

3) If DTC P1260 was retrieved during PCM self-test, go to next step. If DTC P1260 was not retrieved during PCM self-test, check PCM power and ground circuits. See appropriate SELF-DIAGNOSTICS article in ENGINE PERFORMANCE in appropriate MITCHELL® manual.

4) Perform self-diagnostics. See SELF-DIAGNOSTIC SYSTEM. If DTC U1147 is not retrieved, system is okay at this time. If DTC U1147 is retrieved, replace PATS module. If DTC U1147 still exists, replace PCM.

SYSTEM TESTS
SYMPTOM CHART

Symptom	Test
No Communication With Passive Anti-Theft System (PATS) Module	A
THEFT Indicator Always/Never On – No Prove Out	B

TEST A: NO COMMUNICATION WITH PASSIVE ANTI-THEFT SYSTEM MODULE

1) Turn ignition switch to LOCK position. Disconnect PATS module harness connector C255. Turn ignition switch to RUN position. Measure voltage at terminals No. 15 (White/Yellow wire) and No. 16 (Red/Light Green wire) at PATS module harness connector C255. *See Fig. 2.* If battery voltage does not exist, go to next step. If battery voltage exists at both terminals, go to step **3)**.

2) Turn ignition switch to LOCK position. Remove fuses No. 19 (25-amp) and No. 25 (7.5-amp) from instrument panel fuse box. Measure resistance in Light White/Yellow wire between output side of fuse No. 8 in instrument panel fuse box and terminal No. 15 at PATS module harness connector C255. Also, measure resistance in Red/Light Green wire between output side of fuse No. 7 in instrument panel fuse box and terminal No. 16 at PATS module harness connector C255. If both resistance readings are 5 ohms or less, repair power distribution to appropriate fuse. See appropriate wiring diagram in POWER DISTRIBUTION article in WIRING DIAGRAMS. If either resistance reading is greater than 5 ohms, repair open in appropriate wire.

3) Measure resistance between ground and terminal No. 7 (Black/White wire) at PATS module harness connector C255. If resistance is 5 ohms or less, repair module communications concern. See MODULE COMMUNICATIONS NETWORK – RANGER article. If resistance is greater than 5 ohms, repair open in Black/White wire between PATS module and ground.

TEST B: THEFT INDICATOR ALWAYS/NEVER ON – NO PROVE OUT

1) Cycle ignition off then on. If THEFT indicator does not flash every 2 seconds with ignition off but illuminates for 3 seconds when ignition is turned on, repair White/Yellow wire between instrument panel fuse box and PATS module terminal No. 15. If THEFT indicator is not as specified, go to next step.

2) Turn ignition on. If THEFT indicator stays illuminated, perform PATS module self-test. If DTCs are retrieved, go to PASSIVE ANTI-THEFT SYSTEM MODULE DTC INDEX table and perform appropriate test. If no DTCs are retrieved, go to next step. If THEFT indicator does not stay illuminated, go to step **5)**.

3) Turn ignition switch to LOCK position. Disconnect PATS module harness connector C255. If THEFT indicator stays illuminated, repair short to voltage in Dark Blue/Light Green wire between terminal PATS module connector C255 terminal No. 8 and instrument cluster. If THEFT indicator does not stay illuminated, go to next step.

4) Turn ignition off. Reconnect PATS module. Turn ignition on. Using NGS, trigger PATS active command THEFT LMP ON and OFF. If THEFT indicator toggles on and off, perform PATS module self-test. If DTCs are retrieved, go to PASSIVE ANTI-THEFT SYSTEM MODULE DTC INDEX table and perform appropriate test. If no DTCs are retrieved, replace PATS module. See PATS MODULE under REMOVAL & INSTALLATION. If THEFT indicator does not toggle on and off, replace PATS module.

5) Turn ignition on. Using NGS tester, enter PATS module ACTIVE COMMAND MODE. If ACTIVE COMMAND MODE can be entered, go to next step. If ACTIVE COMMAND MODE cannot be entered, perform TEST A: NO COMMUNICATION WITH PATS MODULE.

6) Using NGS tester, trigger active command PATS THEFT LMP ON. If anti-theft indicator light does not illuminate, go to next step. If anti-theft indicator illuminates, system is okay at this time.

7) Turn ignition switch to LOCK position. Disconnect instrument cluster harness connector C214. Turn ignition on. Measure voltage between ground and instrument cluster harness connector C214 terminal No. 6 (Dark Blue/Light Green wire). *See Fig. 3.* If battery voltage does not exist, go to next step. If battery voltage exists, go to step 11).

8) Turn ignition switch to LOCK position. Disconnect PATS module harness connector C255. Measure resistance of Dark Blue/Light Green wire between instrument cluster harness connector C214 terminal No. 6 and PATS module harness connector C255 terminal No. 8. If resistance is 5 ohms or less, go to next step. If resistance is greater than 5 ohms, repair open in Dark Blue/Light Green wire.

9) Measure resistance between ground and PATS module harness connector C255 terminal No. 8 (Dark Blue/Light Green wire). If resistance is greater than 10 k/ohms, go to next step. If resistance is 10 k/ohms or less, repair short to ground in Dark Blue/Light Green wire.

10) Turn ignition off. Reconnect PATS module. Turn ignition on. Using NGS tester, trigger active command PATS THEFT LMP ON. Measure voltage between ground and instrument cluster harness connector C214 terminal No. 6 (Dark Blue/Light Green wire). *See Fig. 3.* If battery voltage exists, go to next step. If battery voltage does not exist, replace PATS module.

11) Ensure theft indicator LED is connected. Measure resistance between top contact of theft indicator and instrument cluster harness connector C214 terminal No. 7 (Black wire). If resistance is less than 5 ohms, replace theft LED. If resistance is 5 ohms or greater, repair or replace instrument cluster.

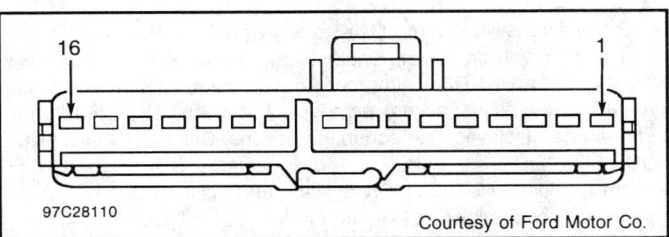

Fig. 3: Identifying Instrument Cluster Connector C214 Terminals

REMOVAL & INSTALLATION

CAUTION: When battery is disconnected, vehicle computer and memory systems may lose memory data. Driveability problems may exist until computer systems have completed a relearn cycle. See COMPUTER RELEARN PROCEDURES article in GENERAL INFORMATION before disconnecting battery.

PATS MODULE

NOTE: Before replacing PATS module, it is necessary to upload module configuration to NGS tester. For reprogramming assistance, refer to help screen on NGS tester configuration card.

Removal & Installation – Disconnect negative battery cable. PATS module is located behind passenger air bag module. Remove passenger air bag module. Remove PATS module assembly with bracket. Disconnect wiring harness connector from PATS module. Release retainer tabs and remove PATS module from bracket. To install, reverse removal procedure.

TRANSCEIVER MODULE

NOTE: If transceiver module is replaced, all existing ignition keys must be reprogrammed. See PROGRAMMING.

Removal & Installation – 1) Disconnect negative battery cable. Transceiver module is located on ignition switch lock cylinder. Insert ignition key into ignition switch lock cylinder. Turn ignition switch lock cylinder to RUN position. Insert a punch in steering column cover hole and press ignition switch lock cylinder release tab while removing ignition switch lock cylinder.

2) Twist and remove tilt handle from column. Remove upper and lower steering column covers. Remove hood release handle. Remove instrument panel lower cover and reinforcement. Remove transceiver module retaining screw from steering column. Carefully pry transceiver over rib on ignition switch lock cylinder housing. Remove transceiver module harness retainers. Disconnect transceiver module harness connector and remove transceiver module. To install, reverse removal procedure.

WIRING DIAGRAMS

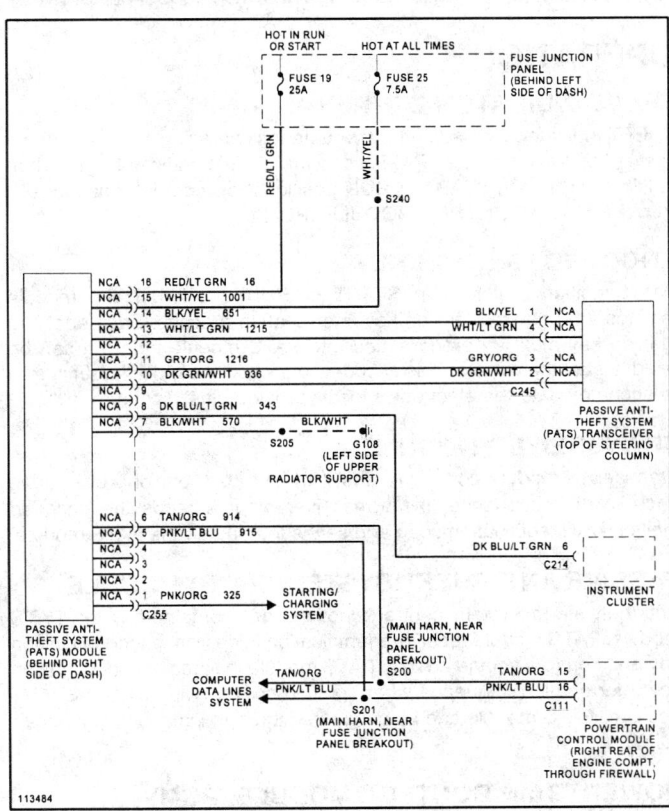

Fig. 4: Passive Anti-Theft System (PATS) Wiring Diagram (Ranger)

DESCRIPTION

The passive anti-theft system is designed to prevent driveaway thefts. The system is passive in that it does not require any activity from the user. System uses radio frequency identification technology to verify proper key is being used to attempt to start the vehicle.

During each starting sequence, the transceiver module reads the encoded ignition key identification code and sends the data to the Passive Anti-Theft System (PATS) module. If the key's identification code is programmed into anti-theft system, vehicle is capable of starting. If key's identification code is incorrect or missing, vehicle is prevented from starting.

PATS module communicates with the Powertrain Control Module (PCM) via Module Communications Network (MCN). PCM then determines if engine will be enabled to start. If the PCM prevents vehicle from starting because of PATS system, a Diagnostic Trouble Code (DTC) will be stored in memory.

PATS vehicle protection system consists of these components: PATS module, THEFT indicator light, transceiver module, encoded ignition key, module communications network and Data Link Connector (DLC).

OPERATION

THEFT INDICATOR LIGHT

THEFT indicator, located in the instrument cluster, is used to prove out system operation status. PATS uses the THEFT indicator light when ignition switch is in START or RUN position. For more information, see POWERTRAIN CONTROL MODULE (PCM).

ENCODED IGNITION KEY

When ignition switch is in START or RUN position, PATS module initiates the encoded ignition key interrogation process. Each encoded ignition key must be programmed into PATS module before it can be used to start the vehicle. This encoded ignition key is much larger in size to accommodate the electronics located inside plastic cover.

TRANSCEIVER MODULE

Transceiver module communicates with encoded ignition key. During each starting sequence, the transceiver module reads the encoded ignition key identification code and sends the data to the PATS module.

PASSIVE ANTI-THEFT SYSTEM (PATS) MODULE

Anti-theft alarm system control functions are contained in the PATS module. PATS module receives identification code from encoded ignition key and controls engine enable. PATS module initiates encoded ignition key interrogation sequence when ignition switch is in RUN or START position. PATS module can be diagnosed through Data Link Connector (DLC).

POWERTRAIN CONTROL MODULE (PCM)

Passive anti-theft system uses PCM to enable or disable vehicle's engine. When system is functioning properly and ignition switch is turned to RUN or START position, THEFT indicator light will turn on for 3 seconds, then turn off. Vehicle will be enabled to start and run. If there is a problem in PATS, THEFT indicator light will flash rapidly or glow constantly for more than 3 seconds when ignition is turned to run or start.

COMPONENT LOCATIONS

COMPONENT LOCATIONS

Component	Location
Data Link Connector	Under Instrument Panel, Below Steering Column
Passive Anti-Theft System Module	Behind Center Of Instrument Panel, Behind Integrated Control Panel

COMPONENT LOCATIONS (Cont.)

Component	Location
Powertrain Control Module	On Right Side Of Firewall In Engine Compartment
Remote Anti-Theft Personality Module	Above Accelerator Pedal

PROGRAMMING

KEY PROGRAMMING – ERASE ALL KEYS & PROGRAM 2 KEYS

NOTE: This procedure is used when a customer needs keys programmed into system and does not have 2 programmed ignition keys available, or when programmed ignition keys have been lost and/or ignition switch assembly has been replaced. This procedure will erase all programmed ignition keys from memory and prevent vehicle from starting until 2 keys have been programmed. Ignition keys must have correct mechanical key cut for vehicle and must be an encoded key. If additional key(s) are to be programmed, perform KEY PROGRAMMING – USING 2 PROGRAMMED KEYS. If remaining keys are with customer and not with vehicle, instruct customer to see owner's manual to program spare key(s).

1) Turn ignition switch from LOCK to RUN position. With NGS tester connected to vehicle, enter function test menu. Select SECURITY ACCESS PROCEDURE. This procedure will take 10 minutes to perform. After the security access procedure has been completed, a new menu will be displayed with command options. Select IGNITION KEY CODE ERASE.

2) Turn ignition switch to LOCK position and disconnect NGS tester. Insert first encoded key into ignition lock cylinder. Turn ignition switch to RUN position for 3 seconds. Turn ignition switch to LOCK position and remove first encoded key.

3) Within 5 seconds, insert second encoded ignition key into ignition lock cylinder. Turn ignition switch to RUN position for 3 seconds. Turn ignition switch to LOCK position and remove second encoded key. Both encoded ignition keys should now start vehicle.

KEY PROGRAMMING – SECURITY ACCESS PROCEDURE

NOTE: Security access must be granted to erase ignition keys, enable/disable spare key programming switch, or perform parameter resets for PATS module and PCM. This procedure has a 10 minute time delay prior to granting security access during which the New Generation Star (NGS) tester must remain connected to vehicle. After security access has been granted, security access command menu is displayed which offers various command options. Multiple security access commands can be executed (if necessary) prior to exiting security access command menu. Execution of all necessary security access commands prior to exiting command menu avoids the performance of an additional security access procedure and the associated 10 minute time delay.

With ignition switch in RUN position and NGS connected to vehicle, enter function test menu. Select SECURITY ACCESS PROCEDURE. This procedure will take 10 minutes to perform. After the security access procedure has been completed, a new menu will be displayed with command options. Select as many functions as required before exiting this menu. Once this menu is exited, security access procedure must be performed again to perform additional commands.

KEY PROGRAMMING – SPARE KEY PROGRAMMING SWITCH

NOTE: The spare key programming switch is a programmable switch which provides the capability to enable/disable the normal customer spare key programming procedure detailed in the owner's manual. This programmable switch is provided as a convenience for rental company fleets or other fleet purchasers who may not want the spare key programming procedure available to the vehicle driver. The spare key programming switch state can be viewed using PATS PID SPARE_KY.

Insert a programmed ignition key into the ignition lock cylinder. Turn ignition switch from LOCK to RUN position. With NGS tester connected to vehicle, enter function test menu. Select SECURITY ACCESS PROCEDURE. This procedure will take 10 minutes to perform. After the security access procedure has been completed, a new menu will be displayed with command options. The default setting on all new vehicles is ENABLE. Select SPARE KEY PROGRAMMING SWITCH. Set SPARE KEY PROGRAMMING SWITCH to ENABLE to allow keys to be programmed or DISABLE to make key programming not accessible.

KEY PROGRAMMING – USING 2 PROGRAMMED KEYS

NOTE: This procedure will only work if 2 or more programmed ignition keys are available and there is a need to program additional keys. If 2 keys are not available, perform KEY PROGRAMMING – ERASE ALL KEYS & PROGRAM 2 KEYS. PID SPARE_KY must be enabled for this procedure to operate. To enable this PID, perform KEY PROGRAMMING – SPARE KEY PROGRAMMING SWITCH and enable spare key programming switch. If programming procedure is successful, new key(s) will start vehicle and THEFT indicator will illuminate for 3 seconds. If programming procedure is not successful, new key(s) will not start vehicle and THEFT indicator will flash for one minute (after flashing for one minute, THEFT indicator will flash fault code). If necessary, repeat programming procedure. If programming of key(s) is still unsuccessful, perform self-diagnostics. See SELF-DIAGNOSTIC SYSTEM. Maximum of 8 keys can be programmed into system. If procedure is not performed as outlined, programming procedure will end. Ignition keys must have correct mechanical key cut for vehicle and must be an encoded key.

1) Insert the first programmed ignition key into ignition lock cylinder. Turn ignition switch from LOCK to RUN position (ignition switch must stay in RUN position for one second). Turn ignition switch to LOCK position and remove ignition key from ignition lock cylinder.

2) Within 5 seconds of turning ignition switch to LOCK position, insert second programmed ignition key into ignition lock cylinder. Turn ignition switch from LOCK to RUN position (ignition switch must stay in RUN position for one second). Turn ignition switch to LOCK position and remove second ignition key from ignition lock cylinder.

3) Within 5 seconds of turning ignition switch to LOCK position, insert a NEW unprogrammed ignition key into ignition lock cylinder. Turn ignition

switch from LOCK to RUN position (ignition switch must stay in RUN position for one second). Turn ignition switch to LOCK position and remove ignition key from ignition lock cylinder. The NEW ignition key should now be programmed. To program additional key(s), repeat key programming procedure from step 1).

KEY PROGRAMMING – WITHOUT USING 2 PROGRAMMED KEYS

NOTE: This procedure is used when customer needs extra keys programmed and 2 programmed keys are not available but system has 2 ignition keys programmed. A maximum of 8 keys can be programmed. If 8 keys are already programmed, this procedure will not allow any more to be programmed. The number of programmed key can be determined by accessing PATS PID NUMKEYS with NGS tester.

Insert unprogrammed key in ignition and turn ignition switch to RUN position. Connect New Generation Star (NGS) tester to Data Link Connector (DLC). Insert Ford Service Function (FSF) card in NGS tester. Perform security access procedure. See KEY PROGRAMMING – SECURITY ACCESS PROCEDURE. Select IGNITION KEY CODE PROGRAM. Turn ignition switch to LOCK position. Disconnect NGS tester. Key should now be programmed and be able to start vehicle.

TROUBLE SHOOTING

Verify customers complaint by operating PATS. Ensure electronically coded ignition key is being used. Check for damaged ignition lock cylinder switch, damaged encoded ignition key or open fuses. Check for loose or corroded connectors, damaged wiring harness, damaged ignition switch or damaged transceiver module. Repair or replace components as necessary. If no problem is found, perform self-diagnostics. See SELF-DIAGNOSTIC SYSTEM.

SELF-DIAGNOSTIC SYSTEM

Connect New Generation Star (NGS) tester to Data Link Connector (DLC), located beneath instrument panel. Using NGS tester, perform data link diagnostics test. See DATA LINK DIAGNOSTIC TEST under COMMUNICATION NETWORK DIAGNOSTICS in MODULE COMMUNICATIONS NETWORK – SABLE & TAURUS article. If NGS tester responds with CKT914, CKT915 or CKT70=ALL ECUS NO RESP/NOT EQUIP, repair module communications concern. See MODULE COMMUNICATIONS NETWORK – SABLE & TAURUS article. If NGS tester displays NO RESP/NOT EQUIP for PASSIVE ANTI-THEFT SYSTEM (PATS) module, perform TEST A: NO COMMUNICATION WITH PASSIVE ANTI-THEFT SYSTEM MODULE under SYSTEM TESTS.

If NGS tester responds with SYSTEM PASSED, retrieve and record continuous DTCs. Erase continuous DTCs. Using NGS tester, perform PATS module self-test. Perform appropriate test in accordance with DTC retrieved. See PASSIVE ANTI-THEFT SYSTEM MODULE DTC INDEX table. Codes listed in this table are only for testing covered in this article. For complete DTC listing, see MODULE COMMUNICATIONS NETWORK – SABLE & TAURUS article. If no DTCs are retrieved, repair by symptom. See SYMPTOM CHART table under SYSTEM TESTS.

PASSIVE ANTI-THEFT SYSTEM MODULE DTC INDEX

DTC [1]	Description	Test
B1213	Anti-Theft Number Of Programmed Keys Is Below Minimum	DTC B1213
B1232 Or B2103	Antenna Not Connected	DTC B1232
B1600	No Key Code Received, Damaged Encoded Ignition Key Or Use Of Non-PATS Key	DTC B1600
B1601	Unprogrammed Encoded Ignition Key (Unprogrammed Ignition Key)	DTC B1601
B1602	Invalid Key Code Format From Ignition Key Transponder (Partial Key Read)	DTC B1602
B1681	Transceiver Defective Or Not Connected	DTC B1681
B2139	Security Key Does Not Match Between PATS & PCM	DTC B2139
B2141	No Security Identification Exchange Between PATS & PCM	DTC B2141
U1147	Vehicle Security Status Missing	DTC U1147

[1] – Codes listed in this table are only for testing covered in this article. For complete DTC listing, see MODULE COMMUNICATIONS NETWORK – SABLE & TAURUS article.

FORD
4-172

1999 ACCESSORIES & EQUIPMENT
Passive Anti-Theft Systems – Sable & Taurus (Cont.)

DIAGNOSTIC TESTS

NOTE: Before performing any testing procedures, self-diagnostics must be performed. See SELF-DIAGNOSTIC SYSTEM.

DTC B1213: ANTI-THEFT NUMBER OF KEYS IS BELOW MINIMUM

1) Using NGS tester, perform Passive Anti-Theft System (PATS) module self-test. If DTC B1213 is the only DTC retrieved, go to next step. If any other DTCs are retrieved, repair all other DTCs first. See PASSIVE ANTI-THEFT SYSTEM MODULE DTC INDEX table under SELF-DIAGNOSTIC SYSTEM.
2) Using NGS tester, access PATS PID NUMKEYS. If PID indicates less than 2 keys, go to next step. If PID indicates 2 or more keys, clear DTCs and retest.
3) Obtain NEW encoded ignition key and insert into ignition lock cylinder. Program NEW encoded ignition key. See KEY PROGRAMMING – ERASE ALL KEYS & PROGRAM 2 KEYS under PROGRAMMING. If THEFT indicator illuminates for 3 seconds and then goes out, clear DTCs and perform PATS module self-test. Verify no DTCs are present. Retest system operation. If THEFT indicator illuminates continuously, repeat step **3)** with the other new encoded ignition key. Retest system operation. If THEFT indicator is flashing, retrieve DTC for new fault. See SELF-DIAGNOSTIC SYSTEM.

DTC B1232: ANTENNA NOT CONNECTED

Turn ignition switch to LOCK position. Verify PATS transceiver module antenna is properly connected, and transceiver module is properly installed. Using NGS tester, perform PATS module self-test. Retrieve and record continuous DTCs. Clear continuous DTCs. If DTC B1232 is retrieved, replace PATS transceiver module. Clear DTCs and repeat PATS module self-test. Retest system operation. If DTC B1232 is not retrieved, system is operating properly.

DTC B1600: NO KEY CODE RECEIVED, DAMAGED ENCODED IGNITION KEY OR USE OF NON-PATS KEY

NOTE: Large metallic objects, a second PATS ignition key, or devices such as electronic credit cards on the same key ring may cause vehicle starting problem and possibly set this code. Ensure customers encoded ignition key is an approved Ford encoded ignition key. Encoded keys from Rotunda, Ilco, and Strattec are also approved keys.

1) Turn ignition switch to LOCK position. Using NGS tester, retrieve and record continuous DTCs. Clear continuous DTCs and perform PATS module self-test. If DTC B1600 is retrieved, go to next step. If any other DTCs are retrieved, repair all other DTCs first. See PASSIVE ANTI-THEFT SYSTEM MODULE DTC INDEX table under SELF-DIAGNOSTIC SYSTEM.
2) Obtain NEW encoded ignition key and insert into ignition lock cylinder. Turn ignition switch to RUN position. Program NEW encoded ignition key. See KEY PROGRAMMING – ERASE ALL KEYS & PROGRAM 2 KEYS under PROGRAMMING. Using NGS tester, perform PATS module self-test. If DTC B1600 is retrieved, go to next step. If any other DTCs are retrieved, go to appropriate DTC test. See PASSIVE ANTI-THEFT SYSTEM MODULE DTC INDEX table under SELF-DIAGNOSTIC SYSTEM. If no DTCs are retrieved, system is operating properly.
3) Turn ignition switch to LOCK position. Replace PATS transceiver module. Using new encoded ignition key from previous step, turn ignition switch to RUN position. Using NGS tester, perform PATS module self-test. If DTC B1600 is retrieved, replace PATS module, then perform DTC B2139: SECURITY KEY DOES NOT MATCH BETWEEN PATS & PCM. If no DTCs are retrieved, system is operating properly.

DTC B1601: UNPROGRAMMED ENCODED IGNITION KEY (UNPROGRAMMED IGNITION KEY)

NOTE: Large metallic objects, a second PATS ignition key, or devices such as electronic credit cards on the same key ring may cause vehicle starting problem and possibly set this code. Ensure customers encoded ignition key is an approved Ford encoded ignition key. Encoded keys from Rotunda, Ilco, and Strattec are also approved keys.

1) Turn ignition switch to LOCK position. Using NGS tester, retrieve and record continuous DTCs. Clear continuous DTCs and perform PATS module self-test. If DTC B1601 is retrieved, go to next step. If DTC B1601 is not retrieved, system is operating properly. Check all other encoded ignition keys with PATS module self-test to verify all other encoded ignition keys are programmed.
2) Using NGS tester, monitor PATS PID NUMKEYS. If PID does not indicate 8 keys, go to next step. If PID indicates 8 keys, erase and reprogram key codes. See KEY PROGRAMMING – ERASE ALL KEYS & PROGRAM 2 KEYS under PROGRAMMING. Clear DTCs and retest system operation.
3) Verify there are at least 2 programmed encoded ignition keys available with vehicle. If at least 2 programmed encoded ignition keys are available with vehicle, go to next step. If at least 2 programmed encoded ignition keys are not available with vehicle, obtain a NEW encoded ignition key so at least 2 keys are available. Program encoded ignition keys. See KEY PROGRAMMING – ERASE ALL KEYS & PROGRAM 2 KEYS under PROGRAMMING and go to step **5)**.
4) Using NGS tester, monitor PATS PID SPARE_KY. If PID indicates YES, program ignition key then go to next step. See KEY PROGRAMMING – USING 2 PROGRAMMED KEYS under PROGRAMMING. If PID indicates NO, enable spare key programming and go to next step. See KEY PROGRAMMING – SPARE KEY PROGRAMMING SWITCH under PROGRAMMING.
5) Using first encoded ignition key, turn ignition switch to RUN position. Turn ignition switch to LOCK position and remove first encoded ignition key. Using second encoded ignition key, turn ignition switch to RUN position. Using both encoded ignition keys, attempt to start vehicle. If vehicle does not start using both encoded ignition keys, go to next step. If vehicle starts using both encoded ignition keys, system is operating properly. If additional encoded ignition keys are needed, see KEY PROGRAMMING – USING 2 PROGRAMMED KEYS under PROGRAMMING.
6) Using NGS tester, retrieve and record continuous DTCs. Clear continuous DTCs and perform PATS module self-test. If DTC B1601 is retrieved, replace PATS module, then perform DTC B2139: SECURITY KEY DOES NOT MATCH BETWEEN PATS & PCM. If DTC B1601 is not retrieved, system is operating properly. If any other DTCs are retrieved, perform appropriate DTC test. See PASSIVE ANTI-THEFT SYSTEM MODULE DTC INDEX table under SELF-DIAGNOSTIC SYSTEM.

1999 ACCESSORIES & EQUIPMENT
Passive Anti-Theft Systems – Sable & Taurus (Cont.)

FORD
4-173

DTC B1602: INVALID KEY-CODE FORMAT FROM IGNITION KEY TRANSPONDER (PARTIAL KEY READ)

NOTE: Large metallic objects, a second PATS ignition key, or devices such as electronic credit cards on the same key ring may cause vehicle starting problem and possibly set this code. Ensure customers encoded ignition key is an approved Ford encoded ignition key. Encoded keys from Rotunda, Ilco, and Strattec are also approved keys.

1) Turn ignition switch to LOCK position. Using NGS tester, retrieve and record continuous DTCs. Clear continuous DTCs and perform PATS module self-test. If DTC B1602 is retrieved, go to next step. If DTC B1602 is not retrieved, system is operating properly. Check all other encoded ignition keys with PATS module self-test to verify all other encoded ignition keys are programmed.

2) Obtain NEW encoded ignition key and insert into ignition lock cylinder. Turn ignition switch to RUN position. Program NEW encoded ignition key. See KEY PROGRAMMING – ERASE ALL KEYS & PROGRAM 2 KEYS under PROGRAMMING. Using NGS tester, perform PATS module self-test. If DTC B1602 is retrieved, go to next step. If DTC B1602 is not retrieved, system is operating properly. If any other DTCs are retrieved, perform appropriate DTC test. See PASSIVE ANTI-THEFT SYSTEM MODULE DTC INDEX table under SELF-DIAGNOSTIC SYSTEM.

3) Turn ignition switch to LOCK position. Replace PATS transceiver module. Turn ignition switch to RUN position. Using NGS tester, perform PATS module self-test. If any DTCs are retrieved, perform appropriate DTC test. See PASSIVE ANTI-THEFT SYSTEM MODULE DTC INDEX table under SELF-DIAGNOSTIC SYSTEM. If no DTCs are retrieved, system is okay at this time.

DTC B1681: TRANSCEIVER DEFECTIVE OR NOT CONNECTED

1) Turn ignition switch to LOCK position. Using NGS tester, retrieve and record continuous DTCs. Clear continuous DTCs and perform PATS module self-test. If DTC B1681 is retrieved, go to next step. If DTC B1681 is not retrieved, system is operating properly.

2) Turn ignition switch to LOCK position. Disconnect PATS transceiver module harness connector C241. Turn ignition switch to RUN position. Measure voltage at terminal No. 2 (Violet/Light Blue wire) at PATS transceiver module harness connector C241. If voltage is greater than 9 volts, go to next step. If voltage is 9 volts or less, repair open in Violet/Light Blue wire between PATS module and PATS transceiver module.

3) Turn ignition switch to LOCK position. Measure resistance between ground and terminal No. 1 (Tan/White wire) at PATS transceiver module harness connector C241. If resistance is 5 ohms or less, go to next step. If resistance is greater than 5 ohms, repair Tan/White wire between PATS module and PATS transceiver module.

4) Connect PATS transceiver module harness connector C241. Turn ignition switch to RUN position. Using a voltmeter, backprobe at terminal No. 3 (Red/Black wire) at PATS transceiver module harness connector C241. If voltage is 9 volts or less, go to next step. If voltage is greater than 9 volts, go to step **6)**.

5) Turn ignition switch to LOCK position. Disconnect PATS transceiver module harness connector C241. Measure resistance between ground and terminal No. 3 (Red/Black wire) at PATS transceiver module harness connector C241. If resistance is greater than 100 ohms, go to next step. If resistance is 100 ohms or less, check for short to ground in Red/Black wire between PATS module and PATS transceiver module. If Red/Black wire is shorted to ground, repair or replace as necessary. If wire is okay, replace PATS module, then perform DTC B2139: SECURITY KEY DOES NOT MATCH BETWEEN PATS & PCM.

6) Disconnect PATS module harness connector C242. Measure resistance in Red/Black wire between terminal No. 3 at PATS transceiver module harness connector C241 and terminal No. 11 at PATS module harness connector C242. *See Fig. 1.* If resistance is 5 ohms or less, go to next step. If resistance is greater than 5 ohms, repair open in Red/Black wire.

7) Turn ignition switch to LOCK position. Connect PATS transceiver module harness connector C241. Connect PATS module harness connector C242. Turn ignition switch to RUN position. Using a voltmeter, backprobe at terminal No. 4 (Brown/Orange wire) at PATS transceiver module harness connector C241. If voltage is 9 volts or less, go to next step. If voltage is greater than 9 volts, go to step **9)**.

8) Turn ignition switch to LOCK position. Disconnect PATS transceiver module harness connector C241. Measure resistance between ground and terminal No. 4 (Brown/Orange wire) at PATS transceiver module harness connector C241. If resistance is greater than 100 ohms, go to next step. If resistance is 100 ohms or less, check for short to ground in Brown/Orange wire between PATS module and PATS transceiver module. If Brown/Orange wire is shorted to ground, repair or replace as necessary. If wire is okay, replace PATS module, then perform DTC B2139: SECURITY KEY DOES NOT MATCH BETWEEN PATS & PCM.

9) Turn ignition switch to LOCK position. Connect PATS transceiver module harness connector C241. Turn ignition switch to RUN position. Using NGS tester, access PATS module active command. Trigger TRANSMIT SIGNAL COMMAND to ON. Transmit signal produces a 2 seconds on, 2 seconds off voltage cycle. Using a voltmeter, backprobe at terminal No. 4 (Brown/Orange wire) at PATS transceiver module harness connector C241. If voltage drops from greater than 9 volts to one volt or less when active command is triggered on, go to next step. If voltage does not drop from greater than 9 volts to one volt or less when active command is triggered on, check for open in Brown/Orange wire between PATS module and PATS transceiver module. Repair or replace Brown/Orange wire as necessary. If Brown/Orange wire is okay, replace PATS module, then perform DTC B2139: SECURITY KEY DOES NOT MATCH BETWEEN PATS & PCM.

10) Turn ignition switch to LOCK position. Replace PATS transceiver module. Turn ignition switch to RUN position. Using NGS tester, perform PATS module self-test. If DTC B1681 is retrieved, go to next step. If DTC B1681 is not retrieved, system is operating properly. If any other DTCs are retrieved, perform appropriate DTC test.

11) Turn ignition switch to LOCK position. Replace PATS module, then perform DTC B2139: SECURITY KEY DOES NOT MATCH BETWEEN PATS & PCM, then return to complete this step. Turn ignition switch to RUN position. Using NGS tester, perform PATS module self-test. If DTC B1681 is retrieved, repair appropriate faulty circuit between PATS module and PATS transceiver module. If no DTCs are retrieved, system is operating properly. If any other DTCs are retrieved, perform appropriate DTC test.

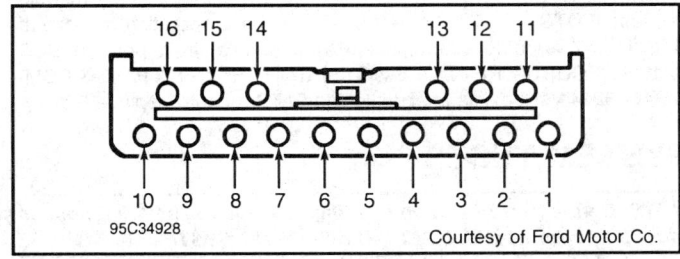

95C34928

Courtesy of Ford Motor Co.

Fig. 1: Identifying PATS Module Harness Connector C242 Terminals

DTC B2139: SECURITY KEY DOES NOT MATCH BETWEEN PATS & PCM

1) Turn ignition switch to LOCK position. Using NGS tester, retrieve and record continuous DTCs. Clear continuous DTCs and perform PATS module self-test. If DTC B2139 is retrieved, go to next step. If DTC B2139 is not retrieved, system is operating properly.

2) Perform security access for PATS module. See KEY PROGRAMMING – SECURITY ACCESS PROCEDURE under PROGRAMMING. Using NGS tester, select PARAMETER RESET command for PATS module. Perform security access for PCM. See KEY PROGRAMMING –

FORD
4-174

1999 ACCESSORIES & EQUIPMENT
Passive Anti-Theft Systems – Sable & Taurus (Cont.)

SECURITY ACCESS PROCEDURE under PROGRAMMING. Using NGS tester, select PARAMETER RESET command for PCM. Turn ignition switch to RUN position for 3 seconds. Turn ignition switch to LOCK position. Using NGS tester, perform PATS self-test. If DTC B2139 is not retrieved, system is operating properly. If DTC B2139 is retrieved, verify PCM calibration is correct for vehicle. If calibration is okay, replace PATS module. If DTC B2139 still exists, replace PCM.

DTC B2141: NO SECURITY IDENTIFICATION EXCHANGE BETWEEN PATS & PCM

1) Turn ignition switch to LOCK position. Using NGS tester, retrieve and record continuous DTCs. Clear continuous DTCs and perform PATS module self-test. If DTC B2141 and DTC U1147 are retrieved together, perform DTC U1147: VEHICLE SECURITY STATUS MISSING. If DTC B2141 is only DTC retrieved, go to next step. If no DTCs are retrieved, system is operating properly.

2) Perform security access for PCM. See KEY PROGRAMMING – SECURITY ACCESS PROCEDURE under PROGRAMMING. Using NGS tester, select PARAMETER RESET command for PCM. Turn ignition switch to RUN position for 3 seconds. Turn ignition switch to LOCK position. Using NGS tester, perform PATS module self-test. If DTC B2141 is not retrieved, system is operating properly. If DTC B2141 is retrieved, verify PCM calibration is correct for vehicle. If calibration is okay, replace PATS module, then perform DTC B2139: SECURITY KEY DOES NOT MATCH BETWEEN PATS & PCM. If DTC B2141 still exists after replacing PATS module, replace PCM.

DTC U1147: VEHICLE SECURITY STATUS MISSING

1) Start engine. If vehicle does not start with THEFT indicator flashing, go to next step. If vehicle starts with THEFT indicator flashing, problem is in PCM. See appropriate SELF-DIAGNOSTICS article in ENGINE PERFORMANCE in appropriate MITCHELL® manual.

2) Turn ignition switch to LOCK position. Using NGS tester, retrieve and record continuous DTCs. Clear continuous DTCs and perform PCM self-test. If NGS tester communicates with PCM, go to next step. If NGS tester does not communicate with NGS tester, problem is in communications network. See MODULE COMMUNICATIONS NETWORK – SABLE & TAURUS article.

3) Using NGS tester, retrieve and record continuous DTCs. Perform PCM self-test. If DTC P1260 is retrieved, go to next step. If DTC P1260 is not retrieved, check PCM power and ground circuits. See appropriate SELF-DIAGNOSTICS article in ENGINE PERFORMANCE in appropriate MITCHELL® manual.

4) Perform self-diagnostics. See SELF-DIAGNOSTIC SYSTEM. Turn ignition switch to LOCK position. Using NGS tester, retrieve and record continuous DTCs. Clear continuous DTCs and perform PATS module self-test. If DTC U1147 is not retrieved, system is operating properly. If DTC U1147 is retrieved, replace PATS module, then perform DTC B2139: SECURITY KEY DOES NOT MATCH BETWEEN PATS & PCM. If DTC B2141 still exists after replacing PATS module, replace PCM.

SYSTEM TESTS

NOTE: Before performing any testing procedures, self-diagnostics must be performed. See SELF-DIAGNOSTIC SYSTEM.

SYMPTOM CHART

Symptom	Test
No Communication With PATS Module	A
No THEFT Indicator Prove Out	B
THEFT Indicator Proves Out For 3 Seconds But Starter Does Not Engage	C

TEST A: NO MODULE COMMUNICATION WITH PASSIVE ANTI-THEFT MODULE

1) Turn ignition switch to LOCK position. Check fuses No. 10 (20-amp) and No. 23 (5-amp) in instrument panel fuse box. If fuses are blown, go to next step. If fuses are okay, go to step **3)**.

2) Disconnect PATS module harness connector C242. Measure resistance between ground and terminal No. 15 (White/Yellow wire) at PATS module harness connector C242. *See Fig. 1.* Also, measure resistance between ground and terminal No. 16 (Black wire) at PATS module harness connector C242. If both resistance reading are greater than 10 k/ohms, replace PATS module and fuses. If resistance is 10 k/ohms or less, repair short to ground in appropriate between instrument panel fuse box and PATS module.

3) Turn ignition switch to LOCK position. Disconnect PATS module harness connector C242. Turn ignition switch to RUN position. Measure voltage at terminals No. 15 (White/Yellow wire) and No. 16 (Black wire) at PATS module harness connector C242. *See Fig. 1.* If battery voltage exists at both terminals, go to next step. If battery voltage does not exist at either terminal, repair appropriate power distribution circuit. See appropriate wiring diagram in POWER DISTRIBUTION article in WIRING DIAGRAMS.

4) Turn ignition switch to LOCK position. Measure resistance between ground and terminal No. 7 (Black/White wire) at PATS module harness connector C242. If resistance is 5 ohms or less, repair module communication concern. See MODULE COMMUNICATIONS NETWORK – SABLE & TAURUS article. If resistance is greater than 5 ohms, repair open in Black/White wire between PATS module and ground.

TEST B: NO THEFT INDICATOR PROVE OUT

1) Observe THEFT indicator with ignition switch in LOCK and RUN positions. If THEFT indicator does not flash when ignition switch is in LOCK position and/or go out after 3 seconds when ignition switch is turned to RUN position, go to next step. If THEFT indicator flashes when ignition switch is in LOCK position and goes out after 3 seconds when ignition switch is turned to RUN position, check power to PATS module (White/Yellow wire). If White/Yellow wire is okay, replace PATS module, then perform DTC B2139: SECURITY KEY DOES NOT MATCH BETWEEN PATS & PCM under DIAGNOSTIC TESTS.

2) Turn ignition switch to RUN position. If THEFT indicator does not remain illuminated, go to step **4)**. If THEFT indicator remains illuminated, perform PATS module self-test. If no DTC were retrieved, go to next step. If any DTCs are retrieved, perform appropriate DTC test. See PASSIVE ANTI-THEFT SYSTEM MODULE DTC INDEX table under SELF-DIAGNOSTIC SYSTEM.

3) Turn ignition switch to LOCK position. Disconnect PATS module harness connector C242. Turn ignition switch to RUN position. If THEFT indicator is not illuminated, replace PATS module, then perform DTC B2139: SECURITY KEY DOES NOT MATCH BETWEEN PATS & PCM under DIAGNOSTIC TESTS. If THEFT indicator is illuminated, repair short to voltage in Dark Blue/Light Green wire between PATS module and instrument cluster harness connector C250.

4) Turn ignition switch to RUN position. Using NGS tester, access PATS active command. If active command can be accessed, go to next step. If active command can not be accessed, perform TEST A: NO MODULE COMMUNICATION WITH PASSIVE ANTI-THEFT MODULE.

5) Trigger PATS active command THEFT LMP to ON. If THEFT indicator does not illuminate, go to next step. If THEFT indicator illuminates, system is okay at this time.

6) Turn ignition switch to LOCK position. Disconnect instrument cluster harness connector C250. Turn ignition switch to RUN position. Trigger PATS active command THEFT LMP to ON. Measure voltage at terminal No. 6 (Dark Blue/Light Green wire) at instrument cluster harness connector C250. *See Fig. 2.* If voltage is 9 volts or less, go to next step. If voltage is greater than 9 volts exists, go to step **10)**.

7) Turn ignition switch to LOCK position. Disconnect PATS module harness connector C242. Measure resistance in Dark Blue/Light Green wire between terminal No. 6 at instrument cluster harness connector C250 and terminal No. 5 at PATS module harness connector C242. *See Figs. 1 and 2.* If resistance is 5 ohms or less, go to next step. If resistance is greater than 5 ohms, repair open in Dark Blue/Light Green wire.

8) Measure resistance between ground and terminal No. 6 (Dark Blue/Light Green wire) at instrument cluster harness connector C250. If

1999 ACCESSORIES & EQUIPMENT
Passive Anti-Theft Systems – Sable & Taurus (Cont.)

FORD
4-175

resistance is greater than 10 k/ohms, go to next step. If resistance is 10 k/ohms or less, repair short to ground in Dark Blue/Light Green wire.

9) Connect PATS module harness connector C242. Turn ignition switch to RUN position. Trigger PATS active command THEFT LMP to ON. Measure voltage at terminal No. 6 (Dark Blue/Light Green wire) at instrument cluster harness connector C250. If voltage is greater than 9 volts, go to next step. If voltage is 9 volts or less, replace PATS module.

10) Turn ignition switch to LOCK position. Remove THEFT indicator LED from instrument cluster. Check LED. If LED is okay, replace instrument cluster. If LED is not okay, replace LED.

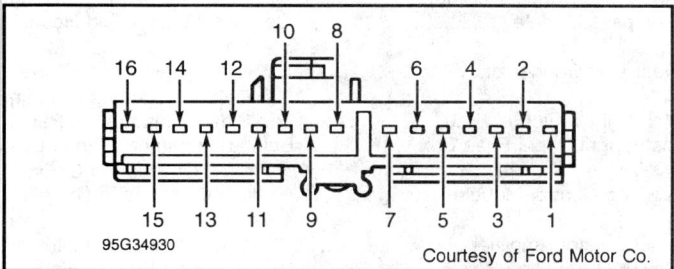

95G34930

Courtesy of Ford Motor Co.

Fig. 2: Identifying Instrument Cluster Harness Connector C250 Terminals

TEST C: THEFT INDICATOR PROVES OUT FOR 3 SECONDS BUT STARTER DOES NOT ENGAGE

1) Turn ignition switch to LOCK position. Using NGS tester, retrieve and record continuous DTCs. Clear continuous DTCs and perform PATS module self-test. If no DTCs are retrieved, go to next step. If any DTCs are retrieved, perform appropriate DTC test. See PASSIVE ANTI-THEFT SYSTEM MODULE DTC INDEX table under SELF-DIAGNOSTIC SYSTEM.

2) Turn ignition switch to LOCK position. Disconnect PATS module harness connector C242. Turn ignition switch to RUN position. Measure voltage at terminal No. 1 (Pink wire) at PATS module harness connector C242. If battery voltage exists, go to next step. If battery voltage does not exist, power distribution circuit. See appropriate wiring diagram in POWER DISTRIBUTION article in WIRING DIAGRAMS.

3) Turn ignition switch to LOCK position. Connect PATS module harness connector C242. Turn ignition switch to RUN position. Using a voltmeter, backprobe at terminal No. 1 (Pink wire) at PATS module connector C242. If voltage is less than one volt, repair Pink wire between PATS module and starter relay. If voltage is one volt or more and THEFT indicator proves out normally, replace PATS module, then perform DTC B2139: SECURITY KEY DOES NOT MATCH BETWEEN PATS & PCM under DIAGNOSTIC TESTS.

REMOVAL & INSTALLATION
PATS MODULE

NOTE: If PATS module is replaced, keys must be programmed. See PROGRAMMING.

Removal & Installation – Disconnect battery ground cable. Remove integrated control panel. See appropriate INSTRUMENT PANELS article. Remove PATS module bracket retaining screw. Disconnect wiring harness connector and remove PATS module. To install, reverse removal procedure.

TRANSCEIVER MODULE

WARNING: To avoid injury from accidental air bag deployment, read and carefully follow all WARNINGS and SERVICE PRECAUTIONS in appropriate AIR BAG RESTRAINT SYSTEMS article.

Removal & Installation – Remove ignition lock cylinder. See appropriate STEERING COLUMN SWITCHES article. Remove screw attaching transceiver to underside of steering column. Using a small screwdriver, gently pry transceiver over key cylinder lower rib. Disconnect wiring harness connector and remove transceiver. To install, reverse removal procedure.

WIRING DIAGRAMS

NOTE: For passive anti-theft system wiring diagram, see ACTIVE ANTI-THEFT SYSTEMS – SABLE & TAURUS article.

DESCRIPTION

Passive Anti-Theft System (PATS) vehicle protection system is designed to prevent driveaway thefts. The system is passive in that it does not require any activity from the user. System uses radio frequency identification technology to verify if proper key is being used to attempt to start the vehicle.

During each starting sequence, the encoded ignition key is interrogated by the instrument cluster. If the key's identification code is programmed into anti-theft system, vehicle is capable of starting. If key's identification code is incorrect or missing, vehicle is prevented from starting.

PATS module communicates with the Powertrain Control Module (PCM) through the Module Communications Network. PCM then determines if engine will be enabled to start.

PATS vehicle protection system consists of these components: anti-theft indicator (THEFT) light, transceiver module, encoded ignition key, instrument cluster, Powertrain Control Module (PCM), module communications network and Lighting Control Module (LCM).

OPERATION

ANTI-THEFT INDICATOR (THEFT) LIGHT

THEFT indicator is used to prove-out system operation status. PATS uses the THEFT indicator light when ignition is in start or run. When system is functioning properly and ignition switch is turned to RUN or START position, THEFT indicator light will turn on for 3 seconds, then turn off. Vehicle will be enabled to start and run. If THEFT indicator light is on continuously for more than 3 seconds or flashes rapidly, a problem exists in passive anti-theft system.

ENCODED IGNITION KEY

The encoded ignition key is much larger in size to accommodate the electronics located inside plastic cover. Each encoded ignition key must be programmed into the instrument cluster. When ignition is in start or run, the instrument cluster initiates the encoded ignition key interrogation process. During each vehicle start sequence, the transceiver module reads the encoded ignition key identification code and sends data to the instrument cluster.

TRANSCEIVER MODULE

Transceiver module communicates with encoded ignition key. During each vehicle start sequence, the transceiver module reads the encoded ignition key identification code and sends data to the instrument cluster.

INSTRUMENT CLUSTER

NOTE: Instrument cluster may also be referred to as Hybrid Electronic Cluster (HEC).

Instrument cluster performs all passive anti-theft system functions. The instrument cluster receives identification code from encoded ignition key and controls engine enable. The instrument cluster initiates the encoded ignition key interrogation process when ignition is in start or run. The instrument cluster communicates with Lighting Control Module (LCM), which controls the anti-theft indicator light.

The Passive Anti-Theft System (PATS) utilizes a self-diagnostic system which stores a Diagnostic Trouble Code (DTC) in instrument cluster or Lighting Control Module (LCM) if a problem exists in PATS. DTCs may be retrieved from instrument cluster or LCM by using New Generation Star (NGS) tester and Data Link Connector (DLC).

POWERTRAIN CONTROL MODULE (PCM)

Passive anti-theft system uses PCM to enable or disable vehicle's engine. The instrument cluster communicates with PCM over the module communications network to enable or disable engine operation.

COMPONENT LOCATIONS

COMPONENT LOCATIONS

Component	Location
Anti-Theft Transceiver Module	Top Of Steering Column
Compass Module	Center Of Windshield Header On Mirror
Data Link Connector	Under Instrument Panel, Right Of Steering Column
Headlight Switch	Left Side Of Instrument Panel
Instrument Panel Fuse Box	Behind Instrument Panel, Left Of Steering Column
Lighting Control Module	Behind Center Of Instrument Panel
Light Sensor Amplifier	Above Instrument Cluster
Power Distribution Box	Left Side Of Engine Compartment, In Front Of Wheel Well
Powertrain Control Module (PCM)	Left Rear Of Engine Compartment On Firewall

PROGRAMMING

KEY PROGRAMMING – SECURITY ACCESS PROCEDURE

NOTE: Security access must be granted to erase ignition keys, enable/disable spare key programming switch, or perform parameter resets for instrument cluster or PCM. This procedure has a 10-minute time delay prior to granting security access during which the New Generation Star (NGS) tester must remain connected to vehicle. After security access has been granted, security access command menu is displayed which offers various command options. Multiple security access commands can be executed (if necessary) prior to exiting security access command menu. Execution of all necessary security access commands prior to exiting command menu avoids the performance of an additional security access procedure and the associated 10-minute time delay. Security access for the instrument cluster and security access for the PCM must be obtained separately as needed (each will require a 10-minute time delay.

With ignition switch in RUN position and NGS tester connected to vehicle, enter function test menu. Select SECURITY ACCESS PROCEDURE. This procedure will take 10 minutes to perform. After the security access procedure has been completed, a new menu will be displayed with command options. Select as many functions as required before exiting this menu. Once this menu is exited, security access procedure must be performed again to perform additional commands.

1999 ACCESSORIES & EQUIPMENT
Passive Anti-Theft Systems – Town Car (Cont.)

FORD
4-177

KEY PROGRAMMING – WITH PROGRAMMED KEYS

NOTE: This procedure will only work if 2 or more programmed ignition keys are available and there is a need to program additional keys. If 2 keys are not available, perform KEY PROGRAMMING – WITHOUT PROGRAMMED KEYS. PID SPARE_KY must be enabled for this procedure to operate. To enable this PID, perform KEY PROGRAMMING – SECURITY ACCESS PROCEDURE and enable spare key programming switch. If programming procedure is successful, new key(s) will start vehicle and THEFT indicator will illuminate for 3 seconds. If programming procedure is not successful, new key(s) will not start vehicle and THEFT indicator will flash for one minute (after flashing for one minute, THEFT indicator will flash fault code). If necessary, repeat programming procedure. If programming of key(s) is still unsuccessful, perform self-diagnostics. See SELF-DIAGNOSTIC SYSTEM. Maximum of eight keys can be programmed into system. If procedure is not performed as outlined, programming procedure will end. Ignition keys must have correct mechanical key cut for vehicle and must be an encoded key.

1) Insert first programmed ignition key into ignition lock cylinder. Turn ignition switch from LOCK to RUN position (ignition switch must stay in RUN position for one second). Turn ignition switch to LOCK position and remove ignition key from ignition lock cylinder.

2) Within 5 seconds of turning ignition switch to LOCK position, insert second programmed ignition key into ignition lock cylinder. Turn ignition switch from LOCK to RUN position (ignition switch must stay in RUN position for one second). Turn ignition switch to LOCK position and remove second ignition key from ignition lock cylinder.

3) Within 10 seconds of turning ignition switch to LOCK position, insert a NEW unprogrammed ignition key into ignition lock cylinder. Turn ignition switch from LOCK to RUN position (ignition switch must stay in RUN position for one second). Turn ignition switch to LOCK position and remove ignition key from ignition lock cylinder. New ignition key should now be programmed. To program additional key(s), repeat key programming procedure from step **1)**.

KEY PROGRAMMING – WITHOUT PROGRAMMED KEYS

NOTE: This procedure is used when a customer needs keys programmed into system and does not have 2 programmed ignition keys available, or when programmed ignition keys have been lost and/or ignition switch assembly has been replaced. This procedure will erase all programmed ignition keys from memory and prevent vehicle from starting until 2 keys have been programmed. Ignition keys must have correct mechanical key cut for vehicle and must be an encoded key. If additional key(s) are to be programmed, perform KEY PROGRAMMING – WITH PROGRAMMED KEYS. If remaining keys are with customer and not with vehicle, instruct customer to see owner's manual to program spare key(s).

1) Turn ignition switch from LOCK to RUN position. With NGS tester connected to vehicle, enter function test menu. Select SECURITY ACCESS PROCEDURE. This procedure will take 10 minutes to perform. After the security access procedure has been completed, a new menu will be displayed with command options. Select IGNITION KEY CODE ERASE.

2) Turn ignition switch to LOCK position and disconnect NGS tester. Insert first encoded ignition key into ignition lock cylinder. Turn ignition switch to RUN position for 3 seconds. Turn ignition switch to LOCK position and remove first encoded key.

3) Insert second encoded ignition key into ignition lock cylinder. Turn ignition switch to RUN position for 3 seconds. Turn ignition switch to LOCK position and remove second encoded key. Both encoded ignition keys should now start vehicle.

KEY PROGRAMMING – SPARE KEY PROGRAMMING SWITCH

NOTE: The spare key programming switch is a programmable switch which provides the capability to enable/disable the normal customer spare key programming procedure detailed in the owner's manual. This programmable switch is provided as a convenience for rental company fleets or other fleet purchasers who may not want the spare key programming procedure available to the vehicle driver. The spare key programming switch state can be viewed using instrument cluster PID SPARE_KY.

Insert a programmed ignition key into ignition lock cylinder. Turn ignition switch from LOCK to RUN position. With NGS tester connected to vehicle, enter function test menu. Select SECURITY ACCESS PROCEDURE. This procedure will take 10 minutes to perform. After security access procedure has been completed, a new menu will be displayed with command options. Default setting on all new vehicles is ENABLE. Select SPARE KEY PROGRAMMING SWITCH. Set SPARE KEY PROGRAMMING SWITCH to ENABLE or DISABLE.

TRANSMITTER

NOTE: After first remote transmitter is programmed, all other remote transmitters will be erased. All remote transmitters must be programmed at the same time. Up to 4 transmitters may be programmed at one time.

1) Cycle ignition switch from LOCK to RUN positions 4 times within 3 seconds. Locks will lock and unlock to confirm programming mode has been entered. Press any button on remote transmitter.

2) If additional remote transmitters are to be programmed, press any button on remaining remote transmitters within 7.5 seconds. To exit programming mode, turn ignition switch to START position or wait 7.5 seconds.

SELF-DIAGNOSTIC SYSTEM

Verify customer's complaint. Ensure electronically coded ignition key is being used. Check for damaged ignition lock cylinder switch, damaged encoded ignition key or open fuses. Check for loose or corroded connectors, damaged wiring harness, damaged ignition switch or damaged transceiver module. Repair or replace components as necessary.

If all components are okay, connect New Generation Star (NGS) tester to Data Link Connector (DLC). Using NGS tester, perform data link diagnostics test. See DATA LINK DIAGNOSTIC TEST under COMMUNICATION NETWORK DIAGNOSTICS in MODULE COMMUNICATIONS NETWORK – TOWN CAR article. If NGS tester responds with CKT914, CKT915 or CKT70=ALL ECUS NO RESP/NOT EQUIP, repair module communications concern. See MODULE COMMUNICATIONS NETWORK – TOWN CAR article. If NGS tester displays NO RESP/NOT EQUIP for instrument cluster, perform TEST A: NO COMMUNICATION WITH INSTRUMENT CLUSTER under SYSTEM TESTS. If NGS tester displays NO RESP/NOT EQUIP for Lighting Control Module (LCM), perform TEST B: NO COMMUNICATION WITH LIGHTING CONTROL MODULE under SYSTEM TESTS.

If NGS tester responds with SYSTEM PASSED, retrieve and record continuous DTCs. Erase continuous DTCs. Using NGS tester, perform instrument cluster and LCM self-test. Perform appropriate test in accordance with DTC retrieved. See INSTRUMENT CLUSTER DTC INDEX and/or LIGHTING CONTROL MODULE DTC INDEX table. Codes listed in these tables are only for testing covered in this article. For complete DTC listing, see MODULE COMMUNICATIONS NETWORK – TOWN CAR article. If no DTCs are retrieved, repair by symptom. See SYMPTOM CHART table under SYSTEM TESTS.

FORD
4-178

1999 ACCESSORIES & EQUIPMENT
Passive Anti-Theft Systems – Town Car (Cont.)

INSTRUMENT CLUSTER DTC INDEX

DTC [1]	Description	Test
B1213	Number Of Programmed Ignition Keys Below Minimum	[2] DTC B1213
B1232/2103	Antenna Not Connected/Defective Transceiver	DTC B1232/2103
B1342	ECU Defective	[3]
B1600	PATS Ignition Key Transponder Signal Not Received (Damaged Key Or Non-PATS Key)	DTC B1600
B1601	PATS Received Incorrect Key-Code From Ignition Key Transponder	DTC B1601
B1602	PATS Received Invalid Key-Code Format From Transponder	DTC B1602
B1681	PATS Transceiver Signal Is Not Received	DTC B1681
B2139	PATS Data Mismatch	DTC B2139
B2141	NVM Configuration Failure	DTC B2141
U1147	Invalid/Missing Data For Vehicle Security	DTC U1147

[1] – Codes listed in this table are only for testing covered in this article. For complete DTC listing, see MODULE COMMUNICATIONS NETWORK – TOWN CAR article.
[2] – If DTCs B1232, B1600, B1601, B1602 OR B1681 are also present, service these DTCs frist then recheck codes.
[3] – Using NGS tester, retrieve and record DTCs. Perform instrument cluster self-test. If DTC B1342 still exists, replace instrument cluster.

LIGHTING CONTROL MODULE DTC INDEX

DTC [1]	Description	Test
B1342	ECU Defective	[2]

[1] – Codes listed in this table are only for testing covered in this article. For complete DTC listing, see MODULE COMMUNICATIONS NETWORK – TOWN CAR article.
[2] – Using NGS tester, retrieve and record DTCs. Perform Lighting Control Module (LCM) self-test. If DTC B1342 still exists, replace LCM.

DIAGNOSTIC TESTS

CAUTION: When battery is disconnected or modules are replaced, vehicle computer and memory systems may lose memory data. Driveability problems may exist until computer systems have completed a relearn cycle. See COMPUTER RELEARN PROCEDURES article in GENERAL INFORMATION before disconnecting battery.

DTC B1213: NUMBER OF PROGRAMMED IGNITION KEYS BELOW MINIMUM

1) Using NGS tester, retrieve and record continuous DTCs. Clear continuous DTCs and perform instrument cluster self-test. If DTC B1213 is the only code retrieved, go to next step. If DTC B1213 is not the only code present, clear DTCs. Repeat instrument cluster self-test. Retest system operation.

2) Using NGS tester, monitor instrument cluster PID NUMKEYS. If PID indicates less than 2 encoded ignition keys programmed, go to next step. If PID indicates more than 2 encoded ignition keys programmed, system is okay at this time.

3) Obtain NEW encoded ignition key(s). Insert key into ignition lock cylinder. Turn ignition switch to RUN position. Program key. See KEY PROGRAMMING – WITHOUT PROGRAMMED KEYS under PROGRAMMING. If THEFT indicator illuminates for 3 seconds and then goes out, clear DTCs and perform instrument cluster self-test to ensure all codes have been cleared. Retest system operation. If THEFT indicator illuminates continuously, repeat this step with a second NEW encoded ignition key. If THEFT indicator flashes, retrieve DTCs for new fault and perform appropriate DTC test.

DTC B1232/2103: ANTENNA NOT CONNECTED/DEFECTIVE TRANSCEIVER

Turn ignition switch to LOCK position. Verify transceiver module is installed properly. See TRANSCEIVER MODULE under REMOVAL & INSTALLATION. Using NGS tester, retrieve and record continuous DTCs. Clear continuous DTCs and perform instrument cluster self-test. If DTC B1232 is retrieved, replace transceiver module. Clear DTCs and repeat instrument cluster self-test. Retest system operation. If DTC B1232 is not retrieved, system is operating properly.

DTC B1600: PATS IGNITION KEY TRANSPONDER SIGNAL NOT RECEIVED (DAMMAGED KEY OR NON-PATS KEY)

NOTE: Large metallic objects, a second PATS ignition key, or devices such as electronic credit cards on the same key ring may cause vehicle starting problem and possibly set this code. Ensure customer's encoded ignition key is an approved Ford encoded ignition key. Encoded keys from Rotunda, Ilco, and Strattec are also approved keys.

1) Using NGS tester, retrieve and record continuous DTCs. Clear continuous DTCs. Perform PATS self-test. If DTC B1600 is retrieved, go to next step. If any other DTCs are retrieved, perform appropriate DTC test. See INSTRUMENT CLUSTER DTC INDEX table under SELF-DIAGNOSTIC SYSTEM. If no DTCs are retrieved, system is okay at this time.

2) Turn ignition switch to LOCK position. Obtain NEW encoded ignition key(s). Insert NEW key into ignition lock cylinder. Turn ignition switch to RUN position. Program key. See KEY PROGRAMMING – WITHOUT PROGRAMMED KEYS under PROGRAMMING. Using NGS tester, perform instrument cluster self-test. If DTC B1600 is still present, go to next step. If any other DTCs are present, perform appropriate test. See INSTRUMENT CLUSTER DTC INDEX table under SELF-DIAGNOSTIC SYSTEM. If no DTCs are present, system is okay at this time.

3) Ensure ignition switch is in LOCK position. Replace transceiver module. Using customer's original encoded ignition key, turn ignition switch to RUN position. Using NGS tester, perform instrument cluster self-test. If DTC B1600 is retrieved, replace instrument cluster and then perform DTC B2139: PATS DATA MISMATCH. If DTC B1600 is not retrieved, system is okay at this time.

DTC B1601: PATS RECEIVED INCORRECT KEY-CODE FROM IGNITION KEY TRANSPONDER

NOTE: Large metallic objects, a second PATS ignition key, or devices such as electronic credit cards on the same key ring may cause vehicle starting problem and possibly set this code. Ensure customer's encoded ignition key is an approved Ford encoded ignition key. Encoded keys from Rotunda, Ilco, and Strattec are also approved keys.

1) Connect NGS tester to Data Link Connector (DLC). Using NGS tester, retrieve and record continuous DTCs. Clear continuous DTCs and perform instrument cluster self-test. If DTC B1601 is retrieved, go to next step. If DTC B1601 is not present, system is okay at this time. Check all customer encoded ignition keys with instrument cluster self-test to verify all other encoded ignition keys are programmed.

2) Using NGS tester, monitor instrument cluster PID NUMKEYS. If instrument cluster PID NUMKEYS does not indicate 8 encoded ignition keys programmed, go to next step. If instrument cluster PID NUMKEYS

1999 ACCESSORIES & EQUIPMENT
Passive Anti-Theft Systems – Town Car (Cont.)

FORD
4-179

indicates 8 encoded ignition keys programmed, erase and reprogram key codes. See KEY PROGRAMMING – WITHOUT PROGRAMMED KEYS under PROGRAMMING.

3) Verify there are at least 2 currently programmed encoded ignition keys available with vehicle. If 2 currently programmed encoded ignition keys are available with vehicle, go to next step. If 2 currently programmed encoded ignition keys are not available with vehicle, obtain 2 NEW encoded ignition keys. Program encoded ignition keys. See KEY PROGRAMMING – WITHOUT PROGRAMMED KEYS under PROGRAMMING. After encoded ignition keys are programmed, go to step 5).

4) Using NGS tester, monitor instrument cluster PID SPARE_KY. If instrument cluster PID SPARE_KEY indicates ENABLE, see KEY PROGRAMMING – WITH PROGRAMMED KEYS under PROGRAMMING. If instrument cluster PID SPARE_KY does not indicate ENABLE, see KEY PROGRAMMING – SPARE KEY PROGRAMMING SWITCH under PROGRAMMING to enable instrument cluster PID SPARE_KY to ENABLE.

5) Turn ignition switch to LOCK position. Using first encoded ignition key, start vehicle. Using second encoded ignition key, start vehicle. If both encoded ignition keys do not start vehicle, go to next step. If both encoded ignition keys start vehicle, system is operating properly. If there is a need to program additional encoded ignition keys, see KEY PROGRAMMING – SPARE KEY PROGRAMMING SWITCH under PROGRAMMING.

6) Using NGS tester, retrieve and record continuous DTCs. Clear continuous DTCs and perform instrument cluster self-test. If DTC B1601 is retrieved, replace instrument cluster. If DTC B1601 is not retrieved, system is okay at this time. If any other DTCs exist, perform appropriate test. See INSTRUMENT CLUSTER DTC INDEX table under SELF-DIAGNOSTIC SYSTEM.

DTC 1602: PATS RECEIVED INVALID KEY-CODE FORMAT FROM IGNITION KEY TRANSPONDER

NOTE: Large metallic objects, a second PATS ignition key, or devices such as electronic credit cards on the same key ring may cause vehicle starting problem and possibly set this code. Ensure customer's encoded ignition key is an approved Ford encoded ignition key. Encoded keys from Rotunda, Ilco, and Strattec are also approved keys.

1) Turn ignition switch to LOCK position. Connect NGS tester to Data Link Connector (DLC). Using NGS tester, retrieve and record continuous DTCs. Clear continuous DTCs and perform instrument cluster self-test. If DTC B1602 is retrieved, go to next step. If DTC B1602 is not retrieved, system is okay at this time. Check all customer encoded ignition keys with instrument cluster self-test to verify all other keys are programmed.

2) Turn ignition switch to LOCK position. Obtain a NEW encoded ignition key. Using encoded ignition key, turn ignition switch to RUN position. Program encoded ignition key. See KEY PROGRAMMING – WITHOUT PROGRAMMED KEYS under PROGRAMMING. Using NGS tester, perform instrument cluster self-test. If DTC B1602 is retrieved, go to next step. If no DTCs are retrieved, system is okay at this time.

3) Ensure ignition switch is in LOCK position. Replace transceiver module. Turn ignition switch to RUN position. Using NGS tester, perform instrument cluster self-test. If no DTCs are retrieved, system is okay at this time. If any other DTCs are retrieved, perform appropriate test. See INSTRUMENT CLUSTER DTC INDEX table under SELF-DIAGNOSTIC SYSTEM.

DTC B1681: PATS TRANSCEIVER SIGNAL IS NOT RECEIVED

1) Turn ignition switch to LOCK position. Connect NGS tester to Data Link Connector (DLC). Using NGS tester, retrieve and record continuous DTCs. Clear DTCs and perform instrument cluster self-test. If DTC B1681 is retrieved, go to next step. If DTC B1681 is not retrieved, system is okay at this time.

2) Ensure ignition switch is in LOCK position. Disconnect transceiver module harness connector C209. Turn ignition switch to RUN position.

Measure voltage at terminal No. 2 (Red/Light Green wire) at transceiver module harness connector C209. *See Fig. 1.* If voltage is 9 volts or greater, go to next step. If voltage is less than 9 volts, repair Red/Light Green wire between instrument panel fuse block fuse No. 12 (15-amp) and transceiver module.

3) Turn ignition switch to LOCK position. Measure resistance between ground and terminal No. 1 (Pink/Orange wire) at transceiver module harness connector C209. If resistance is 5 ohms or less, go to next step. If resistance is greater than 5 ohms, repair open in Pink/Orange wire between transceiver module and ground.

4) Connect transceiver module harness connector C209. Turn ignition switch to RUN position. Using a voltmeter, backprobe at terminal No. 3 (Gray/Orange wire) at transceiver module harness connector C209. If voltage is 9 volts or less, go to next step. If voltage is greater than 9 volts, go to step **7)**.

5) Turn ignition switch to LOCK position. Disconnect transceiver module harness connector C209. Measure resistance between ground and terminal No. 3 (Gray/Orange wire) at transceiver module harness connector C209. If resistance is greater than 100 ohms, go to next step. If resistance is 100 ohms or less, check Gray/Orange wire for short to ground and repair as necessary. If circuit is okay, replace instrument cluster and perform DTC B2139: PATS DATA MISMATCH.

6) Disconnect instrument cluster harness connector C254. Measure resistance in Gray/Orange wire between terminal No. 21 at instrument cluster harness connector C254 and terminal No. 3 at transceiver module harness connector C209. *See Figs. 1 and 2.* If resistance is 5 ohms or less, go to next step. If resistance is greater than 5 ohms, repair open in Gray/Orange wire.

7) Ensure ignition switch is in LOCK position. Connect transceiver module harness connector C209 and instrument cluster harness connector C254. Turn ignition switch to RUN position. Using a voltmeter, backprobe at terminal No. 3 (Gray/Orange wire) at transceiver module harness connector C209. If voltage is 9 volts or less, go to next step. If voltage is greater than 9 volts, go to step **9)**.

8) Turn ignition switch to LOCK position. Disconnect transceiver module harness connector C209. Measure resistance between ground and terminal No. 4 (White/Light Green wire) at transceiver module harness connector C209. If resistance is greater than 100 ohms, go to next step. If resistance is 100 ohms or less, check White/Light Green wire for short to ground and repair as necessary. If circuit is okay, replace instrument cluster.

9) Connect transceiver module harness connector C209. Turn ignition switch to RUN position. Using NGS tester, trigger instrument cluster active command TRANSMIT SIGNAL COMMAND TRANSMIT to ON. Using a voltmeter, backprobe at terminal No. 4 (White/Light Green wire) at transceiver module harness connector C209 while triggering active command from ON to OFF. Voltage should be greater than 9 volts in OFF position and less than one volt in ON position. If voltage is as specified, go to next step. If voltage is not as specified, check for open in White/Light Green wire between transceiver module and instrument cluster and repair as necessary. If circuit is okay, replace instrument cluster.

10) Turn ignition switch to LOCK position. Replace transceiver module. Turn ignition switch to RUN position. Using NGS tester, perform instrument cluster self-test. If DTC B1681 is retrieved, go to next step. If DTC B1681 is not retrieved, system is okay at this time.

11) Turn ignition switch to LOCK position. Replace instrument cluster. Turn ignition switch to RUN position. Using NGS tester, perform instrument cluster self-test. If DTC B1681 is retrieved, repair White/Light Green or Gray/Orange wire(s) between transceiver module and instrument cluster. If no DTCs are retrieved, system is okay at his time. If any other DTCs are retrieved, perform appropriate test. See INSTRUMENT CLUSTER DTC INDEX table under SELF-DIAGNOSTIC SYSTEM.

FORD
4-180

1999 ACCESSORIES & EQUIPMENT
Passive Anti-Theft Systems – Town Car (Cont.)

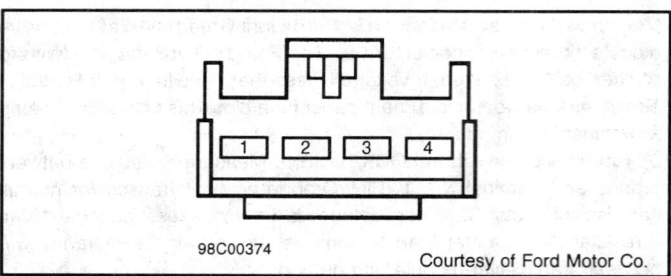

Fig. 1: Identifying Transceiver Module Harness Connector C209 Terminals

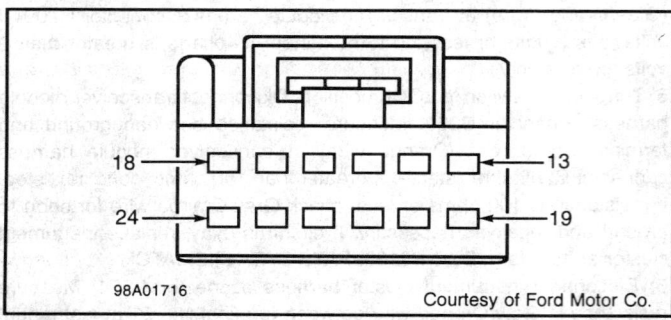

Fig. 2: Identifying Instrument Cluster Harness Connector C254 Terminals

DTC B2139: PATS DATA MISMATCH

1) Turn ignition switch to LOCK position. Connect NGS tester to Data Link Connector (DLC). Using NGS tester, retrieve and record continuous DTCs. Clear continuous DTCs and perform instrument cluster self-test. If DTC B2139 is retrieved, go to next step. If DTC B2139 is not retrieved, system is okay at this time.

2) Perform security access for instrument cluster. See KEY PROGRAMMING – SECURITY ACCESS PROCEDURE under PROGRAMMING. Using NGS tester, select PARAMETER RESET command for instrument cluster. Perform security access for Powertrain Control Module (PCM). See KEY PROGRAMMING – SECURITY ACCESS PROCEDURE under PROGRAMMING. Using NGS tester, select PARAMETER RESET command for PCM. Turn ignition switch to RUN position for 30 seconds. Using NGS tester, clear continuous DTCs. Turn ignition switch to LOCK position. Using NGS tester, perform instrument cluster self-test. If DTC B2139 is not retrieved, system is okay at this time. If DTC B2139 is retrieved, verify PCM calibration is correct for vehicle. If calibration is okay, go to next step.

3) Repeat step 2). If DTC B2139 still exists, replace instrument cluster. If DTC B2139 does not exist, system is okay at this time. If any other DTCs are retrieved, perform appropriate test. See INSTRUMENT CLUSTER DTC INDEX table under SELF-DIAGNOSTIC SYSTEM.

DTC B2141: NVM CONFIGURATION FAILURE

1) Turn ignition switch to LOCK position. Connect NGS tester to Data Link Connector (DLC). Using NGS tester, retrieve and record continuous DTCs. Clear continuous DTCs and perform instrument cluster self-test. If DTC B2141 or no DTCs are retrieved, go to next step. If DTC B2141 and DTC U1147 are retrieved together, perform DTC U1147: INVALID/ MISSING DATA FOR VEHICLE SECURITY test.

2) Insert diagnostic card for PCM active command KEEP ALIVE MEMORY RESET. Turn ignition switch to LOCK position. Turn ignition switch to RUN position for 30 seconds. Turn ignition switch to LOCK position. Attempt to start vehicle. If vehicle does not start, go to next step. If vehicle starts, system is okay at this time.

3) Using NGS tester, clear continuous DTCs. Turn ignition switch to LOCK position. Turn ignition switch to RUN position. Using NGS tester, perform instrument cluster self-test. If DTC B2141 is retrieved, go to next step. If DTC B2141 is not retrieved, repair any other DTCs that are retrieved. See INSTRUMENT CLUSTER DTC INDEX table under SELF-DIAGNOSTIC SYSTEM.

4) Repeat step 3). If DTC B2139 is still exists, ensure PCM calibration is correct. If PCM calibration is correct, replace instrument cluster. If DTC B2139 does not exist, system is okay at this time. If any other DTCs are retrieved, perform appropriate test. See INSTRUMENT CLUSTER DTC INDEX table under SELF-DIAGNOSTIC SYSTEM.

DTC U1147: INVALID/MISSING DATA FOR VEHICLE SECURITY

1) Start engine. If vehicle does not start with THEFT indicator flashing, go to next step. If vehicle starts with THEFT indicator flashing, problem is in PCM. See appropriate SELF-DIAGNOSTICS article in ENGINE PERFORMANCE in appropriate MITCHELL® manual.

2) Connect NGS tester to Data Link Connector (DLC). Using NGS tester, retrieve and record continuous DTCs. Clear DTCs and perform PCM self-test. If NGS tester communicates with PCM, go to next step. If NGS tester does not communicate with NGS tester, repair communications network concern. See MODULE COMMUNICATIONS NETWORK – TOWN CAR article.

3) Using NGS tester, retrieve and record continuous DTCs. If DTC P1260 is retrieved, go to next step. If DTC P1260 is not retrieved, see appropriate SELF-DIAGNOSTICS article in ENGINE PERFORMANCE in appropriate MITCHELL® manual to continue diagnosis.

4) Turn ignition switch to LOCK position. Using NGS tester, retrieve and record continuous DTCs. Clear DTCs and perform instrument cluster self-test. If DTC U1147 is not retrieved, system is okay at this time. If DTC U1147 is retrieved, replace instrument cluster. If DTC U1147 still exists after instrument cluster replacement, replace PCM.

SYSTEM TESTS

CAUTION: When battery is disconnected or modules are replaced, vehicle computer and memory systems may lose memory data. Driveability problems may exist until computer systems have completed a relearn cycle. See COMPUTER RELEARN PROCEDURES article in GENERAL INFORMATION before disconnecting battery.

SYMPTOM CHART

Symptom	Test
No Communication With Instrument Cluster	A
No Communication With Lighting Control Module	B
THEFT Indicator Is Always/Never On Or THEFT Indicator Will Not Prove-Out	C
Vehicle Starts But THEFT Indicator Flashes Fault Code When Ignition Switch Is In RUN Position	1
Vehicle Does Not Start	2

1 – Perform DTC U1147: INVALID/MISSING DATA FOR VEHICLE SECURITY under DIAGNOSTIC TESTS.
2 – Using NGS tester, perform instrument cluster self-test. Retrieve DTCs. If DTCs are present, perform appropriate test. See INSTRUMENT CLUSTER DTC INDEX table under SELF-DIAGNOSTIC SYSTEM. If no DTCs are present, system is okay at this time.

TEST A: NO COMMUNICATION WITH INSTRUMENT CLUSTER

1) Turn ignition switch to LOCK position. Disconnect instrument cluster harness connector C255. Turn ignition switch to RUN position. Measure voltage at terminal No. 9 (Gray/Yellow wire) at instrument cluster harness connector C255. *See Fig. 3.* If voltage is greater than 10 volts, go to next step. If voltage is 10 volts or less, go to step 3).

2) Turn ignition switch to LOCK position. Measure resistance between ground and terminal No. 10 (Pink/Orange wire) at instrument cluster harness connector C255. If resistance is 5 ohms or less, repair module communication concern. See MODULE COMMUNICATIONS NETWORK – TOWN CAR article. If resistance is greater than 5 ohms, repair open in Pink/Orange wire.

3) Turn ignition switch to LOCK position. Check fuse No. 4 (7.5-amp) in instrument panel fuse box. If fuse is okay, go to next step. If fuse is blown, go to step 5).

1999 ACCESSORIES & EQUIPMENT
Passive Anti-Theft Systems – Town Car (Cont.)

FORD
4-181

4) Turn ignition switch to RUN position. Measure voltage at input side of fuse No. 4 in instrument panel fuse box. If voltage is greater than 10 volts, repair open in Gray/Yellow wire between fuse No. 4 (7.5-amp) in instrument panel fuse box and instrument cluster, then repeat DATA LINK DIAGNOSTIC TEST. If voltage is 10 volts or less, repair open in Pink/Black wire between instrument panel fuse block and ignition switch, then repeat DATA LINK DIAGNOSTIC TEST.

5) Measure resistance between ground and terminal No. 9 at instrument cluster harness connector C255. If resistance is 10 k/ohms or less, repair short to ground in Gray/Yellow wire between fuse No. 4 (7.5-amp) in instrument panel fuse box and instrument cluster, then repeat DATA LINK DIAGNOSTIC TEST. If resistance is greater than 10 k/ohms, replace fuse No. 4 (7.5-amp) in instrument panel fuse box, then repeat DATA LINK DIAGNOSTIC TEST. If fuse fails again, replace instrument cluster.

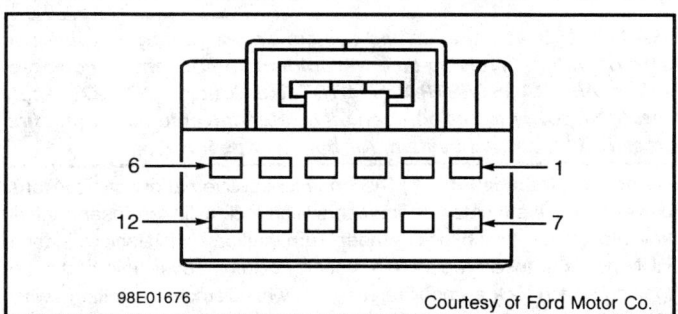

98E01676   Courtesy of Ford Motor Co.

Fig. 3: Identifying Instrument Cluster Harness Connector C255 Terminals

TEST B: NO COMMUNICATION WITH LIGHTING CONTROL MODULE

1) Turn ignition switch to LOCK position. Using NGS tester, monitor LCM PID IGN_LC. If NGS tester does not display UNABLE TO PERFORM TEST/FUNCTION MODULE NOT RESPONDING: LCM CHECK IGNITION STATUS/VERIFY CABLE REQUIREMENTS CHECK CABLE CONNECTION, go to next step. If NGS tester displays UNABLE TO PERFORM TEST/FUNCTION MODULE NOT RESPONDING: LCM CHECK IGNITION STATUS/VERIFY CABLE REQUIREMENTS CHECK CABLE CONNECTION, go to step **8)**.

2) Using NGS tester, monitor LCM PID IGN_LC while rotating ignition switch through ACC, OFF, and RUN positions. If PID IGN_LC does not indicate ACCY while in all positions, go to next step. If PID IGN_LC indicates ACCY while in all positions, go to step **5)**.

3) Measure voltage at output side of fuse No. 14 (7.5-amp) in instrument panel fuse box. If voltage is 10 volts or less, go to next step. If voltage is greater than 10 volts, repair Red/Yellow wire between fuse No. 14 (7.5-amp) instrument panel fuse box and Lighting Control Module (LCM).

4) Check fuse No. 14 (7.5-amp) in instrument panel fuse box. If fuse is okay, repair open in White/Yellow wire between instrument panel fuse block and ignition switch. If fuse is blown, repair short to ground in Red/Yellow wire between fuse No. 14 (7.5-amp) in instrument panel fuse box and Lighting Control Module (LCM).

5) Measure voltage at output side of fuse No. 18 (7.5-amp) in instrument panel fuse box. If voltage is greater than 10 volts, go to step **7)**. If voltage is 10 volts or less, go to step **7)**.

6) Turn ignition switch to LOCK position. Disconnect LCM harness connector C220. Turn ignition switch to RUN position. Measure voltage at terminal No. 7 (Dark Blue/Light Green wire) at LCM harness connector C220. See Fig. 4. If voltage is greater than 10 volts, replace LCM. If voltage is 10 volts or less, repair open in Dark Blue/Light Green wire between fuse No. 18 (7.5-amp) in instrument panel fuse box and LCM.

7) Check fuse No. 18 (7.5-amp) in instrument panel fuse box. If fuse is okay, repair open in Black/Light Green wire between instrument panel fuse box and ignition switch. If fuse is blown, repair short to ground in Dark Blue/Light Green wire between fuse No. 18 (7.5-amp) in instrument panel fuse box and LCM.

8) Measure voltage at output side of fuse No. 31 (7.5-amp) in instrument panel fuse box. If voltage is 10 volts or less, go to next step. If voltage is greater than 10 volts, go to step **10)**.

9) Check fuse No. 31 (7.5-amp) in instrument panel fuse box. If fuse is blown, go to next step. If fuse is okay, repair open in Dark Blue/Orange wire between instrument panel fuse box and power distribution box.

10) Turn ignition switch to LOCK position. Remove and disconnect headlight switch harness connector. Disconnect LCM harness connector C221. Measure resistance between ground and terminal No. 25 (Orange/White wire) at LCM harness connector C221. See Fig. 5. If resistance is greater than 10 k/ohms, go to next step. If resistance is 10 k/ohms or less, repair short to ground in Orange/White wire between fuse No. 31 (7.5-amp) in instrument panel fuse box and LCM.

11) Install and connect headlight switch harness connector. Measure resistance between ground and terminal No. 25 (Orange/White wire) at LCM harness connector C221. If resistance is greater than 10 k/ohms, go to next step. If resistance is 10 k/ohms or less, replace headlight switch.

12) Ensure LCM harness connector C221 is still disconnected. Measure voltage at terminal No. 25 (Orange/White wire) at LCM harness connector C221. If voltage is greater than 10 volts, go to next step. If voltage is 10 volts or less, repair open in Orange/White wire between fuse No. 31 (7.5-amp) in instrument panel fuse box and LCM.

13) Disconnect LCM harness connector C222. Ensure ignition switch is in LOCK position. Measure resistance between ground and terminal No. 23 (Pink/Orange wire) at LCM harness connector C221. Measure resistance between ground and terminal No. 13 (Pink/Orange wire) at LCM harness connector C222. See Fig. 6. If both resistance readings are 5 ohms or less, repair module communication concern. See MODULE COMMUNICATIONS NETWORK – TOWN CAR article. If either resistance reading is greater than 5 ohms, repair open in appropriate Pink/Orange wire between LCM and ground.

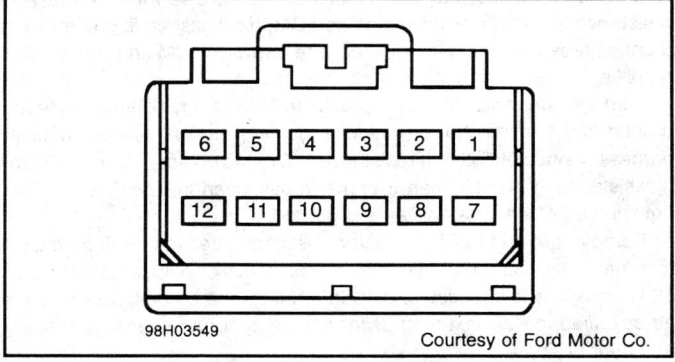

98H03549   Courtesy of Ford Motor Co.

Fig. 4: Identifying Lighting Control Module Harness Connector C220 Terminals

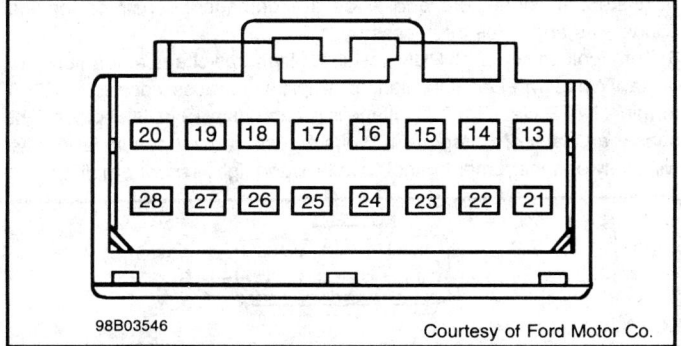

98B03546   Courtesy of Ford Motor Co.

Fig. 5: Identifying Lighting Control Module Harness Connector C221 Terminals

FORD
4-182

1999 ACCESSORIES & EQUIPMENT
Passive Anti-Theft Systems – Town Car (Cont.)

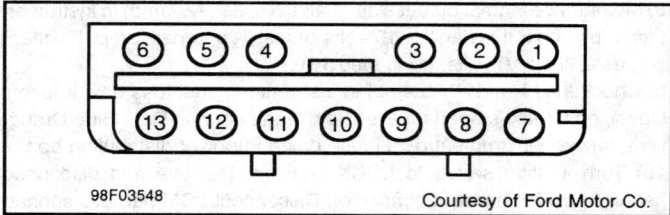

98F03548   Courtesy of Ford Motor Co.

Fig. 6: Identifying Lighting Control Module Harness Connector C222 Terminals

TEST C: THEFT INDICATOR IS ALWAYS/NEVER ON OR THEFT INDICATOR WILL NOT PROVE-OUT

1) Turn ignition switch to LOCK position. Using NGS tester, enter instrument cluster active command mode. If active command mode can be entered, go to next step. If unable to enter active command mode, perform TEST A: NO COMMUNICATION WITH INSTRUMENT CLUSTER.

2) Using NGS tester, trigger LCM active command WARNING LAMPS AND CHIME ANTI-THEFT to ON. If THEFT indicator does not illuminate, go to next step. If THEFT indicator illuminates, system is okay at this time. Verify concern with customer.

3) Turn ignition switch to LOCK position. Disconnect light sensor amplifier harness connector C286. Turn ignition switch to RUN position. Measure voltage at terminal No. 2 (Orange/Red wire) at light sensor amplifier harness connector C286 while triggering LCM active command WARNING LAMPS AND CHIME ANTI-THEFT to ON. *See Fig. 7.* If voltage is 10 volts or less, go to next step. If voltage is greater than 10 volts, go to step **5)**.

4) Turn ignition switch to LOCK position. Disconnect LCM harness connector C221. Measure resistance in Orange/Red wire between terminal No. 18 at LCM harness connector C221 and terminal No. 2 at light sensor amplifier harness connector C286. *See Figs. 5 and 7.* If resistance is 5 ohms or less, replace LCM. If resistance is greater than 5 ohms, repair open in Orange/Red wire between LCM and light sensor amplifier.

5) Turn ignition switch to LOCK position. Measure resistance between ground and terminal No. 1 (Pink/Orange wire) at light sensor amplifier harness connector C286. If resistance is 5 ohms or less, go to next step. If resistance is greater than 5 ohms, repair open in Pink/Orange wire between light sensor amplifier and ground.

6) Remove anti-theft LED. Measure resistance between anti-theft LED terminals. Reverse ohmmeter leads. Resistance should be greater than 10 k/ohms in one direction and 10-20 ohms in the other. If resistance is as specified, go to next step. If resistance is not as specified, replace anti-theft LED and return to step **2)**.

7) Check LCM and light sensor amplifier harness connectors for damaged pins or corroded wires. If connectors and wires are okay, go to next step. If connectors and wires are damaged, repair or replace connectors and wires as necessary.

8) Turn ignition switch to RUN position. Measure voltage at terminal No. 3 (Tan/White wire) at light sensor amplifier harness connector C286 terminal No. 3. *See Fig. 7.* If voltage is greater than 10 volts, replace light sensor amplifier. If voltage is 10 volts or less, repair open in Tan/White wire between instrument panel fuse box and light sensor amplifier.

REMOVAL & INSTALLATION

CAUTION: When battery is disconnected or modules are replaced, vehicle computer and memory systems may lose memory data. Driveability problems may exist until computer systems have completed a relearn cycle. See COMPUTER RELEARN PROCEDURES article in GENERAL INFORMATION before disconnecting battery.

TRANSCEIVER MODULE

NOTE: If transceiver module is replaced, all existing ignition keys must be reprogrammed. See PROGRAMMING.

WARNING: Deactivate air bag system before performing any service operation involving steering column components. See appropriate AIR BAG RESTRAINT SYSTEMS article. DO NOT apply electrical power to any component on steering column without first deactivating air bag system. Air bag may deploy.

Removal & Installation – 1) Disconnect negative battery cable. Transceiver module is located on ignition switch lock cylinder. Insert ignition key into ignition switch lock cylinder. Turn ignition switch lock cylinder to RUN position. Insert a punch in steering column cover hole and press ignition switch lock cylinder release tab while removing ignition switch lock cylinder.

2) Remove tilt wheel lever. Remove parking brake release handle screw and position parking brake release handle aside. Remove lower steering column opening cover. Remove instrument panel steering column opening cover reinforcement.

3) Remove upper and lower steering column covers. Remove transceiver module retaining screw from steering column. Carefully pry transceiver over rib on ignition switch lock cylinder housing. Remove transceiver module harness retainers. Disconnect transceiver module connector and remove transceiver module. To install, reverse removal procedure.

LIGHTING CONTROL MODULE (LCM)

NOTE: The Lighting Control Module (LCM) must be reconfigured if replaced. On Canadian vehicles, refer to NGS tester help screen on the configuration card to program Daytime Running Lamps (DRL).

Removal & Installation – Lighting Control Module (LCM) is located under left side of instrument panel, above brake and accelerator pedals. Disconnect negative battery cable. Remove left instrument panel lower insulator. Remove LCM retaining screws and release locking tab. Disconnect LCM connectors and remove LCM. To install, reverse removal procedure.

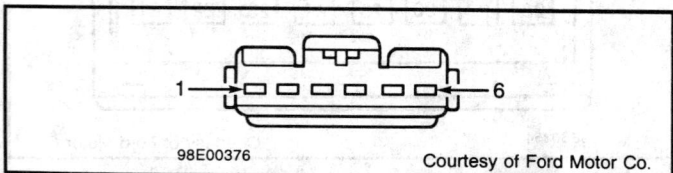

98E00376   Courtesy of Ford Motor Co.

Fig. 7: Identifying Light Sensor Amplifier Connector C286 Terminals

1999 ACCESSORIES & EQUIPMENT
Passive Anti-Theft Systems – Town Car (Cont.)

FORD
4-183

WIRING DIAGRAMS

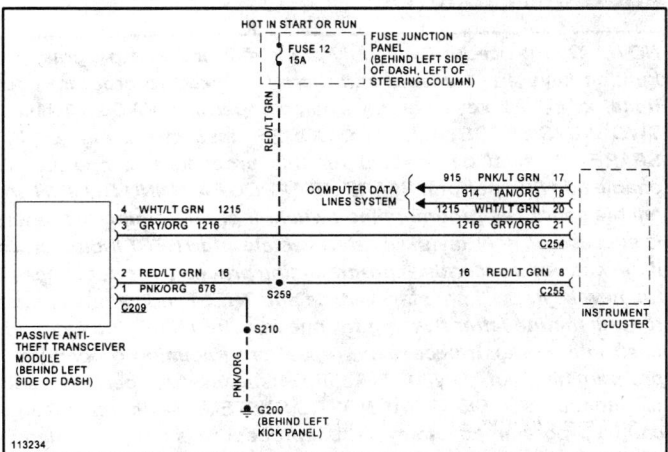

Fig. 8: Passive Anti-Theft System (PATS) Wiring Diagram (Town Car)

DESCRIPTION & OPERATION

NOTE: This system is not compatible with remote start systems, which allow vehicle to be started from outside by driver. Remote system must be removed before any diagnosis or repairs are made to passive anti-theft system related no start issues.

NOTE: All elements of passive anti-theft system must be functional or vehicle will not start.

Passive Anti-Theft System (PATS) contains a theft indicator, encoded ignition key, transceiver module, instrument cluster, Powertrain Control Module (PCM), Standard Corporate Protocol (SCP) communication network and starter relay. PATS uses radio frequency identification technology to deter driveaway theft. Passive means it does not require any activity from user. PATS uses specially encoded keys containing permanently installed transponders. Each transponder contains an identification code. Each replacement encoded ignition key must be programmed into instrument cluster before it is able to start engine. Encoded keys are larger than traditional keys, do not require batteries and should last lifetime of vehicle.

Transceiver module communicates with encoded ignition key and is located behind steering column cover. Transceiver module reads encoded key and sends data to instrument cluster during each vehicle start sequence. Instrument cluster initiates key interrogation sequence when vehicle ignition switch is turned to RUN or START position. PATS uses PCM to enable or disable engine. Instrument cluster and PCM have shared security data, making them a matched pair.

PATS also disables starter motor. If instrument cluster is removed from vehicle, engine will not start. Theft indicator will prove out for 3 seconds when ignition switch is turned to RUN or START position. If PATS is malfunctioning, theft light will flash rapidly or glow steadily. PATS theft indicator flashes every 2 seconds after ignition switch is turned to OFF to act as a visual theft deterrent. PATS will not store DTC or flash theft indicator if valid encoded ignition key is used and a failure occurs in starter relay circuit.

PROGRAMMING

NOTE: All programming procedures are written specifically for New Generation Star (NGS) tester. Most generic scan tools should be able to perform all procedures.

MODULE CONFIGURATION

NOTE: Powertrain Control Module (PCM) has to be flash programmed using a flash cable. See COMPUTER RELEARN PROCEDURES article in GENERAL INFORMATION.

NOTE: Newly released modules will require configuration after being installed on vehicle. All configurable modules will be packaged in a kit which contains a warning label and multi-language sheet reemphasizing requirements to configure replacement modules. A New Generation Star (NGS) tester or Ford compatible scan tool MUST be used to retrieve configuration data from old module before it is removed from vehicle. This information will be transferred into new module so that new module will contain same settings as old module. NGS tester will not retain stored configuration information for longer than 24 hours.

Following manufacturer's instructions, upload old information from old module using Ford Service Function (FSF) card and NGS tester. Install new module and download stored information into new module using FSF card and NGS tester.

PROGRAMMING SPARE KEY(S) WITH TWO PROGRAMMED KEYS

NOTE: This procedure will only work if 2 or more programmed ignition keys are available and there is a need to program additional keys. If 2 keys are not available, perform PROGRAMMING TWO KEYS/ERASE ALL KEY CODES. Instrument cluster PID SPARE_KY must be enabled for this procedure to operate. To enable this PID, perform SPARE KEY PROGRAMMING SWITCH and enable spare key programming switch. If programming procedure is successful, new key(s) will start vehicle and THEFT indicator will illuminate for 3 seconds. If programming procedure is not successful, new key(s) will not start vehicle and THEFT indicator will flash for one minute (after flashing for one minute, THEFT indicator will flash fault code). If necessary, repeat programming procedure. If programming of key(s) is still unsuccessful, perform self-diagnostics. See SELF-DIAGNOSTIC SYSTEM. Maximum of 8 keys can be programmed into system. If procedure is not performed as outlined, programming procedure will end. Ignition keys must have correct mechanical key cut for vehicle and must be an encoded key.

1) Insert the first programmed ignition key into ignition lock cylinder. Turn ignition switch from OFF to RUN position (ignition switch must stay in RUN position for one second). Turn ignition switch to OFF position and remove ignition key from ignition lock cylinder.
2) Within 5 seconds of turning ignition switch to OFF position, insert second programmed ignition key into ignition lock cylinder. Turn ignition switch from OFF to RUN position (ignition switch must stay in RUN position for one second). Turn ignition switch to OFF position and remove second ignition key from ignition lock cylinder.
3) Within 5 seconds of turning ignition switch to OFF position, insert a NEW unprogrammed ignition key into ignition lock cylinder. Turn ignition switch from OFF to RUN position (ignition switch must stay in RUN position for one second). Turn ignition switch to OFF position and remove ignition key from ignition lock cylinder. The NEW ignition key should now be programmed. To program additional key(s), repeat key programming procedure from step 1).

PROGRAMMING SPARE KEY WITHOUT PROGRAMMED KEY(S)

NOTE: This procedure is used when customer needs extra keys programmed and 2 programmed keys are not available, but system has 2 ignition keys programmed. A maximum of 8 keys can be programmed. If 8 keys are already programmed, this procedure will not allow any more keys to be programmed. The number of programmed keys can be determined by accessing instrument cluster PID NUMKEYS with NGS tester.

Insert unprogrammed key in ignition and turn ignition switch to RUN position. Connect New Generation Star (NGS) tester to Data Link Connector (DLC), located under instrument panel next to steering column. Insert Ford Service Function (FSF) card in NGS tester. Perform security access procedure. See SECURITY ACCESS PROCEDURE. Select IGNITION KEY CODE PROGRAM. Turn ignition switch to OFF position. Disconnect NGS tester. Key should now be programmed and be able to start vehicle.

PROGRAMMING TWO KEYS/ERASE ALL KEY CODES

NOTE: This procedure is used when a customer needs keys programmed into system and does not have 2 programmed ignition keys available, or when programmed ignition keys have been lost and/or ignition switch assembly has been replaced. This procedure will erase all programmed ignition keys from memory and prevent vehicle from starting until 2 keys have been programmed. Ignition keys must have correct mechanical key cut for vehicle and must be an encoded key. If additional key(s) are to be programmed, perform PROGRAMMING SPARE KEY(S) WITH TWO PROGRAMMED KEYS. If remaining keys are with customer and not with vehicle, instruct customer to see owner's manual to program spare key(s).

1) Insert Ford Service Function (FSF) card into NGS tester. Turn ignition switch from OFF to RUN position. With NGS tester connected to vehicle, enter instrument cluster then select SECURITY ACCESS PROCEDURE. This procedure will take 10 minutes to perform. After the security access procedure has been completed, a new menu will be displayed with command options. Select IGNITION KEY CODE ERASE.

2) Turn ignition switch to OFF position and disconnect NGS tester. Insert first encoded ignition key into ignition lock cylinder. Turn ignition switch to RUN position for 3 seconds. Turn ignition switch to OFF position and remove first encoded key.

3) Within 5 seconds, insert second encoded ignition key into ignition lock cylinder. Turn ignition switch to RUN position for 3 seconds. Turn ignition switch to OFF position and remove second encoded key. Both encoded ignition keys should now start vehicle.

SECURITY ACCESS PROCEDURE

NOTE: Security access must be granted to erase ignition keys, enable/disable spare key programming switch, or perform parameter resets for instrument cluster and PCM. This procedure has a 10-minute time delay prior to granting security access during which the New Generation Star (NGS) tester must remain connected to vehicle. After security access has been granted, security access command menu is displayed which offers various command options. Multiple security access commands can be executed (if necessary) prior to exiting security access command menu. Execution of all necessary security access commands prior to exiting command menu avoids the performance of an additional security access procedure and the associated 10-minute time delay.

Insert Ford Service Function (FSF) card into NGS tester. Turn ignition switch from OFF to RUN position. With NGS tester connected to vehicle, enter instrument cluster then select SECURITY ACCESS PROCEDURE. This procedure will take 10 minutes to perform. After the security access procedure has been completed, a new menu will be displayed with command options. Select as many functions as required before exiting this menu. Once this menu is exited, security access procedure must be performed again to perform additional commands.

SPARE KEY PROGRAMMING SWITCH

NOTE: The spare key programming switch is a programmable switch which provides the capability to enable/disable the normal customer spare key programming procedure detailed in the owner's manual. This programmable switch is provided as a convenience for rental company fleets or other fleet purchasers who may not want the spare key programming procedure available to the vehicle driver. The spare key programming switch state can be viewed using instrument cluster PID SPARE_KY. Default setting on all new vehicles is ENABLE.

Insert a programmed ignition key into the ignition lock cylinder. Insert Ford Service Function (FSF) card into NGS tester. Turn ignition switch from OFF to RUN position. With NGS tester connected to vehicle, enter

instrument cluster then select SECURITY ACCESS PROCEDURE. This procedure will take 10 minutes to perform. After the security access procedure has been completed, a new menu will be displayed with command options. The default setting on all new vehicles is ENABLE. Select SPARE KEY PROGRAMMING SWITCH. Set SPARE KEY PROGRAMMING SWITCH to ENABLE to allow keys to be programmed or DISABLE to make key programming not accessible.

TROUBLE SHOOTING

Verify customer concern. Check fuses No. 9, 14, 16 and 28 (all 10-amp) in Fuse Junction Box/Panel (FJB). Check PATS transceiver and ignition switch for damage. Check bulbs and wiring harness for damaged, loose or corroded connections/circuitry. Check ignition lock cylinder and encoded ignition key (PATS key). If problem exists, repair as necessary. If problem does not exist, perform self-diagnostics. See SELF-DIAGNOSTIC SYSTEM.

CONNECTOR IDENTIFICATION

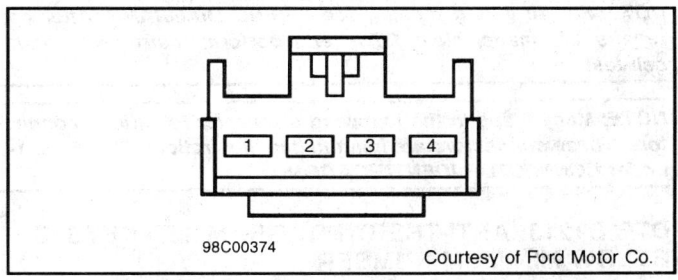

98C00374   Courtesy of Ford Motor Co.

Fig. 1: Identifying Passive Anti-Theft System (PATS) Transceiver 4-Pin Harness Connector

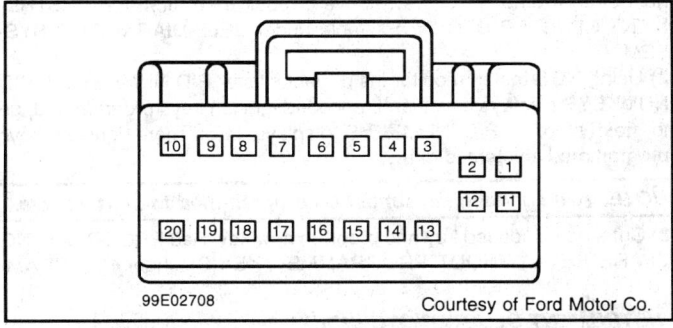

99E02708   Courtesy of Ford Motor Co.

Fig. 2: Identifying Instrument Cluster 20-Pin Harness Connector

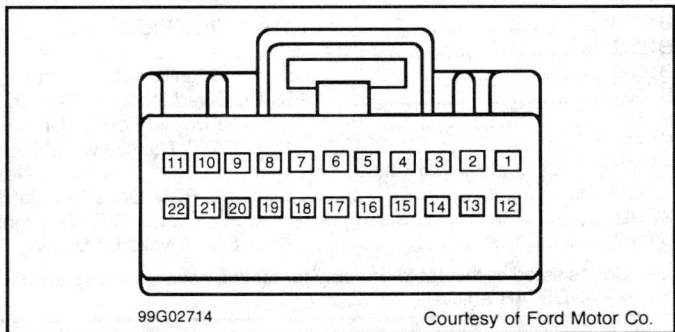

99G02714   Courtesy of Ford Motor Co.

Fig. 3: Identifying Instrument Cluster 22-Pin Harness Connector

SELF-DIAGNOSTIC SYSTEM

NOTE: All diagnostic tests are written specifically for New Generation Star (NGS) tester. Most generic scan tools should be able to perform all test procedures.

Connect New Generation Star (NGS) tester to Data Link Connector (DLC), located beneath instrument panel. Using NGS tester, perform data link diagnostics test. See DATA LINK DIAGNOSTIC TEST under

COMMUNICATION NETWORK DIAGNOSTICS in MODULE COMMUNICATIONS NETWORK – WINDSTAR article. If NGS tester responds with CKT914, CKT915 or CKT70=ALL ECUS NO RESP/NOT EQUIP, repair module communications concern. See MODULE COMMUNICATIONS NETWORK – WINDSTAR article. If NGS tester displays NO RESP/NOT EQUIP for instrument cluster, perform TEST A: NO COMMUNICATION WITH INSTRUMENT CLUSTER under SYSTEM TESTS.

If NGS tester responds with SYSTEM PASSED, retrieve and record continuous DTCs. Erase continuous DTCs. Using NGS tester, perform instrument cluster self-test. Perform appropriate test in accordance with DTC retrieved. See INSTRUMENT CLUSTER DTC INDEX table. Codes listed in these tables are only for testing covered in this article. For complete DTC listing, see MODULE COMMUNICATIONS NETWORK – WINDSTAR article. If no DTCs are retrieved, repair by symptom. See SYMPTOM CHART table under SYSTEM TESTS.

DIAGNOSTIC TESTS

NOTE: For all wiring repairs, see WIRING DIAGRAMS. After any repairs are made, clear DTCs and perform instrument cluster self-test.

NOTE: Many steps in the following tests refer to various connectors. These connectors are identified in illustrations. See Figs. 1-3 under CONNECTOR IDENTIFICATION.

DTC B1213: ANTI-THEFT PROGRAMMED KEYS IS BELOW MINIMUM NUMBER

1) Turn ignition switch to OFF position. Using NGS tester, perform instrument cluster self-test. If DTC B1213 is only DTC retrieved, go to next step. If other DTC are retrieved, repair them first. See INSTRUMENT CLUSTER DTC INDEX table under SELF-DIAGNOSTIC SYSTEM.

2) Using NGS tester, monitor instrument cluster PID NUMKEYS. If PID NUMKEYS displays less than 2 encoded ignition keys programmed, go to next step. If PID NUMKEYS displays 2 or more ignition keys programmed, system is okay.

NOTE: Two encoded keys must be programmed to start vehicle.

3) Cut a new encoded key and program new key. See PROGRAMMING SPARE KEY WITHOUT PROGRAMMED KEY(S) under PROGRAM-

MING. If anti-theft indicator illuminates for 3 seconds and then goes out, clear DTCs and repeat self-test. If theft indicator is on continuously, repeat this step with a second new encoded key. If anti-theft indicator is flashing, retrieve and record DTCs and perform appropriate test. See INSTRUMENT CLUSTER DTC INDEX table under SELF-DIAGNOSTIC SYSTEM.

DTC B1600: PATS IGNITION KEY TRANSPONDER SIGNAL IS NOT RECEIVED

NOTE: Large metallic objects or devices, or a second ignition key on the same ring may cause vehicle starting problems and this DTC under certain conditions. Ensure encoded key is an approved Ford encoded ignition key (encoded keys from Rotunda, Ilco, Curtis and Strattec are approved encoded keys).

1) Using NGS tester, perform instrument cluster self-test. If DTC B1600 is retrieved, go to next step. If other DTCs are retrieved, perform appropriate test. See INSTRUMENT CLUSTER DTC INDEX table under SELF-DIAGNOSTIC SYSTEM. If no DTCs are retrieved, system is okay.

2) Turn ignition switch to OFF position. Ensure customer and replacement encoded keys are Ford approved encoded keys. Cut a new encoded key and program new encoded ignition key. See PROGRAMMING TWO KEYS/ERASE ALL KEY CODES under PROGRAMMING. Using NGS tester, perform instrument cluster self-test. If DTC B1600 is still present, go to next step. If no other DTCs are retrieved, system is okay. If other DTCs are retrieved, perform appropriate test. See INSTRUMENT CLUSTER DTC INDEX table under SELF-DIAGNOSTIC SYSTEM.

3) Turn ignition switch to OFF position. Replace PATS transceiver. See PASSIVE ANTI-THEFT SYSTEM (PATS) TRANSCEIVER MODULE under REMOVAL & INSTALLATION. Turn ignition switch to RUN position. Using customers original encoded key, not encoded key that was cut in previous step, perform instrument cluster self-test. If DTC B1600 is not present, system is okay. If DTC B1600 is retrieved, replace instrument cluster. See ANALOG INSTRUMENT PANELS – WINDSTAR article.

INSTRUMENT CLUSTER DTC INDEX

DTC [1]	Description	Test
B1213	Anti-Theft Programmed Keys Is Below Minimum Number	DTC B1213
B1232	Antenna Not Connected	DTC B2103
B1600	PATS Ignition Key Transponder Signal Is Not Received	DTC B1600
B1601	PATS Received Incorrect Key-Code From Ignition Key Transponder	DTC B1601
B1602	PATS Received Invalid Format Of Key-Code From Ignition Key Transponder	DTC B1602
B1681	PATS Transceiver Module Signal Is Not Received	DTC B1681
B2103	Antenna Not Connected	DTC B2103
B2139	PCM Does Not Match Instrument Cluster	DTC B2139
B2141	NVM Configuration Failure	DTC B2141
U1147	SCP Invalid Or Missing Data For Vehicle Security	DTC U1147

[1] – Codes listed in this table are only for testing covered in this article. For complete DTC listing, see MODULE COMMUNICATIONS NETWORK – WINDSTAR article.

DTC B1601: PATS RECEIVED INCORRECT KEY-CODE FROM IGNITION KEY TRANSPONDER

NOTE: Large metallic objects or devices, or a second ignition key on the same ring may cause vehicle starting problems and this DTC under certain conditions. Ensure encoded key is an approved Ford encoded ignition key (encoded keys from Rotunda, Ilco, Curtis and Strattec are approved encoded keys).

1) Using NGS tester, perform instrument cluster self-test. If DTC B1601 is retrieved, go to next step. If no DTCs are retrieved, system is okay. Perform instrument cluster self-test with all keys to be used with vehicle.

2) Using NGS tester, monitor instrument cluster PID NUMKEYS. If PID NUMKEYS does not display "8", go to next step. If PID NUMKEYS displays "8", erase and reprogram all keys to be used with vehicle. See PROGRAMMING TWO KEYS/ERASE ALL KEY CODES under PROGRAMMING.

3) Ensure there are at least 2 currently programmed encoded ignition keys available with vehicle. If there are 2 currently programmed with vehicle, go to next step. If there are not 2 currently programmed, cut new encoded keys and program new keys. See PROGRAMMING TWO KEYS/ERASE ALL KEY CODES under PROGRAMMING. Go to next step.

4) Using NGS tester, monitor instrument cluster PID SPARE_KY. If instrument cluster PID SPARE_KY indicates ENABLE, perform PROGRAMMING SPARE KEY(S) WITH TWO PROGRAMMED KEYS under PROGRAMMING. Go to next step. If PID SPARE_KY does not indicate ENABLE, enable spare key programming switch. See SPARE KEY PROGRAMMING SWITCH under PROGRAMMING. Go to next step.

5) Turn ignition switch to OFF position, then start vehicle using first encoded ignition key. Turn ignition switch to OFF position, then start vehicle with second encoded ignition key. Turn ignition switch to OFF position. If vehicle starts properly with both encoded ignition keys, system is okay. If there are additional keys that need to be programmed, see PROGRAMMING SPARE KEY(S) WITH TWO PROGRAMMED KEYS under PROGRAMMING. If vehicle does not start properly with both encoded ignition keys, go to next step.

6) Using NGS tester, perform instrument cluster self-test. Clear DTCs and perform self-test using both ignition keys from previous step. If DTC B1601 is not retrieved, system is okay. If other DTCs are retrieved, perform appropriate test. See INSTRUMENT CLUSTER DTC INDEX table under SELF-DIAGNOSTIC SYSTEM. If DTC B1601 is retrieved, replace instrument cluster. See ANALOG INSTRUMENT PANELS – WINDSTAR article. Prior to instrument cluster replacement, see MODULE CONFIGURATION and perform DTC B2139: PCM DOES NOT MATCH INSTRUMENT CLUSTER.

DTC B1602: PATS RECEIVED INVALID FORMAT OF KEY-CODE FROM IGNITION KEY TRANSPONDER

NOTE: Large metallic objects or devices, or a second ignition key on the same ring may cause vehicle starting problems and this DTC under certain conditions. Ensure encoded key is an approved Ford encoded ignition key (encoded keys from Rotunda, Ilco, Curtis and Strattec are approved encoded keys).

1) Using NGS tester, perform instrument cluster self-test. If DTC B1602 is retrieved, go to next step. If DTC B1602 is not retrieved, system is okay. Perform instrument cluster self-test with all keys to be used with vehicle.

2) Turn ignition switch to OFF position. Ensure customer and replacement encoded keys are Ford approved encoded keys. Cut a new encoded key and program new encoded ignition key. See PROGRAMMING TWO KEYS/ERASE ALL KEY CODES under PROGRAMMING. Perform instrument cluster self-test. If DTC B1602 is still present, go to next step. If DTC B1602 is not still present, system is okay. If customer has any additional keys at home, inform them that those keys need to be programmed. This procedure is outlined in owner's manual.

3) Turn ignition switch to OFF position. Replace PATS transceiver. See PASSIVE ANTI-THEFT SYSTEM (PATS) TRANSCEIVER MODULE

under REMOVAL & INSTALLATION. Turn ignition switch to RUN position. Using NGS tester, perform instrument cluster self-test. If any DTCs are retrieved, perform appropriate test. See INSTRUMENT CLUSTER DTC INDEX table under SELF-DIAGNOSTIC SYSTEM. If DTCs are not retrieved, system is okay.

DTC B1681: PATS TRANSCEIVER MODULE SIGNAL IS NOT RECEIVED

1) Using NGS tester, perform instrument cluster self-test. If DTC B1681 is retrieved, go to next step. If DTC B1681 is not retrieved, system is okay.

2) Turn ignition switch to OFF position. Disconnect PATS transceiver 4-pin harness connector C204. Turn ignition switch to RUN position. Measure voltage between PATS transceiver harness connector C204 terminal No. 2 (White/Light Blue wire) and ground. If voltage is more than 9 volts, go to next step. If voltage is 9 volts or less, repair open in White/Light Blue wire.

3) Turn ignition switch to OFF position. Measure resistance between PATS transceiver harness connector C204 terminal No. 1 (Black wire) and ground. If resistance is less than 5 ohms, go to next step. If resistance is 5 ohms or more, repair open in Black wire.

4) Connect PATS transceiver 4-pin harness connector C204. Turn ignition switch to RUN position. Measure voltage by backprobing between PATS transceiver harness connector C204 terminal No. 3 (Gray/Orange wire) and ground. If voltage is 9 volts or less, go to next step. If voltage is more than 9 volts, go to step **7)**.

5) Turn ignition switch to OFF position. Disconnect PATS transceiver 4-pin harness connector C204. Measure resistance between PATS transceiver harness connector C204 terminal No. 3 (Gray/Orange wire) and ground. If resistance is more than 100 ohms, go to next step. If resistance is 100 ohms or less, check Gray/Orange wire for short to ground. If circuit is okay, replace instrument cluster. See ANALOG INSTRUMENT PANELS – WINDSTAR article. Prior to instrument cluster replacement, see MODULE CONFIGURATION. Turn ignition switch to RUN position using 2 encoded ignition keys. Perform DTC B2139: PCM DOES NOT MATCH INSTRUMENT CLUSTER. Clear DTCs and test system for normal operation. If circuit is not okay, repair Gray/Orange wire as necessary. Clear DTCs and test system for normal operation.

6) Turn ignition switch to OFF position. Disconnect PATS transceiver 4-pin harness connector C204 and instrument cluster 22-pin harness connector C239. Measure resistance between PATS transceiver harness connector C204 terminals No. 3 (Gray/Orange wire) and instrument cluster harness connector C239 terminal No. 1 (Gray/Orange wire). If resistance is less than 5 ohms, connect instrument cluster harness connector C239 and go to next step. If resistance is 5 ohms or more, repair open in Gray/Orange wire.

7) Turn ignition switch to OFF position. Connect PATS transceiver 4-pin harness connector C204. Turn ignition switch to RUN position. Measure voltage by backprobing between PATS transceiver harness connector C204 terminal No. 4 (White/Light Green wire) and ground. If voltage is 9 volts or less, go to next step. If voltage is more than 9 volts, go to step **9)**.

8) Turn ignition switch to OFF position. Disconnect PATS transceiver 4-pin harness connector C204. Measure resistance between PATS transceiver harness connector C204 terminal No. 4 (White/Light Green wire) and ground. If resistance is more than 100 ohms, go to next step. If resistance is 100 ohms or less, check White/Light Green wire for short to ground. If circuit is not okay, repair as necessary. If circuit is okay, replace instrument cluster. See ANALOG INSTRUMENT PANELS – WINDSTAR article. Prior to instrument cluster replacement, see MODULE CONFIGURATION. Turn ignition switch to RUN position using 2 encoded ignition keys. Perform DTC B2139: PCM DOES NOT MATCH INSTRUMENT CLUSTER. Clear DTCs and test system for normal operation. If circuit is not okay, repair White/Light Green wire as necessary. Clear DTCs and test system for normal operation.

9) Connect PATS transceiver 4-pin harness connector C204. Turn ignition switch to RUN position. Using NGS tester, trigger instrument cluster active command TRANSMIT SIGNAL COMMAND to RUN. Measure voltage by backprobing between PATS transceiver harness connector C204 terminal No. 4 (White/Light Green wire) and ground. If voltage drops from more than 9 volts to less than one volt when instrument cluster active command TRANSMIT SIGNAL COMMAND is triggered ON, go to next step. If voltage does not drop from more than 9 volts to less than one volt when instrument cluster active command TRANSMIT SIGNAL COMMAND is triggered ON, check circuit for continuity to instrument cluster harness connector C239 terminal No. 6. If circuit is not okay, repair as necessary. If circuit is okay, replace instrument cluster.Prior to instrument cluster replacement, see MODULE CONFIGURATION. Turn ignition switch to RUN position using 2 encoded ignition keys. Perform DTC B2139: PCM DOES NOT MATCH INSTRUMENT CLUSTER. Clear DTCs and test system for normal operation. If circuit is not okay, repair White/Light Green wire as necessary. Clear DTCs and test system for normal operation.

10) Turn ignition switch to OFF position. Replace PATS transceiver. Turn ignition switch to RUN position. Using NGS tester, perform instrument cluster self-test. If DTC B1681 is retrieved, go to next step. If DTCs are not retrieved, system is okay.

11) Turn ignition switch to OFF position. Replace instrument cluster. See ANALOG INSTRUMENT PANELS – WINDSTAR article. Prior to instrument cluster replacement, see MODULE CONFIGURATION. Turn ignition switch to RUN position using 2 encoded ignition keys. Perform DTC B2139: PCM DOES NOT MATCH INSTRUMENT CLUSTER. Turn ignition switch to RUN position. Using NGS tester, perform instrument cluster self-test. If no DTCs are retrieved, system is okay. If other DTCs are retrieved, see INSTRUMENT CLUSTER DTC INDEX table. If DTC B1681 is retrieved, repair White/Light Green wire between instrument cluster and PATS transceiver, Gray/Orange wire between instrument cluster and PATS transceiver, Black wire between PATS transceiver and ground connector G304 (ground connector G304 is located behind left side cowl panel) and/or White/Light Blue wire between instrument cluster harness connector C240 and fuse No. 9 (10-amp) in fuse junction panel.

DTC B2103: ANTENNA NOT CONNECTED

NOTE: After any repairs are made, clear DTCs and perform instrument cluster self-test.

Turn ignition switch to OFF position. Ensure PATS transceiver is properly installed. See PASSIVE ANTI-THEFT SYSTEM (PATS) TRANSCEIVER MODULE under REMOVAL & INSTALLATION. Using NGS tester, perform instrument cluster self-test. Retrieve and record DTCs. Clear DTCs. If DTC B1232 or B2103 is retrieved, replace PATS transceiver module. If no DTCs are retrieved, system is okay.

DTC B2139: PCM DOES NOT MATCH INSTRUMENT CLUSTER

NOTE: After any repairs are made, clear DTCs and perform instrument cluster self-test.

1) Turn ignition switch to OFF position. Using NGS tester, retrieve and record continuous DTCs. Clear continuous DTCs. Turn ignition switch to OFF position. Turn ignition switch to RUN position. Using NGS tester, perform instrument cluster self-test. If DTC B2139 is retrieved, go to next step. If no DTCs are retrieved, system is okay.

NOTE: Do not perform ignition key code erase.

2) Perform security access procedure for instrument cluster. See SECURITY ACCESS PROCEDURE under PROGRAMMING. Using Ford Service Function (FSF) card, select PARAMETER RESET command for instrument cluster. Use diagnostic card for PCM active command KEEP ALIVE MEMORY RESET. Turn ignition switch to OFF position. Turn ignition switch to RUN position for 30 seconds. Clear continuous DTCs. Turn ignition switch to OFF position. Using NGS tester, perform instrument cluster self-test. If DTC B2139 is retrieved, ensure PCM calibration is correct for vehicle. If calibration is correct, repeat this step. If fault code persists, replace instrument cluster. See ANALOG INSTRUMENT PANELS – WINDSTAR article. Prior to instru-

ment cluster replacement, see MODULE CONFIGURATION. Turn ignition switch to RUN position using 2 encoded ignition keys. Perform DTC B2139: PCM DOES NOT MATCH INSTRUMENT CLUSTER. Turn ignition switch to RUN position. Using NGS tester, perform instrument cluster self-test. If no DTCs are retrieved, system is okay. If DTC B2139 still exists, replace PCM.

DTC B2141: NVM CONFIGURATION FAILURE

NOTE: After any repairs are made, clear DTCs and perform instrument cluster self-test.

1) Turn ignition switch to OFF position. Using NGS tester, retrieve and document continuous DTCs. Clear continuous DTCs. Turn ignition switch to OFF position. Turn ignition switch to RUN position. Perform instrument cluster self-test. If only DTC B2141 is retrieved, go to next step. If DTC U1147 and B2141 are retrieved, perform DTC U1147: SCP INVALID OR MISSING DATA FOR VEHICLE SECURITY. If no DTCs are retrieved, system is okay.

2) Using NGS tester, use diagnostic card for PCM active command KEEP ALIVE MEMORY RESET. Turn ignition switch to OFF position. Turn ignitioN switch to RUN position for 30 seconds. Turn ignition switch to OFF position. Turn ignition switch to START position. If vehicle does not start, go to next step. If vehicle starts, system is okay.

3) Using NGS tester, clear continuous DTCs. Turn ignition switch to OFF position. Turn ignition switch to RUN position. Using NGS tester, perform instrument cluster self-test. If DTC B2141 is retrieved, repeat step **2)**. If fault persists, check PCM calibration. If PCM calibration is okay, replace instrument cluster. See ANALOG INSTRUMENT PANELS – WINDSTAR article. Prior to instrument cluster replacement, see MODULE CONFIGURATION. Turn ignition switch to RUN position using 2 encoded ignition keys. Perform DTC B2139: PCM DOES NOT MATCH INSTRUMENT CLUSTER. Turn ignition switch to RUN position. Using NGS tester, perform instrument cluster self-test. If other DTCs are retrieved, perform appropriate test. See INSTRUMENT CLUSTER DTC INDEX table under SELF-DIAGNOSTIC SYSTEM.

DTC U1147: SCP INVALID OR MISSING DATA FOR VEHICLE SECURITY

NOTE: After any repairs are made, clear DTCs and perform instrument cluster self-test.

1) Turn ignition switch to START position. Ensure anti-theft indicator proves out properly. If vehicle does not start, go to next step. If vehicle starts with anti-theft indicator flashing, ensure proper PCM calibration for vehicle.

2) Using NGS tester, retrieve and document continuous DTCs. Clear DTCs and perform PCM KOEO ON-DEMAND SELF-TEST. See SELF-DIAGNOSTICS – EEC-IV article. If NGS communicates with PCM, go to next step. If NGS does not communicate with PCM, repair module communications concern. See MODULE COMMUNICATIONS NETWORK – WINDSTAR article.

3) Using NGS tester, retrieve and document continuous DTCs. If DTC P1260 is retrieved, go to next step. If DTC P1260 is not retrieved, check PCM power and ground circuits. See appropriate wiring diagram in WIRING DIAGRAMS in ENGINE PERFORMANCE in appropriate MITCHELL® manual.

4) Perform the following procedures. Repeat data link diagnostics test. See DATA LINK DIAGNOSTIC TEST in MODULE COMMUNICATIONS NETWORK – WINDSTAR article. If NGS tester displays NO RESP/NOT EQUIP for Instrument Cluster (ICM), perform TEST A: NO COMMUNICATION WITH INSTRUMENT CLUSTER under SYSTEM TESTS. If NGS tester responds with SYSTEM PASSED, go to next step.

5) Clear DTCs. Using NGS tester, perform instrument cluster self-test. Perform appropriate test in accordance with DTC retrieved. See INSTRUMENT CLUSTER DTC INDEX table under SELF-DIAGNOSTIC SYSTEM. If DTC U1147 is retrieved, replace instrument cluster. See ANALOG INSTRUMENT PANELS – WINDSTAR article. Prior to instrument cluster replacement, see MODULE CONFIGURATION. Turn ignition switch to RUN position using 2 encoded ignition keys. Perform DTC B2139: PCM DOES NOT MATCH INSTRUMENT CLUSTER. If DTC U1147 still exists, replace PCM. If no DTCs are retrieved from instrument cluster, FEM or REM self diagnostics, repair by symptom. See SYMPTOM CHART table under SYSTEM TESTS.

SYSTEM TESTS

SYMPTOM CHART

Condition	Test
No Communication With Instrument Cluster	A
Anti-Theft Indicator Always/Never On	B
Anti-Theft Indicator Proves Out Normally (Starter Will Not Crank)	B
Anti-Theft Indicator Flashes (Engine Will Not Start)	1
Anti-Theft Indicator Always On (Engine Will Not Start)	2
Vehicle Starts (Indicator Flashes Fault Code With Key ON)	U1147

1 – Using NGS tester, perform instrument cluster self-test. If DTCs are recorded, perform appropriate test in accordance with DTC retrieved. See INSTRUMENT CLUSTER/ICM DTC INDEX table under SELF-DIAGNOSTIC SYSTEM. If no DTCs are recorded, check for other possible no-start causes.

2 – Clear stored DTCs, cycle ignition switch from OFF to RUN position. Retrieve continuous DTCs. If DTCs are recorded, perform appropriate test in accordance with DTC retrieved. See INSTRUMENT CLUSTER/ICM DTC INDEX table under SELF-DIAGNOSTIC SYSTEM. If no DTCs are recorded, check for other possible no-start causes.

TEST A: NO COMMUNICATION WITH INSTRUMENT CLUSTER

NOTE: After any repairs are made, clear DTCs and perform instrument cluster self-test.

1) Turn ignition switch to OFF position. Disconnect instrument cluster 22-pin harness connectors C239 and C241 and 20-pin harness connector C240. Turn ignition switch to RUN position. Measure voltage between specified instrument cluster harness connector terminals and ground. See INSTRUMENT CLUSTER VOLTAGE table. If all readings are 10 volts or more, go to next step. If any reading is less than 10 volts, repair open in appropriate wire.

INSTRUMENT CLUSTER VOLTAGE

Connector	Terminal	Circuit No. (Wire Color)
C239	11	1001 (WHT/YEL)
C240	7	295 (LT BLU/PNK)
C240	9	1112 (WHT/LT BLU)
C241	19	608 (BLK/YEL)

2) Turn ignition switch to OFF position. Measure resistance between instrument cluster harness connector C240 terminal No. 12 (Black wire) and ground. If resistance is less than 5 ohms, replace instrument cluster. See ANALOG INSTRUMENT PANELS – WINDSTAR article. Prior to instrument cluster replacement, see MODULE CONFIGURATION. Turn ignition switch to RUN position using 2 encoded ignition keys. Perform DTC B2139: PCM DOES NOT MATCH INSTRUMENT CLUSTER. If resistance is 5 ohms or more, repair open in Black wire between instrument cluster and ground connector G304. Ground connector G304 is located behind left kick panel.

TEST B: ANTI-THEFT INDICATOR ALWAYS/NEVER ON

NOTE: After any repairs are made, clear DTCs and perform instrument cluster self-test.

1) Turn ignition switch to RUN position for 10 seconds. Turn ignition switch to OFF position. If anti-theft indicator proves out (illuminates for 3 seconds) but does not flash every 2 seconds when ignition switch is in OFF position, go to next step. If anti-theft indicator is always on, go to step 3). If anti-theft indicator is always off, go to step 4).

2) Disconnect instrument cluster 22-pin harness connector C239. Measure voltage between instrument cluster harness connector C239 terminal No. 11 (White/Yellow wire) and ground. If voltage is more than 10 volts, replace instrument cluster. See ANALOG INSTRUMENT PANELS – WINDSTAR article. Prior to instrument cluster replacement, see MODULE CONFIGURATION. Turn ignition switch to RUN position using 2 encoded ignition keys. Perform DTC B2139: PCM DOES NOT MATCH INSTRUMENT CLUSTER. If voltage is 10 volts or less, repair open in White/Yellow wire.

3) Using NGS tester, perform instrument cluster self-test. If DTC B1213 is retrieved, perform DTC B1213: ANTI-THEFT PROGRAMMED KEYS IS BELOW MINIMUM NUMBER under DIAGNOSTIC TESTS. If DTC B2139 is retrieved, perform DTC B2139: PCM DOES NOT MATCH INSTRUMENT CLUSTER under DIAGNOSTIC TESTS. If DTC B2141 is retrieved, perform DTC B2141: NVM CONFIGURATION FAILURE under DIAGNOSTIC TESTS. If no DTC are retrieved, replace instrument cluster. See ANALOG INSTRUMENT PANELS – WINDSTAR article. Prior to instrument cluster replacement, see MODULE CONFIGURATION. Turn ignition switch to RUN position using 2 encoded ignition keys. Perform DTC B2139: PCM DOES NOT MATCH INSTRUMENT CLUSTER.

4) Measure resistance between terminals of anti-theft LED in both directions. If resistance is more than 10 k/ohms in one direction and 10-20 ohms in the other direction, replace instrument cluster. See ANALOG INSTRUMENT PANELS – WINDSTAR article. Prior to instrument cluster replacement, see MODULE CONFIGURATION. Turn ignition switch to RUN position using 2 encoded ignition keys. Perform DTC B2139: PCM DOES NOT MATCH INSTRUMENT CLUSTER. If resistance is 10 k/ohms or less in one direction and not between 10-20 ohms in the other direction, replace anti-theft LED.

REMOVAL & INSTALLATION

PASSIVE ANTI-THEFT SYSTEM (PATS) TRANSCEIVER MODULE

CAUTION: Electronic modules are sensitive to electrical charges. Proper grounding of technician and workplace is essential to prevent damage.

NOTE: When battery is disconnected and reconnected, some abnormal drive symptoms may occur while vehicle relearns it's adaptive strategy. Vehicle may need to be driven 10 miles or more to learn strategy.

Removal & Installation – 1) Disconnect negative battery cable. Turn ignition switch to RUN position. Insert punch in access hole of steering column and press release tab while pulling out ignition switch lock cylinder. Remove ignition switch lock cylinder. Unscrew tilt wheel handle and shank and remove.

2) Remove 2 screws retaining left side instrument panel steering column opening cover and remove cover. Remove 3 bolts retaining instrument panel steering column opening cover reinforcement and remove reinforcement. Remove 3 screws retaining upper and lower steering column shrouds and remove shrouds. Remove screw from bottom of PATS transceiver module, disconnect electrical connector and remove PATS module. To install, reverse removal procedure.

WIRING DIAGRAMS

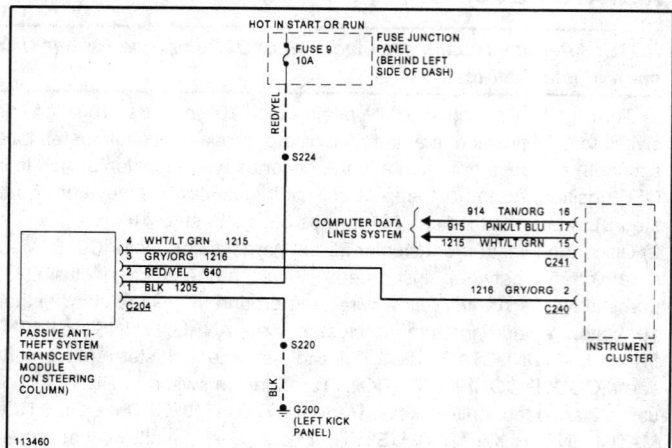

Fig. 4: Passive Anti-Theft System Wiring Diagram (Windstar)

WIRING DIAGRAMS

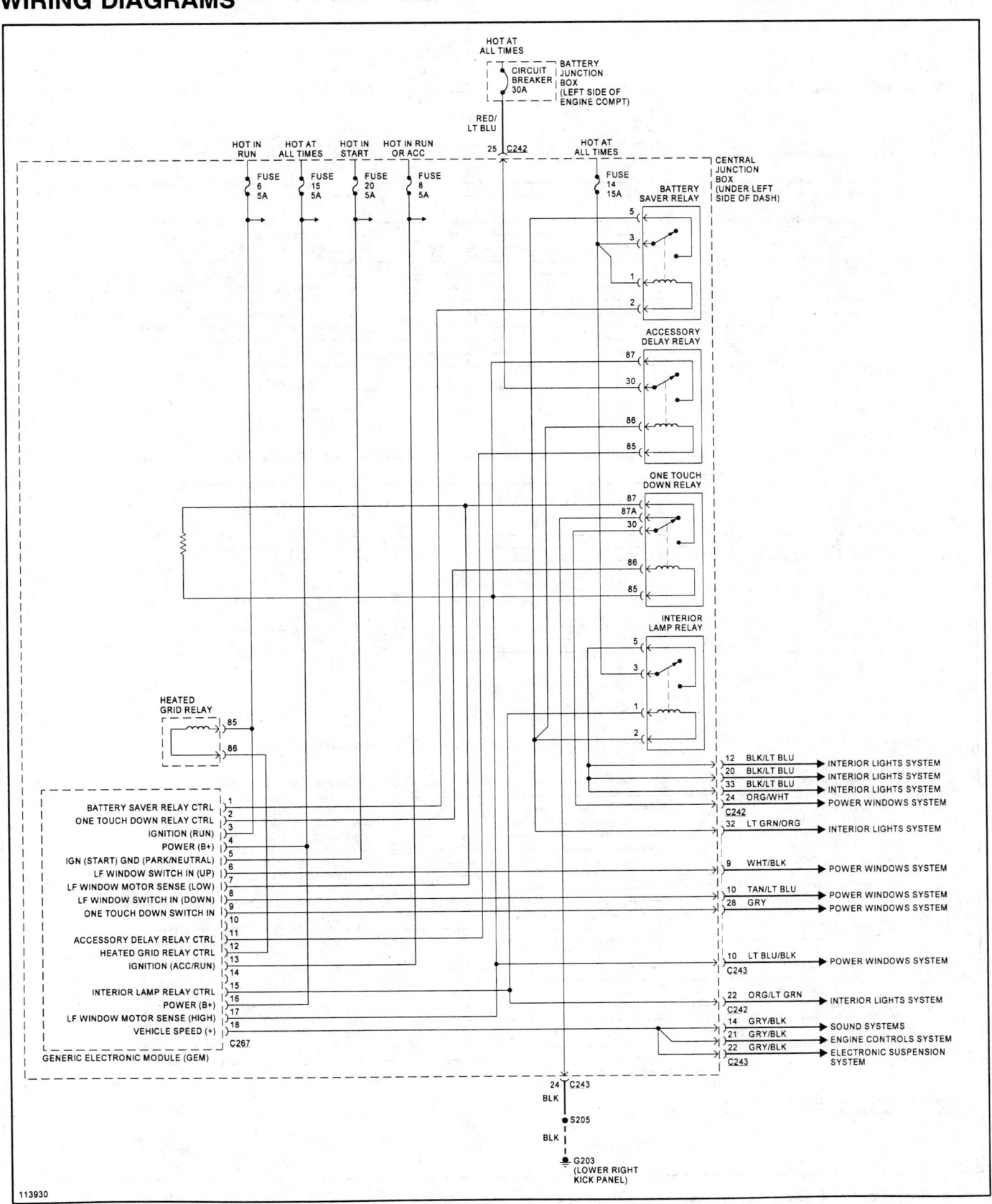

Fig. 1: Body Control Module Wiring Diagram (Expedition & Navigator – 1 Of 2)

113930

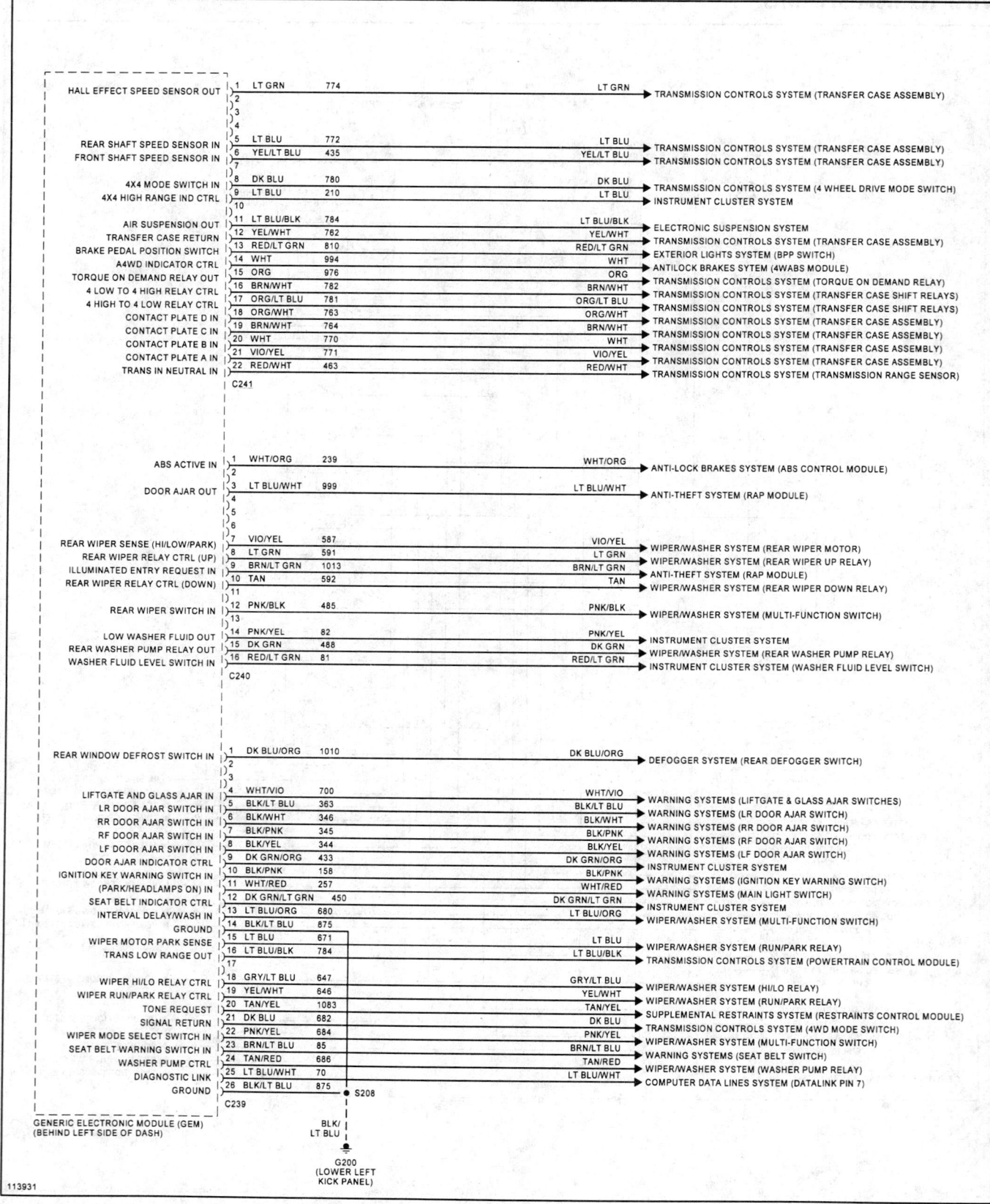

HALL EFFECT SPEED SENSOR OUT	1	LT GRN	774	LT GRN	TRANSMISSION CONTROLS SYSTEM (TRANSFER CASE ASSEMBLY)
	2				
	3				
	4				
REAR SHAFT SPEED SENSOR IN	5	LT BLU	772	LT BLU	TRANSMISSION CONTROLS SYSTEM (TRANSFER CASE ASSEMBLY)
FRONT SHAFT SPEED SENSOR IN	6	YEL/LT BLU	435	YEL/LT BLU	TRANSMISSION CONTROLS SYSTEM (TRANSFER CASE ASSEMBLY)
	7				
4X4 MODE SWITCH IN	8	DK BLU	780	DK BLU	TRANSMISSION CONTROLS SYSTEM (4 WHEEL DRIVE MODE SWITCH)
4X4 HIGH RANGE IND CTRL	9	LT BLU	210	LT BLU	INSTRUMENT CLUSTER SYSTEM
	10				
AIR SUSPENSION OUT	11	LT BLU/BLK	784	LT BLU/BLK	ELECTRONIC SUSPENSION SYSTEM
TRANSFER CASE RETURN	12	YEL/WHT	762	YEL/WHT	TRANSMISSION CONTROLS SYSTEM (TRANSFER CASE ASSEMBLY)
BRAKE PEDAL POSITION SWITCH	13	RED/LT GRN	810	RED/LT GRN	EXTERIOR LIGHTS SYSTEM (BPP SWITCH)
A4WD INDICATOR CTRL	14	WHT	994	WHT	ANTILOCK BRAKES SYTEM (4WABS MODULE)
TORQUE ON DEMAND RELAY OUT	15	ORG	976	ORG	TRANSMISSION CONTROLS SYSTEM (TORQUE ON DEMAND RELAY)
4 LOW TO 4 HIGH RELAY CTRL	16	BRN/WHT	782	BRN/WHT	TRANSMISSION CONTROLS SYSTEM (TRANSFER CASE SHIFT RELAYS)
4 HIGH TO 4 LOW RELAY CTRL	17	ORG/LT BLU	781	ORG/LT BLU	TRANSMISSION CONTROLS SYSTEM (TRANSFER CASE SHIFT RELAYS)
CONTACT PLATE D IN	18	ORG/WHT	763	ORG/WHT	TRANSMISSION CONTROLS SYSTEM (TRANSFER CASE ASSEMBLY)
CONTACT PLATE C IN	19	BRN/WHT	764	BRN/WHT	TRANSMISSION CONTROLS SYSTEM (TRANSFER CASE ASSEMBLY)
CONTACT PLATE B IN	20	WHT	770	WHT	TRANSMISSION CONTROLS SYSTEM (TRANSFER CASE ASSEMBLY)
CONTACT PLATE A IN	21	VIO/YEL	771	VIO/YEL	TRANSMISSION CONTROLS SYSTEM (TRANSFER CASE ASSEMBLY)
TRANS IN NEUTRAL IN	22	RED/WHT	463	RED/WHT	TRANSMISSION CONTROLS SYSTEM (TRANSMISSION RANGE SENSOR)

C241

ABS ACTIVE IN	1	WHT/ORG	239	WHT/ORG	ANTI-LOCK BRAKES SYSTEM (ABS CONTROL MODULE)
	2				
DOOR AJAR OUT	3	LT BLU/WHT	999	LT BLU/WHT	ANTI-THEFT SYSTEM (RAP MODULE)
	4				
	5				
	6				
REAR WIPER SENSE (HI/LOW/PARK)	7	VIO/YEL	587	VIO/YEL	WIPER/WASHER SYSTEM (REAR WIPER MOTOR)
REAR WIPER RELAY CTRL (UP)	8	LT GRN	591	LT GRN	WIPER/WASHER SYSTEM (REAR WIPER UP RELAY)
ILLUMINATED ENTRY REQUEST IN	9	BRN/LT GRN	1013	BRN/LT GRN	ANTI-THEFT SYSTEM (RAP MODULE)
REAR WIPER RELAY CTRL (DOWN)	10	TAN	592	TAN	WIPER/WASHER SYSTEM (REAR WIPER DOWN RELAY)
	11				
REAR WIPER SWITCH IN	12	PNK/BLK	485	PNK/BLK	WIPER/WASHER SYSTEM (MULTI-FUNCTION SWITCH)
	13				
LOW WASHER FLUID OUT	14	PNK/YEL	82	PNK/YEL	INSTRUMENT CLUSTER SYSTEM
REAR WASHER PUMP RELAY OUT	15	DK GRN	488	DK GRN	WIPER/WASHER SYSTEM (REAR WASHER PUMP RELAY)
WASHER FLUID LEVEL SWITCH IN	16	RED/LT GRN	81	RED/LT GRN	INSTRUMENT CLUSTER SYSTEM (WASHER FLUID LEVEL SWITCH)

C240

REAR WINDOW DEFROST SWITCH IN	1	DK BLU/ORG	1010	DK BLU/ORG	DEFOGGER SYSTEM (REAR DEFOGGER SWITCH)
	2				
	3				
LIFTGATE AND GLASS AJAR IN	4	WHT/VIO	700	WHT/VIO	WARNING SYSTEMS (LIFTGATE & GLASS AJAR SWITCHES)
LR DOOR AJAR SWITCH IN	5	BLK/LT BLU	363	BLK/LT BLU	WARNING SYSTEMS (LR DOOR AJAR SWITCH)
RR DOOR AJAR SWITCH IN	6	BLK/WHT	346	BLK/WHT	WARNING SYSTEMS (RR DOOR AJAR SWITCH)
RF DOOR AJAR SWITCH IN	7	BLK/PNK	345	BLK/PNK	WARNING SYSTEMS (RF DOOR AJAR SWITCH)
LF DOOR AJAR SWITCH IN	8	BLK/YEL	344	BLK/YEL	WARNING SYSTEMS (LF DOOR AJAR SWITCH)
DOOR AJAR INDICATOR CTRL	9	DK GRN/ORG	433	DK GRN/ORG	INSTRUMENT CLUSTER SYSTEM
IGNITION KEY WARNING SWITCH IN	10	BLK/PNK	158	BLK/PNK	WARNING SYSTEMS (IGNITION KEY WARNING SWITCH)
(PARK/HEADLAMPS ON) IN	11	WHT/RED	257	WHT/RED	WARNING SYSTEMS (MAIN LIGHT SWITCH)
SEAT BELT INDICATOR CTRL	12	DK GRN/LT GRN	450	DK GRN/LT GRN	INSTRUMENT CLUSTER SYSTEM
INTERVAL DELAY/WASH IN	13	LT BLU/ORG	680	LT BLU/ORG	WIPER/WASHER SYSTEM (MULTI-FUNCTION SWITCH)
GROUND	14	BLK/LT BLU	875		
WIPER MOTOR PARK SENSE	15	LT BLU	671	LT BLU	WIPER/WASHER SYSTEM (RUN/PARK RELAY)
TRANS LOW RANGE OUT	16	LT BLU/BLK	784	LT BLU/BLK	TRANSMISSION CONTROLS SYSTEM (POWERTRAIN CONTROL MODULE)
	17				
WIPER HI/LO RELAY CTRL	18	GRY/LT BLU	647	GRY/LT BLU	WIPER/WASHER SYSTEM (HI/LO RELAY)
WIPER RUN/PARK RELAY CTRL	19	YEL/WHT	646	YEL/WHT	WIPER/WASHER SYSTEM (RUN/PARK RELAY)
TONE REQUEST	20	TAN/YEL	1083	TAN/YEL	SUPPLEMENTAL RESTRAINTS SYSTEM (RESTRAINTS CONTROL MODULE)
SIGNAL RETURN	21	DK BLU	682	DK BLU	TRANSMISSION CONTROLS SYSTEM (4WD MODE SWITCH)
WIPER MODE SELECT SWITCH IN	22	PNK/YEL	684	PNK/YEL	WIPER/WASHER SYSTEM (MULTI-FUNCTION SWITCH)
SEAT BELT WARNING SWITCH IN	23	BRN/LT BLU	85	BRN/LT BLU	WARNING SYSTEMS (SEAT BELT SWITCH)
WASHER PUMP CTRL	24	TAN/RED	686	TAN/RED	WIPER/WASHER SYSTEM (WASHER PUMP RELAY)
DIAGNOSTIC LINK	25	LT BLU/WHT	70	LT BLU/WHT	COMPUTER DATA LINES SYSTEM (DATALINK PIN 7)
GROUND	26	BLK/LT BLU	875		

C239

GENERIC ELECTRONIC MODULE (GEM)
(BEHIND LEFT SIDE OF DASH)

S208

BLK/
LT BLU

G200
(LOWER LEFT
KICK PANEL)

113931

Fig. 2: Body Control Module Wiring Diagram (Expedition & Navigator – 2 Of 2)

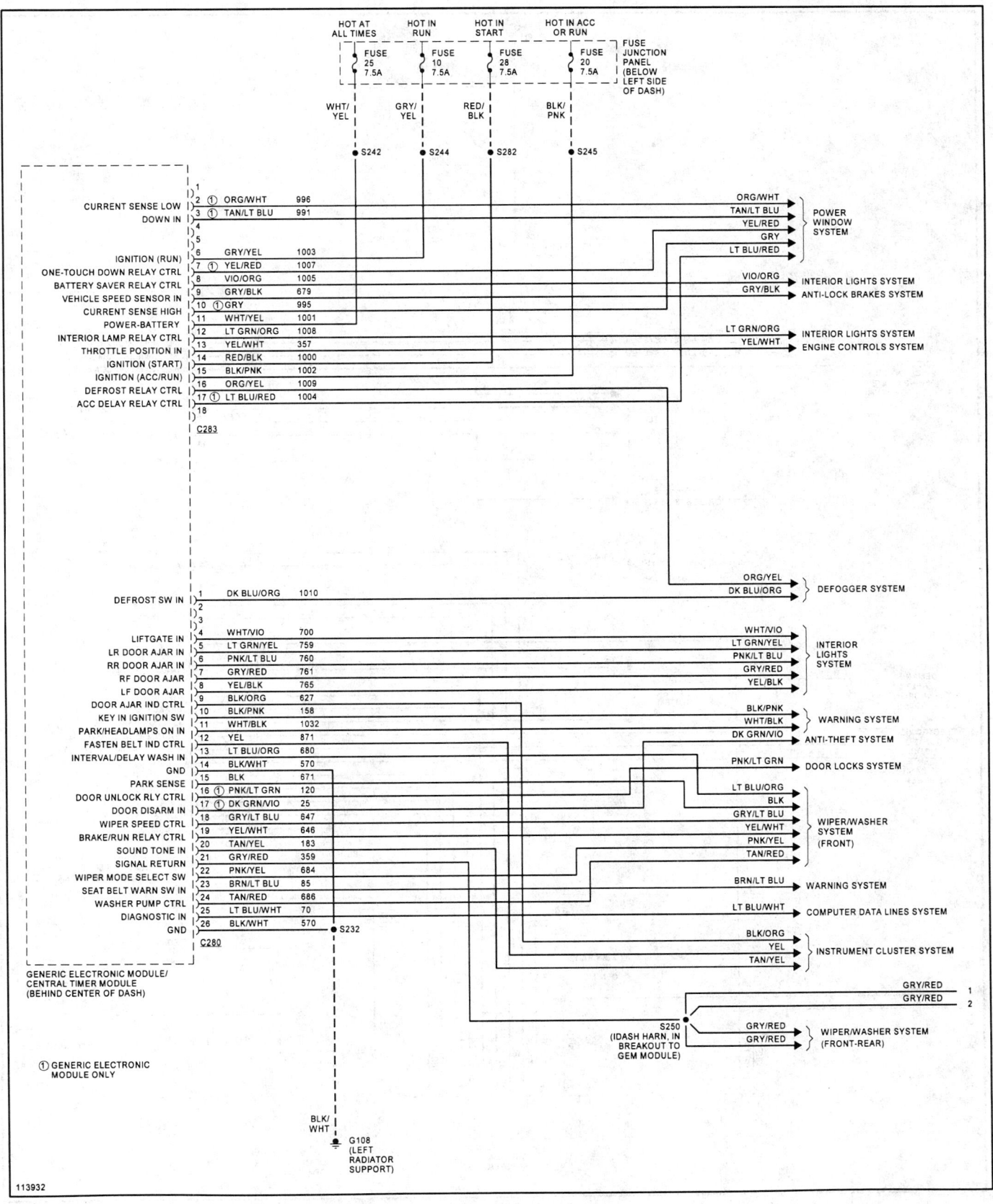

Fig. 3: Body Control Module Wiring Diagram (Explorer & Mountaineer – 1 Of 2)

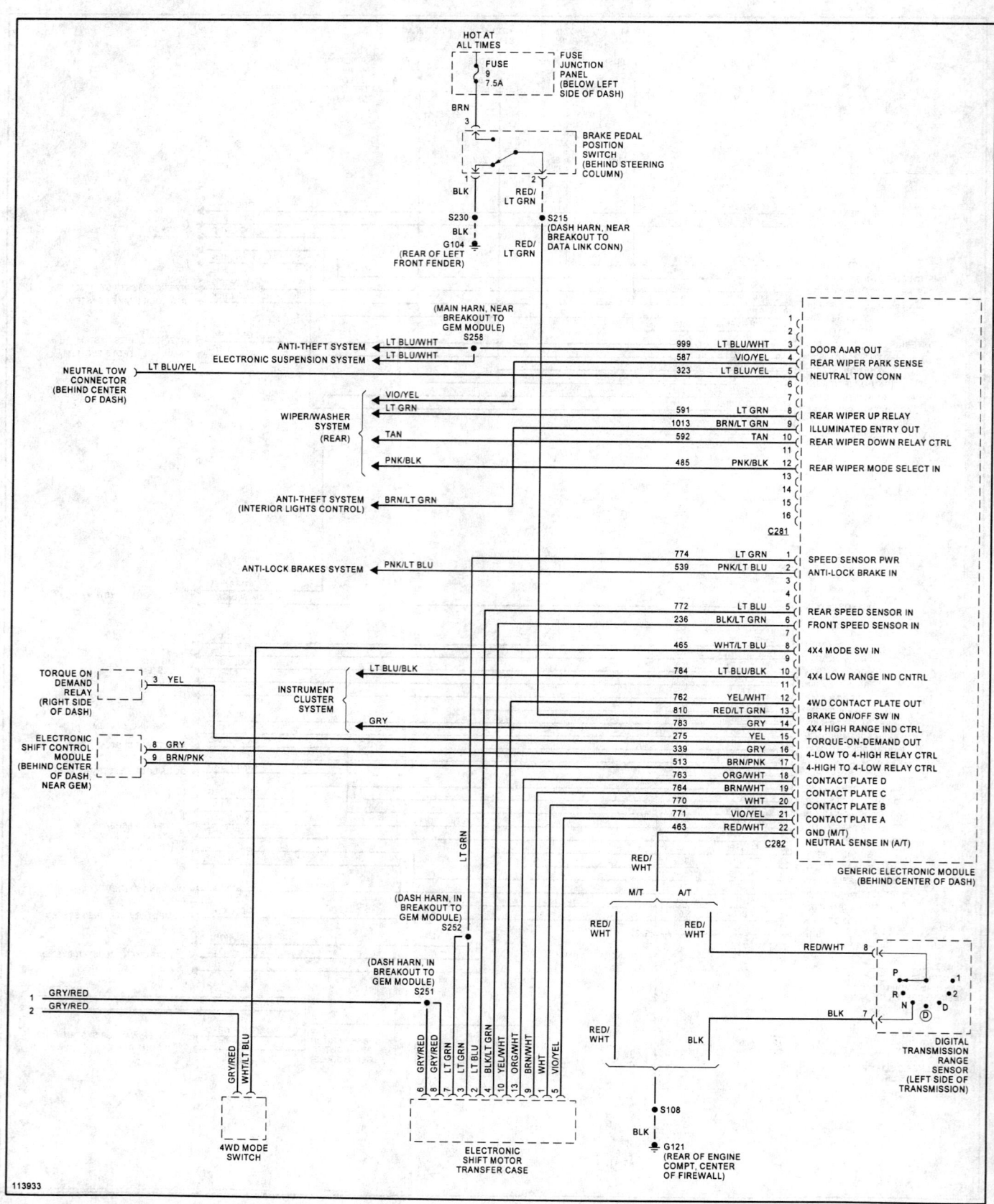

Fig. 4: Body Control Module Wiring Diagram (Explorer & Mountaineer – 2 Of 2)

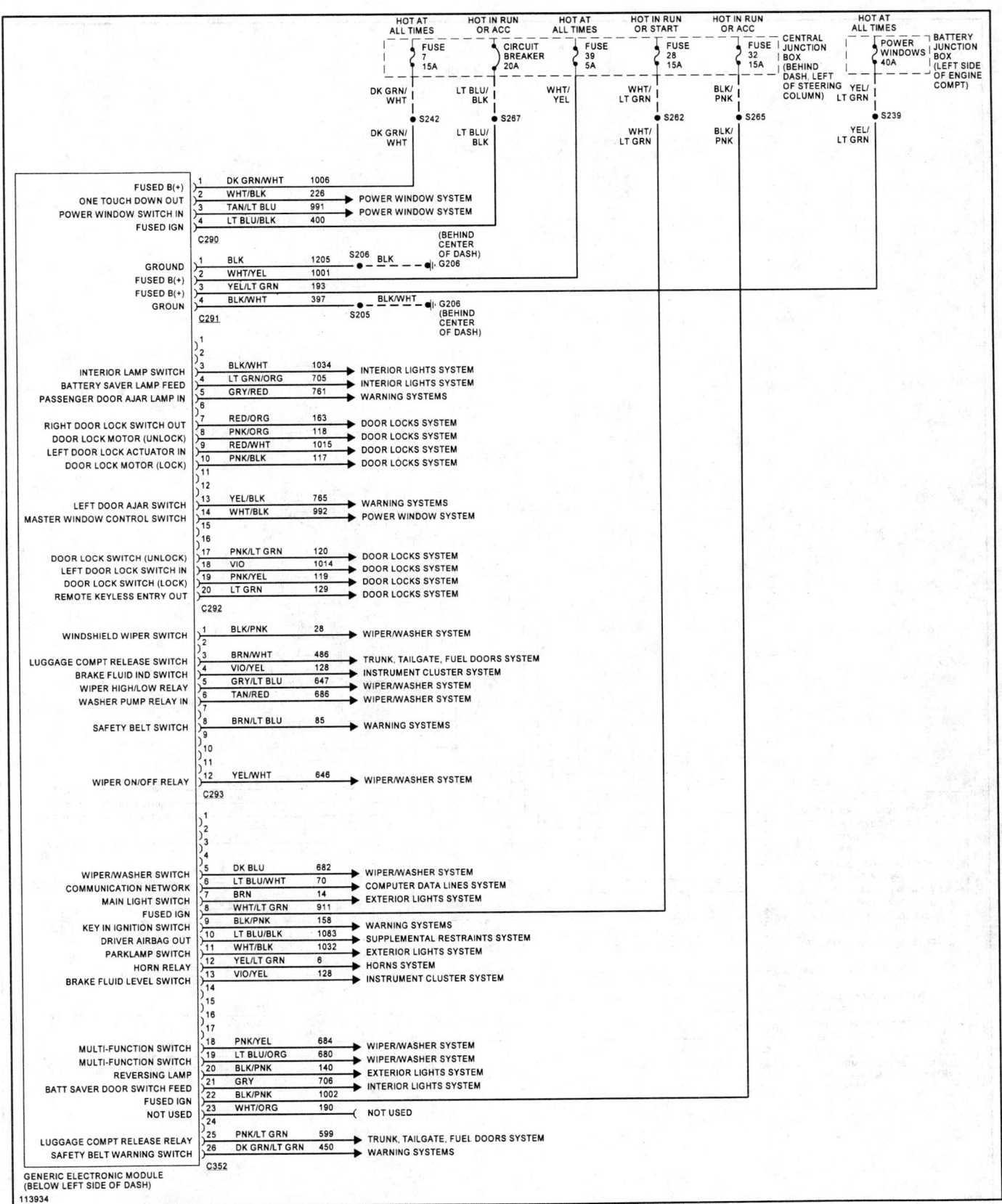

Fig. 5: Body Control Module Wiring Diagram (Mustang)

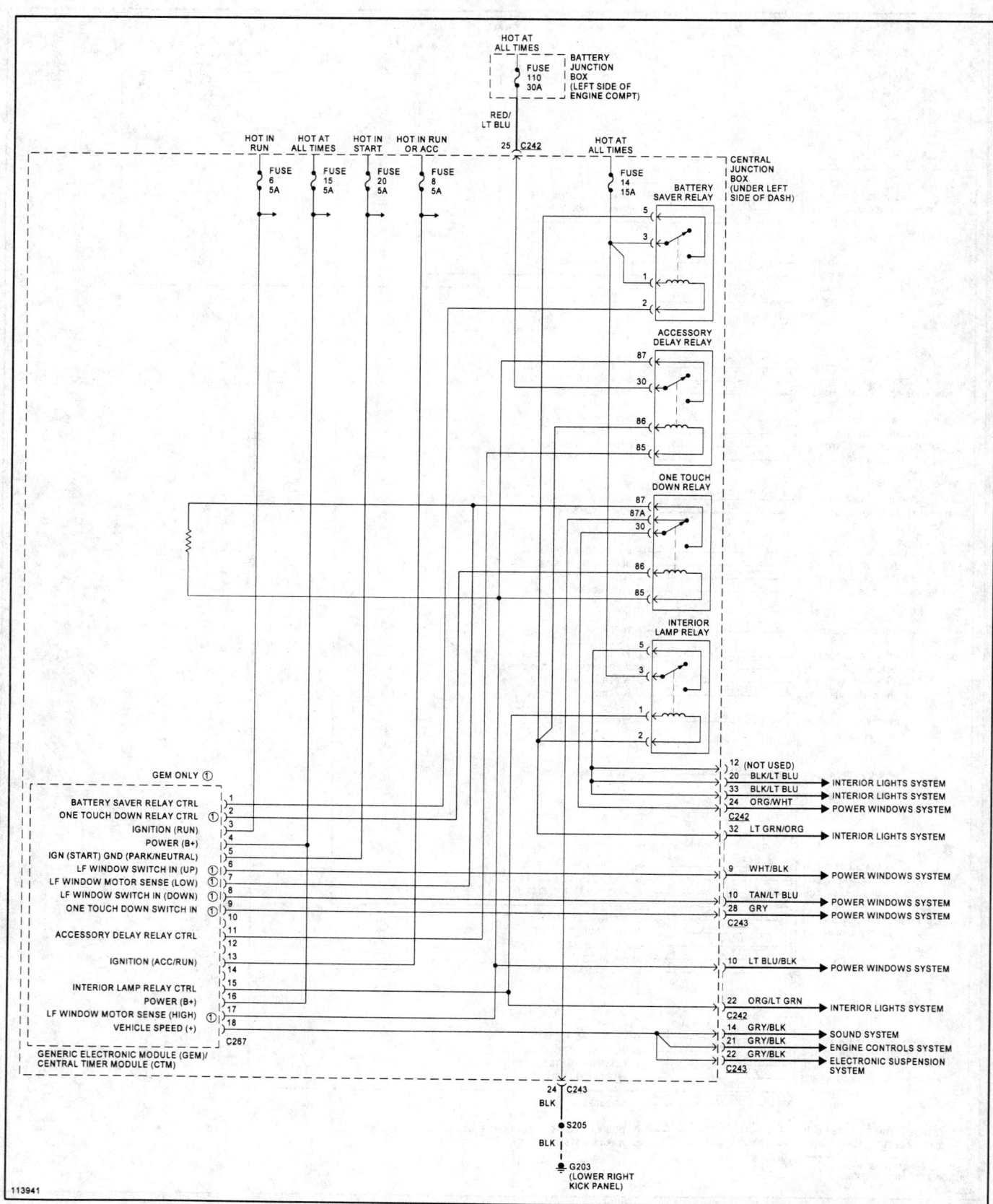

Fig. 6: Body Control Module Wiring Diagram (F150 & F250 Light-Duty Pickup – 1 Of 2)

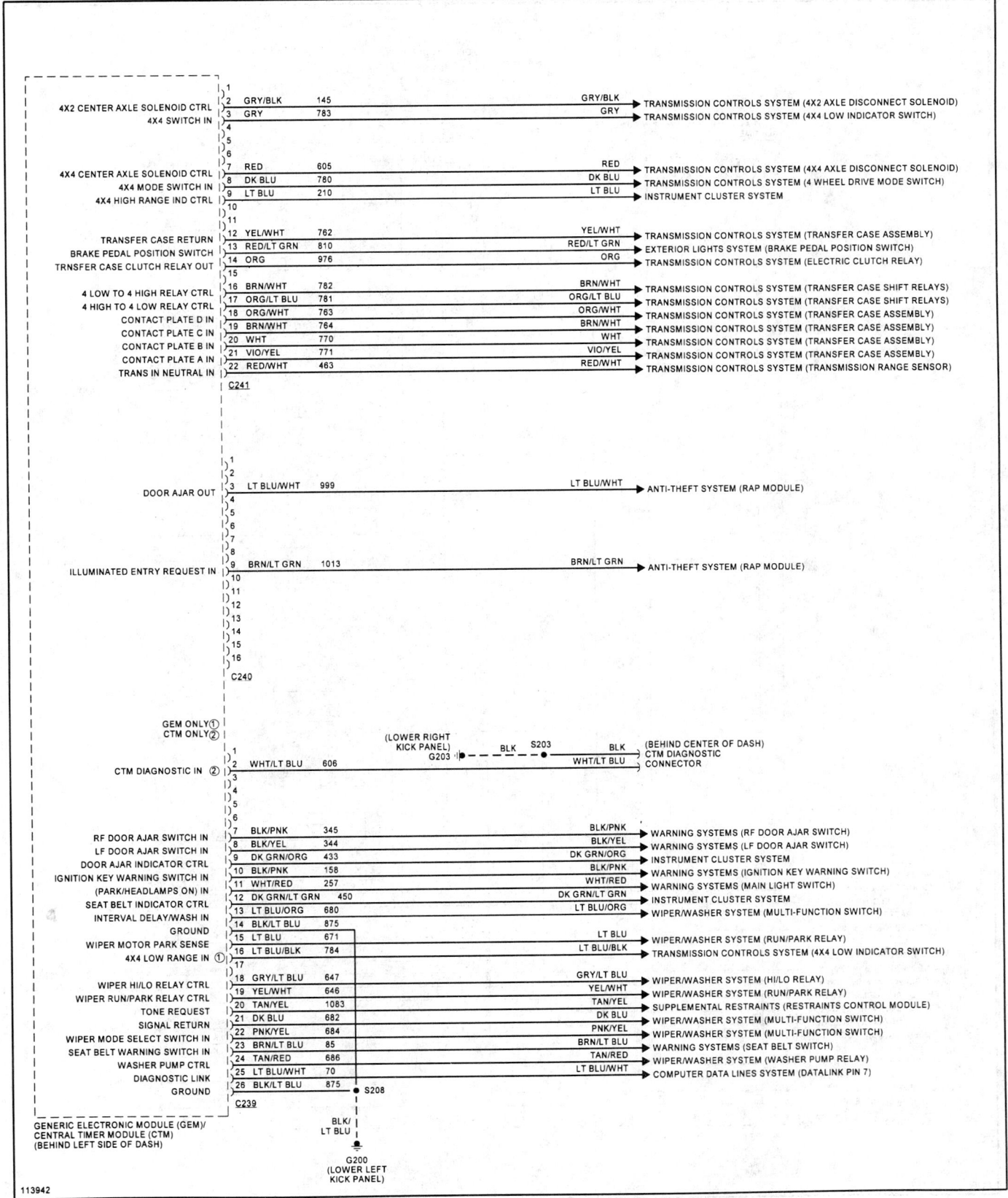

Fig. 7: Body Control Module Wiring Diagram (F150 & F250 Light-Duty Pickup – 2 Of 2)

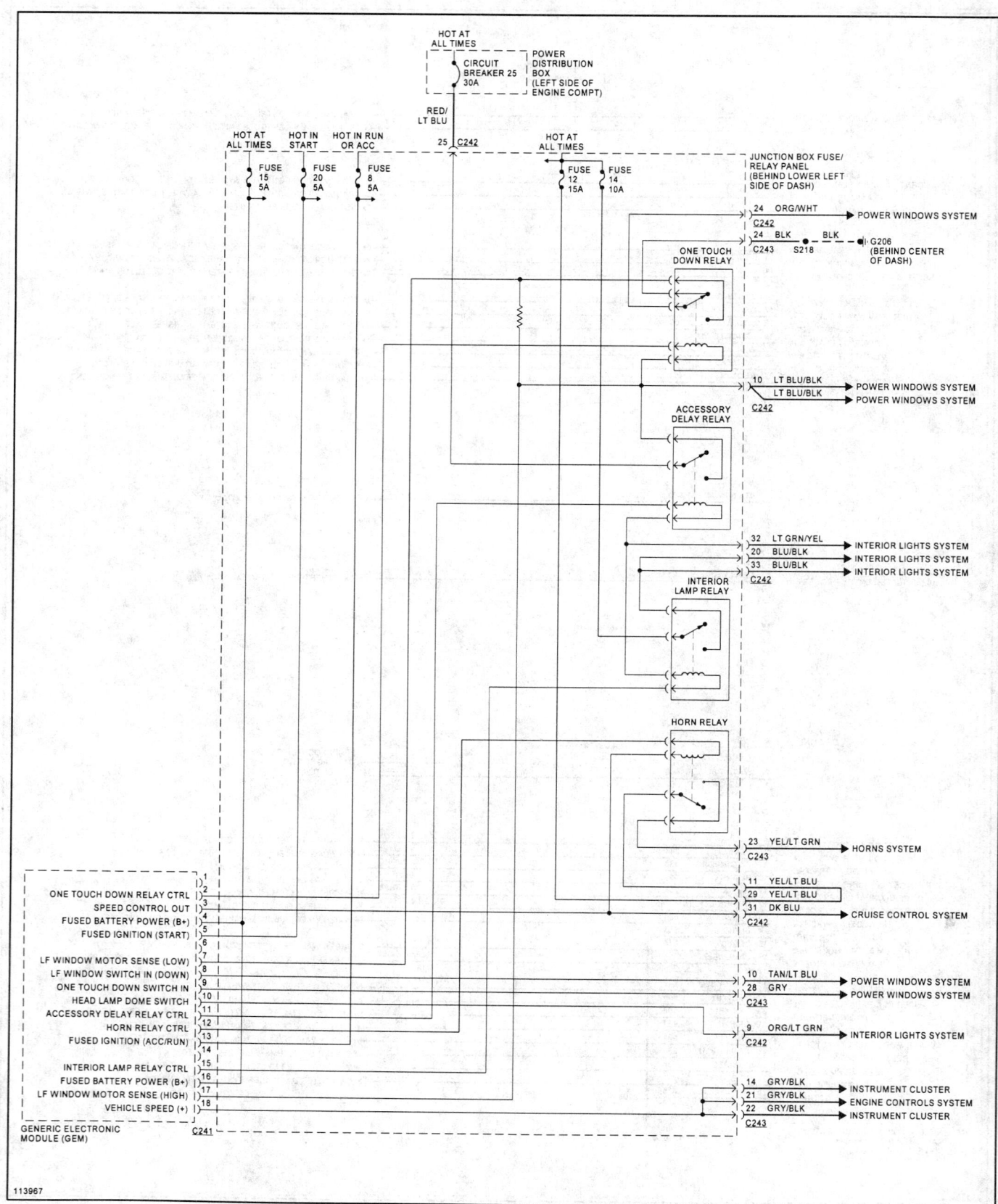

Fig. 8: Body Control Module Wiring Diagram (F250 Super-Duty & F350 Pickup – 1 Of 2)

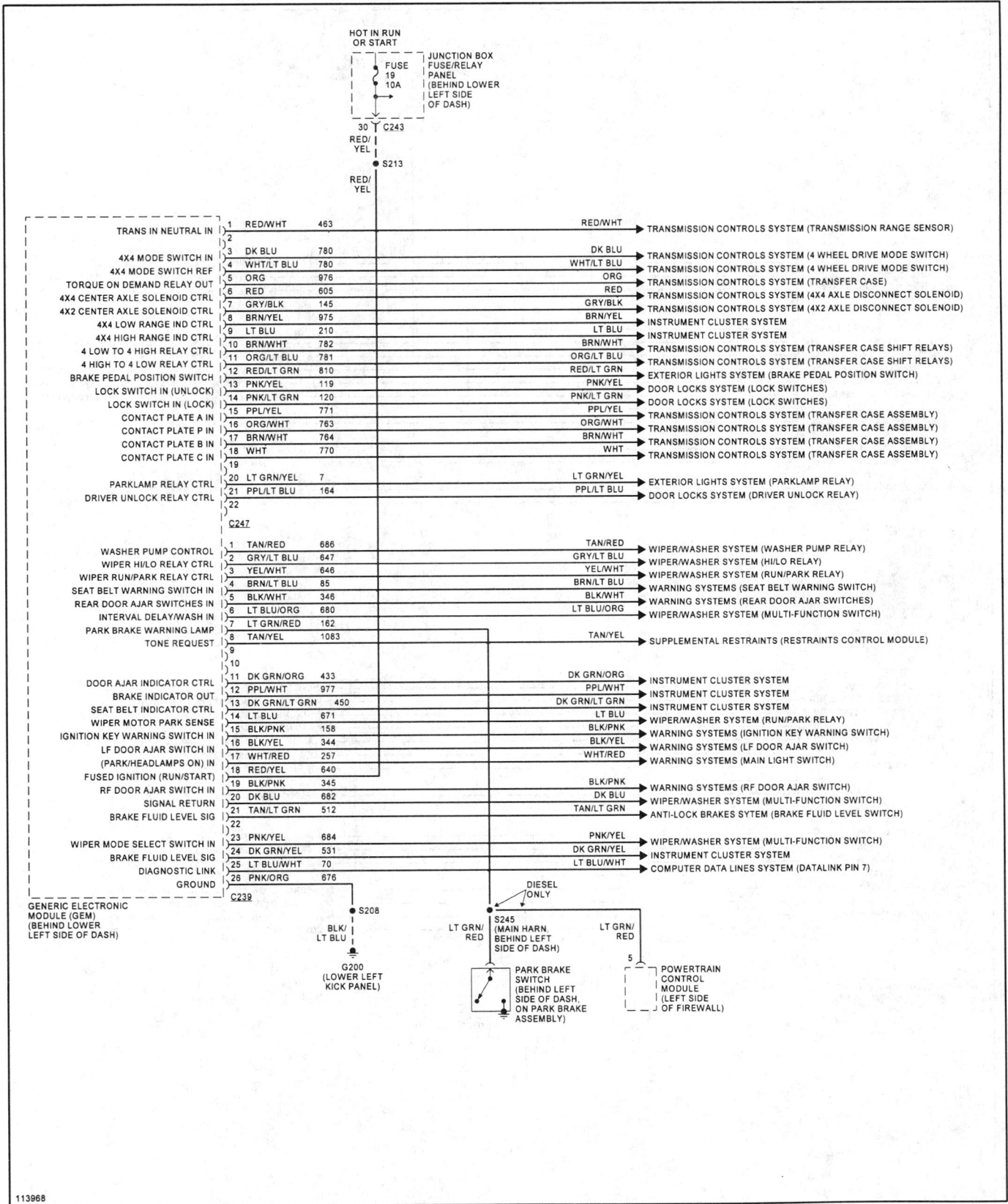

Fig. 9: Body Control Module Wiring Diagram (F250 Super-Duty & F350 Pickup – 2 Of 2)

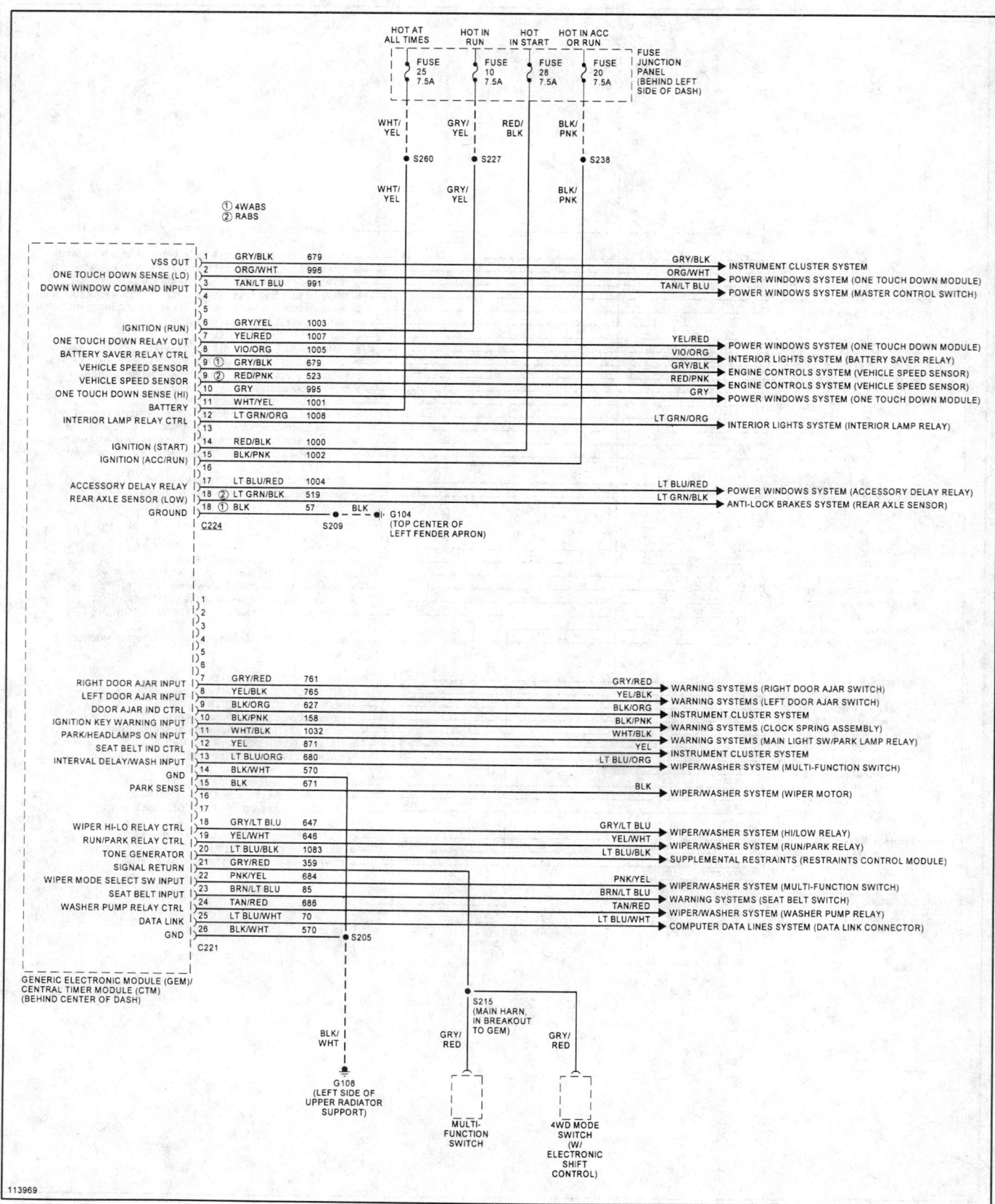

Fig. 10: Body Control Module Wiring Diagram (Ranger – 1 Of 2)

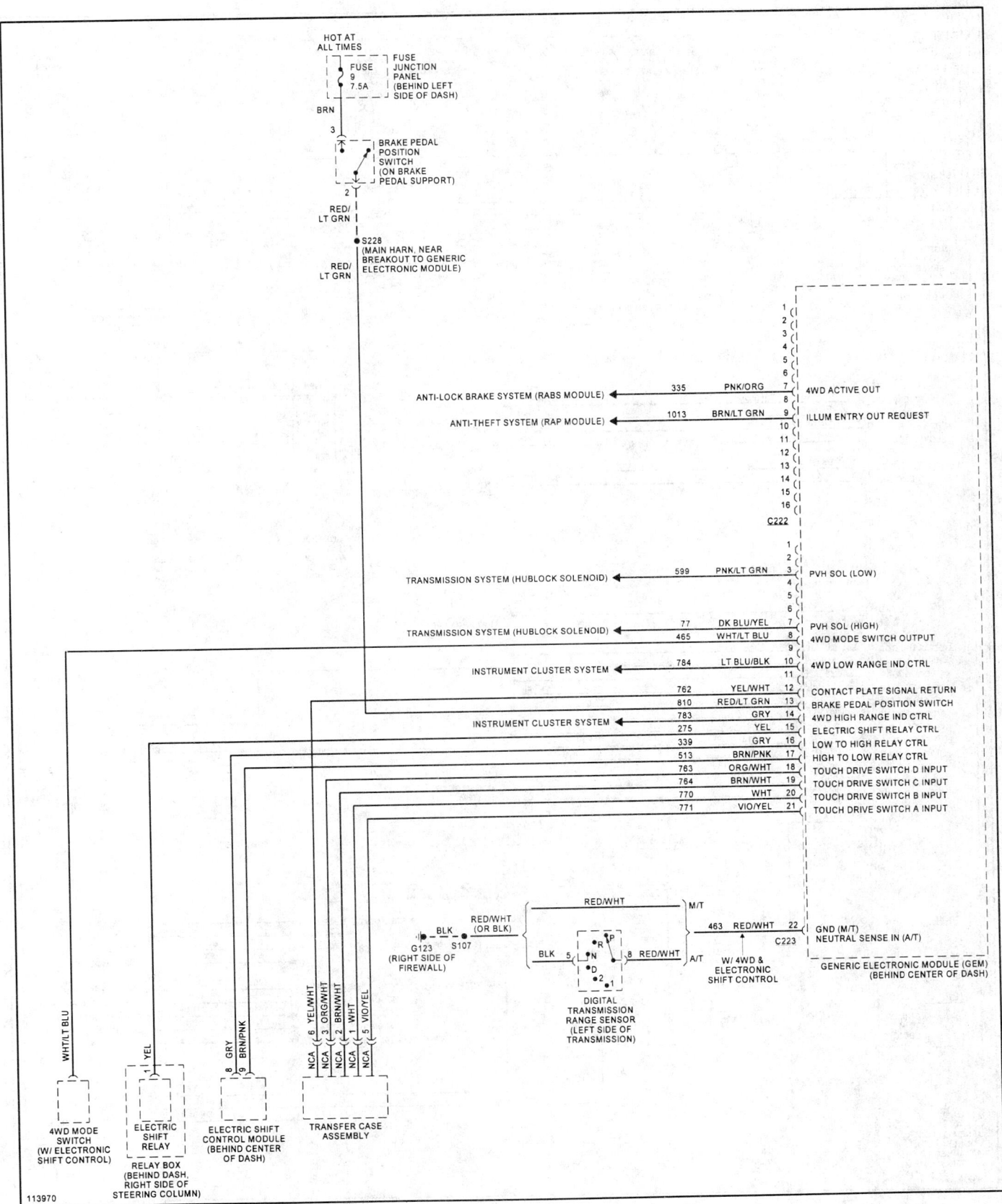

Fig. 11: Body Control Module Wiring Diagram (Ranger – 2 Of 2)

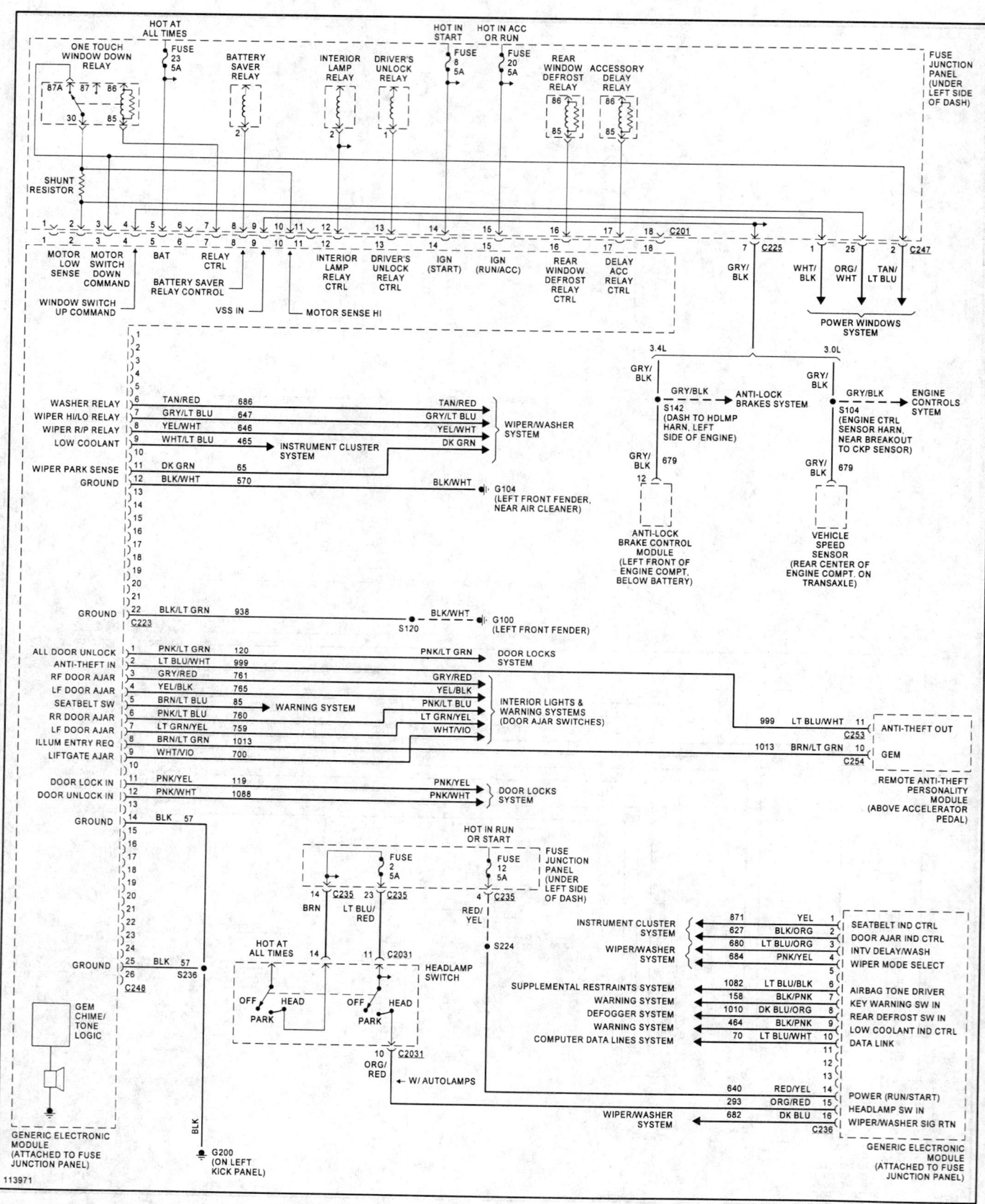

Fig. 12: Body Control Module Wiring Diagram (Sable & Taurus)

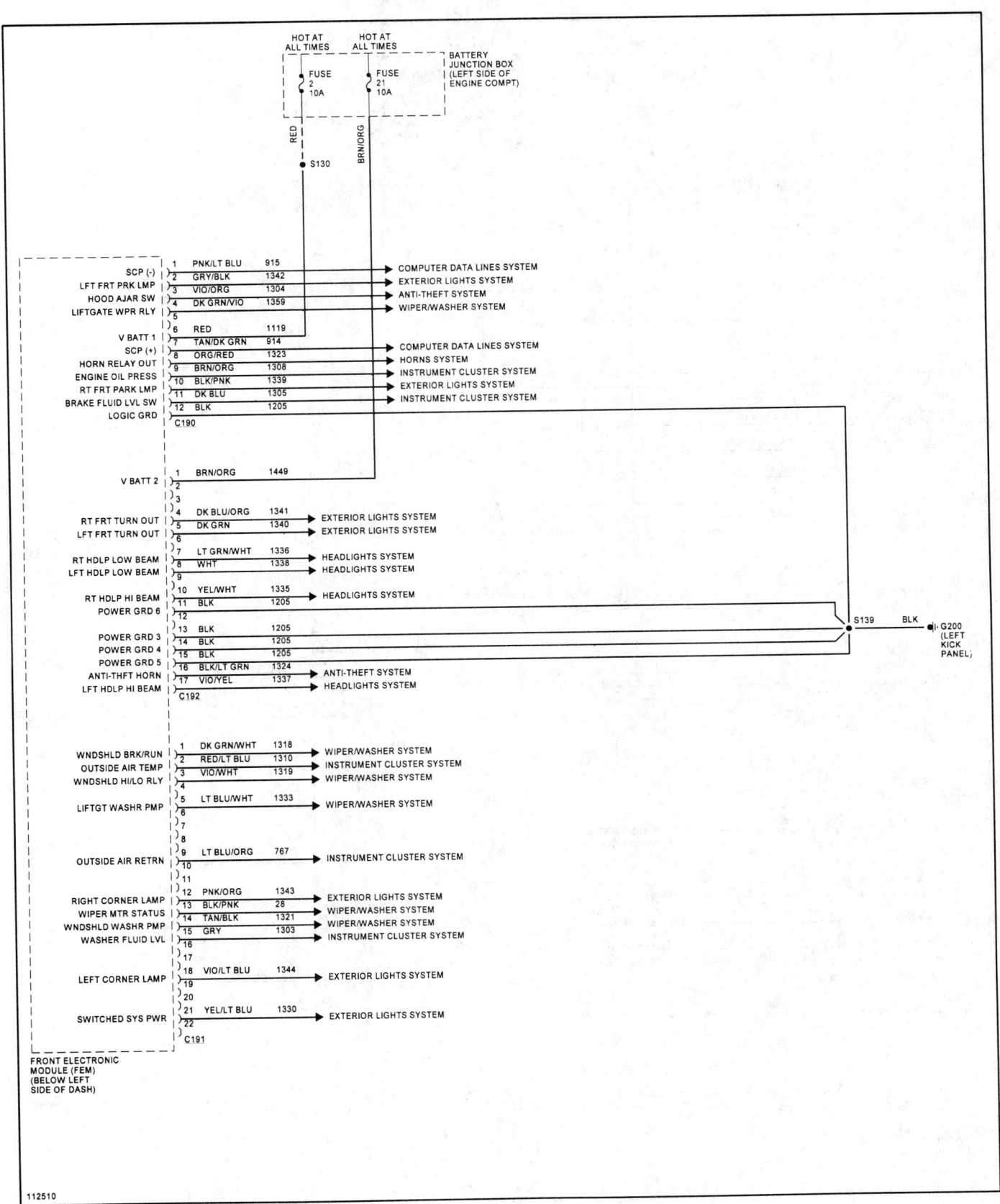

Fig. 13: Body Control Module Wiring Diagram (Windstar – 1 Of 3)

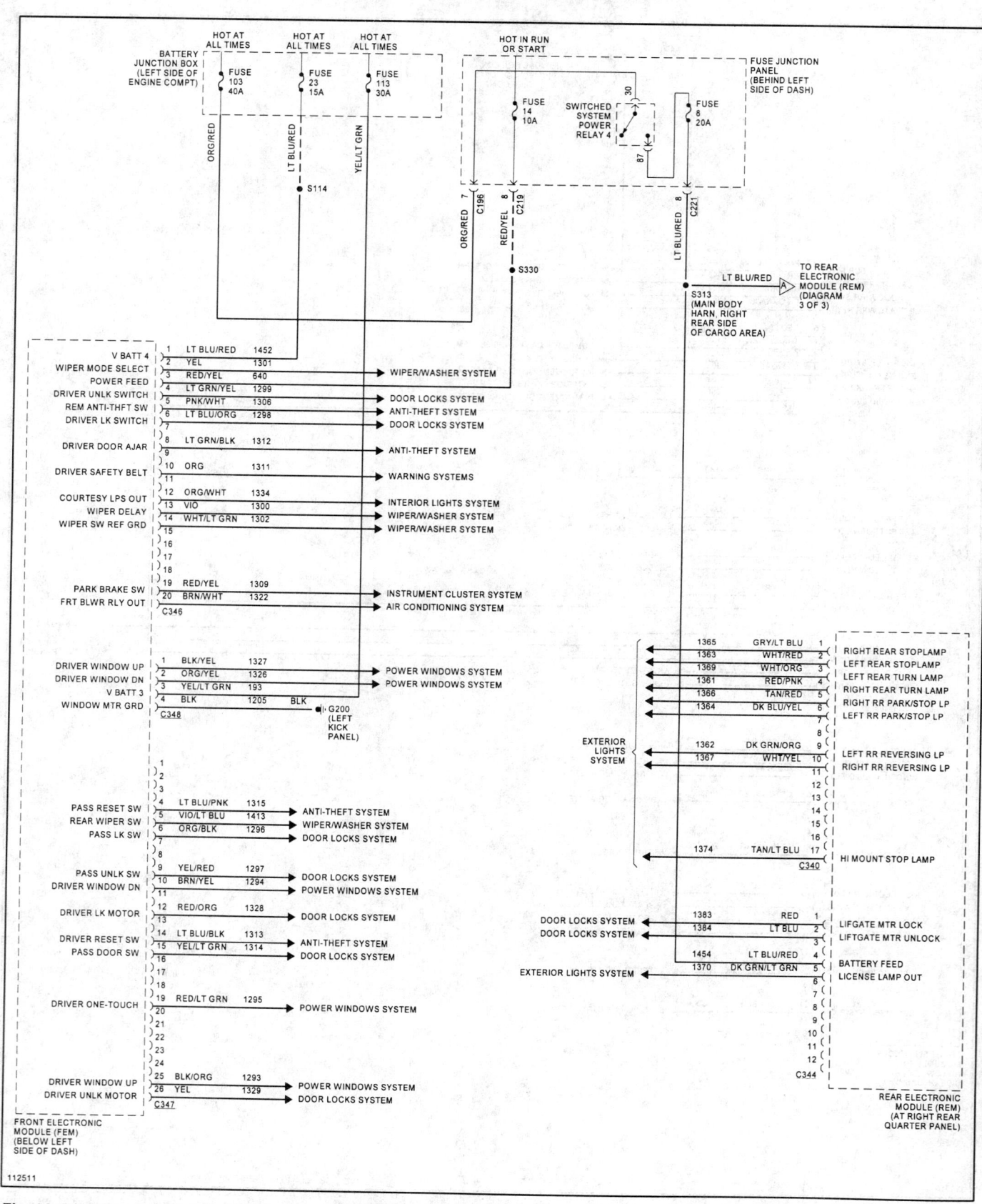

Fig. 14: Body Control Module Wiring Diagram (Windstar – 2 Of 3)

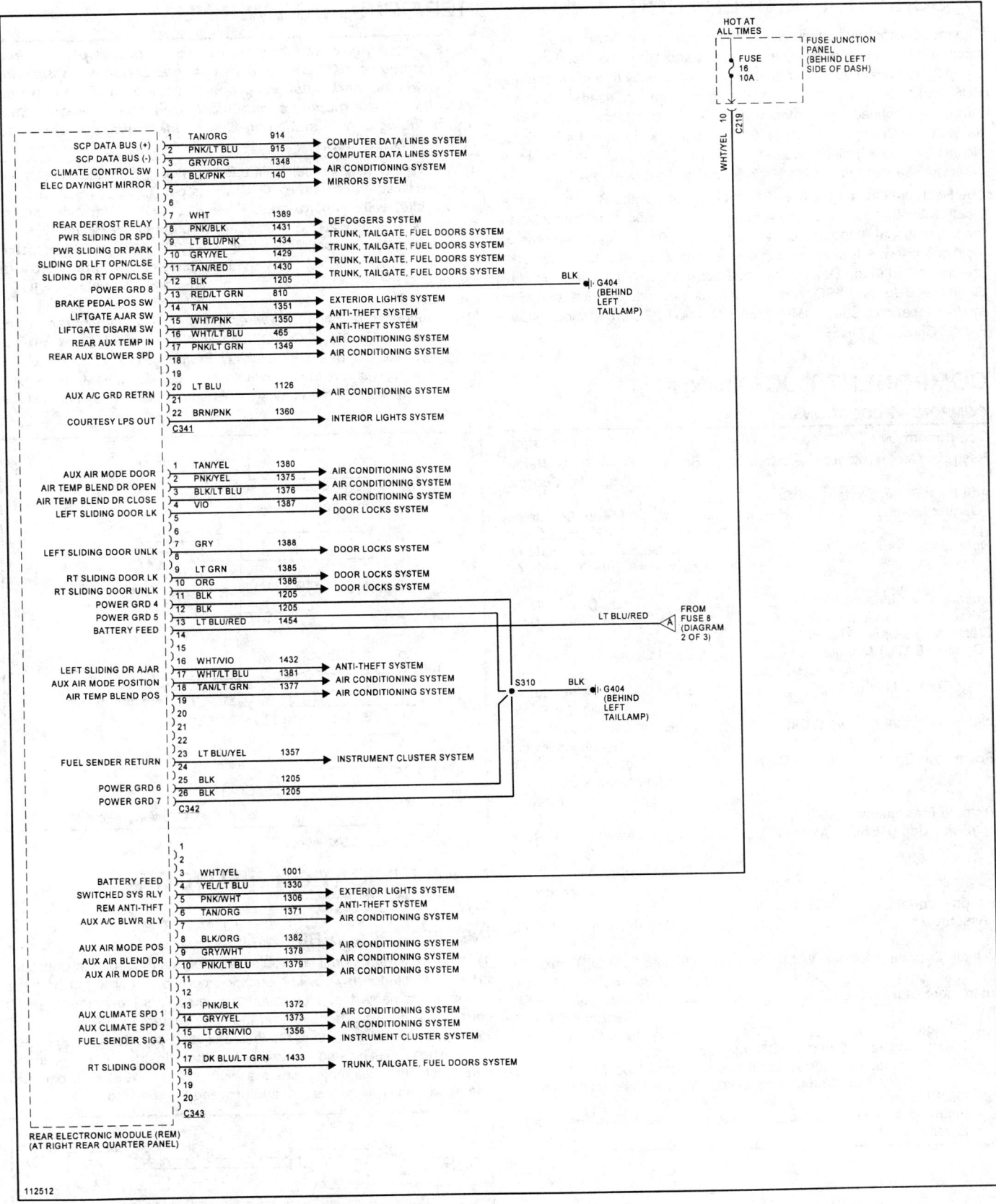

Fig. 15: Body Control Module Wiring Diagram (Windstar – 3 Of 3)

DESCRIPTION & OPERATION

The module communications network provides the ability for module-to-module communication by sharing inputs and outputs instead of each component having an input and output wired directly to each module. A BUS which consists of a pair of twisted wires is used to transfer information between each module. The BUS network is also referred to as Standard Corporate Protocol (SCP). The BUS consists of a (+) circuit No. 914 and a (–) circuit No. 915. The BUS is routed throughout the vehicle to each module except the restraints control module.

The Restraint Control Module (RCM) does not use the BUS to communicate with other modules. The restraints control module is connected to the International Standards Organization (ISO) 9141 diagnostic communications network through a single wire (circuit No. 70). Both networks are connected to the Data Link Connector (DLC). This article is used to diagnose BUS and ISO communications network circuit faults. For module locations, see COMPONENT LOCATIONS table under COMPONENT LOCATIONS.

COMPONENT LOCATIONS

COMPONENT LOCATIONS

Component	Location
Restraint Control Module [1]	Between Front Seats, Below Center Console
Anti-Lock Brake System (ABS) Control Module	Left Front Of Engine Compartment
Data Link Connector (DLC)	Below Driver's Side Of Instrument Panel, To Right Of Steering Column
Driver's Door Module (DDM)	Inside Driver's Door
Driver's Seat Module (DSM)	Under Driver's Seat
Electronic Automatic Temp. Control (EATC) Module	Behind Center Of Instrument Panel
Front Control Unit (FCU) [2]	Behind Center Of Instrument Panel, On Radio
Lighting Control Module (LCM)	On Instrument Panel, Behind Headlight Switch
Powertrain Control Module (PCM)	In Passenger's Side Of Engine Compartment, On Firewall
Remote Emergency Satellite Cellular Unit (RESCU) Module	Passenger's Side Rear Corner Of Trunk, Behind Trim Panel, In Front Of Taillight Assembly
Speed Control Servo/Amplifier Assembly [3]	Mounted On Left Shock Tower
Vehicle Dynamic Module (VDM)	In Driver's Side Of Trunk, On Panel Below Rear Window
Instrument Cluster [4]	Behind Left Side Of Instrument Panel

[1] – Restraint Control Module (RCM) may also be referred to as Electronic Crash Sensor (ECS) module.

[2] – FCU may also be referred to as Audio Control Module (ACM).

[3] – Speed control servo/amplifier assembly may also be referred to as Next Generation Speed Control (NGSC) servo.

[4] – Instrument cluster may also be referred to as Virtual Instrument Cluster (VIC).

REPAIRING BUS WIRING

NOTE: *Following procedure must be used to ensure proper repair is performed on BUS wiring. BUS wiring is sensitive to moisture and oxidation and must be properly sealed to ensure proper operation of the module communications network. Regular heat shrink tubing is NOT sufficient, heat shrink tubing containing hot melt wax is required.*

1) When performing a repair on the BUS wiring, ensure the wires on the BUS are twisted at a rate of 33-40 winds per 3.3 ft. (1 m). The twists should start within approximately 4.9" (124 mm) from any harness connector. Use only 20 AWG standard wire gauge for repairs.

2) If performing a splice in the wiring, strip .75" (19.0 mm) of insulation from one wire and 1.50" (38.1 mm) of insulator from the other wire. Perform STEP 1. See Fig. 1. Place hot melt wax type heat shrink tubing over one wire.

3) Twist stripped portion of the wires together. Solder connection using resin core RMA solder. DO NOT use acid core solder. Bend wires to allow installation of heat shrink tubing. Perform STEP 2. See Fig. 1.

4) Position heat shrink tubing over splice area. Using heat gun, evenly heat the heat shrink tubing until wax flows from both ends of heat shrink tubing.

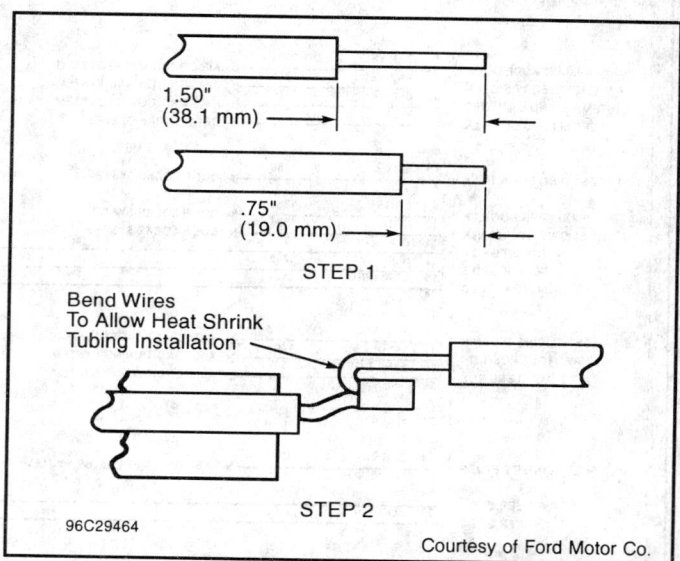

Courtesy of Ford Motor Co.

Fig. 1: Repairing BUS Wiring

COMMUNICATION NETWORK DIAGNOSTICS

INSPECTION & VERIFICATION

1) Verify customer's original problem by operating system in question. Inspect vehicle for any obvious electrical component wiring or harness connector damage. Inspect harness connectors for loose, damaged or corroded terminals. Check related fuses for system in question.

2) Inspect 16-pin Data Link Connector (DLC) pins for damage. See Fig. 2. The DLC is located below driver's side of instrument panel, to the right of steering column. If pins are okay, go to next step. If pins are damaged, repair as necessary and proceed to next step.

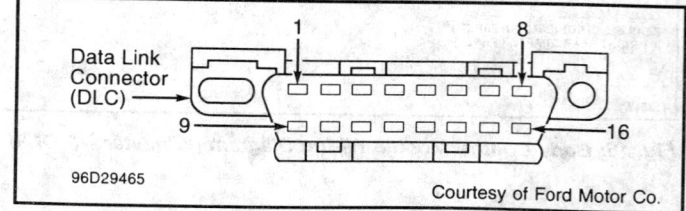

Courtesy of Ford Motor Co.

Fig. 2: Identifying Data Link Connector (DLC) Terminals

3) If problem is still present after performing inspection, connect New Generation Star (NGS) tester to DLC. Select vehicle to be tested from NGS tester menu. If NGS tester does not communicate with vehicle, ensure program card is properly installed. Check NGS tester cable connections and ensure ignition switch is in RUN position. If NGS tester still does not communicate with vehicle, go to TEST P: NO MODULE/NETWORK COMMUNICATION under SYSTEM TESTS. If NGS tester communicates with vehicle, perform data link diagnostic procedure. See DATA LINK DIAGNOSTIC TEST.

DATA LINK DIAGNOSTIC TEST

1) Connect New Generation Star (NGS) tester to Data Link Connector (DLC), if not already connected. Select vehicle to be tested from NGS tester menu.

2) Turn ignition switch to RUN position. Rotate dial on NGS tester to menu item DIAGNOSTIC DATA LINK and press trigger. A test will be performed on the BUS (circuits No. 914 and 915) for the module communications network and the ISO 9141 communication link (circuit No. 70). Circuit No. 70 is the Light Blue/White wire that is between terminal No. 7 on DLC and the restraints control module.

3) If NGS tester displays CKT 914 (+) = SYSTEM PASSED and CKT 915 (−) = SYSTEM PASSED, module communications network is okay at this time. If NGS tester displays CKT 70 = SYSTEM PASSED, ISO 9141 communication link is okay at this time. Return to article that directed you here and continue diagnosis.

4) If NGS tester does not display CKT 914 (+) = SYSTEM PASSED, CKT 915 (−) = SYSTEM PASSED and CKT 70 = SYSTEM PASSED, perform the following as applicable.

- If no response from NGS tester, go to TEST P: NO MODULE/NETWORK COMMUNICATION under SYSTEM TESTS.
- If NGS tester displays CKT 70, CKT 914 and/or CKT 915 = SOME ECUS NO RESP/NOT EQUIP, go to SYMPTOM CHART table and perform appropriate test.
- If NGS tester displays CKT 70 = ALL ECUS NO RESP/NOT EQUIP, go to TEST F: RESTRAINTS CONTROL MODULE DOES NOT RESPOND TO NGS TESTER under SYSTEM TESTS.
- If NGS tester displays CKT 914 = ALL ECUS NO RESP/NOT EQUIP, go to TEST N: NO MODULE/NETWORK COMMUNICATION (BUS LINK) under SYSTEM TESTS.
- If NGS tester displays CKT 915 = ALL ECUS NO RESP/NOT EQUIP, go to TEST N: NO MODULE/NETWORK COMMUNICATION (BUS LINK) under SYSTEM TESTS.
- If module in question is NO RESPONSE/NOT EQUIPPED, go to SYMPTOM CHART table and perform appropriate test.
- If module in question is NO RESPONSE ON CKT 914 (BUS +), go to SYMPTOM CHART table and perform appropriate test.
- If module in question is NO RESPONSE ON CKT 915 (BUS −), go to SYMPTOM CHART table and perform appropriate test.

SYMPTOM CHART

Condition	Test
Anti-Lock Brake System (ABS) Module Does Not Respond To NGS Tester	A
Front Control Unit (FCU) Does Not Respond To NGS Tester [1]	B
Driver's Door Module (DDM) Does Not Respond To NGS Tester	C
Driver's Seat Module (DSM) Does Not Respond To NGS Tester	D
Electronic Automatic Temperature Control (EATC) Module Does Not Respond To NGS Tester	E
Restraint Control Module (RCM) Does Not Respond To NGS Tester [2]	F
Lighting Control Module (LCM) Does Not Respond To NGS Tester	G
Speed Control Servo/Amplifier Assembly Does Not Respond To NGS Tester [3]	H
Powertrain Control Module (PCM) Does Not Respond To NGS Tester	J

SYMPTOM CHART (Cont.)

Condition	Test
Remote Emergency Satellite Cellular Unit (RESCU) Module Does Not Respond To NGS Tester	K
Vehicle Dynamics Module (VDM) Does Not Respond To NGS Tester	L
Instrument Cluster Does Not Respond To NGS Tester [4]	M
No Module/Network Communication (BUS Link)	N
No Module/Network Communication (ISO 9141 Link)	F
No Module/Network Communication	P

[1] — FCU may also be referred to as Audio Control Module (ACM).
[2] — Restraint control module may as be referred to as Electronic Crash Sensor (ECS) module.
[3] — Speed control servo/amplifier assembly may also be referred to as Next Generation Speed Control (NGSC) servo.
[4] — Instrument cluster may also be referred to as Virtual Instrument Cluster (VIC).

RETRIEVING & CLEARING DIAGNOSTIC TROUBLE CODES

Connect New Generation Star (NGS) tester to Data Link Connector (DLC). Following manufacturers instructions to retrieve and clear codes for desired module. See appropriate table under DIAGNOSTIC TROUBLE CODE (DTC) DEFINITIONS for a listing of Diagnostic Trouble Codes (DTCs) and appropriate test procedure.

ACCESSING PARAMETER IDENTIFICATION (PID)

Turn ignition switch to LOCK position. Connect New Generation Star (NGS) tester to Data Link Connector (DLC). Following manufacturers instructions enter PID/DATA MONITOR AND RECORD for desired module. Operate appropriate system and ensure PID expected values are obtained. See appropriate table under PARAMETER IDENTIFICATION (PID) DEFINITIONS.

SYSTEM TESTS

CAUTION: When battery is disconnected or modules are replaced, vehicle computer and memory systems may lose memory data. Driveability problems may exist until computer systems have completed a relearn cycle. See COMPUTER RELEARN PROCEDURES article in GENERAL INFORMATION before disconnecting battery.

NOTE: Always check module power and ground circuits prior to replacing a control module. See appropriate wiring diagram in DATA LINK CONNECTORS, GROUND DISTRIBUTION and/or POWER DISTRIBUTION article in WIRING DIAGRAMS.

TEST A: ANTI-LOCK BRAKE SYSTEM (ABS) MODULE DOES NOT RESPOND TO NGS TESTER

1) Turn ignition switch to LOCK position. Disconnect ABS module harness connector C1012. Disconnect NGS tester. Inspect ABS module harness connector for loose, damaged or corroded terminals. Repair harness connector as necessary and retest system for normal operation. If harness connector is okay, reconnect ABS module harness connector and NGS tester. Turn ignition switch to RUN position. Perform data link diagnostic procedure. See DATA LINK DIAGNOSTIC TEST under COMMUNICATION NETWORK DIAGNOSTICS. If NGS tester indicates ABS: NO RESPONSE ON CKT 914 (BUS +), go to next step. If NGS tester does not indicate ABS: NO RESPONSE ON CKT 914 (BUS +), go to step **5)**.

2) Turn ignition switch to LOCK position. Disconnect ABS module harness connector C1012. Disconnect NGS tester. Measure resistance in Tan/Orange wire between terminal No. 20 at ABS module harness connector C1012 and terminal No. 2 at Data Link Connector (DLC). *See Figs. 2 and 3.* If resistance is greater than 5 ohms, go to next step. If resistance is 5 ohms or less, replace ABS module.

3) Disconnect 84-pin harness connector C217 located behind left side of instrument panel. *See Fig. 4.* Inspect harness connector for loose, damaged or corroded terminals. Repair harness connector as necessary and retest system for normal operation. If harness connector is okay, measure resistance in Tan/Orange wire between terminal No. 55 at harness connector C217 and terminal No. 2 at DLC. *See Figs. 2 and 5.* If resistance is 5 ohms or less, go to next step. If resistance is greater than 5 ohms, repair open in Tan/Orange wire between harness connector C217 and DLC.

4) Disconnect Gray 40-pin harness connector C139 located in left rear of engine compartment. *See Fig. 6.* Inspect harness connector for loose, damaged or corroded terminals. Repair harness connector as necessary and retest system for normal operation. If harness connector is okay, measure resistance in Tan/Orange wire between terminal No. 20 at ABS module harness connector C1012 and terminal No. 19 at harness connector C139. *See Figs. 3 and 7.* If resistance is 5 ohms or less, repair open in Tan/Orange wire between harness connector C217 and female half of harness connector C139. If resistance is greater than 5 ohms, repair open in Tan/Orange wire between male half of harness connector C139 and ABS module harness connector C1012.

5) Turn ignition switch to LOCK position. Disconnect ABS module harness connector C1012. Disconnect NGS tester. Measure resistance in Pink/Light Blue wire between terminal No. 19 at ABS module harness connector and terminal No. 10 at DLC. *See Figs. 2 and 3.* If resistance is greater than 5 ohms, go to next step. If resistance is 5 ohms or less, replace ABS module.

6) Disconnect 84-pin harness connector C217 located behind left side of instrument panel. *See Fig. 4.* Inspect harness connector for loose, damaged or corroded terminals. Repair harness connector as necessary and retest system for normal operation. If harness connector is okay, measure resistance in Pink/Light Blue wire between terminal No. 79 at harness connector C217 and terminal No. 10 at DLC. *See Figs. 2 and 5.* If resistance is 5 ohms or less, go to next step. If resistance is greater than 5 ohms, repair open in Pink/Light Blue wire between harness connector C217 and DLC.

7) Disconnect Gray 40-pin harness connector C139 located in left rear of engine compartment. *See Fig. 6.* Inspect harness connector for loose, damaged or corroded terminals. Repair harness connector as necessary and retest system for normal operation. If harness connector is okay, measure resistance in Pink/Light Blue wire between terminal No. 19 at ABS module harness connector C1012 and terminal No. 23 at harness connector C139. *See Figs. 3 and 7.* If resistance is 5 ohms or less, repair open in Pink/Light Blue wire between harness connector C217 and female half of harness connector C139. If resistance is greater than 5 ohms, repair open in Pink/Light Blue wire between male half of harness connector C139 and ABS module harness connector C1012.

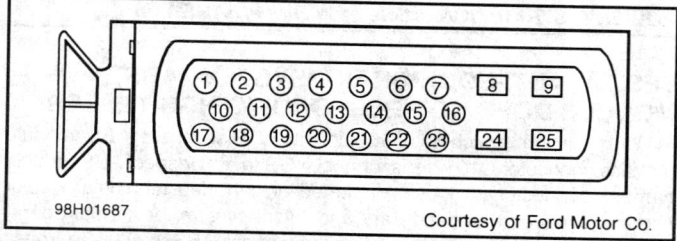

Fig. 3: Identifying ABS Module Harness Connector C1012 Terminals

TEST B: FRONT CONTROL UNIT (FCU) DOES NOT RESPOND TO NGS TESTER

NOTE: Front Control Unit (FCU) may also be referred to as Audio Control Module (ACM).

1) Turn ignition switch to LOCK position. Disconnect FCU 16-pin harness connector C224 located behind center of instrument panel, on radio. Inspect harness connector for loose, damaged or corroded terminals. Repair as necessary and retest system for normal operation.

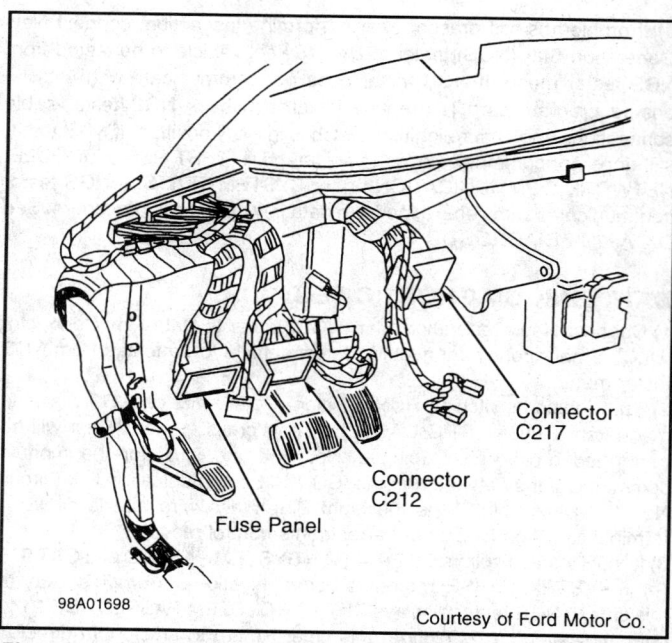

Fig. 4: Locating Bulkhead Harness Connectors C212 & C217

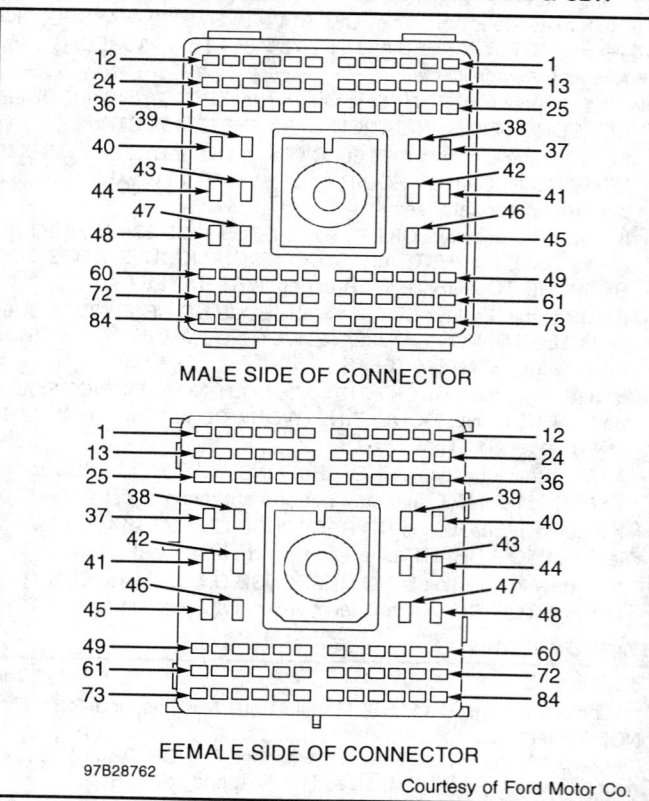

Fig. 5: Identifying Bulkhead Harness Connectors C212 & C217 Terminals

If harness connector is okay, reconnect harness connector. Turn ignition switch to RUN position. Perform data link diagnostic procedure. See DATA LINK DIAGNOSTIC TEST under COMMUNICATION NETWORK DIAGNOSTICS. If NGS tester indicates FCU: NO RESPONSE ON CKT 914 (BUS +), go to next step. If NGS tester does not indicate FCU: NO RESPONSE ON CKT 914 (BUS +), go to step **3)**.

2) Turn ignition switch to LOCK position. Disconnect NGS tester. Measure resistance in Tan/Orange wire between terminal No. 3 at FCU harness connector C224 and terminal No. 2 at Data Link Connector

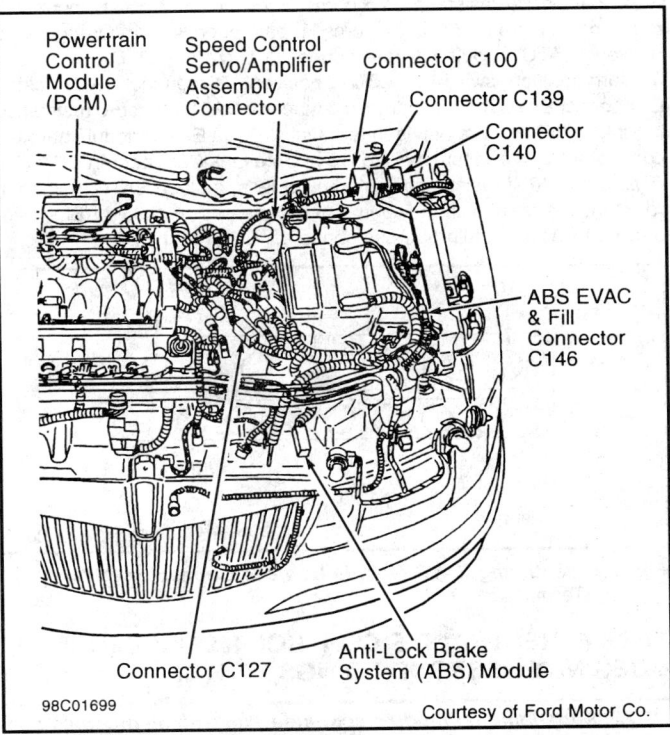

Fig. 6: Locating Engine Compartment Harness Connectors

Powertrain Control Module (PCM)
Speed Control Servo/Amplifier Assembly Connector
Connector C100
Connector C139
Connector C140
ABS EVAC & Fill Connector C146
Connector C127
Anti-Lock Brake System (ABS) Module
98C01699
Courtesy of Ford Motor Co.

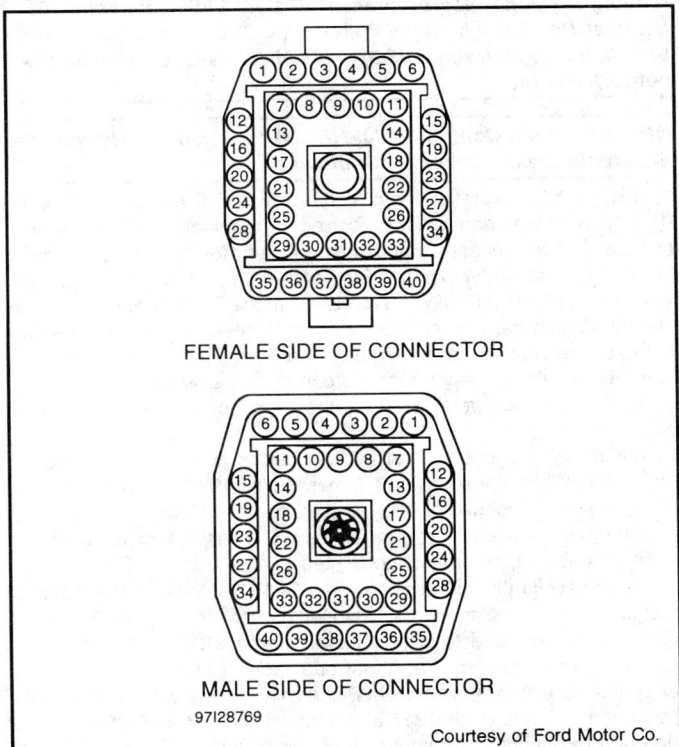

FEMALE SIDE OF CONNECTOR

MALE SIDE OF CONNECTOR
97I28769
Courtesy of Ford Motor Co.

Fig. 7: Identifying Harness Connectors C100 & C139 Terminals

(DLC). If resistance is 5 ohms or less, replace FCU. If resistance is greater than 5 ohms, repair open in Tan/Orange wire between FCU harness connector C224 and DLC.

3) Turn ignition switch to LOCK position. Disconnect NGS tester. measure resistance in Pink/Light Blue wire between terminal No. 4 at FCU harness connector C224 and terminal No. 10 at DLC. If resistance

is 5 ohms or less, replace FCU. If resistance is greater than 5 ohms, repair open in Pink/Light Blue wire between FCU harness connector C224 and DLC.

TEST C: DRIVER'S DOOR MODULE (DDM) DOES NOT RESPOND TO NGS TESTER

1) Turn ignition switch to LOCK position. Disconnect DDM 14-pin harness connector C524 located inside driver's door. Inspect harness connector for loose, damaged or corroded terminals. Repair as necessary and retest system for normal operation. If harness connector is okay, reconnect harness connector. Turn ignition switch to RUN position. Perform data link diagnostic procedure. See DATA LINK DIAGNOSTIC TEST under COMMUNICATION NETWORK DIAGNOSTICS. If NGS tester indicates DDM: NO RESPONSE ON CKT 914 (BUS +), go to next step. If NGS tester does not indicate DDM: NO RESPONSE ON CKT 914 (BUS +), go to step **4)**.

2) Turn ignition switch to LOCK position. Disconnect NGS tester. Disconnect DDM harness connector C524. Measure resistance in Tan/Orange wire between terminal No. 12 at DDM harness connector C524 and terminal No. 2 at Data Link Connector (DLC). *See Figs. 2 and 8*. If resistance is greater than 5 ohms, go to next step. If resistance is 5 ohms or less, replace DDM.

3) Reconnect NGS tester. Turn ignition switch to RUN position. Perform data link diagnostic procedure, to check Driver's Seat Module (DSM) operating state. See DATA LINK DIAGNOSTIC TEST under COMMUNICATION NETWORK DIAGNOSTICS. If NGS tester indicates DSM: NO RESPONSE ON CKT 914 (BUS +), repair open in Tan/Orange wire between female half of bulkhead harness connector C217 and DDM harness connector C524. Harness connector C217 located behind left side of instrument panel. *See Fig. 4*. If NGS tester does not indicate DSM: NO RESPONSE ON CKT 914 (BUS +), repair open in Tan/Orange wire between male half of bulkhead harness connector C217 and DLC.

4) Turn ignition switch to LOCK position. Disconnect NGS tester. Disconnect DDM harness connector C524. Measure resistance in Pink/Light Blue wire between terminal No. 13 at DDM harness connector C524 and terminal No. 10 at DLC. *See Figs. 2 and 8*. If resistance is greater than 5 ohms, go to next step. If resistance is 5 ohms or less, replace DDM.

5) Reconnect NGS tester. Turn ignition switch to RUN position. Perform data link diagnostic procedure, to check Driver's Seat Module (DSM) operating state. See DATA LINK DIAGNOSTIC TEST under COMMUNICATION NETWORK DIAGNOSTICS. If NGS tester indicates DSM: NO RESPONSE ON CKT 915 (BUS −), repair open in Pink/Light Blue wire between female half of bulkhead harness connector C217 and DDM harness connector C524. If NGS tester does not indicate DSM: NO RESPONSE ON CKT 915 (BUS −), repair open in Pink/Light Blue wire between male half of bulkhead harness connector C217 and DLC.

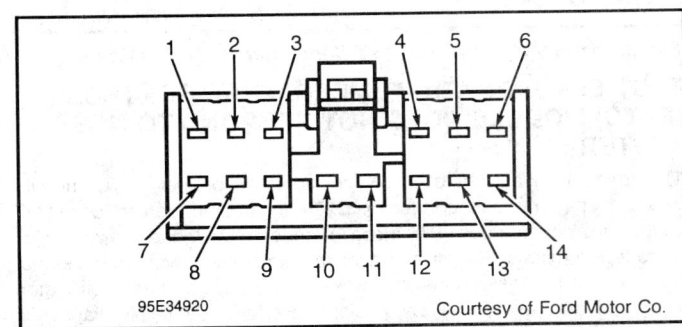

95E34920
Courtesy of Ford Motor Co.

Fig. 8: Identifying DDM Harness Connector C524 Terminals

TEST D: DRIVER'S SEAT MODULE (DSM) DOES NOT RESPOND TO NGS TESTER

1) Turn ignition switch to LOCK position. Disconnect DSM 26-pin harness connector C342 located under driver's front seat. Inspect harness connector for loose, damaged or corroded terminals. Repair as necessary and retest system for normal operation. If harness connector is okay, reconnect harness connector. Turn ignition switch to RUN position. Perform data link diagnostic procedure. See DATA LINK DIAGNOSTIC TEST under COMMUNICATION NETWORK DIAGNOSTICS. If NGS tester indicates DSM: NO RESPONSE ON CKT 914 (BUS +), go to next step. If NGS tester does not indicate DSM: NO RESPONSE ON CKT 914 (BUS +), go to step **4**).

2) Turn ignition switch to LOCK position. Disconnect NGS tester. Disconnect DSM harness connector C342. Measure resistance in Tan/Orange wire between terminal No. 25 at DSM harness connector C342 and terminal No. 2 at Data Link Connector (DLC). See Figs. 2 and 9. If resistance is greater than 5 ohms, go to next step. If resistance is 5 ohms or less, replace DSM.

3) Reconnect NGS tester. Turn ignition switch to RUN position. Perform data link diagnostic procedure, to check Driver's Door Module (DDM) operating state. See DATA LINK DIAGNOSTIC TEST under COMMUNICATION NETWORK DIAGNOSTICS. If NGS tester indicates DDM: NO RESPONSE ON CKT 914 (BUS +), repair open in Tan/Orange wire between female half of bulkhead harness connector C217 and DSM harness connector C342. harness connector C217 located behind left side of instrument panel. See Fig. 4. If NGS tester does not indicate DDM: NO RESPONSE ON CKT 914 (BUS +), repair open in Tan/Orange wire between male half of bulkhead harness connector C217 and DLC.

4) Turn ignition switch to LOCK position. Disconnect NGS tester. Disconnect DSM harness connector C342. Measure resistance in Pink/Light Blue wire between terminal No. 26 at DSM harness connector C342 and terminal No. 10 at DLC. See Figs. 2 and 9. If resistance is greater than 5 ohms, go to next step. If resistance is 5 ohms or less, replace DSM.

5) Reconnect NGS tester. Turn ignition switch to RUN position. Perform data link diagnostic procedure, to check Driver's Door Module (DDM) operating state. See DATA LINK DIAGNOSTIC TEST under COMMUNICATION NETWORK DIAGNOSTICS. If NGS tester indicates DDM: NO RESPONSE ON CKT 915 (BUS –), repair open in Pink/Light Blue wire between female half of bulkhead harness connector C217 and DSM harness connector C342. If NGS tester does not indicate DDM: NO RESPONSE ON CKT 915 (BUS –), repair open in Pink/Light Blue wire between male half of bulkhead harness connector C217 and DLC.

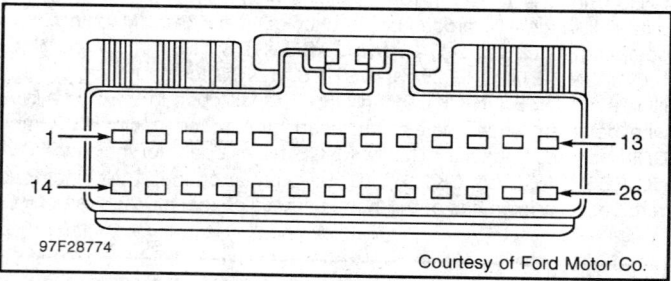

Fig. 9: Identifying DSM Harness Connector C342 Terminals

TEST E: AUTOMATIC TEMPERATURE CONTROL (EATC) MODULE DOES NOT RESPOND TO NGS TESTER

1) Turn ignition switch to LOCK position. Disconnect EATC module White 13-pin harness connector C274 located in behind center of instrument panel. Inspect harness connector for loose, damaged or corroded terminals. Repair as necessary and retest system for normal operation. If harness connector is okay, reconnect harness connector. Turn ignition switch to RUN position. Perform data link diagnostic procedure. See DATA LINK DIAGNOSTIC TEST under COMMUNICATION NETWORK DIAGNOSTICS. If NGS tester indicates EATC: NO RESPONSE ON CKT 914 (BUS +), go to next step. If NGS tester does not indicate EATC: NO RESPONSE ON CKT 914 (BUS +), go to step **3**).

2) Turn ignition switch to LOCK position. Disconnect NGS tester. Disconnect EATC module harness connector C274. Measure resistance in Tan/Orange wire between terminal No. 15 at EATC module harness connector C274 and terminal No. 2 at Data Link Connector (DLC). See Figs. 2 and 10. If resistance is 5 ohms or less, replace EATC module. If resistance is greater than 5 ohms, repair open in Tan/Orange wire between EATC module harness connector C274 and DLC.

3) Turn ignition switch to LOCK position. Disconnect NGS tester. Disconnect EATC module harness connector C274. Measure resistance in Pink/Light Blue wire between terminal No. 1 at EATC module harness connector C274 and terminal No. 10 at Data Link Connector (DLC). See Figs. 2 and 10. If resistance is 5 ohms or less, replace EATC module. If resistance is greater than 5 ohms, repair open in Pink/Light Blue wire between EATC module harness connector C274 and DLC.

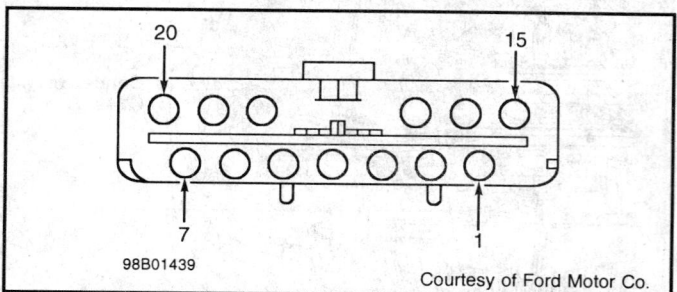

Fig. 10: Identifying EATC Module Harness Connector C274 Terminals

TEST F: RESTRAINTS CONTROL MODULE (RCM) DOES NOT RESPOND TO NGS TESTER

NOTE: Depending on module configuration, with all modules connected and with ignition switch in RUN position or with engine running 2-3 volts may be present at Data Link Connector (DLC) terminal No. 7 (Light Blue/White wire). This is the International Standards Organization (ISO) 9141 diagnostic communications network circuit.

NOTE: Restraint Control Module (RCM) may also be referred to as Electronic Crash Sensor (ECS) module.

1) Inspect NGS tester harness connector and Data Link Connector (DLC) for loose, damaged or corroded terminals. Repair harness connector(s) as necessary and retest system for normal operation. If harness connectors are okay, deactivate air bag system. See appropriate AIR BAG RESTRAINT SYSTEMS article. Disconnect restraints control module harness connector C327 located between front seats, below center console. Inspect harness connector for loose, damaged or corroded terminals. Repair harness connector as necessary and retest system for normal operation. If harness connector is okay, go to next step.

2) Ensure ignition switch is in LOCK position. Measure resistance in Light Blue/White wire between terminal No. 19 at restraints control module harness connector C327 and terminal No. 7 at DLC. See Figs. 2 and 11. If resistance is greater than 5 ohms, go to next step. If resistance is 5 ohms or less, go to step **4**).

3) Disconnect 84-pin harness connector C217 located behind left side of instrument panel. See Fig. 4. Inspect harness connector for loose, damaged or corroded terminals. Repair harness connector as necessary and retest system for normal operation. If harness connector is okay, measure resistance in Light Blue/White wire between terminal No. 59 at harness connector C217 and terminal No. 7 at DLC. See Figs. 2 and 5. If resistance is 5 ohms or less, repair open in Light Blue/White wire between female half of harness connector C217 and restraints control module harness connector C327. If resistance is greater than 5 ohms, repair open in Light Blue/White wire between harness connector C217 and DLC.

4) Turn ignition switch to RUN position. Measure voltage between terminals No. 4 (Black wire) and No. 7 (Light Blue/White) at DLC. Also, measure voltage between terminals No. 7 (Light Blue/White wire) and No. 16 (Light Green/Red wire) at DLC. See Fig. 2. If voltage is indicated, go to next step. If voltage is not indicated, replace restraints control module.

5) Turn ignition switch to LOCK position. Disconnect 84-pin harness connector C217 located behind left side of instrument panel. *See Fig. 4.* Inspect harness connector for loose, damaged or corroded terminals. Repair harness connector as necessary and retest system for normal operation. If harness connector is okay, Turn ignition switch to RUN position. Measure voltage between terminals No. 4 (Black wire) and No. 7 (Light Blue/White) at DLC. Also, measure voltage between terminals No. 7 (Light Blue/White wire) and No. 16 (Light Green/Red wire) at DLC. *See Fig. 2.* If voltage is indicated, repair Light Blue/White wire between harness connector C217 and DLC. If voltage is not indicated, repair open in Light Blue/White wire between female half of harness connector C217 and restraints control module.

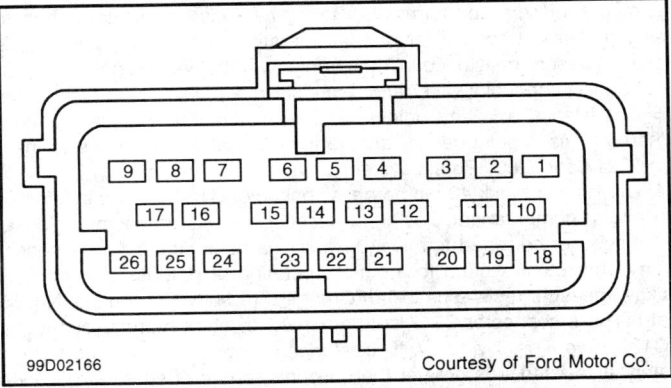

99D02166   Courtesy of Ford Motor Co.

Fig. 11: Identifying Restraint Control Module Harness Connector C327 Terminals

TEST G: LIGHTING CONTROL MODULE (LCM) DOES NOT RESPOND TO NGS TESTER

1) Turn ignition switch to LOCK position. Disconnect LCM 22-pin harness connector C206 located behind left side of instrument panel, behind headlight switch. Inspect harness connector for loose, damaged or corroded terminals. Repair harness connector as necessary and retest system for normal operation. If harness connector is okay, reconnect harness connector. Turn ignition switch to RUN position. Perform data link diagnostic procedure. See DATA LINK DIAGNOSTIC TEST under COMMUNICATION NETWORK DIAGNOSTICS. If NGS tester indicates LCM: NO RESPONSE ON CKT 914 (BUS +), go to next step. If NGS tester does not indicate LCM: NO RESPONSE ON CKT 914 (BUS +), go to step **5**).

2) Turn ignition switch to LOCK position. Disconnect NGS tester. Disconnect LCM harness connector C206. Measure resistance in Tan/Orange wire between terminal No. 2 at LCM harness connector C206 and terminal No. 2 at Data Link Connector (DLC). *See Figs. 2 and 12.* If resistance is greater than 5 ohms, go to next step. If resistance is 5 ohms or less, replace LCM.

3) Disconnect 84-pin harness connector C217 located behind left side of instrument panel. *See Fig. 4.* Inspect harness connector for loose, damaged or corroded terminals. Repair harness connector as necessary and retest system for normal operation. If harness connector is okay, measure resistance in Tan/Orange wire between terminal No. 55 at harness connector C217 and terminal No. 2 at DLC. *See Figs. 2 and 5.* If resistance is 5 ohms or less, go to next step. If resistance is greater than 5 ohms, repair open in Tan/Orange wire between harness connector C217 and DLC.

4) Disconnect 84-pin harness connector C212 located behind left side of instrument panel. *See Fig. 4.* Inspect harness connector for loose, damaged or corroded terminals. Repair harness connector as necessary and retest system for normal operation. If harness connector is okay, measure resistance in Tan/Orange wire between terminal No. 28 at harness connector C212 and terminal No. 2 at LCM harness connector C206. *See Figs. 5 and 12.* If resistance is 5 ohms or less, repair open in Tan/Orange wire between female half of harness connector C217 and harness connector C212. If resistance is greater than 5

ohms, repair open in Tan/Orange wire between male half of harness connector C212 and LCM harness connector C206.

5) Turn ignition switch to LOCK position. Disconnect NGS tester. Disconnect LCM 22-pin harness connector C206. Measure resistance in Pink/Light Blue wire between terminal No. 1 at LCM harness connector C206 and terminal No. 10 at DLC. *See Figs. 2 and 12.* If resistance is greater than 5 ohms, go to next step. If resistance is 5 ohms or less, replace LCM.

6) Disconnect 84-pin harness connector C217 located behind left side of instrument panel. *See Fig. 4.* Inspect harness connector for loose, damaged or corroded terminals. Repair harness connector as necessary and retest system for normal operation. If harness connector is okay, measure resistance in Pink/Light Blue wire between terminal No. 79 at harness connector C217 and terminal No. 10 at DLC. *See Figs. 2 and 5.* If resistance is 5 ohms or less, go to next step. If resistance is greater than 5 ohms, repair open in Pink/Light Blue wire between harness connector C217 and DLC.

7) Disconnect 84-pin harness connector C212 located behind left side of instrument panel. *See Fig. 4.* Inspect harness connector for loose, damaged or corroded terminals. Repair harness connector as necessary and retest system for normal operation. If harness connector is okay, measure resistance in Pink/Light Blue wire between terminal No. 29 at harness connector C212 and terminal No. 1 at LCM harness connector C206. *See Figs. 5 and 12.* If resistance is 5 ohms or less, repair open in Pink/Light Blue wire between female half of harness connector C217 and harness connector C212. If resistance is greater than 5 ohms, repair open in Pink/Light Blue wire between male half of harness connector C212 and LCM harness connector C206.

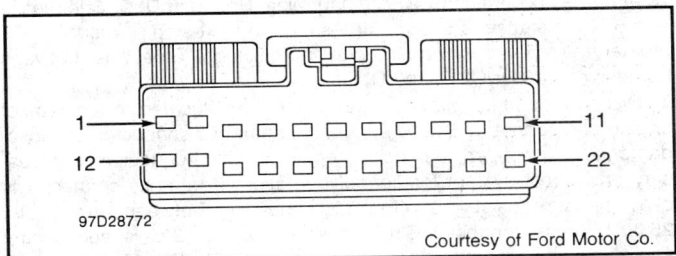

97D28772   Courtesy of Ford Motor Co.

Fig. 12: Identifying LCM Harness Connector C206 Terminals

TEST H: SPEED CONTROL SERVO/AMPLIFIER ASSEMBLY DOES NOT RESPOND TO NGS TESTER

NOTE: Speed control servo/amplifier assembly may also be referred to as Next Generation Speed Control (NGSC) servo.

1) Turn ignition switch to LOCK position. Disconnect speed control servo/amplifier assembly harness connector C152 located in left rear of engine compartment. *See Fig. 6.* Inspect harness connector for loose, damaged or corroded terminals. Repair harness connector as necessary and retest system for normal operation. If harness connector is okay, reconnect harness connector. Turn ignition switch to RUN position. Perform data link diagnostic procedure. See DATA LINK DIAGNOSTIC TEST under COMMUNICATION NETWORK DIAGNOSTICS. If NGS tester indicates NGSC: NO RESPONSE ON CKT 914 (BUS +), go to next step. If NGS tester does not indicate NGSC: NO RESPONSE ON CKT 914 (BUS +), go to step **5**).

2) Turn ignition switch to LOCK position. Disconnect NGS tester. Disconnect speed control servo/amplifier assembly harness connector C152. Measure resistance in Tan/Orange wire between terminal No. 1 at speed control servo/amplifier assembly harness connector C152 and terminal No. 2 at Data Link Connector (DLC). *See Figs. 2 and 13.* If resistance is greater than 5 ohms, go to next step. If resistance is 5 ohms or less, replace speed control servo/amplifier assembly.

3) Disconnect 84-pin harness connector C217 located behind left side of instrument panel. *See Fig. 4.* Inspect harness connector for loose, damaged or corroded terminals. Repair harness connector as necessary and retest system for normal operation. If harness connector is okay, measure resistance in Tan/Orange wire between terminal No. 55

at harness connector C217 and terminal No. 2 at DLC. *See Figs. 2 and 5.* If resistance is 5 ohms or less, go to next step. If resistance is greater than 5 ohms, repair open in Tan/Orange wire between harness connector C217 and DLC.

4) Disconnect Black 40-pin harness connector C100 located in left rear of engine compartment. *See Fig. 6.* Inspect harness connector for loose, damaged or corroded terminals. Repair harness connector as necessary and retest system for normal operation. If harness connector is okay, measure resistance in Tan/Orange wire between terminal No. 1 at speed control servo/amplifier assembly harness connector C152 and terminal No. 18 at harness connector C100. *See Figs. 7 and 13.* If resistance is 5 ohms or less, repair open in Tan/Orange wire between harness connector C217 and female half of harness connector C100. If resistance is greater than 5 ohms, repair open in Tan/Orange wire between male half of harness connector C100 and speed control servo/amplifier assembly harness connector C152.

5) Turn ignition switch to LOCK position. Disconnect speed control servo/amplifier assembly harness connector C152. Disconnect NGS tester. measure resistance in Pink/Light Blue wire between terminal No. 2 speed control servo/amplifier assembly harness connector C152 and terminal No. 10 at DLC. *See Figs. 2 and 13.* If resistance is greater than 5 ohms, go to next step. If resistance is 5 ohms or less, replace speed control servo/amplifier assembly.

6) Disconnect 84-pin harness connector C217 located behind left side of instrument panel. *See Fig. 4.* Inspect harness connector for loose, damaged or corroded terminals. Repair harness connector as necessary and retest system for normal operation. If harness connector is okay, measure resistance in Pink/Light Blue wire between terminal No. 79 at harness connector C217 and terminal No. 10 at DLC. *See Figs. 2 and 5.* If resistance is 5 ohms or less, go to next step. If resistance is greater than 5 ohms, repair open in Pink/Light Blue wire between harness connector C217 and DLC.

7) Disconnect 40-pin harness connector C100 located in left rear of engine compartment. *See Fig. 6.* Inspect harness connector for loose, damaged or corroded terminals. Repair harness connector as necessary and retest system for normal operation. If harness connector is okay, measure resistance in Pink/Light Blue wire between terminal No. 26 at harness connector C100 and terminal No. 2 at speed control servo/amplifier assembly harness connector C152. *See Figs. 7 and 13.* If resistance is 5 ohms or less, repair open in Pink/Light Blue wire between harness connector C217 and harness connector C100. If resistance is greater than 5 ohms, repair open in Pink/Light Blue wire between harness connector C100 and speed control servo/amplifier assembly harness connector C152.

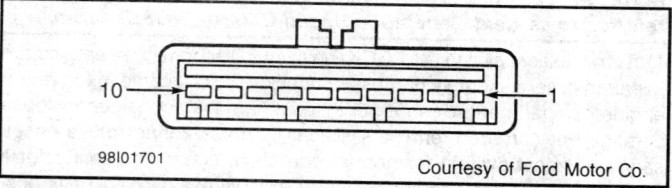

98I01701   Courtesy of Ford Motor Co.

Fig. 13: Identifying Speed Control Servo/Amplifier Assembly Harness Connector C152 Terminals

TEST J: POWERTRAIN CONTROL MODULE (PCM) DOES NOT RESPOND TO NGS TESTER

NOTE: If test results indicate PCM is faulty, always check for any engine performance related Diagnostic Trouble Codes (DTCs) prior to replacing PCM. If any DTCs are present, service DTCs as necessary and retest. See appropriate SELF-DIAGNOSTICS article in ENGINE PERFORMANCE in appropriate MITCHELL® manual.

1) Turn ignition switch to LOCK position. Disconnect PCM harness connector C1032 located in right rear of engine compartment. *See Fig. 6.* Inspect harness connector for loose, damaged or corroded terminals. Repair harness connector as necessary and retest system for normal operation. If harness connector is okay, reconnect harness connector. Turn ignition switch to RUN position. Perform data link

diagnostic procedure. See DATA LINK DIAGNOSTIC TEST under COMMUNICATION NETWORK DIAGNOSTICS. If NGS tester indicates PCM: NO RESPONSE ON CKT 914 (BUS +), go to next step. If NGS tester does not indicate PCM: NO RESPONSE ON CKT 914 (BUS +), go to step **6)**.

2) Turn ignition switch to LOCK position. Disconnect NGS tester. Disconnect PCM harness connector C1032. Measure resistance in Tan/Orange wire between terminal No. 16 at PCM harness connector C1032 and terminal No. 2 at Data Link Connector (DLC). *See Figs. 2 and 14.* If resistance is greater than 5 ohms, go to next step. If resistance is 5 ohms or less, replace PCM.

3) Disconnect 84-pin harness connector C217 located behind left side of instrument panel. *See Fig. 4.* Inspect harness connector for loose, damaged or corroded terminals. Repair harness connector as necessary and retest system for normal operation. If harness connector is okay, measure resistance in Tan/Orange wire between terminal No. 55 at harness connector C217 and terminal No. 2 at DLC. *See Figs. 2 and 5.* If resistance is 5 ohms or less, go to next step. If resistance is greater than 5 ohms, repair open in Tan/Orange wire between harness connector C217 and DLC. Retest system for normal operation.

4) Disconnect Black 40-pin harness connector C139 located in left rear of engine compartment. *See Fig. 6.* Inspect harness connector for loose, damaged or corroded terminals. Repair harness connector as necessary and retest system for normal operation. If harness connector is okay, measure resistance in Tan/Orange wire between terminal No. 55 at harness connector C217 and terminal No. 19 at harness connector C139. *See Figs. 7 and 14.* If resistance is 5 ohms or less, go to next step. If resistance is greater than 5 ohms, repair open in Tan/Orange wire between harness connector C217 and harness connector C139.

5) Disconnect 16-pin harness connector C127 located in left rear of engine compartment. *See Fig. 6.* Inspect harness connector for loose, damaged or corroded terminals. Repair harness connector as necessary and retest system for normal operation. If harness connector is okay, measure resistance in Tan/Orange wire between terminal No. 16 at PCM harness connector C1032 and terminal No. 2 at harness connector C127. *See Figs. 14 and 15.* If resistance is 5 ohms or less, repair open in Tan/Orange wire between harness connector C127 and harness connector C139. If resistance is greater than 5 ohms, repair open in Tan/Orange wire between PCM and harness connector C127.

6) Turn ignition switch to LOCK position. Disconnect PCM harness connector C1032. Disconnect NGS tester. measure resistance in Pink/Light Blue wire between terminal No. 15 at PCM harness connector C1032 and terminal No. 10 at DLC. *See Figs. 2 and 14.* If resistance is greater than 5 ohms, go to next step. If resistance is 5 ohms or less, replace PCM.

7) Disconnect 84-pin harness connector C217 located behind left side of instrument panel. *See Fig. 4.* Inspect harness connector for loose, damaged or corroded terminals. Repair harness connector as necessary and retest system for normal operation. If harness connector is okay, measure resistance in Pink/Light Blue wire between terminal No. 79 at harness connector C217 and terminal No. 10 at DLC. *See Figs. 2 and 5.* If resistance is 5 ohms or less, go to next step. If resistance is greater than 5 ohms, repair open in Pink/Light Blue wire between harness connector C217 and DLC.

8) Disconnect 40-pin harness connector C139 located in left rear of engine compartment. *See Fig. 6.* Inspect harness connector for loose, damaged or corroded terminals. Repair harness connector as necessary and retest system for normal operation. If harness connector is okay, measure resistance in Pink/Light Blue wire between terminal No. 23 at harness connector C139 and terminal No. 79 at female half of harness connector C217. *See Figs. 5 and 7.* If resistance is 5 ohms or less, go to next step. If resistance is greater than 5 ohms, repair open in Pink/Light Blue wire between harness connector C139 and harness connector C217.

9) Disconnect 16-pin harness connector C127 located in left rear of engine compartment. *See Fig. 6.* Inspect harness connector for loose, damaged or corroded terminals. Repair harness connector as necessary and retest system for normal operation. If harness connector is okay, measure resistance in Pink/Light Blue wire between terminal No.

15 at PCM harness connector C1032 and terminal No. 3 at harness connector C127. *See Figs. 14 and 15.* If resistance is 5 ohms or less, repair open in Pink/Light Blue wire between harness connector C127 and harness connector C139. If resistance is greater than 5 ohms, repair open in Pink/Light Blue wire between PCM and harness connector C127.

3) Disconnect 84-pin harness connector C217 located behind left side of instrument panel. *See Fig. 4.* Inspect harness connector for loose, damaged or corroded terminals. Repair harness connector as necessary and retest system for normal operation. If harness connector is okay, measure resistance in Tan/Orange wire between terminal No. 55 at harness connector C217 and terminal No. 2 at DLC. *See Figs. 2 and*

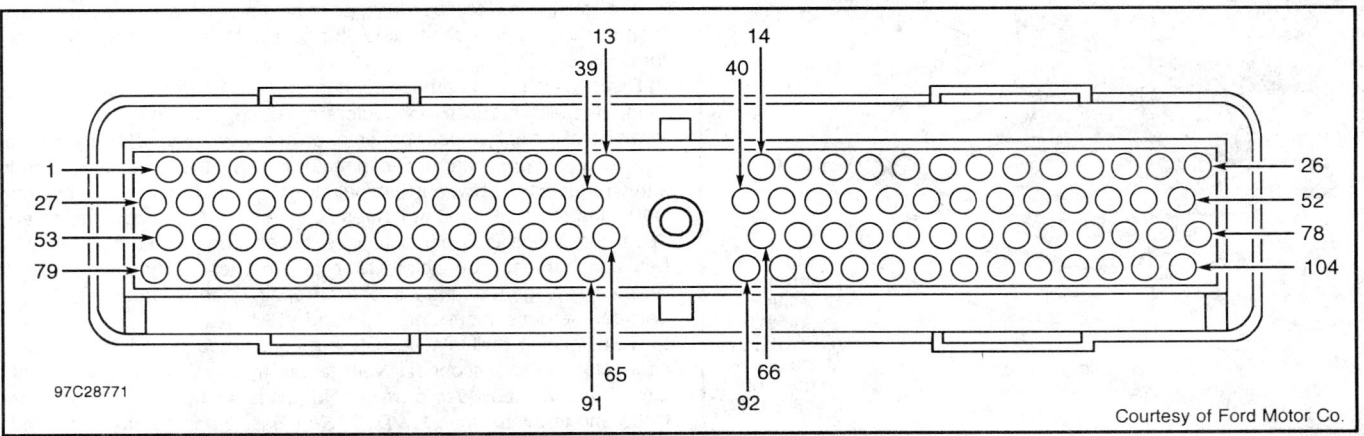

Fig. 14: Identifying PCM Harness Connector C1032 Terminals

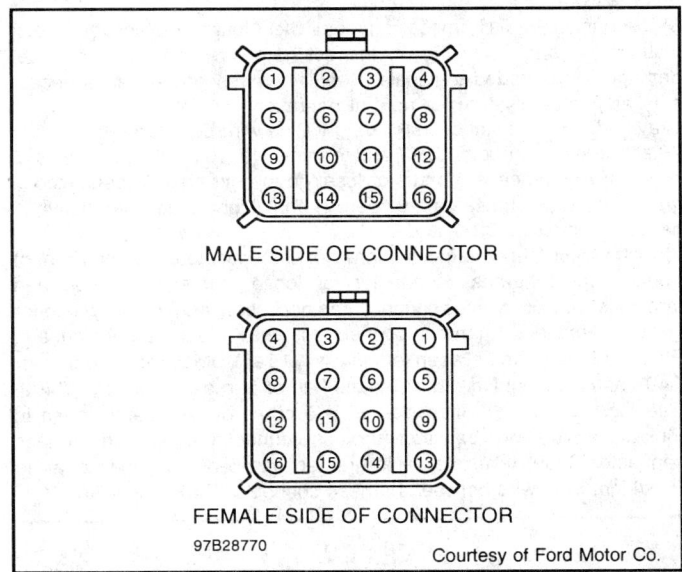

MALE SIDE OF CONNECTOR

FEMALE SIDE OF CONNECTOR

97B28770

Courtesy of Ford Motor Co.

Fig. 15: Identifying Harness Connector C127 Terminals

TEST K: EMERGENCY SATELLITE CELLULAR UNIT (RESCU) MODULE DOES NOT RESPOND TO NGS TESTER

1) Turn ignition switch to LOCK position. Disconnect RESCU module 12-pin harness connector C448 located in right rear of trunk, behind trim panel. *See Fig. 16.* Inspect harness connector for loose, damaged or corroded terminals. Repair harness connector as necessary and retest system for normal operation. If harness connector is okay, reconnect harness connector. Turn ignition switch to RUN position. Perform data link diagnostic procedure. See DATA LINK DIAGNOSTIC TEST under COMMUNICATION NETWORK DIAGNOSTICS. If NGS tester indicates RESCU: NO RESPONSE ON CKT 914 (BUS +), go to next step. If NGS tester does not indicate RESCU: NO RESPONSE ON CKT 914 (BUS +), go to step **5)**.

2) Turn ignition switch to LOCK position. Disconnect NGS tester. Disconnect RESCU module harness connector C448. Measure resistance in Tan/Orange wire between terminal No. 11 at RESCU module harness connector C448 and terminal No. 2 at Data Link Connector (DLC). *See Figs. 2 and 17.* If resistance is greater than 5 ohms, go to next step. If resistance is 5 ohms or less, replace RESCU module.

5. If resistance is 5 ohms or less, go to next step. If resistance is greater than 5 ohms, repair open in Tan/Orange wire between harness connector C217 and DLC.

4) Disconnect 16-pin harness connector C409 located in center front of trunk. Inspect harness connector for loose, damaged or corroded terminals. Repair harness connector as necessary and retest system for normal operation. If harness connector is okay, measure resistance in Tan/Orange wire between terminal No. 11 at RESCU module harness connector C448 and terminal No. 8 at harness connector C409. *See Figs. 17 and 18.* If resistance is 5 ohms or less, repair open in Tan/Orange wire between harness connector C217 and harness connector C409. If resistance is greater than 5 ohms, repair open in Tan/Orange wire between harness connector C409 and RESCU module.

5) Turn ignition switch to LOCK position. Disconnect RESCU module harness connector C448. Disconnect NGS tester. measure resistance in Pink/Light Blue wire between terminal No. 5 at RESCU module harness connector C448 and terminal No. 10 at DLC. *See Figs. 2 and 17.* If resistance is greater than 5 ohms, go to next step. If resistance is 5 ohms or less, replace RESCU.

6) Disconnect 84-pin harness connector C217 located behind left side of instrument panel. *See Fig. 4.* Inspect harness connector for loose, damaged or corroded terminals. Repair harness connector as necessary and retest system for normal operation. If harness connector is okay, measure resistance in Pink/Light Blue wire between terminal No. 79 at harness connector C217 and terminal No. 10 at DLC. *See Figs. 2 and 5.* If resistance is 5 ohms or less, go to next step. If resistance is greater than 5 ohms, repair open in Pink/Light Blue wire between harness connector C217 and DLC.

7) Disconnect 16-pin harness connector C409 located in center front of trunk. Inspect harness connector for loose, damaged or corroded terminals. Repair harness connector as necessary and retest system for normal operation. If harness connector is okay, measure resistance in Pink/Light Blue wire between terminal No. 5 at RESCU module harness connector C448 and terminal No. 16 at female half of harness connector C409. *See Figs. 17 and 18.* If resistance is 5 ohms or less, repair open in Pink/Light Blue wire between harness connector C217 and harness connector C409. If resistance is greater than 5 ohms, repair open in Pink/Light Blue wire between harness connector C409 and RESCU module harness connector C448.

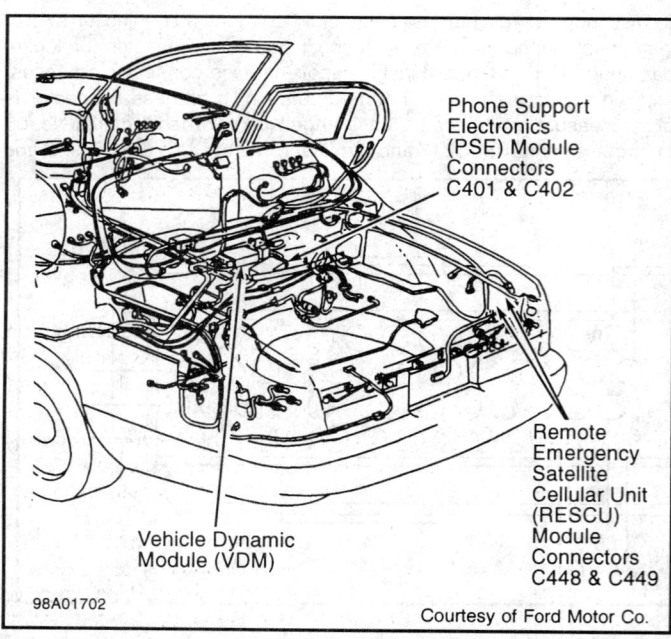

Fig. 16: Locating Phone Support Electronics (PSE) Module & Remote Emergency Satellite Cellular Unit (RESCU) Module

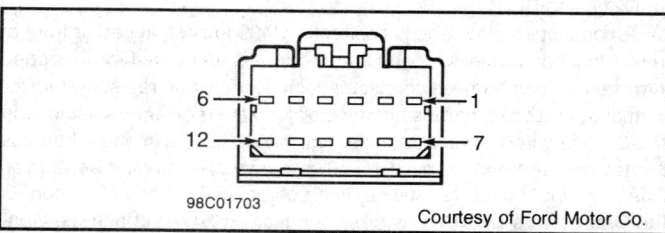

Fig. 17: Identifying RESCU Module Harness Connector C448 Terminals

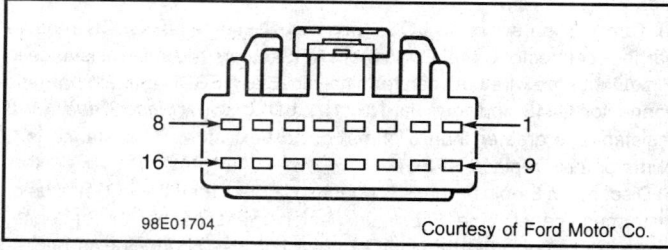

Fig. 18: Identifying Harness Connector C409 Terminals

TEST L: VEHICLE DYNAMICS MODULE (VDM) DOES NOT RESPOND TO NGS TESTER

1) Turn ignition switch to LOCK position. Disconnect VDM 60-pin harness connector C408 located in trunk. *See Fig. 16.* Inspect harness connector for loose, damaged or corroded terminals. Repair harness connector as necessary and retest system for normal operation. If harness connector is okay, reconnect harness connector. Turn ignition switch to RUN position. Perform data link diagnostic procedure. See DATA LINK DIAGNOSTIC TEST under COMMUNICATION NETWORK DIAGNOSTICS. If NGS tester indicates VDM: NO RESPONSE ON CKT 914 (BUS +), go to next step. If NGS tester does not indicate VDM: NO RESPONSE ON CKT 914 (BUS +), go to step 5).

2) Turn ignition switch to LOCK position. Disconnect NGS tester. Disconnect VDM harness connector C408. Measure resistance in Tan/Orange wire between terminal No. 19 at VDM harness connector C408 and terminal No. 2 at Data Link Connector (DLC). *See Figs. 2 and 19.* If resistance is greater than 5 ohms, go to next step. If resistance is 5 ohms or less, replace VDM.

3) Disconnect 84-pin harness connector C217 located behind left side of instrument panel. *See Fig. 4.* Inspect harness connector for loose, damaged or corroded terminals. Repair harness connector as necessary and retest system for normal operation. If harness connector is okay, measure resistance in Tan/Orange wire between terminal No. 55 at harness connector C217 and terminal No. 2 at DLC. *See Figs. 2 and 5.* If resistance is 5 ohms or less, go to next step. If resistance is greater than 5 ohms, repair open in Tan/Orange wire between harness connector C217 and DLC.

4) Disconnect 16-pin harness connector C409 located in center front of trunk. Inspect harness connector for loose, damaged or corroded terminals. Repair harness connector as necessary and retest system for normal operation. If harness connector is okay, measure resistance in Tan/Orange wire between terminal No. 19 at VDM harness connector C408 and terminal No. 8 at harness connector C409. *See Figs. 18 and 19.* If resistance is 5 ohms or less, repair open in Tan/Orange wire between harness connector C217 and harness connector C409. If resistance is greater than 5 ohms, repair open in Tan/Orange wire between harness connector C409 and VDM.

5) Turn ignition switch to LOCK position. Disconnect VDM harness connector C408. Disconnect NGS tester. measure resistance in Pink/Light Blue wire between terminal No. 18 at VDM harness connector C408 and terminal No. 10 at DLC. *See Figs. 2 and 19.* If resistance is greater than 5 ohms, go to next step. If resistance is 5 ohms or less, replace VDM.

6) Disconnect 84-pin harness connector C217 located behind left side of instrument panel. *See Fig. 4.* Inspect harness connector for loose, damaged or corroded terminals. Repair harness connector as necessary and retest system for normal operation. If harness connector is okay, measure resistance in Pink/Light Blue wire between terminal No. 79 at harness connector C217 and terminal No. 10 at DLC. *See Figs. 2 and 5.* If resistance is 5 ohms or less, go to next step. If resistance is greater than 5 ohms, repair open in Pink/Light Blue wire between harness connector C217 and DLC.

7) Disconnect 16-pin harness connector C409 located in center front of trunk. Inspect harness connector for loose, damaged or corroded terminals. Repair harness connector as necessary and retest system for normal operation. If harness connector is okay, measure resistance in Pink/Light Blue wire between terminal No. 18 at VDM harness connector C408 and terminal No. 16 at female half of harness connector C409. *See Figs. 18 and 19.* If resistance is 5 ohms or less, repair open in Pink/Light Blue wire between harness connector C217 and harness connector C409. If resistance is greater than 5 ohms, repair open in Pink/Light Blue wire between harness connector C409 and VDM.

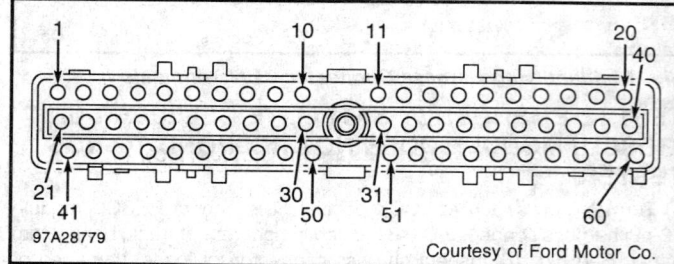

Fig. 19: Identifying VDM Harness Connector C408 Terminals

TEST M: INSTRUMENT CLUSTER DOES NOT RESPOND TO NGS TESTER

NOTE: Instrument cluster may also be referred to as Virtual Instrument Cluster (VIC).

1) Turn ignition switch to LOCK position. Disconnect instrument cluster Gray 20-pin harness connector C256 located behind left side of instrument panel. Inspect harness connector for loose, damaged or corroded terminals. Repair harness connector as necessary and retest system for normal operation. If harness connector is okay, reconnect harness connector. Turn ignition switch to RUN position. Perform data link diagnostic procedure. See DATA LINK DIAGNOSTIC TEST under

COMMUNICATION NETWORK DIAGNOSTICS. If NGS tester indicates VIC: NO RESPONSE ON CKT 914 (BUS +), go to next step. If NGS tester does not indicate VIC: NO RESPONSE ON CKT 914 (BUS +), go to step 3).

2) Turn ignition switch to LOCK position. Disconnect NGS tester. Disconnect instrument cluster harness connector C256. Measure resistance in Tan/Orange wire between terminal No. 11 at instrument cluster harness connector C256 and terminal No. 2 at Data Link Connector (DLC). *See Figs. 2 and 20.* If resistance is 5 ohms or less, replace instrument cluster and retest system for normal operation. If resistance is greater than 5 ohms, repair open in Tan/Orange wire between instrument cluster harness connector C256 and DLC.

3) Turn ignition switch to LOCK position. Disconnect instrument cluster harness connector C256. Disconnect NGS tester. measure resistance in Pink/Light Blue wire between terminal No. 1 at instrument cluster harness connector C256 and terminal No. 10 at DLC. *See Figs. 2 and 20.* If resistance is 5 ohms or less, replace VDM. If resistance is greater than 5 ohms, repair open in Pink/Light Blue wire between instrument cluster harness connector C256 and DLC.

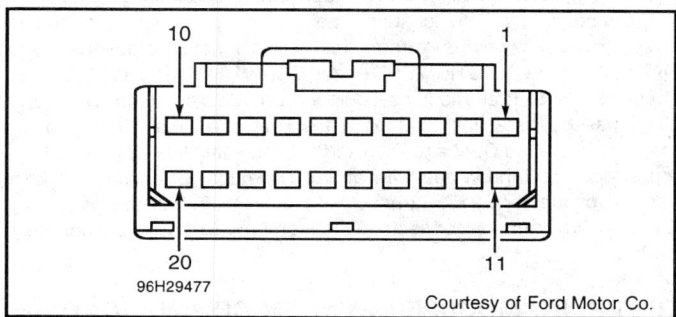

10   1

20   11
96H29477
Courtesy of Ford Motor Co.

Fig. 20: Identifying Instrument Cluster Harness Connector C256 Terminals

TEST N: NO MODULE/NETWORK COMMUNICATION (BUS LINK)

NOTE: Depending on module configuration, with all modules connected and with ignition switch in RUN position or with engine running 2-3 volts may be present at Data Link Connector (DLC) terminals No. 2 (Tan/Orange wire) and No. 10 (Pink/Light Blue wire). These are the Standard Corporate Protocol (SCP) diagnostic communications network circuits.

NOTE: Restraint Control Module (RCM) may also be referred to as Electronic Crash Sensor (ECS) module. Front Control Unit (FCU) may also be referred to as Audio Control Module (ACM). Speed control servo/amplifier assembly may also be referred to as Next Generation Speed Control (NGSC) servo. Instrument cluster may also be referred to as Virtual Instrument Cluster (VIC).

1) Inspect NGS tester harness connector for loose, damaged or corroded terminals. Repair harness connector as necessary and retest system for normal operation. If harness connector is okay, go to next step.

2) Turn ignition switch to LOCK position. Inspect Data Link Connector (DLC) for physical damage, bent terminals or corrosion. Repair harness connector as necessary and retest system for normal operation. If harness connector is okay, go to next step.

3) Turn ignition switch to LOCK position. Disconnect speed control servo/amplifier assembly harness connector C152 located in left rear of engine compartment. *See Fig. 6.* Measure resistance in Tan/Orange wire between terminal No. 1 at speed control servo/amplifier assembly harness connector C152 and terminal No. 2 at DLC. *See Figs. 2 and 13.* Also, measure resistance in Pink/Light Blue wire between terminal No. 2 at speed control servo/amplifier assembly harness connector C152 and terminal No. 10 at DLC. If both resistance readings are 5 ohms or less, go to next step. If any resistance reading is greater than 5 ohms, repair open Tan/Orange wire between DLC and splice S101 and/or

Pink/Light Blue wire between harness connector DLC and splice S118. Splice S101 and splice S118 are located in wiring harness behind instrument cluster.

4) Disconnect 84-pin harness connector C217 located behind left side of instrument panel. *See Fig. 4.* Turn gnition switch to RUN position. Perform data link diagnostic procedure. See DATA LINK DIAGNOSTIC TEST under COMMUNICATION NETWORK DIAGNOSTICS. If instrument cluster, EATC or FCU module did not pass data link diagnostic test, go to next step. If instrument cluster, EATC and FCU modules passed data link diagnostic test, turn ignition switch to LOCK position. Reconnect harness connector C217 and go to step 8).

5) Turn ignition switch to LOCK position. Disconnect Front Control Unit (FCU) 16-pin harness connector C231 located behind center of instrument panel, on radio. Turn ignition switch to RUN position. Perform data link diagnostic procedure. See DATA LINK DIAGNOSTIC TEST under COMMUNICATION NETWORK DIAGNOSTICS. If instrument cluster or EATC module did not pass data link diagnostic test, go to next step. If instrument cluster and EATC modules passed data link diagnostic test, replace FCU.

6) Turn ignition switch to LOCK position. Disconnect EATC module White harness connector C274 located in behind center of instrument panel. Turn ignition switch to RUN position. Perform data link diagnostic procedure. See DATA LINK DIAGNOSTIC TEST under COMMUNICATION NETWORK DIAGNOSTICS. If instrument cluster did not pass data link diagnostic test, go to next step. If instrument cluster passed data link diagnostic test, replace EATC module.

7) Turn ignition switch to LOCK position. Disconnect instrument cluster Gray 20-pin harness connector C256 located behind left side of instrument panel. Turn ignition switch to RUN position. Measure voltage between the following DLC terminals:

- Measure voltage between terminals No. 2 (Tan/Orange wire) and No. 4 (Black wire) at DLC. *See Fig. 2.*
- Measure voltage between terminals No. 2 (Tan/Orange wire) and No. 16 (Light Green/Red wire) at DLC.
- Measure voltage between terminals No. 10 (Pink/Light Blue wire) and No. 4 (Black wire) at DLC.
- Measure voltage between terminals No. 10 (Pink/Light Blue wire) and No. 16 (Light Green/Red wire) at DLC.

If voltage is indicated at any terminals, repair circuit No. 914 (Tan/Orange wire) and/or circuit No. 915 (Pink/Light Blue wire) between harness connector DLC and instrument cluster, EATC and FCU modules. If voltage is not indicated at any terminals, replace instrument cluster.

8) Turn ignition switch to RUN position. Perform data link diagnostic procedure. See DATA LINK DIAGNOSTIC TEST under COMMUNICATION NETWORK DIAGNOSTICS. If any modules did not pass data link diagnostic test, go to next step. If all modules equipped on vehicle passed data link diagnostic test, replace speed control servo/amplifier assembly.

9) Turn ignition switch to LOCK position. Disconnect Black 40-pin harness connector C100 located in left rear of engine compartment. *See Fig. 6.* Turn ignition switch to RUN position. Perform data link diagnostic procedure. See DATA LINK DIAGNOSTIC TEST under COMMUNICATION NETWORK DIAGNOSTICS. If any module, other than speed control servo/amplifier assembly did not pass data link diagnostic test, go to next step. If all modules equipped on vehicle, except speed control servo/amplifier assembly passed data link diagnostic test, repair open in Tan/Orange wire and/or Pink/Light Blue wire between harness connector C100 and speed control servo/amplifier assembly.

10) Turn ignition switch to LOCK position. Disconnect 84-pin harness connector C212 located behind left side of instrument panel. *See Fig. 4.* Turn ignition switch to RUN position. Perform data link diagnostic procedure. See DATA LINK DIAGNOSTIC TEST under COMMUNICATION NETWORK DIAGNOSTICS. If all modules equipped on vehicle, except LCM passed data link diagnostic test, turn ignition switch to LOCK position. Reconnect harness connector C212 and go to next step. If any module, other than LCM did not pass data link diagnostic test, go to step 12).

11) Disconnect LCM 22-pin harness connector C206 located behind left side of instrument panel, behind headlight switch. Turn ignition switch to RUN position. Perform data link diagnostic procedure. See DATA LINK DIAGNOSTIC TEST under COMMUNICATION NETWORK DIAGNOSTICS. If all modules equipped on vehicle, except LCM passed data link diagnostic test, replace LCM. If any module, other than LCM did not pass data link diagnostic test, repair open in Tan/Orange wire and/or Pink/Light Blue wire between harness connector C212 and LCM harness connector C206.

12) Turn ignition switch to LOCK position. Disconnect 16-pin harness connector C409 located in center front of trunk. Turn ignition switch to RUN position. Perform data link diagnostic procedure. See DATA LINK DIAGNOSTIC TEST under COMMUNICATION NETWORK DIAGNOSTICS. If all modules equipped on vehicle, except VDM and RESCU module (if equipped) passed data link diagnostic test, turn ignition switch to LOCK position. Reconnect harness connector C409 and go to next step (models with RESCU module) or go to step 13) (models without RESCU module). If any module, other than VDM and RESCU module (if equipped) did not pass data link diagnostic test, go to step 15).

13) Turn ignition switch to LOCK position. Disconnect RESCU module 12-pin harness connector C448 located in right rear of trunk, behind trim panel. See Fig. 16. Turn ignition switch to RUN position. Perform data link diagnostic procedure. See DATA LINK DIAGNOSTIC TEST under COMMUNICATION NETWORK DIAGNOSTICS. If any module, other than RESCU module did not pass data link diagnostic test, go to next step. If all modules equipped on vehicle, except RESCU module passed data link diagnostic test, replace RESCU module.

14) Turn ignition switch to LOCK position. Disconnect VDM 60-pin harness connector C408 located in trunk. See Fig. 16. Turn ignition switch to RUN position. Perform data link diagnostic procedure. See DATA LINK DIAGNOSTIC TEST under COMMUNICATION NETWORK DIAGNOSTICS. If all modules equipped on vehicle, except VDM and RESCU module (if equipped) passed data link diagnostic test, replace VDM. If any module, other than VDM and RESCU module (if equipped) did not pass data link diagnostic test, repair open in Tan/Orange wire and/or Pink/Light Blue wire between harness connector C409, VDM harness connector and RESCU module harness connector C448 (if equipped).

15) Turn ignition switch to LOCK position. Disconnect Gray 40-pin harness connector C139 located in left rear of engine compartment. See Fig. 6. Turn ignition switch to RUN position. Perform data link diagnostic procedure. See DATA LINK DIAGNOSTIC TEST under COMMUNICATION NETWORK DIAGNOSTICS. If all modules equipped on vehicle, except PCM and ABS passed data link diagnostic test, turn ignition switch to LOCK position. Reconnect C139 and go to next step. If any other module, other than PCM and ABS modules did not pass data link diagnostic test, go to step 18).

16) Turn ignition switch to LOCK position. Disconnect ABS module harness connector, located in left front corner of engine compartment. Turn ignition switch to RUN position. Perform data link diagnostic procedure. See DATA LINK DIAGNOSTIC TEST under COMMUNICATION NETWORK DIAGNOSTICS. If any other module, other than ABS module did not pass data link diagnostic test, go to next step. If all modules equipped on vehicle, except ABS module passed data link diagnostic test, replace ABS module.

17) Turn ignition switch to LOCK position. Disconnect PCM harness connector C1032 located in right rear of engine compartment. See Fig. 6. Turn ignition switch to RUN position. Perform data link diagnostic procedure. See DATA LINK DIAGNOSTIC TEST under COMMUNICATION NETWORK DIAGNOSTICS. If all modules equipped on vehicle, except PCM and ABS module passed data link diagnostic test, replace PCM. If any other module, other than PCM and ABS module did not pass data link diagnostic test, repair open in Tan/Orange wire and/or Pink/Light Blue wire between harness connector C139, PCM harness connector ABS module and evac and fill harness connector C146 (Tan/Orange wire only).

18) Turn ignition switch to LOCK position. Disconnect DDM 14-pin harness connector C524 located inside driver's door. Turn ignition switch to RUN position. Perform data link diagnostic procedure. See DATA LINK DIAGNOSTIC TEST under COMMUNICATION NETWORK DIAGNOSTICS. If any other module, other than DDM did not pass data link diagnostic test, go to next step. If all modules equipped on vehicle, except DDM passed data link diagnostic test, replace DDM.

19) Turn ignition switch to LOCK position. Disconnect DSM 26-pin harness connector C342 located under driver's front seat. Turn ignition switch to RUN position. Perform data link diagnostic procedure. See DATA LINK DIAGNOSTIC TEST under COMMUNICATION NETWORK DIAGNOSTICS. If all modules equipped on vehicle, except DSM and DDM passed data link diagnostic test, replace DSM. If any other module, other than DSM and DDM did not pass data link diagnostic test, repair open in Tan/Orange wire and/or Pink/Light Blue wire between harness connector C217, harness connector C100, harness connector C409, DSM harness connector C342 and DDM harness connector C524.

TEST P: NO MODULE/NETWORK COMMUNICATION

1) Inspect NGS tester harness connector for loose, damaged or corroded terminals. Repair harness connector as necessary and retest system for normal operation. If harness connector is okay, go to next step.

2) Turn ignition switch to LOCK position. Inspect Data Link Connector (DLC) for physical damage, bent terminals or corrosion. Repair as necessary and retest system for normal operation. If harness connector is okay, go to next step.

3) Turn ignition switch to LOCK position. Remove and inspect fuse No. 2 (10-amp) from instrument panel fuse block. If fuse is okay, go to next step. If fuse is blown, replace fuse and retest system for normal operation. Recheck fuse. If fuse is okay, go to next step. If fuse is blown, repair short to ground in circuit No. 1047 (Light Green/Red wire) between instrument panel fuse block and DLC.

4) Measure voltage between ground and terminal No. 16 (Light Green/Red wire) at DLC. See Fig. 2. If battery voltage exists, go to next step. If battery voltage does not exist, repair circuit No. 1047 (Light Green/Red wire) between instrument panel fuse block and DLC.

5) Measure resistance between ground and terminals No. 4 (Black wire) and No. 5 (Black/Light Blue wire) at DLC. If both resistance readings are 5 ohms or less, repair or replace NGS tester. If any resistance reading is greater than 5 ohms, repair open in Black wire or Black/Light Blue wire between ground and DLC.

DIAGNOSTIC TROUBLE CODE (DTC) DEFINITIONS

ANTI-LOCK BRAKE SYSTEM MODULE DTC INDEX

DTC	Description	Test
B1342	ECU Defective	1
B1485	Brake Pedal Input Circuit Open	1
B1676	Battery Voltage Out Of Range	1
C1095	ABS Hydraulic Pump Motor Circuit Failure	1
C1145	Right Front ABS Sensor Input Circuit Failure	1
C1155	Left Front ABS Sensor Input Circuit Failure	1
C1165	Right Rear ABS Sensor Input Circuit Failure	1
C1175	Left Rear ABS Sensor Input Circuit Failure	1

ANTI-LOCK BRAKE SYSTEM MODULE DTC INDEX (Cont.)

DTC	Description	Test
C1233	Left Front ABS Sensor Input Signal Missing	1
C1234	Right Front ABS Sensor Input Signal Missing	1
C1235	Right Rear ABS Sensor Input Signal Missing	1
C1236	Left Rear ABS Sensor Input Signal Missing	1
U1009	Invalid/Missing Data For Engine Torque	2
U1027	Invalid/Missing Data For Engine RPM	2
U1041	Invalid/Missing Data For Vehicle Speed	3
U1051	Invalid/Missing Data For Brakes	4
U1059	Invalid/Missing Data For Transmission Range (PRNDL)	2
U1123	Invalid/Missing Data For Odometer	5

[1] – Repair Anti-Lock Brake System (ABS). See appropriate ANTI-LOCK article in BRAKES in appropriate MITCHELL® manual.

[2] – Caused by Powertrain Control Module (PCM). Using NGS tester, perform PCM self-test and repair powertrain control as necessary. See appropriate SELF-DIAGNOSTICS article in ENGINE PERFORMANCE in appropriate MITCHELL® manual.

[3] – Caused by Vehicle Dynamic Module (VDM), Driver's Door Module (DDM) and/or Lighting Control Module (LCM). Using NGS tester, perform self-test on all these modules.

[4] – Caused by Lighting Control Module (LCM). Using NGS tester, perform LCM self-test.

[5] – Caused by Lighting Control Module (LCM) and/or instrument cluster. Using NGS tester, perform LCM and instrument cluster self-tests.

FRONT CONTROL UNIT DTC INDEX [1]

DTC	Description	Test
B1342	ECU Defective	2
B2401	Audio Tape Deck Mechanical Failure	3
B2402	Audio CD/DJ Thermal Shutdown Fault	4
B2403	Audio CD/DJ Internal Fault	4
B2404	Audio Steering Wheel Switch Circuit Fault	4
B2405	Audio Single Disc Player Thermal Shutdown	5
B2406	Audio Single Disc CD Player Internal Fault	5
U2003	Audio CD/DJ Is Not Responding	4
U2005	Audio Rear Integrated Control Panel Unit Not Responding	6
U2008	Audio Phone Not Responding	7
U2014	Audio Subwoofer Unit Not Responding	4

[1] – Front Control Unit (FCU) may also be referred to as Audio Control Module (ACM).

[2] – Using NGS tester, retrieved and document all continuous DTCs. Clear DTCs. Perform Audio Control Unit (ACU) self-test. If DTC B1342 is retrieved again, replace ACU.

[3] – Remove audio tape. Using NGS tester, perform Audio Control Unit (ACU) self-test. If DTC B2401 is retrieved again, repair or replace ACU.

[4] – Repair audio system as necessary.

[5] – Not applicable to this vehicle.

[6] – This code is retrieved if Rear Integrated Control Panel Unit (RICP) is not present, disconnected or inoperative.

[7] – Repair cellular phone system as necessary.

DRIVER'S DOOR MODULE DTC INDEX

DTC	Description	Test
B1319	Driver's Door Ajar Circuit Failure	1
B1342	ECU Defective	2
B1396	Power Door Lock Circuit Short To Voltage	3
B1397	Power Door Unlock Circuit Short To Voltage	3
B1525	Keyless Entry Circuit Short To Voltage	3
B1541	Driver's Mirror Switch Short To Voltage	4
B1545	Power Seat Switch Short To Voltage	5
B1549	Power Window Master Switch Short To Voltage	6
B1554	Trunk Release Circuit Short To Ground	3
B1562	Door Lock Cylinder Circuit Short To Ground	3
B2425	Remote Keyless Entry Out Of Synchronization	7
U1041	Invalid/Missing Data For Vehicle Speed	8
U1059	Invalid/Missing Data For Transmission Range (PRNDL)	9
U1089	Invalid/Missing Data For Suspension	10
U1181	Invalid/Missing Data For Memory Feature	11
U1262	SCP Bus Communication Fault	12

[1] – Perform TEST Q: COURTESY LIGHTS ON CONTINUOUSLY under SYSTEM TESTS in AUTOLAMP SYSTEMS – CONTINENTAL article.

[2] – Using NGS tester, retrieve and document all continuous DTCs. Clear DTCs. Perform Driver's Door Module (DDM) self-test. If DTC B1342 is retrieved again, replace DDM.

[3] – Repair appropriate keyless entry system circuit. See appropriate wiring diagram in REMOTE KEYLESS ENTRY SYSTEMS article.

[4] – Perform TEST C: SINGLE MIRROR INOPERATIVE under SYSTEM TESTS in POWER MEMORY MIRRORS – CONTINENTAL article.

[5] – Perform TEST C: DRIVER'S SEAT COMPLETELY INOPERATIVE under SYSTEM TESTS in POWER SEATS – CONTINENTAL article.

[6] – Perform TEST C: ALL WINDOWS ARE INOPERATIVE under SYSTEM TESTS in POWER WINDOWS – CONTINENTAL article.

[7] – Check keyless entry system operation. If keyless entry system operates properly, program keypad and remote transmitter. See PROGRAMMING in ACTIVE ANTI-THEFT SYSTEMS – CONTINENTAL article. If keyless entry system does not operate properly, repair keyless entry system as necessary. See appropriate wiring diagram in REMOTE KEYLESS ENTRY SYSTEMS article.

DRIVER'S DOOR MODULE DTC INDEX (Cont.)

8 – Caused by Anti-Lock Brake System (ABS) module. Using NGS tester, perform ABS self-test and repair anti-lock brake system as necessary. See appropriate ANTI-LOCK article in BRAKES in appropriate MITCHELL® manual.

9 – Caused by Powertrain Control Module (PCM). Using NGS tester, perform PCM self-test and repair powertrain control as necessary. See appropriate SELF-DIAGNOSTICS article in ENGINE PERFORMANCE in appropriate MITCHELL® manual.

10 – Caused by Vehicle Dynamic Module (VDM). Using NGS tester, perform VDM self-test and repair electronic suspension as necessary. See appropriate ELECTRONIC article in SUSPENSION in appropriate MITCHELL® manual.

11 – Caused by instrument cluster. Using NGS tester, perform instrument cluster self-test and repair instrument cluster as necessary. See SELF-DIAGNOSTIC SYSTEM in ANALOG INSTRUMENT PANELS – CONTINENTAL article.

12 – Service all other DTCs first. After all other DTC concerns have been repaired, perform TEST N: NO MODULE/NETWORK COMMUNICATION (BUS LINK) under SYSTEM TESTS.

DRIVER'S SEAT MODULE DTC INDEX

DTC	Description	Test
B1342	ECU Defective	1
B1663	Driver's Seat Front Up/Down Circuit Failure	2
B1664	Driver's Seat Rear Up/Down Circuit Failure	2
B1665	Driver's Seat Forward/Backward Circuit Failure	2
B1666	Driver's Seat Recline Circuit Failure	2
B1667	Driver's Mirror Up/Down Circuit Failure	3
B1668	Driver's Mirror Right/Left Circuit Failure	3
B1669	Passenger's Mirror Up/Down Circuit Failure	3
B1670	Passenger's Mirror Right/Left Circuit Failure	3
B1676	Battery Voltage Out Of Range	4
B1950	Rear Up/Down Feedback – Circuit Failure	5
B1953	Rear Up/Down Feedback – Short to Ground	5
B1954	Front Up/Down Feedback – Circuit Failure	5
B1957	Front Up/Down Feedback – Short to Ground	5
B1958	Recline Feedback – Circuit Failure	5
B1961	Recline Feedback – Short To Ground	5
B1962	Horizontal Feedback – Circuit Failure	5
B1965	Horizontal Feedback – Short To Ground	5
B2312	Passenger's Mirror Horizontal Feedback Potentiometer – Circuit Failure	6
B2315	Passenger's Mirror Horizontal Feedback Potentiometer – Short To Ground	6
B2316	Passenger's Mirror Vertical Feedback Potentiometer – Circuit Failure	6
B2319	Passenger's Mirror Vertical Feedback Potentiometer – Short To Ground	6
B2320	Driver's Mirror Horizontal Feedback Potentiometer – Circuit Failure	6
B2323	Driver's Mirror Horizontal Feedback Potentiometer – Shirt To Ground	6
B2324	Driver's Mirror Vertical Feedback Potentiometer – Circuit Failure	6
B2327	Driver's Mirror Vertical Feedback Potentiometer – Short To Ground	6
U1059	Invalid/Missing Data For Transmission Range (PRNDL)	7
U1135	Invalid/Missing Data For Ignition Switch	8
U1181	Invalid/Missing Data For Memory Feature	9
U1181	Invalid/Missing Data For Memory Feature	10
U1194	Invalid/Missing Data For Mirrors	9
U1200	Invalid/Missing Data For Seat Motion/Control	9
U1262	SCP Bus Communication Fault	11

1 – Using NGS tester, retrieve and document all continuous DTCs. Clear DTCs. Perform Driver's Seat Module (DSM) self-test. If DTC B1342 is retrieved again, replace DSM.

2 – Perform TEST C: DRIVER'S SEAT COMPLETELY INOPERATIVE under SYSTEM TEST in POWER SEATS – CONTINENTAL article.

3 – Perform TEST C: SINGLE MIRROR INOPERATIVE under SYSTEM TEST in POWER MEMORY MIRRORS – CONTINENTAL article.

4 – Perform TEST R: BATTERY VOLTAGE OUT OF RANGE (DTC B1676) under SYSTEM TEST in POWER SEATS – CONTINENTAL article.

5 – Perform TEST D: PASSENGER'S SEAT COMPLETELY INOPERATIVE under SYSTEM TEST in POWER SEATS – CONTINENTAL article.

6 – Perform TEST D: MIRROR OPERATES IN ONE SECOND INTERVALS under SYSTEM TEST in POWER MEMORY MIRRORS – CONTINENTAL article.

7 – Caused by Powertrain Control Module (PCM). Using NGS tester, perform PCM self-test and repair powertrain control as necessary. See appropriate SELF-DIAGNOSTICS article in ENGINE PERFORMANCE in appropriate MITCHELL® manual.

8 – Caused by lighting control module. See appropriate STEERING COLUMN SWITCHES article.

9 – Caused by Driver's door module. Using NGS tester, perform DDM self-test and repair power mirror system as necessary. See POWER MEMORY MIRRORS – CONTINENTAL article.

10 – Caused by instrument cluster. Using NGS tester, perform instrument cluster self-test and repair instrument cluster as necessary. See SELF-DIAGNOSTIC SYSTEM in ANALOG INSTRUMENT PANELS – CONTINENTAL article.

11 – Service all other DTCs first. After all other DTC concerns have been repaired, perform TEST N: NO MODULE/NETWORK COMMUNICATION (BUS LINK) under SYSTEM TESTS.

ELECTRONIC AUTOMATIC TEMPERATURE CONTROL MODULE DTC INDEX

DTC	Description	Test
B1249	Blend Door Failure	1
B1252	A/C In-Car Temperature Sensor Open Circuit	1
B1253	A/C In-Car Temperature Sensor Circuit Short To Ground	1
B1255	A/C Ambient Air Temperature Sensor Circuit Open	1
B1257	A/C Ambient Air Temperature Sensor Circuit Short To Ground	1

ELECTRONIC AUTOMATIC TEMPERATURE CONTROL MODULE DTC INDEX (Cont.)

B1261	A/C Solar Radiation Sensor Circuit Short To Ground	1
U1041	Invalid/Missing Data For Vehicle Speed	2
U1073	Invalid/Missing Data For Engine Coolant	3
U1222	Invalid/Missing Data For Interior Lights	4
U1235	Invalid/Missing Data For Displays	5

[1] – Repair A/C system as necessary. See appropriate AUTOMATIC A/C-HEATER SYSTEMS article in appropriate MITCHELL® AIR CONDITIONING & HEATING SERVICE & REPAIR manual.

[2] – Repair vehicle speed sensor circuit. See appropriate SELF-DIAGNOSTICS article in ENGINE PERFORMANCE in appropriate MITCHELL® manual.

[3] – Repair engine coolant temperature sensor circuit. See appropriate SELF-DIAGNOSTICS article in ENGINE PERFORMANCE in appropriate MITCHELL® manual.

[4] – Repair interior lighting as necessary. See SELF-DIAGNOSTIC SYSTEM in AUTOLAMP SYSTEMS – CONTINENTAL article.

[5] – Repair message center as necessary. See SELF-DIAGNOSTIC SYSTEM in INSTRUMENT PANELS – CONTINENTAL article.

INSTRUMENT CLUSTER DTC INDEX [1]

DTC	Description	Test
B1201	Fuel Sender Circuit Failure	2
B1204	Fuel Sender Short To Ground	2
B1205	Instrument Cluster Switch 1 Assembly Circuit Failure	3
B1208	Instrument Cluster Switch 1 Assembly Circuit Short To Ground	3
B1209	Instrument Cluster Switch 2 Assembly Circuit Failure	3
B1212	Instrument Cluster Switch 2 Assembly Circuit Short To Ground	3
B1213	Anti-Theft Number Of Programmed Ignition Keys Is Below Minimum	4 5
B1232 Or B2103	Defective Transceiver	6
B1317	Battery Voltage High	7
B1318	Battery Voltage Low	7
B1342	ECU Defective	8
B1600	PATS Ignition Key Transponder Signal Not Received	9
B1601	PATS Received Incorrect Key Code From Transponder	10
B1602	PATS Received Invalid Key Code Format From Transponder	11
B1681	PATS Transceiver Signal Not Received	12
B2139	Security Identification Does Not Match Between Instrument Cluster & PCM	13
B2141	NVM Configuration Failure	14
U1027	Invalid/Missing Data For Engine RPM	15
U1043	Invalid/Missing Data For Traction Control	16
U1051	Invalid/Missing Data For Brakes	16
U1053	Invalid/Missing Data For Steering	17
U1059	Invalid/Missing Data For Transmission Range (PRNDL)	15
U1073	Invalid/Missing Data For Engine Coolant	15
U1089	Invalid/Missing Data For Suspension	17
U1098	Invalid/Missing Data For Vehicle Speed Control	16
U1123	Invalid/Missing Data For Odometer	16
U1136	Invalid/Missing Data For Telltales	16 18
U1147	SCP Invalid/Missing Data For Vehicle Security	19
U1181	SCP Invalid/Missing Data For Memory Feature	20
U1199	SCP Invalid/Missing Data For External Access (Doors)	18 20
U1211	Invalid/Missing Data For Restraints	18
U1217	Invalid/Missing Data For Exterior Light Outage	18
U1218	Invalid/Missing Data For Exterior Lights	18
U1430	Invalid/Missing Data For Function Red Fuel System	15
U1262	SCP Bus Communications Fault	21

[1] – Instrument cluster may also be referred to as Virtual Instrument Cluster (VIC).

[2] – Perform TEST A: FUEL SENDER CIRCUIT FAILURE (DTC B1201), FUEL SENDER CIRCUIT SHORT TO GROUND (DTC B1204) under SYSTEM TESTS in INSTRUMENT PANELS – CONTINENTAL article.

[3] – Perform TEST U: MESSAGE CENTER NOT OPERATING PROPERLY (DTCS B1205, B1208, B1209 & B1212) under SYSTEM TEST in INSTRUMENT PANELS – CONTINENTAL article.

[4] – If DTCs B1232, B1600, B1601, B1602 OR B1681 are also present, service these DTCs frist then recheck codes.

[5] – Perform DTC B1213: ANTI-THEFT NUMBER OF PROGRAMMED IGNITION KEYS IS BELOW MINIMUM under DIAGNOSTIC TESTS in PASSIVE ANTI-THEFT SYSTEMS – CONTINENTAL article.

[6] – Perform DTC B1232: DEFECTIVE TRANSCEIVER under DIAGNOSTIC TESTS in PASSIVE ANTI-THEFT SYSTEMS – CONTINENTAL article.

[7] – Repair charging system as necessary. See appropriate GENERATORS article in STARTING & CHARGING SYSTEMS.

[8] – Using NGS tester, retrieve and document all continuous DTCs. Clear DTCs. Perform instrument cluster self-test. If DTC B1342 is retrieved again, replace instrument cluster.

[9] – Perform DTC B1600: PATS IGNITION KEY TRANSPONDER SIGNAL NOT RECEIVED under DIAGNOSTIC TESTS in PASSIVE ANTI-THEFT SYSTEMS – CONTINENTAL article.

[10] – Perform DTC B1601: PATS RECEIVED INCORRECT KEY CODE FROM TRANSPONDER under DIAGNOSTIC TESTS in PASSIVE ANTI-THEFT SYSTEMS – CONTINENTAL article.

[11] – Perform DTC B1602: PATS RECEIVED INVALID KEY CODE FORMAT FROM TRANSPONDER under DIAGNOSTIC TESTS in PASSIVE ANTI-THEFT SYSTEMS – CONTINENTAL article.

INSTRUMENT CLUSTER DTC INDEX [1] (Cont.)

[12] – Perform DTC B1681: PATS TRANSCEIVER SIGNAL IS NOT RECEIVED under DIAGNOSTIC TESTS in PASSIVE ANTI-THEFT SYSTEMS – CONTINENTAL article.

[13] – Perform DTC B2139: SECURITY IDENTIFICATION DOES NOT MATCH BETWEEN INSTRUMENT CLUSTER & PCM under DIAGNOSTIC TESTS in PASSIVE ANTI-THEFT SYSTEMS – CONTINENTAL article.

[14] – Perform DTC B2141: NVM CONFIGURATION FAILURE under DIAGNOSTIC TESTS in PASSIVE ANTI-THEFT SYSTEMS – CONTINENTAL article.

[15] – Caused by Powertrain Control Module (PCM). Using NGS tester, perform PCM self-test and repair powertrain control as necessary. See appropriate SELF-DIAGNOSTICS article in ENGINE PERFORMANCE in appropriate MITCHELL® manual.

[16] – Caused by Anti-Lock Brake System (ABS) module. Using NGS tester, perform ABS self-test and repair anti-lock brake system as necessary. See appropriate ANTI-LOCK article in BRAKES in appropriate MITCHELL® manual.

[17] – Caused by Vehicle Dynamic Module (VDM). Using NGS tester, perform VDM self-test and repair electronic suspension as necessary. See appropriate ELECTRONIC article in SUSPENSION in appropriate MITCHELL® manual.

[18] – Caused by Lighting Control Module (LCM). Using NGS tester, perform LCM self-test.

[19] – Perform DTC U1147: SCP INVALID OR MISSING DATA FOR VEHICLE SECURITY under DIAGNOSTIC TESTS in PASSIVE ANTI-THEFT SYSTEMS – CONTINENTAL article.

[20] – Caused by Driver's Door Module (DDM). Using NGS tester, perform DDM self-test.

[21] – Service all other DTCs first. After all other DTC concerns have been repaired, perform TEST N: NO MODULE/NETWORK COMMUNICATION (BUS LINK) under SYSTEM TESTS.

LIGHTING CONTROL MODULE DTC INDEX

DTC	Description	Test
B1312	Headlight Input Circuit Short To Voltage	1
B1334	Decklid Ajar Rear Door Circuit Short To Ground	2
B1342	ECU Defective	3
B1352	Ignition Key-In Circuit Failure	4
B1359	Ignition RUN/ACC Circuit Failure	5
B1462	Seat Belt Switch Circuit Failure	6
B1464	Seat Belt Switch Circuit Short To Voltage	6
B1483	Brake Pedal Input Circuit Failure	7
B1495	Decklid Punch Out Sensor Circuit Failure	8
B1498	Decklid Punch Out Sensor Short To Ground	8
B1509	Flash-To-Pass Switch Circuit Short To Voltage	9
B1522	Hood Switch Circuit Short To Ground	8
B1555	Ignition RUN/START Circuit Failure	10
B1566	Door Ajar Circuit Short To Ground	11
B1569	Headlight High Beam Circuit Short To Voltage	12
B1577	Parking Light Input Circuit Short To Voltage	13
B1582	Dim Panel Increase Input Circuit Short To Ground	14
B1586	Dim Panel Decrease Input Circuit Short To Ground	14
B1590	Autolamp Delay Increase Circuit Short To Ground	15
B1594	Autolamp Delay Decrease Circuit Short To Ground	15
B1676	Battery Voltage Out Of Range	16
B1807	Taillight Output Circuit Open	13
U1041	Invalid/Missing Data For Vehicle Speed	17
U1059	Invalid/Missing Data For Transmission Range (PRNDL)	18
U1123	Invalid/Missing Data For Odometer	17
U1146	Invalid/Missing Data For Vehicle Security	19
U1147	Invalid/Missing Data For Vehicle Security	20
U1181	Invalid/Missing Data For Personalization Features	21
U1198	Invalid/Missing Data For Doors	20
U1222	Invalid/Missing Data For Interior Lights	20
U1262	SCP Bus Communication Fault	22

[1] – Perform TEST B: LOW BEAMS INOPERATIVE under SYSTEM TESTS in AUTOLAMP SYSTEMS – CONTINENTAL article.

[2] – Repair trunk lid release circuit. See appropriate wiring diagram in REMOTE KEYLESS ENTRY SYSTEMS – CONTINENTAL article.

[3] – Using NGS tester, retrieve and document continuous DTCs. Clear all DTCs. Perform Lighting Control Module (LCM) self-test. If DTC B1342 is retrieved again, replace LCM.

[4] – Perform TEST AA: KEY-IN IGNITION CHIME DOES NOT OPERATE PROPERLY under SYSTEM TESTS in ANALOG INSTRUMENT PANELS – CONTINENTAL article.

[5] – Perform TEST B: NO POWER IN ACC POSITION under SYSTEM TESTS in STEERING COLUMN SWITCHES – CONTINENTAL article.

[6] – Perform TEST R: SEAT BELT SWITCH CIRCUIT FAILURE under SYSTEM TESTS in ANALOG INSTRUMENT PANELS – CONTINENTAL article.

[7] – Perform TEST G: BRAKE LIGHTS NEVER/ALWAYS ON under SYSTEM TESTS in AUTOLAMP SYSTEMS – CONTINENTAL article.

[8] – Perform TEST G: ALARM SOUND WITHOUT VIOLATION under SYSTEM TESTS in ACTIVE ANTI-THEFT – CONTINENTAL article.

[9] – Perform TEST E: FLASH-TO-PASS FEATURE INOPERATIVE under SYSTEM TESTS in AUTOLAMP SYSTEMS – CONTINENTAL article.

[10] – Perform TEST S: BATTERY SAVER DOES NOT DEACTIVATE AFTER TIMEOUT under SYSTEM TESTS in AUTOLAMP SYSTEMS – CONTINENTAL article.

[11] – Perform TEST Q: COURTESY LIGHT ON CONTINUOUSLY under SYSTEM TESTS in AUTOLAMP SYSTEMS – CONTINENTAL article.

[12] – Perform TEST C: HIGH BEAMS INOPERATIVE under SYSTEM TESTS in AUTOLAMP SYSTEMS – CONTINENTAL article.

[13] – Perform TEST K: PARKING, REAR OR LICENSE LIGHTS INOPERATIVE under SYSTEM TESTS in AUTOLAMP SYSTEMS – CONTINENTAL article.

[14] – Perform TEST AK: ILLUMINATION CONTROL INOPERATIVE under SYSTEM TESTS in ANALOG INSTRUMENT PANELS – CONTINENTAL article.

LIGHTING CONTROL MODULE DTC INDEX (Cont.)

[15] – Perform TEST F: AUTOLAMPS ARE INOPERATIVE under SYSTEM TESTS in AUTOLAMP SYSTEMS – CONTINENTAL article.

[16] – Check charging system. See appropriate GENERATORS article in STARTING & CHARGING SYSTEMS. If charging system is okay, check power and ground circuits to LCM. See appropriate wiring diagram in POWER DISTRIBUTION article in WIRING DIAGRAMS.

[17] – Caused by Anti-Lock Brake System (ABS) module. Using NGS tester, perform ABS self-test and repair anti-lock brake system as necessary. See appropriate ANTI-LOCK article in BRAKES in appropriate MITCHELL® manual.

[18] – Caused by Powertrain Control Module (PCM). Using NGS tester, perform PCM self-test and repair powertrain control as necessary. See appropriate SELF-DIAGNOSTICS article in ENGINE PERFORMANCE in appropriate MITCHELL® manual.

[19] – Caused by instrument cluster. Using NGS tester, perform instrument cluster self-test and repair instrument cluster as necessary. See SELF-DIAGNOSTIC SYSTEM in ANALOG INSTRUMENT PANELS – CONTINENTAL article.

[20] – Caused by Driver's Door Module (DDM). Using NGS tester, perform DDM self-test.

[21] – Caused by instrument cluster and/or Driver's Door Module (DDM). Using NGS tester, perform DDM and instrument cluster self-test.

[22] – Service all other DTCs first. After all other DTC concerns have been repaired, perform TEST N: NO MODULE/NETWORK COMMUNICATION (BUS LINK) under SYSTEM TESTS.

REMOTE EMERGENCY SATELLITE CELLULAR UNIT DTC INDEX

DTC	Description	Test
B1216	Emergency Or Information Circuit Short To Ground	1
B1342	ECU Defective	2
B1871	Air Bag Activation Circuit Short To Ground	1
B1874	Cellular Phone Connected But Does Not Respond To RESCU	1
B1893	GPS Antenna Circuit Open Or Not Connected	1
B2102	GPS Antenna Circuit Short To Ground	1
B2141	Response Center Phone Numbers Not Programmed Or Invalid	3
B2477	VIN not programmed	4

[1] – Repair appropriate circuit as necessary.

[2] – Using NGS tester, retrieve and document all continuous DTCs. Clear all DTCs. Perform Remote Emergency Satellite Cellular Unit (RESCU) self-test. If DTC B1342 is retrieved again, replace RESCU.

[3] – Using NGS tester, retrieve and document all continuous DTCs. Clear all DTCs. Perform Remote Emergency Satellite Cellular Unit (RESCU) self-test. If DTC B2141 is retrieved again, replace RESCU.

[4] – Using NGS tester, check Remote Emergency Satellite Cellular Unit (RESCU) configuration.

RESTRAINTS CONTROL MODULE DTC INDEX [1]

DTC [2]	Description	Test
B1342	ECU Defective	3
B1231	RCM Crash Data Memory Full	3
B1921	RCM Bracket Ground Resistance High	3
C1414	Incorrect Vehicle Identification Code	3
B1887	Driver's Side Air Bag Circuit Short To Ground	3
B1916	Driver's Side Air Bag Circuit Short To Voltage	3
B1888	Passenger's Side Air Circuit Bag Short To Ground	3
B1925	Passenger's Side Air Bag Circuit Short To Voltage	3
B1932	Driver's Side Air Bag Circuit Resistance High	3
B1933	Passenger's Side Air Bag Circuit Resistance High	3
B1934	Driver's Side Air Bag Circuit Resistance Low	3
B1935	Passenger's Side Air Bag Circuit Resistance Low	3
B2444	Driver's Side Crash Sensor Internal Fault	3
B2445	Passenger's Side Crash Sensor Internal Fault	3
B2441	Driver's Side Crash Sensor Mounting Failure	3
B2440	Passenger's Side Crash Sensor Mounting Failure	3
U2017	Driver's Side Crash Sensor Communication Failure	3
U2018	Passenger's Side Crash Sensor Communication Failure	3
B1993	Driver's Side Air Bag Circuit Shorted To Ground	3
B1992	Driver's Side Air Bag Circuit Shorted To Voltage	3
B1994	Driver's Side Air Bag Circuit Resistance High	3
B1995	Driver's Side Air Bag Circuit Resistance Low	3
B1997	Passenger's Side Air Bag Circuit Shorted To Ground	3
B1996	Passenger's Side Air Bag Circuit Shorted To Voltage	3
B1998	Passenger's Side Air Bag Circuit Resistance High	3
B1999	Passenger's Side Air Bag Circuit Resistance Low	3
B1892	Air Bag Tone Warning Indicator Circuit Short To Ground Or Open	3
B1891	Air Bag Tone Warning Indicator Circuit Short To Voltage	3
B1869	Air Bag Indicator Inoperative	3
B1870	Air Bag Indicator Short To Voltage	3

[1] – Restraint Control Module (RCM) may also be referred to as Electronic Crash Sensor (ECS) module.

[2] – DTCs are listed in order of importance. Repair DTCs in order listed.

[3] – Repair supplemental restraint system as necessary. See DIAGNOSIS & TESTING article in appropriate MITCHELL® AIR BAG SERVICE & REPAIR MANUAL, DOMESTIC & IMPORTED MODELS.

SPEED CONTROL SERVO/ACTUATOR DTC INDEX [1]

DTC	Description	Test
B1318	Battery Voltage Low	2
B1342	ECU Defective	3
C1109	Throttle Position Did Not Return To Idle after Self-Test	4
C1126	Speed Control Switch Stuck For 2 Minutes Or Longer	5
C1127	Deactivator Switch Circuit Failure	6
C1179	Speed Control Servo/Actuator Cable Slack Failure	7
U1027	Invalid/Missing Data For Engine RPM	8
U1041	Invalid/Missing Data For Vehicle Speed	9
U1051	Invalid/Missing Data For Brakes	10
U1059	Invalid/Missing Data For Transmission Range (PRNDL)	8

[1] – Speed control servo/amplifier assembly may also be referred to as Next Generation Speed Control (NGSC) servo.

[2] – Perform TEST C: BATTERY VOLTAGE LOW (DTC B1318) under SYSTEM TESTS in CRUISE CONTROL – CONTINENTAL article.

[3] – Using NGS tester, retrieve and document all continuous DTCs. Clear all DTCs. Perform speed control servo self-test. If DTC B1342 is retrieved again, replace speed control servo.

[4] – Perform TEST D: THROTTLE POSITION DID NOT RETURN TO IDLE AFTER SELF-TEST (DTC C1109) under SYSTEM TESTS in CRUISE CONTROL – CONTINENTAL article.

[5] – Perform TEST E: SPEED CONTROL SWITCH STUCK FOR 2 MINUTES OR LONGER (DTC C1126) under SYSTEM TESTS in CRUISE CONTROL – CONTINENTAL article.

[6] – Perform TEST F: DEACTIVATOR SWITCH CIRCUIT FAILURE (DTC C1127) under SYSTEM TESTS in CRUISE CONTROL – CONTINENTAL article.

[7] – Perform TEST G: SPEED CONTROL SERVO CABLE SLACK FAILURE (DTC C1179) under SYSTEM TESTS in CRUISE CONTROL – CONTINENTAL article.

[8] – Caused by Powertrain Control Module (PCM). Using NGS tester, perform PCM self-test and repair powertrain control as necessary. See appropriate SELF-DIAGNOSTICS article in ENGINE PERFORMANCE in appropriate MITCHELL® manual.

[9] – Caused by Anti-Lock Brake System (ABS) module. Using NGS tester, perform ABS self-test and repair anti-lock brake system as necessary. See appropriate ANTI-LOCK article in BRAKES in appropriate MITCHELL® manual.

[10] – Caused by Lighting Control Module (LCM). Using NGS tester, perform LCM self-test.

VEHICLE DYNAMIC MODULE DTC INDEX

DTC	Description	Test
B1317	Battery Voltage High	1
B1318	Battery Voltage Low	1
B1342	ECU Defective	1
C1722	Air Suspension Height Sensor Power Circuit Short To Voltage	1
C1723	Air Suspension Height Sensor Power Circuit Short To Ground	1
C1735	Air Suspension Left Rear Corner Up Timeout	1
C1736	Air Suspension Left Rear Corner Down Timeout	1
C1737	Air Suspension Right Rear Corner Up Timeout	1
C1738	Air Suspension Right Rear Corner Down Timeout	1
C1770	Air Suspension Vent Solenoid Output Circuit Failure	1
C1773	Air Suspension Vent Solenoid Output Circuit Short To Ground	1
C1790	Air Suspension Left Rear Air Spring/Solenoid Output Circuit Failure	1
C1793	Air Suspension Left Rear Air Spring/Solenoid Output Circuit Short To Ground	1
C1795	Air Suspension Right Rear Air Spring/Solenoid Output Circuit Failure	1
C1798	Air Suspension Right Rear Air Spring/Solenoid Output Circuit Short To Ground	1
C1820	Air Compressor Request Exceeding Maximum Time	1
C1840	Air Suspension Disable Switch Circuit Failure	1
C1842	Air Suspension Disable Switch Circuit Short To Voltage	1
C1881	Air Suspension Right Front Height Sensor Circuit Failure	1
C1884	Air Suspension Right Front Height Sensor Circuit Short To Ground	1
C1885	Air Suspension Right Rear Height Sensor Circuit Failure	1
C1888	Air Suspension Right Rear Height Sensor Circuit Short To Ground	1
C1889	Air Suspension Left Front Height Sensor Circuit Failure	1
C1892	Air Suspension Left Front Height Sensor Circuit Short To Ground	1
C1893	Air Suspension Left Rear Height Sensor Circuit Failure	1
C1896	Air Suspension Left Rear Height Sensor Circuit Short To Ground	1
C1897	Steering VAP II Circuit Loop Failure	2
C1901	Ride Control Right Rear Shock Actuator Circuit Failure	1
C1904	Ride Control Right Rear Shock Actuator Circuit Short To Ground	1
C1905	Ride Control Left Rear Shock Actuator Circuit Failure	1
C1908	Ride Control Left Rear Shock Actuator Circuit Short To Ground	1
C1909	Ride Control Right Front Shock Actuator Circuit Failure	1
C1912	Ride Control Right Front Shock Actuator Circuit Short To Ground	1
C1913	Ride Control Left Front Shock Actuator Circuit Failure	1
C1916	Ride Control Left Front Shock Actuator Circuit Short To Ground	1
C1929	Air Suspension Compressor Relay Circuit Failure	1
C1931	Air Suspension Compressor Relay Circuit Short To Voltage	1
U1027	Invalid/Missing Data For Engine RPM	3
U1041	Invalid/Missing Data For Vehicle Speed	4
U1181	Invalid/Missing Data For Memory Features	5

VEHICLE DYNAMIC MODULE DTC INDEX (Cont.)

U1262 .... SCP Bus Communication Fault 6

[1] – Repair electronic suspension as necessary. See appropriate ELECTRONIC article in SUSPENSION in appropriate MITCHELL® manual.

[2] – Repair electronic steering as necessary. See appropriate ELECTRONIC article in STEERING in appropriate MITCHELL® manual.

[3] – Caused by Powertrain Control Module (PCM). Using NGS tester, perform PCM self-test and repair powertrain control as necessary. See appropriate SELF-DIAGNOSTICS article in ENGINE PERFORMANCE in appropriate MITCHELL® manual.

[4] – Caused by Anti-Lock Brake System (ABS) module. Using NGS tester, perform ABS self-test and repair anti-lock brake system as necessary. See appropriate ANTI-LOCK article in BRAKES in appropriate MITCHELL® manual.

[5] – Caused by instrument cluster. Using NGS tester, perform instrument cluster self-test and repair instrument cluster as necessary. See SELF-DIAGNOSTIC SYSTEM in ANALOG INSTRUMENT PANELS – CONTINENTAL article.

[6] – Service all other DTCs first. After all other DTC concerns have been repaired, perform TEST N: NO MODULE/NETWORK COMMUNICATION (BUS LINK) under SYSTEM TESTS.

PARAMETER IDENTIFICATION (PID) DEFINITIONS

ANTI-LOCK BRAKE SYSTEM MODULE PID INDEX

PID	Description	Expected Value
ABSLF_I	Left Front ABS Inlet Valve	ON, OFF
ABSLF_O	Left Front ABS Outlet Valve	ON, OFF
ABSLR_I	Left Rear ABS Inlet Valve	ON, OFF
ABSLR_O	Left Rear ABS Outlet Valve	ON, OFF
ABSRF_I	Right Front ABS Inlet Valve	ON, OFF
ABSRF_O	Right Front ABS Outlet Valve	ON, OFF
ABSRR_I	Right Rear ABS Inlet Valve	ON, OFF
ABSRR_O	Right Rear ABS Outlet Valve	ON, OFF
BOO_ABS	Brake Switch Input	ON, OFF
CCNTABS	Number Of Continuous DTCs	One Bit Per Count
LF_WSPD	Left Front Wheel Speed Signal	0-255 KPH
LR_WSPD	Left Rear Wheel Speed Signal	0-255 KPH
RF_WSPD	Right Front Wheel Speed Signal	0-255 KPH
RR_WSPD	Right Rear Wheel Speed Signal	0-255 KPH
TC_LVAL	Left T/A Control Valve	ON, OFF
TC_RVAL	Right T/A Control Valve	ON, OFF

DRIVER'S DOOR MODULE PID INDEX

PID	Description	Expected Value
DDMHIGH	High Series DDM	YES, ON
D_DOOR	Driver's Door Ajar Switch	AJAR, CLOSED
DLIDRLS	Trunk Lid Release	ON, OFF
D_PW_SW	Driver's Power Window Switch	UP, DOWN, OFF, SHORT
DRLKCYL	Door Lock Cylinder	ACTIVE, NOTACTIVE
DR_LOCK	Door Lock Output State	YES, ON
DR_UNLK	All Doors Unlocked Output State	YES, ON
D_WINDO	Driver's Window	DOWN, NOTDOWN
KEY_PAD	Driver's Keyless Entry Switch	1, 3, 5, 7, 9
LRPW_SW	Left Rear Power Window Switch	SHORT, UP, DOWN, OFF
MIRH_SW	Power Mirror Position Switch (Horizontal)	SHORT, LEFT, RIGHT, OFF
MIR_SEL	Power Mirror Select Switch	DRVMIR, PSGMIR, OFF
MIRV_SW	Power Mirror Position Switch (Vertical)	SHORT, LEFT, RIGHT, OFF
P_PW_SW	Passenger's Front Window Switch	SHORT, UP, DOWN, OFF
RRPW_SW	Right Rear Power Window Switch	SHORT, UP, DOWN, OFF
SFNT_SW	Power Seat Switch (Front Height)	SHORT, UP, DOWN, OFF
SFWD_SW	Power Seat Switch (Forward/Rearward)	SHORT, UP, DOWN, OFF
SREARSW	Power Seat Switch (Rear Height)	SHORT, UP, DOWN, OFF
SRCL_SW	Power Seat Switch (Recline)	SHORT, UP, DOWN, OFF

DRIVER'S SEAT MODULE PID INDEX

PID	Description	Expected Value
CCNT_DS	Number Of Continuous DTCs In DSM	Number Of DTCs
DMIR_H	Driver's Mirror Horizontal	SENSED, NOTSEN
DMIR_V	Driver's Mirror Vertical	SENSED, NOTSEN
PMIR_H	Passenger's Mirror Horizontal	SENSED, NOTSEN
PMIR_V	Passenger's Mirror Vertical	SENSED, NOTSEN
SFNT_MT	Driver's Seat Front Motor	SENSED, NOTSEN
SFWD_MT	Driver's Seat Forward Motor	SENSED, NOTSEN
SRCL_MT	Driver's Seat Recline Motor	SENSED, NOTSEN
SREARMT	Driver's Seat Rear Motor	SENSED, NOTSEN
VBAT_DS	Battery Voltage	INRANGE, NOTNRANGE

FRONT RADIO CONTROL UNIT PID INDEX

PID	Description	Expected Value
AM_SW	AM Switch	ACTIVE, NOTACT
AS_SW	Autoset Switch	ACTIVE, NOTACT
ASYSON	ASYSON Output State	ACTIVE, NOTACT
BAL_SW	Balance Switch	ACTIVE, NOTACT
BAND_SW	Band Switch	ACTIVE, NOTACT
BASS_SW	Bass Switch	ACTIVE, NOTACT
CD/CJ	CD Disc Jockey	YES, NO
CD_S	Single CD Player	YES, NO
CELLPHN	Cellular Phone	YES, NO
CLKDISP	Clock Display Enable Input State	DISABLE, ENABLE
CLOCK	Clock	YES, NO
CTR_IMG	Center Image Amplifier	YES, NO
DSP_EFF	DSP Effects	YES, NO
EJCT_SW	Eject switch	ACTIVE, NOTACT
FADE_SW	Fade Switch	ACTIVE, NOTACT
FM_SW	FM Switch	ACTIVE, NOTACT
MEM_SW	Memory Switch	ACTIVE, NOTACT
MENU_SW	Steering Wheel Control Input State	VALID, INVALID
MNIDSC	Minidisc Deck	YES, NO
PHONE	Phone Switch (Steering Wheel)	ACTIVE, NOTACT
PRE1_SW	Preset Switch 1	ACTIVE, NOTACT
PRE2_SW	Preset Switch 2	ACTIVE, NOTACT
PRE3_SW	Preset Switch 3	ACTIVE, NOTACT
PRE4_SW	Preset Switch 4	ACTIVE, NOTACT
PRE5_SW	Preset Switch 5	ACTIVE, NOTACT
PRE6_SW	Preset Switch 6	ACTIVE, NOTACT
PTA	PTA Input State	ACTIVE, NOTACT
PWR_SW	Power Switch	ACTIVE, NOTACT
RDBS	RBDS	YES, NO
RBDS_SW	RBDS Switch	ACTIVE, NOTACT
REAR_ST	Rear Seat Controls	YES, ON
SCAN_SW	Scan Switch	ACTIVE, NOTACT
SEEK+	Seek Increase Switch	ACTIVE, NOTACT
SEEK−	Seek Decrease Switch	ACTIVE, NOTACT
STEER_C	Steering Wheel Controls	YES, NO
SUBWOOF	Subwoofer Amplifier	YES, NO
TAPE_SW	Tape Switch	ACTIVE, NOTACT
TAPEDCK	Tape Deck	YES, NO
TREB_SW	Treble Switch	ACTIVE, NOTACT
TUNE+	Tune Increase Switch	ACTIVE, NOTACT
TUNE−	Tune Decrease Switch	ACTIVE, NOTACT
VOL+	Volume Increase Switch	ACTIVE, NOTACT
VOL+_SC	Volume + Switch	ACTIVE, NOTACT
VOL−	Volume Decrease Switch	ACTIVE, NOTACT
VOL−_SC	Volume − Switch	ACTIVE, NOTACT

INSTRUMENT CLUSTER PID INDEX

PID	Description	Expected Value
ACCESS	Security Access Status	TIMED, CODED
ANTISCN	Time-Out For Unprogrammed PATS Key	DISABLE, ENABLE
CCNT_EC	Number Of DTCs In VIC	One Count Per Bit
COOLANT	Engine Coolant Level Status	OK, NOTOK
DISPLAY	Display Switch	ACTIVE, NOTACT
DTE_SW	Distance To Empty Switch	ACTIVE, NOTACT
EM/D_ID	E/M Switch (Driver ID Switch)	ACTIVE, NOTACT
MENU_SW	Menu Switch	ACTIVE, NOTACT
MIN#KEY	Minimum Number Of Programmed Keys Required To Start Vehicle	BCD (Valid Range 2-8)
M_KEY	Programmed Key In Ignition	NOTPRE, PRESENT
NUMKEYS	Number Of Ignition Key Codes Programed	BCD (Valid Range 0-8)
OIL_LVL	Engine Oil Level Status	OK, NOTOK
PCM_ID	Is PCM ID Stored In HEC	STORED, NOTSTR
PCM_VFY	PCM ID Matches Between PCM & VIC	YES, NO
RESETSW	Reset Switch	ACTIVE, NOTACT
SELECT	Select/Mode Switch	ACTIVE, NOTACT
SERVMOD	Service Mode	YES, ON
SPAREKY	Can You Add Spare Keys With 2 Programmed Keys	DISABLE, ENABLE
SYSCKSW	System Check Switch	ACTIVE, NOTACT
TRIP_SW	Trip Switch	ACTIVE, NOTACT
VBAT_EC	System Battery Voltage Potential	NOTOK, OK
V_HDLSW	Vehicle Handling Switch	ACTIVE, NOTACT
WFLUID	Washer Fluid Level	LOW, OK

LIGHTING CONTROL MODULE PID INDEX

PID	Description	Expected Value
ACCDLY	Accessory Delay Driver	ON, OFF
AL_EVT#	Last 8 Alarm Events	[1]
ALP_DLY	Autolamp Delay Time	Seconds
ALP_ON	Autlamp On Driver	[1]
AUTOLMP	Autolamp Switch	INC, DEC, OFF, SHORT
BACK_LT	PWM Output	0.5 Percent/Count
BATSAV	Battery Saver Relay Circuit	ON, OFF
BOO_LC	Brake Switch Input	ON, OFF
CONT_LC	Number Of Continuous DTCs	One Count Per Bit
DECKLID	Deck/Hatch Ajar Switch	AJAR, CLOSED
DIMMER	Panel Dim Switch	INC, DEC, OFF, SHORT
DLIDOUT	Trunk Lid Driver	[1]
DLIDPCH	Trunk Lid Punch-Out	ON, OFF
DRLKCYL	Door Lock Cylinder	ON, OFF
D_SEAT	Driver's Seat Occupied Switch	OCCUPD, NOTOCC
D_SBELT	Driver's Seat Belt	IN, OUT
FLASH	Flash-To-Pass Switch	ON, OFF
FLSHPWR	Turn Signal Power	OPEN, GRN, VBATT
FTURN_L	Left & Right Front Turn Signal Light	R_OPEN, L_OPEN, L/R_OPEN, OK
HBEAMSW	High Beam Switch	ON, OFF
HDLMPSW	Low Beam Switch	ON, OFF
HOOD_SW	Hood Ajar Switch	AJAR, CLOSED
HORNRLY	Horn Control Driver	[1]
IGN_A	Ignition Switch (ACC Position)	YES, NO
IGN_KEY	Ignition Key In/Out	IN, OUT
IGN_LC	Ignition Switch	RUN, START, ACCSSY, OFF
IGN_PCH	Ignition Switch Punch-Out	ON, OFF
IGN_S	Ignition Switch (START Position)	YES, NO
INST_LT	Instrument Panel Lighting	1.6 Percent/Count
INTLMP	Illuminated Entry Relay Circuit	[1]
INTR_LT	Interior Lighting	0.5 Percent/Count
LBEAMSW	Low Beam Switch	ON, OFF
L_HIGH	Left High Beam Output	ON, OFF
LIGHTSN	Ambient Light	DAY, NIGHT
L_LOW	Low Beam Light	[1]
LOWBEAM	Low Beam Light	R_OPEN, L_OPEN, L/R_OPEN, OK
LRDR_SW	Left Rear Door Ajar Switch	AJAR, CLOSED
L_TAIL	Left Rear Tail Light Driver Output State	ON, OFF
PARK_SW	Parking Switch	ON, OFF
PD_HAND	Passenger's Door Handle Switch	ACTIVE, NOTACTIVE
P_DOOR	Passenger's Door Ajar Switch	AJAR, CLOSED
P_DR_LC	Passenger's Door Ajar Switch	AJAR, CLOSED
PWM1DIR	PWM #1 Driver	[1]
R_HIGH	Right High Beam Output	ON, OFF
R_LOW	Right Low Beam Output	ON, OFF
RRDR_SW	Right Rear Door Ajar Switch	AJAR, CLOSED
R_TAIL	Right Rear Tail Light Driver Output State	ON, OFF
RTURN_L	Left & Right Rear Turn Signal Light	R_OPEN, L_OPEN, L/R_OPEN, OK
TAILLMP	Right & Left Tail Light	OPEN, OK
THEFT	Anti-Theft Indicator Driver	[1]
TURNSIG	Turn Signal Driver Output	[1]
TURN_SW	Right & Left Turn Signal Switch	OFF, LEFT, RIGHT, SHORT
VBAT_LC	Battery Voltage	0.1Volt/Count (Volt)
WIPER_M	Wiper Motor Status	ON, OFF

[1] – Expected value should be OFF- - -, OFF- -G, OFF- B-, OFF-BG, OFFO- -, OFFO-G, OFFO-B-, OFFOBG, ON- - -, ON- -G, ON- B-, ON-BG, ONO- -, ONO-G, ONO-B- or ONOBG.

SPEED CONTROL SERVO PID INDEX

PID	Description	Expected Value
CCNT_SC	Number Of Continuous DTCs In Speed Control Servo	One Count Per Bit
COAST	Speed Control Actuator Switch COAST	ACTIVE, NOTACT
RESUME	Speed Control Actuator Switch RESUME	ACTIVE, NOTACT
SC_OFF	Speed Control Actuator Switch OFF	ACTIVE, NOTACT
SC_ON	Speed Control Actuator Switch ON	ACTIVE, NOTACT
SET_ACL	Speed Control Actuator Switch SET/ACCEL	ACTIVE, NOTACT
VS_SET	Set Vehicle Speed	0-255 MPH

VEHICLE DYNAMICS MODULE PID INDEX

PID	Description	Expected Value
AS_COMP	Air Suspension Compressor Status	1
ASDISSW	Air Suspension Inhibit Switch	ACTIVE, NOTACT
ASLRSOL	Left Rear Air Spring Solenoid	1
ASRRSOL	Right Rear Air Spring Solenoid	1
AS_TRIM	Air Suspension Accurate Trim	TRIM, NOTTRIM
AS_VNT	Air Suspension Vent Solenoid Output State	1
CCNTVDM	Number Of Continuous DTCs In VDM	One Count Per Bit
DOORVDM	External Access Door Ajar Switch	AJAR, NOTAJAR
HTG_PWR	Height Sensor Power	Volts
IGN_RUN	Ignition Switch State	RUN, NOTRUN
LF_HGT	Left Front Height Sensor	mm
LFSHOCK	Left Front Shock Actuator State	2
LR_HGT	Left Rear Height Sensor	mm
LRSHOCK	Left Rear Shock Actuator State	2
RF_HGT	Right Front Height Sensor	mm
RFSHOCK	Right Front Shock Actuator State	2
RR_HGT	Right Rear Height Sensor	mm
RRSHOCK	Right Rear Shock Actuator State	2
VAPS_IN	VAPS II Input Current Input	0-100 Percent
VAPSOUT	VAPS II Output Current Set Point	0-100 Percent
VAPSSET	Vehicle Dynamics Feature Option Selection	0, 1
VBATVDM	Battery Voltage	Volts
VSS_VDM	Vehicle Speed Sensor Though SCP Network	1/128

[1] – Expected valve should be ON, OFF, SHORTVBAT, SHORTGRN or OPEN
[2] – Expected value should be FIRM, SOFT, OPEN B+ or GRN.

WIRING DIAGRAMS

NOTE: See appropriate wiring diagrams in DATA LINK CONNECTORS, GROUND DISTRIBUTION and/or POWER DISTRIBUTION article in WIRING DIAGRAMS.

DESCRIPTION & OPERATION

Vehicle has 2 module communications networks. The Powertrain Control Module (PCM) and Anti-Lock Brake System (ABS) module are connected to the multiplex communications network through a pair of twisted wires or BUS. The BUS network is also referred to as Standard Corporate Protocol (SCP). The BUS consists of (+) circuit and a (–) circuit. The ABS module is also connected to the ISO 9141 diagnostic communications network through a single wire along with the Restraint Control Module (RCM). Both networks are connected to the Data Link Connector (DLC). This article is used to diagnose BUS and ISO communications network circuit faults. For module locations, see COMPONENT LOCATIONS table under COMPONENT LOCATIONS.

COMPONENT LOCATIONS

COMPONENT LOCATIONS

Component	Location
Restraint Control Module (RCM)	Under Center Console
Anti-Lock Brake System Module	Left Rear Corner Of Engine Compartment
Central Timer Module	Behind Driver's Side Of Instrument Panel, On Central Junction Box
Data Link Connector	Below Driver's Side Of Instrument Panel, To Right Of Steering Column
Powertrain Control Module	Right Side Of Engine Compartment, On Firewall [1]
Passive Anti-Theft System Module	
In-Line Harness Connector C62	Behind Left Side Of Dash
In-Line Harness Connector C3001	Left Side Of Engine Compartment, On Strut Tower

[1] – Passive Anti-Theft System (PATS) module is built into Powertrain Control Module (PCM).

REPAIRING BUS WIRING

NOTE: *Following procedure must be used to ensure proper repair is performed on BUS wiring. BUS wiring is sensitive to moisture and oxidation and must be properly sealed to ensure proper operation of the module communications network. Regular heat shrink tubing is NOT sufficient, heat shrink tubing containing hot melt wax is required.*

1) When performing a repair on the BUS wiring of the Module Communications Network, ensure the wires on the BUS are twisted at a rate of 33-40 winds per 3.3 ft. (1 m). The twists should start within approximately 4.9" (124 mm) from any connector. Use only 20 AWG standard wire gauge for repairs.

2) If performing a splice in the wiring, strip .75" (19.0 mm) of insulation from one wire and 1.50" (38.1 mm) of insulator from the other wire. Perform STEP 1. *See Fig. 1.* Place hot melt wax heat shrink tubing over one wire.

3) Twist stripped portion of the wires together. Solder connection using resin core RMA solder. DO NOT use acid core solder. Bend wires to allow installation of heat shrink tubing. Perform STEP 2. *See Fig. 1.*

4) Position heat shrink tubing over splice area. Using heat gun, evenly heat the heat shrink tubing until wax flows from both ends of heat shrink tubing.

COMMUNICATION NETWORK DIAGNOSTICS

INSPECTION & VERIFICATION

1) Verify customer's original problem by operating system in question. Inspect vehicle for any obvious electrical component wiring or connector damage. Inspect connectors for loose, damaged or corroded terminals. Check related fuses for system in question.

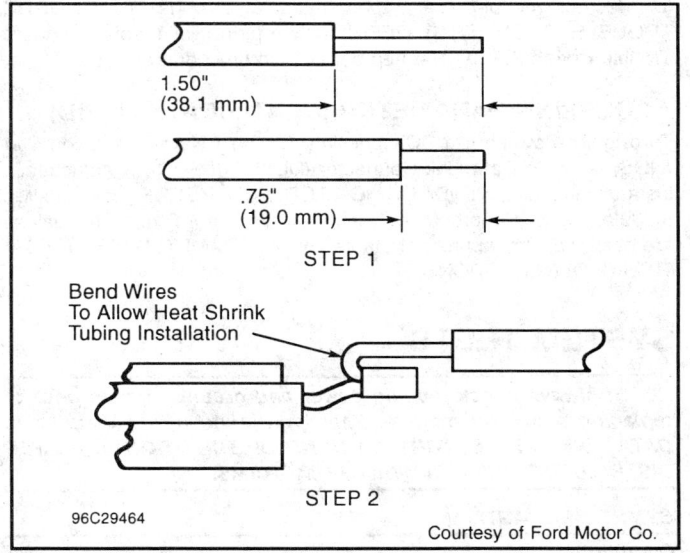

Fig. 1: Repairing Bus Wiring

2) Inspect 16-pin Data Link Connector (DLC) pins for damage. The DLC is located below driver's side of instrument panel, right of steering column. If pins are okay, go to next step. If pins are damaged, repair as necessary and proceed to next step.

3) If problem is still present after performing inspection, connect New Generation Star (NGS) tester to DLC. Select vehicle to be tested from NGS tester menu. If NGS tester does not communicate with vehicle, ensure program card is properly installed. Check NGS tester cable connections and ensure ignition is in RUN position. If NGS tester still does not communicate with vehicle, perform TEST A: NO MODULE/NETWORK COMMUNICATION WITH NGS TESTER under SYSTEM TESTS. If NGS tester communicates with vehicle, perform data link diagnostic procedure. See DATA LINK DIAGNOSTIC TEST.

DATA LINK DIAGNOSTIC TEST

NOTE: *When performing data link diagnostic test, the NGS tester may display BUS circuits 4-PB9 (4-PC28 without ABS) and 5-PB9 (5-PC28 without ABS) as circuits No. 914 and 915. The NGS tester may also display ISO circuit 8-DA1 (8-JA7 without ABS) as circuit No. 70.*

1) Connect New Generation Star (NGS) tester to Data Link Connector (DLC), if not already connected. Select vehicle to be tested from NGS tester menu.

2) Turn ignition switch to RUN position. Rotate dial on NGS tester to menu item DIAGNOSTIC DATA LINK and press trigger. A test will be performed on the BUS for the module communications network and the ISO 9141 communication link.

3) If NGS tester displays CKT 914 = SYSTEM PASSED and CKT 915 = SYSTEM PASSED, module communications network is okay. If NGS tester displays CKT 70 = SYSTEM PASSED, ISO 9141 communication link is operating properly. Return to article that directed you here and continue diagnosis.

4) If NGS tester displays CKT 914 = ALL MODULE NO RESPONSE/NOT EQUIPPED, CKT 915 = ALL MODULE NO RESPONSE/NOT EQUIPPED and CKT 70 = ALL MODULE NO RESPONSE/NOT EQUIPPED, perform TEST A: NO MODULE/NETWORK COMMUNICATION WITH NGS TESTER.

5) If module in question is NO RESPONSE/NOT EQUIPPED, perform appropriate tests. See SYMPTOM CHART table under SYSTEM TESTS.

RETRIEVING & CLEARING DIAGNOSTIC TROUBLE CODES

Connect New Generation Star (NGS) tester to Data Link Connector (DLC). Following manufacturer's instructions to retrieve and clear codes for desired module. See appropriate table under DIAGNOSTIC TROUBLE CODE (DTC) DEFINITIONS for a listing of Diagnostic Trouble Codes (DTCs) and appropriate test procedure.

ACCESSING PARAMETER IDENTIFICATION (PID)

Turn ignition switch to LOCK position. Connect New Generation Star (NGS) tester to Data Link Connector (DLC). Following manufacturer's instructions enter PID/DATA MONITOR AND RECORD for desired module. Operate appropriate system and ensure PID expected values are obtained. See appropriate table under PARAMETER IDENTIFICATION (PID) DEFINITIONS.

SYSTEM TESTS

NOTE: Always check module power and ground circuits prior to replacing a control module. See appropriate wiring diagram in DATA LINK CONNECTORS, GROUND DISTRIBUTION or POWER DISTRIBUTION article in WIRING DIAGRAMS.

SYMPTOM CHART

Condition	Test
No Module/Network Communication With NGS Tester	A
Anti-Lock Brake System (ABS) Module Does Not Respond To NGS Tester	B
Restraint Control Module (RCM) Does Not Respond To NGS Tester	C
Restraint Control Module (RCM) & ABS Module Do Not Respond To NGS Tester (Result Code 70=00000001)	D
Passive Anti-Theft System (PATS) Module Does Not Respond To NGS Tester	[1] E
Powertrain Control Module (PCM) Does Not Respond To NGS Tester	E
Central Timer Module (CTM) Does Not Respond To NGS Tester	F
No Module/Network Communication With NGS Tester (Result Code 00000003)	G

[1] – Passive Anti-Theft System (PATS) module is built into Powertrain Control Module (PCM).

TEST A: NO MODULE/NETWORK COMMUNICATION WITH NGS TESTER

1) Turn ignition switch to LOCK position. Connect New Generation Star (NGS) tester to Data Link Connector (DLC). Turn ignition switch to RUN position. If NGS tester powers up, go to next step. If NGS tester does not power up, go to step **6**).

2) Using NGS tester, perform data link diagnostic procedure. See DATA LINK DIAGNOSTIC TEST under COMMUNICATION NETWORK DIAGNOSTICS. If SYSTEM PASSED is not displayed, go to next step. If SYSTEM PASSED is displayed, return to article that directed you here and continue diagnosis.

3) If ABS:NO RESPONSE/NOT EQUIPPED, AIRBAG MODULE:NO RESPONSE/NOT EQUIPPED or RESULT CODE=00000001 was not retrieved in step **2**), go to next step. If ABS:NO RESPONSE/NOT EQUIPPED was retrieved in step **2**), perform TEST B: ANTI-LOCK BRAKE SYSTEM (ABS) MODULE DOES NOT RESPOND TO NGS TESTER. If AIRBAG MODULE:NO RESPONSE/NOT EQUIPPED was retrieved in step **2**), perform TEST C: RESTRAINT CONTROL MODULE (RCM) DOES NOT RESPOND TO NGS TESTER. If RESULT CODE=00000001 was retrieved in step **2**), perform TEST D: RESTRAINT CONTROL MODULE (RCM) & ABS MODULE DO NOT RESPOND TO NGS TESTER (RESULT CODE 70=00000001).

4) If PCM:NO RESPONSE/NOT EQUIPPED was not retrieved in step **2**), go to next step. If PCM:NO RESPONSE/NOT EQUIPPED was retrieved in step **2**), perform TEST E: POWERTRAIN CONTROL MODULE (PCM) DOES NOT RESPOND TO NGS TESTER.

5) If RESULT CODE for CKT 914 or CKT 915=00000003 was retrieved in step **2**), perform TEST G: NO MODULE/NETWORK COMMUNICATION WITH NGS TESTER (RESULT CODE 00000003). If RESULT

CODE for CKT 914 or CKT 915=00000003 was not retrieved in step **2**), repair by symptom. See SYMPTOM CHART table.

6) Remove and inspect fuse No. 24 (15-amp) from central junction box. If fuse is okay, go to next step. If fuse is blown, reinstall NEW fuse. If fuse blows again, check for short to ground and repair as necessary.

7) Disconnect NGS tester. Turn ignition switch to RUN position. Measure voltage at terminal No. 16 (Orange wire) at Data Link Connector (DLC). *See Fig. 2.* If battery voltage does not exist, go to next step. If battery voltage exists, go to step **9**).

8) Turn ignition switch to LOCK position. Disconnect central junction box harness connector C369. Turn ignition switch to RUN position. Measure voltage at terminal No. 1 at central junction box connector C369 (fuse box side). *See Fig. 3.* If battery voltage exists, repair open in Orange wire. If battery voltage does not exist, replace central junction box.

9) Measure resistance between ground and terminals No. 4 (Black wire) and No. 5 (Black/Orange wire) at DLC. If both resistance readings are 5 ohms or less, repair or replace NGS tester as necessary. If either resistance reading is greater than 5 ohms, repair open in Black wire or Black/Orange wire between ground and DLC.

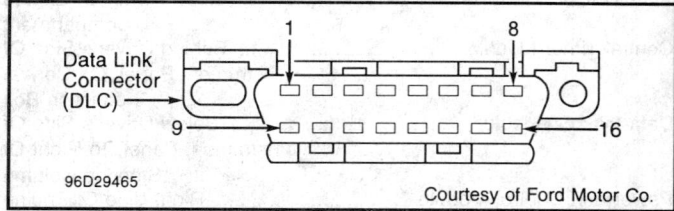

Fig. 2: Identifying Data Link Connector (DLC) Terminals

TEST B: ANTI-LOCK BRAKE SYSTEM (ABS) MODULE DOES NOT RESPOND TO NGS TESTER

1) Turn ignition switch to LOCK position. Disconnect NGS tester (if connected). Disconnect ABS module harness connector C3002. Inspect connector for loose, damaged or corroded terminals. If connector is okay, go to next step. If connector is damaged, repair connector as necessary.

2) Turn ignition switch to RUN position. Measure voltage at terminals No. 24 (White/Violet wire), No. 29 (Blue wire) and No. 30 (Gray wire) at ABS module harness connector C3002. *See Fig. 4.* If zero volts is indicated at all terminals, go to next step. If any voltage is indicated at any terminal, repair short to voltage in appropriate wire between ABS module harness connector and DLC.

3) Measure resistance between terminal No. 24 (White/Violet wire) at ABS module harness connector C3002 and terminal No. 7 (White wire) at Data Link Connector (DLC). *See Figs. 2 and 4.* If resistance is 5 ohms or less, go to next step. If resistance is greater than 5 ohms, repair open in White wire or White/Violet wire between ABS module harness connector and DLC.

4) Measure resistance between terminal No. 29 (Blue wire) at ABS module harness connector C3002 and terminal No. 10 (Blue/White wire) at DLC. If resistance is 5 ohms or less, go to next step. If resistance is greater than 5 ohms, repair open in Blue wire or Blue/White wire between ABS module harness connector and DLC.

5) Measure resistance between terminal No. 30 (Gray wire) at ABS module harness connector C3002 and terminal No. 2 (Gray/Violet wire) at DLC. If resistance is 5 ohms or less, go to next step. If resistance is greater than 5 ohms, repair open in Gray wire or Gray/Violet wire between ABS module harness connector and DLC.

6) Measure resistance between ground and terminal No. 24 (White/Violet wire) at ABS module harness connector C3002. If resistance is greater than 10 k/ohms, go to next step. If resistance is 10 k/ohms or less, repair short to ground in White/Violet wire or White wire between ABS module harness connector and DLC.

7) Measure resistance between ground and terminal No. 29 (Blue wire) at ABS module harness connector C3002. If resistance is greater than 10 k/ohms, go to next step. If resistance is 10 k/ohms or less, repair short to ground in Blue wire or Blue/White wire between ABS module harness connector and DLC.

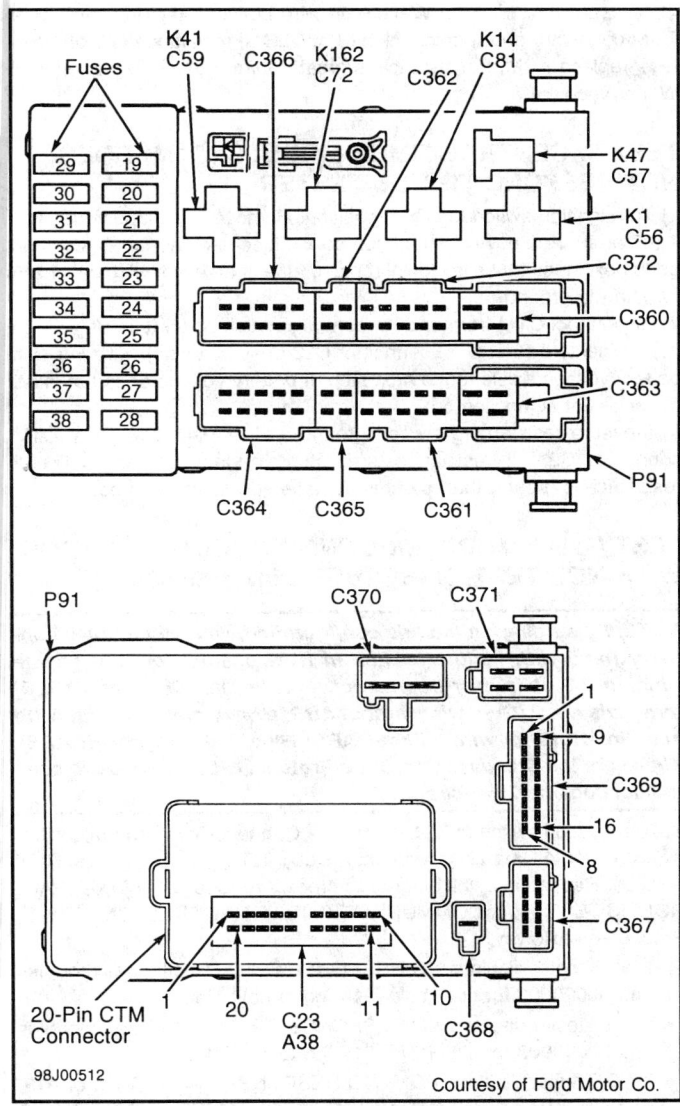

Fig. 3: Identifying Central Junction Box Harness Connectors

8) Measure resistance between ground and terminal No. 30 (Gray wire) at ABS module harness connector C3002. If resistance is greater than 10 k/ohms, replace ABS module. If resistance is 10 k/ohms or less, repair short to ground in Gray wire or Gray/Violet wire between ABS module harness connector and DLC.

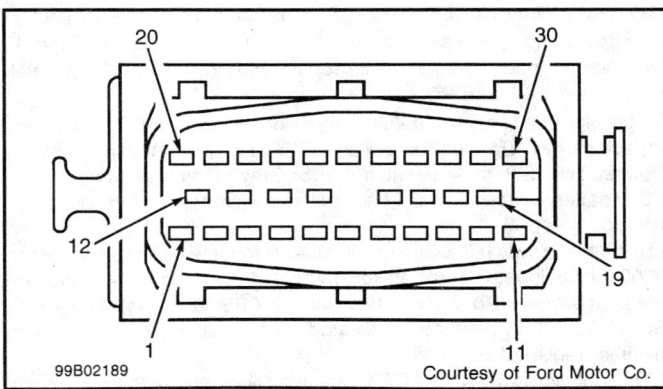

Fig. 4: Identifying ABS Module Harness Connector C3002 Terminals

TEST C: RESTRAINT CONTROL MODULE (RCM) DOES NOT RESPOND TO NGS TESTER

NOTE: Depending on module configuration, with all modules connected and with ignition switch in RUN position or with engine running 2-3 volts may be present at Data Link Connector (DLC) terminal No. 7 (White wire with ABS; White/Red wire without ABS). This is the International Standards Organization (ISO) 9141 diagnostic communications network circuit.

1) Disarm air bag system. See appropriate AIR BAG RESTRAINT SYSTEMS article. Turn ignition switch to LOCK position. Disconnect RCM harness connector C20. Inspect connector for loose, damaged or corroded terminals. If connector is okay, go to next step. If connector is damaged, repair connector as necessary.

2) Turn ignition switch to RUN position. Measure voltage at terminal No. 5 (White/Red wire) at RCM harness connector C20. *See Fig. 5.* If zero volts is indicated, go to next step. If any voltage is indicated, repair short to voltage in White/Red wire between DLC and RCM harness connector.

3) Measure resistance between terminal No. 5 (White/Red wire) at RCM harness connector C20 and terminal No. 7 (White wire with ABS; White/Red wire without ABS) at Data Link Connector (DLC). *See Figs. 2 and 5.* If resistance is 5 ohms or less, go to next step. If resistance is greater than 5 ohms, repair open in White wire or White/Red wire between DLC and RCM harness connector.

4) Measure resistance between ground and terminal No. 5 (White/Red wire) at RCM harness connector C20. If resistance is greater than 10 k/ohms, replace RCM. If resistance is 10 k/ohms or less, repair short to ground in White wire or White/Red wire.

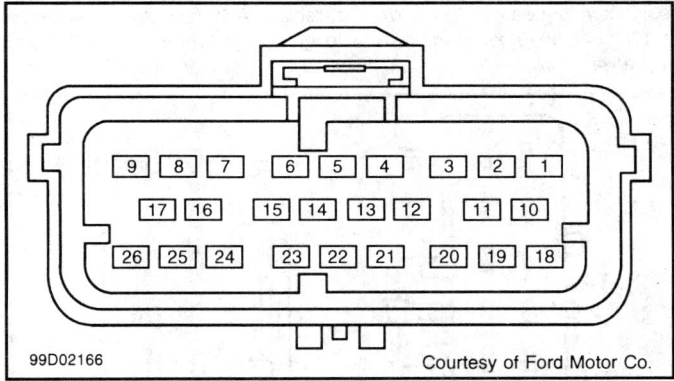

Fig. 5: Identifying RCM Harness Connector C20 Terminals

TEST D: RESTRAINT CONTROL MODULE (RCM) & ABS MODULE DO NOT RESPOND TO NGS TESTER (RESULT CODE 70=00000001)

NOTE: Depending on module configuration, with all modules connected and with ignition switch in RUN position or with engine running 2-3 volts may be present at Data Link Connector (DLC) terminal No. 7 (White wire). This is the International Standards Organization (ISO) 9141 diagnostic communications network circuit.

1) Disarm air bag system. See appropriate AIR BAG RESTRAINT SYSTEMS article. Turn ignition switch to LOCK position. Disconnect NGS tester. Disconnect in-line harness connector C62. Measure resistance between terminal No. 6 (White/Red wire) at in-line harness connector C62 and terminal No. 7 (White wire) at DLC. *See Figs. 2 and 6.* If resistance is 5 ohms or less, go to next step. If resistance is greater than 5 ohms, repair open in White or White/Red wire.

2) Connect in-line harness connector C62. Turn ignition switch to RUN position. Measure voltage between terminals No. 16 (Orange wire) and No. 7 (White wire) at DLC. If approximately 1.5 volts do not exist, go to next step. If approximately 1.5 volts exists, go to step **6)**.

3) Turn ignition switch to LOCK position. Disconnect in-line harness connector C62. Turn ignition switch to RUN position. Measure voltage between terminals No. 16 (Orange wire) and No. 7 (White wire) at DLC. If approximately 1.5 volts exists, go to next step. If approximately 1.5 volts do not exist, go to step **5**).

4) Turn ignition switch to LOCK position. Disconnect RCM harness connector C20. Turn ignition switch to RUN position. Measure voltage at terminal No. 6 (White/Red wire) at in-line harness connector C62. If voltage is indicated, repair short to voltage in White/Red wire. If voltage is not indicated, replace RCM.

5) Turn ignition switch to LOCK position. Disconnect ABS module harness connector C3002. Turn ignition switch to RUN position. Measure voltage at terminal No. 7 (White wire) at DLC. If voltage is indicated, repair short to voltage in White wire. If voltage is not indicated, replace ABS module.

6) Turn ignition switch to LOCK position. Measure resistance between ground and terminal No. 7 (White wire) at DLC. If resistance is 100 ohms or less, go to next step. If resistance is greater than 100 ohms, perform data link diagnostic procedure. See DATA LINK DIAGNOSTIC TEST under COMMUNICATION NETWORK DIAGNOSTICS.

7) Disconnect in-line harness connector C62. Measure resistance between ground and terminal No. 7 (White wire) at DLC. If resistance is greater than 100 ohms, go to next step. If resistance is 100 ohms or less, go to step **9**).

8) Disconnect RCM harness connector C20. Measure resistance between ground and terminal No. 6 (White/Red wire) at in-line harness connector C62. If resistance is greater than 10 k/ohms, replace RCM. If resistance is 10 k/ohms or less, repair short to ground in White/Red wire.

9) Disconnect ABS module harness connector C3002. Measure resistance between ground and terminal No. 7 (White wire) at DLC. If resistance is greater than 10 k/ohms, replace ABS module. If resistance is 10 k/ohms or less, repair short to ground in White, White/Violet or White/Red wire.

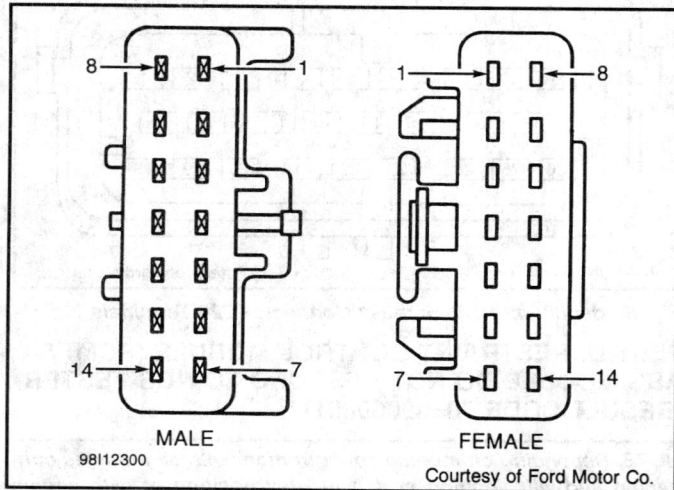

MALE
98112300

FEMALE
Courtesy of Ford Motor Co.

Fig. 6: Identifying In-Line Harness Connector C62 Terminals

TEST E: POWERTRAIN CONTROL MODULE (PCM) DOES NOT RESPOND TO NGS TESTER

1) Turn ignition switch to LOCK position. Disconnect NGS tester. Disconnect PCM harness connector C421. Inspect connector for loose, damaged or corroded terminals. If connector is okay, go to next step. If connector is damaged, repair connector as necessary.

2) Measure resistance between terminal No. 16 (Gray wire) at PCM connector and terminal No. 2 (Gray wire without ABS; Gray/Violet wire with ABS) at Data Link Connector (DLC). See Figs. 2 and 7. If resistance is 5 ohms or less, go to next step. If resistance is greater than 5 ohms, repair open in Gray/Violet and/or Gray wire between DLC and PCM.

3) Measure resistance between terminal No. 15 (Blue wire) at PCM harness connector C421 and terminal No. 10 (Blue wire without ABS; Blue/White wire with ABS) at DLC. If resistance is 5 ohms or less, go to next step. If resistance is greater than 5 ohms, repair open in Blue wire.

4) Measure resistance in White/Blue wire between terminal No. 13 at PCM connector and terminal No. 13 at DLC. If resistance is 5 ohms or less, replace PCM. If resistance is greater than 5 ohms, repair open in White/Blue wire.

TEST F: CENTRAL TIMER MODULE (CTM) DOES NOT RESPOND TO NGS TESTER

1) Turn ignition switch to LOCK position. Remove and inspect fuse No. 1 (80-amp) from power distribution box. If fuse is okay, install fuse and go to next step. If fuse is blown, replace fuse. If fuse blows again, check for short to ground.

2) Disconnect CTM from back of central junction box. Measure voltage at terminal No. 18 at CTM connector C23 (fuse box side). *See Fig. 3.* If battery voltage exists, go to next step. If battery voltage does not exist, replace central junction box.

3) Measure resistance between ground and terminal No. 16 at CTM connector C23. If resistance is 5 ohms or less, replace CTM. If resistance is greater than 5 ohms, replace central junction box.

TEST G: NO MODULE/NETWORK COMMUNICATION WITH NGS TESTER (RESULT CODE 00000003)

NOTE: Depending on module configuration, with all modules connected and with ignition switch in RUN position or with engine running 2-3 volts may be present at Data Link Connector (DLC) terminals No. 2 (Gray wire without ABS; Gray/Violet wire with ABS) and No. 10 (Blue wire without ABS; Blue/White wire with ABS). These are the Standard Corporate Protocol (SCP) diagnostic communications network circuits.

1) Turn ignition switch to LOCK position. Connect New Generation Star (NGS) tester to Data Link Connector (DLC). Turn ignition switch to RUN position. Repeat data link diagnostic procedure. See DATA LINK DIAGNOSTIC TEST under COMMUNICATIONS NETWORK DIAGNOSTICS. Proceed as follows:

- If NGS tester displays NO RESPONSE ON CKT 914 for all modules and 00000003 for circuit No. 914, go to next step.
- If NGS tester displays NO RESPONSE ON CKT 915 for all modules and 00000003 for circuit No. 915, go to step **12**).
- If NGS tester displays PCM: NO RESPONSE ON CKT 914 or 915, go to TEST E: POWERTRAIN CONTROL MODULE (PCM) DOES NOT RESPOND TO NGS TESTER.
- If NGS displays any other message, go to SYMPTOM CHART table under SYSTEM TESTS. Perform appropriate test.

2) Turn ignition switch to LOCK position. Disconnect NGS tester. Disconnect PCM harness connector C421. Measure resistance between terminal No. 16 (Gray wire) and terminal No. 2 (Gray wire without ABS; Gray/Violet wire with ABS) at Data Link Connector (DLC). *See Figs. 2 and 7.* If resistance is 5 ohms or less, go to next step. If resistance is greater than 5 ohms, repair open in Gray or Gray/Violet wire between DCL and PCM.

3) Turn ignition switch to LOCK position. Connect PCM harness connector C421. Turn ignition switch to RUN position. Measure voltage at terminal No. 2 (Gray wire without ABS; Gray/Violet wire with ABS) at DLC. If battery voltage exists, go to next step. If battery voltage does not exist, go to step **7**).

4) Turn ignition switch to LOCK position. ABS module harness connector C3002 (if equipped). Turn ignition switch to RUN position. Measure voltage at terminal No. 2 (Gray wire without ABS; Gray/Violet wire with ABS) at DLC. If any voltage is indicated, go to next step. If zero volts is indicated, replace ABS module.

5) Turn ignition switch to LOCK position. Disconnect PCM harness connector C421. Turn ignition switch to RUN position. Measure voltage between ground and terminal No. 2 (Gray wire without ABS; Gray/Violet wire with ABS) at DLC. If any voltage is indicated, go to next step. If zero volts is indicated, replace PCM.

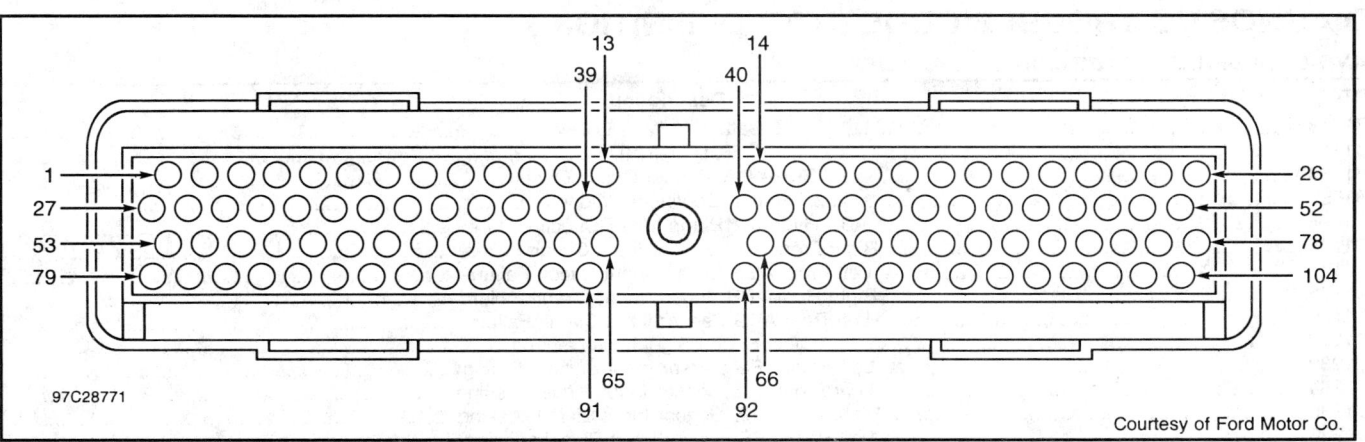

Fig. 7: Identifying PCM Harness Connector C421 Terminals

6) Disconnect in-line harness connector C3001. Turn ignition switch to RUN position. Measure voltage between ground and terminal No. 2 (Gray wire without ABS; Gray/Violet wire with ABS) at DLC. If any voltage is indicated, repair short to power in Gray or Gray/Violet wire between DLC and in-line harness connector C3001. If zero volts is indicated, repair short to power in Gray wire between PCM and in-line harness connector C3001.

7) Turn ignition switch to LOCK position. Measure resistance between ground and terminal No. 2 (Gray wire without ABS; Gray/Violet wire with ABS) at DLC. *See Fig. 2.* If resistance is 100 ohms or less, go to next step. If resistance is greater than 100 ohms, perform TEST E: POWERTRAIN CONTROL MODULE (PCM) DOES NOT RESPOND TO NGS TESTER.

8) Disconnect ABS module harness connector C3002. Measure resistance between ground and terminal No. 2 (Gray wire without ABS; Gray/Violet wire with ABS) at DLC. If resistance is 100 ohms or less, go to next step. If resistance is greater than 100 ohms, replace ABS module.

9) Disconnect PCM harness connector C421. Measure resistance between ground and terminal No. 2 (Gray wire without ABS; Gray/Violet wire with ABS) at DLC. If resistance is 10 k/ohms or less, go to next step. If resistance is greater than 10 k/ohms, replace PCM.

10) Disconnect in-line harness connector C3001. Measure resistance between ground and terminal No. 2 (Gray wire without ABS; Gray/Violet wire with ABS) at DLC. If resistance is 10 k/ohms or less, repair short to ground in Gray wire between PCM and in-line harness connector C3001. If resistance is greater than 10 k/ohms, repair short to ground in Gray or Gray/Red wire between DLC and in-line harness connector C3001.

11) Turn ignition switch to LOCK position. Disconnect NGS tester. Disconnect Powertrain Control Module (PCM) harness connector C421. Measure resistance between terminal No. 10 (Blue wire without ABS; Blue/White wire with ABS) at DLC. If resistance is 5 ohms or less, go to next step. If resistance is greater than 5 ohms, repair open in Blue or Blue/White wire.

12) Connect PCM harness connector C421. Turn ignition switch to RUN position. Measure voltage at terminal No. 10 (Blue wire without ABS; Blue/White wire with ABS) at Data Link Connector (DLC). *See Fig. 2.* If battery voltage exists, go to next step. If battery voltage does not exist, go to step 16).

13) Turn ignition switch to LOCK position. Disconnect ABS module harness connector C20. Turn ignition switch to RUN position. Measure voltage at terminal No. 10 (Blue wire without ABS; Blue/White wire with ABS) at DLC. If battery voltage exists, go to next step. If battery voltage does not exist, replace ABS module.

14) Turn ignition switch to LOCK position. Disconnect PCM harness connector C421. Turn ignition switch to RUN position. Measure voltage at terminal No. 10 (Blue wire without ABS; Blue/White wire with ABS) at DLC. If any voltage is indicated, go to next step. If zero volts is indicated, replace PCM.

15) Turn ignition switch to LOCK position. Disconnect in-line harness connector C3001. Turn ignition switch to RUN position. Measure voltage at terminal No. 10 (Blue wire without ABS; Blue/White wire with ABS) at DLC. If any voltage is indicated, repair short to voltage in Blue or Blue/White wire between DLC and in-line harness connector C3001. If zero volts is indicated, repair short to voltage in Blue wire between PCM and in-line harness connector C3001.

16) Turn ignition switch to LOCK position. Measure resistance between ground and terminal No. 10 (Blue wire without ABS; Blue/White wire with ABS) at DLC. If resistance is 100 ohms or less, go to next step. If resistance is greater than 100 ohms, perform TEST E: POWERTRAIN CONTROL MODULE (PCM) DOES NOT RESPOND TO NGS TESTER.

17) Disconnect ABS module harness connector C3002. Measure resistance between ground and terminal No. 10 (Blue wire without ABS; Blue/White wire with ABS) at DLC. *See Fig. 2.* If resistance is 100 ohms or less, go to next step. If resistance is greater than 100 ohms, replace ABS module.

18) Turn ignition switch to LOCK position. Disconnect PCM harness connector C421. Measure resistance between ground and terminal No. 10 (Blue wire without ABS; Blue/White wire with ABS) at DLC. If resistance is 10 k/ohms or less, go to next step. If resistance is greater than 10 k/ohms, replace PCM.

19) Disconnect in-line harness connector C3001. Measure resistance between ground and terminal No. 10 (Blue wire without ABS; Blue/White wire with ABS) at DLC. If resistance is 10 k/ohms or less, repair short to ground in Blue or Blue/White wire between DLC and in-line harness connector C3001. If resistance is greater than 10 k/ohms, repair short to ground in Blue wire between PCM and in-line harness connector C3001.

DIAGNOSTIC TROUBLE CODE (DTC) DEFINITIONS

ANTI-LOCK BRAKE SYSTEM MODULE DTC INDEX

DTC	Description	Test
B1318	Battery Voltage Low	1
B1342	ECU Defective	2
B1484	Brake Pedal Input Circuit Open	1
B1596	Repair Continuous Codes	1
C1095	ABS Hydraulic Pump Motor Circuit Failure	1
C1145	Right Front ABS Sensor Input Circuit Failure	1
C1155	Left Front ABS Sensor Input Circuit Failure	1
C1165	Right Rear ABS Sensor Input Circuit Failure	1
C1175	Left Rear ABS Sensor Input Circuit Failure	1
C1222	Wheel Speed Signal Mismatched	1
C1233	Left Front ABS Sensor Input Signal Missing	1
C1234	Right Front ABS Sensor Input Signal Missing	1
C1235	Right Rear ABS Sensor Input Signal Missing	1
C1236	Left Rear ABS Sensor Input Signal Missing	1
C1266	ABS Valve Power Relay Circuit Failure	1

[1] – Repair anti-lock brake system concern. See appropriate ANTI-LOCK article in BRAKES in appropriate MITCHELL® manual,
[2] – Using NGS tester, retrieve and document all continuous DTCs. Perform ABS self-test. If DTC B1342 is retrieved again, replace ABS module.

PCM DTC INDEX

DTC [1]	Description	Test
B1213	Anti-Theft Number Of Programmed Keys Is Below Minimum	2 3
B1600	No Key Code Received/Damaged Encoded Ignition Key Or Use Of Non-PATS Key	4
B1601	Incorrect Key Code From Ignition Key Transponder	5
B1602	Invalid Key Code Format From Ignition Key Transponder	6
B1681	Transceiver Defective Or Not Connected	7
B2103	PATS Antenna Not Connected	8

[1] – For a listing of all "P" codes, see appropriate SELF-DIAGNOSTICS article in ENGINE PERFORMANCE in appropriate MITCHELL® manual.
[2] – If DTCs B1232, B1600, B1601, B1602 OR B1681 are also present, service these DTCs frist then recheck codes.
[3] – Perform TEST F: ANTI-THEFT NUMBER OF KEYS IS BELOW MINIMUM under SYSTEM TESTS in PASSIVE ANTI-THEFT SYSTEMS – CONTOUR & MYSTIQUE article.
[4] – Perform TEST B: NO KEY CODE RECEIVED/DAMAGED ENCODED IGNITION KEY OR USE OF NON-PATS KEY under SYSTEM TESTS in PASSIVE ANTI-THEFT SYSTEMS – CONTOUR & MYSTIQUE article.
[5] – Perform TEST C: INCORRECT KEY CODE FROM IGNITION KEY TRANSPONDER under SYSTEM TESTS in PASSIVE ANTI-THEFT SYSTEMS – CONTOUR & MYSTIQUE article.
[6] – Perform TEST D: INVALID KEY CODE FORMAT FROM IGNITION KEY TRANSPONDER under SYSTEM TESTS in PASSIVE ANTI-THEFT SYSTEMS – CONTOUR & MYSTIQUE article.
[7] – Perform TEST E: TRANSCEIVER DEFECTIVE OR NOT CONNECTED under SYSTEM TESTS in PASSIVE ANTI-THEFT SYSTEMS – CONTOUR & MYSTIQUE article.
[8] – Perform TEST A: PATS TRANSCEIVER ANTENNA NOT CONNECTED under SYSTEM TESTS in PASSIVE ANTI-THEFT SYSTEMS – CONTOUR & MYSTIQUE article.

RESTRAINT CONTROL MODULE DTC INDEX

DTC [1]	Description	Test
B1342	ECU Defective	2
B1231	RCM Crash Data Memory Full	3
B1921	RCM Bracket Ground Resistance High	3
B1318	AIR BAG Light On (Low Ignition Feed)	4
C1414	Incorrect Vehicle Identification Code	3
B1887	Driver's Air Bag Circuit Shorted To Ground	3
B1916	Driver's Air Bag Circuit Shorted To Voltage	3
B1888	Passenger's Air Bag Circuit Shorted To Ground	3
B1925	Passenger's Air Bag Circuit Shorted To Voltage	3
B1932	Driver's Air Bag Circuit Resistance High	3
B1933	Passenger's Air Bag Circuit Resistance High	3
B1934	Driver's Air Bag Circuit Resistance Low	3
B1935	Passenger's Air Bag Circuit Resistance Low	3
B1869	Air Bag Indicator Inoperative	3
B1870	Air Bag Indicator Shorted To Voltage	3
B1892	Air Bag Tone Warning Indicator Circuit Shorted To Ground Or Open	3
B1891	Air Bag Tone Warning Indicator Circuit Shorted To Voltage	3

[1] – DTCs are listed in order of importance. Repair DTCs in order listed.
[2] – Using NGS tester, retrieve and document all continuous DTCs. Perform Restraint Control Module (RCM) self-test. If DTC B1342 is retrieved again, replace RCM.
[3] – Repair supplemental restraint system concern. See DIAGNOSIS & TESTING article in appropriate MITCHELL® AIR BAG SERVICE & REPAIR MANUAL, DOMESTIC & IMPORTED MODELS.
[4] – Check RCM power and ground circuit and repair as necessary. If power and ground circuits are okay, repair charging system. See appropriateGENERATORS article in STARTING & CHARGING SYSTEMS.

PARAMETER IDENTIFICATION (PID) DEFINITIONS

ANTI-LOCK BRAKE SYSTEM MODULE PID INDEX

PID	Description	Expected Value
CCNTABS	Number Of Continuous DTC	One Count Per Bit
BOO_ABS	Brake Pedal Position Switch Input	ON, OFF
PMP_MTR	ABS Pump Motor	[1]
VLV_CTR	ABS Valve Control Relay	[1]
ABSRR_O	Right Rear ABS Outlet Valve	[1]
ABSLR_O	Left Rear ABS Outlet Valve	[1]
ABSRF_O	Right Front ABS Outlet Valve	[1]
ABSLF_O	Left Front ABS Outlet Valve	[1]
ABSRF_I	Right Front ABS Inlet Valve	[1]
ABSLF_I	Left Front ABS Inlet Valve	[1]
ABSRR_I	Right Rear ABS Inlet Valve	[1]
ABSLR_I	Left Rear ABS Inlet Valve	[1]
LF_WSPD	Left Front Wheel Speed Signal	0-255 KPH
RF_WSPD	Right Front Wheel Speed Signal	0-255 KPH
LR_WSPD	Left Rear Wheel Speed Signal	0-255 KPH
RR_WSPD	Right Rear Wheel Speed Signal	0-255 KPH

[1] – Expected value should be OFF- - -, OFFO- -, OFF-B-, OFF- - G, OFFO-G, OFFOB-, OFF-BG, OFFOBG, ON- - -, ONO- -, ON-B-, ON- - G, ONO-G, ONOB-, ON-BG or ONOBG.

POWERTRAIN CONTROL MODULE PID INDEX

PID	Description	Expected Value
CCNTABS	Number Of Continuous DTC	One Count Per Bit
NUMKEYS	Number Of Ignition Keys Programmed	0 To 8
M_KEY	Is This A Programmed Key	YES, NO
ENABL_S	Vehicle Starting Status	ENABLED, DISABLED
MIN#KEYS	Minimum Number Of Programmed Keys Required To Start Vehicle	2 To 8
ANTISCAN	20-Second Time-Out After Attempting To Use Unprogrammed Key	ACTIVE, NOTACT
SPARE_KEY	Can You Add Spare Keys With 2 Programmed Keys	YES, NO
SERV_MOD	Is This A Repair Module	YES, NO

RESTRAINT CONTROL MODULE PID INDEX

PID	Description	Expected Value
CCNT	Number Of Continuous DTCs On Speed Control Servo	One Count Per Bit
VBATT	Battery Voltage At RCM	9-16 Volts
D_ABAGR	Driver's Air Bag Module Resistance	1.7-4.1 Ohms
P_ABAGR	Passenger's Air Bag Module Resistance	1.7-3.2 Ohms
BRACKET	Bracket Ground Resistance	Less Than 100 Ohms
VID NO1	Programmed Vehicle ID Pin 10	IGNITION
VID NO2	Programmed Vehicle ID Pin 13	IGNITION
VID NO3	Programmed Vehicle ID Pin 14	NO CONNECTION

WIRING DIAGRAMS

NOTE: See appropriate wiring diagrams in DATA LINK CONNECTORS, GROUND DISTRIBUTION or POWER DISTRIBUTION article in WIRING DIAGRAMS.

DESCRIPTION & OPERATION

NOTE: *Anti-theft/central locking module may also be referred to as Central Security Module (CSM). Hybrid Electronic Cluster (HEC) module is built into instrument cluster. Air bag diagnostic monitor may also be referred to as electronic crash sensor module.*

Vehicle has 2 module communications networks. The Powertrain Control Module (PCM) is connected to the multiplex communications network through a pair of twisted wires or BUS. If vehicle is equipped with traction control, the Anti-Lock Brake System (ABS) module is also connected to BUS. The BUS network is also referred to as Standard Corporate Protocol (SCP). The BUS consists of (+) circuit and a (–) circuit. The ABS module is also connected to the ISO 9141 diagnostic communications network through a single wire along with the air bag diagnostic monitor, anti-theft/central locking module (if equipped) and Hybrid Electronic Cluster (HEC) module. Both networks are connected to the Data Link Connector (DLC). This article is used to diagnose BUS and ISO communications network circuit faults. For module locations, see COMPONENT LOCATIONS table under COMPONENT LOCATIONS.

COMPONENT LOCATIONS

COMPONENT LOCATIONS

Component	Location
Air Bag Diagnostic Monitor [1]	Behind Instrument Panel, On Steering Column
Anti-Lock Brake System Module	Driver's Side Back Corner Of Engine Compartment
Anti-Theft/Central Locking Module [2]	[3] Behind Passenger's Side Kick Panel
Data Link Connector	Under Left Side Of Instrument Panel, Next To Steering Column
In-Line Harness Connector C62	Behind Instrument Cluster
In-Line Harness Connector C58	[3] Behind Passenger's Side Kick Panel
Instrument Panel Fuse Box	Behind Left Side Of Instrument Panel
Hybrid Electronic Cluster Module [4]	Left Side Of Instrument Panel
Powertrain Control Module	Right Rear Corner Of Engine Compartment

[1] – Air bag diagnostic monitor may also be referred to as electronic crash sensor module.
[2] – Anti-theft/central locking module may also be referred to as Central Security Module (CSM).
[3] – See Fig. 1.
[4] – Hybrid Electronic Cluster (HEC) module is built into instrument cluster.

REPAIRING BUS WIRING

NOTE: *Following procedure must be used to ensure proper repair is performed on BUS wiring. BUS wiring is sensitive to moisture and oxidation and must be properly sealed to ensure proper operation of the module communications network. Regular heat shrink tubing is NOT sufficient, heat shrink tubing containing hot melt wax is required.*

1) When performing a repair on the BUS wiring of the Module Communications Network, ensure the wires on the BUS are twisted at a rate of 33-40 winds per 3.3 ft. (1 m). The twists should start within approximately 4.9" (124 mm) from any connector. Use only 20 AWG standard wire gauge for repairs.
2) If performing a splice in the wiring, strip .75" (19.0 mm) of insulation from one wire and 1.50" (38.1 mm) of insulator from the other wire. Perform STEP 1. See Fig. 2. Place hot melt wax heat shrink tubing over one wire.

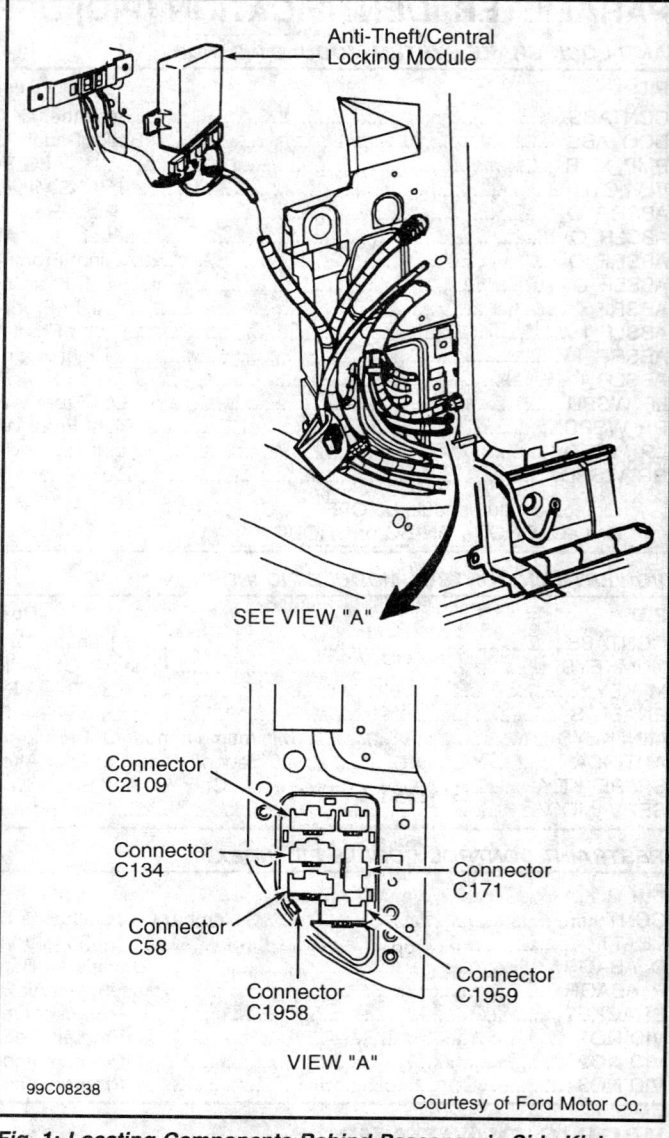

Fig. 1: *Locating Components Behind Passenger's Side Kick Panel*

3) Twist stripped portion of the wires together. Solder connection using resin core RMA solder. DO NOT use acid core solder. Bend wires to allow installation of heat shrink tubing. Perform STEP 2. See Fig. 2.
4) Position heat shrink tubing over splice area. Using heat gun, evenly heat the heat shrink tubing until wax flows from both ends of heat shrink tubing.

COMMUNICATION NETWORK DIAGNOSTICS

INSPECTION & VERIFICATION

1) Verify customer's original problem by operating system in question. Inspect vehicle for any obvious electrical component wiring or connector damage. Inspect connectors for loose, damaged or corroded terminals. Check related fuses for system in question.
2) Inspect Data Link Connector (DLC) pins for damage. The DLC is located below driver's side of instrument panel, right of steering column. If pins are okay, go to next step. If pins are damaged, repair as necessary and proceed to next step.
3) If problem is still present after performing inspection, connect New Generation Star (NGS) tester to DLC. Select vehicle to be tested from NGS tester menu. If NGS tester does not communicate with vehicle,

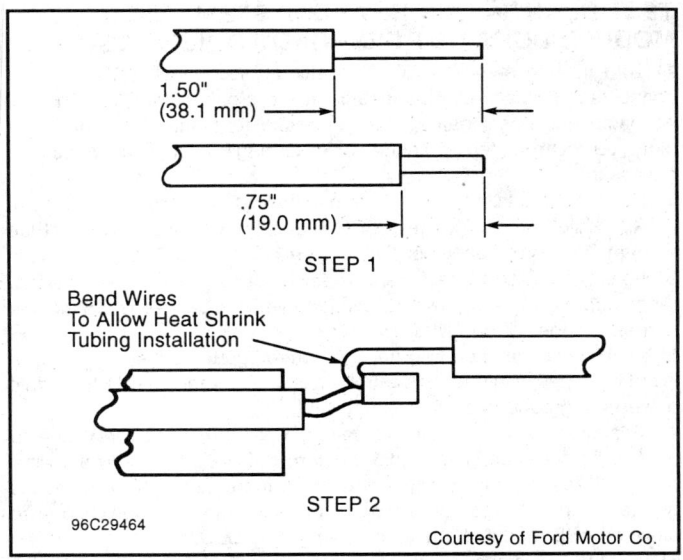

96C29464

Courtesy of Ford Motor Co.

Fig. 2: Repairing Bus Wiring

ensure program card is properly installed. Check NGS tester cable connections and ensure ignition switch is in RUN position. If NGS tester still does not communicate with vehicle, perform TEST G: NO MODULE/ NETWORK COMMUNICATION – NO POWER TO NGS TESTER under SYSTEM TESTS. If NGS tester communicates with vehicle, perform data link diagnostic procedure. See DATA LINK DIAGNOSTIC TEST.

DATA LINK DIAGNOSTIC TEST

NOTE: Circuit No. 70 is the White wire (White/Blue wire if equipped with ABS) connected to terminal No. 7 on DLC. Circuit No. 914 is the Gray wire (Gray/Violet wire if equipped with traction control) connected to terminal No. 2 on DLC. Circuit No. 915 is the Blue wire (Blue/White wire if equipped with traction control) connected to terminal No. 10 on DLC.

1) Connect New Generation Star (NGS) tester to Data Link Connector (DLC), if not already connected. Select vehicle to be tested from NGS tester menu.

2) Turn ignition switch to RUN position. Rotate dial on NGS tester to menu item DIAGNOSTIC DATA LINK and press trigger. A test will be performed on BUS (circuits No. 914 and 915) network and ISO 9141 network (circuit No. 70).

3) If NGS tester displays CKT 914 (+) = SYSTEM PASSED and CKT 915 (−) = SYSTEM PASSED, module communications network is okay. If NGS tester displays CKT 70 = SYSTEM PASSED, ISO 9141 communication link is operating properly. Repair communication concern by symptom. See SYMPTOM CHART table under SYSTEM TESTS.

4) If NGS tester does not display CKT 914 (+) = SYSTEM PASSED, CKT 915 (−) = SYSTEM PASSED and CKT 70 = SYSTEM PASSED, perform the following as applicable:

- If no response from NGS tester, perform TEST G: NO MODULE/ NETWORK COMMUNICATION – NO POWER TO NGS TESTER under SYSTEM TESTS.
- If NGS tester displays CKT 70 = ALL ECUS NO RESP/NOT EQUIP, perform TEST F: NO MODULE/NETWORK COMMUNICATION – ISO 9141 NETWORK under SYSTEM TESTS.
- If NGS tester displays CKT 914 = ALL ECUS NO RESP/NOT EQUIP, perform TEST A: POWERTRAIN CONTROL MODULE (PCM) DOES NOT RESPOND TO NGS TESTER under SYSTEM TESTS.
- If NGS tester displays CKT 915 = ALL ECUS NO RESP/NOT EQUIP, perform TEST A: POWERTRAIN CONTROL MODULE (PCM) DOES NOT RESPOND TO NGS TESTER under SYSTEM TESTS.
- If one of the modules responds NO RESPONSE/NOT EQUIPPED, repair communication concern by symptom. See SYMPTOM CHART table under SYSTEM TESTS.

RETRIEVING & CLEARING DIAGNOSTIC TROUBLE CODES

Connect New Generation Star (NGS) tester to Data Link Connector (DLC). Following manufacturers instructions to retrieve and clear codes for desired module. See appropriate table under DIAGNOSTIC TROUBLE CODE (DTC) DEFINITIONS for a listing of Diagnostic Trouble Codes (DTCs) and appropriate test procedure.

ACCESSING PARAMETER IDENTIFICATION (PID)

Turn ignition switch to LOCK position. Connect New Generation Star (NGS) tester to Data Link Connector (DLC). Following manufacturers instructions enter PID/DATA MONITOR AND RECORD for desired module. Operate appropriate system and ensure PID expected values are obtained. See appropriate table under PARAMETER IDENTIFICA-TION (PID) DEFINITIONS.

SYSTEM TESTS

NOTE: Always check module power and ground circuits prior to replacing a control module. See appropriate wiring diagram in DATA LINK CONNECTORS, GROUND DISTRIBUTION or POWER DISTRIBUTION article in WIRING DIAGRAMS.

SYMPTOM CHART

Symptom	Test
Powertrain Control Module (PCM) Does Not Respond To NGS Tester	A
Anti-Lock Brake System (ABS) Module Does Not Respond To NGS Tester	B
Air Bag Diagnostic Monitor Module Does Not Respond To NGS Tester [1]	C
Hybrid Electronic Cluster (HEC) Module Does Not Respond To NGS Tester [2]	D
Anti-Theft/Central Locking Module Does Not Respond To NGS Tester [3]	E
No Module/Network Communication – ISO 9141 Network	F
No Module/Network Communication – No Power To NGS Tester	G

[1] – Air bag diagnostic monitor may also be referred to as electronic crash sensor module.
[2] – Hybrid Electronic Cluster (HEC) module is built into instrument cluster.
[3] – Anti-theft/central locking module may also be referred to as Central Security Module (CSM) .

TEST A: POWERTRAIN CONTROL MODULE (PCM) DOES NOT RESPOND TO NGS TESTER

NOTE: Depending on module configuration, with all modules connected and with ignition switch in RUN position or with engine running 2-3 volts may be present at Data Link Connector (DLC) terminals No. 2 (Gray wire without traction control; Gray/Violet wire with traction control) and No. 10 (Blue wire without traction control; Blue/White wire with traction control). These are the Standard Corporate Protocol (SCP) diagnostic communications network circuits.

1) Turn ignition switch to LOCK position. Disconnect NGS tester. Disconnect PCM harness connector C421. Inspect connector for loose, damaged or corroded terminals. If connector is okay, go to next step. If connector is damaged, repair connector as necessary.

2) Measure resistance between terminal No. 16 (Gray wire) at PCM harness connector C421 and terminal No. 2 (Gray wire without traction control; Gray/Violet wire with traction control) at Data Link Connector (DLC). *See Figs. 3 and 4.* If resistance is 5 ohms or less, go to next step. If resistance is greater than 5 ohms, repair open in Gray/Violet and/or Gray wire between DLC and PCM.

3) Measure resistance between terminal No. 15 (Blue wire) at PCM harness connector C421 and terminal No. 10 (Blue wire without traction control; Blue/White wire with traction control) at DLC. If resistance is 5 ohms or less, go to next step. If resistance is greater than 5 ohms, open in Blue and/or Blue/White wire.

4) Disconnect Anti-Lock Brake System (ABS) module harness connector C385 (if equipped with traction control). Turn ignition switch to RUN position. Measure voltage at terminal No. 2 (Gray wire without traction control; Gray/Violet wire with traction control) at DLC. If voltage does not exist, go to next step. If voltage exists, repair short to voltage in Gray and/or Gray/Violet wire.

5) Turn ignition switch to LOCK position. Measure resistance between ground and terminal No. 2 (Gray wire without traction control; Gray/Violet wire with traction control) at DLC. If resistance is greater than 10 k/ohms, go to next step. If resistance is 10 k/ohms or less, repair short to ground in Gray and/or Gray/Violet wire.

6) Turn ignition switch to RUN position. Measure voltage at terminal No. 10 (Blue wire without traction control; Blue/White wire with traction control) at DLC. If voltage does not exist, go to next step. If voltage exists, repair short to voltage in Blue and/or Blue/White wire.

7) Turn ignition switch to LOCK position. Measure resistance between ground and terminal No. 10 (Blue wire without traction control; Blue/White wire with traction control) at DLC. If resistance is greater than 10 k/ohms, go to next step. If resistance is 10 k/ohms or less, repair short to ground in Blue and/or Blue/White wire.

8) If vehicle is equipped with traction control, go to next step. If vehicle is not equipped with traction control, replace PCM if PCM power and ground circuits are okay.

9) Connect ABS module harness connector C385. Measure resistance between ground and terminal No. 2 (Gray/Violet wire) at DLC. If resistance is greater than 10 k/ohms, go to next step. If resistance is 10 k/ohms or less, replace ABS module.

10) Measure resistance between ground and terminal No. 10 (Blue/White wire) at DLC. If resistance is greater than 10 k/ohms, go to next step. If resistance is 10 k/ohms or less, replace ABS module.

11) Turn ignition switch to RUN position. Measure voltage at terminal No. 10 (Blue/White wire) at DLC. If voltage is 6 volts or less, go to next step. If voltage is greater than 6 volts, replace ABS module.

12) Measure voltage at terminal No. 2 (Gray/Violet wire) at DLC. If voltage does not exist, replace PCM if PCM power and ground circuits are okay. If voltage exists, replace ABS module.

TEST B: ANTI-LOCK BRAKE SYSTEM (ABS) MODULE DOES NOT RESPOND TO NGS TESTER

1) Turn ignition switch to LOCK position. Disconnect NGS tester (if connected). Disconnect ABS module harness connector C385. Inspect connector for loose, damaged or corroded terminals. If connector is okay, go to next step. If connector is damaged, repair connector as necessary.

2) Measure resistance between terminal No. 24 (White/Violet wire) at ABS module harness connector C385 and terminal No. 7 (White/Blue wire) at Data Link Connector (DLC). *See Figs. 4 and 5.* If resistance is 5 ohms or less, go to next step. If resistance is greater than 5 ohms, repair open in White/Blue and/or White/Violet wire between ABS module harness connector and DLC.

3) If vehicle is equipped with traction control, go to next step. If vehicle is not equipped with traction control, replace ABS module if ABS module power and ground circuits are okay.

4) Measure resistance between terminal No. 29 (Blue wire) at ABS module harness connector C385 and terminal No. 10 (Blue/White wire) at DLC. If resistance is 5 ohms or less, go to next step. If resistance is greater than 5 ohms, repair open in Blue and/or Blue/White wire between ABS module harness connector and DLC.

5) Measure resistance between terminal No. 30 (Gray wire) at ABS module harness connector C385 and terminal No. 2 (Gray/Violet wire) at DLC. If resistance is 5 ohms or less, replace ABS module if ABS module power and ground circuits are okay. If resistance is greater than 5 ohms, repair open in Gray or Gray/Violet wire between ABS module harness connector and DLC.

TEST C: AIR BAG DIAGNOSTIC MONITOR MODULE DOES NOT RESPOND TO NGS TESTER

NOTE: Air bag diagnostic monitor may also be referred to as electronic crash sensor module.

1) Disarm air bag system. See appropriate AIR BAG RESTRAINT SYSTEMS article. Turn ignition switch to LOCK position. Disconnect NGS tester (if connected). Disconnect air bag diagnostic monitor harness connector C20. Inspect connector for loose, damaged or corroded terminals. If connector is okay, go to next step. If connector is

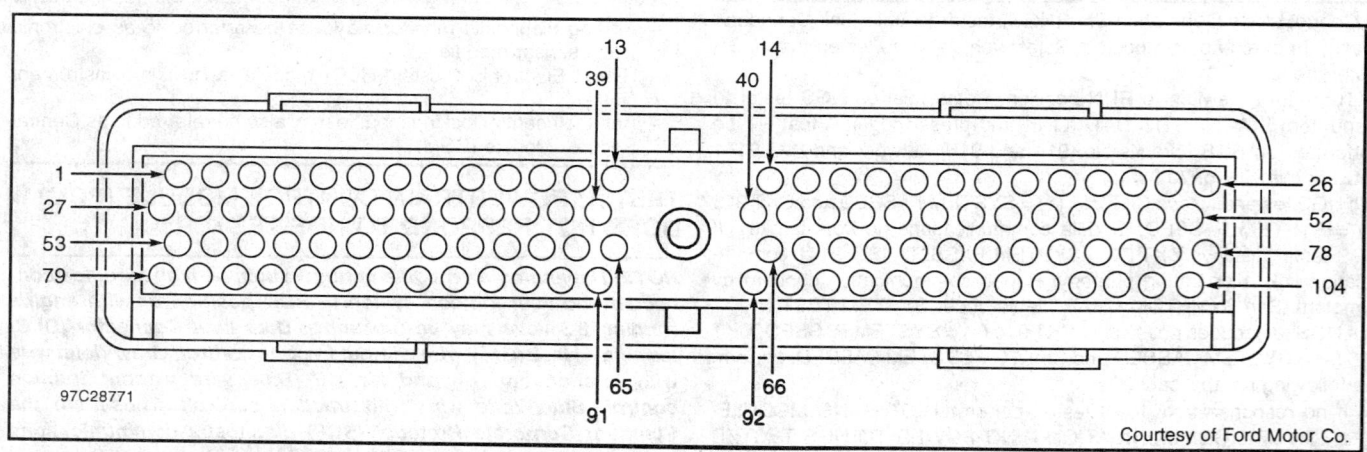

Fig. 3: Identifying PCM Harness Connector C421 Terminals

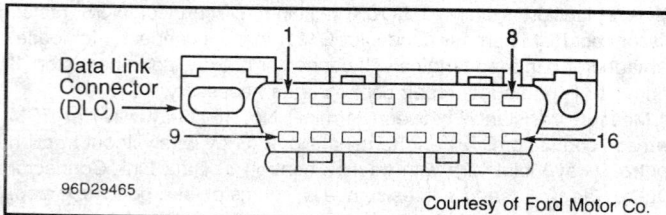

Fig. 4: Identifying Data Link Connector (DLC) Terminals

damaged, repair connector as necessary.

2) Measure resistance between terminal No. 24 (White/Red wire) at air bag diagnostic monitor harness connector C20 and terminal No. 7 (White wire without ABS; White/Blue wire with ABS) at Data Link Connector (DLC). *See Figs. 4 and 6.* If resistance is greater than 5 ohms, go to next step. If resistance is 5 ohms or less, replace air bag diagnostic monitor if air bag diagnostic monitor power and ground circuits are okay.

3) Disconnect in-line harness connector C62. Inspect connector for loose, damaged or corroded terminals. If connector is okay, go to next step. If connector is damaged, repair connector as necessary.

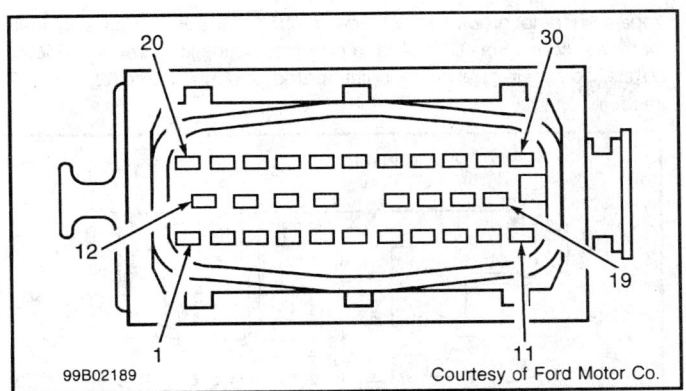

Fig. 5: Identifying ABS Module Harness Connector C385 Terminals

4) Measure resistance between and terminal No. 6 (White wire) at male side of in-line harness connector C62 and terminal No. 7 (White wire without ABS; White/Blue wire with ABS) at DLC. *See Figs. 4 and 7*. If resistance is greater than 5 ohms, repair open in White wire and/or White/Blue wire between DLC and in-line harness connector C62. If resistance is 5 ohms or less, repair open in White/Red wire between in-line harness connector C62 and air bag diagnostic monitor.

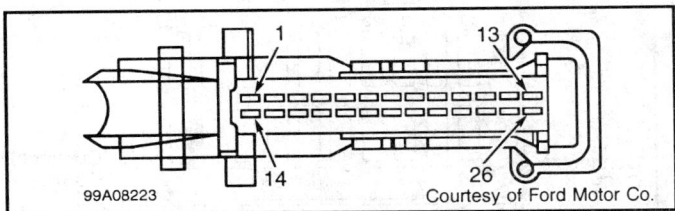

Fig. 6: Identifying Air Bag Diagnostic Monitor Harness Connector C20 & HEC Module Harness Connector C808a Terminals

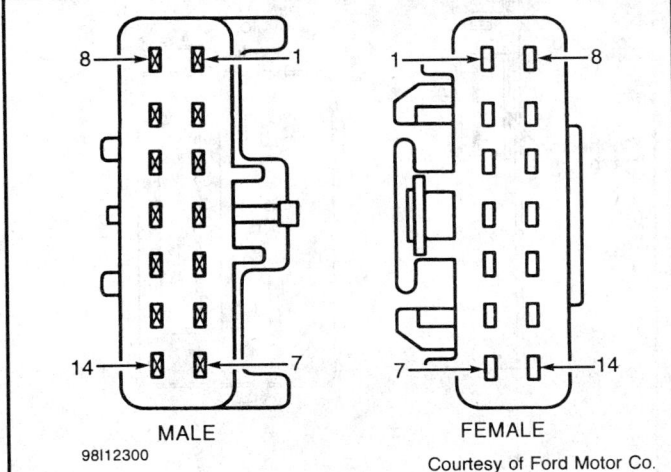

Fig. 7: Identifying In-Line Harness Connector C62 Terminals

TEST D: HYBRID ELECTRONIC CLUSTER (HEC) MODULE DOES NOT RESPOND TO NGS TESTER

NOTE: Hybrid Electronic Cluster (HEC) module is built into instrument cluster.

1) Turn ignition switch to LOCK position. Disconnect NGS tester (if connected). Disconnect HEC module harness connector C808a. Inspect connector for loose, damaged or corroded terminals. If connector is okay, go to next step. If connector is damaged, repair connector as necessary.

2) Measure resistance between terminal No. 9 (White/Violet wire) at HEC module harness connector C808a and terminal No. 7 (White wire

without ABS; White/Blue wire with ABS) at Data Link Connector (DLC). *See Figs. 4 and 6*. If resistance is greater than 5 ohms, go to next step. If resistance is 5 ohms or less, replace HEC module if HEC module power and ground circuits are okay.

3) Disconnect in-line harness connector C62. Inspect connector for loose, damaged or corroded terminals. If connector is okay, go to next step. If connector is damaged, repair connector as necessary.

4) Measure resistance between and terminal No. 6 (White wire) at male side of in-line harness connector C62 and terminal No. 7 (White wire without ABS; White/Blue wire with ABS) at DLC. *See Figs. 4 and 7*. If resistance is greater than 5 ohms, repair open in White wire and/or White/Blue wire between DLC and in-line harness connector C62. If resistance is 5 ohms or less, repair open in White/Violet wire between in-line harness connector C62 and HEC module.

TEST E: ANTI-THEFT/CENTRAL LOCKING MODULE DOES NOT RESPOND TO NGS TESTER

NOTE: Anti-theft/central locking module may also be referred to as Central Security Module (CSM).

1) Turn ignition switch to LOCK position. Disconnect NGS tester (if connected). Disconnect anti-theft/central locking module harness connector C451b. Inspect connector for loose, damaged or corroded terminals. If connector is okay, go to next step. If connector is damaged, repair connector as necessary.

2) Measure resistance between terminal No. 4 (White wire) at anti-theft/central locking module harness connector C451b and terminal No. 7 (White wire without ABS; White/Blue wire with ABS) at Data Link Connector (DLC). *See Figs. 4 and 8*. If resistance is greater than 5 ohms, go to next step. If resistance is 5 ohms or less, replace anti-theft/central locking module if anti-theft/central locking module power and ground circuits are okay.

3) Disconnect in-line harness connector C58. Inspect connector for loose, damaged or corroded terminals. If connector is okay, go to next step. If connector is damaged, repair connector as necessary.

4) Measure resistance between and terminal No. 9 (White wire) at female side of in-line harness connector C58 and terminal No. 7 (White wire without ABS; White/Blue wire with ABS) at DLC. *See Figs. 4 and 8*. If resistance is greater than 5 ohms, go to next step. If resistance is 5 ohms or less, repair open in White between in-line harness connector C58 and anti-theft/central locking module.

5) Disconnect in-line harness connector C62. Inspect connector for loose, damaged or corroded terminals. If connector is okay, go to next step. If connector is damaged, repair connector as necessary.

6) Measure resistance between and terminal No. 6 (White wire) at male side of in-line harness connector C62 and terminal No. 7 (White wire without ABS; White/Blue wire with ABS) at DLC. *See Figs. 4 and 7*. If resistance is greater than 5 ohms, repair open in White wire and/or White/Blue wire between DLC and in-line harness connector C62. If resistance is 5 ohms or less, repair open in White wire between in-line harness connector C62 and in-line harness connector C58.

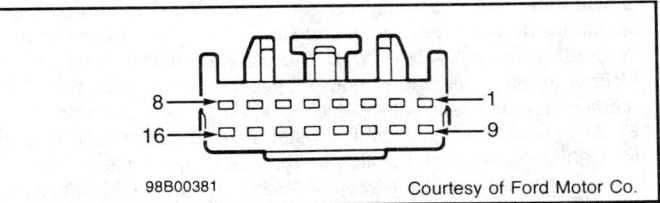

Fig. 8: Identifying In-Line Harness Connector C58 (Female Side Shown) & Anti-Theft/Central Locking Module Harness Connector C451b Terminals

TEST F: NO MODULE/NETWORK COMMUNICATION – ISO 9141 NETWORK

NOTE: Depending on module configuration, with all modules connected and with ignition switch in RUN position or with engine running 2-3 volts may be present at Data Link Connector (DLC) terminal No. 7 (White wire without ABS; White/Blue wire with ABS). This is the International Standards Organization (ISO) 9141 diagnostic communications network circuit.

NOTE: Anti-theft/central locking module may also be referred to as Central Security Module (CSM). Hybrid Electronic Cluster (HEC) module is built into instrument cluster. Air bag diagnostic monitor may also be referred to as electronic crash sensor module.

1) Turn ignition switch to LOCK position. Disconnect NGS tester (if connected). Disconnect in-line harness connector C62. Inspect connector for loose, damaged or corroded terminals. If connector is okay, go to next step. If connector is damaged, repair connector as necessary.
2) Measure resistance between and terminal No. 6 (White wire) at male side of in-line harness connector C62 and terminal No. 7 (White wire without ABS; White/Blue wire with ABS) at DLC. *See Figs. 4 and 7.* If resistance is 5 ohms or less, go to next step. If resistance is greater than 5 ohms, repair open in White wire and/or White/Blue wire between DLC and in-line harness connector C62.
3) Turn ignition switch to RUN position. Measure voltage at terminal No. 7 (White wire without ABS; White/Blue wire with ABS) at DLC. Voltage should not exist. Turn ignition switch to LOCK position. Measure resistance between ground and terminal No. 7 (White wire without ABS; White/Blue wire with ABS) at DLC. Resistance should be greater than 10 k/ohms. If either reading is not as specified, go to next step. If both readings are as specified, go to step 6).
4) If vehicle is equipped with anti-lock brake system (ABS), go to next step. If vehicle is not equipped with ABS, repair short to ground or voltage in White wire between in-line harness connector C62 and DLC.
5) Disconnect ABS module harness connector C385. Turn ignition switch to RUN position. Measure voltage at terminal No. 7 (White/Blue wire) at DLC. Voltage should not exist. Turn ignition switch to LOCK position. Measure resistance between ground and terminal No. 7 (White/Blue wire) at DLC. Resistance should be greater than 10 k/ohms. If either reading is not as specified, repair short to ground or voltage in White/Blue wire between in-line harness connector C62, ABS module and DLC. If both readings are as specified, replace ABS control module.
6) Connect in-line harness connector C62. Turn ignition switch to RUN position. Measure voltage at terminal No. 7 (White wire without ABS; White/Blue wire with ABS) at DLC. Voltage should not exist. Turn ignition switch to LOCK position. Measure resistance between ground and terminal No. 7 (White wire without ABS; White/Blue wire with ABS) at DLC. Resistance should be greater than 10 k/ohms. If either reading is not as specified, go to next step. If both readings are as specified, system is okay at this time.
7) Disconnect air bag diagnostic monitor harness connector C20. Turn ignition switch to RUN position. Measure voltage at terminal No. 7 (White wire without ABS; White/Blue wire with ABS) at DLC. Voltage should not exist. Turn ignition switch to LOCK position. Measure resistance between ground and terminal No. 7 (White wire without ABS; White/Blue wire with ABS) at DLC. Resistance should be greater than 10 k/ohms. If either reading is not as specified, go to next step. If both readings are as specified, replace air bag diagnostic monitor.
8) Disconnect Hybrid Electronic Cluster (HEC) module harness connector C808a. Turn ignition switch to RUN position. Measure voltage at terminal No. 7 (White wire without ABS; White/Blue wire with ABS) at DLC. Voltage should not exist. Turn ignition switch to LOCK position. Measure resistance between ground and terminal No. 7 (White wire without ABS; White/Blue wire with ABS) at DLC. Resistance should be greater than 10 k/ohms. If either reading is not as specified, go to next step. If both readings are as specified, replace HEC module.
9) If vehicle is equipped with anti-theft/central locking module, go to next step. If vehicle is not equipped with anti-theft/central locking module,

repair short to ground or voltage in White/Red wire between in-line harness connector C62 and air bag diagnostic monitor and/or in White/Violet wire between in-line harness connector C62 and HEC module.

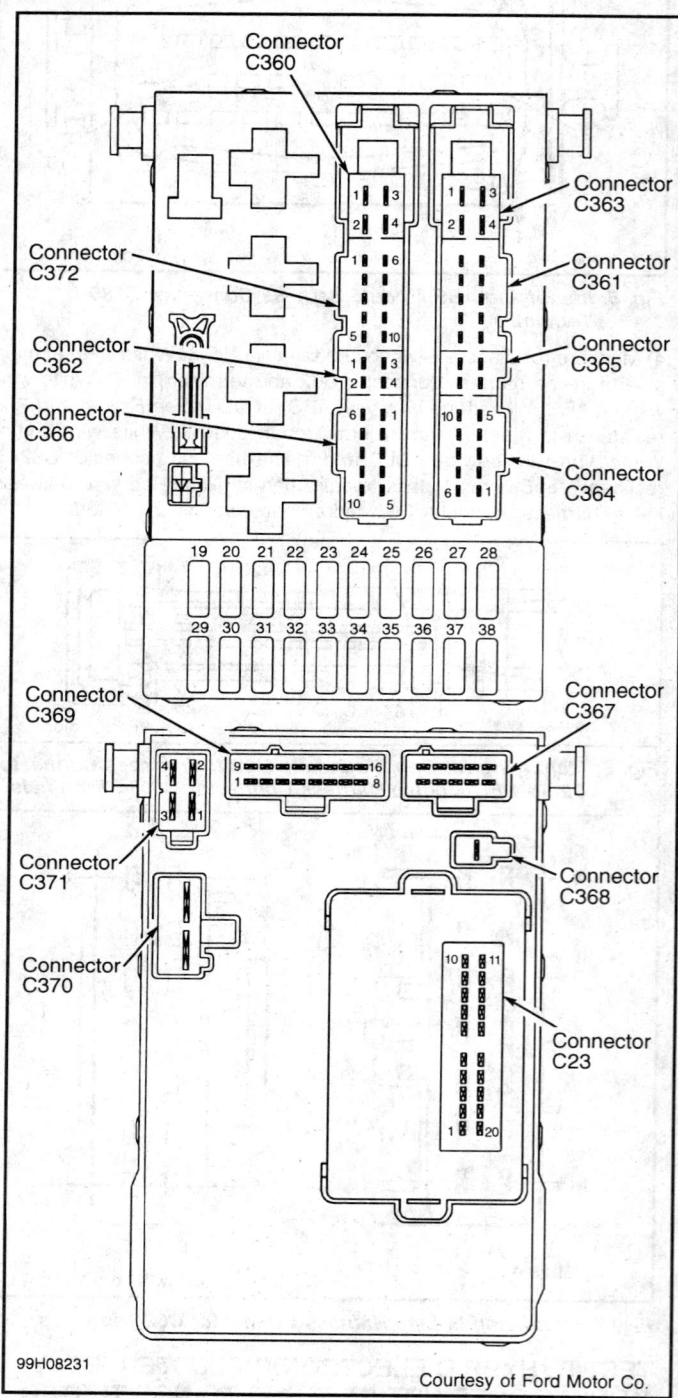

Fig. 9: Identifying Instrument Panel Fuse Box Harness Connectors

10) Disconnect anti-theft/central locking module harness connector C451b. Turn ignition switch to RUN position. Measure voltage at terminal No. 7 (White wire without ABS; White/Blue wire with ABS) at DLC. Voltage should not exist. Turn ignition switch to LOCK position. Measure resistance between ground and terminal No. 7 (White wire without ABS; White/Blue wire with ABS) at DLC. Resistance should be

greater than 10 k/ohms. If either reading is not as specified, go to next step. If both readings are as specified, replace anti-theft/central locking module.

11) Disconnect in-line harness connector C58. Turn ignition switch to RUN position. Measure voltage at terminal No. 7 (White wire without ABS; White/Blue wire with ABS) at DLC. Voltage should not exist. Turn ignition switch to LOCK position. Measure resistance between ground and terminal No. 7 (White wire without ABS; White/Blue wire with ABS) at DLC. Resistance should be greater than 10 k/ohms. If both readings are as specified, repair short to ground or voltage in White wire between in-line harness connector C58 and anti-theft/central locking module. If either reading is not as specified, repair short to ground or voltage in wiring between in-line harness connector C62 and in-line harness connector C58, air bag diagnostic monitor and/or HEC module.

TEST G: NO MODULE/NETWORK COMMUNICATION – NO POWER TO NGS TESTER

1) Turn ignition switch to LOCK position. Measure voltage at terminal No. 16 (Orange wire) at Data Link Connector (DLC). *See Fig. 4.* If battery voltage does not exist, go to next step. If battery voltage exists, go to step **4)**.

2) Remove fuse No. 28 (30-amp) from instrument panel fuse box. Inspect fuse. If fuse is okay, go to next step. If fuse is blown, repair short to ground in power distribution circuit as necessary. See appropriate wiring diagram in POWER DISTRIBUTION article in WIRING DIAGRAMS.

3) Disconnect instrument panel fuse box harness connector C371. *See Fig. 9.* Measure voltage at terminal No. 3 at instrument panel fuse box connect C371 (fuse box side). If battery voltage exists, repair open in Orange wire between instrument panel fuse box and DLC. If battery voltage does not exist, replace instrument panel fuse box.

4) Measure resistance between ground and terminal No. 5 (Black/Orange wire) at DLC. If resistance is 5 ohms or less, go to next step. If resistance is greater than 5 ohms, repair open in Black/Orange wire.

5) Measure resistance between ground and terminal No. 4 (Black wire) at DLC. If resistance is 5 ohms or less, problem is with NGS tester. If resistance is greater than 5 ohms, repair open in Black wire.

DIAGNOSTIC TROUBLE CODE (DTC) DEFINITIONS

NOTE: Anti-theft/central locking module may also be referred to as Central Security Module (CSM). Hybrid Electronic Cluster (HEC) module is built into instrument cluster. Air bag diagnostic monitor may also be referred to as electronic crash sensor module.

AIR BAG DIAGNOSTIC MONITOR DTC INDEX

DTC [1]	Description	Test
B1932	Driver's Air Bag Circuit Open	[2]
B1933	Passenger's Air Bag Circuit Open	[2]
B1934	Driver's Air Bag Inflater Short Circuit	[2]
B1935	Passenger's Air Bag Inflater Short Circuit	[3]
B1231	Longitudinal Acceleration (Crash Data Stored In NVM)	[3]
B1318	Low Battery Voltage	[2]
B1342	ECU Defective	[4]
B1887	Driver's Air Bag Circuit Short To Ground	[2]
B1888	Passenger's Air Bag Circuit Short To Ground	[2]
B1993	Driver's Side Impact Sensor Circuit Short To Ground	[2]
B1997	Passenger's Side Impact Sensor Circuit Short To Ground	[2]
B2122	Driver's Side Satellite Communication Circuit Short To Ground	[2]
B2123	Driver's Side Satellite Communication Circuit Short To Ground	[2]
U2017	Driver's Side Crash Sensor Communication Fault	[2]
U2018	Passenger's Side Crash Sensor Communication Fault	[2]

[1] – DTCs are listed in order of importance. Repair DTCs in order listed.

[2] – Repair supplemental air bag system concern. See DIAGNOSIS & TESTING article in appropriate MITCHELL® AIR BAG SERVICE & REPAIR MANUAL, DOMESTIC & IMPORTED MODELS.

[3] – Replace air bag diagnostic monitor.

[4] – Using NGS tester, retrieve and document all continuous DTCs. Perform electronic crash sensor module self-test. If DTC B1342 is retrieved again, replace electronic crash sensor module.

ANTI-LOCK BRAKE SYSTEM MODULE DTC INDEX

DTC	Description	Test
B1318	Battery Voltage Low	[1]
B1342	ECU Defective	[2]
B1484	Brake Pedal Input Circuit Open	[1]
B1596	Brake Pedal Input Circuit Shorted To Voltage	[1]
C1095	ABS Hydraulic Pump Motor Circuit Failure	[1]
C1145	Right Front ABS Sensor Input Circuit Failure	[1]
C1155	Left Front ABS Sensor Input Circuit Failure	[1]
C1165	Right Rear ABS Sensor Input Circuit Failure	[1]
C1175	Left Rear ABS Sensor Input Circuit Failure	[1]
C1222	Wheel Mismatched	[1]
C1233	Left Front ABS Sensor Input Signal Missing	[1]
C1234	Right Front ABS Sensor Input Signal Missing	[1]
C1235	Right Rear ABS Sensor Input Signal Missing	[1]
C1236	Left Rear ABS Sensor Input Signal Missing	[1]
C1266	ABS Valve Power Circuit Failure	[3]
U1009	SCP Invalid/Missing Data For Engine Torque	[4]

ANTI-LOCK BRAKE SYSTEM MODULE DTC INDEX (Cont.)

DTC	Description	Test
U1027	SCP Invalid/Missing Data For Engine RPM	4
U1262	SCP Communication Fault	5

[1] – Repair anti-lock brake system concern. See appropriate ANTI-LOCK article in BRAKES in appropriate MITCHELL® manual.

[2] – Using NGS tester, retrieve and document all continuous DTCs. Perform ABS self-test. If DTC B1342 is retrieved again, replace ABS module.

[3] – Replace hydraulic control unit. Using NGS tester, perform ABS module self-test after replacement.

[4] – Cause by Powertrain Control Module (PCM). Using NGS tester, perform PCM self-test and perform appropriate test in accordance with DTC retrieved. See appropriate SELF-DIAGNOSTICS article in ENGINE PERFORMANCE in appropriate MITCHELL® manual.

[5] – Repair module communication concern. See MODULE COMMUNICATIONS NETWORK – COUGAR article.

ANTI-THEFT/CENTRAL LOCKING MODULE DTC INDEX

DTC	Description	Test
B1298	Interior Sensor Power Short To Voltage	1
B1299	Interior Sensor Power Short To Ground	1
B1300	Power Door Lock Circuit Failure	2
B1309	Power Door Lock Circuit Short To Ground	3
B1311	Power Door Unlock Circuit Failure	2
B1320	Driver's Door Ajar Circuit Open	4
B1328	Passenger's Door Ajar Circuit Open	4
B1332	Decklid/Rear Door Ajar Circuit Open	4
B1341	Power Door Unlock Circuit Short To Ground	3
B1342	ECU Defective	5
B1520	Hood Switch Circuit Open	1
B1551	Decklid Release Circuit Failure	4
B1553	Decklid Release Circuit Short To Voltage	4
B1554	Decklid Release Circuit Short To Ground	4
B1755	Hazard Flash Output Circuit Short To Voltage	1
B1756	Hazard Flash Output Circuit Short To Ground	1
B2108	Trunk Key Cylinder Switch Failure	1
B2112	Driver's Door Set Switch Stuck Failure	1
B2116	Driver's Door Reset Switch Stuck Failure	6
B2150	Power Supply Circuit Short To Ground (1)	1
B2151	Power Supply Circuit Short To Ground (2)	1
B2153	Rear Echo Sensor Circuit Failure	1
B2154	Front Echo Sensor Circuit Failure	1
B2156	Rear Doppler Sensor Circuit Failure	1
B2157	Rear Doppler Sensor Circuit Failure	1
B2477	Module Configuration Failure	7
B2478	Anti-Theft Input Signal Stuck Failure	1
B2494	Horn/Panic Output Driver Short To Voltage	8
B2496	Horn/Panic Output Driver Short To Ground	8
B2550	Dome Light Output Circuit Short To Voltage	9
B2555	Dome Light Output Circuit Short To Ground	9

[1] – See ACTIVE ANTI-THEFT SYSTEMS – COUGAR article for testing procedures.

[2] – Repair appropriate circuit as necessary. See appropriate wiring diagram in POWER DOOR LOCKS & TRUNK RELEASE article.

[3] – This DTC can be set because of many different reasons. If this DTC is set, repair appropriate system by symptom.

[4] – Repair appropriate circuit as necessary. See appropriate wiring diagram in ILLUMINATION/INTERIOR LIGHTS article.

[5] – Using NGS tester, retrieve and document all continuous DTCs. Perform anti-theft/central locking module self-test. If DTC B1342 is retrieved again, replace anti-theft/central locking module.

[6] – See PASSIVE ANTI-THEFT SYSTEMS – COUGAR article for testing procedures.

[7] – Anti-theft/central locking module requires programming. See COMPUTER RELEARN PROCEDURES article in GENERAL INFORMATION. If DTC B2477 still exists after programming, replace anti-theft/central locking module.

[8] – If remote keyless entry system is operating properly and remote transmitters are programmed, replace anti-theft/central locking module.

[9] – Repair appropriate circuit as necessary. See appropriate wiring diagram in ILLUMINATION/INTERIOR LIGHTS article.

HYBRID ELECTRONIC CLUSTER MODULE DTC INDEX

DTC	Description	Test
B1201	Fuel Sender Circuit Failure	1
B1204	Fuel Sender Short To Ground	1
B1257	Climate Control	1
B1317	Battery voltage High	1
B1318	Battery Voltage Low	1
B1342	ECU Defective	2
B1359	Ignition Switch RUN/ACC Circuit Failure	1
P0115	Engine Coolant Temperature Circuit Malfunction	3

[1] – See INSTRUMENT PANELS – COUGAR article for testing procedures.

[2] – Using NGS tester, retrieve and document all continuous DTCs. Perform Hybrid Electronic Cluster (HEC) module self-test. If DTC B1342 is retrieved again, replace HEC module.

[3] – Repair engine coolant temperature sensor circuit. See appropriate SELF-DIAGNOSTICS article in ENGINE PERFORMANCE in appropriate MITCHELL® manual.

POWERTRAIN CONTROL MODULE DTC INDEX

DTC [1]	Description	Test
B1213	Anti-Theft Number Of Programmed Keys Is Below Minimum	[2]
B1232 Or B2103	Antenna Not Connected	[2]
B1600	No Key Code Received, Damaged Encoded Ignition Key Or Use Of Non-PATS Key	[2]
B1601	Unprogrammed Encoded Ignition Key (Unprogrammed Ignition Key)	[2]
B1602	Invalid Key Code Format From Ignition Key Transponder (Partial Key Read)	[2]
B1681	Transceiver Defective Or Not Connected	[2]

[1] – Codes list in this table are only Powertrain Control Module (PCM) body codes. For a list of all "P" codes, see appropriate SELF-DIAGNOSTICS article in ENGINE PERFORMANCE in appropriate MITCHELL® manual.

[2] – See PASSIVE ANTI-THEFT SYSTEMS – COUGAR article for testing procedures.

PARAMETER IDENTIFICATION (PID) DEFINITIONS

AIR BAG DIAGNOSTIC MONITOR PID INDEX

PID	Description	Expected Value
CCNT	Number Of Continuous DTCs	One Count Per Bit
VBATECS	Battery Voltage	Volts
D_ABAGR	Driver's Air Bag Resistance	2.0-4.1 Ohms
P_ABAGR	Passenger's Air Bag Resistance	1.8-2.2 Ohms
D_ABAGR2	Driver's Side Air Bag Resistance	1.8-2.2 Ohms
P_ABAGR2	Passenger's Air Bag Resistance	1.8-2.2 Ohms

ANTI-LOCK BRAKE SYSTEM MODULE PID INDEX

PID	Description	Expected Value
CCNTABS	Number Of Continuous DTCs	One Count Per Bit
BOO_ABS	Brake Switch Input	ON, OFF
ABSRR_O	Right Rear ABS Outlet Valve	[1]
ABSLR_O	Left Rear ABS Outlet Valve	[1]
ABSRF_O	Right Front ABS Outlet Valve	[1]
ABSLF_O	Left Front ABS Outlet Valve	[1]
ABSRF_I	Right Front ABS Inlet Valve	[1]
ABSLF_I	Left Front ABS Inlet Valve	[1]
ABSRR_I	Right Rear ABS Inlet Valve	[1]
ABSLR_I	Left Rear ABS Inlet Valve	[1]
LF_WSPD	Left Front Wheel Speed Signal	0-255 KPH
RF_WSPD	Right Front Wheel Speed Signal	0-255 KPH
LR_WSPD	Left Rear Wheel Speed Signal	0-255 KPH
RR_WSPD	Right Rear Wheel Speed Signal	0-255 KPH
PMP_MTR	Hydraulic Pump Motor	[1]
VLV_CTR	ABS Valve Control Relay	[1]
LF_TC_P	Left Front Traction Control Primary Valves	ON, OFF
RF_TC_P	Right Front Traction Control Primary Valves	ON, OFF
LR_TC_P	Left Rear Traction Control Primary Valves	ON, OFF
RR_TC_P	Right Rear Traction Control Primary Valves	ON, OFF
LF_TC_S	Left Front Traction Control Switching Valves	ON, OFF
RF_TC_S	Right Front Traction Control Switching Valves	ON, OFF
LR_TC_S	Left Rear Traction Control Switching Valves	ON, OFF
RR_TC_S	Right Rear Traction Control Switching Valves	ON, OFF
T/ALVAL	Left Traction Control Valve Output Status	[1]
T/ARVAL	Right Traction Control Valve Output Status	[1]

[1] – Expected value should be OFF- - -, OFFO- -, OFF-B-, OFF- - G, OFFO-G, OFFOB-, OFF-BG, OFFOBG, ON- - -, ONO- -, ON-B-, ON- - G, ONO-G, ONOB-, ON-BG or ONOBG.

ANTI-THEFT/CENTRAL LOCKING MODULE PID INDEX

PID	Description	Expected Value
AETALRM	Set Alarm Switch	ON, OFF
CCNT	Number Of DTCs Stored	Number
CTL_LK	Central Locking Lock Switch	ON, OFF
CTLUNLK	Central Locking Unlock Switch	ON, OFF
D_DR_CS	Driver's Door Ajar Switch	CLOSED, AJAR
DECKLID	Decklid Ajar Switch	CLOSED, AJAR
DR_LOCK	Driver's Door Lock Output State	NO, YES
DR_UNLK	All Doors Unlock Output State	NO, YES
HOOD_SW	Hood Ajar Switch	CLOSED, AJAR
IGN/SS	Ignition Switch RUN position Or Speed	ON, OFF
P_DR_CS	Passenger's Door Ajar Switch	CLOSED, AJAR
RADIOSW	Radio Remove Switch	ON, OFF
RESETAL	Reset Alarm Switch	ON, OFF
SECSPD	Security Speed Signal	NO, YES

ANTI-THEFT/CENTRAL LOCKING MODULE PID INDEX (Cont.)

PID	Description	Expected Value
TG/HOOD	Tailgate Or Hood ATI	ON, OFF
TRUNK_R	Trunk Release Input Switch	ON, OFF
UNLKSEL	Unlock Select Switch	ON, OFF
VBAT	Battery Voltage	Volts

HYBRID ELECTRONIC CLUSTER MODULE PID INDEX

PID	Description	Expected Value
CCNT_HE	Number Of DTCs Stored	Number
CLOCK	Clock	ON, OFF
COOLANT	Engine Coolant Level Okay	NO, YES
D_DR_HE	Decklid/Hatch Ajar Switch	CLOSED, AJAR
DECKLID	Decklid Ajar Switch	CLOSED, AJAR
PERFECON_SW	Shift Mode	PERF, ECON
ECT	Engine Coolant Temperature	0%-100%
EM/D_IDSW	English/Metric Switch, Driver's ID Switch	ACTIVE, INACTIVE
EXTTEMP	External Temperature Sensor	-40°F-215°F
FUELLVL	Fuel Level Input Status	0%-100%
IGN_HEC	Ignition Switch Status	OFF, ACCY, RUN, START
LIGHTSN	Night/Day	NO, YES
ODOMETR	Vehicle Odometer	Odometer Reading
P_DR_HE	Passenger's Door Ajar Switch	CLOSED, AJAR
RESETSW	Reset Switch	ACTIVE, INACTIVE
RPM	Engine RPM	0-8000 RPM
SELECT	Select Mode Switch	ACTIVE, INACTIVE
TCMCTRL	Transmission Control Button	NO, YES
VBATHEC	Battery Voltage	0-16 Volts
VSS_HEC	Vehicle Speed	0-150 MPH
WEAR_OK	Brake Pad Wear	NO, YES
WFLUID	Washer Fluid Level	LOW, OK

POWERTRAIN CONTROL MODULE PID INDEX

PID	Description	Expected Value
CCNTPCM	Number Of DTCs In PCM	One Count Per DTC
NUMKEYS	Number Of Ignition Key Codes Programed	0-8
M_KEY	Programmed Key In Ignition	NO, YES
ENABL_S	Vehicle Starting Status	ENABLED, DISABLED
MIN#KEYS	Minimum Number Of Programmed Keys Required To Start Vehicle	2-8
ANTISCAN	Time-Out For Unprogrammed PATS Key	ACTIVE, NOTACT
SPARE_KY	Can You Add Spare Keys With 2 Programmed Keys	NO, YES
SERV_MOD	Is This A Repair Module	NO, YES
ACCESS	Security Access Status	Timed/Coded

WIRING DIAGRAMS

NOTE: See appropriate wiring diagrams in DATA LINK CONNECTORS, GROUND DISTRIBUTION and/or POWER DISTRIBUTION article in WIRING DIAGRAMS.

DESCRIPTION & OPERATION

Vehicle has 2 module communications networks. The module communications network provides the ability for module-to-module communication by sharing inputs and outputs instead of each component having an input and output wired directly to each module. A BUS which consists of a pair of twisted wires is used to transfer information between each module. The BUS network is also referred to as Standard Corporate Protocol (SCP) network. The BUS consists of a (+) circuit No. 914 and a (−) circuit No. 915. The BUS is routed throughout the vehicle to Powertrain Control Module (PCM), Electronic Automatic Temperature Control (EATC) module, Anti-Lock Brake System (ABS) module, Passive Anti-Theft System (PATS) module and Natural Gas Vehicle (NGV) module (if equipped). The Lighting Control Module (LCM), Driver's Door Module (DDM), Electronic Crash Sensor (ECS) module do not use the BUS to communicate with other modules. The LCM, DDM and ECS module are connected to the International Standards Organization (ISO) 9141 diagnostic communications network through a single wire (circuit No. 70). Both networks are connected to the Data Link Connector (DLC). This article is used to diagnose BUS and ISO communications network circuit faults.

COMPONENT LOCATIONS

Component	Location
Anti-Lock Brake System Module	Left Front Of Engine Compartment, On Front Of Upper Radiator Support
Data Link Connector	Below Driver's Side Of Instrument Panel, To Right Of Steering Column
Driver's Door Module	Inside Driver's Door
Electronic Automatic Temperature Control Module	Behind Center Of Instrument Panel
Electronic Crash Sensor Module	Behind Right Side Of Instrument Panel, Above Glove Box
Natural Gas Vehicle Module	Front Of Radiator Support
Passive Anti-Theft System Module	Behind Driver's Side Of Instrument Panel
Powertrain Control Module	Left Rear Of Engine Compartment, Near Brake Master Cylinder
Lighting Control Module	Behind Driver's Side Of Instrument Panel, Right Of Steering Column

REPAIRING BUS WIRING

NOTE: Following procedure must be used to ensure proper repair is performed on BUS wiring. BUS wiring is sensitive to moisture and oxidation and must be properly sealed to ensure proper operation of the module communications network. Regular heat shrink tubing is NOT sufficient, heat shrink tubing containing hot melt wax is required.

1) When performing a repair on the BUS wiring, ensure the wires on the BUS are twisted at a rate of 33-40 winds per 3.3 ft. (1 m). The twists should start within approximately 4.9" (124 mm) from any connector. Use only 20 AWG standard wire gauge for repairs.
2) If performing a splice in the wiring, strip .75" (19.0 mm) of insulation from one wire and 1.50" (38.1 mm) of insulator from the other wire. Perform STEP 1. *See Fig. 2.* Place hot melt wax type heat shrink tubing over wire area.
3) Twist stripped portion of the wires together. Solder connection using resin core RMA solder. DO NOT use acid core solder. Bend wires to allow installation of heat shrink tubing. Perform STEP 2. *See Fig. 1.*

4) Position heat shrink tubing over splice area. Using heat gun, evenly heat the heat shrink tubing until wax flows from both ends of heat shrink tubing.

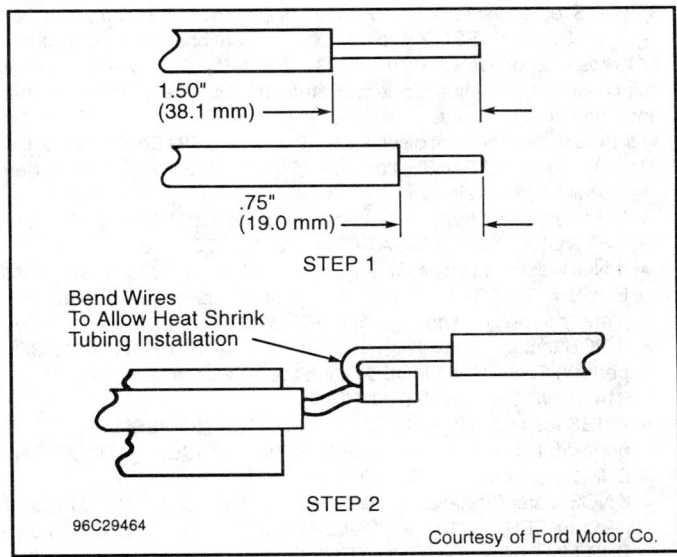

Fig. 1: Repairing BUS Wiring

COMMUNICATION NETWORK DIAGNOSTICS

INSPECTION & VERIFICATION

1) Verify customer's original problem by operating system in question. Inspect vehicle for any obvious electrical component wiring or connector damage. Inspect connectors for loose, damaged or corroded terminals. Check related fuses for system in question.
2) Inspect 16-pin Data Link Connector (DLC) pins for damage. *See Fig. 2.* The DLC is located below driver's side of instrument panel, to the right of steering column. If pins are okay, go to next step. If pins are damaged, repair as necessary and proceed to next step.
3) If problem is still present after performing inspection, connect New Generation Star (NGS) tester to DLC. Select vehicle to be tested from NGS tester menu. If NGS tester does not communicate with vehicle, ensure program card is properly installed. Check NGS tester cable connections and ensure ignition switch is in RUN position. If NGS tester still does not communicate with vehicle, perform TEST K: NO MODULE/NETWORK COMMUNICATION under SYSTEM TESTS. If NGS tester communicates with vehicle, perform data link diagnostic procedure. See DATA LINK DIAGNOSTIC TEST.

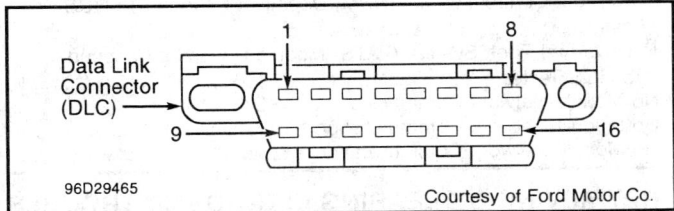

Fig. 2: Identifying Data Link Connector (DLC) Terminals

DATA LINK DIAGNOSTIC TEST

1) Connect New Generation Star (NGS) tester to Data Link Connector (DLC), if not already connected. Select vehicle to be tested from NGS tester menu.
2) Turn ignition switch to RUN position. Rotate dial on NGS tester to menu item DIAGNOSTIC DATA LINK and press trigger. A test will be performed on the BUS (circuits No. 914 and 915) for the module communications network and the ISO 9141 communication link (circuit

FORD
4-244

1999 ACCESSORIES & EQUIPMENT
Module Communications Network
Crown Victoria & Grand Marquis (Cont.)

No. 70). This is the Light Blue/White wire that is between terminal No. 7 on DLC and the electronic crash sensor module, driver's door module and lighting control module.

3) If NGS tester displays CKT 914 (+) = SYSTEM PASSED and CKT 915 (–) = SYSTEM PASSED, module communications network is okay. If NGS tester displays CKT 70 = SYSTEM PASSED, ISO 9141 communication link is operating properly. Return to article that directed you here and continue diagnosis.

4) If NGS tester does not display CKT 914 (+) = SYSTEM PASSED, CKT 915 (–) = SYSTEM PASSED and CKT 70 = SYSTEM PASSED, perform the following as applicable.

- If no response from NGS tester, perform TEST K: NO MODULE/ NETWORK COMMUNICATION under SYSTEM TESTS.
- If NGS tester displays CKT 70, CKT 914 and/or CKT 915 = SOME ECUS NO RESP/NOT EQUIP, perform appropriate test for module(s) not responding. See SYMPTOM CHART table.
- If NGS tester displays CKT 70 = ALL ECUS NO RESP/NOT EQUIP, perform TEST I: NO MODULE/NETWORK COMMUNICATION ISO 9141 LINK under SYSTEM TESTS.
- If NGS tester displays CKT 914 = ALL ECUS NO RESP/NOT EQUIP, perform TEST J: NO MODULE/NETWORK COMMUNICATION – BUS LINK under SYSTEM TESTS.
- If NGS tester displays CKT 915 = ALL ECUS NO RESP/NOT EQUIP, perform TEST J: NO MODULE/NETWORK COMMUNICATION – BUS LINK under SYSTEM TESTS.
- If module in question is NO RESPONSE/NOT EQUIPPED, perform appropriate test for module(s) not responding. See SYMPTOM CHART table.
- If module in question is NO RESPONSE ON CKT 914 (BUS +), perform appropriate test for module(s) not responding. See SYMPTOM CHART table.
- If module in question is NO RESPONSE ON CKT 915 (BUS –), perform appropriate test for module(s) not responding. See SYMPTOM CHART table.

SYMPTOM CHART

Symptom	Test
Anti-Lock Brake System (ABS) Module Does Not Respond To NGS Tester	A
Lighting Control Module (LCM) Does Not Respond To NGS Tester	B
Driver's Door Module (DDM) Does Not Respond To NGS Tester	C
Natural Gas Vehicle (NGV) Module Does Not Respond To NGS Tester	D
Electronic Automatic Temperature Control (EATC) Module Does Not Respond To NGS Tester	E
Electronic Crash Sensor (ECS) Module Does Not Respond To NGS Tester	F
Powertrain Control Module (PCM) Does Not Respond To NGS Tester	G
Passive Anti-Theft System (PATS) Module Does Not Respond To NGS Tester	H
No Module/Network Communication – ISO 9141 Link	I
No Module/Network Communication – BUS Link	J
No Module/Network Communication	K

RETRIEVING & CLEARING DIAGNOSTIC TROUBLE CODES

Connect New Generation Star (NGS) tester to Data Link Connector (DLC). Following manufacturers instructions to retrieve and clear codes for desired module. See appropriate table under DIAGNOSTIC TROUBLE CODE (DTC) DEFINITIONS for a listing of Diagnostic Trouble Codes (DTCs) and appropriate test procedure.

ACCESSING PARAMETER IDENTIFICATION (PID)

Turn ignition switch to LOCK position. Connect New Generation Star (NGS) tester to Data Link Connector (DLC). Following manufacturers

instructions enter PID/DATA MONITOR AND RECORD for desired module. Operate appropriate system and ensure PID expected values are obtained. See appropriate table under PARAMETER IDENTIFICATION (PID) DEFINITIONS.

SYSTEM TESTS

NOTE: Always check module power and ground circuits prior to replacing a control module. See appropriate wiring diagram in DATA LINK CONNECTORS, GROUND DISTRIBUTION and/or POWER DISTRIBUTION article in WIRING DIAGRAMS.

TEST A: ANTI-LOCK BRAKE SYSTEM (ABS) MODULE DOES NOT RESPOND TO NGS TESTER

1) Turn ignition switch to LOCK position. Disconnect ABS module harness connector C162. *See Fig. 3.* Inspect ABS harness connector for loose, damaged or corroded terminals. If problem does not exist, go to next step. If problem exists, repair as necessary and retest system.

2) Connect ABS module harness connector C162. Connect NGS tester to Data Link Connector (DLC). Turn ignition switch to RUN position. Perform data link diagnostic procedure. See DATA LINK DIAGNOSTIC TEST under COMMUNICATION NETWORK DIAGNOSTICS. If NGS tester responds with ABS: NO RESPONSE ON CKT914 (BUS +), go to next step. If NGS tester does not respond with ABS: NO RESPONSE ON CKT915 (BUS –), go to step **6)**.

3) Turn ignition switch to LOCK position. Disconnect NGS tester. Disconnect ABS module harness connector C162. Measure resistance in Tan/Orange wire between terminal No. 20 at ABS module harness connector C162 and terminal No. 2 at DLC. *See Figs. 2 and 4.* If resistance is greater than 5 ohms, go to next step. If resistance is 5 ohms or less, replace ABS module.

4) Disconnect in-line harness connector C107. *See Fig. 3.* Inspect harness connector for loose, damaged or corroded terminals. If problem does not exist, go to next step. If problem exists, repair as necessary and retest system.

5) Measure resistance in Tan/Orange wire between terminal No. 10 at male half of harness connector C107 and terminal No. 2 at DLC. *See Figs. 2 and 5.* If resistance is 5 ohms or less, repair open in Tan/Orange wire between harness connector C107 and ABS module. If resistance is greater than 5 ohms, repair open in Tan/Orange wire between harness connector C107 and DLC.

6) Turn ignition switch to LOCK position. Disconnect NGS tester. Disconnect ABS module harness connector C162. Measure resistance in Pink/Light Blue wire between terminal No. 19 at ABS module harness connector C162 and terminal No. 10 at DLC. *See Figs. 2 and 4.* If resistance is greater than 5 ohms, go to next step. If resistance is 5 ohms or less, replace ABS module.

7) Disconnect in-line harness connector C107. *See Fig. 3.* Inspect harness connector for loose, damaged or corroded terminals. If problem does not exist, go to next step. If problem exists, repair as necessary and retest system.

8) Measure resistance in Pink/Light Blue wire between terminal No. 7 at male half of harness connector C107 and terminal No. 10 at DLC. *See Figs. 2 and 5.* If resistance is 5 ohms or less, repair open in Pink/Light Blue wire between harness connector C107 and ABS module. If resistance is greater than 5 ohms, repair open in Pink/Light Blue wire between harness connector C107 and DLC.

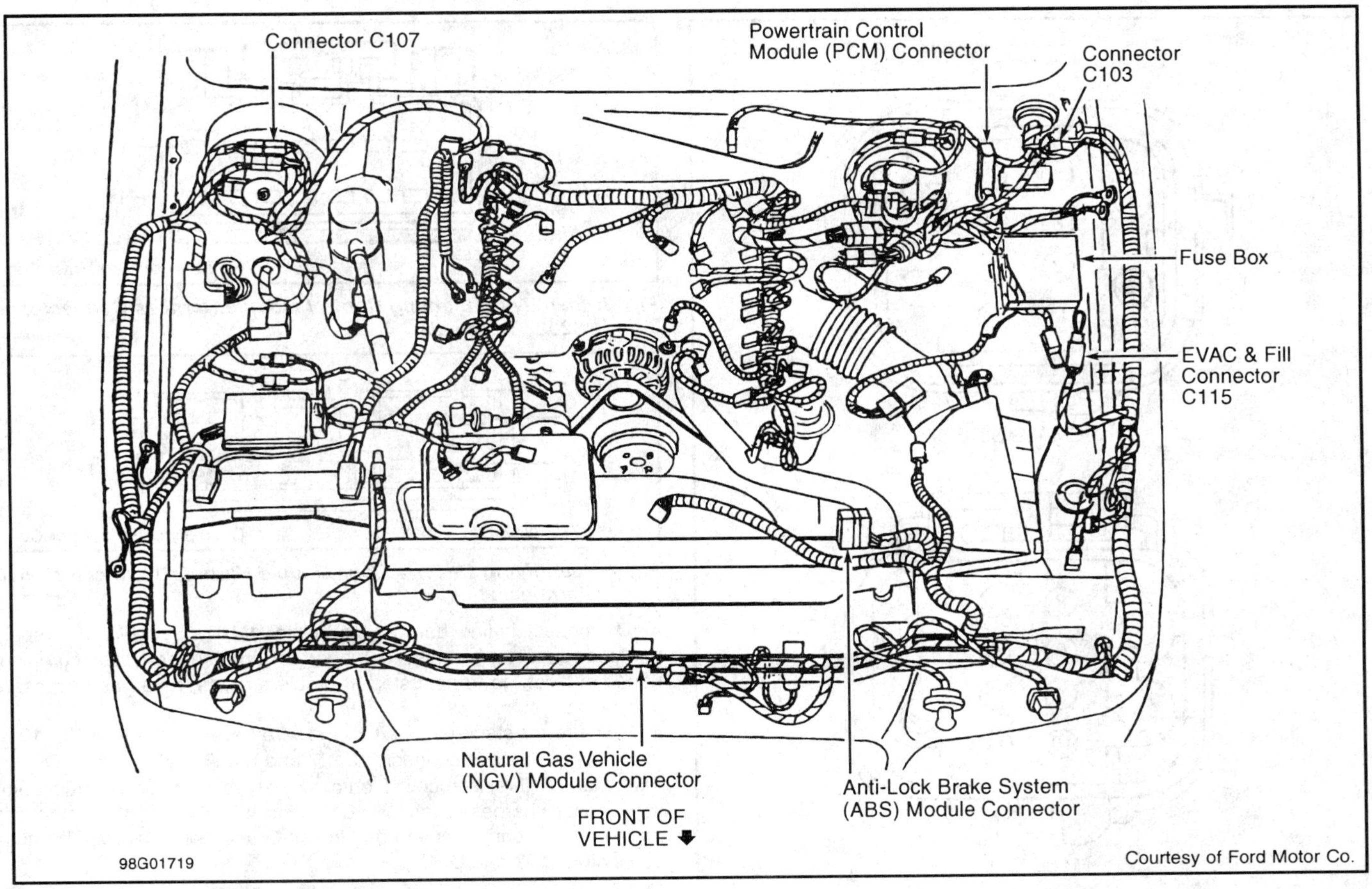

1999 ACCESSORIES & EQUIPMENT
Module Communications Network
Crown Victoria & Grand Marquis (Cont.)

FORD
4-245

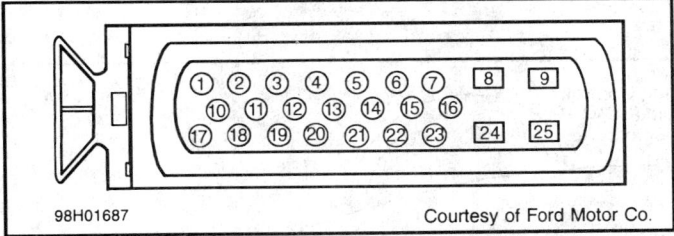

Fig. 3: Locating Engine Compartment Harness Connectors

Fig. 4: Identifying ABS Module Harness Connector C162 Terminals

TEST B: LIGHTING CONTROL MODULE (LCM) DOES NOT RESPOND TO NGS TESTER

1) Turn ignition switch to LOCK position. Disconnect LCM harness connector C2027. *See Fig. 6.* Inspect harness connector for loose, damaged or corroded terminals. If problem does not exist, go to next step. If problem exists, repair as necessary and retest system.

2) Measure resistance in Light Blue/White wire between terminal No. 8 at LCM harness connector C2027 and terminal No. 7 at Data Link Connector (DLC). *See Figs. 2 and 7.* If resistance is 5 ohms or less, replace LCM. If resistance is greater than 5 ohms, repair open in Light Blue/White wire between LCM harness connector C2027 and DLC.

TEST C: DRIVER'S DOOR MODULE (DDM) DOES NOT RESPOND TO NGS TESTER

1) Turn ignition switch to LOCK position. Disconnect DDM harness connector C518. Inspect harness connector for loose, damaged or corroded terminals. If problem does not exist, go to next step. If problem exists, repair as necessary and retest system.

2) Measure resistance in Light Blue/White wire between terminal No. 1 at DDM harness connector C518 and terminal No. 7 at Data Link Connector (DLC). *See Figs. 2 and 8.* If resistance is greater than 5 ohms, go to next step. If resistance is 5 ohms or less, replace DDM.

3) Disconnect in-line harness connector C211. *See Fig. 6.* Inspect harness connector for loose, damaged or corroded terminals. If problem does not exist, go to next step. If problem exists, repair as necessary and retest system.

4) Measure resistance in Light Blue/White wire between terminal No. 4 at male half of harness connector C211 and terminal No. 7 at DLC. *See Figs. 2 and 9.* If resistance is 5 ohms or less, repair open in Light Blue/White wire between harness connector C211 and DDM. If resistance is greater than 5 ohms, repair open in Light Blue/White wire between harness connector C211 and DLC.

TEST D: NATURAL GAS VEHICLE (NGV) MODULE DOES NOT RESPOND TO NGS TESTER

1) Turn ignition switch to LOCK position. Disconnect NGV module harness connector C124. *See Fig. 3.* Inspect harness connector for loose, damaged or corroded terminals. If problem does not exist, go to next step. If problem exists, repair as necessary and retest system.

2) Connect NGV module harness connector C124. Connect NGS tester to Data Link Connector (DLC). Turn ignition switch to RUN position. Perform data link diagnostic procedure. See DATA LINK DIAGNOSTIC TEST under COMMUNICATION NETWORK DIAGNOSTICS. If NGS tester responds with NGV: NO RESPONSE ON CKT914 (BUS +), go to next step. If NGS tester does not respond with NGV: NO RESPONSE ON CKT915 (BUS –), go to step **6)**.

3) Turn ignition switch to LOCK position. Disconnect NGS tester. Disconnect NGV module harness connector C124. Measure resistance in Tan/Orange wire between terminal No. 19 at NGV module harness connector C124 and terminal No. 2 at DLC. *See Figs. 2 and 10.* If resistance is greater than 5 ohms, go to next step. If resistance is 5 ohms or less, replace NGV module.

FORD
4-246

1999 ACCESSORIES & EQUIPMENT
Module Communications Network
Crown Victoria & Grand Marquis (Cont.)

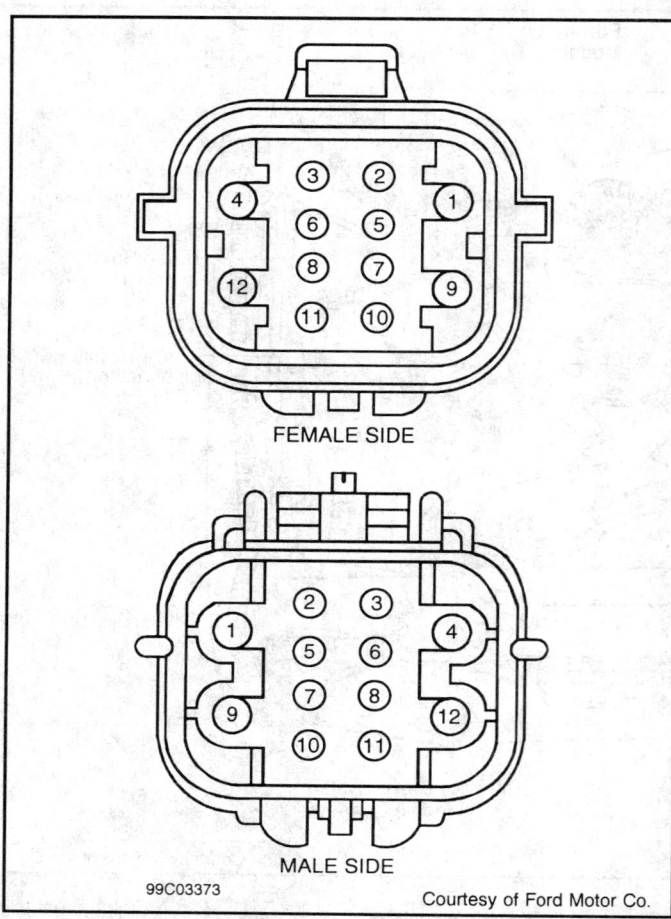

FEMALE SIDE

MALE SIDE

99C03373   Courtesy of Ford Motor Co.

Fig. 5: Identifying In-Line Harness Connector C107 & C103 Terminals

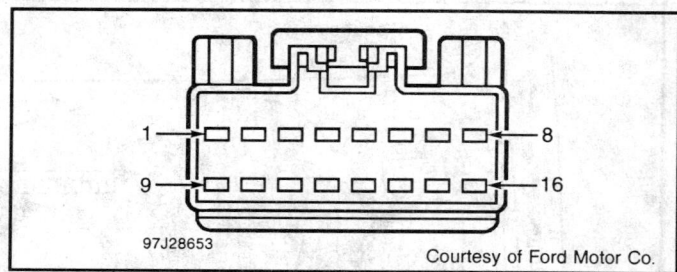

97J28653   Courtesy of Ford Motor Co.

Fig. 7: Identifying Lighting Control Module Harness Connector C2027 Terminals

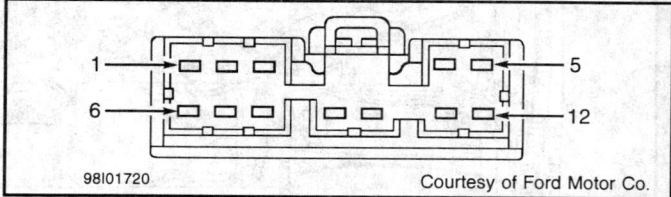

98I01720   Courtesy of Ford Motor Co.

Fig. 8: Identifying Driver's Door Module Harness Connector C518 Terminals

4) Disconnect in-line harness connector C107. *See Fig. 3.* Inspect harness connector for loose, damaged or corroded terminals. If problem does not exist, go to next step. If problem exists, repair as necessary and retest system.

5) Measure resistance in Tan/Orange wire between terminal No. 10 at male half of harness connector C107 and terminal No. 2 at DLC. *See Figs. 2 and 5.* If resistance is 5 ohms or less, repair open in Tan/Orange wire between harness connector C107 and NGV module. If resistance is greater than 5 ohms, repair open in Tan/Orange wire between harness connector C107 and DLC.

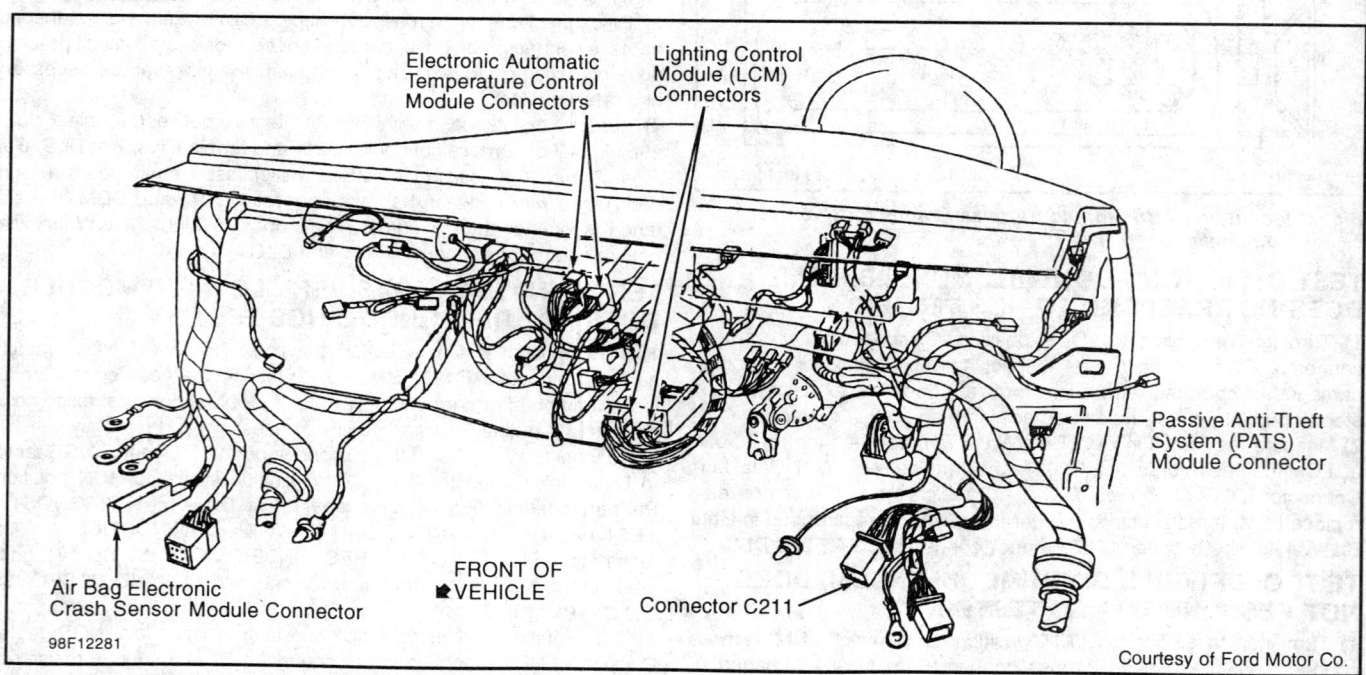

Electronic Automatic Temperature Control Module Connectors

Lighting Control Module (LCM) Connectors

Passive Anti-Theft System (PATS) Module Connector

Air Bag Electronic Crash Sensor Module Connector

FRONT OF VEHICLE

Connector C211

98F12281   Courtesy of Ford Motor Co.

Fig. 6: Locating Harness Connectors Behind Instrument Panel

1999 ACCESSORIES & EQUIPMENT
Module Communications Network
Crown Victoria & Grand Marquis (Cont.)

FORD
4-247

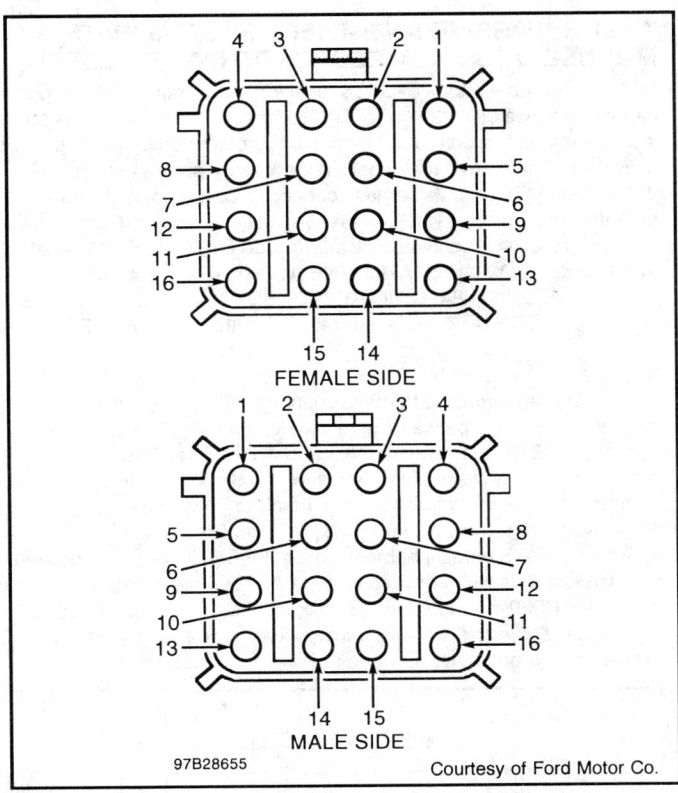

Fig. 9: Identifying In-Line Harness Connector C211 Terminals

6) Turn ignition switch to LOCK position. Disconnect NGS tester. Disconnect NGV module harness connector C124. Measure resistance in Pink/Light Blue wire between terminal No. 18 at NGV module harness connector C124 and terminal No. 10 at DLC. *See Figs. 2 and 10*. If resistance is greater than 5 ohms, go to next step. If resistance is 5 ohms or less, replace NGV module.

7) Disconnect in-line harness connector C107. *See Fig. 3*. Inspect harness connector for loose, damaged or corroded terminals. If problem does not exist, go to next step. If problem exists, repair as necessary and retest system.

8) Measure resistance in Pink/Light Blue wire between terminal No. 7 at male half of harness connector C107 and terminal No. 10 at DLC. *See Figs. 2 and 5*. If resistance is 5 ohms or less, repair open in Pink/Light Blue wire between harness connector C107 and NGV module. If resistance is greater than 5 ohms, repair open in Pink/Light Blue wire between harness connector C107 and DLC.

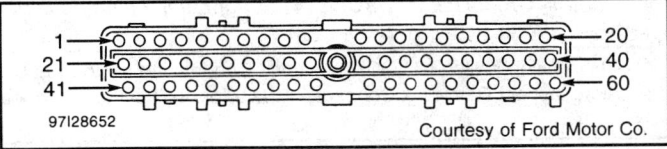

Fig. 10: Identifying Natural Gas Vehicle Module Harness Connector C124 Terminals

TEST E: ELECTRONIC AUTOMATIC TEMPERATURE CONTROL (EATC) MODULE DOES NOT RESPOND TO NGS TESTER

1) Turn ignition switch to LOCK position. Disconnect EATC module harness connector C227. *See Fig. 6*. Inspect harness connector for loose, damaged or corroded terminals. If problem does not exist, go to next step. If problem exists, repair as necessary and retest system.

2) Connect EATC module harness connector C227. Connect NGS tester to Data Link Connector (DLC). Turn ignition switch to RUN position. Perform data link diagnostic procedure. See DATA LINK DIAGNOSTIC

TEST under COMMUNICATION NETWORK DIAGNOSTICS. If NGS tester responds with EATC: NO RESPONSE ON CKT914 (BUS +), go to next step. If NGS tester does not respond with EATC: NO RESPONSE ON CKT915 (BUS –), go to step **4)**.

3) Disconnect NGS tester. Disconnect EATC module harness connector C227. Measure resistance in Tan/Orange wire between terminal No. 15 at EATC module harness connector C227 and terminal No. 2 at DLC. *See Figs. 2 and 11*. If resistance is 5 ohms or less, replace EATC module. If resistance is greater than 5 ohms, repair open in Tan/Orange wire between EATC module and DLC.

4) Disconnect NGS tester. Disconnect EATC module harness connector C227. Measure resistance in Pink/Light Blue wire between terminal No. 1 at EATC module harness connector C227 and terminal No. 10 at DLC. *See Figs. 2 and 11* . If resistance is 5 ohms or less, replace EATC module. If resistance is greater than 5 ohms, repair open in Pink/Light Blue wire between EATC module harness connector and DLC.

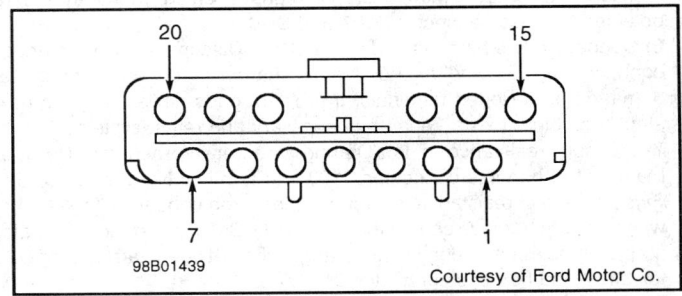

Fig. 11: Identifying EATC Module Harness Connector C227 Terminals

TEST F: ELECTRONIC CRASH SENSOR (ESC) MODULE DOES NOT RESPOND TO NGS TESTER

1) Turn ignition switch to LOCK position. Deactivate air bag system. See appropriate AIR BAG RESTRAINT SYSTEMS article. Disconnect ECS module harness connector C277. Inspect ECS module harness connector for loose, damaged or corroded terminals. If problem does not exist, go to next step. If problem exists, repair as necessary and retest system.

2) Measure resistance in Light Blue/White wire between terminal No. 19 at ECS module harness connector C277 and terminal No. 7 at DLC. *See Figs. 2 and 12*. If resistance is 5 ohms or less, replace ECS module. If resistance is greater than 5 ohms, repair open in Light Blue/White wire between ECS module and DLC.

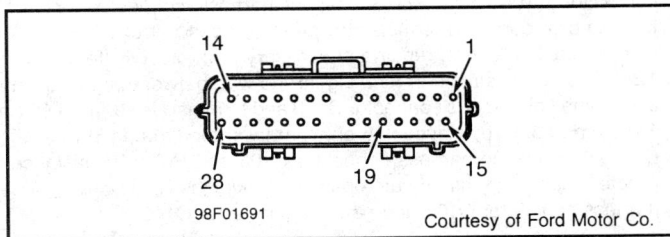

Fig. 12: Identifying Electronic Crash Sensor Module Harness Connector C277 Terminals

TEST G: POWERTRAIN CONTROL MODULE (PCM) DOES NOT RESPOND TO NGS TESTER

1) Turn ignition switch to LOCK position. Disconnect PCM harness connector C185. Inspect harness connector for loose, damaged or corroded terminals. If problem does not exist, go to next step. If problem exists, repair as necessary and retest system.

2) Connect PCM harness connector C185. Connect NGS tester to Data Link Connector (DLC). Turn ignition switch to RUN position. Perform data link diagnostic procedure. See DATA LINK DIAGNOSTIC TEST under COMMUNICATION NETWORK DIAGNOSTICS. If NGS tester

FORD
4-248

1999 ACCESSORIES & EQUIPMENT
Module Communications Network
Crown Victoria & Grand Marquis (Cont.)

responds with PCM: NO RESPONSE ON CKT914 (BUS +), go to next step. If NGS tester does not respond with PCM: NO RESPONSE ON CKT915 (BUS –), go to step **8**).

3) Turn ignition switch to LOCK position. Disconnect NGS tester. Disconnect PCM harness connector C185. Measure resistance in Tan/Orange wire between terminal No. 16 at PCM harness connector C185 and terminal No. 2 at DLC. *See Figs. 2 and 13.* If resistance is greater than 5 ohms, go to next step. If resistance is 5 ohms or less, replace PCM.

4) Disconnect in-line harness connector C107. *See Fig. 3.* Inspect harness connector for loose, damaged or corroded terminals. If problem does not exist, go to next step. If problem exists, repair as necessary and retest system.

5) Measure resistance in Tan/Orange wire between terminal No. 10 at male half of harness connector C107 and terminal No. 2 at DLC. *See Figs. 2 and 5.* If resistance is 5 ohms or less, go to next step. If resistance is greater than 5 ohms, repair open in Tan/Orange wire between harness connector C107 and DLC.

6) Connect in-line harness connector C107. Disconnect in-line harness connector C103. *See Fig. 3.* Inspect harness connector for loose, damaged or corroded terminals. If problem does not exist, go to next step. If problem exists, repair as necessary and retest system.

7) Measure resistance in Tan/Orange wire between terminal No. 2 at male half of harness connector C103 and terminal No. 2 at DLC. *See Figs. 2 and 5.* If resistance is 5 ohms or less, repair open in Tan/Orange wire between harness connector C103 and PCM. If resistance is greater than 5 ohms, repair open in Tan/Orange wire between harness connector C107 and harness connector C103.

8) Turn ignition switch to LOCK position. Disconnect NGS tester. Disconnect PCM harness connector C185. Measure resistance in Pink/Light Blue wire between terminal No. 15 at PCM harness connector C185 and terminal No. 10 at DLC. *See Figs. 2 and 13.* If resistance is greater than 5 ohms, go to next step. If resistance is 5 ohms or less, replace PCM.

9) Disconnect in-line harness connector C107. *See Fig. 3.* Inspect harness connector for loose, damaged or corroded terminals. If problem does not exist, go to next step. If problem exists, repair as necessary and retest system.

10) Measure resistance in Pink/Light Blue wire between terminal No. 7 at male half of harness connector C107 and terminal No. 10 at DLC. *See Figs. 2 and 5.* If resistance is 5 ohms or less, go to next step. If resistance is greater than 5 ohms, repair open in Pink/Light Blue wire between harness connector C107 and DLC.

11) Connect in-line harness connector C107. Disconnect in-line harness connector C103. *See Fig. 3.* Inspect harness connector for loose, damaged or corroded terminals. If problem does not exist, go to next step. If problem exists, repair as necessary and retest system.

12) Measure resistance in Pink/Light Blue wire between terminal No. 3 at male half of harness connector C103 and terminal No. 10 at DLC. *See Figs. 2 and 5.* If resistance is 5 ohms or less, repair open in Pink/Light Blue wire between harness connector C103 and PCM. If resistance is greater than 5 ohms, repair open in Pink/Light Blue wire between harness connector C107 and harness connector C103.

TEST H: PASSIVE ANTI-THEFT SYSTEM (PATS) MODULE DOES NOT RESPOND TO NGS TESTER

1) Turn ignition switch to LOCK position. Disconnect PATS module harness connector C229. *See Fig. 6.* Inspect harness connector for loose, damaged or corroded terminals. If problem does not exist, go to next step. If problem exist, repair as necessary and retest system.

2) Connect PATS module harness connector C229. Connect NGS tester to Data Link Connector (DLC). Turn ignition switch to RUN position. Perform data link diagnostic procedure. See DATA LINK DIAGNOSTIC TEST under COMMUNICATION NETWORK DIAGNOSTICS. If NGS tester responds with PATS: NO RESPONSE ON CKT914 (BUS +), go to next step. If NGS tester does not respond with PATS: NO RESPONSE ON CKT915 (BUS –), go to step **4**).

3) Turn ignition switch to LOCK position. Disconnect NGS tester. Disconnect PATS module harness connector C229. Measure resistance in Tan/Orange wire between terminal No. 6 at PATS module harness connector C229 and terminal No. 2 at DLC. *See Figs. 2 and 14.* If resistance is 5 ohms or less, replace PATS module. If resistance is greater than 5 ohms, repair open in Tan/Orange wire.

4) Turn ignition switch to LOCK position. Disconnect NGS tester. Disconnect PATS module harness connector C229. Measure resistance in Pink/Light Blue wire between terminal No. 5 at PATS module harness connector C229 and terminal No. 10 at DLC. *See Figs. 2 and 14.* If resistance is 5 ohms or less, replace PATS module. If resistance is greater than 5 ohms, repair open in Pink/Light Blue wire.

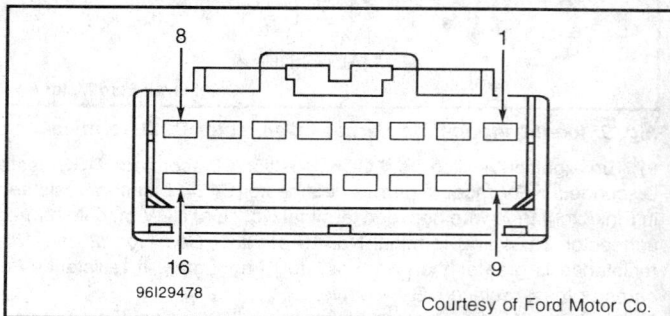

96I29478   Courtesy of Ford Motor Co.

Fig. 14: Identifying Passive Anti-Theft System Harness Connector C229 Terminals

TEST I: NO MODULE/NETWORK COMMUNICATIONS – ISO 9141 LINK

NOTE: Depending on module configuration, with all modules connected and with ignition switch in RUN position or with engine running 2-3 volts may be present at Data Link Connector (DLC) terminal No. 7 (Light Blue/White wire). This is the International Standards Organization (ISO) 9141 diagnostic communications network circuit.

1) Turn ignition switch to LOCK position. Turn ignition switch to LOCK position. Inspect Data Link Connector (DLC) for physical damage, bent

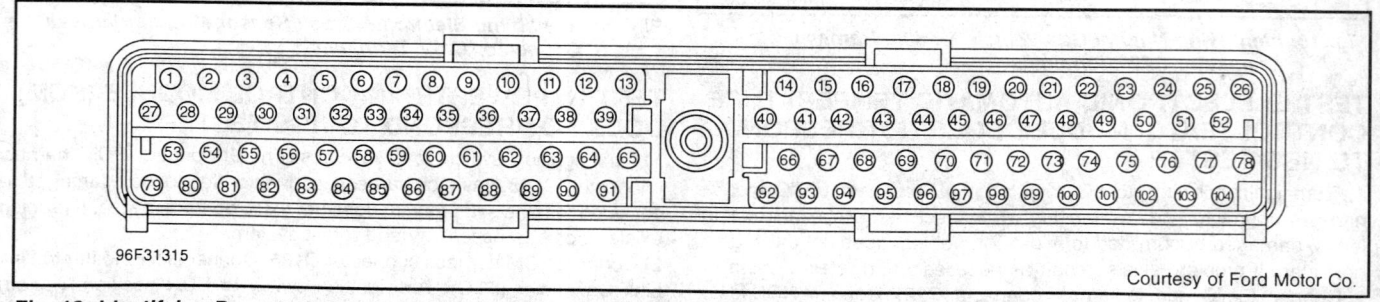

96F31315   Courtesy of Ford Motor Co.

Fig. 13: Identifying Powertrain Control Module Harness Connector C185 Terminals

1999 ACCESSORIES & EQUIPMENT
Module Communications Network
Crown Victoria & Grand Marquis (Cont.)

FORD
4-249

terminals or corrosion. If problem does not exist, go to next step. If problem exists, repair as necessary and retest system.

2) Disconnect Lighting Control Module (LCM) harness connector C2027. *See Fig. 6.* Measure resistance in Light Blue/White wire between terminal No. 8 at LCM harness connector C2027 and terminal No. 7 at DLC. *See Figs. 2 and 7.* If resistance is 5 ohms or less, go to next step. If resistance is greater than 5 ohms, repair open in Light Blue/White wire between LCM harness connector C2027 and DLC.

3) Turn ignition switch to RUN position. Measure voltage between terminals No. 7 (Light Blue/White wire) and No. 16 (Yellow/Black wire) at DLC. *See Fig. 2.* Also, measure voltage between terminals No. 7 (Light Blue/White wire) and No. 4 (Black wire) at DLC. If any reading indicates voltage, go to next step (vehicle with driver's door module) or go to step **7)** (vehicle without driver's door module). If both readings indicate zero volts, replace LCM.

4) Turn ignition switch to LOCK position. Disconnect Driver's Door Module (DDM) harness connector C518. Inspect harness connector for loose, damaged or corroded terminals. *See Fig. 8.* If problem does not exist, go to next step. If problem exists, repair as necessary and retest system.

5) Turn ignition switch to RUN position. Measure voltage between terminals No. 7 (Light Blue/White wire) and No. 16 (Yellow/Black wire) at DLC. *See Fig. 2.* Also, measure voltage between terminals No. 7 (Light Blue/White wire) and No. 4 (Black wire) at DLC. If any reading indicates voltage, go to next step. If both readings indicate zero volts, replace DDM.

6) Turn ignition switch to LOCK position. Disconnect in-line harness connector C211. *See Fig. 6.* Turn ignition switch to RUN position. Measure voltage between terminals No. 7 (Light Blue/White wire) and No. 16 (Yellow/Black wire) at DLC. *See Fig. 2.* Also, measure voltage between terminals No. 7 (Light Blue/White wire) and No. 4 (Black wire) at DLC. If any reading indicates voltage, go to next step. If both readings indicate zero volts, repair short to voltage or ground in Light Blue/White wire between harness connector C211 and DDM.

7) Turn ignition switch to LOCK position. Deactivate air bag system. See appropriate AIR BAG RESTRAINT SYSTEMS article. Connect LCM harness connector C2027. Disconnect Electronic Crash Sensor (ECS) module harness connector C277. Inspect ECS module harness connector for loose, damaged or corroded terminals. If problem does not exist, go to next step. If problem exists, repair as necessary and retest system.

8) Turn ignition switch to LOCK position. Disconnect in-line harness connector C211. *See Fig. 6.* Turn ignition switch to RUN position. Measure voltage between terminals No. 7 (Light Blue/White wire) and No. 16 (Yellow/Black wire) at DLC. *See Fig. 2.* Also, measure voltage between terminals No. 7 (Light Blue/White wire) and No. 4 (Black wire) at DLC. If any reading indicates voltage, repair short to voltage or ground in Light Blue/White wire between DLC, harness connector C211, ECS module and DDM. If both readings indicate zero volts, replace ECS module.

TEST J: NO MODULE/NETWORK COMMUNICATIONS – BUS LINK

NOTE: Powertrain Control Module (PCM), Electronic Automatic Temperature Control (EATC) module, Anti-Lock Brake System (ABS) module, Passive Anti-Theft System (PATS) module and Natural Gas Vehicle (NGV) module (if equipped) are connected to BUS.

NOTE: Depending on module configuration, with all modules connected and with ignition switch in RUN position or with engine running 2-3 volts may be present at Data Link Connector (DLC) terminals No. 2 (Tan/Orange wire) and No. 10 (Pink/Light Blue wire). These are the Standard Corporate Protocol (SCP) diagnostic communications network circuits.

1) Check NGS tester terminals physical damage, bent terminals or corrosion. If problem does not exist, go to next step. If problem exists, repair as necessary and retest system.

2) Turn ignition switch to LOCK position. Inspect Data Link Connector (DLC) for physical damage, bent terminals or corrosion. *See Fig. 2.* If problem does not exist, go to next step. If problem exists, repair as necessary and retest system.

3) Disconnect PCM harness connector C185. *See Fig. 3.* Measure resistance in Tan/Orange wire between terminal No. 16 at PCM harness connector C185 and terminal No. 2 at DLC. *See Figs. 2 and 13.* Also, measure resistance in Pink/Light Blue wire between terminal No. 15 at PCM harness connector C185 and terminal No. 10 at DLC. If both resistance readings are 5 ohms or less and PCM is the only module on BUS, go to next step. If both resistance readings are 5 ohms or less and PCM is not the only module on BUS, go to step **10)**. If either resistance reading is greater than 5 ohms and PCM in the only module on BUS, perform TEST G: POWERTRAIN CONTROL MODULE (PCM) DCES NOT RESPOND TO NGS TESTER. If either resistance reading is greater than 5 ohms and PCM in not the only module on BUS, repair open in Tan/Orange wire and/or Pink/Light Blue wire between PCM harness connector C185 and in-line harness connector C107. *See Fig. 3.*

4) Turn ignition switch to RUN position. Measure voltage at terminal No. 2 (Tan/Orange wire) at DLC. Also, measure voltage at terminal No. 10 (Pink/Light Blue wire) at DLC. If any reading indicates voltage, go to next step. If both readings indicate zero volts, go to step **7)**.

5) Turn ignition switch to LOCK position. Disconnect in-line harness connector C103. *See Fig. 3.* Turn ignition switch to RUN position. Measure voltage at terminal No. 2 (Tan/Orange wire) at DLC. Also, measure voltage at terminal No. 10 (Pink/Light Blue wire) at DLC. If any reading indicates voltage, go to next step. If both readings indicate zero volts, repair short to voltage in Tan/Orange wire and/or Pink/Light Blue wire between in-line harness connector C103 and PCM.

6) Turn ignition switch to LOCK position. Disconnect in-line connector C107. *See Fig. 3.* Turn ignition switch to RUN position. Measure voltage at terminal No. 2 (Tan/Orange wire) at DLC. Also, measure voltage at terminal No. 10 (Pink/Light Blue wire) at DLC. If both readings indicate zero volts, repair short to voltage in Tan/Orange wire and/or Pink/Light Blue wire between in-line harness connector C103 and in-line harness connector C107. If any reading indicates voltage, repair short to voltage in Tan/Orange wire and/or Pink/Light Blue wire between in-line harness connector C107 and DLC.

7) Turn ignition switch to LOCK position. Measure resistance between ground and terminal No. 2 (Tan/Orange wire) at DLC. Also, measure resistance between ground and terminal No. 10 (Pink/Light Blue wire) at DLC. If either resistance reading is 10 k/ohms or less, go to next step. If both resistance readings are greater than 10 k/ohms, repair powertrain control concern. See appropriate SELF-DIAGNOSTICS article in ENGINE PERFORMANCE in appropriate MITCHELL® manual.

8) Disconnect in-line harness connector C103. *See Fig. 3.* Measure resistance between ground and terminal No. 2 (Tan/Orange wire) at

FORD
4-250

1999 ACCESSORIES & EQUIPMENT
Module Communications Network
Crown Victoria & Grand Marquis (Cont.)

DLC. Also, measure resistance between ground and terminal No. 10 (Pink/Light Blue wire) at DLC. If either resistance reading is 10 k/ohms or less, go to next step. If both resistance readings are greater than 10 k/ohms, repair short to ground in Tan/Orange wire and/or Pink/Light Blue wire between in-line harness connector C103 and PCM.

9) Disconnect in-line harness connector C107. *See Fig. 3.* Measure resistance between ground and terminal No. 2 (Tan/Orange wire) at DLC. Also, measure resistance between ground and terminal No. 10 (Pink/Light Blue wire) at DLC. If either resistance reading is 10 k/ohms or less, repair short to ground in Tan/Orange wire and/or Pink/Light Blue wire between in-line harness connector C107 and DLC. If both resistance readings are greater than 10 k/ohms, repair short to ground in Tan/Orange wire and/or Pink/Light Blue wire between in-line harness connector C103 and in-line harness connector C107.

10) Turn ignition switch to RUN position. Measure voltage between terminals No. 2 (Tan/Orange wire) and No. 16 (Yellow/Black wire) at DLC. Measure voltage between terminals No. 2 (Tan/Orange wire) and No. 4 (Black wire) at DLC. Measure voltage between terminals No. 10 (Pink/Light Blue wire) and No. 16 (Yellow/Black wire) at DLC. Measure voltage between terminals No. 10 (Pink/Light Blue wire) and No. 4 (Black wire) at DLC. If any reading indicates voltage, go to next step. If all readings indicate zero volts, repair PCM output concern. See appropriate SELF-DIAGNOSTICS article in ENGINE PERFORMANCE in appropriate MITCHELL® manual.

11) Turn ignition switch to LOCK position. Disconnect in-line harness connector C103. *See Fig. 3.* Turn ignition switch to RUN position. Measure voltage between terminals No. 2 (Tan/Orange wire) and No. 16 (Yellow/Black wire) at DLC. Measure voltage between terminals No. 2 (Tan/Orange wire) and No. 4 (Black wire) at DLC. Measure voltage between terminals No. 10 (Pink/Light Blue wire) and No. 16 (Yellow/Black wire) at DLC. Measure voltage between terminals No. 10 (Pink/Light Blue wire) and No. 4 (Black wire) at DLC. If any reading indicates voltage, go to next step. If all readings indicate zero volts, repair short to ground or voltage in Tan/Orange wire and/or Pink/Light Blue wire between in-line harness connector C103 and PCM.

12) If vehicle is equipped with CNG fuel system, go to next step. If vehicle is not equipped with CNG fuel system, go to step 14).

13) Turn ignition switch to LOCK position. Disconnect Natural Gas Vehicle (NGV) module harness connector C124. *See Fig. 3.* Turn ignition switch to RUN position. Measure voltage between terminals No. 2 (Tan/Orange wire) and No. 16 (Yellow/Black wire) at DLC. Measure voltage between terminals No. 2 (Tan/Orange wire) and No. 4 (Black wire) at DLC. Measure voltage between terminals No. 10 (Pink/Light Blue wire) and No. 16 (Yellow/Black wire) at DLC. Measure voltage between terminals No. 10 (Pink/Light Blue wire) and No. 4 (Black wire) at DLC. If any reading indicates voltage, go to next step. If all readings indicate zero volts, repair NGV module output concern. See appropriate SELF-DIAGNOSTICS article in ENGINE PERFORMANCE in appropriate MITCHELL® manual.

14) If vehicle is equipped with anti-lock brakes, go to next step. If vehicle is not equipped with anti-lock brakes, go to step 16).

15) Turn ignition switch to LOCK position. Disconnect Anti-Lock Brake System (ABS) module harness connector C162. *See Fig. 3.* Turn ignition switch to RUN position. Measure voltage between terminals No. 2 (Tan/Orange wire) and No. 16 (Yellow/Black wire) at DLC. Measure voltage between terminals No. 2 (Tan/Orange wire) and No. 4 (Black wire) at DLC. Measure voltage between terminals No. 10 (Pink/Light Blue wire) and No. 16 (Yellow/Black wire) at DLC. Measure voltage between terminals No. 10 (Pink/Light Blue wire) and No. 4 (Black wire) at DLC. If any reading indicates voltage, go to next step. If all readings indicate zero volts, replace ABS module.

16) If vehicle is equipped with passive anti-theft system, go to next step. If vehicle is not equipped with passive anti-theft system, go to step 18).

17) Turn ignition switch to LOCK position. Disconnect Passive Anti-Theft System (PATS) module harness connector C229. *See Fig. 6.* Turn ignition switch to RUN position. Measure voltage between terminals No. 2 (Tan/Orange wire) and No. 16 (Yellow/Black wire) at DLC. Measure voltage between terminals No. 2 (Tan/Orange wire) and No. 4 (Black wire) at DLC. Measure voltage between terminals No. 10 (Pink/Light Blue wire) and No. 16 (Yellow/Black wire) at DLC. Measure voltage between terminals No. 10 (Pink/Light Blue wire) and No. 4 (Black wire) at DLC. If any reading indicates voltage, go to next step. If all readings indicate zero volts, replace PATS module.

18) If vehicle is equipped with electronic climate control, go to next step. If vehicle is not equipped with electronic climate control, go to step 20).

19) Turn ignition switch to LOCK position. Disconnect Electronic Automatic Temperature Control (EATC) module harness connector C227. *See Fig. 6.* Turn ignition switch to RUN position. Measure voltage between terminals No. 2 (Tan/Orange wire) and No. 16 (Yellow/Black wire) at DLC. Measure voltage between terminals No. 2 (Tan/Orange wire) and No. 4 (Black wire) at DLC. Measure voltage between terminals No. 10 (Pink/Light Blue wire) and No. 16 (Yellow/Black wire) at DLC. Measure voltage between terminals No. 10 (Pink/Light Blue wire) and No. 4 (Black wire) at DLC. If any reading indicates voltage, go to next step. If all readings indicate zero volts, replace EATC module.

20) Turn ignition switch to LOCK position. Disconnect in-line harness connector C107. *See Fig. 3.* Turn ignition switch to RUN position. Measure voltage between terminals No. 2 (Tan/Orange wire) and No. 16 (Yellow/Black wire) at DLC. Measure voltage between terminals No. 2 (Tan/Orange wire) and No. 4 (Black wire) at DLC. Measure voltage between terminals No. 10 (Pink/Light Blue wire) and No. 16 (Yellow/Black wire) at DLC. Measure voltage between terminals No. 10 (Pink/Light Blue wire) and No. 4 (Black wire) at DLC. If any reading indicates voltage, repair short to ground or voltage in between DLC and PATS module and/or EATC module. If all readings indicate zero volts, repair short to ground or voltage in between in-line harness connector C107 and evac and fill connector, ABS module, NGV module and/or in-line harness connector C103.

TEST K: NO MODULE/NETWORK COMMUNICATION

1) Check NGS tester terminals physical damage, bent terminals or corrosion. If problem does not exist, go to next step. If problem exists, repair as necessary.

2) Turn ignition switch to LOCK position. Inspect Data Link Connector (DLC) for physical damage, bent terminals or corrosion. If problem does not exist, go to next step. If problem exists, repair as necessary and retest system.

3) Measure voltage at terminal No. 16 (Yellow/Black wire) at DLC. *See Fig. 2.* If battery voltage exists, go to next step. If battery voltage does not exist, repair open or short to ground in Yellow/Black wire between DLC and fuse No. 12 (30-amp) in power distribution box.

4) Measure resistance between ground and terminals No. 4 (Black wire) and No. 5 (Black/White wire) at DLC. If both resistance readings are 5 ohms or less, repair or replace NGS tester. If either resistance reading is greater than 5 ohms, repair open in appropriate wire.

1999 ACCESSORIES & EQUIPMENT
Module Communications Network
Crown Victoria & Grand Marquis (Cont.)

FORD
4-251

DIAGNOSTIC TROUBLE CODE (DTC) DEFINITIONS

ANTI-LOCK BRAKE SYSTEM MODULE DTC INDEX

DTC	Description	Test
B1342	ECU Defective	1
B1485	Brake Pedal Input Circuit Shorted To Voltage	2
B1676	Battery Voltage Out Of Range	2
C1095	ABS Hydraulic Pump Motor Circuit Failure	2
C1145	Right Front ABS Sensor Input Circuit Failure	2
C1155	Left Front ABS Sensor Input Circuit Failure	2
C1165	Right Rear ABS Sensor Input Circuit Failure	2
C1175	Left Rear ABS Sensor Input Circuit Failure	2
C1233	Left Front ABS Sensor Input Signal Missing	2
C1234	Right Front ABS Sensor Input Signal Missing	2
C1235	Right Rear ABS Sensor Input Signal Missing	2
C1236	Left Rear ABS Sensor Input Signal Missing	3
U1009	SCP Invalid/Missing Data For Engine Torque	3
U1027	SCP Invalid/Missing Data For Engine RPM	3
U1059	SCP Invalid/Missing Data For Transmission Range (PRNDL)	

[1] – Using NGS tester, retrieve and document all continuous DTCs. Perform Anti-Lock Brake System (ABS) module self-test. If DTC B1342 is retrieved again, replace ABS module.

[2] – Repair anti-lock brake system concern. See appropriate ANTI-LOCK article in BRAKES in appropriate MITCHELL® manual.

[3] – Cause by Powertrain Control Module (PCM). Using NGS tester, perform PCM self-test and repair powertrain control concern. See appropriate SELF-DIAGNOSTICS article in ENGINE PERFORMANCE in appropriate MITCHELL® manual.

AUDIO CONTROL MODULE DTC INDEX

DTC	Description	Test
B1342	ECU Defective	1
B2401	Tape Deck Mechanism Fault	2
B2402	CD/DJ Thermal Shutdown	3
B2403	CD/DJ Internal Fault	3
B2405	Single Disc Player Thermal Shutdown	4
B2406	Single Disc Player Internal Fault	4
U2003	CD/DJ Is Not Responding	3
U2005	Rear Integrated Control Panel Is Not Responding	4
U2008	Cellular Phone Is Not Responding	4

[1] – Using NGS tester, clear and document continuous DTCs. Perform Audio Control Module (ACM) self-test. If DTC B1342 is retrieved again, replace ACM.

[2] – Verify No tape is in tape deck. Using NGS tester, clear and document continuous DTCs. Perform Audio Control Module (ACM) self-test. If DTC B2401 is retrieved again, repair or replace ACM as necessary.

[3] – Repair audio system fault.

[4] – DTC does not apply to this vehicle.

DRIVER'S DOOR MODULE DTC INDEX

DTC	Description	Test
B1322	Driver's Door Ajar Circuit Short To Ground	1
B1342	ECU Defective	2
B1396	Door Lock Circuit Short To Voltage	3
B1397	Door Unlock Circuit Short To Voltage	3
B1517	Driver's Seat Occupied Switch Short To Voltage	4
B1525	Keyless Entry Circuit Short To Voltage	4
B1549	Master Window Switch Circuit Short To Voltage	5
B1553	Decklid Release Circuit Short To Voltage	4
B1751	Park/Neutral Switch Short To Voltage	4
B2425	Remote Keyless Entry Out Of Synchronization	4

[1] – Perform DTC B1322: DRIVER'S DOOR AJAR CIRCUIT SHORT TO GROUND under DIAGNOSTIC TESTS in PASSIVE ANTI-THEFT SYSTEMS – CROWN VICTORIA & GRAND MARQUIS article.

[2] – Using NGS tester, retrieve and document all continuous DTCs. Perform Driver's Door Module (DDM) self-test. If DTC B1342 is retrieved again, replace DDM.

[3] – See appropriate wiring diagram in POWER DOOR LOCKS & TRUNK RELEASE article.

[4] – See appropriate wiring diagram in REMOTE KEYLESS ENTRY SYSTEMS article.

[5] – Perform TEST D: DRIVER'S WINDOW IS INOPERATIVE under SYSTEM TESTS in POWER WINDOWS – CROWN VICTORIA & GRAND MARQUIS article.

ELECTRONIC AUTOMATIC TEMPERATURE CONTROL MODULE DTC INDEX

DTC	Description	Test
B1249	Blend Door Circuit Failure	1
B1251	A/C In-Car Temperature Sensor Open Circuit	1

FORD
4-252

1999 ACCESSORIES & EQUIPMENT
Module Communications Network
Crown Victoria & Grand Marquis (Cont.)

ELECTRONIC AUTOMATIC TEMPERATURE CONTROL MODULE DTC INDEX (Cont.)

DTC	Description	Test
B1253	A/C In-Car Temperature Sensor Circuit Short To Ground	1
B1255	A/C Ambient Air Temperature Sensor Circuit Open	1
B1257	A/C Ambient Air Temperature Sensor Circuit Short To Ground	1
B1261	A/C Solar Radiation Sensor Circuit Short To Ground	1
U1041	Invalid/Missing Data For Vehicle Speed	2
U1073	Invalid/Missing Data For Engine Coolant	3
U1222	Invalid/Missing Data For Interior Lights	4

[1] – Repair A/C system as necessary. See appropriate AUTOMATIC A/C-HEATER SYSTEMS article in appropriate MITCHELL® AIR CONDITIONING & HEATING SERVICE & REPAIR manual.

[2] – Repair vehicle speed sensor circuit. See appropriate SELF-DIAGNOSTICS article in ENGINE PERFORMANCE in appropriate MITCHELL® manual.

[3] – Repair engine coolant temperature sensor circuit. See appropriate SELF-DIAGNOSTICS article in ENGINE PERFORMANCE in appropriate MITCHELL® manual.

[4] – Repair interior lighting circuit as necessary. See AUTOLAMP SYSTEMS – CROWN VICTORIA & GRAND MARQUIS article.

ELECTRONIC CRASH SENSOR MODULE DTC INDEX

DTC [1]	Description	Test
B1342	ECU Defective	2
B1231	ECS Module Internal Fault	3
B1921	ECS Module Crash Data Memory Full	3
B1318	Low Battery Voltage	3
C1414	Incorrect Vehicle Identification Code	3
B1887	Driver's Air Bag Circuit Shorted To Ground	3
B1916	Driver's Air Bag Circuit Shorted To Voltage	3
B1925	Passenger's Air Bag Circuit Short To Voltage	3
B1879	Unexpected Feature Present	3
B1878	Unexpected Feature Present	3
B1883	Unexpected Feature Present	3
B1882	Unexpected Feature Present	3
B1932	Driver's Air Bag Circuit Resistance High	3
B1933	Passenger's Air Bag Circuit Resistance High	3
B1934	Driver's Air Bag Circuit Resistance Low	3
B1935	Passenger's Air Bag Circuit Resistance Low	3
B1941	External Crash Sensor Open Circuit Shorted To Voltage	3
B1901	External Crash Sensor Shorted To Ground	3
B1871	Unexpected Feature Present	3
B1889	Unexpected Feature Present	3
B1877	Unexpected Feature Present	3
B1885	Unexpected Feature Present	3
B1881	Unexpected Feature Present	3
B1886	Unexpected Feature Present	3
B1884	Unexpected Feature Present	3
B1890	Unexpected Feature Present	3
B1892	Air Bag Tone Warning Indicator Circuit Shorted To Ground Or Open	3
B1891	Air Bag Tone Warning Indicator Circuit Shorted To Voltage	3
B2141	Nonvolatile Memory Configuration Failure	3
B1869	Air Bag Indicator Inoperative	3
B1870	Air Bag Indicator Shorted To Voltage	3

[1] – DTCs are listed in order of importance. Repair DTCs in order listed.

[2] – Using NGS tester, retrieve and document all continuous DTCs. Perform Electronic Crash Sensor (ECS) module self-test. If DTC B1342 is retrieved again, replace ECS module.

[3] – Repair supplemental air bag system concern. See DIAGNOSIS & TESTING article in appropriate MITCHELL® AIR BAG SERVICE & REPAIR MANUAL, DOMESTIC & IMPORTED MODELS.

LIGHTING CONTROL MODULE DTC INDEX

DTC	Description	Test
B1300	Power Door Lock Circuit Failure	1
B1310	Power Door Unlock Circuit Failure	1
B1312	Headlight Input Short To Battery Voltage	2
B1317	Battery Voltage High	3
B1318	Battery Voltage Low	3
B1319	Driver's Door Ajar Circuit Failure	4
B1322	Driver's Door Ajar Circuit Short To Ground	2
B1331	Decklid Ajar Rear Door Circuit Failure	4
B1334	Decklid Ajar Rear Door Circuit Short To Ground	4
B1340	ECS Tone Request Short To Ground	5
B1342	ECU Defective	6

1999 ACCESSORIES & EQUIPMENT
Module Communications Network
Crown Victoria & Grand Marquis (Cont.)

FORD
4-253

LIGHTING CONTROL MODULE DTC INDEX (Cont.)

DTC	Description	Test
B1343	Heated Rear Window Input Circuit Failure	7
B1345	Heated Rear Window Input Circuit Short To Ground	7
B1352	Ignition Key In Circuit Failure	8
B1354	Ignition Key In Circuit Short To Ground	8
B1359	Ignition RUN/ACC Input Circuit Failure	8
B1361	Ignition RUN/ACC Input Circuit Short To Ground	8
B1396	Power Door Lock Circuit Short To Voltage	1
B1397	Power Door Unlock Circuit Short To Voltage	1
B1442	Door Handle Switch Circuit Failure	2
B1445	Door Handle Switch Circuit Short To Ground	2
B1462	Seat Belt Switch Circuit Failure	5
B1464	Seat Belt Switch Circuit Short To Voltage	5
B1468	Chime Input Request Circuit Failure	5
B1470	Headlight Input Circuit Failure	2
B1555	Ignition RUN/START Circuit Failure	8
B1557	Ignition RUN/START Circuit Short To Voltage	8
B1563	Door Ajar Circuit Failure	2
B1566	Door Ajar Circuit Short To Ground	2
B1575	Parking Light Input Circuit Failure	2
B1577	Parking Light Input Circuit Short To Voltage	2
B1579	Panel Dim Increase Circuit Failure	9
B1581	Panel Dim Increase Circuit Short To Voltage	9
B1583	Panel Dim Decrease Input Circuit Failure	9
B1585	Panel Dim Decrease Input Short To Voltage	9
B1677	Alarm Panic Input Circuit Failure	10
B1679	Alarm Panic Input Circuit Short To Voltage	10
B1685	Dome Light Input Circuit Failure	2
B1687	Dome Light Input Circuit Short To Voltage	2
B1689	Autolamp Delay Circuit Failure	2
B1692	Autolamp Delay Circuit Short To Ground	2
B1693	Autolamp ON Circuit Failure	2
B1695	Autolamp ON Circuit Short To Voltage	2
B1790	Autolamp Sensor Circuit Failure	2
B1792	Autolamp Sensor Circuit Short To Voltage	2
B1872	Turn Signal/Hazard Power Feed Circuit Failure	2
B1873	Turn Signal/Hazard Power Feed Circuit Short To Ground	2

1 – See appropriate wiring diagram in POWER DOOR LOCKS & TRUNK RELEASE article.
2 – See AUTOLAMP SYSTEMS – CROWN VICTORIA & GRAND MARQUIS article.
3 – Check charging system. See appropriate GENERATORS article in STARTING & CHARGING SYSTEMS. If charging system is okay, check power and ground circuits to LCM. See appropriate wiring diagram in POWER DISTRIBUTION article in WIRING DIAGRAMS.
4 – Repair appropriate circuit. See appropriate wiring diagram in REMOTE KEYLESS ENTRY SYSTEMS and ILLUMINATION/INTERIOR LIGHTS articles.
5 – Repair appropriate circuit. See appropriate wiring diagram in WARNING SYSTEMS article.
6 – Using NGS tester, retrieve and document all continuous DTCs. Perform Lighting Control Module (LCM) self-test. If DTC B1342 is retrieved again, replace LCM.
7 – See appropriate wiring diagram in REAR WINDOW DEFOGGERS article.
8 – See STEERING COLUMN SWITCHES – CROWN VICTORIA & GRAND MARQUIS article.
9 – See appropriate INSTRUMENT PANELS article.
10 – Repair Red/Light Blue wire between LCM and DDM. See appropriate wiring diagram in REMOTE KEYLESS ENTRY SYSTEMS article. If wire is okay, replace LCM.

NATURAL GAS VEHICLE MODULE DTC INDEX

DTC	Description	Test
B1291	Fuel Tank Pressure Sensor Circuit Failure	1
B1220	Fuel Tank Pressure Sensor Circuit Short To Voltage	1
B1222	Fuel Tank Temperature Sensor No. 1 Circuit Failure	1
B1223	Fuel Tank Temperature Sensor No. 1 Circuit Open	1
B1224	Fuel Tank Temperature Sensor No. 1 Circuit Short To Voltage	1
B1225	Fuel Tank Temperature Sensor No. 1 Circuit Short To Ground	1
B1226	Fuel Tank Temperature Sensor No. 2 Circuit Failure	1
B1227	Fuel Tank Temperature Sensor No. 2 Circuit Open	1
B1228	Fuel Tank Temperature Sensor No. 2 Circuit Short To Voltage	1
B1229	Fuel Tank Temperature Sensor No. 2 Circuit Short To Ground	1
B1317	Battery Voltage High	1
B1318	Battery Voltage Low	1
B1342	ECU Defective	1

1 – See ANALOG INSTRUMENT PANELS – CROWN VICTORIA & GRAND MARQUIS article.

FORD
4-254

1999 ACCESSORIES & EQUIPMENT
Module Communications Network
Crown Victoria & Grand Marquis (Cont.)

PASSIVE ANTI-THEFT SYSTEM MODULE DTC INDEX

DTC	Description	Test
B1213	Anti-Theft Number Of Programmed Keys Is Below Minimum	1 2
B1232/B2103	PATS Transceiver Antenna Not Connected	2
B1600	PATS Ignition Key Transponder Signal Not Received/Damaged Encoded Ignition Key Or Use Of Non-PATS Key	2
B1601	PATS Received Incorrect Key Code From Ignition Key Transponder	2
B1602	Invalid Key Code Format From Ignition Key Transponder	2
B1681	PATS Transceiver Signal Is Not Received	2
B2139	Security Identification Does Not Match Between PATS & PCM	2
B2141	No Security Identification Exchange Between PATS & PCM	2
U1147	Invalid Or Missing Data For Vehicle Security	2
U1262	SCP Bus Communication Fault	3

[1] – If DTCs B1232, B1600, B1601, B1602 OR B1681 are also present, service these DTCs first then recheck codes.
[2] – See PASSIVE ANTI-THEFT SYSTEMS – CROWN VICTORIA & GRAND MARQUIS article.
[3] – Repair SCP bus communications concern. Perform TEST J: NO MODULE/NETWORK COMMUNICATIONS – BUS LINK under SYSTEM TESTS.

PARAMETER IDENTIFICATION (PID) DEFINITIONS

ANTI-LOCK BRAKE SYSTEM PID INDEX

PID	Description	Expected Value
CCNTABS	Number Of Continuous DTCs	Number Of DTCs
BOO_SW	Brake Peal Position Switch Input	ON, OFF
T/A_VAL	T/A Control Valve	ON, OFF
ABSRR_O	Right Rear ABS Outlet Valve	1
ABSLR_O	Left Rear ABS Outlet Valve	1
ABSRF_O	Right Front ABS Outlet Valve	1
ABSLF_O	Left Front ABS Outlet Valve	1
ABSRF_I	Right Front ABS Inlet Valve	1
ABSLF_I	Left Front ABS Inlet Valve	1
ABSRR_I	Right Rear ABS Inlet Valve	1
ABSLR_I	Left Rear ABS Inlet Valve	1
LF_WSPD	Left Front Wheel Speed Signal	0-255 KPH
RF_WSPD	Right Front Wheel Speed Signal	0-255 KPH
LR_WSPD	Left Rear Wheel Speed Signal	0-255 KPH
RR_WSPD	Right Rear Wheel Speed Signal	0-255 KPH

[1] – Expected value should be OFF- - , OFFO- -, OFF-B-, OFF- - G, OFFO-G, OFFOB-, OFF-BG, OFFOBG, ON- - -, ONO- - -, ON-B-, ON- - G, ONO-G, ONOB-, ON-BG or ONOBG

DRIVER'S DOOR MODULE PID INDEX

PID	Description	Expected Value
CCNT_DD	Number Of Continuous DTCs In DDM	Number Of DTCs
KEYCODE	Factory Keyless Entry Code	5 Digits
D_DR_DD	Driver's Door Ajar Switch	AJAR, CLOSED
DLIDRLS	Deck Lid Release Switch	ON, OFF
D_PW_SW	Driver's Power Window Switch	UP, DOWN, OFF, SHORT
DD_LOCK	Driver's Door Lock Output State	SHORT, LOCK, UNLOCK, OFF
P_DR_DD	Passenger's Door Ajar Switch	CLOSED, AJAR
VBAT_DD	Battery Voltage	UDR0V, OVR5V, ####Volts
D_WINDO	Driver's Window Switch	DOWN, NOT DOWN
IGN_DD	Ignition Switch	ACCY, RUN, START, OFF
KEY_PAD	Driver's Keyless Entry Switch	1, 3, 5, 7, 9
D_SEAT	Driver's Seat Occupied Switch	NOTOCC, OCCUPD
P/N_SW	Transmission Switch Input	NOTP/N, P/N
TRANSGR	Transmission Gear Position	REV, NOTREV

ELECTRONIC CRASH SENSOR MODULE PID INDEX

PID	Description	Expected Value
CCNTECS	Number Of Continuous DTCs	Number Of DTCs
DABAGR	Driver's Air Bag Circuit Resistance	Ohms
PABAGR	Passenger's Air Bag Circuit Resistance	Ohms
BRACKET	Bracket Ground Resistance	Ohms
VBATECS	System Battery Voltage	Volts

LIGHTING CONTROL MODULE PID INDEX

PID	Description	Expected Value
ALARMSW	Security Input	ON, OFF
ALP_INP	Autolamp Analog Input	Percent

1999 ACCESSORIES & EQUIPMENT
Module Communications Network
Crown Victoria & Grand Marquis (Cont.)

FORD
4-255

LIGHTING CONTROL MODULE PID INDEX (Cont.)

PID	Description	Expected Value
AUTOLMP	Autolamp Switch	ON, OFF
CCNT_LC	Number Of Continuous DTCs	Number Of DTCs
CHIMERQ	Chime Request	ON, OFF
D_DR_LC	Driver's Door Ajar Switch	CLOSED, AJAR
D_SBELT	Driver's Seat Belt	IN, OUT
DECKLID	Decklid/Hatch Ajar Switch	CLOSED, AJAR
DOMESW	Dome Light Switch	ON, OFF
DD_LOCK	Driver's Door Lock	OFF, LOCK
DR_UNLK	All Door Unlock Output State	YES, NO
FLSHPWR	Turn Signal Power	NOTACT, ACTIVE
HDLMPSW	Low Beam Switch	ON, OFF
IGN_A	Ignition Switch (ACC Position)	YES, NO
IGN_KEY	Ignition Key In/Out	IN, OUT
IGN_R	Ignition Switch (RUN Position)	YES, NO
IGN_S	Ignition Switch (START Position)	YES, NO
INST_LT	Instrumentation Variable Volume Output	Percent
LATCHIO	Latch Mode Transitions	One Count Per Bit
LIGHTSN	Ambient Light	YES, NO
LR_LOCK	Left Rear Lock	NOTLOC, LOCK
LRDR_SW	Left Rear Door Ajar Switch	CLOSED, AJAR
P_DR_LC	Passenger's Door Ajar Switch	CLOSED, AJAR
PARK_SW	Parking Switch	ON, OFF
PD_LOCK	Passenger's Door Lock	NOTLOC, LOCK
DIM_DEC	Panel Dim Intensity Switch	ON, OFF
DIM_INC	Panel Dim Intensity Switch	ON, OFF
INTR_LT	Interior Lighting	Percent
PWN_DC1	PWM Duty Cycle Switch #1	Percent
RDEF_SW	Rear Defogger Switch	ON, OFF
RR_LOCK	Right Rear Lock	NOTLOC, LOCK
RRDR_SW	Right Rear Door Ajar Switch	CLOSED, AJAR
VBAT_LC	Battery Voltage	Volts

NATURAL GAS VEHICLE MODULE PID INDEX

PID	Description	Expected Value
CCNT_F1	Number Of Continuous DTCs	Number Of DTCs
TANKPR	Fuel Tank Pressure Sensor	0-4000 psi
TEMPS1	Fuel Tank Temperature Sensor No. 1 Input	-40-302°F
TEMPS2	Fuel Tank Temperature Sensor No. 2 Input	-40-302°F
VPWR	Battery Voltage	Voltage
GAUGESG	Instrument Cluster Fuel Gauge Drive Signal	0-4000 mV
GAUGECM	Fuel Gauge Commend Position	[1]

[1] – Fuel Gauge Position In 16ths. 2 equals empty and 18 equals full.

PASSIVE ANTI-THEFT SYSTEM MODULE PID INDEX

PID	Description	Expected Value
ACCESS	Security Access	CODE, TIMED
ANTISCN	Anti-Scan Function	DISABL, ENABLE
CCNTPAT	Number Of Continuous DTCs	One Bit Per Count
ENABL_S	Vehicle Enable Status	DISABL, ENABLE
IGN_R	Ignition Switch (RUN Position)	IN, OUT
M_KEY	Master Key Present	IN, OUT
MIN#KEY	Number Of Keys	One Bit Per Count
NUMKEYS	Number Of Keys Stored	One Bit Per Count
PCM_ID	PCM ID Status Stored	NOTSTR, STORED
PCM_VFY	PCM Verify Okay	YES, ON
SPAREKY	Spare Key Programming	DISABL, ENABLE
SERVMOD	Service Module	YES, ON

WIRING DIAGRAMS

NOTE: See appropriate wiring diagrams in DATA LINK CONNECTORS, GROUND DISTRIBUTION or POWER DISTRIBUTION article in WIRING DIAGRAMS.

DESCRIPTION & OPERATION

Vehicle has 2 module communications networks. The module communications network provides the ability for module-to-module communication by sharing inputs and outputs instead of each component having an input and output wired directly to each module. A BUS which consists of a pair of twisted wires is used to transfer information between each module. The BUS network is also referred to as Standard Corporate Protocol (SCP) network. The BUS consists of a (+) circuit No. 914 and a (–) circuit No. 915. The BUS is routed throughout the vehicle to the Powertrain Control Module (PCM) and on natural gas vehicles, the Natural Gas Vehicle Module (NGVM).

The air bag diagnostic monitor and the 4-Wheel Anti-Lock Brake System (4WABS) module do not use the BUS to communicate with other modules. The air bag diagnostic monitor and 4WABS module are connected to the International Standards Organization (ISO) 9141 diagnostic communications network through a single wire (circuit No. 70). Both networks are connected to the Data Link Connector (DLC). This article is used to diagnose BUS and ISO communications network circuit faults. For module locations, see COMPONENT LOCATIONS table.

COMPONENT LOCATIONS

COMPONENT LOCATIONS

Component	Location
Air Bag Diagnostic Monitor [1]	Behind Right Kick Panel
Auxiliary Powertrain Control Module	Below Left Side Of Instrument Panel
Data Link Connector	Below Driver's Side Of Instrument Panel, To Right Of Steering Column
Natural Gas Vehicle Module	Left Side Of Engine Compartment, On Inner Fender
Powertrain Control Module	Left Rear Of Engine Compartment, Near Brake Master Cylinder
4-Wheel Anti-Lock Brake Module	On Left Front Frame Rail

[1] – Air bag diagnostic monitor may also be referred to as Electronic Crash Sensor (ECS) module.

REPAIRING BUS WIRING

NOTE: *Following procedure must be used to ensure proper repair is performed on BUS wiring. BUS wiring is sensitive to moisture and oxidation and must be properly sealed to ensure proper operation of the module communications network. Regular heat shrink tubing is NOT sufficient, heat shrink tubing containing hot melt wax is required.*

1) When performing a repair on the BUS wiring, ensure the wires on the BUS are twisted at a rate of 33-40 winds per 3.3 ft. (1 m). The twists should start approximately 4.9" (124 mm) from any connector. Use only 20 AWG standard wire gauge for repairs.
2) If performing a splice in the wiring, strip .75" (19.0 mm) of insulation from one wire and 1.50" (38.1 mm) of insulation from the other wire. Perform STEP 1. *See Fig. 1.* Place hot melt wax type heat shrink tubing over one wire.
3) Twist stripped portion of the wires together. Solder connection using resin core RMA solder. DO NOT use acid core solder. Bend wires to allow installation of heat shrink tubing. Perform STEP 2. *See Fig. 1.*
4) Position heat shrink tubing over splice area. Using heat gun, evenly heat the heat shrink tubing until wax flows from both ends of heat shrink tubing.

COMMUNICATION NETWORK DIAGNOSTICS

INSPECTION & VERIFICATION

1) Verify customer's original problem by operating system in question. Inspect vehicle for any obvious electrical component wiring or connector

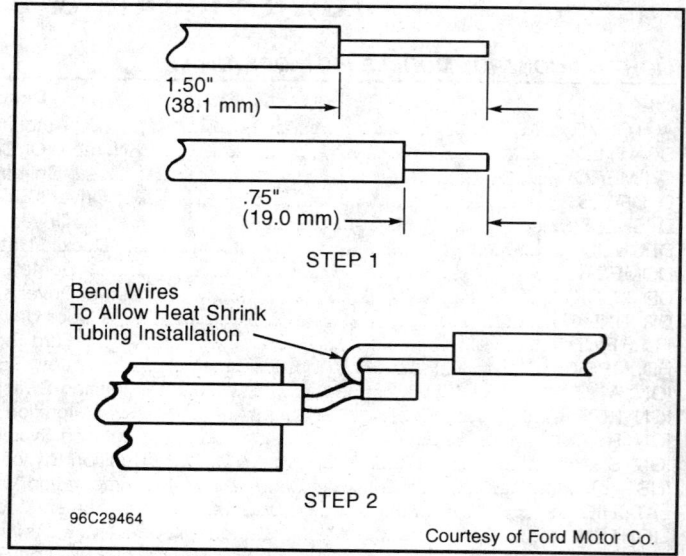

Fig. 1: Repairing BUS Wiring

damage. Inspect connectors for loose, damaged or corroded terminals. Check related fuses for system in question.
2) Inspect 16-pin Data Link Connector (DLC) pins for damage. *See Fig. 2.* The DLC is located below driver's side of instrument panel, to the right of steering column. If pins are okay, go to next step. If pins are damaged, repair as necessary and proceed to next step.
3) If problem is still present after performing inspection, connect New Generation Star (NGS) tester to DLC. Select vehicle to be tested from NGS tester menu. If NGS tester does not communicate with vehicle, ensure program card is properly installed. Check NGS tester cable connections and ensure ignition is on. If NGS tester still does not communicate with vehicle, go to TEST H: NO MODULE/NETWORK COMMUNICATION under TESTING. If NGS tester communicates with vehicle, perform data link diagnostic procedure. See DATA LINK DIAGNOSTIC TEST.

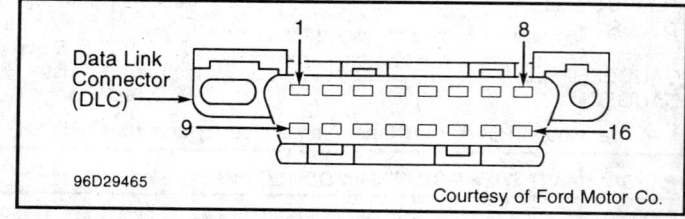

Fig. 2: Identifying Data Link Connector (DLC) Terminals

DATA LINK DIAGNOSTIC TEST

1) Connect New Generation Star (NGS) tester to Data Link Connector (DLC), if not already connected. Select vehicle to be tested from NGS tester menu.
2) Turn ignition on. Rotate dial on NGS tester to menu item DIAGNOSTIC DATA LINK and press trigger. A test will be performed on the BUS (circuits No. 914 and 915) for the module communications network and the ISO 9141 communication network (circuit No. 70). This is the Light Blue/White wire that is between terminal No. 7 on DLC, air bag diagnostic monitor and 4WABS module.
3) If NGS tester displays CKT 914 (+) = SYSTEM PASSED and CKT 915 (–) = SYSTEM PASSED, module communications network is okay. If NGS tester displays CKT 70 = SYSTEM PASSED, ISO 9141 communication network is operating properly. Return to article that directed you here and continue diagnosis.
4) If NGS tester does not display CKT 914 (+) = SYSTEM PASSED, CKT 915 (–) = SYSTEM PASSED and CKT 70 = SYSTEM PASSED, perform the following as applicable:
- If no response from NGS tester, go to TEST H: NO MODULE/ NETWORK COMMUNICATION under TESTING.

- If NGS tester displays CKT 70, CKT 914 and/or CKT 915 = SOME ECUS NO RESP/NOT EQUIP, go to SYMPTOM INDEX table to continue diagnosis.
- If NGS tester displays CKT 70 = ALL ECUS NO RESP/NOT EQUIP, go to TEST F: NO MODULE/NETWORK COMMUNICATION – ISO 9141 NETWORK under TESTING.
- If NGS tester displays CKT 914 = ALL ECUS NO RESP/NOT EQUIP, go to TEST G: NO MODULE/NETWORK COMMUNICATION – SCP NETWORK under TESTING.
- If NGS tester displays CKT 915 = ALL ECUS NO RESP/NOT EQUIP, go to TEST G: NO MODULE/NETWORK COMMUNICATION – SCP NETWORK under TESTING.
- If module in question is NO RESPONSE/NOT EQUIPPED, go to SYMPTOM INDEX table to continue diagnosis.
- If module in question is NO RESPONSE ON CKT 914 (BUS +), go to SYMPTOM INDEX table under SYSTEM TESTING to continue diagnosis.
- If module in question is NO RESPONSE ON CKT 915 (BUS –), go to SYMPTOM INDEX table under SYSTEM TESTING to continue diagnosis.

RETRIEVING & CLEARING DIAGNOSTIC TROUBLE CODES

Connect New Generation Star (NGS) tester to Data Link Connector (DLC). Following manufacturers instructions to retrieve and clear codes for desired module. See appropriate table under DIAGNOSTIC TROUBLE CODE (DTC) DEFINITIONS for a listing of Diagnostic Trouble Codes (DTCs) and appropriate test procedure.

ACCESSING PARAMETER IDENTIFICATION (PID)

Turn ignition switch to LOCK position. Connect New Generation Star (NGS) tester to Data Link Connector (DLC). Following manufacturers instructions enter PID/DATA MONITOR AND RECORD for desired module. Operate appropriate system and ensure PID expected values are obtained. See appropriate table under PARAMETER IDENTIFICATION (PID) DEFINITIONS.

SYSTEM TESTING

NOTE: Always check module power and ground circuits prior to replacing a control module. See appropriate wiring diagram in DATA LINK CONNECTORS, GROUND DISTRIBUTION or POWER DISTRIBUTION article in WIRING DIAGRAMS.

SYMPTOM INDEX

Condition	Test
4-Wheel Anti-Lock Brake System (4WABS) Module Does Not Respond To NGS Tester	A
Air Bag Diagnostic Monitor Does Not Respond To NGS Tester [1]	B
Powertrain Control Module (PCM) Does Not Respond To NGS Tester	C
Auxiliary Powertrain Control Module (APCM) Does Not Respond To NGS Tester	D
Natural Gas Vehicle Module (NGVM) Does Not Respond To NGS Tester	E
No Module/Network Communications – ISO 9141 Network	F
No Module/Network Communications – SCP Network	G
No Module/Network Communication	H

[1] – Air bag diagnostic monitor may also be referred to as air bag Electronic Crash Sensor (ECS) module.

TEST A: 4-WHEEL ANTI-LOCK BRAKE SYSTEM (4WABS) MODULE DOES NOT RESPOND TO NGS TESTER

1) Turn ignition off. Disconnect 4WABS module 24-pin connector, located on left front frame rail. Inspect connector for loose, damaged or corroded terminals. Repair connector as necessary and retest system for normal operation. If connector is okay, go to next step.

2) Measure resistance of Light Blue/White wire between terminal No. 5 at 4WABS module connector and terminal No. 7 at DLC. See Figs. 2 and 3. If resistance is 5 ohms or more, go to next step. If resistance is less than 5 ohms, replace 4WABS module and retest system for normal operation.

3) Disconnect Natural 76-pin connector C234 located on driver's side of engine compartment on firewall. Inspect connector for loose, damaged or corroded terminals. Repair connector as necessary and retest system for normal operation. If connector is okay, go to next step.

4) Measure resistance of Light Blue/White wire between terminal No. 43 at female half of connector C234 and terminal No. 7 at DLC. See Figs. 2 and 4. If resistance is less than 5 ohms, repair open Light Blue/White wire between 4WABS module connector and connector C234. If resistance is 5 ohms or more, repair Light Blue/White wire between DLC and connector C234. Retest system for normal operation.

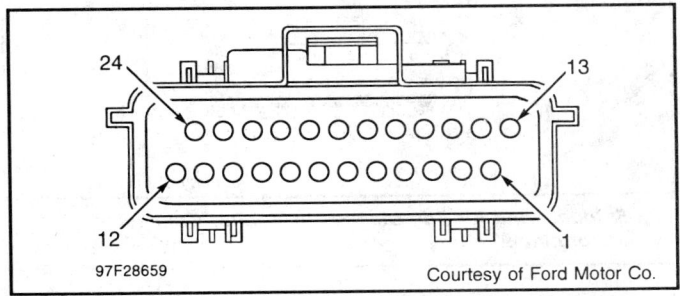

97F28659 Courtesy of Ford Motor Co.

Fig. 3: Identifying 4WABS Module Connector Terminals

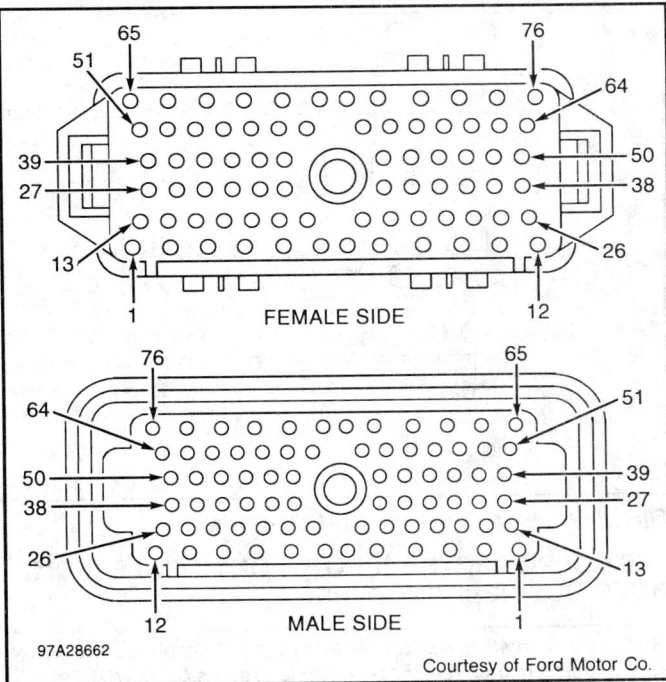

97A28662 Courtesy of Ford Motor Co.

Fig. 4: Identifying Connector C234 Terminals

TEST B: AIR BAG DIAGNOSTIC MONITOR DOES NOT RESPOND TO NGS

1) Turn ignition off. Deactivate air bag system. See AIR BAG RESTRAINT SYSTEMS – ECONOLINE article. Disconnect air bag diagnostic monitor Gray 28-pin connector located behind right kick panel. Inspect connector for loose, damaged or corroded terminals. Repair connector as necessary and retest system for normal operation. If connector is okay, go to next step.

2) Measure resistance of Light Blue/White wire between terminal No. 19 at air bag diagnostic monitor connector and terminal No. 7 at DLC. See

Figs. 2 and 5. If resistance is 5 ohms or more, go to next step. If resistance is less than 5 ohms, replace air bag diagnostic monitor and retest system for normal operation.

3) Disconnect Black 14-pin connector C201 located behind right kick panel. Inspect connector for loose, damaged or corroded terminals. Repair connector as necessary and retest system for normal operation. If connector is okay, go to next step.

4) Measure resistance of Light Blue/White wire between terminal No. 2 at connector C201 and terminal No. 7 at DLC. *See Figs. 2 and 6.* If resistance is less than 5 ohms, repair open Light Blue/White wire between female half of connector C201 and air bag diagnostic monitor connector. Retest system for normal operation. If resistance is 5 ohms or more, repair open Light Blue/White wire between male half of connector C201 and DLC. Retest system for normal operation.

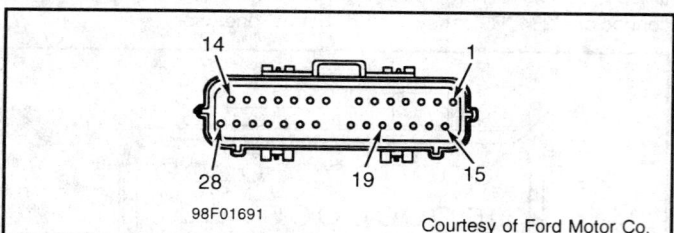

98F01691

Courtesy of Ford Motor Co.

Fig. 5: Identifying Air Bag Diagnostic Monitor Connector Terminals

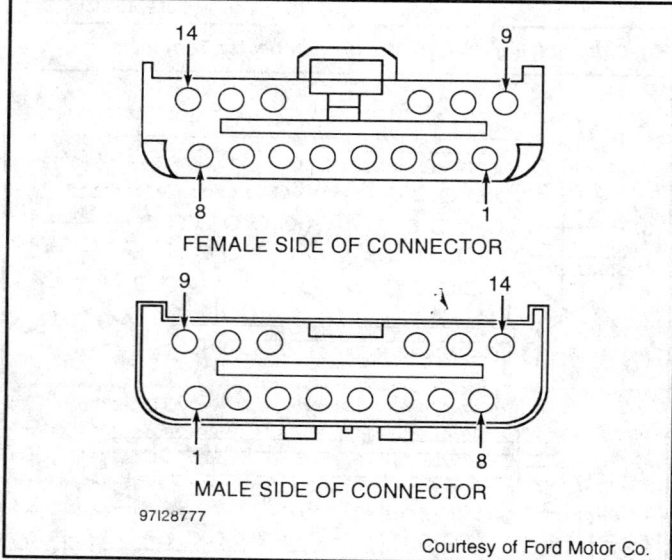

FEMALE SIDE OF CONNECTOR

MALE SIDE OF CONNECTOR

97I28777

Courtesy of Ford Motor Co.

Fig. 6: Identifying Connector C201 Terminals

TEST C: POWERTRAIN CONTROL MODULE (PCM) DOES NOT RESPOND TO NGS

NOTE: If test results indicate PCM is faulty, always check for any engine performance related Diagnostic Trouble Codes (DTCs) prior to replacing PCM. If any DTCs are present, service DTCs as necessary and retest. See appropriate SELF-DIAGNOSTICS article in ENGINE PERFORMANCE in appropriate MITCHELL® manual.

1) Turn ignition off. Disconnect PCM connector located in left rear of engine compartment, near brake master cylinder. Inspect connector for loose, damaged or corroded terminals. Repair connector as necessary and retest system for normal operation. If connector is okay, go to next step.

2) Using an ohmmeter, measure resistance of Tan/Orange wire between terminal No. 16 at PCM connector and terminal No. 2 at Data Link Connector (DLC). *See Figs. 2 and 7.* Also, measure resistance of Pink/Light Blue wire between terminal No. 15 at PCM connector and terminal No. 10 at DLC. If both resistance readings are less than 5

ohms, replace PCM and retest system for normal operation. If any resistance reading is 5 ohms or more, go to next step.

3) Disconnect Natural 76-pin connector C234 located on driver's side of engine compartment on firewall. Inspect connector for loose, damaged or corroded terminals. Repair connector as necessary and retest system for normal operation. If connector is okay, go to next step.

4) Measure resistance of Tan/Orange wire between terminal No. 61 at female half of connector C234 and terminal No. 2 at DLC. *See Figs. 2 and 4.* Also, measure resistance of Pink/Light Blue wire between terminal No. 59 at female half of connector C234 and terminal No. 10 at DLC. If both resistance readings are less than 5 ohms, repair open Tan/Orange wire and/or Pink/Light Blue wire between PCM connector and male half of connector C234. Retest system for normal operation. If any resistance reading is 5 ohms or more, repair open Tan/Orange wire and/or Pink/Light Blue wire between female half of connector C234 and DLC. Retest system for normal operation.

TEST D: AUXILIARY POWERTRAIN CONTROL MODULE (APCM) DOES NOT RESPOND TO NGS

1) Turn ignition off. Disconnect APCM connector located below left side of instrument panel. Inspect connector for loose, damaged or corroded terminals. Repair connector as necessary and retest system for normal operation. If connector is okay, go to next step.

2) Using an ohmmeter, measure resistance of Tan/Orange wire between terminal No. 1 at APCM connector and terminal No. 2 at Data Link Connector (DLC). *See Figs. 2 and 8.* Also, measure resistance of Pink/Light Blue wire between terminal No. 3 at APCM connector and terminal No. 10 at DLC. If both resistance readings are less than 5 ohms, replace APCM and retest system for normal operation. If any resistance reading is 5 ohms or more, repair open Tan/Orange wire and/or Pink/Light Blue wire between APCM connector and DLC. Retest system for normal operation.

TEST E: NATURAL GAS VEHICLE MODULE (NGVM) DOES NOT RESPOND TO NGS

1) Turn ignition off. Disconnect NGVM connector located left side of engine compartment, on inner fender. Inspect connector for loose, damaged or corroded terminals. Repair connector as necessary and retest system for normal operation. If connector is okay, go to next step.

2) Using an ohmmeter, measure resistance of Tan/Orange wire between terminal No. 19 at NGVM connector and terminal No. 2 at Data Link Connector (DLC). *See Figs. 2 and 9.* Also, measure resistance of Pink/Light Blue wire between terminal No. 18 at NGVM connector and terminal No. 10 at DLC. If both resistance readings are less than 5 ohms, replace NGVM and retest system for normal operation. If any resistance reading is 5 ohms or more, go to next step.

3) Disconnect Natural 76-pin connector C234 located on driver's side of engine compartment on firewall. Inspect connector for loose, damaged or corroded terminals. Repair connector as necessary and retest system for normal operation. If connector is okay, go to next step.

4) Measure resistance of Tan/Orange wire between terminal No. 61 at female half of connector C234 and terminal No. 2 at DLC. *See Figs. 2 and 4.* Also, measure resistance of Pink/Light Blue wire between terminal No. 59 at female half of connector C234 and terminal No. 10 at DLC. If both resistance readings are less than 5 ohms, repair open Tan/Orange wire and/or Pink/Light Blue wire between NGVM connector and male half of connector C234. Retest system for normal operation. If any resistance reading is 5 ohms or more, repair open Tan/Orange wire and/or Pink/Light Blue wire between female half of connector C234 and DLC. Retest system for normal operation.

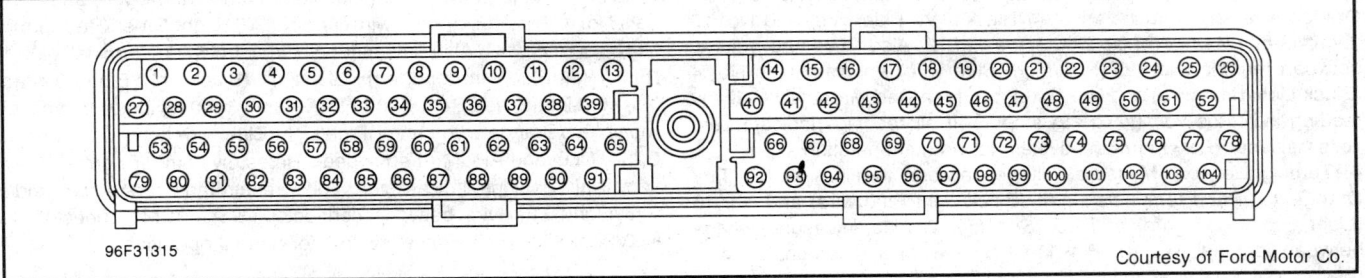

96F31315

Courtesy of Ford Motor Co.

Fig. 7: Identifying PCM Connector Terminals

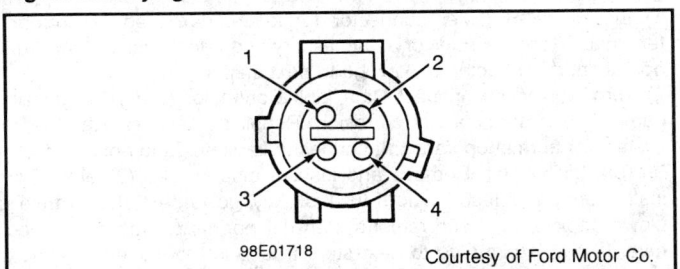

98E01718

Courtesy of Ford Motor Co.

Fig. 8: Identifying APCM Connector Terminals

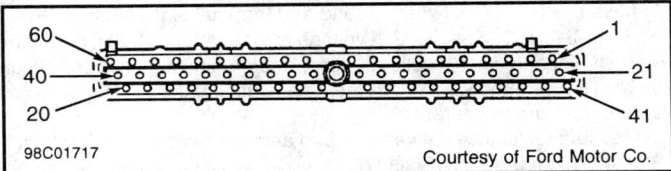

98C01717

Courtesy of Ford Motor Co.

Fig. 9: Identifying NGVM Connector Terminals

TEST F: NO MODULE/NETWORK COMMUNICATIONS – ISO 9141 NETWORK

NOTE: Depending on module configuration, with all modules connected and with ignition switch in RUN position or with engine running 2-3 volts may be present at Data Link Connector (DLC) terminal No. 7 (Light Blue/White wire). This is the International Standards Organization (ISO) 9141 diagnostic communications network circuit.

1) Turn ignition off. Inspect Data Link Connector (DLC) for physical damage, bent terminals or corrosion. Pay particular attention to terminal No. 7 (Light Blue/White wire). Repair connector as necessary and retest system for normal operation. If connector is okay, go to next step.

2) Deactivate air bag system. See AIR BAG RESTRAINT SYSTEMS – ECONOLINE article. Disconnect air bag diagnostic monitor connector located behind right kick panel. Measure resistance of Light Blue/White wire between terminal No. 19 at air bag diagnostic monitor connector and terminal No. 7 at DLC. If resistance is less than 5 ohms, go to next step (if not equipped with 4WABS module) or go to step **5)** (if equipped with 4WABS module).

3) Turn ignition on. Measure voltage between terminals No. 7 (Light Blue/White wire) and No. 16 at DLC. *See Fig. 2.* Also, measure voltage between terminals No. 7 (Light Blue/White wire) and No. 4 (Black/Light Blue wire) at DLC. If any reading indicates voltage, go to next step. If both readings indicate zero volts, replace air bag diagnostic monitor and retest system for normal operation.

4) Turn ignition off. Disconnect Black 14-pin connector C201 located behind right kick panel. Turn ignition on. Measure voltage between terminals No. 7 (Light Blue/White wire) and No. 16 (Light Green/Red wire) at DLC. *See Fig. 2.* Also, measure voltage between terminals No. 7 (Light Blue/White wire) and No. 4 (Black/Light Blue wire) at DLC. If any reading indicates voltage, repair Light Blue/White wire between connector C201, connector C234 (if equipped with 4WABS) and DLC. Retest system for normal operation. If both readings indicate zero volts, repair

Light Blue/White wire between connector C201 and air bag diagnostic monitor. Retest system for normal operation.

5) Turn ignition on. Measure voltage between terminals No. 7 (Light Blue/White wire) and No. 16 (Light Green/Red wire) at DLC. *See Fig. 2.* Also, measure voltage between terminals No. 7 (Light Blue/White wire) and No. 4 (Black/Light Blue wire) at DLC. If any reading indicates voltage, go to next step. If both readings indicate zero volts, replace air bag diagnostic monitor and retest system for normal operation.

6) Turn ignition off. Disconnect 4WABS module 24-pin connector, located on left front frame rail. Turn ignition on. Measure voltage between terminals No. 7 (Light Blue/White wire) and No. 16 (Light Green/Red wire) at DLC. *See Fig. 2.* Also, measure voltage between terminals No. 7 (Light Blue/White wire) and No. 4 (Black/Light Blue wire) at DLC. If any reading indicates voltage, go to next step. If both readings indicate zero volts, replace 4WABS module.

7) Turn ignition off. Disconnect Natural 76-pin connector C234 located on driver's side of engine compartment on firewall. Turn ignition on. Measure voltage between terminals No. 7 (Light Blue/White wire) and No. 16 (Light Green/Red wire) at DLC. *See Fig. 2.* Also, measure voltage between terminals No. 7 (Light Blue/White wire) and No. 4 (Black/Light Blue wire) at DLC. If any reading indicates voltage, go to step **4)**. If both readings indicate zero volts, repair Light Blue/White wire between connector C234 and 4WABS module connector. Retest system for normal operation.

TEST G: NO MODULE/NETWORK COMMUNICATIONS – SCP NETWORK

NOTE: Depending on module configuration, with all modules connected and with ignition switch in RUN position or with engine running 2-3 volts may be present at Data Link Connector (DLC) terminals No. 2 (Tan/Orange wire) and No. 10 (Pink/Light Blue wire). These are the Standard Corporate Protocol (SCP) diagnostic communications network circuits.

1) Turn ignition off. Inspect Data Link Connector (DLC) for physical damage, bent terminals or corrosion. Pay particular attention to terminals No. 2 (Tan/Orange wire) and No. 10 (Pink/Light Blue wire). *See Fig. 2.* Repair connector as necessary and retest system for normal operation. If connector is okay, go to next step.

2) Disconnect PCM connector located in left rear of engine compartment, near brake master cylinder. Measure resistance of Tan/Orange wire between terminal No. 16 at PCM connector and terminal No. 2 at DLC. *See Figs. 2 and 7.* Also, measure resistance of Pink/Light Blue wire between terminal No. 15 at PCM connector and terminal No. 10 at DLC. If both resistance readings are less than 5 ohms, go to next step (vehicles with PCM only) or go to step **4)** (vehicles with natural gas vehicle module or auxiliary powertrain control module). If any resistance reading is 5 ohms or more, proceed as follows.

- On vehicles with Powertrain Control Module (PCM) and/or Natural Gas Vehicle Module (NGVM), go to TEST C: POWERTRAIN CONTROL MODULE (PCM) DOES NOT RESPOND TO NGS.
- On vehicles with Auxiliary Powertrain Control Module (APCM), repair open Tan/Orange wire and/or Pink/Light Blue wire between female half of connector C234 and DLC. Retest system for normal operation.

3) Turn ignition on. Measure voltage between terminal No. 2 (Tan/Orange wire) and terminals No. 4 (Black/Light Blue wire) and No. 16 (Light Green/Red wire) at DLC. *See Fig. 2.* Also, measure voltage between terminal No. 10 (Pink/Light Blue wire) and terminals No. 4 (Black/Light Blue wire) and No. 16 (Light Green/Red wire) at DLC. If any reading indicates voltage, go to step **7)**. If all readings indicate zero volts, replace PCM and retest system for normal operation.

4) Turn ignition on. Measure voltage between terminal No. 2 (Tan/Orange wire) and terminals No. 4 (Black/Light Blue wire) and No. 16 (Light Green/Red wire) at DLC. *See Fig. 2.* Also, measure voltage between terminal No. 10 (Pink/Light Blue wire) and terminals No. 4 (Black/Light Blue wire) and No. 16 (Light Green/Red wire) at DLC. If any reading indicates voltage, go to next step (vehicles with auxiliary powertrain control module) or go to step **6)** (vehicles with natural gas vehicle module). If all readings indicate zero volts, replace PCM and retest system for normal operation.

5) Turn ignition off. Disconnect Auxiliary Powertrain Control Module (APCM) connector located below left side of instrument panel. Turn ignition on. Measure voltage between terminal No. 2 (Tan/Orange wire) and terminals No. 4 (Black/Light Blue wire) and No. 16 (Light Green/Red wire) at DLC. *See Fig. 2.* Also, measure voltage between terminal No. 10 (Pink/Light Blue wire) and terminals No. 4 (Black/Light Blue wire) and No. 16 (Light Green/Red wire) at DLC. If any reading indicates voltage, go to step **7)**. If all readings indicate zero volts, replace APCM and retest system for normal operation.

6) Turn ignition off. Disconnect Natural Gas Vehicle Module (NGVM) connector located on left side of engine compartment, on inner fender. Turn ignition on. Measure voltage between terminal No. 2 (Tan/Orange wire) and terminals No. 4 (Black/Light Blue wire) and No. 16 (Light Green/Red wire) at DLC. *See Fig. 2.* Also, measure voltage between terminal No. 10 (Pink/Light Blue wire) and terminals No. 4 (Black/Light Blue wire) and No. 16 (Light Green/Red wire) at DLC. If any reading indicates voltage, go to next step. If all readings indicate zero volts, replace NGVM and retest system for normal operation.

7) Turn ignition off. Disconnect Natural 76-pin connector C234 located on driver's side of engine compartment on firewall. Turn ignition on.

Measure voltage between terminal No. 2 (Tan/Orange wire) and terminals No. 4 (Black/Light Blue wire) and No. 16 (Light Green/Red wire) at DLC. *See Fig. 2.* Also, measure voltage between terminal No. 10 (Pink/Light Blue wire) and terminals No. 4 (Black/Light Blue wire) and No. 16 (Light Green/Red wire) at DLC. If any reading indicates voltage, repair Tan/Orange wire and/or Pink/Light Blue wire between connector C234, DLC and APCM (if equipped). Retest system for normal operation. If all readings indicate zero volts, repair Tan/Orange wire and/or Pink/Light Blue wire between connector C234, PCM connector and NGVM (if equipped). Retest system for normal operation.

TEST H: NO MODULE/NETWORK COMMUNICATION

1) Inspect NGS tester connector for loose, damaged or corroded terminals. Repair connector as necessary and retest system for normal operation. If connector is okay, go to next step.

2) Turn ignition off. Inspect Data Link Connector (DLC) for physical damage, bent terminals or corrosion. Repair as necessary and retest system for normal operation. If connector is okay, go to next step.

3) Turn ignition off. Remove and inspect fuse No. 23 (20-amp) from instrument panel fuse block. If fuse is okay, go to next step. If fuse is blown, replace fuse and retest system for normal operation. Recheck fuse. If fuse is okay, go to next step. If fuse is blown, repair short to ground in circuit No. 1047 (Light Green/Red wire) between instrument panel fuse block and DLC. Retest system for normal operation.

4) Measure voltage between ground and terminal No. 16 (Light Green/Red wire) at DLC. *See Fig. 2.* If voltage is more than 10 volts, go to next step. If voltage is 10 volts or less, repair circuit No. 1047 (Light Green/Red wire) between instrument panel fuse block and DLC. Retest system for normal operation.

5) Measure resistance between ground and terminals No. 4 (Black/Light Blue wire) and No. 5 (Black/White wire) at DLC. If both resistance readings are less than 5 ohms, repair or replace NGS tester. Retest system for normal operation. If any resistance reading is 5 ohms or more, repair open in Black/Light Blue wire or Black/White wire between ground and DLC. Retest system for normal operation.

DIAGNOSTIC TROUBLE CODE (DTC) DEFINITIONS

AIR BAG DIAGNOSTIC MONITOR DTC INDEX [1]

DTC [2]	Description	Test
B1671	Battery Voltage Out Of Range	3
B1914	Primary Crash Sensor Short To Ground	3
B1915	Driver's Air Bag Circuit Failure	3
B1920	Passenger's Air Bag Circuit Failure	3
B1876	Drive Belt & Buckle Assembly Pretensioner Circuit Short To Ground	3
B1880	Drive Belt & Buckle Assembly Pretensioner Circuit Short To Ground	3
B1231	Crash Event Detected	3
B1921	ECS Bracket Ground Resistance High	3
B1342	ECS Defective	3
C1415	Incorrect Module Configuration	3
B1932	Driver's Side Air Bag Circuit Resistance High	3
B1933	Passenger's Side Air Bag Circuit Resistance High	3
B1887	Driver's Side Air Bag Circuit Short To Ground	3
B1888	Passenger's Side Air Bag Circuit Bag Short To Ground	3
B1941	Primary Crash Sensor Feed/Return Circuit Open	3
B1230	Driver's Drive Belt & Buckle Assembly Pretensioner Circuit Resistance Out Of Range	3
B1232	Passenger's Drive Belt & Buckle Assembly Pretensioner Circuit Resistance Out Of Range	3
B1868	Air Bag Warning Indicator Circuit Failure	3

[1] – Air Bag Diagnostic Monitor may also be referred to as Electronic Crash Sensor (ECS) module.
[2] – DTCs are listed in order of importance. Repair DTCs in order listed.
[3] – Repair supplemental restraint system as necessary. See DIAGNOSIS & TESTING article in appropriate MITCHELL® AIR BAG SERVICE & REPAIR MANUAL, DOMESTIC & IMPORTED MODELS.

AUDIO CONTROL MODULE (ACM) DTC INDEX

DTC	Description	Test
B1342	ECU Defective	1
B2401	Tape Deck Mechanism Fault	2
B2402	CD/DJ Thermal Shutdown	3
B2403	CD/DJ Internal Fault	3
B2404	Steering Wheel Switch Circuit Fault	4
B2405	Single Disc Player Thermal Shutdown	4
B2406	Single Disc Player Internal Fault	4
U2003	CD/DJ Is Not Responding	3
U2005	Rear Integrated Control Panel Is Not Responding	4
U2014	Subwoofer Unit Is Not Responding	4

[1] – Using NGS tester, clear and document continuous DTCs. Perform Audio Control Module (ACM) self-test. If DTC B1342 is retrieved again, replace ACM.

[2] – Verify No tape is in tape deck. Using NGS tester, clear and document continuous DTCs. Perform Audio Control Module (ACM) self-test. If DTC B2401 is retrieved again, repair or replace ACM as necessary.

[3] – Repair audio system fault.

[4] – DTC does not apply to this vehicle.

NATURAL GAS VEHICLE MODULE DTC INDEX

DTC	Description	Test
B1219	Fuel Tank Pressure Sensor Circuit Failure	1
B1220	Fuel Tank Pressure Sensor Circuit Short To Voltage	1
B1222	Fuel Tank Temperature Sensor Circuit Failure	1
B1223	Fuel Tank Temperature Sensor Circuit Open	1
B1224	Fuel Tank Temperature Sensor Circuit Short To Voltage	1
B1225	Fuel Tank Temperature Sensor Circuit Short To Ground	1
B1317	Battery Voltage High	1
B1318	Battery Voltage Low	1
B1342	ECU Circuit Defective	1

[1] – See ANALOG INSTRUMENT PANELS – ECONOLINE article.

4 WHEEL ANTI-LOCK BRAKE SYSTEM (4WABS) MODULE DTC INDEX

DTC	Description	Test
B1342	4WABS Module Defective	1
C1095/C1096	ABS Hydraulic Pump Motor Circuit	1
C1114/C1115	Shorted Anti-Lock Relay	1
C1145	Right Front ABS Sensor Input Circuit Failure	1
C1148/C1234	Right Front ABS Sensor Input Signal Missing	1
C1155	Left Front ABS Sensor Input Circuit Failure	1
C1158/C1233	Left Front ABS Sensor Input Signal Missing	1
C1169	Excessive Dump Time	1
C1185	Open Internal Power Relay	1
C1230	Rear ABS Sensor Input Circuit Failure	1
C1229/C1237	Rear ABS Sensor Input Signal Missing	1
C1220	Anti-Lock Warning Light Shorted	1
C1184/C1222	Wheel Speed Error	1
C1198/C1200	Open Or Shorted LF Isolation Valve Solenoid	1
C1194/C1196	Open Or Shorted LF Dump Valve Solenoid	1
C1214/C1216	Open Or Shorted RF Isolation Valve Solenoid	1
C1210/C1212	Open Or Shorted RF Dump Valve Solenoid	1
C1206/C1208	Open Or Shorted Rear Isolation Valve Solenoid	1
C1202/C1204	Open Or Shorted Rera Dump Valve Solenoid	1
C1226	Faulty Red Brake Warning Indicator	1
C1225	Sorted Red Brake Warning Indicator Relay	1

[1] – Repair 4 Wheel Anti-Lock Brake System (4WABS). See appropriate ANTI-LOCK article in BRAKES in appropriate MITCHELL® manual.

PARAMETER IDENTIFICATION (PID) DEFINITIONS

AIR BAG DIAGNOSTIC MONITOR PID INDEX [1]

PID	Description	Expected Value
CCNTECS	Number Of Continuous DTCs	One Count Per Bit (0–16)
DABAGR	Driver's Air Bag Module Resistance	1.8-4.1 Ohms
PABAGR	Passenger's Air Bag Module Resistance	1.4-3.6 Ohms
CRSHSN1	Primary Crash Sensor No. 1 Resistance	1.4-3.6 Ohms
DPRTNR	Driver's Pentensioner Circuit Resistance	1.4-3.6 Ohms
PPRTNR	Passenger's Pentensioner Circuit Resistance	1.4-3.6 Ohms
BRACKET	Bracket Ground Resistance	Less Than 100 Ohms
VBATECS	System Battery Voltage	9-16 Volts

[1] – Air Bag Diagnostic Monitor may also be referred to as Electronic Crash Sensor (ECS) module.

ANTI-LOCK BRAKE SYSTEM MODULE PID INDEX

PID	Description	Expected Value
ABSLAMP	ABS Warning Light State	ON, OFF
ABSRF_I	Right Front ABS Inlet Valve	ON, OFF
ABSLF_O	Left Front ABS Outlet Valve	ON, OFF
ABSR_I	Rear ABS Inlet Valve	ON, OFF
ABSR_O	Rear ABS Outlet Valve	ON, OFF
ABSRF_I	Right Front ABS Inlet Valve	ON, OFF
ABSRF_O	Right Front ABS Outlet Valve	ON, OFF
BOO_ABS	Brake Pedal Position Switch Input	ON, OFF
BRK_LVL	Brake Fluid Level	OK, notOK
BRKLAMP	Brake Warning Light State	ON, OFF
CCNTABS	Number Of Continuous DTC	One Count Per Bit
LF_WSPI	Left Front Wheel Speed Signal	0-255 KPH
R_WSPI	Rear Wheel Speed Signal	0-255 KPH
RF_WSPI	Right Front Wheel Speed Signal	0-255 KPH
PWR_RLY	Power Relay Feedback Input	ON, OFF

NATURAL GAS VEHICLE MODULE PID INDEX

PID	Description	Expected Value
CCNTF1	Number Of Continuous DTCs	Number Of DTCs
TANKPR	Fuel Tank Pressure Sensor	0-4000 psi
TEMPS1	Fuel Tank Temperature Sensor No. 1 Input	-40-302°F
VBATF1	Battery Voltage	Voltage
GAUGESG	Instrument Cluster Fuel Gauge Drive Signal	0-4000 mV
GAUGECM	Fuel Gauge Commend Position	[1]

[1] – Fuel Gauge Position In 16ths. 2 equals empty and 18 equals full.

WIRING DIAGRAMS

NOTE: See appropriate wiring diagrams in DATA LINK CONNECTORS, GROUND DISTRIBUTION or POWER DISTRIBUTION article in WIRING DIAGRAMS.

DESCRIPTION & OPERATION

Vehicle has 2 module communications networks. The Powertrain Control Module (PCM) is connected to the multiplex communications network through a pair of twisted wires or BUS. The BUS network is also referred to as Standard Corporate Protocol (SCP). The BUS consists of a (+) circuit No. 131 and a (–) circuit No. 132. The air bag diagnostic monitor and all other optional modules (Remote Anti-Theft Personality (RAP) module and Anti-Lock Brake System (ABS) module) are connected to the International Standards Organization (ISO) 9141 diagnostic communications network through a single wire (circuit No. 170). Both networks are connected to the Data Link Connector (DLC). This article is used to diagnose BUS and ISO communications network circuit faults. For module locations, see COMPONENT LOCATIONS table.

COMPONENT LOCATIONS

Component	Location
Air Bag Diagnostic Monitor [1]	Under Front Of Center Console
Anti-Lock Brake (ABS) Module	Under Front Passenger's Seat
Central Junction Box	Below Left Side Of Instrument Panel
Data Link Connector (DLC)	Below Driver's Side Of Instrument Panel, To Left Of Steering Column
Integrated Control Panel (ICP)	Part Of Radio/Air Conditioning Assembly
Power Distribution Box	Left Side Of Engine Compartment, Above Wheelwell
Powertrain Control Module (PCM)	Under Center Console
Remote Anti-Theft Personality (RAP) Module	[2]

[1] – Air bag diagnostic monitor may also be referred to as Electronic Crash Sensor (ECS) module.
[2] – On coupe and sedans, RAP module is behind right rear quarter panel. On station wagons, RAP module is behind left rear quarter panel.

REPAIRING BUS WIRING

NOTE: Following procedure must be used to ensure proper repair is performed on BUS wiring. BUS wiring is sensitive to moisture and oxidation and must be properly sealed to ensure proper operation of the module communications network. Regular heat shrink tubing is NOT sufficient, heat shrink tubing containing hot melt wax is required.

1) When performing a repair on the BUS wiring, ensure the wires on the BUS are twisted at a rate of 33-40 winds per 3.3 ft. (1 m). The twists should start within approximately 4.9" (124 mm) from any connector. Use only 20 AWG standard wire gauge for repairs.

2) If performing a splice in the wiring, strip .75" (19.0 mm) of insulation from one wire and 1.50" (38.1 mm) of insulator from the other wire. Perform STEP 1. *See Fig. 1.* Place hot melt wax type heat shrink tubing over one wire.

3) Twist stripped portion of the wires together. Solder connection using resin core RMA solder. DO NOT use acid core solder. Bend wires to allow installation of heat shrink tubing. Perform STEP 2. *See Fig. 1.*

4) Position heat shrink tubing over splice area. Using heat gun, evenly heat the heat shrink tubing until wax flows from both ends of heat shrink tubing.

COMMUNICATION NETWORK DIAGNOSTICS

INSPECTION & VERIFICATION

1) Verify customer's original problem by operating system in question. Inspect vehicle for any obvious electrical component wiring or connector damage. Inspect connectors for loose, damaged or corroded terminals. Check related fuses for system in question.

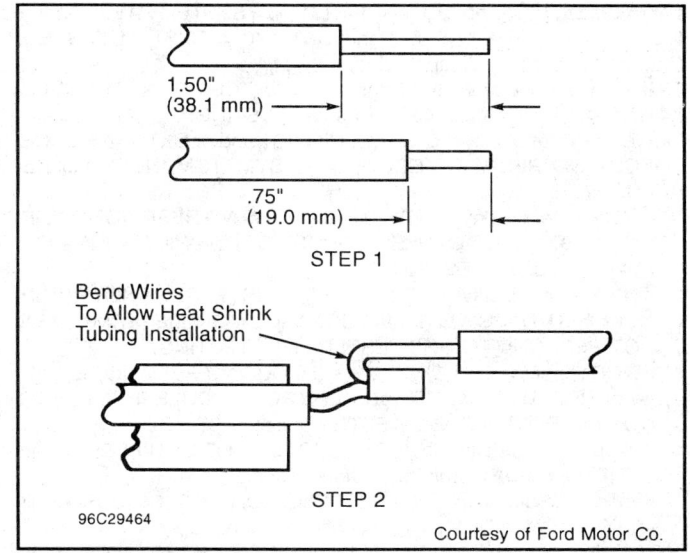

Fig. 1: Repairing BUS Wiring

2) Inspect 16-pin Data Link Connector (DLC) pins for damage. *See Fig. 2.* The DLC is located below driver's side of instrument panel, to the left of steering column. If pins are okay, go to next step. If pins are damaged, repair as necessary and proceed to next step.

3) If problem is still present after performing inspection, connect New Generation Star (NGS) tester to DLC. Select vehicle to be tested from NGS tester menu. If NGS tester does not communicate with vehicle, ensure program card is properly installed. Check NGS tester cable connections and ensure ignition is on. If NGS tester still does not communicate with vehicle, go to TEST F: NO MODULE/NETWORK COMMUNICATION under TESTING. If NGS tester communicates with vehicle, perform data link diagnostic test. See DATA LINK DIAGNOSTIC TEST.

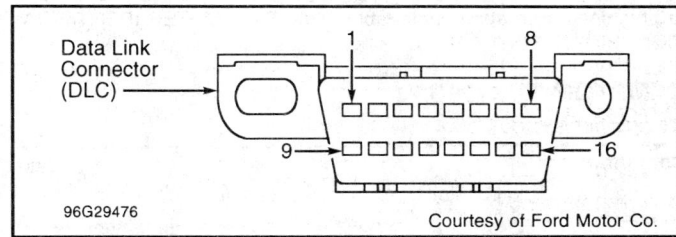

Fig. 2: Identifying Data Link Connector (DLC) Terminals

DATA LINK DIAGNOSTIC TEST

NOTE: When performing Data Link Diagnostic Test, the NGS tester may display BUS circuits No. 131 and 132 as circuits No. 914 and 915. The NGS tester may also display ISO circuit No. 170 as circuit No. 70.

1) Connect New Generation Star (NGS) tester to Data Link Connector (DLC), if not already connected. Select vehicle to be tested from NGS tester menu.

2) Turn ignition on. Rotate dial on NGS tester to menu item DIAGNOSTIC DATA LINK and press trigger. A test will be performed on the BUS (circuits No. 131 and 132) for the module communications network and the ISO 9141 communication link (circuit No. 170). This is the Orange/Blue wire that is between terminal No. 7 on DLC and the air bag diagnostic monitor and other optional modules.

3) If NGS tester displays CKT 131 (+) = SYSTEM PASSED and CKT 132 (–) = SYSTEM PASSED, module communications network is okay. If NGS tester displays CKT 170 = SYSTEM PASSED, ISO 9141 communication link is operating properly. Return to article that directed you here and continue diagnosis.

4) If NGS tester does not display CKT 131 (+) = SYSTEM PASSED, CKT 132 (–) = SYSTEM PASSED and CKT 170 = SYSTEM PASSED, perform the following as applicable:

- If no response from NGS tester, go to TEST F: NO MODULE/ NETWORK COMMUNICATION under TESTING.
- If NGS tester displays CKT 170, CKT 131 and/or CKT 132 = SOME ECUS NO RESP/NOT EQUIP, go to SYMPTOM INDEX table to continue diagnosis.
- If NGS tester displays CKT 170 = ALL ECUS NO RESP/NOT EQUIP, go to TEST E: NO MODULE/NETWORK COMMUNICATIONS – ISO 9141 LINK under TESTING.
- If NGS tester displays CKT 131 = ALL ECUS NO RESP/NOT EQUIP, go to TEST D: POWERTRAIN CONTROL MODULE (PCM) DOES NOT RESPOND TO NGS TESTER under TESTING.
- If NGS tester displays CKT 132 = ALL ECUS NO RESP/NOT EQUIP, go to TEST D: POWERTRAIN CONTROL MODULE (PCM) DOES NOT RESPOND TO NGS TESTER under TESTING.
- If module in question is NO RESPONSE/NOT EQUIPPED, go to SYMPTOM INDEX table to continue diagnosis.
- If module in question is NO RESPONSE ON CKT 131 (BUS +), go to SYMPTOM INDEX table to continue diagnosis.
- If module in question is NO RESPONSE ON CKT 132 (BUS –), go to SYMPTOM INDEX table to continue diagnosis.

RETRIEVING & CLEARING DIAGNOSTIC TROUBLE CODES

Connect New Generation Star (NGS) tester to Data Link Connector (DLC). Following manufacturer's instructions to retrieve and clear codes for desired module. See appropriate table under DIAGNOSTIC TROUBLE CODE (DTC) DEFINITIONS for a listing of Diagnostic Trouble Codes (DTCs) and appropriate test procedure.

ACCESSING PARAMETER IDENTIFICATION (PID)

Turn ignition switch to LOCK position. Connect New Generation Star (NGS) tester to Data Link Connector (DLC). Following manufacturer's instructions enter PID/DATA MONITOR AND RECORD for desired module. Operate appropriate system and ensure PID expected values are obtained. See appropriate table under PARAMETER IDENTIFICATION (PID) DEFINITIONS.

SYMPTOM TESTING

SYMPTOM INDEX

Condition	Test
Air Bag Diagnostic Monitor Does Not Respond To NGS Tester [1]	A
Anti-Lock Brake System (ABS) Module Does Not Respond To NGS Tester	B
Remote Anti-Theft Personality (RAP) Module Does Not Respond To NGS Tester	C
Powertrain Control Module (PCM) Does Not Respond To NGS Tester	D
No Module/Network Communications – ISO 9141 Link	E
No Module/Network Communication	F

[1] – Air bag diagnostic monitor may also be referred to as Electronic Crash Sensor (ECS) module.

SYSTEM TESTING

NOTE: Always check module power and ground circuits prior to replacing a control module. See appropriate wiring diagram in DATA LINK CONNECTORS, GROUND DISTRIBUTION or POWER DISTRIBUTION article in WIRING DIAGRAMS.

TEST A: AIR BAG DIAGNOSTIC MONITOR DOES NOT RESPOND TO NGS TESTER

1) Turn ignition off. Deactivate air bag system. See AIR BAG RESTRAINT SYSTEMS – ESCORT & TRACER article. Disconnect air bag diagnostic monitor connector located under front of center console.

Inspect connector for loose, damaged or corroded terminals. Repair connector as necessary and retest system for normal operation. If connector is okay, go to next step.

2) Measure resistance of Orange/Blue wire between terminal No. 19 at air bag diagnostic monitor connector and terminal No. 7 at Data Link Connector (DLC). *See Figs. 2 and 3.* If resistance is less than 5 ohms, replace air bag diagnostic monitor and retest system for normal operation. If resistance is 5 ohms or more, go to next step.

3) Disconnect White 6-pin in-line connector C233 located behind left side of instrument panel. *See Fig. 4.* Measure resistance of Orange/Blue wire between terminal No. 5 at female half of in-line connector C233 and terminal No. 7 at DLC. *See Figs. 2 and 3.* If resistance is less than 5 ohms, repair open in Orange/Blue wire between in-line connector C233 and air bag diagnostic monitor. Retest system for normal operation. If resistance is 5 ohms or more, repair open in Orange/Blue wire between in-line connector C233 and DLC. Retest system for normal operation.

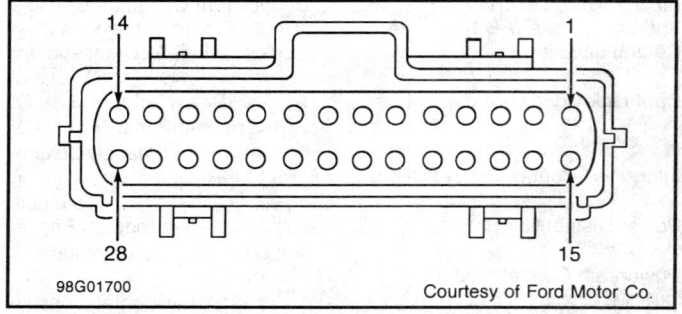

14   1

28   15

98G01700   Courtesy of Ford Motor Co.

Fig. 3: Identifying Air Bag Diagnostic Monitor Connector Terminals

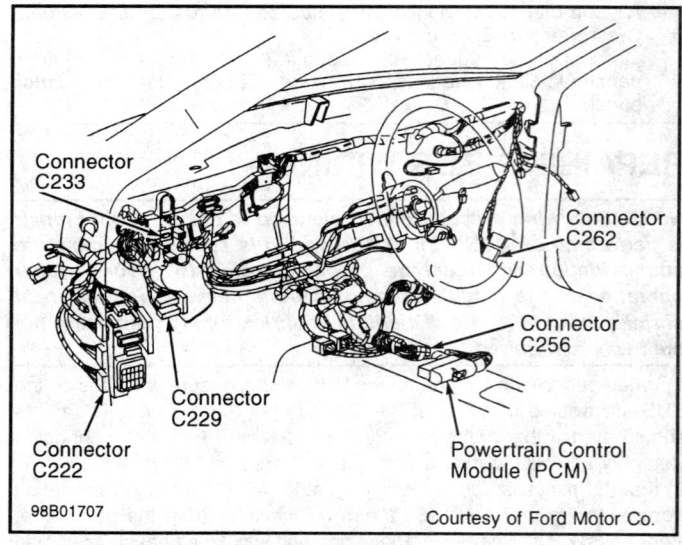

Connector C233

Connector C262

Connector C256

Connector C229

Connector C222

Powertrain Control Module (PCM)

98B01707   Courtesy of Ford Motor Co.

Fig. 4: Locating Connectors & PCM

TEST B: ANTI-LOCK BRAKE SYSTEM (ABS) MODULE DOES NOT RESPOND TO NGS TESTER

1) Turn ignition off. Disconnect ABS control module 40-pin connector located under front passenger's seat. Inspect connector for loose, damaged or corroded terminals. Repair connector as necessary and retest system for normal operation. If connector is okay, go to next step.

2) Measure resistance of Orange/Blue wire between terminal No. 13 at ABS module connector and terminal No. 7 at Data Link Connector (DLC). *See Figs. 2 and 5.* If resistance is less than 5 ohms, replace ABS module and retest system for normal operation. If resistance is 5 ohms or more, go to next step.

3) Disconnect Black 18-pin in-line connector C262. *See Fig. 4.* Measure resistance of Orange/Blue wire between terminal No. 1 at male half of in-line connector C262 and terminal No. 7 at DLC. *See Figs. 2 and 6.* If resistance is less than 5 ohms, repair open in Orange/Blue wire between in-line connector C262 and ABS module connector. Retest system for normal operation. If resistance is 5 ohms or more, repair open in Orange/Blue wire between in-line connector C262 and DLC. Retest system for normal operation.

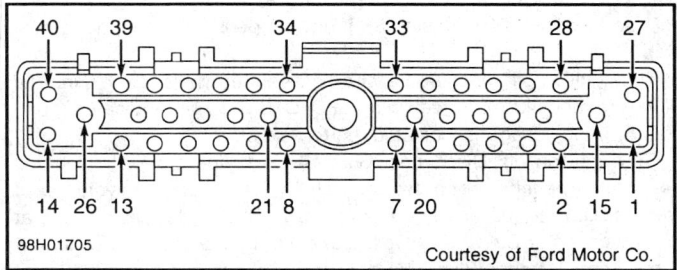

98H01705

Courtesy of Ford Motor Co.

Fig. 5: Identifying ABS Module Connector Terminals

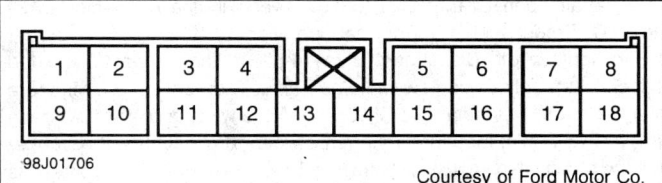

98J01706

Courtesy of Ford Motor Co.

Fig. 6: Identifying Connector C262 Terminals (Male Half Of Connector Shown)

TEST C: REMOTE ANTI-THEFT PERSONALITY (RAP) MODULE DOES NOT RESPOND TO NGS TESTER

1) Turn ignition off. Disconnect RAP module 26-pin connector C405. On coupe and sedans, RAP module is behind right rear quarter panel. On station wagons, RAP module is behind left rear quarter panel. On all models, inspect RAP module 26-pin connector C405 for loose, damaged or corroded terminals. Repair connector as necessary and retest system for normal operation. If connector is okay, go to next step.
2) Using an ohmmeter, measure resistance of Orange/Blue wire between terminal No. 3 at RAP module connector C405 and terminal No. 7 at Data Link Connector (DLC). See Figs. 2 and 7. If resistance is less than 5 ohms, replace RAP module and retest system for normal operation. If resistance is 5 ohms or more, go to next step.
3) Disconnect Black 17-pin in-line connector C222 located behind left side of instrument panel, near fuse block. See Fig. 4. Measure resistance of Orange/Blue wire between terminal No. 6 at in-line connector C222 and terminal No. 7 at DLC. See Figs. 2 and 8. If resistance is less than 5 ohms, repair open in Orange/Blue wire between in-line connector C222 and RAP module connector C405. Retest system for normal operation. If resistance is 5 ohms or more, repair Orange/Blue wire between in-line connector C222 and DLC.

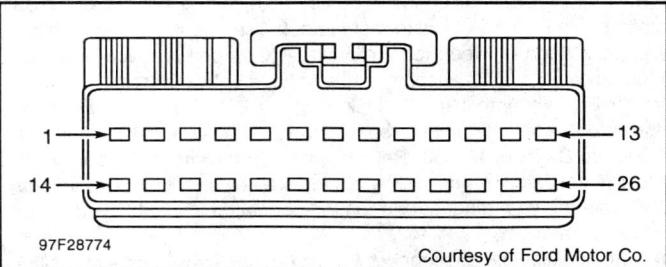

97F28774

Courtesy of Ford Motor Co.

Fig. 7: Identifying RAP Module Connector C405 Terminals

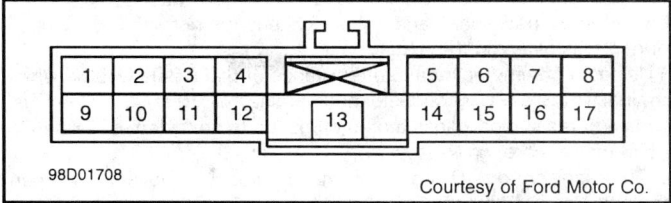

98D01708

Courtesy of Ford Motor Co.

Fig. 8: Identifying Connector C222 Terminals (Male Half Of Connector Shown)

TEST D: POWERTRAIN CONTROL MODULE (PCM) DOES NOT RESPOND TO NGS TESTER

NOTE: If test results indicate PCM is faulty, always check for any engine performance related Diagnostic Trouble Codes (DTCs) prior to replacing PCM. If any DTCs are present, service DTCs as necessary and retest. See appropriate SELF-DIAGNOSTICS article in ENGINE PERFORMANCE in appropriate MITCHELL® manual.

NOTE: Depending on module configuration, with all modules connected and with ignition switch in RUN position or with engine running 2-3 volts may be present at Data Link Connector (DLC) terminals No. 2 (White/Blue wire) and No. 10 (Black/Blue wire). These are the Standard Corporate Protocol (SCP) diagnostic communications network circuits.

1) Turn ignition on. Perform data link diagnostic test. See DATA LINK DIAGNOSTIC TEST under COMMUNICATION NETWORK DIAGNOSTICS. If NGS tester indicates PCM: NO RESPONSE ON CKT 914 (BUS +), go to next step. If NGS tester does not indicate PCM: NO RESPONSE ON CKT 914 (BUS +), go to step 7).
2) Turn ignition off. Disconnect NGS tester. Disconnect PCM connector located under center console. See Fig. 4. Inspect connector for loose, damaged or corroded terminals. Pay particular attention to terminal No. 16. Repair connector as necessary and retest system for normal operation. If connector is okay, inspect Data Link Connector (DLC) for loose, damaged or corroded terminals. Pay particular attention to terminal No. 2 (White/Blue wire) . Repair connector as necessary and retest system for normal operation. If connector is okay, go to next step.
3) Using an ohmmeter, measure resistance of White/Blue wire between terminal No. 16 at PCM connector and terminal No. 2 at DLC. See Figs. 2 and 9. If resistance is less than 5 ohms, go to next step. If resistance is 5 ohms or more, go to step 7).
4) Turn ignition on. Using a voltmeter, measure voltage between terminals No. 2 (White/Blue wire) and No. 16 (Green wire) at DLC. Also, measure voltage between terminals No. 2 (White/Blue wire) and No. 4 (Black wire) at DLC. See Fig. 2. If voltage is indicated at any terminal, go to next step. If voltage is not indicated at any terminal, replace PCM and retest system for normal operation.
5) Turn ignition off. Disconnect White 10-pin in-line connector C256 located near PCM. See Fig. 4. Turn ignition on. Using a voltmeter, measure voltage between terminals No. 2 (White/Blue wire) and No. 16 (Green wire) at DLC. Also, measure voltage between terminals No. 2 (White/Blue wire) and No. 4 (Black wire) at DLC. See Fig. 2. If voltage is indicated at any terminal, repair White/Blue wire between in-line connector C256 and DLC. Retest system for normal operation. If voltage is not indicated at any terminal, repair White/Blue wire between in-line connector C256 and PCM. Retest system for normal operation.
6) Turn ignition off. Disconnect White 10-pin in-line connector C256 located near PCM. See Fig. 4. Using an ohmmeter, measure resistance of White/Blue wire between terminal No. 6 at female half of in-line connector C256 and terminal No. 2 at DLC. See Figs. 2 and 10. If resistance is less than 5 ohms, repair open in White/Blue wire between in-line connector C256 and PCM. Retest system for normal operation. If resistance is 5 ohms or more, repair open in White/Blue wire between in-line connector C256 and DLC. Retest system for normal operation.
7) Disconnect NGS tester. Disconnect PCM connector located under center console. See Fig. 4. Inspect connector for loose, damaged or

corroded terminals. Pay particular attention to terminal No. 10. Repair connector as necessary and retest system for normal operation. If connector is okay, go to next step.

8) Using an ohmmeter, measure resistance of Black/Blue wire between terminal No. 15 at PCM connector and terminal No. 10 at DLC. *See Figs. 2 and 9.* If resistance is less than 5 ohms, go to next step. If resistance is 5 ohms or more, go to step **11**).

9) Turn ignition on. Using a voltmeter, measure voltage between terminals No. 10 (Black/Blue wire) and No. 16 (Green wire) at DLC. Also, measure voltage between terminals No. 10 (Black/Blue wire) and No. 4 (Black wire) at DLC. *See Fig. 2.* If voltage is indicated at any terminals, go to next step. If voltage is not indicated at any terminals, go to appropriate SELF-DIAGNOSTICS article in ENGINE PERFORMANCE in appropriate MITCHELL® manual.

10) Turn ignition off. Disconnect White 10-pin in-line connector C256 located near PCM. *See Fig. 4.* Turn ignition on. Using a voltmeter, measure voltage between terminals No. 10 (Black/Blue wire) and No. 16 (Green wire) at DLC. Also, measure voltage between terminals No. 10 (Black/Blue wire) and No. 4 (Black wire) at DLC. *See Fig. 2.* If voltage is indicated at any terminal, repair Black/Blue wire between in-line connector C256 and DLC. Retest system for normal operation. If voltage is not indicated at any terminal, repair Black/Blue wire between in-line connector C256 and PCM. Retest system for normal operation.

11) Turn ignition off. Disconnect White 10-pin in-line connector C256 located near PCM. *See Fig. 4.* Using an ohmmeter, measure resistance of Black/Blue wire between terminal No. 10 at DLC and terminal No. 1 at female half of in-line connector C256. *See Figs. 2 and 10.* If resistance is less than 5 ohms, repair open in Black/Blue wire between in-line connector C256 and PCM. Retest system for normal operation. If resistance is 5 ohms or more, repair open in Black/Blue wire between in-line connector C256 and DLC. Retest system for normal operation.

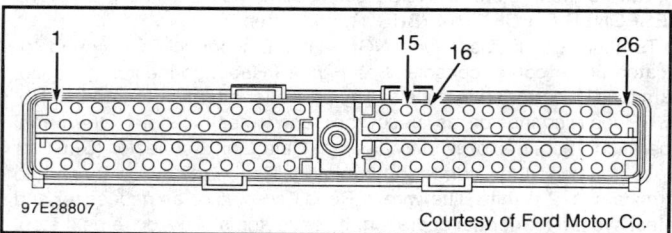

97E28807   Courtesy of Ford Motor Co.

Fig. 9: Identifying Powertrain Control Module (PCM) Terminals

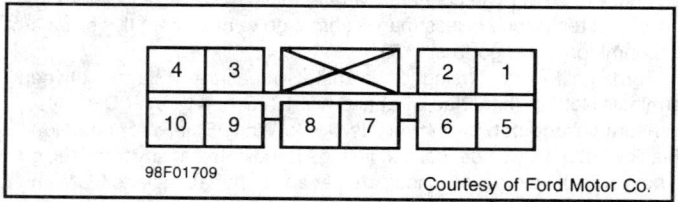

98F01709   Courtesy of Ford Motor Co.

Fig. 10: Identifying Connector C256 Terminals (Female Half Of Connector Shown)

TEST E: NO MODULE/NETWORK COMMUNICATIONS – ISO 9141 LINK

NOTE: Depending on module configuration, with all modules connected and with ignition switch in RUN position or with engine running 2-3 volts may be present at Data Link Connector (DLC) terminal No. 7 (Orange/Blue wire). This is the International Standards Organization (ISO) 9141 diagnostic communications network circuit.

NOTE: When performing the following test, the NGS tester may display ISO circuit No. 170 as circuit No. 70.

1) Inspect NGS tester connector for loose, damaged or corroded terminals. Pay particular attention to terminals No. 4 and 7. Repair as necessary and retest system for normal operation. If connector is okay, inspect Data Link Connector (DLC) for loose, damaged or corroded terminals. Pay particular attention to terminals No. 4 (Black wire) and No. 7 (Orange/Blue wire). Repair as necessary and retest system for normal operation. If connector is okay, go to next step.

2) Turn ignition on. Measure voltage between terminals No. 7 (Orange/Blue wire) and No. 5 (Blue/Orange wire) at DLC. *See Fig. 2.* If any voltage is indicated, go to step **5**). If no voltage is indicated, go to next step.

3) Turn ignition off. Measure voltage between terminals No. 7 (Orange/Blue wire) and No. 16 (Green wire) at DLC. If voltage is indicated, go to step **5**). If no voltage is indicated, go to next step.

4) Turn ignition off. Disconnect Blue 14-pin in-line connector located near clutch pedal position switch. *See Fig. 4.* Measure resistance of Orange/Blue wire between terminal No. 7 at DLC and terminal No. 5 at in-line connector C229. *See Figs. 2 and 11.* If resistance is less than 5 ohms, repair Orange/Blue wire between connectors C229, C222 and C262. Retest system for normal operation. If resistance is 5 ohms or more, repair open Orange/Blue wire between in-line connector C229 and DLC. Retest system for normal operation.

5) Turn ignition off. Disconnect Blue 14-pin in-line connector located near clutch pedal position switch. *See Fig. 4.* Turn ignition on. Measure voltage between terminals No. 7 (Orange/Blue wire) and No. 16 (Green wire) at DLC. Also, measure voltage between terminals No. 7 (Orange/Blue wire) and No. 4 (Black wire) at DLC. *See Fig. 2.* If voltage is indicated at any terminal, repair Orange/Blue wire between DLC and in-line connector C229. Retest system for normal operation. If no voltage is indicated at any terminal, reconnect in-line connector C229 and go to next step.

6) If vehicle is equipped with Anti-Lock Brake System (ABS) module and/or Remote Anti-Theft Personality (RAP) module, go to next step. If vehicle is only equipped with a air bag diagnostic monitor, go to step **8**).

7) Turn ignition off. Deactivate air bag system. See AIR BAG RESTRAINT SYSTEMS – ESCORT & TRACER article. Disconnect air bag diagnostic monitor connector under front of center console. Reconnect positive battery cable and then negative battery cable. Turn ignition on. Perform data link diagnostic test. See DATA LINK DIAGNOSTIC TEST under COMMUNICATION NETWORK DIAGNOSTICS. If NGS tester displays CKT 170 = ALL ECUS NO RESP/NOT EQUIP, go to step **10**). If NGS tester does not display CKT 170 = ALL ECUS NO RESP/NOT EQUIP, replace air bag diagnostic monitor and retest system for normal operation.

8) Turn ignition off. Disconnect NGS tester. Deactivate air bag system. See AIR BAG RESTRAINT SYSTEMS – ESCORT & TRACER article. Disconnect air bag diagnostic monitor connector under front of center console. Reconnect positive battery cable and then negative battery cable. Turn ignition on. Measure voltage between terminals No. 7 (Orange/Blue wire) and No. 16 (Green wire) at DLC. Also, measure voltage between terminals No. 7 (Orange/Blue wire) and No. 4 (Black wire) at DLC. *See Fig. 2.* If voltage is indicated at any terminals, go to next step. If no voltage is indicated, replace air bag diagnostic monitor and retest system for normal operation.

9) Turn ignition off. Disconnect White 6-pin in-line connector C233 located behind left side of instrument panel. *See Fig. 4.* Turn ignition on. Measure voltage between terminals No. 7 (Orange/Blue wire) and No. 16 (Green wire) at DLC. Also, measure voltage between terminals No. 7 (Orange/Blue wire) and No. 4 (Black wire) at DLC. *See Fig. 2.* If voltage is indicated at any terminals, repair Orange/Blue wire between in-line connectors C229 and C233. Retest system for normal operation. If no voltage is indicated, repair Orange/Blue wire between in-line connector C233 and air bag diagnostic monitor connector. Retest system for normal operation.

10) Turn ignition off. Disconnect White 6-pin in-line connector C233 located behind left side of instrument panel. *See Fig. 4.* Turn ignition on. Perform data link diagnostic test. See DATA LINK DIAGNOSTIC TEST under COMMUNICATION NETWORK DIAGNOSTICS. If NGS tester displays CKT 170 = ALL ECUS NO RESP/NOT EQUIP, go to next step. If NGS tester does not display CKT 170 = ALL ECUS NO RESP/NOT EQUIP, repair Orange/Blue wire between in-line connector C233 and air bag diagnostic monitor connector. Retest system for normal operation.

11) If vehicle is equipped with an ABS module and a RAP module, go to next step. If vehicle is only equipped with a RAP module, go to step **13)**.

12) Disconnect RAP module 26-pin connector C405. On coupe and sedans, RAP module is behind right rear quarter panel. On station wagons, RAP module is behind left rear quarter panel. On all models, turn ignition on. Perform data link diagnostic test. See DATA LINK DIAGNOSTIC TEST under COMMUNICATION NETWORK DIAGNOSTICS. If NGS tester displays CKT 170 = ALL ECUS NO RESP/NOT EQUIP, go to step **15)**. If NGS tester does not display CKT 170 = ALL ECUS NO RESP/NOT EQUIP, replace RAP module and retest system for normal operation.

13) Turn ignition off. Disconnect NGS tester and RAP module 26-pin connector C405. On coupe and sedans, RAP module is behind right rear quarter panel. On wagons, RAP module is behind left rear quarter panel. On all models, turn ignition on. Measure voltage between terminals No. 7 (Orange/Blue wire) and No. 16 (Green wire) at DLC. Also, measure voltage between terminals No. 7 (Orange/Blue wire) and No. 4 (Black wire) at DLC. See Fig. 2. If voltage is indicated at any terminal, go to next step. If no voltage is indicated at any terminal, replace RAP module and retest system for normal operation.

14) Turn ignition off. Disconnect Black 17-pin in-line connector C222 located behind left side of instrument panel, near fuse block. See Fig. 4. Turn ignition on. Measure voltage between terminals No. 7 (Orange/Blue wire) and No. 16 (Green wire) at DLC. Also, measure voltage between terminals No. 7 (Orange/Blue wire) and No. 4 (Black wire) at DLC. See Fig. 2. If voltage is indicated at any terminal, repair Orange/Blue wire between connectors C229, C233 and C222. Retest system for normal operation. If no voltage is indicated at any terminal, repair Orange/Blue wire between RAP module connectors C405 and C222. Retest system for normal operation.

15) Turn ignition off. Disconnect Black 17-pin in-line connector C222 located behind left side of instrument panel, near fuse block. See Fig. 4. Disconnect NGS tester. Turn ignition on. Perform data link diagnostic test. See DATA LINK DIAGNOSTIC TEST under COMMUNICATION NETWORK DIAGNOSTICS. If NGS tester displays CKT 170 = ALL ECUS NO RESP/NOT EQUIP (Escort ZX2 may display CKT131=00000003), go to next step. If NGS tester does not display CKT 170 = ALL ECUS NO RESP/NOT EQUIP, repair Orange/Blue wire between in-line connector C222 and RAP module connector C405. Retest system for normal operation.

16) If vehicle is equipped with an ABS module, go to next step. If vehicle is not equipped with an ABS module, system is functioning properly at this time. Testing is complete.

17) Turn ignition off. Disconnect ABS control module 40-pin connector located under front passenger's seat. Disconnect NGS tester. Turn ignition on. Measure voltage between terminals No. 7 (Orange/Blue wire) and No. 16 (Green wire) at DLC. Also, measure voltage between terminals No. 7 (Orange/Blue wire) and No. 4 (Black wire) at DLC. See Fig. 2. If voltage is indicated at any terminal, go to next step. If no voltage is indicated at any terminal, replace ABS module and retest system for normal operation.

18) Turn ignition off. Disconnect Black 18-pin in-line connector C262. See Fig. 4. Turn ignition on. Measure voltage between terminals No. 7 (Orange/Blue wire) and No. 16 (Green wire) at DLC. Also, measure voltage between terminals No. 7 (Orange/Blue wire) and No. 4 (Black wire) at DLC. See Fig. 2. If voltage is indicated at any terminal, repair Orange/Blue wire between in-line connectors C262, C229, C222 (if equipped) and C233. Retest system for normal operation. If no voltage is indicated at any terminal, replace ABS module and retest system for normal operation.

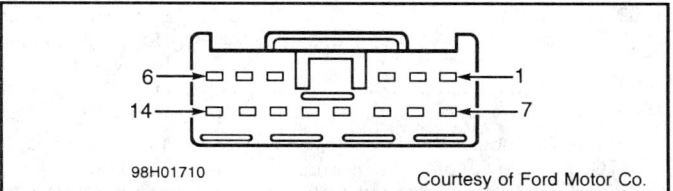

98H01710   Courtesy of Ford Motor Co.

Fig. 11: Identifying Connector C229 Terminals (Male Half Of Connector Shown)

TEST F: NO MODULE/NETWORK COMMUNICATION

1) Turn ignition off. Inspect Data Link Connector (DLC) for physical damage, bent terminals or corrosion. Repair connector as necessary and retest system for normal operation. If connector is okay, go to next step.

2) Inspect NGS tester connector for loose, damaged or corroded terminals. Repair connector as necessary and retest system for normal operation. If connector is okay, go to next step.

3) Turn ignition off. Remove and inspect OBD-II fuse (10-amp) from engine compartment fuse block. If fuse is okay, reinstall fuse and go to next step. If fuse is blown, replace fuse and retest system for normal operation. Recheck fuse. If fuse is blown, repair short to ground in circuit No. 180 (Green wire) between engine compartment fuse block and DLC. Retest system for normal operation.

4) Measure voltage between ground and terminal No. 16 (Green wire) at DLC. See Fig. 2. If voltage is more than 10 volts, go to next step. If voltage is 10 volts or less, repair circuit No. 180 (Green wire) between engine compartment fuse block and DLC. Retest system for normal operation.

5) Measure resistance between ground and terminals No. 4 (Black wire) and No. 5 (Blue/Orange wire) at DLC. If both resistance readings are less than 5 ohms, repair or replace NGS tester. Retest system for normal operation. If any resistance reading is 5 ohms or more, repair open in Black wire or Blue/Orange wire between ground and DLC. Retest system for normal operation.

DIAGNOSTIC TROUBLE CODE (DTC) DEFINITIONS

AIR BAG DIAGNOSTIC MONITOR DTC INDEX [1]

DTC [2]	Description	Test
B1342	ECU Defective	3
B1231	RCM Crash Data Memory Full	3
B1921	RCM Bracket Ground Resistance High	3
B1318	Battery Voltage Low	3
C1414	Incorrect Vehicle Identification Code	3
B1887	Driver's Side Air Bag Circuit Short To Ground	3
B1888	Passenger's Side Air Circuit Bag Short To Ground	3
B1916	Driver's Side Air Bag Circuit Short To Voltage	3
B1925	Passenger's Side Air Bag Circuit Short To Voltage	3
B1879	Unexpected Feature Present	3
B1878	Unexpected Feature Present	3
B1883	Unexpected Feature Present	3
B1882	Unexpected Feature Present	3
B1932	Driver's Side Air Bag Circuit Resistance High	3
B1933	Passenger's Side Air Bag Circuit Resistance High	3
B1934	Driver's Side Air Bag Circuit Resistance Low	3

AIR BAG DIAGNOSTIC MONITOR DTC INDEX [1] (Cont.)

DTC [2]	Description	Test
B1935	Passenger's Side Air Bag Circuit Resistance Low	3
B1941	Unexpected Feature Present	3
B1901	Unexpected Feature Present	3
B1871	Unexpected Feature Present	3
B1889	Unexpected Feature Present	3
B1877	Unexpected Feature Present	3
B1885	Unexpected Feature Present	3
B1881	Unexpected Feature Present	3
B1886	Unexpected Feature Present	3
B1884	Unexpected Feature Present	3
B1890	Unexpected Feature Present	3
B1892	Air Bag Tone Warning Indicator Circuit Short To Ground Or Open	3
B1891	Air Bag Tone Warning Indicator Circuit Short To Voltage	3
B2141	Non-Volatile Memory Configuration Error	3
B1869	Air Bag Indicator Inoperative	3
B1870	Air Bag Indicator Short To Voltage	3

[1] – Air Bag Diagnostic Monitor may also be referred to as Electronic Crash Sensor (ECS) module.
[2] – DTCs are listed in order of importance. Repair DTCs in order listed.
[3] – Repair supplemental restraint system as necessary. See DIAGNOSIS & TESTING article in appropriate MITCHELL® AIR BAG SERVICE & REPAIR MANUAL, DOMESTIC & IMPORTED MODELS.

ANTI-LOCK BRAKE SYSTEM MODULE DTC INDEX

DTC	Description	Test
B1318	Battery Voltage Low	1
B1342	ECU Defective	1
C1095	ABS Hydraulic Pump Motor Circuit Shorted	1
C1096	ABS Hydraulic Pump Motor Circuit Open	1
C1115	Shorted Anti-Lock Relay	1
C1140	Excessive Dump Time Failure	1
C1145	Right Front ABS Sensor Input Circuit Failure	1
C1148/C1234	Right Front ABS Sensor Input Signal Missing	1
C1155	Left Front ABS Sensor Input Circuit Failure	1
C1158/C1233	Left Front ABS Sensor Input Signal Missing	1
C1165	Right Rear ABS Sensor Input Circuit Failure	1
C1168/C1235	Right Rear ABS Sensor Input Signal Missing	1
C1175	Left Rear ABS Sensor Input Circuit Failure	1
C1178/C1236	Left Rear ABS Sensor Input Signal Missing	1
C1184	Excessive ABS Isolation	1
C1185	Open Anti-Lock Relay	1
C1194/C1196	Open Or Shorted LF Dump Valve Solenoid	1
C1198/C1200	Open Or Shorted LF Isolation Valve Solenoid	1
C1220	Anti-Lock Warning Light Shorted	1
C1222	Wheel Speed Error	1
C1210/C1212	Open Or Shorted RF Dump Valve Solenoid	1
C1214/C1216	Open Or Shorted RF Isolation Valve Solenoid	1
C1242/C1244	Open Or Shorted LR Dump Valve Solenoid	1
C1246/C1248	Open Or Shorted RR Dump Valve Solenoid	1
C1250/C1252	Open Or Shorted LR Isolation Valve Solenoid	1
C1254/C1256	Open Or Shorted RR Isolation Valve Solenoid	1

[1] – Repair Anti-Lock Brake System (ABS). See appropriate ANTI-LOCK article in BRAKES in appropriate MITCHELL® manual.

RAP MODULE SELF-TEST DTC INDEX

DTC	Description	Test
B1334	Luggage Compartment/Trunk Lid Door Ajar Circuit Short To Ground	1
B1341	Power Door Unlock Circuit Short To Ground	2
B1522	Hood Switch Circuit Short To Ground	3
B2425	Keyless Entry Out Of Synchronization	4

[1] – Perform TEST B: ALARM SYSTEM DOES NOT ARM under SYSTEM TESTS in ACTIVE ANTI-THEFT SYSTEMS – ESCORT & TRACER article.
[2] – See appropriate REMOTE KEYLESS ENTRY SYSTEMS article for wiring diagram.
[3] – Perform TEST D: ALARM SYSTEM DOES NOT OPERATE PROPERLY under SYSTEM TESTS in ACTIVE ANTI-THEFT SYSTEMS – ESCORT & TRACER article.
[4] – Perform DTC B2425: REMOTE KEYLESS ENTRY OUT OF SYNCHRONIZATION under DIAGNOSTIC TROUBLE CODE TESTS in ACTIVE ANTI-THEFT SYSTEMS – ESCORT & TRACER article.

PARAMETER IDENTIFICATION (PID) DEFINITIONS

AIR BAG DIAGNOSTIC MONITOR PID INDEX [1]

PID	Description	Expected Value
CCNTECS	Number Of Continuous DTCs	One Count Per Bit (0–16)
DABAGR	Driver's Air Bag Module Resistance	1.8-4.1 Ohms
PABAGR	Passenger's Air Bag Module Resistance	1.4-3.6 Ohms
BRACKET	Bracket Ground Resistance	Less Than 100 Ohms
VBATECS	System Battery Voltage	9-16 Volts

[1] – Air Bag Diagnostic Monitor may also be referred to as Electronic Crash Sensor (ECS) module.

ANTI-LOCK BRAKE SYSTEM MODULE PID INDEX

PID	Description	Expected Value
CCNTABS	Number Of Continuous DTC	One Count Per Bit
ABSLAMP	ABS Warning Light State	ON, OFF
BLSHORT	ABS Warning Light State	ON, OFF
BOO_ABS	Brake Pedal Position Switch Input	ON, OFF
BRKLAMP	Brake Warning Light State	ON, OFF
LF_WSPI	Left Front Wheel Speed Signal	0-255 KPH
LR_WSPI	Left Rear Wheel Speed Signal	0-255 KPH
PWR_RLY	Power Relay Feedback Input	ON, OFF
RESETSW	Rear Reset Switch Input	ON, OFF
RF_WSPI	Right Front Wheel Speed Signal	0-255 KPH
RR_WSPI	Right Rear Wheel Speed Signal	0-255 KPH

RAP MODULE PID INDEX

PID	Description	Expected Value
AL_EVT#	Last 8 Alarm Events	HOODDTR, NO_EVT, DROPEN, PANIC, TRAJAR
HOOD-SW	Hood Switch State	PUNCHD, notPUN
DOORRAP	Door Ajar Status Imput	CLOSED, AJAR
IGN_RAP	Ignition Switch	OFF, RUN
DD_RAP	Power Door Unlock Status	OFF, UNLOCK
NOTHEFT	No Theft Jumper	NO, YES
NOREMOTE	No Remote Jumper	NO, YES
DECKLD	Trunk Ajar Status Input	CLOSED, AJAR
LEDFLASH [1]	LED Flash When Armed	ENABLED, DISABLED
HORNCHIRP [2]	Program Chirp Status	ENABLED, DISABLED

[1] – On NGS configuration card.
[2] – Mexico Only.

WIRING DIAGRAMS

NOTE: See appropriate wiring diagrams in DATA LINK CONNECTORS, GROUND DISTRIBUTION or POWER DISTRIBUTION article in WIRING DIAGRAMS.

DESCRIPTION & OPERATION

Vehicle has 2 module communications networks. Both networks can be accessed by using New Generation Star (NGS) tester connected to Data Link Connector (DLC). Standard Corporate Protocol (SCP) network consists of Powertrain Control Module (PCM), Electronic Automatic Temperature Control (EATC) module (Navigator and Expedition Eddie Bauer) and Hybrid Electronic Cluster (HEC) interconnected by a pair of twisted wires (data BUS plus and data BUS minus). SCP network allows intermodule communication. SCP network is robust and will continue to function even if one BUS wire is open, shorted to ground or shorted to power.

International Standards Organization (ISO) 9141 network consists of Restraint Control Module (RCM), Generic Electronic Module (GEM), Driver's Seat Module (DSM) (Navigator with memory seat), Remote Anti-Theft Personality (RAP) module, 4-Wheel Anti-Lock Brake System (4WABS) module and air suspension control module interconnected by a single wire. If that wire is shorted to ground, or power, the network will fail. ISO 9141 network does not permit intermodule communication.

COMPONENT LOCATIONS

Component	Location
Air Suspension Control Module	Behind Center Of Instrument Panel
Central Junction Box (Interior Fuse Panel)	Under Left Side Of Instrument Panel
Data Link Connector (DLC)	Below Left Side Of Instrument Panel, Right Of Steering Column
Driver's Seat Module (DSM)	[1] Under Driver's Seat
Electronic Automatic Temperature Control (EATC) Module	[2] Behind Center Of Instrument Panel
Generic Electronic Module (GEM)	On Back side Of Central Junction Box
Hybrid Electronic Cluster (HEC)	Instrument Cluster
Powertrain Control Module (PCM)	Right Side Of Engine Compartment
Remote Anti-Theft Personality (RAP) Module	Behind Left Side Of Instrument Panel
Restraint Control Module (RCM)	Behind Right Side Of Instrument Panel
4-Wheel Anti-Lock Brake System (ABS) Module	Left Front Of Engine Compartment

[1] – Applies to Navigator with memory seat only.
[2] – Applies to Navigator and Expedition Eddie Bauer only.

REPAIRING NETWORK COMMUNICATIONS WIRING

NOTE: Following procedure must be used to ensure proper repair is performed on network communications wiring. Network communications wiring is sensitive to moisture and oxidation and must be properly sealed to ensure proper operation of the module communications network. Regular heat shrink tubing is not sufficient. Heat shrink tubing containing hot melt wax is required.

NOTE: When performing a repair on Standard Corporate Protocol (SCP) network, ensure the BUS wires are twisted at a rate of 33-40 winds per 3.3 ft. (1 m). The twists should start within approximately 4.9" (124 mm) from any connector. Use only 20 AWG standard wire gauge for repairs.

1) Disconnect battery ground cable. Strip .75" (19.0 mm) of insulation from one wire and 1.50" (38.1 mm) of insulator from the other wire. Perform STEP 1. *See Fig. 1.* Place hot melt wax type heat shrink tubing over one wire.

2) Twist stripped portion of the wires together. Solder connection using rosin core mildly activated (RMA) solder. DO NOT use acid core solder. Bend wires to allow installation of heat shrink tubing. Perform STEP 2. *See Fig. 1.*

3) Position heat shrink tubing over splice area. Using heat gun, evenly heat the heat shrink tubing until wax flows from both ends of heat shrink tubing.

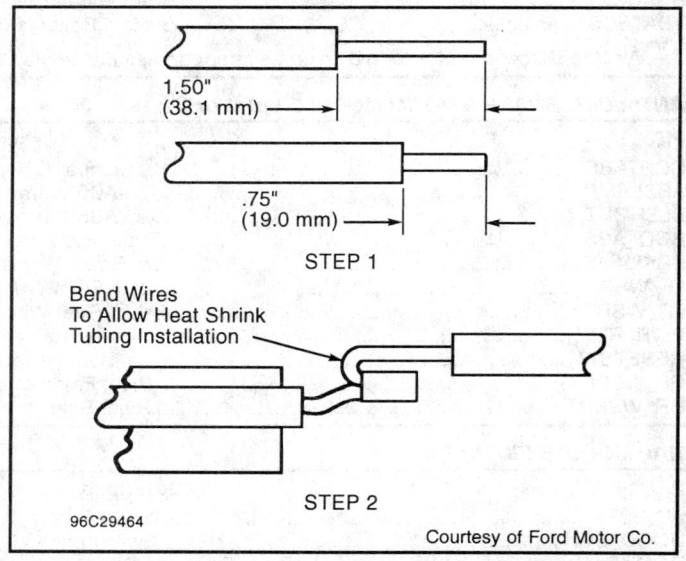

Fig. 1: Repairing Module Communications Network Wiring

COMMUNICATION NETWORK DIAGNOSTICS

INSPECTION & VERIFICATION

1) Verify customer complaint by operating system in question. Inspect vehicle for any obvious electrical component wiring or connector damage. Inspect connectors for loose, damaged or corroded terminals. Check central junction box fuse No. 3 (20-amp) and fuses related to system in question.

2) Inspect 16-pin Data Link Connector (DLC) pins for damage. *See Fig. 2.* DLC is located below driver's side of instrument panel, to right of steering column. If pins are okay, go to next step. If pins are damaged, repair as necessary and proceed to next step.

3) If problem is still present after performing inspection, connect New Generation Star (NGS) tester to DLC. Select vehicle to be tested from NGS tester menu. If NGS tester does not communicate with vehicle, ensure program card is properly installed. Check NGS tester cable connections and ensure ignition switch is in RUN position. If NGS tester still does not communicate with vehicle, go to TEST M: NO MODULE/ NETWORK COMMUNICATION – NO POWER TO NGS TESTER under SYSTEM TESTS. If NGS tester communicates with vehicle, perform data link diagnostic procedure. See DATA LINK DIAGNOSTIC TEST.

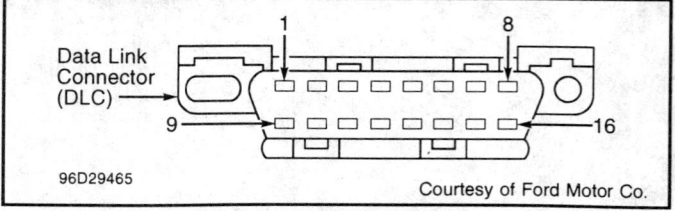

Fig. 2: Identifying Data Link Connector (DLC) Terminals

DATA LINK DIAGNOSTIC TEST

1) Connect New Generation Star (NGS) tester to Data Link Connector (DLC). Select vehicle to be tested from NGS tester menu. Turn ignition switch to RUN position.

2) Rotate dial on NGS tester to menu item DIAGNOSTIC DATA LINK and press trigger. A test will be performed on the BUS (circuits No. 914 and 915) for the module communications network and the ISO 9141 communication link (circuit No. 70).

3) If NGS tester displays SYSTEM PASSED, module communications networks are okay. Return to SYMPTOM TEST INDEX in article of system in question to continue diagnosis.

4) If NGS tester does not display SYSTEM PASSED, perform the following as applicable:

- If no response from NGS tester, go to TEST M: NO MODULE/ NETWORK COMMUNICATION – NO POWER TO NGS TESTER under SYSTEM TESTS.
- If NGS tester displays CKT70, CKT914 and/or CKT915 = SOME ECUS NO RESP/NOT EQUIP, go to SYMPTOM TEST INDEX table to continue diagnosis.
- If NGS tester displays CKT70 = ALL ECUS NO RESP/NOT EQUIP, go to TEST L: NO MODULE/NETWORK COMMUNICATIONS – ISO 9141 NETWORK under SYSTEM TESTS.
- If NGS tester displays CKT914 = ALL ECUS NO RESP/NOT EQUIP, go to TEST K: NO MODULE/NETWORK COMMUNICATIONS – SCP NETWORK under SYSTEM TESTS.
- If NGS tester displays CKT915 = ALL ECUS NO RESP/NOT EQUIP, go to TEST K: NO MODULE/NETWORK COMMUNICATIONS – SCP NETWORK under SYSTEM TESTS.
- If module in question is NO RESPONSE/NOT EQUIPPED, go to SYMPTOM TEST INDEX table to continue diagnosis.
- If module in question is NO RESPONSE ON CKT914 (BUS+), go to SYMPTOM TEST INDEX table to continue diagnosis.
- If module in question is NO RESPONSE ON CKT915 (BUS-), go to SYMPTOM TEST INDEX table to continue diagnosis.

SYMPTOM TEST INDEX

Symptom	Test
4-Wheel Anti-Lock Brake System (4WABS) Module Does Not Respond To NGS Tester	A
Remote Anti-Theft Personality (RAP) Module Does Not Respond To NGS Tester	B
Generic Electronic Module (GEM) Does Not Respond To NGS Tester	C
Restraint Control Module (RCM) Does Not Respond To NGS Tester	D
Air Suspension Control Module Does Not Respond To NGS Tester	E
Driver's Seat Module (DSM) Does Not Respond To NGS Tester [1]	F
Powertrain Control Module (PCM) Does Not Respond To NGS Tester	G
Instrument Cluster Does Not Respond To NGS Tester	H
Electronic Automatic Temperature Control (EATC) Module Does Not Respond To NGS Tester [2]	J
No Module/Network Communications – SCP Network	K
No Module/Network Communications – ISO 9141 Network	L
No Module/Network Communication – No Power To NGS Tester	M

[1] – Applies to Navigator with memory seat/mirrors only.
[2] – Applies to Navigator and Expedition Eddie Bauer only.

RETRIEVING & CLEARING DIAGNOSTIC TROUBLE CODES

Connect New Generation Star (NGS) tester to Data Link Connector (DLC). Following manufacturers instructions to retrieve and clear codes for desired module. See appropriate table under DIAGNOSTIC TROUBLE CODE (DTC) DEFINITIONS for a listing of Diagnostic Trouble Codes (DTCs) and appropriate test procedure.

ACCESSING PARAMETER IDENTIFICATION (PID)

Turn ignition switch to LOCK position. Connect New Generation Star (NGS) tester to Data Link Connector (DLC). Following manufacturers instructions enter PID/DATA MONITOR AND RECORD for desired module. Operate appropriate system and ensure PID expected values are obtained. See appropriate table under PARAMETER IDENTIFICATION (PID) DEFINITIONS.

SYSTEM TESTS

NOTE: Always check module power and ground circuits prior to replacing a control module. See appropriate wiring diagram in DATA LINK CONNECTORS, GROUND DISTRIBUTION or POWER DISTRIBUTION article in WIRING DIAGRAMS.

TEST A: 4-WHEEL ANTI-LOCK BRAKE SYSTEM (4WABS) MODULE DOES NOT RESPOND TO NGS TESTER

NOTE: After making any repair, perform data link diagnostic procedure. See DATA LINK DIAGNOSTIC TEST under COMMUNICATION NETWORK DIAGNOSTICS.

1) Turn ignition switch to LOCK position. Disconnect 4-Wheel Anti-Lock Brake System (4WABS) module Black 24-pin connector. See Fig. 3. Inspect 4WABS connector for loose, damaged or corroded terminals. Repair as necessary. If connectors are okay, go to next step.

2) Measure resistance of Light Blue/White wire between 4WABS module connector terminal No. 5 and DLC terminal No. 7. See Figs. 2 and 3. If resistance is less than 5 ohms, go to next step. If resistance is 5 ohms or more, go to step **4)**.

3) Connect 4WABS module connector. Perform data link diagnostic procedure. See DATA LINK DIAGNOSTIC TEST under COMMUNICATION NETWORK DIAGNOSTICS. If 4WABS module responds to NGS tester, system is functioning properly. If 4WABS module does not respond to NGS tester, replace 4WABS module. See appropriate ANTI-LOCK article in BRAKES in appropriate MITCHELL® manual.

4) Disconnect and inspect both halves of bulkhead Gray 40-pin connector C160 located at left rear of engine compartment. See Fig. 4. Inspect connector for loose, damaged or corroded terminals. Repair connector as necessary. If connector is okay, go to next step.

5) Measure resistance of Light Blue/White wire between DLC terminal No. 7 and bulkhead Gray connector C160 (female half) terminal No. 29. See Figs. 2 and 5. If resistance is less than 5 ohms, repair open in Light Blue/White wire between male half of bulkhead Gray connector C160 and 4WABS module connector. If resistance is 5 ohms or more, repair open in Light Blue/White wire between DLC and female half of bulkhead Gray connector C160.

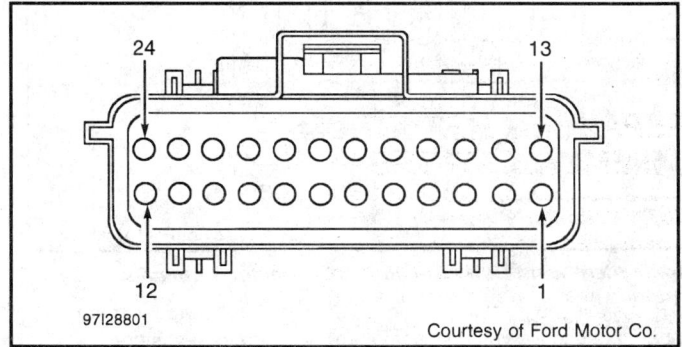

97I28801
Courtesy of Ford Motor Co.

Fig. 3: Identifying 4WABS Module Connector Terminals

TEST B: REMOTE ANTI-THEFT PERSONALITY (RAP) MODULE DOES NOT RESPOND TO NGS TESTER

NOTE: After making any repair, perform data link diagnostic procedure. See DATA LINK DIAGNOSTIC TEST under COMMUNICATION NETWORK DIAGNOSTICS.

1) Turn ignition switch to LOCK position. Disconnect Remote Anti-Theft Personality (RAP) module Black 26-pin connector. See Fig. 6. Inspect

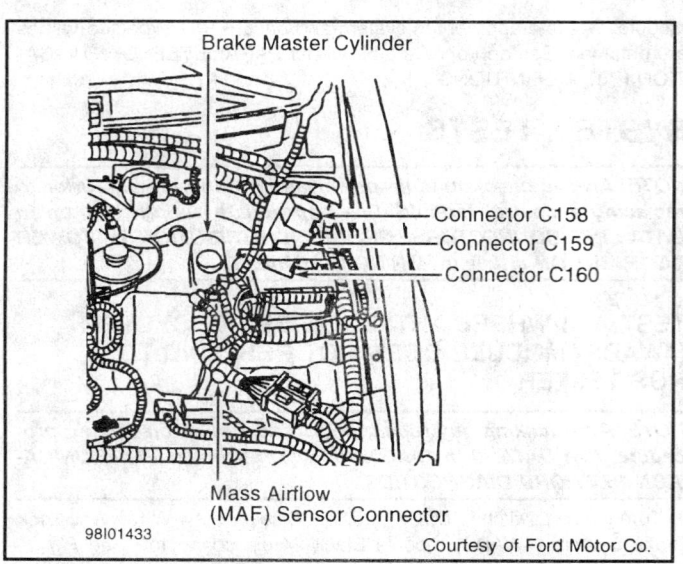

Fig. 4: Locating Bulkhead 40-Pin Connectors

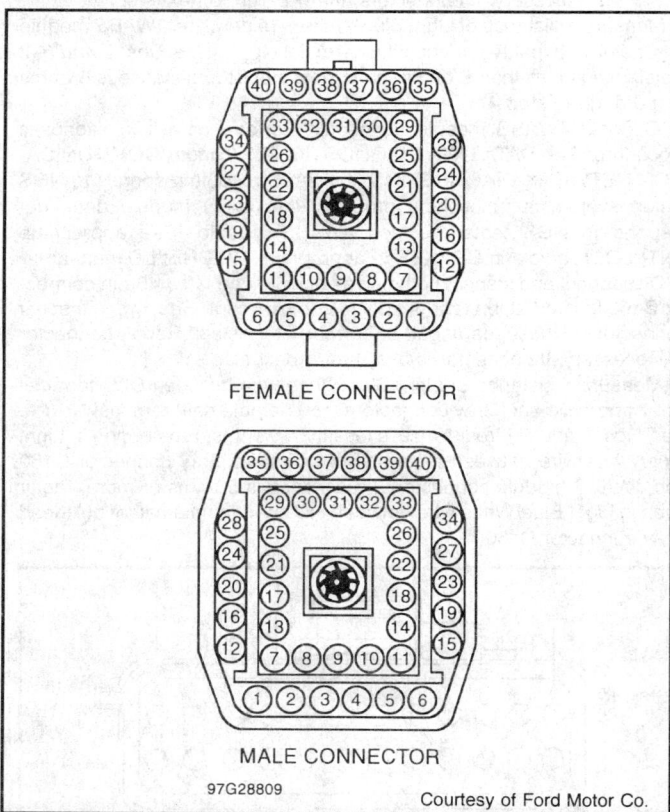

Fig. 5: Identifying Bulkhead 40-Pin Connector Terminals

RAP module connector for loose, damaged or corroded terminals. Repair as necessary. If connectors are okay, go to next step.

2) Measure resistance of Light Blue/White wire between RAP module connector terminal No. 3 and DLC terminal No. 7. *See Figs. 2 and 6.* If resistance is less than 5 ohms, go to next step. If resistance is 5 ohms or more, go to step **4)**.

3) Connect RAP module connector. Perform data link diagnostic procedure. See DATA LINK DIAGNOSTIC TEST under COMMUNICATION NETWORK DIAGNOSTICS. If RAP module responds to NGS tester, system is functioning properly. If RAP module does not respond to NGS tester, replace RAP module. See REMOTE ANTI-THEFT PERSONALITY MODULE under REMOVAL & INSTALLATION.

4) Disconnect and inspect both halves of in-line Gray 16-pin connector C247 located behind left side of instrument panel. *See Fig. 7.* Inspect connector for loose, damaged or corroded terminals. Repair as necessary. If connector is okay, go to next step.

5) Measure resistance of Light Blue/White wire between RAP module 26-pin connector terminal No. 3 and in-line 16-pin connector C247 (male half) terminal No. 16. *See Figs. 6 and 8.* If resistance is less than 5 ohms, repair Light Blue/White wire between female half of in-line connector C247 and DLC. If resistance is 5 ohms or more, repair open in Light Blue/White wire between RAP module connector and male half of in-line connector C247.

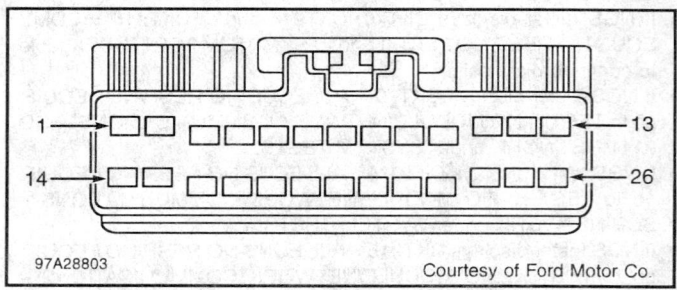

Fig. 6: Identifying GEM & RAP Module 26-Pin Connector Terminals

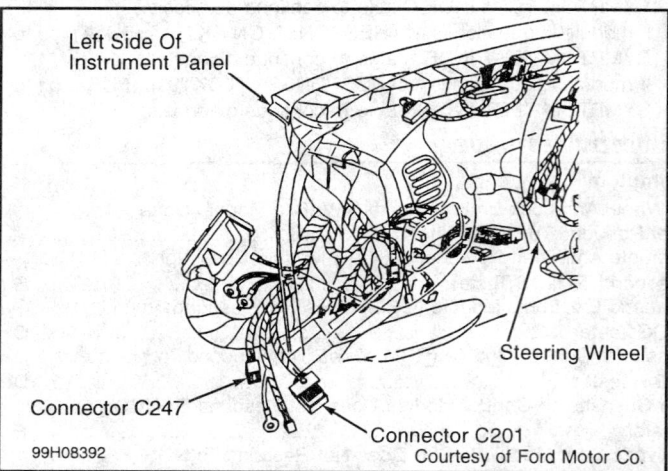

Fig. 7: Locating In-Line 66-Pin Connector C201 & In-Line 16-Pin Connector C247

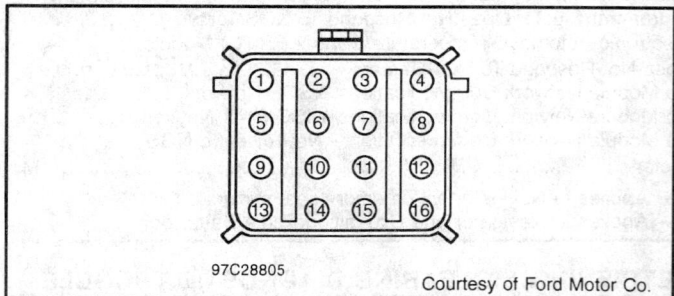

Fig. 8: Identifying In-Line 16-Pin Connector C247 Terminals (Male Side Of Connector Shown)

TEST C: GENERIC ELECTRONIC MODULE (GEM) DOES NOT RESPOND TO NGS TESTER

NOTE: After making any repair, perform data link diagnostic procedure. See DATA LINK DIAGNOSTIC TEST under COMMUNICATION NETWORK DIAGNOSTICS.

1) Turn ignition switch to LOCK position. Disconnect Generic Electronic Module (GEM) Gray 26-pin connector. *See Fig. 6.* Inspect connector

GEM connector for loose, damaged or corroded terminals. Repair as necessary. If connector is okay, go to next step.

2) Measure resistance of Light Blue/White wire between GEM 26-pin connector terminal No. 25 and DLC terminal No. 7. *See Figs. 2 and 6.* If resistance is less than 5 ohms, go to next step. If resistance is 5 ohms or more, repair open in Light Blue/White wire between GEM 26-pin connector and DLC.

3) Connect GEM 26-pin connector. Perform data link diagnostic procedure. See DATA LINK DIAGNOSTIC TEST under COMMUNICATION NETWORK DIAGNOSTICS. If GEM responds to NGS tester, system is functioning properly. If GEM does not respond to NGS tester, replace GEM. See GENERIC ELECTRONIC MODULE/CENTRAL TIMER MODULE (GEM/CTM) under REMOVAL & INSTALLATION in ANALOG INSTRUMENT PANEL – EXPEDITION, F150 & F250 LIGHT-DUTY PICKUP, & NAVIGATOR article.

TEST D: RESTRAINT CONTROL MODULE (RCM) DOES NOT RESPOND TO NGS TESTER

NOTE: After making any repair, perform data link diagnostic procedure. See DATA LINK DIAGNOSTIC TEST under COMMUNICATION NETWORK DIAGNOSTICS.

1) Turn ignition switch to LOCK position. Deactivate air bag system. See appropriate AIR BAG RESTRAINT SYSTEMS article. Disconnect Restraint Control Module (RCM) 26-pin connector. *See Fig. 9.* Inspect RCM connector for loose, damaged or corroded terminals. Repair as necessary. If connector is okay, go to next step.

2) Measure resistance of Light Blue/White wire between RCM connector terminal No. 5 and DLC terminal No. 7. *See Figs. 2 and 9.* If resistance is less than 5 ohms, go to next step. If resistance is 5 ohms or more, repair open in Light Blue/White wire between RCM connector and DLC.

3) Connect RCM connector. Perform data link diagnostic procedure. See DATA LINK DIAGNOSTIC TEST under COMMUNICATION NETWORK DIAGNOSTICS. If RCM responds to NGS tester, system is functioning properly. If RCM does not respond to NGS tester, replace RCM. See RESTRAINT CONTROL MODULE (RCM) under REMOVAL & INSTALLATION in AIR BAG RESTRAINT SYSTEMS – EXPEDITION, EXPLORER, MOUNTAINEER & NAVIGATOR article.

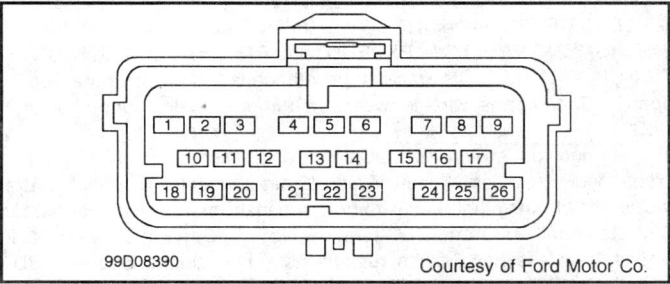

Fig. 9: Identifying Restraint Control Module (RCM) Connector Terminals

TEST E: AIR SUSPENSION CONTROL MODULE DOES NOT RESPOND TO NGS TESTER

NOTE: After making any repair, perform data link diagnostic procedure. See DATA LINK DIAGNOSTIC TEST under COMMUNICATION NETWORK DIAGNOSTICS.

1) Turn ignition switch to LOCK position. Air suspension control module has two 26-pin connectors. Disconnect air suspension control module 26-pin connector C296. Connector C296 has blank terminal No. 13. *See Fig. 10.* Inspect air suspension control module connector C296 for loose, damaged or corroded terminals. Repair as necessary. If connector is okay, go to next step.

2) Measure resistance of Light Blue/White wire between air suspension control module connector C296 terminal No. 29 and DLC terminal No. 7. *See Figs. 2 and 10.* If resistance is less than 5 ohms, go to next step. If

resistance is 5 ohms or more, repair open in Light Blue/White wire between air suspension control module and DLC.

3) Connect air suspension control module connector C296. Perform data link diagnostic procedure. See DATA LINK DIAGNOSTIC TEST under COMMUNICATION NETWORK DIAGNOSTICS. If air suspension control module responds to NGS tester, system is functioning properly. If air suspension control module does not respond to NGS tester, replace air suspension control module. See appropriate ELECTRONIC article in SUSPENSION in appropriate MITCHELL® manual.

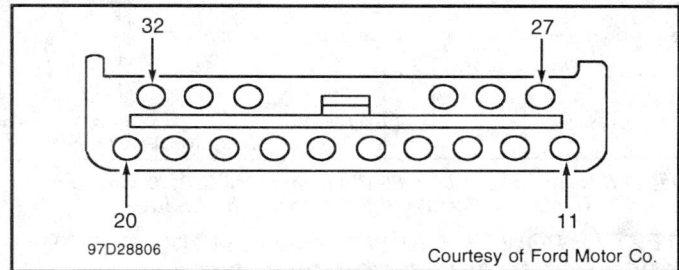

Fig. 10: Identifying Air Suspension Control Module Connector C296 Terminals

TEST F: DRIVER'S SEAT MODULE (DSM) DOES NOT RESPOND TO NGS TESTER

NOTE: After making any repair, perform data link diagnostic procedure. See DATA LINK DIAGNOSTIC TEST under COMMUNICATION NETWORK DIAGNOSTICS.

1) Turn ignition switch to LOCK position. Disconnect Driver's Seat Module (DSM) 22-pin connector. Inspect DSM connector for loose, damaged or corroded terminals. Repair as necessary. If connectors are okay, go to next step.

2) Measure resistance of Light Blue/White wire between DSM connector terminal No. 22 and DLC terminal No. 7. *See Figs. 2 and 11.* If resistance is less than 5 ohms, go next step. If resistance is 5 ohms or more, go to step **4)**.

3) Connect DSM connector. Perform data link diagnostic procedure. See DATA LINK DIAGNOSTIC TEST under COMMUNICATION NETWORK DIAGNOSTICS. If DSM module responds to NGS tester, system is functioning properly. If DSM module does not respond to NGS tester, replace DSM module. See DRIVER'S SEAT MODULE under REMOVAL & INSTALLATION in POWER SEATS – EXPEDITION, PICKUP & NAVIGATOR article.

4) Disconnect and inspect both halves of in-line Black 66-pin connector C201, located behind left side of instrument panel. *See Fig. 7.* Inspect connector for loose, damaged or corroded terminals. Repair as necessary. If connector is okay, go to next step.

5) Measure resistance of Light Blue/White wire between DLC connector terminal No. 7 and in-line 66-pin connector C207 terminal No. 11 (male half). *See Figs. 2 and 12.* If resistance is less than 5 ohms, repair open in Light Blue/White wire between DSM module connector and female half of in-line connector. If resistance is 5 ohms or more, repair open in Light Blue/White wire between male half of in-line connector and DLC.

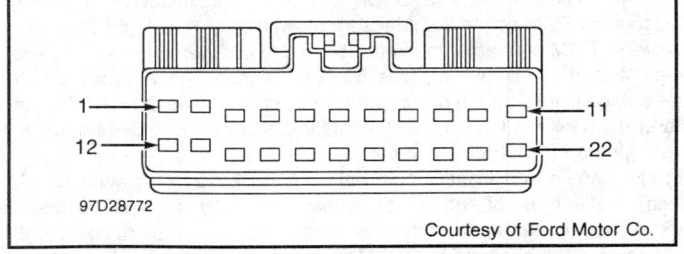

Fig. 11: Identifying DSM 22-Pin Connector Terminals

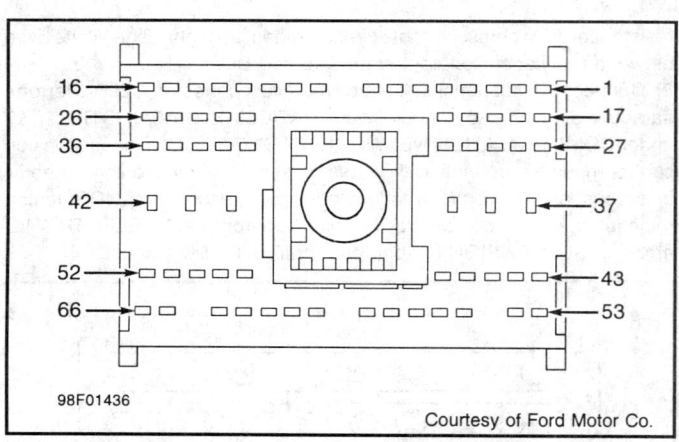

Fig. 12: Identifying In-Line 66-Pin Connector C201 Connector Terminals (Female Side Of Connector Shown)

TEST G: POWERTRAIN CONTROL MODULE (PCM) DOES NOT RESPOND TO NGS TESTER

NOTE: After making any repair, perform data link diagnostic procedure. See DATA LINK DIAGNOSTIC TEST under COMMUNICATION NETWORK DIAGNOSTICS.

NOTE: If test results indicate PCM is faulty, always check for any engine performance related Diagnostic Trouble Codes (DTCs) prior to replacing PCM. If any DTCs are present, service DTCs as necessary. See SELF-DIAGNOSTICS – EEC-V article in ENGINE PERFORMANCE in appropriate MITCHELL® manual.

1) Turn ignition switch to LOCK position. Disconnect Powertrain Control Module (PCM) 104-pin connector. Inspect PCM connector for loose, damaged or corroded terminals. Repair as necessary. Connect PCM connector. Perform data link diagnostic procedure. See DATA LINK DIAGNOSTIC TEST under COMMUNICATION NETWORK DIAGNOSTICS. If NGS tester displays PCM: NO RESPONSE ON CKT914 (BUS+), go to next step. If NGS tester does not display PCM: NO RESPONSE ON CKT 914 (BUS+), go to step 5).

2) Turn ignition switch to LOCK position. Disconnect NGS tester. Disconnect PCM connector. Measure resistance of Tan/Orange wire between PCM connector terminal No. 16 and DLC terminal No. 2. See Figs. 2 and 13. If resistance is less than 5 ohms, perform quick test. See QUICK TEST in SELF-DIAGNOSTICS – EEC-V article in ENGINE PERFORMANCE in appropriate MITCHELL® manual. If resistance is 5 ohms or more, go to next step.

3) Disconnect and inspect both halves of bulkhead Black 40-pin connector C158 located at left rear of engine compartment. See Fig. 4. Inspect connectors for loose, damaged or corroded terminals. Repair as necessary. If connectors are okay, go to next step.

4) Measure resistance of Tan/Orange wire between DLC terminal No. 2 and female half of bulkhead connector C158 terminal No. 25. See Figs. 2 and 5. If resistance is less than 5 ohms, repair open in Tan/Orange wire between male half of bulkhead connector C158 and PCM connector. If resistance is 5 ohms or more, repair open in Tan/Orange wire between female half of bulkhead connector C158 and DLC.

5) Turn ignition switch to LOCK position. Disconnect NGS tester. Disconnect PCM connector. Measure resistance of Pink/Light Blue wire between PCM connector terminal No. 15 and DLC terminal No. 10. See Figs. 2 and 13. If resistance is 5 ohms or more, go to next step. If resistance is less than 5 ohms, perform quick test. See QUICK TEST in SELF-DIAGNOSTICS – EEC-V article in ENGINE PERFORMANCE in appropriate MITCHELL® manual.

6) Disconnect and inspect both halves of bulkhead connector C158, located at left rear of engine compartment. See Fig. 4. Inspect connectors for loose, damaged or corroded terminals. Repair as necessary. If connectors are okay, go to next step.

7) Measure resistance of Pink/Light Blue wire between DLC terminal No. 10 and female half of bulkhead connector C158 terminal No. 29. See Figs. 5 and 13. If resistance is less than 5 ohms, repair open in Pink/Light Blue wire between male half of bulkhead connector C158 and PCM connector. If resistance is 5 ohms or more, repair open in Pink/Light Blue wire between female half of bulkhead connector C158 and DLC.

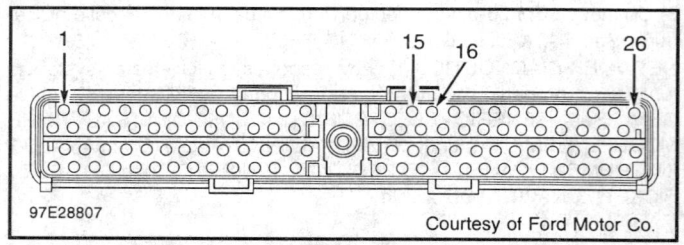

Fig. 13: Identifying PCM Connector Terminals

TEST H: INSTRUMENT CLUSTER DOES NOT RESPOND TO NGS TESTER

NOTE: After making any repair, perform data link diagnostic procedure. See DATA LINK DIAGNOSTIC TEST under COMMUNICATION NETWORK DIAGNOSTICS.

1) Turn ignition switch to LOCK position. Disconnect instrument cluster White 22-pin connector C237. See Fig. 14. Inspect instrument cluster connector C237 for loose, damaged or corroded terminals. Repair as necessary. If connector is okay, go to next step.

2) Connect instrument cluster connector C237. Perform data link diagnostic procedure. See DATA LINK DIAGNOSTIC TEST under COMMUNICATION NETWORK DIAGNOSTICS. If NGS tester displays HEC: NO RESPONSE ON CKT914 (BUS+), go to next step. If NGS tester does not display HEC: NO RESPONSE ON CKT914 (BUS+), go to step 4).

3) Turn ignition switch to LOCK position. Disconnect NGS tester. Disconnect instrument cluster White 22-pin connector C237. Measure resistance of Tan/Orange wire between instrument cluster connector C237 terminal No. 1 and DLC terminal No. 2. See Figs. 2 and 14. If resistance is less than 5 ohms, replace instrument cluster. See INSTRUMENT CLUSTER under REMOVAL & INSTALLATION in ANALOG INSTRUMENT PANELS – EXPEDITION, F150 & F250 LIGHT-DUTY PICKUP, & NAVIGATOR article. If resistance is 5 ohms or more, repair open in Tan/Orange wire between instrument cluster connector and DLC.

4) Turn ignition switch to LOCK position. Disconnect NGS tester. Disconnect instrument cluster White 22-pin connector C237. Measure resistance of Pink/Light Blue wire between instrument cluster connector C237 terminal No. 2 and DLC terminal No. 10. See Figs. 2 and 14. If resistance is less than 5 ohms, replace instrument cluster. See INSTRUMENT CLUSTER under REMOVAL & INSTALLATION in ANALOG INSTRUMENT PANELS – EXPEDITION, F150 & F250 LIGHT-DUTY PICKUP, & NAVIGATOR article. If resistance is 5 ohms or more, repair open in Pink/Light Blue wire.

TEST J: ELECTRONIC AUTOMATIC TEMPERATURE CONTROL (EATC) MODULE DOES NOT RESPOND TO NGS TESTER

NOTE: After making any repair, perform data link diagnostic procedure. See DATA LINK DIAGNOSTIC TEST under COMMUNICATION NETWORK DIAGNOSTICS.

1) Turn ignition switch to LOCK position. Electronic Automatic Temperature Control (EATC) module has two 13-pin connectors. Disconnect EATC module 13-pin connector C280. Connector C280 has a blank terminal No. 5. See Fig. 15. Inspect EATC module connector C280 for loose, damaged or corroded terminals. Repair as necessary. If connectors are okay, go to next step.

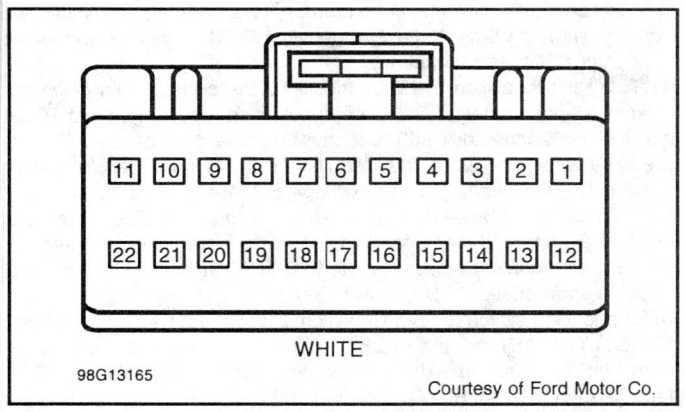

WHITE

98G13165

Courtesy of Ford Motor Co.

Fig. 14: Identifying Instrument Cluster 22-Pin Connector C237 Terminals

2) Perform data link diagnostic procedure. See DATA LINK DIAGNOSTIC TEST under COMMUNICATION NETWORK DIAGNOSTICS. If NGS tester displays EATC: NO RESPONSE ON CKT914 (BUS+), go to next step. If NGS tester does not display EATC: NO RESPONSE ON CKT914 (BUS+), go to step **4**).

3) Turn ignition switch to LOCK position. Disconnect NGS tester. Disconnect EATC module 13-pin connector C280. Measure resistance of Tan/Orange wire between EATC module connector C280 terminal No. 15 and DLC terminal No. 2. See Figs. 2 and 15. If resistance is less than 5 ohms, replace EATC module. See appropriate AUTOMATIC A/C-HEATER SYSTEMS article in appropriate MITCHELL® AIR CONDITIONING & HEATING SERVICE & REPAIR manual. If resistance is 5 ohms or more, repair open in Tan/Orange wire between EATC module connector and DLC.

4) Turn ignition switch to LOCK position. Disconnect NGS tester. Disconnect EATC module 13-pin connector C280. Measure resistance of Pink/Light Blue wire between EATC module connector C280 terminal No. 1 at and DLC terminal No. 10. See Figs. 2 and 15. If resistance is less than 5 ohms, replace EATC module. See appropriate AUTOMATIC A/C-HEATER SYSTEMS article in appropriate MITCHELL® AIR CONDITIONING & HEATING SERVICE & REPAIR manual. If resistance is 5 ohms or more, repair open in Pink/Light Blue wire between EATC module connector and DLC.

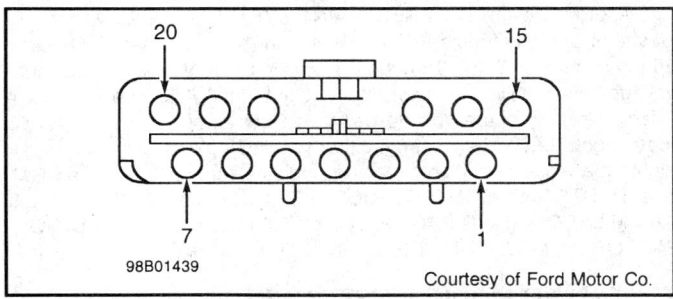

20   15

7   1

98B01439

Courtesy of Ford Motor Co.

Fig. 15: Identifying EATC Module 13-Pin Connector C280 Terminals

TEST K: NO MODULE/NETWORK COMMUNICATIONS – SCP NETWORK

NOTE: *After making any repair, perform data link diagnostic procedure. See DATA LINK DIAGNOSTIC TEST under COMMUNICATION NETWORK DIAGNOSTICS.*

NOTE: *Depending on module configuration, with all modules connected and with ignition switch in RUN position or with engine running 2-3 volts may be present at Data Link Connector (DLC) terminals No. 2 (Tan/Orange wire) and No. 10 (Pink/Light Blue wire). These are the Standard Corporate Protocol (SCP) diagnostic communications network circuits.*

1) Inspect New Generation Star (NGS) tester terminals for loose, damaged or corroded terminals. Repair as necessary. If terminals are okay, go to next step.

2) Turn ignition switch to LOCK position. Inspect Data Link Connector (DLC) terminals for loose, damaged or corroded terminals. Pay particular attention to terminals No. 2 (Tan/Orange wire) and No. 10 (Pink/Light Blue wire). See Fig. 2. Repair as necessary. If terminals are okay, go to next step.

3) Turn ignition switch to LOCK position. Disconnect Powertrain Control Module (PCM) 104-pin connector. Measure resistance of Tan/Orange wire between PCM connector terminal No. 16 and DLC terminal No. 2. See Figs. 2 and 13. Measure resistance of Pink/Light Blue wire between PCM connector terminal No. 15 and DLC terminal No. 10. If resistances are less than 5 ohms, go to next step. If either resistance is 5 ohms or more, repair open in appropriate wire.

4) Turn ignition switch to RUN position. Measure voltage between DLC terminals No. 2 (Tan/Orange wire) and No. 4 (Black wire). Measure voltage between DLC terminals No. 2 (Tan/Orange wire) and No. 16 (Light Blue/White wire). Measure voltage between DLC terminals No. 10 (Pink/Light Blue) and No. 4 (Black wire). Measure voltage between DLC terminals No. 10 (Pink/Light Blue) and No. 16 (Light Blue/White wire). If any reading indicates voltage, go to next step. If all readings indicate zero volts, perform quick test. See QUICK TEST in SELF-DIAGNOSTICS – EEC-V article in ENGINE PERFORMANCE in appropriate MITCHELL® manual.

5) Turn ignition switch to LOCK position. Connect PCM connector. Disconnect bulkhead Black 40-pin connector C158. See Fig. 4. Turn ignition switch to RUN position. Measure voltage between DLC terminals No. 2 (Tan/Orange wire) and No. 4 (Black wire). Measure voltage between DLC terminals No. 2 (Tan/Orange wire) and No. 16 (Light Blue/White wire). Measure voltage between DLC terminals No. 10 (Pink/Light Blue wire) and No. 4 (Black wire). Measure voltage between DLC terminals No. 10 (Pink/Light Blue wire) and No. 16 (Light Blue/White wire). If all readings indicate zero volts, repair appropriate wires between bulkhead C158 and PCM connector. If any reading indicates voltage and vehicle is equipped with Electronic Automatic Temperature Control (EATC) module, connect bulkhead connector C158 and go to next step. If any reading indicates voltage and vehicle is not equipped with EATC module, connect bulkhead connector C158 and go to step **7**).

6) Turn ignition switch to LOCK position. Disconnect Electronic Automatic Temperature Control (EATC) module 13-pin connector C280. EATC module has two 13-pin connectors. Connector C280 has blank terminal No. 5. See Fig. 15. Measure voltage between DLC terminals No. 2 (Tan/Orange wire) and No. 4 (Black wire). Measure voltage between DLC terminals No. 2 (Tan/Orange wire) and No. 16 (Light Blue/White wire). Measure voltage between DLC terminals No. 10 (Pink/Light Blue wire) and No. 4 (Black wire). Measure voltage between DLC terminals No. 10 (Pink/Light Blue wire) and No. 16 (Light Blue/White wire). If any reading indicates voltage, go to next step. If all readings indicate zero volts, replace EATC module. See appropriate AUTOMATIC A/C-HEATER SYSTEMS article in appropriate MITCHELL® AIR CONDITIONING & HEATING SERVICE & REPAIR manual.

7) Turn ignition switch to LOCK position. Disconnect instrument cluster White 22-pin connector C237. See Fig. 14. Turn ignition switch to RUN position. Measure voltage between DLC terminals No. 2 (Tan/Orange

wire) and No. 4 (Black wire). Measure voltage between DLC terminals No. 2 (Tan/Orange wire) and No. 16 (Light Blue/White wire). Measure voltage between DLC terminals No. 10 (Pink/Light Blue wire) and No. 4 (Black wire). Measure voltage between DLC terminals No. 10 (Pink/ Light Blue wire) and No. 16 (Light Blue/White wire). If any reading indicates voltage, repair appropriate wire between bulkhead connector C158 (female side) and instrument cluster connector C237. If all readings indicate zero volts, replace instrument cluster. See INSTRUMENT CLUSTER under REMOVAL & INSTALLATION in ANALOG INSTRUMENT PANELS – EXPEDITION, F150 & F250 LIGHT-DUTY PICKUP, & NAVIGATOR article.

TEST L: NO MODULE/NETWORK COMMUNICATIONS – ISO 9141 NETWORK

NOTE: After making any repair, perform data link diagnostic procedure. See DATA LINK DIAGNOSTIC TEST under COMMUNICATION NETWORK DIAGNOSTICS.

NOTE: Depending on module configuration, with all modules connected and with ignition switch in RUN position or with engine running 2-3 volts may be present at Data Link Connector (DLC) terminal No. 7 (Light Blue/White wire). This is the International Standards Organization (ISO) 9141 diagnostic communications network circuit.

1) Turn ignition switch to LOCK position. Inspect Data Link Connector (DLC) for connector for loose, damaged or corroded terminals. Pay particular attention to terminals No. 4 (Black wire) and No. 7 (Light Blue/White wire). See Fig. 2. Repair as necessary. If connector is okay, go to next step.
2) Disconnect Generic Electronic Module (GEM) Gray 26-pin connector C239. Inspect GEM connector C239 for loose, damaged or corroded terminals. Repair as necessary. If connector is okay, go to next step.
3) Measure resistance of Light Blue/White wire between GEM connector C239 terminal No. 25 and DLC terminal No. 7. See Figs. 2 and 6. If resistance is less than 5 ohms, go to next step. If resistance is 5 ohms or more, repair open in Light Blue/White wire between GEM connector C239 and DLC.
4) Turn ignition switch to RUN position. Measure voltage between DLC terminals No. 7 (Light Blue/White wire) and No. 4 (Black wire). Measure voltage between DLC terminals No. 7 and 16 (both Light Blue/White wires). If both readings indicate zero volts, replace GEM. See GENERIC ELECTRONIC MODULE/CENTRAL TIMER MODULE (GEM/CTM) under REMOVAL & INSTALLATION in ANALOG INSTRUMENT PANELS – EXPEDITION, F150 & F250 LIGHT-DUTY PICKUP, & NAVIGATOR article. If either reading indicates voltage and vehicle is not equipped with Driver's Seat Module (DSM) and air suspension control module, go to step 8). If either reading indicates voltage and vehicle is equipped with DSM and air suspension control module, go to next step. If either reading indicates voltage and vehicle is only equipped with DSM (no air suspension module), go to next step. If either reading indicates voltage and vehicle is only equipped with air suspension control module (no DSM), go to step 7).
5) Turn ignition switch to LOCK position. Disconnect DSM 22-pin connector C356. Turn ignition switch to RUN position. Measure voltage between DLC terminals No. 7 (Light Blue/White wire) and No. 4 (Black wire). Measure voltage between DLC terminals No. 7 and 16 (both Light Blue/White wires). If either reading indicates voltage, go to next step. If both readings indicate zero volts, replace DSM. See DRIVER SEAT MODULE under REMOVAL & INSTALLATION in POWER SEATS – EXPEDITION, PICKUP & NAVIGATOR article.
6) Turn ignition switch to LOCK position. Disconnect in-line Black 66-pin connector C201. See Fig. 7. Turn ignition switch to RUN position. Measure voltage between DLC terminals No. 7 (Light Blue/White wire) and No. 4 (Black wire). Measure voltage between DLC terminals No. 7 and 16 (both Light Blue wires). If either reading indicates voltage and vehicle is equipped with air suspension control module, go to next step. If either reading indicates voltage and vehicle is not equipped with air

suspension control module, go to step 8). If both readings indicate zero volts, repair Light Blue/White wire between DSM connector and in-line connector C201 (female side).
7) Turn ignition switch to LOCK position. Disconnect air suspension module 16-pin connector C296. Air suspension module has two 16-pin connectors. Connector C296 has blank terminal No. 13. See Fig. 10. Measure voltage between DLC terminals No. 7 (Light Blue/White wire) and No. 4 (Black wire). Measure voltage between DLC terminals No. 7 and 16 (both Light Blue/White wires). If either reading indicates voltage, go to next step. If both readings indicate zero volts, replace air suspension module. See appropriate ELECTRONIC article in SUSPENSION in appropriate MITCHELL® manual.
8) Turn ignition switch to LOCK position. Disconnect Remote Anti-Theft Personality (RAP) module Black 26-pin connector C256. See Fig. 6. Turn ignition switch to RUN position. Measure voltage between DLC terminals No. 7 (Light Blue/White wire) and No. 4 (Black wire). Measure voltage between DLC terminals No. 7 and 16 (both are Light Blue wires). If either reading indicates voltage, go to next step. If both readings indicate zero volts, replace RAP module. See REMOTE ANTI-THEFT PERSONALITY MODULE under REMOVAL & INSTALLATION.
9) Turn ignition switch to LOCK position. Disconnect in-line Gray 16-pin connector C247. See Fig. 7. Turn ignition switch to RUN position. Measure voltage between DLC terminals No. 7 (Light Blue/White wire) and 4 (Black wire). Measure voltage between DLC terminals No. 7 and 16 (both Light Blue wires). If either reading indicates voltage, go to next step. If both readings indicate zero volts, repair Light Blue/white wire between in-line connector C247 (male side) and RAP module connector.
10) Turn ignition switch to LOCK position. Disconnect 4-Wheel Anti-Lock Brake System (4WABS) module Black 24-pin connector. Turn ignition switch to RUN position. Measure voltage between DLC terminals No. 7 (Light Blue/White wire) and No. 4 (Black wire). Measure voltage between DLC terminals No. 7 and 16 (both Light Blue/White wires). If either reading indicates voltage, go to next step. If both readings indicate zero volts, replace 4WABS module.
11) Turn ignition switch to LOCK position. Disconnect in-line Gray 40-pin connector C160. See Fig. 4. Turn ignition switch to RUN position. Measure voltage between DLC terminals No. 7 (Light Blue/White wire) and No. 4 (Black wire). Measure voltage between DLC terminals No. 7 and 16 (both Light Blue/White wires). If either reading indicates voltage, go to next step. If both readings indicate zero volts, repair Light Blue/White wire between 4WABS connector and in-line connector C160 (male side).
12) Turn ignition switch to LOCK position. Deactivate air bag system. See appropriate AIR BAG RESTRAINT SYSTEMS article. Disconnect Restraint Control Module (RCM) 26-pin connector. Connect GEM Gray 26-pin connector C239. Turn ignition switch to RUN position. Measure voltage between DLC terminals No. 7 (Light Blue/White wire) and No. 4 (Black wire). Measure voltage between DLC terminals No. 7 and 16 (both Light Blue/White wires). If either reading indicates voltage, repair Light Blue/White wire. If both readings indicate zero volts, replace RCM. See RESTRAINT CONTROL MODULE (RCM) under REMOVAL & INSTALLATION in AIR BAG RESTRAINT SYSTEMS – EXPEDITION, EXPLORER, MOUNTAINEER & NAVIGATOR article.

TEST M: NO MODULE/NETWORK COMMUNICATION – NO POWER TO NGS TESTER

NOTE: After making any repair, perform data link diagnostic procedure. See DATA LINK DIAGNOSTIC TEST under COMMUNICATION NETWORK DIAGNOSTICS.

1) Inspect NGS tester connector for loose, damaged or corroded terminals. Repair as necessary. If connector is okay, go to next step.
2) Turn ignition switch to LOCK position. Inspect Data Link Connector (DLC) for loose, damaged or corroded terminals. Repair as necessary. If connector is okay, go to next step.
3) Measure voltage between DLC terminal No. 16 (Light Blue/White wire) and ground. See Fig. 2. If voltage is more than 10 volts, go to next step. If voltage is 10 volts or less, repair Light Blue/White wire between central junction box and DLC.

4) Measure resistance between DLC terminal No. 4 (Black wire) and ground. Measure resistance between DLC terminal No. 5 (Black/White wire) and ground. If both readings are less than 5 ohms, repair or replace NGS tester. If any resistance reading is 5 ohms or more, repair open in Black wire or Black/White wire between ground and DLC.

DIAGNOSTIC TROUBLE CODE (DTC) DEFINITIONS

NOTE: For Powertrain Control Module (PCM) DTC identification and repair, see SELF-DIAGNOSTICS – EEC-V article in ENGINE PERFORMANCE in appropriate MITCHELL® manual.

AIR SUSPENSION CONTROL MODULE DTC INDEX

DTC	Description	Test
B1318	Battery Voltage Low	1
B1342	Air Suspension Control Module Defective	1
B1485	Brake Pedal Input Circuit Battery Short	2
B1566	Door Ajar Circuit Short To Ground	1
B1749	Park/Neutral Switch Circuit Failure	3
B2140	Initialization Failure (Vehicle Ride Height Not Programmed)	1
C1439	Vehicle Acceleration EEC-V Circuit Failure	1
C1724	Air Suspension Height Sensor Power Circuit Failure	1
C1725	Air Suspension Front Pneumatic Failure	3
C1726	Air Suspension Rear Pneumatic Failure	1
C1756	Air Suspension Front Height Sensor High Signal Circuit Failure	3
C1760	Air Suspension Rear Height Sensor High Signal Circuit Failure	1
C1770	Air Suspension Vent Solenoid Output Circuit Failure	1
C1790	Air Suspension Left Rear Air Spring Solenoid Output Circuit Failure	1
C1795	Air Suspension Right Rear Air Spring Solenoid Output Circuit Failure	1
C1830	Air Suspension Compressor Relay Circuit Failure	1
C1845	Air Suspension Front Inflator Solenoid Output Circuit Failure	3
C1865	Air Suspension Rear Inflator Solenoid Output Circuit Failure	3
C1869	Air Suspension Gate Solenoid Output Circuit Failure	3
C1917	Steering Electronic Variable Orifice (EVO) Out-Of-Range Fault	4
P1807	4x4 High Indicator Circuit Short To Ground	3
P1808	4x4 Low Indicator Circuit Short To Ground	3

[1] – See appropriate ELECTRONIC article in SUSPENSION in appropriate MITCHELL® manual.
[2] – Using NGS tester, perform air suspension control module self-test. Make sure brake pedal is not pressed. If B1485 is retrieved again, repair Brake Pedal Position (BPP) switch circuit. See WIRING DIAGRAMS in appropriate CRUISE CONTROL SYSTEMS article.
[3] – Applies only to 4-Wheel Air Suspension system. See appropriate ELECTRONIC article in SUSPENSION in appropriate MITCHELL® manual.
[4] – See appropriate ELECTRONIC article in STEERING in appropriate MITCHELL® manual.

ANTI-LOCK BRAKE SYSTEM (ABS) MODULE DTC INDEX

DTC	Description	Test
B1342	ECU Defective	1
C1095/C1096	Pump Motor	1
C1113/C1115	Internal Power Relay	1
C1145	Right Front Wheel Speed Sensor (Electrical/Static)	1
C1148/C1234	Right Front Wheel Speed Sensor (Dynamic)	1
C1155	Left Front Wheel Speed Sensor (Electrical/Static)	1
C1158/C1233	Left Front Wheel Speed Sensor (Dynamic)	1
C1169	Excessive Dump Time	1
C1184	ABS System Timeout	1
C1185	Open Internal Power Relay	1
C1194/C1196	Left Front Dump Valve	1
C1198/C1200	Left Front Isolation Valve	1
C1202/C1204	Rear Dump Valve	1
C1206/C1208	Rear isolation Valve	1
C1210/C1212	Right Front Dump Valve	1
C1214/C1216	Right Front Isolation Valve	1
C1220	Yellow Anti-Lock Brake System (ABS) Warning Indicator Failure	1
C1222	Wheel Speed Error (Dynamic)	1
C1229/C1237	Rear Wheel Speed Sensor (Dynamic)	1
C1230	Rear Wheel Speed Sensor (Electrical/Static)	1

[1] – See appropriate ANTI-LOCK article in BRAKES in appropriate MITCHELL® manual.

AUDIO CONTROL MODULE (ACM) DTC INDEX

DTC	Description	Test
B1342	ECU Defective	1
B2401	Audio Tape Deck Mechanism Fault	2
B2402	Audio CD/DJ Thermal Shutdown Fault	3
B2403	Audio CD/DJ Internal Fault	3
B2404	Audio Steering Wheel Switch Circuit Fault	3

AUDIO CONTROL MODULE (ACM) DTC INDEX (Cont.)

DTC	Description	Test
B2405	Audio Single-Disc CD Player Thermal Shutdown Fault	3
B2406	Audio Single-Disc CD Player Internal Fault	3
U2003	Audio Compact Disk/Disk Jockey Not Responding	3
U2005	Audio Rear Integrated Control Panel Unit Not Responding	4
U2008	Audio Phone Not Responding	5
U2014	Audio Subwoofer Unit Not Responding	3

1 – Using NGS tester, retrieve and document all continuous DTCs. Perform Audio Control Module (ACM) self-test. If DTC B1342 is retrieved again, replace ACM.

2 – Verify no tape is in Audio Control Module (ACM). Using NGS tester, retrieve and document all continuous DTCs. Perform ACM self-test. If B2401 is retrieved again, replace or repair ACM.

3 – Repair audio system concern.

4 – RICP is not present, disconnected or inoperative. If vehicle is not equipped with RICP/RSC, code is not applicable.

5 – Repair cellular phone system concern.

DRIVER'S SEAT MODULE (DSM) DTC TEST INDEX

DTC	Description	Test
B1342	ECU Defective	1
B1529	Memory Set Switch Circuit Short To Power	2
B1533	Memory 1 Switch Circuit Short To Power	2
B1537	Memory 2 Switch Circuit Short To Battery	2
B1663	Driver's Seat Front Up/Down Motor Stalled	2 3
B1664	Driver's Seat Rear Up/Down Motor Stalled	2 3
B1665	Driver's Seat Forward/Backward Motor Stalled	2 3
B1667	Driver's Mirror Up/Down Motor Stalled	4
B1668	Driver's Mirror Right/Left Motor Stalled	4
B1669	Passenger's Mirror Up/Down Motor Stalled	4
B1670	Passenger's Mirror Right/Left Motor Stalled	4
B1676	Battery Pack Voltage Out Of Range	5
B1697	Driver's Mirror/Passenger's Switch Circuit Short To Power	6
B1711	Driver's Seat Front Up Switch Circuit Short To Power	3
B1715	Driver's Seat Front Down Switch Circuit Short To Power	3
B1719	Driver's Seat Forward Switch Circuit Short To Power	3
B1723	Driver's Seat Rearward Switch Circuit Short To Power	3
B1727	Driver's Seat Rear Up Switch Circuit Short To Power	3
B1731	Driver's Seat Rear Down Switch Circuit Short To Power	3
B1735	Driver's Mirror Vertical Switch Circuit Short To Battery	6
B1739	Driver's Mirror Horizontal Switch circuit Short To Power	6
B1743	Passenger's Mirror Vertical Switch Circuit Short To Power	6
B1747	Passenger's Mirror Horizontal Switch Circuit Short To Power	6
B1751	Park/Neutral Switch Circuit Short To Power	7
B1950	Seat Rear Up/Down Potentiometer Feedback Circuit Failure	2
B1952	Seat Rear Up/Down Potentiometer Feedback Circuit Short To Power	2
B1954	Seat Front Up/Down Potentiometer Feedback Circuit Failure	2
B1956	Seat Front Up/Down Potentiometer Feedback Circuit Short To Power	2
B1962	Seat Horizontal Forward/Rearward Potentiometer Feedback Circuit Failure	2
B1964	Seat Horizontal Forward/Rearward Potentiometer Feedback Circuit Short To Power	2
B1987	Pedal Forward/Rearward Motor Stalled	8
B1988	Pedal Position Forward Switch Circuit Short To Power	8
B1989	Pedal Position Rearward Switch Circuit Short To Power	8
B1990	Pedal Forward/Rearward Potentiometer Feedback Circuit Failure	8
B1991	Pedal Forward/Rearward Potentiometer Feedback Circuit Short To Power	8

1 – Using NGS tester, retrieve and document all continuous DTCs. Perform Driver's Seat Module (DSM) self-test. If DTC B1342 is retrieved again, replace DSM.

2 – Perform TEST G: MEMORY SEAT DOES NOT OPERATE FROM MEMORY SWITCH under SYSTEM TESTS in POWER SEATS – EXPEDITION, PICKUP & NAVIGATOR article.

3 – Perform TEST F: MEMORY SEAT INOPERATIVE under SYSTEM TESTS in POWER SEATS – EXPEDITION, PICKUP & NAVIGATOR article.

4 – Perform TEST A: MEMORY MIRROR INOPERATIVE or TEST B: MEMORY MIRROR INOPERATIVE AT MEMORY SET SWITCH under SYSTEM TESTS in POWER MEMORY MIRRORS – NAVIGATOR article.

5 – Check charging system concern. See GENERATORS – ECONOLINE, EXPEDITION, EXPLORER (4.0L OHV), PICKUP (GASOLINE), NAVIGATOR & RANGER article in STARTING & CHARGING SYSTEMS. If charging system is okay, repair power and ground circuits to Driver Seat Module (DSM).

6 – Perform TEST A: MEMORY MIRROR INOPERATIVE under SYSTEM TESTS in POWER MEMORY MIRRORS – NAVIGATOR article.

7 – Perform TEST J: NO COMMUNICATION WITH DSM under SYSTEM TESTS in POWER SEATS – EXPEDITION, PICKUP & NAVIGATOR article.

8 – Repair appropriate circuit as necessary. See appropriate wiring diagram in ADJUSTABLE PEDAL ASSEMBLY SYSTEMS article.

ELECTRONIC AUTOMATIC TEMPERATURE CONTROL (EATC) MODULE DTC INDEX

DTC	Description	Test
B1249	Blend Door Short/Failure	1

ELECTRONIC AUTOMATIC TEMPERATURE CONTROL (EATC) MODULE DTC INDEX (Cont.)

DTC	Description	Test
B1251	A/C In-Car Temperature Sensor Open Circuit	1
B1253	A/C In-Car Temperature Sensor Short To Ground	1
B1255	A/C Ambient Temperature Sensor Open Circuit	1
B1257	A/C Ambient Temperature Sensor Short To Ground	1
B1261	A/C Solar Radiation Sensor Circuit Short To Ground	1
U1073	SCP Invalid Or Missing Data For Engine Coolant	2
U1341	SCP Invalid Data For Vehicle Speed	2

[1] – Repair climate control system concern. See appropriate AUTOMATIC A/C-HEATER SYSTEMS article in appropriate MITCHELL® AIR CONDITIONING & HEATING SERVICE & REPAIR manual.

[2] – Perform quick test. See QUICK TEST in SELF-DIAGNOSTICS – EEC-V article in ENGINE PERFORMANCE in appropriate MITCHELL® manual.

GENERIC ELECTRONIC MODULE (GEM) DTC TEST INDEX

DTC	Description	Test
B1240	Rear Washer Pump Relay Coil Circuit Failure	1
B1241	Rear Washer Pump Relay Coil Short To Power	1
B1302	Accessory Delay Relay Coil Circuit Failure	2
B1304	Accessory Delay Relay Coil Circuit Short To Power	2
B1313	Battery Saver Relay Coil Circuit Failure	2
B1315	Battery Saver Relay Coil Circuit Short To Power	2
B1317	Battery Voltage High	3
B1318	Battery Voltage Low	3
B1322	Driver's Door Ajar Circuit Short To Ground	4
B1323	Door Ajar Circuit Failure	5
B1325	Door Ajar Lamp Circuit Short To Power	6
B1330	Passenger's Door Ajar Circuit Short To Ground	4
B1334	Decklid Ajar Rear Door Circuit Short To Ground	4
B1338	Door Ajar Right Rear Circuit Short To Ground	4
B1340	Chime Input Request Circuit Short To Ground	7
B1342	ECU Defective	8
B1345	Heated Backlite Input Circuit Short To Ground	9
B1347	Heated Backlite Relay Circuit Failure	9
B1349	Heated Backlite Relay Short To Power	9
B1352	Ignition Key-In Circuit Failure	7
B1355	Ignition Run Circuit Failure	10
B1359	Ignition Run/Acc Circuit Failure	10
B1365	Ignition Start Circuit Short To Battery	11
B1371	Illuminated Entry Relay Circuit Failure	4
B1373	Illuminated Entry Relay Short To Power	4
B1398	Driver's Window One Touch Down Relay Circuit Failure	12
B1400	Driver's Power Window One Touch Down Relay Circuit Short To Power	12
B1405	Driver's Power Window Down Circuit Short To Power	13
B1410	Driver's Power Window Motor Circuit Failure	13
B1426	Safety Belt Lamp Circuit Short To Power	14
B1428	Safety Belt Lamp Circuit Failure	15
B1431	Front Wiper Brake/Run Relay Circuit Failure	16
B1432	Front Wiper Brake/Run Relay Short To Power	16
B1434	Front Wiper Hi/Low Speed Relay Circuit Failure	17
B1436	Front Wiper Hi/Low Speed Relay Circuit Short To Power	17
B1438	Front Wiper Mode Select Switch Circuit Failure	16
B1441	Front Wiper Mode Select Switch Input Short To Ground	16
B1446	Front Wiper Park Sense Circuit Failure	18
B1450	Front Wiper/Wash Interval Delay Switch Input Circuit Failure	16
B1453	Front Wiper/Wash Interval Delay Switch Input Short To Ground	16
B1454	Low Washer Fluid Indicator Circuit Failure	19
B1456	Low Washer Fluid Indicator Circuit Short To Power	19
B1458	Front Wiper/Washer Pump Motor Relay Circuit Failure	20
B1460	Front Wiper/Washer Pump Motor Relay Coil Short To Power	20
B1462	Safety Belt Switch Circuit Failure	7
B1466	Front Wiper Hi/Low Speed Not Switching	17
B1473	Front Wiper Motor Low Speed Circuit Failure	17
B1476	Front Wiper Motor High Speed Circuit Failure	17
B1482	Wiper Washer Fluid Level Sensor Circuit Short To Ground	19
B1483	Brake Pedal Input Circuit Failure	21
B1485	Brake Pedal Input Circuit Short To Power	21
B1574	Door Ajar Left Rear Circuit Short To Ground	4
B1577	Lamp Park Input Circuit Short To Power	7
B1610	Illuminated Entry Input Short To Ground	4
B1611	Rear Wiper Mode Select Switch Circuit Failure	22
B1614	Rear Wiper Mode Select Switch Circuit Short To Ground	23

GENERIC ELECTRONIC MODULE (GEM) DTC TEST INDEX (Cont.)

DTC	Description	Test
B1814	Rear Wiper Motor Down Relay Circuit Failure	22
B1816	Rear Wiper Motor Down Relay Coil Circuit Short To Power	22
B1818	Rear Wiper Motor Up Relay Coil Circuit Failure	22
B1820	Rear Wiper Motor Up Relay Circuit Short To Power	22
B1839	Rear Wiper Motor Circuit Failure	24
B1840	Front Wiper Power Circuit Failure	16
B1894	Rear Wiper Motor Speed Sense Circuit Failure	22
B2105	Throttle Position Input Out Of Range Low	21
B2106	Throttle Position Input Out Of Range High	21
C1107	ABS Function Enabled Input Circuit Failure	21
P0500	Vehicle Speed Signal Circuit Failure	21 25
P1804	4-Wheel Drive High Indicator Circuit Failure	26
P1806	4-Wheel Drive High Indicator Short To Power	26
P1812	Transmission 4-Wheel Drive Mode Select Circuit Failure	21
P1815	Transmission 4-Wheel Drive Mode Select Short Circuit To Ground	21
P1820	Transmission Transfer Case Clockwise Shift Relay Coil Circuit Failure	21
P1822	Transmission Transfer Case Clockwise Shift Relay Coil Circuit Short To Power	21
P1824	Transmission 4-Wheel Drive Clutch Relay Circuit Failure	21
P1826	Transmission 4-Wheel Drive Low Clutch Relay Short To Power	21
P1828	Transmission Transfer Case Counter Clockwise Shift Relay Coil Circuit Failure	21
P1830	Transmission Transfer Case Counter Clockwise Shift Relay Coil Short To Power	21
P1836	Transmission Transfer Case Front Shaft Speed Sensor Circuit Failure	21
P1837	Transmission Transfer Case Rear Shaft Speed Sensor Circuit Failure	21
P1838	Transmission Transfer Case Shift Motor Circuit Failure	21
P1846	Transmission Transfer Case Contact Plate "A" Circuit Failure	21
P1850	Transmission Transfer Case Contact Plate "B" Circuit Failure	21
P1854	Transmission Transfer Case Contact Plate "C" Circuit Failure	21
P1858	Transmission Transfer Case Contact Plate "D" Circuit Failure	21
P1866	Transmission Transfer Case System Concern – Servicing Required	21
P1867	Transmission Transfer Case Contact Plate General Circuit Failure	21
P1874	Transmission Automatic Hall Effect Sensor Power Circuit Failure	21
P1875	Transmission Automatic Hall Effect Sensor Power Circuit Short To Power	21
P1891	Transmission Transfer Case Contact Plate Ground Return Open Circuit	21
P1892	Transmission Automatic 4-Wheel Drive 4X4 Mechanical Lock Output Circuit Failure	21
P1893	Transmission Automatic 4-Wheel Drive 4X4 Mechanical Lock Output Short To Power	21

[1] – Perform TEST J: REAR WASHER PUMP INOPERATIVE under SYSTEM TESTS in WIPER/WASHER SYSTEMS – EXPEDITION & NAVIGATOR article.

[2] – Perform TEST B: ALL POWER WINDOWS INOPERATIVE under SYSTEM TESTS in POWER WINDOWS – EXPEDITION & NAVIGATOR article.

[3] – Check charging system concern. See GENERATORS – ECONOLINE, EXPEDITION, EXPLORER (4.0L OHV), PICKUP (GASOLINE), NAVIGATOR & RANGER article in STARTING & CHARGING SYSTEMS. If charging system is okay, repair power and ground circuits at Generic Electronic Module (GEM).

[4] – Repair interior illumination concern. See appropriate wiring diagram in ILLUMINATION/INTERIOR LIGHTS article.

[5] – Perform TEST J: DOOR AJAR LAMP INOPERATIVE or TEST K: DOOR AJAR LAMP DOES NOT OPERATE CORRECTLY under SYSTEM TESTS in ANALOG INSTRUMENT PANELS – EXPEDITION, F150 & F250 LIGHT-DUTY PICKUP, & NAVIGATOR article.

[6] – Perform TEST J: DOOR AJAR LAMP INOPERATIVE under SYSTEM TESTS in ANALOG INSTRUMENT PANELS – EXPEDITION, F150 & F250 LIGHT-DUTY PICKUP, & NAVIGATOR article.

[7] – Repair warning chime concern.

[8] – Using NGS tester, retrieve and document all continuous DTCs. Perform Generic Electronic Module (GEM) self-test. If DTC B1342 is retrieved again, replace GEM.

[9] – Repair defogger concern. See appropriate wiring diagram in REAR WINDOW DEFOGGERS article.

[10] – Perform TEST E: NO POWER IN RUN POSITION under SYSTEM TESTS in STEERING COLUMN SWITCHES – EXPEDITION & NAVIGATOR article.

[11] – Perform TEST F: NO POWER IN START POSITION under SYSTEM TESTS in STEERING COLUMN SWITCHES – EXPEDITION & NAVIGATOR article.

[12] – Perform TEST D: ONE TOUCH DOWN FEATURE INOPERATIVE under SYSTEM TESTS in POWER WINDOWS – EXPEDITION & NAVIGATOR article.

[13] – Perform TEST C: SINGLE WINDOW INOPERATIVE under SYSTEM TESTS in POWER WINDOWS – EXPEDITION & NAVIGATOR article.

[14] – Perform TEST H: SAFETY BELT INDICATOR LAMP INOPERATIVE under SYSTEM TESTS in ANALOG INSTRUMENT PANELS – EXPEDITION, F150 & F250 LIGHT-DUTY PICKUP, & NAVIGATOR article.

[15] – Perform TEST H: SAFETY BELT INDICATOR LAMP INOPERATIVE or TEST I: SAFETY BELT INDICATOR LAMP DOES NOT OPERATE CORRECTLY under SYSTEM TESTS in ANALOG INSTRUMENT PANELS – EXPEDITION, F150 & F250 LIGHT-DUTY PICKUP, & NAVIGATOR article.

[16] – Perform TEST A: FRONT WIPERS INOPERATIVE under SYSTEM TESTS in WIPER/WASHER SYSTEMS – EXPEDITION & NAVIGATOR article.

[17] – Perform TEST C: FRONT WIPERS OPERATE AT INTERVAL SETTING, BUT INOPERATIVE AT HIGH &/OR LOW SPEED under SYSTEM TESTS in WIPER/WASHER SYSTEMS – EXPEDITION & NAVIGATOR.

[18] – Perform TEST D: FRONT WIPERS INOPERATIVE AT INTERVAL SETTING, BUT OPERATE AT HIGH & LOW SPEED under SYSTEM TESTS in WIPER/WASHER SYSTEMS – EXPEDITION & NAVIGATOR.

[19] – Perform TEST L: LOW WASHER FLUID INDICATOR DOES NOT OPERATE PROPERLY under SYSTEM TESTS in WIPER/WASHER SYSTEMS – EXPEDITION & NAVIGATOR.

GENERIC ELECTRONIC MODULE (GEM) DTC TEST INDEX (Cont.)

DTC	Description	Test
20	Perform TEST E: FRONT WASHER PUMP INOPERATIVE under SYSTEM TESTS in WIPER/WASHER SYSTEMS – EXPEDITION & NAVIGATOR.	
21	Repair transfer case electronic controls concern. See appropriate BORG-WARNER – ELECTRONIC CONTROLS article in TRANSFER CASES.	
22	Perform TEST G: REAR WIPERS INOPERATIVE under SYSTEM TESTS in WIPER/WASHER SYSTEMS – EXPEDITION & NAVIGATOR article.	
23	Perform TEST K: REAR WIPER STAYS ON CONTINUOUSLY under SYSTEM TESTS in WIPER/WASHER SYSTEMS – EXPEDITION & NAVIGATOR article.	
24	Perform TEST H: REAR WIPER WILL NOT PARK PROPERLY under SYSTEM TESTS in WIPER/WASHER SYSTEMS – EXPEDITION & NAVIGATOR article.	
25	Perform TEST F: FRONT WIPER SPEED DEPENDENT INTERVAL MODE NOT OPERATING PROPERLY under SYSTEM TESTS in WIPER/WASHER SYSTEMS – EXPEDITION & NAVIGATOR article.	
26	Perform TEST N: 4X4 INDICATOR LAMP INOPERATIVE OR ALWAYS ON under SYSTEM TESTS in ANALOG INSTRUMENT PANELS – EXPEDITION, F150 & F250 LIGHT-DUTY PICKUP, & NAVIGATOR article.	

HYBRID ELECTRONIC CLUSTER (HEC) DTC TEST INDEX

DTC	Description	Test
B1201	Fuel Sender Circuit Failure	1
B1202	Fuel Sender Open	1
B1204	Fuel Sender Short To Ground	1
B1213	Anti-Theft Number Of Programmed Keys Below Minimum	2
B1232	Antenna Not Connected Or Damaged Transceiver	3
B1317	Battery Voltage High	4
B1318	Battery Voltage Low	4
B1342	ECU Defective	5
B1356	Ignition RUN Circuit Open	6
B1364	Ignition START Circuit Open	6
B1600	PATS Ignition Key Transponder Signal Not Received	7
B1601	PATS Received Incorrect Key Code (Unprogrammed Encoded Ignition Key)	8
B1602	PATS Received Invalid Key Code Format	9
B1681	PATS Transceiver Signal Not Received	10
B2103	Antenna Not Connected Or Defective Transceiver	3
B2139	PCM ID Mismatch Between PCM And HEC	11
B2141	NVM Configuration Failure	12
B2143	Odometer NVM Memory Failure	13
C1284	Oil Pressure Switch Failure	1
P1197	SELECT/RESET Switch Circuit Failure	13
U1011	SCP Invalid Or Missing Data For Engine Air Intake	14
U1027	SCP Invalid Or Missing Data For Engine RPM	14
U1041	SCP Invalid Or Missing Data For Vehicle Speed	14
U1073	SCP Invalid Or Missing Data For Engine Coolant	14
U1123	SCP Invalid Or Missing Data For Odometer	14
U1131	SCP Invalid Or Missing Data For Fuel System	14
U1147	SCP Invalid Or Missing Data For Vehicle Security For Vehicle Security	15
U1148	SCP Invalid Or Missing Data for audio Control	14
U1262	Missing SCP Message	16

1 – Perform TEST C: FUEL GAUGE INACCURATE under SYSTEM TESTS in ANALOG INSTRUMENT PANELS – EXPEDITION, F150 & F250 LIGHT-DUTY PICKUP, & NAVIGATOR article.

2 – Perform TEST C: ANTI-THEFT NUMBER OF PROGRAMMED KEYS IS BELOW MINIMUM under SYSTEM TESTS in PASSIVE ANTI-THEFT SYSTEMS – EXPEDITION & NAVIGATOR article.

3 – Perform TEST D: ANTENNA NOT CONNECTED under SYSTEM TESTS in PASSIVE ANTI-THEFT SYSTEMS – EXPEDITION & NAVIGATOR article.

4 – Repair charging system concern. See GENERATORS – ECONOLINE, EXPEDITION, EXPLORER (4.0L OHV), PICKUP (GASOLINE), NAVIGATOR & RANGER article in STARTING & CHARGING SYSTEMS. If charging system is okay, repair power and ground circuits to Hybrid Electronic Cluster (HEC).

5 – Using NGS tester, retrieve and document all continuous DTCs. Perform Hybrid Electronic Cluster (HEC) self-test. If DTC B1342 is retrieved again, replace instrument cluster.

6 – Repair ignition circuit concern. See STEERING COLUMN SWITCHES – EXPEDITION & NAVIGATOR article. See appropriate wiring diagram in POWER DISTRIBUTION article in WIRING DIAGRAMS.

7 – Perform TEST E: IGNITION KEY TRANSPONDER SIGNAL NOT RECEIVED under SYSTEM TESTS in PASSIVE ANTI-THEFT SYSTEMS – EXPEDITION & NAVIGATOR article.

8 – Perform TEST F: INCORRECT KEY CODE FROM IGNITION KEY TRANSPONDER under SYSTEM TESTS in PASSIVE ANTI-THEFT SYSTEMS – EXPEDITION & NAVIGATOR article.

9 – Perform TEST G: INVALID FORMAT KEY CODE FROM IGNITION KEY TRANSPONDER under SYSTEM TESTS in PASSIVE ANTI-THEFT SYSTEMS – EXPEDITION & NAVIGATOR article.

10 – Perform TEST H: TRANSCEIVER MODULE SIGNAL NOT RECEIVED under SYSTEM TESTS in PASSIVE ANTI-THEFT SYSTEMS – EXPEDITION & NAVIGATOR article.

11 – Perform TEST I: PCM ID DOES NOT MATCH INSTRUMENT CLUSTER ID under SYSTEM TESTS in PASSIVE ANTI-THEFT SYSTEMS – EXPEDITION & NAVIGATOR article.

12 – Perform TEST J: CONFIGURATION FAILURE, NO PCM ID EXCHANGED under SYSTEM TESTS in PASSIVE ANTI-THEFT SYSTEMS – EXPEDITION & NAVIGATOR article.

HYBRID ELECTRONIC CLUSTER (HEC) DTC TEST INDEX (Cont.)

DTC	Description	Test
[13]	Replace instrument cluster. Clear DTCs and retest system.	
[14]	Using NGS tester, perform Powertrain Control Module (PCM) self-test.	
[15]	Perform TEST K: INVALID OR MISSING VEHICLE SECURITY DATA under SYSTEM TESTS in PASSIVE ANTI-THEFT SYSTEMS – EXPEDITION & NAVIGATOR article.	
[16]	Start diagnostics at INSPECTION & VERIFICATION.	

REMOTE ANTI-THEFT PERSONALITY (RAP) MODULE DTC INDEX

DTC	Description	Test
B1309	Power Door Lock Circuit Short To Ground	1
B1341	Power Door Unlock Circuit Short To Ground	1
B1485	Brake Pedal Input Circuit Short To Power	1
B1629	PRNDL Reverse Input Short To Power	1
B2425	Remote Transmitter Out Of Sync	1

[1] – Repair keyless entry system concern. See appropriate wiring diagram in REMOTE KEYLESS ENTRY article.

RESTRAINT CONTROL MODULE (RCM) DTC INDEX

DTC [1]	Description	Test
B1342	ECU Defective	2
B1231	RCM Crash Data Memory Full	2
B1921	RCM Bracket Ground Resistance High	2
C1414	Incorrect Vehicle Identification Code	2
B1887	Driver's Air Bag Circuit Shorted To Ground	2
B1916	Driver's Air Bag Circuit Shorted To Power Or Ignition	2
B1888	Passenger's Air Bag Circuit Shorted To Ground	2
B1925	Passenger's Air Bag Circuit Shorted To Power	2
B1932	Driver's Air Bag Circuit Resistance High	2
B1933	Passenger's Air Bag Circuit Resistance High	2
B1934	Driver's Air Bag Circuit Resistance Low	2
B1935	Passenger's Air Bag Circuit Resistance Low	2
B1901	External Crash Sensor Shorted To Ground	2
B1941	External Crash Sensor Open Circuit Or Shorted To Power	2
B1892	Air Bag Tone Warning Indicator Circuit Shorted To Ground Or Open	2
B1891	Air Bag Tone Warning Indicator Circuit Shorted To Power	2
B1869	Air Bag Indicator Inoperative	2
B1870	Air Bag Indicator Shorted To Power	2

[1] – DTCs are listed in order of importance. Repair DTCs in order listed.

[2] – Repair supplemental restraint system concern. See appropriate DIAGNOSIS & TESTING article in appropriate MITCHELL® AIR BAG SERVICE & REPAIR MANUAL, DOMESTIC & IMPORTED MODELS.

PARAMETER IDENTIFICATION (PID) DEFINITIONS

REAR AIR SUSPENSION (RAS) CONTROL MODULE PID INDEX

PID	Description	Expected Values
4WDLOW	GEM 4WD Low Signal To Air Suspension Control Module	ON, OFF
4WDSYS	Signal From Electronic Shift Relay And Diode Module To Air Suspension Control Module	YES, NO
ACC_SIG	Acceleration Signal To Air Suspension Control Module	NOTPRE, PRESENT
AS_COMP	Air Suspension Compressor Status	ON, OFF
AS_GATE	Air Suspension Front Solenoid Gate Valve Status	ON, OFF
AS_VENT	Air Suspension Vent Solenoid Valve Status	ON, OFF
ASLRSOL Or LR_SOL	Air Suspension LR Spring Solenoid Valve Status	ON, OFF
ASRRSOL Or RR_SOL	Air Suspension RR Spring Solenoid Valve Status	ON, OFF
BOO_AS	Brake Pedal Position Switch Input To Air Suspension Control Module	ON, OFF
DOOR_AS	Door Ajar Input To Air Suspension Control Module	CLOSED, AJAR
F_FILL	Air Suspension Front Fill Solenoid Valve Status	ON, OFF
FHGTSEN	Value Of Front Air Suspension Height Sensor	DC Voltage Value
IGN_AS	Ignition RUN/START Input To Air Suspension Control Module	NOTRUN, RUN
OPSTRAT	Status Of Air Suspension Operational Strategy	4WAS/2WAS
PK/N_SW	Park/Neutral Switch Input To Air Suspension Control Module	NOTP/N, P/N
R_FILL	Air Suspension Rear Fill Solenoid Valve Status	ON, OFF
RHGTSEN	Value Of Rear Air Suspension Height Sensor	DC Voltage Value
STEER_A	Electronic Steering Sensor A Signal To Air Suspension Control Module	HIGH, LOW
STEER_B	Electronic Steering Sensor B Signal To Air Suspension Control Module	HIGH, LOW
VBAT_AS	Battery Voltage Value To Air Suspension Control Module	DC Voltage Value
VSS_AS Or VSS_ARC	Displays Vehicle Speed Sensor Input To Air Suspension Control Module	VSS Signal In KPH Or MPH
LC_4WDL	Latch Seeing 4WD Low Signal To Air Suspension Control Module	CHANGD/NOCHAG
LC_ACC	Latch Seeing Acceleration Signal To Air Suspension Control Module	CHANGD/NOCHAG

REAR AIR SUSPENSION (RAS) CONTROL MODULE PID INDEX (Cont.)

PID	Description	Expected Values
LC_BOO	Latch Seeing Brake Pedal Position Switch Signal To Air Suspension Control Module	CHANGD/NOCHAG
LC_DOOR	Latch Seeing Door Ajar Signal To Air Suspension Control Module	CHANGD/NOCHAG
LC_IGN	Latch Seeing Ignition RUN/START Signal To Air Suspension Control Module	CHANGD/NOCHAG
LC_PK/N	Latch Seeing Park/Neutral Switch Input To Air Suspension Control Module	CHANGD/NOCHAG
LC_VSS Or VSS_ARC	Latch Seeing Vehicle Speed Sensor Signal Input To Air Suspension Control Module (If Greater Than 56 MPH)	CHANGD/NOCHAG
LCSTR_A	Latch Seeing Electronic Steering Sensor A Signal To Air Suspension Control Module	CHANGD/NOCHAG
LCSTR_B	Latch Seeing Electronic Steering Sensor B Signal To Air Suspension Control Module	CHANGD/NOCHAG

ANTI-LOCK BRAKE CONTROL (ABS) MODULE PID INDEX

PID	Description	Expected Value
4WDABS	4 Wheel Drive Input Switch	2WD, 4WD
ABSLAMP	ABS Warning Lamp State	ON, OFF
ABSLF_I	Left Front ABS Inlet Valve	ON, OFF
ABSLF_O	Left Front ABS Outlet Valve	ON, OFF
ABSR_I	Rear ABS Inlet Valve	ON, OFF
ABSR_O	Rear ABS Outlet Valve	ON, OFF
ABSRF_I	Right Front ABS Inlet Valve	ON, OFF
ABSRF_O	Right Front ABS Outlet Valve	ON, OFF
BOO_ABS	Brake Switch Input	ON, OFF
BRK_LVL	Brake Fluid Level	OK, NOTOK
CCNTABS	Continuous DTCs In ABS Module	Number Of DTCs
LF_WSPD	Left Front Wheel Speed Sensor	0-255 MPH
R_WSPD	Rear Wheel Speed Sensor	0-255 MPH
RF_WSPD	Right Front Wheel Speed Sensor	0-255 MPH
PWR_RLY	Power Relay Feedback Input	ON, OFF

AUDIO CONTROL MODULE (ASM) PID INDEX

PID	Description	Expected Value
+_SW	(+) Switch	ACTIVE, NOTACT
-_SW	(-) Switch	ACTIVE, NOTACT
AM_SW	AM Switch	ACTIVE, NOTACT
AS_SW	Autoset Switch	ACTIVE, NOTACT
ASYSON	ASYSON Output State	ACTIVE, NOTACT
BAL_SW	Balance Switch	ACTIVE, NOTACT
BAND_SW	Band Switch	ACTIVE, NOTACT
BASS_SW	Bass Switch	ACTIVE, NOTACT
CD/DJ	CD Disc Jockey	YES, NO
CD_S	Single CD Player	YES, NO
CELLPHN	Cellular Phone	YES, NO
CLKDISP	Clock Display Enable Input State	DISABLE, ENABLE
CLOCK	Clock	YES, NO
CTR_IMG	Center Image Amplifier	YES, NO
DSP_EFF	DSP Effects	YES, NO
EJCT_SW	Eject Switch	ACTIVE, NOTACT
FADE_SW	Fade Switch	ACTIVE, NOTACT
FM_SW	FM Switch	ACTIVE, NOTACT
MEM_SW	Memory Switch	ACTIVE, NOTACT
MENU_SW	Steering Wheel Controls Inputs State	VALID, INVALID
MNIDSC	Minidisc Deck	YES, NO
PHONE	Phone Switch (Steering Wheel Switches)	ACTIVE, NOTACT
PHONESW	Phone Switch	ACTIVE, NOTACT
PRE1_SW	Preset 1 Switch	ACTIVE, NOTACT
PRE2_SW	Preset 2 Switch	ACTIVE, NOTACT
PRE3_SW	Preset 3 Switch	ACTIVE, NOTACT
PRE4_SW	Preset 4 Switch	ACTIVE, NOTACT
PRE5_SW	Preset 5 Switch	ACTIVE, NOTACT
PRE6_SW	Preset 6 Switch	ACTIVE, NOTACT
PTA	PTA Input State	ACTIVE, NOTACT
PWR_SW	Power Switch	ACTIVE, NOTACT
RBDS	RBDS	YES, NO
RBDS_SW	RBDS Switch	ACTIVE, NOTACT
REAR_ST	Rear Seat Controls	YES, NO
SCAN_SW	Scan Switch	ACTIVE, NOTACT
SEEK+	Seek Increase Switch	ACTIVE, NOTACT
SEEK-	Seek Decrease Switch	ACTIVE, NOTACT
STEER_C	Steering Wheel Controls	YES, NO

AUDIO CONTROL MODULE (ASM) PID INDEX (Cont.)

PID	Description	Expected Value
SUBWOOF	Subwoofer Amplifier	NO, YES
TAPE_SW	Tape Switch	ACTIVE, NOTACT
TAPEDCK	Tape Deck	NO, YES
TREB_SW	Treble Switch	ACTIVE, NOTACT
TUNE+	Tune Increase Switch	ACTIVE, NOTACT
TUNE-	Tune Decrease Switch	ACTIVE, NOTACT
VOL+	Volume Increase Switch	ACTIVE, NOTACT
VOL+_SC	Volume + Switch	ACTIVE, NOTACT
VOL-	Volume Decrease Switch	ACTIVE, NOTACT
VOL-_SC	Volume - Switch	ACTIVE, NOTACT

DRIVER'S SEAT MODULE (DSM) PID INDEX

PID	Description	Expected Value
CCNT	Number Of Continuous DTCs In DSM	Number Of DTCs
MEM1_SW	Memory Recall Switch No. 1	NOTACT, ACTIVE
MEM2_SW	Memory Recall Switch No. 2	NOTACT, ACTIVE
MEMS_SW	Memory Set Switch	NOTACT, ACTIVE
P/N_SW	Park/Neutral Switch	NOTP/N, P/N
PDL_POS	Driver's Pedals Rearward/Forward Position	Percentage
SFNT_FORWARD/REARWARDMT	Driver's Seat Front Motor	NOTSEN, SENSED
SFNT_P	Driver's Seat Front Position Percentage Up	Percentage
SFNT_SW	Front Power Seat Switch	SHORT, UP, DOWN, OFF
SFWD_MT	Driver's Seat Forward/Rearward Motor	NOTSEN, SENSED
SFWD_P	Driver's Seat Position Percentage Forward	Percentage
SFWD_SW	Forward/Rearward Power Seat Switch	SHORT, RWD, FWD, OFF
SREAR_P	Driver's Seat Rear Position Percentage Up	Percent Of Full Up
SREARMT	Driver's Seat Rear Motor	NOTSEN, SENSED
SREARSW	Rear Power Seat Switch	SHORT, UP, DOWN, OFF
DMIR_H	Driver's Side Mirror Horizontal Motor	NOTSEN, SENSED
DMIR_R	Driver's Mirror Position Percentage Right	Percentage
DMIR_UP	Driver's Mirror Position Percentage Up	Percentage
DMIR_V	Driver's Mirror Vertical	NOTSEN, SENSED
MIR_SEL	Power Mirror Select Switch	OFF, DRVMIR, PSGMI
MIRH_SW	Power Mirror Horizontal Position Switch	RIGHT, LEFT
MIRV_SW	Power Mirror Vertical Position Switch	UP, DOWN
PDL_SEN	Pedal Position Sensor Present	NO, YES
PMIR_H	Passenger's Mirror Horizontal Motor	NOTSEN, SENSED
PMIR_R	Passenger's Mirror Position Percentage Right	Percentage
PMIR_UP	Passenger's Mirror Position Percentage Up	Percentage
PMIR_V	Passenger's Mirror Vertical	NOTSEN, SENSED
SFWD_P	Driver's Seat Position Percentage Forward	Percentage
VBATDD	Battery Voltage	VDC

GENERIC ELECTRONIC MODULE (GEM) PID INDEX

PID	Description	Expected Value
4WD_SW	4WD Input Switch	A4WD, 4WDLOW, 4WDHGH, OPEN, GSHORT
4WDCLST	4WD Clutch Output Status	Off- - -, OffO-G, On- - -, On-B-
4WDHIGH	4WD-Wheel High Output State	Off- - -, OffO-G, On- - -, On-B-
ACCDLY	Accessory Delay Relay Circuit	Off- - -, OffO-G, On- - -, On-B-
BATSAV	Battery Saver Relay Circuit	Off- - -, OffO-G, On- - -, On-B-
BOO	Brake Switch Input	OFF, ON
CCNT	Number Of DTCs In GEM	Number Of DTCs
CHIMERQ	Chime Request	OFF, ON
CLTCHSW	Transmission Clutch Interlock Switch	NOTEGD, ENGAGD
D_DN_SW	Driver's Window Down Switch	OFF, DOWN
D_DOOR	Left Front Door Ajar Switch	CLOSED, AJAR
D_PWAMP	Driver's Power Window Motor Current	Amperes
D_PWPK	Driver's Power Window Peak Current	Amperes
D_PWRLY	Driver's Power Window	Off- - -, OffO-G, On- - -, On-B-
D_SBELT	Driver's Seat Belt	OUT, IN
DECKLID	Decklid/Hatch Ajar	CLOSED, AJAR
DRAJR_L	Door Ajar Warning Lamp Circuit	Off- - -, OffO-G, On- - -, On-B-
HALLPWR	Center Axle Hall Power	Off- - -, OffO-G, On- - -, On-B-
IGN_A	Ignition Switch - ACCY Position	NO, YES
IGN_KEY	Ignition Key In/Out	OUT, IN
IGN_O/L	Ignition Switch-OFF/Lock Position	NO, YES
IGN_R	Ignition Switch-RUN Position	NO, YES
IGN_S	Ignition Switch-START Position	NO, YES
INTLMP	Illuminated Entry Relay Circuit	Off- - -, OffO-G, On- - -, On-B-
LRDR_SW	Left Rear Door Ajar Switch	CLOSED, AJAR

GENERIC ELECTRONIC MODULE (GEM) PID INDEX (Cont.)

PID	Description	Expected Value
MECHLCK	Mechanical Lock Output Status	Off- -, OffO-G, On- - -, On-B-
MTR_CCW	Transfer Case Counter Clockwise Motor Output	Off- -, OffO-G, On- - -, On-B-
MTR_CW	Transfer Case Clockwise Motor Output	Off- -, OffO-G, On- - -, On-B-
NTRL_SW	Neutral Safety Switch Input	NOTNTL, NTRL
OTD_SW	One Touch Down Switch	OFF, DOWN
P_DOOR	Passenger's Door Ajar Switch	CLOSED, AJAR
PARK_SW	Parking Switch	OFF, ON
PLATE_A	Transfer Case Contact Plate A	OPEN, CLOSED
PLATE_B	Transfer Case Contact Plate B	OPEN, CLOSED
PLATE_C	Transfer Case Contact Plate C	OPEN, CLOSED
PLATE_D	Transfer Case Contact Plate D	OPEN, CLOSED
PLATEPW	Transfer Case Contact Plate Pulse Width	Off- -, OffO-G, On- - -, On-B-
PWM_DC1	PWM Duty Cycle #1	Percentage
PWR_RLY	Power Relay Feedback Input	OFF, ON
R_WP_DN	Rear Wiper Down Output	Off- -, OffO-G, On- - -, On-B-
R_WP_MD	Rear Wiper Mode Switch	WASH, OPEN, INVLD, INTVL1, INTVL2
R_WP_PK	Rear Wiper Park Sense	NOTPRK, PARKED
R_WP_UP	Rear Wiper Up Output	Off- -, OffO-G, On- - -, On-B-
RDEF_SW	Rear Defrost Switch	OFF, ON
RDEFRLY	Rear Defrost Relay Circuit	Off- -, OffO-G, On- - -, On-B-
RRDR_SW	Right Rear Door Ajar Switch	CLOSED, AJAR
RWASHSW	Rear Washer Switch Position	Off- -, OffO-G, On- - -, On-B-
SBLTLMP	Seat Belt Lamp Circuit	Off- -, OffO-G, On- - -, On-B-
SPEEDWP	Speed Dependent Wiper Function	NOTACT, ACTIVE
TRA_FSP	Transfer Case Front Speed	KPH
TRA_RSP	Transfer Case Rear Speed	KPH
VBAT	Battery Voltage	VDC
VSS	Vehicle Speed	KPH
VSS	Vehicle Speed Low Resolution (MPH)	One Count Per Bit MPH
WASH_SW	Washer Pump Switch	OFF, ON
WASHRLY	Washer Pump Relay Circuit	Off- -, OffO-G, On- - -, On-B-
WFL_LMP	Washer Fluid Lamp Circuit	Off- -, OffO-G, On- - -, On-B-
WFLUID	Washer Fluid Level	LOW, OK
WPHISP	Wiper Two Speed Relay	Off- -, OffO-G, On- - -, On-B-
WPMODE	Wiper Control Mode Select	[1]
WPPK_PK	Wiper Park-To-Park Time	mS
WPPRKSW	Wiper Park Sense	NOTPRK, PARKED
WPRUN	Wiper Run Relay Driver State	Off- -, OffO-G, On- - -, On-B-

[1] – Expected value should be WASH, OPEN, OFF, INTVL1, INTVL2, INTVL3, INTVL4, INTVL5, INTVL6, INTVL7, LOW, HIGH or ?

HYBRID ELECTRONIC CLUSTER (HEC) PID INDEX

PID	Description	Expected Value
ANTISCN	Anti-Scan Function	DISABL, ENABLE
BACK_LT	PWM Output	Percentage
CCNT	Number Of DTCs In HEC	Number Of DTCs
ENABL_S	Vehicle Enable Status	DISABL, ENABLE
FLDLVLI	Brake Fluid Level Input	One Count Per Bit
FUELLVL	Fuel Level Status	Percentage
IGN_O/L	Ignition Switch-OFF/Lock Position	NO, YES
IGN_R	Ignition Switch-RUN Position	NO, YES
IGN_S	Ignition Switch-START Position	NO, YES
M_KEY	Master Key Present	NOTPRE, PRESNT
NUMKEYS	Number Of Keys Stored In Module	One Count Per Bit
OIL_PSW	Oil Pressure Switch Control	One Count Per Bit
PCM_ID	PCM ID Stored In HEC	NOTSTR, STORED
PCM_VFY	PCM ID Matched Between PCM And HEC	NO, YES
RESETSW	Reset Switch	OFF, ON
VBAT	Battery Voltage	VDC

REMOTE ANTI-THEFT PERSONALITY (RAP) MODULE PID INDEX

PID	Description	Expected Values
BOO_RAP	Brake Switch Input	OFF, ON
DD_LOCK	Power Door Lock/Unlock Status	LOCK, UNLOCK, OFF, SHORT
DOORRAP	Door Ajar Switch	AJAR, CLOSED
IGN_RAP	Ignition Switch	RUN/ACC, OFF
TRANSGR	Transmission Gear	REV, NOTREV
AUTOLOCK	Autolock Status	OFF, ON
MEM_SEAT	Memory Seat Movement With Remote Transmitter	OFF, ON
KEY_PAD	Keypad	1/2, 3/4, 5/6, 7/8, 9/10

RESTRAINT CONTROL MODULE (RCM) PID INDEX

PID	Description	Expected Values
CCNT	Number Of DTCs In RCM	Number Of DTCs
VBAT	Battery Feed Voltage At RCM	9.0-16.0 Volts
D_ABAGR	Driver's Air Bag Module Resistance	1.7-3.2 Ohms
P_ABAGR	Passenger's Air Bag Module Resistance	1.7-3.2 Ohms
BRACKET	Bracket Ground Resistance	Less Than 100 Ohms
VID #1	Program Vehicle ID Pin 10	Ignition
VID #2	Program Vehicle ID Pin 13	Ground
VID #3	Program Vehicle ID Pin 14	No Connect

REMOVAL & INSTALLATION

NOTE: For removal and installation procedures of modules referred to in this article, except Anti-Theft Personality (RAP) module, see appropriate articles.

REMOTE ANTI-THEFT PERSONALITY (RAP) MODULE

CAUTION: It is necessary to upload module configuration to New Generation STAR (NGS) tester, or equivalent scan tool, prior to module replacement. Download configuration after new module is installed.

Removal & Installation – Disconnect battery ground cable. Disconnect RAP module electrical connectors (Black 22-pin and Black 26-pin). Remove nuts and RAP module. To install, reverse removal procedure.

WIRING DIAGRAMS

NOTE: See appropriate wiring diagrams in DATA LINK CONNECTORS, GROUND DISTRIBUTION or POWER DISTRIBUTION articles in WIRING DIAGRAMS.

DESCRIPTION & OPERATION

Vehicle has 2 module communications networks. The Powertrain Control Module (PCM), Passive Anti-Theft System (PATS) module and Electronic Automatic Temperature Control (EATC) module are connected to the multiplex communications network through a pair of twisted wires or BUS. The BUS network is also referred to as Standard Corporate Protocol (SCP). The BUS consists of a (+) circuit No. 914 and a (–) circuit No. 915. The Restraint Control Module (RCM), Generic Electronic Module/Central Timer Module (GEM/CTM), Remote Anti-Theft Personality (RAP) module, 4-Wheel Anti-Lock Brake System (4WABS) module, Driver Seat Module (DSM), Parking Aid Module (PAM) and air suspension control module are connected to the International Standards Organization (ISO) 9141 diagnostic communications network through a single wire (circuit No. 70). Both networks are connected to the Data Link Connector (DLC). This article is used to diagnose BUS and ISO communications network circuit faults. For module locations, see COMPONENT LOCATIONS table.

COMPONENT LOCATIONS

Component	Location
Air Suspension Control Module	Behind Left Center Of Instrument Panel
Data Link Connector (DLC)	Below Driver's Side Of Instrument Panel, To Right Of Steering Column
Driver's Seat Module (DSM)	Underneath Driver's Seat
Electronic Automatic Temperature Control Module (EATC)	Behind Center Of Instrument Panel
Generic Electronic Module (GEM)/Central Timer Module (CTM)	Behind Center Of Instrument Panel
Parking Aid Module (PAM)	Behind Spare Tire
Passive Anti-Theft System (PATS) Control Module	Behind Top Right Side Of Instrument Panel
Powertrain Control Module (PCM)	Right Side Of Firewall In Engine Compartment
Remote Anti-Theft Personality (RAP) Module	Behind Left Rear Quarter Panel
Restraint Control Module (RCM)	Behind Right Kick Panel
4-Wheel Anti-Lock Brake System (4WABS) Module	Left Side Of Engine Compartment

REPAIRING BUS WIRING

NOTE: Following procedure must be used to ensure proper repair is performed on BUS wiring. BUS wiring is sensitive to moisture and oxidation and must be properly sealed to ensure proper operation of the module communications network. Regular heat shrink tubing is NOT sufficient, heat shrink tubing containing hot melt wax is required.

1) When performing a repair on the BUS wiring, ensure the wires on the BUS are twisted at a rate of 33-40 winds per 3.3 ft. (1 m). The twists should start within approximately 4.9" (124 mm) from any connector. Use only 20 AWG standard wire gauge for repairs.
2) If performing a splice in the wiring, strip .75" (19.0 mm) of insulation from one wire and 1.50" (38.1 mm) of insulation from the other wire. Perform STEP 1. See Fig. 1. Place hot melt wax heat shrink tubing over one wire.
3) Twist stripped portion of the wires together. Solder connection using resin core RMA solder. DO NOT use acid core solder. Bend wires to allow installation of heat shrink tubing. Perform STEP 2. See Fig. 1.

4) Position heat shrink tubing over splice area. Using heat gun, evenly heat the heat shrink tubing until wax flows from both ends of heat shrink tubing.

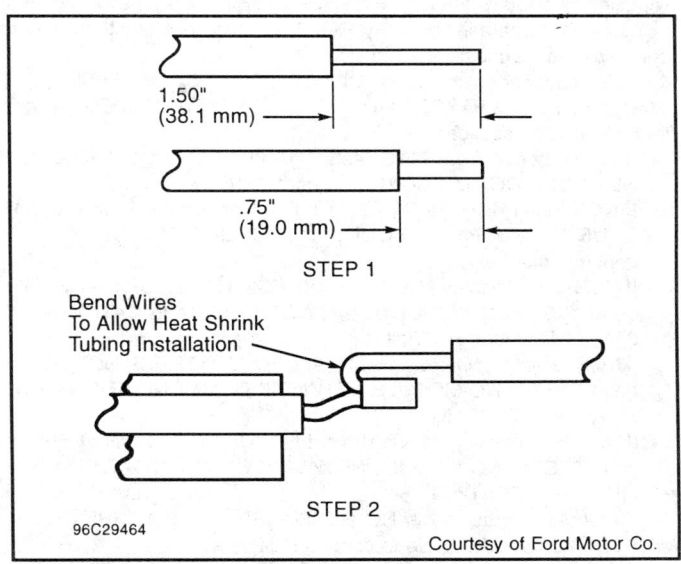

Fig. 1: Repairing BUS Wiring

COMMUNICATION NETWORK DIAGNOSTICS

INSPECTION & VERIFICATION

1) Verify customer's original problem by operating system in question. Inspect vehicle for any obvious electrical component wiring or connector damage. Inspect connectors for loose, damaged or corroded terminals. Check related fuses for system in question.
2) Inspect Data Link Connector (DLC) pins for damage. See Fig. 2. The DLC is located below driver's side of instrument panel, to the right of steering column. If pins are okay, go to next step. If pins are damaged, repair as necessary and proceed to next step.
3) If problem is still present after performing inspection, connect New Generation Star (NGS) tester to DLC. Select vehicle to be tested from NGS tester menu. If NGS tester does not communicate with vehicle, ensure program card is properly installed. Check NGS tester cable connections and ensure ignition is on. If NGS tester still does not communicate with vehicle, go to TEST M: NO MODULE/NETWORK COMMUNICATION under SYSTEM TESTS. If NGS tester communicates with vehicle, perform data link diagnostic procedure. See DATA LINK DIAGNOSTIC TEST.

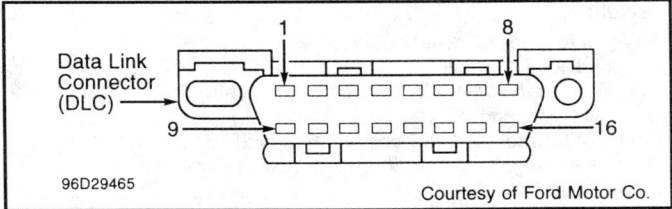

Fig. 2: Identifying Data Link Connector (DLC) Terminals

DATA LINK DIAGNOSTIC TEST

1) Connect New Generation Star (NGS) tester to Data Link Connector (DLC), if not already connected. Select vehicle to be tested from NGS tester menu.
2) Turn ignition on. Rotate dial on NGS tester to menu item DIAGNOSTIC DATA LINK and press trigger. A test will be performed on the BUS (circuits No. 914 and 915) for the module communications network and the ISO 9141 communication link (circuit No. 70).

3) If NGS tester displays CKT 914 (+) = SYSTEM PASSED and CKT 915 (–) = SYSTEM PASSED, module communications network is okay. If NGS tester displays CKT 70 = SYSTEM PASSED, ISO 9141 communication link is operating properly. Return to article that directed you here and continue diagnosis.

4) If NGS tester does not display CKT 914 (+) = SYSTEM PASSED, CKT 915 (–) = SYSTEM PASSED and CKT 70 = SYSTEM PASSED, perform the following as applicable:

- If no response from NGS tester, go to TEST M: NO MODULE/NETWORK COMMUNICATION under TESTING.
- If NGS tester displays CKT 70, CKT 914 and/or CKT 915 = SOME ECUS NO RESP/NOT EQUIP, go to SYMPTOM INDEX table to continue diagnosis.
- If NGS tester displays CKT 70 = ALL ECUS NO RESP/NOT EQUIP, go to TEST K: NO MODULE/NETWORK COMMUNICATION – ISO 9141 LINK under TESTING.
- If NGS tester displays CKT 914 = ALL ECUS NO RESP/NOT EQUIP, go to TEST L: NO MODULE/NETWORK COMMUNICATION – BUS LINK under TESTING.
- If NGS tester displays CKT 915 = ALL ECUS NO RESP/NOT EQUIP, go to TEST L: NO MODULE/NETWORK COMMUNICATION – BUS LINK under TESTING.
- If module in question is NO RESPONSE/NOT EQUIPPED, go to SYMPTOM INDEX table to continue diagnosis.
- If module in question is NO RESPONSE ON CKT 914 (BUS +), go to SYMPTOM INDEX table to continue diagnosis.
- If module in question is NO RESPONSE ON CKT 915 (BUS –), go to SYMPTOM INDEX table to continue diagnosis.

RETRIEVING & CLEARING DIAGNOSTIC TROUBLE CODES

Connect New Generation Star (NGS) tester to Data Link Connector (DLC). Following manufacturer's instructions to retrieve and clear codes for desired module. See appropriate table under DIAGNOSTIC TROUBLE CODE (DTC) DEFINITIONS for a listing of DTCs and location of appropriate test procedure.

ACCESSING PARAMETER IDENTIFICATION (PID)

Turn ignition off. Connect New Generation Star (NGS) tester to Data Link Connector (DLC). Following manufacturer's instructions enter PID/DATA MONITOR AND RECORD for desired module. Operate appropriate system and ensure PID expected values are obtained. See appropriate table under PARAMETER IDENTIFICATION (PID) DEFINITIONS.

SYMPTOM TESTS

SYMPTOM INDEX

Condition	Test
4-Wheel Anti-Lock Brake System (4WABS) Module Does Not Respond To NGS Tester	A
Generic Electronic (GEM) Module/Central Timer Module (CTM) Does Not Respond To NGS Tester	B
Restraint Control Module Does Not Respond To NGS Tester	C
Remote Anti-Theft Personality (RAP) Module Does Not Respond To NGS Tester	D
Powertrain Control Monitor (PCM) Does Not Respond To NGS Tester	E
Air Suspension Control Module Does Not Respond To NGS Tester	F
Electronic Automatic Temperature Control (EATC) Module Does Not Respond To NGS Tester	G
Driver Seat Module (DSM) Module Does Not Respond To NGS Tester	H
Parking Aid Monitor (PAM) Does Not Respond To NGS Tester	I
Passive Anti-Theft System (PATS) Module Does Not Respond To NGS Tester	J

SYMPTOM INDEX (Cont.)

Condition	Test
No Module/Network Communications – ISO 9141 Link	K
No Module/Network Communications – BUS Link	L
No Module/Network Communication	M

SYSTEM TESTS

NOTE: Always check module power and ground circuits prior to replacing a control module. See appropriate wiring diagram in DATA LINK CONNECTORS, GROUND DISTRIBUTION or POWER DISTRIBUTION article in WIRING DIAGRAMS.

TEST A: 4-WHEEL ANTI-LOCK BRAKE SYSTEM (4WABS) MODULE DOES NOT RESPOND TO NGS TESTER

1) Turn ignition off. Disconnect 4WABS module connector located at left side of engine compartment. Inspect connector for physical damage, bent terminals or corrosion. Repair connector as necessary and retest system for normal operation. If connector is okay, go to next step.

2) Measure resistance of Light Blue/White wire between terminal No. 23 at 4WABS module connector and terminal No. 7 at Data Link Connector (DLC). *See Figs. 2 and 3.* If resistance is less than 5 ohms, replace 4WABS module and retest system for normal operation. If resistance is 5 ohms or more, go to next step.

3) Disconnect and inspect both halves of 40-pin bulkhead connector C148 located at left rear of engine compartment, near brake master cylinder. *See Fig. 4.* Inspect connector for physical damage, bent terminals or corrosion. Repair connector as necessary and retest system for normal operation. If connector is okay, go to next step.

4) Measure resistance of Light Blue/White wire between terminal No. 16 at female half of connector C148 and terminal No. 7 at DLC. *See Figs. 2 and 5.* If resistance is less than 5 ohms, go to next step. If resistance is 5 ohms or more, repair open in Light Blue/White wire between DLC and bulkhead connector. Retest system for normal operation.

5) Disconnect and inspect both halves in-line connector C140 located at left front of engine compartment, near 4WABS module connector. Inspect connector for physical damage, bent terminals or corrosion. Repair connector as necessary and retest system for normal operation. If connector is okay, go to next step.

6) Measure resistance of Light Blue/White wire between terminal No. 16 at male half of bulkhead connector C148 and terminal No. 8 at female half of in-line connector C140. *See Figs. 5 and 6.* If resistance is less than 5 ohms, repair open in Light Blue/White wire between in-line connector C140 and 4WABS connector. Retest system for normal operation. If resistance is 5 ohms or more, repair open in Light Blue/White wire between connector C148 and in-line connector C140. Retest system for normal operation.

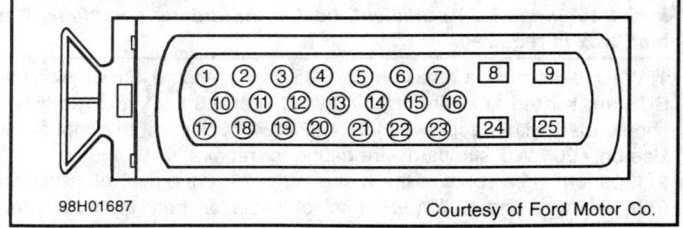

98H01687   Courtesy of Ford Motor Co.

Fig. 3: Identifying 4WABS Module Connector Terminals

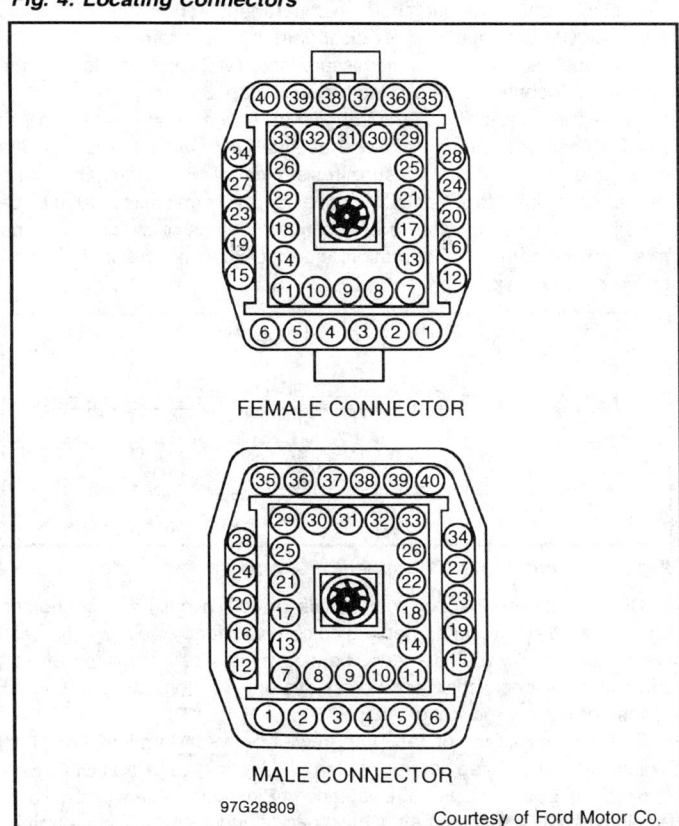

Passive Anti-Theft System (PATS) Module Connector C222

Air Suspension Control Module Connectors

Central Timer Module (CTM), Generic Electronic Module (GEM) Connectors

Instrument Panel

Electronic Automatic Temperature Control (EATC) Module Connectors

Restraint Control Module (RCM) Connectors

FRONT OF VEHICLE

Bulkhead Connector C212

Bulkhead Connector C146

Bulkhead Connector C147

Bulkhead Connector C148

99E02789

Courtesy of Ford Motor Co.

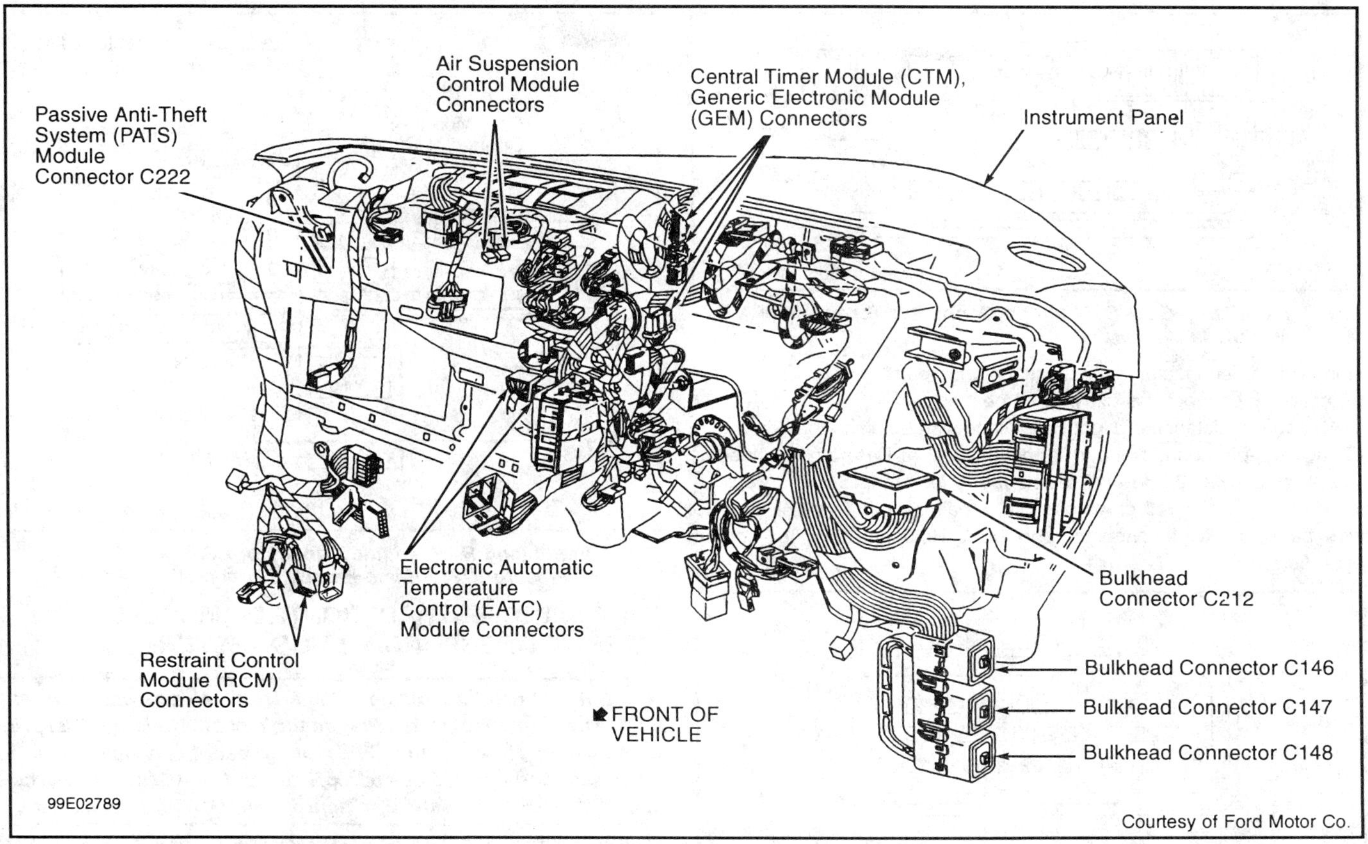

Fig. 4: Locating Connectors

FEMALE CONNECTOR

MALE CONNECTOR

97G28809

Courtesy of Ford Motor Co.

Fig. 5: Identifying 40-Pin Bulkhead Connectors C147 & C148

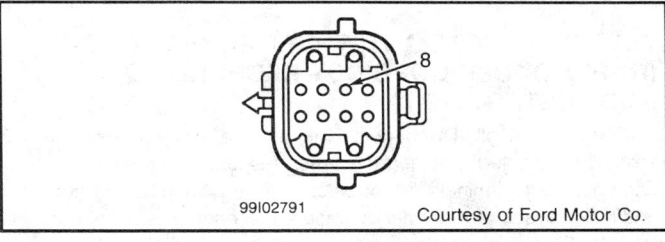

99I02791

Courtesy of Ford Motor Co.

Fig. 6: Identifying In-Line Connector C140 Terminals

TEST B: GENERIC ELECTRONIC MODULE (GEM)/CENTRAL TIMER MODULE (CTM) DOES NOT RESPOND TO NGS TESTER

1) Turn ignition off. Disconnect GEM/CTM 26-pin connector C280 located behind center of instrument panel. *See Fig. 4*. Inspect connector for physical damage, bent terminals or corrosion. Repair connector as necessary and retest system for normal operation. If connector is okay, go to next step.

2) Measure resistance of Light Blue/White wire between terminal No. 25 at GEM/CTM connector and terminal No. 7 at Data Link Connector (DLC). *See Figs. 2 and 7*. If resistance is less than 5 ohms, replace GEM/CTM and retest system for normal operation. If resistance is 5 ohms or more, repair open in Light Blue/White wire between GEM/CTM connector and DLC. Retest system for normal operation.

TEST C: RESTRAINT CONTROL MODULE DOES NOT RESPOND TO NGS TESTER

1) Turn ignition off. Deactivate air bag system. See appropriate AIR BAG RESTRAINT SYSTEMS article. Disconnect Restraint Control Module (RCM) 26-pin connector located behind right kick panel. *See Fig. 4*. Inspect RCM connector for physical damage, bent terminals or corro-

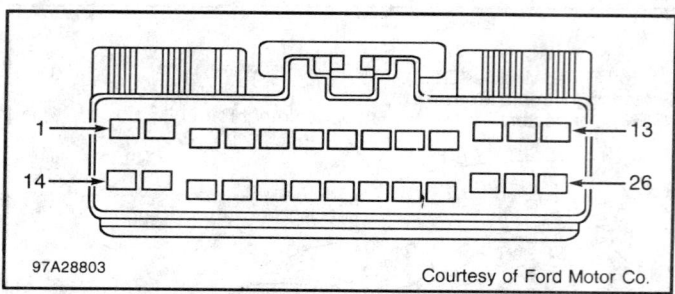

Fig. 7: Identifying GEM/CTM 26-Pin Connector Terminals (RAP Module Is Similar)

sion. Repair connector as necessary and retest system for normal operation. If connector is okay, go to next step.

2) Measure resistance of Light Blue/White wire between terminal No. 5 at RCM 26-pin connector and terminal No. 7 at Data Link Connector (DLC). *See Figs. 2 and 8.* If resistance is less than 5 ohms, replace RCM. If resistance is 5 ohms or more, repair open in Light Blue/White wire between RCM connector and DLC. Retest system for normal operation.

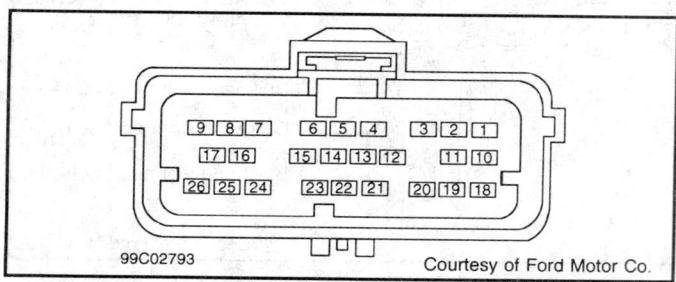

Fig. 8: Identifying Restraint Control Module Connector Terminals

TEST D: REMOTE ANTI-THEFT PERSONALITY (RAP) MODULE DOES NOT RESPOND TO NGS TESTER

1) Turn ignition off. Disconnect RAP module 26-pin connector C336 located behind left rear quarter panel. Inspect connector for physical damage, bent terminals or corrosion. Repair connector as necessary and retest system for normal operation. If connector is okay, go to next step.

2) Measure resistance of Light Blue/White wire between terminal No. 3 at RAP module 26-pin connector and terminal No. 7 at Data Link Connector (DLC). *See Figs. 2 and 6.* If resistance is less than 5 ohms, replace RAP module and retest system for normal operation. If resistance is 5 ohms or more, go to next step.

3) Disconnect and inspect both halves of bulkhead connector C212 located at left corner of instrument panel, near cowl panel grommet. *See Fig. 4.* Inspect connector for physical damage, bent terminals or corrosion. Repair connector as necessary and retest system for normal operation. If connector is okay, go to next step.

4) Measure resistance of Light Blue/White wire between terminal No. 3 at RAP module 26-pin connector and terminal No. 51 at male half of bulkhead connector C212. *See Fig. 9.* If resistance is less than 5 ohms, repair open in Light Blue/White wire between female half of bulkhead connector C212 and DLC. Retest system for normal operation. If resistance is 5 ohms or more, repair open in Light Blue/White wire between RAP module 26-pin connector and male half of bulkhead connector C212. Retest system for normal operation.

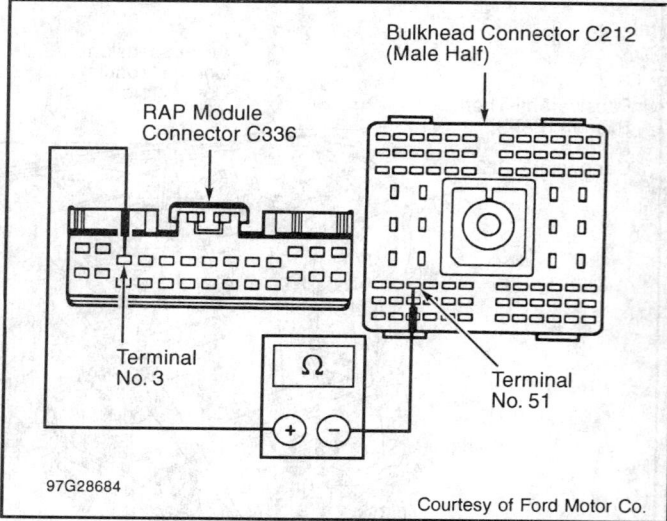

Fig. 9: Identifying RAP Module Connector C336 & Bulkhead Connector C212 (Male Half Of Connector Shown)

TEST E: POWERTRAIN CONTROL MODULE (PCM) DOES NOT RESPOND TO NGS TESTER

NOTE: If test results indicate PCM is faulty, always check for any engine performance related Diagnostic Trouble Codes (DTCs) prior to replacing PCM. If any DTCs are present, service DTCs as necessary and retest. See appropriate SELF-DIAGNOSTICS article in ENGINE PERFORMANCE in appropriate MITCHELL® manual.

1) Turn ignition off. Disconnect Powertrain Control Module (PCM) connector C202 located in engine compartment, at right side of firewall. Inspect PCM connector for physical damage, bent terminals or corrosion. Repair connector as necessary and retest system for normal operation. If connector is okay, go to next step.

2) Measure resistance of Tan/Orange wire between terminal No. 16 at PCM connector and terminal No. 2 at Data Link Connector (DLC) *See Figs. 2 and 10.* Also, measure resistance of Pink/Light Blue wire between terminal No. 15 at PCM connector and terminal No. 10 at DLC. If both resistance readings are less than 5 ohms, replace PCM and retest system for normal operation. If any resistance reading is 5 ohms or more, go to next step.

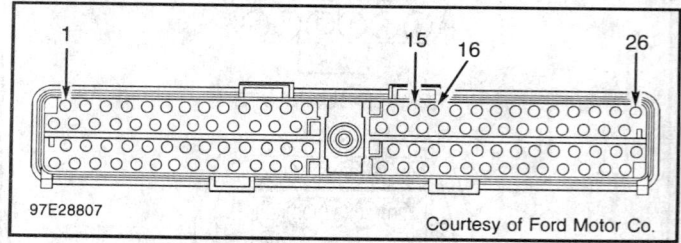

Fig. 10: Identifying PCM Connector Terminals

3) Disconnect and inspect both halves of 40-pin bulkhead connector C147 located at left rear corner engine compartment. *See Fig. 4.* Inspect connector for physical damage, bent terminals or corrosion. Repair connector as necessary and retest system for normal operation. If connector is okay, go to next step.

4) Measure resistance of Tan/Orange wire between terminal No. 21 at female half of bulkhead connector C147 and terminal No. 2 at DLC. *See Figs. 2 and 5.* Also, measure resistance of Pink/Light Blue wire between terminal No. 25 at female half of bulkhead connector C147 and terminal No. 10 at DLC. If both resistance readings are less than 5 ohms, go to next step. If any resistance reading is 5 ohms or more, repair Tan/

Orange wire and/or Pink/Light Blue wire between female half of bulkhead connector C147 and DLC. Retest system for normal operation.

5) Disconnect and inspect both halves of 42-pin bulkhead Gray connector C115. Connector is located at left rear corner engine compartment, right of brake booster. Inspect connector for physical damage, bent terminals or corrosion. *See Fig. 11*. Repair connector as necessary and retest system for normal operation. If connector is okay, go to next step.

6) Measure resistance of Tan/Orange wire between terminal No. 21 at male half of bulkhead connector C147 and terminal No. 11 at male half of bulkhead connector C115. *See Figs. 5 and 11*. Also, measure resistance of Pink/Light Blue wire between terminal No. 25 at male half of bulkhead connector C147 and terminal No. 3 at male half of bulkhead connector C115. If both resistance readings are less than 5 ohms, repair Tan/Orange wire and/or Pink/Light Blue wire between female half of bulkhead connector C115 and PCM connector. Retest system for normal operation. If any resistance reading is 5 ohms or more, repair Tan/Orange wire and/or Pink/Light Blue wire between male half of bulkhead connector C147 and bulkhead connector C115.

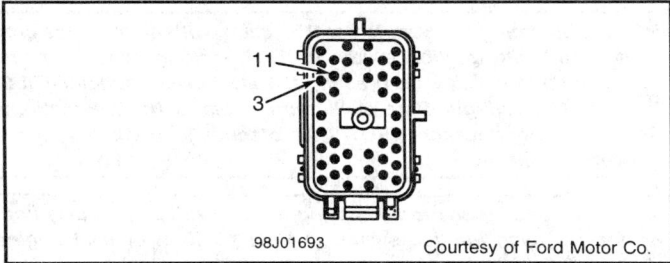

Fig. 11: Identifying Bulkhead Connector C115 Terminals (Male Half Of Connector Shown)

TEST F: AIR SUSPENSION CONTROL MODULE DOES NOT RESPOND TO NGS TESTER

1) Turn ignition off. Disconnect air suspension control module Gray connector C2000 located left center of instrument panel. *See Fig. 4*. Inspect air suspension control module connector for physical damage, bent terminals or corrosion. Repair connector as necessary and retest system for normal operation. If connector is okay, go to next step.

2) Measure resistance of Light Blue/White wire between terminal No. 29 at air suspension control module connector and terminal No. 7 at Data Link Connector (DLC). *See Figs. 2 and 12*. If resistance is less than 5 ohms, replace air suspension control module and retest system for normal operation. If resistance 5 ohms or more, repair open in Light Blue/White wire between air suspension control module connector and DLC. Retest system for normal operation.

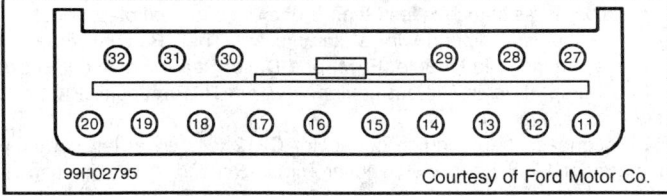

Fig. 12: Identifying Air Suspension Control Module Connector C2000 Terminals

TEST G: AUTOMATIC TEMPERATURE CONTROL (EATC) MODULE DOES NOT RESPOND TO NGS TESTER

1) Turn ignition off. Disconnect Automatic Temperature Control (EATC) module Black connector C297 located left center of instrument panel. *See Fig. 4*. Inspect EATC module connector for physical damage, bent terminals or corrosion. Repair connector as necessary and retest system for normal operation. If connector is okay, go to next step.

2) Measure resistance of Tan/Orange wire between terminal No. 15 at EATC module connector and terminal No. 2 at Data Link Connector

(DLC). *See Figs. 2 and 13*. Also, measure resistance of Light Blue/White wire between terminal No. 1 at EATC module connector and terminal No. 10 at DLC. If both resistance readings are less than 5 ohms, replace EATC module and retest system for normal operation. If any resistance reading is 5 ohms or more, repair Tan/Orange wire and/or Pink/Light Blue wire between DLC and EATC. Retest system for normal operation.

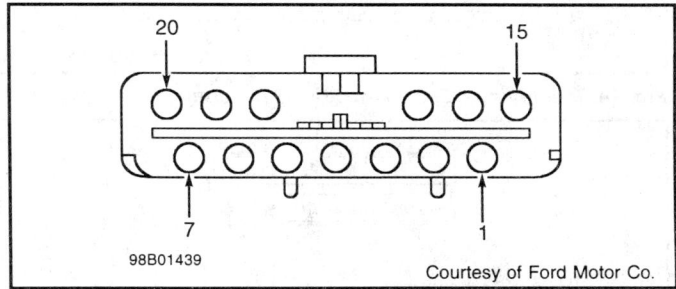

Fig. 13: Identifying EATC Module Black Connector C297 Terminals

TEST H: DRIVER SEAT MODULE (DSM) DOES NOT RESPOND TO NGS TESTER

1) Turn ignition off. Disconnect Driver Seat Module (DSM) 22-pin connector C337 located under driver's seat. Inspect DSM connector for physical damage, bent terminals or corrosion. Repair connector as necessary and retest system for normal operation. If connector is okay, go to next step.

2) Measure resistance of Light Blue/White wire between terminal No. 22 at DSM connector and terminal No. 7 at Data Link Connector (DLC). *See Figs. 2 and 14*. If resistance is less than 5 ohms, replace DSM and retest system for normal operation. If resistance is 5 ohms or more, go to next step.

3) Disconnect in-line connector C346 located under left front of driver's seat. Inspect connector for physical damage, bent terminals or corrosion. Repair connector as necessary and retest system for normal operation. If connector is okay, go to next step.

4) Measure resistance of Light Blue/White wire between terminal No. 22 at DSM connector C337 and terminal No. 11 at in-line connector C346. *See Figs. 14 and 15*. If resistance is less than 5 ohms, go to next step. If resistance is 5 ohms or more, repair open in Light Blue/White wire between DSM connector C337 and in-line connector C346. Retest system for normal operation.

5) Disconnect and inspect both halves of bulkhead connector C212 located at left corner of instrument panel, near cowl panel grommet. *See Fig. 4*. Inspect connector for physical damage, bent terminals or corrosion. Repair connector as necessary and retest system for normal operation. If connector is okay, go to next step.

6) Measure resistance of Light Blue/White wire between terminal No. 7 at DLC and terminal No. 51 at male half of bulkhead connector C212. *See Figs. 2 and 9*. If resistance is less than 5 ohms, repair open in Light Blue/White wire between male half of bulkhead connector C212 and in-line connector C346. Retest system for normal operation. If resistance is 5 ohms or more, repair open in Light Blue/White wire between female half of bulkhead connector C212 and DLC. Retest system for normal operation.

TEST I: PARKING AID MODULE (PAM) DOES NOT RESPOND TO NGS TESTER

1) Turn ignition off. Disconnect Parking Aid Module (PAM) 26-pin connector C440 located behind spare tire. Inspect connector for physical damage, bent terminals or corrosion. Repair connector as necessary and retest system for normal operation. If connector is okay, go to next step.

2) Measure resistance of Light Blue/White wire between terminal No. 5 at PAM connector and terminal No. 7 at Data Link Connector (DLC). *See*

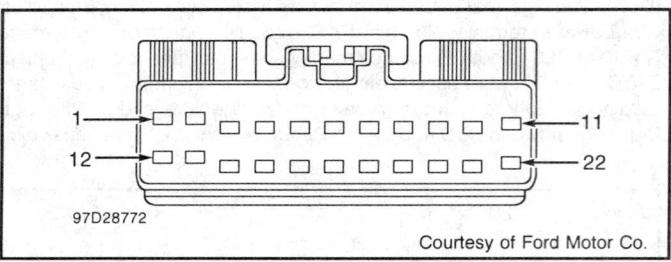

Fig. 14: Identifying DSM Connector C337 Terminals

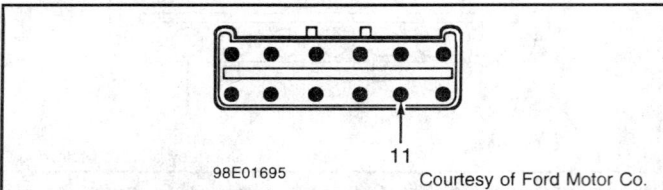

Fig. 15: Identifying In-Line Connector C346 Terminals

Figs. 2 and 16. If resistance is less than 5 ohms, replace PAM and retest system for normal operation. If resistance is 5 ohms or more, go to next step.

3) Disconnect and inspect both halves of bulkhead connector C212 located at left corner of instrument panel, near cowl panel grommet. *See Fig. 4.* Inspect connector for physical damage, bent terminals or corrosion. Repair connector as necessary and retest system for normal operation. If connector is okay, go to next step.

4) Measure resistance of Light Blue/White wire between terminal No. 5 at PAM connector and terminal No. 51 at male half of bulkhead connector C212. *See Figs. 16 and 17.* If resistance is less than 5 ohms, repair open in Light Blue/White wire between female half of bulkhead connector C212 and DLC. Retest system for normal operation. If resistance is 5 ohms or more, repair open in Light Blue/White wire between PAM connector and male half of bulkhead connector C212. Retest system for normal operation.

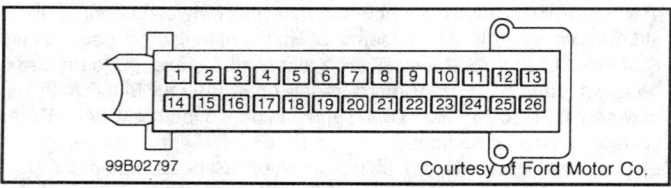

Fig. 16: Identifying Parking Aid Module Connector C440 Terminals

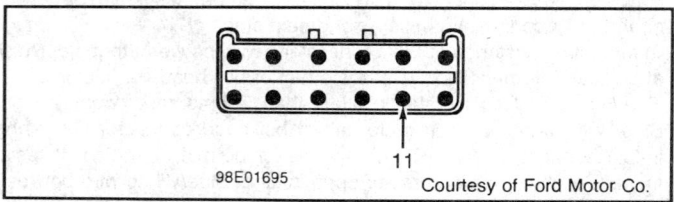

Fig. 17: Identifying Bulkhead Connector C212 Terminals (Male Half Of Connector Shown)

TEST J: PASSIVE ANTI-THEFT SYSTEM (PATS) MODULE DOES NOT RESPOND TO NGS TESTER

1) Turn ignition off. Disconnect PATS module 16-pin connector C222 located behind center of instrument panel. *See Fig. 4.* Inspect PATS module connector for physical damage, bent terminals or corrosion. Repair connector as necessary and retest system for normal operation. If connector is okay, go to next step.

2) Measure resistance of Tan/Orange wire between terminal No. 6 at PATS module connector and terminal No. 2 at DLC. *See Figs. 2 and 18.*

Also, measure resistance of Pink/Light Blue wire between terminal No. 5 at PATS module connector and terminal No. 10 at DLC. If both resistance readings are less than 5 ohms, replace PATS module and retest system for normal operation. If any resistance reading is 5 ohms or more, repair Tan/Orange wire and/or Pink/Light Blue wire between DLC and PATS module. Retest system for normal operation.

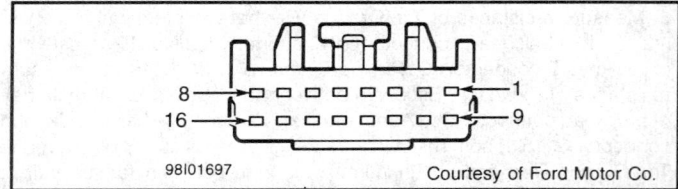

Fig. 18: Identifying PATS Module Connector C222 Terminals

TEST K: NO MODULE/NETWORK COMMUNICATIONS – ISO 9141 LINK

NOTE: Depending on module configuration, with all modules connected and with ignition switch in RUN position or with engine running 2-3 volts may be present at Data Link Connector (DLC) terminal No. 7 (Light Blue/White wire). This is the International Standards Organization (ISO) 9141 diagnostic communications network circuit.

NOTE: Depending on module configuration, with all modules connected and with ignition switch in RUN position or with engine running 2-3 volts may be present at Data Link Connector (DLC) terminal No. 7 (Light Blue/White wire). This is the International Standards Organization (ISO) 9141 diagnostic communications network circuit.

1) Inspect NGS tester connector for loose, damaged or corroded terminals. Pay particular attention to terminal No. 7. Repair connector as necessary and retest system for normal operation. If connector is okay, go to next step.

2) Turn ignition off. Inspect Data Link Connector (DLC) for physical damage, bent terminals or corrosion. Pay particular attention to terminal No. 7 (Light Blue/White wire). Repair connector as necessary and retest system for normal operation. If connector is okay, go to next step.

3) Ensure ignition is off. Disconnect GEM/CTM 26-pin connector C280 located behind center of instrument panel. *See Fig. 4.* Measure resistance of Light Blue/White wire between terminal No. 25 at GEM/CTM 26-pin connector and terminal No. 7 at DLC. *See Figs. 2 and 7.* If resistance is 5 ohms or more, repair open Light Blue/White wire between DLC and GEM/CTM connector. Retest system for normal operation. If resistance is less than 5 ohms, go to next step.

4) If vehicle is equipped with a Remote Anti-Theft Personality (RAP) module, Parking Aid Module (PAM) or a Driver Seat Module (DSM), go to next step. If vehicle is not equipped with a RAP module, PAM or a DSM, go to step **6)**.

5) Disconnect 84-pin in-line connector C212 located at left corner of instrument panel, near cowl panel grommet. *See Fig. 4.* Turn ignition on. Measure voltage between terminals No. 7 (Light Blue/White wire) and No. 16 (Orange wire) at DLC. *See Fig. 2.* Also, measure voltage between terminals No. 7 (Light Blue/White wire) and No. 4 (Black wire) at DLC. If any reading indicates voltage, go to next step. If both readings indicate zero volts, proceed as follows:

- If vehicle is equipped with a combination of RAP module, PAM or DSM, go to step **12)**.
- If vehicle is equipped with a RAP module only, go to step **14)**.
- If vehicle is equipped with a PAM only, go to step **19)**.
- If vehicle is equipped with a DSM only, go to step **20)**.

6) Turn ignition off. Reconnect in-line connector C212. Disconnect 40-pin bulkhead connector C148 located at left rear of engine compartment, near brake master cylinder. *See Fig. 4.* Turn ignition on. Measure voltage between terminals No. 7 (Light Blue/White wire) and No. 16

(Orange wire) at DLC. *See Fig. 2.* Also, measure voltage between terminals No. 7 (Light Blue/White wire) and No. 4 (Black wire) at DLC. If any reading indicates voltage, go to next step. If both readings indicate zero volts, go to step **22**).

7) Turn ignition off. Reconnect bulkhead connector C148. If vehicle is equipped with a air suspension control module, go to next step. If vehicle is not equipped with a air suspension control module, go to step **9**).

8) Disconnect air suspension control module connector C2000 located left center of instrument panel. *See Fig. 4.* Turn ignition on. Measure voltage between terminals No. 7 (Light Blue/White wire) and No. 16 (Orange wire) at DLC. *See Fig. 2.* Also, measure voltage between terminals No. 7 (Light Blue/White wire) and No. 4 (Black wire) at DLC. If any reading indicates voltage, go to next step. If both readings indicate zero volts, replace air suspension control module and retest system for normal operation.

9) Turn ignition off. Reconnect air suspension control module connector C2000. Disconnect GEM/CTM 26-pin connector C280 located behind center of instrument panel. *See Fig. 4.* Turn ignition on. Measure voltage between terminals No. 7 (Light Blue/White wire) and No. 16 (Orange wire) at DLC. *See Fig. 2.* Also, measure voltage between terminals No. 7 (Light Blue/White wire) and No. 4 (Black wire) at DLC. If any reading indicates voltage, go to next step. If both readings indicate zero volts, replace GEM/CTM and retest system for normal operation.

10) Turn ignition off. Reconnect GEM/CTM 26-pin connector C280. Deactivate air bag system. See appropriate AIR BAG RESTRAINT SYSTEMS article. Disconnect Restraint Control Module (RCM) connector, located behind right kick panel. Turn ignition on. Measure voltage between terminals No. 7 (Light Blue/White wire) and No. 16 (Orange wire) at DLC. *See Fig. 2.* Also, measure voltage between terminals No. 7 (Light Blue/White wire) and No. 4 (Black wire) at DLC. If any reading indicates voltage, repair circuit No. 70 (Light Blue/White wire). Retest system for normal operation. If both readings indicate zero volts, replace RCM and retest system for normal operation.

11) Turn ignition off. Reconnect in-line connector C212. Check if vehicle is equipped with Remote Anti-Theft Personality (RAP) module. Rap is located behind left rear quarter panel. If vehicle is equipped with RAP module, go to next step. If vehicle is not equipped with RAP module, go to step **13**).

12) Disconnect RAP module 26-pin connector C336. Turn ignition on. Measure voltage between terminals No. 7 (Light Blue/White wire) and No. 16 (Orange wire) at DLC. *See Fig. 2.* Also, measure voltage between terminals No. 7 (Light Blue/White wire) and No. 4 (Black wire) at DLC. If any reading indicates voltage, go to next step. If both readings indicate zero volts, replace RAP module and retest system for normal operation.

13) Turn ignition off. Reconnect RAP module 26-pin connector C336. Check if vehicle is equipped with Parking Aid Module (PAM). PAM is located behind spare tire. If vehicle is equipped with PAM, go to next step. If vehicle is not equipped with PAM, go to step **15**).

14) Disconnect PAM 24-pin connector C440. Turn ignition on. Measure voltage between terminals No. 7 (Light Blue/White wire) and No. 16 (Orange wire) at DLC. *See Fig. 2.* Also, measure voltage between terminals No. 7 (Light Blue/White wire) and No. 4 (Black wire) at DLC. If any reading indicates voltage, go to next step. If both readings indicate zero volts, replace PAM and retest system for normal operation.

15) Turn ignition off. Reconnect PAM 24-pin connector C440. Check if vehicle is equipped with Driver's Seat Module (DSM). DSM is located under driver's seat. If vehicle is equipped with DSM, go to next step. If vehicle is not equipped with DSM, go to step **17**).

16) Disconnect DSM 22-pin connector C337. Turn ignition on. Measure voltage between terminals No. 7 (Light Blue/White wire) and No. 16 (Orange wire) at DLC. *See Fig. 2.* Also, measure voltage between terminals No. 7 (Light Blue/White wire) and No. 4 (Black wire) at DLC. If any reading indicates voltage, go to next step. If both readings indicate zero volts, replace DSM and retest system for normal operation.

17) Turn ignition off. Reconnect DSM connector C337. Disconnect in-line connector C346 located under of left front of driver's seat. Turn

ignition on. Measure voltage between terminals No. 7 (Light Blue/White wire) and No. 16 (Orange wire) at DLC. *See Fig. 2.* Also, measure voltage between terminals No. 7 (Light Blue/White wire) and No. 4 (Black wire) at DLC. If any reading indicates voltage, repair circuit No. 70 (Light Blue/White wire) between in-line connector C212, in-line connector C346 and RAP module connector. Retest system for normal operation. If both readings indicate zero volts, repair circuit No. 70 (Light Blue/White wire) between in-line connector C346 and DSM connector. Retest system for normal operation.

18) Turn ignition off. Reconnect in-line connector C212. Disconnect RAP module 26-pin connector C336 located behind left rear quarter panel. Turn ignition on. Measure voltage between terminals No. 7 (Light Blue/White wire) and No. 16 (Orange wire) at DLC. *See Fig. 2.* Also, measure voltage between terminals No. 7 (Light Blue/White wire) and No. 4 (Black wire) at DLC. If any reading indicates voltage, repair circuit No. 70 (Light Blue/White wire) between in-line connector C212 and RAP module connector. Retest system for normal operation. If both readings indicate zero volts, replace RAP module and retest system for normal operation.

19) Turn ignition off. Reconnect in-line connector C212. Disconnect PAM 26-pin connector C440 located behind spare tire. Turn ignition on. Measure voltage between terminals No. 7 (Light Blue/White wire) and No. 16 (Orange wire) at DLC. *See Fig. 2.* Also, measure voltage between terminals No. 7 (Light Blue/White wire) and No. 4 (Black wire) at DLC. If any reading indicates voltage, repair circuit No. 70 (Light Blue/White wire) between in-line connector C212 and PAM connector. If both readings indicate zero volts, replace PAM and retest system for normal operation.

20) Turn ignition off. Reconnect PAM 26-pin connector C440. Disconnect DSM 22-pin connector C337 located under driver's seat. Turn ignition on. Measure voltage between terminals No. 7 (Light Blue/White wire) and No. 16 (Orange wire) at DLC. *See Fig. 2.* Also, measure voltage between terminals No. 7 (Light Blue/White wire) and No. 4 (Black wire) at DLC. If any reading indicates voltage, go to next step. If both readings indicate zero volts, replace DSM and retest system for normal operation.

21) Turn ignition off. Disconnect in-line connector C346 located under left front of driver's seat. Turn ignition on. Measure voltage between terminals No. 7 (Light Blue/White wire) and No. 16 (Orange wire) at DLC. *See Fig. 2 .* Also, measure voltage between terminals No. 7 (Light Blue/White wire) and No. 4 (Black wire) at DLC. If any reading indicates voltage, repair circuit No. 70 (Light Blue/White wire) between in-line connector C212 and in-line connector C346. Retest system for normal operation. If both readings indicate zero volts, repair circuit No. 70 (Light Blue/White wire) between in-line connector C346 and DSM connector. Retest system for normal operation.

22) Turn ignition off. Reconnect 40-pin bulkhead connector C148. Disconnect 4WABS module connector located at left front of engine compartment. Turn ignition on. Measure voltage between terminals No. 7 (Light Blue/White wire) and No. 16 (Orange wire) at DLC. *See Fig. 2.* Also, measure voltage between terminals No. 7 (Light Blue/White wire) and No. 4 (Black wire) at DLC. If any reading indicates voltage, go to next step. If both readings indicate zero volts, replace 4WABS module and retest system for normal operation.

23) Turn ignition off. Disconnect in-line 12-pin connector C140 located at left front of engine compartment, near 4WABS module connector. Turn ignition on. Measure voltage between terminals No. 7 (Light Blue/White wire) and No. 16 (Orange wire) at DLC. *See Fig. 2.* Also, measure voltage between terminals No. 7 (Light Blue/White wire) and No. 4 (Black wire) at DLC. If any reading indicates voltage, repair circuit No. 70 (Light Blue/White wire) between in-line connector C148 and in-line connector C140. Retest system for normal operation. If both readings indicate zero volts, repair circuit No. 70 (Light Blue/White wire) between in-line connector C140 and 4WABS. Retest system for normal operation.

TEST L: NO MODULE/NETWORK COMMUNICATIONS – BUS LINK

NOTE: Depending on module configuration, with all modules connected and with ignition switch in RUN position or with engine running 2-3 volts may be present at Data Link Connector (DLC) terminals No. 2 (Tan/Orange wire) and No. 10 (Pink/Light Blue wire). These are the Standard Corporate Protocol (SCP) diagnostic communications network circuits.

NOTE: Depending on module configuration, with all modules connected and with ignition switch in RUN position or with engine running 2-3 volts may be present at Data Link Connector (DLC) terminals No. 2 (Tan/Orange wire) and No. 10 (Pink/Light Blue wire). These are the Standard Corporate Protocol (SCP) diagnostic communications network circuits.

1) Inspect NGS tester connector for physical damage, bent terminals or corrosion. Pay particular attention to terminals No. 2 and 10. Repair connector as necessary and retest system for normal operation. If connector is okay, go to next step.

2) Turn ignition off. Inspect Data Link Connector (DLC) for physical damage, bent terminals or corrosion. Pay particular attention to terminals No. 2 (Tan/Orange wire) and No. 10 (Pink/Light Blue wire). *See Fig. 2.* Repair connector as necessary and retest system for normal operation. If connector is okay, go to next step.

3) Disconnect PATS module 16-pin connector C222 located behind top right center of instrument panel. *See Fig. 4.* Measure resistance of Tan/Orange wire between terminal No. 6 at PATS module connector and terminal No. 2 at DLC. *See Figs. 2 and 18.* Also, measure resistance of Pink/Light Blue wire between terminal No. 5 at PATS module connector and terminal No. 10 at DLC. If both resistance readings are less than 5 ohms, go to next step. If any resistance reading is 5 ohms or more, repair Tan/Orange wire and/or Pink/Light Blue wire between DLC and PATS module. Retest system for normal operation.

4) Turn ignition on. Measure voltage between the following DLC terminals:
- Measure voltage between terminals No. 2 (Tan/Orange wire) and No. 4 (Black wire) at DLC. *See Fig. 2.*
- Measure voltage between terminals No. 2 (Tan/Orange wire) and No. 16 (Orange wire) at DLC.
- Measure voltage between terminals No. 10 (Pink/Light Blue wire) and No. 4 (Black wire) at DLC.
- Measure voltage between terminals No. 10 (Pink/Light Blue wire) and No. 16 (Orange wire) at DLC.

If any reading indicates voltage, go to next step. If all readings indicate zero volts, replace PATS module. Retest system for normal operation.

5) Turn ignition off. Reconnect PATS module 16-pin connector C222. Disconnect Powertrain Control Module (PCM) connector C202 located in engine compartment, at right side of firewall. Turn ignition on. Measure voltage between the following DLC terminals:
- Measure voltage between terminals No. 2 (Tan/Orange wire) and No. 4 (Black wire) at DLC. *See Fig. 2.*
- Measure voltage between terminals No. 2 (Tan/Orange wire) and No. 16 (Orange wire) at DLC.
- Measure voltage between terminals No. 10 (Pink/Light Blue wire) and No. 4 (Black wire) at DLC.
- Measure voltage between terminals No. 10 (Pink/Light Blue wire) and No. 16 (Orange wire) at DLC.

If any reading indicates voltage, on vehicles not equipped with Electronic Automatic Temperature Control (EATC), go to step 7). On vehicles equipped with EATC, go to next step.

If all readings indicate zero volts, replace PCM. Retest system for normal operation.

6) Turn ignition off. Disconnect module Black connector C297 located left center of instrument panel. *See Fig. 4.* Measure voltage between the following DLC terminals:

- Measure voltage between terminals No. 2 (Tan/Orange wire) and No. 4 (Black wire) at DLC. *See Fig. 2.*
- Measure voltage between terminals No. 2 (Tan/Orange wire) and No. 16 (Orange wire) at DLC.
- Measure voltage between terminals No. 10 (Pink/Light Blue wire) and No. 4 (Black wire) at DLC.
- Measure voltage between terminals No. 10 (Pink/Light Blue wire) and No. 16 (Orange wire) at DLC.

If any reading indicates voltage, go to next step. If all readings indicate zero volts, replace EATC module. Retest system for normal operation.

7) Turn ignition off. Disconnect 40-pin bulkhead connector C147 located at left rear corner engine compartment. *See Fig. 4.* Turn ignition on. Measure voltage between the following DLC terminals:

- Measure voltage between terminals No. 2 (Tan/Orange wire) and No. 4 (Black wire) at DLC. *See Fig. 2.*
- Measure voltage between terminals No. 2 (Tan/Orange wire) and No. 16 (Orange wire) at DLC.
- Measure voltage between terminals No. 10 (Pink/Light Blue wire) and No. 4 (Black wire) at DLC.
- Measure voltage between terminals No. 10 (Pink/Light Blue wire) and No. 16 (Orange wire) at DLC.

If all readings indicate zero volts, go to next step. If any reading indicates voltage, repair Tan/Orange wire and/or Pink/Light Blue wire between bulkhead connector C147, DLC, PATS module and EATC. Retest system for normal operation.

8) Turn ignition off. Reconnect bulkhead connector C147. Disconnect 42-pin bulkhead Gray connector C115. Connector is located at left rear corner engine compartment, right of brake booster. Turn ignition on. Measure voltage between the following DLC terminals:
- Measure voltage between terminals No. 2 (Tan/Orange wire) and No. 4 (Black wire) at DLC. *See Fig. 2.*
- Measure voltage between terminals No. 2 (Tan/Orange wire) and No. 16 (Orange wire) at DLC.
- Measure voltage between terminals No. 10 (Pink/Light Blue wire) and No. 4 (Black wire) at DLC.
- Measure voltage between terminals No. 10 (Pink/Light Blue wire) and No. 16 (Orange wire) at DLC.

If all readings indicate zero volts, repair Tan/Orange wire and/or Pink/Light Blue wire between bulkhead connector C115 and PCM. Retest system for normal operation. If any reading indicates voltage, repair Tan/Orange wire and/or Pink/Light Blue wire between bulkhead connector C147 and connector C115. Retest system for normal operation.

TEST M: NO MODULE/NETWORK COMMUNICATION

1) Inspect NGS tester connector for loose, damaged or corroded terminals. Repair as necessary and retest system for normal operation. If connector is okay, go to next step.

2) Turn ignition off. Inspect Data Link Connector (DLC) for physical damage, bent terminals or corrosion. Repair as necessary and retest system for normal operation. If connector is okay, go to next step.

3) Turn ignition off. Remove and inspect fuse No. 5 (10-amp) from instrument panel fuse block. If fuse is blown, go to next step. If fuse is okay, reinstall fuse and go to step 5).

4) Replace fuse and retest system for normal operation. Recheck fuse. If fuse is okay, go to next step. If fuse is blown, repair short to ground in circuit No. 693 (Orange wire) between instrument panel fuse block and DLC. Retest system for normal operation.

5) Measure voltage between ground and terminal No. 16 (Orange wire) at DLC. *See Fig. 2.* If voltage is more than 10 volts, go to next step. If voltage is 10 volts or less, repair circuit No. 693 (Orange wire) between instrument panel fuse block and DLC. Retest system for normal operation.

6) Measure resistance between ground and terminals No. 4 (Black wire) and No. 5 (Black/White wire) at DLC. If both resistance readings are less than 5 ohms, repair or replace NGS tester. Retest system for normal

operation. If any resistance reading is 5 ohms or more, repair open in Black wire or Black/White wire between ground and DLC. Retest system for normal operation.

DIAGNOSTIC TROUBLE CODE (DTC) DEFINITIONS

AIR SUSPENSION CONTROL MODULE DTC INDEX

DTC	Description	Test
B1318	Battery Voltage Low	1
B1342	ECU Defective	1
B1485	Brake Pedal Position Switch Short To Voltage	1
B1565	Door Ajar Input Short To Voltage	1
C1439	Acceleration Input Signal Circuit Failure	1
C1724	Height Sensor Power Circuit Failure	1
C1726	Rear Pneumatic Failure	1
C1760	Rear Height Sensor Circuit Failure	1
C1770	Vent Solenoid Circuit Failure	1
C1830	Air Compressor Relay Circuit Failure	1
C1865	Rear Fill Solenoid Circuit Failure	1
C1869	Rear Gate Solenoid	1

[1] – Repair electronic suspension as necessary. See appropriate ELECTRONIC article in SUSPENSION in appropriate MITCHELL® manual.

DRIVER'S SEAT MODULE (DSM) DTC INDEX

DTC	Description	Test
B1342	ECU Defective	1
B1529	Memory Set Switch Short To Power	2
B1533	Memory 1 Switch Short To Power	2
B1537	Memory 2 Switch Short To Power	2
B1663	Seat Front Up/Down Motor Stalled	2
B1664	Seat Rear Up/Down Motor Stalled	2
B1665	Seat Horizontal Motor Stalled	2
B1676	Battery Voltage Out Or Range	3
B1711	Driver's Seat Front Up Circuit Short To Voltage	2
B1715	Driver's Seat Front Down Circuit Short To Voltage	2
B1719	Driver's Seat Forward Circuit Short To Voltage	2
B1723	Driver's Seat Rearward Circuit Short To Voltage	2
B1727	Driver's Seat Rear Up Circuit Short To Voltage	2
B1731	Driver's Seat Rear Down Circuit Short To Voltage	2
B1950	Driver's Seat Rear Up/Down Feedback Circuit Failure	2
B1952	Driver's Seat Rear Up/Down Feedback Circuit Short To Voltage	2
B1954	Driver's Seat Front Up/Down Feedback Circuit Failure	2
B1956	Driver's Seat Front Up/Down Feedback Circuit Short To Voltage	2
B1962	Driver's Seat Horizontal Feedback Circuit Failure	2
B1964	Driver's Seat Horizontal Feedback Circuit Short To Voltage	2

[1] – Using NGS tester, retrieve and document continuous DTCs. Clear all DTCs. Perform GEM/CTM self-test. If DTC B1342 is retrieved again, replace GEM/CTM.
[2] – Repair power seat system as necessary. See POWER SEATS – EXPLORER & MOUNTAINEER article.
[3] – Check charging system and repair as necessary. See appropriate GENERATORS article in STARTING & CHARGING SYSTEMS. If charging system is okay, repair wiring as necessary. See appropriate wiring diagram in POWER DISTRIBUTION article in WIRING DIAGRAMS.

ELECTRONIC AUTOMATIC TEMPERATURE CONTROL MODULE DTC INDEX

DTC	Description	Test
B1249	Blend Door Failure	1
B1251	A/C In-Car Temperature Sensor Open Circuit	1
B1253	A/C In-Car Temperature Sensor Circuit Short To Ground	1
B1255	A/C Ambient Air Temperature Sensor Circuit Open	1
B1257	A/C Ambient Air Temperature Sensor Circuit Short To Ground	1
B1261	A/C Solar Radiation Sensor Circuit Short To Ground	1
U1073	Invalid/Missing Data For Engine Coolant	2
U1341	Invalid/Missing Data For Vehicle Speed	3

[1] – Repair A/C system as necessary. See appropriate AUTOMATIC A/C-HEATER SYSTEMS article in appropriate MITCHELL® AIR CONDITIONING & HEATING SERVICE & REPAIR manual.
[2] – Repair engine coolant temperature sensor circuit. See SELF-DIAGNOSTICS – EEC-V article in ENGINE PERFORMANCE in appropriate MITCHELL® manual.
[3] – Repair vehicle speed sensor circuit. See appropriate ELECTRONIC CONTROLS article in AUTOMATIC TRANSMISSIONS in appropriate MITCHELL® TRANSMISSION SERVICE & REPAIR manual.

GENERIC ELECTRONIC MODULE/CENTRAL TIMER MODULE (GEM/CTM) DTC INDEX [1]

DTC	Description	Test
B1302 [2]	Accessory Delay Relay Coil Circuit Failure	3
B1304 [2]	Accessory Delay Relay Coil Circuit Open Or Short To Voltage	3
B1313	Battery Saver Relay Coil Circuit Failure	3
B1315	Battery Saver Relay Coil Circuit Short To Voltage	3
B1317	Battery Voltage High	4 5
B1318	Battery Voltage Low	4 5
B1322	Driver's Door Ajar Circuit Short To Ground	5 6
B1323	Door Ajar Light Circuit Failure	7
B1325	Door Ajar Light Circuit Short To Voltage	7
B1330	Passenger's Door Ajar Circuit Short To Ground	5 6
B1334	Deck Lid Ajar Rear Door Circuit Short To Ground	6
B1338	Right Rear Door Ajar Circuit Short To Ground	6
B1340	Chime Input Request Circuit Short To Ground	8
B1342	GEM/CTM Is Defective	9
B1345 [2]	Heated Backlite Input Circuit Short To Ground	10
B1347 [2]	Heated Backlite Relay Circuit Failure	10
B1349 [2]	Heated Backlite Relay Circuit Short To Voltage	10
B1352	Ignition Key-In Circuit Failure	5 8
B1355	Ignition RUN Circuit Failure	11
B1359	Ignition RUN/ACC Circuit Failure	11
B1371	Illuminated Entry Relay Circuit Failure	4
B1373	Interior Light Relay Coil Circuit Short To Voltage	6
B1398 [2]	Driver's Power Window One-Touch Window Relay Circuit Failure	12
B1400 [2]	Driver's Power Window One-Touch Window Relay Coil Circuit Short To Voltage	12
B1404 [2]	Driver Door Power Window Down Circuit Open	12
B1405 [2]	Driver Door Power Window Down Circuit Short To Voltage	12
B1410 [2]	Driver Door Power Window Motor Circuit Failure	5 12
B1426	Seat Belt Light Circuit Short To Voltage	7
B1428	Seat Belt Light Output Circuit Failure	7
B1431	Wiper Brake/Run Relay Circuit Failure	13
B1432	Wiper Brake/Run Relay Short To Voltage	13
B1434	Wiper Hi/Low Speed Relay Circuit Failure	13
B1436	Wiper Hi/Low Speed Relay Circuit Short To Voltage	13
B1438	Wiper Mode Select Switch Circuit Failure	5 13
B1441	Wiper Mode Select Switch Input Short To Ground	5 13
B1446	Wiper Park Sense Circuit Failure	5 13
B1450	Wiper/Wash Interval Delay Switch Input Circuit Failure	5 13
B1453	Wiper/Wash Interval Delay Switch Input Short To Ground	5 13
B1458	Wiper/Washer Pump Motor Relay Circuit Failure	13
B1460	Wiper/Washer Pump Motor Relay Coil Circuit Short To Voltage	13
B1462	Seat Belt Switch Circuit Failure	5 8
B1466	Wiper Hi/Low Speed Not Switching	13
B1467	Wiper Motor Hi/Low Speed Circuit Short To Voltage	13
B1473	Wiper Motor Low Speed Circuit Failure	13
B1475	Delayed Accessory Relay Contacts Short To Voltage	12
B1476	Wiper Motor High Speed Circuit Failure	13
B1483 [2]	Brake Pedal Input Circuit Failure	14
B1485 [2]	Brake Pedal Input Circuit Short To Voltage	14
B1574	Left Rear Door Ajar Circuit Short To Ground	6
B1577 [2]	Parking Light Input Circuit Short To Voltage	5 8
B1610 [2]	Illuminated Entry Input Request Circuit Short To Ground	5 6
B1611 [2]	Rear Wiper Mode Select Switch Circuit Failure	13
B1614 [2]	Rear Wiper Mode Select Switch Circuit Short To Ground	13
B1814 [2]	Rear Wiper Motor Down Relay Circuit Failure	13
B1816 [2]	Rear Wiper Motor Down Relay Coil Circuit Short To Voltage	13
B1818 [2]	Rear Wiper Motor Up Relay Coil Circuit Failure	13
B1820 [2]	Rear Wiper Motor Up Relay Circuit Short To Voltage	13
B1833 [2]	Door Unlock Switch Circuit Short To Ground	5 15
B1834 [2]	Door Unlock Disarm Output Circuit Failure	15
B1836 [2]	Door Unlock Disarm Output Circuit Short To Voltage	15
B1839 [2]	Rear Wiper Motor Circuit Failure	13
B1840	Front Wiper Power Circuit Failure	13
B1894 [2]	Rear Wiper Motor Speed Sense Circuit Failure	13
B2105 [2]	Throttle Position Input Signal Out Of Low Range	14
B2106 [2]	Throttle Position Input Signal Out Of High Range	14
B2141	NVM Configuration Failure	16
P0500 [2]	Vehicle Speed Signal Circuit Failure	14
P1763 [2]	Transmission Neutral In Tow Indicator Circuit Short To Voltage	8
P1764 [2]	Transmission Neutral In Tow Indicator Circuit Failure	8

GENERIC ELECTRONIC MODULE/CENTRAL TIMER MODULE (GEM/CTM) DTC INDEX [1] (Cont.)

DTC	Description	Test
	4-Wheel Drive High Indicator Circuit Failure	7
P1804 [2]	4-Wheel Drive High Indicator Circuit Short To Voltage	7
P1806 [2]	4-Wheel Drive Low Indicator Circuit Failure	7
P1808 [2]	4-Wheel Drive Low Indicator Circuit Short To Voltage	7
P1810 [2]	4-Wheel Drive Mode Select Circuit Failure	14
P1812 [2]	4-Wheel Drive Mode Select Circuit Short To Ground	14
P1815 [2]	Transfer Case Clockwise Shift Relay Coil Circuit Failure	14
P1820 [2]	Transfer Case Clockwise Shift Relay Coil Short To Power	14
P1822 [2]	4-Wheel Drive Electric Clutch Relay Circuit Failure	14
P1824 [2]	4-Wheel Drive Low Clutch Relay Short To Voltage	14
P1826 [2]	Transfer Case Counterclockwise Shift Relay Circuit Failure	14
P1828 [2]	Transfer Case Counterclockwise Shift Relay Coil Short To Voltage	14
P1830 [2]	Transfer Case Front Shaft Speed Sensor Circuit Failure	14
P1836 [2]	Transfer Case Rear Shaft Speed Sensor Circuit Failure	14
P1837 [2]	Transfer Case Shift Motor Circuit Failure	14
P1838 [2]	Transfer Case Contact Plate "A" Circuit Failure	14
P1846 [2]	Transfer Case Contact Plate "B" Circuit Failure	14
P1850 [2]	Transfer Case Contact Plate "C" Circuit Failure	14
P1854 [2]	Transfer Case Contact Plate "D" Circuit Failure	14
P1858 [2]	Transfer Case System Concern	14
P1866 [2]	Transfer Case Contact Plate General Circuit Failure	14
P1867 [2]	Automatic Hall Effect Sensor Power Circuit Failure	14
P1874 [2]	Automatic Hall Effect Sensor Power Circuit Short To Voltage	14
P1875 [2]	Transfer Case Contact Plate Ground Return Open Circuit	14
P1891 [2]		

[1] – Vehicles equipped with 4WD and/or power windows are equipped with a GEM. All other vehicle are equipped with a CTM.

[2] – This code only applies to vehicles equipped with a GEM.

[3] – Perform TEST A: ALL POWER WINDOWS ARE INOPERATIVE in appropriate POWER WINDOWS article for testing procedures.

[4] – Check charging system. See appropriate GENERATORS article in STARTING & CHARGING SYSTEMS. Repair as necessary. If charging system is okay, fault is in power or ground circuits to GEM/CTM. See appropriate wiring diagram in BODY CONTROL MODULES article.

[5] – This DTC may also be present from GEM/CTM wiggle test.

[6] – Check wiring harness for open and/or short circuits and repair as necessary. See appropriate wiring diagram in ILLUMINATION/INTERIOR LIGHTS article.

[7] – Perform appropriate test under SYSTEM TESTS in ANALOG INSTRUMENT CLUSTER – EXPLORER & MOUNTAINEER article.

[8] – Check wiring harness for open and/or short circuits and repair as necessary. See appropriate wiring diagram in WARNING SYSTEMS article.

[9] – Clear DTCs. Retrieve DTCs. If DTC B1342 is retrieved, replace GEM/CTM and retest system operation.

[10] – Check wiring harness for open and/or short circuits and repair as necessary. See appropriate wiring diagram in REAR WINDOW DEFOGGERS article.

[11] – See appropriate STEERING COLUMN SWITCHES article for testing procedures.

[12] – See appropriate POWER WINDOWS article for testing procedures.

[13] – See appropriate WIPER/WASHER SYSTEMS article for testing procedures.

[14] – See appropriate ELECTRONIC CONTROLS article in AUTOMATIC TRANSMISSIONS in appropriate MITCHELL® TRANSMISSION SERVICE & REPAIR manual for testing procedures.

[15] – Check wiring harness for open and/or short circuits and repair as necessary. See appropriate wiring diagram in REMOTE KEYLESS ENTRY SYSTEMS article.

[16] – Vehicle speed calibration data is not programmed into GEM/CTM. Use NGS tester configuration card help screen to program tire size and axle ratio. Retest system operation. If DTC B2141 is still present, replace GEM/CTM and retest system operation.

PARKING AID MODULE DTC (PAM) DTC INDEX

DTC	Description	Test
	Power Supply Sensor Circuit Short To Ground	1
B1299	ECU Defective	2
B1342	LED No. 1 Circuit Short To Voltage	1
B2373	Module Configuration Failure	3
B2477	Left Rear Sensor Circuit Short To Voltage	1
C1699	Left Rear Sensor Circuit Failure	1
C1700	Left Rear Sensor Fault	1
C1701	Right Rear Sensor Circuit Short To Voltage	1
C1702	Right Rear Sensor Circuit Failure	1
C1703	Right Rear Sensor Circuit Fault	1
C1704	Left Rear Center Sensor Circuit Short To Voltage	1
C1705	Left Rear Center Sensor Circuit Failure	1
C1706	Left Rear Center Sensor Circuit Fault	1
C1707	Right Rear Center Sensor Circuit Short To Voltage	1
C1708	Right Rear Center Sensor Circuit Failure	1
C1709	Right Rear Center Sensor Circuit Fault	1
C1710	Rear Sounder Circuit Failure	1
C1742	Rear Sounder Circuit Short To Voltage	1
C1743	Switch Input Circuit Short To Ground	1
C1748		

PARKING AID MODULE DTC (PAM) DTC INDEX (Cont.)

DTC	Description	Test
C1920	LED No. 1 Circuit Failure	1

[1] – See PARKING AID SYSTEM – EXPLORER & MOUNTAINEER article for testing procedure.

[2] – Using NGS tester, retrieve and document all continuous DTCs. Clear DTCs. Perform parking aid module self-test. If DTC B1342 is retrieved again, replace parking aid module.

[3] – Using NGS tester, configure parking aid module module. See COMPUTER RELEARN PROCEDURES article in GENERAL INFORMATION.

PASSIVE ANTI-THEFT SYSTEM (PATS) MODULE DTC INDEX

DTC	Test
B1213 (Number Of Programmed Ignition Keys Below Minimum)	1
B1232 (Defective Transceiver)	1
B1600 (PATS Ignition Key Transponder Signal Not Received)	1
B1601 (PATS Received Incorrect Key Code From Transponder)	1
B1602 (PATS Received Invalid Key Code Format From Transponder)	1
B1681 (PATS Transceiver Signal Is Not Received)	1
B2103 (Antenna Not Connected)	1
B2139 (Security Identification Does Not Match Between PATS Module & PCM)	1
B2141 (No Security Identification Exchange Between PATS Module & PCM)	1
U1147 (Faulty SCP Link Or Incorrect PCM Calibration)	1
U1262 (Missing SCP Message)	2

[1] – Perform appropriate test in PASSIVE ANTI-THEFT SYSTEMS – EXPLORER & MOUNTAINEER article.

[2] – Perform TEST L: NO MODULE/NETWORK COMMUNICATIONS – BUS LINK under SYSTEM TESTS.

REMOTE ANTI-THEFT PERSONALITY (RAP) MODULE DTC INDEX

DTC	Test
B1309 (Door Lock Circuit Short To Ground)	1
B1341 (Door Unlock Circuit Short To Ground)	1
B1485 (Brake Pedal Input Circuit Short To Voltage)	1
B1522 (Hood Switch Circuit Short To Ground)	2
B1526 (Keypad Switch Circuit Short To Ground)	1
B1562 (Door Lock Cylinder Circuit Short To Ground)	2
B1629 (PRNDL Reverse Input Short To Voltage)	1

REMOTE ANTI-THEFT PERSONALITY (RAP) MODULE DTC INDEX (Cont.)

DTC	Test
B1845 (Anti-Theft Ignition Lock Switch Failure)	3
B2425 (Keyless Entry Out Of Synchronization)	1

[1] – Check for open and short circuits. See appropriate wiring diagram in REMOTE KEYLESS ENTRY SYSTEMS article.

[2] – Repair anti-theft system as necessary. See ACTIVE ANTI-THEFT SYSTEMS – EXPLORER & MOUNTAINEER article.

[3] – Disregard DTC B1845. This is an invalid DTC.

RESTRAINT CONTROL MODULE (RCM) DTC INDEX

DTC	Description	Test
B1231	RCM Crash Data Memory Full	1
B1342	ECU Defective	1
B1869	Air Bag Indicator Inoperative	1
B1870	Air Bag Indicator Short To Voltage	1
B1887	Driver's Side Air Bag Circuit Short To Ground	1
B1888	Passenger's Side Air Circuit Bag Short To Ground	1
B1891	Air Bar Tone Warning Indicator Circuit Open Or Short To Ground	1
B1892	Air Bag Tone Warning Indicator Circuit Open Or Short To Ground	1
B1916	Driver's Side Air Bag Circuit Short To Voltage	1
B1921	RCM Bracket Ground Resistance High	1
B1925	Passenger's Side Air Bag Circuit Short To Voltage	1
B1932	Driver's Side Air Bag Circuit Resistance High	1
B1933	Passenger's Side Air Bag Circuit Resistance High	1
B1934	Driver's Side Air Bag Circuit Resistance Low	1
B1935	Passenger's Side Air Bag Circuit Resistance Low	1
B1901	Front External Crash Sensor Short To Ground	1
B1941	Front External Crash Sensor Open Or Short To Voltage	1
B1992	Driver Side Air Bag Circuit Short To Battery Or Ignition	1
B1993	Driver Side Air Bag Circuit Short To Ground	1
B1994	Driver Side Air Bag Circuit High Resistance	1
B1995	Driver Side Air Bag Circuit Low Resistance	1
B1996	Passenger Side Air Bag Circuit Short To Battery Or Ignition	1
B1997	Passenger Side Air Bag Circuit Short To Ground	1
B1998	Passenger Side Air Bag Circuit High Resistance	1
B1999	Passenger Side Air Bag Circuit Low Resistance	1
B2440	Passenger Side Crash Sensor Mounting Failure	1
B2441	Driver Side Crash Sensor Mounting Failure	1
B2444	Driver Side Crash Sensor Internal Fault	1

RESTRAINT CONTROL MODULE (RCM) DTC INDEX (Cont.)

DTC	Description	Test
		1
B2445	Passenger Side Crash Sensor Internal Fault	1
C1414	Incorrect Vehicle Identification Code	1
U2017	Driver Side Crash Sensor Communication Fault	1
U2018	Passenger Side Crash Sensor Communication Fault	1

[1] – Repair supplemental restraint system as necessary. See DIAGNOSIS & TESTING article in appropriate MITCHELL® AIR BAG SERVICE & REPAIR MANUAL, DOMESTIC & IMPORTED MODELS.

4-WHEEL ANTI-LOCK BRAKE SYSTEM (4WABS) MODULE DTC INDEX

DTC	Description	Test
		1
B1342	4WABS Defective	2
B1485	Brake Pedal Position Switch Circuit Failure	3
B1676	Battery Voltage Out Of Range	4
B2141	Vehicle Speed Calibration Data Not Programmed Into Module	3
C1095	Hydraulic Pump Motor Circuit Failure	3
C1102	G-Switch Circuit Failure	3
C1145	Right Front ABS Sensor Circuit Failure	3
C1155	Left Front ABS Sensor Circuit Failure	3
C1230	Rear Front ABS Sensor Circuit Failure	3
C1233	Left Front ABS Sensor Output Signal Missing	3
C1234	Right Front ABS Sensor Output Signal Missing	3
C1237	Rear ABS Sensor Output Signal Missing	

[1] – Using NGS tester, retrieve and document all continuous. Perform Anti-Lock Brake System (ABS) module self-test. If DTC B1342 is retrieved again, replace ABS module.
[2] – Disregard DTC B1485. This is an invalid DTC.
[3] – Repair Anti-Lock Brake System (ABS). See appropriate ANTI-LOCK article in BRAKES in appropriate MITCHELL® manual.
[4] – Using NGS tester, perform calibration procedure. Repeat self-test.

PARAMETER IDENTIFICATION (PID) DEFINITIONS

AIR SUSPENSION CONTROL MODULE PID INDEX

PID	Description	Expected Values
AS_COMP	Air Suspension Compressor Status	ON, OFF
AS_GATE	Air Suspension Front Solenoid Gate Valve Status	ON, OFF
AS_VENT	Air Suspension Vent Solenoid Valve Status	ON, OFF
BOO_ARC	Brake Pedal Position Switch Input	ON, OFF
CCNTARC	Number Of Continuous DTCs Counted By Air Suspension Control Module	One Count Per Bit
DR_OPEN	Door Ajar Input	CLOSED, CLOSED
F_FILL	Air Suspension Front Fill Solenoid Valve Status	ON, OFF
HGTSENS	Height Sensor	ON, OFF
IGN_RUN	Detection Of Ignition Switch In RUN Position	notRUN, RUN
OFFROAD	Vehicle Off Road Status	ON, OFF
PCM_ACC	Acceleration Signal From PCM	YES, NO
R_FILL	Rear Fill Solenoid Valve Status	1
RASGATE	Rear Gate Solenoid Valve Status	1
RHGTSEN	Value Of Rear Height Sensor	DC Voltage Value
STEER_A	Electronic Steering Sensor A Signal	HIGH, LOW
STEER_B	Electronic Steering Sensor B Signal	HIGH, LOW
VBATARC	Battery Voltage Value To Air Suspension Control Module	DC Voltage Value
VSS_ARC	Displays Vehicle Speed Sensor Input To Air Suspension Control Module	VSS Signal In KPH Or MPH

[1] – Expected value should be OFF- - -, OFFO- -, OFF-B-, OFF- - G, ON- - -, ONO- -, ON-B-, ON- -G

GENERIC ELECTRONIC MODULE/CENTRAL TIMER MODULE (GEM/CTM) PID INDEX [1]

PID	Description	Expected Value
R_WP_MD	Rear Wiper Mode Switch Status (GEM Only)	OFF, INTVL 1-2, LOW WASH
VSS_GEM	Vehicle Speed Input	0-255 KPH
PARK_SW	External Access Ajar Switch Status	OFF, ON
D_DR_SW	Left Front Door Ajar Switch Status	CLOSED, AJAR
DR_DSRM	Door Disarm Switch Status	L_DOOR, R_DOOR, LIFT_G, OFF
DR_UNLK	All Doors Unlock Ouput State	ON- - -, OFF- - -, ON-B-, OFFO-G
P_DR_SW	Right Passenger Door Ajar Switch Status	CLOSED, AJAR
IGN_KEY	Key In Ignition Input	IN, OUT
IGN_GEM	Ignition Switch Status	START, RUN, OFF, ACC
BATSAV	Battery Saver Relay Circuit	ON- - -, OFF- - -, ON-B-, OFFO-G
VBATGEM	Battery Voltage	0.0 VDC - 14.3 VDC
LGATESW	Liftgate Ajar Switch Status	CLOSED, AJAR
LRDR_SW	Left Rear Door Ajar Switch Status	CLOSED, AJAR

GENERIC ELECTRONIC MODULE/CENTRAL TIMER MODULE (GEM/CTM) PID INDEX [1] (Cont.)

PID	Description	Expected Value
RRDR_SW	Right Rear Door Ajar Switch Status	CLOSED, AJAR
INTLMP	Illuminated Entry Relay Circuit	ON- - -, OFF- - -, ON-B-, OFFO-G
CLTCHSW	Trans Clutch Interlock Switch (GEM Only)	ENGAGED, NOT ENGAGED
NTRL_SW	Neutral Safety Switch Input	NTRL, notNTRL
MTR_CCW	Trans Transfer CCW Motor Output	ON- - -, OFF- - -, ON-B-, OFFO-G
MTR_CW	CW Shift Relay Coil Status	ON- - -, OFF- - -, ON-B-, OFFO-G
4WD_SW	4WD Switch Status (GEM Only)	AUTO, 4WDLOW, 4WDHIGH
4WDELCL	4WD Electronic Clutch	ON- - -, OFF- - -, ON-B-, OFFO-G
TRANSGR	Transmission Gear Status	REV, notREV
4WDCLCH	4WD Electronic Clutch Output Status (GEM Only)	ON- - -, OFF- - -, ON-B-, OFFO-G
4WDLOW	4WD Low Indicator Status (GEM Only)	ON- - -, OFF- - -, ON-B-, OFFO-G
4WDHIGH	4WD High Indicator Status (GEM Only)	ON- - -, OFF- - -, ON-B-, OFFO-G
PLATE_A	Transfer Case Contact Plate Switch A (GEM Only)	OPEN, CLOSED
PLATE_B	Transfer Case Contact Plate Switch B (GEM Only)	OPEN, CLOSED
PLATE_C	Transfer Case Contact Plate Switch C (GEM Only)	OPEN, CLOSED
PLATE_D	Transfer Case Contact Plate Switch D (GEM Only)	OPEN, CLOSED
BOO_GEM	Brake Pedal Position Switch Input (GEM Only)	ON, OFF
HALLPWR	Hall Effect Speed Sensor Power (GEM Only)	ON, OFF, ON-B-, OFFO-G
4WDCLST	FWD Clutch PWM Output Status (GEM Only)	ON, OFF, ON-B-, OFFO-G
TRA_RSP	Rear Shaft Speed (GEM Only)	0-255 MPH
TRA_FSP	Front Shaft Speed (GEM Only)	0-255 MPH
PLATEPW	Transfer Case Contact Plate Ground Output (GEM Only)	ON, OFF, ON-B-, OFFO-G
PWR_RLY	ABS Active Input	ON, OFF
NTF	Neutral Tow Function (GEM Only)	ON, OFF
NTF_LMP	Neutral Tow Light (GEM Only)	ON, OFF
D_SBLT	Driver's Seat Belt Status	IN, OUT
IPCHIME	External Chime Request	ON, OFF
SBLTMP	Seat Belt Indicator Status	ON, OFF, ON-B-, OFFO-G
DRAJR_L	Door Ajar Warning Light Circuit	ON, OFF
D_PWRLY	On Touch Down Relay Coil Circuit Status (GEM Only)	ON- - -, OFF- - -, ON-B-, OFFO-G
D_PWAMP	Driver's Power Window Motor Current (GEM Only)	.25 Amp Increments
D_PWPK	Driver's Power Window Motor Peak Current (GEM Only)	.25 Amp Increments
ACCDLY	Accessory Delay Relay Coil Circuit (GEM Only)	ON- - -, OFF- - -, ON-B-, OFFO-G
RDEF_SW	Rear Defrost Control Switch Status	ON- - -, OFF- - -, ON-B-, OFFO-G
RDEFRLY	Rear Window Defrost Relay Coil Circuit	ON- - -, OFF- - -, ON-B-, OFFO-G
WASHRLY	Washer Relay Status	ON- - -, OFF- - -, ON-B-, OFFO-G
WPPK_PK	Wiper Park-To-Park Time	0-6.5 Seconds
WPMODE	Wiper Control Mode Status	WASH, OPEN INVLD, OFF, INTVL 1-7, LOW, HIGH
WPPRKSW	Wiper Motor Status	PARKED, notPRK
WPRUN	Wiper Mode Run Relay	ON- - -, OFF- - -, ON-B-, OFFO-G
WPHISP	Wiper HI/LO Relay Status	ON- - -, OFF- - -, ON-B-, OFFO-G
WASH_SW	Washer Pump Relay Switch Status	ON, OFF, ON-B-, OFFO-G
R_WP_UP	Rear Wiper Up Relay Staus (GEM Only)	ON, OFF, ON-B-, OFFO-G
R_WP_DN	Rear Wiper Down Relay Staus (GEM Only)	ON, OFF, ON-B-, OFFO-G
R_WP_SW	Rear Wiper Input Switch Staus (GEM Only)	WPLOW, OFF, WPHIGH
R_WP_PK	Rear Wiper Park Staus (GEM Only)	PARKED, notPRK

[1] – Vehicles equipped with 4WD and/or power windows are equipped with a GEM. All other vehicle are equipped with a CTM.

PASSIVE ANTI-THEFT SYSTEM (PATS) MODULE PID INDEX

PID	Description	Expected Value
CCNTPATS	Number Of Continuous DTCs	On count Per Bit
IGN_PAT	Ignition Switch Position	RUN/ACC, OFF
NUMKEYS	Number Of Ignition Keys Programmed	0-8
M_KEYS	Programmed Key In Ignition	YES, ON
ENABL_S	Has PATS Enable Vehicle	ENABLE, DISABLED
ACCESS	Security Access Status	TIMED, CODED
MIN#KEYS	Minimum Number Of Keys Required To Start Vehicle	2-8
ANTISCN	Time Out For Unprogrammed PATS Key	ACTIVE, notACT
PCM_ID	Is PCM ID Stored In PATS	STORED, notSTR
SPAREKY	Can You Add Spare Key With 2 Programmed Keys	YES, NO
PCM_VFY	PCM ID Matches Between PCM & PATS	YES, NO

REMOTE ANTI-THEFT PERSONALITY (RAP) MODULE PID INDEX

PID	Description	Expected Values
AL_EVT#	Last Eight Alarm Events	NO_EVT, DROPEN, HOODTR, IGNTAM, PANIC
BOO_RAP	Brake Switch Input	OFF, ON
HOOD_SW	Hood Switch Input	notPUN, PUNCHED
IGN_RES	Ignition Lock Anti-Theft Switch	HIGH

REMOTE ANTI-THEFT PERSONALITY (RAP) MODULE PID INDEX (Cont.)

PID	Description	Expected Values
KEYCODE	Factory 5 Digit Unlock Code For Keypad	5 Digit#, INVLD
KEY_PAD	Keypad Switch Input	1/2, 3/4, 5/6, 7/8, 9/0
DOORRAP	Door Ajar Status Input From GEM	CLOSED, AJAR
DR_DARM	Door Disarm Input	notACTIVE, ACTIVE
IGN_RAP	Ignition Switch	RUN, OFF
DD_LOCK	Power Door Lock/Unlock Status	LOCK, UNLOCK, OFF, SHORT
NOTHEFT	Theft Only State	NO, YES
NOREMOT	Remote Only Input State	NO, YES
TRANSGR	Transmission Gear	notREV, REV

RESTRAINT CONTROL MODULE (RCM) PID INDEX

PID	Description	Expected Value
CCNT	Number Of Continuous DTCs In RCM	DTCS
DABAGR	Driver Air Bag Circuit Resistance	1.8-4.1 Ohms
PABAGR	Passenger Air Bag Circuit Resistance	1.4-3.6 Ohms
DABAG2	Driver Side Impact Air Bag Circuit Resistance	1.4-3.6 Ohms
PABAG2	Passenger Side Impact Air Bag Circuit Resistance	1.4-3.6 Ohms
BRACKET	Bracket Ground Resistance	Less Than 100 Ohms
VID#1	Program Vehicle ID Pin 10	No Connection
VID#2	Program Vehicle ID Pin 13	Ignition
VID#3	Program Vehicle ID Pin 14	No Connection

4-WHEEL ANTI-LOCK BRAKE SYSTEM (4WABS) MODULE PID INDEX

PID	Description	Expected Value
ABSLF_I	Left Front ABS Inlet Valve	ON, OFF
ABSLF_O	Left Front ABS Outlet Valve	ON, OFF
ABSRF_I	Right Front ABS Inlet Valve	ON, OFF
ABSRF_O	Right Front ABS Outlet Valve	ON, OFF
ABSR_I	Rear ABS Inlet Valve	ON, OFF
ABSR_O	Rear ABS Outlet Valve	ON, OFF
BOO_ABS	Brake Switch Input	ON/OFF
CONTABS	Number Of Continuous DTCs	One Bit Per Count
LF_WSPD	Left Front Wheel Speed Signal	0-255 KPH
R_WSPD	Rear Wheel Speed Signal	0-255 KPH
RF_WSPD	Right Front Wheel Speed Signal	0-255 KPH
ACCLSW1	Acceleration Switch Position 1 Input	ACT, notACT
ACCLSW2	Acceleration Switch Position 2 Input	ACT, notACT
4WDLOW	4WD Low Input	ON, OFF

WIRING DIAGRAMS

NOTE: See appropriate wiring diagrams in DATA LINK CONNECTORS, GROUND DISTRIBUTION or POWER DISTRIBUTION article in WIRING DIAGRAMS.

DESCRIPTION & OPERATION

Vehicle has 2 module communications networks. The module communications network provides the ability for module-to-module communication by sharing inputs and outputs instead of each component having an input and output wired directly to each module. A BUS which consists of a pair of twisted wires is used to transfer information between each module. The BUS network is also referred to as Standard Corporate Protocol (SCP) network. The BUS consists of a (+) circuit No. 914 and a (–) circuit No. 915. The BUS is routed throughout the vehicle to the Anti-Lock Brake System (ABS) module (with traction control), Powertrain Control Module (PCM) and instrument cluster.

The Restraint Control Module (RCM) and Generic Electronic Module (GEM) do not use the BUS to communicate with other modules. The ABS (without traction control), RCM and GEM module are connected to the International Standards Organization (ISO) 9141 diagnostic communications network through a single wire (circuit No. 70). Both networks are connected to the Data Link Connector (DLC). This article is used to diagnose BUS and ISO communications network circuit faults. For module locations, see COMPONENT LOCATIONS table under COMPONENT LOCATIONS.

COMPONENT LOCATIONS

COMPONENT LOCATIONS

Component	Location
Anti-Lock Brake System Module	Right Front Of Engine Compartment, Behind Radiator
Central Junction Box	Behind Left Side Of Instrument Panel
Data Link Connector	Below Driver's Side Of Instrument Panel, Right Of Steering Column
Generic Electronic Module	Behind Instrument Panel, Next To Central Junction Box
In-Line Harness Connector C107	Left Rear Corner Of Engine Compartment
In-Line Harness Connector C108	Right Front Corner Of Engine Compartment
In-Line Harness Connector C216	Behind Right Front Kick Panel
In-Line Harness Connector C331	Behind Left Side Of Instrument Panel
Powertrain Control Module	Behind Right Front Kick Panel
Restraint Control Module	Behind Left Center Of Instrument Panel

REPAIRING BUS WIRING

NOTE: *Following procedure must be used to ensure proper repair is performed on BUS wiring. BUS wiring is sensitive to moisture and oxidation and must be properly sealed to ensure proper operation of the module communications network. Regular heat shrink tubing is NOT sufficient, heat shrink tubing containing hot melt wax is required.*

1) When performing a repair on the BUS wiring, ensure the wires on the BUS are twisted at a rate of 33-40 winds per 3.3 ft. (1 m). The twists should start approximately 4.9" (124 mm) from any connector. Use only 20 AWG standard wire gauge for repairs.
2) If performing a splice in the wiring, strip .75" (19.0 mm) of insulation from one wire and 1.50" (38.1 mm) of insulation from the other wire. Perform STEP 1. *See Fig. 1.* Place hot melt wax type heat shrink tubing over one wire.
3) Twist stripped portion of the wires together. Solder connection using resin core RMA solder. DO NOT use acid core solder. Bend wires to allow installation of heat shrink tubing. Perform STEP 2. *See Fig. 1.*
4) Position heat shrink tubing over splice area. Using heat gun, evenly heat the heat shrink tubing until wax flows from both ends of heat shrink tubing.

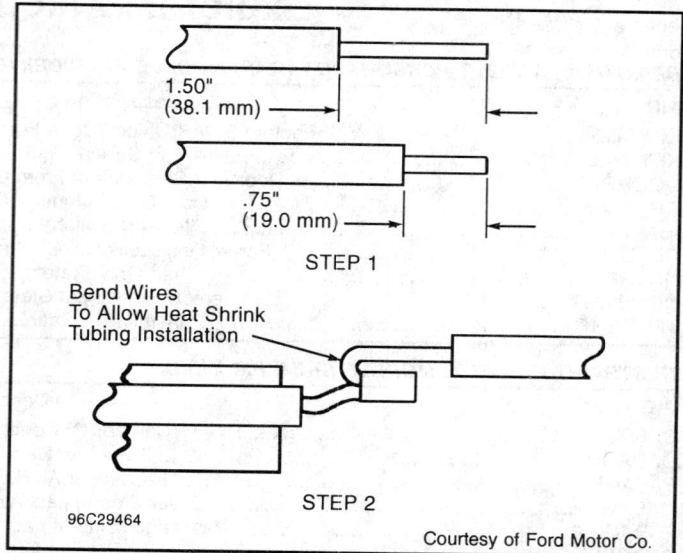

1.50"
(38.1 mm)

.75"
(19.0 mm)

STEP 1

Bend Wires
To Allow Heat Shrink
Tubing Installation

STEP 2

96C29464

Courtesy of Ford Motor Co.

Fig. 1: Repairing BUS Wiring

COMMUNICATION NETWORK DIAGNOSTICS

NOTE: *Before checking for any communication concern, inspect Data Link Connector (DLC) for loose, damaged or corroded terminals. Pay particular attention to terminals No. 2 (Tan/Orange wire), No. 7 (Light Blue/White wire) and No. 10 (Pink/Light Blue wire).*

INSPECTION & VERIFICATION

1) Verify customer's original problem by operating system in question. Inspect vehicle for any obvious electrical component wiring or connector damage. Inspect connectors for loose, damaged or corroded terminals. Check related fuses for system in question.
2) Inspect Data Link Connector (DLC) pins for damage. *See Fig. 2.* The DLC is located below driver's side of instrument panel, right of steering column. If pins are okay, go to next step. If pins are damaged, repair as necessary and proceed to next step.
3) If problem is still present after performing inspection, connect New Generation Star (NGS) tester to DLC. Select vehicle to be tested from NGS tester menu. If NGS tester does not communicate with vehicle, ensure program card is properly installed. Check NGS tester cable connections and ensure ignition is on. If NGS tester still does not communicate with vehicle, perform TEST H: NO MODULE/NETWORK COMMUNICATION under SYSTEM TESTS. If NGS tester communicates with vehicle, perform data link diagnostic procedure. See DATA LINK DIAGNOSTIC TEST.

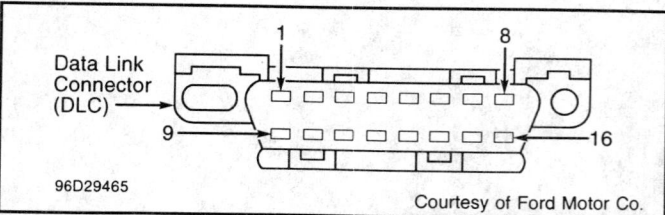

Data Link
Connector
(DLC)

1   8

9   16

96D29465

Courtesy of Ford Motor Co.

Fig. 2: Identifying Data Link Connector (DLC) Terminals

DATA LINK DIAGNOSTIC TEST

1) Connect New Generation Star (NGS) tester to Data Link Connector (DLC), if not already connected. Select vehicle to be tested from NGS tester menu.
2) Turn ignition switch to RUN position. Rotate dial on NGS tester to menu item DIAGNOSTIC DATA LINK and press trigger. A test will be

performed on the BUS (circuits No. 914 and 915) for the module communications network and the ISO 9141 communication link (circuit No. 70).

3) If NGS tester displays CKT 914 (+) = SYSTEM PASSED and CKT 915 (−) = SYSTEM PASSED, module communications network is okay. If NGS tester displays CKT 70 = SYSTEM PASSED, ISO 9141 communication link is operating properly. Return to article that directed you here and continue diagnosis.

4) If NGS tester does not display CKT 914 (+) = SYSTEM PASSED, CKT 915 (−) = SYSTEM PASSED and CKT 70 = SYSTEM PASSED, perform the following as applicable.

- If no response from NGS tester, perform TEST H: NO MODULE/ NETWORK COMMUNICATION under SYSTEM TESTS.
- If NGS tester displays CKT 70, CKT 914 and/or CKT 915 = SOME ECUS NO RESP/NOT EQUIP, perform appropriate test. See SYMPTOM INDEX table under SYSTEM TESTS.
- If NGS tester displays CKT 70 = ALL ECUS NO RESP/NOT EQUIP, perform TEST F: NO MODULE/NETWORK COMMUNICATION – ISO 9141 LINK under SYSTEM TESTS.
- If NGS tester displays CKT 914 = ALL ECUS NO RESP/NOT EQUIP, perform TEST G: NO MODULE/NETWORK COMMUNICATION – BUS LINK under SYSTEM TESTS.
- If NGS tester displays CKT 915 = ALL ECUS NO RESP/NOT EQUIP, perform TEST G: NO MODULE/NETWORK COMMUNICATION – BUS LINK under SYSTEM TESTS.
- If module in question is NO RESPONSE/NOT EQUIPPED, perform appropriate test. See SYMPTOM INDEX table under SYSTEM TESTS.
- If module in question is NO RESPONSE ON CKT 914 (BUS +), perform appropriate test. See SYMPTOM INDEX table under SYSTEM TESTS.
- If module in question is NO RESPONSE ON CKT 915 (BUS −), perform appropriate test. See SYMPTOM INDEX table under SYSTEM TESTS.

RETRIEVING & CLEARING DIAGNOSTIC TROUBLE CODES

NOTE: It is also possible to retrieve instrument cluster DTCs using instrument cluster. See ANALOG INSTRUMENT PANELS – MUSTANG article.

Connect New Generation Star (NGS) tester to Data Link Connector (DLC). Following manufacturer's instructions to retrieve and clear codes for desired module. See appropriate table under DIAGNOSTIC TROUBLE CODE (DTC) DEFINITIONS for a listing of DTCs and location of appropriate test procedure.

ACCESSING PARAMETER IDENTIFICATION (PID)

Turn ignition switch to LOCK position. Connect New Generation Star (NGS) tester to Data Link Connector (DLC). Following manufacturer's instructions enter PID/DATA MONITOR AND RECORD for desired module. Operate appropriate system and ensure PID expected values are obtained. See appropriate table under PARAMETER IDENTIFICATION (PID) DEFINITIONS.

SYSTEM TESTS

NOTE: Before performing any system tests, inspect Data Link Connector (DLC) for loose, damaged or corroded terminals. Pay particular attention to terminals No. 2 (Tan/Orange wire), No. 7 (Light Blue/White wire) and No. 10 (Pink/Light Blue wire).

NOTE: Always check module power and ground circuits prior to replacing a control module. See appropriate wiring diagram in DATA LINK CONNECTORS, GROUND DISTRIBUTION or POWER DISTRIBUTION article in WIRING DIAGRAMS.

SYMPTOM INDEX

Symptom	Test
Anti-Lock Brake System (ABS) Module Does Not Respond To NGS Tester	A
Generic Electronic Module Does Not Respond To NGS Tester	B
Restraint Control Module Does Not Respond To NGS Tester	C
Instrument Cluster Does Not Respond To NGS Tester	D
Powertrain Control Module (PCM) Does Not Respond To NGS Tester	E
No Module/Network Communication – ISO 9141 Link	F
No Module/Network Communication – Bus Link	G
No Module/Network Communication	H

TEST A: ANTI-LOCK BRAKE SYSTEM (ABS) MODULE DOES NOT RESPOND TO NGS TESTER

1) If vehicle is equipped with traction control, go to next step. If vehicle is not equipped with traction control, go to step **14)**.

2) Turn ignition switch to LOCK position. Disconnect ABS module harness connector C141. Inspect connector for loose, damaged or corroded terminals. If connector is okay, go to next step. If problem exists, repair connector as necessary.

3) Turn ignition switch to LOCK position. Connect ABS module harness connector C141. Perform data link diagnostic procedure. See DATA LINK DIAGNOSTIC TEST. If ABS:NO RESPONSE ON CKT 914 (BUS+) was retrieved, go to next step. If ABS: NO RESPONSE ON CKT 915 (BUS−) was retrieved, go to step **9)**.

4) Turn ignition switch to LOCK position. Disconnect NGS tester. Disconnect ABS module harness connector C141. Measure resistance in Tan/Orange wire between terminal No. 30 at ABS module harness connector C141 and terminal No. 2 at DLC. *See Figs. 2 and 3*. If resistance is greater than 5 ohms, go to next step. If resistance is 5 ohms or less, replace ABS module.

5) Disconnect in-line harness connector C108. *See Fig. 4*. Inspect connector for loose, damaged or corroded terminals. If connector is okay, go to next step. If problem exists, repair connector as necessary.

6) Measure resistance in Tan/Orange wire between terminal No. 6 at female side of in-line harness connector C108 and terminal No. 2 at DLC. *See Figs. 2 and 5*. If resistance is greater than 5 ohms, go to next step. If resistance is 5 ohms or less, repair open in Tan/Orange wire between in-line harness connector C108 and ABS module.

7) Disconnect in-line harness connector C216. *See Fig. 6*. Inspect connector for loose, damaged or corroded terminals. If connector is okay, go to next step. If problem exists, repair connector as necessary.

8) Measure resistance in Tan/Orange wire between terminal No. 10 at female side of in-line harness connector C216 and terminal No. 2 at DLC. *See Figs. 2 and 7*. If resistance is 5 ohms or less, repair open in Tan/Orange wire between in-line harness connector C216 and in-line harness connector C108. If resistance is greater than 5 ohms, repair open in Tan/Orange wire between in-line harness connector C216 and DLC.

9) Turn ignition switch to LOCK position. Disconnect NGS tester. Disconnect ABS module harness connector C141. Measure resistance in Pink/Light Blue wire between terminal No. 29 at ABS module harness connector C141 and terminal No. 10 at DLC. *See Figs. 2 and 3*. If resistance is greater than 5 ohms, go to next step. If resistance is 5 ohms or less, replace ABS module.

10) Disconnect in-line harness connector C108. *See Fig. 4*. Inspect connector for loose, damaged or corroded terminals. If connector is okay, go to next step. If problem exists, repair connector as necessary.

11) Measure resistance in Pink/Light Blue wire between terminal No. 13 at female side of in-line harness connector C108 and terminal No. 10 at DLC. *See Figs. 2 and 5*. If resistance is greater than 5 ohms, go to next step. If resistance is 5 ohms or less, repair open in Pink/Light Blue wire between in-line harness connector C108 and ABS module.

12) Disconnect in-line harness connector C216. *See Fig. 6.* Inspect connector for loose, damaged or corroded terminals. If connector is okay, go to next step. If problem exists, repair connector as necessary.

13) Measure resistance in Pink/Light Blue wire between terminal No. 13 at female side of in-line harness connector C216 and terminal No. 10 at DLC. *See Figs. 2 and 7.* If resistance is 5 ohms or less, repair open in Pink/Light Blue wire between in-line harness connector C216 and in-line harness connector C108. If resistance is greater than 5 ohms, repair open in Pink/Light Blue wire between in-line harness connector C216 and DLC.

14) Turn ignition switch to LOCK position. Disconnect ABS module harness connector C141. Inspect connector for loose, damaged or corroded terminals. If connector is okay, go to next step. If problem exists, repair connector as necessary.

15) Measure resistance in Light Blue/White wire between terminal No. 24 at ABS module harness connector C141 and terminal No. 7 at DLC. *See Figs. 2 and 3.* If resistance is greater than 5 ohms, go to next step. If resistance is 5 ohms or less, replace ABS module.

16) Disconnect in-line harness connector C107. *See Fig. 4.* Inspect connector for loose, damaged or corroded terminals. If connector is okay, go to next step. If problem exists, repair connector as necessary.

17) Measure resistance in Light Blue/White wire between terminal No. 7 at male half of connector C107 and terminal No. 7 at DLC. *See Figs. 2 and 5.* If resistance is greater than 5 ohms, go to next step. If resistance is less than 5 ohms, repair open in Light Blue/White wire between harness connector C107 and ABS module.

18) Disconnect in-line harness connector C331. *See Fig. 8.* Inspect connector for loose, damaged or corroded terminals. If connector is okay, go to next step. If problem exists, repair connector as necessary.

19) Measure resistance in Light Blue/White wire between terminal No. 1 at male half of harness connector C331 and terminal No. 7 at DLC. If resistance is 5 ohms or less, repair open in Light Blue/White wire between in-line harness connector C107 and in-line harness connector C331. If resistance is greater than 5 ohms, repair open in Light Blue/White wire between in-line harness connector C331 and DLC.

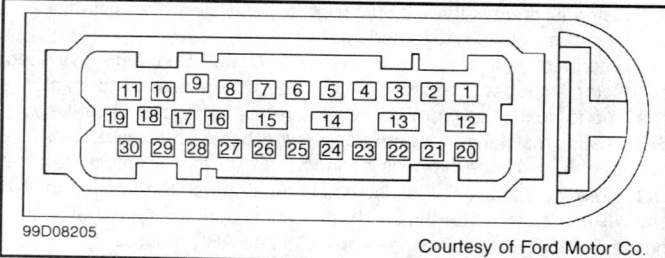

99D08205

Courtesy of Ford Motor Co.

Fig. 3: Identifying ABS Module Harness Connector C141 Terminals

TEST B: GENERIC ELECTRONIC MODULE DOES NOT RESPOND TO NGS TESTER

1) Turn ignition switch to LOCK position. Disconnect GEM module harness connector C352. Inspect connector for loose, damaged or corroded terminals. If connector is okay, go to next step. If problem exists, repair connector as necessary.

2) Measure resistance in Light Blue/White wire between terminal No. 6 at GEM module harness connector C352 and terminal No. 7 at DLC. *See Figs. 2 and 9.* If resistance is 5 ohms or less, replace GEM. If resistance is greater than 5 ohms, repair open in Light Blue/White wire.

TEST C: RESTRAINT CONTROL MODULE DOES NOT RESPOND TO NGS TESTER

1) Turn ignition switch to LOCK position. Disable air bag system. See appropriate AIR BAG RESTRAINT SYSTEMS article. Disconnect Restraint Control Module (RCM) harness connector C276. Inspect

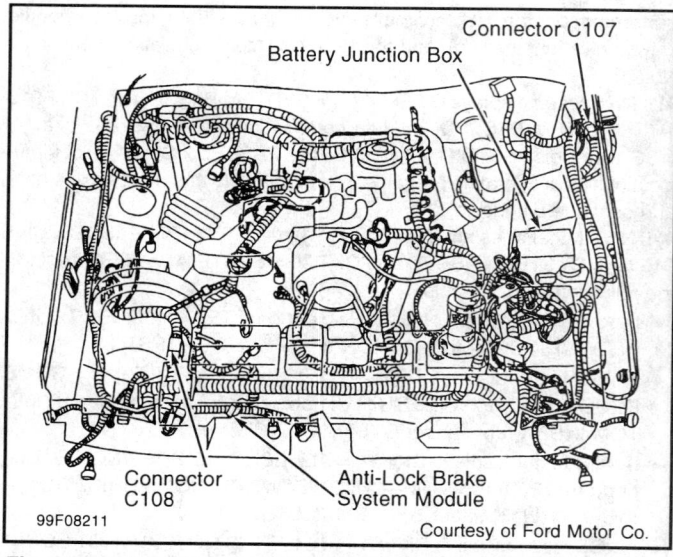

Courtesy of Ford Motor Co.

Fig. 4: Locating Engine Compartment Harness Connectors

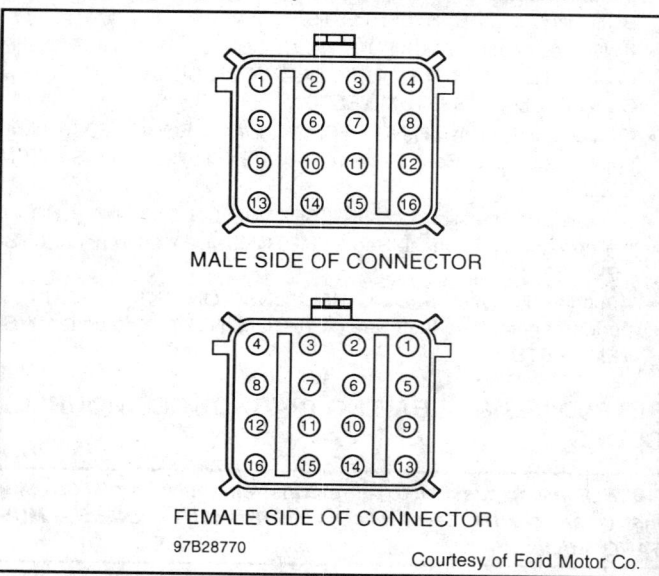

97B28770

Courtesy of Ford Motor Co.

Fig. 5: Identifying In-Line Harness Connectors C107 & C108 Terminals

connector for loose, damaged or corroded terminals. If connector is okay, go to next step. If problem exists, repair connector as necessary.

2) Measure resistance in Light Blue/White wire between terminal No. 5 at RCM harness connector C276 and terminal No. 7 at DLC. *See Figs. 2 and 10.* If resistance is 5 ohms or less, replace RCM. If resistance is greater than 5 ohms, repair open in Light Blue/White wire.

TEST D: INSTRUMENT CLUSTER DOES NOT RESPOND TO NGS TESTER

1) Turn ignition switch to LOCK position. Disconnect instrument cluster harness connector C250. Inspect connector for loose, damaged or corroded terminals. If connector is okay, go to next step. If problem exists, repair connector as necessary.

2) Turn ignition switch to LOCK position. Connect instrument cluster harness connector C250. Perform data link diagnostic procedure. See DATA LINK DIAGNOSTIC TEST. If instrument cluster: NO RESPONSE ON CKT 914 (BUS+) was retrieved, go to next step. If instrument cluster: NO RESPONSE ON CKT 915 (BUS–) was retrieved, go to step 4) .

3) Turn ignition switch to LOCK position. Disconnect NGS tester. Disconnect instrument cluster harness connector C250. Measure resistance in Tan/Orange wire between terminal No. 1 at instrument cluster harness connector C250 and terminal No. 2 at DLC. *See Figs. 2 and 11.*

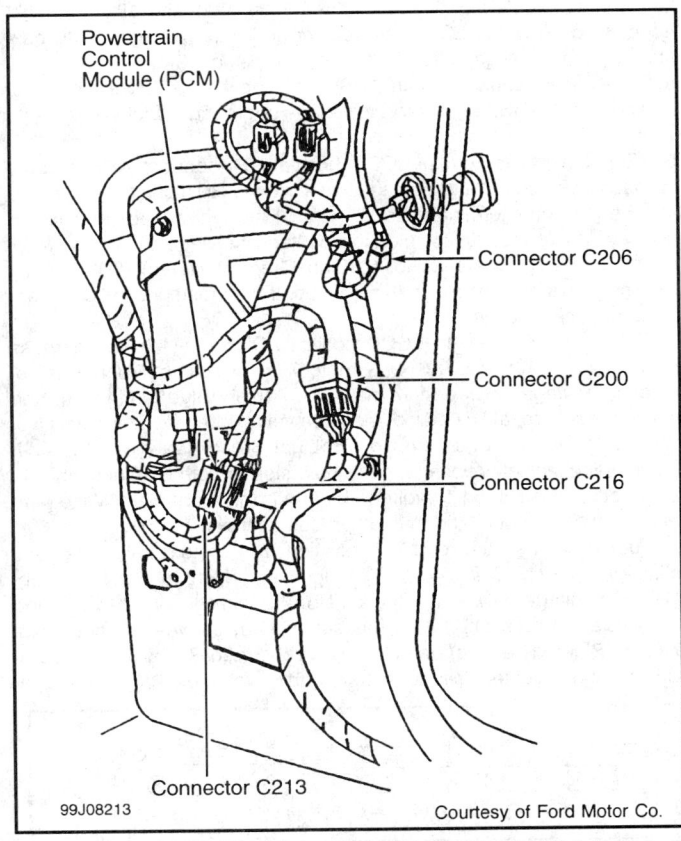

Powertrain
Control
Module (PCM)

Connector C206

Connector C200

Connector C216

Connector C213

99J08213   Courtesy of Ford Motor Co.

Fig. 6: Locating Harness Connectors Behind Right Kick Panel

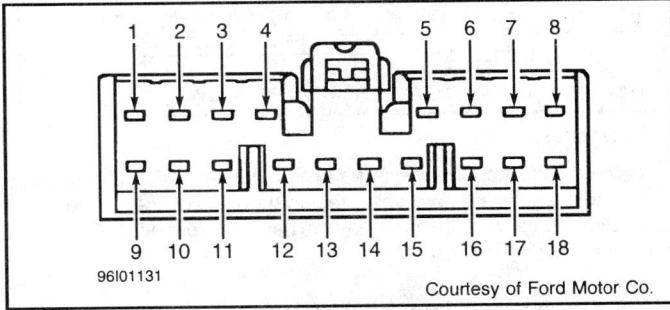

96I01131   Courtesy of Ford Motor Co.

**Fig. 7: Identifying In-Line Harness Connector C216 Terminals
(Female Half Of Connector Shown)**

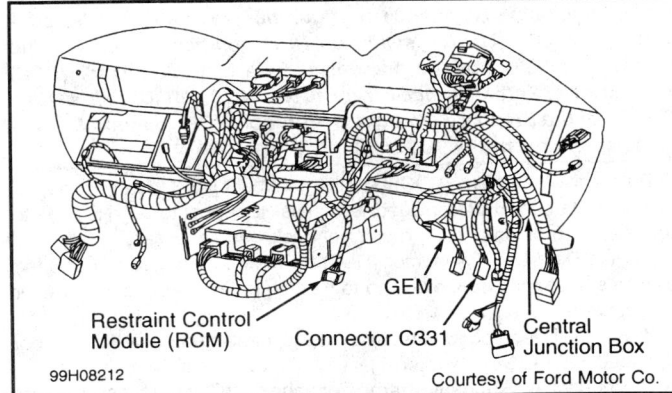

Restraint Control
Module (RCM)   Connector C331

GEM

Central
Junction Box

99H08212   Courtesy of Ford Motor Co.

Fig. 8: Locating Harness Connectors Behind Instrument Panel

If resistance is greater than 5 ohms, repair open in Tan/Orange wire. If resistance is 5 ohms or less, replace instrument cluster.

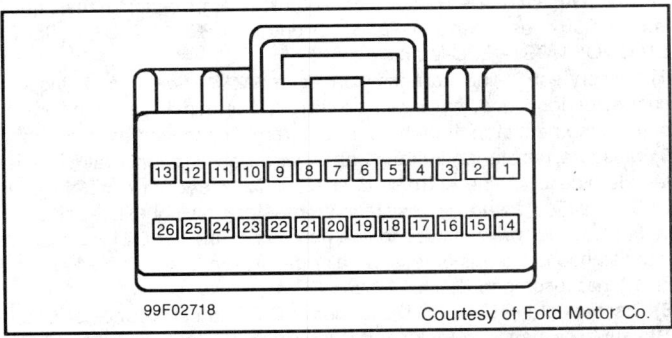

99F02718   Courtesy of Ford Motor Co.

**Fig. 9: Identifying GEM Module Harness Connector C352
Terminals**

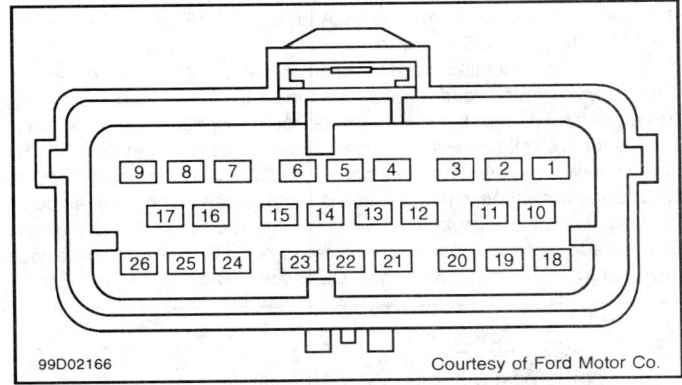

99D02166   Courtesy of Ford Motor Co.

Fig. 10: Identifying RCM Harness Connector C276 Terminals

4) Turn ignition switch to LOCK position. Disconnect NGS tester. Disconnect instrument cluster harness connector C250. Measure resistance in Pink/Light Blue wire between terminal No. 2 at instrument cluster harness connector C250 and terminal No. 10 at DLC. See Figs. 2 and 11. If resistance is greater than 5 ohms, repair open in Pink/Light Blue wire. If resistance is 5 ohms or less, replace instrument cluster.

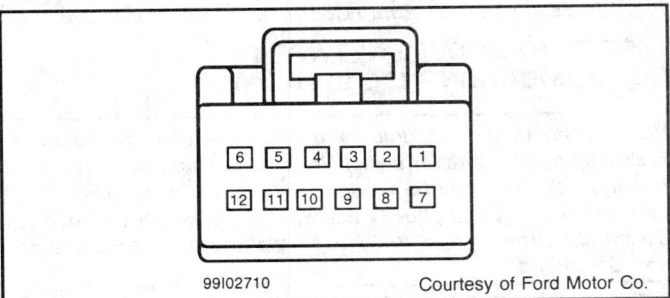

99I02710   Courtesy of Ford Motor Co.

**Fig. 11: Identifying Instrument Cluster Harness Connector C250
Terminals**

TEST E: POWERTRAIN CONTROL MODULE (PCM) DOES NOT RESPOND TO NGS TESTER

1) Turn ignition switch to LOCK position. Disconnect PCM harness connector C294. Inspect connector for loose, damaged or corroded terminals. If connector is okay, go to next step. If problem exists, repair connector as necessary.

2) Turn ignition switch to LOCK position. Connect PCM harness connector C294. Perform data link diagnostic procedure. See DATA LINK DIAGNOSTIC TEST. If PCM:NO RESPONSE ON CKT 914 (BUS+) was retrieved, go to next step. If PCM:NO RESPONSE ON CKT 915 (BUS–) was retrieved, go to step **6**).

3) Disconnect NGS tester. Disconnect PCM harness connector C294. Measure resistance in Tan/Orange wire between terminal No. 16 at PCM harness connector C294 and terminal No. 2 at DLC. See Figs. 2

and 12. If resistance is greater than 5 ohms, go to next step. If resistance is 5 ohms or less, perform TEST QA under SYSTEM TEST in SELF-DIAGNOSTICS – ECC-V article.

4) Disconnect in-line harness connector C216. *See Fig. 6.* Inspect connector for loose, damaged or corroded terminals. If connector is okay, go to next step. If problem exists, repair connector as necessary.

5) Measure resistance in Tan/Orange wire between terminal No. 6 at female side of in-line harness connector C216 and terminal No. 2 at DLC. *See Figs. 2 and 7.* If resistance is greater than 5 ohms, repair open in Tan/Orange wire between in-line harness connector C216 and DLC. If resistance is 5 ohms or less, repair open in Tan/Orange wire between in-line harness connector C216 and PCM.

6) Disconnect NGS tester. Disconnect PCM harness connector C294. Measure resistance in Pink/Light Blue wire between terminal No. 15 at PCM harness connector C294 and terminal No. 10 at DLC. *See Figs. 2 and 12.* If resistance is greater than 5 ohms, go to next step. If resistance is 5 ohms or less, perform TEST QA under SYSTEM TEST in SELF-DIAGNOSTICS – ECC-V article.

7) Disconnect in-line harness connector C216. *See Fig. 6.* Inspect connector for loose, damaged or corroded terminals. If connector is okay, go to next step. If problem exists, repair connector as necessary.

8) Measure resistance in Pink/Light Blue wire between terminal No. 13 at female side of in-line harness connector C216 and terminal No. 10 at DLC. *See Figs. 2 and 7.* If resistance is greater than 5 ohms, repair open in Pink/Light Blue wire between in-line harness connector C216 and DLC. If resistance is 5 ohms or less, repair open in Pink/Light Blue wire between in-line harness connector C216 and PCM.

between terminals No. 7 (Light Blue/White wire) and No. 16 (Light Green/Red wire) at DLC. If any reading indicates voltage, go to next step. If both readings indicate zero volts, replace RCM.

5) If vehicle is equipped with ABS, go to next step. If vehicle is not equipped with ABS, repair short to voltage or ground in Light Blue/White wire.

6) Turn ignition switch to LOCK position. Disconnect ABS module harness connector C141. Turn ignition switch to RUN position. Measure voltage between terminals No. 7 (Light Blue/White wire) and No. 4 (Black wire) at DLC. Also, measure voltage between terminals No. 7 (Light Blue/White wire) and No. 16 (Light Green/Red wire) at DLC. If any reading indicates voltage, go to next step. If both readings indicate zero volts, replace ABS.

7) Turn ignition switch to LOCK position. Disconnect in-line harness connector C107. *See Fig. 4.* Turn ignition switch to RUN position. Measure voltage between terminals No. 7 (Light Blue/White wire) and No. 4 (Black wire) at DLC. Also, measure voltage between terminals No. 7 (Light Blue/White wire) and No. 16 (Light Green/Red wire) at DLC. If any reading indicates voltage, go to next step. If both readings indicate zero volts, repair short to voltage or ground in Light Blue/White wire between ABS module and in-line harness connector C107.

8) Turn ignition switch to LOCK position. Disconnect in-line harness connector C331. *See Fig. 8.* Turn ignition switch to RUN position. Measure voltage between terminals No. 7 (Light Blue/White wire) and No. 4 (Black wire) at DLC. Also, measure voltage between terminals No. 7 (Light Blue/White wire) and No. 16 (Light Green/Red wire) at DLC. If any reading indicates voltage, repair short to voltage or ground in Light

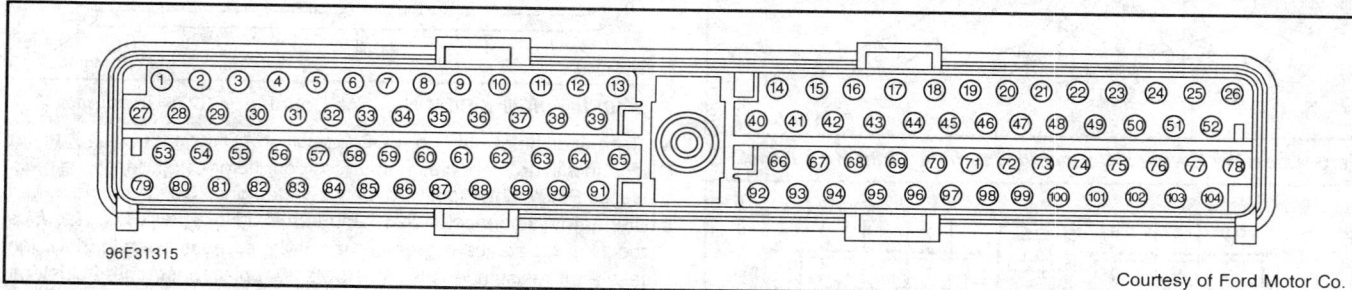

Fig. 12: Identifying Powertrain Control Module Harness Connector C294 Terminals

Courtesy of Ford Motor Co.

TEST F: NO MODULE/NETWORK COMMUNICATION – ISO 9141 LINK

NOTE: Depending on module configuration, with all modules connected and with ignition switch in RUN position or with engine running 2-3 volts may be present at Data Link Connector (DLC) terminal No. 7 (Light Blue/White wire). This is the International Standards Organization (ISO) 9141 diagnostic communications network circuit.

1) Turn ignition switch to LOCK position. Inspect NGS tester connector for loose, damaged or corroded terminals. If connector is okay, go to next step. If problem exists, repair connector as necessary.

2) Disconnect GEM module harness connector C352. Measure resistance in Light Blue/White wire between terminal No. 6 at GEM module harness connector C352 and terminal No. 7 at DLC. *See Figs. 2 and 9.* If resistance is 5 ohms or less, go to next step. If resistance is greater than 5 ohms, repair open in Light Blue/White wire.

3) Turn ignition switch to RUN position. Measure voltage between terminals No. 7 (Light Blue/White wire) and No. 4 (Black wire) at DLC. *See Fig. 2.* Also, measure voltage between terminals No. 7 (Light Blue/White wire) and No. 16 (Light Green/Red wire) at DLC. If any reading indicates voltage, go to next step. If both readings indicate zero volts, replace GEM.

4) Turn ignition switch to LOCK position. Disable air bag system. See appropriate AIR BAG RESTRAINT SYSTEMS article. Disconnect Restraint Control Module (RCM) harness connector C276. Turn ignition switch to RUN position. Measure voltage between terminals No. 7 (Light Blue/White wire) and No. 4 (Black wire) at DLC. Also, measure voltage

Blue/White wire between in-line harness connector C331 and DLC. If both readings indicate zero volts, repair short to voltage or ground in Light Blue/White wire between in-line harness connector C331 and in-line harness connector C107.

TEST G: NO MODULE/NETWORK COMMUNICATION – BUS LINK

NOTE: Depending on module configuration, with all modules connected and with ignition switch in RUN position or with engine running 2-3 volts may be present at Data Link Connector (DLC) terminals No. 2 (Tan/Orange wire) and No. 10 (Pink/Light Blue wire). These are the Standard Corporate Protocol (SCP) diagnostic communications network circuits.

1) Turn ignition switch to LOCK position. Inspect NGS tester connector for loose, damaged or corroded terminals. If connector is okay, go to next step. If problem exists, repair connector as necessary.

2) Inspect Data Link Connector (DLC) for loose, damaged or corroded terminals. If connector is okay, go to next step. If problem exists, repair connector as necessary.

3) If vehicle is equipped with ABS, go to next step. If vehicle is not equipped with ABS, go to step 7).

4) Disconnect ABS module harness connector C141. Measure resistance in Tan/Orange wire between terminal No. 30 at ABS module harness connector C141 and terminal No. 2 at DLC. *See Figs. 2 and 3.* Also, measure resistance in Pink/Light Blue wire between terminal No. 29 at ABS module harness connector C141 and terminal No. 10 at DLC. If both resistance readings are 5 ohms or less, go to next step. If either resistance reading is greater than 5 ohms, repair open in appropriate wire between ABS module and DLC.

5) Turn ignition switch to RUN position. Measure voltage between terminals No. 2 (Tan/Orange wire) and No. 4 (Black wire) at DLC. Also, measure voltage between terminals No. 2 (Tan/Orange wire) and No. 16 (Light Green/Red wire) at DLC. Also, measure voltage between terminals No. 10 (Pink/Light Blue wire) and No. 16 (Light Green/Red wire) at DLC. Also, measure voltage between terminals No. 10 (Pink/Light Blue wire) and No. 16 (Light Green/Red wire) at DLC. If any reading indicates voltage, go to next step. If all readings indicate zero volts, replace ABS module.

6) Turn ignition switch to LOCK position. Disconnect in-line harness connector C108. *See Fig. 4.* Turn ignition switch to RUN position. Measure voltage between terminals No. 2 (Tan/Orange wire) and No. 4 (Black wire) at DLC. Also, measure voltage between terminals No. 2 (Tan/Orange wire) and No. 16 (Light Green/Red wire) at DLC. Also, measure voltage between terminals No. 10 (Pink/Light Blue wire) and No. 16 (Light Green/Red wire) at DLC. Also, measure voltage between terminals No. 10 (Pink/Light Blue wire) and No. 16 (Light Green/Red wire) at DLC. If any reading indicates voltage, go to next step. If all readings indicate zero volts, repair short to voltage or ground in appropriate wire between in-line harness connector C108 and ABS module.

7) Turn ignition switch to LOCK position. Disconnect PCM harness connector C294. Measure resistance in Tan/Orange wire between terminal No. 16 at PCM harness connector C294 and terminal No. 2 at DLC. *See Figs. 2 and 12.* Also, measure resistance in Pink/Light Blue wire between terminal No. 15 at PCM harness connector C294 and terminal No. 10 at DLC. If both resistance readings are 5 ohms or less, go to next step. If either resistance reading is greater than 5 ohms, repair open in appropriate wire between PCM and DLC.

8) Turn ignition switch to RUN position. Measure voltage between terminals No. 2 (Tan/Orange wire) and No. 4 (Black wire) at DLC. Also, measure voltage between terminals No. 2 (Tan/Orange wire) and No. 16 (Light Green/Red wire) at DLC. Also, measure voltage between terminals No. 10 (Pink/Light Blue wire) and No. 16 (Light Green/Red wire) at DLC. Also, measure voltage between terminals No. 10 (Pink/Light Blue wire) and No. 16 (Light Green/Red wire) at DLC. If any reading indicates voltage, go to next step. If all readings indicate zero volts, replace PCM.

9) Turn ignition switch to LOCK position. Disconnect in-line harness connector C216. *See Fig. 6.* Turn ignition switch to RUN position.

Measure voltage between terminals No. 2 (Tan/Orange wire) and No. 4 (Black wire) at DLC. Also, measure voltage between terminals No. 2 (Tan/Orange wire) and No. 16 (Light Green/Red wire) at DLC. Also, measure voltage between terminals No. 10 (Pink/Light Blue wire) and No. 16 (Light Green/Red wire) at DLC. Also, measure voltage between terminals No. 10 (Pink/Light Blue wire) and No. 16 (Light Green/Red wire) at DLC. If any reading indicates voltage, go to next step. If all readings indicate zero volts, repair short to voltage or ground in appropriate wire between in-line harness connector C216 and PCM.

10) Turn ignition switch to LOCK position. Disconnect instrument cluster harness connector C250. Measure voltage between terminals No. 2 (Tan/Orange wire) and No. 4 (Black wire) at DLC. Also, measure voltage between terminals No. 2 (Tan/Orange wire) and No. 16 (Light Green/Red wire) at DLC. Also, measure voltage between terminals No. 10 (Pink/Light Blue wire) and No. 16 (Light Green/Red wire) at DLC. Also, measure voltage between terminals No. 10 (Pink/Light Blue wire) and No. 16 (Light Green/Red wire) at DLC. If any reading indicates voltage, repair short to voltage or ground in appropriate wire between instrument cluster and DLC. If all readings indicate zero volts, replace instrument cluster.

TEST H: NO MODULE/NETWORK COMMUNICATION

1) Turn ignition switch to LOCK position. Inspect NGS tester connector for loose, damaged or corroded terminals. If connector is okay, go to next step. If problem exists, repair connector as necessary.

2) Inspect Data Link Connector (DLC) for loose, damaged or corroded terminals. If connector is okay, go to next step. If problem exists, repair connector as necessary.

3) Measure voltage at terminal No. 16 (Light Green/Red wire) at DLC. *See Fig. 2.* If battery voltage exists, go to next step. If battery voltage does not exist, repair power distribution circuit as necessary. See appropriate wiring diagram in POWER DISTRIBUTION article in WIRING DIAGRAMS.

4) Measure resistance between ground and terminals No. 4 (Black wire) and No. 5 (Blue/Yellow wire) at DLC. If both resistance readings are 5 ohms or less, repair or replace NGS tester. If either resistance reading is greater than 5 ohms, repair open in appropriate wire between ground and DLC.

DIAGNOSTIC TROUBLE CODE (DTC) DEFINITIONS

ANTI-LOCK BRAKE SYSTEM MODULE DTC INDEX

DTC	Description	Test
B1318	Battery Voltage Low	1
B1342	ECU Defective	2
B1484	Brake Pedal Input Circuit Open	1
B1596	Repair Continuous DTCs	3
C1095	ABS Hydraulic Pump Motor Circuit Failure	1
C1145	Right Front ABS Sensor Input Circuit Failure	1
C1155	Left Front ABS Sensor Input Circuit Failure	1
C1165	Right Rear ABS Sensor Input Circuit Failure	1
C1175	Left Rear ABS Sensor Input Circuit Failure	1
C1222	Anti-Lock Brake Sensor Mismatch	1
C1233	Left Front ABS Sensor Input Signal Missing	1
C1234	Right Front ABS Sensor Input Signal Missing	1
C1235	Right Rear ABS Sensor Input Signal Missing	1
C1236	Left Rear ABS Sensor Input Signal Missing	4
C1266	ABS Valve Power Relay Circuit Failure	5
C1805	Mismatched PCM And/Or ABS Module	6
U1009	Invalid/Missing Data For Engine Torque	6
U1027	Invalid/Missing Data For Engine RPM	6
U1059	Invalid/Missing Data For Transmission Range Switch	6
U1083	Invalid/Missing Data For Engine System	6
U1262	SCP Bus Communication Fault	7

[1] – Repair Anti-Lock Brake System (ABS). See appropriate ANTI-LOCK article in BRAKES in appropriate MITCHELL® manual.

ANTI-LOCK BRAKE SYSTEM MODULE DTC INDEX (Cont.)

[2] – Using NGS tester, retrieve and document all continuous. Perform Anti-Lock Brake System (ABS) module self-test. If DTC B1342 is retrieved again, replace ABS module.

[3] – Repair all DTC retrieved.

[4] – Replace ABS module.

[5] – Using NGS tester, retrieve and document all continuous. Perform Anti-Lock Brake System (ABS) module self-test. If DTC C1805 is retrieved again, replace PCM and/or ABS module as necessary.

[6] – Cause by Powertrain Control Module (PCM). Using NGS tester, perform PCM self-test. For PCM DTC testing procedures, see appropriate SELF-DIAGNOSTICS article in ENGINE PERFORMANCE in appropriate MITCHELL® manual.

[7] – Perform TEST G: NO MODULE/NETWORK COMMUNICATION – BUS LINK under SYSTEM TESTS.

GENERIC ELECTRONIC MODULE DTC INDEX

DTC	Description	Test
B1217	Horn Relay Coil Circuit Failure	1
B1218	Horn Relay Coil Circuit Short To Voltage	1
B1312	Headlight Input Circuit Short To Voltage	2
B1317	Battery Voltage High	3
B1318	Battery Voltage Low	3
B1322	Driver's Door Ajar Circuit Short To Ground	4
B1330	Passenger's Door Ajar Circuit Short To Ground	4
B1334	Trunk Lid/Rear Door Ajar Circuit Short To Ground	4
B1340	Chime Input Request Circuit Short To Ground	5
B1342	ECU Defective	6
B1353	Key-In-Ignition Circuit Open	5
B1359	Ignition Switch RUN/ACC Circuit Failure	1
B1396	Power Door Lock Circuit Short To Voltage	4
B1397	Power Door Unlock Circuit Short To Voltage	4
B1405	Driver's Power Window Down Circuit Short To Voltage	7
B1408	Driver's Power Window Up Circuit Short To Voltage	7
B1410	Driver's Power Window Motor Circuit Short To Voltage	7
B1426	Seat Belt Switch Circuit Short To Voltage	5
B1428	Seat Belt Indicator Circuit Failure	5
B1431	On/Off Relay Circuit Failure	8
B1432	On/Off Relay Circuit Short To Power	8
B1434	High/Low Relay Coil Circuit Failure	8
B1436	High/Low Relay Coil Circuit Short To Power	8
B1438	Wiper Switch Circuit Failure	8
B1441	Wiper Switch Circuit Short To Ground	8
B1446	Park Sense Circuit Failure	8
B1448	Park Sense Circuit Short To Power	8
B1450	Wash/Delay Switch Circuit Failure	8
B1453	Wash/Delay Switch Circuit Short To Ground	8
B1458	Washer Pump Relay Circuit Failure	8
B1460	Washer Pump Relay Coil Circuit Short To Power	8
B1462	Seat Belt Switch Circuit Failure	5
B1466	High & Low Speeds Not Switching	8
B1473	Motor Low Speed Circuit Failure	8
B1476	Motor High Speed Circuit Failure	8
B1498	Trunk Lid Punch-Out Sensor Short To Ground	4
B1551	Trunk Lid Release Circuit Failure	4
B1553	Trunk Lid Release Circuit Short To Voltage	4
B1555	Ignition RUN/START Circuit Failure	1
B1603	Anti-Theft Indicator Circuit Failure	9
B1605	Anti-Theft Indicator Circuit Short To Voltage	9
B1687	Dome Light Input Circuit Short To Voltage	10
B1833	Door Unlock Disarm Switch Circuit Short To Ground	9
B2486	Parking Light Output Relay Circuit Failure	9
B2488	Parking Light Output Relay Circuit Short To Voltage	9
C1189	Brake Fluid Level Sensor Input Short To Voltage	5
C1223	Brake Light Warning Output Circuit Failure	5
C1225	Brake Light Warning Output Circuit Short To Voltage	5

[1] – See STEERING COLUMN SWITCHES – MUSTANG article for testing procedure.

[2] – See appropriate wiring diagram in HEADLIGHT SYSTEMS article.

[3] – Check charging system. See appropriate GENERATORS article in STARTING & CHARGING SYSTEMS. If charging system is okay, check power and ground circuits to GEM. See appropriate wiring diagram in POWER DISTRIBUTION article in WIRING DIAGRAMS.

[4] – See appropriate wiring diagram in REMOTE KEYLESS ENTRY SYSTEMS and/or POWER DOOR LOCK & REMOTE TRUNK RELEASE article.

[5] – See INSTRUMENT PANELS – MUSTANG article for testing procedure.

[6] – Using NGS tester, retrieve and document all continuous. Perform Generic Electronic Module (GEM) self-test. If DTC B1342 is retrieved again, replace GEM.

[7] – See POWER WINDOWS – MUSTANG article for testing procedure.

[8] – See WIPER/WASHER SYSTEMS – MUSTANG article for testing procedure.

GENERIC ELECTRONIC MODULE DTC INDEX (Cont.)

[9] – See PASSIVE ANTI-THEFT SYSTEMS – MUSTANG article for testing procedure.
[10] – See appropriate wiring diagram in ILLUMINATION/INTERIOR LIGHTS article.

INSTRUMENT CLUSTER DTC INDEX

Scan Tool DTC	Dealer Test Mode DTC	Description	Test
B1202	9202	Fuel Sender Circuit Open	1
B1204	9204	Fuel Sender Short To Ground	1
B1213	9213	Anti-Theft Number Of Programmed Ignition Keys Is Below Minimum	2
B1232 Or B2103	A103 Or 9232	Defective Transceiver	2
B1317	9317	Battery Voltage High	3
B1318	9318	Battery Voltage Low	3
B1342	9342	ECU Defective	4
B1356	9356	Ignition Run Circuit Open	5
B1364	9364	Ignition Start Circuit Open	5
B1600	9600	PATS Ignition Key Transponder Signal Not Received	2
B1601	9601	PATS Received Incorrect Key-Code From Transponder	2
B1602	9602	PATS Received Invalid Key-Code Format From Transponder	2
B1681	9681	PATS Transceiver Signal Not Received	2
B2139	A139	Security Identification Does Not Match Between Instrument Cluster & PCM	2
B2141	A141	NVM Configuration Failure	2
B2143	A143	NVM Memory Failure	6
C1284	5284	Oil Pressure Switch Failure	1
U1027	D027	Invalid/Missing Data For Engine RPM	7
U1041	D041	Invalid/Missing Data For Vehicle Speed	7
U1043	D043	Invalid/Missing Data For Traction Control	8
U1073	D073	Invalid/Missing Data For Engine Coolant	7
U1123	D123	Invalid/Missing Data For Odometer	7
U1147	D147	SCP Invalid/Missing Data For Vehicle Security	2
U1262	D262	SCP Bus Communications Fault	9

[1] – See INSTRUMENT PANELS – MUSTANG article for testing procedure.
[2] – See PASSIVE ANTI-THEFT SYSTEMS – MUSTANG article for testing procedure.
[3] – Check charging system. See appropriate GENERATORS article in STARTING & CHARGING SYSTEMS. If charging system is okay, check power and ground circuits to instrument cluster. See appropriate wiring diagram in POWER DISTRIBUTION article in WIRING DIAGRAMS.
[4] – Using NGS tester, retrieve and document all continuous. Perform instrument cluster self-test. If DTC B1342 is retrieved again, replace instrument cluster.
[5] – See STEERING COLUMN SWITCHES – MUSTANG article for testing procedure.
[6] – Replace instrument cluster.
[7] – Cause by PCM. Repair communication circuit between instrument cluster and PCM.
[8] – Cause by ABS module. Repair communication circuit between instrument cluster and ABS module.
[9] – Service all other DTCs first. After all other DTC concerns have been repaired, perform TEST G: NO MODULE/NETWORK COMMUNICATION – BUS LINK under SYSTEM TESTS.

RESTRAINTS CONTROL MODULE DTC INDEX

DTC [1]	Description	Test
B1342	ECU Defective	2
B1231	RCM Crash Data Memory Full	2
B1921	RCM Bracket Ground Resistance High	2
C1414	Incorrect Vehicle Identification Code	2
B1887	Driver's Side Air Bag Circuit Short To Ground	2
B1916	Driver's Side Air Bag Circuit Short To Voltage	2
B1888	Passenger's Side Air Circuit Bag Short To Ground	2
B1925	Passenger's Side Air Bag Circuit Short To Voltage	2
B1932	Driver's Side Air Bag Circuit Resistance High	2
B1933	Passenger's Side Air Bag Circuit Resistance High	2
B1934	Driver's Side Air Bag Circuit Resistance Low	2
B1935	Passenger's Side Air Bag Circuit Resistance Low	2
B1892	Air Bag Tone Warning Indicator Circuit Short To Ground Or Open	2
B1891	Air Bag Tone Warning Indicator Circuit Short To Voltage	2
B1869	Air Bag Indicator Inoperative	2
B1870	Air Bag Indicator Short To Voltage	2

[1] – DTCs are listed in order of importance. Repair DTCs in order listed.
[2] – Repair supplemental restraint system as necessary. See DIAGNOSIS & TESTING article in appropriate MITCHELL® AIR BAG SERVICE & REPAIR MANUAL, DOMESTIC & IMPORTED MODELS.

PARAMETER IDENTIFICATION (PID) DEFINITIONS

ANTI-LOCK BRAKE SYSTEM MODULE PID INDEX

PID	Description	Expected Value
ABSLF_I	Left Front ABS Inlet Valve	1
ABSLF_O	Left Front ABS Outlet Valve	1

ANTI-LOCK BRAKE SYSTEM MODULE PID INDEX (Cont.)

PID	Description	Expected Value
ABSLR_I	Left Rear ABS Inlet Valve	1
ABSLR_O	Left Rear ABS Outlet Valve	1
ABSRF_I	Right Front ABS Inlet Valve	1
ABSRF_O	Right Front ABS Outlet Valve	1
ABSRR_I	Right Rear ABS Inlet Valve	1
ABSRR_O	Right Rear ABS Outlet Valve	1
BOO_ABS	Brake Switch Input	ON/OFF
CCNTABS	Number Of Continuous DTCs	One Bit Per Count
LF_WSPD	Left Front Wheel Speed Signal	0-255 KPH
LR_WSPD	Left Rear Wheel Speed Signal	0-255 KPH
RF_WSPD	Right Front Wheel Speed Signal	0-255 KPH
RR_WSPD	Right Rear Wheel Speed Signal	0-255 KPH
LF_TC_P	Left Front Traction Control Priming Valve	ON/OFF
RF_TC_P	Right Front Traction Control Priming Valve	ON/OFF
LR_TC_P	Left Rear Traction Control Priming Valve	ON/OFF
RR_TC_P	Right Rear Traction Control Priming Valve	ON/OFF
LF_TC_S	Left Front Traction Control Switching Valve	ON/OFF
RF_TC_S	Right Front Traction Control Switching Valve	ON/OFF
LR_TC_S	Left Rear Traction Control Switching Valve	ON/OFF
RR_TC_S	Right Rear Traction Control Switching Valve	ON/OFF
T/ALVAL	Left Traction Control Valve Output State	1
T/ARVAL	Right Traction Control Valve Output State	1
PMP_MTR	ABS Pump Motor	1
VLV_CTR	ABS Valve Control Relay	1

[1] – Expected value should be OFF- - -, OFFO- -, OFF-B-, OFF- - G, OFFO-G, OFFOB-, OFF-BG, OFFOBG, ON- - -, ONO- -, ON-B-, ON- - G, ONO-G, ONOB-, ON-BG or ONOBG

GENERIC ELECTRONIC MODULE PID INDEX

PID	Description	Expected Value
CCNT	Number Of DTCs In VIC	One Count Per Bit
ABCHIME	Air Bag Chime	ON, OFF
AL_EVT#	Last 8 Alarm Events	1
BRK_LVL	Brake Fluid Level	NOTOK, OK
BRKLAMP	Brake Warning Light State	2
D_DN_SW	Driver's Window Down Switch	OFF, DOWN
D_DOOR	Driver's Door Ajar Switch	CLOSED, AJAR
D_DSRM	Driver's Door Unlock Disarm Switch	NO, YES
D_SBELT	Driver's Seat Belt	OUT, IN
D_UP_SW	Driver's Window Up Switch	OFF, UP
DECKLID	Trunk Lid/Hatch Ajar	CLOSED, AJAR
DOMESW	Dome Light Switch	OFF, ON
DR_LOCK	Driver's Door Lock Output State	NO, YES
DR_UNLK	All Doors Unlock Output State	NO, YES
HOOD_SW	Trunk Lid/Hatch Or Hood Punchout	NOTPUN, PUNCHD
HORNRLY	Horn Control Driver	2
IGN_A	Ignition Switch (ACC Position)	NO, YES
IGN_KEY	Ignition Key In/Out	OUT, IN
IGN_R	Ignition Switch (RUN Position)	NO, YES
IGN_S	Ignition Switch (START Position)	NO, YES
MTU	Measurement Time Unit	MS
P_DOOR	Passenger's Door Ajar Switch	CLOSED, AJAR
PARK_SW	Parking Switch	OFF, ON
PD_LOCK	Passenger's Door Lock	NO, YES
PD_UNLK	Passenger's Door Unlock	NO, YES
PRK_BRK	Parking Brake Switch Input	OFF, ON
SBLTLMP	Seat Belt Indicator Circuit	2
THEFT	Anti-Theft Indicator Driver	2
TRANSGR	Transmission Gear Position	NOTREV, REV
VBAT	Battery Voltage	Volts
WASHRLY	Washer Pump Relay Circuit	2
WPHISP	Wiper 2 Speed Relay	2
WPMODE	Wiper Control Mode Select	3
WPPK_PK	Wiper Park-To-Park Time	MS
WPPRKSW	Wiper Park Sense	NOTPRK, PARKED
WPRUN	Wiper Run Relay Driver State	2

[1] – Expected value should be DROPEN, HOODTR, IGNTAM, PANIC, T_AJAR, RR_SD, LR_SD, P_DOOR, D_DOOR, RADIO, WINDO, ULTRS, DLID_P, HOOD and/or NOEVNT.
[2] – Expected value should be OFF- - -, OFF-B-, ON- - - or ON-B-.
[3] – Expected value should be WASH, OPEN, INVLD, OFF, INTVL1, INTVL2, INTVL3, INTVL4, INTVL5, INTVL6, INTVL7, LOW or HIGH.

INSTRUMENT CLUSTER PID INDEX

PID	Description	Expected Value
CCNT	Number Of DTCs In VIC	One Count Per Bit
COOLANT	Engine Coolant Level Status	OK/NOTOK
NUMKEYS	Number Of Ignition Key Codes Programed	BCD (Valid Range 0-8)
RESETSW	Reset Switch	ACTIVE/NOTACT
VBAT	System Battery Voltage Potential	Volts
FUELLVL	Fuel Level Status	Percent
IGN_O/L	Ignition Switch (LOCK Position)	NO/YES
IGN_R	Ignition Switch (RUN Position)	NO/YES
IGN_S	Ignition Switch (START Position)	NO/YES
OIL_PSW	Oil Pressure Switch Control	One Count Per Bit
PANLDIM	Panel Dim Intensity	Percent
TRAC_SW	T/A Disable Switch	[1]

[1] – Expected value should be OFF- - -, OFFO- -, OFF-B-, OFF- - G, OFFO-G, OFFOB-, OFF-BG, OFFOBG, ON- - -, ONO- -, ON-B-, ON- - G, ONO-G, ONOB-, ON-BG or ONOBG

RESTRAINT CONTROL MODULE PID INDEX

PID	Description	Expected Value
CCNT	Number Of Continuous DTCs In RCM	One Count Per Bit
VBAT	Battery Voltage Feed To RCM	Volts
D_ABAGR	Driver's Air Bag Module Resistance	1.7-4.1 Ohms
P_ABAGR	Passenegr's Air Bag Module Resistance	1.7-3.2 Ohms
BRACKET	Bracket Ground Resistance	100 Ohms Or Less
VID#1	Program Vehicle ID Pin 10	No Connection
VID#2	Program Vehicle ID Pin 13	No Connection
VID#3	Program Vehicle ID Pin 14	Ignition

WIRING DIAGRAMS

NOTE: See appropriate wiring diagrams in DATA LINK CONNECTORS, GROUND DISTRIBUTION or POWER DISTRIBUTION article in WIRING DIAGRAMS.

DESCRIPTION & OPERATION

Vehicle has 2 module communications networks. The Powertrain Control Module (PCM), Hybrid Electronic Instrument Cluster (HEC) and Natural Gas Vehicle Module (NGVM) are connected to the multiplex communications network through a pair of twisted wires or BUS. The BUS network is also referred to as Standard Corporate Protocol (SCP). The BUS consists of a (+) circuit and a (−) circuit (circuits No. 914 and 915 respectively). The Generic Electronic (GEM) Module/Central Timer Module (CTM), Remote Anti-Theft Personality (RAP) module, Restraint Control Module (RCM) and 4-Wheel Anti-Lock Brake System (4WABS) module are connected to the International Standards Organization (ISO) 9141 diagnostic communications network through a single wire (circuit No. 70). Both networks are connected to the Data Link Connector (DLC). This article is used to diagnose BUS and ISO communications network circuit faults. For module locations, see COMPONENT LOCATIONS.

COMPONENT LOCATIONS

COMPONENT LOCATIONS

Component	Location
Restraint Control Module	Behind Right Side Of Instrument Panel
Data Link Connector	Below Driver's Side Of Instrument Panel, Right Of Steering Column
Generic Electronic Module/Central Timer Module [1]	Below Driver's Side Of Instrument Panel, To Left Of Steering Column
Natural Gas Vehicle Module	Front Of Engine Compartment, Near Hood Latch Assembly
Powertrain Control Module	Right Side Of Engine Compartment, On Fenderwell
Remote Anti-Theft Personality Module	Behind Driver's Side Of Instrument Panel, To Left Of Steering Column
4-Wheel Anti-Lock Brake System Module	Left Front Of Engine Compartment, On Front Of Upper Radiator Support

[1] – GEM is equipped on vehicles with 4WD and/or power windows. CTM is equipped on vehicles with 2WD or vehicles without power windows.

REPAIRING BUS WIRING

NOTE: The following procedure must be used to ensure proper repair is performed on BUS wiring. BUS wiring is sensitive to moisture and oxidation and must be properly sealed to ensure proper operation of the module communications network. Regular heat shrink tubing is NOT sufficient, heat shrink tubing containing hot melt wax is required.

1) When performing a repair on the BUS wiring, ensure the wires on the BUS are twisted at a rate of 33-40 winds per 3.3 ft. (1 m). The twists should start within approximately 4.9" (124 mm) from any connector. Use only 20 AWG standard wire gauge for repairs.

2) If performing a splice in the wiring, strip .75" (19.0 mm) of insulation from one wire and 1.50" (38.1 mm) of insulation from the other wire. Perform STEP 1. *See Fig. 1.* Place hot melt wax heat shrink tubing over one wire.

3) Twist stripped portion of the wires together. Solder connection using resin core RMA solder. DO NOT use acid core solder. Bend wires to allow installation of heat shrink tubing. Perform STEP 2. *See Fig. 1.*

4) Position heat shrink tubing over splice area. Using heat gun, evenly heat the heat shrink tubing until wax flows from both ends of heat shrink tubing.

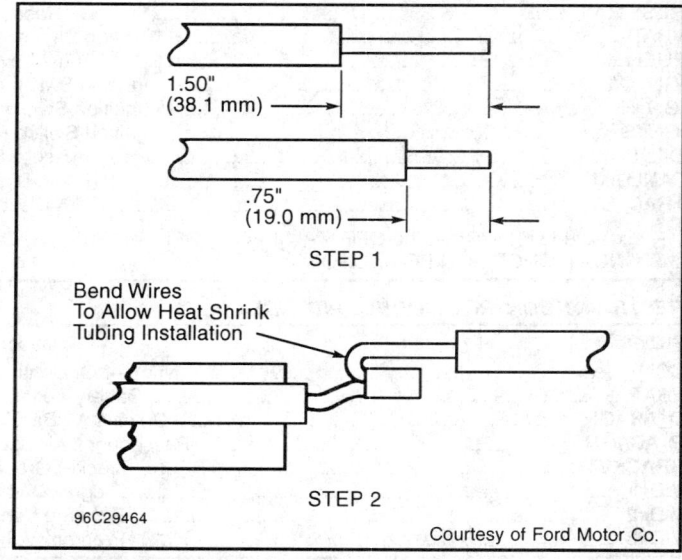

Fig. 1: Repairing BUS Wiring

COMMUNICATION NETWORK DIAGNOSTICS

INSPECTION & VERIFICATION

1) Verify customer's original problem by operating system in question. Inspect vehicle for any obvious electrical component wiring or connector damage. Inspect connectors for loose, damaged or corroded terminals. Inspect related fuses for system in question.

2) Inspect Data Link Connector (DLC) pins for damage. *See Fig. 2.* DLC is located below driver's side of instrument panel, to the right of steering column. If pins are okay, go to next step. If pins are damaged, repair as necessary and proceed to next step.

3) If problem is still present after performing inspection, connect New Generation Star (NGS) tester to DLC. Select vehicle to be tested from NGS tester menu. If NGS tester does not communicate with vehicle, ensure program card is properly installed. Inspect NGS tester cable connections and ensure ignition switch is in ON position. If NGS tester still does not communicate with vehicle, go to TEST J: NO MODULE/ NETWORK COMMUNICATION under SYSTEM TESTS. If NGS tester communicates with vehicle, perform data link diagnostic test. See DATA LINK DIAGNOSTIC TEST.

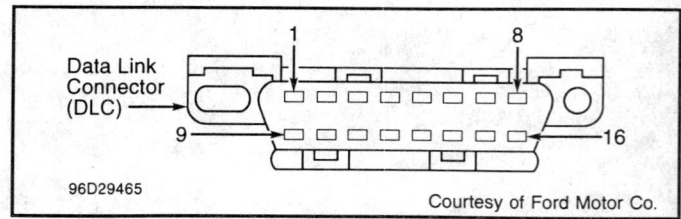

Fig. 2: Identifying Data Link Connector (DLC) Terminals

DATA LINK DIAGNOSTIC TEST

1) Connect New Generation Star (NGS) tester to Data Link Connector (DLC), if not already connected. Select vehicle to be tested from NGS tester menu.

2) Turn ignition switch to ON position. Rotate dial on NGS tester to menu item DIAGNOSTIC DATA LINK and press trigger. A test will be performed on the BUS (circuits No. 914 and 915) for the module communications network and the ISO 9141 communication link (circuit No. 70).

1999 ACCESSORIES & EQUIPMENT
Module Communications Network
F150 & F250 Light-Duty Pickup (Cont.)

FORD
4-313

3) If NGS tester displays CKT 914 (+) = SYSTEM PASSED and CKT 915 (−) = SYSTEM PASSED, or if NGS tester displays CKT 70 = SYSTEM PASSED, ISO 9141, module communications network is okay. Return to article that directed you here and continue diagnosis.

4) If no response from NGS tester, go to TEST J: NO MODULE/ NETWORK COMMUNICATION under SYSTEM TESTS. Perform the following as applicable. If NGS tester displays:

- CKT 70, CKT 914 and/or CKT 915 = SOME ECUS NO RESP/NOT EQUIP, go to SYMPTOM INDEX under SYSTEM TESTS to continue diagnosis for module in question.
- CKT 70 = ALL ECUS NO RESP/NOT EQUIP, go to TEST G: NO MODULE/NETWORK COMMUNICATION – ISO 9141 LINK under SYSTEM TESTS.
- CKT 914 = ALL ECUS NO RESP/NOT EQUIP, go to TEST H: NO MODULE/NETWORK COMMUNICATION – BUS LINK under SYSTEM TESTS.
- CKT 915 = ALL ECUS NO RESP/NOT EQUIP, go to TEST H: NO MODULE/NETWORK COMMUNICATION – BUS LINK under SYSTEM TESTS.
- NO RESPONSE/NOT EQUIPPED, go to SYMPTOM INDEX under SYSTEM TEST to continue diagnosis for module in question.
- NO RESPONSE ON CKT 914 (BUS +), go to SYMPTOM INDEX under SYSTEM TESTS to continue diagnosis for module in question.
- NO RESPONSE ON CKT 915 (BUS −), go to SYMPTOM INDEX under SYSTEM TESTS to continue diagnosis for module in question.

RETRIEVING & CLEARING DIAGNOSTIC TROUBLE CODES

Connect New Generation Star (NGS) tester to Data Link Connector (DLC). Following manufacturers instructions to retrieve and clear codes for desired module. See appropriate table under DIAGNOSTIC TROUBLE CODE (DTC) DEFINITIONS for a listing of Diagnostic Trouble Codes (DTCs) and appropriate test procedure.

ACCESSING PARAMETER IDENTIFICATION (PID)

Turn ignition switch to LOCK position. Connect New Generation Star (NGS) tester to Data Link Connector (DLC). Following manufacturers instructions enter PID/DATA MONITOR AND RECORD for desired module. Operate appropriate system and ensure PID expected values are obtained. See appropriate table under PARAMETER IDENTIFICATION (PID) DEFINITIONS.

SYSTEM TESTS

NOTE: *Always check module power and ground circuits prior to replacing a control module. See appropriate wiring diagram in* DATA LINK CONNECTORS, GROUND DISTRIBUTION *or* POWER DISTRIBUTION *article in* WIRING DIAGRAMS.

NOTE: *If repairs to a Module Communications Network circuit is required, see* REPAIRING BUS WIRING. *After any repairs are made to vehicle always perform data link diagnostic test. See* DATA LINK DIAGNOSTIC TEST.

SYMPTOM INDEX

Condition	Test
4-Wheel Anti-Lock Brake System (4WABS) Module Does Not Respond To NGS Tester	A
Remote Anti-Theft Personality (RAP) Module Does Not Respond To NGS Tester	B
Generic Electronic (GEM) Module/Central Timer Module (CTM) Does Not Respond To NGS Tester	C
Restraint Control Module (RCM) Does Not Respond To NGS Tester	D

SYMPTOM INDEX (Cont.)

Condition	Test
Powertrain Control Module (PCM) Does Not Respond To NGS Tester	E
Natural Gas Vehicle (NGV) Module Does Not Respond To NGS Tester	F
No Module/Network Communications – ISO 9141 Link	G
No Module/Network Communication – Bus Link	H
Instrument Cluster (HEC) Module Does Not Respond To NGS Tester	I
No Module/Network Communication	J

TEST A: 4-WHEEL ANTI-LOCK BRAKE SYSTEM (4WABS) MODULE DOES NOT RESPOND TO NGS TESTER

1) Turn ignition switch to OFF position. Disconnect 4WABS module Black 24-pin connector C146 located at left front of engine compartment, on front of upper radiator support. Inspect ABS connector for loose, damaged or corroded terminals. If connector is damaged, repair as necessary. If connector is okay, go to next step.

2) Using ohmmeter, measure resistance of Light Blue/White wire between terminal No. 5 at 4WABS module connector C146 and terminal No. 7 at Data Link Connector (DLC). *See Figs. 2 and 3.* If resistance is 5 ohms or more, go to next step. If resistance is less than 5 ohms, replace 4WABS module.

3) Disconnect Gray 40-pin connector C160 located in left rear corner of engine compartment, near firewall. Inspect connector for loose, damaged or corroded terminals. If connector is damaged, repair as necessary. If connector is okay, go to next step.

4) Measure resistance of Light Blue/White wire between terminal No. 29 at female half of connector C160 and terminal No. 7 at DLC. *See Figs. 2 and 4.* If resistance is less than 5 ohms, repair open in Light Blue/White wire between 4WABS module connector C146 and male half of connector C160. If resistance is 5 ohms or more, repair open in Light Blue/White wire between female half of connector C160 and DLC.

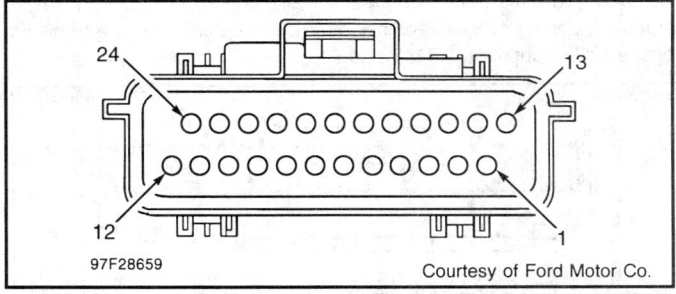

97F28659   Courtesy of Ford Motor Co.

Fig. 3: *Identifying 4WABS Control Module Connector C146 Terminals*

TEST B: REMOTE ANTI-THEFT PERSONALITY (RAP) MODULE DOES NOT RESPOND TO NGS TESTER

1) Turn ignition switch to OFF position. Disconnect Remote Anti-theft Personality (RAP) module 26-pin connector C256 located behind driver's side of instrument panel, left of steering column. Inspect connector for loose, damaged or corroded terminals. If connector is damaged, repair as necessary. If connector is okay, go to next step.

2) Measure resistance of Light Blue/White wire between terminal No. 3 at RAP module connector C256 and terminal No. 7 at Data Link Connector (DLC). *See Figs. 2 and 5.* If resistance is 5 ohms or more, go to next step. If resistance is less than 5 ohms, replace RAP module.

3) Disconnect 16-pin harness connector C247 located behind left side of instrument panel. *See Fig. 6.* Inspect connector for loose, damaged or corroded terminals. If connector is damaged, repair as necessary. If connector is okay, go to next step.

FORD
4-314

1999 ACCESSORIES & EQUIPMENT
Module Communications Network
F150 & F250 Light-Duty Pickup (Cont.)

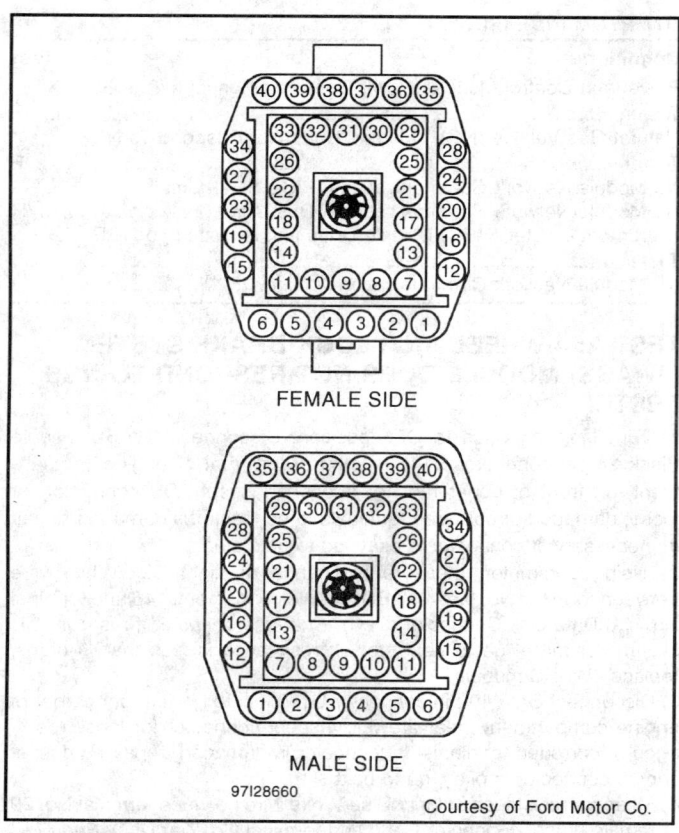

FEMALE SIDE

MALE SIDE

97I28660

Courtesy of Ford Motor Co.

Fig. 4: Identifying Connector C158 & C160 Terminals

4) Measure resistance of Light Blue/White wire between terminal No. 16 at male half of connector C247 and terminal No. 7 at DLC. *See Figs. 2 and 7.* If resistance is less than 5 ohms, repair open in Light Blue/White wire between male half of connector C247 and RAP module. If resistance is 5 ohms or more, repair open in Light Blue/White wire between female half of connector C247 and DLC.

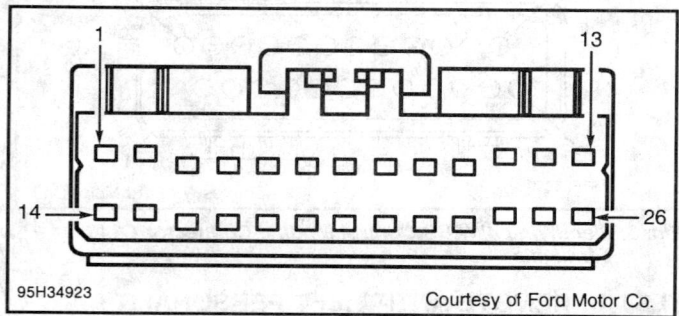

95H34923

Courtesy of Ford Motor Co.

Fig. 5: Identifying RAP Module Connector C256 & GEM/CTM C239 Connector Terminals

TEST C: GENERIC ELECTRONIC MODULE (GEM)/CENTRAL TIMER MODULE (CTM) DOES NOT RESPOND TO NGS TESTER

1) Turn ignition switch to OFF position. Disconnect Generic Electronic Module (GEM)/Central Timer Module (CTM) 26-pin connector C239 located below driver's side of instrument panel, left of steering column. *See Fig. 6.* Inspect connector for loose, damaged or corroded terminals. If connector is damaged, repair as necessary. If connector is okay, go to next step.

2) Measure resistance of Light Blue/White wire between terminal No. 25 at GEM/CTM connector C239 and terminal No. 7 at DLC. *See Figs. 2*

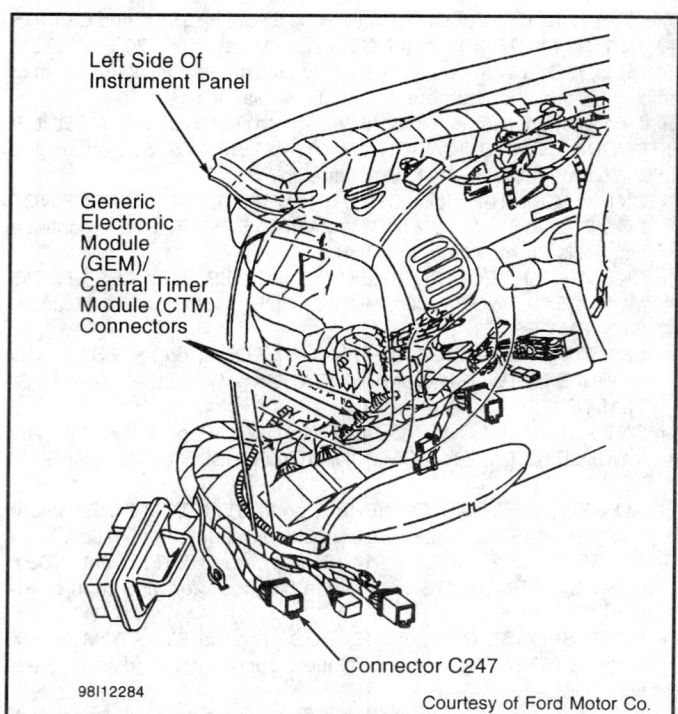

Left Side Of Instrument Panel

Generic Electronic Module (GEM)/ Central Timer Module (CTM) Connectors

Connector C247

98I12284

Courtesy of Ford Motor Co.

Fig. 6: Locating Connectors Behind Left Side Of Instrument Panel

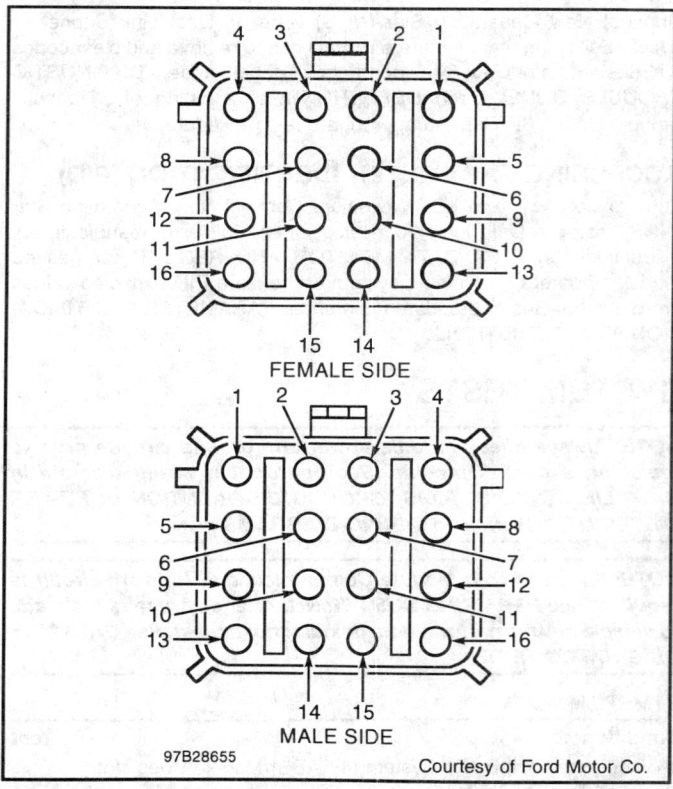

FEMALE SIDE

MALE SIDE

97B28655

Courtesy of Ford Motor Co.

Fig. 7: Identifying Connector C247 Terminals

and 5. If resistance is less than 5 ohms, replace GEM. If resistance is 5 ohms or more, repair Light Blue/White wire between GEM/CTM connector C239 and DLC.

Module Communications Network
F150 & F250 Light-Duty Pickup (Cont.)

TEST D: RESTRAINT CONTROL MODULE (RCM) DOES NOT RESPOND TO NGS TESTER

1) Turn ignition switch to OFF position. Deactivate air bag system. See appropriate AIR BAG RESTRAINT SYSTEMS article. Disconnect Restraint Control Module (RCM) 26-pin connector C208 located behind right side of instrument panel. Inspect connector for loose, damaged or corroded terminals. If connector is damaged, repair as necessary. If connector is okay, go to next step.

2) Measure resistance of Light Blue/White wire between terminal No. 5 at RCM connector C208 and terminal No. 7 at DLC. *See Figs. 2 and 8.* If resistance is less than 5 ohms, replace RCM. If resistance is 5 ohms or more, repair Light Blue/White wire between RCM connector C208 and DLC.

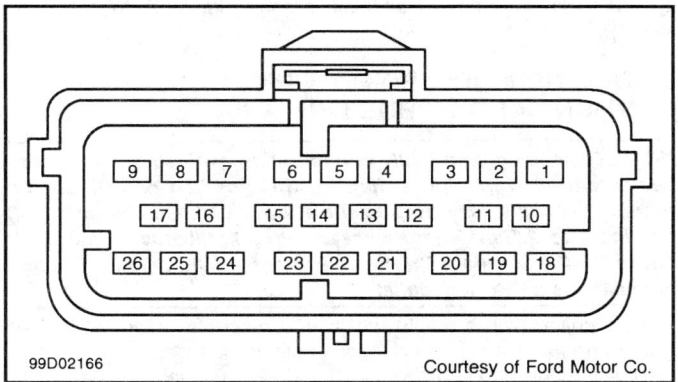

99D02166   Courtesy of Ford Motor Co.

Fig. 8: Identifying Restraint Control Module (RCM) Connector C208 Terminals

TEST E: POWERTRAIN CONTROL MODULE (PCM) DOES NOT RESPOND TO NGS TESTER

1) Turn ignition switch to OFF position. Disconnect Powertrain Control Module (PCM) 104-pin connector located in right side of engine compartment, on fenderwell. Inspect connector for loose, damaged or corroded terminals. If connector is damaged, repair as necessary. If connector is okay, go to next step.

2) Measure resistance of Tan/Orange wire between terminal No. 16 at PCM connector and terminal No. 2 at DLC. *See Figs. 2 and 9.* Also, measure resistance of Pink/Light Blue wire between terminal No. 15 at PCM connector and terminal No. 10 at DLC. If either resistance reading is 5 ohms or more, go to next step. If both resistance readings are less than 5 ohms, replace PCM.

3) Disconnect Black 40-pin connector C158 located in left rear corner of engine compartment, on firewall. Inspect connector for loose, damaged or corroded terminals. If connector is damaged, repair as necessary. If connector is okay, go to next step.

4) Measure resistance of Tan/Orange wire between terminal No. 25 at female half of connector C158 and terminal No. 2 at DLC. *See Figs. 2 and 4.* Also, measure resistance of Pink/Light Blue wire between terminal No. 29 at female half of connector C158 and terminal No. 10 at DLC. If either resistance reading is 5 ohms or more, repair open in Tan/Orange wire and/or Pink/Light Blue wire between female half of connector C158 and DLC. If both resistance readings are less than 5 ohms, repair open in Tan/Orange wire and/or Pink/Light Blue wire between male half of connector C158 and PCM.

TEST F: NATURAL GAS VEHICLE (NGV) MODULE DOES NOT RESPOND TO NGS TESTER

1) Turn ignition switch to OFF position. Disconnect NGV module 60-pin connector located in front of engine compartment, near hood latch assembly. Inspect connector for loose, damaged or corroded terminals. If connector is damaged, repair as necessary. If connector is okay, go to next step.

2) Measure resistance of Tan/Orange wire between terminal No. 19 at NGV module connector and terminal No. 2 at DLC. *See Figs. 2 and 10.* Also, measure resistance of Pink/Light Blue wire between terminal No. 18 at NGV module connector and terminal No. 10 at DLC. If either resistance reading is 5 ohms or more, go to next step. If both resistance readings are less than 5 ohms, replace NGV module.

3) Disconnect Black 40-pin connector C158 located in left rear corner of engine compartment, on firewall. Inspect connector for loose, damaged or corroded terminals. If connector is damaged, repair as necessary. If connector is okay, go to next step.

4) Measure resistance of Tan/Orange wire between terminal No. 25 at female half of connector C158 and terminal No. 2 at DLC. *See Figs. 2 and 4.* Also, measure resistance of Pink/Light Blue wire between terminal No. 29 at female half of connector C158 and terminal No. 10 at DLC. If either resistance reading is 5 ohms or more, repair open in Tan/Orange wire and/or Pink/Light Blue wire between female half of connector C158 and DLC. If both resistance readings are less than 5 ohms, repair open in Tan/Orange wire and/or Pink/Light Blue wire between male half of connector C158 and NGV module.

TEST G: NO MODULE/NETWORK COMMUNICATIONS – ISO 9141 LINK

NOTE: Depending on module configuration, with all modules connected and with ignition switch in RUN position or with engine running 2-3 volts may be present at Data Link Connector (DLC) terminal No. 7 (Light Blue/White wire). This is the International Standards Organization (ISO) 9141 diagnostic communications network circuit.

1) Turn ignition switch to OFF position. Inspect Data Link Connector (DLC) for connector for loose, damaged or corroded terminals. Pay particular attention to terminal No. 7 (Light Blue/White wire). If connector is damaged, repair as necessary. If connector is okay, go to next step.

2) Disconnect Generic Electronic Module (GEM)/Central Timer Module (CTM) 26-pin connector C239 located below driver's side of instrument panel, to left of steering column. *See Fig. 6.* Measure resistance of Light Blue/White wire between terminal No. 25 at GEM/CTM connector C239 and terminal No. 7 at DLC. *See Figs. 2 and 5.* If resistance is less than 5 ohms, go to next step. If resistance is 5 ohms or more, repair open in Light Blue/White wire between GEM/CTM connector C239 and DLC.

3) Turn ignition switch to ON position. Measure voltage between terminals No. 7 (Light Blue/White wire) and No. 4 (Black wire) at DLC. *See Fig. 2.* Also, measure voltage between terminals No. 7 (Light Blue/White wire) and No. 16 (Light Blue/White wire) at DLC. If either reading is zero volts, replace GEM/CTM. If either reading indicates voltage, reconnect GEM/CTM connector and proceed if follows:

- If vehicle is not equipped with a Remote Anti-Theft Personality (RAP) module or a 4WABS module, go to next step.
- If vehicle is equipped with a RAP module and/or a 4-Wheel Anti-Lock Brake System (4WABS) module, go to step **5)**.
- If vehicle is equipped with a 4WABS module only, go to step **7)**.

NOTE: ISO 9141 communication network (circuit No. 70) will not function if circuit No. 70 (Light Blue/White wire) is shorted to ground or voltage. Steps 4)-8) are used for locating a short in circuit No. 70.

4) Turn ignition switch to OFF position. Deactivate air bag system. See appropriate AIR BAG RESTRAINT SYSTEMS article. Disconnect Restraint Control Module (RCM) 26-pin connector C208 located behind

FORD
4-316

1999 ACCESSORIES & EQUIPMENT
Module Communications Network
F150 & F250 Light-Duty Pickup (Cont.)

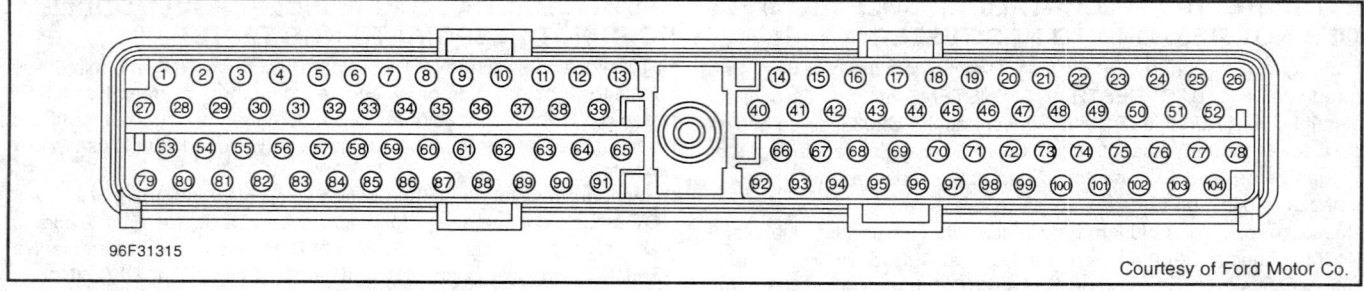

96F31315

Courtesy of Ford Motor Co.

Fig. 9: Identifying PCM Connector Terminals

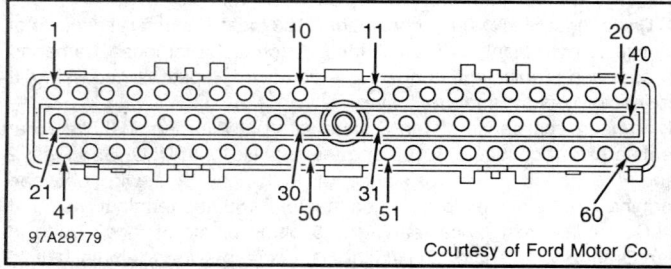

97A28779

Courtesy of Ford Motor Co.

Fig. 10: Identifying NGV Module Connector Terminals

right side of instrument panel. Turn ignition switch to ON position. Measure voltage between terminals No. 7 (Light Blue/White wire) and No. 4 (Black wire) at DLC. Also, measure voltage between terminals No. 7 (Light Blue/White wire) and No. 16 (Light Blue/White wire) at DLC. If both readings indicate zero volts, replace RCM. If either reading indicates voltage, repair Light Blue/White wire between DLC, GEM/CTM, RCM connector C208, connector C247 (if equipped with RAP module) and connector C160 (if equipped with 4WABS module).

5) Turn ignition switch to OFF position. Disconnect RAP module 26-pin connector C256 located behind driver's side of instrument panel, left of steering column. Turn ignition switch to ON position. Measure voltage between terminals No. 7 (Light Blue/White wire) and No. 4 (Black wire) at DLC. Also, measure voltage between terminals No. 7 (Light Blue/White wire) and No. 16 (Light Blue/White wire) at DLC. If both readings indicate zero volts, replace RAP module. If either reading indicates voltage, go to next step.

6) Turn ignition switch to OFF position. Disconnect 16-pin connector C247 located behind left side of instrument panel. *See Fig. 6.* Turn ignition switch to ON position. Measure voltage between terminals No. 7 (Light Blue/White wire) and No. 4 (Black wire) at DLC. Also, measure voltage between terminals No. 7 (Light Blue/White wire) and No. 16 (Light Blue/White wire) at DLC. If both readings indicate zero volts, repair Light Blue/White wire between male half of connector C247 and RAP module connector C256. If either reading indicates voltage, go to step **4)** for vehicles not equipped with 4WABS module or go to next step for vehicles equipped with 4WABS module.

7) Turn ignition switch to OFF position. Disconnect 4WABS module Black 24-pin connector C146 located at left front of engine compartment, on front of upper radiator support. Turn ignition switch to ON position. Measure voltage between terminals No. 7 (Light Blue/White wire) and No. 4 (Black wire) at DLC. Also, measure voltage between terminals No. 7 (Light Blue/White wire) and No. 16 (Light Blue/White wire) at DLC. If both readings indicate zero volts, replace 4WABS module. If either reading indicates voltage, go to next step.

8) Turn ignition switch to OFF position. Disconnect Gray 40-pin connector C160 located in left rear corner of engine compartment near firewall. Turn ignition switch to ON position. Measure voltage between terminals No. 7 (Light Blue/White wire) and No. 4 (Black wire) at DLC. Also, measure voltage between terminals No. 7 (Light Blue/White wire) and No. 16 (Light Blue/White wire) at DLC. If both readings indicate zero

volts, repair Light Blue/White wire between male half of connector C160 and 4WABS module connector. If either reading indicates voltage, go to step **4)**.

TEST H: NO MODULE/NETWORK COMMUNICATION – BUS LINK

NOTE: Depending on module configuration, with all modules connected and with ignition switch in RUN position or with engine running 2-3 volts may be present at Data Link Connector (DLC) terminals No. 2 (Tan/Orange wire) and No. 10 (Pink/Light Blue wire). These are the Standard Corporate Protocol (SCP) diagnostic communications network circuits.

1) Turn ignition switch to OFF position. Inspect Next Generation Star (NGS) tester connector for loose, damaged or corroded terminals. Pay particular attention to terminals No. 2 and 10. If connector is damaged, repair as necessary. If connector is okay, go to next step.

2) Inspect Data Link Connector (DLC) for loose, damaged or corroded terminals. Pay particular attention to terminals No. 2 (Tan/Orange wire) and No. 10 (Pink/Light Blue wire). *See Fig. 2.* If connector is damaged, repair as necessary. If connector is okay, go to next step.

3) Disconnect Powertrain Control Module (PCM) 104-pin connector located in right side of engine compartment, on fenderwell. Measure resistance of Tan/Orange wire between terminal No. 16 at PCM connector and terminal No. 2 at DLC. *See Figs. 2 and 9.* Also, measure resistance of Pink/Light Blue wire between terminal No. 15 at PCM connector and terminal No. 10 at DLC. If both resistance readings are less than 5 ohms, go to next step for vehicles without natural gas module or go to step **5)** for vehicles with natural gas module. If either resistance reading is 5 ohms or more, repair Tan/Orange wire between wiring harness splice S157 and DLC and/or repair Pink/Light Blue wire between wiring harness splice S156 and DLC.

4) Turn ignition switch to ON position. Measure voltage between terminals No. 2 (Tan/Orange wire) and No. 4 (Black wire) at DLC. Measure voltage between terminals No. 2 (Tan/Orange wire) and No. 16 (Light Green/Red wire) at DLC. Measure voltage between terminals No. 10 (Pink/Light Blue wire) and No. 4 (Black wire) at DLC. Measure voltage between terminals No. 10 (Pink/Light Blue wire) and No. 16 (Light Green/Red wire) at DLC. If all readings indicate zero volts, replace PCM. If any reading indicates voltage, go to step **6)**.

5) Turn ignition switch to OFF position. Disconnect Natural Gas Vehicle (NGV) module 60-pin connector located in front of engine compartment, near hood latch assembly. Turn ignition switch to ON position. Measure voltage between terminals No. 2 (Tan/Orange wire) and No. 4 (Black wire) at DLC. Measure voltage between terminals No. 2 (Tan/Orange wire) and No. 16 (Light Green/Red wire) at DLC. Measure voltage between terminals No. 10 (Pink/Light Blue wire) and No. 4 (Black wire) at DLC. Measure voltage between terminals No. 10 (Pink/Light Blue wire) and No. 16 (Light Green/Red wire) at DLC. If all readings indicate zero volts, replace NGV module. If any reading indicates voltage, go to step **4)**.

6) Turn ignition switch to OFF position. Disconnect Black 40-pin connector C158 located in left rear corner of engine compartment, on firewall. Turn ignition switch to ON position. Measure voltage between

1999 ACCESSORIES & EQUIPMENT
Module Communications Network
F150 & F250 Light-Duty Pickup (Cont.)

FORD
4-317

terminals No. 2 (Tan/Orange wire) and No. 4 (Black wire) at DLC. Measure voltage between terminals No. 2 (Tan/Orange wire) and No. 16 (Light Green/Red wire) at DLC. Measure voltage between terminals No. 10 (Pink/Light Blue wire) and No. 4 (Black wire) at DLC. Measure voltage between terminals No. 10 (Pink/Light Blue wire) and No. 16 (Light Green/Red wire) at DLC. If all readings indicate zero volts, repair Tan/Orange wire and/or Pink/Light Blue wire between male half of connector C158 and PCM. If any reading indicates voltage, repair Tan/Orange wire and/or Pink/Light Blue wire between female half of connector C158 and DLC.

TEST I: INSTRUMENT CLUSTER (HEC) MODULE DOES NOT RESPOND TO NGS TESTER

1) Turn ignition switch to OFF position. Disconnect instrument cluster White 22-pin connector C237. Inspect connector for damage. If connector is damaged, repair as necessary. If connector is okay, go to next step.

2) Measure resistance between instrument cluster harness connector C237 terminal No. 1 (Tan/Orange wire) and DLC connector terminal No. 2 (Tan/Orange wire). Also, measure resistance between instrument cluster harness connector C237 terminal No. 2 (Pink/Light Blue wire) and DLC connector terminal No. 10 (Pink/Light Blue wire). *See Figs. 2 and 11.* If both resistances are less than 5 ohms, replace instrument cluster. If either resistance is 5 ohms or more, repair Tan/Orange wire and/or Pink/Light Blue wire between instrument cluster connector C237 and DLC.

TEST J: NO MODULE/NETWORK COMMUNICATION

1) Turn ignition switch to OFF position. Inspect Next Generation Star (NGS) tester connector for loose, damaged or corroded terminals. If connector is damaged, repair as necessary. If connector is okay, go to next step.

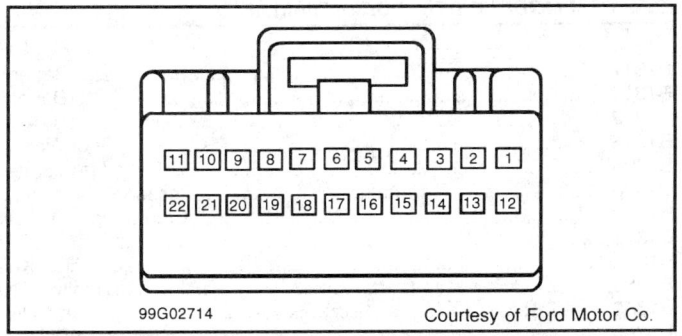

99G02714   Courtesy of Ford Motor Co.

Fig. 11: Identifying Instrument Cluster 22-Pin Connector C237 Terminals

2) Inspect Data Link Connector (DLC) for physical damage, bent terminals or corrosion. If connector is damaged, repair as necessary. If connector is okay, go to next step.

3) Remove and inspect fuse No. 3 (20-amp) from Central Junction Box (CJB). If fuse is okay, reinstall fuse and go to next step. If fuse is blown, check for short to ground in Light Blue/White wire between CJB and DLC and replace fuse No. 3.

4) Measure voltage between ground and terminal No. 16 (Light Blue/White wire) at DLC. *See Fig. 2.* If voltage is more than 10 volts, go to next step. If voltage is 10 volts or less, repair open in Light Blue/White wire between CJB and DLC.

5) Measure resistance between ground and terminals No. 4 (Black wire) and No. 5 (Black/White wire) at DLC. If both resistance readings are less than 5 ohms, repair or replace NGS tester. If either resistance reading is 5 ohms or more, repair open in Black wire or Black/White wire between ground and DLC.

DIAGNOSTIC TROUBLE CODE (DTC) DEFINITIONS

ANTI-LOCK BRAKE SYSTEM MODULE DTC INDEX

DTC	Description	Test
B1342	ECU Defective	1
C1095/C1096	ABS Hydraulic Pump Motor Circuit Failure	2
C1113/C1115	Internal Power Relay	2
C1145	Right Front ABS Sensor (Electrical/Static)	2
C1148/C1234	Right Front ABS Sensor (Dynamic)	2
C1155	Left Front ABS Sensor (Electrical/Static)	2
C1158/C1233	Left Front ABS Sensor (Dynamic)	2
C1169	Excessive Dump Time	2
C1175	Left Rear ABS Sensor Input Circuit Failure	2
C1184	ABS System Time-out	2
C1185	Open Internal Power Relay	2
C1194/C1196	Left Front Dump valve	2
C1198/C1200	Left Front Isolation Valve	2
C1202/C1204	Rear Dump Valve	2
C1206/C1208	Rear Isolation Valve	2
C1210/C1212	Right Front Dump Valve	2
C1214/C1216	Right Front Isolation Valve	2
C1220	Yellow ABS Warning Indicator Failure	2
C1222	Wheel Speed Error (Dynamic)	2
C1229/C1237	Rear ABS Sensor (Dynamic)	2
C1230	Rear ABS Sensor (Electrical/Static)	2

[1] – Using NGS tester, retrieve and document all continuous DTCs. Perform Anti-Lock Brake System (ABS) module self-test. If DTC B1342 is retrieved again, replace ABS module.

[2] – Repair anti-lock brake system concern. See appropriate ANTI-LOCK article in BRAKES in appropriate MITCHELL® manual.

GEM/CTM MODULE DTC INDEX

DTC	Description	Test
B1302	Accessory Delay Relay Coil Circuit Failure	1
B1304	Accessory Delay Relay Coil Circuit Short To Voltage	1
B1313	Battery Saver Relay Coil Circuit Failure	2
B1315	Battery Saver Relay Coil Circuit Short To Voltage	2

FORD
4-318

1999 ACCESSORIES & EQUIPMENT
Module Communications Network
F150 & F250 Light-Duty Pickup (Cont.)

GEM/CTM MODULE DTC INDEX (Cont.)

DTC	Description	Test
B1317	Battery Voltage High	3
B1318	Battery Voltage Low	3
B1322	Driver's Door Ajar Circuit Short To Ground	2
B1323	Door Ajar Lamp Circuit Failure	4
B1325	Door Ajar Lamp Circuit Short To Voltage	4
B1330	Passenger's Door Ajar Circuit Short To Ground	2
B1340	Chime Input Request Circuit Short To Ground	6
B1342	ECU Defective	7
B1352	Ignition Key-In Circuit Failure	9
B1355	Ignition RUN Circuit Failure	9
B1359	Ignition RUN/ACC Circuit Failure	9
B1365	Ignition START Circuit Short To Voltage	9
B1371	Illuminated Entry Relay Circuit Failure	2
B1373	Illuminated Entry Relay Short To Voltage	2
B1398	Driver's Power Window One-Touch Window Relay Circuit Failure	1
B1400	Driver's Power Window One-Touch Window Relay Circuit Short To Voltage	1
B1405	Driver's Power Window Down Short To Voltage	1
B1410	Driver's Power Window Motor Circuit Failure	1
B1426	Lamp Safety Belt Circuit Short To Voltage	4
B1428	Lamp Safety Belt Circuit Failure	4
B1431	Wiper Brake/Run Relay Circuit Failure	5
B1432	Wiper Brake/Run Relay Circuit Short To Voltage	5
B1434	Wiper Hi/Low Speed Relay Coil Circuit Failure	5
B1436	Wiper Hi/Low Speed Relay Circuit Short To Voltage	5
B1438	Wiper Mode Select Switch Circuit Failure	5
B1441	Wiper Mode Select Switch Circuit Short To Ground	5
B1446	Wiper Park Sense Circuit Failure	5
B1450	Wiper Wash/Delay Switch Circuit Failure	5
B1453	Wiper Wash/Delay Switch Circuit Short To Ground	5
B1458	Wiper Washer Pump Motor Relay Circuit Failure	5
B1460	Wiper Washer Pump Motor Relay Coil Circuit Short To Voltage	5
B1462	Safety Belt Switch Circuit Failure	6
B1466	Wiper Hi/Low Speed Not Switching	5
B1467	Wiper Hi/Low Speed Circuit Motor Short To Voltage	5
B1473	Wiper Low Speed Circuit Motor Failure	5
B1476	Wiper High Speed Circuit Motor Failure	5
B1483	Brake Pedal Input Circuit Failure	8
B1485	Brake Pedal Input Circuit Short To Voltage	8
B1577	Parking Light Input Circuit Short To Voltage	6
B1610	Illuminated Entry Input Short Circuit To Ground	2
B1840	Wiper Front Power Circuit Failure	5

[1] – See appropriate POWER WINDOWS article for testing procedure.

[2] – See appropriate AUTOLAMP SYSTEMS article for testing procedure.

[3] – Check charging system. See appropriate GENERATORS article in STARTING & CHARGING SYSTEMS. If charging system is okay, check power and ground circuits to GEM/CTM. See appropriate wiring diagram in POWER DISTRIBUTION article in WIRING DIAGRAMS.

[4] – See appropriate INSTRUMENT PANELS article for testing procedure.

[5] – See appropriate WIPER/WASHER SYSTEMS article for testing procedure.

[6] – Repair appropriate circuit. See appropriate wiring diagram in WARNING SYSTEMS article.

[7] – Using NGS tester, retrieve and document all continuous DTCs. Perform GEM/CTM self-test. If DTC B1342 is retrieved again, replace GEM/CTM.

[8] – See appropriate TRANSFER CASE ELECTRONIC CONTROLS article in TRANSMISSIONS in appropriate MITCHELL® TRANSMISSION SERVICE & REPAIR manual for testing procedure.

[9] – See appropriate STEERING COLUMN SWITCHES article for testing procedure.

INSTRUMENT CLUSTER DTC TEST INDEX

DTC	Description	Test
B1202	Fuel Sender Open	1
B1204	Fuel Sender Short To Ground	1
B1213	Anti-Theft Number Of Programmed Keys Below Minimum	2
B1317	Battery Voltage High	3
B1318	Battery Voltage Low	3
B1342	ECU Defective	4
B1356	Ignition RUN Circuit Open	5
B1364	Ignition START Circuit Open	5
B1600	PATS Ignition Key Transponder Signal Not Received	2
B1604	PATS Received Incorrect Key Code	2
B1602	PATS Received Invalid Key Code Format	2
B1681	PATS Transceiver Signal Not Received	2

1999 ACCESSORIES & EQUIPMENT
Module Communications Network
F150 & F250 Light-Duty Pickup (Cont.)

FORD
4-319

INSTRUMENT CLUSTER DTC TEST INDEX (Cont.)

DTC	Description	Test
B1232	Antenna Not Connected Or Damaged Transceiver	2
B2103	Antenna Not Connected Or Defective Transceiver	2
B2139	PCM ID Mismatch Between PCM & HEC	2
B2141	NVM Configuration Failure	2
B2143	Odometer NVM Memory Failure	6
C1284	Oil Pressure Switch Failure	1
P1197	SELECT/RESET Switch Circuit Failure	6
U1011	SCP Invalid Or Missing Data For Engine Air Intake	7
U1027	SCP Invalid Or Missing Data For Engine RPM	7
U1041	SCP Invalid Or Missing Data For Vehicle Speed	7
U1073	SCP Invalid Or Missing Data For Engine Coolant	7
U1123	SCP Invalid Or Missing Data For Odometer	7
U1131	SCP Invalid Or Missing Data For Fuel System	7
U1147	SCP Invalid Or Missing Data For Vehicle Security For Vehicle Security	2
U1148	SCP Invalid Or Missing Data for audio Control	7
U1262	Missing SCP Message	8

[1] – See appropriate ANALOG INSTRUMENT PANELS article for testing procedure.
[2] – See appropriate PASSIVE ANTI-THEFT SYSTEMS article for testing procedure.
[3] – Check charging system. See appropriate GENERATORS article in STARTING & CHARGING SYSTEMS. If charging system is okay, check power and ground circuits to instrument cluster. See appropriate wiring diagram in POWER DISTRIBUTION article in WIRING DIAGRAMS.
[4] – Using NGS tester, retrieve and document all continuous DTCs. Perform instrument cluster self-test. If DTC B1342 is retrieved again, replace instrument cluster.
[5] – See appropriate STEERING COLUMN SWITCHES article for testing procedures and appropriate wiring diagram in POWER DISTRIBUTION article in WIRING DIAGRAMS.
[6] – Replace instrument cluster. Clear DTCs and retest system.
[7] – Using NGS tester, perform PCM self-test.
[8] – Perform TEST H: NO MODULE/NETWORK COMMUNICATION – BUS LINK under SYSTEM TESTS.

NATURAL GAS VEHICLE MODULE DTC INDEX

DTC	Description	Test
B1219	Fuel Tank Pressure Sensor Circuit Failure	1
B1220	Fuel Tank Pressure Sensor Circuit Short To Voltage	1
B1222	Fuel Tank Temperature Sensor Circuit Failure	1
B1223	Fuel Tank Temperature Sensor Circuit Open	1
B1224	Fuel Tank Temperature Sensor Circuit Short To Voltage	1
B1225	Fuel Tank Temperature Sensor Circuit Short To Ground	1
B1317	Battery Voltage High	1
B1318	Battery Voltage Low	1
B1342	ECU Defective	1

[1] – See appropriate ANALOG INSTRUMENT PANELS article for testing procedure.

PASSIVE ANTI-THEFT SYSTEM (PATS) DTC INDEX

DTC	Description	Test
B1202	Fuel Sender Open	1
B1204	Fuel Sender Short To Ground	1
B1213	Anti-Theft Number Of Programmed Keys Is Below Minimum	1
B1232	Antenna Not Connected Or Defective Transceiver	1
B1317	Battery Voltage High	2
B1318	Battery Voltage Low	2
B1342	ECU Defective	3
B1356	Ignition RUN Circuit Open	4
B1364	Ignition START Circuit Open	4
B1600	No Key Code Received/Damaged Encoded Ignition Key Or Use Of Non-PATS Key	1
B1601	Incorrect Key Code From Ignition Key Transponder	1
B1602	Invalid Key Code Format From Ignition Key Transponder	1
B1681	Transceiver Defective Or Not Connected	1
B2103/B1232	PATS Antenna Not Connected	1
B2139	PCM ID Does Not Match Between Instrument Cluster & PCM	1
B2141	No PCM ID Exchange Between Instrument Cluster & PCM	1
B2143	Odometer NVM Memory Failure	1
C1284	Oil Pressure Switch Failure	1
U1147	Invalid Or Missing Vehicle Security Data	1

[1] – Repair anti-theft system concern. See appropriate PASSIVE ANTI-THEFT SYSTEMS article for testing procedure.
[2] – Check charging system. See appropriate GENERATORS article in STARTING & CHARGING SYSTEMS. If charging system is okay, check power and ground circuits to PATS module. See appropriate wiring diagram in POWER DISTRIBUTION article in WIRING DIAGRAMS.

FORD
4-320

1999 ACCESSORIES & EQUIPMENT
Module Communications Network
F150 & F250 Light-Duty Pickup (Cont.)

PASSIVE ANTI-THEFT SYSTEM (PATS) DTC INDEX (Cont.)

[3] – Using NGS tester, retrieve and document all continuous DTCs. Perform Passive Anti-Theft System (PATS) module self-test. If DTC B1342 is retrieved again, replace PATS module.
[4] – Repair steering column switch concern. See appropriate STEERING COLUMN SWITCHES article for testing procedure.

REMOTE ANTI-THEFT PERSONALITY (RAP) MODULE DTC INDEX

DTC	Description	Test
B1309	Door Lock Circuit Short To Ground	1
B1341	Door Unlock Circuit Short To Ground	1
B1485	Brake Pedal Input Circuit Short To Voltage	1
B1562	Door Lock Cylinder Circuit Short To Ground	2
B1629	PRNDL Reverse Input Short To Voltage	1
B1845	Ignition Tamper Circuit Failure	3
B2425	Remote Keyless Entry Out Of Synchronization	1

[1] – Repair remote keyless entry system concern. See appropriate wiring diagram in REMOTE KEYLESS ENTRY SYSTEMS article.
[2] – Repair power door lock concern. See appropriate wiring diagram in POWER DOOR LOCKS article.
[3] – Repair ignition switch concern. See appropriate PASSIVE ANTI-THEFT SYSTEMS article.

RESTRAINTS CONTROL MODULE (RCM) DTC INDEX

DTC [1]	Description	Test
B1342	ECU Defective	2
B1231	RCM Crash Data Memory Full	3
B1921	RCM Bracket Ground Resistance High	3
C1414	Incorrect Vehicle Identification Code	3
B1887	Driver's Air Bag Circuit Shorted To Ground	3
B1916	Driver's Air Bag Circuit Shorted To Voltage	3
B1888	Passenger's Air Bag Circuit Short To Ground	3
B1925	Passenger's Air Bag Circuit Short To Voltage	3
B1932	Driver's Air Bag Circuit Resistance High	3
B1933	Passenger's Air Bag Circuit Resistance High	3
B1934	Driver's Air Bag Circuit Resistance Low	3
B1935	Passenger's Air Bag Circuit Resistance Low	3
B1871	Passenger's Air Bag Deactivation (PAD) Switch Fault	3
B1884	Passenger's Air Bag Deactivation (PAD) Warning Lamp Inoperative	3
B1890	Passenger's Air Bag Deactivation (PAD) Warning Lamp Short To Voltage	3
B1892	Air Bag Tone Warning Indicator Circuit Shorted To Ground Or Open	3
B1891	Air Bag Tone Warning Indicator Circuit Shorted To Voltage	3
B1869	Air Bag Indicator Inoperative	3
B1870	Air Bag Indicator Shorted To Voltage	3

[1] – DTCs are listed in order of importance. Repair DTCs in order listed.
[2] – Using NGS tester, retrieve and document all continuous DTCs. Perform Restraints Control Module (RCM) self-test. If DTC B1342 is retrieved again, replace RCM.
[3] – Repair air bag system concern. See DIAGNOSIS & TESTING article in appropriate MITCHELL® AIR BAG SERVICE & REPAIR MANUAL, DOMESTIC & IMPORTED MODELS.

PARAMETER IDENTIFICATION (PID) DEFINITIONS

ANTI-LOCK BRAKE SYSTEM PID INDEX

PID	Description	Expected Value
4WDABS	4Wheel Drive Input Switch	2WD-4WD
ABSLAMP	ABS Warning Lamp State	ON, OFF
BRK_LVL	Brake Fluid Level	OK, NOTOK
PWR_RLY	Power Relay Feedback Input	ON, OFF
CCNTABS	Number Of Continuous DTCs	Number Of DTCs
BOO_ABS	Brake Pedal Position Switch Input	ON, OFF
TRAC_SW	Traction Control Disable Switch	N/A
TRACACT	Traction Control Active Indicator Lamp	N/A
TRACOFF	Traction Control OFF Indicator Lamp	1/128
ABSR_O	Rear ABS Outlet Valve	ON, OFF
ABSRF_O	Right Front ABS Outlet Valve	ON, OFF
ABSLF_O	Left Front ABS Outlet Valve	ON, OFF
ABSRF_I	Right Front ABS Inlet Valve	ON, OFF
ABSLF_I	Left Front ABS Inlet Valve	ON, OFF
ABSR_I	Rear ABS Inlet Valve	ON, OFF
ABSLR_I	Left Rear ABS Inlet Valve	ON, OFF
LF_WSPD	Left Front Wheel Speed Signal	0-255 KPH
RF_WSPD	Right Front Wheel Speed Signal	0-255 KPH
R_WSPD	Rear Wheel Speed Signal	0-255 KPH

1999 ACCESSORIES & EQUIPMENT
Module Communications Network
F150 & F250 Light-Duty Pickup (Cont.)

FORD
4-321

GEM/CTM MODULE PID INDEX

PID	Description	Expected Value
2WDSOL	2 Wheel Drive Solenoid Status	[1]
4WD_SW	4 WD Input Switch	[2]
4WDDELCL	4WD Electronic Clutch Output	[1]
4WDHIGH	4WD-Wheel High Output State	[1]
4WDSOL	4Wheel Drive Solenoid Status	[1]
ACCDLY	Accessory Delay Relay Circuit	[1]
BATSAV	Battery Saver Relay Circuit	[1]
BOO	Brake Switch Input	ON, OFF
CCNT	Number Of Continuous DTCs	Number Of DTCs
CHIMERQ	Chime Request	ON, OFF
CLTCHSW	Trans. Clutch Interlock Sw.	NOTEGD, ENGAGD
D_DN_SW	Driver's Window Down Switch	ON, OFF
D_DOOR	Left Front Door Ajar Switch	CLOSED, AJAR
D_PWAMP	Driver's Power Window Motor Current	AMP
D_PWPK	Driver's Power Window Peak Current	AMP
D_PWRLY	Driver's Power Window	[1]
D_SBELT	Driver's Seat Belt	IN, OUT
DRAJR_L	Door Ajar Warning Lamp Circuit	[1]
IGN_A	Ignition Switch (ACC Position)	YES, NO
IGN_KEY	Ignition Key In/Out	IN, OUT
IGN_O/L	Ignition Switch (OFF/Lock Position)	YES, NO
IGN_R	Ignition Switch (RUN Position)	YES, NO
IGN_S	Ignition Switch (START Position)	YES, NO
INTLMP	Illumination Entry Relay Circuit	[1]
MTR_CCW	Trans. Xfer Counter Cw Motor Output	[1]
MTR_CW	Trans. Xfer Clockwise Motor Output	[1]
NTRL_SW	Neutral Safety Switch Input	NOTNTL, NTRL
OTD_SW	One Touch Down Switch	DOWN, OFF
OVERSPD	Vehicle Overspeed Warning Status	DISABL, ENABLE
P_DOOR	Passenger's Door Ajar Switch	CLOSED, AJAR
PARK_SW	Parking Switch	ON, OFF
PLATE_A	Trans. Xfer Case Contact Plate A	OPEN, CLOSED
PLATE_B	Trans. Xfer Case Contact Plate B	OPEN, CLOSED
PLATE_C	Trans. Xfer Case Contact Plate C	OPEN, CLOSED
PLATE_D	Trans. Xfer Case Contact Plate D	OPEN, CLOSED
PLATEPW	Trans. Xfer Case Contact Plt Pul Wid	[1]
SBLTLMP	Seat Belt Lamp Circuit	[1]
SPEEDWP	Speed Dependent Wiper Function	NOTACT, ACTIVE
VSS	Vehicle Speed	KPH
VSS	Vehicle Speed Low Resolution (MPH)	MPH
WASH_SW	Washer Pump Switch	ON, OFF
WASHRLY	Washer Pump Relay Circuit	[1]
WPHISP	Wiper 2 Speed Relay	[1]
WPMODE	Wiper Control Mode Select	[3]
WPPK_PK	Wiper Park-To-Park Time	mS
WPPRKSW	Windshield Wiper Park Sense	NOTPRK, PARKED
WPRUN	Wiper Run Relay Driver State	[1]
VBAT	Battery Voltage	Voltage Range

[1] – Expected values shold be Off- - -, OffO-G, On- - - or On-B-.
[2] – Expected values should be 2WD, 4WDLOW, 4WDHGH, OPEN or GSHORT
[3] – Expected values should be WASH, OPEN, OFF, INTVL1, INTVL2, INTVL3, INTVL4, INTVL5, INTVL6, INTVL7, LOW, HIGH or ?.

INSTRUMENT CLUSTER PID INDEX

PID	Description	Expected Value
CCNT_ICM	Number Of Continuous DTCs	Number Of DTCs
SPARE_KY	Spare Keys	DISABL, ENABLE
PCM_VFY	PCM ID Matches Between PCM & HEC	YES, NO
NUMKEYS	No. Of Ignition Key Codes Programmed	0-8 BCD
M_KEY	Master Key Present	NOTPRE, PRESNT
ANTISCN	Anti-Scan Function	DISABL, ENABLE
ENABLE_S	Has PATS Enabled The Vehicle	DISABL, ENABLE
PCM_ID	PCM ID	NOTSTR, STORED
VBAT_EC	System Battery Voltage Potential	OK, NOTOK
GAUGESG_EC	Fuel Level Status	OK, NOTOK
IGN_O/L	Ignition Switch- OFF/Lock Position	YES, NO
IGN_R	Ignition Switch- RUN Position	YES, NO
IGN_S	Ignition Switch- START Position	YES, NO
ODOMETR	Vehicle Odometer-English	Number Of Miles

1999 ACCESSORIES & EQUIPMENT
Module Communications Network
F150 & F250 Light-Duty Pickup (Cont.)

INSTRUMENT CLUSTER PID INDEX (Cont.)

PID	Description	Expected Value
OIL_PSW	Oil Pressure Switch Count	One Count Per Bit
PANLDIM	Panel Dim Intensity Switch	0-100%
OD_CODE_CNT	No. Of DTCs Set Due To Diagnostic Test	One Count Per Bit
RESETSW	Select/Reset Switch	ON, OFF
PWM_DC1	PWM Duty Cycle #1	0-100%

NATURAL GAS VEHICLE MODULE PID INDEX

PID	Description	Expected Value
CCNTF1	Number Of Continuous DTCs	Number Of DTCs
TANKPR	Fuel Tank Pressure Sensor	0-4000 psi
TEMPS1	Fuel Tank Temperature Sensor No. 1 Input	-40-302°F
VBAT_FI	Battery Voltage	0-16 Volts DC
GAUGESG	Instrument Cluster Fuel Gauge Drive Signal	0-4000 mV
GAUGECM	Fuel Gauge Command Position	1

[1] – Fuel gauge position in 16ths. 2 equals empty and 18 equals full.

PASSIVE ANTI-THEFT SYSTEM MODULE PID INDEX

PID	Description	Expected Value
ACCESS	Security Access	CODE, TIMED
ANTISCN	Anti-Scan Function	DISABL, ENABLE
CCNTPAT	Number Of Continuous DTCs	Number Of DTCs
ENABL_S	Vehicle Enable Status	DISABL, ENABLE
IGN_R	Ignition Switch (RUN Position)	IN, OUT
M_KEY	Master Key Present	IN, OUT
MIN#KEY	Number Of Keys	One Bit Per Count
NUMKEYS	Number Of Keys Stored	One Bit Per Count
PCM_ID	PCM ID Status Stored	NOTSTR, STORED
PCM_VFY	PCM Verify Okay	YES, ON
SPAREKY	Spare Key Programming	DISABL, ENABLE
SERVMOD	Service Module	YES, ON

REMOTE ANTI-THEFT PERSONALITY (RAP) MODULE PID INDEX

PID	Description	Expected Value
AL_EVT#	Last 8 Alarm Events	1
BOO_RAP	Brake Switch Input	OFF, ON
DOORRAP	Door Ajar Status Input From GEM	AJAR, CLOSED
DR_DARM	Door Disarm Input	NOTACT, ACTIVE
IGN_A	Ignition Switch (ACCY Position)	NO, YES
IGN_R	Ignition Switch (RUN Position)	NO, YES
IGN_RES	Ignition Tamper Sensor	2
DD_LOCK	Power Door Lock/Unlock Status	OFF, LOCK, UNLOCK, SHORT
NOTHEFT	Theft Only State	NO, YES
NOREMOT	Remote Only Input State	NO, YES
TRANSGR	Transmission Gear	NOTREV, REV

[1] – Expected values should be No_EVNT, DR OPEN, PANIC or IGNTAMP.
[2] – Expected values should be 162 OHM, 0 OHM or HIGH OHM.

RESTRAINTS CONTROL MODULE (RCM) PID INDEX

PID	Description	Expected Value
CCNT	Number Of Continuous DTCs	Number Of DTCs
D_ABAGR	Driver's Air Bag Module Resistance	1.7-4.1 Ohms
P_ABAGR	Passenger's Air Bag Circuit Resistance	1.7-3.2 Ohms
BRACKET	Bracket Ground Resistance	Less Than 100 Ohms
VBAT	System Battery Voltage At RCM	9.0-16.0 Volts
VID #1	Program Vehicle ID Pin 10	N/A
VID #2	Program Vehicle ID Pin 13	N/A
VID #3	Program Vehicle ID Pin 14	N/A

WIRING DIAGRAMS

NOTE: See appropriate wiring diagrams in DATA LINK CONNECTORS, GROUND DISTRIBUTION or POWER DISTRIBUTION article in WIRING DIAGRAMS.

NOTE: This article includes Cab & Chassis.

DESCRIPTION & OPERATION

NOTE: Electronic Crash Sensor (ECS) module may also be referred to as air bag diagnostic module, air bag diagnostic monitor or Restraints Control Module (RCM).

Vehicle has 2 module communications networks. Both networks can be accessed by New Generation Star (NGS) tester through the Data Link Connector (DLC). Standard Corporate Protocol (SCP) network consists of Powertrain Control Module (PCM) and, if equipped, Auxiliary Powertrain Control Module (APCM) interconnected by a pair of twisted wires (data BUS plus and data BUS minus). SCP network allows intermodule communication. SCP network is robust and will continue to function even if one BUS wire is open, shorted to ground or shorted to power.

International Standards Organization (ISO) 9141 network consists of Electronic Crash Sensor (ECS) module, Generic Electronic Module (GEM), Overhead Trip Computer (OTC) and 4-wheel anti-lock brake system module, or rear wheel anti-lock brake system module. GEM controls windshield wipers, courtesy lights, 4-wheel shift on the fly and one-touch down power windows. These modules are interconnected by a single wire. If Light Blue/White wire is shorted to ground, or power, ISO 9141 network will fail. ISO 9141 network does not permit intermodule communication.

COMPONENT LOCATIONS

COMPONENT LOCATIONS

Component	Location
Anti-Lock Brake Module	Left Front Engine Compartment, Near Air Cleaner
Electronic Crash Sensor (ECS) Module	Behind Center Of Instrument Panel
Auxiliary Powertrain Control Module (APCM)	Behind Lower Right Hand Side Of Instrument Panel
Data Link Connector (DLC)	Behind Center Bottom Of Instrument Panel
Generic Electronic Module (GEM)	Lower Left Hand Side Of Instrument Panel
Overhead Trip Computer (OTC)	Front Center Of Headliner
Powertrain Control Module (PCM)	Behind Left Wheel Well Apron

REPAIRING NETWORK COMMUNICATIONS WIRING

NOTE: Following procedure must be used to ensure proper repair is performed on network communications wiring. Network communications wiring is sensitive to moisture and oxidation and must be properly sealed to ensure proper operation of the module communications network. Regular heat shrink tubing is NOT sufficient, heat shrink tubing containing hot melt glue is required.

NOTE: When performing a repair on Standard Corporate Protocol (SCP) network, ensure the BUS wires are twisted at a rate of 33-40 winds per 3.3 ft. (1 m). The twists should start within approximately 4.9" (124 mm) from any connector. Use only 20 AWG standard wire gauge for repairs.

1) Disconnect battery ground cable. Strip .75" (19.0 mm) of insulation from one wire and 1.50" (38.1 mm) of insulator from the other wire. Perform STEP 1. See Fig. 1. Place hot melt glue type heat shrink tubing over one wire.

2) Twist stripped portion of the wires together. Solder connection using rosin core mildly activated (RMA) solder. DO NOT use acid core solder. Bend wires to allow installation of heat shrink tubing. Perform STEP 2. See Fig. 1.

3) Position heat shrink tubing over splice area. Using heat gun, evenly heat the heat shrink tubing until glue flows from both ends of heat shrink tubing.

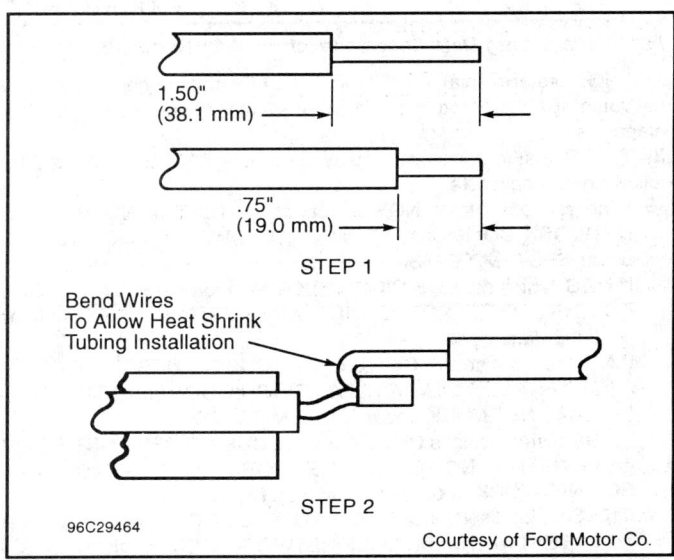

Fig. 1: Repairing Module Communications Network Wiring

COMMUNICATION NETWORK DIAGNOSTICS

NOTE: When performing Generic Electronic Module (GEM) self-test, vehicles built prior to February 5, 1998 must have power windows completely up and headlights and parking lights off. Failure to do so will result in DTCs B1577 and B2357 being set. Vehicles built after February 5, 1998 must have headlights and parking lights on. Failure to do so will result in B1575 being set.

INSPECTION & VERIFICATION

1) Verify customer complaint by operating system in question. Inspect vehicle for any obvious electrical component wiring or connector damage. Inspect connectors for loose, damaged or corroded terminals. Check fuse junction panel fuse No. 3 (20-amp) and fuses related to system in question.

2) If problem is still present after performing inspection, connect New Generation Star (NGS) tester to DLC. Select vehicle to be tested from NGS tester menu. If NGS tester does not communicate with vehicle, ensure program card is properly installed. Check NGS tester cable connections and ensure ignition switch is in RUN position. If NGS tester still does not communicate with vehicle, go to TEST J: NO MODULE/ NETWORK COMMUNICATION – NO POWER TO NGS TESTER under SYSTEM TESTS. If NGS tester communicates with vehicle, perform data link diagnostics network test. See DATA LINK DIAGNOSTICS NETWORK TEST.

DATA LINK DIAGNOSTICS NETWORK TEST

1) Connect New Generation Star (NGS) tester to Data Link Connector (DLC). Select vehicle to be tested from NGS tester menu. Turn ignition switch to RUN position. Rotate dial on NGS tester to menu item DIAGNOSTIC DATA LINK and press trigger. A test will be performed on the BUS (circuits No. 914 and 915) network and the ISO 9141 network (circuit No. 70).

FORD
4-324

1999 ACCESSORIES & EQUIPMENT
Module Communications Network
F250 Super-Duty & F350 Pickup (Cont.)

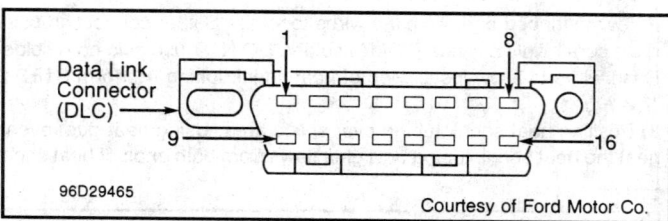

Fig. 2: Identifying Data Link Connector (DLC) Terminals

2) If NGS tester displays SYSTEM PASSED, module communications networks are okay. Return to article of system in question to continue diagnosis.

3) If NGS tester does not display SYSTEM PASSED, perform the following as applicable:

- If no response from NGS tester, go to TEST J: NO MODULE/ NETWORK COMMUNICATION – NO POWER TO NGS TESTER under SYSTEM TESTS.
- If NGS tester displays CKT70, CKT914 and/or CKT915 = SOME ECUS NO RESP/NOT EQUIP, see SYMPTOM INDEX table to continue diagnosis.
- If NGS tester displays CKT70 = ALL ECUS NO RESP/NOT EQUIP, go to TEST G: NO MODULE/NETWORK COMMUNICATIONS – ISO 9141 NETWORK under SYSTEM TESTS.
- If NGS tester displays CKT914 = ALL ECUS NO RESP/NOT EQUIP, go to TEST H: NO MODULE/NETWORK COMMUNICATIONS – SCP NETWORK under SYSTEM TESTS.
- If NGS tester displays CKT915 = ALL ECUS NO RESP/NOT EQUIP, go to TEST H: NO MODULE/NETWORK COMMUNICATIONS – SCP NETWORK under SYSTEM TESTS.
- If module in question is NO RESPONSE/NOT EQUIPPED, see SYMPTOM INDEX table to continue diagnosis.
- If module in question is NO RESPONSE ON CKT914 (BUS+) or NO RESPONSE ON CKT915 (BUS-), see SYMPTOM INDEX table to continue diagnosis.

SYMPTOM INDEX

Condition	Test
Anti-Lock Brake System (ABS) Module Does Not Respond To NGS Tester	A
Electronic Crash Sensor (ECS) Module Does Not Respond To NGS Tester	B
Powertrain Control Module (PCM) Does Not Respond To NGS Tester	C
Auxiliary Powertrain Control Module (APCM) Does Not Respond To NGS Tester	D
Overhead Trip Computer (OTC) Module Does Not Respond To NGS Tester	E
Generic Electronic Module (GEM) Does Not Respond To NGS Tester	F
No Module/Network Communications – ISO 9141 Network	G
No Module/Network Communications – SCP Network	H
No Module/Network Communication – No Power To NGS Tester	J

SYSTEM TESTS

NOTE: Always check module power and ground circuits prior to replacing a control module. See appropriate wiring diagram in DATA LINK CONNECTORS, GROUND DISTRIBUTION or POWER DISTRIBUTION article in WIRING DIAGRAMS.

TEST A: ANTI-LOCK BRAKE SYSTEM (ABS) MODULE DOES NOT RESPOND TO NGS TESTER

1) Turn ignition switch to LOCK position. Disconnect Anti-Lock Brake System (ABS) module 24-pin connector. Inspect ABS module connector for loose, damaged or corroded terminals. Repair as necessary. If ABS module connector is okay, go to next step.

2) Measure resistance of Light Blue/White wire between ABS module connector terminal No. 5 and Data Link Connector (DLC) terminal No. 7. *See Figs. 2 and 3.* If resistance is less than 5 ohms, replace ABS module. See appropriate ANTI-LOCK article in BRAKES in appropriate MITCHELL® manual for removal and installation procedure. If resistance is 5 ohms or more, go to next step.

3) Disconnect in-line 40-pin connector C1050. *See Fig. 4.* Inspect both halves of in-line 40-pin connector C1050 for loose, damaged or corroded terminals. Repair as necessary. If in-line connector C1050 is okay, go to next step.

4) Measure resistance of Light Blue/White wire between in-line connector C1050 (female side) terminal No. 32 and DLC terminal No. 7. *See Figs. 2 and 5.* If resistance is less than 5 ohms, repair open in Light Blue/White wire between in-line connector C1050 (male side) and ABS module. If resistance is 5 ohms or more, repair open in Light Blue/White wire between DLC and in-line connector C1050 (female side).

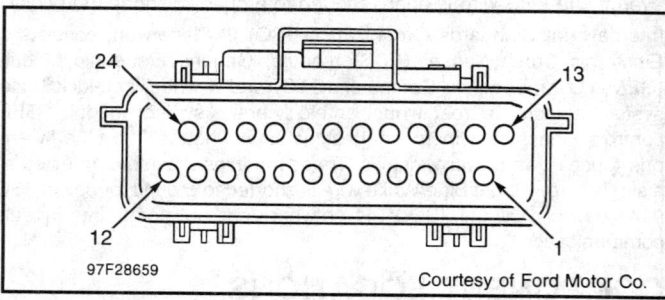

Fig. 3: Identifying Anti-Lock Brake System (ABS) Module Connector Terminals

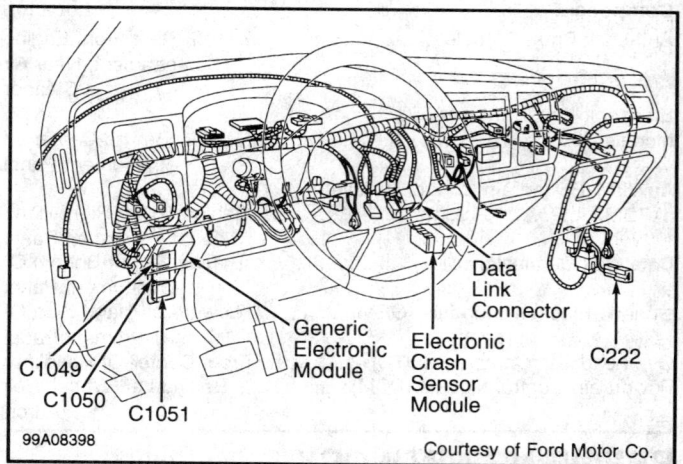

Fig. 4: Locating Components and Connectors Behind Instrument Panel

TEST B: ELECTRONIC CRASH SENSOR (ECS) MODULE DOES NOT RESPOND TO NGS TESTER

NOTE: Electronic Crash Sensor (ECS) module may also be referred to as air bag diagnostic module, air bag diagnostic monitor or Restraints Control Module (RCM).

1) Turn ignition switch to LOCK position. Deactivate air bag system. See appropriate AIR BAG RESTRAINT SYSTEMS article. Disconnect Electronic Crash Sensor (ESC) module connector. Inspect ESC module connector for loose, damaged or corroded terminals. Repair as necessary. If ESC module connector is okay, go to next step.

2) Measure resistance of Light Blue/White wire between ECS module terminal No. 19 and Data Link Connector (DLC) terminal No. 7. *See Figs. 2 and 6.* If resistance is less than 5 ohms, replace ECS module. See AIR BAG DIAGNOSTIC MONITOR under REMOVAL & INSTALLATION in ANALOG INSTRUMENT PANELS – F250 SUPER-DUTY &

1999 ACCESSORIES & EQUIPMENT
Module Communications Network
F250 Super-Duty & F350 Pickup (Cont.)

FORD
4-325

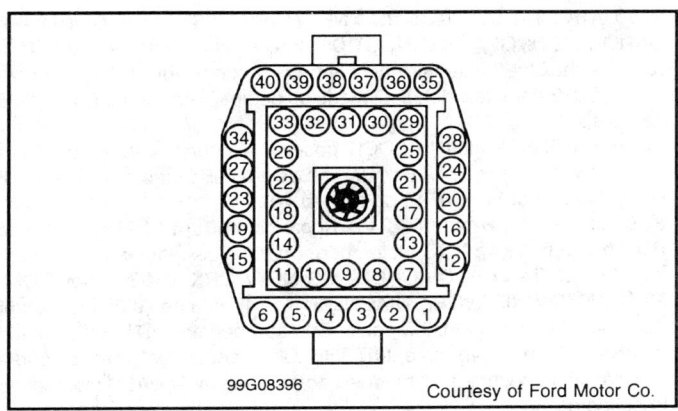

Fig. 5: Identifying In-Line 40-Pin Connector Terminals (Female Side)

F350 PICKUP article. If resistance is 5 ohms or more, repair open in Light Blue/White wire between DLC and ECS module.

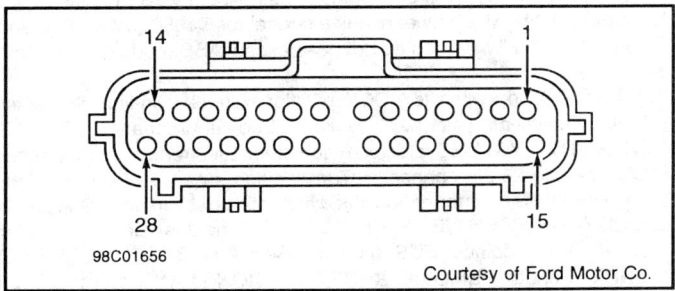

Fig. 6: Identifying Electronic Crash Sensor (ECS) Module Connector Terminals

TEST C: POWERTRAIN CONTROL MODULE (PCM) DOES NOT RESPOND TO NGS TESTER

1) Turn ignition switch to LOCK position. Disconnect Powertrain Control Module (PCM) 104-pin connector. Inspect PCM connector for loose, damaged or corroded terminals. Repair as necessary. If PCM terminals are okay, go to next step.

2) Measure resistance of Tan/Orange wire between PCM connector terminal No. 16 and Data Link Connector (DLC) terminal No. 2. *See Figs. 2 and 7.* Also measure resistance if Pink/Light Blue wire between PCM connector terminal No. 15 and DLC terminal No. 10. If each resistance is less than 5 ohms, problem is in PCM. On gasoline engine, perform quick test. See QUICK TEST in SELF-DIAGNOSTICS – EEC-V article or QUICK TEST in SELF-DIAGNOSTICS – 7.3L DIESEL article in ENGINE PERFORMANCE in appropriate MITCHELL® manual. If either resistance is 5 ohms or more, go to next step.

3) Disconnect in-line 40-pin connector C1049. *See Fig. 4.* Inspect both halves of in-line 40-pin connector C1049 for loose, damaged or corroded terminals. Repair as necessary. If in-line connector C1049 is okay, go to next step.

4) Measure resistance of Tan/Orange wire between in-line connector C1049 (female side) terminal No. 25 and DLC terminal No. 2. *See Figs. 2 and 5.* Also measure resistance of Pink/Light Blue wire between in-line connector C1049 (female side) terminal No. 29 and DLC terminal No. 10. If each resistance is less than 5 ohms, repair open in Tan/Orange wire and/or Pink/Light blue wire between PCM connector and in-line C1049 connector (male side). If either resistance is 5 ohms or more, repair open in appropriate wire between in-line connector C1049 (female side) and DLC.

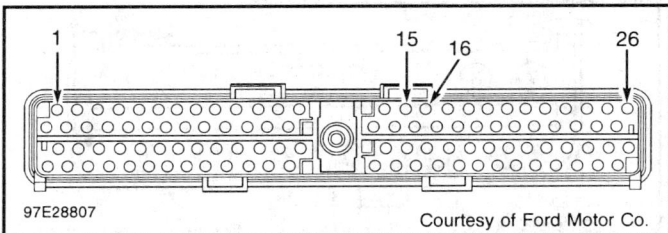

Fig. 7: Identifying Powertrain Control Module (PCM) Connector Terminals

TEST D: AUXILIARY POWERTRAIN CONTROL MODULE (APCM) DOES NOT RESPOND TO NGS TESTER

1) Turn ignition switch to LOCK position. Disconnect 4-pin Auxiliary Powertrain Control Module (APCM) connector. Inspect APCM connector for loose, damaged or corroded terminals. Repair as necessary. If APCM connector is okay, go to next step.

2) Measure resistance of Tan/Orange wire between APCM connector and Data Link Connector (DLC) terminal No. 2. *See Fig. 2.* Also measure resistance of Pink/Light Blue wire between APCM connector and DLC terminal No. 10. If each resistance is less than 5 ohms, replace APCM. If either resistance is 5 ohms or more, repair open in appropriate wire between APCM and DLC.

TEST E: OVERHEAD TRIP COMPUTER (OTC) MODULE DOES NOT RESPOND TO NGS TESTER

1) Turn ignition switch to LOCK position. Disconnect Overhead Trip Computer (OTC) connector. Inspect OTC connector for loose, damaged or corroded terminals. Repair as necessary. If OTC connector is okay, go to next step.

2) Measure resistance of Light Blue/White wire between OTC connector terminal No. 4 and Data Link Connector (DLC) terminal No. 7. *See Figs. 2 and 8.* If resistance is less than 5 ohms, replace OTC. If resistance is 5 ohms or more, go to next step.

3) Disconnect in-line 10-pin connector C222. *See Fig. 4.* Inspect in-line 10-pin connector C222 for loose, damaged or corroded terminals. Repair as necessary. If in-line connector C222 is okay, go to next step.

4) Measure resistance of Light Blue/White wire between DLC terminal No. 7 and in-line connector C222 (male side) terminal No. 5. *See Figs. 2 and 9.* If resistance is less than 5 ohms, repair open in Light Blue/White wire between in-line connector C222 (female side) and OTC connector. If resistance is 5 ohms or more, repair open in Light Blue/White wire between DLC and in-line connector C222 (male side).

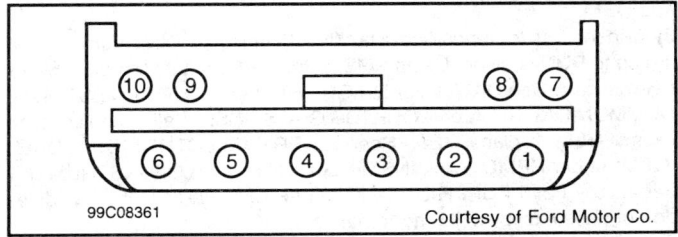

Fig. 8: Identifying Overhead Trip Computer (OTC) Connector Terminals

TEST F: GENERIC ELECTRONIC MODULE (GEM) DOES NOT RESPOND TO NGS TESTER

1) Turn ignition switch to LOCK position. Disconnect GEM 26-pin connector C239. Inspect GEM connector C239 for loose, damaged or corroded terminals. Repair as necessary. If GEM connector C239 is okay, go to next step.

2) Measure resistance of Light Blue/White wire between GEM connector C239 terminal No. 25 and Data Link Connector (DLC) terminal No. 7.

FORD
4-326

1999 ACCESSORIES & EQUIPMENT
Module Communications Network
F250 Super-Duty & F350 Pickup (Cont.)

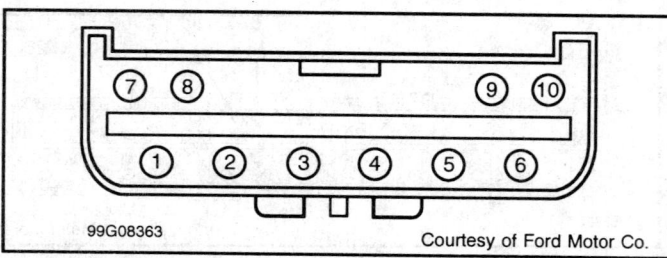

99G08363   Courtesy of Ford Motor Co.

Fig. 9: Identifying In-Line 10-Pin Connector C222 Terminals (Male Side)

See Figs. 2 and 10. If resistance is less than 5 ohms, replace GEM. See GENERIC ELECTRONIC MODULE under REMOVAL & INSTALLATION in ANALOG INSTRUMENT PANELS – F250 SUPER-DUTY & F350 PICKUP article. If resistance is 5 ohms or more, repair open in Light Blue/White wire between DLC and GEM connector C239.

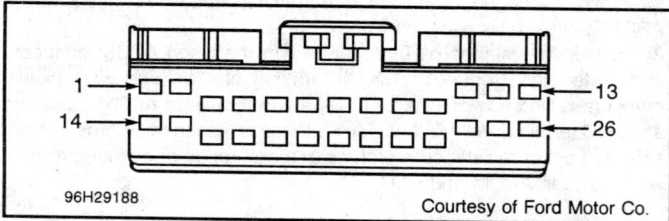

96H29188   Courtesy of Ford Motor Co.

Fig. 10: Identifying GEM Connector C239 Terminals

TEST G: NO MODULE/NETWORK COMMUNICATIONS – ISO 9141 NETWORK

NOTE: Depending on module configuration, with all modules connected and with ignition switch in RUN position or with engine running 2-3 volts may be present at Data Link Connector (DLC) terminal No. 7 (Light Blue/White wire). This is the International Standards Organization (ISO) 9141 diagnostic communications network circuit.

1) Turn ignition switch to LOCK position. Inspect Data Link Connector (DLC) for loose, damaged or corroded terminals. Repair as necessary. If DLC is okay, go to next step.
2) Disconnect Generic Electronic Module (GEM) 26-pin connector C239. Measure resistance of Light Blue/White wire between GEM connector C239 terminal No. 25 and DLC terminal No. 7. See Figs. 2 and 10. If resistance is less than 5 ohms, go to next step. If resistance is 5 ohms or more, repair open in Light Blue/White wire between DLC and GEM.
3) Connect New Generation Star (NGS) tester to DLC. Turn ignition switch to RUN position. Using NGS tester, perform data link diagnostics network test. See DATA LINK DIAGNOSTICS NETWORK TEST under COMMUNICATION NETWORK DIAGNOSTICS. If all modules pass except GEM, replace GEM. See GENERIC ELECTRONIC MODULE (GEM) under REMOVAL & INSTALLATION in ANALOG INSTRUMENT PANELS – F250 SUPER-DUTY & F350 PICKUP article. If all modules do not pass except GEM, go to next step.
4) Turn ignition switch to LOCK position. Connect GEM connector C239. If vehicle has Overhead Trip Computer (OTC), to next step. If vehicle does not have OTC, go to step 7).
5) Turn ignition switch to LOCK position. Disconnect OTC 10-pin connector. Turn ignition switch to RUN position. Using NGS tester, perform data link diagnostics network test. See DATA LINK DIAGNOSTICS NETWORK TEST under COMMUNICATION NETWORK DIAGNOSTICS. If all modules pass except OTC, replace OTC. If all modules do not pass except OTC, go to next step.
6) Turn ignition switch to LOCK position. Disconnect in-line 10-pin connector C222. See Fig. 4. Connect OTC. Turn ignition switch to RUN position. Using NGS tester, perform data link diagnostics network test.

See DATA LINK DIAGNOSTICS NETWORK TEST under COMMUNICATION NETWORK DIAGNOSTICS. If all modules pass except OTC, repair Light Blue/White wire between OTC connector and in-line connector C222 (female side). If all modules do not pass except OTC, go to next step.
7) Turn ignition switch to LOCK position. Connect in-line connector C222. If vehicle has Anti-Lock Brake System (ABS), go to next step. If vehicle does not have ABS, go to step 10).
8) Disconnect ABS module 24-pin connector. Turn ignition switch to RUN position. Using NGS tester, perform data link diagnostics network test. See DATA LINK DIAGNOSTICS NETWORK TEST under COMMUNICATION NETWORK DIAGNOSTICS. If all modules pass except ABS module, replace ABS module. See appropriate ANTI-LOCK article in BRAKES in appropriate MITCHELL® manual for removal and installation procedure. If all modules do not pass except ABS module, go to next step.
9) Turn ignition switch to LOCK position. Connect ABS module connector. Disconnect in-line 40-pin connector C1050. See Fig. 4. Using NGS tester, perform data link diagnostics network test. See DATA LINK DIAGNOSTICS NETWORK TEST under COMMUNICATION NETWORK DIAGNOSTICS. If all modules pass except ABS module, repair Light Blue/White wire between in-line connector C1050 (male side) and ABS module. If all modules do not pass except ABS module, go to next step.
10) Turn ignition switch to LOCK position. Connect in-line connector C1050. Deactivate air bag system. See appropriate AIR BAG RESTRAINT SYSTEMS article. Disconnect Electronic Crash Sensor (ECS) module 28-pin connector. Turn ignition switch to RUN position. Using NGS tester, perform data link diagnostics network test. See DATA LINK DIAGNOSTICS NETWORK TEST. If all modules pass except for ECS module, replace ECS module. See AIR BAG DIAGNOSTIC MONITOR under REMOVAL & INSTALLATION in ANALOG INSTRUMENT PANELS – F250 SUPER-DUTY & F350 PICKUP article. If all modules do not pass except for ECS module, repair Light Blue/White wire between ECS module, GEM, in-line connector C222 (male side if equipped with OTC), in-line connector C1050 (female side if equipped with ABS module) and DLC.

TEST H: NO MODULE/NETWORK COMMUNICATIONS – SCP NETWORK

NOTE: Depending on module configuration, with all modules connected and with ignition switch in RUN position or with engine running 2-3 volts may be present at Data Link Connector (DLC) terminals No. 2 (Tan/Orange wire) and No. 10 (Pink/Light Blue wire). These are the Standard Corporate Protocol (SCP) diagnostic communications network circuits.

1) Turn ignition switch to LOCK position. Inspect Data Link Connector (DLC) for loose, damaged or corroded terminals. Repair as necessary. If DLC is okay, go to next step.
2) Disconnect Powertrain Control Module (PCM) 104-pin connector. Measure resistance of Tan/Orange wire between PCM connector terminal No. 16 and DLC terminal No. 2. See Figs. 2 and 7. Also measure resistance of Pink/Light Blue wire between PCM connector terminal No. 15 and DLC terminal No. 10. If each resistance is less than 5 ohms, and vehicle is equipped with Auxiliary Powertrain Control Module (APCM), go to next step. If each resistance is less than 5 ohms, and vehicle is equipped with only PCM, go to step 6). If either resistance is 5 ohms or more, and vehicle is equipped with APCM, repair appropriate wire between in-line 40-pin connector C1049 and DLC. See Fig. 4. If either resistance is 5 ohms or more, and vehicle is equipped only with PCM, go to TEST C: POWERTRAIN CONTROL MODULE (PCM) DOES NOT RESPOND TO NGS TESTER.
3) Turn ignition switch to RUN position. Measure voltage between DLC terminals No. 2 (Tan/Orange wire) and No. 4 (Black wire). See Fig. 2. Measure voltage between DLC terminals No. 2 (Tan/Orange wire) and No. 16 (Light Blue/White wire). Measure voltage between DLC terminals

1999 ACCESSORIES & EQUIPMENT
Module Communications Network
F250 Super-Duty & F350 Pickup (Cont.)

FORD
4-327

No. 10 (Pink/Light Blue wire) and No. 4 (Black wire). Measure voltage between DLC terminals No. 10 (Pink/Light Blue wire) and No. 16 (Light Blue/White wire). If any reading indicates voltage, go to next step. If all readings indicate zero volts, perform quick test. See QUICK TEST in SELF-DIAGNOSTICS – EEC-V article or QUICK TEST in SELF-DIAGNOSTICS – 7.3L DIESEL article in ENGINE PERFORMANCE in appropriate MITCHELL® manual.

4) Turn ignition switch to LOCK position. Disconnect APCM 4-pin connector. Turn ignition switch to RUN position. Measure voltage between DLC terminals No. 2 (Tan/Orange wire) and No. 4 (Black wire). Measure voltage between DLC terminals No. 2 (Tan/Orange wire) and No. 16 (Light Blue/White wire). Measure voltage between DLC terminals No. 10 (Pink/Light Blue wire) and No. 4 (Black wire). Measure voltage between DLC terminals No. 10 (Pink/Light Blue wire) and No. 16 (Light Blue/White wire). If any reading indicates voltage, go to next step. If all readings are zero volts, replace APCM. See .

5) Turn ignition switch to LOCK position. Disconnect in-line 40-pin connector C1049. *See Fig. 4.* Turn ignition switch to RUN position. Measure voltage between DLC terminals No. 2 (Tan/Orange wire) and No. 4 (Black wire). Measure voltage between DLC terminals No. 2 (Tan/Orange wire) and No. 16 (Light Blue/White wire). Measure voltage between DLC terminals No. 10 (Pink/Light Blue wire) and No. 4 (Black wire). Measure voltage between DLC terminals No. 10 (Pink/Light Blue wire) and No. 16 (Light Blue/White wire). If any reading indicates voltage, repair appropriate wire between in-line connector C1049 (female side), DLC and APCM connector. If all readings indicate zero volts, repair appropriate wire between in-line connector C1049 (male side) and PCM.

6) Turn ignition switch to RUN position. Measure voltage between DLC terminals No. 2 (Tan/Orange wire) and No. 4 (Black wire). Measure voltage between DLC terminals No. 2 (Tan/Orange wire) and No. 16 (Light Blue/White wire). Measure voltage between DLC terminals No. 10 (Pink/Light Blue wire) and No. 4 (Black wire). Measure voltage between DLC terminals No. 10 (Pink/Light Blue wire) and No. 16 (Light Blue/White wire). If any reading indicates voltage, go to next step. If all readings indicates zero volts, perform quick test. See QUICK TEST in

SELF-DIAGNOSTICS – EEC-V article or QUICK TEST in SELF-DIAGNOSTICS – 7.3L DIESEL article in ENGINE PERFORMANCE in appropriate MITCHELL® manual.

7) Turn ignition switch to LOCK position. Disconnect in-line 40-pin connector C1049. *See Fig. 4.* Turn ignition switch to RUN position. Measure voltage between DLC terminals No. 2 (Tan/Orange wire) and No. 4 (Black wire). Measure voltage between DLC terminals No. 2 (Tan/Orange wire) and No. 16 (Light Blue/White wire). Measure voltage between DLC terminals No. 10 (Pink/Light Blue wire) and No. 4 (Black wire). Measure voltage between DLC terminals No. 10 (Pink/Light Blue wire) and No. 16 (Light Blue/White wire). If any reading indicates voltage, repair appropriate wire between in-line connector C1049 (female side) and DLC. If all readings indicate zero volts, repair appropriate wire between in-line connector C1049 (male side) and PCM connector.

TEST J: NO MODULE/NETWORK COMMUNICATION – NO POWER TO NGS TESTER

1) Inspect New Generation Star (NGS) tester connector for loose, damaged or corroded terminals. Repair as necessary. If connector is okay, go to next step.

2) Turn ignition switch to LOCK position. Inspect Data Link Connector (DLC) for loose, damaged or corroded terminals. Repair as necessary. If DLC is okay, go to next step.

3) Check fuse junction panel fuse No. 3 (20-amp). Replace as necessary. If fuse blows again, check for short to ground. Repair as necessary. If fuse is okay, reinstall fuse and go to next step.

4) Measure voltage between DLC terminal No. 16 (Light Blue/White wire) and ground. *See Fig. 2.* If voltage is more than 10 volts, go to next step. If voltage is 10 volts or less, repair Light Blue/White wire.

5) Measure resistance between DLC terminal No. 4 (Black wire) and ground. *See Fig. 2.* Also measure resistance between DLC terminal No. 5 (Black/White wire) and ground. If each resistance if less than 5 ohms, check NGS tester. If any resistance is 5 ohms or more, repair open in appropriate wire(s).

DIAGNOSTIC TROUBLE CODE (DTC) DEFINITIONS

NOTE: For Powertrain Control Module (PCM) DTC identification and repair, see SELF-DIAGNOSTICS – EEC-V in ENGINE PERFORMANCE.

ELECTRONIC CRASH SENSOR (ECS) MODULE DTC INDEX [1]

DTC [2]	Description	Test
B1342	ECU Defective	3
B1231	ECS Crash Data Memory Full	3
B1921	ECS Bracket High Resistance/Incorrect Mounting	3
B1318	Low Battery Voltage	3
C1414	Incorrect Module Design Level	3
B1887	Driver's Air Bag Circuit Short To Ground	3
B1916	Driver's Air Bag Circuit Short To Power	3
B1888	Passenger's Air Bag Circuit Short To Ground	3
B1925	Passenger's Air Bag Circuit Short To Power	3
B1932	Driver's Air Bag Resistance High	3
B1933	Passenger's Air Bag Resistance High	3
B1934	Driver's Air Bag Circuit Resistance Low	3
B1935	Passenger's Air Bag Circuit Resistance Low	3
B1941	Unexpected Feature Present	3
B1901	Unexpected Feature Present	3
B1871	Passenger's Air Bag Deactivation (PAD) Switch Fault	3
B1885	Unexpected Feature Present	3
B1886	Unexpected Feature Present	3
B1884	Passenger's Air Bag Deactivation (PAD) Switch Warning Light Inoperative	3
B1890	Passenger's Air Bag Deactivation (PAD) Switch Warning Light Short To Power	3
B1892	Air Bag tone Warning Indicator Circuit Short To Ground Or Open	3
B1891	Air Bag Tone Warning Indicator Circuit Short To Power	3
B2141	Non-Volatile Memory Configuration Failure	3
B1869	Air Bag Indicator Inoperative	3

FORD
4-328

1999 ACCESSORIES & EQUIPMENT
Module Communications Network
F250 Super-Duty & F350 Pickup (Cont.)

ELECTRONIC CRASH SENSOR (ECS) MODULE DTC INDEX[1] (Cont.)

DTC[2]	Description	Test
B1870	Air Bag Indicator Shorted To Power	3

[1] – Electronic Crash Sensor (ECS) module may also be referred to as air bag diagnostic module, air bag diagnostic monitor or Restraints Control Module (RCM).
[2] – DTCs are listed in order of importance. Repair DTCs in order listed.
[3] – Repair supplemental restraint system concern. For information on air bag DIAGNOSIS & TESTING, see MITCHELL® AIR BAG SERVICE & REPAIR MANUAL, DOMESTIC & IMPORTED MODELS.

ANTI-LOCK BRAKE CONTROL (ABS) MODULE DTC INDEX[1]

DTC	Description	Test
B1342	ECU Defective	2
B2141/B2477	NV Memory Configuration Failure	2
C1095/C1096	Pump Motor	2
C1115	Internal Power Relay	2
C1145[3]	Right Front Wheel Speed Sensor (Electrical/Static)	2
C1148/C1234[3]	Right Front Wheel Speed Sensor (Dynamic)	2
C1155[3]	Left Front Wheel Speed Sensor (Electrical/Static)	2
C1158/C1233[3]	Left Front Wheel Speed Sensor (Dynamic)	2
C1169	Excessive Dump Time	2
C1184	ABS System Time-Out	2
C1185	Open Internal Power Relay	2
C1194/C1196[3]	Left Front Dump Valve	2
C1198/C1200[3]	Left Front Isolation Valve	2
C1202/C1204	Rear Dump Valve	2
C1206/C1208	Rear Isolation Valve	2
C1210/C1212[3]	Right Front Dump Valve	2
C1214/C1216[3]	Right Front Isolation Valve	2
C1222	Wheel Speed Error (Dynamic)	2
C1226	Brake Warning Light Output Short To Ground	2
C1229/C1237	Rear Wheel Speed Sensor (Dynamic)	2
C1230	Rear Wheel Speed Sensor (Electrical/Static)	2

[1] – Rear wheel anti-lock brake and 4-wheel anti-lock brake systems have same DTCs except where noted.
[2] – See appropriate ANTI-LOCK article in BRAKES in appropriate MITCHELL® manual.
[3] – DTC for 4-wheel anti-lock brake system only.

GENERIC ELECTRONIC MODULE (GEM) DTC TEST INDEX

DTC	Description	Test
B1217	Horn Relay Coil Circuit Failure	1
B1218	Horn Relay Coil Circuit Short To Power	1
B1243	One-Touch Down Window Switch Circuit Short To Power	1
B1300	Power Door Lock Circuit Failure	1
B1302	Accessory Delay Relay Coil Circuit Failure	3
B1304	Accessory Delay Relay Coil Circuit Short To Power	3
B1310	Power Door Unlock Circuit Failure	1
B1317	Battery Voltage High	4
B1318	Battery Voltage Low	4
B1322	Driver's Door Ajar Circuit Short To Ground	5
B1323	Door Ajar Light Circuit Failure	6
B1325	Door Ajar Light Circuit Short To Power	6
B1330	Passenger's Door Ajar Circuit Short To Ground	5
B1338	Right Rear Or Left Rear Door Ajar Circuit Short To Ground	5
B1340	Chime Input Request Circuit Short To Ground	7
B1342	ECU Defective	8
B1352	Ignition Key-In Circuit Failure	7
B1355	Ignition RUN Circuit Failure	9
B1359	Ignition RUN/ACC Circuit Failure	9
B1366	Ignition START Circuit Short To Ground	10
B1371	Illuminated Entry Relay Circuit Failure	5
B1373	Illuminated Entry Relay Short To Power	5
B1396	Power Door Lock Circuit Short To Power	1
B1397	Power Door Unlock Circuit Short To Power	1
B1398	Driver's Window One-Touch Down Relay Circuit Failure	11
B1400	Driver's Power Window One-Touch Down Relay Circuit Short To Power	11
B1405	Driver's Power Window Down Circuit Short To Power	11
B1410	Driver's Power Window Motor Circuit Failure	2
B1426	Safety Belt Light Circuit Short To Power	12
B1428	Safety Belt Light Circuit Failure	12
B1431	Wiper Run/Park Relay Circuit Failure	13

1999 ACCESSORIES & EQUIPMENT
Module Communications Network
F250 Super-Duty & F350 Pickup (Cont.)

FORD
4-329

GENERIC ELECTRONIC MODULE (GEM) DTC TEST INDEX (Cont.)

DTC	Description	Test
B1432	Wiper Run/Park Relay Short To Power	13
B1434	Wiper Hi/Low Speed Relay Circuit Failure	14
B1436	Wiper Hi/Low Speed Relay Circuit Short To Power	14
B1438	Wiper Mode Select Switch Circuit Failure	13
B1441	Wiper Mode Select Switch Circuit Short To Ground	15
B1446	Wiper Park Sense Circuit Failure	13
B1450	Wiper/Wash Delay Switch Circuit Failure	16
B1453	Wiper/Wash Delay Switch Circuit Short To Ground	15
B1458	Washer Pump Motor Relay Coil Circuit Failure	17
B1460	Washer Pump Motor Relay Coil Short To Power	17
B1462	Seat Belt Switch Circuit Failure	7
B1473	Wiper Motor Low Speed Circuit Failure	13
B1475	Accessory Delay Relay Contact Short To Power	18
B1476	Wiper Motor High Speed Circuit Failure	13
B1483	Brake Pedal Input Circuit Failure	19
B1485	Brake Pedal Input Circuit Short To Power	19
B1574	Left Rear Door Ajar Circuit Short To Ground	5
B1577 [20]	Park Light Input Circuit Short To Power	7
B1840	Wiper Power Circuit Failure	13
B1982	Driver's Door Unlock Relay Circuit Failure	1
B1983	Driver's Door Unlock Relay Circuit Short To Power	1
B2132	Dimmer Switch Short To Ground	5
B2141	NVM Configuration Failure	21
B2357 [20]	Driver's Window Down Current Sense (Low) Circuit Failure	11
B2425	Remote Keyless Entry Out Of Synchronization	1
C1125	Brake Fluid Level Sensor Input Circuit Failure	22
C1182	Park Light Flash Relay Circuit Failure	1
C1183	Park Light Flash Relay Circuit Short To Power	1
C1189	Brake Fluid Level Sensor Input Circuit Short To ground	22
C1223	Brake Light Warning Output Circuit Failure	22
C1225	Brake Light Warning Output Circuit short To Power	22
C1230	Speed Wheel Sensor Rear Center Input Circuit Failure	23
C1446	Park Brake Switch Circuit Failure	22
C1728	Unable To Transition Between 4H & 2H	19
C1729	Unable To Transition Between 4H & 4L	19
C1751	Vehicle Speed Sensor No. 1 Output Circuit Short To Power	24
C1752	Vehicle Speed Sensor No. 1 Output Circuit Short To Ground	24
P0500	Vehicle Speed Signal Circuit Failure	25
P1804	4-Wheel Drive High Indicator Circuit Failure	19
P1806	4-Wheel Drive High Indicator Short To Power	19
P1808	4-Wheel Drive Low Indicator Circuit Failure	19
P1810	4-Wheel Drive Low Indicator Short To Power	19
P1812	4-Wheel Drive Mode Select Circuit Failure	19
P1815	4-Wheel Drive Mode Select Short Circuit To Ground	19
P1819	Transmission Neutral Safety Switch Short To Ground	19
P1820	Transmission Transfer Case Clockwise Shift Relay Coil Circuit Failure	19
P1822	Transmission Transfer Case Clockwise Shift Relay Coil Short To Power	19
P1828	Transmission Transfer Case Counterclockwise Shift Relay Coil Circuit Failure	19
P1830	Transmission Transfer Case Counterclockwise Shift Relay Coil Short To Power	19
P1832	Transmission Transfer Case Differential Lockup Solenoid Circuit Failure	19
P1834	Transmission Transfer Case Differential Lockup Solenoid Short To Power	19
P1838	Transmission Transfer Case Shift Motor Circuit Failure	19
P1865	Transmission Transfer Case Contact Plate Power Short To Ground	19
P1866	Transmission Transfer Case System Concern	19
P1867	Transmission Transfer Case Contact Plate General Circuit Failure	19
P1876	Transmission Transfer Case 2-Wheel Drive Solenoid Circuit Failure	19
P1877	Transmission Transfer Case 2-Wheel Drive Solenoid Short To Power	19

[1] – Repair remote keyless entry concern. See appropriate wiring diagram in REMOTE KEYLESS ENTRY SYSTEMS article.

[2] – Perform TEST G: ONE-TOUCH DOWN FEATURE INOPERATIVE under SYSTEM TESTS in POWER WINDOWS – F250 SUPER-DUTY & F350 PICKUP article.

[3] – Perform TEST B: ALL WINDOWS INOPERATIVE under SYSTEM TESTS in POWER WINDOWS – F250 SUPER-DUTY & F350 PICKUP article.

[4] – Repair charging system concern. See appropriate GENERATORS article in STARTING & CHARGING SYSTEMS.

[5] – Repair interior illumination concern. See appropriate wiring diagram in ILLUMINATION/INTERIOR LIGHTS article.

[6] – Perform TEST V: DOOR AJAR LIGHT INOPERATIVE, CHIME OKAY under SYSTEM TESTS in ANALOG INSTRUMENT PANELS – F250 SUPER-DUTY & F350 PICKUP article.

[7] – Repair warning chime concern. See appropriate wiring diagram in WARNING SYSTEMS article.

[8] – Using NGS tester, clear DTCs. Retrieve DTCs. If B1342 is retrieved again, replace GEM. See GENERIC ELECTRONIC MODULE (GEM) under REMOVAL & INSTALLATION in ANALOG INSTRUMENT PANELS – F250 SUPER-DUTY & F350 PICKUP article.

1999 ACCESSORIES & EQUIPMENT
Module Communications Network
F250 Super-Duty & F350 Pickup (Cont.)

GENERIC ELECTRONIC MODULE (GEM) DTC TEST INDEX (Cont.)

DTC   **Description**   **Test**

[9] – Perform TEST C: NO POWER IN RUN POSITION under SYSTEM TESTS in STEERING COLUMN SWITCHES – EXCEPT F150 & F250 LIGHT-DUTY PICKUP article.

[10] – Perform TEST D: NO POWER IN START POSITION under SYSTEM TESTS in STEERING COLUMN SWITCHES – EXCEPT F150 & F250 LIGHT-DUTY PICKUP article.

[11] – Perform TEST C: DRIVER WINDOW INOPERATIVE under SYSTEM TESTS in POWER WINDOWS – F250 SUPER-DUTY & F350 PICKUP article.

[12] – Perform TEST W: SAFETY BELT LIGHT INOPERATIVE, CHIME OKAY under SYSTEM TESTS in ANALOG INSTRUMENT PANELS – F250 SUPER-DUTY & F350 PICKUP article.

[13] – Perform TEST B: WIPERS INOPERATIVE under SYSTEM TESTS in WIPER/WASHER SYSTEMS – F250 SUPER-DUTY & F350 PICKUP article.

[14] – Perform TEST D: WIPER HIGH/LOW SPEEDS DO NOT OPERATE PROPERLY under SYSTEM TESTS in WIPER/WASHER SYSTEMS – F250 SUPER-DUTY & F350 PICKUP article.

[15] – Perform TEST C: WIPERS STAY ON CONTINUOUSLY under SYSTEM TESTS in WIPER/WASHER SYSTEMS – F250 SUPER-DUTY & F350 PICKUP article.

[16] – Perform TEST E: INTERVAL MODE DOES NOT OPERATE PROPERLY under SYSTEM TESTS in WIPER/WASHER SYSTEMS – F250 SUPER-DUTY & F350 PICKUP article.

[17] – Perform TEST F: WASHER/WIPER MODE DOES NOT OPERATE PROPERLY under SYSTEM TESTS in WIPER/WASHER SYSTEMS – F250 SUPER-DUTY & F350 PICKUP article.

[18] – Perform TEST H: DELAYED ACCESSORY DOES NOT TURN OFF under SYSTEM TESTS in POWER WINDOWS – F250 SUPER-DUTY & F350 PICKUP article.

[19] – Repair transfer case electronic controls concern. See NEW VENTURE 271 – ELECTRONIC CONTROLS article in TRANSFER CASES.

[20] – When performing Generic Electronic Module (GEM) self-test, vehicles built prior to February 5, 1998 must have power windows completely up and headlights and parking lights off. Failure to do so will result in DTCs B1577 and B2357 being set. Vehicles built after February 5, 1998 must have headlights and parking lights on. Failure to do so will result in B1575 being set.

[21] – Check module configuration. Refer to NGS Ford Service Function card to verify proper module configuration. Clear DTCs. Retrieve DTCs. If DTC B2141 is retrieved again, replace GEM. See GENERIC ELECTRONIC MODULE (GEM) under REMOVAL & INSTALLATION in ANALOG INSTRUMENT PANELS – F250 SUPER-DUTY & F350 PICKUP article.

[22] – Perform TEST M: RED BRAKE LIGHT INOPERATIVE OR ALWAYS ON under SYSTEM TESTS in ANALOG INSTRUMENT PANELS – F250 SUPER-DUTY & F350 PICKUP article.

[23] – Perform TEST H: SPEEDOMETER INOPERATIVE under SYSTEM TESTS in ANALOG INSTRUMENT PANELS – F250 SUPER-DUTY & F350 PICKUP article.

[24] – Repair cruise control system concern. See CRUISE CONTROL SYSTEMS – F250 SUPER-DUTY & F350 PICKUP article.

[25] – Perform TEST G: SPEED DEPENDENT INTERVAL MODE DOES NOT OPERATE PROPERLY under SYSTEM TESTS in WIPER/WASHER SYSTEMS – F250 SUPER-DUTY & F350 PICKUP article.

OVERHEAD TRIP COMPUTER (OTC) DTC INDEX

DTC	Description	Test
B1201	Fuel Level Sensor Circuit Open Or Short To Ground	1
B1203	Fuel Level Sensor Circuit Short To Power	1
B1208	Message Center MODE Or E/M Button Stuck Closed	2
B1342	ECU Defective	1
B2141	Message Center Module Configuration Failure	3
B2148	Pulse Width Modulated Signal Open Or Short To Ground	1
C1123	Vehicle Speed Signal Short To Power	1
P0500	Vehicle Speed Signal Input Malfunction	1
U2015	Powertrain Control Module (PCM) Signal Open Or Short To Power	1
U2016	PCM Short To Ground	1

[1] – Repair OTC system concern. See appropriate wiring diagram in OVERHEAD CONSOLES article.

[2] – Check for proper assembly of outer/inner message center console.

[3] – Check module configuration. Refer to NGS tester Ford Service Function card to verify proper module configuration. Clear DTCs. Retrieve DTCs. If DTC B2141 is present again, replace GEM. See GENERIC ELECTRONIC MODULE (GEM) under REMOVAL & INSTALLATION in ANALOG INSTRUMENT PANELS – F250 SUPER-DUTY & F350 PICKUP article.

1999 ACCESSORIES & EQUIPMENT
Module Communications Network
F250 Super-Duty & F350 Pickup (Cont.)

FORD
4-331

PARAMETER IDENTIFICATION (PID) DEFINITIONS

AIR BAG ELECTRONIC CRASH SENSOR (ECS) MODULE PID INDEX [1]

PID	Description	Expected Values
CCNTECS	Number of DTCs In Module	Number of DTCs
DABAGR	Driver's Air Bag Module Resistance	1.8-4.1 Ohms
PABAGR	Passenger's Air Bag Module Resistance	1.4-3.6 Ohms
BRACKET	Bracket Ground Resistance	Less Than 100 Ohms
VBATECS	System Battery Voltage	9.0-16.0 Volts

[1] – Electronic Crash Sensor (ECS) module may also be referred to as air bag diagnostic module, air bag diagnostic monitor or Restraints Control Module (RCM).

ANTI-LOCK BRAKE CONTROL (ABS) MODULE PID INDEX [1]

PID	Description	Expected Value
4WDABS	4 Wheel Drive Input Switch	2WD, 4WD
ABSLAMP	ABS Warning Light State	ON, OFF
ABSLF_I [2]	Left Front ABS Inlet Valve	ON, OFF
ABSLF_O [2]	Left Front ABS Outlet Valve	ON, OFF
ABSR_I	Rear ABS Inlet Valve	ON, OFF
ABSR_O	Rear ABS Outlet Valve	ON, OFF
ABSRF_I [2]	Right Front ABS Inlet Valve	ON, OFF
ABSRF_O [2]	Right Front ABS Outlet Valve	ON, OFF
BOO_ABS	Brake Switch Input	ON, OFF
BRKLAMP	Brake Warning Light State	ON, OFF
CCNTABS	Number of DTCs In Module	Number Of DTCs
LF_WSPD [2]	Left Front Wheel Speed Sensor	0-255 KPH
R_WSPD	Rear Wheel Speed Sensor	0-255 KPH
RF_WSPD [2]	Right Front Wheel Speed Sensor	0-255 KPH
PWR_RLY	Power Relay Feedback Input	ON, OFF

[1] – Rear wheel anti-lock brake and 4-wheel anti-lock brakes systems have same PIDs except where otherwise noted.
[2] – 4-wheel anti-lock brakes system only.

GENERIC ELECTRONIC MODULE (GEM) PID INDEX

PID	Description	Expected Value
ACCDLY	Accessory Delay Relay Circuit	ON, OFF
BATSAV	Battery Saver Output Status	ON, OFF
BOO_GEM	Brake Input Switch Status	ON, OFF
CLTCHSW	Transmission Clutch Interlock Switch	ENGAGED, NOTENGD
D_DN_SW	Driver's Window Down Switch	OFF, DOWN
D_PWRLY	Driver's Power Window Status	OFF, ON
D_PWAMP	Driver's Power Window Motor Current	0.25-63.75 Amps
DRAJR_L	Door Ajar Warning Light Status	ON, OFF
D_DR_SW	Left External Access Ajar Switch Status	CLOSED, AJAR
D_SBELT	Driver's Seat Belt Status	IN, OUT
IGN_GEM	Ignition Switch Status	START, RUN, OFF, ACC
IGN_KEY	Ignition Key In/Out	IN, OUT
MTR_CCW	Transfer Case Counter Clockwise Motor Output	ON, OFF, OFFO-G
MTR_CW	Transfer Case Clockwise Motor Output	ON, OFF
NTRL_SW	Neutral Safety Switch Input	NTRL, NOTNTRL
OTD_SW	One-Touch Down Switch Status	OFF, DOWN
P_DR_SW	Right External Access Ajar Switch Status	CLOSED, AJAR
RRDR_SW	Right Rear Door Ajar Switch	CLOSED, AJAR
LRDR_SW	Left Rear Door Ajar Switch	CLOSED, AJAR
PARK_SW	Park Brake Switch Status	ON, OFF
BRKLAMP	Brake Warning Light Status	ON, OFF
FLUID_1	Brake Fluid Level Switch No. 1 Status	[1]
FLUIDSW_2	Brake Fluid Level Switch No. 2 Status	[1]
PLATE_A	Transfer Case Contact Plate A	OPEN, CLOSED
PLATE_B	Transfer Case Contact Plate B	OPEN, CLOSED
PLATE_C	Transfer Case Contact Plate C	OPEN, CLOSED
PLATE_D	Transfer Case Contact Plate D	OPEN, CLOSED
PLATEPW	Transfer Case Contact Plate Pull	ON, OFF
SBLTMP	Seat Belt Light Circuit	ON, OFF
SPEEDWP	Speed Dependent Wiper Function	ACTIVE, NOTACT
VBATGEM	Battery Voltage	0.0-25.5 VDC
VSS_GEM	Vehicle Speed Input	0-225 KPH
WASHRLY	Washer Pump Relay Circuit	ON, OFF-
WASH_SW	Washer Pump Switch	ON, OFF
WPHISP	Wiper High/Low Speed Relay	ON, OFF

FORD
4-332

1999 ACCESSORIES & EQUIPMENT
Module Communications Network
F250 Super-Duty & F350 Pickup (Cont.)

GENERIC ELECTRONIC MODULE (GEM) PID INDEX (Cont.)

PID	Description	Expected Value
WPMODE	Wiper Control Mode Select	2
WPPRKSW	Wiper Park Sense	PARKED, NOTPRK
WPRUN	Wiper Run Relay Driver State	ON, OFF
2WDSOL	2WD Hub Lock Solenoid Output Status	ON, OFF
4WDHIGH	4WD High Output State	ON, OFF
4WDLOW	4WD Low Output State	ON, OFF
4WDSGEM	4WD Input Switch Status	3
4WDSOL	4WD Hub Lock Solenoid Output Status	ON, OFF
IPCHIME	External Chime Request	ON, OFF
PARK_SW	Exterior Light Control Input Park Lights Switch Status	ON, OFF
HDL_DIM	Headlight Dimmer Switch	ON, OFF
PRKFRLY	Park Light Flash Relay	ON, OFF
HORNRLY	Horn Control Relay Output Status	ON, OFF
DR_UNLK	All Doors Unlock Output Status	ON, OFF
DD_UNLK	Driver's Door Unlock Output Status	ON, OFF
ALL_RLY	All Door Lock Output Status	ON, OFF
INTLMP	Illuminated Entry Relay Circuit	ON, OFF

[1] – Information not available from manufacturer.
[2] – Expected value should be WASH, OPEN, OFF, INTVL1, INTVL2, INTVL3, INTVL4, INTVL5, INTVL6, INTVL7, LOW or HIGH.
[3] – Expected value should be 2WD, 4WD LOW, 4WD HIGH, OPEN or SHORT TO GND.

OVERHEAD TRIP COMPUTER (OTC) PID INDEX

PID	Description	Expected Values
CCNT_OT	Number of DTCs In Module	Number of DTCs
VSS2OTC	Vehicle Speed Signal Input To Message Center	0-128 MPH
VBATOTC	System Battery Voltage	0-25.5 Volts
FUELIN3	Fuel Level Analog Input	0-51.2 Gallons
FUELUSE	Fuel Usage (Cumulative)	0-89478.49 Gallons (48000 Counts Per Gallon)
PWM_DC1	Pulse Width Modulated Duty Cycle	0-100%

WIRING DIAGRAMS

NOTE: See appropriate wiring diagrams in DATA LINK CONNECTORS, GROUND DISTRIBUTION or POWER DISTRIBUTION article in WIRING DIAGRAMS.

DESCRIPTION & OPERATION

Vehicle has 2 module communications networks. The Powertrain Control Module (PCM) is connected to the multiplex communications network through a pair of twisted wires or BUS. The BUS network is also referred to as Standard Corporate Protocol (SCP). The BUS consists of a (+) circuit and a (–) circuit (circuit No. 914 and 915 respectively).

The air bag diagnostic monitor and all other optional modules, the Generic Electronic Module (GEM), Passive Anti-Theft (PAT) module and 4-Wheel Anti-Lock Brake System (4WABS) module, are connected to the International Standards Organization (ISO) 9141 diagnostic communications network through a single wire (circuit No. 70). Both networks are connected to the Data Link Connector (DLC). This article is used to diagnose BUS and ISO communications network circuit faults. For module locations, see COMPONENT LOCATIONS table.

COMPONENT LOCATIONS

Component	Location
Air Bag Diagnostic Monitor [1]	Behind Right Kick Panel
Data Link Connector (DLC)	Below Driver's Side Of Instrument Panel, To Right Of Steering Column
Generic Electronic Module (GEM)	Behind Center Of Instrument Panel
Passive Anti-Theft (PAT) Module	Behind Passenger Air Bag Module
Powertrain Control Module (PCM)	Mounted Through Firewall, On Passenger's Side
4-Wheel Anti-Lock Brake System (4WABS) Module	Left Side Of Engine Compartment

[1] – Air bag diagnostic monitor may also be known as Restraint Control Module (RCM).

REPAIRING BUS WIRING

NOTE: The following procedure must be used to ensure proper repair is performed on BUS wiring. BUS wiring is sensitive to moisture and oxidation and must be properly sealed to ensure proper operation of the module communications network. Regular heat shrink tubing is NOT sufficient, heat shrink tubing containing hot melt wax is required.

1) When performing a repair on the BUS wiring, ensure the wires on the BUS are twisted at a rate of 33-40 winds per 3.3 ft. (1 m). The twists should start within approximately 4.9" (124 mm) from any connector. Use only 20 AWG standard wire gauge for repairs.

2) If performing a splice in the wiring, strip .75" (19.0 mm) of insulation from one wire and 1.50" (38.1 mm) of insulation from the other wire. Perform STEP 1. *See Fig. 1.* Place hot melt wax heat shrink tubing over one wire.

3) Twist stripped portion of the wires together. Solder connection using resin core RMA solder. DO NOT use acid core solder. Bend wires to allow installation of heat shrink tubing. Perform STEP 2. *See Fig. 1.*

4) Position heat shrink tubing over splice area. Using heat gun, evenly heat the heat shrink tubing until wax flows from both ends of heat shrink tubing.

COMMUNICATION NETWORK DIAGNOSTICS

INSPECTION & VERIFICATION

1) Verify customer's original problem by operating system in question. Inspect vehicle for any obvious electrical component wiring or connector damage. Inspect connectors for loose, damaged or corroded terminals. Check related fuses for system in question.

2) Inspect 16-pin Data Link Connector (DLC) pins for damage. *See Fig. 2.* The DLC is located below driver's side of instrument panel, to the right of steering column. If pins are okay, go to next step. If pins are damaged, repair as necessary and proceed to next step.

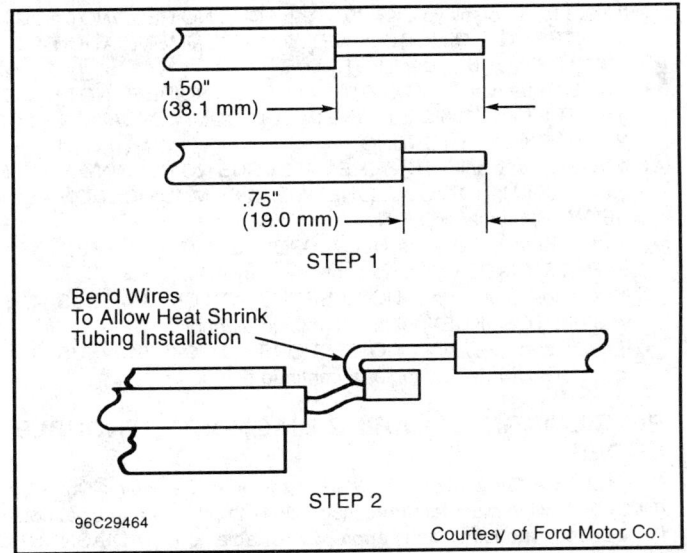

Fig. 1: Repairing BUS Wiring

3) If problem is still present after performing inspection, connect New Generation Star (NGS) tester to DLC. Select vehicle to be tested from NGS tester menu. If NGS tester does not communicate with vehicle, ensure program card is properly installed. Check NGS tester cable connections and ensure ignition is on. If NGS tester still does not communicate with vehicle, go to TEST I: NO MODULE/NETWORK COMMUNICATION – NO POWER TO NGS THROUGH DLC under TESTING. If NGS tester communicates with vehicle, perform data link diagnostic procedure. See DATA LINK DIAGNOSTIC TEST.

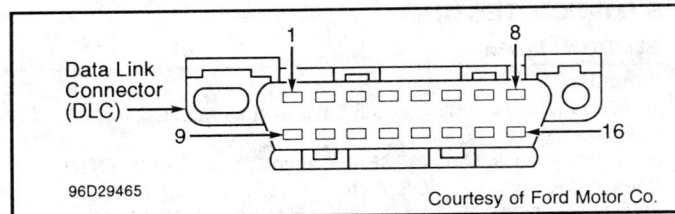

Fig. 2: Identifying Data Link Connector (DLC) Terminals

DATA LINK DIAGNOSTIC TEST

1) Connect New Generation Star (NGS) tester to Data Link Connector (DLC), if not already connected. Select vehicle to be tested from NGS tester menu.

2) Turn ignition on. Rotate dial on NGS tester to menu item DIAGNOSTIC DATA LINK and press trigger. A test will be performed on the BUS (circuits No. 914 and 915) for the module communications network and the ISO 9141 communication link (circuit No. 70). This is the Light Blue/White wire that is between terminal No. 7 on DLC and the air bag diagnostic monitor and other optional modules.

3) If NGS tester displays CKT 914 (+) = SYSTEM PASSED and CKT 915 (–) = SYSTEM PASSED, module communications network is okay. If NGS tester displays CKT 70 = SYSTEM PASSED, ISO 9141 communication link is operating properly. Return to article that directed you here and continue diagnosis.

4) If NGS tester does not display CKT 914 (+) = SYSTEM PASSED, CKT 915 (–) = SYSTEM PASSED and CKT 70 = SYSTEM PASSED, perform the following as applicable.

- If no response from NGS tester, go to TEST I: NO MODULE/NETWORK COMMUNICATION – NO POWER TO NGS THROUGH DLC under TESTING.

- If NGS tester displays CKT 70, CKT 914 and/or CKT 915 = SOME ECUS NO RESP/NOT EQUIP, go to SYMPTOM INDEX table to continue diagnosis.

- If NGS tester displays CKT 70 = ALL ECUS NO RESP/NOT EQUIP, go to TEST G: NO MODULE/NETWORK COMMUNICATION – ISO 9141 NETWORK under TESTING.
- If NGS tester displays CKT 914 = ALL ECUS NO RESP/NOT EQUIP, go to TEST H: NO MODULE/NETWORK COMMUNICATION – SCP NETWORK under TESTING.
- If NGS tester displays CKT 915 = ALL ECUS NO RESP/NOT EQUIP, go to TEST H: NO MODULE/NETWORK COMMUNICATION – SCP NETWORK under TESTING.
- If module in question is NO RESPONSE/NOT EQUIPPED, go to SYMPTOM INDEX table to continue diagnosis.
- If module in question is NO RESPONSE ON CKT 914 (BUS +), go to SYMPTOM INDEX table to continue diagnosis.
- If module in question is NO RESPONSE ON CKT 915 (BUS –), go to SYMPTOM INDEX table to continue diagnosis.

RETRIEVING & CLEARING DIAGNOSTIC TROUBLE CODES

Connect New Generation Star (NGS) tester to Data Link Connector (DLC). Following manufacturers instructions to retrieve and clear codes for desired module. See appropriate table under DIAGNOSTIC TROUBLE CODE (DTC) DEFINITIONS for a listing of Diagnostic Trouble Codes (DTCs) and appropriate test procedure.

ACCESSING PARAMETER IDENTIFICATION (PID)

Turn ignition switch to LOCK position. Connect New Generation Star (NGS) tester to Data Link Connector (DLC). Following manufacturers instructions enter PID/DATA MONITOR AND RECORD for desired module. Operate appropriate system and ensure PID expected values are obtained. See appropriate table under PARAMETER IDENTIFICATION (PID) DEFINITIONS.

SYMPTOM TESTING

SYMPTOM INDEX

Condition	Test
4-Wheel Anti-Lock Brake System (4WABS) Module Does Not Respond To NGS Tester	A
Generic Electronic Module (GEM)/Central Timer Module (CTM) Does Not Respond To NGS Tester	B
Air Bag Diagnostic Monitor Does Not Respond To NGS Tester [1]	C
Remote Anti-Theft Personality (RAP) Module Does Not Respond To NGS Tester	D
Powertrain Control Module (PCM) Does Not Respond To NGS Tester	E
Passive Anti-Theft System (PATS) Module Does Not Respond To NGS Tester	F
No Module/Network Communications – ISO 9141 Network	G
No Module/Network Communications – SCP Network	H
No Module/Network Communication – No Power To NGS Through DLC	I

[1] – May be referred to as Restraint Control Module (RCM).

SYSTEM TESTING

NOTE: *Always check module power and ground circuits prior to replacing a control module. See appropriate wiring diagram in* DATA LINK CONNECTORS, GROUND DISTRIBUTION *or* POWER DISTRIBUTION *article in* WIRING DIAGRAMS.

TEST A: 4-WHEEL ANTI-LOCK BRAKE SYSTEM (4WABS) MODULE DOES NOT RESPOND TO NGS TESTER

1) Turn ignition off. Disconnect 25-pin 4WABS module connector located at left side of engine compartment. See Fig. 3, 4 or 5. Inspect 4WABS connector and Data Link Connector (DLC) for physical damage, bent

terminals or corrosion. Repair connectors as necessary and retest system for normal operation. If connectors are okay, go to next step.
2) Measure resistance of Light Blue/White wire between terminal No. 23 at 4WABS module connector and terminal No. 7 at DLC. See Figs. 2 and 6. If resistance is less than 5 ohms, replace 4WABS module and retest system for normal operation. If resistance is 5 ohms or more, go to next step.
3) Disconnect and inspect both halves of 40-pin bulkhead connector C134 located at left rear of engine compartment. See Fig. 3, 4 or 5. Inspect connector for physical damage, bent terminals or corrosion. Repair connector as necessary and retest system for normal operation. If connector is okay, go to next step.
4) Measure resistance of Light Blue/White wire between terminal No. 16 at female half of bulkhead connector C134 and terminal No. 7 at DLC. See Figs. 2 and 7. If resistance is less than 5 ohms, go to next step. If resistance is 5 ohms or more, repair open in Light Blue/White wire between DLC and 40-pin bulkhead connector. Retest system for normal operation.
5) Disconnect and inspect both halves in-line connector C179 located at left rear of engine compartment. See Fig. 3, 4 or 5. Inspect connector for physical damage, bent terminals or corrosion. Repair connector as necessary and retest system for normal operation. If connector is okay, go to next step.
6) Measure resistance of Light Blue/White wire between terminal No. 16 at male half of bulkhead connector C134 and terminal No. 8 at female half of in-line connector C179. See Figs. 7 and 8. If resistance is less than 5 ohms, repair open in Light Blue/White wire between in-line connector C179 and 4WABS connector. If resistance is 5 ohms or more, repair open in Light Blue/White wire between male half of 40-pin bulkhead connector and in-line connector C179. Retest system for normal operation.

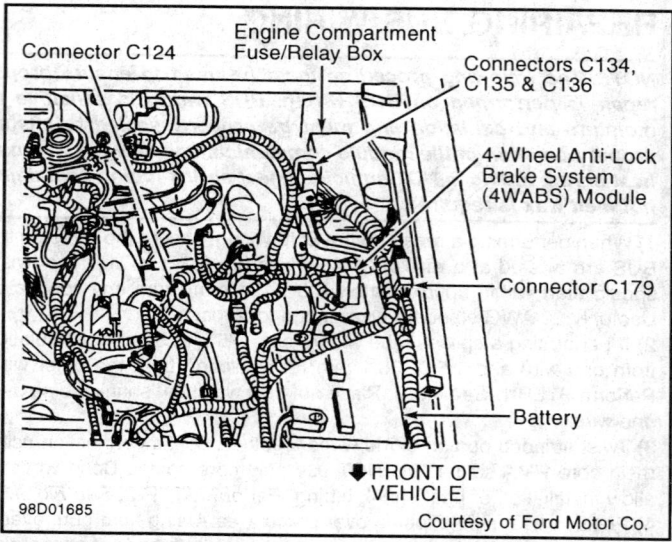

Fig. 3: *Identifying Connectors In Left Side Of Engine Compartment (2.5L)*

TEST B: GENERIC ELECTRONIC MODULE (GEM)/CENTRAL TIMER MODULE (CTM) DOES NOT RESPOND TO NGS TESTER

1) Turn ignition off. Disconnect GEM 26-pin connector located behind center of instrument panel. Inspect GEM connector and Data Link Connector (DLC) for physical damage, bent terminals or corrosion. Repair connectors as necessary and retest system for normal operation. If connectors are okay, go to next step.
2) Measure resistance of Light Blue/White wire between terminal No. 25 at GEM 26-pin connector and terminal No. 7 at DLC. See Figs. 2 and 9. If resistance is less than 5 ohms, replace GEM and retest system for

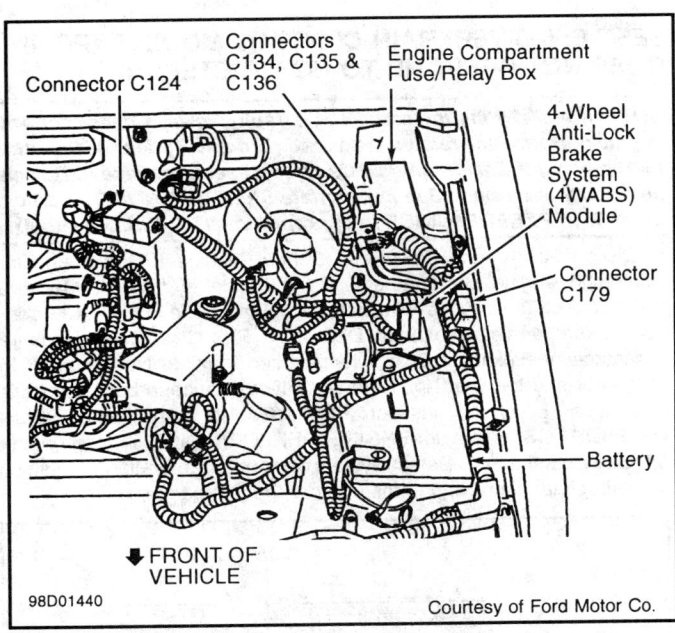

Fig. 4: Identifying Connectors In Left Side Of Engine Compartment (3.0L)

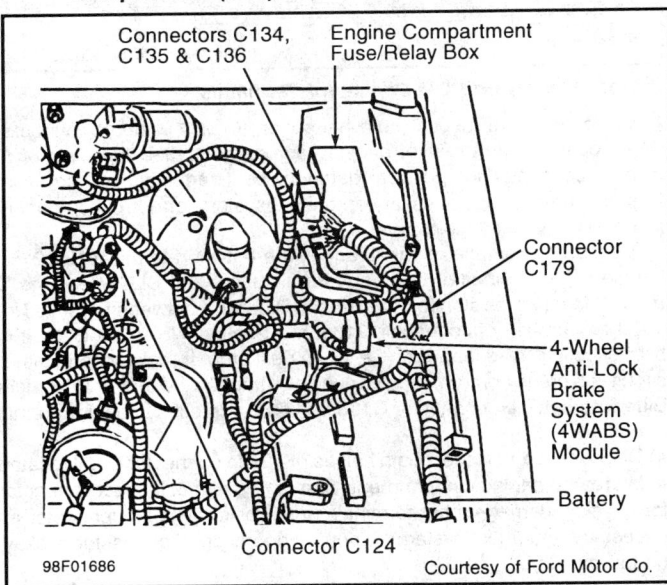

Fig. 5: Identifying Connectors In Left Side Of Engine Compartment (4.0L)

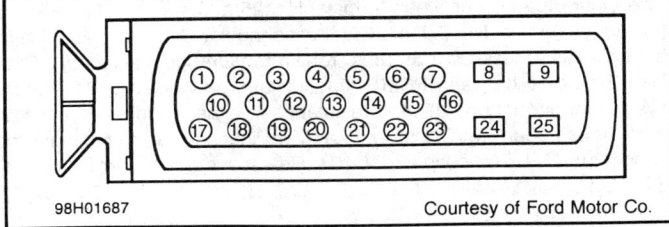

Fig. 6: Identifying 4WABS Module Connector Terminals

normal operation. If resistance is 5 ohms or more, repair open in Light Blue/White wire between GEM connector and DLC and retest system for normal operation.

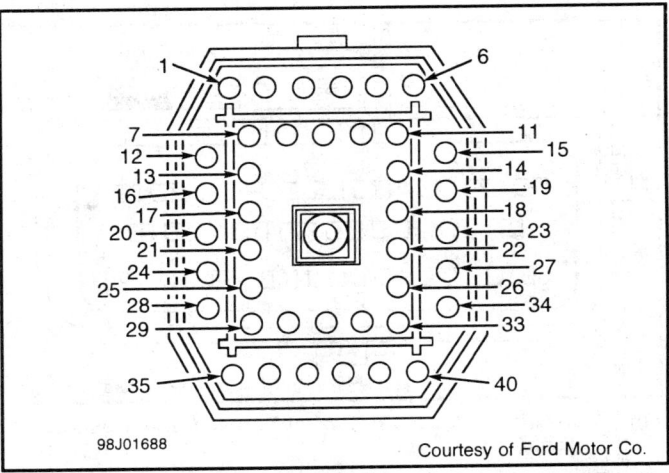

Fig. 7: Identifying Bulkhead 40-pin Connectors C134 & C136 (Female Side Of Connector Shown)

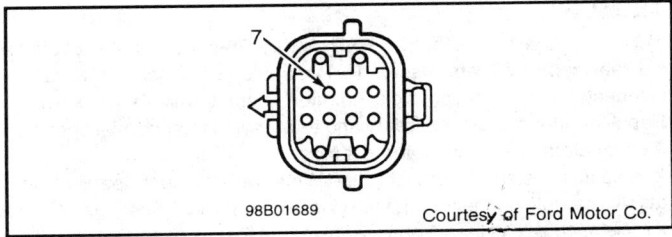

Fig. 8: Identifying In-Line Connector C179 Terminals

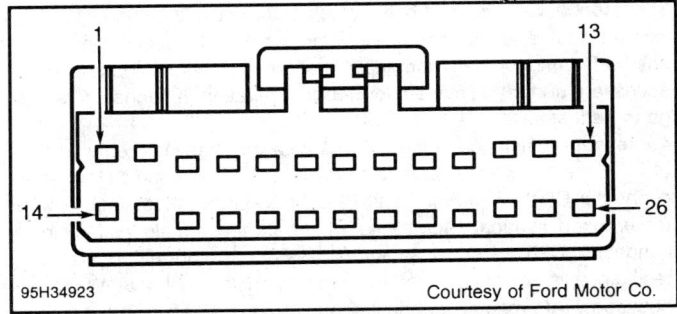

Fig. 9: Identifying GEM 26-Pin & RAP Module 26-Pin Connector Terminals

TEST C: AIR BAG DIAGNOSTIC MONITOR DOES NOT RESPOND TO NGS TESTER

NOTE: Air bag diagnostic monitor may be referred to as Restraint Control Module (RCM).

1) Turn ignition off. Deactivate air bag system. See AIR BAG RESTRAINT SYSTEMS – RANGER article. Disconnect Restraint Control Module (RCM) connector located behind right kick panel. Inspect RCM connector and Data Link Connector (DLC) for physical damage, bent terminals or corrosion. Repair connectors as necessary and retest system for normal operation. If connectors are okay, go to next step.

2) Measure resistance of Light Blue/White wire between terminal No. 5 at RCM connector and terminal No. 7 at DLC. *See Figs. 2 and 10.* If resistance is less than 5 ohms, replace RCM and retest system for normal operation. If resistance is 5 ohms or more, repair open in Light Blue/White wire between RCM connector and DLC. Retest system for normal operation.

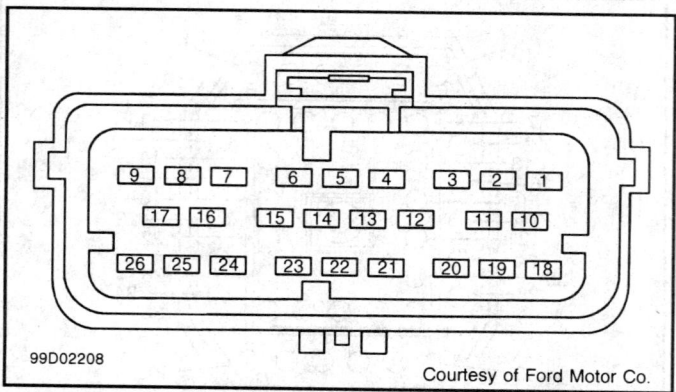

Fig. 10: Identifying Restraint Control Module (RCM) Connector Terminals

TEST D: REMOTE ANTI-THEFT PERSONALITY (RAP) MODULE DOES NOT RESPOND TO NGS TESTER

1) Turn ignition off. Disconnect RAP module 26-pin connector located at left rear corner of cab. Inspect RAP module connector and Data Link Connector (DLC) for physical damage, bent terminals or corrosion. Repair connectors as necessary and retest system for normal operation. If connectors are okay, go to next step.

2) Measure resistance of Light Blue/White wire between terminal No. 3 at RAP module connector and terminal No. 7 at DLC. *See Figs. 2 and 9.* If resistance is less than 5 ohms, replace RAP module and retest system for normal operation. If resistance is 5 ohms or more, go to next step.

3) Disconnect and inspect both halves of 84-pin in-line connector C201 located behind left corner of instrument panel. Inspect connector for physical damage, bent terminals or corrosion. Repair connector as necessary and retest system for normal operation. If connector is okay, go to next step.

4) Measure resistance of Light Blue/White wire between terminal No. 3 at RAP module connector and terminal No. 51 at male half of in-line connector C201. *See Figs. 9 and 11.* If resistance is less than 5 ohms, repair open in Light Blue/White wire between female half of in-line connector C201 and DLC. Retest system for normal operation. If resistance is 5 ohms or more, repair open in Light Blue/White wire between RAP module connector and male half of in-line connector C201. Retest system for normal operation.

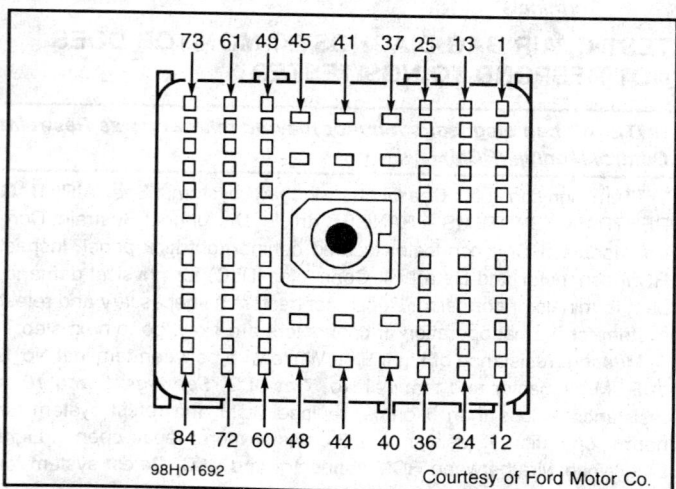

Fig. 11: Identifying In-Line Connector C201 Terminals (Male Half Of Connector Shown)

TEST E: POWERTRAIN CONTROL MODULE (PCM) DOES NOT RESPOND TO NGS TESTER

NOTE: *If test results indicate PCM is faulty, always check for any engine performance related Diagnostic Trouble Codes (DTCs) prior to replacing PCM. If any DTCs are present, service DTCs as necessary and retest. See appropriate SELF-DIAGNOSTICS article in ENGINE PERFORMANCE in appropriate MITCHELL® manual.*

1) Disconnect 104-pin Powertrain Control Module (PCM) connector located in engine compartment, at right side of firewall. Measure resistance of Tan/Orange wire between terminal No. 16 at PCM connector and terminal No. 2 at DLC. *See Figs. 2 and 12.* Measure resistance of Pink/Light Blue wire between terminal No. 15 at PCM connector and terminal No. 10 at DLC. If resistance in both circuits is less than 5 ohms, inspect PCM. Go to appropriate SELF-DIAGNOSTICS article in ENGINE PERFORMANCE in appropriate MITCHELL® manual. Retest system for normal operation. If resistance in either circuit is 5 ohms or more, go to next step.

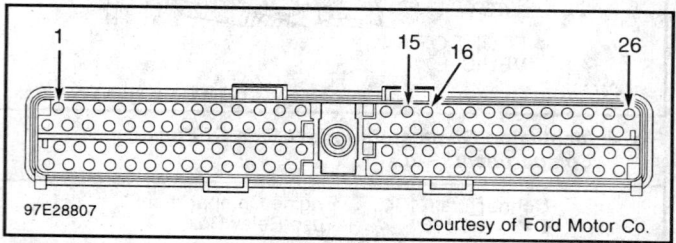

Fig. 12: Identifying PCM Connector Terminals

2) Disconnect and inspect both halves of 40-pin bulkhead connector C136 located at left rear of engine compartment. *See Fig. 3, 4 or 5.* Inspect connector for physical damage, bent terminals or corrosion. Repair connector as necessary and retest system for normal operation. If connector is okay, go to next step.

3) Measure resistance of Tan/Orange wire between terminal No. 21 at female half of connector C136 and terminal No. 2 at DLC. *See Figs. 2 and 7.* Measure resistance of Pink/Light Blue wire between terminal No. 25 at female half of connector C136 and terminal No. 10 at DLC. If in both circuits is less than 5 ohms, go to next step. If resistance in either circuit is 5 ohms or more, repair open Tan/Orange wire and/or Pink/Light Blue wire between connector C136 and DLC. Retest system for normal operation.

4) Disconnect and inspect both halves of 42-pin connector C124 located at left rear of engine compartment. *See Fig. 3, 4 or 5.* Inspect connector for physical damage, bent terminals or corrosion. Repair connector as necessary and retest system for normal operation. If connector is okay, go to next step.

5) Measure resistance of Tan/Orange wire between terminal No. 21 at male half of connector C136 and terminal No. 11 at male half of connector C124. *See Figs. 7 and 13.* Also, measure resistance of Pink/Light Blue wire between terminal No. 25 at male half of connector C136 and terminal No. 3 at male half of connector C124. If resistance in both circuits is less than 5 ohms, repair Tan/Orange wire and/or Pink Light/Blue wire between PCM connector and connector C124. Retest system for normal operation. If resistance in either circuit is 5 ohms or more, repair open Tan/Orange wire and/or Pink/Light Blue wire between connector C136 and connector C124. Retest system for normal operation.

TEST F: PASSIVE ANTI-THEFT SYSTEM (PATS) MODULE DOES NOT RESPOND TO NGS TESTER

1) Turn ignition switch to LOCK position. Disconnect Passive Anti-Theft System (PATS) module harness connector C255. *See Fig. 14.* Inspect harness connector for loose, damaged or corroded terminals. If problem does not exist, go to next step. If problem exist, repair as necessary and retest system.

2) Measure resistance in Tan/Orange wire between terminal No. 6 at PATS module harness connector C255 and terminal No. 2 at DLC. *See*

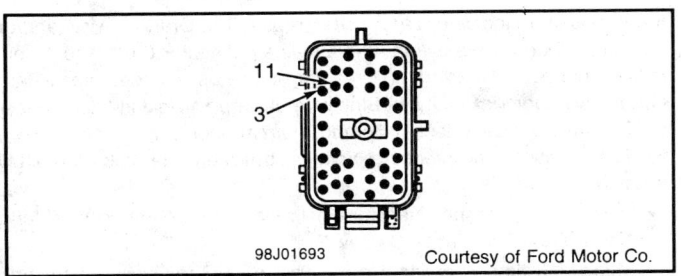

Fig. 13: Identifying Connector C124 Terminals (Male Half Of Connector Shown)

Figs. 2 and 14. Measure resistance in Pink/Light Blue wire between terminal No. 5 at PATS module harness connector C255 and terminal No. 10 at DLC. If resistance in both circuits is 5 ohms or less, replace PATS module. If resistance in either circuit is more than 5 ohms, repair open in Pink/Light Blue wire and/or Tan/Orange wire.

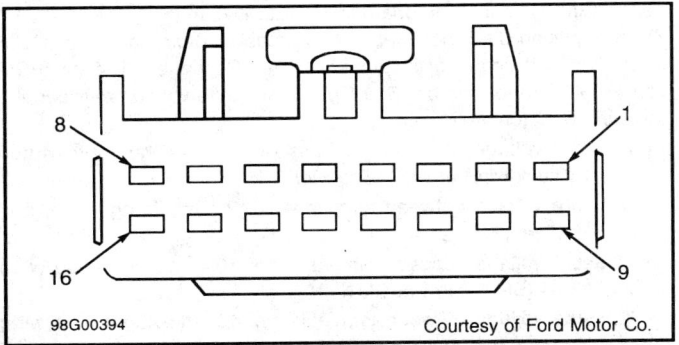

Fig. 14: Identifying PATS Module Connector C255 Terminals

TEST G: NO MODULE/NETWORK COMMUNICATIONS – ISO 9141 NETWORK

NOTE: Depending on module configuration, with all modules connected and with ignition switch in RUN position or with engine running 2-3 volts may be present at Data Link Connector (DLC) terminal No. 7 (Light Blue/White wire). This is the International Standards Organization (ISO) 9141 diagnostic communications network circuit.

1) Turn ignition off. Inspect Data Link Connector (DLC) for physical damage, bent terminals or corrosion. Pay particular attention to terminal No. 7 (Light Blue/White wire). Repair connector as necessary and retest system for normal operation. If connector is okay, go to next step.

2) Ensure ignition is off. Disconnect GEM 26-pin connector located behind center of instrument panel. Measure resistance of Light Blue/White wire between terminal No. 25 at GEM 26-pin connector and terminal No. 7 at DLC. *See Figs. 2 and 9.* If resistance is 5 ohms or more, repair open Light Blue/White wire between DLC and splice and wiring harness splice S225. Splice is located in main wiring harness near breakout to GEM. Retest system for normal operation. If resistance is less than 5 ohms, reconnect GEM connector. Proceed as follows:

- If vehicle is equipped with a Remote Anti-Theft Personality (RAP) module and a 4-Wheel Anti-Lock Brake System (4WABS) module, go to next step.
- If vehicle is equipped with a RAP module only, go to next step.
- If vehicle is equipped with a 4WABS module only, go to step **4)**.
- If vehicle is not equipped with a RAP module or a 4WABS module, go to step **5)**.

NOTE: ISO 9141 communication network will not function if circuit No. 70 (Light Blue/White wire) is shorted to ground or power. Steps 3) - 9) are used for locating a short in circuit No. 70.

3) Disconnect 84-pin in-line connector C201 located behind left corner of instrument panel. Turn ignition on. Measure voltage between terminals No. 7 (Light Blue/White wire) and No. 16 (Orange wire) at DLC. *See Fig. 2.* Also, measure voltage between terminals No. 7 (Light Blue/White wire) and No. 4 (Black wire) at DLC. Both readings should indicate zero volts. If any reading indicates voltage, go to next step (vehicles with 4WABS) or go to step 5) (vehicles without 4WABS). If both readings indicate zero volts, go to step 7).

4) Turn ignition off. Disconnect 40-pin bulkhead connector C134 located at left rear of engine compartment. *See Fig. 3, 4 or 5.* Turn ignition on. Measure voltage between terminals No. 7 (Light Blue/White wire) and No. 16 (Orange wire) at DLC. *See Fig. 2.* Also, measure voltage between terminals No. 7 (Light Blue/White wire) and No. 4 (Black wire) at DLC. If any reading indicates voltage, go to next step. If both readings indicate zero volts, go to step 8).

5) Turn ignition off. Disconnect GEM/CTM 26-pin connector C221 located behind center of instrument panel. *See Fig. 9.* Turn ignition on. Measure voltage between terminals No. 7 (Light Blue/White wire) and No. 16 (Orange wire) at DLC. *See Fig. 2.* Also, measure voltage between terminals No. 7 (Light Blue/White wire) and No. 4 (Black wire) at DLC. If any reading indicates voltage, go to next step. If both readings indicate zero volts, replace GEM and retest system for normal operation.

6) Turn ignition off. Deactivate air bag system. See AIR BAG RESTRAINT SYSTEMS – RANGER article. Disconnect Restraint Control Module (RCM) connector. Reconnect GEM/CTM connector C221. Turn ignition on. Measure voltage between terminals No. 7 (Light Blue/White wire) and No. 16 (Orange wire) at DLC. *See Fig. 2.* Also, measure voltage between terminals No. 7 (Light Blue/White wire) and No. 4 (Black wire) at DLC. If any reading indicates voltage, repair circuit No. 70 (Light Blue/White wire) between DLC and RCM connector, GEM connector, 84-pin in-line connector C201 or 40-pin bulkhead connector C134. Retest system for normal operation. If both readings indicate zero volts, replace RCM and retest system for normal operation.

7) Turn ignition off. Reconnect connector C201. Disconnect RAP module 26-pin connector located at left rear corner of cab. Turn ignition on. Measure voltage between terminals No. 7 (Light Blue/White wire) and No. 16 (Orange wire) at DLC. *See Fig. 2.* Also, measure voltage between terminals No. 7 (Light Blue/White wire) and No. 4 (Black wire) at DLC. If any reading indicates voltage, repair circuit No. 70 (Light Blue/White wire) between connector C201 and RAP module connector. If both readings indicate zero volts, replace RAP module and retest system for normal operation.

8) Turn ignition off. Reconnect 40-pin bulkhead connector C134. Disconnect 25-pin 4WABS module connector located at left side of engine compartment. *See Fig. 3, 4 or 5.* Turn ignition on. Measure voltage between terminals No. 7 (Light Blue/White wire) and No. 16 (Orange wire) at DLC. *See Fig. 2.* Also, measure voltage between terminals No. 7 (Light Blue/White wire) and No. 4 (Black wire) at DLC. If any reading indicates voltage, go to next step. If both readings indicate zero volts, replace 4WABS module and retest system for normal operation.

9) Turn ignition off. Disconnect 40-pin bulkhead connector C179 located at left rear of engine compartment. *See Fig. 3, 4 or 5.* Turn ignition on. Measure voltage between terminals No. 7 (Light Blue/White wire) and No. 16 (Orange wire) at DLC. *See Fig. 2.* Also, measure voltage between terminals No. 7 (Light Blue/White wire) and No. 4 (Black wire) at DLC. If any reading indicates voltage, repair circuit No. 70 (Light Blue/White wire) between connector C134 and connector C179. Retest system for normal operation. If both readings indicate zero volts, repair circuit No. 70 (Light Blue/White wire) between connector C179 and 4WABS module. Retest system for normal operation.

TEST H: NO MODULE/NETWORK COMMUNICATIONS – SCP NETWORK

NOTE: Depending on module configuration, with all modules connected and with ignition switch in RUN position or with engine running 2-3 volts may be present at Data Link Connector (DLC) terminals No. 2 (Tan/Orange wire) and No. 10 (Pink/Light Blue wire). These are the Standard Corporate Protocol (SCP) diagnostic communications network circuits.

1) Turn ignition off. Inspect Data Link Connector (DLC) for physical damage, bent terminals or corrosion. Pay particular attention to terminals No. 2 (Tan/Orange wire) and No. 10 (Pink/Light Blue wire). *See Fig. 2.* Repair connector as necessary and retest system for normal operation. If connector is okay, go to next step.

2) Turn ignition off. Disconnect 104–pin Powertrain Control Module (PCM) connector located in engine compartment, at right side of firewall. Turn ignition on. Measure resistance of Tan/Orange wire between terminal No. 16 at PCM connector and terminal No. 2 at DLC. *See Figs. 2 and 12.* Measure resistance of Pink/Light Blue wire between terminal No. 15 at PCM connector and terminal No. 10 at DLC. If resistance in both circuits is less than 5 ohms and evehicle is equiped with a PATS module, go to step 6). If resistance in both circuits is less than 5 ohms and vehicle is not equiped with a PATS module, go to next step. If resistance is either circuit is 5 ohms or more and vehicle is not equiped with a PATS module, go to POWERTRAIN CONTROL MODULE (PCM) DOES NOT RESPOND TO NGS TESTER test. If resistance is either circuit is 5 ohms or more and vehicle is equiped with a PATS module, repair Pink/Light Blue wire or Tan/Orange wire.

3) Turn ignition on. Measure voltage between the following DLC terminals:
- Measure voltage between terminals No. 2 (Tan/Orange wire) and No. 4 (Black wire) at DLC. *See Fig. 2.*
- Measure voltage between terminals No. 2 (Tan/Orange wire) and No. 16 (Orange wire) at DLC.
- Measure voltage between terminals No. 10 (Pink/Light Blue wire) and No. 4 (Black wire) at DLC.
- Measure voltage between terminals No. 10 (Pink/Light Blue wire) and No. 16 (Orange wire) at DLC.

If any reading indicates voltage, go to next step. If all readings indicate zero volts, go to appropriate SELF-DIAGNOSTICS article in ENGINE PERFORMANCE in appropriate MITCHELL® manual.

4) Turn ignition off. Disconnect 42-pin in-line connector C124 located at left rear of engine compartment. *See Fig. 3, 4 or 5.* Turn ignition on. Measure voltage between the following DLC terminals:
- Measure voltage between terminals No. 2 (Tan/Orange wire) and No. 4 (Black wire) at DLC. *See Fig. 2.*
- Measure voltage between terminals No. 2 (Tan/Orange wire) and No. 16 (Orange wire) at DLC.
- Measure voltage between terminals No. 10 (Pink/Light Blue wire) and No. 4 (Black wire) at DLC.
- Measure voltage between terminals No. 10 (Pink/Light Blue wire) and No. 16 (Orange wire) at DLC.

If any reading indicates voltage, go to next step. If all readings indicate zero volts, repair Tan/Orange wire and/or Pink/Light Blue wire between 42-pin in-line connector C124 and PCM. Retest system for normal operation.

5) Turn ignition off. Disconnect 40-pin bulkhead connector C136 located at left rear of engine compartment. *See Fig. 3, 4 or 5.* Turn ignition on. Measure voltage between the following DLC terminals:
- Measure voltage between terminals No. 2 (Tan/Orange wire) and No. 4 (Black wire) at DLC. *See Fig. 2.*
- Measure voltage between terminals No. 2 (Tan/Orange wire) and No. 16 (Orange wire) at DLC.
- Measure voltage between terminals No. 10 (Pink/Light Blue wire) and No. 4 (Black wire) at DLC.
- Measure voltage between terminals No. 10 (Pink/Light Blue wire) and No. 16 (Orange wire) at DLC.

If all readings indicate zero volts, repair Tan/Orange wire and/or Pink/Light Blue wire between 40-pin in-line connector C136 and 42-pin in-line connector C124. If any reading indicates voltage, repair Tan/Orange wire and/or Pink/Light Blue wire between 40-pin in-line connector C136 and DLC. Retest system for normal operation.

6) Turn ignition on. Measure voltage between the following DLC terminals:
- Measure voltage between terminals No. 2 (Tan/Orange wire) and No. 4 (Black wire) at DLC. *See Fig. 2.*
- Measure voltage between terminals No. 2 (Tan/Orange wire) and No. 16 (Orange wire) at DLC.
- Measure voltage between terminals No. 10 (Pink/Light Blue wire) and No. 4 (Black wire) at DLC.
- Measure voltage between terminals No. 10 (Pink/Light Blue wire) and No. 16 (Orange wire) at DLC.

If any reading indicates zero volts, go to next step. If all readings indicate voltage, go to appropriate SELF-DIAGNOSTICS article in ENGINE PERFORMANCE in appropriate MITCHELL® manual.

7) Turn ignition off. Disconnect PATS module 16-pin connector C255 located behind center of instrument panel. Reconnect 104–pin PCM connector. Turn ignition on. *See Fig. 14.* Measure voltage between the following DLC terminals:
- Measure voltage between terminals No. 2 (Tan/Orange wire) and No. 4 (Black wire) at DLC. *See Fig. 2.*
- Measure voltage between terminals No. 2 (Tan/Orange wire) and No. 16 (Orange wire) at DLC.
- Measure voltage between terminals No. 10 (Pink/Light Blue wire) and No. 4 (Black wire) at DLC.
- Measure voltage between terminals No. 10 (Pink/Light Blue wire) and No. 16 (Orange wire) at DLC.

If any reading indicates voltage, go to next step. If all readings indicate voltage, replace PATS module. Retest system for normal operation.

8) Turn ignition off. Reconnect PATS module. Disconnect 42-pin in-line connector C124 located at left rear of engine compartment. *See Fig. 3, 4 or 5.* Turn ignition on. Measure voltage between the following DLC terminals:
- Measure voltage between terminals No. 2 (Tan/Orange wire) and No. 4 (Black wire) at DLC. *See Fig. 2.*
- Measure voltage between terminals No. 2 (Tan/Orange wire) and No. 16 (Orange wire) at DLC.
- Measure voltage between terminals No. 10 (Pink/Light Blue wire) and No. 4 (Black wire) at DLC.
- Measure voltage between terminals No. 10 (Pink/Light Blue wire) and No. 16 (Orange wire) at DLC.

If any reading indicates zero volts, go to next step. If all readings indicate voltage, repair Tan/Orange wire and/or Pink/Light Blue wire between PCM and 42-pin in-line connector C124.

9) Turn ignition off. Disconnect 40-pin bulkhead connector C136 located at left rear of engine compartment. *See Fig. 3, 4 or 5.* Turn ignition on. Measure voltage between the following DLC terminals:
- Measure voltage between terminals No. 2 (Tan/Orange wire) and No. 4 (Black wire) at DLC. *See Fig. 2.*
- Measure voltage between terminals No. 2 (Tan/Orange wire) and No. 16 (Orange wire) at DLC.
- Measure voltage between terminals No. 10 (Pink/Light Blue wire) and No. 4 (Black wire) at DLC.
- Measure voltage between terminals No. 10 (Pink/Light Blue wire) and No. 16 (Orange wire) at DLC.

If any reading indicates zero volts, repair Tan/Orange wire and/or Pink/Light Blue wire between 40-pin in-line connector C136 and PATS module. If all readings indicate voltage, repair Tan/Orange wire and/or Pink/Light Blue wire between 40-pin in-line connector C136 and 42-pin in-line connector C124. Retest system for normal operation.

TEST I: NO MODULE/NETWORK COMMUNICATION – NO POWER TO NGS THROUGH DLC

1) Inspect NGS tester connector for loose, damaged or corroded terminals. Repair as necessary and retest system for normal operation. If connector is okay, go to next step.

2) Turn ignition off. Inspect Data Link Connector (DLC) for physical damage, bent terminals or corrosion. Repair as necessary and retest system for normal operation. If connector is okay, go to next step.

3) Measure voltage between ground and terminal No. 16 (Orange wire) at DLC. *See Fig. 2*. If voltage is more than 10 volts, go to next step. If voltage is 10 volts or less, repair Orange wire between instrument panel fuse block and DLC. Retest system for normal operation.

4) Measure resistance between ground and terminals No. 4 (Black wire) and No. 5 (Black/White wire) at DLC. If both resistance readings are less than 5 ohms, repair or replace NGS tester. Retest system for normal operation. If any resistance reading is 5 ohms or more, repair open in Black wire or Black/White wire between ground and DLC. Retest system for normal operation.

DIAGNOSTIC TROUBLE CODE (DTC) DEFINITIONS

GENERIC ELECTRONIC MODULE/CENTRAL TIMER MODULE (GEM/CTM) DTC DEFINITIONS

DTC	Definition	Test
B1302	Accessory Delay Relay Coil Circuit Failure	1
B1304	Accessory Delay Relay Coil Circuit Short To Battery	1
B1313	Battery Saver Relay Coil Circuit Failure	2
B1315	Battery Saver Relay Coil Circuit Short To Battery	2
B1317	Battery Voltage High	3 4
B1318	Battery Voltage Low	3 4
B1322	Driver Door Ajar Circuit Short To Ground	2 4
B1323	Driver Door Ajar Light Circuit Failure	5
B1325	Door Ajar Light Circuit Short To Battery	5
B1330	Passenger Door Ajar Circuit Short To Ground	2 4
B1340	Chime Input Request Circuit Short To Ground	6
B1342	GEM/CTM Is Defective	7
B1352	Ignition Key-In Circuit Failure	6 4
B1355	Ignition RUN Circuit Failure	8
B1359	Ignition RUN/ACC Circuit Failure	8
B1371	Illuminated Entry Relay Circuit Failure	2
B1373	Illuminated Entry Relay Short To Battery	2
B1398	Driver Door One-Touch Window Relay Circuit Failure	1
B1400	Driver Door One-Touch Window Relay Coil Circuit Short To Battery	1
B1404	Driver Door Window Down Switch Input Circuit Open	1
B1405	Driver Door Window Down Switch Input Circuit Short To Battery	1 4
B1410	Driver Door Window Motor Circuit Failure	4
B1426	Seat Belt Light Circuit Short To Battery	5
B1428	Seat Belt Light Circuit Failure	5
B1431	Wiper Brake/Run Relay Circuit Failure	9
B1432	Wiper Brake/Run Relay Circuit Short To Battery	9
B1434	Wiper High/Low Speed Relay Circuit Failure	9
B1436	Wiper High/Low Speed Relay Circuit Short To Battery	9 4
B1438	Wiper Mode Select Switch Circuit Failure	9 4
B1441	Wiper Mode Select Switch Short To Ground	9 4
B1446	Wiper Park Sense Circuit Failure	9 4
B1450	Wiper/Wash Interval Delay Switch Input Failure	9 4
B1453	Wiper/Wash Interval Delay Switch Input Short To Ground	9
B1458	Wiper/Washer Pump Motor Relay Circuit Failure	9
B1460	Wiper/Washer Pump Motor Relay Coil Short To Battery	6 4
B1462	Seat Belt Switch Circuit Failure	9
B1466	Wiper High/Low Speed Not Switching	9
B1467	Wiper Motor Hi/Low Speed Circuit Short To Battery	9
B1473	Wiper Motor Low Speed Circuit Failure	1
B1475	Delayed Accessory Relay Contacts Short To Battery	9
B1476	Wiper Motor High Speed Circuit Failure	10
B1483	Brake Pedal Input Circuit Failure	10
B1485	Brake Pedal Input Circuit Short To Battery	6 4
B1577	Parking Light Input Circuit Short To Battery	2 4
B1610	Illuminated Entry Input Circuit Short To Ground	11
B1833	Door Unlock Switch Circuit Short To Ground	9
B1840	Wiper Power Circuit Failure	12
B2141	NVM Configuration Failure	5
C1751	VSS Output Short To Battery	5
C1752	VSS Output Short To Ground	10
P0500	Vehicle Speed Signal Circuit Failure	10
P1804	4WD High Indicator Circuit Failure	10
P1806	4WD High Indicator Circuit Short To Battery	10
P1808	4WD Low Indicator Circuit Failure	10
P1810	4WD Low Indicator Circuit Short To Battery	10

GENERIC ELECTRONIC MODULE/CENTRAL TIMER MODULE (GEM/CTM) DTC DEFINITIONS (Cont.)

DTC	Definition	Test
P1812	4WD Mode Select Switch Circuit Failure	10
P1815	4WD Mode Select Switch Circuit Short To Ground	10
P1820	Transfer Case Clockwise Shift Relay Coil Circuit Failure	10
P1822	Transfer Case Clockwise Shift Relay Coil Short To Battery	10
P1824	4WD Electric Clutch Relay Circuit Failure	10
P1826	4WD Low Clutch Relay Circuit Short To Battery	10
P1828	Transfer Case Counterclockwise Shift Relay Coil Circuit Failure	10
P1830	Transfer Case Counterclockwise Shift Relay Coil Short To Battery	10
P1832	Transfer Case Differential Lock-Up Solenoid Failure	10
P1833	Transfer Case Differential Lock-Up Solenoid Open Circuit	10
P1834	Transfer Case Differential Lock-Up Solenoid Short To Battery	10
P1835	Transfer Case Differential Lock-Up Solenoid Short To Ground	10
P1838	Transfer Case Shift Motor Circuit Failure	10
P1846	Transfer Case Contact Plate "A" Circuit Failure	10
P1850	Transfer Case Contact Plate "B" Circuit Failure	10
P1854	Transfer Case Contact Plate "C" Circuit Failure	10
P1858	Transfer Case Contact Plate "D" Circuit Failure	10
P1863	Transfer Case Contact Plate Power Circuit Open	10
P1866	Transfer Case System Concern	10
P1867	Transfer Case Contact Plate General Circuit Failure	10
P1878	Transfer Case Disengage Solenoid Circuit Failure	10
P1879	Transfer Case Disengage Solenoid Open Circuit	10
P1880	Transfer Case Disengage Solenoid Short To Battery	10
P1885	Transfer Case Disengage Solenoid Short To Ground	10
P1891	Transfer Case Contact Plate Ground Return Circuit Open	10

[1] – See POWER WINDOWS – RANGER article for testing procedures.

[2] – Test wiring for opens and/or shorts and repair as necessary. See appropriate wiring diagram in ILLUMINATION/INTERIOR LIGHTS article.

[3] – See GENERATORS – RANGER article in STARTING & CHARGING SYSTEMS for testing procedures.

[4] – This DTC may also be present from GEM/CTM wiggle test.

[5] – See ANALOG INSTRUMENT PANELS – RANGER article for testing procedures.

[6] – Test wiring for opens and/or shorts and repair as necessary. See appropriate wiring diagram in WARNING SYSTEMS article.

[7] – Using NGS tester, clear DTCs. Retrieve DTCs. If DTC B1342 is retrieved, replace GEM/CTM and retest system operation.

[8] – See STEERING COLUMN SWITCHES – RANGER article for testing procedures.

[9] – See WIPER/WASHER SYSTEMS – RANGER article for testing procedures.

[10] – See appropriate TRANSFER CASES article in TRANSMISSIONS in appropriate MITCHELL® TRANSMISSION SERVICE & REPAIR manual for testing procedures.

[11] – See wiring diagram in appropriate REMOTE KEYLESS ENTRY SYSTEMS article for testing procedures.

[12] – Vehicle speed calibration data is not programmed into GEM/CTM. Use NGS tester configuration card help screen to program tire size and axle ratio. Retest system operation. If DTC B2141 is still present, replace GEM/CTM and retest system operation.

PASSIVE ANTI-THEFT SYSTEM MODULE DTC INDEX

DTC	Description	[1] Test
B1213	Anti-Theft Number Of Programmed Keys Is Below Minimum	[2] B1213
B1232/B2103	PATS Transceiver Antenna Not Connected	B1232
B1600	PATS Ignition Key Transponder Signal Not Received/Damaged Encoded Ignition Key Or Use Of Non-PATS Key	B1600
B1601	PATS Received Incorrect Key Code From Ignition Key Transponder	B1601
B1602	Invalid Key Code Format From Ignition Key Transponder	B1602
B1681	PATS Transceiver Signal Is Not Received	B1681
B2139	Security Identification Does Not Match Between PATS & PCM	B2139
B2141	No Security Identification Exchange Between PATS & PCM	B2141
U1147	Invalid Or Missing Data For Vehicle Security	U1147
U1262	SCP Bus Communication Fault	3

[1] – In PASSIVE ANTI-THEFT SYSTEMS – RANGER article.

[2] – If DTCs B1232, B1600, B1601, B1602 OR B1681 are also present, service these DTCs first then recheck codes.

[3] – Repair SCP bus communications concern.

REMOTE ANTI-THEFT PERSONALITY (RAP) MODULE DTC INDEX

DTC	Description	[1] Test
B1309	Power Door Lock Circuit Short To Ground	1
B1341	Power Door Unlock Circuit Short To Ground	1
B1522	Hood Switch Circuit Short To Ground	1
B1562	Door Lock Cylinder Circuit Short To Ground	1
B2425	Keyless Entry Out Of Synchronization	1

[1] – See wiring diagram in appropriate REMOTE KEYLESS ENTRY SYSTEMS article.

RESTRAINT CONTROL MODULE (RCM) DTC INDEX

DTC [1]	Description	Test
B1342	ECU Defective	2

RESTRAINT CONTROL MODULE (RCM) DTC INDEX (Cont.)

DTC [1]	Description	Test
B1231	RCM Internal Fault	3
B1921	RCM Crash Data Memory Full	3
C1414	Incorrect Vehicle Identification Code	3
B1887	Driver's Air Bag Circuit Shorted To Ground	3
B1916	Driver's Air Bag Circuit Shorted To Voltage	3
B1888	Passenger's Air Bag Circuit Shorted To Ground	3
B1925	Passenger's Air Bag Circuit Shorted To Voltage	3
B1932	Driver's Air Bag Circuit Resistance High	3
B1933	Passenger's Air Bag Circuit Resistance High	3
B1934	Driver's Air Bag Circuit Resistance Low	3
B1935	Passenger's Air Bag Circuit Resistance Low	3
B1871	Passenger's Air Bag Deactivation (PAD) Switch Fault	3
B1884	Passenger's Air Bag Deactivation (PAD) Warning Light Inoperative	3
B1890	Passenger's Air Bag Deactivation (PAD) Warning Light Short To Battery	3
B1892	Air Bag Tone Warning Indicator Circuit Shorted To Ground Or Open	3
B1891	Air Bag Tone Warning Indicator Circuit Shorted To Voltage	3
B1869	Air Bag Indicator Inoperative	3
B1870	Air Bag Indicator Shorted To Voltage	3

[1] – DTCs are listed in order of importance. Repair DTCs in order listed.

[2] – Using NGS tester, retrieve and document all continuous DTCs. Perform Restraint Control Module (RCM) self-test. If DTC B1342 is retrieved again, replace RCM.

[3] – Repair supplemental restraint system concern. See DIAGNOSIS & TESTING article in appropriate MITCHELL® AIR BAG SERVICE & REPAIR MANUAL, DOMESTIC & IMPORTED MODELS.

4 WHEEL ANTI-LOCK BRAKE SYSTEM (4WABS) MODULE DTC INDEX

DTC	Description	Test
B1342	ECU Defective	1
B1485	Brake Pedal Input Circuit Shorted To Voltage	2
B1676	Battery Voltage Out Of Range	2
B2141	Vehicle Speed Calibration Data Not Programmed Into Module	2
C1095	ABS Hydraulic Pump Motor Circuit Failure	2
C1102	G-Switch Circuit Failure	2
C1145	Right Front ABS Sensor Input Circuit Failure	2
C1155	Left Front ABS Sensor Input Circuit Failure	2
C1230	Rear ABS Sensor Input Circuit Failure	2
C1233	Left Front ABS Sensor Input Signal Missing	2
C1234	Right Front ABS Sensor Input Signal Missing	2
C1237	Rear ABS Sensor Input Signal Missing	

[1] – Using NGS tester, retrieve and document all continuous DTCs. Perform ABS self-test. If DTC B1342 is retrieved again, replace ABS module.

[2] – Repair anti-lock brake system concern. See appropriate ANTI-LOCK article in BRAKES in appropriate MITCHELL® manual.

PARAMETER IDENTIFICATION (PID) DEFINITIONS

GEM/CTM PID INDEX

PID	Description	Expected Value
VSS_GEM	Vehicle Speed Input	0–255 KPH
PARK_SW	External Access Ajar Switch Status	OFF, ON
D_DR_SW	Left Front Door Ajar Switch Status	CLOSED, AJAR
P_DR_SW	Right Passenger Door Ajar Switch Status	CLOSED, AJAR
IGN_KEY	Key In Ignition Status	IN, OUT
IGN_GEM	Ignition Switch Status	START, RUN, OFF, ACC
BATSAV	Battery Saver Relay Circuit	ON- - -, OFF- - -, ON-B-, OFFO-G
VBATGEM	Battery Voltage	0.0 VDC - 14.3 VDC
INTLMP	Illuminated Entry Relay Circuit	ON- - -, OFF- - -, ON-B-, OFFO-G
CLTCHSW	Trans Clutch Interlock Switch	ENGAGED, NOT ENGAGED
NTRL_SW	Neutral Saftey Switch Input	NTRL, notNTRL
MTR_CCW	Trans Transfer CCW Motor Output	ON- - -, OFF- - -, ON-B-, OFFO-G
MTR_CW	CW Shift Relay Coil Status	ON- - -, OFF- - -, ON-B-, OFFO-G
4WDCLCH	4WD Electronic Clutch Output Status	ON- - -, OFF- - -, ON-B-, OFFO-G
4WDLOW	4WD Low Indicator Status	ON- - -, OFF- - -, ON-B-, OFFO-G
4WDHIGH	4WD High Indicator Status	ON- - -, OFF- - -, ON-B-, OFFO-G
4WD_SW	4WD Switch Status	2WD, 4WD HIGH, 4WD LOW
PLATE_A	Transfer Case Contact Plate Switch A	OPEN, CLOSED
PLATE_B	Transfer Case Contact Plate Switch B	OPEN, CLOSED
PLATE_C	Transfer Case Contact Plate Switch C	OPEN, CLOSED
PLATE_D	Transfer Case Contact Plate Switch D	OPEN, CLOSED
BOO_GEM	Brake Pedal Position Switch Input	ON, OFF
PLATEPW	Transfer Case Contact Plate Ground Output	ON - - -, OFF- - -
D_SBLT	Driver's Seat Belt Status	IN, OUT

GEM/CTM PID INDEX (Cont.)

PID	Description	Expected Value
IPCHIME	External Chime Request	ON, OFF
SBLTMP	Seat Belt Indicator Status	ON, OFF, ON-B-, OFFO-G
DRAJR_L	Door Ajar Warning Light Circuit	ON, OFF
D_PWRLY	On Touch Down Relay Coil Circuit Status	ON- -, OFF- -, ON-B-, OFFO-G
D_PWAMP	Driver's Power Window Motor Current	.25 Amp Increments
D_PWPK	Driver's Power Window Motor Peak Current	.25 Amp Increments
ACCDLY	Accessory Delay Relay Coil Circuit	ON- -, OFF- -, ON-B-, OFFO-G
WPPK_PK	Wiper Park-To-Park Time	0-6.5 Seconds
WPMODE	Wiper Control Mode Status	WASH, OPEN INVLD, OFF, INTVL 1–7, LOW, HIGH
WPPRKSW	Wiper Motor Status	PARKED, notPRK
WPRUN	Wiper Mode Run Relay	ON- -, OFF- -, ON-B-, OFFO-G
WPHISP	Wiper HI/LO Relay Status	ON- -, OFF- -, ON-B-, OFFO-G
WASH_SW	Washer Pump Relay Switch Status	ON, OFF, ON-B-, OFFO-G

PATS MODULE PID INDEX

PID	Description	Expected Value
CCNTPATS	Number Of Continuous DTC	One Count Per Bit
IGN_PAT	Ignition Switch	OFF, RUN
NUMKEYS	Number Of Ignition Key Codes Programed	BCD (Valid Range 0-8)
ENABL_S	Has PATS Enabled Vehicle	DISABLED, ENABLED
ACCESS	Security Access Status	TIMED, CODED
MIN#KEY	Minimum Number Of Programmed Keys Required To Start Vehicle	BCD (Valid Range 2-8)
ANTISCN	Time-Out For Unprogrammed PATS Key	notACT, ACTIVE
PCM_ID	Is PCM ID Stored In PATS Module	STORED, /notSTR
SPARE_KY	Can You Add Spare Keys With 2 Programmed Keys	YES, NO
PCM_VFY	PCM ID Matches Between PCM & PATS Module	YES, NO

RAP MODULE PID INDEX

PID	Description	Expected Value
AL_EVT#	Last 8 Alarm Events	HOODDTR, NO_EVT, DROPEN, PANIC, TRAJAR
DD_LOCK	Power Door Lock/Unlock Status	OFF, LOCK, UNLOCK, SHORT
DOORRAP	Door Ajar Status Input	CLOSED, AJAR
DR_DARM	Door Disarm Input	notACT, ACTIVE
HOOD_SW	Hood Switch Input	PUNCHD, notPUN
IGN_RAP	Ignition Switch	OFF, RUN/ACC
IGN_RES	Ignition Lock Anti-Theft Switch	162, 0, HIGH

RESTRAINT CONTROL MODULE (RCM) PID INDEX

PID	Description	Expected Value
CCNT	Number Of Continuous DTCs On Speed Control Servo	0–10
VBAT	Battery Feed Voltage At RCM	9-16 Volts
D_ABAGR	Driver's Air Bag Module Resistance	1.7-4.1 Ohms
P_ABAGR	Passenger's Air Bag Module Resistance	1.7-3.2 Ohms
BRACKET	Bracket Ground Resistance	Less Than 100 Ohms
VID #1	Programmed Vehicle ID Pin 10	Ground
VID #2	Programmed Vehicle ID Pin 13	NO CONNECT
VID #3	Programmed Vehicle ID Pin 14	NO CONNECT

4 WHEEL ANTI-LOCK BRAKE SYSTEM (4WABS) PID INDEX

PID	Description	Expected Value
CCNTABS	Number Of Continuous DTC	One Count Per Bit
BOO_ABS	Brake Pedal Position Switch Input	ON, OFF
ACCLSW1	Acceleration Switch Position 1 Input	ACT, notACT
ACCLSW2	Acceleration Switch Position 2 Input	ACT, notACT
ABSR_O	Rear ABS Outlet Valve	ON, OFF
ABSRR_O	Right Rear ABS Outlet Valve	ON, OFF
ABSLF_O	Left Front ABS Outlet Valve	ON, OFF
ABSR_I	Rear ABS Inlet Valve	ON, OFF
ABSRF_I	Right Front ABS Inlet Valve	ON, OFF
ABSLF_I	Left Front ABS Inlet Valve	ON, OFF
LF_WSPD	Left Front Wheel Speed Signal	0-255 KPH
RF_WSPD	Right Front Wheel Speed Signal	0-255 KPH
R_WSPD	Rear Wheel Speed Signal	0-255 KPH
4WDLOW	4WD LOW Input	ON, OFF

WIRING DIAGRAMS

NOTE: See appropriate wiring diagrams in DATA LINK CONNEC-
TORS, GROUND DISTRIBUTION or POWER DISTRIBUTION article
in WIRING DIAGRAMS.

DESCRIPTION & OPERATION

Vehicle has 2 module communications networks. The module communications network provides the ability for module-to-module communication by sharing inputs and outputs instead of each component having an input and output wired directly to each module. A BUS which consists of a pair of twisted wires is used to transfer information between each module. The BUS network is also referred to as Standard Corporate Protocol (SCP). The BUS consists of a (+) circuit No. 914 and a (–) circuit No. 915. The BUS is routed throughout the vehicle to Powertrain Control Module (PCM), Remote Climate Control (RCC) module and Passive Anti-Theft System (PATS) module (if equipped). The Generic Electronic Module (GEM), Anti-lock Brake System (ABS) control module, Remote Anti-theft Personality (RAP) module, electronic crash sensor module and Semi-Active Ride Control (SARC) module do not use the BUS to communicate with other modules. These modules are connected to the International Standards Organization (ISO) 9141 diagnostic communications network through a single wire (circuit No. 70). Both networks are connected to the Data Link Connector (DLC). This article is used to diagnose BUS and ISO communications network circuit faults. For module locations, see COMPONENT LOCATIONS.

COMPONENT LOCATIONS

COMPONENT LOCATIONS

Component	Location
Anti-Lock Brake System Module	In Engine Compartment, Below Battery
Data Link Connector	[1] Under Instrument Panel, Below Steering Column
Electronic Crash Sensor Module	[1] Behind Center Of Instrument Panel, On Tunnel
Generic Electronic Module	[1] Attached To Under Side Of Instrument Panel Fuse Box
In-Line Harness Connector C130	Left Side Of Engine Compartment, On Top Of Transmission
In-Line Harness Connector C214	[1] Behind Left Side Of Instrument Panel
In-Line Harness Connector C221	[1] Behind Left Side Of Instrument Panel
In-Line Harness Connector C243	[1] Behind Right Side Of Instrument Panel, Behind Glove Box
Passive Anti-Theft System Module	[1] Behind Center Of Instrument Panel, Behind Integrated Control Panel
Powertrain Control Module	On Right Side Of Firewall In Engine Compartment
Remote Anti-Theft Personality Module	[1] Above Accelerator Pedal
Remote Climate Control Module	[1] Behind Right Side Of Instrument Panel, Behind Glove Box
Semi-Active Ride Control Module	Right Side Of Luggage Compartment

[1] – See Fig. 4.

REPAIRING BUS WIRING

NOTE: Following procedure must be used to ensure proper repair is performed on BUS wiring. BUS wiring is sensitive to moisture and oxidation and must be properly sealed to ensure proper operation of the module communications network. Regular heat shrink tubing is NOT sufficient, heat shrink tubing containing hot melt wax is required.

1) When performing a repair on the BUS wiring, ensure the wires on the BUS are twisted at a rate of 33-40 winds per 3.3 ft. (1 m). The twists should start approximately 4.9" (124 mm) from any connector. Use only 20 AWG standard wire gauge for repairs.

2) If performing a splice in the wiring, strip .75" (19.0 mm) of insulation from one wire and 1.50" (38.1 mm) of insulation from the other wire. Perform STEP 1. See Fig. 1. Place hot melt wax type heat shrink tubing over one wire.

3) Twist stripped portion of the wires together. Solder connection using resin core RMA solder. DO NOT use acid core solder. Bend wires to allow installation of heat shrink tubing. Perform STEP 2. See Fig. 1.

4) Position heat shrink tubing over splice area. Using heat gun, evenly heat the heat shrink tubing until wax flows from both ends of heat shrink tubing.

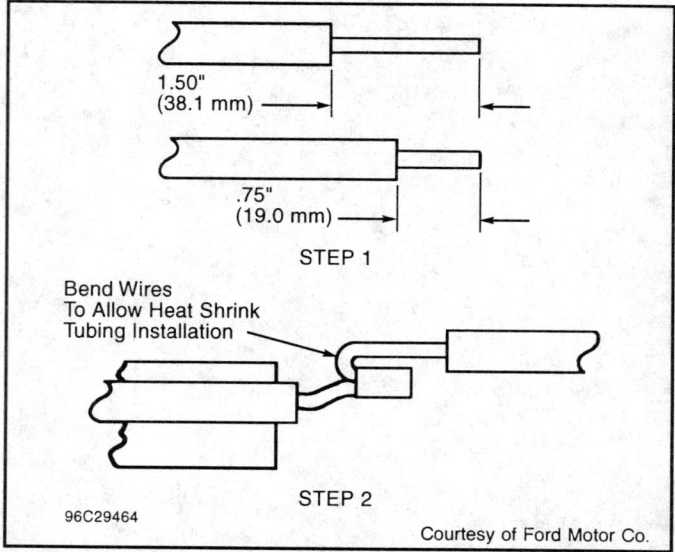

Fig. 1: Repairing BUS Wiring

COMMUNICATION NETWORK DIAGNOSTICS

INSPECTION & VERIFICATION

1) Verify customer's original problem by operating system in question. Inspect vehicle for any obvious electrical component wiring or connector damage. Inspect connectors for loose, damaged or corroded terminals. Check related fuses for system in question.

2) Inspect Data Link Connector (DLC) pins for damage. See Fig. 2. The DLC is located below driver's side of instrument panel, right of steering column. If pins are okay, go to next step. If pins are damaged, repair as necessary and proceed to next step.

3) If problem is still present after performing inspection, connect New Generation Star (NGS) tester to DLC. Select vehicle to be tested from NGS tester menu. If NGS tester does not communicate with vehicle, ensure program card is properly installed. Check NGS tester cable connections and ensure ignition is on. If NGS tester still does not communicate with vehicle, perform TEST L: NO MODULE/NETWORK COMMUNICATION under SYSTEM TESTS. If NGS tester communicates with vehicle, perform data link diagnostic procedure. See DATA LINK DIAGNOSTIC TEST.

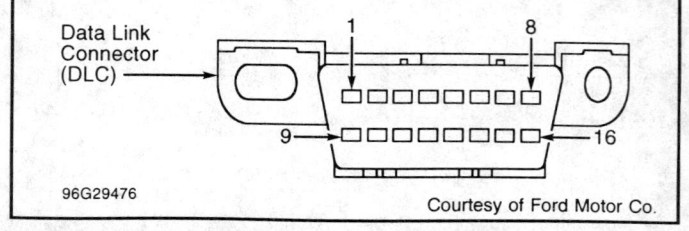

Fig. 2: Identifying Data Link Connector (DLC) Terminals

DATA LINK DIAGNOSTIC TEST

1) Connect New Generation Star (NGS) tester to Data Link Connector (DLC), if not already connected. Select vehicle to be tested from NGS tester menu.

2) Turn ignition on. Rotate dial on NGS tester to menu item DIAGNOSTIC DATA LINK and press trigger. A test will be performed on the BUS (circuits No. 914 and 915) for the module communications network and the ISO 9141 communication link (circuit No. 70).

3) If NGS tester displays CKT 914 (+) = SYSTEM PASSED and CKT 915 (–) = SYSTEM PASSED, module communications network is okay. If NGS tester displays CKT 70 = SYSTEM PASSED, ISO 9141 communication link is operating properly. Return to article that directed you here and continue diagnosis.

4) If NGS tester does not display CKT 914 (+) = SYSTEM PASSED, CKT 915 (–) = SYSTEM PASSED and CKT 70 = SYSTEM PASSED, perform the following as applicable.

- If no response from NGS tester, perform TEST L: NO MODULE/ NETWORK COMMUNICATION under SYSTEM TESTS.
- If NGS tester displays CKT 70, CKT 914 and/or CKT 915 = SOME ECUS NO RESP/NOT EQUIP, perform appropriate test for module not responding. See SYMPTOM CHART table.
- If NGS tester displays CKT 70 = ALL ECUS NO RESP/NOT EQUIP, perform TEST B: NO MODULE/NETWORK COMMUNICATION – ISO 9141 LINK under SYSTEM TESTS.
- If NGS tester displays CKT 914 = ALL ECUS NO RESP/NOT EQUIP, perform TEST A: NO MODULE/NETWORK COMMUNICATION – BUS LINK under SYSTEM TESTS.
- If NGS tester displays CKT 915 = ALL ECUS NO RESP/NOT EQUIP, perform TEST A: NO MODULE/NETWORK COMMUNICATION – BUS LINK under SYSTEM TESTS.
- If module in question is NO RESPONSE/NOT EQUIPPED, perform appropriate test for module not responding. See SYMPTOM CHART table.
- If module in question is NO RESPONSE ON CKT 914 (BUS +), perform appropriate test for module not responding. See SYMPTOM CHART table.
- If module in question is NO RESPONSE ON CKT 915 (BUS –), perform appropriate test for module not responding. See SYMPTOM CHART table.

SYMPTOM CHART

Symptom	Test
No Module/Network Communication – BUS Link	A
No Module/Network Communication – ISO 9141 Link	B
Anti-Lock Brake System (ABS) Does Not Respond To NGS Tester	C
Generic Electronic Module (GEM) Does Not Respond To NGS Tester	D
Electronic Crash Sensor Module Does Not Respond To NGS Tester	E
Passive Anti-Theft System (PATS) Module Does Not Respond To NGS Tester	F
Powertrain Control Module (PCM) Does Not Respond To NGS Tester	G
Remote Anti-Theft System Personality (RAP) Module Does Not Respond To NGS Tester	H
Remote Climate Control (RCC) Module Does Not Respond To NGS Tester	J
Semi-Active Ride Control (SARC) Module Does Not Respond To NGS Tester	K
No Module/Network Communication	L

RETRIEVING & CLEARING DIAGNOSTIC TROUBLE CODES

Connect New Generation Star (NGS) tester to Data Link Connector (DLC). Following manufacturer's instructions to retrieve and clear codes for desired module. See appropriate table under DIAGNOSTIC TROUBLE CODE (DTC) DEFINITIONS for a listing of Diagnostic Trouble Codes (DTCs) and appropriate test procedure.

ACCESSING PARAMETER IDENTIFICATION (PID)

Turn ignition switch to LOCK position. Connect New Generation Star (NGS) tester to Data Link Connector (DLC). Following manufacturer's instructions enter PID/DATA MONITOR AND RECORD for desired module. Operate appropriate system and ensure PID expected values are obtained. See appropriate table under PARAMETER IDENTIFICATION (PID) DEFINITIONS.

WIGGLE TEST

The wiggle test is designed to help identify and locate intermittent failures in vehicle wiring harness and system components. Once wiggle test is entered, several inputs and outputs of the module are monitored for a change of state. When a state change is encountered, a tone will sound and/or a DTC will be displayed on New Generation Star (NGS) tester. For modules that store DTCs, DTC description will determine an open circuit, short to ground, or short to voltage. By performing wiggle test and pulling on different areas of wiring harness, intermittent open and short circuits can be located and serviced.

1) Connect New Generation Star (NGS) scan tester to Data Link Connector (DLC). Turn ignition switch to ON position. Rotate dial on scan tester to DIAGNOSTIC DATA LINK menu and press trigger.

2) Rotate dial on scan tester to highlight the desired module you wish to access and press trigger. Rotate dial on scan tester to highlight DIAGNOSTIC TEST MODES and press trigger. Rotate dial on scan tester to highlight WIGGLE TEST. Press trigger, then press START (button 3).

SYSTEM TESTS

NOTE: Always check module power and ground circuits prior to replacing a control module. See appropriate wiring diagram in DATA LINK CONNECTORS, GROUND DISTRIBUTION or POWER DISTRIBUTION article in WIRING DIAGRAMS.

TEST A: NO MODULE/NETWOR COMMUNICATION – BUS LINK

NOTE: Depending on module configuration, with all modules connected and with ignition switch in RUN position or with engine running 2-3 volts may be present at Data Link Connector (DLC) terminals No. 2 (Tan/Orange wire) and No. 10 (Pink/Light Blue wire). These are the Standard Corporate Protocol (SCP) diagnostic communications network circuits.

NOTE: After making any repair, perform data link diagnostic procedure. See DATA LINK DIAGNOSTIC TEST under COMMUNICATION NETWORK DIAGNOSTICS.

1) Turn ignition switch to LOCK position. Disconnect Powertrain Control Module (PCM) harness connector C191. Disconnect Passive Anti-Theft System (PATS) module harness connector C242 (if equipped). Disconnect Remote Climate Control (RCC) module harness connector C2044 (if equipped). Measure resistance in Tan/Orange wire between terminal No. 16 at PCM harness connector C191 and terminal No. 2 at DLC. *See Figs. 2 and 3.* Also, measure voltage in Pink/Light Blue wire between terminal No. 15 at PCM harness connector C191 and terminal No. 10 at DLC. If both resistance readings are 5 ohms or less, go to next step. If either resistance reading is greater than 5 ohms, repair open in appropriate wire.

2) Turn ignition switch to RUN position. Measure voltage at terminals No. 2 (Tan/Orange wire) and No. 10 (Pink/Light Blue wire) at DLC. If voltage does not exist at both terminals, go to next step. If voltage exists at either terminal, repair short to voltage in appropriate wire.

3) Turn ignition switch to LOCK position. Measure resistance between ground and terminals No. 2 (Tan/Orange wire) and No. 10 (Pink/Light Blue wire) at DLC. If both resistance readings are greater than 10 k/ohms, go to next step. If either resistance reading is 10 k/ohms or less, repair short to ground in appropriate wire.

4) Measure resistance between terminals No. 2 (Tan/Orange wire) and No. 10 (Pink/Light Blue wire) at DLC. If resistance is greater than 10 k/ohms, go to next step. If resistance is 10 k/ohms or less, repair short between Tan/Orange wire and Pink/Light Blue wire.

5) Connect PCM harness connector C191. Turn ignition switch to RUN position. Measure voltage at terminals No. 2 (Tan/Orange wire) and No. 10 (Pink/Light Blue wire) at DLC. If voltage does not exist at both terminals, go to next step. If voltage exists at either terminal, replace PCM.

6) Turn ignition switch to LOCK position. Measure resistance between ground and terminals No. 2 (Tan/Orange wire) and No. 10 (Pink/Light Blue wire) at DLC. If both resistance readings are greater than 10 k/ohms, go to next step. If either resistance reading is 10 k/ohms or less, replace PCM.

7) Measure resistance between terminals No. 2 (Tan/Orange wire) and No. 10 (Pink/Light Blue wire) at DLC. If resistance is greater than 10 k/ohms and not equipped with PATS and climate control, system is okay at this time. If resistance is greater than 10 k/ohms and equipped with PATS and climate control or just PATS, go to next step. If resistance is greater than 10 k/ohms and equipped climate control without PATS, go to step **11)**. If resistance is 10 k/ohms or less, replace PCM.

8) Connect PATS module harness connector C242. Turn ignition switch to RUN position. Measure voltage at terminals No. 2 (Tan/Orange wire) and No. 10 (Pink/Light Blue wire) at DLC. If voltage does not exist at both terminals, go to next step. If voltage exists at either terminal, replace PATS module.

9) Turn ignition switch to LOCK position. Measure resistance between ground and terminals No. 2 (Tan/Orange wire) and No. 10 (Pink/Light Blue wire) at DLC. If both resistance readings are greater than 10 k/ohms, go to next step. If either resistance reading is 10 k/ohms or less, replace PATS module.

10) Measure resistance between terminals No. 2 (Tan/Orange wire) and No. 10 (Pink/Light Blue wire) at DLC. If resistance is greater than 10 k/ohms and not equipped with climate control, system is okay at this time. If resistance is greater than 10 k/ohms and equipped climate control, go to next step. If resistance is 10 k/ohms or less, replace PATS module.

11) Connect Remote Climate Control (RCC) module harness connector C2044. Turn ignition switch to RUN position. Measure voltage at terminals No. 2 (Tan/Orange wire) and No. 10 (Pink/Light Blue wire) at DLC. If voltage does not exist at both terminals, go to next step. If voltage exists at either terminal, replace RCC module.

12) Turn ignition switch to LOCK position. Measure resistance between ground and terminals No. 2 (Tan/Orange wire) and No. 10 (Pink/Light Blue wire) at DLC. If both resistance readings are greater than 10 k/ohms, go to next step. If either resistance reading is 10 k/ohms or less, replace RCC module.

13) Measure resistance between terminals No. 2 (Tan/Orange wire) and No. 10 (Pink/Light Blue wire) at DLC. If resistance is greater than 10 k/ohms, system is okay at this time. If resistance is 10 k/ohms or less, replace RCC module.

TEST B: NO MODULE/NETWORK COMMUNICATION – ISO 9141 LINK

NOTE: Depending on module configuration, with all modules connected and with ignition switch in RUN position or with engine running 2-3 volts may be present at Data Link Connector (DLC) terminal No. 7 (Light Blue/White wire). This is the International Standards Organization (ISO) 9141 diagnostic communications network circuit.

NOTE: After making any repair, perform data link diagnostic procedure. See DATA LINK DIAGNOSTIC TEST under COMMUNICATION NETWORK DIAGNOSTICS.

1) Turn ignition switch to LOCK position. Inspect NGS tester connector for loose, damaged or corroded terminals. If connector is okay, go to next step. If problem exists, repair connector as necessary.

2) Inspect Data Link Connector (DLC) for physical damage, bent terminals or corrosion. If connector is okay, go to next step. If problem exists, repair as necessary.

3) Disconnect Generic Electronic Module (GEM) harness connector C236. *See Fig. 4.* Measure resistance in Light Blue/White wire between terminal No. 10 at GEM harness connector C236 and terminal No. 7 at DLC. *See Figs. 2 and 5.* If resistance is 5 ohms or less, go to next step. If resistance is greater than 5 ohms, repair open in Light Blue/White wire between GEM and DLC.

4) If vehicle is equipped with Anti-Lock Brake System (ABS), go to next step. If vehicle is not equipped with ABS, go to step **7)**.

5) Disconnect Anti-Lock Brake System (ABS) module harness connector C1057. Turn ignition switch to RUN position. Perform data link diagnostic procedure. See DATA LINK DIAGNOSTIC TEST under COMMUNICATION NETWORK DIAGNOSTICS. If NGS tester displays CKT 70 = ALL ECUS NO RESP/NOT EQUIP, go to next step. If NGS tester does not display CKT 70 = ALL ECUS NO RESP/NOT EQUIP, replace ABS module.

6) Turn ignition switch to LOCK position. Disconnect in-line harness connector C221. *See Fig. 4.* Turn ignition switch to RUN position. Perform data link diagnostic procedure. See DATA LINK DIAGNOSTIC TEST under COMMUNICATION NETWORK DIAGNOSTICS. If NGS tester displays CKT 70 = ALL ECUS NO RESP/NOT EQUIP, go to next step. If NGS tester does not display CKT 70 = ALL ECUS NO RESP/NOT EQUIP, repair Light Blue/White wire between in-line harness connector C221 and ABS module.

7) Turn ignition switch to LOCK position. Connect ABS module connector C1057 (if disconnected). Disconnect GEM harness connector C236. *See Fig. 4.* Turn ignition switch to RUN position. Perform data link diagnostic procedure. See DATA LINK DIAGNOSTIC TEST under COMMUNICATION NETWORK DIAGNOSTICS. If NGS tester displays CKT 70 = ALL ECUS NO RESP/NOT EQUIP, go to next step. If NGS tester does not display CKT 70 = ALL ECUS NO RESP/NOT EQUIP, replace GEM module.

8) Turn ignition switch to LOCK position. Disconnect in-line harness connector C214. *See Fig. 4.* Turn ignition switch to RUN position. Perform data link diagnostic procedure. See DATA LINK DIAGNOSTIC TEST under COMMUNICATION NETWORK DIAGNOSTICS. If NGS tester does not display CKT 70 = ALL ECUS NO RESP/NOT EQUIP, go to next step. If NGS tester displays CKT 70 = ALL ECUS NO RESP/NOT EQUIP, repair Light Blue/White wire between GEM, in-line harness connector C214, in-line harness connector C221 and DLC.

9) Turn ignition switch to LOCK position. Connect GEM harness connector and in-line harness connector C214. Deactivate air bag system. See appropriate AIR BAG RESTRAINT SYSTEMS article. Disconnect electronic crash sensor module harness connector C277. *See Fig. 4.* Turn ignition switch to RUN position. Perform data link diagnostic procedure. See DATA LINK DIAGNOSTIC TEST under COMMUNICATION NETWORK DIAGNOSTICS. If NGS tester displays CKT 70 = ALL ECUS NO RESP/NOT EQUIP, go to next step. If NGS tester does not display CKT 70 = ALL ECUS NO RESP/NOT EQUIP, replace electronic crash sensor module.

10) Turn ignition switch to LOCK position. If vehicle is equipped with Remote Anti-Theft Personality (RAP) module, go to next step. If vehicle is not equipped with RAP module, go to step **12)**.

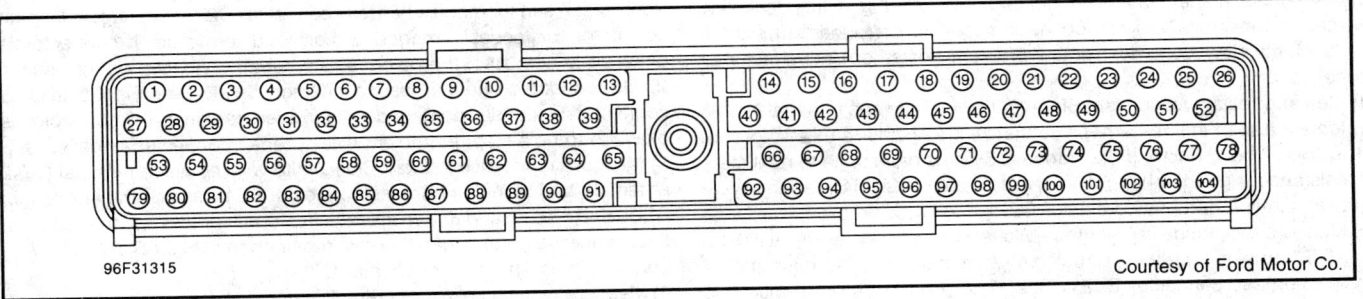

Fig. 3: Identifying PCM Harness Connector C191 Terminals

11) Turn ignition switch to LOCK position. Disconnect Remote Anti-Theft Personality (RAP) module harness connector C253. *See Fig. 4.* Turn ignition switch to RUN position. Perform data link diagnostic procedure. See DATA LINK DIAGNOSTIC TEST under COMMUNICATION NETWORK DIAGNOSTICS. If NGS tester displays CKT 70 = ALL ECUS NO RESP/NOT EQUIP, go to next step. If NGS tester does not display CKT 70 = ALL ECUS NO RESP/NOT EQUIP, replace RAP module.

12) Turn ignition switch to LOCK position. If vehicle is equipped with Semi-Active Ride Control (SARC) module, go to next step. If vehicle is not equipped with SARC module, repair Light Blue/White wire between in-line harness connector C214, RAP module and electronic crash sensor module.

13) Turn ignition switch to LOCK position. Disconnect Semi-Active Ride Control (SARC) module harness connector C451. Turn ignition switch to RUN position. Perform data link diagnostic procedure. See DATA LINK DIAGNOSTIC TEST under COMMUNICATION NETWORK DIAGNOSTICS. If NGS tester displays CKT 70 = ALL ECUS NO RESP/NOT EQUIP, repair Light Blue/White wire between in-line harness connector C214, RAP module, electronic crash sensor module and SARC module. If NGS tester does not display CKT 70 = ALL ECUS NO RESP/NOT EQUIP, replace SARC module.

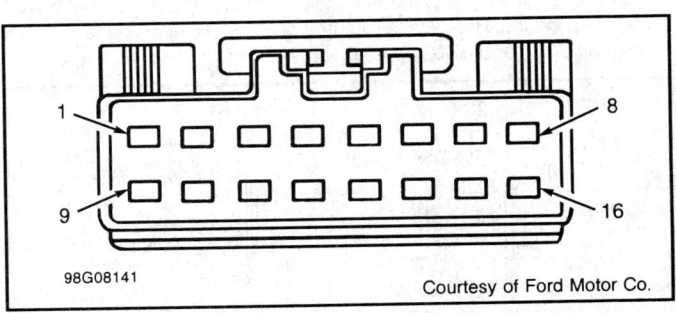

Fig. 5: Identifying GEM Harness Connector C236 Terminals

TEST C: ANTI-LOCK BRAKE SYSTEM (ABS) MODULE DOES NOT RESPOND TO NGS TESTER

NOTE: After making any repair, perform data link diagnostic procedure. See DATA LINK DIAGNOSTIC TEST under COMMUNICATION NETWORK DIAGNOSTICS.

1) Turn ignition switch to LOCK position. Disconnect ABS module

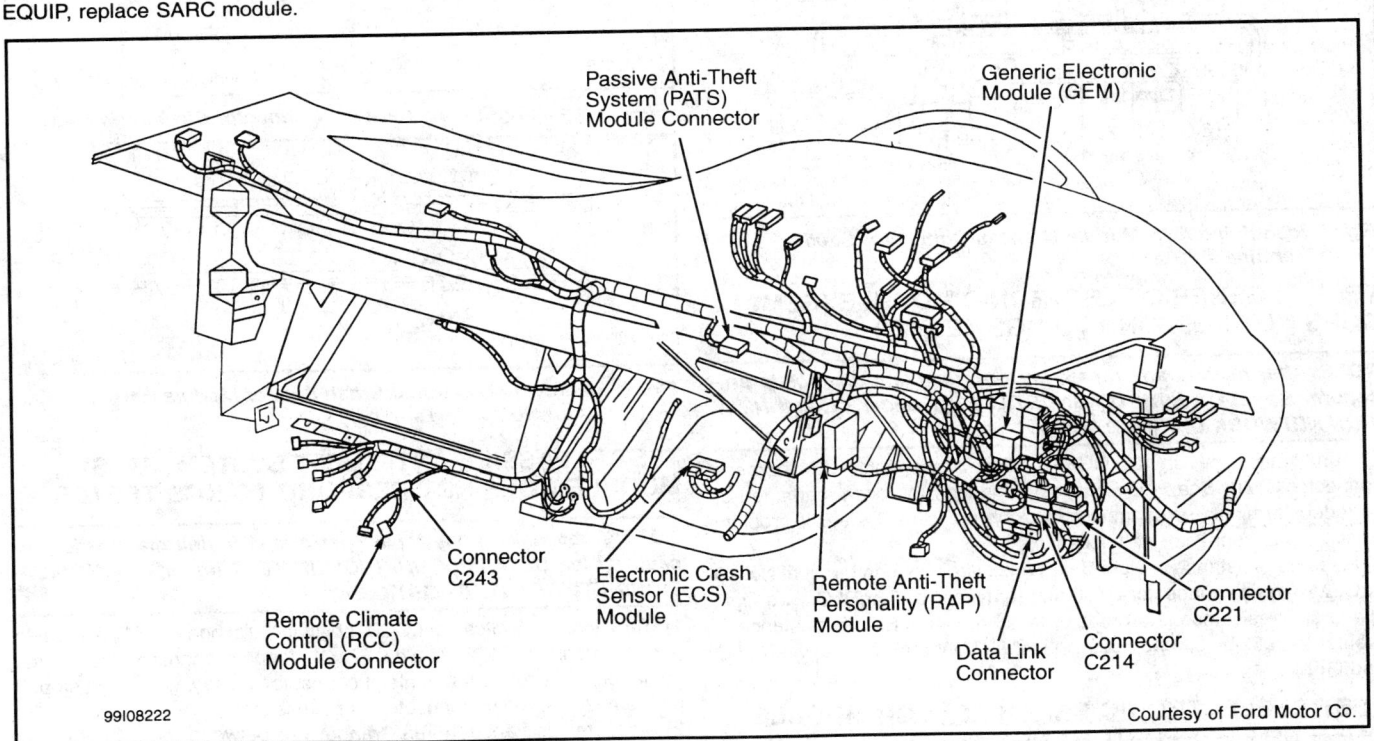

Fig. 4: Locating Harness Connectors Behind Instrument Panel

harness connector C1057. Inspect connector for loose, damaged or corroded terminals. If connector is okay, go to next step. If problem exists, repair connector as necessary.

2) Disconnect in-line harness connector C221. *See Fig. 4.* Inspect in-line harness connector C221 for loose, damaged or corroded terminals. If connector is okay, go to next step. If problem exists, repair connector as necessary.

3) Measure resistance in Light Blue/White wire between terminal No. 25 at female half of in-line harness connector C221 and terminal No. 7 at DLC. *See Figs. 2 and 6.* If resistance is 5 ohms or less, go to next step. If resistance is greater than 5 ohms, repair open in Light Blue/White wire between in-line harness connector C221 and DLC.

4) Measure resistance in Light Blue/White wire between terminal No. 23 at ABS harness connector C1057 and terminal No. 25 at male half of in-line harness connector C221. *See Figs. 6 and 7.* If resistance is 5 ohms or less, replace ABS module. If resistance is greater than 5 ohms, repair open in Light Blue/White wire between male half of in-line harness connector C221 and ABS module.

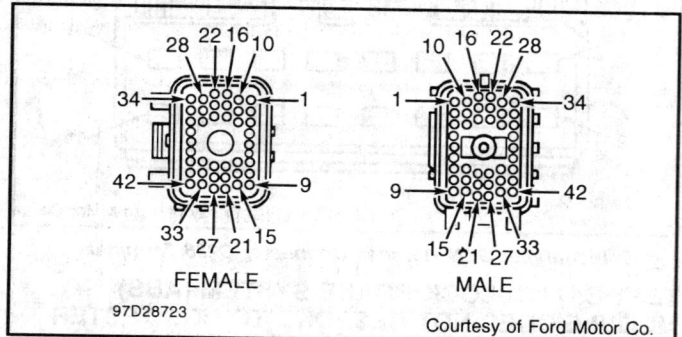

Fig. 6: Identifying In-Line Harness Connector C221 & C130 Terminals

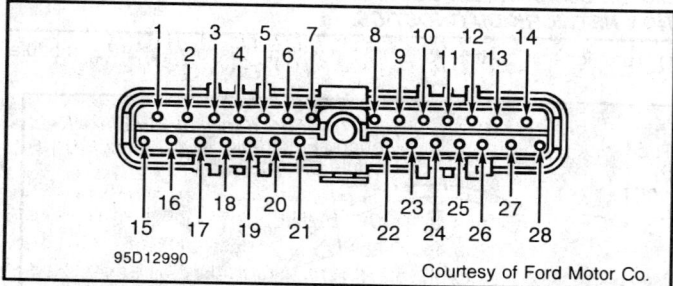

Fig. 7: Identifying ABS Module Harness Connector C1057 Terminals

TEST D: GENERIC ELECTRONIC MODULE (GEM) DOES NOT RESPOND TO NGS TESTER

NOTE: After making any repair, perform data link diagnostic procedure. See DATA LINK DIAGNOSTIC TEST under COMMUNICATION NETWORK DIAGNOSTICS.

1) Turn ignition switch to LOCK position. Disconnect GEM harness connector C236. *See Fig. 4.* Inspect connector for loose, damaged or corroded terminals. If connector is okay, go to next step. If problem exists, repair connector as necessary.

2) Measure resistance in Light Blue/White wire between terminal No. 10 at GEM harness connector C236 and terminal No. 7 at DLC. *See Figs. 2 and 5.* If resistance is 5 ohms or less, replace GEM. If resistance is greater than 5 ohms, repair open in Light Blue/White wire between DLC and GEM.

TEST E: ELECTRONIC CRASH SENSOR MODULE DOES NOT RESPOND TO NGS TESTER

NOTE: After making any repair, perform data link diagnostic procedure. See DATA LINK DIAGNOSTIC TEST under COMMUNICATION NETWORK DIAGNOSTICS.

1) Turn ignition switch to LOCK position. Disable air bag system. See appropriate AIR BAG RESTRAINT SYSTEMS article. Disconnect elec-

tronic crash sensor module harness connector C277. *See Fig. 4.* Inspect connector for loose, damaged or corroded terminals. If connector is okay, go to next step. If problem exists, repair connector as necessary.

2) Disconnect in-line harness connector C214. *See Fig. 4.* Inspect connector for loose, damaged or corroded terminals. If connector is okay, go to next step. If problem exists, repair connector as necessary.

3) Measure resistance in Light Blue/White wire between terminal No. 2 at female half of in-line harness connector C214 and terminal No. 7 at DLC. *See Figs. 2 and 8.* If resistance is 5 ohms or less, go to next step. If resistance is greater than 5 ohms, repair open in Light Blue/White wire between in-line harness connector C214 and DLC.

4) Measure resistance in Light Blue/White wire between terminal No. 19 at electronic crash sensor module harness connector C277 and terminal No. 2 at male half of in-line harness connector C214. *See Figs. 8 and 9.* If resistance is 5 ohms or less, replace electronic crash sensor module. If resistance is greater than 5 ohms, repair open in Light Blue/White wire between electronic crash sensor module and in-line harness connector C214.

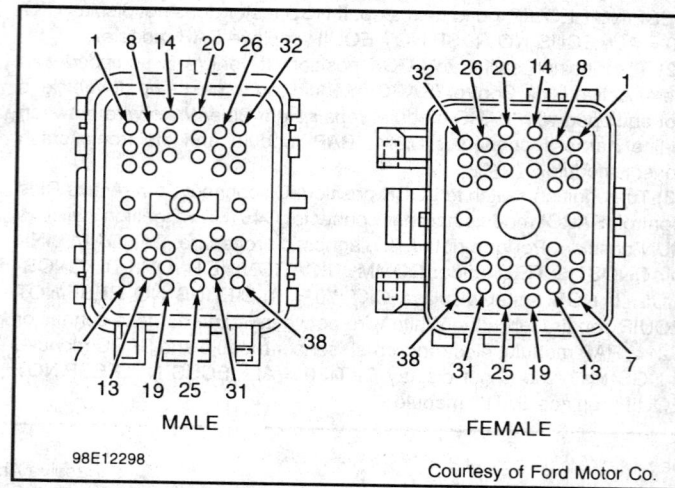

Fig. 8: Identifying In-Line Harness Connector C214 Terminals

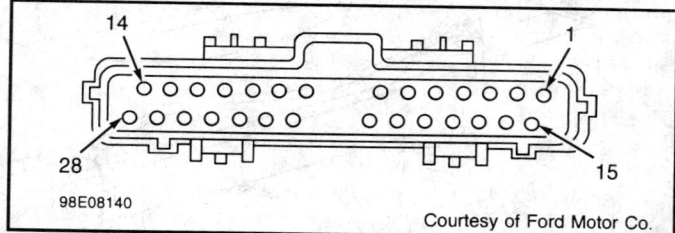

Fig. 9: Identifying Electronic Crash Sensor Module Harness Connector C277 Terminals

TEST F: PASSIVE ANTI-THEFT SYSTEM (PATS) MODULE DOES NOT RESPOND TO NGS TESTER

NOTE: After making any repair, perform data link diagnostic procedure. See DATA LINK DIAGNOSTIC TEST under COMMUNICATION NETWORK DIAGNOSTICS.

1) Turn ignition switch to LOCK position. Disconnect PATS module harness connector C242. *See Fig. 4.* Inspect connector for loose, damaged or corroded terminals. If connector is okay, go to next step. If problem exists, repair connector as necessary.

2) Measure resistance in Tan/Orange wire between terminal No. 6 at PATS module harness connector C242 and terminal No. 2 at DLC. *See Figs. 2 and 10.* Also, measure resistance in Pink/Light Blue wire between terminal No. 5 at PATS module harness connector C242 and terminal No. 10 at DLC. If both resistance readings are 5 ohms or less, replace PATS module. If any resistance reading is greater than 5 ohms, repair open in Tan/Orange wire and/or Light Blue/White wire between PATS module and DLC.

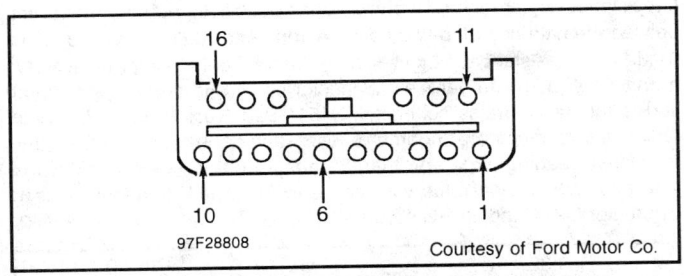

Fig. 10: Identifying PATS Module Harness Connector C242 Terminals

TEST G: POWERTRAIN CONTROL MODULE (PCM) DOES NOT RESPOND TO NGS TESTER

NOTE: After making any repair, perform data link diagnostic procedure. See DATA LINK DIAGNOSTIC TEST under COMMUNICATION NETWORK DIAGNOSTICS.

1) Turn ignition switch to LOCK position. Disconnect PCM harness connector C191. Inspect connector for loose, damaged or corroded terminals. Pay particular attention to terminals No. 16 (Tan/Orange wire) and No. 15 (Pink/Light Blue wire). If connector is okay, go to next step. If problem exists, repair connector as necessary.
2) Disconnect in-line harness connector C221. *See Fig. 4.* Inspect connector for loose, damaged or corroded terminals. If connector is okay, go to next step. If problem exists, repair connector as necessary.
3) Measure resistance in Tan/Orange wire between terminal No. 22 at female half of in-line harness connector C221 and terminal No. 2 at DLC. *See Figs. 2 and 6.* Also, measure resistance in Pink/Light Blue wire between terminal No. 24 at female half of in-line harness connector C221 and terminal No. 10 at DLC. If both resistance readings are 5 ohms or less, go to next step. If any resistance reading is greater than 5 ohms, repair open in Tan/Orange wire and/or Pink/Light Blue wire between female half of in-line harness connector C221 and DLC.
4) Disconnect in-line harness connector C130. Inspect connector for loose, damaged or corroded terminals. If connector is okay, go to next step. If problem exists, repair connector as necessary.
5) Measure resistance in Tan/Orange wire between terminal No. 22 at male half of in-line harness connector C221 and terminal No. 5 at male half of in-line harness connector C130. *See Fig. 6.* Also, measure resistance in Pink/Light Blue wire between terminal No. 24 at male half of in-line harness connector C221 and terminal No. 6 at male half of in-line harness connector C130. If both resistance readings are 5 ohms or less, go to next step. If any resistance reading is greater than 5 ohms, repair open in Tan/Orange wire and/or Pink/Light Blue wire between male half of in-line harness connector C221 and male half of in-line harness connector C130.
6) Measure resistance in Tan/Orange wire between terminal No. 5 at female half of in-line harness connector C130 and terminal No. 16 at PCM harness connector C191. *See Figs. 3 and 6.* Also, measure resistance in Pink/Light Blue wire between terminal No. 6 at female half of in-line harness connector C130 and terminal No. 15 at PCM connector harness connector C191. If both resistance readings are 5 ohms or less, replace PCM. If any resistance reading is greater than 5 ohms, repair open in Tan/Orange wire and/or Pink/Light Blue wire between female half of in-line harness connector C130 and PCM.

TEST H: REMOTE ANTI-THEFT PERSONALITY (RAP) MODULE DOES NOT RESPOND TO NGS TESTER

NOTE: After making any repair, perform data link diagnostic procedure. See DATA LINK DIAGNOSTIC TEST under COMMUNICATION NETWORK DIAGNOSTICS.

1) Turn ignition switch to LOCK position. Disconnect RAP module harness connector C253. *See Fig. 4.* Inspect connector for loose,

damaged or corroded terminals. If connector is okay, go to next step. If problem exists, repair connector as necessary.
2) Disconnect in-line harness connector C214. *See Fig. 4.* Inspect connector for loose, damaged or corroded terminals. If connector is okay, go to next step. If problem exists, repair connector as necessary.
3) Measure resistance in Light Blue/White wire between terminal No. 2 at female half of in-line harness connector C214 and terminal No. 7 at DLC. *See Figs. 2 and 8.* If resistance is 5 ohms or less, go to next step. If resistance is greater than 5 ohms, repair open in Light Blue/White wire between female half of in-line harness connector C214 and DLC.
4) Measure resistance in Light Blue/White wire between terminal No. 2 at male half of in-line harness connector C214 and terminal No. 3 at RAP module harness connector C253. *See Figs. 8 and 11.* If both resistance readings are 5 ohms or less, replace RAP module. If any resistance reading is greater than 5 ohms, repair open in Tan/Orange wire and/or Pink/Light Blue wire between male half of in-line harness connector C214 and RAP module.

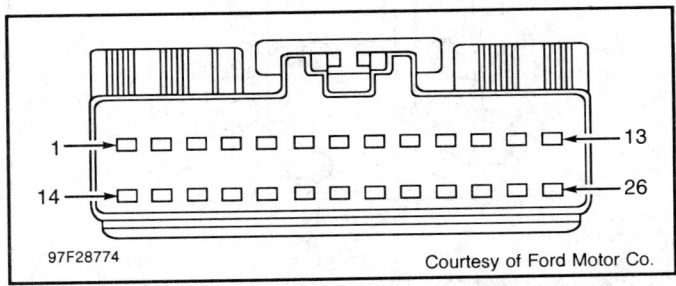

Fig. 11: Identifying RAP Module Harness Connector C253 & RCC Module Harness Connector C2044 Terminals

TEST J: REMOTE CLIMATE CONTROL (RCC) MODULE DOES NOT RESPOND TO NGS TESTER

NOTE: After making any repair, perform data link diagnostic procedure. See DATA LINK DIAGNOSTIC TEST under COMMUNICATION NETWORK DIAGNOSTICS.

1) Turn ignition switch to LOCK position. Disconnect RCC module harness connector C2044. *See Fig. 4.* Inspect connector for loose, damaged or corroded terminals. If connector is okay, go to next step. If problem exists, repair connector as necessary.
2) Disconnect in-line harness connector C243. *See Fig. 4.* Inspect connector for loose, damaged or corroded terminals. If connector is okay, go to next step. If problem exists, repair connector as necessary.
3) Measure resistance in Tan/Orange wire between terminal No. 6 at male half of in-line harness connector C243 and terminal No. 2 at DLC. *See Figs. 2 and 11.* Also, measure resistance in Pink/Light Blue wire between terminal No. 2 at male half of in-line harness connector C243 and terminal No. 10 at DLC. If both resistance readings are 5 ohms or less, go to next step. If any resistance reading is greater than 5 ohms, repair open in Tan/Orange and/or Pink/Light Blue wire between male half of in-line harness connector C243 and DLC.
4) Measure resistance in Tan/Orange wire between terminal No. 6 at female half of in-line harness connector C243 and terminal No. 3 at RCC module harness connector C2044. *See Figs. 11 and 12.* Also, measure resistance in Pink/Light Blue wire between terminal No. 2 at female half of in-line harness connector C243 and terminal No. 4 at RCC module harness connector C2044. If both resistance readings are 5 ohms or less, replace RCC module. If any resistance reading is greater than 5 ohms, repair open in Tan/Orange and/or Pink/Light Blue wire between female half of in-line harness connector C243 and RCC module.

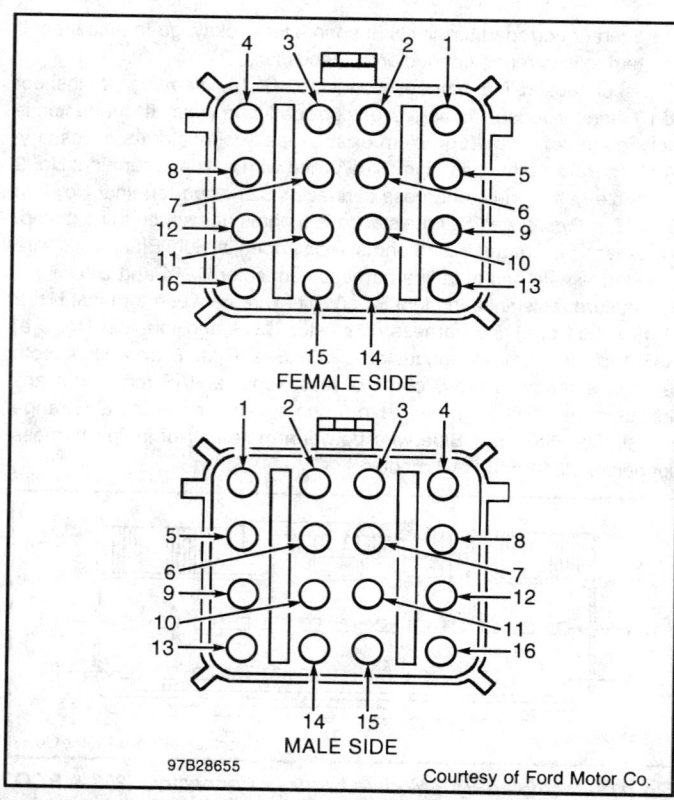

Fig. 12: Identifying In-Line Harness Connector C243 Terminals

TEST K: SEMI-ACTIVE RIDE CONTROL (SARC) MODULE DOES NOT RESPOND TO NGS TESTER

NOTE: After making any repair, perform data link diagnostic procedure. See DATA LINK DIAGNOSTIC TEST under COMMUNICATION NETWORK DIAGNOSTICS.

1) Turn ignition switch to LOCK position. Disconnect SARC module harness connector C451. Inspect connector for loose, damaged or corroded terminals. If connector is okay, go to next step. If problem exists, repair connector as necessary.
2) Disconnect in-line harness connector C214. *See Fig. 4.* Inspect connector for loose, damaged or corroded terminals. If connector is okay, go to next step. If problem exists, repair connector as necessary.
3) Measure resistance in Light Blue/White wire between terminal No. 2 at female half of in-line harness connector C214 and terminal No. 7 at DLC. *See Figs. 2 and 8.* If resistance is 5 ohms or less, go to next step.

If resistance is greater than 5 ohms, repair open in Light Blue/White wire between female half of in-line harness connector C214 and DLC.
4) Measure resistance in Light Blue/White wire between terminal No. 2 at male half of in-line harness connector C214 and terminal No. 29 at SARC module harness connector C451. *See Figs. 8 and 13.* If both resistance readings are 5 ohms or less, replace SARC module. If any resistance reading is greater than 5 ohms, repair open in Tan/Orange wire and/or Pink/Light Blue wire between male half of in-line harness connector C214 and SARC module.

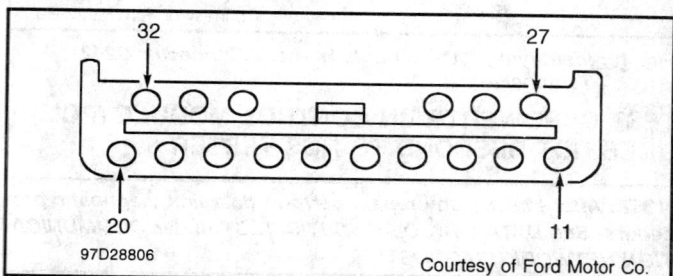

Fig. 13: Identifying SARC Module Harness Connector C451 Terminals

TEST L: NO MODULE/NETWORK COMMUNICATION

NOTE: After making any repair, perform data link diagnostic procedure. See DATA LINK DIAGNOSTIC TEST under COMMUNICATION NETWORK DIAGNOSTICS.

1) Turn ignition switch to LOCK position. Inspect NGS tester connector for loose, damaged or corroded terminals. If connector is okay, go to next step. If problem exists, repair connector as necessary.
2) Inspect Data Link Connector (DLC) for loose, damaged or corroded terminals. If connector is okay, go to next step. If problem exists, repair connector as necessary.
3) Turn ignition switch to LOCK position. Remove and inspect fuse No. 25 (10-amp) from instrument panel fuse box. If fuse is okay, install fuse and go to next step. If fuse is blown, replace fuse and retest system for normal operation. Recheck fuse. If fuse is blown, repair short to ground in Light Green/Red wire between instrument panel fuse block and DLC.
4) Measure voltage between ground and terminal No. 16 (Light Green/Red wire) at DLC. *See Fig. 2.* If battery voltage exists, go to next step. If battery voltage does not exist, repair Light Green/Red wire between instrument panel fuse box and DLC.
5) Measure resistance between ground and terminals No. 4 (Black wire) and No. 5 (Blue/Orange wire) at DLC. If both resistance readings are 5 ohms or less, repair or replace NGS tester. If any resistance reading is more than 5 ohms, repair open in Black wire and/or Blue/Orange wire between ground and DLC.

DIAGNOSTIC TROUBLE CODE (DTC) DEFINITIONS

ELECTRONIC CRASH SENSOR MODULE DTC INDEX

DTC [1]	Description	Test
B1342	ECU Defective	2
B1231	Crash Data Memory Full	3
B1921	ECS Ground Resistance Too High	3
B1318	Low Battery Voltage	3
C1414	Incorrect Vehicle Identification Code	3
B1887	Driver's Air Bag Circuit Short To Ground	3
B1916	Driver's Air Bag Circuit Short To Voltage	3
B1888	Passenger's Air Bag Circuit Short To Ground	3
B1925	Passenger's Air Bag Circuit Short To Voltage	3
B1879	Unexpected Feature Present	3
B1878	Unexpected Feature Present	3
B1883	Unexpected Feature Present	3
B1882	Unexpected Feature Present	3
B1932	Driver's Air Bag Circuit Resistance High	3
B1933	Passenger's Air Bag Circuit Resistance High	3

ELECTRONIC CRASH SENSOR MODULE DTC INDEX (Cont.)

DTC [1]	Description	Test
B1934	Driver's Air Bag Circuit Resistance Low	3
B1935	Passenger's Air Bag Circuit Resistance Low	3
B1941	Unexpected Feature Present	3
B1901	Unexpected Feature Present	3
B1871	Unexpected Feature Present	3
B1889	Unexpected Feature Present	3
B1877	Unexpected Feature Present	3
B1885	Unexpected Feature Present	3
B1881	Unexpected Feature Present	3
B1886	Unexpected Feature Present	3
B1884	Unexpected Feature Present	3
B1890	Air Bag Tone Warning Indicator Circuit Short To Ground Or Open	3
B1892	Air Bag Tone Warning Indicator Circuit Short To Voltage	3
B1891	Nonvolatile Memory Configuration Failure	3
B2141	Air Bag Indicator Inoperative	3
B1869	Air Bag Indicator Short To Voltage	3
B1870		

[1] – DTCs are listed in order of importance. Repair DTCs in order listed.
[2] – Using NGS tester, retrieve and document all continuous DTCs. Perform air bag electronic crash sensor module self-test. If DTC B1342 is retrieved again, replace air bag electronic crash sensor module.
[3] – Repair supplemental air bag system concern. See DIAGNOSIS & TESTING article in appropriate MITCHELL® AIR BAG SERVICE & REPAIR MANUAL, DOMESTIC & IMPORTED MODELS.

ANTI-LOCK BRAKE SYSTEM MODULE DTC INDEX

DTC	Description	Test
B1318	Battery Voltage Low	1
B1342	ECU Defective	2
B1596	Brake Pedal Input Circuit Shorted To Voltage	1
C1095	ABS Hydraulic Pump Motor Circuit Failure	1
C1145	Right Front ABS Sensor Input Circuit Failure	1
C1155	Left Front ABS Sensor Input Circuit Failure	1
C1165	Right Rear ABS Sensor Input Circuit Failure	1
C1175	Left Rear ABS Sensor Input Circuit Failure	1
C1194	Left Front Dump Valve Coil Circuit Failure	3
C1198	Left Front ISOL Valve Coil Circuit Failure	3
C1214	Right Front Inlet Valve Circuit Failure	3
C1222	Wheel Mismatched	1
C1233	Left Front ABS Sensor Input Signal Missing	1
C1234	Right Front ABS Sensor Input Signal Missing	1
C1235	Right Rear ABS Sensor Input Signal Missing	1
C1236	Left Rear ABS Sensor Input Signal Missing	1
C1242	Left Rear Dump Valve Coil Circuit Failure	3
C1246	Right Rear Dump Valve Coil Circuit Failure	3
C1250	Left Rear ISOL Valve Coil Circuit Failure	3
C1254	Right Rear ISOL Valve Coil Circuit Failure	3
C1266	ABS Valve Power Circuit Failure	1

[1] – Repair anti-lock brake system concern. See appropriate ANTI-LOCK article in BRAKES in appropriate MITCHELL® manual.
[2] – Using NGS tester, retrieve and document all continuous DTCs. Perform ABS self-test. If DTC B1342 is retrieved again, replace ABS module.
[3] – Replace ABS module.

GENERIC ELECTRONIC MODULE DTC INDEX

DTC	Description	Test
B1300	Power Door Lock Circuit Failure	1 2
B1302	Delayed Accessory Relay Coil Circuit Failure	1 3
B1304	Delayed Accessory Relay Coil Circuit Short To Voltage	1 3
B1309	Power Door Lock Sense Circuit Short To Ground	1 2
B1310	Power Door Unlock Circuit Failure	2
B1314	Battery Saver Relay Coil Circuit Open	4
B1315	Battery Saver Relay Coil Circuit Short To Voltage	4
B1316	Battery Saver Relay Coil Circuit Short To Ground	4
B1317	Battery Voltage High	1 5
B1318	Battery Voltage Low	1 5
B1319	Driver's Door Ajar Circuit Failure	1 4
B1322	Driver's Door Ajar Circuit Short To Ground	1 4
B1323	Door Ajar Indicator Circuit Failure	6
B1325	Door Ajar Indicator Circuit Short To Voltage	6
B1327	Passenger's Door Ajar Circuit Failure	1 4
B1330	Passenger's Door Ajar Circuit Short To Ground	1 4
B1331	Decklid Ajar Rear Door Circuit Failure	

GENERIC ELECTRONIC MODULE DTC INDEX (Cont.)

DTC	Description	Test
B1334	Decklid Ajar Rear Door Circuit Short To Ground	1 4
B1335	Right Rear Door Ajar Circuit Short To Ground	1 4
B1338	Right Rear Door Ajar Circuit Short To Ground	1 4
B1342	ECU Failure	7
B1343	Rear Window Defogger Switch Input Circuit Failure	1 8
B1345	Rear Window Defogger Switch Input Circuit Short To Ground	1 8
B1347	Rear Window Defogger Switch Relay Circuit Failure	8
B1349	Rear Window Defogger Switch Relay Circuit Short To Voltage	8
B1352	Ignition Key-In Circuit Failure	1 6
B1354	Ignition Key-In Circuit Short To Ground	1 6
B1359	Ignition RUN/ACC Circuit Failure	1 9
B1361	Ignition RUN/ACC Circuit Short To Voltage	1
B1363	Ignition Start Circuit Failure	1
B1365	Ignition Start Circuit Short To Voltage	1 9
B1371	Illuminated Entry Relay Circuit Failure	10
B1373	Illuminated Entry Relay Short To Voltage	10
B1397	Power Door Unlock Circuit Short To Voltage	2
B1398	Driver's Door Window One-Touch Relay Circuit Failure	3
B1400	Driver's Door Window One-Touch Relay Circuit Short To Voltage	3
B1402	Driver's Door Window Down Switch Circuit Failure	1
B1403	Driver's Door Window Up Switch Circuit Failure	1
B1405	Driver's Door Window Down Circuit Short To Voltage	1 3
B1408	Driver's Door Window Up Circuit Short To Voltage	1 3
B1410 [11]	Driver's Door Window Motor Circuit Failure	1 3
B1426	Seat Belt Indicator Circuit Short To Voltage	6
B1428	Seat Belt Indicator Circuit Failure	6
B1430	Seat Belt Switch Circuit Short To Ground	1 6
B1432	Wiper Park Relay Circuit Short To Power	12
B1433	Wiper Park Relay Circuit Short To Ground	12
B1434	Wiper High/Low Speed Relay Circuit Failure	12
B1436	Wiper High/Low Speed Relay Short To Power	12
B1438	Wiper Mode Select Switch Circuit Failure	1 12
B1441	Wiper Mode Select Switch Short To Ground	1 12
B1446	Wiper Park Sense Circuit Failure	1 12
B1448	Wiper Park Sense Circuit Short To Power	1 12
B1450	Wiper/Washer Delay Switch Circuit Failure	1 12
B1453	Wiper/Washer Delay Switch Circuit Short To Ground	1 12
B1458	Wiper/Washer Pump Motor Relay Circuit Failure	12
B1460	Wiper Washer Pump Motor Relay Coil Short To Power	12
B1462	Seat Belt Switch Circuit Failure	1 6
B1465	Wiper Park Relay Circuit Open	12
B1466	Wiper High/Low Speed Not Switching	12
B1473	Wiper Motor Low Speed Circuit Failure	12
B1474	Battery Saver Power Relay Circuit Short To Voltage	4
B1475	Delayed Accessory Relay Contact Short To Voltage	3
B1476	Wiper Motor High Speed Circuit Failure	12
B1555	Ignition RUN/START Circuit Failure	1 9
B1557	Ignition RUN/START Circuit Short To Voltage	1
B1571	Left Rear Door Ajar Circuit Failure	1
B1574	Left Rear Door Ajar Circuit Short To Ground	1
B1575	Parking Light Input Circuit Failure	1 6
B1577	Parking Light Input Circuit Short To Voltage	1 6
B1607	Illuminated Entry Input Circuit Failure	1
B1610	Illuminated Entry Input Circuit Short To Ground	1 10
B1830	Door Unlock/Disarm Switch Circuit Failure	1 2
B1833	Door Unlock/Disarm Switch Circuit Short To Ground	1 2
B1834	Door Unlock/Disarm Switch Output Circuit Failure	2
B1836	Door Unlock/Disarm Switch Output Circuit Short To Voltage	2
B1838	Battery Saver Power Relay Circuit Failure	4
B1840	Front Wiper Power Circuit Failure	12
B1898	VAPS II Circuit Open	1 13
C1899	VAPS II Circuit Short To Voltage	1 13
C1928	VAPS II Solenoid Actuator Return Circuit Short To Ground	13
P1881	Engine Coolant Level Switch Input Circuit Failure	6
P1882	Engine Coolant Level Switch Circuit Short To Ground	6
P1883	Engine Coolant Level Indicator Circuit Failure	6
P1884	Engine Coolant Level Indicator Circuit Short To Voltage	6

[1] – This code can be set by performing wiggle test. See WIGGLE TEST under COMMUNICATION NETWORK DIAGNOSTICS.
[2] – Repair appropriate circuit as necessary. See appropriate wiring diagram in REMOTE KEYLESS ENTRY SYSTEMS article.
[3] – See POWER WINDOWS – SABLE & TAURUS article for testing procedures.
[4] – Repair appropriate circuit as necessary. See appropriate wiring diagram in ILLUMINATION/INTERIOR LIGHTS article.

GENERIC ELECTRONIC MODULE DTC INDEX (Cont.)

DTC	Description	Test
5	Check charging system. See appropriate GENERATORS article in STARTING & CHARGING SYSTEMS. If charging system is okay, check power and ground circuits to GEM. See appropriate wiring diagram in POWER DISTRIBUTION article in WIRING DIAGRAMS.	
6	See ANALOG INSTRUMENT PANELS – SABLE & TAURUS for testing procedures.	
7	Using NGS tester, retrieve and document all continuous. Perform Generic Electronic Module (GEM) self-test. If DTC B1342 is retrieved again, replace GEM.	
8	Repair appropriate circuit as necessary. See appropriate wiring diagram in REAR WINDOW DEFOGGERS article.	
9	See STEERING COLUMN SWITCHES – SABLE & TAURUS article for testing procedures.	
10	See AUTOLAMP SYSTEMS – SABLE & TAURUS article for testing procedures.	
11	If DTC B1474 is retrieved with any other DTC and B1410, repair DTC B1474 first before repairing DTC B1410. If any other DTC is retrieved with B1410, repair those first.	
12	See WIPER/WASHER SYSTEMS – SABLE & TAURUS article for testing procedures.	
13	See appropriate ELECTRONIC article in STEERING in appropriate MITCHELL® manual for testing procedures.	

PASSIVE ANTI-THEFT SYSTEM MODULE DTC INDEX

DTC	Description	Test
B1213	Anti-Theft Number Of Programmed Keys Is Below Minimum	1
B1232 Or		1
B2103	Antenna Not Connected	1
B1600	No Key Code Received, Damaged Encoded Ignition Key Or Use Of Non-PATS Key	1
B1601	Unprogrammed Encoded Ignition Key (Unprogrammed Ignition Key)	1
B1602	Invalid Key Code Format From Ignition Key Transponder (Partial Key Read)	1
B1681	Transceiver Defective Or Not Connected	1
B2139	Security Key Does Not Match Between PATS & PCM	1
B2141	No Security Identification Exchange Between PATS & PCM	1
U1147	Vehicle Security Status Missing	2
U1262	SCP Bus Communication Fault	1

1 – See PASSIVE ANTI-THEFT SYSTEMS – SABLE & TAURUS article for testing procedures.
2 – Perform TEST A: NO MODULE/NETWORK COMMUNICATION – BUS LINK under SYSTEM TESTS.

REMOTE ANTI-THEFT PERSONALITY MODULE DTC INDEX

DTC	Description	Test
B1309	Power Door Lock Circuit Short To Ground	1
B1341	Power Door Unlock Circuit Short To Ground	1
B1485	Brake Pedal Input Short To Voltage	1
B1522	Hood Switch Circuit Short To Ground	2
B1526	Keypad Short To Ground	1
B1562	Door Lock Cylinder Circuit Short To Ground	1
B1629	PRNDL Reverse In/Out Short To Voltage	1
B2425	Remote Keyless Entry Out Of Synchronization	3

1 – Repair appropriate circuit as necessary. See appropriate wiring diagram in REMOTE KEYLESS ENTRY SYSTEMS article.
2 – See ACTIVE ANTI-THEFT SYSTEMS – SABLE & TAURUS article for testing procedures.
3 – Reprogram all remote transmitters. See COMPUTER RELEARN PROCEDURES article in GENERAL INFORMATION.

REMOTE CLIMATE CONTROL MODULE DTC INDEX

DTC	Description	Test
B1239	Blend Door Circuit Short	1
B1249	Blend Door Circuit Failure	1
B1251	A/C In-Car Temperature Sensor Open Circuit	1
B1253	A/C In-Car Temperature Sensor Circuit Short To Ground	1
B1255	A/C Ambient Air Temperature Sensor Circuit Open	1
B1257	A/C Ambient Air Temperature Sensor Circuit Short To Ground	1
B1261	A/C Solar Radiation Sensor Circuit Short To Ground	1
C2767/U2005	Communication Error Between Instrument Control Panel & RCC	2
U1073	Invalid/Missing Data For Engine Coolant	3
U1341	Invalid/Missing Data For Vehicle Speed	

1 – Repair A/C system as necessary. See appropriate AUTOMATIC A/C-HEATER SYSTEMS article in appropriate MITCHELL® AIR CONDITIONING & HEATING SERVICE & REPAIR manual.
2 – Repair engine coolant temperature sensor circuit. See appropriate SELF-DIAGNOSTICS article in ENGINE PERFORMANCE in appropriate MITCHELL® manual.
3 – Repair vehicle speed sensor circuit. See appropriate SELF-DIAGNOSTICS article in ENGINE PERFORMANCE in appropriate MITCHELL® manual.

PARAMETER IDENTIFICATION (PID) DEFINITIONS

AIR BAG ELECTRONIC CRASH SENSOR MODULE PID INDEX

PID	Description	Expected Value
CCNTECS	Number Of Continuous DTCs	One Count Per Bit
VBATECS	Battery Voltage	Volts
D_ABAGR	Driver's Air Bag Resistance	1.8-4.1 Ohms
P_ABAGR	Passenger's Air Bag Resistance	1.4-3.6 Ohms
BRACKET	Bracket Ground Resistance	Less Than 100 Ohms

ANTI-LOCK BRAKE SYSTEM MODULE PID INDEX

PID	Description	Expected Value
CCNTABS	Number Of Continuous DTCs	One Count Per Bit
BOO_ABS	Brake Switch Input	ON, OFF
ABSRR_O	Right Rear ABS Outlet Valve	1
ABSLR_O	Left Rear ABS Outlet Valve	1
ABSRF_O	Right Front ABS Outlet Valve	1
ABSLF_O	Left Front ABS Outlet Valve	1
ABSRF_I	Right Front ABS Inlet Valve	1
ABSLF_I	Left Front ABS Inlet Valve	1
ABSRR_I	Right Rear ABS Inlet Valve	1
ABSLR_I	Left Rear ABS Inlet Valve	1
LF_WSPD	Left Front Wheel Speed Signal	0-255 KPH
RF_WSPD	Right Front Wheel Speed Signal	0-255 KPH
LR_WSPD	Left Rear Wheel Speed Signal	0-255 KPH
RR_WSPD	Right Rear Wheel Speed Signal	0-255 KPH
PMP_MTR	Hydraulic Pump Motor	ON, OFF

[1] – Expected value should be ON, OFF, SHORTVBAT, SHORTGND or OPEN.

GENERIC ELECTRONIC MODULE PID INDEX

PID	Description	Expected Value
VSS_GEM	Vehicle Speed Input To GEM	1-255 KPH
CLNTLMP	Engine Coolant Light Output State	1
VAPS_IN	VAPSII Input Current ID	
VAPSOUT	VAPSII Output Current Set Point	0-100%
DR_UNLK	All Door Unlock Output State	0-100%
DD_UNLK	Driver's Door Unlock Output State	1
D_PWRLY	Driver's Power Window Relay	1
DDPWAMP	Driver's Power Window Motor Current	.25-63.75 Amps
WPPK_PK	Wiper Park-To-Park Time	0-65 mS
WPMODE	Wiper Control Mode Select	2
SBLTLMP	Seat Belt Light Circuit	1
WPHISP	Wiper 2 Speed Relay	1
WPRUN	Wiper Run Relay Driver State	1
WASH_SW	Washer Pump Switch	ON, OFF
WASHRLY	Washer Pump Relay Circuit	1
DRAJR_L	Door Ajar Warning Light Circuit	1
BATSAV	Battery Saver Relay Circuit	1
INTLMP	Illuminated Entry Relay Circuit	1
ACCDLY	Accessory Delay Relay Circuit	1
RDEFRLY	Rear Defogger Relay Circuit	1
DECKLID	Decklid Ajar Switch	CLOSED, AJAR
IGN_KEY	Ignition Key In/Out	IN, OUT
HDLMPSW	Low Beams	ON, OFF
COOLANT	Engine Coolant Level	OK, NOTOK
DDPW_SW	Driver's Power Window Up Switch	3
DDLCK	Driver's Door Lock	ACTIVE, NOTACT
CDR_ULK	Central Door Unlock Switch	ACTIVE, NOTACT
WPPRKSW	Windshield Wiper	PARKED, NOTPRK
IGN_GEM	Ignition Switch Position	START, RUN/ACC, OFF
D_SBELT	Driver's Seat Beat	FSTND, UNFSTD
RDEF_SW	Rear Defogger Switch	ACTIVE, NOTACT
ILLE_V	Illuminated Entry Input	4
LRDR_SW	Left Rear Door Ajar Switch	CLOSED, AJAR
RRDR_SW	Right Rear Door Ajar Switch	CLOSED, AJAR
TONE_RQ	Tone Request	ON, OFF
D_DR_SW	Driver's Door Ajar Switch	CLOSED, AJAR
P_DR_SW	Passenger's Door Ajar Switch	CLOSED, AJAR
VBATGEM	Battery Voltage	Volts

[1] – Expected value should be ON, OFF or SHORTVBAT.
[2] – Expected value should be WASH, OPEN, INVLD, OFF, INTVL1, INTVL2, INTVL3, INTVL4, INTVL5, INTVL6, INTVL7, LOW or HIGH.

GENERIC ELECTRONIC MODULE PID INDEX (Cont.)

PID	Description	Expected Value

[3] – Expected value should be UP, DOWN, OFF or SHORT.
[4] – Expected value should be between 20 and 80 percent of battery voltage.

PASSIVE ANTI-THEFT SYSTEM MODULE PID INDEX

PID	Description	Expected Value
CCNTPATS	Number Of Continuous DTCs	On count Per Bit
IGN_RAP	Ignition Switch Position	RUN/ACC, OFF
NUMKEYS	Number Of Ignition Keys Programmed	0-8
M_KEYS	Programmed Key In Ignition	YES, ON
ENABL_S	Has PATS Enable Vehicle	ENABLE, DISABLED
ACCESS	Security Access Status	TIMED, CODED
MIN#KEYS	Minimum Number Of Keys Required To Start Vehicle	2-8
ANTISCN	Time Out For Unprogrammed PATS Key	ACTIVE, NOTACT
PCM_ID	Is PCM ID Stored In PATS	STORED, NOTSTR
SPAREKY	Can You Add Spare Key With 2 Programmed Keys	YES, NO
SERVMOD	Service Module	YES, NO
PCM_VFY	PCM ID matches Between PCM & PATS	YES, NO

REMOTE ANTI-THEFT PERSONALITY MODULE PID INDEX

PID	Description	Expected Value
TRANSGR	Transmission Gear	REV. NOTREV
BOO_ABS	Brake Switch Input	ON, OFF
KEYCODE	Factory Keyless Entry Keycode	[1]
DOORRAP	Door Ajar Switch	AJAR, CLOSED
DD_LOCK	Power Door Lock Output State	[2]
IGN_RAP	Ignition Switch Position	RUN/ACC, OFF
KEY_PAD	Number Pressed On Keypad	1, 3, 5, 7, 9
AL_EVT#	Last 8 Alarm Events	[3]
HOOD_SW	Hood Switch	PUNCHED, NOTPUN
DR_DARM	Door Disarm Input	ACTIVE, NOTACT
NOTTHEFT	Theft Only State	YES, ON
NOREMOTE	Remote Only Input State	YES, ON
KEYLOCK	Central Lock	ACTIVE, NOTACT

[1] – Displays factory key code.
[2] – Expected valve should be LOCK, UNLOCK, OFF or SHORT.
[3] – Expected value should be DROPEN, HOODTR, IGNTAM, NOEVNT, PANIC or DLID_P.

WIRING DIAGRAMS

NOTE: See appropriate wiring diagrams in DATA LINK CONNECTORS, GROUND DISTRIBUTION or POWER DISTRIBUTION article in WIRING DIAGRAMS.

DESCRIPTION & OPERATION

The module communications network provides the ability for module-to-module communication by sharing inputs and outputs instead of each component having an input and output wired directly to each module. The BUS network, which consists of a pair of twisted wires, is used to transfer information between each module. The BUS network is routed throughout the vehicle to each module except the Restraint Control Module (RCM).

The RCM does not use the BUS to communicate with other modules. The RCM is connected to the ISO 9141 network. Both networks are connected to the Data Link Connector (DLC). For module locations, see COMPONENT LOCATIONS.

COMPONENT LOCATIONS

For component locations refer to illustration and table. See COMPONENT LOCATIONS table. *See Figs. 1 and 2.*

COMPONENT LOCATIONS

Component	Location
Restraint Control Module (RAM)	Behind Passenger's Side Kick Panel
Air Suspension/Electronic Variable Orifice (EVO) Steering Module [1]	Behind Instrument Panel Next To Glove Box
Anti-Lock Brake System (ABS) Module	Right Front Of Engine Compartment, Under Upper Radiator Support
Data Link Connector (DLC)	Below Left Side Of Instrument Panel, To Right Of Steering Column
Driver's Door Module (DDM)	Inside Driver's Door
Driver's Seat Module	Under Driver's Seat
Electronic Automatic Temperature Control (EATC) Module	Center Of Instrument Panel
Front Radio Control Unit [2]	Behind Center Of Instrument Panel, On Radio
Powertrain Control Module (PCM)	In Engine Compartment On Left Side Of Firewall
Lighting Control Module (LCM)	Behind Left Side Of Instrument Panel, To Right Of Steering Column

[1] – Air suspension/EVO steering module may also be referred to as Rear Air Suspension Module (RASM).

[2] – Front radio control unit may also be referred to as Audio Control Module (ACM).

REPAIRING BUS WIRING

NOTE: Following procedure must be used to ensure proper repair is performed on BUS wiring. BUS wiring is sensitive to moisture and oxidation and must be properly sealed to ensure proper operation of the module communications network. Regular heat shrink tubing is NOT sufficient, heat shrink tubing containing hot melt wax is required.

1) When performing a repair on the BUS wiring, ensure the wires on the BUS are twisted at a rate of 33-40 winds per 3.3 ft. (1 m). The twists should start within approximately 4.9" (124 mm) from any harness connector. Use only 20 AWG standard wire gauge for repairs.

2) If performing a splice in the wiring, strip .75" (19.0 mm) of insulation from one wire and 1.50" (38.1 mm) of insulator from the other wire. Perform STEP 1. *See Fig. 3.* Place hot melt wax type heat shrink tubing over one wire.

3) Twist stripped portion of the wires together. Solder connection using resin core RMA solder. DO NOT use acid core solder. Bend wires to allow installation of heat shrink tubing. Perform STEP 2. *See Fig. 3.*

4) Position heat shrink tubing over splice area. Using heat gun, evenly heat the heat shrink tubing until wax flows from both ends of heat shrink tubing.

COMMUNICATION NETWORK DIAGNOSTICS

INSPECTION & VERIFICATION

1) Verify customer's original problem by operating system in question. Inspect vehicle for any obvious electrical component wiring or connector damage. Inspect harness connectors for loose, damaged or corroded terminals. Check fuse No. 23 (20-amp) in instrument panel fuse box and related fuses for system in question.

2) Inspect 16-pin Data Link Connector (DLC) pins for damage. *See Fig. 4.* The DLC is located below driver's side of instrument panel, to the right of steering column. If pins are okay, go to next step. If pins are damaged, repair as necessary and proceed to next step.

3) If problem is still present after performing inspection, connect New Generation Star (NGS) tester to DLC. Select vehicle to be tested from NGS tester menu. If NGS tester does not communicate with vehicle, ensure program card is properly installed. Check NGS tester cable connections and ensure ignition switch is in RUN position. If NGS tester still does not communicate with vehicle, go to TEST N: NO MODULE/NETWORK COMMUNICATION under SYSTEM TESTING. If NGS tester communicates with vehicle, perform data link diagnostic procedure. See DATA LINK DIAGNOSTIC TEST.

DATA LINK DIAGNOSTIC TEST

NOTE: Circuit No. 70 is the Light Blue/White wire connected to terminal No. 7 on DLC. Circuit No. 914 is the Tan/Orange wire connected to terminal No. 2 on DLC. Circuit No. 915 is the Pink/Light Blue wire connected to terminal No. 10 on DLC.

1) Connect New Generation Star (NGS) tester to Data Link Connector (DLC), if not already connected. Select vehicle to be tested from NGS tester menu.

2) Turn ignition switch to RUN position. Rotate dial on NGS tester to menu item DIAGNOSTIC DATA LINK and press trigger. A test will be performed on the BUS (circuits No. 914 and 915) network and the ISO 9141 network (circuit No. 70).

3) If NGS tester displays CKT 914 (+) = SYSTEM PASSED and CKT 915 (−) = SYSTEM PASSED, module communications network is kay. If NGS tester displays CKT 70 = SYSTEM PASSED, ISO 9141 communication link is operating properly. Repair communication concern by symptom. See SYMPTOM INDEX table to continue diagnosis.

4) If NGS tester does not display CKT 914 (+) = SYSTEM PASSED, CKT 915 (−) = SYSTEM PASSED and CKT 70 = SYSTEM PASSED, perform the following as applicable.

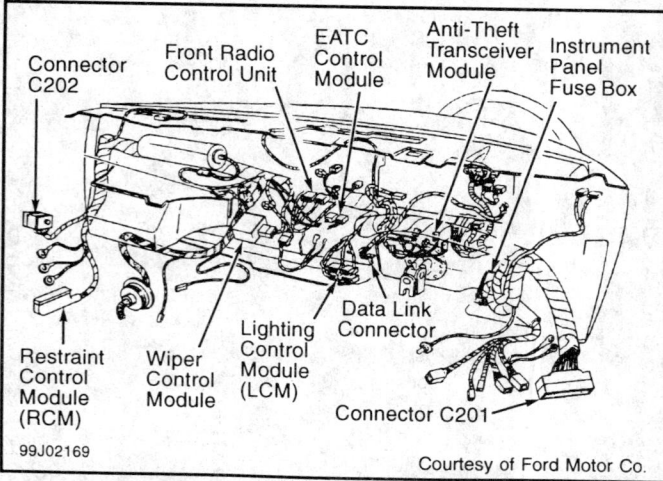

Connector C202 · Front Radio Control Unit · EATC Control Module · Anti-Theft Transceiver Module · Instrument Panel Fuse Box · Restraint Control Module (RCM) · Wiper Control Module · Lighting Control Module (LCM) · Data Link Connector · Connector C201

99J02169

Courtesy of Ford Motor Co.

Fig. 1: Locating Components & Harness Connectors Behind Instrument Panel

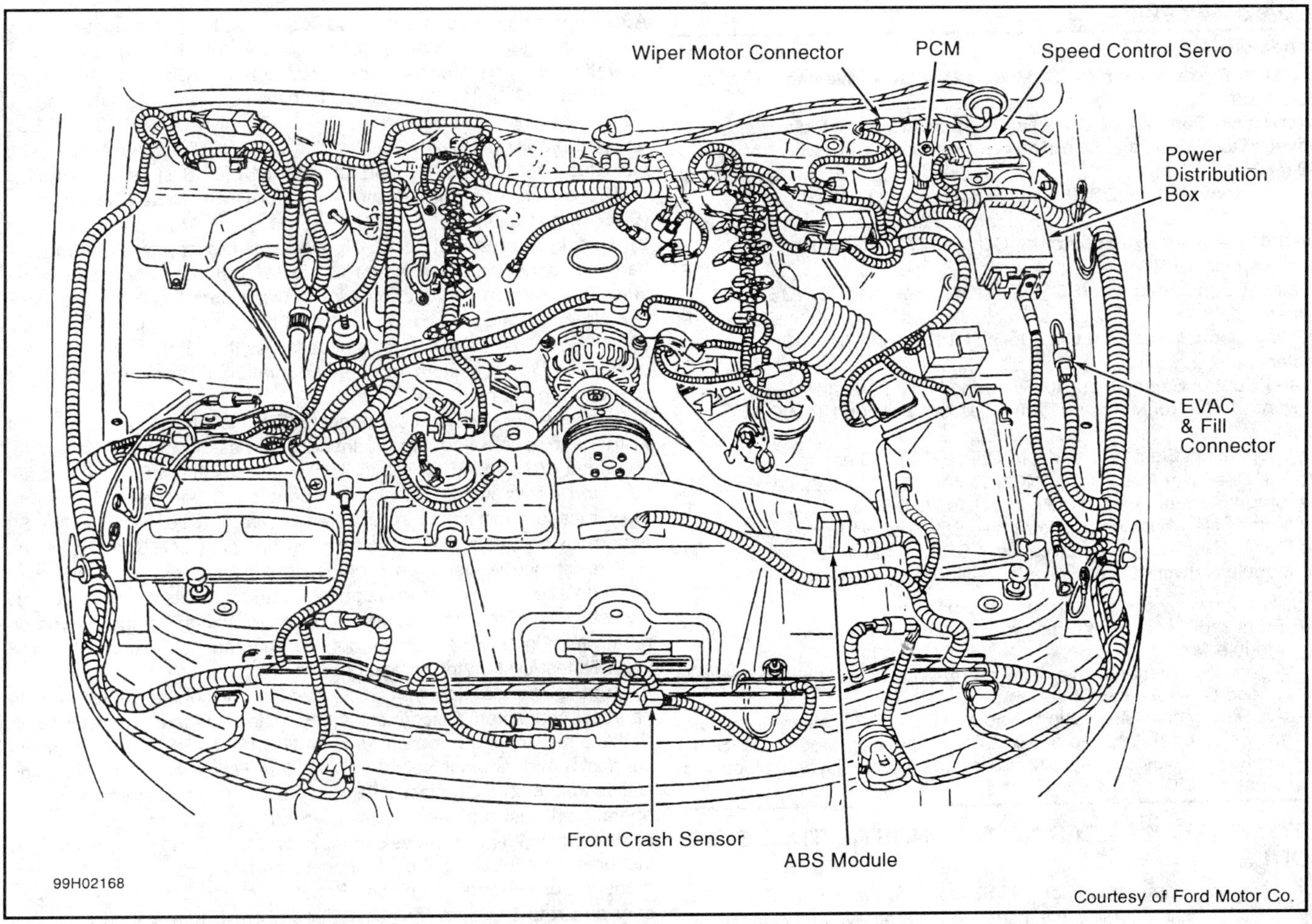

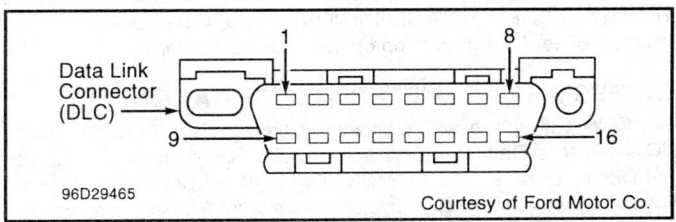

Fig. 2: Locating Engine Compartment Components & Harness Connectors

Wiper Motor Connector
PCM
Speed Control Servo
Power Distribution Box
EVAC & Fill Connector
Front Crash Sensor
ABS Module

99H02168

Courtesy of Ford Motor Co.

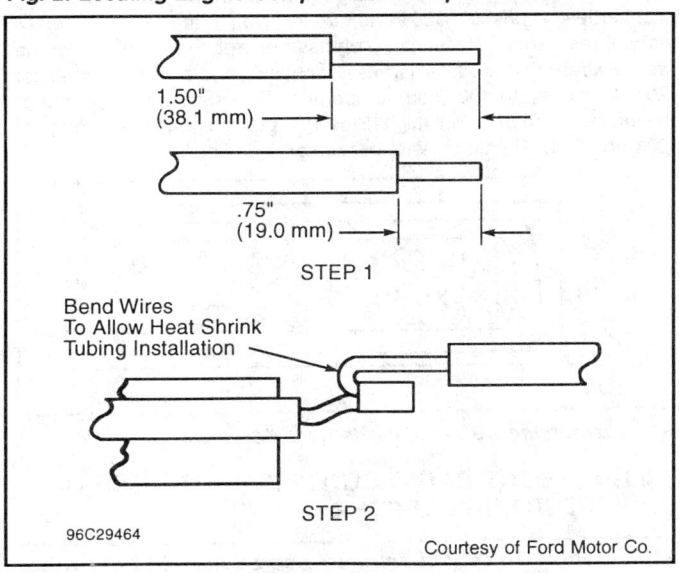

Fig. 3: Repairing BUS Wiring

1.50" (38.1 mm)

.75" (19.0 mm)

STEP 1

Bend Wires To Allow Heat Shrink Tubing Installation

STEP 2

96C29464

Courtesy of Ford Motor Co.

- If no response from NGS tester, perform TEST N: NO MODULE/ NETWORK COMMUNICATION under SYSTEM TESTS.
- If NGS tester displays CKT 70, CKT 914 and/or CKT 915 = SOME ECUS NO RESP/NOT EQUIP, repair communication concern by symptom. See SYMPTOM INDEX table to continue diagnosis.

Data Link Connector (DLC)

1

8

9

16

96D29465

Courtesy of Ford Motor Co.

Fig. 4: Identifying Data Link Connector (DLC) Terminals

- If NGS tester displays CKT 70 = ALL ECUS NO RESP/NOT EQUIP, perform TEST F: RESTRAINT CONTROL MODULE (RCM) DOES NOT RESPOND TO NGS TESTER under SYSTEM TESTS.
- If NGS tester displays CKT 914 = ALL ECUS NO RESP/NOT EQUIP, perform TEST M: NO MODULE/NETWORK COMMUNICATION – BUS LINK under SYSTEM TESTS.
- If NGS tester displays CKT 915 = ALL ECUS NO RESP/NOT EQUIP, perform TEST M: NO MODULE/NETWORK COMMUNICATION – BUS LINK under SYSTEM TESTS.
- If module in question is NO RESPONSE/NOT EQUIPPED, repair communication concern by symptom. See SYMPTOM INDEX table to continue diagnosis.
- If module in question is NO RESPONSE ON CKT 914 (BUS +), repair communication concern by symptom. See SYMPTOM INDEX table to continue diagnosis.
- If module in question is NO RESPONSE ON CKT 915 (BUS –), repair communication concern by symptom. See SYMPTOM INDEX table to continue diagnosis.

SYMPTOM INDEX

[1] – Front radio control unit may also be referred to as Audio Control Module (ACM).

[2] – Speed control servo may also be referred to as Next Generation Speed Control (NGSC) servo.

[3] – Air Suspension/Electronic Variable Orifice (EVO) steering module may also be referred to as Rear Air Suspension Module (RASM).

[4] – Instrument cluster may also be referred to as Hybrid Electronic Cluster (HEC).

RETRIEVING & CLEARING DIAGNOSTIC TROUBLE CODES

Connect New Generation Star (NGS) tester to Data Link Connector (DLC). Following manufacturers instructions to retrieve and clear codes for desired module. See appropriate table under DIAGNOSTIC TROUBLE CODE (DTC) DEFINITIONS for a listing of Diagnostic Trouble Codes (DTCs) and appropriate test procedure.

ACCESSING PARAMETER IDENTIFICATION (PID)

Turn ignition switch to LOCK position. Connect New Generation Star (NGS) tester to Data Link Connector (DLC). Following manufacturers instructions enter PID/DATA MONITOR AND RECORD for desired module. Operate appropriate system and ensure PID expected values are obtained. See appropriate table under PARAMETER IDENTIFICATION (PID) DEFINITIONS.

SYSTEM TESTS

CAUTION: When battery is disconnected or modules are replaced, vehicle computer and memory systems may lose memory data. Driveability problems may exist until computer systems have completed a relearn cycle. See COMPUTER RELEARN PROCEDURES article in GENERAL INFORMATION before disconnecting battery.

NOTE: Always check module power and ground circuits prior to replacing a control module. See appropriate wiring diagram in DATA LINK CONNECTORS, GROUND DISTRIBUTION or POWER DISTRIBUTION article in WIRING DIAGRAMS.

TEST A: ANTI-LOCK BRAKE SYSTEM (ABS) MODULE DOES NOT RESPOND TO NGS TESTER

1) Turn ignition switch to LOCK position. Disconnect ABS module harness connector, located in right front of engine compartment, under upper radiator support. Disconnect NGS tester (if connected). Inspect

ABS harness connector for loose, damaged or corroded terminals. Repair harness connector as necessary and retest system for normal operation. If harness connector is okay, connect ABS module harness connector and connect NGS tester. Turn ignition switch to RUN position. Perform data link diagnostic test. See DATA LINK DIAGNOSTIC TEST under COMMUNICATION NETWORK DIAGNOSTICS. If NGS tester indicates ABS: NO RESPONSE ON CKT 914 (BUS +), go to next step. If NGS tester does not indicate ABS: NO RESPONSE ON CKT 914 (BUS +), go to step 4).

2) Turn ignition switch to LOCK position. Disconnect ABS module harness connector. Disconnect NGS tester. Using an ohmmeter, measure resistance in Tan/Orange wire between terminal No. 20 at ABS module harness connector and terminal No. 2 at Data Link Connector (DLC). See Figs. 4 and 5. If resistance is less than 5 ohms, replace ABS module and retest system for normal operation. If resistance is 5 ohms or greater, go to next step.

3) Disconnect 76-pin harness connector C201 located behind left side of instrument panel. See Fig. 1. Inspect harness connector for loose, damaged or corroded terminals. Repair harness connector as necessary and retest system for normal operation. If harness connector is okay, measure resistance in Tan/Orange wire between terminal No. 59 at harness connector C201 and terminal No. 2 at DLC. See Figs. 4 and 6. If resistance is less than 5 ohms, repair open in Tan/Orange wire between ABS module harness connector and harness connector C201. Retest system for normal operation. If resistance is 5 ohms or greater, repair open in Tan/Orange wire between harness connector C201 and DLC. Retest system for normal operation.

4) Turn ignition switch to LOCK position. Disconnect ABS module harness connector. Disconnect NGS tester. Measure resistance in Pink/Light Blue wire between terminal No. 19 at ABS module harness connector and terminal No. 10 at DLC. See Figs. 4 and 5. If resistance is less than 5 ohms, replace ABS module and retest system for normal operation. If resistance is 5 ohms or greater, go to next step.

5) Disconnect 76-pin harness connector C201 located behind left side of instrument panel. See Fig. 1. Inspect harness connector for loose, damaged or corroded terminals. Repair harness connector as necessary and retest system for normal operation. If harness connector is okay, measure resistance in Pink/Light Blue wire between terminal No. 60 at harness connector C201 and terminal No. 10 at DLC. See Figs. 4 and 6. If resistance is less than 5 ohms, repair open in Pink/Light Blue wire between ABS module harness connector and harness connector C201. Retest system for normal operation. If resistance is 5 ohms or greater, repair open in Pink/Light Blue wire between harness connector C201 and DLC. Retest system for normal operation.

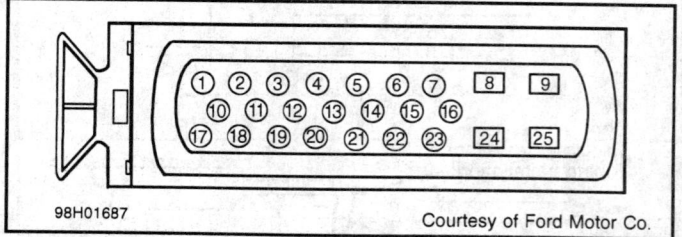

98H01687   Courtesy of Ford Motor Co.

Fig. 5: Identifying ABS Module Harness Connector Terminals

TEST B: FRONT RADIO CONTROL UNIT DOES NOT RESPOND TO NGS TESTER

NOTE: Front radio control unit may also be referred to as Audio Control Module (ACM).

1) Turn ignition switch to LOCK position. Disconnect front radio control unit 20-pin harness connector C258 located behind center of instrument panel, on radio. See Fig. 1. Inspect harness connector for loose, damaged or corroded terminals. Repair as necessary and retest system for normal operation. If harness connector is okay, reconnect harness connector C258. Turn ignition switch to RUN position. Perform data link diagnostic test. See DATA LINK DIAGNOSTIC TEST under COMMUNICATION NETWORK DIAGNOSTICS. If NGS tester indicates FCM:

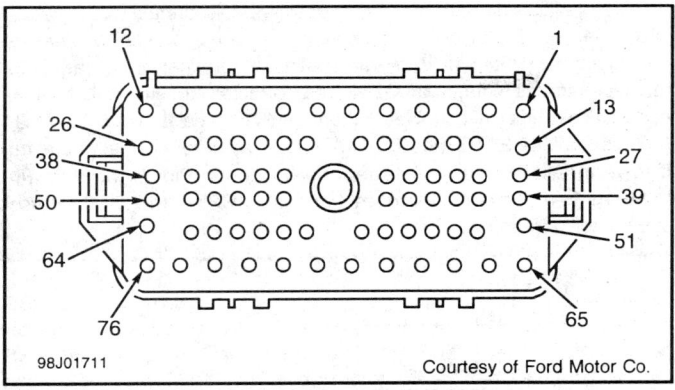

Fig. 6: Identifying Harness Connector C201 Terminals

NO RESPONSE ON CKT 914 (BUS +), go to next step. If NGS tester does not indicate FCM: NO RESPONSE ON CKT 914 (BUS +), go to step **3**).

2) Turn ignition switch to LOCK position. Disconnect NGS tester. Disconnect front radio control unit 20-pin harness connector C258. Measure resistance in Tan/Orange wire between terminal No. 3 at front radio control unit harness connector C258 and terminal No. 2 at Data Link Connector (DLC). See Figs. 4 and 7. If resistance is less than 5 ohms, replace front radio control unit and retest system for normal operation. If resistance is 5 ohms or greater, repair open Tan/Orange wire between front radio control unit harness connector and DLC. Retest system for normal operation.

3) Turn ignition switch to LOCK position. Disconnect NGS tester. Disconnect front radio control unit 20-pin harness connector C258. Measure resistance in Pink/Light Blue wire between terminal No. 4 at front radio control unit harness connector C258 and terminal No. 10 at DLC. See Figs. 4 and 7. If resistance is less than 5 ohms, replace front radio control unit and retest system for normal operation. If resistance is 5 ohms or more, repair open in Pink/Light Blue wire between front radio control unit harness connector and DLC.

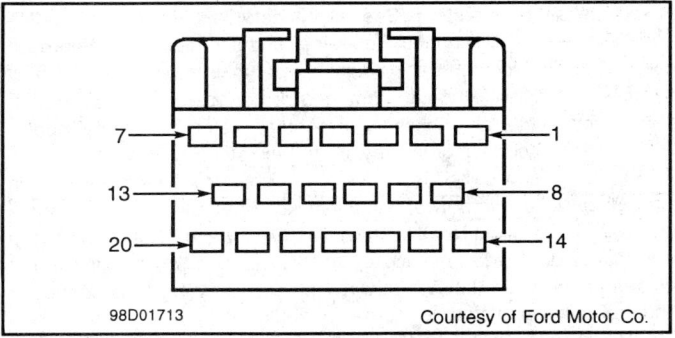

Fig. 7: Identifying Front Radio Control Unit Harness Connector C258 Terminals

TEST C: DRIVER'S DOOR MODULE (DDM) DOES NOT RESPOND TO NGS TESTER

1) Turn ignition switch to LOCK position. Disconnect DDM 22-pin harness connector C520 located inside driver's door. Inspect harness connector for loose, damaged or corroded terminals. Repair as necessary and retest system for normal operation. If harness connector is okay, reconnect harness connector. Turn ignition switch to RUN position. Perform data link diagnostic test. See DATA LINK DIAGNOSTIC TEST under COMMUNICATION NETWORK DIAGNOSTICS. If NGS tester indicates DDM: NO RESPONSE ON CKT 914 (BUS +), go to next step. If NGS tester does not indicate DDM: NO RESPONSE ON CKT 914 (BUS +), go to step **4**).

2) Turn ignition switch to LOCK position. Disconnect NGS tester. Disconnect DDM harness connector C520. Measure resistance in Tan/Orange wire between terminal No. 35 at DDM harness connector C520 and terminal No. 2 at Data Link Connector (DLC). See Figs. 4 and

8. If resistance is less than 5 ohms, replace DDM and retest system for normal operation. If resistance is 5 ohms or greater, go to next step.

3) Disconnect 42-pin harness connector C202 located behind right side of instrument panel. See Fig. 1. Inspect harness connector for loose, damaged or corroded terminals. Repair as necessary and retest system for normal operation. If harness connector is okay, measure resistance in Tan/Orange wire between terminal No. 6 at male half of harness connector C202 and terminal No. 2 at DLC. See Figs. 4 and 9. If resistance is less than 5 ohms, repair open in Tan/Orange wire between DDM harness connector C520 and harness connector C202. Retest system for normal operation. If resistance is 5 ohms or greater, repair open in Tan/Orange wire between harness connector C202 and DLC. Retest system for normal operation.

4) Turn ignition switch to LOCK position. Disconnect NGS tester. Disconnect DDM harness connector C520. Measure resistance in Pink/Light Blue wire between terminal No. 36 at DDM harness connector C520 and terminal No. 10 at DLC. See Figs. 4 and 9. If resistance is less than 5 ohms, replace DDM and retest system for normal operation. If resistance is 5 ohms or greater, go to next step.

5) Disconnect 42-pin harness connector C202 located behind right side of instrument panel. See Fig. 1. Inspect harness connector for loose, damaged or corroded terminals. Repair as necessary and retest system for normal operation. If harness connector is okay, measure resistance in Pink/Light Blue wire between terminal No. 7 at male half of harness connector C202 and terminal No. 10 at DLC. See Figs. 4 and 9. If resistance is less than 5 ohms, repair open in Pink/Light Blue wire between DDM harness connector C520 and harness connector C202. Retest system for normal operation. If resistance is 5 ohms or greater, repair open in Pink/Light Blue wire between harness connector C202 and DLC. Retest system for normal operation.

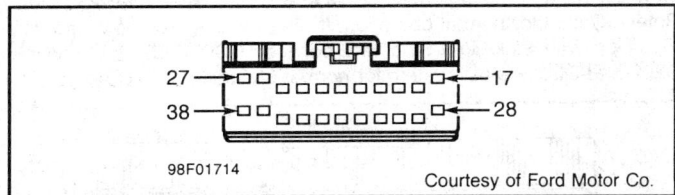

Fig. 8: Identifying DDM Harness Connector C520 Terminals

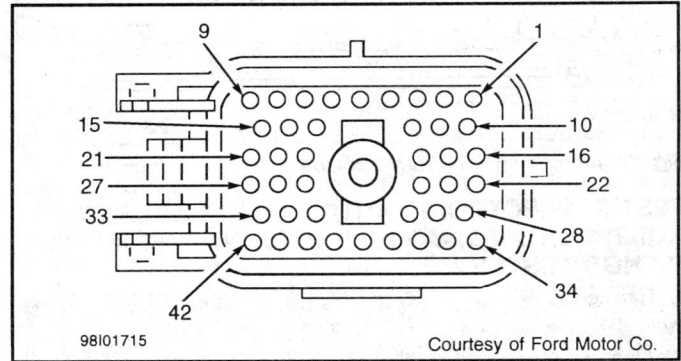

Fig. 9: Identifying Harness Connector C202 Terminals (Male Half Shown)

TEST D: DRIVER'S SEAT MODULE (DSM) DOES NOT RESPOND TO NGS TESTER

1) Turn ignition switch to LOCK position. Disconnect DSM 26-pin harness connector C313 located under driver's front seat. Inspect harness connector for loose, damaged or corroded terminals. Repair as necessary and retest system for normal operation. If harness connector is okay, reconnect harness connector. Turn ignition switch to RUN position. Perform data link diagnostic test. See DATA LINK DIAGNOSTIC TEST under COMMUNICATION NETWORK DIAGNOSTICS. If NGS tester indicates DSM: NO RESPONSE ON CKT 914 (BUS +), go to next step. If NGS tester does not indicate DSM: NO RESPONSE ON CKT 914 (BUS +), go to step **4**).

2) Turn ignition switch to LOCK position. Disconnect NGS tester. Disconnect DSM harness connector C313. Measure resistance in Tan/Orange wire between terminal No. 25 at DSM harness connector C313 and terminal No. 2 at Data Link Connector (DLC). *See Figs. 4 and 10.* If resistance is less than 5 ohms, replace DSM and retest system for normal operation. If resistance is 5 ohms or greater, go to next step.

3) Disconnect 42-pin harness connector C202 located behind right side of instrument panel. *See Fig. 1.* Inspect harness connector for loose, damaged or corroded terminals. Repair as necessary and retest system for normal operation. If harness connector is okay, measure resistance in Tan/Orange wire between terminal No. 6 at male half of harness connector C202 and terminal No. 2 at DLC. *See Figs. 4 and 9.* If resistance is less than 5 ohms, repair open in Tan/Orange wire between DSM harness connector C313 and harness connector C202. Retest system for normal operation. If resistance is 5 ohms or greater, repair open in Tan/Orange wire between harness connector C202 and DLC. Retest system for normal operation.

4) Turn ignition switch to LOCK position. Disconnect NGS tester. Disconnect DSM harness connector C313. Measure resistance in Pink/Light Blue wire between terminal No. 26 at DSM harness connector C313 and terminal No. 10 at DLC. *See Figs. 4 and 10.* If resistance is less than 5 ohms, replace DSM and retest system for normal operation. If resistance is 5 ohms or greater, go to next step.

5) Disconnect 42-pin harness connector C202 located behind right side of instrument panel. *See Fig. 1.* Inspect harness connector for loose, damaged or corroded terminals. Repair as necessary and retest system for normal operation. If harness connector is okay, measure resistance in Pink/Light Blue wire between terminal No. 7 at male half of harness connector C202 and terminal No. 10 at DLC. *See Figs. 4 and 9.* If resistance is less than 5 ohms, repair open in Pink/Light Blue wire between DSM harness connector C313 and harness connector C202. Retest system for normal operation. If resistance is 5 ohms or greater, repair open in Pink/Light Blue wire between DSM harness connector C202 and DLC. Retest system for normal operation.

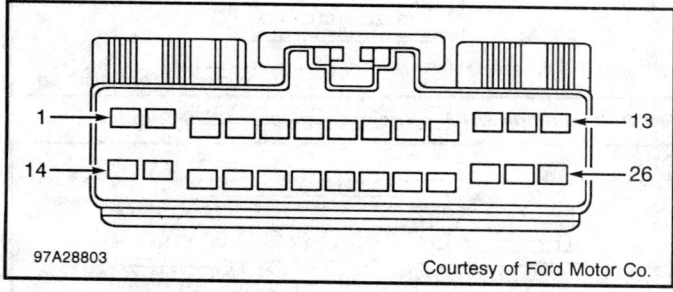

97A28803   Courtesy of Ford Motor Co.

Fig. 10: Identifying DSM Harness Connector C313 Terminals

TEST E: ELECTRONIC AUTOMATIC TEMPERATURE CONTROL (EATC) MODULE DOES NOT RESPOND TO NGS TESTER

1) Turn ignition switch to LOCK position. Disconnect EATC module White harness connector C281 located behind center of instrument panel. *See Fig. 1.* Inspect harness connector for loose, damaged or corroded terminals. Repair as necessary and retest system for normal operation. If harness connector is okay, reconnect harness connector. Turn ignition switch to RUN position. Perform data link diagnostic test. See DATA LINK DIAGNOSTIC TEST under COMMUNICATION NETWORK DIAGNOSTICS. If NGS tester indicates EATC: NO RESPONSE ON CKT 914 (BUS +), go to next step. If NGS tester does not indicate EATC: NO RESPONSE ON CKT 914 (BUS +), go to step **3)**.

2) Turn ignition switch to LOCK position. Disconnect NGS tester. Disconnect EATC module White harness connector C281. Measure resistance in Tan/Orange wire between terminal No. 15 at EATC module harness connector C281 and terminal No. 2 at Data Link Connector (DLC). *See Figs. 4 and 11.* If resistance is less than 5 ohms, replace EATC module and retest system for normal operation. If resistance is 5 ohms or greater, repair open in Tan/Orange wire between EATC module harness connector C274 and DLC. **Retest** system for normal operation.

3) Turn ignition switch to LOCK position. Disconnect NGS tester. Disconnect EATC module White harness connector C281. Measure resistance in Pink/Light Blue wire between terminal No. 1 at EATC module harness connector C281 and terminal No. 10 at Data Link harness connector (DLC). *See Figs. 4 and 11.* If resistance is less than 5 ohms, replace EATC module and retest system for normal operation. If resistance is 5 ohms or greater, repair open in Pink/Light Blue wire between EATC module harness connector C281 and DLC. Retest system for normal operation.

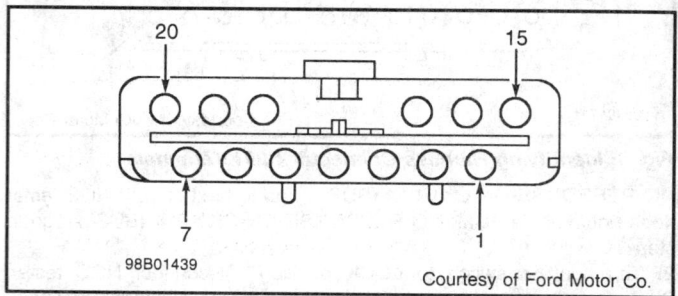

98B01439   Courtesy of Ford Motor Co.

Fig. 11: Identifying EATC Module Harness Connector C281 Terminals

TEST F: RESTRAINT CONTROL MODULE (RCM) DOES NOT RESPOND TO NGS TESTER

NOTE: Depending on module configuration, with all modules connected and with ignition switch in RUN position or with engine running 2-3 volts may be present at Data Link Connector (DLC) terminal No. 7 (Light Blue/White wire). This is the International Standards Organization (ISO) 9141 diagnostic communications network circuit.

1) Inspect NGS tester connector and Data Link Connector (DLC) for loose, damaged or corroded terminals. Repair connector(s) as necessary and retest system for normal operation. If connectors are okay, deactivate air bag system. See appropriate AIR BAG RESTRAINT SYSTEMS article. Disconnect Restraint Control Module (RCM) harness connector C276 located behind right side of instrument panel. Inspect harness connector for loose, damaged or corroded terminals. Repair harness connector as necessary and retest system for normal operation. If harness connector is okay, go to next step.

2) Ensure ignition switch is in LOCK position. Measure resistance in Light Blue/White wire between terminal No. 7 at RCM harness connector C276 and terminal No. 7 at DLC. *See Figs. 4 and 12.* If resistance is less than 5 ohms, go to next step. If resistance is 5 ohms or greater, repair open in Light Blue/White wire between RCM harness connector and DLC. Retest system for normal operation.

3) Turn ignition switch to RUN position. Measure voltage between terminals No. 4 (Black wire) and No. 7 (Light Blue/White wire) at DLC. Also, measure voltage between terminals No. 7 (Light Blue/White wire) and No. 16 (Light Blue/White wire) at DLC. *See Fig. 4.* If voltage is indicated at any terminals, repair Light Blue/White wire between RCM harness connector and DLC. Retest system for normal operation. If voltage is not indicated at any terminals, replace RCM and retest system for normal operation.

TEST G: LIGHTING CONTROL MODULE (LCM) DOES NOT RESPOND TO NGS TESTER

1) Turn ignition switch to LOCK position. Disconnect LCM 16-pin harness connector C221 located behind left side of instrument panel, right of steering column. Inspect harness connector for loose, damaged or corroded terminals. Repair harness connector as necessary and retest system for normal operation. If harness connector is okay, reconnect harness connector. Turn ignition switch to RUN position. Perform data link diagnostic test. See DATA LINK DIAGNOSTIC TEST under COMMUNICATION NETWORK DIAGNOSTICS. If NGS tester

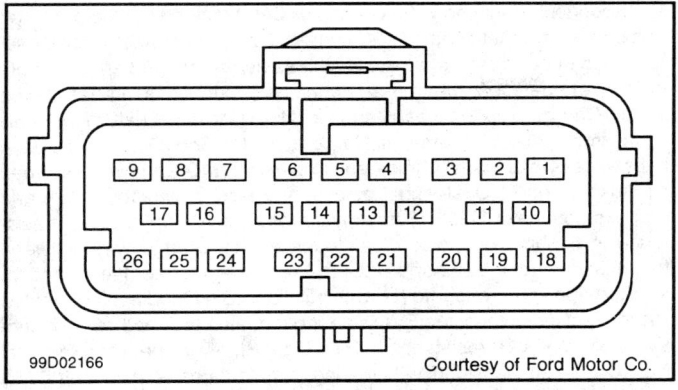

Fig. 12: Identifying Restraint Control Module Harness Connector C276 Terminals

indicates LCM: NO RESPONSE ON CKT 914 (BUS +), go to next step. If NGS tester does not indicate LCM: NO RESPONSE ON CKT 914 (BUS +), go to step **3**).

2) Turn ignition switch to LOCK position. Disconnect NGS tester. Disconnect LCM harness connector C221. Measure resistance in Tan/Orange wire between terminal No. 20 at LCM harness connector C221 and terminal No. 2 at Data Link Connector (DLC). *See Figs. 4 and 13*. If resistance is less than 5 ohms, replace LCM and retest system for normal operation. If resistance is 5 ohms or greater, repair open in Tan/Orange wire between LCM harness connector and DLC. Retest system for normal operation.

3) Turn ignition switch to LOCK position. Disconnect NGS tester. Disconnect LCM harness connector C221. Measure resistance in Pink/Light Blue wire between terminal No. 28 at LCM harness connector C221 and terminal No. 10 at DLC. *See Figs. 4 and 13*. If resistance is less than 5 ohms, replace LCM and retest system for normal operation. If resistance is 5 ohms or greater, repair open in Pink/Light Blue wire between LCM harness connector C221 and DLC. Retest system for normal operation.

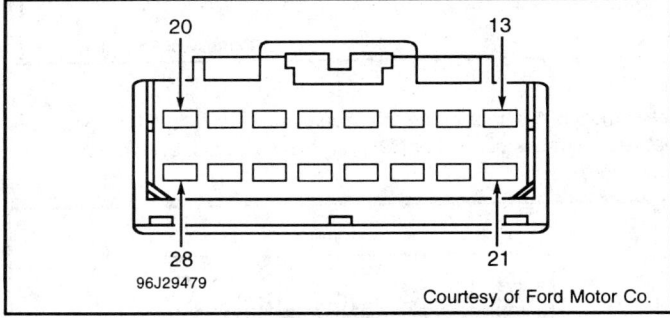

Fig. 13: Identifying LCM Harness Connector C221 Terminals

TEST H: SPEED CONTROL SERVO DOES NOT RESPOND TO NGS TESTER

NOTE: Speed control servo may also be referred to as Next Generation Speed Control (NGSC) servo.

1) Turn ignition switch to LOCK position. Disconnect speed control servo 10-pin harness connector located in left rear of engine compartment. Inspect harness connector for loose, damaged or corroded terminals. Repair harness connector as necessary and retest system for normal operation. If harness connector is okay, reconnect harness connector. Turn ignition switch to RUN position. Perform data link diagnostic test. See DATA LINK DIAGNOSTIC TEST under COMMUNICATION NETWORK DIAGNOSTICS. If NGS tester indicates NGSC: NO RESPONSE ON CKT 914 (BUS +), go to next step. If NGS tester does not indicate NGSC: NO RESPONSE ON CKT 914 (BUS +), go to step **4**).

2) Turn ignition switch to LOCK position. Disconnect NGS tester. Disconnect speed control servo 10-pin harness connector. Measure

resistance in Tan/Orange wire between terminal No. 1 at speed control servo harness connector and terminal No. 2 at Data Link Connector (DLC). *See Figs. 4 and 14*. If resistance is less than 5 ohms, replace speed control servo and retest system for normal operation. If resistance is 5 ohms or greater, go to next step.

3) Disconnect 76-pin harness connector C201 located behind left side of instrument panel. *See Fig. 1*. Inspect harness connector for loose, damaged or corroded terminals. Repair harness connector as necessary and retest system for normal operation. If harness connector is okay, measure resistance in Tan/Orange wire between terminal No. 59 at harness connector C201 and terminal No. 2 at DLC. *See Figs. 4 and 6*. If resistance is less than 5 ohms, repair open in Tan/Orange wire between speed control servo harness connector and harness connector C201. Retest system for normal operation. If resistance is 5 ohms or greater, repair open in Tan/Orange wire between harness connector C201 and DLC. Retest system for normal operation.

4) Turn ignition switch to LOCK position. Disconnect NGS tester. Disconnect speed control servo harness connector. Measure resistance in Pink/Light Blue wire between terminal No. 2 at speed control servo harness connector and terminal No. 10 at DLC. *See Figs. 4 and 14*. If resistance is less than 5 ohms, replace speed control servo and retest system for normal operation. If resistance is 5 ohms or greater, go to next step.

5) Disconnect 76-pin harness connector C201 located behind left side of instrument panel. *See Fig. 1*. Inspect harness connector for loose, damaged or corroded terminals. Repair harness connector as necessary and retest system for normal operation. If harness connector is okay, measure resistance in Pink/Light Blue wire between terminal No. 60 at harness connector C201 and terminal No. 10 at DLC. *See Figs. 4 and 6*. If resistance is less than 5 ohms, repair open in Pink/Light Blue wire between speed control servo harness connector and harness connector C201. Retest system for normal operation. If resistance is 5 ohms or greater, repair open in Pink/Light Blue wire between harness connector C201 and DLC. Retest system for normal operation.

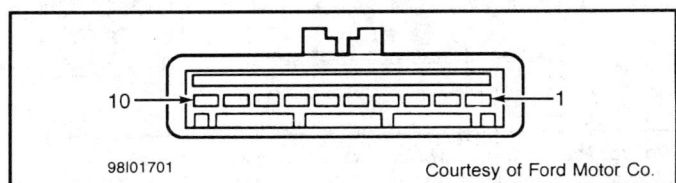

Fig. 14: Identifying Speed Control Servo Harness Connector Terminals

TEST J: POWERTRAIN CONTROL MODULE (PCM) DOES NOT RESPOND TO NGS TESTER

NOTE: If test results indicate PCM is faulty, always check for any engine performance related Diagnostic Trouble Codes (DTCs) prior to replacing PCM. If any DTCs are present, service DTCs as necessary and retest. See appropriate SELF-DIAGNOSTICS article in ENGINE PERFORMANCE in appropriate MITCHELL® manual.

1) Turn ignition switch to LOCK position. Disconnect PCM harness connector located in engine compartment on left side of firewall. Inspect harness connector for loose, damaged or corroded terminals. Repair harness connector as necessary and retest system for normal operation. If harness connector is okay, reconnect harness connector. Turn ignition switch to RUN position. Perform data link diagnostic test. See DATA LINK DIAGNOSTIC TEST under COMMUNICATION NETWORK DIAGNOSTICS. If NGS tester indicates PCM: NO RESPONSE ON CKT 914 (BUS +), go to next step. If NGS tester does not indicate PCM: NO RESPONSE ON CKT 914 (BUS +), go to step **4**).

2) Turn ignition switch to LOCK position. Disconnect NGS tester. Disconnect PCM harness connector. Measure resistance in Tan/Orange wire between terminal No. 16 at PCM harness connector and terminal No. 2 at Data Link Connector (DLC). *See Figs. 4 and 15*. If resistance is less than 5 ohms, replace PCM and retest system for normal operation. If resistance is 5 ohms or greater, go to next step.

3) Disconnect 76-pin harness connector C201 located behind left side of instrument panel. *See Fig. 1.* Inspect harness connector for loose, damaged or corroded terminals. Repair harness connector as necessary and retest system for normal operation. If harness connector is okay, measure resistance in Tan/Orange wire between terminal No. 59 at harness connector C201 and terminal No. 2 at DLC. *See Figs. 4 and 6.* If resistance is less than 5 ohms, repair open in Tan/Orange wire between PCM harness connector and harness connector C201. Retest system for normal operation. If resistance is 5 ohms or greater, repair open in Tan/Orange wire between harness connector C201 and DLC. Retest system for normal operation.

4) Turn ignition switch to LOCK position. Disconnect NGS tester. Disconnect PCM harness connector. Measure resistance in Pink/Light Blue wire between terminal No. 15 at PCM harness connector and terminal No. 10 at DLC. *See Figs. 4 and 15.* If resistance is less than 5 ohms, replace PCM and retest system for normal operation. If resistance is 5 ohms or greater, go to next step.

5) Disconnect 76-pin harness connector C201 located behind left side of instrument panel. *See Fig. 1.* Inspect harness connector for loose, damaged or corroded terminals. Repair harness connector as necessary and retest system for normal operation. If harness connector is okay, measure resistance in Pink/Light Blue wire between terminal No. 60 at harness connector C201 and terminal No. 10 at DLC. *See Figs. 4 and 6.* If resistance is less than 5 ohms, repair open in Pink/Light Blue wire between PCM harness connector and harness connector C201. Retest system for normal operation. If resistance is 5 ohms or greater, repair open in Pink/Light Blue wire between harness connector C201 and DLC. Retest system for normal operation.

3) Disconnect 42-pin harness connector C202 located behind right side of instrument panel. *See Fig. 1.* Inspect harness connector for loose, damaged or corroded terminals. Repair as necessary and retest system for normal operation. If harness connector is okay, measure resistance in Tan/Orange wire between terminal No. 6 at male half of harness connector C202 and terminal No. 2 at DLC. *See Figs. 4 and 9.* If resistance is less than 5 ohms, repair open in Tan/Orange wire between air suspension/EVO steering module harness connector C251 and harness connector C202. Retest system for normal operation. If resistance is 5 ohms or more, repair open in Tan/Orange wire between harness connector C202 and DLC. Retest system for normal operation.

4) Turn ignition switch to LOCK position. Disconnect NGS tester. Disconnect air suspension/EVO steering module Black harness connector C251. Measure resistance in Pink/Light Blue wire between terminal No. 10 at air suspension/EVO steering module harness connector C251 and terminal No. 10 at Data Link Connector (DLC). *See Figs. 4 and 16.* If resistance is less than 5 ohms, replace air suspension/EVO steering module and retest system for normal operation. If resistance is 5 ohms or greater, go to next step.

5) Disconnect 42-pin harness connector C202 located behind right side of instrument panel. *See Fig. 1.* Inspect harness connector for loose, damaged or corroded terminals. Repair as necessary and retest system for normal operation. If harness connector is okay, measure resistance in Pink/Light Blue wire between terminal No. 7 at male half of harness connector C202 and terminal No. 10 at DLC. *See Figs. 4 and 9.* If resistance is less than 5 ohms, repair open in Pink/Light Blue wire between air suspension/EVO steering module harness connector C251 and harness connector C202. Retest system for normal operation. If

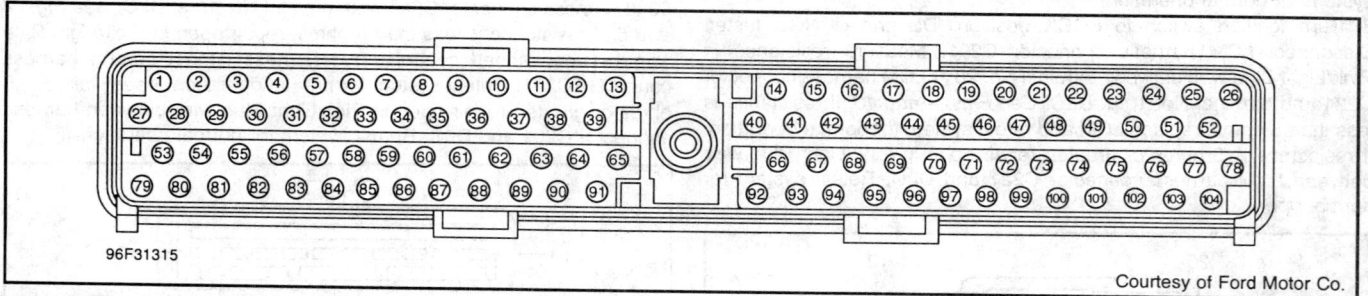

96F31315

Courtesy of Ford Motor Co.

Fig. 15: Identifying PCM Harness Connector Terminals

TEST K: AIR SUSPENSION/ELECTRONIC VARIABLE ORIFICE (EVO) STEERING MODULE DOES NOT RESPOND TO NGS TESTER

NOTE: Air Suspension/Electronic Variable Orifice (EVO) steering module may also be referred to as Rear Air Suspension Module (RASM).

1) Turn ignition switch to LOCK position. Disconnect air suspension/EVO steering module Black harness connector C251. Air suspension/EVO steering module is located below right side of instrument panel. Inspect harness connector for loose, damaged or corroded terminals. Repair harness connector as necessary and retest system for normal operation. If harness connector is okay, reconnect harness connector. Turn ignition switch to RUN position. Perform data link diagnostic test. See DATA LINK DIAGNOSTIC TEST under COMMUNICATION NETWORK DIAGNOSTICS. If NGS tester indicates RASM: NO RESPONSE ON CKT 914 (BUS +), go to next step. If NGS tester does not indicate RASM: NO RESPONSE ON CKT 914 (BUS +), go to step **4)**.

2) Turn ignition switch to LOCK position. Disconnect NGS tester. Disconnect air suspension/EVO steering module Black harness connector C251. Measure resistance in Tan/Orange wire between terminal No. 9 at air suspension/EVO steering module harness connector C251 and terminal No. 2 at Data Link Connector (DLC). *See Figs. 4 and 16.* If resistance is less than 5 ohms, replace air suspension/EVO steering module and retest system for normal operation. If resistance is 5 ohms or greater, go to next step.

resistance is 5 ohms or greater, repair open in Pink/Light Blue wire between harness connector C202 and DLC. Retest system for normal operation.

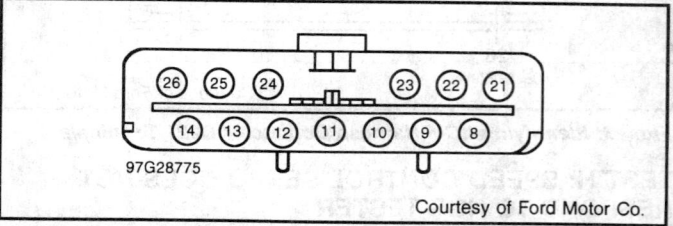

97G28775

Courtesy of Ford Motor Co.

Fig. 16: Identifying Air Suspension/EVO Steering Module Harness Connector C251 Terminals

TEST L: INSTRUMENT CLUSTER DOES NOT RESPOND TO NGS TESTER

NOTE: Instrument cluster may also be referred to as Hybrid Electronic Cluster (HEC).

1) Turn ignition switch to LOCK position. Disconnect instrument cluster 12-pin harness connector C254. Inspect harness connector for loose, damaged or corroded terminals. Repair harness connector as necessary and retest system for normal operation. If harness connector is okay, reconnect harness connector. Turn ignition switch to RUN position. Perform data link diagnostic test. See DATA LINK DIAGNOSTIC TEST under COMMUNICATION NETWORK DIAGNOSTICS. If NGS tester indicates VIC: NO RESPONSE ON CKT 914 (BUS +), go to next step. If NGS tester does not indicate VIC: NO RESPONSE ON CKT 914 (BUS +), go to step 3).

2) Turn ignition switch to LOCK position. Disconnect NGS tester. Disconnect instrument cluster harness connector C254. Using an ohmmeter, measure resistance in Tan/Orange wire between terminal No. 18 at instrument cluster harness connector C254 and terminal No. 2 at Data Link Connector (DLC). See Figs. 4 and 17. If resistance is less than 5 ohms, replace instrument cluster and retest system for normal operation. If resistance is 5 ohms or greater, repair open in Tan/Orange wire between instrument cluster harness connector C254 and DLC. Retest system for normal operation.

3) Turn ignition switch to LOCK position. Disconnect NGS tester. Disconnect instrument cluster harness connector C254. Measure resistance in Pink/Light Blue wire between terminal No. 17 at instrument cluster harness connector C254 and terminal No. 10 at DLC. See Figs. 4 and 17. If resistance is less than 5 ohms, replace instrument cluster and retest system for normal operation. If resistance is 5 ohms or greater, repair open in Pink/Light Blue wire between instrument cluster harness connector C254 and DLC. Retest system for normal operation.

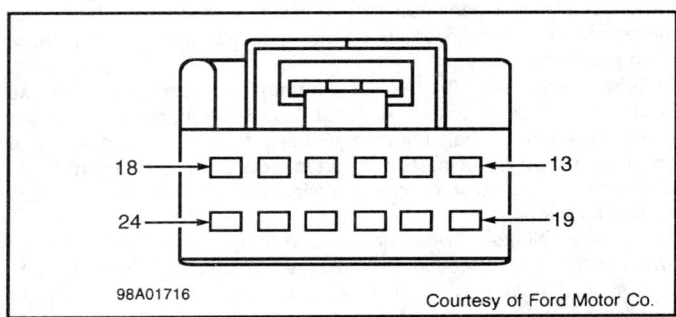

98A01716   Courtesy of Ford Motor Co.

Fig. 17: Identifying Instrument Cluster Harness Connector C254 Terminals

TEST M: NO MODULE/NETWORK COMMUNICATION – SCP BUS LINK

NOTE: *Depending on module configuration, with all modules connected and with ignition switch in RUN position or with engine running 2-3 volts may be present at Data Link Connector (DLC) terminals No. 2 (Tan/Orange wire) and No. 10 (Pink/Light Blue wire). These are the Standard Corporate Protocol (SCP) diagnostic communications network circuits.*

NOTE: *Front radio control unit may also be referred to as Audio Control Module (ACM). Speed control servo may also be referred to as Next Generation Speed Control (NGSC) servo. Air Suspension/ Electronic Variable Orifice (EVO) steering module may also be referred to as Rear Air Suspension Module (RASM). Instrument cluster may also be referred to as Hybrid Electronic Cluster (HEC).*

1) Inspect NGS tester connector for loose, damaged or corroded terminals. Repair connector as necessary and retest system for normal operation. If connector is okay, go to next step.

2) Turn ignition switch to LOCK position. Inspect Data Link Connector (DLC) for physical damage, bent terminals or corrosion. Repair connector as necessary and retest system for normal operation. If connector is okay, go to next step.

3) Turn ignition switch to LOCK position. Disconnect speed control servo 10-pin harness connector located in left rear of engine compartment. Measure resistance in Tan/Orange wire between terminal No. 1 at speed control servo harness connector and terminal No. 2 at DLC. See Figs. 4 and 14. Also, measure resistance in Pink/Light Blue wire between terminal No. 2 at speed control servo harness connector and terminal No. 10 at DLC. If both resistance readings are less than 5 ohms, go to next step. If either resistance reading is 5 ohms or greater, repair open

in Tan/Orange wire and/or Pink/Light Blue wire between harness connector C201 and DLC. Retest system for normal operation.

4) Connect NGS tester. Turn ignition switch to RUN position. Perform data link diagnostic test. See DATA LINK DIAGNOSTIC TEST under COMMUNICATION NETWORK DIAGNOSTICS. If all modules equipped on vehicle passed data link diagnostic test, except speed control servo, replace speed control servo and retest system for normal operation. If any module other than speed control servo did not pass data link diagnostic test, go to next step.

5) Turn ignition switch to LOCK position. Disconnect 76-pin harness connector C201 located behind left side of instrument panel. See Fig. 1. Turn ignition switch to RUN position. Perform data link diagnostic test. See DATA LINK DIAGNOSTIC TEST under COMMUNICATION NETWORK DIAGNOSTICS. If all modules equipped on vehicle except PCM, ABS module and speed control servo passed data link diagnostic test, reconnect harness connector C201 and go to next step. If any module other than PCM, ABS module and speed control servo did not pass data link diagnostic test, reconnect harness connector C201 and go to step 8).

6) Turn ignition switch to LOCK position. Disconnect ABS module harness connector, located in right front of engine compartment, under upper radiator support. Turn ignition switch to RUN position. Perform data link diagnostic test. See DATA LINK DIAGNOSTIC TEST under COMMUNICATION NETWORK DIAGNOSTICS. If all modules equipped on vehicle except ABS module and speed control servo passed data link diagnostic test, replace ABS module and retest system for normal operation. If any module other than ABS module and speed control servo did not pass data link diagnostic test, go to next step.

7) Turn ignition switch to LOCK position. Disconnect PCM harness connector located in engine compartment on left side of firewall. Perform data link diagnostic test. See DATA LINK DIAGNOSTIC TEST under COMMUNICATION NETWORK DIAGNOSTICS. If all modules equipped on vehicle except ABS module, PCM and speed control servo passed data link diagnostic test, replace PCM and retest system for normal operation. If any module other than ABS module, PCM and speed control servo did not pass data link diagnostic test, repair circuit No. 914 (Tan/Orange wire) and/or circuit No. 915 (Pink/Light Blue wire) between harness connector C201 and ABS module, PCM, speed control servo and evac and fill harness connector C133 (Tan/Orange wire only). Retest system for normal operation.

8) Turn ignition switch to LOCK position. Disconnect 42-pin harness connector C202 located behind right side of instrument panel. See Fig. 1. Turn ignition switch to RUN position. Perform data link diagnostic test. See DATA LINK DIAGNOSTIC TEST under COMMUNICATION NETWORK DIAGNOSTICS. If all modules equipped on vehicle except air suspension/Electronic Variable Orifice (EVO) steering module, Driver's Door Module (DDM) and Driver's Seat Module (DSM) (if equipped) passed data link diagnostic test, reconnect harness connector C202 and go to next step. If any module other than air suspension/EVO steering module, DDM and DSM (if equipped) did not pass data link diagnostic test, reconnect harness connector C202 and go to step 12).

9) Turn ignition switch to LOCK position. Disconnect DDM 22-pin harness connector C520 located inside driver's door. Turn ignition switch to RUN position. Perform data link diagnostic test. See DATA LINK DIAGNOSTIC TEST under COMMUNICATION NETWORK DIAGNOSTICS. If all modules equipped on vehicle except DDM passed data link diagnostic test, replace DDM and retest system for normal operation. If any module other than DDM did not pass data link diagnostic test, go to next step (if equipped with a DSM) or go to step 11) (if not equipped with a DSM).

10) Turn ignition switch to LOCK position. Disconnect DSM 26-pin harness connector C313 located under driver's front seat. Turn ignition switch to RUN position. Perform data link diagnostic test. See DATA LINK DIAGNOSTIC TEST under COMMUNICATION NETWORK DIAGNOSTICS. If all modules equipped on vehicle except DSM and DDM passed data link diagnostic test, replace DSM and retest system for normal operation. If any module other than DSM and DDM did not pass data link diagnostic test, go to next step

11) Disconnect air suspension/EVO steering module Black harness connector C251. Air suspension/EVO steering module is located below right side of instrument panel. Turn ignition switch to RUN position. Perform data link diagnostic test. See DATA LINK DIAGNOSTIC TEST under COMMUNICATION NETWORK DIAGNOSTICS. If all modules equipped on vehicle except DSM, DDM and air suspension/EVO steering module passed data link diagnostic test, replace air suspension/EVO steering module and retest system for normal operation. If any module other than DSM, DDM and air suspension/EVO steering module did not pass data link diagnostic test, repair circuit No. 914 (Tan/Orange wire) and/or circuit No. 915 (Pink/Light Blue wire) between harness connector C202 and DSM (if equipped), DDM and air suspension/EVO steering module and retest system for normal operation.

12) Turn ignition switch to LOCK position. Disconnect LCM 16-pin harness connector C221 located behind left side of instrument panel, right of steering column. Turn ignition switch to RUN position. Perform data link diagnostic test. See DATA LINK DIAGNOSTIC TEST under COMMUNICATION NETWORK DIAGNOSTICS. If all modules equipped on vehicle except LCM passed data link diagnostic test, replace LCM and retest system for normal operation. If any module other than LCM did not pass data link diagnostic test, go to next step (if equipped with front radio control unit) or go to step **14)** (if not equipped with front radio control unit).

13) Turn ignition switch to LOCK position. Disconnect front radio control unit 20-pin harness connector C258 located behind center of instrument panel, on radio. *See Fig. 1.* Turn ignition switch to RUN position. Perform data link diagnostic test. See DATA LINK DIAGNOSTIC TEST under COMMUNICATION NETWORK DIAGNOSTICS. If all modules equipped on vehicle except LCM and front radio control unit passed data link diagnostic test, replace front radio control unit and retest system for normal operation. If any module other than LCM and front radio control unit did not pass data link diagnostic test, go to next step.

14) Turn ignition switch to LOCK position. Disconnect instrument cluster 12-pin harness connector C254. Turn ignition switch to RUN position. Perform data link diagnostic test. See DATA LINK DIAGNOSTIC TEST under COMMUNICATION NETWORK DIAGNOSTICS. If all modules equipped on vehicle except instrument cluster, LCM and front radio control unit (if equipped) passed data link diagnostic test, replace instrument cluster and retest system for normal operation. If any module other than instrument cluster, LCM and front radio control unit (if equipped) did not pass data link diagnostic test, go to next step.

15) Turn ignition switch to LOCK position. Disconnect Electronic Automatic Temperature Control (EATC) module White harness connector C281 located behind center of instrument panel. Turn ignition switch to RUN position. Perform data link diagnostic test. See DATA LINK DIAGNOSTIC TEST under COMMUNICATION NETWORK DIAGNOSTICS. If all modules equipped on vehicle except EATC module, instrument cluster, LCM and front radio control unit (if equipped) passed data link diagnostic test, replace EATC module and retest system for normal operation. If any module other than EATC module, instrument cluster, LCM and front radio control unit (if equipped) did not pass data link diagnostic test, repair circuit No. 914 (Tan/Orange wire) and/or circuit No. 915 (Pink/Light Blue wire) between harness connector C202 and LCM, front radio control unit (if equipped), instrument cluster and EATC module. Retest system for normal operation.

TEST N: NO MODULE/NETWORK COMMUNICATION – NO POWER TO NGS TESTER

1) Inspect NGS tester connector for loose, damaged or corroded terminals. Repair connector as necessary and retest system for normal operation. If connector is okay, go to next step.
2) Turn ignition switch to LOCK position. Inspect Data Link Connector (DLC) for physical damage, bent terminals or corrosion. Repair as necessary and retest system for normal operation. If connector is okay, go to next step.
3) Remove and inspect fuse No. 23 (20-amp) from instrument panel fuse block. If fuse is okay, go to next step. If fuse is blown, replace fuse and retest system for normal operation. Recheck fuse. If fuse is okay, go to next step. If fuse is blown, repair short to ground in circuit No. 40 (Light Blue/White wire) between instrument panel fuse block and DLC. Retest system for normal operation.
4) Measure voltage between ground and terminal No. 16 (Light Blue/White wire) at DLC. *See Fig. 4.* If voltage is greater than 10 volts, go to next step. If voltage is 10 volts or less, repair circuit No. 40 (Light Blue/White wire) between instrument panel fuse block and DLC. Retest system for normal operation.
5) Measure resistance between ground and terminals No. 4 (Black wire) and No. 5 (Black/White wire) at DLC. If both resistance readings are less than 5 ohms, repair or replace NGS tester. Retest system for normal operation. If either resistance reading is 5 ohms or greater, repair open in Black wire or Black/White wire between ground and DLC. Retest system for normal operation.

DIAGNOSTIC TROUBLE CODE (DTC) DEFINITIONS

NOTE: *Front radio control unit may also be referred to as Audio Control Module (ACM). Speed control servo may also be referred to as Next Generation Speed Control (NGSC) servo. Air Suspension/Electronic Variable Orifice (EVO) steering module may also be referred to as Rear Air Suspension Module (RASM). Instrument cluster may also be referred to as Hybrid Electronic Cluster (HEC).*

NOTE: *For Powertrain Control Module (PCM) DTC identification and repair, see appropriate SELF-DIAGNOSTICS article in ENGINE PERFORMANCE in appropriate MITCHELL® manual.*

AIR SUSPENSION/ELECTRONIC VARIABLE ORIFICE STEERING MODULE DTC INDEX

DTC	Description	Test
B1317	Battery Voltage High	1
B1318	Battery Voltage Low	1
B1342	ECU Defective	2
C1441	Steering Sensor Channel A Circuit Failure	3
C1442	Steering Sensor Channel B Circuit Failure	3
C1722	Air Suspension Height Sensor Power Circuit Short To Voltage	1
C1723	Air Suspension Height Sensor Power Circuit Short To Ground	1
C1760	Air Suspension Rear Height Sensor High Signal Circuit Failure	1
C1763	Air Suspension Rear Height Sensor High Signal Circuit Short To Ground	1
C1765	Air Suspension Rear Height Sensor Low Signal Circuit Failure	1
C1768	Air Suspension Rear Height Sensor Low Signal Circuit Short To Ground	1
C1770	Air Suspension Vent Solenoid Output Circuit Failure	1
C1773	Air Suspension Vent Solenoid Output Circuit Short To Ground	1
C1790	Air Suspension Left Rear Air Spring Solenoid Output Circuit Failure	1

AIR SUSPENSION/ELECTRONIC VARIABLE ORIFICE STEERING MODULE DTC INDEX (Cont.)

DTC	Description	Test
C1793	Air Suspension Left Rear Air Spring Solenoid Output Circuit Short To Ground	1
C1795	Air Suspension Right Rear Air Spring Solenoid Output Circuit Failure	1
C1798	Air Suspension Right Rear Air Spring Solenoid Output Circuit Short To Ground	1
C1813	Air Suspension Vent Request Exceeded Maximum Time	1
C1818	Air Suspension Air Compressor Request Exceeded Maximum Time	1
C1830	Air Compressor Relay Circuit Failure	1
C1832	Air Compressor Relay Circuit Short To Voltage	1
C1840	Air Suspension Switch Circuit Failure	1
C1842	Air Suspension Switch Circuit Short To Voltage	1
C1897	Steering VAPS Circuit Loop Failure	3
U1041	SCP Invalid/Missing Data For Vehicle Speed	4

[1] – Repair electronic suspension concern. See appropriate ELECTRONIC article in SUSPENSION in appropriate MITCHELL® manual.
[2] – Using NGS tester, retrieve and document all continuous DTCs. Perform air suspension/electronic variable orifice steering module self-test. If DTC B1342 is retrieved again, replace air suspension/electronic variable orifice steering module.
[3] – Repair electronic steering concern. See appropriate ELECTRONIC article in STEERING in appropriate MITCHELL® manual.
[4] – Cause By Anti-Lock Brake System (ABS) module. Using NGS tester, perform ABS self-test and repair anti-lock brake system concern. See appropriate ANTI-LOCK article in BRAKES in appropriate MITCHELL® manual.

ANTI-LOCK BRAKE SYSTEM MODULE DTC INDEX

DTC	Description	Test
B1342	ECU Defective	1
B1485	Brake Pedal Input Circuit Shorted To Voltage	2
B1676	Battery Voltage Out Of Range	2
C1095	ABS Hydraulic Pump Motor Circuit Failure	2
C1145	Right Front ABS Sensor Input Circuit Failure	2
C1155	Left Front ABS Sensor Input Circuit Failure	2
C1165	Right Rear ABS Sensor Input Circuit Failure	2
C1175	Left Rear ABS Sensor Input Circuit Failure	2
C1233	Left Front ABS Sensor Input Signal Missing	2
C1234	Right Front ABS Sensor Input Signal Missing	2
C1235	Right Rear ABS Sensor Input Signal Missing	2
C1236	Left Rear ABS Sensor Input Signal Missing	2
U1009	SCP Invalid/Missing Data For Engine Torque	3
U1027	SCP Invalid/Missing Data For Engine RPM	3
U1041	SCP Invalid/Missing Data For Vehicle Speed	4
U1043	SCP Invalid/Missing Data For Traction Control	5
U1059	SCP Invalid/Missing Data For Transmission Range (PRNDL)	3
U1123	SCP Invalid/Missing Data For Odometer	6

[1] – Using NGS tester, retrieve and document all continuous DTCs. Perform ABS self-test. If DTC B1342 is retrieved again, replace ABS module.
[2] – Repair anti-lock brake system concern. See appropriate ANTI-LOCK article in BRAKES in appropriate MITCHELL® manual.
[3] – Cause by Powertrain Control Module (PCM). Using NGS tester, perform PCM self-test and repair powertrain control concern. See appropriate SELF-DIAGNOSTICS article in ENGINE PERFORMANCE in appropriate MITCHELL® manual.
[4] – Caused by instrument cluster, Driver's Door Module (DDM), Lighting Control Module (LCM), Restraint Control Module (RCM) and/or speed control servo control module. Using NGS tester, perform self-test on all these modules.
[5] – Cause by instrument cluster. Using NGS tester, perform instrument cluster self-test.
[6] – Caused by instrument cluster and/or air suspension/electronic variable orifice steering module. Using NGS tester, perform instrument cluster and air suspension/electronic variable orifice steering module self-test.

DRIVER'S DOOR MODULE DTC INDEX

DTC	Description	Test
B1322	Driver's Door Ajar Circuit Failure	1
B1342	ECU Defective	2
B1396	Power Door Lock Circuit Short To Voltage	3
B1397	Power Door Unlock Circuit Short To Voltage	3
B1402	Driver's Door Window Switch Down Circuit Open	4
B1529	Memory Set Switch Circuit Short To Voltage	5
B1533	Memory "1" Switch Circuit Short To Voltage	5
B1537	Memory "2" Switch Short To Voltage	5
B1545	Power Seat Switch Short To Voltage	6
B1549	Power Window Switch Short To Voltage	4
B1553	Trunk Release Switch Circuit Short To Voltage	5
B1566	Passenger's And/Or Rear Door Ajar Circuits Short To Ground	1
B2338	Mirror Switch Assembly Circuit Short To Voltage	7
B2368	Memory LED Output Short To Voltage	5
B2373	LED "1" Circuit Short To Voltage	8
B2425	Remote Keyless Entry Out Of Synchronization	9
C1920	LED "1" Circuit Failure	5
U1041	SCP Invalid/Missing Data For Vehicle Speed	10
U1059	SCP Invalid/Missing Data For Transmission Range (PRNDL)	11

DRIVER'S DOOR MODULE DTC INDEX (Cont.)

DTC	Description	Test
U1089	SCP Invalid/Missing Data For Suspension	12
U1135	SCP Invalid/Missing Data For Ignition Switch	13
U1181	SCP Invalid/Missing Data For Personalization (Memory) Features	14
U1199	SCP Invalid/Missing Data For External Access (Doors)	15
U1222	SCP Invalid/Missing Data For Interior Lights	15
U1262	SCP Bus Communication Fault	16

[1] – Perform TEST Q: COURTESY LIGHTS STAY ON CONTINUOUSLY under SYSTEM TESTS in AUTOLAMP SYSTEMS article.

[2] – Using NGS tester, retrieve and document all continuous DTCs. Perform DDM self-test. If DTC B1342 is retrieved again, replace DDM.

[3] – Repair appropriate keyless entry system circuit. See appropriate wiring diagram in REMOTE KEYLESS ENTRY SYSTEMS article.

[4] – Perform TEST B: SINGLE WINDOW INOPERATIVE under SYSTEM TESTS in POWER WINDOWS – CONTINENTAL article.

[5] – Perform TEST D: MIRROR OPERATES IN ONE SECOND INTERVALS under SYSTEM TESTS in POWER MIRRORS – TOWN CAR article.

[6] – Perform TEST C: DRIVER'S SEAT COMPLETELY INOPERATIVE (WITH MEMORY) under SYSTEM TESTS in POWER SEATS – TOWN CAR article.

[7] – Perform TEST C: SINGLE MIRROR INOPERATIVE under SYSTEM TESTS in POWER MIRRORS – TOWN CAR article.

[8] – Perform TEST G: MEMORY MIRRORS INOPERATIVE under SYSTEM TESTS in POWER MIRRORS – TOWN CAR article.

[9] – Program transmitter. See TRANSMITTER under PROGRAMMING in PASSIVE ANTI-THEFT SYSTEMS – TOWN CAR article.

[10] – Caused by Anti-Lock Brake System (ABS) module. Using NGS tester, perform ABS self-test and repair anti-lock brake system concern. See appropriate ANTI-LOCK article in BRAKES in appropriate MITCHELL® manual.

[11] – Caused by Powertrain Control Module (PCM). Using NGS tester, perform PCM self-test and repair powertrain control concern. See appropriate SELF-DIAGNOSTICS article in ENGINE PERFORMANCE in appropriate MITCHELL® manual.

[12] – Caused by air suspension/electronic variable orifice steering module. Using NGS tester, perform air suspension/electronic variable orifice steering module self-test and repair electronic suspension concern. See appropriate ELECTRONIC article in SUSPENSION in appropriate MITCHELL® manual.

[13] – Caused by Lighting Control Module (LCM). Using NGS tester, perform LCM self-test and repair steering column switch concern. See SELF-DIAGNOSTIC SYSTEM in STEERING COLUMN SWITCHES – TOWN CAR article.

[14] – Cause by Driver's Door Module (DDM). Using NGS tester, perform DDM self-test.

[15] – Caused by Lighting Control Module (LCM). Using NGS tester, perform LCM self-test.

[16] – Service all other DTCs first. After all other DTC concerns have been repaired, perform TEST M: NO MODULE/NETWORK COMMUNICATION – SCP BUS LINK under SYSTEM TESTS.

DRIVER'S SEAT MODULE DTC INDEX

DTC	Description	Test
B1342	ECU Defective	1
B1663	Driver's Seat Front Up/Down Circuit Failure	2
B1664	Driver's Seat Rear Up/Down Circuit Failure	2
B1665	Driver's Seat Forward/Backward Circuit Failure	2
B1666	Driver's Seat Recline Circuit Failure	2
B1667	Driver's Mirror Up/Down Circuit Failure	3
B1668	Driver's Mirror Right/Left Circuit Failure	3
B1669	Passenger's Mirror Up/Down Circuit Failure	3
B1670	Passenger's Mirror Right/Left Circuit Failure	3
B1676	Battery Voltage Out Of Range	4
B1950	Driver's Seat Rear Up/Down Potentiometer – Circuit Failure	5
B1953	Driver's Seat Rear Up/Down Potentiometer – Short to Ground	5
B1954	Driver's Seat Front Up/Down Potentiometer – Circuit Failure	5
B1957	Driver's Seat Front Up/Down Potentiometer – Short to Ground	5
B1958	Driver's Seat Recline Potentiometer – Circuit Failure	5
B1961	Driver's Seat Recline Potentiometer – Short To Ground	5
B1962	Driver's Seat Horizontal Potentiometer – Circuit Failure	5
B1965	Driver's Seat Horizontal Potentiometer – Short To Ground	5
B2312	Passenger's Mirror Right/Left Potentiometer – Circuit Failure	6
B2315	Passenger's Mirror Right/Left Potentiometer – Short To Ground	6
B2316	Passenger's Mirror Up/Down Potentiometer – Circuit Failure	6
B2319	Passenger's Mirror Up/Down Potentiometer – Short To Ground	6
B2320	Driver's Mirror Right/Left Potentiometer – Circuit Failure	6
B2323	Driver's Mirror Right/Left Potentiometer – Shirt To Ground	6
B2324	Driver's Mirror Up/Down Potentiometer – Circuit Failure	6
B2327	Driver's Mirror Up/Down Potentiometer – Short To Ground	6
U1059	SCP Invalid/Missing Data For Transmission Range (PRNDL)	7
U1135	SCP Invalid/Missing Data For Ignition Switch	8
U1180	SCP Invalid/Missing Data For Memory Feature	9
U1181	SCP Invalid/Missing Data For Memory Feature	9
U1194	SCP Invalid/Missing Data For Mirrors	9
U1200	SCP Invalid/Missing Data For Seat Motion/Control	10
U1262	SCP Bus Communication Fault	11

[1] – Using NGS tester, retrieve and document all continuous DTCs. Perform Driver's Seat Module (DSM) self-test. If DTC B1342 is retrieved again, replace DSM.

[2] – Perform TEST C: DRIVER'S SEAT COMPLETELY INOPERATIVE (WITH MEMORY) under SYSTEM TESTS in POWER SEATS – TOWN CAR article.

[3] – Perform TEST C: SINGLE MIRROR INOPERATIVE under SYSTEM TESTS in POWER MIRRORS – TOWN CAR article.

DRIVER'S SEAT MODULE DTC INDEX (Cont.)

DTC	Description	Test

[4] – Perform TEST P: BATTERY VOLTAGE OUT OF RANGE (DTC B1676) under SYSTEM TESTS in POWER SEATS – TOWN CAR article.
[5] – Perform TEST E: SEAT MOTORS OPERATE IN ONE SECOND INTERVALS under SYSTEM TESTS in POWER SEATS – TOWN CAR article.
[6] – Perform TEST D: MIRROR OPERATES IN ONE SECOND INTERVALS under SYSTEM TESTS in POWER MIRRORS – TOWN CAR article.
[7] – Caused by Powertrain Control Module (PCM). Using NGS tester, perform PCM self-test and repair powertrain control concern. See appropriate SELF-DIAGNOSTICS article in ENGINE PERFORMANCE in appropriate MITCHELL® manual.
[8] – Caused by Lighting Control Module (LCM). Using NGS tester, perform LCM self-test and repair steering column switch concern. See SELF-DIAGNOSTIC SYSTEM in STEERING COLUMN SWITCHES – TOWN CAR article.
[9] – Caused by Driver's Door Module (DDM). Using NGS tester, perform DDM self-test and repair power mirror system concern. See SELF-DIAGNOSTIC SYSTEM in POWER MIRRORS – TOWN CAR article.
[10] – Caused by Driver's Door Module (DDM). Using NGS tester, perform DDM self-test and repair power seat system concern. See SELF-DIAGNOSTIC SYSTEM in POWER SEATS – TOWN CAR article.
[11] – Service all other DTCs first. After all other DTC concerns have been repaired, perform TEST M: NO MODULE/NETWORK COMMUNICATION – SCP BUS LINK under SYSTEM TESTS.

ELECTRONIC AUTOMATIC TEMPERATURE CONTROL MODULE DTC INDEX

DTC	Description	Test
B1249	Blend Door Short	1
B1251	A/C In-Car Temperature Sensor Open Circuit	1
B1253	A/C In-Car Temperature Sensor Short To Ground	1
B1255	A/C Ambient Temperature Sensor Open Circuit	1
B1257	A/C Ambient Temperature Sensor Short To Ground	1
B1261	A/C Solar Radiation Sensor Circuit Short To Ground	1
B2416	Recirculated Air Door Circuit Failure	1
U1041	SCP Invalid/Missing Data For Vehicle Speed	2
U1073	SCP Invalid/Missing Data For Engine Coolant	2
U1222	SCP Invalid/Missing Data For Interior Lights	3
U1235	SCP Invalid/Missing Data For Displays	4

[1] – Repair climate control concern. See appropriate AUTOMATIC A/C-HEATER SYSTEMS article in appropriate MITCHELL® AIR CONDITIONING & HEATING SERVICE & REPAIR.
[2] – Caused by Powertrain Control Module (PCM). Using NGS tester, perform PCM self-test and repair powertrain control concern. See appropriate SELF-DIAGNOSTICS article in ENGINE PERFORMANCE in appropriate MITCHELL® manual.
[3] – Cause by Lighting Control Module (LCM). Using NGS tester, perform LCM self-test and repair interior lighting concern. See SELF-DIAGNOSTIC SYSTEM in AUTOLAMP SYSTEMS – TOWN CAR article.
[4] – Caused by instrument cluster module. Using NGS tester, perform instrument cluster self-test and repair instrument cluster concern. See SELF-DIAGNOSTIC SYSTEM in INSTRUMENT PANELS – TOWN CAR article.

FRONT RADIO CONTROL UNIT DTC INDEX

DTC	Description	Test
B1342	ECU Defective	1
B2401	Audio Tape Deck Mechanical Fault	2
B2402	Audio CD/DJ Thermal Shutdown	3
B2403	Audio CD/DJ Internal Fault	3
B2404	Audio Steering Wheel Switch Circuit Failure	3
B2405	Audio Single-Disc CD Player Thermal Shutdown Fault	3
B2406	Audio Single-Disc CD Player Internal Fault	3
U2003	Audio CD/DJ Is Not Responding	3
U2005	Audio Rear Integrated Control Panel Unit Is Not Responding	5
U2008	Audio Phone Is Not Responding	4
U2014	Audio Subwoofer Unit Is Not Responding	3

[1] – Using NGS tester, retrieve and document all continuous DTCs. Perform front radio control unit self-test. If DTC B1342 is retrieved again, replace front radio control unit.
[2] – Remove audio tape. Using NGS tester, clear DTCs. Perform front radio control unit self-test. If B2401 is retrieved, repair or replace front radio control unit.
[3] – Repair audio system concern.
[4] – Repair cellular phone system concern.
[5] – This DTC is retrieved if vehicle is not equipped with Rear Audio Control Panel (RACP) or RACP is disconnected or inoperative.

INSTRUMENT CLUSTER DTC INDEX

DTC	Description	Test
B1201	Fuel Sender Circuit Failure	1
B1204	Fuel Sender Short To Ground	1
B1205	Instrument Cluster Switch 1 Assembly Circuit Failure (Open Or Short To Voltage)	2
B1208	Instrument Cluster Switch 1 Assembly Circuit Short To Ground	2
B1213	Number Of Programmed Ignition Keys Below Minimum	3 4
B1232/2103	Antenna Not Connected/Defective Transceiver	5
B1317	Battery Voltage High (Greater Than 19 Volts)	6
B1318	Battery Voltage Low (Less Than 9 Volts)	6
B1342	ECU Defective	7
B1600	PATS Ignition Key Transponder Signal Not Received (Damaged Key Or Non-PATS Key)	8

INSTRUMENT CLUSTER DTC INDEX (Cont.)

DTC	Description	Test
B1601	PATS Received Incorrect Key-Code From Ignition Key Transponder	9
B1602	PATS Received Invalid Key Code Format From Transponder	10
B1681	PATS Transceiver Signal Is Not Received	11
B2139	PATS Data Mismatch	12
B2141	NVM Configuration Failure	13
B2143	NVM Memory Failure	14
U1147	Invalid/Missing Data For Vehicle Security	15
U1262	SCP Bus Communication Fault	16
U2013	No Response From Compass Module	17

[1] – Perform TEST B: FUEL GAUGE INACCURATE under SYSTEM TESTS in INSTRUMENT PANELS – TOWN CAR article.

[2] – Perform TEST AA: MESSAGE CENTER SWITCH NOT OPERATING PROPERLY under SYSTEM TESTS in INSTRUMENT PANELS – TOWN CAR article.

[3] – If DTCs B1232, B1600, B1601, B1602 OR B1681 are also present, service these DTCs frist then recheck codes.

[4] – Perform DTC B1213: ANTI-THEFT NUMBER OF PROGRAMED KEYS IS BELOW MINIMUM under DIAGNOSTIC TESTS in PASSIVE ANTI-THEFT SYSTEMS – TOWN CAR article.

[5] – Perform DTC B1232/2103: DEFECTIVE TRANSCEIVER under DIAGNOSTIC TESTS in PASSIVE ANTI-THEFT SYSTEMS – TOWN CAR article.

[6] – Check charging system. See appropriate GENERATORS article in STARTING & CHARGING SYSTEMS. If charging system is okay, check power and ground circuits to instrument cluster. See appropriate wiring diagram in POWER DISTRIBUTION article in WIRING DIAGRAMS.

[7] – Using NGS tester, retrieve and record all continuous DTCs. Perform instrument cluster self-test. If DTC B1342 still exists, replace instrument cluster.

[8] – Perform DTC B1600: PATS IGNITION KEY TRANSPONDER SIGNAL NOT RECEIVED under DIAGNOSTIC TESTS in PASSIVE ANTI-THEFT SYSTEMS – TOWN CAR article.

[9] – Perform DTC B1601: PATS RECEIVED INCORRECT KEY CODE FROM IGNITION KEY TRANSPONDER under DIAGNOSTIC TESTS in PASSIVE ANTI-THEFT SYSTEMS – TOWN CAR article.

[10] – Perform DTC B1602: PATS RECEIVED INVALID KEY CODE FORMAT FROM IGNITION KEY TRANSPONDER under DIAGNOSTIC TESTS in PASSIVE ANTI-THEFT SYSTEMS – TOWN CAR article.

[11] – Perform DTC B1681: PATS TRANSCEIVER SIGNAL IS NOT RECEIVED under DIAGNOSTIC TESTS in PASSIVE ANTI-THEFT SYSTEMS – TOWN CAR article.

[12] – Perform DTC B2139: PATS DATA MISMATCH under DIAGNOSTIC TESTS in PASSIVE ANTI-THEFT SYSTEMS – TOWN CAR article.

[13] – Perform DTC B2141: NVM CONFIGURATION FAILURE under DIAGNOSTIC TESTS in PASSIVE ANTI-THEFT SYSTEMS – TOWN CAR article.

[14] – Perform TEST V: ODOMETER INOPERATIVE under SYSTEM TESTS in INSTRUMENT PANELS – TOWN CAR article.

[15] – Perform DTC U1147: INVALID OR MISSING DATA FOR VEHICLE SECURITY under DIAGNOSTIC TESTS in PASSIVE ANTI-THEFT SYSTEMS – TOWN CAR article.

[16] – Service all other DTCs first. After all other DTC concerns have been repaired, perform TEST M: NO MODULE/NETWORK COMMUNICATION – SCP BUS LINK under SYSTEM TESTS.

[17] – Repair compass module circuits and/or replace compass module as necessary. See WIRING DIAGRAMS in INSTRUMENT PANELS – TOWN CAR article.

LIGHTING CONTROL MODULE DTC INDEX

DTC	Description	Test
B1312	Headlight Input Short To Battery Voltage	1
B1334	Trunk Lid Ajar Rear Door Circuit Short To Ground	2
B1340	ECS Tone Request Short To Ground	3
B1342	ECU Defective	4
B1352	Ignition Key-In Circuit Failure	5
B1359	Ignition RUN/ACC Input Circuit Failure	6
B1462	Seat Belt Switch Circuit Failure	7
B1485	Brake Pedal Input Circuit Short To Voltage	8
B1555	Ignition RUN/START Circuit Failure	9
B1569	High Beam Short To Battery Voltage	10
B1577	Parking Lamp Input Short To Voltage	11
B1581	Panel Dim Increase Input Circuit Short To Voltage	12
B1585	Panel Dim Decrease Input Short To Voltage	12
B1676	Battery Voltage Out Of Range	13
B1687	Dome Light Input Short To Voltage	14
B1689	Autolamp Delay Input Circuit Failure	15
B1691	Autolamp Delay Input Circuit Short To Voltage	15
B1695	Autolamp ON/OFF Short To Voltage	15
B1873	Turn Signal/Hazard Power Feed Short To Ground	16
U1041	SCP Invalid/Missing Data For Vehicle Speed	17
U1059	SCP Invalid/Missing Data For Transmission Range (PRNDL)	18
U1197	SCP Invalid/Missing Data For Door Locks	19
U1199	SCP Invalid/Missing Data For External Access (Doors)	19

[1] – Perform TEST D: LOW BEAMS ARE ON CONTINUOUSLY (DAYTIME RUNNING LIGHTS ARE DISABLED) under SYSTEM TESTS in AUTOLAMP SYSTEMS – TOWN CAR article.

[2] – See appropriate wiring diagram in REMOTE KEYLESS ENTRY SYSTEMS article.

[3] – Repair short to ground in Electronic Crash Sensor (ECS) circuit. See DIAGNOSIS & TESTING in MITCHELL® AIR BAG SERVICE & REPAIR MANUAL, DOMESTIC & IMPORTED MODELS.

LIGHTING CONTROL MODULE DTC INDEX (Cont.)

DTC	Description	Test

4 – Using NGS tester, retrieve and document all continuous DTCs. Perform LCM self-test. If DTC B1342 is retrieved again, replace LCM.

5 – Perform TEST P: COURTESY LIGHTS INOPERATIVE under SYSTEM TESTS in AUTOLAMP SYSTEMS – TOWN CAR article.

6 – Perform TEST G: IGNITION RUN/ACC CIRCUIT FAILURE (DTC 1359) under SYSTEM TESTS in STEERING COLUMN SWITCHES – TOWN CAR article.

7 – Perform TEST N: NO COMMUNICATION WITH DRIVER'S DOOR MODULE under SYSTEM TESTS in AUTOLAMP SYSTEMS – TOWN CAR article.

8 – Perform TEST G: STOPLIGHTS INOPERATIVE under SYSTEM TESTS in AUTOLAMP SYSTEMS – TOWN CAR article.

9 – Perform TEST H: IGNITION RUN/START CIRCUIT FAILURE (DTC 1555) under SYSTEM TESTS in STEERING COLUMN SWITCHES – TOWN CAR article.

10 – Perform TEST C: HIGH BEAMS INOPERATIVE under SYSTEM TESTS in AUTOLAMP SYSTEMS – TOWN CAR article.

11 – Perform TEST M: PARKING, TAIL OR LICENSE LIGHTS ON CONTINUOUSLY under SYSTEM TESTS in AUTOLAMP SYSTEMS – TOWN CAR article.

12 – Perform TEST AJ: DASH DIMMING CONTROL INOPERATIVE under SYSTEM TESTS in INSTRUMENT PANELS – TOWN CAR article.

13 – Check charging system. See appropriate GENERATORS article in STARTING & CHARGING SYSTEMS. If charging system is okay, check power and ground circuits to LCM. See appropriate wiring diagram in POWER DISTRIBUTION article in WIRING DIAGRAMS.

14 – Perform TEST Q: COURTESY LIGHTS STAY ON CONTINUOUSLY under SYSTEM TESTS in AUTOLAMP SYSTEMS – TOWN CAR article.

15 – Perform TEST F: AUTOLAMP SYSTEM IS INOPERATIVE under SYSTEM TESTS in AUTOLAMP SYSTEMS – TOWN CAR article.

16 – Perform TEST H: TURN SIGNAL & HAZARD LIGHTS ARE INOPERATIVE under SYSTEM TESTS in AUTOLAMP SYSTEMS – TOWN CAR article.

17 – Caused by Anti-Lock Brake System (ABS) module. Using NGS tester, perform ABS self-test and repair anti-lock brake system concern. See appropriate ANTI-LOCK article in BRAKES in appropriate MITCHELL® manual.

18 – Caused by Powertrain Control Module (PCM). Using NGS tester, perform PCM self-test and repair powertrain control concern. See appropriate SELF-DIAGNOSTICS article in ENGINE PERFORMANCE in appropriate MITCHELL® manual.

19 – Caused by Driver's Door Module (DDM). Using NGS tester, perform DDM self-test.

RESTRAINT CONTROL MODULE DTC INDEX

DTC [1]	Description	Test
B1342	ECU Defective	[2]
B1231	RCM Internal Fault	[3]
B1921	RCM Crash Data Memory Full	[3]
C1414	Incorrect Vehicle Identification Code	[3]
B1887	Driver's Air Bag Circuit Shorted To Ground	[3]
B1916	Driver's Air Bag Circuit Shorted To Voltage	[3]
B1888	Passenger's Air Bag Circuit Shorted To Ground	[3]
B1925	Passenger's Air Bag Circuit Shorted To Voltage	[3]
B1932	Driver's Air Bag Circuit Resistance High	[3]
B1933	Passenger's Air Bag Circuit Resistance High	[3]
B1934	Driver's Air Bag Circuit Resistance Low	[3]
B1935	Passenger's Air Bag Circuit Resistance Low	[3]
B1901	External Crash Sensor Shorted To Ground	[3]
B1941	External Crash Sensor Open Circuit Shorted To Voltage	[3]
B2444	Driver's Side Crash Sensor Internal Fault	[3]
B2445	Passenger's Side Crash Sensor Internal Fault	[3]
B2441	Driver's Side Crash Sensor Mounting Fault	[3]
B2440	Passenger's Side Crash Sensor Mounting Fault	[3]
U2017	Driver's Side Crash Sensor Communication Fault	[3]
U2018	Passenger's Side Crash Sensor Communication Fault	[3]
B1993	Driver's Side Air Bag Circuit Shorted To Ground	[3]
B1992	Driver's Side Air Bag Circuit Shorted To Voltage	[3]
B1994	Driver's Side Air Bag Circuit Resistance High	[3]
B1995	Driver's Side Air Bag Circuit Resistance Low	[3]
B1997	Passenger's Side Air Bag Circuit Shorted To Ground	[3]
B1996	Passenger's Side Air Bag Circuit Shorted To Voltage	[3]
B1998	Passenger's Side Air Bag Circuit Resistance High	[3]
B1999	Passenger's Side Air Bag Circuit Resistance Low	[3]
B1892	Air Bag Tone Warning Indicator Circuit Shorted To Ground Or Open	[3]
B1891	Air Bag Tone Warning Indicator Circuit Shorted To Voltage	[3]
B1869	Air Bag Indicator Inoperative	[3]
B1870	Air Bag Indicator Shorted To Voltage	[3]

1 – DTCs are listed in order of importance. Repair DTCs in order listed.

2 – Using NGS tester, retrieve and document all continuous DTCs. Perform Restraint Control Module (RCM) self-test. If DTC B1342 is retrieved again, replace RCM.

3 – Repair supplemental restraint system concern. See DIAGNOSIS & TESTING article in appropriate MITCHELL® AIR BAG SERVICE & REPAIR MANUAL, DOMESTIC & IMPORTED MODELS.

SPEED CONTROL SERVO DTC INDEX

DTC	Description	Test
B1318	Battery Voltage Low	[1]
B1342	ECU Defective	[2]
C1109	Throttle Position Did Not Return To Idle After Self-Test	[3]

SPEED CONTROL SERVO DTC INDEX (Cont.)

DTC	Description	Test
C1126	Speed Control Switch Stuck For 2 Minutes Or Longer	4
C1127	Deactivator Switch Circuit Failure	5
C1179	Speed Control Cable Slack Failure	6
U1027	SCP Invalid/Missing Data For Engine RPM	7
U1041	SCP Invalid/Missing Data For Vehicle Speed	8
U1051	SCP Invalid/Missing Data For Brakes	9
U1059	SCP Invalid/Missing Data For Transmission Range (PRNDL)	7

[1] – Perform TEST C: BATTERY VOLTAGE LOW (DTC B1318) under SYSTEM TESTS in CRUISE CONTROL SYSTEMS – TOWN CAR article.

[2] – Using NGS tester, retrieve and document all continuous DTCs. Perform air suspension/electronic variable orifice steering module self-test. If DTC B1342 is retrieved again, replace air suspension/electronic variable orifice steering module.

[3] – Perform TEST D: THROTTLE POSITION DID NOT RETURN TO IDLE AFTER SELF-TEST (DTC C1109) under SYSTEM TESTS in CRUISE CONTROL SYSTEMS – TOWN CAR article.

[4] – Perform TEST E: SPEED CONTROL SWITCH STUCK FOR 2 MINUTES OR LONGER (DTC C1126) under SYSTEM TESTS in CRUISE CONTROL SYSTEMS – TOWN CAR article.

[5] – Perform TEST F: DEACTIVATOR SWITCH CIRCUIT FAILURE (DTC C1127) under SYSTEM TESTS in CRUISE CONTROL SYSTEMS – TOWN CAR article.

[6] – Perform TEST G: SPEED CONTROL SERVO/ACTUATOR CABLE SLACK FAILURE (DTC C1179) under SYSTEM TESTS in CRUISE CONTROL SYSTEMS – TOWN CAR article.

[7] – Cause by Powertrain Control Module (PCM). Using NGS tester, perform PCM self-test and repair powertrain control concern. See appropriate SELF-DIAGNOSTICS article in ENGINE PERFORMANCE in appropriate MITCHELL® manual.

[8] – Cause by Anti-Lock Brake System (ABS) module. Using NGS tester, perform ABS self-test and repair anti-lock brake system concern. See appropriate ANTI-LOCK article in BRAKES in appropriate MITCHELL® manual.

[9] – Caused by Lighting Control Module (LCM). Using NGS tester, perform LCM self-test.

PARAMETER IDENTIFICATION (PID) DEFINITIONS

NOTE: Front radio control unit may also be referred to as Audio Control Module (ACM). Speed control servo may also be referred to as Next Generation Speed Control (NGSC) servo. Air uspension/Electronic Variable Orifice (EVO) steering module may also be referred to as Rear Air Suspension Module (RASM). Instrument cluster may also be referred to as Hybrid Electronic Cluster (HEC).

AIR SUSPENSION/ELECTRONIC VARIABLE ORIFICE STEERING MODULE PID INDEX

PID	Description	Expected Value
AS_COMP	Air Suspension Compressor Status	1
AS_TRIM	Air Suspension Accurate Trim	TRIM, NOTTRIM
AS_VENT	Air Suspension Vent Solenoid Status	1
AS_WARN	Air Suspension Warning Indicator	ON, OFF
ASR_HGT	Rear Digital Height Sensor	TRIM, HIGH, LOW, HGND, LGND, H_LGND, L_HGND
CCNTRAS	Number Of Continuous DTCs In Rear Suspension Control Module	# Of DTCs
D_DRRAS	Driver's Door Input To Rear Suspension Control Module	AJAR, CLOSED
FUEL_DR	Fuel Door Ajar	AJAR, CLOSED
IGN_RAS	Ignition Switch Input To Rear Suspension Control Module	ACCY, RUN, START, OFF
LR_SOL	Air Suspension Left Rear Air Spring Solenoid Status	1
P_DRRAS	Passenger's Door Input To Rear Suspension Control Module	AJAR, CLOSED
RR_SOL	Air Suspension Right Rear Air Spring Solenoid Status	1
VAPS_IN	VAPSII Input Current Loop	100/255
VAPSDRV	VAPSII Driver Output State	1
VAPSOUT	VAPSII Output Current Set Point	100/255
VBATRAS	Battery Voltage Value To Rear Suspension Control Module	UDR 0V, OVR 5V, #####Volts
VSS_RSS	Vehicle Speed Input To Rear Suspension Control Module	1/128

[1] – Expected value should be OFF- -, OFFO- -, OFF-B-, OFF- - G, OFFO-G, OFFOB-, OFF-BG, OFFOBG, ON- - -, ONO- -, ON-B-, ON- - G, ONO-G, ONOB-, ON-BG or ONOBG

ANTI-LOCK BRAKE SYSTEM PID INDEX

PID	Description	Expected Value
TRAC_SW	T/A Disable Switch	1
TC_LVAL	Left T/A Control Valve	ON, OFF
TC_RVAL	Right T/A Control Valve	ON, OFF
ABSRR_O	Right Rear ABS Outlet Valve	1
ABSLR_O	Left Rear ABS Outlet Valve	1
ABSRF_O	Right Front ABS Outlet Valve	1
ABSLF_O	Left Front ABS Outlet Valve	1
ABSRF_I	Right Front ABS Inlet Valve	1
ABSLF_I	Left Front ABS Inlet Valve	1
ABSRR_I	Right Rear ABS Inlet Valve	1
ABSLR_I	Left Rear ABS Inlet Valve	1
LF_WSPD	Left Front Wheel Speed Signal	0-255 KPH
RF_WSPD	Right Front Wheel Speed Signal	0-255 KPH
LR_WSPD	Left Rear Wheel Speed Signal	0-255 KPH
RR_WSPD	Right Rear Wheel Speed Signal	0-255 KPH

ANTI-LOCK BRAKE SYSTEM PID INDEX (Cont.)

PID	Description	Expected Value
[1] – Expected value should be OFF- - -, OFFO- -, OFF- B-, OFF- - G, OFFO-G, OFFOB-, OFF-BG, OFFOBG, ON- - -, ONO- -, ON-B-, ON- - G, ONO-G, ONOB-, ON-BG or ONOBG		

DRIVER'S DOOR MODULE PID INDEX

PID	Description	Expected Value
CCNT_DD	Number Of Continuous DTCs In DDM	Number Of DTCs
KEYCODE	Factory Keyless Entry Code	5 Digits
D_DR_DD	Driver's Door Ajar Switch	AJAR, CLOSED
DLIDRLS	Deck Lid Release Switch	ON, OFF
D_PW_SW	Driver's Power Window Switch	UP, DOWN, OFF, SHORT
DR_LOCK	Door Lock Output State	SHORT, LOCK, UNLOCK, OFF
MIRV_SW	Power Mirror Position Switch (Vertical)	SHORT, LEFT, RIGHT, OFF
MIRH_SW	Power Mirror Position Switch (Horizontal)	PSSNGR, DRIVER
SRCL_SW	Power Seat Switch (Recline)	SHORT, UP, DOWN, OFF
SFWD_SW	Power Seat Switch (Forward/Rearward)	SHORT, UP, DOWN, OFF
SREARSW	Power Seat Switch (Rear Height)	SHORT, UP, DOWN, OFF
SFNT_SW	Power Seat Switch (Front Height)	SHORT, UP, DOWN, OFF
P_DR_DD	Passenger's Door Ajar Switch	CLOSED, AJAR
VBAT_DD	Battery Voltage	UDR0V, OVR5V, ####Volts
D_PWRLY	Left Power Window Output State	[1]
DD_UNLK	Driver's Door Unlock Output	[1]
DLIDOUT	Trunk Lid Driver Output State	[1]
MEM_LED	Memory LED Status	[1]
MEM1_SW	Memory Recall Switch 1	ACTIVE, NOTACT
MEM2_SW	Memory Recall Switch 2	ACTIVE, NOTACT
MEM3_SW	Memory Recall Switch 3	ACTIVE, NOTACT
MEMS_SW	Memory Set Switch	ACTIVE, NOTACT
OTD_SW	One Touch Down Switch	ACTIVE, NOTACT
NONE(FT)	Recall Last TIC Data	UNLOCK, LOCK, DECKLID, PANIC

[1] – Expected value should be OFF- - -, OFFO- -, OFF- B-, OFF- - G, OFFO-G, OFFOB-, OFF-BG, OFFOBG, ON- - -, ONO- -, ON-B-, ON- - G, ONO-G, ONOB-, ON-BG or ONOBG

DRIVER'S SEAT MODULE PID INDEX

PID	Description	Expected Value
CCNT_DS	Number Of Continuous DTCs In DSM	Number Of DTCs
PMIR_H	Passenger's Mirror Horizontal	SENSEED, NOTSEN
PMIR_V	Passenger's Mirror Vertical	SENSEED, NOTSEN
DMIR_H	Driver's Mirror Horizontal	SENSEED, NOTSEN
DMIR_V	Driver's Mirror Vertical	SENSEED, NOTSEN
SRCL_MT	Driver's Seat Recline Motor	SENSEED, NOTSEN
SFWD_MT	Driver's Seat Forward Motor	SENSEED, NOTSEN
SREARMT	Driver's Seat Rear Motor	SENSEED, NOTSEN
SFNT_MT	Driver's Seat Front Motor	SENSEED, NOTSEN
VBAT_DS	Battery Voltage	INRANGE, NOTNRANGE

FRONT RADIO CONTROL UNIT PID INDEX

PID	Description	Expected Value
+_SW	(+) Switch	ACTIVE, NOTACT
–_SW	(–) Switch	ACTIVE, NOTACT
AM_SW	AM Switch	ACTIVE, NOTACT
AS_SW	Autoset Switch	ACTIVE, NOTACT
ASYSON	ASYSON Output State	ACTIVE, NOTACT
BAL_SW	Balance Switch	ACTIVE, NOTACT
BAND_SW	Band Switch	ACTIVE, NOTACT
BASS_SW	Bass Switch	ACTIVE, NOTACT
CD/CJ	CD Disc Jockey	YES, NO
CD_S	Single CD Player	YES, NO
CELLPHN	Cellular Phone	YES, NO
CLKDISP	Clock Display Enable Input State	DISABLE, ENABLE
CLOCK	Clock	ACTIVE, NOTACT
CTR_IMG	Center Image Amplifier	ACTIVE, NOTACT
DSP_EFF	DSP Effects	ACTIVE, NOTACT
EJCT_SW	Eject Switch	ACTIVE, NOTACT
FADE_SW	Fade Switch	ACTIVE, NOTACT
FM_SW	FW Switch	ACTIVE, NOTACT
MEM_SW	Memory Switch	ACTIVE, NOTACT
MENU_SW	Steering Wheel Control Input State	VALID, INVALID
MNIDSC	Minidisc Deck	YES, NO
PHONE	Phone Switch (Steering Wheel)	ACTIVE, NOTACT

FRONT RADIO CONTROL UNIT PID INDEX (Cont.)

PID	Description	Expected Value
PRE1_SW	Preset 1 Switch	ACTIVE, NOTACT
PRE2_SW	Preset 2 Switch	ACTIVE, NOTACT
PRE3_SW	Preset 3 Switch	ACTIVE, NOTACT
PRE4_SW	Preset 4 Switch	ACTIVE, NOTACT
PRE5_SW	Preset 5 Switch	ACTIVE, NOTACT
PRE6_SW	Preset 6 Switch	ACTIVE, NOTACT
PTA	PTA Input State	ACTIVE, NOTACT
PWR_SW	Power Switch	ACTIVE, NOTACT
RBDS	RBDS	YES, NO
RBDS_SW	RBDS Switch	ACTIVE, NOTACT
REAR_ST	Rear Seat Controls	YES, NO
SCAN_SW	Scan Switch	ACTIVE, NOTACT
SEEK+	Seek Increase Switch	ACTIVE, NOTACT
SEEK–	Seek Decrease Switch	ACTIVE, NOTACT
STEER_C	Steering Wheel Controls	YES, NO
SUBWOOF	Subwoofer Amplifier	NO, YES
TAPE_SW	Tape Switch	ACTIVE, NOTACT

INSTRUMENT CLUSTER PID INDEX

PID	Description	Expected Value
CCNT_EC	Number Of DTCs In HEC	One Count Per Bit
IGN_HEC	Ignition Switch Status	YES, NO
NUMKEYS	Number Of Ignition Key Codes Programed	BCD (Valid Range 0-8)
M_KEY	Programmed Key In Ignition	NOTPRE, PRESENT
ACCESS	Security Access Status	TIMED, CODED
MIN#KEY	Minimum Number Of Programmed Keys Required To Start Vehicle	BCD (Valid Range 2-8)
ANTISCN	Time-Out For Unprogrammed PATS Key	DISABLE, ENABLE
PCM_ID	Is PCM ID Stored In HEC	STORED, NOTSTR
SPAREKY	Can You Add Spare Keys With 2 Programmed Keys	DISABLE, ENABLE
SERVMOD	Service Mode	YES, ON
WFLUID	Washer Fluid Level	LOW, OK
VBAT_EC	System Battery Voltage Potential	NOTOK, OK
ODOMETR	Vehicle Odometer English	Miles
FUELLVL	Fuel Level Analog Input Status	%FULL
PCM_VFY	PCM	YES, NO
MC_SW	Message Center Switch Module Input Status	ENABLE, DISABLE
ENABL_S	Has PATS Enabled Vehicle	One Count Per Bit
OIL_PSW	Oil Pressure Switch Count	

LIGHTING CONTROL MODULE PID INDEX

PID	Description	Expected Value
BOO_LC	Brake Switch Input	ON, OFF
D_SBELT	Driver's Seat Belt	IN, OUT
HBEAMSW	High Beam Switch	ON, OFF
PARK_SW	Parking Switch	ON, OFF
LIGHTSN	Ambient Light	ON, OFF
L_LOW	Left Low Beam Light	OPEN, OK
AUTOLMP	Autolamp Switch	NC, DEC, OFF, SHORT
DIMMER	Panel Dim Switch	NC, DEC, OFF, SHORT
DECKLID	Deck/Hatch Ajar Switch	AJAR, CLOSED
IGN_KEY	Ignition Key In/Out	IN, OUT
IGN_LC	Ignition Switch	RUN, START, ACCSSY, OFF
VBAT_LC	Battery Voltage	0.1Volt/Count (Volt)
DOMESW	Dome Light Switch	100/64 Percent/Count
CHIMERQ	External Tone Request	ON, OFF
INTR_LT	Interior Lighting	0.005 Percent/Count
TURNSIG	Turn Signal Driver Output	ON, OFF
BACK_LT	PWM Output	%ON, %OFF
ALP_DLY	Autolamp Delay Time	Seconds
FLSHPWR	Turn Signal Power	OPEN, GRN, VBATT
ACCDLY	Accessory Delay Driver	ON, OFF
L_HIGH	Left High Beam Output	ON, OFF
R_HIGH	Right High Beam Output	ON, OFF
R_LOW	Right Low Beam Output	ON, OFF
BATSAV	Demand Lighting Status	ON, OFF

SPEED CONTROL SERVO PID INDEX

PID	Description	Expected Value
CCNT_SC	Number Of Continuous DTCs On Speed Control Servo	One Count Per Bit
COAST	Speed Control Actuator Switch COAST	ACTIVE, NOTACT
RESUME	Speed Control Actuator Switch RESUME	ACTIVE, NOTACT
SC_OFF	Speed Control Actuator Switch OFF	ACTIVE, NOTACT
SC_ON	Speed Control Actuator Switch ON	ACTIVE, NOTACT
SET_ACL	Speed Control Actuator Switch SET, ACCEL	ACTIVE, NOTACT
VS_SET	Set Vehicle Speed	0-255 MPH

WIRING DIAGRAMS

NOTE: See appropriate wiring diagrams in DATA LINK CONNECTORS, GROUND DISTRIBUTION or POWER DISTRIBUTION article in WIRING DIAGRAMS.

DESCRIPTION & OPERATION

The module communications network provides the ability for module-to-module communication by sharing inputs and outputs instead of each component having an input and output wired directly to each module. The communications network is routed throughout the vehicle to the Powertrain Control Module (PCM), anti-lock brake control module, transmission Control Module (TCM) and air bag diagnostic monitor. This article is used to diagnose communications network circuit faults. Lighting Control Module (LCM) and Smart Entry Control (SEC) Timer/Module are not part of communications network. For module locations, see COMPONENT LOCATIONS table.

COMPONENT LOCATIONS

COMPONENT LOCATIONS

Component	Location
Air Bag Diagnostic Monitor	In Bottom Of Center Console
Air Bag Sliding Contact	In Steering Wheel
Anti-Lock Brake Control Module	Behind Center Of Dash
Battery Junction Box (BJB)	In Engine Compartment, Next To Battery
Data Link Connector (DLC) C2018	Below Driver's Side Of Instrument Panel, To Right Of Steering Column
Data Link Connector (DLC) C252	Below Driver's Side Of Instrument Panel, To Left Of Steering Column Above Fuse Junction Panel
Engine Compartment Relay Box	Left Front Side Of Engine Compartment
Fuse Junction Panel	Below Left Side Of Instrument Panel
Lighting Control Module (LCM)	Bottom Of Center Console, Below Dash Panel
Powertrain Control Module (PCM)	Behind Glove Box
Smart Entry Control (SEC) Timer/Module	Behind Center Top Of Dash Panel
Transaxle Control Module (TCM)	Behind Instrument Cluster

COMMUNICATION NETWORK DIAGNOSTICS

INSPECTION & VERIFICATION

1) Verify customer's original problem by operating system in question. Inspect vehicle for any obvious electrical component wiring or connector damage. Inspect connectors for loose, damaged or corroded terminals. Check related fuses for system in question.

2) If problem is still present after performing inspection, connect New Generation Star (NGS) tester to appropriate Data Link Connector (DLC). DLC C2018 is for OBDII diagnostics and power to NGS. DLC C252 is for all module diagnostics. DLC C2018 is located below driver's side of instrument panel, to right of steering column. DLC C252 is located below driver's side of instrument panel, to left of steering column above fuse junction panel. Select vehicle to be tested from NGS tester menu. If NGS tester does not communicate with vehicle, ensure program card is properly installed. Check NGS tester cable connections and ensure ignition is on. If NGS tester still does not communicate with vehicle and NGS does not power up, go to TEST E: NO MODULE/NETWORK COMMUNICATIONS & NO POWER TO DLC C2018 under TESTING. If NGS tester still does not communicate with vehicle and NGS powers up, go to TEST D: NO MODULE/NETWORK COMMUNICATIONS & UNABLE TO COMMUNICATE WITH ANY MODULE under TESTING. If NGS tester communicates with vehicle, perform system precheck. See SYSTEM PRECHECK – CHECKING COMMUNICATIONS WITH ALL MODULES.

SYSTEM PRECHECK – CHECKING COMMUNICATIONS WITH ALL MODULES

1) Turn ignition off. Connect New Generation Star (NGS) tester to Data Link Connector (DLC) C252, if not already connected. DLC C252 is located below driver's side of instrument panel, to left of steering column above fuse junction panel. Turn ignition on. Run DIAGNOSTIC TEST MODE RESULTS for Anti-lock Brake System (ABS). If the results are:
- LINK COMMUNICATION ERROR
- MODULE NOT RESPONDING
- CHECK IGNITION STATUS
- CHECK CABLE (DDL ADAPTER) CONNECTIONS

Go to next step. If results are not as listed, see SYMPTOM INDEX under SYSTEM TESTING.

2) Run DIAGNOSTIC TEST MODE RESULTS for Powertrain Control Module (PCM). If the results are:
- LINK COMMUNICATION ERROR
- MODULE NOT RESPONDING
- CHECK IGNITION STATUS
- CHECK CABLE (DDL ADAPTER) CONNECTIONS

Go to next step. If results are not as listed, see SYMPTOM INDEX under SYSTEM TESTING.

3) Run DIAGNOSTIC TEST MODE RESULTS for Transmission Control Module (TCM). If the results are:
- LINK COMMUNICATION ERROR
- MODULE NOT RESPONDING
- CHECK IGNITION STATUS
- CHECK CABLE (DDL ADAPTER) CONNECTIONS

Go to TEST D: NO MODULE/NETWORK COMMUNICATIONS & UNABLE TO COMMUNICATE WITH ANY MODULE under TESTING. If results are not as listed, see SYMPTOM INDEX under SYSTEM TESTING.

RETRIEVING DIAGNOSTIC TROUBLE CODES

All diagnostic codes for anti-lock brakes and air bag are retrieved using flash codes. See appropriate article. PCM or TCM code retrieval is discussed in appropriate SELF-DIAGNOSTICS article in ENGINE PERFORMANCE in appropriate MITCHELL® manual.

ACCESSING PARAMETER IDENTIFICATION (PID)

Turn ignition switch to LOCK position. Connect New Generation Star (NGS) tester to Data Link Connector (DLC) C252. DLC C252 is located below driver's side of instrument panel, to left of steering column above fuse junction panel. Following manufacturer's instructions, enter PID/DATA MONITOR AND RECORD for desired module. Operate appropriate system and ensure PID expected values are obtained. See table under PARAMETER IDENTIFICATION (PID) DEFINITIONS.

SYSTEM TESTING

NOTE: Always check module power and ground circuits prior to replacing a control module. See appropriate wiring diagram in DATA LINK CONNECTORS, GROUND DISTRIBUTION or POWER DISTRIBUTION article in WIRING DIAGRAMS.

SYMPTOM INDEX

Condition	Test
Anti-Lock Brake Control Module Does Not Respond To NGS Tester	A
Powertrain Control Module (PCM) Does Not Respond To NGS Tester	B
Transmission Control Module (TCM) Does Not Respond To NGS Tester	C
No Module/Network Communications – Unable To Communicate With Any Module	D
No Module/Network Communications – No Power To DLC C2018	E

TEST A: ANTI-LOCK BRAKE CONTROL MODULE DOES NOT RESPOND TO NGS TESTER

1) Turn ignition off. Connect New Generation Star (NGS) tester to Data Link Connector (DLC) C252. DLC C252 is located below driver's side of instrument panel, to left of steering column above fuse junction panel. Disconnect ABS module connector C249, located behind center of dash. Inspect connector for loose, damaged or corroded terminals. Repair connector as necessary and retest system for normal operation. Measure resistance of Yellow/Red wire between terminal No. 22 at ABS module connector and terminal No. 1 at DLC C252. *See Figs. 1 and 2.* If resistance is 5 ohms or more, go to next step. If resistance is less than 5 ohms, go to step **3)**.

2) Measure resistance of Yellow/Red wire between female side of in-line connector C170 terminal No. 51 and DLC C252 terminal No. 1. In-line connector C170 is located behind left side of dash above fuse junction panel. *See Fig. 3.* If resistance is less than 5 ohms, repair open Yellow/Red wire between ABS module connector C249 and in-line connector C170. Retest system. If resistance is 5 ohms or more, repair open Yellow/Red wire between in-line connector C170 and DLC C252. Retest system.

3) Measure resistance of Yellow/Black wire between terminal No. 11 at ABS module connector C249 and terminal No. 2 at DLC C252. If resistance is 5 ohms or more, go to next step. If resistance is less than 5 ohms, replace ABS module. Retest system.

4) Measure resistance of Yellow/Black wire between female side of in-line connector C170 terminal No. 63 and DLC C252 terminal No. 2. In-line connector C170 is located behind left side of dash above fuse junction panel. *See Fig. 3.* If resistance is less than 5 ohms, repair open Yellow/Black wire between ABS module connector C249 and in-line connector C170. Retest system. If resistance is 5 ohms or more, repair open Yellow/Black wire between in-line connector C170 and DLC C252. Retest system.

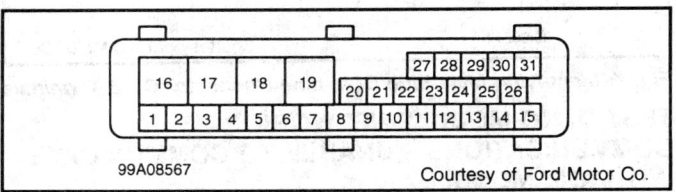

Fig. 1: Identifying ABS Module Connector C249 Terminals

TEST B: POWERTRAIN CONTROL MODULE (PCM) DOES NOT RESPOND TO NGS

NOTE: If test results indicate PCM is faulty, always check for any engine performance related Diagnostic Trouble Codes (DTCs) prior to replacing PCM. If any DTCs are present, service DTCs as necessary and retest. See appropriate SELF-DIAGNOSTICS article in ENGINE PERFORMANCE in appropriate MITCHELL® manual.

1) Turn ignition off. Disconnect PCM connector is located behind glove box. Inspect connector for loose, damaged or corroded terminals. Repair connector as necessary and retest system for normal operation. If connector is okay, measure resistance of Yellow/Red wire between terminal No. 74 at PCM connector and terminal No. 1 at Data Link Connector (DLC) C252. *See Figs. 2 and 4.* If resistance is 5 ohms or more, go to next step. If resistance is less than 5 ohms, go to step **3)**.

2) Measure resistance of Yellow/Red wire between female side of in-line connector C272 terminal No. 2 and DLC C252 terminal No. 1. In-line connector C272 is located behind center top of dash. *See Fig. 5.* If resistance is less than 5 ohms, repair open Yellow/Red wire between PCM connector and in-line connector C272. Retest system. If resistance is 5 ohms or more, repair open Yellow/Red wire between in-line connector C272 and DLC C252. Retest system.

3) Measure resistance of Yellow/Black wire between terminal No. 75 at PCM connector and terminal No. 2 at DLC C252. If resistance is 5 ohms or more, go to next step. If resistance is less than 5 ohms, see

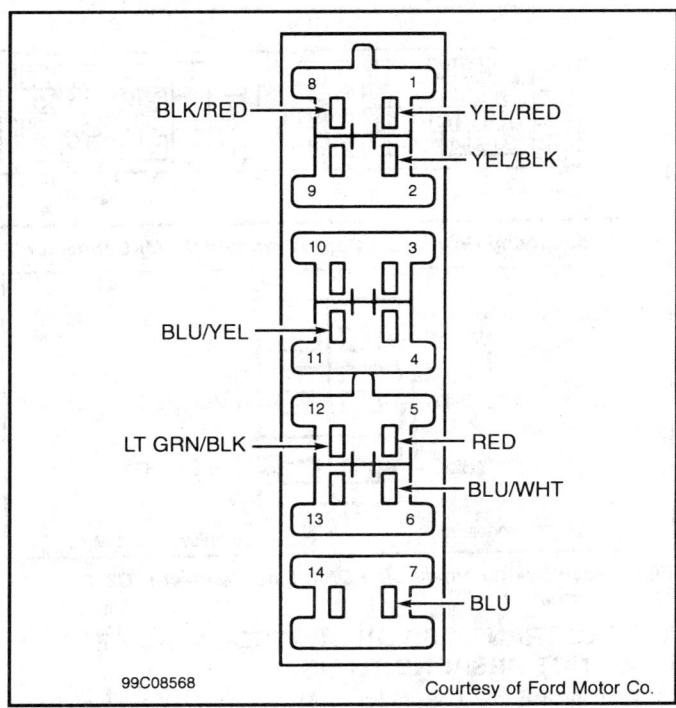

Fig. 2: Identifying DLC C252 Terminals

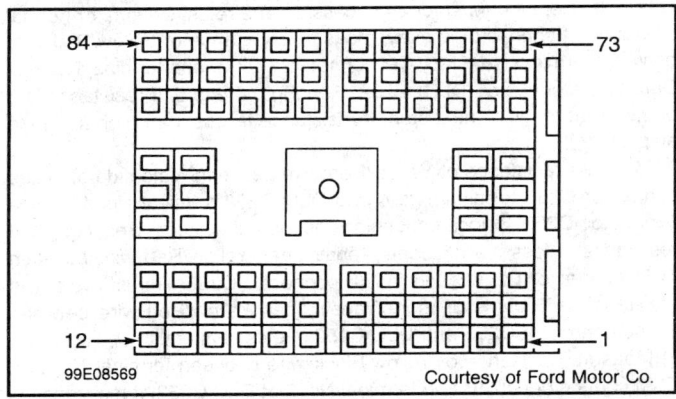

Fig. 3: Identifying Female Side Of In-Line Connector C170 Terminals

SELF-DIAGNOSTICS – VILLAGER article in ENGINE PERFORMANCE in appropriate MITCHELL® manual and perform PCM system test.

4) Measure resistance of Yellow/Black wire between female side of in-line connector C272 terminal No. 5 and DLC C252 terminal No. 2. In-line connector C272 is located behind center top of dash. *See Fig. 5.* If resistance is less than 5 ohms, repair open Yellow/Black wire between PCM connector and in-line connector C272. Retest system. If resistance is 5 ohms or more, repair open Yellow/Black wire between in-line connector C272 and DLC C252. Retest system.

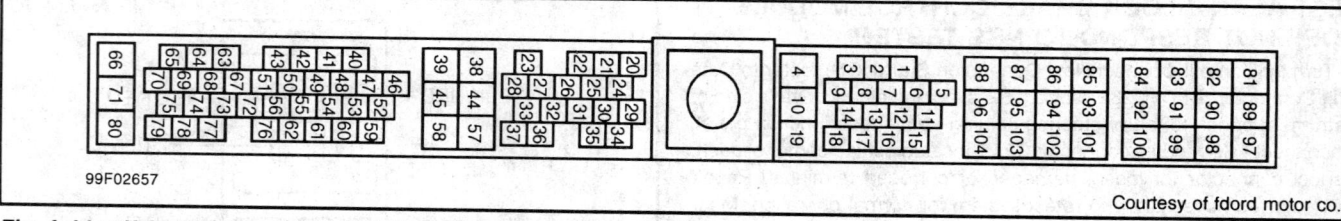

99F02657

Courtesy of fdord motor co.

Fig. 4: Identifying Powertrain Control Module (PCM) Connector Terminals

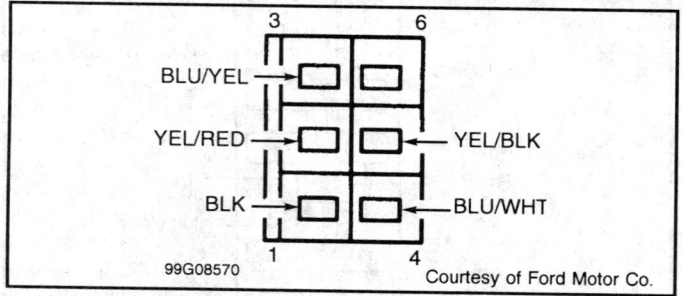

99G08570

Courtesy of Ford Motor Co.

Fig. 5: Identifying Female Side Of In-Line Connector C272 Terminals

TEST C: TRANSMISSION CONTROL MODULE (TCM) DOES NOT RESPOND TO NGS

1) Turn ignition off. Disconnect TCM connector is located behind instrument cluster. Inspect connector for loose, damaged or corroded terminals. Repair connector as necessary and retest system for normal operation. If connector is okay, measure resistance of Yellow/Red wire between terminal No. 6 at TCM connector C277B and terminal No. 1 at Data Link Connector (DLC) C252. *See Figs. 2 and 6.* If resistance is 5 ohms or more, go to next step. If resistance is less than 5 ohms, go to step **3)**.

2) Measure resistance of Yellow/Red wire between male side of in-line connector C255 terminal No. 4 and DLC C252 terminal No. 1. In-line connector C255 is located behind instrument cluster. *See Fig. 7.* If resistance is less than 5 ohms, repair open Yellow/Red wire between TCM connector C277B and in-line connector C255. Retest system. If resistance is 5 ohms or more, repair open Yellow/Red wire between in-line connector C255 and DLC C252. Retest system.

3) Measure resistance of Yellow/Black wire between terminal No. 7 at TCM connector C277B and terminal No. 2 at DLC C252. If resistance is 5 ohms or more, go to next step. If resistance is less than 5 ohms, replace TCM. Retest system.

4) Measure resistance of Yellow/Black wire between male side of in-line connector C255 terminal No. 9 and DLC C252 terminal No. 2. In-line connector C255 is located behind instrument cluster. *See Fig. 7.* If resistance is less than 5 ohms, repair open Yellow/Black wire between TCM connector C277B and in-line connector C255. Retest system. If resistance is 5 ohms or more, repair open Yellow/Black wire between in-line connector C255 and DLC C252. Retest system.

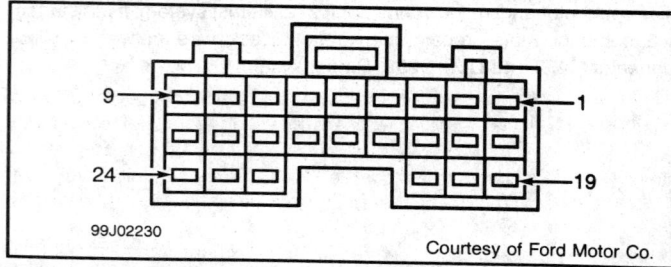

99J02230

Courtesy of Ford Motor Co.

Fig. 6: Identifying Transmission Control Module (TCM) Connector C277B Terminals

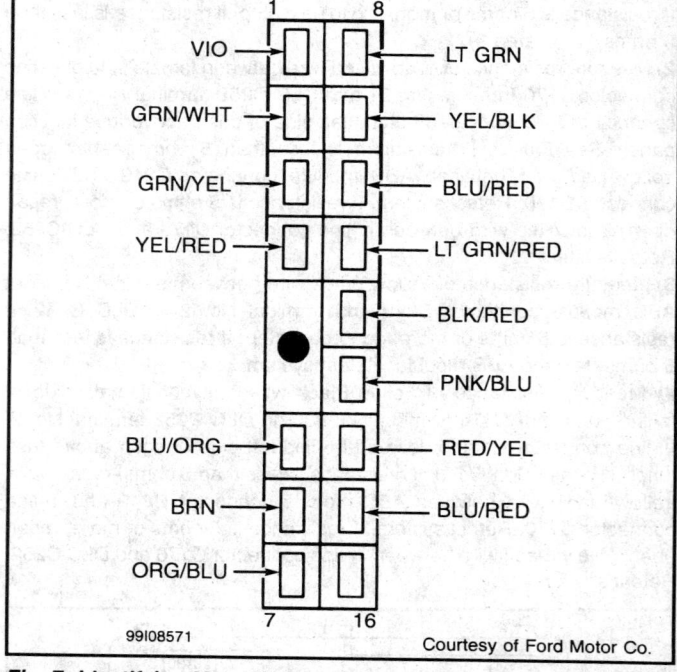

99I08571

Courtesy of Ford Motor Co.

Fig. 7: Identifying Male Side Of In-Line Connector C255 Terminals

TEST D: NO MODULE/NETWORK COMMUNICATIONS – UNABLE TO COMMUNICATE WITH ANY MODULE

1) Turn ignition off. Inspect NGS tester connector for loose, damaged or corroded terminals. Repair connector as necessary and retest system for normal operation. If connector is okay, go to next step.

2) Inspect Data Link Connector (DLC) C252 for physical damage, bent terminals or corrosion. C252 is located below driver's side of instrument panel, to left of steering column above fuse junction panel. Repair connector as necessary and retest system for normal operation. If connector is okay, go to next step.

3) Disconnect TCM connector is located behind instrument cluster. Inspect connector for loose, damaged or corroded terminals. Repair connector as necessary and retest system for normal operation. If connector is okay, measure resistance of Yellow/Red wire between terminal No. 6 at TCM connector C277B and terminal No. 1 at Data Link Connector (DLC) C252. *See Figs. 2 and 6.* If resistance is 5 ohms or more, repair open Yellow/Red wire. If resistance is less than 5 ohms, go to next step.

4) Measure resistance of Yellow/Black wire between terminal No. 7 at TCM connector C277B and terminal No. 2 at DLC C252. If resistance is 5 ohms or more, repair open Yellow/Black wire. If resistance is less than 5 ohms, go to next step.

5) Connect New Generation Star (NGS) tester to Data Link Connector (DLC) C252, if not already connected. Turn ignition on. Run DIAGNOSTIC TEST MODE RESULTS for Powertrain Control Module (PCM). If the results are:

- LINK COMMUNICATION ERROR
- MODULE NOT RESPONDING
- CHECK IGNITION STATUS

- CHECK CABLE (DDL ADAPTER) CONNECTIONS

Go to next step. If results are not as listed, replace TCM. Retest system.

6) Turn ignition off. Disconnect ABS module connector C249, located behind center of dash. Turn ignition on. Run DIAGNOSTIC TEST MODE RESULTS for PCM. If the results are:

- LINK COMMUNICATION ERROR
- MODULE NOT RESPONDING
- CHECK IGNITION STATUS
- CHECK CABLE (DDL ADAPTER) CONNECTIONS

Go to next step. If results are not as listed, replace ABS module. Retest system.

7) Turn ignition off. Deactivate air bag system. See AIR BAG RESTRAINT SYSTEMS – VILLAGER article. Disconnect air bag diagnostic monitor. Air bag diagnostic monitor is located in bottom of center console. Turn ignition on. Run DIAGNOSTIC TEST MODE RESULTS for PCM. If the results are:

- LINK COMMUNICATION ERROR
- MODULE NOT RESPONDING
- CHECK IGNITION STATUS
- CHECK CABLE (DDL ADAPTER) CONNECTIONS

Go to next step. If results are not as listed, replace ABS air bag diagnostic monitor. Retest system.

8) Turn ignition off. Disconnect PCM connector. PCM is located behind glove box. Turn ignition on. Measure voltage between ground and DLC C252 terminal No. 1 (Yellow/Red wire). If any voltage is present, go to step 24). If no voltage is present, go to next step.

9) Measure voltage between ground and DLC C252 terminal No. 2 (Yellow/Black wire). If any voltage is present, go to step 20). If no voltage is present, go to next step.

10) Turn ignition off. Measure resistance between ground and DLC C252 terminal No. 1 (Yellow/Red wire). If resistance is more than 10 k/ohms, go to next step. If resistance is 10 k/ohms or less, go to step 16).

11) Measure resistance between ground and DLC C252 terminal No. 2 (Yellow/Black wire). If resistance is more than 10 k/ohms, see SELF-DIAGNOSTICS – VILLAGER article in ENGINE PERFORMANCE in appropriate MITCHELL® manual. If resistance is 10 k/ohms or less, go to next step.

12) Disconnect in-line 84-pin connector C170. In-line connector C170 is located behind left side of dash above fuse junction panel. Measure resistance between ground and DLC C252 terminal No. 2 (Yellow/Black wire). If resistance is more than 10 k/ohms, repair short to ground in Yellow/Black wire between in-line connector C170 and ABS module. ABS module behind center of dash. If resistance is 10 k/ohms or less, go to next step.

13) Disconnect in-line 16-pin connector C255. In-line connector C255 is located behind instrument cluster. Measure resistance between ground and DLC C252 terminal No. 2 (Yellow/Black wire). If resistance is more than 10 k/ohms, repair short to ground in Yellow/Black wire between in-line connector C255 and TCM. TCM is located behind instrument cluster. If resistance is 10 k/ohms or less, go to next step.

14) Disconnect in-line 12-pin connector C2021. In-line connector C2021 is located behind center top of dash. Measure resistance between ground and DLC C252 terminal No. 2 (Yellow/Black wire). If resistance is more than 10 k/ohms, repair short to ground in Yellow/Black wire between in-line connector C2021 and air bag diagnostic monitor. Air bag diagnostic monitor is located in bottom of center console. If resistance is 10 k/ohms or less, go to next step.

15) Disconnect in-line 6-pin connector C272. In-line connector C272 is located behind center top of dash. Measure resistance between ground and DLC C252 terminal No. 2 (Yellow/Black wire). If resistance is more than 10 k/ohms, repair short to ground in Yellow/Black wire between in-line connector C272 and PCM. PCM is located behind glove box. If resistance is 10 k/ohms or less, repair short to ground in Yellow/Black wire between in-line connector C272, in-line connector C2021, in-line connector C255, in-line connector C170 and DLC C252.

16) Disconnect in-line 84-pin connector C170. In-line connector C170 is located behind left side of dash above fuse junction panel. Measure resistance between ground and DLC C252 terminal No. 1 (Yellow/Red wire). If resistance is more than 10 k/ohms, repair short to ground in Yellow/Red wire between in-line connector C170 and ABS module. ABS module behind center of dash. If resistance is 10 k/ohms or less, go to next step.

17) Disconnect in-line 16-pin connector C255. In-line connector C255 is located behind instrument cluster. Measure resistance between ground and DLC C252 terminal No. 1 (Yellow/Red wire). If resistance is more than 10 k/ohms, repair short to ground in Yellow/Red wire between in-line connector C255 and TCM. TCM is located behind instrument cluster. If resistance is 10 k/ohms or less, go to next step.

18) Disconnect in-line 12-pin connector C2021. In-line connector C2021 is located behind center top of dash. Measure resistance between ground and DLC C252 terminal No. 1 (Yellow/Red wire). If resistance is more than 10 k/ohms, repair short to ground in Yellow/Red wire between in-line connector C2021 and air bag diagnostic monitor. Air bag diagnostic monitor is located in bottom of center console. If resistance is 10 k/ohms or less, go to next step.

19) Disconnect in-line 6-pin connector C272. In-line connector C272 is located behind center top of dash. Measure resistance between ground and DLC C252 terminal No. 1 (Yellow/Red wire). If resistance is more than 10 k/ohms, repair short to ground in Yellow/Red wire between in-line connector C272 and PCM. PCM is located behind glove box. If resistance is 10 k/ohms or less, repair short to ground in Yellow/Red wire between in-line connector C272, in-line connector C2021, in-line connector C255, in-line connector C170 and DLC C252.

20) Disconnect in-line 84-pin connector C170. In-line connector C170 is located behind left side of dash above fuse junction panel. Measure voltage between ground and DLC C252 terminal No. 2 (Yellow/Black wire). If voltage is zero volts, repair short to voltage in Yellow/Black wire between in-line connector C170 and ABS module. ABS module behind center of dash. If voltage is present, go to next step.

21) Disconnect in-line 16-pin connector C255. In-line connector C255 is located behind instrument cluster. Measure voltage between ground and DLC C252 terminal No. 2 (Yellow/Black wire). If voltage is zero volts, repair short to voltage in Yellow/Black between in-line connector C255 and TCM. TCM is located behind instrument cluster. If voltage is present, go to next step.

22) Disconnect in-line 12-pin connector C2021. In-line connector C2021 is located behind center top of dash. Measure voltage between ground and DLC C252 terminal No. 2 (Yellow/Black wire). If voltage is zero volts, repair short to voltage in Yellow/Black between in-line connector C2021 and air bag diagnostic monitor. Air bag diagnostic monitor is located in bottom of center console. If voltage is present, go to next step.

23) Disconnect in-line 6-pin connector C272. In-line connector C272 is located behind center top of dash. Measure voltage between ground and DLC C252 terminal No. 2 (Yellow/Black wire). If voltage is zero volts, repair short to voltage in Yellow/Black between in-line connector C272 and PCM. PCM is located behind glove box. If voltage is present, repair short to voltage in Yellow/Black between in-line connector C272, in-line connector C2021, in-line connector C255, in-line connector C170 and DLC C252.

24) Disconnect in-line 84-pin connector C170. In-line connector C170 is located behind left side of dash above fuse junction panel. Measure voltage between ground and DLC C252 terminal No. 1 (Yellow/Red wire). If voltage is zero volts, repair short to voltage in Yellow/Red wire between in-line connector C170 and ABS module. ABS module behind center of dash. If voltage is present, go to next step.

25) Disconnect in-line 16-pin connector C255. In-line connector C255 is located behind instrument cluster. Measure voltage between ground and DLC C252 terminal No. 1 (Yellow/Red wire). If voltage is zero volts, repair short to voltage in Yellow/Red wire between in-line connector C255 and TCM. TCM is located behind instrument cluster. If voltage is present, go to next step.

26) Disconnect in-line 12-pin connector C2021. In-line connector C2021 is located behind center top of dash. Measure voltage between ground and DLC C252 terminal No. 1 (Yellow/Red wire). If voltage is zero volts, repair short to voltage in Yellow/Red wire between in-line connector C2021 and air bag diagnostic monitor. Air bag diagnostic monitor is located in bottom of center console. If voltage is present, go to next step.

27) Disconnect in-line 6-pin connector C272. In-line connector C272 is located behind center top of dash. Measure voltage between ground and DLC C252 terminal No. 1 (Yellow/Red wire). If voltage is zero volts, repair short to voltage in Yellow/Red wire between in-line connector C272, in-line connector C2021, in-line connector C255, in-line connector C170 and DLC C252.

TEST E: NO MODULE/NETWORK COMMUNICATIONS – NO POWER TO DLC C2018

1) Inspect NGS tester connector for loose, damaged or corroded terminals. Repair connector as necessary and retest system for normal operation. If connector is okay, go to next step.
2) Turn ignition off. Inspect Data Link Connector (DLC) C2018 for physical damage, bent terminals or corrosion. DLC C2018 is located below driver's side of instrument panel, to right of steering column. Repair as necessary and retest system for normal operation. If connector is okay, go to next step.
3) Measure voltage between ground and terminal No. 16 (Red wire) at DLC. See Fig. 8. If voltage is more than 10 volts, go to next step. If

voltage is 10 volts or less, repair Red wire between instrument panel fuse block and DLC C2018. Retest system for normal operation.
4) Measure resistance between ground and terminals No. 4 (Black wire) and No. 5 (Black/Red wire) at DLC. If both resistance readings are less than 5 ohms, repair or replace NGS tester. Retest system for normal operation. If any resistance reading is 5 ohms or more, repair open in Black wire or Black/Red wire between ground and DLC C2018. Retest system for normal operation.

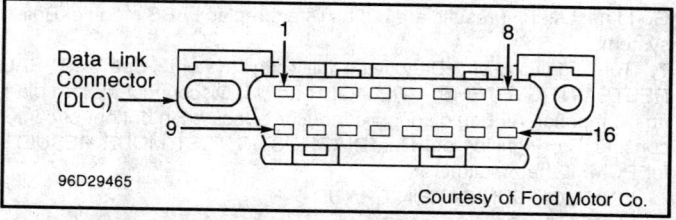

Fig. 8: Identifying Data Link Connector (DLC) Terminals

PARAMETER IDENTIFICATION (PID) DEFINITIONS
ANTI-LOCK BRAKE SYSTEM MODULE PID INDEX

PID	Description	Expected Value
ABSLF_O	Left Front ABS Outlet Valve	ON, OFF
ABSRF_O	Right Front ABS Outlet Valve	ON, OFF
ABSRR_O	Right Rear ABS Outlet Valve	ON, OFF
ABSLR_O	Left Rear ABS Outlet Valve	ON, OFF
ABSLF_I	Left Front ABS Inlet Valve	ON, OFF
ABSRF_I	Right Front ABS Inlet Valve	ON, OFF
ABSRR_I	Right Rear ABS Inlet Valve	ON, OFF
ABSLR_I	Left Rear ABS Inlet Valve	ON, OFF
LF_WSPD	Left Front Wheel Speed Signal	0-255 MPH
RF_WSPD	Right Front Wheel Speed Signal	0-255 MPH
RR_WSPD	Right Rear Wheel Speed Signal	0-255 MPH
LR_WSPD	Left Rear Wheel Speed Signal	0-255 MPH
PWRSUP	Battery Voltage To Anti-Lock Control Module	#.## V
ABSLAMP	ABS Warning Light State	ON, OFF
ABS_IN	ABS Status In	ON, OFF
BOO_ABS	Brake Pedal Position Switch Input	ON, OFF
VLV_CTR	ABS Valve Control Relay	ON, OFF
LIMITSIG	Limit Signals	OK, notOK
MOTORLYI	ABS Pump Motor Relay Input	ON, OFF

WIRING DIAGRAMS

NOTE: See appropriate wiring diagrams in DATA LINK CONNECTORS, GROUND DISTRIBUTION or POWER DISTRIBUTION article in WIRING DIAGRAMS.

DESCRIPTION & OPERATION

Vehicle has 2 module communications networks. The module communications network provides the ability for module-to-module communication by sharing inputs and outputs instead of each component having an input and output wired directly to each module. A BUS which consists of a pair of twisted wires is used to transfer information between each module. The BUS network is also referred to as Standard Corporate Protocol (SCP). The BUS consists of a (+) circuit No. 914 and a (–) circuit No. 915. The BUS is routed throughout the vehicle to Powertrain Control Module (PCM), Anti-lock Brake System (ABS) control module, Front Electronics Module (FEM), Rear Electronics Module (REM), Instrument Cluster Module (ICM), Next Generation Speed Control (NGSC) module and Remote Keyless Entry (RKE) module (if equipped). The Parking Aid Module (PAM), Restraint Control Module (RCM), Left Power Sliding Door Module (LPSDM) and Right Power Sliding Door Module (RPSDM) do not use the BUS to communicate with other modules. These modules are connected to the International Standards Organization (ISO) 9141 diagnostic communications network through a single wire (circuit No. 70). Both networks are connected to the Data Link Connector (DLC). This article is used to diagnose BUS and ISO communications network circuit faults. For module locations, see COMPONENT LOCATIONS.

COMPONENT LOCATIONS

COMPONENT LOCATIONS

Component	Location
Anti-Lock Brake Control Module	1
Data Link Connector (DLC)	Located Below Driver's Side Of Instrument Panel, Right Of Steering Column
Front Electronics Module (FEM)	1
In-Line 14-Pin Harness Connector C432	Located Rear Right Side Of Cargo Area, Behind Panel
In-Line 16-Pin Harness Connector C180	Located Behind Instrument Panel, Above Front Electronics Module (FEM)
In-Line 16-Pin Harness Connector C292	Located Behind Driver's Side Kick Panel
In-Line 42-Pin Harness Connector C100	Located At Left Side Rear Of Engine Compartment
Instrument Cluster	1
Next Generation Speed Control (NGSC) Servo	1
Parking Aid Module (PAM)	1
Rear Electronics Module (REM)	1
Remote Keyless Entry (RKE) Module	1
Restraint Contol Module	1
Powertrain Control Module (PCM)	1

1 – See Fig. 1.

REPAIRING BUS WIRING

NOTE: *Following procedure must be used to ensure proper repair is performed on BUS wiring. BUS wiring is sensitive to moisture and oxidation and must be properly sealed to ensure proper operation. Regular heat shrink tubing is NOT sufficient, heat shrink tubing containing hot melt wax is required.*

1) When performing a repair on the BUS wiring of the Module Communications Network, ensure the wires on the BUS are twisted at a rate of 33-40 winds per 3.3 ft. (1 m). The twists should start within approximately 4.9" (124 mm) from any connector. Use only 20 AWG standard wire gauge for repairs.

2) If performing a splice in the wiring, strip .75" (19.0 mm) of insulation from one wire and 1.50" (38.1 mm) of insulator from the other wire. Perform STEP 1. See Fig. 2. Place hot melt wax heat shrink tubing over one wire.

3) Twist stripped portion of the wires together. Solder connection using resin core RMA solder. DO NOT use acid core solder. Bend wires to allow installation of heat shrink tubing. Perform STEP 2. See Fig. 2.

4) Position heat shrink tubing over splice area. Using heat gun, evenly heat the heat shrink tubing until wax flows from both ends of heat shrink tubing.

PROGRAMMING

MODULE CONFIGURATION

NOTE: *Powertrain Control Module (PCM) has to be flash programmed using a flash cable. See COMPUTER RELEARN PROCEDURES article in GENERAL INFORMATION.*

NOTE: *Newly released modules will require configuration after being installed on vehicle. All configurable modules will be packaged in a kit which contains a warning label and multi-language sheet reemphasizing requirements to configure replacement modules. A New Generation Star (NGS) tester or Ford compatible scan tool MUST be used to retrieve configuration data from old module before it is removed from vehicle. This information will be transferred into new module so that new module will contain same settings as old module. NGS tester will not retain stored configuration information for longer than 24 hours.*

Following manufacturer's instructions, upload old information from old module using Ford Service Function (FSF) card and NGS tester. Install new module and download stored information into new module using FSF card and NGS tester.

COMMUNICATION NETWORK DIAGNOSTICS

INSPECTION & VERIFICATION

1) Verify customer's original problem by operating system in question. Inspect vehicle for any obvious electrical component wiring or connector damage. Inspect connectors for loose, damaged or corroded terminals. Inspect related fuses for system in question.

2) Inspect Data Link Connector (DLC) pins for damage. See Fig. 6. The DLC is located below driver's side of instrument panel, right of steering column. If pins are okay, go to next step. If pins are damaged, repair as necessary and proceed to next step.

3) If problem is still present after performing inspection, connect New Generation Star (NGS) tester to DLC. Select vehicle to be tested from NGS tester menu. If NGS tester does not communicate with vehicle, ensure program card is properly installed. Inspect NGS tester cable connections and ensure ignition is on. If NGS tester still does not communicate with vehicle, perform TEST N: NO MODULE/NETWORK COMMUNICATION – NO POWER TO NGS TESTER under SYSTEM TESTS. If NGS tester communicates with vehicle, perform data link diagnostic test. See DATA LINK DIAGNOSTIC TEST.

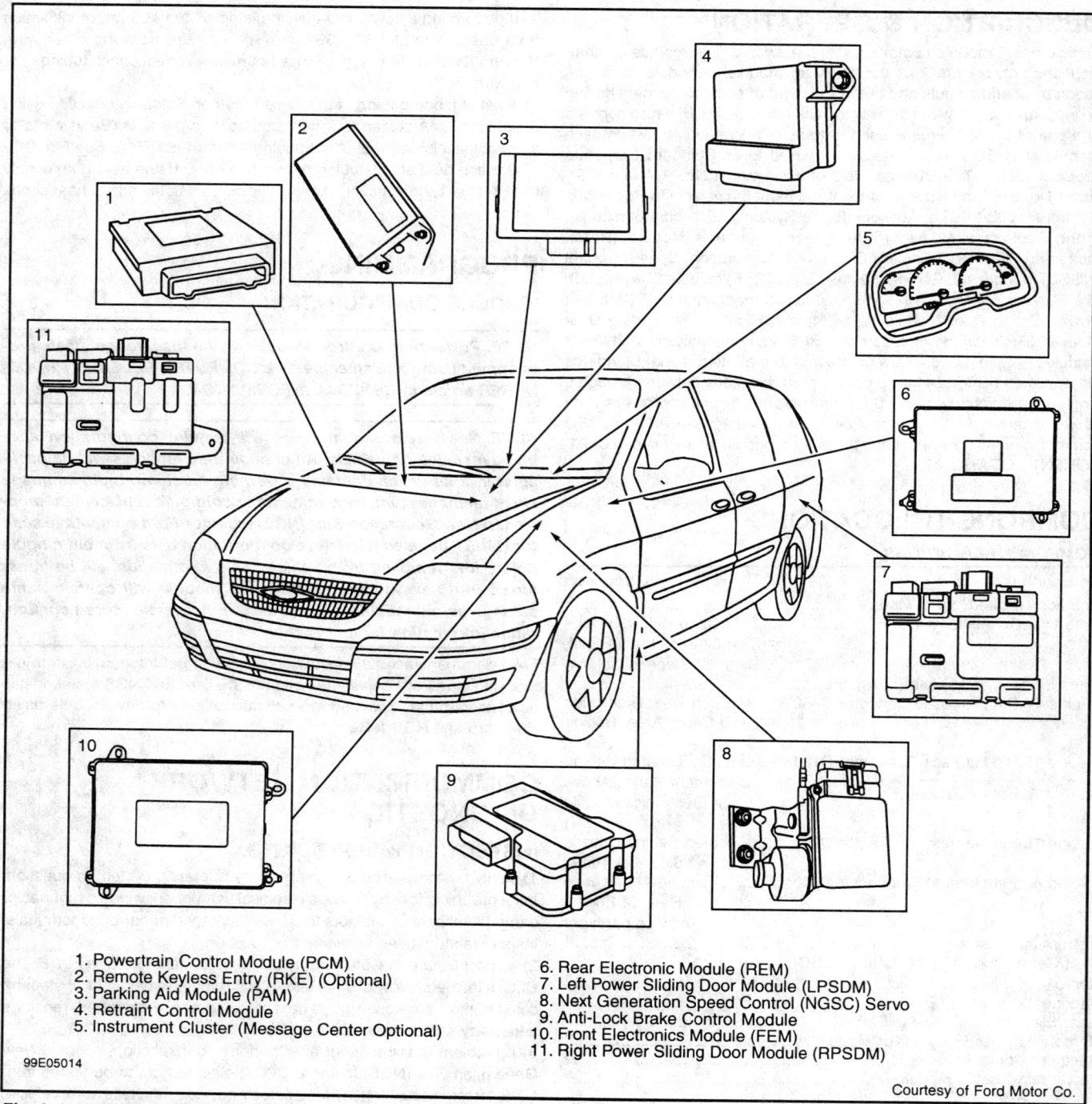

1. Powertrain Control Module (PCM)
2. Remote Keyless Entry (RKE) (Optional)
3. Parking Aid Module (PAM)
4. Retraint Control Module
5. Instrument Cluster (Message Center Optional)
6. Rear Electronic Module (REM)
7. Left Power Sliding Door Module (LPSDM)
8. Next Generation Speed Control (NGSC) Servo
9. Anti-Lock Brake Control Module
10. Front Electronics Module (FEM)
11. Right Power Sliding Door Module (RPSDM)

99E05014

Courtesy of Ford Motor Co.

Fig. 1: Locating Vehicle Communication Network Modules

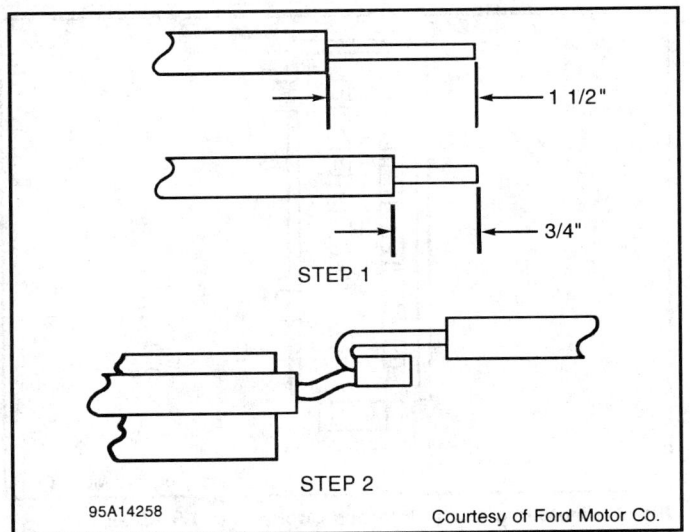

95A14258   Courtesy of Ford Motor Co.

Fig. 2: Repairing Bus Wiring

DATA LINK DIAGNOSTIC TEST

1) Connect New Generation Star (NGS) tester to Data Link Connector (DLC), if not already connected. Select vehicle to be tested from NGS tester menu.

2) Turn ignition switch to ON position. Rotate dial on NGS tester to menu item DIAGNOSTIC DATA LINK and press trigger. A test will be performed on the BUS (circuits No. 914 and 915) for the module communications network and the ISO 9141 communication link (circuit No. 70). If NGS tester displays, SYSTEM PASSED, module communications network is operating properly. Return to article that directed you here and continue diagnosis. If NGS tester does not display SYSTEM PASSED, perform appropriate test. See DATA LINK DIAGNOSTICS NETWORK TEST table.

DATA LINK DIAGNOSTICS NETWORK TEST

Scan Tool Readout	Test
CKT70 = ALL ECUS NO RESP / NOT EQUIP	L
CKT914 = ALL ECUS NO RESP / NOT EQUIP	M
CKT915 = ALL ECUS NO RESP / NOT EQUIP	M
CKT70, CKT914, CKT915 = SOME ECUS NO RESP / NOT EQUIP	1
NO RESPONSE ON CKT914 (BUS +)	1
NO RESPONSE ON CKT915 (BUS –)	1
NO RESPONSE / NOT EQUIPPED	1

[1] – Repair communication concern for appropriate module(s). See SYMPTOM CHART table.

SYMPTOM CHART

Condition	Test
Anti-Lock Brake Control Module Does Not Respond To NGS Tester	A
Parking Aid Module Does Not Respond To NGS Tester	B
Left Power Sliding Door Module Does Not Respond To NGS Tester	C
Right Power Sliding Door Module Does Not Respond To NGS Tester	D
Remote Keyless Entry Module Does Not Respond To NGS Tester	E
Restraint Control Module Does Not Respond To NGS Tester	F
Rear Electronics Module Does Not Respond To NGS Tester	G
Next Generation Speed Control Servo Does Not Respond To NGS Tester	H
Front Electonics Module Does Not Respond To NGS Tester	I
Powertrain Control Module Does Not Respond To NGS Tester	J
Instrument Cluster Does Not Respond To NGS Tester	K
No Module/Network Communication – ISO 9141	L

SYMPTOM CHART (Cont.)

Condition	Test
No Module/Network Communication – SCP Data Bus	M
No Module/Network Communication – No Power To NGS Tester	N

RETRIEVING & CLEARING DIAGNOSTIC TROUBLE CODES

Connect New Generation Star (NGS) tester to Data Link Connector (DLC). Following manufacturers instructions to retrieve and clear codes for desired module. See appropriate table under DIAGNOSTIC TROUBLE CODE (DTC) DEFINITIONS for a listing of Diagnostic Trouble Codes (DTCs) and appropriate test procedure.

ACCESSING PARAMETER IDENTIFICATION (PID)

Turn ignition switch to LOCK position. Connect New Generation Star (NGS) tester to Data Link Connector (DLC). Following manufacturers instructions enter PID/DATA MONITOR AND RECORD for desired module. Operate appropriate system and ensure PID expected values are obtained. See appropriate table under PARAMETER IDENTIFICATION (PID) DEFINITIONS.

WIGGLE TEST

The wiggle test is designed to help identify and locate intermittent failures in vehicle wiring harness and system components. Once wiggle test is entered, several inputs and outputs of the module are monitored for a change of state. When a state change is encountered, a tone will sound and/or a DTC will be displayed on New Generation Star (NGS) tester. For modules that store DTCs, DTC description will determine an open circuit, short to ground, or short to voltage. By performing wiggle test and pulling on different areas of wiring harness, intermittent open and short circuits can be located and serviced.

1) Connect NGS scan tester to Data Link Connector (DLC). Turn ignition switch to ON position. Rotate dial on scan tester to DIAGNOSTIC DATA LINK menu and press trigger.

2) Rotate dial on scan tester to highlight the desired module you wish to access and press trigger. Rotate dial on scan tester to highlight DIAGNOSTIC TEST MODES and press trigger. Rotate dial on scan tester to highlight WIGGLE TEST. Press trigger, then press START (button 3).

CONNECTOR IDENTIFICATION

CONNECTOR IDENTIFICATION

Connector	See Fig.
Anti-Lock Brake Control Module Harness Connector (C111)	11
Data Link Connector (C216)	6
Front Electronics Module Harness Connector (C190)	4
Front Electronics Module Harness Connector (C191)	10
Front Electronics Module Harness Connector (C192)	8
Front Electronics Module Harness Connector (C346)	9
In-Line Harness Connector (C100)	13
In-Line Harness Connectors (C180 & C292)	7
In-Line Harness Connector (C432)	5
Instrument Cluster Harness Connector (C239 & C241)	10
Instrument Cluster Harness Connector (C240)	9
Left Power Sliding Door Module Harness Connector (C355)	4
Next Generation Speed Control Servo Harness Connector (C116)	3
Powertrain Control Module Harness Connector (C103)	14
Rear Electronics Module Harness Connector (C340)	8
Rear Electronics Module Harness Connector (C341)	10
Rear Electronics Module Harness Connector (C343)	9
Rear Electronics Module Harness Connector (C344)	4
Remote Keyless Entry Module Harness Connector (C200)	4
Restraint Control Module Harness Connector (C231)	12

CONNECTOR IDENTIFICATION (Cont.)

Connector	See Fig.
Right Power Sliding Door Module Harness Connector (C352)	4

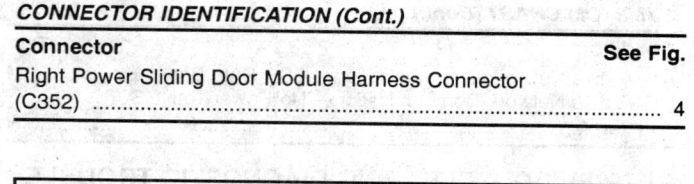

Fig. 3: Identifying 10-Pin Harness Connector Terminals (C116)

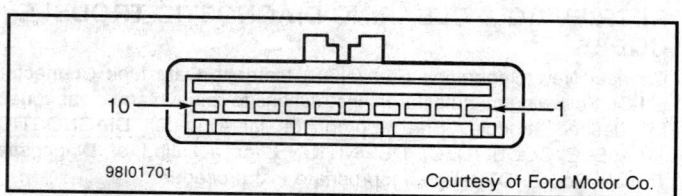

Fig. 4: Identifying 12-Pin Harness Connector Terminals (C190, C200, C344, C352 & C355)

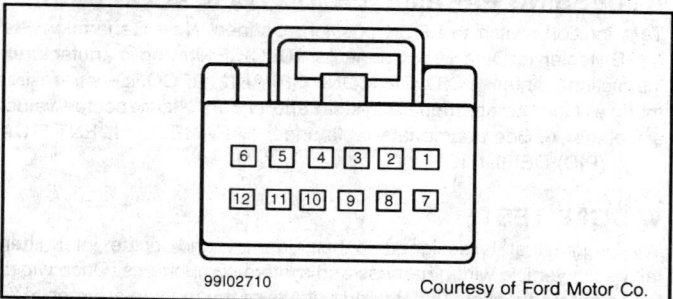

Fig. 5: Identifying 14-Pin Harness Connector Terminals (C432)

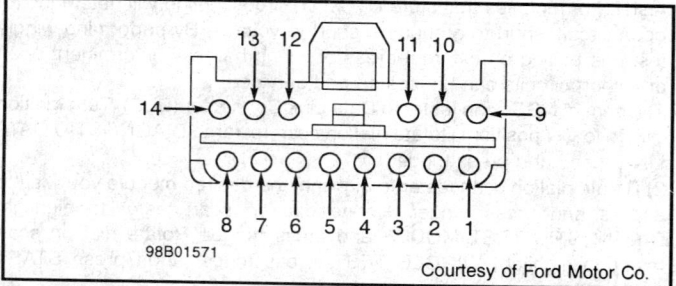

Fig. 6: Identifying 16-Pin Harness Connector Terminals (C216)

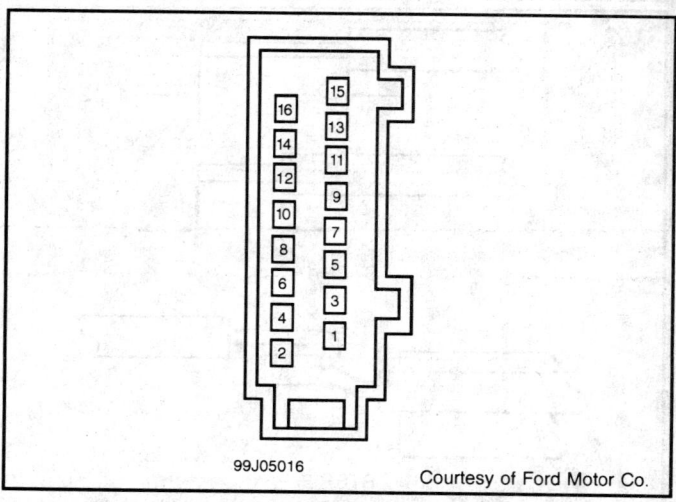

Fig. 7: Identifying 16-Pin Harness Connectors Terminals (C180 & 292)

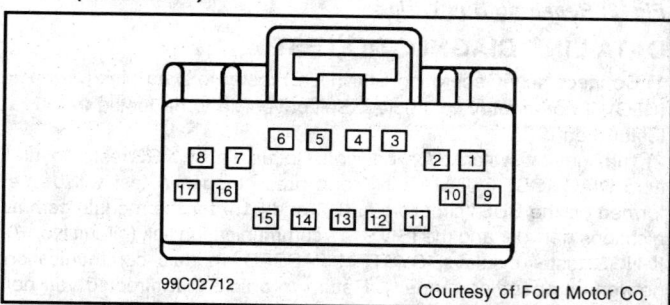

Fig. 8: Identifying 17-Pin Harness Connector Terminals (C192 & 340)

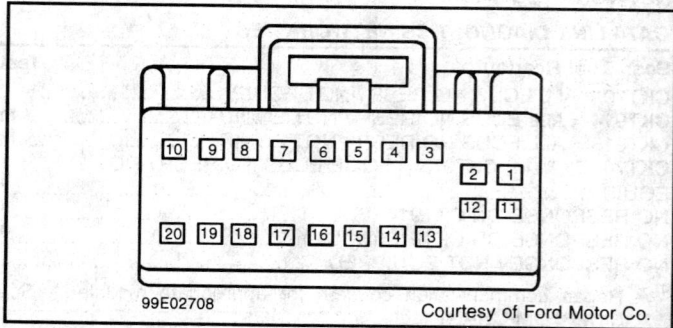

Fig. 9: Identifying 20-Pin Harness Connector Terminals (C240, C343 & 346)

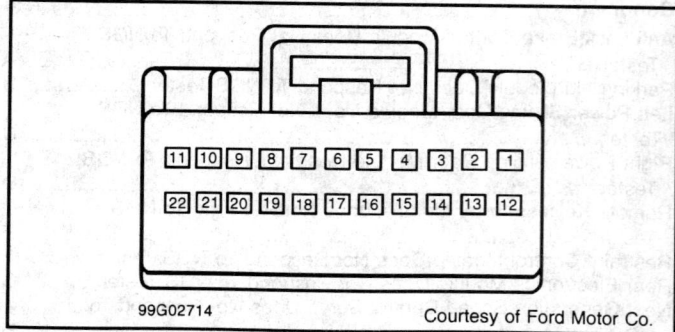

Fig. 10: Identifying 22-Pin Harness Connector Terminals (C191, C239, C241 & C341)

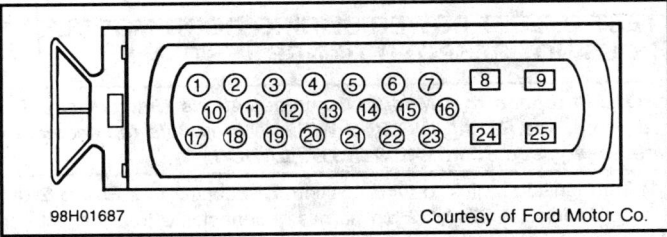

98H01687   Courtesy of Ford Motor Co.

Fig. 11: Identifying 25-Pin Harness Connector Terminals (C111)

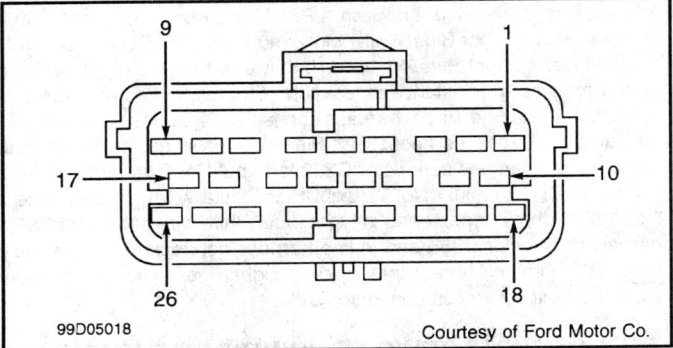

99D05018   Courtesy of Ford Motor Co.

Fig. 12: Identifying 26-Pin Harness Connector Terminals (C231)

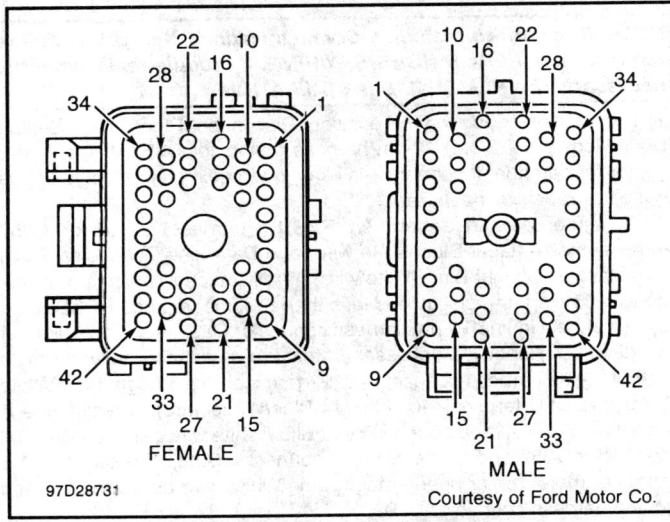

97D28731   Courtesy of Ford Motor Co.

Fig. 13: Identifying 42-Pin Harness Connector Terminals (C100)

SYSTEM TESTS

NOTE: All diagnostic tests are written specifically for New Generation Star (NGS) tester. Most generic scan tools should be able to perform all test procedures. Many steps in the following tests refer to various connectors. These connector and terminal identifications are in illustrations. See Figs. 3-14 under CONNECTOR IDENTIFICATION. Always check module power and ground circuits prior to replacing a control module. See appropriate wiring diagram in GROUND DISTRIBUTION and/or POWER DISTRIBUTION articles in WIRING DIAGRAMS.

NOTE: After repairs are made to vehicle always perform data link diagnostic test. See DATA LINK DIAGNOSTIC TEST under COMMUNICATION NETWORK DIAGNOSTICS.

CAUTION: Be careful when probing fuse junction box, power distribution box or any connectors. Damage will result to connector receptacle if probe or terminal being used is too large. Electronic modules are sensitive to static electrical charges. If exposed to these charges, damage may result.

TEST A: ANTI-LOCK BRAKE CONTROL MODULE DOES NOT RESPOND TO NGS TESTER

NOTE: If repairs to a Module Communications Network circuit is required, see REPAIRING BUS WIRING. If module replacement is necessary, see REMOVAL & INSTALLATION.

1) Turn ignition switch to OFF position. Inspect Data Link Connector (DLC) for damage. Repair as necessary. Disconnect anti-lock brake control module 25-pin harness connector C111. Inspect connector for damage. Repair as necessary. Connect anti-lock brake control module harness connector C111. Connect NGS tester to DLC. Turn ignition switch to ON position. Perform data link diagnostic test. See DATA LINK DIAGNOSTIC TEST under COMMUNICATION NETWORK DIAGNOSTICS. If result was ABS: NO RESPONSE ON CKT914 (BUS+), go to next step. If result was ABS: NO RESPONSE ON CKT915 (BUS–), go to step **5)**.

2) Turn ignition switch to OFF position. Disconnect NGS tester. Disconnect anti-lock brake control module 25-pin harness connector C111. Measure resistance between anti-lock brake control module harness connector C111 terminal No. 15 (Tan/Orange wire) and DLC terminal No. 2 (Tan/Orange wire). If resistance is 5 ohms or more, go to next step. If resistance is less than 5 ohms, replace anti-lock brake control module.

3) Disconnect in-line 16-pin harness connector C292. Inspect connector for damage. Repair as necessary. Measure resistance between male

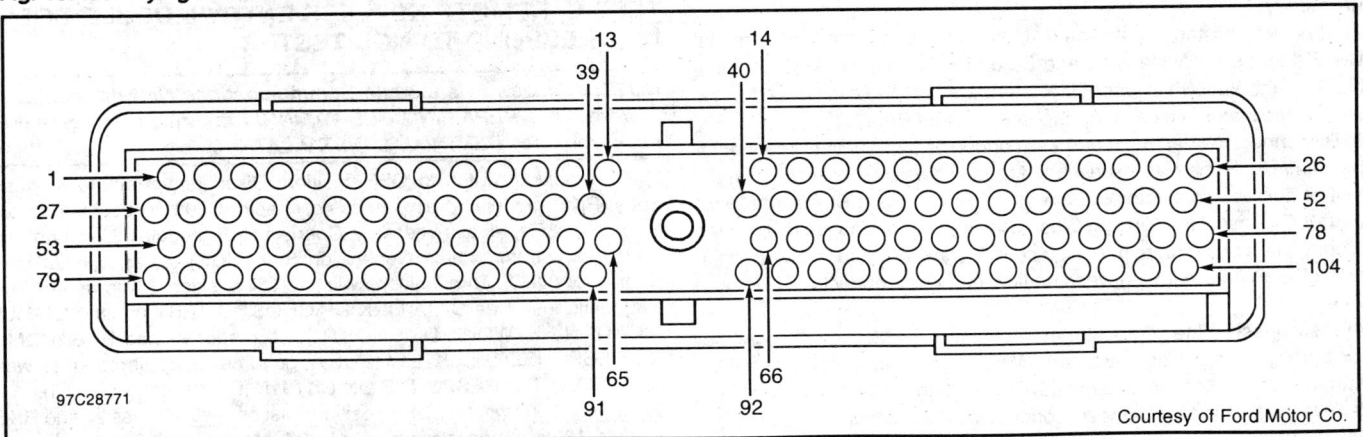

97C28771   Courtesy of Ford Motor Co.

Fig. 14: Identifying 104-Pin Harness Connector Terminals (C103)

half of in-line harness connector C292 terminal No. 4 (Tan/Orange wire) and DLC terminal No. 2 (Tan/Orange wire). If resistance is less than 5 ohms, go to next step. If resistance is 5 ohms or more, repair open in Tan/Orange wire between in-line harness connector C292 and DLC.

4) Disconnect in-line 16-pin harness connector C180. Inspect connector for damage. Repair as necessary. Measure resistance between female half of in-line harness connector C292 terminal No. 4 (Tan/Orange wire) and male half of in-line harness connector C180 terminal No. 4 (Tan/Orange wire). If resistance is less than 5 ohms, repair open in Tan/Orange wire between of in-line harness connector C180 and anti-lock brake control module harness connector C111. If resistance is 5 ohms or more, repair open in Tan/Orange wire between in-line harness connector C292 and in-line harness connector C180.

5) Turn ignition switch to OFF position. Disconnect NGS tester. Disconnect anti-lock brake control module 25-pin harness connector C111. Measure resistance between anti-lock brake control module harness connector C111 terminal No. 6 (Pink/Light Blue wire) and DLC terminal No. 10 (Pink/Light Blue wire). If resistance is 5 ohms or more, go to next step. If resistance is less than 5 ohms, replace anti-lock brake control module.

6) Disconnect in-line 16-pin harness connector C292. Inspect connector for damage. Repair as necessary. Measure resistance between male half of in-line harness connector C292 terminal No. 2 (Pink/Light Blue wire) and DLC terminal No. 10 (Pink/Light Blue wire). If resistance is less than 5 ohms, go to next step. If resistance is 5 ohms or more, repair open in Pink/Light Blue wire between in-line harness connector C292 and DLC.

7) Disconnect in-line 16-pin harness connector C180. Inspect connector for damage. Repair as necessary. Measure resistance between female half of in-line harness connector C292 terminal No. 2 (Pink/Light Blue wire) and male half of in-line harness connector C180 terminal No. 6 (Pink/Light Blue wire). If resistance is less than 5 ohms, repair open in Pink/Light Blue wire between in-line harness connector C180 and anti-lock brake control module harness connector C111. If resistance is 5 ohms or more, repair open in Pink/Light Blue wire between in-line harness connector C292 and in-line harness connector C180.

TEST B: PARKING AID MODULE DOES NOT RESPOND TO NGS TESTER

NOTE: If repairs to a Module Communications Network circuit is required, see REPAIRING BUS WIRING. If module replacement is necessary, see REMOVAL & INSTALLATION.

1) Turn ignition switch to OFF position. Disconnect Parking Aid Module (PAM) 26-pin harness connector C445. Inspect connector for damage. If connector is okay, go to next step. If connector is not okay, repair as necessary.

2) Measure resistance between PAM harness connector C445 terminal No. 5 (Light Blue/White wire) and Data Link Connector (DLC) terminal No. 7 (Light Blue/White wire). If resistance is 5 ohms or more, go to next step. If resistance is less than 5 ohms, replace PAM.

3) Disconnect in-line 16-pin harness connector C292. Inspect connector for damage. Repair as necessary. Measure resistance between male half of harness connector C292 terminal No. 5 (Light Blue/White wire) and DLC terminal No. 7 (Light Blue/White wire). If resistance is less than 5 ohms, go to next step. If resistance is 5 ohms or more, repair open in Light Blue/White wire between in-line harness connector C292 and DLC.

4) Disconnect in-line 14-pin harness connector C432. Inspect connector for damage. Repair as necessary. Measure resistance between PAM harness connector C445 terminal No. 5 (Light Blue/White wire) and female half of in-line harness connector C432 terminal No. 9 (Light Blue/White wire). If resistance is less than 5 ohms, repair open in Light Blue/White wire between in-line harness connector C292 and in-line harness connector C432. If resistance is 5 ohms or more, repair open in Light Blue/White wire between PAM harness connector C445 and in-line harness connector C432.

TEST C: LEFT POWER SLIDING DOOR MODULE DOES NOT RESPOND TO NGS TESTER

NOTE: If repairs to a Module Communications Network circuit is required, see REPAIRING BUS WIRING. If module replacement is necessary, see REMOVAL & INSTALLATION.

1) Turn ignition switch to OFF position. Disconnect Left Power Sliding Door Module (LPSDM) 12-pin harness connector C355. Inspect connector for damage. If connector is okay, go to next step. If connector is not okay, repair as necessary.

2) Measure resistance between LPSDM harness connector C355 terminal No.10 (Light Blue/White wire) and Data Link Connector (DLC) terminal No. 7 (Light Blue/White wire). If resistance is 5 ohms or more, go to next step. If resistance is less than 5 ohms, replace LPSDM.

3) Disconnect in-line 16-pin harness connector C292. Inspect connector for damage. Repair as necessary. Measure resistance between male half of in-line harness connector C292 terminal No. 5 (Light Blue/White wire) and DLC terminal No. 7 (Light Blue/White wire). If resistance is less than 5 ohms, repair open in Light Blue/White wire between LPSDM harness connector C355 and in-line harness connector C292. If resistance is 5 ohms or more, repair open in Light Blue/White wire between DLC and in-line harness connector C292.

TEST D: RIGHT POWER SLIDING DOOR MODULE DOES NOT RESPOND TO NGS TESTER

NOTE: If repairs to a Module Communications Network circuit is required, see REPAIRING BUS WIRING. If module replacement is necessary, see REMOVAL & INSTALLATION.

1) Turn ignition switch to OFF position. Disconnect Right Power Sliding Door Module (RPSDM) 12-pin harness connector C352. Inspect connector for damage. If connector is okay, go to next step. If connector is not okay, repair as necessary.

2) Measure resistance between RPSDM harness connector C352 terminal No.10 (Light Blue/White wire) and Data Link Connector (DLC) terminal No. 7 (Light Blue/White wire). If resistance is 5 ohms or more, go to next step. If resistance is less than 5 ohms, replace RPSDM.

3) Disconnect in-line 16-pin harness connector C292. Inspect connector for damage. Repair as necessary. Measure resistance between male half of in-line harness connector C292 terminal No. 5 (Light Blue/White wire) and DLC terminal No. 7 (Light Blue/White wire). If resistance is less than 5 ohms, repair open in Light Blue/White wire between RPSDM connector C352 and in-line harness connector C292. If resistance is 5 ohms or more, repair open in Light Blue/White wire between DLC and in-line harness connector C292.

TEST E: REMOTE KEYLESS ENTRY MODULE DOES NOT RESPOND TO NGS TESTER

NOTE: If repairs to a Module Communications Network circuit is required, see REPAIRING BUS WIRING. If module replacement is necessary, see REMOVAL & INSTALLATION.

1) Turn ignition switch to OFF position. Disconnect Remote Keyless Entry (RKE) module 12-pin harness connector C200. Inspect connector for damage. Repair as necessary. Connect RKE module 12-pin harness connector. Connect Next Generation Star (NGS) tester to Data Link Connector (DLC). Turn ignition switch to ON position. Perform data link diagnostic test. See DATA LINK DIAGNOSTIC TEST under COMMUNICATION NETWORK DIAGNOSTICS. If response was RKE (DDM): NO RESPONSE ON CKT914 (BUS+), go to next step. If response was RKE (DDM): NO RESPONSE ON CKT915 (BUS-), go to step **3)**.

2) Turn ignition switch to OFF position. Disconnect NGS tester and RKE module 12-pin harness connector C200. Measure resistance between RKE module harness connector C200 terminal No. 3 (Tan/Orange wire) and DLC terminal No. 2 (Tan/Orange wire). If resistance was less than 5 ohms, replace RKE. If resistance is 5 ohms or more, repair open in Tan/Orange wire between RKE module harness connector C200 and DLC.

3) Turn ignition switch to OFF position. Disconnect NGS tester and RKE module 12-pin harness connector C200. Measure resistance between RKE module harness connector C200 terminal No. 4 (Pink/Light Blue wire) and DLC terminal No. 10 (Pink/Light Blue wire). If resistance is less than 5 ohms, replace RKE. If resistance was 5 ohms or more, repair open in Pink/Light Blue wire between RKE module harness connector C200 and DLC.

TEST F: RESTRAINT CONTROL MODULE DOES NOT RESPOND TO NGS TESTER

NOTE: If repairs to a Module Communications Network circuit is required, see REPAIRING BUS WIRING. If module replacement is necessary, see REMOVAL & INSTALLATION.

1) Turn ignition switch to OFF position. Deactivate air bag system. See appropriate AIR BAG RESTRAINT SYSTEMS article. Disconnect Restraint Control Module (RCM) 26-pin harness connector. Inspect connector for damage. If connector is okay, go to next step. If connector is not okay, repair as necessary.

2) Turn ignition switch to OFF position. Measure resistance between RCM harness connector C231 terminal No. 5 (Light Blue/White wire) and Data Link Connector (DLC) terminal No. 7 (Light Blue/White wire). If resistance is less than 5 ohms, replace RCM. If resistance is 5 ohms or more, repair open in Light Blue/White wire between RCM harness connector C231 and DLC.

TEST G: REAR ELECTRONICS MODULE DOES NOT RESPOND TO NGS TESTER

NOTE: If repairs to a Module Communications Network circuit is required, see REPAIRING BUS WIRING. If module replacement is necessary, see REMOVAL & INSTALLATION.

1) Turn ignition switch to OFF position. Disconnect Rear Electronics Module (REM) 22-pin harness connector C341. Inspect connector for damage. Repair as necessary. Connect REM connector C341. Connect Next Generation Star (NGS) tester to Data Link Connector (DLC). Turn ignition switch to ON position. Perform data link diagnostic test. See DATA LINK DIAGNOSTIC TEST under COMMUNICATION NETWORK DIAGNOSTICS. If response was REM: NO RESPONSE ON CKT914 (BUS+), go to next step. If response was REM: NO RESPONSE ON CKT915 (BUS-), go to step **4**).

2) Turn ignition switch to OFF position. Disconnect NGS tester. Disconnect REM 22-pin harness connector C341. Measure resistance between REM harness connector C341 terminal No. 1 (Tan/Orange wire) and DLC terminal No. 2 (Tan/Orange wire). If resistance is 5 ohms or more, go to next step. If resistance is less than 5 ohms, replace REM.

3) Disconnect in-line 16-pin harness connector C292. Inspect connector for damage. Repair as necessary. Measure resistance between male half of in-line harness connector C292 terminal No. 4 (Tan/Orange wire) and DLC terminal No. 2 (Tan/Orange wire). If resistance is less than 5 ohms, repair open in Tan/Orange wire between in-line connector C292 and REM. If resistance is 5 ohms or more, repair open in Tan/Orange wire between in-line harness connector C292 and DLC.

4) Turn ignition switch to OFF position. Disconnect NGS tester. Disconnect REM 22-pin harness connector C341. Measure resistance between REM harness connector C341 terminal No. 2 (Pink/Light Blue wire) and DLC terminal No. 10 (Pink/Light Blue wire). If resistance is 5 ohms or more, go to next step. If resistance is less than 5 ohms, replace REM.

5) Disconnect in-line 16-pin harness connector C292. Inspect connector for damage. Repair as necessary. Measure resistance between male half of in-line harness connector C292 terminal No. 2 (Pink/Light Blue wire) and DLC terminal No.10 (Pink/Light Blue wire). If resistance is less than 5 ohms, repair open in Pink/Light Blue wire between in-line harness connector C292 and REM. If resistance is 5 ohms or more, repair open in Pink/Light Blue wire between in-line harness connector C292 and DLC.

TEST H: NEXT GENERATION SPEED CONTROL SERVO DOES NOT RESPOND TO NGS TESTER

NOTE: If repairs to a Module Communications Network circuit is required, see REPAIRING BUS WIRING. If module replacement is necessary, see REMOVAL & INSTALLATION.

1) Turn ignition switch to OFF position. Disconnect Next Generation Speed Control (NGSC) servo 10-pin harness connector C116. Inspect connector for damage. Repair as necessary. Connect NGSC servo harness connector C116. Connect NGS tester to Data Link Connector (DLC). Turn ignition switch to ON position. Perform data link diagnostic test. See DATA LINK DIAGNOSTIC TEST under COMMUNICATION NETWORK DIAGNOSTICS. If response is NGSC: NO RESPONSE ON CKT914 (BUS+), go to next step. If response is NGSC: NO RESPONSE ON CKT915 (BUS-), go to step **5**).

2) Turn ignition switch to OFF position. Disconnect NGS tester. Disconnect NGSC servo harness connector C116. Measure resistance between NGSC servo harness connector C116 terminal No. 1 (Tan/Orange wire) and DLC terminal No. 2 (Tan/Orange wire). If resistance is 5 ohms or more, go to next step. If resistance is less than 5 ohms, replace NGSC servo.

3) Disconnect in-line 16-pin harness connector C292. Inspect connector for damage. Repair as necessary. Measure resistance between male half of in-line harness connector C292 terminal No. 4 (Tan/Orange wire) and DLC terminal No. 2 (Tan/Orange wire). If resistance is less than 5 ohms, go to next step. If resistance is 5 ohms or more, repair open in Tan/Orange wire between in-line harness connector C292 and DLC.

4) Disconnect in-line 16-pin harness connector C180. Inspect connector for damage. Repair as necessary. Measure resistance between female half of harness connector C292 terminal No. 4 (Tan/Orange wire) and male half of in-line harness connector C180 (Tan/Orange wire). If resistance is less than 5 ohms, repair open in Tan/Orange wire between in-line harness connector C180 and NGSC servo harness connector C116. If resistance is 5 ohms or more, repair open in Tan/Orange wire between in-line harness connector C292 and in-line harness connector C180.

5) Turn ignition switch to OFF position. Disconnect NGS tester. Disconnect NGSC servo harness connector C116. Measure resistance between NGSC servo harness connector C116 terminal No. 2 (Pink/Light Blue wire) and DLC terminal No. 10 (Pink/Light Blue wire). If resistance is 5 ohms or more, go to next step. If resistance is less than 5 ohms, replace NGSC servo.

6) Disconnect in-line 16-pin harness connector C292. Inspect connector for damage. Repair as necessary. Measure resistance between male half of in-line harness connector C292 terminal No. 1 (Pink/Light Blue wire) and DLC terminal No. 10 (Pink/Light Blue wire). If resistance is less than 5 ohms, go to next step. If resistance is 5 ohms or more, repair open in Pink/Light Blue wire between in-line harness connector C292 and DLC.

7) Disconnect in-line 16-pin harness connector C180. Inspect connector for damage. Repair as necessary. Measure resistance between female half of in-line harness connector C292 terminal No. 1 (Pink/Light Blue wire) and male half of in-line harness connector C180 (Pink/Light Blue wire). If resistance is less than 5 ohms, repair open in Pink/Light Blue wire between in-line harness connector C180 and NGSC servo harness connector C116. If resistance is 5 ohms or more, repair open in Pink/Light Blue wire between in-line harness connector C292 and in-line harness connector C180.

TEST I: FRONT ELECTRONICS MODULE DOES NOT RESPOND TO NGS TESTER

NOTE: If repairs to a Module Communications Network circuit is required, see REPAIRING BUS WIRING. If module replacement is necessary, see REMOVAL & INSTALLATION.

1) Turn ignition switch to OFF position. Disconnect Front Electronics Module (FEM) 12-pin harness connector C190. Inspect connector for damage. Repair as necessary. Connect FEM 12-pin harness connector

C190. Connect Next Generation Star (NGS) tester to Data Link Connector (DLC). Turn ignition switch to ON position. Perform data link diagnostic test. See DATA LINK DIAGNOSTIC TEST under COMMUNICATION NETWORK DIAGNOSTICS. If response is FEM: NO RESPONSE ON CKT914 (BUS+), go to next step. If response is FEM: NO RESPONSE ON CKT915 (BUS-), go to step 5).

2) Turn ignition switch to OFF position. Disconnect NGS tester. Disconnect FEM 12-pin harness connector C190. Measure resistance between FEM harness connector C190 terminal No. 7 (Tan/Orange wire) and DLC terminal No. 2 (Tan/Orange wire). If resistance is 5 ohms or more, go to next step. If resistance is less than 5 ohms, replace FEM.

3) Disconnect in-line 16-pin harness connector C292. Inspect connector for damage. Repair as necessary. Measure resistance between male half of in-line harness connector C292 terminal No. 4 (Tan/Orange wire) and DLC terminal No. 2 (Tan/Orange wire). If resistance is less than 5 ohms, go to next step. If resistance is 5 ohms or more, repair open in Tan/Orange wire between in-line harness connector C292 and DLC.

4) Disconnect in-line 16-pin harness connector C180. Inspect connector for damage. Repair as necessary. Measure resistance between female half of harness connector C292 terminal No. 4 (Tan/Orange wire) and male half of in-line harness connector C180 terminal No. 4 (Tan/Orange wire). If resistance is less than 5 ohms, repair open in Tan/Orange wire between in-line harness connector C180 and FEM harness connector C190. If resistance is 5 ohms or more, repair open in Tan/Orange wire between in-line harness connector C292 and in-line harness connector C180.

5) Turn ignition switch to OFF position. Disconnect NGS tester. Disconnect FEM 12-pin harness connector C190. Measure resistance between FEM harness connector C190 terminal No. 1 (Pink/Light Blue wire) and DLC terminal No. 10 (Pink/Light Blue wire). If resistance is 5 ohms or more, go to next step. If resistance is less than 5 ohms, replace FEM.

6) Disconnect in-line 16-pin harness connector C292. Inspect connector for damage. Repair as necessary. Measure resistance between male half of in-line harness connector C292 terminal No. 1 (Pink/Light Blue wire) and DLC terminal No. 10 (Pink/Light Blue wire). If resistance is less than 5 ohms, go to next step. If resistance is 5 ohms or more, repair open in Pink/Light Blue wire between male half of in-line harness connector C292 and DLC.

7) Disconnect in-line 16-pin harness connector C180. Inspect connector for damage. Repair as necessary. Measure resistance between female half of harness connector C292 terminal No. 1 (Pink/Light Blue wire) and male half of in-line harness connector C180 (Pink/Light Blue wire). If resistance is less than 5 ohms, repair open in Pink/Light Blue wire between in-line harness connector C180 and FEM harness connector C190. If resistance is 5 ohms or more, repair open in Pink/Light Blue wire between in-line harness connector C292 and in-line harness connector C180.

TEST J: POWERTRAIN CONTROL MODULE DOES NOT RESPOND TO NGS TESTER

NOTE: If repairs to a Module Communications Network circuit is required, see REPAIRING BUS WIRING. If module replacement is necessary, see REMOVAL & INSTALLATION.

1) Turn ignition switch to OFF position. Disconnect Powertrain Control Module (PCM) 104-pin harness connector C103. Inspect connector for damage. Repair as necessary. Connect PCM harness connector C103. Connect Next Generation Star (NGS) tester to Data Link Connector (DLC). Turn ignition switch to ON position. Perform data link diagnostic test. See DATA LINK DIAGNOSTIC TEST under COMMUNICATION NETWORK DIAGNOSTICS. If response is PCM: NO RESPONSE ON CKT914 (BUS+), go to next step. If response is PCM: NO RESPONSE ON CKT915 (BUS-), go to step 6).

2) Turn ignition switch to OFF position. Disconnect NGS tester. Disconnect PCM 104-pin harness connector C103. Measure resistance between PCM harness connector C103 terminal No. 16 (Tan/Orange wire) and DLC terminal No. 2 (Tan/Orange wire). If resistance is 5 ohms or more, go to next step. If resistance is less than 5 ohms, replace PCM.

3) Disconnect in-line 16-pin harness connector C292. Inspect connector for damage. Repair as necessary. Measure resistance between male half of in-line harness connector C292 terminal No. 4 (Tan/Orange wire) and DLC terminal No. 2 (Tan/Orange wire). If resistance is less than 5 ohms, go to next step. If resistance is 5 ohms or more, repair open in Tan/Orange wire between in-line harness connector C292 and DLC.

4) Disconnect in-line 16-pin harness connector C180. Inspect connector for damage. Repair as necessary. Measure resistance between female half of harness connector C292 terminal No. 4 (Tan/Orange wire) and male half of in-line harness connector C180 terminal No. 4 (Tan/Orange wire). If resistance is less than 5 ohms, go to next step. If resistance is 5 ohms or more, repair open in Tan/Orange wire between in-line harness connector C292 and in-line harness connector C180.

5) Disconnect in-line 42-pin harness connector C100. Inspect connector for damage. Repair as necessary. Measure resistance between female half of harness connector C100 terminal No. 18 (Tan/Orange wire) and female half of harness connector C180 terminal No. 4 (Tan/Orange wire). If resistance is less than 5 ohms, repair open in Tan/Orange wire between in-line harness connector C100 and PCM harness connector C103. If resistance is 5 ohms or more, repair open in Tan/Orange wire between in-line harness connector C100 and in-line harness connector C180.

6) Turn ignition switch to OFF position. Disconnect NGS tester. Disconnect PCM 104-pin harness connector C103. Measure resistance between PCM harness connector C103 terminal No. 15 (Pink/Light Blue wire) and DLC terminal No. 10 (Pink/Light Blue wire). If resistance is 5 ohms or more, go to next step. If resistance is less than 5 ohms, replace PCM.

7) Disconnect in-line 16-pin harness connector C292. Inspect connector for damage. Repair as necessary. Measure resistance between male half of in-line harness connector C292 terminal No. 2 (Pink/Light Blue wire) and DLC terminal No. 10 (Pink/Light Blue wire). If resistance is less than 5 ohms, go to next step. If resistance is 5 ohms or more, repair open in Pink/Light Blue wire between in-line harness connector C292 and DLC.

8) Disconnect in-line 16-pin harness connector C180. Inspect connector for damage. Repair as necessary. Measure resistance between female half of harness connector C292 terminal No. 2 (Pink/Light Blue wire) and male half of in-line harness connector C180 terminal No. 6 (Pink/Light Blue wire). If resistance is less than 5 ohms, go to next step. If resistance is 5 ohms or more, repair open in Pink/Light Blue wire between in-line harness connector C292 and in-line harness connector C180.

9) Disconnect in-line 42-pin harness connector C100. Inspect connector for damage. Repair as necessary. Measure resistance between female half of harness connector C100 terminal No. 17 (Pink/Light Blue wire) and female half of harness connector C180 terminal No. 6 (Pink/Light Blue wire). If resistance is less than 5 ohms, repair open in Pink/Light Blue wire between in-line harness connector C100 and PCM harness connector C103. If resistance is 5 ohms or more, repair open in Pink/Light Blue wire between in-line harness connector C100 and in-line harness connector C180.

TEST K: INSTRUMENT CLUSTER DOES NOT RESPOND TO NGS TESTER

NOTE: If repairs to a Module Communications Network circuit is required, see REPAIRING BUS WIRING. If module replacement is necessary, see REMOVAL & INSTALLATION.

1) Turn ignition switch to OFF position. Disconnect instrument cluster 22-pin harness connector C241. Inspect connector for damage. Repair as necessary. Connect instrument cluster harness connector C241. Connect Next Generation Star (NGS) tester to Data Link Connector (DLC). Turn ignition switch to ON position. Perform data link diagnostic test. See DATA LINK DIAGNOSTIC TEST under COMMUNICATION NETWORK DIAGNOSTICS. If response is ICM: NO RESPONSE ON CKT914 (BUS+) or MCM: NO RESPONSE ON CKT914 (BUS+), go to next step. If response is either ICM: NO RESPONSE ON CKT914 (BUS+) or MCM: NO RESPONSE ON CKT914 (BUS+), replace instrument cluster. If response is ICM: NO RESPONSE ON CKT915 (BUS-)

and MCM: NO RESPONSE ON CKT915 (BUS-), go to step **3**). If response is either ICM: NO RESPONSE ON CKT915 (BUS-) or MCM: NO RESPONSE ON CKT915 (BUS-), replace instrument cluster.

2) Turn ignition switch to OFF position. Disconnect NGS tester. Disconnect instrument cluster 22-pin harness connector C241. Measure resistance between instrument cluster harness connector C241 terminal No. 16 (Tan/Orange wire) and DLC terminal No. 2 (Tan/Orange wire). If resistance is less than 5 ohms, replace instrument cluster. If resistance is 5 ohms or more, repair open in Tan/Orange wire between instrument cluster harness connector C241 and DLC.

3) Turn ignition switch to OFF position. Disconnect NGS tester. Disconnect instrument cluster 22-pin harness connector C241. Measure resistance between instrument cluster harness connector C241 terminal No. 17 (Pink/Light Blue wire) and DLC terminal No. 10 (Pink/Light Blue wire). If resistance is less than 5 ohms, replace instrument cluster. If resistance is 5 ohms or more, repair open in Pink/Light Blue wire between instrument cluster harness connector C241 and DLC.

TEST L: NO MODULE/NETWORK COMMUNICATION – ISO 9141

NOTE: Depending on module configuration, with all modules connected and with ignition switch in RUN position or with engine running 2-3 volts may be present at Data Link Connector (DLC) terminal No. 7 (Light Blue/White wire). This is the International Standards Organization (ISO) 9141 diagnostic communications network circuit.

NOTE: If repairs to a Module Communications Network circuit is required, see REPAIRING BUS WIRING. If module replacement is necessary, see REMOVAL & INSTALLATION.

1) Turn ignition switch to OFF position. Inspect Data Link Connector (DLC) terminal No. 7 for damage. If DLC is okay, go to next step. If DLC is damaged, repair as necessary.

2) Turn ignition switch to OFF position. Deactivate air bag system. See appropriate AIR BAG RESTRAINT SYSTEMS article. Disconnect Restraint Control Module (RCM) 26-pin harness connector C231. Inspect connector for damage. Repair as necessary. Measure resistance between RCM harness connector C231 terminal No. 5 (Light Blue/White wire) and DLC terminal No. 7 (Light Blue/White wire). If resistance is less than 5 ohms and vehicle is equipped with Parking Aid Module (PAM) or Right Power Sliding Door Module (RPSDM), go to next step. If resistance is less than 5 ohms and vehicle is only equipped with RCM, go to step **14**). If resistance 5 ohms or more, repair open in Light Blue/White wire between RCM harness connector C231 and DLC.

3) Turn ignition switch to ON position. Measure voltage between DLC terminals No. 7 (Light Blue/White wire) and No. 4 (Black wire). Also, measure voltage between DLC terminals No. 7 (Light Blue/White wire) and No. 16 (Light Blue/White wire). If voltage is present at either measurement and vehicle is equipped with PAM only, go to next step. If voltage is present at either measurement and vehicle is equipped with RPSDM or Left Power Sliding Door Module (LPSDM), go to step **7**). If voltage is present at either measurement and vehicle is equipped with RPSDM and PAM, go to step **12**). If voltage is not present at both measurements, replace RCM.

4) Turn ignition switch to OFF position. Disconnect PAM 26-pin harness connector C445. Turn ignition switch to ON position. Measure voltage between DLC terminals No. 7 (Light Blue/White wire) and No. 4 (Black wire). Also, measure voltage between DLC terminals No. 7 (Light Blue/White wire) and No. 16 (Light Blue/White wire). If voltage is present at either measurement, go to next step. If voltage is not present at both measurement, replace PAM.

5) Turn ignition switch to OFF position. Disconnect in-line 14-pin harness connector C432. Turn ignition switch to ON position. Measure voltage between DLC terminals No. 7 (Light Blue/White wire) and No. 4 (Black wire). Also, measure voltage between DLC terminals No. 7 (Light Blue/White wire) and No. 16 (Light Blue/White wire). If voltage is present

at either measurement, go to next step. If voltage is not present at both measurements, repair open in Light Blue/White wire between PAM and in-line harness connector C432.

6) Turn ignition switch to OFF position. Disconnect in-line 16-pin harness connector C292. Turn ignition switch to ON position. Measure voltage between DLC terminals No. 7 (Light Blue/White wire) and No. 4 (Black wire). Also, measure voltage between DLC terminals No. 7 (Light Blue/White wire) and No. 16 (Light Blue/White wire). If voltage is present at either measurement, repair short to ground or voltage in Light Blue/White wire between DLC and male half of in-line harness connector C292. If voltage is not present at both measurements, repair short to ground or voltgae in Light Blue/White wire between in-line harness connector C432 and in-line harness connector C292.

7) If vehicle is not equipped with LPSDM, go to next step. If vehicle is equipped with LPSDM, go to step **10**).

8) Turn ignition switch to OFF position. Disconnect RPSDM 12-pin harness connector C352. Turn ignition switch to ON position. Measure voltage between DLC terminals No. 7 (Light Blue/White wire) and No. 4 (Black wire). Also, measure voltage between DLC terminals No. 7 (Light Blue/White wire) and No. 16 (Light Blue/White wire). If voltage is present at either measurement, go to next step. If voltage is not present at both measurements, replace RPSDM.

9) Turn ignition switch to OFF position. Disconnect in-line 16-pin harness connector C292. Turn ignition switch to ON position. Measure voltage between DLC terminals No. 7 (Light Blue/White wire) and No. 4 (Black wire). Also, measure voltage between DLC terminals No. 7 (Light Blue/White wire) and No. 16 (Light Blue/White wire). If voltage is more than 10 volts, repair open in Light Blue/White wire between DLC and male half of in-line harness connector C292. If voltage is 10 volts or less, repair short to ground between RPSDM C352, LPSDM C355 (if equipped), in-line harness connector C432 (if equipped with PAM) and in-line harness connector C292.

10) Turn ignition switch to OFF position. Disconnect RPSDM 12-pin harness connector C352. Turn ignition switch to ON position. Measure voltage between DLC terminals No. 7 (Light Blue/White wire) and No. 4 (Black wire). Also, measure voltage between DLC terminals No. 7 (Light Blue/White wire) and No. 16 (Light Blue/White wire). If voltage is present at either measurement, go to next step. If voltage is not present at both measurements, replace RPSDM.

11) Turn ignition switch to OFF position. Disconnect LPSDM 12-pin harness connector C355. Turn ignition switch to ON position. Measure voltage between DLC terminals No. 7 (Light Blue/White wire) and No. 4 (Black wire). Also, measure voltage between DLC terminals No. 7 (Light Blue/White wire) and No. 16 (Light Blue/White wire). If voltage is present at either measurement, go to step **9**). If voltage is not present at both measurements, replace LPSDM.

12) Turn ignition switch to OFF position. Disconnect PAM 26-pin connector C445. Turn ignition switch to ON position. Measure voltage between DLC terminals No. 7 (Light Blue/White wire) and No. 4 (Black wire). Also, measure voltage between DLC terminals No. 7 (Light Blue/White wire) and No. 16 (Light Blue/White wire). If voltage is present at either measurement, go to next step. If voltage is not present at both measurements, replace PAM.

13) Turn ignition switch to OFF position. Disconnect in-line 14-pin harness connector C432. Turn ignition switch to ON position. Measure voltage between DLC terminals No. 7 (Light Blue/White wire) and No. 4 (Black wire). Also, measure voltage between DLC terminals No. 7 (Light Blue/White wire) and No. 16 (Light Blue/White wire). If voltage is present at either measurement, go to step **7**). If voltage is not present at both measurements, repair short to ground or voltage between PAM and in-line harness connector C432.

14) Turn ignition switch to ON position. Measure voltage between DLC terminals No. 7 (Light Blue/White wire) and No. 4 (Black wire). Also measure voltage between DLC terminals No. 7 (Light Blue/White wire) and No. 16 (Light Blue/White wire). If voltage is present at either measurement, repair short to ground or voltage between DLC and RCM. If voltage is not present at both measurements, replace RCM.

TEST M: NO MODULE/NETWORK COMMUNICATION – SCP DATA BUS

NOTE: Depending on module configuration, with all modules connected and with ignition switch in RUN position or with engine running 2-3 volts may be present at Data Link Connector (DLC) terminals No. 2 (Tan/Orange wire) and No. 10 (Pink/Light Blue wire). These are the Standard Corporate Protocol (SCP) diagnostic communications network circuits.

NOTE: If repairs to a Module Communications Network circuit is required, see REPAIRING BUS WIRING. If module replacement is necessary, see REMOVAL & INSTALLATION.

1) Inspect NGS tester terminals for damage. If terminals are okay, go to next step. If terminals are not okay, repair as necessary.

2) Turn ignition switch to OFF position. Inspect Data Link Connector (DLC) terminals for damage. If terminals are okay, go to next step. If terminals are not okay, repair as necessary.

3) Turn ignition switch to OFF position. Disconnect Next Generation Speed Control (NGSC) servo 10-pin harness connector C116. Measure resistance between NGSC servo harness connector C116 terminal No. 1 (Tan/Orange wire) and DLC terminal No. 2 (Tan/Orange wire). Also, measure resistance between NGSC servo harness connector C116 terminal No. 2 (Pink/Light Blue wire) and DLC terminal No. 10 (Pink/Light Blue wire). If resistances are less than 5 ohms, go to next step. If either resistance is 5 ohms or more, repair open in Tan/Orange wire and/or Pink/Light Blue wire.

4) Connect NGS tester to DLC. Turn ignition switch to ON position. Perform data link diagnostic test. See DATA LINK DIAGNOSTIC TEST. If all modules equipped on vehicle pass test, go to next step. If all modules equipped on vehicle pass, except NGSC servo, replace NGSC servo.

5) Turn ignition switch to OFF position. Disconnect in-line 16-pin harness connector C180. Turn ignition switch to ON position. Perform data link diagnostic test. See DATA LINK DIAGNOSTIC TEST. If all modules equipped on vehicle pass, except NGSC servo and anti-lock brake control module, connect connector C180 and go to next step. If all modules equipped on vehicle pass test, connect connector C180 and go to step 10).

6) Turn ignition switch to OFF position. Disconnect anti-lock brake control module 25-pin harness connector C111. Turn ignition switch to ON position. Perform data link diagnostic test. See DATA LINK DIAGNOSTIC TEST. If all modules equipped on vehicle pass test, go to next step. If all modules equipped on vehicle pass, except NGSC servo and anti-lock brake control module, replace anti-lock brake control module.

7) Turn ignition switch to OFF position. Disconnect Powertrain Control Module (PCM) 104-pin harness connector C103. Turn ignition switch to ON position. Perform data link diagnostic test. See DATA LINK DIAGNOSTIC TEST. If all modules equipped on vehicle pass test, go to next step. If all modules equipped on vehicle pass, except NGSC servo, PCM and anti-lock brake control module, replace PCM. See appropriate REMOVAL, OVERHAUL & INSTALLATION article in ENGINE PERFORMANCE in appropriate MITCHELL® manual.

8) Turn ignition switch to OFF position. Disconnect in-line 42-pin harness connector C100. Turn ignition switch to ON position. Perform data link diagnostic test. See DATA LINK DIAGNOSTIC TEST. If Front Electronics Module (FEM) does not pass test, go to next step. If FEM passes test, repair Tan/Orange wire if damaged and/or Pink/Light Blue wire if damaged, between in-line male connector C100 and PCM.

9) Turn ignition switch to OFF position. Disconnect FEM 12-pin harness connector C190. Turn ignition switch to ON position. Perform data link diagnostic test. See DATA LINK DIAGNOSTIC TEST. If all modules equipped on vehicle pass, except NGSC servo, PCM, FEM and anti-lock brake control module, replace FEM. If all modules equipped on vehicle pass, repair Tan/Orange wire and/or Pink/Light Blue wire if damaged, between in-line female connector C100, anti-lock brake control module, FEM and in-line female connector C180.

10) Turn ignition switch to OFF position. Disconnect Rear Electronics Module (REM) 22-pin harness connector C341. Turn ignition switch to ON position. Perform data link diagnostic test. See DATA LINK DIAGNOSTIC TEST. If all modules on vehicle pass test, go to next step. If all modules on vehicle pass test, except NGSC servo and REM, replace REM.

11) Turn ignition switch to OFF position. Disconnect in-line 16-pin harness connector C292. Turn ignition switch to ON position. Perform data link diagnostic test. See DATA LINK DIAGNOSTIC TEST. If instrument cluster does not pass test, reconnect connector C292 and go to next step. If instrument cluster passes test, repair Tan/Orange wire and/or Pink/Light Blue wire if damaged, between in-line female connector C292, REM and in-line male connector C180.

12) Turn ignition switch to OFF position. Disconnect instrument cluster 22-pin harness connector C241. Turn ignition switch to ON position. Perform data link diagnostic test. See DATA LINK DIAGNOSTIC TEST. If all modules on vehicle pass test and vehicle is equipped with Remote Keyless Entry (RKE), go to next step. If all modules on vehicle pass test and vehicle is not equipped with RKE, repair Tan/Orange wire and/or Pink/Light Blue wire if damaged, between in-line male connector C292, instrument cluster and DLC. If all modules on vehicle pass test, except instrument cluster and message center (if equipped), NGSC servo and REM, replace instrument cluster.

13) Turn ignition switch to OFF position. Disconnect RKE 12-pin harness connector C200. Turn ignition switch to ON position. Perform data link diagnostic test. See DATA LINK DIAGNOSTIC TEST. If all modules on vehicle pass test, except RKE, NGSC servo, REM and instrument cluster, replace RKE. If all modules on vehicle pass test, repair Tan/Orange wire and/or Pink/Light Blue wire if damaged, between in-line male connector C292, RKE, instrument cluster and DLC.

TEST N: NO MODULE/NETWORK COMMUNICATION – NO POWER TO NGS TESTER

1) Inspect NGS tester terminals for damage. If terminals are okay, go to next step. If terminals are not okay repair as necessary.

2) Turn ignition switch to OFF position. Inspect Data Link Connector (DLC) terminals for damage. If terminals are okay, go to next step. If terminals are not okay, repair as necessary.

3) Measure voltage between DLC terminal No. 16 (Light Blue/White wire) and ground. If voltage is more than 10 volts, go to next step. If voltage is 10 volts or less, repair open in Light Blue/White wire between DLC and Fuse Junction Box (FJB).

4) Measure resistance between DLC terminal No. 4 (Black wire) and ground. Also, measure resistance between DLC terminal No. 5 (Black/White wire) and ground. If resistances are less than 5 ohms, check NGS tester. If resistance is 5 ohms or more, repair open in Black wire and/or Black/White wire.

DIAGNOSTIC TROUBLE CODE (DTC) DEFINITIONS

ANTI-LOCK BRAKE SYSTEM MODULE DTC INDEX

DTC	Description	Test
B1317	Battery Voltage High	1
B1318	Battery Voltage Low	1
B1342	ECU Defective	2
B2477	Module Configuration Failure	3
C1095	ABS Hydraulic Pump Motor Circuit Failure	1

ANTI-LOCK BRAKE SYSTEM MODULE DTC INDEX (Cont.)

DTC	Description	Test
		1
C1096	ABS Hydraulic Pump Motor Circuit Open	1
C1103	Hydraulic Brake Switch Circuit Failure	1
C1115	Power Relay Short To Voltage	1
C1145	Right Front Wheel Speed Input Circuit Failure	1
C1155	Left Front Wheel Speed Input Circuit Failure	1
C1165	Right Rear Wheel Speed Input Circuit Failure	1
C1175	Left Rear Wheel Speed Input Circuit Failure	1
C1184	ABS System Time-out	1
C1185	Power Relay Output Circuit Failure	1
C1194	Left Front Dump Valve Circuit Failure	1
C1198	Left Front Isolation Valve Circuit Failure	1
C1210	Right Front Dump Valve Circuit Failure	1
C1214	Right Front Isolation Valve Circuit Failure	1
C1233	Left Front Wheel Speed Sensor Signal Missing Or Erratic	1
C1234	Right Front Wheel Speed Sensor Signal Missing Or Erratic	1
C1235	Right Rear Wheel Speed Sensor Signal Missing Or Erratic	1
C1236	Left Rear Wheel Speed Sensor Signal Missing Or Erratic	1
C1242	Left Rear Dump Valve Circuit Failure	1
C1246	Right Rear Dump Valve Circuit Failure	1
C1250	Left Rear Isolation Valve Circuit Failure	1
C1254	Right Rear Isolation Valve Circuit Failure	4
C1404	Right Front Traction Control Valve Circuit Failure	4
C1410	Left Front Traction Control Valve Circuit Failure	5
C1446	Brake Pedal Position (BPP)	6
U1009	Invalid Or Missing Data For Engine Torque	6
U1027	Invalid Or Missing Data For Engine RPM	6
U1059	Invalid Or Missing Data For Transaxle/Gear Position	

[1] – Repair anti-lock brake system concern. See appropriate ANTI-LOCK article in BRAKES in appropriate MITCHELL® manual.
[2] – Using NGS tester, perform Anti-Lock Brake System (ABS) module self-test. If DTC B1342 is retrieved again, replace ABS module.
[3] – Program ABS module. See MODULE CONFIGURATION under PROGRAMMING.
[4] – Replace anti-lock brake control module. See ANTI-LOCK BRAKE CONTROL MODULE under REMOVAL & INSTALLATION.
[5] – See AUTOLAMP SYSTEMS – WINDSTAR article for testing procedure.
[6] – Using NGS tester, perform Powertrain Control Module (PCM) self-test.

FRONT ELECTRONIC MODULE DTC INDEX

DTC	Description	Test
		1
B1241	Wiper Washer Rear Pump Relay Circuit Short To Voltage	2
B1243	Express Window Down Switch Circuit Short To Voltage	1
B1244	Wiper Rear Motor Run Relay Circuit Failure	1
B1245	Wiper Rear Motor Run Relay Circuit Short To Voltage	3
B1254	Air Temperature External Sensor Circuit Failure	4
B1294	Battery Power Relay Circuit Short To Voltage	2
B1304	Accessory Delay Relay Coil Circuit Short To Voltage	3
B1308	Oil Level Switch Circuit Short To Ground	5
B1309	Power Door Lock Circuit Short To Ground	6
B1319	Driver's Door Ajar Circuit Failure	6
B1327	Passenger's Door Ajar Circuit Failure	5
B1341	Power Door Unlock Circuit Short To Ground	7
B1342	ECU Defective	2
B1404	Driver's Power Window Down Circuit Open	2
B1405	Driver's Power Window Down Circuit Short To Voltage	2
B1407	Driver's Power Window Up Circuit Open	2
B1408	Driver's Power Window Up Circuit Short To Voltage	1
B1431	Wiper Brake/Run Relay Circuit Failure	1
B1432	Wiper Brake/Run Relay Circuit Short To Voltage	1
B1436	Wiper Hi/Low Speed Relay Coil Circuit Short To Voltage	1
B1438	Wiper Mode Select Switch Circuit Failure	1
B1446	Wiper Park Sense Circuit Failure	1
B1448	Wiper Park Sense Circuit Short To Voltage	1
B1450	Wiper Wash/Delay Switch Circuit Failure	1
B1460	Wiper Washer Pump Motor Relay Coil Circuit Short To Voltage	3
B1462	Seat Belt Switch Circuit Failure	3
B1482	Wiper Washer Fluid Level Sensor Circuit Short To Ground	4
B1499	Left Turn Signal Circuit Failure	4
B1501	Left Turn Signal Circuit Short To Voltage	4
B1503	Right Turn Signal Circuit Failure	4
B1505	Right Turn Signal Circuit Short To Voltage	8
B1519	Hood Switch Circuit Failure	9
B1558	Ignition Run/Start Circuit Short To Ground	1
B1611	Wiper Rear Mode Select Switch Circuit Failure	

FRONT ELECTRONIC MODULE DTC INDEX (Cont.)

DTC	Description	Test
B1676	Battery Pack Voltage Out Of Range	10
B1833	Door Unlock Disarm Switch Circuit Short To Ground	8
B2473	Passenger's Door Disarm Switch Circuit Short To Ground	8
B2474	Passenger's Door Lock Switch Circuit Short To Ground	5
B2475	Passenger's Door Unlock Switch Circuit Short To Ground	5
B2477	Module Configuration Failure	11
B2479	Brake Park Switch Circuit Short To Ground	3
B2480	Left Front Corner Lamp Output Circuit Short To Voltage	4
B2482	Right Front Corner Lamp Output Circuit Short To Voltage	4
B2491	Right Front Park Lamp Output Circuit Short To Voltage	4
B2493	Left Front Park Lamp Output Circuit Short To Voltage	4
B2496	Anti Theft Horn Output Circuit Short To Ground	8
B2499	Courtesy Lamp Output Failure – Stepwell/Puddle Lamps [12]	6
B2500	Courtesy Lamp Output Circuit Short To Voltage	6
B2501	Left Front Low Beam Circuit Failure	4
B2502	Left Front Low Beam Circuit Short To Voltage	4
B2503	Right Front Low Beam Circuit Failure	4
B2504	Right Front Low Beam Circuit Short To Voltage	4
B2505	Left Front High Beam Circuit Failure	4
B2506	Left Front High Beam Circuit Short To Voltage	4
B2507	Right Front High Beam Circuit Failure	4
B2508	Right Front High Beam Circuit Short To Voltage	4
B2510	Main Blower Motor Relay Circuit Short To Voltage	13
B2511	Horn Output Relay Circuit Short To Voltage	6
B2595	Anti-Theft Input Signal Circuit Failure	8
C1189	Brake Fluid Level Sensor Input Short Circuit To Ground	3
U1041	SCP Invalid Or Missing Data For Vehicle Speed	14
U1059	SCP Invalid Or Missing Data For Transaxle/PRNDL	15
U1135	SCP Invalid Or Missing Data For Ignition Switch/Starter	16
U1178	SCP Invalid Or Missing Data For Climate Control (HVAC)	16
U1262	SCP Communication Bus Fault	M

[1] – See WIPER/WASHER SYSTEMS – WINDSTAR article for testing procedure.
[2] – See POWER WINDOWS – WINDSTAR article for testing procedure.
[3] – See ANALOG INSTRUMENT PANELS – WINDSTAR article for testing procedure.
[4] – See AUTOLAMP SYSTEMS – WINDSTAR article for testing procedure.
[5] – Repair appropriate circuit as necessary. See appropriate wiring diagram in POWER DOOR LOCKS article.
[6] – See appropriate wiring diagram in ILLUMINATION/INTERIOR LIGHTS article.
[7] – Using NGS tester, perform Front Electronic Module (FEM) self-test. If DTC B1342 is retrieved again, replace FEM module.
[8] – See ACTIVE ANTI-THEFT SYSTEMS – WINDSTAR article for testing procedures.
[9] – See STEERING COLUMN SWITCHES – WINDSTAR article for testing procedures.
[10] – Check charging system. See appropriate GENERATORS article in STARTING & CHARGING SYSTEMS. If charging system is okay, check power and ground circuits to Front Electronic Module (FEM). See appropriate wiring diagram in POWER DISTRIBUTION article in WIRING DIAGRAMS.
[11] – See MODULE CONFIGURATION under PROGRAMMING.
[12] – DTC will be recorded if vehicle is not equipped with stepwell/puddle lamps. Check vehicle for these options.
[13] – Repair A/C system as necessary. See appropriate AUTOMATIC A/C-HEATER SYSTEMS article in appropriate MITCHELL® AIR CONDITIONING & HEATING SERVICE & REPAIR manual.
[14] – Using NGS tester, perform Anti-lock Brake System (ABS) self-test.
[15] – Using NGS tester, perform Powertrain Control Module (PCM) self-test.
[16] – Using NGS tester, perform Instrument Cluster Module (ICM) self-test.

INSTRUMENT CLUSTER DTC INDEX

DTC	Description	Test
B1202	Fuel Sender Circuit Open	1
B1204	Fuel Sender Circuit Short To Ground	1
B1205	ICM Switch 1 Assembly Circuit Failure (Open Or Short To Voltage)	1
B1213	Number Of Programmed Ignition Keys Is Below Minimum	2
B1232	Antenna Not Connected Defective Transceiver	2
B1246	Dim Panel Potentiometer Switch Circuit Failure	3
B1249	Blend Door Failure	4
B1342	ECU Defective	5
B1346	Heated Backlite Input Circuit Short To Ground	6
B1352	Ignition Key-In Circuit Failure	3
B1470	Headlamp Input Circuit Failure	7
B1600	PATS Ignition Key Transponder Signal Is Not Received – Non PATS Key Or Damaged Key	2
B1601	PATS Received Incorrect Key-Code From Ignition Key Transponder – Unprogrammed Encoded Ignition Key	2
B1602	PATS Received Invalid Format Of Key-Code From Ignition Key Transponder – Partial Key Read	2
B1676	Battery Voltage Out Of Range	3
B1681	PATS Transceiver Signal Is Not Received – Not Connected, Damaged Or Damaged Wiring	2
B1875	Turn Signal/Hazard Switch Signal Circuit Failure	7

INSTRUMENT CLUSTER DTC INDEX (Cont.)

DTC	Description	Test
B2103	Antenna Not Connected Defective Transceiver	2
B2139	PCM ID Does Not Match Between Instrument Cluster & PCM	8
B2141	NVM Configuration Failure – No PCM ID Exchanged Between Instrument Cluster & PCM	2
B2175	A/C Signal Circuit Short To Ground	4
B2176	Overdrive Switch Circuit Short To Voltage	9
B2472	Fog Lamp Switch Failure	7
B2477	Module Configuration Failure	10
B2513	Blower (Fan) Circuit Failure	4
B2586	Headlamp Mode Circuit Failure	7
C1779	Blower Switch Failure	4
U1041	SCP Invalid Or Missing Data For Vehicle Speed	11
U1043	SCP Invalid Or Missing Data For Traction Control	12
U1051	SCP Invalid Or Missing Data For Brakes	12
U1073	SCP Invalid Or Missing Data For Brakes	11
U1123	SCP Invalid Or Missing Data For Engine Coolant	12
U1131	SCP Invalid Or Missing Data For Fuel System	3
U1147	Invalid Or Missing Data For Vehicle Security	2
U1262	Missing SCP Message	M
U2013	Compass Module – No Response	1

[1] – See ANALOG INSTRUMENT PANELS – WINDSTAR article for testing procedure.
[2] – See PASSIVE ANTI-THEFT SYSTEMS – WINDSTAR article for testing procedure.
[3] – See ANALOG INSTRUMENT PANELS – WINDSTAR article for testing procedure.
[4] – Repair A/C system as necessary. See appropriate AUTOMATIC A/C-HEATER SYSTEMS article in appropriate MITCHELL® AIR CONDITIONING & HEATING SERVICE & REPAIR manual for testing procedure.
[5] – Using NGS tester, perform instrument cluster self-test. If DTC B1342 is retrieved again, replace instrument cluster.
[6] – See POWER WINDOWS – WINDSTAR article for testing procedure.
[7] – See AUTOLAMP SYSTEMS – WINDSTAR article for testing procedure.
[8] – See ACTIVE ANTI-THEFT SYSTEMS – WINDSTAR article for testing procedure.
[9] – See FORD AX4S ELECTRONIC CONTROLS article in AUTOMATIC TRANSMISSIONS in appropriate MITCHELL® TRANSMISSION SERVICE & REPAIR manual for testing procedure.
[10] – See MODULE CONFIGURATION under PROGRAMMING.
[11] – Using NGS tester, perform PCM self-test.
[12] – Using NGS tester, perform ABS/Traction Control self-test.

LEFT POWER SLIDING DOOR MODULE DTC INDEX

DTC	Description	Test
B1342	ECU Defective	1
B2238	Broken Cable Detected	2
B2270	PSD Exceeded Time Allowed To Cinch Door [3]	2
B2271	PSD Did Not Reach Full Open Position During Self-Test	2
B2362	Remote Key Fob Open/Close Signal Circuit Short To Ground	2
B2363	Position Sensor System Failure	2
B2364	Fuel Filler Door Open Circuit	2
B2365	"B" Pillar Power Sliding Door Open/Close Switch Circuit Short To Ground	2
B2366	Power Sliding Door Open/Close Switch Circuit Short To Ground	2
B2374	Power Sliding Door Latch Switch Circuit Short To Ground	2
B2483	Enable Signal Open Circuit (Park)	2
B2589	No Power Sliding Door Latch Switch Detected On Closing & Door Reversed	2
B2591	No Power Sliding Door Latch Switch Detected On Unlatch	2
B2592	Door Not Pulled Into Primary During Power Close & High Duty Cycles	2
B2593	Door Reversed While Closing Due To An Obstacle	2
B2594	No Movement Detected After An Unlatch During Power Open Operation	2
B2603	Power Sliding Door Not Fully Closed During Power Close During Self-Test When Pulled To Primary Latch Position.	2
B2604	Power Sliding Door On/Off Switch Open Circuit	2
B2605	Disable Signal Open Circuit – Vehicle Speed Over 6 MPH	2

[1] – Using NGS tester, perform Left Power Sliding Door Module (LPSDM) self-test. If DTC B1342 is retrieved again, replace LPSDM.
[2] – See POWER SLIDING DOORS – WINDSTAR article for testing procedure.
[3] – Exceeded the time allowed to reach primary latch position after reaching secondary latch position.

MESSAGE CENTER MODULE (MCM) DTC INDEX

DTC	Description	Test
B1205	Message Center Compass Inoperative	1
B1342	ECU Defective	2
B1676	Battery Voltage Out Of Range	1
B2477	Module Configuration Failure	3
U1073	Invalid Or Missing Data For Engine Coolant	4
U1097	Invalid Or Missing Data For Fuel Flow	5
U1131	Invalid Or Missing Data For Fuel Level	6
U1222	Invalid Or Missing Data For Backlighting Intesity	

MESSAGE CENTER MODULE (MCM) DTC INDEX (Cont.)

DTC	Description	Test
U2013	Message Center Compass Inoperative	1

[1] – See ANALOG INSTRUMENT PANELS – WINDSTAR article for testing procedures.
[2] – Using NGS tester, perform Message Center Module (MCM) self-test. If DTC B1342 is retrieved again, replace instrument cluster.
[3] – See MODULE CONFIGURATION under PROGRAMMING.
[4] – Using NGS tester, perform Powertrain Control Module (PCM) self-test.
[5] – Using NGS tester, perform Rear Electronics Module (REM) self-test.
[6] – Using NGS tester, perform Instrument Cluster Module (ICM) self-test.

PARKING AID MODULE DTC INDEX

DTC	Description	Test
B1299	Power Supply Sensor Circuit Short To Ground	1
B1342	Defective ECU	2
B2373	LED #1 Circuit Short To Voltage	1
B2477	Module Configuration Failure	3
C1699	Left Rear Sensor Short To Voltage	1
C1700	Left Rear Sensor Circuit Failure	1
C1701	Left Rear Sensor Circuit Fault	1
C1702	Right Rear Sensor Short To Voltage	1
C1703	Right Rear Sensor Circuit Failure	1
C1704	Right Rear Sensor Circuit Fault	1
C1705	Left Rear Center Sensor Circuit Short To Voltage	1
C1706	Left Rear Center Sensor Circuit Failure	1
C1707	Left Rear Center Sensor Fault	1
C1708	Right Rear Center Sensor Circuit Short To Voltage	1
C1709	Right Rear Center Sensor Circuit Failure	1
C1710	Right Rear Center Sensor Fault	1
C1742	Rear Sounder Circuit Failure	1
C1743	Rear Sounder Circuit Short To Voltage	1
C1748	Switch Input Circuit Short To Ground	1
C1902	LED #1 Circuit Failure	1

[1] – See PARKING AID SYSTEM – WINDSTAR article for testing procedure.
[2] – Using NGS tester, perform Parking Aid Module (PAM) self-test. If DTC B1342 is retrieved again, replace PAM.
[3] – See MODULE CONFIGURATION under PROGRAMMING.

REAR ELECTRONIC MODULE DTC INDEX

DTC	Description	Test
B1201	Fuel Sender Circuit Failure	1
B1332	Decklid Ajar Rear Door Circuit Open	2
B1338	Right Rear Door Ajar Circuit Short To Ground	2
B1342	ECU Defective	3
B1349	Heated Backlite Relay Short To Voltage	4
B1485	Brake Pedal Input Circuit Short To Voltage	5
B1574	Left Rear Door Ajar Circuit Short To Ground	5
B1676	Battery Pack Voltage Out Of Range	6
B1806	Tail Lamp Output Circuit Failure	5
B1808	Tail Lamp Output Circuit Short To Voltage	5
B2477	Module Configuration Failure	7
B2519	High Mount Stop Lamp Circuit Failure	5
B2520	High Mount Stop Lamp Circuit Battery	5
B2523	License Lamp Circuit Failure	5
B2524	License Lamp Circuit Short To Voltage	5
B2527	Left Rear Stop Lamp Circuit Failure	5
B2528	Left Rear Stop Lamp Circuit Short To Voltage	5
B2529	Left Rear Turn Lamp Circuit Failure	5
B2530	Left Rear Turn Lamp Circuit Short To Voltage	5
B2531	Right Rear Reversing Lamp Circuit Failure	5
B2532	Right Rear Reversing Lamp Circuit Short To Voltage	5
B2533	Right Rear Stop Lamp Circuit Failure	5
B2534	Right Rear Stop Lamp Circuit Short To Voltage	5
B2535	Right Rear Turn Lamp Circuit Failure	5
B2536	Right Rear Turn Lamp Circuit Short To Voltage	5
B2539	Auxililiary A/C Mode Position Reference Circuit Short To Ground	8
B2540	Auxililiary A/C Mode Position Reference Circuit Short To Voltage	8
B2543	Auxililiary A/C Control Switch Reference Circuit Short To Ground	8
B2544	Auxililiary A/C Control Switch Reference Circuit Short To Voltage	8
B2545	System Power Relay Circuit Short To Voltage	5
B2553	Disable Signal Output Circuit Short To Voltage	9
B2554	Dome Lamp Output Circuit Failure	2
B2555	Dome Lamp Output Circuit Short To Voltage	2

REAR ELECTRONIC MODULE DTC INDEX (Cont.)

DTC	Description	Test
B2556	Enable Signal Circuit Short To Voltage	9
B2557	Left Power Sliding Door Open/Close Output Circuit Short To Voltage	10
B2558	Right Power Sliding Door Open/Close Output Circuit Short To Voltage	10
B2559	Auxililiary A/C Blower Motor Relay Circuit Short To Voltage	8
B2560	Auxililiary A/C Blower Motor Relay Circuit Short To Ground	8
B2561	Auxililiary A/C Blower Speed 1 Circuit Failure	8
B2562	Auxililiary A/C Blower Speed 1 Circuit Short To Ground	8
B2563	Auxililiary A/C Blower Speed 2 Circuit Failure	8
B2564	Auxililiary A/C Blower Speed 2 Circuit Short To Ground	8
B2565	Right Tail Lamp Circuit Failure	5
B2566	Right Tail Lamp Circuit Short To Ground	5
B2568	Reverse Mirror Output Circuit Short To Ground	11
B2569	Liftgate Disarm Switch Circuit Short To Ground	12
B2570	Right Lamp Outage Signal Circuit Short To Ground	13
B2571	Left Lamp Outage Signal Circuit Short To Ground	13
U1041	SCP Invalid Or Missing Data For Vehicle Speed	14
U1059	SCP Invalid Or Missing Data For Transaxle/PRNDL	15
U1178	SCP Invalid Or Missing Data For Climate Control (HVAC)	16
U1262	SCP Communication Bus Fault	M

1 – See ANALOG INSTRUMENT PANELS – WINDSTAR article for testing procedure.
2 – Repair appropriate circuit as necessary. See appropriate wiring diagram in ILLUMINATION/INTERIOR LIGHTS article.
3 – Using NGS tester, perform Rear Electronic Module (REM) self-test. If DTC B1342 is retrieved again, replace REM.
4 – See POWER WINDOWS – WINDSTAR article for testing procedure.
5 – See AUTOLAMP SYSTEMS – WINDSTAR article for testing procedure.
6 – Check charging system. See appropriate GENERATORS article in STARTING & CHARGING SYSTEMS. If charging system is okay, check power and ground circuits to REM. See appropriate wiring diagram in POWER DISTRIBUTION article in WIRING DIAGRAMS.
7 – See MODULE CONFIGURATION under PROGRAMMING.
8 – Repair A/C system as necessary. See appropriate AUTOMATIC A/C-HEATER SYSTEMS article in appropriate MITCHELL® AIR CONDITIONING & HEATING SERVICE & REPAIR manual.
9 – Repair other DTCs or see SYMPTOM CHART under SYSTEM TESTS in POWER SLIDING DOORS – WINDSTAR article.
10 – See POWER SLIDING DOOR – WINDSTAR article for testing procedure.
11 – See POWER MIRRORS – WINDSTAR article for testing procedure.
12 – See ACTIVE ANTI-THEFT SYSTEMS – WINDSTAR article for testing procedure.
13 – Repair appropriate circuit as necessary. See appropriate wiring diagram in MESSAGE CENTER article.
14 – Using NGS tester, perform ABS self-test.
15 – Using NGS tester, perform PCM self-test.
16 – Using NGS tester, perform ICM self-test

RESTRAINTS CONTROL MODULE (RCM) DTC INDEX

DTC [1]	Description	Test
B1342	ECU Defective	2
B1231	RCM Crash Data Memory Full	3
B1921	RCM Bracket Ground Resistance High	3
C1414	Incorrect Vehicle Identification Code	3
B1887	Driver's Air Bag Circuit Shorted To Ground	3
B1916	Driver's Air Bag Circuit Shorted To Voltage	3
B1888	Passenger's Air Bag Circuit Short To Ground	3
B1925	Passenger's Air Bag Circuit Short To Voltage	3
B1932	Driver's Air Bag Circuit Resistance High	3
B1933	Passenger's Air Bag Circuit Resistance High	3
B1934	Driver's Air Bag Circuit Resistance Low	3
B1935	Passenger's Air Bag Circuit Resistance Low	3
B2444	Driver's Side Crash Sensor Internal Fault	3
B2440	Passenger's Side Crash Sensor Mounting Failure	3
B2441	Driver's Side Crash Sensor Mounting Failure	3
B2445	Passenger's Side Crash Sensor Internal Fault	3
U2017	Driver's Side Crash Sensor Communication Fault	3
U2018	Passenger's Side Crash Sensor Communication Fault	3
B1993	Driver's Side Air Bag Circuit Short To Ground	3
B1997	Passenger's Side Air Bag Circuit Short To Ground	3
B1992	Driver's Side Air Bag Circuit Short To Voltage Or Ignition	3
B1996	Passenger's Side Air Bag Circuit Short To Voltage Or Ignition	3
B1994	Driver's Side Air Bag Circuit High Resistance	3
B1998	Passenger's Side Air Bag Circuit High Resistance	3
B1995	Driver's Side Air Bag Circuit Low Resistance	3
B1999	Passenger's Side Air Bag Circuit Low Resistance	3
B1892	Air Bag Tone Warning Indicator Circuit Short To Ground Or Open	3
B1891	Air Bag Tone Warning Indicator Circuit Short To Voltage	3
B1869	Air Bag Indicator Inoperative	3
B1870	Air Bag Indicator Short To Voltage	3

RESTRAINTS CONTROL MODULE (RCM) DTC INDEX (Cont.)

DTC [1]	Description	Test

[1] – DTCs are listed in order of importance. Repair DTCs in order listed.
[2] – Using NGS tester, perform Restraints Control Module (RCM) self-test. If DTC B1342 is retrieved again, replace RCM.
[3] – Repair air bag system concern. See DIAGNOSIS & TESTING article in appropriate MICHELL® AIR BAG SERVICE & REPAIR MANUAL, DOMESTIC & IMPORTED MODELS.

RIGHT POWER SLIDING DOOR MODULE DTC INDEX

DTC	Description	Test
B1342	ECU Defective	1
B2238	Broken Cable Detected	2
B2270	Power Sliding Door Exceeded Time Allowed To Cinch Door [3]	2
B2271	Power Sliding Door Did Not Reach Full Open Position During Self-Test	2
B2362	Remote Key Fob Open/Close Signal Circuit Short To Ground	2
B2363	Position Sensor System Failure	2
B2365	"B" Pillar Power Sliding Door Open/Close Switch Circuit Short To Ground	2
B2366	Power Sliding Door Open/Close Switch Circuit Short To Ground	2
B2374	Power Sliding Door Latch Switch Circuit Short To Ground	2
B2483	Enable Signal Open Circuit (Park)	2
B2589	No Power Sliding Door Latch Switch detected On Closing & Door Reversed	2
B2591	No Power Sliding Door Latch Switch Detected On Unlatch	2
B2592	Door Not Pulled Into Primary During Power Close & High Duty Cycles	2
B2593	Door Reversed While Closing Due To An Obstacle	2
B2594	No Movement Detected After An Unlatch During Power Open Operation	2
B2603	Power Sliding Door Not Fully Closed During Power Close During Self-Test When Pulled To Primary Latch Position	2
B2604	Power Sliding Door On/Off Switch Open Circuit	2
B2605	Disable Signal Open Circuit – Vehicle Speed Over 6 MPH	2

[1] – Using NGS tester, clear and document all continuous DTCs. Perform Right Power Sliding Door Module (RPSDM) self-test. If DTC B1342 is retrieved again, replace RPSDM.
[2] – See POWER SLIDING DOORS – WINDSTAR article for testing procedure.
[3] – Exceeded the time allowed to reach primary latch position after reaching secondary latch position.

PARAMETER IDENTIFICATION (PID) DEFINITIONS

ANTI-LOCK BRAKE SYSTEM PID INDEX

PID	Description	Expected Value
ABSLAMP	ABS Warning Lamp State	ON, OFF
BRKLAMP	Brake Warning Lamp State	ON, OFF
PWR_RLY	Power Relay Feedback Input	ON, OFF
CCNTABS	Number Of Continuous DTCs	Number Of DTCs
BOO_ABS	Brake Pedal Position Switch Input	ON, OFF
ABSRR_I	Right Rear ABS Inlet Valve	ON, OFF
ABSRR_O	Right Rear ABS Outlet Valve	ON, OFF
ABSLF_I	Left Front ABS Inlet Valve	ON, OFF
ABSLF_O	Left Front ABS Outlet Valve	ON, OFF
ABSRF_I	Right Front ABS Inlet Valve	ON, OFF
ABSRF_O	Right Front ABS Outlet Valve	ON, OFF
ABSLR_I	Left Rear ABS Inlet Valve	ON, OFF
ABSLR_O	Left Rear ABS Outlet Valve	ON, OFF
LF_WSPD	Left Front Wheel Speed Signal	ON, OFF
RF_WSPD	Right Front Wheel Speed Signal	0-255 KPH
RR_WSPD	Right Rear Wheel Speed Signal	0-255 KPH
LR_WSPD	Left Rear Wheel Speed Signal	0-255 KPH

FRONT ELECTRONICS MODULE PID INDEX

PID	Description	Expected Value
ACCDLY	Accessory Delay Relay Circuit	1
AL_EVT1	Last 8 Alarm Events	2
AL_EVT2	Last 8 Alarm Events	2
AL_EVT3	Last 8 Alarm Events	2
AL_EVT4	Last 8 Alarm Events	2
AL_EVT5	Last 8 Alarm Events	2
AL_EVT6	Last 8 Alarm Events	2
AL_EVT7	Last 8 Alarm Events	2
AL_EVT8	Last 8 Alarm Events	2
ATHFTSW	Security Speed Signal	NOTACT, ACTIVE
BLWRMTR	Blower Motor	NOTACT, ACTIVE
BRK_LVL	Brake Fluid Level	NOTOK, OK
CCNT	Number Of DTCs Stored In Module	One Count Per Bit
D_DN_SW	Driver's Window Down Switch	OFF, DOWN
D_DOOR	Left Front Door Ajar Switch	CLOSED, AJAR

FRONT ELECTRONICS MODULE PID INDEX (Cont.)

PID	Description	Expected Value
D_DSRM	Driver's Door Unlock Disarm Switch	NO, YES
D_PWPK	Driver's Power Window Peak Current	Amps
D_PWRLY	Driver's Power Window	[1]
D_SBELT	Driver's Seat Belt	OUT, IN
D_UP_SW	Driver's Up Window Switch	OFF, UP
DD_UNLK	Driver's Door Unlock Output	[1]
DR_LOCK	Driver's Door Lock Output State	NO, YES
DR_UNLK	All Doors Unlock Output State	NO, YES
DU_WRLY	Window Driver Output State	NOTACT, ACTIVE
EXTTEMP	External Temperature Sensor Unfiltered Data	Degrees In Celsius
HOOD_SW	Hood Ajar Switch	CLOSED, AJAR
HORNRLY	Horn Control Driver	[1]
IGN_R	Ignition Switch – RUN Position	NO, YES
L_HIGH	Left High Beam Lamp Driver	[1]
L_LOW	Low Beam Lamp	[1]
LF_TURN	Left & Right Front Turn Lamp	[1]
OIL_LVL	Engine Oil Level	NOTOK, OK
OTD_SW	One Touch Down Switch	OFF, DOWN
P_DOOR	Passenger's Door Ajar Switch	CLOSED, AJAR
P_DSRM	Passenger's Door Unlock Disarm Switch	NO, YES
PARKLMP	Park Lamp Output	NOTACT, ACTIVE
PD_LOCK	Passenger'ss Door Lock	NO, YES
PD_UNLK	Passenger's Unlock Activated	NO, YES
PRK_BRK	Parking Brake Switch Input	OFF, ON
R_HIGH	Right High Beam Lamp Driver	[1]
R_LOW	Low Beam Lamp	[1]
R_WPRUN	Rear Wiper Run Switch	[1]
RADIOSW	Radio Remove Switch	OFF, ON
RF_TURN	Left & Right Front Turn Lamp	[1]
RWASHSW	Rear Washer Switch Position	[1]
VBAT	Battery Voltage	Voltage
WASHRLY	Washer Pump Relay Circuit	[1]
WFLUID	Washer Fluid Level	LOW, OK
WPHISP	Wiper 2 Speed Relay	[1]
WPMODE	Wiper Control Mode Select	[3]
WPPRKSW	Windshield Wiper Park Sense	NOTPRK, PARKED
WPRUN	Wiper Run Relay Driver State	[1]

[1] – Expected values should be Off- -, Off- -G, Off-B-, Off-BG, OffO- -, OffO-G, OffOB-, OffOBG, On- -, On- -G, On-B-, On-BG, OnO- -, OnO-G, OnOB- or OnOBG.

[2] – Expected values should be DROPEN, HOODTR, IGNTAM, PANIC, T_AJAR, D_DOOR, RADIO or NOEVNT.

[3] – Expected values should be WASH, OPEN, INVLD, OFF, INTVL1, INTVL2, INTVL3, INTVL4, INTVL5, INTVL6, INTVL7, LOW, HIGH or ?.

INSTRUMENT CLUSTER/ICM PID INDEX

PID	Description	Expected Value
A/C	A/C	OFF, ON
A/C_DMD	A/C Demand Switch Input	OFF, ON
ABCHIME	Air Bag Chime	OFF, ON
ANTISCN	Anti-Scan Function	DISABL, ENABLE
BLENDDR	Blend Door Position	% ?????
C_KEYMD	Clear Keys Mode Status	NOTACT, ACTIVE
CCNT	Number Of Continuous DTCs Stored In ICM	One Count Per Bit
DIM_SW	Dimmer Switch Input Status 2	[1]
DOMESW	Dome Lamp Switch	OFF, ON
ENABL_S	Vehicle Enable Status	DISABL, ENABLE
FBLWR_S	Front Auxiliary Blower Status	[2]
HORN_SW	Horn Input Switch	OFF, ON
IGN_A	Ignition Switch – ACCY Position	NO, YES
IGN_KEY	Ignition Key In/Out	OUT, IN
IGN_O/U	Ignition Switch- OFF/Unlock Position	NO, YES
IGN_R	Ignition Switch- RUN Position	NO, YES
IGN_S	Ignition Switch- START Position	[3]
L_MODE	Lighting Mode Input Switch Status	[4]
LAMP_SW	Headlamp Switch Status	NO, YES
LIGHTSN	Night(True)/Day(False)	[5]
LSWMODE	Headlamp Switch Mode Status	NO, YES
M_BLWR	Main Blower Status	NO, YES
M_KEY	Master Key Present	NOTPRE, PRESNT
NUMKEYS	Number Of Ignition Key Codes Programmed	0-8 BCD
PCM_ID	PCM ID Status Stored	NOTST, STORED
PCM_VFY	PCM Verify OK	NO, YES

INSTRUMENT CLUSTER/ICM PID INDEX (Cont.)

PID	Description	Expected Value
RDEF_SW	Rear Defrost Switch	OFF, ON
RESETSW	Select/Reset Switch	OFF, ON
RFOG_SW	Rear Fog Lamp Switch Signal	OFF, ON
TRACOFF	T/A Off Indicator Lamp	OFF- - -, ON- - -
TRANS_I	Transmission Control Indicator Light	OFF- - -, ON- - -
TURN_SW	Left & Right Turn Signal Switch	OFF, ON
VBAT	System Battery Voltage Potential	6
		OK, notOK

[1] – Expected values should be GND, LVL2I, LVL1, OPEN or INVLD.
[2] – Expected values should be S_GND, OFF, REAR, M_LOW, M_HI, HIGH or S_BAT.
[3] – Expected values should be S_GND, ALL_L, LOW_L, OFF or S_BAT.
[4] – Expected values should be OFF, ON, PARK, A_LMP or INVLD.
[5] – Expected values should be PASS, HIGH_B, LOW_B or INVLD.
[6] – Expected values should be SHORT, RIGHT, LEFT or OFF.

LEFT POWER SLIDING DOOR MODULE PID INDEX

PID	Description	Expected Value
CCNT	Number Of Continuous DTCs Stored In Module	Number Of DTCs
SD_ONSW	Overhead Console On/Off Switch	NOTACT, ACTIVE
SD_OPSW	Overhead Console Open/Close Switch	NOTACT, ACTIVE
SD_B_SW	"B" Pillar Open/Close Switch Input	NOTACT, ACTIVE
SD_OPSG	Rear Electronics Module Open/Close Signal	NOTACT, ACTIVE
PARK/IG	Park/Ignition Signal	NOTACT, ACTIVE
LATCHSW	Power Sliding Door Latch Switch	NOTACT, ACTIVE
VSS_OK	Vehicle Speed Over 6 MPH	NOTACT, ACTIVE
FUEL_DR	Fuel Filler Door Switch	NOTACT, ACTIVE
OPEN_M	Driver Motor Open Status	NOTACT, ACTIVE
UNLATCH	Unlatch Actuator Status	NOTACT, ACTIVE
OPTIC_P	Position Sensor Power Status	NOTACT, ACTIVE
CLOSE_M	Drive Motor Closed Status	NOTACT, ACTIVE
MCLUTCH	Motor Clutch Status	NOTACT, ACTIVE
PSD_POS	Sliding Door Position	1

[1] – Expected values should be 1-5 (1= Closed, 2= Unlatched, 4= Open).

MESSAGE CENTER MODULE PID INDEX

PID	Description	Expected Value
RESETSW	Reset Switch	OFF, ON
INFOSW	Info Switch	OFF, ON
SETUPSW	Setup Switch	OFF, ON

REAR ELECTRONICS MODULE PID INDEX

PID	Description	Expected Value
CCNT	Number Of Continuous DTCs	Number Of DTCs
VBAT	Battery Voltage	Volts
BLNDPOS	Blend Door Position Status	1
BOO	Brake Pedal Switch	ON, OFF
DR_DSRM	Decklid/Hatch Unlock Disarm Switch	NO/YES
LRDR_SW	Left Rear Door Ajar	AJAR, CLOSED
RRDR_SW	Right Rear/Sliding Door Ajar	AJAR, CLOSED
DECKLID	Decklid/Hatch Ajar	AJAR, CLOSED
LR_TURN	Left Rear Turn/Stop Driver Output State	2
RR_TURN	Right Rear Turn/Stop Driver Output State	2
L_TAIL	Left Tail Lamp Output State	2
R_TAIL	Right Tail Lamp Output State	2
L_BRK_L	Left Rear Stop Lamp	2
R_BRK_L	Right Rear Stop Lamp	2
LR_BKUP	Left Rear Backup Lamp	ON, OFF
RR_BKUP	Right Rear Backup Lamp	ON, OFF
LCNC_LP	License Lamp	ON, OFF
HMNTSTP	High Mount Stop Lamp	ON, OFF
RDEFRLY	Heated Backlite Driver Output State	2
A/CMT_R	A/C Blower Motor Output Relay	ON, OFF
A/CSPD1	A/C Blower Motor Output Speed 1	LOW, HIGH
A/CBL_P	A/C Blend Door Output Position	OPEN, CLOSED
A/CMD_P	A/C Mode Door Output Status	OPEN, CLOSED
A/CSPD2	A/C Blower Motor Output Speed 2	LOW, HIGH
P_LCKO	Passenger's/Liftgate Lock Activated	NOT, ACTIVE
P_ULKO	Passenger's/Liftgate Unlock Activated	NOT, ACTIVE
LR_LCKO	Left Rear Lock Activated	NOT, ACTIVE

REAR ELECTRONICS MODULE PID INDEX (Cont.)

PID	Description	Expected Value
LR_ULKO	Left Rear Unlock Activated	NOT, ACTIVE
RR_LCKO	Right Rear Lock Activated	NOT, ACTIVE
RR_ULKO	Right Rear Unlock Activated	NOT, ACTIVE

[1] – Expected values should be MVG, NotMVG, FL HOT, FL COLD, H_FAIL or C_FAIL.

[2] – Expected values should be Off- - -, Off- -G, Off-B-, Off-BG, OffO- -, OffO-G, OffOB-, OffOBG, On- - -, On- -G, On-B-, On-BG, OnO- -, OnO-G, OnOB- or OnOBG.

RESTRAINTS CONTROL MODULE (RCM) PID INDEX

PID	Description	Expected Value
CCNT	Number Of Continuous DTCs	Number Of DTCs
D_ABAGR	Driver Air Bag Module Resistance	1.7-4.1 Ohms
P_ABAGR	Passenger's Air Bag Circuit Resistance	1.7-3.2 Ohms
DABAG2	Driver Side Impact Air Bag Resistance	1.7-3.2 Ohms
PABAG2	Passenger's Side Impact Air Bag Resistance	1.7-3.2 Ohms
BRACKET	Bracket Ground Resistance	Less Than 100 Ohms
VID #1	Program Vehicle ID Pin 10	N/A
VID #2	Program Vehicle ID Pin 13	N/A
VID #3	Program Vehicle ID Pin 14	N/A

RIGHT POWER SLIDING DOOR MODULE PID INDEX

PID	Description	Expected Value
CCNT	Number Of Continuous DTCs Stored In Module	Number Of DTCs
SD_ONSW	Overhead Console On/Off Switch	NOTACT, ACTIVE
SD_OPSW	Overhead Console Open/Close Switch	NOTACT, ACTIVE
SD_B_SW	B-Pillar Open/Close Switch Input	NOTACT, ACTIVE
SD_OPSG	REM Open/Close Signal	NOTACT, ACTIVE
PARK/IG	Park/Ignition Signal	NOTACT, ACTIVE
LATCHSW	PSD Latch Switch	NOTACT, ACTIVE
VSS_OK	Vehicle Speed Over 6 MPH	NOTACT, ACTIVE
OPEN_M	Driver Motor Open Status	NOTACT, ACTIVE
UNLATCH	Unlatch Actuator Status	NOTACT, ACTIVE
OPTIC_P	Position Sensor Power Status	NOTACT, ACTIVE
CLOSE_M	Drive Motor Closed Status	NOTACT, ACTIVE
MCLUTCH	Motor Clutch Status	[1]
PSD_POS	Sliding Door Position	

[1] – Expected values should be 1-5 (1= Closed, 2= Unlatched, 4= Open).

REMOVAL & INSTALLATION

CAUTION: *Electronic modules are sensitive to static electrical charges. Proper grounding of technician and workplace is essential to prevent damage. Prior to removal of modules, it is necessary to upload module configuration information to New Generation Star (NGS) tester. This information needs to be downloaded into new module once installed. See MODULE CONFIGURATION under PROGRAMMING.*

NOTE: *When battery is disconnected, vehicle computer and memory systems may lose memory data. Driveability problems may exist until computer systems have completed a relearn cycle. See COMPUTER RELEARN PROCEDURES article in GENERAL INFORMATION before disconnecting battery.*

ANTI-LOCK BRAKE CONTROL MODULE

Removal & Installation – 1) Disconnect negative battery cable. Raise and support vehicle. Remove screw and 3 bolts retaining Hydraulic Control Unit (HCU) dust shield. Disconnect anti-lock brake control module electrical connector by sliding connector lock rearward.

2) Remove 3 bolts retaining HCU bracket to frame. Lift bracket hooks from frame and lower HCU to access anti-lock brake control module. Be sure to lift straight up to avoid damage to HCU components. Remove 4 bolts retaining anti-lock brake control module and remove module. Clean top of HCU before installing new module. To install, reverse removal procedure.

FRONT ELECTRONICS MODULE (FEM)

Removal & Installation – Disconnect negative battery cable. Remove 2 bolts holding instrument panel lower steering column opening cover. Remove cover. Remove 3 bolts holding instrument panel opening cover reinforcement. Remove reinforcement. Disconnect 6 electrical connectors to FEM, remove 3 bolts holding FEM and remove FEM. To install FEM, reverse removal procedures.

INSTRUMENT CLUSTER

NOTE: *After instrument cluster replacement, anti-theft system must be reprogrammed. See PASSIVE ANTI-THEFT SYSTEMS – WINDSTAR article.*

Removal & Installation – 1) Disconnect negative battery cable. Remove 2 screws and remove instrument panel steering column cover ("D") from below steering column. See Fig. 15.

2) Remove 3 bolts and remove instrument panel steering column cover reinforcement from below steering column. Loosen 4 bolts retaining steering column. Lower steering column. Remove lower steering column shroud from steering column. Using a punch, push button below ignition lock cylinder and pull ignition switch lock cylinder out.

3) Remove upper steering column shroud from steering column. Remove light switch knob and gently pry instrument panel finish panel ("E") away from instrument panel ("A"). See Fig. 16. Disconnect headlight switch miniature bulb socket from instrument panel finish panel.

4) Remove 2 retaining screws at bottom of cluster opening panel and gently pry from instrument panel. See Fig. 16. Disconnect electrical connectors. Remove 2 retaining screws and gently pry instrument panel

finish panel ("F") from instrument panel. *See Fig. 17.* Disconnect transaxle range indicator cable from column by removing retaining screw and cable loop.

5) Remove 4 screws retaining instrument cluster. Pull instrument cluster forward to gain access to electrical connectors. Disconnect electrical connectors. Remove instrument cluster. To install, reverse removal procedure. Tighten instrument cluster retaining screws to 18-26 INCH lbs. (2-3 N.m). Tighten instrument panel steering column cover reinforcement retaining screws to 106 INCH lbs. (12 N.m).

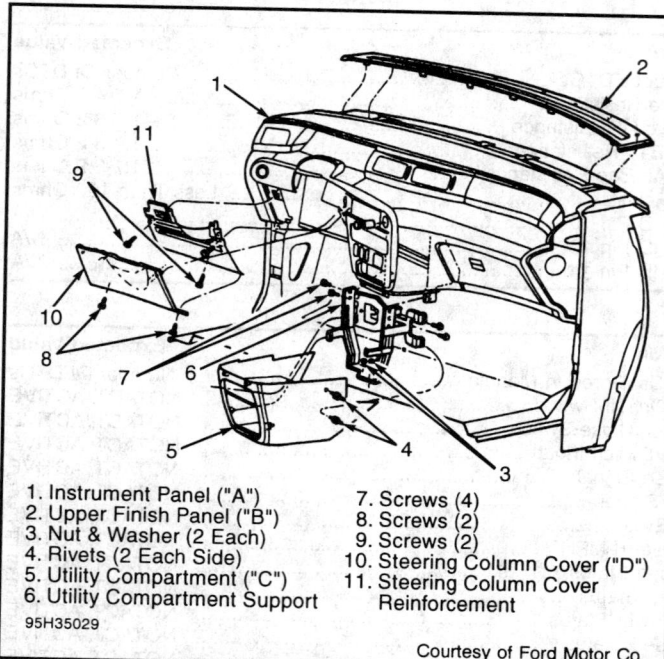

1. Instrument Panel ("A")
2. Upper Finish Panel ("B")
3. Nut & Washer (2 Each)
4. Rivets (2 Each Side)
5. Utility Compartment ("C")
6. Utility Compartment Support
7. Screws (4)
8. Screws (2)
9. Screws (2)
10. Steering Column Cover ("D")
11. Steering Column Cover Reinforcement

95H35029

Courtesy of Ford Motor Co.

Fig. 15: Exploded View Of Instrument Panel

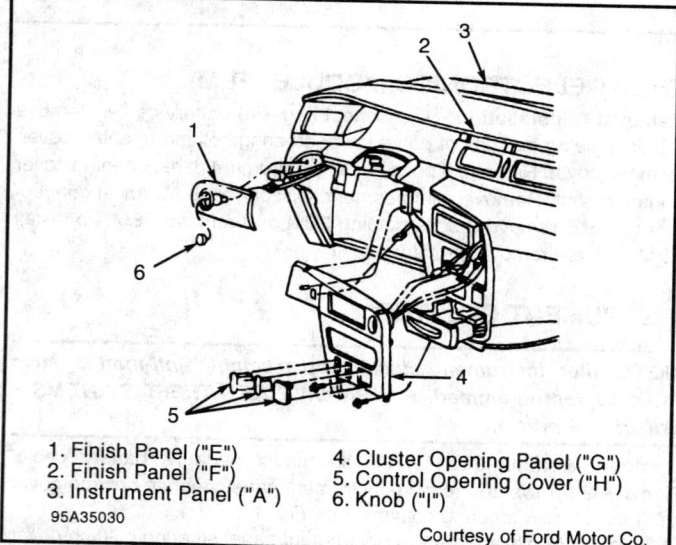

1. Finish Panel ("E")
2. Finish Panel ("F")
3. Instrument Panel ("A")
4. Cluster Opening Panel ("G")
5. Control Opening Cover ("H")
6. Knob ("I")

95A35030

Courtesy of Ford Motor Co.

Fig. 16: Removing Cluster Opening Panel

LEFT POWER SLIDING DOOR MODULE (LPSDM)

NOTE: After installation of LPSDM, ensure power sliding doors are fully closed, latched and unlocked.

Removal & Installation – 1) Remove Fuse Junction Box (FJB) 15-amp fuse No. 6. Remove left rear upper and lower quarter trim panel. Remove upper and lower A/C ducts. Disconnect 5 electrical connectors

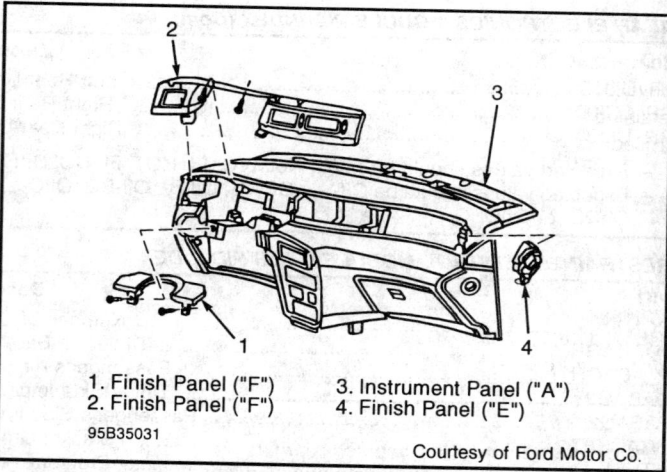

1. Finish Panel ("F")
2. Finish Panel ("F")
3. Instrument Panel ("A")
4. Finish Panel ("E")

95B35031

Courtesy of Ford Motor Co.

Fig. 17: Removing Instrument Panel Finish Panel

from module. Remove bolt retaining LPSDM, unsnap control module hinge from actuator assembly and remove module.

2) To install, reverse removal procedure. Install FJB 15-amp fuse No. 6. Initialize both power sliding doors by pressing overhead control switch to open left power sliding door to full open position and then close power sliding door to full close position.

NEW GENERATION SPEED CONTROL (NGSC) SERVO

Removal – 1) Disconnect negative battery cable. Remove air cleaner assembly. Disconnect speed control servo/actuator electrical connector. Remove 2 speed control servo/actuator mounting bolts. Lift and remove speed control servo/actuator.

NOTE: Opening throttle will remove speed control actuator cable tension during this step.

2) Disconnect speed control cable from throttle body. Depress locking tab on speed control servo/actuator cap and rotate counterclockwise while lifting cap outward. Remove speed control cable slug from speed control servo/actuator pulley and remove speed control actuator cable from speed control servo/actuator pulley.

NOTE: Incorrect wrapping of speed control actuator cable around speed control servo/actuator pulley may result in a high idle condition.

Installation – To install, make sure locking spring snaps into place on speed control cable slug. Insert speed control cable slug into speed control servo/actuator pulley slot. Ensure rubber seal is fully seated on servo/actuator cable cap. Align speed control actuator cable cap tabs with slots in speed control servo/actuator housing and seat speed control cable cap. Rotate cap clockwise until locking tab engages. Install speed control servo/actuator bracket bolts and connect electrical connector to speed control servo/actuator.

PARKING AID MODULE (PAM)

Removal & Installation – Remove right side rear quarter trim panel and position sound insulator aside. Disconnect electrical connector. Remove module retaining nut and remove Parking Aid Module (PAM). To install reverse removal procedure.

REAR ELECTRONICS MODULE (REM)

Removal & Installation – Disconnect negative battery cable. Remove right quarter trim panel. Remove 3 bolts holding service jack mounting bracket and remove bracket. Disconnect 5 electrical connectors to REM, remove 3 nuts holding REM and remove REM. To install, reverse removal procedure.

REMOTE KEYLESS ENTRY (RKE) MODULE

Removal & Installation – Disconnect negative battery cable. Lower glove box and disconnect RKE electrical connector. Remove 3 nuts retaining RKE module and remove module. To install, reverse removal procedure.

RESTRAINT CONTROL MODULE (RCM)

WARNING: To avoid accidental deployment and possible personal injury, backup power supply must be depleted before repairing or replacing any air bag restraint system components. Disconnect battery and, if equipped, auxiliary power supplies. Wait one minute for backup power supply energy to deplete.

CAUTION: For proper operation, it is critical to tighten restraint control module bolts to specification.

Removal & Installation – **1)** Disconnect negative battery cable. Wait one minute for backup power supply energy to deplete. Remove 4 pushpins, pull utility compartment straight out to release retaining clips and remove utility compartment. Roll carpet back and remove 2 retaining bolts on passenger's side for restraint control module bracket.
2) With carpeting rolled back, disengage 2 RCM connector locking clips. Disconnect 2 electrical connectors, remove 2 retaining bolts on driver side for RCM bracket and remove RCM and bracket. To install, reverse removal procedure. Tighten RCM retaining bolts to 106 INCH lbs. (12 N.m). and prove out air bag system.

RIGHT POWER SLIDING DOOR MODULE (RPSDM)

NOTE: After installation of RPSDM, ensure power sliding doors are fully closed, latched and unlocked.

Removal & Installation – **1)** Remove Fuse Junction Box (FJB) 15-amp fuse No. 6. Remove right rear quarter trim panel. Disconnect 5 electrical connectors from module. Remove RPSDM retaining bolt, unsnap control module hinge from actuator assembly and remove module.
2) To install, reverse removal procedure. Install FJB 15-amp fuse. Initialize both power sliding doors by pressing overhead control switch to open left power sliding door to full open position and then close power sliding door to full close position.

WIRING DIAGRAMS

NOTE: See appropriate wiring diagrams in DATA LINK CONNECTORS, GROUND DISTRIBUTION or POWER DISTRIBUTION article in WIRING DIAGRAMS.

1999 ACCESSORIES & EQUIPMENT
Cruise Control Systems – Continental

DESCRIPTION & OPERATION

Major components of the cruise control system are speed control switches, servo/actuator, horn relay, Brake Pedal Position (BPP) switch, deactivator switch, ABS control module, Lighting Control Module (LCM), and related wiring. This system does not require engine vacuum. An electronic servo/actuator actuates the throttle.

The system is operational only at speeds greater than 30 MPH. The system is activated when ON/OFF switch is switched on and SET/ACCEL button is pressed and released. Vehicle will maintain set speed until new speed is set, brake pedal is pressed, or ON/OFF switch is switched off. If system has been deactivated by pressing brake pedal, set speed can be regained by pressing and releasing RESUME button. When brake pedal is pressed, a signal from switch is sent to the speed control servo to deactivate the system. A deactivator switch acts as a redundant brake signal.

COMPONENT LOCATIONS

COMPONENT LOCATIONS

Component	Location
Data Link Connector (DLC)	Below Driver's Side Of Instrument Panel, To Right Of Steering Column
Instrument Panel Fuse Box	Below Left Instrument Panel
Lighting Control Module (LCM)	On Instrument Panel, Behind Headlight Switch
Power Distribution Box	Left Side Of Engine Compartment, Above Wheelwell
Powertrain Control Module (PCM)	In Passenger's Side Of Engine Compartment, On Firewall
Speed Control Servo/Amplifier Assembly [1]	Mounted On Left Shock Tower

[1] – Speed control servo/amplifier assembly may also be referred to as Next Generation Speed Control (NGSC) servo.

ADJUSTMENTS

SPEED CONTROL SERVO ACTUATOR CABLE

Remove cable retaining clip from cable adjuster. Ensure throttle is fully closed. Pull servo cable to take up any slack. Loosen at least one notch so there is 0.04-0.12" (1-3 mm) of slack in cable. Insert cable retaining clip and snap into place. Ensure throttle linkage operates freely and smoothly.

TROUBLE SHOOTING

Verify customer complaint. Check for faulty fuses. Check for loose or corroded connections. Check for damaged wiring harness. Check for damaged switches. Check for damaged or binding servo/actuator cable. Check for incorrect servo/actuator cable adjustment. Verify horn and stoplights function properly. Repair as necessary. Inspect actuator and throttle linkage for smooth operation. Unbind as necessary. If no problems are found, go to SELF-DIAGNOSTIC SYSTEM.

SELF-DIAGNOSTIC SYSTEM

Verify customers complaint. Verify horn system is operating properly and repair as necessary. Verify speedometer is operating properly and repair as necessary. Inspect for obvious signs of mechanical and electrical damage. Repair or replace components as necessary.

If all components are okay, connect New Generation Star (NGS) tester to Data Link Connector (DLC), located beneath instrument panel. Using NGS tester, preform data link diagnostics test. See DATA LINK DIAGNOSTIC TEST under COMMUNICATION NETWORK DIAGNOSTICS in MODULE COMMUNICATIONS NETWORK – CONTINENTAL article. If NGS tester responds with CKT914, CKT915 or CKT70=ALL ECUS NO RESP/NOT EQUIP, repair module communications concern. See MODULE COMMUNICATIONS NETWORK – CONTINENTAL article. If NGS tester displays NO RESP/NOT EQUIP for speed control servo, perform TEST A: NO COMMUNICATION WITH SPEED CONTROL SERVO under SYSTEM TESTS.

If NGS tester responds with SYSTEM PASSED, retrieve and record continuous DTCs. Erase continuous DTCs. Using NGS tester, perform speed control servo self-test. Perform appropriate test in accordance with DTC retrieved. See SPEED CONTROL SERVO DTC INDEX table. Codes listed in this table are only for testing covered in this article. For complete DTC listing, see MODULE COMMUNICATIONS NETWORK – CONTINENTAL article. If no DTCs are retrieved, repair by symptom. See SYMPTOM CHART table under SYSTEM TESTS.

SPEED CONTROL SERVO DTC INDEX

DTC [1]	Description	Test
B1318	Battery Voltage Low	C
B1342	ECU Defective	[2]
C1109	Throttle Position Did Not Return To Idle after Self-Test	D
C1126	Speed Control Switch Stuck For 2 Minutes Or Longer	E
C1127	Deactivator Switch Circuit Failure	F
C1179	Speed Control Servo Cable Slack Failure	G

[1] – Codes listed in this table are only for testing covered in this article. For complete DTC listing, see MODULE COMMUNICATIONS NETWORK – CONTINENTAL article.

[2] – Using NGS tester, retrieve and document all continuous DTCs. Perform speed control servo self-test. If DTC B1342 is retrieved again, replace speed control servo.

SYSTEM TESTS

CAUTION: *When battery is disconnected or modules are replaced, vehicle computer and memory systems may lose memory data. Driveability problems may exist until computer systems have completed a relearn cycle. See COMPUTER RELEARN PROCEDURES article in GENERAL INFORMATION before disconnecting battery.*

SYMPTOM CHART

Symptom	Test
No Communication With Speed Control Servo	A
Unable To Enter Self-Test	B
Battery Voltage Low (DTC B1318)	C
Throttle Position Did Not Return To Idle After Self-Test (DTC C1109)	D
Speed Control Switch Stuck For 2 Minutes Or Longer (DTC C1126)	E
Deactivator Switch Circuit Failure (DTC C1127)	F
Speed Control Servo Cable Slack Failure (DTC C1179)	G
Speed Control Is Inoperative – No Diagnostic Trouble Codes	H
Set Speed Fluctuates	I
Coast Switch Is Inoperative	J
Set/Accel Switch Is Inoperative	K
Resume Switch Is Inoperative	L
Off Switch Is Inoperative	M

TEST A: NO COMMUNICATION WITH SPEED CONTROL SERVO

1) Check fuse No. 28 (10-amp) in instrument panel fuse box fuse No. 34 (15-amp). If fuse is okay, go to next step. If fuse is blown, replace fuse and retest system operation. If fuse fails again, repair short to ground in Light Green/Violet wire.

2) Turn ignition switch to LOCK position. Disconnect speed control servo harness connector C152. Turn ignition switch to RUN position. Measure voltage at terminal No. 7 (Light Green/Violet wire) at speed control servo harness connector C152. See Fig. 1. If voltage is greater than 10 volts, go to next step. If voltage is 10 volts or less, repair open in Light Green/Violet wire.

3) Measure resistance between ground and terminal No. 10 (Black wire) at speed control servo harness connector C152. If resistance is 5 ohms or less, repair module communication concern. See MODULE COMMUNICATIONS NETWORK – CONTINENTAL article. If resistance is greater than 5 ohms, repair open in Black wire.

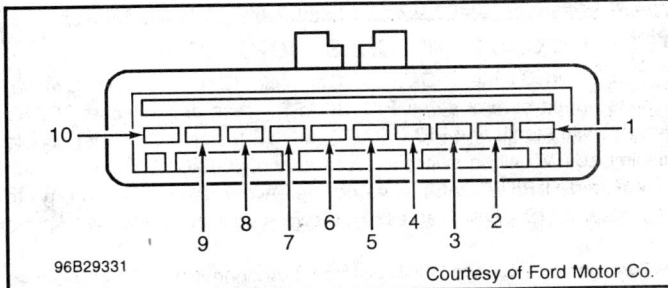

96B29331   Courtesy of Ford Motor Co.

Fig. 1: Identifying Speed Control Servo Harness Connector C152 Terminals

TEST B: UNABLE TO ENTER SELF-TEST

Connect NGS tester to Data Link Connector (DLC). Check communication with speed control servo. If NGS tester communicates with speed control servo, replace speed control servo. If NGS tester does not communicate with speed control servo, perform TEST A: NO COMMUNICATION WITH SPEED CONTROL SERVO.

TEST C: BATTERY VOLTAGE LOW (DTC B1318)

Turn ignition switch to LOCK position. Disconnect speed control servo harness connector C152. Measure voltage at terminal No. 7 (Light Green/Violet wire) at speed control servo harness connector C152. See

Fig. 1. If voltage is 10 volts or less, repair charging system. See appropriate GENERATORS article in STARTING & CHARGING SYSTEMS. If voltage is greater than 10 volts, repair open in Black wire between speed control servo and ground.

TEST D: THROTTLE POSITION DID NOT RETURN TO IDLE AFTER SELF-TEST (DTC C1109)

1) Check speed control servo cable for binding or sticking. If cable is okay, go to next step. If cable is not okay, repair or replace cable as necessary.

2) Check throttle lever for binding or sticking. If throttle lever is okay, go to next step. If throttle lever is not okay, repair or replace throttle lever as necessary.

3) Check speed control servo cable adjustment. See SPEED CONTROL SERVO ACTUATOR CABLE under ADJUSTMENTS. Using NGS tester, retrieve and document DTCs. Clear continuous DTCs. Perform speed control servo self-test. If DTC C1109 is retrieved, replace speed control servo. If DTC C1109 is not retrieved, system is okay at this time.

TEST E: SPEED CONTROL SWITCH STUCK FOR 2 MINUTES OR LONGER (DTC C1126)

1) Turn ignition switch to LOCK position. Disconnect speed control switch harness connector. Turn ignition switch to RUN position. Using NGS tester, clear continuous DTCs. Wait 3 minutes. Retrieve and document continuous DTCs. If DTC C1126 is retrieved, go to next step. If DTC C1126 is not retrieved, replace speed control switch.

2) Turn ignition switch to LOCK position. Disconnect speed control servo harness connector C152. Measure resistance between ground and terminal No. 5 (Light Blue/Black wire) at speed control servo harness connector C152. See Fig. 1. If resistance is 10 k/ohms or less, go to next step. If resistance is greater than 10 k/ohms, replace speed control servo.

3) Disconnect air bag sliding contact harness connector C2012. Measure resistance between ground and terminal No. 5 (Light Blue/Black wire) at speed control servo harness connector C152. If resistance is greater than 10 k/ohms, replace air bag sliding contact. If resistance is 10 k/ohms or less, repair short to ground in Light Blue/Black wire between speed control servo and air bag sliding contact.

TEST F: DEACTIVATOR SWITCH CIRCUIT FAILURE (DTC C1127)

1) Check fuse No. 32 (15-amp) in instrument panel fuse box. If fuse is okay, go to next step. If fuse is blown, replace fuse and retest system operation. If fuse fails again, repair short to ground in Light Green/Red wire.

2) Turn ignition switch to LOCK position. Disconnect speed control servo harness connector C152. Measure voltage at terminal No. 9 (Orange wire) at speed control servo harness connector C152 while pressing and releasing brake pedal. See Fig. 1. Voltage should be greater than 10 volts with brake pedal released and zero volts with brake pedal pressed. If voltage is as specified, replace speed control servo. If voltage is not as specified, go to next step.

3) Disconnect deactivator switch harness connector C218. Measure voltage at Light Green/Red wire terminal at deactivator switch harness connector C218. If voltage is greater than 10 volts, go to next step. If voltage is 10 volts or less, repair open in Light Green/Red wire.

4) Measure resistance in Orange wire between terminal No. 9 at speed control servo harness connector C152 and deactivator switch harness connector C218. If resistance is 5 ohms or less, replace deactivator switch. If resistance is greater than 5 ohms, repair open in Orange wire.

TEST G: SPEED CONTROL SERVO CABLE SLACK FAILURE (DTC C1179)

Check speed control servo cable adjustment. See SPEED CONTROL SERVO/ACTUATOR CABLE under ADJUSTMENTS. Using NGS tester, clear continuous DTCs. Retrieve and document DTCs. If DTC C1179 is retrieved, replace speed control servo. If DTC C1179 is not retrieved, system is okay at this time.

TEST H: SPEED CONTROL IS INOPERATIVE – NO DIAGNOSTIC TROUBLE CODES

1) Check horn operation by pressing steering wheel horn switch. If horn operates properly, go to next step. If horn does not operate properly, repair horn as necessary. See WIRING DIAGRAMS in STEERING COLUMN SWITCHES – CONTINENTAL article.

2) Turn ignition switch to LOCK position. Disconnect speed control servo harness connector C152. Turn ignition switch to RUN position. Measure voltage at terminal No. 5 (Light Blue/Black wire) at speed control servo harness connector C152 while pressing speed control switch ON. See Fig. 1. If voltage is greater than 10 volts, go to next step. If voltage is 10 volts or less, go to step 4).

3) Ensure ignition switch is in LOCK position. Measure resistance between terminals No. 5 (Light Blue/Black wire) and No. 6 (Black wire) at speed control servo harness connector C152 while pressing speed control SET/ACCEL switch. Resistance should be 612-748 ohms when switch is pressed and greater than 10 k/ohms when switch is released. If resistance is as specified, replace speed control servo. If resistance is not as specified, replace speed control switch.

4) Turn ignition switch to LOCK position. Disconnect air bag sliding contact harness connector C2012. Measure resistance in Light Blue/Black wire between terminal No. 5 at speed control servo harness connector C152 and terminal No. 6 at air bag sliding contact harness connector C2012 (female side). See Figs. 1 and 2. If resistance is 5 ohms or less, go to next step. If resistance is greater than 5 ohms, repair open in Light Blue/Black wire.

5) Disable and remove driver's side air bag. See appropriate AIR BAG RESTRAINT SYSTEMS article. On models without remote audio/climate controls, check resistance between terminal No. 1 at air bag sliding contact and terminal No. 6 at air bag sliding contact connector C2012. See Fig. 3. On models with remote audio/climate controls, check resistance between terminal No. 6 at air bag sliding contact and terminal No. 6 at air bag sliding contact harness connector C2012 (male side). If resistance is one ohm or less and vehicle is not equipped with remote audio/climate controls, replace speed control switches. If resistance is one ohm or less and vehicle is equipped with remote audio/climate controls, go to next step. If resistance is greater than one ohm, replace air bag sliding contact.

6) Measure resistance between terminal No. 4 at air bag sliding contact harness connector and terminal No. 2 at speed control switch harness connector. See Fig. 4. Measure resistance between terminal No. 6 at air bag sliding contact harness connector and terminal No. 1 at speed control switch harness connector. If both resistance readings are 5 ohms or less, replace speed control switches. If either resistance reading is greater than 5 ohms, replace speed control switch wiring harness.

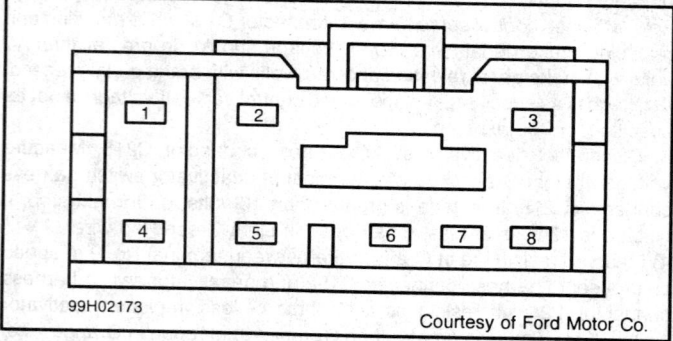

99H02173   Courtesy of Ford Motor Co.

Fig. 2: Identifying Air Bag Sliding Contact Harness Connector C2012 Terminals

TEST I: SET SPEED FLUCTUATES

Check throttle lever and speed control servo cable operation while performing speed control servo slack test with NGS tester. If throttle lever operates properly, replace speed control servo. If throttle lever does not operate properly, repair or replace components as necessary.

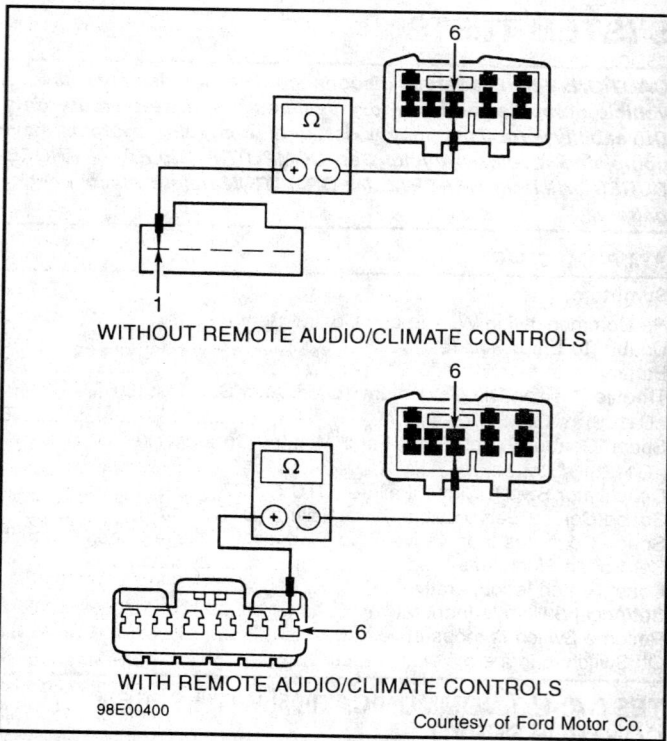

WITHOUT REMOTE AUDIO/CLIMATE CONTROLS

WITH REMOTE AUDIO/CLIMATE CONTROLS

98E00400   Courtesy of Ford Motor Co.

Fig. 3: Checking Air Bag Sliding Contact

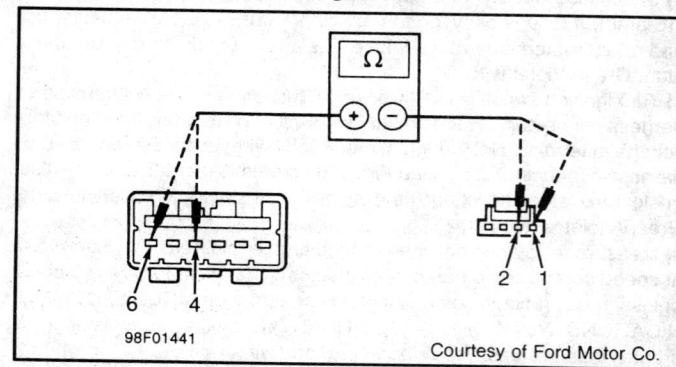

98F01441   Courtesy of Ford Motor Co.

Fig. 4: Checking Speed Control Switch Wiring Harness

TEST J: COAST SWITCH IS INOPERATIVE

1) Connect NGS tester to Data Link Connector (DLC). Using NGS tester, access speed control servo PID COAST. Press and release COAST switch while monitoring PID COAST on NGS tester. NGS tester should display ACTIVE when switch is pressed and NOTACTIVE when switch is released. If PID COAST does not agree with switch position, go to next step. If PID COAST agrees with switch position, system is okay at this time.

2) Turn ignition switch to LOCK position. Disconnect speed control servo harness connector C152. Measure resistance between terminals No. 5 (Light Blue/Black wire) and No. 6 (Black wire) at speed control servo harness connector C152 while pressing speed control COAST switch. See Fig. 1. Resistance should be 108-132 ohms when switch is pressed and greater than 10 k/ohms when switch is not pressed. If resistance is as specified, replace speed control servo. If resistance is not as specified, replace speed control switch.

TEST K: SET/ACCEL SWITCH IS INOPERATIVE

1) Connect NGS tester to Data Link Connector (DLC). Using NGS tester, access speed control servo PID SET_ACL. Press and release SET/ACCEL switch while monitoring PID SET_ACL on NGS tester. NGS tester should display ACTIVE when switch is pressed and NOTACTIVE

when switch is released. If PID SET_ACL does not agree with switch position, go to next step. If PID SET_ACL agrees with switch position, system is okay at this time.

2) Turn ignition switch to LOCK position. Disconnect speed control servo harness connector C152. Measure resistance between speed control terminals No. 5 (Light Blue/Black wire) and No. 6 (Black wire) at servo harness connector C152 while pressing speed control SET/ACCEL switch. See Fig. 1. Resistance should be 612-748 ohms when switch is pressed and greater than 10 k/ohms when switch is not pressed. If resistance is as specified, replace speed control servo. If resistance is not as specified, replace speed control switch.

TEST L: RESUME SWITCH IS INOPERATIVE

1) Connect NGS tester to Data Link Connector (DLC). Using NGS tester, access speed control servo PID RESUME. Press and release RESUME switch while monitoring PID SET_ACL on NGS tester. NGS tester should display ACTIVE when switch is pressed and NOTACTIVE when switch is released. If PID RESUME does not agree with switch position, go to next step. If PID RESUME agrees with switch position, system is okay at this time.

2) Turn ignition switch to LOCK position. Disconnect speed control servo harness connector C152. Measure resistance between speed control terminals No. 5 (Light Blue/Black wire) and No. 6 (Black wire) at servo harness connector C152 while pressing speed control RESUME switch. See Fig. 1. Resistance should be 1980-2420 ohms when switch is pressed and greater than 10 k/ohms when switch is not pressed. If resistance is as specified, replace speed control servo. If resistance is not as specified, replace speed control switch.

TEST M: OFF SWITCH IS INOPERATIVE

1) Connect NGS tester to Data Link Connector (DLC). Using NGS tester, access speed control servo PID SC_OFF. Press and release OFF switch while monitoring PID SC_OFF on NGS tester. NGS tester should display ACTIVE when switch is pressed and NOTACTIVE when switch is released. If PID SC_OFF does not agree with switch position, go to next step. If PID SC_OFF agrees with switch position, system is okay at this time.

2) Turn ignition switch to LOCK position. Disconnect speed control servo harness connector C152. Measure resistance between speed control terminals No. 5 (Light Blue/Black wire) and No. 6 (Black wire) at servo harness connector C152 while pressing speed control OFF switch. See Fig. 1. Resistance should be 5 ohms or less when switch is pressed and greater than 10 k/ohms when switch is not pressed. If resistance is as specified, replace speed control servo. If resistance is not as specified, replace speed control switch.

REMOVAL & INSTALLATION

WARNING: Deactivate air bag system before working around steering column. See appropriate AIR BAG RESTRAINT SYSTEMS article.

CAUTION: When battery is disconnected or modules are replaced, vehicle computer and memory systems may lose memory data. Driveability problems may exist until computer systems have completed a relearn cycle. See COMPUTER RELEARN PROCEDURES article in GENERAL INFORMATION before disconnecting battery.

SPEED CONTROL SWITCHES

Removal & Installation (With Remote Audio/Climate Controls) – Disconnect negative battery cable. Carefully pry speed control switches from steering wheel. Disconnect speed control switches harness connector and remove switches. To install, reverse removal procedure.

Removal & Installation (Without Remote Audio/Climate Controls) – Disable air bag system and remove driver side air bag module. See appropriate AIR BAG RESTRAINT SYSTEMS article. Ensure front wheels are in straight ahead position. Remove steering wheel retaining bolt and remove steering wheel. Tape air bag sliding contact to steering column to prevent misalignment. Remove steering wheel trim. Remove switches from steering wheel. To install, reverse removal procedure.

DEACTIVATOR SWITCH

Removal – Disconnect negative battery cable. Disconnect deactivator switch harness connector. Rotate deactivator switch counterclockwise. Remove deactivator switch.

Installation – Pull deactivator switch plunger out to its full travel. Fully depress brake pedal. Install deactivator switch and rotate clockwise. Connect deactivator switch harness connector. Slowly release brake pedal. Reconnect negative battery cable.

SPEED CONTROL SERVO ASSEMBLY

Removal & Installation – Disconnect speed control servo harness connector. Press cable cap locking tab and rotate cap counterclockwise to remove. Remove cable ball slug from pulley. Remove retaining nuts and servo. Separate speed control servo from bracket if necessary. To install, reverse removal procedure.

WIRING DIAGRAMS

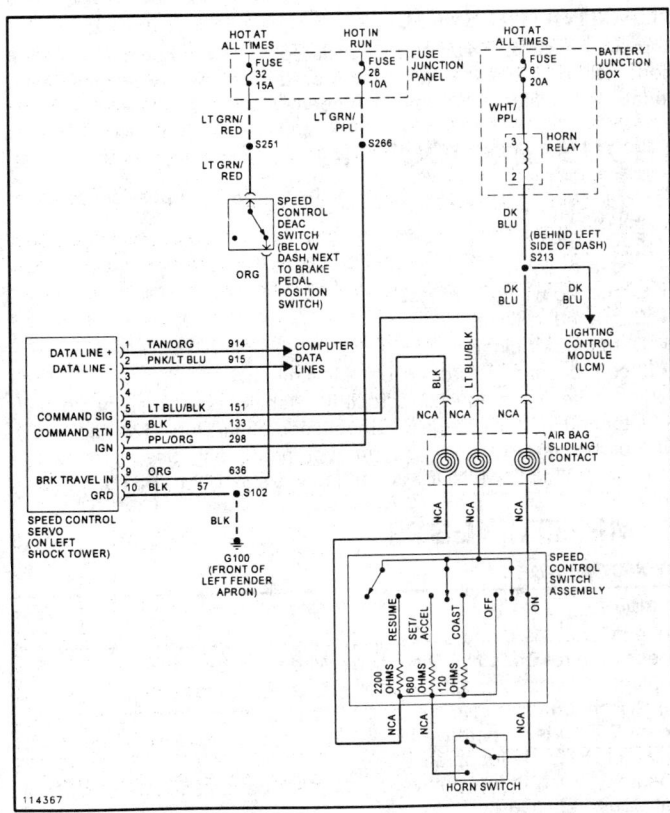

Fig. 5: Cruise Control System Wiring Diagram (Continental)

DESCRIPTION & OPERATION

Major components of the cruise control system are speed control switches, servo/actuator, vehicle speed sensor, stoplight switch, deactivator switch, clutch pedal position switch, and related wiring. This system does not require engine vacuum. An electronic servo/actuator actuates the throttle. All electronic control components are contained within the servo/actuator assembly.

The system is operational only at speeds greater than 25 MPH. The system is activated when ON/OFF switch is switched on and SET/ACCEL button is pressed and released. Vehicle will maintain set speed until new speed is set, brake pedal is pressed, clutch pedal is pressed, or ON/OFF switch is switched off. If system has been deactivated by pressing brake pedal or clutch pedal, set speed can be regained by pressing and releasing RESUME button. When brake pedal or clutch pedal is pressed, a signal from switch is sent to the servo/actuator to deactivate the system. A deactivator switch acts as a redundant brake signal.

COMPONENT LOCATIONS

COMPONENT LOCATIONS

Component	Location
Brake Pedal Deactivator Switch	On Brake Pedal Bracket
Clutch Pedal Position (CPP) Switch	On Clutch Pedal Bracket
Speed Control Servo/Actuator	Right Front Of Engine Compartment, On Strut Tower
Vehicle Speed Sensor	On Side Of Transmission

ADJUSTMENTS

DEACTIVATOR SWITCH

Remove deactivator switch. Pull switch plunger out completely until it stops. Depress brake pedal. Install switch and slowly release brake pedal. Deactivator switch is now properly adjusted.

TROUBLE SHOOTING

Before performing any testing, check the following for possible cause of system malfunction:
- Faulty fuses.
- Loose or corroded connections.
- Damaged wiring harness.
- Damaged switches.
- Damaged or binding servo/actuator cable.
- Incorrect servo/actuator cable adjustment.

Verify brake lights function properly. Repair as necessary. Inspect actuator and throttle linkage for smooth operation. Unbind as necessary. If no problems are found, perform appropriate test based upon symptom. See SYMPTOM INDEX table under SYMPTOM TESTS.

SYMPTOM TESTS

SYMPTOM INDEX

Symptom	Test
Speed Control Is Inoperative	A
Speed Control Does Not Disengage When Brakes Are Applied	B
Off Switch Is Inoperative	C
Coast Switch Is Inoperative	D
Set/Accl Switch Is Inoperative	E
Resume Switch Is Inoperative	F
Set Speed Fluctuates	G
Speed Control Does Not Disengage When Clutch Is Applied	H

TEST A: SPEED CONTROL IS INOPERATIVE

1) Turn ignition switch to LOCK position. Disconnect speed control servo/actuator harness connector C833. Turn ignition switch to RUN position. Measure voltage between terminals No. 7 (Violet/White wire) and No. 10 (Black/White wire) at speed control servo/actuator harness connector C833. See Fig. 1. If battery voltage exists, go to next step. If battery voltage does not exist, go to step **13**).

2) Measure voltage between terminals No. 4 (Orange/Blue wire) and No. 10 (Black/White wire) at speed control servo/actuator harness connector C833. If any voltage exists, repair brake light switch circuit for short to voltage or replace brake light switch. See appropriate wiring diagram in EXTERIOR LIGHTS article. If voltage does not exist and vehicle is equipped with M/T, go to next step. If voltage does not exist and vehicle is equipped with A/T, go to step **4**).

3) Turn ignition switch to LOCK position. Disconnect Clutch Pedal Position (CPP) switch harness connector C825. Measure resistance between terminals No. 1 and No. 3 at CPP switch (component side). See Fig. 2. If resistance is 5 ohms or less, go to next step. If resistance is greater than 5 ohms, replace CPP switch.

4) Turn ignition switch to RUN position. Measure voltage between terminals No. 9 (Orange/Yellow wire) and No. 10 (Black/White wire) at speed control servo/actuator harness connector C833. If battery voltage exists, go to next step. If battery voltage does not exist, go to step **15**).

5) Turn ignition switch to LOCK position. Measure resistance between terminals No. 5 (White wire) and 6 (Black wire) at speed control servo/actuator harness connector C833. If resistance is greater than 10 k/ohms, go to next step. If resistance is 10 k/ohms or less, replace speed control/horn switch.

6) Turn ignition switch to RUN position. Measure voltage between terminals No. 5 (White wire) and 10 (Black/White wire) at speed control servo/actuator harness connector C833. If no voltage exists, go to next step. If any voltage exists, repair short to voltage in White wire between speed control servo/actuator and clockspring.

7) Turn ignition switch to LOCK position. Measure resistance between terminals No. 5 (White wire) and 10 (Black/White wire) at speed control servo/actuator harness connector C833. If resistance is greater than 10 k/ohms, go to next step. If resistance is 10 k/ohms or less, repair short to ground in White wire between speed control servo/actuator and clockspring.

8) Measure resistance between terminals No. 6 (Black wire) and 10 (Black/White wire) at speed control servo/actuator harness connector C833. If resistance is greater than 10 k/ohms, go to next step. If resistance is 10 k/ohms or less, repair short to ground in Black wire between speed control servo/actuator and clockspring.

9) Turn ignition switch to RUN position. Measure voltage between ground and terminal No. 6 (Black wire) at speed control servo/actuator harness connector C833. If no voltage exists, go to next step. If any voltage exists, repair short to voltage in Black wire between speed control servo/actuator and clockspring.

10) Measure voltage between ground and terminal No. 5 (White wire) at speed control servo/actuator harness connector C833 while pressing speed control ON switch. If battery voltage exists, go to next step. If battery voltage does not exist, check horn operation. If horn does not operate, repair horn system as necessary. If horn operates properly, go to step **14**).

11) Turn ignition switch to LOCK position. Measure resistance between terminals No. 5 (White wire) and No. 6 (Black wire) at speed control servo/actuator harness connector C833 while pressing speed control SET/ACC switch. If resistance is 640-720 ohms, go to next step. If resistance is not 640-720 ohms, replace speed control/horn switch.

12) Disconnect instrument cluster harness connector C808b. Measure resistance between terminal No. 3 (White/Violet wire) at speed control servo/actuator harness connector C833 and terminal No. 8 (White/Light Blue wire) at instrument cluster harness connector C808b. If resistance is 5 ohms or less and speedometer operates properly, replace speed control servo/actuator. If resistance is 5 ohms or less and speedometer does not operate properly, repair speedometer. See appropriate INSTRUMENT PANELS article. If resistance is greater than 5 ohms, repair open in White/Violet or White/Light Blue wire as necessary.

13) Measure voltage at terminal No. 7 (Violet/White wire) at speed control servo/actuator harness connector C833. If battery voltage exists, repair open in Black/White wire. If battery voltage does not exists, repair open in Violet/White wire.

14) Measure resistance between terminals No. 5 (White wire) and No. 6 (Black wire) at speed control servo/actuator harness connector C833 while pressing speed control OFF switch. If resistance is 5 ohms or less, replace speed control/horn switch. If resistance is greater than 5 ohms, repair open in White wire.

15) Ensure ignition switch is in LOCK position. Disconnect brake pedal deactivator switch harness connector C824. Measure resistance between brake pedal deactivator switch terminals (component side). If resistance is 5 ohms or less, go to next step. If resistance is greater than 5 ohms, replace brake pedal deactivator switch.

16) Turn ignition switch to RUN position. Measure voltage at terminal No. 1 (Orange/Yellow wire) at brake pedal deactivator switch harness connector C824. See Fig. 3. If battery voltage exists, go to next step. If battery voltage does not exist, repair open in Orange/Yellow wire.

17) Ensure ignition is in LOCK position. Disconnect speed control servo/actuator harness connector C833. Measure resistance in Orange/Yellow wire between terminal No. 9 at speed control servo/actuator harness connector C833 and terminal No. 2 at brake pedal deactivator switch harness connector C824. If resistance is 5 ohms or less, replace speed control servo/actuator. If resistance is greater than 5 ohms, repair open in Orange/Yellow wire.

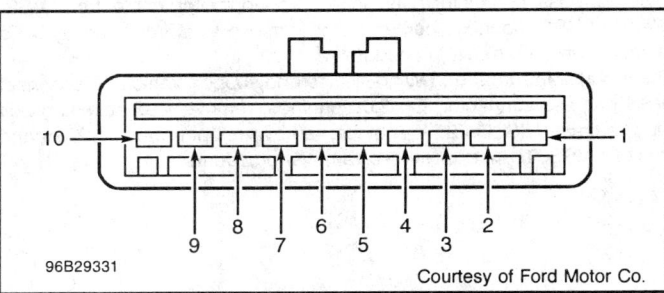

Fig. 1: Identifying Speed Control Servo/Actuator Harness Connector C833 Terminals

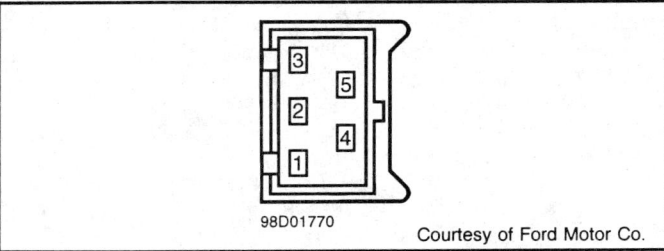

Fig. 2: Identifying Clutch Pedal Position Switch Terminals

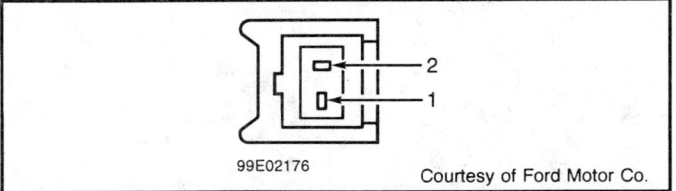

Fig. 3: Identifying Brake Pedal Deactivator Switch Harness Connector C824 Terminals

TEST B: SPEED CONTROL DOES NOT DISENGAGE WHEN BRAKES ARE APPLIED

1) Turn ignition switch to RUN position. Press brake pedal and observe brake light operation. If brake lights operate properly, go to next step. If brake lights do not operate properly, repair brake lights as necessary. See appropriate wiring diagram in EXTERIOR LIGHTS article.

2) Ensure ignition switch is in LOCK position. Disconnect brake pedal deactivator switch harness connector C824. Measure resistance between brake pedal deactivator switch terminals. Resistance should be 5 ohms or less when brake pedal is released and greater than 10

k/ohms when brake pedal is depressed. If resistance is as specified, go to next step. If resistance is no as specified, replace brake pedal deactivator switch.

3) Ensure ignition switch is in LOCK position. Disconnect speed control servo/actuator harness connector C833. Measure voltage between terminals No. 9 (Orange/Yellow wire) and No. 10 (Black/White wire) at speed control servo/actuator harness connector C833. See Fig. 1. If no voltage exists, go to next step. If any voltage exists, repair short to voltage in Orange/Yellow wire.

4) Disconnect Brake Pedal Position (BPP) switch harness connector C444. Measure resistance in Orange/Blue wire between terminal No. 4 at speed control servo/actuator harness connector C833 and BPP switch harness connector C444. If resistance is 5 ohms or less, replace speed control servo/actuator. If resistance is greater than 5 ohms, repair open in Orange/Blue wire.

TEST C: OFF SWITCH IS INOPERATIVE

Turn ignition switch to LOCK position. Disconnect speed control servo/actuator harness connector C833. Measure resistance between terminals No. 5 (White wire) and No. 6 (Black wire) at speed control servo/actuator harness connector C833 while pressing speed control OFF switch. See Fig. 1. If resistance is 5 ohms or less, replace speed control servo/actuator. If resistance is greater than 5 ohms, replace speed control/horn switch.

TEST D: COAST SWITCH IS INOPERATIVE

Turn ignition switch to LOCK position. Disconnect speed control servo/actuator harness connector C833. Measure resistance between terminals No. 5 (White wire) and No. 6 (Black wire) at speed control servo/actuator harness connector C833 while pressing speed control COAST switch. See Fig. 1. If resistance is 114-126 ohms, replace speed control servo/actuator. If resistance is not 114-126 ohms, replace speed control/horn switch.

TEST E: SET/ACCL SWITCH IS INOPERATIVE

Turn ignition switch to LOCK position. Disconnect speed control servo/actuator harness connector C833. Measure resistance between terminals No. 5 (White wire) and No. 6 (Black wire) at speed control servo/actuator harness connector C833 while pressing speed control SET/ACCL switch. See Fig. 1. If resistance is 646-714 ohms, replace speed control servo/actuator. If resistance is not 646-714 ohms, replace speed control/horn switch.

TEST F: RESUME SWITCH IS INOPERATIVE

Turn ignition switch to LOCK position. Disconnect speed control servo/actuator harness connector C833. Measure resistance between terminals No. 5 (White wire) and No. 6 (Black wire) at speed control servo/actuator harness connector C833 while pressing speed control RESUME switch. See Fig. 1. If resistance is 2090-2310 ohms, replace speed control servo/actuator. If resistance is not 2090-2310 ohms, replace speed control/horn switch.

TEST G: SET SPEED FLUCTUATES

Turn ignition switch to LOCK position. Disconnect speed control servo/actuator harness connector C833. Disconnect vehicle speed sensor harness connector. Measure resistance between White/Blue terminal at vehicle speed sensor harness connector and terminal No. 3 (White/Violet wire) at speed control servo/actuator harness connector C833. If resistance is 5 ohms or less and speedometer operates properly, replace speed control servo/actuator. If resistance is 5 ohms or less and speedometer does not operate properly, repair speedometer as necessary. See appropriate INSTRUMENT PANELS article. If resistance is greater than 5 ohms, repair open in White/Violet or White/Blue wire.

TEST H: SPEED CONTROL DOES NOT DISENGAGE WHEN CLUTCH IS APPLIED

Ensure ignition switch is in LOCK position. Disconnect Clutch Pedal Position (CPP) switch harness connector C825. Measure resistance between terminals No. 1 and 3 at CPP switch (component side). See

Fig. 2. Resistance should be greater than 10 k/ohms when clutch pedal is depressed and less than 5 ohms when clutch pedal is released. If resistance is as specified, replace speed control servo/actuator. If resistance is not as specified, replace CPP switch.

REMOVAL & INSTALLATION

WARNING: Deactivate air bag system before working around steering column. See appropriate AIR BAG RESTRAINT SYSTEMS article.

CAUTION: When battery is disconnected, vehicle computer and memory systems may lose memory data. Driveability problems may exist until computer systems have completed a relearn cycle. See COMPUTER RELEARN PROCEDURES article in GENERAL INFORMATION before disconnecting battery.

SPEED CONTROL SWITCHES

Removal & Installation – Disable air bag system and remove driver side air bag. See appropriate AIR BAG RESTRAINT SYSTEMS article. Disconnect speed control switches harness connector and remove switches. To install, reverse removal procedure.

DEACTIVATOR SWITCH

Removal & Installation – Remove driver side lower instrument panel. Disconnect deactivator switch harness connector (located above stoplight switch) and remove deactivator switch. To install, reverse removal procedure. Adjust deactivator switch. See DEACTIVATOR SWITCH under ADJUSTMENTS.

SERVO/ACTUATOR ASSEMBLY

Removal & Installation (2.0L Engine) – Remove intake air resonator. Disconnect actuating cable from throttle body cam. Remove throttle cable from throttle bracket. Push retaining clip from throttle bracket and pull cable out. Disconnect speed control servo/actuator harness connector. Remove actuator retaining bolt and separate actuator. Depress and hold cable cap locking clip while turning cap counterclockwise. Remove cable from actuator pulley. To install, reverse removal procedure.

Removal & Installation (2.5L Engine) – Disconnect actuating cable from throttle body cam. Pull actuating cable through throttle bracket. Push retaining clip from throttle bracket and pull cable out. Disconnect air temperature sensor electrical connector. Disconnect speed control servo/actuator electrical connector. Remove actuator retaining bolt and separate actuator. Remove outer cowl top vent panel/screen. Depress and hold cable cap locking clip while turning cap counterclockwise. Remove cable from actuator pulley. To install, reverse removal procedure.

VEHICLE SPEED SENSOR (VSS)

Removal & Installation (A/T) – Raise and support vehicle. Disconnect VSS harness connector. Disconnect speedometer cable from VSS. Remove VSS mounting bolt and clip. Remove VSS from transaxle. To install, reverse removal procedure.

Removal & Installation (M/T) – Raise and support vehicle. Disconnect VSS harness connector. On 2.0L engines, remove VSS retaining bolt and remove VSS. On 2.5L engines, remove roll pin retaining VSS and remove VSS. To install, reverse removal procedure.

WIRING DIAGRAMS

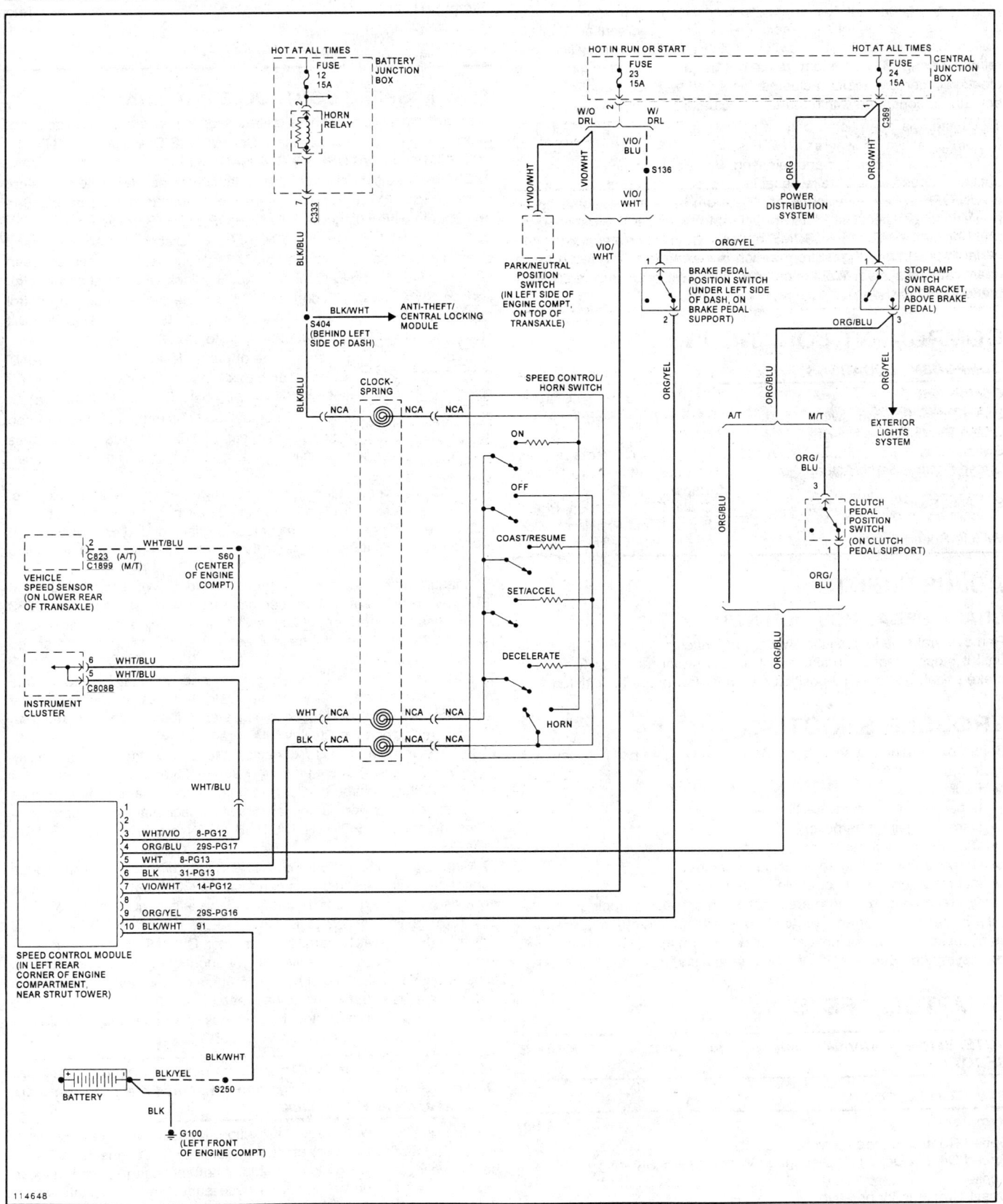

Fig. 4: Cruise Control System Wiring Diagram (Contour & Mystique)

114648

DESCRIPTION & OPERATION

Major components of the cruise control system are speed control switches, speed control servo/actuator, vehicle speed sensor, stoplight switch, brake pedal position switch, clutch pedal position switch, and related wiring. This system does not require engine vacuum. An electronic servo/actuator actuates the throttle. Speed control servo/actuator is contained within the servo/actuator assembly.

The system is operational only at speeds greater than 25 MPH. The system is activated when ON/OFF switch is switched on and SET/ACCEL button is pressed and released. Vehicle will maintain set speed until new speed is set, brake pedal is pressed, clutch pedal is pressed, or ON/OFF switch is switched off. If system has been deactivated by pressing brake pedal or clutch pedal, set speed can be regained by pressing and releasing RESUME button. When brake pedal or clutch pedal is pressed, a signal from switch is sent to the servo/actuator to deactivate the system. A brake pedal position switch acts as a redundant brake signal.

COMPONENT LOCATIONS

COMPONENT LOCATIONS

Component	Location
Brake Pedal Position Switch	On Brake Pedal Bracket
Clutch Pedal Position (CPP) Switch	On Clutch Pedal Bracket
Speed Control Servo/Actuator	Left Rear Of Engine Compartment, On Strut Tower
Stoplight Switch	On Brake Pedal Bracket, Below Brake Pedal Position Switch
Vehicle Speed Sensor	On Side Of Transmission

ADJUSTMENTS

BRAKE PEDAL POSITION SWITCH

Remove brake pedal position switch. Pull switch plunger out completely until it stops. Depress brake pedal. Install switch and slowly release brake pedal. brake pedal position switch is now properly adjusted.

TROUBLE SHOOTING

Before performing any testing, check the following for possible cause of system malfunction:
- Faulty fuses.
- Loose or corroded connections.
- Damaged wiring harness.
- Damaged switches.
- Damaged or binding servo/actuator cable.
- Incorrect servo/actuator cable adjustment.

Verify brake lights and horn are functioning properly. Repair as necessary. Inspect actuator and throttle linkage for smooth operation. Repair as necessary. If no problems are found, perform appropriate test based upon symptom. See SYMPTOM INDEX table under SYMPTOM TESTS.

SYMPTOM TESTS

NOTE: Before performing any symptom test, see TROUBLE SHOOTING.

SYMPTOM INDEX

Symptom	Test
Speed Control Is Inoperative	A
Speed Control Does Not Disengage When Brakes Are Applied	B
Coast Switch Is Inoperative	C
Resume Switch Is Inoperative	D
Speed Control Does Not Disengage When Clutch Is Applied	E
Set Speed Fluctuates	F

SYMPTOM INDEX (Cont.)

Symptom	Test
Off Switch Is Inoperative	1

[1] – Replace speed control servo/actuator.

TEST A: SPEED CONTROL IS INOPERATIVE

1) Press horn switches. If horn operates, go to next step. If horn does not operate, repair horn as necessary. See WIRING DIAGRAMS in STEERING COLUMN SWITCHES – COUGAR article.

2) Check brake light operation. If brake lights operate, go to next step. If brake lights do not operate, repair brake lights as necessary. See appropriate wiring diagram in EXTERIOR LIGHTS article.

3) Turn ignition switch to LOCK position. Disconnect speed control servo/actuator harness connector C833. Measure resistance between terminals No. 5 (White wire) and No. 6 (Black wire) at speed control servo/actuator harness connector C833 while pressing speed control ON switch. See Fig. 1. If resistance is not 260-280 ohms, go to next step. If resistance is 260-280 ohms, go to step 6).

4) Deactivate air bag system. See appropriate AIR BAG RESTRAINT SYSTEMS article. Disconnect air bag sliding contact harness connector C896. Measure resistance is White wire between terminal No. 3 at air bag sliding contact harness connector C896 and terminal No. 5 at speed control servo/actuator harness connector C833. If resistance is 5 ohms or less, go to next step. If resistance is greater than 5 ohms, repair open in White wire.

5) Remove driver's side air bag. Measure resistance in Black wire, Red/Orange wire and Black/Blue wire of air bag sliding contact. If all resistance readings are 5 ohms or less, replace speed control switch. If any resistance reading is greater than 5 ohms, replace air bag sliding contact.

6) Measure resistance between terminals No. 5 (White wire) and No. 6 (Black wire) at speed control servo/actuator harness connector C833 while pressing speed control OFF switch. If resistance is 5 ohms or less, go to next step. If resistance is greater than 5 ohms, replace speed control switch.

7) Measure resistance between ground and terminal No. 10 (Black/White wire) at speed control servo/actuator harness connector C833. If resistance is 5 ohms or less, go to next step. If resistance is greater than 5 ohms, repair open in Black/White wire.

8) Turn ignition switch to RUN position. Measure voltage at terminal No. 7 (Violet/White wire) at speed control servo/actuator harness connector C833. If battery voltage exists, go to next step. If battery voltage does not exist, repair power distribution circuit as necessary. See appropriate wiring diagram in POWER DISTRIBUTION article in WIRING DIAGRAMS.

9) Measure voltage at terminal No. 9 (Orange/Yellow wire) at speed control servo/actuator harness connector C833. If battery voltage does not exist, go to next step. If battery voltage exists, go to step 13).

10) Turn ignition switch to LOCK position. Disconnect Brake Pedal Position (BPP) switch harness connector C824. Measure resistance between terminals at BPP switch (component side). When brake pedal is not pressed, resistance should be 5 ohms or less. When brake pedal is depressed, resistance should be greater than 10 k/ohms. If resistance is as specified, go to next step. If resistance is not as specified, adjust or replace BPP switch as necessary.

NOTE: Both wires at BPP switch harness connector C824 are Orange/Yellow. Ensure voltage and resistance measurements are made at appropriate terminal.

11) Turn ignition switch to RUN position. Measure voltage at terminal No. 2 (Orange/Yellow wire) at BPP switch harness connector C824. If battery voltage exists, go to next step. If battery voltage does not exist, repair power distribution circuit as necessary. See appropriate wiring diagram in POWER DISTRIBUTION article in WIRING DIAGRAMS.

12) Turn ignition switch to LOCK position. Measure resistance in Orange/Yellow wire between terminal No. 1 at BPP switch harness connector and terminal No. 9 at speed control servo/actuator harness connector C833. If resistance is 5 ohms or less, adjust BPP switch. If resistance is greater than 5 ohms, repair open in Orange/Yellow wire.

13) Measure voltage at terminal No. 4 (Orange/Blue wire) at speed control servo/actuator harness connector C833 while depressing brake pedal. If battery voltage does not exist and equipped with M/T, go to next step. If battery voltage does not exist and equipped with A/T, repair open in Orange/Blue wire. If battery voltage exists, go to step **16)**.

NOTE: CPP switch harness connector C824 has 2 Orange/Blue wires. Ensure voltage measurement is made at appropriate terminal.

14) Turn ignition switch to LOCK position. Disconnect Clutch Pedal Position (CPP) switch harness connector C825. Measure voltage at Orange/Blue wire terminal at CPP switch harness connector C825 while depressing brake pedal. If battery voltage exists, go to next step. If battery voltage does not exist, repair open in Orange/Blue wire.

15) Measure resistance between terminals No. 1 and 3 at CPP switch (component side). *See Fig. 2.* When clutch pedal is not depressed, resistance should be 5 ohms or less. When clutch pedal is depressed, resistance should be greater than 10 k/ohms. If resistance is as specified, repair open in Orange/Blue wire between CPP switch and speed control servo/actuator. If resistance is not as specified, adjust or replace CPP switch as necessary.

16) Disconnect Hybrid Electronic Cluster (HEC) harness connector C808b. Measure resistance in White/Blue wire between terminal No. 26 at HEC harness connector C808b and terminal No. 3 at speed control servo/actuator harness connector C833. *See Figs. 1 and 3.* If resistance is 5 ohms or less, go to next step. If resistance is greater than 5 ohms, repair open in White/Blue wire.

17) Connect all disconnected harness connectors and restore vehicle to normal operating condition. Using New Generation Star (NGS) tester, perform HEC self-test. If no DTCs exist, replace speed control servo/actuator. If any DTCs exist, repair as necessary. For a complete list of HEC DTCs and location of testing procedures, see MODULE COMMUNICATIONS NETWORK – COUGAR article.

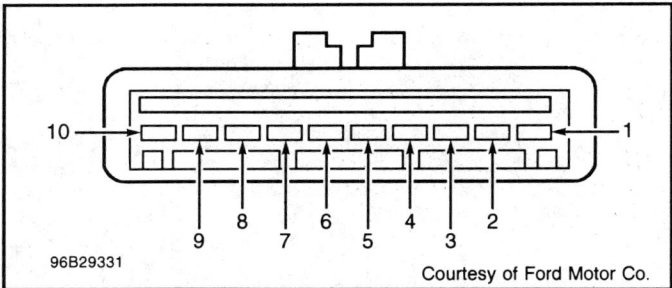

Fig. 1: Identifying Speed Control Servo/Actuator Harness Connector C833 Terminals

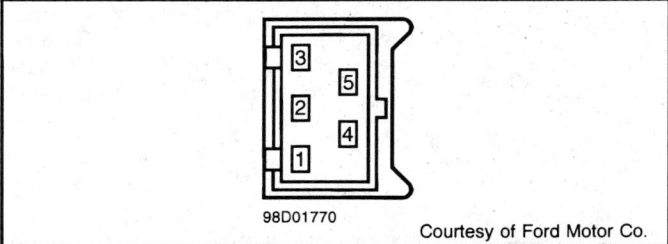

Fig. 2: Identifying Clutch Pedal Position Switch Terminals (Component Side)

TEST B: SPEED CONTROL DOES NOT DISENGAGE WHEN BRAKES ARE APPLIED

1) Turn ignition switch to RUN position. Press brake pedal and observe brake light operation. If brake lights operate properly, go to next step. If brake lights do not operate properly, repair brake lights as necessary. See appropriate wiring diagram in EXTERIOR LIGHTS article.

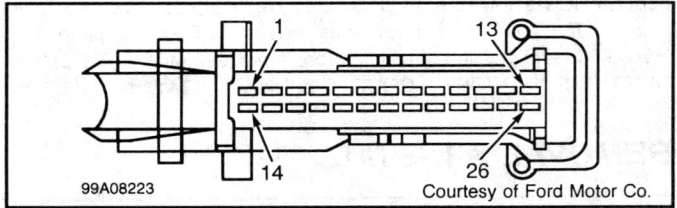

Fig. 3: Identifying Hybrid Electronic Cluster Harness Connector C808b Terminals

2) Ensure ignition switch is in LOCK position. Disconnect Brake Pedal Position (BPP) switch harness connector C824. Measure resistance between BPP switch terminals (component side). Resistance should be 5 ohms or less when brake pedal is released and greater than 10 k/ohms when brake pedal is depressed. If resistance is as specified, go to next step. If resistance is no as specified, replace BPP switch.

3) Ensure ignition switch is in LOCK position. Disconnect speed control servo/actuator harness connector C833. Turn ignition switch to RUN position. Measure voltage at terminal No. 9 (Orange/Yellow wire) at speed control servo/actuator harness connector C833. *See Fig. 1.* If no voltage exists, go to next step. If any voltage exists, repair short to voltage in Orange/Yellow wire.

4) Disconnect stop light switch harness connector C444. Measure resistance in Orange/Blue wire between terminal No. 4 at speed control servo/actuator harness connector C833 and stop light switch connector C444. If resistance is 5 ohms or less, replace speed control servo/actuator. If resistance is greater than 5 ohms, repair open in Orange/Blue wire.

TEST C: COAST SWITCH IS INOPERATIVE

Turn ignition switch to LOCK position. Disconnect speed control servo/actuator harness connector C833. Measure resistance between terminals No. 5 (White wire) and No. 6 (Black wire) at speed control servo/actuator harness connector C833 while pressing speed control COAST switch. *See Fig. 1.* If resistance is 110-130 ohms, replace speed control servo/actuator. If resistance is not 110-130 ohms, replace speed control/horn switch.

TEST D: RESUME SWITCH IS INOPERATIVE

Turn ignition switch to LOCK position. Disconnect speed control servo/actuator harness connector C833. Measure resistance between terminals No. 5 (White wire) and No. 6 (Black wire) at speed control servo/actuator harness connector C833 while pressing speed control RESUME switch. *See Fig. 1.* If resistance is approximately 2200 ohms, replace speed control servo/actuator. If resistance is not approximately 2200 ohms, replace speed control/horn switch.

TEST E: SPEED CONTROL DOES NOT DISENGAGE WHEN CLUTCH IS APPLIED

Ensure ignition switch is in LOCK position. Disconnect Clutch Pedal Position (CPP) switch harness connector C825. Measure resistance between terminals No. 1 and 3 at CPP switch (component side). *See Fig. 2.* Resistance should be greater than 10 k/ohms when clutch pedal is depressed and less than 5 ohms when clutch pedal is released. If resistance is as specified, replace speed control servo/actuator. If resistance is not as specified, replace CPP switch.

TEST F: SET SPEED FLUCTUATES

1) Turn ignition switch to LOCK position. Disconnect speed control servo/actuator harness connector C833. Disconnect Hybrid Electronic Cluster (HEC) harness connector C808b. Measure resistance in White/Blue wire between terminal No. 26 at HEC harness connector C808b and terminal No. 3 at speed control servo/actuator harness connector C833. *See Figs. 1 and 3.* If resistance is 5 ohms or less, go to next step. If resistance is greater than 5 ohms, repair open in White/Blue wire.

2) Connect all disconnected harness connectors and restore vehicle to normal operating condition. Using New Generation Star (NGS) tester, perform HEC self-test. If no DTCs exist, replace speed control servo/actuator. If any DTCs exist, repair as necessary. For a complete list of HEC DTCs and location of testing procedures, see MODULE COMMUNICATIONS NETWORK – COUGAR article.

REMOVAL & INSTALLATION

WARNING: *Deactivate air bag system before working around steering column. See appropriate AIR BAG RESTRAINT SYSTEMS article.*

CAUTION: *When battery is disconnected, vehicle computer and memory systems may lose memory data. Driveability problems may exist until computer systems have completed a relearn cycle. See COMPUTER RELEARN PROCEDURES article in GENERAL INFORMATION before disconnecting battery.*

SPEED CONTROL SWITCHES

Removal & Installation – Disable air bag system and remove driver side air bag. See appropriate AIR BAG RESTRAINT SYSTEMS article. Disconnect speed control switches harness connector and remove switches. To install, reverse removal procedure.

BRAKE PEDAL POSITION SWITCH

Removal & Installation – Remove driver's side instrument panel under cover. Disconnect brake pedal position switch harness connector (located above stoplight switch) and remove brake pedal position switch. To install, reverse removal procedure. Adjust brake pedal position switch. See BRAKE PEDAL POSITION SWITCH under ADJUSTMENTS.

SERVO/ACTUATOR ASSEMBLY

Removal & Installation (2.0L Engine) – Remove intake air resonator. Disconnect actuating cable from throttle body cam. Remove throttle cable from throttle bracket. Push retaining clip from throttle bracket and pull cable out. Disconnect speed control servo/actuator harness connector. Remove actuator retaining bolt and separate actuator. Depress and hold cable cap locking clip while turning cap counterclockwise. Remove cable from actuator pulley. To install, reverse removal procedure.

Removal & Installation (2.5L Engine) – Disconnect actuating cable from throttle body cam. Pull actuating cable through throttle bracket. Push retaining clip from throttle bracket and pull cable out. Disconnect air temperature sensor electrical connector. Disconnect speed control servo/actuator electrical connector. Remove actuator retaining bolt and separate actuator. Remove outer cowl top vent panel/screen. Depress and hold cable cap locking clip while turning cap counterclockwise. Remove cable from actuator pulley. To install, reverse removal procedure.

VEHICLE SPEED SENSOR (VSS)

Removal & Installation (A/T) – Raise and support vehicle. Disconnect VSS harness connector. Disconnect speedometer cable from VSS. Remove VSS mounting bolt and clip. Remove VSS from transaxle. To install, reverse removal procedure.

Removal & Installation (M/T) – Raise and support vehicle. Disconnect VSS harness connector. On 2.0L engines, remove VSS retaining bolt and remove VSS. On 2.5L engines, remove roll pin retaining VSS and remove VSS. To install, reverse removal procedure.

WIRING DIAGRAMS

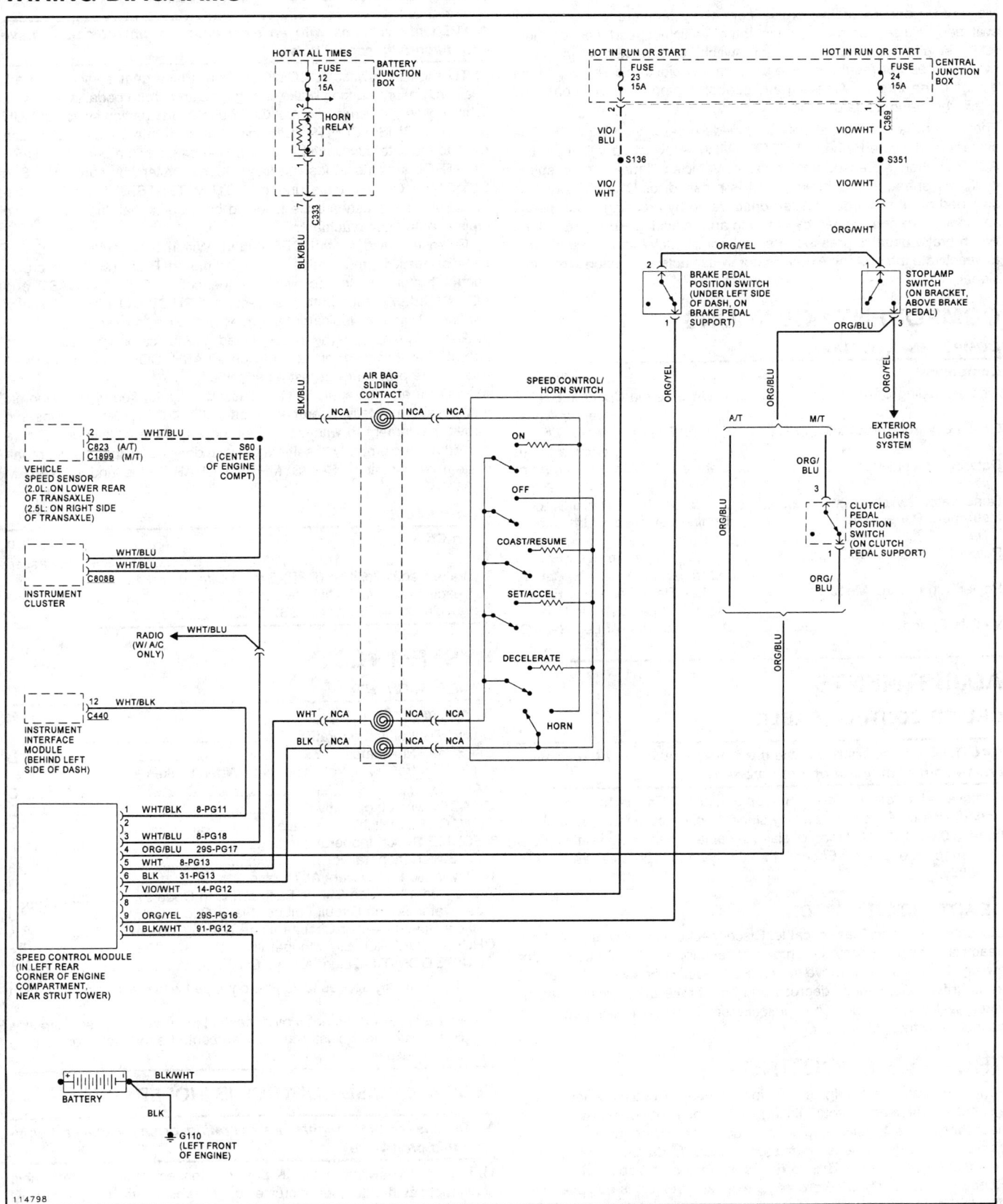

Fig. 4: Cruise Control System Wiring Diagram (Cougar)

DESCRIPTION & OPERATION

Major components of the cruise control system are cruise control switches, cruise control servo/actuator, vehicle speed sensor, horn relay, stoplight switch, deactivator switch, and related wiring. This system does not require engine vacuum. An electronic servo/actuator actuates the throttle. All electronic control components are contained within the servo/actuator assembly.

The system is operational only at speeds greater than 30 MPH. The system is activated when ON/OFF switch is switched on and SET/ACCEL button is pressed and released. Vehicle will maintain set speed until new speed is set, brake pedal is pressed, or ON/OFF switch is switched off. If system has been deactivated by pressing brake pedal, set speed can be regained by pressing and releasing RESUME button. When brake pedal is pressed, a signal from switch is sent to the servo to deactivate the system. A deactivator switch acts as a redundant brake signal.

COMPONENT LOCATIONS

COMPONENT LOCATIONS

Component	Location
Air Bag Sliding Contact	On Steering Column, Behind Steering Wheel
Cruise Control Servo/Actuator	Left Rear Corner Of Engine Compartment
Data Link Connector	Behind Left Side Of Instrument Panel
Deactivator Switch	On Brake Pedal Bracket
Instrument Panel Fuse Box	Behind Left Side Of Instrument Panel
Power Distribution Box	Right Front Of Engine Compartment Next To Battery
Powertrain Control Module	Left Rear Corner Of Engine Compartment, In Firewall
Vehicle Speed Sensor	Located At Left Rear Of Transmission

ADJUSTMENTS

CRUISE CONTROL CABLE

CAUTION: Cruise control cable must not be pulled tight, otherwise cruise control may not operate properly.

Remove cable retaining clip from cable adjuster. Ensure throttle is fully closed. Pull cable to take up any slack. Loosen at least one notch so there is 0.04-0.12" (1-3 mm) of slack in cable. Insert cable retaining clip and snap into place. Ensure throttle linkage operates freely and smoothly.

DEACTIVATOR SWITCH

Disconnect negative battery cable. Disconnect electrical connector from deactivator switch (located on brake pedal support). Rotate deactivator switch clockwise and remove switch. Pull deactivator switch plunger out to full travel. Completely depress and hold brake pedal. Install deactivator switch and rotate counterclockwise. Release brake pedal and connect electrical connector.

TROUBLE SHOOTING

Verify horn and brake lights function properly. Repair as necessary. Inspect actuator and throttle linkage for smooth operation. Unbind as necessary. Check for faulty fuses, loose or corroded connections, damaged wiring harness, damaged switches, damaged or binding servo/actuator cable and incorrect servo/actuator cable adjustment. Repair as necessary. If no problems exist and vehicle is equipped with an electronic instrument cluster, perform self-diagnostics. See SELF-DIAGNOSTIC SYSTEM. If no problems exist and vehicle is equipped with an analog instrument cluster, repair by symptom. See SYMPTOM CHART table under SYSTEM TESTS.

SELF-DIAGNOSTIC SYSTEM

NOTE: Only vehicles with an electronic instrument cluster have self-diagnostic capabilities.

1) Turn ignition switch to LOCK position. Place gear selector in Park position. Ensure parking brake is engaged and brake pedal is released. While holding the cruise control OFF button, turn ignition switch to RUN position. CRUISE CONTROL indicator on instrument cluster will flash once to indicate successful entry into self-diagnostic mode. If CRUISE CONTROL indicator does not flash, repair system by symptom. See SYMPTOM CHART table under SYSTEM TESTS. If CRUISE CONTROL indicator flashes once followed by 5 additional flashes, replace cruise control servo/actuator.
2) Release cruise control OFF button. Within 5 seconds of entering self-diagnostics, press cruise control ON button. Press remaining cruise control buttons in the following sequence: RESUME, COAST and SET/ACCEL. As each button is pressed, CRUISE CONTROL indicator will flash. Wait until indicator light goes out to press next button.
3) After sequence has been completed, the indicator light will flash to indicate test passed or failed. See FLASH CODE table. Perform appropriate procedure or test as specified.
4) Immediately after static test has passed, actuator performs a dynamic test by automatically operating throttle .04-.40" (1-10 mm). Observe throttle movement to witness any sticking of cable or linkage. Ensure throttle returns properly. If self-diagnostics does not pinpoint fault, repair system by symptom. See SYMPTOM CHART table under SYSTEM TESTS.

FLASH CODE

Flash Code	Test
1	System Passed
2 (Brake Pedal Position (BPP) Switch Circuit)	I
3 (Deactivator Switch Circuit)	J
4 (Vehicle Speed Sensor (VSS) Circuit)	K

SYSTEM TESTS

SYMPTOM CHART

Symptom	Test
Cruise Control Is Inoperative	A
Set Speed Fluctuates	B
Cruise Control Does Not Disengage When Brakes Are Applied	C
COAST Switch Inoperative	D
SET/ACCEL Switch Inoperative	E
RESUME Switch Inoperative	F
OFF Switch Inoperative	G
No Dynamic Pull Occurs At Throttle	[1] H
Brake Pedal Position Switch Failure (Flash Code 2)	[1] I
Deactivator Switch Circuit Failure (Flash Code 3)	[1] J
Vehicle Speed Sensor Circuit Failure (Flash Code 4)	[1] K
CRUISE CONTROL Light Inoperative	[1 2]
CRUISE CONTROL Light Always On	[1 2]

[1] – This test only applies to vehicle equipped with electronic instrument clusters.
[2] – Manufacturer does not provide testing information. Check circuitry, bulb, instrument cluster and cruise control servo/actuator as possible causes.

TEST A: CRUISE CONTROL IS INOPERATIVE

NOTE: Ensure brake lights are operating properly before beginning this procedure.

1) Turn igniton switch to LOCK position. Inspect cruise control cable attachment at throttle body. If cruise control cable is attached, go to next step. If cruise control cable is not attached, attach cable and retest system.
2) Disconnect cruise control servo/actuator harness connector C234. Turn ignition switch to RUN position. Measure voltage between termi-

1999 ACCESSORIES & EQUIPMENT
Cruise Control Systems – Crown Victoria & Grand Marquis (Cont.)

FORD
4-413

nals No. 7 (White/Violet wire) and No. 10 (Pink/Orange wire) at cruise control servo/actuator harness connector C234. *See Fig. 1.* If battery voltage does not exist, go to next step. If battery voltage exists, go to step **4**).

3) Measure resistance between ground and terminal No. 10 (Pink/Orange wire) at cruise control servo/actuator harness connector C234. If resistance is 5 ohms or less, repair open or short to ground in White/Violet wire. If resistance is greater than 5 ohms, repair open in Pink/Orange wire.

4) Ensure brake pedal is not depressed. Measure voltage between terminals No. 4 (Light Green wire) and No. 10 (Pink/Orange wire) at cruise control servo/actuator harness connector C234. If voltage does not exist, go to next step. If voltage exists, repair short to voltage in Light Green wire.

5) Measure resistance between terminals No. 4 (Light Green wire) and No. 10 (Pink/Orange wire) at cruise control servo/actuator harness connector C234. If resistance is 20 ohms or less, go to next step. If resistance is greater than 20 ohms, repair open in Light Green wire.

6) Measure voltage between terminals No. 9 (Orange wire) and No. 10 (Pink/Orange wire) at cruise control servo/actuator harness connector C234. If battery voltage does not exist, go to next step. If battery voltage exists, go to step **9**).

7) Disconnect cruise control deactivator switch harness connector C233. Measure resistance between cruise control deactivator switch terminals (component side). If resistance is 5 ohms or less, go to next step. If resistance is greater than 5 ohms, replace cruise control deactivator switch.

8) Measure voltage at Light Green/Red wire terminal at cruise control deactivator switch harness connector C233. If battery voltage exists, repair open in Orange wire. If battery voltage does not exist, repair open in Light Green/Red wire.

9) Ensure cruise control switch is off. Measure voltage between terminals No. 5 (Light Blue/Black wire) and No. 10 (Pink/Orange wire) at cruise control servo/actuator harness connector C234. If battery voltage does not exist, go to next step. If battery voltage exists, replace cruise control switch.

10) Measure voltage between terminals No. 5 (Light Blue/Black wire) and No. 10 (Pink/Orange wire) at cruise control servo/actuator harness connector C234 while depressing cruise control switch to ON position. If battery voltage does not exist, go to next step. If battery voltage exists, go to step **13**).

11) Disarm air bags. See appropriate AIR BAG RESTRAINT SYSTEMS article. Disconnect air bag sliding contact harness connector C238 (Gray 4–pin connector). Measure resistance in Dark Green/Orange wire between terminal No. 4 at air bag sliding contact harness connector C238 and terminal No. 6 at cruise control servo/actuator harness connector C234. If resistance is 5 ohms or less, go to next step. If resistance is greater than 5 ohms, repair open in Dark Green/Orange wire.

12) Remove driver's side air bag. See appropriate AIR BAG RESTRAINT SYSTEMS article. Measure resistance in air bag sliding contact. *See Fig. 2.* If resistance is one ohm or less, replace cruise control switch. If resistance is greater than one ohm, replace air bag sliding contact.

13) Measure resistance between terminals No. 5 (light Blue/Black wire) and No. 6 (Dark Green/Orange wire) at cruise control servo/actuator harness connector C234 while pressing SET/ACCEL switch. If resistance is 640–720 ohms, go to next step. If resistance is not 640–720 ohms, replace cruise control switch.

14) Install driver's side air bag. Connect all disconnected harness connectors. Activate air bag system. See appropriate AIR BAG RESTRAINT SYSTEMS article. Test drive vehicle and observe speedometer operation. If speedometer operates properly, go to next step. If speedometer does not operate properly, repair speedometer as necessary. See appropriate INSTRUMENT PANELS article.

15) Turn ignition switch to LOCK position. Disconnect Vehicle Speed Sensor (VSS) harness connector C1020. Disconnect cruise control servo/actuator harness connector C234. Measure resistance in Gray/Black wire between VSS harness connector C1020 and terminal No. 3

at cruise control servo/actuator harness connector C234. If resistance is 5 ohms or less, replace cruise control servo/actuator. If resistance is greater than 5 ohms, repair open in Gray/Black wire.

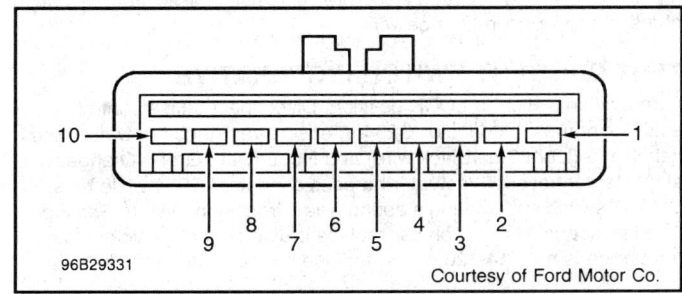

Fig. 1: Identifying Cruise Control Servo/Actuator Harness
Connector C234 Terminals

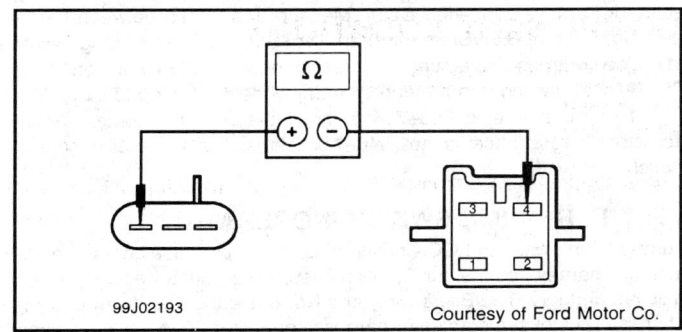

Fig. 2: Testing Air Bag Sliding Contact Cruise Control Circuit

TEST B: SET SPEED FLUCTUATES

1) Check for binding or sticking cruise control servo/actuator cable, throttle linkage and/or throttle plate. Ensure throttle cable bracket and cruise control servo/actuator bracket are not loose. Repair as necessary. Test drive vehicle to check operation. If all components are okay, go to next step.

2) Driver vehicle and observe speedometer operation. If speedometer operates properly, replace cruise control servo/actuator. If speedometer does not operate properly, repair speedometer as necessary. See appropriate INSTRUMENT PANELS article.

TEST C: CRUISE CONTROL DOES NOT DISENGAGE WHEN BRAKES ARE APPLIED

1) Check brake lights for proper operation. If brake lights operate properly, go to next step. If brake lights do not operate properly, repair brake lights as necessary. See appropriate wiring diagram in EXTERIOR LIGHTS article.

2) Disconnect cruise control servo/actuator harness connector C234. Measure voltage between terminals No. 4 (Light Green wire) and No. 10 (Pink/Orange wire) at cruise control servo/actuator harness connector C234 while depressing brake pedal. *See Fig. 1.* If battery voltage exists, go to next step. If battery voltage does not exist, repair open in Light Green wire.

3) Measure voltage between terminals No. 9 (Orange wire) and No. 10 (Pink/Orange wire) at cruise control servo/actuator harness connector C234. Without brake pedal depressed, battery voltage should exist. With brake pedal depressed, zero volts should exist. If voltage is not as specified, go to next step. If voltage is as specified, replace cruise control servo/actuator.

4) Disconnect cruise control deactivator switch harness connector C233. Using a fused jumper wire, connect terminals at cruise control deactivator switch harness connector C233. Measure voltage between terminals No. 9 (Orange wire) and No. 10 (Pink/Orange wire) at cruise control servo/actuator harness connector C234. If battery voltage does not exist, go to next step. If battery voltage exists, replace cruise control deactivator switch.

FORD
4-414

1999 ACCESSORIES & EQUIPMENT
Cruise Control Systems – Crown Victoria & Grand Marquis (Cont.)

5) Measure resistance in Orange wire between cruise control deactivator switch harness connector C233 and terminal No. 9 at cruise control servo/actuator harness connector C234. If resistance is 5 ohms or less, repair open in Light Green/Red wire. If resistance is greater than 5 ohms, repair open in Orange wire.

TEST D: COAST SWITCH INOPERATIVE

Turn ignition switch to LOCK position. Disconnect cruise control servo/actuator harness connector C234. Measure resistance between terminals No. 5 (Light Blue/Black wire) and No. 6 (Dark Green/Orange wire) at cruise control servo/actuator harness connector C234 while pressing COAST switch and rotating steering wheel from stop to stop. See Fig. 1. If resistance is 114-126 ohms, replace cruise control servo/actuator. If resistance is not 114-126 ohms, replace cruise control switch.

TEST E: SET/ACCEL SWITCH INOPERATIVE

Turn ignition switch to LOCK position. Disconnect cruise control servo/actuator harness connector C234. Measure resistance between terminals No. 5 (Light Blue/Black wire) and No. 6 (Dark Green/Orange wire) at cruise control servo/actuator harness connector C234 while pressing SET/ACCEL switch and rotating steering wheel from stop to stop. See Fig. 1. If resistance is 646–714 ohms, replace cruise control servo/actuator. If resistance is not 646–714 ohms, replace cruise control switch.

TEST F: RESUME SWITCH INOPERATIVE

Turn ignition switch to LOCK position. Disconnect cruise control servo/actuator harness connector C234. Measure resistance between terminals No. 5 (Light Blue/Black wire) and No. 6 (Dark Green/Orange wire) at cruise control servo/actuator harness connector C234 while pressing RESUME switch and rotating steering wheel from stop to stop. See Fig. 1. If resistance is 2090–2310 ohms, replace cruise control servo/actuator. If resistance is not 2090–2310 ohms, replace cruise control switch.

TEST G: OFF SWITCH INOPERATIVE

Turn ignition switch to LOCK position. Disconnect cruise control servo/actuator harness connector C234. Measure resistance between terminals No. 5 (Light Blue/Black wire) and No. 6 (Dark Green/Orange wire) at cruise control servo/actuator harness connector C234 while pressing OFF switch and rotating steering wheel from stop to stop. See Fig. 1. If resistance is 5 ohms or less, replace cruise control servo/actuator. If resistance greater than 5 ohms, replace cruise control switch.

TEST H: NO DYNAMIC PULL OCCURS AT THROTTLE

NOTE: This test only applies to vehicle equipped with electronic instrument clusters.

1) Ensure cruise control cable is attached. If cruise control cable is attached, go to next step. If cruise control cable is not attached, attach cruise control cable and retest system.
2) Disconnect cruise control cable from throttle linkage. Check slack in cruise control cable. If slack is approximately 0.12" (3 mm), go to next step. If slack is not approximately 0.12" (3 mm), adjust cruise control cable. See CRUISE CONTROL CABLE under ADJUSTMENTS.
3) Inspect cruise control cable for sticking and binding. If cruise control cable is okay, replace cruise control servo/actuator. If cruise control cable is not okay, replace cruise control cable.

TEST I: BRAKE PEDAL POSITION SWITCH FAILURE (FLASH CODE 2)

NOTE: This test only applies to vehicle equipped with electronic instrument clusters.

1) Check brake light operation. If brake lights operate, go to next step. If brake lights do not operate, repair brake lights as necessary. See appropriate wiring diagram in EXTERIOR LIGHTS article.

2) Turn ignition switch to LOCK position. Disconnect cruise control servo/actuator harness connector C234. Turn ignition switch to RUN position. Measure voltage between terminals No. 4 (White/Violet wire) and No. 10 (Pink/Orange wire) at cruise control servo/actuator harness connector C234. See Fig. 1. If battery voltage exists, replace cruise control servo/actuator. If battery voltage does not exist, repair open in White/Violet or Pink/Orange wire.

TEST J: DEACTIVATOR SWITCH CIRCUIT FAILURE (FLASH CODE 3)

NOTE: This test only applies to vehicle equipped with electronic instrument clusters.

1) Check brake light operation. If brake lights operate, go to next step. If brake lights do not operate, repair brake lights as necessary. See appropriate wiring diagram in EXTERIOR LIGHTS article.
2) Turn ignition switch to LOCK position. Disconnect cruise control servo/actuator harness connector C234. Turn ignition switch to RUN position. Measure voltage between terminals No. 9 (Orange wire) and No. 10 (Pink/Orange wire) at cruise control servo/actuator harness connector C234. See Fig. 1. If battery voltage does not exist, go to next step. If battery voltage exists, replace cruise control servo/actuator.
3) Turn ignition switch to LOCK position. Disconnect cruise control deactivator switch harness connector C233. Turn ignition switch to RUN position. Using a fused jumper wire, connect terminals at cruise control deactivator switch harness connector C233. Measure voltage between terminals No. 9 (Orange wire) and No. 10 (Pink/Orange wire) at cruise control servo/actuator harness connector C234. If battery voltage does not exist, go to next step. If battery voltage exists, replace cruise control deactivator switch.
4) Measure resistance in Orange wire between cruise control deactivator switch harness connector C233 and terminal No. 9 at cruise control servo/actuator harness connector C234. If resistance is 5 ohms or less, repair open in Light Green/Red wire. If resistance is greater than 5 ohms, repair open in Orange wire.

TEST K: VEHICLE SPEED SENSOR CIRCUIT FAILURE (FLASH CODE 4)

NOTE: This test only applies to vehicle equipped with electronic instrument clusters.

1) Test drive vehicle and observe speedometer operation. If speedometer operates properly, go to next step. If speedometer does not operate properly, repair speedometer as necessary. See appropriate INSTRUMENT PANELS article.
2) Turn ignition switch to LOCK position. Disconnect Vehicle Speed Sensor (VSS) harness connector C1020. Disconnect cruise control servo/actuator harness connector C234. Measure resistance in Gray/Black wire between VSS harness connector C1020 and terminal No. 3 at cruise control servo/actuator harness connector C234. See Fig. 1. If resistance is 5 ohms or less, replace cruise control servo/actuator. If resistance is greater than 5 ohms, repair open in Gray/Black wire.

REMOVAL & INSTALLATION

WARNING: Deactivate air bag system before working around steering column. See appropriate AIR BAG RESTRAINT SYSTEMS article.

CAUTION: When battery is disconnected, vehicle computer and memory systems may lose memory data. Driveability problems may exist until computer systems have completed a relearn cycle. See COMPUTER RELEARN PROCEDURES article in GENERAL INFORMATION before disconnecting battery.

CRUISE CONTROL SWITCHES

Removal & Installation – Disable air bag system. See DISABLING & ACTIVATING AIR BAG SYSTEM in appropriate AIR BAG RESTRAINT SYSTEMS article. Disconnect battery cables. Remove upper and lower

Cruise Control Systems – Crown Victoria & Grand Marquis (Cont.)

steering column covers. Remove air bag module retaining nuts. Unplug air bag module electrical connector from air bag sliding contact connector. Remove air bag. Disconnect cruise control switch connectors. Remove retaining screws and switch assembly. To install, reverse removal procedure.

DEACTIVATOR SWITCH

Removal – Disconnect negative battery cable. Disconnect electrical connector from deactivator switch (located on brake pedal support). Rotate deactivator switch clockwise and remove switch.

Installation – Pull deactivator switch plunger out to full travel. Completely depress and hold brake pedal. Install deactivator switch and rotate counterclockwise. Release brake pedal and connect electrical connector.

SERVO/ACTUATOR ASSEMBLY

Removal & Installation – 1) Disconnect cruise control cable from throttle body lever by pulling upwards at location shown. *See Fig. 3.* Disconnect cruise control servo/actuator connector. Remove 2 nuts securing cruise control servo/actuator to fenderwell.

2) Remove cruise control cable cap from servo/actuator by depressing cap locking arm and rotating cap counterclockwise. Remove cable ball slug from pulley. To install, reverse removal procedure. Ensure rubber seal is fully seated onto cruise control servo/actuator cable cap and throttle lever is at idle position after cruise control cable is installed.

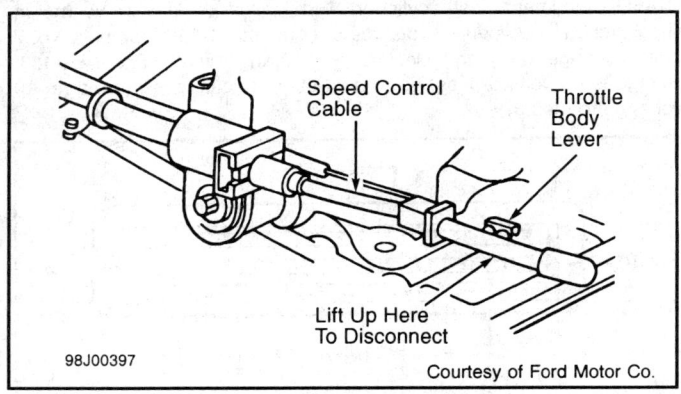

Fig. 3: Removing Cruise Control Cable From Throttle Body Lever

VEHICLE SPEED SENSOR (VSS)

Removal & Installation – Raise and support vehicle. Disconnect electrical connector from VSS (located at left rear of transmission). Remove VSS mounting bolt and VSS. To install, reverse removal procedure.

WIRING DIAGRAMS

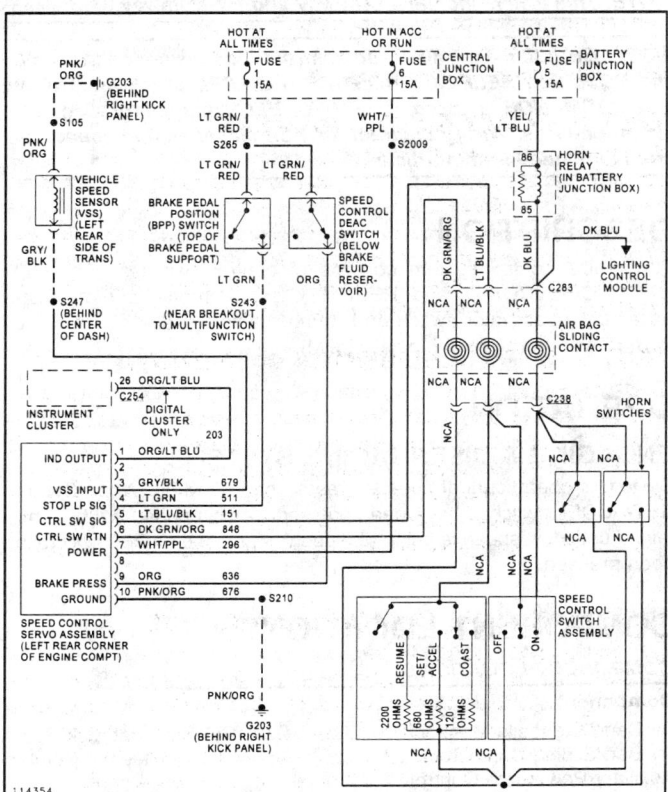

*Fig. 4: Cruise Control System Wiring Diagram
(Crown Victoria & Grand Marquis)*

NOTE: This article includes Cutaway and RV Cutaway.

NOTE: On 7.3L diesel, all speed control functions are controlled by the PCM. See SELF-DIAGNOSTICS – DIESEL article in ENGINE PERFORMANCE in appropriate MITCHELL® manual for diagnostic procedures. Wiring diagram for 7.3L diesel engine speed control is included in this article.

DESCRIPTION

The cruise control system consists of control switches (ON, OFF, SET-ACCEL, COAST and RESUME), servo throttle servo/actuator assembly, deactivator switch and wiring. Vehicle speed signal comes from Powertrain Control Module (PCM).

OPERATION

ENGAGING & DISENGAGING SYSTEM

System is operational at speeds greater than 30 MPH. When ON and SET-ACCEL switches have been pressed, vehicle speed will be maintained until new speed is set, brake pedal is pressed or OFF switch has been pressed.

COMPONENT LOCATIONS

COMPONENT LOCATIONS

Component	Location
Air Bag Diagnostic Monitor [1]	Behind Right Kick Panel
Air Bag Sliding Contact	Top Of Steering Column
Auxiliary Powertrain Control Module	Below Left Side Of Instrument Panel
Data Link Connector	Below Driver's Side Of Instrument Panel, To Right Of Steering Column
Deactivator Switch	Bottom Of Brake master cylinder
Natural Gas Vehicle Module	Left Side Of Engine Compartment, On Inner Fender
Powertrain Control Module	Left Rear Of Engine Compartment, Near Brake Master Cylinder
Speed Control Switches	Either Side Of Driver Air Bag
Speed Control Servo	Left Side Of Engine Compartment Near Master Cylinder
Vehicle Speed Sensor	Left Side Of Transmission

[1] – Air bag diagnostic monitor may also be referred to as Electronic Crash Sensor (ECS) module.

ADJUSTMENTS

ACTUATOR CABLE

Gasoline Models – Remove cable adjustment clip. Set throttle plate to closed position. Pull actuator cable to take up slack. Back off actuator cable one notch. While holding cable, insert cable adjustment clip.
Diesel Models – No adjustment is possible.

TROUBLE SHOOTING

Before performing any testing, check the following for possible cause of system malfunction:
- Faulty fuses.
- Loose or corroded connections.
- Damaged wiring harness.
- Damaged switches.
- Damaged or binding actuator cable.
- Incorrect actuator cable adjustment.

Verify horn and stoplights function properly. Repair as necessary. Inspect actuator and throttle linkage for smooth operation. Unbind as necessary. If no problems are found, perform appropriate test based **upon symptom. See SYSTEM TESTS.**

SYSTEM TESTS

NOTE: Before performing any testing, perform TROUBLE SHOOTING. Repair as necessary. Check PCM for stored Diagnostic Trouble Codes (DTCs). See appropriate SELF-DIAGNOSTICS article in ENGINE PERFORMANCE in appropriate MITCHELL® manual for diagnostic procedures.

NOTE: On 7.3L diesel, speed control functions are controlled by the PCM. See SELF-DIAGNOSTICS – DIESEL article in ENGINE PERFORMANCE in appropriate MITCHELL® manual for diagnostic procedures.

SYMPTOM INDEX

Symptom	Test
Speed Control Inoperative	A
Set Speed Fluctuates	B
Speed Control Does Not Disengage When Brakes Are Applied	C
Coast Switch Is Inoperative	D
Set/Accl Switch Is Inoperative	E
Resume Switch Is Inoperative	F
Off Switch Is Inoperative	G

TEST A: SPEED CONTROL IS INOPERATIVE

1) Turn ignition off. Disconnect speed control servo/actuator connector C146 (located near master cylinder). Turn ignition on. Using a voltmeter, check voltage between servo/actuator connector C146 terminals No. 7 (Violet/Orange wire) and No. 10 (Pink/Orange wire). *See Fig. 1.* If voltage is 10 volts or less, go to next step. If voltage is more than 10 volts, go to step **3)**.

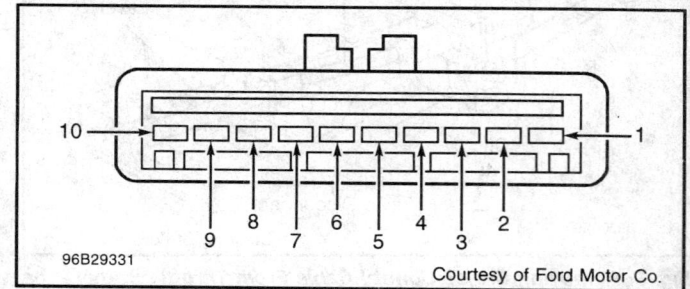

96B29331   Courtesy of Ford Motor Co.

Fig. 1: Identifying Servo/Actuator Connector C146 Terminals

2) Turn ignition off. Using an ohmmeter, check resistance between ground and speed control servo/actuator connector C146 terminal No. 10 (Pink/Orange wire). *See Fig. 1.* If resistance is less than 5 ohms, repair Violet/Orange wire between instrument panel fuse block and speed control servo/actuator. Retest system operation. If resistance is 5 ohms or more, repair open Pink/Orange wire between speed control servo/actuator and ground. Retest system operation.
3) Check stoplight operation while pressing and releasing brake pedal. If stoplights operate properly, go to next step. If stoplights do not operate properly, see appropriate wiring diagram in EXTERIOR LIGHTS article to continue diagnosis.
4) Turn ignition off. Disconnect speed control servo/actuator connector C146 (located near master cylinder). Using an ohmmeter, check resistance between speed control servo/actuator connector C146 terminals No. 4 (Light Green wire) and No. 10 (Pink/Orange wire). *See Fig. 1.* If resistance is less than 20 ohms, go to next step. If resistance is 20 ohms or more, repair open Light Green wire. Retest system operation.
5) Ensure ignition is off. Using a voltmeter, check voltage between speed control servo/actuator connector C146 terminals No. 9 (Red/Light Green wire) and No. 10 (Pink/Orange wire). *See Fig. 1.* If voltage is 10 volts or less, go to next step. If voltage is more than 10 volts, go to step **8)**.
6) Ensure ignition is off. Disconnect deactivator switch connector C151 (located on bottom of brake master cylinder). Using an ohmmeter, check

resistance between deactivator switch terminals (component side). If resistance is less than 5 ohms, go to next step. If resistance is 5 ohms or more, replace deactivator switch and bleed brake system. Retest system operation.

7) Ensure ignition is off. Using a voltmeter, check voltage between ground and deactivator switch connector C151 Light Green/Red wire terminal. If voltage is more than 10 volts, repair open Red/Light Green wire between deactivator switch and speed control servo/actuator. Retest system operation. If voltage is 10 volts or less, repair open Light Green/Red wire between instrument panel fuse block and deactivator switch. Retest system operation.

8) Turn ignition on. Using a voltmeter, check voltage between speed control servo/actuator connector C146 terminals No. 5 (Light Blue/Black wire) and No. 10 (Pink/Orange wire). *See Fig. 1.* If voltage is present, go to next step. If no voltage is present, go to step **11).**

9) Disconnect speed control switch connector from steering wheel. Turn ignition on. Using a voltmeter, check voltage between speed control servo/actuator connector C146 terminals No. 5 (Light Blue/Black wire) and No. 10 (Pink/Orange wire). *See Fig. 1.* If any voltage is present, go to next step. If no voltage is present, replace speed control switch and retest system operation.

10) Disconnect air bag sliding contact connector C223 (located on top of steering column, near clockspring assembly). Turn ignition on. Using a voltmeter, check voltage between speed control servo/actuator connector C146 terminals No. 5 (Light Blue/Black wire) and No. 10 (Pink/Orange wire). *See Fig. 1.* If any voltage is present, repair Light Blue/Black wire. Retest system operation. If no voltage is present, replace air bag sliding contact and retest system operation. See AIR BAG RESTRAINT SYSTEMS – ECONOLINE article.

11) Using an ohmmeter, check resistance between speed control servo/actuator connector C146 terminals No. 5 (Light Blue/Black wire) and No. 6 (Dark Green/Orange wire) while pressing speed control SET/ACCEL switch. If resistance is not 612-748 ohms, go to next step. If resistance is 640-720 ohms, go to step **14).**

12) Ensure ignition is off. Disconnect air bag sliding contact connector C223 (located on top of steering column, near clockspring assembly). Using an ohmmeter, check resistance in Light Blue/Black wire between speed control servo/actuator connector C146 terminal No. 5 and air bag sliding contact connector C223. If resistance is less than 5 ohms, go to next step. If resistance is 5 ohms or more, repair open in Light Blue/Black wire. Retest system operation.

13) Remove driver side air bag. See AIR BAG RESTRAINT SYSTEMS – ECONOLINE article. Using an ohmmeter, check resistance between air bag sliding contact 5-pin male connector C253 terminal No. 1 and air bag sliding contact 6-pin male connector C223 terminal No. 1. *See Fig. 2.* If resistance is less than one ohm, replace speed control switch and retest system operation. If resistance is one ohm or more, replace air bag sliding contact and retest system operation.

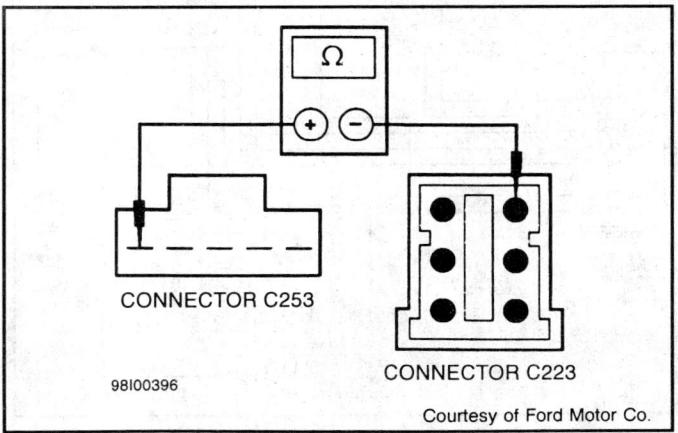

98I00396

Courtesy of Ford Motor Co.

Fig. 2: Checking Air Bag Sliding Contact

14) Disconnect vehicle speed sensor connector C108 (located on left side of transmission). Using an ohmmeter, check resistance in Gray/

Black wire between speed control servo/actuator connector C146 terminal No. 3 and vehicle speed sensor connector C108. If resistance is less than 5 ohms, go to next step. If resistance is 5 ohms or more, repair open in Gray/Black wire. Retest system operation.

15) Ensure ignition is off. Disengage speed control servo/actuator cable from servo/actuator. Inspect cable by pulling end of cable and observing throttle movement. Replace cable if broken or binding and retest system operation. If cable is okay, replace servo/actuator and retest system operation.

TEST B: SET SPEED FLUCTUATES

1) Ensure ignition is off. Disengage speed control servo/actuator cable from servo/actuator. Inspect cable by pulling end of cable and observing throttle movement. If cable is okay, go to next step. Replace cable if broken or binding and retest system operation.

2) Drive vehicle and observe speedometer operation without using speed control. If speedometer needle fluctuates, see ANALOG INSTRUMENT PANELS – ECONOLINE article to continue diagnosis. If speedometer needle does not fluctuate, replace speed control servo/actuator and retest system operation.

TEST C: SPEED CONTROL DOES NOT DISENGAGE WHEN BRAKES ARE APPLIED

1) Ensure ignition is off. Disengage speed control servo/actuator cable from servo/actuator. Inspect cable by pulling end of cable and observing throttle movement. If cable is okay, go to next step. Replace cable if broken or binding and retest system operation.

2) Check stoplight operation while pressing and releasing brake pedal. If stoplights operate properly, go to next step. If stoplights do not operate properly, see appropriate wiring diagram in EXTERIOR LIGHTS article to continue diagnosis.

3) Ensure ignition is off. Disconnect speed control servo/actuator connector C146 (located near master cylinder). Press and hold brake pedal. Using a voltmeter, check voltage between speed control servo/actuator connector C146 terminals No. 4 (Light Green wire) and No. 10 (Pink/Orange wire) . *See Fig. 1.* If voltage is more than 10 volts, replace speed control servo/actuator and retest system operation. If voltage is 10 volts or less, repair Light Green wire between speed control servo/actuator and BPP switch. Retest system operation.

TEST D: COAST SWITCH IS INOPERATIVE

Turn ignition off. Disconnect speed control servo/actuator connector C146 (located near master cylinder). While pressing COAST switch and rotating steering wheel from stop to stop, check resistance between speed control servo/actuator connector C146 terminals No. 5 (Light Blue/Black wire) and 6. *See Fig. 1.* If resistance is 108-132 ohms, replace speed control servo/actuator and retest system operation. If resistance is not 108-132 ohms, replace speed control switch and retest system operation.

TEST E: SET/ACCEL SWITCH IS INOPERATIVE

Turn ignition off. Disconnect speed control servo/actuator connector C146 (located near master cylinder). While pressing SET/ACCEL switch and rotating steering wheel from stop to stop, check resistance between speed control servo/actuator connector C146 terminals No. 5 (Light Blue/Black wire) and No. 6 (Dark Green/Orange wire). *See Fig. 1.* If resistance is 612-748 ohms, replace speed control servo/actuator and retest system operation. If resistance is not 612-748 ohms, replace speed control switch and retest system operation.

TEST F: RESUME FUNCTION INOPERATIVE

Turn ignition off. Disconnect speed control servo/actuator connector C146 (located near master cylinder). While pressing RESUME switch and rotating steering wheel from stop to stop, check resistance between speed control servo/actuator connector C146 terminals No. 5 (Light Blue/Black wire) and No. 6 (Dark Green/Orange wire). *See Fig. 1.* If resistance is 1980-2420 ohms, replace speed control servo/actuator and retest system operation. If resistance is not 1980-2420 ohms, replace speed control switch and retest system operation.

TEST G: OFF SWITCH IS INOPERATIVE

Turn ignition off. Disconnect speed control servo/actuator connector C146 (located near master cylinder). While pressing OFF switch and rotating steering wheel from stop to stop, check resistance between speed control servo/actuator connector C146 terminals No. 5 (Light Blue/Black wire) and No. 6 (Dark Green/Orange wire). *See Fig. 1.* If resistance is 5 ohms or less, replace speed control servo/actuator and retest system operation. If resistance is more than 5 ohms, replace speed control switch and retest system operation.

REMOVAL & INSTALLATION

WARNING: Disable air bag system before working around steering column or removing any air bag system component. See AIR BAG RESTRAINT SYSTEMS – ECONOLINE article.

CAUTION: When battery is disconnected, vehicle computer and memory systems may lose memory data. Driveability problems may exist until computer systems have completed a relearn cycle. See COMPUTER RELEARN PROCEDURES article in GENERAL INFORMATION before disconnecting battery.

SPEED CONTROL SERVO/ACTUATOR

Removal & Installation – 1) Remove air cleaner assembly. Remove accelerator control splash shield. Remove coolant recovery reservoir and position aside. Remove speed control bracket mounting bolts. Unplug connector from speed control servo/actuator.
2) Press locking tab, rotate speed control actuator cable cap and disconnect speed control servo/actuator cable. Remove speed control servo/actuator. Remove speed control servo/actuator from bracket. To install, reverse removal procedure. Adjust cable. See ACTUATOR CABLE under ADJUSTMENTS.

SPEED CONTROL SWITCHES

WARNING: Observe all air bag service precautions when working around air bag components. Disable air bag system. See SERVICE PRECAUTIONS and DISABLING & ACTIVATING AIR BAG SYSTEM in AIR BAG RESTRAINT SYSTEMS – ECONOLINE article.

Removal – 1) Disable air bag system. See DISABLING & ACTIVATING AIR BAG SYSTEM in AIR BAG RESTRAINT SYSTEMS – ECONOLINE article. Remove air bag nuts and washers from steering wheel. Unplug air bag connector from clockspring (contact assembly). Remove air bag module.

WARNING: Place air bag module on bench with trim cover facing upward.

2) Unplug horn/speed control harness connector from clockspring. Remove speed control switches. Disconnect switch wires.
Installation – Install switches. Connect air bag module wiring connector to clockspring (contact assembly). Position air bag module onto steering wheel. Install air bag module nuts and washers. Tighten nuts to 84-120 INCH lbs. (10-14 N.m). Activate air bag system. Observe AIR BAG warning light to verify system is functioning properly. See SYSTEM OPERATION CHECK in AIR BAG RESTRAINT SYSTEMS – ECONOLINE article.

DEACTIVATOR (BRAKE PRESSURE) SWITCH

Removal & Installation – Deactivator switch is located on master cylinder. Disconnect electrical connector. Unscrew switch. To install, reverse removal procedure. Bleed brake system. See appropriate article in BRAKES in appropriate MITCHELL® manual.
WIRING DIAGRAMS

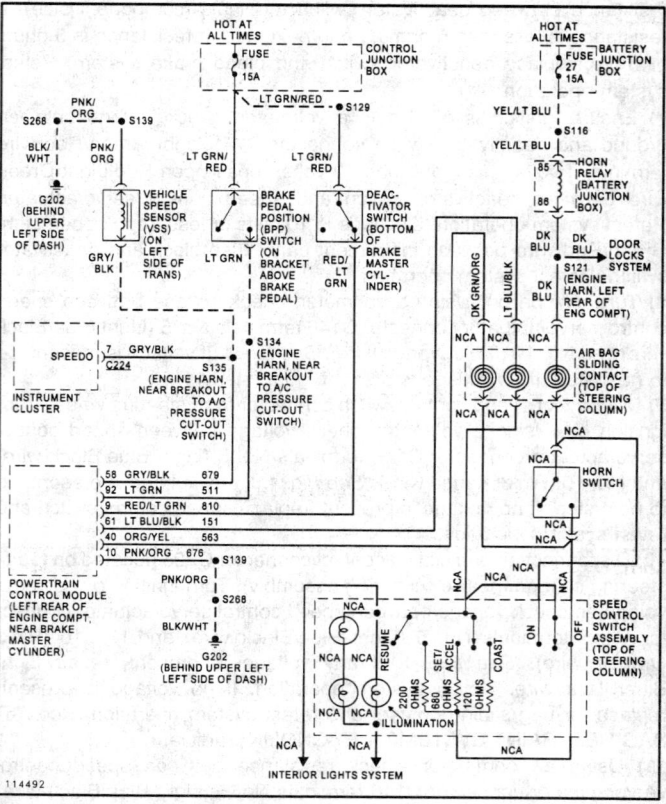

Fig. 3: Cruise Control System Wiring Diagram (Econoline – Diesel)

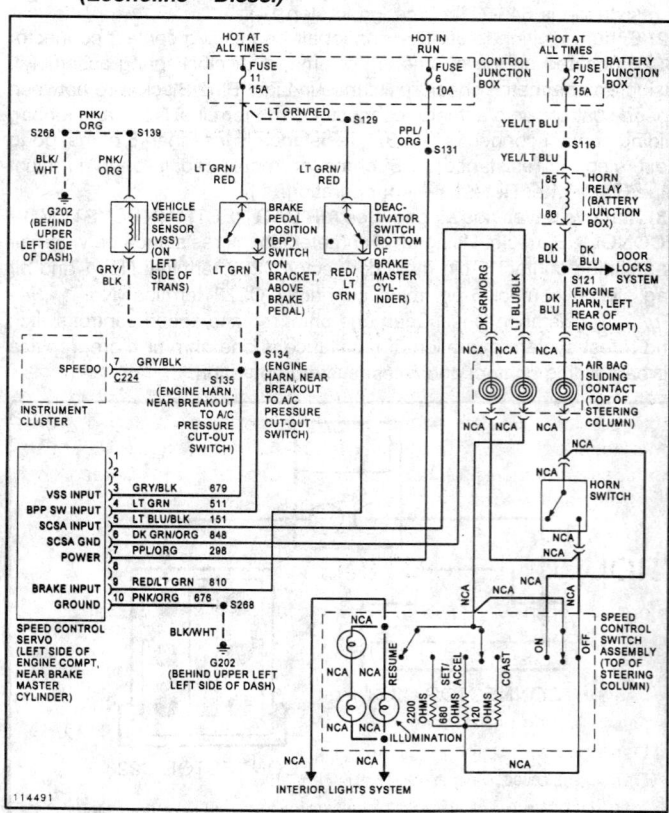

Fig. 4: Cruise Control System Wiring Diagram (Econoline – Gasoline)

DESCRIPTION & OPERATION

Major components of the cruise control system are speed control switches, servo/actuator, vehicle speed sensor, Brake Pedal Position (BPP) switch, deactivator switch, Clutch Pedal Position (CPP) switch, and related wiring. This system does not require engine vacuum. An electronic servo/actuator actuates the throttle. All electronic control components are contained within the servo/actuator assembly.

The system is operational only at speeds greater than 30 MPH. The system is activated when ON/OFF switch is switched on and SET/ACCEL button is pressed and released. Vehicle will maintain set speed until new speed is set, brake pedal is pressed, clutch pedal is pressed, or ON/OFF switch is switched off. If system has been deactivated by pressing brake pedal or clutch pedal, set speed can be regained by pressing and releasing RESUME button. When brake pedal or clutch pedal is pressed, a signal from switch is sent to the servo to deactivate the system. A deactivator switch acts as a redundant brake signal.

COMPONENT LOCATIONS

COMPONENT LOCATIONS

Component	Location
Air Bag Sliding Contact	Below Steering Wheel
Brake Pedal Position (BPP) Switch	Top Of Brake Pedal Support
Clutch Pedal Position (CPP) Switch	Top Of Brake Pedal Support
Data Link Connector (DLC)	Below Driver's Side Of Instrument Panel, To Right Of Steering Column
Deactivator Switch	Top Of Brake Pedal Support
Instrument Cluster [1]	Behind Left Side Of Instrument Panel
Central Junction Box	Below Left Instrument Panel
Power Distribution Box	Left Side Of Engine Compartment, Above Wheelwell
Powertrain Control Module (PCM)	In Center Console Below Shifter

[1] – Instrument cluster may also be referred to as Virtual Instrument Cluster (VIC).

ADJUSTMENTS

SERVO/ACTUATOR CABLE

NOTE: *The speed control servo/actuator cable is not adjustable on vehicles equipped with ZETEC engine. Cable adjustment is for vehicles equipped with 2.0L SPI engine only.*

Disconnect speed control servo/actuator cable from throttle control lever. Remove speed control servo/actuator cable adjuster clip from cable adjuster. Ensure throttle is fully closed. Adjust speed control servo/actuator cable until freeplay is .04-.12″ (1-3 mm). Install speed control servo/actuator cable adjuster clip. Ensure throttle linkage operates freely and smoothly.

TROUBLE SHOOTING

Before performing any testing, check the following for possible cause of system malfunction:

- Faulty fuses.
- Loose or corroded connections.
- Damaged wiring harness.
- Damaged switches.
- Damaged or binding servo/actuator cable.
- Incorrect servo/actuator cable adjustment.

Verify speedometer and stoplights function properly. Repair as necessary. Inspect actuator and throttle linkage for smooth operation. Unbind as necessary. If no problems are found, perform appropriate test based upon symptom. See SYSTEM TESTS.

SYSTEM TESTS

WARNING: *Deactivate air bag system before working around steering column. See appropriate AIR BAG RESTRAINT SYSTEMS article.*

CAUTION: *When battery is disconnected or modules are replaced, vehicle computer and memory systems may lose memory data. Driveability problems may exist until computer systems have completed a relearn cycle. See COMPUTER RELEARN PROCEDURES article in GENERAL INFORMATION before disconnecting battery.*

NOTE: *Before beginning system tests, perform TROUBLE SHOOTING.*

NOTE: *After repairs are complete, ensure all component are properly installed and all harness connectors are connected properly and repeat data link diagnostic test. See DATA LINK DIAGNOSTIC TEST under COMMUNICATIONS NETWORK DIAGNOSTICS in MODULE COMMUNICATIONS NETWORK – ESCORT & TRACER article.*

Verify the customer complaint by operating speed control. Visually inspect for obvious sign of mechanical and electrical damage. If no visual damage is evident, perform appropriate system test. See SYSTEM TEST INDEX table. A digital volt-ohmmeter is required to test the cruise control system. See WIRING DIAGRAMS for terminal numbers.

SYSTEM TEST INDEX

Symptom	Go To
Speed Control Inoperative	TEST A
Set Speed Fluctuates	TEST B
Speed Control Does Not Disengage When Brakes Are Applied	TEST C
Speed Control Does Not Disengage When Clutch Is Applied	TEST D
Coast Switch Is Inoperative	TEST E
Set/Accl Switch Is Inoperative	TEST F
Resume Switch Is Inoperative	TEST G
Off Switch Is Inoperative	TEST H

TEST A: SPEED CONTROL IS INOPERATIVE

1) Turn ignition off. Disconnect speed control servo/actuator connector C177 (located on left front side of engine compartment). Turn ignition switch to RUN position. Using a voltmeter, check voltage between speed control servo/actuator connector C177 terminal No. 7 (Yellow wire) and terminal No. 10 (Blue wire). *See Fig. 1.* If voltage is more than 10 volts, go to step **4)**. If voltage is 10 volts or less, go to next step.

2) Turn ignition off. Check central junction box ASC fuse (10-amp). If fuse is okay, go to next step. If fuse is not okay, replace fuse and retest system operation. If fuse fails again, check for short to ground in Yellow wire between central junction box and speed control servo/actuator. Repair as necessary and retest system operation.

3) Using an ohmmeter, check resistance between ground and speed control servo/actuator connector C177 terminal No. 10 (Blue wire). *See Fig. 1.* If resistance is less than 5 ohms, repair open in Yellow wire between central junction box and speed control servo/actuator. Retest system operation. If resistance is 5 ohms or more, repair open in Blue wire between speed control servo/actuator and ground.

4) Check stoplight operation while pressing brake pedal. If stoplights operate properly, go to next step. If stoplights do not operate properly, see appropriate wiring diagram in EXTERIOR LIGHTS article to continue diagnosis.

5) Using an ohmmeter, check resistance between speed control servo/actuator connector C177 terminal No. 4 (Gren wire) and terminal No. 10 (Blue wire). If resistance is less than 20 ohms, go to step **8)**. If resistance is 20 ohms or more and vehicle is equipped with M/T, go to next step. If resistance is 20 ohms or more and vehicle is equipped with A/T, repair

Green wire between speed control servo/actuator and Brake Pedal Position (BPP) switch. Retest system operation.

6) Ensure ignition is off. Disconnect Clutch Pedal Position (CPP) switch connector C292 (located on top of clutch pedal support). Using an ohmmeter, check resistance between CPP switch terminals (switch side). If resistance is less than 5 ohms, go to next step. If resistance is 5 ohms or more, replace CPP switch and retest system operation.

7) Ensure ignition is off. Disconnect BPP switch connector C245 (located on top of brake pedal support). Using an ohmmeter, check resistance in Green wire between CPP switch connector C292 and BPP switch connector C245. If resistance is less than 5 ohms, repair White or Green wire between speed control servo/actuator and CPP switch. Retest system operation. If resistance is 5 ohms or more, repair open in Green wire between CPP switch and BPP switch. Retest system operation.

8) Ensure ignition is off. Using a voltmeter, check voltage between speed control servo/actuator connector C177 terminal No. 9 (Green/Yellow wire) and terminal No. 10 (Black wire). See Fig. 1. If voltage is 10 volts or less, go to next step. If voltage is more than 10 volts, go to step **11)**.

9) Ensure ignition is off. Disconnect deactivator switch connector C208 (located on top of brake pedal support). Using an ohmmeter, check resistance between deactivator switch terminals (switch side). If resistance is less than 5 ohms, go to next step. If resistance is 5 ohms or more, replace deactivator switch and retest system operation.

10) Using a voltmeter, check voltage between ground and deactivator switch connector C208 Green/White wire terminal. If voltage is more than 10 volts, repair Green/Yellow wire between deactivator switch and speed control servo/actuator. Retest system operation. If voltage is 10 volts or less, repair Green/White wire between central junction box and deactivator switch. Retest system operation.

11) Ensure ignition is off. Using a voltmeter, check voltage between speed control servo/actuator connector C177 terminal No. 5 (Red/Yellow wire) and terminal No. 10 (Blue wire). See Fig. 1. If voltage is indicated, go to next step. If no voltage is indicated, go to step **14)**.

12) Disconnect speed control switch connector C269 (located in steering wheel, under air bag module). Turn ignition switch to RUN position. Using a voltmeter, check voltage between speed control servo/actuator connector C177 terminal No. 5 (Red/Yellow wire) and terminal No. 10 (Blue wire). See Fig. 1. If voltage is indicated, go to next step. If no voltage is indicated, replace speed control switches and retest system operation.

13) Ensure ignition is off. Disconnect air bag sliding contact connector C248 (located under steering wheel). Turn ignition switch to RUN position. Using a voltmeter, check voltage between speed control servo/actuator connector C177 terminal No. 5 (Red/Yellow wire) and terminal No. 10 (Blue wire). See Fig. 1. If voltage is indicated, repair short to power in Red/Yellow wire between air bag sliding contact and speed control servo/actuator. Retest system operation. If no voltage is indicated, replace air bag sliding contact and retest system operation.

14) Using an ohmmeter, check resistance between speed control servo/actuator connector C177 terminal No. 5 (Red/Yellow wire) and terminal No. 6 (Red/Blue wire) while pressing speed control SET/ACCEL switch. If resistance is 640-720 ohms, go to next step. If resistance is not 640-720 ohms, go to step **16)**.

15) Turn ignition switch to RUN position. Using a voltmeter, check voltage between speed control servo/actuator connector C177 terminal No. 5 (Red/Yellow wire) and terminal No. 10 (Blue wire) while pressing speed control ON switch. If voltage is more than 10 volts, go to step **19)**. If voltage is 10 volts or less, replace speed control switch and retest system operation.

16) Ensure ignition is off. Disconnect air bag sliding contact connector C248 (located under steering wheel). Using an ohmmeter, check resistance in Red/Yellow wire between air bag sliding contact connector C248 (male side) and speed control servo/actuator connector C177 terminal No. 5. If resistance is less than 5 ohms, go to next step. If resistance is 5 ohms or more, repair open in Red/Yellow wire and retest system operation.

17) Using an ohmmeter, check resistance in Red/Blue wire between air bag sliding contact connector C248 (male side) and speed control servo/actuator connector C177 terminal No. 6. If resistance is less than 5 ohms, go to next step. If resistance is 5 ohms or more, repair open in Red/Blue wire and retest system operation.

18) Disconnect speed control switch connector C269 (located in steering wheel, under air bag module). Using an ohmmeter, check resistance between speed control switch connector C269 (female side) terminals No. 1 and 2 while pressing speed control SET/ACCEL switch. See Fig. 2. If resistance is 640-720 ohms, replace air bag sliding contact and retest system operation. If resistance is not 640-720 ohms, replace speed control switch and retest system operation.

19) Test drive vehicle and observe speedometer operation. If speedometer operates properly, go to next step. If speedometer does not operate properly, see appropriate INSTRUMENT PANELS article to continue diagnosis.

20) Ensure ignition is off. Remove speed control servo/actuator cable from speed control servo/actuator. Inspect cable by pulling end of cable and observing throttle movement. Replace cable if broken or binding. Retest system operation. If cable is okay, replace servo/actuator and retest system operation.

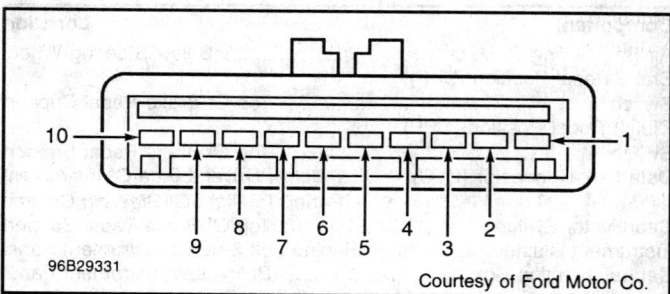

Fig. 1: Identifying Speed Control Servo/Actuator Connector C177 Terminals

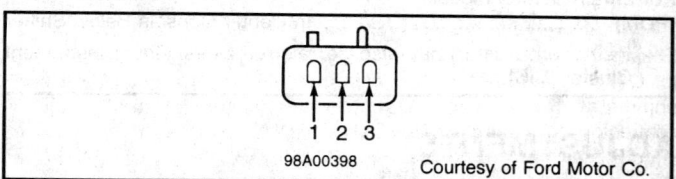

Fig. 2: Identifying Speed Control Switch Connector C269 Terminals

TEST B: SET SPEED FLUCTUATES

1) Ensure ignition is off. Disengage speed control servo/actuator cable from servo/actuator. Inspect cable by pulling end of cable and observing throttle movement. If cable is okay, go to next step. Replace cable if broken or binding and retest system operation. Repair throttle body linkage if necessary, and retest system operation.

2) Drive vehicle and observe speedometer operation without using speed control. If speedometer needle fluctuates, see appropriate INSTRUMENT PANELS article to continue diagnosis. If speedometer needle does not fluctuate, replace speed control servo/actuator and retest system operation.

TEST C: SPEED CONTROL DOES NOT DISENGAGE WHEN BRAKES ARE APPLIED

1) Press brake pedal and observe stoplight operation. If stoplights operate properly, go to next step. If stoplights do not operate properly, see appropriate wiring diagram in EXTERIOR LIGHTS article to continue diagnosis.

2) Ensure ignition is off. Disconnect speed control servo/actuator connector C177 (located on left front side of engine compartment). Using an ohmmeter, check resistance between speed control servo/actuator connector C177 terminal No. 4 (Green wire) and terminal No. 10 (Blue wire). See Fig. 1. If resistance is less than 20 ohms, replace speed control servo/actuator and retest system operation. If resistance is 20 ohms or more and vehicle is equipped with M/T, go to next step. If resistance is 20 ohms or more and vehicle is equipped with A/T, repair Green wire between speed control servo/actuator and Brake Pedal Position (BPP) switch. Retest system operation.

3) Ensure ignition is off. Disconnect Clutch Pedal Position (CPP) switch connector C292 (located on top of clutch pedal support). Using an ohmmeter, check resistance between CPP switch terminals (switch side). If resistance is less than 5 ohms, go to next step. If resistance is 5 ohms or more, replace CPP switch and retest system operation.

4) Ensure ignition is off. Disconnect BPP switch connector C245 (located on top of brake pedal support). Using an ohmmeter, check resistance in Green wire between CPP switch connector C292 and BPP switch connector C245. If resistance is less than 5 ohms, repair White or Green wire between speed control servo/actuator and CPP switch. Retest system operation. If resistance is 5 ohms or more, repair open in Green wire between CPP switch and BPP switch. Retest system operation.

TEST D: SPEED CONTROL DOES NOT DISENGAGE WHEN CLUTCH IS APPLIED

1) Ensure ignition is off. Disconnect Clutch Pedal Position (CPP) switch connector C292 (located on top of clutch pedal support). Using an ohmmeter, check resistance between CPP switch terminals (switch side) while pressing clutch pedal. If resistance is more than 10 k/ohms, go to next step. If resistance measurement is 10 k/ohms or less, replace CPP switch and retest system operation.

2) Ensure ignition is off. Disconnect speed control servo/actuator connector C177 (located on left front side of engine compartment). Using an ohmmeter, check resistance between ground and speed control servo/actuator connector C177 terminal No. 4 (Green wire). See Fig. 1. If resistance is more than 10 k/ohms, replace speed control servo/actuator and retest system operation. If resistance is 10 k/ohms or less, repair short to ground in Green wire or White wire. Retest system operation.

TEST E: COAST SWITCH IS INOPERATIVE

Ensure ignition is off. Disconnect speed control servo/actuator connector C177 (located on left front side of engine compartment). Using an ohmmeter, check resistance between speed control servo/actuator connector C177 terminal No. 5 (Red/Yellow wire) and terminal No. 6 (Red/Blue wire) while pressing speed control COAST switch. See Fig. 1. If resistance is 114-126 ohms, replace speed control servo/actuator and retest system operation. If resistance is not 114-126 ohms, replace speed control switches and retest system operation.

TEST F: SET/ACCL SWITCH IS INOPERATIVE

Turn ignition off. Disconnect speed control servo/actuator connector C177 (located on left front side of engine compartment). Using an ohmmeter, check resistance between speed control servo/actuator connector C177 terminal No. 5 (Red/Yellow wire) and terminal No. 6 (Red/Blue wire) while pressing speed control SET/ACCL switch. See Fig. 1. If resistance is 646-714 ohms, replace speed control servo/actuator and retest system operation. If resistance is not 646-714 ohms, replace speed control switches and retest system operation.

TEST G: RESUME SWITCH IS INOPERATIVE

Turn ignition off. Disconnect speed control servo/actuator connector C177 (located on left front side of engine compartment). Using an ohmmeter, check resistance between speed control servo/actuator connector C177 terminal No. 5 (Red/Yellow wire) and terminal No. 6 (Red/Blue wire) while pressing speed control RESUME switch. See Fig. 1 . If resistance is 2090-2310 ohms, replace speed control servo/actuator and retest system operation. If resistance is not 2090-2310 ohms, replace speed control switches and retest system operation.

TEST H: OFF SWITCH IS INOPERATIVE

Turn ignition off. Disconnect speed control servo/actuator connector C177 (located on left front side of engine compartment). Using an ohmmeter, check resistance between speed control servo/actuator connector C177 terminal No. 5 (Red/Yellow wire) and terminal No. 6 (Red/Blue wire) while pressing speed control OFF switch. See Fig. 1. If resistance is less than 5 ohms, replace speed control servo/actuator and retest system operation. If resistance is 5 ohms or more, replace speed control switches and retest system operation.

REMOVAL & INSTALLATION

WARNING: Deactivate air bag system before working around steering column. See appropriate AIR BAG RESTRAINT SYSTEMS article.

CAUTION: When battery is disconnected, vehicle computer and memory systems may lose memory data. Driveability problems may exist until computer systems have completed a relearn cycle. See COMPUTER RELEARN PROCEDURES article in GENERAL INFORMATION before disconnecting battery.

SPEED CONTROL SWITCHES

Removal & Installation – Disable air bag system and remove driver side air bag module. See appropriate AIR BAG RESTRAINT SYSTEMS article. Ensure front wheels are in straight-ahead position. Remove steering wheel retaining bolt and remove steering wheel. Tape air bag sliding contact to steering column to prevent misalignment. Remove steering wheel trim. Remove switch retaining screws and switch assembly. To install, reverse removal procedure.

DEACTIVATOR SWITCH

Removal & Installation – Deactivator switch is located on brake pedal support. Disconnect deactivator switch electrical connector and unscrew deactivator switch. To install, reverse removal procedure.

SPEED CONTROL SERVO/ACTUATOR

Removal & Installation – 1) Disconnect negative battery cable. Disconnect speed control servo/actuator cable from throttle body. On coupe, remove speed control servo/actuator cable sleeve from retainer and remove retainer. On all models, disconnect speed control servo/actuator connector.

2) Press speed control servo/actuator cable cap locking tab in, rotate cap and remove cap from servo/actuator. Remove cable ball slug from pulley and disconnect cable. Remove retaining bolts/nuts and remove speed control servo/actuator assembly. To install, reverse removal procedure.

VEHICLE SPEED SENSOR (VSS)

Removal & Installation – Raise and support vehicle. Disconnect electrical connector from VSS (located on lower rear of transaxle). On vehicles equipped with A/T, remove heated oxygen sensor wire retainer from VSS bracket. On all models, remove VSS mounting bolt and VSS. To install, reverse removal procedure.

WIRING DIAGRAMS

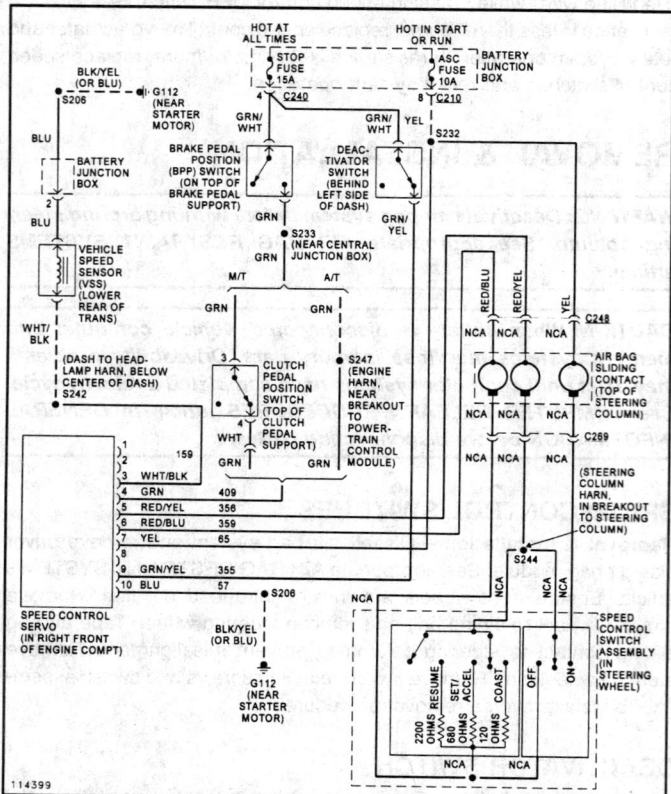

Fig. 3: Cruise Control System Wiring Diagram (Escort & Tracer)

DESCRIPTION

The cruise control system consists of control switches (ON, OFF, SET-ACCEL, COAST and RESUME), servo/actuator assembly, Vehicle Speed Sensor (VSS), deactivator switch and wiring.

OPERATION

ENGAGING & DISENGAGING SYSTEM

System is operational at speeds greater than 30 MPH. When ON and SET-ACCEL switches have been pressed, vehicle speed will be maintained until new speed is set, brake pedal is pressed or OFF switch is pressed.

SYMPTOM TESTS

NOTE: If Malfunction Indicator Light (MIL) is lit or flashes, check PCM for stored Diagnostic Trouble Codes (DTCs). See appropriate SELF-DIAGNOSTICS article in ENGINE PERFORMANCE in appropriate MITCHELL® manual.

Before trouble shooting system, perform complete visual inspection of system. Check all fuses. Check operation of stoplights including high mounted stoplight. Check speedometer operation. Repair as necessary.

CRUISE CONTROL INOPERATIVE

1) Remove splash shield from throttle linkage. Ensure actuator cable is properly connected to throttle body and speed control servo. Pull on cable at throttle linkage side and note accelerator pedal movement. Check for smooth operation of cable. Correct as necessary and test operation.

2) Unplug harness connector from servo located near master cylinder. Turn ignition switch to RUN position. Measure voltage between servo harness connector terminal No. 7 (Light Blue/Pink wire) and terminal No. 10 (Black wire). *See Fig. 1.* If battery voltage is present, go to step **4)**. If battery voltage is not present, check fuse No. 5. Replace fuse if necessary. If fuse is okay, go to next step.

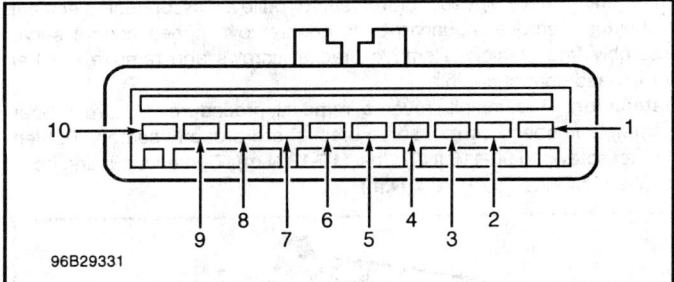

Fig. 1: Identifying Servo/Actuator Harness Connector Terminals

3) Turn ignition off. Measure resistance between harness connector terminal No. 10 (Black wire) and ground. If resistance is less than 5 ohms, repair Light Blue/Pink wire. If resistance is 5 ohms or greater, repair Black wire to ground. See WIRING DIAGRAMS.

4) With brake pedal released, measure voltage between servo harness connector terminal No. 4 (Red/Light Green) and terminal No. 10 (Black wire). If no voltage is present, go to step **6)**. If voltage is present, go to next step.

5) Disconnect Brake Pedal Position (BPP) switch harness connector. Measure voltage between servo harness connector terminal No. 4 (Red/Light Green) and terminal No. 10 (Black wire). If no voltage is present, replace BPP switch and check system for normal operation. If voltage is present, repair short to power between BPP switch connector and servo harness connector terminal No. 4. See WIRING DIAGRAMS. Check system for normal operation.

6) Turn ignition off. Measure resistance between servo harness connector terminal No. 4 (Red/Light Green) and terminal No. 10 (Black wire). If resistance is less than 5 ohms, go to next step. If resistance is 5 ohms or greater, repair open or high resistance in circuit between servo

harness connector terminal No. 4 and ground, (including BPP). See WIRING DIAGRAMS. Check system for normal operation.

7) With brake pedal released, measure voltage between servo harness connector terminal No. 9 (Black/Yellow wire) and terminal No. 10 (Black wire). If battery voltage is not present, go to next step. If battery voltage is present, go to step **10)**.

8) Unplug connector from brake pressure switch, located on master cylinder. Measure resistance between switch terminals with brake pedal released. If resistance is less than 5 ohms, go to next step. If resistance is 5 ohms or greater, replace switch and check system for normal operation.

9) Measure voltage between brake pressure switch harness connector terminal (Light Green/Red wire) and ground. If battery voltage is present, repair open in Black/Yellow wire. If battery voltage is not present, repair open fuse or Light Green/Red wire. See WIRING DIAGRAMS.

10) Disable air bag restraint system. See appropriate AIR BAG RESTRAINT SYSTEMS article. Disconnect air bag sliding contact connector at base of steering column. Measure resistance of Light Blue/Black wire between servo harness connector terminal No. 5 and corresponding air bag sliding contact connector terminal (harness side). If resistance is less than 5 ohms, go to next step. If resistance is 5 ohms or greater, repair open or high resistance in Light Blue/Black wire. See WIRING DIAGRAMS. Check system for normal operation.

11) With Driver's air bag module removed, measure resistance of air bag sliding contact between column side of connector at base of steering column and sliding contact. Connect one ohmmeter lead to column side connector terminal corresponding to Light Blue/Black wire in harness side of connector, and other ohmmeter lead to appropriate sliding contact pin at top of steering column. See WIRING DIAGRAMS. If resistance is less than 1 ohm, go to next step. If resistance is one ohm or greater, replace air bag sliding contact and check system operation. See appropriate AIR BAG RESTRAINT SYSTEMS article.

12) With speed control ON switch depressed, check for voltage between servo harness connector terminal No. 5 (Light Blue/Black wire) and terminal No. 10 (Black wire). If voltage is present, go to next step. If no voltage is present, install new speed control actuator switch and check for normal system operation. See COMMAND SWITCHES under REMOVAL & INSTALLATION.

13) While depressing SET/ACCEL button on steering wheel, measure resistance between servo harness connector terminal No. 5 (Light Blue/Black wire) and terminal No. 6 (Dark Green/Orange wire). Resistance should be between 640 ohms and 720 ohms. If resistance is as specified, go to next step. If resistance is not as specified, install new speed control servo switch and check system for normal operation. See SPEED CONTROL SERVO under REMOVAL & INSTALLATION.

14) Disconnect Powertrain Control Module (PCM) 104-pin connector. Measure resistance of Gray/Black wire between PCM connector terminal No. 68 and servo harness connector terminal No. 3. *See Figs. 1 and 2.* If resistance is less than 5 ohms, install new speed control servo and check system for normal operation. If resistance is 5 ohms or greater, repair open or high resistance in Gray/Black wire and check system for normal operation. See WIRING DIAGRAMS.

SET SPEED FLUCTUATES

Turn ignition off. Disengage cable from speed control servo. Inspect actuator cable and throttle linkage for binding. Pull on cable and observe resistance and verify throttle pedal movement. Repair as necessary. If no binding exists, replace speed control servo. See SPEED CONTROL SERVO under REMOVAL & INSTALLATION.

SYSTEM DOES NOT TURN OFF WHEN BRAKES ARE APPLIED

1) Turn ignition off. Disengage cable from speed control servo. Inspect actuator cable and throttle linkage for binding. Pull on cable and observe resistance and verify throttle pedal movement. Repair as necessary. If cable is okay, go to next step.

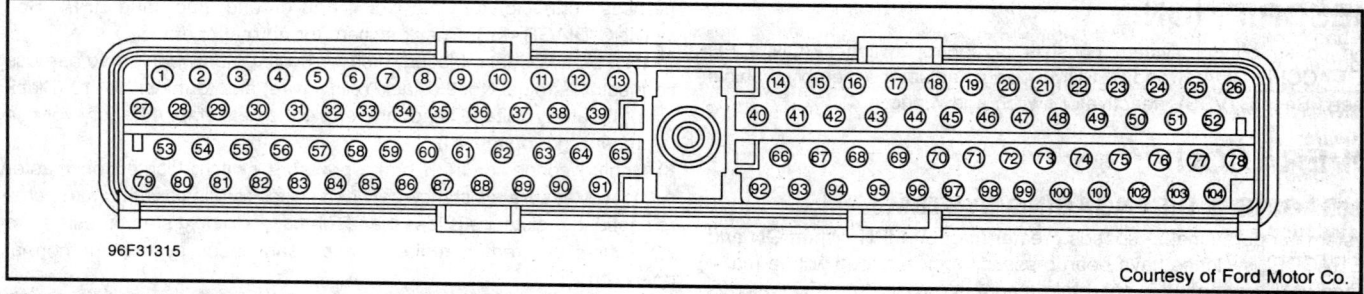

96F31315

Courtesy of Ford Motor Co.

Fig. 2: Identifying Powertrain Control Module (PCM) Connector Terminals

2) Disconnect speed control servo harness connector. While depressing brake pedal, measure voltage between servo harness connector terminal No. 4 (Red/Light Green wire) and terminal No. 10 (Black wire). If voltage is greater than 10 volts, replace speed control servo. See SPEED CONTROL SERVO under REMOVAL & INSTALLATION. If voltage is 10 volts or less, go to next step.

3) Disconnect Brake Pedal Position (BPP) switch harness connector. Measure voltage of White/Yellow wire between BPP switch harness connector and ground. If voltage is greater than 10 volts, go to next step. If voltage is 10 volts or less, repair White/Yellow wire circuit and check system for normal operation. See WIRING DIAGRAMS.

4) Measure resistance of Red/Light Green wire between BPP switch harness connector and speed control servo harness connector terminal No. 4. If resistance is 5 ohms or greater, repair Red/Light Green wire or connections. If resistance is less than 5 ohms, replace BPP switch and check system for normal operation.

COAST FUNCTION INOPERATIVE

Turn ignition off. Disconnect 10-pin connector from speed control servo. While pressing COAST switch and rotating steering wheel from stop to stop, measure resistance between speed control servo harness connector terminal No. 5 (Light Blue/Black wire) and terminal No. 6 (Dark Green/Orange wire). If resistance is 114-126 ohms, install new speed control servo. See SPEED CONTROL SERVO under REMOVAL & INSTALLATION. If resistance is not 114-126 ohms, install new speed control actuator switch. See COMMAND SWITCHES under REMOVAL & INSTALLATION. Check system for normal operation.

ACCEL FUNCTION INOPERATIVE

Turn ignition off. Disconnect 10-pin connector from speed control servo. While pressing SET/ACCEL switch and rotating steering wheel from stop to stop, measure resistance between speed control servo harness connector terminal No. 5 (Light Blue/Black wire) and terminal No. 6 (Dark Green/Orange wire). If resistance is 646-714 ohms, install new speed control servo. See SPEED CONTROL SERVO under REMOVAL & INSTALLATION. If resistance is not 646-714 ohms, install new speed control actuator switch. See COMMAND SWITCHES under REMOVAL & INSTALLATION. Check system for normal operation.

RESUME FUNCTION INOPERATIVE

Turn ignition off. Disconnect 10-pin connector from speed control servo. While pressing RESUME switch and rotating steering wheel from stop to stop, measure resistance between speed control servo harness connector terminal No. 5 (Light Blue/Black wire) and terminal No. 6 (Dark Green/Orange wire). If resistance is 2090-2310 ohms, install new speed control servo. See SPEED CONTROL SERVO under REMOVAL & INSTALLATION. If resistance is not 2090-2310 ohms, install new speed control actuator switch. See COMMAND SWITCHES under REMOVAL & INSTALLATION. Check system for normal operation.

SPEED CONTROL WILL NOT TURN OFF WITH OFF SWITCH

Turn ignition off. Disconnect 10-pin connector from speed control servo. While pressing OFF switch and rotating steering wheel from stop to stop, check for continuity between speed control servo harness connec-

tor terminal No. 5 (Light Blue/Black wire) and terminal No. 6 (Dark Green/Orange wire). If resistance is less than 5 ohms, install new speed control servo. See SPEED CONTROL SERVO under REMOVAL & INSTALLATION. If resistance is 5 ohms or greater, install new speed control actuator switch. See COMMAND SWITCHES under REMOVAL & INSTALLATION. Check system for normal operation.

REMOVAL & INSTALLATION

WARNING: Disable air bag system before working around steering column or removing any air bag system component. See appropriate AIR BAG RESTRAINT SYSTEMS article.

CAUTION: When battery is disconnected, vehicle computer and memory systems may lose memory data. Driveability problems may exist until computer systems have completed a relearn cycle. See COMPUTER RELEARN PROCEDURES article in GENERAL INFORMATION before disconnecting battery.

SPEED CONTROL SERVO

Removal – Push in locking arm on speed control actuator cable cap. Rotate speed control actuator cable cap counterclockwise and separate from speed control servo. *See Fig. 3.* Depress spring retainer and slide cable end out of speed control servo pulley. Disconnect electrical connector. Remove mounting bolts and remove speed control servo assembly from vehicle. Remove bracket screws and remove bracket from speed control servo.

Installation – To install, reverse removal procedure. Ensure rubber grommets in speed control servo bracket are properly seated. Tighten bracket screws to 90-115 INCH lbs. (10-13 N.m). Tighten mounting bolts to 67-92 INCH lbs. (7.6-10.4 N.m).

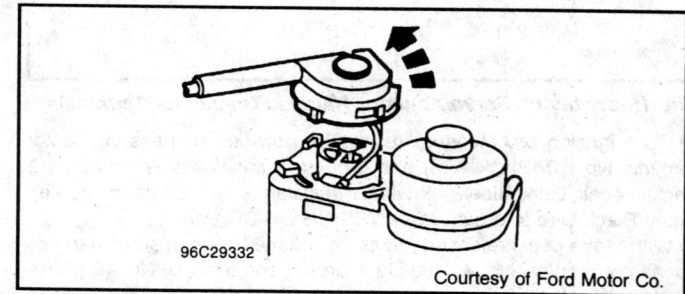

96C29332

Courtesy of Ford Motor Co.

Fig. 3: Removing Cable From Servo

COMMAND SWITCHES

WARNING: Observe all air bag service precautions. Disable air bag system. See SERVICE PRECAUTIONS and DISABLING & ACTIVATING AIR BAG SYSTEM in appropriate AIR BAG RESTRAINT SYSTEMS article.

Removal – 1) Disable air bag system. See DISABLING & ACTIVATING AIR BAG SYSTEM in appropriate AIR BAG RESTRAINT SYSTEMS article. Remove air bag nuts and washers from steering wheel. Unplug air bag connector from clockspring (contact assembly). Remove air bag module.

WARNING: Place air bag module on bench with trim cover facing upward.

---

2) Release 4 retaining clips from switches. Disconnect switch harness connectors. Remove switch assembly from steering wheel.

Installation – Install switches in steering wheel. Connect air bag module wiring connector to clockspring (contact assembly). Position air bag module onto steering wheel. Install air bag module nuts and washers. Activate air bag system. Observe AIR BAG warning light to verify system is functioning properly. See SYSTEM OPERATION CHECK in appropriate AIR BAG RESTRAINT SYSTEMS article.

DEACTIVATOR (BRAKE PRESSURE) SWITCH

Removal & Installation – Deactivator switch is located on master cylinder. Disconnect negative battery cable. Unplug harness connector. Unscrew switch. To install, reverse removal procedure. Torque switch to 11-15 ft. lbs. (15-20 N.m). Bleed brake system. See appropriate DISC & DRUM article in BRAKES in appropriate MITCHELL® manual. Wash any brake fluid from painted or plastic surfaces.

WIRING DIAGRAMS

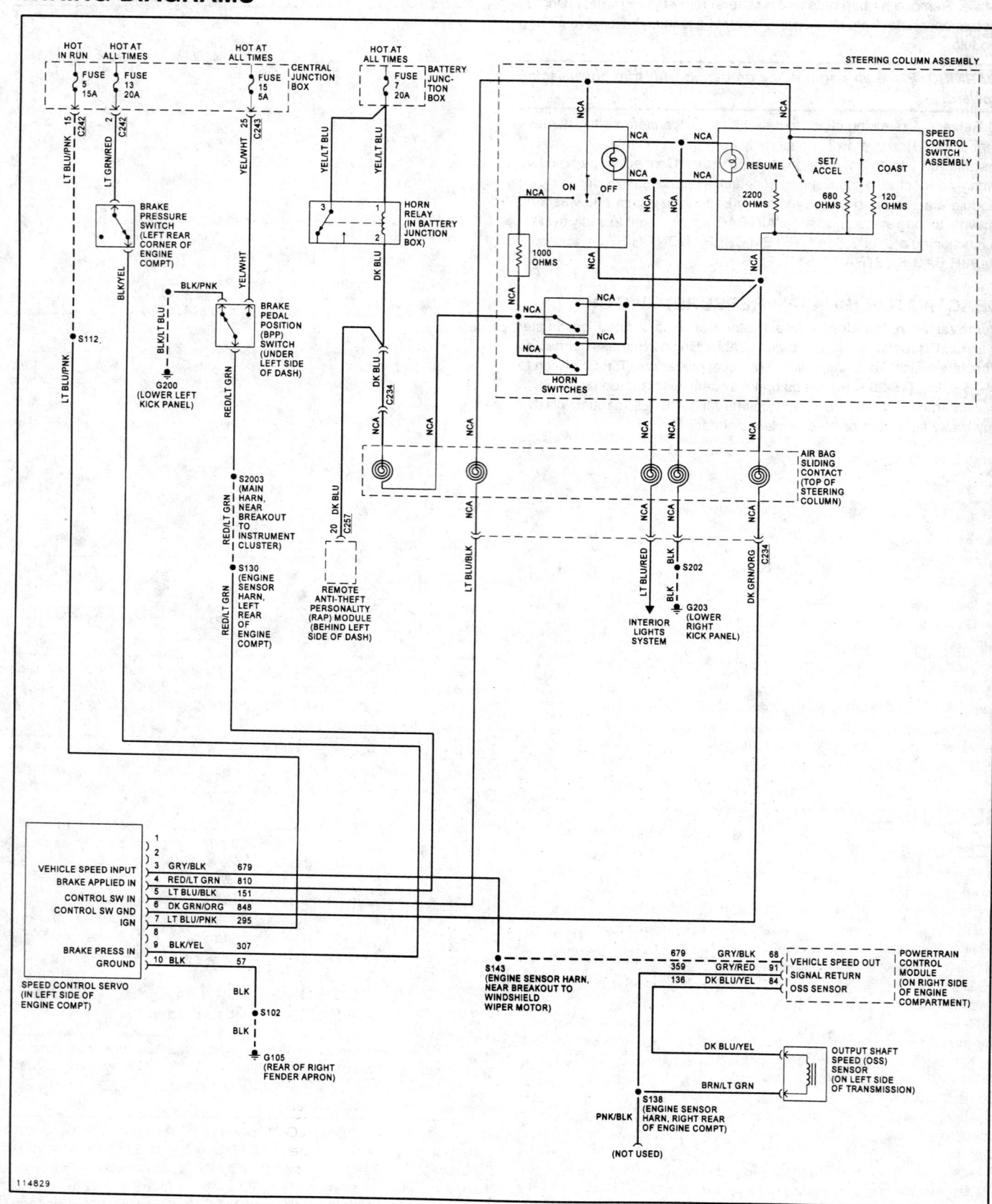

Fig. 4: Cruise Control System Wiring Diagram (Expedition & Navigator)

DESCRIPTION & OPERATION

Major components of the cruise control system are speed control switches, servo/actuator, horn relay, Brake Pedal Position (BPP) switch, deactivator switch, and related wiring. This system does not require engine vacuum. An electronic servo/actuator actuates the throttle. All electronic control components are contained within the speed control servo/actuator.

The system is operational only at speeds greater than 30 MPH. The system is activated when ON/OFF switch is switched on and SET/ACCEL button is pressed and released. Vehicle will maintain set speed until new speed is set, brake pedal is pressed, clutch pedal is pressed, or ON/OFF switch is switched off. If system has been deactivated by pressing brake or clutch pedal, set speed can be regained by pressing and releasing RESUME button. When brake or clutch pedal is pressed, a signal from switch is sent to the servo to deactivate the system. A deactivator switch acts as a redundant brake signal.

ADJUSTMENTS

SERVO/ACTUATOR CABLE

Remove cable housing retaining clip. Ensure throttle plate is in closed position. Pull actuator cable to take up slack. Back off at least one notch. While holding cable, insert cable retaining clip. Check throttle operation.

TROUBLE SHOOTING

Before performing any testing, check following for possible cause of system malfunction.
- Faulty fuses.
- Loose or corroded connections.
- Damaged wiring harness.
- Damaged switches.
- Damaged or binding servo/actuator cable.
- Incorrect servo/actuator cable adjustment.

Verify horn and stoplights function properly. Repair as necessary. Inspect actuator and throttle linkage for smooth operation. Unbind as necessary. If no problems are found, perform SELF-DIAGNOSTIC TEST under SELF-DIAGNOSTIC SYSTEM.

SELF-DIAGNOSTIC SYSTEM

SELF-DIAGNOSTIC TEST

1) Place gear selector in Park. Ensure parking brake is engaged and brake pedal is released. While holding speed control OFF button, turn ignition switch to RUN position. CRUISE indicator on instrument cluster should flash once to indicate successful entry into self-diagnostic mode. If CRUISE indicator does not flash, repeat step **1)**. If CRUISE indicator still does not flash, repair system by symptom. See SYMPTOM DIAGNOSIS table. If CRUISE CONTROL indicator flashes once followed by 5 additional flashes, replace cruise control servo/actuator.
2) Release speed control OFF button. Within 5 seconds of entering self-diagnostics, press speed control ON button. Press remaining speed control buttons in the following sequence; ON, RES, COAST and SET/ACCEL. As each button is pressed, CRUISE indicator will flash. Wait until indicator light goes out to press next button.
3) After sequence has been completed, indicator light will flash to indicate test passed or failed. See FLASH CODES table and perform appropriate test.
4) Immediately after static test has passed, actuator performs a dynamic test by automatically operating throttle .04-.40" (1-10 mm). Observe throttle movement to witness any sticking of cable or linkage. Ensure throttle returns properly. Turn ignition switch to LOCK position. If self-diagnostics does not pinpoint fault, see SYMPTOM DIAGNOSIS table and perform appropriate test under SYSTEM TESTS.

FLASH CODES

Flash Code	Test
Flash Code 1 (With Throttle Pull)	Test Passed
(No Throttle Pull At Throttle Body)	1
(No Throttle Pull At Servo/Actuator)	A
(Speed Control Inoperative)	D
Flash Code 2 (Brake Pedal Position (BPP) Switch Circuit)	B
Flash Code 3 (Deactivator Switch Circuit)	C
Flash Code 4 (Vehicle Speed Sensor (VSS) Circuit)	D
Flash Code 5 (Servo/Actuator)	2

[1] – Replace speed control servo/actuator cable and perform SELF-DIAGNOSTIC TEST.
[2] – Replace speed control servo/actuator and perform SELF-DIAGNOSTIC TEST.

SYMPTOM DIAGNOSIS

Symptom	Test
Speed Control Indicator Light Inoperative	1
Speed Control Inoperative - No Flash Codes	E
Speed Control Does Not Disengage When Clutch Is Applied	F
Coast Switch Is Inoperative	G
SET/ACCEL Switch Is Inoperative	H
Resume Switch Is Inoperative	J
Off Switch Is Inoperative	K
Speed Control Indicator Does Not Turn Off	L
Set Speed Fluctuates	M

[1] – For diagnosis and repair, go to ANALOG INSTRUMENT PANELS – EXPLORER & MOUNTAINEER article.

SYSTEM TESTS

TEST A: NO DYNAMIC PULL AT SPEED CONTROL SERVO/ACTUATOR (FLASH CODE 1)

NOTE: After each service or repair procedure has been completed, reconnect all components. Clear DTCs and repeat SELF-DIAGNOSTIC TEST under SELF-DIAGNOSTIC SYSTEM to ensure system is funtioning properly.

1) Turn ignition switch to LOCK position. Check if speed control servo/actuator cable is attached at servo/actuator and throttle. If cable is attached properly, go to next step. If cable is not attached properly, connect cable.
2) Check speed control servo/actuator cable adjustment. See SERVO/ACTUATOR CABLE under ADJUSTMENTS. If cable is adjusted properly, go to next step. If cable is not adjusted properly, adjust as necessary.
3) Disconnect speed control servo/actuator cable from servo/actuator. Check speed control servo/actuator cable for sticking or binding. If cable is okay, replace speed control servo/actuator. If cable is not okay, replace speed control servo/actuator cable.

TEST B: BRAKE PEDAL POSITION (BPP) SWITCH CIRCUIT FAILURE (FLASH CODE 2)

NOTE: After each service or repair procedure has been completed, reconnect all components. Clear DTCs and repeat SELF-DIAGNOSTIC TEST under SELF-DIAGNOSTIC SYSTEM to ensure system is funtioning properly.

1) Turn ignition switch to LOCK position. Disconnect speed control servo/actuator harness connector C171 located at right rear of engine compartment. Turn ignition switch to RUN position. Measure voltage between terminals No. 4 (Tan/Light Blue wire) and No. 10 (Black wire) at speed control servo/actuator connector C171. *See Fig. 1.* If voltage exists, go to step **7)**. If voltage does not exist and vehicle is equipped with M/T, go to next step. If voltage does not exist and vehicle is equipped with A/T, go to step **5)**.

2) Turn ignition switch to LOCK position. Disconnect Clutch Pedal Position (CPP) switch harness connector C209. Measure resistance between Red/Light Green wire terminal and Tan/Light Blue wire terminal at CPP switch (component side). If resistance is less than 5 ohms, go to next step. If resistance is 5 ohms or more, replace CPP switch.

3) Using an ohmmeter, measure resistance between speed control servo/actuator connector C171 terminal No. 4 and CPP switch connector C209 or jumper Tan/Light Blue wire terminal. *See Fig. 1.* If resistance is less than 5 ohms, go to next step. If resistance is 5 ohms or more, repair open in Tan/Light Blue wire.

4) Disconnect Brake Pedal Position (BPP) switch connector C224 (located on brake pedal support). Using an ohmmeter, measure resistance between CPP switch connector C209 or jumper Red/Light Green wire terminal and BPP switch connector C224 Red/Light green wire terminal. If resistance is less than 5 ohms, go to step 6). If resistance is 5 ohms or more, repair open in Red/Light Green wire.

5) Disconnect Brake Pedal Position (BPP) switch connector C224 (located on brake pedal support). Using an ohmmeter, measure resistance between speed control servo/actuator connector C171 terminal No. 4 (Tan/Light Blue wire) and BPP switch connector C224 Red/Light green wire terminal. *See Fig. 1.* If resistance is less than 5 ohms, go to next step. If resistance is 5 ohms or more, repair open in Red/Light Green or Tan/Light Blue wire.

6) Using an ohmmeter, measure resistance between ground and BPP switch connector C224 Black wire terminal. If resistance is less than 5 ohms, replace BPP switch. If resistance is 5 ohms or more, repair open in Black wire between BPP switch and ground.

7) Disconnect Brake Pedal Position (BPP) switch connector C224 (located on brake pedal support). Using a voltmeter, measure voltage between speed control servo/actuator connector C171 terminals No. 4 and 10. *See Fig. 1.* If no voltage is present, replace BPP switch. If voltage is present and vehicle is equipped with A/T, repair Red/Light Green and/or Tan/Light Blue wire. If voltage is present and vehicle is equipped with M/T, go to next step.

8) Disconnect CPP switch connector C209 or jumper (located on clutch pedal arm). Using a voltmeter, measure voltage between speed control servo/actuator connector C171 terminals No. 4 (Tan/Light Blue wire) and 10 (Black wire) . *See Fig. 1.* If voltage is present, repair Red/Light Green wire. If no voltage is present, repair Tan/Light Blue wire.

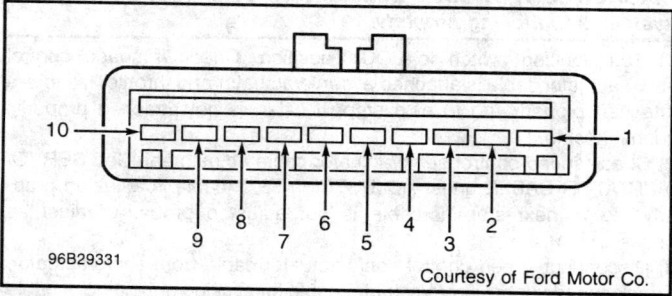

96B29331   Courtesy of Ford Motor Co.

Fig. 1: Identifying Servo/Actuator Connector C171 Terminals

TEST C: DEACTIVATOR SWITCH CIRCUIT FAILURE (FLASH CODE 3)

NOTE: After each service or repair procedure has been completed, reconnect all components. Clear DTCs and repeat SELF-DIAGNOSTIC TEST under SELF-DIAGNOSTIC SYSTEM to ensure system is funtioning properly.

1) Turn ignition switch to LOCK position. Disconnect speed control servo/actuator connector C171 located at right rear of engine compartment. Turn ignition switch to RUN position. Using a voltmeter, measure voltage between speed control servo/actuator connector C171 terminals No. 9 (Black/Yellow wire) and 10 (Black wire). See. 1. If voltage is 10 volts or less, go to next step. If voltage is more than 10 volts, replace speed control servo/actuator.

2) Turn ignition switch to LOCK position. Disconnect deactivator switch connector C102. Switch is located in front of brake master cylinder. Turn

ignition switch to RUN position. Connect a jumper wire between deactivator switch connector C102 terminals. Using a voltmeter, check voltage between speed control servo/actuator connector C171 terminals No. 9 (Black/Yellow wire) and 10 (Black wire). If voltage is 10 volts or less, go to next step. If voltage is more than 10 volts, replace deactivator switch.

3) Using an ohmmeter, check resistance between speed control servo/actuator connector C171 terminal No. 9 and deactivator switch connector C103 Black/Yellow wire terminal. If resistance is less than 5 ohms, repair Light Green/Red wire between deactivator switch and instrument panel fuse block. If resistance is 5 ohms or more, repair Black/Yellow wire between speed control servo/actuator and deactivator switch.

TEST D: VEHICLE SPEED SENSOR (VSS) CIRCUIT FAILURE (FLASH CODE 4)

NOTE: After each service or repair procedure has been completed, reconnect all components. Clear DTCs and repeat SELF-DIAGNOSTIC TEST under SELF-DIAGNOSTIC SYSTEM to ensure system is funtioning properly.

1) Test drive vehicle and while observing speedometer operation. If speedometer operates properly, go to next step. If speedometer does not operate properly, see ANALOG INSTRUMENT PANELS – EXPLORER & MOUNTAINEER article to continue diagnosis.

2) Turn ignition switch to LOCK position. Disconnect speed control servo/actuator connector C171 located at right rear of engine compartment. Disconnect ABS control module connector C186 located near left front fenderwell). Using an ohmmeter, check resistance in Gray/Black wire between speed control servo/actuator connector C171 terminal No. 3 and ABS control module connector C186 terminal No. 10. *See Figs. 1 and 2.* If resistance is less than 5 ohms, replace speed control servo/actuator and perform. If resistance is 5 ohms or more, repair open in Gray/Black wire.

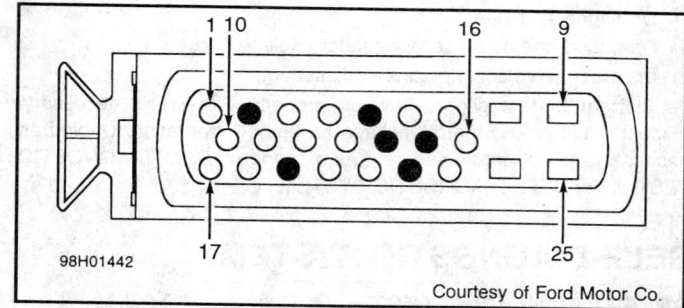

98H01442   Courtesy of Ford Motor Co.

Fig. 2: Identifying ABS Control Module Connector C186 Terminals

TEST E: SPEED CONTROL INOPERATIVE (NO FLASH CODES)

NOTE: After each service or repair procedure has been completed, reconnect all components. Clear DTCs and repeat SELF-DIAGNOSTIC TEST under SELF-DIAGNOSTIC SYSTEM to ensure system is funtioning properly.

1) Ensure ignition is off. Disconnect speed control servo/actuator connector C171 located at right rear of engine compartment. Turn ignition switch to RUN position. Using a voltmeter, measure voltage between ground and speed control servo/actuator connector C171 terminal No. 7 (Gray/Yellow wire). If voltage is more than 10 volts, go to next step. If voltage is 10 volts or less, repair open in Gray/Yellow wire between instrument panel fuse block and speed control servo/actuator.

2) Turn ignition off. Using an ohmmeter, measure resistance between ground and speed control servo/actuator connector C171 terminal No. 10 (Black wire) . *See Fig. 1.* If resistance is less than 5 ohms, go to next step. If resistance is 5 ohms or more, repair open in Black wire between speed control servo/actuator and ground.

3) Turn ignition switch to RUN position. Using a voltmeter, measure voltage between ground and speed control servo/actuator connector C171 terminal No. 5 (Light Blue/Black wire while pressing speed control ON switch. *See Fig. 1.* If voltage is more than 10 volts, go to step **6)**. If voltage is 10 volts or less, go to next step.

4) Ensure ignition is off. Disconnect air bag sliding contact connector C220 (located at base of steering column). Using an ohmmeter, measure resistance of Light Blue/Black wire between speed control servo/actuator connector C171 terminal No. 5 and air bag sliding contact connector C220 (female side). *See Fig. 1.* If resistance is less than 5 ohms, go to next step. If resistance is 5 ohms or more, repair open in Light Blue/Black wire between speed control servo/actuator and air bag sliding contact.

5) Disable and remove driver side air bag. See appropriate AIR BAG RESTRAINT SYSTEMS article. On models without remote audio/climate controls, measure resistance between air bag sliding contact terminal No. 1 and air bag sliding contact 6-pin male connector C220 terminal No. 1. *See Fig. 3.* On models with remote audio/climate controls, measure resistance between air bag sliding contact terminal No. 6 and air bag sliding contact 8-pin connector C220, terminal No. 1. If resistance is less than one ohm and vehicle is not equipped with remote audio/climate controls, replace speed control switches. If resistance is less than one ohm and vehicle is equipped with remote audio/climate controls, go to step **7)**. On all models, if resistance is one ohm or more, replace air bag sliding contact.

6) Using an ohmmeter, measure resistance between speed control servo/actuator connector C171 terminals No. 5 (Light Blue/Black wire) and No. 6 (Dark Green/Orange wire) while pressing speed control OFF switch. If resistance is less than 5 ohms and vehicle is not equipped with remote audio/climate controls, replace speed control switches. If resistance is less than 5 ohms and vehicle is equipped with remote audio/climate controls, go to next step. On all models, if resistance is 5 ohms or more, replace speed control servo/actuator.

7) Using an ohmmeter, measure resistance between air bag sliding contact connector terminal No. 4 and speed control switch connector terminal No. 2. *See Fig. 4.* Check resistance between air bag sliding contact connector terminal No. 6 and speed control switch connector terminal No. 1. If resistances are less than 5 ohms, replace speed control switches. If resistances are 5 ohms or more, replace speed control switch wiring harness.

TEST F: SPEED CONTROL DOES NOT DISENGAGE WHEN CLUTCH IS APPLIED

NOTE: After each service or repair procedure has been completed, reconnect all components. Clear DTCs and repeat SELF-DIAGNOSTIC TEST under SELF-DIAGNOSTIC SYSTEM to ensure system is funtioning properly.

1) Turn ignition switch to LOCK position. Disconnect Clutch Pedal Position (CPP) switch connector C209 or jumper (located on clutch pedal arm). Using an ohmmeter, measure resistance between CPP switch terminals No. 3 and 4 while pressing clutch pedal. *See Fig. 5.* If resistance is more than 10 k/ohms, go to next step. If resistance is 10 k/ohms or less, replace CPP switch.

2) Ensure ignition is off. Disconnect speed control servo/actuator connector C171 located at right rear of engine compartment. Using an ohmmeter, CHECK RESISTANCE BETWEEN GROUND AND SPEED CONTROL SERVO/ACTUATOR CONNECTOR C171 TERMINAL NO. 4 (Tan/Light Blue wire). *See Fig. 1.* If resistance is more than 10 k/ohms, replace speed control servo/actuator. If resistance is 10 k/ohms or less, repair short to ground in Tan/Light Blue wire between speed control servo/actuator and CPP switch.

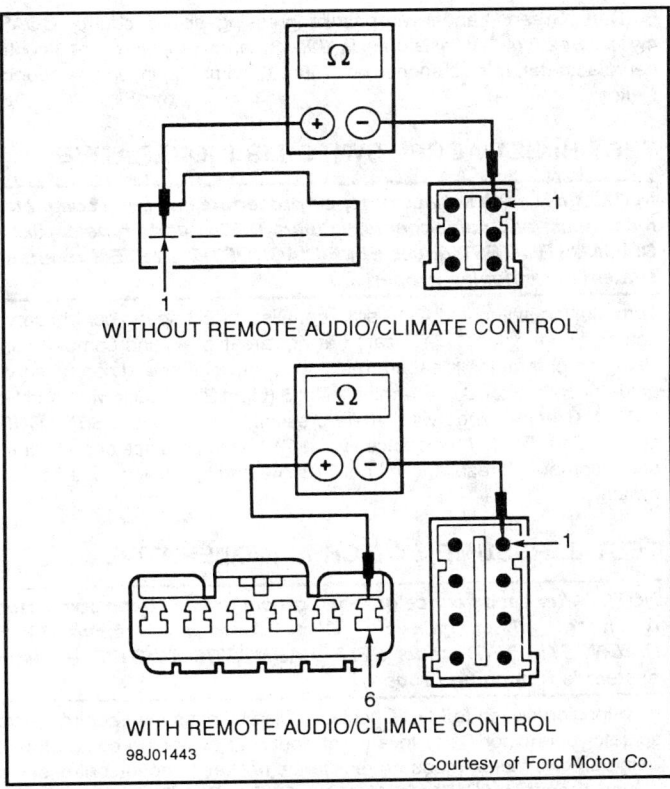

WITHOUT REMOTE AUDIO/CLIMATE CONTROL

WITH REMOTE AUDIO/CLIMATE CONTROL

98J01443   Courtesy of Ford Motor Co.

Fig. 3: Testing Air Bag Sliding Contact

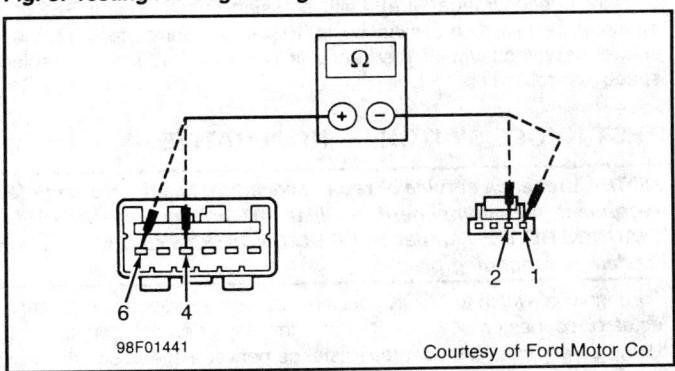

98F01441   Courtesy of Ford Motor Co.

Fig. 4: Testing Speed Control Switch Wiring Harness

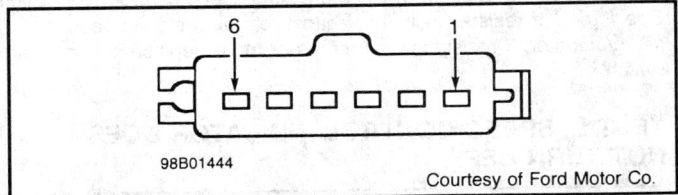

98B01444   Courtesy of Ford Motor Co.

Fig. 5: Identifying CPP Switch Terminals

TEST G: COAST SWITCH IS INOPERATIVE

NOTE: After each service or repair procedure has been completed, reconnect all components. Clear DTCs and repeat SELF-DIAGNOSTIC TEST under SELF-DIAGNOSTIC SYSTEM to ensure system is funtioning properly.

Turn ignition switch to LOCK position. Disconnect speed control servo/actuator connector C171 located at right rear of engine compartment. Using an ohmmeter, measure resistance between speed control servo/actuator connector C171 terminals No. 5 (Light Blue/Black wire) and No.

6 (Dark Green/Orange wire) while pressing speed control COAST switch. See Fig. 1. If resistance is 108-132 ohms, replace speed control servo/actuator. If resistance is not 108-132 ohms, replace speed control switch.

TEST H: SET/ACCEL SWITCH IS INOPERATIVE

NOTE: *After each service or repair procedure has been completed, reconnect all components. Clear DTCs and repeat SELF-DIAGNOSTIC TEST under SELF-DIAGNOSTIC SYSTEM to ensure system is funtioning properly.*

Turn ignition switch to LOCK position. Disconnect speed control servo/actuator connector C171 located at right rear of engine compartment. Using an ohmmeter, measure resistance between speed control servo/actuator connector C171 terminals No. 5 (Light Blue/Black wire) and No. 6 (Dark Green/Orange wire) while pressing speed control SET/ACCEL switch. See Fig. 1. If resistance is 612-748 ohms, replace speed control servo/actuator. If resistance is not 612-748 ohms, replace speed control switch.

TEST J: RESUME SWITCH IS INOPERATIVE

NOTE: *After each service or repair procedure has been completed, reconnect all components. Clear DTCs and repeat SELF-DIAGNOSTIC TEST under SELF-DIAGNOSTIC SYSTEM to ensure system is funtioning properly.*

Turn ignition switch to LOCK position. Disconnect speed control servo/actuator connector C171 located at right rear or engine compartment. Using an ohmmeter, measure resistance between speed control servo/actuator connector C171 terminals No. 5 (Light Blue/Black wire) and No. 6 (Dark Green/Orange wire) while pressing speed control RESUME switch. See Fig. 1. If resistance is 1980-2420 ohms, replace speed control servo/actuator. If resistance is not 1980-2420 ohms, replace speed control switch.

TEST K: OFF SWITCH IS INOPERATIVE

NOTE: *After each service or repair procedure has been completed, reconnect all components. Clear DTCs and repeat SELF-DIAGNOSTIC TEST under SELF-DIAGNOSTIC SYSTEM to ensure system is funtioning properly.*

Turn ignition switch to LOCK position. Disconnect speed control servo/actuator connector C171 located at right rear of engine compartment. Using an ohmmeter, measure resistance between speed control servo/actuator connector C171 terminals No. 5 (Light Blue/Black wire) and No. 6 (Dark Green/Orange wire) while pressing speed control OFF switch. See Fig. 1. If resistance is less than 5 ohms, replace speed control servo/actuator. If resistance is 5 ohms or more, replace speed control switch.

TEST L: SPEED CONTROL INDICATOR DOES NOT TURN OFF

NOTE: *After each service or repair procedure has been completed, reconnect all components. Clear DTCs and repeat SELF-DIAGNOSTIC TEST under SELF-DIAGNOSTIC SYSTEM to ensure system is funtioning properly.*

1) Turn ignition switch to LOCK position. Disconnect speed control servo/actuator connector C171 located at right rear of engine compartment. Turn ignition switch to RUN position. If speed control indicator illuminates, go to next step. If speed control indicator does not illuminate, replace speed control servo/actuator.
2) Ensure ignition is off. Disconnect instrument cluster White 16-pin connector C286 (located behind instrument cluster) . Using an ohmmeter, measure resistance between ground and speed control servo/actuator connector C171 terminal No. 1 (Orange/Light Blue wire). See Fig. 1. If resistance is more than 10 k/ohms, replace instrument cluster

printed circuit. If resistance is 10 k/ohms or less, repair short to ground in Orange/Light Blue wire between instrument cluster and speed control servo/actuator.

TEST M: SET SPEED FLUCTUATES

NOTE: *After each service or repair procedure has been completed, reconnect all components. Clear DTCs and repeat SELF-DIAGNOSTIC TEST under SELF-DIAGNOSTIC SYSTEM to ensure system is funtioning properly.*

1) Turn ignition switch to LOCK position. Remove speed control servo/actuator cable from servo/actuator. Check for binding or sticking speed control servo/actuator cable, throttle linkage and/or throttle plate. Ensure throttle cable bracket and speed control servo/actuator bracket are not loose. Repair or replace as necessary. If all components are okay, go to next step.
2) Test drive vehicle and observe speedometer operation. If speedometer operates properly, replace speed control servo/actuator. If speedometer does not operate properly, see ANALOG INSTRUMENT PANELS – EXPLORER & MOUNTAINEER article to continue diagnosis.

REMOVAL & INSTALLATION

WARNING: *Disable air bag system before working around steering column or removing any air bag system component. See appropriate AIR BAG RESTRAINT SYSTEMS article.*

CAUTION: *When battery is disconnected, vehicle computer and memory systems may lose memory data. Driveability problems may exist until computer systems have completed a relearn cycle. See COMPUTER RELEARN PROCEDURES article in GENERAL INFORMATION before disconnecting battery.*

SPEED CONTROL SERVO/ACTUATOR

Removal & Installation – Disconnect speed control servo/actuator electrical connector located at right rear of engine compartment.. Press in locking tab arm on cable cap and rotate cap counterclockwise. Disengage cable slug from servo pulley. Gently push slug past retaining spring with a small screwdriver. Separate bracket from servo. To install, reverse removal procedure.

VEHICLE SPEED SENSOR

Removal & Installation – Powertrain Control Module (PCM) receives vehicle speed input signal from 4-Wheel Anti-Lock (4WAL) module. 4WAL module receives its input signal from rear axle sensor. If equipped with air suspension, turn air suspension switch off. Disconnect negative battery cable. Raise and support vehicle. Unplug rear axle sensor electrical connector. Remove rear axle sensor retaining bolt from axle housing and remove sensor. To install, reverse removal procedure. Lubricate NEW sensor "O" ring and install sensor. Tighten switch to 25-30 ft. lbs. (34-41 N.m).

DEACTIVATOR SWITCH

Removal & Installation – Disconnect negative battery cable. Disconnect deactivator switch connector located at front of brake master cylinder. Unscrew switch. To install, reverse removal procedure. Tighten switch to 12-14 ft. lbs. (16-20 N.m). Bleed brake system. See appropriate article in BRAKES in appropriate MITCHELL® manual.

SPEED CONTROL SWITCHES

NOTE: *Right and left switch assemblies can be replaced individually.*

Removal & Installation – Disconnect negative battery cable. Disable air bag system. See appropriate AIR BAG RESTRAINT SYSTEMS article. Carefully separate speed control switches from steering wheel. Disconnect wiring at switches to be replaced. Remove switches. To install, reverse removal procedure.

WIRING DIAGRAMS

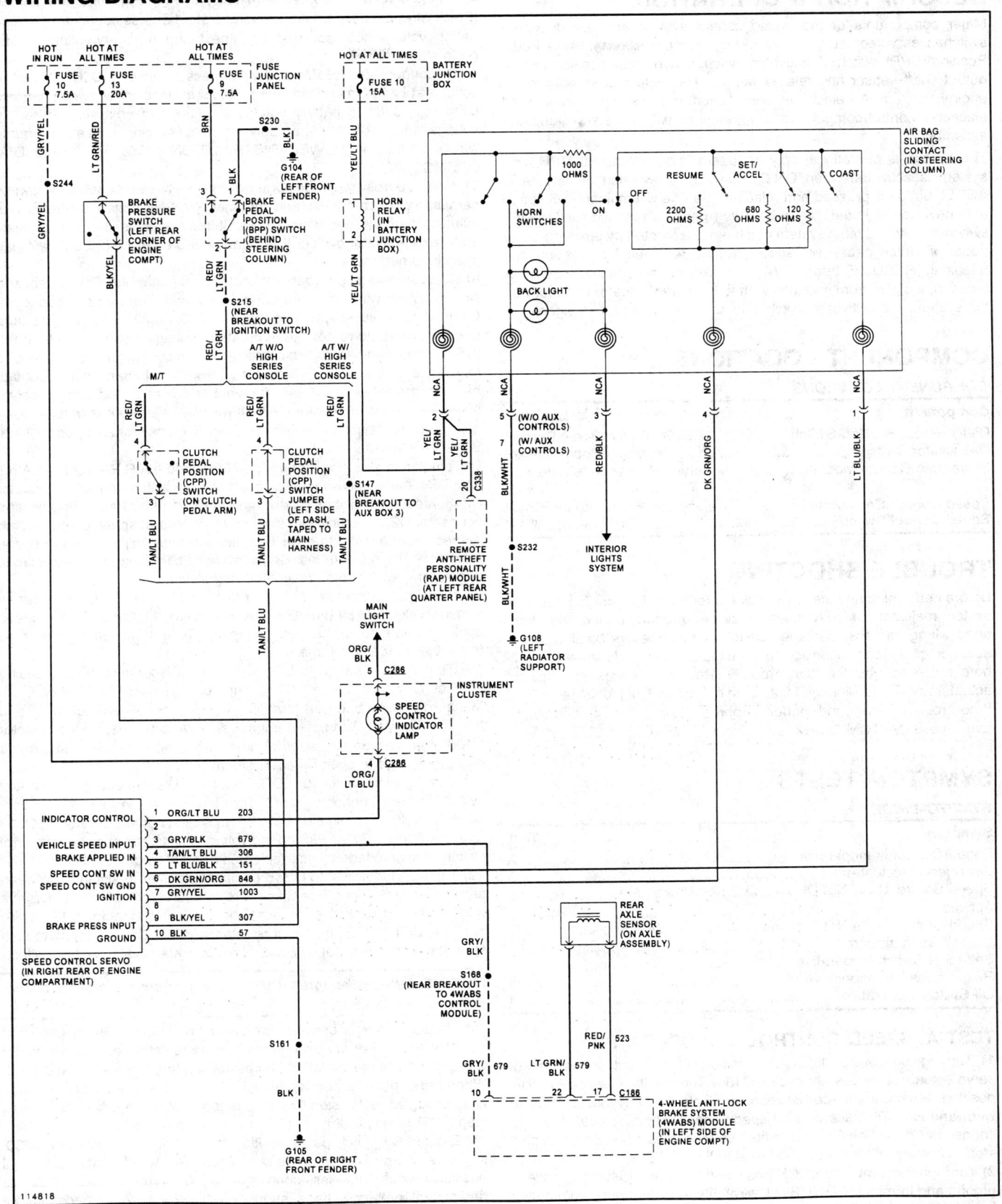

Fig. 6: Cruise Control System Wiring Diagram (Explorer & Mountaineer)

1999 ACCESSORIES & EQUIPMENT
Cruise Control Systems – Mustang

DESCRIPTION & OPERATION

Major components of the cruise control system are speed control switches, servo/actuator, vehicle speed sensor, horn relay, Brake Pedal Position (BPP) switch, deactivator switch, clutch pedal position switch, output shaft sensor and related wiring. This system does not require engine vacuum. An electronic servo/actuator actuates the throttle. All electronic control components are contained within the servo/actuator assembly.

The system is operational only at speeds greater than 30 MPH. The system is activated when ON/OFF switch is switched on and SET/ACCEL button is pressed and released. Vehicle will maintain set speed until new speed is set, brake or clutch pedal is pressed, or ON/OFF switch is switched off. If system has been deactivated by pressing brake pedal or clutch pedal, set speed can be regained by pressing and releasing RESUME button. When brake pedal or clutch pedal is pressed, a signal from switch is sent to the servo/actuator to deactivate the system. A deactivator switch acts as a redundant brake signal.

COMPONENT LOCATIONS

COMPONENT LOCATIONS

Component	Location
Clutch Pedal Position Switch	On Clutch Pedal Bracket
Deactivator Switch	On Brake Pedal Bracket
Powertrain Control Module	Behind Passenger's Side Kick Panel
Speed Control Servo/Actuator	Behind Left Front Fender Wheel
Speed Control Switch	On Steering Wheel

TROUBLE SHOOTING

Before performing any testing, check the following for possible cause of system malfunction: faulty fuses, loose or corroded connections, damaged wiring harness, damaged switches, damaged or binding servo/actuator cable and incorrect servo/actuator cable adjustment. Verify horn and stoplights function properly. Repair as necessary. Inspect actuator and throttle linkage for smooth operation. Unbind as necessary. If no problems are found, perform appropriate test based upon symptom. See SYMPTOM INDEX table under SYMPTOM TESTS.

SYMPTOM TESTS

SYMPTOM INDEX

Symptom	Test
Speed Control Is Inoperative	A
Set Speed Fluctuates	B
Speed Control Does Not Disengage When Brakes Are Applied	C
Speed Control Does Not Disengage When Clutch Is Applied	D
Coast Switch Inoperative	E
Set/Accel Switch Inoperative	F
Resume Switch Inoperative	G
Off Switch Inoperative	H

TEST A: SPEED CONTROL IS INOPERATIVE

1) Turn ignition switch to LOCK position. Disconnect speed control servo/actuator harness connector C136. Turn ignition switch to RUN position. Measure voltage between terminals No. 7 (White/Light Blue wire) and No. 10 (Black wire) at speed control servo/actuator harness connector C136. See Fig. 1. If battery voltage does not exist, go to next step. If battery voltage exists, go to step **3)**.

2) Turn ignition switch to LOCK position. Measure resistance between ground and terminal No. 10 (Black wire) at speed control servo/actuator harness connector C136. If resistance is 5 ohms or less, repair power distribution circuit. See appropriate wiring diagram in POWER DISTRIBUTION article in WIRING DIAGRAMS. If resistance is greater than 5 ohms, repair open in Black wire.

3) Measure voltage between terminals No. 9 (Orange wire) and No. 10 (Black wire) at speed control servo/actuator harness connector C136. If battery voltage does not exist, go to next step. If battery voltage exists, go to step **6)**.

4) Disconnect deactivator switch harness connector C261. Measure voltage at Light Green/Red wire terminal at deactivator switch harness connector C261. If battery voltage exists, go to next step. If battery voltage does not exist, repair power distribution circuit. See appropriate wiring diagram in POWER DISTRIBUTION article in WIRING DIAGRAMS.

5) Measure resistance in Orange wire between deactivator switch harness connector C261 and terminal No. 9 at speed control servo/actuator harness connector C136. If resistance is 5 ohms or less, replace deactivator switch. If resistance is greater than 5 ohms, repair open in Orange wire.

6) Measure voltage between terminals No. 5 (Light Blue/Black wire) and No. 10 (Black wire) at speed control servo/actuator harness connector C136 while pressing speed control switch ON button. If battery voltage does not exist, go to next step. If battery voltage exists, go to step **9)**.

7) Disconnect air bag sliding contact harness connector C233. Measure resistance in Light Blue/Black wire between air bag sliding contact harness connector C233 and terminal No. 5 at speed control servo/actuator harness connector C136. If resistance is 5 ohms or less, go to next step. If resistance is greater than 5 ohms, repair open in Light Blue/Black wire.

8) Remove driver's side air bag. See appropriate AIR BAG RESTRAINT SYSTEMS article. Disconnect speed control switch harness connector C243. Measure resistance between pin No. 1 at air bag sliding contact connector C233 (component side) and pin No. 1 at speed control switch harness connector C243 (air bag sliding contact side). See Fig. 2. If resistance is 5 ohms or less, replace speed control switch. If resistance is greater than 5 ohms, replace air bag sliding contact.

9) Turn ignition switch to RUN position. Measure voltage between terminals No. 5 (Light Blue/Black wire) and No. 10 (Black wire) at speed control servo/actuator harness connector C136. If no voltage exists, go to next step. If any voltage exists, go to step **12)**.

10) Turn ignition switch to LOCK position. Disconnect air bag sliding contact harness connector C233. Turn ignition switch to RUN position. Measure voltage between terminals No. 5 (Light Blue/Black wire) and No. 10 (Black wire) at speed control servo/actuator harness connector C136. If no voltage exists, go to next step. If any voltage exists, repair short to voltage in Light Blue/Black wire.

11) Turn ignition switch to LOCK position. Disconnect speed control switch harness connector C243. Turn ignition switch to RUN position. Measure voltage at pin No. 1 at air bag sliding contact connector C233 (component side). See Fig. 2. If no voltage exists, replace speed control switch. If any voltage exists, replace air bag sliding contact.

12) Turn ignition switch to LOCK position. Measure resistance between terminals No. 5 (Light Blue/Black wire) and No. 6 (Dark Green/Orange wire) at speed control servo/actuator harness connector C136 while pressing SET/ACCEL button. If resistance is 612-748 ohms, go to next step. If resistance is not 612-748 ohms, replace speed control switch.

NOTE: Ensure brake lights are operating properly before proceeding.

13) Measure voltage between terminals No. 4 (Light Green wire) and No. 10 (Black wire) at speed control servo/actuator harness connector C136. When brake pedal is depressed, battery voltage should exist. When brake pedal is not depressed, no voltage should exist. If voltage is as specified, go to step **16)**. If voltage is not as specified, go to next step (M/T) or repair open in Light Green wire (A/T).

14) Disconnect clutch pedal position switch harness connector C260. Measure voltage at appropriate Light Green wire terminal at clutch pedal position switch harness connector C260. When brake pedal is depressed, battery voltage should exist. When brake pedal is not depressed, no voltage should exist. If voltage is as specified, go to next step. If voltage is not as specified, repair open in Light Green wire.

15) Measure resistance in Light Green wire between clutch pedal position switch harness connector C260 and terminal No. 4 at speed control servo/actuator harness connector C136. If resistance is 5 ohms or less, replace clutch pedal position switch. If resistance is greater than 5 ohms, repair open in Light Green wire.

16) Turn ignition switch to LOCK position. Disconnect Powertrain Control Module (PCM) harness connector C294. Measure resistance in White/Orange wire between terminal No. 3 at speed control servo/actuator harness connector C136 and terminal No. 68 at PCM harness connector C294. *See Figs. 2 and 3.* If resistance is 5 ohms or less, go to next step. If resistance is greater than 5 ohms, repair open in White/Orange wire.

17) Install known good speed control servo/actuator. Test drive vehicle and check for proper speed control operation. If speed control operates properly, replace speed control servo/actuator. If speed control does not operate properly, replace PCM.

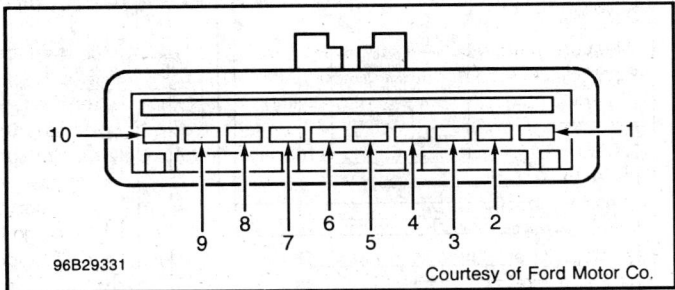

Fig. 1: Identifying Servo/Actuator harness connector C136 Terminals

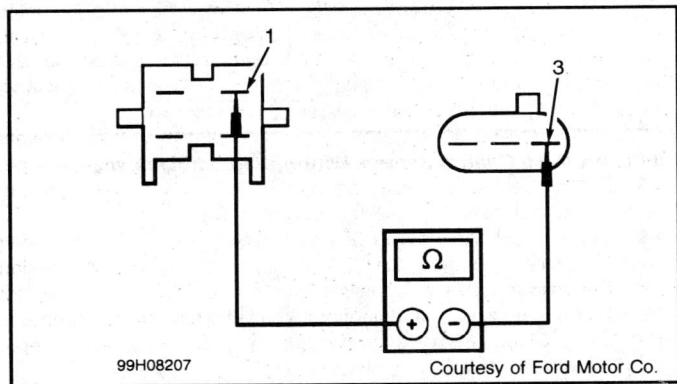

Fig. 2: Testing Air Bag Sliding Contact Resistance

TEST B: SET SPEED FLUCTUATES

1) Ensure engine is properly tuned. Ensure problem does not occur while driving vehicle without speed control activated. If problem occurs only with speed control activated, go to next step. If problem occurs without speed control activated, repair engine performance problem as necessary.

2) Check for binding or sticking speed control servo/actuator cable, throttle linkage and/or throttle plate. Ensure throttle cable bracket and speed control servo/actuator bracket are not loose. If problem does not exist, go to next step. If problem exists, repair as necessary.

3) Install known good speed control servo/actuator. Test drive vehicle and check for proper speed control operation. If speed control operates properly, replace speed control servo/actuator. If speed control does not operate properly, replace Powertrain Control Module (PCM).

TEST C: SPEED CONTROL DOES NOT DISENGAGE WHEN BRAKES ARE APPLIED

NOTE: Ensure brake lights are operating properly before proceeding.

Turn ignition switch to LOCK position. Disconnect speed control servo/actuator harness connector C136. Measure voltage between terminals No. 4 (Light Green wire) and No. 10 (Black wire) at speed control servo/actuator harness connector C136. *See Fig. 1.* When brake pedal is depressed, battery voltage should exist. When brake pedal is not depressed, no voltage should exist. If voltage is as specified, replace speed control servo/actuator. If voltage is not as specified, repair open in Light Green wire between speed control servo/actuator and instrument panel fuse box.

TEST D: SPEED CONTROL DOES NOT DISENGAGE WHEN CLUTCH IS APPLIED

Turn ignition switch to LOCK position. Disconnect clutch pedal position switch harness connector C260. Measure resistance between Measure resistance between clutch pedal position switch terminals (component side). When clutch pedal is depressed, resistance should be greater than 1o k/ohms. When clutch pedal is not depressed, resistance should be 5 ohms or less. If resistance is as specified, replace speed control servo/actuator. If resistance is not as specified, replace clutch pedal position switch.

TEST E: COAST SWITCH INOPERATIVE

Turn ignition switch to LOCK position. Disconnect speed control servo/actuator harness connector C136. Measure resistance between terminals No. 5 (Light Blue/Black wire) and No. 6 (Dark Green/Orange wire) at speed control servo/actuator harness connector C136 while pressing holding COAST button. *See Fig. 1.* If resistance is 108-132 ohms, replace speed control servo/actuator. If resistance is not 108-132 ohms, replace speed control switch.

TEST F: SET/ACCEL SWITCH INOPERATIVE

Turn ignition switch to LOCK position. Disconnect speed control servo/actuator harness connector C136. Measure resistance between termi-

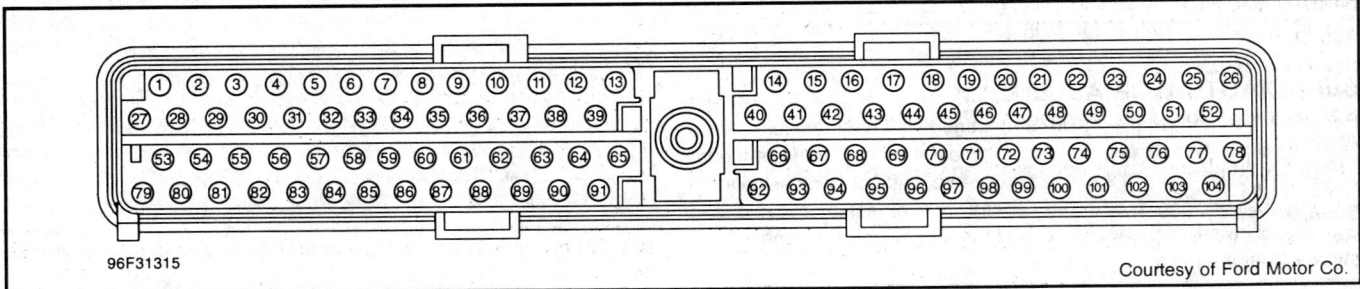

Fig. 3: Identifying PCM Harness Connector C294 Terminals

nals No. 5 (Light Blue/Black wire) and No. 6 (Dark Green/Orange wire) at speed control servo/actuator harness connector C136 while pressing holding SET/ACCEL button. *See Fig. 1.* If resistance is 612-748 ohms, replace speed control servo/actuator. If resistance is not 612-748 ohms, replace speed control switch.

TEST G: RESUME SWITCH INOPERATIVE

Turn ignition switch to LOCK position. Disconnect speed control servo/actuator harness connector C136. Measure resistance between terminals No. 5 (Light Blue/Black wire) and No. 6 (Dark Green/Orange wire) at speed control servo/actuator harness connector C136 while pressing holding RESUME button. *See Fig. 1.* If resistance is 1980-2420 ohms, replace speed control servo/actuator. If resistance is not 1980-2420 ohms, replace speed control switch.

TEST H: OFF SWITCH INOPERATIVE

Turn ignition switch to LOCK position. Disconnect speed control servo/actuator harness connector C136. Measure resistance between terminals No. 5 (Light Blue/Black wire) and No. 6 (Dark Green/Orange wire) at speed control servo/actuator harness connector C136 while pressing holding OFF button. *See Fig. 1.* If resistance is 5 ohms or less, replace speed control servo/actuator. If resistance is greater than 5 ohms, replace speed control switch.

REMOVAL & INSTALLATION

WARNING: Deactivate air bag system before working around steering column. See appropriate AIR BAG RESTRAINT SYSTEMS article.

CAUTION: When battery is disconnected, vehicle computer and memory systems may lose memory data. Driveability problems may exist until computer systems have completed a relearn cycle. See COMPUTER RELEARN PROCEDURES article in GENERAL INFORMATION before disconnecting battery.

SPEED CONTROL SWITCHES

Removal & Installation – Disable air bag system. Remove driver's side air bag module. See appropriate AIR BAG RESTRAINT SYSTEMS article. Remove steering wheel. Remove steering wheel rear cover. Remove ribbon harness from clips. Disconnect horn contacts electrical connectors. Remove right side horn contract. Remove speed control switch retaining screws. Remove speed control switches. To install, reverse removal procedure. Ensure all wiring is positioned so no interference will occur when installing steering wheel.

DEACTIVATOR SWITCH

Removal & Installation – Deactivator switch is located above Brake Pedal Position (BPP) switch, connected to brake pedal arm. Disconnect deactivator switch harness connector. Disconnect deactivator switch push rod from brake pedal arm. Disengage locking tabs securing switch. To install, reverse removal procedure.

SERVO/ACTUATOR ASSEMBLY

Removal & Installation – 1) Disconnect negative battery cable. Raise and support vehicle. Remove left front wheel. Remove left front fender splash shield. Disconnect speed control servo/actuator harness connector. Depress locking tab, rotate speed control actuator cable cap counterclockwise and remove cap. Disconnect actuator cable from servo/actuator assembly.

2) Remove 3 speed control servo/actuator retaining bolts. Remove speed control servo/actuator. To install, reverse removal procedure. Ensure rubber seal is fully seated onto speed control servo/actuator cable cap and throttle lever is at idle position after speed control cable is installed and adjusted. Proper assembly of speed control servo/actuator can be verified by a white band on speed control cable being visible.

WIRING DIAGRAMS

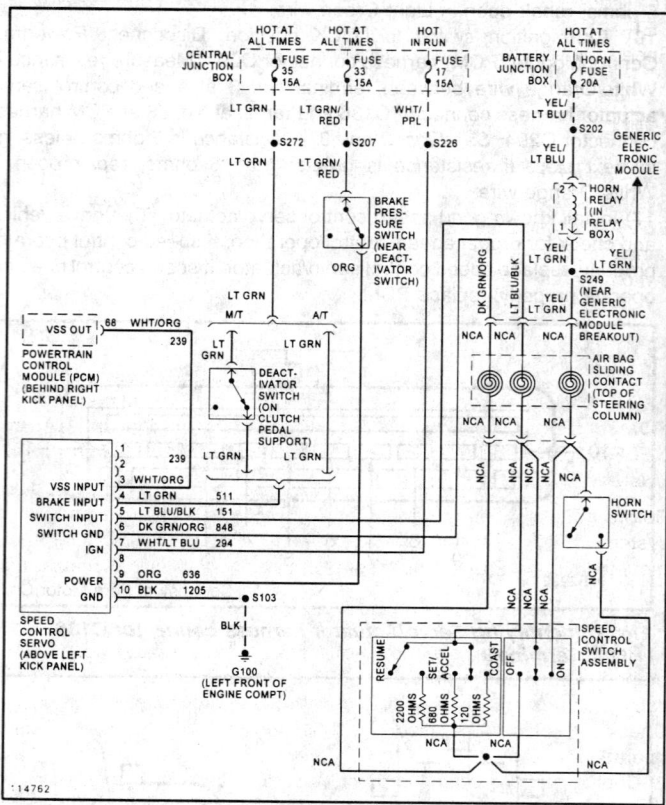

Fig. 4: Cruise Control System Wiring Diagram (Mustang)

DESCRIPTION

The cruise control system consists of control switches (ON, OFF, SET-ACCEL, COAST and RESUME), servo/actuator assembly, Vehicle Speed Sensor (VSS), deactivator switch and wiring.

OPERATION

ENGAGING & DISENGAGING SYSTEM

System is operational at speeds greater than 30 MPH. When ON and SET-ACCEL switches have been pressed, vehicle speed will be maintained until new speed is set, brake or clutch pedal is pressed or OFF switch is pressed.

SYMPTOM TESTS

NOTE: If Malfunction Indicator Light (MIL) is lit or flashes, check PCM for stored Diagnostic Trouble Codes (DTCs). See appropriate SELF-DIAGNOSTICS article in ENGINE PERFORMANCE in appropriate MITCHELL® manual.

Before trouble shooting system, perform complete visual inspection of system. Check all fuses. Check operation of stoplights including high mounted stoplight. Check speedometer operation. Repair as necessary.

CRUISE CONTROL INOPERATIVE

1) Remove splash shield from throttle linkage. Ensure actuator cable is properly connected to throttle body and speed control servo. Pull on cable at throttle linkage side and note accelerator pedal movement. Check for smooth operation of cable. Correct as necessary and test operation.

2) Unplug harness connector from servo located near master cylinder. Turn ignition switch to RUN position. Measure voltage between servo harness connector terminal No. 7 (Light Blue/Pink wire) and terminal No. 10 (Black wire). *See Fig. 1.* If battery voltage is present, go to step **4)**. If battery voltage is not present, check fuse No. 5. Replace fuse if necessary. If fuse is okay, go to next step.

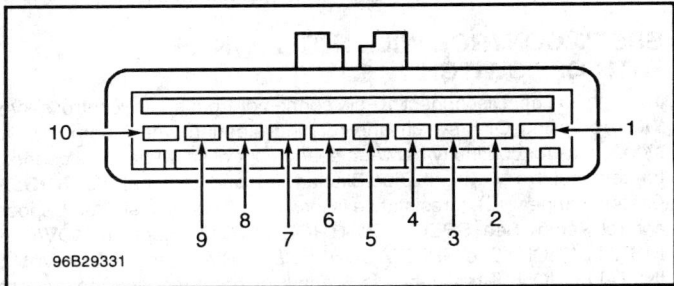

Fig. 1: Identifying Servo/Actuator Harness Connector Terminals

3) Turn ignition off. Measure resistance between harness connector terminal No. 10 (Black wire) and ground. If resistance is less than 5 ohms, repair Light Blue/Pink wire. If resistance is 5 ohms or greater, repair Black wire to ground. See WIRING DIAGRAMS.

4) With brake pedal released and ignition off, measure voltage between servo harness connector terminal No. 4 (Tan/Light Blue) and terminal No. 10 (Black wire). If no voltage is present, go to next step. If voltage is present, install new BPP switch and check system for normal operation.

5) Turn ignition off. Measure resistance between servo harness connector terminal No. 4 (Tan/Light Blue) and terminal No. 10 (Black wire). If resistance is less than 20 ohms, go to next step. If resistance is 20 ohms or greater, go to step **15)**.

6) Measure voltage between servo harness connector terminal No. 9 (Black/Yellow wire) and terminal No. 10 (Black wire). If battery voltage is not present, go to next step. If battery voltage is present, go to step **9)**.

7) Unplug connector from brake pressure switch, located on master cylinder. Measure resistance between switch terminals with brake pedal

released. If resistance is less than 5 ohms, go to next step. If resistance is 5 ohms or greater, replace switch and check system for normal operation.

8) Measure voltage between brake pressure switch harness connector terminal (Light Green/Red wire) and ground. If battery voltage is present, repair open in Black/Yellow wire. If battery voltage is not present, repair open in fuse or Light Green/Red wire between fuse and switch. See WIRING DIAGRAMS. Check system for normal operation.

9) Check for voltage between servo harness connector terminal No. 5 (Light Blue/Black wire) and terminal No. 10 (Black wire). If voltage is present, speed control actuator switch is stuck on. Install new speed control actuator switch and check for normal system operation. See COMMAND SWITCHES under REMOVAL & INSTALLATION. If no voltage is present, go to next step.

10) With speed control ON switch depressed, check for voltage between servo harness connector terminal No. 5 (Light Blue/Black wire) and terminal No. 10 (Black wire). If voltage is present, go to step **13)**. If no voltage is present, go to next step.

11) Disable air bag restraint system. See appropriate AIR BAG RESTRAINT SYSTEMS article. Disconnect air bag sliding contact connector at base of steering column. Measure resistance of Dark Green/Orange wire between servo harness connector terminal No. 6 and air bag sliding contact connector (harness side). If resistance is less than 5 ohms, go to next step. If resistance is 5 ohms or greater, repair open or high resistance in Dark Green/Orange wire. See WIRING DIAGRAMS. Check system for normal operation.

12) With Driver's air bag module removed, measure resistance of air bag sliding contact between column side of connector at base of steering column and sliding contact. Connect one ohmmeter lead to connector terminal corresponding to Light Blue/Black wire in harness side of connector, and other ohmmeter lead to appropriate sliding contact pin. See WIRING DIAGRAMS. If resistance is less than 1 ohm, install new speed control actuator switch and check system for normal operation. See COMMAND SWITCHES under REMOVAL & INSTALLATION. If resistance is one ohm or greater, replace air bag sliding contact and check system operation. See appropriate AIR BAG RESTRAINT SYSTEMS article.

13) While depressing SET/ACCEL button on steering wheel, measure resistance between servo harness connector terminal No. 5 (Light Blue/Black wire) and terminal No. 6 (Dark Green/Orange wire). Resistance should be between 640 ohms and 720 ohms. If resistance is as specified, go to next step. If resistance is not as specified, install new speed control actuator switch and check system for normal operation. See COMMAND SWITCHES under REMOVAL & INSTALLATION.

14) Test drive vehicle and observe speedometer operation. If speedometer operates properly, repair circuit (Gray/Black wire) between servo connector terminal No. 3 and PCM 104-pin connector terminal No. 68. See WIRING DIAGRAMS. If speedometer does not operate properly, see appropriate INSTRUMENT PANELS article.

15) Turn igniton off. Disconnect Brake Pedal Position (BPP) switch. Measure resistance between BPP switch harness connector terminal No. 1 (Black/Pink wire) and ground. If resistance is less than 5 ohms, go to next step. If resistance is 5 ohms or greater, repair Black/Pink wire between BPP switch and ground connection. See WIRING DIAGRAMS. Check system for normal operation.

16) Measure resistance between BPP switch terminals No. 1 and No. 2. *See Fig. 2.* If resistance is less than 5 ohms, go to next step. If resistance is 5 ohms or greater, install new BPP switch and check system for normal operation.

17) Disconnect Clutch Pedal Position (CPP) switch or jumper. Measure resistance of Red/Light Green wire between CPP connector and BPP connector. If resistance is less than 5 ohms, go to next step. If resistance is 5 ohms or greater, repair Red/Light Green wire or connections and check system operation. See WIRING DIAGRAMS.

18) Measure resistance of Tan/Light Blue wire between CPP connector and speed control servo connector terminal No. 4. *See Fig. 1.* If resistance is less than 5 ohms, install new CPP switch or jumper. If resistance is 5 ohms or greater, repair Tan/Light Blue wire or connections and check system operation. See WIRING DIAGRAMS.

FORD
4-436

1999 ACCESSORIES & EQUIPMENT
Cruise Control Systems – F150 & F250 Light-Duty Pickup (Cont.)

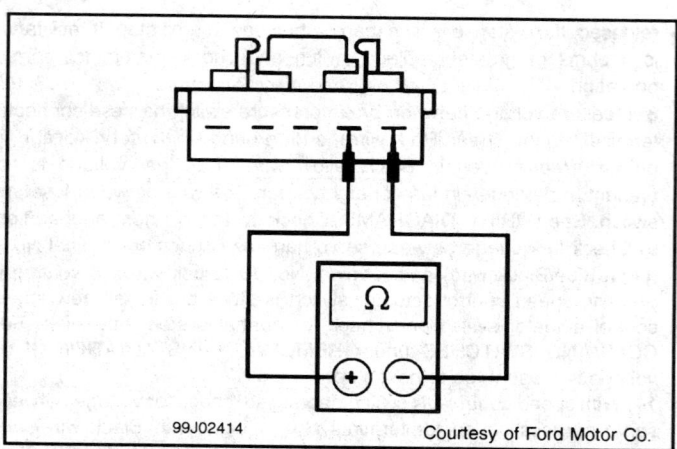

Fig. 2: Testing Brake Pedal Position (BPP) Switch

99J02414   Courtesy of Ford Motor Co.

SET SPEED FLUCTUATES

Turn ignition off. Disengage cable from speed control servo. Inspect actuator cable and throttle linkage for binding. Pull on cable and observe resistance and verify throttle pedal movement. Repair or replace as necessary. If no binding exists, test drive vehicle and observe speedometer operation. If speedometer fluctuates, see appropriate INSTRUMENT PANELS article. If speedometer does not fluctuate, replace speed control servo and check system for normal operation. See SPEED CONTROL SERVO under REMOVAL & INSTALLATION.

SYSTEM DOES NOT TURN OFF WHEN BRAKES ARE APPLIED

1) Disconnect Brake Pedal Position (BPP) switch. Turn ignition switch to RUN position. Measure voltage between BPP switch harness connector terminal No. 3 (White/Yellow wire) and ground. If voltage is greater than 10 volts, go to next step. If voltage is 10 volts or less, repair circuit or fuse. See WIRING DIAGRAMS.

2) Turn ignition off. Measure resistance between BPP switch terminals No. 1 and No. 2. *See Fig. 2.* Resistance should be greater than 10 k/ohms with brake pedal depressed, and less than 5 ohms with brake pedal released. If resistance is as specified, go to next step. If resistance is not as specified, install new BPP switch and check system for normal operation.

3) Measure voltage between speed control servo harness connector terminal No. 9 (Black/Yellow wire) and terminal No. 10 (Black wire). *See Fig. 1.* Voltage should be 0 volts with brake pedal depressed, and greater than 10 volts with brake pedal released. If voltage is not as specified, go to next step. If voltage is as specified, install new speed control servo and check system for normal operation. See SPEED CONTROL SERVO under REMOVAL & INSTALLATION.

4) Disconnect brake pressure switch harness connector. (Switch is located on master cylinder). Connect a 10-amp fused jumper wire between harness connector terminals. Measure voltage between speed control servo harness connector terminal No. 9 (Black/Yellow wire) and terminal No. 10 (Black wire). *See Fig. 1.* If voltage is 10 volts or less, go to next step. If voltage is greater than 10 volts, install new brake pressure switch. See DEACTIVATOR (BRAKE PRESSURE) SWITCH under REMOVAL & INSTALLATION.

5) Measure resistance of Black/Yellow wire between speed control servo harness connector terminal No. 9 and brake pressure switch terminal (Black/Yellow wire). If resistance is less than 5 ohms, repair circuit to switch (Light Green/Red wire) or fuse. If resistance is 5 ohms or greater, repair circuit between switch and speed control servo (Black/Yellow wire). See WIRING DIAGRAMS. Check system for normal operation.

SYSTEM DOES NOT TURN OFF WHEN CLUTCH IS APPLIED

Disconnect speed control servo harness connector. Depress clutch pedal while measuring voltage between speed control servo harness connector terminal No. 4 (Tan/Light Blue wire) and terminal No. 10

(Black wire). If voltage is greater than 10 volts, install new speed control servo and check system for normal operation. See SPEED CONTROL SERVO under REMOVAL & INSTALLATION. If voltage 10 volts or less, replace clutch pedal position switch and check system for normal operation.

COAST FUNCTION INOPERATIVE

Turn ignition off. Disconnect 10-pin connector from speed control servo. While pressing COAST switch and rotating steering wheel from stop to stop, measure resistance between speed control servo harness connector terminal No. 5 (Light Blue/Black wire) and terminal No. 6 (Dark Green/Orange wire). If resistance is 108-132 ohms, install new speed control servo. See SPEED CONTROL SERVO under REMOVAL & INSTALLATION. If resistance is not 108-132 ohms, install new speed control actuator switch. See COMMAND SWITCHES under REMOVAL & INSTALLATION. Check system for normal operation.

ACCEL FUNCTION INOPERATIVE

Turn ignition off. Disconnect 10-pin connector from speed control servo. While pressing SET/ACCEL switch and rotating steering wheel from stop to stop, measure resistance between speed control servo harness connector terminal No. 5 (Light Blue/Black wire) and terminal No. 6 (Dark Green/Orange wire). If resistance is 612-748 ohms, install new speed control servo. See SPEED CONTROL SERVO under REMOVAL & INSTALLATION. If resistance is not 612-748 ohms, install new speed control actuator switch. See COMMAND SWITCHES under REMOVAL & INSTALLATION. Check system for normal operation.

RESUME FUNCTION INOPERATIVE

Turn ignition off. Disconnect 10-pin connector from speed control servo. While pressing RESUME switch and rotating steering wheel from stop to stop, measure resistance between speed control servo harness connector terminal No. 5 (Light Blue/Black wire) and terminal No. 6 (Dark Green/Orange wire). If resistance is 1980-2420 ohms, install new speed control servo. See SPEED CONTROL SERVO under REMOVAL & INSTALLATION. If resistance is not 1980-2420 ohms, install new speed control actuator switch. See COMMAND SWITCHES under REMOVAL & INSTALLATION. Check system for normal operation.

SPEED CONTROL WILL NOT TURN OFF WITH OFF SWITCH

Turn ignition off. Disconnect 10-pin connector from speed control servo. While pressing OFF switch and rotating steering wheel from stop to stop, check for continuity between speed control servo harness connector terminal No. 5 (Light Blue/Black wire) and terminal No. 6 (Dark Green/Orange wire). If resistance is less than 5 ohms, install new speed control servo. See SPEED CONTROL SERVO under REMOVAL & INSTALLATION. See SPEED CONTROL SERVO under REMOVAL & INSTALLATION. If resistance is 5 ohms or greater, install new speed control actuator switch. See COMMAND SWITCHES under REMOVAL & INSTALLATION. Check system for normal operation.

REMOVAL & INSTALLATION

WARNING: Disable air bag system before working around steering column or removing any air bag system component. See appropriate AIR BAG RESTRAINT SYSTEMS article.

CAUTION: When battery is disconnected, vehicle computer and memory systems may lose memory data. Driveability problems may exist until computer systems have completed a relearn cycle. See COMPUTER RELEARN PROCEDURES article in GENERAL INFORMATION before disconnecting battery.

SPEED CONTROL SERVO

Removal – Push in locking arm on speed control actuator cable cap. Rotate speed control actuator cable cap counterclockwise and separate from speed control servo. *See Fig. 3.* Depress spring retainer and slide cable end out of speed control servo pulley. Disconnect electrical connector. Remove mounting bolts and remove speed control servo assembly from vehicle. Remove bracket screws and remove bracket from speed control servo.

Installation – To install, reverse removal procedure. Ensure rubber grommets in speed control servo bracket are properly seated. Torque bracket screws to 90-115 INCH lbs. (10-13 N.m). Torque mounting bolts to 67-92 INCH lbs. (7.6-10.4 N.m).

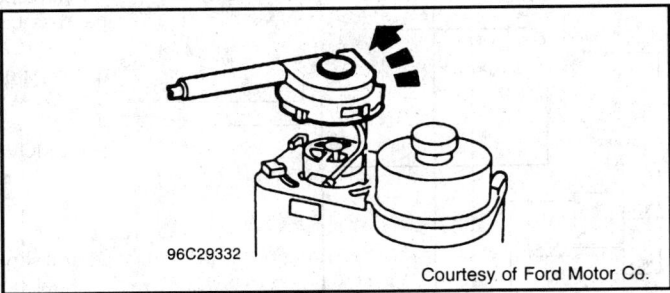

96C29332

Courtesy of Ford Motor Co.

Fig. 3: Removing Cable From Servo

COMMAND SWITCHES

WARNING: Observe all air bag service precautions. Disable air bag system. See SERVICE PRECAUTIONS and DISABLING & ACTIVATING AIR BAG SYSTEM in appropriate AIR BAG RESTRAINT SYSTEMS article.

Removal – 1) Disable air bag system. See DISABLING & ACTIVATING AIR BAG SYSTEM in appropriate AIR BAG RESTRAINT SYSTEMS article. Remove air bag nuts and washers from steering wheel. Unplug air bag connector from clockspring (contact assembly). Remove air bag module.

WARNING: Place air bag module on bench with trim cover facing upward.

2) Release 4 retaining clips from switches. Disconnect switch harness connectors. Remove switch assembly from steering wheel.

Installation – Install switches in steering wheel. Connect air bag module wiring connector to clockspring (contact assembly). Position air bag module onto steering wheel. Install air bag module nuts and washers. Activate air bag system. Observe AIR BAG warning light to verify system is functioning properly. See SYSTEM OPERATION CHECK in appropriate AIR BAG RESTRAINT SYSTEMS article.

DEACTIVATOR (BRAKE PRESSURE) SWITCH

Removal & Installation – Deactivator switch is located on master cylinder. Disconnect negative battery cable. Unplug harness connector. Unscrew switch. To install, reverse removal procedure. Tighten switch to 11-15 ft. lbs. (15-20 N.m). Bleed brake system. See appropriate DISC & DRUM article in BRAKES in appropriate MITCHELL® manual. Wash any brake fluid from painted or plastic surfaces.

FORD
4-438

1999 ACCESSORIES & EQUIPMENT
Cruise Control Systems – F150 & F250 Light-Duty Pickup (Cont.)

WIRING DIAGRAMS

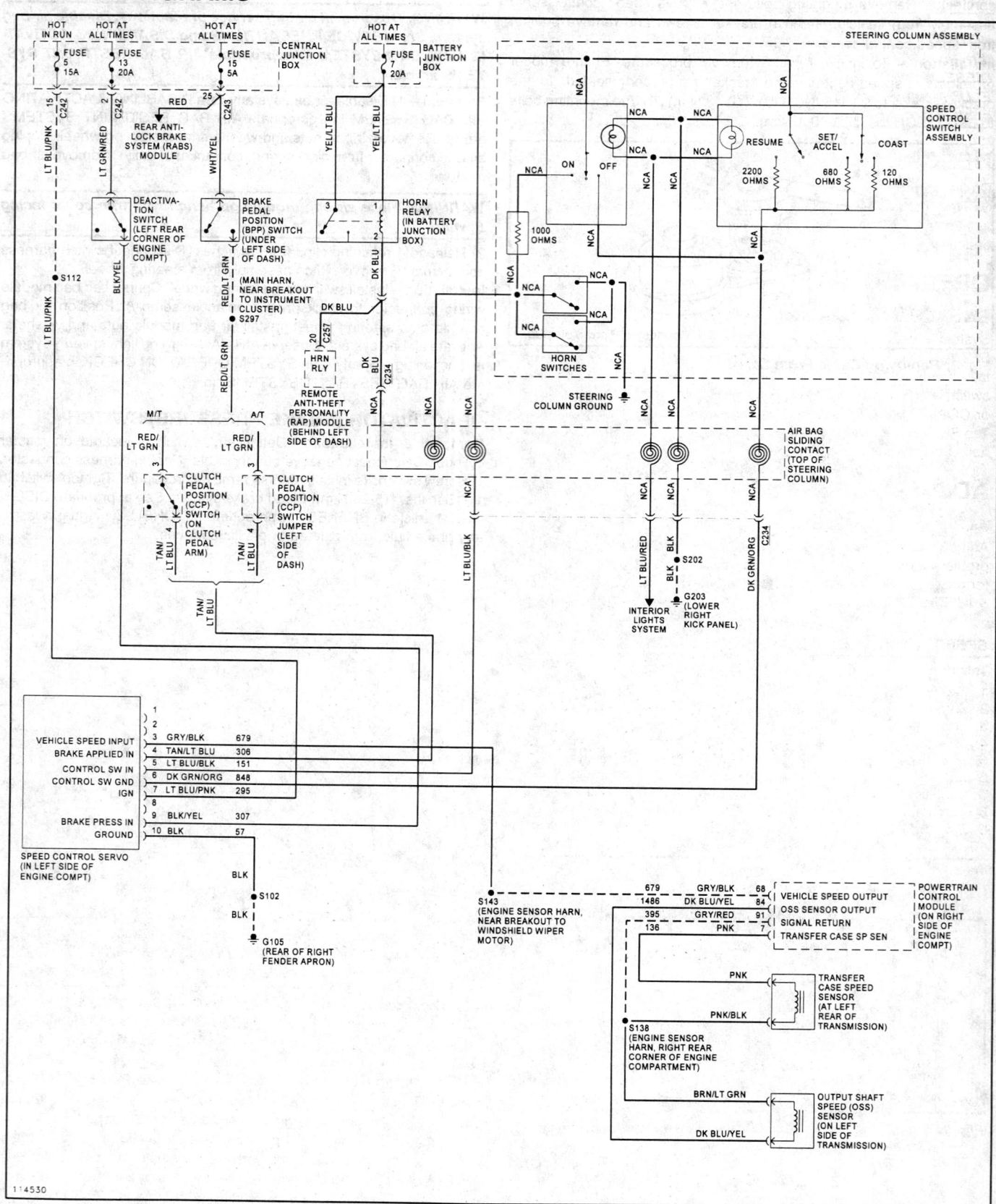

Fig. 4: Cruise Control System Wiring Diagram (F150 & F250 Light-Duty Pickup)

NOTE: This article includes Cab & Chassis.

NOTE: On 7.3L diesel, all speed control functions are controlled by the Powertrain Control Module (PCM). See SELF-DIAGNOSTICS – DIESEL article in ENGINE PERFORMANCE in appropriate MITCHELL® manual for diagnostic procedures. For diesel engine cruise control system wiring diagrams, see WIRING DIAGRAMS.

DESCRIPTION

Cruise control system consists of speed control switches (ON, OFF, SET/ACCEL, COAST and RESUME), speed control servo/actuator assembly, brake pedal position switch, clutch pedal position switch, deactivator switch (brake pressure switch) and related wiring.

OPERATION

ENGAGING & DISENGAGING SYSTEM

System is operational at speeds greater than 30 MPH. When ON and SET/ACCEL switches have been pressed, vehicle speed will be maintained until new speed is set, brake or clutch pedal is depressed, or OFF switch is pressed. To increase or decrease set speed, hold SET/ACCEL or COAST switch until desired speed is reached, then release switch. Tap SET/ACCEL or COAST switch for one MPH incremental increase or decrease in speed.

ADJUSTMENTS

ACTUATOR CABLE

Adjustment procedure not available from manufacturer. If there is a problem with high idle due to not enough length in actuator cable, check for proper cable installation. See ACTUATOR CABLE under REMOVAL & INSTALLATION.

TROUBLE SHOOTING

Perform complete visual inspection of system. Repair as necessary. Ensure speedometer and horn are operating properly. If there are any problems with speedometer or horn, repair those first. See ANALOG INSTRUMENT PANELS – F250 SUPER-DUTY & F350 PICKUP article and/or STEERING COLUMN SWITCHES – F250 SUPER-DUTY & F350 PICKUP article. If Malfunction Indicator Light (MIL) is lit or flashes, check Powertrain Control Module (PCM) for stored Diagnostic Trouble Codes (DTCs). See appropriate SELF-DIAGNOSTICS article in ENGINE PERFORMANCE in appropriate MITCHELL® manual for diagnostic procedures.

SYSTEM TESTS

WARNING: Deactivate air bag system before performing any service operation involving steering column components. See appropriate AIR BAG RESTRAINT SYSTEMS article. Do not apply electrical power to any component on steering column without first deactivating air bag system. Air bag may deploy.

CAUTION: When battery is disconnected, vehicle computer and memory systems may lose memory data. Driveability problems may exist until computer systems have completed a relearn cycle. See COMPUTER RELEARN PROCEDURES article in GENERAL INFORMATION before disconnecting battery.

SPEED CONTROL SERVO/ACTUATOR ASSEMBLY CONNECTOR TERMINAL IDENTIFICATION

The following test procedures reference various terminals on speed control servo/actuator assembly connector. For terminal number, circuit description and wire color, see SPEED CONTROL SERVO/ACTUATOR ASSEMBLY CONNECTOR TERMINAL IDENTIFICATION table. *See Fig. 1.*

SPEED CONTROL SERVO/ACTUATOR ASSEMBLY CONNECTOR TERMINAL IDENTIFICATION

Terminal	Circuit Description	Wire Color
1	Not Used	Not Used
2	Not Used	Not Used
3	Vehicle Speed Input	GRY/BLK
4	Brake/Clutch Position Switch Input	TAN/LT BLU
5	Speed Control Switch Input	LT BLU/BLK
6	Speed Control Switch Return	DK GRN/ORG
7	Vehicle Power	LT BLU/PNK
8	Not Used	Not Used
9	Brake Pressure Input	BLK/YEL
10	Ground	BLK

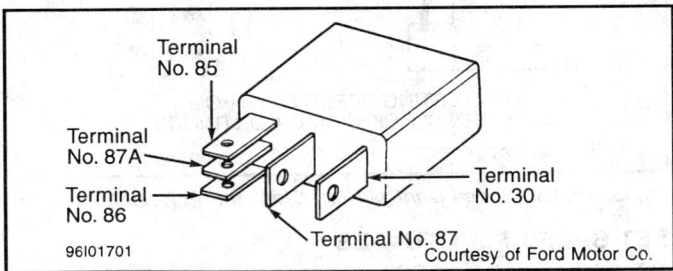

Fig. 1: Identifying Speed Control Servo/Actuator Assembly Connector Terminals

Terminal No. 85
Terminal No. 87A
Terminal No. 86
Terminal No. 87
Terminal No. 30
96I01701
Courtesy of Ford Motor Co.

SPEED CONTROL INOPERATIVE

NOTE: Ensure horn operates properly before performing this test. Repair as necessary. See WIRING DIAGRAMS in STEERING COLUMN SWITCHES – F250 SUPER-DUTY & F350 PICKUP article.

1) Turn ignition switch to LOCK position. Remove accelerator control splash shield. Inspect speed control actuator cable attachment. Pull on actuator cable and note throttle movement. If actuator cable is okay, go to next step. If cable is not okay, reattach or replace actuator cable. See ACTUATOR CABLE under REMOVAL & INSTALLATION.

2) Disconnect speed control servo/actuator assembly 10-pin connector located at right side of engine compartment near starter motor relay. Turn ignition switch to RUN position. Measure voltage between speed control servo/actuator assembly connector terminals No. 7 (Light Blue/Pink wire) and No. 10 (Black wire). *See Fig. 1.* If battery voltage does not exist, go to next step. If battery voltage exists, go to step **5)**.

FORD
4-440

1999 ACCESSORIES & EQUIPMENT
Cruise Control Systems – F250 Super-Duty & F350 Pickup (Cont.)

3) Turn ignition switch to LOCK position. Check fuse junction panel fuse No. 28 (10-amp). If fuse is okay, go to next step. If fuse is blown, replace fuse. Test system. If fuse blows again, repair short to ground in Light Blue/Pink wire.

4) Measure resistance between speed control servo/actuator assembly connector terminal No. 10 (Black wire) and ground. *See Fig. 1.* If resistance is less than 5 ohms, repair open in Light Blue/Pink wire. If resistance is 5 ohms or more, repair open in Black wire.

5) Turn ignition switch to LOCK position. Measure voltage between speed control servo/actuator assembly connector terminals No. 4 (Tan/Light Blue wire) and No. 10 (Black wire). *See Fig. 1.* If battery voltage exists, replace brake pedal position switch. If battery voltage does not exist, go to next step.

6) Measure resistance between speed control servo/actuator assembly connector terminals No. 4 (Tan/Light Blue wire) and No. 10 (Black wire). If resistance is less than 5 ohms, go to next step. If resistance is 5 ohms or more, go to step 16).

7) Measure voltage between speed control servo/actuator assembly connector terminals No. 9 (Black/Yellow wire) and No. 10 (Black wire). If battery voltage exists, go to step 10). If battery voltage does not exist, go to next step.

8) Disconnect deactivator switch (brake pressure switch) 2-pin connector located at brake master cylinder. Measure resistance between switch terminals. If resistance is less than 5 ohms, go to next step. If resistance is 5 ohms or more, replace switch.

9) Measure voltage between deactivator switch connector Light Green/Red wire terminal and ground. If battery voltage exists, repair open in Black/Yellow wire. If battery voltage does not exist, repair open in Light Green/Red wire. See WIRING DIAGRAMS.

10) Measure voltage between speed control servo/actuator assembly connector terminals No. 5 (Light Blue/Black wire) and No. 10 (Black wire). *See Fig. 1.* If battery voltage exists, go to step 17). If battery voltage does not exist, go to next step.

11) Measure voltage between speed control servo/actuator assembly harness connector terminals No. 5 (Light Blue/Black wire) and No. 10 (Black wire) while pressing speed control actuator ON switch. If battery voltage exists, go to step 14). If battery voltage does not exist, go to next step.

12) Disconnect speed control/horn switch assembly 6-pin connector in steering wheel. Measure resistance in Light Blue/Black wire between speed control servo/actuator assembly connector terminal No. 5 and speed control/horn switch assembly connector terminal No. 1. *See Figs. 1 and 2.* If resistance is less than 5 ohms, go to next step. If resistance is 5 ohms or more, repair open in Light Blue/Black wire.

13) Remove driver's air bag. See appropriate AIR BAG RESTRAINT article. Disconnect speed control switches connector. Measure resistance between speed control/horn clockspring connector terminal No. 1 and top of speed control/horn clockspring terminal No. 5. *See Fig. 3.* If resistance is less than one ohm, replace speed control actuator switch. See SPEED CONTROL SWITCHES under REMOVAL & INSTALLATION. If resistance is one ohm or more, replace speed control/horn clockspring. See CLOCKSPRING under REMOVAL & INSTALLATION.

14) With SET/ACCEL switch pressed, measure resistance between speed control servo/actuator assembly connector terminals No. 5 (Light Blue/Black wire) and No. 6 (Dark Green/Orange wire). *See Fig. 1.* If resistance is 612-748 ohms, go to next step. If resistance is not 612-748 ohms, replace speed control actuator switch. See SPEED CONTROL SWITCHES under REMOVAL & INSTALLATION.

15) Drive vehicle and observe speedometer. If speedometer operates properly, repair open in Gray/Black wire. See WIRING DIAGRAMS. If speedometer does not operate properly, repair speedometer as necessary. See appropriate ANALOG INSTRUMENT PANELS article for diagnostic procedures.

16) Disconnect Brake Pedal Position (BPP) switch 5-pin connector. Measure resistance between BPP switch connector Pink/Orange wire terminal and ground. If resistance is less than 5 ohms, go to step 19). If resistance is 5 ohms or more, repair open in Pink/Orange wire.

17) Turn ignition switch to LOCK position. Disconnect speed control/horn switch assembly 6-pin connector. Turn ignition switch to RUN position. Measure voltage between speed control servo/actuator assembly connector terminals No. 5 (Light Blue/Black wire) and No. 10 (Black wire). *See Fig. 1.* If battery voltage exists, go to next step. If battery voltage does not exist, replace speed control actuator switches. See SPEED CONTROL SWITCHES under REMOVAL & INSTALLATION.

18) Turn ignition switch to LOCK position. Disconnect speed control/horn switch assembly 6-pin connector. Turn ignition switch to RUN position. Measure voltage between speed control servo/actuator assembly connector terminals No. 5 (Light Blue/Black wire) and No. 10 (Black wire). If voltage exists, repair short to power in Light Blue/Black wire. If no voltage exists, replace clockspring. See CLOCKSPRING under REMOVAL & INSTALLATION.

19) Turn ignition switch to RUN position. Measure voltage between BPP switch connector Light Blue/Black wire terminal and ground. If battery voltage exists, go to next step. If battery voltage does not exist, repair open in Light Blue/Black wire.

20) Disconnect Clutch Pedal Position (CPP) switch (M/T) or jumper (A/T) 6-pin connector. Measure resistance of Red/Light Green wire between BPP switch connector and CPP switch (jumper on A/T) connector. If resistance is less than 5 ohms, go to next step. If resistance is 5 ohms or more, repair open in Red/Light Green wire.

21) Measure resistance of Tan/Light Blue wire between CPP switch (jumper on A/T) connector and speed control servo/actuator assembly connector terminal No. 4. If resistance is less than 5 ohms, go to next step. If resistance is 5 ohms or more, repair open in Tan/Light Blue wire.

22) Measure resistance between CPP switch (jumper on A/T) terminals No. 3 and 4 (center terminals). If resistance is less than 5 ohms, replace BPP switch. If resistance is 5 ohms or more, replace CPP switch or jumper.

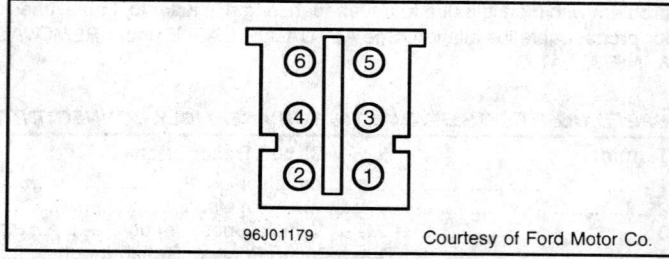

96J01179   Courtesy of Ford Motor Co.

Fig. 2: Identifying Speed Control/Horn Switch Assembly Connector Terminals (Female Side Shown)

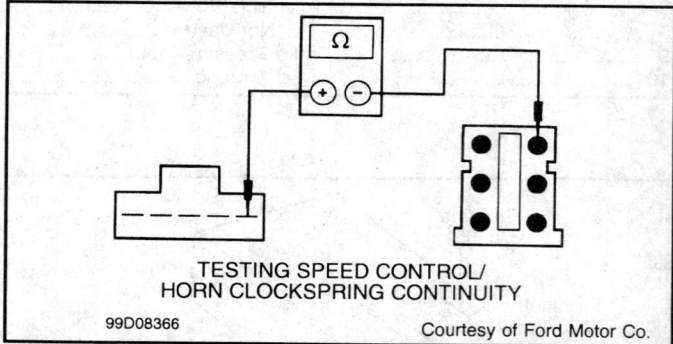

TESTING SPEED CONTROL/
HORN CLOCKSPRING CONTINUITY

99D08366   Courtesy of Ford Motor Co.

Fig. 3: Testing Speed Control/Horn Clockspring Resistance

SET SPEED FLUCTUATES

1) Turn ignition switch to LOCK position. Remove speed control actuator cable from speed control servo/actuator assembly. Inspect core wire and check actuator cable by pulling on cable and noting throttle movement. If actuator cable is okay, go to next step. If actuator cable is faulty, replace actuator cable and/or repair throttle body linkage as necessary.

2) Drive vehicle and observe speedometer operation. If speedometer fluctuates, repair speedometer as necessary. See appropriate ANALOG INSTRUMENT CLUSTER article for further diagnosis. If speedometer is

1999 ACCESSORIES & EQUIPMENT
Cruise Control Systems – F250 Super-Duty & F350 Pickup (Cont.)

FORD
4-441

steady, replace speed control servo/actuator assembly. See SPEED CONTROL SERVO/ACTUATOR ASSEMBLY under REMOVAL & INSTALLATION.

CRUISE DOES NOT TURN OFF WHEN BRAKES ARE APPLIED

1) Disconnect speed control servo/actuator assembly 10-pin connector, located at right side of engine compartment near starter motor relay. Measure voltage between speed control servo/actuator assembly connector terminals No. 4 (Tan/Light Blue wire) and No. 10 (Black wire) while pressing and releasing brake pedal. *See Fig. 1.* Battery voltage should exist when brake pedal is pressed and no voltage should exist when brake pedal is released. If voltage is as specified, go to step **7)**. If voltage is not as specified, go to next step.

2) Check fuse junction panel fuse No. 15 (5-amp). If fuse is okay, go to next step. If fuse is blown, replace fuse. Test system. If fuse blows again, repair short to ground. See WIRING DIAGRAMS.

3) Turn ignition switch to LOCK position. Disconnect Brake Pedal Position (BPP) switch 5-pin connector. Turn ignition switch to RUN position. Measure voltage between BPP switch connector Light Blue/Black wire terminal and ground. If battery voltage exists, go to next step. If battery voltage does not exist, repair open in Light Blue/Black wire.

4) Disconnect Clutch Pedal Position (CPP) switch (M/T) or jumper (A/T) 6-pin connector. Measure resistance of Red/Light Green wire between BPP switch connector and CPP switch (jumper on A/T) connector. If resistance is less than 5 ohms, go to next step. If resistance is 5 ohms or more, repair open in Red/Light Green wire.

5) Measure resistance of Tan/Light Blue wire between CPP switch (jumper A/T) connector and speed control servo/actuator assembly connector terminal No. 4. If resistance is less than 5 ohms, go to next step. If resistance is 5 ohms or more, repair open in Tan/Light Blue wire.

6) Measure resistance between CPP switch (jumper A/T) terminal No. 3 and 4 (center terminals). If resistance is less than 5 ohms, replace BPP switch. If resistance is 5 ohms or more, replace CPP switch or jumper.

7) Measure voltage between speed control servo/actuator assembly connector terminal No. 9 (Black/Yellow wire) and ground while firmly pressing and releasing brake pedal. *See Fig. 1.* No voltage should exist with brake pedal firmly pressed and battery voltage should exist with brake released. If voltage is as specified, replace speed control servo/actuator assembly. See SPEED CONTROL SERVO/ACTUATOR ASSEMBLY under REMOVAL & INSTALLATION. If voltage is not as specified, go to next step.

8) Disconnect deactivator switch (brake pressure switch) 2-pin connector located at front of master cylinder. Connect jumper wire between deactivator switch connector terminals. Measure voltage between speed control servo/actuator assembly connector terminals No. 9 (Black/Yellow wire) and No. 10 (Black wire). *See Fig. 1.* If battery voltage exists, replace deactivator switch. If battery voltage does not exist, go to next step.

9) Measure resistance of Black/Yellow wire between deactivator switch connector and speed control servo/actuator assembly connector terminal No. 9. If resistance is less than 5 ohms, repair open in Light Green/Red wire. If resistance is 5 ohms or more, repair open in Black/Yellow wire.

CRUISE DOES NOT TURN OFF WHEN CLUTCH PEDAL IS APPLIED

1) Turn ignition switch to LOCK position. Disconnect speed control servo/actuator assembly 10-pin connector, located at right side of engine compartment near starter motor relay. Measure resistance between speed control servo/actuator assembly connector terminals No. 4 (Tan/Light Blue wire) and No. 10 (Black wire). *See Fig. 1.* If resistance is less than 5 ohms, go to next step. If resistance is 5 ohms or more, go to SPEED CONTROL INOPERATIVE.

2) Measure resistance between speed control servo/actuator assembly connector terminals No. 4 (Tan/Light Blue wire) and No. 10 (Black wire) while depressing clutch pedal. If resistance is more than 10 k/ohms, replace speed control servo/actuator assembly. See SPEED CONTROL

SERVO/ACTUATOR ASSEMBLY under REMOVAL & INSTALLATION. If resistance is 10 k/ohms or less, replace CPP switch.

COAST FUNCTION INOPERATIVE

Turn ignition switch to LOCK position. Disconnect speed control servo/actuator assembly 10-pin connector, located at right side of engine compartment near starter motor relay. Measure resistance between speed control servo/actuator assembly connector terminals No. 5 (Light Blue/Black wire) and No. 6 (Dark Green/Orange wire) while rotating steering wheel from stop to stop with COAST switch depressed. *See Fig. 1.* If resistance is 108-132 ohms, replace speed control servo/actuator assembly. See SPEED CONTROL SERVO/ACTUATOR ASSEMBLY under REMOVAL & INSTALLATION. If resistance is not 108-132 ohms, replace speed control switches. See SPEED CONTROL SWITCHES under REMOVAL & INSTALLATION.

SET/ACCEL FUNCTION INOPERATIVE

Turn ignition switch to LOCK position. Disconnect speed control servo/actuator assembly 10-pin connector, located at right side of engine compartment near starter motor relay. Measure resistance between speed control servo/actuator assembly connector terminals No. 5 (Light Blue/Black wire) and No. 6 (Dark Green/Orange wire) while rotating steering wheel from stop to stop with SET/ACCEL switch depressed. *See Fig. 1.* If resistance is 612-748 ohms, replace speed control servo/actuator assembly. See SPEED CONTROL SERVO/ACTUATOR ASSEMBLY under REMOVAL & INSTALLATION. If resistance is not 612-748 ohms, replace speed control switches. See SPEED CONTROL SWITCHES under REMOVAL & INSTALLATION.

RESUME FUNCTION INOPERATIVE

Turn ignition switch to LOCK position. Disconnect speed control servo/actuator assembly 10-pin connector, located at right side of engine compartment near starter motor relay. Measure resistance between speed control servo/actuator assembly connector terminals No. 5 (Light Blue/Black wire) and No. 6 (Dark Green/Orange wire) while rotating steering wheel from stop to stop with RESUME switch depressed. *See Fig. 1.* If resistance is 1980-2420 ohms, replace speed control servo/actuator assembly. See SPEED CONTROL SERVO/ACTUATOR ASSEMBLY under REMOVAL & INSTALLATION. If resistance is not 1980-2420 ohms, replace speed control switches. See SPEED CONTROL SWITCHES under REMOVAL & INSTALLATION.

SPEED CONTROL WILL NOT TURN OFF WITH OFF SWITCH

Turn ignition switch to LOCK position. Disconnect speed control servo/actuator assembly 10-pin connector, located at right side of engine compartment near starter motor relay. Measure resistance between speed control servo/actuator assembly connector terminals No. 5 (Light Blue/Black wire) and No. 6 (Dark Green/Orange wire) while rotating steering wheel from stop to stop with OFF switch depressed. *See Fig. 1.* If resistance is less than 5 ohms, replace speed control servo/actuator assembly. See SPEED CONTROL SERVO/ACTUATOR ASSEMBLY under REMOVAL & INSTALLATION. If resistance is 5 ohms or more, replace speed control switches. See SPEED CONTROL SWITCHES under REMOVAL & INSTALLATION.

FORD
4-442

1999 ACCESSORIES & EQUIPMENT
Cruise Control Systems – F250 Super-Duty & F350 Pickup (Cont.)

REMOVAL & INSTALLATION

WARNING: Disable air bag system before working around steering column or removing any air bag system component. See appropriate AIR BAG RESTRAINT SYSTEMS article.

CAUTION: When battery is disconnected, vehicle computer and memory systems may lose memory data. Driveability problems may exist until computer systems have completed a relearn cycle. See COMPUTER RELEARN PROCEDURES article in GENERAL INFORMATION before disconnecting battery.

ACTUATOR CABLE

Removal – Remove air cleaner outlet tube. Remove accelerator control splash shield. Disconnect actuator cable from throttle body cam and bracket. Push in locking arm on actuator cable cap and rotate cap counterclockwise to remove. Disconnect actuator cable core wire end from servo pulley.

NOTE: Incorrect wrapping of actuator cable around servo pulley may result in high idle condition.

Installation – Gently compress servo spring and insert cable slug into servo pulley slot. Make sure rubber seal is fully seated onto actuator cable cap. Release compressed spring while aligning actuator cable cap tabs with slots in servo housing. Rotate actuator cable cap until locking arm engages. Connect actuator cable to throttle body cam. Position cable in bracket. Install accelerator control splash shield. Install air cleaner outlet tube.

CLOCKSPRING

Removal & Installation – 1) Remove steering wheel. See STEERING WHEEL. Apply 2 strips of masking tape across air bag sliding contact to prevent clockspring rotation.
2) Twist and remove tilt wheel handle and shank. Remove lower steering column shroud. Turn ignition switch to RUN position. Using a punch, push upward on lock cylinder release tab while pulling out lock cylinder.
3) Remove upper steering column shroud. Remove key-in-ignition warning indicator switch. Turn instrument panel steering column cover retaining clips counterclockwise to release. Remove instrument panel steering column cover.
4) Disconnect clockspring electrical connectors. Remove 3 retaining clips and remove clockspring. To install, reverse removal procedure. Remove anti-rotation tab on new clockspring.

DEACTIVATOR (BRAKE PRESSURE) SWITCH

Removal & Installation – Deactivator switch is located on master cylinder. Disconnect electrical connector. Unscrew switch. To install, reverse removal procedure. Bleed brake system. See appropriate DISC & DRUM article in BRAKES in appropriate MITCHELL® manual.

SPEED CONTROL SERVO/ACTUATOR ASSEMBLY

Removal & Installation. – Remove actuator cable. See ACTUATOR CABLE. Disconnect electrical connector. Remove servo and bracket. To install, reverse removal procedure. Tighten bolts/screws to 72-89 INCH lbs. (8-10 N.m).

SPEED CONTROL SWITCHES

WARNING: Observe all air bag service precautions. Disable air bag system. See SERVICE PRECAUTIONS and DISABLING & ACTIVATING AIR BAG SYSTEMS in appropriate AIR BAG RESTRAINT SYSTEMS article.

Removal & Installation – 1) Disconnect battery ground cable. Disconnect auxiliary power sources, if any. Wait one minute for air bag diagnostic monitor module energy reserves to deplete.
2) Remove 2 back cover plugs and bolts holding driver's air bag module. Remove driver's air bag module. Release 4 speed control switch clips and remove speed control switches. Disconnect electrical connector. To install, reverse removal procedure.

STEERING WHEEL

Removal & Installation – 1) Disconnect battery ground cable. Disconnect auxiliary power sources, if any. Wait one minute for air bag diagnostic monitor module energy reserves to deplete. Make sure wheels are straight ahead.
2) Remove 2 back cover plugs and bolts holding driver's air bag module. Remove driver's air bag module. Remove and discard steering wheel retaining bolt.
3) Use 2-jaw puller to remove steering wheel. Remove steering wheel while routing wires from air bag sliding contact through steering wheel. To install, reverse removal procedure. Use new steering wheel bolt. Tighten to 23-32 ft. lbs. (31-44 N.m).

FORD
4-443

1999 ACCESSORIES & EQUIPMENT
Cruise Control Systems – F250 Super-Duty & F350 Pickup (Cont.)

WIRING DIAGRAMS

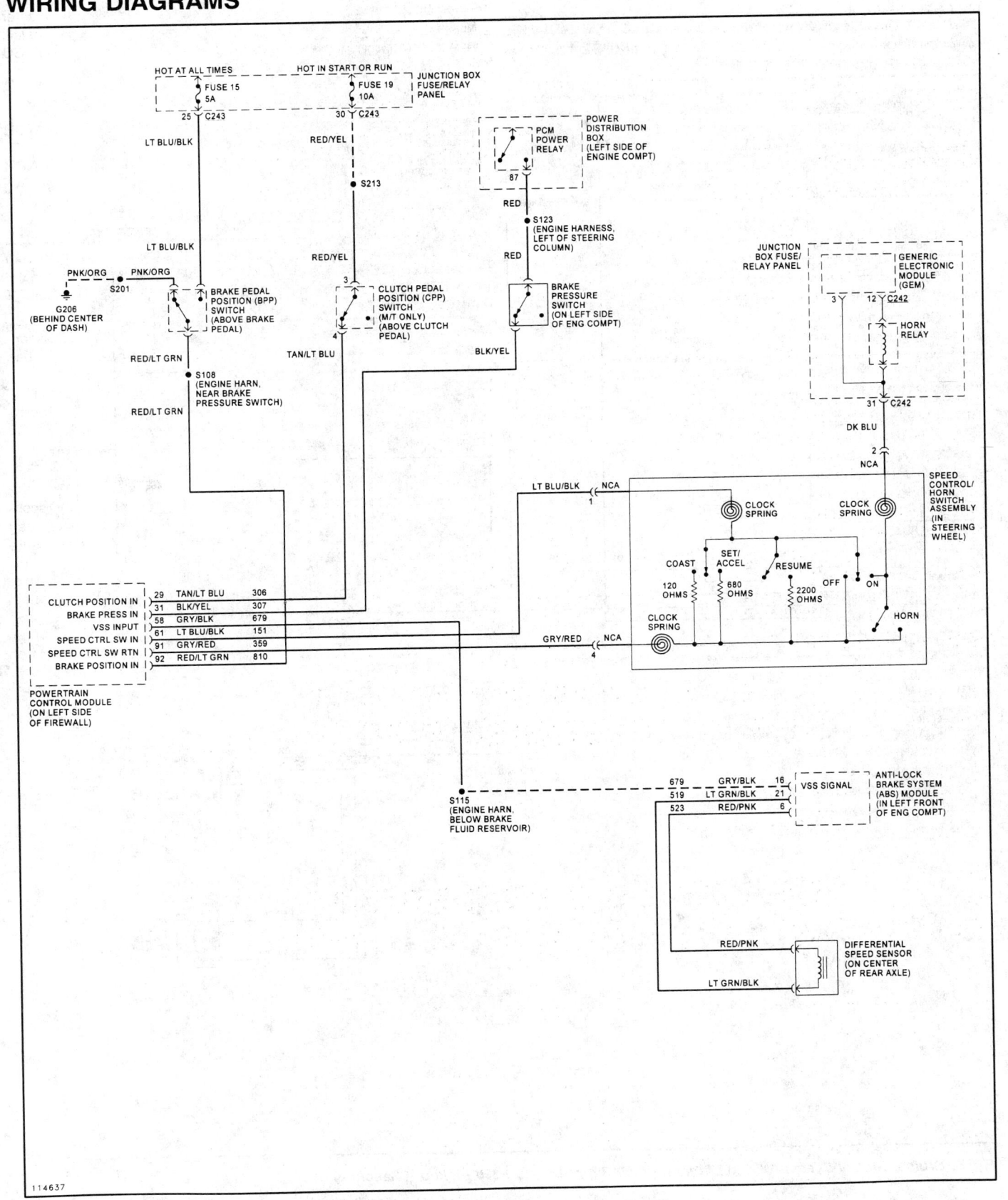

Fig. 4: Cruise Control System Wiring Diagram (F250 Super-Duty & F350 Pickup – Diesel)

114637

FORD
4-444

1999 ACCESSORIES & EQUIPMENT
Cruise Control Systems – F250 Super-Duty & F350 Pickup (Cont.)

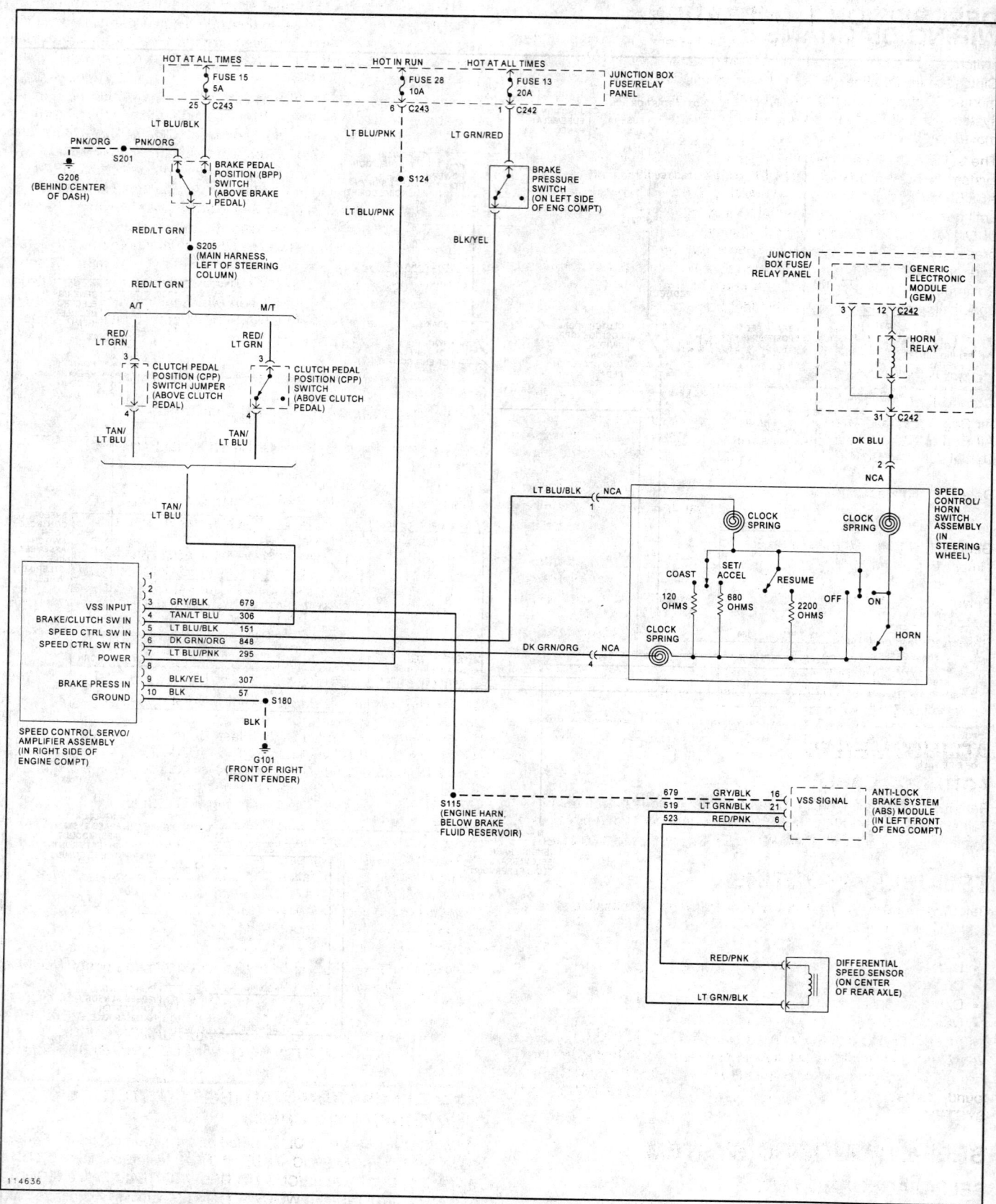

Fig. 5: Cruise Control System Wiring Diagram (F250 Super-Duty & F350 Pickup – Gasoline)

DESCRIPTION & OPERATION

Major components of the cruise control system are speed control switches, servo/actuator, horn relay, Brake Pedal Position (BPP) switch, Clutch Pedal Position (CPP) switch, deactivator switch, ABS control module, Generic Electronic Module (GEM), and related wiring. This system does not require engine vacuum. An electronic servo/actuator moves the throttle.

The system is operational only at speeds greater than 30 MPH. The system is activated when ON/OFF switch is switched on and SET/ACCEL button is pressed and released. Vehicle will maintain set speed until new speed is set, brake pedal is pressed, clutch pedal is pressed, or ON/OFF switch is switched off. If system has been deactivated by pressing brake or clutch pedal, set speed can be regained by pressing and releasing RESUME button. When brake or clutch pedal is pressed, a signal from switch is sent to the servo to deactivate the system. A deactivator switch acts as a redundant brake signal.

COMPONENT LOCATIONS

COMPONENT LOCATIONS

Component	Location
Air Bag Diagnostic Monitor [1]	Behind Right Kick Panel
Air Bag Sliding Contact	Base Of Steering Column
Cental Junction Box	Behind Left Side Of instrument Panel
Data Link Connector (DLC)	Below Driver's Side Of Instrument Panel, To Right Of Steering Column
Generic Electronic Module/Central Timer Module (GEM/CTM)	Behind Center Of Instrument Panel
Powertrain Control Module (PCM)	Mounted Through Firewall, On Passenger's Side
Speed Control Servo	Right Rear Of Engine Compartment
Speed Control Switches	In Steering Wheel

[1] – Air bag diagnostic monitor may also be known as Electronic Crash Sensor (ECS) module.

ADJUSTMENTS

ACTUATOR CABLE

Remove cable retaining clip. Ensure throttle plate is in closed position. Pull actuator cable to take up slack. Back off at least one notch. While holding cable, insert cable retaining clip. Check throttle operation.

TROUBLE SHOOTING

Before performing any testing, check following for possible cause of system malfunction.
- Faulty fuses.
- Loose or corroded connections.
- Damaged wiring harness.
- Damaged switches.
- Damaged or binding servo/actuator cable.
- Incorrect servo/actuator cable adjustment.

Verify horn and stoplights function properly. Inspect actuator and throttle linkage for smooth operation. Repair as necessary. If no problems are found, perform SELF-DIAGNOSTIC TEST under SELF-DIAGNOSTIC SYSTEM.

SELF-DIAGNOSTIC SYSTEM

SELF-DIAGNOSTIC TEST

1) Place gear selector in Park. Ensure parking brake is engaged and brake pedal is released. While depressing speed control OFF button, turn ignition switch to RUN position. Speed control indicator on instrument cluster should flash once to indicate successful entry into self-diagnostic mode. If speed control indicator does not flash, repeat

step 1). If speed control indicator still does not flash, see appropriate INSTRUMENT PANELS article to continue diagnosis. If speed control indicator flashes 5 times when diagnostics is entered, replace speed control servo. See SPEED CONTROL SERVO/ACTUATOR under REMOVAL & INSTALLATION.

2) Release speed control OFF button. Within 5 seconds of entering self-diagnostics, press speed control ON button. Press remaining speed control buttons in the following sequence; ON, RES, COAST and SET/ACCEL. As each button is pressed, speed control indicator will flash. Wait until indicator light goes out before pressing next button.

3) After sequence has been completed, indicator light will flash to indicate test passed or failed. See FLASH CODE table. Perform appropriate procedure or test as specified under SYSTEM TESTS.

4) Immediately after static test has passed, actuator performs a dynamic test by automatically operating throttle .04-.40" (1-10 mm). Observe throttle movement to witness any sticking of cable or linkage. Ensure throttle returns properly. Turn ignition off. If self-diagnostics does not pinpoint fault, see SYMPTOM table. Perform appropriate test as specified under SYSTEM TESTS.

FLASH CODE

Flash Code	Test
1 (With Correct Throttle Actuation At End Of Test) [1]	System Passed
2 (Brake Pedal Position (BPP) Or Clutch Pedal Position (CPP) Switch Circuit)	D
3 (Deactivator Switch Circuit)	E
4 (Vehicle Speed Sensor (VSS) Circuit)	[2]

[1] – See SYMPTOM table for Flash Code 1 and incorrect throttle actuation at end of test.

[2] – If vehicle is equipped with 4-wheel ABS, proceed to TEST F: FLASH CODE 4 – VEHICLE SPEED SENSOR (VSS) CIRCUIT FAILURE. If vehicle is equipped with rear ABS only, perform NEW GENERATION STAR (NGS) TESTER COMMUNICATION CHECK.

SYMPTOM

Symptom	Test
No Communication With Module – GEM/CTM	A
Unable To Enter Self-Test	B [1]
No Throttle Pull At Throttle Body (Flash Code 1)	C
No Throttle Pull At Servo/Actuator (Flash Code 1)	C [2]
Speed Control Inoperative (Flash Code 1)	
Speed Control Inoperative – No Flash Codes	G
Speed Control Does Not Disengage When Clutch Is Applied	H
Coast Switch Is Inoperative	I
SET/ACCEL Switch Is Inoperative	J
Resume Switch Is Inoperative	K
OFF Switch Is Inoperative	L
Speed Control Indicator Always On	M [3]
Speed Control Indicator Inoperative	
Set Speed Fluctuates	N

[1] – Replace speed control servo/actuator cable and perform self-test diagnostics using NGS tester.

[2] – If vehicle is equipped with 4-wheel ABS, perform SYSTEM TEST D. If vehicle is equipped with rear ABS only, perform NEW GENERATION STAR (NGS) TESTER COMMUNICATION CHECK.

[3] – Go to ANALOG INSTRUMENT PANELS – RANGER article for diagnosis.

NEW GENERATION STAR (NGS) TESTER COMMUNICATION CHECK

1) Connect NGS tester to DLC located below instrument panel. Perform DATA LINK DIAGNOSTIC TEST. If NGS tester displays CKT914, CKT915 or CKT70=ALL ECUS NO RESP/NOT EQUIP, see MODULE COMMUNICATIONS NETWORK – RANGER article to continue diagnosis. If NGS tester displays NO RESP/NOT EQUIP for GEM/CTM, go to TEST A: NO COMMUNICATION MODULE – GEM/CTM under SYSTEM TESTS.

2) If NGS tester displays SYSTEM PASSED, retrieve and record continuous DTCs. Erase continuous DTCs and perform self-test diagnostics for GEM/CTM. If GEM/CTM DTCs are retrieved, see GENERIC ELECTRONIC MODULE/CENTRAL TIMER MODULE (GEM/CTM) DTC DEFINITIONS table to continue diagnosis. If GEM/CTM DTCs are retrieved, that are not listed in table, go to MODULE COMMUNICATIONS NETWORK – RANGER article. If no DTCs are retrieved, diagnose by symptom. See SYMPTOM table.

GENERIC ELECTRONIC MODULE/CENTRAL TIMER MODULE (GEM/CTM) DTC DEFINITIONS

DTC	Description
B1342	[1] GEM/CTM Is Defective
B2141	[2] NVM Configuration Failure
C1751	[3] VSS Output Short To Battery
C1752	[3] VSS Output Short To Ground

[1] – Using NGS tester, clear DTCs. Retrieve DTCs. If DTC B1342 is retrieved, replace GEM/CTM and retest system operation.

[2] – Vehicle speed calibration data is not programmed into GEM/CTM. Use NGS tester configuration card help screen to program tire size and axle ratio. Retest system operation. If DTC B2141 is still present, replace GEM/CTM and retest system operation.

[3] – Go to TEST F: FLASH CODE 4 – VEHICLE SPEED SIGNAL CIRCUIT FAILURE.

SYSTEM TESTS

CAUTION: When battery is disconnected or modules are replaced, vehicle computer and memory systems may lose memory data. Driveability problems may exist until computer systems have completed a relearn cycle. See COMPUTER RELEARN PROCEDURES article in GENERAL INFORMATION before disconnecting battery.

TEST A: NO COMMUNICATION WITH MODULE – GEM/CTM

1) Using a voltmeter, check voltage between ground and central junction box fuse No. 25 (7.5-amp) input terminal (right terminal). If voltage is more than 10 volts, go to next step. If voltage is 10 volts or less, repair power supply circuit. See appropriate wiring diagram in POWER DISTRIBUTION article in WIRING DIAGRAMS. Clear DTCs and retest system operation.

2) Turn ignition off. Disconnect GEM/CTM 18-pin connector C224 (located behind center of instrument cluster). Using a voltmeter, check voltage between ground and GEM/CTM connector C224 terminal No. 11 (White/Yellow wire). *See Fig. 1.* If voltage is more than 10 volts, go to next step. If voltage is 10 volts or less, repair White/Yellow wire between central junction box and GEM/CTM. Retest system operation.

3) Disconnect GEM/CTM 26-pin connector C221 (located behind center of instrument cluster). Using an ohmmeter, check resistance between ground and GEM/CTM connector C221 terminal No. 14 (Black/White wire). *See Fig. 1.* Check resistance between ground and GEM/CTM connector C221 terminal No. 26. If either resistance is less than 5 ohms, replace GEM/CTM. Clear DTCs and retest system operation. If resistance(s) are 5 ohms or more, repair open in appropriate Black/White wire between GEM/CTM and ground. Clear DTCs and retest system operation.

TEST B: UNABLE TO ENTER SELF-TEST

If NGS tester communicates with GEM/CTM, replace GEM/CTM and retest system. If NGS tester does not communicate with GEM/CTM, go to TEST A: NO COMMUNICATION WITH MODULE – GEM/CTM.

TEST C: FLASH CODE 1 – NO DYNAMIC PULL AT SPEED CONTROL SERVO/ACTUATOR

NOTE: After repair procedure has been completed, reconnect all components and preform SELF-DIAGNOSTIC TEST under SELF-DIAGNOSTIC SYSTEM.

Turn ignition off. Disconnect speed control servo/actuator cable from servo/actuator. Check speed control servo/actuator cable for sticking or

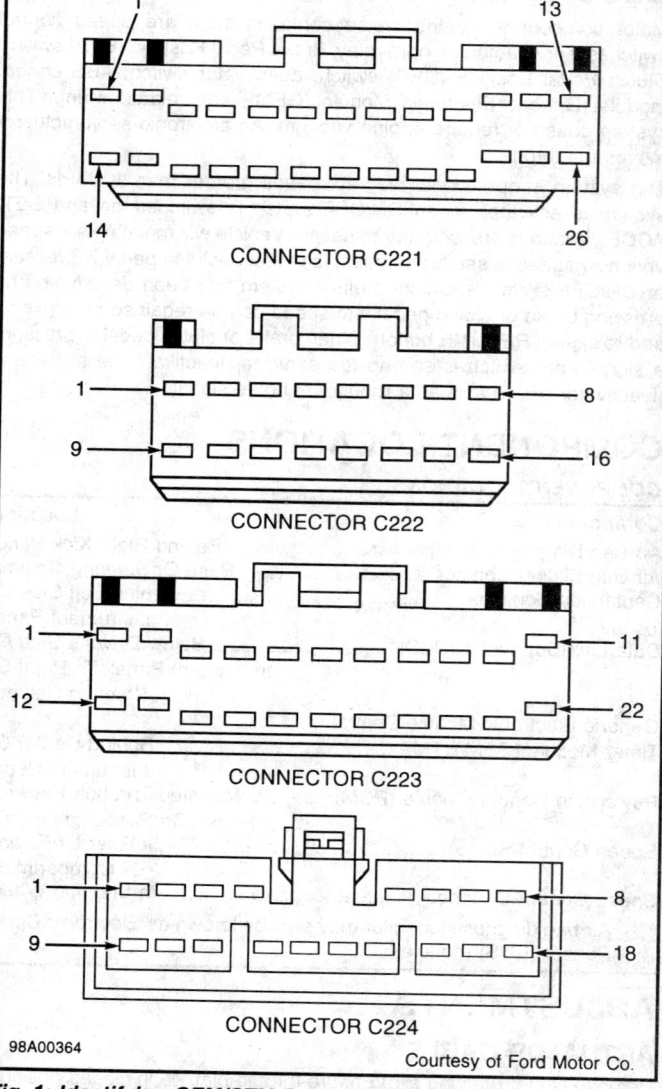

CONNECTOR C221

CONNECTOR C222

CONNECTOR C223

CONNECTOR C224

98A00364   Courtesy of Ford Motor Co.

Fig. 1: Identifying GEM/CTM Connector Terminals

binding. If speed control servo/actuator cable is okay, replace speed control servo/actuator. If speed control servo/actuator cable is not okay, replace speed control servo/actuator cable and perform self-test diagnostics using NGS tester.

TEST D: FLASH CODE 2 – BRAKE PEDAL POSITION (BPP) SWITCH CIRCUIT FAILURE

NOTE: After repair procedure has been completed, reconnect all components and preform SELF-DIAGNOSTIC TEST under SELF-DIAGNOSTIC SYSTEM.

1) Turn ignition off. Disconnect speed control servo/actuator connector C165 (located in right rear of engine compartment). Turn ignition on. Using a voltmeter, check voltage between speed control servo/actuator connector C165 terminal No. 4 (Tan/Light Blue wire) and terminal No. 10 (Pink/Orange wire). *See Fig. 2.* If voltage is present, go to step **6)**. If no voltage is present, go to next step.

2) Ensure ignition is off. Disconnect Clutch Pedal Position (CPP) switch connector C206 (located under left side of instrument panel, near clutch pedal arm). Using an ohmmeter, check resistance between CPP switch terminals No. 3 and 4. *See Fig. 3.* If resistance is less than 5 ohms, go to next step. If resistance is 5 ohms or more, replace CPP switch.

3) Using an ohmmeter, check resistance in Tan/Light Blue wire between speed control servo/actuator connector C165 terminal No. 4 and CPP switch connector C206 terminal No. 3. *See Fig. 2.* If resistance is less than 5 ohms, go to next step. If resistance is 5 ohms or more, repair open in Tan/Light Blue wire.

4) Disconnect Brake Pedal Position (BPP) switch connector C210 (located under left side of instrument panel, near brake pedal support). Using an ohmmeter, check resistance in Red/Light Green wire between CPP switch connector C206 terminal No. 4 and BPP switch connector C210 terminal No. 2. If resistance is less than 5 ohms, go to next step. If resistance is 5 ohms or more, repair open in Red/Light Green wire.

5) Using an ohmmeter, check resistance between ground and BPP switch connector C210 terminal No. 1 (Black wire). If resistance is less than 5 ohms, replace BPP switch. If resistance is 5 ohms or more, repair open in Black wire between BPP switch and ground.

6) Disconnect Brake Pedal Position (BPP) switch connector C210 (located under left side of instrument panel, near brake pedal support). Using a voltmeter, check voltage between speed control servo/actuator connector C165 terminal No. 4 (Tan/Light Blue wire) and terminal No. 10 (Pink/Orange wire). *See Fig. 2.* If voltage is present, go to next step. If no voltage is present, replace BPP switch.

7) Disconnect Clutch Pedal Position (CPP) switch connector C206 (located under left side of instrument panel, near clutch pedal arm). Using a voltmeter, check voltage between speed control servo/actuator connector C165 terminal No. 4 (Tan/Light Blue wire) and terminal No. 10 (Pink/Orange wire). *See Fig. 2.* If voltage is present, repair Tan/Light Blue wire. If no voltage is present, repair Red/Light Green wire.

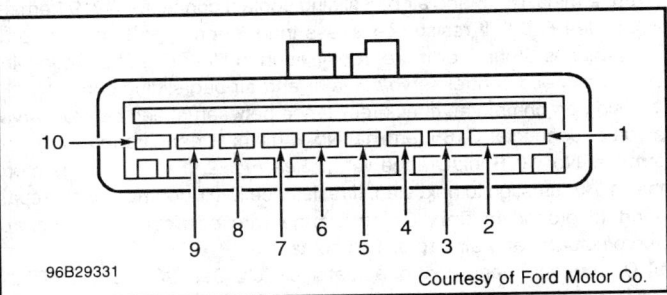

Fig. 2: Identifying Servo/Actuator Connector C165 Terminals

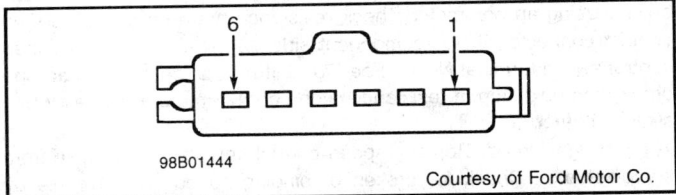

Fig. 3: Identifying CPP Switch Terminals

TEST E: FLASH CODE 3 – DEACTIVATOR SWITCH CIRCUIT FAILURE

NOTE: After repair procedure has been completed, reconnect all components and preform SELF-DIAGNOSTIC TEST under SELF-DIAGNOSTIC SYSTEM. Deactivator switch may also be referred to as brake pressure switch.

1) Press brake pedal and check stoplight operation. If stoplights operate properly, go to next step. If stoplights do not operate properly, see appropriate wiring diagram in EXTERIOR LIGHTS article to continue diagnosis.

2) Turn ignition off. Disconnect speed control servo/actuator connector C165 (located in right rear of engine compartment). Turn ignition switch to RUN position. Using a voltmeter, check voltage between speed control servo/actuator connector C165 terminal No. 9 (Black/Yellow wire) and terminal No. 10 (Pink/Orange wire). *See Fig. 2.* If voltage is 10 volts or less, go to next step. If voltage is more than 10 volts, replace speed control servo/actuator.

3) Turn ignition off. Disconnect deactivator switch connector C138 (located on brake master cylinder). Turn ignition switch to RUN position. Using a voltmeter, check voltage between ground and deactivator switch

connector C138 Red/Light Green wire. If voltage is 10 volts or less, repair open Red/Light Green wire. If voltage is more than 10 volts, go to next step.

4) Using an ohmmeter, check resistance in Black/Yellow wire between speed control servo/actuator connector C165 terminal No. 9 and deactivator switch connector C138 terminal. If resistance is less than 5 ohms, replace deactivator switch. If resistance is 5 ohms or more, repair open Black/Yellow wire between speed control servo/actuator and deactivator switch.

TEST F: FLASH CODE 4 – VEHICLE SPEED SENSOR (VSS) CIRCUIT FAILURE

NOTE: After repair procedure has been completed, reconnect all components and preform SELF-DIAGNOSTIC TEST under SELF-DIAGNOSTIC SYSTEM. Deactivator switch may also be referred to as brake pressure switch.

1) Check to see if vehicle is equipped with rear wheel ABS or 4-wheel ABS. If vehicle is equipped with rear wheel ABS, go to next step. If vehicle is equipped with 4-wheel ABS, go to step 11).

2) Using NGS tester, monitor GEM/CTM PID IGN_GEM while rotating ignition switch through all positions. If vehicle is equipped with manual transmission, press clutch pedal when ignition switch is in START position. If PID values agree with ignition switch positions, go to next step. If PID values do not agree with ignition switch positions, check ignition switch. See STEERING COLUMN SWITCHES – RANGER article. If ignition switch is okay, check ignition switch circuits. See appropriate wiring diagram in POWER DISTRIBUITION article in WIRING DIAGRAM.

3) Using NGS tester, retrieve continuous DTCs. Clear continuous DTCs and perform self-test for GEM/CTM. If DTC P0500 or no DTCs are retrieved, go to next step. If DTC C1752 is retrieved, go to step 8). If DTC C1751 is retrieved, go to step 10).

4) Disconnect GEM/CTM 18-pin connector C224 (located behind center of instrument cluster). Disconnect ABS control module 14-pin connector C238 (located behind lower center of instrument panel). Disconnect rear ABS sensor connector C1010 (located on inside of left front frame rail). Using an ohmmeter, check resistance between ground and GEM/CTM connector C224 terminal No. 9 (Black/Yellow wire). *See Fig. 1.* Check resistance between ground and GEM/CTM connector C224 terminal No. 18 (Light Green/Black wire). If resistances are more than 10 k/ohms, go to next step. If either resistance is 10 k/ohms or less, repair short to ground in appropriate circuit(s).

5) Using an ohmmeter, check resistance in Red/Pink wire between GEM/CTM connector C224 terminal No. 9 and rear ABS sensor connector C1010 terminal. Check resistance in Light Green/Black wire between GEM/CTM connector C224 terminal No. 18 and rear ABS sensor connector C1010 terminal. *See Fig. 1.* If either resistance is less than 5 ohms, go to next step. If resistances are 5 ohms or more, repair open in appropriate circuit(s).

6) Using a voltmeter, check voltage between ground and GEM/CTM connector C224 terminal No. 9 (Black/Yellow wire). Check voltage between ground and GEM/CTM connector C224 terminal No. 18 (Light Green/Black wire). If no voltage is present, go to next step. If voltage is present, repair short to voltage in appropriate circuit(s).

7) Using NGS tester, monitor GEM/CTM PID VSS_GEM while driving vehicle between 0-55 MPH. If GEM/CTM PID VSS_GEM value and speedometer indicate more than zero MPH, go to next step. If GEM/CTM PID VSS_GEM value and speedometer do not indicate more than zero MPH, repair or replace rear ABS sensor. See appropriate ANTI-LOCK article in BRAKES in appropriate MITCHELL® manual.

8) Disconnect instrument cluster 12-pin connector C215 (located behind instrument cluster). Disconnect PCM 104-pin connector C111 (located near center of safety wall). Disconnect speed control servo/actuator connector C165 (located in right rear of engine compartment). Disconnect GEM/CTM 18-pin connector C224 (located behind center of instrument cluster). Using an ohmmeter, check resistance between ground and GEM/CTM connector C224 terminal No. 1 (Gray/Black

wire). *See Fig. 1*. If resistance is more than 10 k/ohms, go to next step. If resistance is 10 k/ohms or less, repair short to ground in Gray/Black wire.

9) Using an ohmmeter, check resistance in Gray/Black wire between GEM/CTM connector C224 terminal No. 1 and speed control servo/actuator connector C165 terminal No. 3. *See Figs. 2 and 1*. If resistance is less than 5 ohms, go to next step. If resistance is 5 ohms or more, repair open in Gray/Black wire.

10) Disconnect speed control servo/actuator connector C165 (located in right rear of engine compartment). Disconnect GEM/CTM 18-pin connector C224 (located behind center of instrument cluster). Disconnect PCM 104-pin connector C111 (located near center of safety wall). Using a voltmeter, check voltage between ground and GEM/CTM connector C224 terminal No. 1 (Gray/Black wire). If voltage is present, repair short to power in Gray/Black wire. If no voltage is present, replace speed control servo/actuator.

11) Test drive vehicle while observing speedometer operation. If speedometer operates properly, go to next step. If speedometer does not operate properly, see ANALOG INSTRUMENT PANELS – RANGER article to continue diagnosis.

12) Turn ignition off. Disconnect ABS control module connector C154 (located near left front fenderwell). Using an ohmmeter, check resistance in Gray/Black wire between speed control servo/actuator connector C165 terminal No. 3 and ABS control module connector C154 terminal No. 10. *See Figs. 2 and 4*. If resistance is less than 5 ohms, replace speed control servo/actuator. If resistance is 5 ohms or more, repair open in Gray/Black wire.

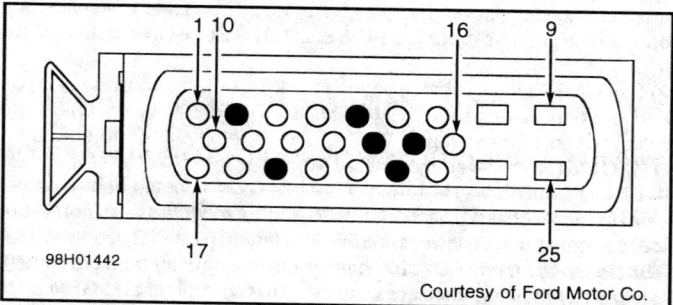

98H01442

Courtesy of Ford Motor Co.

Fig. 4: Identifying ABS Control Module Connector C154 Terminals

TEST G: SPEED CONTROL INOPERATIVE – NO FLASH CODES

NOTE: After repair procedure has been completed, reconnect all components and preform SELF-DIAGNOSTIC TEST under SELF-DIAGNOSTIC SYSTEM. Deactivator switch may also be referred to as brake pressure switch.

1) Disconnect speed control servo/actuator connector C165 (located in right rear of engine compartment). Turn ignition switch to RUN position. Using a voltmeter, check voltage between speed control servo/actuator connector C165 terminal No. 7 (Gray/Yellow wire) and terminal No. 10 (Pink/Orange wire). *See Fig. 2*. If voltage is more than 10 volts, go to next step. If voltage is 10 volts or less, repair Gray/Yellow or Pink/Orange wire(s).

2) Using a voltmeter, check voltage between speed control servo/actuator connector C165 terminal No. 5 (Light Blue/Black wire) and terminal No. 10 (Pink/Orange wire). *See Fig. 2*. If voltage is 10 volts or less, go to next step. If voltage is more than 10 volts, go to step **11**).

3) Using a voltmeter, check voltage between speed control servo/actuator connector C165 terminal No. 5 (Light Blue/Black wire) and terminal No. 10 (Pink/Orange wire) while pressing speed control ON switch. *See Fig. 2*. If voltage is more than 10 volts, go to step **6**). If voltage is 10 volts or less, go to next step.

4) Turn ignition off. Disconnect air bag sliding contact connector C219 (located at base of steering column). Using an ohmmeter, check resistance in Light Blue/Black wire between speed control servo/

actuator connector C165 terminal No. 5 and air bag sliding contact connector C219 (female side). *See Fig. 2*. If resistance is less than 5 ohms, go to next step. If resistance is 5 ohms or more, repair open in Light Blue/Black wire between speed control servo/actuator and air bag sliding contact.

5) Disconnect speed control actuator switch. See SPEED CONTROL SWITCHES under REMOVAL & INSTALLATION. Disable and remove driver side air bag. See appropriate AIR BAG RESTRAINT SYSTEMS – RANGER article. Using an ohmmeter, check resistance between air bag sliding contact connector C219 (component side) terminal No. 1 and speed control switch terminal No. 2. *See Fig. 5*. If resistance is less than one ohm, replace speed control switch. If resistance is one ohm or more, replace air bag sliding contact.

6) Using an ohmmeter, check resistance between speed control servo/actuator connector C165 terminal No. 5 (Light Blue/Black wire) and terminal No. 6 (Dark Green/Orange wire) while first pressing speed control OFF switch and then SET/ACCEL switch. *See Fig. 2*. If resistance is less than 5 ohms with speed control OFF switch pressed and 612-748 ohms with speed control SET/ACCEL switch pressed, go to step **10**). If resistance is 5 ohms or more with speed control OFF switch pressed and not 612-748 ohms with speed control SET/ACCEL switch pressed, go to next step.

7) Ensure ignition is off. Using an ohmmeter, check resistance in Dark Green/Orange wire between speed control servo/actuator connector C165 terminal No. 6 and air bag sliding contact connector C219 (female side). *See Fig. 2*. If resistance is less than 5 ohms, go to next step. If resistance is 5 ohms or more, repair open in Dark Green/Orange wire between speed control servo/actuator and air bag sliding contact.

8) Using an ohmmeter, check resistance between speed control servo/actuator connector C165 terminal No. 6 (Dark Green/Orange wire) and terminal No. 10 (Pink/Orange wire). *See Fig. 2*. If resistance is more than 10 k/ohms, go to next step. If resistance is 10 k/ohms or less, repair short to ground in Dark Green/Orange wire between speed control servo/actuator and air bag sliding contact.

9) Disconnect speed control actuator switch. See SPEED CONTROL SWITCHES under REMOVAL & INSTALLATION. Disable and remove driver side air bag. See AIR BAG RESTRAINT SYSTEMS – RANGER article. Using an ohmmeter, check resistance between air bag sliding contact connector C219 (component side) terminal No. 4 and speed control switch terminal No. 3. *See Fig. 5*. If resistance is less than one ohm, go to next step. If resistance is one ohm or more, replace air bag sliding contact.

10) Turn ignition off. Remove speed control servo/actuator cable from servo/actuator. Check for broken or binding speed control cable by pulling cable ball slug to ensure throttle moves freely. If speed control cable is okay, replace speed control servo/actuator. Repair or replace speed control cable as necessary.

11) Disconnect speed control ON/OFF switch connector. See SPEED CONTROL SWITCHES under REMOVAL & INSTALLATION. Turn ignition switch to RUN position. Using a voltmeter, check voltage between speed control servo/actuator connector C165 terminal No. 5 (Light Blue/Black wire) and terminal No. 10 (Pink/Orange wire). If voltage is present, go to next step. If no voltage is present, replace speed control ON/OFF switch.

12) Disconnect air bag sliding contact connector C219 (located at base of steering column). Turn ignition switch to RUN position. Using a voltmeter, check voltage between speed control servo/actuator connector C165 terminal No. 5 (Light Blue/Black wire) and terminal No. 10 (Pink/Orange wire). *See Fig. 2*. If voltage is present, repair short to voltage in appropriate circuit. If no voltage is present, replace air bag sliding contact.

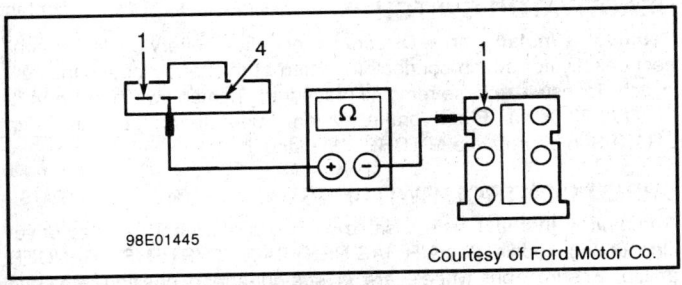

98E01445

Courtesy of Ford Motor Co.

Fig. 5: Checking Air Bag Sliding Contact

TEST H: SPEED CONTROL DOES NOT DISENGAGE WHEN CLUTCH IS APPLIED

NOTE: After repair procedure has been completed, reconnect all components and preform SELF-DIAGNOSTIC TEST under SELF-DIAGNOSTIC SYSTEM. Deactivator switch may also be referred to as brake pressure switch.

1) Turn ignition off. Disconnect Clutch Pedal Position (CPP) switch connector C206 (located on clutch pedal support). Using an ohmmeter, check resistance between CPP switch terminals No. 3 and 4 (component side) while pressing clutch pedal. *See Fig. 3.* If resistance is more than 10 k/ohms, go to next step. If measured resistance is 10 k/ohms or less, replace CPP switch and perform self-test diagnostics using NGS tester.

2) Ensure ignition is off. Disconnect speed control servo/actuator connector C165 (located in right rear of engine compartment). Using an ohmmeter, check resistance between ground and speed control servo/actuator connector C165 terminal No. 4 (Tan/Light Blue wire). *See Fig. 2.* If resistance is more than 10 k/ohms, replace speed control servo/actuator and perform self-test diagnostics using NGS tester. If resistance is 10 k/ohms or less, repair short to ground in Tan/Light Blue wire between speed control servo/actuator and CPP switch. Perform self-test diagnostics using NGS tester.

TEST I: COAST SWITCH IS INOPERATIVE

NOTE: After repair procedure has been completed, reconnect all components and preform SELF-DIAGNOSTIC TEST under SELF-DIAGNOSTIC SYSTEM. Deactivator switch may also be referred to as brake pressure switch.

Turn ignition off. Disconnect speed control servo/actuator connector C165 (located in right rear of engine compartment). Using an ohmmeter, check resistance between speed control servo/actuator connector C165 terminal No. 5 (Light Blue/Black wire) and terminal No. 6 (Dark Green/Orange wire) while pressing speed control COAST switch. *See Fig. 2.* If resistance is 108-132 ohms, replace speed control servo/actuator. If resistance is not 108-132 ohms, replace speed control COAST switch.

TEST J: SET/ACCEL SWITCH IS INOPERATIVE

NOTE: After repair procedure has been completed, reconnect all components and preform SELF-DIAGNOSTIC TEST under SELF-DIAGNOSTIC SYSTEM. Deactivator switch may also be referred to as brake pressure switch.

Turn ignition off. Disconnect speed control servo/actuator connector C165 (located in right rear of engine compartment). Using an ohmmeter, check resistance between speed control servo/actuator connector C165 terminal No. 5 (Light Blue/Black wire) and terminal No. 6 (Dark Green/Orange wire) while pressing speed control SET/ACCEL switch. *See Fig. 2.* If resistance is 612-748 ohms, replace speed control servo/actuator. If resistance is not 612-748 ohms, replace speed control SET/ACCEL switch.

TEST K: RESUME SWITCH IS INOPERATIVE

NOTE: After repair procedure has been completed, reconnect all components and preform SELF-DIAGNOSTIC TEST under SELF-DIAGNOSTIC SYSTEM. Deactivator switch may also be referred to as brake pressure switch.

Turn ignition off. Disconnect speed control servo/actuator connector C165 (located in right rear of engine compartment). Using an ohmmeter, check resistance between speed control servo/actuator connector C165 terminal No. 5 (Light Blue/Black wire) and terminal No. 6 (Dark Green/Orange wire) while pressing speed control RESUME switch. *See Fig. 2.* If resistance is 1980-2420 ohms, replace speed control servo/actuator and perform self-test diagnostics using NGS tester. If resistance is not 1980-2420 ohms, replace speed control RESUME switch and perform self-test diagnostics using NGS tester.

TEST L: OFF SWITCH IS INOPERATIVE

NOTE: After repair procedure has been completed, reconnect all components and preform SELF-DIAGNOSTIC TEST under SELF-DIAGNOSTIC SYSTEM. Deactivator switch may also be referred to as brake pressure switch.

Turn ignition off. Disconnect speed control servo/actuator connector C165 (located in right rear of engine compartment). Using an ohmmeter, check resistance between speed control servo/actuator connector C165 terminal No. 5 (Light Blue/Black wire) and terminal No. 6 (Dark Green/Orange wire) while pressing speed control OFF switch. *See Fig. 2.* If resistance is less than 5 ohms, replace speed control servo/actuator. If resistance is 5 ohms or more, replace speed control ON/OFF switch.

TEST M: SPEED CONTROL INDICATOR ALWAYS ON

NOTE: After repair procedure has been completed, reconnect all components and preform SELF-DIAGNOSTIC TEST under SELF-DIAGNOSTIC SYSTEM. Deactivator switch may also be referred to as brake pressure switch.

1) Turn ignition off. Disconnect speed control servo/actuator connector C165 (located in right rear of engine compartment). Turn ignition switch to RUN position. If speed control indicator illuminates, go to next step. If speed control indicator does not illuminate, replace speed control servo/actuator.

2) Ensure ignition is off. Disconnect instrument cluster connector C214 (located behind instrument cluster). Using an ohmmeter, check resistance between ground and speed control servo/actuator connector C165 terminal No. 1 (Orange/Light Blue wire). *See Fig. 2.* If resistance is more than 10 k/ohms, replace instrument cluster printed circuit. If resistance is 10 k/ohms or less, repair short to ground in Orange/Light Blue wire between instrument cluster and speed control servo/actuator.

TEST N: SET SPEED FLUCTUATES

NOTE: After repair procedure has been completed, reconnect all components and preform SELF-DIAGNOSTIC TEST under SELF-DIAGNOSTIC SYSTEM. Deactivator switch may also be referred to as brake pressure switch.

1) Ensure engine is properly tuned. Ensure problem does not occur while driving vehicle without speed control activated. If problem occurs without speed control activated, repair engine as necessary. If problem occurs only with speed control activated, go to next step.

2) Check for binding or sticking speed control servo/actuator cable, throttle linkage and/or throttle plate. Ensure throttle cable bracket and speed control servo/actuator bracket are not loose. Repair as necessary. If all components are okay, repair Gray/Black and/or Pink/Orange wire. See WIRING DIAGRAMS.

REMOVAL & INSTALLATION

WARNING: Disable air bag system before working around steering column or removing any air bag system component. See AIR BAG RESTRAINT SYSTEMS – RANGER article.

CAUTION: When battery is disconnected, vehicle computer and memory systems may lose memory data. Driveability problems may exist until computer systems have completed a relearn cycle. See COMPUTER RELEARN PROCEDURES article in GENERAL INFORMATION before disconnecting battery.

SPEED CONTROL SERVO/ACTUATOR

Removal & Installation – Disconnect negative battery cable. Disconnect speed control servo/actuator electrical connector. Press in locking tab arm on cable cap and rotate cap counterclockwise. Disengage cable slug from servo pulley. Gently push slug past retaining spring with a small screwdriver. Remove speed control servo/actuator bracket bolt and remove servo/actuator. Separate bracket from servo. To install, reverse removal procedure.

DEACTIVATOR SWITCH

Removal & Installation – Disconnect negative battery cable. Disconnect deactivator switch connector located at master cylinder. Unscrew switch. To install, reverse removal procedure. Tighten switch to 12-14 ft. lbs. (16-20 N.m). Bleed brake system. See appropriate article in BRAKES in appropriate MITCHELL® manual.

SPEED CONTROL SWITCHES

Removal & Installation – Disable air bag system and remove driver side air bag module. See AIR BAG RESTRAINT SYSTEMS – RANGER article. Ensure front wheels are in straight-ahead position. Remove steering wheel retaining bolt and remove steering wheel. Tape air bag sliding contact to steering column to prevent misalignment. Remove steering wheel rear cover. Separate ribbon harness from retaining clips. Disconnect horn contact electrical connectors. Remove right side horn contact. Remove switch retaining screws and switch assembly. To install, reverse removal procedure.

WIRING DIAGRAMS

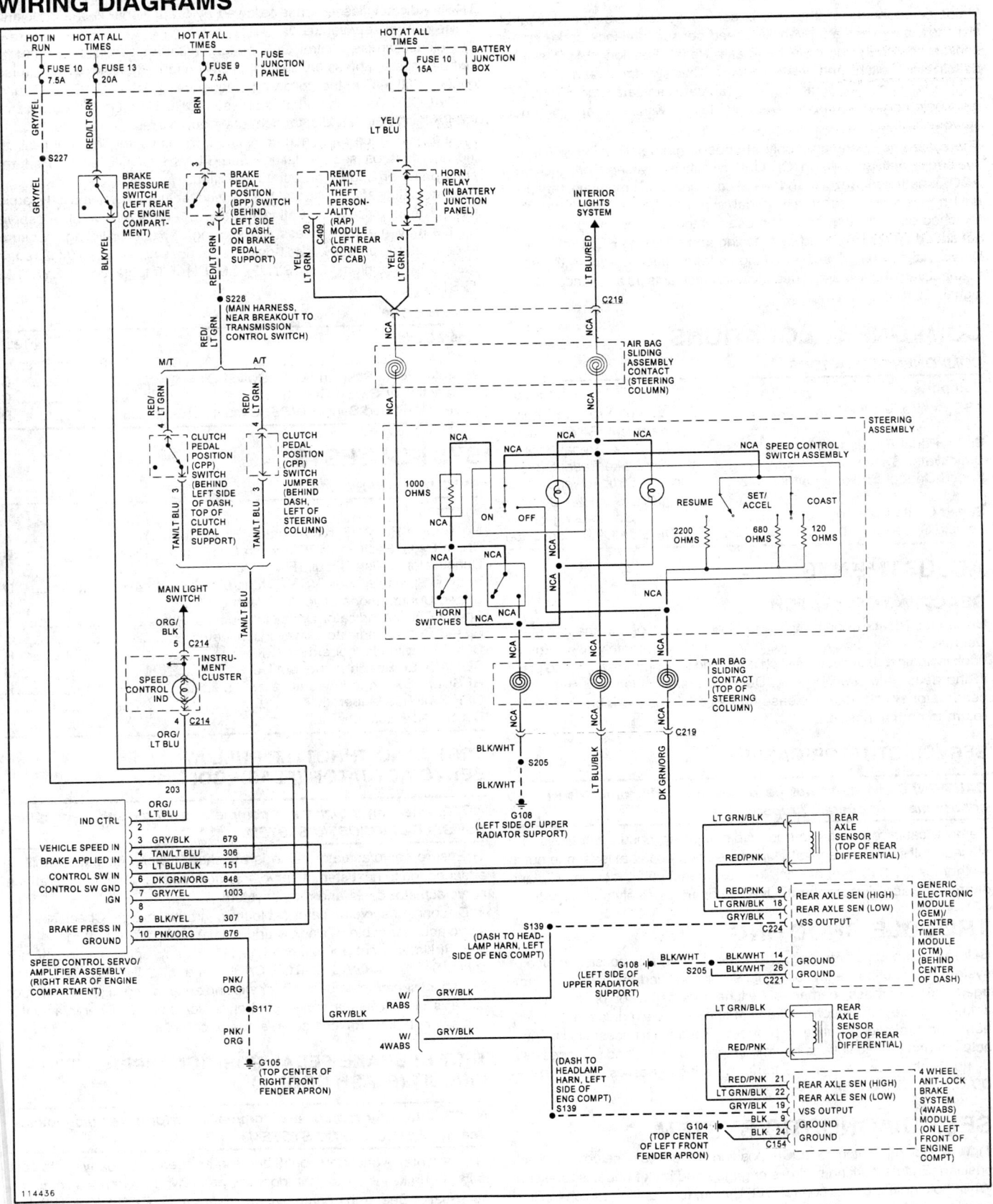

Fig. 6: Cruise Control System Wiring Diagram (Ranger)

114436

1999 ACCESSORIES & EQUIPMENT
Cruise Control Systems – Sable & Taurus

DESCRIPTION & 3OPERATION

Major components of the cruise control system are speed control switches, servo/actuator, vehicle speed sensor (anti-lock brake speed sensor on SHO), horn relay, Brake Pedal Position (BPP) switch, deactivator switch, and related wiring. This system does not require engine vacuum. An electronic servo/actuator actuates the throttle. All electronic control components are contained within the speed control servo/actuator.

The system is operational only at speeds greater than 30 MPH. The system is activated when ON/OFF switch is switched on and SET/ACCEL button is pressed and released. Vehicle will maintain set speed until new speed is set, brake pedal is pressed, or ON/OFF switch is switched off. If system has been deactivated by pressing brake pedal, set speed can be regained by pressing and releasing RESUME button. When brake pedal is pressed, a signal from switch is sent to the servo to deactivate the system. A deactivator switch acts as a redundant brake signal.

COMPONENT LOCATIONS

COMPONENT LOCATIONS

Component	Location
ABS Control Module	Left Front Of Engine Compartment, Below Battery
Brake Pedal Position Switch	On Brake Pedal Bracket
Deactivator Switch	On Brake Pedal Bracket
Speed Control Servo/Actuator	On Left Strut Tower, Left Of Brake Master Cylinder
Speed Control Switch	On Steering Wheel
Vehicle Speed Sensor	On Side Of Transmission

ADJUSTMENTS

DEACTIVATOR SWITCH

Disconnect deactivator switch hook from plastic pedal adapter stem. Depress deactivator switch hook and plunger assembly fully. Ensure hook is against deactivator switch body and locking tab snaps into place in the deactivator switch hook. Depress brake pedal fully and attach deactivator switch hook. Release brake pedal and allow brake pedal to return to normal position.

SERVO/ACTUATOR CABLE

CAUTION: Cable must not be pulled too tight, otherwise speed control may not operate properly.

Remove cable retaining clip from cable adjuster. Ensure throttle is fully closed. Pull servo cable to take up any slack. Loosen at least one notch so there is 0.12" (3 mm) of slack in cable. Insert cable retaining clip and snap into place. Ensure throttle linkage operates freely and smoothly.

TROUBLE SHOOTING

Before performing any testing, check the following for possible cause of system malfunction: faulty fuses, loose or corroded connections, damaged wiring harness, damaged switches, damaged or binding servo/actuator cable and incorrect servo/actuator cable adjustment. Verify horn and brakelights function properly. Repair as necessary. Inspect actuator and throttle linkage for smooth operation. Unbind as necessary. If no problems are found, perform self-diagnostics. See SELF-DIAGNOSTIC SYSTEM.

SELF-DIAGNOSTIC SYSTEM

1) Turn ignition switch to LOCK position. Place gear selector in Park position. Ensure parking brake is engaged and brake pedal is released. While holding the cruise control OFF button, turn ignition switch to RUN position. CRUISE CONTROL indicator on instrument cluster will flash once to indicate successful entry into self-diagnostic mode. If CRUISE CONTROL indicator does not flash, repair system by symptom. See

SYMPTOM CHART table under SYSTEM TESTS. If CRUISE CONTROL indicator flashes once followed by 5 additional flashes, replace cruise control servo/actuator.

2) Release cruise control OFF button. Within 5 seconds of entering self-diagnostics, press cruise control ON button. Press remaining cruise control buttons in the following sequence: RESUME, COAST and SET/ACCEL. As each button is pressed, CRUISE CONTROL indicator will flash. Wait until indicator light goes out to press next button.

3) After sequence has been completed, the indicator light will flash to indicate test passed or failed. See FLASH CODE table. Perform appropriate procedure or test as specified.

4) Immediately after static test has passed, actuator performs a dynamic test by automatically operating throttle .04-.40" (1-10 mm). Observe throttle movement to witness any sticking of cable or linkage. Ensure throttle returns properly. If self-diagnostics does not pinpoint fault, repair system by symptom. See SYMPTOM CHART table under SYSTEM TESTS.

FLASH CODE

Flash Code	Test
1	System Passed
2 (Brake Pedal Position (BPP) Switch Circuit)	B
3 (Deactivator Switch Circuit)	C
4 (Vehicle Speed Sensor (VSS) Circuit)	D

SYSTEM TESTS

SYMPTOM CHART

Symptom	Test
No Throttle Pull At Servo/Actuator (Flash Code 1)	A
Brake Pedal Position (BPP) Switch Circuit (Flash Code 2)	B
Deactivator Switch Circuit (Flash Code 3)	C
Vehicle Speed Sensor (VSS) Circuit (Flash Code 4)	D
Speed Control Inoperative (No Flash Codes)	E
Speed Control Indicator Does Not Illuminate	F
Speed Control Indicator Always Illuminated	G
COAST Switch Is Inoperative	H
SET/ACCEL Switch Is Inoperative	J
RESUME Switch Is Inoperative	K
OFF Switch Is Inoperative	L
Set Speed Fluctuates	M

TEST A: NO THROTTLE PULL AT SERVO/ACTUATOR (FLASH CODE 1)

NOTE: After any repairs are complete, perform self-diagnostics. See SELF-DIAGNOSTIC SYSTEM.

1) Ensure servo/actuator cable is attached. If servo/actuator cable is attached, go to next step. If servo/actuator cable is not attached, attach servo/actuator cable and retest system.

2) Disconnect servo/actuator cable from throttle linkage. Check slack in servo/actuator cable. If slack is approximately 0.12" (3 mm), go to next step. If slack is not approximately 0.12" (3 mm), adjust servo/actuator cable. See SERVO/ACTUATOR CABLE under ADJUSTMENTS.

3) Inspect servo/actuator cable for sticking and binding. If servo/actuator cable is okay, replace cruise control servo/actuator. If servo/actuator cable is not okay, replace servo/actuator cable.

TEST B: BRAKE PEDAL POSITION (BPP) SWITCH CIRCUIT (FLASH CODE 2)

NOTE: After any repairs are complete, perform self-diagnostics. See SELF-DIAGNOSTIC SYSTEM.

1) Check brakelight operation. If brakelights operate properly, go to next step. If brakelights do not operate properly, repair brakelights as necessary. See appropriate wiring diagram in EXTERIOR LIGHTS article.

2) Disconnect speed control servo/actuator harness connector C102. Measure voltage at terminal No. 4 (Red/Light Green wire) at speed

control servo/actuator harness connector C102 while pressing and releasing brake pedal. *See Fig. 1.* Battery voltage should exist when brake pedal is depressed and zero volts should exist when brake pedal is not depressed. If voltage is as specified, replace speed control servo/actuator. If voltage is not as specified, repair open in Red/Light Green wire.

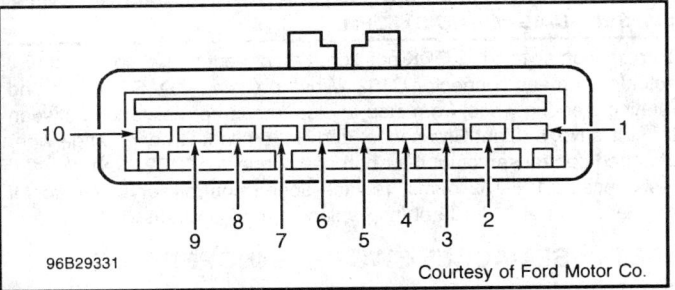

Fig. 1: Identifying Servo/Actuator Harness Connector C102 Terminals

TEST C: DEACTIVATOR SWITCH CIRCUIT (FLASH CODE 3)

NOTE: After any repairs are complete, perform self-diagnostics. See SELF-DIAGNOSTIC SYSTEM.

1) Check brakelight operation. If brakelights operate properly, go to next step. If brakelights do not operate properly, repair brakelights as necessary. See appropriate wiring diagram in EXTERIOR LIGHTS article.

2) Disconnect speed control servo/actuator harness connector C102. Measure voltage at terminal No. 9 (Tan/Orange wire) at speed control servo/actuator harness connector C102 while pressing and releasing brake pedal. *See Fig. 1 .* Battery voltage should exist when brake pedal is released and zero volts should exist when brake pedal is depressed. If voltage is not as specified, go to next step. If voltage is as specified, replace speed control servo/actuator.

3) Disconnect deactivator switch harness connector C246. Measure voltage at Light Green/Red wire terminal at deactivator switch harness connector C246. If battery voltage exists, go to next step. If battery voltage does not exist, repair power distribution circuit. See appropriate wiring diagram in POWER DISTRIBUTION article in WIRING DIAGRAMS.

4) Measure resistance in Tan/Orange wire between deactivator switch harness connector C246 and terminal No. 9 at speed control servo/actuator harness connector C102. If resistance is 5 ohms or less, replace deactivator switch. If resistance is greater than 5 ohms, repair open in Tan/Orange wire.

TEST D: VEHICLE SPEED SENSOR (VSS) CIRCUIT (FLASH CODE 4)

NOTE: After any repairs are complete, perform self-diagnostics. See SELF-DIAGNOSTIC SYSTEM.

1) Test drive vehicle and observe speedometer operation. If speedometer operates properly, go to next step. If speedometer does not operate properly, repair speedometer as necessary. See INSTRUMENT PANELS – SABLE & TAURUS article.

2) On Taurus SHO models, go to next step. On all other models, go to step **4)**.

3) Disconnect ABS control module harness connector C1057. Measure resistance in Gray/Black wire between terminal No. 3 at speed control servo/actuator harness connector C102 and terminal No. 12 at ABS control module harness connector C1057. *See Figs. 1 and 2.* If resistance is 5 ohms or less, replace speed control servo/actuator. If resistance is greater than 5 ohms, repair open in Gray/Black wire.

4) Disconnect vehicle speed sensor harness connector C1043. Measure resistance in Gray/Black wire between terminal No. 3 at speed control servo/actuator connector C102 and vehicle speed sensor harness connector C1043. If resistance is 5 ohms or less, replace speed control servo/actuator. If resistance is greater than 5 ohms, repair open in Gray/Black wire.

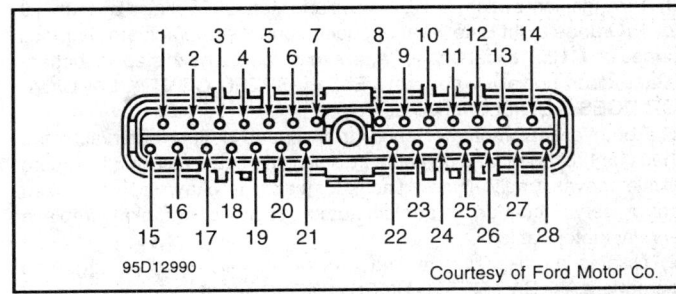

Fig. 2: Identifying ABS Control Module Harness Connector C1057 Terminals

TEST E: SPEED CONTROL INOPERATIVE (NO FLASH CODES)

NOTE: After any repairs are complete, perform self-diagnostics. See SELF-DIAGNOSTIC SYSTEM.

1) Turn ignition switch to LOCK position. Disconnect speed control servo/actuator harness connector C102. Turn ignition switch to RUN position. Measure voltage between terminals No. 7 (Orange wire) and No. 10 (Black wire) at speed control servo/actuator harness connector C102. *See Fig. 1.* If batter voltage does not exist, go to next step. If battery voltage exists, go to step **3)**.

2) Turn ignition switch to LOCK position. Measure resistance between ground and terminal No. 10 (Black wire) at speed control servo/actuator harness connector C102. If resistance is greater than 5 ohms, repair open in Black wire. If resistance is 5 ohms or less, repair power distribution circuit. See appropriate wiring diagram in POWER DISTRIBUTION article in WIRING DIAGRAMS.

3) Turn ignition switch to RUN position. With no speed control switches depressed, measure voltage between terminals No. 5 (Orange wire) and No. 10 (Black wire) at speed control servo/actuator harness connector C102. If zero volts exists, go to next step. If any voltage exists, go to step **12)**.

4) Measure voltage between terminals No. 5 (Orange wire) and No. 10 (Black wire) at speed control servo/actuator harness connector C102 while pressing speed control ON switch. If battery voltage exists, go to next step. If battery voltage does not exist, go to step **6)**.

5) Check horn operation. If horn operates properly, go to step **8)**. If horn does not operate properly, repair horn as necessary, See WIRING DIAGRAMS in STEERING COLUMN SWITCHES – SABLE & TAURUS article.

6) Disable air bag system and remove driver's side air bag. See appropriate AIR BAG RESTRAINT SYSTEMS article. Disconnect air bag sliding contact harness connector C228. Disconnect speed control switch harness connector C230. Measure resistance across each of air bag sliding contact windings between terminals of air bag sliding contact harness connector C228 (male side) and speed control switch harness connector C230. If each resistance reading is .25-.50 ohm, go to next step. If each resistance reading is not .25-.50 ohm, replace air bag sliding contact.

7) Measure resistance in Light Green wire between terminal No. 5 at speed control servo/actuator harness connector C102 and air bag sliding contact harness connector C228 (female side). If resistance is 5 ohms or less, replace speed control switches. If resistance is greater than 5 ohms, repair open in Light Green wire.

8) Measure resistance between terminals No. 5 (Light Green wire) and No. 6 (Dark Green/Orange wire) at speed control servo/actuator connector C102 while pressing speed control SET/ACCEL switch. If resistance is 612-748 ohms, go to next step. If resistance is not 612-748 ohms, replace speed control switches.

9) Measure resistance between terminals No. 5 (Light Green wire) and No. 6 (Dark Green/Orange wire) at speed control servo/actuator connector C102 while pressing speed control OFF switch. If resistance is 5 ohms or less, go to next step. If resistance is greater than 5 ohms, replace speed control switches.

10) Turn ignition switch to RUN position. Measure voltage at terminal No. 1 (Orange/Light Blue wire) at speed control servo/actuator harness connector C102. If battery voltage exists, go to next step. If battery voltage does not exist, perform TEST F: SPEED CONTROL INDICATOR DOES NOT ILLUMINATE.

11) Remove servo/actuator cable from speed control servo/actuator. Check for broken or binding cable by pulling on cable ball slug to ensure throttle moves freely. If servo/actuator cable is okay, replace speed control servo/actuator. If servo/actuator cable is not okay, replace servo/actuator cable.

12) Disable air bag system and remove driver's side air bag. See appropriate AIR BAG RESTRAINT SYSTEMS article. Disconnect speed control switch harness connector C230. Measure voltage between terminals 5 (Light Green wire) and No. 10 (Black wire) at speed control servo/actuator harness connector C102. If any voltage exists, go to next step. If zero volts exists, replace speed control switch.

13) Disconnect air bag sliding contact harness connector C228. Measure voltage between terminals 5 (Light Green wire) and No. 10 (Black wire) at speed control servo/actuator harness connector C102. If any voltage exists, repair short to voltage in Light Green wire. If zero volts exists, replace air bag sliding contact.

TEST F: SPEED CONTROL INDICATOR DOES NOT ILLUMINATE

NOTE: *After any repairs are complete, perform self-diagnostics. See SELF-DIAGNOSTIC SYSTEM.*

1) Turn ignition switch to LOCK position. Disconnect speed control servo/actuator harness connector C102. Turn ignition switch to RUN position. Measure voltage between terminals No. 1 (Orange/Light Blue wire) and No. 10 (Black wire) at speed control servo/actuator harness connector C102. *See Fig. 1.* If battery voltage does not exist, go to next step. If battery voltage exists, replace speed control servo/actuator.

2) Disconnect instrument cluster harness connector C251. Measure resistance in Orange/Light Blue wire between terminal No. 5 at instrument cluster harness connector C251 and terminal No. 1 at speed control servo/actuator harness connector C102. *See Figs. 1 and 3.* If resistance is 5 ohms or less, replace instrument cluster. If resistance is greater than 5 ohms, repair open in Orange/Light Blue wire.

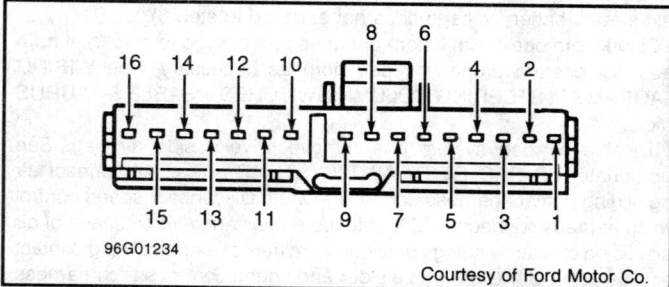

96G01234   Courtesy of Ford Motor Co.

Fig. 3: Identifying Instrument Cluster Harness Connector C251 Terminals

TEST G: SPEED CONTROL INDICATOR ALWAYS ILLUMINATED

NOTE: *After any repairs are complete, perform self-diagnostics. See SELF-DIAGNOSTIC SYSTEM.*

1) Turn ignition switch to LOCK position. Disconnect speed control servo/actuator harness connector C102. Turn ignition switch to RUN position. If speed control indicator illuminates, go to next step. If speed control indicator does not illuminate, replace speed control servo/actuator.

2) Disconnect instrument cluster harness connector C251. Measure resistance between ground and terminal No. 5 at instrument cluster

harness connector C251. *See Fig. 3.* If resistance is greater than 10 k/ohms, replace instrument cluster. If resistance is 10 k/ohms or less, repair short to ground in Orange/Light Blue wire.

TEST H: COAST SWITCH IS INOPERATIVE

NOTE: *After any repairs are complete, perform self-diagnostics. See SELF-DIAGNOSTIC SYSTEM.*

Turn ignition switch to LOCK position. Disconnect speed control servo/actuator harness connector C102. While pressing COAST switch and rotating steering wheel from stop to stop, measure resistance between terminals No. 5 (Light Green wire) and No. 6 (Dark Green/Orange wire) at speed control servo/actuator harness connector C102. *See Fig. 1.* If resistance is 108-132 ohms, replace speed control servo/actuator. If resistance is not 108-132 ohms, replace speed control switch.

TEST J: SET/ACCEL SWITCH IS INOPERATIVE

NOTE: *After any repairs are complete, perform self-diagnostics. See SELF-DIAGNOSTIC SYSTEM.*

Turn ignition switch to LOCK position. Disconnect speed control servo/actuator harness connector C102. While pressing SET/ACCEL switch and rotating steering wheel from stop to stop, measure resistance between terminals No. 5 (Light Green wire) and No. 6 (Dark Green/Orange wire) at speed control servo/actuator harness connector C102. *See Fig. 1.* If resistance is 612-748 ohms, replace speed control servo/actuator. If resistance is not 612-748 ohms, replace speed control switch.

TEST K: RESUME SWITCH IS INOPERATIVE

NOTE: *After any repairs are complete, perform self-diagnostics. See SELF-DIAGNOSTIC SYSTEM.*

Turn ignition switch to LOCK position. Disconnect speed control servo/actuator harness connector C102. While pressing RESUME switch and rotating steering wheel from stop to stop, measure resistance between terminals No. 5 (Light Green wire) and No. 6 (Dark Green/Orange wire) at speed control servo/actuator harness connector C102. *See Fig. 1.* If resistance is 1980-2420 ohms, replace speed control servo/actuator. If resistance is not 1980-2420 ohms, replace speed control switch.

TEST L: OFF SWITCH IS INOPERATIVE

NOTE: *After any repairs are complete, perform self-diagnostics. See SELF-DIAGNOSTIC SYSTEM.*

Turn ignition switch to LOCK position. Disconnect speed control servo/actuator harness connector C102. While pressing OFF switch and rotating steering wheel from stop to stop, measure resistance between terminals No. 5 (Light Green wire) and No. 6 (Dark Green/Orange wire) at speed control servo/actuator harness connector C102. *See Fig. 1.* If resistance is 5 ohms or less, replace speed control servo/actuator. If resistance greater than 5 ohms, replace speed control switch.

TEST M: SET SPEED FLUCTUATES

NOTE: *After any repairs are complete, perform self-diagnostics. See SELF-DIAGNOSTIC SYSTEM.*

1) Ensure engine is properly tuned. Ensure problem does not occur while driving vehicle without speed control activated. If problem occurs only with speed control activated, go to next step. If problem occurs without speed control activated, repair engine as necessary.

2) Check for binding or sticking speed control servo/actuator cable, throttle linkage and/or throttle plate. Ensure throttle cable bracket and speed control servo/actuator bracket are not loose. If problem does not exist, go to next step. If problem exists, repair as necessary.

3) Test drive vehicle and observe speedometer operation. If speedometer operates properly, go to next step. If speedometer does not operate properly, repair speedometer as necessary. See INSTRUMENT PANELS – SABLE & TAURUS article.

4) On Taurus SHO models, go to next step. On all other models, go to step **6)**.

5) Disconnect speed control servo/actuator harness connector C102. Disconnect ABS control module harness connector C1057. Measure resistance in Gray/Black wire between terminal No. 3 at speed control servo/actuator harness connector C102 and terminal No. 12 at ABS control module harness connector C1057. *See Figs. 1 and 2.* If resistance is 5 ohms or less, replace speed control servo/actuator. If resistance is greater than 5 ohms, repair open in Gray/Black wire.

6) Disconnect speed control servo/actuator harness connector C102. Disconnect vehicle speed sensor harness connector C1043. Measure resistance in Gray/Black wire between terminal No. 3 at speed control servo/actuator connector C102 and vehicle speed sensor harness connector C1043. If resistance is 5 ohms or less, replace speed control servo/actuator. If resistance is greater than 5 ohms, repair open in Gray/Black wire.

REMOVAL & INSTALLATION

WARNING: Deactivate air bag system before working around steering column. See appropriate AIR BAG RESTRAINT SYSTEMS article.

CAUTION: When battery is disconnected, vehicle computer and memory systems may lose memory data. Driveability problems may exist until computer systems have completed a relearn cycle. See COMPUTER RELEARN PROCEDURES article in GENERAL INFORMATION before disconnecting battery.

SPEED CONTROL SWITCHES

Removal & Installation (Except SHO) – Disable air bag system and remove driver side air bag module. See appropriate AIR BAG RESTRAINT SYSTEMS article. Disconnect electrical connectors from speed control switches. Remove retaining screws and switches. To install, reverse removal procedure.

Removal & Installation (SHO) – Disable air bag system and remove driver side air bag module. See appropriate AIR BAG RESTRAINT SYSTEMS article. Ensure front wheels are in straight ahead position. Remove steering wheel retaining bolt and remove steering wheel. Tape air bag sliding contact to steering column to prevent misalignment. Remove steering wheel trim. Remove switch retaining screws and switch assembly. To install, reverse removal procedure.

DEACTIVATOR SWITCH

Removal & Installation – Deactivator switch is located above brake-light switch, connected to brake pedal arm. Disconnect deactivator switch electrical connector. Disconnect deactivator switch push rod from brake pedal arm. Disengage locking tabs securing switch. To install, reverse removal procedure.

SERVO/ACTUATOR ASSEMBLY

Removal & Installation – Remove accelerator control splash shield. Remove speed control servo/actuator cable-to-accelerator cable bracket retaining screw. Disconnect speed control servo/actuator cable from throttle body. Press speed control servo/actuator cable cap locking tab in and rotate cap counterclockwise. Remove speed control servo/actuator cable ball slug from pulley. Remove speed control servo/actuator retaining nuts. Remove speed control servo/actuator. If necessary, separate speed control servo/actuator from bracket. To install, reverse removal procedure.

VEHICLE SPEED SENSOR (VSS)

Removal & Installation – Raise and support vehicle. Remove exhaust "Y" pipe. Remove VSS heat shield. Disconnect VSS harness connector. Remove VSS retaining bolt. Remove VSS assembly from transaxle. To install, reverse removal procedure.

WIRING DIAGRAMS

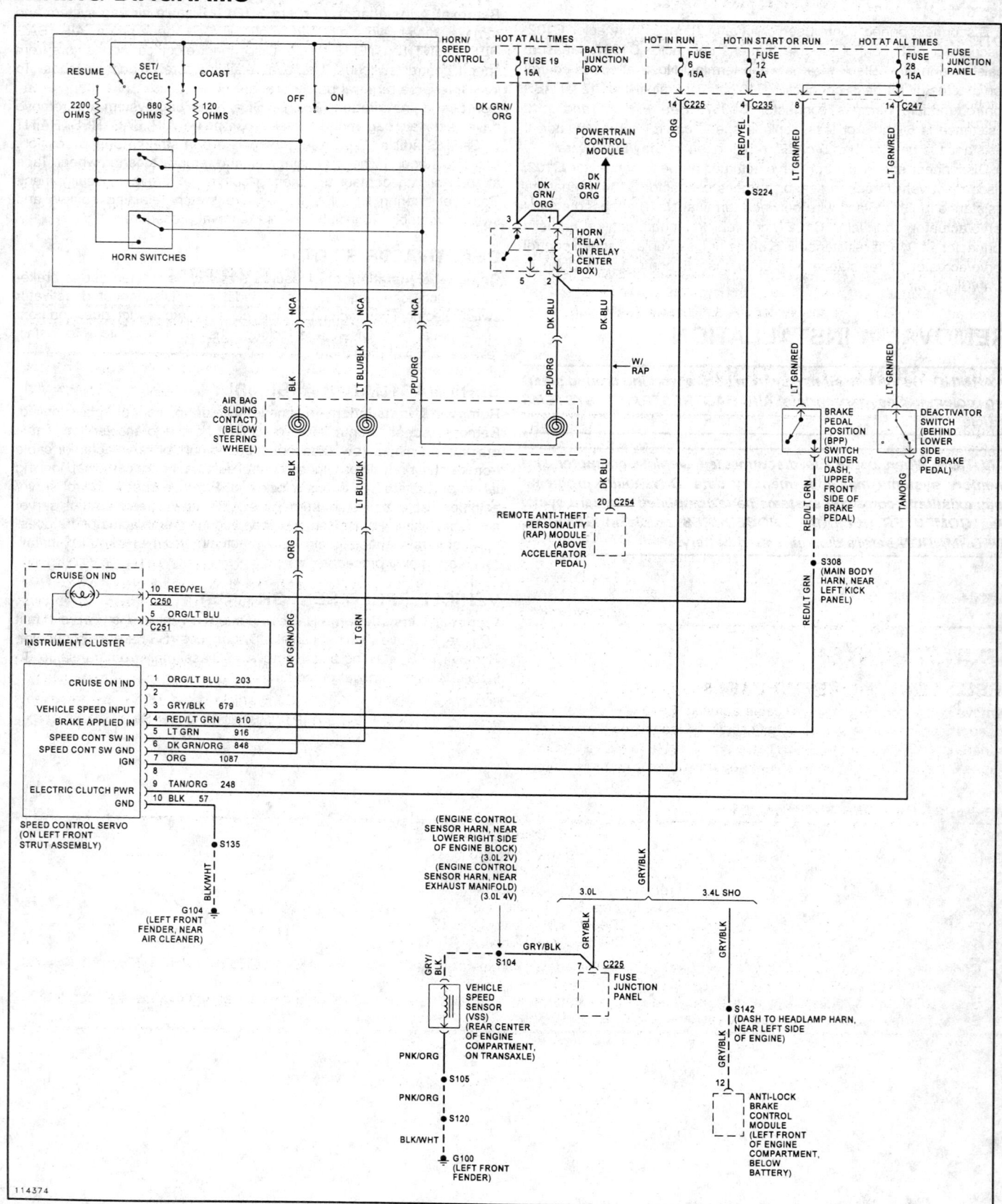

Fig. 4: Cruise Control System Wiring Diagram (Sable & Taurus)

DESCRIPTION & OPERATION

NOTE: Ensure speedometer and horn systems are operating properly before testing speed control system.

Major components of the cruise control system are the speed control switches, speed control servo, horn relay, deactivator switch, Lighting Control Module (LCM), ABS module, message center display and related wiring. This system does not require engine vacuum. An electronic servo/actuator actuates the throttle.

The system is operational only at speeds greater than 30 MPH. The system is activated when ON/OFF switch is switched on and SET/ACCEL button is pressed and released. Vehicle will maintain set speed until new speed is set, brake pedal is pressed, or ON/OFF switch is switched off. If system has been deactivated by pressing brake pedal, set speed can be regained by pressing and releasing RESUME button. When brake pedal is pressed, a signal from switch is sent to the speed control servo to deactivate the system. A deactivator switch acts as a redundant brake signal.

COMPONENT LOCATIONS

COMPONENT LOCATIONS

Component	Location
Deactivator Switch	On Brake Pedal Support
Data Link Connector	Under Instrument Panel, Right Of Steering Column
Instrument Panel Fuse Box	Behind Instrument Panel, Left Of Steering Column
Power Distribution Box	Left Side Of Engine Compartment, In Front Of Wheelwell
Speed Control Servo	Left Rear Of Engine Compartment

ADJUSTMENTS

SPEED CONTROL SERVO CABLE

Remove cable retaining clip from cable adjuster. Ensure throttle is fully closed. Pull servo cable to take up any slack. Loosen at least one notch so there is 0.12" (3 mm) of slack in cable. Insert cable retaining clip and snap into place. Ensure throttle linkage operates freely and smoothly.

TROUBLE SHOOTING

NOTE: Ensure speedometer and horn systems are operating properly before testing speed control system.

Verify customer complaint. Check for blown fuses and replace as necessary. Check for loose or corroded connections. Check for damaged wiring harness. Check for damaged switches. Check for damaged or binding servo/actuator cable. Incorrect servo/actuator cable adjustment. Verify horn and stoplights function properly. Repair as necessary. Inspect actuator and throttle linkage for smooth operation. Unbind as necessary. If no problems are found, go to SELF-DIAGNOSTIC SYSTEM.

SELF-DIAGNOSTIC SYSTEM

NOTE: Ensure speedometer and horn systems are operating properly before testing speed control system.

Verify customers complaint by operating speed control system. Check for damaged speed control servo cable, damaged throttle lever, or damaged switches. Check for blown fuse(s), loose or corroded connectors, or damaged wiring harness. Repair or replace components as necessary. If all components are okay, connect NGS tester to DLC located below instrument panel. Using NGS tester, perform DATA LINK DIAGNOSTIC TEST. If NGS tester displays CKT914, CKT915 or CKT70=ALL ECUS NO RESP/NOT EQUIP, repair communication concern. See MODULE COMMUNICATIONS NETWORK – TOWN CAR article. If NGS tester displays NO RESP/NOT EQUIP for speed control servo, perform TEST A: NO COMMUNICATION WITH SPEED CONTROL SERVO under SYSTEM TESTS. If NGS tester displays SYSTEM PASSED, retrieve and record continuous DTCs. Erase continuous DTCs. Perform speed control servo self-test. Perform appropriate DTC test in accordance with DTC retrieved. See SPEED CONTROL SERVO DTC INDEX table. Codes listed in table are only for testing covered in this article. For complete DTC listing, see MODULE COMMUNICATIONS NETWORK – TOWN CAR article. If no DTCs are retrieved, repair by symptom. See SYMPTOM CHART under SYSTEM TESTS.

SPEED CONTROL SERVO DTC INDEX

DTC [1]	Description	Test
B1318	Battery Voltage Low	C
B1342	ECU Defective	[2]
C1109	Throttle Position Did Not Return To Idle After Self-Test	D
C1126	Speed Control Switch Stuck For 2 Minutes Or Longer	E
C1127	Deactivator Switch Circuit Failure	F
C1179	Speed Control Cable Slack Failure	G

[1] – Codes listed in this table are only for testing covered in this article. For complete DTC listing, see MODULE COMMUNICATIONS NETWORK – TOWN CAR article.

[2] – Using NGS tester, retrieve and document all continuous. Perform air suspension/electronic variable orifice steering module self-test. If DTC B1342 is retrieved again, replace air suspension/electronic variable orifice steering module.

SYSTEM TESTS

CAUTION: When battery is disconnected or modules are replaced, vehicle computer and memory systems may lose memory data. Driveability problems may exist until computer systems have completed a relearn cycle. See COMPUTER RELEARN PROCEDURES article in GENERAL INFORMATION before disconnecting battery.

NOTE: Ensure speedometer and horn systems are operating properly before testing speed control system.

NOTE: After completing any repair, use NGS tester to clear DTCs and repeat speed control servo self-test.

WARNING: Deactivate air bag system before working around steering column. See appropriate AIR BAG RESTRAINT SYSTEMS article.

CAUTION: When battery is disconnected, vehicle computer and memory systems may lose memory data. Driveability problems may exist until computer systems have completed a relearn cycle. See COMPUTER RELEARN PROCEDURES article in GENERAL INFORMATION before disconnecting battery.

SYMPTOM CHART

Symptom	Test
No Communication With Speed Control Servo	A
Unable To Enter Self-Test	B
Speed Control Inoperative – No Diagnostic Trouble Codes	H
Set Speed Fluctuates	I
Coast Switch Inoperative	J
Set/Accel Switch Inoperative	K
Resume Switch Inoperative	L
Off Switch Inoperative	M

TEST A: NO COMMUNICATION WITH SPEED CONTROL SERVO

1) Check condition of fuse No. 8 (10-amp) in instrument panel fuse box. If fuse is okay, go to next step. If fuse is blown, replace fuse and retest system operation. If fuse fails again, repair short to ground in White/Violet wire.

2) Turn ignition switch to LOCK position. Disconnect speed control servo harness connector C123 (located in left rear of engine compartment). Turn ignition switch to RUN position. Measure voltage at terminal No. 7 (White/Violet wire) at speed control servo harness connector C123. *See Fig. 1.* If battery voltage exists, go to next step. If battery voltage does not exist, repair open in White/Violet wire.

3) Measure resistance between ground and terminal No. 10 (Pink/Orange wire) at speed control servo harness connector C123. If resistance is less than 5 ohms, repair communication concern. See MODULE COMMUNICATIONS NETWORK – TOWN CAR article. If resistance is 5 ohms or greater, repair open in Pink/Orange wire.

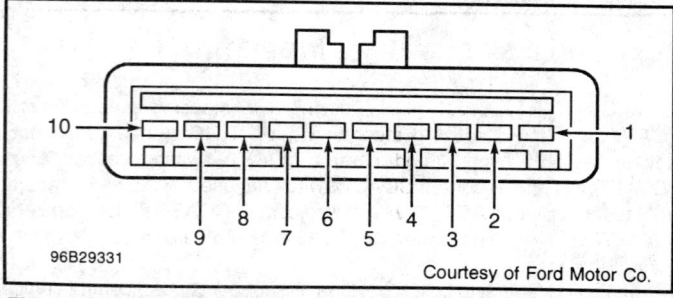

96B29331   Courtesy of Ford Motor Co.

Fig. 1: Identifying Servo/Actuator Harness Connector C152 Terminals

TEST B: UNABLE TO ENTER SELF-TEST

Connect New Generation Star (NGS) tester to Data Link Connector (DLC). Using NGS tester, perform speed control servo self-test. If NGS tester communicates with speed control servo, replace speed control servo. If NGS tester does not communicate with speed control servo, perform TEST A: NO COMMUNICATION WITH SPEED CONTROL SERVO.

TEST C: BATTERY VOLTAGE LOW (DTC B1318)

Turn ignition switch to LOCK position. Disconnect speed control servo harness connector C123 (located in left rear of engine compartment). Turn ignition switch to RUN position. Measure voltage at terminal No. 7 (White/Violet wire) at speed control servo harness connector C123. *See Fig. 1.* If battery voltage does not exist, repair open in White/Violet wire or repair charging as necessary. See appropriate article in STARTING & CHARGING SYSTEMS. If battery voltage exists, repair open in Pink/Orange wire.

TEST D: THROTTLE POSITION DID NOT RETURN TO IDLE AFTER SELF-TEST (DTC C1109)

1) Check speed control servo cable for binding or sticking. If cable is okay, go to next step. If cable is not okay, repair or replace cable as necessary.

2) Check throttle lever for binding or sticking. If throttle lever is okay, go to next step. If throttle lever is no okay, repair or replace throttle lever as necessary.

3) Check speed control servo cable adjustment. See SPEED CONTROL SERVO CABLE under ADJUSTMENTS. Using NGS tester, clear continuous DTCs. Retrieve and document DTCs. If DTC C1109 is retrieved, replace speed control servo and repeat speed control servo self-test. If DTC C1109 is not retrieved, system is okay at this time.

TEST E: SPEED CONTROL SWITCH STUCK FOR 2 MINUTES OR LONGER (DTC C1126)

1) Using NGS tester, monitor speed control servo PIDs COAST, RESUME, SC_OFF, SC_ON, and SET/ACL. Press and release speed control switches. If NGS tester does not indicate ACTIVE with speed control switches pressed and NOTACT with speed control switches released, go to next step. If NGS tester indicates ACTIVE with speed control switches pressed and NOTACT with speed control switches released, system is okay at this time.

2) Turn ignition switch to LOCK position. Disconnect speed control switch harness connector. Turn ignition switch to RUN position. Using NGS tester, clear continuous DTCs. Wait 3 minutes. Retrieve and document continuous DTCs. If DTC C1126 is retrieved, go to next step. If DTC C1126 is not retrieved, replace speed control switch.

3) Turn ignition switch to LOCK position. Disconnect speed control servo harness connector C123 (located in left rear of engine compartment). Measure resistance between ground and terminal No. 5 (Light Blue/Black wire) at speed control servo harness connector C123. *See Fig. 1.* If resistance is 10 k/ohms or less, go to next step. If resistance is greater than 10 k/ohms, replace speed control servo.

NOTE: Disable air bag system. See DISABLING & ACTIVATING AIR BAG SYSTEM in appropriate AIR BAG RESTRAINT SYSTEMS article.

4) Disconnect clockspring harness connector C283 (located near base of steering column). Measure resistance between ground and terminal No. 5 (Light Blue/Black wire) at speed control servo harness connector C123. If resistance is greater than 10 k/ohms, replace air bag sliding contact. If resistance is 10 k/ohms or less, repair short to ground in Light Blue/Black wire.

TEST F: DEACTIVATOR SWITCH CIRCUIT FAILURE (DTC C1127)

NOTE: Deactivator switch may also be referred to as brake pressure switch.

1) Turn ignition switch to LOCK position. Disconnect speed control servo harness connector C123 (located in left rear of engine compartment). Measure voltage at terminal No. 9 (Orange wire) at speed control servo harness connector C123 while pressing and releasing brake pedal. *See Fig. 1.* Battery voltage should exist with brake pedal released and zero volts should exist with brake pedal depressed. If voltage is not as specified, go to next step. If voltage is as specified, replace speed control servo.

2) Disconnect deactivator switch harness connector C219 (located on brake pedal support). Measure voltage at terminal Light Green/Red wire at deactivator switch harness connector C219. If battery voltage exists, go to next step. If battery voltage does not exist, repair open or short in Light Green/Red wire.

3) Measure resistance in Orange wire between terminal No. 9 at speed control servo harness connector C123 and deactivator switch harness connector C219. If resistance is less than 5 ohms, replace deactivator switch. If resistance is 5 ohms or greater, repair open in Orange wire.

TEST G: SPEED CONTROL SERVO CABLE SLACK FAILURE (DTC C1179)

Check speed control servo cable adjustment. See SPEED CONTROL SERVO CABLE under ADJUSTMENTS. Using NGS tester, clear continuous DTCs. Retrieve and document DTCs. If DTC C1179 is retrieved, replace speed control servo. If DTC C1179 is not retrieved, system is okay at this time.

TEST H: SPEED CONTROL IS INOPERATIVE – NO DIAGNOSTIC TROUBLE CODES

1) Check horn operation by pressing steering wheel horn switch. If horn operates properly, go to next step. If horn does not operate properly, repair horn system as necessary. See appropriate wiring diagram in appropriate STEERING COLUMN SWITCHES article.

2) Turn ignition switch to LOCK position. Disconnect speed control servo harness connector C123 (located in left rear of engine compartment). Turn ignition switch to RUN position. Measure voltage at terminal No. 5 (Light Blue/Black wire) at speed control servo harness connector C123 while pressing speed control ON switch. *See Fig. 1.* If battery voltage exists, go to next step. If battery voltage does not exist, go to step **4)**.

3) Ensure ignition switch is in LOCK position. Measure resistance between terminals No. 5 (Light Blue/Black wire) and No. 6 (Dark Green/Orange wire) at speed control servo harness connector C123. *See Fig. 1.* Resistance should be 612-748 ohms when SET/ACCEL switch is pressed and greater than 10 k/ohms when SET/ACCEL switch is released. If resistance is as specified, replace speed control servo. If resistance is not as specified, repair wiring or replace speed control switch as necessary.

NOTE: Disable air bag system. See DISABLING & ACTIVATING AIR BAG SYSTEM in appropriate AIR BAG RESTRAINT SYSTEMS article.

4) Turn ignition switch to LOCK position. Disconnect clockspring harness connector C283. Measure resistance in Light Blue/Black wire between terminal No. 6 at clockspring harness connector and terminal No. 5 at speed control servo harness connector C123. If resistance is less than 5 ohms, go to next step. If resistance is 5 ohms or greater, repair open in Light Blue/Black wire.

5) Remove driver's side air bag. See appropriate AIR BAG RESTRAINT SYSTEMS article. If equipped with redundant steering wheel controls, measure resistance between terminal No. 6 at clockspring harness connector C283 (clockspring side) and terminal No. 6 at driver's side air bag connector (clockspring side). *See Fig. 2.* If not equipped with redundant steering wheel controls, measure resistance between terminal No. 6 at clockspring harness connector C283 (clockspring side) and

terminal No. 1 at driver's side air bag connector (clockspring side). *See Fig. 3.* If resistance is less than 1 ohm and equipped with redundant steering wheel controls, repair steering wheel harness or replace speed control switch as necessary. If resistance is less than 1 ohm and not equipped with redundant steering wheel controls, replace speed control switch. If resistance is 1 ohm or greater, replace clockspring.

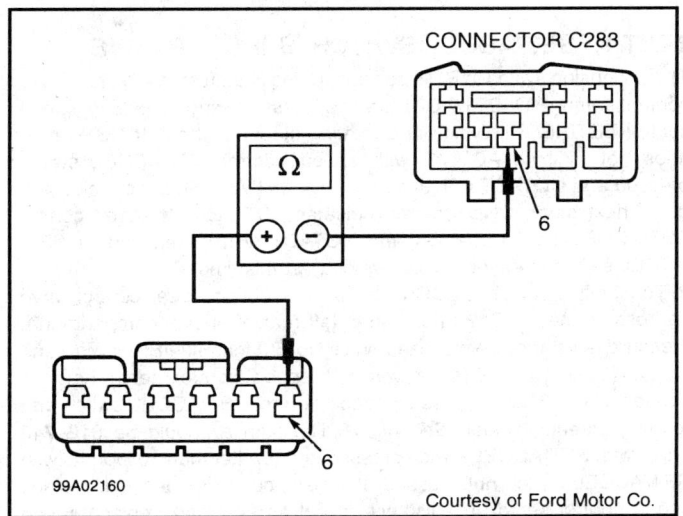

Fig. 2: Testing Clockspring With Redundant Steering Wheel Control

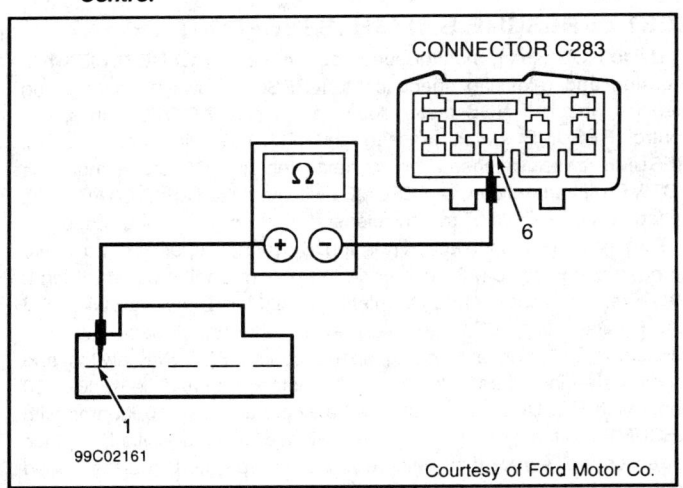

Fig. 3: Testing Clockspring Without Redundant Steering Wheel Control

TEST I: SET SPEED FLUCTUATES

Turn ignition switch to RUN position. Check throttle lever and speed control servo cable operation while performing speed control servo slack test using NGS tester. If throttle lever operates properly, replace speed control servo. If throttle lever does not operate properly, repair or replace components as necessary.

TEST J: COAST SWITCH IS INOPERATIVE

1) Turn ignition switch to RUN position. Using NGS tester, monitor speed control servo PID COAST while pressing and releasing speed control COAST switch and rotating steering wheel. If NGS tester does not indicate ACTIVE with speed control COAST switch pressed and NOTACT with speed control COAST switch released, go to next step. If NGS tester indicates ACTIVE with speed control COAST switch pressed and NOTACT with speed control COAST switch released, system is okay at this time.

2) Turn ignition switch to LOCK position. Disconnect speed control servo harness connector C123 (located in left rear of engine compartment). Measure resistance between terminals No. 5 (Light Blue/Black wire) and

No. 6 (Dark Green/Orange wire) at speed control servo harness connector C123 while pressing speed control COAST switch and rotating steering wheel. *See Fig. 1.* Resistance should be 105-135 ohms with COAST switch pressed and greater than 10 k/ohms with COAST switch not pressed. If resistance is as specified, replace speed control servo. If resistance is not as specified, replace speed control switch.

TEST K: SET/ACCEL SWITCH IS INOPERATIVE

1) Turn ignition switch to RUN position. Using NGS tester, monitor speed control servo PID SET/ACCEL while pressing and releasing speed control SET/ACCEL switch and rotating steering wheel. If NGS tester does not indicate ACTIVE with speed control SET/ACCEL switch pressed and NOTACT with speed control SET/ACCEL switch released, go to next step. If NGS tester indicates ACTIVE with speed control SET/ACCEL switch pressed and NOTACT with speed control SET/ACCEL switch released, system is okay at this time.

2) Turn ignition switch to LOCK position. Disconnect speed control servo harness connector C123 (located in left rear of engine compartment). Measure resistance between terminals No. 5 (Light Blue/Black wire) and No. 6 (Dark Green/Orange wire) at speed control servo harness connector C123 while pressing speed control SET/ACCEL switch and rotating steering wheel. *See Fig. 1.* Resistance should be 612–748 ohms with SET/ACCEL switch pressed and greater than 10 k/ohms with SET/ACCEL switch not pressed. If resistance is as specified, replace speed control servo. If resistance is not as specified, replace speed control switch.

TEST L: RESUME SWITCH IS INOPERATIVE

1) Using NGS tester, monitor speed control servo PID RESUME while pressing and releasing speed control RESUME switch and rotating steering wheel. If NGS tester does not indicate ACTIVE with speed control RESUME switch pressed and NOTACT with speed control RESUME switch released, go to next step. If NGS tester indicates ACTIVE with speed control RESUME switch pressed and NOTACT with speed control RESUME switch released, system is perating properly.

2) Turn ignition switch to LOCK position. Disconnect speed control servo harness connector C123 (located in left rear of engine compartment). Measure resistance between terminals No. 5 (Light Blue/Black wire) and No. 6 (Dark Green/Orange wire) at speed control servo harness connector C123 while pressing speed control RESUME switch and rotating steering wheel. *See Fig. 1.* Resistance should be 1980-2420 ohms with RESUME switch pressed and greater than 10 k/ohms with RESUME switch not pressed. If resistance is as specified, replace speed control servo. If resistance is not as specified, replace speed control switch.

TEST M: OFF SWITCH IS INOPERATIVE

1) Using NGS tester, monitor speed control servo PID SC_OFF while pressing and releasing speed control OFF switch and rotating steering wheel. If NGS tester does not indicate ACTIVE with speed control OFF switch pressed and NOTACT with speed control OFF switch released, go to next step. If NGS tester indicates ACTIVE with speed control OFF switch pressed and NOTACT with speed control OFF switch released, system is operating properly.

2) Turn ignition switch to LOCK position. Disconnect speed control servo harness connector C123 (located in left rear of engine compartment). Measure resistance between terminals No. 5 (Light Blue/Black wire) and No. 6 (Dark Green/Orange wire) at speed control servo harness connector C123 while pressing speed control OFF switch and rotating steering wheel. *See Fig. 1.* Resistance should be less than 5 ohms with OFF switch pressed and greater than 10 k/ohms with OFF switch not pressed. If resistance is as specified, replace speed control servo. If resistance is not as specified, replace speed control switch.

REMOVAL & INSTALLATION

WARNING: Deactivate air bag system before working around steering column. See appropriate AIR BAG RESTRAINT SYSTEMS article.

CAUTION: When battery is disconnected or modules are replaced, vehicle computer and memory systems may lose memory data. Driveability problems may exist until computer systems have completed a relearn cycle. See COMPUTER RELEARN PROCEDURES article in GENERAL INFORMATION before disconnecting battery.

SPEED CONTROL SWITCHES

Removal & Installation (With Redundant Steering Wheel Controls) – Disconnect negative battery cable. Carefully pry speed control switches from steering wheel. Disconnect harness connectors from speed control switches, and remove switches. To install, reverse removal procedure.

Removal & Installation (Without Redundant Steering Wheel Controls) – Disable air bag system and remove driver side air bag module. See appropriate AIR BAG RESTRAINT SYSTEMS article. Ensure front wheels are in straight-ahead position. Remove steering wheel retaining bolt and remove steering wheel. Tape air bag sliding contact to steering column to prevent misalignment. Remove steering wheel trim. Remove switches from steering wheel. To install, reverse removal procedure.

DEACTIVATOR SWITCH

Removal – Disconnect negative battery cable. Disconnect deactivator switch harness connector. Rotate deactivator switch counterclockwise. Remove deactivator switch.

Installation – Pull deactivator switch plunger out to its full travel. Fully depress brake pedal. Install deactivator switch and rotate clockwise. Connect deactivator switch harness connector. Slowly release brake pedal. Reconnect negative battery cable.

SPEED CONTROL SERVO

Removal & Installation – Disconnect negative battery cable. Remove engine cover. Remove speed control servo cable from throttle lever. Press cable cap locking tab and rotate cap counterclockwise to remove. Remove cable ball slug from pulley. Disconnect speed control servo harness connector. Remove retaining nuts and servo. Separate speed control servo from bracket if necessary. To install, reverse removal procedure.

WIRING DIAGRAMS

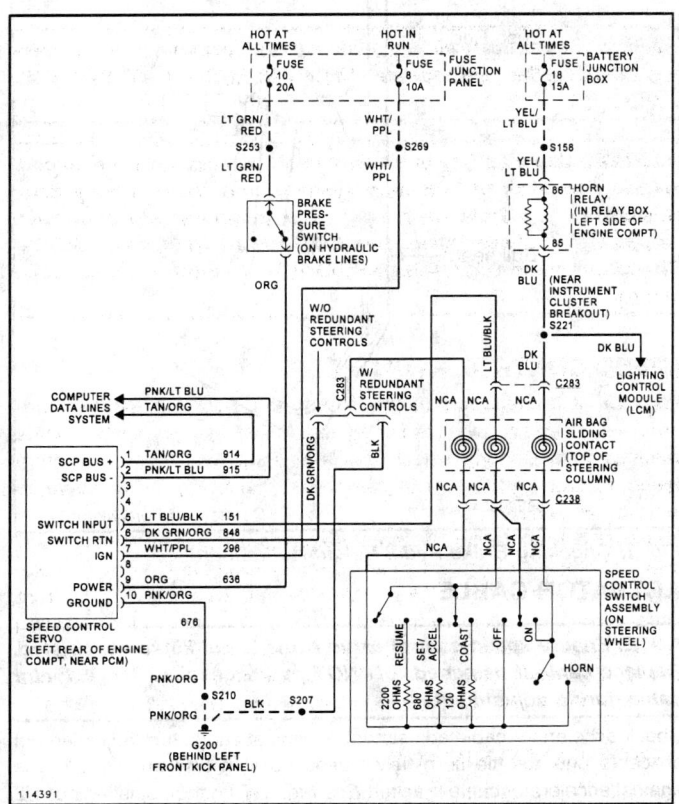

Fig. 4: Cruise Control System Wiring Diagram (Town Car)

DESCRIPTION

Speed control system is electronically controlled and vacuum operated. Major components of speed control system include actuator, servo, amplifier, relays, control switches, Brake Pedal Position (BPP) switch, deactivator switch, air bag sliding contact (clockspring), Transmission Range (TR) switch, and Vehicle Speed Sensor (VSS). Speed control system is operational only at speeds greater than 30 MPH.

OPERATION

Speed control system is activated when ON switch is pressed and COAST/SET button is pressed. Vehicle will maintain set speed until new speed is set, brake pedal is depressed, CANCEL button is pressed, gear selector is placed in Neutral, or OFF switch is pressed. If system has been deactivated by process other than pressing OFF switch, set speed can be regained by pressing and releasing RES/ACCEL button.

If a malfunction is detected in speed control system, system will automatically cancel. CRUISE indicator on instrument cluster will flash, warning driver of problem. Speed control deactivator switch provides an additional safety feature. When brake pedal is depressed, a signal is sent from deactivator switch to amplifier to deactivate operation.

COMPONENT LOCATIONS

COMPONENT LOCATIONS

Component	Location
Air Bag Sliding Contact	In Steering Wheel
Data Link Connector (DLC)	Below Driver's Side Of Instrument Panel, To Right Of Steering Column
Deactivator Switch	At Brake Pedal
Engine Compartment Relay Box	Left Front Side Of Engine Compartment
Fuse Junction Panel	Below Left Side Of Instrument Panel
Horn Relay	Engine Compartment Relay Box
INHIBIT Relay	Engine Compartment Relay Box
Power Distribution Box	In Engine Compartment, Next To Battery
Powertrain Control Module (PCM)	Behind Glove Box
Smart Entry Control (SEC) Timer/Module	Behind Center Top Of Dash Panel
Speed Control Actuator	Left Side Of Engine Compartment
Speed Control Actuator Module	Below Left Side Of Instrument Panel
Speed Control HOLD Relay	Engine Compartment Relay Box
Transaxle Control Module (TCM)	Behind Instrument Cluster
Vehicle Speed Sensor (VSS)	Center Of Engine Compartment

ADJUSTMENTS

BRAKE PEDAL HEIGHT

1) Check brake pedal height by measuring from center of rubber brake pedal pad to bulkhead below carpet. See Fig. 1. Brake pedal height should be 7.68-8.07″ (195-205 mm).
2) If brake pedal height is not as specified, loosen brake pedal push rod lock nut. Turn push rod until pedal height is as specified. Tighten brake pedal push rod lock nut to 12-16 ft. lbs. (16-22 N.m).

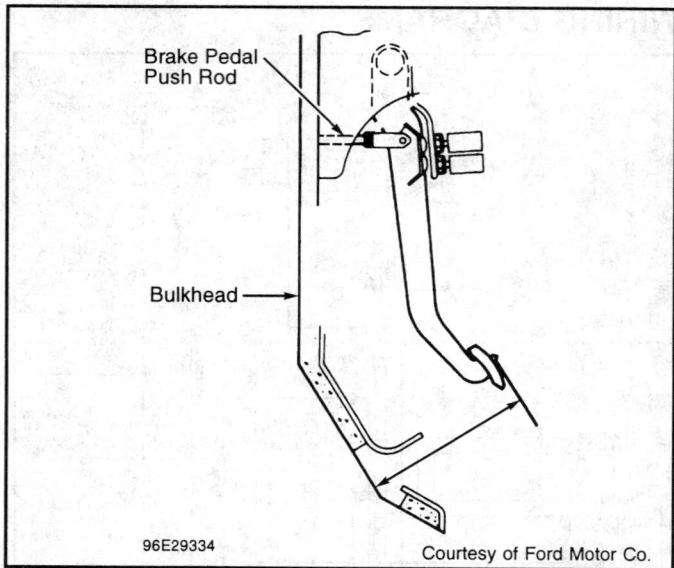

Fig. 1: Checking Brake Pedal Height Adjustment

ACTUATOR CABLE

NOTE: Ensure speed control servo cable is not kinked or twisted. Replace cable if damaged. DO NOT pull excessively on actuator cable during adjustment.

Check accelerator cable adjustment. To adjust cable, turn adjusting nut on cable until throttle is in fully closed position and adjusting nut is against accelerator cable bracket. See Fig. 2. Turn the adjusting nut 1/2 to 1 turn counterclockwise. Tighten speed control actuator cable lock nut to 71-97 INCH lbs. (8-11 N.m). A slight amount of slack should exist with throttle fully closed. Test speed control system for proper operation.

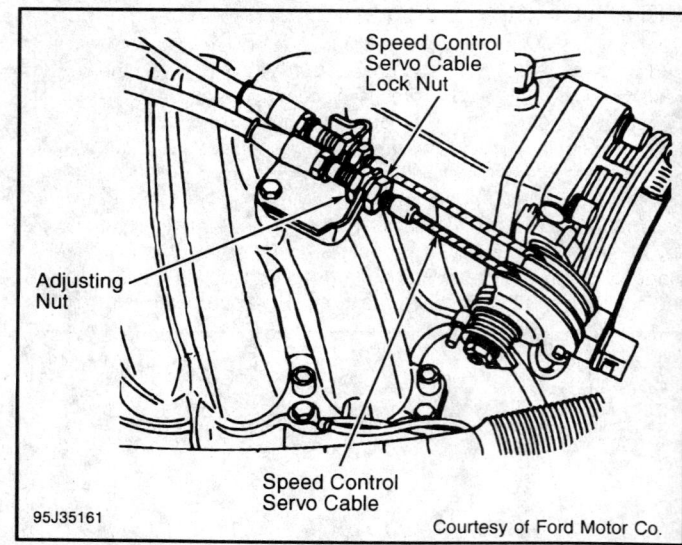

Fig. 2: Adjusting Speed Control Servo Cable

SPEED CONTROL DEACTIVATOR SWITCH & BRAKE ON/OFF SWITCH

Adjust brake pedal height. See BRAKE PEDAL HEIGHT. Measure distance between brake pedal stopper and threaded end of speed control deactivator or BPP switch. See Fig. 3. Distance should be .012-.039″ (0.3-1.0 mm). If distance is not as specified, loosen appropriate switch lock nut. Adjust switch until distance is as specified. Tighten lock nut to 9-11 ft. lbs. (12-15 N.m).

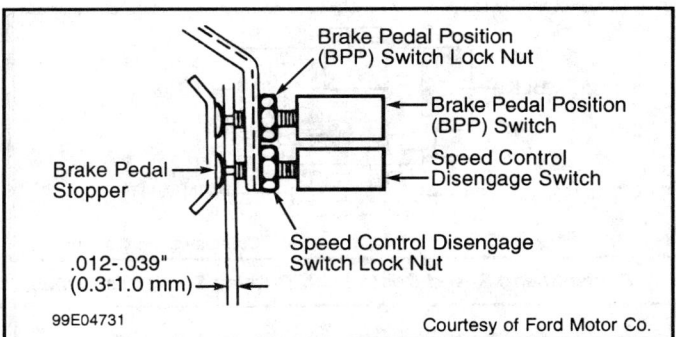

Fig. 3: Adjusting BPP & Speed Control Deactivator Switches

TROUBLE SHOOTING

Before proceeding with testing, perform a visual check of the following:
- Vacuum leaks at actuator.
- Incorrect actuator cable adjustment.
- Damaged or binding actuator cable.
- Faulty fuses.
- Loose or corroded connections.
- Damaged wiring harness.
- Damaged or misadjusted switches.
- Damaged or corroded relays.
- Damaged or misadjusted brake pedal.
- Damaged or misadjusted Transmission Range (TR) switch.

Verify speedometer, horn and stoplights function properly. Repair as necessary. Inspect actuator cable and throttle cable/linkage for smooth operation. Repair as necessary. If no problems are found, perform road test to verify problem. Perform appropriate system test. See SYMPTOM INDEX table under SYSTEM TESTS.

COMPONENT TESTS

SPEED CONTROL HOLD OR INHIBIT RELAY

1) Using an ohmmeter, measure resistance between relay terminals No. 1 and 2. *See Fig. 4 or 5.* If resistance is 100-150 ohms, go to next step. If resistance is not 100-150 ohms, replace appropriate relay.

2) Check continuity between all other terminals, except terminal No. 1 and 2. If continuity exists in any measurement, replace relay. If continuity does not exist in any measurement, go to next step.

3) Remove ohmmeter and apply battery voltage to relay terminals No. 1, 3 and 6. Apply ground to relay terminal No. 2. Check for voltage between relay terminals No. 2 and 7 and between No. 2 and 5 or 4. If battery voltage exists in both measurements, relay is okay. If battery voltage does not exist at either measurement, replace appropriate relay.

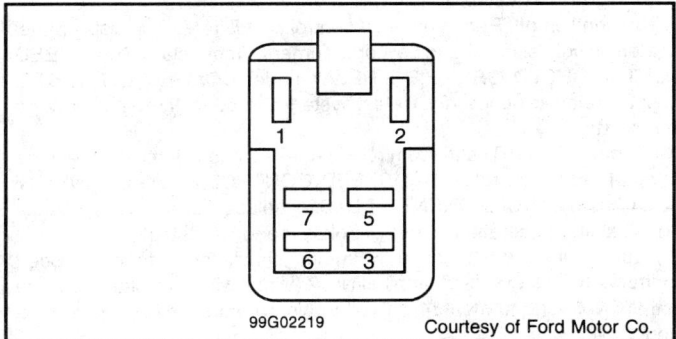

Fig. 4: Identifying Speed Control HOLD Relay Terminals

SPEED CONTROL SWITCH ASSEMBLY

Turn ignition off. Access speed control switch electrical connector but do not disconnect connector. Check for voltage at Purple/Orange wire and Yellow/Blue wire terminals of speed control switch while pressing buttons as specified. See SPEED CONTROL SWITCH VOLTAGE

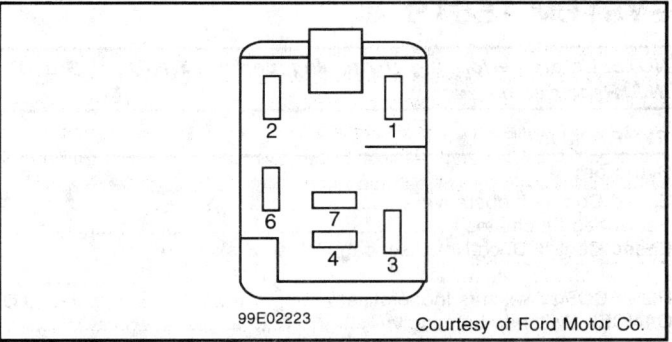

Fig. 5: Identifying INHIBIT Relay Terminals

SPECIFICATIONS table. Press only one button at a time. If voltages are as specified, go to SYMPTOM TESTS and resume testing at last step completed. If voltages are not as specified, replace speed control switch.

SPEED CONTROL SWITCH VOLTAGE SPECIFICATIONS

Button	Volts
No Button Pressed	
Purple/Orange Wire	Less Than One
Yellow/Blue Wire	Less Than One
CANCEL Pressed	
Purple/Orange Wire	More Than 5
Yellow/Blue Wire	More Than 5
COAST/SET Pressed	
Purple/Orange Wire	Less Than One
Yellow/Blue Wire	More Than 10
RES/ACCEL Pressed	
Purple/Orange Wire	More Than 10
Yellow/Blue Wire	Less Than One

SPEED CONTROL ACTUATOR

1) Turn ignition off. Disconnect speed control actuator 4-pin connector. Using a jumper wire, connect terminal No. 2 of speed control actuator component to positive battery terminal. *See Fig. 6.* Connect a second jumper wire from terminal No. 3 of actuator component to negative battery terminal. Speed control actuator should operate.

2) With terminal No. 2 still connected to positive battery terminal, connect terminals No. 1, 3 and 4 to negative battery terminal. Speed control actuator should pull in. Leaving all other jumpers connected, remove jumper wire from terminal No. 3 of actuator connector. Speed control actuator should remain pulled in.

3) Leaving all other jumpers connected, remove jumper wire from terminal No. 2 of actuator connector. Speed control actuator should release immediately. If speed control actuator operates as specified, if sent here from a system test, return to appropriate test and resume testing at last step completed. If speed control actuator does not operate as specified, replace speed control actuator.

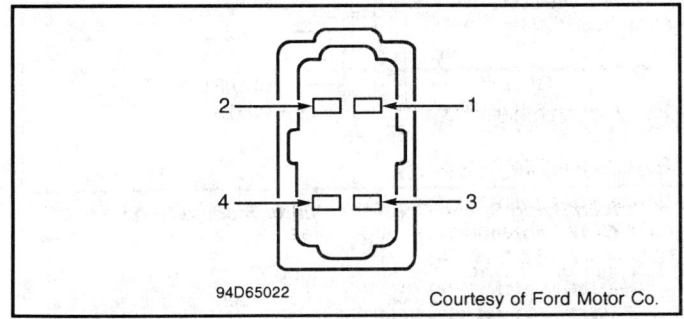

Fig. 6: Identifying Speed Control Actuator Terminals

SYSTEM TESTS

NOTE: Before performing any testing, perform TROUBLE SHOOTING. Repair as necessary.

SYMPTOM INDEX

Symptom	Test
Speed Control Inoperative	A
Set Speed Fluctuates	
Speed Control Does Not Disengage When Brakes Are Applied	1
RES/ACCEL Switch Is Inoperative	C
CANCEL Switch Is Inoperative	D
OFF Switch Is Inoperative	2
CRUISE Light Always ON	E
Cruise Switch Indicator Light Always On Or Off	F

1 – Ensure voltage exists with brake pedal depressed at speed control actuator module connector terminal No. 20 (Yellow/Black wire) and not at terminal No. 16 (Blue/White wire). If voltage is not as specified, repair appropriate circuit. See WIRING DIAGRAMS. If voltage is as specified, replace speed control actuator module.
2 – Install NEW speed control actuator switch. See SPEED CONTROL SWITCH ASSEMBLY under REMOVAL & INSTALLATION.

TEST A: SPEED CONTROL INOPERATIVE

WARNING: Disable air bag system before working around steering column or removing any air bag system component. See AIR BAG RESTRAINT SYSTEMS – VILLAGER article.

1) Turn ignition off. Disconnect speed control actuator module connector C247 located under center of dash. Turn ignition on. Using a voltmeter, check voltage between ground and speed control actuator module connector C247 terminal No. 15 (Green/White wire) while pressing buttons of speed control (ON/OFF) switch. Press ON switch. *See Fig. 7.* Voltage should be more than 10 volts. Press OFF switch. Voltage should be less than one volt. If voltages are as specified, go to step **8)**. If voltages are not as specified, go to next step.
2) Turn ignition off. Remove speed control HOLD relay from relay panel located in left side of engine compartment. Test relay. See SPEED CONTROL HOLD RELAY under COMPONENT TESTS. Replace relay as necessary. Retest system operation. If relay is okay, go to next step.
3) Turn ignition on. Check voltage between ground and speed control HOLD relay socket terminal No. 5 (Blue wire). *See Fig. 8.* If voltage is more than 10 volts, go to next step. If voltage is 10 volts or less, repair Blue wire between speed control HOLD relay and power distribution box.

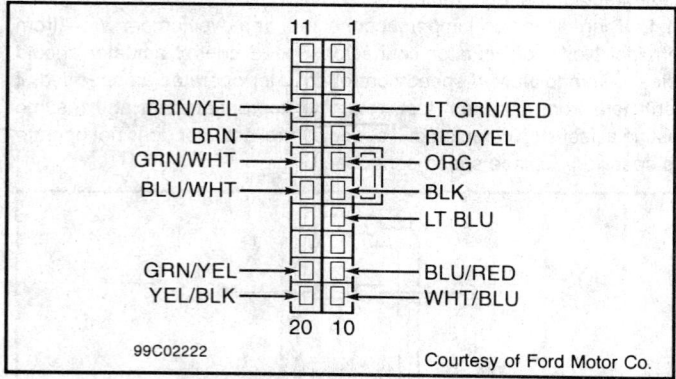

99C02222   Courtesy of Ford Motor Co.

Fig. 7: Identifying Speed Control Actuator Module Connector C247 Terminals

4) Turn ignition off. Disconnect speed control ON/OFF switch connector C262. Turn ignition on. Check voltage between ground and speed control (ON/OFF) switch connector C262 terminal No. 7 (Blue wire). *See Fig. 9.* If voltage is more than 10 volts, go to next step. If voltage is 10 volts or less, repair Blue wire between speed control (ON/OFF) switch fuse junction panel.

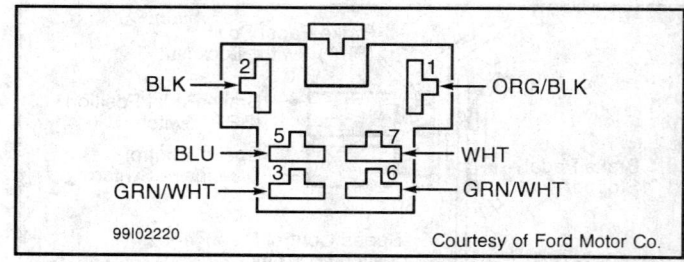

99I02220   Courtesy of Ford Motor Co.

Fig. 8: Identifying Speed Control HOLD Relay Socket Terminals

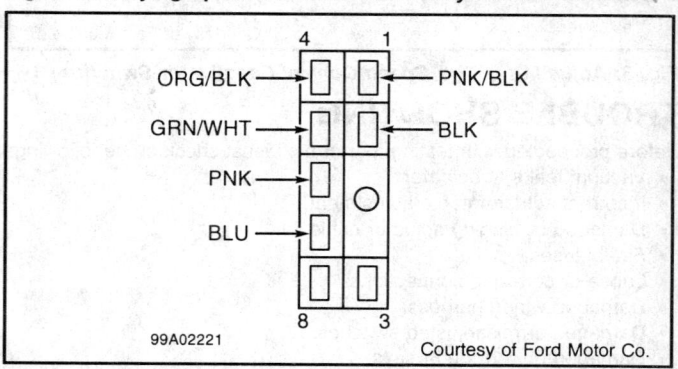

99A02221   Courtesy of Ford Motor Co.

Fig. 9: Identifying Speed Control ON/OFF Switch Connector Terminals

5) Turn ignition off. Using an ohmmeter, check resistance in Orange/Black wire between speed control HOLD relay socket terminal No. 1 and speed control ON/OFF switch connector C262 terminal No. 4. If resistance is less than 5 ohms, go to next step. If resistance is 5 ohms or more, repair open Orange/Black wire.
6) Check resistance in Green/White wire between speed control HOLD relay socket terminal No. 3 and speed control ON/OFF switch connector C262 terminal No. 5. Check resistance in Green/White wire between speed control actuator module connector C247 terminal No. 15 and speed control ON/OFF switch connector C262 terminal No. 5. *See Figs. 7-9.* If resistance is less than 5 ohms in both measurements, go to next step. If resistance is 5 ohms or more in either measurement, repair open in appropriate Green/White wire. Retest system operation.
7) Check resistance between ground and speed control HOLD relay socket terminal No. 2 (Black wire). If resistance is less than 5 ohms, replace speed control ON/OFF switch. If resistance is 5 ohms or more, repair open in Black wire. See WIRING DIAGRAMS.
8) Ensure ignition is on. Check voltage between ground and speed control actuator module connector C247 terminal No. 16 (Blue/White wire). If voltage is more than 10 volts, go to step **16)**. If voltage is 10 volts or less, go to next step.
9) Turn ignition off. Remove speed control HOLD relay from relay panel located in left side of engine compartment. Test relay. See SPEED CONTROL HOLD OR INHIBIT RELAY under COMPONENT TESTS. Replace relay as necessary. Retest system operation. If relay is okay, go to next step.
10) Remove INHIBIT relay from relay panel located in left side of engine compartment. Test relay. See SPEED CONTROL HOLD OR INHIBIT RELAY under COMPONENT TESTS. Replace relay as necessary. Retest system operation. If relay is okay, go to next step.
11) Turn ignition on. Using a voltmeter, check for voltage at speed control HOLD relay socket terminal No. 7 (White wire) . If voltage is more than 10 volts, go to step **14)**. If voltage is not as specified, go to next step.
12) Turn ignition off. Disconnect speed control deactivator switch connector. Deactivator switch connector is located at brake pedal support. Using a ohmmeter, check resistance of White wire between speed control deactivator switch connector and speed control HOLD relay socket terminal No. 7. If resistance is less than 5 ohms, go to next step. If resistance 5 ohms or more, repair White wire. Retest system operation.

13) Turn ignition on. Using a voltmeter, check for voltage between ground and speed control deactivator switch connector Blue wire terminal. If voltage is more than 10 volts, replace speed control deactivator switch. Retest system operation. If voltage is 10 volts or less, repair Blue wire. Retest system operation.

14) Turn ignition off. Using an ohmmeter, check resistance in Green/White wire between speed control HOLD relay socket terminal No. 6 and INHIBIT relay socket terminal No. 4. *See Figs. 4 and 5.* If resistance is less than 5 ohms, go to next step. If resistance is 5 ohms or more, repair Green/White wire. Retest system operation.

15) Check resistance in Blue/White wire between INHIBIT relay socket terminal No. 3 and speed control actuator module connector C247 terminal No. 16. If resistance is less than 5 ohms, check starting circuit wiring, see STARTERS – VILLAGER article in STARTING & CHARGING SYSTEMS to continue diagnosis. If resistance is 5 ohms or more, repair Blue/White wire. Retest system operation.

16) Turn ignition off. Disconnect instrument cluster connector C266B (C267A on electronic instrument clusters). Using an ohmmeter, check resistance in Green/Yellow wire between instrument cluster connector C266B terminal No. 4 (C267A terminal No. 6 on electronic instrument clusters) and speed control actuator module connector C247 terminal No. 19. *See Fig. 10 or 11.* If resistances is less than 5 ohms, go to next step. If resistance is 5 ohms or more, repair Green/Yellow wire. Retest system operation.

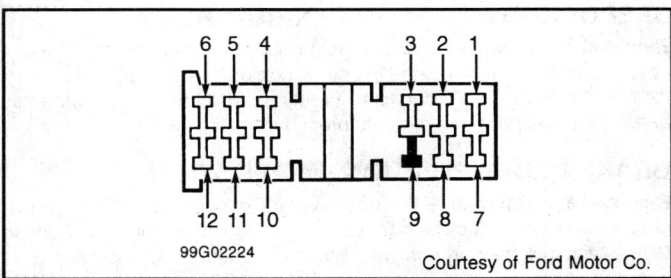

Fig. 10: Identifying Instrument Cluster Connector C266B Terminals

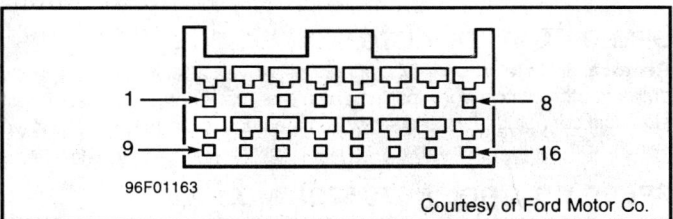

Fig. 11: Identifying Electronic Instrument Cluster Connector C267A Terminals

17) Disconnect speed control actuator connector C127. Check resistance of wires between speed control actuator connector C127 and speed control actuator module connector C247. See SPEED CONTROL ACTUATOR CIRCUITS table. *See Figs. 6 and 7.* If all resistances are less than 5 ohms between module and actuator, go to next step. If any resistance measurement is 5 ohms or more, repair open in appropriate circuit. Retest system operation.

SPEED CONTROL ACTUATOR CIRCUITS

Wire Color	Module Terminal	Actuator Terminal
Brown	14	2
Light Blue	7	3
Brown/Yellow	13	4
Orange/Green	5	1

18) Check resistance of speed control actuator circuits between speed control actuator module connector C247 and ground. See SPEED CONTROL ACTUATOR CIRCUITS table for terminal and wire color

identification. If all resistance measurements are more than 10 k/ohms, go to next step. If all resistance measurements are not more than 10 k/ohms, repair short to ground in appropriate circuit. Retest system operation.

19) Disconnect inlet port vacuum line from speed control vacuum canister (located underneath vacuum canister). Connect fused jumper between positive battery terminal and speed control actuator connector pin No. 2 (component side). Attach ground to speed control actuator connector pin No. 3 (component side). Speed control actuator should operate. If speed control actuator operates, go to next step. If speed control actuator does not operate, replace speed control actuator.

20) With pin No. 2 still connected to positive battery terminal, connect pins No. 1, 3 and 4 to ground. Speed control actuator should pull in. If speed control actuator pulls in, go to next step. If speed control actuator does not pull in, replace speed control actuator.

21) Leaving all other jumpers connected, remove jumper wire from pin No. 3 of actuator. Speed control actuator should remain pulled in. If speed control actuator remains pulled in, go to next step. If speed control actuator does not remain pulled in, replace speed control actuator.

22) Leaving all other jumpers connected, remove jumper wire from pin No. 2 of actuator. Speed control actuator should release immediately. If speed control actuator operates as specified, go to next step. If speed control actuator does not operate as specified, replace speed control actuator.

23) Turn ignition on. Check voltage between ground and speed control actuator module connector C247 terminal No. 10 (White/Blue wire). If voltage is more than 10 volts with SET/COAST switch pressed and zero volts with SET/COAST switch released, go to step **26)**. If voltage is not more than 10 volts with SET/COAST switch pressed or not zero volts with SET/COAST switch released, go to next step

24) Turn ignition off. Remove driver's air bag. See AIR BAG RESTRAINTS SYSTEMS – VILLAGER article. Disconnect speed control actuator switch in steering wheel. Check resistance of White/Blue wire between speed control actuator switch and speed control actuator module connector terminal No. 10. If resistance is less than 5 ohms, replace speed control actuator switch. If resistance is 5 ohms or more, go to next step.

25) Disconnect air bag sliding contact connector C214. Using an ohmmeter, check resistance in White/Blue wire between speed control actuator module connector C247 terminal No. 10 and air bag sliding contact connector C214. If resistance is less than 5 ohms, replace air bag sliding contact. If resistance is 5 ohms or more, repair White/Blue wire. Retest system operation.

26) Disconnect Brake Pedal Position (BPP) switch. Check resistance between ground and speed control actuator module connector C247 terminal No. 20 (Yellow/Black wire). If resistance is less than 20 ohms, replace speed control actuator module. If resistance is 20 ohms, repair open Yellow/Black wire. Retest system operation.

TEST B: SET SPEED FLUCTUATES

1) Observe speedometer while test driving vehicle at a constant speed of 40-55 MPH. If speedometer does not display a constant speed, diagnose and repair speedometer as necessary. See appropriate INSTRUMENT PANELS article. If speedometer displays a constant speed, go to next step.

2) Test speed control actuator. See SPEED CONTROL ACTUATOR under COMPONENT TESTS. If speed control actuator is okay, replace speed control actuator module and retest system operation. If speed control actuator is not okay, replace speed control actuator and retest system operation.

TEST C: RES/ACCEL SWITCH IS INOPERATIVE

WARNING: Disable air bag system before working around steering column or removing any air bag system component. See AIR BAG RESTRAINT SYSTEMS – VILLAGER article.

1) Turn ignition off. Disconnect speed control actuator module connector C247. Check voltage between ground and speed control actuator module connector C247 terminal No. 9 (Blue/Red wire) while pushing and releasing RES/ACCEL switch. *See Fig. 7.* If voltage is more than 10 volts with RES/ACCEL switch pressed and zero volts with RES/ACCEL switch released, replace speed control actuator module and retest system operation. If voltage is not more than 10 volts with RES/ACCEL switch pressed or not zero volts with RES/ACCEL switch released, go to next step.

2) Remove driver's air bag. See AIR BAG RESTRAINT SYSTEMS – VILLAGER article. Disconnect speed control actuator switch in steering wheel. Check resistance of Blue/Red wire between speed control actuator switch and speed control actuator module connector terminal No. 9. If resistance is less than 5 ohms, replace speed control actuator switch. If resistance is 5 ohms or more, go to next step.

3) Disconnect air bag sliding contact connector C214. Using an ohmmeter, check resistance in Blue/Red wire between speed control actuator module connector C247 terminal No. 9 and air bag sliding contact connector C214. If resistance is less than 5 ohms, replace air bag sliding contact. If resistance is 5 ohms or more, repair Blue/Red wire. Retest system operation.

TEST D: CANCEL SWITCH IS INOPERATIVE

WARNING: Disable air bag system before working around steering column or removing any air bag system component. See AIR BAG RESTRAINT SYSTEMS – VILLAGER article.

1) Turn ignition off. Disconnect speed control actuator module connector. Check voltage between ground and speed control actuator module connector terminal No. 9 (Blue/Red wire) and No. 10 (White/Blue wire) while pushing and releasing CANCEL switch. *See Fig. 7.* If voltage is more than 10 volts with CANCEL switch pressed and zero volts with CANCEL switch released in both measurements, replace speed control actuator module and retest system operation. If voltage is not more than 10 volts with CANCEL switch pressed or not zero volts with CANCEL switch released in either measurements, go to next step.

2) Remove driver's air bag. See AIR BAG RESTRAINT SYSTEMS – VILLAGER article. Disconnect speed control actuator switch in steering wheel. Check resistance of Blue/Red wire between speed control actuator switch and speed control actuator module connector terminal No. 9. If resistance is less than 5 ohms, replace speed control actuator switch. If resistance is 5 ohms or more, go to next step.

3) Disconnect air bag sliding contact connector C214. Using an ohmmeter, check resistance in Blue/Red wire between speed control actuator module connector C247 terminal No. 9 and air bag sliding contact connector C214. If resistance is less than 5 ohms, replace air bag sliding contact. If resistance is 5 ohms or more, repair Blue/Red wire. Retest system operation.

TEST E: CRUISE LIGHT ALWAYS ON

1) Turn ignition off. Disconnect speed control actuator module connector. Turn ignition on. If CRUISE light is illuminated, go to next step. If CRUISE light goes out, replace speed control actuator module.

2) Turn ignition off. Disconnect instrument cluster connector C266B (C267A on electronic instrument clusters). Check voltage between ground and speed control actuator module connector terminal No. 4 (Red/Yellow wire). *See Fig. 7.* If any voltage is present, repair short to voltage in Red/Yellow wire. If no voltage is present, go to appropriate INSTRUMENT PANELS article.

TEST F: SPEED CONTROL ACTUATOR SWITCH INDICATOR LIGHT ALWAYS ON OR OFF

1) If speed control actuator switch light is always on, replace speed control actuator switch and retest system. If speed control actuator switch light is always off, go to next step.

2) Turn ignition off. Disconnect speed control actuator switch connector C262. Depress brake pedal. Using an ohmmeter, check resistance between ground and speed control actuator switch connector C262 terminal No. 2 (Black wire). If resistance is less than 5 ohms, replace speed control actuator switch and retest system. If resistance is 5 ohms or more, repair open Black wire.

REMOVAL & INSTALLATION

WARNING: Disable air bag system before working around steering column or removing any air bag system component. See AIR BAG RESTRAINT SYSTEMS – VILLAGER article.

CAUTION: When battery is disconnected, vehicle computer and memory systems may lose memory data. Driveability problems may exist until computer systems have completed a relearn cycle. See COMPUTER RELEARN PROCEDURES article in GENERAL INFORMATION before disconnecting battery.

AIR BAG SLIDING CONTACT

Removal & Installation – 1) Disconnect negative battery cable and wait 10 minutes for back-up power supply to be depleted. Remove steering wheel. Place match marks and tape inner and outer elements of air bag sliding contact in place. Remove 2 lower steering column shroud screws and remove lower steering column shroud. Loosen gear selector boot and position upper steering column shroud aside.

2) Remove air bag sliding contact screws. Pull air bag sliding contact off steering column shaft, and position aside. Disconnect air bag sliding contact electrical connectors and remove air bag sliding contact from steering column. To install, reverse removal procedure. Ensure match marks on inner and outer elements are properly aligned.

SPEED CONTROL HOLD & INHIBIT RELAYS

Removal & Installation – Disconnect negative battery cable. Remove cover from relay panel located in engine compartment in front of battery. Remove SPEED CONTROL HOLD relay and INHIBIT relay from relay panel. To install, reverse removal procedure.

BRAKE PEDAL POSITION (BPP) SWITCH

Removal & Installation – Squeeze Brake Pedal Position (BPP) switch electrical connector lock tabs to disconnect electrical connector. Loosen BPP switch lock nut and remove switch from brake pedal. *See Fig. 3.* To install, reverse removal procedure. Adjust BPP switch. See SPEED CONTROL DEACTIVATOR SWITCH & BRAKE ON/OFF SWITCH under ADJUSTMENTS.

SPEED CONTROL ACTUATOR SWITCH

Removal & Installation – Disconnect negative battery cable. Carefully pull actuator switch from instrument panel just enough to disconnect electrical connector. Disconnect switch electrical connector and remove switch from instrument panel. To install, reverse removal procedure.

SPEED CONTROL ACTUATOR MODULE

Removal & Installation – 1) Disconnect negative battery cable. Remove front seat trim panels. Slide front seats fully forward to gain access to rear seat tract bolts. Remove rear seat tract bolts. Slide front seats to rear to gain access to front seat tract bolts. Remove front seat tract bolts.

2) Disconnect seat module and sensor connectors, if equipped. Remove front seats. Remove right and left scuff plates. Remove right and left "A" pillar lower trim moldings. Remove console covers.

3) Remove both side kick panels. Remove accelerator stopper cover. Remove rear seat center air flow ducts. Move aside front carpet. Remove 10 bolts and heat duct cover. Remove rear seat right air flow duct.

4) Remove rear seat air flow duct outlet. Remove speed control actuator module connector and module. To install, reverse removal procedure.

SPEED CONTROL DEACTIVATOR SWITCH

Removal & Installation – Squeeze deactivator switch electrical connector lock tabs to disconnect electrical connector. Loosen deactivator switch lock nut and remove switch from brake pedal. *See Fig. 3.* To install, reverse removal procedure. Adjust deactivator switch. See SPEED CONTROL DEACTIVATOR SWITCH & BRAKE ON/OFF SWITCH under ADJUSTMENTS.

SPEED CONTROL ACTUATOR

Removal & Installation – Disconnect negative battery cable. Loosen actuator (servo) cable lock nut. *See Fig. 2*. Remove actuator cable from throttle lever. Disconnect actuator electrical connector. Remove actuator mounting bracket bolts. Remove actuator from vehicle. To install, reverse removal procedure. Adjust actuator cable. See ACTUATOR CABLE under ADJUSTMENTS.

SPEED CONTROL SWITCH ASSEMBLY

Removal & Installation – Remove speed control switch assembly cover from left rear side of steering wheel. Remove 2 speed control switch mounting screws from steering wheel. Control switch electrical connector is mounted to steering wheel. Gently move switch up and down, while pulling it away from steering wheel, to disconnect electrical connector. Remove speed control switch from steering wheel. To install, reverse removal procedure.

VEHICLE SPEED SENSOR (VSS)

Removal & Installation – Locate Vehicle Speed Sensor (VSS) on upper rear portion of transaxle housing. Disconnect negative battery cable. Raise and support vehicle. Disconnect VSS electrical connector. Remove VSS hold-down bracket bolt and remove hold-down bracket. Remove VSS from transaxle. To install, reverse removal procedure.

WIRING DIAGRAMS

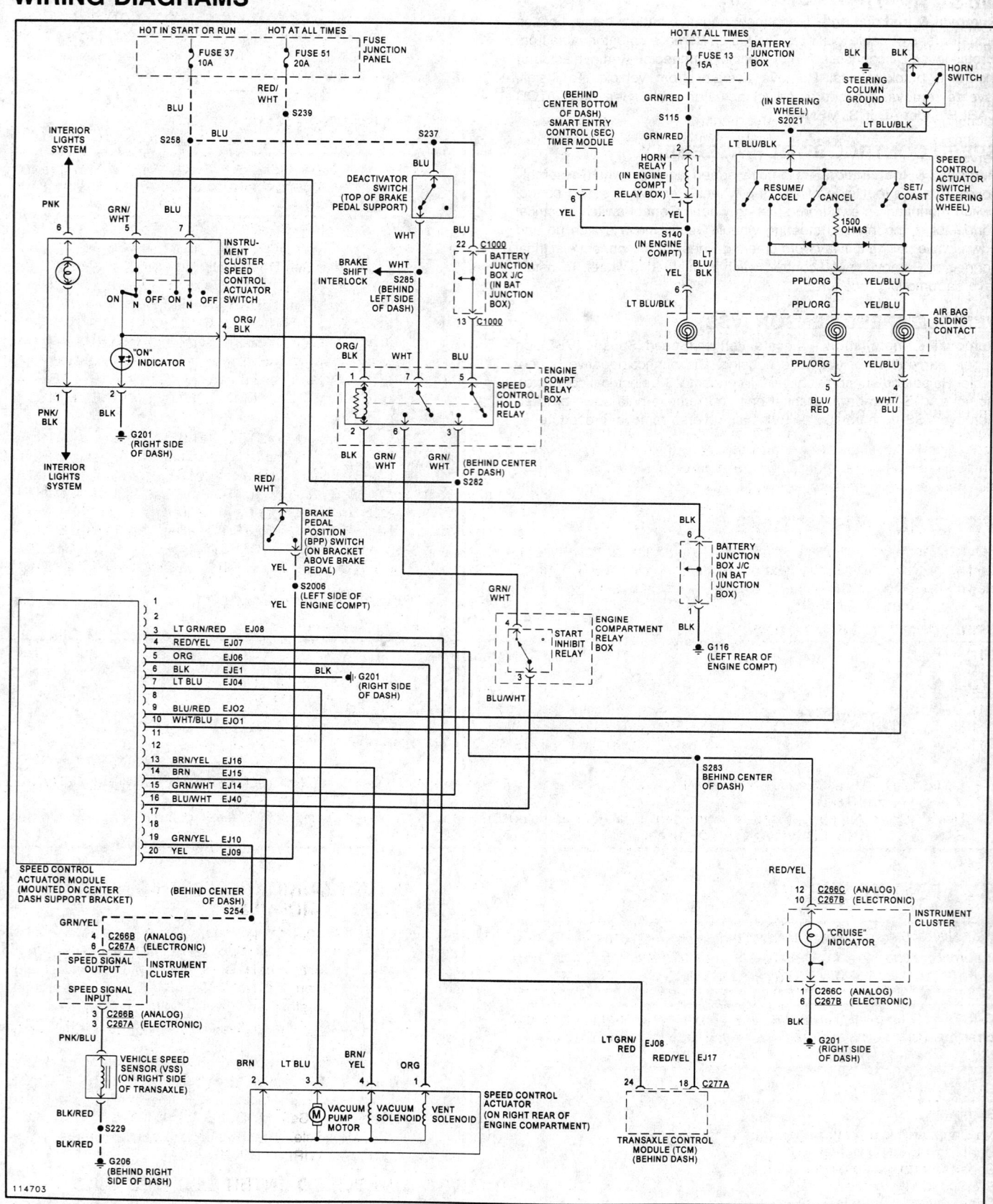

Fig. 12: Cruise Control System Wiring Diagram (Villager)

DESCRIPTION

Speed control system is electronically controlled. Major components of speed control system include speed control actuator cable, speed control servo/actuator, Rear Electronics Module (REM), speed control actuator switch, brake pressure switch, anti-lock brake control module and air bag sliding contact. This system does not require engine vacuum. An electronic servo actuates the throttle. Speed control system is operational only at speeds greater than 30 MPH. Speed control servo/actuator communicates with Anti-Lock Brake System (ABS) module, Powertrain Control Module (PCM) and REM using Standard Corporate Protocol (SCP) bus link.

OPERATION

Speed control system is activated when ON button is pressed and SET/ACCEL button is pressed. Vehicle will maintain speed until new speed is set, brake pedal is depressed or OFF button is pressed. To decrease from a set speed, COAST button can be pressed and held until desired reduced speed is reached or, momentarily tapping COAST button for one MPH deceleration increments. If system has been deactivated by process other than pressing OFF button, set speed can be regained by pressing and releasing RESUME button.

Under normal braking conditions, when brake pedal is depressed, a signal from stoplight switch to servo deactivates operation. Speed control brake pressure switch provides an additional safety feature. Under increased brake pedal effort, brake pressure switch will open and eliminate power to servo, releasing throttle from servo control.

TROUBLE SHOOTING

Before performing any testing, check speed control actuator cable stuck, binding or seized. Check for bent or breaking throttle lever. Check for blown Fuse Junction Box/Panel (FJB) fuse No. 10 (10-amp). Check for loose or corroded connections. Check for open or shorted circuits. Verify speedometer, horn and stoplights are functioning properly. Inspect actuator and throttle linkage for smooth operation. If any problems are found, repair as necessary. If no problems are found, perform self-diagnostics. See SELF-DIAGNOSTIC SYSTEM.

SELF-DIAGNOSTIC SYSTEM

NOTE: All diagnostic tests are written specifically for New Generation Star (NGS) tester. Most generic scan tools should be able to perform all test procedures.

Connect New Generation Star (NGS) tester to Data Link Connector (DLC), located beneath instrument panel. Using NGS tester, perform data link diagnostics test. See DATA LINK DIAGNOSTIC TEST under COMMUNICATION NETWORK DIAGNOSTICS in MODULE COMMUNICATIONS NETWORK – WINDSTAR article. If NGS tester responds with CKT914, CKT915 or CKT70=ALL ECUS NO RESP/NOT EQUIP, repair module communications concern. See MODULE COMMUNICATIONS NETWORK – WINDSTAR article. If NGS tester displays NO RESP/NOT EQUIP for speed control servo/actuator, perform TEST A: NO COMMUNICATION WITH SPEED CONTROL SERVO MODULE under SYSTEM TESTS.

If NGS tester responds with SYSTEM PASSED, retrieve and record continuous DTC. Erase continuous DTC. Using NGS tester, perform speed control servo/actuator self-test. If any DTC are retrieved, perform appropriate test in accordance with DTC retrieved. See SPEED CONTROL SERVO DTC INDEX. Codes listed in this table are only for testing covered in this article. For complete DTC listing, see MODULE COMMUNICATIONS NETWORK – WINDSTAR article. If no DTC are retrieved, repair by symptom. See SYMPTOM CHART under SYSTEM TESTS.

SPEED CONTROL SERVO DTC INDEX

DTC [1]	Description	Test
B1318	Battery Voltage Low	C
B1342	ECU Defective	[2]
C1109	Throttle Position Did Not Return To Idle After Self-Test	F
C1126	Speed Control Switch Stuck For 2 Minutes Or Longer	D
C1127	Brake Pressure Switch Circuit Failure	E
C1179	Speed Control Cable Slack Failure	F

[1] – Codes listed in this table are only for testing covered in this article. For complete DTC listing, see MODULE COMMUNICATIONS NETWORK – WINDSTAR article.

[2] – Using NGS tester, perform speed control servo/actuator self-test. If DTC B1342 is retrieved again, replace speed control servo/actuator. See SPEED CONTROL SERVO/ACTUATOR under REMOVAL & INSTALLATION.

SYSTEM TESTS

WARNING: Disable air bag system before working around steering column or removing any air bag system component. See appropriate AIR BAG RESTRAINT SYSTEMS article.

CAUTION: Electronic modules are sensitive to static electrical charges. Proper grounding of technician and component is essential to prevent damage.

SYMPTOM CHART

Symptom	Test
No Communication With Speed Control Servo Module	A
Unable To Enter Self-Test	B
Speed Control Inoperative – No DTC	G
Set Speed Fluctuates	H
Coast Switch Inoperative	J
SET/ACCEL Switch Inoperative	K
RESUME Switch Inoperative	L
OFF Switch Inoperative	M

TEST A: NO COMMUNICATION WITH SPEED CONTROL SERVO MODULE

1) Turn ignition switch to OFF position. Disconnect speed control servo/actuator 10-pin harness connector C116. Turn ignition switch to ON position. Measure voltage between speed control servo/actuator harness connector C116 terminal No. 7 (Red/Black wire) and ground. *See Fig. 1.* If voltage is greater than 10 volts, go to next step. If voltage is 10 volts or more, repair power source circuit. See WIRING DIAGRAMS.

2) Turn ignition switch to OFF position. Measure resistance between speed control servo/actuator harness connector C116 terminal No. 10 (Black wire) and ground. If resistance is less than 5 ohms, repair module communication concern. See MODULE COMMUNICATIONS NETWORK – WINDSTAR article. If resistance is 5 ohms or more, repair open in Black wire. See WIRING DIAGRAMS.

TEST B: UNABLE TO ENTER SELF-TEST

Using NGS tester, perform speed control servo/actuator self-test. If NGS tester communicates with speed control servo/actuator, replace speed control servo/actuator. See SPEED CONTROL SERVO/ACTUATOR under REMOVAL & INSTALLATION. If NGS tester does not communi-

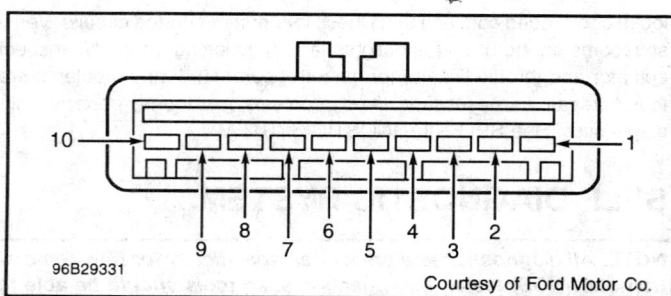

96B29331   Courtesy of Ford Motor Co.

**Fig. 1: Identifying Speed Control Servo/Actuator & Air Bag
Sliding Contact 10-Pin Harness Connector Terminals**

cate with speed control servo/actuator, perform TEST A: NO COMMU-
NICATION WITH SPEED CONTROL SERVO MODULE.

TEST C: BATTERY VOLTAGE LOW (DTC B1318)

Turn ignition switch to OFF position. Disconnect speed control servo/
actuator 10-pin harness connector C116. Turn ignition switch to ON
position. Measure resistance between speed control servo/actuator
harness connector C116 terminal No. 10 (Black wire) and ground. *See
Fig. 1.* If resistance is less than 5 ohms, repair charging system as
necessary. See appropriate GENERATORS article in STARTING &
CHARGING SYSTEMS. If resistance is 5 ohms or more, repair open in
Black wire. See WIRING DIAGRAMS.

TEST D: SPEED CONTROL SWITCH STUCK FOR
TWO MINUTES OR LONGER (DTC C1126)

1) Using NGS tester, monitor speed control servo/actuator PIDs COAST,
RESUME, SC_OFF, SC_ON and SET_ACL while depressing and
releasing each speed control actuator switch. If NGS tester indicates
ACTIVE with speed control actuator switch depressed and NOTACT
with speed control actuator switch released, system is okay. If NGS
tester does not indicate ACTIVE with speed control actuator switch
depressed and NOT with speed control actuator switch released, go to
next step.

2) Turn ignition switch to OFF position. Disconnect speed control
actuator switch. Using NGS tester, clear continuous DTC. Wait 3
minutes and perform speed control servo/actuator self-test. If DTC
C1126 is retrieved, go to next step. If DTC C1126 is not retrieved,
replace speed control actuator switch. See SPEED CONTROL ACTUA-
TOR SWITCH under REMOVAL & INSTALLATION.

3) Turn ignition switch to OFF position. Disconnect speed control
servo/actuator 10-pin harness connector C116. Measure resistance
between speed control servo/actuator harness connector C116 terminal
No. 5 (Light Blue/Black wire) and ground. *See Fig. 1.* If resistance is 10
k/ohms or less, go to next step. If resistance is more than 10 k/ohms,
replace speed control servo/actuator. See SPEED CONTROL SERVO/
ACTUATOR under REMOVAL & INSTALLATION.

4) Disconnect air bag sliding contact. Measure resistance between
speed control servo/actuator harness connector C116 terminal No. 5
(Light Blue/Black wire) and ground. If resistance is more than 10
k/ohms, replace air bag sliding contact. See AIR BAG SLIDING CON-
TACT under REMOVAL & INSTALLATION. If resistance is 10 k/ohms or
less, repair short to ground in Light Blue/Black wire. See WIRING
DIAGRAMS.

TEST E: BRAKE PRESSURE SWITCH CIRCUIT
FAILURE (DTC C1127)

1) Turn ignition switch to ON position. Disconnect speed control
servo/actuator 10-pin harness connector C116. Measure voltage
between speed control servo/actuator harness connector C116 terminal
No. 9 (Light Blue/Red wire) and ground while applying and releasing
brake pedal. *See Fig. 1.* If voltage is not more than 10 volts with brake
pedal released or not zero volts with brake pedal applied, go to next
step. If voltage is more than 10 volts when brake pedal released and

zero volts when brake pedal is applied, replace speed control servo/
actuator. See SPEED CONTROL SERVO/ACTUATOR under
REMOVAL & INSTALLATION.

2) Disconnect brake pressure switch 2-pin harness connector C127.
Measure voltage between brake pressure switch harness connector
C127 Red/Black wire terminal and ground. If voltage is more than 10
volts, go to next step. If voltage is 10 volts or less, repair open in
Red/Black wire. See WIRING DIAGRAMS.

3) Measure resistance between speed control servo/actuator harness
connector C116 terminal No. 9 (Light Blue/Red wire) and brake pressure
switch harness connector Light Blue/Red wire terminal. If resistance is
less than 5 ohms, replace brake pressure switch. See SPEED CON-
TROL BRAKE PRESSURE SWITCH under REMOVAL & INSTALLA-
TION. If resistance is 5 ohms or more, repair open in Light Blue/Red
wire.

TEST F: SPEED CONTROL CABLE SLACK FAILURE
(DTC C1179)

Check throttle lever and speed control actuator cable for correct
operation while measuring speed control cable slack. If cable slack is
0-.24" (0-6 mm) and throttle lever operates correctly, replace speed
control servo/actuator. See SPEED CONTROL SERVO/ACTUATOR
under REMOVAL & INSTALLATION. If cable slack is not 0-.24" (0-6 mm)
and throttle lever operates correctly and cable bracket is not bent,
replace speed control actuator cable. See SPEED CONTROL ACTUA-
TOR CABLE under REMOVAL & INSTALLATION.

TEST G: SPEED CONTROL INOPERATIVE (NO DTC)

1) Check horn system operation by pressing horn switch. If horn
operates correctly, go to next step. If horn does not operate correctly,
repair horn as necessary. See WIRING DIAGRAMS in STEERING
COLUMN SWITCHES – WINDSTAR article.

2) Turn ignition switch to OFF position. Disconnect speed control
servo/actuator 10-pin harness connector C116. Measure voltage
between speed control servo/actuator harness connector C116 terminal
No. 5 (Light Blue/Black wire) and ground while pressing speed control
actuator switch ON switch. *See Fig. 1.* If voltage is more than 10 volts,
go to next step. If voltage is 10 volts or less, replace speed control
actuator switch. See SPEED CONTROL ACTUATOR SWITCH under
REMOVAL & INSTALLATION.

3) Measure resistance between speed control servo/actuator harness
connector C116 terminals No. 5 (Light Blue/Black wire) and No. 6 (Dark
Green/Orange wire) while pressing speed control actuator switch SET/
ACCEL. If resistance is 612-748 ohms with switched pressed and more
than 10 k/ohms with switch released, replace speed control servo/
actuator. See SPEED CONTROL SERVO/ACTUATOR under
REMOVAL & INSTALLATION. If resistance is not 612-748 ohms with
switch is pressed and more than 10 k/ohms or less with switch released,
replace speed control actuator switch. See SPEED CONTROL ACTUA-
TOR SWITCH under REMOVAL & INSTALLATION.

TEST H: SET SPEED FLUCTUATES

*NOTE: There must not be any loose components when performing
speed control servo slack test.*

Check throttle lever, speed control actuator cable and accelerator cable
bracket for correct operation while performing speed control servo slack
test with NGS tester. If throttle lever components operate correctly,
system is okay. If throttle lever components do not operate correctly,
replace faulty component(s).

TEST J: COAST SWITCH INOPERATIVE

1) Using NGS tester, monitor speed control servo/actuator PID COAST.
Depress and release speed control actuator switch COAST button while
slightly turning steering wheel from side to side. If NGS tester does not
indicate ACTIVE with COAST button depressed and NOTACT with
COAST button released, go to next step. If NGS tester indicates ACTIVE
with COAST button depressed and NOTACT with COAST button
released, system is okay.

2) Turn ignition switch to OFF position. Disconnect speed control servo/actuator 10-pin harness connector C116. Measure resistance between speed control servo/actuator harness connector C116 terminals No. 5 (Light Blue/Black wire) and No. 6 (Dark Green/Orange wire) while pressing speed control actuator switch COAST button and slightly turning steering wheel from side to side. *See Fig. 1.* If resistance is 108-132 ohms with COAST button pressed and more than 10 k/ohms with COAST button released, replace speed control servo/actuator. See SPEED CONTROL SERVO/ACTUATOR under REMOVAL & INSTALLATION. If resistance is not 108-132 ohms with COAST button pressed and more than 10 k/ohms with COAST button released, replace speed control actuator switch. See SPEED CONTROL ACTUATOR SWITCH under REMOVAL & INSTALLATION.

TEST K: SET/ACCEL SWITCH INOPERATIVE

1) Using NGS tester, monitor speed control servo/actuator PID SET-_ACL. Depress and release speed control actuator switch SET/ACCEL button while slightly turning steering wheel from side to side. If NGS tester does not indicate ACTIVE with SET/ACCEL button depressed and NOTACT with SET/ACCEL button released, go to next step. If NGS tester indicates ACTIVE with SET/ACCEL button depressed and NOTACT with SET/ACCEL button released, system is okay.

2) Turn ignition switch to OFF position. Disconnect speed control servo/actuator 10-pin harness connector C116. Measure resistance between speed control servo/actuator harness connector C116 terminals No. 5 (Light Blue/Black wire) and No. 6 (Dark Green/Orange wire) while pressing speed control actuator switch SET/ACCEL button and slightly turning steering wheel from side to side. *See Fig. 1.* If resistance is 612-748 ohms with SET/ACCEL button pressed and more than 10 k/ohms with SET/ACCEL button released, replace speed control servo/actuator. See SPEED CONTROL SERVO/ACTUATOR under REMOVAL & INSTALLATION. If resistance is not 612-748 ohms with SET/ACCEL button pressed and is more than 10 k/ohms with SET/ACCEL button released, replace speed control actuator switch. See SPEED CONTROL ACTUATOR SWITCH under REMOVAL & INSTALLATION.

TEST L: RESUME SWITCH INOPERATIVE

1) Using NGS tester, monitor speed control servo/actuator PID RESUME. Depress and release speed control actuator switch RESUME button while slightly turning steering wheel from side to side. If NGS tester does not indicate ACTIVE with RESUME button depressed and NOTACT with RESUME button released, go to next step. If NGS tester indicates ACTIVE with RESUME button depressed and NOTACT with RESUME button released, system is okay.

2) Turn ignition switch to OFF position. Disconnect speed control servo/actuator 10-pin harness connector C116. Measure resistance between speed control servo/actuator harness connector C116 terminals No. 5 (Light Blue/Black wire) and No. 6 (Dark Green/Orange wire) while pressing speed control actuator switch RESUME button and slightly turning steering wheel from side to side. *See Fig. 1.* If resistance is 1980-2420 ohms with RESUME button pressed and more than 10 k/ohms with RESUME button released, replace speed control servo/actuator. See SPEED CONTROL SERVO/ACTUATOR under REMOVAL & INSTALLATION. Clear DTC and repeat self-test. If resistance is not 1980-2420 ohms with RESUME button pressed and not than 10 k/ohms with RESUME button released, replace speed control actuator switch. See SPEED CONTROL ACTUATOR SWITCH under REMOVAL & INSTALLATION.

TEST M: OFF SWITCH INOPERATIVE

1) Using NGS tester, monitor speed control servo/actuator PID SC_OFF. Depress and release speed control actuator switch OFF button while slightly turning steering wheel from side to side. If NGS tester does not indicate ACTIVE with OFF button depressed and NOTACT with OFF button released, go to next step. If NGS tester indicates ACTIVE with OFF button depressed and NOTACT with OFF button released, system is okay.

2) Turn ignition switch to OFF position. Disconnect speed control servo/actuator 10-pin harness connector C116. Measure resistance between speed control servo/actuator harness connector C116 terminals No. 5 (Light Blue/Black wire) and No. 6 (Dark Green/Orange wire) while pressing speed control actuator switch OFF button and slightly turning steering wheel from side to side. *See Fig. 1.* If resistance is less than 5 ohms with OFF button pressed and more than 10 k/ohms with OFF button released, replace speed control servo/actuator. See SPEED CONTROL SERVO/ACTUATOR under REMOVAL & INSTALLATION. Clear DTC and repeat self-test. If resistance is not less than 5 ohms with OFF button pressed and more than 10 k/ohms with OFF button released, replace speed control actuator switch. See SPEED CONTROL ACTUATOR SWITCH under REMOVAL & INSTALLATION.

REMOVAL & INSTALLATION

WARNING: Disable air bag system before working around steering column or removing any air bag system component. See appropriate AIR BAG RESTRAINT SYSTEMS article.

CAUTION: When battery is disconnected, vehicle computer and memory systems may lose memory data. Driveability problems may exist until computer systems have completed a relearn cycle. See COMPUTER RELEARN PROCEDURES article in GENERAL INFORMATION before disconnecting battery.

AIR BAG SLIDING CONTACT

WARNING: Always wear safety glasses when repairing Supplement Restraint System (SRS) vehicle. Carry live air bag module with air bag and trim pointed away from body. Never set a live air bag module down with trim facing down. This will reduce risk of injury in event of accidental deployment.

Removal – 1) Ensure front wheels are in straight-ahead position and steering column shaft alignment mark is at 12 o'clock position. Disconnect negative battery cable and wait one minute for back-up power supply to be depleted. Remove steering wheel. Mark air bag sliding contact to prevent accidental rotation when air bag sliding contact is removed. Hub should not turn more than 45 degrees in either direction to prevent damage.

CAUTION: Do not stretch or damage transmission shift indicator cable performing following steps.

2) Remove 2 screws to remove steering column lower finish panel. Remove 3 retaining bolts holding steering column lower finish panel reinforcement. Loosen but DO NOT remove 4 nuts holding steering column, allowing column to drop slightly. Remove 2 finish panels on either side of steering column on instrument panel.

3) Disconnect headlight switch harness connector. Remove steering column lower shroud. Remove ignition lock cylinder by turning ignition switch to RUN position. Using pin punch or equivalent, press on tab and pull out on ignition lock cylinder and remove.

4) Place transmission shift lever in its lowest position. Remove instrument cluster finish panel 4 retaining screws and remove finish panel. Place transmission shift lever in park position. Remove upper steering column shroud. Remove screw holding Passive Anti-Theft System (PATS) transmitter on side of lock cylinder housing and remove PATS transmitter.

5) Disconnect 2 air bag sliding contact harness connectors from main wiring harness. Remove air bag sliding contact by pushing snap back at 6 o'clock position, then 3 o'clock position, then 12 o'clock position and remove from steering shaft.

Installation – To install, reverse removal procedure. Ensure front wheels are in straight ahead position and steering column shaft alignment mark is at 12 o'clock position. Prove out air bag system.

SPEED CONTROL ACTUATOR CABLE

NOTE: Ensure throttle lever and brackets are free of damage prior to replacement of speed control cable. Speed control cable is not adjustable. If slack on new cable is more than 7/32″ (6 mm), check for bent or broken throttle lever or brackets. After installation of speed control cable, ensure speed control cable does not interfere with throttle travel.

Remove speed control servo/actuator. See SPEED CONTROL SERVO/ACTUATOR. Remove speed control actuator cable from throttle lever and squeeze speed control cable housing mounting locking tabs and remove from bracket. To install, reverse removal procedure.

SPEED CONTROL ACTUATOR SWITCH

CAUTION: When separating speed control actuator switch from steering wheel, it is necessary to take precautions not to damage steering wheel.

NOTE: When battery is disconnected, vehicle computer and memory systems may lose memory data. Driveability problems may exist until computer systems have completed a relearn cycle. See COMPUTER RELEARN PROCEDURES article in GENERAL INFORMATION before disconnecting battery.

Removal & Installation – Disconnect negative battery cable. Pry speed control actuator switch out of steering wheel. Disconnect speed control actuator switch harness connector and remove speed control actuator switch. To install, reverse removal procedure.

SPEED CONTROL BRAKE PRESSURE SWITCH

NOTE: When battery is disconnected, vehicle computer and memory systems may lose memory data. Driveability problems may exist until computer systems have completed a relearn cycle. See COMPUTER RELEARN PROCEDURES article in GENERAL INFORMATION before disconnecting battery.

Removal & Installation – Disconnect negative battery cable. Remove air cleaner assembly. Disconnect speed control brake pressure switch harness connector. Unscrew and remove speed control brake pressure switch. To install, reverse removal procedure. Bleed hydraulic brake system.

SPEED CONTROL SERVO/ACTUATOR

NOTE: When battery is disconnected, vehicle computer and memory systems may lose memory data. Driveability problems may exist until computer systems have completed a relearn cycle. See COMPUTER RELEARN PROCEDURES article in GENERAL INFORMATION before disconnecting battery.

Removal – 1) Disconnect negative battery cable. Remove air cleaner assembly. Disconnect speed control servo/actuator harness connector. Remove 2 speed control servo/actuator mounting bolts. Lift and remove servo/actuator. Disconnect speed control cable from throttle body.

2) Depress locking tab on speed control servo/actuator cap and rotate counterclockwise while lifting cap outward. Remove speed control cable slug from speed control servo/actuator pulley. Remove speed control actuator cable from speed control servo/actuator pulley.

NOTE: Incorrect wrapping of speed control actuator cable around speed control servo/actuator pulley may result in a high idle condition.

Installation – To install, make sure locking spring snaps into place on speed control cable slug. Insert speed control cable slug into speed control servo/actuator pulley slot. Ensure rubber seal is fully seated on servo/actuator cable cap. Align speed control actuator cable cap tabs with slots in speed control servo/actuator housing and seat speed control cable cap. Rotate cap clockwise until locking tab engages. Install speed control servo/actuator bracket bolts and connect harness connector to speed control servo/actuator.

WIRING DIAGRAMS

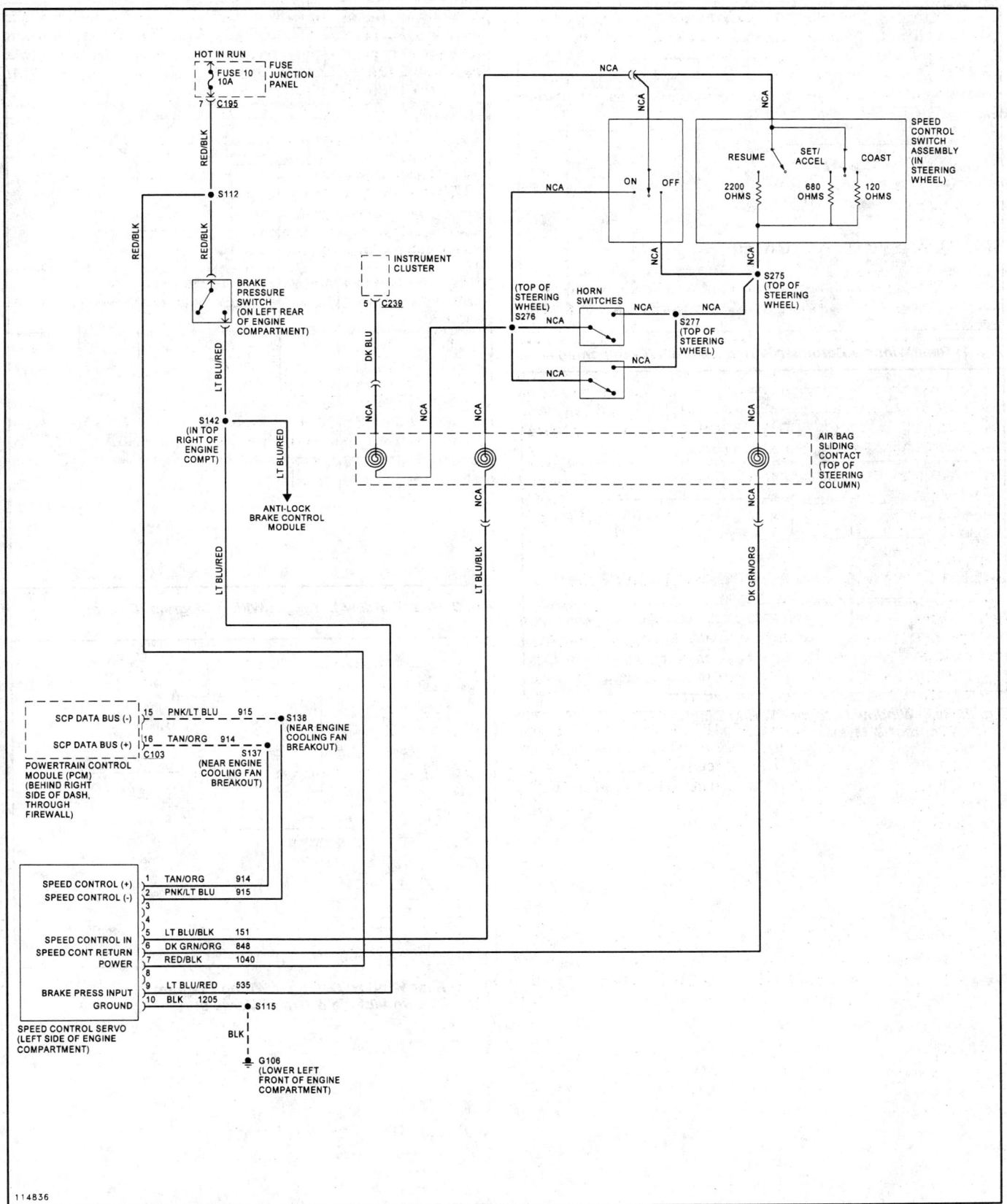

Fig. 2: Cruise Control System Wiring Diagram (Windstar)

114836

WIRING DIAGRAMS

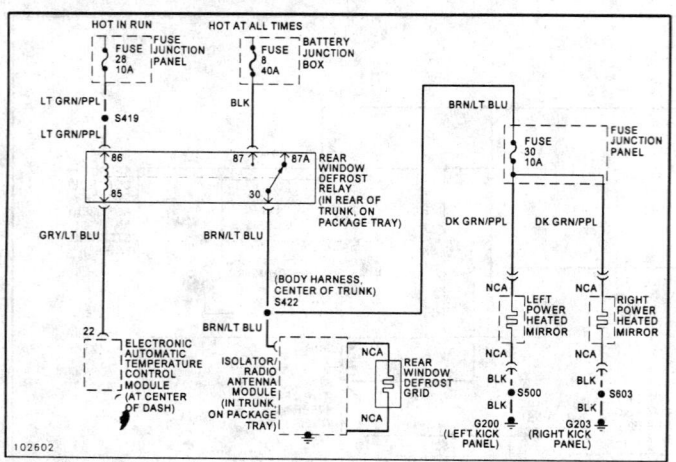

Fig. 1: Rear Window Defogger Wiring Diagram (Continental)

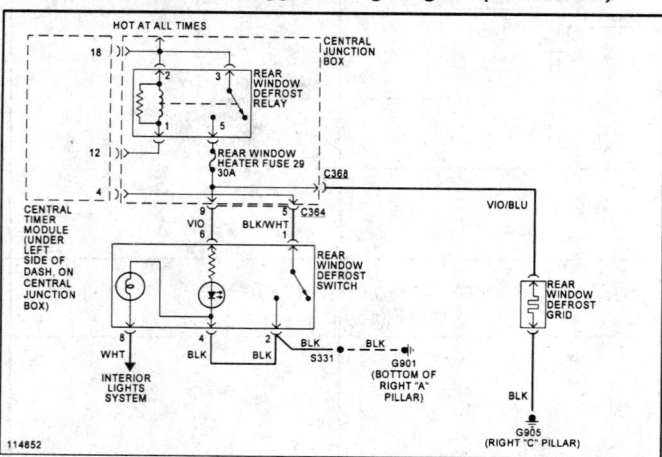

Fig. 2: Rear Window Defogger Wiring Diagram (Contour & Mystique)

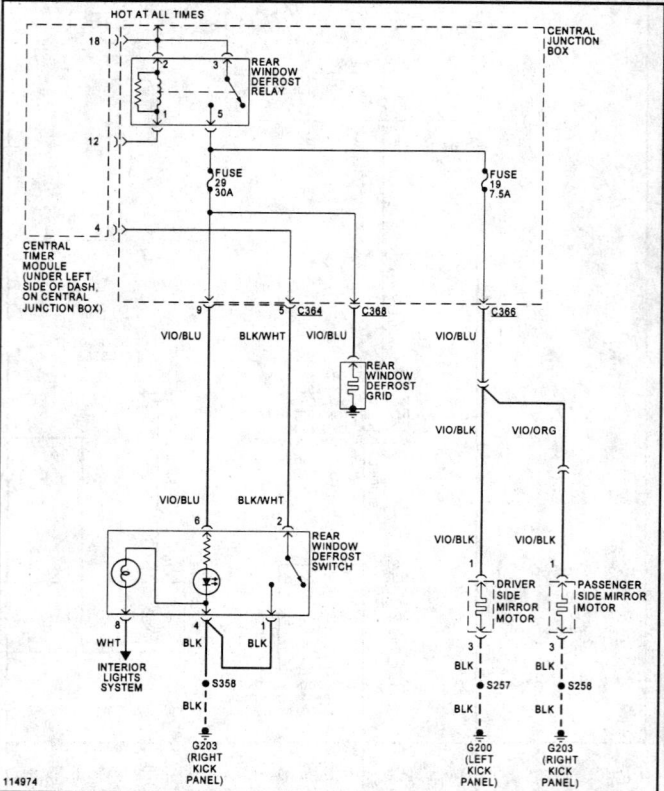

Fig. 3: Rear Window Defogger Wiring Diagram (Cougar)

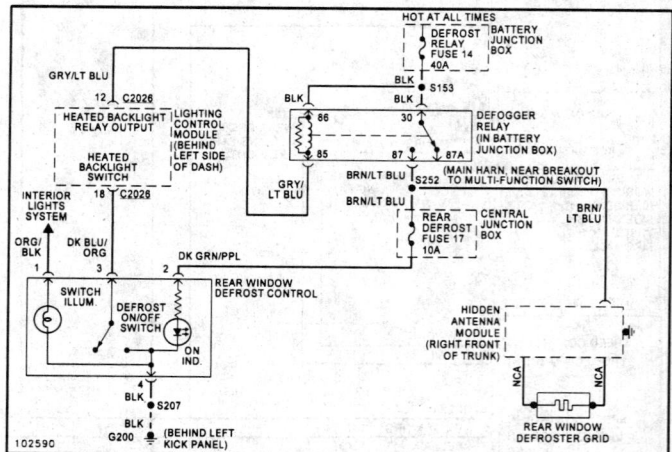

Fig. 4: Rear Window Defogger Wiring Diagram (Crown Victoria & Grand Marquis)

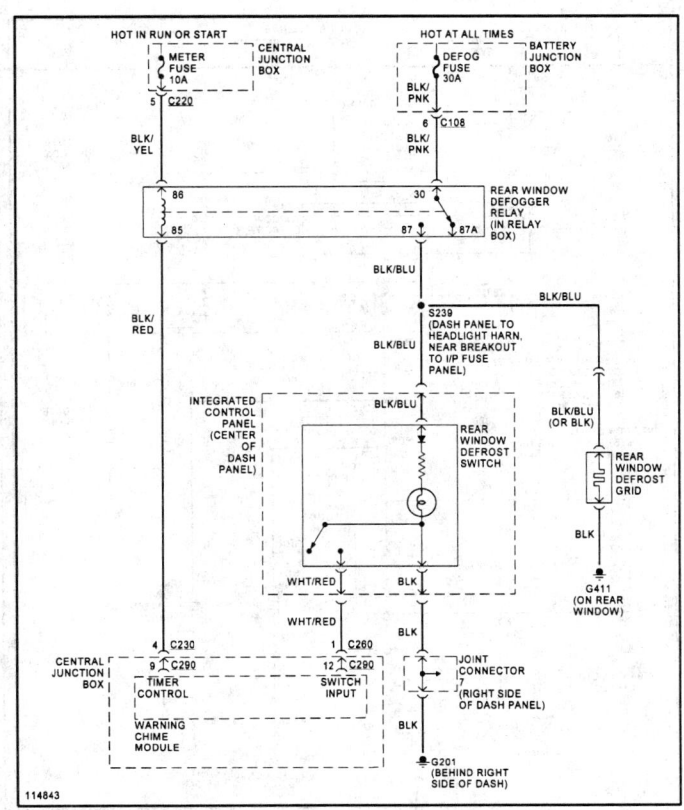

Fig. 5: Rear Window Defogger Wiring Diagram (Escort & Tracer)

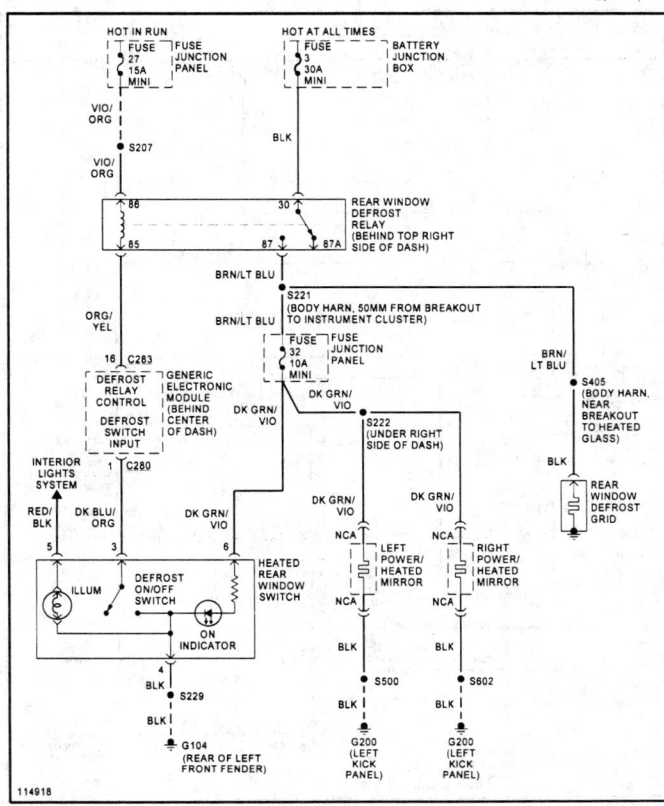

Fig. 7: Rear Window Defogger Wiring Diagram (Explorer & Mountaineer)

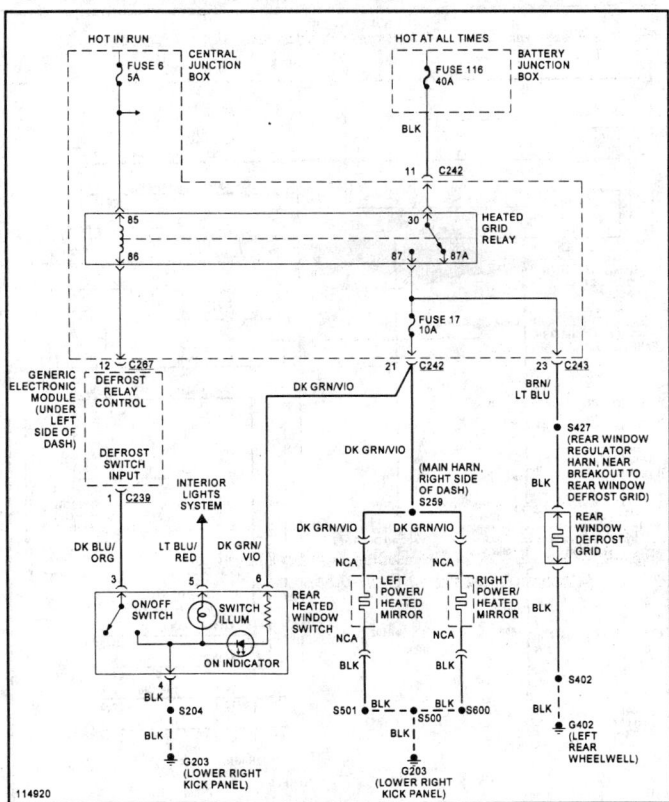

Fig. 6: Rear Window Defogger Wiring Diagram (Expedition & Navigator)

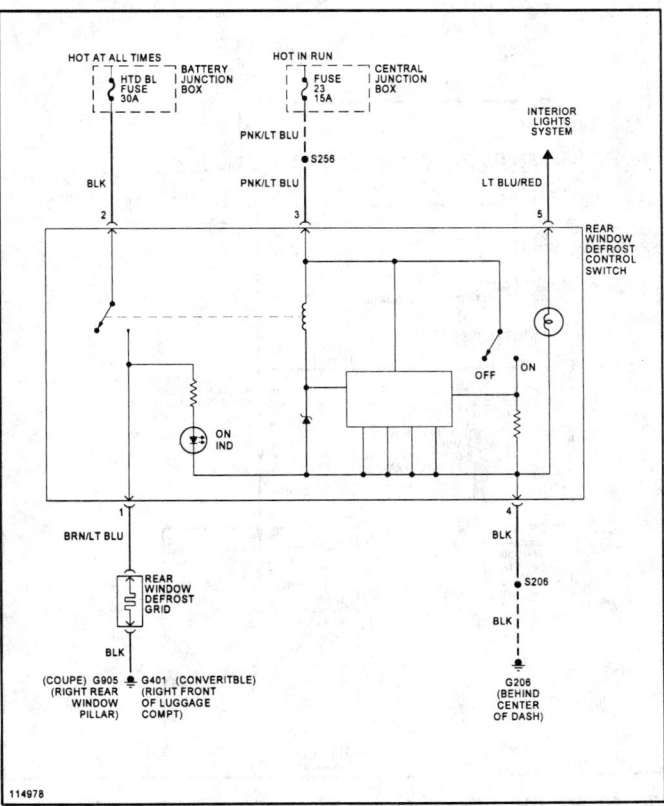

Fig. 8: Rear Window Defogger Wiring Diagram (Mustang)

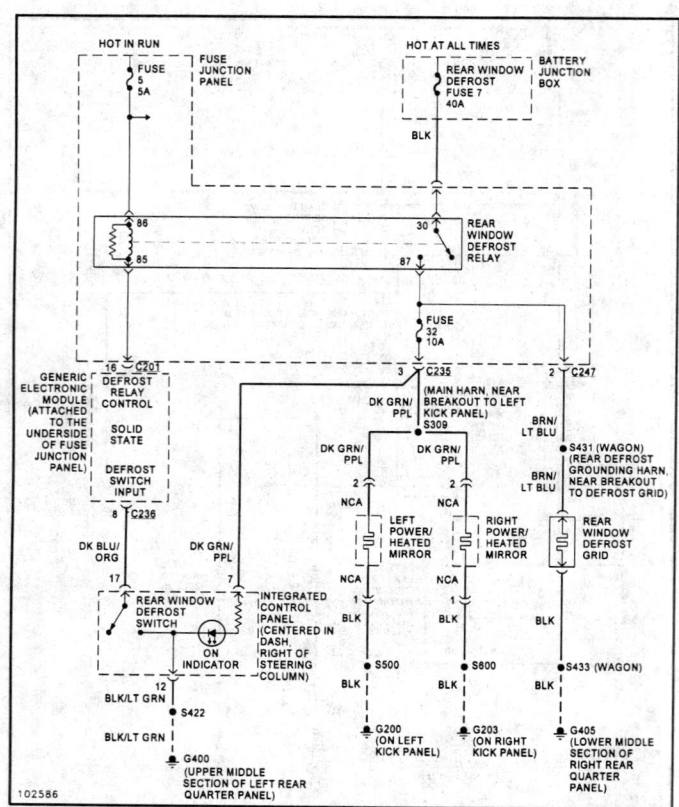

Fig. 9: Rear Window Defogger Wiring Diagram (Sable & Taurus)

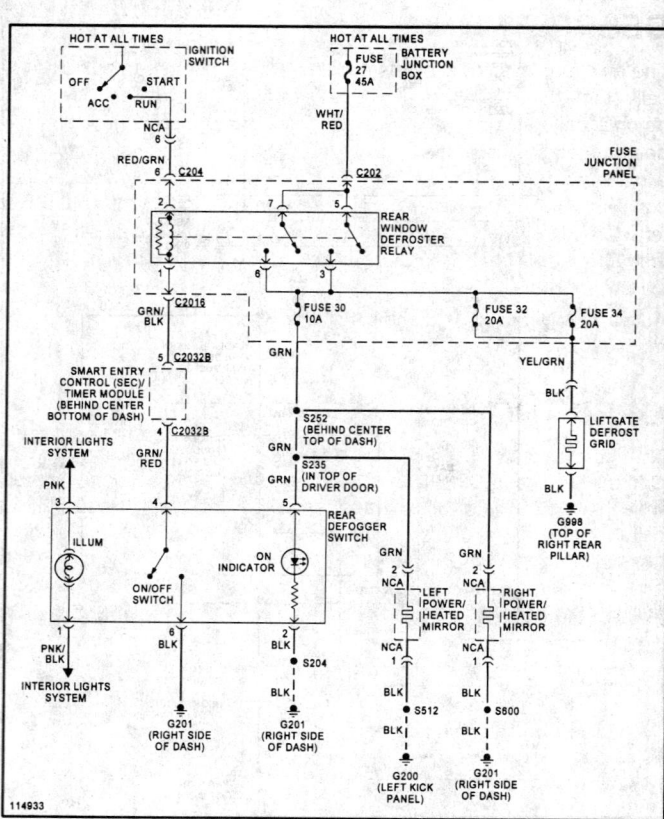

Fig. 11: Rear Window Defogger Wiring Diagram (Villager)

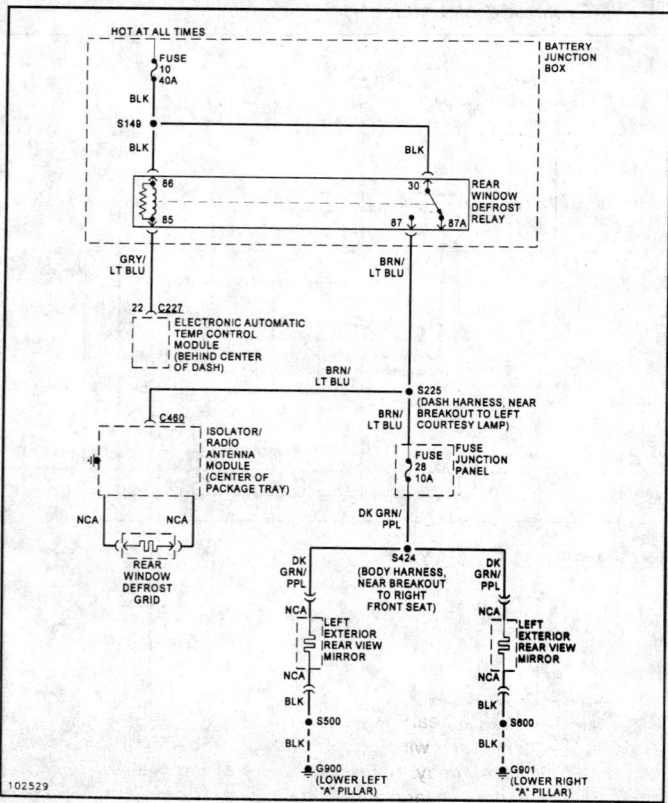

Fig. 10: Rear Window Defogger Wiring Diagram (Town Car)

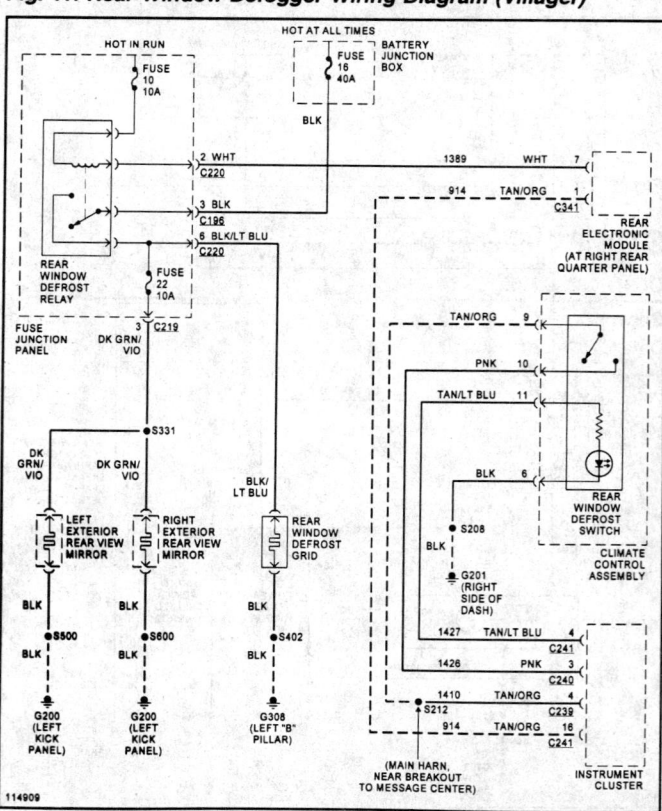

Fig. 12: Rear Window Defogger Wiring Diagram (Windstar)

DESCRIPTION

The autolamp system is a light-sensitive, on-off control. It will automatically turn the headlights on and off. The system can be set to automatically turn off interior and exterior lights after the ignition has been turned off. This feature is adjustable and can be turned off or has a maximum time delay setting of up to 3 minutes. Autolamp system consists of the light sensor amplifier, located in the defroster grille on top left dash, Lighting Control Module (LCM), located under left side of instrument panel and time delay switch which is integral with headlight switch.

Autolamp system LCM communicates with other control modules via module communications network.

OPERATION

The autolamp system activates various lights through the Lighting Control Module (LCM). The system also includes autolamp feature which keeps the headlights on after ignition is turned off, then automatically turns lights off after a pre-selected time period. The delay period can be lengthened by holding time delay control in MAX delay position. See Fig. 1. Autolamp feature also automatically turns headlights and taillights on at night.

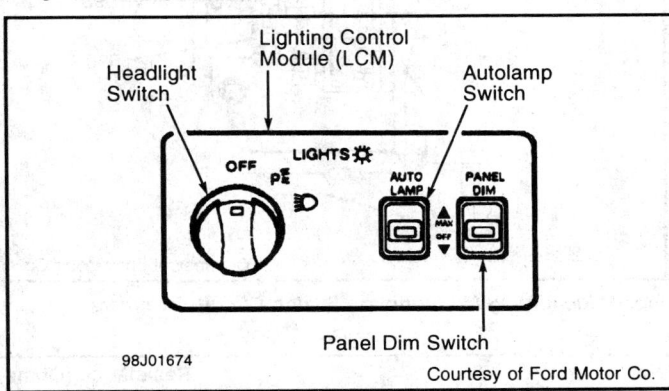

Fig. 1: Identifying Lighting Control Module (LCM) Controls

COMPONENT LOCATIONS

COMPONENT LOCATIONS

Component	Location
Data Link Connector (DLC)	Below Driver's Side Of Instrument Panel, To Right Of Steering Column
Door Lock Switch	Appropriate Door Panel Arm Rest
Driver's Door Module (DDM)	Behind Driver's Door Panel, Lower Front Corner
Driver's Seat Module (DSM)	Under Driver's Seat
Heated Seat Module	Under Appropriate Seat
Heated Seat Switch	Center Of Instrument Panel, Under Heater Controls
Instrument Cluster [1]	Behind Left Side Of Instrument Panel
Instrument Panel Fuse Box	Below Left Instrument Panel
Keyless Entry Keypad	Driver's Door Below Exterior Door Handle
Lighting Control Module (LCM)	On Instrument Panel, Behind Headlight Switch
Light Sensor Amplifier	Top Left Side Of Instrument Panel
Lumbar Switch	Side Of Seat Cushion
Power Distribution Box	Left Side Of Engine Compartment, Above Wheelwell
Power Mirror Switch	Driver's Door Panel Arm Rest

COMPONENT LOCATIONS (Cont.)

Component	Location
Powertrain Control Module (PCM)	In Passenger's Side Of Engine Compartment, On Firewall

[1] – Instrument cluster may also be referred to as Virtual Instrument Cluster (VIC).

TROUBLE SHOOTING

Verify customers complaint. Check all system fuses. See AUTOLAMP SYSTEM FUSE LOCATIONS table. Check or replace any suspect bulbs. Check for a damaged light sensor amplifier and for mechanical damage to headlight switch. Check battery condition and battery terminals. Check for good clean connections at chassis ground point locations. See appropriate wiring diagram in HEADLIGHT SYSTEMS article. Correct any obvious problems before continuing testing. If no problems are found, go to SELF-DIAGNOSTIC SYSTEM.

AUTOLAMP SYSTEM FUSE LOCATIONS

Application	Fuse No. (Amp Rating)
Power Distribution Box	7 (15) & 10 (60)
Fuse Junction Panel	1 (10), 4 (10), 5 (10), 19 (10), 20 (10), 25 (10), 31 (15) & 40 (10)

COMPONENT TESTS

DOOR LOCK SWITCH

Using an ohmmeter, check for continuity between indicated switch connector terminals when switch is operated as specified. See POWER DOOR LOCK SWITCH CONTINUITY TEST table. See Fig. 2. Replace switch if it does not test as specified.

POWER DOOR LOCK SWITCH CONTINUITY TEST

Switch Position	Continuity Between Pins
Lock	1 & 6
Unlock	5 & 6

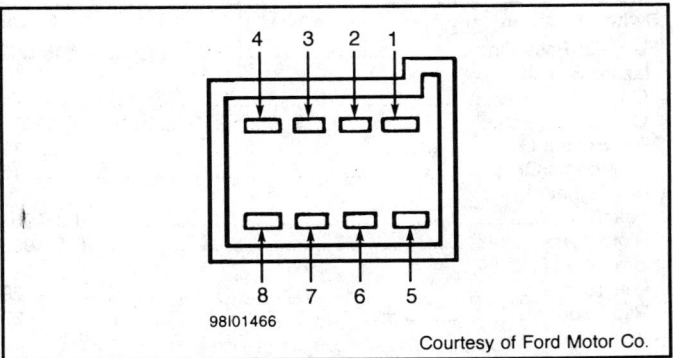

Fig. 2: Identifying Power Door Lock Switch Connector & Mirror Control Switch Connector Terminals

HIGH BEAM RELAY

1) Remove high beam relay from power distribution box in engine compartment. Measure resistance between terminal No. 2 and all other terminals of high beam relay. See Fig. 3. If resistance is greater than 5 ohms between terminal No. 2 and all other terminals, go to next step. If resistance is 5 ohms or less between terminal No. 2 and any other terminal, replace high beam relay.

2) Using 2 fused jumper wires, apply battery voltage to terminals No. 1 and 3 of high beam relay. Measure voltage at terminal No. 4 of high beam relay. If battery voltage exists, leave jumper wires connected and go to next step. If battery voltage does not exist, replace high beam relay.

3) Ground terminal No. 2 of high beam relay. Measure voltage at terminal No. 5 of high beam relay. If battery voltage exists, relay is okay at this time. If battery voltage does not exist, replace high beam relay.

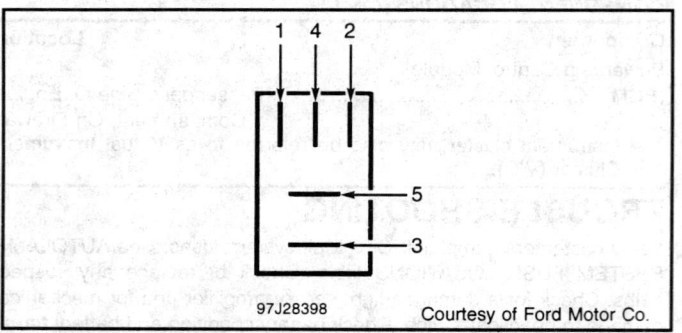

Fig. 3: Identifying High Beam Relay Terminals

MIRROR CONTROL SWITCH

Using an ohmmeter, check for continuity between indicated switch connector terminals when switch is activated as specified. See POWER MIRROR SWITCH CONTINUITY TEST table. *See Fig. 2.* Replace switch if it does not test as specified.

POWER MIRROR SWITCH CONTINUITY TEST

Switch Position	Continuity Between Pins
Left Mirror	
Up	1 & 6; 3 & 5
Down	1 & 3; 5 & 6
Left	1 & 6; 4 & 5
Right	1 & 4; 5 & 6
Right Mirror	
Up	1 & 6; 5 & 7
Down	1 & 7; 5 & 6
Left	1 & 6; 5 & 8
Right	1 & 8; 5 & 6

MULTIFUNCTION SWITCH

Disconnect multifunction switch harness connectors. Set hazard flasher switch to OFF position unless specified otherwise. Resistance should exist between terminals with switch in specified position. See MULTI-FUNCTION SWITCH RESISTANCE table. *See Fig. 4.* If resistance is not as specified, or is poor in any switch position, replace multifunction switch.

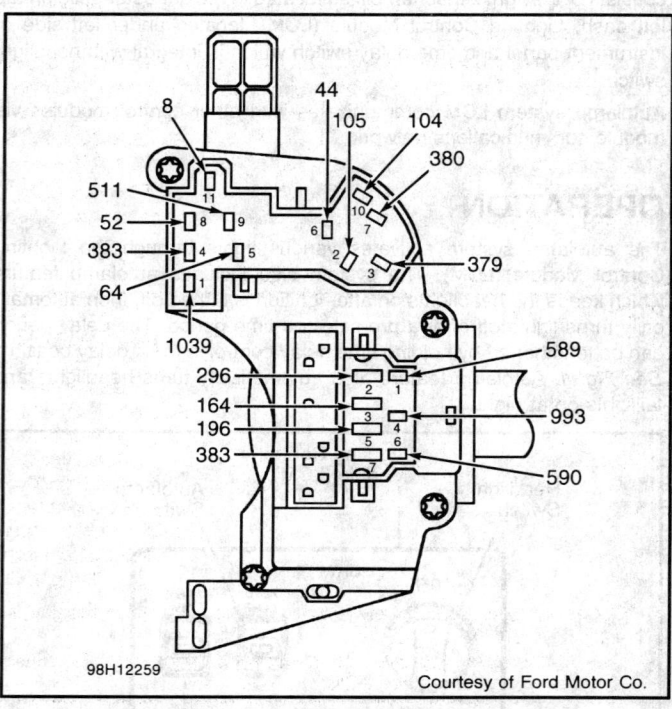

Fig. 4: Identifying Multifunction Switch Circuit Terminals

MULTIFUNCTION SWITCH RESISTANCE

Switch Position	Circuit No.	Resistance (Ohms)
Flash-To-Pass On	196 & 383; 164 & 296	[1]
Hazard Switch		
On	44, 52, 64, 104 & 105; 383 & 1039	[1]
Off	8 & 1039; [2] 44, 104 & 105	[1]
High Beams On	196 & 296	[1]
Low Beams On	164 & 296	[1]
Turn Signals [3]		
Left Turn	8 & 1039; 44, 52 & 105	[1]
Right Turn	8 & 1039; 44, 64 & 104	[1]
Cornering Lights [3]		
Left Turn	296 & 380	[1]
Right Turn	296 & 379	[1]
Washer		
On	590 & 993	[1]
Off	590 & 993	[4] 103,300
Wipers		
Off	589 & 993	[4] 47,600
Low Speed	589 & 993	[4] 4080
High Speed	589 & 993	[1]
Interval	589 & 993	[4] 11,330
Interval Delay [5] [6]		
MAX	590 & 993	[4] 103,300
MIN	590 & 993	[4] 3300

[1] – Resistance should be less than 5 ohms.
[2] – Brake light trough circuit.
[3] – Hazard switch MUST be off.
[4] – Resistance may vary by as much as 5 percent.
[5] – Resistance should vary smoothly between specified limits as knob is rotated between MIN and MAX positions.
[6] – These values are with wiper switch in OFF position. If wiper switch is in LOW or HIGH position, resistance between terminals No. 590 and 993 should be within 10 percent of 3300 ohms.

SELF-DIAGNOSTIC SYSTEM

NOTE: *Lighting Control Module (LCM) controls more than just autolamp system. A non-autolamp LCM fault may effect the autolamp system.*

Verify customers complaint. Check for loose or corroded connectors and damaged wiring harness. Check for a damaged light sensor amplifier and for mechanical damage to headlight switch. Repair or replace components as necessary.

If all components are okay, connect New Generation Star (NGS) tester to Data Link Connector (DLC), located beneath instrument panel. Using NGS tester, perform data link diagnostics test. See DATA LINK DIAGNOSTIC TEST under COMMUNICATION NETWORK DIAGNOSTICS in MODULE COMMUNICATIONS NETWORK – CONTINENTAL article. If NGS tester responds with CKT914, CKT915 or CKT70=ALL ECUS NO RESP/NOT EQUIP, repair module communications concern. See

MODULE COMMUNICATIONS NETWORK – CONTINENTAL article. If NGS tester displays NO RESP/NOT EQUIP for Lighting Control Module (LCM), perform TEST A: NO COMMUNICATION WITH LIGHTING CONTROL MODULE under SYSTEM TESTS. If NGS tester displays NO RESP/NOT EQUIP for Driver's Door Module (DDM), perform TEST O: NO COMMUNICATION WITH DRIVER'S DOOR MODULE under SYSTEM TESTS.

If NGS tester responds with SYSTEM PASSED, retrieve and record continuous DTCs. Erase continuous DTCs. Using NGS tester, perform DDM and LCM self-test. Perform appropriate test in accordance with DTC retrieved. See DRIVER'S DOOR MODULE DTC INDEX and/or LIGHTING CONTROL MODULE DTC INDEX table. Codes listed in these tables are only for testing covered in this article. For complete DTC listing, see MODULE COMMUNICATIONS NETWORK – CONTINENTAL article. If no DTCs are retrieved, repair by symptom. See SYMPTOM CHART table under SYSTEM TESTS.

LIGHTING CONTROL MODULE DTC INDEX

DTC [1]	Description	Test
B1312	Headlight Input Circuit Short To Voltage	B
B1342	ECU Defective	[2]
B1483	Brake Pedal Input Circuit Failure	G
B1509	Flash-To-Pass Switch Circuit Short To Voltage	E
B1555	Ignition RUN/START Circuit Failure	S
B1566	Door Ajar Circuit Short To Ground	Q
B1569	Headlight High Beam Circuit Short To Voltage	C
B1577	Parking Light Input Circuit Short To Voltage	K
B1590	Autolamp Delay Increase Circuit Short To Ground	F
B1594	Autolamp Delay Decrease Circuit Short To Ground	F
B1807	Taillight Output Circuit Open	K

[1] – Codes listed in this table are only for testing covered in this article. For complete DTC listing, see MODULE COMMUNICATIONS NETWORK – CONTINENTAL article.

[2] – Using NGS tester, retrieve and document continuous DTCs. Clear all DTCs. Perform Lighting Control Module (LCM) self-test. If DTC B1342 is retrieved again, replace LCM.

DRIVER'S DOOR MODULE DTC INDEX

DTC [1]	Description	Test
B1319	Driver's Door Ajar Circuit Failure	Q
B1342	ECU Defective	[2]

[1] – Codes listed in this table are only for testing covered in this article. For complete DTC listing, see MODULE COMMUNICATIONS NETWORK – CONTINENTAL article.

[2] – Using NGS tester, retrieve and document all continuous DTCs. Clear DTCs. Perform Driver's Door Module (DDM) self-test. If DTC B1342 is retrieved again, replace DDM.

SYSTEM TESTS

CAUTION: *When battery is disconnected or modules are replaced, vehicle computer and memory systems may lose memory data. Driveability problems may exist until computer systems have completed a relearn cycle. See COMPUTER RELEARN PROCEDURES article in GENERAL INFORMATION before disconnecting battery.*

SYMPTOM CHART

Symptom	Test
No Communication With Lighting Control Module	A
Low Beams Inoperative	B
High Beams Inoperative	C
Low Beams On Continuously (Daytime Running Lights Disabled)	D
Flash-To-Pass Feature Inoperative	E
Autolamps Are Inoperative	F
Brake Lights Never/Always On	G
Turn Signal/Hazard Lights Never/Always On	H
Cornering Lights Never/Always On	J
Parking, Rear Or License Lights Inoperative	K

SYMPTOM CHART (Cont.)

Symptom	Test
Parking, Rear Or License Lights On Continuously	L
Back-Up Light Inoperative	M
Back-Up Light On Continuously	N
No Communication With Driver's Door Module	O
Courtesy Lights Inoperative	P
Courtesy Light On Continuously	Q
Demand Lighting Inoperative	R
Battery Saver Does Not Deactivate After Timeout	S
Keypad Illumination Malfunction	T

TEST A: NO COMMUNICATION WITH LIGHTING CONTROL MODULE

1) Turn ignition switch to LOCK position. Connect New Generation Star (NGS) tester to Data Link Connector (DLC). Monitor Lighting Control Module (LCM) PID IGN_LC. If NGS tester does not display UNABLE TO PERFORM TEST/FUNCTION or MODULE NOT RESPONDING: LCM or CHECK IGNITION STATUS/VERIFY CABLE REQUIREMENTS or CHECK CABLE CONNECTIONS, go to next step. If NGS tester displays UNABLE TO PERFORM TEST/FUNCTION or MODULE NOT RESPONDING: LCM or CHECK IGNITION STATUS/VERIFY CABLE REQUIREMENTS or CHECK CABLE CONNECTIONS, go to step **16**.

2) Turn ignition switch to RUN position. Monitor LCM PID IGN_LC while turning key to each position. If PID IGN_LC shows ACCY while in ACCESSORY position and OFF in all other positions, replace LCM. If PID IGN_LC shows ACCY while in RUN position, go to next step. If PID IGN_LC shows OFF in all positions, go to step 7).

3) Turn ignition switch to RUN position. Measure voltage at output side of fuse No. 5 (10-amp) in instrument panel fuse box. If battery voltage does not exist, go to next step. If battery voltage exists, repair open in Red/Yellow wire between instrument panel fuse box and LCM.

4) Check fuse No. 5 in instrument panel fuse box. If fuse is blown, go to next step. If fuse is okay, repair open in Brown/Pink wire between instrument panel fuse box and ignition switch.

5) Turn ignition switch to LOCK position. Disconnect LCM harness connector C206. Disconnect light sensor amplifier harness connector C243. Measure resistance between ground and terminal No. 17 (Red/Yellow wire) at LCM harness connector C206. *See Fig. 5.* If resistance is 20 ohms or less, go to next step. If resistance is greater than 20 ohms, repair short to ground in Red/Yellow wire.

6) Turn ignition switch to LOCK position. Connect LCM harness connector C206. Remove fuse No. 5 (10-amp) in instrument panel fuse box. Measure resistance between ground and output side of fuse No. 5 in instrument panel fuse box. If resistance is 20 ohms or less, perform TEST F: AUTOLAMPS ARE INOPERATIVE. If resistance is greater than 20 ohms, replace LCM.

7) Turn ignition switch to RUN position. Measure voltage at output side of fuse No. 4 (10-amp) in instrument panel fuse box. If battery voltage exists, go to next step. If battery voltage does not exist, go to step 9).

8) Turn ignition switch to LOCK position. Disconnect LCM harness connector C208. Turn ignition switch to RUN position. Measure voltage at terminal No. 2 (Black/Pink wire) at LCM harness connector C208. *See Fig. 6.* If battery voltage exists, replace LCM. If battery voltage does not exist, repair open in Black/Pink wire.

9) Turn ignition switch to LOCK position. Check fuse No. 4 (10-amp) in instrument panel fuse box. If fuse is blown, go to next step. If fuse is okay, repair open in Black/Light Green wire between instrument panel fuse box and ignition switch.

10) Disconnect driver's door lock switch harness connector C505. Measure resistance between ground and terminal No. 2 (Black/Pink wire) at LCM harness connector C208. If resistance is 10 k/ohms or less, go to next step. If resistance is greater than 10 k/ohms, replace driver's door lock switch.

11) Disconnect passenger's door lock switch harness connector C602. Measure resistance between ground and terminal No. 2 (Black/Pink wire) at LCM harness connector C208. If resistance is 10 k/ohms or less, go to next step. If resistance is greater than 10 k/ohms, replace passenger's door lock switch.

12) Disconnect passenger's power window switch harness connector C600. Measure resistance between ground and terminal No. 2 (Black/Pink wire) at LCM harness connector C208. If resistance is 10 k/ohms or less, go to next step. If resistance is greater than 10 k/ohms, replace passenger's power window switch.

13) Disconnect left rear power window switch harness connector C709. Measure resistance between ground and terminal No. 2 (Black/Pink wire) at LCM harness connector C208. If resistance is 10 k/ohms or less, go to next step. If resistance is greater than 10 k/ohms, replace left rear power window switch.

14) Disconnect right rear power window switch harness connector C809. Measure resistance between ground and terminal No. 2 (Black/Pink wire) at LCM harness connector C208. If resistance is 10 k/ohms or less, go to next step. If resistance is greater than 10 k/ohms, replace right rear power window switch.

15) Ensure ignition switch is in LOCK position. Connect LCM harness connector C208. Using and ohmmeter, measure resistance by back-probing between ground and terminal No. 2 (Black/Pink wire) at LCM harness connector C208. If resistance is greater than 2 k/ohms, replace LCM. If resistance is 2 k/ohms or less, repair Black/Pink wire.

16) Turn ignition switch to LOCK position. Disconnect LCM harness connectors. Measure resistance between ground and terminal No. 13 (Black wire) at LCM harness connector C206. *See Fig. 5.* Measure

resistance between ground and terminal No. 1 (Black wire) at LCM harness connector C207. *See Fig. 7.* Measure resistance between ground and terminal No. 9 (Black wire) at LCM harness connector C211. *See Fig. 8.* If all resistance readings are 5 ohms or less, go to next step. If any resistance reading is greater than 5 ohms, repair appropriate Black wire.

17) Measure resistance between ground and terminal No. 15 (Black/Light Blue wire) at LCM harness connector C207. If resistance is 5 ohms or less, repair module communication concern. See appropriate MODULE COMMUNICATIONS NETWORK article. If resistance is greater than 5 ohms, repair open in Black/Light Blue wire.

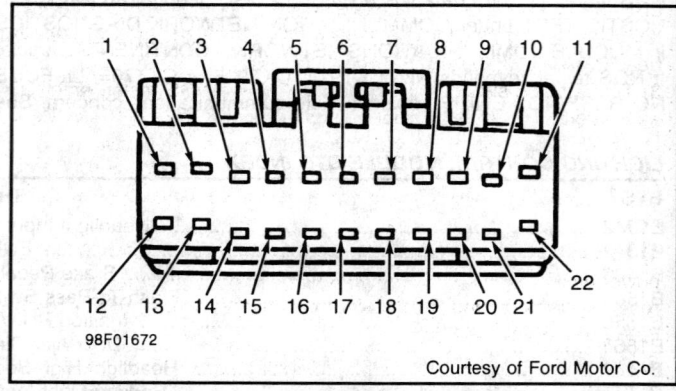

Courtesy of Ford Motor Co.

Fig. 5: Identifying Lighting Control Module Harness Connector C206 Terminals

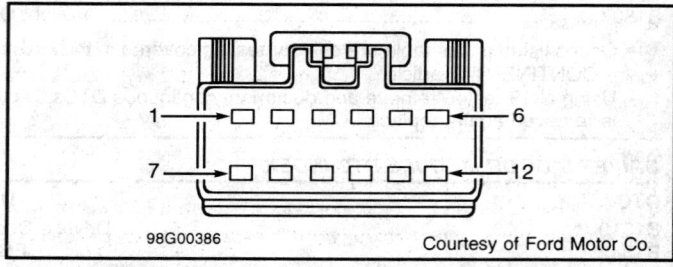

Courtesy of Ford Motor Co.

Fig. 6: Identifying Lighting Control Module Harness Connector C208 Terminals

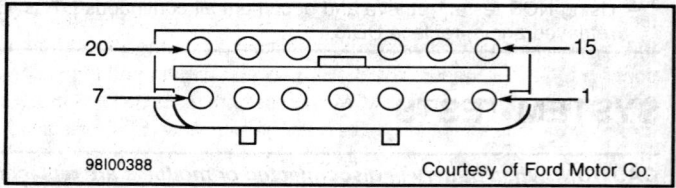

Courtesy of Ford Motor Co.

Fig. 7: Identifying Lighting Control Module Harness Connector C207 Terminals

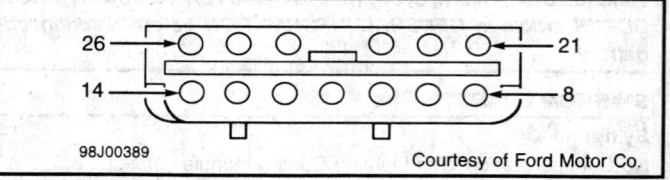

Courtesy of Ford Motor Co.

Fig. 8: Identifying Lighting Control Module Harness Connector C211 Terminals

TEST B: LOW BEAMS INOPERATIVE

NOTE: Due to varying wattage ratings and resulting current draw, certain aftermarket bulbs may cause Lighting Control Module (LCM) to shut down. Verify that bulbs meet Ford specifications.

1) Ensure headlight switch is off. Connect NGS tester to Data Link Connector (DLC). Perform Lighting Control Module (LCM) self-test. If no DTCs are retrieved, go to next step. If DTC B1312 is retrieved, replace LCM.

2) Ensure autolamps and headlights are off. Ensure multifunction switch is not in high beam position. Using NGS tester, monitor LCM PID LBEAMSW while turning headlight switch on and off. If PID agrees with headlight switch position, go to next step. If PID does not agree with headlight switch position, replace LCM.

3) Turn ignition switch to RUN position. Using NGS tester, enter LCM active command for headlight control. Trigger LEFT LOW and RIGHT LOW active commands on. If both low beams are inoperative, go to next step. If only left low beam is inoperative, go to step **6)**. If only right low beam is inoperative, go to step **14)**. If both low beams operate, replace LCM.

4) Turn ignition switch to LOCK position. Check fuse No. 10 (60-amp) in power distribution box. If fuse is okay, go to next step. If fuse is blown, repair short to ground in Tan wire between power distribution box and instrument panel fuse box.

5) Measure voltage at input side of fuse No. 10 in power distribution box. If battery voltage exists, repair open in Tan wire between power distribution box and instrument panel fuse box. If battery voltage does not exist, repair voltage supply to fuse No. 10 in power distribution box as necessary.

6) Disconnect left headlight switch harness connector C1037. Turn ignition switch to RUN position. Using NGS tester, enter LCM active command for headlight control. Trigger LEFT LOW active command on. Measure voltage at Dark Green/Orange wire terminal at left headlight harness connector C1037. If battery voltage exists, go to next step. If battery voltage does not exist, go to step **8)**.

7) Turn ignition switch to LOCK position. Measure resistance between ground and Black wire terminal at left headlight harness connector C1037. If resistance is 5 ohms or less, replace left headlight bulb. If resistance is greater than 5 ohms, repair open in Black wire.

8) Remove fuse No. 19 (10-amp) in instrument panel fuse box. Check fuse. If fuse is blown, go to next step. If fuse is okay, go to step **11)**.

9) Ensure ignition switch is in LOCK position. Disconnect LCM harness connector C211. Measure resistance between ground and terminal No. 24 (Pink/Light Green wire) at LCM harness connector C211. *See Fig. 8.* If resistance is greater than 10 k/ohms, go to next step. If resistance is 10 k/ohms or less, repair short to ground in Pink/Light Green wire.

NOTE: Left headlight wire changes color between LCM and right headlight. It is a Dark Blue/White wire at LCM and a Dark Green/Orange wire at left headlight.

10) Measure resistance between ground and terminal No. 12 (Dark Blue/White wire) at LCM harness connector C211. If resistance is greater than 10 k/ohms, replace LCM. If resistance is 10 k/ohms or less, repair short to ground in Dark Blue/White wire and/or Dark Green/Orange wire between LCM and left headlight.

11) Ensure fuse No. 10 is installed in power distribution box. Measure voltage at input side of fuse No. 19 in instrument panel fuse box. If battery voltage exists, go to next step. If battery voltage does not exist, repair open in Tan wire between instrument panel fuse box and power distribution box.

12) Ensure ignition switch is in LOCK position. Disconnect LCM harness connector C211. Measure resistance in Pink/Light Green wire between output side of fuse No. 19 and terminal No. 24 at LCM harness

connector C211. *See Fig. 8.* If resistance is 5 ohms or less, go to next step. If resistance is greater than 5 ohms, repair open in Pink/Light Green wire.

NOTE: Left headlight wire changes color between LCM and right headlight. It is a Dark Blue/White wire at LCM and a Dark Green/Orange wire at left headlight.

13) Measure resistance in wiring between dark green/Orange wire terminal at left headlight harness connector C1037 and terminal No. 24 (Dark Blue/White wire) at LCM harness connector C211. If resistance is 5 ohms or less, replace LCM. If resistance is greater than 5 ohms, repair open in Dark Blue/White wire and/or Dark Green/Orange wire between LCM and left headlight.

14) Disconnect right headlight switch harness connector C1038. Turn ignition switch to RUN position. Using NGS tester, enter LCM active command for headlight control. Trigger RIGHT LOW active command on. Measure voltage at Dark Green/Orange wire terminal at right headlight harness connector C1038. If battery voltage exists, go to next step. If battery voltage does not exist, go to step **16)**.

15) Turn ignition switch to LOCK position. Measure resistance between ground and Black wire terminal at right headlight harness connector C1038. If resistance is 5 ohms or less, replace right headlight bulb. If resistance is greater than 5 ohms, repair open in Black wire.

16) Remove fuse No. 25 (10-amp) in instrument panel fuse box. Check fuse. If fuse is blown, go to next step. If fuse is okay, go to step **19)**.

17) Ensure ignition switch is in LOCK position. Disconnect LCM harness connector C211. Measure resistance between ground and terminal No. 25 (Tan/Red wire) at LCM harness connector C211. *See Fig. 8.* If resistance is greater than 10 k/ohms, go to next step. If resistance is 10 k/ohms or less, repair short to ground in Tan/Red wire.

18) Measure resistance between ground and terminal No. 26 (Dark Green/Orange wire) at LCM harness connector C211. If resistance is greater than 10 k/ohms, replace LCM. If resistance is 10 k/ohms or less, repair short to ground in Dark Green/Orange wire between LCM and right headlight.

19) Ensure fuse No. 10 is installed in power distribution box. Measure voltage at input side of fuse No. 25 in instrument panel fuse box. If battery voltage exists, go to next step. If battery voltage does not exist, repair open in Tan wire between instrument panel fuse box and power distribution box.

20) Remove fuse No. 25 from instrument panel fuse box. Ensure ignition switch is in LOCK position. Disconnect LCM harness connector C211. Measure resistance in Tan/Red wire between output side of fuse No. 25 and terminal No. 25 at LCM harness connector C211. *See Fig. 8.* If resistance is 5 ohms or less, go to next step. If resistance is greater than 5 ohms, repair open in Tan/Red wire.

21) Measure resistance in Dark Green/Orange wire between right headlight harness connector C1037 and terminal No. 24 at LCM harness connector C211. If resistance is 5 ohms or less, replace LCM. If resistance is greater than 5 ohms, repair open in Dark Green/Orange wire between LCM and right headlight.

TEST C: HIGH BEAMS INOPERATIVE

1) Using NGS tester, perform Lighting Control Module (LCM) self-test. If no DTCs were retrieved, go to next step. If DTC B1569 is retrieved, go to step **3)**.

2) Ensure autolamps and headlights are off. Ensure multifunction switch is not in high beam position. Using NGS tester, monitor LCM PID LBEAMSW while turning headlight switch on and off. If PID agrees with headlight switch position, go to next step. If PID does not agree with headlight switch position, replace LCM.

3) Turn headlights on. Using NGS tester, monitor LCM PID HIBEAMSW while moving multifunction switch to high beam position and low beam position. If PID does not agree with switch position, go to next step. If PID agrees with switch position, go to step **12)**.

4) Disconnect multifunction switch harness connectors. Test multifunction switch. See MULTIFUNCTION SWITCH under COMPONENT TESTS. If multifunction switch is okay, go to next step if LCM PID

HIBEAMSW always displayed OFF or go to step **11)** if LCM PID HIBEAMSW always read ON. If multifunction switch is defective, replace multifunction switch.

5) Turn ignition switch to LOCK position. Remove fuse No. 40 (10-amp) in instrument panel fuse box. Check fuse. If fuse is okay, go to next step. If fuse is blown, go to step **8)**.

6) Turn ignition switch to RUN position. Measure voltage at input side of fuse No. 40 in instrument panel fuse box. If battery voltage exists, go to next step. If battery voltage does not exist, repair open in Gray/Yellow wire between instrument panel fuse box and ignition switch.

NOTE: Wire between output side of fuse No. 40 and multifunction switch harness connector C268 changes color. It is a Brown/Orange wire at output side of fuse No. 40 and White/Violet wire at multifunction switch harness connector C268.

7) Turn ignition switch to LOCK position. Ensure multifunction switch harness connector C268 is still disconnected and fuse No. 40 is still removed. Measure resistance in wiring between output side of fuse No. 40 in instrument panel fuse box and terminal No. 2 at multifunction switch harness connector C268. *See Fig. 9.* If resistance is 5 ohms or less, go to step **10)**. If resistance is greater than 5 ohms, repair open in Brown/Orange wire and/or White/Violet wire.

NOTE: Wire between output side of fuse No. 40 and multifunction switch harness connector C268 changes color. It is a Brown/Orange at output side of fuse No. 40 and White/Violet at multifunction switch harness connector C268.

8) Ensure multifunction switch harness connector C268 is still disconnected and fuse No. 40 is still removed. Measure resistance between ground and terminal No. 2 (Brown/Orange wire) at multifunction switch harness connector C268. *See Fig. 9.* If resistance is greater than 10 k/ohms, go to next step. If resistance is 10 k/ohms or less, repair short to ground in Brown/Orange wire and/or White/Violet wire.

9) Turn ignition switch to LOCK position. Disconnect LCM harness connector C206. Measure resistance between ground and terminal No. 6 (Violet/Light Blue wire) at LCM harness connector C206. *See Fig. 5.* If resistance is greater than 10 k/ohms, replace LCM. If resistance is 10 k/ohms or less, repair short to ground in Violet/Light Blue wire between LCM and multifunction switch.

10) Turn ignition switch to LOCK position. Disconnect LCM harness connector C206. Measure resistance in Violet/Light Blue wire between terminal No. 3 at multifunction switch harness connector C268 and terminal No. 6 at LCM harness connector C206. *See Figs. 5 and 9.* If resistance is 5 ohms or less, replace LCM. If resistance is greater than 5 ohms, repair open in Violet/Light Blue wire.

11) Connect multifunction switch harness connectors. Turn ignition switch to LOCK position. Disconnect LCM harness connector C206. Turn ignition switch to RUN position. Place multifunction switch in high beam position. Measure voltage at terminal No. 6 (Violet/Light Blue wire) at LCM harness connector C206. *See Fig. 5.* If battery voltage exists, replace LCM. If battery voltage does not exist, repair open in Violet/Light Blue wire.

12) Turn ignition switch to RUN position. Using NGS tester, trigger HIGH BEAM active command to ON. If high beams do not turn on, go to next step. If high beams turn on, replace LCM.

13) Turn ignition switch to LOCK position. Remove high beam relay in power distribution box. Turn ignition switch to RUN position. Using NGS tester, trigger HIGH BEAM active command to ON. Measure resistance between ground and terminal No. 2 (Brown wire) at high beam relay socket. *See Fig. 10.* If resistance is greater than 5 ohms, go to next step. If resistance is 5 ohms or less, go to step **15)**.

14) Turn ignition switch to LOCK position. Disconnect LCM harness connector C208. Measure resistance in Brown wire between terminal No. 2 at high beam relay socket and terminal No. 1 at LCM harness connector C208. *See Figs. 6 and 10.* If resistance is 5 ohms or less, go to next step. If resistance is greater than 5 ohms, repair open in Brown wire.

15) Measure voltage at terminal No. 5 at high beam relay socket. If battery voltage does not exist, go to next step. If battery voltage exists, go to step **20)**.

16) Remove fuse No. 7 (15-amp) in power distribution box. Check fuse. If fuse is okay, go to next step. If fuse is blown, go to step **18)**.

17) Measure voltage at input side of fuse No. 7 in power distribution box. If battery voltage exists, repair open in Dark Blue/Orange wire under power distribution box. If battery voltage does not exist, repair or replace power distribution box as necessary.

18) Ensure fuse No. 7 is still removed. Measure resistance between ground and terminal No. 5 (Dark Blue/Orange wire) at high beam relay socket. If resistance is greater than 10 k/ohms, go to next step. If resistance is 10 k/ohms or less, repair short to ground in Dark Blue/Orange wire under power distribution box.

19) Test high beam relay. See HIGH BEAM RELAY under COMPONENT TESTS. If relay is defective, replace high beam relay. If relay is okay, repair open in Light Green/Black wire between high beam relay and headlights.

20) Test high beam relay. See HIGH BEAM RELAY under COMPONENT TESTS. If relay is okay, go to next step. If relay is defective, replace high beam relay.

21) Turn ignition switch to LOCK position. Disconnect left and right headlight harness connectors. Measure resistance in Light Green/Black wire between terminal No. 3 at high beam relay socket and both headlight harness connectors. If both resistance readings are 5 ohms or less, replace appropriate headlight bulb(s). If either resistance reading is greater than 5 ohms, repair open in appropriate Light Green/Black wire.

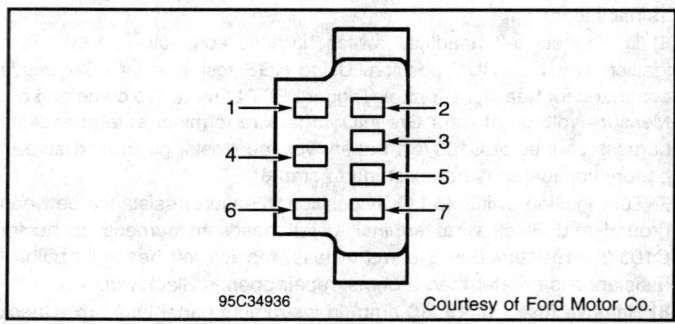

95C34936   Courtesy of Ford Motor Co.

Fig. 9: Identifying Multifunction Switch Harness Connector C268 Terminals

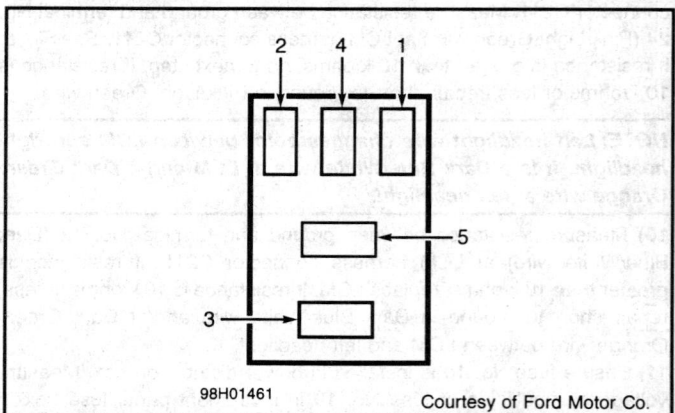

98H01461   Courtesy of Ford Motor Co.

Fig. 10: Identifying High Beam Relay Socket Terminals

TEST D: LOW BEAMS ON CONTINUOUSLY (DAYTIME RUNNING LIGHTS DISABLED)

1) Ensure headlight switch is off. Connect NGS tester to Data Link Connector (DLC). Perform Lighting Control Module (LCM) self-test. If no DTCs are retrieved, go to next step. If DTC B1312 is retrieved, replace LCM.

2) Turn ignition switch to RUN position. Ensure autolamps and headlights are off. Ensure multifunction switch is not in high beam position. Using NGS tester, monitor LCM PID LBEAMSW while turning headlight switch on and off. If PID agrees with headlight switch position, go to next step. If PID does not agree with headlight switch position, replace LCM.
3) Turn ignition switch to LOCK position. If low beams are on, go to next step. Place gear selector in Park. If low beams are off, system is okay at this this.
4) Disconnect Lighting Control Module (LCM) harness connector C211. Measure voltage at terminals No. 12 (Dark Blue/White wire) and No. 26 (Dark Green/Orange wire) at LCM harness connector C211. *See Fig. 8.* If voltage exists, repair short to voltage in appropriate wire. If voltage does not exist, replace LCM.

TEST E: FLASH-TO-PASS FEATURE INOPERATIVE

1) Connect NGS tester to Data Link Connector (DLC). Using NGS tester, perform Lighting Control Module (LCM) self-test. If no DTCs were retrieved, go to next step. If DTC B1509 is retrieved, go to step **8)**.
2) Turn headlights on. Place multifunction switch in high beam position. If high beams operate, go to next step. If high beams do not operate, perform TEST C: HIGH BEAMS INOPERATIVE.
3) Turn headlights on. Using NGS tester, monitor LCM PID FLASH while moving multifunction switch to flash-to-pass position and back. If PID does not agree with switch position, go to next step. If PID agrees with switch position, replace LCM.
4) Turn ignition switch to LOCK position. Disconnect multifunction switch harness connectors. Test multifunction switch. See MULTIFUNCTION SWITCH under COMPONENT TEST. If multifunction switch is okay, go to next step. If multifunction switch is defective, replace multifunction switch.
5) Turn ignition switch to RUN position. Measure voltage at input side of fuse No. 20 (15-amp) in instrument panel fuse box. If battery voltage exists, remove fuse and go to next step. If battery voltage does not exist, repair open in Tan/Black wire.
6) Ensure multifunction switch harness connector C268 is still disconnected. Measure resistance in Dark Blue/Orange wire between output side of fuse No. 20 in instrument panel fuse box and terminal No. 7 at multifunction switch harness connector C268. *See Fig. 9.* If resistance is 5 ohms or less, go to next step. If resistance is greater than 5 ohms, repair open in Dark Blue/Orange wire.
7) Connect multifunction switch harness connectors. Disconnect LCM harness connector C206. Turn ignition switch to RUN position. Measure at terminal No. 5 (Dark Blue/Orange wire) at LCM harness connector C206. *See Fig. 5.* When multifunction switch is in flash-to-pas position battery voltage should exist. When multifunction switch is not in flash-to-pass position battery voltage should not exist. If voltage is as specified, replace LCM. If voltage is not as specified, repair open or short in Dark Blue/Orange wire.
8) Disconnect multifunction switch harness connector C268 and LCM harness connector C206. Turn ignition switch to RUN position. Measure voltage at terminal No. 5 (Dark Blue/Orange wire) at LCM harness connector C206. *See Fig. 5.* If voltage exists, repair short to voltage in Dark Blue/Orange wire. If voltage does not exist, replace multifunction switch.

TEST F: AUTOLAMPS ARE INOPERATIVE

NOTE: Ensure all other headlight system operation is okay before proceeding with this test.

1) Ensure headlight switch and autolamp switches are off. Connect NGS tester to Data Link Connector (DLC). Perform Lighting Control Module (LCM) self-test. If no DTCs are retrieved, go to next step. If DTC B1590 is retrieved, replace LCM.
2) Turn ignition switch to RUN position. Using NGS tester, monitor LCM PID LIGHTSN while applying a bright light source and covering light sensor/amplifier. PID should display DAY with light source apply and NIGHT when covered. If PID display is not as specified, go to next step. If PID display is as specified, go to step **6)**.

3) Turn ignition switch to LOCK position. Disconnect light sensor/amplifier harness connector C243. Measure resistance between ground and terminal No. 4 (White/Purple wire) at light sensor/amplifier harness connector C243. *See Fig. 11.* If resistance is greater than 10 k/ohms, go to next step. If resistance is 10 k/ohms or less, repair short to ground in White/Purple wire between light sensor/amplifier and LCM.
4) Using NGS tester, monitor LCM PID LIGHTSN while connecting a fused jumper wire between terminal No. 4 (White/Purple wire) and No. 6 (Red/Yellow wire) at light sensor/amplifier harness connector C243. LCM PID LIGHTSN should display DAY with ignition switch in RUN position and NIGHT with ignition switch in LOCK position. If PID display is not as specified, go to next step. If PID display is as specified, replace light sensor/amplifier.
5) Ensure jumper wire is still connected as in step **4)**. Turn ignition switch to LOCK position. Disconnect LCM harness connector C206. Measure voltage between ground and terminal No. 19 (White/Purple wire) at LCM harness connector C206. *See Fig. 5.* Battery voltage should exist with ignition switch in RUN position and battery voltage should not exist with ignition switch in LOCK position. If voltage is as specified, go to next step. If voltage is not as specified, repair open in White/Purple wire.
6) Turn ignition switch to LOCK position. Connect LCM harness connector C206 and light sensor/amplifier harness connector C243. Turn autolamp switch on and headlight switch off. Turn ignition switch to RUN position. Cover light sensor/amplifier. Headlights should turn on after 15 seconds. Uncover light sensor/amplifier and apply a bright light source. Headlight should turn off after 15 seconds. If headlights operate as specified, system is okay at this time. If headlights do not operate as specified, replace LCM.

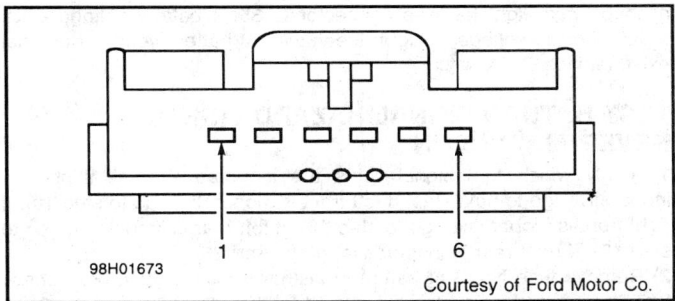

98H01673   Courtesy of Ford Motor Co.

Fig. 11: Identifying Light Sensor/Amplifier Harness Connector C243 Terminals

TEST G: BRAKE LIGHTS NEVER/ALWAYS ON

1) Connect NGS tester to Data Link Connector (DLC). Perform Lighting Control Module (LCM) self-test. If no DTCs are retrieved, go to next step. If DTC B1483 is retrieved, go to next step.
2) Turn ignition switch to RUN position. Operate both turn signals. If both turn signal operate, go to next step. If either turn signal does not operate, perform TEST H: TURN SIGNAL/HAZARD LIGHTS NEVER/ALWAYS ON.
3) Ensure ignition switch is in RUN position. Using NGS tester, monitor LCM PID BOO_LCM while depressing and releasing brake pedal. If PID agrees with brake pedal position, replace LCM. If PID does not agree with brake pedal position, go to next step if brake lights are inoperative, go to step **11)** if only third brake light is inoperative or go to step **12)** if brake lights are always on.
4) Measure voltage at output side of fuse No. 32 (15-amp) in instrument panel fuse box. If battery voltage does not exist, go to next step. If battery voltage exists, go to step **8)**.
5) Remove fuse No. 32 in instrument panel fuse box. Check fuse. If fuse is blown, go to next step. If fuse is okay, repair open in Tan/Black wire between instrument panel fuse box and power distribution box.
6) Ensure fuse No. 32 is still removed. Disconnect Brake Pedal Position (BPP) switch harness connector C253. Measure resistance between ground and Light Green/Red wire terminal at BPP switch harness connector C253. If resistance is greater than 10 k/ohms, go to next step. If resistance is 10 k/ohms or less, repair short to ground in Light Green/Red wire.

7) Turn ignition switch to LOCK position. Disconnect LCM harness connector C206. Measure resistance between ground and terminal No. 8 (Light Green wire) at LCM harness connector C206. *See Fig. 5.* If resistance is greater than 10 k/ohms, replace BPP switch. If resistance is 10 k/ohms or less, repair short to ground in Light Green wire.

8) Disconnect Brake Pedal Position (BPP) switch harness connector C253. Measure voltage at Light Green/Red wire terminal at BPP switch harness connector C253. If battery voltage exists, go to next step. If battery voltage does not exist, repair open in Light Green/Red wire.

9) Turn ignition switch to LOCK position. Using a fused jumper wire, connect Light Green and Light Green/Red wire terminals at BPP switch harness connector C253. If brake lights do not illuminate, remove jumper wire and go to next step. If brake lights illuminate, replace BPP switch.

10) Ensure igniton switch is in LOCK position. Disconnect LCM harness connector C206. Measure resistance in Light Green wire between BPP switch harness connector and terminal No. 8 at LCM harness connector C206. *See Fig. 5.* If resistance is 5 ohms or less, replace LCM. If resistance is greater than 5 ohms, repair open in Light Green wire.

11) Turn igniton switch to LOCK position. Disconnect third brake light harness connector C435. Measure voltage at Light Green wire terminal at third brake light harness connector C435 while depressing brake pedal. If battery voltage exist, repair open in Black wire or replace bulb as necessary. If battery voltage does not exist, repair open in Light Green wire between third brake light and brake pedal position switch.

12) Turn ignition switch to LOCK position. Disconnect third brake light harness connector C435. Disconnect Brake Pedal Position (BPP) switch harness connector C253. Measure voltage at Light Green wire terminal at third brake light harness connector C435. If battery voltage exist, repair short to voltage in Light Green wire. If battery voltage does not exist, replace BPP switch.

TEST H: TURN SIGNAL/HAZARD LIGHTS NEVER/ALWAYS ON

1) Verify which turn signal lights are inoperative. If all lights are inoperative, go to next step. If left front is inoperative, go to step 10). If right front is inoperative, go to step 13). If left rear is inoperative, go to step 16). If right rear is inoperative, go to step 25).

2) Remove fuse No. 3 (15-amp) in instrument panel fuse box. Check fuse. If fuse is okay, go to next step. If fuse is blown, go to step 7).

3) Install fuse No. 3 in instrument panel fuse box. Turn ignition switch to RUN position. Measure voltage at output side of fuse No. 3 in instrument panel fuse box. If battery voltage exists, go to next step. If battery voltage does not exist, repair open in Gray/Yellow wire between instrument panel fuse box and ignition switch.

4) Disconnect multifunction switch harness connector C269. Turn ignition switch to RUN position. Measure voltage at terminal No. 1 (Black/Yellow wire) at multifunction switch harness connector C269. *See Fig. 12.* If battery voltage exists, go to next step. If battery voltage does not exist, repair open in Black/Yellow wire between multifunction switch and instrument panel fuse box.

5) Turn ignition switch to LOCK position. Disconnect LCM harness connector C207. Measure resistance in Orange/Yellow wire between terminal No. 19 at LCM harness connector C207 and terminal No. 11 at multifunction switch harness connector C269. *See Figs. 7 and 12.* If resistance is 5 ohms or less, go to next step. If resistance is greater than 5 ohms, repair open in Orange/Yellow wire.

6) Measure resistance in Light Blue wire between terminal No. 20 at LCM harness connector C207 and terminal No. 6 at multifunction switch harness connector C269. If resistance is 5 ohms or less, replace multifunction switch. If resistance is greater than 5 ohms, repair open in Light Blue wire.

7) Ensure fuse No. 3 is still removed. Disconnect multifunction switch harness connector C269. Measure resistance between ground and terminal No. 1 (Black/Yellow wire) at multifunction switch harness connector C269. *See Fig. 12.* If resistance is greater than 10 k/ohms, go to next step. If resistance is 10 k/ohms or less, repair short to ground in Black/Yellow wire between multifunction switch and instrument panel fuse box.

8) Turn ignition switch to LOCK position. Disconnect LCM harness connector C207. Measure resistance between ground and terminal No. 19 (Orange/Yellow wire) at LCM harness connector C207. *See Fig. 7.* If resistance is greater than 10 k/ohms, go to next step. If resistance is 10 k/ohms or less, repair short to ground in Orange/Yellow wire between multifunction switch and LCM.

9) Measure resistance between ground and terminal No. 20 (Light Blue wire) at LCM harness connector C207. If resistance is greater than 10 k/ohms, replace multifunction switch. If resistance is 10 k/ohms or less, repair short to ground in Light Blue wire between multifunction switch and LCM.

10) Turn ignition switch to LOCK position. Remove fuse No. 24 (10-amp) in instrument panel fuse box. Check fuse. If fuse is okay, go to next step. If fuse is blown, repair short to ground in Light Green/White wire between instrument panel fuse box and left front turn signal or instrument cluster.

11) Turn ignition switch to RUN position. Place multifunction switch in left turn position. Measure voltage and input side of fuse No. 24 in instrument panel fuse box. If voltage does not fluctuate between 3 and 10 volts, go to next step. If voltage fluctuates between 3 and 10 volts, repair open in Light Green/White wire, ground (Black wire) or replace blub as necessary.

12) Turn ignition switch to LOCK position. Disconnect multifunction switch harness connector C269. Measure resistance in Yellow wire between input side of fuse No. 24 in instrument panel fuse box and terminal No. 8 at multifunction switch harness connector C296. *See Fig. 12.* If resistance is 5 ohms or less, replace multifunction switch. If resistance is greater than 5 ohms, repair open in Yellow wire.

13) Turn ignition switch to LOCK position. Remove fuse No. 6 (10-amp) in instrument panel fuse box. Check fuse. If fuse is okay, go to next step. If fuse is blown, repair short to ground in White/Light Blue wire between instrument panel fuse box and right front turn signal or instrument cluster.

14) Turn ignition switch to RUN position. Place multifunction switch in right turn position. Measure voltage and input side of fuse No. 6 in instrument panel fuse box. If voltage does not fluctuate between 3 and 10 volts, go to next step. If voltage fluctuates between 3 and 10 volts, repair open in White/Light Blue wire, ground (Black wire) or replace blub as necessary.

15) Turn ignition switch to LOCK position. Disconnect multifunction switch harness connector C269. Measure resistance in Dark Green wire between input side of fuse No. 6 in instrument panel fuse box and terminal No. 5 at multifunction switch harness connector C296. *See Fig. 12.* If resistance is 5 ohms or less, replace multifunction switch. If resistance is greater than 5 ohms, repair open in Dark Green wire.

16) Turn ignition switch to LOCK position. Disconnect left rear turn signal harness connector C439. Turn igniton switch to RUN position. Place multifunction switch in left turn position. Measure voltage at Orange/Light Blue wire terminal at left rear turn signal harness connector C439. If voltage fluctuates between 3 and 10 volts, go to next step. If voltage does not fluctuate between 3 and 10 volts, go to step 18).

17) Measure resistance between ground and Black wire terminal at left rear turn signal harness connector C439. If resistance is 5 ohms or less, replace bulb. If resistance is greater than 5 ohms, repair open in Black wire.

18) Remove fuse No. 12 (10-amp) in instrument panel fuse box. Check fuse. If fuse is okay, go to next step. If fuse is blown, go to step 23).

19) Turn igniton switch to RUN position. Place multifunction switch in left turn position. Measure voltage at input side of fuse No. 12 in instrument panel fuse box. If voltage does not fluctuate between 3 and 10 volts, go to next step. If voltage fluctuates between 3 and 10 volts, go to step 21).

20) Turn ignition switch to LOCK position. Disconnect multifunction switch harness connector C269. Measure resistance in Red/White wire between input side of fuse No. 12 in instrument panel fuse box and terminal No. 2 at multifunction switch harness connector C269. *See Fig. 12.* If resistance is 5 ohms or less, replace multifunction switch. If resistance is greater than 5 ohms, repair open in Red/White wire.

21) Install fuse No. 18 in instrument panel fuse box. Disconnect LCM harness connector C211. Turn ignition switch to RUN position. Place

multifunction switch in left turn position. Measure voltage at terminal No. 22 (Light Blue/Black wire) at LCM harness connector C211 *See Fig. 8.* If voltage fluctuates between 3 and 10 volts, go to next step. If voltage does not fluctuate between 3 and 10 volts, repair open in Light Blue/Black wire.

NOTE: Wire between LCM and left rear turn signal changes color. It is a Light Green/Orange wire at LCM and Orange/Light Blue wire at left rear turn signal.

22) Disconnect LCM harness connector C207. Remove both left rear turn signal bulbs. Measure resistance between Orange/Light Blue wire terminal at left rear turn signal light harness connector C439 and terminal No. 7 (Light Green/Orange wire) at LCM harness connector C207. *See Fig. 7.* If resistance 5 ohms or less, replace LCM. If resistance is greater than 5 ohms, repair open in Light Green/Orange wire or Orange/Light Blue wire between LCM and left rear turn signal.

23) Disconnect LCM harness connector C211. Measure resistance between ground and terminal No. 22 (Light Blue/Black wire) at LCM harness connector C211. *See Fig. 8.* If resistance is greater than 10 k/ohms, go to next step. If resistance is 10 k/ohms or less, repair short to ground in Light Blue/Black wire.

NOTE: Wire between LCM and left rear turn signal changes color. It is a Light Green/Orange wire at LCM and Orange/Light Blue wire at left rear turn signal.

24) Turn igniton switch to LOCK position. Disconnect LCM harness connector C207. Remove both left turn signal bulbs. Measure resistance between ground and terminal No. 7 (Light Green/Orange wire) at LCM harness connector C207. *See Fig. 7.* If resistance is greater than 10 k/ohms, replace LCM. If resistance is 10 k/ohms or less, repair short to ground in Light Green/Orange wire or Orange/Light Blue wire between LCM and left rear turn signal.

25) Turn ignition switch to LOCK position. Disconnect right rear turn signal harness connector C440. Turn igniton switch to RUN position. Place multifunction switch in right turn position. Measure voltage at Orange/Light Blue wire terminal at right rear turn signal harness connector C440. If voltage fluctuates between 3 and 10 volts, go to next step. If voltage does not fluctuate between 3 and 10 volts, go to step 27).

26) Measure resistance between ground and Black wire terminal at right rear turn signal harness connector C439. If resistance is 5 ohms or less, replace bulb. If resistance is greater than 5 ohms, repair open in Black wire.

27) Remove fuse No. 18 (10-amp) in instrument panel fuse box. Check fuse. If fuse is okay, go to next step. If fuse is blown, go to step 32).

28) Turn igniton switch to RUN position. Place multifunction switch in right turn position. Measure voltage at input side of fuse No. 18 in instrument panel fuse box. If voltage does not fluctuate between 3 and 10 volts, go to next step. If voltage fluctuates between 3 and 10 volts, go to step 30).

29) Turn ignition switch to LOCK position. Disconnect multifunction switch harness connector C269. Measure resistance in Light Blue/Orange wire between input side of fuse No. 18 in instrument panel fuse box and terminal No. 10 at multifunction switch harness connector C269. *See Fig. 12.* If resistance is 5 ohms or less, replace multifunction switch. If resistance is greater than 5 ohms, repair open in Red/White wire.

30) Install fuse No. 18 in instrument panel fuse box. Disconnect LCM harness connector C211. Turn ignition switch to RUN position. Place multifunction switch in right turn position. Measure voltage at terminal No. 8 (Dark Blue wire) at LCM harness connector C211. *See Fig. 8.* If voltage fluctuates between 3 and 10 volts, go to next step. If voltage does not fluctuate between 3 and 10 volts, repair open in Dark Blue wire.

31) Remove both right rear turn signal bulbs. Measure resistance in Orange/Light Blue wire between right rear turn signal light harness connector C439 and terminal No. 21 at LCM harness connector C211. If resistance 5 ohms or less, replace LCM. If resistance is greater than 5 ohms, repair open in Orange/Light Blue wire between LCM and right rear turn signal.

32) Disconnect LCM harness connector C211. Measure resistance between ground and terminal No. 8 (Dark Blue wire) at LCM harness connector C211. *See Fig. 8.* If resistance is greater than 10 k/ohms, go to next step. If resistance is 10 k/ohms or less, repair short to ground in Dark Blue wire.

33) Turn igniton switch to LOCK position. Remove both right turn signal bulbs. Measure resistance between ground and terminal No. 21 (Orange/Light Blue wire) at LCM harness connector C211. If resistance is greater than 10 k/ohms, replace LCM. If resistance is 10 k/ohms or less, repair short to ground in Orange/Light Blue wire between LCM and right rear turn signal.

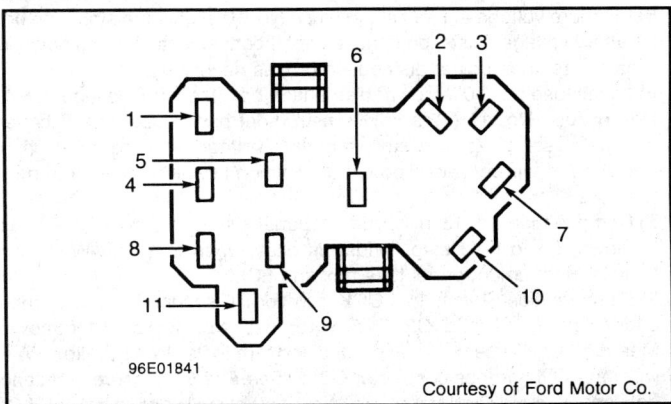

96E01841
Courtesy of Ford Motor Co.

Fig. 12: Identifying Multifunction Switch Harness Connector C269 Terminals

TEST J: CORNERING LIGHTS NEVER/ALWAYS ON

1) Turn ignition switch to RUN position. Turn headlights switch on. Place multifunction switch to high beam position. If high beams operate, go to next step. If high beams do not operate, perform TEST C: HIGH BEAMS INOPERATIVE.

2) Turn ignition switch to LOCK position. Disconnect multifunction switch harness connectors. Test multifunction switch. See MULTIFUNCTION SWITCH under COMPONENT TESTS. If multifunction switch is okay, go to next step. If multifunction switch is defective, replace multifunction switch.

NOTE: Wire between multifunction switch and left front cornering light changes color. It is a Violet/Yellow wire at multifunction switch harness connector C269 and Brown/White wire at left cornering light.

3) Connect multifunction switch harness connectors. Disconnect right and left cornering light harness connectors. Turn ignition switch to RUN position. Measure voltage at Brown/White wire terminal at appropriate cornering light with multifunction switch in appropriate position. If battery voltage exists, go to next step. If battery voltage does not exist, repair open in appropriate wire.

4) Turn igniton switch to LOCK position. Measure resistance between ground and Black wire terminal at both cornering light harness connectors. If resistance is 5 ohms or less, replace bulb. If resistance is greater than 5 ohms, repair open in Black wire.

TEST K: PARKING, REAR OR LICENSE LIGHTS INOPERATIVE

1) Ensure headlight switch and autolamp switches are off. Connect NGS tester to Data Link Connector (DLC). Perform Lighting Control Module (LCM) self-test. If no DTCs are retrieved, go to next step. If DTC B1807 is retrieved, go to step 14) if parking lights are not always on or perform TEST L: PARKING, REAR OR LICENSE LIGHTS ON CONTINUOUSLY if parking lights are always on. If DTC B1577 is retrieved, replace LCM.

2) Turn ignition switch to RUN position. Using NGS tester, monitor LCM PID PARKSW and LCM PID LBEAMSW while turning headlight switch on and off. If PIDs agree with switch position, go to next step. If PIDs do not agree with switch position, replace LCM.

3) Using NGS tester, select LCM active command TURN SIGNALS AND MARKER LAMPS. Trigger PARKLAMPS and TAILLAMPS on. If parking lights, marker lights and tail lights are all inoperative, go to next step. If only front parking lights and marker lights are inoperative, to step 9). If only right rear tail lights are inoperative, go to step 14). If only left rear tail lights are inoperative, go to step 17). If both rear tail lights and parking lights are inoperative, go to step 10). If parking lights and marker lights operate, replace LCM.

4) Remove fuse No. 10 (60-amp) in power distribution box. Check fuse. If fuse is okay, go to next step. If fuse is blown, repair short to ground in Tan wire between power distribution box and instrument panel fuse box.

5) Measure voltage at input side of fuse No. 10 in power distribution box. If battery voltage exists, go to next step. If battery voltage does not exist, repair or replace power distribution box as necessary.

6) Install fuse No. 10 in power distribution box. Measure voltage at input side of fuse No. 13 (15-amp) in instrument panel fuse box. If battery voltage exists, go to next step. If battery voltage does not exist, repair open in Tan wire between power distribution box and instrument panel fuse box.

7) Remove fuse No. 13 in instrument panel fuse box. Check fuse. If fuse is blown, go to next step. If fuse is okay, open in Yellow/White wire between instrument panel fuse box and LCM.

8) Turn ignition switch to LOCK position. Disconnect LCM harness connectors C211 and C207. Ensure fuse No. 13 is still removed. Measure resistance between ground and terminals No. 11 (Yellow/White wire) at LCM harness connector C211. See Fig. 8. Measure resistance between ground and terminals No. 4 (Yellow/White wire) at LCM harness connector C207. See Fig. 7. If both resistance readings are greater than 10 k/ohms, replace LCM. If either resistance reading is 10 k/ohms or less, repair short to ground in Yellow/White wire between instrument panel fuse box and LCM.

9) Disconnect LCM harness connector C211. Remove all marker light, licence plate light and front parking light bulbs. Measure resistance between ground and terminal No. 10 (Orange/Black wire) at LCM harness connector C211. See Fig. 8. If resistance is greater than 10 k/ohms, go to step 12). If resistance is 10 k/ohms or less, repair short to ground in Orange/Black wire.

10) Disconnect LCM harness connector C207. Remove all rear tail lights and rear parking light bulbs. Measure resistance between ground and terminal No. 5 (White/Red wire) at LCM harness connector C207. See Fig. 7. If resistance is greater than 10 k/ohms, go to next step. If resistance is 10 k/ohms or less, repair short to ground in White/Red wire.

11) Ensure all rear tail light and rear parking light bulbs are still removed. Measure resistance between ground and terminal No. 18 (White wire) at LCM harness connector C207. If resistance is greater than 10 k/ohms, replace LCM. If resistance is 10 k/ohms or less, repair short to ground in White wire.

12) Turn ignition switch to LOCK position. Measure voltage at terminal No. 11 (Yellow/White wire) at LCM harness connector C211. If battery voltage exists, go to next step. If battery voltage does not exist, repair open in Yellow/White wire between instrument panel fuse box and LCM.

13) Connect LCM harness connector C211. Turn parking lights on. Using a voltmeter, backprobe at terminal No. 10 (Orange/Black wire) at LCM harness connector C211. If battery voltage exists, repair open in Orange/Black wire. If battery voltage does not exist, replace LCM.

14) Turn igniton switch to LOCK position. Disconnect both right rear tail light harness connectors. Turn ignition switch to RUN position. Using NGS tester, select LCM active command TURN SIGNAL AND MARKERLAMPS. Trigger TAILLAMPS on. Measure voltage at White/Red wire terminal at both right rear tail light harness connectors. If battery voltage exists, go to next step. If battery voltage does not exist, go to step 16).

15) Turn ignition switch to LOCK position. Measure resistance between ground and Black wire terminal at both right rear tail light harness connectors. If either resistance reading is greater than 5 ohms, repair open in Black wire. If both resistance readings are 5 ohms or less, replace bulb(s).

16) Turn ignition switch to LOCK position. Disconnect LCM harness connector C207. Measure resistance in White/Red wire between right rear tail light harness connectors and terminal No. 5 at LCM harness

connector C207. See Fig. 7. If resistance is 5 ohms or less, replace LCM. If resistance is greater than 5 ohms, repair open in White/Red wire.

17) Turn igniton switch to LOCK position. Disconnect both left rear tail light harness connectors. Turn ignition switch to RUN position. Using NGS tester, select LCM active command TURN SIGNAL AND MARKERLAMPS. Trigger TAILAMPS on. Measure voltage at White wire terminal at both left rear tail light harness connectors. If battery voltage exists, go to next step. If battery voltage does not exist, go to step 19).

18) Turn ignition switch to LOCK position. Measure resistance between ground and Black wire terminal at both left rear tail light harness connectors. If either resistance reading is greater than 5 ohms, repair open in Black wire. If both resistance readings are 5 ohms or less, replace bulb(s).

19) Turn ignition switch to LOCK position. Disconnect LCM harness connector C207. Measure resistance in White wire between left rear tail light harness connectors and terminal No. 18 at LCM harness connector C207. See Fig. 7. If resistance is 5 ohms or less, replace LCM. If resistance is greater than 5 ohms, repair open in White wire.

TEST L: PARKING, REAR OR LICENSE LIGHTS ON CONTINUOUSLY

1) Ensure headlight switch and autolamp switches are off. Connect NGS tester to Data Link Connector (DLC). Perform Lighting Control Module (LCM) self-test. If no DTCs are retrieved, go to next step. If DTC B1807 is retrieved, go to step 5). If DTC B1577 is retrieved, replace LCM.

2) Turn ignition switch to RUN position. Using NGS tester, monitor LCM PID PARKSW and LCM PID LBEAMSW while turning headlight switch on and off. If PIDs agree with switch position, go to next step. If PIDs do not agree with switch position, replace LCM.

3) Using NGS tester, select LCM active command TURN SIGNALS AND MARKER LAMPS. Trigger PARKLAMPS and TAILLAMPS on then off. If parking and tail lights turn on and off, replace LCM. If parking lights do not turn off, go to next step. If tail lights do not turn off, go to step 5).

4) Turn ignition switch to LOCK position. Disconnect LCM harness connector C211. Measure voltage at terminal No. 10 (Orange/Black wire) at LCM harness connector C211. See Fig. 8. If voltage exists, repair short to voltage in Orange/Black wire. If voltage does not exist, replace LCM.

5) Turn ignition switch to LOCK position. Disconnect LCM harness connector C207. Measure voltage at terminals No. 5 (White/Red wire) and No. 18 (White wire) at LCM harness connector C207. See Fig. 7. If voltage does not exist, go to next step. If voltage exists, repair short to voltage in appropriate wire.

6) Turn ignition switch to LOCK position. Disconnect LCM harness connector C211. Measure voltage at terminals No. 7 (Light Green/Orange wire) and No. 21 (Orange/Light Blue wire) at LCM harness connector C211. See Fig. 8. If voltage does not exist, replace LCM. If voltage exists, repair short to voltage in appropriate wire.

TEST M: BACK-UP LIGHT INOPERATIVE

1) Turn ignition switch to LOCK position. Disconnect Digital Transmission Range (DTR) sensor harness connector C180. Turn ignition switch to RUN position. Measure voltage at terminal No. 9 (Red/Black wire) at DTR sensor harness connector C180. See Fig. 13. If battery voltage does not exist, go to next step. If battery voltage exists, go to step 5).

2) Remove fuse No. 34 (15-amp) in instrument panel fuse box. Check fuse. If fuse is okay, go to next step. If fuse is blown, go to step 4).

3) Measure voltage at input side of fuse No. 34 in instrument panel fuse box. If battery voltage exists, repair open in Red/Black wire between instrument panel fuse box and DTR sensor. If battery voltage does not exist, repair open in Gray/Yellow wire between instrument panel fuse box and ignition switch.

4) Ensure fuse No. 34 is still remove. Measure resistance between ground and terminal No. 9 (Red/Black wire) at DTR sensor harness connector C180. If resistance is greater than 10 k/ohms, go to next step. If resistance is 10 k/ohms or less, repair short to ground in Red/Black wire.

5) Remove backup light bulbs. Measure resistance between ground and terminal No. 11 (Black/Red wire) at DTR sensor harness connector C180. If resistance is greater than 10 k/ohms, adjust or replace DTR sensor as necessary. If resistance is 10 k/ohms or less, repair short to ground in Black/Pink wire.

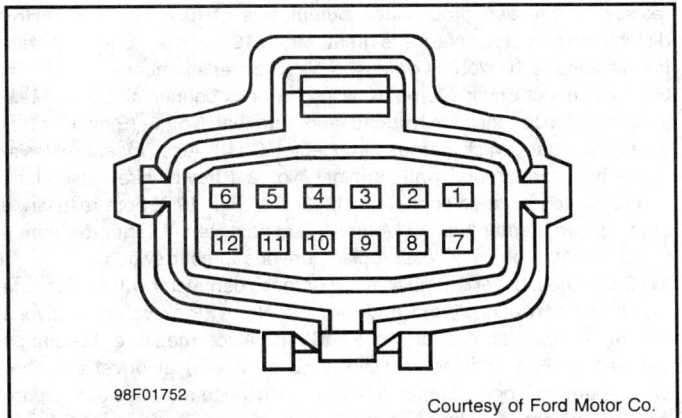

98F01752 · Courtesy of Ford Motor Co.

Fig. 13: Identifying Digital Transmission Range Sensor Harness Connector C180 Terminals

TEST N: BACK-UP LIGHT ON CONTINUOUSLY

Disconnect Digital Transmission Range (DTR) sensor harness connector. Turn ignition switch to RUN position. If back-up lights illuminate, repair short to voltage in Black/Pink wire. If reverse lights do not illuminate, adjust or replace DTR sensor as necessary.

TEST O: NO COMMUNICATION WITH DRIVER'S DOOR MODULE

NOTE: After any repairs are complete, ensure all component are properly installed and all harness connectors are connected properly and repeat data link diagnostic test.

NOTE: Connectors C315 and C362 are 2 terminal connectors. Identify connectors by wire color. See WIRING DIAGRAMS.

1) Connect NGS tester to Data Link Connector (DLC). Turn ignition switch to RUN position. Monitor Driver's Door Module (DDM) PIDs SFWD_SW, SREAR_SW, SFNT_SW and SRCL_SW while activating power seat control switch. If UNABLE TO PERFORM TEST FUCTION MODULE NOT RESPONDING: DDM CHECK IGNITION STATUS/VERIFY CABLE REQUIREMENTS CHEK CABLE CONNECTIONS? is not displayed, go to next step. If UNABLE TO PERFORM TEST FUCTION MODULE NOT RESPONDING: DDM CHECK IGNITION STATUS/VERIFY CABLE REQUIREMENTS CHEK CABLE CONNECTIONS? is displayed, perform TEST A: NO COMMUNICATION WITH LIGHTING CONTROL MODULE.

2) Turn ignition switch to LOCK position. Remove fuse No. 39 (10-amp) in instrument panel fuse box. Check fuse. If fuse is okay, go to next step. If fuse is blown, go to step **6)**.

3) Measure voltage at input side of fuse No. 39 in instrument panel fuse box. If battery voltage exists, go to next step. If battery voltage does not exist, go to step **24)**.

4) Install fuse No. 39. Disconnect Driver's Door Module (DDM) harness connector C524. Measure voltage at terminal No. 6 (Black/White wire) at DDM harness connector C524. *See Fig. 14.* If battery voltage exists, go to next step. If battery voltage does not exist, repair open in Black/White wire between instrument panel fuse box and DDM.

5) Measure resistance between ground and terminal No. 14 (Black/Light Blue wire) at DDM harness connector C524. If resistance is greater than 5 ohms, repair open in Black/Light Blue wire. If resistance is 5 ohms or less, repair module communication concern. See MODULE COMMUNICATIONS NETWORK – CONTINENTAL article.

6) Replace fuse No. 39. DO NOT operate any switches. If fuse blows, go to next step. If fuse does not blow, go to step **14)**.

7) Remove fuse No. 39. Disconnect DDM harness connector C524, Driver's Seat Module (DSM) harness connector C342, keyless entry keypad harness connector C525, driver's seat control switch harness connector C520, driver's door lock switch harness connector C505, passenger's door lock switch harness connector C602 and power mirror control switch harness connector C550. Measure resistance between ground and terminal No. 6 (Black/White wire) at DDM harness connector C524. If resistance is greater than 10 k/ohms, go to next step. If resistance is 10 k/ohms or less, repair short to ground in Black/White wire.

8) Connect keyless entry keypad harness connector C525. Measure resistance between ground and terminal No. 6 (Black/White wire) at DDM harness connector C524. If resistance is greater than 10 k/ohms, go to next step. If resistance is 10 k/ohms or less, replace keyless entry keypad.

9) Connect driver's seat control switch harness connector C520. Measure resistance between ground and terminal No. 6 (Black/White wire) at DDM harness connector C524. If resistance is greater than 10 k/ohms, go to next step. If resistance is 10 k/ohms or less, replace driver's seat control switch.

10) Connect DSM harness connector C342. Measure resistance between ground and terminal No. 6 (Black/White wire) at DDM harness connector C524. If resistance is greater than 10 k/ohms, go to next step. If resistance is 10 k/ohms or less, replace driver's seat module.

11) Connect DDM harness connector C524. Measure resistance between ground and terminal No. 6 (Black/White wire) at driver's door lock switch harness connector C505. *See Fig. 15.* If resistance is greater than 10 k/ohms, go to next step. If resistance is 10 k/ohms or less, replace driver's door module.

12) Connect passenger's door lock switch harness connector C602. Measure resistance between ground and terminal No. 6 (Black/White wire) at driver's door lock switch harness connector C505. If resistance is greater than 10 k/ohms, go to next step. If resistance is 10 k/ohms or less, replace passenger's door lock switch.

13) Connect power mirror control switch harness connector C550. Measure resistance between ground and terminal No. 6 (Black/White wire) at driver's door lock switch harness connector C505. If resistance is greater than 10 k/ohms, replace driver's door lock switch. If resistance is 10 k/ohms or less, replace power mirror control switch.

14) Lock and unlock doors at all door lock switches. If fuse No. 39 blows, go to next step. If fuse No. 39 does not blow, go to step **17)**.

15) Remove driver's and passenger's door lock switches. Test both door lock switches. See DOOR LOCK SWITCH under COMPONENT TESTS. If both door lock switches are okay, go to next step. If either door lock switch is defective, replace appropriate door lock switch.

16) Disconnect Driver's Door Module (DDM) harness connector C506. Measure resistance between ground and terminal No. 1 (Pink/Yellow wire) at driver's door lock switch harness connector C505. Also, measure resistance between ground and terminal No. 5 (Pink/Light Green wire) at driver's door lock switch harness connector C505. *See Fig. 15.* If either resistance reading is 10 k/ohms or less, repair short to ground in appropriate wire(s). If both resistance readings are greater than 10 k/ohms, replace driver's door module.

17) Press each number on keyless entry pad one at a time. If fuse No. 39 blows, go to next step. If fuse No. 39 does not blow, go to step **19)**.

18) Disconnect Driver's Door Module (DDM) harness connector C523. Disconnect keyless entry keypad harness connector C525. Measure resistance between ground and appropriate terminals at remote keyless entry keypad harness connector C525. See REMOTE KEYLESS ENTRY TERMINAL IDENTIFICATION table. *See Fig. 16.* If all resistance readings are greater than 10 k/ohms, replace driver's door module. If any resistance readings are 10 k/ohms or less, repair short to ground in appropriate wire.

REMOTE KEYLESS ENTRY TERMINAL IDENTIFICATION

Terminal	Wire Color
1	Red
2	Yellow
3	Yellow/Black

REMOTE KEYLESS ENTRY TERMINAL IDENTIFICATION (Cont.)

Terminal	Wire Color
4	Light Green/Red
5	Light Blue/Yellow
9	Light Blue

19) Activate mirrors in all directions. If fuse No. 39 blows, go to next step. If fuse No. 39 does not blow, go to step **22)**.

20) Remove mirror control switch. Test mirror control switch. See MIRROR CONTROL SWITCH under COMPONENT TESTS. If mirror control switch is okay, go to next step. If mirror control switch is defective, replace mirror control switch.

21) Disconnect Driver's Door Module (DDM) harness connector C506. Disconnect mirror control switch harness connector C550. Measure resistance between ground and appropriate terminals at mirror control switch harness connector C550. See MIRROR CONTROL SWITCH TERMINAL IDENTIFICATION table. *See Fig. 17.* If all resistance readings are greater than 10 k/ohms, replace driver's door module. If any resistance reading are 10 k/ohms or less, repair short to ground in appropriate wire.

MIRROR CONTROL SWITCH TERMINAL IDENTIFICATION

Terminal	Wire Color
3	Dark Blue/Orange
4	Red/Orange
6	Yellow/Black
7	Purple/Orange
8	Dark Green/Orange

22) Activate driver's seat control switch in all directions. If fuse No. 39 blows, go to next step. If fuse No. 39 does not blow, system is operating properly at this time.

23) Disconnect Driver's Door Module (DDM) harness connector C506. Disconnect driver's seat control switch harness connector C520. Measure resistance between ground and appropriate terminals at driver's seat control switch harness connector C520. See DRIVER'S SEAT CONTROL SWITCH TERMINAL IDENTIFICATION table. *See Fig. 18.* If all resistance readings are greater than 10 k/ohms, replace driver's door module. If any resistance readings are 10 k/ohms or less, repair short to ground in appropriate wire.

DRIVER'S SEAT CONTROL SWITCH TERMINAL IDENTIFICATION

Terminal	Wire Color
2	Red/White
3	Red/Light Green
4	Red/Light Blue
5	Gray
7	Yellow/White
8	Yellow/Light Green
9	Yellow/Light Blue
10	Gray/Black

24) Turn ignition switch to LOCK position. Remove fuse No. 1 (30-amp) in power distribution box. Check fuse. If fuse is okay, go to next step. If fuse is blown, go to step **26)**.

25) Measure voltage at input side of fuse No. 1 in power distribution box. If battery voltage exists, repair open in Red wire between power distribution box and instrument panel fuse box. If battery voltage does not exist, repair or replace power distribution box as necessary.

26) Ensure fuse No. 1 in power distribution box is still removed. Disconnect Driver's Seat Module (DSM) harness connector C362. Disconnect driver's heated seat module harness connector C352. Disconnect driver's lumbar switch harness connector C348. Measure resistance between ground and terminal No. 1 (Red wire) at DSM harness connector C362. If resistance is greater than 10 k/ohms, go to next step. If resistance is 10 k/ohms or less, repair short to ground in Red wire.

27) Connect DSM harness connector C362. Measure resistance between ground and output side of fuse No. 1 in power distribution box. If resistance is greater than 10 k/ohms, go to next step. If resistance is 10 k/ohms or less, replace driver's seat module.

28) Replace fuse No. 1 (30-amp) in power distribution box. Connect driver's lumbar switch harness connector C348. Operate driver's lumbar switch in both directions. If fuse No. 1 blows, go to next step. If fuse No. 1 does not blow, go to step **32)**.

29) Remove fuse No. 1 (30-amp) from power distribution box. Measure resistance between ground and output side of fuse No. 1 in power distribution box. If resistance is greater than 10 k/ohms, go to next step. If resistance is 10 k/ohms or less, replace driver's lumbar switch.

30) Disconnect driver's lumbar switch harness connector C348. Measure resistance between ground and terminal No. 4 (Pink wire) at driver's lumbar switch harness connector C348. Also, measure resistance between ground and terminal No. 2 (Brown wire) at driver's lumbar switch harness connector C348. *See Fig. 19.* If both resistance readings are greater than 10 k/ohms, go to next step. If either resistance reading is 10 k/ohms or less, replace driver's lumbar switch.

31) Disconnect driver's lumbar motor harness connector C315. Measure resistance between ground and terminal No. 4 (Pink wire) at driver's lumbar switch harness connector C348. Also, measure resistance between ground and terminal No. 2 (Brown wire) at driver's lumbar switch harness connector C348. If both resistance readings are greater than 10 k/ohms, replace power lumbar motor. If either resistance reading is 10 k/ohms or less, repair short to ground in appropriate wire.

32) Disconnect driver's heated seat module harness connector C352. Measure resistance between ground and appropriate terminals at driver's heated seat module harness connector C352. See HEATED SEAT MODULE CONNECTOR TERMINAL IDENTIFICATION table. *See Fig. 14.* If all resistance readings are greater than 10 k/ohms, replace driver's heated seat module. If any resistance readings are 10 k/ohms or less, repair short to ground in appropriate wire.

HEATED SEAT MODULE CONNECTOR TERMINAL IDENTIFICATION

Terminal	Wire Color
5	Black/Light Blue
6	Brown/Light Blue
8	Yellow/Light Blue
9	Gray/Light Blue
10	Red/Light Blue
11	Orange/Light Blue
12	Purple/Light Blue
13	White/Light Blue

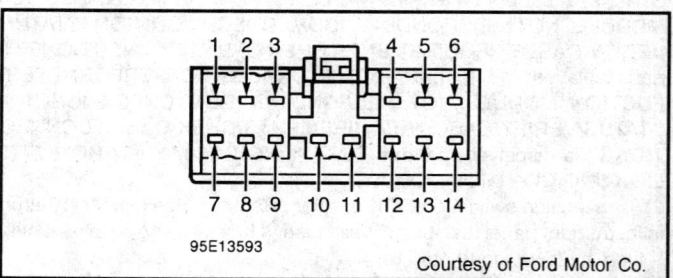

95E13593

Courtesy of Ford Motor Co.

Fig. 14: Identifying Driver's Door Module Harness Connector C524 & Driver's Heated Seat Module Harness Connector C352 Terminals

TEST P: COURTESY LIGHTS INOPERATIVE

1) Connect NGS tester to Data Link Connector (DLC). Using NGS tester, monitor Driver's Door Module (DDM) PID D_DOOR while opening and closing driver's door. If PID agrees with door position, go to next step. If PID does not agree with door position, go to step **15)**.

2) Using NGS tester, monitor Lighting Control Module (LCM) PIDs LRDR_SW, P_DOOR, and RRDR_SW while opening and closing passenger's, right rear and left rear doors. If PID agrees with door position, go to next step. If PID does not agree with door position, go to step **18)**.

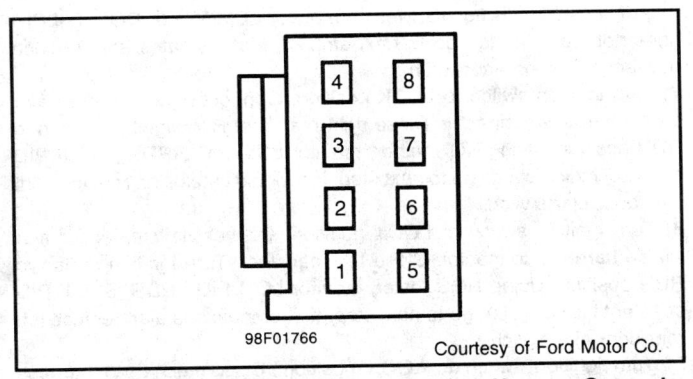

Fig. 15: Identifying Driver's Door Lock Switch Harness Connector C505 Terminals

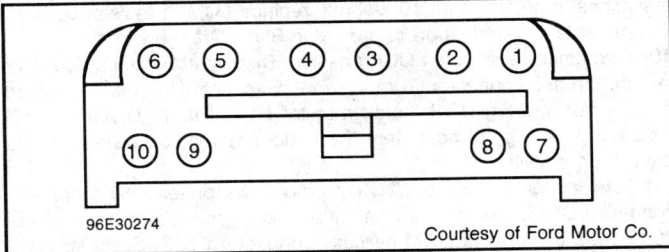

Fig. 16: Identifying Remote Keyless Entry Keypad Harness Connector C525 Terminals

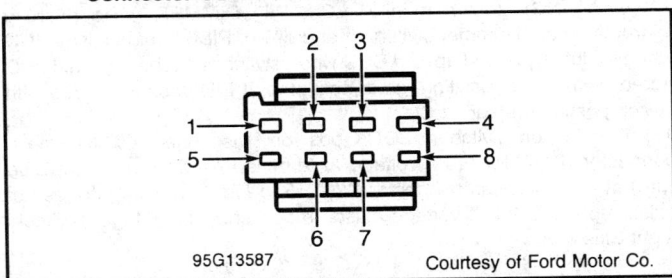

Fig. 17: Identifying Mirror Control Switch Harness Connector C550 Terminals

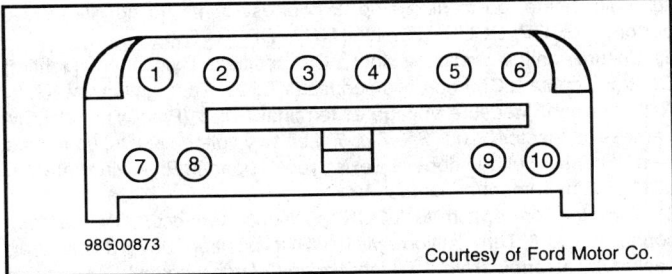

Fig. 18: Identifying Driver's Seat Control Switch Harness Connector C520 Terminals

3) Using NGS tester, select LCM active command BATTERY SAVER & COURTESY ENTRY. Trigger COURTESYL on. If courtesy lights do no illuminate, go to next step. If courtesy lights illuminate, replace LCM.

4) Open glove box. If glove box light does not illuminate, go to next step. If glove box light illuminates, go to step **13)**.

5) Turn igniton switch to LOCK position. Remove fuse No. 9 (60-amp) in power distribution box. If fuse is okay, go to next step. If fuse is blown, repair short to ground in Tan/Black wire between power distribution box and instrument panel fuse box.

6) Measure voltage at input side of fuse No. 9 in power distribution box. If battery voltage exists, go to next step. If battery voltage does not exist, repair or replace power distribution box as necessary.

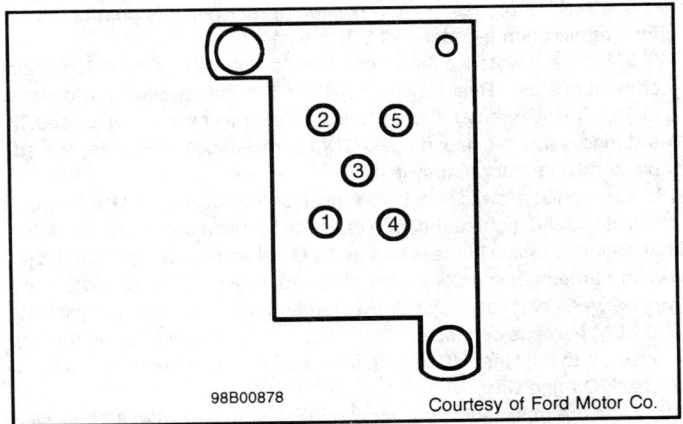

Fig. 19: Identifying Driver's Lumbar Switch Harness Connector C348 Terminals

7) Install fuse No. 9 in power distribution box. Measure voltage at input side of fuse No. 31 (15-amp) in instrument panel fuse box. If battery voltage exists, go to next step. If battery voltage does not exist, repair open in Tan/Black wire between power distribution box and instrument panel fuse box.

8) Remove fuse No. 31 (15-amp) in instrument panel fuse box. Check fuse. If fuse is okay, go to next step. If fuse is blown, go to step **10)**.

9) Install fuse No. 31 in instrument panel fuse box. Turn ignition switch to LOCK position. Disconnect LCM harness connectors C207 and C208. Measure voltage at terminal No. 17 (Pink wire) at LCM harness connector C207. See Fig. 7. Measure voltage at terminal No. 6 (Pink wire) at LCM harness connector C208. See Fig. 6. If battery voltage exists at both terminals, replace LCM. If battery voltage does not exists at both terminals, repair open in appropriate Pink wire.

10) Ensure fuse No. 31 in instrument panel fuse box is still removed. Turn ignition switch to LOCK position. Disconnect LCM harness connectors C207 and C208. Measure resistance between ground and terminal No. 17 (Pink wire) at LCM harness connector C207. See Fig. 7. Measure resistance between ground and terminal No. 6 (Pink wire) at LCM harness connector C208. See Fig. 6. If both resistance reading are greater than 10 k/ohms, go to next step. If either resistance reading is 10 k/ohms or less, repair short to ground in appropriate Pink wire.

11) Remove all courtesy lights. Measure resistance between ground and terminal No. 3 (Black/Light Blue wire) at LCM harness connector C207. If resistance is greater than 10 k/ohms, go to next step. If resistance is 10 k/ohms or less, repair short to ground in Black/Light Blue wire.

12) Ensure all courtesy lights are still removed. Measure resistance between ground and terminal No. 10 (Light Green/Orange wire) at LCM harness connector C208. If resistance is greater than 10 k/ohms, replace LCM. If resistance is 10 k/ohms or less, repair short to ground in Light Green/Orange wire.

13) Turn ignition switch to LOCK position. Disconnect LCM harness connector C207. Measure voltage at terminal No. 17 (Pink wire) at LCM harness connector C207. See Fig. 7. If battery voltage exists, go to next step. If battery voltage does not exist, repair open in Pink wire between LCM and instrument panel fuse box.

14) Connect LCM harness connector C207. Turn igniton switch to RUN position. Using NGS tester, select LCM active command BATTERY SAVER & COURTESY ENTRY. Trigger COURTESYL on. Using a voltmeter, backprobe at terminal No. 3 (Black/Light Blue wire) at LCM harness connector C207. If battery voltage exists, repair open in Black/Light Blue wire. If battery voltage does not exist, replace LCM.

15) Turn ignition switch to LOCK position. Disconnect DDM harness connector C523 and driver's door ajar switch harness connector C513. Measure resistance in Dark Blue wire between driver's door ajar switch harness connector C513 and terminal No. 20 at DDM harness connector C523. See Fig. 20. If resistance is 5 ohms or less, go to next step. If resistance is greater than 5 ohms, repair open in Dark Blue wire.

16) Measure resistance between ground and Black/Light Blue wire terminal at driver's door ajar switch harness connector C513. If resistance is 5 ohms or less, go to next step. If resistance is greater than 5 ohms, repair open in Black/Light Blue wire.

17) Measure resistance between driver's door ajar switch terminals (component side). Resistance should be 5 ohms or less with driver's door open and greater than 5 ohms with driver's door is closed. If resistance is as specified, replace DDM. If resistance is not as specified, replace driver's door ajar switch.

18) Turn ignition switch to LOCK position. Disconnect LCM harness connector C206, right rear door ajar switch harness connector C804, left rear door ajar switch harness connector C704 and passenger's door ajar switch harness connector C611. Measure resistance in Black/Orange wire between each door ajar switch harness connector and terminal No. 9 at LCM harness connector C206. *See Fig. 5.* If resistance is 5 ohms or less, go to next step. If resistance is greater than 5 ohms, repair open in Black/Orange wire.

19) Measure resistance between ground and Black/Light Blue wire terminal at each door ajar switch harness connector. If resistance is 5 ohms or less, go to next step. If resistance is greater than 5 ohms, repair open in Black/Light Blue wire.

20) Measure resistance between door ajar switch terminals (component side). Resistance should be 5 ohms or less with door open and greater than 5 ohms with door is closed. If resistance is as specified, replace DDM. If resistance is not as specified, replace appropriate door ajar switch.

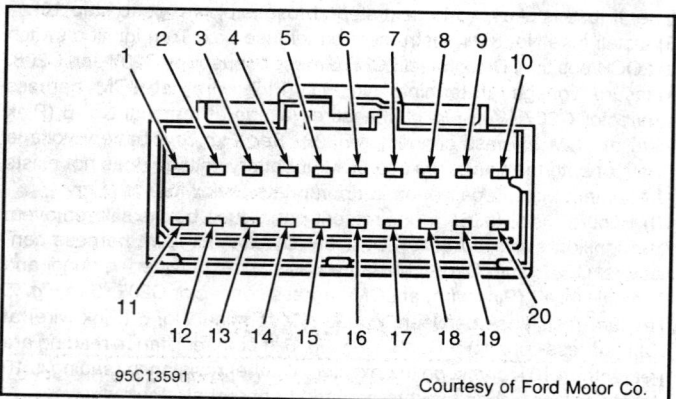

95C13591
Courtesy of Ford Motor Co.

Fig. 20: Identifying Driver's Door Module Harness Connector C523 Terminals

TEST Q: COURTESY LIGHTS ON CONTINUOUSLY

1) Ensure dimmer switch is not stuck up or down. Connect NGS tester to Data Link Connector (DLC). Perform Lighting Control Module (LCM) self-test. If no DTCs are retrieved, go to next step. If DTC B1566 is retrieved, go to step 4). If DTCs B1582 and/or B1586 is retrieved, replace LCM.

2) Using NGS tester, perform Driver's Door Module (DDM) self-test. If no DTCs or DTC B1319 are retrieved, go to next step. If any other DTCs are retrieved, perform appropriate test. See DRIVER'S DOOR MODULE DTC INDEX table under SELF-DIAGNOSTIC SYSTEM.

3) Using NGS tester, monitor DDM PID D_DOOR while opening and closing driver's door. If PID agrees with door position, go to next step. If PID does not agree with door position, go to step 10).

4) Using NGS tester, monitor Lighting Control Module (LCM) PIDs LRDR_SW, P_DOOR, and RRDR_SW while opening and closing passenger's, right rear and left rear doors. If PID does not agree with door position, go to next step. If PID agrees with door position, go to step 12).

5) Turn igniton switch to LOCK position. Disconnect passenger's, right rear and left rear door ajar switch harness connectors. Turn ignition switch to RUN position. Using NGS tester, monitor LCM PIDs LRDR_SW, P_DOOR, and RRDR_SW. If PID does not indicate ajar, go to next step. If door indicates ajar, go to step 9).

6) Turn ignition switch to LOCK position. Connect passenger's door ajar switch harness connector. Close passenger's door. Turn ignition switch

to RUN position. Using NGS tester, monitor LCM PID P_DOOR. If PID does not indicate ajar, go to next step. If door indicates ajar, replace passenger's door ajar switch.

7) Turn ignition switch to LOCK position. Connect right rear door ajar switch harness connector. Close right rear door. Turn ignition switch to RUN position. Using NGS tester, monitor LCM PID RRDR_SW. If PID does not indicate ajar, go to next step. If door indicates ajar, replace right rear door ajar switch.

8) Turn ignition switch to LOCK position. Connect left rear door ajar switch harness connector. Close left rear door. Turn ignition switch to RUN position. Using NGS tester, monitor LCM PID LRDR_SW. If PID does not indicate ajar, go to next step. If door indicates ajar, replace left rear door ajar switch.

9) Turn ignition switch to LOCK position. Disconnect LCM harness connector C206. Measure resistance between ground and terminal No. 9 (Black/Orange wire) at LCM harness connector C206. *See Fig. 5.* If resistance is greater than 10 k/ohms, replace LCM. If resistance is 10 k/ohms or less, repair short to ground in Black/Orange wire.

10) Turn igniton switch to LOCK position. Disconnect driver's door ajar switch harness connector. Turn ignition switch to RUN position. Close driver's door. Using NGS tester, monitor DDM PID D_DOOR. If PID indicates AJAR, go to next step. If PID does not indicate ajar, replace driver's door ajar switch.

11) Turn igniton switch to LOCK position. Disconnect DDM harness connector C523. Measure resistance between ground and terminal No. 20 (Dark Blue wire) at DDM harness connector C523. *See Fig. 20.* If resistance is greater than 10 k/ohms, replace DDM. If resistance is 10 k/ohms or less, repair short to ground in Dark Blue wire.

12) Using NGS tester, monitor LCM PID DIMMER while pushing instrument panel dimmer switch up and down. PID should indicate INC when switch is pushed up and DEC when switch is pushed down. If PID agrees with switch position, go to next step. If PID does not agree with switch position, replace LCM.

13) Turn igniton switch to LOCK position. Disconnect LCM harness connector C207. Measure voltage at terminal No. 3 (Black/Light Blue wire) at LCM harness connector C207. *See Fig. 7.* If voltage does not exist, replace LCM. If voltage exists, repair short to voltage in Black/Light Blue wire.

TEST R: DEMAND LIGHTING INOPERATIVE

1) Turn ignition switch to LOCK position. Open driver's door. If courtesy lights illuminate, go to next step. If courtesy lights do not illuminate, perform TEST P: COURTESY LIGHTS INOPERATIVE.

2) Ensure ignition switch is in LOCK position. Disconnect Lighting Control Module (LCM) harness connector C208. Turn ignition switch to RUN position. Measure voltage at terminal No. 6 (Pink wire) at LCM harness connector C208. *See Fig. 6.* If battery voltage exists, go to next step. If battery voltage does not exist, repair open in Pink wire between LCM and instrument panel fuse box.

3) Turn ignition switch to LOCK position. Connect LCM harness connector C208. Turn ignition switch to RUN position. Using a voltmeter, backprobe at terminal No. 10 (Light Green/Orange wire) at LCM harness connector C208. If battery voltage exists and all demand lights are inoperative, go to next step. If battery voltage exists and trunk light is inoperative, go to step 8). If battery voltage exists and glove box light is inoperative, go to step 6). If battery voltage does not exist, replace LCM.

4) Turn ignition switch to LOCK position. Disconnect in-line harness connector C900. Connector C900 is located behind headliner near upper left corner of windshield. Turn ignition switch to RUN position. Measure voltage at terminal No. 3 (Light Green/Orange wire) at in-line harness connector C900 (male side). *See Fig. 21.* If battery voltage exists, go to next step. If battery voltage does not exist, repair open in Light Green/Orange wire.

NOTE: *Wiring between in-line harness connector C900 and roof-mounted lights runs through headliner.*

5) Turn ignition switch to LOCK position. Measure resistance between ground and terminal No. 9 (Black wire) at in-line harness connector

C900 (male side). If resistance is 5 ohms or less, replace headliner. If resistance is greater than 5 ohms, repair open in Black wire.

6) Turn ignition switch to LOCK position. Disconnect glove box light harness connector C241. Measure voltage at Light Green/Orange wire terminal at glove box light harness connector C241. If battery voltage exists, go to next step. If battery voltage does not exists, repair open in Light Green/Orange wire.

7) Measure resistance between ground and Black wire terminal at glove box light harness connector C241. If resistance is greater than 5 ohms, repair open in Black wire. If resistance is 5 ohms or less, replace bulb.

8) Turn ignition switch to LOCK position. Disconnect trunk light harness connector C438. Measure voltage at Light Green/Orange wire terminal at trunk light harness connector C438. If battery voltage exists, go to next step. If battery voltage does not exists, repair open in Light Green/Orange wire.

9) Measure resistance between ground and Black wire terminal at trunk light harness connector C438. If resistance is greater than 5 ohms, repair open in Black wire or repair trunk lid ajar switch circuit as necessary. If resistance is 5 ohms or less, replace bulb.

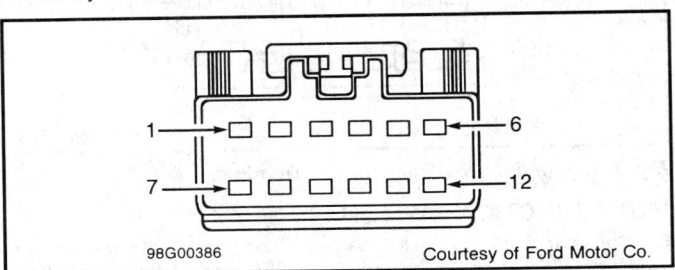

98G00386   Courtesy of Ford Motor Co.

Fig. 21: Identifying In-Line Harness Connector C900 Terminals

TEST S: BATTERY SAVER DOES NOT DEACTIVATE AFTER TIMEOUT

1) Connect New Generation Star (NGS) tester to Data Link Connector (DLC). Using NGS tester, perform Lighting Control Module (LCM) self-test. If no DTCs are retrieved, go to next step. If DTC B1555 is retrieved, go to step 5) . If any other DTCs are retrieved, perform appropriate test. See LIGHTING CONTROL MODULE DTC INDEX table under SELF-DIAGNOSTIC SYSTEM.

2) Activate all demand lights. If all demand lights operate properly, go to next step. If any demand light(s) do not operate properly, repair by symptom. See SYMPTOM CHART table.

3) Open and close all doors while monitoring courtesy lights. If all courtesy lights operate properly, go to next step. If any courtesy light(s) do not operate properly, repair by symptom. See SYMPTOM CHART table.

4) Ensure headlight switch is not in autolamp position. Turn headlights on and off. If headlights operate properly, go to next step. If headlights do not operate properly, repair by symptom. See SYMPTOM CHART table.

NOTE: Voltage at terminal No. 2 (Black/Pink wire) at LCM harness connector C208 should only exist when ignition switch is in ACC and RUN positions.

5) Turn ignition switch to LOCK position. Disconnect LCM harness connector C208. Measure voltage at terminal No. 2 (Black/Pink wire) at LCM harness connector C208. See Fig. 6. If voltage does not exist, go to next step. If voltage exists, repair short to voltage in Black/Pink wire.

NOTE: Voltage at terminal No. 17 (Red/Yellow wire) at LCM harness connector C206 should only exist when ignition switch is in RUN and START positions.

6) Ensure ignition switch is in LOCK position. Disconnect LCM harness connector C206. Measure voltage at terminal No. 17 (Red/Yellow wire) at LCM harness connector C206. See Fig. 5. If voltage does not exist, replace LCM. If voltage exists, repair short to voltage in Red/Yellow wire.

TEST T: KEYPAD ILLUMINATION MALFUNCTION

1) Connect New Generation Star (NGS) tester to Data Link Connector (DLC). Using NGS tester, perform Driver's Door Module (DDM) self-test. If no DTCs are retrieved, go to next step if keypad is illumination inoperative or go to step 6) if keypad illuminates continuously . If any other DTCs are retrieved, perform appropriate test. See DRIVER'S DOOR MODULE DTC INDEX table under SELF-DIAGNOSTIC SYSTEM.

2) Using NGS tester, select DDM active command KEYPAD BACKLIGHTING. Trigger KEYPAD BACKLIGHTING on and off. If keypad illumination does not turn on and off, go to next step. If keypad illumination turns on and off, repair remote keyless entry concern. See appropriate wiring diagram in REMOTE KEYLESS ENTRY SYSTEMS article.

3) Turn ignition switch to LOCK position. Disconnect DDM harness connector C523. Turn ignition switch to RUN position. Measure voltage at terminal No. 11 (Light Blue wire) at DDM harness connector C523. See Fig. 20. If battery voltage exists, go to next step. If battery voltage does not exist, go to step 5).

4) Using a jumper wire, ground terminal No. 11 (Light Blue wire) at DDM harness connector C523. If keypad does not illuminate, go to next step. If keypad illuminates, replace DDM.

5) Disconnect keypad harness connector C525. Measure voltage at terminal No. 6 (Black/White wire) at keypad harness connector C525. See Fig. 16. If battery voltage exists, replace keypad. If battery voltage does not exist, repair open in Black/White wire between keypad and instrument panel fuse box.

6) Turn ignition switch to LOCK position. Disconnect DDM harness connector C523. If keypad is still illuminated, go to next step. If keypad illumination turns off, replace DDM.

7) Disconnect keypad harness connector C525. If keypad illumination turns off, go to next step. If keypad is still illuminated, replace keypad.

8) Measure resistance between ground and terminal No. 11 (Light Blue wire) at LCM harness connector C523. If resistance is greater than 10 k/ohms, system is okay at this time. If resistance is 10 k/ohms or less, repair short to ground in Light Blue wire.

REMOVAL & INSTALLATION

CAUTION: When battery is disconnected or modules are replaced, vehicle computer and memory systems may lose memory data. Driveability problems may exist until computer systems have completed a relearn cycle. See COMPUTER RELEARN PROCEDURES article in GENERAL INFORMATION before disconnecting battery.

HEADLIGHT SWITCH

NOTE: Autolamp switch is integral to Lighting Control Module (LCM). See LIGHTING CONTROL MODULE (LCM).

LIGHT SENSOR AMPLIFIER

Removal & Installation – Remove upper panel from dash. Unclip amplifier assembly and disconnect harness connector. To install, reverse removal procedure.

LIGHTING CONTROL MODULE (LCM)

Removal & Installation – Disconnect battery ground. Remove 3 screws and lower steering column finish panel. Remove 3 LCM mounting screws. Carefully pull LCM from dash panel and disconnect 3 harness connectors. To install, reverse removal procedure.

WIRING DIAGRAMS

See appropriate wiring diagram in HEADLIGHT SYSTEMS, EXTERIOR LIGHTS, ILLUMINATION/INTERIOR LIGHTS and LIGHTING CONTROL MODULES articles. Also see appropriate wiring diagram in POWER DISTRIBUTION article in WIRING DIAGRAMS.

DESCRIPTION

The autolamp system is a light-sensitive, on-off control. It will automatically turn the headlights on. The system can be set to automatically turn off interior and exterior lights after the ignition has been turned off. This time delay feature is adjustable and has a maximum time delay setting of up to 3 minutes.

Autolamp system consists of the light sensor amplifier, located in the defroster grille on top left dash, Lighting Control Module (LCM), located underneath dash on right side of steering column and time delay switch which is integral with headlight switch.

Autolamp system LCM communicates with other control modules thought module communications network.

OPERATION

Autolamp system is activated by turning dash mounted headlight switch counterclockwise to AUTOLAMP position. A small AUTOLAMP indicator light on the switch will light when lights are energized. When AUTO-LAMP feature is selected, lights will turn on and off automatically based on the amount of ambient light monitored by the Light Sensor Amplifier. Time delay (delayed turn-off function) is selected by the position of the lighting switch when it is turned counterclockwise from the OFF position. Maximum time delay of 3 minutes is obtained when the switch is rotated fully counterclockwise.

COMPONENT LOCATIONS

COMPONENT LOCATIONS

Component	Location
Brake Pedal Position Switch	On Brake Pedal Bracket
Data Link Connector	Behind Left Side Of Instrument Panel
Driver's Door Module	Behind Driver's Door Panel
Headlight Switch	Left Side Of Instrument Panel
Light Sensor Amplifier	Behind Instrument Panel, Above Instrument Cluster
Lighting Control Module	Behind Instrument Panel, Right Of Steering Column

TROUBLE SHOOTING

Verify customers complaint. Check fuses No. 1, 4, 5, 6, 8 and 13 (all 15-amp), located instrument panel fuse box. Check circuit breakers No. 12 (18-amp) and No. 14 (20-amp), located in instrument panel fuse box. Check all fuses in power distribution box. Check or replace any suspect bulbs. Check for a damaged or obstructed light sensor amplifier, damaged door ajar switches and for mechanical damage to headlight switch. Check for damaged brake pedal position switch and damaged multifunction switch. Check circuits for opens or shorts. Check for good clean connections at chassis ground point locations. See appropriate wiring diagram in HEADLIGHT SYSTEMS article. Correct any obvious problems before continuing test. If all checks are okay, perform self-diagnostics. See SELF-DIAGNOSTIC SYSTEM.

COMPONENT TESTS

HEADLIGHT SWITCH

Disconnect headlight switch harness connectors. Check resistance between indicated terminal with switch in specified position. See HEADLIGHT SWITCH CONTINUITY TEST table. See Fig. 1. If resistance is not as specified, replace headlight switch.

HEADLIGHT SWITCH CONTINUITY TEST

Switch Position	Terminals	Resistance
Headlight Circuit		
Off	7 & 8	1
Park	7 & 8	1
Head	7 & 8	2
Parking Light Circuit		
Off	7 & 3	1

HEADLIGHT SWITCH CONTINUITY TEST (Cont.)

Switch Position	Terminals	Resistance
Park	7 & 3	2
Head	7 & 3	2
Dome Light Circuit		
Off	6 & 7	1
On	6 & 7	2
Autolamp Circuit		
Off	4 & 7	1
On	4 & 7	2
Rheostat	7 & 9	3

1 – Resistance should be greater than 10 k/ohms.
2 – Resistance should be 5 ohms or less.
3 – Rotate dial clockwise from off to max. Resistance should increase smoothly from 3 k/ohms to 200 k/ohms.

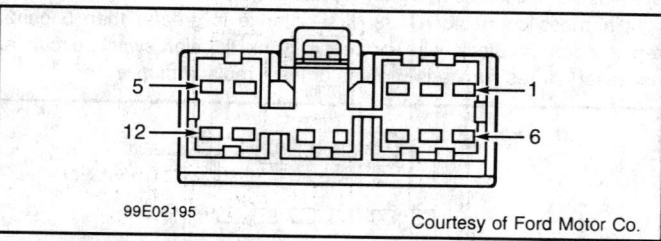

99E02195   Courtesy of Ford Motor Co.

Fig. 1: Identifying Headlight Switch Terminals

MULTIFUNCTION SWITCH

Disconnect multifunction switch harness connectors. Set hazard flasher switch to OFF position unless specified otherwise. Measure resistance between terminals with switch in specified position. See MULTIFUNCTION SWITCH RESISTANCE table. See Fig. 2. If resistance is not as specified, or is poor in any switch position, replace multifunction switch.

MULTIFUNCTION SWITCH RESISTANCE

Switch Position	Terminals	Ohms
Brakelight Feed Through [1]	2, 9 & 10	2
Flash-To-Pass On	1 & 3; 5 & 7	2
Hazard Switch		
Off	1 & 11	2
On	4 & 11; 2, 5, 6 & 10	2
Headlight Dimmer		
High Beam	1 & 5	2
Low Beam	1 & 3	2
Turn Signals [3]		
Left Turn	6, 8 & 10	2
Left Cornering Light	1 & 7	2
Right Turn	2, 5 & 6	2
Right Cornering Light	1 & 3	2
Washer		
On	4 & 6	2
Off	4 & 6	[4] 103,300
Wipers		
Off	2 & 4	[5] 47,600
Low Speed	2 & 4	[5] 4080
High Speed	2 & 4	2
Interval	2 & 4	[5] 11,330
Interval Delay [6] [7]		
MAX	4 & 6	[4] 103,300
MIN	4 & 6	[4] 3300

1 – Hazard switch off and turn signal switch in neutral position.
2 – Resistance should be 5 ohms or less.
3 – Hazard switch MUST be off.
4 – Resistance may vary by as much as 10 percent.
5 – Resistance may vary by as much as 5 percent.
6 – Resistance should vary smoothly between specified limits as knob is rotated between MIN and MAX positions.
7 – These values are with wiper switch in off position. If wiper switch is in low or high position, resistance between terminals No. 4 and 6 should be within 10 percent of 3300 ohms.

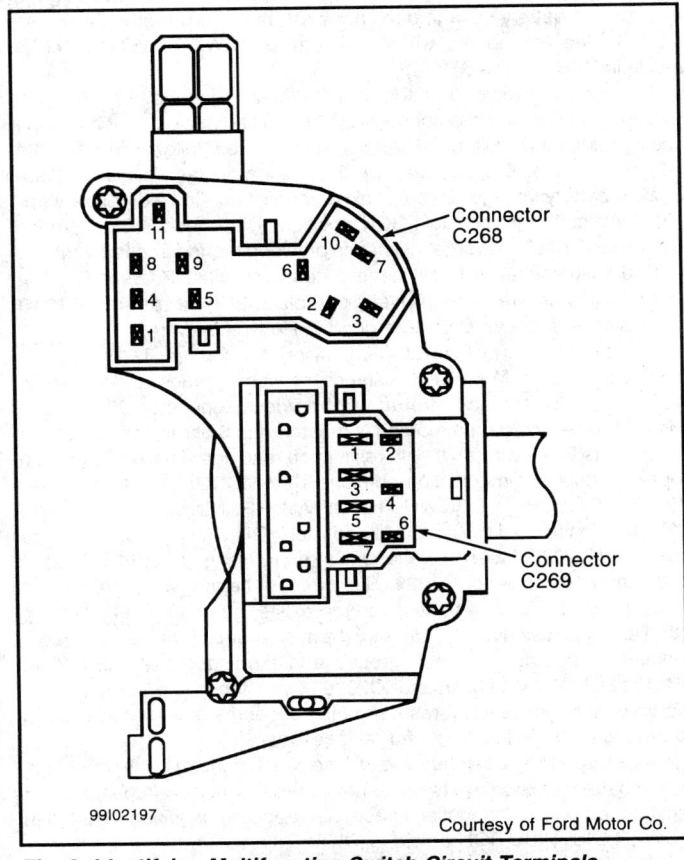

Fig. 2: Identifying Multifunction Switch Circuit Terminals

Connector C268

Connector C269

99I02197

Courtesy of Ford Motor Co.

SELF-DIAGNOSTIC SYSTEM

Connect New Generation Star (NGS) tester to Data Link Connector (DLC), located beneath instrument panel. Using NGS tester, perform data link diagnostics test. See DATA LINK DIAGNOSTIC TEST under COMMUNICATION NETWORK DIAGNOSTICS in MODULE COMMUNICATIONS NETWORK – CROWN VICTORIA & GRAND MARQUIS article. If NGS tester responds with CKT914, CKT915 or CKT70=ALL ECUS NO RESP/NOT EQUIP, repair module communications concern. See MODULE COMMUNICATIONS NETWORK – CROWN VICTORIA & GRAND MARQUIS article. If NGS tester displays NO RESP/NOT EQUIP for Lighting Control Module (LCM), perform TEST A: NO COMMUNICATION WITH LIGHTING CONTROL MODULE under SYSTEM TESTS. If NGS tester displays NO RESP/NOT EQUIP for Driver's Door Module (DDM), perform TEST X: NO COMMUNICATION WITH DRIVER'S DOOR MODULE under SYSTEM TESTS.

If NGS tester responds with SYSTEM PASSED, retrieve and record continuous DTCs. Erase continuous DTCs. Using NGS tester, perform DDM and LCM self-test. Perform appropriate test in accordance with DTC retrieved. See DRIVER'S DOOR MODULE DTC INDEX and/or LIGHTING CONTROL MODULE DTC INDEX table. Codes listed in these tables are only for testing covered in this article. For complete DTC listing, see MODULE COMMUNICATIONS NETWORK – CROWN VICTORIA & GRAND MARQUIS article. If no DTCs are retrieved, repair by symptom. See SYMPTOM CHART table under SYSTEM TESTS.

DRIVER'S DOOR MODULE DTC INDEX

DTC [1]	Description	Test
B1342	ECU Defective	[2]

[1] – Codes listed in this table are only for testing covered in this article. For complete DTC listing, see MODULE COMMUNICATIONS NETWORK – CROWN VICTORIA & GRAND MARQUIS article.

[2] – Using NGS tester, clear and document continuous DTCs. Perform Driver's Door Module (DDM) self-test. If DTC B1342 is retrieved again, replace DDM.

LIGHTING CONTROL MODULE DTC INDEX

DTC [1]	Description	Test
B1312	Headlight Input Short To Battery Voltage	C
B1322	Driver's Door Ajar Circuit Short To Ground	T
B1342	ECU Defective	2
B1442	Door Handle Switch Circuit Failure	U
B1445	Door Handle Switch Circuit Short To Ground	U
B1470	Headlight Input Circuit Failure	B
B1563	Door Ajar Circuit Failure	S
B1566	Door Ajar Circuit Short To Ground	V
B1575	Parking Light Input Circuit Failure	P
B1577	Parking Light Input Circuit Short To Voltage	P
B1685	Dome Light Input Circuit Failure	W
B1687	Dome Light Input Circuit Short To Voltage	W
B1689	Autolamp Delay Circuit Failure	I
B1692	Autolamp Delay Circuit Short To Ground	I
B1693	Autolamp ON Circuit Failure	H
B1695	Autolamp ON Circuit Short To Voltage	H
B1790	Autolamp Sensor Circuit Failure	H
B1792	Autolamp Sensor Circuit Short To Voltage	H
B1872	Turn Signal/Hazard Power Feed Circuit Failure	K
B1873	Turn Signal/Hazard Power Feed Circuit Short To Ground	L

[1] – Codes listed in this table are only for testing covered in this article. For complete DTC listing, see MODULE COMMUNICATIONS NETWORK – CROWN VICTORIA & GRAND MARQUIS article.

[2] – Using NGS tester, clear and document continuous DTCs. Perform Lighting Control Module (LCM) self-test. If DTC B1342 is retrieved again, replace LCM.

FORD
4-494

1999 ACCESSORIES & EQUIPMENT
Autolamp Systems – Crown Victoria & Grand Marquis (Cont.)

SYSTEM TESTS

SYMPTOM CHART

Symptom	Test
No Communication With Lighting Control Module	A
Headlights Inoperative	B
Headlights On Continuously	C
High Beams Inoperative	D
Low Beams Inoperative	E
One Low Beam Inoperative	F
One High Beam Inoperative	G
Autolamps Inoperative	H
Autolamp Time Delay Inoperative	I
Brakelights Inoperative	J
Turn/Hazard Power Feed Circuit Short To Voltage (DTC B1872)	K
Turn/Hazard Power Feed Circuit Short To Ground (DTC B1873)	L
Turn Signals & Hazards Inoperative	M
Turn Signals Inoperative (Hazards Operate)	N
Hazards Inoperative (Turn Signals Operate)	O
Parking Light Input Short To Voltage (DTC B1575 Or B1577)	P
Parking Lights Inoperative	Q
Parking Lights On Continuously	R
Courtesy Lights Inoperative	S
Driver's Door Ajar Circuit Failure (DTC B1322)	T
Door Handle Switch Circuit Failure (DTC B1442 Or B1445)	U
Door Ajar Circuit Short To Ground (DTC B1566)	V
Dome Light Input Circuit Failure (DTC B1687 Or B1685)	W
No Communication With Driver's Door Module	X

TEST A: NO COMMUNICATION WITH LIGHTING CONTROL MODULE

1) Turn ignition switch to RUN position. Using NGS tester, monitor Lighting Control Module (LCM) PID IGN_LC. If NGS tester does not indicate UNABLE TO PERFORM TEST FUNCTION, MODULE NOT RESPONDING, CHECK IGNITION STATUS/VERIFY CABLE REQUIREMENTS, OR CHECK CABLE CONNECTIONS, go to next step. If NGS tester indicates UNABLE TO PERFORM TEST FUNCTION, MODULE NOT RESPONDING, CHECK IGNITION STATUS/VERIFY CABLE REQUIREMENTS, OR CHECK CABLE CONNECTIONS, go to step **11)**.

2) Turn ignition switch to RUN position. Using NGS tester, monitor LCM PID IGN_LC while rotating ignition switch through ACCY, OFF and RUN positions. If PID indicates START while ignition switch is in RUN position, go to next step. If PID indicates RUN while ignition switch is in RUN position, go to step **12)**. If PID indicates ACCY while ignition switch is in RUN position, go to step **7)**.

3) Turn ignition switch to LOCK position. Remove fuse No. 6 (15-amp) from instrument panel fuse box. Check fuse. If fuse is okay, go to next step. If fuse is blown, go to step **6)**.

4) Turn ignition switch to RUN position. Measure voltage at input side of fuse No. 6 in instrument panel fuse box. If battery voltage exists, go to next step. If battery voltage does not exist, repair power supply to fuse No. 6. See appropriate wiring diagram in POWER DISTRIBUTION article in WIRING DIAGRAMS.

5) Turn ignition switch to LOCK position. Install fuse No. 6. Disconnect LCM harness connector C2027. Turn ignition switch to RUN position. Measure voltage at terminal No. 1 (White/Violet wire) at LCM harness connector C2027. *See Fig. 3.* If battery voltage exists, replace LCM. If battery voltage does not exist, repair open in White/Violet wire.

6) Turn ignition switch to LOCK position. Disconnect Lighting Control Module (LCM) harness connector C2027. Measure resistance between ground and terminal No. 1 (White/Violet wire) at LCM harness connector C2027. *See Fig. 3* . If resistance is greater than 10 k/ohms, replace LCM. If resistance is 10 k/ohms or less, repair short to ground in White/Violet wire.

7) Turn ignition switch to LOCK position. Remove fuse No. 13 (15-amp) from instrument panel fuse box. Check fuse. If fuse is okay, go to next step. If fuse is blown, go to step **10)**.

8) Turn ignition switch to RUN position. Measure voltage at input side of fuse No. 13 in instrument panel fuse box. If battery voltage exists, go to next step. If battery voltage does not exist, repair power supply to fuse No. 13. See appropriate wiring diagram in POWER DISTRIBUTION article in WIRING DIAGRAMS.

9) Turn ignition switch to LOCK position. Install fuse No. 13 (15-amp). Disconnect LCM harness connector C2027. Turn ignition switch to RUN position. Measure voltage at terminal No. 9 (Red/Yellow wire) at LCM 16-pin connector C2027. *See Fig. 3.* If battery voltage exists, replace LCM. If battery voltage does not exist, repair open in Red/Yellow wire.

10) Turn ignition switch to LOCK position. Disconnect LCM harness connector C2027. Measure resistance between ground and terminal No. 9 (Red/Yellow wire) at LCM harness connector C2027. *See Fig. 3*. If resistance is greater than 10 k/ohms, replace LCM. If resistance is 10 k/ohms or less, repair short to ground in Red/Yellow wire.

11) Turn ignition switch to LOCK position. Disconnect LCM harness connector C2029. Measure resistance between ground and terminals No. 4 and 9 (both Black wire) at LCM harness connector C2029. *See Fig. 4.* If either resistance reading is greater than 5 ohms, repair open in appropriate Black wire(s). If both resistance readings are 5 ohms or less, repair module communication concern. See MODULE COMMUNICATIONS NETWORK – CROWN VICTORIA & GRAND MARQUIS article.

12) Turn ignition switch to LOCK position. Disconnect LCM harness connector C2029. Measure voltage at terminal No. 6 (Tan/White wire) at LCM harness connector C2029. *See Fig. 4.* If battery voltage does not exist, go to next step. If battery voltage exists, go to step **16)**.

13) Remove fuse No. 4 (15-amp) from instrument panel fuse box. Measure resistance between ground and terminal No. 6 (Tan/White wire) at LCM harness connector C2029. If resistance is greater than 10 k/ohms, go to next step. If resistance is 10 k/ohms or less, repair short to ground in Tan/White wire and replace fuse.

14) Measure voltage at input side of fuse No. 4 in instrument panel fuse box. If battery voltage exists, go to next step. If battery voltage does not exist, repair power distribution circuit. See appropriate wiring diagram in POWER DISTRIBUTION article in WIRING DIAGRAMS.

15) Measure resistance in Tan/White wire between output side of fuse No. 4 and terminal No. 6 at LCM harness connector C2029. If resistance is 5 ohms or less, system is okay at this time. If resistance is greater than 5 ohms, repair open in Tan/White wire.

16) Measure voltage at terminal No. 11 (Light Green/Yellow wire) at LCM harness connector C2029. If battery voltage does not exist, go to next step. If battery voltage exists, go to step **20)**.

17) Remove fuse No. 8 (15-amp) from instrument panel fuse box. Measure resistance between ground and terminal No. 11 (Light Green/Yellow wire) at LCM harness connector C2029. If resistance is greater than 10 k/ohms, go to next step. If resistance is 10 k/ohms or less, repair short to ground in Light Green/Yellow wire and replace fuse.

18) Measure voltage at input side of fuse No. 8. If battery voltage exists, go to next step. If battery voltage does not exist, repair power distribution circuit. See appropriate wiring diagram in POWER DISTRIBUTION article in WIRING DIAGRAMS.

19) Measure resistance in Light Green/Yellow wire between output side of fuse No. 8 and terminal No. 11 at LCM harness connector C2029. If resistance is 5 ohms or less, system is okay at this time. If resistance is greater than 5 ohms, repair open in Light Green/Yellow wire.

20) Measure resistance between ground and terminal No. 9 (Black wire) at LCM harness connector C2029. If resistance is 5 ohms or less, repair communication concern. See MODULE COMMUNICATIONS NETWORK – CROWN VICTORIA & GRAND MARQUIS article. If resistance is greater than 5 ohms, repair open in Black wire.

TEST B: HEADLIGHTS INOPERATIVE

NOTE: Due to varying wattage ratings and resulting current draw, certain aftermarket bulbs may cause Lighting Control Module (LCM) to shut down. Verify that bulbs meet Ford specifications.

1) Using NGS tester, perform Lighting Control Module (LCM) self-test. If no DTCs are retrieved and autolamps operate, go to next step. If no DTCs are retrieved and autolamps do not operate, perform TEST H:

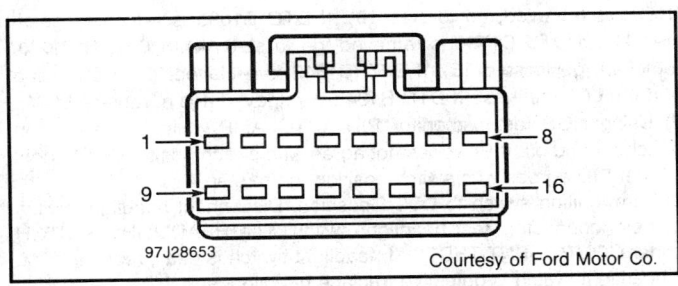

Fig. 3: Identifying Lighting Control Module Harness Connector C2027 Terminals

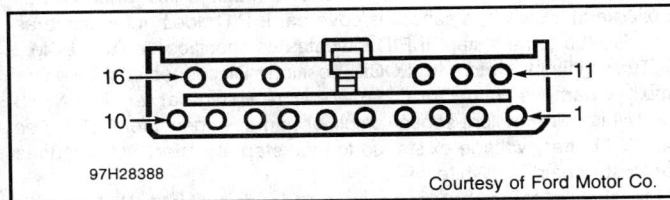

Fig. 4: Identifying Lighting Control Module Harness Connector C2029 Terminals

AUTOLAMPS INOPERATIVE. If DTC B1470 is retrieved, go to step **8**). If any other DTCs are retrieved, perform appropriate test. See LIGHTING CONTROL MODULE DTC INDEX table under SELF-DIAGNOSTIC SYSTEM. If DTC B1342 is retrieved, clear DTC and perform LCM self-test. If DTC B1342 is retrieved again, replace LCM.

2) Turn ignition switch to RUN position. Using NGS tester, trigger LCM active command HEAD/CORNERING LAMP LOW BEAM to ON. If headlights turn on, go to next step. If headlights do not turn on, go to step **5**).

3) Using NGS tester, monitor LCM PID HDLMPSW while turning headlight switch to ON position. If PID does not indicate ON, go to next step. If PID indicates ON, replace LCM.

4) Test headlight switch. See HEADLIGHT SWITCH under COMPONENT TESTS. If headlight switch is defective, replace headlight switch. If headlight switch is defective, repair open in Red/Yellow wire between headlight switch and LCM.

5) Turn ignition switch to LOCK position. Disconnect LCM harness connector C2029. Turn ignition switch to RUN position. Measure voltage at terminal No. 16 (Orange/White wire) at LCM harness connector C2029. *See Fig. 4.* If battery voltage exists, go to next step. If battery voltage does not exist, repair Orange/White wire from fuse panel to LCM and retest system.

6) Using a fused jumper wire, connect terminals No. 10 (Gray wire) and No. 16 (Orange/White wire) at LCM harness connector C2029. If headlights do not turn on, leave jumper wire connected and go to next step. If headlights turn on, replace LCM.

7) Disconnect multifunction switch harness connector C269. Measure voltage at terminal No. 1 (Gray wire) at multifunction switch harness connector C269. *See Fig. 5.* If battery voltage exists, replace multifunction switch. If battery voltage does not exist, repair open in Gray wire.

NOTE: LCM harness connector C2027 has 2 Red/Yellow wires next to each other. Terminal No. 9 is hot in RUN and START. Terminal No. 10 is headlight switch input.

8) Turn ignition switch to LOCK position. Disconnect LCM harness connector C2027. Disconnect headlight switch harness connector C262. Measure resistance in Red/Yellow wire between terminal No. 8 at headlight switch harness connector C262 and terminal No. 10 at LCM harness connector C2027. *See Figs. 3 and 6.* Resistance should be 5 ohms or less. Also, measure resistance between ground and terminal No. 10 (Red/Yellow wire) at LCM harness connector C2027. Resistance should be greater than 10 k/ohms. If both resistance readings are as specified, replace LCM. If either resistance reading is not as specified, repair open or short to ground in Red/Yellow wire.

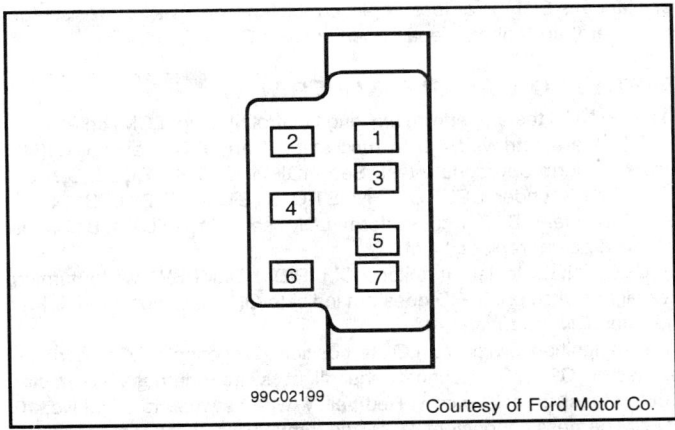

Fig. 5: Identifying Multifunction Switch Harness Connector C269 Terminals

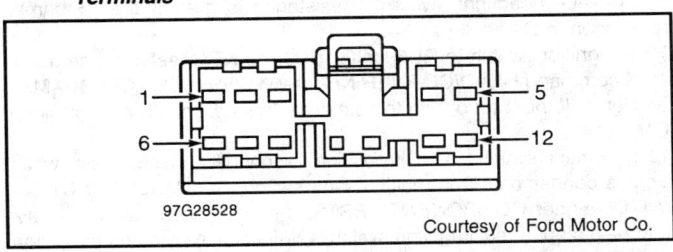

Fig. 6: Identifying Headlight Switch Harness Connector C262 & Driver's Door Module Harness Connector C518 Terminals

TEST C: HEADLIGHTS ON CONTINUOUSLY

1) Using NGS tester, perform Lighting Control Module (LCM) self-test. If no DTCs are retrieved, go to next step. If DTC B1312 is retrieved, go to step **3**). If DTC B1693 and/or B1790 are retrieved, perform TEST H: AUTOLAMPS INOPERATIVE. If DTC B1342 is retrieved, clear DTC and perform LCM self-test. If DTC B1342 is retrieved again, replace LCM.

2) Using NGS tester, monitor LCM PID HDLMPSW. If PID indicates ON, go to next step. If PID does not indicate ON, go to step **5**).

3) Test headlight switch. See HEADLIGHT SWITCH under COMPONENT TESTS. If headlight switch is defective, replace headlight switch. If headlight switch is defective, repair open in Red/Yellow wire between headlight switch and LCM.

NOTE: LCM harness connector C2027 has 2 Red/Yellow wires next to each other. Terminal No. 9 is hot in RUN and START. Terminal No. 10 is headlight switch input.

4) Ensure headlight switch is off. Turn ignition switch to LOCK position. Disconnect LCM harness connector C2027. Measure voltage at terminal No. 10 (Red/Yellow wire) at LCM harness connector C2027. *See Fig. 3.* If voltage does not exist, replace LCM. If voltage exists, repair short to voltage in Red/Yellow wire.

5) Turn ignition switch to LOCK position. Disconnect LCM harness connector C2029. If headlights are still on, repair short to voltage in Gray wire between LCM and multifunction switch. If headlights are not on, replace LCM.

TEST D: HIGH BEAMS INOPERATIVE

NOTE: Due to varying wattage ratings and resulting current draw, certain aftermarket bulbs may cause Lighting Control Module (LCM) to shut down. Verify that bulbs meet Ford specifications.

1) Turn ignition switch to LOCK position. Disconnect multifunction switch harness connector C269. Measure voltage at terminal No. 7 (Orange/White wire) at multifunction switch harness connector C269. *See Fig. 5.* If battery voltage exists, go to next step. If battery voltage does not exist, repair open in Orange/White wire.

2) Measure resistance between ground and terminal No. 5 (Light Green/Black wire) at multifunction switch harness connector C269. If

FORD
4-496

1999 ACCESSORIES & EQUIPMENT
Autolamp Systems – Crown Victoria & Grand Marquis (Cont.)

resistance is 5 ohms or less, replace multifunction switch. If resistance is greater than 5 ohms, repair open in Light Green/Black wire.

TEST E: LOW BEAMS INOPERATIVE

1) Using NGS tester, perform Lighting Control Module (LCM) self-test. If no DTCs are retrieved, go to next step. If any DTCs except B1342 exists. perform appropriate test. See LIGHTING CONTROL MODULE DTC INDEX under SELF-DIAGNOSTIC SYSTEM. If DTC B1342 is retrieved, clear DTC and perform LCM self-test. If DTC B1342 is retrieved again, replace LCM.

2) Using NGS tester, monitor LCM PID HDLMPSW while turning headlight switch on. If PID does not indicate ON, go to next step. If PID indicates ON, go to step 4).

3) Turn ignition switch to LOCK position. Disconnect LCM harness connector C2027. Disconnect headlight switch harness connector C262. Measure resistance in Red/Yellow wire between terminal No. 10 at LCM harness connector C2027 and terminal No. 8 at headlight switch harness connector C262. See Figs. 3 and 6. If resistance is 5 ohms or less, replace headlight switch. If resistance is greater than 5 ohms, repair open in Red/Yellow wire.

4) Turn ignition switch to RUN position. Using NGS tester, trigger LCM active command HEAD/CORNERING LAMP CONTROL LOW BEAM. If headlights do not turn on, go to next step. If headlights turn on, replace LCM.

5) Turn ignition switch to LOCK position. Disconnect multifunction switch harness connectors. Test multifunction switch. See MULTIFUNCTION SWITCH under COMPONENT TESTS. If multifunction switch is okay, go to next step. If multifunction switch is defective, replace multifunction switch.

6) Turn ignition switch to LOCK position. Disconnect LCM harness connector C2029. Measure resistance in Gray wire between terminal No. 10 at LCM harness connector and terminal No. 1 at multifunction switch harness connector C269. See Figs. 4 and 5. If resistance is 5 ohms or less, repair open in Red/Black wire between multifunction switch and headlights. If resistance is greater than 5 ohms, repair open in Gray wire.

TEST F: ONE LOW BEAM INOPERATIVE

1) Turn ignition switch to LOCK position. Disconnect inoperative headlight harness connector. Turn ignition switch to RUN position. Turn low beams on. Measure voltage at Red/Black wire terminal of inoperative headlight harness connector. If battery voltage exists, go to next step. If battery voltage does not exist, repair open in Red/Black wire.

2) Turn headlights off. Turn ignition switch to LOCK position. Measure resistance between ground and Black wire terminal of inoperative headlight harness connector. If resistance is 5 ohms or less, replace headlight bulb. If resistance is greater than 5 ohms, repair open in Black wire.

TEST G: ONE HIGH BEAM INOPERATIVE

1) Turn ignition switch to LOCK position. Disconnect inoperative headlight harness connector. Turn ignition switch to RUN position. Turn high beams on. Measure voltage at Light Green/Black wire terminal of inoperative headlight harness connector. If battery voltage exists, go to next step. If battery voltage does not exist, repair open in Light Green/Black wire.

2) Turn headlights off. Turn ignition switch to LOCK position. Measure resistance between ground and Black wire terminal of inoperative headlight harness connector. If resistance is 5 ohms or less, replace headlight bulb. If resistance is greater than 5 ohms, repair open in Black wire.

TEST H: AUTOLAMPS INOPERATIVE

1) Using NGS tester, perform LCM self-test. If no DTCs are retrieved and autolamps are inoperative, go to next step. If no DTCs are retrieved and autolamps are always on, go to step 7). If DTC B1312 is retrieved, perform TEST C: HEADLIGHTS ON CONTINUOUSLY. If DTC B1470 is retrieved, perform TEST B: HEADLIGHTS INOPERATIVE. If DTC

B1693 is retrieved, go to step 10). If DTC B1695 is retrieved, go to step 12). If DTC B1790 is retrieved, go to step 14). If DTC B1792 is retrieved, go to step 15). If DTC B1342 is retrieved, clear DTC and perform LCM self-test. If DTC B1342 is retrieved again, replace LCM.

2) Using NGS tester, monitor PID AUTOLAMP while turn autolamp switch on and off. If PID does not agree with switch position, go to next step. If PID agrees with switch position, go to step 4).

3) Turn ignition switch to LOCK position. Disconnect headlight switch harness connector. Test headlight switch. See HEADLIGHT SWITCH under COMPONENT TESTS. If headlight switch is okay, replace LCM. If headlight switch is defective, replace headlight switch.

4) Using NGS tester, monitor LCM PID LIGHTSN while illuminating and covering light sensor amplifier. PID should indicate NO when light is applied and YES when sensor is covered. If PID does not indicate as specified, go to next step. If PID indicates as specified, replace LCM.

5) Turn ignition switch to LOCK position. Disconnect light sensor amplifier harness connector C286. Measure voltage at terminal No. 3 (Tan/White wire) at light sensor amplifier harness connector C286. See Fig. 7. If battery voltage exists, go to next step. If battery voltage does not exist, repair Tan/White wire.

6) Measure resistance between ground and terminal No. 1 (Pink/Orange wire) at light sensor amplifier harness connector C286. If resistance is 5 ohms or less, replace light sensor amplifier. If resistance is greater than 5 ohms, repair open in Pink/Orange wire.

7) Using NGS tester, monitor PID AUTOLAMP while turn autolamp switch on and off. If PID does not agree with switch position, go to next step. If PID agrees with switch position, go to step 9).

8) Turn ignition switch to LOCK position. Disconnect headlight switch harness connectors. Test headlight switch. See HEADLIGHT SWITCH under COMPONENT TESTS. If headlight switch is okay, replace LCM. If headlight switch is defective, replace headlight switch.

9) Using NGS tester, monitor LCM PID LIGHTSN while illuminating and covering light sensor amplifier. PID should indicate NO when light is applied and YES when sensor is covered. If PID does not indicate as specified, go to next step. If PID indicates as specified, replace LCM.

10) Turn ignition switch to LOCK position. Disconnect LCM harness connector C2026. Disconnect headlight switch harness connector C262. Measure resistance in Violet/Orange wire between terminal No. 6 at LCM harness connector C2026 and terminal No. 4 at headlight switch harness connector C262. See Figs. 6 and 8. Resistance should be 5 ohms or less. Also, measure resistance between ground and terminal No. 6 (Violet/Orange wire) at LCM harness connector C2026. Resistance should be greater than 10 k/ohms. If both resistance readings are as specified, go to next step. If resistance readings are not as specified, repair open or short to ground in Violet/Orange wire.

11) Test headlight switch. See HEADLIGHT SWITCH under COMPONENT TESTS. If headlight switch is okay, replace LCM. If headlight switch is defective, replace headlight switch.

12) Turn ignition switch to LOCK position. Disconnect LCM harness connector C2026. Disconnect headlight switch harness connector C262. Measure voltage at terminal No. 4 (Violet/Orange wire) at headlight switch harness connector C262. See Fig. 6. If voltage does not exist, go to next step. If voltage exists, repair short to voltage in Violet/Orange wire.

13) Test headlight switch. See HEADLIGHT SWITCH under COMPONENT TESTS. If headlight switch is okay, replace LCM. If headlight switch is defective, replace headlight switch.

14) Turn ignition switch to LOCK position. Disconnect LCM harness connector C2026. Disconnect light sensor amplifier harness connector C286. Measure resistance in White/Violet wire between terminal No. 7 at LCM harness connector C2026 and terminal No. 4 at light sensor amplifier harness connector C286. See Figs. 7 and 8. Resistance should be 5 ohms or less. Also, measure resistance between ground and terminal No. 7 (White/Violet wire) at LCM harness connector C2026. Resistance should be greater than 10 k/ohms. If both resistance readings are as specified, replace LCM. If resistance readings are not as specified, repair open or short to ground in White/Violet wire.

15) Turn ignition switch to LOCK position. Disconnect LCM harness connector C2026. Disconnect light sensor amplifier harness connector

1999 ACCESSORIES & EQUIPMENT
Autolamp Systems – Crown Victoria & Grand Marquis (Cont.)

FORD
4-497

C282. Measure voltage at terminal No. 4 (White/Violet wire) at light sensor amplifier harness connector C282. *See Fig. 7.* If voltage does not exist, replace LCM. If voltage exists, repair short to voltage in White/Violet wire.

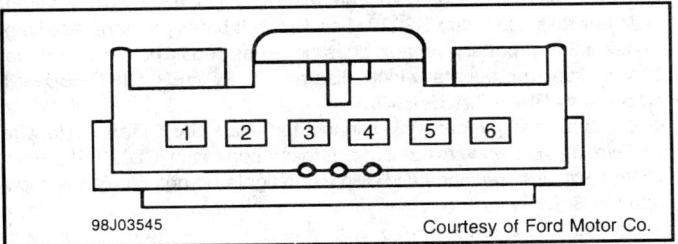

Fig. 7: Identifying Light Sensor Amplifier Harness Connector C286 Terminals

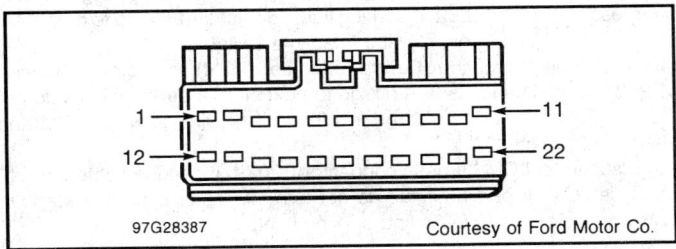

Fig. 8: Identifying Lighting Control Module Harness Connector C2026 Terminals

TEST I: AUTOLAMP TIME DELAY INOPERATIVE

1) Using NGS tester, perform Lighting Control Module (LCM) self-test. If no DTCs are retrieved, go to next step. If DTC B1689 or B1692 are retrieved, go to step **3)**. If DTC B1342 is retrieved, clear DTC and perform LCM self-test. If DTC B1342 is retrieved again, replace LCM.
2) Turn ignition switch to LOCK position. Disconnect headlight switch harness connectors. Test headlight switch. See HEADLIGHT SWITCH under COMPONENT TESTS. If headlight switch is okay, replace LCM. If headlight switch is defective, replace headlight switch.
3) Turn ignition switch to LOCK position. Disconnect LCM harness connector C2026. Measure voltage at terminal No. 9 (Dark Blue/Orange wire) at LCM harness connector C2026. *See Fig. 8.* If voltage does not exist, go to next step. If voltage exists, repair short to voltage in Dark Blue/Orange wire.
4) Disconnect headlight switch harness connector C262. Measure resistance in Dark Blue/Orange wire between terminal No. 8 at LCM harness connector C2026 and terminal No. 9 at headlight switch harness connector C262. *See Figs. 6 and 8.* Resistance should be 5 ohms or less. Also, measure resistance between ground and terminal No. 8 (Dark Blue/Orange wire) at LCM harness connector C2026. Resistance should be greater than 10 k/ohms. If both resistance readings are as specified, go to next step. If resistance readings are not as specified, repair open or short to ground in Dark Blue/Orange wire.
5) Disconnect headlight switch harness connectors. Test headlight switch. See HEADLIGHT SWITCH under COMPONENT TESTS. If headlight switch is okay, replace LCM. If headlight switch is defective, replace headlight switch.

TEST J: BRAKELIGHTS INOPERATIVE

NOTE: On Grand Marquis brakelight circuit runs through multi-function switch.

1) Turn ignition switch to LOCK position. Disconnect Brake Pedal Position (BPP) switch harness connector C2002. Measure voltage at Light Green/Red wire terminal at BPP switch harness connector C2002. If battery voltage exists, go to next step. If battery voltage does not exist, repair open or short to ground in power distribution circuit. See appropriate wiring diagram in POWER DISTRIBUTION article in WIRING DIAGRAMS.

2) Using a fused jumper wire, connect Light Green/Red wire terminal and Light Green wire terminal at BPP switch harness connector C2002. If brakelights illuminate, replace BPP switch. If brakelights do not illuminate, repair open in Light Green wire on Crown Victoria or go to next step on Grand Marquis.
3) Connect BPP switch harness connector C2002. Disconnect multifunction switch harness connector C268. Measure voltage at terminal No. 9 (Light Green wire) at multifunction switch harness connector C268 while pressing brake pedal. *See Fig. 9.* If battery voltage exists, go to next step. If battery voltage does not exist, check for open in Light Green wire. If wire is okay, replace BPP switch.
4) Test multifunction switch. See MULTIFUNCTION SWITCH under COMPONENT TESTS. If multifunction switch is defective, replace multifunction switch. If multifunction switch is okay, repair open in Light Green/Orange wire for left brakelight or Orange/Light Blue wire for right brakelight.

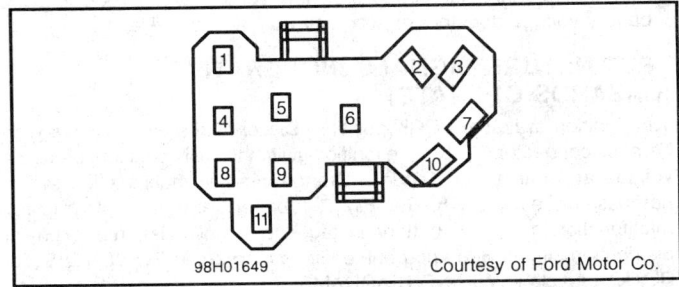

Fig. 9: Identifying Multifunction Switch Harness Connector C268 Terminals

TEST K: TURN/HAZARD POWER FEED CIRCUIT SHORT TO VOLTAGE (DTC B1872)

1) Turn ignition switch to LOCK position. Disconnect Lighting Control Module (LCM) harness connector C2029. Disconnect multifunction switch harness connector C268. Measure voltage at terminal No. 15 (White/Red wire) at LCM harness connector C2029. *See Fig. 4.* If voltage does not exist, go to next step. If voltage exists, repair short to voltage in White/Red wire.
2) Test multifunction switch. See MULTIFUNCTION SWITCH under COMPONENT TESTS. If multifunction switch is okay, replace LCM. If multifunction switch is defective, replace multifunction switch.

TEST L: TURN/HAZARD POWER FEED CIRCUIT SHORT TO GROUND (DTC B1873)

1) Using NGS tester, perform Lighting Control Module (LCM) self-test. If no DTC are retrieved, go to next step. If DTC B1873 is retrieved, go to step **3)**. If DTC B1342 is retrieved, clear DTC and perform LCM self-test. If DTC B1342 is retrieved again, replace LCM.
2) Using NGS tester, monitor LCM PID FLSHPWR while turning flashers on and off. If PID indicates ACTIVE when hazards are on and NOTACT when hazards are off, system is okay at this time. If PID does not indicate ACTIVE when hazards are on and NOTACT when hazards are off, replace multifunction switch.
3) Ensure hazard switch is off. Using NGS tester, monitor LCM PID FLSHPWR. If PID does not indicate ACTIVE, go to next step. If PID indicates ACTIVE, replace LCM.
4) Turn hazard switch on. Using NGS tester, monitor LCM PID FLSHPWR. If PID does not indicate ACTIVE, repair White/Red wire between multifunction switch and LCM. If PID indicates ACTIVE, repair Violet/Orange wire between multifunction switch and fuse No. 5 (15-amp) in instrument panel fuse box.

TEST M: TURN SIGNALS & HAZARDS INOPERATIVE

1) Turn ignition switch to LOCK position. Disconnect multifunction switch harness connector C268. Turn ignition switch to RUN position. Measure voltage at terminals No. 1 (Violet/Orange wire) and No. 4 (Light Green/Red wire) at multifunction switch harness connector C268. *See*

FORD
4-498

1999 ACCESSORIES & EQUIPMENT
Autolamp Systems – Crown Victoria & Grand Marquis (Cont.)

Fig. 9. If battery voltage exists at both terminals, go to next step. If battery voltage does not exist at either terminal, repair appropriate power distribution circuit. See appropriate wiring diagram in POWER DISTRIBUTION article in WIRING DIAGRAMS.

2) Test multifunction switch. See MULTIFUNCTION SWITCH under COMPONENT TESTS. If multifunction switch is okay, go to next step. If multifunction switch is defective, replace multifunction switch.

3) Turn ignition switch to LOCK position. Ensure multifunction switch harness connectors are still disconnected. Disconnect Lighting Control Module (LCM) harness connector C2029. Measure resistance in Light Blue wire between terminal No. 13 at LCM harness connector C2029 and terminal No. 6 at multifunction switch harness connector C268. See Figs. 4 and 9. If resistance is 5 ohms or less, go to next step. If resistance is greater than 5 ohms, repair open in Light Blue wire.

4) Connect multifunction switch harness connectors. Turn ignition switch to RUN position. Measure voltage at terminal No. 15 (White/Red wire) at LCM harness connector C2029. If battery voltage exists, replace LCM. If battery voltage does not exist, repair open in White/Red wire.

TEST N: TURN SIGNALS INOPERATIVE (HAZARDS OPERATE)

Turn ignition switch to LOCK position. Disconnect multifunction switch harness connector C268. Turn ignition switch to RUN position. Measure voltage at terminal No. 1 (Violet/Orange wire) at multifunction switch harness connector C268. See Fig. 9. If battery voltage exists, replace multifunction switch. If battery voltage does not exist, repair power distribution circuit. See appropriate wiring diagram in POWER DISTRIBUTION article in WIRING DIAGRAMS.

TEST O: HAZARDS INOPERATIVE (TURN SIGNALS OPERATE)

Turn ignition switch to LOCK position. Disconnect multifunction switch harness connector C268. Turn ignition switch to RUN position. Measure voltage at terminal No. 4 (Light Green/Red wire) at multifunction switch harness connector C268. See Fig. 9. If battery voltage exists, replace multifunction switch. If battery voltage does not exist, repair power distribution circuit. See appropriate wiring diagram in POWER DISTRIBUTION article in WIRING DIAGRAMS.

TEST P: PARKING LIGHT INPUT SHORT TO VOLTAGE (DTC B1575 OR B1577)

1) Using NGS tester, perform Lighting Control Module (LCM) self-test. If no DTCs or DTC B1577 is retrieved, go to next step. If DTC B1575 is retrieved, go to step 4). If DTC B1342 is retrieved, clear DTC and perform LCM self-test. If DTC B1342 is retrieved again, replace LCM.

2) Turn ignition switch to LOCK position. Disconnect headlight switch harness connector C262. Using NGS tester, monitor LCM PID PARK_SW. If PID indicates ON, go to next step. If PID does not indicate ON, replace headlight switch.

3) Disconnect LCM harness connector C2027. Measure voltage at terminal No. 13 (White/Black wire) at LCM harness connector C2027. See Fig. 3. If voltage exists, repair short to voltage in White/Black wire. If voltage does not exist, replace LCM.

4) Turn ignition switch to LOCK position. Disconnect LCM harness connector C2027. Disconnect headlight switch harness connector C262. Measure resistance in White/Black wire between terminal No. 13 at LCM harness connector C2027 and terminal No. 3 at headlight switch harness connector C262. See Figs. 3 and 6. Resistance should be 5 ohms or less. Also, measure resistance between ground and terminal No. 13 (White/Black wire) at LCM harness connector C2027. Resistance should be greater than 10 k/ohms. If both resistance readings are as specified, replace LCM. If resistance readings are not as specified, repair open or short to ground in White/Black wire.

TEST Q: PARKING LIGHTS INOPERATIVE

1) Using NGS tester, monitor Lighting Control Module (LCM) PID PARK_SW while turning parking lights on and off. If PID does not agree with switch position, go to next step. If PID agrees with switch position, go to step 3).

2) Test headlight switch. See HEADLIGHT SWITCH under COMPONENT TESTS. If headlight switch is okay, go to next step. If headlight switch is defective, replace headlight switch.

3) Turn ignition switch to LOCK position. Disconnect LCM harness connector C2029. Measure voltage at terminal No. 6 (Tan/White wire) at LCM harness connector C2029. See Fig. 4. If battery voltage exists, go to next step. If battery voltage does not exist, repair power distribution circuit. See appropriate wiring diagram in POWER DISTRIBUTION article in WIRING DIAGRAMS.

4) Using a fused jumper wire, connect terminals No. 6 (Tan/White wire) and No. 14 (Brown wire) at LCM harness connector C2029. If parking lights illuminate, replace LCM. If parking lights do not illuminate, repair open in Brown wire.

TEST R: PARKING LIGHTS ON CONTINUOUSLY

1) Turn ignition switch to LOCK position. Disconnect headlight switch harness connector C262. If parking lights do not turn off, go to next step. If parking lights turn off, replace headlight switch.

2) Disconnect Lighting Control Module (LCM) harness connector C2027. If parking lights turn off, go to next step. If parking lights do not turn off, repair short to voltage in White/Black wire between LCM and headlight switch.

3) Disconnect LCM harness connector C2029. If parking lights turn off, replace LCM. If parking lights do not turn off, repair short to voltage in Brown wire between LCM and parking lights.

TEST S: COURTESY LIGHTS INOPERATIVE

1) Using NGS tester, trigger Lighting Control Module (LCM) active command PWM OUTPUT COMMAND 2 to 100 percent. If courtesy lights illuminate, go to next step. If courtesy lights do not illuminate, go to step 13).

2) Turn dome light switch on. If courtesy lights illuminate, go to next step. If courtesy lights do not illuminate, go to step 5).

3) Open driver's door. If courtesy lights illuminate, go to next step. If courtesy lights do not illuminate, go to step 9).

4) Open passenger's, right rear and left rear doors one at a time. If courtesy lights illuminate, system is okay at this time. If courtesy lights do not illuminate, go to step 11).

5) Using NGS tester, monitor LCM PID DOMESW while turning dome light switch on and off. If PID does not agree with switch position, go to next step. If PID agrees with switch position, replace LCM.

6) Turn ignition switch to LOCK position. Disconnect LCM harness connector C2027. Measure voltage at terminal No. 2 (Black/White wire) at LCM harness connector C2027 while turning dome light switch on and off. See Fig. 3. Voltage should exists when dome light is on and should not exist when switch is off. If voltage is not as specified, go to next step. If voltage is as specified, replace LCM.

7) Disconnect negative battery cable. Disconnect headlight switch harness connector C262. Measure resistance in Black/White wire between terminal No. 2 at LCM harness connector C2027 and terminal No. 6 at headlight switch harness connector C262. See Figs. 3 and 6. If resistance is 5 ohms or less, go to next step. If resistance is greater than 5 ohms, repair open in Black/White wire.

8) Connect negative battery cable. Measure voltage at terminal No. 7 (Orange/White wire) at headlight switch harness connector C262. If battery voltage exists, replace headlight switch. If battery voltage does not exist, repair power distribution circuit. See appropriate wiring diagram in POWER DISTRIBUTION article in WIRING DIAGRAMS.

9) Using NGS tester, monitor LCM PID D_DR_LC while opening and closing driver's door. If PID does not agree with door position, go to next step. If PID agrees with door position, replace LCM.

10) Turn ignition switch to LOCK position. Disconnect LCM harness connector C2026. Disconnect driver's door ajar switch harness connector C500. Measure resistance in Dark Blue wire between terminal No. 11 at LCM harness connector C2026 and driver's door ajar switch harness connector C500. See Fig. 8. If resistance is 5 ohms or less, replace driver's door ajar switch. If resistance is greater than 5 ohms, repair open in Dark Blue wire.

1999 ACCESSORIES & EQUIPMENT
Autolamp Systems – Crown Victoria & Grand Marquis (Cont.)

FORD
4-499

11) Using NGS tester, monitor LCM PID P_DR_LC while opening and closing appropriate door. If PID does not agree with door position, go to next step. If PID agrees with door position, replace LCM.

12) Turn ignition switch to LOCK position. Disconnect LCM harness connector C2027. Disconnect appropriate door ajar switch harness connector C500. Measure resistance in Black/Orange wire between terminal No. 11 at LCM harness connector C2027 and appropriate door ajar switch harness connector. *See Fig. 3.* If resistance is 5 ohms or less, replace appropriate door ajar switch. If resistance is greater than 5 ohms, repair open in Black/Orange wire.

13) Turn ignition switch to LOCK position. Disconnect LCM harness connector C2029. Measure voltage at terminal No. 11 (Light Green/Yellow wire) at LCM harness connector C2029. *See Fig. 4.* If battery voltage exists, go to next step. If battery voltage does not exist, repair power distribution circuit. See appropriate wiring diagram in POWER DISTRIBUTION article in WIRING DIAGRAMS.

14) Using a fused jumper wire, connect terminals No. 11 (Light Green/Yellow wire) and No. 5 (Black/Light Blue wire) at LCM harness connector C2029. If courtesy lights illuminate, replace LCM. If courtesy lights do not illuminate, repair open or short to ground in Black/Light Blue wire.

TEST T: DRIVER'S DOOR AJAR CIRCUIT FAILURE (DTC B1322)

1) Turn ignition switch to LOCK position. Disconnect Driver's Door Module (DDM) harness connector C518. Close all doors. Measure resistance between ground and terminal No. 9 (Black/Yellow wire) at DDM harness connector C518. *See Fig. 6.* If resistance is 5 ohms or less, go to next step. If resistance is greater than 5 ohms, replace DDM.

2) Disconnect Lighting Control Module (LCM) harness connector C2026. Measure resistance between ground and terminal No. 10 (Black/Yellow wire) at LCM connector C2026. *See Fig. 8.* If resistance is 5 ohms or less, repair short to ground in Black/Yellow wire. If resistance is greater than 5 ohms, replace LCM.

TEST U: DOOR HANDLE SWITCH CIRCUIT FAILURE (DTC B1442 OR B1445)

1) Turn ignition switch to LOCK position. Disconnect Lighting Control Module (LCM) harness connector C2027. Measure resistance between ground and terminal No. 12 (White/Light Blue wire) at LCM harness connector C2027. *See Fig. 3.* If resistance is 10 k/ohms or less, go to next step. If resistance is greater than 10 k/ohms, go to step **4)**.

2) Disconnect driver's door handle switch harness connector C504. Measure resistance between ground and terminal No. 12 (White/Light Blue wire) at LCM harness connector C2027. If resistance is 10 k/ohms or less, go to next step. If resistance is greater than 10 k/ohms, replace driver's door handle switch.

3) Disconnect passenger's door handle switch harness connector C604. Measure resistance between ground and terminal No. 12 (White/Light Blue wire) at LCM harness connector C2027. If resistance is 10 k/ohms or less, repair short to ground in White/Light Blue wire. If resistance is greater than 10 k/ohms, replace passenger's door handle switch.

4) Disconnect driver's and passenger's door handle switch harness connectors. Measure resistance in White/Light Blue wire between each door handle switch harness connector and terminal No. 12 at LCM harness connector C2027. If both resistance readings are 5 ohms or less, go to next step. If either resistance reading is greater than 5 ohms, repair open in White/Light Blue wire.

5) Turn ignition switch to RUN position. Measure voltage at terminal No. 12 (White/Light Blue wire) at LCM harness connector C2027. If voltage exists, repair short to voltage in White/Light Blue wire. If voltage does not exist, replace LCM.

TEST V: DOOR AJAR CIRCUIT SHORT TO GROUND (DTC B1566)

1) Using NGS tester, monitor LCM PID P_DR_LC while opening and closing all passenger's doors one at a time. If PID does not agree with door position, go to next step. If PID agrees with door position, replace LCM.

2) Disconnect all door ajar switch harness connectors. Using NGS tester, monitor LCM PID P_DR_LC. If PID indicates CLOSED, go to next step. If PID indicates OPEN, repair short to ground in Black/Orange wire.

3) Connect right rear door ajar switch harness connector. Using NGS tester, monitor LCM PID P_DR_LC while opening and closing right rear door. If PID agrees with door position, go to next step. If PID does not agree with door position, replace right rear door ajar switch.

4) Close right rear door. Connect left rear door ajar switch harness connector. Using NGS tester, monitor LCM PID P_DR_LC while opening and closing left rear door. If PID agrees with door position, go to next step. If PID does not agree with door position, replace left rear door ajar switch.

5) Close left rear door. Connect passenger's door ajar switch harness connector. Using NGS tester, monitor LCM PID P_DR_LC while opening and closing passenger's door. If PID agrees with door position, system is okay at this time. If PID does not agree with door position, replace passenger's door ajar switch.

TEST W: DOME LIGHT INPUT CIRCUIT FAILURE (DTC B1687 OR B1685)

1) Using NGS tester, monitor Lighting Control Module (LCM) PID DOMESW. If PID indicates ON, go to next step. If PID indicates OFF, go to step **3)**.

2) Turn ignition switch to LOCK position. Disconnect headlight switch harness connector C262. Using NGS tester, monitor LCM PID DOMESW. If PID indicates ON, repair short to voltage in Black/White wire between headlight switch and LCM. If PID indicates OFF, replace headlight switch.

3) Turn ignition switch to LOCK position. Disconnect LCM harness connector C2027. Disconnect headlight switch harness connector C262. Measure resistance in Black/White wire between terminal No. 2 at LCM harness connector C2027 and terminal No. 6 at headlight switch harness connector C262. *See Figs. 3 and 6.* If resistance is 5 ohms or less, go to next step. If resistance is greater than 5 ohms, repair open in Black/White wire.

4) Measure resistance between ground and terminal No. 2 (Black/White wire) at LCM harness connector C2027. If resistance is greater than 10 k/ohms, replace LCM. If resistance is 10 k/ohms or less, repair short to ground in Black/White wire.

TEST X: NO COMMUNICATION WITH DRIVER'S DOOR MODULE

1) Turn ignition switch to LOCK position. Disconnect Driver's Door Module (DDM) harness connector C520. Turn ignition switch to RUN position. Measure voltage at terminals No. 3 (Yellow/Light Green wire) and No. 4 (Black/White wire) at DDM harness connector C520. *See Fig. 10.* If battery voltage exists at both terminals, go to next step. If battery voltage does not exist and either terminal, repair appropriate power distribution circuit. See appropriate wiring diagram in POWER DISTRIBUTION article in WIRING DIAGRAMS.

2) Turn ignition switch to LOCK position. Disconnect DDM harness connector C519. Measure resistance between ground and terminals No. 4 (Pink/Orange wire) and No. 15 (Black wire) at DDM harness connector C519. *See Fig. 11.* If either resistance reading is greater than 5 ohms, repair open in appropriate wire. If both resistance readings are 5 ohms or less, repair module communications concern. See MODULE COMMUNICATIONS NETWORK – CROWN VICTORIA & GRAND MARQUIS article.

REMOVAL & INSTALLATION

HEADLIGHT SWITCH

Removal & Installation – Disconnect negative battery cable. Remove instrument panel trim panels by pulling up and unsnapping from retainers. Remove knobs from headlight switch. Remove nut from headlight switch. Disconnect headlight switch connectors. Remove headlight switch. To install, reverse removal procedure. Tighten switch retaining nut to 26 INCH lbs. (3 N.m).

FORD
4-500

1999 ACCESSORIES & EQUIPMENT
Autolamp Systems – Crown Victoria & Grand Marquis (Cont.)

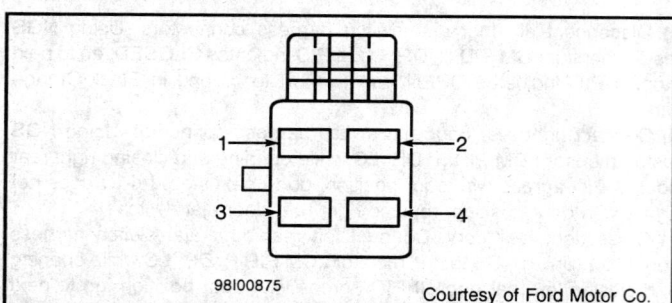

98I00875 — Courtesy of Ford Motor Co.

Fig. 10: Identifying Driver's Door Module Harness Connector C520 Terminals

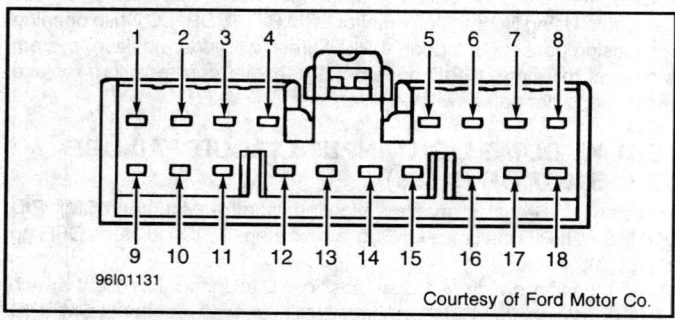

96I01131 — Courtesy of Ford Motor Co.

Fig. 11: Identifying Driver's Door Module Harness Connector C519 Terminals

LIGHTING CONTROL MODULE (LCM)

Removal & Installation – Remove driver side underdash panel. Locate LCM above accelerator pedal. Disconnect LCM connectors. Unclip module from mounting bracket. To install, reverse removal procedure.

LIGHT SENSOR AMPLIFIER

Removal & Installation – Pry up and unsnap instrument panel upper finish panel. Remove retaining screws and light sensor amplifier. Disconnect electrical connector. To install, reverse removal procedure.

WIRING DIAGRAMS

See appropriate wiring diagram in HEADLIGHT SYSTEMS, EXTERIOR LIGHTS, ILLUMINATION/INTERIOR LIGHTS and LIGHTING CONTROL MODULES articles. Also see appropriate wiring diagram in POWER DISTRIBUTION article in WIRING DIAGRAMS.

DESCRIPTION & OPERATION

Autolamp system provides light-sensitive automatic on-off control of exterior lights normally controlled by regular headlight switch. Autolamp system keeps lights on for a pre-selected period of time after ignition switch is turned off. Pre-selected time lapse is adjustable up to approximately 3 minutes.

COMPONENT LOCATIONS

COMPONENT LOCATIONS

Component	Location
Autolamp Module	Located Behind Center Of Instrument Panel
Central Junction Box (CJB)	Located Under Left Side Of Instrument Panel
Fog Light Relay	Located In Battery Junction Box (BJB), On Left Side Of Engine Compartment
Headlight & Parking Light Relays	Located In No. 1 Relay Block, Above Passenger's Air Bag
Remote Anti-Theft Personality (RAP) Module	Located Behind Left Side Of Instrument Panel

TROUBLE SHOOTING

Manufacturer's sequence for diagnosing and repairing autolamp system is as follows:

- Verify Customer's Complaint
- Perform Visual Inspection
- Perform Appropriate SYMPTOM TESTS

INITIAL CHECKS

If concern is not visually evident following initial checks, determine affected system and perform appropriate test. See SYMPTOM CHART under SYMPTOM TESTS.

Autolamps System – Check Central Junction Box (CJB) fuses No. 4 and 29 (both 5-amp), headlight bulb and headlight relay. Check wiring harness for damaged, loose or corroded connectors. Check headlight switch and autolamp time delay switch (part of headlight switch) for damage.

Fog Lights – Check Battery Junction Box (BJB) fuse No. 9 (15-amp), Central Junction Box (CJB) fuse No. 27 (5-amp), fog light relay and fog light bulbs. Check wiring harness for damaged, loose or corroded connectors. Check headlight switch for damage.

Headlights System – Check Battery Junction Box (BJB) fuse No. 8 (30-amp). Check Central Junction Box (CJB) fuses No. 16 (20-amp), No. 26 (10-amp) and No. 28 (10-amp). Check headlight bulb. Check wiring harness for damaged, loose or corroded connectors. Check headlight switch and multifunction switch for damage.

Parking, Rear or License Lights – Check Battery Junction Box (BJB) fuse No. 7 (15-amp) and Central Junction Box (CJB) fuse No. 4 (5-amp). Check parking light relay, parking lights, rear lights and license light. Check wiring harness for damaged, loose or corroded connectors. Check headlight switch and multifunction switch for damage.

Reverse Lights – Check Central Junction Box (CJB) fuse No. 5 (15-amp). Check reverse lights and Digital Transmission Range (DTR) sensor. Check wiring harness for damaged, loose or corroded connectors. Check reverse light switch for damage.

Stoplights System – Check Central Junction Box (CJB) fuse No. 13 (15-amp). Check stoplight bulb. Check wiring harness for damaged, loose or corroded connectors. Check for damaged Brake Pedal Position (BPP) switch.

Turn Signal & Hazard Lights – Check Central Junction Box (CJB) fuses No. 1 (15-amp) and No. 23 (10-amp). Check electronic flasher and turn signal/hazard light. Check wiring harness for damaged, loose or corroded connectors. Check multifunction switch for damage.

COMPONENT TESTS

MICRO ISO RELAY

1) Remove relay to be tested. Measure resistance between relay terminal No. 2 and all other terminals. If resistance is 5 ohms or less between relay terminal No. 2 and any other terminals, replace relay. If all resistances are more than 5 ohms, go to next step.

2) Using a jumper wire, connect between positive battery terminal and relay terminal No. 3. Using a test light, check for voltage at relay terminal No. 4. If voltage is present, go to next step. If voltage is not present, replace relay.

3) Using 3 jumper wires, connect one jumper between positive battery terminal and relay terminal No. 1. Connect another jumper wire between positive battery terminal and relay terminal No. 3. Connect the last jumper wire between negative battery terminal and relay terminal No. 2. Using a test light, check for voltage at relay terminal No. 4. If battery voltage is present, replace relay. If battery voltage is not present, using a test light, check for voltage at relay terminal No. 5. If battery voltage is not present, replace relay. If battery voltage is present, relay is okay.

CONNECTOR IDENTIFICATION

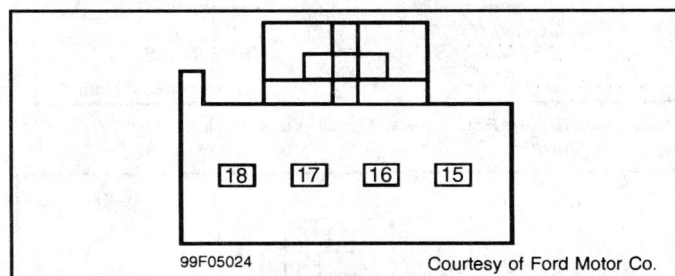

Fig. 1: Identifying Headlight Switch 4-Pin Harness Connector C244

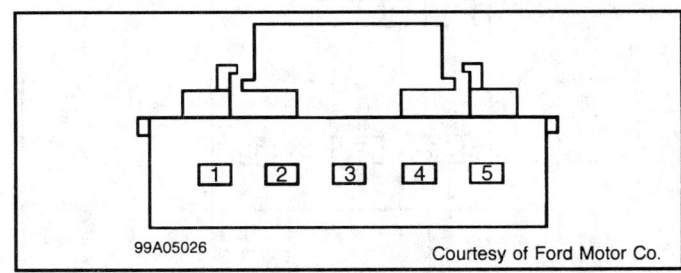

Fig. 2: Brake Pedal Position (BPP) Switch Harness 5-Pin Connector C252

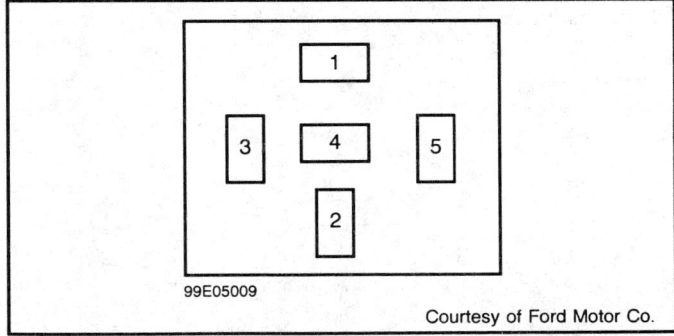

Fig. 3: Identifying Electronic Flasher 5-Pin Connector Terminals

FORD
4-502

1999 ACCESSORIES & EQUIPMENT
Autolamp Systems – Expedition, F150 & F250 Light-Duty Pickup & Navigator (Cont.)

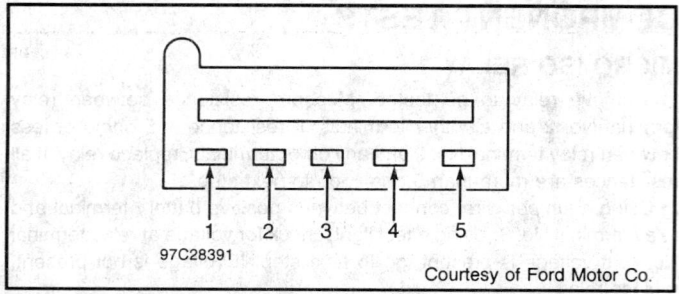

97C28391

Courtesy of Ford Motor Co.

Fig. 4: Identifying Autolamp Module 5-Pin Connector C216 Terminals

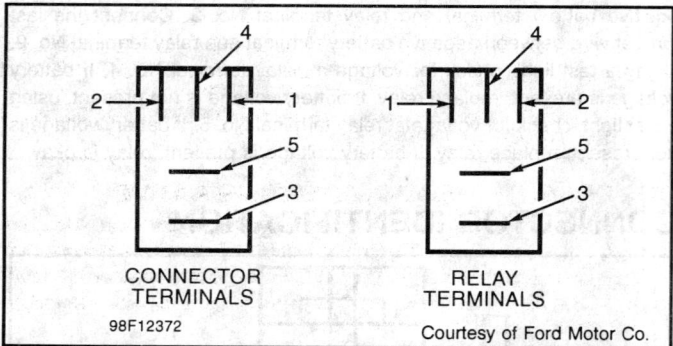

98F12372

Courtesy of Ford Motor Co.

Fig. 5: Identifying Fog Lights, Headlight & Parking Light Relay Terminals

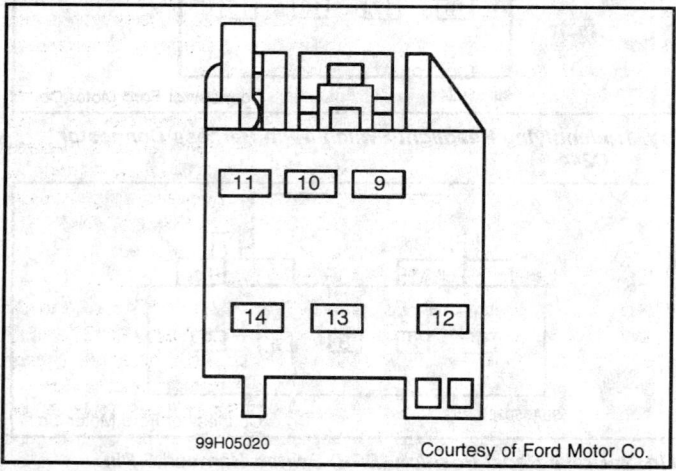

99H05020

Courtesy of Ford Motor Co.

Fig. 6: Headlight Switch 6-Pin (Gray) Harness Connector C245

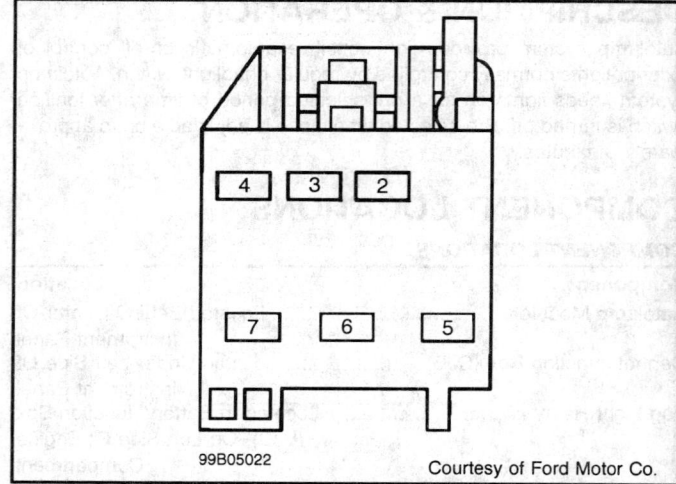

99B05022

Courtesy of Ford Motor Co.

Fig. 7: Headlight Switch 6-Pin (Black) Harness Connector C246

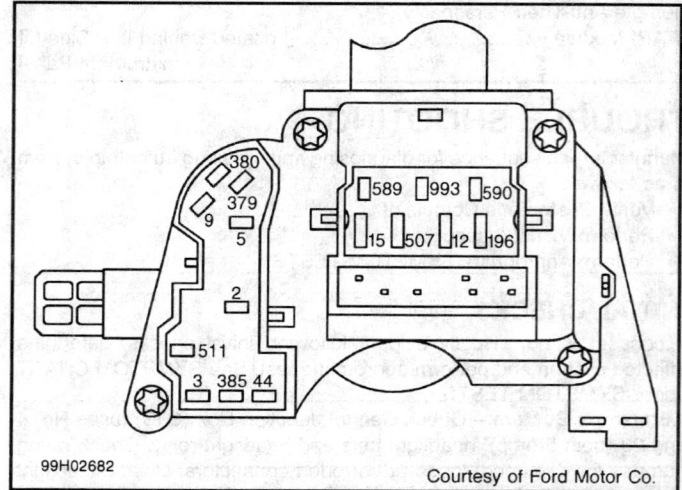

99H02682

Courtesy of Ford Motor Co.

Fig. 8: Identifying Multifunction Switch Terminals

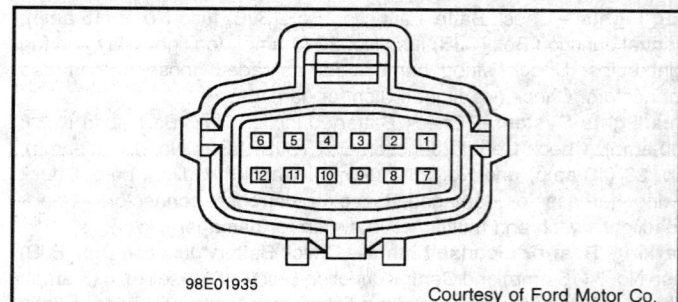

98E01935

Courtesy of Ford Motor Co.

Fig. 9: Digital Transmission Range (DTR) Sensor 12-Pin Harness Connector C182

1999 ACCESSORIES & EQUIPMENT
Autolamp Systems – Expedition, F150 & F250 Light-Duty Pickup & Navigator (Cont.)

FORD
4-503

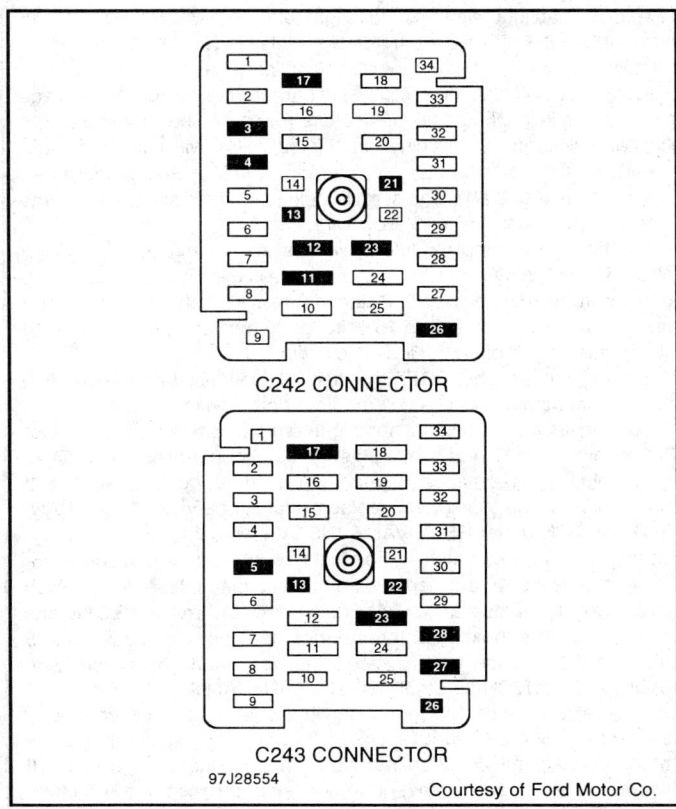

Fig. 10: Identifying Central Junction Box 34-Pin Connector Terminals

SYMPTOM TESTS

NOTE: Perform initial checks before performing any symptom test. See INITIAL CHECKS under TROUBLE SHOOTING.

NOTE: Many steps in the following symptom tests refer to various connectors. These connectors are identified in illustrations. See Figs. 1-10 under CONNECTOR IDENTIFICATION.

CAUTION: Electronic modules are sensitive to static electrical charges. Proper grounding of technician and component is essential to prevent damage.

SYMPTOM CHART

Symptom	Test
Both Headlights Inoperative	A
Low Beams Inoperative	B
High Beams Inoperative	C
One Low Beam Headlight Inoperative	D
One High Beam Headlight Inoperative	E
Headlights Always On	F[1]
Flash-To-Pass Feature Inoperative	F
Autolamps Inoperative	G
Autolamps Always On	H
Autolamp Time Delay Inoperative	I
Headlights Inoperative With Autolamps On	JJ
Stoplights Inoperative	K
One Or More Stoplights Inoperative	L
Stoplights Always On	M
Turn Signals Never On	N
Hazard Flasher Lights Never On	O
One Turn Signal/Hazard Flasher Never On	P
Turn Signal Lights Always On	P[2]

SYMPTOM CHART (Cont.)

Symptom	Test
Hazard Flasher Lights Always On	2
Signal Mirrors Never On	Q
Parking, Rear Or License Lights Inoperative	R
Parking, Rear Or License Lights Inoperative (Autolamps Okay)	S
One Or More Parking, Rear Or License Light(s) Inoperative	T
Parking, Rear Or License Lights Always On	U
Fog Lights Inoperative	V
Individual Fog Light Inoperative	W
Fog Lights Always On	X
Reverse Lights Inoperative	Y
Individual Reverse Light Inoperative	Z
Reverse Lights Always On	AA

[1] – Check Dark Blue/Orange wire for an open and repair as necessary. If okay, replace multifunction switch. See MULTIFUNCTION SWITCH under REMOVAL & INSTALLATION.

[2] – Replace multifunction switch. See MULTIFUNCTION SWITCH under REMOVAL & INSTALLATION.

TEST A: BOTH HEADLIGHTS INOPERATIVE

1) Disconnect headlight switch 6-pin harness connector C246. Measure voltage between headlight switch harness connector C246 terminal No. 7 (Dark Blue/Orange wire) and ground. If voltage is more than 10 volts, go to next step. If voltage is 10 volts or less, repair power distribution circuit as necessary.

2) Disconnect multifunction switch 7-pin harness connector C259. Measure resistance between headlight switch harness connector C246 terminal No. 6 (Red/Yellow wire) and multifunction switch harness connector C259 terminal No. 15 (Red/Yellow wire). If resistance is less than 5 ohms, connect headlight switch and go to next step. If resistance is 5 ohms or more, repair open in Red/Yellow wire.

3) Place headlight switch in ON position. Measure voltage between multifunction switch harness connector C259 terminal No. 15 (Red/Yellow wire) and ground. If voltage is more than 10 volts, replace multifunction switch. See MULTIFUNCTION SWITCH under REMOVAL & INSTALLATION. If voltage is 10 volts or less, replace headlight switch. See HEADLIGHT SWITCH under REMOVAL & INSTALLATION.

TEST B: LOW BEAMS INOPERATIVE

1) Turn ignition switch to OFF position. Place multifunction switch in low beam position. Remove Central Junction Box (CJB) fuses No. 26 and 28 (both 10-amp). Place headlight switch in ON position. Measure voltage between CJB fuses No. 26 and 28 input terminals and ground. If voltages are more than 10 volts, perform TEST D: ONE LOW BEAM HEADLIGHT INOPERATIVE. If voltage is 10 volts or less, go to next step.

2) Disconnect CJB 34-pin harness connector C243. Measure voltage between CJB harness connector C243 terminal No. 7 (Red/Black wire) and ground. If voltage is 10 volts or less, go to next step. If voltage is more than 10 volts, replace CJB.

3) Disconnect multifunction switch 7-pin harness connector C259. Measure resistance between multifunction switch harness connector C259 terminal No. 13 (Red/Black wire) and CJB harness connector C243 terminal No. 7 (Red/Black wire). If resistance is less than 5 ohms, replace multifunction switch. See MULTIFUNCTION SWITCH under REMOVAL & INSTALLATION. If resistance is 5 ohms or more, repair open in Red/Black wire.

TEST C: HIGH BEAMS INOPERATIVE

1) Disconnect left hand headlight 3-pin harness connector C143. Measure resistance between left hand headlight harness connector C143 terminal No. 2 (Light Green/Black wire) and fuse No. 16 output terminal No. 1 (Light Green/Black wire). If resistance is 5 ohms or more, go to next step. If resistance is less than 5 ohms, connect left hand headlight and go to step **3)**.

FORD
4-504

1999 ACCESSORIES & EQUIPMENT
Autolamp Systems – Expedition, F150 & F250 Light-Duty Pickup & Navigator (Cont.)

2) Disconnect Central Junction Box (CJB) 34-pin harness connector C242. Measure resistance between CJB harness connector C242 terminal No. 5 (Light Green/Black wire) and left hand headlight harness connector C143 terminal No. 2 (Light Green/Black wire). If resistance is less than 5 ohms, replace CJB. If resistance is 5 ohms or more, repair open in Light Green/Black wire.

3) Place headlight switch in ON position. Place multifunction switch in high beam position. Measure voltage between fuse No. 16 input terminal No. 2 (Gray/Orange wire) and ground. If voltage is 10 volts or less, go to next step. If voltage is more than 10 volts, perform TEST E: ONE HIGH BEAM HEADLIGHT INOPERATIVE.

4) Disconnect Central Junction Box (CJB) 34-pin harness connector C242. Measure voltage between CJB harness connector C242 terminal No. 30 (Gray/Orange wire) and ground. If voltage is 10 volts or less, go to next step. If voltage is more than 10 volts, replace CJB.

5) Disconnect multifunction switch 7-pin harness connector C259. Measure resistance between multifunction switch harness connector C259 terminal No. 12 (Gray/Orange wire) and CJB harness connector C242 terminal No. 30 (Gray/Orange wire). If resistance is less than 5 ohms, replace multifunction switch. See MULTIFUNCTION SWITCH under REMOVAL & INSTALLATION. If resistance is 5 ohms or more, repair open in Gray/Orange wire.

TEST D: ONE LOW BEAM HEADLIGHT INOPERATIVE

Disconnect inoperative headlight harness connector. Place headlight switch in ON position and multifunction switch in low beam position. Measure voltage between right hand headlight harness connector C133 terminal No. 3 (Dark Green/Orange wire) or left hand headlight harness connector C143 terminal No. 3 (Dark Blue/Orange wire) and ground. If voltage is more than 10 volts, replace headlight bulb. See appropriate HEADLIGHT BULB under REMOVAL & INSTALLATION. If voltage is 10 volts or less, repair open in appropriate wire.

TEST E: ONE HIGH BEAM HEADLIGHT INOPERATIVE

Disconnect inoperative headlight harness connector. Place headlight switch in ON position and multifunction switch in high beam position. Measure voltage between right hand headlight harness connector C133 terminal No. 2 (Light Green/Black wire) or left hand headlight harness connector C143 terminal No. 2 (Light Green/Black wire) and ground. If voltage is more than 10 volts, replace headlight bulb. See appropriate HEADLIGHT BULB under REMOVAL & INSTALLATION. If voltage is 10 volts or less, repair open in appropriate wire.

TEST F: HEADLIGHTS ALWAYS ON

1) Turn ignition switch to OFF position. Disconnect headlight switch 6-pin harness connector C246. If headlights are on, go to next step. If headlights are off, replace headlight switch. See HEADLIGHT SWITCH under REMOVAL & INSTALLATION.

2) Disconnect multifunction switch 7-pin harness connector C259. If headlights are off, go to next step. If headlights are on, go to step **4)**.

3) Measure voltage between multifunction switch harness connector C259 terminal No. 15 (Red/Yellow wire) and ground. If voltage is more than zero volts, repair short to voltage in Red/Yellow wire. If voltage is zero volts, replace multifunction switch. See MULTIFUNCTION SWITCH under REMOVAL & INSTALLATION.

4) Disconnect Central Junction Box (CJB) 34-pin harness connector C243. Measure voltage between multifunction switch harness connector C259 terminal No. 507 (Red/Black wire) and ground. If voltage is more than zero volts, repair short to voltage in Red/Black wire. If voltage is zero volts, replace CJB.

TEST G: AUTOLAMPS INOPERATIVE

1) Turn ignition switch to OFF position. Place headlight switch in ON position. If headlights turn on, place headlight switch in OFF position and go to next step. If headlights do not turn on, perform TEST A: BOTH HEADLIGHTS INOPERATIVE.

2) Remove headlight relay. Test headlight relay. See MICRO ISO RELAY under COMPONENT TESTS. If headlight relay is okay, go to next step. If headlight relay is not okay, replace headlight relay.

3) Disconnect multifunction switch 7-pin harness connector C259. Place headlight switch in OFF position. Measure resistance between headlight relay harness connector terminal No. 5 (Red/Yellow wire) and multifunction switch harness connector C259 terminal No. 15 (Red/Yellow wire). If resistance is less than 5 ohms, go to next step. If resistance is 5 ohms or more, repair open in Red/Yellow wire.

4) Disconnect autolamp module 5-pin harness connector C216. Turn ignition switch to ON position. Measure voltage between autolamp module harness connector C216 terminal No. 1 (Red/Yellow wire) and ground. If voltage is more than 10 volts, go to next step. If voltage is 10 volts or less, repair open in Red/Yellow wire.

5) Turn ignition switch to OFF position. Disconnect headlight switch harness connectors. Place autolamp time delay switch in ON position. Measure resistance between headlight switch component connector C244 terminal No. 17 and headlight switch component connector C246 terminal No. 1. If resistance is less than 5 ohms, go to next step. If resistance is 5 ohms or more, replace headlight switch. See HEADLIGHT SWITCH under REMOVAL & INSTALLATION.

6) Measure resistance between headlight switch component connector C244 terminals No. 17 and 16 while rotating autolamp time delay switch from stop to stop. If resistance varies between 225 ohms and 3.3 k/ohms while rotated, go to next step. If resistance does not vary between 225 ohms and 3.3 k/ohms while rotated, replace headlight switch. See HEADLIGHT SWITCH under REMOVAL & INSTALLATION.

7) Measure resistance between headlight switch harness connector C244 terminal No. 16 (Dark Blue/Orange wire) and autolamp module harness connector C216 terminal No. 5 (Dark Blue/Orange wire). If resistance is less than 5 ohms, go to next step. If resistance is 5 ohms or more, repair open in Dark Blue/Orange wire.

8) Measure resistance between headlight switch harness connector C244 terminal No. 17 (Purple/Orange wire) and autolamp module harness connector C216 terminal No. 2 (Purple/Orange wire). If resistance is less than 5 ohms, go to next step. If resistance is 5 ohms or more, repair open in Purple/Orange wire.

9) Measure resistance between headlight switch harness connector C246 terminal No. 4 (Black wire) and ground. If resistance is less than 5 ohms, go to next step. If resistance is 5 ohms or more, repair open in Black wire.

10) Measure voltage between headlight relay harness connector terminal No. 1 (Orange/Light Green wire) and ground. If voltage is more than 10 volts, go to next step. If voltage is 10 volts or less, repair open in Orange/Light Green wire.

11) Measure voltage between autolamp module harness connector C216 terminal No. 4 (Orange/Light Green wire) and ground. If voltage is more than 10 volts, go to next step. If voltage is 10 volts or less, repair open in Orange/Light Green wire.

12) Measure voltage between headlight relay harness connector terminal No. 3 (Dark Blue/Orange wire) and ground. If voltage is more than 10 volts, go to next step. If voltage is 10 volts or less, repair open in Dark Blue/Orange wire.

13) Measure resistance between headlight relay harness connector terminal No. 2 (Light Green/Yellow wire) and autolamp module harness connector C216 terminal No. 3 (Light Green/Yellow wire). If resistance is less than 5 ohms, replace autolamp module. If resistance is 5 ohms or more, repair open in Light Green/Yellow wire.

TEST H: AUTOLAMPS ALWAYS ON

1) Turn ignition switch to OFF position. Place autolamp time delay switch in OFF position and headlight switch in OFF position. If headlights are on, go to next step. If headlights are off, perform TEST I: AUTOLAMP TIME DELAY INOPERATIVE.

2) Disconnect autolamp module 5-pin harness connector C216. If headlights do not turn off, go to next step. If headlights turn off, replace autolamp module.

1999 ACCESSORIES & EQUIPMENT
Autolamp Systems – Expedition, F150 & F250 Light-Duty Pickup & Navigator (Cont.)

FORD
4-505

3) Remove headlight relay. Measure resistance between headlight relay component terminals No. 3 and 5. If resistance is more than 10 k/ohms, repair short to voltage in Light Green/Yellow wire. If resistance is 10 k/ohms or less, replace headlight relay.

TEST I: AUTOLAMP TIME DELAY INOPERATIVE

1) Disconnect autolamp module 5-pin harness connector C216. Turn ignition switch to ON position. Measure voltage between autolamp module harness connector C216 terminal No. 1 (Red/Yellow wire) and ground. If voltage is more than 10 volts, go to next step. If voltage is 10 volts or less, repair open in Red/Yellow wire.

2) Turn ignition switch to OFF position. Disconnect headlight switch harness connectors. Place autolamp switch in ON position. Measure resistance between headlight switch component connector C244 terminal No. 17 and headlight switch component connector C246 terminal No. 1. If resistance is less than 5 ohms, go to next step. If resistance is 5 ohms or more, replace headlight switch. See HEADLIGHT SWITCH under REMOVAL & INSTALLATION.

3) Measure resistance between headlight switch harness connector C246 terminal No. 4 (Black wire) and ground. If resistance is less than 5 ohms, go to next step. If resistance is 5 ohms or more, repair open in Black wire.

4) Measure resistance between headlight switch harness connector C244 terminal No. 17 (Purple/Orange wire) and autolamp module harness connector C216 terminal No 2 (Purple/Orange wire). If resistance is less than 5 ohms, go to next step. if resistance is 5 ohms or more, repair open in Purple/Orange wire.

5) Measure resistance between headlight switch component connector C244 terminals No. 17 and 16 while rotating autolamp time delay switch from stop to stop. If resistance varies between 225 ohms and 3.3 k/ohms while rotated, go to next step. If resistance does not vary between 225 ohms and 3.3 k/ohms while rotated, replace headlight switch. See HEADLIGHT SWITCH under REMOVAL & INSTALLATION.

6) Measure resistance between headlight switch harness connector C244 terminal No. 16 (Dark Blue/Orange wire) and autolamp module harness connector C216 terminal No. 5 (Dark Blue/Orange wire). If resistance is less than 5 ohms, replace autolamp module. If resistance is 5 ohms or more, repair open in Dark Blue/Orange wire.

TEST J: HEADLIGHTS INOPERATIVE WITH AUTOLAMPS ON

Place autolamp time delay switch in OFF position and headlight switch in ON position. If headlights illuminate, perform TEST G: AUTOLAMPS INOPERATIVE. If headlights do not illuminate, perform TEST A: BOTH HEADLIGHTS INOPERATIVE.

TEST K: STOPLIGHTS INOPERATIVE

1) Disconnect Brake Pedal Position (BPP) switch 5-pin harness connector C252. Measure voltage between BPP switch harness connector C252 terminal No. 5 (Light Green/Red wire) and ground. If voltage is more than 10 volts, go to next step. If voltage is 10 volts or less, repair open in Light Green/Red wire.

2) Connect a 10-amp fused jumper between BPP switch harness connector C252 terminals No. 5 (Light Green/Red wire) and No. 4 (Light Green wire). If stoplights operate correctly, replace BPP switch. See BRAKE PEDAL POSITION (BPP) SWITCH under REMOVAL & INSTALLATION. If stoplights do not operate correctly, repair open in Light Green wire.

TEST L: ONE OR MORE STOPLIGHTS INOPERATIVE

1) Remove inoperative stoplight. Apply brake pedal. Measure voltage between appropriate stoplight light harness connector terminal (Light Green/Orange wire on left side; Orange/Light Blue wire on right side; Light Green wire on high mounted stoplight) and ground. If voltage is 10 volts or less for rear stoplight, go to next step. If voltage is 10 volts or less for high mounted stoplight, repair open in Light Green wire. If voltage is 10 volts or more, replace stoplight bulb.

2) Disconnect Brake Pedal Position (BPP) switch harness connector C252 and multifunction switch 10-pin harness connector C258. Measure resistance between inoperative stoplight harness connector (Light Green/Orange wire) on left hand side, (Orange/Light Blue wire) on right hand side and multifunction switch harness connector C258 terminal No. 9 (Light Green/Orange wire) for left hand side, or terminal No. 5 (Orange/Light Blue wire) for right hand side. If resistance is less than 5 ohms, replace multifunction switch. See MULTIFUNCTION SWITCH under REMOVAL & INSTALLATION. If resistance is 5 ohms or more, repair open in appropriate wire.

TEST M: STOPLIGHTS ALWAYS ON

1) Turn ignition switch to OFF position. If rear mounted stoplight is illuminated, go to next step. If rear mounted stoplight is not illuminated, system is okay.

2) Disconnect Brake Pedal Position (BPP) switch 5-pin harness connector C252. If stoplights are still illuminated, go to next step. If stoplights are not still illuminated, replace BPP switch. See BRAKE PEDAL POSITION (BPP) SWITCH under REMOVAL & INSTALLATION.

3) Disconnect multifunction switch. If any stoplights are illuminated, repair voltage in Light Green wire for high mounted stoplight, Light Green/Orange wire for left hand stoplight or Orange/Light Blue wire for right hand stoplight. If no stoplights are illuminated, replace multifunction switch. See MULTIFUNCTION SWITCH under REMOVAL & INSTALLATION.

TEST N: TURN SIGNALS NEVER ON

1) Remove electronic flasher. Turn ignition switch to ON position. Measure voltage between electronic flasher harness connector terminal No 2 and ground. Measure voltage between electronic flasher harness connector terminal No. 3 and ground. If voltages are more than 10 volts, go to next step. If either voltage is 10 volts or less, repair open in appropriate circuit.

2) Turn ignition switch to OFF position. Disconnect multifunction switch 10-pin harness connector C258. Measure resistance between multifunction switch harness connector C258 terminal No. 44 (Light Blue wire) and electronic flasher harness connector terminal No. 1 (Light Blue wire). Resistance should be less than 5 ohms. Measure resistance between multifunction switch harness connector C258 terminal No. 44 (Light Blue wire) and ground. Resistance should be more than 10 k/ohms. If resistance is as specified, go to next step. If resistance is not as specified, repair open and/or short to ground in Light Blue wire.

3) Place multifunction switch in right turn position. Measure resistance between multifunction switch component connector terminals No. 44 and 5. If resistance is less than 5 ohms, replace electronic flasher. If resistance is 5 ohms or more, replace multifunction switch. See MULTIFUNCTION SWITCH under REMOVAL & INSTALLATION.

TEST O: HAZARD FLASHER LIGHTS NEVER ON

1) Remove electronic flasher. Measure voltage between electronic flasher harness connector terminal No. 3 (Red/White wire) and ground. If voltage is more than 10 volts, go to next step. If voltage is 10 volts or less, repair open in Red/White wire.

2) Turn ignition switch to OFF position. Disconnect multifunction switch 10-pin harness connector C258. Measure resistance between multifunction switch harness connector C258 terminal No. 385 (White/Red wire) and electronic flasher harness connector terminal No. 4 (White/Red wire). Resistance should be less than 5 ohms. Measure resistance between multifunction switch harness connector C258 terminal No. 385 (White/Red wire) and ground. Resistance should be more than 10 k/ohms. If resistance is as specified, go to next step. If resistance is not as specified, repair open and/or short to ground in White/Red wire.

3) Place hazard flasher light switch in ON position. Measure resistance between multifunction switch component connector C258 terminals No.

FORD
4-506

1999 ACCESSORIES & EQUIPMENT
Autolamp Systems – Expedition, F150 & F250 Light-Duty Pickup & Navigator (Cont.)

385 and 5. If resistance is less than 5 ohms, replace electronic flasher. If resistance is 5 ohms or more, replace multifunction switch. See MULTIFUNCTION SWITCH under REMOVAL & INSTALLATION.

TEST P: ONE TURN SIGNAL/HAZARD FLASHER NEVER ON

Turn ignition switch to OFF position. Remove inoperative turn signal/hazard flasher light. Place hazard flasher light switch in ON position. Measure voltage between appropriate light harness connector terminal and ground. See TURN SIGNAL/HAZARD LIGHT CIRCUIT TESTS. If voltage alternates between less than 1 volt and more than 10 volts, replace appropriate turn signal/hazard light bulb. If voltage does alternate between less than 1 volt and more than 10 volts, repair open in appropriate wire.

TURN SIGNAL/HAZARD LIGHT CIRCUIT TESTS

Inoperative Light	Wire Color
Left Front	Light Green/White
Right Front	White/Light Blue
Left Rear	Light Green/Orange
Right Rear	Orange/Light Blue

TEST Q: SIGNAL MIRRORS NEVER ON

1) Turn ignition switch to ON position. Check signal mirror operation. If signal mirrors operate correctly, system is okay. If left hand signal mirror does not operate correctly, go to next step. If right hand signal mirror does not operate correctly, go to step **3)**.

2) Turn ignition switch to OFF position. Disconnect left hand outside rear view mirror 10-pin harness connector C507. Turn ignition switch to ON position. Place multifunction switch in left turn position. Measure voltage between left hand outside rear view mirror harness connector C507 terminal No. 7 (Light Green/White wire) and ground. If voltage varies between zero and more than 10 volts, replace left hand outside rear view mirror. See OUTSIDE REAR VIEW MIRROR under REMOVAL & INSTALLATION. If voltage does not vary between zero and more than 10 volts, repair open in Light Green/White wire.

3) Turn ignition switch to OFF position. Disconnect right hand outside rear view mirror 10-pin harness connector C607. Turn ignition switch to ON position. Place multifunction switch in right turn position. Measure voltage between right hand outside rear view mirror harness connector C607 terminal No. 7 (White/Light Blue wire) and ground. If voltage varies between zero and more than 10 volts, replace right hand outside rear view mirror. See OUTSIDE REAR VIEW MIRROR under REMOVAL & INSTALLATION. If voltage does not vary between zero and more than 10 volts, repair open in White/Light Blue wire.

TEST R: PARKING, REAR OR LICENSE LIGHTS INOPERATIVE

1) Disconnect headlight switch 6-pin harness connector C245. Measure voltage between headlight switch harness connector C245 terminal No. 13 (Tan/White wire) and ground. If voltage is more than 10 volts, go to next step. If voltage is 10 volts or less, repair open in Tan/White wire.

2) Measure resistance between headlight switch harness connector C245 terminal No. 14 (Brown wire) and ground. If resistance is less than 5 ohms, replace headlight switch. See HEADLIGHT SWITCH under REMOVAL & INSTALLATION. If resistance is 5 ohms or more, repair open in Brown wire.

TEST S: PARKING, REAR OR LICENSE LIGHTS INOPERATIVE (AUTOLAMPS OKAY)

1) Turn ignition switch to OFF position. Place headlight switch in parking lights ON position. If parking lights illuminate, go to next step. If parking lights do not illuminate, perform TEST R: PARKING, REAR OR LICENSE LIGHTS INOPERATIVE.

2) Remove parking light relay. Measure voltage between parking light relay harness connector terminal No. 1 (Orange/Light Green wire) and ground. If voltage is more than 10 volts, go to next step. If voltage is 10 volts or less, repair open in Orange/Light Green wire.

3) Test parking light relay. See MICRO ISO RELAY under COMPONENT TESTS. If parking light relay is okay, go to next step. If parking light relay is not okay, replace parking light relay.

4) Disconnect autolamp module 5-pin harness connector C216. Measure resistance between parking light relay harness connector terminal No. 2 (Light Green/Yellow wire) and autolamp module harness connector C216 terminal No. 3 (Light Green/Yellow wire). If resistance is less than 5 ohms, replace autolamp module. If resistance is 5ohms or more, repair open in Light Green/Yellow wire.

TEST T: ONE OR MORE PARKING, REAR OR LICENSE LIGHT(S) INOPERATIVE

1) Turn ignition switch to OFF position. Disconnect inoperative light. Place headlight switch in parking lights ON position. Measure voltage between light harness connector Brown wire terminal and ground. If voltage is more than 10 volts, go to next step. If voltage is 10 volts or less, repair open in Brown wire.

2) Measure resistance between inoperative light harness connector Black wire terminal and ground. If resistance is less than 5 ohms, replace appropriate light. If resistance is 5 ohms or more, repair open in Black wire.

TEST U: PARKING, REAR OR LICENSE LIGHTS ALWAYS ON

1) Turn ignition switch to OFF position. Remove parking light relay. Measure resistance between parking light relay component terminals No. 5 and 3. If resistance is more than 10 k/ohms, go to next step. If resistance is 10 k/ohms or less, replace parking light relay.

2) Disconnect autolamp module harness connectors, Remote Anti-theft Personality (RAP) module 22-pin harness connector C257 and remove parking light relay. Measure resistance between parking light relay harness connector terminal No. 2 (Light Green/Yellow wire) and ground. If resistance is more than 10 k/ohms, go to next step. If resistance is 10 k/ohms or less, repair short to ground in Light Green/Yellow wire.

3) Disconnect headlight switch 6-pin harness connector C245. Measure resistance between headlight switch component connector C245 terminals No. 13 and 14. If resistance is more than 10 k/ohms, replace autolamp module. If resistance is 10 k/ohms or less, replace headlight switch. See HEADLIGHT SWITCH under REMOVAL & INSTALLATION.

TEST V: FOG LIGHTS INOPERATIVE

1) Turn ignition switch to OFF position. Place headlight switch in ON position and multifunction switch in low beam position. If headlights illuminate, go to next step. If headlights do not illuminate, perform TEST A: BOTH HEADLIGHTS INOPERATIVE.

2) Remove fog light relay. Measure voltage between fog light relay harness connector terminal No. 1 (White/Black wire) and ground. If voltage is more than 10 volts, go to next step. If voltage is 10 volts or less, repair open in White/Black wire.

3) Measure voltage between fog light relay harness connector terminal No. 3 (Orange/Light Green wire) and ground. If voltage is more than 10 volts, go to next step. If voltage is 10 volts or less, repair open in Orange/Light Green wire.

4) Measure resistance between fog light relay harness connector terminal No. 5 (Tan/Orange wire) and ground. If resistance is 5 ohms or more, go to next step. If resistance is less than 5 ohms, go to step **6)**.

5) Disconnect inoperative fog light. Measure resistance between inoperative fog light harness connector terminal No. 1 (Black wire) and ground. If resistance is less than 5 ohms, repair Tan/Orange wire. If resistance is 5 ohms or more, repair open in Black wire.

6) Place fog light switch in ON position. Measure resistance between fog light relay harness connector terminal No. 2 (Yellow wire) and ground. If resistance is 5 ohms or more, go to next step. If resistance is less than 5 ohms, replace fog light relay.

1999 ACCESSORIES & EQUIPMENT

FORD
4-507

Autolamp Systems – Expedition, F150 & F250 Light-Duty Pickup & Navigator (Cont.)

7) Place headlight switch in OFF position. Disconnect headlight switch harness connector. Place fog light switch in ON position. Measure resistance between headlight component connector C246 terminals No. 4 and 3. If resistance is less than 5 ohms, go to next step. If resistance is 5 ohms or more, replace headlight switch. See HEADLIGHT SWITCH under REMOVAL & INSTALLATION.

8) Measure resistance between headlight switch harness connector C246 terminal No. 4 (Black wire) and ground. If resistance is less than 5 ohms, repair Yellow wire. If resistance is 5 ohms or more, repair open in Black wire.

TEST W: INDIVIDUAL FOG LIGHT INOPERATIVE

1) Turn ignition switch to OFF position. Disconnect inoperative fog light harness connector. Place headlight switch in ON position, multifunction switch in low beam position and fog light switch in ON position. Measure voltage between inoperative fog light harness connector terminal No. 2 (Tan/Orange wire) and ground. If voltage is more than 10 volts, go to next step. If voltage is 10 volts or less, repair open in Tan/Orange wire.

2) Measure resistance between inoperative fog light harness connector terminal No. 1 (Black wire) and ground. If resistance is less than 5 ohms, replace fog light bulb. See FOG LIGHT BULB under REMOVAL & INSTALLATION. If resistance is 5 ohms or more, repair open in Black wire.

TEST X: FOG LIGHTS ALWAYS ON

1) Turn ignition switch to OFF position. Remove fog light relay. Measure resistance between fog light relay component terminals No. 3 and 5. If resistance is more than 10 k/ohms, go to next step. If resistance is 10 k/ohms or less, replace fog light relay.

2) Disconnect headlight switch 6-pin harness connector C246. Measure resistance between fog light relay harness connector terminal No. 2 (Yellow wire) and ground. If resistance is more than 10 k/ohms, replace headlight switch. See HEADLIGHT SWITCH under REMOVAL & INSTALLATION. If resistance is 10 k/ohms or less, repair short to ground in Yellow wire.

TEST Y: REVERSE LIGHTS INOPERATIVE

1) Turn ignition switch to OFF position. Disconnect Digital Transmission Range (DTR) sensor 12-pin harness connector C182 on vehicles equipped with A/T or reverse light switch 2-pin harness connector C188 on vehicles equipped with M/T. Turn ignition switch to ON position. If vehicle is equipped with A/T, measure voltage between DTR sensor harness connector C182 terminal No. 9 (Light Blue/Pink wire) and ground. If vehicle is equipped with M/T, measure voltage between reverse light switch harness connector C188 Light Blue/Pink wire terminal and ground. If voltage is more than 10 volts, go to next step. If voltage is 10 volts or less, repair open in appropriate wire.

2) Turn ignition switch to OFF position. If vehicle is equipped with A/T, measure resistance between DTR sensor harness connector C182 terminal No. 11 (Black/Pink wire) and ground. If vehicle is equipped with M/T, measure resistance between reverse light switch harness connector C188 Black/Pink wire terminal and ground. If resistance is 5 ohms or more, go to next step. If resistance is less than 5 ohms, replace DTR sensor on vehicles equipped with A/T. If vehicle is equipped with M/T, replace reverse light switch.

3) Disconnect inoperative reverse light. Measure resistance between reverse light harness connector Black wire terminal and ground. If resistance is less than 5 ohms, repair open in Black/Pink wire. If resistance is 5 ohms or more, repair open in Black wire.

TEST Z: INDIVIDUAL REVERSE LIGHT INOPERATIVE

1) Turn ignition switch to OFF position. Disconnect inoperative reverse light. Turn ignition switch to ON position. Set parking brake. Place transmission shift lever in Reverse. Measure voltage between inoperative reverse light harness connector Black/Pink wire terminal and

ground. If voltage is more than 10 volts, go to next step. If voltage is 10 volts or less, repair open in Black/Pink wire.

2) Turn ignition switch to OFF position. Measure resistance between inoperative reverse light harness connector Black wire terminal and ground. If resistance is less than 5 ohms, replace reverse light bulb. If resistance is 5 ohms or more, repair open in Black wire.

TEST AA: REVERSE LIGHTS ALWAYS ON

Turn ignition switch to OFF position. Disconnect Digital Transmission Range (DTR) sensor 12-pin harness connector C182 on vehicles equipped with A/T or reverse light switch 2-pin harness connector C188 on vehicles equipped with M/T. On all models, set parking brake. Turn ignition switch to ON position. Place transmission shift lever in Reverse. If vehicle is equipped with A/T, measure resistance between DTR sensor component connector C182 terminals No. 9 and 11. If vehicle is equipped with M/T, measure resistance between reverse light switch component connector C188 terminal No. 1 and 2. If resistance is less than 5 ohms, replace DTR sensor (A/T) or reverse light switch (M/T). If resistance is 5 ohms or more, repair short to voltage in Black/Pink wire.

REMOVAL & INSTALLATION

BRAKE PEDAL POSITION (BPP) SWITCH

Removal & Installation – Disconnect BPP switch harness connector. Remove self-locking pin, spacer and BPP switch. To install, reverse removal procedure.

FOG LIGHT BULB

WARNING: Halogen bulbs contain gas under pressure. Bulb may shatter if glass envelope is scratched or if bulb is dropped. Handle bulb carefully. Grasp bulb by base only and avoid touching glass envelope.

NOTE: Fog light bulb should not be removed from fog light until just before replacement bulb is installed. Removing bulb from fog light assembly for extended periods of time may effect performance of new bulb. Contaminants may enter fog light where they may settle on lens or reflector. Never turn on fog lights with bulb removed from fog light.

NOTE: When battery is disconnected and reconnected, some abnormal drive symptoms may occur while vehicle relearns it's adaptive strategy. Vehicle may need to be driven 10 miles or more to learn strategy.

Removal & Installation – Disconnect battery ground cable. Disconnect fog light bulb harness connector and rotate fog light socket counterclockwise and remove. To install, reverse removal procedure.

FORD
4-508

1999 ACCESSORIES & EQUIPMENT
Autolamp Systems – Expedition, F150 & F250 Light-Duty Pickup & Navigator (Cont.)

HEADLIGHT BULB

WARNING: Halogen bulbs contain gas under pressure. Bulb may shatter if glass envelope is scratched or if bulb is dropped. Handle bulb carefully. Grasp bulb by base only and avoid touching glass envelope.

NOTE: Headlight bulb should not be removed from headlight until just before replacement bulb is installed. Removing bulb from headlight assembly for extended periods of time may effect performance of new bulb. Contaminants may enter headlight where they may settle on lens or reflector. never turn on headlights with bulb removed from headlight.

NOTE: When battery is disconnected and reconnected, some abnormal drive symptoms may occur while vehicle relearns it's adaptive strategy. Vehicle may need to be driven 10 miles or more to learn strategy.

Removal & Installation (Expedition, & F150 & F250 Light-Duty Pickup) – 1) Raise and support vehicle hood. Disconnect battery ground cable. Remove headlight assembly retainers by pushing rearward and lifting up. Pull headlight forward slightly to expose harness connectors. Disconnect harness connectors and remove headlight assembly.

2) Rotate headlight bulb retainer counterclockwise and remove. Remove headlight bulb by pulling straight out with a gentle up-and-down motion. To install, reverse removal procedure. Ensure correct headlight adjustment after installation.

Removal & Installation (Navigator) – 1) Raise and support vehicle hood. Disconnect battery ground cable. Remove headlight assembly retainers by pushing rearward and lifting up. Pull headlight forward slightly to expose protective covers for harness connectors. Rotate headlight bulb protective cover counterclockwise and remove.

2) Disconnect headlight harness connector. Rotate headlight bulb retainer counterclockwise and remove. Remove headlight bulb by pulling straight out with a gentle up-and-down motion. To install, reverse removal procedure. Ensure correct headlight adjustment after installation.

HEADLIGHT SWITCH

NOTE: When battery is disconnected and connected, some abnormal drive symptoms may occur while vehicle relearns it's adaptive strategy. Vehicle may need to be driven 10 miles or more to learn strategy.

Removal & Installation – 1) Disconnect battery ground cable. Turn headlight switch knob to headlight ON position and pull knob. Insert a thin tool behind headlight switch knob at 7 o'clock position to release knob and remove. Rotate headlight switch knob 180 degrees and install onto switch.

2) Turn knob counterclockwise until back of headlight switch knob is in OFF position. Turn headlight knob fully clockwise, approximately 180 degrees. Pull headlight switch from instrument panel and disconnect harness connectors. To install, reverse removal procedure.

MULTIFUNCTION SWITCH

NOTE: When battery is disconnected and reconnected, some abnormal drive symptoms may occur while vehicle relearns it's adaptive strategy. Vehicle may need to be driven 10 miles or more to learn strategy.

Removal & Installation – Disconnect battery ground cable. Turn ignition switch to RUN position. Insert punch through hole in lower steering column shroud and push ignition switch lock cylinder release tab while pulling out ignition switch lock cylinder. Twist tilt wheel handle and remove. Set gear selector to lowest position. Remove steering column opening cover. Remove upper and lower steering column shrouds. Disconnect harness connectors. Remove multifunction switch. To install, reverse removal procedure.

OUTSIDE REAR VIEW MIRROR

Removal & Installation – Remove front inside door trim panel. Disconnect harness connector and harness clips. Remove 3 nuts retaining mirror body and remove exterior rear view mirror. Feed mirror wiring through opening in front door. To install, reverse removal procedure.

WIRING DIAGRAMS

NOTE: See appropriate wiring diagram in HEADLIGHT SYSTEMS, EXTERIOR LIGHTS, ILLUMINATION/INTERIOR LIGHTS and LIGHTING CONTROL MODULES articles. Also see appropriate wiring diagram in POWER DISTRIBUTION article in WIRING DIAGRAMS.

DESCRIPTION

The autolamp system provides automatic on-off control of the headlights in addition to normal headlight switch operation. The headlights will automatically turn on when outside light dims. The system also includes a delay feature which keeps the headlights on for a pre-selected time period after ignition is turned off. Major components of the system are a light sensor amplifier assembly, located on backside of interior rear view mirror, headlight relay, parking light relay and headlight switch.

OPERATION

The headlight switch must be in the OFF position for automatic operation. The light sensor must be exposed to ambient light to operate properly. Time delay can be varied up to 3 minutes before lights turn off automatically. Time delay is controlled by delay switch knob on bottom of inside rear view mirror. Sliding delay switch knob to the right increases time headlights are on after ignition switch is turned off.

TROUBLE SHOOTING

Verify customer's complaint. Check fuse No. 11 in instrument panel fuse box. Fuse box is located on left side of instrument panel. Also, check fuses No. 11 and 12 in Power Distribution Center (PDC). PDC is located in left side of engine compartment near brake master cylinder. Replace fuse(s) as necessary and recheck system operation. Check or replace any suspect bulbs. Visual inspect for damaged wiring harness and loose or corroded connector terminals. Check for good clean connections at chassis ground point locations. See appropriate wiring diagram in HEADLIGHT SYSTEMS article. Correct any obvious problems before proceeding. If no problems are found, go to SYMPTOM DIAGNOSIS table.

SYMPTOM DIAGNOSIS

Symptom	Test
Autolamps Inoperative	A
Autolamps Always On	B
Autolamp Time Delay Inoperative	C

COMPONENT TESTS

HEADLIGHT SWITCH

Remove headlight switch. Check continuity between appropriate terminals with switch in specified position. See HEADLIGHT SWITCH TEST table. See Fig. 1. If continuity is not as specified, replace headlight switch.

HEADLIGHT SWITCH TEST

Switch Position	Between Terminals	Continuity
Indicator Bulb Circuit		
Park	7 & 9	Yes
Head	7 & 9	Yes
Ignition On, Lights Off Circuit		
Off	4 & 8	Yes
Park	4 & 8	No
Head	4 & 8	No
Headlight Circuit		
Off	2 & 6	No
Park	2 & 6	No
Head	2 & 6	Yes
Parking Lights Circuit		
Off	3 & 5	No
Park	3 & 5	Yes
Head	3 & 5	Yes

HEADLIGHT RELAY & PARKING LIGHT RELAY

1) Remove headlight relay from relay box. Relay box is located below center of instrument panel. Measure resistance between terminal No. 2 and all other relay terminals. See Fig. 2. If all resistance readings are more than 5 ohms, go to next step. If any resistance reading is 5 ohms or less, replace relay.

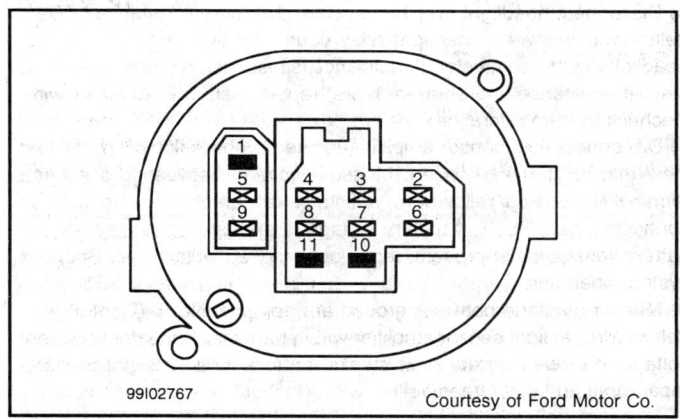

99I02767   Courtesy of Ford Motor Co.

Fig. 1: Identifying Headlight Switch Terminals

2) Using 2 jumper wires, connect positive battery voltage to relay terminals No. 1 and 3. Measure voltage between ground and terminal No. 4. If battery voltage is present, go to next step. If battery voltage is not present, replace relay. Connect another jumper wire between ground and relay terminal No. 5. If battery voltage is present, relay is okay. If battery voltage is not present, replace relay.

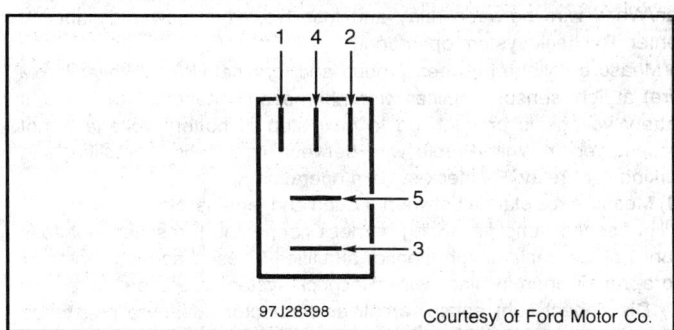

97J28398   Courtesy of Ford Motor Co.

Fig. 2: Identifying Headlight Relay & Parking Light Relay Terminals

SYSTEM TESTS

NOTE: Always perform visual inspection and basic checks before performing any system test. See TROUBLE SHOOTING.

TEST A: AUTOLAMPS INOPERATIVE

NOTE: Autolamp time delay switch and panel dim switch are integral to headlight switch. If autolamp time delay switch or panel dim switch is defective, headlight switch assembly must be replaced.

1) Turn ignition off. Turn headlight switch on. If headlights are on, go to next step. If headlights are off, check headlight switch. See HEADLIGHT SWITCH under COMPONENT TESTS. Replace switch as necessary and recheck system operation. If headlight switch is okay, check and repair headlight circuits as necessary. See appropriate wiring diagram in HEADLIGHT SYSTEMS article. Recheck system operation.
2) If autolamp system related fuses have already been checked, go to next step. If fuses have not been checked, inspect fuse No. 11 in instrument panel fuse box. Also, check fuses No. 11 and 12 in power distribution center. If fuses are okay, go to next step. If fuse(s) is blown, replace fuse(s) as necessary and recheck system operation. If instrument panel No. 11 blows again, go to step **11**). If power distribution box fuse No. 11 blows again, go to step **12**). If fuse No. 12 blows again repair short to ground in Light Blue/Orange wire. Recheck system operation.
3) Remove headlight relay from relay box located below center of instrument panel. Test headlight relay. See HEADLIGHT RELAY & PARKING LIGHT RELAY under COMPONENT TESTS. Replace relay as necessary. If relay is okay, go to next step.

4) Disconnect headlight switch connector. Measure resistance of Red/Yellow wire between headlight relay connector and terminal No. 2 at headlight switch connector. If resistance is less then 5 ohms, go to next step. If resistance is 5 ohms or more, repair open in Red/Yellow wire. Recheck system operation.

5) Disconnect light sensor amplifier, located on backside of inside rear view mirror. Turn ignition on. Measure voltage between ground and terminal No. 6 (Red/Yellow wire) at light sensor amplifier wiring harness connector. *See Fig. 3.* If battery voltage is present, go to next step. If battery voltage is not present, repair open in Red/Yellow wire. Recheck system operation.

6) Measure voltage between ground and terminal No. 5 (Light Green/Yellow wire) at light sensor amplifier wiring harness connector. If battery voltage is present, go to next step. If battery voltage is not present, repair open in Light Green/Yellow wire. Recheck system operation.

7) Measure voltage between ground and terminal No. 3 (Dark Blue/Orange wire) at headlight relay wiring harness connector. *See Fig. 2.* If battery voltage is present, go to next step. If battery voltage is not present, repair open in Dark Blue/Orange wire between headlight relay and power distribution center. Recheck system operation.

8) Measure voltage between ground and terminal No. 1 (Tan/White wire) at headlight relay wiring harness connector. If battery voltage is present, install relay and go to next step. If battery voltage is not present, repair Tan/White wire between relay and fuse No. 11 in power distribution center. Recheck system operation.

9) Measure voltage between ground and terminal No. 2 (White/Purple wire) at light sensor amplifier wiring harness connector. *See Fig. 3.* If battery voltage is present, go to next step. If battery voltage is not present, repair White/Purple wire between light sensor amplifier and parking light relay. Recheck system operation.

10) Measure resistance between ground and terminal No. 4 (Black wire) at light sensor amplifier wiring harness connector. If resistance is less than 5 ohms, replace light sensor amplifier. If resistance is 5 ohms or more, repair open in Black wire. Recheck system operation.

11) Disconnect light sensor amplifier connector. Measure resistance between ground and terminal No. 5 (Light Green/Yellow wire) at light sensor amplifier wiring harness connector. If resistance is more than 10,000 ohms, circuit is okay. Replace light sensor amplifier. Replace fuse and recheck system operation. If resistance is 10,000 ohms or less, repair short to ground in Light Green/Yellow wire). Replace fuse and recheck system operation.

12) Disconnect light sensor amplifier connector. Measure resistance between ground and terminal No. 6 (Red/Yellow wire) at light sensor amplifier wiring harness connector. If resistance is more than 10,000 ohms, replace light sensor amplifier. Replace fuse and recheck system operation. If resistance is 10,000 ohms or less, repair short to ground in Red/Yellow wire. Replace fuse and recheck system operation.

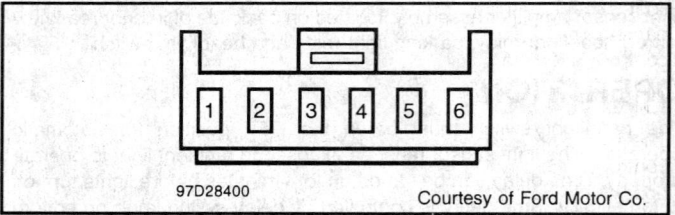

97D28400   Courtesy of Ford Motor Co.

Fig. 3: Identifying Autolamp Light Sensor Amplifier Connector Terminals

TEST B: AUTOLAMPS ALWAYS ON

1) Turn ignition off. Set autolamp time delay switch in OFF position. Disconnect headlight switch connector. If headlights are on, go to next step. If headlights are off, replace headlight switch and recheck system operation.

2) Remove headlight relay from relay box located below center of instrument panel. Measure resistance between relay terminals No. 3 and 5. *See Fig. 2.* If resistance is more than 10,000 ohms, go to next step. If resistance is 10,000 ohms or less, replace relay. Recheck system operation.

3) Disconnect light sensor amplifier, located on backside of inside rear view mirror. Remove parking light relay from relay box located below center of instrument panel.. Measure resistance between ground and terminal No. 2 (White/Purple wire) at headlight relay wiring harness connector. *See Fig. 2.* If resistance is more than 10, 000 ohms, replace light sensor amplifier. Recheck system operation. If resistance is 10,000 ohms or less, replace short to ground in White/Purple wire between light sensor amplifier and parking light relay. Recheck system operation.

TEST C: AUTOLAMP TIME DELAY INOPERATIVE

Check parking light operation. If parking lights are functioning properly, replace light sensor amplifier assembly. If parking lights are not functioning properly, check headlight switch. See HEADLIGHT SWITCH under COMPONENT TESTS. Repair as necessary and recheck system operation. If headlight switch is okay, check and repair headlight switch circuits as necessary. See appropriate wiring diagram in HEADLIGHT SYSTEMS article.

WIRING DIAGRAMS

NOTE: For autolamp system wiring diagram, see appropriate wiring diagram in HEADLIGHT SYSTEMS article.

DESCRIPTION

The autolamp system provides automatic on-off control of the headlights in addition to normal headlight switch operation. The headlights will automatically turn on when outside light dims. The system also includes a delay feature which keeps the headlights on for a pre-selected time period after ignition is turned off. Major components of the system are a light sensor amplifier assembly, autolamp headlight relay, autolamp parking light relay, and an on-off switch with an integral time delay control (potentiometer).

OPERATION

The headlight switch must be in the OFF position and the autolamp control switch (thumb wheel) must be in the ON position for automatic operation. The light sensor must be exposed to ambient light to operate properly. Time delay can be varied up to about 3 minutes before lights turn off automatically. Turning autolamp control switch toward MAX delay position increases time headlights are on after ignition is turned off.

COMPONENT LOCATIONS

COMPONENT LOCATIONS

Component	Location
Generic Electronic Module	Connected To Back Of Instrument Panel Fuse Box
Instrument Panel Fuse Box	Under Left Side Of Instrument Panel
Light Sensor/Amplifier	Right Top Side Of Instrument Panel, Near Windshield
Passive Anti-Theft System Module	Behind Left Center Of Instrument panel, Behind Integrated Control Panel
Remote Anti-Theft Personality Module	Above Accelerator Pedal

ADJUSTMENTS

LIGHT SENSOR AMPLIFIER

Light sensor amplifier can be adjusted to turn headlights on earlier or later than original manufacturer's calibration. Light sensor amplifier is located in defroster grille, top left of dash and has an adjustment feature which adjusts amplifiers operational range. Based on average light available during sunrise and sunset hours, turning adjustment screw located on the amplifier 1/16 turn counterclockwise will turn on headlights about 15 minutes later. *See Fig. 1.*

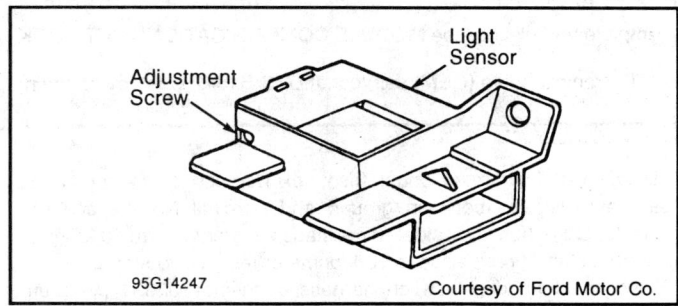

95G14247   Courtesy of Ford Motor Co.

Fig. 1: Locating Light Sensor Adjustment Screw

TROUBLE SHOOTING

CAUTION: Electronic modules are sensitive to static electrical charges. Proper grounding of technician and workpiece is essential to prevent damage.

Verify customer concern by operating system in question. Inspect wiring harness for obvious signs of shorts, opens, bad connections or damage. Visually inspect for blown fuses, damaged light sensor/amplifier, damaged relays damaged headlight switch and defective bulbs. If all checks are okay, perform self-diagnostics. See SELF-DIAGNOSTIC SYSTEM.

COMPONENT TESTS

HEADLIGHT SWITCH

Remove headlight switch. Check continuity or resistance between appropriate terminals with switch in specified position. See HEADLIGHT SWITCH TEST table. *See Fig. 2.* If continuity or resistance is not as specified, replace headlight switch.

HEADLIGHT SWITCH TEST

Switch Position	Between Terminals	Continuity
Autolamp Feed Circuit		
Off	4 & 17	No
Park	4 & 17	No
Head	9 & 17	No
Autolamp On/Off Circuit		
Off	4 & 17	No
Off	4 & 16	[1]
On	4 & 17	Yes
On	4 & 16	[2]
Instrument Cluster Illumination Circuit		[3]
Dome Light Circuit		
Off	4 & 12	No
On	4 & 12	Yes
Headlight Circuit		
Off	6 & 7	No
Park	6 & 7	No
Head	6 & 7	Yes
Parking Lights Circuit		
Off	13 & 14	No
Park	13 & 14	Yes
Head	13 & 14	Yes
Warning Chime Circuit		
Off	10 & 11	No
Park	10 & 11	Yes
Head	10 & 11	Yes

[1] – Resistance should be 3.4-3.7 k/ohms.
[2] – Resistance should be 193-214 k/ohms.
[3] – Resistance should smoothly decrease as thumbwheel is rotated from up to down positions.

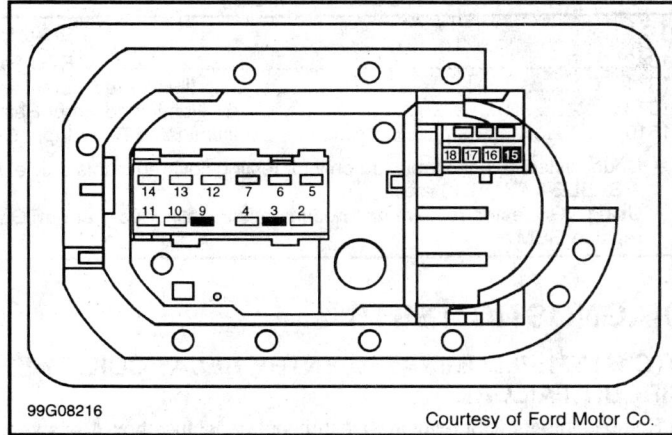

99G08216   Courtesy of Ford Motor Co.

Fig. 2: Identifying Headlight Switch Terminals

MINI ISO RELAY

1) Remove mini ISO relay. Measure resistance between appropriate relay terminals. See MINI ISO RELAY RESISTANCE SPECIFICATIONS table. *See Fig. 3.* If resistance is as specified, go to next step. If resistance is not as specified, replace relay.

MINI ISO RELAY RESISTANCE SPECIFICATIONS

Between Terminals	Resistance
85 & 86	50-100 Ohms
30 & 87a	5 Ohms Or Less

MINI ISO RELAY RESISTANCE SPECIFICATIONS (Cont.)

Between Terminals	Resistance
30 & 87	Greater Than 10 K/Ohms
30 & 86	Greater Than 10 K/Ohms
86 & 87a	Greater Than 10 K/Ohms
86 & 87	Greater Than 10 K/Ohms

2) Using a fused jumper wire, connect positive battery voltage to terminal No. 85. Using another jumper wire, ground terminal No. 86. Resistance should now be 5 ohms or less between terminals No. 30 and 87 and greater than 10 k/ohms between terminals 30 and 87a. If resistance is as specified, relay is okay at this time. If resistance is not as specified, replace horn relay.

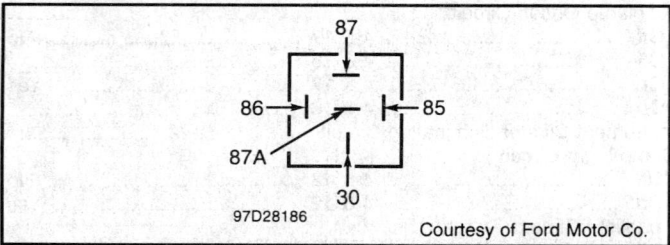

Fig. 3: Identifying Mini ISO Relay Terminals

MICRO ISO RELAY

1) Remove relay to be tested. Measure resistance between terminal No. 5 and all other terminals. *See Fig. 4.* If all resistance reading are greater than 5 ohms, go to next step. If any resistance reading is 5 ohms or less, replace relay.

2) Measure resistance between terminals No. 3 and 4. If resistance is 5 ohms or less, go to next step. If resistance is greater than 5 ohms, replace relay.

3) Apply battery voltage and ground between terminals No. 1 and 2. Measure resistance between terminals No. 3 and 5. Resistance should be 5 ohms or less. Measure resistance between terminals No. 3 and 4.

Resistance should be greater than 5 ohms. If resistance is not as specified, replace relay. If resistance is as specified, relay is okay at this time.

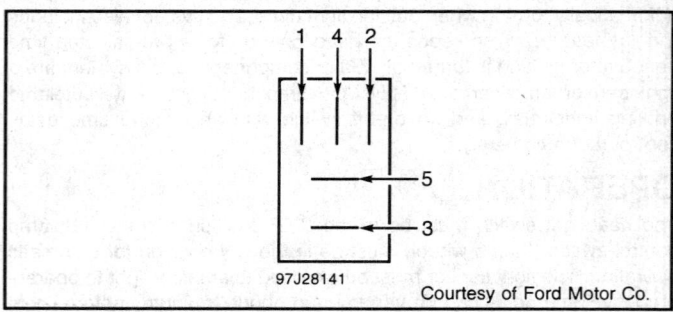

Fig. 4: Identifying Micro ISO Relay Terminals

SELF-DIAGNOSTIC SYSTEM

Connect New Generation Star (NGS) tester to Data Link Connector (DLC), located beneath instrument panel. Using NGS tester, perform data link diagnostics test. See DATA LINK DIAGNOSTIC TEST under COMMUNICATION NETWORK DIAGNOSTICS in MODULE COMMUNICATIONS NETWORK – SABLE & TAURUS article. If NGS tester responds with CKT914, CKT915 or CKT70=ALL ECUS NO RESP/NOT EQUIP, repair module communications concern. See MODULE COMMUNICATIONS NETWORK – SABLE & TAURUS article. If NGS tester displays NO RESP/NOT EQUIP for Generic Electronic Module (GEM), perform TEST A: NO COMMUNICATION WITH GENERIC ELECTRONIC MODULE under SYSTEM TESTS.

If NGS tester responds with SYSTEM PASSED, retrieve and record continuous DTCs. Erase continuous DTCs. Using NGS tester, perform GEM self-test. Perform appropriate test in accordance with DTC retrieved. See GENERIC ELECTRONIC MODULE DTC INDEX table. Codes listed in this table are only for testing covered in this article. For complete DTC listing, see MODULE COMMUNICATIONS NETWORK – SABLE & TAURUS article. If no DTCs are retrieved, repair by symptom. See SYMPTOM CHART table under SYSTEM TESTS.

GENERIC ELECTRONIC MODULE DTC INDEX

DTC [1]	Description	Test
B1342	ECU Failure	[2]
B1371	Illuminated Entry Relay Circuit Failure	DTC B1371
B1373	Illuminated Entry Relay Short To Battery	DTC B1373
B1610	Illuminated Entry Input Circuit Short To Ground	DTC B1610

[1] – Codes listed in these table are only for testing covered in this article. For complete DTC listing, see MODULE COMMUNICATIONS NETWORK – SABLE & TAURUS article.

[2] – Using NGS tester, retrieve and document all continuous. Perform Generic Electronic Module (GEM) self-test. If DTC B1342 is retrieved again, replace GEM.

DIAGNOSTIC TESTS

DTC B1371: ILLUMINATED ENTRY RELAY COIL CIRCUIT FAILURE

1) Remove interior light relay from instrument panel fuse box. Measure resistance between terminals No. 1 and 2 at interior light relay (component side). *See Fig. 4.* If resistance is 10 k/ohms or less, go to next step. If resistance is greater than 10 k/ohms, replace interior light relay.

2) Disconnect Generic Electronic Module (GEM) from back of instrument panel fuse box (connector C201). Measure resistance between terminal No. 2 at interior light relay socket and terminal No. 12 at GEM connector C201 (fuse box side). *See Figs. 5 and 6.* If resistance is 5 ohms or less, go to next step. If resistance is greater than 5 ohms, replace instrument panel fuse box.

3) Measure resistance between ground and terminal No. 12 at GEM connector C201 (fuse box side). If resistance is 10 k/ohms or less, go to next step. If resistance is greater than 10 k/ohms, replace GEM.

4) Disconnect instrument panel fuse box harness connector C235. Measure resistance between ground and terminal No. 12 at GEM connector C201 (fuse box side). If resistance is greater than 10 k/ohms, go to next step. If resistance is 10 k/ohms or less, go to step **6)**.

5) Disconnect headlight switch harness connector C2031. Measure resistance between ground and terminal No. 27 (Light Green/Orange wire) at instrument panel fuse box harness connector C235. *See Fig. 7.* If resistance is 10 k/ohms or less, repair short to ground in Light Green/Orange wire. If resistance is greater than 10 k/ohms, replace headlight switch.

6) Ensure interior light relay is still removed. Measure resistance between ground and terminal No. 12 at GEM connector C201 (fuse box side). If resistance is greater than 10 k/ohms, replace interior light relay. If resistance is 10 k/ohms or less, replace instrument panel fuse box.

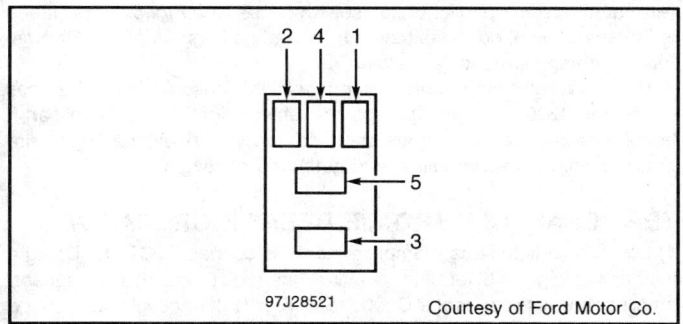

Fig. 5: Identifying Autolamp Headlight, Battery Saver Relay, Interior Light Relay & Parking Light Relay Socket Terminals

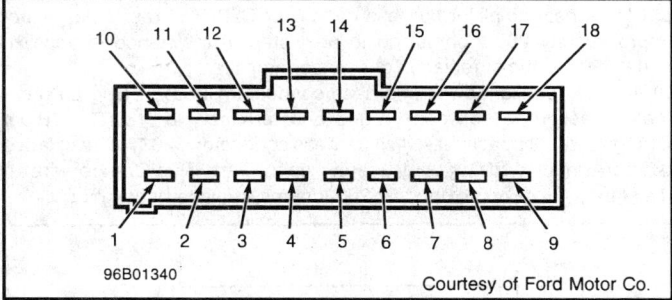

Fig. 6: Identifying GEM Connector C201 Terminals (Fuse Box Side)

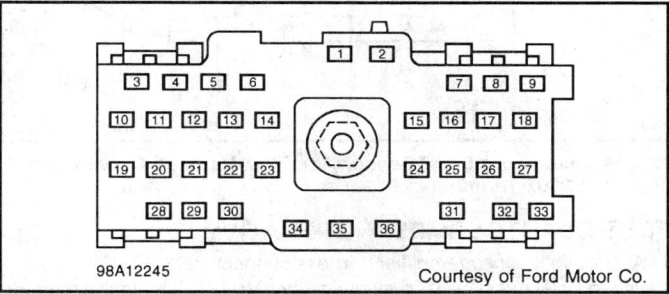

Fig. 7: Identifying Instrument Panel Fuse Box Harness Connector C235 Terminals

DTC B1373: ILLUMINATED ENTRY RELAY CIRCUIT SHORT TO VOLTAGE

1) Remove interior light relay from instrument panel fuse box. Turn ignition switch to RUN position. Measure voltage at terminal No. 2 at interior light relay socket C207. See Fig. 5. If voltage exists, go to next step. If no voltage exists, replace interior light relay.

2) Turn ignition switch to LOCK position. Disconnect Generic Electronic Module (GEM) from back of instrument panel fuse box (connector C201). Measure voltage at terminal No. 2 at interior light relay socket C207. If voltage exists, go to next step. If no voltage exists, replace GEM.

3) Disconnect instrument panel fuse box harness connector C235. Measure voltage at terminal No. 2 at interior light relay socket C207. If no voltage exists, go to next step. If voltage exists, replace instrument panel fuse box.

4) Disconnect headlight switch harness connector C2031. Measure voltage at terminal No. 27 (Light Green/Orange wire) at instrument panel fuse box harness connector C235. See Fig. 7. If voltage exists, repair short to voltage in Light Green/Orange wire. If no voltage exists, replace headlight switch.

DTC B1610: ILLUMINATED ENTRY RELAY CIRCUIT SHORT TO GROUND

1) Disconnect Generic Electronic Module (GEM) harness connector C248. Measure resistance between ground and terminal No. 8 (Brown/Light Green wire) at GEM harness connector C248. See Fig. 8. If resistance is 5 ohms or less, go to next step. If resistance is greater than 5 ohms, go to step 3).

2) Disconnect Remote Anti-Theft Personality (RAP) module harness connector C254. Measure resistance between ground and terminal No. 8 (Brown/Light Green wire) at GEM harness connector C248. If resistance is 5 ohms or less, repair short to ground in Brown/Light Green wire. If resistance is greater than 5 ohms, replace RAP module.

3) Connect New Generation Star (NGS) tester to Data Link Connector (DLC). Connect any disconnected harness connectors. Turn ignition switch to RUN position. Perform wiggle test while flexing wiring harness between RAP module and GEM. If DTC B1607 or B1610 are retrieved during wiggle test, repair intermittent short in Brown/Light Green wire. If DTC B1607 or B1610 are not retrieved during wiggle test, perform GEM self-test. If DTC B1610 is retrieved again, replace GEM

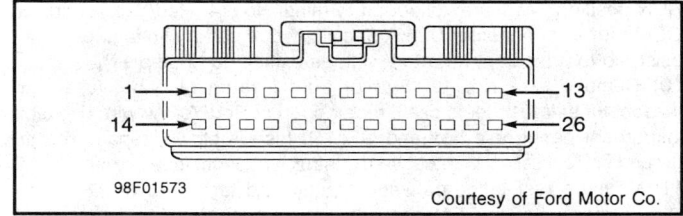

Fig. 8: Identifying GEM Harness Connector C248 Terminals

SYSTEM TESTS

NOTE: After a repair is completed, always recheck system operation to ensure repair procedure has corrected the problem.

SYMPTOM CHART

Symptom	Test
No Communication With Generic Electronic Module	A
Headlights Always On [1]	B
Autolamp Time Delay Inoperative	C
Autolamps Inoperative	D
Instrument Panel Lights Inoperative With Autolamps On	E

[1] – This test only applies to vehicles with autolamps.

TEST A: NO COMMUNICATION WITH GENERIC ELECTRONIC MODULE

1) Remove fuse No. 23 from instrument panel fuse box. Measure resistance between ground and output side of fuse No. 23 in instrument panel fuse box. Resistance should start at greater than one m/ohm and drop steadily to less than 3 k/ohms. If resistance is not as specified, go to next step. If resistance is as specified, go to step 7).

2) If resistance in step 1) read greater than 10 ohms, go to next step. If resistance in step 1) read 10 ohms or less, go to step 4).

3) Remove Generic Electronic Module (GEM) from instrument panel fuse box. Disconnect and reconnect ohmmeter as in step 1). If resistance is not greater than one m/ohm (may drop steadily to less than 3 k/ohms), go to next step. If resistance is greater than one m/ohm (may drop steadily to less than 3 k/ohms), replace GEM.

4) Disconnect instrument panel fuse box harness connector C247. Measure resistance between ground and output side of fuse No. 23. If resistance is 10 k/ohms or less, replace instrument panel fuse box. If resistance is greater than 10 k/ohms and equipped with anti-theft system, connect instrument panel fuse box harness connector C247 and go to next step. If resistance is greater than 10 k/ohms and not equipped with anti-theft system, connect instrument panel fuse box harness connector C247 and go to step 7).

5) Disconnect Passive Anti-Theft System (PATS) module harness connector C242. Disconnect and reconnect ohmmeter as in step 1). If

resistance does not read greater than one m/ohm and drops steadily to less than 3 k/ohms, go to next step. If resistance reads greater than one m/ohm and drops steadily to less than 3 k/ohms, replace PATS module.

6) Disconnect Remote Anti-Theft Personality (RAP) module harness connector C254. Disconnect and reconnect ohmmeter as in step **1)**. If resistance reads greater than one m/ohm, replace RAP module. If resistance reads one m/ohm or less, repair short to ground in White/ Yellow wire between fuse No. 23 and RAP module.

7) Disconnect Generic Electronic Module (GEM) harness connector C248. Measure resistance between ground and terminals No. 14 and 25 (both Black wires) at GEM harness connector C248. *See Fig. 8.* If both resistance readings are 5 ohms or less, go to next step. If either resistance reading is greater than 5 ohms, repair open in appropriate wire(s).

8) Disconnect GEM harness connector C223. Measure resistance between ground and terminal No. 12 (Black/White wire) at GEM harness connector C223. *See Fig. 9.* If resistance is 5 ohms or less, go to next step. If resistance is greater than 5 ohms, repair open in Black/White wire.

9) Disconnect GEM harness connector C236. Turn ignition switch to RUN position. Measure voltage at terminal No. 14 (Red/Yellow wire) at GEM harness connector C236. *See Fig. 10.* If battery voltage does not exist, go to next step. If battery voltage exists, go to step **11)**.

10) Remove fuse No. 12 (5-amp) from instrument panel fuse box. Inspect fuse. If fuse tests okay, repair open in Red/Yellow wire between instrument panel fuse box and GEM. If fuse is blown, repair short to ground in Red/Yellow wire between instrument panel fuse box and GEM.

11) Measure resistance between ground and terminal No. 22 (Black/ Light Green wire) at GEM harness connector C223. If resistance is 5 ohms or less, repair module communication concern. See MODULE COMMUNICATIONS NETWORK – SABLE & TAURUS article. If resistance is greater than 5 ohms, repair open in Black/Light Green wire.

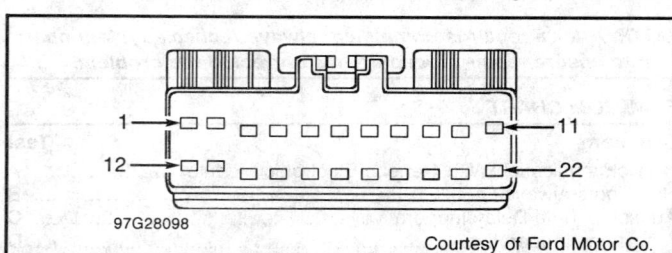

97G28098
Courtesy of Ford Motor Co.

Fig. 9: Identifying GEM Harness Connector C223 Terminals

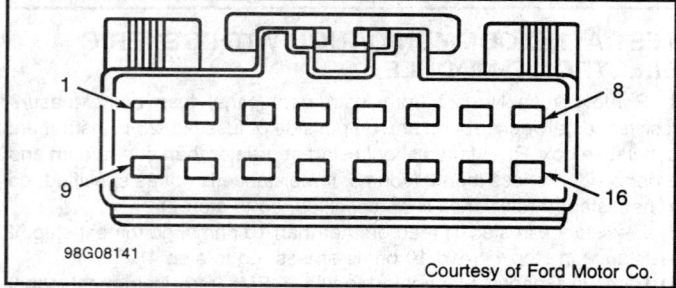

98G08141
Courtesy of Ford Motor Co.

Fig. 10: Identifying GEM Harness Connector C236 Terminals

TEST B: HEADLIGHTS ALWAYS ON

NOTE: This test only applies to vehicles equipped with autolamps.

1) Ensure headlight switch is off. Disconnect headlight switch connectors C2031 and C2032. If headlights are still on, go to next step. If headlights are off, replace headlight switch.

2) Remove autolamp headlight relay from engine compartment fuse box. If headlights are off, go to next step. If headlights are still on, repair short to voltage in Red/Yellow wire between headlight switch and multifunction switch.

3) Remove parking light relay from engine compartment fuse box. Measure resistance between ground and terminal No. 1 (White/Violet

wire) at autolamp headlight relay socket C132. *See Fig. 5.* If resistance is 5 ohms or less, go to next step. If resistance is greater than 5 ohms, replace autolamp headlight relay.

4) Reconnect all components. Disconnect light sensor/amplifier harness connector C2007. If headlights go off, replace light sensor amplifier. If headlights remain on, repair short to ground in White/Violet wire between light sensor/amplifier and autolamp headlight relay.

TEST C: AUTOLAMP TIME DELAY INOPERATIVE

1) Disconnect light sensor/amplifier harness connector C2007. Using a jumper wire, ground terminal No. 3 White/Violet wire at light sensor/ amplifier harness connector C2007. *See Fig. 11.* If headlights are on, go to next step. If headlights are not on, perform TEST D: AUTOLAMPS INOPERATIVE.

2) Set autolamp time delay thumb wheel to MAX position. Measure resistance between ground and terminal No. 5 (Dark Blue/Orange wire) at light sensor/amplifier harness connector C2007. If resistance is not approximately 200 k/ohms, go to next step. If resistance is approximately 200 k/ohms, replace light sensor/amplifier.

3) Access headlight switch harness connector C2037. Using an ohmmeter, backprobe between ground and terminal No. 16 (Dark Blue/ Orange wire) at headlight switch harness connector C2037. If resistance is approximately 200 k/ohms, repair open Dark Blue/Orange wire. If resistance is not approximately 200 k/ohms, replace headlight switch.

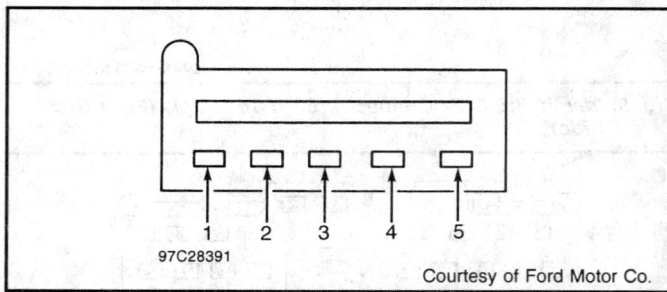

97C28391
Courtesy of Ford Motor Co.

Fig. 11: Identifying Light Sensor/Amplifier Harness Connector C2007 Terminals

TEST D: AUTOLAMPS INOPERATIVE

1) Access light sensor/amplifier harness connector C2007. Turn ignition switch to RUN position. Turn autolamp system on. Using an ohmmeter, backprobe between ground and terminal No. 3 (White/Purple wire) at light sensor/amplifier harness connector C2007. *See Fig. 11.* Cover light sensor/amplifier with a dark cloth to simulate darkness. Wait 15 seconds. If resistance is greater than 5 ohms, go to next step. If resistance is 5 ohms or less, go to step **5)**.

2) Ensure autolamp system is on. Using an ohmmeter, backprobe between ground and terminal No. 2 (Purple/Orange wire) at light sensor/amplifier harness connector C2007. If resistance is greater than 5 ohms, go to next step. If resistance is 5 ohms or less, replace light sensor amplifier.

3) Access headlight switch harness connectors. Ensure autolamp system is still on. Using an ohmmeter, backprobe between ground and terminal No. 17 (Purple/Orange wire) at headlight switch harness connector C2037. If resistance is greater than 5 ohms, go to next step. If resistance is 5 ohms or less, repair open in Purple/Orange wire.

4) Disconnect headlight switch harness connector C2032. Measure resistance between ground and terminal No. 4 (Black wire) at headlight switch harness connector C2032. If resistance is 5 ohms or less, replace headlight switch. If resistance is greater than 5 ohms, repair open Black wire.

5) Remove autolamp headlight and parking light relays from engine compartment fuse box. Measure resistance between ground and terminal No. 5 (White/Purple wire) at autolamp headlight relay socket C123. *See Fig. 5.* If resistance is 5 ohms or less, go to next step. If resistance is greater than 5 ohms, repair open in White/Purple wire.

6) Measure voltage at terminals No. 2 and 3 (both Dark Blue/Orange wires) at autolamp headlight relay socket C123. If battery voltage exists at both terminals, go to next step. If battery voltage does not exist at both terminals, repair power distribution circuit(s) as necessary. See appropriate wiring diagram in POWER DISTRIBUTION article in WIRING DIAGRAMS.

7) Turn headlight switch on. Measure voltage at terminal No. 5 (Red/Yellow wire) at autolamp headlight relay socket C123. If battery voltage exists, replace autolamp headlight relay. If battery voltage does not exist, repair open Red/Yellow wire.

TEST E: INSTRUMENT PANEL LIGHTS INOPERATIVE WITH AUTOLAMPS ON

1) Turn headlight switch to PARK position. If instrument panel and parking lights are on, turn headlight switch off and go to next step. If instrument panel and parking lights are not on, repair instrument cluster panel lighting and parking lights as necessary. See appropriate wiring diagram in ILLUMINATION/INTERIOR LIGHTS and/or EXTERIOR LIGHTS article.

2) Turn autolamp system on. Cover light sensor/amplifier with a dark cloth to simulate darkness. Wait 15 seconds. If headlights are on, go to next step. If headlights are off, go to TEST D: AUTOLAMPS INOPERATIVE.

3) Remove autolamp headlight and parking light relays from engine compartment fuse box. Measure resistance in White/Violet wire between terminal No. 1 at autolamp headlight relay socket C123 and terminal No. 1 at autolamp parking light relay socket C122. See Fig. 5. If resistance is 5 ohms or less, go to next step. If resistance is greater than 5 ohms, repair open in White/Violet wire.

4) Measure voltage at terminal No. 3 (Purple/White wire) at autolamp parking light relay socket C122. If battery voltage exists, go to next step. If battery voltage does not exist, power distribution circuit as necessary. See appropriate wiring diagram in POWER DISTRIBUTION article in WIRING DIAGRAMS.

5) Turn headlight switch to PARK position. Measure voltage at terminal No. 5 (Brown wire) at autolamp parking light relay socket C122. If battery voltage exists, replace autolamp parking light relay. If battery voltage does not exist, repair open in Brown wire.

REMOVAL & INSTALLATION

CAUTION: When battery is disconnected, vehicle computer and memory systems may lose memory data. Driveability problems may exist until computer systems have completed a relearn cycle. See COMPUTER RELEARN PROCEDURES article in GENERAL INFORMATION before disconnecting battery.

LIGHT SENSOR AMPLIFIER ASSEMBLY

Removal & Installation – Light sensor amplifier is located in defroster grille, top left of dash. Remove instrument panel upper finish panel. Remove retaining screws and light sensor amplifier assembly. Unplug connector. To install, reverse removal procedure.

WIRING DIAGRAMS

NOTE: See appropriate wiring diagram in HEADLIGHT SYSTEMS, EXTERIOR LIGHTS, ILLUMINATION/INTERIOR LIGHTS and LIGHTING CONTROL MODULES articles. Also see appropriate wiring diagram in POWER DISTRIBUTION article in WIRING DIAGRAMS.

DESCRIPTION

The autolamp system is a light-sensitive, on-off control. It will automatically turn the headlights on. The system can be set to automatically turn off interior and exterior lights after the ignition has been turned off. This time delay feature is adjustable and has a maximum time delay setting of up to 3 minutes.

Autolamp system consists of the light sensor amplifier, located in the defroster grille on top left dash, Lighting Control Module (LCM), located underneath dash on left side of steering column and time delay switch which is integral with headlight switch.

Autolamp system LCM communicates with other control modules via module communications network.

OPERATION

Autolamp system is activated by turning dash mounted headlight switch counterclockwise to AUTOLAMP position. A small AUTOLAMP indicator light on the switch will light when lights are energized. When AUTO-LAMP feature is selected, lights will turn on and off automatically based on the amount of ambient light monitored by the light sensor amplifier. Time delay (delayed turn-off function) is selected by the position of the lighting switch when it is turned counterclockwise from the OFF position. Maximum time delay of 3 minutes is obtained when the switch is rotated fully counterclockwise.

COMPONENT LOCATIONS

COMPONENT LOCATIONS

Component	Location
Accessory Delay Relay	In Instrument Panel Fuse Box
Brake Pedal Position Switch	On Brake Pedal Support
Data Link Connector	Under Instrument Panel, Right Of Steering Column
Dimmer Switch	Left Side Of Instrument Panel
Door Ajar Switch	Part Of Latch Assembly
Door Lock Switch	Appropriate Door Panel Arm Rest
Driver's Door Module (DDM)	Behind Driver's Door Panel, Lower Front Corner
Driver Seat Module	Under Driver's Seat
Headlight Switch	Left Side Of Instrument Panel
Instrument Panel Fuse Box	Behind Instrument Panel, Left Of Steering Column
Lighting Control Module	Behind Center Of Instrument Panel
Light Sensor Amplifier	Above Instrument Cluster
Mirror Control Switch	Driver's Door Panel Arm Rest
Power Distribution Box	Left Side Of Engine Compartment, In Front Of Wheel Well
Seat Control Switch	
With Memory	On Appropriate Door
Without Memory	Side Of Appropriate Seat

TROUBLE SHOOTING

Verify customer complaint. Check instrument panel fuse panel fuses No. 7 (15-amp), No. 9 (20-amp) and No. 31 (7.5-amp). Replace fuse(s) as necessary. Check or replace any suspect bulbs. Check for a damaged light sensor amplifier and for mechanical damage to headlight switch. Check circuits for opens or shorts. Check for good clean connections at chassis ground point locations. See appropriate wiring diagram in HEADLIGHT SYSTEMS article. Correct any obvious problems before continuing test. If all checks are okay, go to SELF-DIAGNOSTIC SYSTEM.

COMPONENT TESTS

HEADLIGHT SWITCH

Disconnect headlight switch harness connector. Continuity should be as specified between terminals with switch in specified position. See HEADLIGHT SWITCH TEST table. *See Fig. 1.* If continuity is not as specified, replace headlight switch.

HEADLIGHT SWITCH TEST

Switch Position	Between Terminals	Continuity
All	1 & 2	[1] Yes
Autolamp		
Off	4 & 7	No
On	4 & 7	Yes
Rheostat	9 & 7	[2]
Dome Light		
Off	6 & 7	No
On	6 & 7	Yes
Headlights		
Off	3 & 7; 7 & 8	No
Park	7 & 8	No
Park	3 & 7	Yes
On	3 & 7; 7 & 8	Yes

[1] – Backlighting illumination circuit.
[2] – Resistance should smoothly increase from 3000 to 200,000 ohms as headlight switch is rotated counterclockwise from OFF position toward AUTOLAMP position.

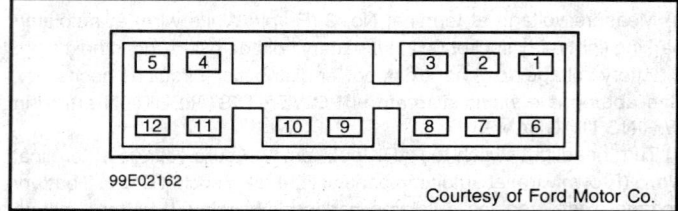

99E02162   Courtesy of Ford Motor Co.

Fig. 1: Identifying Headlight Switch Terminals

DIMMER SWITCH

Disconnect dimmer switch harness connector. Continuity should be as specified between terminals with switch in specified position. See DIMMER SWITCH TEST table. *See Fig. 2.* If continuity is not as specified, replace dimmer switch.

DIMMER SWITCH TEST

Switch Position	Between Terminals	Continuity
Dimmer		
Down	1 & 2	Yes
Neutral	1 & 2; 2 & 4	No
Up	2 & 4	Yes

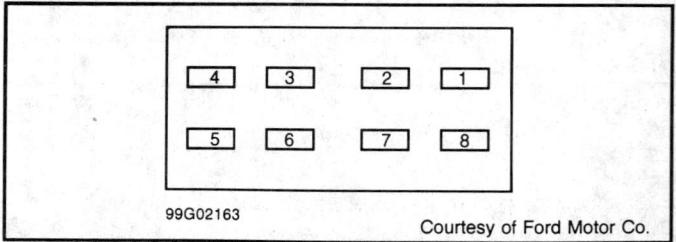

99G02163   Courtesy of Ford Motor Co.

Fig. 2: Identifying Dimmer Switch Terminals

SELF-DIAGNOSTIC SYSTEM

NOTE: All Diagnostic Trouble Code (DTC) tests are for use with New Generation Star (NGS) tester. If a generic scan tool is used, ensure scan tool is certified OBD-II standard. Refer to manufacturer's instructions as necessary.

NOTE: Lighting Control Module (LCM) controls more than just autolamp system. A non-autolamp LCM fault in may effect the autolamp system.

Verify customers complaint by operating autolamp system and all other lights. Check for blown fuse(s), loose or corroded connectors, or damaged wiring harness. Repair or replace components as necessary. If all components are okay, connect NGS tester to Data Link Connector (DLC) located below instrument panel. Using NGS tester, perform DATA LINK DIAGNOSTIC TEST. If NGS tester displays CKT914, CKT915 or CKT70=ALL ECUS NO RESP/NOT EQUIP, repair communication concern. See MODULE COMMUNICATIONS NETWORK – TOWN CAR article. If NGS tester displays NO RESP/NOT EQUIP for Lighting Control Module (LCM), perform TEST A: NO COMMUNICATION WITH LIGHTING CONTROL MODULE under SYSTEM TESTS. If NGS tester displays NO RESP/NOT EQUIP for Driver's Door Module (DDM), perform TEST N: NO COMMUNICATION WITH DRIVER'S DOOR MODULE under SYSTEM TESTS. If NGS tester displays SYSTEM PASSED, retrieve and record continuous DTCs. Erase continuous DTCs. Perform LCM and DDM self-test. Perform appropriate test in accordance with DTC retrieved. See LIGHTING CONTROL MODULE DTC INDEX and/or DRIVER'S DOOR MODULE DTC INDEX table. Codes listed in these tables are only for testing covered in this article. For complete DTC listing, see MODULE COMMUNICATIONS NETWORK – TOWN CAR article. If no DTCs are retrieved, repair by symptom. See SYMPTOM CHART table under SYSTEM TESTS.

LIGHTING CONTROL MODULE DTC INDEX

DTC [1]	Description	Test
B1312	Headlight Input Short To Battery Voltage	D
B1342	ECU Defective	[2]
B1352	Ignition Key-In Circuit Failure	P
B1462	Seat Belt Switch Circuit Failure	N
B1485	Brake Pedal Input Circuit Short To Voltage	G
B1569	High Beam Short To Battery Voltage	C
B1577	Parking Lamp Input Short To Voltage	M
B1687	Dome Light Input Short To Voltage	Q
B1689	Autolamp Delay Input Circuit Failure	F
B1691	Autolamp Delay Input Circuit Short To Voltage	F
B1695	Autolamp ON/OFF Short To Voltage	F
B1873	Turn Signal/Hazard Power Feed Short To Ground	H

[1] – Codes listed in this table are only for testing covered in this article. For complete DTC listing, see MODULE COMMUNICATIONS NETWORK – TOWN CAR article.
[2] – Using NGS tester, retrieve and document all continuous. Perform LCM self-test. If DTC B1342 is retrieved again, replace LCM.

DRIVER'S DOOR MODULE DTC INDEX

DTC [1]	Description	Test
B1322	Driver's Door Ajar Circuit Failure	Q
B1342	ECU Defective	[2]
B1566	Passenger's And/Or Rear Door Ajar Circuits Short To Ground	Q

[1] – Codes listed in this table are only for testing covered in this article. For complete DTC listing, see MODULE COMMUNICATIONS NETWORK – TOWN CAR article.
[2] – Using NGS tester, retrieve and document all continuous. Perform DDM self-test. If DTC B1342 is retrieved again, replace DDM.

SYSTEM TESTS

CAUTION: When battery is disconnected or modules are replaced, vehicle computer and memory systems may lose memory data. Driveability problems may exist until computer systems have completed a relearn cycle. See COMPUTER RELEARN PROCEDURES article in GENERAL INFORMATION before disconnecting battery.

SYMPTOM CHART

Symptom	Test
No Communication With Lighting Control Module	A
Low Beams Inoperative	B
High Beams Inoperative	C
Low Beams Are On Continuously (Daytime Running Lights Are Disabled)	D
Flash-To-Pass Feature Inoperative	E
Autolamp System Is Inoperative	F
Stoplights Inoperative	G
Turn Signal & Hazard Lights Are Inoperative	H
One Turn Signal/Hazard Light Inoperative	J
Cornering Lighting Never/Always On	K

SYMPTOM CHART (Cont.)

Symptom	Test
Parking, Rear Or License Lights Are Inoperative	L
Parking, Tail Or License Lights On Continuously	M
No Communication With Driver's Door Module	N
Courtesy Lights Inoperative	P
Courtesy Lights Stay On Continuously	Q
On-Demand Lighting Inoperative	R
Battery Saver Does Not Deactivate After Timeout	S
Individual Courtesy Light Inoperative	T

TEST A: NO COMMUNICATION WITH LIGHTING CONTROL MODULE

1) Turn ignition switch to LOCK position. Connect New Generation Star (NGS) tester to Data Link Connector (DLC). Turn ignition switch to RUN position. Monitor LCM PID IGN_LC. If UNABLE TO PERFORM TEST/FUNCTION MODULE NOT RESPONDING:LCM CHECK IGNITION STATUS/VERIFY CABLE REQUIREMENTS CHECK CABLE CONNECTIONS? is not displayed, go to next step. If UNABLE TO PERFORM TEST/FUNCTION MODULE NOT RESPONDING:LCM CHECK IGNITION STATUS/VERIFY CABLE REQUIREMENTS CHECK CABLE CONNECTIONS? is displayed, go to step **8)**.

2) Monitor LCM PID IGN_LC on NGS tester while turn ignition switch to all positions except START. If OFF is not displayed in all positions, go to next step. If OFF is displayed in all positions, go to step **5)**.

3) Remove fuse No. 14 (7.5-amp) from instrument panel fuse box. Measure voltage at input side of fuse No. 14. If battery voltage exists, go to next step. If battery voltage does not exist, repair power distribution circuit. See appropriate wiring diagram in POWER DISTRIBUTION article in WIRING DIAGRAMS.

4) Inspect fuse No. 14. If fuse is blown, repair short to ground in Red/Yellow wire. If fuse is okay, repair open in Red/Yellow wire.

5) Remove fuse No. 18 (7.5-amp) from instrument panel fuse box. Turn ignition switch to RUN position. Measure voltage at input side of fuse No. 18. If battery voltage exists, go to next step. If battery voltage does not exist, repair power distribution circuit and/or replace ignition switch as necessary. See appropriate wiring diagram in POWER DISTRIBU-TION article in WIRING DIAGRAMS.

6) Inspect fuse No. 18. If fuse is blown, repair short to ground in Dark Blue/Light Green wire. If fuse is okay, install fuse and go to next step.

7) Turn ignition switch to LOCK position. Disconnect LCM harness connector C220. Turn ignition switch to RUN position. Measure voltage at terminal No. 6 (Dark Blue/Light Green wire) at LCM harness connec-tor C220. *See Fig. 3.* If battery voltage exists, replace LCM. If battery voltage does not exist, repair open in Dark Blue/Light Green wire.

8) Remove fuse No. 31 (7.5-amp) from instrument panel fuse box. Measure voltage at input side of fuse No. 31. If battery voltage exists, go to next step. If battery voltage does not exist, repair power distribution circuit. See appropriate wiring diagram in POWER DISTRIBUTION article in WIRING DIAGRAMS.

9) Inspect fuse No. 31. If fuse is blown, go to next step. If fuse is okay, repair open in Orange/White wire.

10) Ensure fuse No. 31 is still removed. Turn ignition switch to LOCK position. Disconnect headlight switch harness connector and LCM harness connector C221. Measure resistance between ground and terminal No. 25 (Orange/White wire) at LCM harness connector C221. *See Fig. 4.* If resistance is greater than 10 k/ohms, go to next step. If resistance is 10 k/ohms or less, repair short to ground in Orange/White wire.

11) Connect headlight switch harness connector. Measure resistance between ground and terminal No. 25 (Orange/White wire) at LCM harness connector C221. If resistance is greater than 10 k/ohms, go to next step. If resistance is 10 k/ohms or less, replace headlight switch.

12) Install fuse No. 31. Measure voltage at terminal No. 25 (Orange/White wire) at LCM harness connector C221. If battery voltage exists, go to next step. If battery voltage does not exist, repair open in Orange/White wire.

13) Disconnect LCM harness connector C222. Measure resistance between ground and terminal No. 23 (Pink/Orange wire) at LCM harness connector C221. Measure resistance between ground and terminal No. 13 (Pink/Orange wire) at LCM harness connector C222. *See Fig. 5.* If either resistance reading is greater than 5 ohms, repair open in Pink/Orange wire. If both resistance readings are 5 ohms or less, repair communication concern. See MODULE COMMUNICA-TIONS NETWORK – TOWN CAR article.

TEST B: LOW BEAMS INOPERATIVE

NOTE: Due to varying wattage ratings and resulting current draw, certain aftermarket bulbs may cause Lighting Control Module (LCM) to shut down. Verify that bulbs meet Ford specifications.

1) Using NGS tester, perform Lighting Control Module (LCM) self-test. If no DTCs are retrieved, go to next step. If DTC B1342 is retrieved, clear DTC and repeat LCM self-test. If DTC B1342 is retrieved again, replace LCM.

2) Ensure autolamp and high beams are off. Using NGS tester, monitor LCM PID LBEAMSW while turning headlight switch on and off. If PID does not agree with headlight switch position, go to next step. If PID agrees with headlight switch position, go to step **5)**.

3) Turn ignition switch to LOCK position. Disconnect LCM harness connector C221. Turn ignition switch to RUN position. Turn low beams

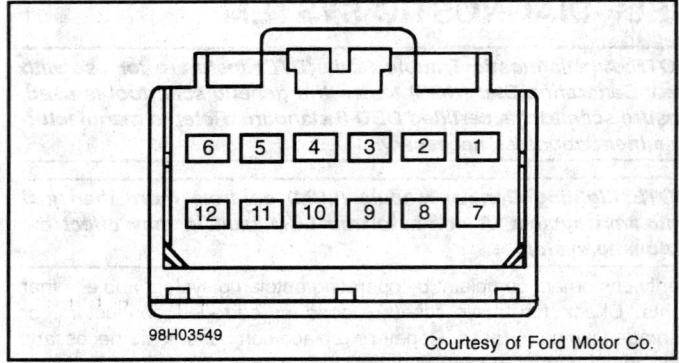

98H03549   Courtesy of Ford Motor Co.

Fig. 3: Identifying Lighting Control Module Connector C220 Terminals

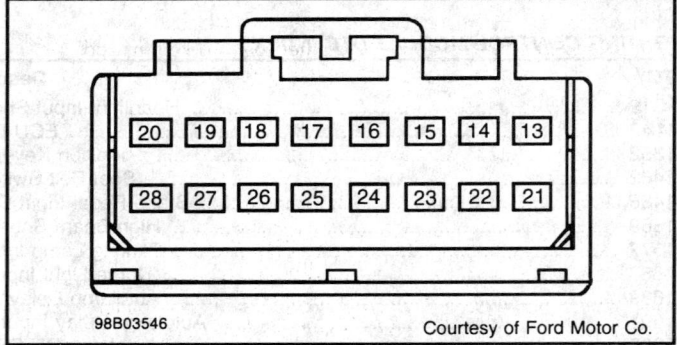

98B03546   Courtesy of Ford Motor Co.

Fig. 4: Identifying Lighting Control Module Connector C221 Terminals

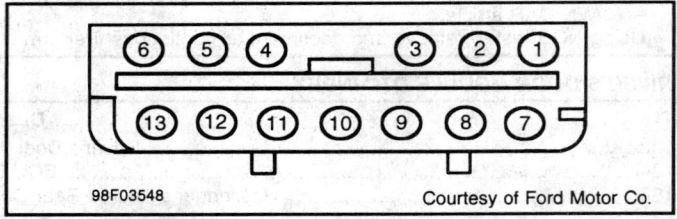

98F03548   Courtesy of Ford Motor Co.

Fig. 5: Identifying Lighting Control Module Connector C222 Terminals

on. Measure voltage at terminal No. 15 (Red/Yellow wire) at LCM harness C221. *See Fig. 4.* If battery voltage does not exist, go to next step. If battery voltage exists, replace LCM.

4) Turn ignition switch to LOCK position. Disconnect headlight switch harness connector C234 and LCM harness connectors. Using a fused jumper wire, connect terminals No. 7 (Orange/White wire) and No. 8 (Red/Yellow wire) at headlight switch harness connector C234. *See Fig. 6.* Measure voltage at terminal No. 15 (Red/Yellow wire) at LCM harness connector C221. If battery voltage does not exist, repair open in Red/Yellow wire. If battery voltage exist, replace headlight switch.

5) Turn ignition switch to RUN position. Ensure gear selector is in PARK position. Using NGS tester, trigger LCM active command LEFT LOW and RIGHT LOW. If both low beams illuminate, replace LCM. If both low beams do not illuminate, go to next step. If only left low beam does not illuminate, go to step **8)**. If only right low beam does not illuminate, go to step **16)**.

6) Turn ignition switch to LOCK position. Inspect fuse No. 7 (50-amp) in power distribution box. If fuse is okay, go to next step. If fuse is blown, repair short to ground in Dark Blue/Orange wire between power distribution box and instrument panel fuse box. See appropriate wiring diagram in POWER DISTRIBUTION article in WIRING DIAGRAMS.

7) Measure voltage to input side of fuse No. 7 (50-amp) in power distribution box. If battery voltage exists, repair open in Dark Blue/Orange wire between power distribution box and instrument panel fuse box. See appropriate wiring diagram in POWER DISTRIBUTION article in WIRING DIAGRAMS. If battery voltage does not exist, repair or replace power distribution box as necessary.

8) Disconnect left headlight harness connector. Turn ignition switch to RUN position. Using NGS tester, trigger LCM active command LEFT LOW to ON. Measure voltage at Light Green/Black wire terminal at left headlight harness connector. If battery voltage exists, go to next step. If battery voltage does not exist, go to step **10)**.

9) Measure resistance between ground and Black wire terminal at left headlight harness connector. If resistance is 5 ohms or less, replace left headlight bulb. If resistance is greater than 5 ohms, repair open in Black wire.

10) Remove fuse No. 1 (10–amp) from instrument panel fuse box. Inspect fuse. If fuse is blown, go to next step. If fuse is okay, install fuse and go to step **13)**.

11) Turn ignition switch to LOCK position. Ensure fuse No. 1 is still removed. Disconnect left headlight harness connector. Disconnect LCM harness connector C200. Measure resistance between ground and terminal No. 14 (White/Light Green wire) at LCM harness connector C200. *See Fig. 7.* If resistance is greater than 10 k/ohms, go to next step. If resistance is 10 k/ohms or less, repair short to ground in White/Light Green wire.

12) Turn ignition switch to LOCK position. Disconnect left headlight harness connector. Disconnect LCM harness connector C222. *See Fig. 5.* Measure resistance between ground and terminal No. 15 (Dark Blue/White wire) at LCM harness connector C200. If resistance is greater than 10 k/ohms, replace LCM. If resistance is 10 k/ohms or less, repair short to ground in Dark Blue/White wire.

13) Measure voltage at input side of fuse No. 1 (10–amp) in instrument panel box. If battery voltage exists, go to next step. If battery voltage does not exist, repair open in Dark Blue/Orange wire between power distribution box and instrument panel fuse box.

14) Turn ignition switch to LOCK position. Disconnect LCM harness connector C200. Ensure fuse No. 1 is installed. Measure voltage at terminal No. 14 (White/Light Green wire) at LCM harness connector C200. If battery voltage exists, go to next step. If battery voltage does not exist, repair open in White/Light Green wire.

15) Using a fused jumper wire, connect terminal No. 14 (White/Light Green wire) and No. 15 (Dark Blue/White wire) at LCM harness connector C200. If left low beam illuminates, replace LCM. If left low beam does not illuminate, repair open in Dark Blue/White wire.

NOTE: Right headlight wire changes color between LCM and right headlight. It is a Dark Green/Orange wire at LCM and a Dark Blue/White wire at right headlight.

16) Disconnect right headlight harness connector. Turn ignition switch to RUN position. Using NGS tester, trigger LCM active command RIGHT LOW to ON. Measure voltage at Dark Blue/White wire terminal at right headlight harness connector. If battery voltage exists, go to next step. If battery voltage does not exist, go to step **18)**.

17) Measure resistance between ground an Black wire terminal at right headlight harness connector. If resistance is 5 ohms or less, replace right headlight bulb. If resistance is greater than 5 ohms, repair open in Black wire.

18) Remove fuse No. 3 (10–amp) from instrument panel fuse box. Inspect fuse. If fuse is blown, go to next step. If fuse is okay, install fuse and go to step **21)**.

19) Ensure fuse No. 3 is still removed. Turn ignition switch to LOCK position. Disconnect LCM harness connector C222. Measure resistance between ground and terminal No. 5 (Dark Blue/Light Green wire) at LCM harness connector C222. *See Fig. 5.* If resistance is greater than 10 k/ohms, go to next step. If resistance is 10 k/ohms or less, repair short to ground in Dark Blue/Light Green wire.

20) Disconnect right headlight harness connector. Measure resistance between ground terminal No. 6 (Dark Green/Orange wire) and LCM harness connector C222. If resistance is greater than 10 k/ohms, replace LCM. If resistance is 10 k/ohms or less, repair short to ground in Dark Green/Orange wire.

21) Measure voltage at input side of fuse No. 3 in instrument panel fuse box. If battery voltage exists, go to next step. If battery voltage does not

exist, repair open in Dark Blue/Orange wire between power distribution box and instrument panel fuse box.

22) Turn ignition switch to LOCK position. Disconnect LCM harness connector C222. Measure voltage at terminal No. 5 (Dark Blue/Light Green wire) at LCM harness connector C222. If battery voltage exists, go to next step. If battery voltage does not exist, repair open Dark Blue/Light Green wire.

NOTE: Dark Green/Orange wire changes to Dark Blue/White wire between LCM and right headlight.

23) Connect headlight switch harness connector C234. Using a fused jumper wire, connect terminals No. 5 (Dark Blue/Light Green wire) and No. 6 (Dark Green/Orange wire) at LCM harness connector C222 . If left low beam illuminates, replace LCM. If left low beam does not illuminate, repair open in Dark Green/Orange wire.

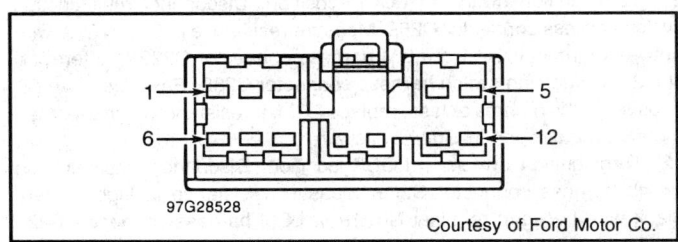

Fig. 6: Identifying Headlight Switch Harness Connector C234 Terminals

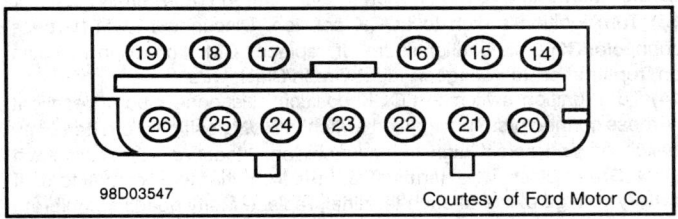

Fig. 7: Identifying Lighting Control Module Connector C200 Terminals

TEST C: HIGH BEAMS INOPERATIVE

1) Using NGS tester, perform LCM self-test. If no DTCs are retrieved, go to next step or step **12)** if only high beam indicator is inoperative. If DTC B1569 is retrieved, go to step **4)**. If DTC B1342 is retrieved, clear DTC and repeat LCM self-test. If DTC B1342 is retrieved again, replace LCM.

2) Turn headlight switch on. If low beams operate, go to next step. If low beams do not operate, perform TEST B: LOW BEAMS INOPERATIVE.

3) Turn headlight switch on. Using NGS tester, monitor LCM PID HIBEAMSW. Turn multifunction switch high beam on then off several times. If PID does not agree with switch position, go to next step or step **12)** if only high beam indicator is inoperative. If PID agrees with switch position, go to step **14)**.

4) Disconnect multifunction switch harness connectors. Test multifunction switch. See MULTIFUNCTION SWITCH under COMPONENT TEST in STEERING COLUMN SWITCHES – TOWN CAR article. If multifunction switch is defective, replace multifunction switch. If multifunction switch is okay, recheck LCM PID HIBEAMSW. If PID reads OFF continuously, go to next step. If PID reads ON continuously, reconnect multifunction switch and go to step **13)**.

5) Remove fuse No. 9 (20-amp) from instrument panel fuse panel. Inspect fuse. If fuse is okay, install fuse and go to next step. If fuse is blown, go to step **8)**.

6) Measure voltage at input side of fuse No. 9. If battery voltage exists, go to next step. If battery voltage does not exist, repair open Dark Blue/Orange wire between power distribution box and instrument panel fuse box.

7) Disconnect LCM harness connector C222. Measure voltage at terminal No. 7 (Pink wire) at LCM harness connector C222. *See Fig. 5.* If battery voltage exists, go to step **11)**. If battery voltage does not exist, repair open in Pink wire.

8) Turn ignition switch to LOCK position. Disconnect LCM harness connector C222. Measure resistance between ground and terminal No. 7 (Pink wire) at LCM harness connector C222. See Fig. 5. If resistance is greater than 10 k/ohms, go to next step. If resistance is 10 k/ohms or less, repair short to ground in Pink wire.

9) Turn ignition switch to LOCK position. Place multifunction switch in low beam position. Measure resistance between ground and terminal No. 1 (Gray/White wire) at LCM harness connector C222. If resistance is greater than 10 k/ohms, go to next step. If resistance is 10 k/ohms or less, repair short to ground in Gray/White wire.

10) Turn ignition switch to LOCK position. Disconnect LCM harness connector C200. Measure resistance between ground and terminal No. 19 (Light Green/Black wire) at LCM harness connector C220. See Fig. 7. If resistance is greater than 10 k/ohms, replace LCM. If resistance is 10 k/ohms or less, repair short to ground in Light Green/Black wire.

11) Turn ignition switch to LOCK position. Disconnect multifunction switch harness connector C269. Measure resistance in Gray/White wire between terminal No. 1 at LCM harness connector C222 and terminal No. 2 multifunction switch harness connector C269. See Figs. 5 and 8. If resistance is 5 ohms or less, replace LCM. If resistance is greater than 5 ohms, repair open in Gray/White wire.

12) Turn ignition switch to LOCK position. Disconnect multifunction switch harness connector C269. Measure resistance in Light Green/Black wire between terminal No. 19 at LCM harness connector C220 and terminal No. 5 at multifunction switch harness connector. See Figs. 7 and 8. If resistance is 5 ohms or less, replace LCM. If resistance is greater than 5 ohms, repair open in Light Green/Black wire.

13) Turn ignition switch to LOCK position. Disconnect LCM harness connector C200. If headlights turn off, replace LCM. If headlights remain on, repair short to voltage in Light Green/Black wire.

14) Turn ignition switch to LOCK position. Disconnect both headlight harness connectors. Turn ignition switch to RUN position. Turn headlight switch on and select high beam operation. Measure voltage at each Light Green/Black wire terminal at headlight harness connectors. If battery voltage exists at each terminal, replace faulty headlight bulb(s). If battery voltage does not exist at connector(s), repair open in appropriate Light Green/Black wire.

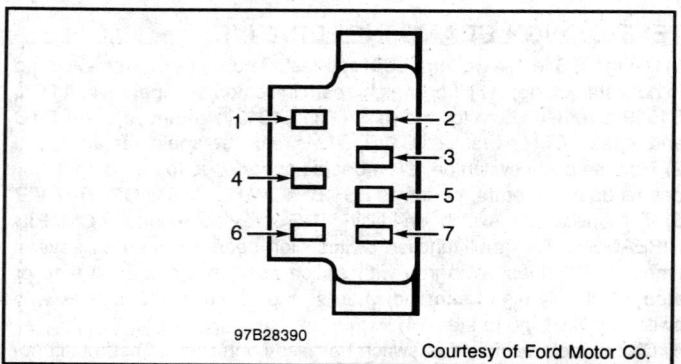

Fig. 8: Identifying Multifunction Switch Connector C269 Terminals

TEST D: LOW BEAMS ARE ON CONTINUOUSLY (DAYTIME RUNNING LIGHTS ARE DISABLED)

1) Using NGS tester, perform LCM self-test. If no DTCs are retrieved or DTC B1689 is retrieved, go to next step. If DTC B1312 is retrieved, go to step 5). If DTC U1059 is retrieved, repair powertrain control malfunction. See appropriate SELF-DIAGNOSTICS article in ENGINE PERFORMANCE in appropriate MITCHELL® manual.

2) Ensure headlight switch, high beam switch and autolamp switch are off. Turn ignition switch to RUN position. Ensure gear selector is in PARK position. If headlights remain on, go to next step. If headlights turn off, system is okay at this time.

3) Turn ignition switch to LOCK position. Disconnect headlight switch harness connector C234. Measure voltage at terminal No. 7 (Orange/

White wire) at headlight switch harness connector C234. See Fig. 6. If battery voltage exists, go to next step. If battery voltage does not exist, repair open in Orange/White wire.

4) Disconnect LCM harness connector C220. Measure resistance in Orange/White wire between terminal No. 11 at LCM harness connector C220 and terminal No. 6 at headlight switch connector C234. See Figs. 3 and 6. If resistance is 5 ohms or less, go to next step. If resistance is greater than 5 ohms, repair open in Orange/White wire.

5) Turn ignition switch to LOCK position. Disconnect headlight switch harness connectors. Test headlight switch. See HEADLIGHT SWITCH under COMPONENT TESTS. If headlight switch is okay, go to next step. If headlight switch is defective, replace headlight switch.

6) Turn ignition switch to LOCK position. Disconnect LCM harness connectors. Measure voltage at terminal No. 15 (White/Black wire) at LCM harness connector C221. See Fig. 4. If battery voltage does not exist, go to next step. If battery voltage exists, repair short to voltage in White/Black wire.

7) Turn ignition switch to LOCK position. Measure voltage at terminal No. 15 (Dark Blue/White wire) at LCM harness connector C200. See Fig. 7. Measure voltage at terminal No. 6 (Dark Green/Orange wire) at LCM harness connector C222. See Fig. 5. If battery voltage exists at either terminal, repair short to voltage in appropriate wire(s). If battery voltage does not exist, replace LCM.

TEST E: FLASH-TO-PASS FEATURE INOPERATIVE

1) Turn ignition switch to LOCK position. Turn headlights on. Place multifunction switch in high beam position. If high beams operate, go to next step. If high beams do not operate, perform TEST C: HIGH BEAMS INOPERATIVE.

2) Turn ignition switch to LOCK position. Disconnect multifunction switch harness connector C269. Turn ignition switch to RUN position. Measure voltage at terminal No. 7 (Pink wire) at multifunction switch harness connector C269. See Fig. 8. If battery voltage exists, replace multifunction switch. If battery voltage does not exist, repair open in Pink wire.

TEST F: AUTOLAMP SYSTEM IS INOPERATIVE

1) Using NGS tester, perform LCM self-test. If no DTCs are retrieved, go to next step. If DTC B1689, B1691 and/or B1695 is retrieved, go to step 3). If DTC B1342 is retrieved, clear DTC and repeat LCM self-test. If DTC B1342 is retrieved again, replace LCM.

2) Using NGS tester, monitor LCM PID LIGHTSN while illuminating light sensor, then remove light source. PID should read OFF when light is applied and ON when light is removed. If PID reads as specified, go to next step. If PID does not read as specified, go to step 8).

3) Monitor PID AUTOLMP while turning autolamp switch on and off. If PID does not agree with switch position, go to next step. If PID agrees with switch position, replace LCM.

4) Turn ignition switch to LOCK position. Disconnect headlight switch harness connectors. Test headlight switch. See HEADLIGHT SWITCH under COMPONENT TESTS. If headlight switch is okay, go to next step. If headlight switch is defective, replace headlight switch.

5) Turn ignition switch to LOCK position. Disconnect LCM and headlight switch harness connectors. Measure voltage at terminal No. 2 (Dark Blue/Orange wire) at LCM harness connector C220. See Fig. 3. Measure voltage at terminal No. 27 (Violet/Orange wire) at LCM harness connector C221. See Fig. 4. If battery voltage does not exist at both terminals, go to next step. If battery voltage exists at either terminal, repair short to voltage in appropriate wire(s).

6) Measure resistance between ground and terminal No. 2 (Dark Blue/Orange wire) at LCM harness connector C220. Measure resistance between ground and terminal No. 27 (Violet/Orange wire) LCM harness connector C221. If both resistance readings are greater than 10 k/ohms, go to next step. If either resistance reading is 10 k/ohms or less, repair short to ground in appropriate wire(s).

7) Measure resistance in Dark Blue/Orange wire between terminal No. 2 at LCM harness connector C220 and terminal No. 9 at headlight switch harness connector C234. See Figs. 3 and 6. Measure resistance in Purple/Orange wire between terminal No. 27 at LCM harness connector C221 and terminal No. 4 at headlight switch harness connector C234. If

both resistance readings are 5 ohms or less, replace LCM. If either resistance reading is greater than 5 ohms, repair open in appropriate wire.

8) Turn ignition switch to LOCK position. Disconnect light sensor amplifier harness connector C286. Measure resistance between ground and terminal No. 4 (White/Violet wire) at light sensor amplifier harness connector C286. *See Fig. 9.* If resistance is greater than 10 k/ohms, go to next step. If resistance is 10 k/ohms or less, repair short to ground in White/Violet wire.

9) Turn ignition switch to RUN position. Using NGS tester, monitor LCM PID LIGHTSN. Using a fused jumper wire, connect terminals No. 3 (Tan/White wire) and No. 4 (White/Violet wire) at light sensor amplifier harness connector C286. If PID LIGHTSN does not read ON, leave jumper wire connected and go to next step. If PID LIGHTSN reads ON, replace light sensor amplifier.

10) Turn ignition switch to LOCK position. Disconnect LCM harness connector C221. Turn ignition switch to RUN position. Measure voltage at terminal No. 12 (White/Violet wire) at LCM harness connector C221. *See Fig. 4.* If battery voltage exists, replace LCM. If battery voltage does not exist, repair open in White/Violet wire.

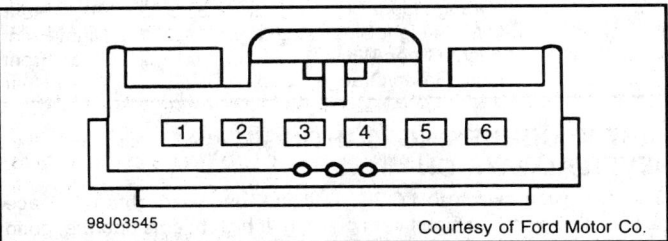

98J03545 — Courtesy of Ford Motor Co.

Fig. 9: Identifying Light Sensor Amplifier Control Harness Connector C286 Terminals

TEST G: STOPLIGHTS INOPERATIVE

NOTE: Brake Pedal Position (BPP) switch may also be referred to as brakelight or stoplight switch.

1) While observing stoplight operation, have assistant depress brake pedal. If stoplights illuminate, system is okay at this time. If stoplights do not illuminate, go to next step. If only rear hi-mount stoplight is inoperative, go to step **12)**. If stoplights illuminate continuously, go to step **13)**.

2) Measure voltage at output side of fuse No. 10 (20-amp) in instrument panel fuse box. If battery voltage does not exist, go to next. If battery voltage exists, go to step **6)**.

3) Remove fuse No. 10 (20-amp) from instrument panel fuse panel. Inspect fuse. If fuse is blown, go to next step. If fuse is okay, repair open in Tan/Black wire between power distribution box and instrument panel fuse box.

4) Disconnect Brake Pedal Position (BPP) switch harness connector. Measure resistance between ground and Light Green/Red wire terminal at BPP switch harness connector. If resistance is greater than 10 k/ohms, go to next step. If resistance is 10 k/ohms or less, repair short to ground in Light Green/Red wire.

5) Turn ignition switch to LOCK position. Remove fuses No. 20 (7.5-amp) and No. 22 (20-amp) from instrument panel fuse box. Measure resistance between ground and Light Green wire terminal at BPP switch harness connector. If resistance is greater than 10 k/ohms, replace BPP switch. If resistance is 10 k/ohms or less, repair short to ground in Light Green wire.

6) Disconnect Brake Pedal Position (BPP) switch harness connector. Measure voltage between ground and Light Green/Red wire terminal at BPP switch harness connector. If battery voltage exists, go to next step. If battery voltage does not exist, repair open in Light Green/Red wire.

7) Using a fused jumper wire, connect BPP switch harness connector terminals. If stoplights do not illuminate, leave jumper wire connected and go to next step. If stoplights illuminate, replace BPP switch.

8) Turn ignition switch to LOCK position. Measure voltage at input side of fuse No. 22 (20-amp) in instrument panel fuse box. If battery voltage

exists, leave jumper wire connected and go to next step. If battery voltage does not exist, repair open in Light Green wire.

9) Inspect instrument panel fuse panel fuse No. 22 (20-amp). If fuse is okay, leave jumper wire connected and go to next step. If fuse is faulty, remove jumper wire and go to step **11)**.

10) Turn ignition switch to LOCK position. Disconnect multifunction switch harness connector C268. Measure voltage at terminal No. 9 (Dark Green wire) at multifunction switch harness connector C268. *See Fig. 10.* If battery voltage exists, replace multifunction switch. If battery voltage does not exist, repair open in Dark Green wire.

11) Disconnect multifunction switch harness connector C268. Measure resistance between ground and terminal No. 9 (Dark Green wire) at multifunction switch harness connector C268. *See Fig. 10.* If resistance is greater than 10 k/ohms, replace multifunction switch. If resistance is 10 k/ohms or less, repair short to ground in Dark Green wire.

12) Apply brake pedal. Measure voltage at Dark Green wire terminal at hi-mount stoplight harness connector. If battery voltage exists, check Black wire as necessary. If wire is okay, replace bulb(s). If battery voltage does not exist, repair open in Dark Green wire.

13) Disconnect BPP switch harness connector. If stoplights turn off, replace BPP switch. If stoplights do not turn off, go to next step.

14) Remove fuse No. 22 (20-amp) from instrument panel fuse box. Measure voltage at Light Green wire terminal at BPP switch harness connector. If battery voltage does not exist, go to next step. If battery voltage exists, repair short to voltage in Light Green wire.

15) Remove fuse No. 20 (7.5-amp) from instrument panel fuse box. Measure voltage at output side of fuse No. 20. If battery voltage does not exist, go to next step. If battery voltage exists, go to step **17)**.

16) Remove instrument panel fuse panel fuse No. 22 (20-amp). Disconnect multifunction switch harness connector C268. Measure voltage at terminal No. 9 (Dark Green wire) at multifunction switch harness connector C268. *See Fig. 10.* If battery voltage does not exist, replace multifunction switch. If battery voltage exists, repair short to voltage in Dark Green wire.

17) Disconnect Lighting Control Module (LCM) harness connector C220. Measure voltage at terminal No. 8 (Red/Light Green wire) at LCM harness connector C220. *See Fig. 3.* If battery voltage does not exist, replace LCM. If battery voltage exists, repair short to voltage in Red/Light Green wire.

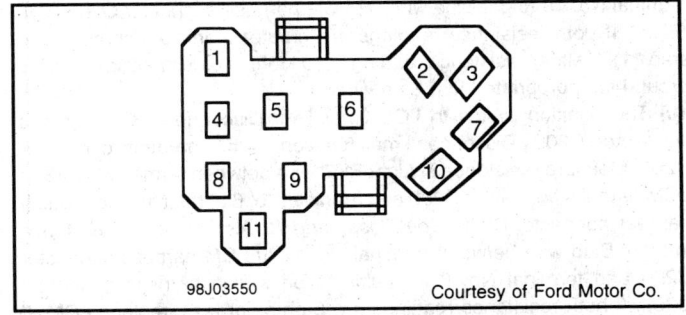

98J03550 — Courtesy of Ford Motor Co.

Fig. 10: Identifying Multifunction Switch Connector C268 Terminals

TEST H: TURN SIGNAL & HAZARD LIGHTS ARE INOPERATIVE

1) Using NGS tester, perform LCM self-test. If DTC B1873 or no DTCs are retrieved, go to next step. If DTC B1342 is retrieved, clear DTC and repeat LCM self-test. If DTC B1342 is retrieved again, replace LCM and retest system.

2) Inspect fuse No. 15 (20-amp) in instrument panel fuse box. If fuse is okay, install fuse and go to next step. If fuse is blown, go to step **4)**.

3) Turn ignition switch to RUN position. Measure voltage at input side of fuse No. 15 (20-amp) in instrument panel fuse box. If battery voltage exists, go to step **5)**. If battery voltage does not exist, repair open in Gray/Yellow wire between instrument panel fuse box and ignition switch.

4) Remove fuse No. 15 (20-amp) from instrument panel fuse panel. Disconnect multifunction switch harness connector C268. Measure resistance between ground and terminal No. 1 (Black/Yellow wire) at multifunction switch harness connector C268. See Fig. 10. If resistance is greater than 10 k/ohms, go to step 6). If resistance is 10 k/ohms or less, repair short to ground in Black/Yellow wire.

5) Disconnect multifunction switch harness connector C268. Measure voltage at terminal No. 1 (Black/Yellow wire) at multifunction switch harness connector C268. See Fig. 10. If battery voltage exists, go to next step. If battery voltage does not exist, repair open in Black/Yellow wire.

6) Disconnect multifunction switch harness connectors. Test multifunction switch. See MULTIFUNCTION SWITCH under COMPONENT TESTS in STEERING COLUMN SWITCHES – TOWN CAR article. If multifunction switch is okay and referral was from previous step, go to step 8). If multifunction switch is okay and referral was NOT from previous step, go to next step. If multifunction switch is defective, replace multifunction switch.

7) Turn ignition switch to LOCK position. Disconnect LCM harness connector C200. Disconnect multifunction switch harness connector C268. Measure resistance between ground and terminal No. 23 (White/Red wire) at LCM harness connector C200 and between ground and terminal No. 23 (White/Red wire) at LCM harness connector C200. See Fig. 7. If both resistance readings are greater than 10 k/ohms, go to step 9). If either resistance reading is 10 k/ohms or less, repair short to ground in appropriate White/Red wire.

8) Turn ignition switch to LOCK position. Disconnect LCM harness connector C200. Disconnect multifunction switch harness connector C268. Measure resistance in White/Red wire between terminal No. 23 at LCM harness connector C200 and terminal No. 11 at multifunction switch harness connector C268. See Figs. 7 and 10. Also measure resistance in White/Red wire between terminal No. 24 at LCM harness connector C200 and terminal No. 11 at multifunction switch harness connector C268. If both resistance readings are 5 ohms or less, go to step 10). If either resistance reading is greater than 5 ohms, repair open in appropriate White/Red wire.

9) Turn ignition switch to LOCK position. Disconnect LCM harness connector C200. Disconnect multifunction switch harness connector C269. Measure resistance between ground and terminal No. 17 (Light Blue wire) at LCM harness connector C200 and between ground and terminal No. 18 (Light Blue wire) at LCM harness connector C200. See Fig. 7. If both resistance readings are greater than 10 k/ohms, go to step 11). If either resistance reading is 10 k/ohms or less, repair short to ground in appropriate Light Blue wire.

10) Turn ignition switch to LOCK position. Disconnect LCM harness connector C200. Disconnect multifunction switch harness connector C269. Measure resistance in Light Blue wire between terminal No. 18 at LCM harness connector C200 and terminal No. 6 at multifunction switch harness connector C268. See Figs. 7 and 10. Also measure resistance in Light Blue wire between terminal No. 17 at LCM harness connector C200 and terminal No. 6 at multifunction switch harness connector C268. If both resistance readings are 5 ohms or less, replace LCM. If either resistance reading is greater than 5 ohms, repair open in appropriate Light Blue wire.

11) Disconnect multifunction switch harness connector C268. Measure resistance between ground and indicated terminals at multifunction switch harness connector C268. See TURN SIGNAL & HAZARD LIGHT CIRCUIT TEST table. See Fig. 10 . If any resistance readings is less than 2 ohms, repair short to ground in appropriate wire(s). If all resistance readings are greater than 2 ohms, replace LCM.

TURN SIGNAL & HAZARD LIGHT CIRCUIT TEST

Terminal	Wire Color
2	Orange/Light Blue
5	White/Light Blue
8	Light Green/White
10	Light Green/Orange

TEST J: ONE TURN SIGNAL/HAZARD LIGHT INOPERATIVE

1) Access multifunction switch harness connector C268. Turn ignition switch to RUN position. Place multifunction switch in inoperative position. Using a voltmeter, backprobe appropriate terminal at multifunction switch harness connector C268. See TURN SIGNAL OUTPUT table. See Fig. 10. If battery pulsing voltage exists, leave multifunction switch in inoperative position and go to next step. If battery pulsing voltage does not exist, replace multifunction switch. xx

2) Disconnect inoperative light harness connector. Measure voltage at appropriate wire at inoperative light harness connector. See TURN SIGNAL OUTPUT table. If battery pulsing voltage exists, go to next step. If battery pulsing voltage does not exist, repair open in appropriate wire.

3) Measure resistance between ground and Black wire terminal at inoperative light harness connector. If resistance is 5 ohms or less, replace defective bulb. If resistance is greater than 5 ohms, repair open in Black wire.

TURN SIGNAL OUTPUT

Terminal	Wire Color	Inoperative Light
2	Orange/Light Blue	Right Rear
5	White/Light Blue	Right Front
8	Light Green/White	Left Front
9	Light Green/Orange	Left Rear

TEST K: CORNERING LIGHTING NEVER/ALWAYS ON

1) Turn ignition switch to LOCK position. Turn headlights on. Place multifunction switch in high beam position. If high beams operate, go to next step. If high beams do not operate, perform TEST C: HIGH BEAMS INOPERATIVE.

2) Turn ignition switch to LOCK position. Disconnect multifunction switch harness connectors. Test multifunction switch. See MULTIFUNCTION SWITCH under COMPONENT TESTS in STEERING COLUMN SWITCHES – TOWN CAR article. If multifunction switch is okay, go to next step. If multifunction switch is defective, replace multifunction switch.

3) Connect multifunction switch harness connectors. Disconnect left and right cornering light harness connectors. Turn ignition switch to RUN position. Place multifunction switch in left turn position. Measure voltage at Violet/Yellow wire at left cornering light harness connector. Place multifunction switch in right turn position. Measure voltage at Violet/Yellow wire at right cornering light harness connector. If battery voltage exists at both wires, go to next step. If battery voltage does not exist at either wire, repair open in appropriate Violet/Yellow wire.

4) Turn ignition switch to LOCK position. Measure resistance between ground and Black wire at both cornering light harness connectors. If both resistance readings are 5 ohms or less, replace appropriate bulb. If either resistance reading is greater than 5 ohms, repair open in appropriate Black wire.

TEST L: PARKING, REAR OR LICENSE LIGHTS ARE INOPERATIVE

1) Connect NGS tester to Data Link Connector (DLC). Turn ignition switch to RUN position. Using NGS tester, monitor LCM PID PARK_SW while turning headlight switch on and off. If PID agrees with headlight switch position, go to next step. If PID agrees with headlight switch position, go to step 6).

2) Turn headlight switch on. If low beams operate, go to next step. If low beams do not operate, perform TEST B: LOW BEAMS INOPERATIVE.

3) Turn ignition switch to LOCK position. Disconnect LCM harness connector C221. Measure voltage at terminal No. 21 (White/Black wire) at LCM harness connector C221. See Fig. 4. Battery voltage should exist when headlight switch is in park and headlight positions. If voltage is as specified, replace LCM. If voltage is not as specified, go to next step.

4) Disconnect headlight switch harness connector C234. Measure resistance between ground and terminal No. 21 (White/Black wire) at

LCM harness connector C221. If resistance is greater than 10 k/ohms, go to next step. If resistance is 10 k/ohms or less, repair short to ground in White/Black wire.

5) Measure resistance in White/Black wire between terminal No. 21 at LCM harness connector C221 and terminal No. 3 at headlight switch harness connector C234. *See Figs. 4 and 6.* If resistance is 5 ohms or less, replace headlight switch. If resistance is greater than 5 ohms, repair open in White/Black wire.

6) Turn ignition switch to RUN position. Using NGS tester, select LCM active command. Trigger PARKLAMPS and TAILLAMPS on. If parking and tail lights do not illuminate, go to next step. If only individual tail or parking light does not illuminate, go to step **13)**. If parking and tail lights illuminate, replace LCM.

7) Measure voltage at input side of fuse No. 7 (15-amp) in instrument panel fuse box. If battery voltage exists, go to next step. If battery voltage does not exist, repair open in Dark Blue/Orange wire between power distribution box and instrument panel fuse box.

8) Remove fuse No. 7 from instrument panel fuse box. Inspect fuse, If fuse is blown, go to next step. If fuse is okay, install fuse and go to step **11)**.

9) Turn ignition switch to LOCK position. Disconnect LCM harness connector C200. Measure resistance between ground and terminal No. 16 (Tan/White wire) at LCM harness connector. *See Fig. 7.* If resistance is greater than 10 k/ohms, go to next step. If resistance is 10 k/ohms or less, repair short to ground in Tan/White wire.

10) Ensure LCM harness connector is disconnected. Using a fused jumper wire, connect terminals No. 22 (Brown wire) and No. 23 (White/Red wire) at LCM harness connector C200. If jumper wire fuse blows, repair short to ground in Brown wire. If jumper wire fuse does not blow, replace LCM.

11) Turn ignition switch to LOCK position. Disconnect LCM harness connector C200. Measure voltage at terminal No. 16 (Tan/White wire) at LCM harness connector C200. *See Fig. 7.* If battery voltage exists, go to next step. If battery voltage does not exist, repair open in Tan/White wire.

12) Turn ignition switch to LOCK position. Disconnect LCM harness connector C200. Using a fused jumper wire, connect terminals No. 16 (Tan/White wire) and No. 14 (Brown wire) at LCM harness connector. If parking and tail lights do not illuminate, go to next step. If parking and tail lights illuminate, replace LCM.

13) Turn ignition switch to LOCK position. Connect all disconnected connectors. Disconnect inoperative light harness connector(s). Turn ignition switch to RUN position. Using NGS tester, trigger TAILAMPS active command on. Measure voltage at Brown wire at inoperative light harness connector. If battery voltage exists, go to next step. If battery voltage does not exist, repair open in appropriate Brown wire.

14) Turn ignition switch to LOCK position. Measure resistance between ground and Black wire at inoperative light harness connector. If resistance is 5 ohms or less, replace blub. If resistance is greater than 5 ohms, repair open in appropriate Black wire.

TEST M: PARKING, TAIL OR LICENSE LIGHTS ON CONTINUOUSLY

1) Using NGS tester, perform LCM self-test. If DTC B1577 is retrieved or no DTCs are retrieved, go to next step. If DTC B1342 is retrieved, clear DTC and repeat LCM self-test. If DTC B1342 is retrieved again, replace LCM.

2) Using NGS tester, monitor LCM PID PARK_SW while turning headlight switch on and off. If PID does not agree with switch position, go to next step. If PID agrees with switch position, go to step **5)**.

3) Disconnect headlight switch harness connector C234. Test headlight switch. See HEADLIGHT SWITCH under COMPONENT TESTS. If headlight switch is okay, go to next step. If headlight switch is defective, replace headlight switch.

4) Turn ignition switch to LOCK position. Disconnect LCM harness connector C221. Measure voltage at terminal No. 21 (White/Black wire) at LCM harness connector C221. *See Fig. 4.* If battery voltage exists, repair short to voltage in White/Black wire. If battery voltage does not exist, replace LCM.

5) Turn ignition switch to LOCK position. Disconnect LCM harness connector C200. *See Fig. 7.* Measure voltage at terminal No. 22 (Brown wire) at LCM harness connector C200. If battery voltage exists, repair short to voltage in Brown wire. If battery voltage does not exist, replace LCM.

TEST N: NO COMMUNICATION WITH DRIVER'S DOOR MODULE

1) Ensure transmission is in Park. Turn ignition switch to LOCK position. Check fuse No. 30 (7.5-amp) in instrument panel fuse box. If fuse is okay, go to next step. If fuse is blown, go to step **5)**.

2) Measure voltage at input side of fuse No. 30. If battery voltage exists, go to next step. If battery voltage does not exist, go to step **20)**.

3) Ensure fuse No. 30 is removed from instrument panel fuse box. Disconnect DDM harness connector C520. Measure resistance in Light Green/Violet wire between terminal No. 29 at DDM harness connector C520 and output side of fuse No. 30. *See Fig. 11.* If resistance is 5 ohms or less, go to next step. If resistance is greater than 5 ohms, repair open in Light Green/Violet wire between instrument panel fuse box and DDM.

4) Measure resistance between ground and terminal No. 23 (Pink/Orange wire) at DDM harness connector C520. If resistance is greater than 5 ohms, repair open in Pink/Orange wire. If resistance is 5 ohms or less, replace driver's door module.

5) Replace fuse No. 30. DO NOT operate any switches. If fuse blows, go to next step. If fuse does not blow, go to step **9)**.

6) Remove fuse No. 30. Disconnect DDM harness connector C520 and Driver's Seat Module (DSM) harness connector C313. Measure resistance between ground and terminal No. 29 (Light Green/Violet wire) at DDM harness connector C520. *See Fig. 11.* If resistance is 10 k/ohms or less, go to next step. If resistance is greater than 10 k/ohms, go to step **8)**.

7) Test door lock switches, remote trunk release switch, mirror control switch and seat control switches. See appropriate test under COMPONENT TESTS in POWER MIRRORS – TOWN CAR article. If no switch is defective, repair short to ground in Light Green/Violet wire. If any switch is defective, replace appropriate switch.

8) Connect DSM harness connector C313. Measure resistance between ground and terminal No. 29 (Light Green/Violet wire) at DDM harness connector C520. If resistance is greater than 10 k/ohms, replace driver's door module. If resistance is 10 k/ohms or less, replace driver's seat module.

9) Lock and unlock doors at all door lock switches. If fuse No. 30 blows, go to next step. If fuse No. 30 does not blow, go to step **12)**.

10) Remove door lock switches. Test all door lock switches. See DOOR LOCK SWITCH under COMPONENT TESTS in POWER MIRRORS – TOWN CAR article. If all door lock switches are okay, go to next step. If any door lock switch is defective, replace appropriate door lock switch.

11) Disconnect Driver's Door Module (DDM) harness connector C520. Disconnect driver's door lock switch harness connector C503. Disconnect passenger's door lock switch harness connector C603. Measure resistance between ground and terminal No. 2 (Pink/Yellow wire) at driver's door lock switch harness connector C503. Also, measure resistance between ground and terminal No. 6 (Pink/Light Green wire) at driver's door lock switch harness connector C503. *See Fig. 12 .* If either or both resistance reading are 10 k/ohms or less, repair short to ground in appropriate wire(s). If both resistance readings are greater than 10 k/ohms, replace driver's door module.

12) Activate mirrors in all directions. If fuse No. 30 blows, go to next step. If fuse No. 30 does not blow, go to step **15)**.

13) Remove mirror control switch. Test mirror control switch. See MIRROR CONTROL SWITCH under COMPONENT TESTS in POWER MIRRORS – TOWN CAR article. If mirror control switch is okay, go to next step. If mirror control switch is defective, replace mirror control switch.

14) Disconnect Driver's Door Module (DDM) harness connector C520. Disconnect mirror control switch harness connector C550. Measure resistance between ground and appropriate terminals at DDM harness connector C520. See MIRROR CONTROL SWITCH CIRUCIT IDENTIFICATION table. *See Fig. 11.* If all resistance readings are greater than

10 k/ohms, replace driver's door module. If any resistance reading are 10 k/ohms or less, repair short to ground in appropriate wire.

MIRROR CONTROL SWITCH CIRCUIT IDENTIFICATION

Terminal	Wire Color
18	Yellow/Black
19	Dark Blue/Orange
30	Red/Orange
31	Violet/Orange
32	Dark Green/Orange

15) Activate memory switch through all positions. If fuse No. 30 blows, go to next step. If fuse No. 30 does not blow, go to step **18)**.

16) Remove driver's seat control switch. Test memory portion of driver's seat control switch. See DRIVER'S SEAT CONTROL SWITCH (WITH MEMORY) under COMPONENT TESTS in POWER MIRRORS – TOWN CAR article. If memory switch is okay, go to next step. If memory switch is defective, replace driver's seat control switch.

17) Disconnect Driver's Door Module (DDM) harness connectors C520 and C521. Measure resistance between ground and appropriate terminals at driver's seat control switch harness connector C509. See SEAT SWITCH CIRCUIT TERMINAL IDENTIFICATION table. *See Fig. 13.* If all resistance readings are greater than 10 k/ohms, replace driver's door module. If any resistance readings are 10 k/ohms or less, repair short to ground in appropriate wire.

SEAT SWITCH CIRCUIT TERMINAL IDENTIFICATION

Terminal	Wire Color
4	White/Orange
5	Brown/Orange
6	Brown/Light Green
7	Black/Orange

18) Activate driver's seat control switch in all directions. If fuse No. 30 blows, go to next step. If fuse No. 30 does not blow, system is operating properly at this time.

19) Disconnect Driver's Door Module (DDM) harness connector C521. Disconnect driver's seat control switch harness connector C509. Measure resistance between ground and appropriate terminals at driver's seat control switch harness connector C509. See DRIVER'S SEAT CONTROL SWITCH TERMINAL IDENTIFICATION table. *See Fig. 13.* If all resistance readings are greater than 10 k/ohms, replace driver's door module. If any resistance readings are 10 k/ohms or less, repair short to ground in appropriate wire.

DRIVER'S SEAT CONTROL SWITCH TERMINAL IDENTIFICATION

Terminal	Wire Color
1	Yellow/White
2	Red/Light Blue
3	Yellow/Light Blue
9	Red/White
11	Yellow/Light Green
12	Red/Light Green
13	Gray
14	Gray/Black

20) Turn ignition switch to LOCK position. Remove maxi-fuse No. 8 (30-amp) from power distribution box. Measure voltage at input side of maxi-fuse No. 8 at power distribution box. If battery voltage exists, go to next step. If battery voltage does not exist, repair power supply to maxi-fuse No. 8.

21) Ensure maxi-fuse No. 8 is still removed. Remove fuse No. 30 (7.5-amp) from instrument panel fuse box. Disconnect Driver's Seat Module (DSM) harness connector C337. Measure resistance in Red wire between output side of maxi-fuse No. 8 and input side of fuse No. 30. If resistance is 5 ohms or less, go to next step. If resistance is greater than 5 ohms, repair open in Red wire.

22) Measure resistance between ground and output side of maxi-fuse No. 8 at power distribution box. If resistance is greater than 10 k/ohms, replace driver's door module. If resistance is 10 k/ohms or less, repair short to ground in Red wire.

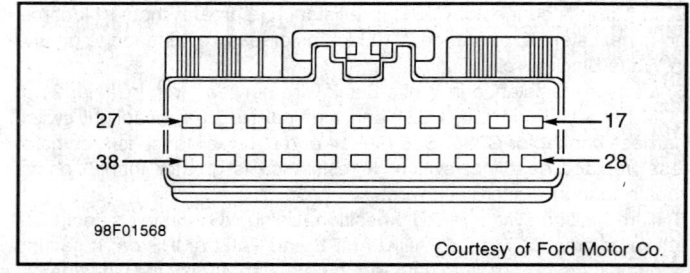

Fig. 11: Identifying DDM Harness Connector C520 Terminals

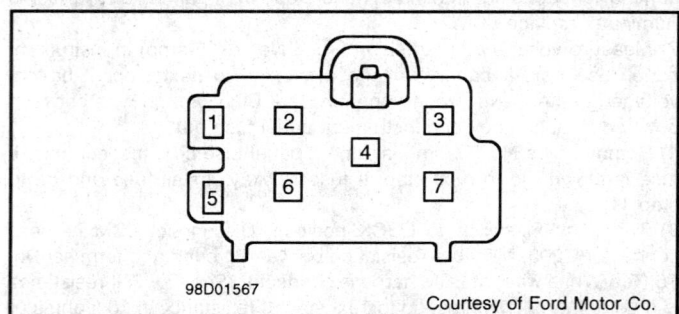

Fig. 12: Identifying Driver's Door Lock Switch Harness Connector C503 Terminals

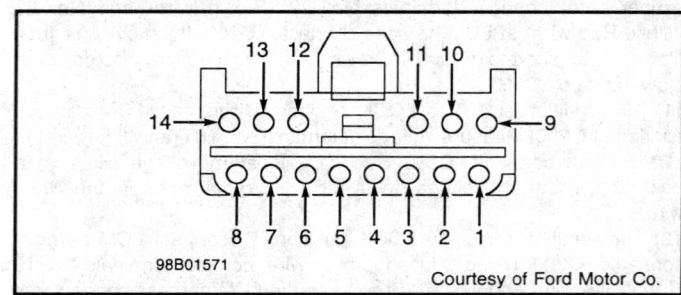

Fig. 13: Identifying Driver's Seat Control Switch Harness Connector C509 Terminals

TEST P: COURTESY LIGHTS INOPERATIVE

1) Connect New Generation Star (NGS) tester to Data Link Connector (DLC). Using NGS tester, perform Lighting Control Module (LCM) self-test. If DTC B1342 is not retrieved, go to next step. If DTC B1342 is retrieved, retrieve and record all continuous DTCs. Perform LCM self-test. If DTC B1342 is retrieved again, replace LCM.

2) Using NGS tester, monitor DDM PID D_DR_DD while opening and closing driver's door. If PID agrees with driver's door position, go to next step. If PID does not agree with driver's door position, go to step **15)**.

3) Using NGS tester, monitor DDM PID P_DR_DD while opening and closing passenger's door. If PID agrees with passenger's door position, go to next step. If PID does not agree with passenger's door position, go to step **17)**.

4) Turn ignition switch to RUN position. Using NGS tester, access active command BATTERY SAVER & COURTESY ENTRY. Trigger LCM active command COURTESY LAMPS ON. If courtesy lights do not illuminate, go to next step. If courtesy lights illuminate, replace LCM.

5) Open glove box. If glove box light does not illuminate, go to next step. If glove box light illuminates, go to step **14)**.

6) Turn ignition switch to LOCK position. Remove fuse No. 5 (40-amp) from power distribution box. Inspect fuse. If fuse is okay, go to next step. If fuse is blown, repair short to ground in Tan/Black wire between power distribution box and instrument panel fuse box.

7) Measure voltage at input side of fuse No. 5 at power distribution box. If battery voltage exists, go to next step. If battery voltage does not exist, repair or replace power distribution box as necessary.

8) Install fuse No. 5 in power distribution box. Measure voltage at input side of fuse No. 25 (15-amp) in instrument panel fuse box. If battery voltage exists, go to next step. If battery voltage does not exist, repair open in Tan/Black wire between power distribution box and instrument panel fuse box.

9) Remove fuse No. 25 from instrument panel fuse box. Inspect fuse. If fuse is okay, go to next step. If fuse is blown, go to step **11**).

10) Disconnect LCM harness connector C222. Install fuse No. 25 in instrument panel fuse box. Measure voltage at terminal No. 9 (Light Green/Yellow wire) at CM harness connector C222. *See Fig. 5.* If battery voltage exists, replace LCM. If battery voltage does not exist, repair open in Light Green/Yellow wire.

11) Ensure fuse No. 25 in instrument panel fuse box is still removed. Disconnect LCM harness connector C222. Measure resistance between ground and terminal No. 9 (Light Green/Yellow wire) at CM harness connector C222. See Fig. 5. If resistance is greater than 10 k/ohms, go to next step. If resistance is 10 k/ohms or less, repair short to ground in Light Green/Yellow wire.

12) Remove all courtesy light bulbs including one in trunk. Measure resistance between ground and terminal No. 10 (Black/Light Blue wire) at LCM harness connector C222. If resistance is greater than 10 k/ohms, go to next step. If resistance is 10 k/ohms or less, repair short to ground in Black/Light Blue wire.

13) Ensure all courtesy light bulbs including one in trunk are still removed. Measure resistance between ground and terminal No. 4 (Light Green/Orange wire) at LCM harness connector C222. If resistance is greater than 10 k/ohms, replace LCM. If resistance is 10 k/ohms or less, repair short to ground in Light Green/Orange wire.

14) Turn ignition switch to RUN position. Using NGS tester, access active command BATTERY SAVER & COURTESY ENTRY. Trigger LCM active command COURTESYL ON. Using a voltmeter, backprobe at terminal No. 10 (Black/Light Blue wire) at LCM harness connector C222. *See Fig. 5.* If battery voltage exists, open in Black/Light Blue wire. If battery voltage does not exist, replace LCM.

15) Turn ignition switch to LOCK position. Disconnect Driver's Door Module (DDM) harness connector C521. Disconnect driver's door ajar switch harness connector. Measure resistance in Dark Blue wire between driver's door ajar switch harness connector terminal and terminal No. 5 at DDM harness connector C521. *See Fig. 14.* If resistance is 5 ohms or less, go to next step. If resistance is greater than 5 ohms, repair open in Dark Blue wire.

16) Measure resistance between ground and terminal at driver's door ajar switch (component side). Resistance should be 5 ohms or less when switch is released. Resistance should be greater than 10 k/ohms when switch is depressed. If resistance is not as specified, replace driver's door ajar switch. If resistance is as specified, replace DDM.

17) Turn ignition switch to LOCK position. Disconnect Driver's Door Module (DDM) harness connector C521. Disconnect passenger's, right rear, and left rear door ajar switch harness connectors. Measure resistance in Black/Orange wire between each door ajar switch harness connector terminal and terminal No. 6 at DDM harness connector C521. *See Fig. 14.* If all resistance readings are 5 ohms or less, go to next step. If any resistance reading is greater than 5 ohms, repair open in appropriate Black/Orange wire.

18) Measure resistance between ground and terminal at each door ajar switch (component side). Resistance should be 5 ohms or less when switch is released. Resistance should be greater than 10 k/ohms when switch is depressed. If resistance is not as specified, replace appropriate door ajar switch. If resistance is as specified, replace DDM.

TEST Q: COURTESY LIGHTS STAY ON CONTINUOUSLY

1) Connect New Generation Star (NGS) tester to Data Link Connector (DLC). Using NGS tester, perform Lighting Control Module (LCM) self-test. If DTC B1342 and/or B1687 are not retrieved, go to next step. If DTC B1687 is not retrieved, go to step **13**). If DTC B1342 is retrieved, retrieve and record all continuous DTCs. Perform LCM self-test. If DTC B1342 is retrieved again, replace LCM.

2) Using NGS tester, perform Driver's Door Module (DDM) self-test. If any DTCs except B1566 is retrieved, go to next step. If DTC B1566 is retrieved, go to step **4**).

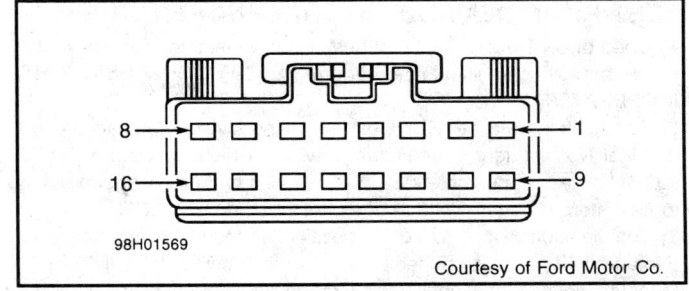

98H01569

Courtesy of Ford Motor Co.

Fig. 14: Identifying DDM Harness Connector C521 Terminals

3) Using NGS tester, monitor DDM PID D_DR_DD while opening and closing driver's door. If PID agrees with driver's door position, go to next step. If PID does not agree with driver's door position, go to step **10**).

4) Using NGS tester, monitor DDM PID P_DR_DD while opening and closing passenger's door. If PID does not agree with passenger's door position, go to next step. If PID agrees with passenger's door position, go to step **12**).

5) Disconnect passenger's, right rear, and left rear door ajar switch harness connectors. Using NGS tester, monitor DDM PID P_DR_DD. If PID does not indicate AJAR, go to next step. If PID indicates AJAR, go to step **9**).

6) Turn ignition switch to LOCK position. Connect passenger's door ajar switch harness connector. Close passenger's door. Turn ignition switch to RUN position. Using NGS tester, monitor DDM PID P_DR_DD. If PID does not indicate AJAR, go to next step. If PID indicates AJAR, replace passenger's door ajar switch.

7) Turn ignition switch to LOCK position. Connect right rear door ajar switch harness connector. Ensure passenger's door is closed. Close right rear door. Turn ignition switch to RUN position. Using NGS tester, monitor DDM PID P_DR_DD. If PID does not indicate AJAR, go to next step. If PID indicates AJAR, replace right rear door ajar switch.

8) Turn ignition switch to LOCK position. Connect left rear door ajar switch harness connector. Ensure passenger's and right rear doors are closed. Close left rear door. Turn ignition switch to RUN position. Using NGS tester, monitor DDM PID P_DR_DD. If PID does not indicate AJAR, replace DDM. If PID indicates AJAR, replace left rear door ajar switch.

9) Turn ignition switch to LOCK position. Disconnect DDM harness connector C521. Measure resistance between ground and terminal No. 6 (Black/Orange wire) at DDM harness connector C521. *See Fig. 14.* If resistance is 10 k/ohms or less, repair short to ground in Black/Orange wire. If resistance is greater than 10 k/ohms, replace DDM.

10) Disconnect driver's door ajar switch harness connector. Turn ignition switch to RUN position. Using NGS tester, monitor DDM PID D_DR_DD. If PID indicates AJAR, go to next step. If PID does not indicate AJAR, replace driver's door ajar switch.

11) Turn ignition switch to LOCK position. Disconnect DDM harness connector C521. Measure resistance between ground and terminal No. 5 (Dark Blue wire) at DDM harness connector C521. *See Fig. 14.* If resistance is 10 k/ohms or less, repair short to ground in Dark Blue wire. If resistance is greater than 10 k/ohms, replace DDM.

12) Turn ignition switch to LOCK position. Disconnect LCM harness connector C222. Turn ignition switch to RUN position. Measure voltage at terminal No. 10 (Black/Light Blue wire) at LCM harness connector C222. *See Fig. 5.* If voltage exists, repair short to voltage in Black/Light Blue wire. If voltage does not exist, replace LCM.

13) Using NGS tester, monitor LCM PID DOMESW while turn dome light on and off at headlight switch. If PID does not agree with switch position, go to next step. If PID agrees with switch position, replace LCM.

14) Turn ignition switch to LOCK position. Disconnect headlight switch harness connector. Using NGS tester, monitor LCM PID DOMESW. IF PID indicates OFF, replace headlight switch. If PID does not indicate OFF, repair short to voltage in Black/White wire between headlight switch and LCM.

TEST R: ON-DEMAND LIGHTING INOPERATIVE

1) Open driver's door. If any courtesy lights illuminate, go to next step. If no courtesy lights illuminate, perform TEST P: COURTESY LIGHTS INOPERATIVE.

2) Turn ignition switch to RUN position. Using a voltmeter, backprobe at terminal No. 4 (Light Green/Orange wire) at Lighting Control Module (LCM) harness connector C222. *See Fig. 5*. If battery voltage exists, go to next step. If battery voltage does not exist, replace LCM.

3) Turn ignition switch to LOCK position. Disconnect inoperative on-demand light harness connector. Turn ignition switch to RUN position. Measure voltage at Light Green/Orange wire terminal at inoperative on-demand light harness connector. If battery voltage exists, go to next step. If battery voltage does not exist, repair open in Light Green/Orange wire.

4) Measure resistance between ground and Black wire terminal at inoperative on-demand light harness connector. If resistance is 5 ohms or less, replace blub. If resistance is greater than 5 ohms, repair open in Black wire.

TEST S: BATTERY SAVER DOES NOT DEACTIVATE AFTER TIMEOUT

1) Connect New Generation Star (NGS) tester to Data Link Connector (DLC). Using NGS tester, perform Lighting Control Module (LCM) self-test. If no DTCs are retrieved, go to next step. If any DTCs are retrieved, perform appropriate test. See LIGHTING CONTROL MODULE DTC INDEX table under SELF-DIAGNOSTIC SYSTEM.

2) Activate all demand lights. If all demand lights operate properly, go to next step. If any demand light(s) do not operate properly, repair by symptom. See SYMPTOM CHART table.

3) Open and close all doors while monitoring courtesy lights. If all courtesy lights operate properly, go to next step. If any courtesy light(s) do not operate properly, repair by symptom. See SYMPTOM CHART table.

4) Ensure headlight switch is not in autolamp position. Turn headlights on and off. If headlights operate properly, replace LCM. If headlights do not operate properly, repair by symptom. See SYMPTOM CHART table.

TEST T: INDIVIDUAL COURTESY LIGHT INOPERATIVE

1) Turn ignition switch to LOCK position. Disconnect inoperative courtesy light harness connector. Connect New Generation Star (NGS) tester to Data Link Connector (DLC). Using NGS tester, access active command BATTERY SAVER & COURTESY ENTRY. Trigger LCM active command COURTESYL ON. Measure voltage Black/Light Blue wire terminal at inoperative courtesy light harness connector. If battery voltage exists, go to next step. If battery voltage does not exist, repair open in appropriate Black/Light Blue wire.

2) Turn ignition switch to LOCK position. Measure resistance between ground and Black wire terminal at inoperative courtesy light harness connector. If resistance is 5 ohms or less, replace bulb. If resistance is greater than 5 ohms, repair open in appropriate Black wire.

REMOVAL & INSTALLATION

CAUTION: When battery is disconnected or modules are replaced, vehicle computer and memory systems may lose memory data. Driveability problems may exist until computer systems have completed a relearn cycle. See COMPUTER RELEARN PROCEDURES article in GENERAL INFORMATION before disconnecting battery.

BRAKE PEDAL POSITION (BPP) SWITCH

Removal & Installation – Disconnect negative battery cable. Remove lower instrument panel insulator. Disconnect BPP switch harness connector. Remove cotter pin and disconnect power booster push rod from brake pedal. Remove push rod sleeve. Remove BPP switch. To install, reverse removal procedure.

HEADLIGHT SWITCH

Removal & Installation – Disconnect negative battery cable. Remove instrument panel trim panels by pulling up and unsnapping from retainers. Remove knobs from headlight switch. Remove nut from headlight switch. Disconnect headlight switch connectors. Remove headlight switch. To install, reverse removal procedure. Tighten switch retaining nut to 26 INCH lbs. (3 N.m).

LIGHTING CONTROL MODULE (LCM)

Removal & Installation – Remove driver side underdash panel. Locate LCM on left side of instrument panel. Disconnect LCM connectors. Unclip module from mounting bracket. To install, reverse removal procedure.

LIGHT SENSOR AMPLIFIER ASSEMBLY

Removal & Installation – Pry up and unsnap instrument panel upper finish panel. Remove instrument panel defroster grille. Remove retaining screws and light sensor amplifier. Disconnect electrical connector. To install, reverse removal procedure.

MULTIFUNCTION SWITCH

See appropriate STEERING COLUMN SWITCHES article.

WIRING DIAGRAMS

NOTE: See appropriate wiring diagram in HEADLIGHT SYSTEMS, EXTERIOR LIGHTS, ILLUMINATION/INTERIOR LIGHTS and LIGHTING CONTROL MODULES articles. Also see appropriate wiring diagram in POWER DISTRIBUTION article in WIRING DIAGRAMS.

DESCRIPTION

Controlled by the Lighting Control Module (LCM), the autolamp system provides automatic on-off control of the headlights in addition to normal headlight switch operation. The headlights will automatically turn on when outside light dims. The system also includes a delay feature which keeps the headlights on for a pre-selected time period after ignition is turned off. Major components of the system are an LCM, autolamp switch (integral to headlight switch) and a light sensor.

OPERATION

The headlight switch must be in AUTO1 or AUTO2 position for automatic operation. The light sensor must be exposed to ambient light to operate properly. Time delay is varied by switch position; 25 seconds in AUTO1 and 2.5 minutes in AUTO2 position before lights turn off automatically. Turning headlight switch to OFF position shuts autolamps off.

COMPONENT LOCATIONS

COMPONENT LOCATIONS

Component	Location
Air Bag Sliding Contact	In Steering Wheel
Autolamp Sensor	Right Side Of Instrument Panel, Near Lower Right Corner
Data Link Connector (DLC)	Below Driver's Side Of Instrument Panel, To Right Of Steering Column
Engine Compartment Relay Box	Left Front Side Of Engine Compartment
Fuse Junction Panel	Below Left Side Of Instrument Panel
Headlight Switch	Left Side Of Instrument Panel
Power Distribution Box	In Engine Compartment, Next To Battery
Powertrain Control Module (PCM)	Behind Glove Box
Lighting Control Module (LCM)	Bottom Of Center Console, Below Dash Panel
Transaxle Control Module (TCM)	Behind Instrument Cluster

TROUBLE SHOOTING

Manufacturer's sequence for diagnosing and repairing autolamp system is as follows:

- Verify Customer's Complaint
- Perform Visual Inspection
- Perform appropriate test under SYSTEM TESTS

INITIAL CHECKS

Verify customer's complaint. Check autolamp system related fuses. See WIRING DIAGRAMS. Replace fuse(s) as necessary and recheck system operation. Check or replace any suspect bulbs. Check for damaged headlight switch or Lighting Control Module (LCM). Check for a covered light sensor. Sensor is located on right side of instrument panel, near lower right corner of instrument panel. Check for loose or corroded wiring harness connectors. Check for good clean connections at chassis ground point locations. See WIRING DIAGRAMS. Correct any obvious problems before continuing test. If all checks are okay, go to SYSTEM TESTS.

COMPONENT TESTS

HEADLIGHT SWITCH

Disconnect headlight switch harness connector. Continuity should be as specified between terminals with switch in specified position. See HEADLIGHT SWITCH TEST table. *See Fig. 1.* If continuity is not as specified, replace headlight switch.

HEADLIGHT SWITCH TEST

Switch Position	Between Terminals	Continuity
Autolamp		
OFF	9 & 10	Yes
AUTO1	9 & 10	[1] Yes
AUTO2	9 & 10	[1] Yes
Dome Light		
Switch Normal	6 & 7	No
Switch Depressed	6 & 7	Yes
Headlights		
OFF	3 & 8	No
Park	3 & 8	No
On	3 & 8	Yes
Parklights		
OFF	3 & 7	No
Park	3 & 7	Yes
On	3 & 7	Yes
Switch Illumination		
Head	1 & 2	Yes
Park	1 & 2	Yes

[1] – Resistance will increase from OFF to AUTO1 to AUTO2.

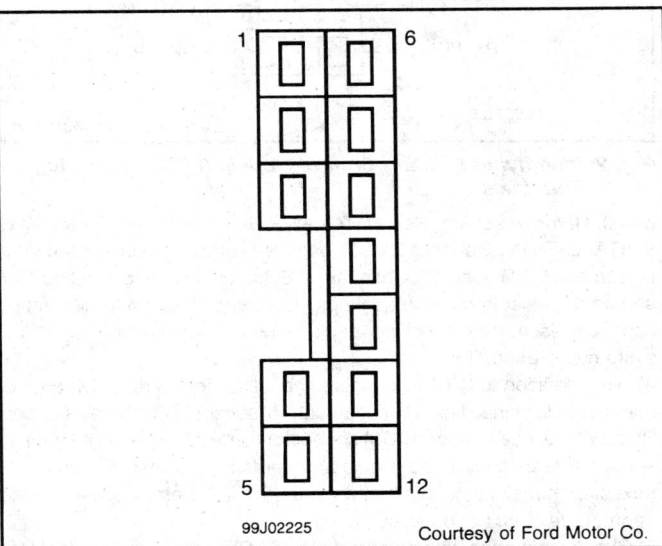

99J02225   Courtesy of Ford Motor Co.

Fig. 1: Identifying Headlight Switch Terminals

SYSTEM TESTS

SYMPTOM CHART

Symptom	Test
Autolamps Inoperative	A
Autolamp Time Delay Inoperative	B

NOTE: After a repair is completed, always recheck system operation to ensure repair procedure has corrected the problem.

TEST A: AUTOLAMPS INOPERATIVE

1) Turn ignition off. Turn headlight switch to ON position. Ensure high beam and low beam headlights work correctly. If headlights work correctly, turn headlight switch to OFF position and go to next step. If headlights do not work correctly, repair headlights. See appropriate wiring diagram in HEADLIGHT SYSTEMS article.
2) Disconnect Lighting Control Module (LCM). LCM is located in bottom of center console, below dash panel. Turn ignition on. Check voltage between ground and LCM connector terminal No. 9 (Light Green wire). *See Fig. 2.* If voltage is more than 10 volts, go to next step. If voltage is 10 volts or less, repair open or short to ground in Light Green wire.
3) Disconnect autolamp light sensor 2-pin connector. Sensor is located on right side of instrument panel, near lower right corner of instrument

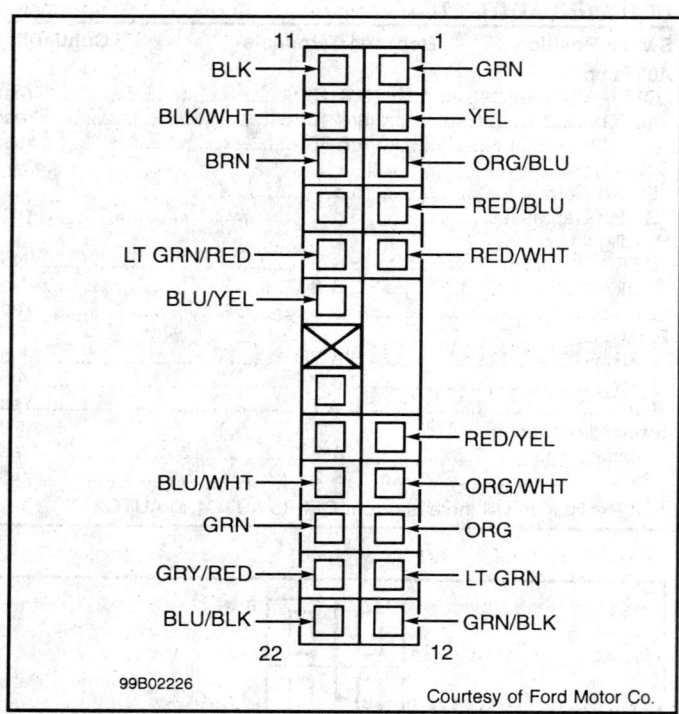

Fig. 2: Identifying Lighting Control Module (LCM) Connector Terminals

panel. Remove sensor. See AUTOLAMP SENSOR under REMOVAL & INSTALLATION. Connect DVOM between autolamp sensor terminals. Reverse DVOM leads. Continuity should exist in one direction and should not exist in other. If continuity is as specified, go to next step. If continuity is not as specified, replace autolamp sensor and recheck system operation.

4) Turn ignition off. Check resistance of Green wire between LCM connector terminal No. 1 and autolamp sensor. Check resistance of Black/White wire between LCM connector terminal No. 12 and autolamp sensor. If resistance in both measurements is less than 5 ohms, go to next step. If resistance in either measurement is 5 ohms or more, repair appropriate circuit and retest system.

5) Check resistance between ground and LCM connector terminal No. 1 (Green wire). Check resistance between ground and LCM connector terminal No. 12 (Black/White wire). If resistance in both measurements is more than 10 k/ohms, replace LCM and retest system. If resistance in either measurement is less than 10 k/ohms, repair short to ground in appropriate circuit. Retest system.

TEST B: AUTOLAMP TIME DELAY INOPERATIVE

1) Turn ignition on. Cover autolamp light sensor. Sensor is located on right side of instrument panel, near lower right corner of instrument panel. Turn headlight switch to either AUTO position. If headlights illuminate, turn headlight switch to OFF position and go to next step. If do not headlights illuminate, go to TEST A: AUTOLAMPS INOPERATIVE test.

2) Turn ignition off. Check headlight switch. See HEADLIGHT SWITCH under COMPONENT TESTS. Replace switch as necessary and recheck system operation. If switch is okay, go to next step.

3) Turn ignition off. Disconnect Lighting Control Module (LCM). LCM is located in bottom of center console, below dash panel. Measure resistance of Blue/White wire between LCM connector terminal No. 19 and headlight switch wiring harness connector terminal No. 9. *See Figs. 2 and 3.* If resistance is less than 5 ohms, go to next step. If resistance is 5 ohms or more, repair open Blue/White wire and recheck system operation.

4) Measure resistance between ground and LCM connector terminal No. 19 (Blue/White wire). If resistance is more than 10 k/ohms, replace LCM

and retest system. If resistance is 10 k/ohms or less, repair short to ground in Blue/White wire. Recheck system operation.

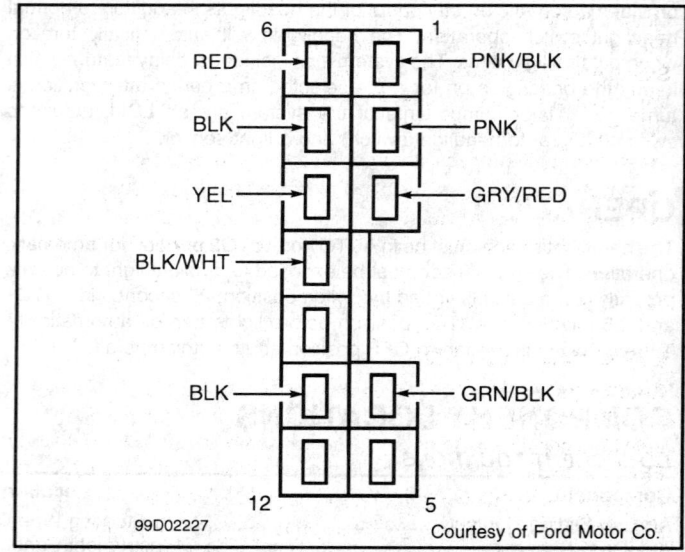

Fig. 3: Identifying Headlight Switch Connector Terminals

REMOVAL & INSTALLATION

CAUTION: When battery is disconnected, vehicle computer and memory systems may lose memory data. Driveability problems may exist until computer systems have completed a relearn cycle. See COMPUTER RELEARN PROCEDURES article in GENERAL INFORMATION before disconnecting battery.

AUTOLAMP SENSOR

Removal & Installation – Sensor is located on right side of instrument panel, near lower right corner of instrument panel. Gently pry instrument panel upper molding from instrument panel. Turn and pull sensor from instrument panel. Disconnect sensor connector. To install, reverse removal procedure.

HEADLIGHT SWITCH

NOTE: headlight switch can be replaced separately from headlight switch, but to replace headlight switch, headlight switch assembly must be removed.

Removal & Installation – Disconnect negative battery cable. Carefully pull headlight switch assembly from instrument panel. Disconnect switch connectors. Remove headlight switch retaining screws. Remove headlight switch from headlight switch assembly. To install, reverse removal procedure.

WIRING DIAGRAMS

NOTE: For autolamp system wiring diagram, see HEADLIGHT SYSTEMS article.

DESCRIPTION & OPERATION

Vehicle's electronic functions are divided into zones. Front Electronic Module (FEM) controls front portion of vehicle, Rear Electronic Module (REM) controls rear portion of vehicle. These systems rely heavily on Standard Corporate Protocol (SCP) communication network in order to transmit and receive signals. It is very important to understand:

- Where input originates from.
- All information necessary in order for a feature to operate.
- Which module(s) receive(s) input or command message.
- Does module which received input, control output of feature, or does it output a message over SCP communication network to another module.
- Which module controls output of feature.

LIGHTING SYSTEMS

Autolamps – Autolamps are controlled by headlamp switch, autolamp sensor, instrument cluster and FEM. When headlamp switch is in autolamp position, instrument cluster sends an ON or OFF command to FEM, depending on signal from autolamp sensor. FEM will process this information and output appropriate command to headlamps. Autolamps will remain on approximately 20 seconds after ignition switch is turned from RUN position to ACC or OFF position. Autolamps and Daytime Running Lights (DRL) may be configured to be controlled by FEM.

Exterior Lighting – The front exterior lights are controlled by the FEM and the rear exterior lights are controlled by the REM. An additional function of lighting system is a lamp outage function which provides indication to driver if certain bulbs are not functioning. With a bulb out, FEM or REM will send a message to instrument cluster and message center (if equipped). All exterior lights are powered by Switched System Power (SSP), see SWITCHED SYSTEM POWER (SSP). A failure of all or any of SSP features will cause inoperative exterior lighting. When diagnosing exterior lighting, it is essential to determine if all related symptoms and DTC are controlled by SSP feature.

Headlamps – Headlamps are controlled by FEM and Instrument Cluster Module (ICM). Headlamp and multifunction switches. When headlamp switch is in any position, instrument cluster module will send a command to FEM through SCP communication network. FEM will process this information and command appropriate command to headlamps. High beams and flash-to-pass functions are also controlled by multifunction switch. Left and right low and high beam will provide a lamp outage signal. In case of multifunction switch, all headlamp switch or ignition switch invalid or missing data failures, low beams will be illuminated.

Parking, Rear Or License Lamps – Left and right front parking lamps are controlled by FEM. Left and right rear park and license lamps are controlled by REM. When headlamp switch is in headlamp or park position, it sends a signal to instrument cluster. Instrument cluster then sends a command through SCP to FEM or REM, which applies signals to appropriate lamps. Only left and right rear tail lamps provide lamp outage indication. In case of certain headlamp switch, ignition switch or REM failures, rear park lamps will be provided.

Reversing Lamps – Reversing lamps are controlled by REM and PCM. When transmission is placed in reverse, PCM sends a message through SCP to REM. REM processes this information and sends a command to reversing lamps.

Stoplamps – Brake lighting is controlled by REM and Brake Pedal Position (BPP) switch. BPP switch inputs information to REM when brake pedal is depressed. REM then processes information and output to right, left and high mounted stoplamps. Only left and right stoplamps provide lamp outage indication.

Switched System Power (SSP) – SSP is invoked by FEM and REM, and removes power function from relays that provides power to exterior lamps, interior lamps and power door locks. This is only accomplished when FEM and REM are in sleep mode. FEM and REM are in sleep mode when ignition switch is in OFF position and no wake up (inputs) occur for 30 minutes. Modules will not sleep if parking or hazard lamps are active. SSP1, SSP2, SSP3 and SSP4 relays are controlled by SSP function. SSP relays will be energized when FEM or REM are not in sleep mode, and each relay will supply power to multiple features/functions.

Turn Signal, Cornering & Hazard Lamps – FEM controls front left and right turn signals, hazard lamps and cornering lamps. REM controls rear turn signals and hazard lamps When multifunction switch is in left or right turn position or hazard switch is in ON position, they send signals to instrument cluster. Instrument cluster then sends a command through SCP to FEM or REM, which applies signals to appropriate lamps. When a turn signal is commanded ON by instrument cluster, FEM commands appropriate cornering lamp ON.

COMPONENT LOCATIONS

COMPONENT LOCATIONS

Component	Location
Autolamp Sensor	Left Side Of Instrument Panel
Battery Junction Box (BJB)	Left Side Of Engine Compartment
Brake Pedal Position (BPP) Switch	Behind Instrument Panel, On Top Of Brake Pedal
Front Electronics Module (FEM)	[1] Below Left Side Of Instrument Panel.
Fuse Junction Box/Panel (FJB	Behind Left Side Of Instrument Panel
Rear Electronics Module (REM)	[2] Behind Right Side Rear Interior Quarter Panel.
Switched System Power (SSP) Relays – SSP1 & SSP2	In Battery Junction Box (BJB)
Switched System Power (SSP) Relays – SSP3 & SSP4	In Fuse Junction Box/Panel (FJB)

[1] – See Fig. 1.
[2] – See Fig. 2.

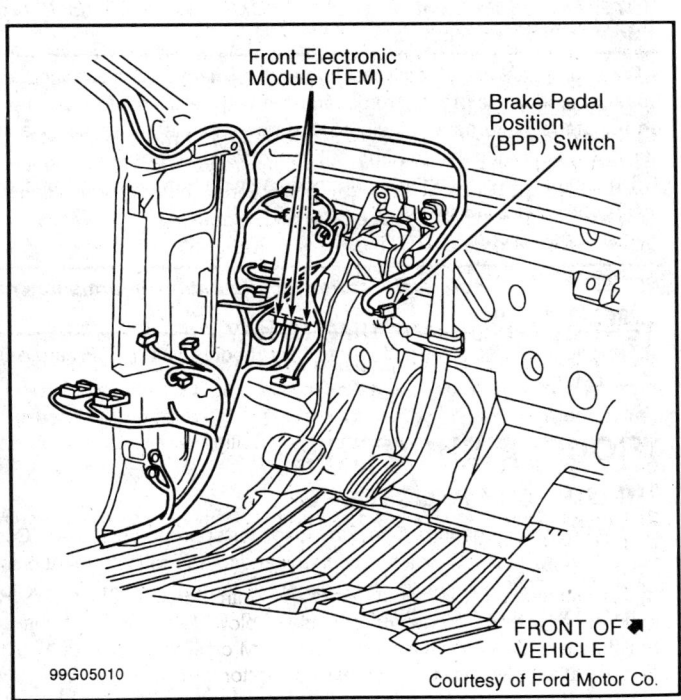

99G05010   Courtesy of Ford Motor Co.

Fig. 1: Front Electronics Module (FEM)

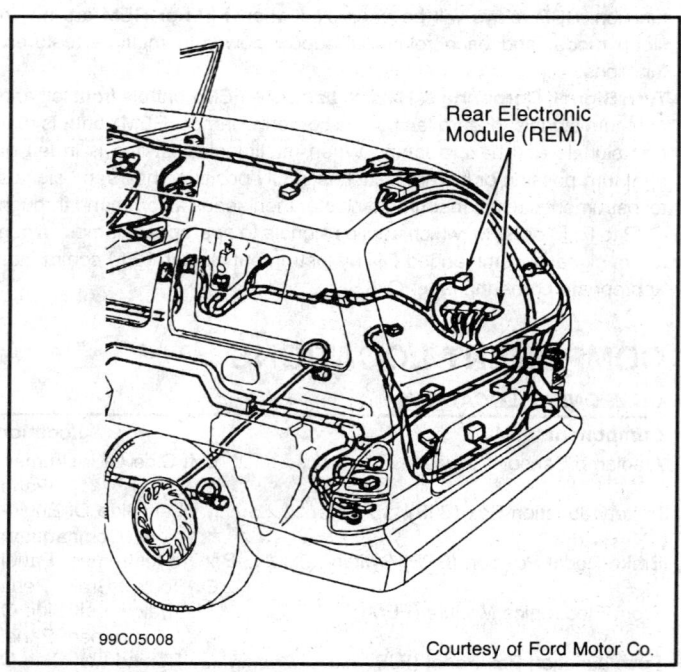

Fig. 2: Rear Electronics Module (REM)

PROGRAMMING

MODULE CONFIGURATION

NOTE: Newly released modules will require configuration after being installed on vehicle. All configurable modules will be packaged in a kit which contains a warning label and multi-language sheet reemphasizing requirements to configure replacement modules.

NOTE: Powertrain Control Module (PCM) has to be flash programmed using a flash cable.

A Ford compatible scan tool must be used to retrieve configuration data from old module before it is removed from vehicle. This information will be transferred into new module so that new module will contain same settings as old module. To carry out configuration process:
1) Upload old information from old module using Ford Service Function (FSF) card and NGS tester.
2) Install new module.

NOTE: NGS will not retain stored configuration information for longer than 24 hours.

3) Download stored information into new module using FSF card and NGS tester.

TROUBLE SHOOTING

PRELIMINARY PROCEDURE

Ensure customer concern. Check all fuses for appropriate system. See FUSE LOCATIONS. Check for mechanical damage to instrument cluster, FEM, REM, multifunction, headlamp or ignition switch. Check for damaged wiring harness, bulbs and/or loose, corroded connections.

FUSE LOCATIONS

System & Fuse Location	Fuse No. (Amp Rating)
Autolamps	
Battery Junction Box	109 (40), 108 (40), 114 (40), 103 (40), 2 (10), 23 (15), 22 (15), 16 (15) & 15 (15)
Central Junction Box	13 (15) & 7 (15)
Headlamps	
Battery Junction Box	109 (40), 108 (40), 114 (40), 103 (40), 2 (10), 23 (15), 16 (15) & 15 (15)
Central Junction Box	8 (20), 16 (10), 9 (10), 28 (10) & 14 (10)
Parking, Rear Or License Lamps	
Battery Junction Box	22 (15) & 23 (15)
Central Junction Box	12 (15) & 13 (15)
Reversing Lamps	
Battery Junction Box	22 (15) & 23 (15)
Central Junction Box	12 (15) & 13 (15)
Stoplamps	
Central Junction Box	13 (15), 7 (15), 12 (20) & 11 (10)
Turn Signal, Cornering & Hazard Lamps	
Battery Junction Box	22 (15) & 23 (15)
Central Junction Box	12 (15) & 13 (15)

CONNECTOR IDENTIFICATION

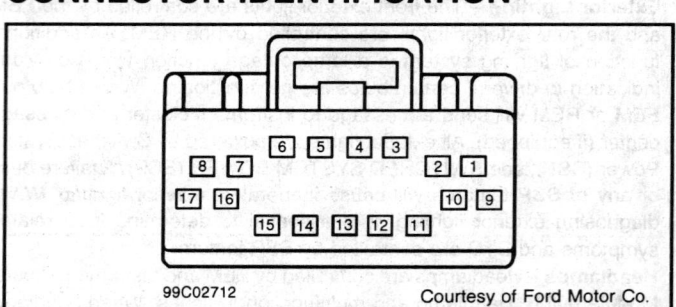

Fig. 3: Front/Rear Electronics Module 17-Pin Connector

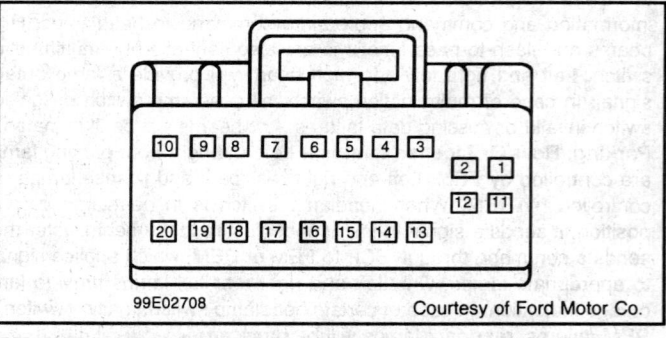

Fig. 4: Front/Rear Electronics Module & Instrument Cluster 20-Pin Connector

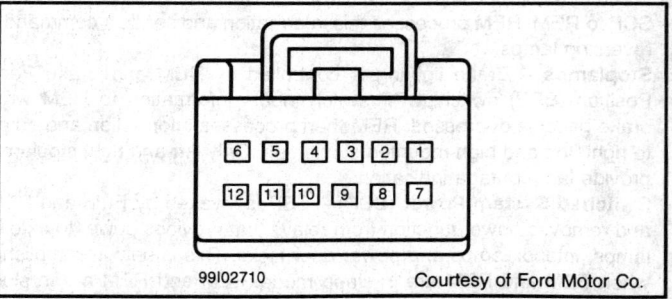

Fig. 5: Front/Rear Electronics Module 12-Pin Connector

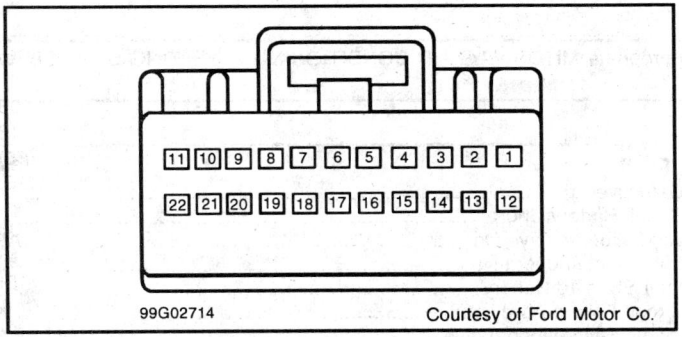

99G02714   Courtesy of Ford Motor Co.

Fig. 6: Front/Rear Electronics Module & Instrument Cluster 22-Pin Connector

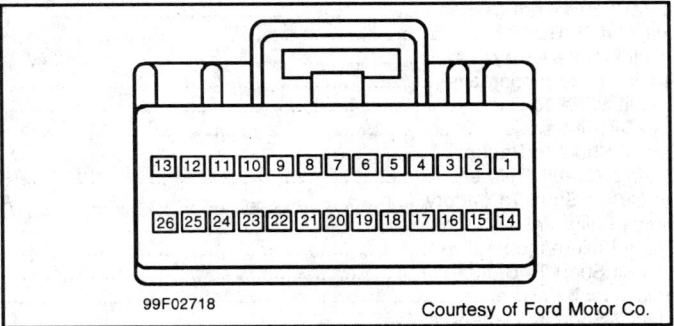

99F02718   Courtesy of Ford Motor Co.

Fig. 7: Front/Rear Electronics Module 26-Pin Connector

SELF-DIAGNOSTICS

NOTE: Many steps in the following tests refer to various connectors. These connectors are identified in illustrations under CONNECTOR IDENTIFICATION. See Figs. 3-7.

RETRIEVING CODES (SCAN TOOL)

NOTE: All diagnostic tests are written specifically for New Generation Star (NGS) tester. Most generic scan tools should be able to perform all test procedures.

Connect New Generation Star (NGS) tester to Data Link Connector (DLC), located beneath instrument panel. Using NGS tester, perform data link diagnostics test. See DATA LINK DIAGNOSTIC TEST under COMMUNICATION NETWORK DIAGNOSTICS in MODULE COMMUNICATIONS NETWORK – WINDSTAR article. If NGS tester responds with CKT914, CKT915 or CKT70=ALL ECUS NO RESP/NOT EQUIP, repair module communications concern. See MODULE COMMUNICATIONS NETWORK – WINDSTAR article. If NGS tester displays NO RESP/NOT EQUIP for Front Electronics Module (FEM), perform TEST A: NO COMMUNICATION WITH FRONT ELECTRONICS MODULE (FEM) under SYSTEM TESTS. If NGS tester displays NO RESP/NOT EQUIP for Rear Electronic Module (REM), perform TEST B: NO COMMUNICATION WITH REAR ELECTRONICS MODULE (REM) under SYSTEM TESTS. If NGS tester displays NO RESP/NOT EQUIP for Instrument Cluster (ICM), perform TEST C: NO COMMUNICATION WITH INSTRUMENT CLUSTER (ICM) under SYSTEM TESTS.

If NGS tester responds with SYSTEM PASSED, retrieve and record continuous DTCs. Erase continuous DTCs. Using NGS tester, perform instrument cluster, FEM and REM self-test. Perform appropriate test in accordance with DTC retrieved. Go to FRONT ELECTRONIC MODULE DTC INDEX, REAR ELECTRONIC MODULE DTC INDEX and/or INSTRUMENT CLUSTER DTC INDEX. Codes listed in these tables are only for testing covered in this article. For complete DTC listing, see MODULE COMMUNICATIONS NETWORK – WINDSTAR article.

If no DTCs are retrieved though instrument cluster, FEM or REM self diagnostics, repair by symptom. See SYMPTOM CHART.

FRONT ELECTRONIC MODULE DTC INDEX

DTC [1]	Description	Test
B1294	Battery Power Relay Circuit Short To Battery	J
B1342	ECU Defective	[2]
B1499	Left Turn Signal Circuit Failure	AA
B1501	Left Turn Signal Circuit Short To Battery	AA
B1503	Right Turn Signal Circuit Failure	Z
B1505	Right Turn Signal Circuit Short To Battery	Z
B2480	LF Corner Lamp Output Short To Battery	AH
B2482	RF Corner Lamp Output Short To Battery	AG
B2491	RF Park Lamp Output Short To Battery	AN
B2493	LF Park Lamp Output Short To Battery	AO
B2501	LF Lamp Low Beam Circuit Failure/Inoperative	F
B2501	LF Lamp Low Beam Circuit Failure/Always On	G
B2502	LF Lamp Low Beam Circuit Short To Battery	F
B2503	RF Lamp Low Beam Circuit Failure	D
B2504	RF Lamp Low Beam Circuit Short To Battery	D
B2505	LF Lamp High Beam Circuit Failure	F
B2506	LF Lamp High Beam Circuit Short To Battery	F
B2507	RF Lamp High Beam Circuit Failure	D
B2508	RF Lamp High Beam Circuit Short To Battery	D
U1041	Invalid Or Missing Data For Vehicle Speed	[3]
U1059	Invalid Or Missing Data For Transaxle/PRNDL	[4]
U1135	Invalid Or Missing Data For Ignition Switch/Starter	[5]
U1178	Invalid Or Missing Data For Climate Control	[6]

[1] – Codes listed in this table are only for testing covered in this article. For complete DTC listing, see MODULE COMMUNICATIONS NETWORK – WINDSTAR article in ACCESSORIES & EQUIPMENT.

[2] – Clear and document all DTC. Perform FEM self-test. If DTC B1342 is retrieved again, replace Front Electronic Module (FEM).

[3] – See appropriate ANTI-LOCK – 4WAL article in BRAKES in appropriate MITCHELL® manual.

[4] – See appropriate ELECTRONIC CONTROLS article in AUTOMATIC TRANSMISSIONS in appropriate MITCHELL® TRANSMISSION SERVICE & REPAIR manual.

[5] – See appropriate STEERING COLUMN SWITCHES article.

FRONT ELECTRONIC MODULE DTC INDEX (Cont.)

[6] – See appropriate AUTOMATIC A/C-HEATER SYSTEMS article in appropriate MITCHELL® AIR CONDITIONING & HEATING SERVICE & REPAIR manual.

REAR ELECTRONIC MODULE DTC INDEX

DTC [1]	Description	Test
B1342	ECU Is Defective	[2]
B1485	Brake Pedal Input Circuit Battery Short	T
B1806	Tail Lamp Output Circuit Failure/Always On	AR
B1806	Tail Lamp Output Circuit Failure/Inoperative	AQ
B1808	Tail Lamp Output Circuit Short To Battery	AQ
B2519	High Mount Stop Lamp Circuit Failure/Always On	W
B2519	High Mount Stop Lamp Circuit Failure/Inoperative	S
B2520	High Mount Stop Lamp Circuit Short To Battery	S
B2523	License Lamp Circuit Failure/Always On	AU
B2523	License Lamp Circuit Failure/Inoperative	AT
B2524	License Lamp Circuit Shrt To Battery	AT
B2527	Left Rear Stop Lamp Circuit Failure/Always On	V
B2527	Left Rear Stop Lamp Circuit Failure/Inoperative	R
B2528	Left Rear Stop Lamp Circuit Short To Battery	R
B2529	Left Rear Turn Lamp Circuit Failure	Y
B2530	Left Rear Turn Lamp Circuit Short To Battery	Y
B2531	Right Rear Reversing Lamp Circuit Failure	AV
B2532	Right Rear Reversing Lamp Circuit Short To Battery	AV
B2533	Right Rear Stop Lamp Circuit Failure/Always On	U
B2533	Right Rear Stop Lamp Circuit Failure/Inoperative	Q
B2534	Right Rear Stop Lamp Circuit Short To Battery	Q
B2535	Right Rear Turn Lamp Circuit Failure	X
B2536	Right Rear Turn Lamp Circuit Short To Battery	X
B2545	System Power Relay Circuit Short To Battery	J
B2565	Right Tail Lamp Circuit Failure/Always On	AR
B2565	Right Tail Lamp Circuit Failure/Inoperative	AP
B2566	Right Tail Lamp Circuit Short To Ground	AP
U1041	Invalid Or Missing Data For Vehicle Speed	[3]
U1059	Invalid Or Missing Data For Transaxle/PRNDL	[4]
U1178	Invalid Or Missing Data For Climate Control	[5]

[1] – Codes listed in this table are only for testing covered in this article. For complete DTC listing, see MODULE COMMUNICATIONS NETWORK – WINDSTAR article.
[2] – Clear and document all DTC. Perform REM self-test. If DTC B1342 is retrieved again, replace Rear Electronic Module (REM).
[3] – See appropriate ANTI-LOCK – 4WAL article in BRAKES in appropriate MITCHELL® manual.
[4] – See appropriate ELECTRONIC CONTROLS article in AUTOMATIC TRANSMISSIONS in appropriate MITCHELL® TRANSMISSION SERVICE & REPAIR manual.
[5] – See appropriate AUTOMATIC A/C-HEATER SYSTEMS article in appropriate MITCHELL® AIR CONDITIONING & HEATING SERVICE & REPAIR manual.

INSTRUMENT CLUSTER DTC INDEX

DTC [1]	Description	Test
B1342	ECU Defective	[2]
B1470	Headlamp Circuit Failure	I
B1875	Turn Signal/Hazard Switch Signal Circuit Failure	AK For (RH) Or AL For (LH)
B2586	Headlamp Mode Circuit Failure	I
U1041	Invalid Or Missing Data For Vehicle Speed	[3]
U1043	Invalid Or Missing Data For Traction Control	[4]
U1123	Invalid Or Missing Data For Odometer	[4]

[1] – Codes listed in this table are only for testing covered in this article. For complete DTC listing, see MODULE COMMUNICATIONS NETWORK – WINDSTAR article.
[2] – Clear and document all DTC. Perform instrument cluster self-test. If DTC B1342 is retrieved again, replace instrument cluster.
[3] – See appropriate SELF-DIAGNOSTICS – EEC-V article in ENGINE PERFORMANCE in appropriate MITCHELL® manual.
[4] – See appropriate ANTI-LOCK – 4WAL article in BRAKES in appropriate MITCHELL® manual.

SYMPTOM CHART

Condition	Test
No Communication With FEM	A
No Communication With REM	B
No Communication With Instrument Cluster	C
RH High/Low Beam Are Inoperative	D
RH High/Low Beam Are Always On	E
LH High/Low Beam Are Inoperative	F
LH High/Low Beam Are Always On	G
Low Beams Are Inoperative	H

SYMPTOM CHART (Cont.)

Condition	Test
High Beams Are Inoperative	I
Power Supply Relay/All SSP Features Are Inoperative	J
Power Supply Relay/SSP1	K
Power Supply Relay/SSP2	L
Power Supply Relay/SSP3	M
Power Supply Relay/SSP4	N
Autolamps Are Inoperative	O
Autolamp Time Delay Inoperative	[1]

SYMPTOM CHART (Cont.)

Condition	Test
Stoplamps Are Inoperative	P
RR Stoplamp Inoperative	Q
LR Stoplamp Inoperative	R
High Mounted Stoplamp Inoperative	S
All Stoplamps Are On Continuously	T
RR Stoplamp On Continuously	U
LR Stoplamp On Continuously	V
High Mounted Stoplamp On Continuously	W
RR Turn Lamp Never/Always On	X
LR Turn Lamp Never/Always On	Y
RF Turn Lamp Never/Always On	Z
LF Turn Lamp Never/Always On	AA
RF Turn Signal & Park Lamps/Never On	AB
LF Turn Signal & Park Lamps/Never On	AC
RF Turn Signal/Park & Cornering Lamps/Never On	AD
LF Turn Signal/Park & Cornering Lamps/Never On	AE
Both Cornering Lamps are Inoperative	AF
RH Cornering Lamp Is Never/Always On	AG
LH Cornering Lamp Is Never/Always On	AH
Rear Hazard Lamps Are Never/Always On	AI
Front Hazard Lamps Are Never/Always On	AJ
RH Turn Signal Lamp Never/Always On	AK
LH Turn Signal Lamp Never/Always On	AL
Hazard Flashers Are Never/Always On	AM
Rear Hazard Flashers Never/Always On & Turn Signals Operate Correctly	1
Front Hazard Flashers Never/Always On & Turn Signals Operate Correctly	2
RF Parking Lamp Inoperative	AN
LF Parking Lamp Inoperative	AO
RR Park & Stop Lamp Inoperative	AP
LR Park & Stop Lamp Inoperative	AQ
RR Parking Lamp On Continuously	AR
LR Parking Lamp On Continuously	AS
License Lamps Inoperative	AT
License Lamps Always On	AU
Reversing Lamps Inoperative	AV
Reversing Lamps Always On	AW
One Reversing Lamp Inoperative	AX
Trailer Lamps Inoperative/Always On Or Electric Trailer Brakes Inoperative	3

1 – Replace FEM and retest system for normal operation.
2 – Replace REM and retest system for normal operation.
3 – For trailer light diagnosis, see appropriate WIRING DIAGRAMS in EXTERIOR LIGHTS article.

CAUTION: Electronic modules are sensitive to static electrical charges. Proper grounding of technician and component is essential to prevent damage.

TEST A: NO COMMUNICATION WITH FRONT ELECTRONICS MODULE (FEM)

NOTE: Cycle ignition switch from OFF to RUN position to enable SSP feature.

1) Turn ignition switch to OFF position. Remove Battery Junction Box (BJB) 10-amp fuse No. 2 and 15-amp fuse No. 23. Ensure both fuses are okay. If either or both fuse(s) are blown, replace fuse(s). If fuses are okay, turn ignition switch to ON position and check voltage between BJB fuses No. 2 input side and No. 23 input side and ground. If voltages are more than 10 volts, reinstall BJB fuses No. 2 and No. 23 and go to next step. If voltages are 10 volts or less, repair BJB power supply circuit(s). See WIRING DIAGRAMS. Clear DTC and repeat FEM self-test.
2) Turn ignition switch to OFF position. Disconnect FEM. Check voltage between FEM harness connectors C346 terminal No. 1 (Light Blue/Red wire), C190 terminal No. 6 (Red wire) and ground. If voltages are more than 10 volts, go to next step. If voltages are 10 volts or less, repair circuit(s). See WIRING DIAGRAMS. Clear DTC and repeat FEM self-test.

3) Turn ignition switch to OFF position. Check resistance between FEM 12-pin connector C190 terminal No. 12 (Black wire), FEM 17-pin connector C192 terminal No's. 11, 13, 14 and 15 (Black wires) and ground. If resistance is less than 5 ohms at every terminal, go to MODULE COMMUNICATIONS NETWORK – WINDSTAR article. If resistance is 5 ohms or more at any terminal, repair circuit(s). See WIRING DIAGRAMS. Repeat self-test and clear DTC.

TEST B: NO COMMUNICATION WITH REAR ELECTRONICS MODULE (REM)

NOTE: Cycle ignition switch from OFF to RUN position to enable system power feature.

1) Turn ignition switch to OFF position. Remove 10-amp fuse No. 16 from Fuse Junction Box/Panel (FJB). Turn ignition switch to ON position. Check voltage between FJB fuse No. 16 input terminal and ground. If voltage is more than 10 volts, reinstall fuse No. 16 and go to next step. If voltage is 10 volts or less, repair FJB power supply circuit. See WIRING DIAGRAMS. Repeat self-test and clear DTC.
2) Turn ignition switch to OFF position. Disconnect REM 20-pin harness connector C343. Check voltage between terminal No. 3 (White/Yellow wire) and ground. Turn ignition switch to ON position. If voltage is more than 10 volts go to next step. If voltage is 10 volts or less, repair circuit. See WIRING DIAGRAMS. Repeat self-test and clear DTC.
3) Turn ignition switch to OFF position. Disconnect REM harness connectors C341 (22-pin) and C342 (26-pin). Check resistances between REM connector C341 terminal No. 12 (Black wire), REM connector C342 terminals No. 11,12, 25 and 26 (Black wires) and ground. If all connector terminal resistances are less than 5 ohms, go to MODULE COMMUNICATIONS NETWORK – WINDSTAR article. If any of the terminals have 5 ohms or more, repair circuit(s). See WIRING DIAGRAMS. Repeat self-test and clear DTC.

TEST C: NO COMMUNICATION WITH INSTRUMENT CLUSTER

1) Turn ignition switch to OFF position. Disconnect instrument cluster 22-pin connector C239, and 20-pin connector C240. Turn igniton switch to ON position. Check voltage between specified harness connector terminals and ground. See INSTRUMENT CLUSTER VOLTAGE. If all readings are 10 volts or more, go to next step. If any reading is less than 10 volts, repair circuit and retest system.

INSTRUMENT CLUSTER VOLTAGE

IC Connector	Pin	Circuit No.
C239	11	1001 (WH/YE)
C240	7	295 (LB/PK)
C240	8 & 9	1112 (WH/LB)

2) Turn ignition switch to OFF position. Check the resistance between instrument cluster harness connector C240 terminal 12 (Black wire) and ground. If resistance is less than 5 ohms, go to MODULE COMMUNICATIONS NETWORK – WINDSTAR article. If resistance is 5 ohms or more, repair open circuit or poor connection in Black wire to ground connector G304, located behind left kick panel.

TEST D: RH HIGH/LOW BEAM ARE INOPERATIVE

NOTE: Cycle ignition switch from OFF to RUN position to enable SSP feature.

1) Retrieve DTC from FEM. If DTC B2503 is retrieved , go to next step. If DTC B2504 is retrieved, go to step 3) . If DTC B2507 is retrieved, go to step 4). If DTC B2508 is retrieved, go to step 5). If no DTC were retrieved, go to step 6).
2) Turn ignition switch to OFF position. Disconnect right side headlamp 3-pin connector C122 and FEM 17-pin connector C192. Check resistance between FEM harness connector C192 terminal No. 7 (Light Green/White wire) and right side headlamp harness connector C122 terminal No. 3 (Light Green/White wire). If resistance is less than 5

ohms, replace FEM. See FRONT ELECTRONICS MODULE (FEM), under REMOVAL & INSTALLATION. Clear DTC and repeat self-test. If resistance is 5 ohms or more, repair circuit. See WIRING DIAGRAMS. Clear DTC and repeat self-test.

3) Turn ignition switch to OFF position. Disconnect right side headlamp 3-pin connector C122 and FEM 17-pin connector C192. Check voltage between right side headlamp harness connector C122 terminal No. 3 (Light Green/White wire) and ground. If voltage is present, repair circuit for short to power. See WIRING DIAGRAMS. Clear DTC and repeat self-test. If no voltage is present, replace FEM. See FRONT ELECTRONICS MODULE (FEM), under REMOVAL & INSTALLATION.

4) Turn ignition switch to OFF position. Disconnect right side headlamp 3-pin connector C122 and FEM 17-pin connector C192. Check resistance between FEM harness connector C192 terminal No. 10 (Yellow/White wire) and right side headlamp harness connector C122 terminal No. 1 (Yellow/White wire). If resistance is less than 5 ohms, replace FEM. See FRONT ELECTRONICS MODULE (FEM), under REMOVAL & INSTALLATION. Clear DTC and repeat self-test. If resistance is 5 ohms or more, repair circuit. See WIRING DIAGRAMS. Clear DTC and repeat self-test.

NOTE: Cycle ignition switch from OFF to RUN position to enable SSP feature.

5) Turn ignition switch to OFF position. Disconnect right side headlamp 3-pin connector C122 and FEM 17-pin connector C192. Check voltage between right side headlamp harness connector C122 terminal No. 10 (Yellow/White wire) and ground. If voltage is present, repair circuit for short to power. See WIRING DIAGRAMS. Clear DTC and repeat self-test. If no voltage is present, replace FEM. See FRONT ELECTRONICS MODULE (FEM), under REMOVAL & INSTALLATION. Clear DTC and repeat self-test.

NOTE: Cycle ignition switch from OFF to RUN position to enable SSP feature.

6) Using NGS tester, select and monitor FEM PIDs R_HIGH and R_LOW ON. Place headlamp switch in ON position. Place high beams ON and then OFF. If FEM PIDs are correct, go to next step. If FEM PIDs are not correct, replace FEM. See FRONT ELECTRONICS MODULE (FEM), under REMOVAL & INSTALLATION. Clear DTC and repeat self-test.

7) Trigger FEM active commands RIGHT LOW and RGHT HIGH ON. If right high and low beams do not operate correctly, trigger FEM active commands RIGHT LOW and RGHT HIGH OFF and go to next step. If right high and low beams operate correctly, replace FEM. See FRONT ELECTRONICS MODULE (FEM), under REMOVAL & INSTALLATION. Clear DTC and repeat self-test.

8) Remove BJB 15-amp fuse No.15. Check voltage between BJB fuse No. 15 input side and ground. If voltage is more than 10 volts, repair circuit (Light Green/Red wire). See WIRING DIAGRAMS. Retest system. If voltage is 10 volts or less, repair power source to BJB. See WIRING DIAGRAMS. Retest system.

TEST E: RH HIGH/LOW BEAM ARE ALWAYS ON

NOTE: Cycle ignition switch from OFF to RUN position to enable SSP feature.

1) Retrieve DTC from FEM. If no DTC are recorded, go to next step. If any DTC are recorded, go to FRONT ELECTRONIC MODULE DTC INDEX.

2) Disconnect FEM 17–pin connector C192. If right side high beam is still illuminated, repair circuit (Yellow/White wire). See WIRING DIAGRAMS. Retest system. If right side low beam is still illuminated, repair circuit (Light Green/White wire). See WIRING DIAGRAMS. Retest system. If headlamps do not remain illuminated, replace FEM. See FRONT ELECTRONICS MODULE (FEM), under REMOVAL & INSTALLATION. Clear DTC and repeat self-test.

TEST F: LH HIGH/LOW BEAM ARE INOPERATIVE

NOTE: Cycle ignition switch from OFF to RUN position to enable SSP feature.

1) Retrieve DTC from FEM. If DTC B2501 is recorded, go to next step. If DTC B2502 is recorded, go to step **3)**. If DTC B2504 is recorded, go to step **4)**. If DTC B2506 is recorded, go to step **5)**. If no DTC are recorded, go to step **6)**.

2) Turn ignition switch to OFF position. Disconnect left side headlamp connector C110 and FEM 17-pin connector C192. Check resistance between FEM harness connector C192 terminal No. 8 (White wire) and left side headlamp harness connector C110 terminal No. 3 (White wire). If resistance is less than 5 ohms, replace FEM. See FRONT ELECTRONICS MODULE (FEM), under REMOVAL & INSTALLATION. Clear DTC and repeat self-test. If resistance is 5 ohms or more, repair circuit. See WIRING DIAGRAMS Clear DTC and repeat self-test.

NOTE: Cycle ignition switch from OFF to RUN position to enable SSP feature.

3) Turn ignition switch to OFF position. Disconnect left side headlamp connector C110 and FEM 17-pin connector C192. Check voltage between left side headlamp connector C110 terminal No. 3 (White wire) and ground. If voltage is present, repair circuit for short to power. See WIRING DIAGRAMS. Clear DTC and repeat self-test. If voltage is not present, replace FEM. See FRONT ELECTRONICS MODULE (FEM), under REMOVAL & INSTALLATION. Clear DTC and repeat self-test.

NOTE: Cycle ignition switch from OFF to RUN position to enable SSP feature.

4) Turn ignition switch to OFF position. Disconnect left side headlamp connector C110 and FEM 17-pin connector C192. Check resistance between FEM harness connector C192 terminal No. 17 (Violet/Yellow wire) and left side headlamp harness connector C110 terminal No. 1 (Violet/Yellow wire). If resistance is less than 5 ohms, replace FEM. See FRONT ELECTRONICS MODULE (FEM), under REMOVAL & INSTALLATION. Clear DTC and repeat self-test. If resistance is 5 ohms or more, repair circuit. See WIRING DIAGRAMS. Clear DTC and repeat self-test.

NOTE: Cycle ignition switch from OFF to RUN position to enable SSP feature.

5) Turn ignition switch to OFF position. Disconnect left side headlamp connector C110 and FEM 17-pin connector C192. Check voltage between FEM harness connector C192 terminal No. 17 (Violet/Yellow wire) and ground. If voltage is present, repair circuit for short to power. See WIRING DIAGRAMS. Clear DTC and repeat self-test. If voltage is not present, replace FEM. See FRONT ELECTRONICS MODULE (FEM), under REMOVAL & INSTALLATION. Clear DTC and repeat self-test. If resistance is 5 ohms or more, repair circuit. Clear DTC and repeat self-test.

NOTE: Cycle ignition switch from OFF to RUN position to enable SSP feature.

6) Using NGS tester, select and monitor FEM PIDs L_HIGH and L_LOW ON. Place headlamp switch in ON position. Place high beams ON and then OFF. If FEM PIDs are correct, go to next step. If FEM PIDs are not correct, replace FEM. See FRONT ELECTRONICS MODULE (FEM), under REMOVAL & INSTALLATION. Clear DTC and repeat self-test.

7) Trigger FEM active commands LEFT HIGH and LEFT LOW ON. If right high and low beams do not operate correctly, trigger FEM active commands LEFT HIGH and LEFT LOW OFF and go to next step. If right high and low beams operate correctly, replace FEM. See FRONT ELECTRONICS MODULE (FEM), under REMOVAL & INSTALLATION. Clear DTC and repeat self-test.

8) Remove Battery Junction Box (BJB) 15-amp fuse No. 16. Check voltage between BJB fuse No. 16 input side and ground. If voltage is more than 10 volts, repair circuit (Yellow/Red wire). See WIRING DIAGRAMS. Retest system. If voltage is 10 volts or less, repair power source to BJB. See WIRING DIAGRAMS. Retest system.

TEST G: LH HIGH/LOW BEAM ARE ALWAYS ON

NOTE: Cycle ignition switch from OFF to RUN position to enable SSP feature.

1) Retrieve DTC from FEM. If no DTC are recorded, go to next step. If any DTC are recorded, go to FRONT ELECTRONIC MODULE DTC INDEX.

NOTE: Cycle ignition switch from OFF to RUN position to enable SSP feature.

2) Disconnect FEM 17–pin connector C192. If left side high beam is still illuminated, repair circuit (Violet/Yellow wire). See WIRING DIAGRAMS. Retest system. If left side low beam is still illuminated, repair circuit (White wire). See WIRING DIAGRAMS. Retest system. If headlamps do not remain illuminated, replace FEM. See FRONT ELECTRONICS MODULE (FEM), under REMOVAL & INSTALLATION. Clear DTC and repeat self-test.

TEST H: LOW BEAMS ARE INOPERATIVE

NOTE: Cycle ignition switch from OFF to RUN position to enable SSP feature.

1) Retrieve DTC from FEM. If no DTC are recorded, go to next step. If any DTC are recorded, go to FRONT ELECTRONIC MODULE DTC INDEX.
2) Place headlamp switch in ON position. If tail lamps are okay, go to next step. If tail lamps are inoperative, go to step **5)**.
3) Place headlamp switch in ON position. Using NGS tester, monitor PIDs L_LOW and R_LOW. If FEM PIDs are correct, go to next step. If FEM PIDs are not correct, go to step **5)**.
4) Trigger FEM active commands LEFT LOW and RIGHT LOW ON and OFF. If headlamps come on and then go off, replace FEM. See FRONT ELECTRONICS MODULE (FEM), under REMOVAL & INSTALLATION. Retest system. If headlamps do not come on and go off, verify symptom. See SYMPTOM CHART.
5) Turn ignition switch to OFF position. Disconnect headlamp switch 8-pin connector C253 and instrument cluster 22-pin connector C239. Check resistance between headlamp switch harness connector C253 terminal No. 4 (Red/White wire) and instrument cluster harness connector C239 terminal No. 10 (Red/White wire). If resistance is less than 5 ohms, go to next step. If resistance is 5 ohms or more, repair circuit. See WIRING DIAGRAMS.
6) Check headlamp switch. See HEADLAMP SWITCH under COMPONENT TESTING. If headlamp switch is okay, replace instrument cluster. See INSTRUMENT CLUSTER/ICM under REMOVAL & INSTALLATION. Retest system. If headlamp switch is not okay, replace headlamp switch. See HEADLAMP SWITCH under REMOVAL & INSTALLATION. Retest system.

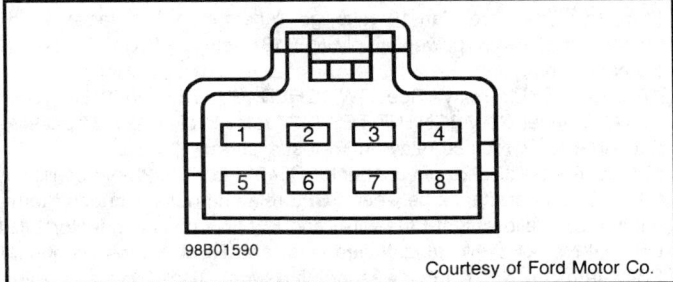

98B01590
Courtesy of Ford Motor Co.

Fig. 8: Headlamp Switch 8-Pin Connector

TEST I: HIGH BEAMS ARE INOPERATIVE

NOTE: Cycle ignition switch from OFF to RUN position to enable SSP feature.

1) Retrieve DTC from FEM. If no DTC are recorded, go to next step. If any DTC are recorded, go to FRONT ELECTRONIC MODULE DTC INDEX.

NOTE: Cycle ignition switch from OFF to RUN position to enable SSP feature.

2) Place high beams in ON position. Using NGS tester, monitor FEM PIDs L_HIGH and R_HIGH. If FEM PIDs are correct, go to next step. If FEM PIDs are not correct, go to step **4)**.
3) Trigger FEM active commands LEFT HIGH and RGHT HIGH ON and then OFF. If headlamps come on and then go off, replace FEM. See FRONT ELECTRONICS MODULE (FEM), under REMOVAL & INSTALLATION. Retest system. If headlamps do not come on and then go off, verify symptom. See SYMPTOM CHART.
4) Disconnect multifunction switch 10-pin connector C263 and instrument cluster 22-pin connector. Check resistance between multifunction switch harness connector C263 terminal No. 7 (Red/Pink wire) and instrument cluster connector C241 terminal No. 20 (Red/Pink wire). If resistance is less than 5 ohms, go to next step. If resistance is 5 ohms or more, repair circuit. See WIRING DIAGRAMS. Retest system.
5) Check multifunction switch, see MULTIFUNCTION SWITCH under COMPONENT TESTS. If multifunction switch is okay, replace instrument cluster. See INSTRUMENT CLUSTER/ICM under REMOVAL & INSTALLATION. Retest system. If multifunction switch is not okay, replace multifunction switch. See MULTIFUNCTION SWITCH under REMOVAL & INSTALLATION. Retest system.

TEST J: POWER SUPPLY RELAY/ALL SSP FEATURES ARE INOPERATIVE

NOTE: Cycle ignition switch from OFF to RUN position to enable SSP feature.

NOTE: Refer to SWITCHED SYSTEM POWER (SSP) under DESCRIPTION & OPERATION and SWITCHED SYSTEM POWER (SSP) RELAYS under COMPONENT TESTS.

1) Retrieve DTC from FEM. If no DTC are recorded, go to next step. If DTC B1294 is recorded, go to step **3)**. If any other DTC are recorded, go to FRONT ELECTRONIC MODULE DTC INDEX.
2) Retrieve DTC from REM. If DTC B2545 is recorded, go to next step. If no DTC are recorded, go to step **9)**. If any other DTC are recorded, go to FRONT ELECTRONIC MODULE DTC INDEX.

NOTE: Cycle ignition switch from OFF to RUN position to enable SSP feature.

3) Turn ignition switch to OFF position. Remove SSP1 relay. Check voltage between SSP1 relay harness connector terminal No. 85 (Yellow/Light Blue wire) and ground. *See Fig. 11.* If voltage is present, go to next step. If voltage is not present, replace SSP1 relay. Clear DTC and repeat self-test.

NOTE: Cycle ignition switch from OFF to RUN position to enable SSP feature.

4) Remove SSP2 relay. Check voltage between SSP2 relay harness connector terminal No. 85 (Yellow/Light Blue wire) and ground. *See Fig. 11.* If voltage is present, go to next step. If voltage is not present, replace SSP2 relay. Clear DTC and repeat self-test.

NOTE: Cycle ignition switch from OFF to RUN position to enable SSP feature.

5) Remove SSP3 relay. Check voltage between SSP3 relay harness connector terminal No. 85 (Yellow/Light Blue wire) and ground. *See*

Fig. 11. If voltage is present, go to next step. If voltage is not present, replace SSP3 relay. Clear DTC and repeat self-test.

NOTE: *Cycle ignition switch from OFF to RUN position to enable SSP feature.*

6) Remove SSP4 relay. Check voltage between SSP4 relay harness connector terminal No. 85 (Yellow/Light Blue wire) and ground. *See Fig. 11.* If voltage is present, go to next step. If voltage is not present, replace SSP4 relay. Clear DTC and repeat self-test.

NOTE: *Cycle ignition switch from OFF to RUN position to enable SSP feature.*

7) Disconnect FEM 22-pin connector C191. Check voltage between FEM harness connector C191 terminal No. 19 (Yellow/Light Blue wire) and ground. If voltage is present, go to next step. If voltage is not present, replace FEM. See FRONT ELECTRONICS MODULE (FEM), under REMOVAL & INSTALLATION. Clear DTC and repeat self-test.

8) Disconnect REM 20-pin connector C343. Check voltage between REM harness connector C343 terminal No. 4 (Yellow/Light Blue wire) and ground. If voltage is present, repair circuit. See WIRING DIAGRAMS. Clear DTC and repeat self-test. If voltage is not present, replace REM. See REAR ELECTRONICS MODULE (REM), under REMOVAL & INSTALLATION. Clear DTC and repeat self-test.

9) Turn ignition switch to OFF position. Disconnect FEM 22-pin connector C191 and REM 20-pin connector C343. Check resistance between REM harness connector C343 terminal No. 4 (Yellow/Light Blue wire) and FEM harness connector C191 terminal No. 21 C. If resistance is less than 5 ohms, go to next step. If resistance is 5 ohms or more, repair circuit. See WIRING DIAGRAMS. Clear DTC and repeat self-test.

10) Remove SSP1, SSP2, SSP3 and SSP4 relays. check resistance between FEM harness connector C191 terminal No. 21 (Yellow/Light Blue wire) and SSP relays harness connectors terminal No. 85 (Yellow/Light Blue wire). If resistances are less than 5 ohms, replace REM. See REAR ELECTRONICS MODULE (REM), under REMOVAL & INSTALLATION. Clear DTC and repeat self-test. If resistances are 5 ohms or more, repair circuit. See WIRING DIAGRAMS. Clear DTC and repeat self-test.

TEST K: POWER SUPPLY RELAY/SSP1

NOTE: *Cycle ignition switch from OFF to RUN position to enable SSP feature.*

NOTE: *Refer to SWITCHED SYSTEM POWER (SSP) under DESCRIPTION & OPERATION and SWITCHED SYSTEM POWER (SSP) RELAYS under COMPONENT TESTS.*

1) Retrieve DTC from FEM. If no DTC are recorded, go to next step. If DTC B1294 is recorded, go to TEST J: POWER SUPPLY RELAY/ALL SSP FEATURES ARE INOPERATIVE. If any other DTC are recorded, go to FRONT ELECTRONIC MODULE DTC INDEX.

2) Remove SSP1 relay. Check voltage between SSP1 relay harness connector terminals No. 86 & No. 30 (Red/Light Green wires) and ground. If voltages are more than 10 volts, go to next step. If voltages are 10 volts or less, repair power supply to BJB. See WIRING DIAGRAMS. Retest system.

3) Check SSP1 relay. See SWITCHED SYSTEM POWER (SSP) RELAYS under COMPONENT TESTS. If relay is okay, go to next step. If it is not okay, replace relay and retest system.

4) Disconnect REM 20-pin connector C343 and FEM 22-pin connector C191. Check resistance between SSP1 relay harness connector terminal No. 85 (Yellow/Light Blue wire), and FEM harness connector C191 terminal No. 21 (Yellow/Light Blue wire) and REM harness connector C343 terminal No. 4 (Yellow/Light Blue wire). If resistance in either circuit is less than 5 ohms, check all SSP controlled features for correct operation. See SWITCHED SYSTEM POWER (SSP) under DESCRIPTION & OPERATION. If all features are inoperative go to TEST J: POWER SUPPLY RELAY/ALL SSP FEATURES ARE INOPERATIVE. If resistances are 5 ohms or more repair circuit. See WIRING DIAGRAMS. Clear DTC and repeat self-test.

TEST L: POWER SUPPLY RELAY/SSP2

NOTE: *Cycle ignition switch from OFF to RUN position to enable SSP feature.*

NOTE: *Refer to SWITCHED SYSTEM POWER (SSP) under DESCRIPTION & OPERATION and SWITCHED SYSTEM POWER (SSP) RELAYS under COMPONENT TESTS.*

1) Retrieve DTC from FEM. If no DTC are recorded, go to next step. If DTC B1294 is recorded, go to TEST J: POWER SUPPLY RELAY/ALL SSP FEATURES ARE INOPERATIVE. If any other DTC are recorded, go to FRONT ELECTRONIC MODULE DTC INDEX.

2) Remove SSP2 relay. Check voltage between SSP2 relay harness connector terminal No. 86 and terminal No. 30 (Red/Light Green wires) and ground. If voltages are more than 10 volts, go to next step. If voltages are 10 volts or less, repair power supply to BJB, see WIRING DIAGRAMS. Retest system.

3) Check SSP2 relay. See SWITCHED SYSTEM POWER (SSP) RELAYS under COMPONENT TESTS. If relay is okay, go to next step. If it is not okay, replace relay and retest system.

4) Disconnect REM 20-pin connector C343 and FEM 22-pin connector C191. Check resistance between SSP2 relay harness connector terminal No. 85 (Yellow/Light Blue wire) and FEM harness connector C191 terminal No. 21 (Yellow/Light Blue wire) and REM harness connector C343 terminal No. 4 (Yellow/Light Blue wire). If resistance in either circuit is less than 5 ohms, check all SSP controlled features for correct operation. See SWITCHED SYSTEM POWER (SSP) under DESCRIPTION & OPERATION. If all features are inoperative go to TEST J: POWER SUPPLY RELAY/ALL SSP FEATURES ARE INOPERATIVE. If resistances are 5 ohms or more repair circuit. See WIRING DIAGRAMS. Clear DTC and repeat self-test.

TEST M: POWER SUPPLY RELAY/SSP3

NOTE: *Cycle ignition switch from OFF to RUN position to enable SSP feature.*

NOTE: *Refer to SWITCHED SYSTEM POWER (SSP) under DESCRIPTION & OPERATION and SWITCHED SYSTEM POWER (SSP) RELAYS under COMPONENT TESTS.*

1) Retrieve DTC from FEM. If no DTC are recorded, go to next step. If DTC B1294 is recorded, go to TEST J: POWER SUPPLY RELAY/ALL SSP FEATURES ARE INOPERATIVE. If any other DTC are recorded, go to FRONT ELECTRONIC MODULE DTC INDEX.

2) Retrieve DTC from REM. If no DTC are recorded, go to next step. If DTC B2545 is recorded, go to TEST J: POWER SUPPLY RELAY/ALL SSP FEATURES ARE INOPERATIVE. If any other DTC are recorded, go to REAR ELECTRONIC MODULE DTC INDEX.

3) Remove SSP3 relay. Check voltage between SSP3 relay harness connector terminal No. 86 and terminal No. 30 (Red wires) and ground. If voltages are more than 10 volts, go to next step. If voltages are 10 volts or less, repair power supply to BJB, see WIRING DIAGRAMS. Retest system.

4) Check SSP3 relay. See SWITCHED SYSTEM POWER (SSP) RELAYS under COMPONENT TESTS. If relay is okay, go to next step. If it is not okay, replace relay and retest system.

5) Disconnect REM 20-pin connector C343 and FEM 22-pin connector C191. Check resistance between SSP3 relay harness connector terminal No. 85 (Yellow/Light Blue wire) and FEM harness connector C191 terminal No. 21 (Yellow/Light Blue wire) and REM harness connector C343 terminal No. 4 (Yellow/Light Blue wire). If resistance in either circuit is less than 5 ohms, check all SSP controlled features for correct operation. See SWITCHED SYSTEM POWER (SSP) under DESCRIPTION & OPERATION. If all features are inoperative go to TEST J: POWER SUPPLY RELAY/ALL SSP FEATURES ARE INOPERATIVE. If resistances are 5 ohms or more repair circuit. See WIRING DIAGRAMS. Clear DTC and repeat self-test.

TEST N: POWER SUPPLY RELAY/SSP4

NOTE: Cycle ignition switch from OFF to RUN position to enable SSP feature.

NOTE: Refer to SWITCHED SYSTEM POWER (SSP) under DESCRIPTION & OPERATION and SWITCHED SYSTEM POWER (SSP) RELAYS under COMPONENT TESTS.

1) Retrieve DTC from FEM. If no DTC are recorded, go to next step. If DTC B1294 is recorded, go to TEST J: POWER SUPPLY RELAY/ALL SSP FEATURES ARE INOPERATIVE. If any other DTC are recorded, go to FRONT ELECTRONIC MODULE DTC INDEX.

2) Retrieve DTC from REM. If no DTC are recorded, go to next step. If DTC B2545 is recorded, go to TEST J: POWER SUPPLY RELAY/ALL SSP FEATURES ARE INOPERATIVE. If any other DTC are recorded, go to REAR ELECTRONIC MODULE DTC INDEX.

3) Remove SSP4 relay. Check voltage between SSP4 relay harness connector terminal No. 86 and terminal No. 30 (Orange/Red wires) and ground. If voltages are more than 10 volts, go to next step. If voltages are 10 volts or less, repair power supply to BJB, see WIRING DIAGRAMS. Retest system.

4) Check SSP4 relay. See SWITCHED SYSTEM POWER (SSP) RELAYS under COMPONENT TESTS. If relay is okay, go to next step. If it is not okay, replace relay and retest system.

5) Disconnect REM 20-pin connector C343 and FEM 22-pin connector C191. Check resistance between SSP4 relay harness connector terminal No. 85 (Yellow/Light Blue wire) and FEM harness connector C191 terminal No. 21 (Yellow/Light Blue wire) and REM harness connector C343 terminal No. 4 (Yellow/Light Blue wire). If resistance in either circuit is less than 5 ohms, check all SSP controlled features for correct operation. See SWITCHED SYSTEM POWER (SSP) under DESCRIPTION & OPERATION. If all features are inoperative go to TEST J: POWER SUPPLY RELAY/ALL SSP FEATURES ARE INOPERATIVE. If resistances are 5 ohms or more repair circuit. See WIRING DIAGRAMS. Clear DTC and repeat self-test.

TEST O: AUTOLAMPS ARE INOPERATIVE

NOTE: Cycle ignition switch from OFF to RUN position to enable SSP feature.

1) Place headlamp switch in ON position. If low beams illuminate, go to next step. If low beams do not illuminate, go to TEST H: LOW BEAMS ARE INOPERATIVE.

2) Check headlamp switch, see HEADLAMP SWITCH under COMPONENT TESTS. If headlamp switch is okay, go to next step. If headlamp switch is not okay, replace headlamp switch. See HEADLAMP SWITCH under REMOVAL & INSTALLATION. Retest system.

3) Place headlamp switch in autolamps position. Using NGS tester, monitor instrument cluster PID LIGHTSN while illuminating light sensor amplifier, then remove light source. If PID indicates NO with light source applied and YES with light source removed, go to next step. If PID does not indicate NO with light source applied and YES with light source removed, go to step **8)**.

4) Turn ignition switch to OFF position. Disconnect autolamp sensor 6-pin connector C260, *see Fig. 9*. Turn ignition switch to ON position. Check voltage between autolamp sensor harness connector C260 terminal No. 6 (Red/Yellow wire) and ground. If voltage is more than 10 volts, go to next step. If volts are 10 volts or less, repair circuit. See WIRING DIAGRAMS. Retest system.

5) Check resistance between autolamp sensor harness connector C260 terminal No. 1 (Black wire). If resistance is less than 5 ohms, go to next step. If resistance is 5 ohms or more, repair circuit. See WIRING DIAGRAMS. Retest system.

6) Turn ignition switch to OFF position. Disconnect instrument cluster 20-pin connector C240. Turn ignition switch to ON position. Check voltage between instrument cluster harness connector C240 terminal No. 2 (Yellow/White wire) and ground. If voltage is not present, go to next step. If voltage is present, repair circuit. See WIRING DIAGRAMS. Retest system.

7) Turn ignition switch to OFF position. Check resistance between instrument cluster harness connector C240 terminal No. 2 (Yellow/White wire) and autolamp sensor harness connector C260 terminal No. 4 (Yellow/White wire), and ground. If resistance is more than 10 k/ohms between instrument cluster C240 terminal No. 2 (Yellow/White wire) and ground and less than 5 ohms between instrument cluster harness connector C240 terminal No. 2 (Yellow/White wire) and autolamp sensor harness connector C260 terminal No. 4 (Yellow/White wire), replace autolamp sensor. Retest system. If resistance is 10 k/ohms or less between instrument cluster C240 terminal No. 2 (Yellow /White wire) and ground, and 5 ohms or more between instrument cluster harness connector C240 terminal No. 2 (Yellow /White wire) and autolamp sensor harness connector C260 terminal No. 4 (Yellow/White wire), Repair circuit. See WIRING DIAGRAMS. Retest system.

8) Disconnect headlamp switch 8-pin connector C253. Turn ignition switch to ON position. Check voltage between headlamp switch harness connector C253 terminal No. 5 (Dark Blue/White wire) and ground. If voltage is not present, go to next step. If voltage is present, repair circuit. See WIRING DIAGRAMS. Retest system.

9) Disconnect instrument cluster 22-pin connector C241. Check resistance between headlamp switch harness connector C253 terminal No. 5 (Dark Blue/White wire) and ground; and between headlamp switch harness connector C253 terminal No. 5 (Dark Blue/White wire) and instrument cluster harness connector C241 terminal No. 3 (Dark Blue/White wire). If resistance is more than 10 k/ohms between headlamp switch harness connector C253 terminal No. 5 (Dark Blue/White wire) and ground; and less than 5 ohms between headlamp switch harness connector C253 terminal No. 5 (Dark Blue/White wire) and instrument cluster harness connector C241 terminal No. 3 (Dark Blue/White wire), replace instrument cluster. See INSTRUMENT CLUSTER/ICM under REMOVAL & INSTALLATION. Clear DTC and repeat self-test. If resistance is 10 k/ohms or less between headlamp switch harness connector C253 terminal No. 5 (Dark Blue/White wire) and ground; and 5 ohms or more between headlamp switch harness connector C253 terminal No. 5 (Dark Blue/White wire) and instrument cluster harness connector C241 terminal No. 3 (Dark Blue/White wire), repair circuit. See WIRING DIAGRAMS. Retest system.

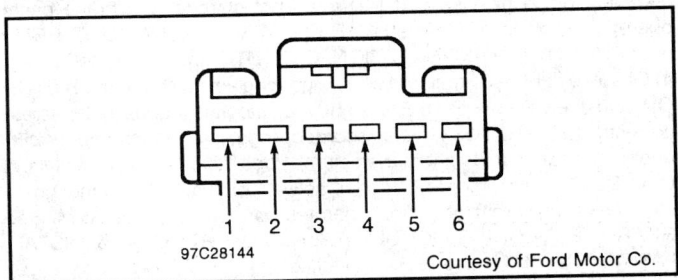

97C28144   Courtesy of Ford Motor Co.

Fig. 9: Autolamp Sensor 6-pin Connector

TEST P: STOPLAMPS ARE INOPERATIVE

NOTE: Cycle ignition switch from OFF to RUN position to enable SSP feature.

1) Retrieve DTC from REM. If no DTC are recorded, go to next step. If DTC are recorded, go to REAR ELECTRONIC MODULE DTC INDEX. Refer to headlamps.

2) Using NGS tester, observe stoplamps while triggering REM active commands; L STOP,R STOP and H MNT STP, ON and OFF. If all stoplamps operate correctly, TRIGGER REM active commands OFF and go to next step. If any stoplamps do not operate correctly, see SYMPTOM CHART under SELF-DIAGNOSTICS. If no stoplamps operate, replace REM. See REAR ELECTRONICS MODULE (REM), under REMOVAL & INSTALLATION. Clear DTC and repeat self-test.

3) Monitor REM PID BOO while depressing and releasing brake pedal. If PID changed value when pedal was depressed and released, go to next step. If PID did not change value while depressing and releasing pedal, TRIGGER PID OFF and go to step 5.

4) Monitor REM PIDs L_BRK_L, R_BRK_L and HMNTSTP WHILE depressing and releasing brake pedal. If PIDs change when brake pedal is operated, see SYMPTOM CHART under SELF-DIAGNOSTICS. If PIDs do not change with brake pedal operation, replace REM. See REAR ELECTRONICS MODULE (REM), under REMOVAL & INSTALLATION. Clear DTC and repeat self-test.

5) Disconnect Brake Pedal Position (BPP) switch 2-pin connector C251. Check voltage between BPP switch harness connector Terminal No. 2 (Light Green/Red wire) and ground. If voltage is more than 10 volts, go to next step. If voltage is 10 volts or less, repair circuit. See WIRING DIAGRAMS. Retest system.

6) Check resistance between BPP switch terminal No. 1 and terminal No. 2 while depressing and releasing brake pedal. If resistance is more than 10 k/ohms with brake pedal released and less than 5 ohms with brake pedal depressed, go to next step. If resistance is 10 k/ohms or less with brake pedal released and more than 5 ohms with brake pedal depressed, replace BPP. See BRAKE PEDAL POSITION (BPP) SWITCH under REMOVAL & INSTALLATION. Retest system.

7) Disconnect REM 22-pin connector C341. Check resistance between BPP switch harness connector C251 terminal No.1 (Red/Light Green wire) and REM harness connector C341 terminal No.13 (Red/Light Green wire). If resistance is less than 5 ohms, replace REM. See REAR ELECTRONICS MODULE (REM), under REMOVAL & INSTALLATION. Clear DTC and repeat self-test. If resistance is 5 ohms or more, repair circuit. See WIRING DIAGRAMS. Retest system.

TEST Q: RR STOPLAMP INOPERATIVE

NOTE: Cycle ignition switch from OFF to RUN position to enable SSP feature.

1) Retrieve DTC from REM. If no DTC are recorded, go to next step. If DTC B2534 or B2533 are recorded, go to step **3)**. For all other DTC, go to REAR ELECTRONIC MODULE DTC INDEX. Refer to headlamps.

2) Place headlamp switch in parking lamp position. If right rear parking lamp illuminates, go to next step. If right rear parking lamp does not illuminate, go to step **5)**.

3) Using NGS tester, monitor REM PID R_BRK_L. Depress and release brake pedal. If PID changes value when brake pedal is depressed and released, go to next step. If PID does not change with brake pedal operation, replace REM. See REAR ELECTRONICS MODULE (REM), under REMOVAL & INSTALLATION. Clear DTC and repeat self-test.

4) Observe right rear stoplamp while triggering active command R STOP ON and then R STOP OFF. If right rear stoplamp does not operate correctly and DTC B2533 was recorded, trigger active command OFF and go to next step. If right rear stoplamp does not operate correctly and DTC B2534 was recorded, trigger active command OFF and go to step **7)** . If right rear stoplamp operates correctly, replace REM. See REAR ELECTRONICS MODULE (REM), under REMOVAL & INSTALLATION. Clear DTC and repeat self-test.

NOTE: Cycle ignition switch from OFF to RUN position to enable SSP feature.

5) Remove right rear stoplamp bulb and check voltage between right rear stop/park lamp harness socket (Gray/Light Blue wire) and ground. If voltage is more than 10 volts, go to next step. If voltage is 10 volts or less, repair as necessary. Clear DTC and repeat self-test.

6) Disconnect REM 17-pin connector C340. Check resistance between REM harness connector C340 terminal No.1 (Gray/Light Blue wire) and right rear stop/park lamp harness connector C401 terminal No. 3 (Gray/Light Blue wire). If resistance is less than 5 ohms, go to next step. If resistance is 5 ohms or more, repair circuit. See WIRING DIAGRAMS. Retest system.

NOTE: Cycle ignition switch from OFF to RUN position to enable SSP feature.

7) Check voltage between REM harness connector C340 terminal No. 1 (Gray/Light Blue wire) and ground. If voltage is present, repair circuit.

See WIRING DIAGRAMS. Clear DTC and repeat self-test. If voltage is not present, replace REM. See REAR ELECTRONICS MODULE (REM), under REMOVAL & INSTALLATION. Clear DTC and repeat self-test.

TEST R: LR STOPLAMP INOPERATIVE

NOTE: Cycle ignition switch from OFF to RUN position to enable SSP feature.

1) Retrieve DTC from REM. If no DTC are recorded, go to next step. If DTC B2528 or B2527 are recorded, go to step **3)**. For all other DTC, go to REAR ELECTRONIC MODULE DTC INDEX. Refer to headlamps.

2) Place headlamp switch in parking lamp position. If left rear parking lamp illuminates, go to next step. If left rear parking lamp does not illuminate, go to step **5)**.

3) Using NGS tester, monitor REM PID L_BRK_L. Depress and release brake pedal. If PID changes value when brake pedal is depressed and released, go to next step. If PID does not change with brake pedal operation, replace REM. See REAR ELECTRONICS MODULE (REM), under REMOVAL & INSTALLATION. Clear DTC and repeat self-test.

4) Observe left rear stoplamp while triggering active command L STOP ON and then L STOP OFF. If DTC B2527 was recorded and left rear stoplamp does not operate correctly, trigger active command OFF and go to next step. If DTC B2528 was recorded and left rear stoplamp does not operate correctly, trigger active command OFF and go to step **7)**. If left rear stoplamp operates correctly, replace REM. See REAR ELECTRONICS MODULE (REM), under REMOVAL & INSTALLATION. Clear DTC and repeat self-test.

NOTE: Cycle ignition switch from OFF to RUN position to enable SSP feature.

5) Remove left rear stoplamp bulb and check voltage between left rear stop/park lamp harness socket (White/Red wire) and ground. If voltage is more than 10 volts, go to next step. If voltage is 10 volts or less, repair as necessary. Clear DTC and repeat self-test.

6) Disconnect REM 17-pin connector C340. Check resistance between REM harness connector C340 terminal No.2 (White/Red wire) and left rear stop/park lamp harness connector C404 terminal No. 3 (White/Red wire). If resistance is less than 5 ohms, go to next step. If resistance is 5 ohms or more, repair circuit. See WIRING DIAGRAMS. Retest system.

NOTE: Cycle ignition switch from OFF to RUN position to enable SSP feature.

7) Check voltage between REM harness connector C340 terminal No. 2 (White/Red wire) and ground. If voltage is present, repair circuit. See WIRING DIAGRAMS. Clear DTC and repeat self-test. If voltage is not present, replace REM. See REAR ELECTRONICS MODULE (REM), under REMOVAL & INSTALLATION. Clear DTC and repeat self-test.

TEST S: HIGH MOUNTED STOPLAMP INOPERATIVE

NOTE: Cycle ignition switch from OFF to RUN position to enable SSP feature.

1) Retrieve DTC from REM. If no DTC are recorded, go to next step. If DTC B2520 or B2519 are recorded, go to step **3)**. For all other DTC, go to REAR ELECTRONIC MODULE DTC INDEX. Refer to headlamps.

2) Observe stoplamps while depressing brake pedal If both stoplamps illuminate, go to next step. If neither stoplamp illuminates, see SYMPTOM CHARTunder SELF-DIAGNOSTICS.

3) Using NGS tester, monitor REM PID HMNTSTP. Depress and release brake pedal. If PID changes value when brake pedal is depressed and released, go to next step. If PID does not change with brake pedal operation, replace REM. See REAR ELECTRONICS MODULE (REM), under REMOVAL & INSTALLATION. Clear DTC and repeat self-test.

4) Observe high mounted stoplamp while triggering active command H MNT STP ON and then H MNT STP OFF. If high mounted stoplamp does not operate correctly and DTC B2519 was recorded, trigger active

command OFF and go to next step. If high mounted stoplamp does not operate correctly and DTC B2520 was recorded, trigger active command OFF and go to step 7). If high mount stoplamp operates correctly, replace REM. See REAR ELECTRONICS MODULE (REM), under REMOVAL & INSTALLATION. Clear DTC and repeat self-test.

NOTE: Cycle ignition switch from OFF to RUN position to enable SSP feature.

5) Remove high mount stoplamp bulbs and check voltage between high mounted stop/park lamp harness socket (Tan/Light Blue wire) and ground. If voltage is more than 10 volts, go to next step. If voltage is 10 volts or less, repair as necessary. Clear DTC and repeat self-test.

6) Disconnect REM 17-pin connector C340. Check resistance between REM harness connector C340 terminal No.17 (Tan/Light Blue wire) and high mounted stoplamp harness connector C903 terminal No. 2 (Tan/Light Blue wire). If resistance is less than 5 ohms, go to next step. If resistance is 5 ohms or more, repair circuit. See WIRING DIAGRAMS. Retest system.

NOTE: Cycle ignition switch from OFF to RUN position to enable SSP feature.

7) Check voltage between REM harness connector C340 terminal No. 17 (Tan/Light Blue wire) and ground. If voltage is present, repair circuit. See WIRING DIAGRAMS. Clear DTC and repeat self-test. If voltage is not present, replace REM. See REAR ELECTRONICS MODULE (REM), under REMOVAL & INSTALLATION. Clear DTC and repeat self-test.

TEST T: ALL STOPLAMPS ARE ON CONTINUOUSLY

NOTE: Cycle ignition switch from OFF to RUN position to enable SSP feature.

1) Retrieve DTC from REM. If DTC B1485 is recorded, go to next step. For all other DTC, go to REAR ELECTRONIC MODULE DTC INDEX, refer to headlamps. If no DTC are recorded, go to step 5.

2) Using NGS tester, monitor REM PID BOO while depressing and releasing brake pedal. If PID does not change value when brake pedal is depressed and then released, go to next step. If PID changes value when brake pedal is depressed and then released, go to step 5.

3) Disconnect Brake Pedal Position (BPP) switch connector C251. If stoplamps do not turn OFF, go to next step. If stoplamps turn OFF, repair circuit. See WIRING DIAGRAMS. Clear DTC and repeat self-test.

NOTE: Cycle ignition switch from OFF to RUN position to enable SSP feature.

4) Disconnect REM 22-pin connector C341. Check voltage between REM harness connector C341 terminal 13 (Red/Light Green wire) and ground. If voltage is present, repair circuit. See WIRING DIAGRAMS. Clear DTC and repeat self-test. If voltage is not present, replace REM. See REAR ELECTRONICS MODULE (REM), under REMOVAL & INSTALLATION. Clear DTC and repeat self-test.

5) Using NGS tester, monitor REM PIDs L_BRK_L, R_BRK_L and HMNTSTP, while depressing and releasing brake pedal. If PIDs change when brake pedal is depressed and then released, go to SYMPTOM CHART. If PIDs do not change when brake pedal is depressed and then released, replace REM. See REAR ELECTRONICS MODULE (REM), under REMOVAL & INSTALLATION. Clear DTC and repeat self-test.

TEST U: RR STOPLAMP ON CONTINUOUSLY

NOTE: Cycle ignition switch from OFF to RUN position to enable SSP feature.

1) Retrieve DTC from REM. If no DTC are recorded, go to next step. If DTC B2533 is recorded, go to step 3). For all other DTC, go to REAR ELECTRONIC MODULE DTC INDEX. Refer to headlamps.

2) Using NGS tester, monitor REM PID R_BRK_L while depressing and releasing brake pedal. If PID does not change value when brake pedal is operated, trigger REM PIDs OFF and go to next step. If PID changes

value when brake pedal is operated, replace REM. See REAR ELECTRONICS MODULE (REM), under REMOVAL & INSTALLATION. Clear DTC and repeat self-test.

3) Disconnect REM 17-pin connector and remove right rear stop/park lamp bulb. Check resistance between REM harness connector C340 terminal No. 1 (Gray/Light Blue wire) and ground. If resistance is more than 10 k/ohms, replace REM. See REAR ELECTRONICS MODULE (REM), under REMOVAL & INSTALLATION. Clear DTC and repeat self-test. If resistance is 10 k/ohms or less, repair circuit. See WIRING DIAGRAMS. Clear DTC and repeat self-test.

TEST V: LR STOPLAMP ON CONTINUOUSLY

NOTE: Cycle ignition switch from OFF to RUN position to enable SSP feature.

1) Retrieve DTC from REM. If no DTC are recorded, go to next step. If DTC B2527 is recorded, go to step 3). For all other DTC, go to REAR ELECTRONIC MODULE DTC INDEX. Refer to headlamps.

2) Using NGS tester, monitor REM PID L_BRK_L while depressing and releasing brake pedal. If PID does not change value when brake pedal is operated, trigger REM PIDs OFF and go to next step. If PID changes value when brake pedal is operated, replace REM. See REAR ELECTRONICS MODULE (REM), under REMOVAL & INSTALLATION. Clear DTC and repeat self-test.

3) Disconnect REM 17-pin connector 340 and remove left rear stop/park lamp bulb. Check resistance between REM harness connector C340 terminal No. 2 (White/Red wire) and ground. If resistance is more than 10 k/ohms, replace REM. See REAR ELECTRONICS MODULE (REM), under REMOVAL & INSTALLATION. Clear DTC and repeat self-test. If resistance is 10 k/ohms or less, repair circuit. See WIRING DIAGRAMS. Clear DTC and repeat self-test.

TEST W: HIGH MOUNTED STOPLAMP ON CONTINUOUSLY

NOTE: Cycle ignition switch from OFF to RUN position to enable SSP feature.

1) Retrieve DTC from REM. If no DTC are recorded, go to next step. If DTC B2519 is recorded, go to step 3). For all other DTC, go to REAR ELECTRONIC MODULE DTC INDEX. Refer to headlamps.

2) Using NGS tester, monitor REM PID HMNTSTP while depressing and releasing brake pedal. If PID does not change value when brake pedal is operated, trigger REM PIDs OFF and go to next step. If PID changes value when brake pedal is operated, replace REM. See REAR ELECTRONICS MODULE (REM), under REMOVAL & INSTALLATION. Clear DTC and repeat self-test.

3) Disconnect REM 17-pin connector 340 and remove high mounted stoplamp bulbs. Check resistance between REM harness connector C340 terminal No. 17 (Tan/Light Blue wire) and ground. If resistance is more than 10 k/ohms, replace REM. See REAR ELECTRONICS MODULE (REM), under REMOVAL & INSTALLATION. Clear DTC and repeat self-test. If resistance is 10 k/ohms or less, repair circuit. See WIRING DIAGRAMS. Clear DTC and repeat self-test.

TEST X: RR TURN LAMP NEVER/ALWAYS ON

NOTE: Cycle ignition switch from OFF to RUN position to enable SSP feature.

1) Retrieve DTC from REM. If no DTC are recorded and right rear turn signal is never on, go to next step. If no DTC are recorded and right rear turn signal is always on, go to step 4). If DTC B2535 is recorded, go to step 5). If DTC B2536 is recorded, go to step 8). For all other DTC, go to REAR ELECTRONIC MODULE DTC INDEX. Refer to headlamps.

2) Place right side turn signal ON using turn signal switch. If right front turn signal lamp illuminates, go to next step. If right front turn signal lamp does not illuminate, go to TEST AK: RH TURN SIGNAL LAMP NEVER/ALWAYS ON under SYSTEM TESTS.

3) Using NGS tester, monitor REM PID RR_TURN. Place right side turn signal in ON position. If PID changes value with turn signal switch ON, go to next step. If PID does not change value with turn signal switch in ON position, replace REM. See REAR ELECTRONICS MODULE (REM), under REMOVAL & INSTALLATION. Clear DTC and repeat self-test.

4) Observe right rear turn signal lamp while triggering REM active command RR TURN ON and then RR TURN OFF. If right rear turn signal does not operate correctly, go to next step. If right rear turn signal operates correctly, replace REM. See REAR ELECTRONICS MODULE (REM), under REMOVAL & INSTALLATION. Clear DTC and repeat self-test.

NOTE: Cycle ignition switch from OFF to RUN position to enable SSP feature.

5) Remove right rear turn signal bulb. Check voltage between right rear turn signal lamp socket (Gray/Red wire) and ground. If voltage is more than 10 volts, go to next step. If voltage is 10 volts or less, repair circuit. See WIRING DIAGRAMS. Clear DTC and repeat self-test.

6) Disconnect REM 17-pin connector C340. Check resistance between REM harness connector C340 terminal No. 4 (Red/Pink wire) and right rear turn signal lamp socket (Red/Pink wire). If resistance is less than 5 ohms, go to next step. If resistance is 5 ohms or more, repair circuit. See WIRING DIAGRAMS. Clear DTC and repeat self-test.

7) Check resistance between REM harness connector C340 terminal No. 4 (Red/Pink wire) and ground. If resistance is more than 10 k/ohms, go to next step. If resistance is 10 k/ohms or less, repair circuit. See WIRING DIAGRAMS. Clear DTC and repeat self-test.

NOTE: Cycle ignition switch from OFF to RUN position to enable SSP feature.

8) Disconnect REM 17-pin connector C340 and remove right rear turn signal bulb. Check voltage between REM harness connector C340 terminal No. 4 (Red/Pink wire) and ground. If voltage is present, repair circuit. See WIRING DIAGRAMS. Clear DTC and repeat self-test. If voltage is not present, replace REM. See REAR ELECTRONICS MODULE (REM), under REMOVAL & INSTALLATION. Clear DTC and repeat self-test.

TEST Y: LR TURN LAMP NEVER/ALWAYS ON

NOTE: Cycle ignition switch from OFF to RUN position to enable SSP feature.

1) Retrieve DTC from REM. If no DTC are recorded and left rear turn signal is never on, go to next step. If no DTC are recorded and left rear turn signal is always on, go to step 4). If DTC B2529 is recorded, go to step 5). If DTC B2530 is recorded, go to step 8). For all other DTC, go to REAR ELECTRONIC MODULE DTC INDEX. Refer to headlamps.

2) Place left side turn signal ON using turn signal switch. If left front turn signal lamp illuminates, go to next step. If left front turn signal lamp does not illuminate, go to TEST AL: LH TURN SIGNAL LAMP NEVER/ALWAYS ON under SYSTEM TESTS.

3) Using NGS tester, monitor REM PID LR_TURN. Place left side turn signal in ON position. If PID changes value with turn signal switch ON, go to next step. If PID does not change value with turn signal switch in ON position, replace REM. See REAR ELECTRONICS MODULE (REM), under REMOVAL & INSTALLATION. Clear DTC and repeat self-test.

4) Observe left rear turn signal lamp while triggering REM active command LR TURN ON and then LR TURN OFF. If left rear turn signal does not operate correctly, go to next step. If left rear turn signal operates correctly, replace REM. See REAR ELECTRONICS MODULE (REM), under REMOVAL & INSTALLATION. Clear DTC and repeat self-test.

NOTE: Cycle ignition switch from OFF to RUN position to enable SSP feature.

5) Remove left rear turn signal bulb. Check voltage between left rear turn signal lamp socket (Gray/Red wire) and ground. If voltage is more than 10 volts, go to next step. If voltage is 10 volts or less, repair circuit. See WIRING DIAGRAMS. Clear DTC and repeat self-test.

6) Disconnect REM 17-pin connector C340. Check resistance between REM harness connector C340 terminal No.3 (White/Orange wire) and left rear turn signal lamp socket (White/Orange wire). If resistance is less than 5 ohms, go to next step. If resistance is 5 ohms or more, repair circuit. See WIRING DIAGRAMS. Clear DTC and repeat self-test.

7) Check resistance between REM harness connector C340 terminal No. 3 (White/Orange wire) and ground. If resistance is more than 10 k/ohms, go to next step. If resistance is 10 k/ohms or less, repair circuit. See WIRING DIAGRAMS. Clear DTC and repeat self-test.

NOTE: Cycle ignition switch from OFF to RUN position to enable SSP feature.

8) Disconnect REM 17-pin connector C340 and remove left rear turn signal bulb. Check voltage between REM harness connector C340 terminal No. 3 (White/Orange wire) and ground. If voltage is present, repair circuit. See WIRING DIAGRAMS. Clear DTC and repeat self-test. If voltage is not present, replace REM. See REAR ELECTRONICS MODULE (REM), under REMOVAL & INSTALLATION. Clear DTC and repeat self-test.

TEST Z: RF TURN LAMP NEVER/ALWAYS ON

NOTE: Cycle ignition switch from OFF to RUN position to enable SSP feature.

1) Retrieve DTC from FEM. If DTC B1503 is recorded, go to next step. If DTC B1505 is recorded, go to step 4). If no DTC are recorded, go to step 5). For all other DTC, go to FRONT ELECTRONIC MODULE DTC INDEX. Refer to headlamps.

2) Remove right front turn signal bulb and disconnect FEM 17-pin connector C192. Check resistance between right front turn signal lamp socket (Dark Blue/Orange wire) and ground. If resistance is more than 10 k/ohms, go to next step. If resistance is 10 k/ohms or less, repair circuit. See WIRING DIAGRAMS. Clear DTC and repeat self-test.

3) Check resistance between FEM harness connector C192 terminal No. 4 (Dark Blue/Orange wire) and right front turn signal lamp socket (Dark Blue/Orange wire). If resistance is less than 5 ohms, replace FEM. See FRONT ELECTRONICS MODULE (FEM), under REMOVAL & INSTALLATION. Clear DTC and repeat self-test. If resistance is 5 ohms or more, repair circuit. See WIRING DIAGRAMS. Clear DTC and repeat self-test.

NOTE: Cycle ignition switch from OFF to RUN position to enable SSP feature.

4) Remove right front turn signal bulb and disconnect FEM 17-pin connector C192. Check voltage between right front turn signal lamp socket (Dark Blue/Orange wire) and ground. If voltage is present repair circuit. See WIRING DIAGRAMS. Clear DTC and repeat self-test. If voltage is not present, replace FEM. See FRONT ELECTRONICS MODULE (FEM), under REMOVAL & INSTALLATION. Clear DTC and repeat self-test.

5) Place right side turn signal in ON position. If right rear turn signal does not operate correctly, go to TEST AK: RH TURN SIGNAL LAMP NEVER/ALWAYS ON. If right rear turn signal operates correctly, replace FEM. See FRONT ELECTRONICS MODULE (FEM), under REMOVAL & INSTALLATION. Clear DTC and repeat self-test.

TEST AA: LF TURN LAMP NEVER/ALWAYS ON

NOTE: Cycle ignition switch from OFF to RUN position to enable SSP feature.

1) Retrieve DTC from FEM. If DTC B1499 is recorded, go to next step. If DTC B1501 is recorded, go to step 4). If no DTC are recorded, go to step 5). For all other DTC, go to FRONT ELECTRONIC MODULE DTC INDEX. Refer to headlamps.

2) Remove left front turn signal bulb and disconnect FEM 12-pin connector C190. Check resistance between left front turn signal lamp socket (Gray/Black wire) and ground. If resistance is more than 10 k/ohms, go to next step. If resistance is 10 k/ohms or less, repair circuit. See WIRING DIAGRAMS. Clear DTC and repeat self-test.

3) Check resistance between FEM harness connector C190 terminal No. 2 (Gray/Black wire) and left front turn signal lamp socket (Gray/Black wire). If resistance is less than 5 ohms, replace FEM. See FRONT ELECTRONICS MODULE (FEM), under REMOVAL & INSTALLATION. Clear DTC and repeat self-test. If resistance is 5 ohms or more, repair circuit. See WIRING DIAGRAMS. Clear DTC and repeat self-test.

NOTE: Cycle ignition switch from OFF to RUN position to enable SSP feature.

4) Remove left front turn signal bulb and disconnect FEM 12-pin connector C190. Check voltage between left front turn signal lamp socket (Gray/Black wire) and ground. If voltage is present repair circuit. See WIRING DIAGRAMS. Clear DTC and repeat self-test. If voltage is not present, replace FEM. See FRONT ELECTRONICS MODULE (FEM), under REMOVAL & INSTALLATION. Clear DTC and repeat self-test.

5) Place left side turn signal in ON position. If left rear turn signal does not operate correctly, go to TEST AL: LH TURN SIGNAL LAMP NEVER/ALWAYS ON. If left rear turn signal operates correctly, replace FEM. See FRONT ELECTRONICS MODULE (FEM), under REMOVAL & INSTALLATION. Clear DTC and repeat self-test.

TEST AB: RF TURN SIGNAL & PARK LAMPS/NEVER ON

NOTE: Cycle ignition switch from OFF to RUN position to enable SSP feature.

1) Place right side turn signal in ON position and headlamp to parking lamp position. If right rear turn signal and park lamps operate correctly, go to next step. If right rear turn signal and park lamps do not operate correctly, go to TEST AK: RH TURN SIGNAL LAMP NEVER/ALWAYS ON.

2) Check voltage between right front turn signal lamp socket (White/Red wire) and ground. If voltage is more than 10 volts, replace FEM. See FRONT ELECTRONICS MODULE (FEM), under REMOVAL & INSTALLATION. Clear DTC and repeat self-test. If voltage is 10 volts or less, repair circuit. See WIRING DIAGRAMS. Clear DTC and repeat self-test.

TEST AC: LF TURN SIGNAL & PARK LAMPS/NEVER ON

NOTE: Cycle ignition switch from OFF to RUN position to enable SSP feature.

1) Place left side turn signal in ON position and headlamp to parking lamp position. If left rear turn signal and park lamps operate correctly, go to next step. If left rear turn signal and park lamps do not operate correctly, go to TEST AL: LH TURN SIGNAL LAMP NEVER/ALWAYS ON.

2) Check voltage between left front turn signal lamp socket (Light Blue/Red wire) and ground. If voltage is more than 10 volts, replace FEM. See FRONT ELECTRONICS MODULE (FEM), under REMOVAL & INSTALLATION. Clear DTC and repeat self-test. If voltage is 10 volts or less, repair circuit. See WIRING DIAGRAMS. Clear DTC and repeat self-test.

TEST AD: RF TURN SIGNAL/PARK & CORNERING LAMPS/NEVER ON

NOTE: Cycle ignition switch from OFF to RUN position to enable SSP feature.

1) Place right side turn signal in ON position and headlamp to parking lamp position. If right rear turn signal and park lamps operate correctly, go to next step. If right rear turn signal and park lamps do not operate correctly, go to TEST AK: RH TURN SIGNAL LAMP NEVER/ALWAYS ON.

2) Remove Battery Junction Box (BJB) 15-amp fuse No. 22. Check voltage between BJB fuse No. 22 input side and ground. If voltage is more than 10 volts, reinstall BJB fuse No. 22 and go to next step. If voltage is 10 volts or less, repair power source to BJB. Clear DTC and repeat self-test.

3) Remove right front turn signal bulb and measure voltage between right front turn signal lamp socket (White/Red wire) and ground. If voltage is more than 10 volts, replace FEM. See FRONT ELECTRONICS MODULE (FEM), under REMOVAL & INSTALLATION. Clear DTC and repeat self-test. If voltage is 10 volts or less, repair circuit. See WIRING DIAGRAMS. Clear DTC and repeat self-test.

TEST AE: LF TURN SIGNAL/PARK & CORNERING LAMPS/NEVER ON

NOTE: Cycle ignition switch from OFF to RUN position to enable SSP feature.

1) Place left side turn signal in ON position and headlamp to parking lamp position. If left rear turn signal and park lamps operate correctly, go to next step. If left rear turn signal and park lamps do not operate correctly, go to TEST AL: LH TURN SIGNAL LAMP NEVER/ALWAYS ON.

2) Remove Battery Junction Box (BJB) 15-amp fuse No. 23. Check voltage between BJB fuse No. 23 input side and ground. If voltage is more than 10 volts, reinstall BJB fuse No. 23 and go to next step. If voltage is 10 volts or less, repair power source to BJB. Clear DTC and repeat self-test.

3) Remove left front turn signal bulb and check voltage between left front turn signal lamp socket (Light Blue/Red wire) and ground. If voltage is more than 10 volts, replace FEM. See FRONT ELECTRONICS MODULE (FEM), under REMOVAL & INSTALLATION. Clear DTC and repeat self-test. If voltage is 10 volts or less, repair circuit. See WIRING DIAGRAMS. Clear DTC and repeat self-test.

TEST AF: BOTH CORNERING LAMPS ARE INOPERATIVE

NOTE: Cycle ignition switch from OFF to RUN position to enable SSP feature.

1) Turn ignition switch to OFF position. Disconnect FEM 20-pin connector C346 and check voltage between FEM harness connector C346 terminal No. 3 (Red/Yellow wire) and ground.

2) If voltage is more than 10 volts, repair circuit. See WIRING DIAGRAMS. Clear DTC and repeat self-test. If voltage is 10 volts or less, replace FEM. See FRONT ELECTRONICS MODULE (FEM), under REMOVAL & INSTALLATION. Clear DTC and repeat self-test.

TEST AG: RH CORNERING LAMP IS NEVER/ALWAYS ON

NOTE: Cycle ignition switch from OFF to RUN position to enable SSP feature.

1) Retrieve DTC from FEM. If DTC B2482 is recorded, go to next step. If no DTC are recorded, go to step **3)**.

NOTE: Cycle ignition switch from OFF to RUN position to enable SSP feature.

2) Remove right side cornering lamp bulb and disconnect FEM 22-pin connector C191. Check voltage between right side cornering lamp socket (Pink/Orange wire) and ground. If voltage is present, repair circuit. See WIRING DIAGRAMS. Clear DTC and repeat self-test. If voltage is not present, replace FEM. See FRONT ELECTRONICS MODULE (FEM), under REMOVAL & INSTALLATION. Clear DTC and repeat self-test.

3) Remove right side cornering lamp bulb. Check voltage between right side cornering lamp socket (White/Red wire) and ground. If voltage is more than 10 volts, go to next step. If voltage is 5 volts or less, repair circuit. See WIRING DIAGRAMS. Clear DTC and repeat self-test.

4) Disconnect FEM 22-pin connector C191. Check resistance between right side cornering lamp socket (Pink/Orange wire) and ground. If resistance is more than 10 k/ohms, go to next step. If resistance is 10 k/ohms or less, repair circuit. See WIRING DIAGRAMS. Clear DTC and repeat self-test.

5) Check resistance between FEM harness connector C191 terminal No. 12 (Pink/Orange wire) and right side cornering lamp socket (Pink/Orange wire). If resistance is less than 5 ohms, replace FEM. See FRONT ELECTRONICS MODULE (FEM), under REMOVAL & INSTALLATION. Clear DTC and repeat self-test. If resistance is 5 ohms or more, repair circuit. See WIRING DIAGRAMS. Clear DTC and repeat self-test.

TEST AH: LH CORNERING LAMP IS NEVER/ALWAYS ON

NOTE: Cycle ignition switch from OFF to RUN position to enable SSP feature.

1) Retrieve DTC from FEM. If DTC B2480 is recorded, go to next step. If no DTC are recorded, go to step 3).

NOTE: Cycle ignition switch from OFF to RUN position to enable SSP feature.

2) Remove left side cornering lamp bulb and disconnect FEM 22-pin connector C191. Check voltage between left side cornering lamp socket (Violet/Light Blue wire) and ground. If voltage is present, repair circuit. See WIRING DIAGRAMS. Clear DTC and repeat self-test. If voltage is not present, replace FEM. See FRONT ELECTRONICS MODULE (FEM), under REMOVAL & INSTALLATION. Clear DTC and repeat self-test.

3) Remove left side cornering lamp bulb. Check voltage between left side cornering lamp socket (Light Blue/Red wire) and ground. If voltage is more than 10 volts, go to next step. If voltage is 5 volts or less, repair circuit. See WIRING DIAGRAMS. Clear DTC and repeat self-test.

4) Disconnect FEM 22-pin connector C191. Check resistance between left side cornering lamp socket (Violet/Light Blue wire) and ground. If resistance is more than 10 k/ohms, go to next step. If resistance is 10 k/ohms or less, repair circuit. See WIRING DIAGRAMS. Clear DTC and repeat self-test.

5) Check resistance between FEM harness connector C191 terminal No. 18 (Violet/Light Blue wire) and left side cornering lamp socket (Violet/Light Blue wire). If resistance is less than 5 ohms, replace FEM. See FRONT ELECTRONICS MODULE (FEM), under REMOVAL & INSTALLATION. Clear DTC and repeat self-test. If resistance is 5 ohms or more, repair circuit. See WIRING DIAGRAMS. Clear DTC and repeat self-test.

TEST AI: REAR HAZARD LAMPS ARE NEVER/ALWAYS ON

NOTE: Cycle ignition switch from OFF to RUN position to enable SSP feature.

1) Retrieve DTC from FEM. If no DTC are recorded, go to next step. If any DTC are recorded, go to REAR ELECTRONIC MODULE DTC INDEX. Refer to headlamps.

2) Place hazard lamp switch in ON position. If hazard lamps operate correctly, go to next step. If hazard lamps do not operate correctly, go to TEST AM: HAZARD FLASHERS ARE NEVER/ALWAYS ON.

3) Place turn signal switch in right turn signal ON position and then left turn signal ON position, while observing rear turn signal lamps. If rear turn signals operate correctly, replace REM. See REAR ELECTRONICS MODULE (REM), under REMOVAL & INSTALLATION. Clear DTC and repeat self-test. If rear turn signals do not operate correctly, go to SYMPTOM CHART under SELF-DIAGNOSTICS. Refer to rear turn signals.

TEST AJ: FRONT HAZARD LAMPS ARE NEVER/ALWAYS ON

NOTE: Cycle ignition switch from OFF to RUN position to enable SSP feature.

1) Retrieve DTC from FEM. If no DTC are recorded, go to next step. If any DTC are recorded, go to REAR ELECTRONIC MODULE DTC INDEX. Refer to headlamps.

2) Place hazard lamp switch in ON position. If hazard lamps operate correctly, go to next step. If hazard lamps do not operate correctly, go to TEST AM: HAZARD FLASHERS ARE NEVER/ALWAYS ON.

3) Place turn signal switch in right turn signal ON position and then left turn signal ON position, while observing rear turn signal lamps. If front turn signals operate correctly, replace FEM. See FRONT ELECTRONICS MODULE (FEM), under REMOVAL & INSTALLATION. Clear DTC and repeat self-test. If front turn signals do not operate correctly, go to SYMPTOM CHART under SELF-DIAGNOSTICS. Refer to front turn signals.

TEST AK: RH TURN SIGNAL LAMP NEVER/ALWAYS ON

NOTE: Cycle ignition switch from OFF to RUN position to enable SSP feature.

1) Using NGS tester, monitor ICM PID TURN_SW. Place right side turn signal in ON position. If ICM PID TURN_SW does not indicate RIGHT, go to next step. If ICM PID TURN_SW indicates RIGHT, replace instrument cluster. See INSTRUMENT CLUSTER/ICM under REMOVAL & INSTALLATION. Retest system.

2) Test multifunction switch. See MULTIFUNCTION SWITCH under COMPONENT TESTS. If multifunction switch is okay, go to next step. If multifunction switch is not okay, replace multifunctioin switch. See MULTIFUNCTION SWITCH under REMOVAL & INSTALLATION.

NOTE: Cycle ignition switch from OFF to RUN position to enable SSP feature.

3) Turn ignition switch to OFF position. Remove instrument cluster 20-pin connector C240 and multifunction switch 10-pin connector C263. Turn ignition switch to ON position. Check voltage between multifunction switch harness connector C263 terminal No. 9 (Light Blue/Orange wire) and ground. If voltage is not present, go to next step. If voltage is present, repair circuit. See WIRING DIAGRAMS. Clear DTC and repeat self-test.

4) Check resistance between multifunction switch harness connector C263 terminal No. 9 (Light Blue/Orange wire) and instrument cluster harness connector C240 terminal No.14 (Light Blue/Orange wire); and between instrument cluster harness connector C240 terminal No. 14 (Light Blue/Orange wire) and ground. If resistances are less than 5 ohms between multifunction switch and instrument cluster, and more than 10 k/ohms between instrument cluster and ground, repair circuit. See WIRING DIAGRAMS. Clear DTC and repeat self-test. If resistance is 5 ohms or more between multifunction switch and instrument cluster and 10 k/ohms or less between instrument cluster and ground, replace instrument cluster. See INSTRUMENT CLUSTER/ICM under REMOVAL & INSTALLATION. Clear DTC and repeat self-test.

TEST AL: LH TURN SIGNAL LAMP NEVER/ALWAYS ON

NOTE: Cycle ignition switch from OFF to RUN position to enable SSP feature.

1) Using NGS tester, monitor ICM PID TURN_SW. Place left side turn signal in ON position. If ICM PID TURN_SW does not indicate LEFT, go to next step. If ICM PID TURN_SW indicates LEFT, replace instrument cluster. See INSTRUMENT CLUSTER/ICM under REMOVAL & INSTALLATION. Retest system.

2) Test multifunction switch. See MULTIFUNCTION SWITCH under COMPONENT TESTS. If multifunction switch is okay, go to next step. If

multifunction switch is not okay, replace multifunctioin switch. See MULTIFUNCTION SWITCH under REMOVAL & INSTALLATION.

NOTE: Cycle ignition switch from OFF to RUN position to enable SSP feature.

3) Turn ignition switch to OFF position. Remove instrument cluster 20-pin connector C240 and multifunction switch 10-pin connector C263. Turn ignition switch to ON position. Check voltage between multifunction switch harness connector C263 terminal No. 8 (Light Blue/Red wire) and ground. If voltage is not present, go to next step. If voltage is present, repair circuit. See WIRING DIAGRAMS. Clear DTC and repeat self-test.

4) Check resistance between multifunction switch harness connector C263 terminal No. 8 (Light Blue/Red wire) and instrument cluster harness connector C240 terminal No.13 (Light Blue/Red wire); and between instrument cluster harness connector C240 terminal No. 13 (Light Blue/Red wire) and ground. If resistances are less than 5 ohms between multifunction switch and instrument cluster, and more than 10 k/ohms between instrument cluster and ground, repair circuit. See WIRING DIAGRAMS. Clear DTC and repeat self-test. If resistance is 5 ohms or more between multifunction switch and instrument cluster and 10 k/ohms or less between instrument cluster and ground, replace instrument cluster. See INSTRUMENT CLUSTER/ICM under REMOVAL & INSTALLATION. Clear DTC and repeat self-test.

TEST AM: HAZARD FLASHERS ARE NEVER/ALWAYS ON

NOTE: Cycle ignition switch from OFF to RUN position to enable SSP feature.

1) Place turn signal switch in left turn signal ON position and then right turn signal ON position, while observing turn signal lamps. If turn signals operate correctly, go to next step. If turn signals do not operate correctly, go to TEST AK: RH TURN SIGNAL LAMP NEVER/ALWAYS ON for right side and TEST AL: LH TURN SIGNAL LAMP NEVER/ALWAYS ON for left side signals.

2) Test multifunction switch. See MULTIFUNCTION SWITCH under COMPONENT TESTS. If multifunction switch is okay, replace instrument cluster. See INSTRUMENT CLUSTER/ICM under REMOVAL & INSTALLATION. Clear DTC and repeat self-test. If multifunction switch is not okay, replace multifunctioin switch. See MULTIFUNCTION SWITCH under REMOVAL & INSTALLATION.

TEST AN: RF PARKING LAMP INOPERATIVE

NOTE: Cycle ignition switch from OFF to RUN position to enable SSP feature.

1) Retrieve DTC from FEM. If DTC B2491 is recorded, go to next step. If no DTC are recorded, go to step **3)**.

2) Remove right front park lamp bulb and disconnect FEM 12-pin connector C190. Check voltage between right front parking lamp assembly (Black/Pink wire) and ground. If voltage is present, repair circuit. See WIRING DIAGRAMS. Clear DTC and repeat self-test. If voltage is not present, replace FEM. See FRONT ELECTRONICS MODULE (FEM) under REMOVAL & INSTALLATION. Clear DTC and repeat self-test.

NOTE: Cycle ignition switch from OFF to RUN position to enable SSP feature.

3) Place headlamp switch in parking lamps ON position. If right front parking lamp is always ON, go to next step. If right front parking lamp is always off, go to step **5)**. If right front and right rear parking lamps do not illuminate, go to step **6)**.

4) Remove right front park lamp bulb and disconnect FEM 12-pin connector C190. Check resistance between right front parking lamp socket assembly (Black/Pink wire) and ground. If resistance is more than 10 k/ohms, replace FEM. See FRONT ELECTRONICS MODULE (FEM), under REMOVAL & INSTALLATION. Clear DTC and repeat self-test. If resistance is 10 k/ohms or less, repair circuit. See WIRING DIAGRAMS. Clear DTC and repeat self-test.

5) Remove right front park lamp bulb and disconnect FEM 12-pin connector C190. Check resistance between right front parking lamp socket assembly (Black/Pink wire) and FEM harness connector C190 terminal No. 10 (Black/Pink wire). If resistance is less than 5 ohms, replace FEM. See FRONT ELECTRONICS MODULE (FEM), under REMOVAL & INSTALLATION. Clear DTC and repeat self-test. If resistance is 5 ohms or more, repair circuit. See WIRING DIAGRAMS. Clear DTC and repeat self-test.

6) Test headlamp switch. See HEADLAMP SWITCH under COMPONENT TESTS. If headlamp switch is okay, go to next step. If headlamp switch is not okay, replace headlamp switch. See HEADLAMP SWITCH under REMOVAL & INSTALLATION. Retest system.

7) Turn ignition switch to OFF position. Disconnect headlamp switch 8-pin connector C253 and instrument cluster 20-pin connector C240. Turn ignition switch to ON position. Check voltage between headlamp switch harness connector C253 terminal No. 8 (Black/Light Green wire) and ground. If voltage is not present, go to next step. If voltage is present, repair circuit. See WIRING DIAGRAMS. Clear DTC and repeat self-test.

8) Check resistance between headlamp switch harness connector C253 terminal No. 8 (Black/Light Green wire) and instrument cluster harness connector C240 terminal No.16 (Black/Light Green wire); and between headlamp switch connector C253 terminal No. 8 (Black/Light Green wire) and ground. If resistances are less than 5 ohms between headlamp switch and instrument cluster, and more than 10 k/ohms between headlamp switch and ground, replace instrument cluster. See INSTRUMENT CLUSTER/ICM under REMOVAL & INSTALLATION. Clear DTC and repeat self-test. If resistance is 5 ohms or more between headlamp switch and instrument cluster, and 10 k/ohms or less between headlamp switch and ground, repair circuit. See WIRING DIAGRAMS. Clear DTC and repeat self-test.

TEST AO: LF PARKING LAMP INOPERATIVE

NOTE: Cycle ignition switch from OFF to RUN position to enable SSP feature.

1) Retrieve DTC from FEM. If DTC B2493 is recorded, go to next step. If no DTC are recorded, go to step **3)**.

2) Remove left front park lamp bulb and disconnect FEM 12-pin connector C190. Check voltage between left front parking lamp assembly (Dark Green wire) and ground. If voltage is present, repair circuit. See WIRING DIAGRAMS. Clear DTC and repeat self-test. If voltage is not present, replace FEM. See FRONT ELECTRONICS MODULE (FEM), under REMOVAL & INSTALLATION. Clear DTC and repeat self-test.

NOTE: Cycle ignition switch from OFF to RUN position to enable SSP feature.

3) Place headlamp switch in parking lamps ON position. If left front parking lamp is always ON, go to next step. If left front parking lamp is always off, go to step **5)**. If left front and left rear parking lamps do not illuminate, go to step **6)**.

4) Remove left front park lamp bulb and disconnect FEM 12-pin connector C190. Check resistance between left front parking lamp socket assembly (Dark Green wire) and ground. If resistance is more than 10 k/ohms, replace FEM. See FRONT ELECTRONICS MODULE (FEM), under REMOVAL & INSTALLATION. Clear DTC and repeat self-test. If resistance is 10 k/ohms or less, repair circuit. See WIRING DIAGRAMS. Clear DTC and repeat self-test.

5) Remove left front park lamp bulb and disconnect FEM 12-pin connector C190. Check resistance between left front parking lamp socket assembly (Dark Green wire) and FEM harness connector C190 terminal No. 2 (Dark Green wire). If resistance is less than 5 ohms, replace FEM. See FRONT ELECTRONICS MODULE (FEM), under REMOVAL & INSTALLATION. Clear DTC and repeat self-test. If resistance is 5 ohms or more, repair circuit. See WIRING DIAGRAMS. Clear DTC and repeat self-test.

6) Test headlamp switch. See HEADLAMP SWITCH under COMPONENT TESTS. If headlamp switch is okay, go to next step. If headlamp switch is not okay, replace headlamp switch. See HEADLAMP SWITCH under REMOVAL & INSTALLATION. Retest system.

7) Turn ignition switch to OFF position. Disconnect headlamp switch 8-pin connector C253 and instrument cluster 20-pin connector C240. Turn ignition switch to ON position. Check voltage between headlamp switch harness connector C253 terminal No. 8 (Black/Light Green wire) and ground. If voltage is not present, go to next step. If voltage is present, repair circuit. See WIRING DIAGRAMS. Clear DTC and repeat self-test.

8) Check resistance between headlamp switch harness connector C253 terminal No. 8 (Black/Light Green wire) and instrument cluster harness connector C240 terminal No.16 (Black/Light Green wire); and between headlamp switch connector C253 terminal No. 8 (Black/Light Green wire) and ground. If resistances are less than 5 ohms between headlamp switch and instrument cluster, and more than 10 k/ohms between headlamp switch and ground, replace instrument cluster. See INSTRUMENT CLUSTER/ICM under REMOVAL & INSTALLATION. Clear DTC and repeat self-test. If resistance is 5 ohms or more between headlamp switch and instrument cluster, and 10 k/ohms or less between headlamp switch and ground, repair circuit. See WIRING DIAGRAMS. Clear DTC and repeat self-test.

TEST AP: RR PARK & STOP LAMP INOPERATIVE

1) Retrieve DTC from FEM. If no DTC are recorded, go to next step. If DTC B2565 or B2566 are recorded, go to step 3). For all other DTC, go toFRONT ELECTRONIC MODULE DTC INDEX. Refer to headlamps.
2) Depress brake pedal, while observing right rear stoplamp. If right rear stoplamp operates correctly, go to next step. If right rear stoplamp does not operate correctly, go to step 5).
3) Using NGS tester, monitor REM PID R_TAIL. Place headlamp switch in parking lamp position. If PID changes when headlamp switch is placed in parking lamp position, go to next step. If PID does not change when headlamp switch is placed in parking lamp position, replace REM. See REAR ELECTRONICS MODULE (REM)-test.
4) Observe right rear lamp bulb while triggering REM active commands R/TAILMPS ON and then OFF. If right rear lamp does not operate correctly and DTC B2565 was recorded, go to next step. If right rear lamp does not operate correctly and DTC B2566 was recorded, go to step 7). If right rear lamp operates correctly, replace REM. See REAR ELECTRONICS MODULE (REM), under REMOVAL & INSTALLATION. Clear DTC and repeat self-test.

NOTE: Cycle ignition switch from OFF to RUN position to enable SSP feature.

5) Remove right rear lamp bulb. Check voltage between right rear lamp socket (Tan/Red wire) and ground. If voltage is more than 10 volts, go to next step. If voltage is 10 volts or less, repair circuit. See WIRING DIAGRAMS. Clear DTC and repeat self-test.
6) Disconnect REM 17-pin connector C340. Check resistance between REM harness connector C340 terminal No. 5 (Tan/Red wire) and right rear lamp socket (Tan/Red wire). If resistance is less than 5 ohms, go to next step. If resistance is 5 ohms or more, repair circuit. See WIRING DIAGRAMS. Clear DTC and repeat self-test.

NOTE: Cycle ignition switch from OFF to RUN position to enable SSP feature.

7) Remove right rear lamp bulb and disconnect REM 17-pin connector C340. Check voltage between REM harness connector C340 terminal No. 5 (Tan/Red wire) and ground. If voltage is present, repair circuit. See WIRING DIAGRAMS. Clear DTC and repeat self-test. If voltage is not present, replace REM. See REAR ELECTRONICS MODULE (REM), under REMOVAL & INSTALLATION. Clear DTC and repeat self-test.

TEST AQ: LR PARK & STOP LAMP INOPERATIVE

NOTE: Cycle ignition switch from OFF to RUN position to enable SSP feature.

1) Retrieve DTC from FEM. If no DTC are recorded, go to next step. If DTC B1808 or B1806 are recorded, go to step 3). For all other DTC, go to REAR ELECTRONIC MODULE DTC INDEX. Refer to headlamps.
2) Depress brake pedal, while observing left rear stoplamp. If left rear stoplamp operates correctly, go to next step. If left rear stoplamp does not operate correctly, go to step 5).
3) Using NGS tester, monitor REM PID L_TAIL. Place headlamp switch in parking lamp position. If PID changes when headlamp switch is placed in parking lamp position, go to next step. If PID does not change when headlamp switch is placed in parking lamp position, replace REM. See REAR ELECTRONICS MODULE (REM), under REMOVAL & INSTALLATION. Clear DTC and repeat self-test.
4) Observe left rear lamp bulb while triggering REM active commands L/TAILMPS ON and then OFF. If left rear lamp does not operate correctly and DTC B1806 was recorded, go to next step. If left rear lamp does not operate correctly and DTC B1808 was recorded, go to step 7). If left rear lamp operates correctly, replace REM. See REAR ELECTRONICS MODULE (REM), under REMOVAL & INSTALLATION. Clear DTC and repeat self-test.

NOTE: Cycle ignition switch from OFF to RUN position to enable SSP feature.

5) Remove left rear lamp bulb. Check voltage between left rear lamp socket (Dark Blue/Yellow wire) and ground. If voltage is more than 10 volts, go to next step. If voltage is 10 volts or less, repair circuit. See WIRING DIAGRAMS. Clear DTC and repeat self-test.
6) Disconnect REM 17-pin connector C340. Check resistance between REM harness connector C340 terminal No. 6 (Dark Blue/Yellow wire) and left rear lamp socket (Dark Blue/Yellow wire). If resistance is less than 5 ohms, go to next step. If resistance is 5 ohms or more, repair circuit. See WIRING DIAGRAMS. Clear DTC and repeat self-test.

NOTE: Cycle ignition switch from OFF to RUN position to enable SSP feature.

7) Remove left rear lamp bulb and disconnect REM 17-pin connector C340. Check voltage between REM harness connector C340 terminal No. 6 (Dark Blue/Yellow wire) and ground. If voltage is present, repair circuit. See WIRING DIAGRAMS. Clear DTC and repeat self-test. If voltage is not present, replace REM. See REAR ELECTRONICS MODULE (REM), under REMOVAL & INSTALLATION. Clear DTC and repeat self-test.

TEST AR: RR PARKING LAMP ON CONTINUOUSLY

NOTE: Cycle ignition switch from OFF to RUN position to enable SSP feature.

1) Retrieve DTC from REM. If no DTC are recorded, go to next step. If DTC B2565 is recorded, go to step 3). For all other DTC, go to REAR ELECTRONIC MODULE DTC INDEX. Refer to headlamps.
2) Using NGS tester, monitor REM PID R_TAIL. Place headlamp switch in parking lamp position. If PID does not change value when headlamp switch is placed in parking lamp position, go to next step. If PID changes value when headlamp switch is placed in parking lamp position, replace REM. See REAR ELECTRONICS MODULE (REM), under REMOVAL & INSTALLATION. Clear DTC and repeat self-test.
3) Remove right rear lamp bulb and disconnect REM 17-pin connector C340. Check resistance between REM harness connector C340 terminal No. 5 (Tan/Red wire) and ground. If resistance is more than 10 k/ohms, replace REM. See REAR ELECTRONICS MODULE (REM), under REMOVAL & INSTALLATION. Clear DTC and repeat self-test. If resistance is 10 k/ohms or less, repair circuit. See WIRING DIAGRAMS. Clear DTC and repeat self-test.

TEST AS: LR PARKING LAMP ON CONTINUOUSLY

NOTE: Cycle ignition switch from OFF to RUN position to enable SSP feature.

1) Retrieve DTC from REM. If no DTC are recorded, go to next step. If DTC B1806 is recorded, go to step **3)**. For all other DTC, go to REAR ELECTRONIC MODULE DTC INDEX. Refer to headlamps.

2) Using NGS tester, monitor REM PID L_TAIL. Place headlamp switch in parking lamp position. If PID does not change value when headlamp switch is placed in parking lamp position, go to next step. If PID changes value when headlamp switch is placed in parking lamp position, replace REM. See REAR ELECTRONICS MODULE (REM), under REMOVAL & INSTALLATION. Clear DTC and repeat self-test.

3) Remove left rear lamp bulb and disconnect REM 17-pin connector C340. Check resistance between REM harness connector C340 terminal No. 6 (Dark Blue/Yellow wire) and ground. If resistance is more than 10 k/ohms, replace REM. See REAR ELECTRONICS MODULE (REM), under REMOVAL & INSTALLATION. Clear DTC and repeat self-test. If resistance is 10 k/ohms or less, repair circuit. See WIRING DIAGRAMS. Clear DTC and repeat self-test.

TEST AT: LICENSE LAMPS INOPERATIVE

NOTE: Cycle ignition switch from OFF to RUN position to enable SSP feature.

1) Retrieve DTC from REM. If no DTC are recorded, go to next step. If DTC B2523 or B2524 are recorded, go to step **4)**. For all other DTC, go to REAR ELECTRONIC MODULE DTC INDEX. Refer to headlamps.

2) Place headlamp in parking lamp position. If rear lamps illuminate, go to next step. If rear lamps do not illuminate, go to SYMPTOM CHART under SELF-DIAGNOSTICS.

3) Using NGS tester, monitor REM PID LCNC_LP. Place headlamp switch in parking lamp position. If PID changes value when headlamp switch is placed in parking lamp position, go to next step. If PID does not change value when headlamp switch is placed in parking lamp position, replace REM. See REAR ELECTRONICS MODULE (REM), under REMOVAL & INSTALLATION. Clear DTC and repeat self-test.

NOTE: Cycle ignition switch from OFF to RUN position to enable SSP feature.

4) Remove inoperative license lamp bulb. Check voltage between inoperative license lamp socket (Gray/Red wire) and ground. If voltage is more than 10 volts, go to next step. If voltage is 10 volts or less, repair circuit. See WIRING DIAGRAMS. Clear DTC and repeat self-test.

5) Disconnect REM 12-pin connector C344. Check resistance between REM harness connector C344 terminal No. 5 (Dark Green/Light Green wire), and inoperative license lamp socket (Dark Green/Light Green wire). If resistance is less than 5 ohms, go to next step. If resistance is 5 ohms or more, repair circuit. See WIRING DIAGRAMS. Clear DTC and repeat self-test.

NOTE: Cycle ignition switch from OFF to RUN position to enable SSP feature.

6) Check voltage between REM harness connector C344 terminal No. 5 (Dark Green/Light Green wire) and ground. If voltage is present, repair circuit. See WIRING DIAGRAMS. Clear DTC and repeat self-test. If voltage is not present, replace REM. See REAR ELECTRONICS MODULE (REM), under REMOVAL & INSTALLATION. Clear DTC and repeat self-test.

TEST AU: LICENSE LAMPS ALWAYS ON

NOTE: Cycle ignition switch from OFF to RUN position to enable SSP feature.

1) Retrieve DTC from REM. If no DTC are recorded, go to next step. If DTC B2523 is recorded, go to step **3)**. For all other DTC, go to REAR ELECTRONIC MODULE DTC INDEX. Refer to headlamps.

2) Using NGS tester, monitor REM PID LCNC_LP. Place headlamp switch in parking lamp position. If PID does not change value when headlamp switch is placed in parking lamp position, go to next step. If PID changes value when headlamp switch is placed in parking lamp position, replace REM. See REAR ELECTRONICS MODULE (REM), under REMOVAL & INSTALLATION. Clear DTC and repeat self-test.

3) Disconnect REM 12-pin connector C344 and remove license lamp bulbs. Check resistance between REM harness connector C344 terminal NO. 5 (Dark Green/Light Green wire) and ground. If resistance is more than 10 k/ohms, replace REM. See REAR ELECTRONICS MODULE (REM), under REMOVAL & INSTALLATION. Clear DTC and repeat self-test. If resistance is 10 k/ohms or less, repair circuit. See WIRING DIAGRAMS. Clear DTC and repeat self-test.

TEST AV: REVERSING LAMPS INOPERATIVE

NOTE: Cycle ignition switch from OFF to RUN position to enable SSP feature.

1) Retrieve DTC from REM. If no DTC are recorded, go to next step. If DTC B2532 is recorded, go to step **3)**. For all other DTC, go to REAR ELECTRONIC MODULE DTC INDEX. Refer to headlamps.

2) Using NGS tester, monitor REM PID RR_BKUP. Set parking brake. If PID changes value when gear shift lever is placed in REVERSE, go to next step. If PID does not change value when gear shift lever is placed in REVERSE, replace REM. See REAR ELECTRONICS MODULE (REM), under REMOVAL & INSTALLATION. Clear DTC and repeat self-test.

3) Using NGS tester, observe reversing lamps, while triggering REM active commands BACKUPLMP ON and then OFF. If reversing lamps do not operate correctly, go to next step. If reversing lamps operate correctly, replace REM. See REAR ELECTRONICS MODULE (REM), under REMOVAL & INSTALLATION. Clear DTC and repeat self-test.

4) Remove reversing lamp bulbs. Check voltage between left side, and right side reversing lamp sockets (Gray/Red wires) and ground. If voltages are more than 10 volts, go to next step. If voltage(s) are 10 volts or less, repair circuit(s) . See WIRING DIAGRAMS. Clear DTC and repeat self-test.

5) Disconnect REM 17-pin connector C340. Check resistance between REM harness connector C340 terminal No. 9 (Dark Green/Orange wire) and left side reversing lamp socket (Dark Green/Orange wire): and between REM harness connector C340 terminal No. 10 (White/Yellow wire) and right side reversing lamp socket (White/Yellow wire). If resistances are less than 5 ohms, go to next step. If resistance(s) are 5 ohms or more, repair circuit(s). See WIRING DIAGRAMS. Clear DTC and repeat self-test.

NOTE: Cycle ignition switch from OFF to RUN position to enable SSP feature.

6) Check voltage between REM harness connector C340 terminals No. 9 (Dark Green/Orange wire), No. 10 (White/Yellow wire) and ground. If voltage is present, repair circuit(s). See WIRING DIAGRAMS. Clear DTC and repeat self-test. If voltage is not present, replace REM. See REAR ELECTRONICS MODULE (REM), under REMOVAL & INSTALLATION. Clear DTC and repeat self-test.

TEST AW: REVERSING LAMPS ALWAYS ON

NOTE: Cycle ignition switch from OFF to RUN position to enable SSP feature.

1) Retrieve DTC from REM. If no DTC are recorded, go to next step. If DTC B2531 is recorded, go to step **3)**. For all other DTC, go to REAR ELECTRONIC MODULE DTC INDEX. Refer to headlamps.

2) Using NGS tester, monitor REM PID RR_BKUP. Set parking brake. If PID changes value when gear shift lever is placed in reverse, go to next step. If PID does not change value when gear shift lever is placed in reverse, replace REM. See REAR ELECTRONICS MODULE (REM), under REMOVAL & INSTALLATION. Clear DTC and repeat self-test.

3) Disconnect REM 17-pin connector C340. Check resistances between REM harness connector C340 terminals No. 9 (Dark Green/Orange wire), No. 10 (White/Yellow wire) and ground. If resistances are more than 10 k/ohms, replace REM. See REAR ELECTRONICS MODULE (REM), under REMOVAL & INSTALLATION. Clear DTC and repeat self-test. If resistances are 10 k/ohms or less, repair circuit(s). See WIRING DIAGRAMS. Clear DTC and repeat self-test.

TEST AX: ONE REVERSING LAMP INOPERATIVE

NOTE: Cycle ignition switch from OFF to RUN position to enable SSP feature.

1) Retrieve DTC from REM. If no DTC are recorded, go to next step. If any DTC are recorded, go to REAR ELECTRONIC MODULE DTC INDEX. Refer to headlamps.

2) Remove inoperative reversing lamp. Check voltage between left side reversing lamp socket (Gray/Red wire) or right side reversing lamp socket (Gray/Red wire) and ground. If voltage is more than 10 volts, go to next step. If voltage is 10 volts or less, repair circuit(s). See WIRING DIAGRAMS. Clear DTC and repeat self-test.

3) Disconnect REM 17-pin connector C340. Check resistance between REM harness connector C340 terminal No. 9 (Dark Green/Orange wire) and left side reversing lamp socket (Dark Green/Orange wire); or between REM harness connector C340 terminal No. 10 (White/Yellow wire) and right side reversing lamp socket (White/Yellow wire). If resistance(s) are more than 10 k/ohms, replace REM. See REAR ELECTRONICS MODULE (REM), under REMOVAL & INSTALLATION. Clear DTC and repeat self-test. If resistances are 10 k/ohms or less, repair circuit(s). See WIRING DIAGRAMS. Clear DTC and repeat self-test.

COMPONENT TESTS

HEADLAMP SWITCH

Disconnect headlamp switch. Check for continuity between headlamp switch terminals as specified with switch in indicated position. For headlamp connector terminal identification, *see Fig. 8.* Replace headlamp switch if continuity is not as specified.

HEADLAMP SWITCH RESISTANCE

Switch Position	Between Terminals	Continuity
Headlamp circuit		
Autolamp	4 & 2	NO
Off	4 & 2	NO
Park	4 & 2	NO
Head Light	4 & 2	1.2 k/ohms
Parking Light Circuit		
Autolamp	8 & 2	NO
Off	8 & 2	NO
Park	8 & 2	1.2 k/ohms
Head Light	8 & 2	1.2 k/ohms
Off Circuit		
Autolamp	7 & 2	NO
Off	7 & 2	1.2 k/ohms
Park	7 & 2	NO
Head Light	7 & 2	NO
Autolamp Circuit		
Autolamp	5 & 2	1.2 k/ohms
Off	5 & 2	NO
Park	5 & 2	NO
Head Light	5 & 2	NO

MULTIFUNCTION SWITCH

Disconnect multifunction switch. Check for continuity between multifunction switch terminals as specified with switch in indicated position. See MULTIFUNCTION SWITCH CONTINUITY. *See Fig. 10* MULTIFUNCTION SWITCH CONNECTOR for identification. Replace multifunction switch if resistance is not as specified.

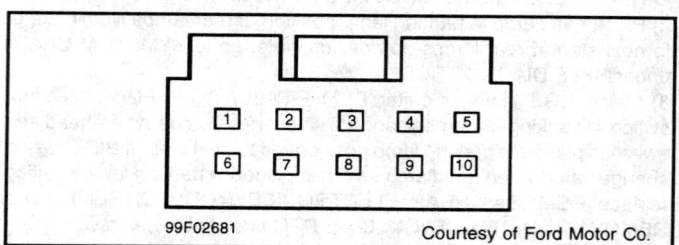

99F02681   Courtesy of Ford Motor Co.

Fig. 10: Multifunction Switch Connector

MULTIFUNCTION SWITCH CONTINUITY

Switch Positions	Terminals	Continuity
Flash To Pass		
Pull & Hold Lever Toward Steering Wheel	10 & 7; 10 & 6	YES
Dimmer High Beam		
Lever Away From Steering Wheel	10 & 7	YES
Dimmer Low Beam		
Lever In Detent Closest To Steering Wheel	10 & 6	YES
Turn Switch		
Left Turn/Hazard OFF	10 & 8	YES
Right Turn/Hazard OFF	10 & 9	YES
Hazard Switch		
Hazard ON	10 & 8; 10 & 9	YES

SWITCHED SYSTEM POWER (SSP) RELAYS

NOTE: For SSP Relay Harness Connector & Relay Terminals identification, refer to 11.

1) Remove relay. Measure resistance between relay terminal No. 85 and 30, 86, 87, and 87a. If resistance is 5 ohms or less between relay terminal No. 85 and any other terminals, replace relay. If all resistances are more than 5 ohms, go to next step.

2) Using a jumper wire, connect between positive battery terminal and relay terminal No. 30. Using a self-powered test lamp, check for voltage at relay terminal No. 87a. If voltage is present, go to next step. If voltage is not present, replace relay.

3) Using 3 jumper wires, connect one jumper between positive battery terminal and relay terminal No. 30. Connect another jumper wire between positive battery terminal and relay terminal No. 86. Connect the last jumper wire between negative battery terminal and relay terminal No. 85. Using a test light, check for voltage at relay terminal No. 87. If battery voltage is present, replace relay. If battery voltage is not present, using a test light, check for voltage at relay terminal No. 5. If battery voltage is not present, replace relay. If battery voltage is present, relay is okay.

NOTE: When diagnosing a SSP relay, ensure all systems for that relay are inoperative. See SYMPTOM CHART if all systems for one SSP relay are inoperative, or if all systems for all SSP relays are inoperative. Relays, fuses which power them and systems they control are as follows:

SSP1 – Powered By Battery Junction Box (BJB) 40-amp Fuse No. 109.
- Driver Power Door Lock (FEM)
- LH headlamp (FEM)

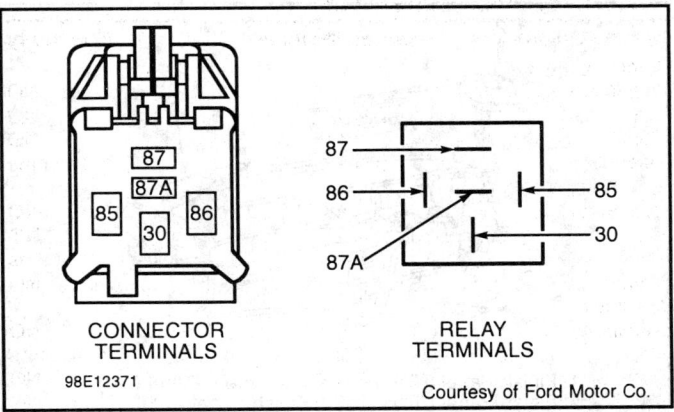

CONNECTOR TERMINALS

RELAY TERMINALS

98E12371

Courtesy of Ford Motor Co.

Fig. 11: Switched System Power (SSP) Relay Harness Connector & Relay Terminals

- RF Park/Turn/Cornering Lamps (FEM)

SSP2 – Powered By Battery Junction Box (BJB) 40-amp Fuse No. 108.
- RH Headlamp (FEM)
- LF Park/Turn/Cornering Lamps (FEM)

SSP3 – Powered By Battery Junction Box (BJB) 40-amp Fuse No. 114.
- High Mounted Stoplamp (REM)
- Right Rear Park/Stoplamps (REM)
- Stepwell/Puddle Lamps (FEM)
- Reversing Lamps (REM)
- All Overhead Courtesy/Demand Lamps (REM)
- Left Rear Turn Signals (REM)
- License Lamps (REM)
- Trailer Stoplamps/Turn Signals (If Equipped With Trailer Tow)

SSP4 – Powered By Battery Junction Box (BJB) 40-amp Fuse No. 103.
- Left Rear Park/Stoplamps (REM)
- Right Rear Turn Signals (REM)
- Passenger Door/Side/Liftgate Locks (REM)
- Trailer Park Lamps (If Equipped With Trailer Tow)

REMOVAL & INSTALLATION

BRAKE PEDAL POSITION (BPP) SWITCH

Removal & Installation – Disconnect Brake Pedal Position (BPP) switch 2-pin connector. Remove self-locking pin, spacer and BPP switch. To install, reverse removal procedure.

FRONT ELECTRONICS MODULE (FEM)

CAUTION: Electronic modules are sensitive to static electrical charges. Proper grounding of technician and workplace is essential to prevent damage.

CAUTION: Prior to removal of Module, it is necessary to upload module configuration information to New Generation Star (NGS) tester. This information needs to be downloaded into new module once installed. See INSTRUMENT CLUSTER MODULE/FEM/REM PROGRAMMING.

NOTE: When battery is disconnected and reconnected, some abnormal drive symptoms may occur while vehicle relearns it's adaptive strategy. Vehicle may need to be driven 10 miles or more to learn strategy.

Removal & Installation – 1) Disconnect battery ground cable. Remove 2 bolts holding instrument panel lower steering column opening cover. Remove cover. Remove 3 bolts holding instrument panel opening cover reinforcement. Remove reinforcement. Disconnect six electrical connectors to FEM, remove 3 bolts holding FEM and remove FEM.
2) To install FEM, reverse removal procedures.

HEADLAMP ASSEMBLY

Removal & Installation – Raise headlamp retainers, disconnect electrical connectors and remove headlamp assembly. To install headlamp assembly, reverse removal procedures.

HEADLAMP BULB

WARNING: Halogen bulbs contain gas under pressure. Bulb may shatter if glass envelope is scratched or if bulb is dropped. Grasp bulb only by it's base. Avoid touching glass envelope.

NOTE: Headlamp bulb should not be removed from headlamp assembly until replacement bulb is ready to be installed. Contaminants may enter headlamp assembly where they can settle on lens or reflector, possibly affecting headlamp bulb performance. Never turn on headlamps with bulb removed.

Removal & Installation – Remove headlamp assembly. See HEADLAMP ASSEMBLY under REMOVAL & INSTALLATION. Remove protective cover from rear of headlamp assembly. Depress spring clips and remove bulb by pulling it straight out of headlamp assembly. To install headlamp bulb, reverse removal procedure.

HEADLAMP SWITCH

NOTE: When battery is disconnected and reconnected, some abnormal drive symptoms may occur while vehicle relearns it's adaptive strategy. Vehicle may need to be driven 10 miles or more to relearn strategy.

Removal & Installation – Disconnect battery ground cable. Unclip headlamp switch with integral instrument panel cover. Disconnect electrical connectors and remove headlamp switch. To install headlamp switch, reverse removal procedure.

INSTRUMENT CLUSTER/ICM

CAUTION: Electronic modules are sensitive to static electrical charges. Proper grounding of technician and workplace is essential to prevent damage.

CAUTION: Prior to removal of module, it is necessary to upload module configuration information to New Generation Star (NGS) tester. This information needs to be downloaded into new module once installed. See INSTRUMENT CLUSTER MODULE/FEM/REM PROGRAMMING.

NOTE: After instrument cluster replacement, see PASSIVE ANTI-THEFT SYSTEMS – WINDSTAR article in ACCESSORIES & EQUIPMENT for anti-theft system programming.

Removal & Installation – 1) Disconnect negative battery cable. Remove 2 screws and remove instrument panel steering column cover ("D") from below steering column. *See Fig. 12.*
2) Remove 4 nuts and remove instrument panel steering column cover reinforcement from below steering column. Loosen 4 bolts retaining steering column. Lower steering column. Remove lower steering column shroud from steering column. Using a punch, push button below ignition lock cylinder and pull ignition switch lock cylinder out.
3) Remove upper steering column shroud from steering column. Remove light switch knob and gently pry instrument panel finish panel ("E") away from instrument panel ("A"). *See Fig. 13.* Disconnect headlight switch miniature bulb socket from instrument panel finish panel.
4) Remove 2 retaining screws at bottom of cluster opening panel and gently pry from instrument panel. *See Fig. 13.* Disconnect electrical connectors. Remove 2 retaining screws and gently pry instrument panel finish panel ("F") from instrument panel. *See Fig. 14.* Disconnect transaxle range indicator cable from column by removing retaining screw and cable loop.
5) Remove 4 screws retaining instrument cluster. Pull instrument cluster forward to gain access to electrical connectors. Disconnect electrical

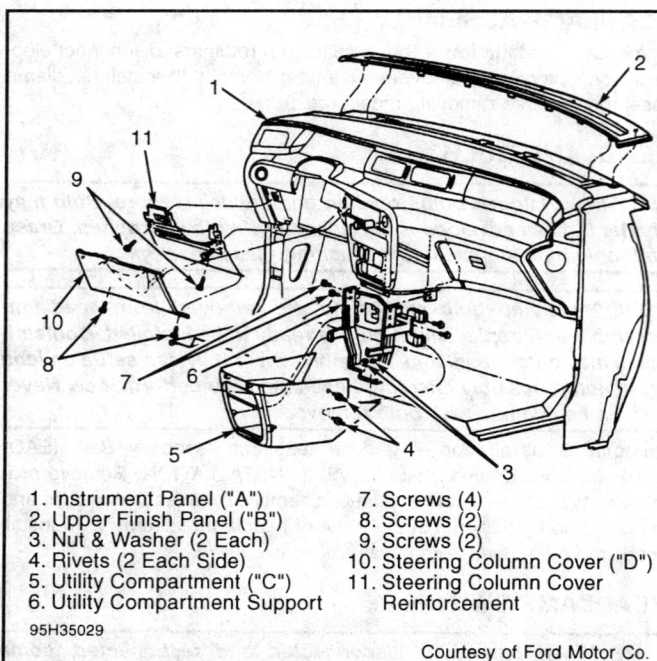

1. Instrument Panel ("A")
2. Upper Finish Panel ("B")
3. Nut & Washer (2 Each)
4. Rivets (2 Each Side)
5. Utility Compartment ("C")
6. Utility Compartment Support
7. Screws (4)
8. Screws (2)
9. Screws (2)
10. Steering Column Cover ("D")
11. Steering Column Cover Reinforcement

95H35029

Courtesy of Ford Motor Co.

Fig. 12: Exploded View Of Instrument Panel

connectors. Remove instrument cluster. To install, reverse removal procedure. Tighten instrument cluster retaining screws to 18-26 INCH lbs. (2-3 N.m). Tighten instrument panel steering column cover reinforcement retaining screws to 106 INCH lbs. (12 N.m).

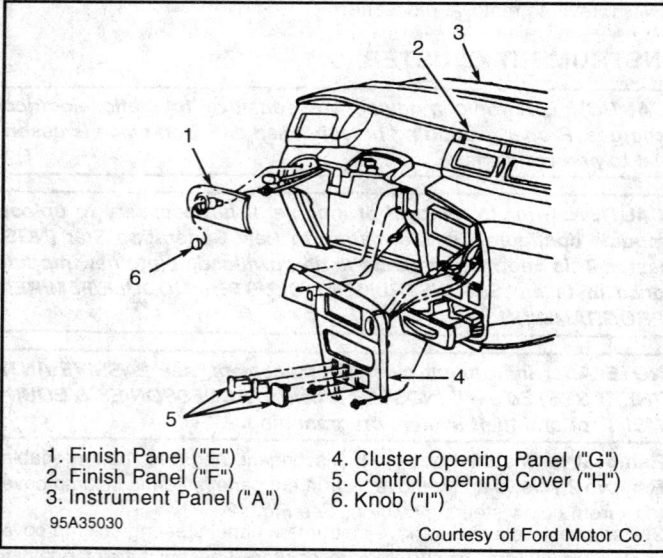

1. Finish Panel ("E")
2. Finish Panel ("F")
3. Instrument Panel ("A")
4. Cluster Opening Panel ("G")
5. Control Opening Cover ("H")
6. Knob ("I")

95A35030

Courtesy of Ford Motor Co.

Fig. 13: Removing Cluster Opening Panel

MULTIFUNCTION SWITCH

Removal & Installation – Disconnect battery ground cable. Twist tilt wheel handle counterclockwise and remove. Remove upper and lower steering column shrouds. Remove switch screws. Disconnect electrical connectors. Remove switch. To install, reverse removal procedure.

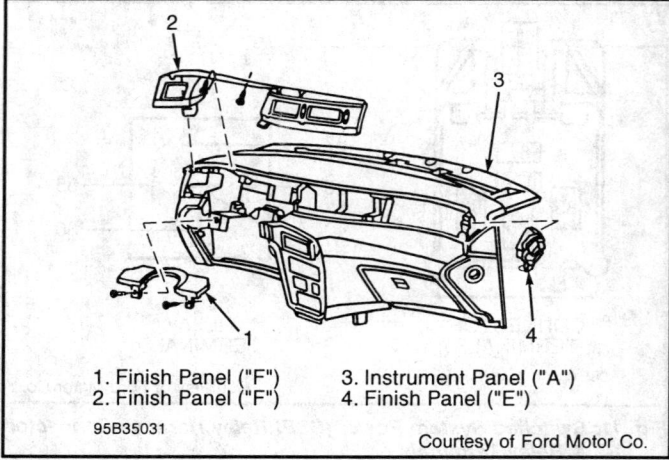

1. Finish Panel ("F")
2. Finish Panel ("F")
3. Instrument Panel ("A")
4. Finish Panel ("E")

95B35031

Courtesy of Ford Motor Co.

Fig. 14: Removing Instrument Panel Finish Panel

REAR ELECTRONICS MODULE (REM)

CAUTION: Electronic modules are sensitive to static electrical charges. Proper grounding of technician and workplace is essential to prevent damage.

CAUTION: Prior to removal of module, it is necessary to upload module configuration information to New Generation Star (NGS) tester. This information needs to be downloaded into new module once installed. See INSTRUMENT CLUSTER MODULE/FEM/REM PROGRAMMING.

NOTE: When battery is disconnected and reconnected, some abnormal drive symptoms may occur while vehicle relearns its adaptive strategy. Vehicle may need to be driven 10 miles or more to learn strategy.

Removal & Installation – Disconnect battery ground cable. Remove right quarter trim panel. Remove 3 bolts holding service jack mounting bracket and remove bracket. Disconnect five electrical connectors to REM, remove 3 nuts holding REM and remove REM. To install REM, reverse removal procedure.

WIRING DIAGRAMS

NOTE: See HEADLIGHT SYSTEMS article for wiring diagrams.

WIRING DIAGRAMS

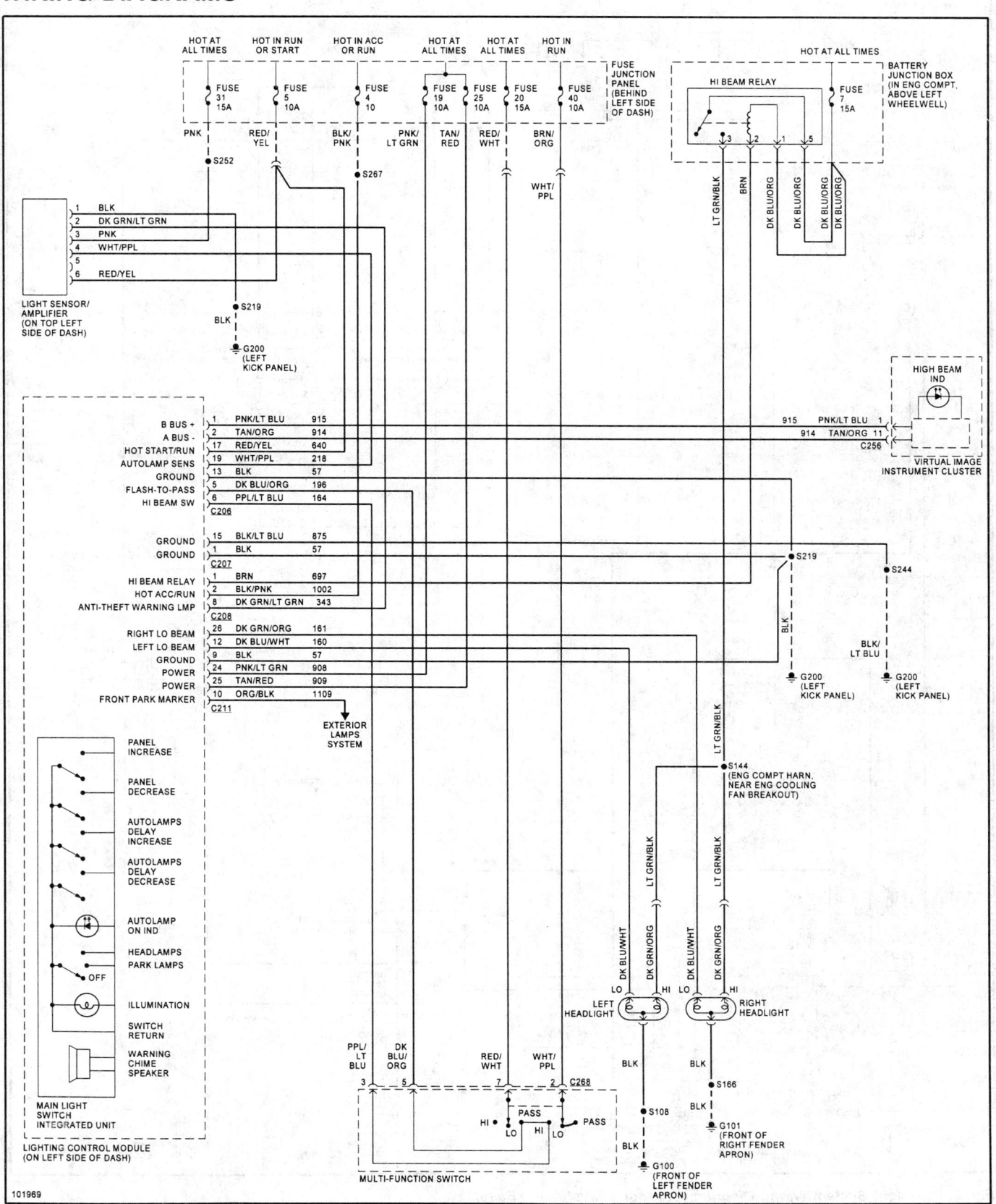

Fig. 1: Headlight System Wiring Diagram (Continental)

101969

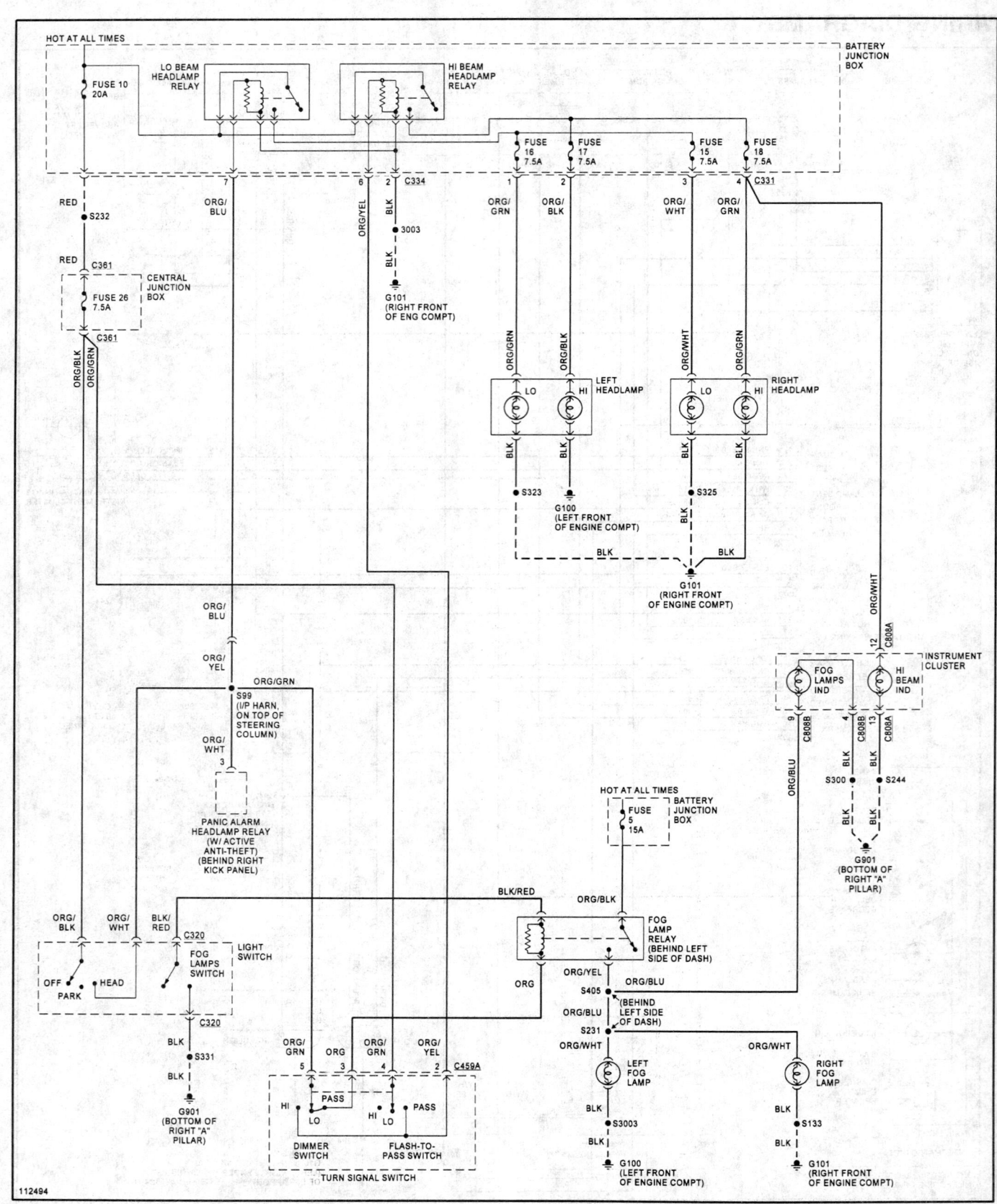

Fig. 2: Headlight System Wiring Diagram (Contour & Mystique – Base)

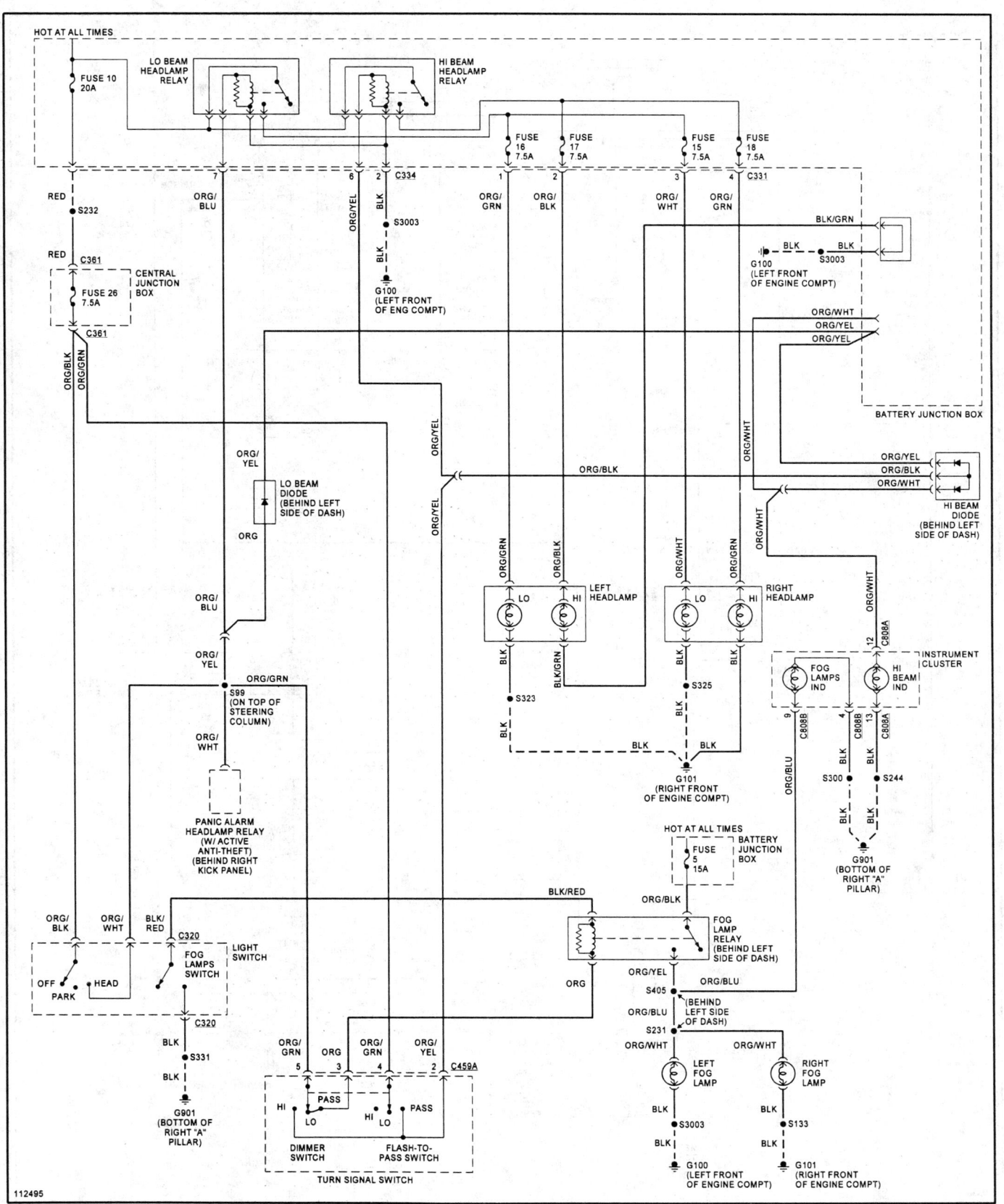

Fig. 3: Headlight System Wiring Diagram (Contour & Mystique – Highline)

112495

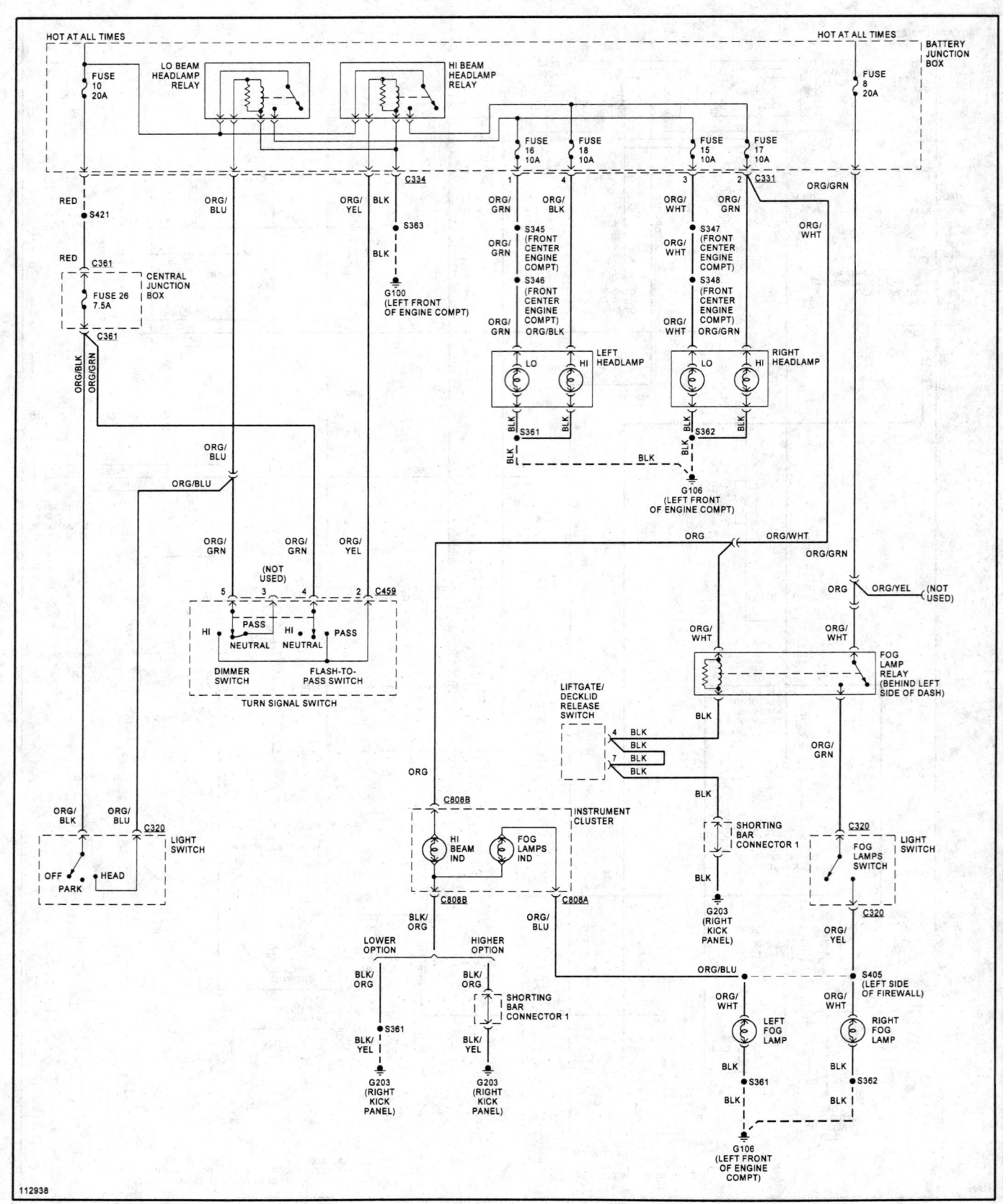

Fig. 4: Headlight System Wiring Diagram (Cougar – Without DRL & Without Bulb Outage Module)

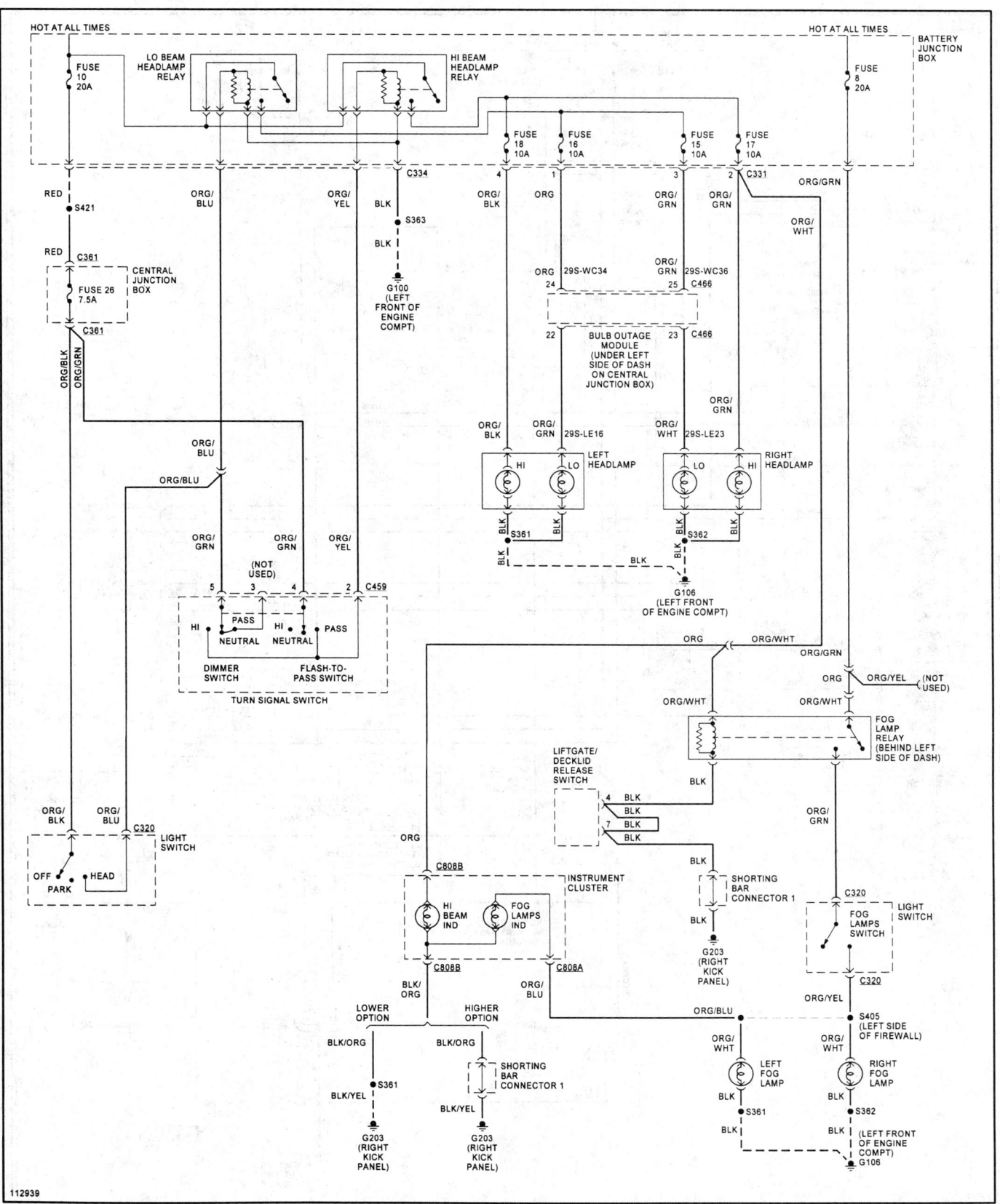

Fig. 5: Headlight System Wiring Diagram (Cougar – With Bulb Outage Module)

112939

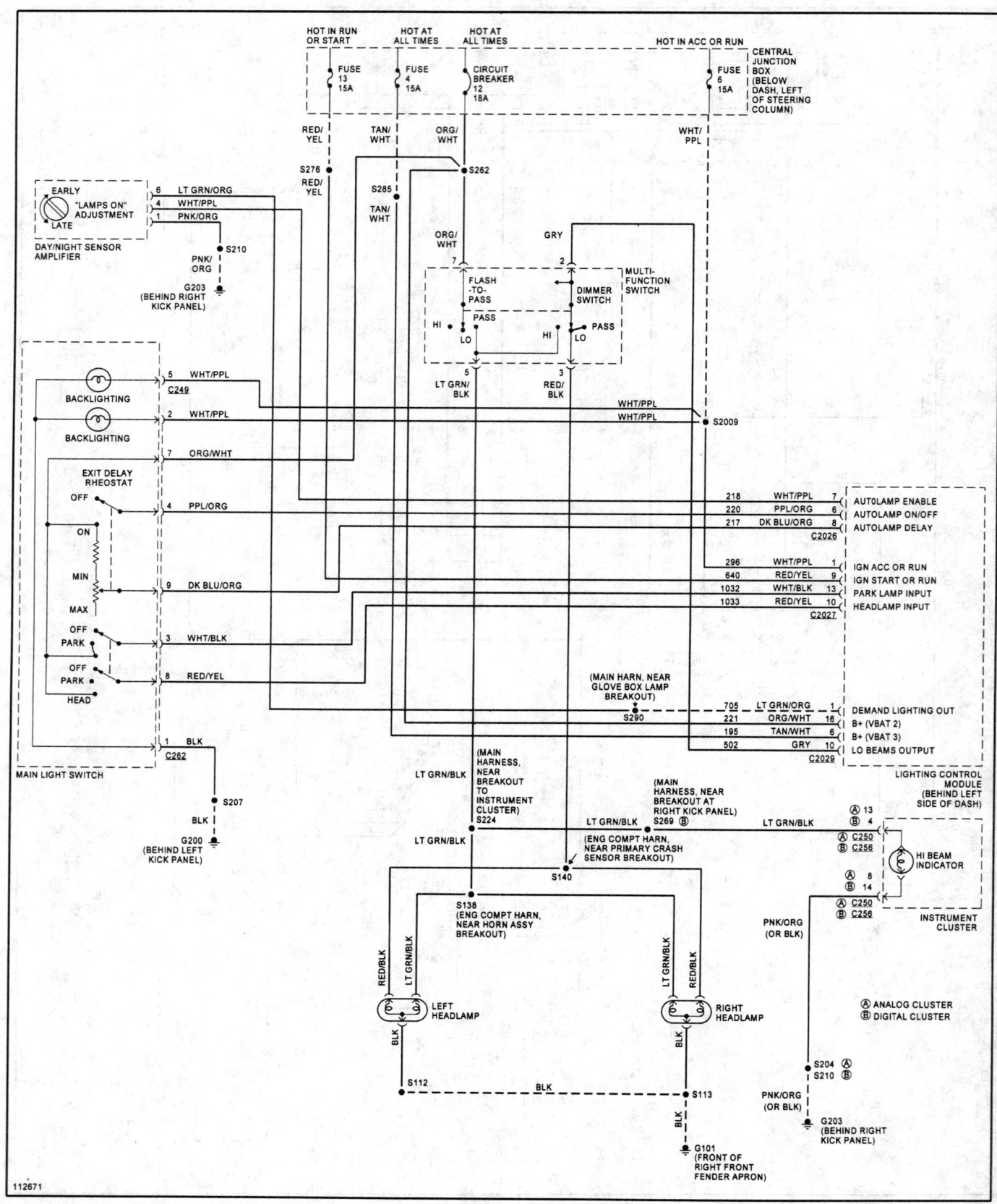

Fig. 6: Headlight System Wiring Diagram (Crown Victoria & Grand Marquis – Without DRL)

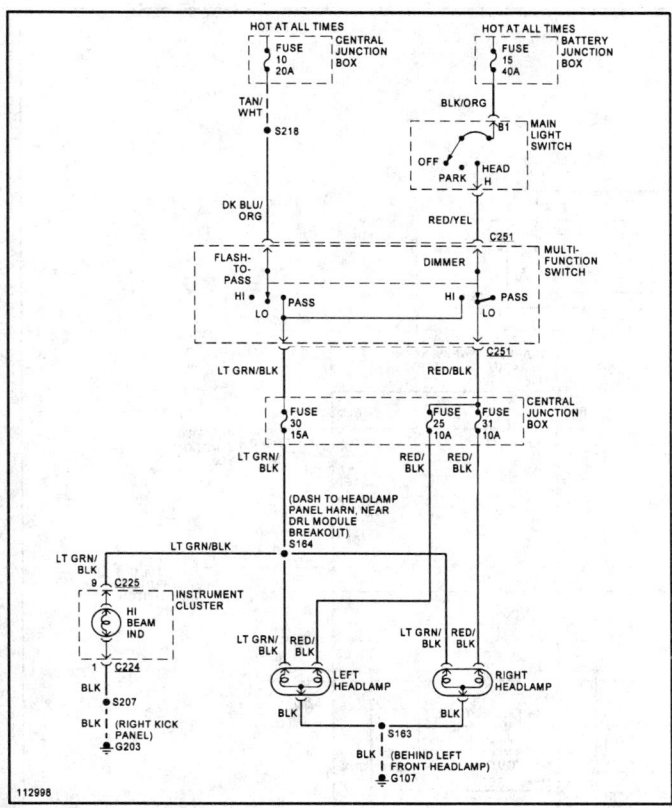

**Fig. 7: Headlight System Wiring Diagram
(Econoline – Without DRL)**

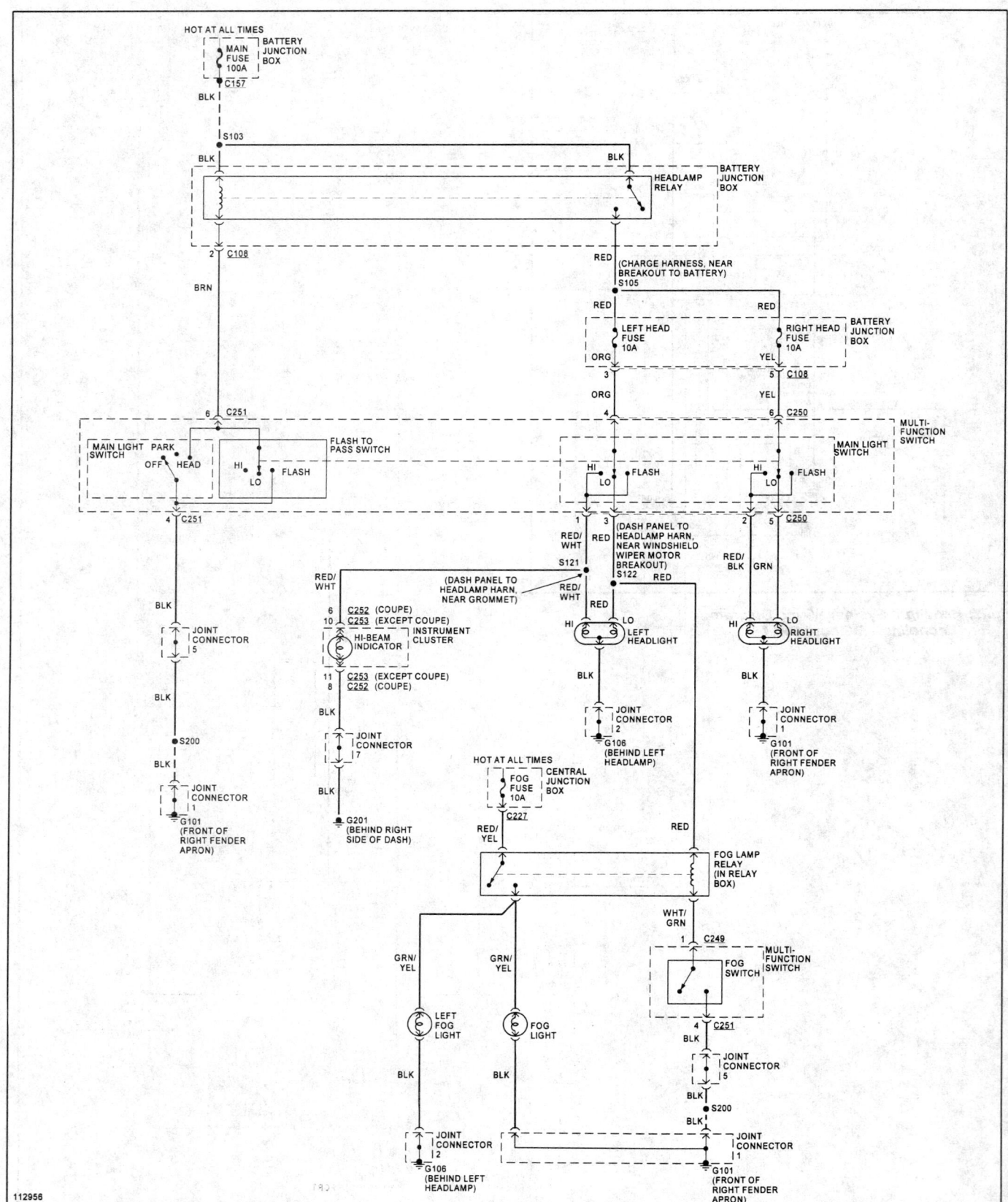

Fig. 8: Headlight System Wiring Diagram (Escort & Tracer – Without DRL)

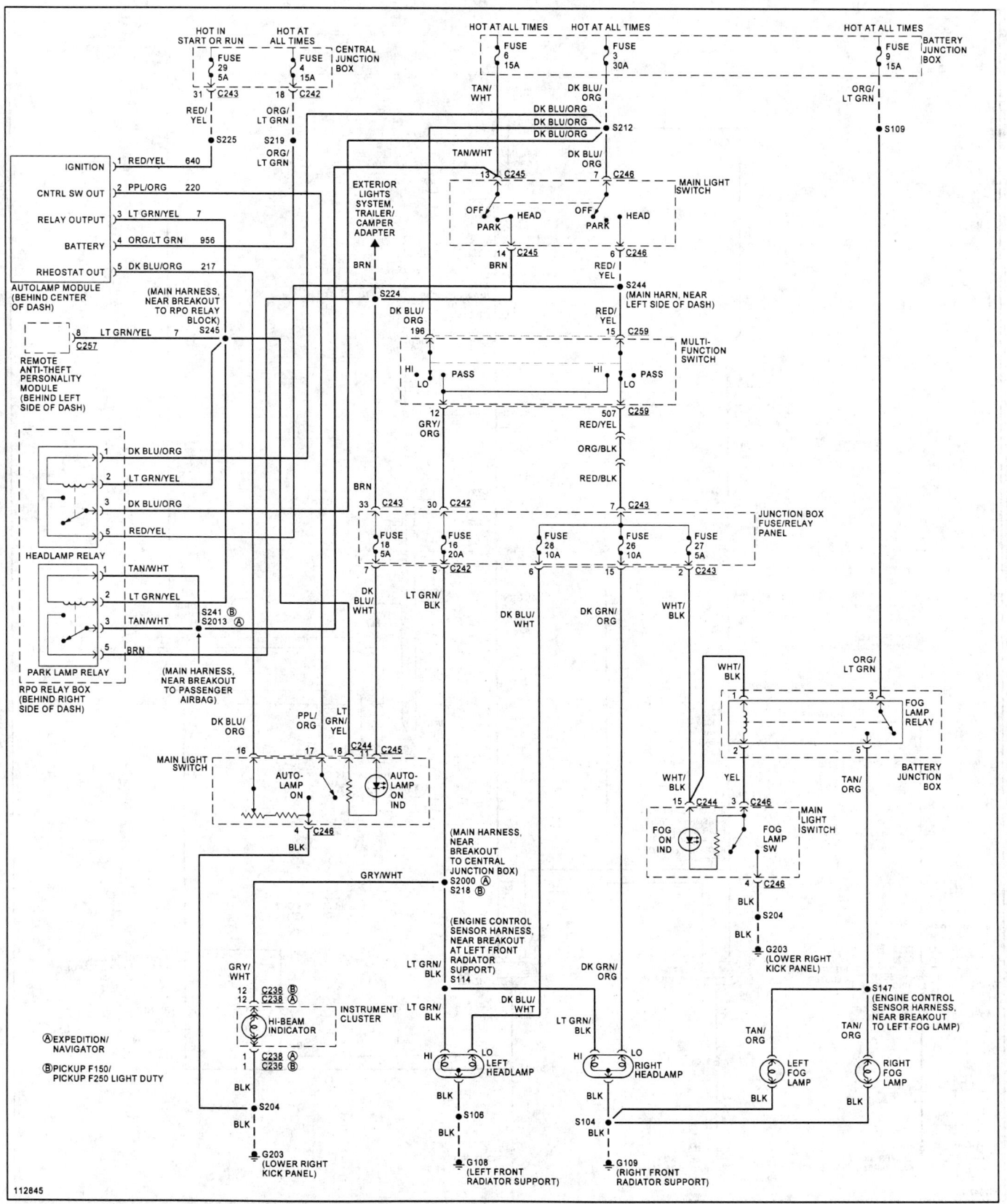

Fig. 9: Headlight System Wiring Diagram (Expedition, F150 & F250 Light-Duty Pickup, & Navigator – Without DRL – Autolamps & Fog Lights Circuits)

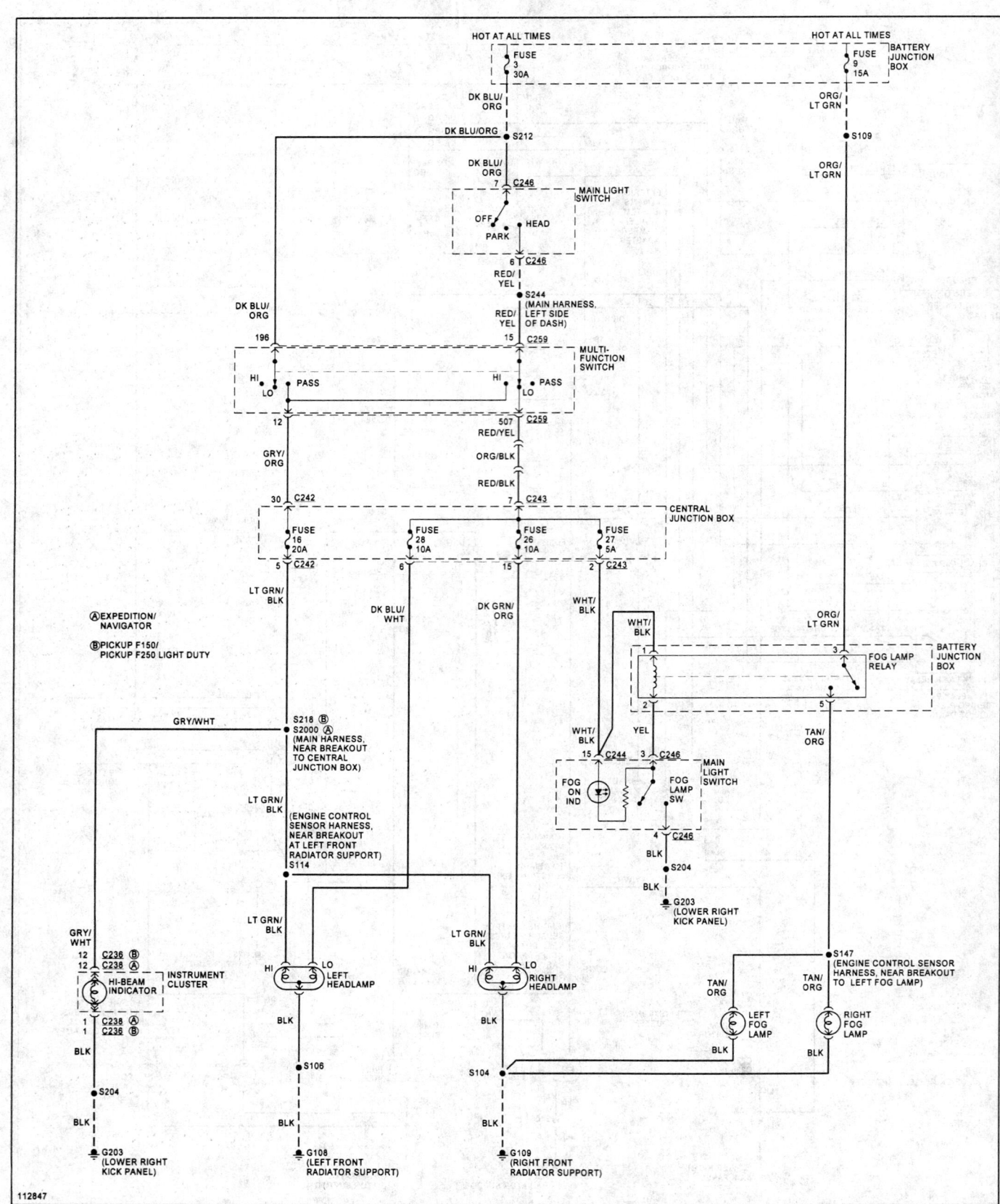

Fig. 10: Headlight System Wiring Diagram (Expedition, F150 & F250 Light-Duty Pickup, & Navigator – Without DRL – Headlights & Fog Lights Circuits)

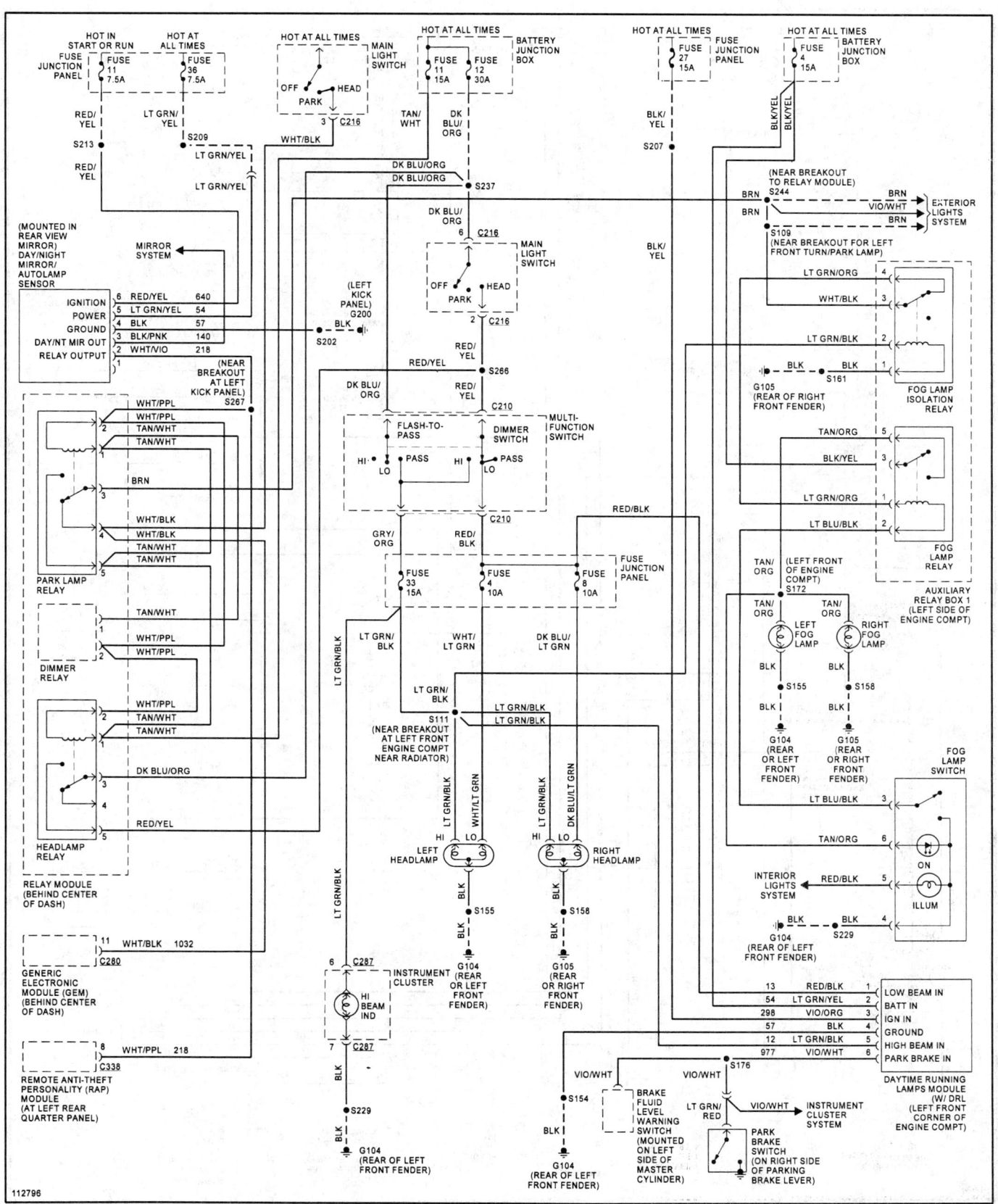

Fig. 11: Headlight System Wiring Diagram (Explorer & Mountaineer – Autolamps Circuit)

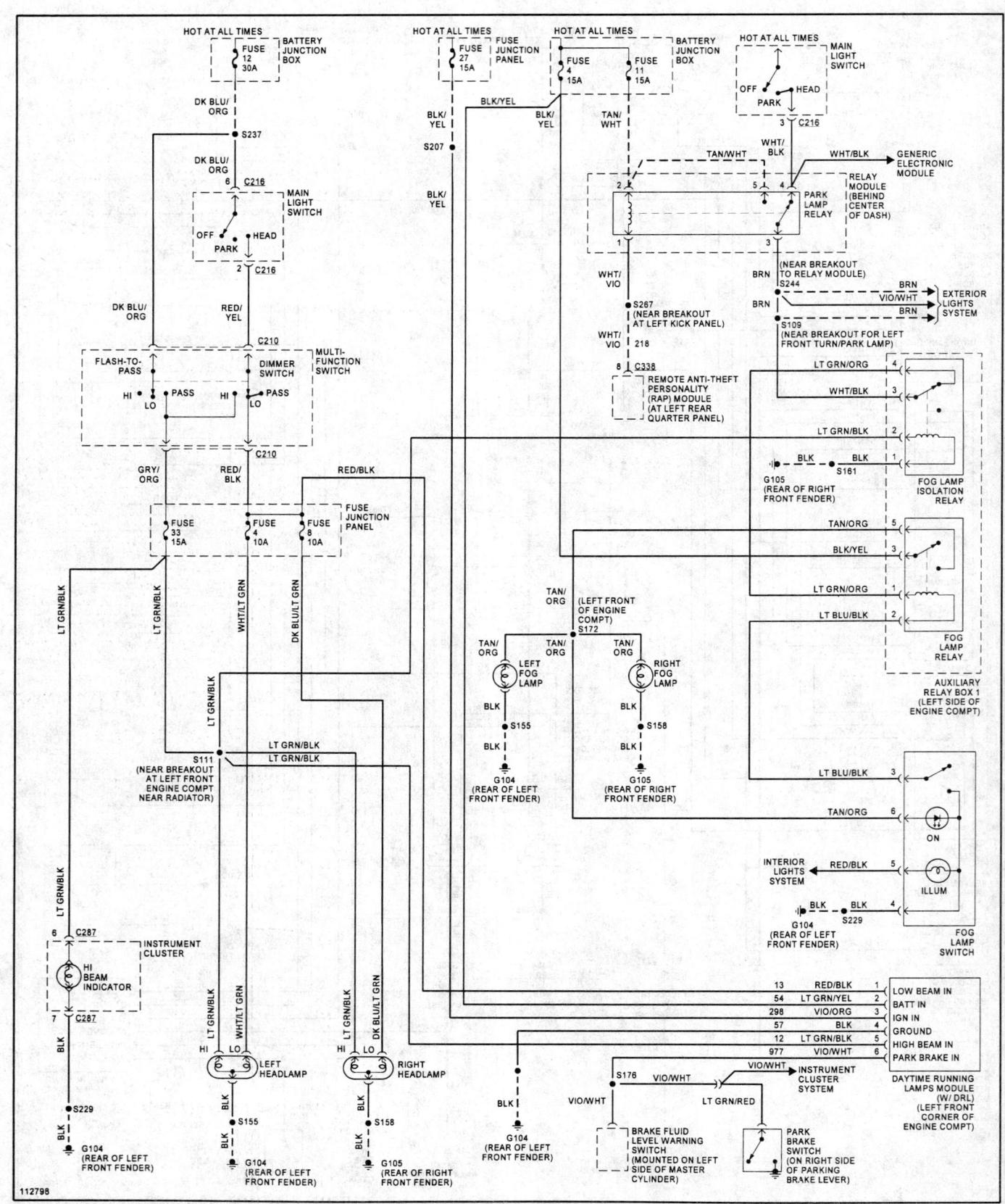

Fig. 12: Headlight System Wiring Diagram (Explorer & Mountaineer – Headlights Circuit)

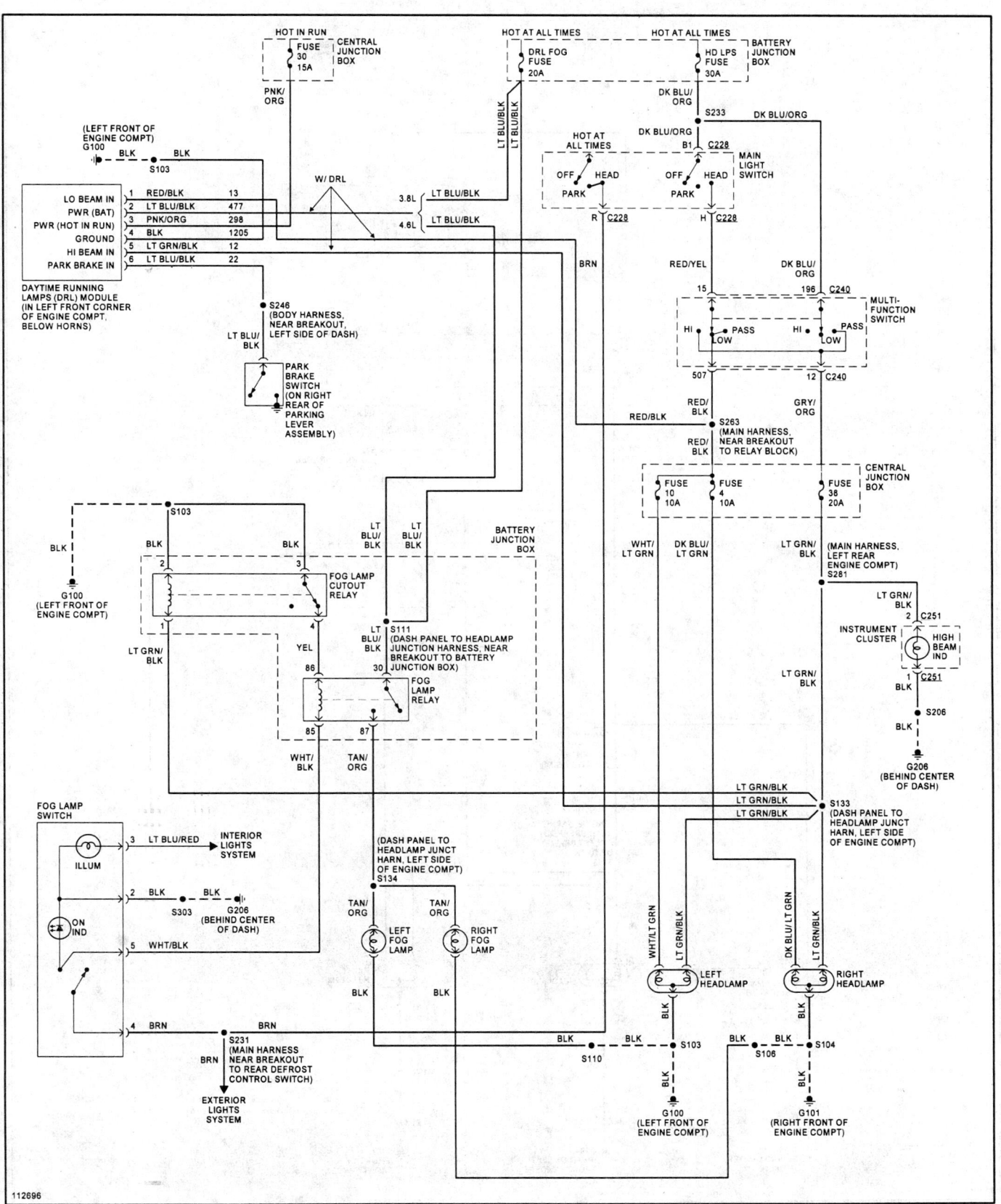

Fig. 13: Headlight System Wiring Diagram (Mustang)

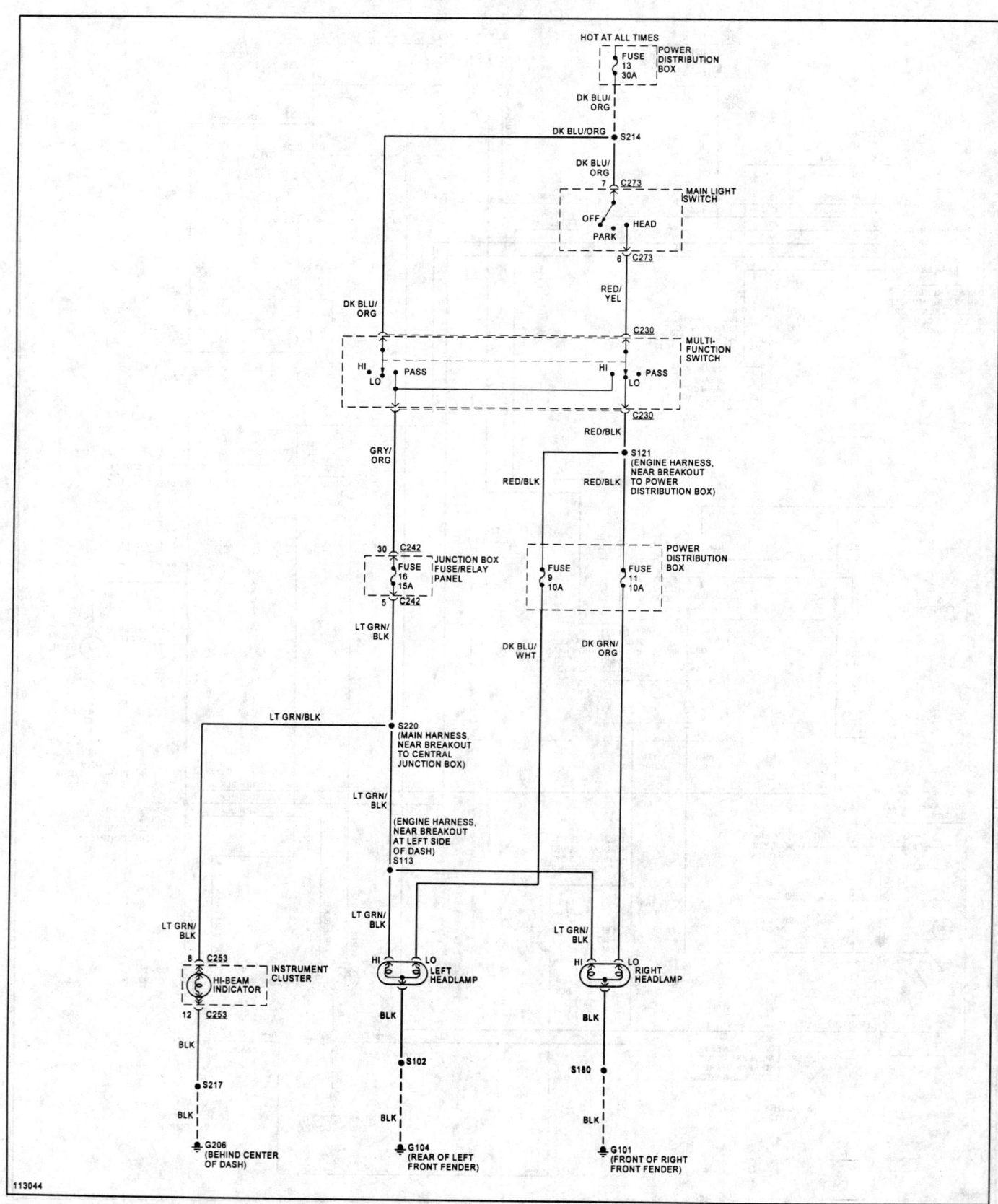

Fig. 14: Headlight System Wiring Diagram (F250 & F350 Super-Duty Pickup – Without DRL)

113044

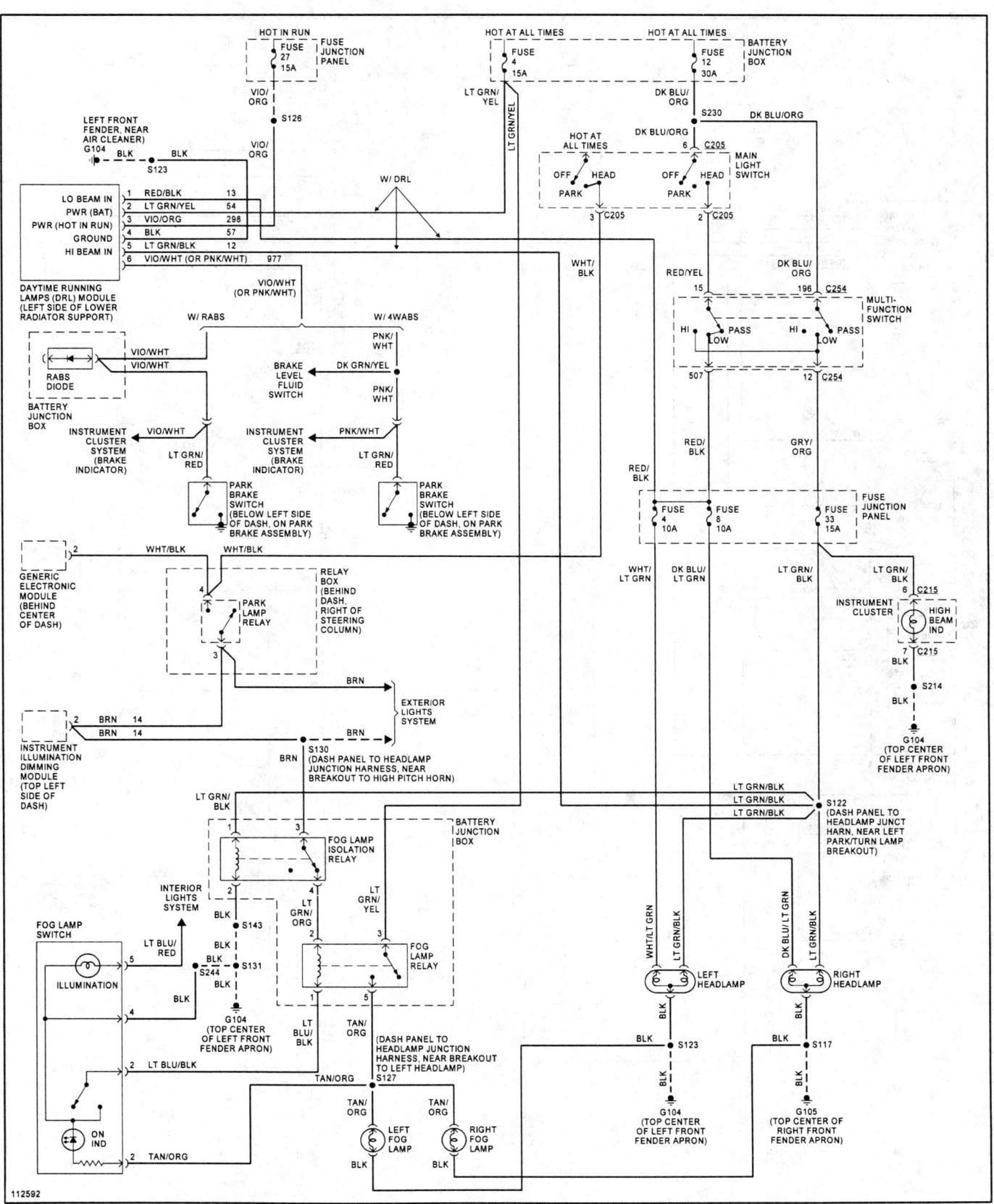

Fig. 15: Headlight System Wiring Diagram (Ranger)

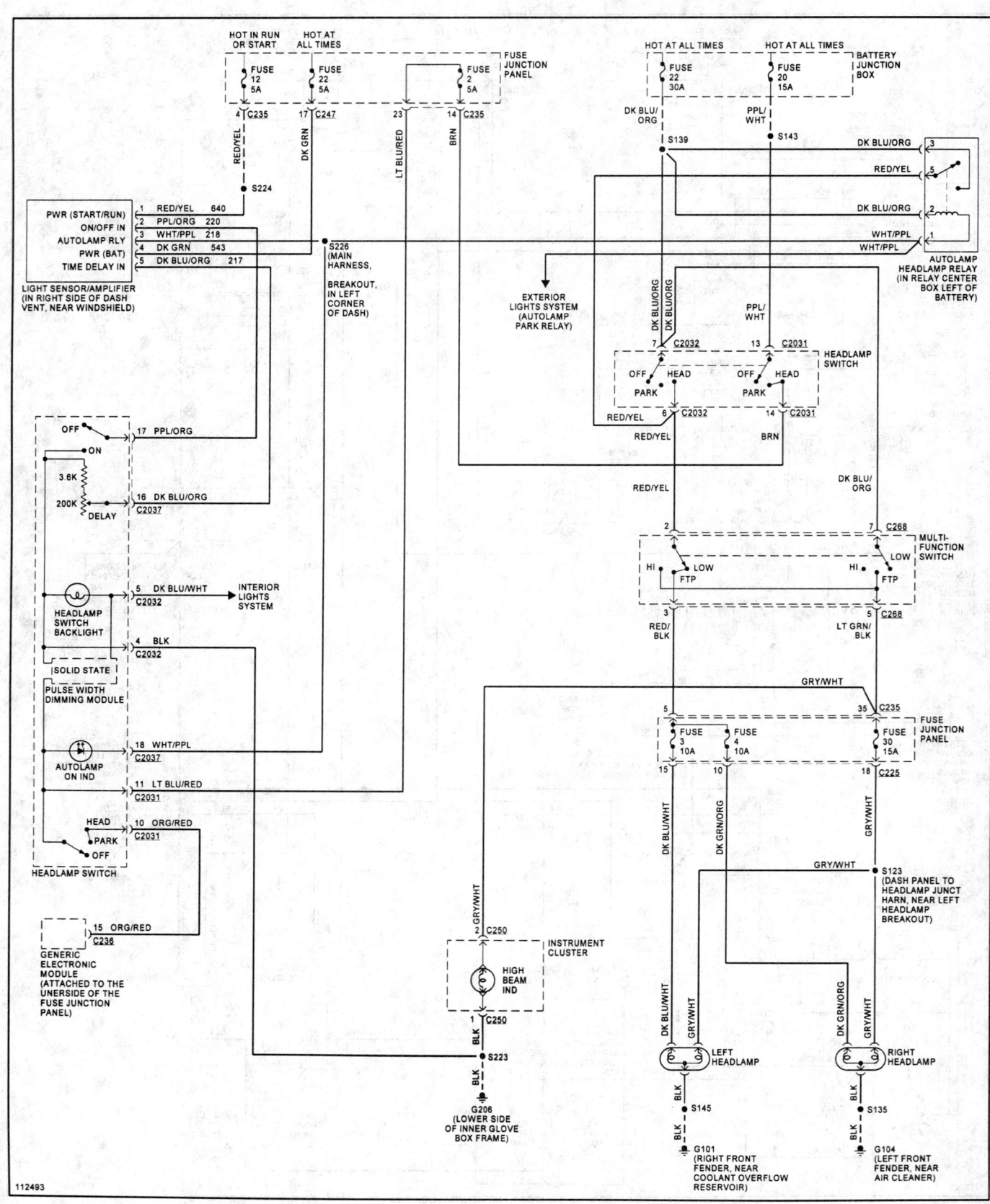

Fig. 16: Headlight System Wiring Diagram (Sable & Taurus – Without DRL – Autolamps Circuit)

112493

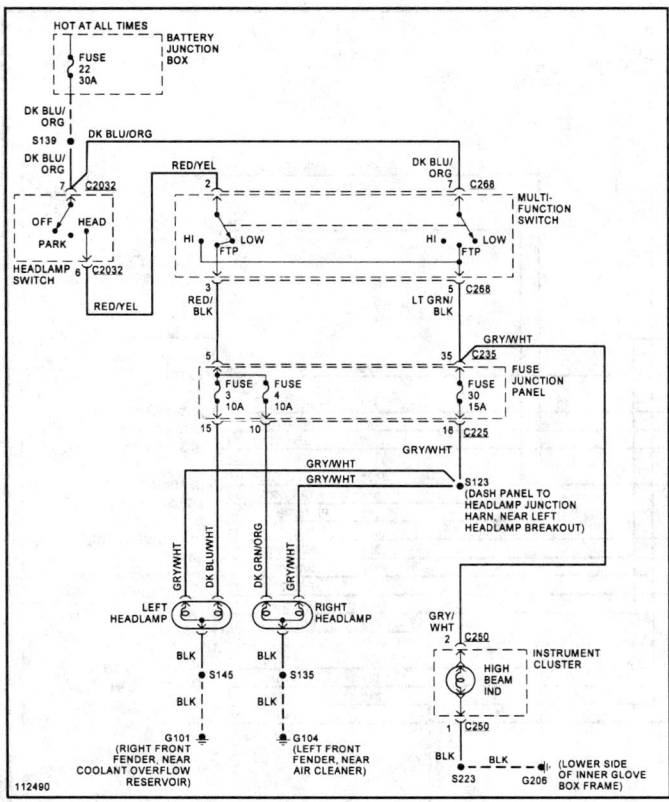

*Fig. 17: Headlight System Wiring Diagram (Sable & Taurus –
Without DRL – Headlights Circuit)*

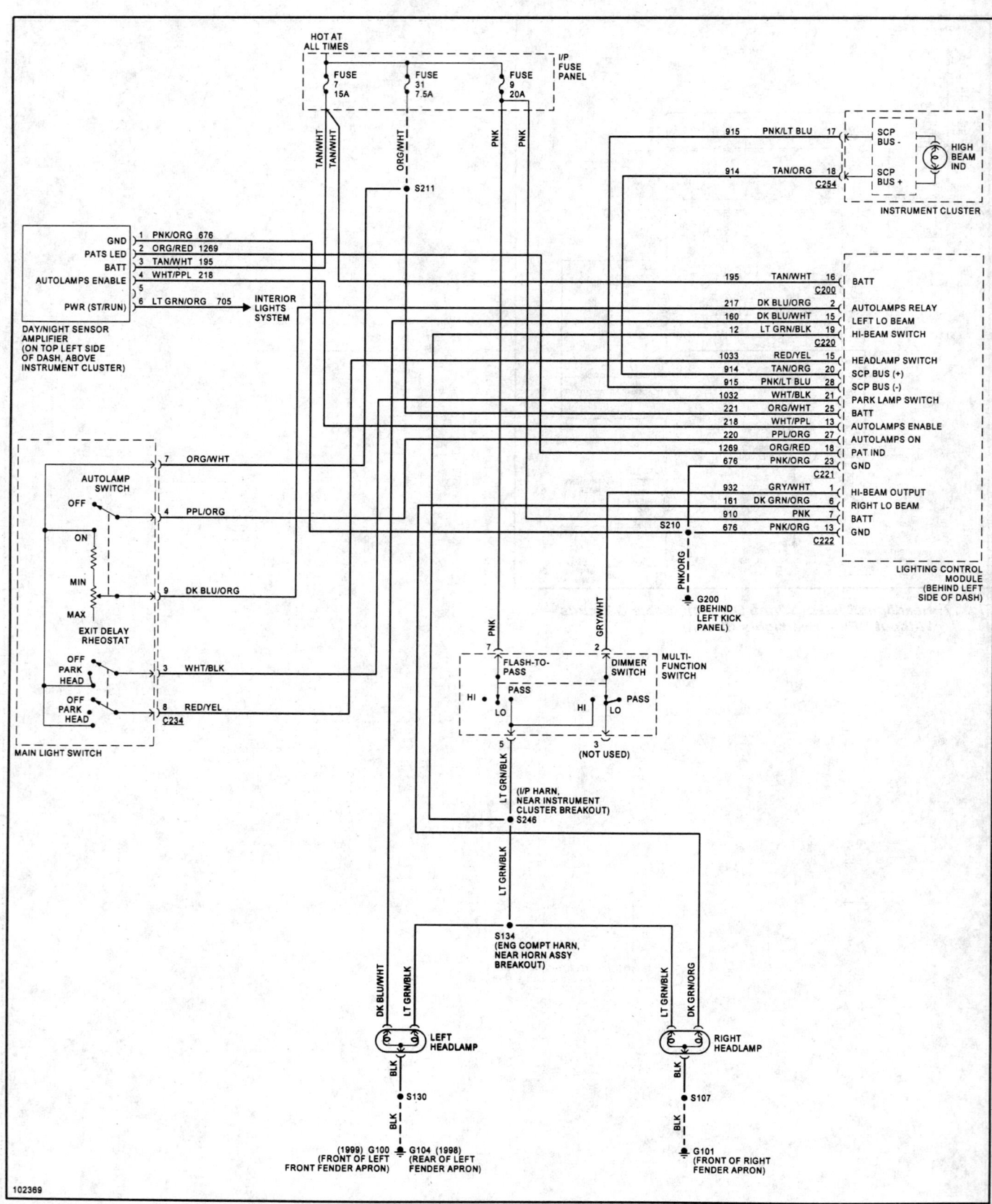

Fig. 18: Headlight System Wiring Diagram (Town Car – Autolamps & Delayed Exit Circuit)

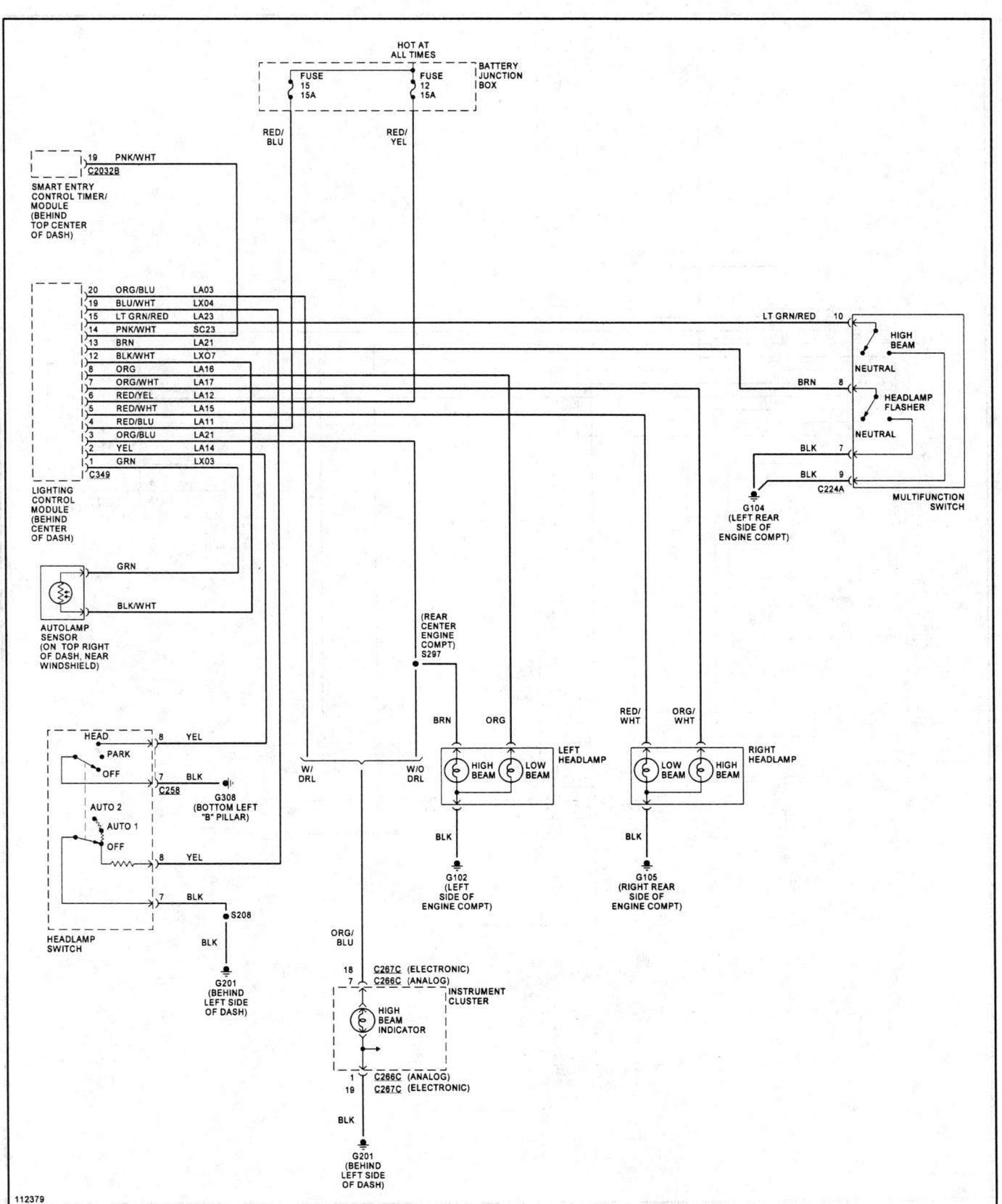

Fig. 19: Headlight System Wiring Diagram (Villager – With Autolamps)

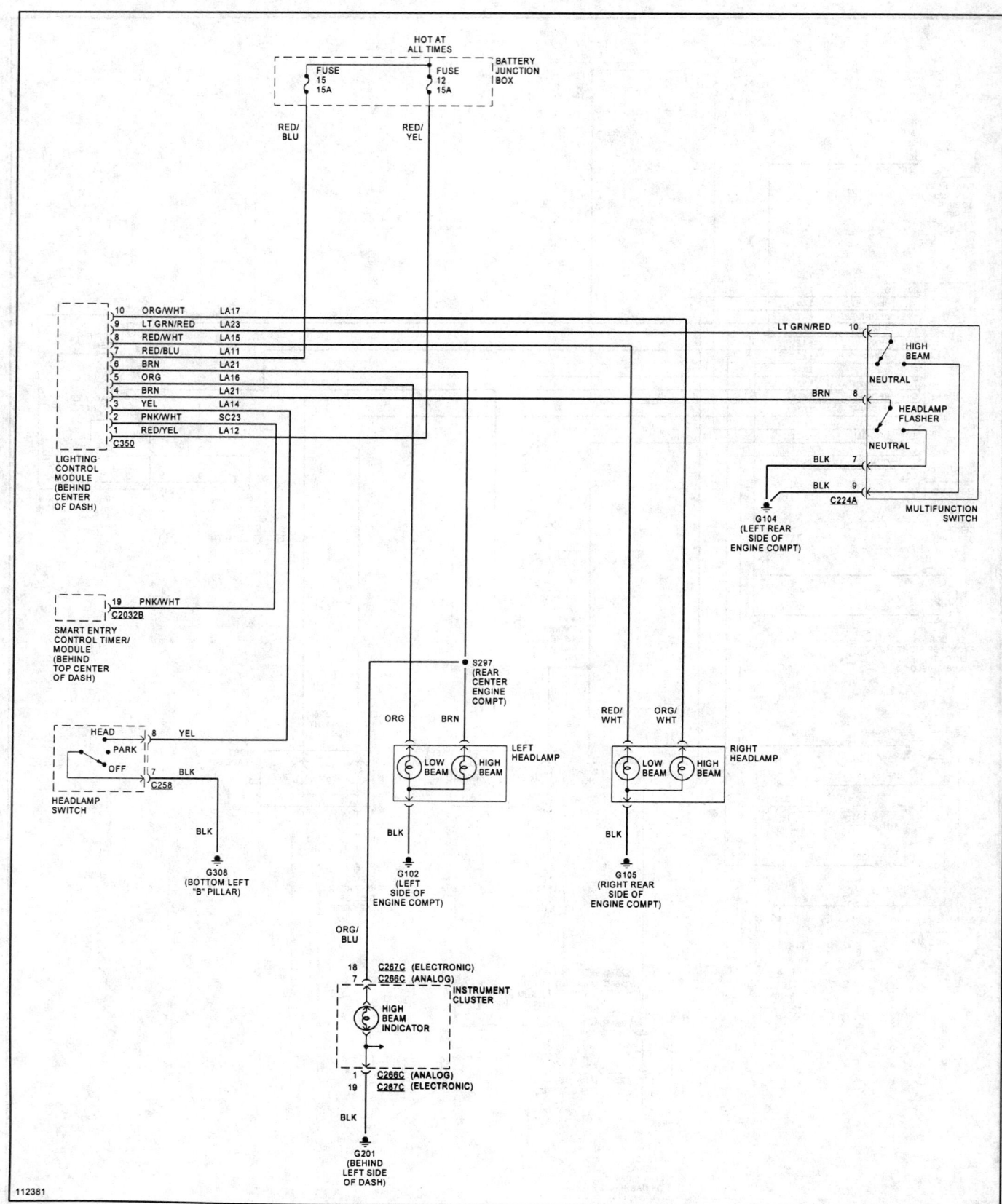

Fig. 20: Headlight System Wiring Diagram (Villager – Without Autolamps)

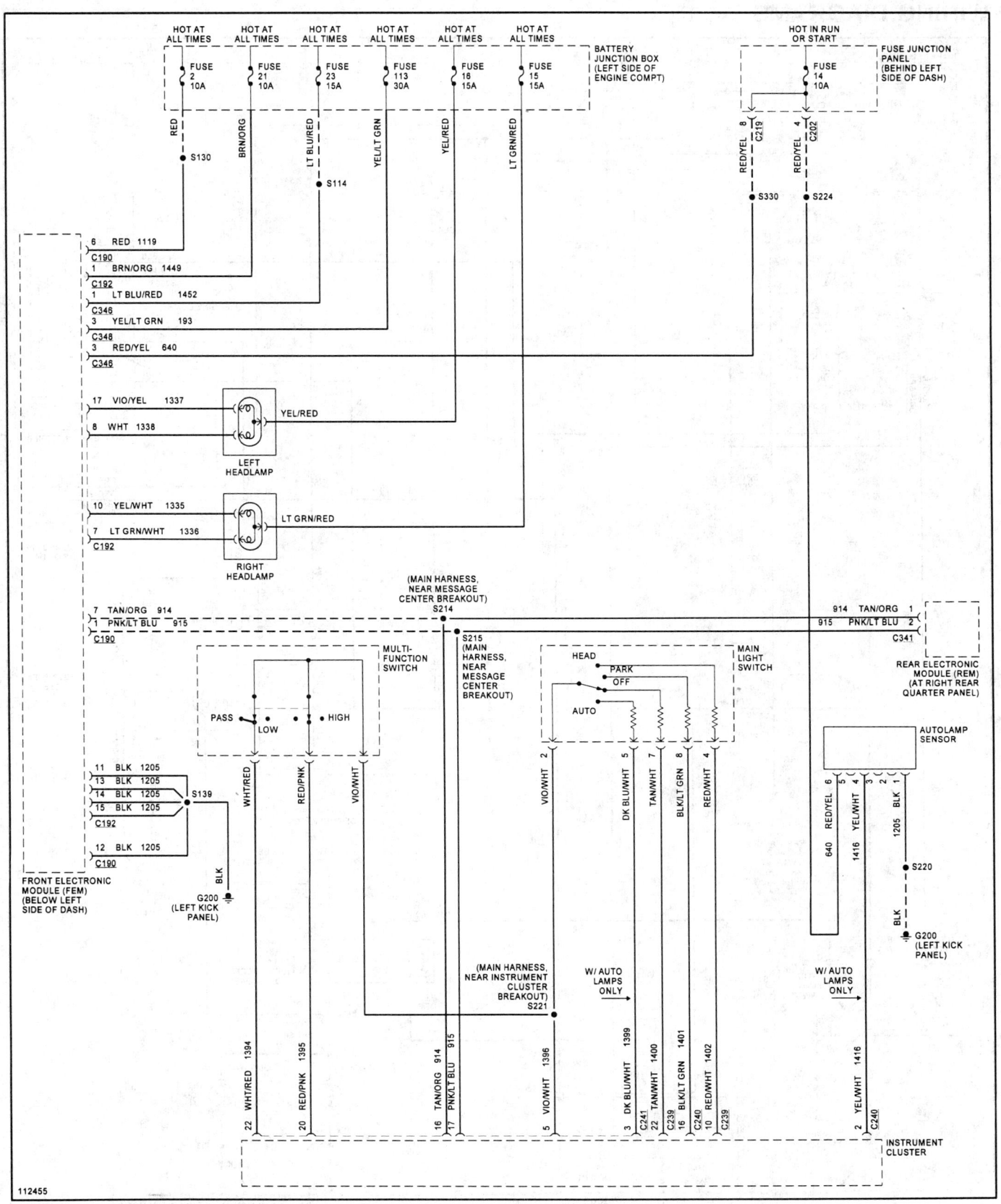

Fig. 21: Headlight System Wiring Diagram (Windstar)

WIRING DIAGRAMS

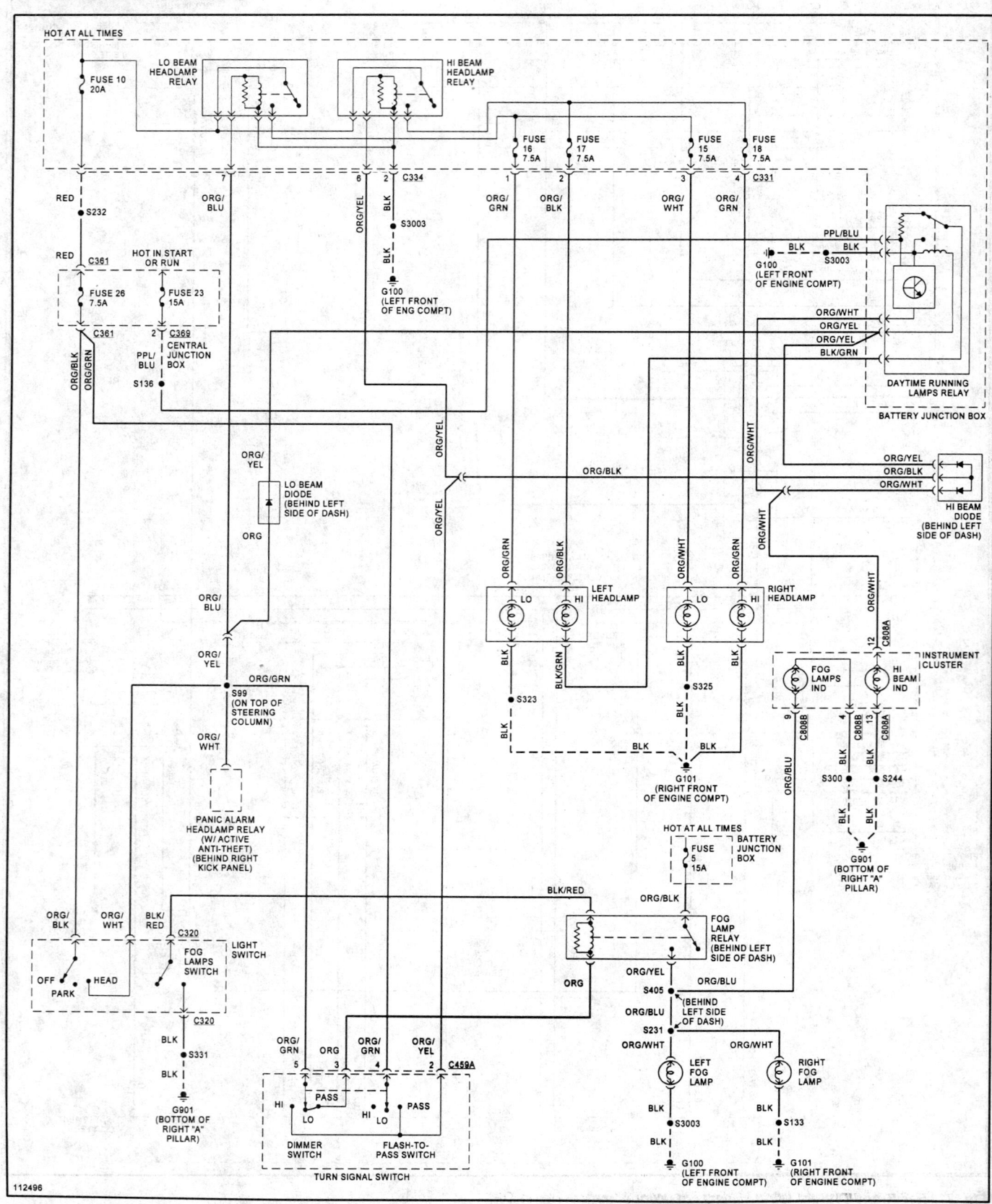

Fig. 1: Daytime Running Lights Wiring Diagram (Contour & Mystique – With DRL)

112496

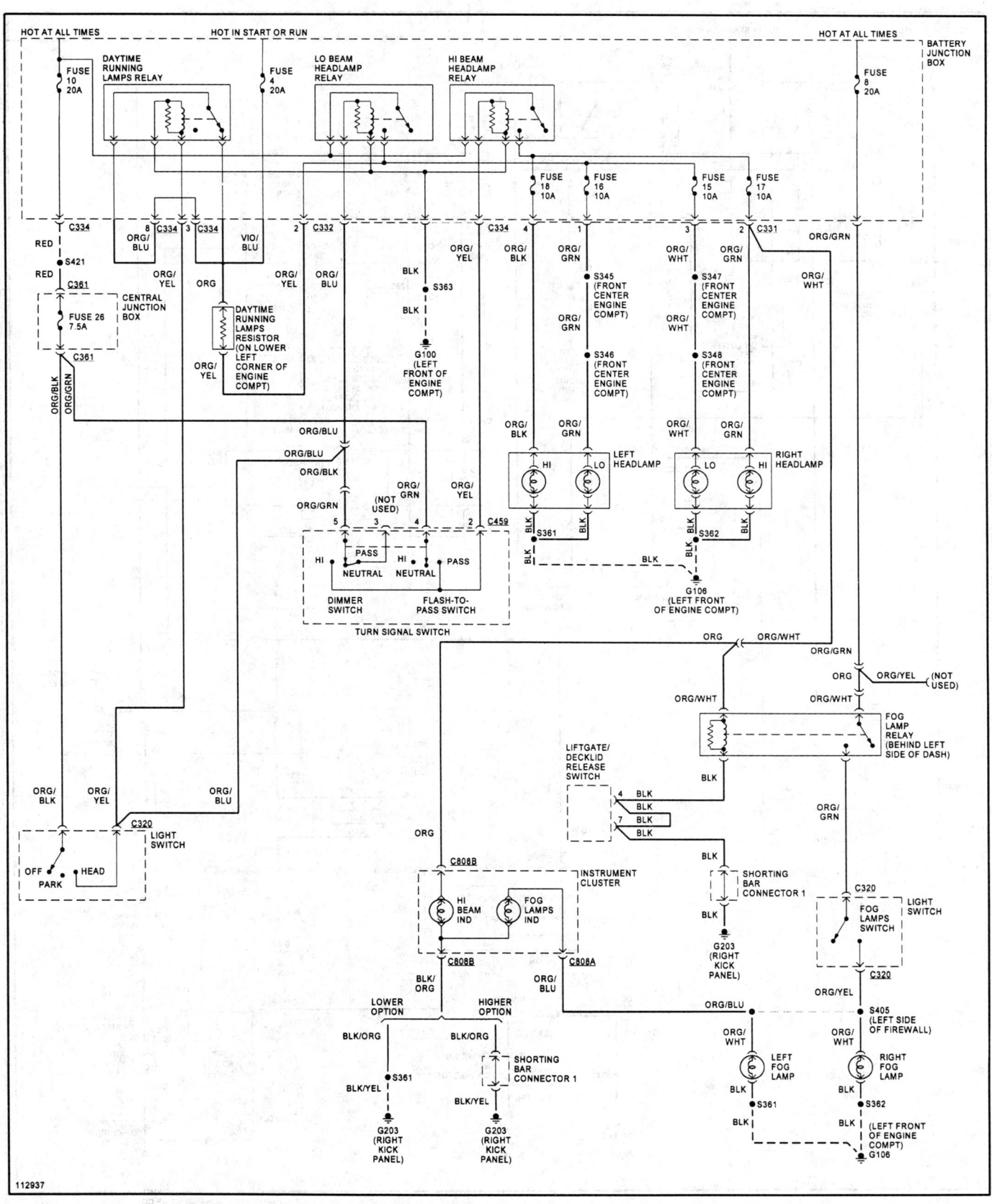

Fig. 2: Daytime Running Lights Wiring Diagram (Cougar – With DRL)

112937

HOT AT ALL TIMES | HOT IN START OR RUN | HOT AT ALL TIMES

BATTERY JUNCTION BOX

FUSE 10 20A | DAYTIME RUNNING LAMPS RELAY | FUSE 4 20A | LO BEAM HEADLAMP RELAY | HI BEAM HEADLAMP RELAY | FUSE 8 20A

FUSE 18 10A | FUSE 16 10A | FUSE 15 10A | FUSE 17 10A

C334 | 8 C334 | 3 C334 | VIO/BLU | 2 C332 | C334 | 4 | 1 | 3 | 2 C331 | ORG/GRN

RED | ORG/BLU | ORG/YEL | ORG | ORG/YEL | ORG/BLU | BLK | ORG/YEL | ORG/BLK | ORG | ORG/GRN | ORG/GRN | ORG/WHT

S421

RED

C361

CENTRAL JUNCTION BOX

FUSE 26 7.5A

C361

29S-WC34 | ORG/GRN | 29S-WC36

S363

BLK

G100 (LEFT FRONT OF ENGINE COMPT)

ORG | 24 | 25 | C466

DAYTIME RUNNING LAMPS RESISTOR (ON LOWER LEFT CORNER OF ENGINE COMPT)

ORG/YEL

22 | BULB OUTAGE MODULE (UNDER LEFT SIDE OF DASH ON CENTRAL JUNCTION BOX) | 23 | C466

ORG/BLK | ORG/GRN

ORG/BLU | ORG/BLK | ORG/GRN | ORG/GRN | 29S-LE16 | ORG/WHT | 29S-LE23 | ORG/WHT

LEFT HEADLAMP | RIGHT HEADLAMP

HI | LO | LO | HI

ORG/BLU | ORG/BLK | ORG/GRN

5 | 3 | 4 | 2 C459

HI NEUTRAL | HI NEUTRAL | PASS

PASS

DIMMER SWITCH | FLASH-TO-PASS SWITCH

TURN SIGNAL SWITCH

(NOT USED) ORG/GRN | ORG/YEL

BLK | BLK | S361 | BLK | BLK | S362 | BLK

BLK

G106 (LEFT FRONT OF ENGINE COMPT)

ORG | ORG/WHT | ORG/GRN

ORG | ORG/YEL (NOT USED)

ORG/WHT | ORG/WHT | FOG LAMP RELAY (BEHIND LEFT SIDE OF DASH)

LIFTGATE/DECKLID RELEASE SWITCH

4 BLK | BLK | BLK

BLK | 7 BLK | BLK

ORG/BLK | ORG/YEL | ORG/BLU

LIGHT SWITCH

C320

OFF | HEAD

PARK

ORG

SHORTING BAR CONNECTOR 1

BLK

C808B

INSTRUMENT CLUSTER

HI BEAM IND | FOG LAMPS IND

ORG/GRN

G203 (RIGHT KICK PANEL)

C320 LIGHT SWITCH

FOG LAMPS SWITCH

C808B | C808A

BLK/ORG | ORG/BLU

C320

LOWER OPTION | HIGHER OPTION

ORG/GRN

ORG/YEL

BLK/ORG | BLK/ORG

SHORTING BAR CONNECTOR 1

ORG/BLU | S405 (LEFT SIDE OF FIREWALL)

BLK/YEL | BLK/YEL

ORG/WHT | ORG/WHT

LEFT FOG LAMP | RIGHT FOG LAMP

S361 | G203 (RIGHT KICK PANEL) | G203 (RIGHT KICK PANEL)

BLK | BLK | S361 | S362

BLK | BLK (LEFT FRONT OF ENGINE COMPT)

G106

112940

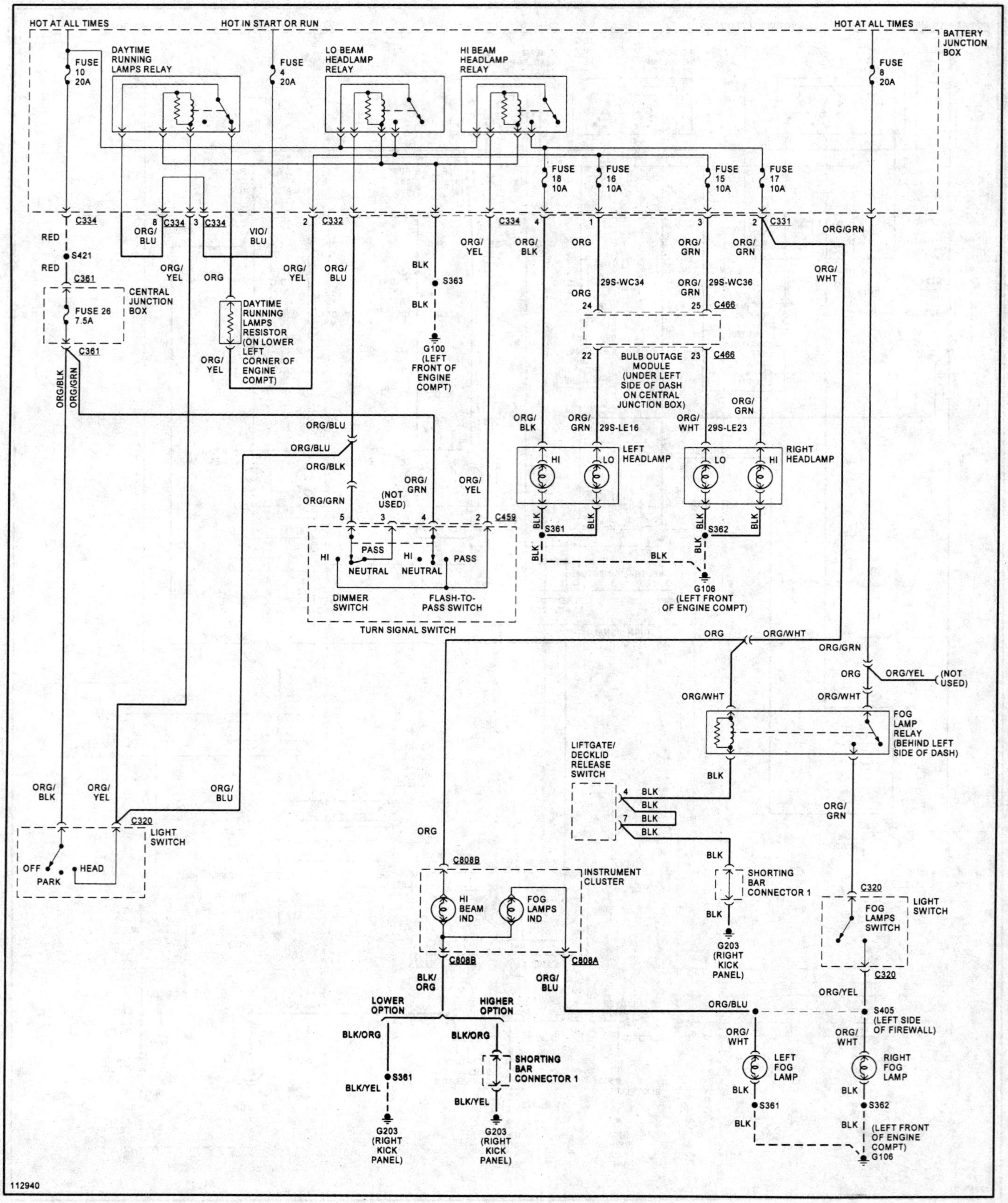

Fig. 3: Daytime Running Lights Wiring Diagram (Cougar – With DRL & Bulb Outage Module)

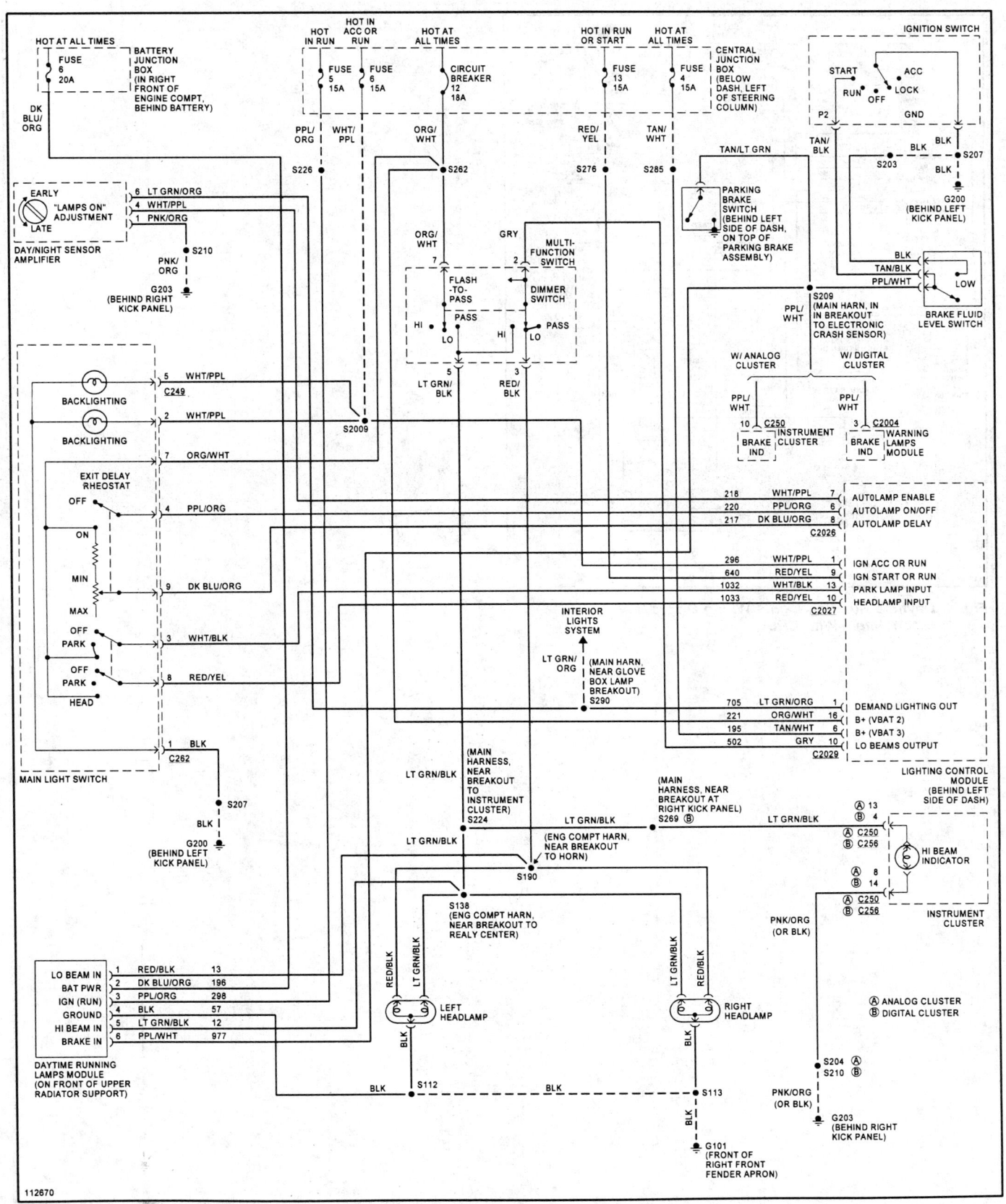

Fig. 4: Daytime Running Lights Wiring Diagram (Crown Victoria & Grand Marquis – With DRL – Headlights Circuit)

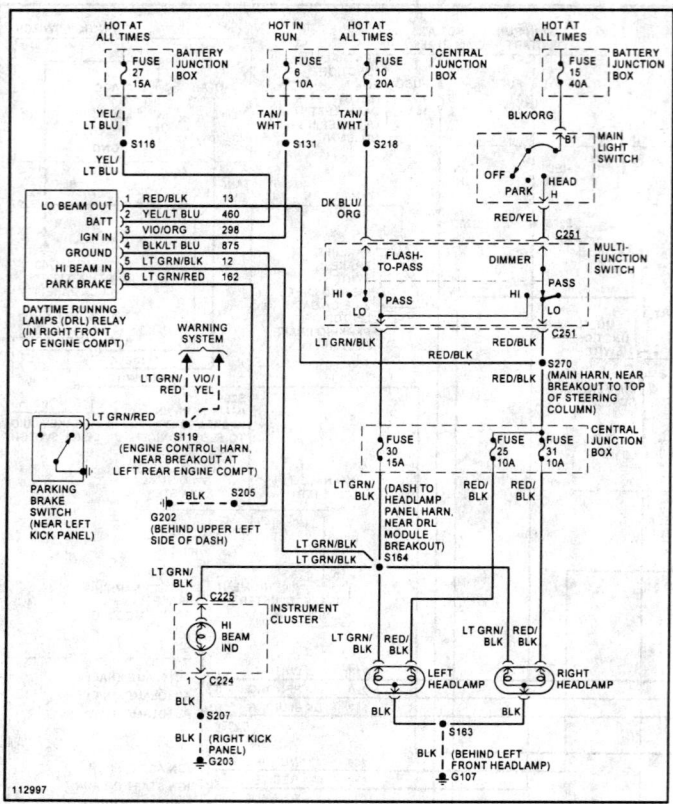

Fig. 5: Daytime Running Lights Wiring Diagram
(Econoline – With DRL)

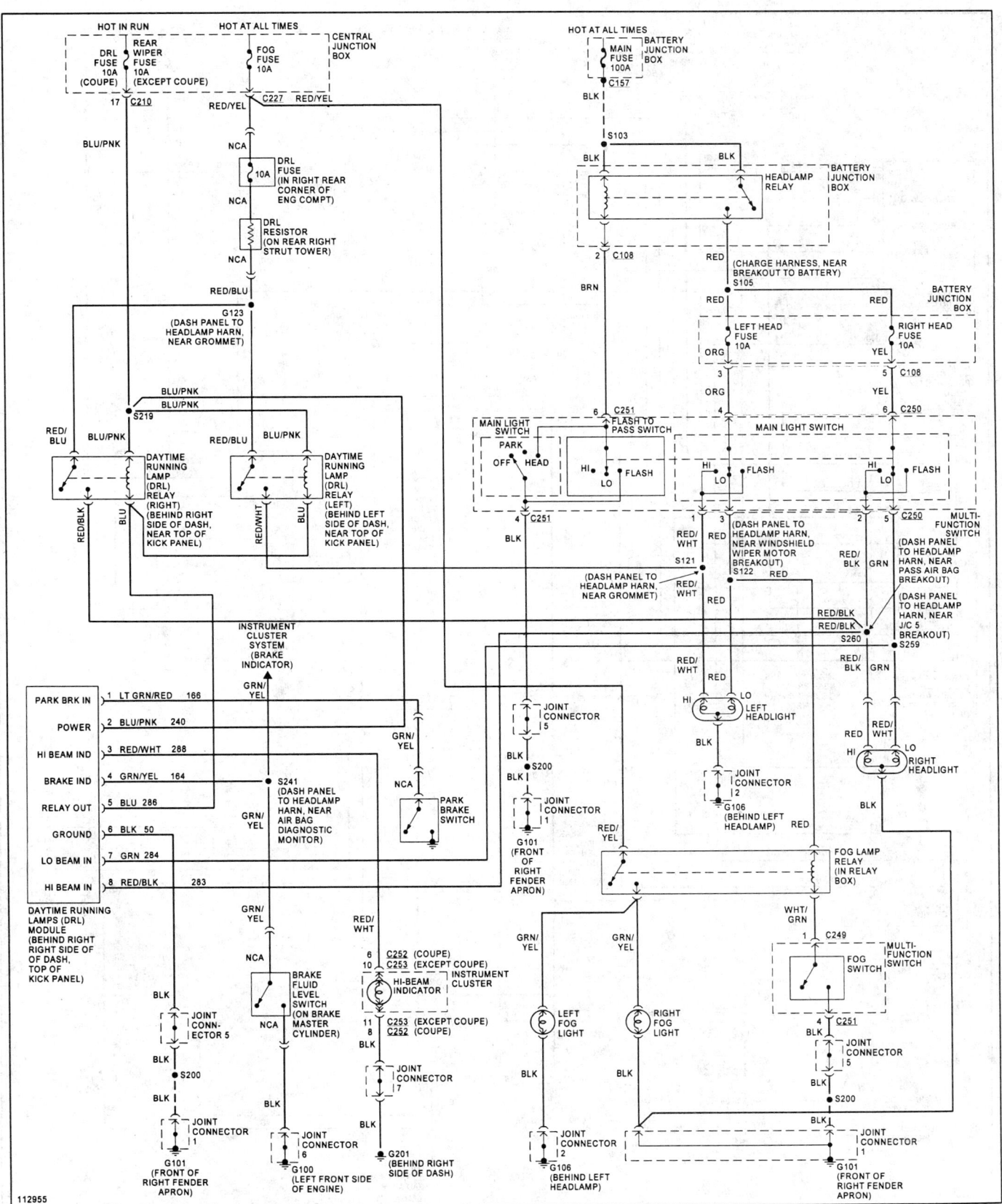

Fig. 6: Daytime Running Lights Wiring Diagram (Escort & Tracer – With DRL)

112955

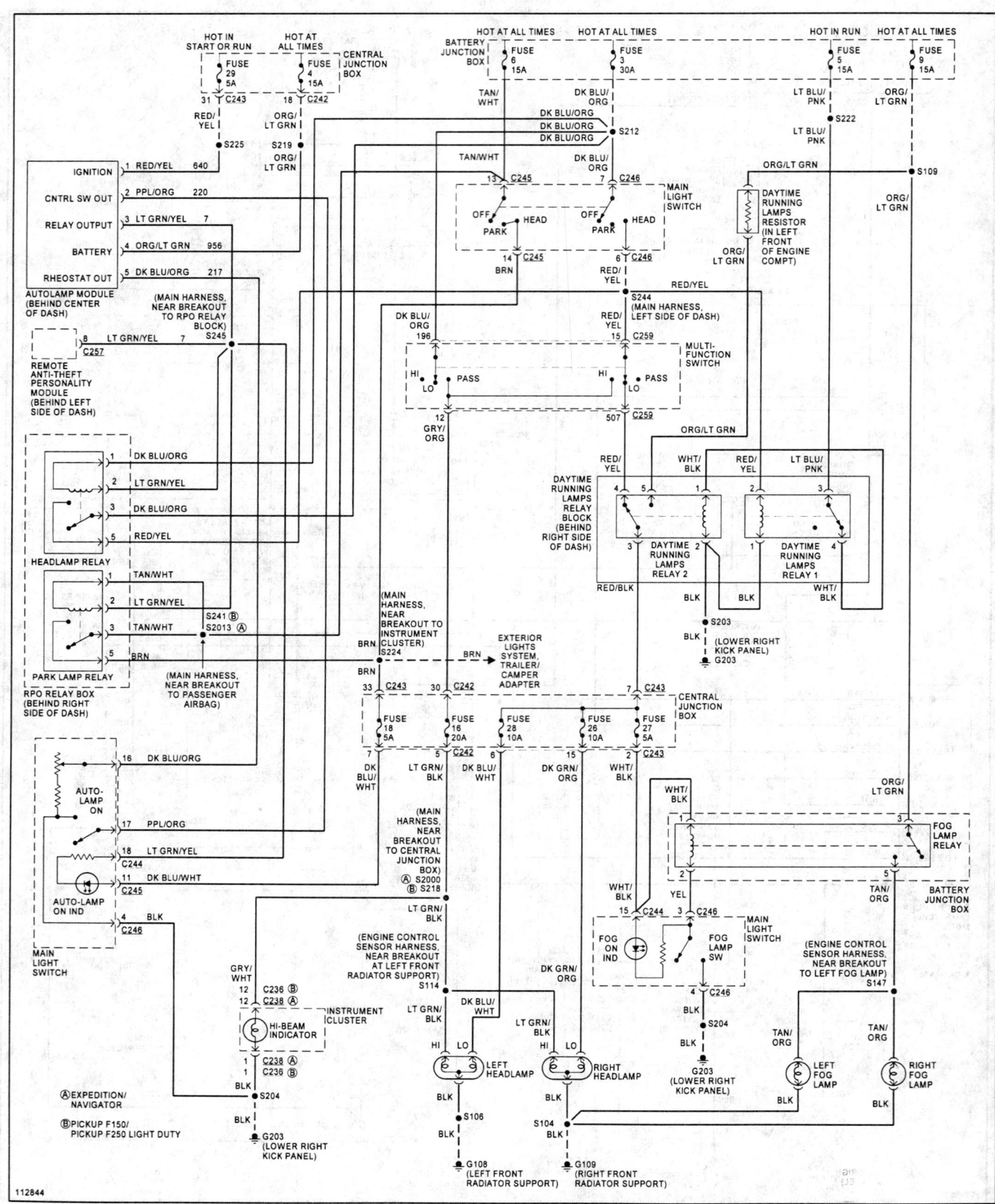

Fig. 7: Daytime Running Lights Wiring Diagram (Expedition, F150 & F250 Light-Duty Pickup, & Navigator – With DRL – Autolamps & Fog Lights Circuits)

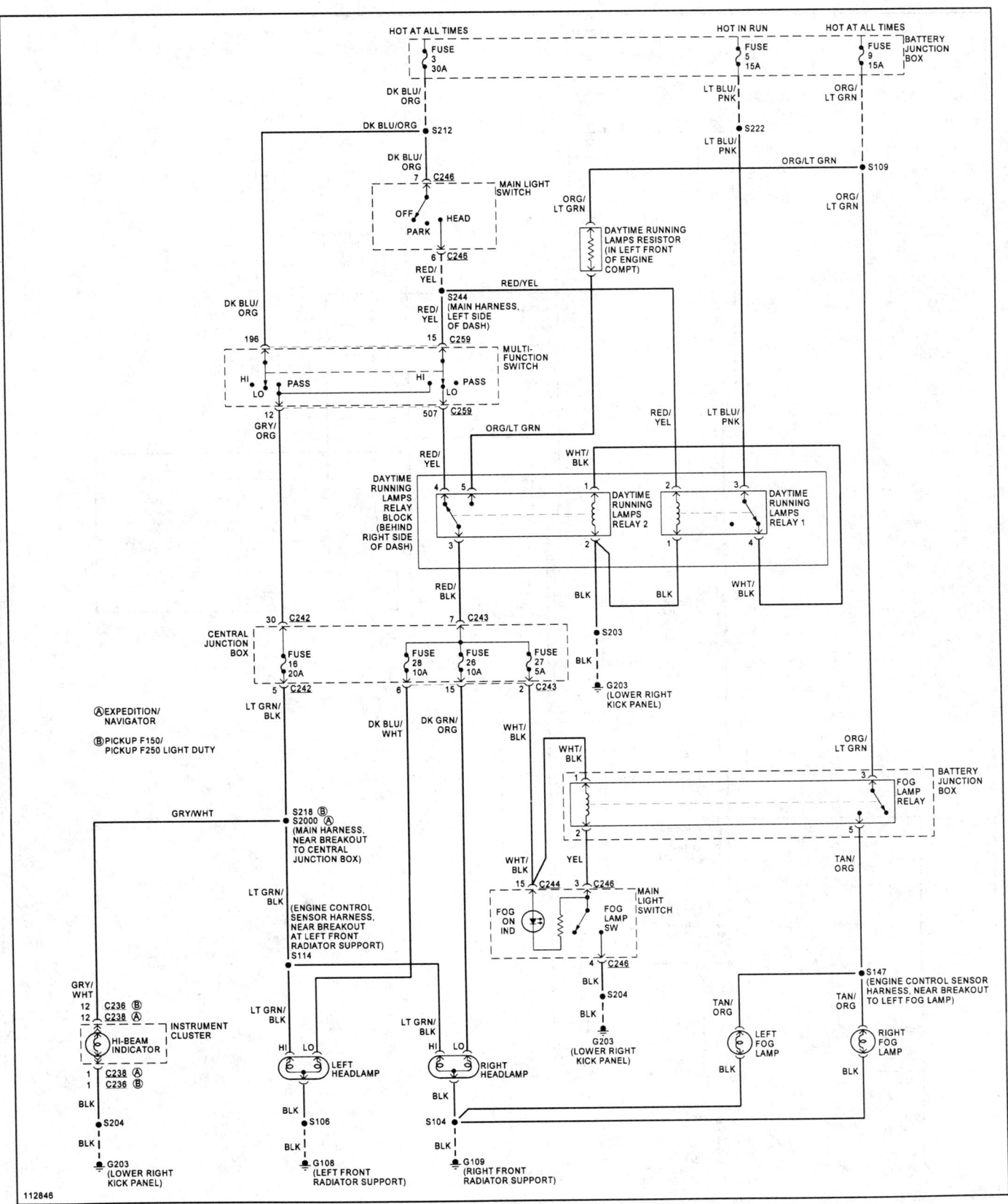

Fig. 8: Daytime Running Lights Wiring Diagram (Expedition, F150 & F250 Light-Duty Pickup, & Navigator – With DRL – Headlights & Fog Lights Circuits)

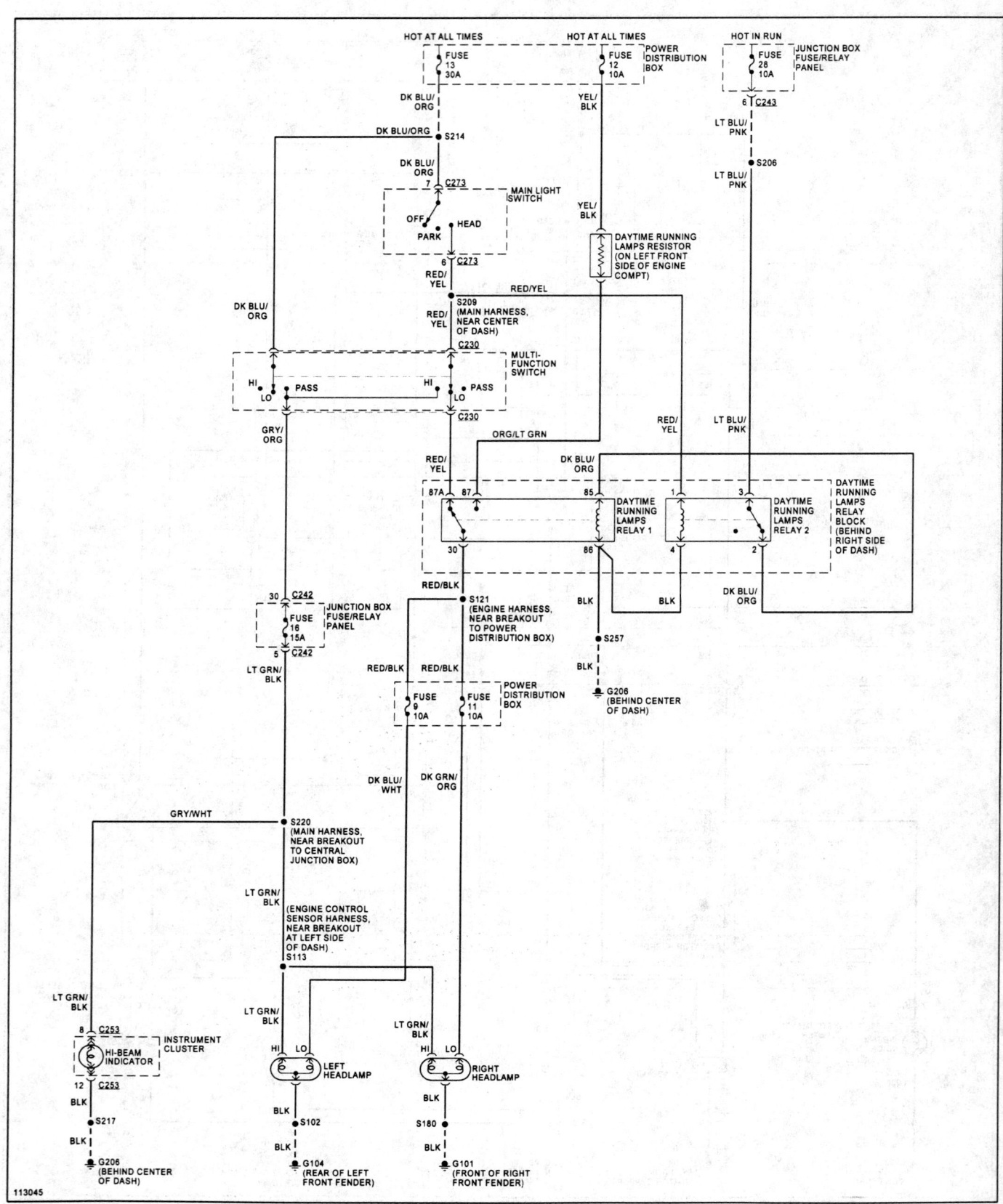

Fig. 9: Daytime Running Lights Wiring Diagram (F250 & F350 Super-Duty Pickup – With DRL)

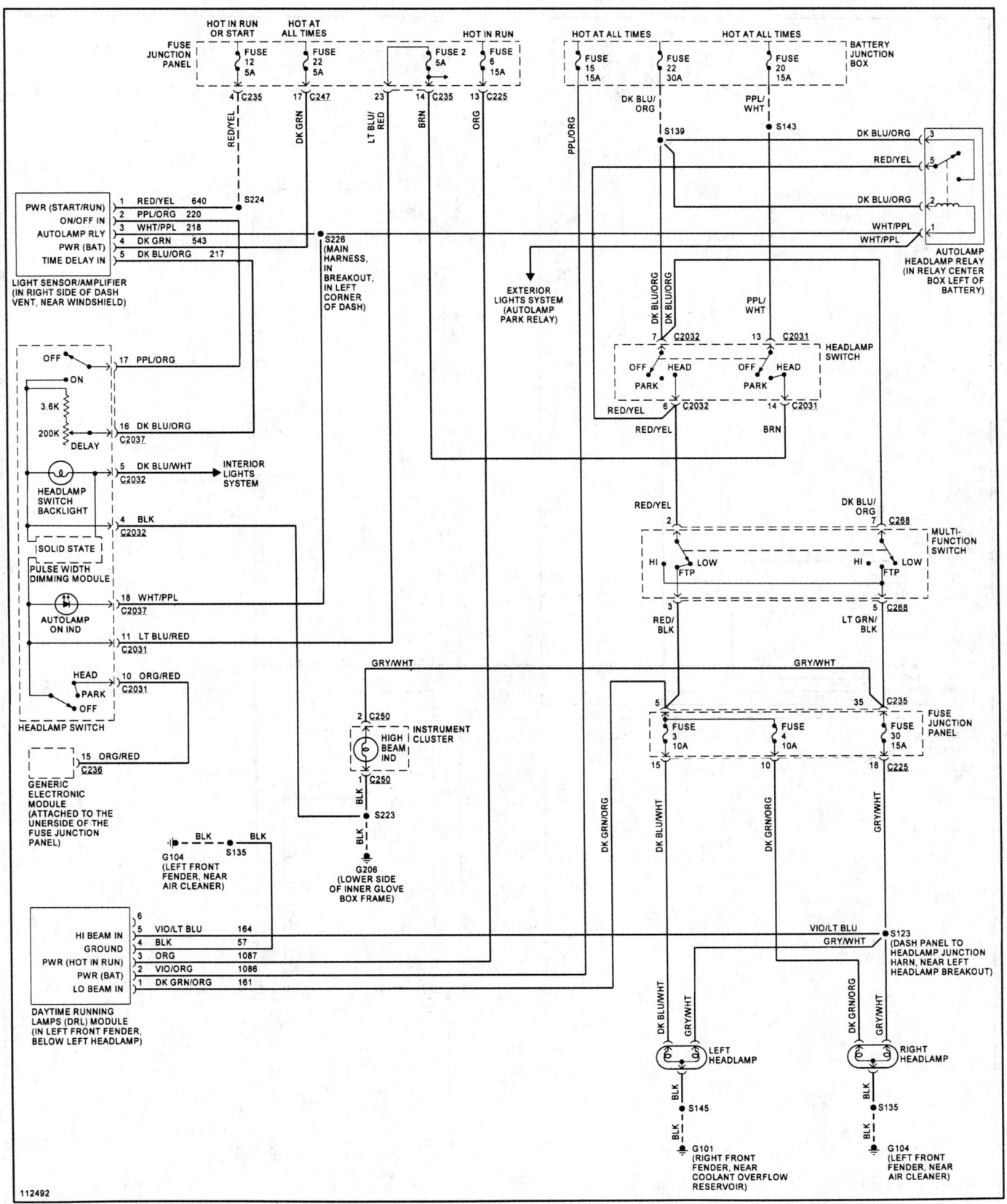

Fig. 10: Daytime Running Lights Wiring Diagram (Sable & Taurus – With DRL – Autolamps Circuit)

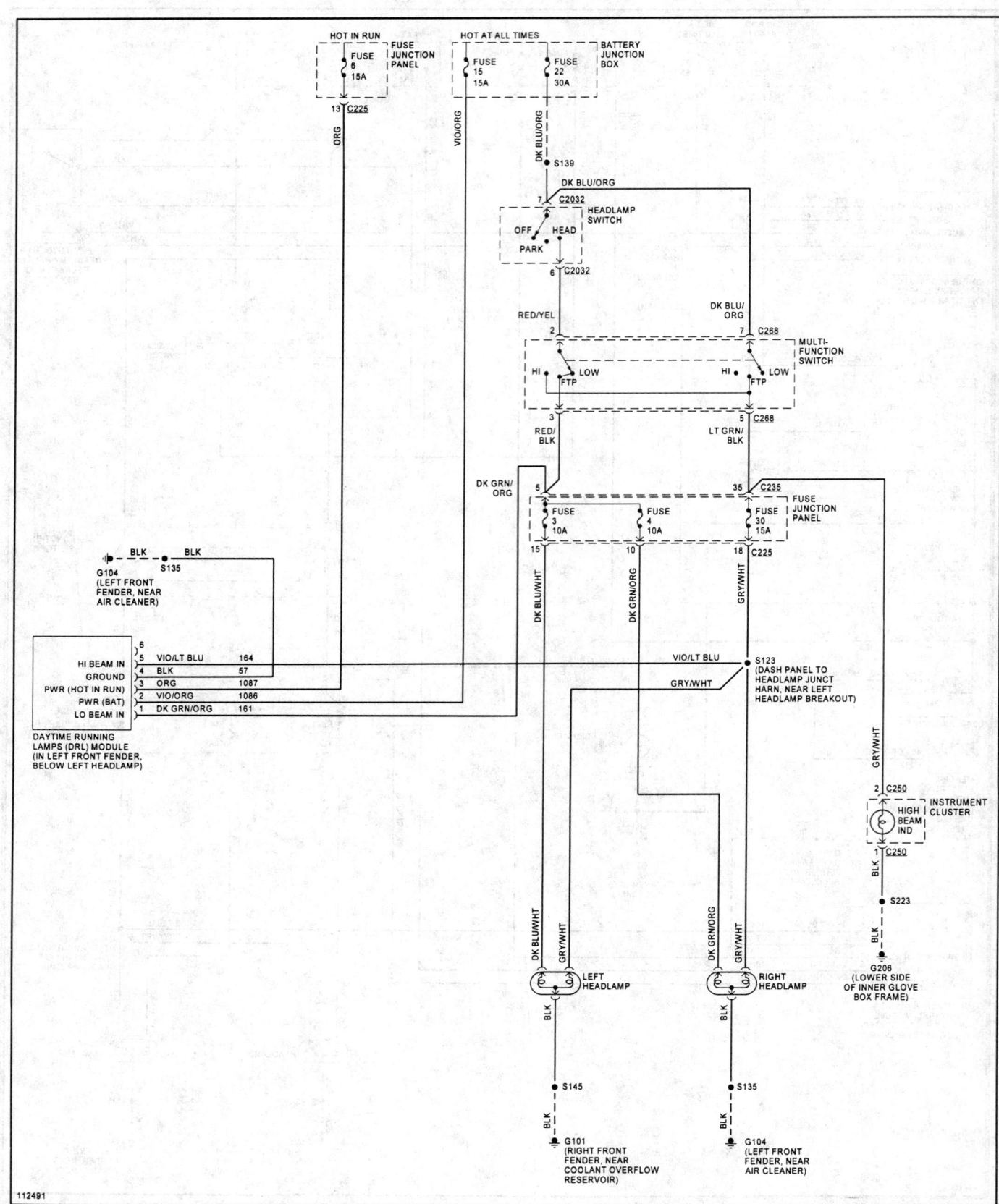

Fig. 11: Daytime Running Lights Wiring Diagram (Sable & Taurus – With DRL – Headlights Circuit)

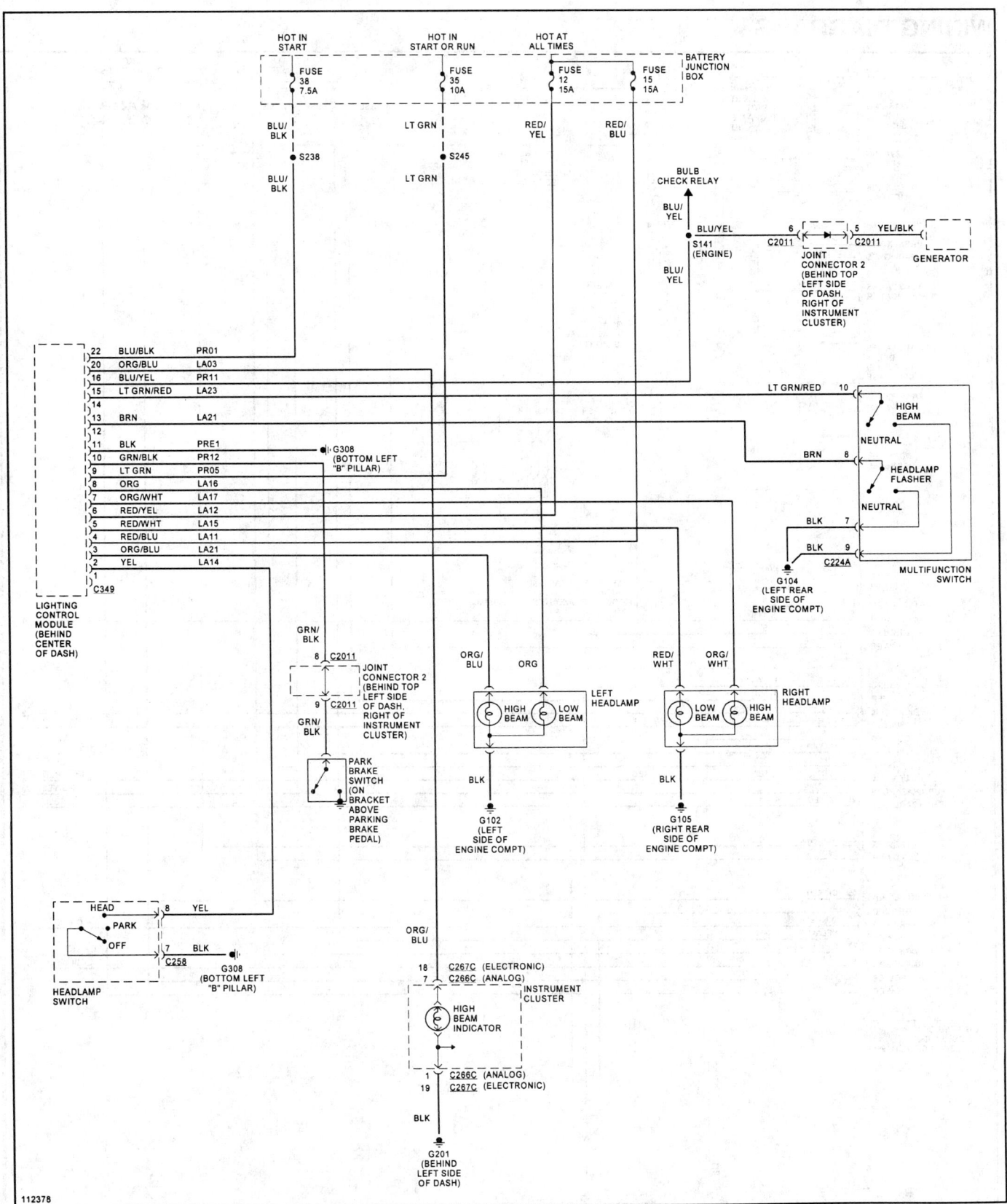

Fig. 12: Daytime Running Lights Wiring Diagram (Villager – With DRL)

WIRING DIAGRAMS

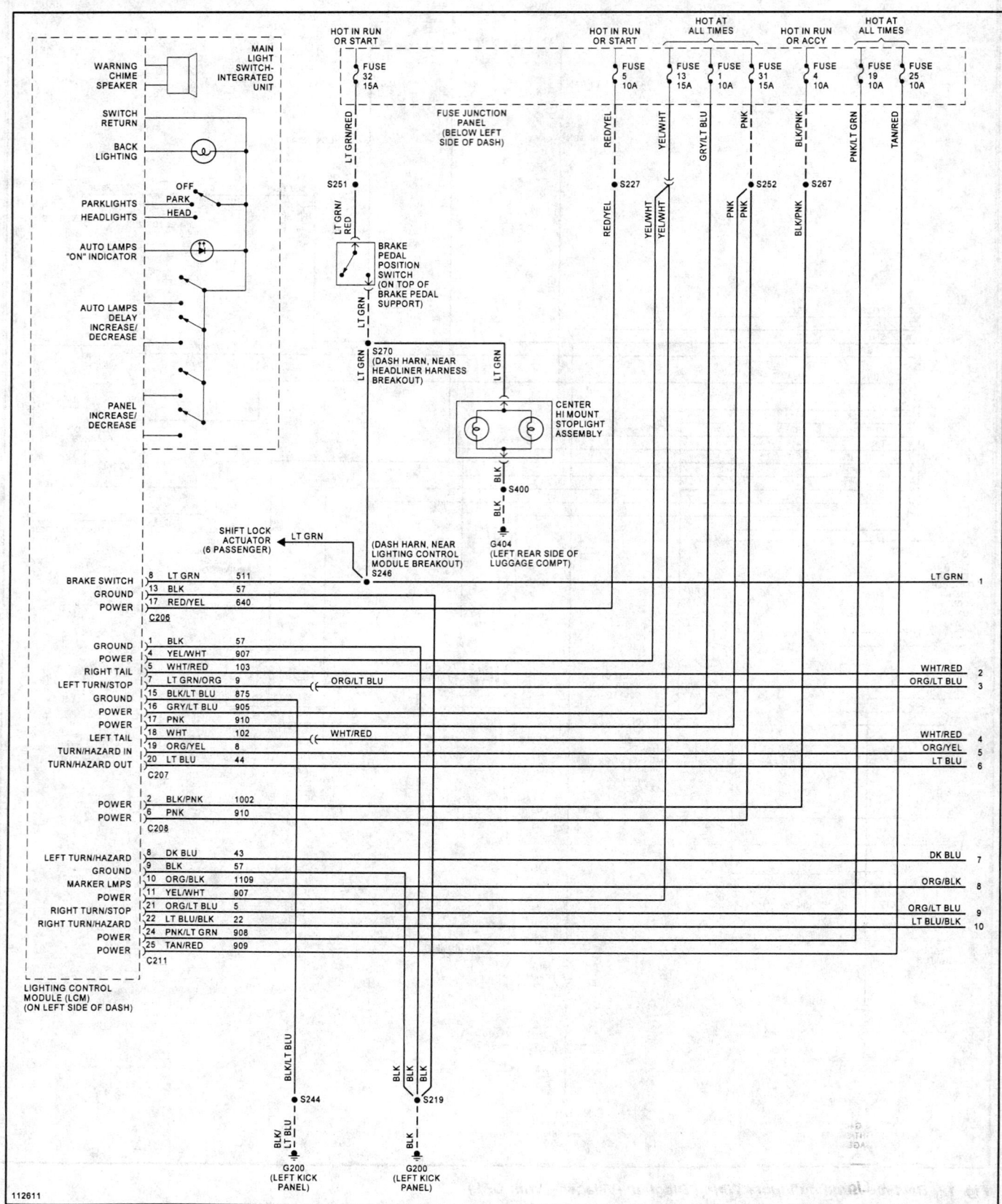

Fig. 1: Exterior Lights Wiring Diagram (Continental – 1 Of 2)

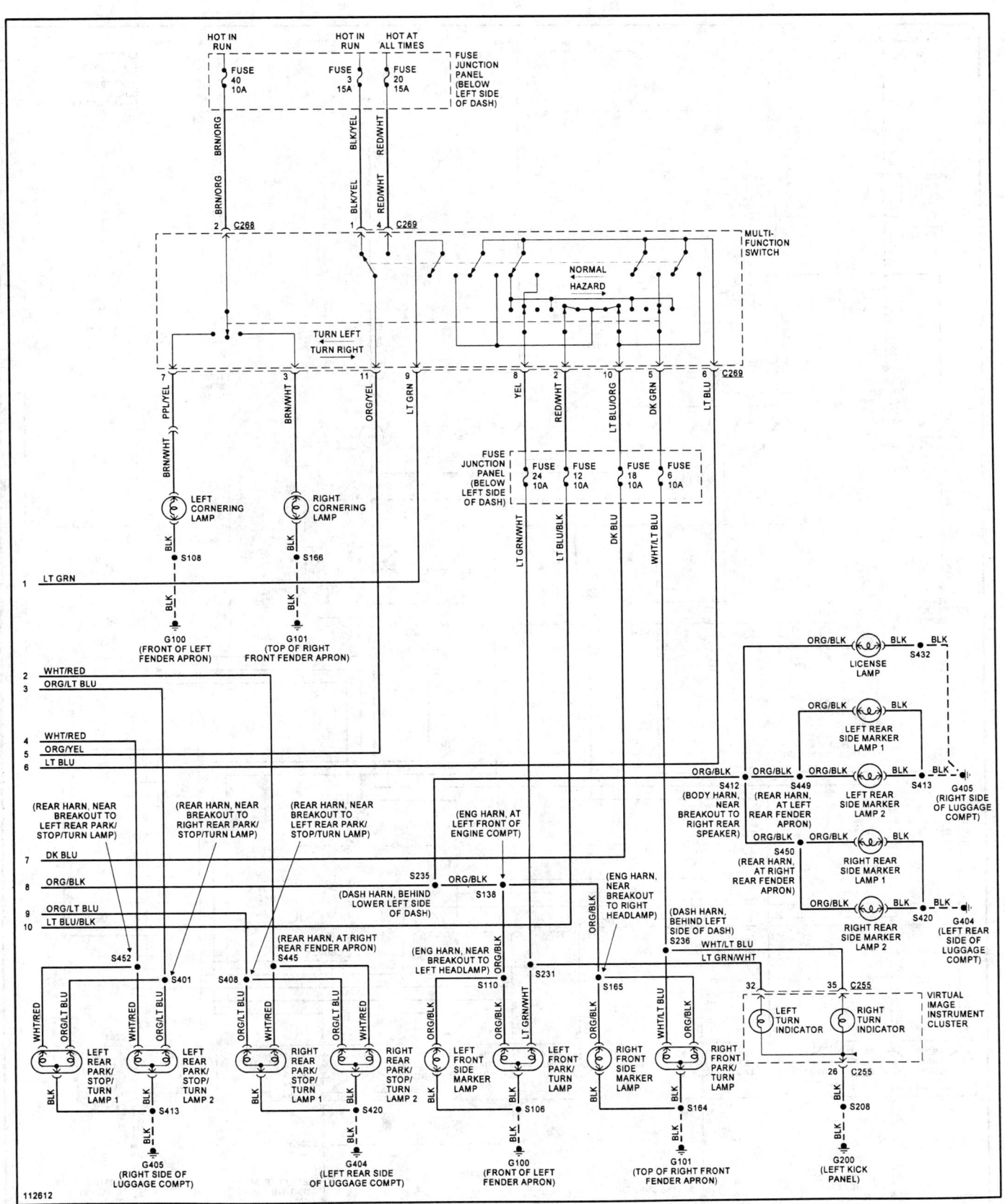

Fig. 2: Exterior Lights Wiring Diagram (Continental – 2 Of 2)

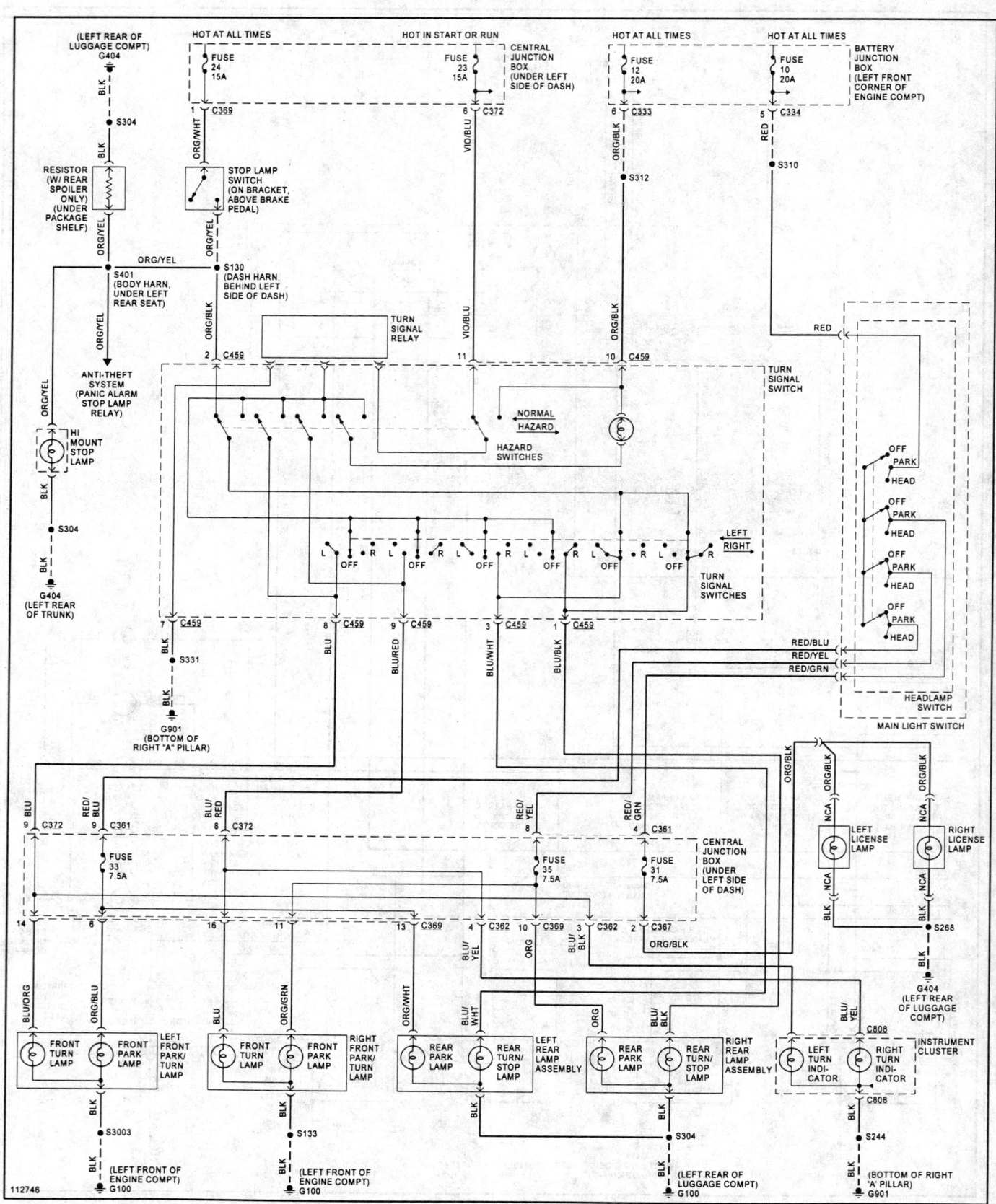

Fig. 3: Exterior Lights Wiring Diagram (Contour & Mystique)

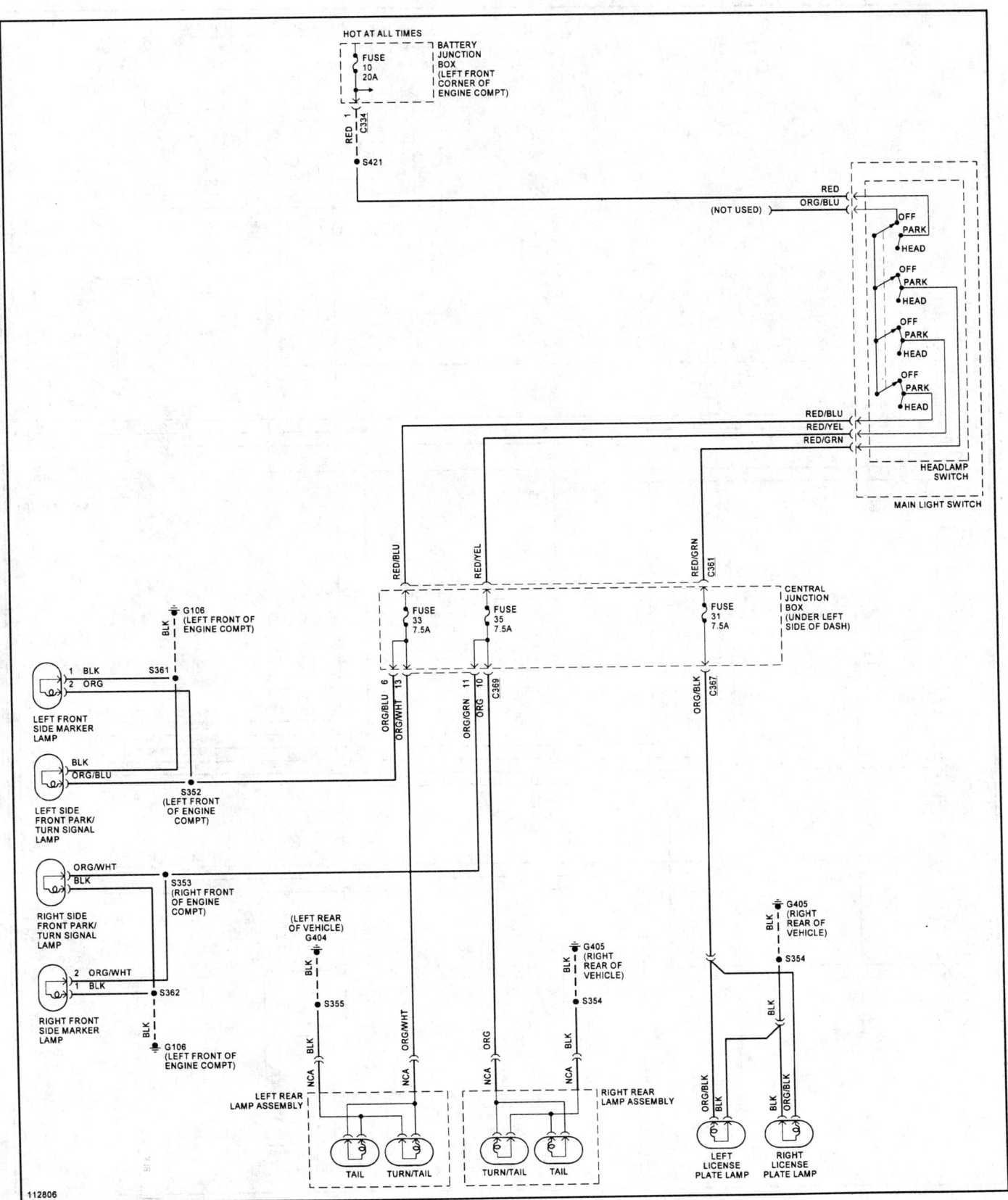

Fig. 4: Park & License Lights Wiring Diagram (Cougar – Low Option Content)

112806

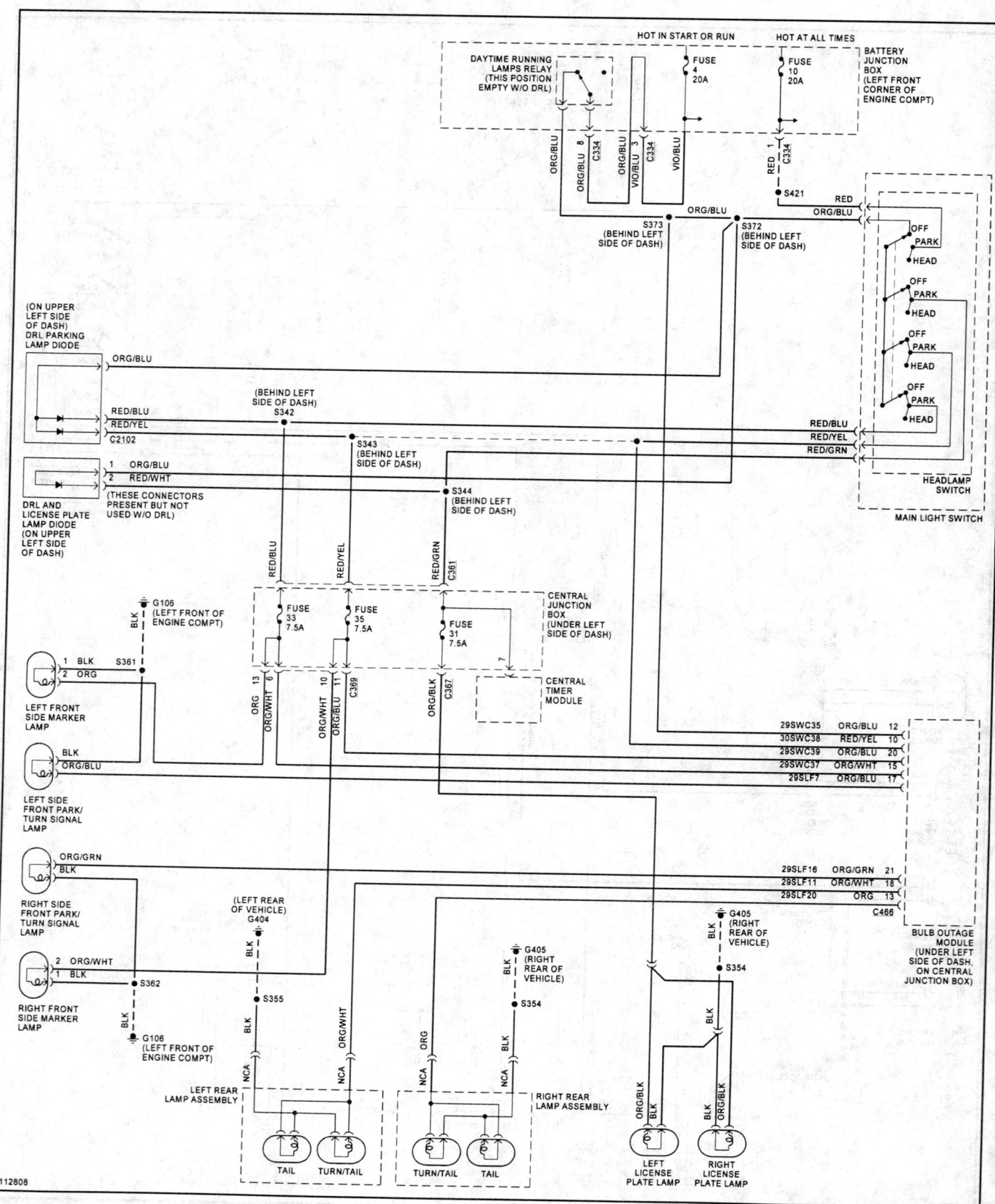

Fig. 5: Park & License Lights Wiring Diagram (Cougar – High Option Content With Auxiliary Warning)

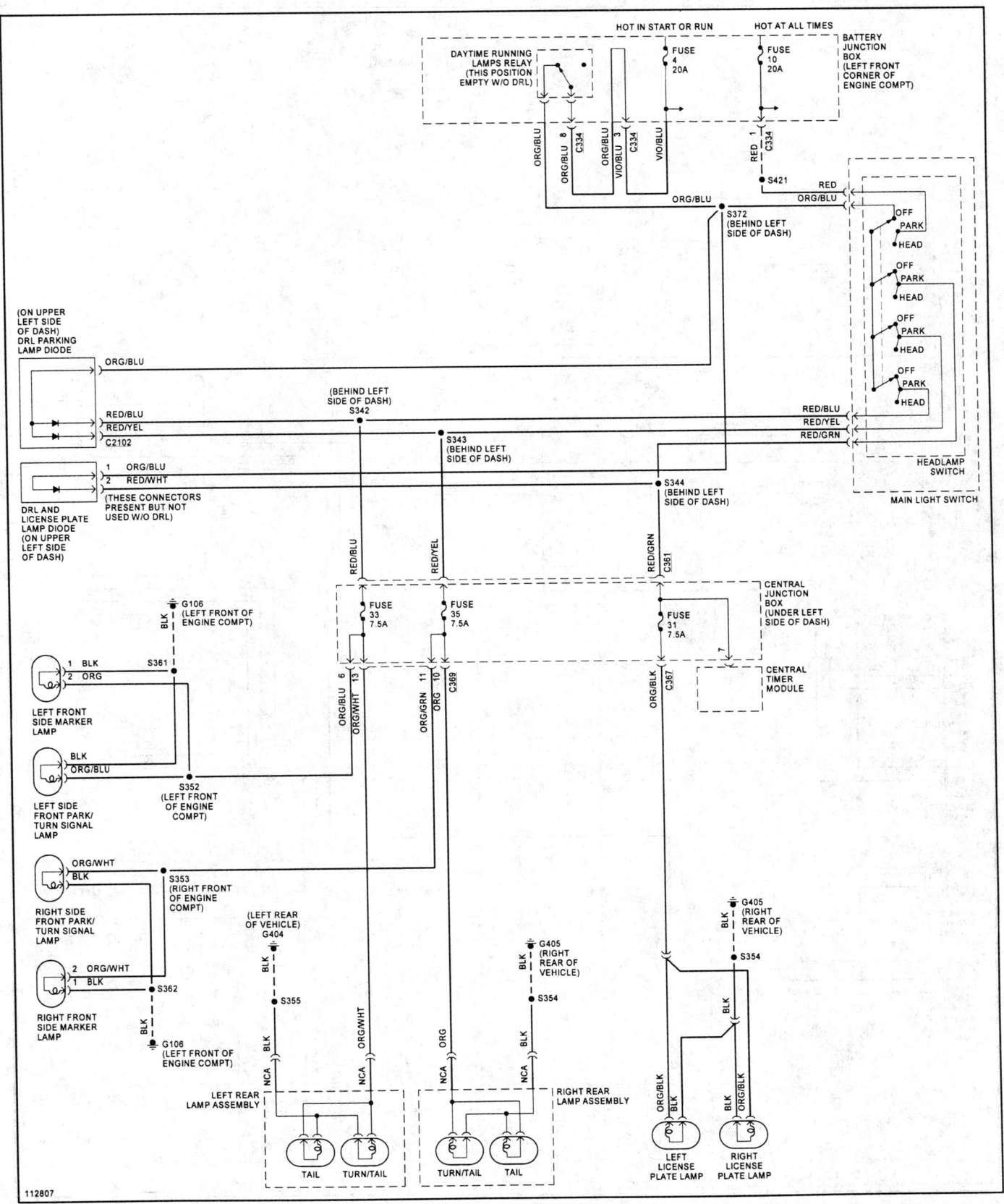

Fig. 6: Park & License Lights Wiring Diagram (Cougar – High Option Content Without Auxiliary Warning)

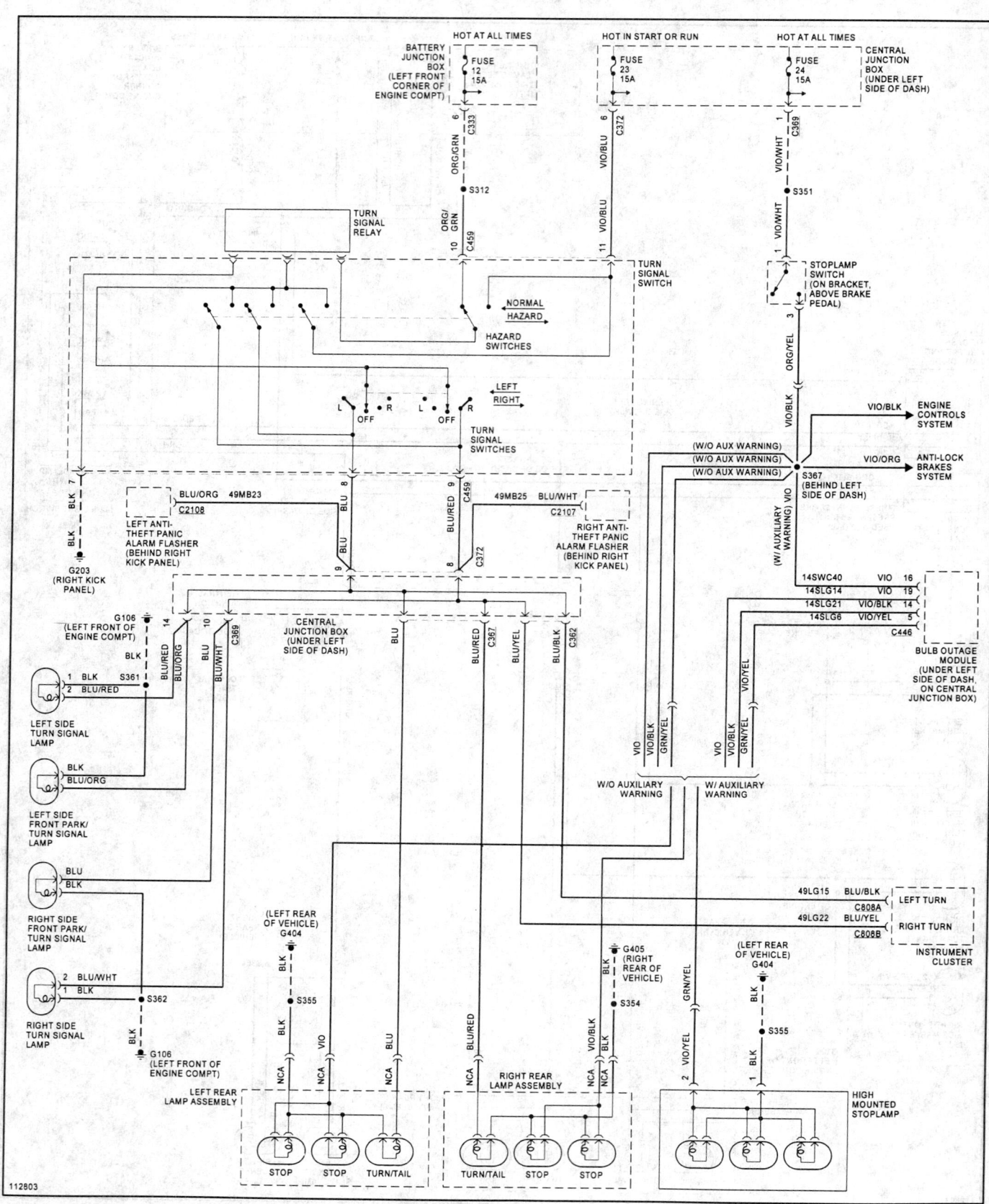

Fig. 7: Turn Signal, Hazard & Stoplights Circuit Wiring Diagram (Cougar)

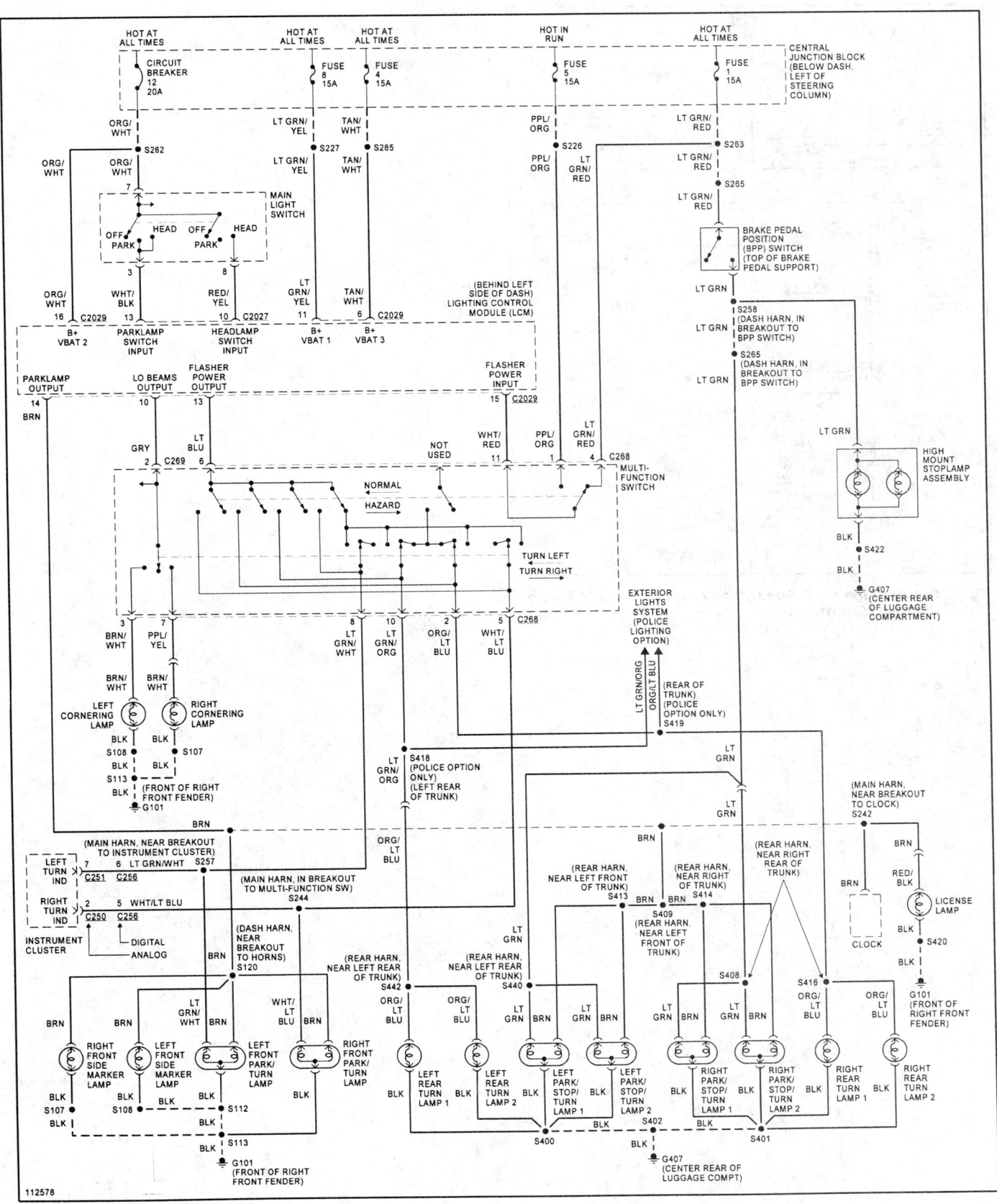

Fig. 8: Exterior Lights Wiring Diagram (Crown Victoria)

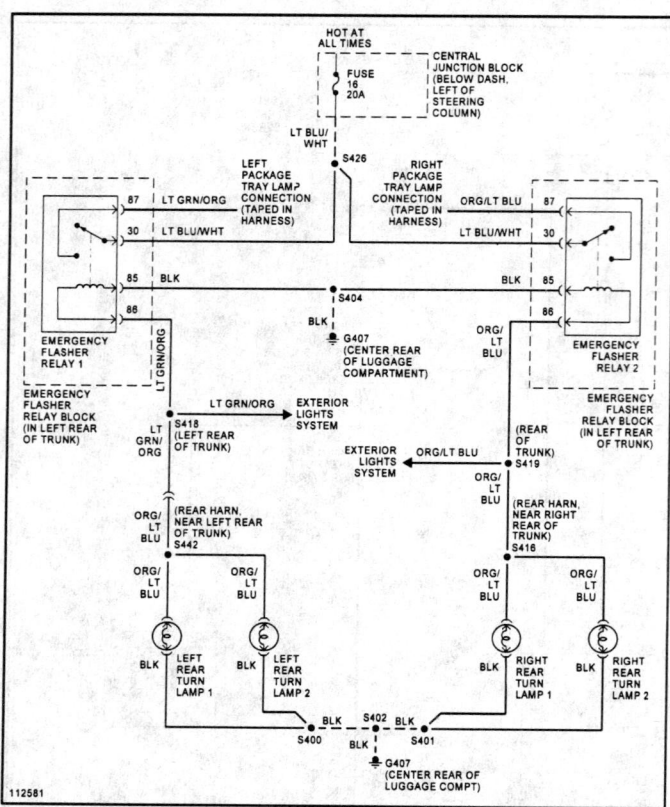

Fig. 9: Exterior Lights – Police Option Accessory Lights Wiring Diagram (Crown Victoria)

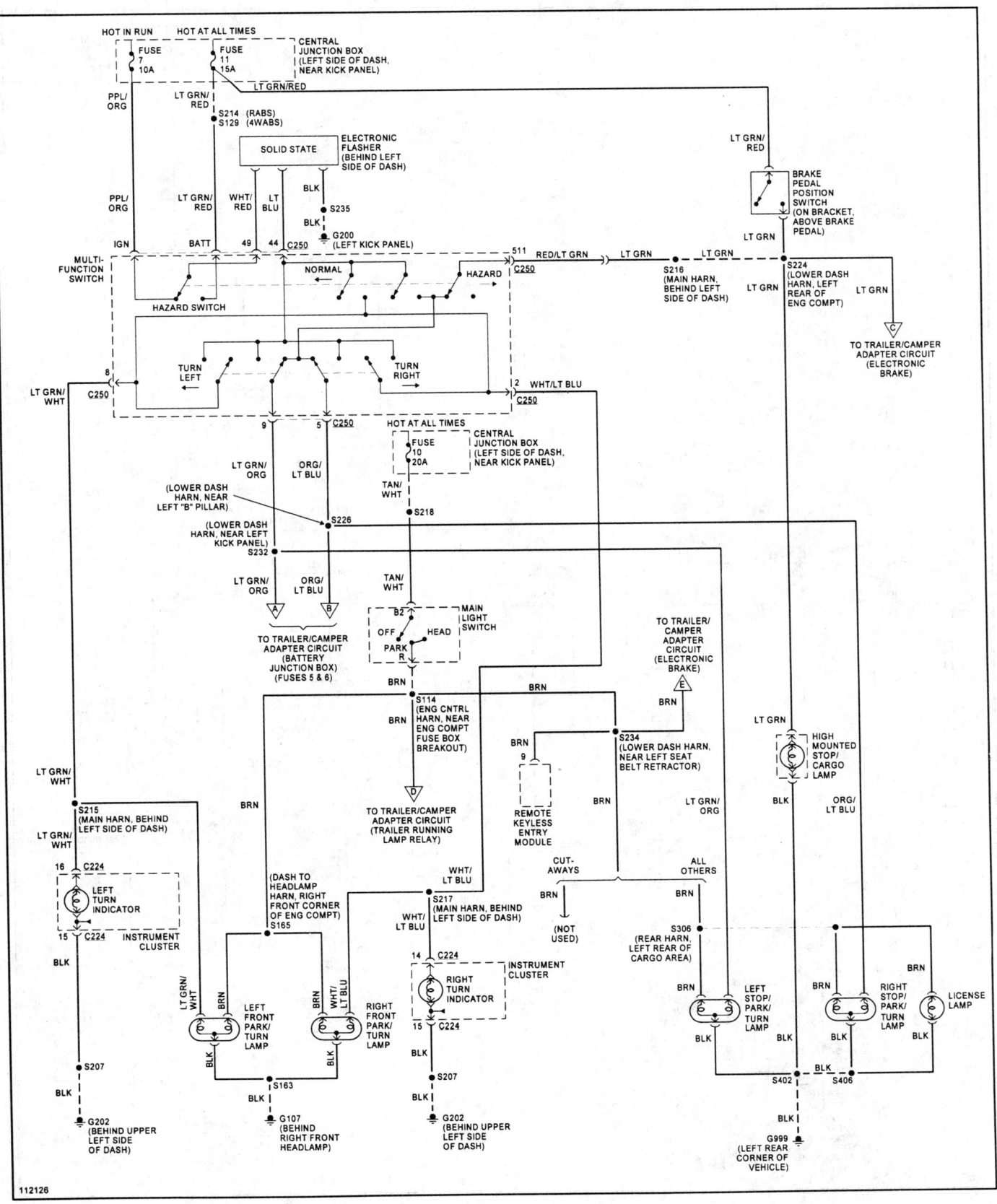

Fig. 10: Exterior Lights Wiring Diagram (Econoline)

112126

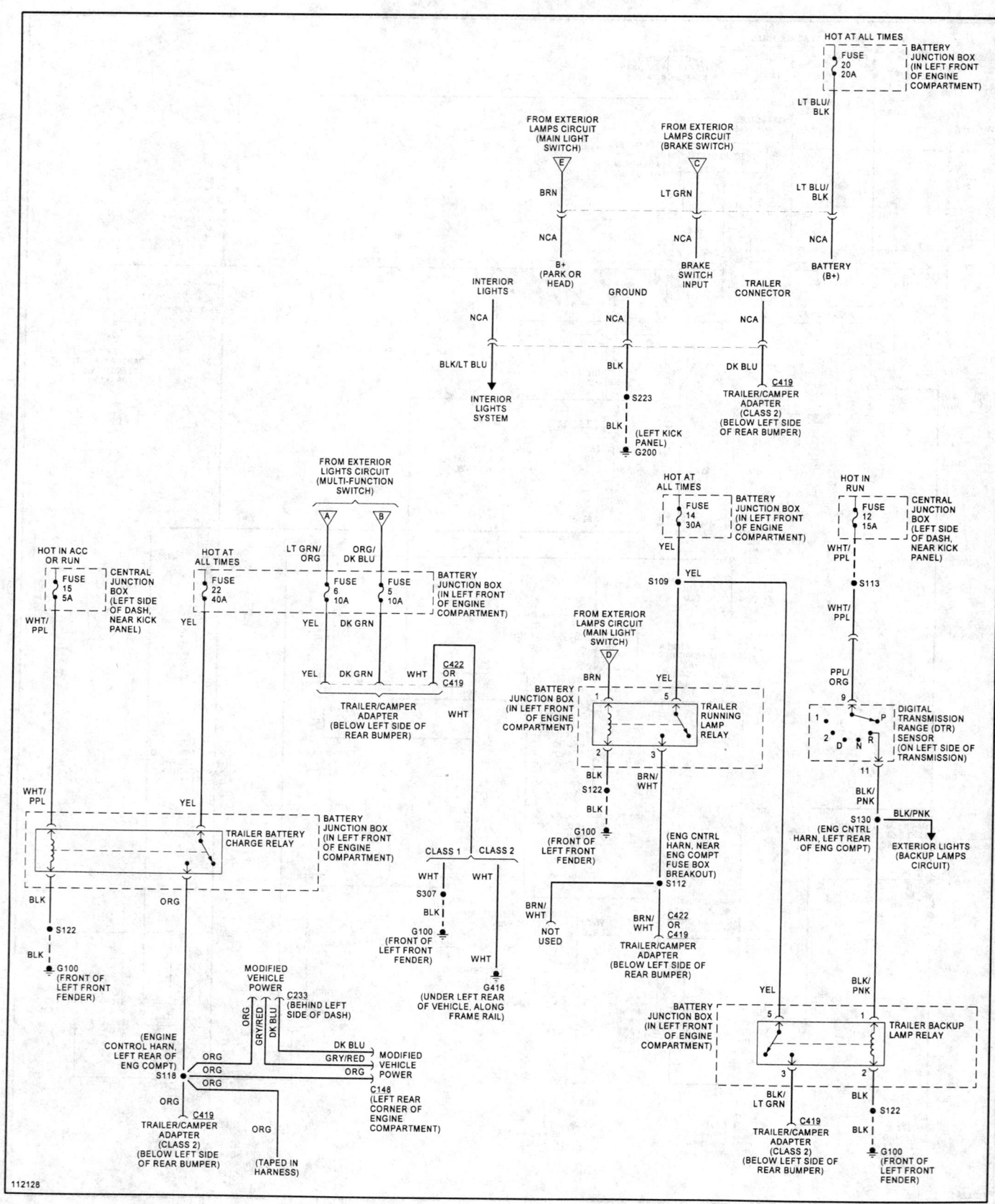

Fig. 11: Trailer/Camper Adapter Wiring Diagram (Econoline)

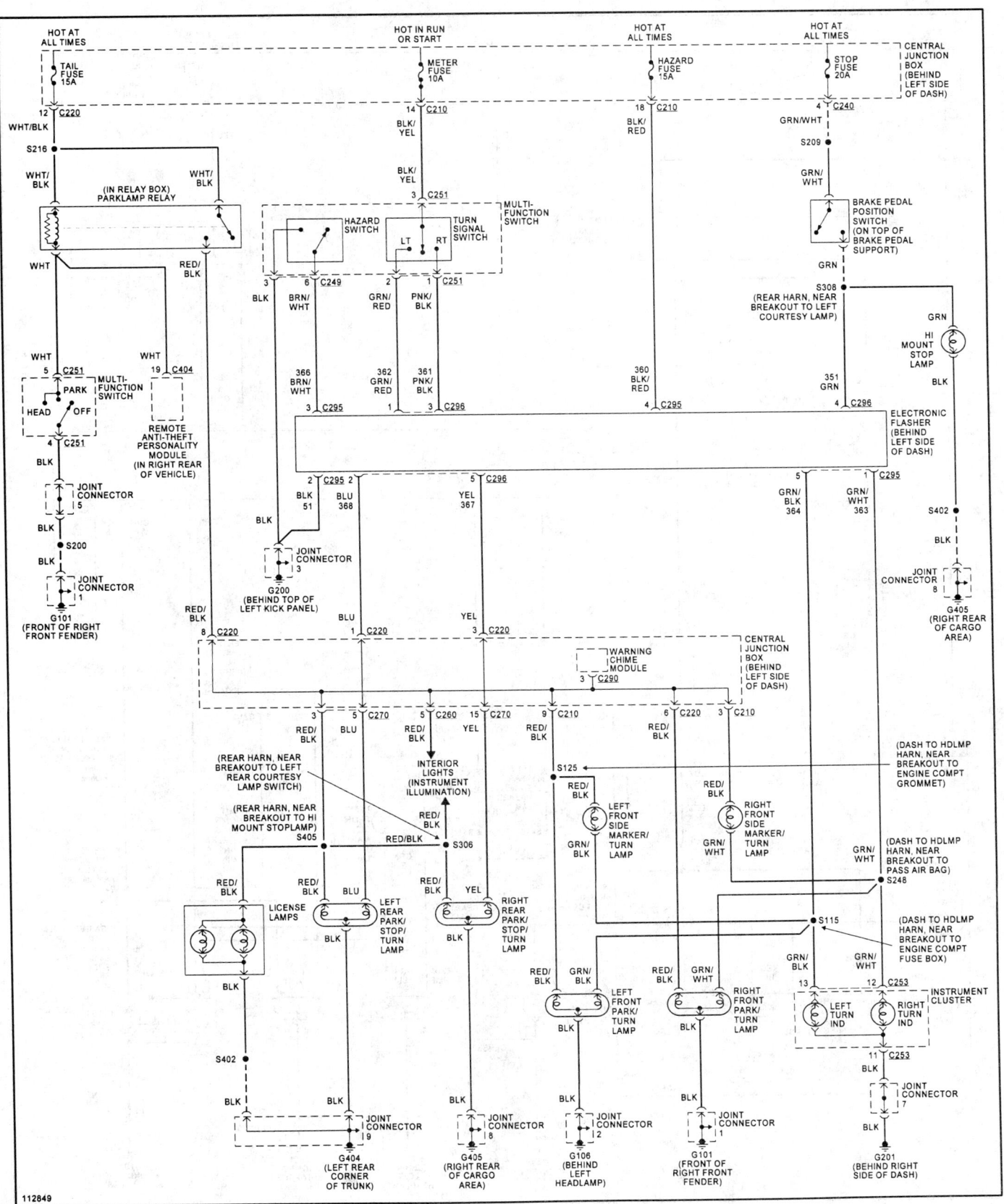

Fig. 12: Exterior Lights Wiring Diagram (Escort & Tracer – Sedan)

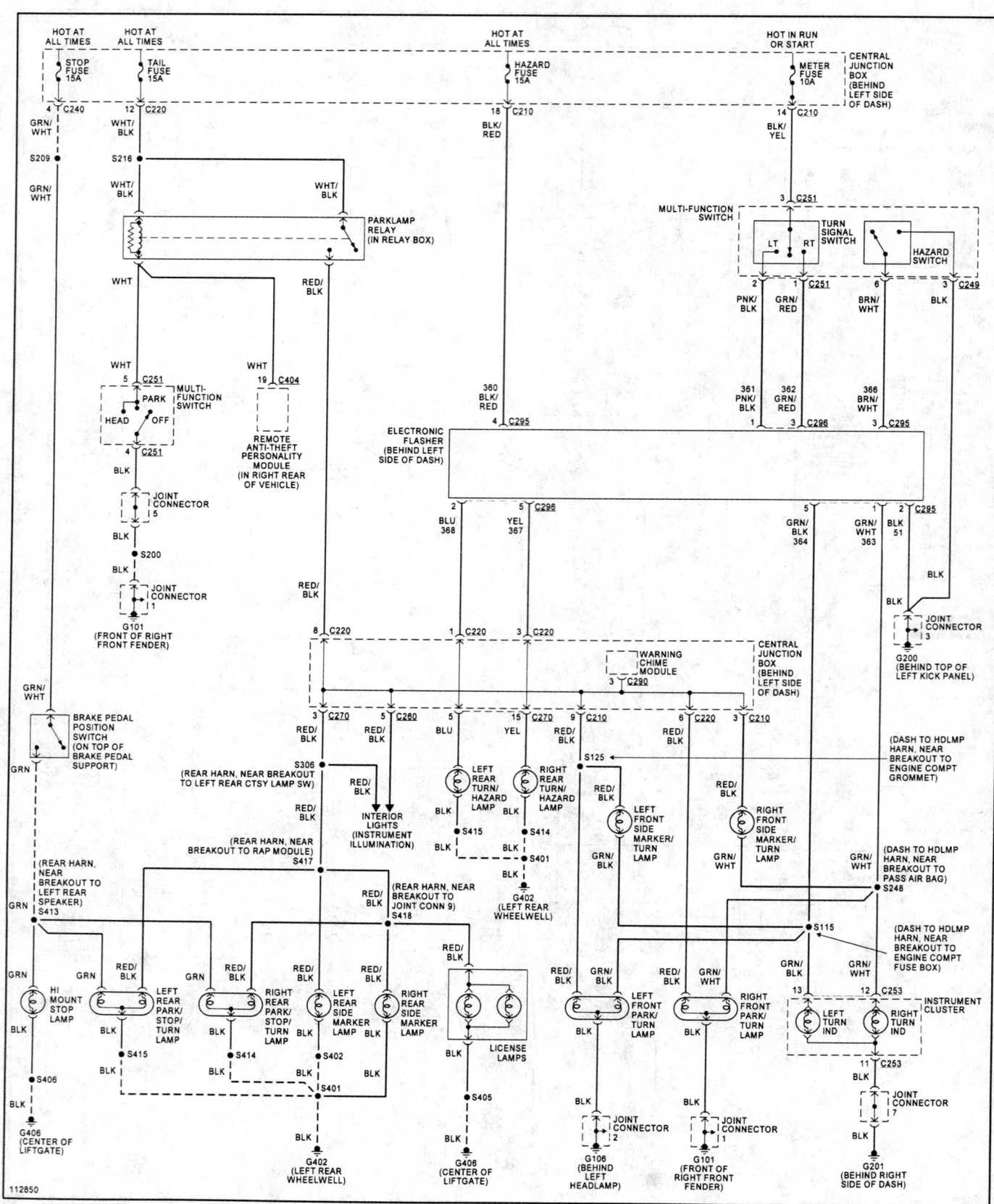

Fig. 13: Exterior Lights Wiring Diagram (Escort & Tracer – Wagon)

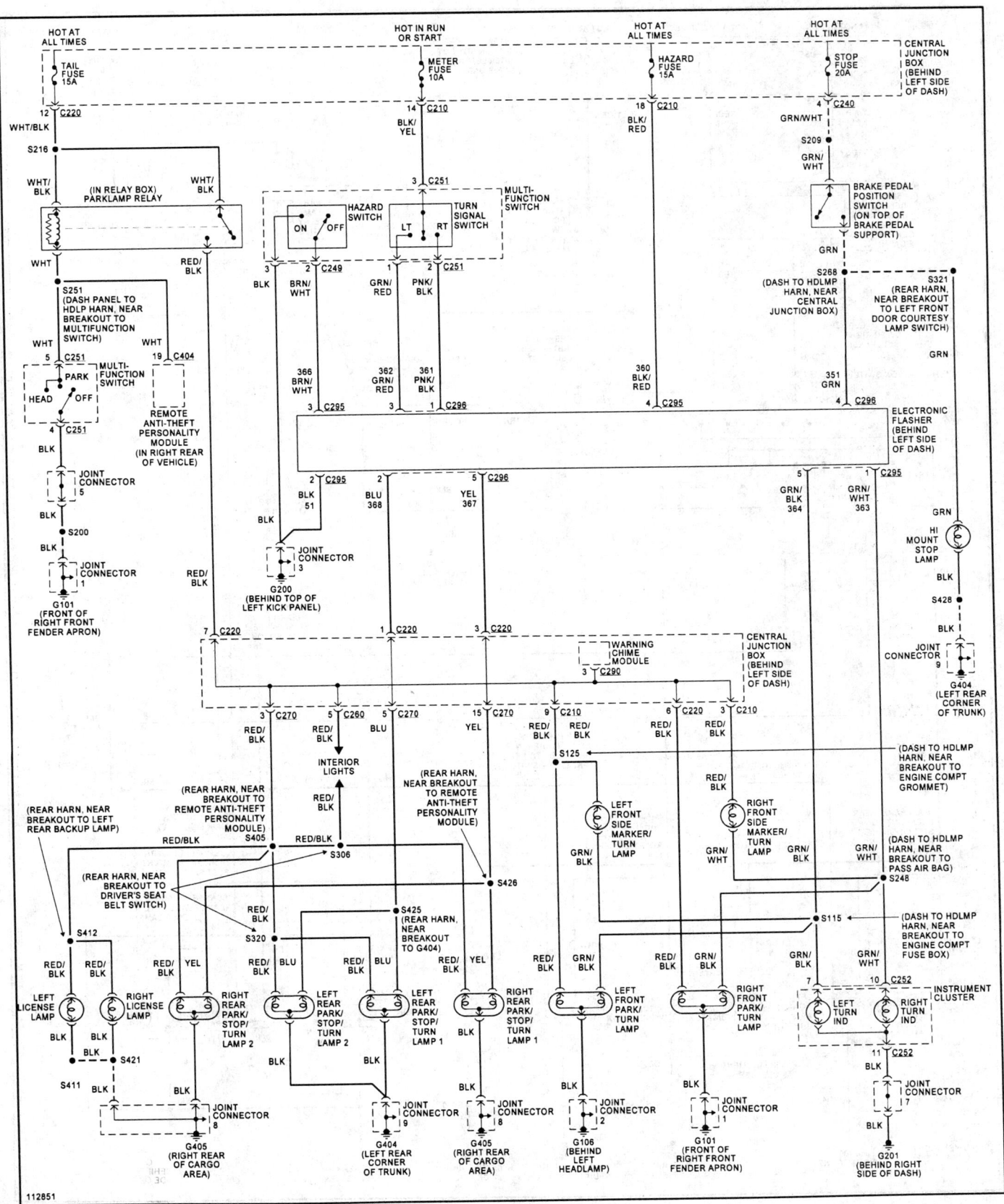

Fig. 14: Exterior Lights Wiring Diagram (Escort ZX2)

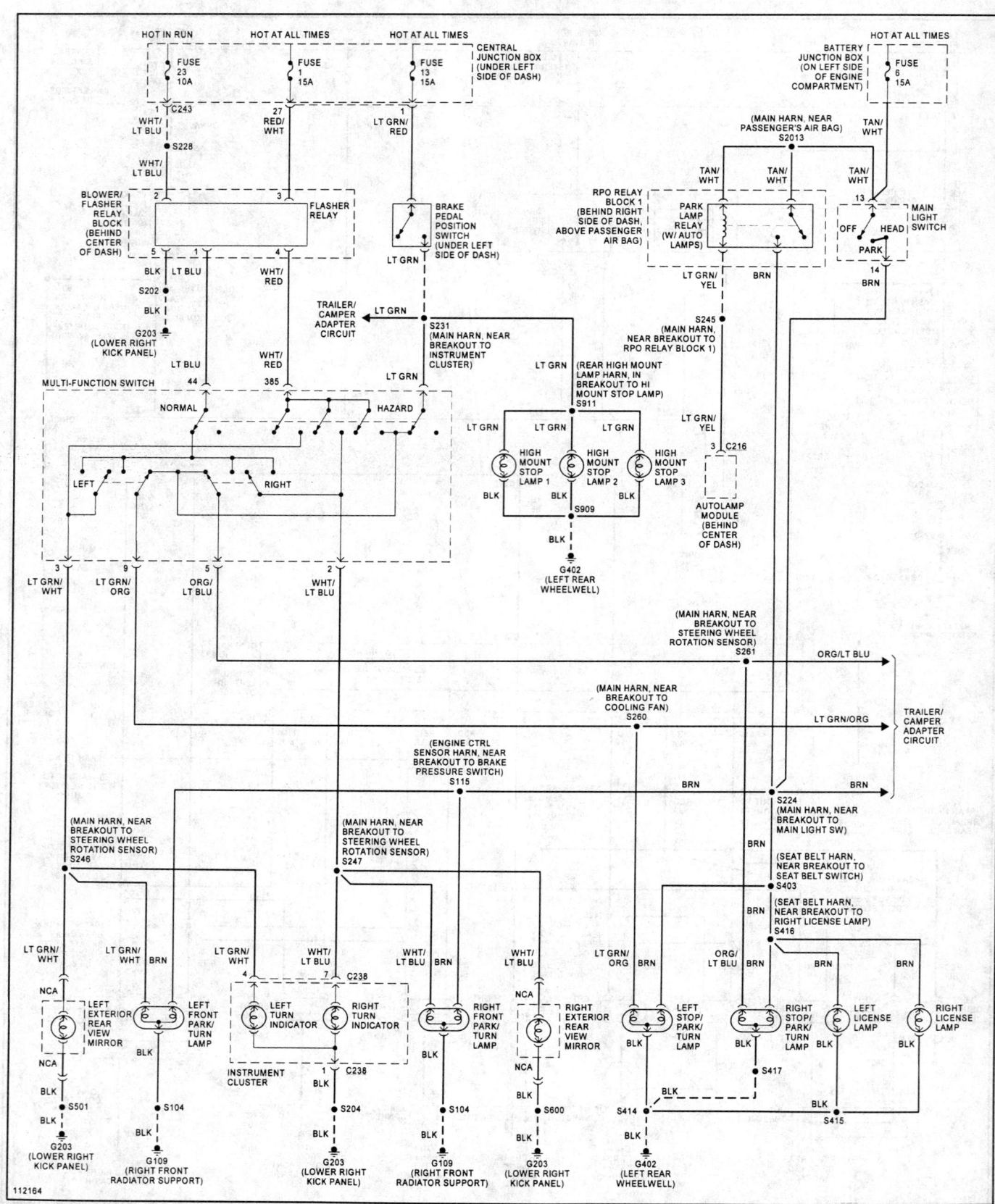

Fig. 15: Exterior Lights Wiring Diagram (Expedition)

112164

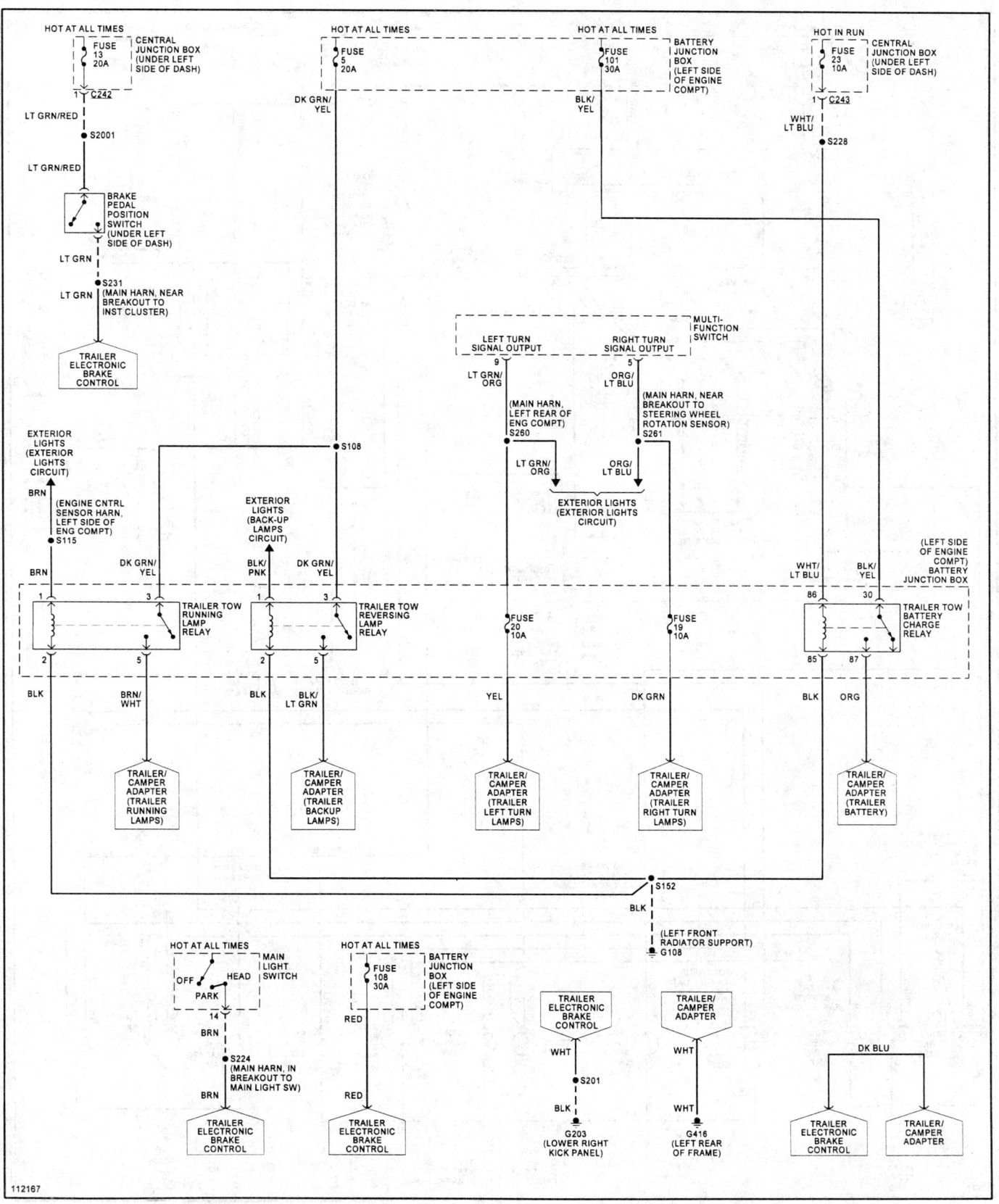

Fig. 16: Trailer/Camper Adapter Wiring Diagram (Expedition & Navigator)

112167

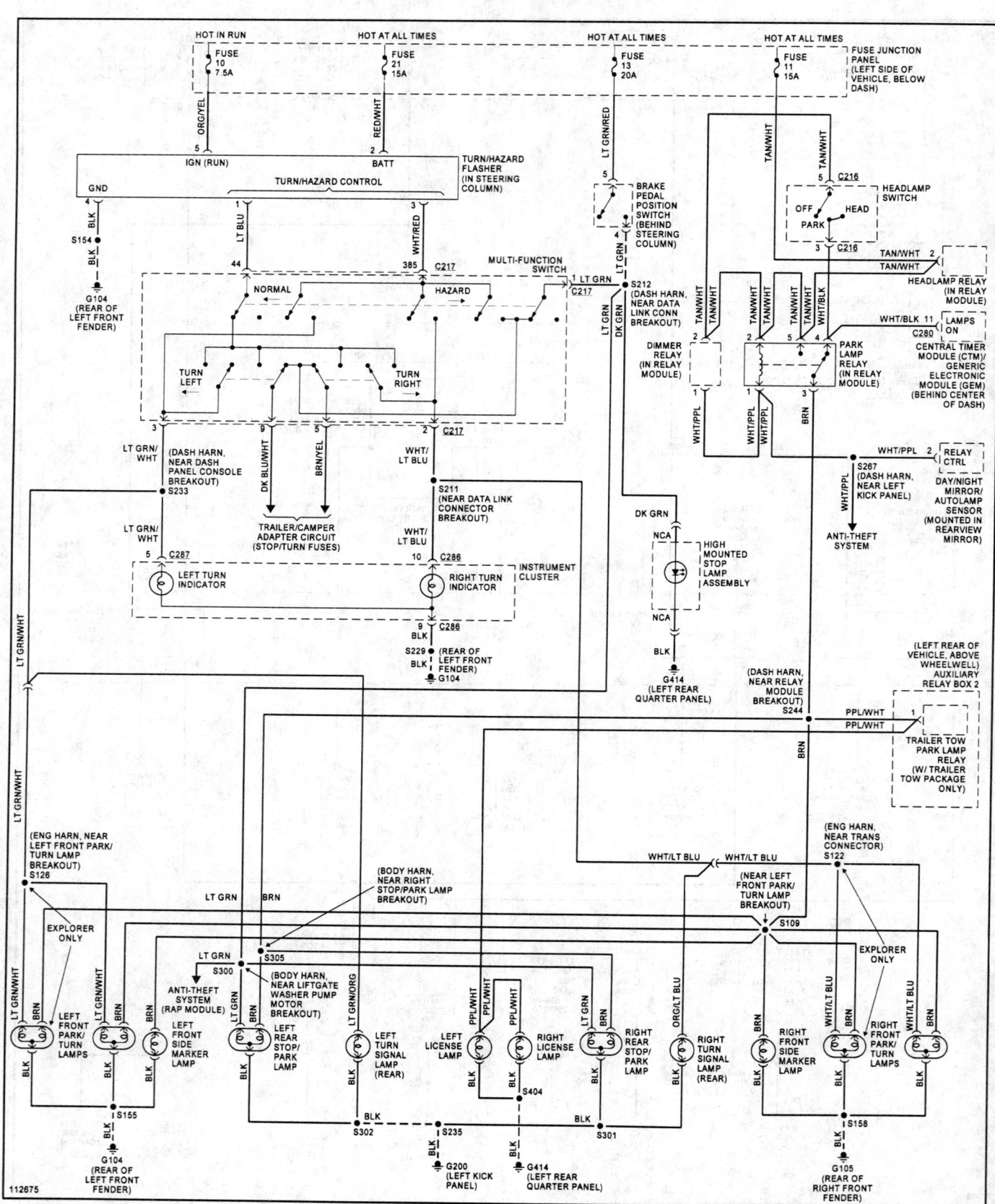

Fig. 17: Exterior Lights Wiring Diagram (Explorer & Mountaineer)

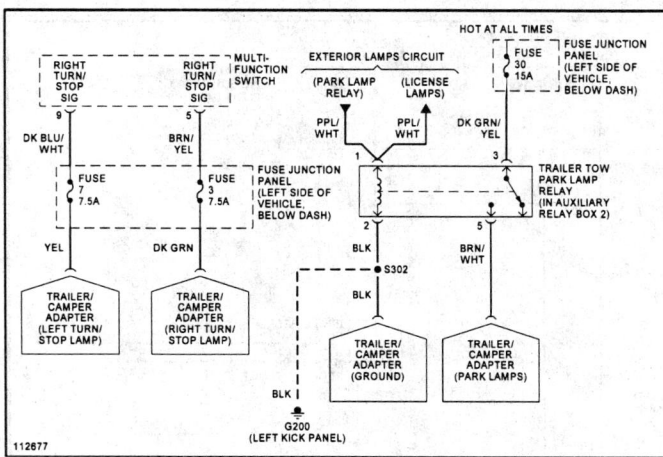

**Fig. 18: Trailer/Camper Adapter Wiring Diagram
(Explorer & Mountaineer)**

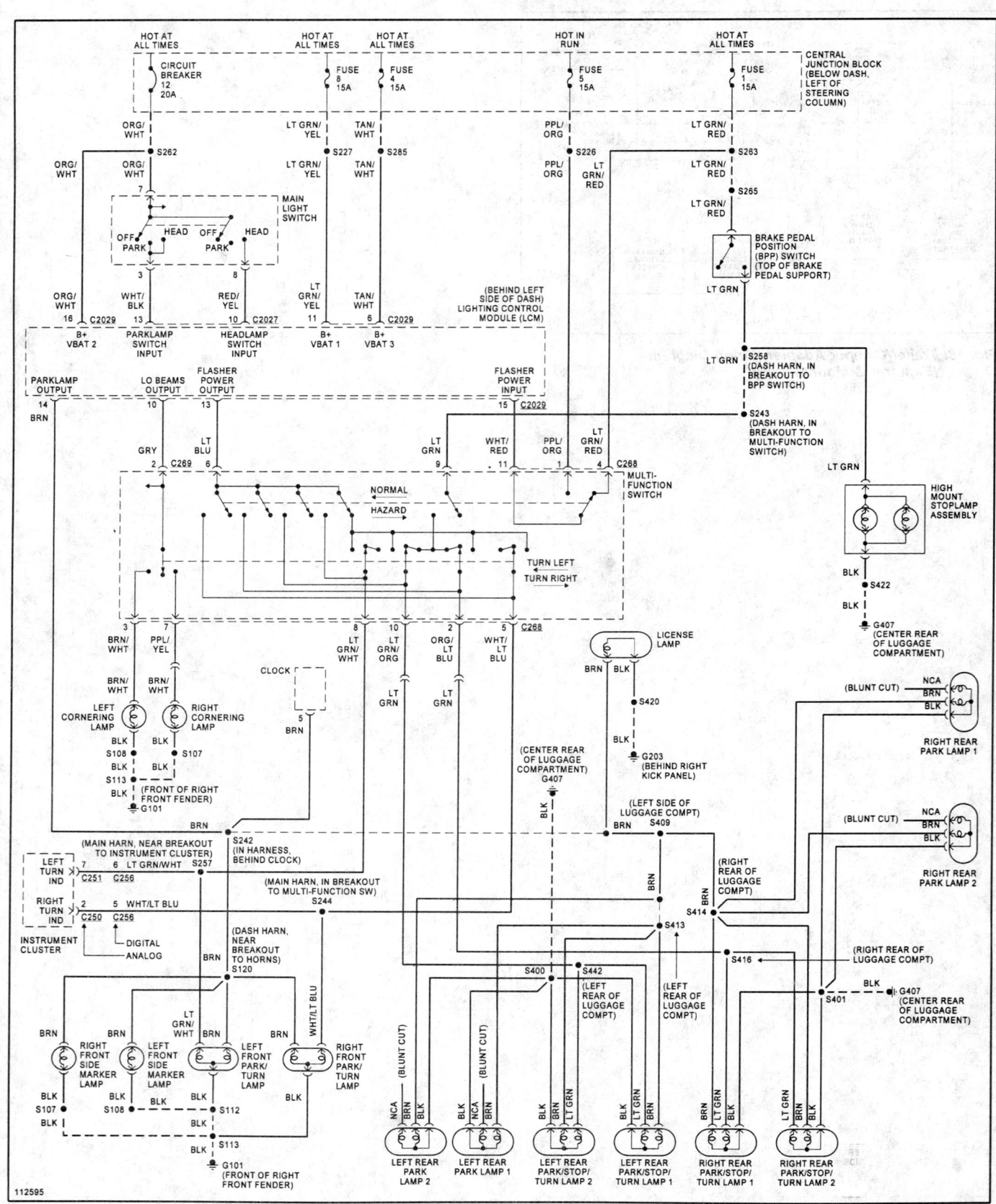

Fig. 19: Exterior Lights Wiring Diagram (Grand Marquis)

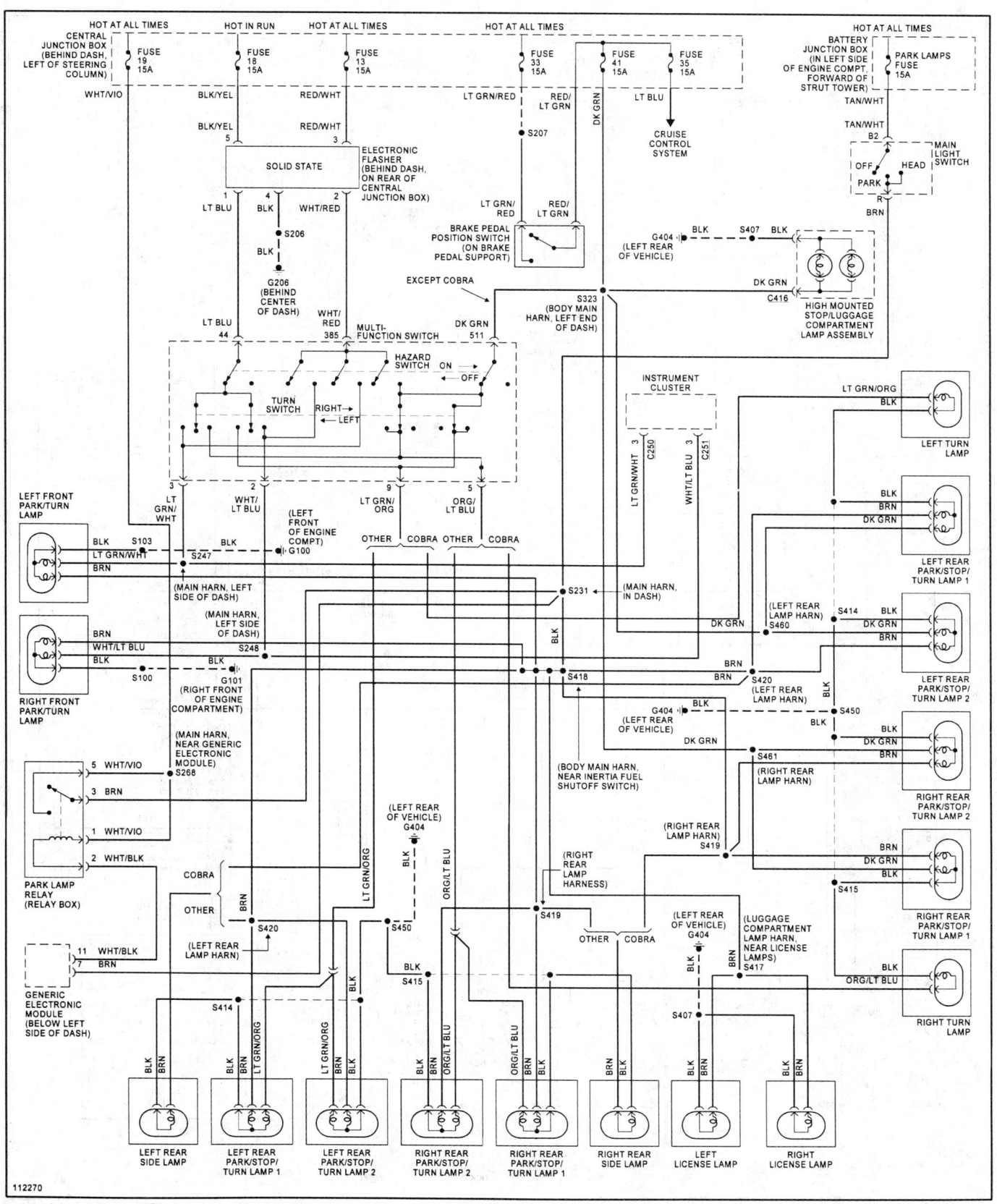

Fig. 20: Exterior Lights Wiring Diagram (Mustang)

112270

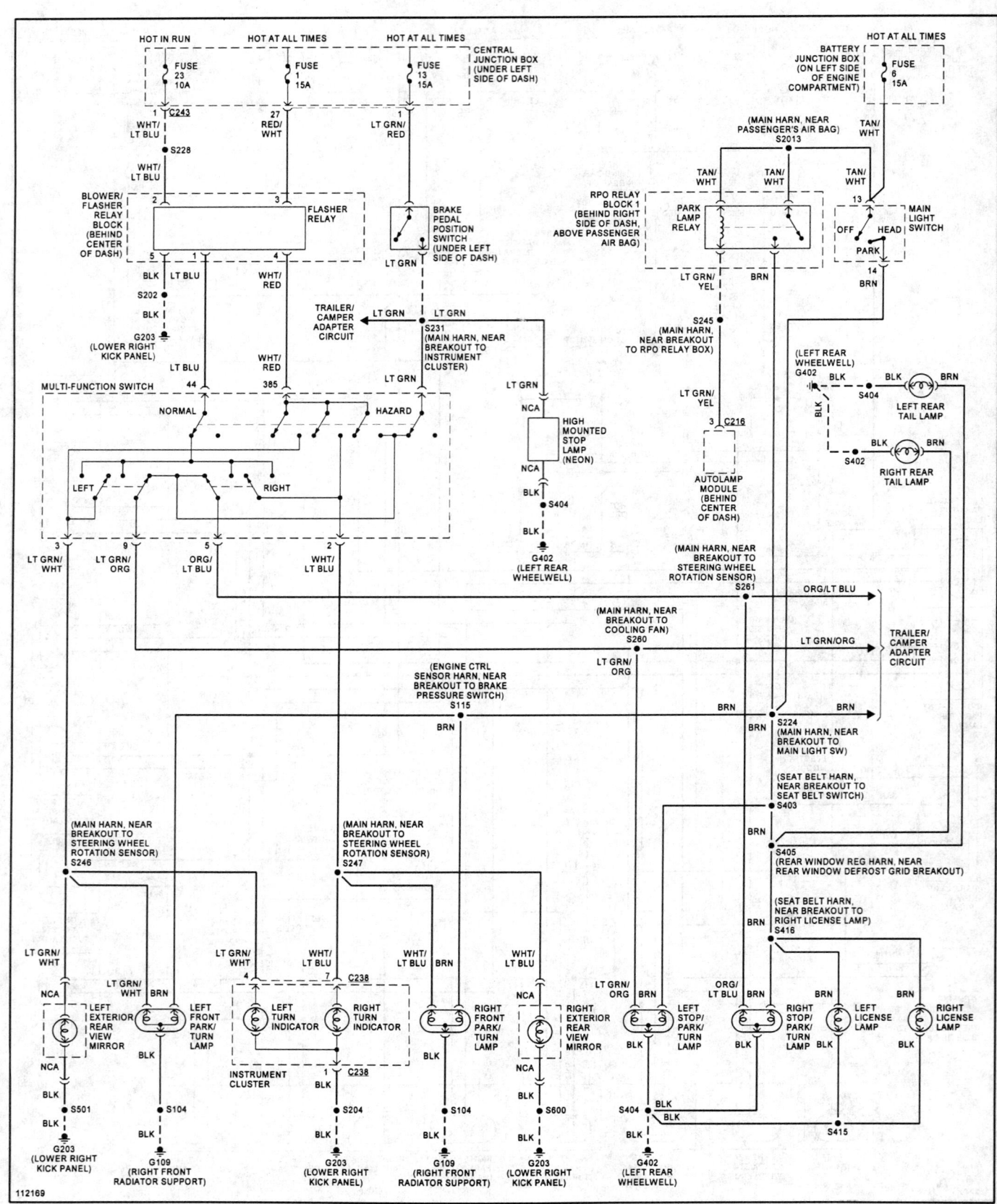

Fig. 21: Exterior Lights Wiring Diagram (Navigator)

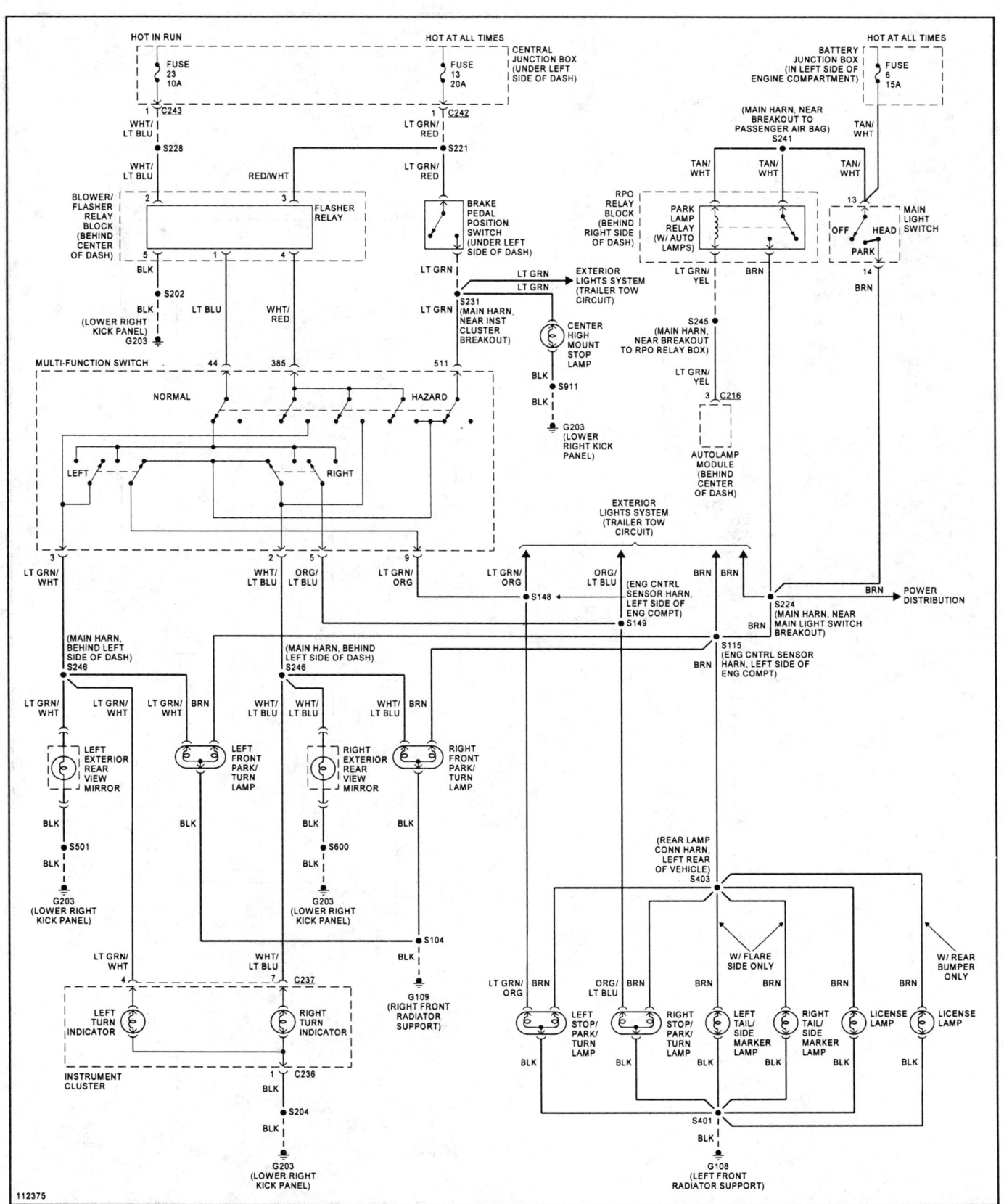

Fig. 22: Exterior Lights Wiring Diagram (F150 & F250 Light-Duty Pickup)

112375

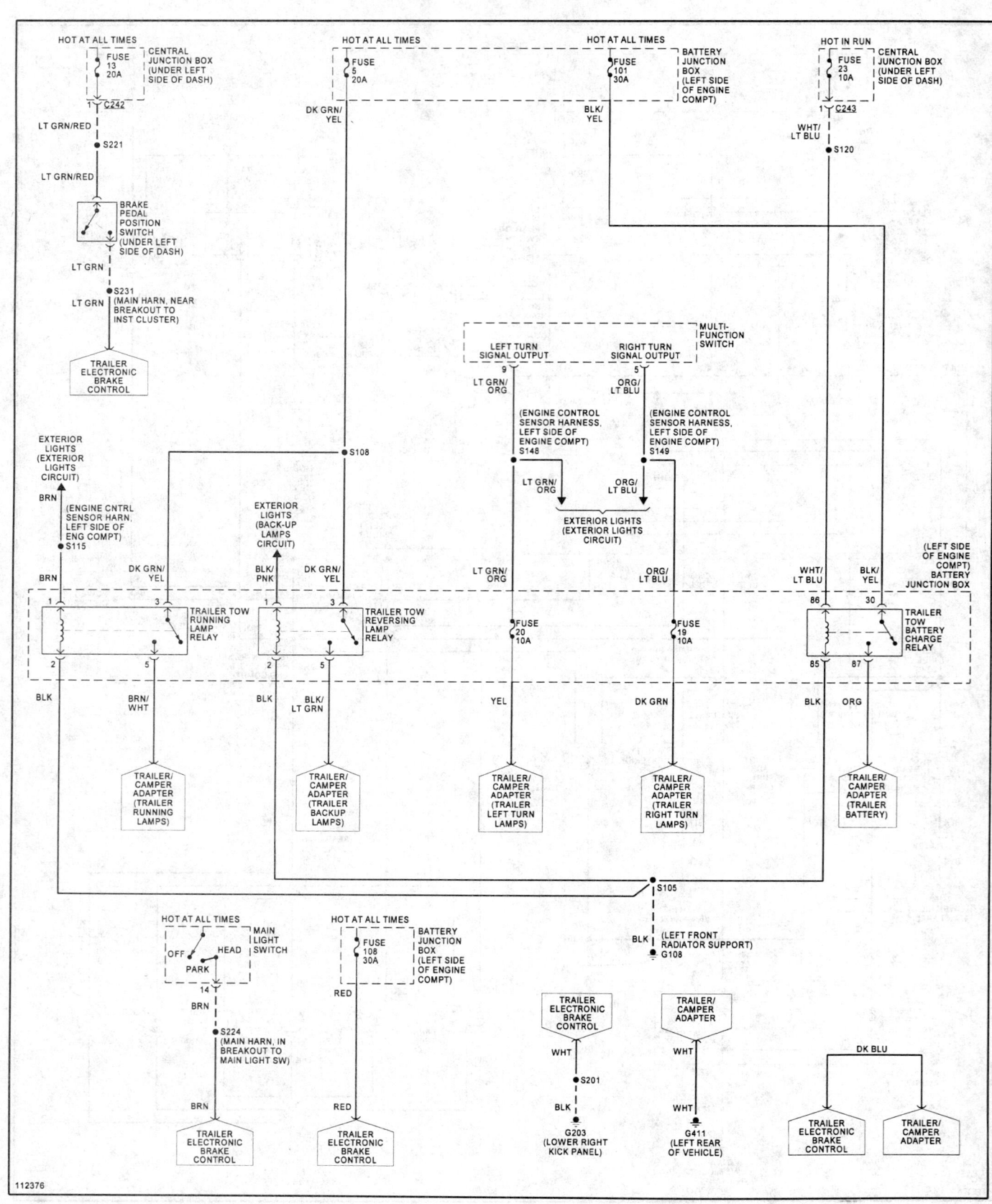

Fig. 23: Trailer/Camper Adapter Wiring Diagram (F150 & F250 Light-Duty Pickup)

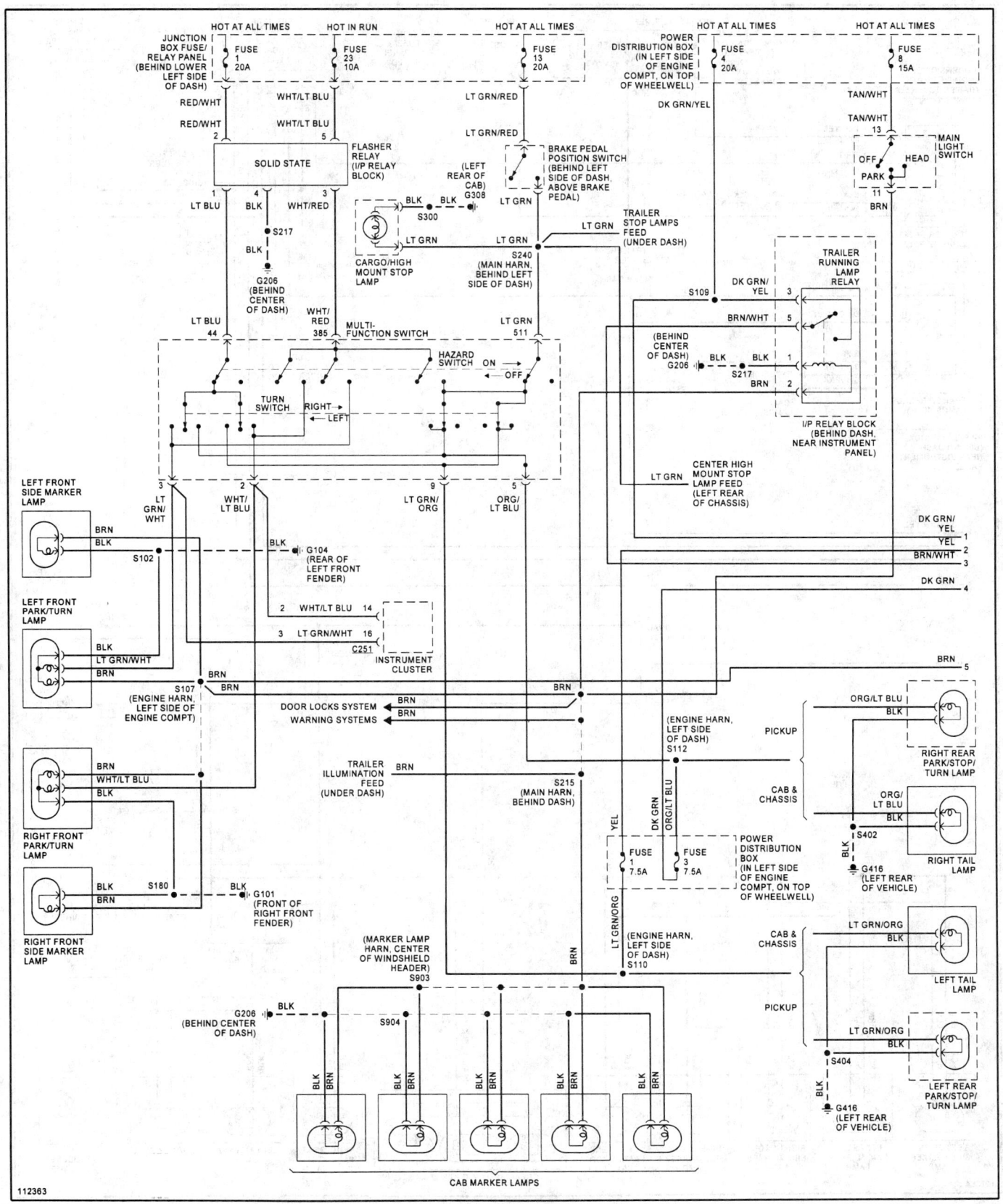

Fig. 24: Exterior Lights & Trailer Connector Wiring Diagram (F250 & F350 Super-Duty Pickup – 1 Of 2)

112363

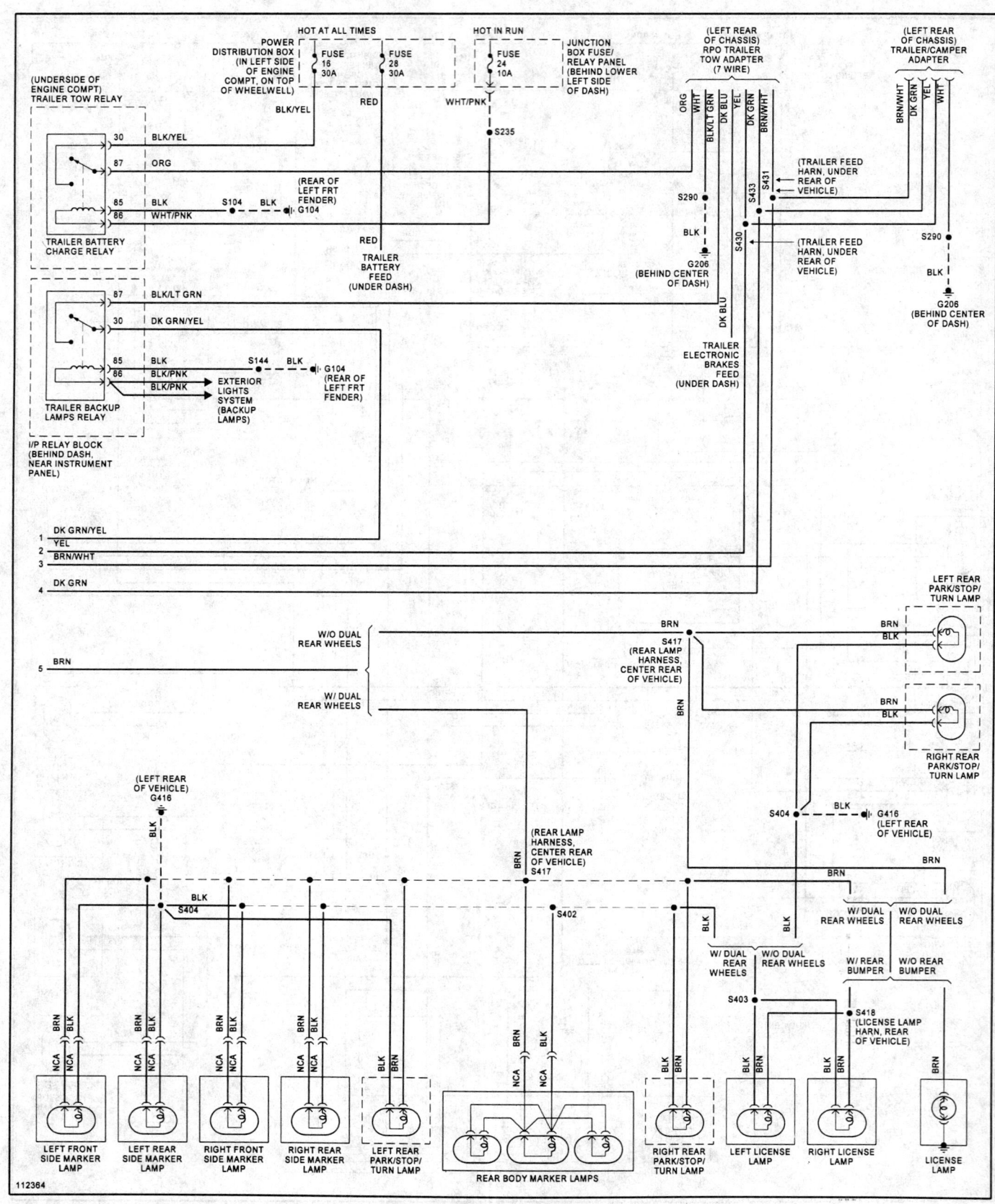

Fig. 25: Exterior Lights & Trailer Connector Wiring Diagram (F250 & F350 Super-Duty Pickup – 2 Of 2)

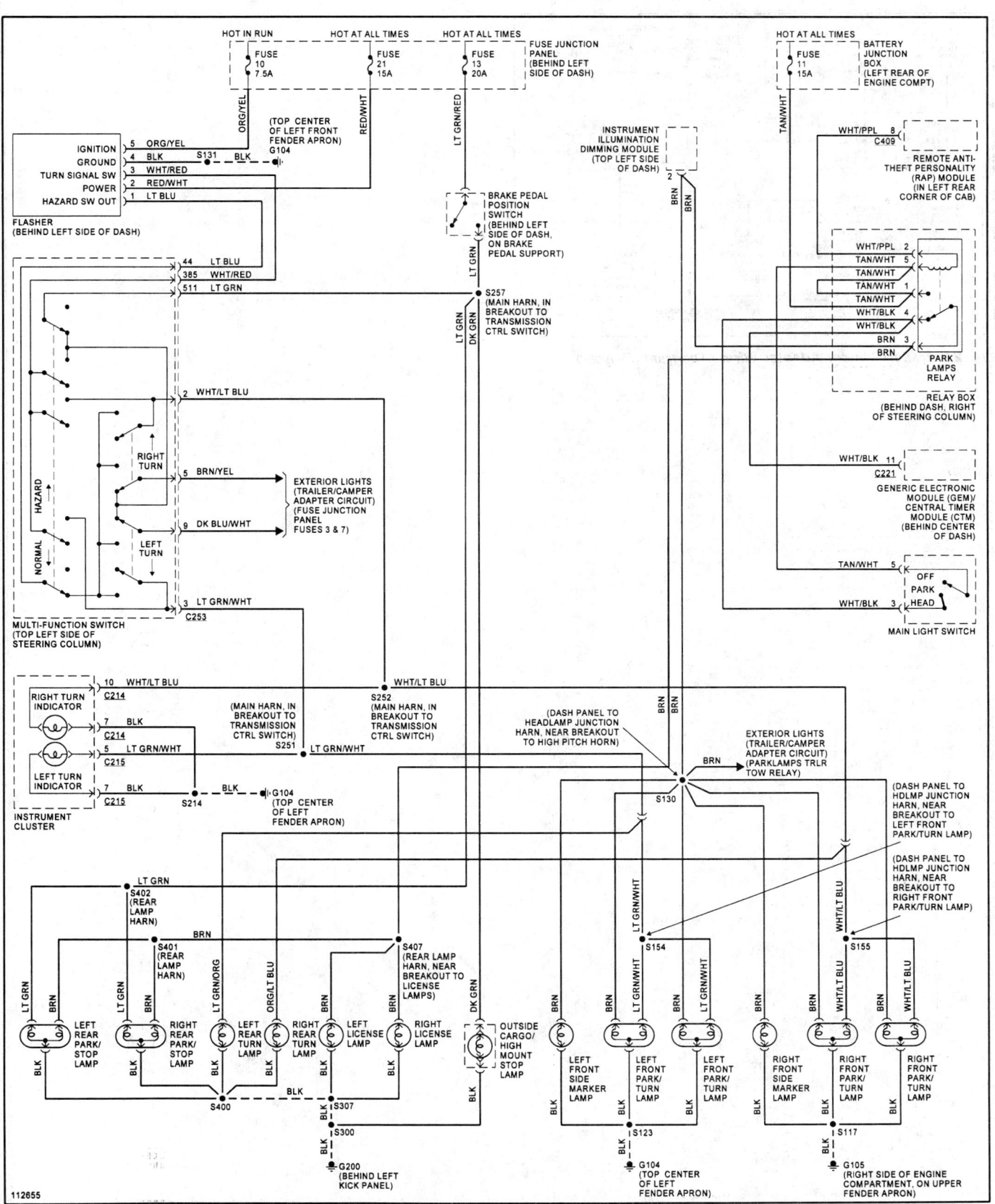

Fig. 26: Exterior Lights Wiring Diagram (Ranger)

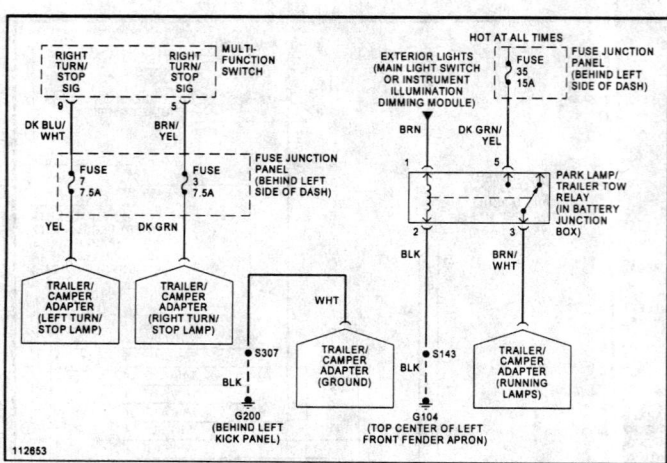

Fig. 27: Trailer/Camper Adapter Wiring Diagram (Ranger)

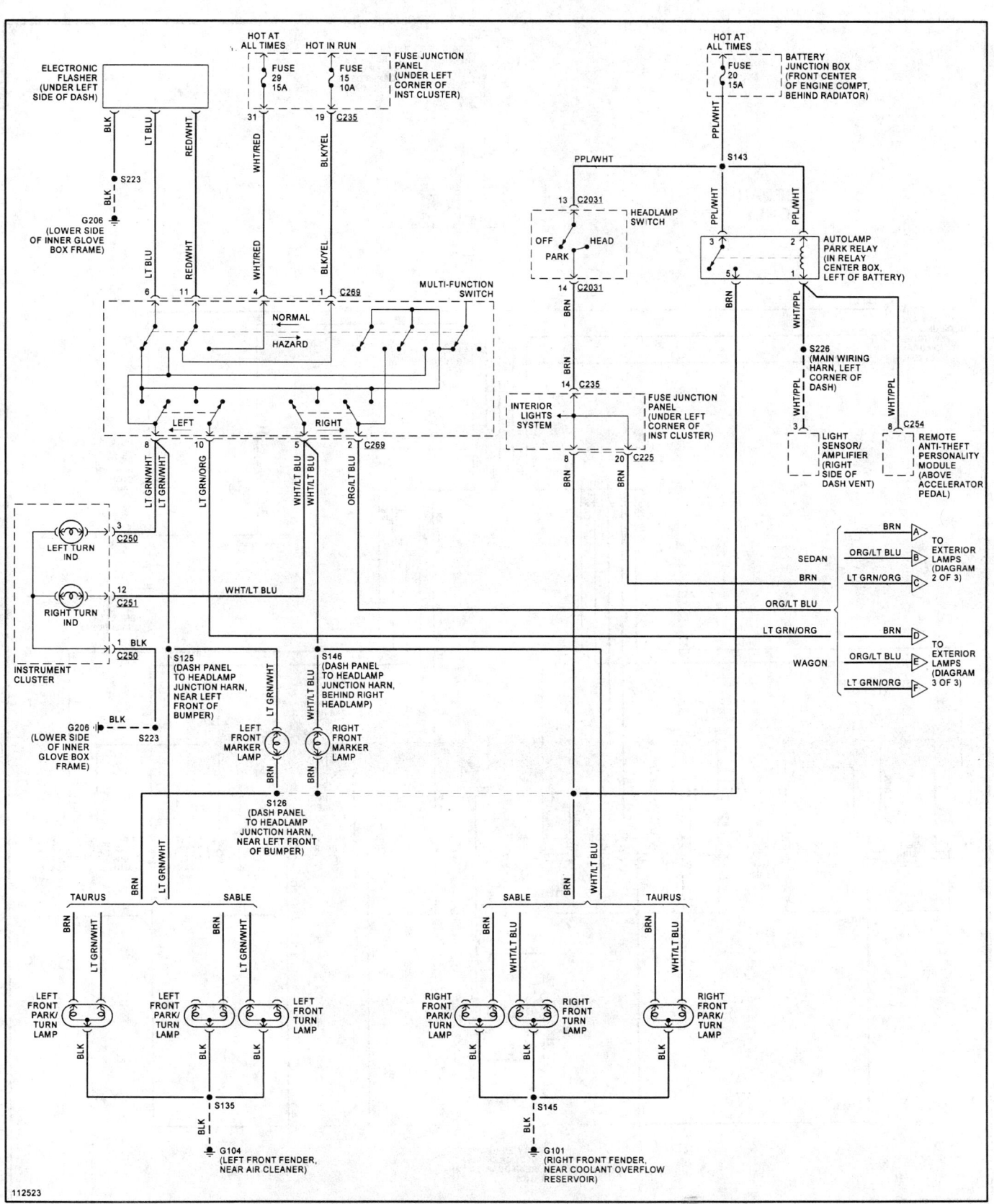

Fig. 28: Exterior Lights Wiring Diagram (Sable & Taurus – 1 Of 3)

112523

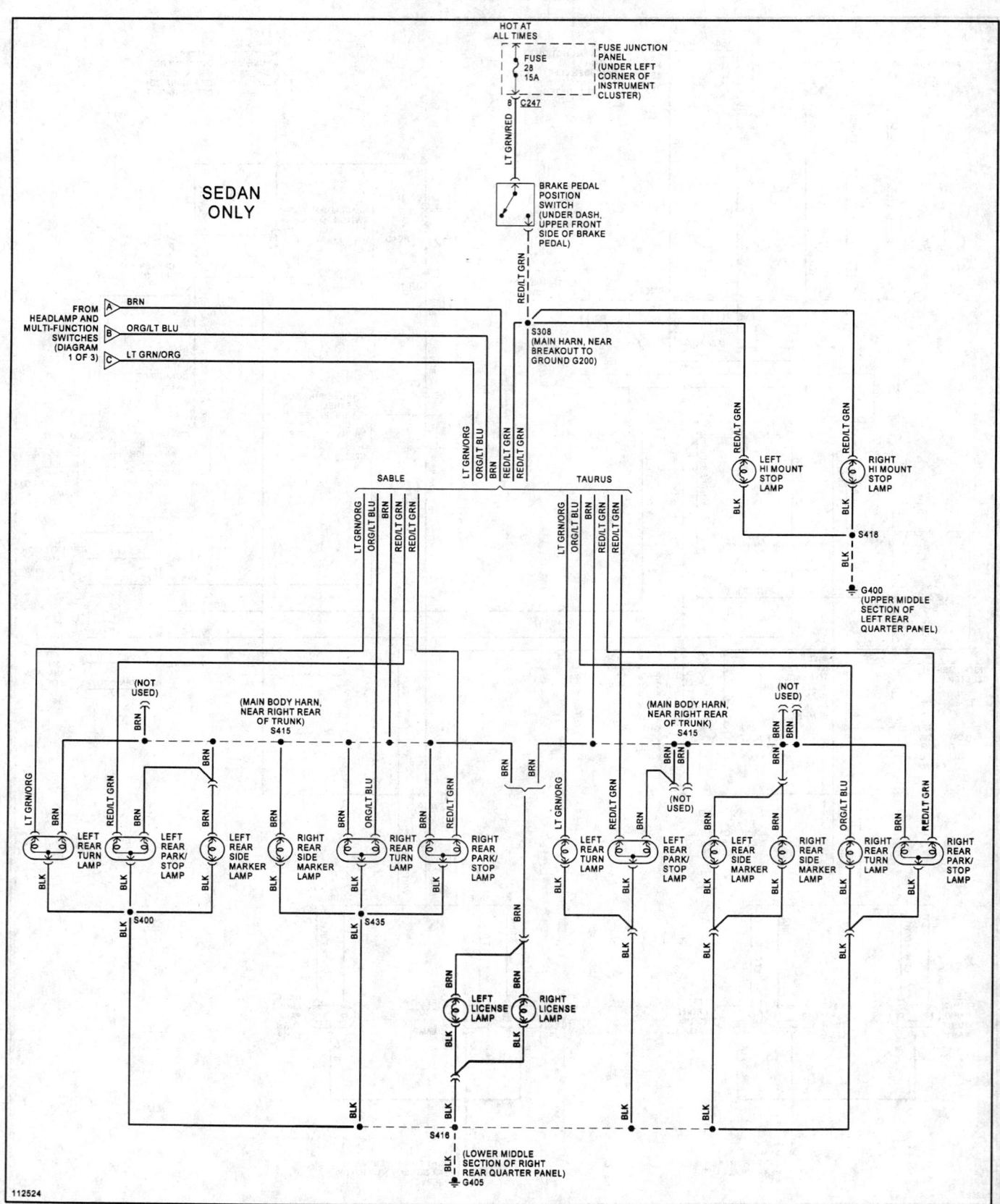

Fig. 29: Exterior Lights Wiring Diagram (Sable & Taurus – 2 Of 3)

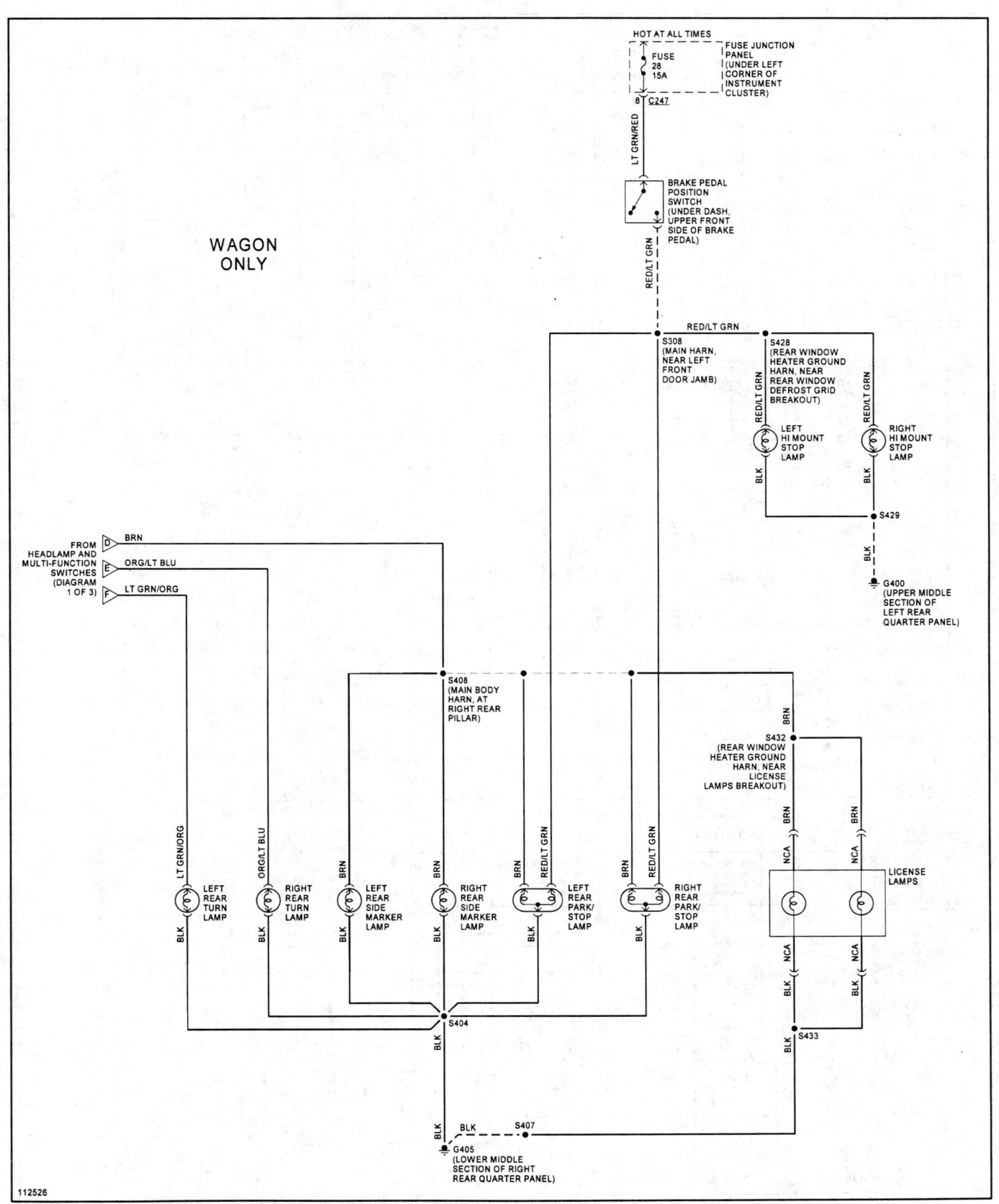

Fig. 30: Exterior Lights Wiring Diagram (Sable & Taurus – 3 Of 3)

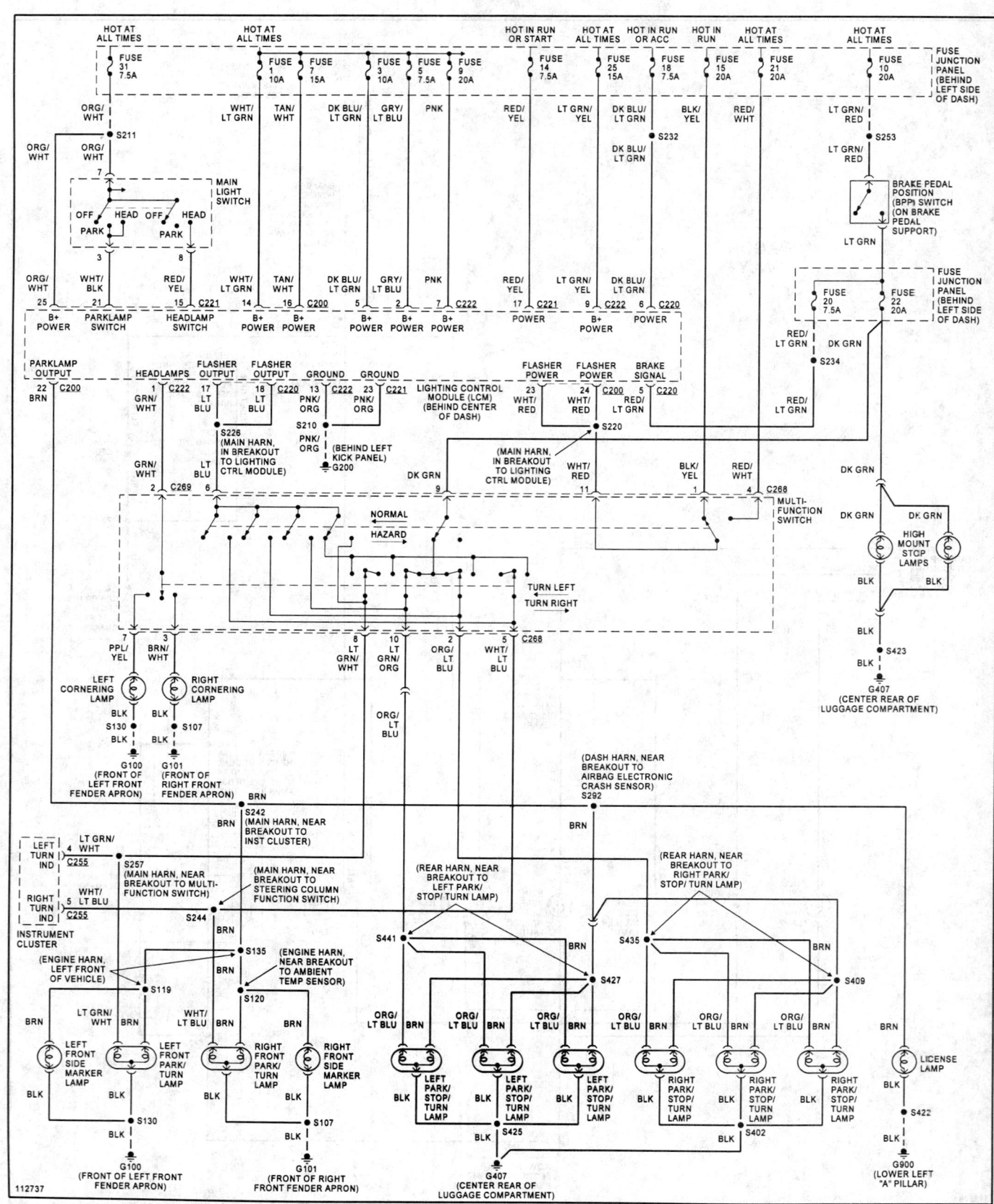

Fig. 31: Exterior Lights Wiring Diagram (Town Car)

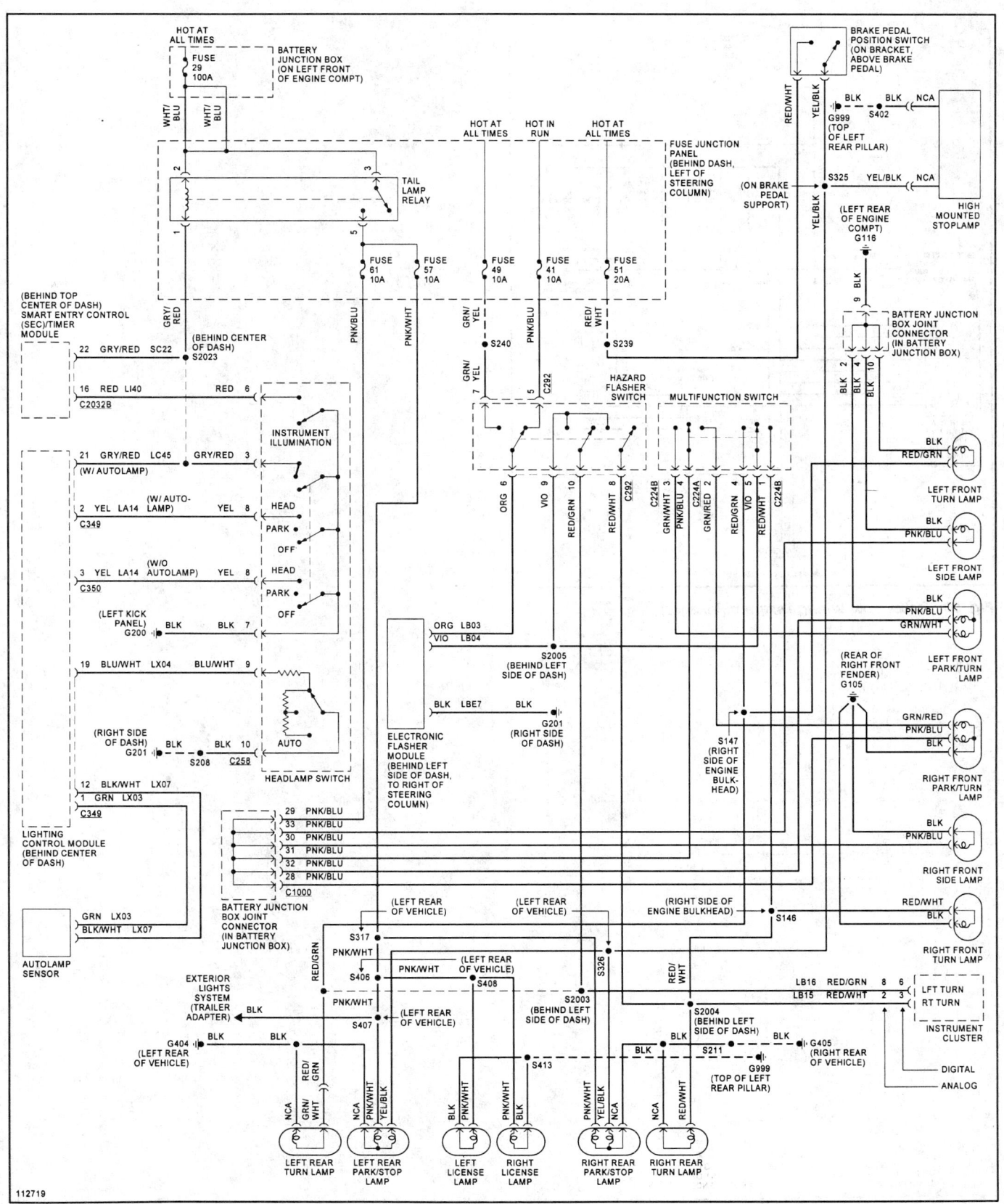

Fig. 32: Exterior Lights Wiring Diagram (Villager)

112719

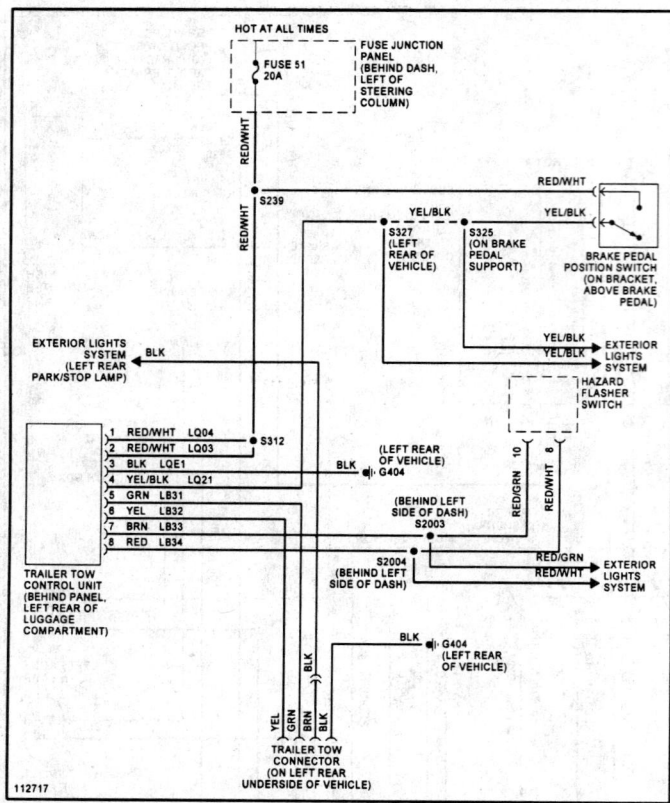

Fig. 33: Trailer Tow Wiring Diagram (Villager)

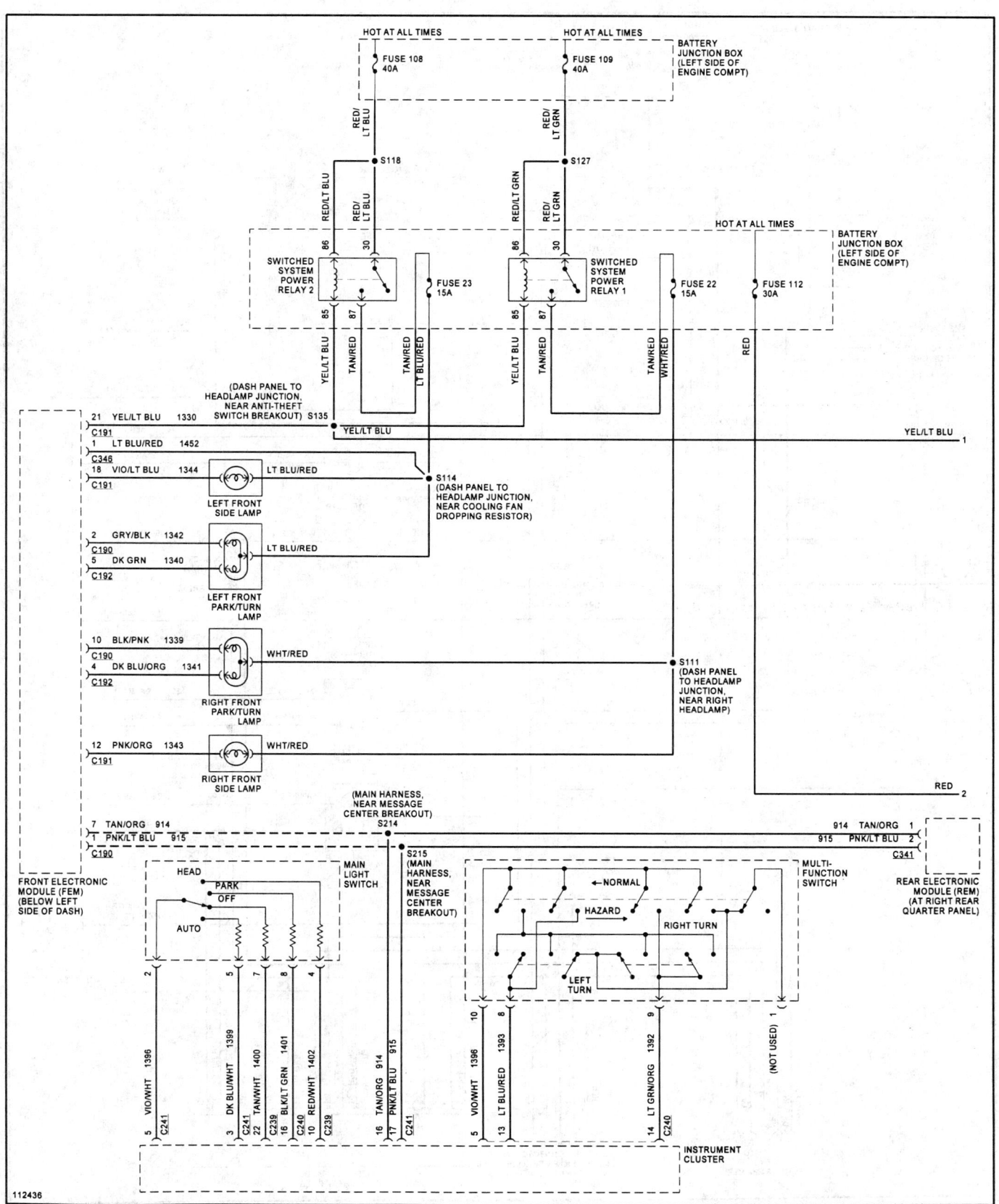

Fig. 34: Exterior Lights & Trailer Connector Wiring Diagram (Windstar – 1 Of 2)

112436

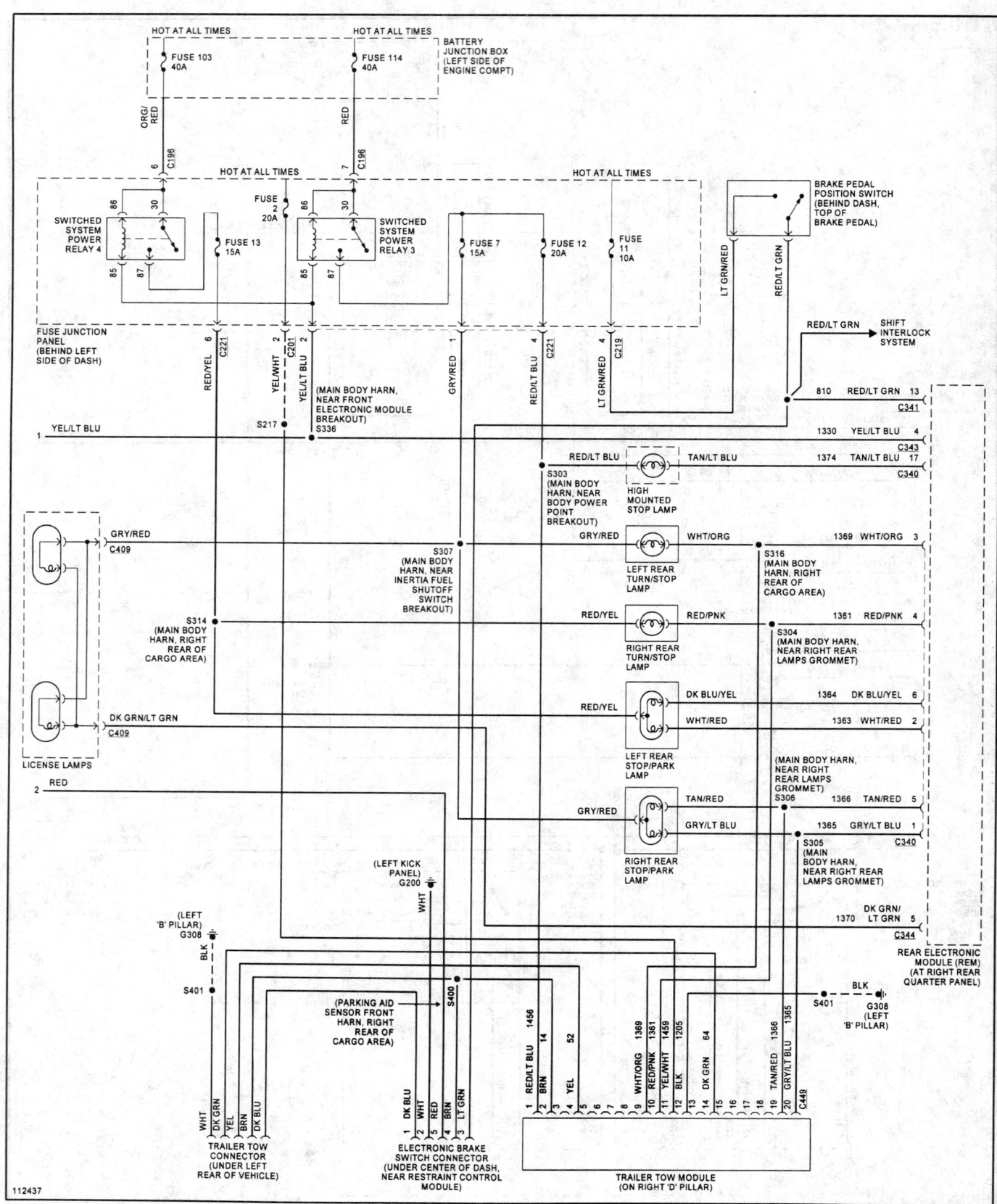

Fig. 35: Exterior Lights & Trailer Connector Wiring Diagram (Windstar – 2 Of 2)

WIRING DIAGRAMS

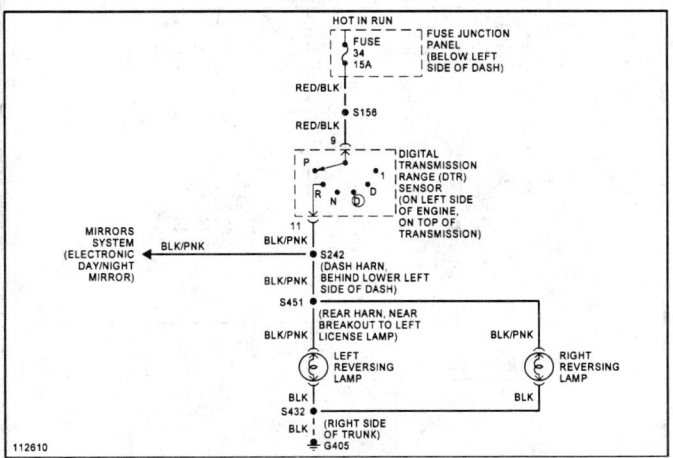

Fig. 1: Back-Up Lights Wiring Diagram (Continental)

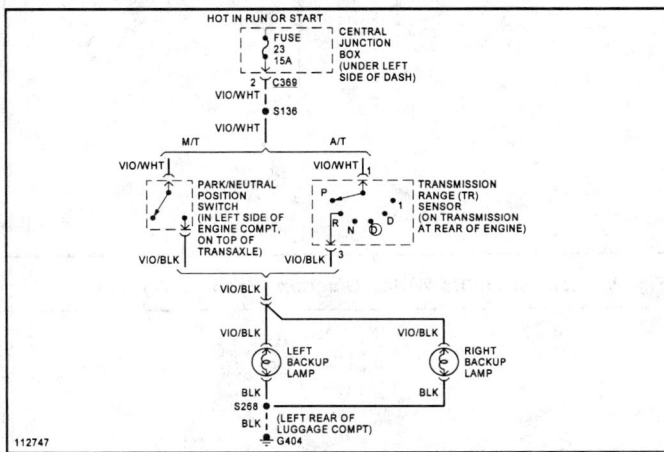

Fig. 2: Back-Up Lights Wiring Diagram (Contour & Mystique)

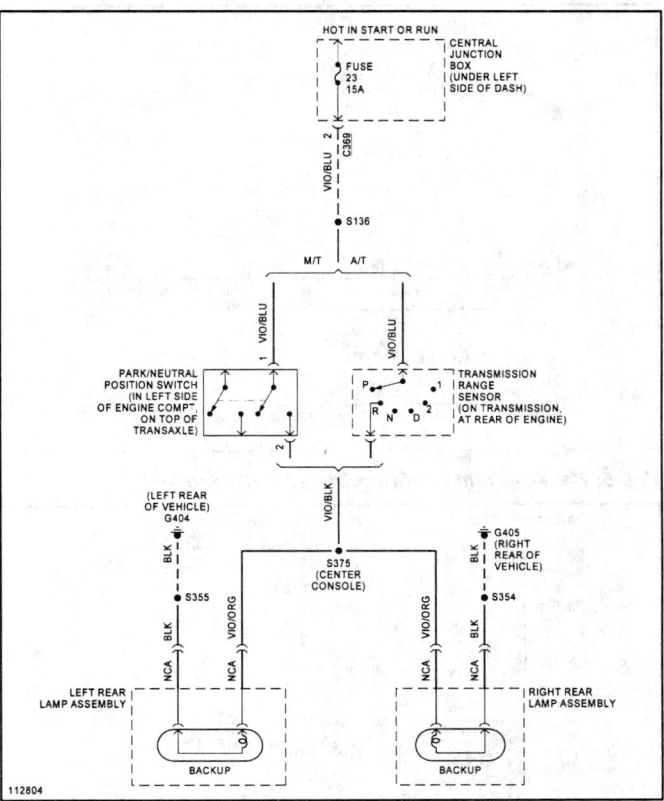

Fig. 3: Back-Up Lights Wiring Diagram (Cougar)

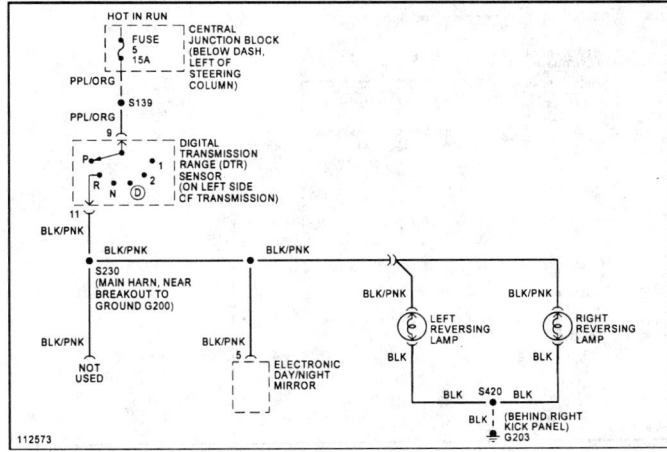

Fig. 4: Back-Up Lights Wiring Diagram (Crown Victoria & Grand Marquis)

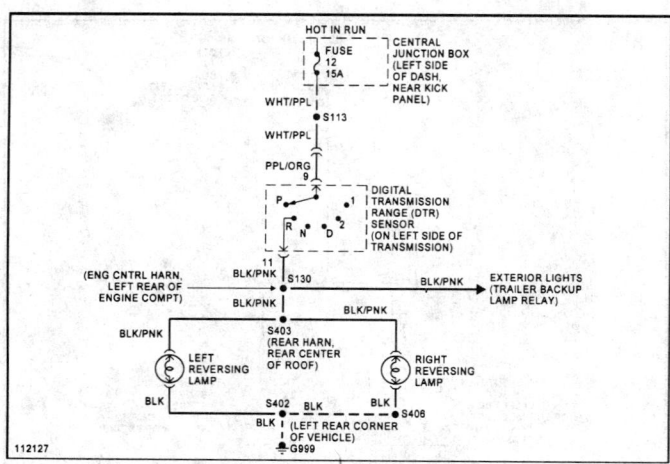

Fig. 5: Back-Up Lights Wiring Diagram (Econoline)

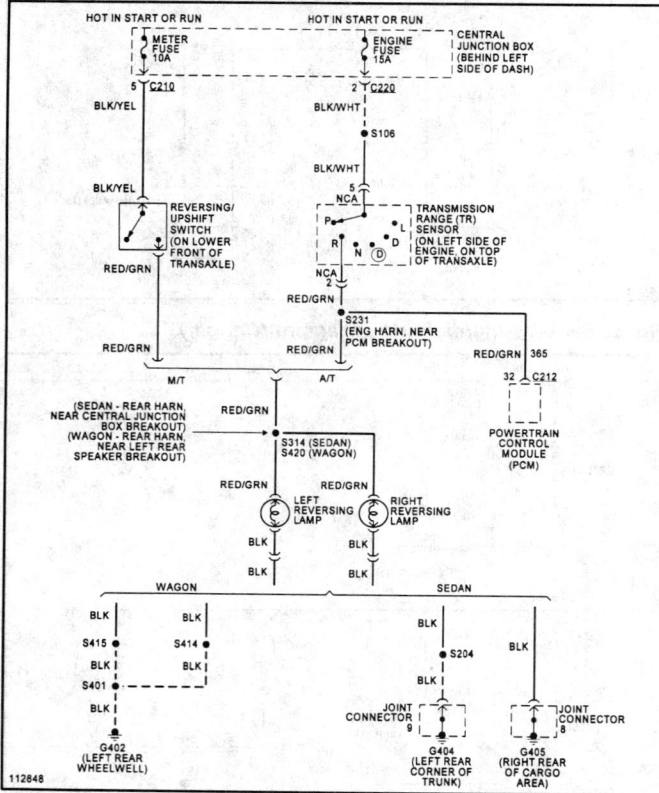

Fig. 6: Back-Up Lights Wiring Diagram (Escort & Tracer)

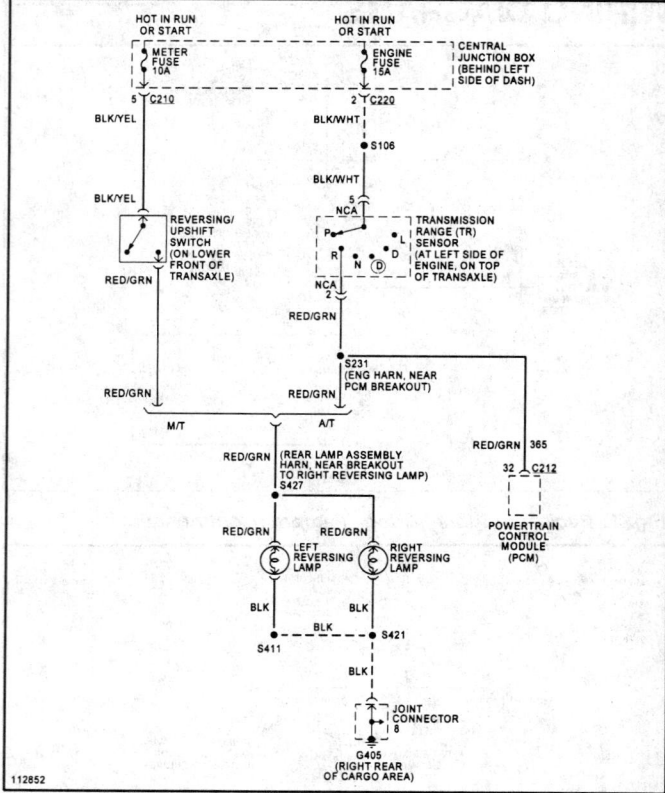

Fig. 7: Back-Up Lights Wiring Diagram (Escort ZX2)

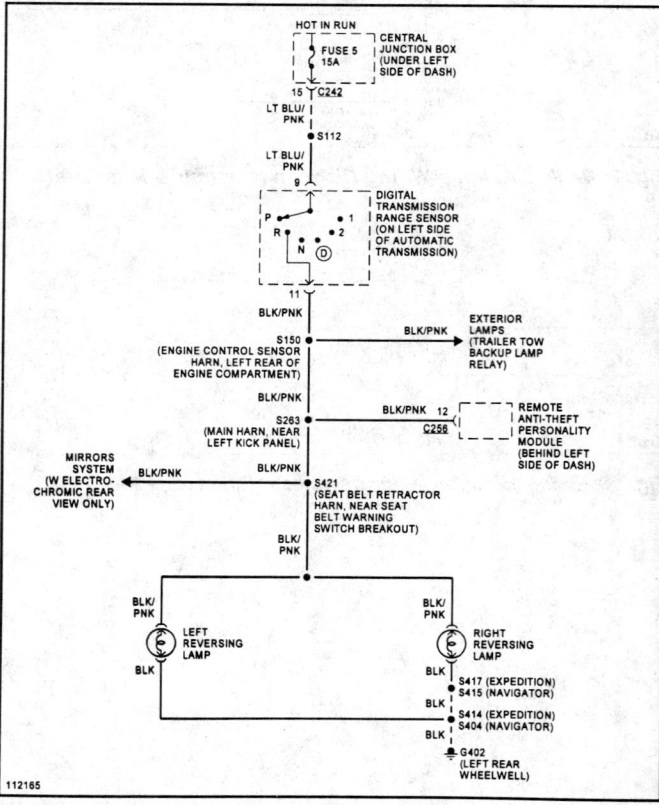

Fig. 8: Back-Up Lights Wiring Diagram (Expedition & Navigator)

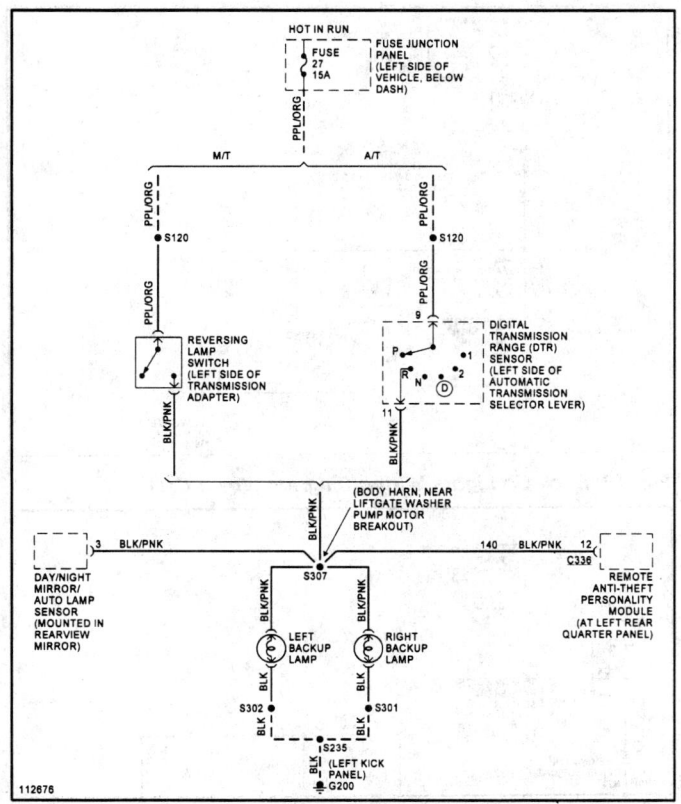

Fig. 9: Back-Up Lights Wiring Diagram (Explorer & Mountaineer)

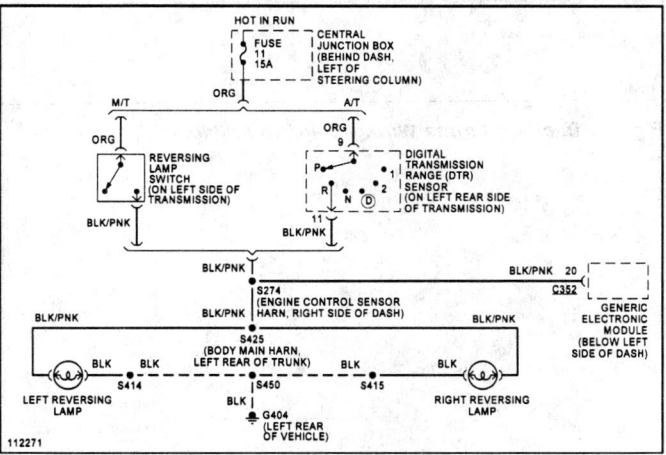

Fig. 10: Back-Up Lights Wiring Diagram (Mustang)

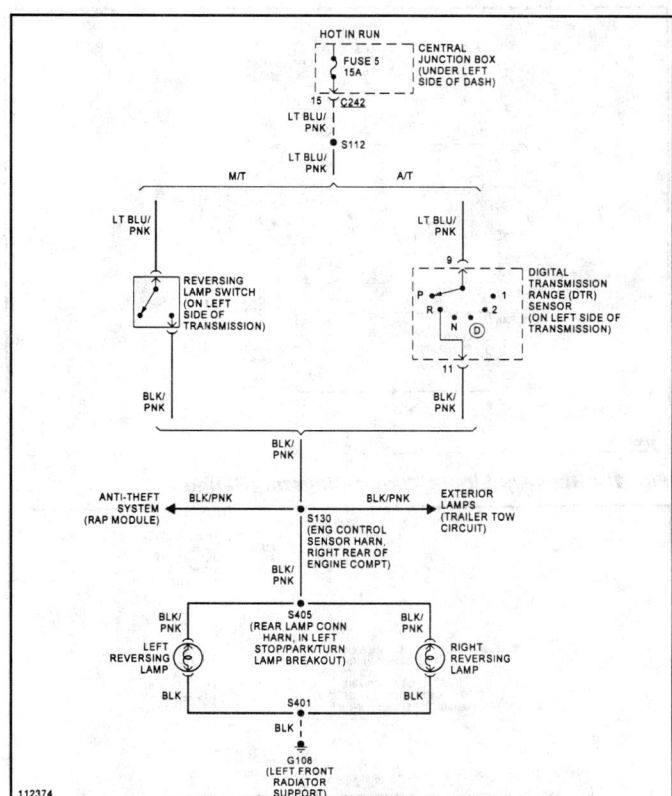

Fig. 11: Back-Up Lights Wiring Diagram (F150 & F250 Light-Duty Pickup)

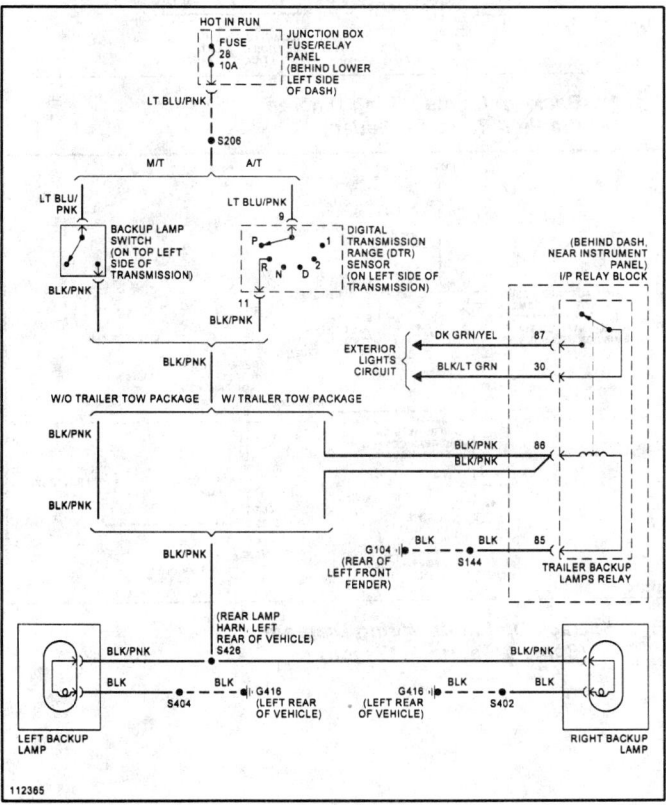

Fig. 12: Back-Up Lights Wiring Diagram (F250 & F350 Super-Duty Pickup)

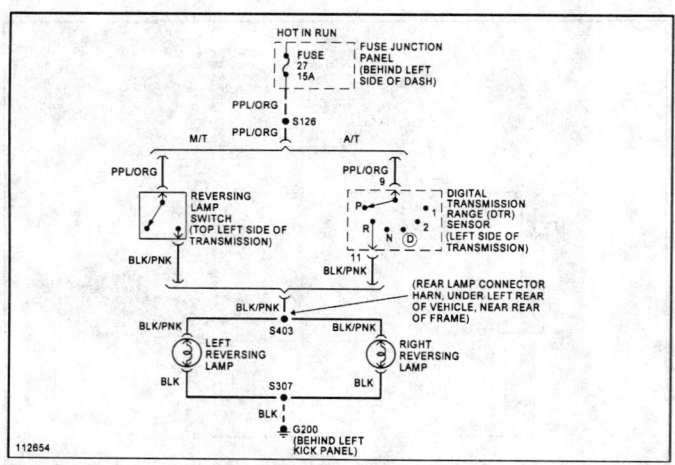

Fig. 13: Back-Up Lights Wiring Diagram (Ranger)

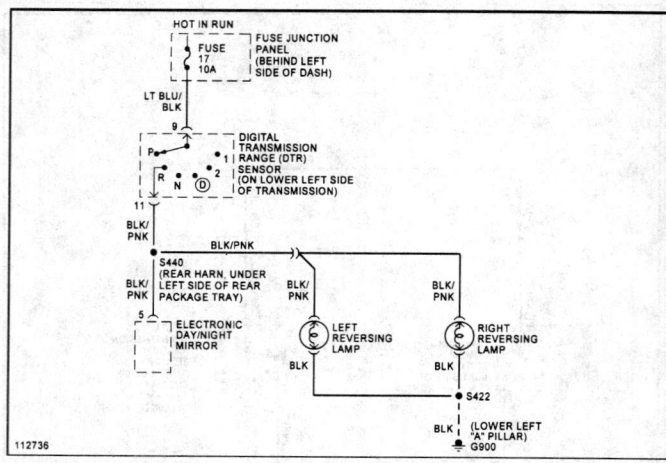

Fig. 16: Back-Up Lights Wiring Diagram (Town Car)

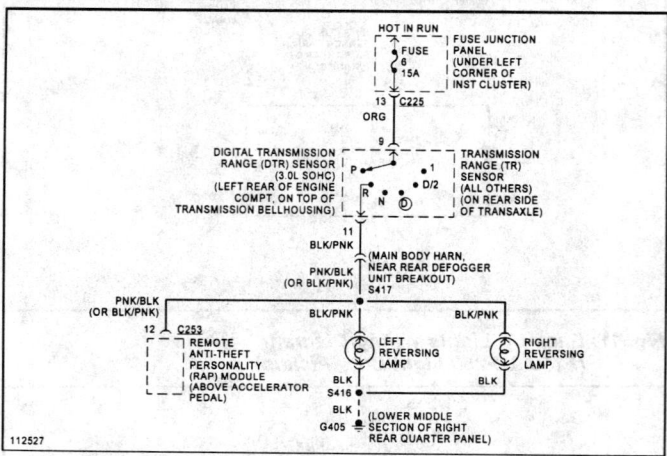

Fig. 14: Back-Up Lights Wiring Diagram (Sable & Taurus – Sedan)

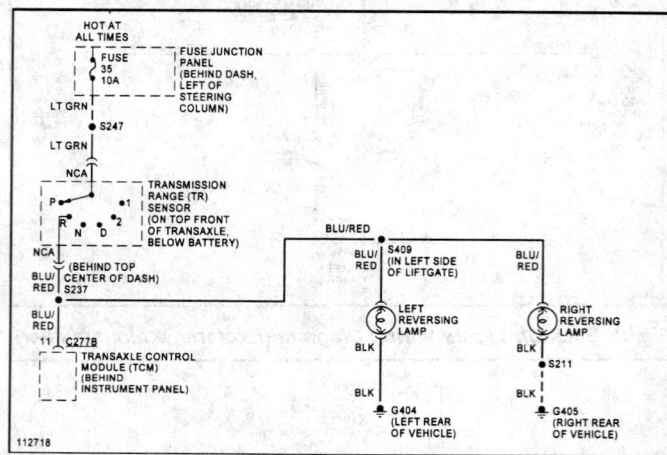

Fig. 17: Back-Up Lights Wiring Diagram (Villager)

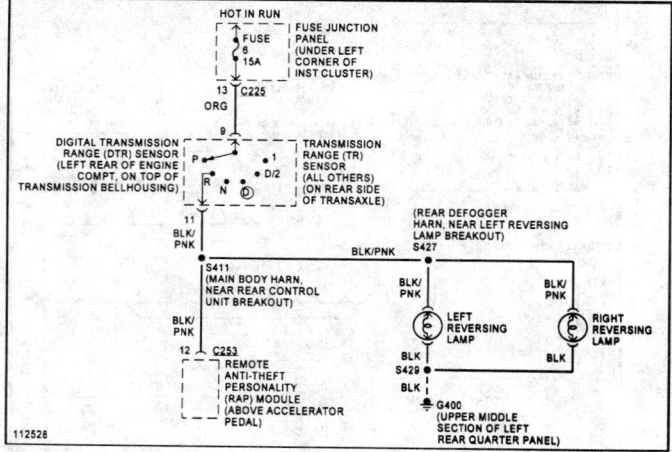

Fig. 15: Back-Up Lights Wiring Diagram (Sable & Taurus – Wagon)

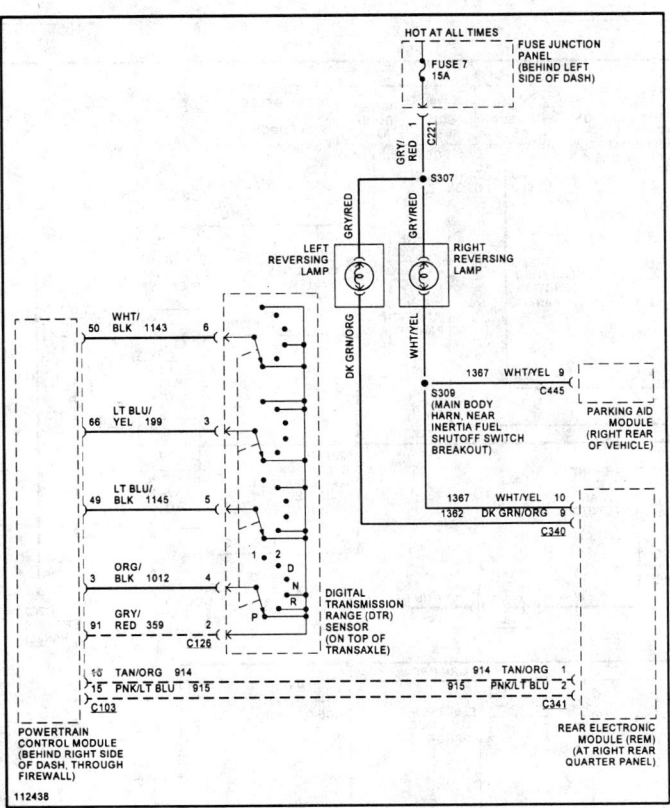

Fig. 18: Back-Up Lights Connector Wiring Diagram (Windstar)

WIRING DIAGRAMS

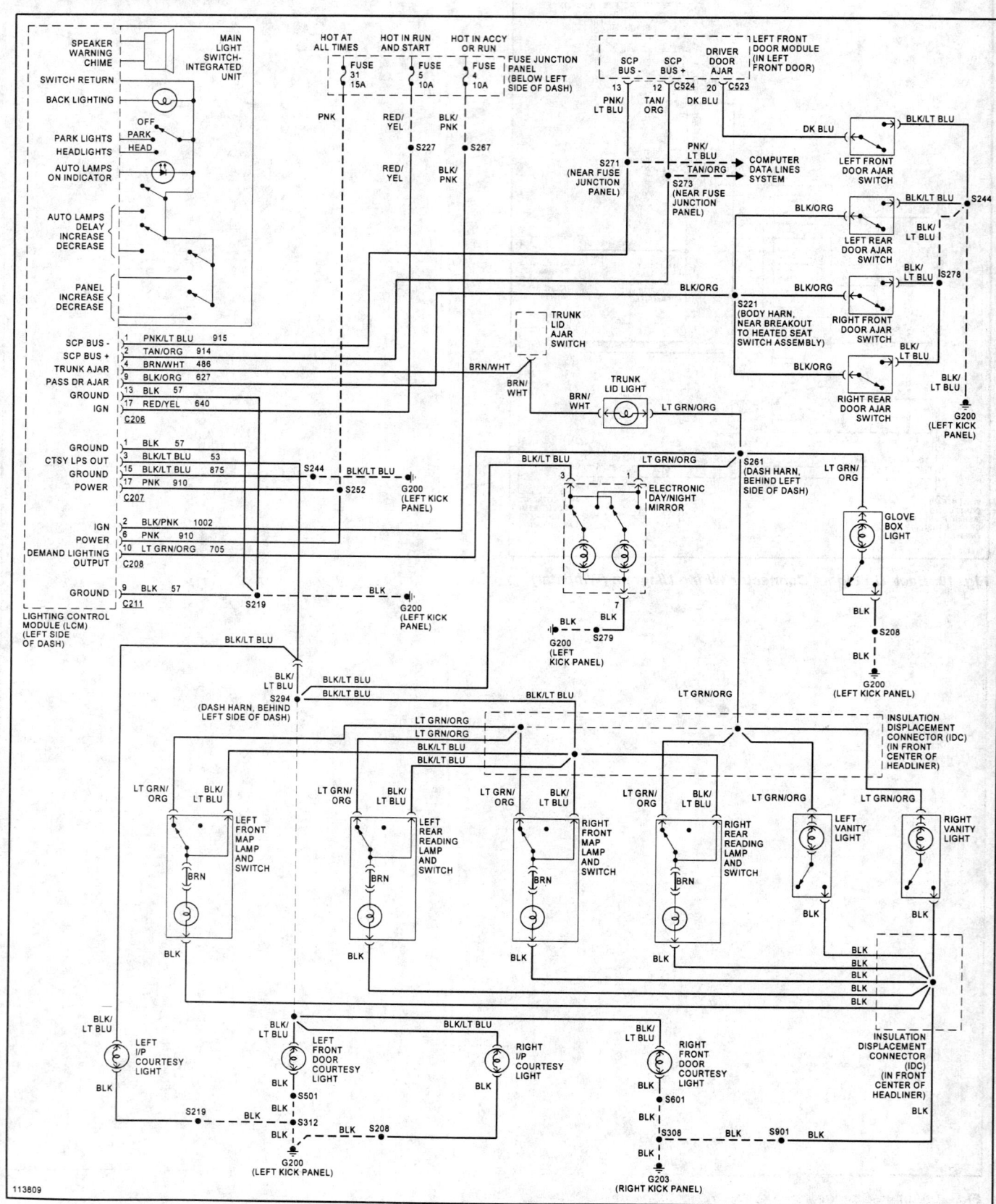

Fig. 1: Illumination/Interior Lights Wiring Diagram (Continental – 1 Of 2)

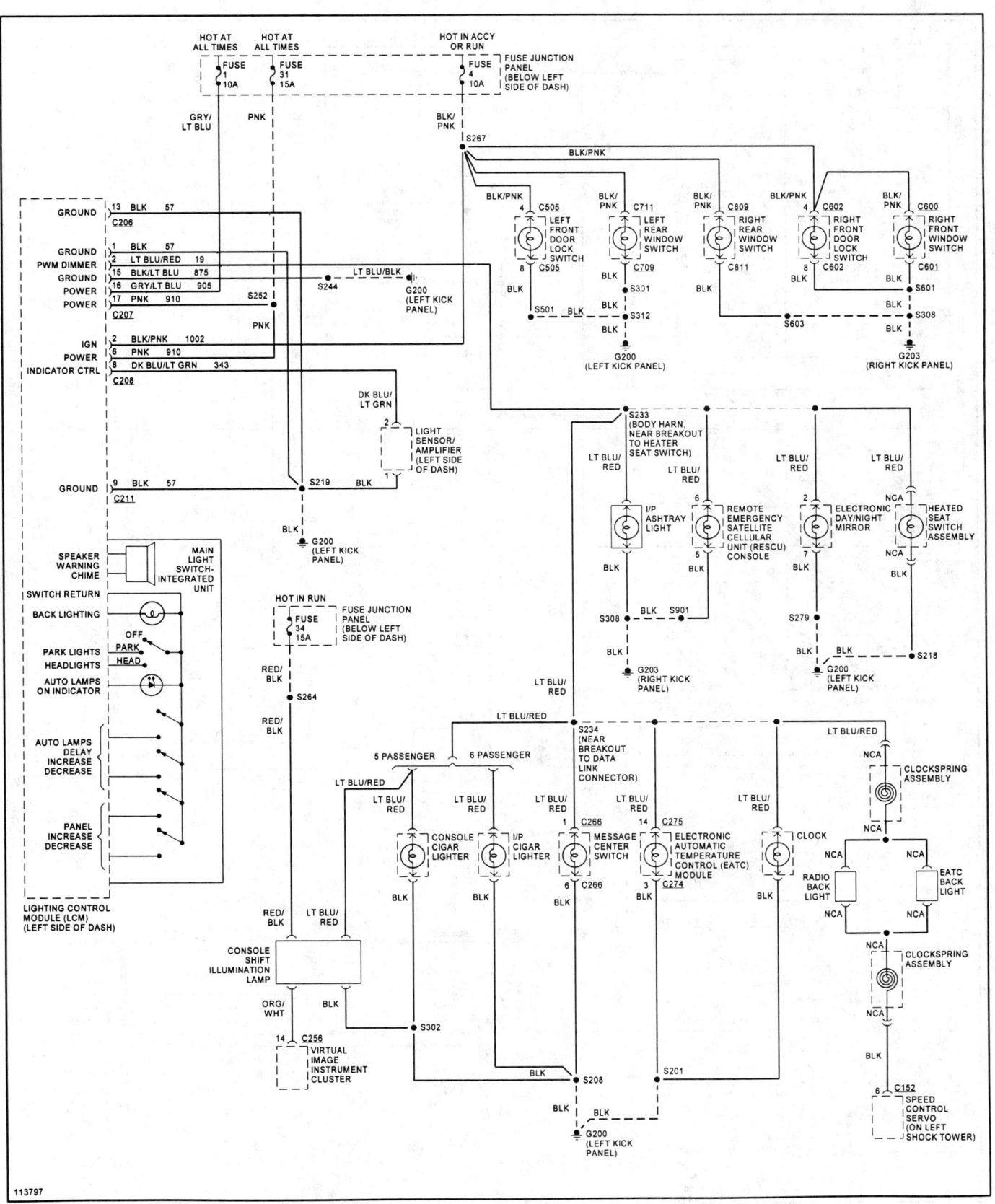

Fig. 2: Illumination/Interior Lights Wiring Diagram (Continental – 2 Of 2)

113797

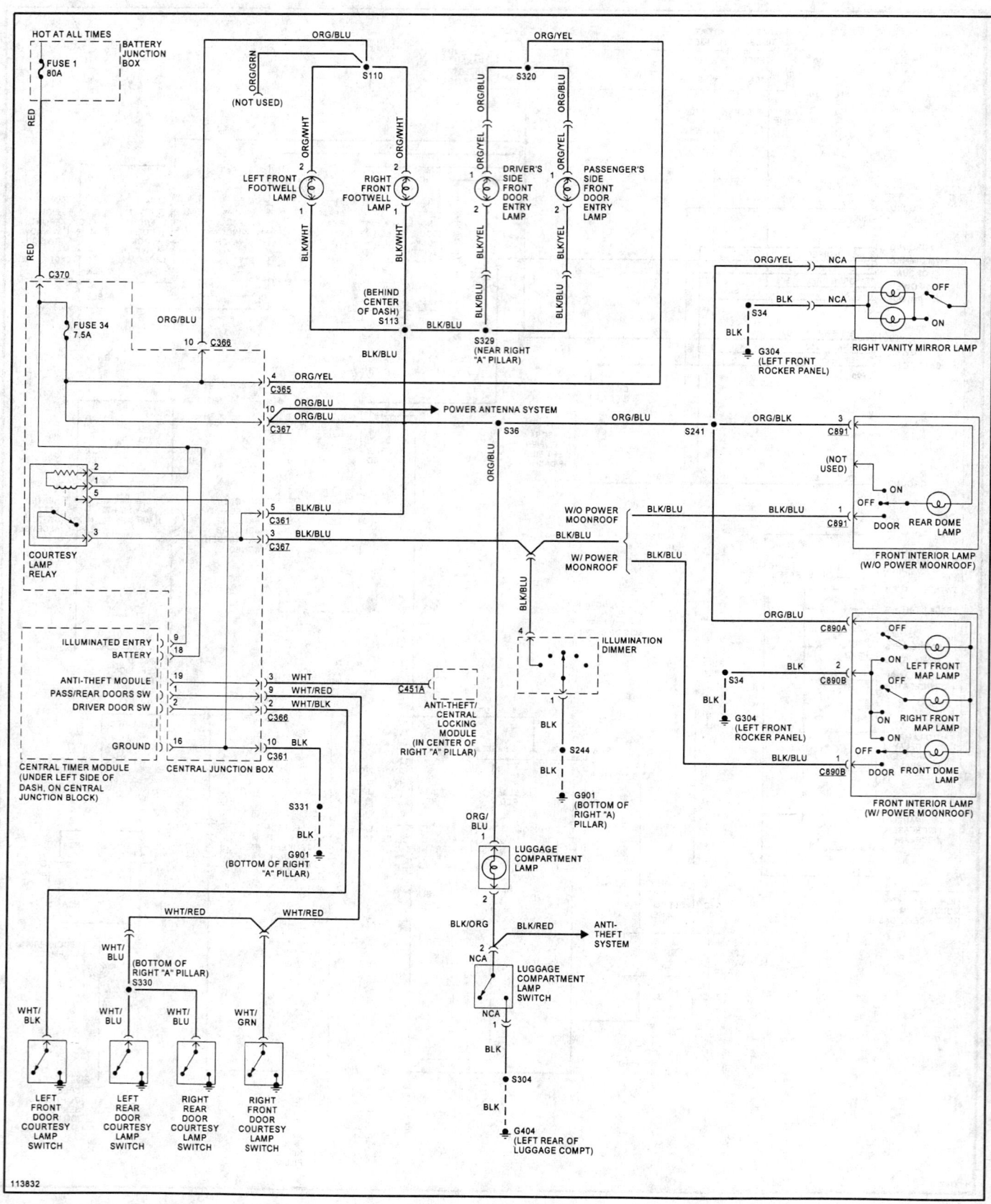

Fig. 3: Illumination/Interior Lights Wiring Diagram (Contour & Mystique – 1 Of 2)

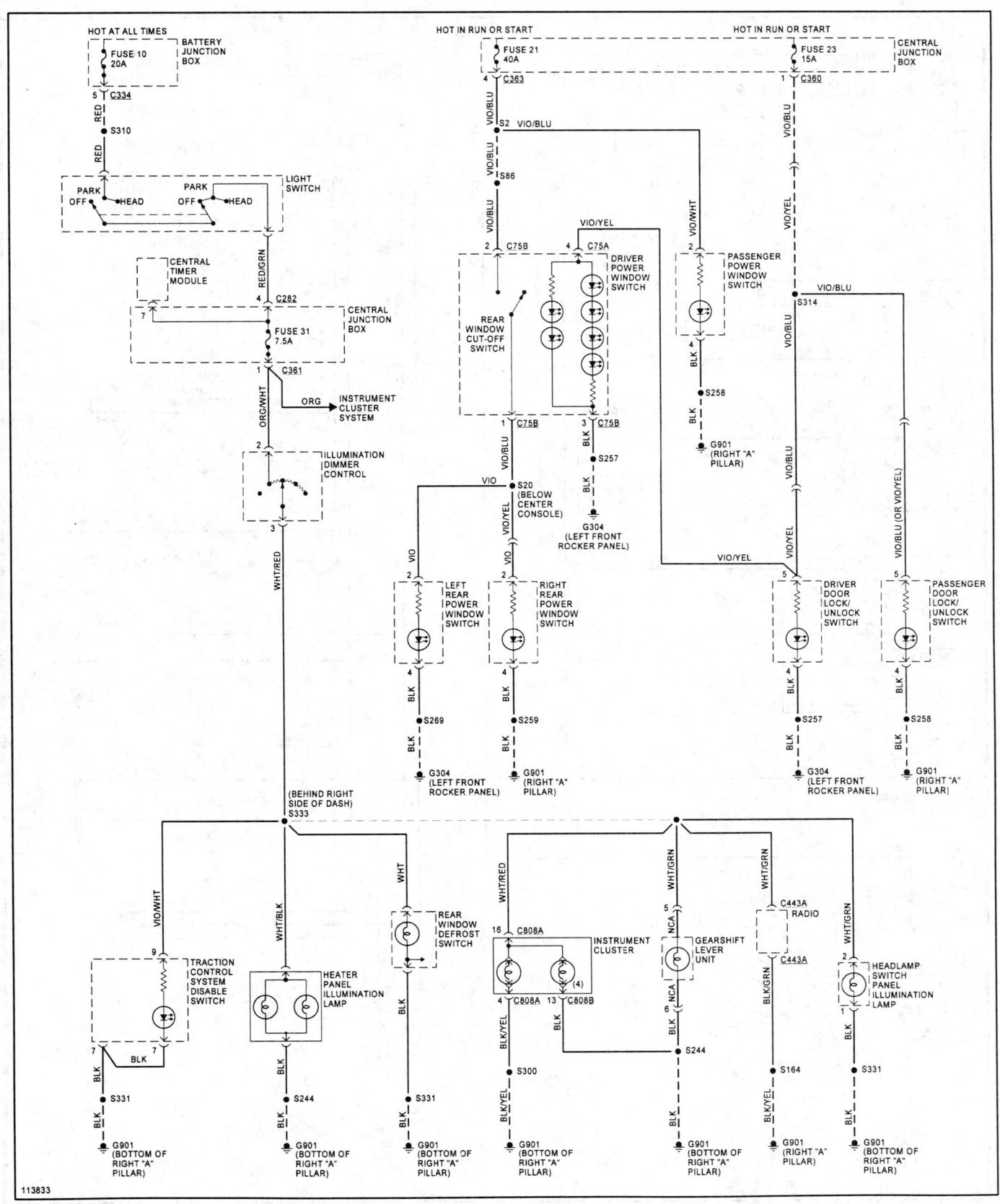

Fig. 4: Illumination/Interior Lights Wiring Diagram (Contour & Mystique – 2 Of 2)

113833

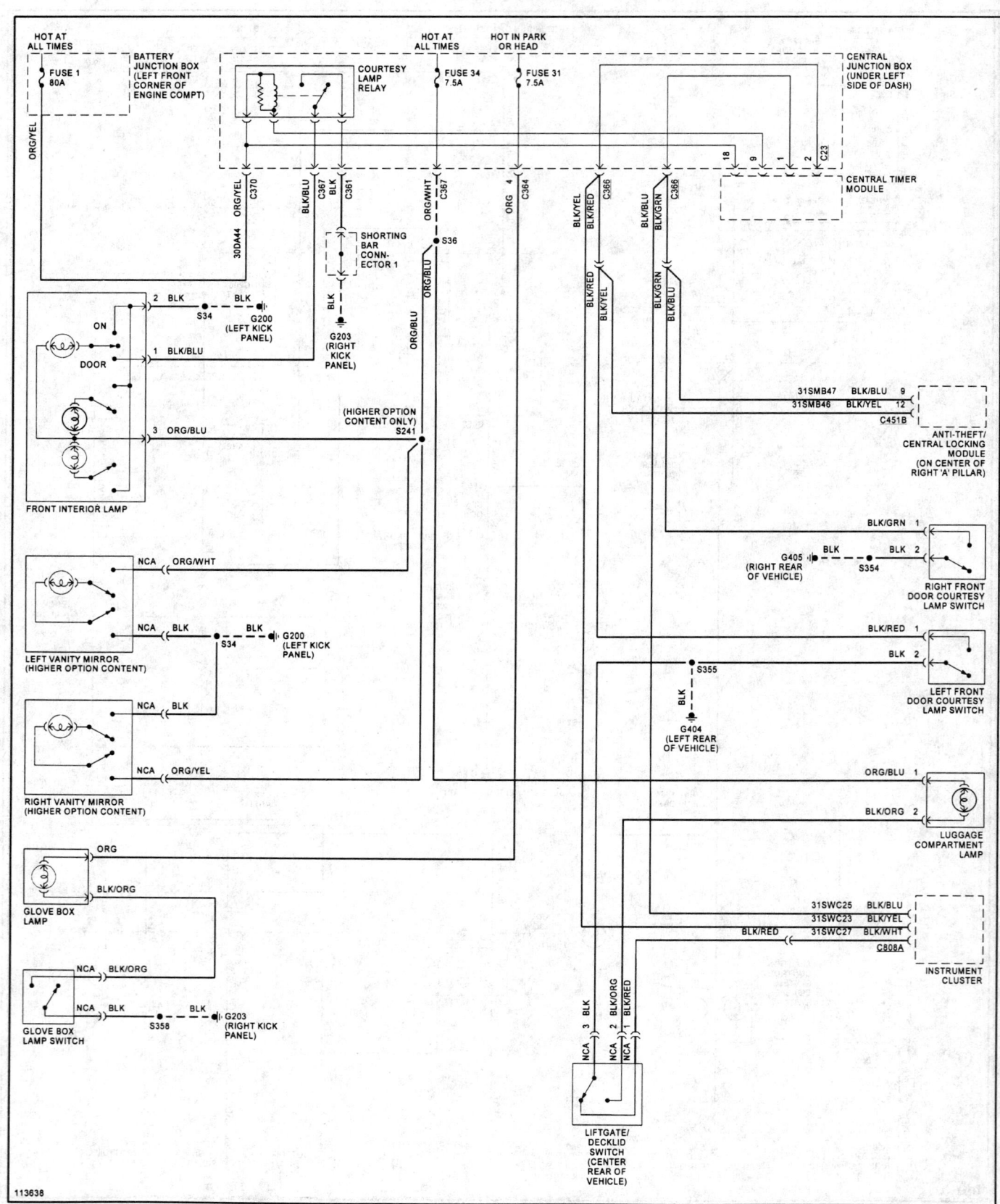

Fig. 5: Illumination/Interior Lights Wiring Diagram (Cougar – High Option Content – 1 Of 2)

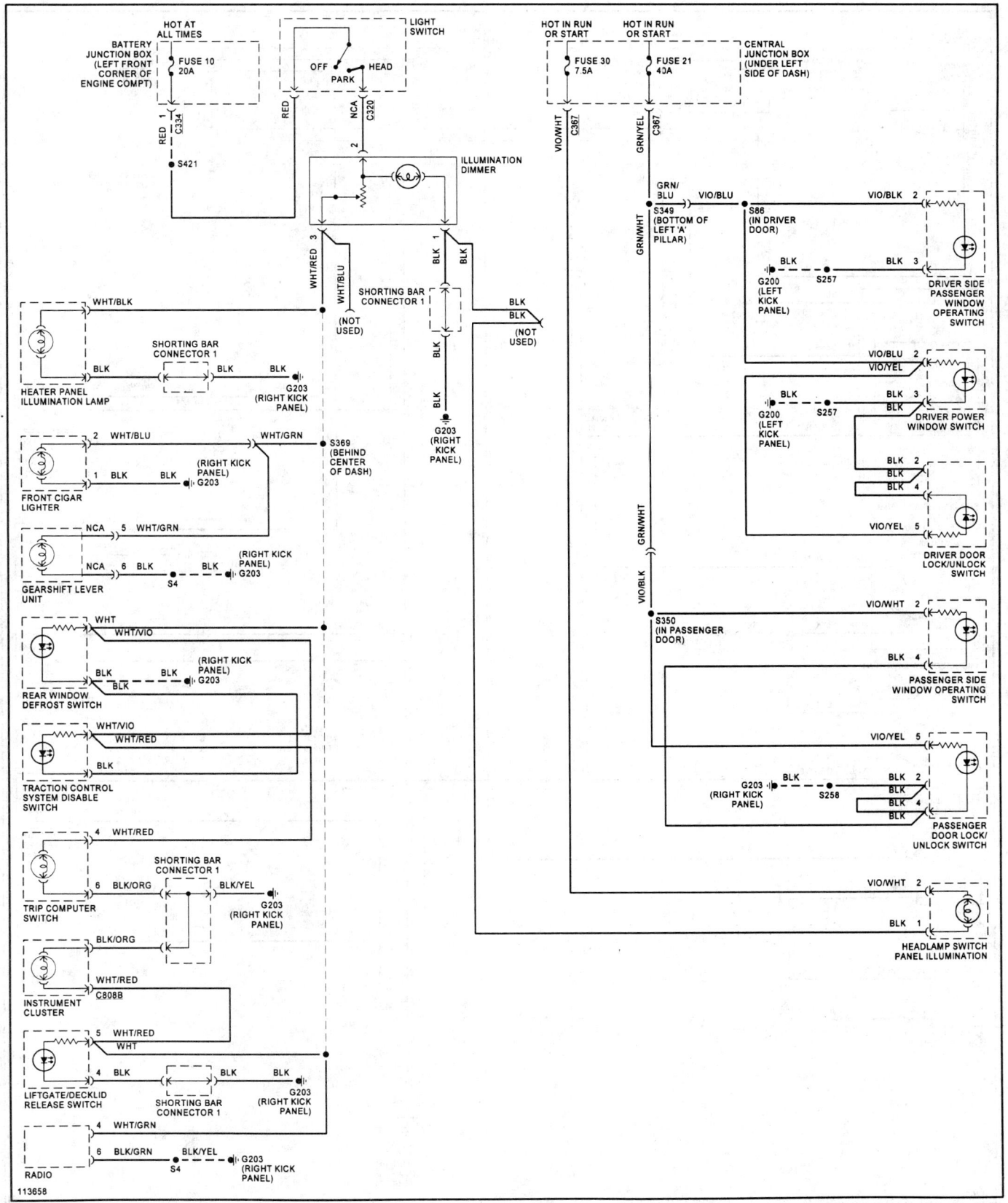

Fig. 6: Illumination/Interior Lights Wiring Diagram (Cougar – High Option Content – 2 Of 2)

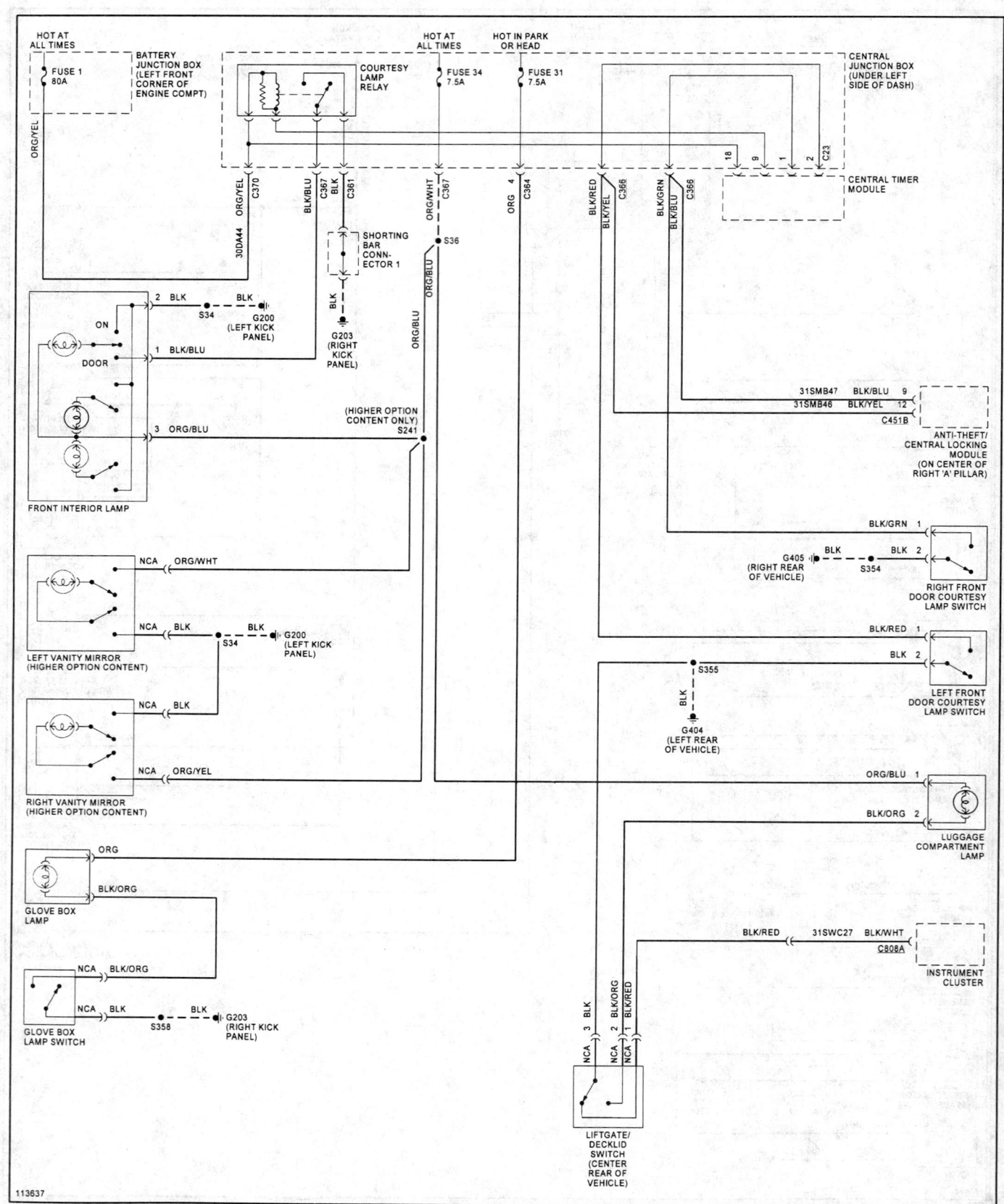

Fig. 7: Illumination/Interior Lights Wiring Diagram (Cougar – Low Option Content – 1 Of 2)

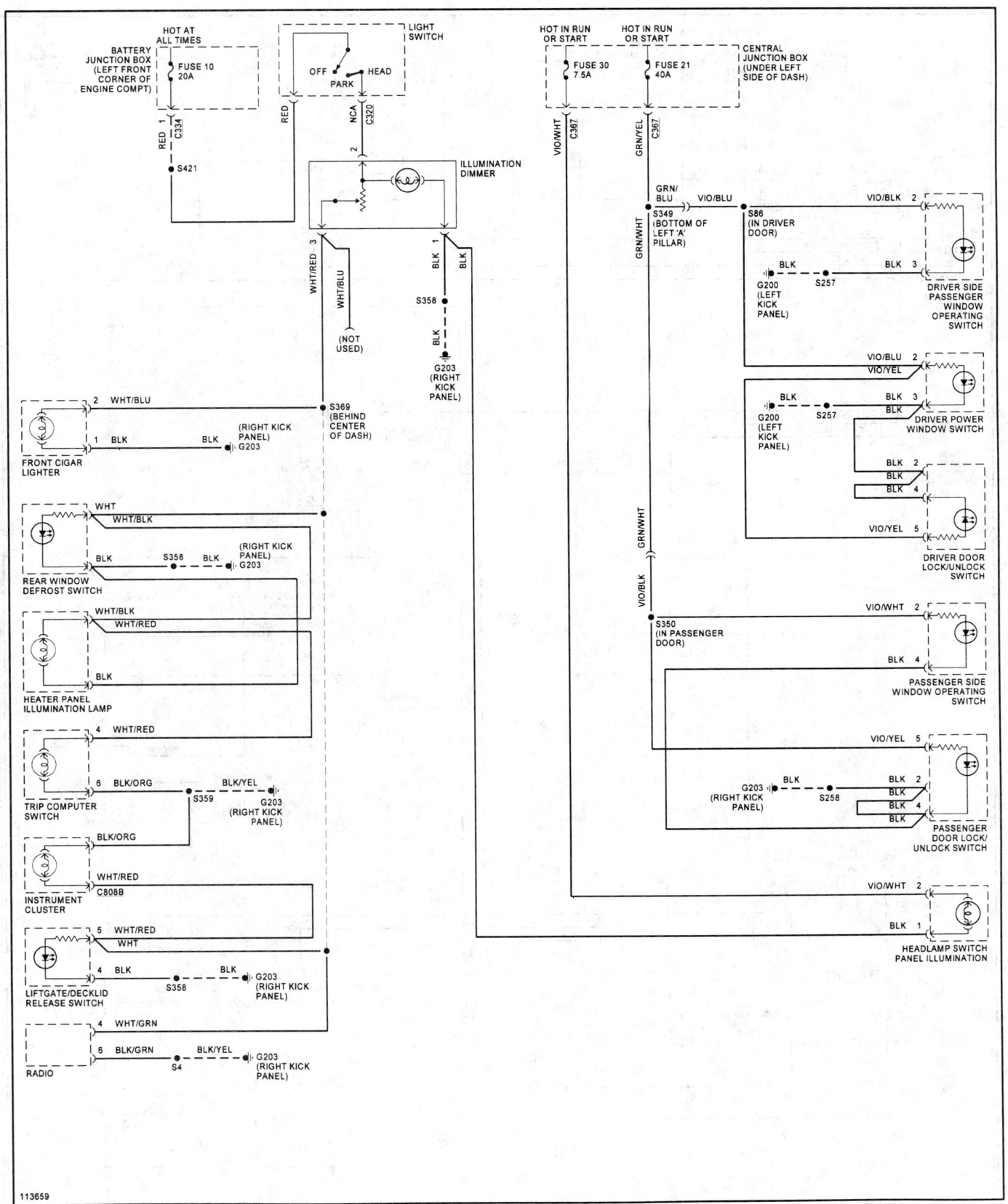

Fig. 8: Illumination/Interior Lights Wiring Diagram (Cougar – Low Option Content – 2 Of 2)

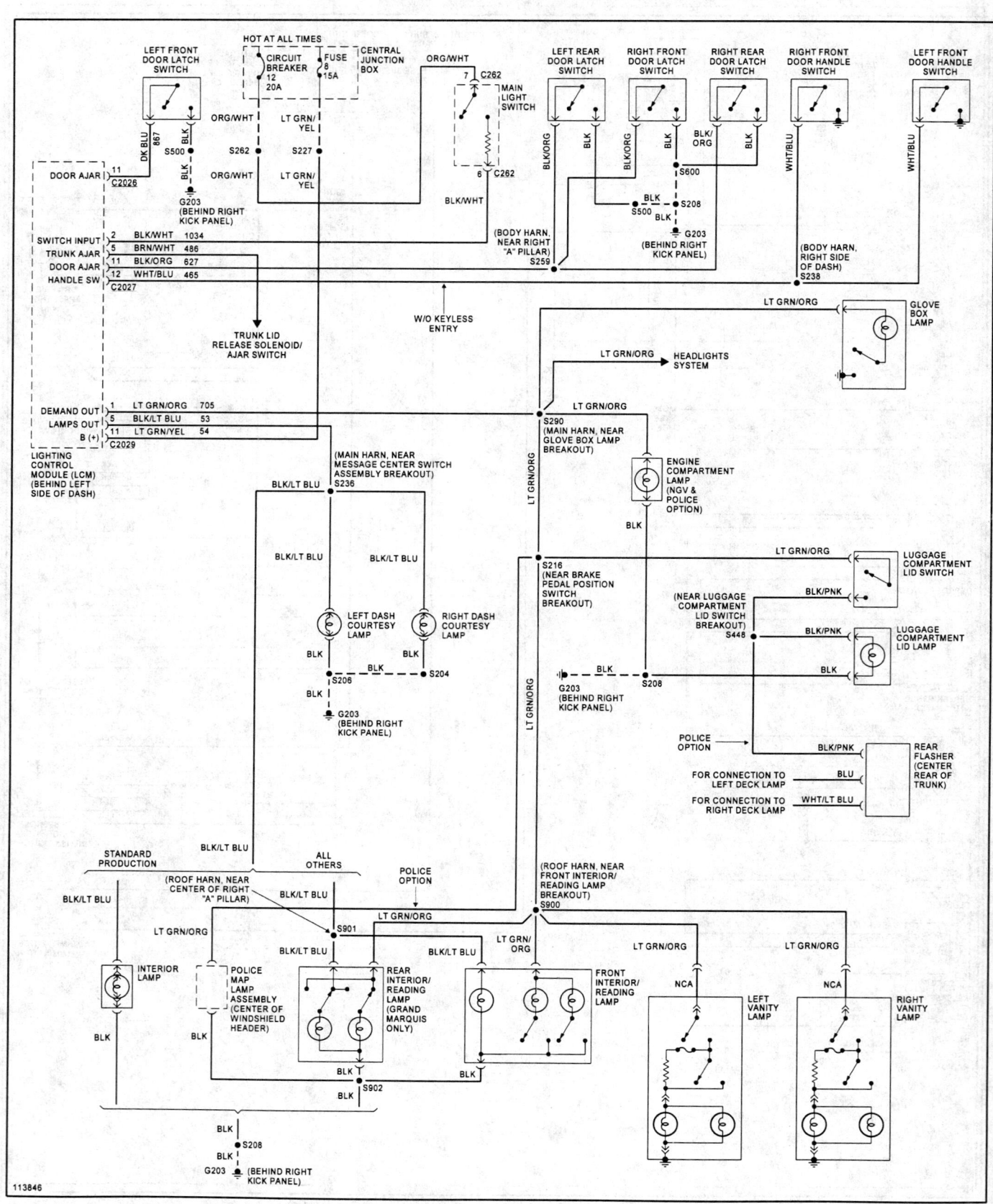

Fig. 9: Illumination/Interior Lights Wiring Diagram (Crown Victoria & Grand Marquis – 1 Of 2)

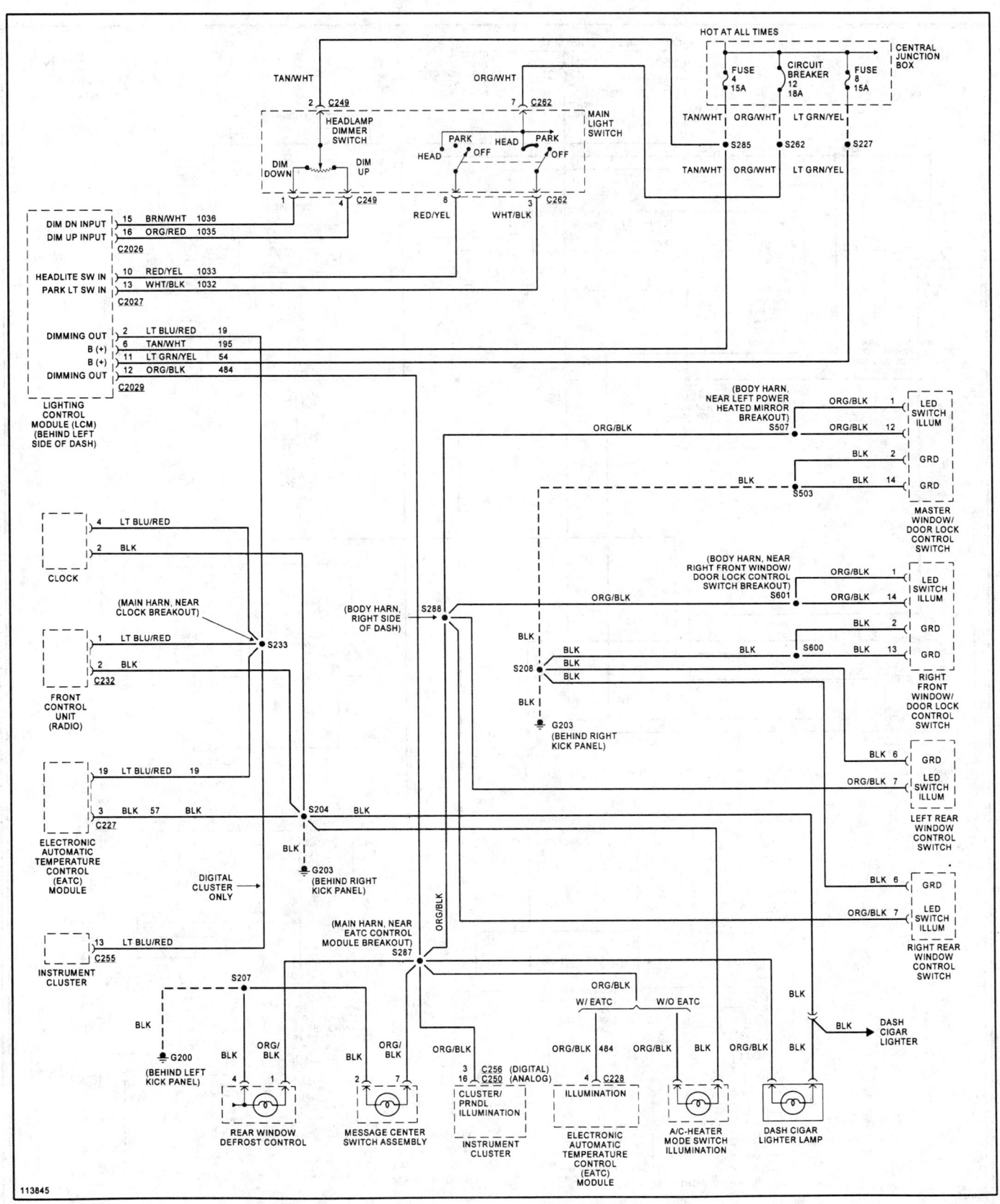

Fig. 10: Illumination/Interior Lights Wiring Diagram (Crown Victoria & Grand Marquis – 2 Of 2)

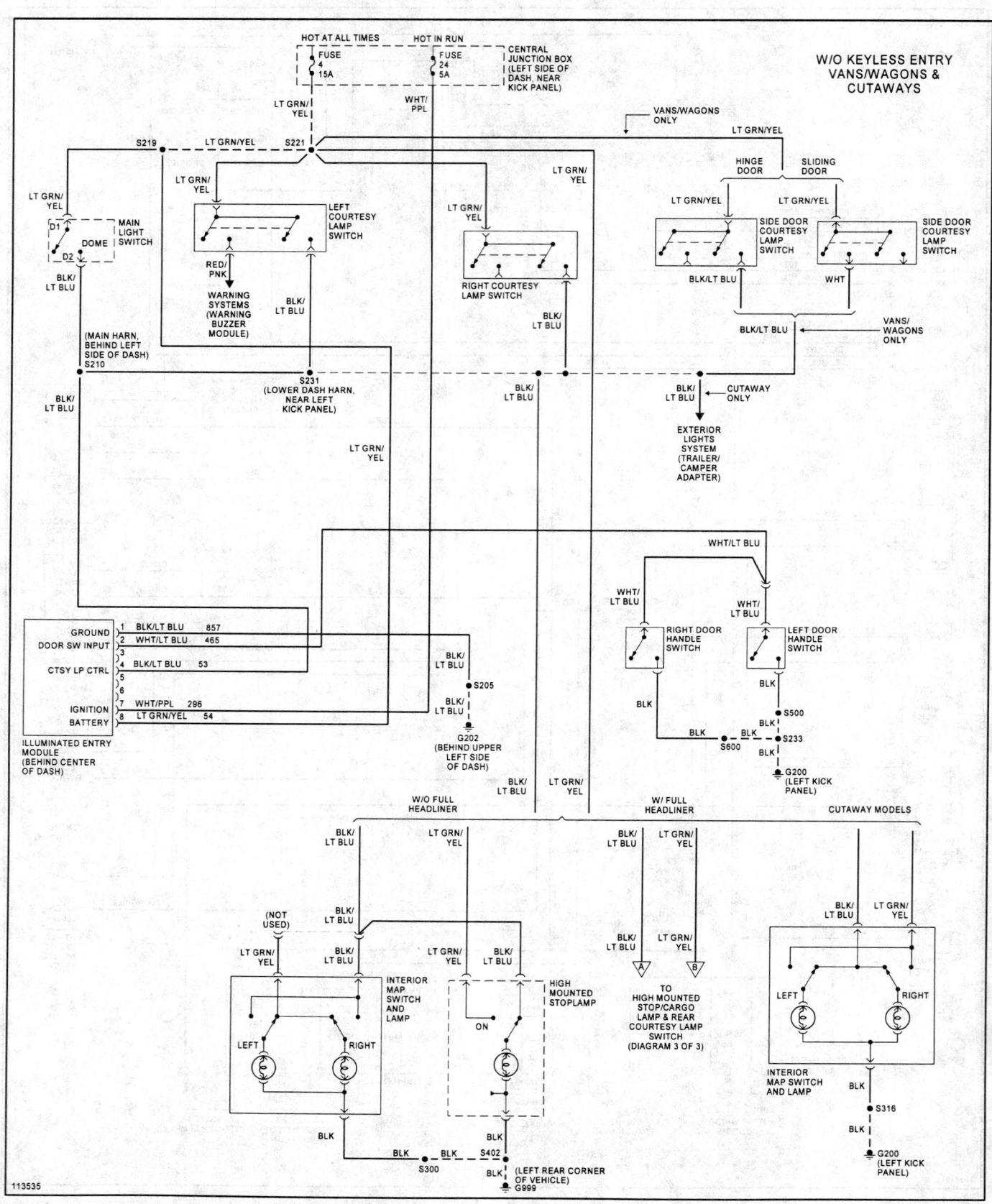

Fig. 11: Illumination/Interior Lights Wiring Diagram (Econoline – 1 Of 4)

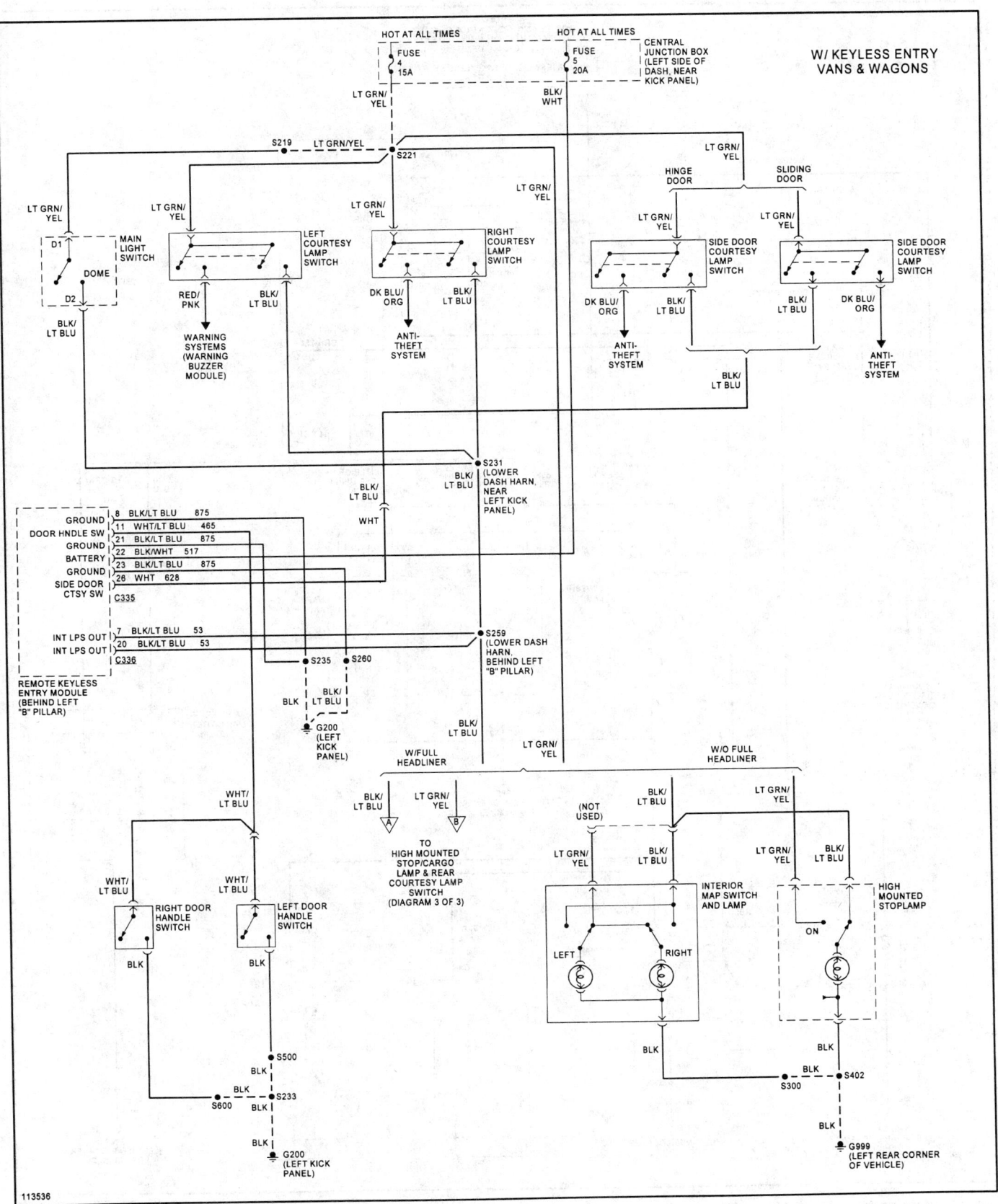

Fig. 12: Illumination/Interior Lights Wiring Diagram (Econoline – 2 Of 4)

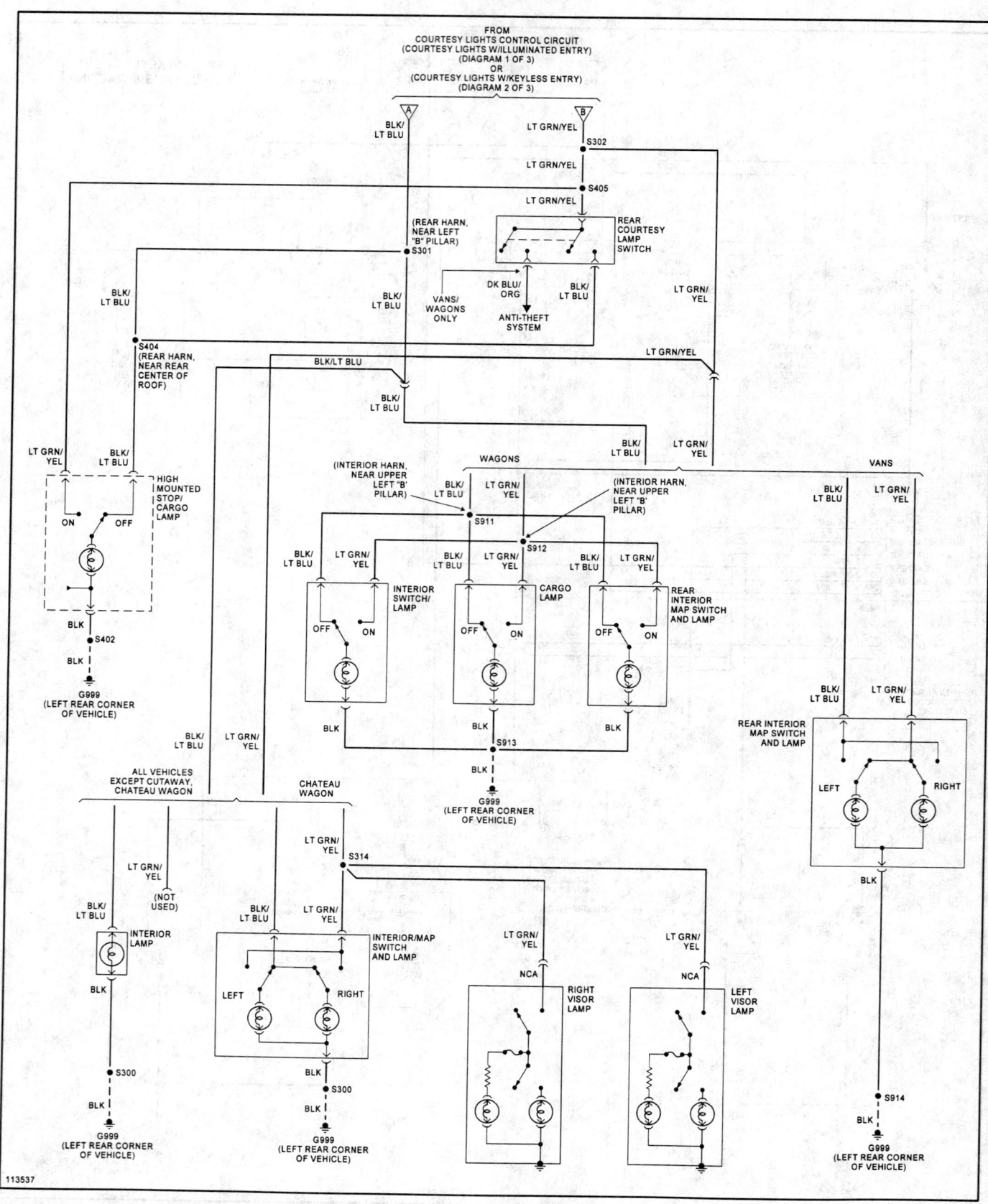

Fig. 13: Illumination/Interior Lights Wiring Diagram (Econoline – 3 Of 4)

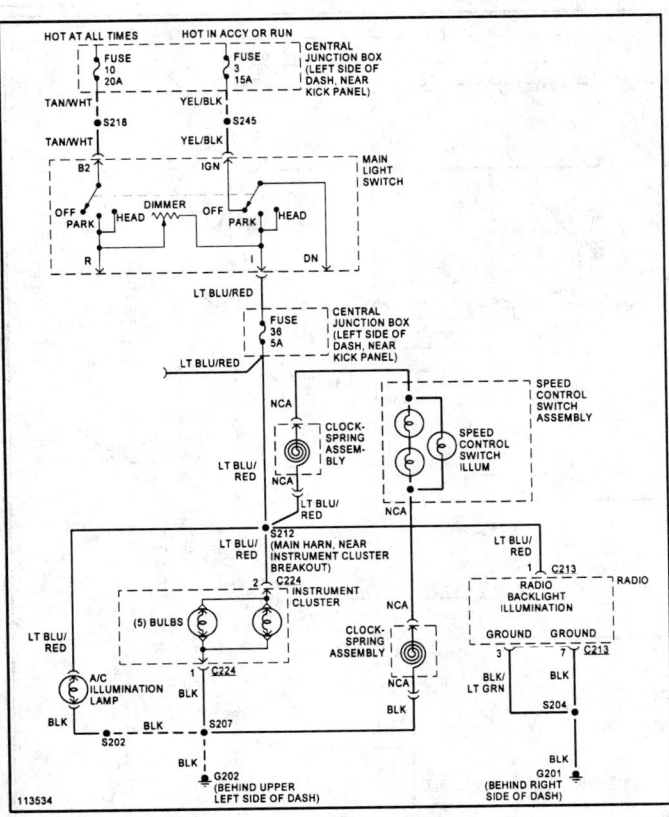

**Fig. 14: Illumination/Interior Lights Wiring Diagram
(Econoline – 4 Of 4)**

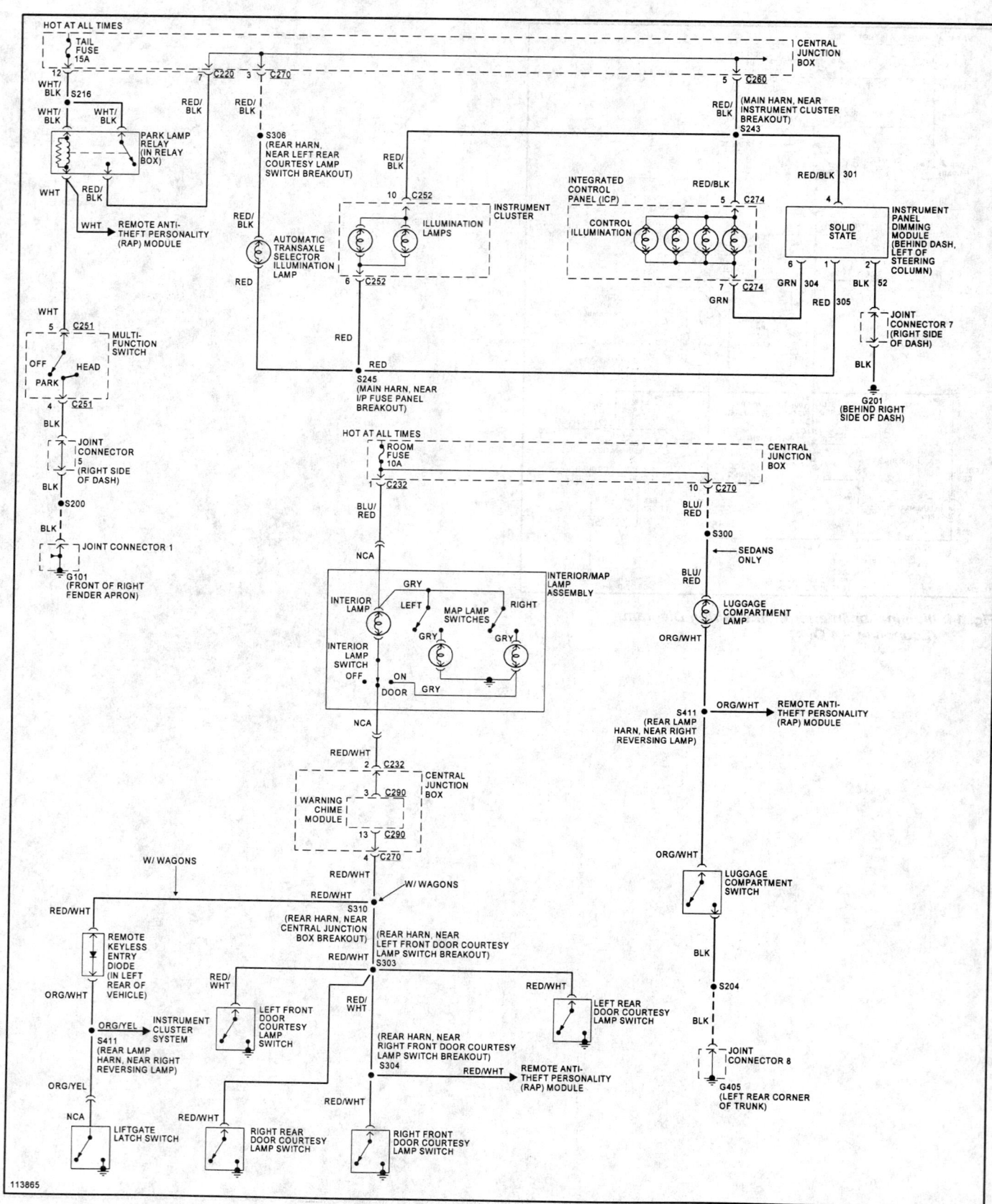

Fig. 15: Illumination/Interior Lights Wiring Diagram (Escort & Tracer)

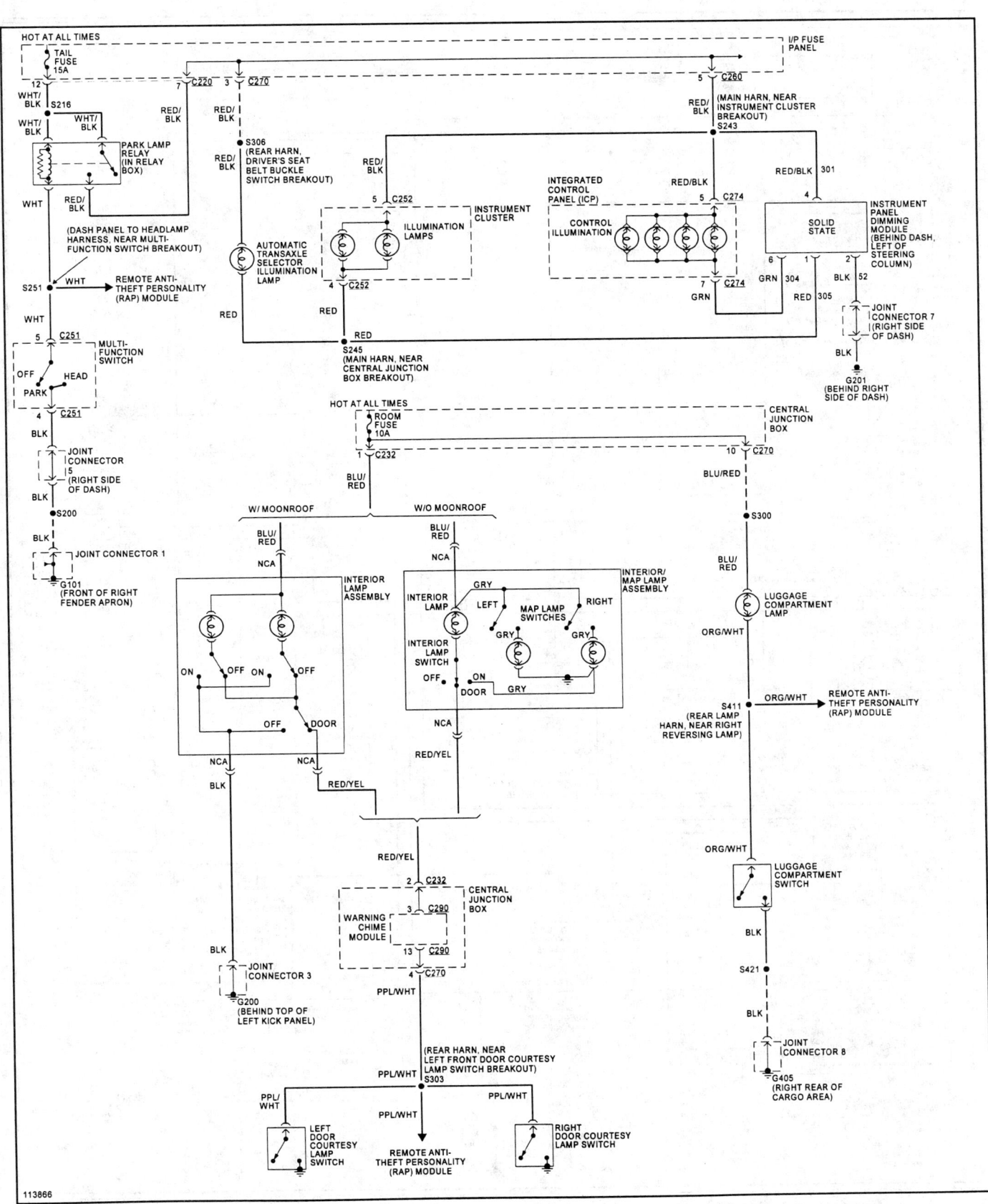

Fig. 16: Illumination/Interior Lights Wiring Diagram (Escort ZX2)

113866

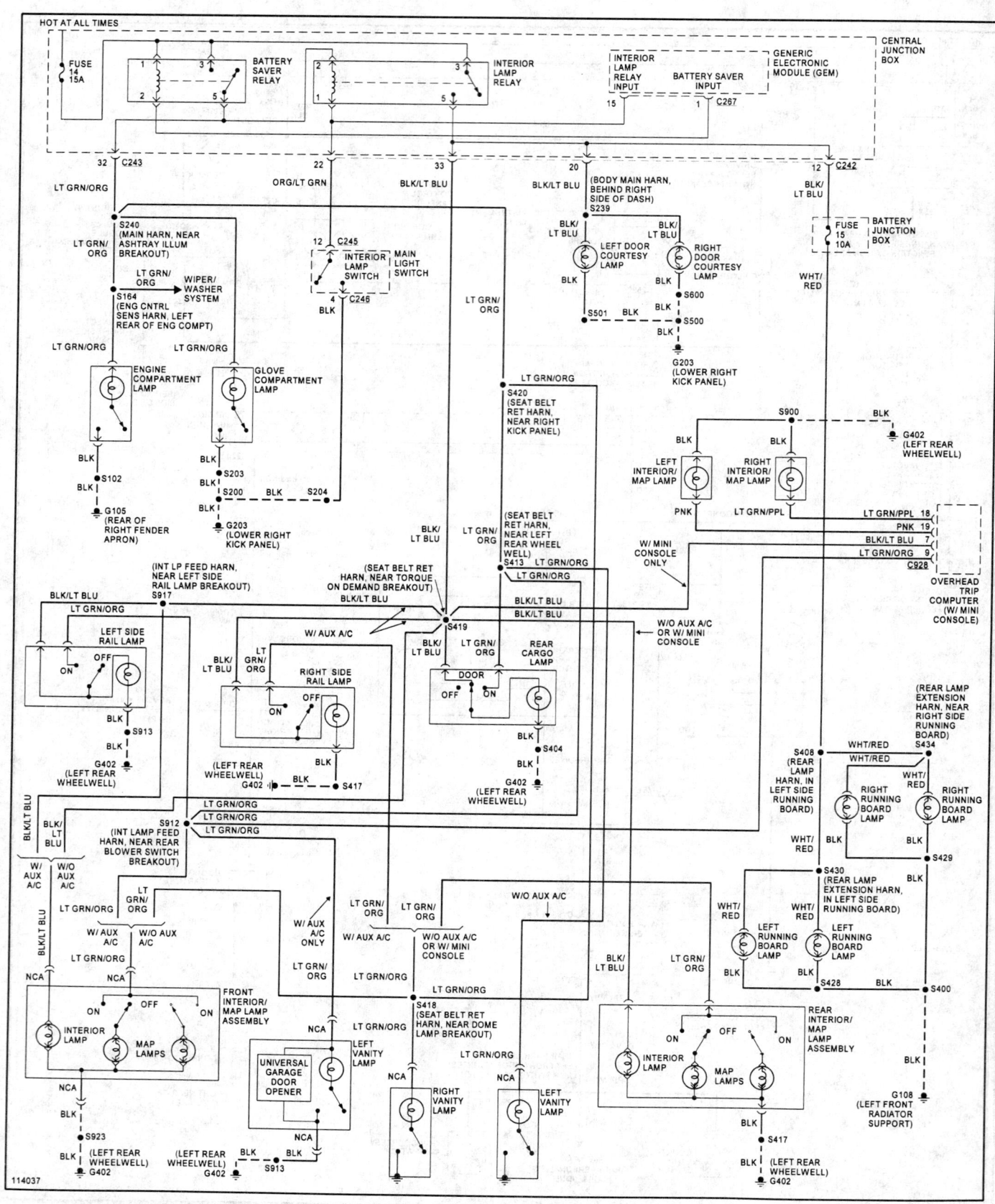

Fig. 17: Illumination/Interior Lights Wiring Diagram (Expedition & Navigator – 1 Of 2)

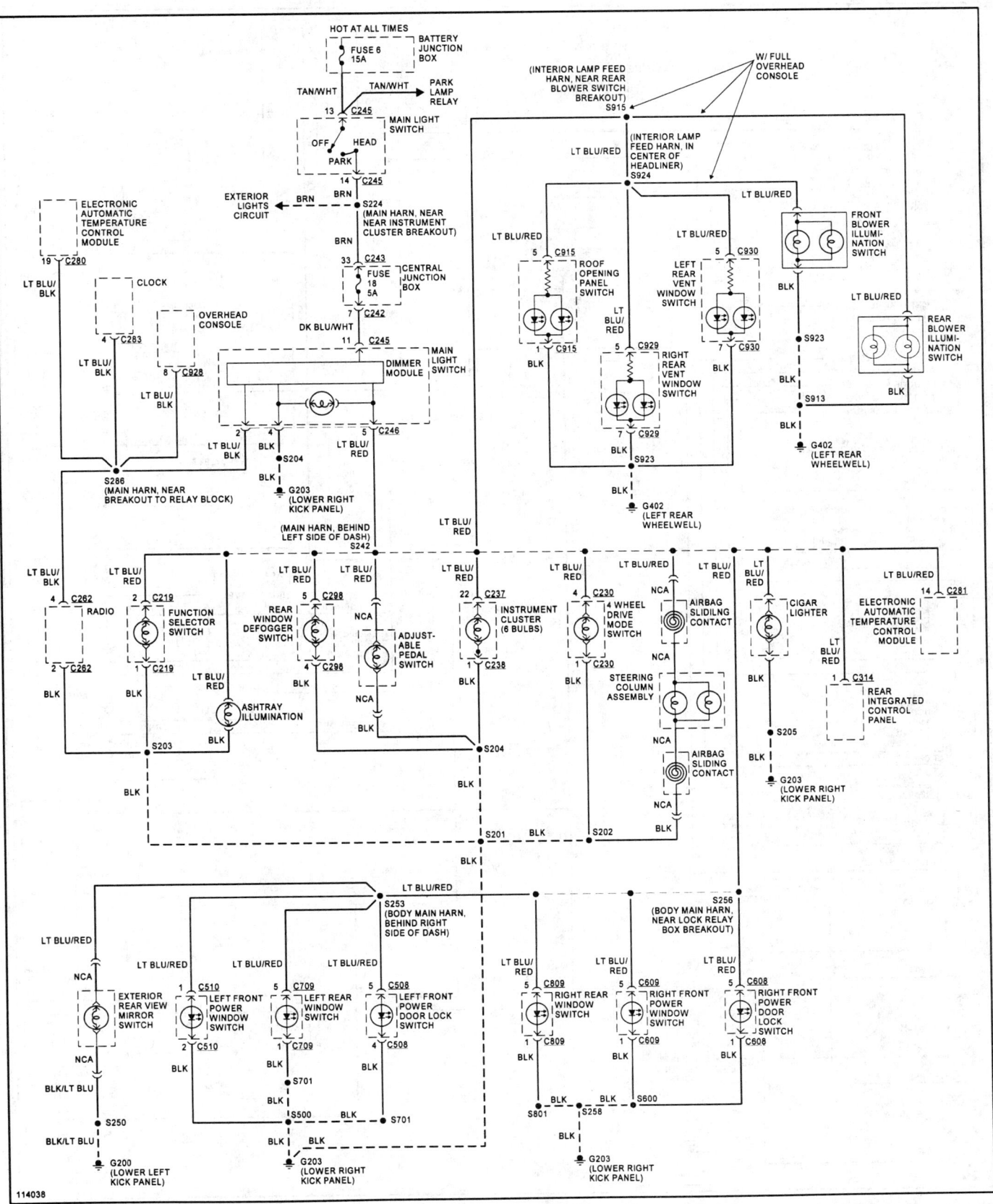

Fig. 18: Illumination/Interior Lights Wiring Diagram (Expedition & Navigator – 2 Of 2)

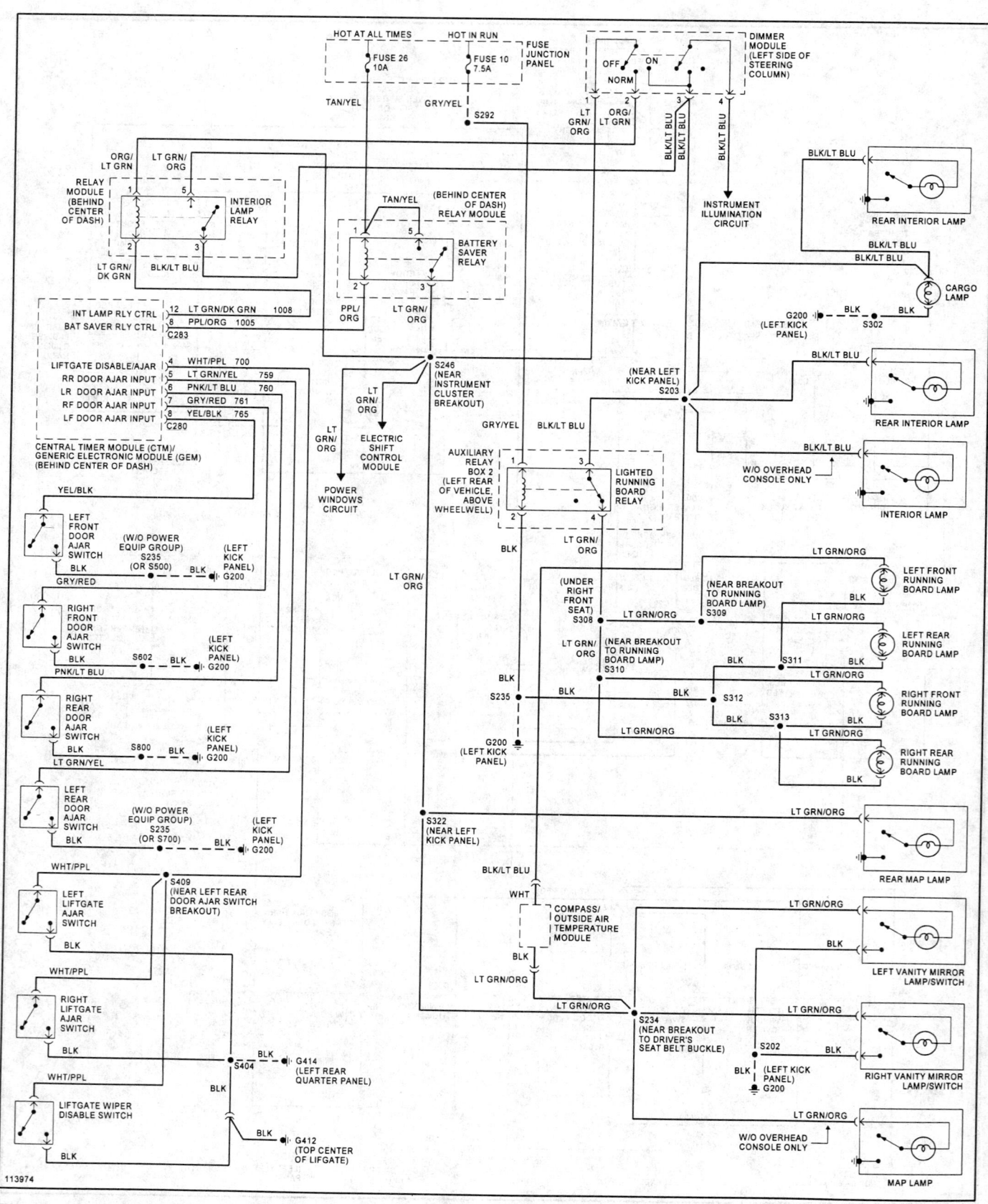

Fig. 19: Illumination/Interior Lights Wiring Diagram (Explorer & Mountaineer – 1 Of 3)

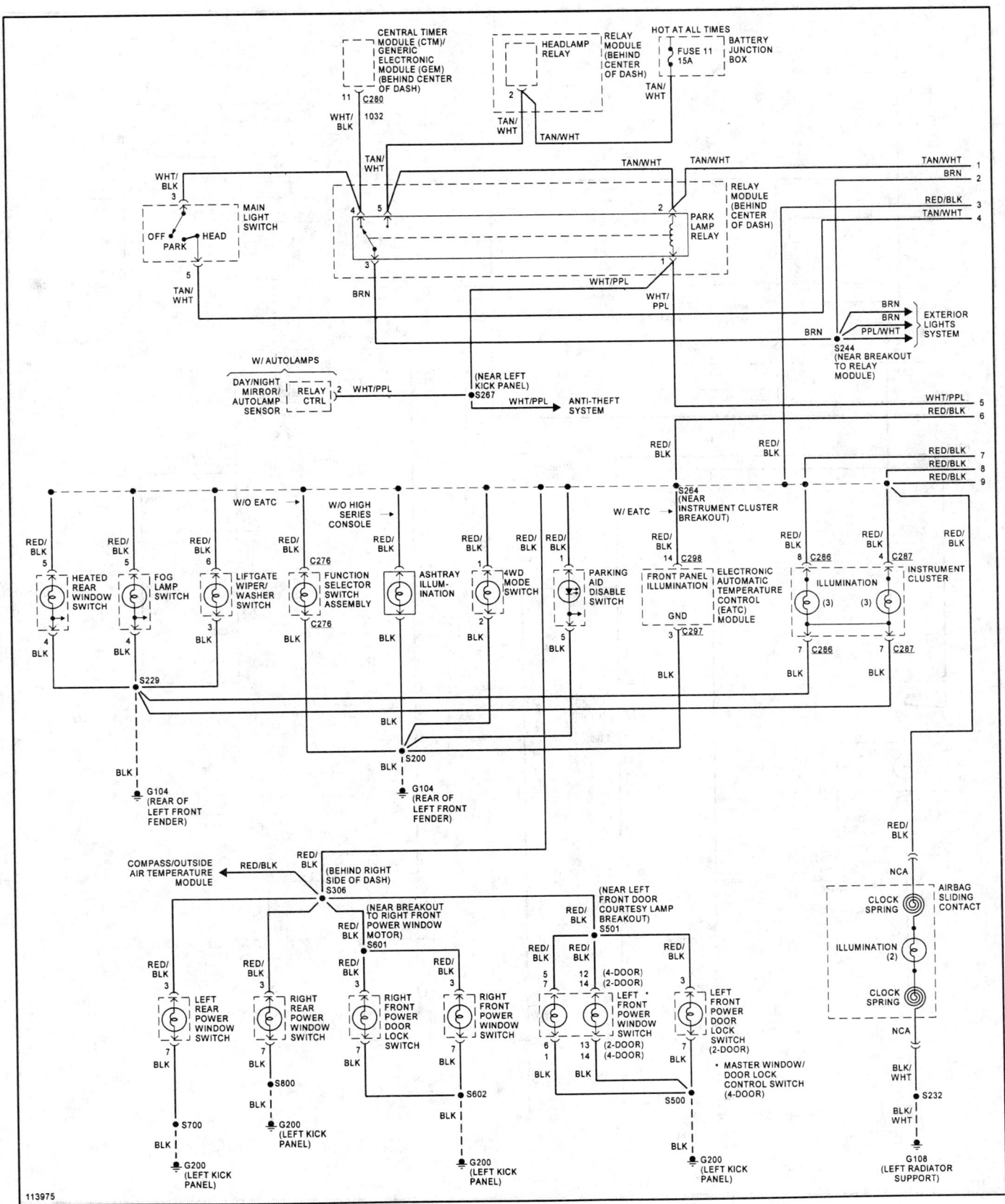

Fig. 20: Illumination/Interior Lights Wiring Diagram (Explorer & Mountaineer – 2 Of 3)

113975

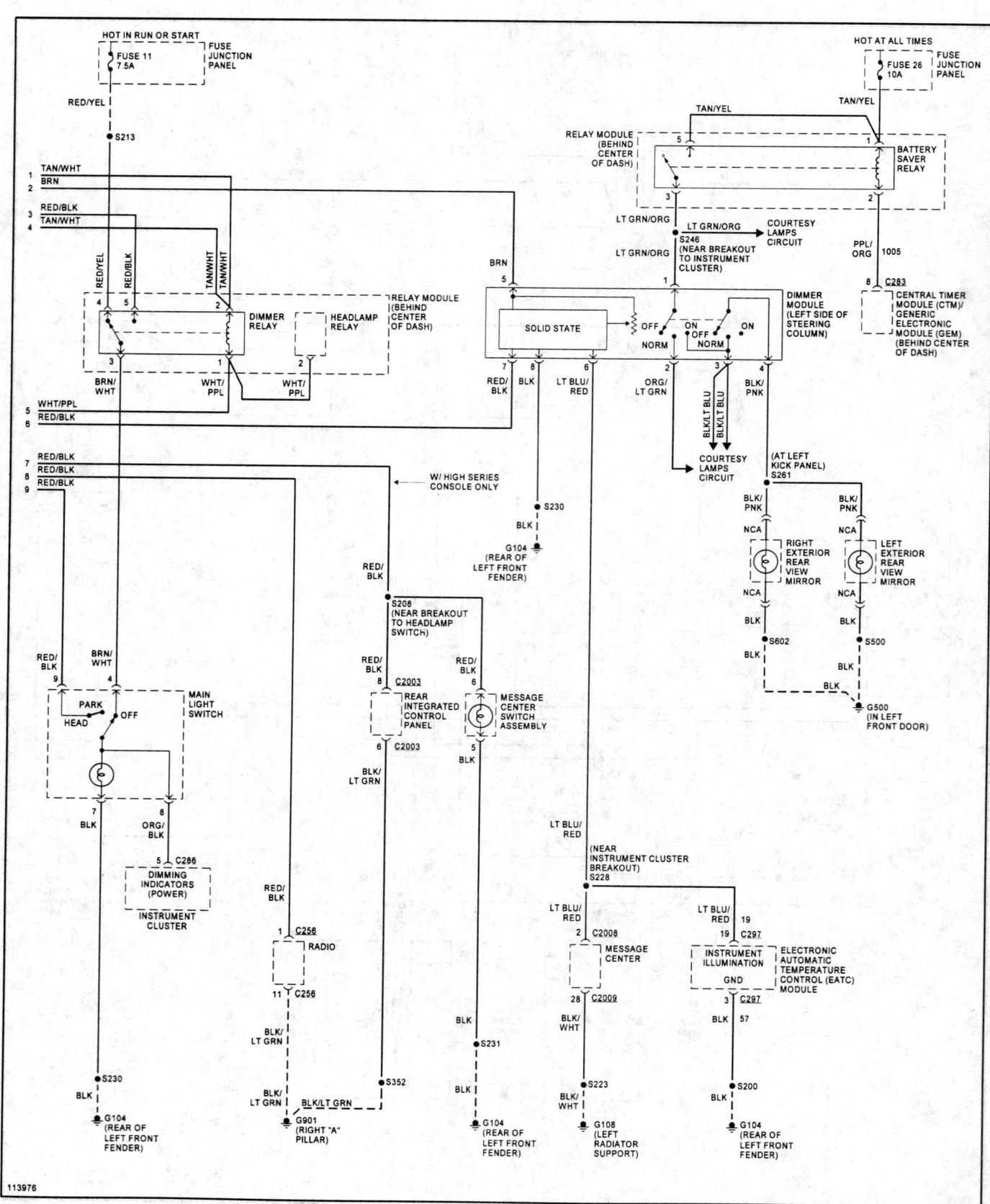

Fig. 21: Illumination/Interior Lights Wiring Diagram (Explorer & Mountaineer – 3 Of 3)

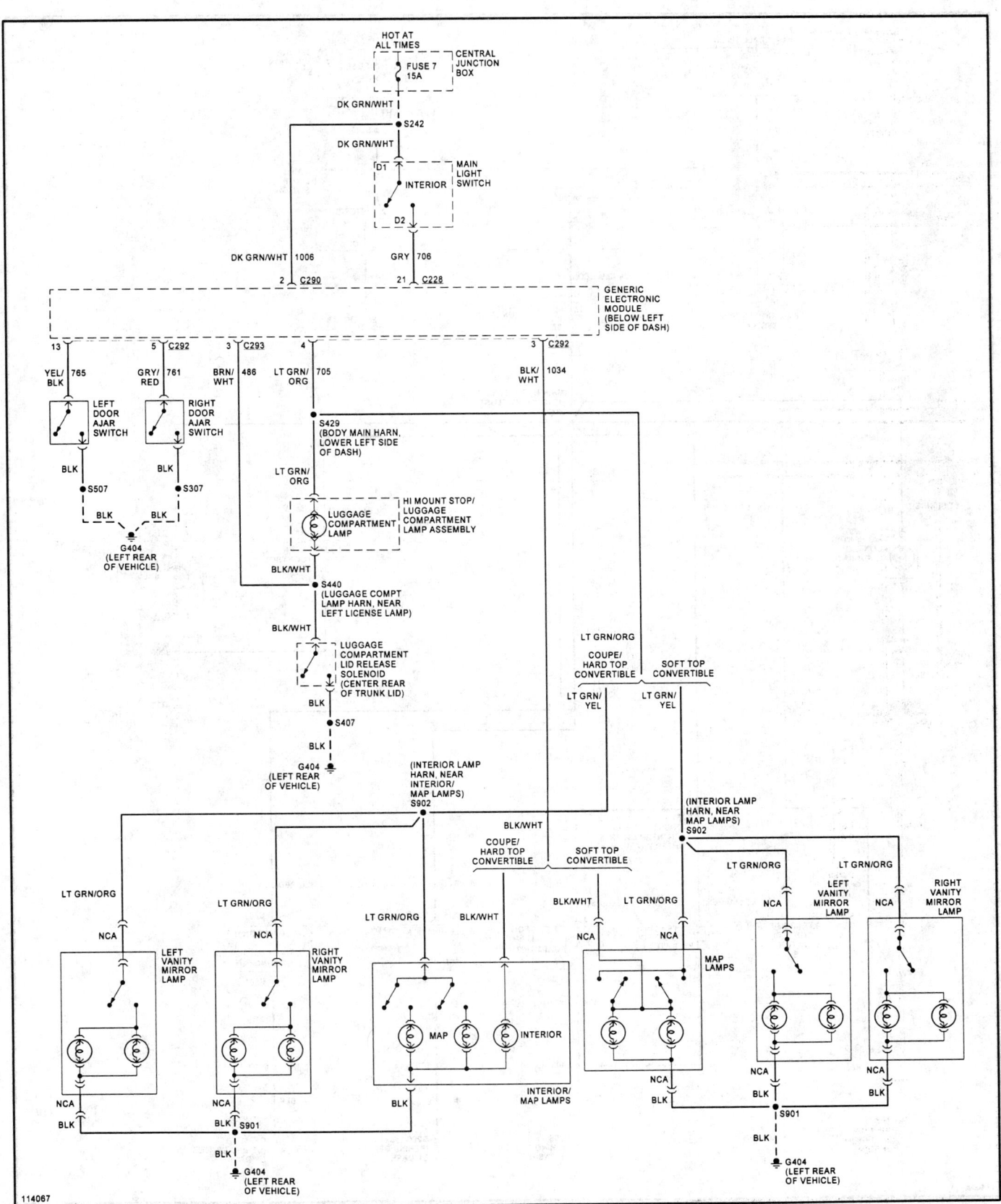

Fig. 22: Illumination/Interior Lights Wiring Diagram (Mustang – 1 Of 2)

114067

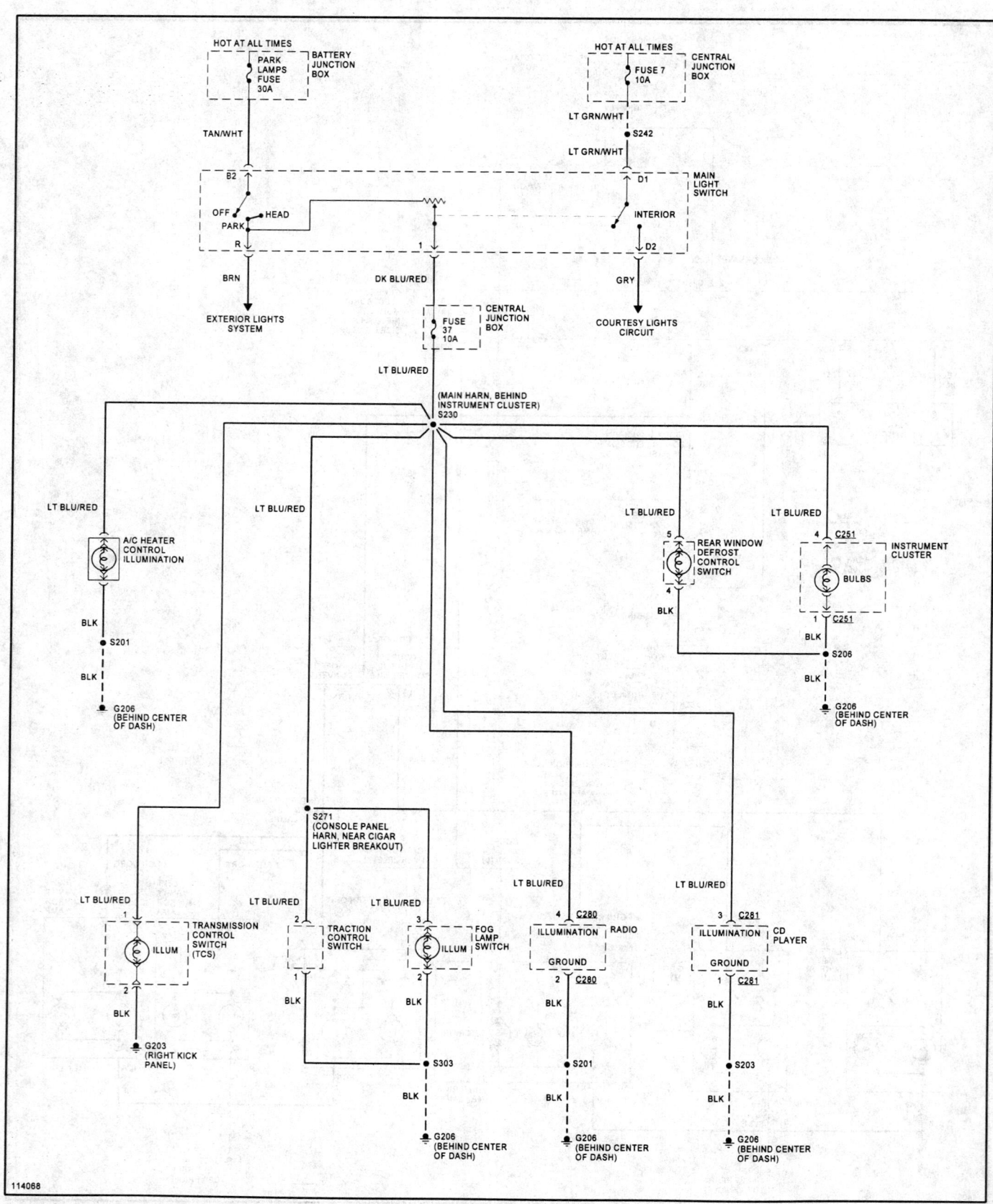

Fig. 23: Illumination/Interior Lights Wiring Diagram (Mustang – 2 Of 2)

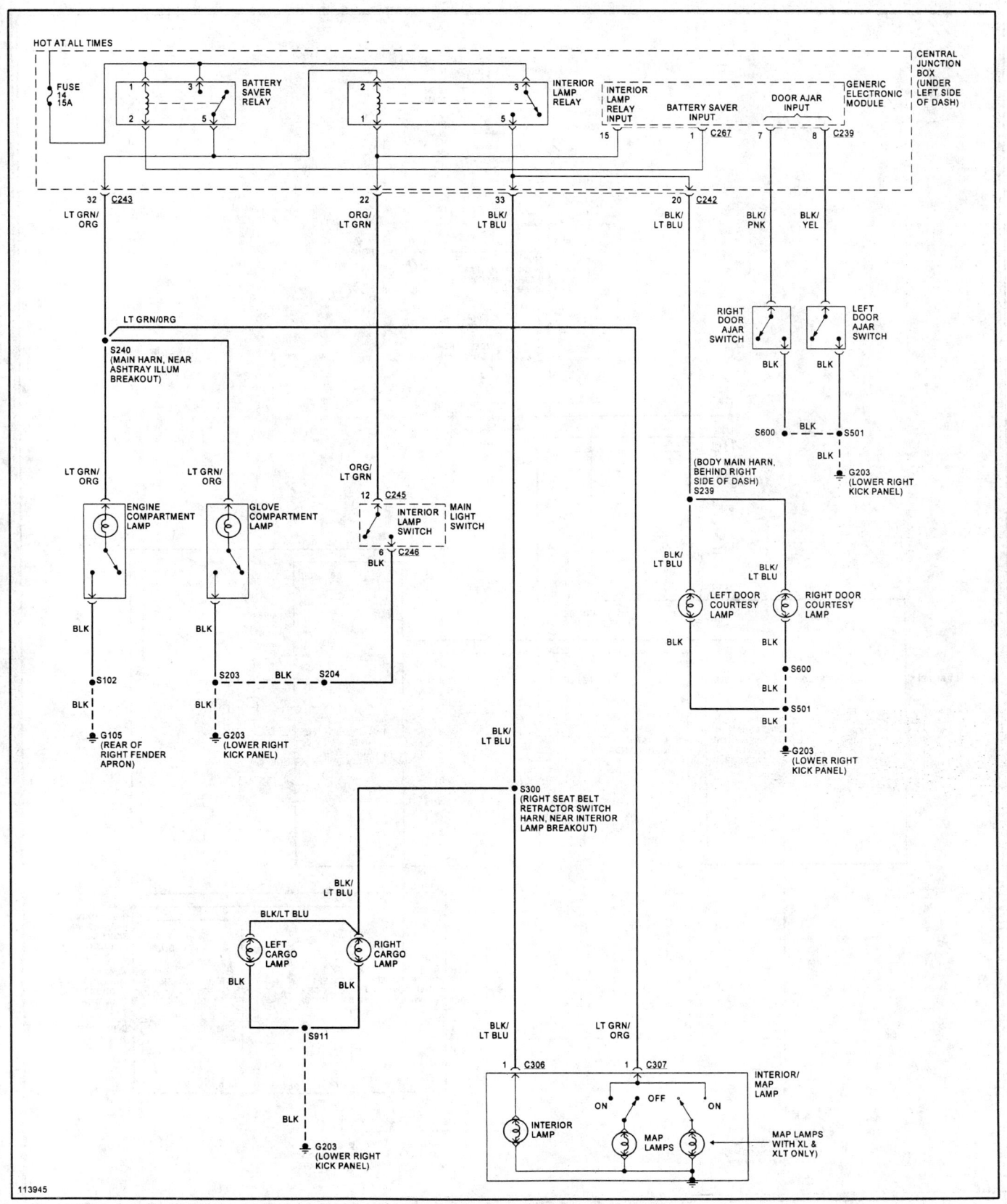

Fig. 24: Illumination/Interior Lights Wiring Diagram (F150 & F250 Light-Duty Pickup – 1 Of 2)

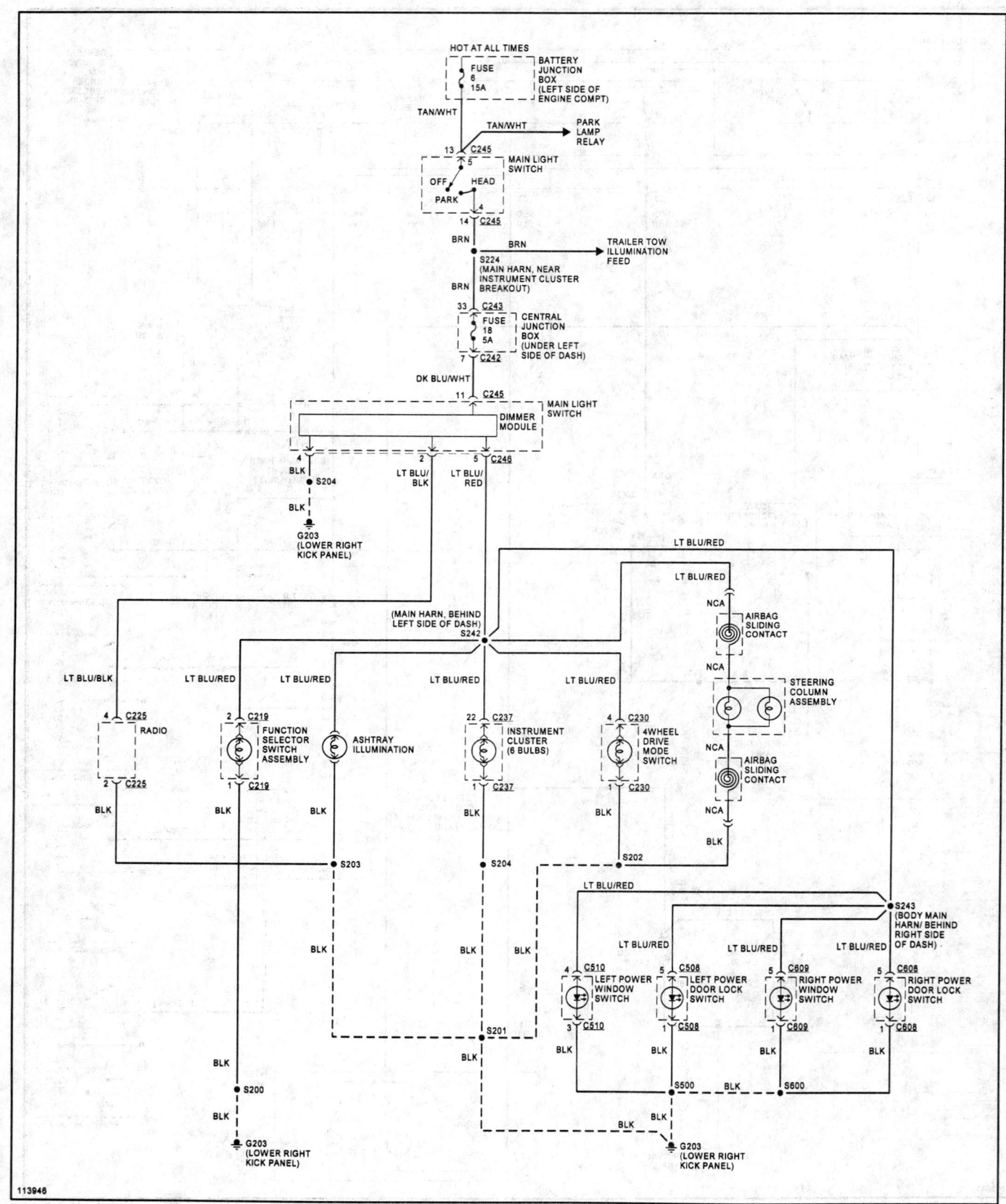

Fig. 25: Illumination/Interior Lights Wiring Diagram (F150 & F250 Light-Duty Pickup – 2 Of 2)

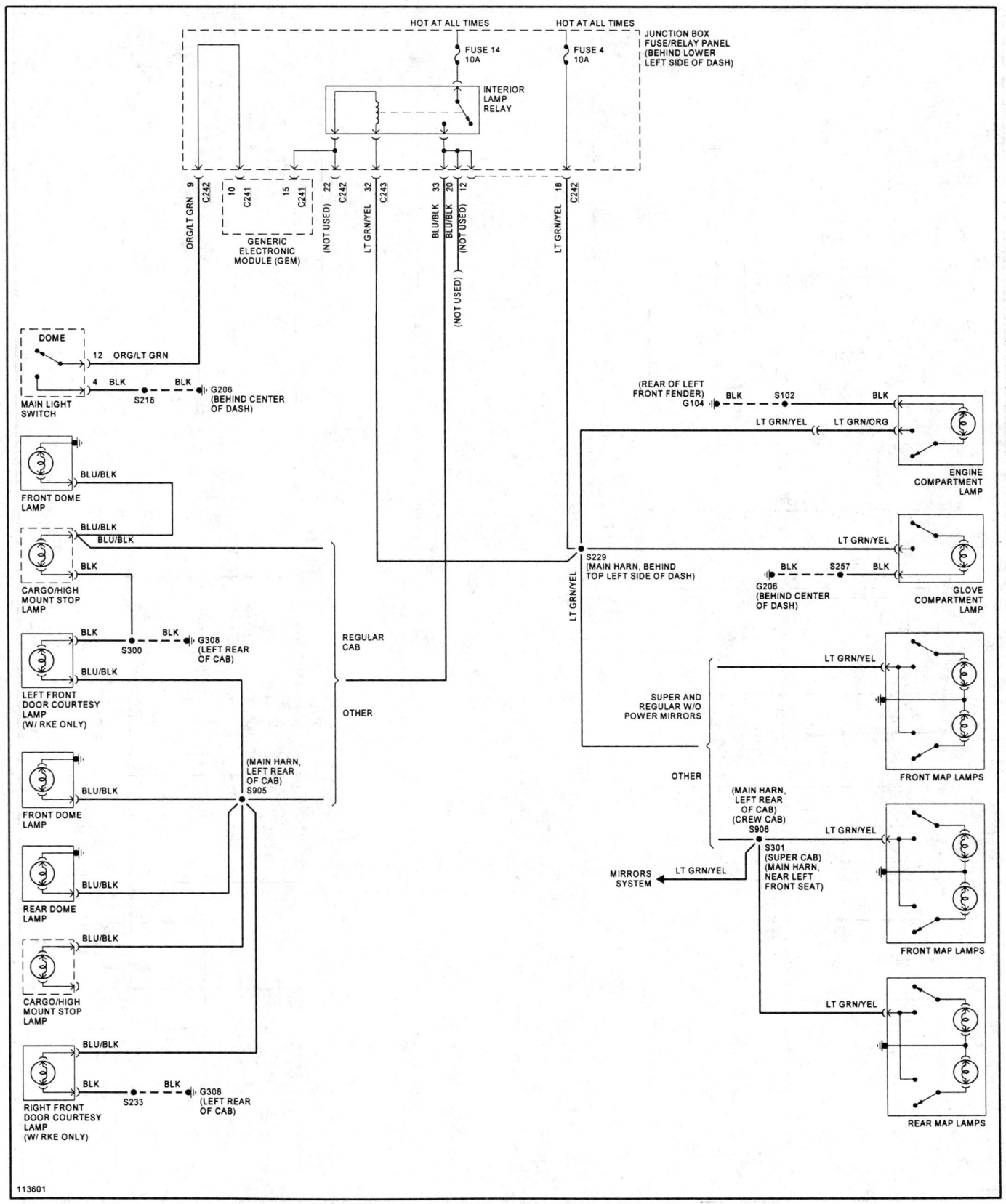

Fig. 26: Illumination/Interior Lights Wiring Diagram (F250 & F350 Super-Duty Pickup – 1 Of 2)

113601

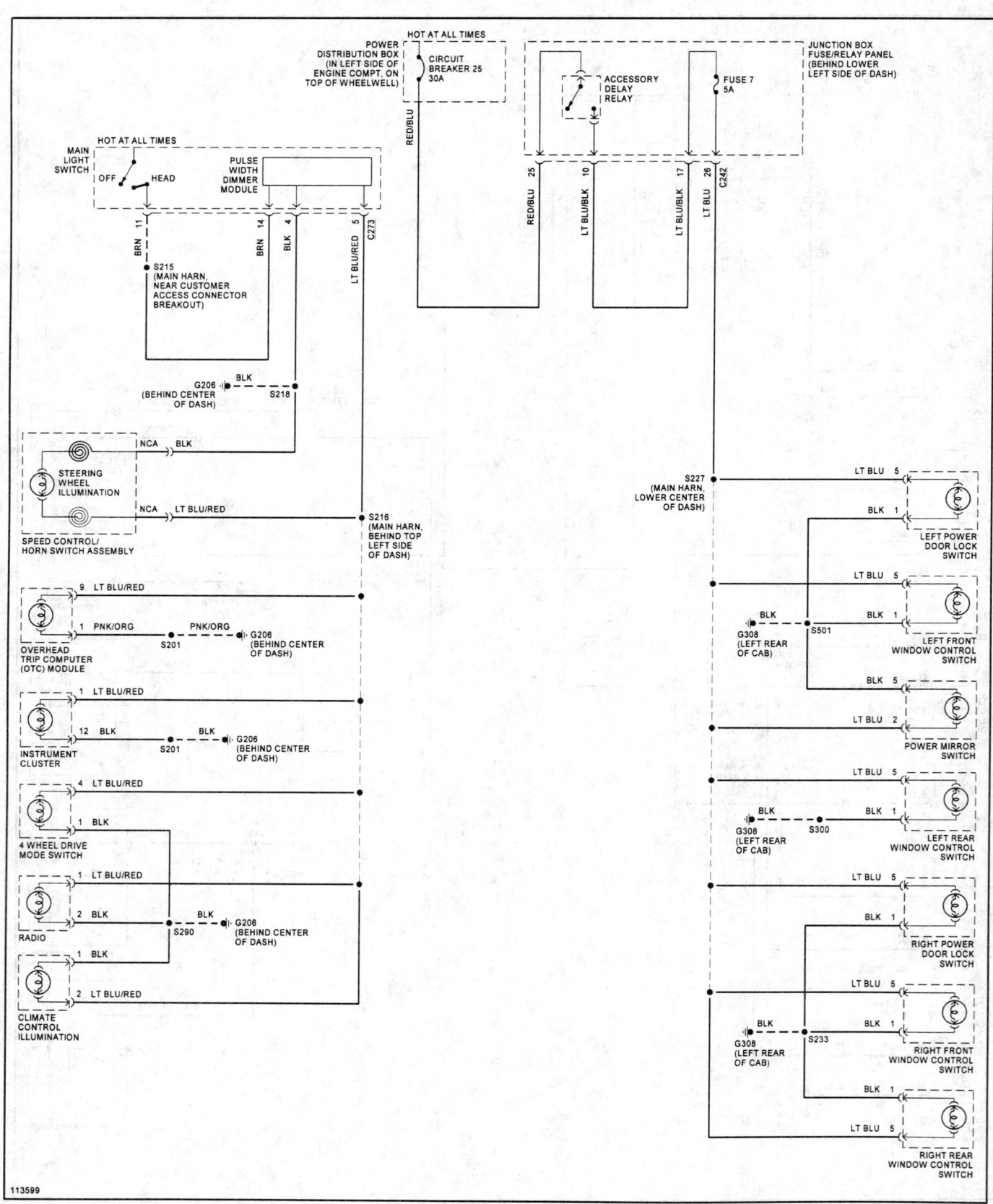

Fig. 27: Illumination/Interior Lights Wiring Diagram (F250 & F350 Super-Duty Pickup – 2 Of 2)

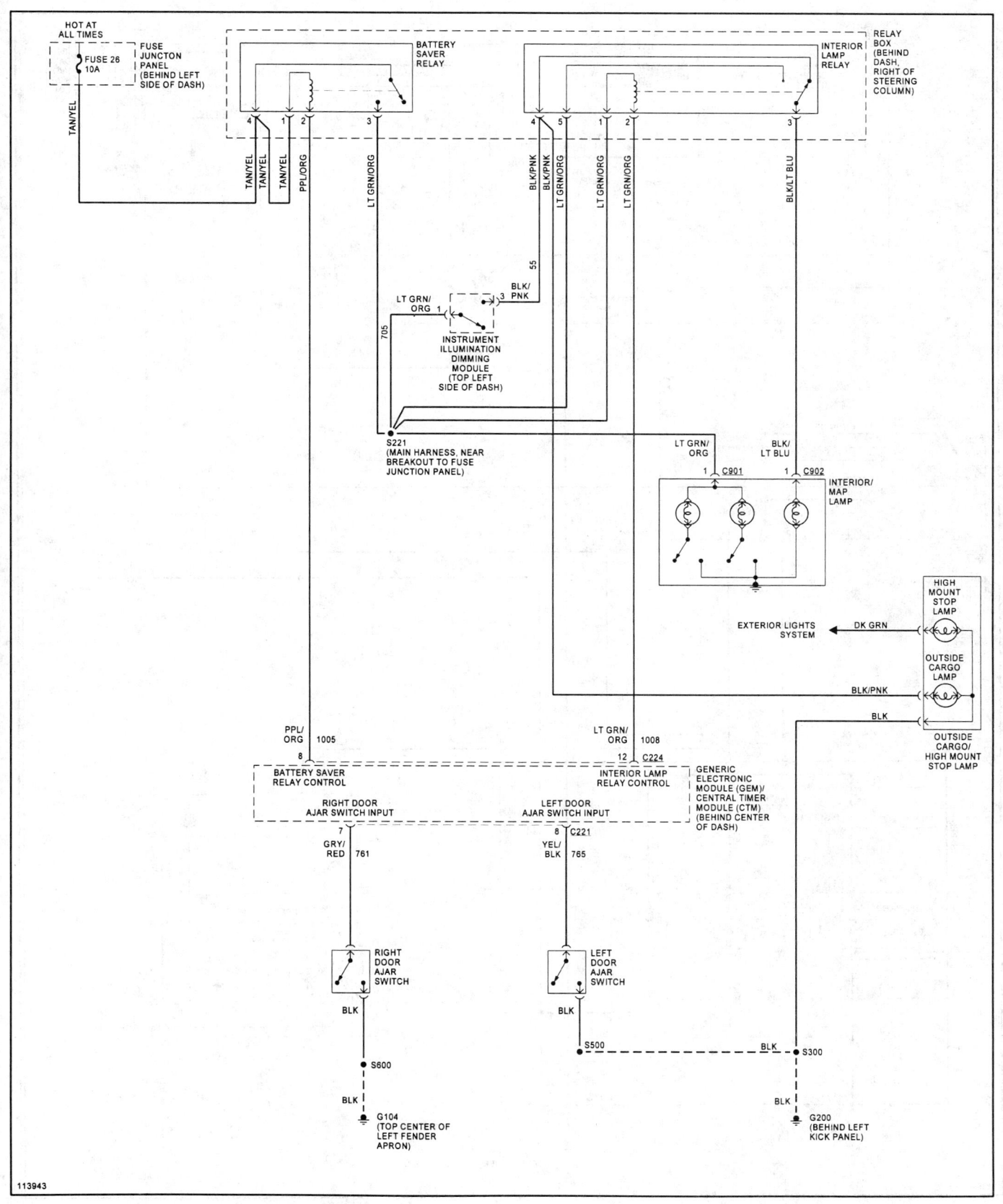

Fig. 28: Illumination/Interior Lights Wiring Diagram (Ranger – 1 Of 2)

113943

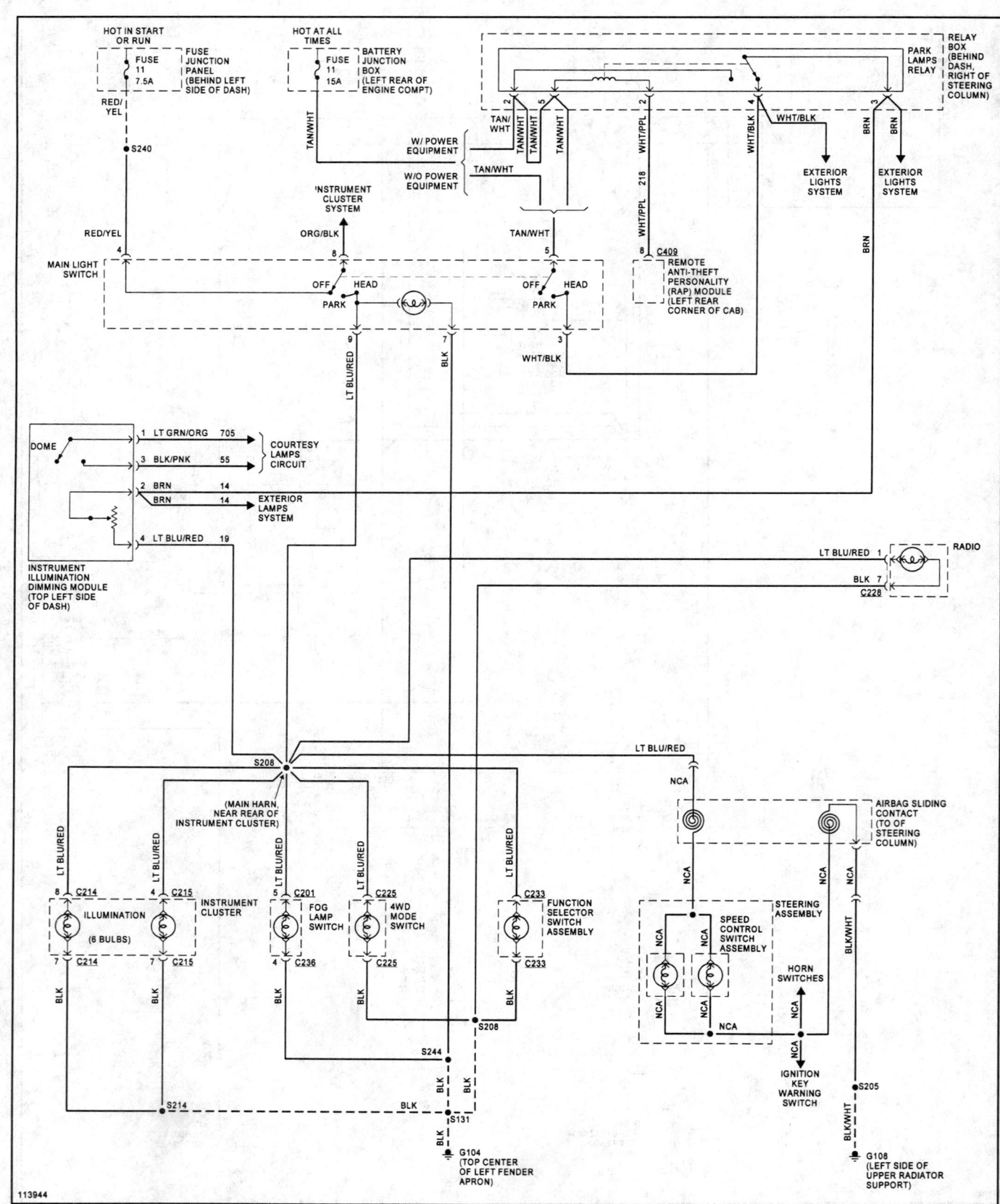

Fig. 29: Illumination/Interior Lights Wiring Diagram (Ranger – 2 Of 2)

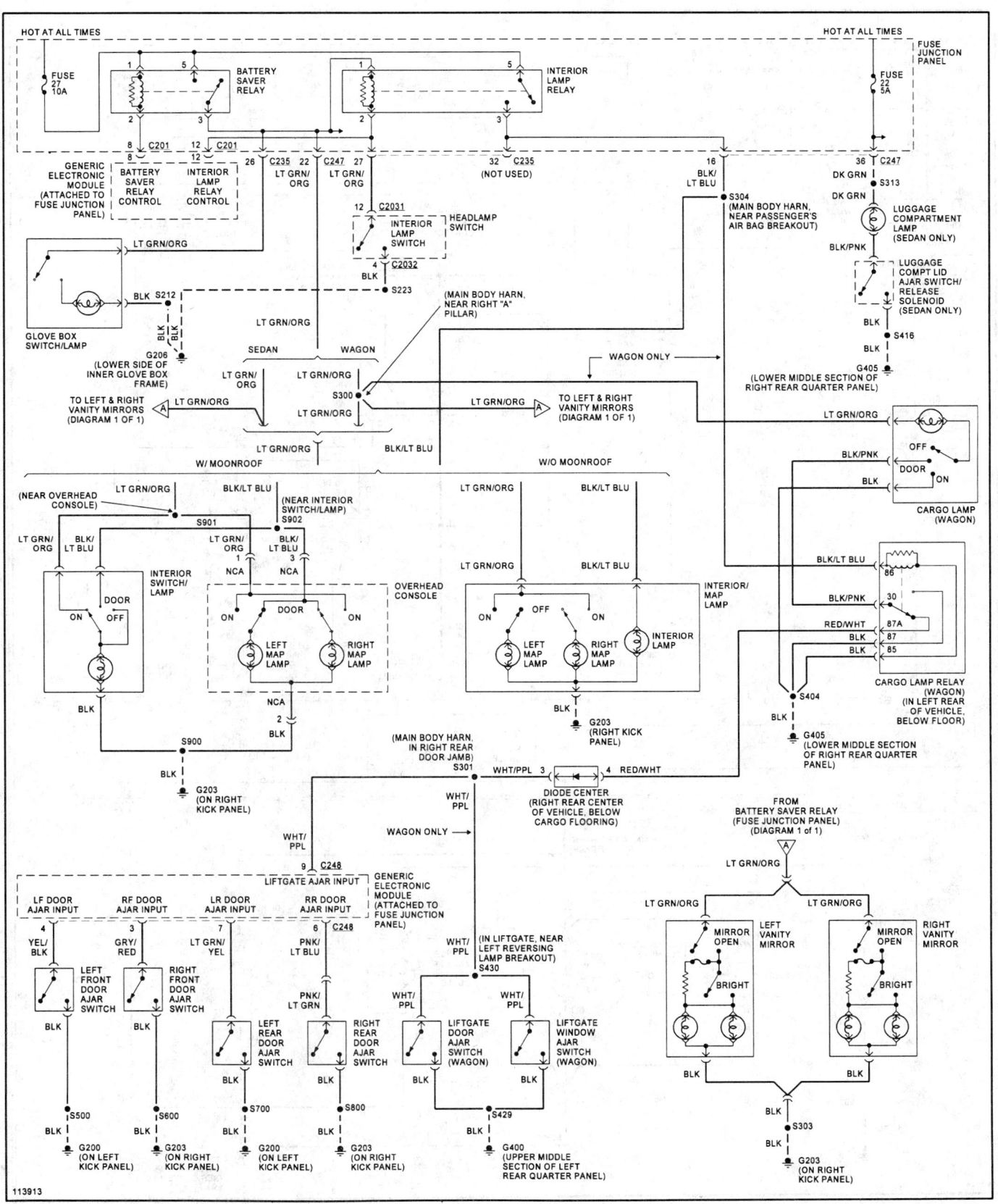

Fig. 30: Illumination/Interior Lights Wiring Diagram (Sable & Taurus – 1 Of 2)

113913

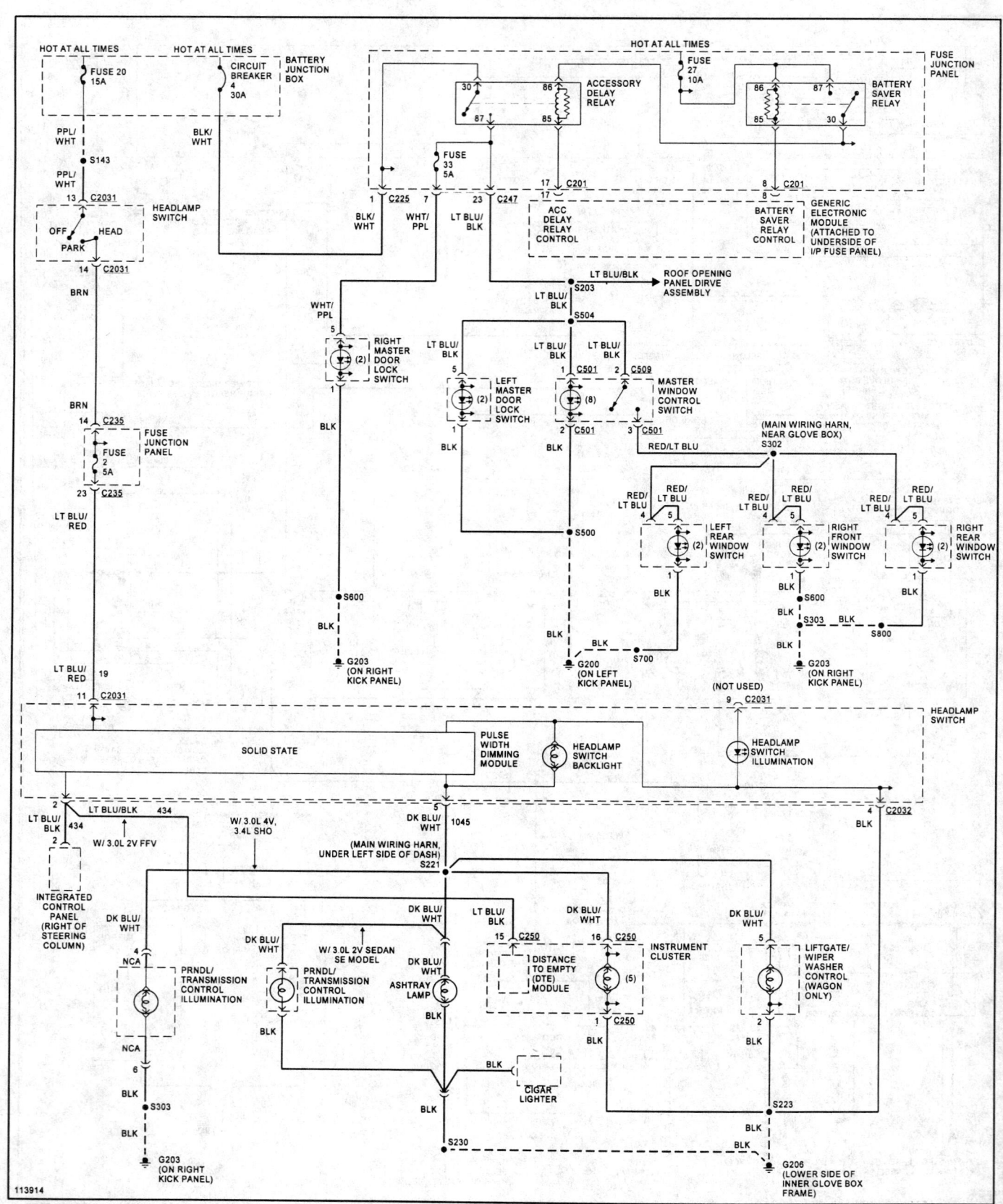

Fig. 31: Illumination/Interior Lights Wiring Diagram (Sable & Taurus – 2 Of 2)

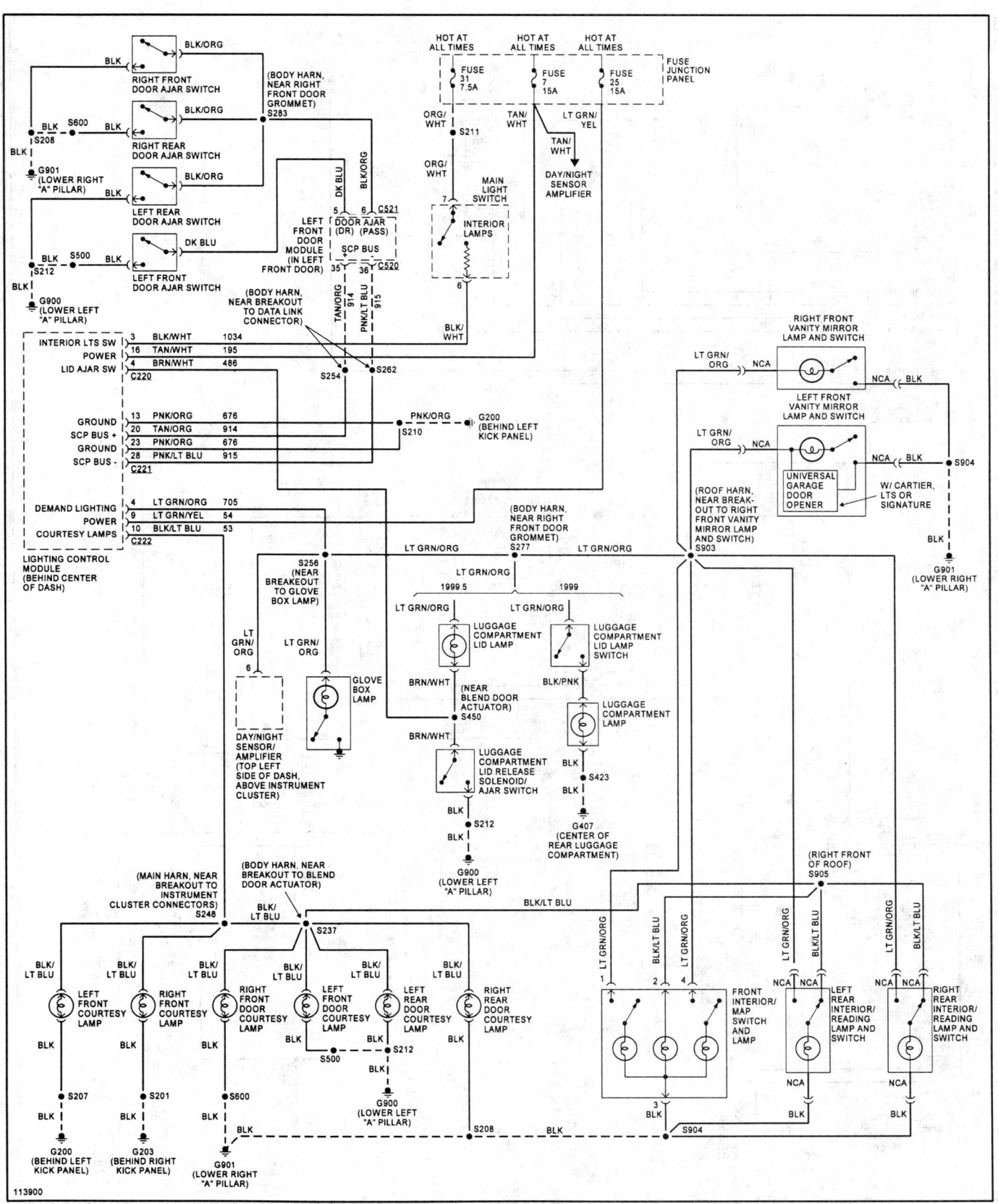

Fig. 32: Illumination/Interior Lights Wiring Diagram (Town Car – 1 Of 2)

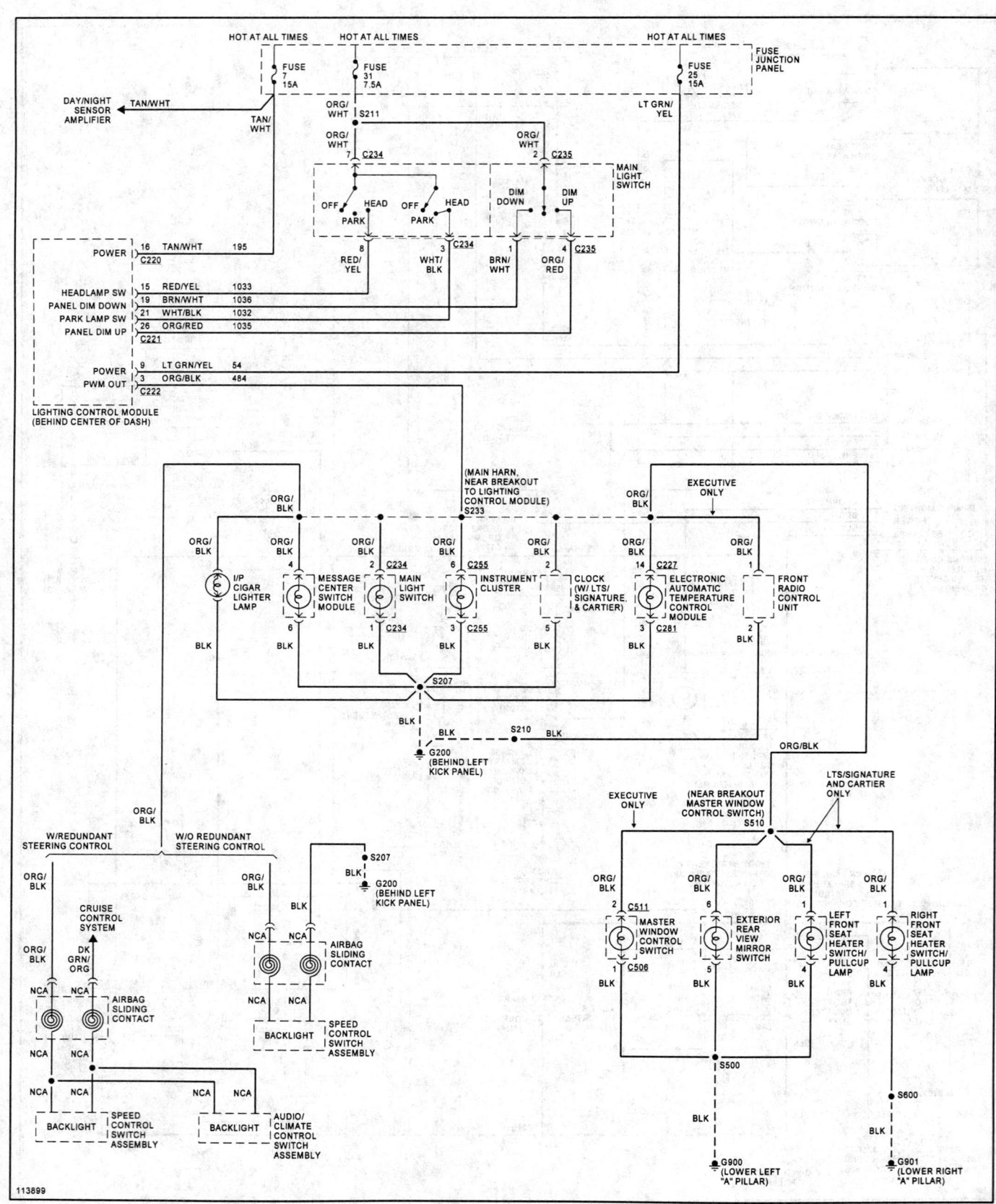

Fig. 33: Illumination/Interior Lights Wiring Diagram (Town Car – 2 Of 2)

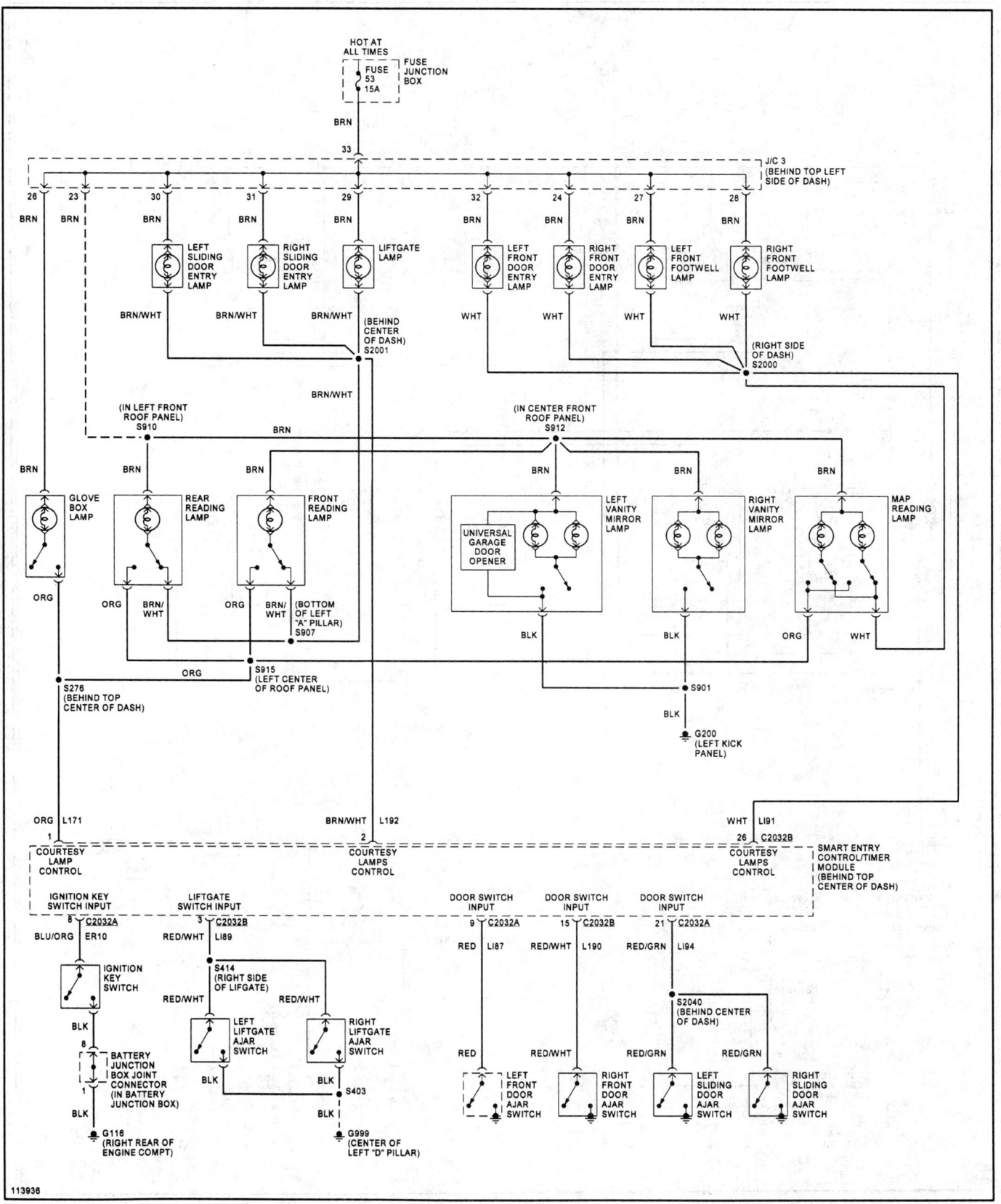

Fig. 34: Illumination/Interior Lights Wiring Diagram (Villager – With Reading Lights – 1 Of 3)

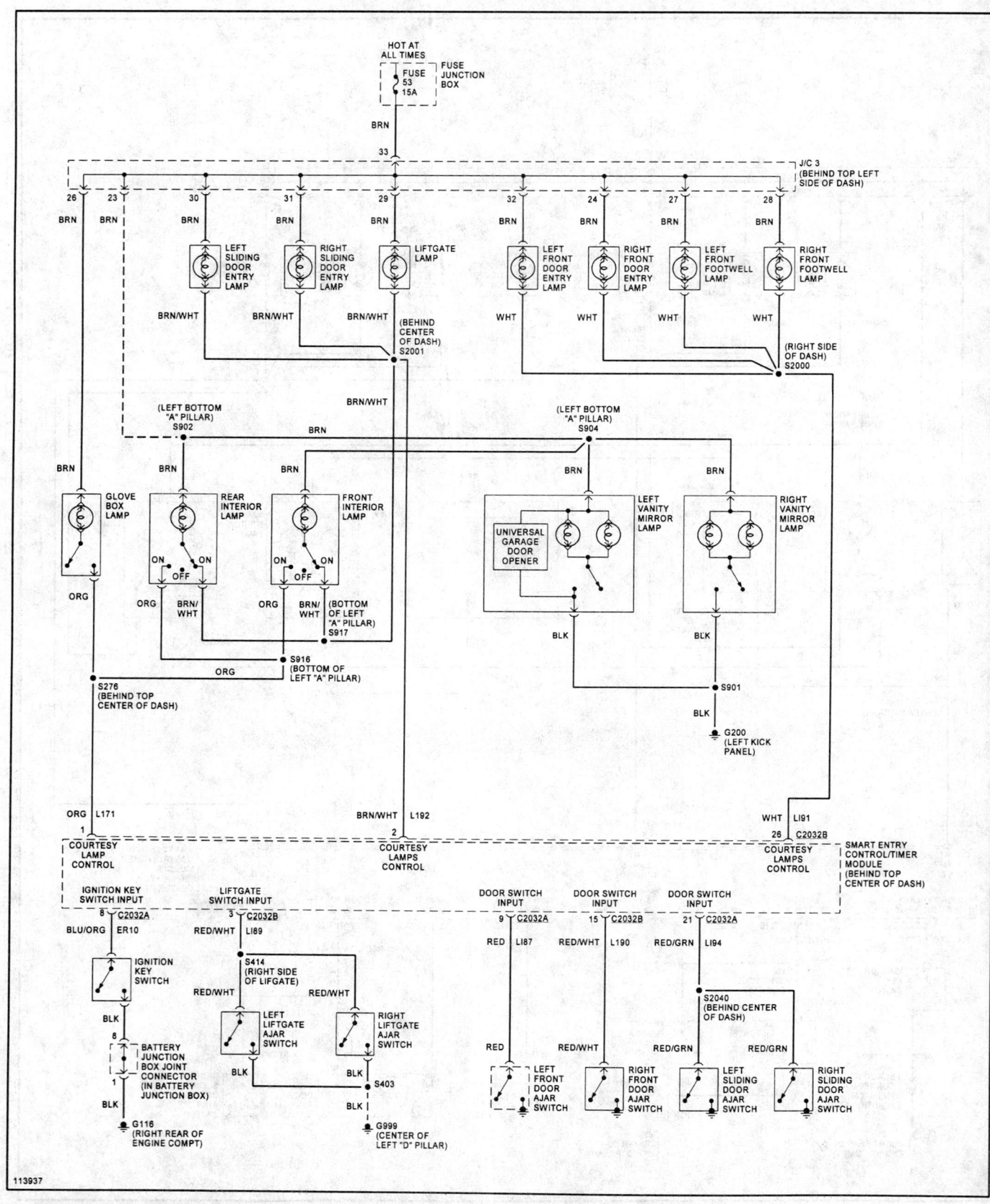

Fig. 35: Illumination/Interior Lights Wiring Diagram (Villager – Without Reading Lights – 2 Of 3)

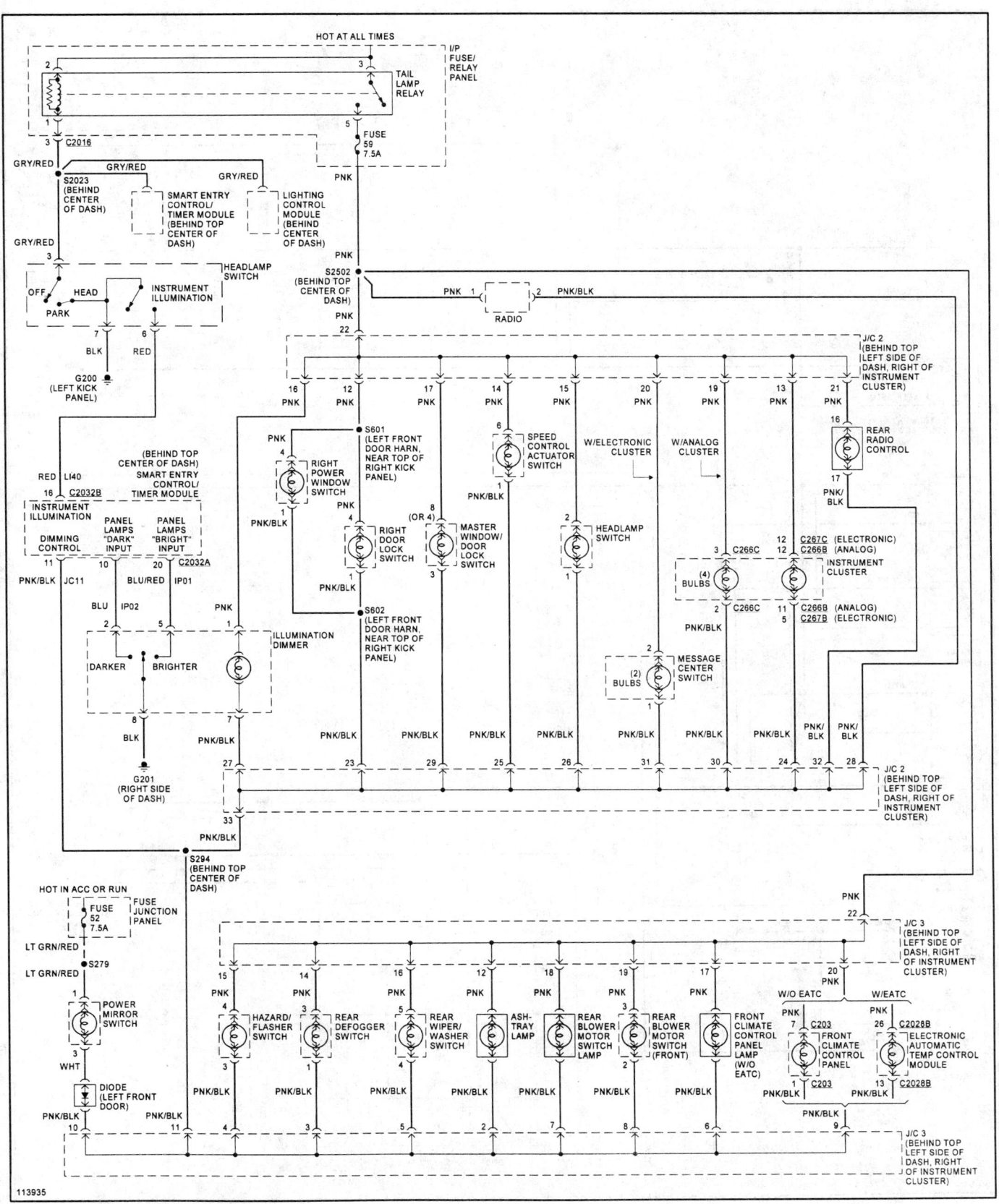

Fig. 36: Illumination/Interior Lights Wiring Diagram (Villager – 3 Of 3)

113935

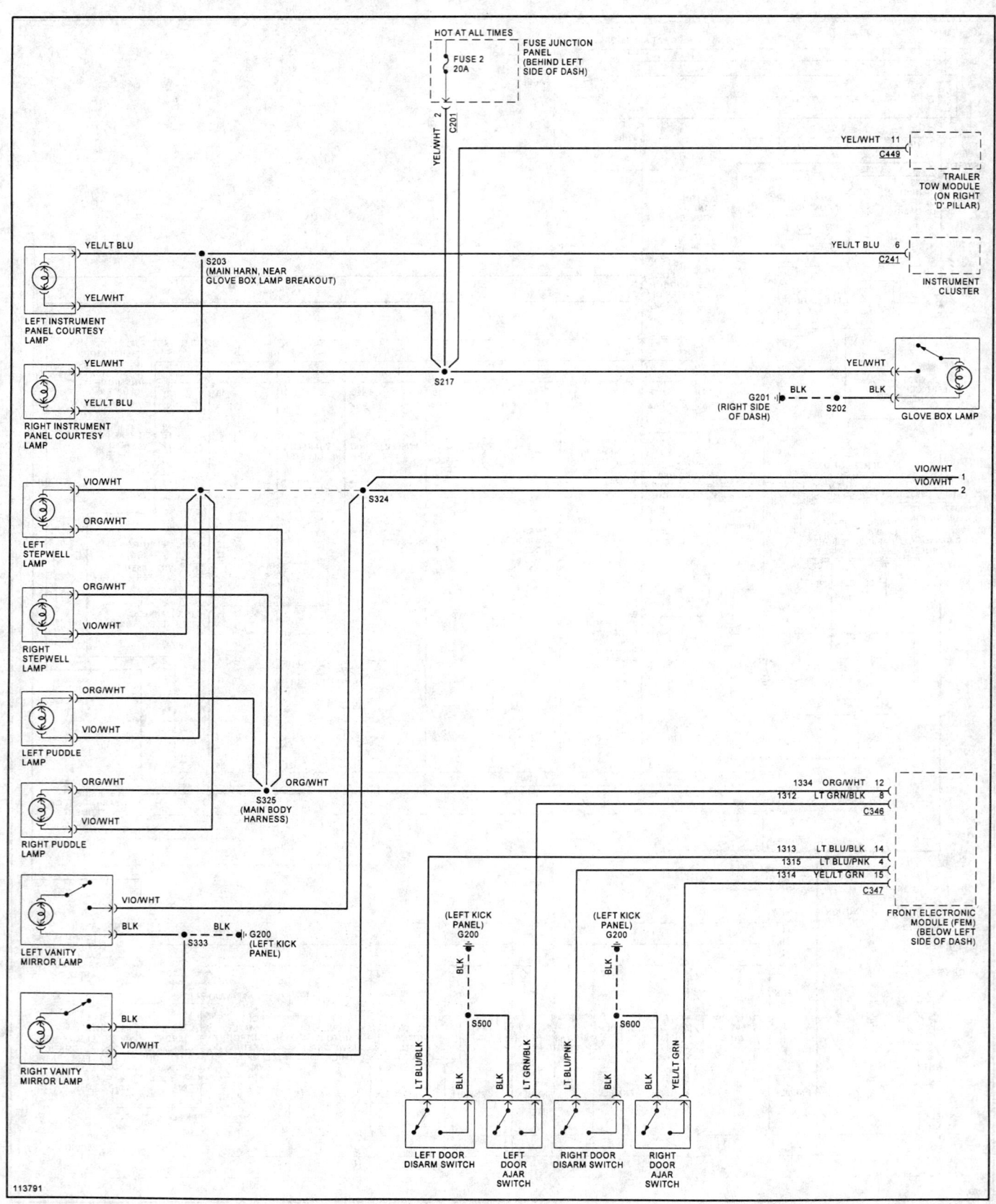

Fig. 37: Illumination/Interior Lights Connector Wiring Diagram (Windstar – 1 Of 3)

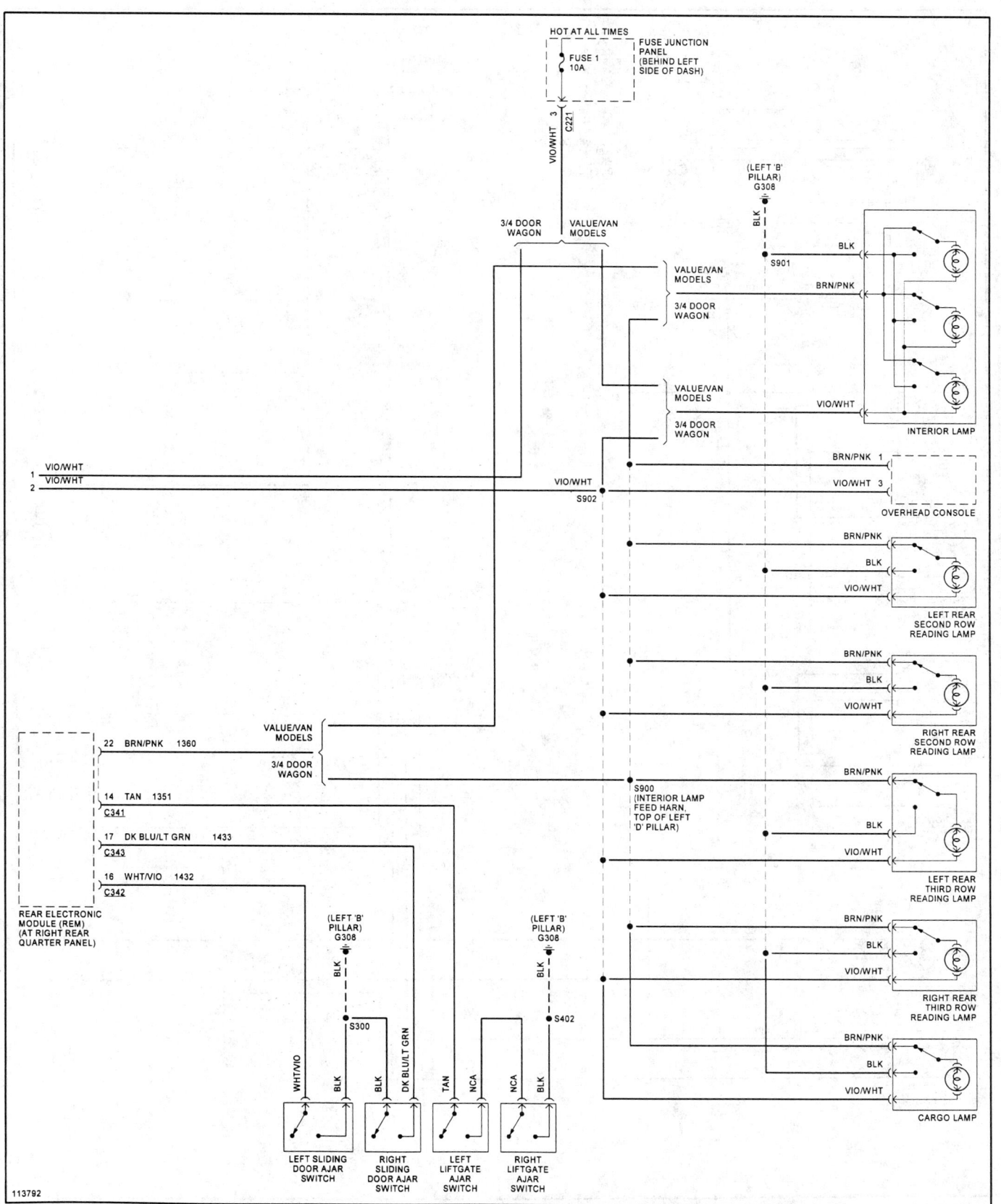

Fig. 38: Illumination/Interior Lights Connector Wiring Diagram (Windstar – 2 Of 3)

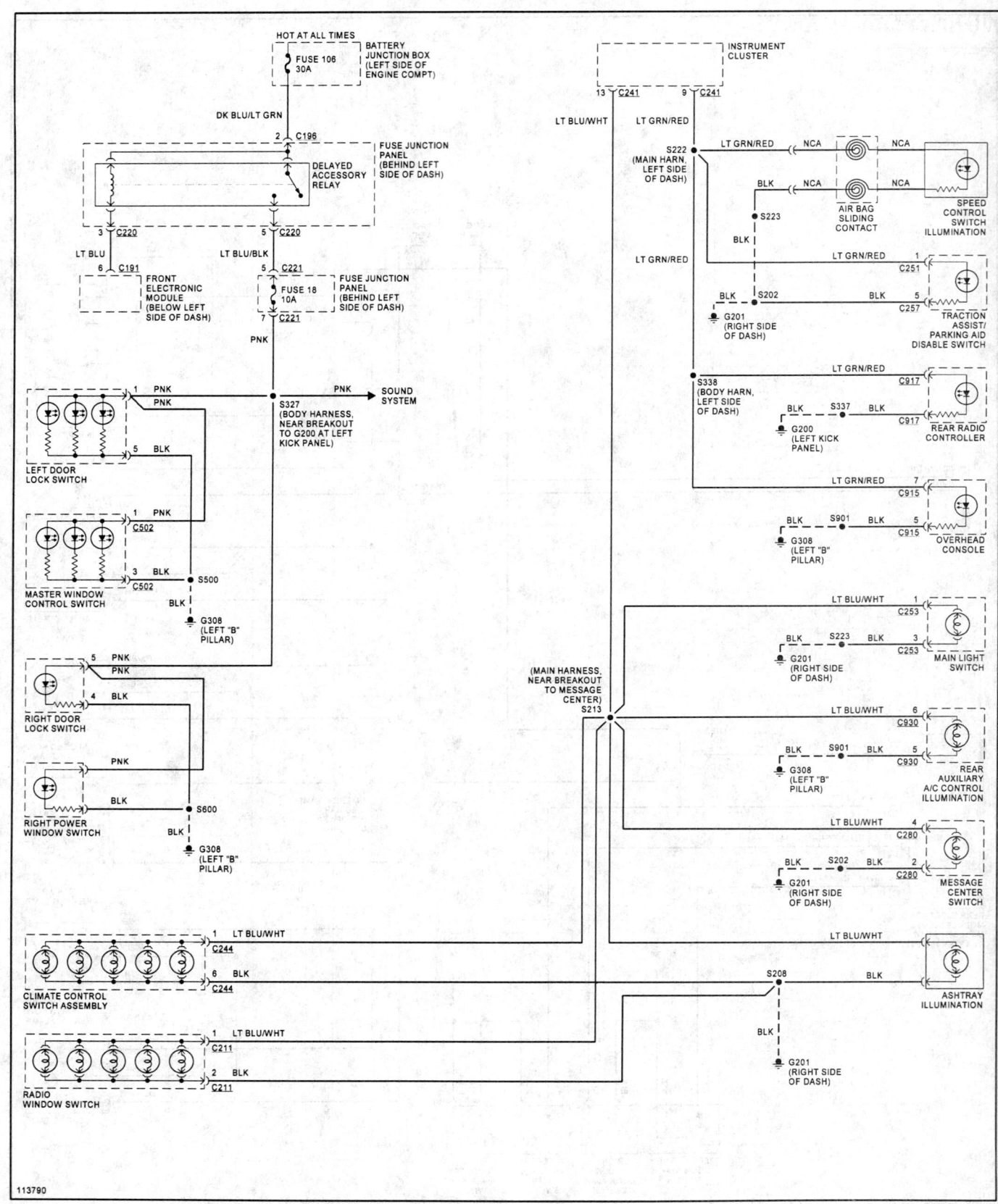

Fig. 39: Illumination/Interior Lights Connector Wiring Diagram (Windstar – 3 Of 3)

WIRING DIAGRAMS

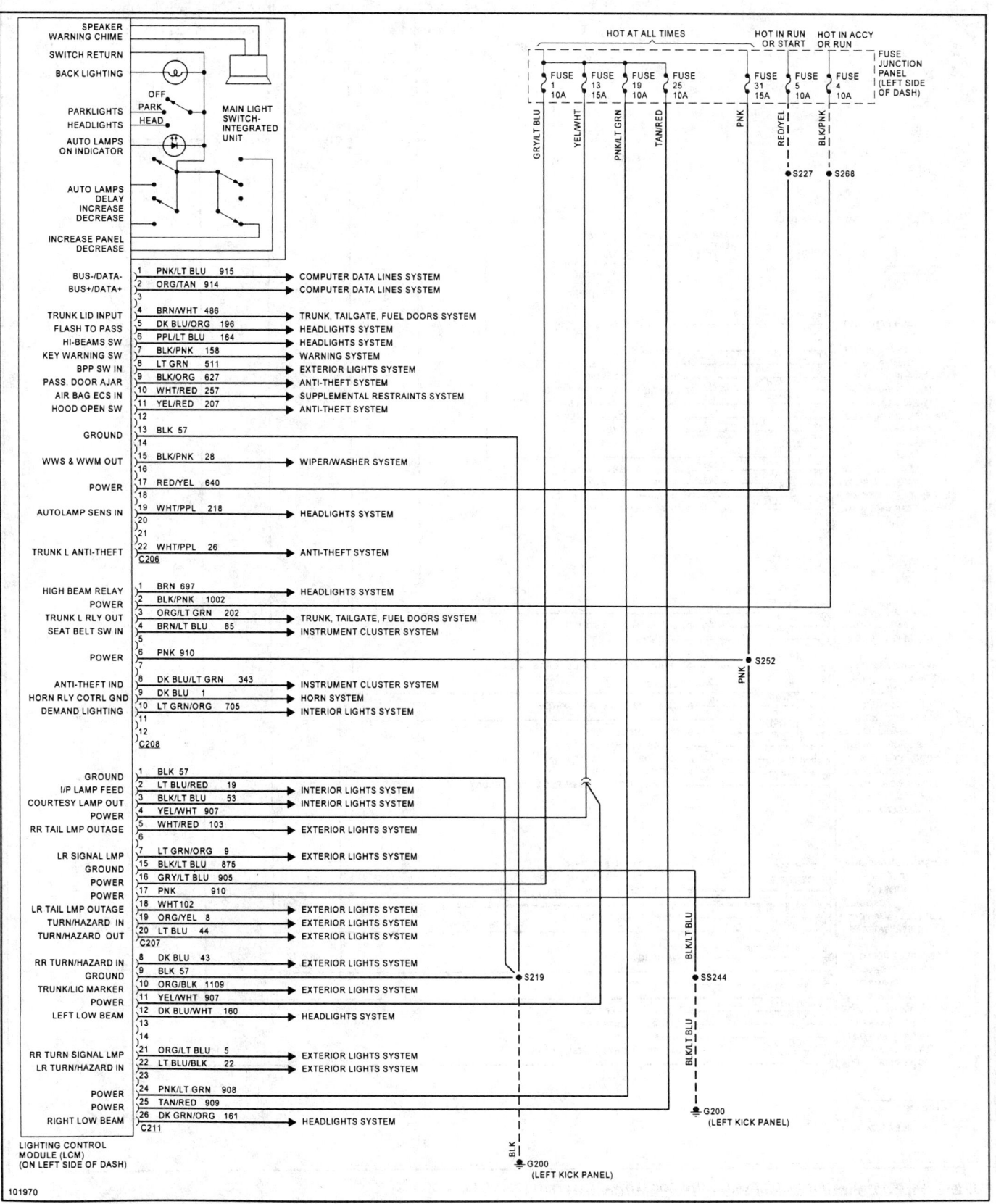

Fig. 1: Lighting Control Modules Wiring Diagram (Contour & Mystique)

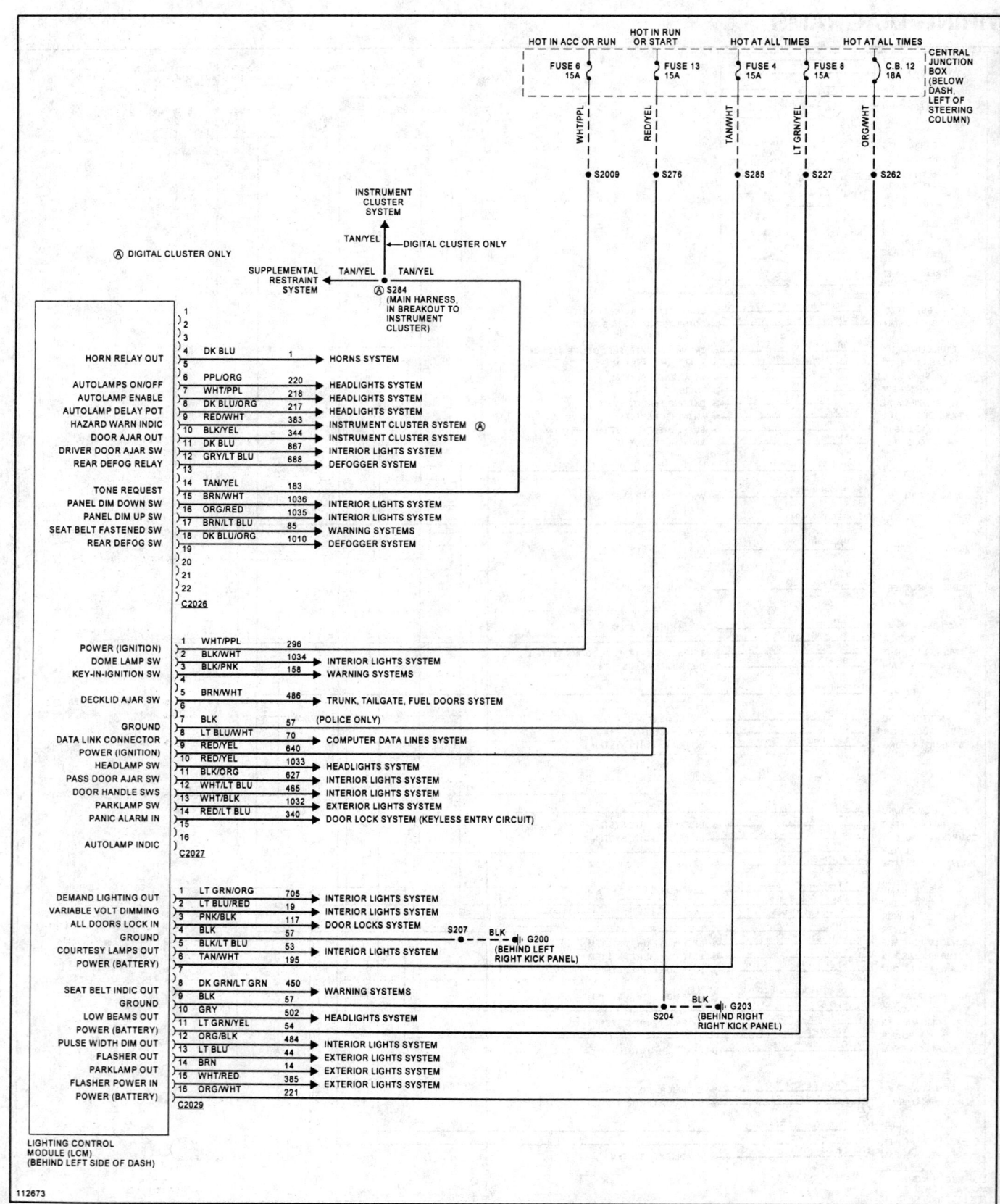

Fig. 2: Lighting Control Modules Wiring Diagram (Cougar)

112673

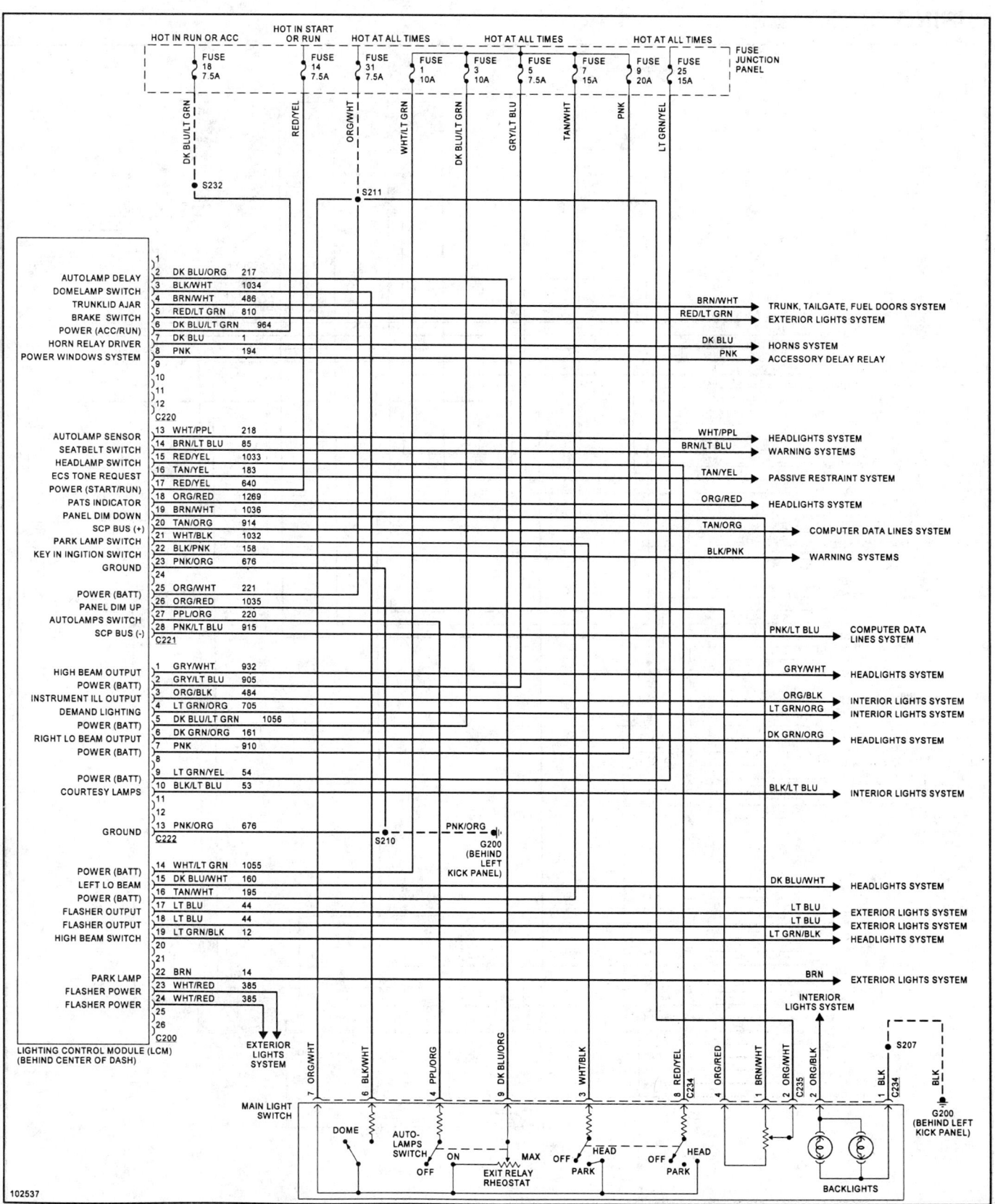

Fig. 3: Lighting Control Modules Wiring Diagram (Town Car)

102537

WIRING DIAGRAMS

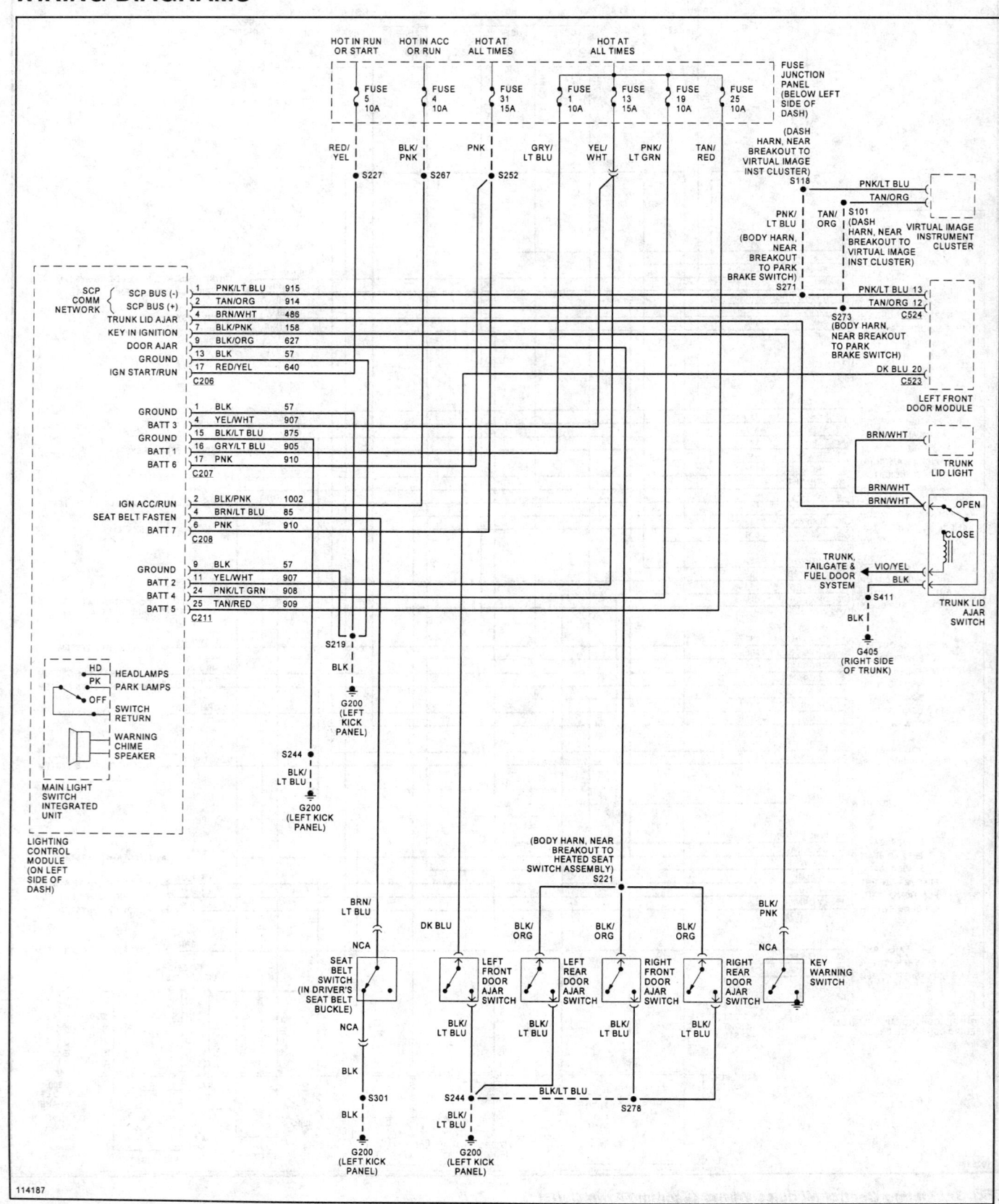

Fig. 1: Warning System Wiring Diagram (Continental)

114187

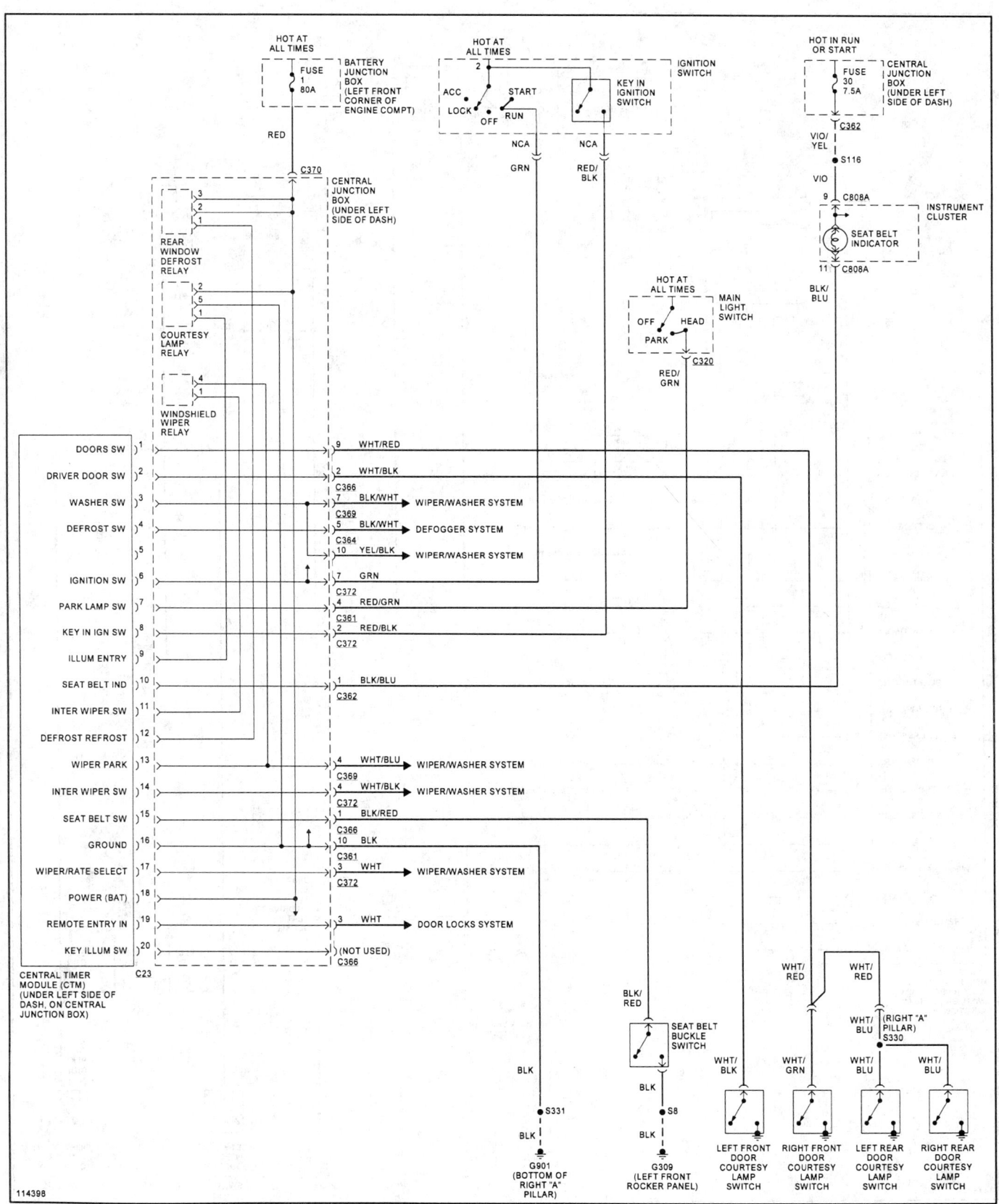

Fig. 2: Warning System Wiring Diagram (Contour & Mystique)

114398

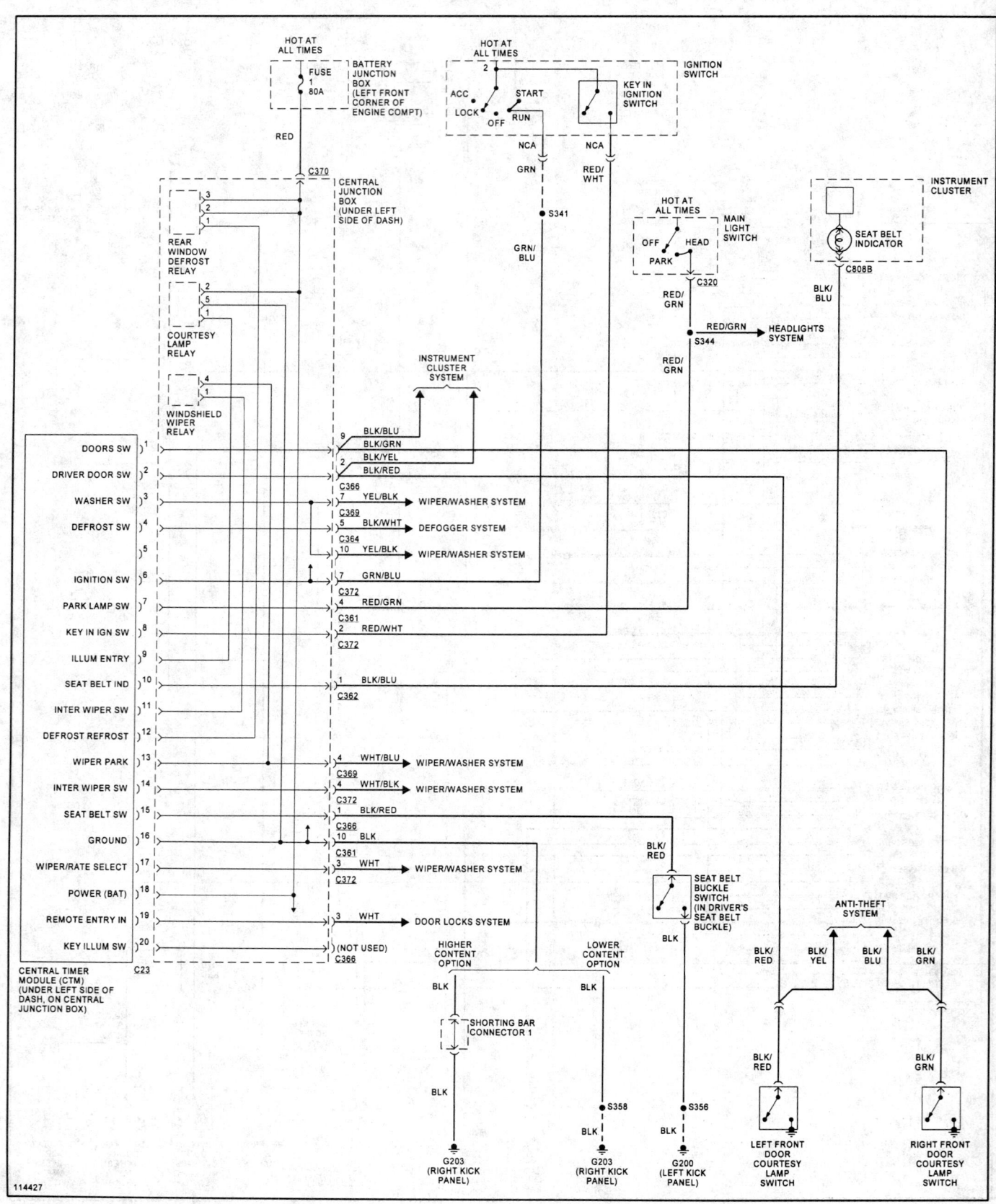

Fig. 3: Warning System Wiring Diagram (Cougar)

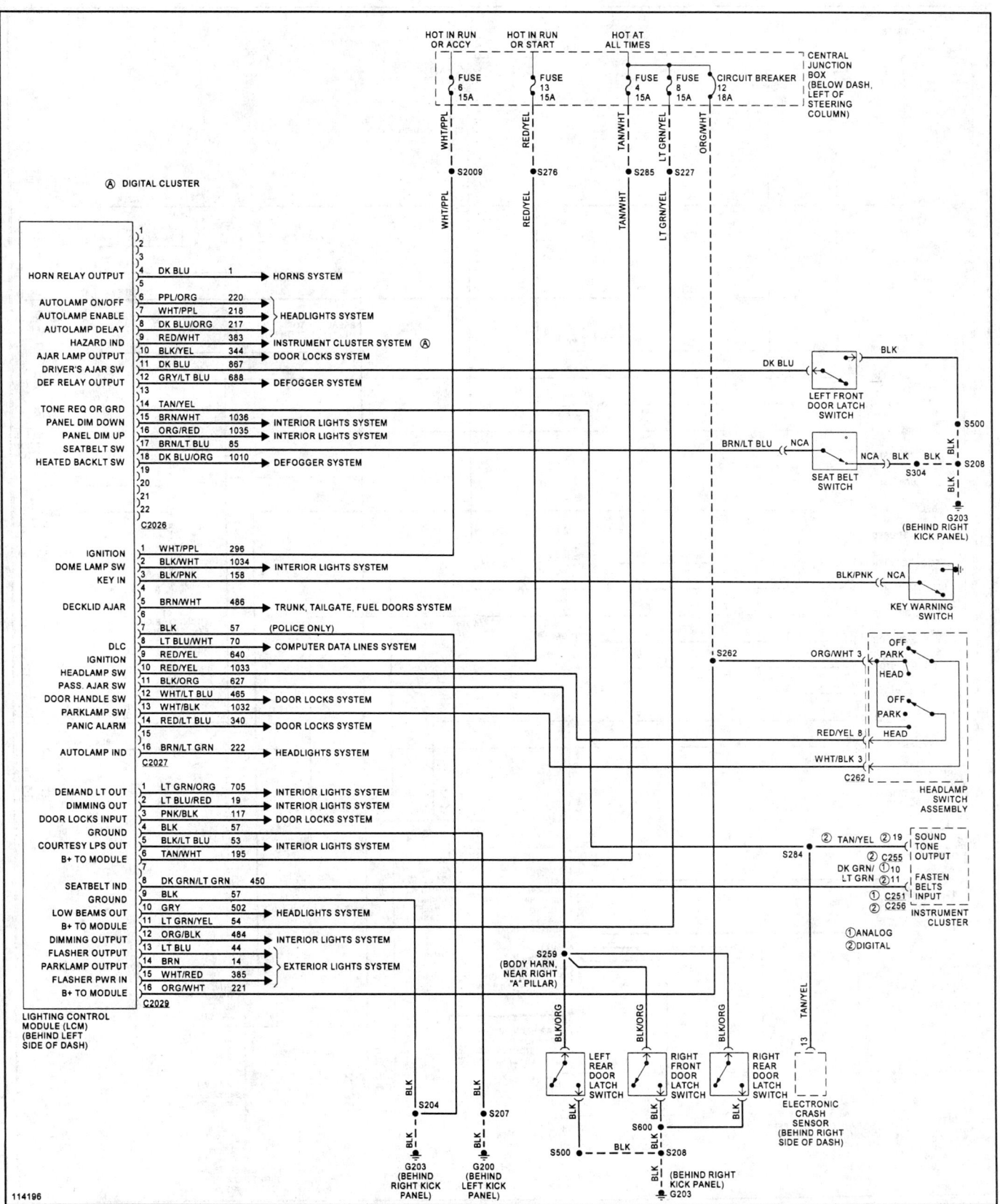

Fig. 4: Warning System Wiring Diagram (Crown Victoria & Grand Marquis)

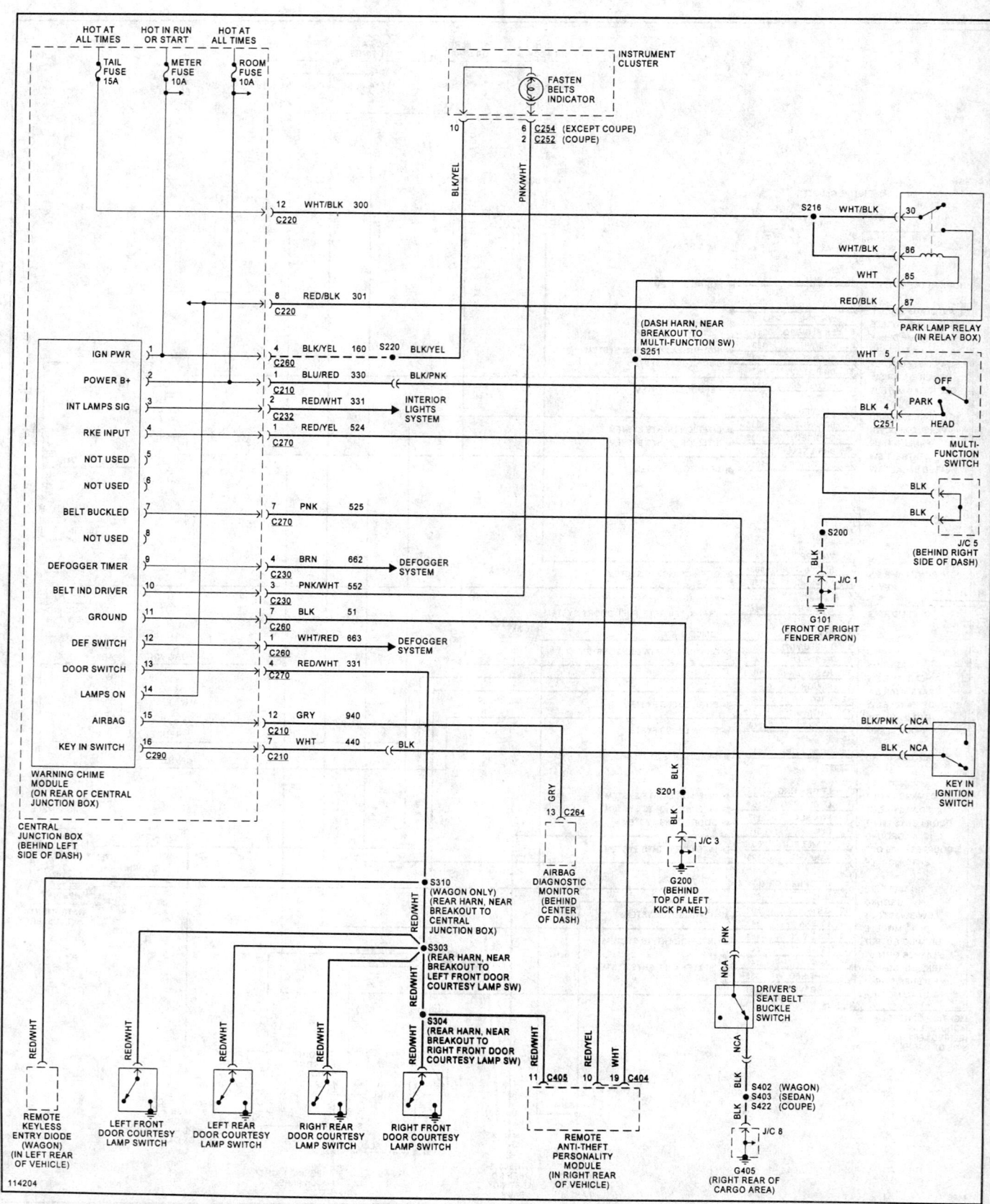

Fig. 5: Warning System Wiring Diagram (Escort & Tracer)

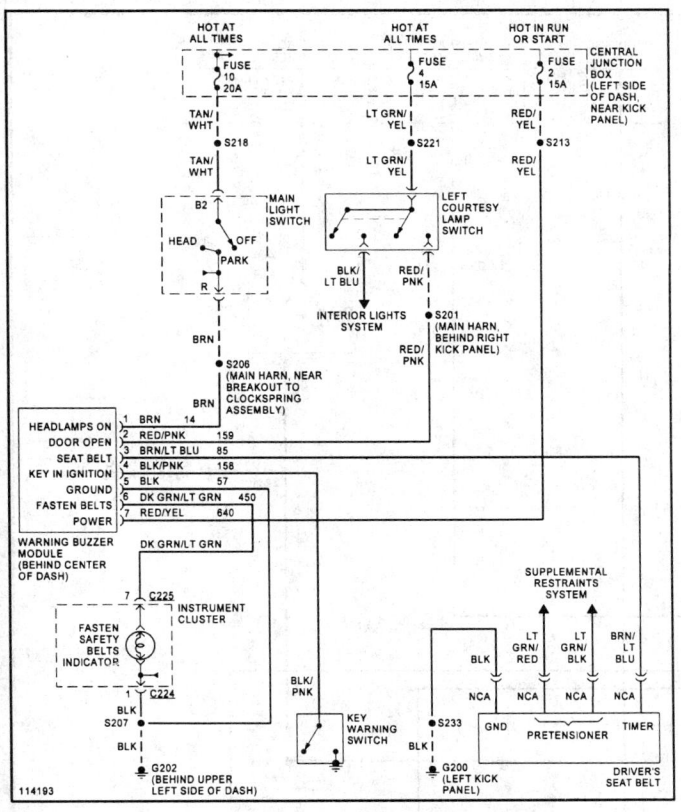

Fig. 6: Warning System Wiring Diagram (Econoline)

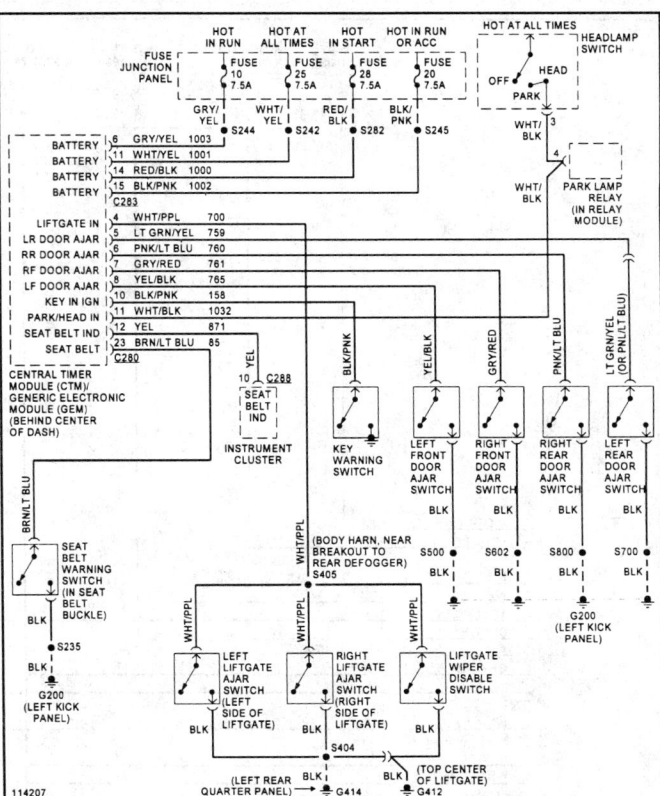

Fig. 8: Warning System Wiring Diagram
(Explorer & Mountaineer)

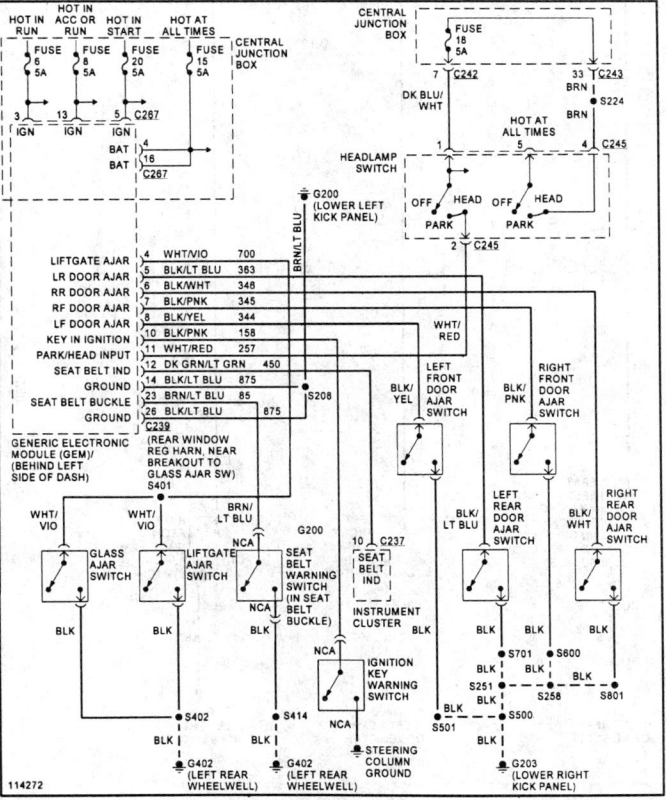

Fig. 7: Warning System Wiring Diagram (Expedition & Navigator)

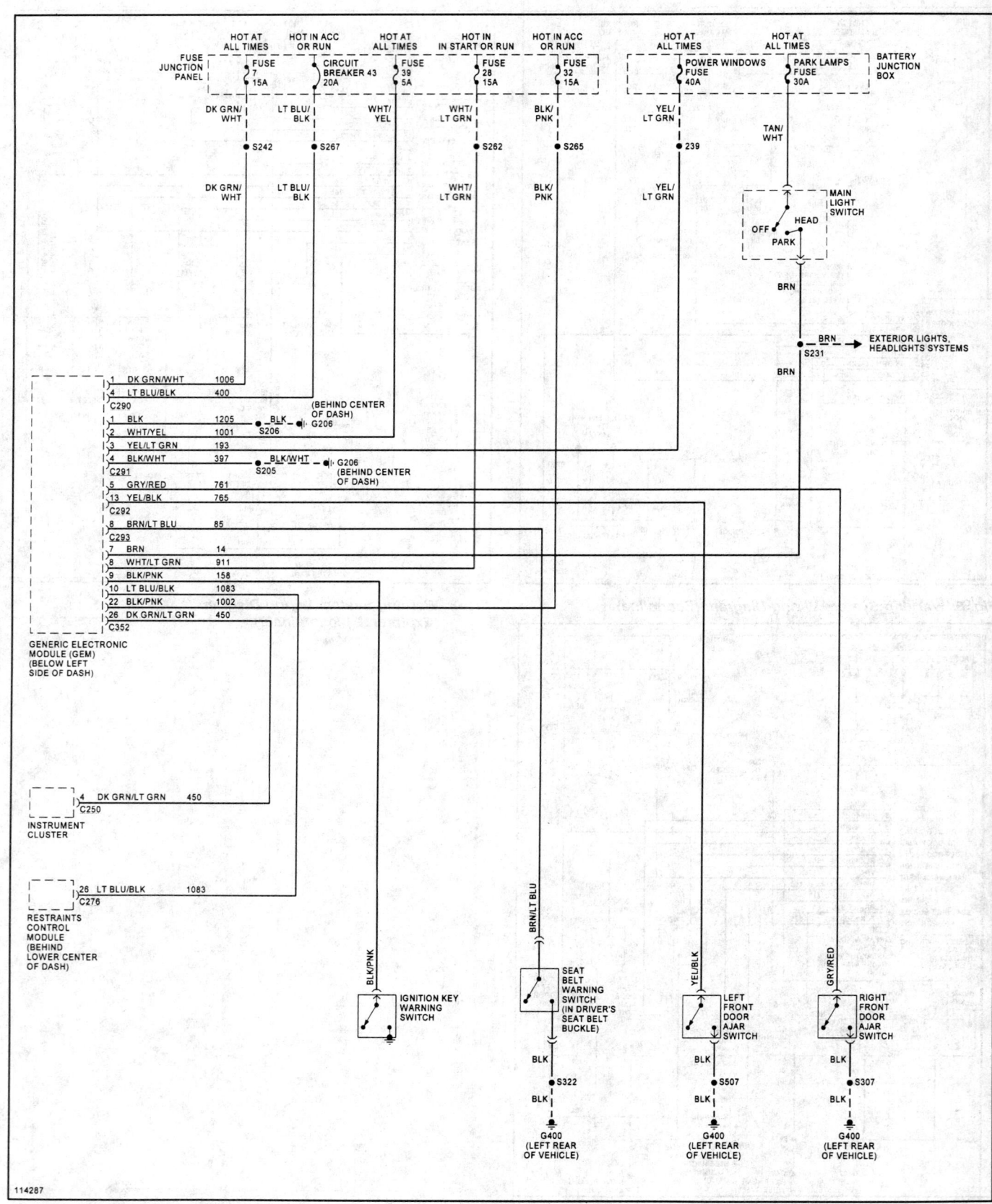

Fig. 9: Warning System Wiring Diagram (Mustang)

114287

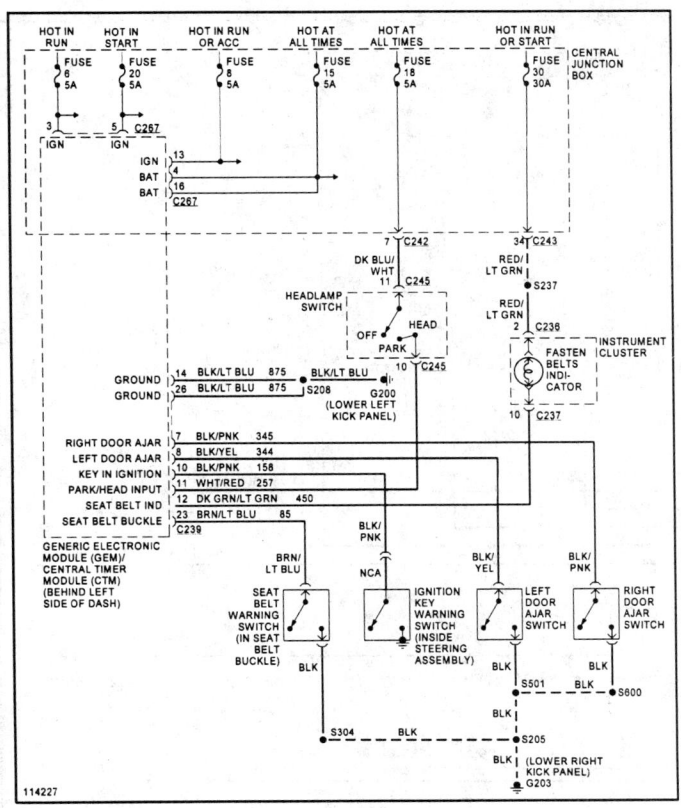

Fig. 10: Warning System Wiring Diagram (F150 & F250 Light-Duty Pickup)

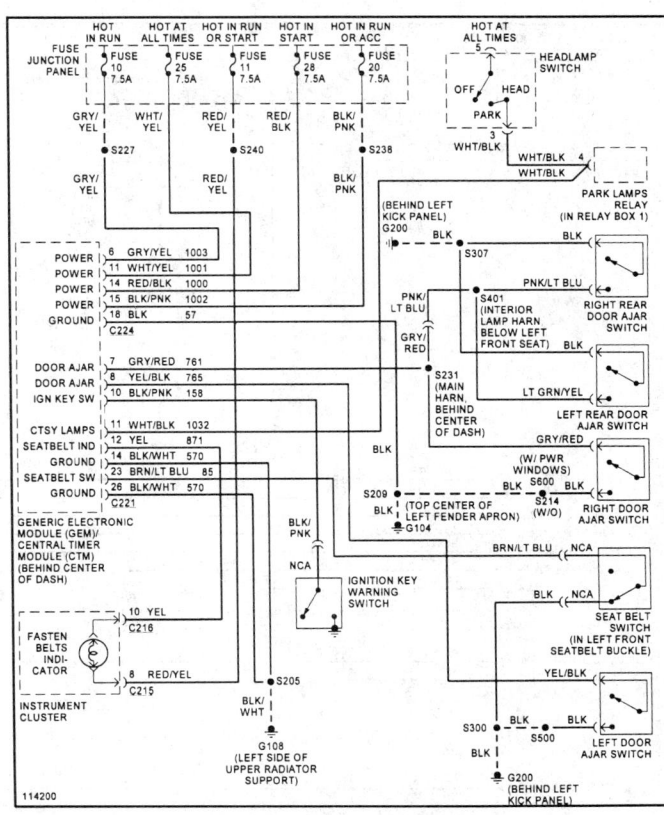

Fig. 12: Warning System Wiring Diagram (Ranger)

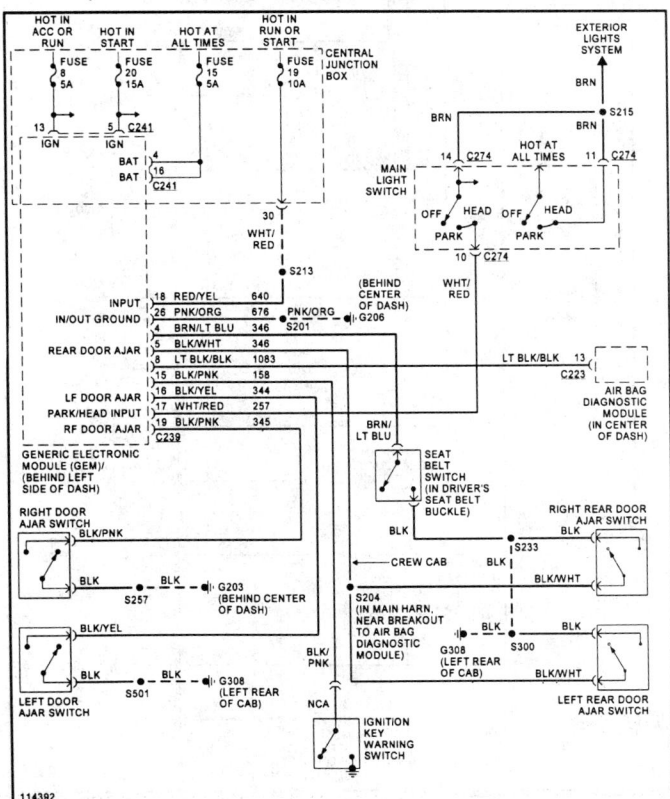

Fig. 11: Warning System Wiring Diagram (F250 Super-Duty & F350 Pickup)

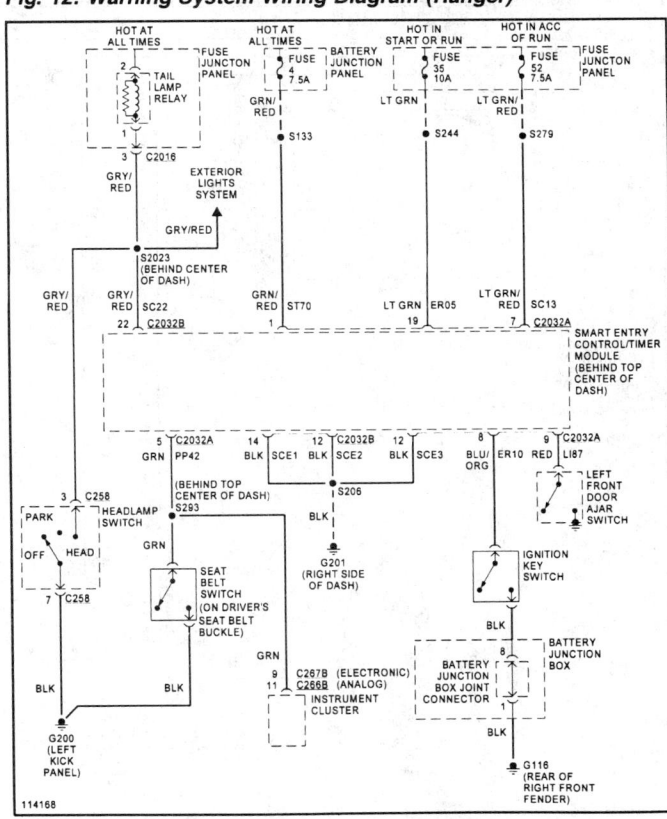

Fig. 13: Warning System Wiring Diagram (Villager)

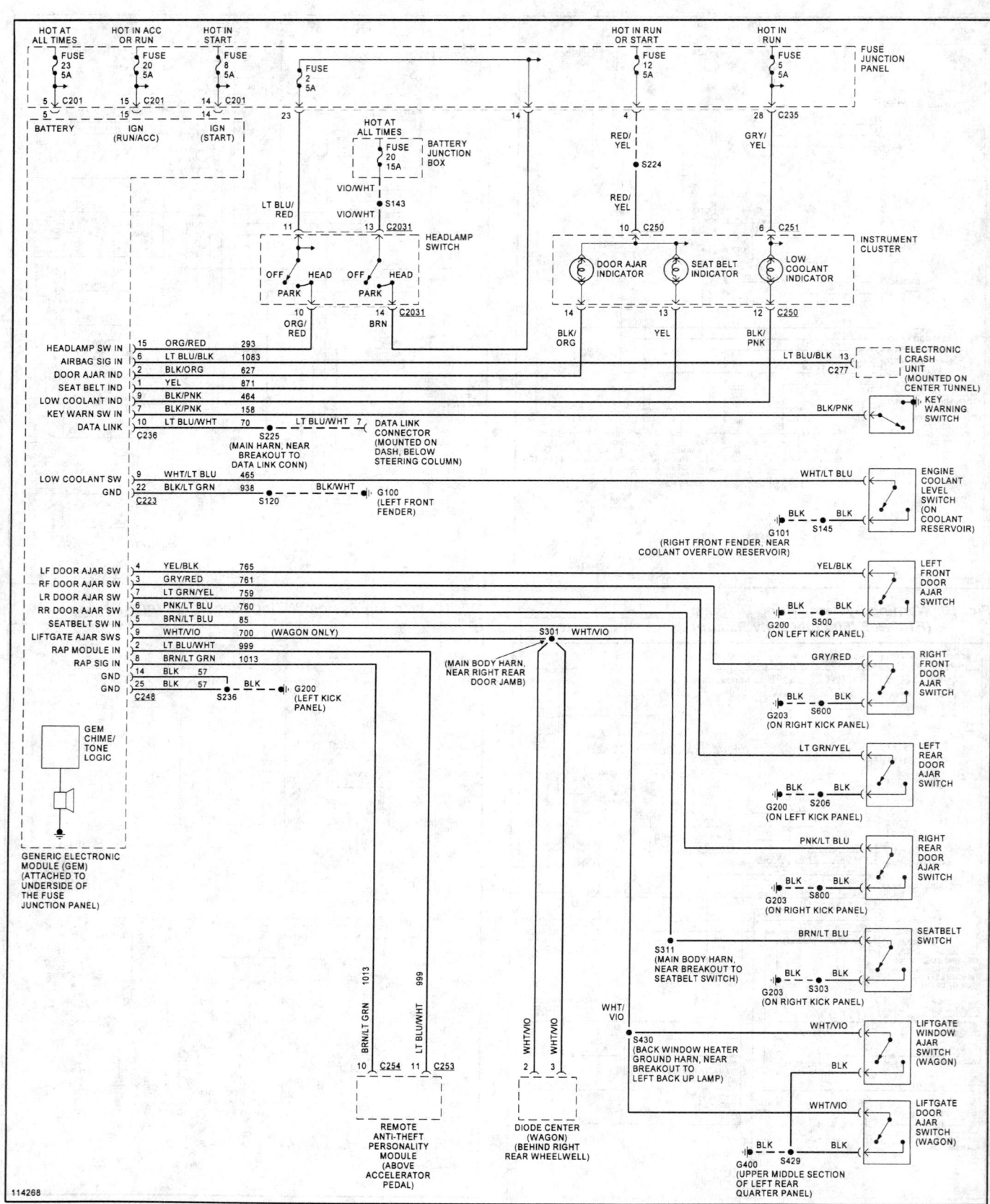

Fig. 14: Warning System Wiring Diagram (Sable & Taurus)

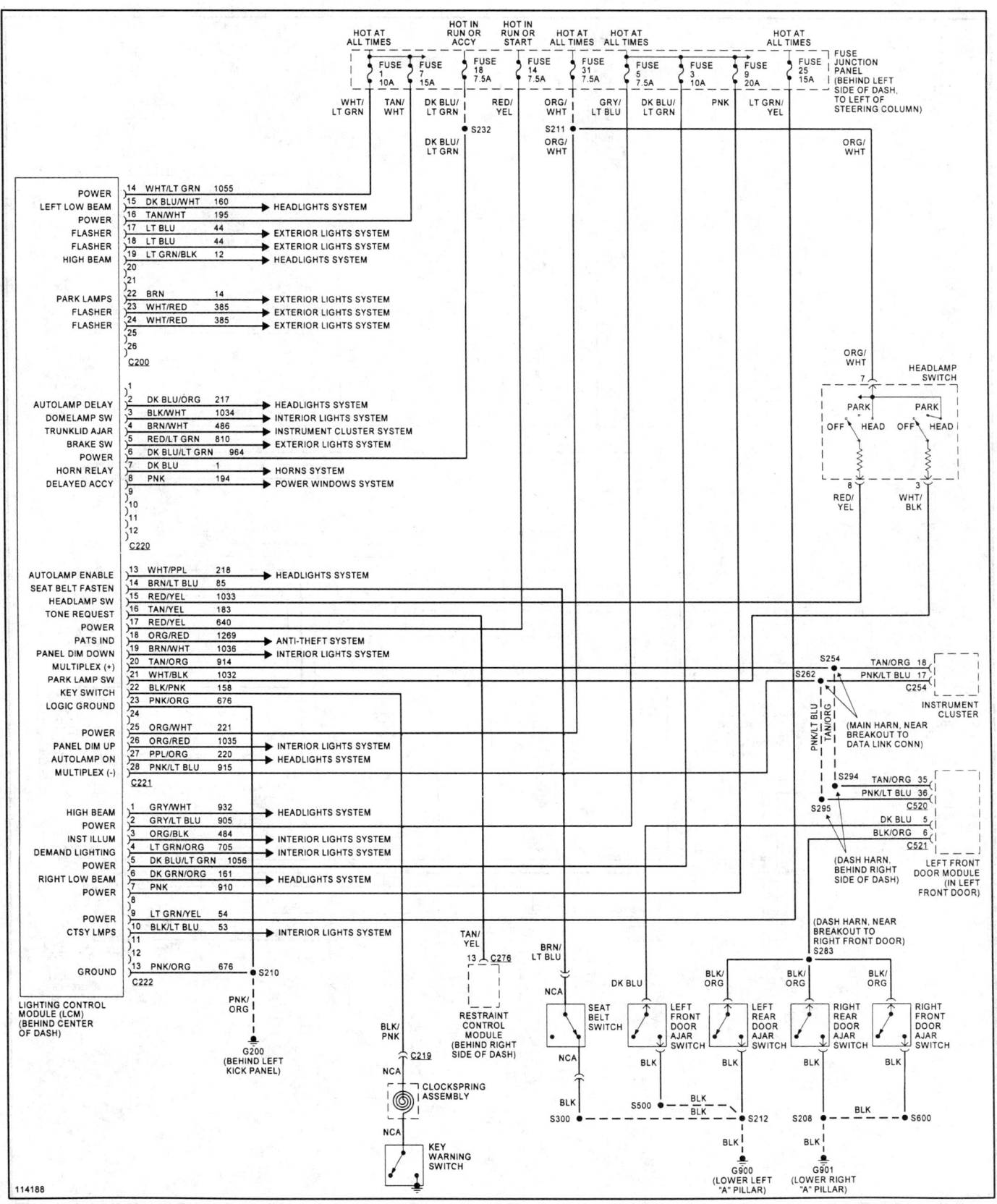

Fig. 15: Warning System Wiring Diagram (Town Car)

114188

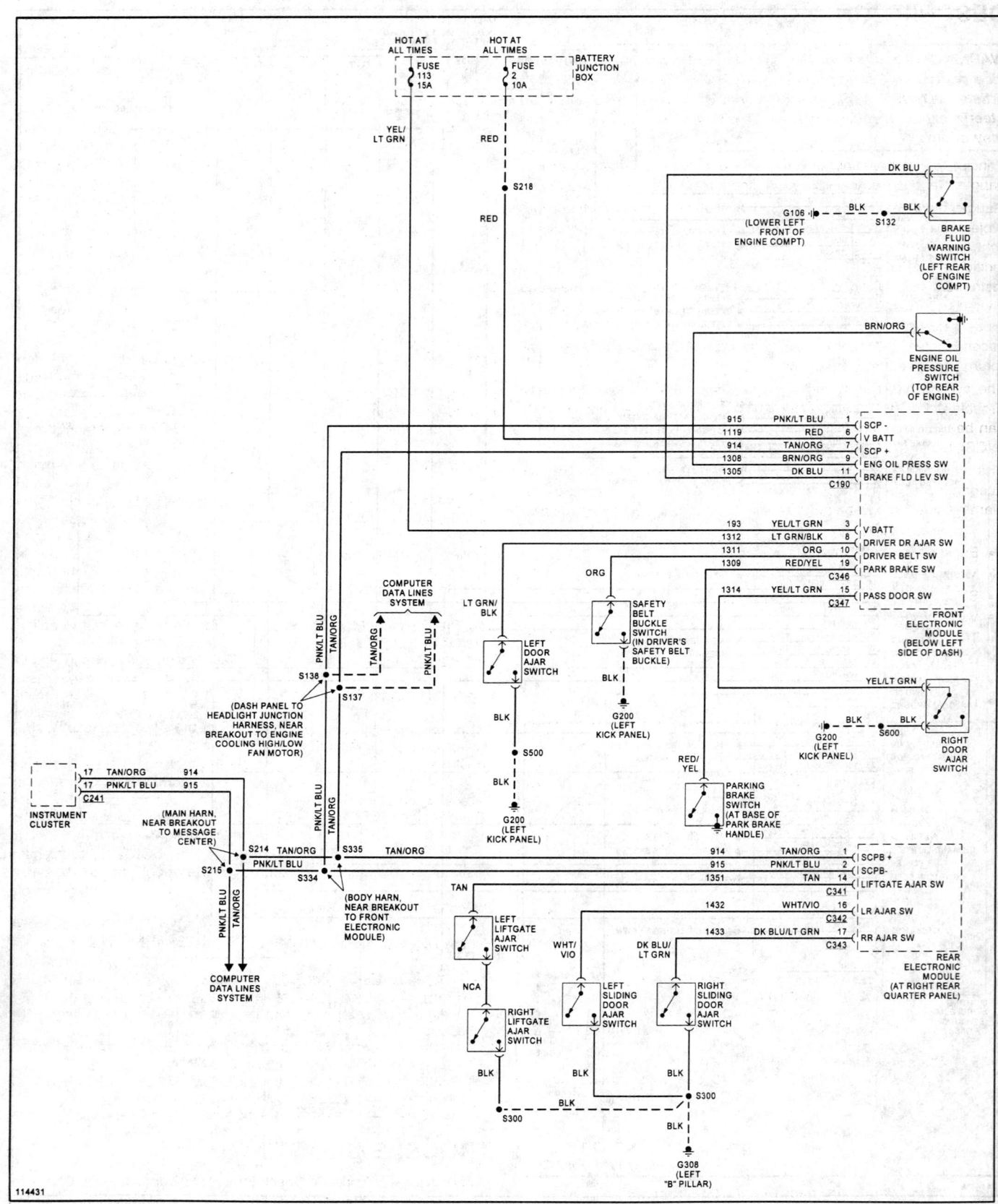

Fig. 16: Warning System Wiring Diagram (Windstar)

DESCRIPTION & OPERATION

WARNING: Deactivate air bag system before performing any service operation. See appropriate AIR BAG RESTRAINT SYSTEMS article. DO NOT apply electrical power to any component on steering column without first deactivating air bag system. Air bag may deploy.

Principal components of the virtual image instrument panel are analog gauges, various warning indicators, and a message center. *See Fig. 1.* Gauges have analog needles and a virtual instrument cluster mask that projects gauge faces and graduation using a cold cathode fluorescent light to present a 3 dimensional effect. Displays appear whenever the ignition switch is in RUN position. When ignition is first turned on, the instrument cluster will go through a prove-out cycle. The message center and instrument pointers will come on at full intensity, and the message center will display PLEASE FASTEN YOUR SEAT BELT. A few seconds later, the graphics will come on and the gauge pointers will return to their appropriate positions.

The system has self-diagnostic capabilities. One or more Diagnostic Trouble Codes (DTC) will be stored in the event of a malfunction. DTCs can be retrieved from instrument cluster using a New Generation Star (NGS) Tester (007-00500). See SELF-DIAGNOSTIC SYSTEM.

The message center is a green vacuum fluorescent dot matrix display integrated into right side of instrument cluster. Message center provides warning status messages and access to various features, including:

- System Check
- English/Metric Or Driver I.D.
- Menu
- Select
- Vehicle Handling
- Trip
- Display
- Reset
- DTE/Economy

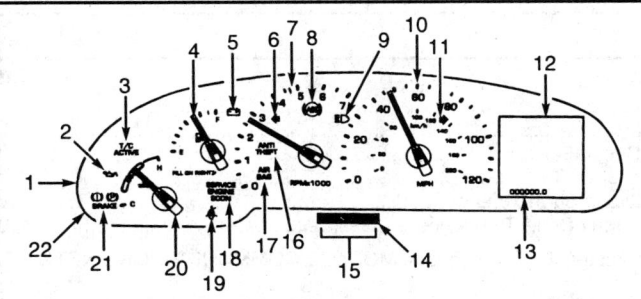

1. EIC
2. Low Oil Warning
3. Traction Control Warning
4. Fuel Gauge
5. Charge Warning
6. Turn Signal Warning
7. Tachometer
8. Anti-Lock Warning
9. High Beam Indicator
10. Speedometer
11. Turn Signal Warning
12. Message Center
13. Odometer
14. PRNDL Light
15. PRNDL
16. Anti-Theft Warning
17. Air Bag Warning
18. MIL Light
19. Seat Belt Warning
20. Temperature Gauge
21. Brake Warning
22. Housing

95A13524

Courtesy of Ford Motor Co.

Fig. 1: Identifying Instrument Cluster Components

COMPONENT LOCATIONS

COMPONENT LOCATIONS

Component	Location
Anti-Lock Brake System (ABS) Control Module	Left Front Of Engine Compartment
Data Link Connector (DLC)	Below Driver's Side Of Instrument Panel, To Right Of Steering Column
Door Lock Switch	Appropriate Door Panel Arm Rest
Driver's Door Module (DDM)	Behind Driver's Door Panel, Lower Front Corner
Driver's Heated Seat Module	Under Driver's Seat
Driver's Seat Module (DSM)	Under Driver's Seat
Electronic Automatic Temp. Control (EATC) Module	Behind Center Of Instrument Panel
Front Control Unit (FCU) [1]	Behind Center Of Instrument Panel, On Radio
Front Seat Track Assembly	[2] Under Appropriate Seat
Heated Seat Module	Under Appropriate Seat
Heated Seat Switch	Center Of Instrument Panel, Under Heater Controls
Instrument Cluster [3]	Behind Left Side Of Instrument Panel
Instrument Panel Fuse Box	Below Left Instrument Panel
Keyless Entry Keypad	Driver's Door Below Exterior Door Handle
Lighting Control Module (LCM)	On Instrument Panel, Behind Headlight Switch
Light Sensor Amplifier	Top Left Side Of Instrument Panel
Low Tire Pressure Module	Top Front Center Of Headliner
Lumbar Switch	Side Of Seat Cushion
Message Center Switches	On Instrument Panel, Right Of Instrument Cluster
Power Distribution Box	Left Side Of Engine Compartment, Above Wheelwell
Power Mirror Switch	Driver's Door Panel Arm Rest
Powertrain Control Module (PCM)	In Passenger's Side Of Engine Compartment, On Firewall
Remote Emergency Satellite Cellular Unit (RESCU) Module	Passenger's Side Rear Corner Of Trunk, Behind Trim Panel, In Front Of Taillight Assembly
Restraint Control Module [4]	Between Front Seats, Below Center Console
Speed Control Servo/Amplifier Assembly [5]	Mounted On Left Shock Tower
Vehicle Dynamic Module (VDM)	In Driver's Side Of Trunk, On Panel Below Rear Window

[1] – FCU may also be referred to as Audio Control Module (ACM).

[2] – Front seat track and adjustment motors are a complete assembly.

[3] – Instrument cluster may also be referred to as Virtual Instrument Cluster (VIC).

[4] – Restraint Control Module (RCM) may also be referred to as Electronic Crash Sensor (ECS) module.

[5] – Speed control servo/amplifier assembly may also be referred to as Next Generation Speed Control (NGSC) servo.

TROUBLE SHOOTING

Verify customer complaint. Check for low washer fluid level. Check for low engine coolant level. Check for low engine oil level. Check for low brake fluid level. Check for loose accessory drive belt. Check for loose or corroded connectors. Check for damaged wiring. Check for blown fuses. Check for faulty switches. If no problem is found, go to SELF-DIAGNOSTIC SYSTEM.

SELF-DIAGNOSTIC SYSTEM

NOTE: Before beginning self-diagnostics, perform TROUBLE SHOOTING.

NOTE: A New Generation Star (NGS) tester is required to test the power mirror system. If NGS tester does not communicate with vehicle, refer to NGS tester manual.

Connect New Generation Star (NGS) Tester (007-00500) to Data Link Connector (DLC) located below instrument panel. Using NGS tester, perform data link diagnostic test. If NGS tester displays CKT914, CKT915 or CKT70=ALL ECUS NO RESP/NOT EQUIP, repair communications concern. See MODULE COMMUNICATIONS NETWORK – CONTINENTAL article. If NGS tester displays NO RESP/NOT EQUIP for instrument cluster, perform TEST B: NO COMMUNICATION WITH INSTRUMENT CLUSTER under SYSTEM TESTS. If NGS tester dis-

plays NO RESP/NOT EQUIP for Driver's Door Module (DDM), perform TEST AJ: NO COMMUNICATION WITH DRIVER'S DOOR MODULE under SYSTEM TESTS. If NGS tester displays NO RESP/NOT EQUIP for Lighting Control Module (LCM), perform TEST C: NO COMMUNICATION WITH LIGHTING CONTROL MODULE under SYSTEM TESTS. If NGS tester displays SYSTEM PASSED, retrieve and record DTCs from all modules. Erase DTCs from all modules. Perform instrument cluster, DDM and LCM self-test. Perform appropriate test in accordance with DTC retrieved. See INSTRUMENT CLUSTER DTC INDEX, DRIVER'S DOOR MODULE DTC INDEX and/or LIGHTING CONTROL MODULE DTC INDEX table. Codes listed in these tables are only for testing covered in this article. For complete DTC listing, see MODULE COMMUNICATIONS NETWORK – CONTINENTAL article. If self-test is passed and no DTCs are retrieved, repair by symptom. See SYMPTOM CHART under SYSTEM TESTS.

INSTRUMENT CLUSTER DTC INDEX

DTC [1]	Description	Test
B1201	Fuel Sender Circuit Failure	A
B1204	Fuel Sender Short To Ground	A
B1205	Instrument Cluster Switch 1 Assembly Circuit Failure	U
B1208	Instrument Cluster Switch 1 Assembly Circuit Short To Ground	U
B1209	Instrument Cluster Switch 2 Assembly Circuit Failure	U
B1212	Instrument Cluster Switch 2 Assembly Circuit Short To Ground	U
B1342	ECU Defective	[2]

[1] – Codes listed in this table are only for testing covered in this article. For complete DTC listing, see MODULE COMMUNICATIONS NETWORK – CONTINENTAL article.
[2] – Using NGS tester, retrieve and record DTCs. Perform instrument cluster self-test. If DTC B1342 still exists, replace instrument cluster.

DRIVER'S DOOR MODULE DTC INDEX

DTC [1]	Description	Test
B1342	ECU Defective	[2]

[1] – Codes listed in this table are only for testing covered in this article. For complete DTC listing, see MODULE COMMUNICATIONS NETWORK – CONTINENTAL article.
[2] – Using NGS tester, retrieve and document all continuous. Perform Driver's Door Module (DDM) self-test. If DTC B1342 is retrieved again, replace DDM.

LIGHTING CONTROL MODULE DTC INDEX

DTC [1]	Description	Test
B1342	ECU Defective	[2]
B1352	Ignition Key-In Circuit Failure	AA
B1462	Seat Belt Switch Circuit Failure	R
B1464	Seat Belt Switch Circuit Short To Voltage	R
B1582	Dim Panel Increase Input Circuit Short To Ground	AK
B1586	Dim Panel Decrease Input Circuit Short To Ground	AK

[1] – Codes listed in this table are only for testing covered in this article. For complete DTC listing, see MODULE COMMUNICATIONS NETWORK – CONTINENTAL article.
[2] – Using NGS tester, retrieve and document continuous DTCs. Clear all DTCs. Perform Lighting Control Module (LCM) self-test. If DTC B1342 is retrieved again, replace LCM.

SYSTEM TESTS

CAUTION: When battery is disconnected or modules are replaced, vehicle computer and memory systems may lose memory data. Driveability problems may exist until computer systems have completed a relearn cycle. See COMPUTER RELEARN PROCEDURES article in GENERAL INFORMATION before disconnecting battery.

NOTE: Before beginning system tests, perform TROUBLE SHOOTING.

NOTE: After repairs are complete, ensure all component are properly installed and all harness connectors are connected properly and repeat data link diagnostic test. See DATA LINK DIAGNOSTIC TEST under COMMUNICATIONS NETWORK DIAGNOSTICS in MODULE COMMUNICATIONS NETWORK – TOWN CAR article.

SYMPTOM CHART

Symptom	Test
Fuel Sender Circuit Failure (DTC B1201); Fuel Sender Short To Ground (DTC B1204)	A
No Communication With Instrument Cluster	B
No Communication With Lighting Control Module	C
Temperature Gauge Inaccurate	D
Low Coolant Warning Never/Always On	E

SYMPTOM CHART (Cont.)

Symptom	Test
Oil Pressure Warning Never/Always On	F
Speedometer Inaccurate	G
Tachometer Inaccurate	H
Charge Warning Never/Always On	J
Low Washer Fluid Warning Never/Always On	K
Brake Warning Never/Always On	L
High Beam Warning Never/Always On	M
Seat Belt Warning Is Inoperative (Chime Is Operative)	N
Decklid Ajar Circuit Short To Ground	P
ECU Is Defective	Q
Seat Belt Switch Circuit Failure	R
Turn On Headlamps Warning Never/Always On	S
Transmission Range Indicator Never On (5 Passenger With Redundant Park Switch Only)	T
Message Center Not Operating Properly (DTCs B1205, B1208, B1209 & B1212)	U
Oil Level Warning Inoperative	V
Low Tire Pressure Warning Never On	W
Speed Control Messages Not Displayed	Y
Seat Belt Warning Chime Inoperative	Z
Key-In-Ignition Chime Does Not Operate Properly	AA
Door Ajar Chime Does Not Operate Properly	AB
Headlight Chime Does Not Operate Properly	AC
Chime Sounds When Driver's Door Is Closed (Headlights Off & Key Removed)	AD
Low Tire Pressure Warning Always On Or Flashing	AE
Low Tire Pressure Warning Light Never On	AF
Air Bag Warning Chime Does Not Operate Properly	AG
Trunk Lid Ajar Chime Does Not Operate Properly	AH
Turn Signal Warning Chime Does Not Operate Properly	AI
No Communication With Driver's Door Module	AJ
Dash Illumination Control Inoperative	AK

TEST A: FUEL SENDER CIRCUIT FAILURE (DTC B1201); FUEL SENDER SHORT TO GROUND (DTC B1204)

1) Connect NGS tester to Data Link Connector (DLC). Turn ignition switch to RUN position. Select and trigger instrument cluster active command FUELLEVEL. Adjust scroll knob to read 50 percent. Fuel gauge reading should be at half tank. Adjust scroll knob to read 100 percent. Fuel gauge reading should be full. If fuel gauge responded as specified, go to next step. If fuel gauge did not respond as specified, replace instrument cluster.

2) Turn ignition switch to LOCK position. Disconnect fuel tank sender harness connector C415. Connect one lead of Instrument Gauge System Tester (014-R1063) to terminal No. 8 (Yellow/White wire) at fuel tank sender harness connector C415. Connect the other lead of tester to terminal No. 5 (Orange/Yellow wire) at fuel tank sender harness connector C415. See Fig. 2. Set tester to 15 ohms. Turn ignition switch to RUN position. Turn ignition switch to LOCK position. Turn ignition switch to RUN position and wait one minute. If fuel gauge reads empty or below, go to next step. If fuel gauge does not read empty or below, go to step **5)**.

3) Turn ignition switch to LOCK position. Set tester to 160 ohms. Turn ignition switch to RUN position and wait one minute. Fuel gauge should started at empty and go to full or above. If fuel gauge did not respond as specified, go to next step. If fuel gauge responded as specified, replace fuel tank sender.

4) Inspect fuel tank. If fuel tank is okay, repair or replace fuel sender assembly as necessary. If fuel tank is damaged, repair or replace fuel tank as necessary.

5) Turn ignition switch to LOCK position. Disconnect instrument cluster harness connector C256. Measure resistance between ground and terminal No. 4 (Yellow/White wire) at instrument cluster harness connector C256. Resistance should be greater than 10 k/ohms. Measure resistance in Yellow/White wire between terminal No. 4 at instrument cluster harness connector C256 and terminal No. 8 at fuel tank sender harness connector. See Figs. 2 and 3. Resistance should be 5 ohms or

less. If resistance is as specified, go to next step. If resistance is not as specified, repair short or open in Yellow/White wire.

6) Disconnect instrument cluster harness connector C255. Measure resistance between ground and terminal No. 28 (Orange/Yellow wire) at instrument cluster harness connector C255. Resistance should be greater than 10 k/ohms. Measure resistance in Orange/Yellow wire between terminal No. 28 at instrument cluster harness connector C255 and terminal No. 5 at fuel tank sender harness connector. Resistance should be 5 ohms or less. If resistance is as specified, replace instrument cluster. If resistance is not as specified, repair short or open in Orange/Yellow wire.

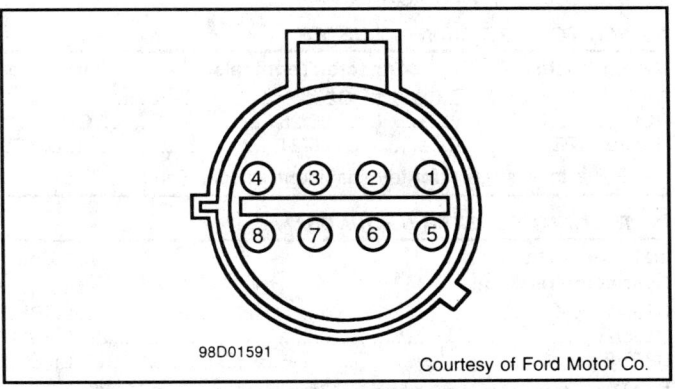

Fig. 2: Identifying Fuel Tank Sender Harness Connector C415 Terminals

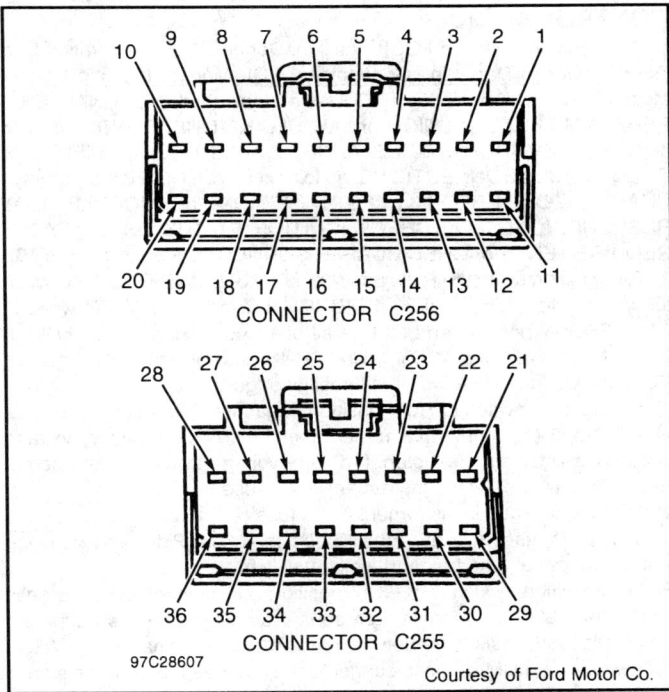

Fig. 3: Identifying Instrument Cluster Harness Connector Terminals

TEST B: NO COMMUNICATION WITH INSTRUMENT CLUSTER

1) Turn ignition switch to LOCK position. Remove fuses No. 5 (10-amp), No. 26 (10-amp) and No. 28 (10-amp) in instrument panel fuse box. Check fuses. If fuses are okay, install fuses and go to next step. If any fuse is blown, replace fuse and retest system. If fuse blows again, check for short to ground and repair as necessary. See appropriate wiring diagram in POWER DISTRIBUTION article in WIRING DIAGRAMS.

2) Disconnect instrument cluster harness connectors C255 and C256. Measure voltage at appropriate terminal at appropriate instrument cluster harness connector with key in appropriate condition. See POWER TO INSTRUMENT CLUSTER table. *See Fig. 3.* If all voltage measurements are greater than 10 volts, go to next step. If any voltage measurement is 10 volts or less, repair open in appropriate circuit. See WIRING DIAGRAMS.

3) Turn ignition switch to LOCK position. Measure resistance between ground and appropriate instrument cluster harness connector terminals. See INSTRUMENT CLUSTER GROUNDS table. If all resistance readings are 5 ohms or less, repair module communication concern. See MODULE COMMUNICATIONS NETWORK – CONTINENTAL article. If any resistance reading is greater than 5 ohms, repair open in appropriate wire. See WIRING DIAGRAMS.

POWER TO INSTRUMENT CLUSTER [1]

Switch Position	Connector/Terminals	Wire Color
OFF	C256/9	PPL
RUN	C256/20	LT GRN/PPL
RUN/START	C255/21	RED/YEL

[1] – Refer to illustration for terminal identification. *See Fig. 3.*

INSTRUMENT CLUSTER GROUNDS [1]

Instrument Cluster Connector/Terminal	Wire Color
C256/10	BLK/LT BLU
C255/26	BLK
C255/27	BLK/LT BLU

[1] – Refer to illustration for terminal identification. *See Fig. 3.*

TEST C: NO COMMUNICATION WITH LIGHTING CONTROL MODULE

1) Turn ignition switch to LOCK position. Connect New Generation Star (NGS) tester to Data Link Connector (DLC). Monitor Lighting Control Module (LCM) PID IGN_LC. If NGS tester does not display UNABLE TO PERFORM TEST/FUNCTION or MODULE NOT RESPONDING: LCM or CHECK IGNITION STATUS/VERIFY CABLE REQUIREMENTS or CHECK CABLE CONNECTIONS, go to next step. If NGS tester displays UNABLE TO PERFORM TEST/FUNCTION or MODULE NOT RESPONDING: LCM or CHECK IGNITION STATUS/VERIFY CABLE REQUIREMENTS or CHECK CABLE CONNECTIONS, go to step **16)**.

2) Turn ignition switch to RUN position. Monitor LCM PID IGN_LC while turning key to each position. If PID IGN_LC indicates ACCY while in ACCESSORY position and OFF in all other positions, replace LCM. If PID IGN_LC indicates ACCY while in RUN position, go to next step. If PID IGN_LC indicates OFF in all positions, go to step **7)**.

3) Turn ignition switch to RUN position. Measure voltage at output side of fuse No. 5 (10-amp) in instrument panel fuse box. If battery voltage does not exist, go to next step. If battery voltage exists, repair open in Red/Yellow wire between instrument panel fuse box and LCM.

4) Check fuse No. 5 in instrument panel fuse box. If fuse is blown, go to next step. If fuse is okay, repair open in Brown/Pink wire between instrument panel fuse box and ignition switch.

5) Turn ignition switch to LOCK position. Disconnect LCM harness connector C206. Disconnect light sensor amplifier harness connector C243. Measure resistance between ground and terminal No. 17 (Red/Yellow wire) at LCM harness connector C206. *See Fig. 4.* If resistance is 20 ohms or less, go to next step. If resistance is greater than 20 ohms, repair short to ground in Red/Yellow wire.

6) Turn ignition switch to LOCK position. Connect LCM harness connector C206. Remove fuse No. 5 (10-amp) in instrument panel fuse box. Measure resistance between ground and output side of fuse No. 5 in instrument panel fuse box. If resistance is 20 ohms or less, repair autolamp concern. See AUTOLAMP SYSTEMS – CONTINENTAL article. If resistance is greater than 20 ohms, replace LCM.

7) Turn ignition switch to RUN position. Measure voltage at output side of fuse No. 4 (10-amp) in instrument panel fuse box. If battery voltage exists, go to next step. If battery voltage does not exist, go to step **9)**.

8) Turn ignition switch to LOCK position. Disconnect LCM harness connector C208. Turn ignition switch to RUN position. Measure voltage at terminal No. 2 (Black/Pink wire) at LCM harness connector C208. See

Fig. 5. If battery voltage exists, replace LCM. If battery voltage does not exist, repair open in Black/Pink wire.

9) Turn ignition switch to LOCK position. Check fuse No. 4 (10-amp) in instrument panel fuse box. If fuse is blown, go to next step. If fuse is okay, repair open in Black/Light Green wire between instrument panel fuse box and ignition switch.

10) Disconnect driver's door lock switch harness connector C505. Measure resistance between ground and terminal No. 2 (Black/Pink wire) at LCM harness connector C208. If resistance is 10 k/ohms or less, go to next step. If resistance is greater than 10 k/ohms, replace driver's door lock switch.

11) Disconnect passenger's door lock switch harness connector C602. Measure resistance between ground and terminal No. 2 (Black/Pink wire) at LCM harness connector C208. If resistance is 10 k/ohms or less, go to next step. If resistance is greater than 10 k/ohms, replace passenger's door lock switch.

12) Disconnect passenger's power window switch harness connector C600. Measure resistance between ground and terminal No. 2 (Black/Pink wire) at LCM harness connector C208. If resistance is 10 k/ohms or less, go to next step. If resistance is greater than 10 k/ohms, replace passenger's power window switch.

13) Disconnect left rear power window switch harness connector C709. Measure resistance between ground and terminal No. 2 (Black/Pink wire) at LCM harness connector C208. If resistance is 10 k/ohms or less, go to next step. If resistance is greater than 10 k/ohms, replace left rear power window switch.

14) Disconnect right rear power window switch harness connector C809. Measure resistance between ground and terminal No. 2 (Black/Pink wire) at LCM harness connector C208. If resistance is 10 k/ohms or less, go to next step. If resistance is greater than 10 k/ohms, replace right rear power window switch.

15) Ensure ignition switch is in LOCK position. Connect LCM harness connector C208. Using and ohmmeter, measure resistance by back-probing between ground and terminal No. 2 (Black/Pink wire) at LCM harness connector C208. If resistance is greater than 2 k/ohms, replace LCM. If resistance is 2 k/ohms or less, repair Black/Pink wire.

16) Turn ignition switch to LOCK position. Disconnect LCM harness connectors. Measure resistance between ground and terminal No. 13 (Black wire) at LCM harness connector C206. *See Fig. 4.* Measure resistance between ground and terminal No. 1 (Black wire) at LCM harness connector C207. *See Fig. 6.* Measure resistance between ground and terminal No. 9 (Black wire) at LCM harness connector C211. *See Fig. 7.* If all resistance readings are 5 ohms or less, go to next step. If any resistance reading is greater than 5 ohms, repair appropriate Black wire.

17) Measure resistance between ground and terminal No. 15 (Black/Light Blue wire) at LCM harness connector C207. If resistance is 5 ohms or less, repair module communication concern. See MODULE COMMUNICATIONS NETWORK – CONTINENTAL article. If resistance is greater than 5 ohms, repair open in Black/Light Blue wire.

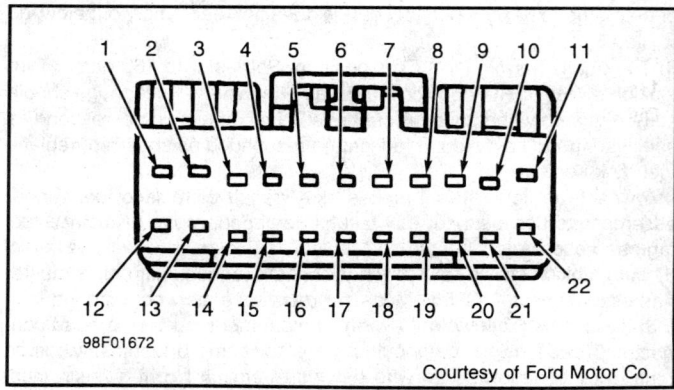

98F01672

Courtesy of Ford Motor Co.

Fig. 4: Identifying Lighting Control Module Harness Connector C206 Terminals

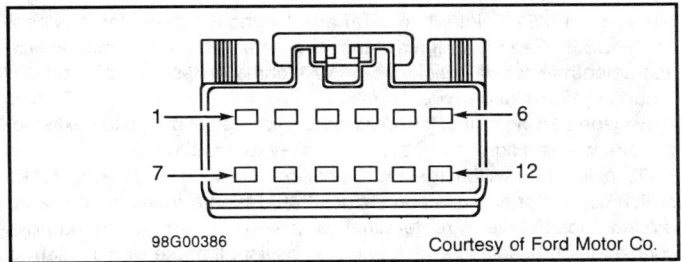

98G00386   Courtesy of Ford Motor Co.

Fig. 5: Identifying Lighting Control Module Harness Connector C208 Terminals

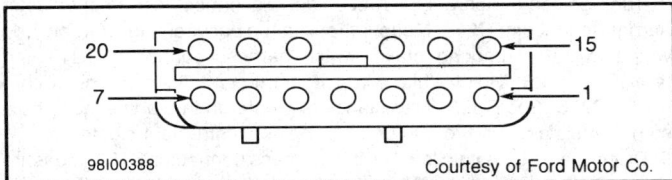

98I00388   Courtesy of Ford Motor Co.

Fig. 6: Identifying Lighting Control Module Harness Connector C207 Terminals

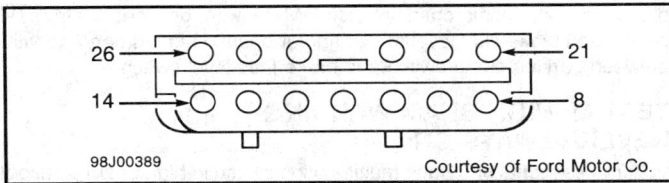

98J00389   Courtesy of Ford Motor Co.

Fig. 7: Identifying Lighting Control Module Harness Connector C211 Terminals

TEST D: TEMPERATURE GAUGE INACCURATE

1) Connect New Generation Star (NGS) tester to Data Link Connector (DLC). Turn ignition switch to RUN position. Perform data link diagnostics. See DATA LINK DIAGNOSTIC TEST under COMMUNICATION NETWORK DIAGNOSTICS in MODULE COMMUNICATIONS NETWORK – CONTINENTAL article. If vehicle passes, go to next step. If vehicle does not pass, repair module communication concern. See MODULE COMMUNICATIONS NETWORK – CONTINENTAL article.

2) Using NGS tester, select instrument cluster active command ENGCOOLNT. Trigger ENGCOOLNT on. Adjust scroll knob to zero percent. Temperature gauge reading should be at C (cold). Adjust scroll knob to 50 percent. Temperature gauge reading should be between to O and R in the word NORM. Adjust scroll knob to 100 percent. Temperature gauge reading should be at H (hot). If temperature gauge responds as specified, repair temperature sensor circuit. See appropriate SELF-DIAGNOSTICS article in ENGINE PERFORMANCE in appropriate MITCHELL® manual. If temperature gauge did not respond as specified, replace instrument cluster.

TEST E: LOW COOLANT WARNING NEVER/ALWAYS ON

1) Ensure coolant reservoir is full. Turn ignition switch to LOCK position. Disconnect coolant level sensor harness connector C148. Turn ignition switch to RUN position. Measure voltage at Light Blue wire terminal at coolant level sensor harness connector C148. If voltage is greater than 4 volts, go to next step. If voltage is 4 volts or less, go to step **3)**.

2) Turn ignition switch to LOCK position. Measure resistance between ground and Black wire terminal at engine coolant level sensor harness connector C148. If resistance is 5 ohms or less, go to step **4)**. If resistance is greater than 5 ohms, repair open in Black wire.

3) Disconnect instrument cluster harness connector C256. Measure resistance in Light Blue wire between engine coolant level sensor harness connector C148 and terminal No. 7 at instrument cluster connector C256. *See Fig. 3.* If resistance is 5 ohms or less, go to next step. If resistance is greater than 5 ohms, repair open in Light Blue wire.

4) Measure resistance between coolant level sensor terminals (component side). If resistance is greater than 5 ohms, replace coolant level sensor. If resistance is 5 ohms or less, replace instrument cluster.

TEST F: OIL PRESSURE WARNING NEVER/ALWAYS ON

1) Turn ignition switch to RUN position. If oil pressure warning light is not on, go to next step. If warning light is on, go to step **3)**.

2) Disconnect oil pressure switch harness connector C1020. Using a fused jumper wire, ground White/Red wire terminal at oil pressure switch harness connector C1020. If oil pressure warning light does not come on, go to next step. If oil pressure warning light comes on, replace oil pressure switch.

3) Start engine. If oil pressure warning light does not go through prove-out and go out, go to next step. If oil pressure warning light goes through prove-out and goes out, system is okay at this time.

4) Turn ignition switch to LOCK position. Disconnect oil pressure switch connector. Turn ignition switch to RUN position. If oil pressure warning light goes out, go to next step. If oil pressure warning light remains on, go to step **6)**.

5) Connect external oil pressure gauge. Start and idle engine. If oil pressure is greater than 5 psi ($.35$ kg/cm^2), go to next step. If oil pressure is 5 psi ($.35$ kg/cm^2) or less, repair engine oiling concern. See appropriate article in ENGINES.

6) Turn ignition switch to LOCK position. Disconnect instrument cluster harness connector C255. Measure resistance between ground and terminal No. 24 (White/Red wire) at instrument cluster harness connector C255. *See Fig. 3.* If resistance is greater than 10 k/ohms, go to next step. If resistance is 10 k/ohms or less, repair short to ground in White/Red wire.

7) Measure resistance in White/Red wire between terminal No. 24 at instrument cluster connector C255 and oil pressure switch harness connector C1020. If resistance is 5 ohms or less, replace instrument cluster. If resistance is greater than 5 ohms, repair open in White/Red wire.

TEST G: SPEEDOMETER INACCURATE

1) Connect New Generation Star (NGS) tester to Data Link Connector (DLC). Turn ignition switch to RUN position. Perform data link diagnostics. See DATA LINK DIAGNOSTIC TEST under COMMUNICATION NETWORK DIAGNOSTICS in MODULE COMMUNICATIONS NETWORK – CONTINENTAL article. If vehicle passes, go to next step. If vehicle does not pass, repair module communication concern. See MODULE COMMUNICATIONS NETWORK – CONTINENTAL article.

2) Test drive vehicle above 5 MPH. Using NGS tester, monitor ABS module speed signal. Compare speed indicated on speedometer with speed indicated on NGS tester. If speed indications agree, repair vehicle speed signal concern. See appropriate ANTI-LOCK article in BRAKES in appropriate MITCHELL® manual. If speed indications do not agree, replace instrument cluster.

TEST H: TACHOMETER INACCURATE

1) Connect New Generation Star (NGS) tester to Data Link Connector (DLC). Turn ignition switch to RUN position. Using NGS tester, perform data link diagnostics. See DATA LINK DIAGNOSTIC TEST under COMMUNICATION NETWORK DIAGNOSTICS in MODULE COMMUNICATIONS NETWORK – CONTINENTAL article. If vehicle passes, go to next step. If vehicle does not pass, repair module communication concern. See MODULE COMMUNICATIONS NETWORK – CONTINENTAL article.

2) Using NGS tester, select instrument cluster active command TCHOMETER. Trigger TCHOMETER on. Adjust scroll knob to zero percent. Tachometer reading should be approximately zero RPM. Adjust scroll knob to 50 percent. Tachometer reading should be approximately 3500 RPM. Adjust scroll knob to 100 percent. Tachometer reading should be approximately 7000 RPM. If tachometer did not respond as specified, go to next step. If tachometer responds as specified, system is okay at this time.

3) Check For Clean Tach Out (CTO) circuit open or short, see appropriate SELF-DIAGNOSTICS article in ENGINE PERFORMANCE in appropriate MITCHELL® manual. If CTO circuit is okay, replace instrument cluster. If CTO circuit is faulty, repair as necessary. See appropriate SELF-DIAGNOSTICS article in ENGINE PERFORMANCE in appropriate MITCHELL® manual.

TEST J: CHARGE WARNING NEVER/ALWAYS ON

1) Check charging system operation. See appropriate GENERATORS article in STARTING & CHARGING SYSTEMS. If charging system is operating properly, go to next step. If charging system is not operating properly, repair as necessary.

2) Turn ignition switch to RUN position. If charging warning indicator is not on, go to next step. If charging warning indicator is on, go to step 4).

3) Turn ignition switch to LOCK position. Disconnect instrument cluster harness connector C256. Disconnect generator voltage regulator harness connector C154. Measure resistance in Light Green/Red wire between generator voltage regulator harness connector C154 and terminal No. 18 at instrument cluster harness connector C256. See Fig. 3. If resistance is 5 ohms or less, replace instrument cluster. If resistance is greater than 5 ohms, repair open in Light Green/Red wire.

4) Turn ignition switch to LOCK position. Disconnect instrument cluster harness connector C256. Disconnect generator voltage regulator harness connector C154. Measure resistance between ground and Light Green/Red wire terminal at generator voltage regulator harness connector C154. If resistance is greater than 10 k/ohms, replace instrument cluster. If resistance is 10 k/ohms or less, repair short to ground in Light Green/Red wire.

TEST K: LOW WASHER FLUID WARNING NEVER/ALWAYS ON

1) Ensure washer reservoir is full. Turn ignition switch to LOCK position. Disconnect washer fluid level sensor harness connector. Turn ignition switch to RUN position. If washer warning is on, go to next step. If washer warning is not on, go to step 3).

2) Turn ignition switch to LOCK position. Measure resistance between ground and Black wire terminal at washer fluid level sensor harness connector. If resistance is 5 ohms or less, go to step 4). If resistance is greater than 5 ohms, repair open in Black wire.

3) Disconnect instrument cluster harness connector C256. Measure resistance in Pink/Yellow wire between washer fluid level sensor harness connector and terminal No. 17 at instrument cluster harness connector C256. See Fig. 3 . If resistance is 5 ohms or less, go to next step. If resistance is greater than 5 ohms, repair open in Pink/Yellow wire.

4) Measure resistance between washer fluid level sensor terminals (component side) If resistance is greater than 5 ohms, replace washer fluid level sensor. If resistance is 5 ohms or less, replace instrument cluster.

TEST L: BRAKE WARNING NEVER/ALWAYS ON

1) Ensure brake fluid reservoir is full and parking brake is released. Turn ignition switch to RUN position. If brake warning light is on, go to next step. If brake warning light is not on, go to step 6).

2) Connect New Generation Star (NGS) tester to Data Link Connector (DLC). Turn ignition switch to RUN position. Using NGS tester, monitor LCM PID PARK_SW while applying parking brake. If PID does not agree with parking brake position, go to next step. If PID agrees with parking brake position, repair parking brake signal from LCM as necessary.

3) Turn ignition switch to LOCK position. Disconnect parking brake switch harness connector C246. Turn ignition switch to RUN position. If brake warning light is on, go to next step. If warning light is not on, replace parking brake switch.

4) Turn ignition switch to LOCK position. Disconnect brake fluid level switch harness connector C182. Turn ignition switch to RUN position. If brake warning light is on, go to next step. If warning light is not on, replace brake fluid level switch.

5) Turn ignition switch to LOCK position. Disconnect instrument cluster harness connector C255. Measure resistance between ground and terminal No. 25 (Violet/White wire) at instrument cluster harness connector C255. See Fig. 3. If resistance is greater than 10 k/ohms, replace instrument cluster. If resistance is 10 k/ohms or less, repair short to ground in Violet/White wire.

6) Engage parking brake. If brake warning light is not on, go to next step. If brake warning light is on, system is okay at this time.

7) Turn ignition switch to LOCK position. Disconnect parking brake switch connector harness connector C246. Using a fused jumper wire, ground Violet/White wire terminal at parking brake switch harness connector. Turn ignition switch to RUN position. If brake warning light is not on, go to next step. If warning light is on, replace parking brake switch.

8) Turn ignition switch to LOCK position. Disconnect instrument cluster harness connector C255. Measure resistance between Light Green/Red wire terminal at parking brake switch harness connector C246 and terminal No. 25 (Violet/White wire) at instrument cluster harness connector C255. See Fig. 3. If resistance is greater than 5 ohms, go to next step. If resistance is 5 ohms or less, replace instrument cluster.

9) Disconnect brake fluid level switch harness connector C182. Measure resistance between Violet/White wire terminal and Light Green/Red wire terminal at brake fluid level switch (component side). If resistance is greater than 5 ohms, replace brake fluid level switch. If resistance is 5 ohms or less, repair open in Violet/White wire between instrument cluster and brake fluid level switch and/or open in Light green/Red wire between parking brake switch and brake fluid level switch.

TEST M: HIGH BEAM WARNING NEVER/ALWAYS ON

1) Turn headlights on. Place multifunction switch in high beam position. If high beam are on, go to next step. If high beam are not on, repair headlight system concern. See AUTOLAMP SYSTEMS – CONTINENTAL article.

2) Connect New Generation Star (NGS) tester to Data Link Connector (DLC). Turn ignition switch to RUN position. Using NGS tester, select Lighting Control Module (LCM) active command HIGHBEAM. Trigger HIGHBEAM on. If high beam warning light is on, replace LCM. If high beam warning light is not on, replace instrument cluster.

TEST N: SEAT BELT WARNING IS INOPERATIVE (CHIME IS OPERATIVE)

1) Ensure driver's seat belt is not fastened. Turn ignition switch to RUN position. If seat belt warning chime sounds, go to next step. If warning chime does not sound, repair seat belt warning chime. Perform TEST Z: SEAT BELT WARNING CHIME INOPERATIVE.

2) Ensure driver's seat belt is not fastened. Turn ignition switch to RUN position and wait one minute. If seat belt warning light does not prove out, go to next step. If seat belt warning light proves out, system is okay at this time.

3) Connect New Generation Star (NGS) tester to Data Link Connector (DLC). Turn ignition switch to RUN position. Using NGS tester, select LCM active command SEATBELT. Trigger SEATBELT on. If seat belt warning light is on, replace LCM. If seat belt warning light is not on, replace instrument cluster.

TEST P: DECKLID AJAR CIRCUIT SHORT TO GROUND

1) Turn ignition switch to LOCK position. Connect NGS tester to Data Link Connector (DLC). Turn ignition switch to RUN position. Ensure all doors are fully closed. Using NGS tester, perform LCM self-test. If DTC B1334 exists, go to next step. If DTC B1334 does not exist, perform appropriate test. See LIGHTING CONTROL MODULE DTC INDEX table under SELF-DIAGNOSTIC SYSTEM.

2) Using NGS tester, monitor PID DECKLID. If PID indicates AJAR, repair short to ground in Brown/White wire or replace trunk ajar switch as necessary. If PID does not indicate AJAR, replace LCM.

TEST Q: ECU IS DEFECTIVE

Turn ignition switch to LOCK position. Connect New Generation Star (NGS) tester to Data Link Connector (DLC). Turn ignition switch to RUN position. Clear DTCs. Perform self-test. If DTC B1342 is retrieved, replace ECU in question. If DTC B1342 is not retrieved, repair any other DTCs.

TEST R: SEAT BELT SWITCH CIRCUIT FAILURE

1) Turn ignition switch to LOCK position. Connect NGS tester to Data Link Connector (DLC). Ensure all doors are fully closed. Using NGS tester, perform Lighting Control Module (LCM) self-test. If DTC B1462 exists, go to next step. If DTC B1462 does not exist, perform appropriate test. See LIGHTING CONTROL MODULE DTC INDEX table under SELF-DIAGNOSTIC SYSTEM.

2) Buckle driver's seat belt. Using NGS tester, monitor PID D_SBELT. If PID does not indicate IN, go to next step. If PID indicates IN, replace LCM.

3) Turn ignition switch to LOCK position. Disconnect LCM harness connector C208. Measure voltage at terminal No. 4 (Brown/Light Blue wire) at LCM harness connector C208. See Fig. 5. If voltage does not exist, go to next step. If voltage exists, repair short to voltage in Brown/Light Blue wire.

4) Turn ignition switch to RUN position. Measure resistance between ground and terminal No. 4 (Brown/Light Blue wire) at LCM harness connector C208. See Fig. 5. If resistance is greater than 5 ohms, go to next step. If resistance is 5 ohms or less, replace LCM.

5) Turn ignition switch to LOCK position. Disconnect driver's seat belt switch harness connector C308. Measure resistance in Brown/Light Blue wire between driver's seat belt switch harness connector C308 and terminal No. 4 at LCM harness connector C208. If resistance is 5 ohms or less, replace driver's seat belt switch. If resistance is greater than 5 ohms, repair open in Brown/Light Blue wire.

TEST S: TURN ON HEADLAMPS WARNING NEVER/ALWAYS ON

1) Start engine. Turn autolamps on. Monitor autolamp operation. Increase autolamp delay time. Turn ignition switch to LOCK position. If autolamps operate properly, go to next step. If autolamps do not operate properly, repair autolamp system. See AUTOLAMP SYSTEMS – CONTINENTAL article.

2) Turn ignition switch to RUN position. Cover light sensor amplifier. Ensure headlight switch is off. If TURN ON HEADLAMPS indicator is off, go to next step. If TURN ON HEADLAMPS indicator is on, system is okay at this time.

3) Connect NGS tester to Data Link Connector (DLC). Turn ignition switch to RUN position. Using NGS tester, select LCM active command WARNING LAMPS AND CHIME. Trigger daytime running lights active command and observe TURN ON HEADLAMPS indicator. Using NGS tester, select instrument cluster active command WARNING LAMPS AND CHIME. Trigger turn on headlamps indicator active command. Observe TURN ON HEADLAMPS indicator. If indicator is on, replace LCM. If indicator is not on, replace instrument cluster.

TEST T: TRANSMISSION RANGE INDICATOR NEVER ON (5 PASSENGER WITH REDUNDANT PARK SWITCH ONLY)

1) Connect NGS tester to Data Link Connector (DLC). Turn ignition switch to RUN position. Perform instrument cluster self-test. If DTC U1059 is not present, go to next step. If DTC U1059 is retrieved, repair transmission range switch circuit. See appropriate SELF-DIAGNOSTICS article in ENGINE PERFORMANCE in appropriate MITCHELL® manual.

2) Place shift lever in Park. Select instrument cluster active command INSTRUMENT CLUSTER LAMP CONTROL. Trigger PRNDL LAMP. Scroll and select PARK then trigger ON. If PARK indicator does not turn on, go to next step. If PARK indicator turns on, go to step 6).

3) Turn ignition switch to LOCK position. Disconnect instrument cluster harness connector C256. Turn ignition switch to RUN position. Measure voltage at terminal No. 14 (Orange/White wire) at instrument cluster harness connector C256. See Fig. 3. If battery voltage exists, go to next step. If battery voltage exists, check PARK indicator light bulb and replace as necessary. If light bulb is okay, replace instrument cluster.

4) Turn ignition switch to LOCK position. Disconnect console shift illumination light harness connector C334. Measure resistance in Orange/White wire between console shift illumination light harness connector C334 and terminal No. 14 at instrument cluster harness connector C256. If resistance is 5 ohms or less, go to next step. If resistance is greater than 5 ohms, repair open in Orange/White wire.

5) Turn ignition switch to RUN position. Measure voltage at Red/Black wire terminal at console shift illumination light harness connector C334. If battery voltage exists, replace redundant park switch. If battery voltage does not exist, repair open in Red/Black wire.

6) Using NGS tester, select instrument cluster active command INSTRUMENT CLUSTER LAMP CONTROL. Trigger PRNDL LAMP. Scroll and select each individual range. If each range indicator illuminates, system is okay at this time. If each range indicator does not illuminate, replace light bulb in question.

TEST U: MESSAGE CENTER NOT OPERATING PROPERLY (DTCS B1205, B1208, B1209 & B1212)

1) Turn ignition switch to RUN position. Press each message center button and listen for tone. If tone does not sound when each button is pressed, go to next step. If tone sounds when each button is pressed, system is okay at this time.

2) Turn ignition switch to LOCK position. Disconnect message center switch module harness connector. Measure resistance between terminals at message center switch module (component side) while pressing each button. See MESSAGE CENTER SWITCH MODULE RESISTANCE table. See Fig. 8. If resistance readings are as specified, go to next step. If resistance readings are not as specified, replace message center switch module.

3) Disconnect instrument cluster harness connector C256. Measure resistance in Light Green wire between terminal No. 3 at instrument cluster harness connector C256 and terminal No. 4 at message center switch module harness connector C266. See Figs. 3 and 9. Measure resistance in Light Blue/Yellow wire between terminal No. 13 at instrument cluster harness connector C256 and terminal No. 5 at message center switch module harness connector C266. Measure resistance in Pink/Orange wire between terminal No. 15 at instrument cluster harness connector C256 and terminal No. 2 at message center switch module harness connector C266. If resistance readings are 5 ohms or less, replace instrument cluster. Is any resistance reading is greater than 5 ohms, repair appropriate open circuit(s).

MESSAGE CENTER SWITCH MODULE RESISTANCE

Terminals	Press Button	Ohms
2 & 4	None	16,900–17,900
2 & 4	DTE ECON	5400–5800
2 & 4	TRIP	2900–3100
2 & 4	DISPLAY	900–1000
2 & 4	RESET	300–400
2 & 5	None	16,900–17,900
2 & 5	MENU	5400–5800
2 & 5	SELECT	2900–3100
2 & 5	SYSTEM CHECK	1700–1850
2 & 5	DRIVER ID/E/M	900–1000
2 & 5	VEHICLE HANDLING	300–400

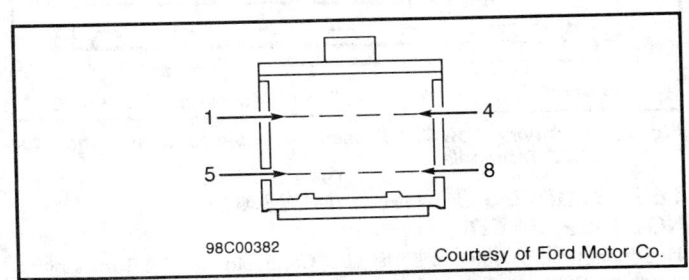

98C00382   Courtesy of Ford Motor Co.

Fig. 8: Identifying Message Center Switch Module Terminals

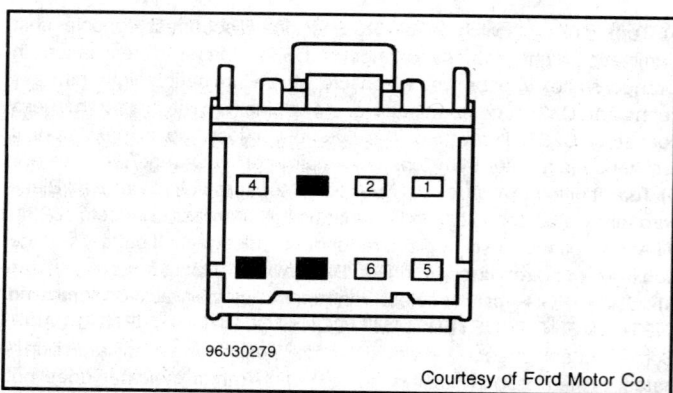

Courtesy of Ford Motor Co.

Fig. 9: Identifying Message Center Switch Harness Connector C266 Terminals

TEST V: OIL LEVEL WARNING INOPERATIVE

1) Turn ignition switch to LOCK position. Disconnect low oil level switch harness connector C1019. Turn ignition switch to RUN position. Measure voltage at White/Pink wire terminal at low oil level switch harness connector C1019. If 4 volts or less exists, go to next step. If greater than 4 volts exists, replace low oil level switch.

2) Turn ignition switch to LOCK position. Disconnect instrument cluster harness connector C256. Measure resistance between ground and White/Pink wire terminal at low oil level switch harness connector C1019. Resistance should be greater than 10 k/ohms. Measure resistance in White/Pink wire between low oil level switch harness connector C1019 and terminal No. 8 at instrument cluster harness connector C256. *See Fig. 3.* Resistance should be less than 5 ohms. If resistance is not as specified, repair open or short in White/Pink wire. If resistance is as specified, replace instrument cluster.

TEST W: LOW TIRE PRESSURE WARNING NEVER ON

1) Turn ignition switch to RUN position. Observer low tire pressure indicator in overhead console. If low tire pressure indicator proves out, go to next step. If low tire pressure indicator does not prove out, perform TEST AE: LOW TIRE PRESSURE WARNING ALWAYS ON OR FLASHING.

2) Turn ignition switch to LOCK position. Disconnect instrument cluster harness connector C256. Disconnect low tire pressure module harness connector C927. Measure resistance between ground and terminal No. 2 (Dark Green wire) at low tire pressure module harness connector C927. Resistance should be greater than 10 k/ohms. Measure resistance in Dark Green wire between terminal No. 2 at low tire pressure module harness connector C927 and terminal No. 2 at instrument cluster harness connector C256. *See Figs. 3 and 10.* Resistance should be less than 5 ohms. If resistance is not as specified, repair open or short in Dark Green wire. If resistance is as specified, replace instrument cluster.

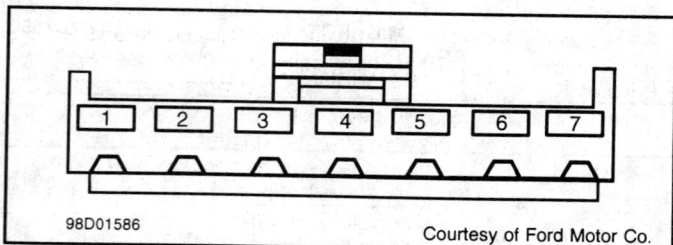

Courtesy of Ford Motor Co.

Fig. 10: Identifying Low Tire Pressure Module Harness Connector C927 Terminals

TEST Y: SPEED CONTROL MESSAGES NOT DISPLAYED

1) Connect NGS tester to Data Link Connector (DLC). Turn ignition switch to RUN position. Using NGS tester, select instrument cluster

active commend MESSAGE CENTER. Trigger MSGCENTER on. If all segments of message center illuminate, go to next step. If all segments of message center do not illuminate, replace instrument cluster.

2) Check cruise control system operation. If cruise control operates properly, replace instrument cluster. If cruise control does not operate properly, repair cruise control concern. See CRUISE CONTROL SYSTEMS – CONTINENTAL article.

TEST Z: SEAT BELT WARNING CHIME INOPERATIVE

1) Connect NGS tester to Data Link Connector (DLC). Using NGS tester, monitor Lighting Control Module (LCM) PID D_SBELT while buckling and unbuckling driver's seat belt. Id PID agrees with seat belt position, replace LCM. If PID always indicates OUT, go to next step. If PID always indicates IN, go to step **4)**.

2) Turn igniton switch to LOCK position. Disconnect driver's seat belt switch harness connector C308. Using NGS tester, monitor LCM PID D_SBELT. If PID indicates OUT, go to next step. If PID does not indicate OUT, replace driver's seat belt switch.

3) Turn igniton switch to LOCK position. Disconnect LCM harness connector C208. Measure resistance between ground and terminal No. 4 (Brown/Light Blue wire) at LCM harness connector C208. *See Fig. 5.* If resistance is greater than 10 k/ohms, replace LCM. If resistance is 10 k/ohms or less, repair short to ground in Brown/Light Blue wire.

4) Turn igniton switch to LOCK position. Disconnect driver's seat belt switch harness connector C308. Using a fused jumper wire, ground Brown/Light Blue wire terminal at driver's seat belt switch harness connector C308. Using NGS tester, monitor LCM PID D_SBELT. If PID indicates IN, go to next step. If PID does not indicate IN, go to step **6)**.

5) Disconnect LCM harness connector C208. Measure resistance in Brown/Light Blue wire between driver's seat belt switch harness connector C308 and terminal No. 4 at LCM harness connector C208. *See Fig. 5.* If resistance is 5 ohms or less, replace LCM. If resistance is greater than 5 ohms, repair open in Brown/Light Blue wire.

6) Measure resistance between ground and Black wire terminal at driver's seat belt switch harness connector C308. If resistance is 5 ohms or less, replace driver's seat belt switch. If resistance is greater than 5 ohms, repair open in Black wire.

TEST AA: KEY-IN-IGNITION CHIME DOES NOT OPERATE PROPERLY

WARNING: Vehicle is equipped with an air bag system. To prevent air bag deployment, system must be disabled before working near steering column and instrument cluster. See appropriate AIR BAG RESTRAINT SYSTEMS article.

1) Turn ignition switch to LOCK position. Using NGS tester, monitor Driver's Door Module (DDM) PID D_DOOR while opening and closing driver's door. If DDM PID D_DOOR indicates AJAR with driver door open and CLOSED with driver door closed, go to next step. If DDM PID D_DOOR does not indicate AJAR with driver door open and does not indicate CLOSED with driver door closed, repair driver door ajar switch circuit. See appropriate wiring diagram in ILLUMINATION/INTERIOR LIGHTS article.

2) Turn ignition switch to LOCK position. Using NGS tester, retrieve and record LCM DTCs. Clear continuous DTCs. Perform LCM self-test. If DTC B1352 is retrieved, go to next step. If DTC B1352 is not retrieved, replace LCM.

3) Ensure ignition switch is in LOCK position. Disconnect key-in-ignition switch harness connector C2012. Measure voltage at terminal No. 5 (Black/Pink wire) at key-in-ignition switch harness connector C2012. *See Fig. 11.* If no voltage exists, go to next step. If any voltage exists, repair open in Black/Pink wire between LCM and key-in-ignition warning switch.

4) Using a fused jumper wire, ground terminal No. 5 (Black/Pink wire) at key-in-ignition switch harness connector C2012. Using NGS tester, monitor Lighting Control Module (LCM) PID IGN_KEY. If LCM PID IGN_KEY indicates IN, replace key-in-ignition switch. If LCM PID

IGN_KEY does not indicate IN, repair open in Black/Pink wire between LCM and key-in-ignition warning switch.

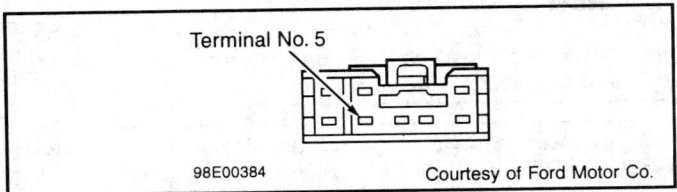

Terminal No. 5

98E00384   Courtesy of Ford Motor Co.

Fig. 11: Identifying Key-In-Ignition Switch Harness Connector C2012 Terminals

TEST AB: DOOR AJAR CHIME DOES NOT OPERATE PROPERLY

1) Turn ignition switch to LOCK position. Connect NGS tester to Data Link Connector (DLC). Using NGS tester, retrieve and record Lighting Control Module (LCM) DTCs. Clear continuous DTCs. Perform LCM self-test. If DTC U1198 is not retrieved, go to next step. If DTC U1198 is retrieved, perform Driver's Door Module (DDM) self-test and perform appropriate test. See DRIVER'S DOOR MODULE DTC INDEX table under SELF-DIAGNOSTIC SYSTEM.

2) Using NGS tester, monitor LCM PID P_DOOR while opening and closing passenger's, right rear and left rear doors one at a time. Using NGS tester, monitor DDM PID D_DOOR while opening and closing driver's door. If PIDs agree with door positions, go to next step. If PIDs do not agree with door positions, repair appropriate door ajar switch circuit. See appropriate wiring diagram in ILLUMINATION/INTERIOR LIGHTS article.

3) Turn ignition switch to LOCK position. Using NGS tester, monitor LCM PID IGN_LC. Turn ignition switch to RUN position. If PID indicates RUN, replace LCM. If PID does not indicate RUN, repair open in Red/Yellow wire between LCM and instrument panel fuse box.

TEST AC: HEADLIGHT CHIME DOES NOT OPERATE PROPERLY

1) Turn headlights on. If headlights an parking lights operate properly, go to next step. If headlights and parking lights do not operate properly, repair exterior lights. See AUTOLAMP SYSTEMS – CONTINENTAL article.

2) Using NGS tester, monitor Driver's Door Module (DDM) PID D_DOOR while opening and closing driver's door. If PID agrees with door position, replace LCM. If PID does not agree with door position, repair driver's door ajar switch circuit. See appropriate wiring diagram in ILLUMINATION/INTERIOR LIGHTS article.

TEST AD: CHIME SOUNDS WHEN DRIVER'S DOOR IS CLOSED (HEADLIGHTS OFF & KEY REMOVED)

WARNING: Vehicle is equipped with an air bag system. To prevent air bag deployment, system must be disabled before working near steering column and instrument cluster. See appropriate AIR BAG RESTRAINT SYSTEMS article.

1) Remove key from ignition. Ensure headlights are off. Using NGS tester, monitor Lighting Control Module (LCM) PID IGN_KEY. If PID does not indicate IN, go to next step. If PID indicates IN, replace LCM.

2) Disconnect LCM harness connector C206. Measure resistance between ground and terminal No. 7 (Black/Pink wire) at LCM harness connector C206. See Fig. 4. If resistance is 5 ohms or less, go to next step. If resistance is greater than 5 ohms, replace LCM.

3) Disconnect key-in-ignition switch harness connector C2012. Measure resistance between ground and terminal No. 5 (Black/Pink wire) at key-in-ignition switch harness connector C2012. See Fig. 11. If resistance is 5 ohms or less, repair Black/Pink wire. If resistance is greater than 5 ohms, replace key-in-ignition switch.

TEST AE: LOW TIRE PRESSURE WARNING ALWAYS ON OR FLASHING

1) Turn ignition switch to LOCK position. Turn ignition switch to RUN position. LOW TIRE PRESSURE warning light should illuminate and then turn off after a few seconds. If light does not operate as specified, go to next step. If light operates as specified, go to step 4).

2) If light stay on continuously, go to next step. If light is never on, perform TEST AF: LOW TIRE PRESSURE WARNING LIGHT NEVER ON.

3) Turn ignition switch to LOCK position. Disconnect low tire pressure module harness connector C927. Remove low tire pressure warning light blub. Measure resistance between ground and terminal No. 4 (Black/Yellow wire) at low tire pressure module harness connector C927. See Fig. 10. If resistance is 5 ohms or less, replace low tire pressure module. If resistance is greater than 5 ohms, repair open in Black/Yellow wire.

4) Check tire pressure. If tire pressure is okay, go to next step. If tire pressure is incorrect, adjust tire pressure as necessary.

NOTE: Perform this step on each tire one at a time.

5) Adjust tire pressure on one tire to 5 psi. Test drive vehicle for 2 minutes at 10 MPH. Low tire pressure warning light should flash and LOW TIRE PRESSURE should be displayed in message center. Adjust pressure in same tire to 15 psi. Test drive vehicle for 2 minutes at 10 MPH. Low tire pressure warning light should stay on and LOW TIRE PRESSURE should not be displayed in message center. Adjust pressure in same tire to normal operating pressure. Test drive vehicle for 2 minutes at 10 MPH. Low tire pressure warning light should stay off and LOW TIRE PRESSURE should not be displayed in message center. If no warning is given for any tire, replace low tire pressure module. If warning operates properly on at least one tire, replace appropriate low tire pressure sensor(s). If only low tire pressure warning light does not operate properly, replace low tire pressure module. If only message center does not operate properly, perform TEST U: MESSAGE CENTER NOT OPERATING PROPERLY (DTCS B1205, B1208, B1209 & B1212).

TEST AF: LOW TIRE PRESSURE WARNING LIGHT NEVER ON

1) Turn ignition switch to LOCK position. Turn ignition switch to RUN position. Low tire pressure warning light should illuminate and then turn off after a few seconds. If light never illuminates, go to next step. If light is always on or flashing, perform TEST AE: LOW TIRE PRESSURE WARNING ALWAYS ON OR FLASHING. If light operates as specified, system is okay at this time.

2) Remove fuse No. 28 (10-amp) in instrument panel fuse box. Check fuse. If fuse is okay, go to next step. If fuse is blown, repair short to ground in Light Green/Violet wire between instrument panel fuse box and low tire pressure module.

3) Turn ignition switch to LOCK position. Ensure fuse No. 28 is still removed. Disconnect low tire pressure module harness connector C927. Measure resistance in Light Green/Violet wire between output side of fuse No. 28 in instrument panel fuse box and terminal No. 6 at low tire pressure module harness connector C927. See Fig. 10. If resistance is 5 ohms or less, go to next step. If resistance is greater than 5 ohms, repair open in Light Green/Violet wire.

4) Measure resistance between ground and terminal No. 7 (Black/Light Blue wire) at low tire pressure module harness connector C927. If resistance is 5 ohms or less, go to next step. If resistance is greater than 5 ohms, repair open in Black/Light Blue wire.

5) Remove low tire pressure warning light bulb. Check bulb. If bulb is okay, go to next step. If bulb is not okay, replace bulb.

NOTE: Both low tire pressure bulb control circuits are Black/Yellow wires.

6) Measure resistance in both Black/Yellow wires between low tire pressure bulb harness connector and terminals No. 4 and 5 at low tire pressure module harness connector C927. If both resistance readings

are 5 ohms or less, replace low tire pressure module. If either resistance reading is greater than 5 ohms, repair open in appropriate Black/Yellow wire.

TEST AG: AIR BAG WARNING CHIME DOES NOT OPERATE PROPERLY

1) Turn ignition switch to LOCK position. Connect NGS tester to Data Link Connector (DLC). Retrieve and document Restraints Control Module (RCM) continuous DTCs. If no DTCs exists, go to next step. If any DTCs exist, repair restraint system concern. See DIAGNOSIS & TESTING in MITCHELL® AIR BAG SERVICE & REPAIR MANUAL, DOMESTIC & IMPORTED MODELS.

2) Ensure ignition switch is in LOCK position. Deactivate air bag system. See appropriate AIR BAG RESTRAINT SYSTEMS article. Disconnect Lighting Control Module (LCM) harness connector C206. Disconnect RCM harness connector C327. Turn ignition switch to RUN position. Measure voltage at terminal No. 10 (White/Red wire) at LCM harness connector C206. *See Fig. 4.* If voltage does not exist, go to next step. If voltage exists, repair short to voltage in White/Red wire.

3) Turn ignition switch to LOCK position. Measure resistance between ground and terminal No. 10 (White/Red wire) at LCM harness connector C206. If resistance is greater than 10 k/ohms, go to next step. If resistance is 10 k/ohms or less, repair short to ground in White/Red wire.

4) Measure resistance in White/Red wire between terminal No. 10 at LCM harness C206 and terminal No. 26 at RCM harness connector C327. *See Figs. 4 and 12.* If resistance is 5 ohms or less, replace LCM. If resistance is greater than 5 ohms, repair open in Red/White wire.

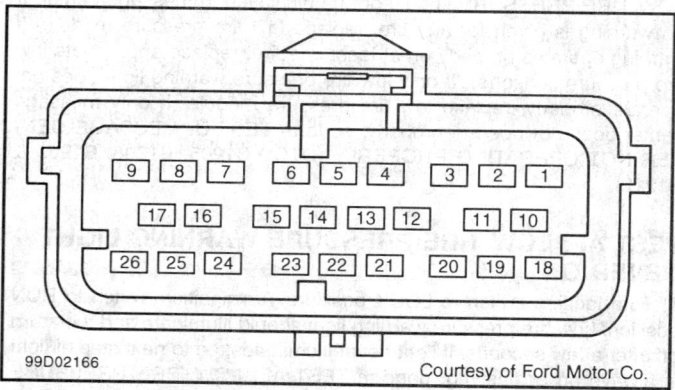

99D02166   Courtesy of Ford Motor Co.

Fig. 12: Identifying Restraints Control Module Harness Connector C327 Terminals

TEST AH: TRUNK LID AJAR CHIME DOES NOT OPERATE PROPERLY

Close trunk lid. Turn ignition switch to RUN position. If trunk lid ajar light is illuminated, replace LCM. If trunk lid ajar light is not illuminated, repair open in Brown/White wire.

TEST AI: TURN SIGNAL WARNING CHIME DOES NOT OPERATE PROPERLY

1) Turn ignition switch to RUN position. Operate turn signals. If turn signals operate properly, go to next step. If turn signals do not operate properly, repair turn signal concern. Perform TEST H: TURN SIGNAL/HAZARD LIGHTS NEVER/ALWAYS ON under SYSTEM TESTS in AUTOLAMP SYSTEMS – CONTINENTAL article.

2) Turn ignition switch to LOCK position. Connect NGS tester to Data Link Connector (DLC). Using NGS tester, retrieve and document Lighting Control Module DTCs. If DTC U1123 is not retrieved, replace LCM. If DTC U1123 is retrieved, repair anti-lock brake system concern. See appropriate ANTI-LOCK article in BRAKES in appropriate MITCH-ELL® manual.

TEST AJ: NO COMMUNICATION WITH DRIVER'S DOOR MODULE

NOTE: After any repairs are complete, ensure all component are properly installed and all harness connectors are connected properly and repeat data link diagnostic test.

NOTE: Connectors C315 and C362 are 2 terminal connectors. Identify connectors by wire color. See WIRING DIAGRAMS.

1) Connect NGS tester to Data Link Connector (DLC). Turn ignition switch to RUN position. Monitor Driver's Door Module (DDM) PIDs SFWD_SW, SREAR_SW, SFNT_SW and SRCL_SW while activating power seat control switch. If UNABLE TO PERFORM TEST FUNCTION MODULE NOT RESPONDING: DDM CHECK IGNITION STATUS/VERIFY CABLE REQUIREMENTS CHECK CABLE CONNECTIONS? is not displayed, go to next step. If UNABLE TO PERFORM TEST FUNCTION MODULE NOT RESPONDING: DDM CHECK IGNITION STATUS/VERIFY CABLE REQUIREMENTS CHECK CABLE CONNECTIONS? is displayed, perform TEST C: NO COMMUNICATION WITH LIGHTING CONTROL MODULE.

2) Turn ignition switch to LOCK position. Remove fuse No. 39 (10-amp) in instrument panel fuse box. Check fuse. If fuse is okay, go to next step. If fuse is blown, go to step **6)**.

3) Measure voltage at input side of fuse No. 39 in instrument panel fuse box. If battery voltage exists, go to next step. If battery voltage does not exist, go to step **24)**.

4) Install fuse No. 39. Disconnect Driver's Door Module (DDM) harness connector C524. Measure voltage at terminal No. 6 (Black/White wire) at DDM harness connector C524. *See Fig. 13.* If battery voltage exists, go to next step. If battery voltage does not exist, repair open in Black/White wire between instrument panel fuse box and DDM.

5) Measure resistance between ground and terminal No. 14 (Black/Light Blue wire) at DDM harness connector C524. If resistance is greater than 5 ohms, repair open in Black/Light Blue wire. If resistance is 5 ohms or less, repair module communication concern. See MODULE COMMUNICATIONS NETWORK – CONTINENTAL article.

6) Replace fuse No. 39. DO NOT operate any switches. If fuse blows, go to next step. If fuse does not blow, go to step **14)**.

7) Remove fuse No. 39. Disconnect DDM harness connector C524, Driver's Seat Module (DSM) harness connector C342, keyless entry keypad harness connector C525, driver's seat control switch harness connector C520, driver's door lock switch harness connector C505, passenger's door lock switch harness connector C602 and power mirror control switch harness connector C550. Measure resistance between ground and terminal No. 6 (Black/White wire) at DDM harness connector C524. If resistance is greater than 10 k/ohms, go to next step. If resistance is 10 k/ohms or less, repair short to ground in Black/White wire.

8) Connect keyless entry keypad harness connector C525. Measure resistance between ground and terminal No. 6 (Black/White wire) at DDM harness connector C524. If resistance is greater than 10 k/ohms, go to next step. If resistance is 10 k/ohms or less, replace keyless entry keypad.

9) Connect driver's seat control switch harness connector C520. Measure resistance between ground and terminal No. 6 (Black/White wire) at DDM harness connector C524. If resistance is greater than 10 k/ohms, go to next step. If resistance is 10 k/ohms or less, replace driver's seat control switch.

10) Connect DSM harness connector C342. Measure resistance between ground and terminal No. 6 (Black/White wire) at DDM harness connector C524. If resistance is greater than 10 k/ohms, go to next step. If resistance is 10 k/ohms or less, replace driver's seat module.

11) Connect DDM harness connector C524. Measure resistance between ground and terminal No. 6 (Black/White wire) at driver's door lock switch harness connector C505. *See Fig. 14.* If resistance is greater than 10 k/ohms, go to next step. If resistance is 10 k/ohms or less, replace driver's door module.

12) Connect passenger's door lock switch harness connector C602. Measure resistance between ground and terminal No. 6 (Black/White wire) at driver's door lock switch harness connector C505. If resistance is greater than 10 k/ohms, go to next step. If resistance is 10 k/ohms or less, replace passenger's door lock switch.

13) Connect power mirror control switch harness connector C550. Measure resistance between ground and terminal No. 6 (Black/White wire) at driver's door lock switch harness connector C505. If resistance is greater than 10 k/ohms, replace driver's door lock switch. If resistance is 10 k/ohms or less, replace power mirror control switch.

14) Lock and unlock doors at all door lock switches. If fuse No. 39 blows, go to next step. If fuse No. 39 does not blow, go to step **17**).

15) Remove driver's and passenger's door lock switches. Test both door lock switches. See DOOR LOCK SWITCH under COMPONENT TESTS in POWER MIRRORS – CONTINENTAL article. If both door lock switches are okay, go to next step. If either door lock switch is defective, replace appropriate door lock switch.

16) Disconnect Driver's Door Module (DDM) harness connector C506. Measure resistance between ground and terminal No. 1 (Pink/Yellow wire) at driver's door lock switch harness connector C505. Also, measure resistance between ground and terminal No. 5 (Pink/Light Green wire) at driver's door lock switch harness connector C505. *See Fig. 14.* If either resistance reading is 10 k/ohms or less, repair short to ground in appropriate wire(s). If both resistance readings are greater than 10 k/ohms, replace driver's door module.

17) Press each number on keyless entry pad one at a time. If fuse No. 39 blows, go to next step. If fuse No. 39 does not blow, go to step **19**).

18) Disconnect Driver's Door Module (DDM) harness connector C523. Disconnect keyless entry keypad harness connector C525. Measure resistance between ground and appropriate terminals at remote keyless entry keypad harness connector C525. See REMOTE KEYLESS ENTRY TERMINAL IDENTIFICATION table. *See Fig. 15.* If all resistance readings are greater than 10 k/ohms, replace driver's door module. If any resistance readings are 10 k/ohms or less, repair short to ground in appropriate wire.

REMOTE KEYLESS ENTRY TERMINAL IDENTIFICATION

Terminal	Wire Color
1	Red
2	Yellow
3	Yellow/Black
4	Light Green/Red
5	Light Blue/Yellow
9	Light Blue

19) Activate mirrors in all directions. If fuse No. 39 blows, go to next step. If fuse No. 39 does not blow, go to step **22**).

20) Remove mirror control switch. Test mirror control switch. See MIRROR CONTROL SWITCH under COMPONENT TESTS in POWER MIRRORS – CONTINENTAL article. If mirror control switch is okay, go to next step. If mirror control switch is defective, replace mirror control switch.

21) Disconnect Driver's Door Module (DDM) harness connector C506. Disconnect mirror control switch harness connector C550. Measure resistance between ground and appropriate terminals at mirror control switch harness connector C550. See MIRROR CONTROL SWITCH TERMINAL IDENTIFICATION table. *See Fig. 14.* If all resistance readings are greater than 10 k/ohms, replace driver's door module. If any resistance reading are 10 k/ohms or less, repair short to ground in appropriate wire.

MIRROR CONTROL SWITCH TERMINAL IDENTIFICATION

Terminal	Wire Color
3	Dark Blue/Orange
4	Red/Orange
6	Yellow/Black
7	Purple/Orange
8	Dark Green/Orange

22) Activate driver's seat control switch in all directions. If fuse No. 39 blows, go to next step. If fuse No. 39 does not blow, system is operating properly at this time.

23) Disconnect Driver's Door Module (DDM) harness connector C506. Disconnect driver's seat control switch harness connector C520. Measure resistance between ground and appropriate terminals at driver's seat control switch harness connector C520. See DRIVER'S SEAT CONTROL SWITCH TERMINAL IDENTIFICATION table. *See Fig. 16.* If all resistance readings are greater than 10 k/ohms, replace driver's door module. If any resistance readings are 10 k/ohms or less, repair short to ground in appropriate wire.

DRIVER'S SEAT CONTROL SWITCH TERMINAL IDENTIFICATION

Terminal	Wire Color
2	Red/White
3	Red/Light Green
4	Red/Light Blue
5	Gray
7	Yellow/White
8	Yellow/Light Green
9	Yellow/Light Blue
10	Gray/Black

24) Turn ignition switch to LOCK position. Remove fuse No. 1 (30-amp) in power distribution box. Check fuse. If fuse is okay, go to next step. If fuse is blown, go to step **26**).

25) Measure voltage at input side of fuse No. 1 in power distribution box. If battery voltage exists, repair open in Red wire between power distribution box and instrument panel fuse box. If battery voltage does not exist, repair or replace power distribution box as necessary.

26) Ensure fuse No. 1 in power distribution box is still removed. Disconnect Driver's Seat Module (DSM) harness connector C362. Disconnect driver's heated seat module harness connector C352. Disconnect driver's lumbar switch harness connector C348. Measure resistance between ground and terminal No. 1 (Red wire) at DSM harness connector C362. If resistance is greater than 10 k/ohms, go to next step. If resistance is 10 k/ohms or less, repair short to ground in Red wire.

27) Connect DSM harness connector C362. Measure resistance between ground and output side of fuse No. 1 in power distribution box. If resistance is greater than 10 k/ohms, go to next step. If resistance is 10 k/ohms or less, replace driver's seat module.

28) Replace fuse No. 1 (30-amp) in power distribution box. Connect driver's lumbar switch harness connector C348. Operate driver's lumbar switch in both directions. If fuse No. 1 blows, go to next step. If fuse No. 1 does not blow, go to step **32**).

29) Remove fuse No. 1 (30-amp) from power distribution box. Measure resistance between ground and output side of fuse No. 1 in power distribution box. If resistance is greater than 10 k/ohms, go to next step. If resistance is 10 k/ohms or less, replace driver's lumbar switch.

30) Disconnect driver's lumbar switch harness connector C348. Measure resistance between ground and terminal No. 4 (Pink wire) at driver's lumbar switch harness connector C348. Also, measure resistance between ground and terminal No. 2 (Brown wire) at driver's lumbar switch harness connector C348. *See Fig. 17.* If both resistance readings are greater than 10 k/ohms, go to next step. If either resistance reading is 10 k/ohms or less, replace driver's lumbar switch.

31) Disconnect driver's lumbar motor harness connector C315. Measure resistance between ground and terminal No. 4 (Pink wire) at driver's lumbar switch harness connector C348. Also, measure resistance between ground and terminal No. 2 (Brown wire) at driver's lumbar switch harness connector C348. If both resistance readings are greater than 10 k/ohms, replace power lumbar motor. If either resistance reading is 10 k/ohms or less, repair short to ground in appropriate wire.

32) Disconnect driver's heated seat module harness connector C352. Measure resistance between ground and appropriate terminals at driver's heated seat module harness connector C352. See HEATED SEAT MODULE CONNECTOR TERMINAL IDENTIFICATION table. *See Fig. 13.* If all resistance readings are greater than 10 k/ohms, replace driver's heated seat module. If any resistance readings are 10 k/ohms or less, repair short to ground in appropriate wire.

HEATED SEAT MODULE CONNECTOR TERMINAL IDENTIFICATION

Terminal	Wire Color
5	Black/Light Blue
6	Brown/Light Blue
8	Yellow/Light Blue
9	Gray/Light Blue
10	Red/Light Blue
11	Orange/Light Blue
12	Purple/Light Blue
13	White/Light Blue

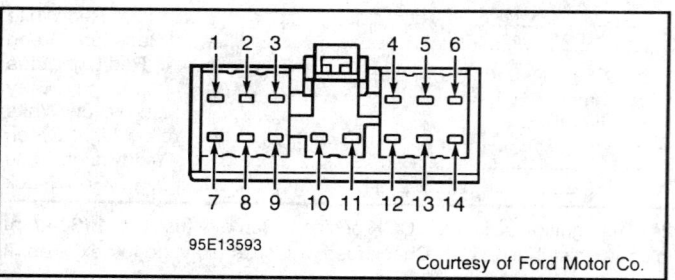

Fig. 13: Identifying Driver's Door Module Harness Connector C524 & Driver's Heated Seat Module Harness Connector C352 Terminals

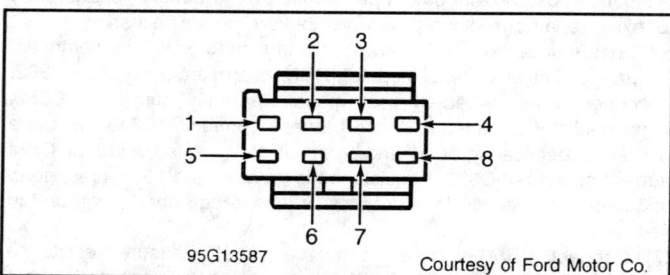

Fig. 14: Identifying Driver's Door Lock Switch Harness Connector C505 & Mirror Control Switch Harness Connector C550 Terminals

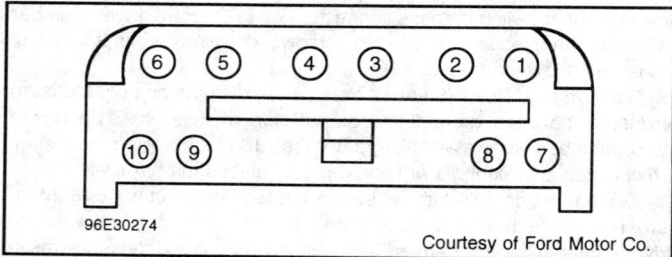

Fig. 15: Identifying Remote Keyless Entry Keypad Harness Connector C525 Terminals

TEST AK: DASH ILLUMINATION CONTROL INOPERATIVE

1) Place gear selector in Park. Ensure dimmer switch is not stuck in up or down position. Connect NGS tester to Data Link Connector (DLC). Using NGS tester, retrieve and document continuous DTCs. Clear DTCs. Perform Lighting Control Module (LCM) self-test. If neither DTC B1582 or B1586 are retrieved, go to next step. If DTC B1582 or B1586 is retrieved, replace LCM.

2) Remove fuse No. 1 (10-amp) in instrument panel fuse box. Check fuse. If fuse is okay, go to next step. If fuse is blown, go to step **5)**.

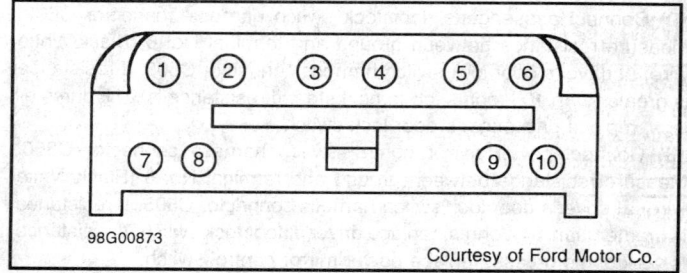

Fig. 16: Identifying Driver's Seat Control Switch Harness Connector C520 Terminals

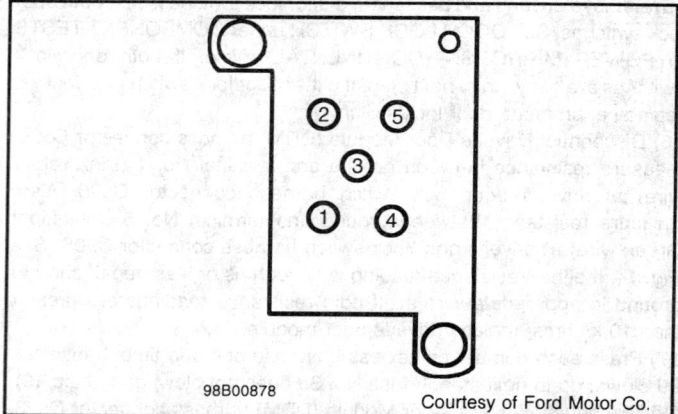

Fig. 17: Identifying Driver's Lumbar Switch Harness Connector C348 Terminals

3) Measure voltage at input side of fuse No. 1 in instrument panel fuse box. If battery voltage exists, go to next step. If battery voltage does not exist, repair open in Tan wire between instrument panel fuse box and power distribution box.

4) Install fuse No. 1 in instrument panel fuse box. Turn ignition switch to LOCK position. Disconnect LCM harness connector C207. Measure voltage at terminal No. 16 (Gray/Light Blue wire) at LCM harness connector C207. *See Fig. 6.* If battery voltage exists, go to step **7)**. If battery voltage does not exist, repair open in Gray/Light Blue wire.

5) Ensure fuse No. 1 in instrument panel fuse box is still removed. Turn ignition switch to LOCK position. Disconnect LCM harness connector C207. Measure resistance between ground and terminal No. 16 (Gray/Light Blue wire) at LCM harness connector C207. *See Fig. 6.* If resistance is greater than 10 k/ohms, go to next step. If resistance is 10 k/ohms or less, repair short to ground in Gray/Light Blue wire.

6) Check for short to ground in Light Blue/Red wire between terminal No. 2 at LCM harness connector C207 and the following lights: ashtray, electronic day/night mirror, remote emergency satellite cellular unit console, heated seat switch assembly, clockspring harness connector C2012, clock, message center switch, electronic automatic temperature control module, console shift illumination, console cigarette lighter and instrument panel cigarette lighter. See appropriate wiring diagram in ILLUMINATION/INTERIOR LIGHTS article. If short exists, repair as necessary. If short does not exist, check listed components for internal shorts and repair as necessary. If components are okay, replace LCM.

7) Using a fused jumper wire, connect terminals No. 16 and No. 2 at LCM harness connector C207. If dash lights illuminate, replace LCM. If dash lights do not illuminate, repair open in Light Blue/Red wire.

REMOVAL & INSTALLATION

WARNING: Vehicle is equipped with an air bag system. To prevent air bag deployment, system must be disabled before working near steering column and instrument cluster. See appropriate AIR BAG RESTRAINT SYSTEMS article.

CAUTION: When battery is disconnected or modules are replaced, vehicle computer and memory systems may lose memory data. Driveability problems may exist until computer systems have completed a relearn cycle. See COMPUTER RELEARN PROCEDURES article in GENERAL INFORMATION before disconnecting battery.

INSTRUMENT CLUSTER

Removal & Installation – 1) Position vehicle on level surface to prevent movement when transmission selector is out of Park. Set parking brake. Disable air bag system. See appropriate AIR BAG RESTRAINT SYSTEMS article. Unlock ignition switch. Set shift lever to Low (column shift only).

2) Using Radio Remover (T87P-19061-A), remove radio front control unit. Remove instrument panel lower cover. Unsnap and remove panel center woodgrain strips. Remove steering column cover.

3) Remove instrument panel brace. Disconnect shift indicator cable (column shift only). Lower steering column. Protect upper bowl of steering column trim. Tilt steering column downward as far as possible.

4) Remove instrument cluster finish panel. Remove instrument cluster retaining screws. Pull left side of instrument cluster outward enough to unplug harness connectors.

5) On 6-passenger models with console shift, disconnect transmission range indicator. On all models, remove instrument cluster. To install, reverse removal procedure. Activate air bag system. See appropriate AIR BAG RESTRAINT SYSTEMS article.

WIRING DIAGRAMS

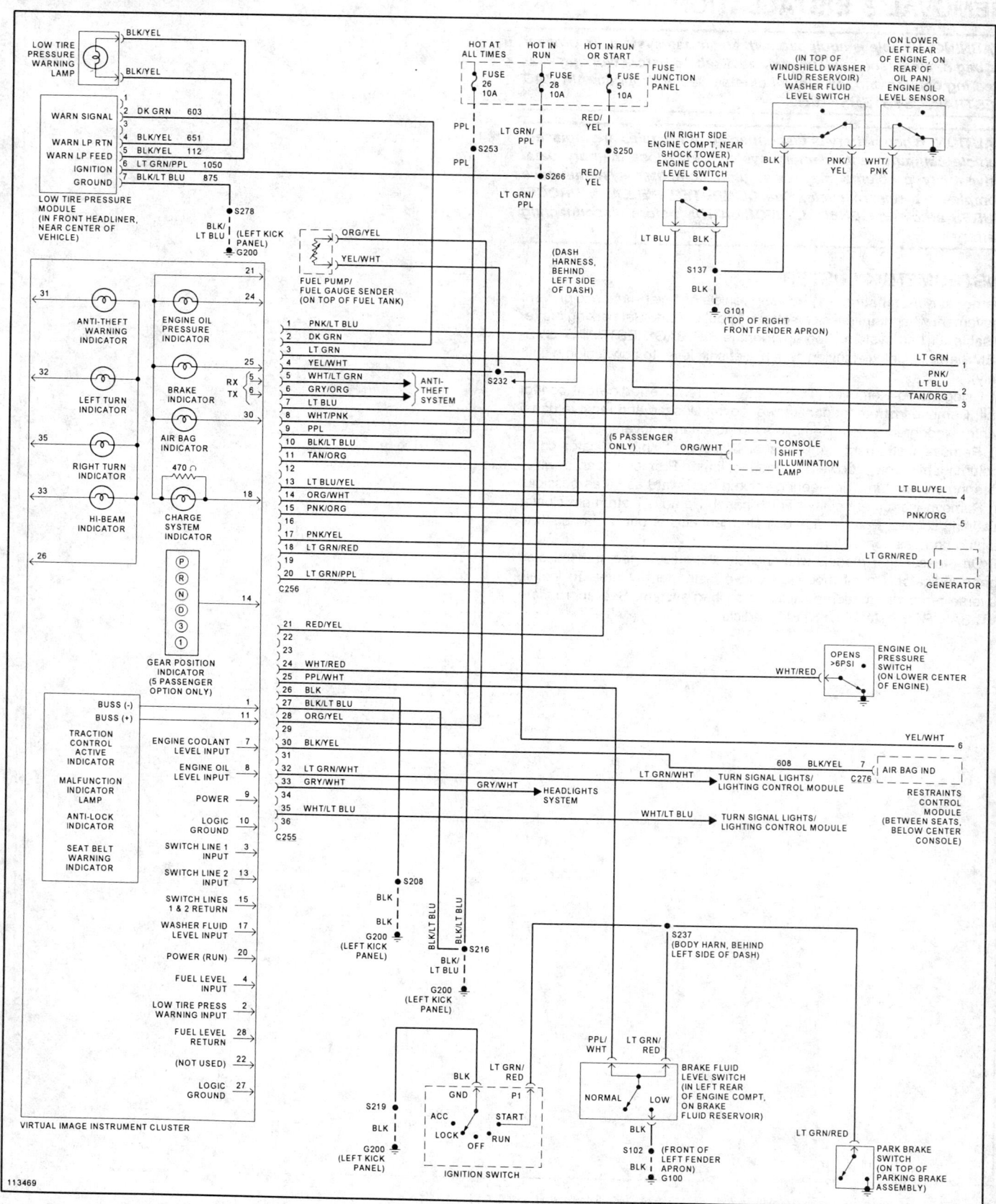

Fig. 18: Analog Instrument Panel Wiring Diagram (Continental – 1 Of 2)

113469

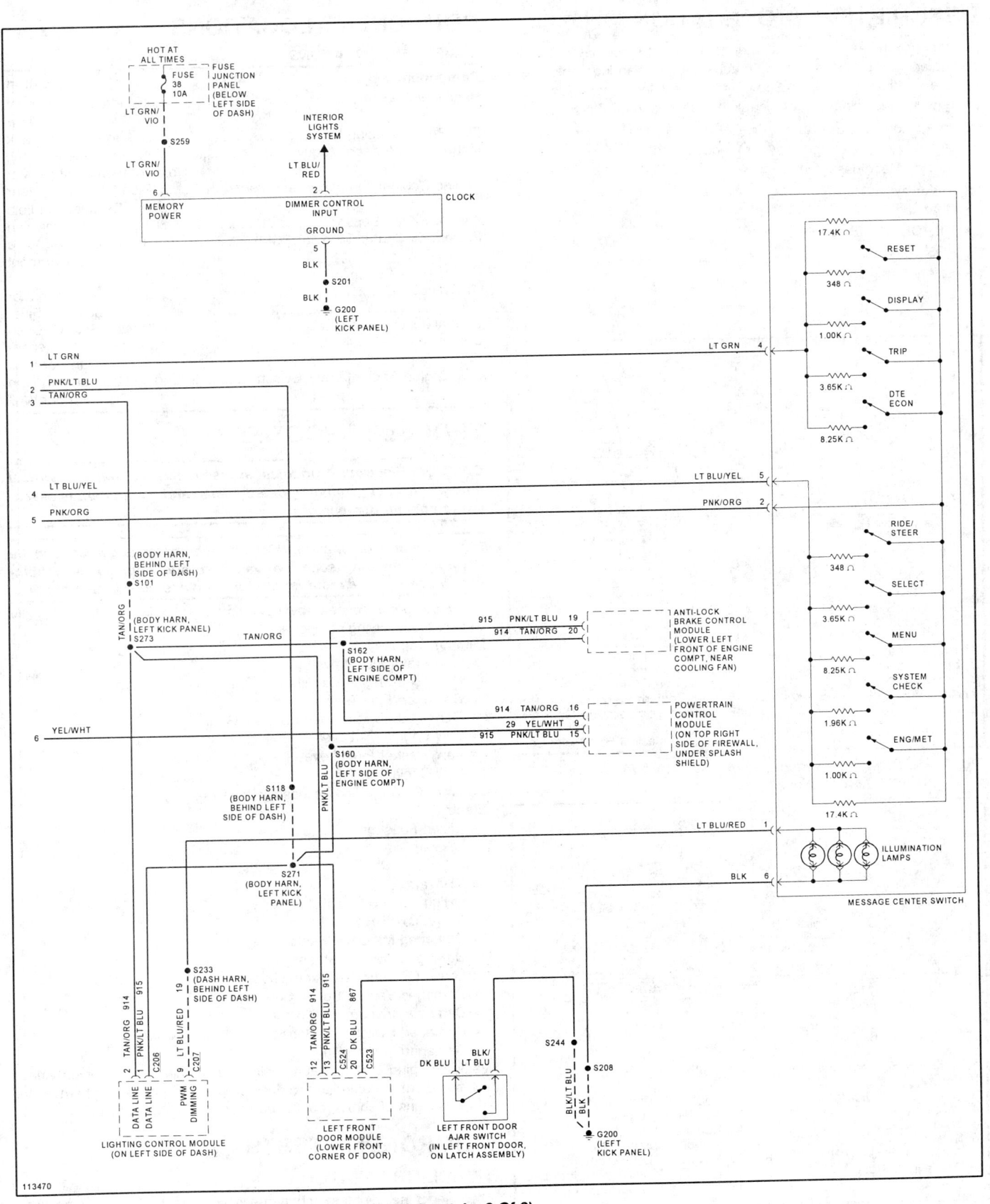

Fig. 19: Analog Instrument Panel Wiring Diagram (Continental – 2 Of 2)

113470

DESCRIPTION & OPERATION

Instrument cluster contains a speedometer with odometer and trip odometer, fuel gauge and temperature gauge. Warning lights are in various locations on cluster. *See Figs. 1 and 2.* Instrument cluster and panel will not illuminate when headlight switch is in OFF position.

When ignition switch is turned to ON position, the following warning indicators will light momentarily for function proof:

- Air Bag Readiness
- Brake System
- Charging System
- MIL (CHECK ENGINE)
- ABS
- Safety Belt
- Overdrive OFF
- Oil Pressure Warning

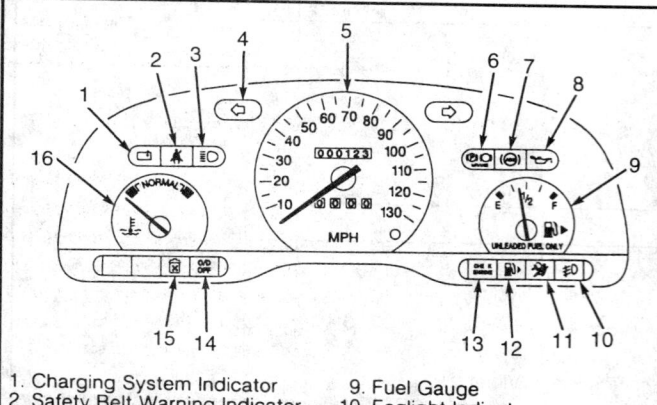

1. Charging System Indicator
2. Safety Belt Warning Indicator
3. High Beam Indicator
4. Turn Indicator
5. Speedometer
6. Brake Indicator
7. Anti-Lock Brake (ABS) Indicator
8. Oil Pressure Gauge
9. Fuel Gauge
10. Foglight Indicator
11. Air Bag Indicator
12. Low Fuel Indicator
13. Check Engine Light
14. Overdrive Off Indicator
15. Low Coolant Warning Indicator
16. Coolant Temperature Gauge

98E00509

Courtesy of Ford Motor Co.

Fig. 1: Identifying Instrument Cluster Gauges & Indicators – Without Tachometer

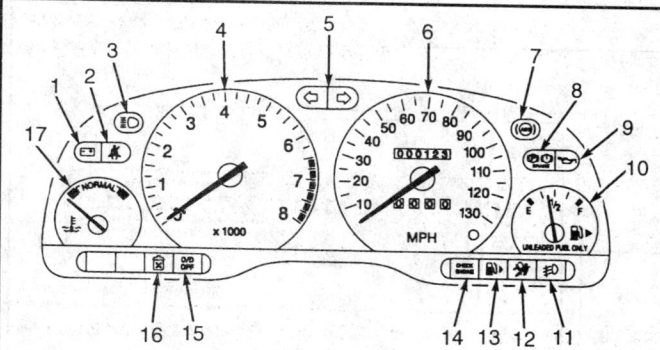

1. Charging System Indicator
2. Safety Belt Warning Indicator
3. High Beam Indicator
4. Tachometer
5. Turn Indicators
6. Speedometer
7. Anti-Lock Brake (ABS) Indicator
8. Brake Indicator
9. Oil Pressure Gauge
10. Fuel Gauge
11. Foglight Indicator
12. Air Bag Indicator
13. Low Fuel Indicator
14. Check Engine Light
15. Overdrive Off Indicator
16. Low Coolant Warning Indicator
17. Coolant Temperature Gauge

98H00510

Courtesy of Ford Motor Co.

Fig. 2: Identifying Instrument Cluster Gauges & Indicators – With Tachometer

COMPONENT LOCATIONS

COMPONENT LOCATIONS

Component	Location
Headlight Switch	Left Side Of Instrument Panel
Fuel Pump Sending Unit	Top Of Fuel Tank
Instrument Interface Module	Behind Instrument Panel, Next To Instrument Cluster
Engine Coolant Temperature Sensor	Side Of Engine, Near Exhaust Manifold
Vehicle Speed Sensor	On Transmission
Powertrain Control Module (PCM)	Right Rear Of Engine Compartment
Oil Pressure Switch	
4 Cylinder	Above Generator
V6	Above Oil Filter
Central Junction Box	Under Left Side Of Dash
Central Timer Module (CTM)	On Back Of Central Junction Box
Low Engine Coolant Level Switch	In Engine Compartment, On Right Fender Well

TROUBLE SHOOTING

CAUTION: Electronic modules are sensitive to static electrical charges. Proper grounding of technician and component is essential to prevent damage.

NOTE: Testing of speedometer or tachometer accuracy can be done by comparing scan tool values to speedometer or tachometer. If scan tool readout is different, replace appropriate meter.

Verify customer concern by operating system in question. Visually inspect the following components:

Mechanical:
- Low Brake Fluid Level
- Damaged Engine Oil Filter
- Damaged Fuel Tank
- Damaged Vehicle Speed Sensor Gear
- Low Engine Oil Level
- Low Washer Fluid Level
- Low Coolant Level
- Worn Or Damaged Accessory Drive Belt

Electrical:
- Blown Fuse(s):
  Relay Feed
  Turn
  Hazard
  High/Low LH Headlights
  High/Low RH Headlights
- Damaged Miniature Bulbs
- Damaged Wiring Harness
- Loose Or Corroded Connections
- Damaged Vehicle Speed Sensor
- Damaged Instrument Cluster
- Damaged Switches & Sensors
- Damaged Ignition Relay

Verify charging system, safety belt warning chime, turn signals, headlights and cruise control are working properly. Inspect wiring harness for obvious signs of shorts, opens, bad connections or damage.

COMPONENT TESTS

HEADLIGHT SWITCH

Disconnect headlight switch harness connector. Continuity between terminals should be as specified with switch in specified position. See HEADLIGHT SWITCH CONTINUITY table. *See Fig. 3.* If resistance is not as specified, or is poor in any switch position, replace headlight switch.

HEADLIGHT SWITCH CONTINUITY

Terminals	Switch Position	Normal Condition
Headlight Circuit		
11 & 12	Off	No Continuity
11 & 12	Park	No Continuity
11 & 12	Head	Continuity
Licence Plate Light Circuit		
14 & 15	Off	No Continuity
14 & 15	Park	Continuity
14 & 15	Head	Continuity
Left Parking Light Circuit		
2 & 15	Off	No Continuity
2 & 15	Park	Continuity
2 & 15	Head	Continuity
Right Parking Light Circuit		
13 & 15	Off	No Continuity
13 & 15	Park	Continuity
13 & 15	Head	Continuity
Fog Light Circuit		
8 & 10	Off	No Continuity
8 & 10	On	Continuity

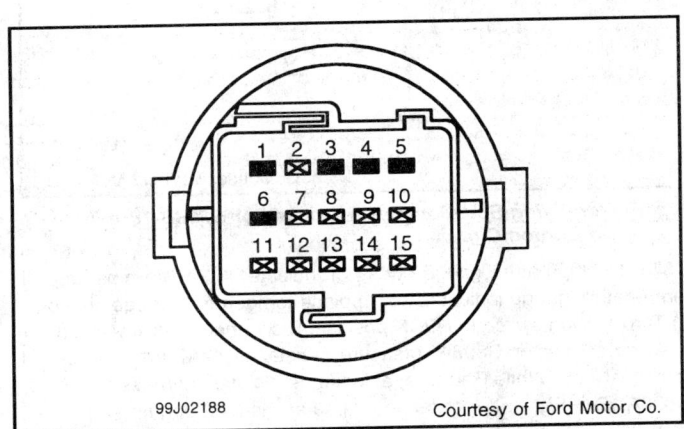

Fig. 3: Identifying Headlight Switch Terminals

99J02188   Courtesy of Ford Motor Co.

SYSTEM TESTS

SYMPTOM CHART

Symptom	Test
Warning Lights & Gauges Inoperative	A
Fuel Gauge Reads Inaccurately	B
Temperature Gauge Inaccurate	C
Tachometer Inoperative	D
Oil Pressure Warning Inoperative	E
Oil Pressure Warning Always On	F
Seat Belt Warning Indicator Inoperative (Chime Operative)	G
Seat Belt Warning Indicator Always On (Chime Operative)	H
Brake Warning Inoperative	I
Low Fuel Indicator Inoperative	J
Low Fuel Indicator Always On	K
Low Coolant Indicator Inoperative	L
Low Coolant Indicator Always On	M
Speedometer Inoperative	N
Odometer Inoperative	O
Speedometer Inaccurate	P
Tachometer Inaccurate	Q
High Beam Indicator Inoperative	R
Turn Indicator Inoperative	S
Charge Warning Never On	T
Check Engine Light Inoperative	U
Check Engine Light Always On	V
ABS Light Inoperative	W

TEST A: WARNING LIGHTS & GAUGES INOPERATIVE

1) Turn ignition switch to LOCK position. Remove fuse No. 30 (7.5-amp) from central junction box. Check fuse. If fuse is blown, replace fuse and retest. If fuse is okay, go to next step. If fuse blows again, go to step **4)**.

2) Disconnect instrument cluster harness connector C808A. Turn ignition switch to RUN position. Measure voltage at terminal No. 14 (Violet wire) at instrument cluster harness connector C808A. *See Fig. 4*. If battery voltage exists, go to next step. If battery voltage does not exist, repair open in Violet wire.

3) Turn ignition switch to LOCK position. Disconnect instrument cluster harness connector C808B. Measure resistance between ground and terminal No. 4 (Black wire) at instrument cluster harness connector C808A. Measure resistance between terminal No. 7 (Black/Yellow wire) at instrument cluster harness connector C808B. *See Fig. 5*. If both resistance readings are 5 ohms or less, replace instrument cluster printed circuit. If either resistance reading is greater than 5 ohms, repair open in Black or Black/Yellow wire.

4) Ensure fuse No. 30 is still removed. Measure resistance between terminal No. 14 (Violet wire) and No. 4 (Black wire) at instrument cluster harness connector C808A. If resistance is greater than 10 k/ohms, replace instrument cluster printed circuit. If resistance is 10 k/ohms or less, repair short to ground in Violet wire.

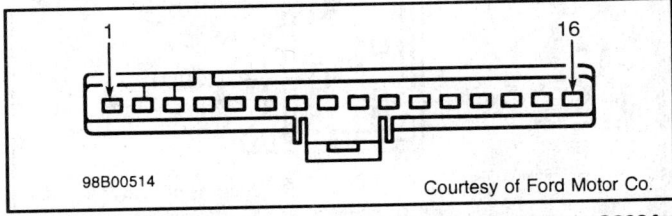

98B00514   Courtesy of Ford Motor Co.

Fig. 4: Identifying Instrument Cluster Harness Connector C808A Terminals

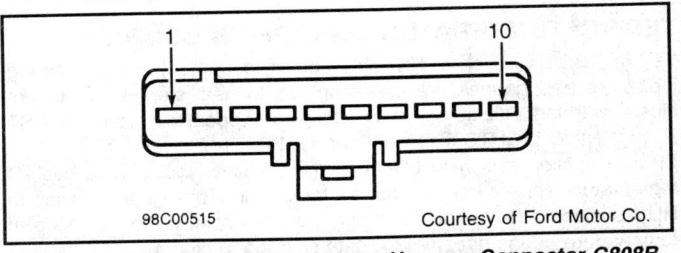

98C00515   Courtesy of Ford Motor Co.

Fig. 5: Identifying Instrument Cluster Harness Connector C808B Terminals

TEST B: FUEL GAUGE READS INACCURATELY

1) Turn ignition switch to RUN position. If instrument cluster warning indicators and gauges are not operating, perform TEST A: WARNING LIGHTS & GAUGES INOPERATIVE. If instrument cluster warning indicators and gauges are operating, go to next step.

2) Turn ignition switch to LOCK position. Disconnect fuel pump sending unit harness connector C732. Turn ignition switch to RUN position. If fuel gauge indicates full, go to next step. If fuel gauge does not indicate full, go to step **4)**.

3) Turn ignition switch to LOCK position. Using a jumper wire, ground terminal No. 5 (White/Red wire) at fuel pump sending unit harness connector terminal C732. See Fig. 6. If fuel gauge does not indicate empty, go to step **8)**. If fuel gauge indicates empty, replace fuel pump sending unit.

4) Turn ignition switch to LOCK position. Disconnect instrument cluster harness connector C808B. Measure resistance between ground and terminal No. 7 (White/Red wire) at instrument cluster harness connector C808B. See Fig. 5. If resistance is greater than 10 k/ohms, go to next step. If resistance is less than 10 k/ohms, repair short to ground in White/Red wire.

5) Disconnect remaining instrument cluster harness connectors. Remove instrument cluster. Measure resistance between terminal No. 7 at instrument cluster connector C808B (component side) and fuel gauge terminal F3 on printed circuit. See Fig. 7. If resistance is 5 ohms or less, go to next step. If resistance is greater than 5 ohms, replace printed circuit.

6) Measure resistance between terminal No. 4 at instrument cluster connector C808B (component side) and fuel gauge terminal F2 on printed circuit. If resistance is 5 ohms or less, go to next step. If resistance is greater than 5 ohms, replace printed circuit.

7) Measure resistance between speedometer terminal S2 on printed circuit and fuel gauge terminal F1 on printed circuit. See Fig. 8. If resistance is 5 ohms or less, replace instrument cluster or fuel gauge as necessary. If resistance is greater than 5 ohms, replace printed circuit.

8) Turn ignition switch to LOCK position. Measure resistance in White/Red wire between terminal No. 7 at instrument cluster harness connector C808B and terminal No. 5 at fuel pump sending unit harness connector C732. See Figs. 5 and 6. If resistance is 5 ohms or less, check Black/Blue wire between fuel pump sending unit harness connector terminal No. 4 and ground for an open and repair as necessary. If Black/Blue wire is okay, replace instrument cluster. If resistance is 5 ohms or more, repair open White/Red wire.

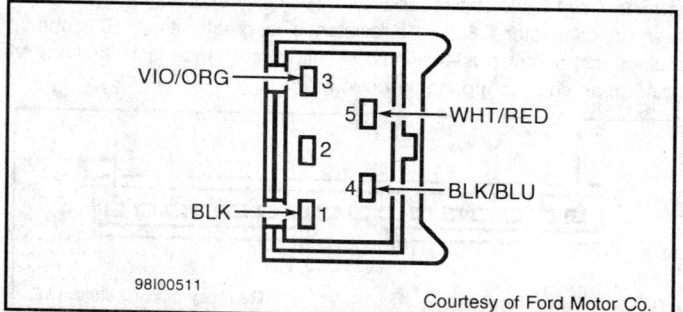

Fig. 6: Identifying Fuel Sending Unit Harness Connector C732 Terminals

TEST C: TEMPERATURE GAUGE INACCURATE

1) Turn ignition switch to RUN position. If instrument cluster warning indicators and gauges are operating, go to next step. If instrument cluster warning indicators and gauges are not operating, perform TEST A: WARNING LIGHTS & GAUGES INOPERATIVE.

2) Turn ignition switch to LOCK position. Disconnect engine coolant temperature sensor harness connector C1886. Turn ignition switch to RUN position. If temperature gauge indicates cold, go to next step. If temperature gauge does not indicate cold, go to step **4)**.

3) Turn ignition switch to LOCK position. Using a jumper wire, ground White/Red wire terminal at temperature sensor harness connector

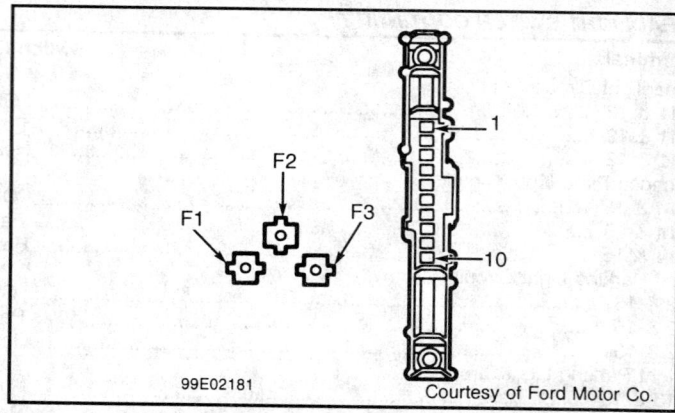

Fig. 7: Identifying Fuel Gauge & Connector C808B Terminals On Printed Circuit

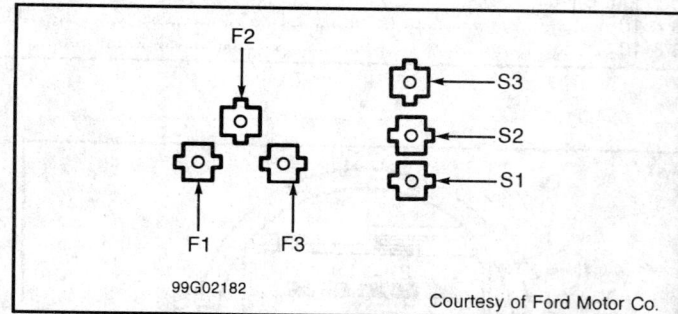

Fig. 8: Identifying Speedometer & Connector C808B Terminals On Printed Circuit

C845. If temperature gauge does not indicate hot, go to next step. If temperature gauge indicates hot, replace temperature gauge sensor.

4) Turn ignition switch to LOCK position. Disconnect instrument cluster harness connector C808A. Measure resistance between ground and terminal No. 6 (White/Red wire) at instrument cluster harness connector C808A. See Fig. 4. If resistance is greater than 10 k/ohms, go to next step. If resistance is less than 10 k/ohms, repair short to ground in White/Red wire.

5) Turn ignition switch to LOCK position. Measure resistance in White/Red wire between terminal No. 6 at instrument cluster harness connector C808A and temperature gauge sending unit harness connector C845. If resistance is 5 ohms or less, go to next step. If resistance is greater than 5 ohms, repair open White/Red wire.

6) Disconnect remaining instrument cluster harness connectors. Remove instrument cluster. Measure resistance between terminal No. 6 at instrument cluster connector C808A (component side) and temperature gauge terminal C1 on printed circuit. See Fig. 9. If resistance is 5 ohms or less, go to next step. If resistance is greater than 5 ohms, replace printed circuit.

7) Measure resistance between terminal No. 9 at instrument cluster connector C808A (component side) and temperature gauge terminal C3 on printed circuit. If resistance is 5 ohms or less, go to next step. If resistance is greater than 5 ohms, replace printed circuit.

8) Measure resistance between terminal No. 13 at instrument cluster connector C808A (component side) and temperature gauge terminal C2 on printed circuit. If resistance is 5 ohms or less, replace temperature gauge or instrument cluster as necessary. If resistance is greater than 5 ohms, replace printed circuit.

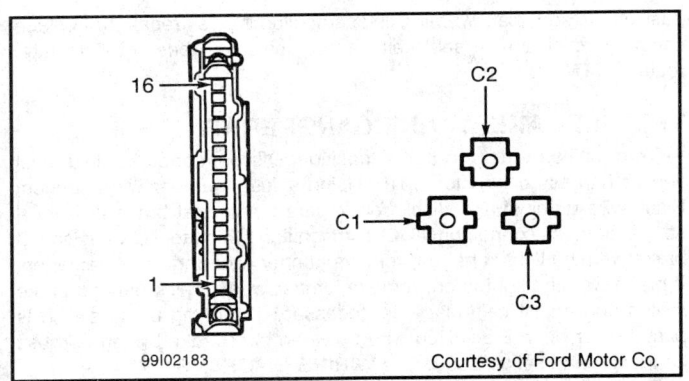

99I02183

Courtesy of Ford Motor Co.

Fig. 9: Identifying Temperature Gauge & Connector C808A Terminals On Printed Circuit

TEST D: TACHOMETER INOPERATIVE

NOTE: If PCM is replaced, PCM MUST be programmed. If vehicle is equipped with passive anti-theft system, all ignition keys MUST be programmed into PCM. See Appropriate Computer Relearn Procedures in GENERAL INFORMATION.

1) Turn ignition switch to RUN position. If instrument cluster warning indicators and gauges are operating, go to next step. If instrument cluster warning indicators and gauges are not operating, perform TEST A: WARNING LIGHTS & GAUGES INOPERATIVE.

2) Turn ignition switch to LOCK position. Disconnect instrument cluster harness connector C808A. Turn ignition switch to RUN position. Using external tachometer, measure RPM between ground and terminal No. 8 (White/Black wire) at instrument cluster harness connector C808A. *See Fig. 4.* If external tachometer shows engine RPM, go to next step. If external tachometer does not show engine RPM, go to step **6**).

3) Disconnect remaining instrument cluster harness connectors. Remove instrument cluster. Measure resistance between terminal No. 13 at instrument cluster connector C808A (component side) and tachometer terminal T1 on printed circuit. *See Fig. 10.* If resistance is 5 ohms or less, go to next step. If resistance is greater than 5 ohms, replace printed circuit.

4) Measure resistance between terminal No. 8 at instrument cluster connector C808A (component side) and tachometer terminal T3 on printed circuit. If resistance is 5 ohms or less, go to next step. If resistance is greater than 5 ohms, replace printed circuit.

5) Measure resistance between terminal No. 9 at instrument cluster connector C808A (component side) and tachometer terminal T2 on printed circuit. If resistance is 5 ohms or less, replace tachometer or instrument cluster as necessary. If resistance is greater than 5 ohms, replace printed circuit.

6) Disconnect Powertrain Control Module (PCM) harness connector C421. PCM is located at right rear of engine compartment. Install EEC-V 104-Pin Breakout Box (014-00950) following manufacturer's instructions to PCM harness connector C421. Measure resistance between terminal No. 8 (White/Black wire) at instrument cluster harness connector C808A and terminal No. 48 at breakout box. *See Fig. 4.* If resistance is 5 ohms or less, go to next step. If resistance is greater than 5 ohms, repair open in White/Black wire.

7) Measure resistance between terminals No. 48 and 24 at breakout box. If resistance is greater than 10 k/ohms, go to next step. If resistance is 10 k/ohms or less, repair short to ground in White/Black wire.

8) Turn ignition switch to RUN position. Measure voltage between terminals No. 48 and 97 at breakout box. If voltage is one volt or less, replace PCM. If voltage is greater than one volt, repair short to voltage in White/Black wire.

TEST E: OIL PRESSURE WARNING INOPERATIVE

1) Turn ignition switch to RUN position. If instrument cluster warning indicators and gauges are operating, go to next step. If instrument cluster warning indicators and gauges are not operating, perform TEST A: WARNING LIGHTS & GAUGES INOPERATIVE.

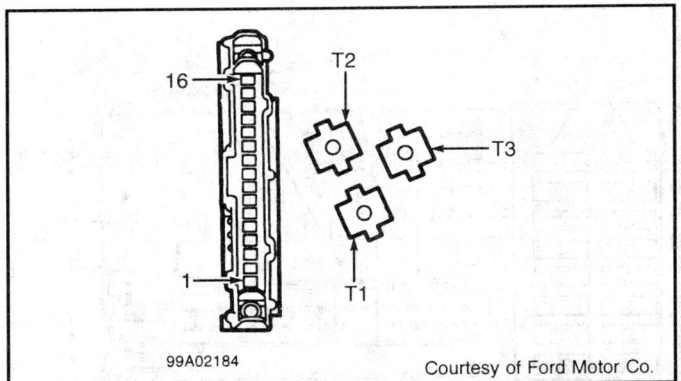

99A02184

Courtesy of Ford Motor Co.

Fig. 10: Identifying Tachometer & Connector C808A Terminals On Printed Circuit

2) Turn ignition switch to LOCK position. Disconnect oil pressure switch harness connector C953. Turn ignition switch to RUN position. Measure voltage at Black/Green wire terminal at oil pressure switch harness connector C953. If battery voltage does not exist, go to next step. If battery voltage exists, replace oil pressure switch.

3) Turn ignition switch to LOCK position. Disconnect instrument cluster harness connector C808B. Measure resistance in Black/Green wire between oil pressure switch harness connector C953 and terminal No. 1 at instrument cluster harness connector C808B. If resistance is 5 ohms or less, check oil pressure indicator bulb and replace as necessary. If bulb is okay, replace instrument cluster printed circuit. If resistance is greater than 5 ohms, repair open in Black/Green wire.

TEST F: OIL PRESSURE WARNING ALWAYS ON

1) Turn ignition switch to LOCK position. Disconnect oil pressure switch harness connector C953. Turn ignition switch to RUN position. If instrument cluster oil pressure warning indicator is on, go to next step. If instrument cluster oil pressure warning indicator is off, verify oil pressure with mechanical gauge. If oil pressure is okay, replace oil pressure switch.

2) Turn ignition switch to LOCK position. Disconnect instrument cluster harness connector C808B. Measure resistance between ground and Black/Green wire terminal at oil pressure switch harness connector C953. If resistance is greater than 10 k/ohms, replace instrument cluster printed circuit. If resistance is 10 k/ohms or less, repair short to ground in Black/Green wire.

TEST G: SEAT BELT WARNING INDICATOR INOPERATIVE (CHIME OPERATIVE)

1) Turn ignition switch to LOCK position. Disconnect central junction box harness connector C362. *See Fig. 11 .* Turn ignition switch to RUN position. Using a fused jumper wire, ground terminal No. 1 (Black/Blue wire) at central junction box harness connector C362. If seat belt warning indicator is no on, go to next step. If seat belt warning indicator is on, go to step **3**).

2) Turn ignition switch to LOCK position. Disconnect instrument cluster harness connector C808A. Measure resistance in Black/Blue wire between terminal No. 1 at central junction box harness connector C362 and terminal No. 11 at instrument cluster harness connector C808A. *See Fig. 4.* If resistance is 5 ohms or less, check seat belt warning indicator bulb in cluster and replace as necessary. If bulb is okay, replace instrument cluster printed circuit. If resistance is greater than 5 ohms, repair open in Black/Blue wire.

3) Turn ignition switch to LOCK position. Disconnect Central Timer Module (CTM) from rear of central junction box. Measure resistance between terminal No. 10 at central timer module connector (fuse box side) and terminal No. 1 at central junction box connector C362 (fuse box side). *See Fig. 11.* If resistance is 5 ohms or less, replace CTM. If resistance is greater than 5 ohms, replace central junction box.

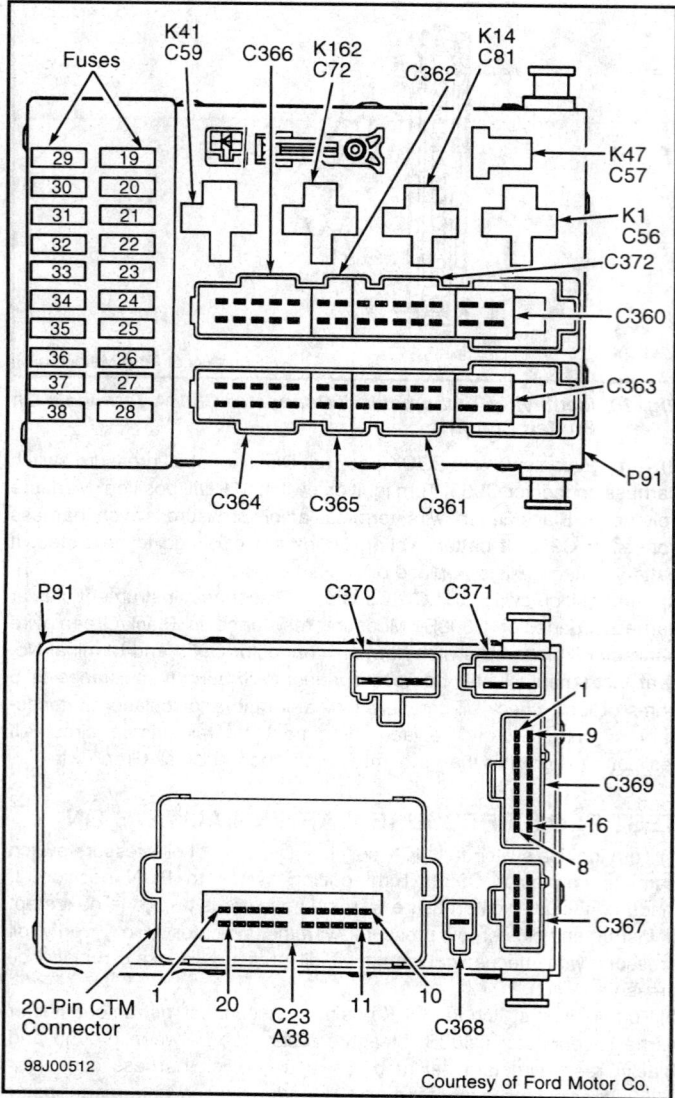

Fig. 11: Identifying Central Junction Box Fuses & Harness Connectors

TEST H: SEAT BELT WARNING INDICATOR ALWAYS ON (CHIME OPERATIVE)

1) Turn ignition switch to RUN position. Ensure seat belt is buckled. If seat belt chime is off and seat belt warning indicator is illuminated, go to next step. If seat belt chime is on and seat belt warning indicator is illuminated, repair chime module circuit. See appropriate wiring diagram in WARNING SYSTEMS article. If seat belt chime is off and seat belt warning indicator is not illuminated, system is okay.

2) Turn ignition switch to LOCK position. Disconnect central junction box harness connector C362. *See Fig. 11 .* Turn ignition switch to RUN position. If seat belt warning indicator does not illuminate, go to next step. If seat belt warning indicator illuminates, go to step **4)**.

3) Turn ignition switch to LOCK position. Disconnect instrument cluster harness connector C808A. Measure resistance between ground and terminal No. 11 (Black/Blue wire) at instrument cluster harness connector C808A. *See Fig. 4.* If resistance is greater than 10 k/ohms, replace instrument cluster printed circuit. If resistance is 10 k/ohms or less, repair short to ground in Black/Blue wire.

4) Turn ignition switch to LOCK position. Connect central junction box harness connector C362. Remove Central Timer Module (CTM) from back of central junction box. *See Fig. 11.* Turn ignition switch to RUN

position. If seat belt warning indicator illuminates, repair or replace central junction box. If seat belt warning indicator does not illuminate, replace CTM.

TEST I: BRAKE WARNING INOPERATIVE

1) Turn ignition switch to LOCK position. Disconnect brake fluid level sensor harness connector C810. Using a fused jumper wire, connect Black wire terminal and Black/Yellow wire terminal at brake fluid level sensor harness connector C810. Turn ignition switch to RUN position. If brake warning light is not on, remove jumper wire and go to next step. If brake warning light is on, remove jumper wire. Check parking brake switch and adjust or replace as necessary. If parking brake switch is okay, repair open Black/Red wire between park brake switch harness connector and splice S308. See WIRING DIAGRAMS.

2) Turn ignition switch to LOCK position. Measure resistance between ground and Black wire terminal at brake fluid level sensor harness connector C810. If resistance is 5 ohms or less, go to next step. If resistance is greater than 5 ohms, repair open Black wire.

3) Turn ignition switch to LOCK position. Disconnect instrument cluster harness connector C808B. Measure resistance in Black/Yellow wire between terminal No. 3 at instrument cluster harness connector C808B and brake fluid level sensor harness connector C810. *See Fig. 5.* If resistance is 5 ohms or less, inspect brake warning bulb and replace as necessary. If bulb is okay, replace instrument cluster printed circuit. If resistance is greater than 5 ohms, repair open in Black/Yellow wire.

TEST J: LOW FUEL INDICATOR INOPERATIVE

Turn ignition switch to LOCK position. Disconnect fuel pump sending unit harness connector C732. Turn ignition switch to RUN position. If low fuel indicator go on, system is okay at this time. If low fuel indicator is illuminated and fuel gauge is not operating properly, perform TEST B: FUEL GAUGE READS INACCURATELY test. If low fuel indicator is not illuminated, check LED. If LED is okay, replace instrument cluster.

TEST K: LOW FUEL INDICATOR ALWAYS ON

Turn ignition switch to LOCK position. Disconnect fuel pump sending unit harness connector C732. Turn ignition switch to RUN position. Connect jumper wire between ground and terminal No. 5 (White/Red wire) at fuel pump sending unit harness connector C732. *See Fig. 6.* If low fuel indicator is illuminated and fuel gauge is operating properly, replace instrument cluster and retest system. If low fuel indicator is illuminated and fuel gauge is not operating properly, perform TEST B: FUEL GAUGE READS INACCURATELY test. If low fuel indicator is not illuminated, system is okay.

TEST L: LOW COOLANT INDICATOR INOPERATIVE

1) Turn ignition switch to LOCK position. Disconnect low engine coolant level switch harness connector C812. Using a fused jumper wire, connect Black wire terminal and White/Green wire terminal at low engine coolant level switch harness connector C812. If low engine coolant level indicator illuminates for 5 seconds or less, go to next step. If low engine coolant level indicator illuminates for more than 5 seconds and coolant level is below switch in reservoir, replace low engine coolant level switch. If low engine coolant level indicator illuminates for more than 5 seconds and coolant level is above switch in reservoir, lower engine coolant level and retest system.

2) Measure resistance between ground and Black wire terminal at low engine coolant level switch harness connector C812. If resistance is 5 ohms or less, go to next step. If resistance is greater than 5 ohms, repair open in Black wire.

3) Disconnect instrument interface module harness connector C440. Measure resistance in White/Green wire between terminal No. 12 at instrument interface module harness connector C440 and low engine coolant level switch harness connector C812. *See Fig. 12.* If resistance is 5 ohms or less, go to next step. If resistance is greater than 5 ohms, repair open in White/Green wire.

4) Using a fused jumper wire, ground terminal No. 13 (Black/Yellow wire) at instrument interface module harness connector C440. If low engine coolant level indicator does not illuminate, go to next step. If low engine coolant level indicator illuminates, replace instrument interface module.

5) Turn ignition switch to LOCK position. Disconnect instrument cluster harness connector C808A. Measure resistance in lack/Yellow wire between terminal No. 13 at instrument interface module harness connector C440 and terminal No. 3 at instrument cluster harness connector C808A. *See Figs. 4 and 12*. If resistance is 5 ohms or less, check low engine coolant level indicator bulb and replace as necessary. If bulb is okay, replace instrument cluster printed circuit. If resistance is greater than 5 ohms, repair open in Black/Yellow wire.

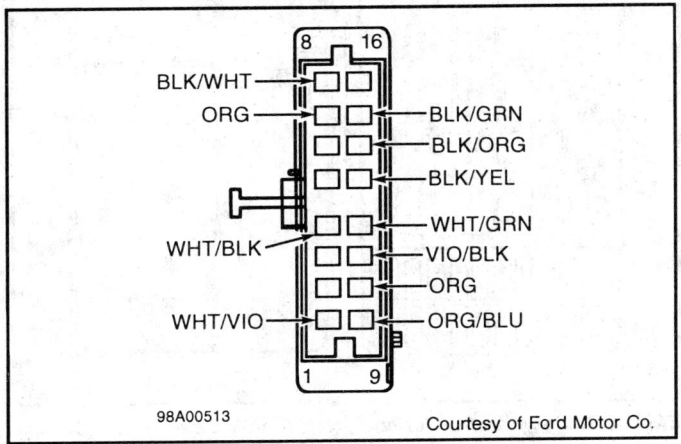

98A00513   Courtesy of Ford Motor Co.

Fig. 12: Identifying Instrument Interface Module Harness Connector C440 Terminals

TEST M: LOW COOLANT INDICATOR ALWAYS ON

1) Turn ignition switch to LOCK position. Ensure coolant reservoir is full. Turn ignition switch to RUN position. If low engine coolant level indicator stays illuminated. go to next step. If low engine coolant level indicator illuminates for about 5 seconds and turns off, system is okay.

2) Turn ignition switch to LOCK position. Disconnect low engine coolant level switch harness connector C812. Turn ignition switch to RUN position. If low engine coolant level indicator does not illuminate for about 5 seconds and turn off, go to next step. If low engine coolant level indicator illuminates for about 5 seconds and turns off, replace low engine coolant level switch.

3) Disconnect instrument interface module harness connector C440. Measure resistance between ground and terminal No. 12 (White/Green wire) at instrument interface module harness connector C440. *See Fig. 12*. If resistance is greater than 10 k/ohms, go to next step. If resistance is 10 k/ohms or less, repair short to ground in White/Green wire.

4) Disconnect instrument cluster harness connector C808A. Measure resistance between ground and terminal No. 3 (Black/Yellow wire) at instrument cluster harness connector C808A. *See Fig. 4*. If resistance is greater than 10 k/ohms, inspect instrument cluster printed circuit. If instrument cluster printed circuit is okay, replace instrument interface module. If resistance is 10 k/ohms or less, repair short to ground in Black/Yellow wire.

TEST N: SPEEDOMETER INOPERATIVE

1) Turn ignition switch to LOCK position. Connect NGS tester to Data Link Connector (DLC). Retrieve and document continuous DTCs. Clear continuous DTCs. Test drive vehicle for 5 minutes. Retrieve continuous DTCs. If DTC P0500, P0501, P0502 or P0503 are not retrieved, go to next step. If DTC P0500, P0501, P0502 or P0503 are retrieved, repair vehicle speed sensor concern. See appropriate SELF-DIAGNOSTICS article in ENGINE PERFORMANCE in appropriate MITCHELL® manual.

2) Turn ignition switch to LOCK position. Disconnect vehicle speed sensor harness connector C903 (C1899 on M/T). Disconnect instrument cluster harness connector C808B. Measure resistance in White/Blue wire between terminal No. 6 at instrument cluster harness connector

C808B and terminal No. 2 at vehicle speed sensor harness connector. *See Figs. 5 and 13*. If resistance is 5 ohms or less, repair or replace instrument cluster as necessary. If resistance is greater than 5 ohms, repair open in White/Blue wire.

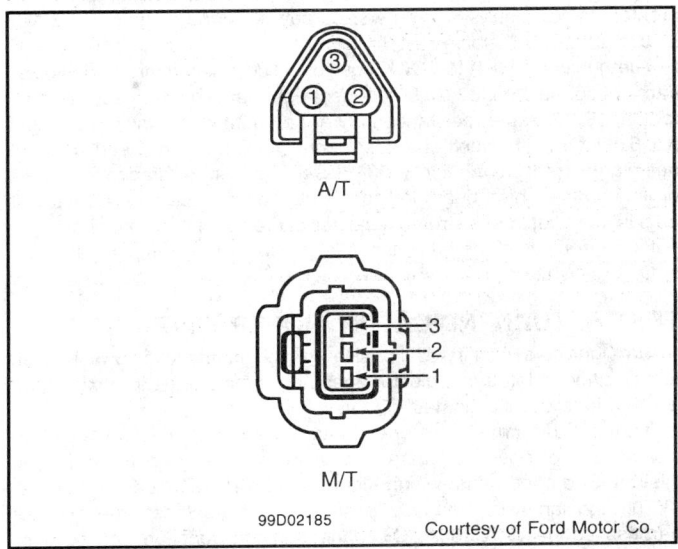

A/T

M/T

99D02185   Courtesy of Ford Motor Co.

Fig. 13: Identifying Vehicle Speed Sensor Harness Connectors

TEST O: ODOMETER INOPERATIVE

Test driver vehicle and observe speedometer operation. If speedometer is operative, repair or replace instrument cluster as necessary. If speedometer is inoperative, perform TEST N: SPEEDOMETER INOPERATIVE test.

TEST P: SPEEDOMETER INACCURATE

1) Turn ignition switch to LOCK position. Connect NGS tester to Data Link Connector (DLC). Using NGS tester, monitor PCM PID VSS(+). Start vehicle. Test driver vehicle and compare PID value on NGS tester to speedometer. If speeds do not match, go to next step. If speeds match, system is okay at this time.

2) Turn ignition switch to LOCK position. Disconnect vehicle speed sensor harness connector C903 (C1899 on M/T). Measure resistance between ground and terminal No. 2 (White/Blue wire) at vehicle speed sensor harness connector. *See Fig. 13*. If resistance is greater than 10 k/ohms, repair or replace instrument cluster as necessary. If resistance is 10 k/ohms or less, repair short to ground in White/Blue wire between vehicle speed sensor and instrument cluster and/or short to ground in White/Violet wire between PCM and splice S60. See WIRING DIAGRAMS.

TEST Q: TACHOMETER INACCURATE

1) Turn ignition switch to LOCK position. Connect NGS tester to Data Link harness connector (DLC). Using NGS tester, monitor PCM PID RPM. Start vehicle. With engine running compare PID value on NGS tester to tachometer. If RPM matches, system is okay at this time. If RPM does not match, repair or replace instrument cluster as necessary.

2) Disconnect instrument cluster harness connectors. Remove instrument cluster. Measure resistance between terminal No. 13 at instrument cluster connector C808A (component side) and tachometer terminal T1 on printed circuit. *See Fig. 10*. If resistance is 5 ohms or less, go to next step. If resistance is greater than 5 ohms, replace printed circuit.

3) Measure resistance between terminal No. 8 at instrument cluster connector C808A (component side) and tachometer terminal T3 on printed circuit. If resistance is 5 ohms or less, go to next step. If resistance is greater than 5 ohms, replace printed circuit.

4) Measure resistance between terminal No. 9 at instrument cluster connector C808A (component side) and tachometer terminal T2 on printed circuit. If resistance is 5 ohms or less, replace tachometer or instrument cluster as necessary. If resistance is greater than 5 ohms, replace printed circuit.

TEST R: HIGH BEAM INDICATOR INOPERATIVE

1) Turn ignition switch to RUN position. Turn headlights on. Place multifunction switch to high beam position. If high beam headlights are on, go to next step. If high beam headlights are not on, locate and repair problem in headlight system. See appropriate wiring diagram in HEADLIGHT SYSTEMS article.

2) Turn ignition switch to LOCK position. Disconnect instrument cluster harness connector C808A. Disconnect right headlight harness connector C834B. Measure resistance in Orange/White wire between terminal No. 5 at instrument cluster harness connector C808A and headlight right headlight harness connector C834B. See Fig. 4. If resistance is 5 ohms or less, inspect high beam indicator bulb and replace as necessary. If bulb is okay, replace instrument cluster printed circuit. If continuity does not exist, replace bulb. If resistance is greater than 5 ohms, repair open in Orange/White wire.

TEST S: TURN INDICATOR INOPERATIVE

1) Turn ignition switch in RUN position. Place multifunction switch in left turn position. If left turn indicator does not illuminate, go to next step. If left turn indicator illuminates, go to step **5)**.

2) If left outside turn signals operate, go to next step. If left outside turn signals do not operate, locate and repair problem in exterior lighting system. See appropriate wiring diagram in EXTERIOR LIGHTS article.

3) Turn ignition switch to LOCK position. Disconnect instrument cluster harness connector C808A. Disconnect central junction box harness connector C362. See Fig. 11. Measure resistance in Blue/Black wire between terminal No. 3 at central junction box harness connector C362 and terminal No. 2 at instrument cluster harness connector C808A. See Fig. 4. If resistance is 5 ohms or less, go to next step. If resistance is greater than 5 ohms, repair open in Blue/Black wire.

4) Disconnect central timer module back of central junction box. See Fig. 11. Measure resistance between terminal No. 14 at central timer module connector (fuse box side) and terminal No. 3 at central junction box connector C362 (fuse box side). See Fig. 14. If resistance is 5 ohms or less, inspect left turn signal indicator bulb and replace as necessary. If bulb is okay, replace instrument cluster printed circuit. If resistance is greater than 5 ohms, repair or replace central junction box as necessary.

5) Turn ignition switch to RUN position. Place multifunction switch in right turn position. If right turn indicator does not illuminate, go to next step. If right turn indicator illuminates, system is okay at this time.

6) If right outside turn signals operate, go to next step. If right outside turn signals do not operate, locate and repair problem in exterior lighting system. See appropriate wiring diagram in EXTERIOR LIGHTS article.

7) Turn ignition switch to LOCK position. Disconnect instrument cluster harness connector C808A. Disconnect central junction box harness connector C362. See Fig. 11. Measure resistance in Blue/Yellow wire between terminal No. 4 at central junction box harness connector C362 and terminal No. 3 at instrument cluster harness connector C808A. See Fig. 4. If resistance is 5 ohms or less, go to next step. If resistance is greater than 5 ohms, repair open in Blue/Yellow wire.

8) Disconnect central timer module from back of instrument panel. See Fig. 11. Measure resistance between terminal No. 16 at central timer module connector (fuse box side) at terminal No. 4 at central junction box connector C362 (fuse box side). See Fig. 15. If resistance is 5 ohms or less, inspect right turn signal indicator bulb and replace as necessary. If bulb is okay, replace instrument cluster printed circuit. If resistance is greater than 5 ohms, repair or replace central junction box as necessary.

TEST T: CHARGE WARNING NEVER ON

1) Turn ignition switch to LOCK position. Disconnect generator harness connector C1885A. Turn ignition switch to RUN position. Using a fused jumper wire, ground terminal No. 1 (Green/Black wire) at generator harness connector C1885A. If charge warning indicator does not illuminate, go to next step. If charge warning indicator illuminates, repair charging system concern. See appropriate GENERATORS article in CHARGING & STARTING SYSTEMS.

2) Turn ignition switch to LOCK position. Disconnect instrument cluster harness connector C808A. Measure resistance in Green/Black wire

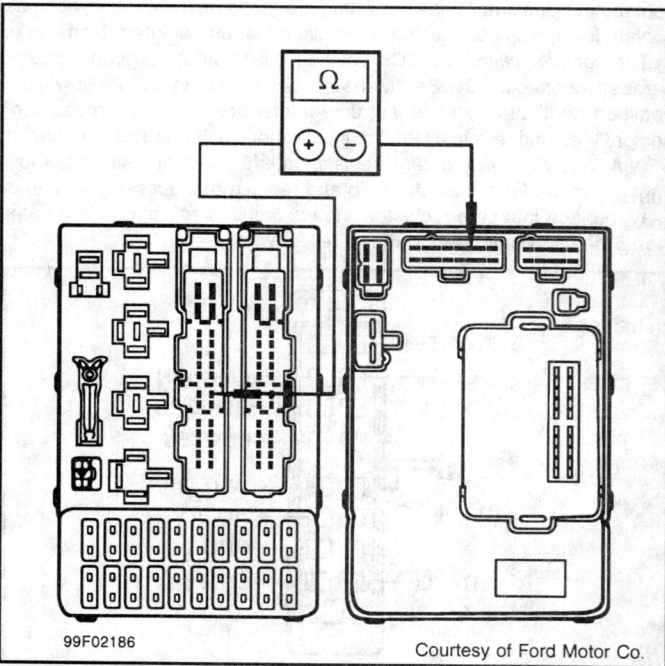

99F02186 · Courtesy of Ford Motor Co.

Fig. 14: Testing Central Junction Box (Left Turn Indicator Circuit)

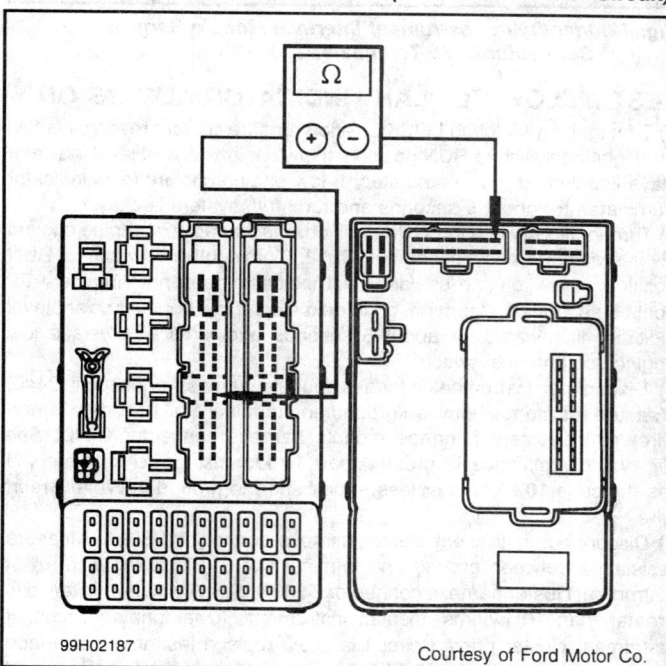

99H02187 · Courtesy of Ford Motor Co.

Fig. 15: Testing Central Junction Box (Right Turn Indicator Circuit)

between terminal No. 1 at generator harness connector C1885A and terminal No. 7 at instrument cluster harness connector C808A. See Fig. 4. If resistance is 5 ohms or less, inspect charge warning indicator bulb and replace as necessary. If bulb is okay, replace instrument cluster printed circuit. If resistance is greater than 5 ohms, repair open in Green/Black wire.

TEST U: CHECK ENGINE LIGHT INOPERATIVE

NOTE: CHECK ENGINE light may also be referred to as Malfunction Indicator Light (MIL).

1) Turn ignition switch to LOCK position. Disconnect PCM harness connector C421. Connect breakout box to PCM harness connector

C421. Using a fused jumper wire, connect terminals No. 2 and 24 at breakout box. Turn ignition switch to RUN position. If CHECK ENGINE light does not illuminate, go to next step. If CHECK ENGINE light illuminates, repair powertrain control concern. See appropriate SELF-DIAGNOSTICS article in ENGINE PERFORMANCE in appropriate MITCHELL® manual.

2) Turn ignition switch to LOCK position. Disconnect instrument cluster harness connector C808B. Measure resistance in Black/Orange wire between terminal No. 2 at breakout box and terminal No. 3 at instrument cluster harness connector C808B. *See Fig. 5.* If resistance is 5 ohms or less, inspect CHECK ENGINE indicator bulb and replace as necessary. If bulb is okay, replace instrument cluster printed circuit. If resistance is greater than 5 ohms, repair open in Black/Orange wire.

TEST V: CHECK ENGINE LIGHT ALWAYS ON

NOTE: CHECK ENGINE light may also be referred to as Malfunction Indicator Light (MIL).

1) Start engine. If CHECK ENGINE light illuminates and then goes out after engine is started, system is okay at this time. If CHECK ENGINE light illuminates and remains on after engine is started, repair powertrain control concern. See appropriate SELF-DIAGNOSTICS article in ENGINE PERFORMANCE in appropriate MITCHELL® manual. If no powertrain control concern exists, go to next step.

2) Turn ignition switch to LOCK position. Disconnect PCM harness connector C421. Turn ignition switch to RUN position. If CHECK ENGINE light does not illuminate, replace PCM. If CHECK ENGINE light illuminates, check for short to ground in Black/Orange wire. If short to ground does not exists, replace instrument cluster printed circuit.

TEST W: ABS LIGHT INOPERATIVE

Turn ignition switch to LOCK position. Disconnect instrument cluster harness connector C808A. Disconnect ABS module harness connector C3002. Measure resistance in Black/Red wire between terminal No. 25 at ABS module harness connector C3002 and terminal No. 2 at instrument cluster harness connector C808A. *See Figs. 5 and 16.* If resistance is greater than 5 ohms, repair open in Black/Red wire. If resistance is 5 ohms or less, inspect ABS indicator bulb and replace as necessary. If bulb is okay, check instrument cluster printed circuit and replace as necessary. If printed circuit is okay, repair ABS concern. See appropriate ANTI-LOCK article in BRAKES in appropriate MITCHELL® manual.

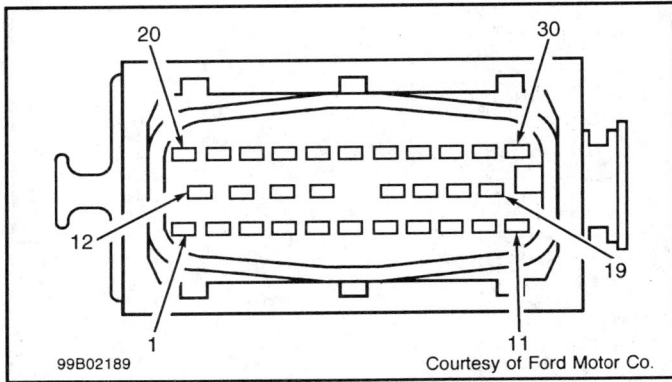

99B02189   Courtesy of Ford Motor Co.

Fig. 16: Identifying ABS Module Harness Connector C3002 Terminals

REMOVAL & INSTALLATION

FUEL PRESSURE RELIEF

Turn ignition switch to LOCK position. Remove air cleaner assembly. Connect Fuel Pressure Gauge (T80L-9974-B) to fuel pressure relief cap on fuel injection supply manifold. Open manual valve on fuel pressure gauge to relieve fuel system pressure.

COOLANT TEMPERATURE GAUGE

Removal & Installation – 1) Disconnect negative battery cable. Remove instrument cluster. See INSTRUMENT CLUSTER.

2) Separate instrument cluster housing from instrument cluster back plate. Remove speedometer and tachometer. See SPEEDOMETER/ODOMETER and TACHOMETER.

3) Carefully remove temperature gauge retaining screw and temperature gauge assembly by pulling gauge assembly away from instrument cluster back plate. To install, reverse removal procedure.

FUEL GAUGE

Removal & Installation – 1) Disconnect negative battery cable. Remove instrument cluster. See INSTRUMENT CLUSTER.

2) Separate instrument cluster housing from instrument cluster back plate. Remove speedometer. See SPEEDOMETER/ODOMETER.

3) Carefully remove fuel gauge retaining screw and fuel gauge assembly by pulling fuel gauge assembly away from instrument cluster back plate. To install, reverse removal procedure.

FUEL GAUGE SENDING UNIT

Removal & Installation – 1) Depressurize fuel system. See FUEL PRESSURE RELIEF.

2) Remove rear seat cushion. Remove plastic grommet from floor pan. Disconnect fuel pump module electrical harness connector.

3) Disconnect fuel and vapor tubes from fuel pump module.

NOTE: To disconnect fuel tubes from pump module, compress tabs on both sides of each nylon push-connect fitting and ease fuel tube out of fuel pump module.

4) Before removing fuel pump module, clean area around module of any dirt or debris. Using Fuel Tank Sender Wrench (D84P-9275-A), turn fuel pump locking retainer ring counterclockwise and remove retainer ring.

5) Remove fuel pump module. Remove and discard pump module "O" ring seal. Cover opening in fuel tank to prevent contamination of fuel while fuel pump module is absent.

6) To install, carefully clean fuel pump module mounting surfaces and "O" ring seal groove on fuel tank. Apply a light coat of long-life grease on NEW "O" ring seal to hold it in place, and install "O" ring into seal groove on fuel tank. To complete installation, reverse removal procedure.

INSTRUMENT CLUSTER

Removal & Installation – 1) Disconnect negative battery cable. Remove 3 instrument panel finish panel retaining screw covers. Remove 5 screws retaining instrument panel finish panel to instrument panel. *See Fig. 17.*

2) Pull instrument panel finish panel away from instrument panel. Disconnect wiring harness connectors from instrument cluster and heated rear window switch and light, if equipped. Remove instrument panel finish panel.

3) Remove 5 screws retaining instrument cluster. On non-tilt models, lower steering column to gain clearance to remove instrument cluster.

4) Pull instrument cluster away from instrument panel. Disconnect 2 instrument cluster printed circuit harness connectors from instrument cluster back plate. Remove instrument cluster. To install, reverse removal procedure.

PRINTED CIRCUIT

NOTE: When battery has been disconnected and reconnected, some abnormal drive symptoms may occur while powertrain control module relearns its adaptive strategy. Vehicle may need to be driven 10 or more miles to relearn strategy.

Removal & Installation – 1) Disconnect negative battery cable. Remove instrument cluster. See INSTRUMENT CLUSTER.

2) Remove instrument panel light sockets and miniature bulbs by twisting counterclockwise and pulling out. Separate instrument cluster housing from instrument cluster back plate.

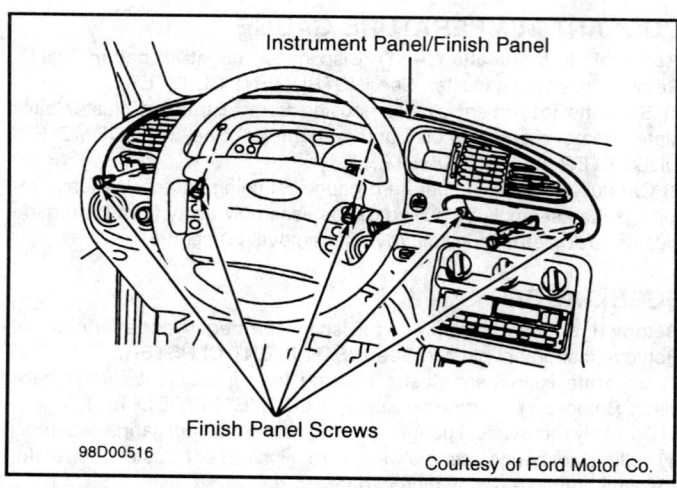

Instrument Panel/Finish Panel

Finish Panel Screws

98D00516

Courtesy of Ford Motor Co.

Fig. 17: Removing Instrument Panel Finish Panel

3) Remove instrument cluster warning light lenses from posts on instrument cluster back plate. Remove gauges. See SPEEDOMETER/ODOMETER, TACHOMETER, FUEL GAUGE and COOLANT TEMPERATURE GAUGE.

4) Remove and discard all snap-in harness connector clips. Remove 2 instrument cluster printed circuit retainers. *See Fig. 18.*

NOTE: From front side of instrument cluster back plate, use a small flat-nosed drift to push in pins to release printed circuit retainers.

5) Carefully remove instrument cluster printed circuit without bending. To install, reverse removal procedure, using NEW snap-in harness connector clips.

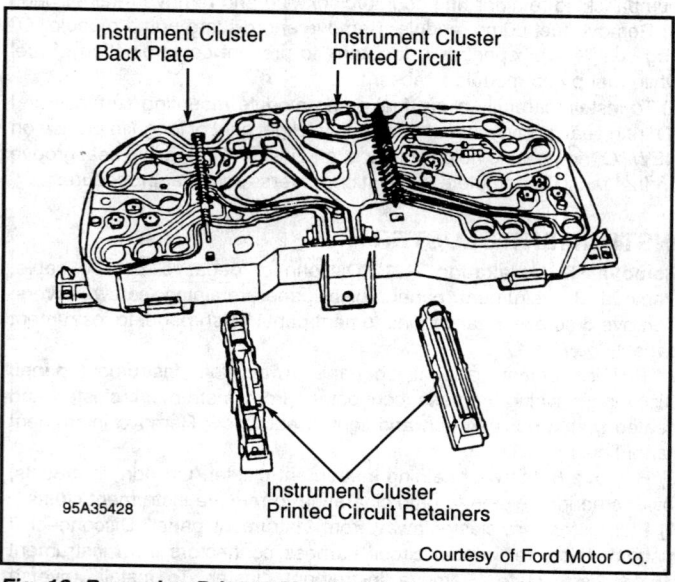

Instrument Cluster
Back Plate

Instrument Cluster
Printed Circuit

Instrument Cluster
Printed Circuit Retainers

95A35428

Courtesy of Ford Motor Co.

Fig. 18: Removing Printed Circuit

SPEEDOMETER/ODOMETER

Removal & Installation – 1) Disconnect negative battery cable. Remove instrument cluster. See INSTRUMENT CLUSTER.

2) Separate instrument cluster housing from instrument cluster back plate. Remove 3 speedometer retaining screws.

3) Grasp speedometer at top and bottom using fingers only. Carefully pull speedometer away from instrument cluster back plate. To install, reverse removal procedure

TACHOMETER

Removal & Installation – 1) Disconnect negative battery cable. Remove instrument cluster. See INSTRUMENT CLUSTER.

2) Separate instrument cluster housing from instrument cluster back plate. Remove speedometer. See SPEEDOMETER/ODOMETER.

CAUTION: Tachometer is calibrated at factory. Rough handling can disturb calibration.

3) Remove tachometer retaining screw and remove tachometer. Grasp tachometer at top and bottom using fingers only. Carefully pull tachometer away from instrument cluster back plate. To install, reverse removal procedure.

WIRING DIAGRAMS

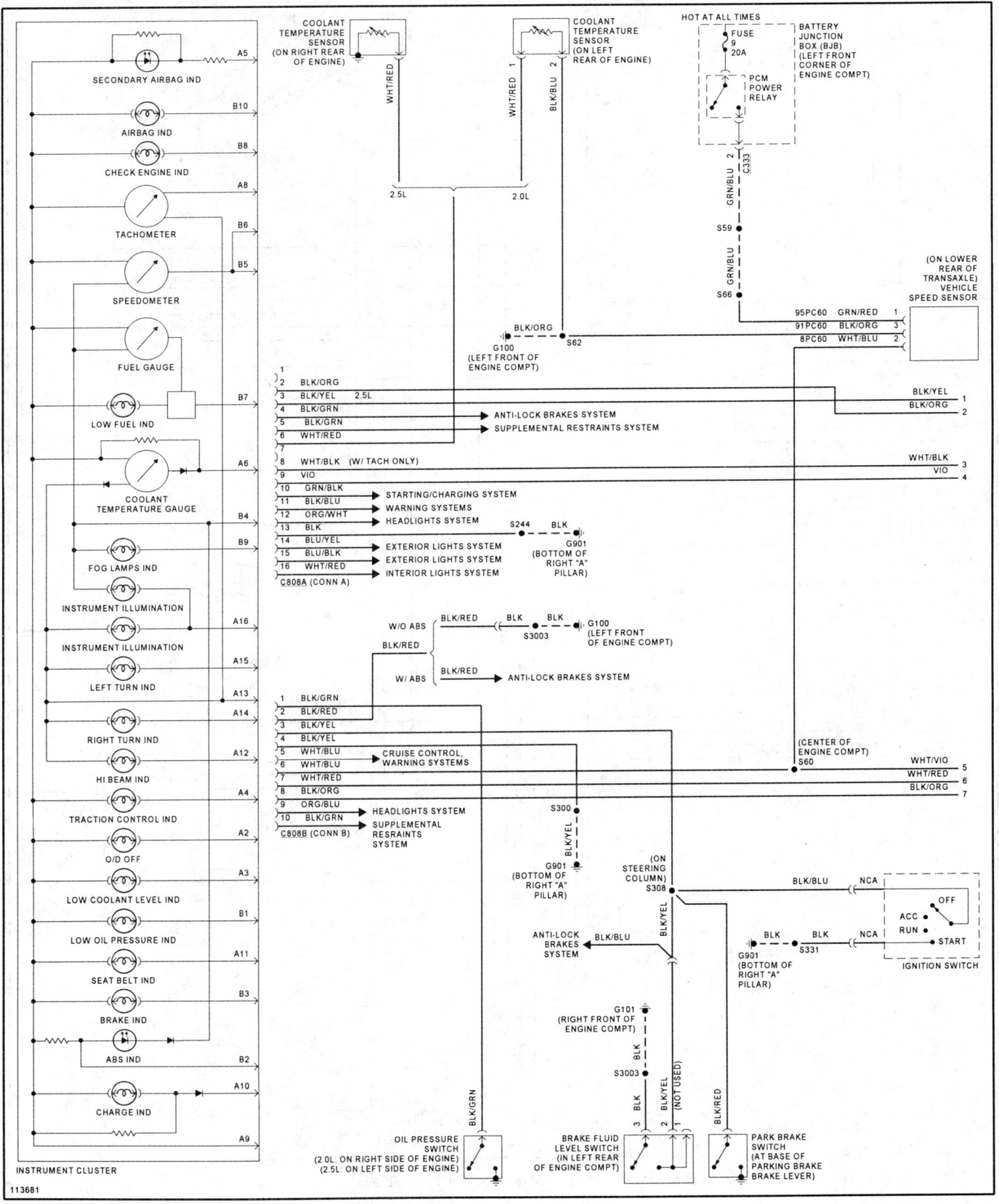

Fig. 19: Analog Instrument Panel Wiring Diagram (Contour & Mystique – A/T – 1 Of 2)

113681

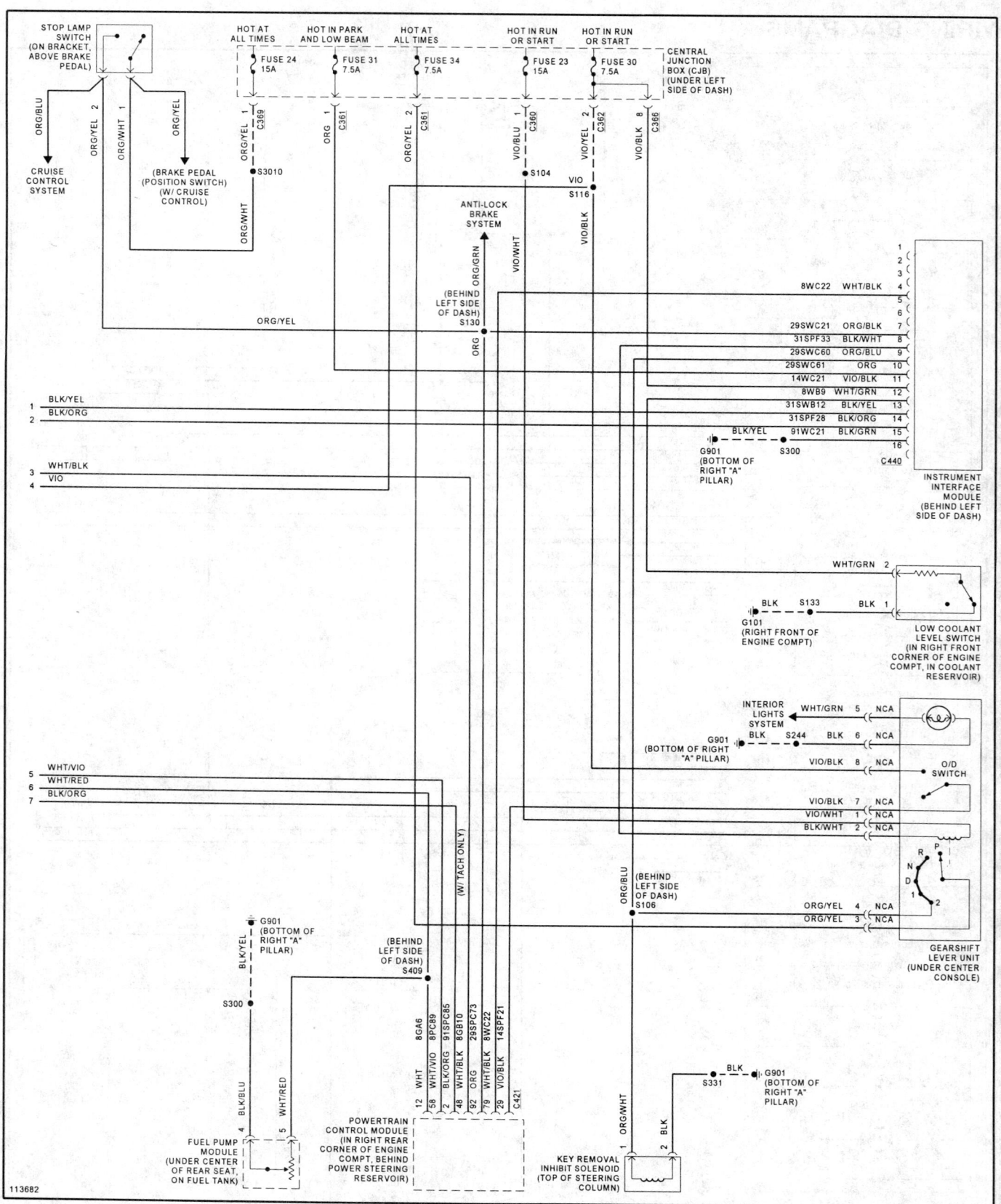

Fig. 20: Analog Instrument Panel Wiring Diagram (Contour & Mystique – A/T – 2 Of 2)

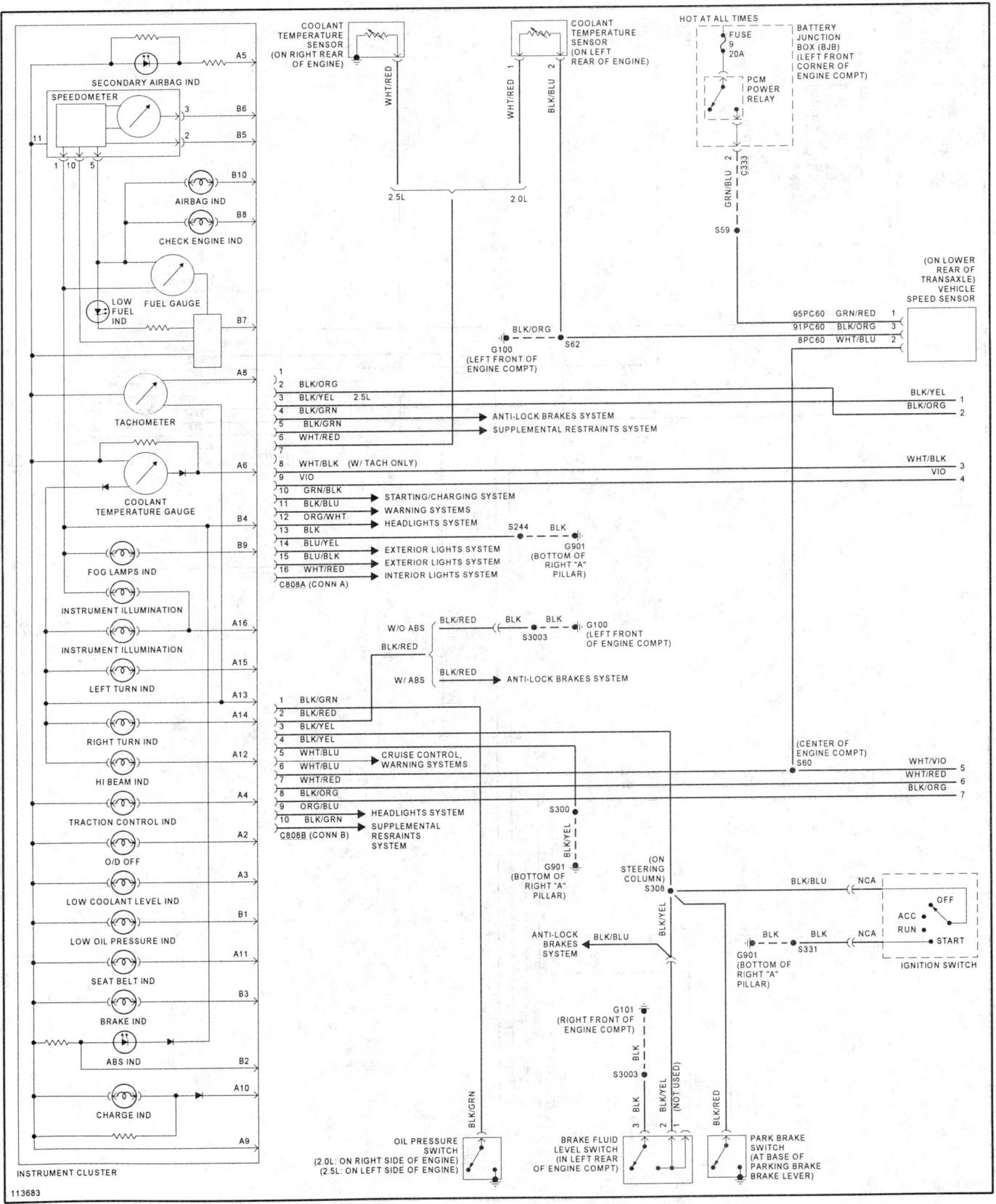

Fig. 21: Analog Instrument Panel Wiring Diagram (Contour & Mystique – M/T – 1 Of 2)

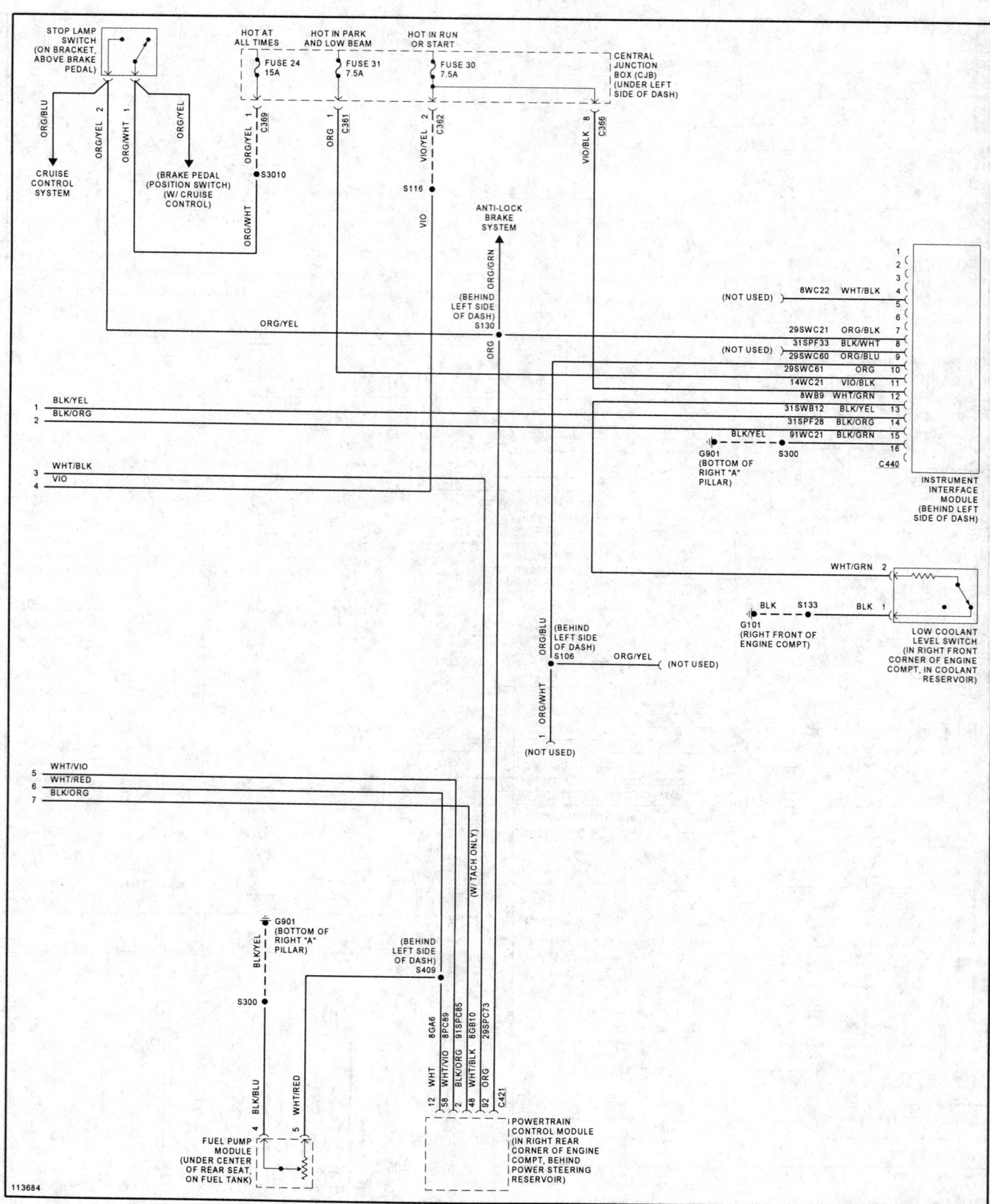

Fig. 22: Analog Instrument Panel Wiring Diagram (Contour & Mystique – M/T – 1 Of 2)

DESCRIPTION & OPERATION

NOTE: Hybrid Electronic Cluster (HEC) module is built into instrument cluster.

Instrument cluster contains Hybrid Electronic Cluster (HEC) module, speedometer, tachometer, message center, fuel gauge, temperature gauge and warning indicators. Warning indicators are in various locations on cluster. Instrument cluster and panel will not illuminate when headlight switch is in OFF position.

HEC receives its input and output signals hardwired or over International Standards Organization (ISO) 9141 bus line. HEC carries out a display proveout to verify warning indicators are operating properly. When ignition switch is turned to RUN position, the following indicators will illuminate or be displayed: anti-lock brake system, air bag, charging system, brake system, low fuel, low washer, seat belt (60 second proveout) and malfunction indicator light (CHECK ENGINE).

HEC also controls illumination of the following indicator light module warning indicators: maintenance interval warning, frost warning, ice warning, brake pad wear and door/decklid ajar. Bulb warning indicator is controlled by bulb outage module.

COMPONENT LOCATIONS

COMPONENT LOCATIONS

Component	Location
Anti-Lock Brake System Module	On Hydraulic Unit
Brake Fluid Level Sensor	On Brake Fluid Reservoir
Bulb Outage Module	On Instrument Panel Fuse Box
Central Timer Module	Connect To Rear Of Instrument Panel Fuse Box
Engine Coolant Temperature Sensor	Left Rear Of Engine
Fuel Pump Module	[1] Top Of Fuel Tank
Hybrid Electronic Cluster Module	[2]
Ice Warning Sensor	Front Center Of Engine Compartment, On Radiator Support
Indicator Light Module	Top Center Of Head Liner
Instrument Panel Fuse Box	Under Left Side Of Instrument Panel
Interface Module	Behind Instrument Cluster
Low Engine Coolant Level Switch	Right Front Corner Of Engine Compartment
Low Washer Fluid Level Switch	On Washer Reservoir
Oil Pressure Switch	
4-Cylinder	Above Generator
V6	Side Of Block, Next To Oil Filter
Powertrain Control Module	Right Rear Corner Of Engine Compartment
Message Center Switch	Center Of Instrument Panel
Vehicle Speed Sensor	Top Of Transmission, Above Axle Shaft

[1] – Accessible through floor of trunk.
[2] – Built into instrument cluster.

TROUBLE SHOOTING

CAUTION: Electronic modules are sensitive to static electrical charges. Proper grounding of technician and component is essential to prevent damage.

Verify customer concern by operating system in question. Visually inspect the following components:

Mechanical:
- Low Brake Fluid Level
- Damaged Engine Oil Filter
- Damaged Engine Oil Pump
- Struck Gauges
- Damaged Fuel Tank
- Low Washer Fluid Level
- Low Coolant Level
- Worn Or Damaged Accessory Drive Belt

Electrical:
- Blown Fuse(s)
- Damaged Miniature Bulbs
- Damaged Wiring Harness
- Loose Or Corroded Connections
- Damaged Instrument Cluster
- Damaged Switches & Sensors

Verify charging system, safety belt warning chime, turn signals, headlights and cruise control are working properly. Inspect wiring harness for obvious signs of shorts, opens, bad connections or damage. If problem exists, repair as necessary. If no problem exists, perform self-diagnostics. See SELF-DIAGNOSTIC SYSTEM.

COMPONENT TESTS

HEADLIGHT SWITCH

Disconnect headlight switch harness connector. Continuity between terminals should be as specified with switch in specified position. See HEADLIGHT SWITCH CONTINUITY table. *See Fig. 1.* If resistance is not as specified, or is poor in any switch position, replace headlight switch.

HEADLIGHT SWITCH CONTINUITY

Terminals	Switch Position	Normal Condition
Headlight Circuit		
11 & 12	Off	No Continuity
11 & 12	Park	No Continuity
11 & 12	Head	Continuity
Licence Plate Light Circuit		
14 & 15	Off	No Continuity
14 & 15	Park	Continuity
14 & 15	Head	Continuity
Left Parking Light Circuit		
2 & 15	Off	No Continuity
2 & 15	Park	Continuity
2 & 15	Head	Continuity
Right Parking Light Circuit		
13 & 15	Off	No Continuity
13 & 15	Park	Continuity
13 & 15	Head	Continuity
Fog Light Circuit		
8 & 10	Off	No Continuity
8 & 10	On	Continuity

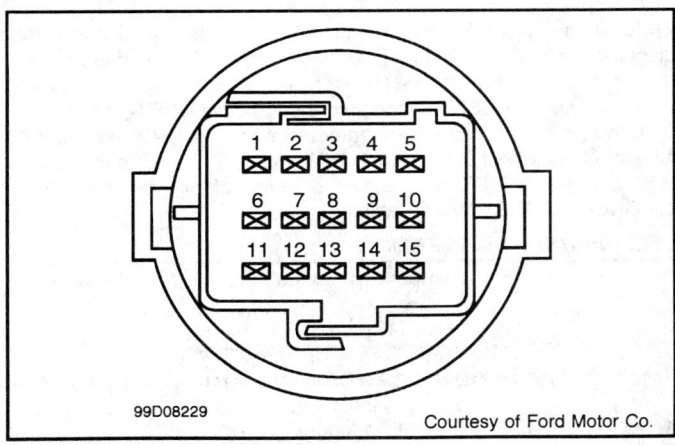

99D08229　　　　Courtesy of Ford Motor Co.

Fig. 1: Identifying Headlight Switch Terminals

SELF-DIAGNOSTIC SYSTEM

NOTE: *Hybrid Electronic Cluster (HEC) module is built into instrument cluster.*

USING NEW GENERATION STAR TESTER

Connect New Generation Star (NGS) tester to Data Link Connector (DLC), located beneath instrument panel. Using NGS tester, perform data link diagnostics test. See DATA LINK DIAGNOSTIC TEST under COMMUNICATION NETWORK DIAGNOSTICS in MODULE COMMUNICATIONS NETWORK – COUGAR article. If NGS tester responds with CKT914, CKT915 or CKT70=ALL ECUS NO RESP/NOT EQUIP, repair module communications concern. See MODULE COMMUNICATIONS NETWORK – COUGAR article. If NGS tester displays NO RESP/NOT EQUIP for Hybrid Electronic Cluster (HEC) module, perform TEST A: NO COMMUNICATION WITH HYBRID ELECTRONIC CLUSTER MODULE under SYSTEM TESTS.

If NGS tester responds with SYSTEM PASSED, retrieve and record continuous DTCs. Erase continuous DTCs. Using NGS tester, perform HEC module self-test. Perform appropriate test in accordance with DTC retrieved. See HYBRID ELECTRONIC CLUSTER MODULE DTC INDEX table. If no DTCs are retrieved, repair by symptom. See SYMPTOM CHART table under SYSTEM TESTS.

HYBRID ELECTRONIC CLUSTER MODULE DTC INDEX

NGS DTC	Display DTC	Description	Test
B1201	9201	Fuel Sender Circuit Failure	B
B1204	9204	Fuel Sender Short To Ground	B
B1257	9257	Climate Control	H
B1317	9317	Battery voltage High	A
B1318	9318	Battery Voltage Low	A
B1342	9324	ECU Defective	[1]
B1359	9359	Ignition Switch RUN/ACC Circuit Failure	A
P0115	0115	Engine Coolant Temp. Circuit Malfunction	[2]

[1] – Using NGS tester, retrieve and document all continuous DTCs. Perform Hybrid Electronic Cluster (HEC) module self-test. If DTC B1342 is retrieved again, replace HEC module.
[2] – Repair engine coolant temperature sensor circuit. See appropriate SELF-DIAGNOSTICS article in ENGINE PERFORMANCE in appropriate MITCHELL® manual.

ON-BOARD SELF-DIAGNOSTIC TEST MODE

1) To enter Hybrid Electronic Cluster (HEC) module on-board self-diagnostic mode with engine off, simultaneously depress and message center switch UNITS and RESET buttons while turning ignition switch from LOCK to RUN position. Release RESET button first, then release UNITS button.

2) To enter Hybrid Electronic Cluster (HEC) module on-board self-diagnostic mode with engine running, simultaneously depress and message center switch UNITS and RESET buttons while starting vehicle. Release RESET button first, then release UNITS button.

3) At this point HEC module will enter test No. 1 (gauge sweep test). To navigate to next test, depress SELECT button. To navigate to previous test, depress RESET button. For a listing of all test, see SELF-DIAGNOSTIC TEST MODE table.

SELF-DIAGNOSTIC TEST MODE

Test	Component Tested	Description
1	Tachometer & Speedometer	1
2	HEC Red Only Memory (ROM)	2
3	Message Center Displays, Indicator Light Module & Warning Indicators	3
4	HEC Non Volatile Memory (NVM)	4
5	Battery	5

SELF-DIAGNOSTIC TEST MODE (Cont.)

Test	Component Tested	Description
6	HEC Input/Output	6
7	Speedometer	7
8	Tachometer	8
9	Engine Coolant Temperature	9
10	Engine Coolant Temperature Gauge, Tachometer, Speedometer & Fuel Gauge	10
11	Fuel	11
12	Diagnostic Trouble Codes	12

[1] – This test checks gauge sweep. All gauges should sweep smoothly; five seconds up, then 5 seconds down.
[2] – This test checks HEC module ROM version level.
[3] – This test checks indicator bulbs and displays. All indicators and displays that are controlled by HEC module should illuminate.
[4] – This test checks NVM revision.
[5] – This test checks A/D. For engineering use only.
[6] – This test checks port. For engineering use only.
[7] – This test checks speed signal input. To toggle between MPH and km/h depress UNITS button.
[8] – This test checks engine speed input signal.
[9] – This test checks engine coolant temperature. To toggle between °F and °C depress UNITS button.
[10] – This test checks gauge counts. Checks HEC gauges and determines gauge angle. Also, displays a 4 digit hexadecimal value.
[11] – This test checks fuel pulses. For engineering use only.
[12] – This test retrieves DTCs test. To list DTCs, depress UNITS button after entering test. For DTC listing and appropriate test procedure, see HYBRID ELECTRONIC CLUSTER MODULE DTC INDEX table under USING NEW GENERATION STAR TESTER.

SYSTEM TESTS

NOTE: *Hybrid Electronic Cluster (HEC) module is built into instrument cluster.*

SYMPTOM CHART

Symptom	Test
No Communication With Hybrid Electronic Cluster Module	A
Fuel Gauge Inaccurate	B
Speedometer Inoperative	C
Tachometer Inoperative	D
Temperature Gauge Inaccurate	E
High Beam Indicator Inoperative	F
Maintenance Interval Indicator Inoperative/Always On	G
Ice Warning Indicator Inoperative/Always On	H
Frost Warning Indicator Inoperative/Always On	I
Brake Pad Warning Indicator Inoperative/Always On	J
Low Washer Fluid Warning Indicator Inoperative/Always On	K
Door Ajar Warning Indicator Inoperative/Always On	L
Bulb Out Warning Indicator Always On	M
Oil Pressure Warning Indicator Inoperative	N
Oil Pressure Warning Indicator Always On	O
Seat Belt Warning Indicator Inoperative (Chime Operative)	P
Seat Belt Warning Indicator Always On (Chime Operative)	Q
Brake Warning Indicator Inoperative	R
Low Fuel Warning Indicator Inoperative	S
Low Fuel Warning Indicator Always On	T
Low Coolant Warning Indicator Inoperative	U
Low Coolant Warning Indicator Always On	V
Turn Signal Indicator Inoperative	W
Charge Warning Indicator Never On	X
Check Engine Light Always On	Y
Check Engine Light Always On	Z
ABS Warning Indicator Inoperative	AA
Message Center Switch Not Operating Correctly	AB
Message Center Not Operating Correctly	AC

TEST A: NO COMMUNICATION WITH HYBRID ELECTRONIC CLUSTER MODULE

NOTE: Hybrid Electronic Cluster (HEC) module is built into instrument cluster.

1) Turn ignition switch to LOCK position. Disconnect Hybrid Electronic Cluster (HEC) module harness connector C808b. Measure voltage at terminal No. 14 (Orange wire) at HEC module harness connector C808b. *See Fig. 2.* If battery voltage exists, go to next step. If battery voltage does not exist, repair power distribution circuit as necessary. See appropriate wiring diagram in POWER DISTRIBUTION article in WIRING DIAGRAMS.

2) Turn ignition switch to RUN position. Measure voltage at terminal No. 15 (Violet wire) at HEC module harness connector C808b. If battery voltage exists, go to next step. If battery voltage does not exist, repair power distribution circuit as necessary. See appropriate wiring diagram in POWER DISTRIBUTION article in WIRING DIAGRAMS.

3) Turn ignition switch to LOCK position. Measure resistance between ground and terminal No. 2 (Black/Orange wire) at HEC module harness connector C808b. Also, measure resistance between ground and terminal No. 16 (Black/Orange wire) at HEC module harness connector C808b. If both resistance readings are 5 ohms or less, repair module communication concern. See MODULE COMMUNICATIONS NETWORK – COUGAR article. If either resistance reading is greater than 5 ohms, repair open in Black/Orange wire.

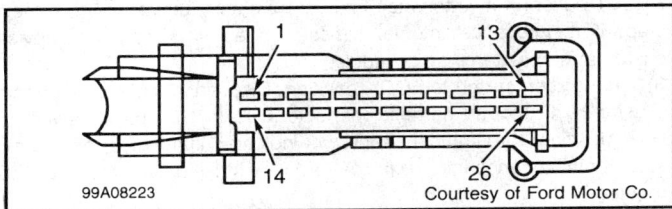

Fig. 2: Identifying HEC Module Harness Connector C808a & C808b Terminals

TEST B: FUEL GAUGE INACCURATE

1) Connect New Generation Star (NGS) tester to Data Link Connector (DLC). Turn ignition switch to RUN position. Using NGS tester, clear continuous DTCs and perform Hybrid Electronic Cluster (HEC) module self-test. If DTC B1201 or B1204 are not retrieved, go to next step. If DTC B1201 or B1204 is retrieved, go to step **3)**.

2) Using NGS tester, access HEC module active command FUEL LEVEL CONTROL. Trigger, monitor and scroll FUELLEVEL to 0%, 50% and 100%. Fuel gauge should indicate empty at 0%, half at 50% and full at 100%. If fuel gauge responds as specified, go to next step. If fuel gauge does not respond as specified, replace HEC module.

3) Turn ignition switch to LOCK position. Disconnect fuel pump module harness connector C732. Disconnect HEC module harness connector C808b. Measure resistance in White/Red wire between terminal No. 21 at HEC module harness connector C808b and terminal No. 5 at fuel pump module harness connector C732. *See Figs. 2 and 3.* Resistance should be 5 ohms or less. Also, measure resistance between ground and terminal No. 21 (White/Red wire) at HEC module harness connector C808b. Resistance should be greater than 10 k/ohms. If both resistance readings are as specified, go to next step. If either resistance reading is not as specified, repair open and/or short to ground in White/Red wire.

4) Measure resistance between ground and terminal No. 1 (Black wire) at fuel pump module harness connector C732. If resistance is 5 ohms or less, replace fuel pump module. If resistance is greater than 5 ohms, repair open in Black wire.

TEST C: SPEEDOMETER INOPERATIVE

1) Turn ignition switch to LOCK position. Connect New Generation Star (NGS) tester to Data Link Connector (DLC). Using NGS tester, access Hybrid Electronic Cluster (HEC) module active command SPEEDOMETER COMMAND. Trigger and scroll SPDOMETER in 5% increments.

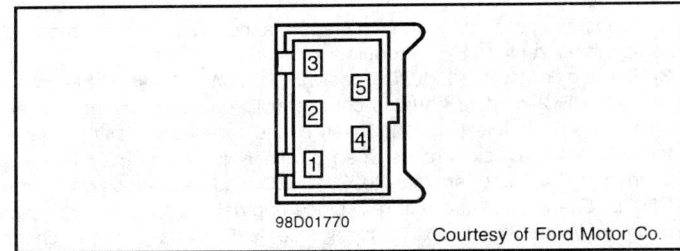

Fig. 3: Identifying Fuel Pump Module Harness Connector C732 Terminals

Speedometer should be increase 12 MPH for each 5%. If speedometer responds as specified, go to next step. If speedometer does not respond as specified, replace HEC module.

2) Using NGS tester, monitor HEC module PID VSS_HEC while driving vehicle. If PID does not agree with vehicle speed, go to next step. If PID agrees with vehicle speed, replace HEC module.

3) Turn ignition switch to LOCK position. Disconnect HEC module harness connector C808b. Disconnect Vehicle Speed Sensor (VSS) harness connector. Measure resistance in White/Blue wire between terminal No. 2 at VSS harness connector and terminal No. 9 at HEC module harness connector C808b. *See Figs. 2 and 4.* If resistance is 5 ohms or less, go to next step. If resistance is greater than 5 ohms, repair open in White/Blue wire.

4) Measure resistance between ground and terminal No. 1 (Black/Orange wire) at VSS harness connector. If resistance is 5 ohms or less, go to next step. If resistance is greater than 5 ohms, repair open in Black/Orange wire.

5) Turn ignition switch to RUN position. Measure voltage at terminal No. 3 (Green/Red wire) at VSS harness connector. If battery voltage exists, replace VSS. If battery voltage does not exist, repair power distribution circuit to VSS. See appropriate wiring diagram in POWER DISTRIBUTION article in WIRING DIAGRAMS.

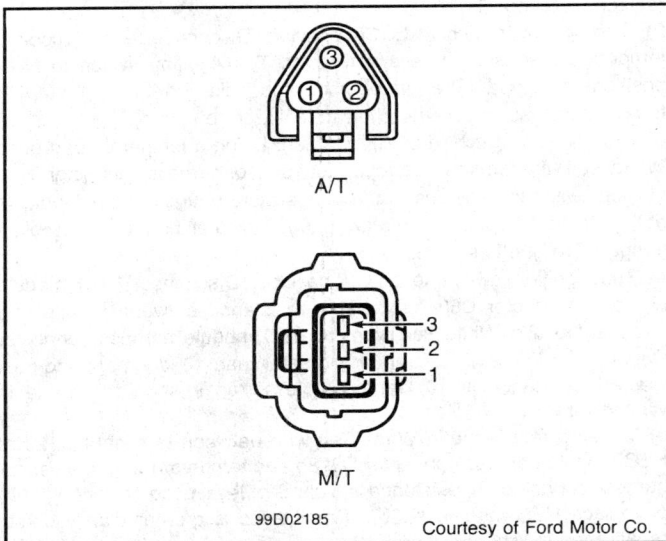

Fig. 4: Identifying Vehicle Speed Sensor Harness Connectors

TEST D: TACHOMETER INOPERATIVE

NOTE: If Powertrain Control Module (PCM) is replace, PCM MUST be programmed. If vehicle is equipped with passive anti-theft system, all ignition keys MUST be programmed into PCM. See COMPUTER RELEARN PROCEDURES article in GENERAL INFORMATION.

1) Turn ignition switch to LOCK position. Connect New Generation Star (NGS) tester to Data Link Connector (DLC). Using NGS tester, access Hybrid Electronic Cluster (HEC) module active command TACHOMETER. Trigger, monitor and scroll TACHOMETER in 5% increments.

Tachometer should be increase 450 RPM for each 5%. If tachometer responds as specified, go to next step. If tachometer does not respond as specified, replace HEC module.

2) Turn ignition switch to LOCK position. Disconnect Hybrid Electronic Cluster (HEC) module harness connector C808a. Disconnect Power-train Control Module (PCM) harness connector C421. Measure resistance in White/Black wire between terminal No. 48 at PCM harness connector C421 and terminal No. 7 at HEC module harness connector C808a. *See Figs. 2 and 5.* If resistance is greater than 5 ohms, repair open in White/Black wire. If resistance is 5 ohms or less, check tachometer CTO circuit. Perform TEST JH under SYSTEM TEST in SELF-DIAGNOSTICS – EEC-V article in ENGINE PERFORMANCE in appropriate MITCHELL® manual.

2) Measure resistance between ground and terminals No. 2 and 16 (both Black/Orange wire). If both resistance readings are 5 ohms or less, replace HEC module. If either resistance reading is greater than 5 ohms, repair open in appropriate wire.

TEST G: MAINTENANCE INTERVAL INDICATOR INOPERATIVE/ALWAYS ON

1) Turn ignition switch to RUN position. If maintenance interval indicator is always illuminated, go to next step. If aintenance interval indicator is inoperative, go to step 5). If maintenance interval indicator illuminates for 3 seconds then turns off, system is okay at this time.

2) Depress SELECT button for trip odometer to be displayed. Depress

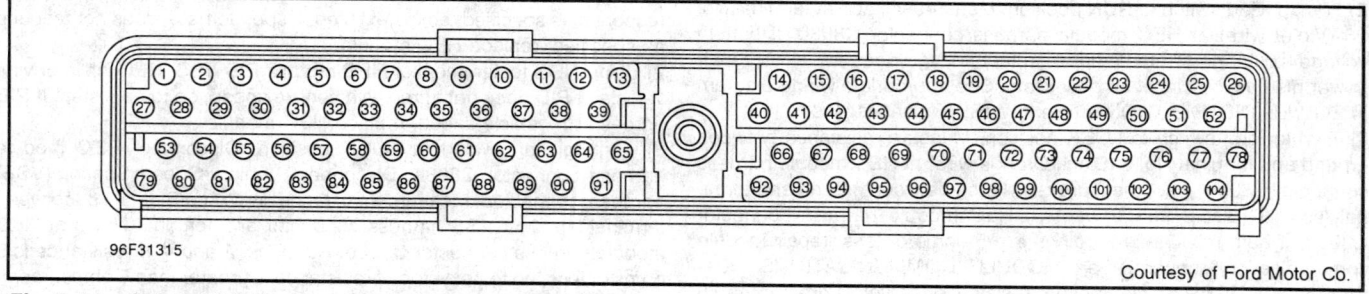

Fig. 5: Identifying PCM Harness Connector C421 Terminals

96F31315

Courtesy of Ford Motor Co.

TEST E: TEMPERATURE GAUGE INACCURATE

1) Turn ignition switch to LOCK position. Connect New Generation Star (NGS) tester to Data Link Connector (DLC). Using NGS tester, access Hybrid Electronic Cluster (HEC) module active command ENGINE COOLANT CONTROL. Trigger, monitor and scroll ENGCOOLANT to 0%, 50% and 100%. Temperature gauge should indicate cold at 0%, half at 50% and hot at 100% . If temperature gauge responds as specified, go to next step. If temperature gauge does not respond as specified, replace HEC module.

2) Turn ignition switch to LOCK position. Disconnect engine coolant temperature sensor harness connector. Turn ignition switch to RUN position. If temperature gauge indicates cold, go to next step. If temperature gauge does not indicate cold, go to step 4).

3) Turn ignition switch to LOCK position. Using a jumper wire, ground White/Red wire terminal at temperature sensor harness connector. Turn ignition switch to RUN position. If temperature gauge does not indicate hot, go to next step. If temperature gauge indicates hot, replace coolant temperature gauge sensor.

4) Turn ignition switch to LOCK position. Disconnect HEC module harness connector C808b. Measure resistance between ground and terminal No. 23 (White/Red wire) at HEC module harness connector C808b. *See Fig. 2.* If resistance is greater than 10 k/ohms, go to next step. If resistance is 10 k/ohms or less, repair short to ground in White/Red wire.

5) Measure resistance in White/Red wire between terminal No. 23 at HEC module harness connector C808b and temperature gauge sensor harness connector. If resistance is 5 ohms or less, go to next step (2.0L) or replace HEC module (2.5L). If resistance is greater than 5 ohms, repair open in White/Red wire.

6) Measure resistance between ground and Black/Blue wire terminal at temperature gauge sensor harness connector. If resistance is 5 ohms or less, replace HEC module. If resistance is greater than 5 ohms, repair open in Black/Blue wire.

TEST F: HIGH BEAM INDICATOR INOPERATIVE

1) Turn ignition switch to LOCK position. Disconnect Hybrid Electronic Cluster (HEC) module harness connector C808b. Turn headlights on. Turn high beams on. Measure voltage at terminal No. 25 (Orange/White wire) at HEC module harness connector C808b. If battery voltage exists, go to next step. If battery voltage does not exist, repair open in Orange/White wire.

RESET button. If maintenance interval indicator illuminates, go to next step. If maintenance interval indicator does not illuminate, advise customer of maintenance schedule.

3) Turn ignition switch to LOCK position. Disconnect Hybrid Electronic Cluster (HEC) module harness connector C808b. Turn ignition switch to RUN position. If maintenance interval indicator illuminates, go to next step. If maintenance interval indicator does not illuminate, replace HEC module.

4) Turn ignition switch to LOCK position. Disconnect indicator light module harness connector C467. Measure resistance between ground and terminal No. 8 (Black/Blue wire) at indicator light module harness connector C467. *See Fig. 6.* If resistance is greater than 10 k/ohms, replace indicator light module. If resistance is 10 k/ohms or less, repair short to ground in Black/Blue wire.

5) Turn ignition switch to LOCK position. Connect New Generation Star (NGS) tester to Data Link Connector (DLC). Turn ignition switch to RUN position. Using NGS tester, access Hybrid Electronic Cluster (HEC) module active command WARNING LAMPS AND CHIME COMMAND. Trigger ALLWARNING LAMPS to ON. If maintenance interval indicator does not illuminate, go to next step. If maintenance interval indicator illuminates, replace HEC module.

6) Turn ignition switch to LOCK position. Disconnect indicator light module harness connector C467. Turn ignition switch to RUN position. Measure voltage at terminal No. 6 (Violet wire) at indicator light module harness connector C467. *See Fig. 6.* If battery voltage exists, go to next step. If battery voltage does not exist, repair power distribution circuit as necessary. See appropriate wiring diagram in POWER DISTRIBUTION article in WIRING DIAGRAMS.

7) Turn ignition switch to LOCK position. Disconnect HEC module harness connector C808b. Measure resistance in Black/Blue wire between terminal No. 8 at indicator light module harness connector C467 and terminal No. 23 at HEC module harness connector C808b. *See Figs. 2 and 6.* If resistance is 5 ohms or less, replace indicator light module. If resistance is greater than 5 ohms, repair open in Black/Blue wire.

TEST H: ICE WARNING INDICATOR INOPERATIVE/ALWAYS ON

1) Turn ignition switch to RUN position. If ice warning indicator is always illuminated, go to next step. If ice warning indicator is inoperative, go to step 4). If ice warning indicator illuminate for 3 seconds then turns off, system is okay at this time.

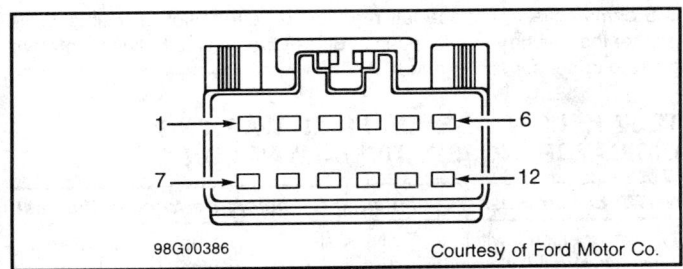

98G00386   Courtesy of Ford Motor Co.

Fig. 6: Identifying Indicator Light Module Harness Connector C467 Terminals

2) Turn ignition switch to LOCK position. Disconnect Hybrid Electronic Cluster (HEC) module harness connector C808a. Turn ignition switch to RUN position. If ice warning indicator illuminates, go to next step. If ice warning indicator does not illuminate, go to step **8)**.

3) Turn ignition switch to LOCK position. Disconnect indicator light module harness connector C467. Measure resistance between ground and terminal No. 10 (Black/Red wire) at indicator light module harness connector C467. *See Fig. 6*. If resistance is greater than 10 k/ohms, replace indicator light module. If resistance is 10 k/ohms or less, repair short to ground in Black/Red wire.

4) Turn ignition switch to LOCK position. Disconnect indicator light module harness connector C467. Turn ignition switch to RUN position. Measure voltage at terminal No. 6 (Violet wire) at indicator light module harness connector C467. *See Fig. 6*. If battery voltage exists, go to next step. If battery voltage does not exist, repair power distribution circuit as necessary. See appropriate wiring diagram in POWER DISTRIBUTION article in WIRING DIAGRAMS.

5) Turn ignition switch to LOCK position. Disconnect HEC module harness connector C808a. Turn ignition switch to RUN position. Measure voltage at terminal No. 10 (Black/Red wire) at indicator light module harness connector C467. If voltage does not exist, go to next step. If voltage exists, repair short to voltage in Black/Red wire.

6) Turn ignition switch to LOCK position. Measure resistance in Black/Red wire between terminal No. 10 at indicator light module harness connector C467 and terminal No. 18 at HEC module harness connector C808a. *See Figs. 2 and 6*. If resistance is 5 ohms or less, go to next step. If resistance is greater than 5 ohms, repair open in Black/Red wire.

7) Connect indicator light module harness connector C467. Turn ignition switch to RUN position. Using a fused jumper wire, ground terminal No. 18 (Black/Red wire) at HEC module harness connector C808a. If ice warning indicator illuminates, go to next step. If ice warning indicator does not illuminate, replace indicator light module.

8) Turn ignition switch to LOCK position. Connect HEC module harness connector C808a. Connect New Generation Star (NGS) tester to Data Link Connector (DLC). Turn ignition switch to RUN position. Using NGS tester, monitor HEC module PID EXTTEMP. If PID does not agree with air temperature, go to next step. If PID agrees with air temperature, replace HEC module.

9) Turn ignition switch to LOCK position. Disconnect HEC module harness connector 808b. Disconnect ice warning sensor harness connector C974. Measure resistance in Brown/Yellow wire between ice warning sensor harness connector C974 and terminal No. 9 at HEC module harness connector C808b. *See Fig. 2*. Also, measure resistance in White/Black wire between ice warning sensor harness connector C974 and terminal No. 20 at HEC module harness connector C808b. If both resistance readings are 5 ohms or less, replace ice warning sensor. If either resistance reading is greater than 5 ohms, repair open in appropriate wire.

TEST I: FROST WARNING INDICATOR INOPERATIVE/ALWAYS ON

1) Turn ignition switch to RUN position. If frost warning indicator is always illuminated, go to next step. If frost warning indicator is inoperative, go to step **4)**. If frost warning indicator illuminates for 3 seconds then turns off, system is okay at this time.

2) Turn ignition switch to LOCK position. Disconnect Hybrid Electronic Cluster (HEC) module harness connector C808a. Turn ignition switch to RUN position. If frost warning indicator illuminates, go to next step. If frost warning indicator does not Illuminate, go to step **8)**.

3) Turn ignition switch to LOCK position. Disconnect indicator light module harness connector C467. Measure resistance between ground and terminal No. 9 (Black/Blue wire) at indicator light module harness connector C467. *See Fig. 6*. If resistance is greater than 10 k/ohms, replace indicator light module. If resistance is 10 k/ohms or less, repair short to ground in Black/Blue wire.

4) Turn ignition switch to LOCK position. Disconnect indicator light module harness connector C467. Turn ignition switch to RUN position. Measure voltage at terminal No. 6 (Violet wire) at indicator light module harness connector C467. *See Fig. 6*. If battery voltage exists, go to next step. If battery voltage does not exist, repair power distribution circuit as necessary. See appropriate wiring diagram in POWER DISTRIBUTION article in WIRING DIAGRAMS.

5) Turn ignition switch to LOCK position. Disconnect HEC module harness connector C808a. Turn ignition switch to RUN position. Measure voltage at terminal No. 9 (Black/Blue wire) at indicator light module harness connector C467. If voltage does not exist, go to next step. If voltage exists, repair short to voltage in Black/Blue wire.

6) Turn ignition switch to LOCK position. Measure resistance in Black/Blue wire between terminal No. 9 at indicator light module harness connector C467 and terminal No. 19 at HEC module harness connector C808a. *See Figs. 2 and 6*. If resistance is 5 ohms or less, go to next step. If resistance is greater than 5 ohms, repair open in Black/Blue wire.

7) Connect indicator light module harness connector C467. Turn ignition switch to RUN position. Using a fused jumper wire, ground terminal No. 19 (Black/Blue wire) at HEC module harness connector C808a. If frost warning indicator illuminates, go to next step. If frost warning indicator does not illuminate, replace indicator light module.

8) Turn ignition switch to LOCK position. Connect HEC module harness connector C808a. Connect New Generation Star (NGS) tester to Data Link Connector (DLC). Turn ignition switch to RUN position. Using NGS tester, monitor HEC module PID EXTTEMP. If PID does not agree with air temperature, go to next step. If PID agrees with air temperature, replace HEC module.

9) Turn ignition switch to LOCK position. Disconnect HEC module harness connector 808b. Disconnect ice warning sensor harness connector C974. Measure resistance in Brown/Yellow wire between ice warning sensor harness connector C974 and terminal No. 9 at HEC module harness connector C808b. *See Fig. 2*. Also, measure resistance in White/Black wire between ice warning sensor harness connector C974 and terminal No. 20 at HEC module harness connector C808b. If both resistance readings are 5 ohms or less, replace ice warning sensor. If either resistance reading is greater than 5 ohms, repair open in appropriate wire.

TEST J: BRAKE PAD WARNING INDICATOR INOPERATIVE/ALWAYS ON

1) Turn ignition switch to RUN position. If brake pad warning indicator is always illuminated, go to next step. If brake pad warning indicator is inoperative, go to step **4)**. If brake pad warning indicator illuminate for 3 seconds then turns off, system is okay at this time.

2) Turn ignition switch to LOCK position. Disconnect Hybrid Electronic Cluster (HEC) module harness connector C808b. Turn ignition switch to RUN position. If brake pad warning indicator illuminates, go to next step. If brake pad warning indicator does not illuminate, go to step **8)**.

3) Turn ignition switch to LOCK position. Disconnect indicator light module harness connector C467. Measure resistance between ground and terminal No. 11 (Black/Orange wire) at indicator light module harness connector C467. *See Fig. 6*. If resistance is greater than 10 k/ohms, replace indicator light module. If resistance is 10 k/ohms or less, repair short to ground in Black/Orange wire.

4) Turn ignition switch to LOCK position. Disconnect indicator light module harness connector C467. Turn ignition switch to RUN position. Measure voltage at terminal No. 6 (Violet wire) at indicator light module harness connector C467. *See Fig. 6*. If battery voltage exists, go to next

step. If battery voltage does not exist, repair power distribution circuit as necessary. See appropriate wiring diagram in POWER DISTRIBUTION article in WIRING DIAGRAMS.

5) Turn ignition switch to LOCK position. Disconnect HEC module harness connector C808a. Turn ignition switch to RUN position. Measure voltage at terminal No. 11 (Black/Orange wire) at indicator light module harness connector C467. If voltage does not exist, go to next step. If voltage exists, repair short to voltage in Black/Orange wire.

6) Turn ignition switch to LOCK position. Measure resistance in Black/Orange wire between terminal No. 11 at indicator light module harness connector C467 and terminal No. 24 at HEC module harness connector C808a. See Figs. 2 and 6. If resistance is 5 ohms or less, go to next step. If resistance is greater than 5 ohms, repair open in Black/Orange wire.

7) Connect indicator light module harness connector C467. Turn ignition switch to RUN position. Using a fused jumper wire, ground terminal No. 24 (Black/Orange wire) at HEC module harness connector C808a. If brake pad warning indicator illuminates, go to next step. If brake pad warning indicator does not illuminate, replace indicator light module.

8) Turn ignition switch to LOCK position. Connect HEC module harness connector C808a. Connect New Generation Star (NGS) tester to Data Link Connector (DLC). Turn ignition switch to RUN position. Using NGS tester, monitor HEC module WEAR_OK. If PID does not indicate YES, go to next step. If PID indicates YES, replace HEC module.

9) Turn ignition switch to LOCK position. Disconnect HEC module harness connector C808a. Measure resistance between ground and terminal No. 12 (Black/Yellow wire) at HEC module harness connector C808a. See Fig. 2. If resistance is greater than 10 k/ohms, go to next step. If resistance is 10 k/ohms or less, go to step 12).

10) Disconnect left front brake pad sensor harness connector C723. Measure resistance in Black/Yellow wire between left front brake pad sensor harness connector C723 and terminal No. 12 at HEC module harness connector C808a. Resistance should be 5 ohms or less. Also, measure resistance between ground and terminal No. 12 (Black/Yellow wire) at HEC module harness connector C808a. Resistance should be greater than 10 k/ohms. If resistance is as specified, go to next step. If resistance is not as specified, repair open and/or short to ground in Black/Yellow wire.

11) Measure resistance between ground and Black wire terminal at left front brake pad sensor harness connector C723. If resistance is 5 ohms or less, replace left front brake pad sensor. If resistance is greater than 5 ohms, repair open in Black wire.

12) Measure resistance between ground and terminal No. 13 (Black/Orange wire) at HEC module harness connector C808a. If resistance is greater than 10 k/ohms, go to next step. If resistance is 10 k/ohms or less, replace HEC module.

NOTE: Left and right rear brake sensor harness connector have 2 Black/Orange wires connected to then. Ensure all resistance measurements are made at appropriate wire.

13) Disconnect left rear brake pad sensor harness connector C725. Measure resistance in Black/Orange wire between left rear brake pad sensor harness connector C725 and terminal No. 13 at HEC module harness connector C808a. If resistance is greater than 5 ohms, go to next step. If resistance is 5 ohms or less, go to step 16).

14) Disconnect right rear brake pad sensor harness connector C1866. Measure resistance in Black/Orange wire between right rear brake pad sensor harness connector C1866 and terminal No. 13 at HEC module harness connector C808a. If resistance is 5 ohms or less, go to next step. If resistance is greater than 5 ohms, repair open in Black/Orange wire between HEC and right rear brake pad sensor.

15) Measure resistance in Black/Orange wire between right rear brake pad sensor harness connector C1866 and left rear brake pad sensor harness connector C725. If resistance is 5 ohms or less, replace right rear brake pad sensor. If resistance is greater than 5 ohms, repair open in Black/Orange wire between right rear brake pad sensor and left rear brake pad sensor.

16) Measure resistance between ground and Black/Orange wire terminal at left rear brake pad sensor harness connector C725. If resistance

is 5 ohms or less, replace left rear brake pad sensor. If resistance is greater than 5 ohms, repair open in Black/Orange wire between left rear brake pad sensor and ground.

TEST K: LOW WASHER FLUID WARNING INDICATOR INOPERATIVE/ALWAYS ON

NOTE: Ensure washer reservoir is full before performing this test.

1) Turn ignition switch to RUN position. Low washer fluid warning indicator should illuminate. Start engine. Low washer fluid warning indicator should turn off. If fluid warning indicator is always illuminated, go to next step. If fluid warning indicator is inoperative, go to step 6). If fluid warning indicator operates as specified, system is okay at this time.

2) Turn ignition switch to LOCK position. Connect New Generation Star (NGS) tester to Data Link Connector (DLC). Turn ignition switch to RUN position. Using NGS tester, monitor Hybrid Electronic Cluster (HEC) module PID WFLUID. If PID indicates LOW, go to next step. If PID does not indicate LOW, replace HEC module.

3) Turn ignition switch to LOCK position. Disconnect HEC module harness connector C808a. Turn ignition switch to RUN position. Measure voltage at terminal No. 10 (White/Blue wire) at HEC module harness connector C808a. See Fig. 2. If voltage does not exist, go to next step. If voltage exists, repair short to voltage in White/Blue wire.

4) Turn ignition switch to LOCK position. Disconnect low washer fluid level switch harness connector C803. Measure resistance in White/Blue wire between low washer fluid level switch harness connector C803 and terminal No. 10 at HEC module harness connector C808a. If resistance is 5 ohms or less, go to next step. If resistance is greater than 5 ohms, repair open in White/Blue wire.

5) Measure resistance between ground and Black wire terminal at low washer fluid level switch harness connector C803. If resistance is 5 ohms or less, replace low washer fluid level switch. If resistance is greater than 5 ohms, repair open in Black wire.

6) Turn ignition switch to LOCK position. Disconnect HEC module harness connector C808a. Disconnect indicator light module harness connector C467. Measure resistance in Black/Red wire between terminal No. 1 at indicator light module harness connector C467 and terminal No. 20 at HEC module harness connector C808a. See Figs. 2 and 6. Resistance should be 5 ohms or less. Also, measure resistance between ground and terminal No. 1 (Black/Red wire) at indicator light module harness connector C467. Resistance should be greater than 10 k/ohms. If resistance is as specified and indicator is inoperative, go to next step. If resistance is as specified and indicator is always illuminated, replace indicator light module. If resistance is not as specified, repair open and/or short to ground in Black/Red wire.

7) Connect indicator light module harness connector C467. Turn ignition switch to RUN position. Using a fused jumper wire, ground terminal No. 20 (Black/Red wire) at HEC module harness connector C808a. If fluid warning indicator illuminates, replace HEC module. If fluid warning indicator does not illuminate, replace indicator light module.

TEST L: DOOR AJAR WARNING INDICATOR INOPERATIVE/ALWAYS ON

1) Turn ignition switch to RUN position. If door ajar warning indicator is always illuminated, go to next step. If door ajar warning indicator is inoperative, go to step 6). If door ajar warning indicator illuminate for 3 seconds then turns off, system is okay at this time.

2) Turn ignition switch to LOCK position. Connect New Generation Star (NGS) tester to Data Link Connector (DLC). Turn ignition switch to RUN position. Using NGS tester, monitor Hybrid Electronic Cluster (HEC) module PIDs D_DR_HE, P_DR_HE and DECKLID while opening each door and decklid. If PID DECKLID does not agree decklid position, go to next step. If PID D_DR_HE does not agree driver's door position, go to step 4). If PID P_DR_HE does not agree passenger's door position, go to step 5). If PID agrees with door/decklid positions, replace HEC module.

3) Turn ignition switch to LOCK position. Disconnect HEC module harness connector C808a. Disconnect decklid ajar switch harness connector C798. Measure resistance between ground and terminal No. 5 (Black/White wire) at HEC module harness connector C808a. *See Fig. 2.* If resistance is greater than 10 k/ohms, replace decklid ajar switch. If resistance is 10 k/ohms or less, repair short to ground in Black/White wire.

4) Turn ignition switch to LOCK position. Disconnect HEC module harness connector C808a. Disconnect driver's door ajar switch harness connector C685. Disconnect central timer module from back of fuse box. Measure resistance between ground and terminal No. 6 (Black/Yellow wire) at HEC module harness connector C808a. *See Fig. 2.* If resistance is greater than 10 k/ohms, replace driver's door ajar switch. If resistance is 10 k/ohms or less, repair short to ground in Black/Yellow wire.

5) Turn ignition switch to LOCK position. Disconnect HEC module harness connector C808a. Disconnect passenger's door ajar switch harness connector C684. Disconnect central timer module from back of fuse box. Measure resistance between ground and terminal No. 11 (Black/Blue wire) at HEC module harness connector C808a. *See Fig. 2.* If resistance is greater than 10 k/ohms, replace passenger's door ajar switch. If resistance is 10 k/ohms or less, repair short to ground in Black/Blue wire.

6) Turn ignition switch to LOCK position. Disconnect HEC module harness connector C808a. Disconnect indicator light module harness connector C467. Measure resistance in Black/Yellow wire between terminal No. 2 at indicator light module harness connector C467 and terminal No. 11 at HEC module harness connector C808a. *See Figs. 2 and 6.* Resistance should be 5 ohms or less. Also, measure resistance between ground and terminal No. 2 (Black/Yellow wire) at indicator light module harness connector C467. Resistance should be greater than 10 k/ohms. If resistance is as specified and indicator is inoperative, go to next step. If resistance is as specified and indicator is always illuminated, replace indicator light module. If resistance is not as specified, repair open and/or short to ground in Black/Yellow wire.

7) Connect indicator light module harness connector C467. Turn ignition switch to RUN position. Using a fused jumper wire, ground terminal No. 11 (Black/Yellow wire) at HEC module harness connector C808a. If door ajar warning indicator illuminates, replace HEC module. If door ajar warning indicator does not illuminate, replace indicator light module.

TEST M: BULB OUT WARNING INDICATOR ALWAYS ON

NOTE: Under normal operating conditions, bulb out warning indicator will illuminate until vehicle is started and brake pedal is depressed.

1) Turn ignition switch to RUN position. Check all exterior lights for proper operation. If all exterior lights operate properly, go to next step. If any exterior light does not operate properly, fix appropriate exterior light as necessary. See appropriate wiring diagram in HEADLIGHT SYSTEMS article, DAYTIME RUNNING LIGHTS article and/or EXTERIOR LIGHTS article.

2) Turn ignition switch to LOCK position. Disconnect bulb outage module harness connector C466. Turn ignition switch to RUN position. If bulb out warning indicator illuminates, go to next step. If bulb out warning indicator is not illuminated, go to step **4)**.

3) Turn ignition switch to LOCK position. Disconnect indicator light module harness connector C467. Measure resistance between ground and terminal No. 3 (Violet/Blue wire) at indicator light module harness connector C467. *See Fig. 6.* If resistance is greater than 10 k/ohms, replace indicator light module. If resistance is 10 k/ohms or less, repair short to ground in Violet/Blue wire.

4) Turn ignition switch to LOCK position. Disconnect Hybrid Electronic Cluster (HEC) module C808a. Measure resistance between ground and terminal No. 7 (White/Black wire) at bulb outage module harness connector C466. *See Fig. 7.* If resistance is greater than 10 k/ohms, replace bulb outage module. If resistance is 10 k/ohms or less, repair short to ground in White/Black wire.

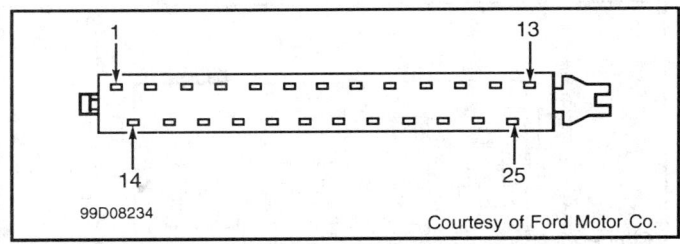

Fig. 7: Identifying Bulb Outage Module Harness Connector C466 Terminals

TEST N: OIL PRESSURE WARNING INDICATOR INOPERATIVE

1) Turn ignition switch to RUN position. If instrument cluster warning indicators and gauges are operating, go to next step. If instrument cluster warning indicators and gauges are not operating, perform TEST A: NO COMMUNICATION WITH HYBRID ELECTRONIC CLUSTER MODULE.

2) Turn ignition switch to LOCK position. Disconnect oil pressure switch harness connector C953. Turn ignition switch to RUN position. Measure voltage at Black/Green wire terminal at oil pressure switch harness connector C953. If battery voltage does not exist, go to next step. If battery voltage exists, replace oil pressure switch.

3) Turn ignition switch to LOCK position. Disconnect Hybrid Electronic Cluster (HEC) module harness connector C808b. Measure resistance in Black/Green wire between oil pressure switch harness connector C953 and terminal No. 5 at Hybrid Electronic Cluster (HEC) module harness connector C808b. *See Fig. 2.* If resistance is 5 ohms or less, replace HEC module. If resistance is greater than 5 ohms, repair open in Black/Green wire.

TEST O: OIL PRESSURE WARNING INDICATOR ALWAYS ON

1) Turn ignition switch to LOCK position. Disconnect oil pressure switch harness connector C953. Turn ignition switch to RUN position. If oil pressure warning indicator illuminates, go to next step. If instrument cluster oil pressure warning indicator does not illuminate, verify oil pressure with mechanical gauge. If oil pressure is okay, replace oil pressure switch.

2) Turn ignition switch to LOCK position. Disconnect Hybrid Electronic Cluster (HEC) module harness connector C808b. Measure resistance between ground and Black/Green wire terminal at oil pressure switch harness connector C953. If resistance is greater than 10 k/ohms, replace HEC module. If resistance is 10 k/ohms or less, repair short to ground in Black/Green wire.

TEST P: SEAT BELT WARNING INDICATOR INOPERATIVE (CHIME OPERATIVE)

1) Turn ignition switch to LOCK position. Disconnect instrument panel fuse box harness connector C362. *See Fig. 8.* Turn ignition switch to RUN position. Using a fused jumper wire, ground terminal No. 1 (Black/Blue wire) at instrument panel fuse box harness connector C362. If seat belt warning indicator does not illuminate, go to next step. If seat belt warning indicator illuminates, go to step **3)**.

2) Turn ignition switch to LOCK position. Disconnect Hybrid Electronic Cluster (HEC) module harness connector C808b. Measure resistance in Black/Blue wire between terminal No. 1 at instrument panel fuse box harness connector C362 and terminal No. 18 at HEC module harness connector C808b. *See Fig. 2.* If resistance is 5 ohms or less, replace HEC module. If resistance is greater than 5 ohms, repair open in Black/Blue wire.

3) Turn ignition switch to LOCK position. Disconnect Central Timer Module (CTM) from rear of instrument panel fuse box. Measure resistance between terminal No. 10 at central timer module connector (fuse box side) and terminal No. 1 at instrument panel fuse box connector C362 (fuse box side). *See Fig. 8.* If resistance is 5 ohms or less, replace CTM. If resistance is greater than 5 ohms, replace instrument panel fuse box.

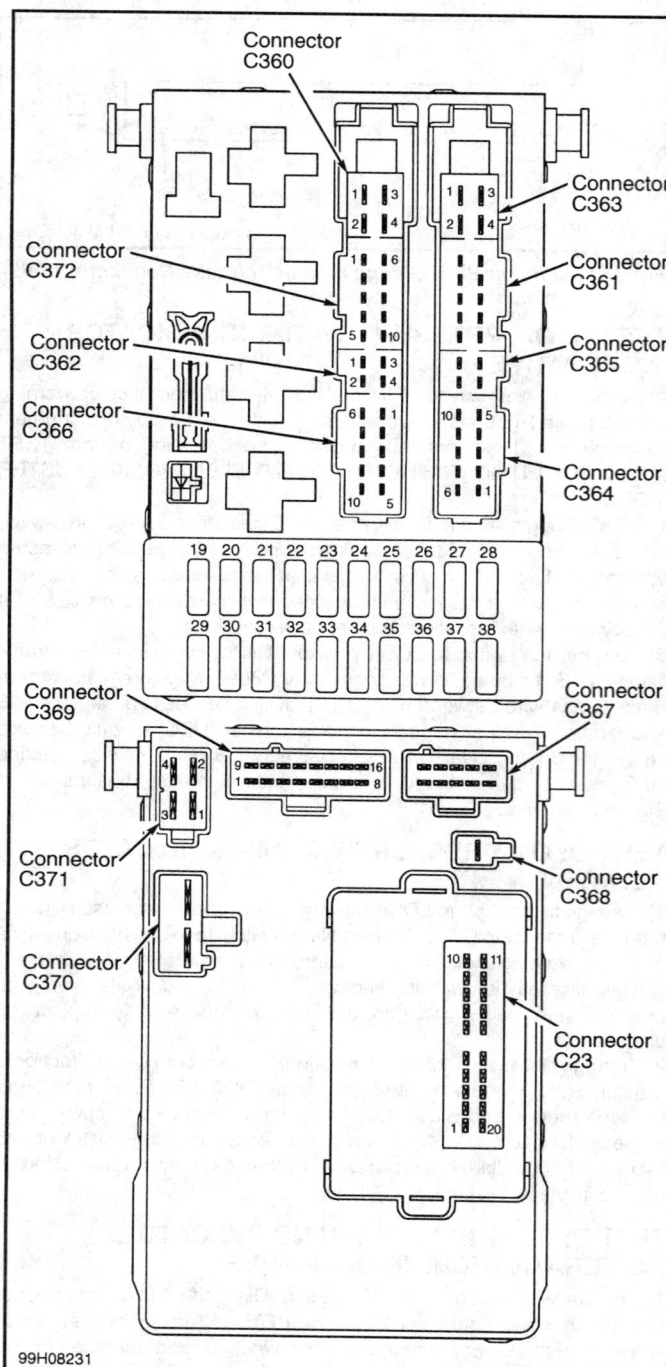

99H08231

Courtesy of Ford Motor Co.

Fig. 8: Identifying Instrument Panel Fuse Box Harness Connectors

TEST Q: SEAT BELT WARNING INDICATOR ALWAYS ON (CHIME OPERATIVE)

1) Turn ignition switch to RUN position. Buckle seat belt. If seat belt chime is off and seat belt warning indicator is illuminated, go to next step. If seat belt chime is on and seat belt warning indicator is illuminated, repair chime module circuit. See appropriate wiring diagram in WARNING SYSTEMS article. If seat belt chime is off and seat belt warning indicator is not illuminated, system is okay.
2) Turn ignition switch to LOCK position. Disconnect instrument panel fuse box harness connector C362. See Fig. 8. Turn ignition switch to RUN position. If seat belt warning indicator illuminates, go to next step. If seat belt warning indicator does not illuminate, go to step 4).

3) Turn ignition switch to LOCK position. Disconnect Hybrid Electronic Cluster (HEC) module harness connector C808a. Measure resistance between ground and terminal No. 18 (Black/Blue wire) at HEC module harness connector C808a. See Fig. 2. If resistance is greater than 10 k/ohms, replace HEC module. If resistance is 10 k/ohms or less, repair short to ground in Black/Blue wire.
4) Turn ignition switch to LOCK position. Connect instrument panel fuse box harness connector C362. Remove Central Timer Module (CTM) from back of instrument panel fuse box. See Fig. 8. Turn ignition switch to RUN position. If seat belt warning indicator illuminates, repair or replace instrument panel fuse box as necessary. If seat belt warning indicator does not illuminate, replace CTM.

TEST R: BRAKE WARNING INDICATOR INOPERATIVE

1) Turn ignition switch to LOCK position. Disconnect brake fluid level sensor harness connector C810. Using a fused jumper wire, connect Black wire terminal and Black/Yellow wire terminal at brake fluid level sensor harness connector C810. Turn ignition switch to RUN position. If brake warning light does not illuminate, remove jumper wire and go to next step. If brake warning light illuminates, remove jumper wire. Check parking brake switch and adjust or replace as necessary. If parking brake switch is okay, repair open Black/Red wire between parking brake switch harness connector and splice S308. See WIRING DIAGRAMS.
2) Turn ignition switch to LOCK position. Measure resistance between ground and Black wire terminal at brake fluid level sensor harness connector C810. If resistance is 5 ohms or less, go to next step. If resistance is greater than 5 ohms, repair open in Black wire.
3) Turn ignition switch to LOCK position. Disconnect Hybrid Electronic Cluster (HEC) module harness connector C808b. Measure resistance in Black/Yellow wire between terminal No. 6 at Hybrid Electronic Cluster (HEC) module harness connector C808b and brake fluid level sensor harness connector C810. See Fig. 2. If resistance is 5 ohms or less, replace HEC module. If resistance is greater than 5 ohms, repair open in Black/Yellow wire.

TEST S: LOW FUEL WARNING INDICATOR INOPERATIVE

Turn ignition switch to LOCK position. Disconnect fuel pump module harness connector C732. Turn ignition switch to RUN position. If low fuel warning indicator illuminates, system is okay at this time. If low fuel warning indicator does not illuminate and fuel gauge is not operating properly, perform TEST B: FUEL GAUGE INACCURATE. If low fuel warning indicator does not illuminate and fuel gauge is operating properly, replace Hybrid Electronic Cluster (HEC) module.

TEST T: LOW FUEL WARNING INDICATOR ALWAYS ON

Turn ignition switch to LOCK position. Disconnect fuel pump module harness connector C732. Turn ignition switch to RUN position. Using a fused jumper wire, ground White/Red wire terminal at fuel pump module harness connector C732. If low fuel indicator is illuminated and fuel gauge is operating properly, replace Hybrid Electronic Cluster (HEC) module. If low fuel indicator is illuminated and fuel gauge is not operating properly, perform TEST B: FUEL GAUGE INACCURATE. If low fuel indicator is not illuminated, system is okay.

TEST U: LOW COOLANT WARNING INDICATOR INOPERATIVE

1) Turn ignition switch to LOCK position. Disconnect low engine coolant level switch harness connector C812. Turn ignition switch to RUN position. Using a fused jumper wire, connect Black wire terminal and White/Green wire terminal at low engine coolant level switch harness connector C812. If low engine coolant level indicator illuminates for 5 seconds or less, go to next step. If low engine coolant level indicator illuminates for greater than 5 seconds and coolant level is below switch in reservoir, replace low engine coolant level switch. If low engine

coolant level indicator illuminates for more than 5 seconds and coolant level is above switch in reservoir, lower engine coolant level and retest system.

2) Measure resistance between ground and Black wire terminal at low engine coolant level switch harness connector C812. If resistance is 5 ohms or less, go to next step. If resistance is greater than 5 ohms, repair open in Black wire.

3) Disconnect Hybrid Electronic Cluster (HEC) module harness connector C808a. Measure resistance in White/Green wire between terminal No. 8 at HEC module harness connector C808a and low engine coolant level switch harness connector C812. *See Fig. 2.* If resistance is 5 ohms or less, replace HEC module. If resistance is greater than 5 ohms, repair open in White/Green wire.

TEST V: LOW COOLANT WARNING INDICATOR ALWAYS ON

1) Turn ignition switch to LOCK position. Ensure coolant reservoir is full. Turn ignition switch to RUN position. If low engine coolant level indicator stays illuminated. go to next step. If low engine coolant level indicator illuminates for about 5 seconds and turns off, system is okay.

2) Turn ignition switch to LOCK position. Disconnect low engine coolant level switch harness connector C812. Turn ignition switch to RUN position. If low engine coolant level indicator does not illuminate for about 5 seconds and turn off, go to next step. If low engine coolant level indicator illuminates for about 5 seconds and turns off, replace low engine coolant level switch.

3) Disconnect Hybrid Electronic Cluster (HEC) module harness connector C808a. Measure resistance between ground and terminal No. 8 (White/Green wire) at HEC module harness connector C808a. *See Fig. 2.* If resistance is greater than 10 k/ohms, replace HEC module and/or instrument cluster interface module as necessary. If resistance is 10 k/ohms or less, repair short to ground in White/Green wire.

TEST W: TURN SIGNAL INDICATOR INOPERATIVE

1) Turn ignition switch in RUN position. Place multifunction switch in left turn position. If left turn indicator does not illuminate, go to next step. If left turn indicator illuminates, go to step **5)**.

2) If left outside turn signals operate, go to next step. If left outside turn signals do not operate, locate and repair problem in exterior lighting system. See appropriate wiring diagram in EXTERIOR LIGHTS article.

3) Turn ignition switch to LOCK position. Disconnect Hybrid Electronic Cluster (HEC) module harness connector C808a. Disconnect instrument panel fuse box harness connector C362. *See Fig. 8.* Measure resistance in Blue/Black wire between terminal No. 3 at instrument panel fuse box harness connector C362 and terminal No. 1 at Hybrid Electronic Cluster (HEC) module harness connector C808a. *See Fig. 2.* If resistance is 5 ohms or less, go to next step. If resistance is greater than 5 ohms, repair open in Blue/Black wire.

4) Disconnect instrument cluster harness connector C369. Measure resistance between terminal No. 14 at instrument cluster connector C396 (fuse box side) and terminal No. 3 at instrument panel fuse box connector C362 (fuse box side). *See Fig. 8.* If resistance is 5 ohms or less, replace HEC module. If resistance is greater than 5 ohms, repair or replace instrument panel fuse box as necessary.

5) Turn ignition switch to RUN position. Place multifunction switch in right turn position. If right turn indicator does not illuminate, go to next step. If right turn indicator illuminates, system is okay at this time.

6) If right outside turn signals operate, go to next step. If right outside turn signals do not operate, locate and repair problem in exterior lighting system. See appropriate wiring diagram in EXTERIOR LIGHTS article.

7) Turn ignition switch to LOCK position. Disconnect Hybrid Electronic Cluster (HEC) module harness connector C808a. Disconnect instrument panel fuse box harness connector C362. *See Fig. 8.* Measure resistance in Blue/Yellow wire between terminal No. 4 at instrument panel fuse box connector C362 and terminal No. 19 at HEC module harness connector C808a. *See Fig. 2.* If resistance is 5 ohms or less, go to next step. If resistance is greater than 5 ohms, repair open in Blue/Yellow wire.

8) Disconnect instrument panel fuse box harness connector C369. Measure resistance between terminal No. 16 at instrument panel fuse box connector C369 (fuse box side) at terminal No. 4 at instrument panel fuse box connector C362 (fuse box side). *See Fig. 8.* If resistance is 5 ohms or less, replace HEC module. If resistance is greater than 5 ohms, repair or replace instrument panel fuse box as necessary.

TEST X: CHARGE WARNING INDICATOR NEVER ON

1) Turn ignition switch to LOCK position. Disconnect generator harness connector. Turn ignition switch to RUN position. Using a fused jumper wire, ground Green/Black wire terminal at generator harness connector. If charge warning indicator does not illuminate, go to next step. If charge warning indicator illuminates, repair charging system concern. See appropriate GENERATORS article in CHARGING & STARTING SYSTEMS.

2) Turn ignition switch to LOCK position. Disconnect Hybrid Electronic Cluster (HEC) module harness connector C808b. Measure resistance in Green/Black wire between generator harness connector and terminal No. 4 at HEC module harness connector C808b. *See Fig. 2.* If resistance is 5 ohms or less, replace HEC module. If resistance is greater than 5 ohms, repair open in Green/Black wire.

TEST Y: CHECK ENGINE LIGHT INOPERATIVE

NOTE: CHECK ENGINE light may also be referred to as Malfunction Indicator Light (MIL).

1) Turn ignition switch to LOCK position. Disconnect Powertrain Control Module (PCM) harness connector C421. Connect breakout box to PCM harness connector C421. Using a fused jumper wire, connect terminals No. 2 and 24 at breakout box. Turn ignition switch to RUN position. If CHECK ENGINE light does not illuminate, go to next step. If CHECK ENGINE light illuminates, repair powertrain control concern. See appropriate SELF-DIAGNOSTICS article in ENGINE PERFORMANCE in appropriate MITCHELL® manual.

2) Turn ignition switch to LOCK position. Disconnect Hybrid Electronic Cluster (HEC) module harness connector C808a. Measure resistance in Black/Orange wire between terminal No. 2 at breakout box and terminal No. 16 at HEC module harness connector C808a. *See Fig. 2.* If resistance is 5 ohms or less, replace HEC module. If resistance is greater than 5 ohms, repair open in Black/Orange wire.

TEST Z: CHECK ENGINE LIGHT ALWAYS ON

NOTE: If Powertrain Control Module (PCM) is replace, PCM MUST be programmed. If vehicle is equipped with passive anti-theft system, all ignition keys MUST be programmed into PCM. See COMPUTER RELEARN PROCEDURES article in GENERAL INFORMATION.

NOTE: CHECK ENGINE light may also be referred to as Malfunction Indicator Light (MIL).

1) Start engine. If CHECK ENGINE light illuminates and then goes out after engine is started, system is okay at this time. If CHECK ENGINE light illuminates and remains on after engine is started, repair powertrain control concern. See appropriate SELF-DIAGNOSTICS article in ENGINE PERFORMANCE in appropriate MITCHELL® manual. If no powertrain control concern exists, go to next step.

2) Turn ignition switch to LOCK position. Disconnect Powertrain Control Module (PCM) harness connector C421. Turn ignition switch to RUN position. If CHECK ENGINE light does not illuminate, replace PCM. If CHECK ENGINE light illuminates, check for short to ground in Black/Orange wire. If short to ground does not exists, replace Hybrid Electronic Cluster (HEC) module.

TEST AA: ABS WARNING INDICATOR INOPERATIVE

1) Turn ignition switch to LOCK position. Disconnect Anti-Lock Brake System (ABS) module harness connector C385. Using a fused jumper wire, ground terminal No. 20 (Black/Red wire) at ABS module harness connector C385. *See Fig. 9*. Turn ignition switch to RUN position. If ABS warning indicator does not illuminate, go to next step. If ABS warning indicator illuminates, repair ABS concern. See appropriate ANTI-LOCK article in BRAKES in appropriate MITCHELL® manual.

2) Turn ignition switch to LOCK position. Disconnect Hybrid Electronic Cluster (HEC) module harness connector C808b. Measure resistance in Black/Red wire between terminal No. 16 at ABS module harness connector C385 and terminal No. 7 at HEC module harness connector C808b. *See Figs. 2 and 9*. If resistance is greater than 5 ohms, repair open in Black/Red wire. If resistance is 5 ohms or less, replace HEC module.

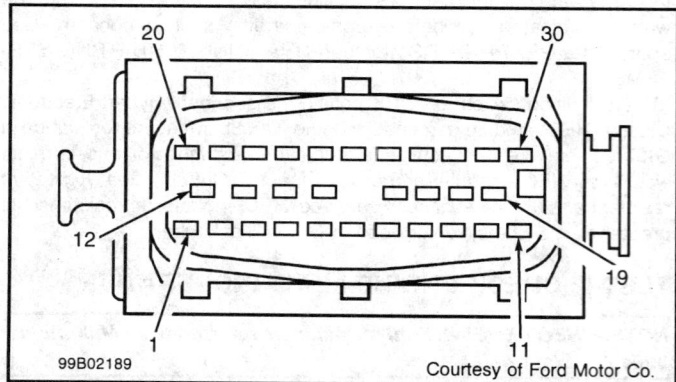

99B02189   Courtesy of Ford Motor Co.

Fig. 9: Identifying ABS Module Harness Connector C385 Terminals

TEST AB: MESSAGE CENTER SWITCH NOT OPERATING CORRECTLY

1) Connect New Generation Star (NGS) tester to Data Link Connector (DLC). Turn ignition switch to RUN position. Using NGS tester, monitor Hybrid Electronic Cluster (HEC) module PID RESETSW while pressing RESET button. Also, monitor HEC PID SELECT while pressing SELECT button. Also, monitor message center while pressing UNITS button. If SELECT button was not acknowledged, go to next step. If RESET button was not acknowledged, go to step **3)**. If UNITS button was not acknowledged, go to step **4)**. If PIDs agree with switch position and UNITS button toggles message center between English and metric, go to step **5)**.

2) Turn ignition switch to LOCK position. Disconnect message center switch harness connector C422. Measure resistance between terminals No. 2 and 6 at message center switch (component side). *See Fig. 10*. Resistance should be 5 ohms or less when SELECT button is pressed and greater than 10 k/ohms when SELECT button in not pressed. If resistance is not as specified, replace message center switch. If resistance is as specified, repair White/Green wire between message center switch and HEC module.

3) Turn ignition switch to LOCK position. Disconnect message center switch harness connector C422. Measure resistance between terminals No. 1 and 6 at message center switch (component side). *See Fig. 10*. Resistance should be 5 ohms or less when RESET button is pressed and greater than 10 k/ohms when RESET button in not pressed. If resistance is not as specified, replace message center switch. If resistance is as specified, repair White/Blue wire between message center switch and HEC module.

4) Turn ignition switch to LOCK position. Disconnect message center switch harness connector C422. Measure resistance between terminals No. 3 and 6 at message center switch (component side). *See Fig. 10*. Resistance should be 5 ohms or less when UNITS button is pressed and greater than 10 k/ohms when UNITS button in not pressed. If resistance is not as specified, replace message center switch. If resistance is as specified, repair White/Violet wire between message center switch and HEC module.

5) Turn ignition switch to LOCK position. Disconnect message center switch harness connector C422. Measure resistance between ground and Black wire terminal at message center switch harness connector C422. If resistance is 5 ohms or less, replace message center switch. If resistance is greater than 5 ohms, repair open in Black wire.

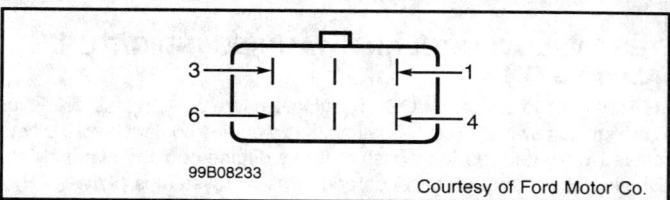

99B08233   Courtesy of Ford Motor Co.

Fig. 10: Identifying Message Center Switch Terminals

TEST AC: MESSAGE CENTER NOT OPERATING CORRECTLY

Connect New Generation Star (NGS) tester to Data Link Connector (DLC). Using NGS tester, perform Hybrid Electronic Cluster (HEC) module self-test. If any DTCs are retrieved, perform appropriate test in accordance with DTC retrieved. See HYBRID ELECTRONIC CLUSTER MODULE DTC INDEX table under SELF-DIAGNOSTIC SYSTEM. If no DTC are retrieved and fuel gauge and speedometer are operating properly, replace HEC module. If no DTC are retrieved and fuel gauge and/or speedometer are not operating properly, perform TEST B: FUEL GAUGE INACCURATE and/or TEST C: SPEEDOMETER INOPERATIVE.

REMOVAL & INSTALLATION

CAUTION: When battery is disconnected, vehicle computer and memory systems may lose memory data. Driveability problems may exist until computer systems have completed a relearn cycle. See COMPUTER RELEARN PROCEDURES article in GENERAL INFORMATION before disconnecting battery.

INSTRUMENT CLUSTER

Removal & Installation – 1) Remove ashtray and cigarette light bezel. Disconnect negative battery cable. Using Radio Remover (T87P-19061-A), detach radio from instrument panel. Pull radio out and disconnect radio harness connectors. Remove switch assembly, above heater controls, and disconnect harness connectors.

2) Remove 5 heater controls/radio bezel retaining screws. Detach bezel from clips at top of bezel. Disconnect heater controls harness connectors and disconnect vacuum line. Remove driver's side lower instrument panel trim panel. Remove headlight switch bezel retaining screws. Detach bezel from clips at top of bezel.

3) Disconnect headlight switch harness connectors. Remove instrument cluster bezel retaining screws. Detach bezel from clips at top of bezel and remove. Remove instrument cluster retaining screws. Pull instrument cluster back and disconnect harness connectors. Remove instrument cluster. To install, reverse removal procedures.

WIRING DIAGRAMS

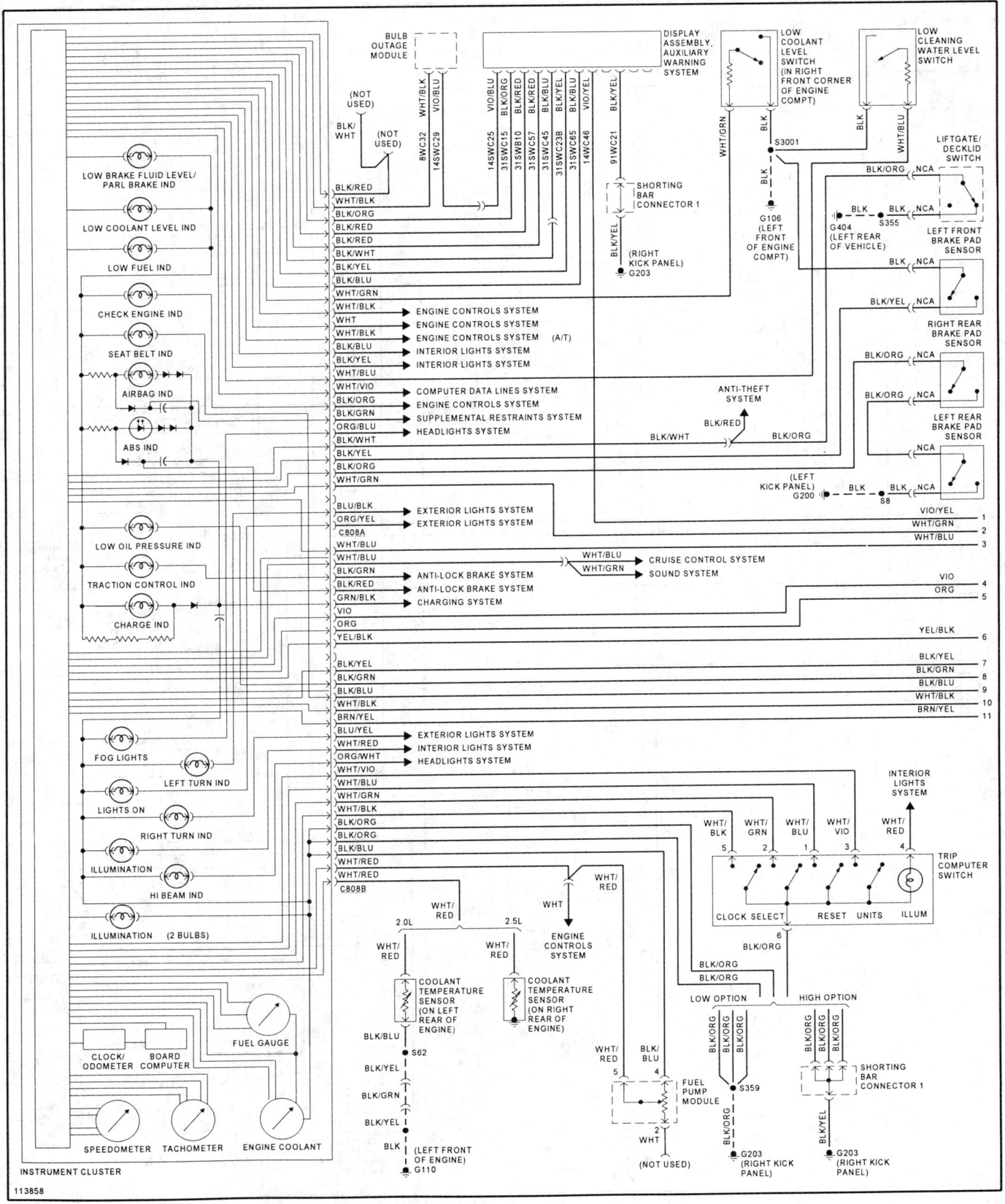

Fig. 11: Analog Instrument Panel Wiring Diagram (Cougar – 1 Of 2)

113858

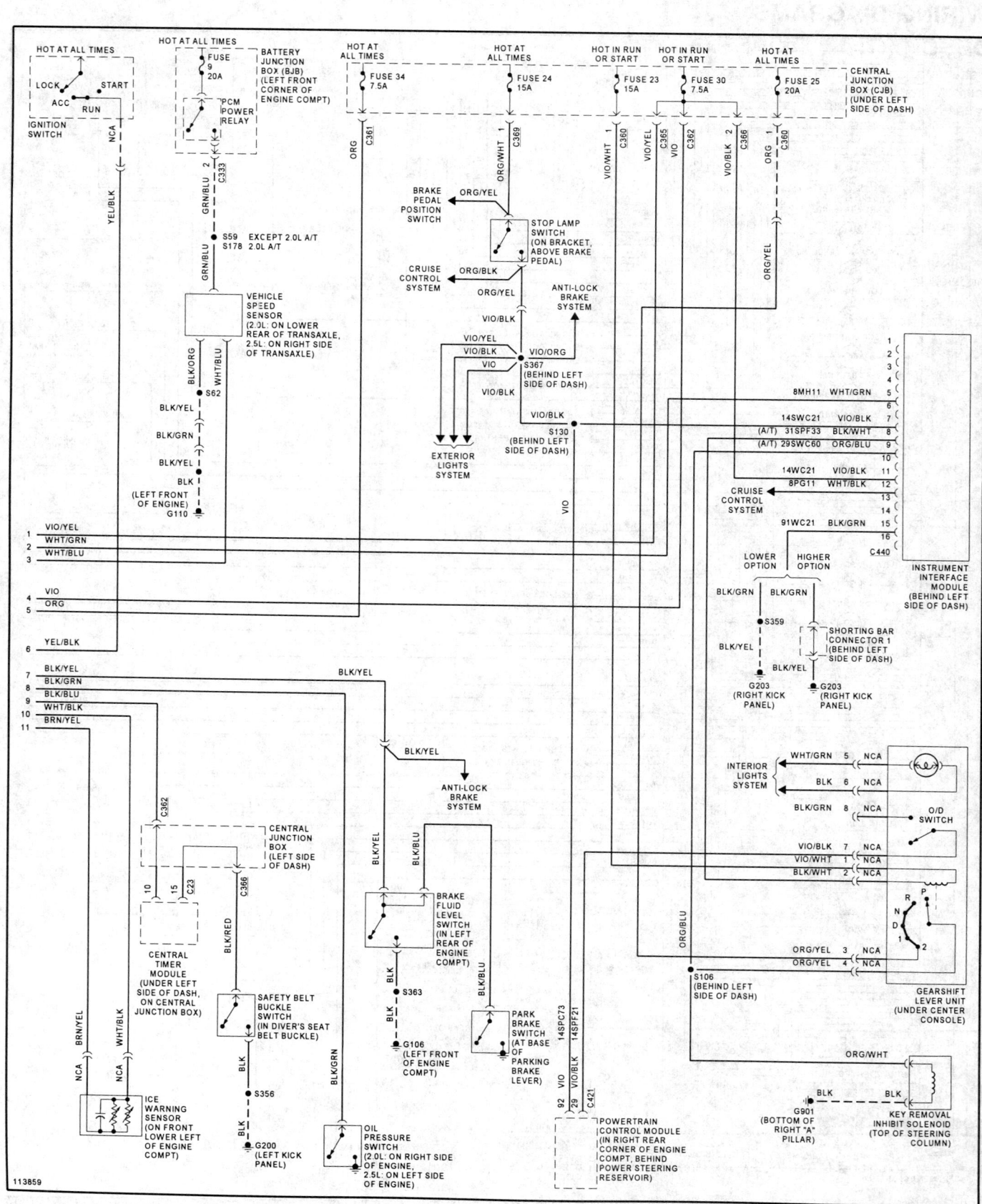

Fig. 12: Analog Instrument Panel Wiring Diagram (Cougar – 2 Of 2)

113859

1999 ACCESSORIES & EQUIPMENT
Analog Instrument Panels
Crown Victoria & Grand Marquis

DESCRIPTION & OPERATION

Instrument cluster contains a speedometer/odometer, fuel gauge/voltmeter assembly, temperature gauge/oil pressure gauge assembly, transmission range indicator and various warning indicators placed across top of instrument cluster. See Figs. 1 and 2.

Anti-slosh module is part of low fuel level warning and provides delay in fuel gauge to prevent fluctuation in fuel gauge pointer as a result of fuel movement in tank. The module is a small printed circuit board which latches into a pocket on back of instrument cluster. There are no provisions for calibration or adjustment of anti-slosh/low fuel level warning module. On vehicle equipped with CNG fuel system, fuel gauge and voltmeter inputs are receive from Natural Gas Vehicle (NGV) module.

When ignition switch is turned to ON position, the following warning indicators will light momentarily for function proof:

- ABS
- AIR BAG
- BRAKE
- Charging System
- Coolant Temperature
- LOW FUEL
- MIL (CHECK ENGINE)
- OD OFF
- Safety Belt
- TRAC CNTL

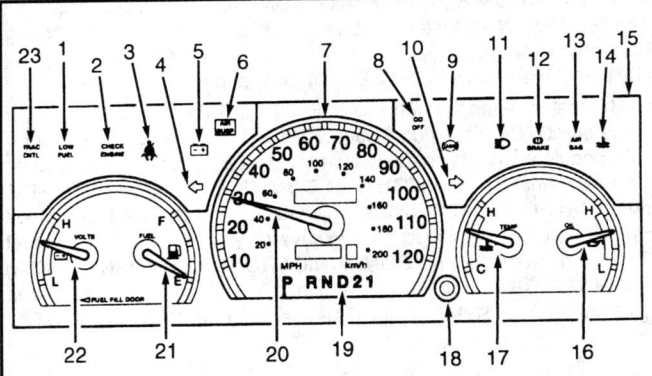

1. Low Fuel Indicator
2. Check Engine Light
3. Safety Belt Warning Indicator
4. Left Turn Indicator
5. Charging System Indicator
6. Air Suspension Indicator
7. Speedometer
8. Overdrive Off Indicator
9. Anti-Lock Brake (ABS) Indicator
10. Right Turn Indicator
11. High Beam Indicator
12. Brake Indicator
13. Air Bag Indicator
14. Coolant System Warning Indicator
15. Instrument Cluster
16. Oil Pressure Gauge
17. Coolant Temperature Gauge
18. Trip Reset
19. Transmission Range Indicator
20. Speedometer Pointer
21. Fuel Gauge
22. Battery Voltage Gauge
23. Traction Control Indicator

98A00505
Courtesy of Ford Motor Co.

Fig. 1: Identifying Instrument Cluster Gauges & Indicators (Front View)

COMPONENT LOCATIONS

COMPONENT LOCATIONS

Component	Location
Air Suspension Control Module	Behind Instrument Panel, Above Glove Box
Anti-Lock Brake System Module	Left Front Of Vehicle, On Radiator Support
Data Link Connector	Behind Left Side Of Instrument Panel

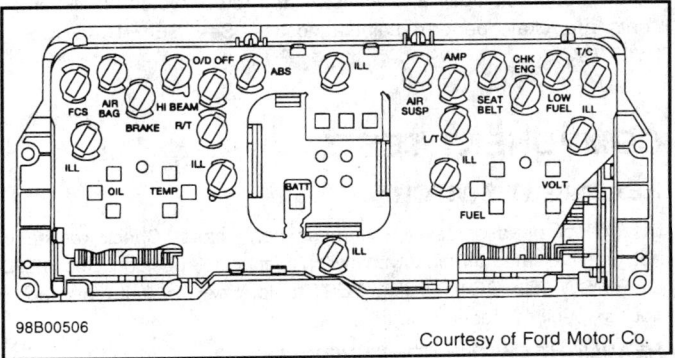

98B00506
Courtesy of Ford Motor Co.

Fig. 2: Identifying Instrument Cluster Gauges & Indicators (Rear View)

COMPONENT LOCATIONS (Cont.)

Component	Location
Daytime Running Light Module	Front Center Of Radiator Support
Engine Coolant Temperature Sender	Top Front Right Of Engine
Fuel Pump Module	On Rear Of Fuel Tank
Fuel Tank Pressure Sensor (CNG)	On Upper Fuel Tank Assembly
Fuel Tank Temperature Sensor No. 1 (CNG)	On Upper Fuel Tank Assembly
Fuel Tank Temperature Sensor No. 2 (CNG)	On Lower Fuel Tank Assembly
Headlight Switch	Left Side Of Instrument Panel
Ignition Switch	On Steering Column
Instrument Panel Fuse Box	Behind Left Side Of Instrument Panel
Lighting Control Module	Behind Instrument Panel, Right Of Steering Column
Natural Gas Vehicle Module	On Front Radiator Support
Powertrain Control Module	Left Rear Corner Of Engine Compartment, In Firewall
Vehicle Speed Sensor	Located At Left Rear Of Transmission

TROUBLE SHOOTING

Verify customer concern by operating system in question. Attempt to duplicate condition with ignition switch in RUN position, in START position before ignition switch is released, and in RUN position with engine running. Visually inspect components. If inspection reveals an obvious concern which can be easily serviced, correct malfunction before continuing.

Mechanical Inspection:
- Damaged Fuel Tank
- Low Engine Coolant Level
- Low Engine Oil Level
- Worn Or Damaged Accessory Drive Belt

Electrical Inspection:
- Blown Fuses
- Damaged Indicator Bulbs
- Damaged Wiring Harness
- Loose Or Corroded Connections
- Damaged Switches, Sensors Or Modules
- Damaged VSS
- Damaged Instrument Cluster

Verify charging system, fuel system, cooling system, safety belt warning chime, turn signals, headlights and cruise control are working properly. Inspect wiring harness for obvious signs of shorts, opens, bad connections or damage. If inspection reveals obvious concerns that can be

FORD
4-716

1999 ACCESSORIES & EQUIPMENT
Analog Instrument Panels
Crown Victoria & Grand Marquis (Cont.)

readily identified, repair as necessary and retest system. If all components are okay, perform self-diagnostics. See SELF-DIAGNOSTIC SYSTEM.

COMPONENT TESTS

HEADLIGHT SWITCH

Disconnect headlight switch harness connectors. Check resistance between indicated terminal with switch in specified position. See HEADLIGHT SWITCH CONTINUITY TEST table. *See Fig. 3*. If resistance is not as specified, replace headlight switch.

HEADLIGHT SWITCH CONTINUITY TEST

Switch Position	Terminals	Resistance
Headlight Circuit		
Off	7 & 8	1
Park	7 & 8	1
Head	7 & 8	2
Parking Light Circuit		
Off	7 & 3	1
Park	7 & 3	2
Head	7 & 3	2
Dome Light Circuit		
Off	6 & 7	1
On	6 & 7	2
Autolamp Circuit		
Off	4 & 7	1
On	4 & 7	2
Rheostat	7 & 9	3

[1] – Resistance should be greater than 10 k/ohms.
[2] – Resistance should be 5 ohms or less.
[3] – Rotate dial clockwise from off to max. Resistance should increase smoothly from 3 k/ohms to 200 k/ohms.

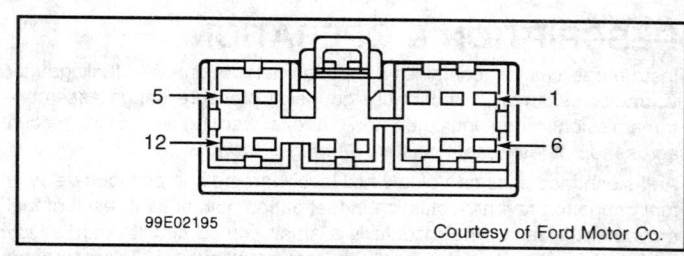

99E02195   Courtesy of Ford Motor Co.

Fig. 3: Identifying Headlight Switch Terminals

SELF-DIAGNOSTIC SYSTEM

CAUTION: Electronic modules are sensitive to static electrical charges. Proper grounding of technician and workpiece is essential to prevent damage.

Connect New Generation Star (NGS) tester to Data Link Connector (DLC), located beneath instrument panel. Using NGS tester, perform data link diagnostics test. See DATA LINK DIAGNOSTIC TEST under COMMUNICATION NETWORK DIAGNOSTICS in MODULE COMMUNICATIONS NETWORK – CROWN VICTORIA & GRAND MARQUIS article. If NGS tester responds with CKT914, CKT915 or CKT70=ALL ECUS NO RESP/NOT EQUIP, repair module communications concern. See MODULE COMMUNICATIONS NETWORK – CROWN VICTORIA & GRAND MARQUIS article. If NGS tester displays NO RESP/NOT EQUIP for Lighting Control Module (LCM), perform TEST A: NO COMMUNICATION WITH LIGHTING CONTROL MODULE under SYSTEM TESTS. If NGS tester displays NO RESP/NOT EQUIP for Natural Gas Vehicle (NGV) module, perform TEST T: NO COMMUNICATION WITH NATURAL GAS VEHICLE MODULE under SYSTEM TESTS.

If NGS tester responds with SYSTEM PASSED, retrieve and record continuous DTCs. Erase continuous DTCs. Using NGS tester, perform NGV module and LCM self-test. Perform appropriate test in accordance with DTC retrieved. See LIGHTING CONTROL MODULE DTC INDEX and/or NATURAL GAS VEHICLE MODULE DTC INDEX table. Codes listed in this table are only for testing covered in this article. For complete DTC listing, see MODULE COMMUNICATIONS NETWORK – CROWN VICTORIA & GRAND MARQUIS article. If no DTCs are retrieved, repair by symptom. See SYMPTOM CHART table under SYSTEM TESTS.

LIGHTING CONTROL MODULE DTC INDEX

DTC [1]	Description	Test
B1342	ECU Defective	2
B1579	Panel Dim Increase Circuit Failure	AH
B1581	Panel Dim Increase Circuit Short To Voltage	AI
B1583	Panel Dim Decrease Input Circuit Failure	AJ
B1585	Panel Dim Decrease Input Short To Voltage	AK

[1] – Codes listed in this table are only for testing covered in this article. For complete DTC listing, see MODULE COMMUNICATIONS NETWORK – CROWN VICTORIA & GRAND MARQUIS article.
[2] – Using NGS tester, clear and document continuous DTCs. Perform Driver's Door Module (DDM) self-test. If DTC B1342 is retrieved again, replace DDM.

NATURAL GAS VEHICLE MODULE DTC INDEX

DTC	Description	Test
B1219	Fuel Tank Pressure Sensor Circuit Failure	U
B1220	Fuel Tank Pressure Sensor Circuit Short To Voltage	V
B1222	Fuel Tank Temperature Sensor No. 1 Circuit Failure	W
B1223	Fuel Tank Temperature Sensor No. 1 Circuit Open	X
B1224	Fuel Tank Temperature Sensor No. 1 Circuit Short To Voltage	Y
B1225	Fuel Tank Temperature Sensor No. 1 Circuit Short To Ground	Z
B1226	Fuel Tank Temperature Sensor No. 2 Circuit Failure	AA
B1227	Fuel Tank Temperature Sensor No. 2 Circuit Open	AB
B1228	Fuel Tank Temperature Sensor No. 2 Circuit Short To Voltage	AC
B1229	Fuel Tank Temperature Sensor No. 2 Circuit Short To Ground	AD
B1317	Battery Voltage High	AE
B1318	Battery Voltage Low	AF

1999 ACCESSORIES & EQUIPMENT
Analog Instrument Panels
Crown Victoria & Grand Marquis (Cont.)

FORD
4-717

NATURAL GAS VEHICLE MODULE DTC INDEX (Cont.)

DTC	Description	Test
B1342	ECU Defective	AG

SYSTEM TESTS

CAUTION: Electronic modules are sensitive to static electrical charges. Proper grounding of technician and workpiece is essential to prevent damage.

SYMPTOM CHART

Symptom	Test
No Communication With Lighting Control Module	A
Instrument Cluster Inoperative	B
Fuel Gauge Inaccurate (Gasoline)	C
Coolant Temperature Gauge Inaccurate	D
Oil Pressure Gauge Inaccurate	E
Speedometer/Odometer Inoperative	F
Low Fuel Warning Light Never/Always On	G
Charge Warning Light Never On	H
Brake Warning Light Never On	I
Check Engine Light Inoperative	J
Seat Belt Warning Light Inoperative (Chime Operative)	K
Air Suspension Warning Light Never/Always On	L
Left Turn Indicator Never/Always On	M
Right Turn Indicator Never/Always On	N
High Beam Warning Never/Always On	O
Traction Control Indicator Inoperative	P
Overdrive Off Indicator Inoperative	Q
ABS Indicator Inoperative	R
Fail-Safe Cooling Indicator Inoperative	S
No Communication With Natural Gas Vehicle Module	T [1]
Fuel Gauge Inaccurate (CNG)	AL
Panel Illumination Control Inoperative	AM
Instrument Cluster Illumination Inoperavtive	AM
Instrument Panel Illmination Does Not Dim	AN

[1] – Using NGS tester, perform NGV module self-test. If any DTCs exist, perform appropriate test in accordance with DTC retrieved. See NATURAL GAS VEHICLE MODULE DTC INDEX table under SELF-DIAGNOSTIC SYSTEM. If no DTCs exist, perform TEST AG: FUEL GAUGE INACCURATE (CNG) OR ECU DEFECTIVE (DTC B1342).

TEST A: NO COMMUNICATION WITH LIGHTING CONTROL MODULE

1) Turn ignition switch to RUN position. Using NGS tester, monitor Lighting Control Module (LCM) PID IGN_LC. If NGS tester does not indicate UNABLE TO PERFORM TEST FUNCTION, MODULE NOT RESPONDING, CHECK IGNITION STATUS/VERIFY CABLE REQUIREMENTS, OR CHECK CABLE CONNECTIONS, go to next step. If NGS tester indicates UNABLE TO PERFORM TEST FUNCTION, MODULE NOT RESPONDING, CHECK IGNITION STATUS/ VERIFY CABLE REQUIREMENTS, OR CHECK CABLE CONNECTIONS, go to step **11)**.

2) Turn ignition switch to RUN position. Using NGS tester, monitor LCM PID IGN_LC while rotating ignition switch through ACCY, OFF and RUN positions. If PID indicates START while ignition switch is in RUN position, go to next step. If PID indicates RUN while ignition switch is in RUN position, go to step **12)**. If PID indicates ACCY while ignition switch is in RUN position, go to step **7)**.

3) Turn ignition switch to LOCK position. Remove fuse No. 6 (15-amp) from instrument panel fuse box. Check fuse. If fuse is okay, go to next step. If fuse is blown, go to step **6)**.

4) Turn ignition switch to RUN position. Measure voltage at input side of fuse No. 6 in instrument panel fuse box. If battery voltage exists, go to next step. If battery voltage does not exist, repair power supply to fuse No. 6. See appropriate wiring diagram in POWER DISTRIBUTION article in WIRING DIAGRAMS.

5) Turn ignition switch to LOCK position. Install fuse No. 6. Disconnect LCM harness connector C2027. Turn ignition switch to RUN position. Measure voltage at terminal No. 1 (White/Violet wire) at LCM harness connector C2027. *See Fig. 4*. If battery voltage exists, replace LCM. If battery voltage does not exist, repair open in White/Violet wire.

6) Turn ignition switch to LOCK position. Disconnect Lighting Control Module (LCM) harness connector C2027. Measure resistance between ground and terminal No. 1 (White/Violet wire) at LCM harness connector C2027. *See Fig. 4* . If resistance is greater than 10 k/ohms, replace LCM. If resistance is 10 k/ohms or less, repair short to ground in White/Violet wire.

7) Turn ignition switch to LOCK position. Remove fuse No. 13 (15-amp) from instrument panel fuse box. Check fuse. If fuse is okay, go to next step. If fuse is blown, go to step **10)**.

8) Turn ignition switch to RUN position. Measure voltage at input side of fuse No. 13 in instrument panel fuse box. If battery voltage exists, go to next step. If battery voltage does not exist, repair power supply to fuse No. 13. See appropriate wiring diagram in POWER DISTRIBUTION article in WIRING DIAGRAMS.

9) Turn ignition switch to LOCK position. Install fuse No. 13 (15-amp). Disconnect LCM harness connector C2027. Turn ignition switch to RUN position. Measure voltage at terminal No. 9 (Red/Yellow wire) at LCM harness connector C2027. *See Fig. 4*. If battery voltage exists, replace LCM. If battery voltage does not exist, repair open in Red/Yellow wire.

10) Turn ignition switch to LOCK position. Disconnect LCM harness connector C2027. Measure resistance between ground and terminal No. 9 (Red/Yellow wire) at LCM harness connector C2027. *See Fig. 4*. If resistance is greater than 10 k/ohms, replace LCM. If resistance is 10 k/ohms or less, repair short to ground in Red/Yellow wire.

11) Turn ignition switch to LOCK position. Disconnect LCM harness connector C2029. Measure resistance between ground and terminals No. 4 and 9 (both Black wire) at LCM harness connector C2029. *See Fig. 5*. If either resistance reading is greater than 5 ohms, repair open in appropriate Black wire(s). If both resistance readings are 5 ohms or less, repair module communication concern. See MODULE COMMUNICATIONS NETWORK – CROWN VICTORIA & GRAND MARQUIS article.

12) Turn ignition switch to LOCK position. Disconnect LCM harness connector C2029. Measure voltage at terminal No. 6 (Tan/White wire) at LCM harness connector C2029. *See Fig. 5*. If battery voltage does not exist, go to next step. If battery voltage exists, go to step **16)**.

13) Remove fuse No. 4 (15-amp) from instrument panel fuse box. Measure resistance between ground and terminal No. 6 (Tan/White wire) at LCM harness connector C2029. If resistance is greater than 10 k/ohms, go to next step. If resistance is 10 k/ohms or less, repair short to ground in Tan/White wire and replace fuse.

14) Measure voltage at input side of fuse No. 4 in instrument panel fuse box. If battery voltage exists, go to next step. If battery voltage does not exist, repair power distribution circuit. See appropriate wiring diagram in POWER DISTRIBUTION article in WIRING DIAGRAMS.

15) Measure resistance in Tan/White wire between output side of fuse No. 4 and terminal No. 6 at LCM harness connector C2029. If resistance is 5 ohms or less, system is okay at this time. If resistance is greater than 5 ohms, repair open in Tan/White wire.

FORD
4-718

1999 ACCESSORIES & EQUIPMENT
Analog Instrument Panels
Crown Victoria & Grand Marquis (Cont.)

16) Measure voltage at terminal No. 11 (Light Green/Yellow wire) at LCM harness connector C2029. If battery voltage does not exist, go to next step. If battery voltage exists, go to step **20)**.

17) Remove fuse No. 8 (15-amp) from instrument panel fuse box. Measure resistance between ground and terminal No. 11 (Light Green/Yellow wire) at LCM harness connector C2029. If resistance is greater than 10 k/ohms, go to next step. If resistance is 10 k/ohms or less, repair short to ground in Light Green/Yellow wire and replace fuse.

18) Measure voltage at input side of fuse No. 8. If battery voltage exists, go to next step. If battery voltage does not exist, repair power distribution circuit. See appropriate wiring diagram in POWER DISTRIBUTION article in WIRING DIAGRAMS.

19) Measure resistance in Light Green/Yellow wire between output side of fuse No. 8 and terminal No. 11 at LCM harness connector C2029. If resistance is 5 ohms or less, system is okay at this time. If resistance is greater than 5 ohms, repair open in Light Green/Yellow wire.

20) Measure resistance between ground and terminal No. 9 (Black wire) at LCM harness connector C2029. If resistance is 5 ohms or less, repair module communication concern. See MODULE COMMUNICATIONS NETWORK – CROWN VICTORIA & GRAND MARQUIS article. If resistance is greater than 5 ohms, repair open in Black wire.

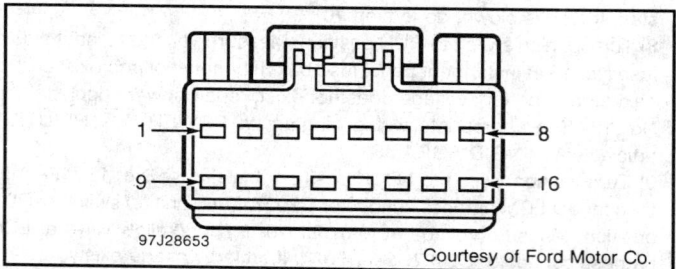

96B01236

Courtesy of Ford Motor Co.

Fig. 6: Identifying Instrument Cluster Connector C251 Terminals

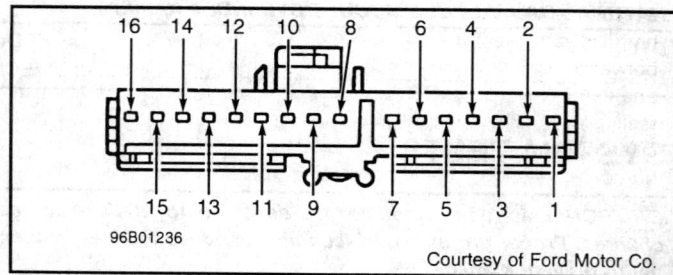

96G01234

Courtesy of Ford Motor Co.

Fig. 7: Identifying Instrument Cluster Connector C250 Terminals

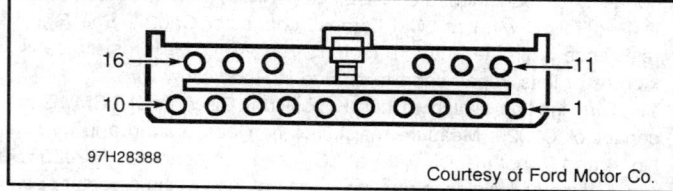

97J28653

Courtesy of Ford Motor Co.

Fig. 4: Identifying Lighting Control Module Harness Connector C2027 Terminals

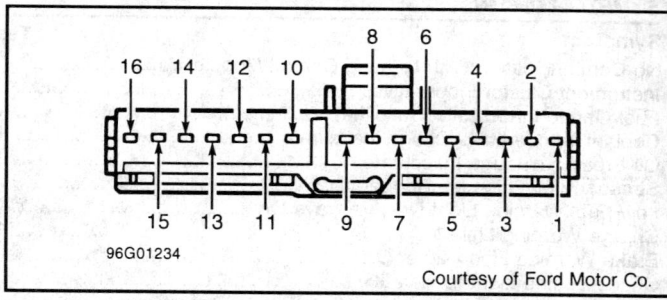

97H28388

Courtesy of Ford Motor Co.

Fig. 5: Identifying Lighting Control Module Harness Connector C2029 Terminals

TEST B: INSTRUMENT CLUSTER INOPERATIVE

Gasoline Vehicle – 1) Turn ignition switch to LOCK position. Disconnect instrument cluster harness connectors C250 and C251. Turn ignition switch to RUN position. Measure voltage at terminal No. 3 (Red/Yellow wire) at instrument cluster harness connector C251. *See Fig. 6.* Measure voltage at terminal No. 6 (Red/Yellow wire) at instrument cluster harness connector C250. *See Fig. 7.* If battery voltage exists at both terminals, go to next step. If battery voltage does not exist at both terminals, repair appropriate power distribution circuit. See appropriate wiring diagram in POWER DISTRIBUTION article in WIRING DIAGRAMS.

2) Turn ignition switch to LOCK position. Measure resistance between ground and terminals No. 2 and 14 (both Pink/Orange wires) at instrument cluster harness connector C251. Measure resistance between ground and terminals No. 4 and 8 (both Pink/Orange wires) at instrument cluster harness connector C250. *See Fig. 7.* If all resistance readings are 5 ohms or less, replace instrument cluster printed circuit. If any resistance reading is greater than 5 ohms, repair open in appropriate circuit.

Natural Gas Vehicle – 1) Turn ignition switch to LOCK position. Disconnect Natural Gas Vehicle (NGV) module harness connector C124. Measure voltage at terminals No. 37 and 57 (both Red wires) at

NGV module harness connector C124. *See Fig. 8.* If battery voltage exists at both terminals, go to next step. If battery voltage does not exist at both terminals, repair appropriate power distribution circuit. See appropriate wiring diagram in POWER DISTRIBUTION article in WIRING DIAGRAMS.

2) Turn ignition switch to LOCK position. Disconnect instrument cluster harness connectors. Disconnect fuel tank pressure sensor harness connector C422. Measure resistance between terminals No. 12 (Black/Yellow wire) and No. 26 (White/Red wire) at NGV module harness connector C124. If resistance is greater than 10 k/ohms, go to next step. If resistance is 10 k/ohms or less, repair short between White/Red and Black/Yellow wires.

3) Measure resistance between terminals No. 26 and 37 (both Red wires) at NGV module harness connector C124. If resistance is greater than 10 k/ohms, go to next step. If resistance is 10 k/ohms or less, repair short between Red wires.

4) Measure resistance between ground and terminals No. 40 and 60 (both Black/White wire) at NGV module harness connector C124. If both resistance readings are 5 ohms or less, go to next step. If either resistance reading is greater than 5 ohms, repair open in appropriate Black/White wire.

5) Measure resistance between terminals No. 26 (White/Red wire) and No. 40 (Black/White wire) at NGV module harness connector C124. If resistance is greater than 10 k/ohms, go to next step. If resistance is 10 k/ohms or less, repair short to ground in White/Red wire.

6) Connect NGV module harness connector C124. Measure resistance between ground and terminal No. 2 (Black/White wire) at instrument panel harness connector C251. *See Fig. 6.* If resistance is greater than 5 ohms, go to next step. If resistance is 5 ohms or less, go to step **8)**.

7) Disconnect NGV module harness connector C124. Measure resistance in Black/White wire between terminal No. 2 at instrument cluster harness connector C251 and terminal No. 31 at NGV module harness connector C124. If resistance is 5 ohms or less, replace NGV module. If resistance is greater than 5 ohms, repair open in Black/White wire.

8) Connect NGV module harness connector C124. Turn ignition switch to RUN position. Measure voltage at terminal No. 6 (Black/Yellow wire) at instrument cluster harness connector C250. *See Fig. 7.* Measure voltage at terminal No. 3 (Black/Yellow wire) at instrument cluster harness connector C251. If battery voltage does not exist at both terminals, go to next step. If battery voltage exists at both terminals, replace instrument cluster printed circuit.

1999 ACCESSORIES & EQUIPMENT
Analog Instrument Panels
Crown Victoria & Grand Marquis (Cont.)

FORD
4-719

9) Turn ignition switch to LOCK position. Disconnect NGV module harness connector C124. Measure resistance in Black/Yellow wire between terminal No. 6 at instrument cluster harness connector C250 and terminal No. 12 at NGV module harness connector C124. Measure resistance in Black/Yellow wire between terminal No. 3 at instrument cluster harness connector C251 and terminal No. 12 at NGV module harness connector C124. If both resistance readings are 5 ohms or less, replace NGV module. If either resistance reading is greater than 5 ohms, repair open in appropriate Black/Yellow wire.

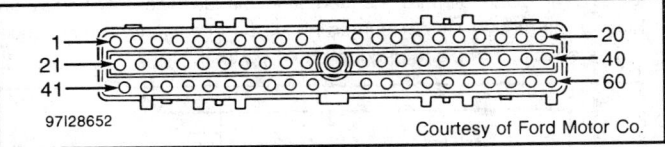

97I28652   Courtesy of Ford Motor Co.

Fig. 8: Identifying Natural Gas Vehicle Module Harness Connector C124 Terminals

TEST C: FUEL GAUGE INACCURATE (GASOLINE)

1) Turn ignition switch to LOCK position. Disconnect fuel pump module harness connector C464. Connect Instrument Gauge System Tester (014–R1063) to ground and terminal No. 5 (Yellow/White wire) at fuel pump module harness connector C464. *See Fig. 9.* Set tester to 160 ohms. Turn ignition switch to RUN position. Turn tester on. Wait one minute. Fuel gauge should indicate full or above. Turn ignition switch to LOCK position. Set tester to 15 ohms. Turn ignition switch to RUN position. Wait one minute. Fuel gauge should indicate empty or below. Turn ignition switch to LOCK position. If fuel gauge responded as specified, go to next step. If fuel gauge did not respond as specified, go to step **4)**.

2) Inspect fuel tank for damage or distortion. If there is no damage, go to next step. If there is damage or distortion, replace fuel tank.

3) Visually inspect fuel pump assembly and wiring for damage. If damage exists, repair or replace as necessary. If damage does not exist, replace fuel level sensor.

4) Turn ignition switch to LOCK position. Disconnect instrument cluster harness connector C251. Measure resistance in Yellow/White wire between terminal No. 1 at instrument cluster harness connector C251 and terminal No. 5 at fuel pump module harness connector C464. *See Figs. 6 and 9.* Resistance should be 5 ohms or less. Measure resistance between ground and terminal No. 5 (Yellow/White wire) at fuel pump module harness connector C464. Resistance should be greater than 10 k/ohms. If both resistance readings are as specified, go to next step. If either resistance readings is not as specified, repair open or short to ground in Yellow/White wire.

5) Measure resistance between ground and terminal No. 8 (Pink/Orange wire) at fuel pump module harness connector C464. If resistance is 5 ohms or less, go to next step. If resistance is greater than 5 ohms, repair open in Pink/Orange wire.

6) Inspect instrument cluster printed circuit. If printed circuit is okay, replace fuel gauge. If printed circuit is damaged, replace printed circuit.

TEST D: COOLANT TEMPERATURE GAUGE INACCURATE

1) Turn ignition switch to LOCK position. Disconnect engine coolant temperature sender harness connector C189. Using a fused jumper wire, ground Red/White wire terminal at engine coolant temperature sender harness connector C189. Turn ignition switch to RUN position. If coolant temperature gauge indicates hot, go to next step. If coolant temperature gauge does not indicate hot, go to step **3)**.

2) Turn ignition switch to LOCK position. Measure resistance between ground and Pink/Orange wire terminal at engine coolant temperature sender harness connector C189. If resistance is 5 ohms or less, replace engine coolant temperature sender. If resistance is greater than 5 ohms, repair open in Pink/Orange wire.

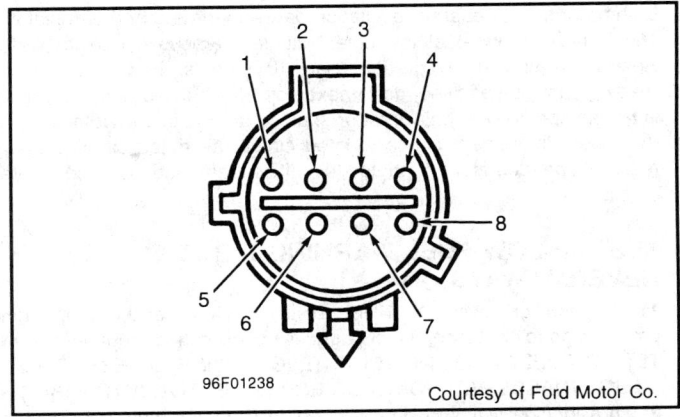

96F01238   Courtesy of Ford Motor Co.

Fig. 9: Identifying Fuel Pump Module Connector C464 Terminals

3) Turn ignition switch to LOCK position. Disconnect instrument cluster harness connector C250. Measure resistance in Red/White wire between engine coolant temperature sender harness connector C189 and terminal No. 5 at instrument cluster harness connector C250. *See Fig. 7.* Resistance should be 5 ohms or less. Measure resistance between ground and terminal No. 5 (Red/White wire) at instrument cluster harness connector C250. Resistance should be greater than 10 k/ohms. If both resistance readings are as specified, go to next step. If either resistance readings is not as specified, repair open or short to ground in Red/White wire.

4) Inspect instrument cluster printed circuit. If printed circuit is okay, replace coolant temperature gauge. If printed circuit is damaged, replace printed circuit.

TEST E: OIL PRESSURE GAUGE INACCURATE

1) Turn ignition switch to LOCK position. Disconnect oil pressure sender harness connector C1014. Using a fused jumper wire, ground White/Red wire terminal at oil pressure sender harness connector C1014. Turn ignition switch to RUN position. If oil pressure gauge indicates normal, go to next step. If oil pressure gauge does not indicate normal, go to step **3)**.

2) Using a mechanical oil pressure gauge, check engine oil pressure. If oil pressure is 40-70 psi at normal operating temperature, replace oil pressure sender. If oil pressure is not 40-70 psi at normal operating temperature, repair engine oiling system as necessary.

3) Turn ignition switch to LOCK position. Disconnect instrument cluster harness connector C250. Measure resistance in White/Red wire between oil pressure sender harness connector C1014 and terminal No. 7 at instrument cluster harness connector C250. *See Fig. 7.* Resistance should be 5 ohms or less. Measure resistance between ground and terminal No. 7 (White/Red wire) at instrument cluster harness connector C250. Resistance should be greater than 10 k/ohms. If both resistance readings are as specified, go to next step. If either resistance readings is not as specified, repair open or short to ground in Red/White wire.

4) Inspect instrument cluster printed circuit. If printed circuit is okay, replace oil pressure gauge. If printed circuit is damaged, replace printed circuit.

TEST F: SPEEDOMETER/ODOMETER INOPERATIVE

1) Turn ignition switch to LOCK position. Disconnect Vehicle Speed Sensor (VSS) harness connector C1020. Start engine. Raise and support vehicle. Place gear selector in Drive. Using a voltmeter set to AC range, measure voltage between VSS terminals (component side). If voltage is 1.3–6.1 volts AC, go to next step. If voltage is not 1.3–1.6 volts AC, replace speedometer drive gear and/or VSS as necessary.

2) Turn ignition switch to LOCK position. Disconnect instrument cluster harness connector C251. Measure resistance in Gray/Black wire between VSS harness connector C1020 and terminal No. 16 at instrument cluster harness connector C251. *See Fig. 6.* Resistance should be

FORD
4-720

1999 ACCESSORIES & EQUIPMENT
Analog Instrument Panels
Crown Victoria & Grand Marquis (Cont.)

5 ohms or less. Measure resistance between ground and terminal No. 16 (Gray/Black wire) at instrument cluster harness connector C251. Resistance should be greater than 10 k/ohms. If both resistance readings are as specified, go to next step. If either resistance readings is not as specified, repair open or short to ground in Gray/Black wire.

3) Inspect instrument cluster printed circuit. If printed circuit is okay, replace speedometer. If printed circuit is damaged, replace printed circuit.

TEST G: LOW FUEL WARNING LIGHT NEVER/ALWAYS ON

1) Turn ignition switch to RUN position. If fuel gauge is operating properly, go to next step. If fuel gauge is not operating properly, perform TEST C: FUEL GAUGE INACCURATE (GASOLINE) or TEST AG: FUEL GAUGE INACCURATE (CNG) OR ECU DEFECTIVE (DTC B1342).

2) Turn ignition switch to LOCK position. Remove instrument cluster. Inspect instrument cluster printed circuit. If printed circuit is okay, replace fuel gauge. If printed circuit is damaged, replace printed circuit.

TEST H: CHARGE WARNING LIGHT NEVER ON

1) Turn ignition switch to LOCK position. Disconnect generator harness connector C154. Using a fused jumper wire, ground Light Green/Red wire terminal at generator harness connector C154. Start engine. If charge warning light does not illuminate, go to next step. If charging warning light illuminates, repair charging system. See appropriate GENERATORS article in STARTING & CHARGING SYSTEMS.

2) Turn ignition switch to LOCK position. Disconnect instrument cluster harness connector C251. Measure resistance in Light Green/Red wire between generator harness connector and terminal No. 9 at instrument cluster harness connector C251. See Fig. 6. If resistance is 5 ohms or less, go to next step. If resistance is greater than 5 ohms, repair open in Light Green/Red wire.

3) Turn ignition switch to RUN position. Measure voltage at terminal No. 8 (Black/White wire) at instrument cluster harness connector C251. If battery voltage exists, replace bulb or instrument cluster printed circuit as necessary. If battery voltage does not exist, repair power distribution circuit. See appropriate wiring diagram in POWER DISTRIBUTION article in WIRING DIAGRAMS.

TEST I: BRAKE WARNING LIGHT NEVER ON

NOTE: Ensure brake fluid is at correct level in reservoir.

1) Turn ignition switch to LOCK position. Disconnect brake fluid level switch harness connector C170. Using a fused jumper wire, ground Violet/White terminal at brake fluid level switch harness connector C170. Turn ignition switch to RUN. If brake warning light does not illuminate, go to next step. If brake warning light illuminates, go to step 3).

2) Turn ignition switch to LOCK position. Disconnect instrument cluster harness connector C250. Disconnect daytime running light module harness connector C180. Disconnect parking brake switch harness connector C296. Measure resistance in Violet/White wire between brake fluid level switch harness connector C170 and terminal No. 10 at instrument cluster harness connector C250. See Fig. 7. Measure resistance between Tan/Light Green wire terminal at parking brake switch harness connector C296 and terminal No. 10 (Violet/White wire) at instrument cluster harness connector C250. If both resistance readings are 5 ohms or less, go to step 6). If either resistance reading is greater than 5 ohms, repair open in appropriate wire.

3) Turn ignition switch to LOCK position. Measure resistance between Tan/Black wire terminal and Violet/White wire terminal at brake fluid level switch (component side). If resistance is 5 ohms or less, go to next step. If resistance is greater than 5 ohms, replace brake fluid level switch.

4) Disconnect ignition switch harness connector C292. Measure resistance in Tan/Black wire between brake fluid level switch harness connector C170 and terminal P2 at ignition switch harness connector

C292. See Fig. 10. If resistance is 5 ohms or less, go to next step. If resistance is greater than 5 ohms, replace open in Tan/Black wire.

5) Measure resistance between ground and terminal GND (Black wire) at ignition switch harness connector C292. If resistance is 5 ohms or less, replace ignition switch. If resistance is greater than 5 ohms, replace open in Black wire.

6) Measure resistance between Tan/Light Green wire terminal at parking brake switch (component side). Resistance should be 5 ohms or less with parking brake applied. Resistance should be greater than 10 k/ohms with parking brake released. If resistance is as specified, replace bulb or instrument cluster printed circuit as necessary. If resistance is not as specified, replace parking brake switch.

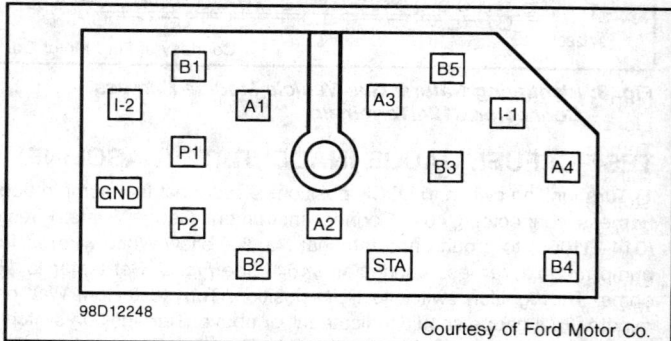

98D12248   Courtesy of Ford Motor Co.

Fig. 10: Identifying Ignition Switch Harness Connector C292 Terminals

TEST J: CHECK ENGINE LIGHT INOPERATIVE

Turn ignition switch to LOCK position. Disconnect Powertrain Control Module (PCM) harness connector C185. Disconnect instrument cluster harness connector C251. Measure resistance is Pink/Light Green wire between terminal No. 2 at PCM harness connector C185 and terminal No. 4 at instrument cluster harness connector C251. See Figs. 6 and 11. If resistance is 5 ohms or less, repair powertrain concern. See appropriate SELF-DIAGNOSTICS article in ENGINE PERFORMANCE in appropriate MITCHELL® manual. If resistance is greater than 5 ohms, repair open in Pink/Light Green wire.

1999 ACCESSORIES & EQUIPMENT
Analog Instrument Panels
Crown Victoria & Grand Marquis (Cont.)

FORD
4-721

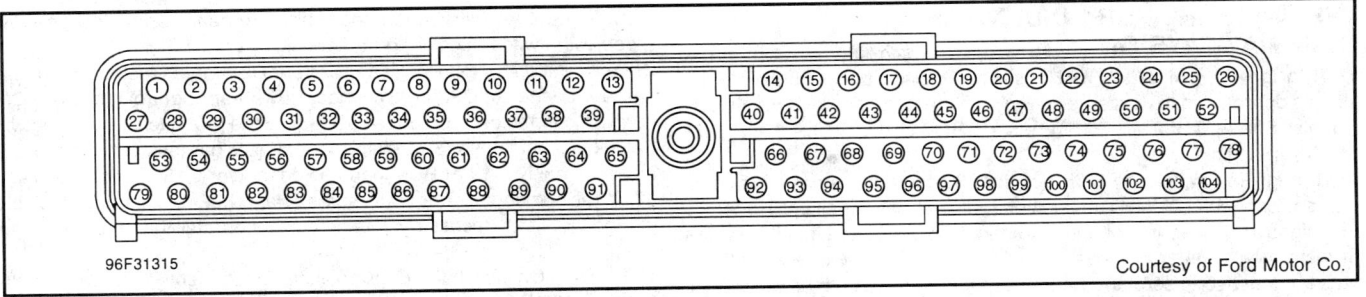

96F31315
Courtesy of Ford Motor Co.

Fig. 11: Identifying Powertrain Control Module Harness Connector C185 Terminals

TEST K: SEAT BEAT WARNING LIGHT INOPERATIVE (CHIME OPERATIVE)

1) Turn ignition switch to LOCK position. Disconnect seat belt switch harness connector C304. Using a fused jumper wire, ground Brown/Light Blue wire terminal at seat belt switch harness connector C304. Turn ignition switch to RUN position. If seat belt warning light does not illuminate, go to next step. If seat beat warning light illuminates, go to step **3)**.

2) Turn ignition switch to LOCK position. Disconnect Lighting Control Module (LCM) harness connector C2026. Measure resistance in Brown/Light Blue wire between seat belt switch harness connector C304 and terminal No. 17 at LCM harness connector C2026. *See Fig. 12.* If resistance is 5 ohms or less, go to step **4)**. If resistance is greater than 5 ohms, repair open in Brown/Light Blue wire.

3) Turn ignition switch to LOCK position. Measure resistance between ground and Black wire terminal at seat belt switch harness connector C304. If resistance is 5 ohms or less, replace seat belt switch. If resistance is greater than 5 ohms, repair open in Black wire.

4) Disconnect instrument cluster harness connector C251. Measure resistance in Dark Green/Light Green wire between terminal No. 10 at instrument cluster harness connector C251 and terminal No. 8 at LCM harness connector C2029. *See Figs. 5 and 6.* Resistance should be 5 ohms or less. Measure resistance between ground and terminal No. 10 (Dark Green/Light Green wire) at instrument cluster harness connector C251. Resistance should be greater than 10 k/ohms. If both resistance readings are as specified, replace bulb or instrument cluster printed circuit as necessary. If either resistance readings is not as specified, repair open or short to ground in Dark Green/Light Green wire.

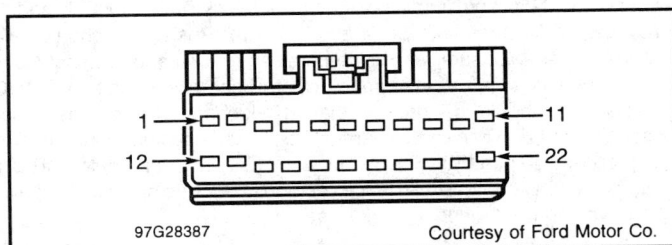

97G28387
Courtesy of Ford Motor Co.

Fig. 12: Lighting Control Module Harness Connector C2026 Terminals

TEST L: AIR SUSPENSION WARNING LIGHT NEVER/ALWAYS ON

1) Start engine. If air suspension warning light is always on, go to next step. If air suspension warning light is not always on, go to step **4)**.

2) Check air suspension service switch. Air suspension service switch is located on right side in trunk. If air suspension service switch is on, go to next step. If air suspension service switch is off turn air suspension service switch to ON position.

3) Turn ignition switch to LOCK position. Disconnect air suspension control module harness connector C215. Disconnect instrument cluster harness connector C251. Measure resistance in Dark Green/Light Green wire between terminal No. 11 at instrument cluster harness connector C251 and terminal No. 11 at air suspension control module

harness connector C215. *See Figs. 6 and 13.* Resistance should be 5 ohms or less. Measure resistance between ground and terminal No. 11 (Dark Green/Light Green wire) at instrument cluster harness connector C251. Resistance should be greater than 10 k/ohms. If both resistance readings are as specified, replace air suspension control module. If either resistance readings is not as specified, repair open or short to ground in Dark Green/Light Green wire.

4) Turn ignition switch to LOCK position. Disconnect instrument cluster connector C251. Turn ignition switch to RUN position. Measure voltage between terminals No. 11 (Dark Green/Light Green wire) and No. 12 (Light Blue/Pink wire) at instrument cluster connector C251. *See Fig. 6.* If battery voltage does not exist, go to next step. If battery voltage exists, replace bulb or instrument cluster printed circuit as necessary.

5) Measure voltage at terminal No. 12 (Light Blue/Pink wire) at instrument cluster connector C251. If battery voltage exists, repair air suspension concern. See appropriate ELECTRONIC article in SUSPENSION in appropriate MITCHELL® manual. If battery voltage does not exist, repair power distribution circuit. See appropriate wiring diagram in POWER DISTRIBUTION article in WIRING DIAGRAMS.

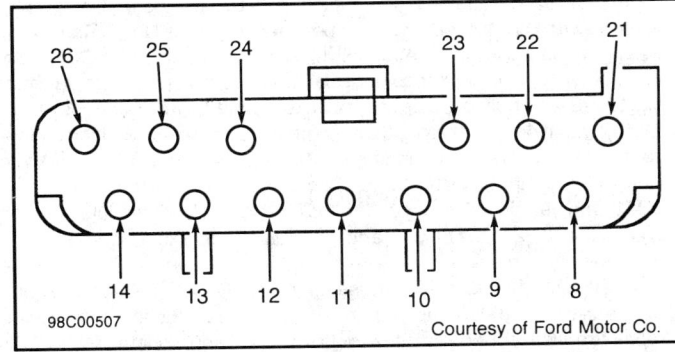

98C00507
Courtesy of Ford Motor Co.

Fig. 13: Identifying Air Suspension Control Module Harness Connector C215 Terminals

TEST M: LEFT TURN INDICATOR NEVER/ALWAYS ON

1) Turn ignition switch to RUN position. Operate turn signals. If turn signals operate, go to next step. If turn signals do not operate, repair turn signals. See AUTOLAMP SYSTEMS – CROWN VICTORIA & GRAND MARQUIS article.

2) Turn ignition switch to LOCK position. Disconnect instrument cluster harness connector C251. Turn ignition switch to RUN position. Turn left turn signal on. Measure voltage at terminal No. 7 (Light Green/White wire) at instrument cluster harness connector C251. *See Fig. 6.* If voltage fluctuates between zero and battery voltage, replace bulb or instrument cluster printed circuit as necessary. If voltage does not fluctuate between zero and battery voltage, repair open or short in Light Green/White wire.

FORD
4-722

1999 ACCESSORIES & EQUIPMENT
Analog Instrument Panels
Crown Victoria & Grand Marquis (Cont.)

TEST N: RIGHT TURN INDICATOR NEVER/ALWAYS ON

1) Turn ignition switch to RUN position. Operate turn signals. If turn signals operate, go to next step. If turn signals do not operate, repair turn signals. See AUTOLAMP SYSTEMS – CROWN VICTORIA & GRAND MARQUIS article.

2) Turn ignition switch to LOCK position. Disconnect instrument cluster harness connector C250. Turn ignition switch to RUN position. Turn right turn signal on. Measure voltage at terminal No. 2 (White/Light Blue wire) at instrument cluster harness connector C250. *See Fig. 7*. If voltage fluctuates between zero and battery voltage, replace bulb or instrument cluster printed circuit as necessary. If voltage does not fluctuate between zero and battery voltage, repair open or short in White/Light Blue wire.

TEST O: HIGH BEAM WARNING NEVER/ALWAYS ON

1) Turn ignition switch to RUN position. Turn on high beams. If high beams operate, go to next step. If high beams do not operate, repair high beams. See AUTOLAMP SYSTEMS – CROWN VICTORIA & GRAND MARQUIS article.

2) Turn ignition switch to LOCK position. Disconnect instrument cluster harness connector C250. Turn ignition switch to RUN position. Turn high beams on. Measure voltage at terminal No. 13 (Light Green/Black wire) at instrument cluster harness connector C250. *See Fig. 7*. If battery voltage exists, replace bulb or instrument cluster printed circuit as necessary. If battery voltage does not exist, repair open or short in Light Green/Black wire.

TEST P: TRACTION CONTROL INDICATOR INOPERATIVE

1) Turn ignition switch to LOCK position. Disconnect instrument cluster connector C251. Turn ignition switch to RUN position. Turn traction control switch on. Measure voltage between terminals No. 3 (Red/Yellow wire) and No. 5 (Violet wire) at instrument cluster connector C251. *See Fig. 6*. If battery voltage does not exist, go to next step. If battery voltage exists, replace bulb or instrument cluster printed circuit as necessary.

2) Turn ignition switch to LOCK position. Disconnect anti-lock brake control module harness connector C162. Measure resistance in Violet wire between terminal No. 5 at instrument cluster harness connector C251 and terminal No. 5 at anti-lock brake control module harness connector C162. *See Figs. 6 and 14*. Resistance should be 5 ohms or less. Measure resistance between ground and terminal No. 5 (Violet wire) at instrument cluster harness connector C251. Resistance should be greater than 10 k/ohms. If both resistance readings are as specified, repair traction control system concern. See appropriate ANTI-LOCK article in BRAKES in appropriate MITCHELL® manual. If either resistance readings is not as specified, repair open or short to ground in Violet wire.

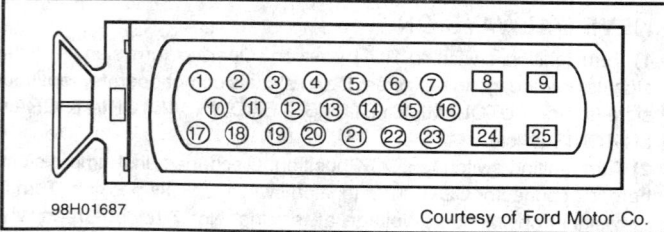

98H01687   Courtesy of Ford Motor Co.

Fig. 14: Identifying Anti-Lock Brake Control Module Harness Connector C162 Terminals

TEST Q: OVERDRIVE OFF INDICATOR INOPERATIVE

1) Turn ignition switch to LOCK position. Connect NGS tester to Data Link Connector (DLC). Turn ignition switch to RUN position. Using NGS tester, monitor PCM PID TCIL while pressing overdrive switch on and

off. If PID agrees with switch position, go to next step. If PID does not agree with switch position, go to step **3)**.

2) Turn ignition switch to LOCK position. Disconnect instrument cluster harness connector C250. Disconnect Powertrain Control Module (PCM) harness connector C185. Measure resistance in White/Light Green wire between terminal No. 3 at instrument cluster harness connector C250 and terminal No. 12 at PCM harness connector C185. *See Figs. 7 and 11*. If resistance is 5 ohms or less, replace bulb or instrument cluster printed circuit as necessary. If resistance is greater than 5 ohms, repair open in White/Light Green wire.

3) Turn ignition switch to LOCK position. Disconnect Powertrain Control Module (PCM) harness connector C185. Turn ignition switch to RUN position. Turn overdrive switch on. Measure voltage at terminal No. 29 (Tan/White wire) at PCM harness connector C185. *See Fig. 11*. If battery voltage does not exist, go to next step. If battery voltage exists, replace PCM.

4) Turn ignition switch to LOCK position. Disconnect overdrive switch harness connector C202. Turn ignition switch to RUN position. Measure voltage at Red/Yellow wire terminal at overdrive switch harness connector C202. If battery voltage exists, go to next step. If battery voltage does not exist, repair power distribution circuit. See appropriate wiring diagram in POWER DISTRIBUTION article in WIRING DIAGRAMS.

5) Turn ignition switch to LOCK position. Measure resistance in Tan/White wire between overdrive switch harness connector C202 and terminal No. 29 at PCM harness connector C185. Resistance should be 5 ohms or less. Measure resistance between ground and terminal No. 29 (Tan/White wire) at PCM harness connector C185. Resistance should be greater than 10 k/ohms. If both resistance readings are as specified, replace overdrive switch. If either resistance readings is not as specified, repair open or short to ground in Tan/White wire.

TEST R: ABS INDICATOR INOPERATIVE

1) Turn ignition switch to LOCK position. Disconnect instrument cluster connector C250. Turn ignition switch to RUN position. Measure voltage between terminals No. 6 (Red/Yellow wire) and No. 9 (Dark Green wire) at instrument cluster connector C250. *See Fig. 7*. If battery voltage does not exist, go to next step. If battery voltage exists, replace bulb or instrument cluster printed circuit as necessary.

2) Turn ignition switch to LOCK position. Disconnect anti-lock brake control module harness connector C162. Measure resistance in Dark Green wire between terminal No. 9 at instrument cluster harness connector C250 and terminal No. 9 at anti-lock brake control module harness connector C162. *See Figs. 7 and 14*. Resistance should be 5 ohms or less. Measure resistance between ground and terminal No. 9 (Dark Green wire) at instrument cluster harness connector C250. Resistance should be greater than 10 k/ohms. If both resistance readings are as specified, repair anti-lock brake system concern. See appropriate ANTI-LOCK article in BRAKES in appropriate MITCHELL® manual. If either resistance readings is not as specified, repair open or short to ground in Dark Green wire.

TEST S: FAIL-SAFE COOLING INDICATOR INOPERATIVE

1) Turn ignition switch to LOCK position. Disconnect instrument cluster connector C250. Turn ignition switch to RUN position. Measure voltage between terminals No. 6 (Red/Yellow wire) and No. 12 (Orange/Red wire) at instrument cluster connector C250. *See Fig. 7*. If battery voltage does not exist, go to next step. If battery voltage exists, replace bulb or instrument cluster printed circuit as necessary.

2) Turn ignition switch to LOCK position. Disconnect Powertrain Control Module (PCM) harness connector C185. Measure resistance in Orange/Red wire between terminal No. 12 at instrument cluster harness connector C250 and terminal No. 45 at PCM harness connector C185. *See Figs. 7 and 11*. Resistance should be 5 ohms or less. Measure resistance between ground and terminal No. 12 (Orange/Red wire) at instrument cluster harness connector C250. Resistance should be greater than 10 k/ohms. If both resistance readings are as specified,

1999 ACCESSORIES & EQUIPMENT
Analog Instrument Panels
Crown Victoria & Grand Marquis (Cont.)

FORD
4-723

repair powertrain control concern. See appropriate SELF-DIAGNOSTICS article in ENGINE PERFORMANCE in appropriate MITCHELL® manual. If either resistance readings is not as specified, repair open or short to ground in Orange/Red wire.

TEST T: NO COMMUNICATION WITH NATURAL GAS VEHICLE MODULE

1) Turn ignition switch to LOCK position. Disconnect Natural Gas Vehicle (NGV) module harness connector C124. Measure voltage at terminal No. 1 (Yellow/Black wire) at NGV module harness connector C124. *See Fig. 8.* If battery voltage exists, go to next step. If battery voltage does not exist, repair power distribution circuit. See appropriate wiring diagram in POWER DISTRIBUTION article in WIRING DIAGRAMS.

2) Turn ignition switch to RUN position. Measure voltage at terminals No. 37 (Red wire) and No. 57 (Red wire) at NGV module harness connector C124. If battery voltage exists at both terminals, go to next step. If battery voltage does not exist at both terminals, repair appropriate power distribution circuit. See appropriate wiring diagram in POWER DISTRIBUTION article in WIRING DIAGRAMS.

3) Turn ignition switch to LOCK position. Measure resistance between ground and terminals No. 40 (Black/White wire) and No. 60 (Black/White wire) at NGV module harness connector C124. If either resistance reading is greater than 5 ohms, repair open in appropriate Black/White wire. If both resistance readings are 5 ohms or less, repair module communications concern. See MODULE COMMUNICATIONS NETWORK – CROWN VICTORIA & GRAND MARQUIS article.

TEST U: FUEL TANK SENSOR CIRCUIT FAILURE (DTC B1219)

1) Turn ignition switch to RUN position. Using NGS tester, monitor Natural Gas Vehicle (NGV) module PID TANKPR. If PID indicates zero psi, go to next step. If PID does not indicate zero psi, check connectors for loose and corroded pins. If all connections are clean and tight, clear DTCs. Using NGS tester, perform NGV module self-test. If DTC B1219 is retrieved again, replace NGV module.

2) Turn ignition switch to LOCK position. Disconnect NGV module harness connector C124. Disconnect fuel tank pressure sensor harness connector C422. Measure resistance between terminals No. 2 (Black/Light Blue wire) and No. 4 (Red/Pink wire) at fuel tank pressure sensor harness connector C422. *See Fig. 15.* If resistance is greater than 10 k/ohms, go to next step. If resistance is 10 k/ohms or less, repair short between Black/Light Blue and Red/Pink wires.

3) Connect NGV module harness connector C124. Measure voltage between terminals No. 1 (White/Red wire) and No. 2 (Black/Light Blue wire) at fuel tank pressure sensor harness connector C422. If 4-6 volts exists, go to next step. If 4-6 volts does not exist, go to step **6)**.

4) Turn ignition switch to LOCK position. Using a fused jumper wire, connect terminals No. 1 (White/Red wire) and No. 4 (Red/Pink wire) at fuel tank pressure sensor harness connector C422. Turn ignition switch to RUN position. Using a voltmeter, backprobe between terminals No. 7 (Red/Pink wire) and No. 26 (White/Red wire) at NGV module harness connector C124. *See Fig. 8.* If 4.61 volts or less exists, go to next step. If greater than 4.61 volts exists, go to step **6)**.

5) Turn ignition switch to LOCK position. Measure resistance in White/Red wire between terminal No. 26 at NGV module harness connector C124 and terminal No. 1 at fuel tank pressure sensor harness connector C422. If resistance is greater than 5 ohms, repair open in White/Red wire. If resistance is 5 ohms or less, repair open in Red/Pink wire.

6) Turn ignition switch to LOCK position. Disconnect NGV module harness connector C124. Measure resistance in Black/Light Blue wire between terminal No. 46 at NGV module harness connector C124 and terminal No. 2 at fuel tank pressure sensor harness connector C422. *See Figs. 8 and 15.* If resistance is 5 ohms or less, go to next step. If resistance is greater than 5 ohms, repair open in Black/Light Blue wire.

7) Measure resistance between terminals No. 40 (Black/White wire) and No. 26 (White/Red wire) at NGV module harness connector C124. If resistance is greater than 10 k/ohms, go to next step. If resistance is 10 k/ohms or less, repair short to ground in White/Red wire.

8) Measure resistance between terminals No. 40 (Black/White wire) and No. 46 (Black/Light Blue wire) at NGV module harness connector C124. If resistance is greater than 10 k/ohms, go to next step. If resistance is 10 k/ohms or less, repair short to ground in Black/Light Blue wire.

9) Measure resistance in White/Red wire between terminal No. 26 at NGV module harness connector C124 and terminal No. 1 at fuel tank pressure sensor harness connector C422. If resistance is 5 ohms or less, go to next step. If resistance is greater than 5 ohms, repair open in White/Red wire.

10) Measure voltage at terminal No. 1 (White/Red wire) at fuel tank pressure sensor harness connector C422. If voltage does not exist, go to next step. If voltage exists, repair short to voltage in White/Red wire.

11) Check fuel tank solenoids operation. See appropriate SYSTEM & COMPONENT TESTING article in ENGINE PERFORMANCE in appropriate MITCHELL® manual. If fuel tank solenoids operate properly, go to next step. If fuel tank solenoid(s) do not operate properly, repair fuel tank solenoid(s) as necessary.

12) Check fuel system for leaks. See appropriate SYSTEM & COMPONENT TESTING article in ENGINE PERFORMANCE in appropriate MITCHELL® manual. If fuel system leaks, repair as necessary. If fuel system does not leak, replace NGV module.

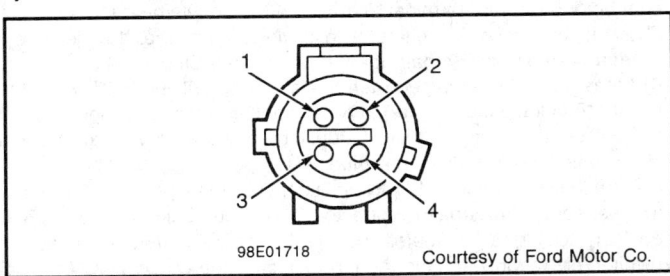

98E01718   Courtesy of Ford Motor Co.

Fig. 15: Identifying Fuel Tank Pressure Sensor Harness Connector C422 Terminals

TEST V: FUEL TANK SENSOR CIRCUIT SHORT TO VOLTAGE (DTC B1220)

1) Turn ignition switch to RUN position. Using NGS tester, monitor Natural Gas Vehicle (NGV) module PID TANKPR. If PID indicates zero psi, go to next step. If PID does not indicate zero psi, check connectors for loose and corroded pins. If all connections are clean and tight, clear DTCs. Using NGS tester, perform NGV module self-test. If DTC B1220 is retrieved again, replace NGV module.

2) Turn ignition switch to LOCK position. Disconnect NGV module harness connector C124. Disconnect fuel tank pressure sensor harness connector C422. Turn ignition switch to RUN position. Measure voltage between terminals No. 7 (Red/Pink wire) and No. 46 (Black/Light Blue wire) at NGV module harness connector C124. *See Fig. 8.* If greater than .61 volt exists, go to next step. If .61 volt or less exists, replace fuel tank pressure sensor.

3) Turn ignition switch to LOCK position. Measure resistance between terminals No. 7 (Red/Pink wire) and No. 26 (White/Red wire) at NGV module harness connector C124. If resistance is greater than 10 k/ohms, go to next step. If resistance is 10 k/ohms or less, repair short between Red/Pink and White/Red wires.

4) Turn ignition switch to RUN position. Measure voltage at terminal No. 7 (Red/Pink wire) at NGV module harness connector C124. If voltage does not exist, go to next step. If voltage exists, repair short to voltage in Red/Pink wire.

5) Check fuel tank solenoids operation. See appropriate SYSTEM & COMPONENT TESTING article in ENGINE PERFORMANCE in appropriate MITCHELL® manual. If fuel tank solenoids operate properly, go to next step. If fuel tank solenoid(s) do not operate properly, repair fuel tank solenoid(s) as necessary.

FORD
4-724

1999 ACCESSORIES & EQUIPMENT
Analog Instrument Panels
Crown Victoria & Grand Marquis (Cont.)

6) Check fuel system for leaks. See appropriate SYSTEM & COMPONENT TESTING article in ENGINE PERFORMANCE in appropriate MITCHELL® manual. If fuel system leaks, repair as necessary. If fuel system does not leak, replace NGV module.

TEST W: FUEL TANK TEMPERATURE SENSOR NO. 1 CIRCUIT FAILURE (DTC B1222)

1) Turn ignition switch to RUN position. Using a voltmeter, backprobe between terminals No. 47 (White/Yellow wire) and No. 46 (Black/Light Blue wire) at Natural Gas Vehicle (NGV) module harness connector C124. *See Fig. 8.* If greater than 4.55 volts exists, go to next step. If 4.55 volts or less exists, go to step **5)**.

2) Turn ignition switch to LOCK position. Disconnect fuel tank temperature sensor No. 1 harness connector C418. Using a fused jumper wire, connect Black/Light Blue wire terminal and White/Yellow wire terminal at fuel tank temperature sensor No. 1 harness connector C418. Turn ignition switch to RUN position. Using a voltmeter, backprobe between terminals No. 47 (White/Yellow wire) and No. 46 (Black/Light Blue wire) at NGV module harness connector C124. If greater than .12 volt exists, go to next step. If .12 volt or less exists, replace fuel tank temperature sensor No. 1.

3) Turn ignition switch to LOCK position. Measure resistance in Black/Light Blue wire between fuel tank temperature sensor No. 1 harness connector C418 and terminal No. 46 at NGV module harness connector C124. If resistance is 5 ohms or less, go to next step. If resistance is greater than 5 ohms, repair open in Black/Light Blue wire.

4) Measure voltage between terminals No. 40 (Black/White wire) and No. 46 (Black/Light Blue wire) at NGV module harness connector C124. If .5 volt or less exists, go to next step. If greater than .5 volt exists, repair short to voltage in Black/Light Blue wire.

5) Turn ignition switch to LOCK position. Disconnect fuel tank temperature sensor No. 1 harness connector C418. Turn ignition switch to RUN position. Using a voltmeter, backprobe between terminals No. 47 (White/Yellow wire) and No. 46 (Black/Light Blue wire) at NGV module harness connector C124. If 4.55 volts or less exists, go to next step. If greater than 4.55 volts, replace fuel tank temperature sensor No. 1.

6) Turn ignition switch to LOCK position. Using an ohmmeter, backprobe between terminals No. 40 (Black/White wire) and No. 46 (Black/Light Blue wire) at NGV module harness connector C124. If resistance is greater than 10 k/ohms, go to next step. If resistance is 10 k/ohms or less, repair short to ground in Black/Light Blue wire.

CAUTION: NGS tester MUST be used in this procedure to measure voltage. Using a standard DVOM to carry out this test will cause an inaccurate reading, possibly leading to inaccurate repairs.

7) Connect fuel tank temperature sensor No. 1 harness connector C418. Connect accessory voltmeter leads to NGS tester. Connect positive lead on NGS tester to terminal No. 47 (White/Yellow wire) and negative lead to terminal No. 40 (Black/White wire) at NGV module harness connector C124 (backprobing). Turn ignition switch to RUN position. Enter DIGITAL MEASUREMENT SYSTEM on NGS tester. Select VOLTMETER, then LINK. Select PID/DATA, then NGV. Select TEMPS1, then START. Select REC, then press TRIGGER to capture data. Press TRIGGER again to store data, then select VIEW to examine data. If voltage varies rapidly between .2-4.9 volts, repair intermittent contact condition. If voltage does not vary rapidly between .2-4.9 volts, replace NGV module.

TEST X: FUEL TANK TEMPERATURE SENSOR NO. 1 CIRCUIT OPEN (DTC B1223)

1) Using NGS tester, monitor Natural Gas Vehicle (NGV) module PID TEMPS1. If PID indicates 199°F (93°C), go to next step. If PID does not indicate 199°F (93°C), check connectors for loose and corroded pins. If all connections are clean and tight, clear DTCs. Using NGS tester, perform NGV module self-test. If DTC B1223 is retrieved again, replace NGV module.

2) Turn ignition switch to LOCK position. Disconnect fuel tank temperature sensor No. 1 harness connector C418. Disconnect NGV module harness connector C124. Measure resistance in Black/Light Blue wire between fuel tank temperature sensor No. 1 harness connector C418 and terminal No. 46 at NGV module harness connector C124. *See Fig. 8.* If resistance is 5 ohms or less, go to next step. If resistance is greater than 5 ohms, repair open in Black/Light Blue wire.

3) Measure resistance in White/Yellow wire between fuel tank temperature sensor No. 1 harness connector C418 and terminal No. 47 at NGV module harness connector C124. If resistance is 5 ohms or less, replace fuel tank temperature sensor No. 1. If resistance is greater than 5 ohms, repair open in White/Yellow wire.

TEST Y: FUEL TANK TEMPERATURE SENSOR NO. 1 CIRCUIT SHORT TO VOLTAGE (DTC B1224)

1) Using NGS tester, monitor Natural Gas Vehicle (NGV) module PID TEMPS1. If PID indicates 199°F (93°C), go to next step. If PID does not indicate 199°F (93°C), check connectors for loose and corroded pins. If all connections are clean and tight, clear DTCs. Using NGS tester, perform NGV module self-test. If DTC B1224 is retrieved again, replace NGV module.

2) Turn ignition switch to LOCK position. Disconnect fuel tank temperature sensor No. 1 harness connector C418. Disconnect NGV module harness connector C124. Measure voltage between terminals No. 46 (Black/Light Blue wire) and No. 40 (Black/White wire) at NGV module harness connector C124. *See Fig. 8.* If .5 volt or less exists, go to next step. If greater than .5 volt exists, repair short to voltage in Black/Light Blue wire.

3) Measure voltage between terminals No. 47 (White/Yellow wire) and No. 40 (Black/White wire) at NGV module harness connector C124. If .5 volt or less exists, replace NGV module. If greater than .5 volt exists, repair short to voltage in White/Yellow wire.

TEST Z: FUEL TANK TEMPERATURE SENSOR NO. 1 CIRCUIT SHORT TO GROUND (DTC B1225)

1) Using NGS tester, monitor Natural Gas Vehicle (NGV) module PID TEMPS1. If PID indicates 199°F (93°C), go to next step. If PID does not indicate 199°F (93°C), check connectors for loose and corroded pins. If all connections are clean and tight, clear DTCs. Using NGS tester, perform NGV module self-test. If DTC B1225 is retrieved again, replace NGV module.

2) Turn ignition switch to LOCK position. Disconnect fuel tank temperature sensor No. 1 harness connector C418. Disconnect NGV module harness connector C124. Measure resistance between terminals No. 47 (White/Yellow wire) and No. 40 (Black/White wire) at NGV module harness connector C124. *See Fig. 8.* If resistance is greater than 10 k/ohms, go to next step. If resistance is 10 k/ohms or less, repair short to ground in White/Yellow wire.

3) Measure resistance between terminals No. 46 (Black/Light Blue wire) and No. 47 (White/Yellow wire) at NGV module harness connector C124. If resistance is greater than 10 k/ohms, replace fuel tank temperature sensor No. 1. If resistance is 10 k/ohms or less, repair short between White/Yellow and Black/Light Blue wires.

TEST AA: FUEL TANK TEMPERATURE SENSOR NO. 2 CIRCUIT FAILURE (DTC B1226)

1) Turn ignition switch to RUN position. Using a voltmeter, backprobe between terminals No. 28 (Light Blue/Pink wire) and No. 46 (Black/Light Blue wire) at Natural Gas Vehicle (NGV) module harness connector C124. *See Fig. 8.* If greater than 4.55 volts exists, go to next step. If 4.55 volts or less exists, go to step **5)**.

2) Turn ignition switch to LOCK position. Disconnect fuel tank temperature sensor No. 2 harness connector C419. Using a fused jumper wire, connect Black/Light Blue wire terminal and Light Blue/Pink wire terminal at fuel tank temperature sensor No. 2 harness connector C419. Turn ignition switch to RUN position. Using a voltmeter, backprobe between

1999 ACCESSORIES & EQUIPMENT
Analog Instrument Panels
Crown Victoria & Grand Marquis (Cont.)

FORD
4-725

terminals No. 28 (Light Blue/Pink wire) and No. 46 (Black/Light Blue wire) at NGV module harness connector C124. If greater than .12 volt exists, go to next step. If .12 volt or less exists, replace fuel tank temperature sensor No. 2.

3) Turn ignition switch to LOCK position. Measure resistance in Black/Light Blue wire between fuel tank temperature sensor No. 2 harness connector C419 and terminal No. 46 at NGV module harness connector C124. If resistance is 5 ohms or less, go to next step. If resistance is greater than 5 ohms, repair open in Black/Light Blue wire.

4) Measure voltage between terminals No. 40 (Black/White wire) and No. 46 (Black/Light Blue wire) at NGV module harness connector C124. If .5 volt or less exists, go to next step. If greater than .5 volt exists, repair short to voltage in Black/Light Blue wire.

5) Turn ignition switch to LOCK position. Disconnect fuel tank temperature sensor No. 2 harness connector C419. Turn ignition switch to RUN position. Using a voltmeter, backprobe between terminals No. 28 (Light Blue/Pink wire) and No. 46 (Black/Light Blue wire) at NGV module harness connector C124. If 4.55 volts or less exists, go to next step. If greater than 4.55 volts exists, replace fuel tank temperature sensor No. 2.

6) Turn ignition switch to LOCK position. Using an ohmmeter, backprobe between terminals No. 40 (Black/White wire) and No. 46 (Black/Light Blue wire) at NGV module harness connector C124. If resistance is greater than 10 k/ohms, go to next step. If resistance is 10 k/ohms or less, repair short to ground in Black/Light Blue wire.

CAUTION: NGS tester MUST be used in this procedure to measure voltage. Using a standard DVOM to carry out this test will cause an inaccurate reading, possibly leading to inaccurate repairs.

---

7) Connect fuel tank temperature sensor No. 2 harness connector C419. Connect accessory voltmeter leads to NGS tester. Connect positive lead on NGS tester to terminal No. 28 (Light Blue/Pink wire) and negative lead to terminal No. 40 (Black/White wire) at NGV module harness connector C124 (backprobing). Turn ignition switch to RUN position. Enter DIGITAL MEASUREMENT SYSTEM on NGS tester. Select VOLTMETER, then LINK. Select PID/DATA, then NGV. Select TEMPS2, then START. Select REC, then press TRIGGER to capture data. Press TRIGGER again to store data, then select VIEW to examine data. If voltage varies rapidly between .2-4.9 volts, repair intermittent contact condition. If voltage does not vary rapidly between .2-4.9 volts, replace NGV module.

TEST AB: FUEL TANK TEMPERATURE SENSOR NO. 2 CIRCUIT OPEN (DTC B1227)

1) Using NGS tester, monitor Natural Gas Vehicle (NGV) module PID TEMPS2. If PID indicates 199°F (93°C), go to next step. If PID does not indicate 199°F (93°C), check connectors for loose and corroded pins. If all connections are clean and tight, clear DTCs. Using NGS tester, perform NGV module self-test. If DTC B1227 is retrieved again, replace NGV module.

2) Turn ignition switch to LOCK position. Disconnect fuel tank temperature sensor No. 2 harness connector C419. Disconnect NGV module harness connector C124. Measure resistance in Black/Light Blue wire between fuel tank temperature sensor No. 2 harness connector C419 and terminal No. 46 at NGV module harness connector C124. *See Fig. 8.* If resistance is 5 ohms or less, go to next step. If resistance is greater than 5 ohms, repair open in Black/Light Blue wire.

3) Measure resistance in Light Blue/Pink wire between fuel tank temperature sensor No. 2 harness connector C418 and terminal No. 28 at NGV module harness connector C124. If resistance is 5 ohms or less, replace fuel tank temperature sensor No. 2. If resistance is greater than 5 ohms, repair open in Light Blue/Pink wire.

TEST AC: FUEL TANK TEMPERATURE SENSOR NO. 2 CIRCUIT SHORT TO VOLTAGE (DTC B1228)

1) Using NGS tester, monitor Natural Gas Vehicle (NGV) module PID TEMPS2. If PID indicates 199°F (93°C), go to next step. If PID does not

indicate 199°F (93°C), check connectors for loose and corroded pins. If all connections are clean and tight, clear DTCs. Using NGS tester, perform NGV module self-test. If DTC B1228 is retrieved again, replace NGV module.

2) Turn ignition switch to LOCK position. Disconnect fuel tank temperature sensor No. 2 harness connector C419. Disconnect NGV module harness connector C124. Measure voltage between terminals No. 46 (Black/Light Blue wire) and No. 40 (Black/White wire) at NGV module harness connector C124. *See Fig. 8.* If .5 volt or less exists, go to next step. If greater than .5 volt exists, repair short to voltage in Black/Light Blue wire.

3) Measure voltage between terminals No. 28 (Light Blue/Pink wire) and No. 40 (Black/White wire) at NGV module harness connector C124. If .5 volt or less exists, replace NGV module. If greater than .5 volt exists, repair short to voltage in Light Blue/Pink wire.

TEST AD: FUEL TANK TEMPERATURE SENSOR NO. 2 CIRCUIT SHORT TO GROUND (DTC B1229)

1) Using NGS tester, monitor Natural Gas Vehicle (NGV) module PID TEMPS2. If PID indicates 199°F (93°C), go to next step. If PID does not indicate 199°F (93°C), check connectors for loose and corroded pins. If all connections are clean and tight, clear DTCs. Using NGS tester, perform NGV module self-test. If DTC B1229 is retrieved again, replace NGV module.

2) Turn ignition switch to LOCK position. Disconnect fuel tank temperature sensor No. 2 harness connector C419. Disconnect NGV module harness connector C124. Measure resistance between terminals No. 28 (Light Blue/Pink wire) and No. 40 (Black/White wire) at NGV module harness connector C124. *See Fig. 8.* If resistance is greater than 10 k/ohms, go to next step. If resistance is 10 k/ohms or less, repair short to ground in Light Blue/Pink wire.

3) Measure resistance between terminals No. 46 (Black/Light Blue wire) and No. 28 (Light Blue/Pink wire) at NGV module harness connector C124. If resistance is greater than 10 k/ohms, replace fuel tank temperature sensor No. 2. If resistance is 10 k/ohms or less, repair short between Light Blue/Pink and Black/Light Blue wires.

TEST AE: BATTERY VOLTAGE HIGH (DTC B1317)

1) Using NGS tester, clear continuous DTCs. Connect voltmeter to battery terminals. Using NGS tester, perform Natural Gas Vehicle (NGV) module self-test while monitoring battery voltage. If battery voltage does not raise above 17 volts during self-test, go to next step. If battery voltage raise above 17 volts during self-test, repair charging system. See appropriate GENERATORS article in STARTING & CHARGING SYSTEMS.

2) Start vehicle. Using NGS tester, perform NGV self-test while monitoring battery voltage. If battery voltage is not greater than 17 volts during self-test, go to next step. If battery voltage is greater than 17 volts during self-test, repair charging system. See appropriate GENERATORS article in STARTING & CHARGING SYSTEMS.

3) Turn ignition switch to LOCK position. Using NGS tester, retrieve and clear continuous DTCs. Repeat NGV self-test. If DTC B1317 is retrieved again, replace NGV module. If DTC B1317 is not retrieved again, system is okay at this time.

TEST AF: BATTERY VOLTAGE LOW (DTC B1318)

1) Using NGS tester, clear continuous DTCs. Connect voltmeter to battery terminals. Using NGS tester, perform Natural Gas Vehicle (NGV) module self-test while monitoring battery voltage. If battery voltage does not drop below 8 volts during self-test, go to next step. If battery voltage drops below 8 volts during self-test, repair charging system. See appropriate GENERATORS article in STARTING & CHARGING SYSTEMS.

2) Start vehicle. Using NGS tester, perform NGV self-test while monitoring battery voltage. If battery voltage does not drop below 8 volts during self-test, go to next step. If battery voltage drops below 8 volts

FORD
4-726

1999 ACCESSORIES & EQUIPMENT
Analog Instrument Panels
Crown Victoria & Grand Marquis (Cont.)

during self-test, repair charging system. See appropriate GENERATORS article in STARTING & CHARGING SYSTEMS.

3) Turn ignition switch to LOCK position. Using NGS tester, retrieve and clear continuous DTCs. Repeat NGV self-test. If DTC B1318 is retrieved again, replace NGV module. If DTC B1318 is not retrieved again, system is okay at this time.

TEST AG: FUEL GAUGE INACCURATE (CNG) OR ECU DEFECTIVE (DTC B1342)

1) Turn ignition switch to LOCK position. Disconnect Natural Gas Vehicle (NGV) module harness connector C124. Inspect harness and module connectors for loose, damaged or corroded connections. If problem does not exist, go to next step. If problem exists, repair or replace as necessary.

2) Turn ignition switch to RUN position. Measure voltage at terminals No. 37 and 57 (both Red wires) at NGV module harness connector C124. *See Fig. 8.* If battery voltage exists at both terminals, go to next step. If battery voltage does not exits at both terminals, repair open in appropriate power distribution circuit. See appropriate wiring diagram in POWER DISTRIBUTION article in WIRING DIAGRAMS.

3) Measure resistance between ground and terminals No. 40 and 60 (both Black/White wires) at NGV module harness connector C124. If both resistance readings are 5 ohms or less, go to next step. If either resistance reading in greater than 5 ohms, repair open in appropriate Black/White wire. See appropriate wiring diagram in GROUND DISTRIBUTION article in WIRING DIAGRAMS.

4) Turn ignition switch to LOCK position. Connect NGV module harness connector C124. Using a ohmmeter, backprobe between terminals No. 40 and 31 (both Black/White wires) at NGV module harness connector C124. If resistance is 5 ohms or less, go to next step. If resistance is greater than 5 ohms, replace NGV module.

5) Disconnect instrument cluster harness connectors. Turn ignition switch to RUN position. Measure voltage between terminal No. 6 (Black/Yellow wire) at instrument cluster harness connector C250 and terminal No. 2 (Black/White wire) at instrument cluster harness connector C251. *See Figs. 6 and 7.* Also, measure voltage between terminals No. 2 (Black/White wire) and No. 3 (Black/Pink wire) at instrument cluster harness connector C251. If battery voltage does not exist in both measurements, go to next step. If battery voltage exists in both measurements, go to step **8)**.

6) Turn ignition switch to LOCK position. Disconnect NGV module harness connector C124. Measure resistance in Black/Yellow wire between terminal No. 6 at instrument cluster harness connector C250 and terminal No. 12 at NGV module harness connector C124. Resistance should be 5 ohms or less. Measure resistance in Black/Yellow wire between terminal No. 3 at instrument cluster harness connector C251 and terminal No. 12 at NGV module harness connector C124. Resistance should be 5 ohms or less. Measure resistance between ground and terminal No. 6 (Black/Yellow wire) at instrument cluster harness connector C250. Resistance should be greater than 10 k/ohms. Measure resistance between ground and terminal No. 3 (Black/Yellow wire) at instrument cluster harness connector C251. Resistance should be greater than 10 k/ohms. If all resistance readings are as specified, go to next step. If any resistance reading is not as specified, repair open or short to ground in Black/Yellow wire.

7) Measure resistance in Black/White wire between terminal No. 2 at instrument cluster harness connector C251 and terminal No. 31 at NGV module harness connector C124. If resistance is 5 ohms or less, replace NGV module. If resistance is greater than 5 ohms, repair open in Black/White wire.

8) Disconnect NGV module harness connector C124. Measure resistance in Yellow/White wire between terminal No. 1 at instrument cluster harness connector C251 and terminal No. 38 at NGV module harness connector C124. If resistance is 5 ohms or less, go to next step. If resistance is greater than 5 ohms, repair open in Yellow/White wire.

9) Measure voltage at terminal No. 1 (Yellow/White wire) at instrument cluster harness connector C251. If voltage does not exist, go to next step. If voltage exists, repair short to voltage in Yellow/White wire.

10) Measure resistance between ground and terminal No. 1 (Yellow/White wire) at instrument cluster harness connector C251. If resistance is greater than 10 k/ohms, go to next step. If resistance is 10 k/ohms or less, repair short to ground in Yellow/White wire.

11) Using a fused jumper wire, connect terminals No. 12 (Black/Yellow wire) and No. 37 (Red wire) at NGV module harness connector C124. Using another fused jumper wire, connect terminals No. 31 and 40 (both Black/White wires) at NGV module harness connector C124. Connect Instrument Gauge Tester (014–R1063) leads to terminals No. 38 (Yellow/White wire) and No. 60 (Black/White wire) at NGV module harness connector C124. Adjust tester to 22 ohms. Turn ignition switch to RUN position. Wait 60 seconds. If fuel gauge does not indicate empty, go to next step. If fuel gauge indicates empty, go to step **14)**

12) Turn ignition switch to LOCK position. Turn ignition switch to RUN position. Tap lightly on instrument cluster. Wait 60 seconds. If fuel gauge does not indicate empty, go to next step. If fuel gauge indicates empty, replace fuel gauge.

13) Turn ignition switch to LOCK position. Adjust tester to 145 ohms. Turn ignition switch to RUN position. Wait 60 seconds. If fuel gauge indicates full, system is okay at this time. If fuel gauge does not indicate full, replace fuel gauge.

14) Turn ignition switch to LOCK position. Measure resistance in Yellow/White wire between terminal No. 1 at instrument cluster harness connector C251 and terminal No. 38 at NGV module harness connector C124. If resistance is 5 ohms or less, replace instrument cluster printed circuit. If resistance is greater than 5 ohms, repair open in Yellow/White wire.

TEST AH: PANEL DIMMING INCREASE INPUT CIRCUIT FAILURE (DTC B1579)

1) Turn ignition switch to LOCK position. Disconnect headlight switch harness connectors. Test headlight switch. See HEADLIGHT SWITCH under COMPONENT TESTS. If headlight switch is okay, go to next step. If headlight switch is defective, replace headlight switch.

2) Disconnect Lighting Control Module (LCM) harness connector C2026. Measure resistance in Orange/Red wire between terminal No. 4 at headlight switch harness connector C249 and terminal No. 16 at LCM harness connector C2026. *See Figs. 12 and 16.* Resistance should be 5 ohms or less. Measure resistance between ground and terminal No. 16 (Orange/Red wire) at LCM harness connector C2026. Resistance should be greater than 10 k/ohms. If both resistance readings are as specified, replace LCM. If either resistance reading is not as specified, repair open or short to ground in Orange/Red wire.

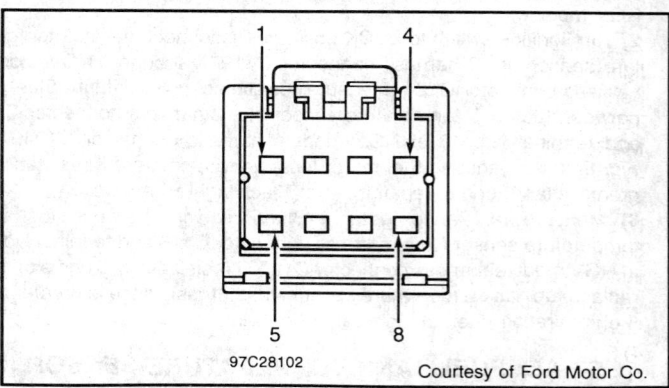

97C28102   Courtesy of Ford Motor Co.

Fig. 16: Identifying Headlight Switch Harness Connector C249 Terminals

1999 ACCESSORIES & EQUIPMENT
Analog Instrument Panels
Crown Victoria & Grand Marquis (Cont.)

FORD
4-727

TEST AI: PANEL DIMMING INCREASE INPUT CIRCUIT SHORT TO VOLTAGE (DTC B1581)

1) Turn ignition switch to LOCK position. Disconnect headlight switch harness connector C249. Turn ignition switch to RUN position. Measure voltage at terminal No. 4 (Orange/Red wire) at headlight switch harness connector C249. *See Fig. 16.* If any voltage exists, go to next step. If zero volts exists, replace headlight switch.

2) Turn ignition switch to LOCK position. Disconnect Lighting Control Module (LCM) harness connector C2026. Turn ignition switch to RUN position. Measure voltage at terminal No. 4 (Orange/Red wire) at headlight switch harness connector C249. If zero volts exists, replace LCM. If any voltage exists, repair short to voltage in Orange/Red wire.

TEST AJ: PANEL DIMMING DECREASE INPUT CIRCUIT FAILURE (DTC B1583)

1) Turn ignition switch to LOCK position. Disconnect headlight switch harness connectors. Test headlight switch. See HEADLIGHT SWITCH under COMPONENT TESTS. If headlight switch is okay, go to next step. If headlight switch is defective, replace headlight switch.

2) Disconnect Lighting Control Module (LCM) harness connector C2026. Measure resistance in Brown/White wire between terminal No. 1 at headlight switch harness connector C249 and terminal No. 15 at LCM harness connector C2026. *See Figs. 12 and 16.* Resistance should be 5 ohms or less. Measure resistance between ground and terminal No. 15 (Brown/White wire) at LCM harness connector C2026. Resistance should be greater than 10 k/ohms. If both resistance readings are as specified, replace LCM. If either resistance reading is not as specified, repair open or short to ground in Brown/White wire.

TEST AK: PANEL DIMMING DECREASE INPUT CIRCUIT SHORT TO VOLTAGE (DTC B1585)

1) Turn ignition switch to LOCK position. Disconnect headlight switch harness connector C249. Turn ignition switch to RUN position. Measure voltage at terminal No. 1 (Brown/White wire) at headlight switch harness connector C249. *See Fig. 16.* If any voltage exists, go to next step. If zero volts exists, replace headlight switch.

2) Turn ignition switch to LOCK position. Disconnect Lighting Control Module (LCM) harness connector C2026. Turn ignition switch to RUN position. Measure voltage at terminal No. 1 (Brown/White wire) at headlight switch harness connector C249. If zero volts exists, replace LCM. If any voltage exists, repair short to voltage in Brown/White wire.

TEST AL: PANEL ILLUMINATION CONTROL INOPERATIVE

1) Using NGS tester, perform Lighting Control Module (LCM) self-test. If not DTC are retrieved, go to next step. If any DTC are retrived, perform appropriate test. See LIGHTING CONTROL MODULE DTC INDEX table under SELF-DIAGNOSTIC SYSTEM.

2) Turn ignition switch to RUN position. Turn parking lights on. If parking lights illuminate, go to next step. If pearking lights do not illuminate, perform TEST Q: PARKING LIGHTS INOPERATIVE under SYSTEM TESTS in AUTOLAMP SYSTEM – CROWN VICTORIA & GRAND MARQUIS article.

3) Turn ignition switch to LOCK position. Disconnect LCM harness connector C2029. Using a fused jumper wire, connect terminals No. 2 (Light Blue/Red wire) and No. 6 (Tan/White wire) at LCM harness connector C2029. *See Fig. 5 .* Turn ignition switch to RUN position. If instrument cluster panel lights do not illuminate, remove jumper wire and go to next step. If instrument cluster panel lights illuminate, replace LCM.

4) Ensure ignition switch is in RUN position. Measure voltage at terminal No. 6 (Tan/White wire) at LCM harness connector C2029. If battery voltage exists, repair open in Light Blue/Red wire. If battery voltage does not exist, repair power diatribution circuit. See appropriate wiring diagram in POWER DISTRIBUTION article in WIRING DIAGRAMS.

TEST AM: INSTRUMENT CLUSTER ILLUMINATION INOPERATIVE

1) Operate turn signals. If turn signal indicators operate, go to next step. If turn signal indicators do not operate, repair open in Black wire between instrument cluster and ground. See appropriate wiring diagram in GROUND DISTRIBUTION article in WIRING DIAGRAMS.

2) Turn ignition switch to LOCK position. Disconnect instrument cluster harness connector C250. Turn headlights on. Measure voltage at terminal No. 16 (Orange/Black wire) at instrument cluster harness connector C250. *See Fig. 7.* If battery voltage exists, replace instrument cluster printed circuit. If battery voltage does not exist, repair open in Orange/Black wire.

TEST AN: INSTRUMENT PANEL ILLMINATION DOES NOT DIM

1) Turn ignition switch to RUN position. Turn headlights on. Using NGS tester, monitor Lighting Control Module (LCM) PID DIM_DEC while holding dim switch down. If PID indicates ON, go to next step. If PID does not indicate ON, go to step **3)**.

2) Turn ignition switch to LOCK position. Disconnect LCM harness connector C2026. Disconnect headlight switch harness connector C249. Measure resistance in Brown/White wire between terminal No. 15 at LCM harness connector C2026 and terminal No. 1 at headlight switch harness connector C249. *See Figs. 12 and 16.* If resistance is 5 ohms or less, go to next step. If resistance is greater than repair open in Brown/White wire.

3) Using NGS tester, monitor LCM PID DIM_INC while holding dim switch up. If PID does not indicate ON, go to next step. If PID indicates ON, replace LCM.

4) Turn ignition switch to LOCK position. Disconnect LCM harness connector C2026. Disconnect headlight switch harness connector C249. Measure resistance in Orange/Red wire between terminal No. 16 at LCM harness connector C2026 and terminal No. 4 at headlight switch harness connector C249. *See Figs. 12 and 16.* If resistance is 5 ohms or less, go to next step. If resistance is greater than repair open in Orange/Red wire.

5) Measure resistance between ground and terminal No. 2 (Tan/White wire) at headlight switch harness connector C249. If resistance is greater than 10 k/ohms, go to next step. If resistance is 10 k/ohms or less, repair short to ground in Tan/White wire.

6) Test headlight switch. See HEADLIGHT SWITCH under COMPONENT TESTS. If headlight switch is okay, replace LCM. If headlight switch is defective, replace headlight switch.

REMOVAL & INSTALLATION

CAUTION: When battery is disconnected, vehicle computer and memory systems may lose memory data. Driveability problems may exist until computer systems have completed a relearn cycle. See COMPUTER RELEARN PROCEDURES article in GENERAL INFORMATION before disconnecting battery.

CAUTION: Electronic modules are sensitive to static electrical charges. Proper grounding of technician and workpiece is essential to prevent damage.

NATURAL GAS VEHICLE MODULE

Removal & Installation – 1) Disconnect negative battery cable. Remove upper radiator sight shield. Remove Natural Gas Vehicle (NGV) module harness connector cover. Loosen NGV harness connector retaining bolt. Disconnect NGV module harness connector.

2) Remove NGV module bracket retaining bolts. Remove NGV module-to-bracket retaining bolts. Remove NGV module. To install, reverse removal procedures.

FORD
4-728

1999 ACCESSORIES & EQUIPMENT
Analog Instrument Panels
Crown Victoria & Grand Marquis (Cont.)

INSTRUMENT CLUSTER

Removal – 1) Disconnect negative battery cable. Remove left side instrument panel molding. Remove right side instrument panel molding. **2)** On Crown Victoria, remove 6 screws and remove lower instrument panel steering column cover. On Grand Marquis, remove 5 screws and remove instrument panel steering column cover.
3) On all models, remove screw fastening transmission range indicator column bracket to steering column. Detach cable loop from terminal and shift lever. Remove column bracket from column.
4) Remove 4 cluster retaining screws. Disconnect cluster connectors from instrument cluster back plate and remove instrument cluster.
Installation – 1) Position instrument cluster to instrument panel. Connect cluster connectors. Ensure transmission range cable is routed properly. Install 4 cluster retaining screws and tighten to 8-12 ft. lbs. (0.8-1.4 N.m).
2) Position transmission range indicator column bracket to steering column tube (locate terminal in column slot) and use following sequence to adjust transmission range indicator:

- Place transmission selector lever arm and support on steering column tube in "1" position.
- Place loop on indicator cable assembly over retainer terminal on shift lever.
- Secure cable bracket with screw.
- Shift transmission selector lever arm and support into "D" position. Adjust thumb wheel on steering column tube so entire width of pointer falls within letter "D".
- When properly adjusted, entire width of pointer must fall within width of letter "D" and must touch remaining letters or numerals when viewed parallel to center line of steering column tube from driver's position.

3) Position lower steering column shroud and install retaining screws. Connect negative battery cable and check operation of instruments.

ANTI-SLOSH MODULE (GAUGE AMPLIFIER)

NOTE: Anti-slosh module and gauge must be serviced together.

Removal – Remove instrument cluster. See INSTRUMENT CLUSTER. Depress tang and remove instrument cluster gauge amplifier from rear of instrument cluster.
Installation – Position module in guides, line up terminals over center of printed circuit connections, and push until module clicks into place. To complete installation, reverse removal procedure.

PRINTED CIRCUIT

CAUTION: When removing gauge contact clips, DO NOT damage instrument cluster printed circuit.

Removal & Installation – Remove instrument cluster. See INSTRUMENT CLUSTER. Remove indicator and illumination bulbs from rear of instrument cluster. Remove gauge contact clips from rear of cluster by compressing clip ends together and pulling out. Discard clips. Carefully remove printed circuit from rear of instrument cluster. To install, reverse removal procedure using NEW gauge contact clips.

FUEL GAUGE/VOLTMETER

CAUTION: Gauges are factory calibrated. Excessive rough handling can disturb calibration. DO NOT remove pointers.

NOTE: Gauge and anti-slosh module must be serviced together.

Removal & Installation – Disconnect negative battery cable. Remove instrument cluster. See INSTRUMENT CLUSTER. Remove screws retaining cluster back plate. Remove cluster main lens. Remove instrument cluster mask. Remove fuel gauge/voltmeter assembly and anti-slosh module. To install, reverse removal procedure.

TEMPERATURE GAUGE/OIL PRESSURE GAUGE

Removal & Installation – 1) Disconnect negative battery cable. Remove instrument cluster. See INSTRUMENT CLUSTER.
2) Remove screws retaining cluster back plate. Remove cluster main lens. Remove instrument cluster mask. Remove temperature gauge/oil pressure gauge assembly. To install, reverse removal procedure.

SPEEDOMETER/ODOMETER

CAUTION: During service, it is important to keep speedometer face up. Speedometer function will be affected by storage in face down position.

Removal & Installation – Disconnect negative battery cable. Remove instrument cluster. See INSTRUMENT CLUSTER. Remove 7 screws retaining instrument cluster mask and main lens assembly. Remove speedometer assembly. To install, reverse removal procedure.

TRANSMISSION RANGE INDICATOR

Removal & Installation – 1) Remove instrument cluster. See INSTRUMENT CLUSTER. Remove 8 screws from instrument cluster main lens and cluster mask.
2) Remove temperature gauge/oil pressure gauge assembly. Releasing snaps, remove transmission range indicator from speedometer. Remove transmission range indicator. To install, reverse removal procedure.

INDICATOR/WARNING BULBS

WARNING: Bulbs are pressurized and may shatter if improperly handled. Wear eye protection when servicing bulbs.

Removal & Installation – Disconnect negative battery cable. Remove instrument cluster. See INSTRUMENT CLUSTER. Remove indicator/ warning bulbs. To install, reverse removal procedure.

FUEL TANK TEMPERATURE SENSORS

See appropriate REMOVAL, OVERHAUL & INSTALLATION article in ENGINE PERFORMANCE in appropriate MITCHELL® manual.

FUEL TANK PRESSURE SENSOR

See appropriate REMOVAL, OVERHAUL & INSTALLATION article in ENGINE PERFORMANCE in appropriate MITCHELL® manual.

1999 ACCESSORIES & EQUIPMENT
Analog Instrument Panels
Crown Victoria & Grand Marquis (Cont.)

FORD
4-729

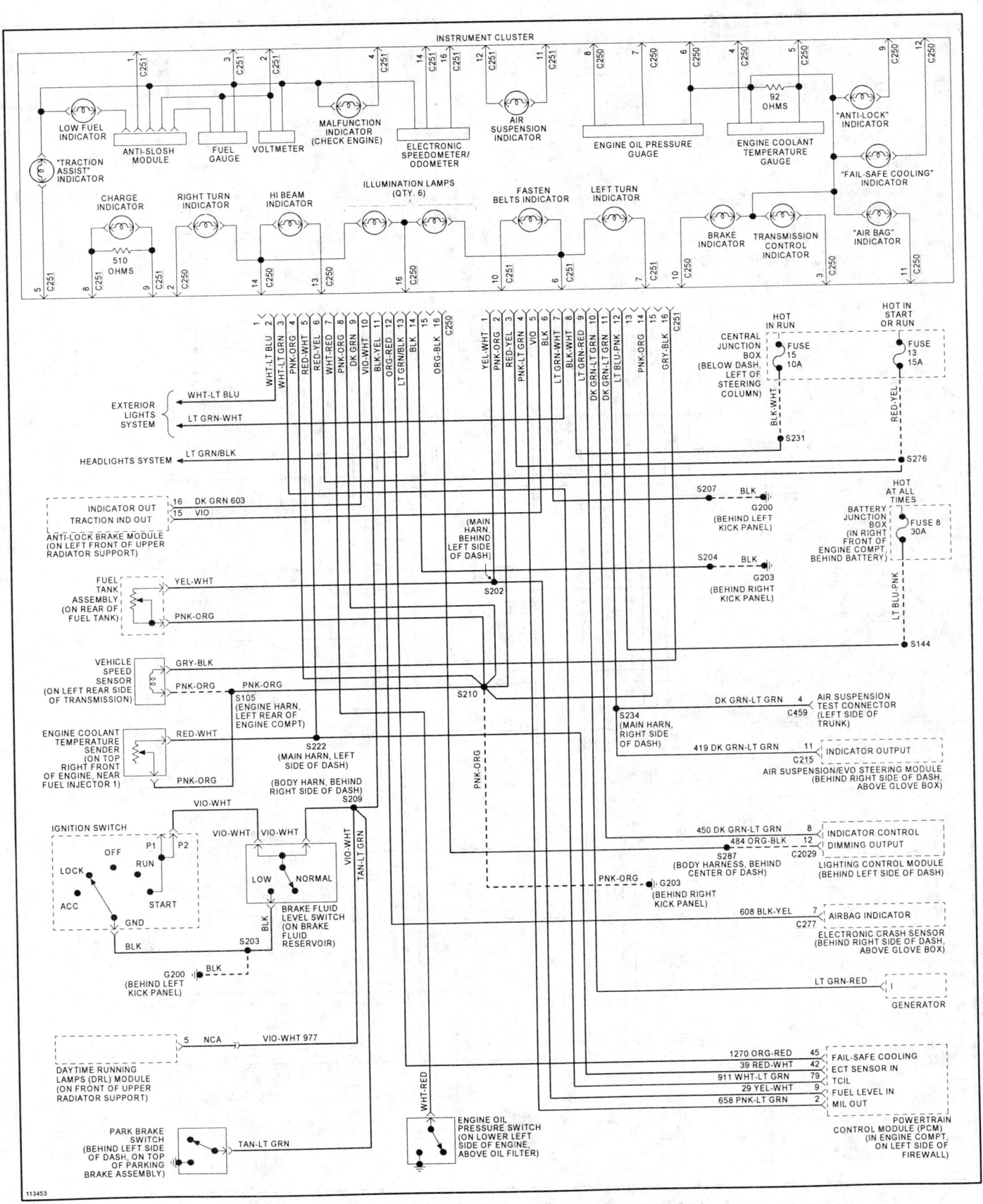

Fig. 17: Analog Instrument Panel Wiring Diagram (Crown Victoria & Grand Marquis – Gasoline)

113453

FORD
4-730

1999 ACCESSORIES & EQUIPMENT
Analog Instrument Panels
Crown Victoria & Grand Marquis (Cont.)

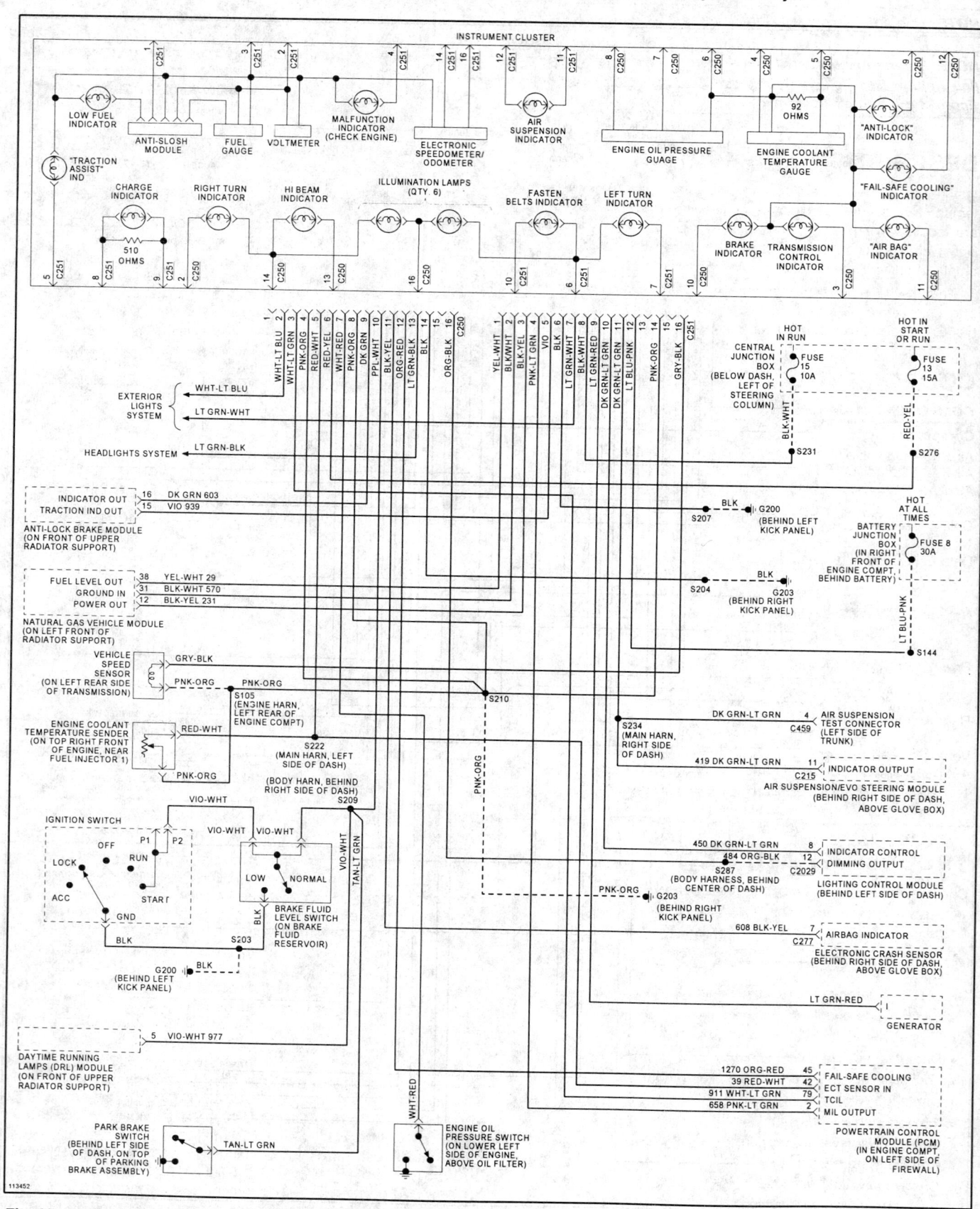

Fig. 18: Analog Instrument Panel Wiring Diagram (Crown Victoria – CNG)

NOTE: This article includes Cutaway and RV Cutaway.

NOTE: For instrument panel fuel system related testing of Econoline Natural Gas Vehicle (NGV), see Analog Instrument Panels – Econoline – Natural Gas Vehicle.

DESCRIPTION & OPERATION

Instrument cluster contains a speedometer, odometer, fuel gauge, temperature gauge, oil pressure gauge and a voltmeter. Warning lights are located in instrument cluster face panel. *See Fig. 1.* Intensity of illumination is controlled by rotating headlight switch knob, controlling output of pulse width module.

The gauges within the instrument cluster are not separately replaceable. The only serviceable parts within instrument cluster are illumination bulbs, indicator bulbs and cluster mask.

COMPONENT LOCATIONS

COMPONENT LOCATIONS

Component	Location
Air Bag Diagnostic Monitor [1]	Behind Right Kick Panel
Air Bag Sliding Contact	Top Of Steering Column
Auxiliary Powertrain Control Module	Below Left Side Of Instrument Panel
Chime Module	Behind Center Of Instrument Cluster
Data Link Connector	Below Driver's Side Of Instrument Panel, To Right Of Steering Column
Natural Gas Vehicle Module	Left Side Of Engine Compartment, On Inner Fender
Powertrain Control Module	Left Rear Of Engine Compartment, Near Brake Master Cylinder
Rear Anti-Lock Brake (RABS) Module	Behind Center Of Instrument Panel
Vehicle Speed Sensor	Left Side Of Transmission
4-Wheel Anti-Lock Brake Module	On Left Front Frame Rail

[1] – Air bag diagnostic monitor may also be referred to as Electronic Crash Sensor (ECS) module.

TROUBLE SHOOTING

Check the following items before proceeding with testing:

- Fuse No. 2 (15-amp) and No. 14 (5-amp) in instrument panel fuse panel.
- Fuse No. 4 (10-amp) in engine compartment Power Distribution Center (PDC).
- Loose or damaged harness connectors.
- Stuck gauge needle.
- Tripped inertia fuel cut-off switch.
- Damaged vehicle speed sensor.
- Low oil level.
- Damaged oil filter or oil pump.
- Tripped inertia fuel shutoff switch.
- Engine oiling system function.
- Cooling system function.
- Charging system function.
- Fuel delivery system function.

SYSTEM TESTS

CAUTION: When battery is disconnected or modules are replaced, vehicle computer and memory systems may lose memory data. Driveability problems may exist until computer systems have completed a relearn cycle. See COMPUTER RELEARN PROCEDURES article in GENERAL INFORMATION before disconnecting battery.

NOTE: Before beginning system tests, perform TROUBLE SHOOTING.

SYMPTOM CHART

Symptom	Test
Fuel Gauge Inaccurate	A
Voltage Gauge Inaccurate	B
Oil Pressure Gauge Inaccurate	C
Temperature Gauge Inaccurate	D
Temperature Warning Light Flickers & Gauge Reads Fully Hot	E [1]
Speedometer Inoperative But Odometer Functions Properly	[2]
Trip Odometer Inoperative, Speedometer Okay	F [2]
Safety Belt Warning Inoperative	G
Speedometer Inaccurate	G
Speedometer/Odometer Inoperative	H
Brake Warning Indicator Inoperative	J
Charge Warning Inoperative	K
Anti-Lock Brake Warning Indicator Inoperative	L
CHECK ENGINE Light (MIL) Inoperative	M
High Beam Warning Inoperative	N
Left Turn Indicator Inoperative	P
Right Turn Indicator Inoperative	Q
Air Bag Warning Imperative	R
Low Oil Pressure/High Coolant Temperature Indicator Inoperative	S
Water In Fuel Indicator Inoperative	T
Wait To Start Indicator Inoperative	[3]
Brake Warning Indicator Always On	

[1] – Replace instrument cluster.
[2] – Ensure trip lever is not binding, repair as necessary. If trip lever is okay, replace instrument cluster.
[3] – See appropriate article in BRAKES in appropriate MITCHELL® manual.

TEST A: FUEL GAUGE INACCURATE

NOTE: Anti-slosh circuitry will cause fuel gauge to take about 20 minutes to go from empty to full if fueled with ignition on.

1) Turn ignition off. Disconnect fuel gauge sending unit. Using Instrument Gauge System Tester (014-R-1063), connect one tester lead to fuel sending unit Yellow/White wire. Connect second lead to ground. Set instrument gauge system tester to 160 ohms. Turn instrument gauge system tester on. Turn ignition on. Wait one minute and read fuel gauge. Fuel gauge should read "F" or above. Set tester to 15 ohms. Wait one minute and read fuel gauge. Fuel gauge should read "E" or below. If fuel gauge reads as specified, disconnect tester and go to next step. If fuel gauge does not read as specified, disconnect tester and go to step **4)**.

2) Visually inspect fuel tank for damage. If fuel tank is okay, go to next step. If fuel tank is damaged, repair or replace as necessary.

3) Visually inspect fuel pump assembly for damage or corroded connections. Inspect float and float rod. If fuel pump assembly is okay, replace fuel level sender. See FUEL LEVEL SENDER under REMOVAL & INSTALLATION. If fuel pump assembly is damaged, replace assembly and retest system.

4) Turn ignition off. Remove instrument cluster. See INSTRUMENT CLUSTER under REMOVAL & INSTALLATION. Measure resistance of Yellow/White wire between instrument cluster connector C224 terminal No. 10 and fuel level sending unit connector. *See Fig. 2.* Resistance should be less than 5 ohms. Measure resistance between ground and instrument cluster connector C224 terminal No. 10 (Yellow/White wire).

Resistance should be more than 10 k/ohms. If resistance is as specified, go to next step. If resistance is not as specified, repair open or short to ground in Yellow/White wire. See WIRING DIAGRAMS.

5) Measure resistance between ground and fuel level sending unit connector Black/Yellow wire. If resistance is less than 5 ohms, replace instrument cluster. If resistance is more than 5 ohms, repair open in Black/Yellow wire. See WIRING DIAGRAMS.

than 10 volts, repair open or short in Red/White wire between instrument cluster connector and fuse No. 4 in PDC.

4) Start engine. If gauge is in normal range, system is okay. If gauge is not in normal range, check for poor connection at bulkhead connector and instrument cluster ground connections. See WIRING DIAGRAMS. Repair as necessary. Retest system.

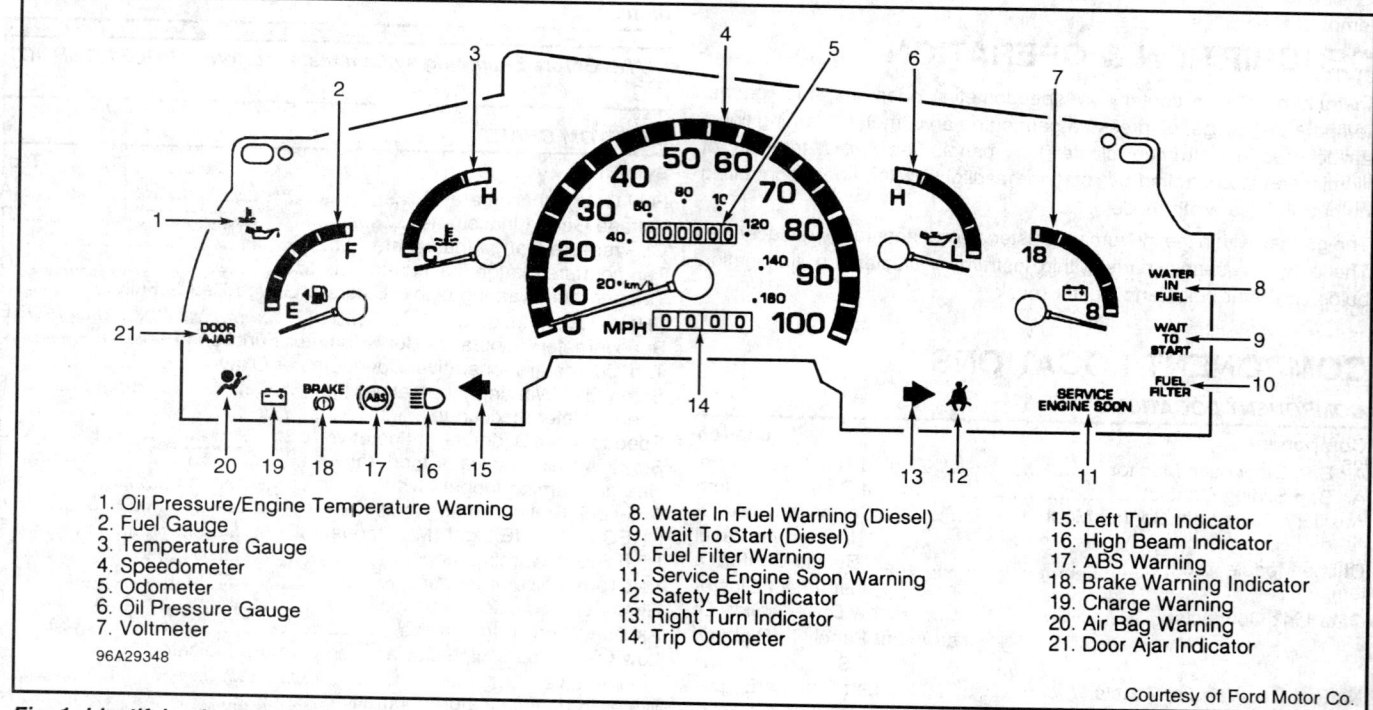

1. Oil Pressure/Engine Temperature Warning
2. Fuel Gauge
3. Temperature Gauge
4. Speedometer
5. Odometer
6. Oil Pressure Gauge
7. Voltmeter

8. Water In Fuel Warning (Diesel)
9. Wait To Start (Diesel)
10. Fuel Filter Warning
11. Service Engine Soon Warning
12. Safety Belt Indicator
13. Right Turn Indicator
14. Trip Odometer

15. Left Turn Indicator
16. High Beam Indicator
17. ABS Warning
18. Brake Warning Indicator
19. Charge Warning
20. Air Bag Warning
21. Door Ajar Indicator

96A29348

Courtesy of Ford Motor Co.

Fig. 1: Identifying Instrument Panel

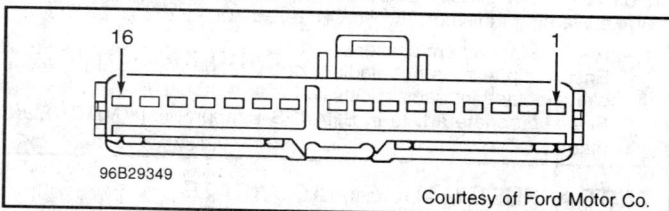

96B29349

Courtesy of Ford Motor Co.

Fig. 2: Identifying Instrument Cluster Connector C224 Terminals

TEST B: VOLTMETER INACCURATE

NOTE: Ensure charging system is operating properly before proceeding with this test. See appropriate GENERATORS article in STARTING & CHARGING SYSTEMS.

1) Turn ignition on. Observe voltmeter. If voltmeter registers in normal range, go to step 4). If voltmeter registers higher than normal range, replace instrument cluster. If voltmeter registers lower than normal range, go to next step.

NOTE: Power feed to voltmeter from fuse No. 4 in PDC changes wire colors at junction connector where harness enters passenger compartment. This circuit is a Yellow wire at PDC and Red/White wire at instrument cluster.

2) Inspect fuse No. 4 in PDC. If fuse is okay, go to next step. If fuse is blown, install new fuse and retest. If fuse blows again, repair circuit for short to ground. See WIRING DIAGRAMS.

3) Remove instrument cluster. See INSTRUMENT CLUSTER under REMOVAL & INSTALLATION. Disconnect instrument cluster harness connector C224. See Fig. 2. Measure voltage between ground and connector C224 terminal No. 3 (Red/White wire). If voltage is more than 10 volts, replace instrument cluster. Retest system. If voltage is less

TEST C: OIL PRESSURE GAUGE INACCURATE

1) Ensure oil level is okay. Ensure oil pressure switch wire is securely connected. Turn ignition on, engine off. If oil pressure gauge indicates about zero, go to next step. If oil pressure gauge does not indicate about zero, go to step 5).

2) Start engine. If oil pressure gauge indicates normal oil pressure, check for intermittent problem. If oil pressure gauge does not indicate normal oil pressure, go to next step.

3) Turn ignition off. Remove instrument cluster. See INSTRUMENT CLUSTER under REMOVAL & INSTALLATION. Start engine. Measure resistance between instrument cluster harness connector C224 terminal No. 6 (White/Red wire) and No. 5 (Black/White wire). See Fig. 2. If resistance is less than 5 ohms, replace instrument cluster. If resistance is more than 5 ohms, go to next step.

4) Turn ignition off. Disconnect oil pressure switch. Connect jumper wire between oil pressure switch connector and ground. Measure resistance between ground and instrument cluster harness connector C224 terminal No. 6 (White/Red wire). If resistance is less than 5 ohms, replace oil pressure switch. If resistance is more than 5 ohms, repair open White/Red wire.

5) Turn ignition off. Remove instrument cluster. See INSTRUMENT CLUSTER under REMOVAL & INSTALLATION. Disconnect instrument cluster harness connector C224. Measure resistance between instrument cluster harness connector C224 terminal No. 6 and ground. If resistance is less than 5 ohms, go to next step. If resistance is more than 5 ohms, replace instrument cluster.

6) Turn ignition off. Disconnect oil pressure switch harness connector. Measure resistance between instrument cluster harness connector C224 terminal No. 6 and ground. If resistance is less than 5 ohms, repair short to ground in White/Red wire. Retest system. If resistance is more than 5 ohms, replace oil pressure switch. Retest system.

TEST D: TEMPERATURE GAUGE INACCURATE

1) Start and run engine until it reaches operating temperature. If temperature gauge indicates normal operating temperature, check for an intermittent problem. If temperature gauge reads high, go to next step. If temperature gauge reads low, go to step **4)**.

2) Turn ignition off. Disconnect temperature gauge sending unit connector. Turn ignition on. If temperature gauge reads high, go to next step. If temperature gauge does not read high, replace temperature sending unit and recheck gauge operation.

3) Turn ignition off. Remove instrument cluster. See INSTRUMENT CLUSTER under REMOVAL & INSTALLATION. Disconnect instrument cluster harness connector C224. *See Fig. 2.* Measure resistance between instrument cluster harness connector C224 terminal No. 9 (Red/White wire) and ground. If resistance is more than 10 k/ohms, replace instrument cluster. Retest system. If resistance is less than 10 k/ohms, repair short to ground in Red/White wire between temperature sending unit and instrument cluster.

4) Turn ignition off. Disconnect temperature sending unit harness connector. Connect a jumper wire across temperature sending unit harness connector terminals. Turn ignition on. If temperature gauge does not indicate HOT, go to next step. If temperature gauge indicates HOT, replace temperature sending unit. Retest system.

5) Turn ignition off. Measure resistance between Yellow/Red wire at temperature sending unit harness connector and ground. If resistance is less than 5 ohms, go to next step. If resistance is more than 5 ohms, repair open Yellow/Red or Pink/Orange wire. Check gauge operation.

6) Remove instrument cluster. See INSTRUMENT CLUSTER under REMOVAL & INSTALLATION. Measure resistance or Red/White wire between instrument cluster harness connector C224 terminal No. 9 and temperature sending unit harness connector. *See Fig. 2.* If resistance is less than 5 ohms, replace instrument cluster. If resistance is more than 5 ohms, repair open Red/White wire. Check gauge operation.

TEST E: TEMPERATURE WARNING LIGHT FLICKERS & GAUGE READS FULLY HOT

NOTE: Ensure engine coolant level is full and temperature sending unit connector is securely attached.

1) Turn ignition on. Wiggle Red/White and Yellow/Red wires at temperature sending unit harness connector. If temperature gauge and light remains steady, go to next step. If gauge fluctuates or light flickers, repair open temperature sending unit wire.

2) Turn ignition off. Disconnect temperature sending unit. Connect a jumper wire between temperature sending unit harness connector terminals. Turn ignition on. Temperature gauge should indicate fully HOT with jumper wire installed and fully COLD with jumper wire removed. If gauge indicates as specified, replace temperature sending unit. If gauge does not indicate as specified, go to TEST D: TEMPERATURE GAUGE INACCURATE test.

TEST F: SEAT BELT WARNING INDICATOR INOPERATIVE

1) Turn ignition off. Remove instrument cluster. See INSTRUMENT CLUSTER under REMOVAL & INSTALLATION. Turn ignition on. Measure voltage between ground and instrument cluster connector C225 terminal No. 7 (Dark Green/Light Green wire). *See Fig. 3.* If voltage is 10 volts or less, go to step **3)**. If voltage is more than 10 volts, go to next step.

2) Remove seat belt warning indicator bulb from instrument cluster. Check continuity between bulb terminals. If continuity exists, replace instrument cluster. If continuity does not exist, replace bulb and retest system.

3) Cycle ignition key off and back on. Measure voltage between ground and instrument cluster connector C225 terminal No. 7 (Dark Green/Light Green wire). *See Fig. 3.* This is a prove out circuit test and voltage will only last for a few seconds. If voltage is less than 10 volts, go to next step. If voltage is more than 10 volts, repair open Black wire between instrument cluster connector C224 terminal No. 1 and ground.

4) Turn ignition off. Disconnect chime module. Chime module is located behind center of instrument cluster. Measure resistance of Dark Green/Light Green wire between instrument cluster connector C225 terminal No. 7 and chime module connector C214 terminal No. 6. *See Figs. 3 and 4.* If resistance is less than 5 ohms, see appropriate wiring diagram in WARNING SYSTEMS article to diagnosis circuits to chime module. If resistance is 5 ohms or more, repair open Dark Green/Light Green wire.

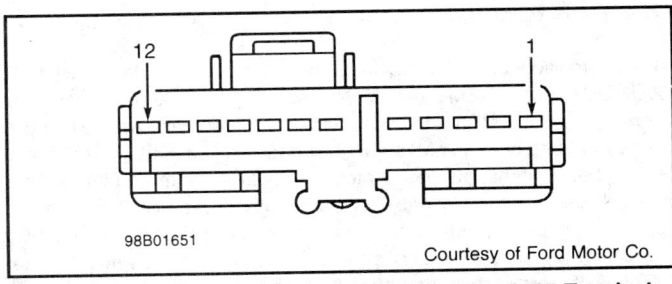

Fig. 3: Identifying Instrument Cluster Connector C225 Terminals

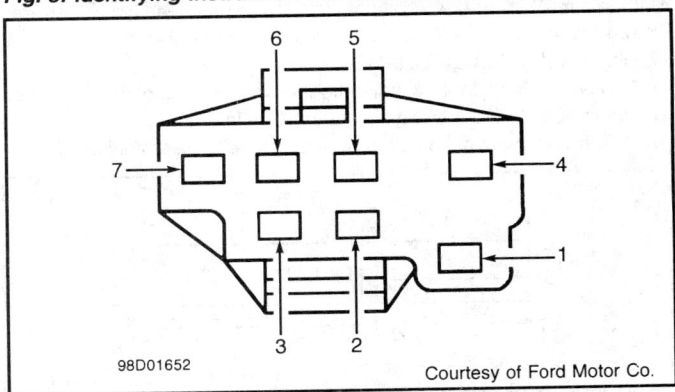

Fig. 4: Identifying Chime Module Connector C214 Terminals

TEST G: SPEEDOMETER READING INACCURATE

1) Using New Generation Star (NGS) tester or equivalent, drive vehicle at a steady speed until Powertrain Control Module (PCM) VSS PID indicates 30 MPH (48 km/h). If speedometer indication is 28-35 (45-57 km/h), go to next step. If speedometer indication is not 28-35 (45-57 km/h), see appropriate SELF-DIAGNOSTICS article in ENGINE PERFORMANCE in appropriate MITCHELL® manual to diagnosis VSS circuit.

2) Drive vehicle at a steady speed until VSS PID indicates 60 MPH (97 km/h). If speedometer indication is 58-62 (94-100 km/h), speedometer is okay at this time, go to next step. If speedometer indication is not 58-62 (94-100 km/h), see appropriate SELF-DIAGNOSTICS article in ENGINE PERFORMANCE in appropriate MITCHELL® manual.

3) Turn ignition off. Remove instrument cluster. See INSTRUMENT CLUSTER under REMOVAL & INSTALLATION. Install EEC-V 104-Pin Breakout Box (014-00950) following manufacturer's instructions. Measure resistance between breakout box pin No. 48 and instrument cluster connector C224 terminal No. 7 (Gray/Black wire). Resistance should be more than 10 k/ohms. Measure resistance between ground and instrument cluster connector C224 terminal No. 7 (Gray/Black wire). Resistance should be less than 5 ohms. If resistance is as specified, go to next step. If resistance is not as specified, repair open or short in Gray/Black wire.

4) Measure voltage between ground and instrument cluster connector C224 terminal No. 3 (Red/White wire). If voltage is more than 10 volts, replace instrument cluster and retest system. If voltage is 10 volts or less, repair Red/White wire between instrument cluster and PDC.

TEST H: BRAKE WARNING INDICATOR INOPERATIVE

1) Set parking brake. Turn ignition on. If Red brake warning indicator does not illuminate, go to next step. If Red brake warning indicator illuminates, system is okay.

2) Disconnect parking brake switch connector. Connect jumper wire between ground and parking brake switch connector. If Red brake warning indicator illuminates, replace parking brake switch. Retest system. If Red brake warning indicator does not illuminate, go to next step.

3) Turn ignition off. Remove instrument cluster. See INSTRUMENT CLUSTER under REMOVAL & INSTALLATION. Measure resistance between instrument cluster connector C226 terminal No. 4 (Purple/White wire) and parking brake switch connector. See Fig. 5. If resistance is less than 5 ohms, go to next step. If resistance is more than 5 ohms and vehicle is equipped with Rear Anti-Lock Brakes System (RABS), repair open circuit between instrument cluster, dual brake warning diode/resister assembly and park brake switch. See WIRING DIAGRAMS. If resistance is more than 5 ohms and vehicle is equipped with 4 Wheel Anti-Lock Brakes System (4WABS), repair open circuit between instrument cluster, 4WABS relay, 4WABS module and park brake switch. See WIRING DIAGRAMS.

4) Remove brake system warning light bulb. Check continuity between terminals of bulb. If continuity exists, replace instrument cluster. Retest system. If continuity does not exist, replace bulb. Retest system.

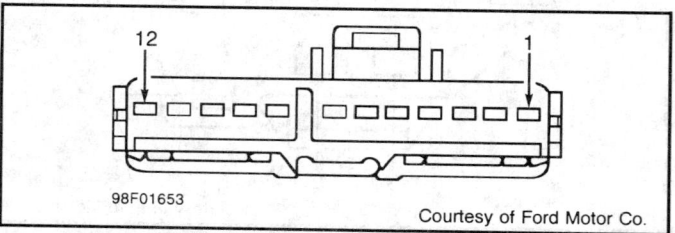

```
12                              1
```
98F01653   Courtesy of Ford Motor Co.

Fig. 5: Identifying Instrument Cluster Connector C226 Terminals

TEST J: CHARGE WARNING INDICATOR INOPERATIVE

1) Turn ignition on. Using a voltmeter, measure voltage by backprobing between instrument cluster connector C226 terminals No. 5 (Light Green/Red wire) and No. 7 (White/Yellow wire). If voltage is more than 9 volts, go to next step. If voltage is 9 volts or less, go to step 3).

2) Turn ignition off. Remove instrument cluster. See INSTRUMENT CLUSTER under REMOVAL & INSTALLATION. Remove charge system warning light bulb. Check continuity between terminals of bulb. If continuity exists, replace instrument cluster. Retest system. If continuity does not exist, replace bulb. Retest system.

3) Remove instrument cluster. See INSTRUMENT CLUSTER under REMOVAL & INSTALLATION. Turn ignition on. Measure voltage between ground and instrument cluster connector C226 terminal No. 7 (White/Yellow wire). If voltage is more than 10 volts and vehicle is equipped with a single generator, go to next step. If voltage is more than 10 volts and vehicle is equipped with dual generators, go to step 5). If voltage is less than 10 volts, repair open White/Yellow wire. Retest system.

4) Turn ignition off. Disconnect generator harness 3-pin connector. Measure resistance of Light Green/Red wire between generator harness 3-pin connector and instrument cluster connector C226 terminal No. 5. If resistance is less than 5 ohms, refer to generator diagnosis in appropriate GENERATORS article in STARTING & CHARGING SYSTEMS. If resistance is 5 ohms or more, repair open in Light Green/Red wire. Retest system.

5) Install EEC-V 104-Pin Breakout Box (014-00950) following manufacturer's instructions. Measure resistance between breakout box pin No. 67 and instrument cluster connector C226 terminal No. 5 (Light Green/Red wire). If resistance is less than 5 ohms, refer to generator diagnosis in appropriate GENERATORS article in STARTING & CHARGING SYSTEMS. If resistance is 5 ohms or more, repair open in Light Green/Red wire. Retest system.

TEST K: ANTI-LOCK BRAKE WARNING LIGHT INOPERATIVE

NOTE: Voltage measurement is step 1) is for prove-out circuit. Voltage will only exist for a few seconds after key returns to RUN position.

1) Start engine. Using a voltmeter, measure voltage by backprobing between instrument cluster connector C225 terminal No. 8 (Dark Green wire) and connector C226 terminal No. 12 (Red/Yellow wire). See Figs. 3 and 5. If voltage is 9 volts or less, go to step 3). If voltage is more than 9 volts, go to next step.

2) Turn ignition off. Remove instrument cluster. See INSTRUMENT CLUSTER under REMOVAL & INSTALLATION. Remove anti-lock brake warning light bulb. Check continuity between terminals of bulb. If continuity exists, replace instrument cluster. Retest system. If continuity does not exist, replace bulb. Retest system.

3) Turn ignition off. Remove instrument cluster. See INSTRUMENT CLUSTER under REMOVAL & INSTALLATION. Disconnect Rear Anti-Lock Brakes System (RABS) module connector C217, if equipped. Disconnect 4 Wheel Anti-Lock Brakes System (4WABS) module connector C144, if equipped. RABS module is located behind center of instrument panel to right of lighter. 4WABS module is located of left front frame rail. On RABS models, measure resistance of Dark Green wire between RABS module connector C217 terminal No. 7 and instrument cluster connector C225 terminal No. 8. On 4WABS models, measure resistance of Dark Green wire between 4WABS module connector C144 terminal No. 1 and instrument cluster connector C225 terminal No. 8. On all models, if resistance is less than 5 ohms, see appropriate ANTI-LOCK article in BRAKES in appropriate MITCHELL® manual. If resistance is 5 ohms or more, repair open in Dark Green wire. Retest system.

TEST L: SERVICE ENGINE SOON LIGHT INOPERATIVE

NOTE: Voltage measurement is step 1) is for prove-out circuit. Voltage will only exist for a few seconds when key is turned to RUN position.

1) Turn ignition on. Using a voltmeter, measure voltage by backprobing between instrument cluster connector C225 terminal No. 5 (Pink/Light Green wire) and connector C226 terminal No. 12 (Red/Yellow wire). See Figs. 3 and 5. If voltage is 9 volts or less, go to step 3). If voltage is more than 9 volts, go to next step.

2) Turn ignition off. Remove instrument cluster. See INSTRUMENT CLUSTER under REMOVAL & INSTALLATION. Remove anti-lock brake warning light bulb. Check continuity between terminals of bulb. If continuity exists, replace instrument cluster. Retest system. If continuity does not exist, replace bulb. Retest system.

3) Turn ignition off. Remove instrument cluster. See INSTRUMENT CLUSTER under REMOVAL & INSTALLATION. Install EEC-V 104-Pin Breakout Box (014-00950) following manufacturer's instructions. Measure resistance between breakout box pin No. 2 and instrument cluster connector C225 terminal No. 5 (Pink/Light Green wire). If resistance is less than 5 ohms, see appropriate SELF-DIAGNOSTICS article in ENGINE PERFORMANCE in appropriate MITCHELL® manual, for Powertrain Control Module (PCM) diagnostics. If resistance 5 ohms or more, repair open in Pink/Light Green wire. Retest system.

TEST M: HIGH BEAM INDICATOR INOPERATIVE

1) Turn ignition off. Remove instrument cluster. See INSTRUMENT CLUSTER under REMOVAL & INSTALLATION. Disconnect instrument cluster connector C225. See Fig. 3. Turn ignition on. Turn multifunction switch to high beam lights on position. Measure voltage between ground

and instrument cluster connector C225 terminal No. 9 (Gray/White wire). If voltage is more than 10 volts, go to next step. If voltage is less than 10 volts, go to step **3)**.

2) Remove high beam indicator bulb. Check for continuity across high beam indicator bulb terminals. If continuity exists, replace instrument cluster. Retest system. If continuity does not exist, replace bulb and retest system.

3) Disconnect multifunction switch 7-pin connector C251. Measure resistance between multifunction switch 7-pin connector C251 terminal No. 5 (Light Green/Black wire) and instrument cluster connector C225 terminal No. 5 (Gray/White wire). See Figs. 3 and 6. If resistance is less than 5 ohms, see appropriate wiring diagram in HEADLIGHT SYSTEMS article. If resistance is 5 ohms or more, repair open in Gray/White or Light Green/Black wire. High beam indicator wire changes from Gray/White to Light Green/Black at bulkhead connector near blower motor. Retest system.

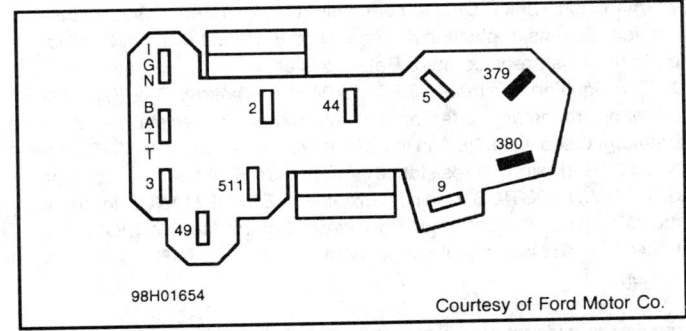

Fig. 7: Identifying Multifunction Switch 11-pin Connector C250 Terminals

terminal No. 14. See Figs. 2 and 7. If resistance is less than 5 ohms, see appropriate wiring diagram in EXTERIOR LIGHTS article to diagnosis power to multifunction switch. If resistance 5 ohms or more, repair open in White/Light Blue wire.

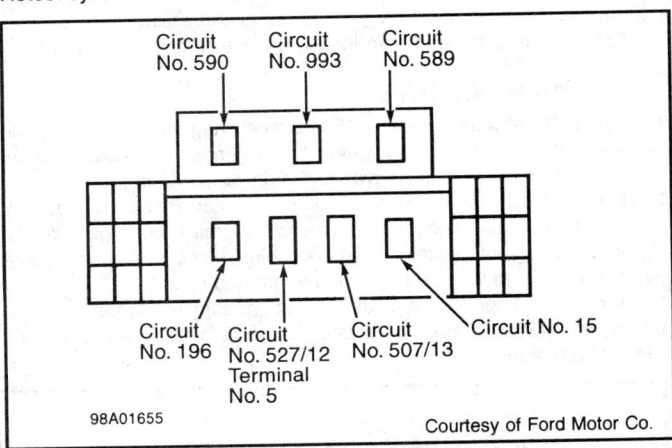

Fig. 6: Identifying Multifunction Switch 7-pin Connector C251 Terminals

TEST N: LEFT TURN INDICATOR INOPERATIVE

1) Turn ignition off. Remove instrument cluster. See appropriate INSTRUMENT CLUSTER under REMOVAL & INSTALLATION. Place multifunction is left turn position. Measure voltage between ground and instrument cluster connector C224 terminal No. 16 (Light Green/White wire). See Fig. 2. If voltage is more than 10 volts, go to next step. If voltage is 10 volts or less, go to step **3)**.

2) Turn ignition off. Check for continuity across left turn indicator bulb. If continuity exists, replace instrument cluster. See INSTRUMENT CLUSTER under REMOVAL & INSTALLATION. Retest system. If continuity does not exist, replace bulb. Retest system.

3) Disconnect multifunction switch 11-pin connector C250. Measure resistance of Light Green/White wire between multifunction switch 11-pin connector C250 circuit No. 3 and instrument cluster connector C224 terminal No. 16. See Figs. 2 and 7. If resistance is less than 5 ohms, see appropriate wiring diagram in EXTERIOR LIGHTS article to diagnosis power to multifunction switch. If resistance 5 ohms or more, repair open in Light Green/White wire.

TEST P: RIGHT TURN INDICATOR INOPERATIVE

1) Turn ignition off. Remove instrument cluster. See appropriate INSTRUMENT CLUSTER under REMOVAL & INSTALLATION. Place multifunction is right turn position. Measure voltage between ground and instrument cluster connector C224 terminal No. 14 (White/Light Blue wire). See Fig. 2. If voltage is 10 volts or less, go to step **3)**. If voltage is more than 10 volts, go to next step.

2) Turn ignition off. Check for continuity across right turn indicator bulb. If continuity exists, replace instrument cluster. See INSTRUMENT CLUSTER under REMOVAL & INSTALLATION. Retest system. If continuity does not exist, replace bulb. Retest system.

3) Disconnect multifunction switch 11-pin connector C250. Measure resistance of White/Light Blue wire between multifunction switch 11-pin connector C250 circuit No. 2 and instrument cluster connector C224

TEST Q: AIR BAG INDICATOR INOPERATIVE

1) Turn ignition on. Using a voltmeter, measure voltage by backprobing between instrument cluster connector C226 terminals No. 6 (Black/Yellow wire) and No. 7 (White/Yellow wire). If voltage is 9 volts or less, go to step **3)**. If voltage is more than 9 volts, go to next step.

2) Turn ignition off. Remove air bag indicator bulb. See INSTRUMENT CLUSTER under REMOVAL & INSTALLATION. Check for continuity between air bag indicator bulb terminals. If continuity exists, replace instrument cluster. Retest system. If continuity does not exist, replace bulb. Retest system.

3) Turn ignition off. Disconnect air bag diagnostic monitor connector C200. C200 is located under right side of instrument panel. Measure resistance of Black/Yellow wire between instrument cluster connector C226 terminal No. 6 and air bag diagnostic monitor connector C200 terminal No. 7. See Figs. 3 and 8. If resistance is less than 5 ohms, see AIR BAG RESTRAINT SYSTEMS – ECONOLINE article. If resistance is 5 ohms or more, repair open in Black/Yellow wire. Retest system.

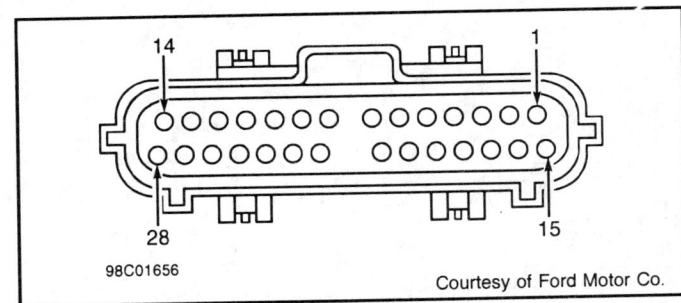

Fig. 8: Identifying Air Bag Diagnostic Monitor Connector C200 Terminals

TEST R: LOW OIL PRESSURE/HIGH COOLANT TEMPERATURE WARNING INDICATOR INOPERATIVE

Remove indicator bulb. See INSTRUMENT CLUSTER under REMOVAL & INSTALLATION. Check for continuity between indicator bulb terminals. If continuity exists, replace instrument cluster. Retest system. If continuity does not exist, replace bulb. Retest system.

TEST S: WATER IN FUEL WARNING INDICATOR INOPERATIVE

1) Using a voltmeter, measure voltage by backprobing between instrument cluster connector C225 terminal No. 12 (Red wire) and connector C226 terminal No. 12 (Red/Yellow wire). See Figs. 3 and 5. If voltage is more than 9 volts, go to next step. If voltage is 9 volts or less, go to step **3)**.

2) Turn ignition off. Remove instrument cluster. See INSTRUMENT CLUSTER under REMOVAL & INSTALLATION. Remove water in fuel warning light bulb. Check continuity between terminals of bulb. If continuity exists, replace instrument cluster. Retest system. If continuity does not exist, replace bulb. Retest system.

3) Turn ignition off. Install EEC-V 104-Pin Breakout Box (014-00950) following manufacturer's instructions. Measure resistance between breakout box pin No. 28 and instrument cluster connector C225 terminal No. 12 (Red wire). If resistance is less than 5 ohms, see appropriate SELF-DIAGNOSTICS article in ENGINE PERFORMANCE in appropriate MITCHELL® manual for Powertrain Control Module (PCM) diagnostics. If resistance 5 ohms or more, repair open in Red wire. Retest system.

TEST T: WAIT TO START INDICATOR INOPERATIVE

1) Using a voltmeter, measure voltage by backprobing between instrument cluster connector C225 terminal No. 12 (Red wire) and connector C226 terminal No. 12 (Red/Yellow wire). *See Figs. 2 and 3.* If voltage is more than 9 volts, go to next step. If voltage is 9 volts or less, go to step **3)**.

2) Turn ignition off. Remove instrument cluster. See INSTRUMENT CLUSTER under REMOVAL & INSTALLATION. Remove wait-to-start indicator bulb. Check continuity between terminals of bulb. If continuity exists, replace instrument cluster. Retest system. If continuity does not exist, replace bulb. Retest system.

3) Turn ignition off. Disconnect instrument cluster connector C225. Install EEC-V 104-Pin Breakout Box (014-00950) following manufacturer's instructions. Measure resistance between breakout box pin No. 70 and instrument cluster connector C225 terminal No. 11 (Black/Pink wire). *See Fig. 3.* If resistance is less than 4 ohms, see appropriate SELF-DIAGNOSTICS article in ENGINE PERFORMANCE in appropriate MITCHELL® manual, for Powertrain Control Module (PCM) diagnostics. If resistance is 4 ohms or more, repair open in Black/Pink wire.

REMOVAL & INSTALLATION
FUEL LEVEL SENDER

CAUTION: Fuel system is under high pressure. Fuel system pressure must be relieved before any fuel system repair is tempted. To receive fuel pressure, attach fuel pressure gauge to Schrader valve. Slowly open manual valve on fuel pressure gauge to receive fuel pressure gauge.

Removal & Installation – 1) Disconnect negative battery cable. Ensure fuel pressure is relieved. On aft fuel tank, remove drain plug and remove fuel. On midship fuel tank, remove rear fuel vapor plug and siphon fuel from tank.

2) On all models, raise and support vehicle. Disconnect fuel tank filler pipe and vent hose. Place jack under fuel tank. Remove fuel tank straps. Partially lower tank. Disconnect fuel level sender and pump assembly connectors. Remove fuel tank. Remove retaining screws and fuel level sender and pump assembly. To install, reverse removal procedure.

INSTRUMENT CLUSTER

Removal & Installation – 1) Disconnect negative battery cable. Remove headlight switch knob and bezel. Remove 2 screws above cluster lens. *See Fig. 9.* Remove instrument cluster bezel.

2) Remove 4 screws retaining instrument cluster. Pull cluster out and disconnect harness connectors. Remove transmission range indicator. Remove instrument cluster. To disassemble cluster, remove all cluster warning and illumination bulbs. Remove printed circuit.

3) Disengage 4 locking tabs at top and bottom of cluster. Remove instrument cluster mask. To install, reassemble cluster and reverse removal procedure.

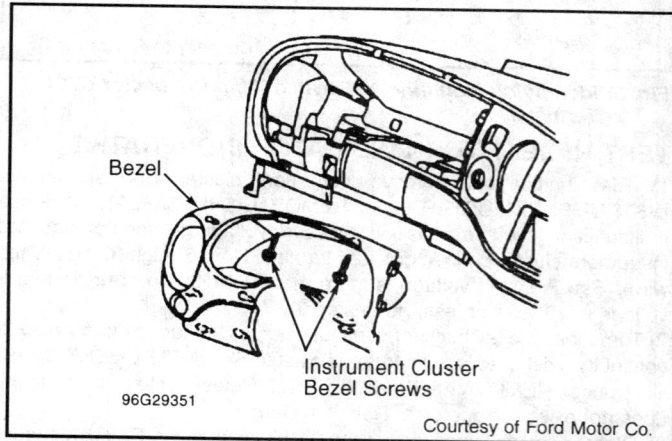

Bezel

Instrument Cluster Bezel Screws

96G29351

Courtesy of Ford Motor Co.

Fig. 9: Removing Instrument Cluster Bezel

WIRING DIAGRAMS

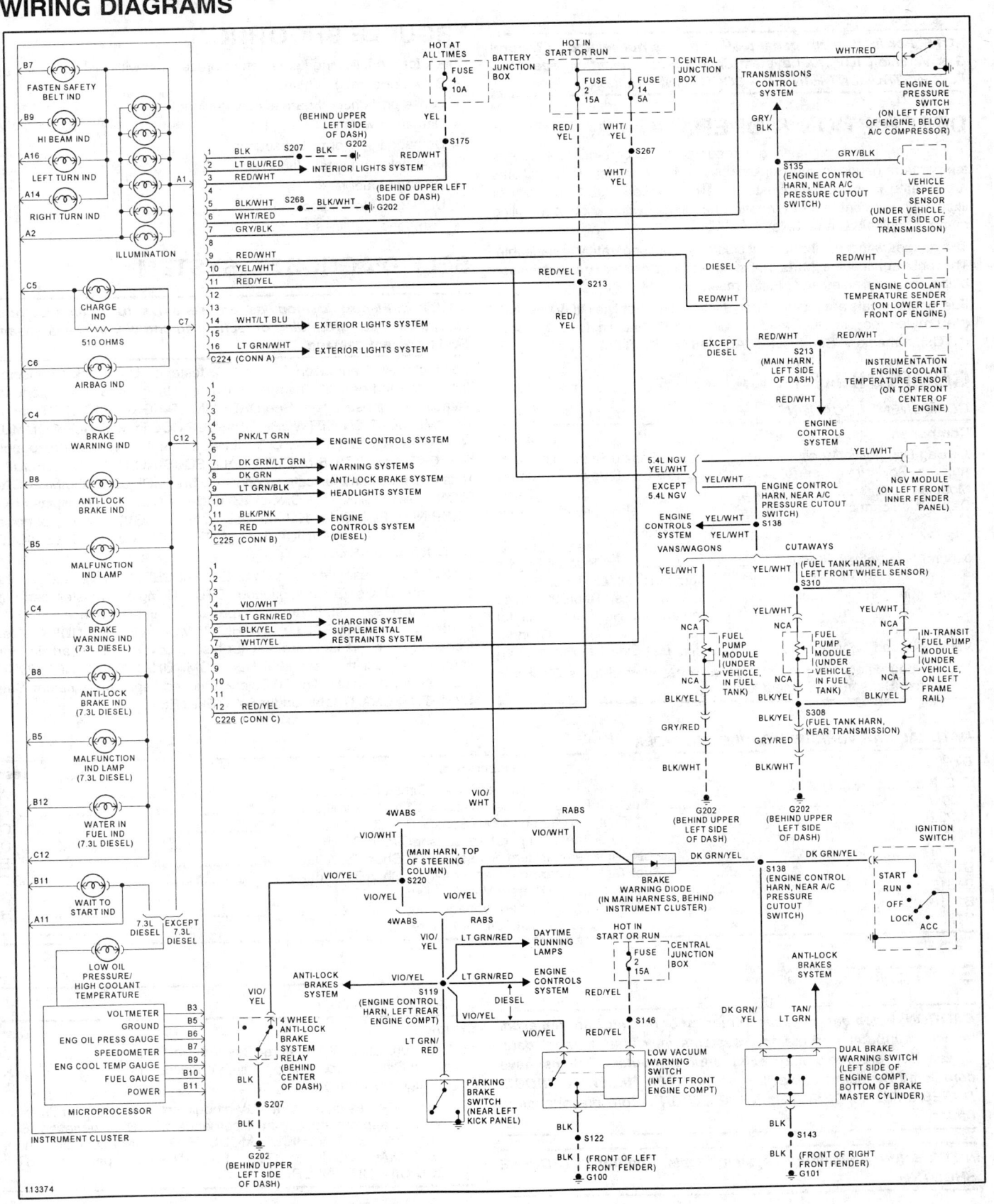

Fig. 10: Analog Instrument Panel Wiring Diagram (Econoline)

113374

1998-99 ACCESSORIES & EQUIPMENT
Analog Instrument Panels
Econoline – Natural Gas Vehicle

NOTE: *For instrument panel testing that is not related to Natural Gas Vehicle (NGV) fuel system or fuel level indication, see ANALOG INSTRUMENT PANELS – ECONOLINE article.*

DESCRIPTION & OPERATION

Instrument cluster contains a speedometer, odometer, fuel gauge, temperature gauge, oil pressure gauge and a voltmeter. Warning lights are located in instrument cluster face panel. *See Fig. 1.* Intensity of illumination is controlled by rotating headlight switch knob, controlling output of pulse width module.

The gauges within the instrument cluster are not separately replaceable. The only serviceable parts within instrument cluster are illumination bulbs, indicator bulbs and cluster mask.

Fuel gauge inputs are received from Natural Gas Vehicle (NGV) module. If a problem occurs NGV module will store Diagnostic Trouble Codes (DTCs) in memory. See SELF-DIAGNOSTIC SYSTEM.

COMPONENT LOCATIONS

COMPONENT LOCATIONS

Component	Location
Air Bag Diagnostic Monitor [1]	Behind Right Kick Panel
Auxiliary Powertrain Control Module	Below Left Side Of Instrument Panel
Data Link Connector	Below Driver's Side Of Instrument Panel, To Right Of Steering Column
Natural Gas Vehicle Module	Left Side Of Engine Compartment, On Inner Fender
Powertrain Control Module	Left Rear Of Engine Compartment, Near Brake Master Cylinder
Vehicle Speed Sensor	Left Side Of Transmission

[1] – Air bag diagnostic monitor may also be referred to as Electronic Crash Sensor (ECS) module.

TROUBLE SHOOTING

Check for the following items before proceeding with testing:
- Blown or damaged fuses.
- Loose or damaged harness connectors.
- Damaged wiring.
- Damaged sensor or transducer.
- Fuel delivery system function.
- Damaged fuel tank.
- Damaged fuel solenoid(s).
- Damaged fuel lines.

SELF-DIAGNOSTIC SYSTEM

CAUTION: *Electronic modules are sensitive to static electrical charges. Proper grounding of technician and workpiece is essential to prevent damage.*

Connect New Generation Star (NGS) tester to Data Link Connector (DLC), located beneath instrument cluster. Using NGS tester, perform data link diagnostics test. See DATA LINK DIAGNOSTIC TEST under COMMUNICATION NETWORK DIAGNOSTICS in MODULE COMMUNICATIONS NETWORK – ECONOLINE article. If NGS tester responds with CKT914, CKT915 or CKT70=ALL ECUS NO RESP/NOT EQUIP, repair module communications concern. See MODULE COMMUNICATIONS NETWORK – ECONOLINE article. If NGS tester displays NO RESP/NOT EQUIP for Natural Gas Vehicle (NGV) module, perform TEST J: NO COMMUNICATION WITH NATURAL GAS VEHICLE MODULE under SYSTEM TESTS.

If NGS tester responds with SYSTEM PASSED, retrieve and record continuous DTCs. Erase continuous DTCs. Using NGS tester, perform NGV module self-test. Perform appropriate test in accordance with DTC retrieved. See NATURAL GAS VEHICLE MODULE DTC INDEX table. Codes listed in this table are only for testing covered in this article. For complete DTC listing, see MODULE COMMUNICATIONS NETWORK – ECONOLINE article. If no DTCs are retrieved, repair by symptom. See SYMPTOM CHART table under SYSTEM TESTS.

NATURAL GAS VEHICLE MODULE DTC INDEX

DTC	Description	Test
B1219	Fuel Tank Pressure Sensor Circuit Failure	A
B1220	Fuel Tank Pressure Sensor Circuit Short To Voltage	B
B1222	Fuel Tank Temperature Sensor Circuit Failure	C
B1223	Fuel Tank Temperature Sensor Circuit Open	D
B1224	Fuel Tank Temperature Sensor Circuit Short To Voltage	E
B1225	Fuel Tank Temperature Sensor Circuit Short To Ground	F
B1317	Battery Voltage High	G
B1318	Battery Voltage Low	H
B1342	ECU Circuit Failure	I

SYSTEM TESTS

CAUTION: *When battery is disconnected or modules are replaced, vehicle computer and memory systems may lose memory data. Driveability problems may exist until computer systems have completed a relearn cycle. See COMPUTER RELEARN PROCEDURES article in GENERAL INFORMATION before disconnecting battery.*

NOTE: *Before beginning system tests, perform TROUBLE SHOOTNG.*

SYMPTOM CHART

Symptom	Test
No Communication With Natural Gas Vehicle Module	J
Integrated Circuit Display Inoperative Or Inaccurate	K
Fuel Gauge Inaccurate (NGV)	[1]

[1] – Using NGS tester, perform NGV module self-test. If any DTCs exist, perform appropriate test in accordance with DTC retrieved. See NATURAL GAS VEHICLE MODULE DTC INDEX table under SELF-DIAGNOSTIC SYSTEM. If no DTCs exist, perform TEST I: ECU CIRCUIT FAILURE.

1998-99 ACCESSORIES & EQUIPMENT
Analog Instrument Panels
Econoline – Natural Gas Vehicle (Cont.)

FORD
4-739

TEST A: FUEL TANK SENSOR CIRCUIT FAILURE (DTC B1219)

1) Turn ignition switch to RUN position. Using New Generation Star (NGS) tester, monitor Natural Gas Vehicle (NGV) module PID TANKPR. If PID indicates zero psi, go to next step. If PID does not indicate zero psi, check connectors for loose and corroded pins. If all connections are clean and tight, clear DTCs. Using NGS tester, perform NGV module self-test. If DTC B1219 is retrieved again, replace NGV module.

2) Turn ignition switch to LOCK position. Disconnect NGV module harness connector C1012. Install 60-pin Breakout Box (014-00322) following manufacturer's instructions. Leave NGV module disconnected. Disconnect fuel tank pressure sensor harness connector C349. C349 is located on left center of vehicle on fuel tank. Measure resistance between breakout box pin No. 7 and 46. If resistance is more than 10 k/ohms, go to next step. If resistance is 10 k/ohms or less, repair short between Red/Pink and Gray/Red wires of fuel tank pressure sensor circuit.

3) Connect NGV module harness connector C1012 to 60-pin Breakout Box. Turn ignition switch to RUN position. Measure voltage between Brown/White wire and Gray/Red wire terminals at fuel tank pressure sensor harness connector C349. If voltage is 4-6 volts, go to next step. If voltage is not 4-6 volts, go to step **6**).

If resistance is 5 ohms or less, go to next step. If resistance is more than 5 ohms, repair open in Gray/Red wire.

7) Measure resistance between breakout box pins No. 40 or 60 and No. 26. If resistance is more than 10 k/ohms, go to next step. If resistance is 10 k/ohms or less, repair short to ground in Brown/White wire.

8) Measure resistance between breakout box pins No. 40 or 60 and No. 46. If resistance is more than 10 k/ohms, go to next step. If resistance is 10 k/ohms or less, repair short to ground in Gray/Red wire.

9) Measure resistance in Brown/White wire between breakout box pin No. 26 and fuel tank pressure sensor harness connector C349. If resistance is 5 ohms or less, go to next step. If resistance is more than 5 ohms, repair open in Brown/White wire.

10) Measure voltage of Brown/White wire at fuel tank pressure sensor harness connector C349. If voltage does not exist, go to next step. If voltage exists, repair short to voltage in Brown/White wire.

11) Check fuel tank solenoids operation. See appropriate SYSTEM & COMPONENT TESTING article in ENGINE PERFORMANCE in appropriate MITCHELL® manual. If fuel tank solenoids operate properly, go to next step. If fuel tank solenoid(s) do not operate properly, repair fuel tank solenoid(s) as necessary.

12) Check fuel system for leaks. See appropriate SYSTEM & COMPONENT TESTING article in ENGINE PERFORMANCE in appropriate

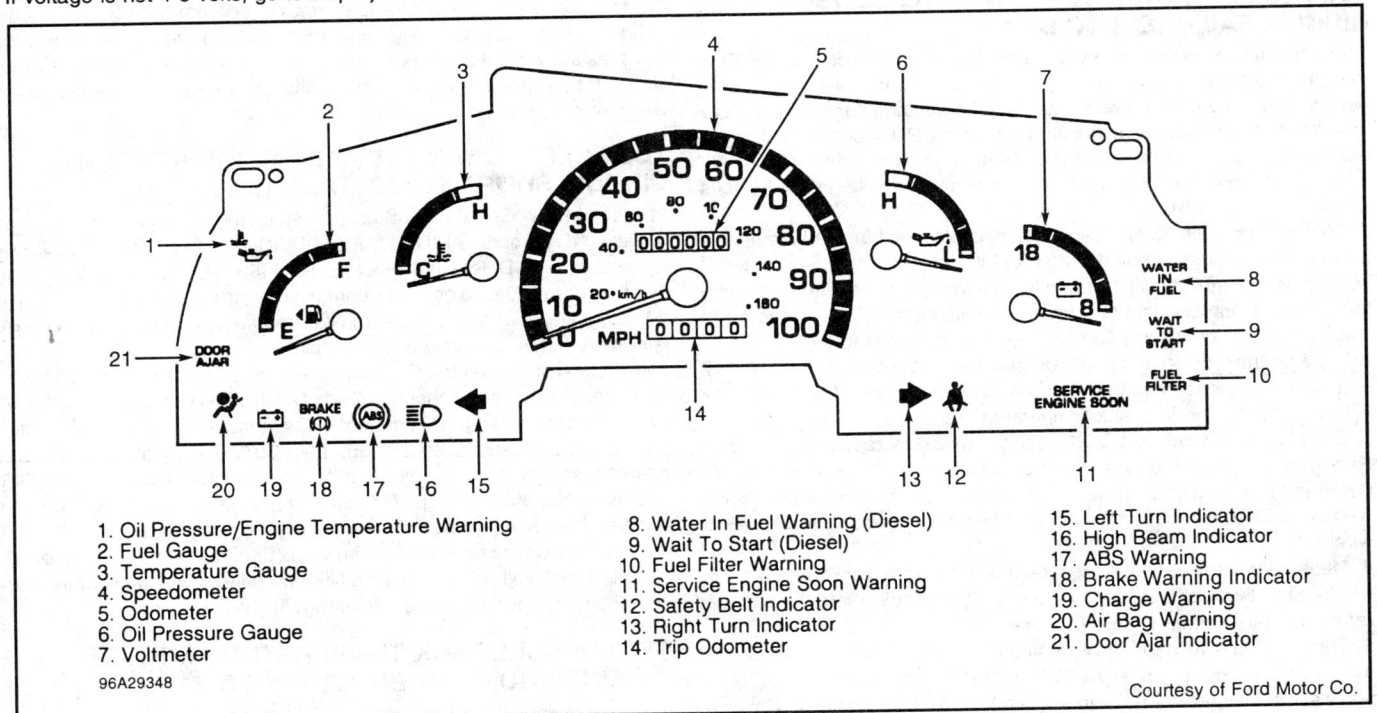

1. Oil Pressure/Engine Temperature Warning
2. Fuel Gauge
3. Temperature Gauge
4. Speedometer
5. Odometer
6. Oil Pressure Gauge
7. Voltmeter

8. Water In Fuel Warning (Diesel)
9. Wait To Start (Diesel)
10. Fuel Filter Warning
11. Service Engine Soon Warning
12. Safety Belt Indicator
13. Right Turn Indicator
14. Trip Odometer

15. Left Turn Indicator
16. High Beam Indicator
17. ABS Warning
18. Brake Warning Indicator
19. Charge Warning
20. Air Bag Warning
21. Door Ajar Indicator

96A29348

Courtesy of Ford Motor Co.

Fig. 1: Identifying Instrument Panel

4) Turn ignition switch to LOCK position. Using a fused jumper wire, connect Brown/White wire and Red/Pink wire terminals at fuel tank pressure sensor harness connector C349. Turn ignition switch to RUN position. Using a voltmeter, measure voltage between breakout box pin No. 7 and 26. If voltage is 4.61 volts or less, go to next step. If voltage is more than 4.61 volts, go to step **6**).

5) Turn ignition switch to LOCK position. Disconnect breakout box from NGV module. Measure resistance in Brown/White wire between breakout box pin No. 26 fuel tank pressure sensor harness connector C349. If resistance is more than 5 ohms, repair open in Brown/White wire. If resistance is 5 ohms or less, repair open in Red/Pink wire.

6) Turn ignition switch to LOCK position. Disconnect breakout box from NGV module. Measure resistance in Gray/Red wire between breakout box pin No. 46 and fuel tank pressure sensor harness connector C349.

MITCHELL® manual. If fuel system leaks, repair as necessary. If fuel system does not leak, replace NGV module.

TEST B: FUEL TANK SENSOR CIRCUIT SHORT TO VOLTAGE (DTC B1220)

1) Turn ignition switch to RUN position. Using New Generation Star (NGS) tester, monitor Natural Gas Vehicle (NGV) module PID TANKPR. If PID indicates zero psi, go to next step. If PID does not indicate zero psi, check connectors for loose and corroded pins. If all connections are clean and tight, clear DTCs. Using NGS tester, perform NGV module self-test. If DTC B1220 is retrieved again, replace NGV module.

2) Turn ignition switch to LOCK position. Disconnect NGV module harness connector C1012. Install 60-pin Breakout Box (014-00322) following manufacturer's instructions. Leave NGV module disconnected. Disconnect fuel tank pressure sensor harness connector C349. C349 is

FORD
4-740

1998-99 ACCESSORIES & EQUIPMENT
Analog Instrument Panels
Econoline – Natural Gas Vehicle (Cont.)

located on left center of vehicle on fuel tank. Turn ignition switch to RUN position. Measure voltage between breakout box pins No. 7 and No. 46. If voltage is more than .61 volt, go to next step. If voltage is .61 volt or less, replace fuel tank pressure sensor. See FUEL TANK PRESSURE SENSOR under REMOVAL & INSTALLATION.

3) Turn ignition switch to LOCK position. Measure resistance between breakout box pins No. 7 and 26. If resistance is more than 10 k/ohms, go to next step. If resistance is 10 k/ohms or less, repair short between Red/Pink and Brown/White wires.

4) Turn ignition switch to RUN position. Measure voltage at breakout box pins No. 7 and 37 or 57. If voltage does not exist, go to next step. If voltage exists, repair short to voltage in Red/Pink wire.

5) Check fuel tank solenoids operation. See appropriate SYSTEM & COMPONENT TESTING article in ENGINE PERFORMANCE in appropriate MITCHELL® manual. If fuel tank solenoids operate properly, go to next step. If fuel tank solenoid(s) do not operate properly, repair fuel tank solenoid(s) as necessary.

6) Check fuel system for leaks. See appropriate SYSTEM & COMPONENT TESTING article in ENGINE PERFORMANCE in appropriate MITCHELL® manual. If fuel system leaks, repair as necessary. If fuel system does not leak, replace NGV module.

TEST C: FUEL TANK TEMPERATURE SENSOR CIRCUIT FAILURE (DTC B1222)

1) Turn ignition switch to LOCK position. Disconnect Natural Gas Vehicle (NGV) module harness connector C1012. Install 60-pin Breakout Box (014-00322) following manufacturer's instructions. Leave NGV module disconnected. Turn ignition switch to RUN position. Using a voltmeter, measure voltage between breakout box pins No. 47 and 46. If voltage is more than 4.55 volts, go to next step. If voltage is 4.55 volts or less, go to step 5).

2) Turn ignition switch to LOCK position. Disconnect fuel tank temperature sensor harness connector C351. C351 is located on left center of vehicle on fuel tank. Using a fused jumper wire, connect Gray/Red wire terminal and Orange/Light Green wire terminal at fuel tank temperature sensor harness connector C351. Turn ignition switch to RUN position. Using a voltmeter, measure voltage between breakout box pins No. 47 and 46. If voltage is more than .12 volt, go to next step. If voltage is .12 volt or less, replace fuel tank temperature sensor.

3) Turn ignition switch to LOCK position. Measure resistance in Gray/Red wire between fuel tank temperature sensor harness connector C351 and breakout box pin No. 46. If resistance is 5 ohms or less, go to next step. If resistance is more than 5 ohms, repair open in Gray/Red wire.

4) Measure voltage between breakout box pins No. 40 or 60 and No. 46. If voltage is .5 volt or less, go to next step. If voltage is more than .5 volt, repair short to voltage in Gray/Red wire.

5) Turn ignition switch to LOCK position. Disconnect fuel tank temperature sensor harness connector C351. C351 is located on left center of vehicle on fuel tank. Turn ignition switch to RUN position. Using a voltmeter, measure voltage between breakout box pins No. 47 and 46. If voltage is 4.55 volts or less, go to next step. If voltage is more than 4.55 volts, replace fuel tank temperature sensor.

6) Turn ignition switch to LOCK position. Using an ohmmeter, measure resistance between breakout box pins No. 40 and 46. If resistance is more than 10 k/ohms, go to next step. If resistance is 10 k/ohms or less, repair short to ground in Gray/Red wire.

CAUTION: New Generation Star (NGS) tester must be used in this procedure to measure voltage. Using a standard DVOM to carry out this test will cause an inaccurate reading, possibly leading to inaccurate repairs.

---

7) Connect fuel tank temperature sensor harness connector C351. Connect accessory voltmeter leads to NGS tester. Connect positive lead on NGS tester to breakout box pin No. 47 and negative lead to pin No. 40. Turn ignition switch to RUN position. Enter DIGITAL MEASUREMENT SYSTEM on NGS tester. Select VOLTMETER, then LINK. Select

PID/DATA, then NGV. Select TEMPS1, then START. Select REC, then press TRIGGER to capture data. Press TRIGGER again to store data, then select VIEW to examine data. If voltage varies rapidly between .2-4.9 volts, repair intermittent contact condition. If voltage does not vary rapidly between .2-4.9 volts, replace NGV module.

TEST D: FUEL TANK TEMPERATURE SENSOR CIRCUIT OPEN (DTC B1223)

1) Using New Generation Star (NGS) tester, monitor Natural Gas Vehicle (NGV) module PID TEMPS1. If PID indicates 199°F (93°C), go to next step. If PID does not indicate 199°F (93°C), check connectors for loose and corroded pins. If all connections are clean and tight, clear DTCs. Using NGS tester, perform NGV module self-test. If DTC B1223 is retrieved again, replace NGV module.

2) Turn ignition switch to LOCK position. Disconnect fuel tank temperature sensor harness connector C351. C351 is located on left center of vehicle on fuel tank. Disconnect NGV module harness connector C1012. Install 60-pin Breakout Box (014-00322) following manufacturer's instructions. Measure resistance in Gray/Red wire between fuel tank temperature sensor harness connector C351 and breakout box pin No. 46. If resistance is 5 ohms or less, go to next step. If resistance is more than 5 ohms, repair open in Gray/Red wire.

3) Measure resistance in Orange/Light Green wire between fuel tank temperature sensor harness connector C351 and breakout box pin No. 47. If resistance is 5 ohms or less, replace fuel tank temperature sensor No. 1. If resistance is more than 5 ohms, repair open in Orange/Light Green wire.

TEST E: FUEL TANK TEMPERATURE SENSOR CIRCUIT SHORT TO VOLTAGE (DTC B1224)

1) Using New Generation Star (NGS) tester, monitor Natural Gas Vehicle (NGV) module PID TEMPS1. If PID indicates 199°F (93°C), go to next step. If PID does not indicate 199°F (93°C), check connectors for loose and corroded pins. If all connections are clean and tight, clear DTCs. Using NGS tester, perform NGV module self-test. If DTC B1224 is retrieved again, replace NGV module.

2) Turn ignition switch to LOCK position. Disconnect fuel tank temperature sensor harness connector C351. C351 is located on left center of vehicle on fuel tank. Disconnect NGV module harness connector C1012. Install 60-pin Breakout Box (014-00322) following manufacturer's instructions. Measure voltage between breakout box pins No. 46 and 40 or No. 60. If voltage is .5 volt or less, go to next step. If voltage is more than .5 volt, repair short to voltage in Gray/Red wire.

3) Measure voltage between breakout box pins No. 47 and 40 or No. 60. If voltage is .5 volt or less, replace NGV module. If voltage is more than .5 volt, repair short to voltage in Orange/Light Green wire.

TEST F: FUEL TANK TEMPERATURE SENSOR CIRCUIT SHORT TO GROUND (DTC B1225)

1) Using New Generation Star (NGS) tester, monitor Natural Gas Vehicle (NGV) module PID TEMPS1. If PID indicates 199°F (93°C), go to next step. If PID does not indicate 199°F (93°C), check connectors for loose and corroded pins. If all connections are clean and tight, clear DTCs. Using NGS tester, perform NGV module self-test. If DTC B1225 is retrieved again, replace NGV module.

2) Turn ignition switch to LOCK position. Disconnect fuel tank temperature sensor harness connector C351. C351 is located on left center of vehicle on fuel tank. Disconnect NGV module harness connector C1012. Install 60-pin Breakout Box (014-00322) following manufacturer's instructions. Measure resistance between breakout box pins No. 47 and 40 or No. 60. If resistance is more than 10 k/ohms, go to next step. If resistance is 10 k/ohms or less, repair short to ground in Orange/Light Green wire.

3) Measure resistance between breakout box pins No. 46 and 47. If resistance is more than 10 k/ohms, replace fuel tank temperature sensor. If resistance is 10 k/ohms or less, repair short between Orange/Light Green and Gray/Red wires.

1998-99 ACCESSORIES & EQUIPMENT
Analog Instrument Panels
Econoline – Natural Gas Vehicle (Cont.)

FORD
4-741

TEST G: BATTERY VOLTAGE HIGH (DTC B1317)

1) Using New Generation Star (NGS) tester, clear continuous DTCs. Connect voltmeter to battery terminals. Using NGS tester, perform Natural Gas Vehicle (NGV) module self-test while monitoring battery voltage. If battery voltage is less than 17 volts during self-test, go to next step. If battery voltage is more than 17 volts during self-test, repair charging system. See GENERATORS article in STARTING & CHARGING SYSTEMS.

2) Start vehicle. Using NGS tester, perform NGV self-test while monitoring battery voltage. If battery voltage is not more than 17 volts during self-test, go to next step. If battery voltage is more than 17 volts during self-test, repair charging system. See appropriate GENERATORS article in STARTING & CHARGING SYSTEMS.

3) Turn ignition switch to LOCK position. Using NGS tester, retrieve and clear continuous DTCs. Repeat NGV self-test. If DTC B1317 is retrieved again, replace NGV module. If DTC B1317 is not retrieved again, system is okay at this time.

TEST H: BATTERY VOLTAGE LOW (DTC B1318)

1) Using New Generation Star (NGS) tester, clear continuous DTCs. Connect voltmeter to battery terminals. Using NGS tester, perform Natural Gas Vehicle (NGV) module self-test while monitoring battery voltage. If battery voltage is not less than 8 volts during self-test, go to next step. If battery voltage is less than 8 volts during self-test, repair charging system. See GENERATORS article in STARTING & CHARGING SYSTEMS.

2) Start vehicle. Using NGS tester, perform NGV self-test while monitoring battery voltage. If battery voltage is not less than 8 volts during self-test, go to next step. If battery voltage is less than 8 volts during self-test, repair charging system. See appropriate GENERATORS article in STARTING & CHARGING SYSTEMS.

3) Turn ignition switch to LOCK position. Using NGS tester, retrieve and clear continuous DTCs. Repeat NGV self-test. If DTC B1318 is retrieved again, replace NGV module. If DTC B1318 is not retrieved again, system is okay at this time.

TEST I: ECU CIRCUIT FAILURE (DTC B1342)

1) Turn ignition switch to LOCK position. Disconnect Natural Gas Vehicle (NGV) module harness connector C1012. Inspect harness and module connectors for loose, damaged or corroded connections. If problem does not exist, go to next step. If problem exists, repair or replace as necessary.

2) Turn ignition switch to RUN position. Install 60-pin Breakout Box (014-00322) following manufacturer's instructions. Measure voltage between breakout box pins No. 37 or 57 (Red wires) and No. 40 or 60 (Black wires). If battery voltage exists, go to step **4)**. If battery voltage does not exist, go to next step.

3) Turn ignition switch to LOCK position. Measure resistance between ground and breakout pins No. 40 or 60. If resistance is less than 5 ohms, repair open Red wires between Powertrain Control Module (PCM) power relay and NGV module. If resistance is 5 ohms or more, repair appropriate Black wire.

4) Turn ignition switch to LOCK position. Connect NGV module connector C1012 to 60-pin breakout box. Measure resistance between breakout box pins No. 40 or 60 and No. 16. If resistance reading is 5 ohms or less, go to next step. If resistance reading is more than 5 ohms, replace NGV module. See NATURAL GAS VEHICLE (NGV) MODULE under REMOVAL & INSTALLATION.

5) Disconnect instrument cluster harness connectors. Measure resistance between terminal No. 12 (Black/White wire) at instrument cluster harness connector C224 and breakout box pin No. 16. See Fig. 2. If resistance is less than 5 ohms, go to next step. If resistance is 5 ohms or more, repair open Black/White wire.

6) Measure resistance in Yellow/White wire between terminal No. 7 at instrument cluster harness connector C224 and breakout box pin No. 38. If resistance is 5 ohms or less, go to next step. If resistance is more than 5 ohms, repair open in Yellow/White wire.

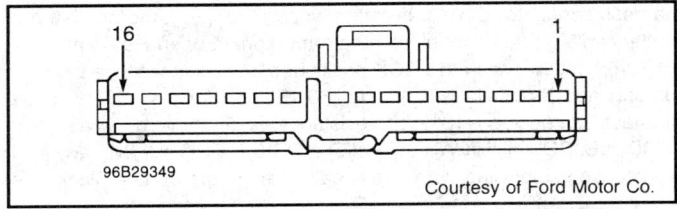

96B29349

Courtesy of Ford Motor Co.

Fig. 2: Identifying Instrument Cluster Connector C224 Terminals

7) Measure voltage between breakout box pins No. 38 and 40 or No. 60. If voltage is .5 volt or less, go to next step. If voltage is more than .5 volt, repair short to voltage in Yellow/White wire.

8) Disconnect NGV module harness connector C1012 from 60-pin breakout box. Measure resistance in Yellow/White wire between ground and terminal No. 7 at instrument cluster harness connector C224. If resistance is more than 10 k/ohms, go to next step. If resistance is 10 k/ohms or less, repair short to ground in Yellow/White wire.

9) Connect Instrument Gauge Tester (014-R1063) leads to breakout box pins No. 38 and 60. Adjust tester to 22 ohms. Turn ignition switch to RUN position. Wait 60 seconds. If fuel gauge does not indicate empty, go to next step. If fuel gauge indicates empty, go to step **11)**. Measure voltage at terminal No. 1 (Yellow/White wire) at instrument cluster harness connector C224. If voltage does not exist, go to next step. If voltage exists, repair short to voltage in Yellow/White wire.

10) Turn ignition switch to LOCK position. Turn ignition switch to RUN position. Tap lightly on instrument cluster. Wait 60 seconds. If fuel gauge does not indicate empty, go to next step. If fuel gauge indicates empty, replace fuel gauge.

11) Turn ignition switch to LOCK position. Adjust tester to 145 ohms. Turn ignition switch to RUN position. Wait 60 seconds. If fuel gauge indicates full, system is okay at this time. If fuel gauge does not indicate full, replace fuel gauge.

TEST J: NO COMMUNICATION WITH NATURAL GAS VEHICLE MODULE

1) Turn ignition switch to LOCK position. Disconnect Natural Gas Vehicle (NGV) module harness connector C1012. Measure voltage between ground and terminal No. 1 (Yellow/Black wire) at NGV module harness connector C1012. See Fig. 3. If battery voltage exists, go to next step. If battery voltage does not exist, go to step **5)**.

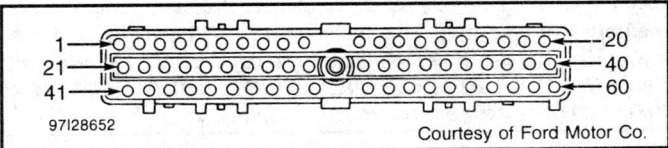

97I28652

Courtesy of Ford Motor Co.

Fig. 3: Identifying Natural Gas Vehicle Module Harness Connector C124 Terminals

2) Remove mini-fuse No. 25 (20-amp) from power distribution box. Measure resistance between ground and terminal No. 1 (Yellow/Black wire) at NGV module harness connector C1012. If resistance is more than 10 k/ohms, go to next step. If resistance is 10 k/ohms or less, repair short to ground in Yellow wire.

3) Measure voltage between ground and input side (inside terminal) of mini-fuse No. 25 (20-amp). If battery voltage exists, go to next step. If battery voltage does not exist, repair open Yellow wire between NGV module and power distribution box.

4) Measure resistance between terminal No. 1 (Yellow wire) at NGV module harness connector C1012 and output side terminal of mini-fuse No. 25. If resistance is 5 ohms or less, replace mini-fuse No. 25 (20-amp) and retest system. If resistance is more than 5 ohms, repair open in Yellow wire.

5) Turn ignition switch to RUN position. Measure voltage between ground and terminals No. 37 and 57 (Red wires) at NGV module

FORD
4-742

1998-99 ACCESSORIES & EQUIPMENT
Analog Instrument Panels
Econoline – Natural Gas Vehicle (Cont.)

harness connector C1012. If battery voltage exists, go to next step. If battery voltage does not exist, repair appropriate open Red wire.

6) Turn ignition switch to LOCK position. Measure resistance between ground and terminals No. 40 and 60 (Black wires) at NGV module harness connector C1012. If resistance is 5 ohms or less, go to MODULE COMMUNICATIONS NETWORK – ECONOLINE article. If resistance is more than 5 ohms, repair open in appropriate Black wire.

TEST K: INTEGRATED CIRCUIT DISPLAY INOPERATIVE OR INACCURATE

1) Turn ignition switch to LOCK position. Disconnect Natural Gas Vehicle (NGV) module harness connector C1012. Install 60-pin Breakout Box (014-00322) following manufacturer's instructions. Turn ignition switch to RUN position. Measure voltage between breakout box pins No. 37 or 57 (Red wires) and No. 40 or 60 (Black wires). If battery voltage exists, go to step 5). If battery voltage does not exist, go to next step.

2) Turn ignition switch to LOCK position. Measure resistance between breakout pins No. 26 and 37. If resistance is less than 5 ohms, repair short between Red and Brown/White wires of NGV module. If resistance is 5 ohms or more, go to next step.

3) Measure resistance between breakout box pins No. 40 or 60 and No. 26. If resistance reading is 5 ohms or less, repair short to ground in Brown/White wire. If resistance reading is more than 5 ohms, go to next step.

4) Measure resistance between ground and breakout box pins No. 40 or 60. If resistance is less than 5, repair open in Red wire to terminal No. 37 or 57 at NGV module harness connector C1012. If resistance is 5 ohms or more, replace NGV module.

5) Measure resistance between breakout box pins No. 40 or 60 and No. 16. If resistance reading is 5 ohms or less, go to next step. If resistance reading is more than 5 ohms, replace NGV module.

6) Disconnect instrument cluster harness connectors. Measure resistance between terminal No. 12 (Black/White wire) at instrument cluster harness connector C224 and breakout box pin No. 16. See Fig. 2. If resistance is less than 5 ohms, replace instrument cluster. If resistance is 5 ohms or more, repair Black/White wire.

REMOVAL & INSTALLATION

CAUTION: When battery is disconnected, vehicle computer and memory systems may lose memory data. Driveability problems may exist until computer systems have completed a relearn cycle. See COMPUTER RELEARN PROCEDURES article in GENERAL INFORMATION before disconnecting battery.

CAUTION: Electronic modules are sensitive to static electrical charges. Proper grounding of technician and workpiece is essential to prevent damage.

NATURAL GAS VEHICLE (NGV) MODULE

Removal & Installation – 1) Disconnect negative battery cable. Remove coolant recovery tank. Remove Natural Gas Vehicle (NGV) module harness connector cover. Loosen NGV harness connector retaining bolt. Disconnect NGV module harness connector.

2) Remove NGV module bracket retaining bolts. Remove NGV module-to-bracket retaining bolts. Remove NGV module. To install, reverse removal procedures.

FUEL TANK PRESSURE SENSOR

CAUTION: Fuel tank system pressure must be vented before any fuel system component replacement is started. If fuel system solenoids are not operating properly, see REMOVAL, OVERHAUL & INSTALLATION – Natural Gas Vehicle article in ENGINE PERFORMANCE in appropriate MITCHELL® manual.

Removal & Installation – 1) Release fuel pressure from lines. See FUEL SYSTEM PRESSURE RELEASE (FUEL LINE VENTING). Disconnect negative battery cable.

2) Raise and support vehicle. Disconnect fuel tank pressure sensor connector. Fuel tank pressure sensor connector is located on left center of vehicle on fuel tank. Remove fuel tank pressure sensor. See Fig. 4. To install, replace "O" rings on fuel tank pressure sensor and spacer. Ensure new "O" rings are lubricated with motor oil. To complete installation, reverse removal procedures.

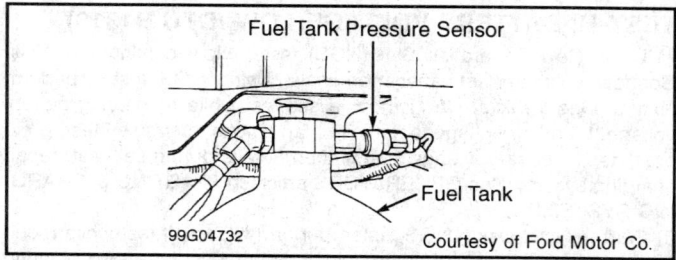

Fuel Tank Pressure Sensor

Fuel Tank

99G04732

Courtesy of Ford Motor Co.

Fig. 4: Removing Fuel Tank Pressure Sensor

WARNING: Fuel supply lines remain pressurized after engine shutdown. Ensure no open flame of any type is present. Flammable gases may be present and ignite, resulting in possible injury. Always release (vent) fuel pressure before disconnecting any fuel injection-related component downstream of fuel tank shutoff solenoids. DO NOT vent fuel system indoors. Manufacturer recommends venting fuel through a vent stack that allows natural gas to be vented outside of repair shop. Vent stack must be approved by local authorities.

NOTE: To perform fuel system pressure release, use Fuel Rail Test and Venting Kit (134-00116), Grounding Cable (134-00121) and Venting Hose (134-00118). Manufacturer recommends venting fuel through a vent stack that allows natural gas to be vented outside of repair shop. Vent stack must be approved by local authorities.

Fuel System Pressure Release (Fuel Line Venting) – 1) Insert grounding spike into earth. Connect grounding cable between grounding spike and fuel injection supply manifold. See Fig. 5.

2) Turn manual lockdown valve jackscrew on each fuel tank solenoid valve. See Fig. 6. Connect fuel rail test and vent kit hose to Schrader valve on fuel rail. Ensure valve on tester is closed. Connect Venting Hose (134-00118) to Fuel Pressure Test And Venting Kit (134-00121) manifold.

3) Remove fuel pump relay from power distribution box. Construct a jumper wire approximately 6″ long with spade terminals on each end. Jump fuel pump relay terminals. See Fig. 7.

4) Slowly open bleed valve on fuel pressure vent and test kit manifold and allow fuel to vent to atmosphere for one minute. Close bleed valve and remove pressure test and venting kit from vehicle.

1998-99 ACCESSORIES & EQUIPMENT
Analog Instrument Panels
Econoline – Natural Gas Vehicle (Cont.)

FORD
4-743

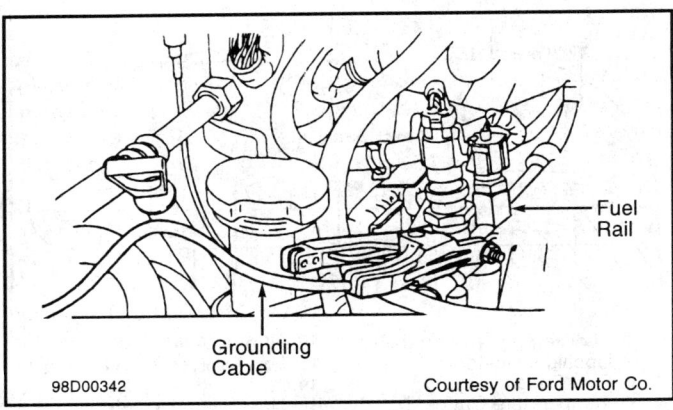

Fuel Rail

Grounding Cable

98D00342

Courtesy of Ford Motor Co.

Fig. 5: Connecting Grounding Cable To Fuel Rail

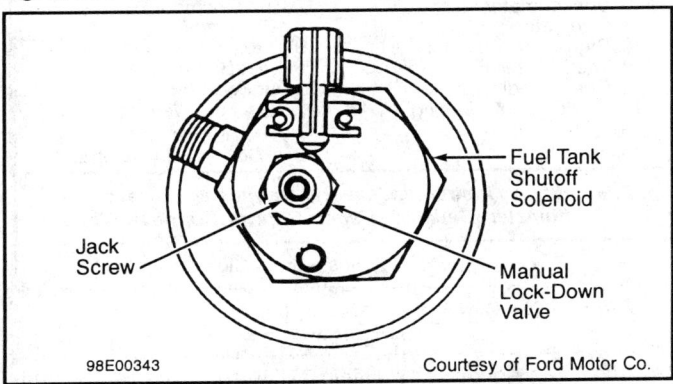

Fuel Tank Shutoff Solenoid

Jack Screw

Manual Lock-Down Valve

98E00343

Courtesy of Ford Motor Co.

Fig. 6: Identifying Fuel Tank Solenoid Components

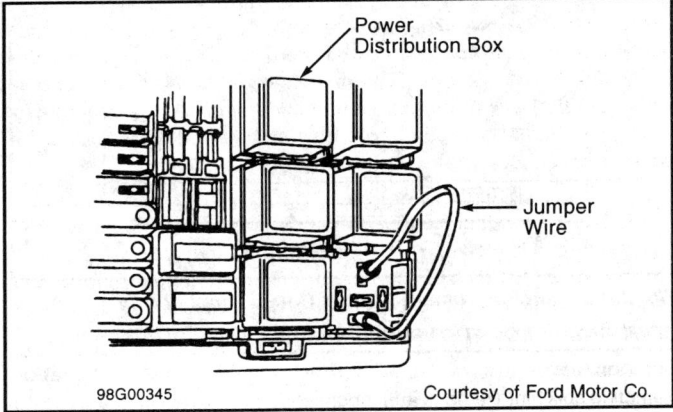

Power Distribution Box

Jumper Wire

98G00345

Courtesy of Ford Motor Co.

Fig. 7: Jumpering Fuel Pump Relay (Econoline)

WIRING DIAGRAMS

NOTE: See ANALOG INSTRUMENT PANELS – ECONOLINE article.

DESCRIPTION & OPERATION

WARNING: Deactivate air bag system before performing any service operation. See appropriate AIR BAG RESTRAINT SYSTEMS article. DO NOT apply electrical power to any component on steering column without first deactivating air bag system. Air bag may deploy.

Instrument cluster contains a speedometer/odometer, tachometer (if equipped), fuel gauge, temperature gauge and various warning lights placed in groups at bottom of instrument cluster. *See Figs. 1 and 2.*

Instrument cluster gauge amplifier is part of low fuel level warning/anti-slosh module and provides delay in fuel gauge to prevent fluctuation in fuel gauge pointer as a result of fuel movement in tank. The module is a small printed circuit board which latches into a pocket on back of instrument cluster. *See Fig. 3.* There are no provisions for calibration or adjustment of low fuel level warning/anti-slosh module.

When ignition switch is turned to ON position, the following warning indicators will light momentarily for function proof:

- ABS Warning
- Air Bag Warning
- BRAKE Warning
- Charging Indicator
- CHECK COOLANT Warning
- Low Oil Warning
- SERVICE ENGINE SOON (MIL) Light
- Safety Belt Warning

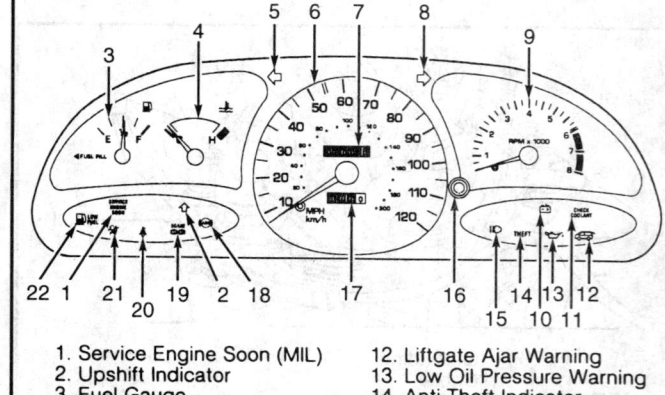

1. Service Engine Soon (MIL)
2. Upshift Indicator
3. Fuel Gauge
4. Temperature Gauge
5. Left Turn Indicator
6. Speedometer
7. Odometer
8. Right Turn Indicator
9. Tachometer
10. Charge Indicator
11. Low Coolant Warning
12. Liftgate Ajar Warning
13. Low Oil Pressure Warning
14. Anti-Theft Indicator
15. High Beam Indicator
16. Trip Odometer Reset
17. Trip Odometer
18. ABS Warning
19. Brake Warning
20. Seat Belt Warning
21. Air Bag Warning
22. Low Fuel Warning

97E28047

Courtesy of Ford Motor Co.

Fig. 2: Identifying Instrument Cluster Gauges & Indicators With Tachometer (Sedan & Wagon Shown; Coupe Is Similar)

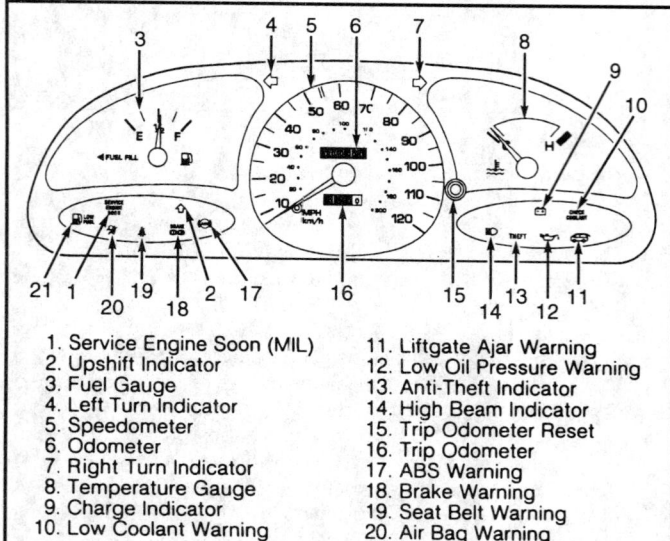

1. Service Engine Soon (MIL)
2. Upshift Indicator
3. Fuel Gauge
4. Left Turn Indicator
5. Speedometer
6. Odometer
7. Right Turn Indicator
8. Temperature Gauge
9. Charge Indicator
10. Low Coolant Warning
11. Liftgate Ajar Warning
12. Low Oil Pressure Warning
13. Anti-Theft Indicator
14. High Beam Indicator
15. Trip Odometer Reset
16. Trip Odometer
17. ABS Warning
18. Brake Warning
19. Seat Belt Warning
20. Air Bag Warning
21. Low Fuel Warning

97D28046

Courtesy of Ford Motor Co.

Fig. 1: Identifying Instrument Cluster Gauges & Indicators Without Tachometer

COMPONENT LOCATIONS

COMPONENT LOCATIONS

Component	Location
Air Bag Sliding Contact	Below Steering Wheel
Central Junction Box	Below Left Side Of Instrument Panel
Instrument Cluster	Behind Left Side Of Instrument Panel
Multifunction Switch	Part Of Upper Steering Column
Power Distribution Box	Left Side Of Engine Compartment, Above Wheelwell
Powertrain Control Module (PCM)	In Center Console, Below Shifter

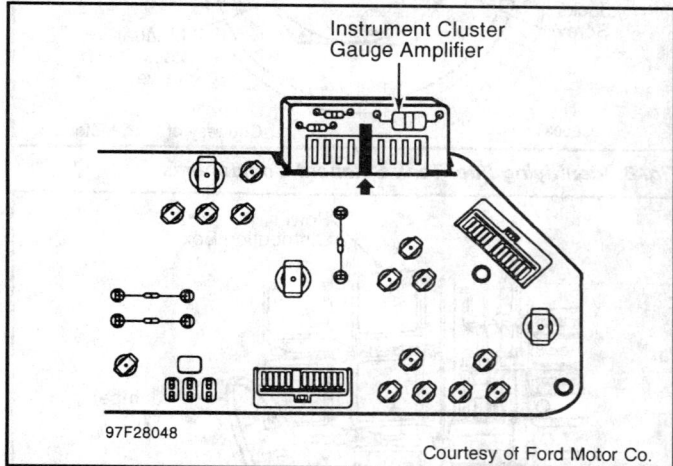

97F28048

Courtesy of Ford Motor Co.

Fig. 3: Locating Instrument Cluster Gauge Amplifier

COMPONENT LOCATIONS (Cont.)

Component	Location
Remote Anti-Theft Personality Module	
Coupe & Sedan	In Luggage Compartment, Behind Right Trim Panel
Wagon	In Luggage Compartment, Behind Left Trim Panel
Turn Signal/Hazard Flasher	Underdash, Near Left Cowl Side Trim

TROUBLE SHOOTING

WARNING: Vehicle is equipped with an air bag system. System MUST be disabled before working near steering column and instrument cluster to prevent air bag deployment. See appropriate AIR BAG RESTRAINT SYSTEMS article.

Before performing any tests on instrument cluster, check the following items to eliminate common problems: If fault is not evident, go to SYSTEM TESTS.

Mechanical:
- Failed engine lubrication system.

- Low engine oil.
- Damaged speedometer drive or driven gear.

Electrical:
- Blown fuses.
- Burnt out bulb.
- Loose or corroded connections.
- Damaged wiring harness.
- Damaged vehicle speed sensor.
- Damaged instrument cluster printed circuit.

COMPONENT TESTS

TEMPERATURE GAUGE

1) Turn ignition off. Disconnect engine coolant temperature indicator sender unit. Connect one lead of Instrument Gauge System Tester (014-R1063) to Red/White wire terminal at water temperature indicator sender unit harness connector and other lead to ground.

2) Set tester to 300 ohms. Turn ignition on. Wait one minute and read gauge. Gauge should read "C" (cold). Turn ignition off.

3) Set tester to 45 ohms. Turn ignition on. Wait one minute and read gauge. Gauge should read one fourth of mid-range. Turn ignition off.

4) Set tester to 18.3 ohms. Turn ignition on. Wait one minute and read gauge. Gauge should read "H" (hot). Turn ignition off. If gauge does not operate as specified, replace temperature gauge.

FUEL GAUGE

1) Disconnect 6-pin fuel level sensor/pump connector. Connect one lead of Instrument Gauge System Tester (014-R1063) to Yellow/Brown wire at fuel level sensor and pump harness connector, and other tester lead to ground.

2) Set tester to 15 ohms. Turn ignition on. Wait one minute and read fuel gauge. Gauge should read "E" (empty). Turn ignition off. Set tester to 160 ohms. Turn ignition on. Wait one minute and read gauge. Gauge should read "F" (full). Turn ignition off. If gauge does not operate as indicated, replace fuel gauge.

SYSTEM TESTS

CAUTION: Electronic modules are sensitive to static electrical charges. Proper grounding of technician and workpiece is essential to prevent damage.

Verify charging system, fuel system, safety belt warning chime, turn signals, headlights and cruise control are working properly. Inspect wiring harness for obvious signs of shorts, opens, bad connections or damage. If no visual damage is evident, perform appropriate system test. See SYSTEM TEST SYMPTOM INDEX table. A digital volt-ohmmeter is required to test the power mirror system. See WIRING DIAGRAMS for terminal numbers.

SYSTEM TEST SYMPTOM INDEX

Symptom	Test
Instrument Cluster Display(s) Inoperative Or Erratic	A
Fuel Gauge Inaccurate	B
Temperature Gauge Inaccurate	C
Speedometer/Odometer Inaccurate	D
Tachometer Inaccurate	E
Improper Brake Warning Operation	F
Improper Low Fuel Warning Operation	G
Improper Anti-Theft Warning Operation	H
Improper Charge Warning Operation	J
Improper Oil Pressure Warning Operation	K
Improper Air Bag Warning Operation	L
Improper ABS Warning Operation	M
Turn, High Beam & Theft Indicators Never On	N
Improper LH Turn Indicator Operation	P
Improper RH Turn Indicator Operation	Q
Improper High Beam Indicator Operation	R
Improper SERVICE ENGINE SOON (MIL) Operation	[1]
Improper CHECK COOLANT Indicator Operation	S

[1] – See appropriate SELF-DIAGNOSTICS article in ENGINE PERFORMANCE in appropriate MITCHELL® manual.

TEST A: INSTRUMENT CLUSTER DISPLAY(S) INOPERATIVE OR ERRATIC

Coupe – 1) Check 10-amp METER fuse. *See Fig. 4.* If fuse is okay, go to next step. If fuse is blown, go to next step. Turn ignition off. Replace 10-amp METER fuse. Turn ignition on and inspect fuse. If fuse fails again, check and repair short to ground as necessary. See WIRING DIAGRAMS.

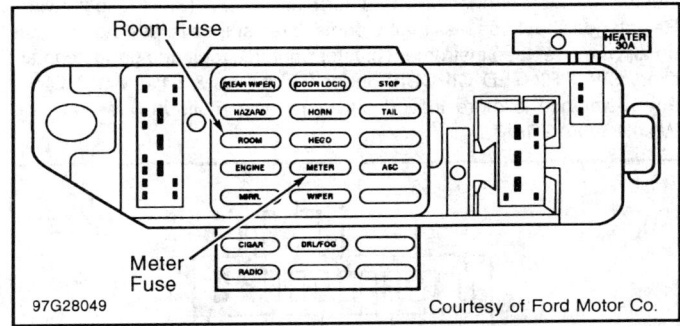

Fig. 4: Identifying Fuses

2) Turn ignition on. Measure voltage between ground and top terminal (right terminal) of METER fuse holder (Blue wire). If voltage is more than 10 volts, reinstall fuse and go to next step. If voltage is less than 10 volts, repair power feed for METER fuse. See WIRING DIAGRAMS.

3) Turn ignition off. Remove instrument cluster. See INSTRUMENT CLUSTER under REMOVAL & INSTALLATION. Disconnect all (3) instrument cluster electrical connectors. Measure voltage between ground and instrument cluster harness connector C254 terminal No. 6 (Black/Yellow wire). *See Fig. 5.* Measure voltage between ground and instrument cluster harness connector C252 terminal No. 12 (Black/Yellow wire). *See Fig. 6.* Measure voltage between ground and instrument cluster harness connector C253 terminals No. 4 and 12 (Black/Yellow wire). *See Fig. 7.* Voltage should be more than 10 volts at each Black/Yellow wire. If voltage is more than 10 volts, go to next step. If voltage is less than 10 volts, repair Black/Yellow wire(s) in question. See WIRING DIAGRAMS.

4) Turn ignition off. Measure resistance between ground and instrument cluster harness connector C254 terminal No. 5 (Black/Green wire). Measure resistance between ground and instrument cluster harness connector C252 terminals No. 11 (Blue wire) and No. 8 (Black wire). Measure resistance between ground and instrument cluster harness connector C253 terminal No. 6 (Black/Green wire). Resistance should be less than 5 ohms. If resistance is less than 5 ohms on all wires, replace instrument cluster printed circuit and gauge contact clips. See PRINTED CIRCUIT under REMOVAL & INSTALLATION. If any resistance is more than 5 ohms, repair circuit(s) in question. See WIRING DIAGRAMS.

Sedan & Wagon – 1) Check 10-amp METER fuse. *See Fig. 4.* If fuse is okay, go to next step. If fuse is blown, go to next step. Turn ignition off. Replace 10-amp METER fuse. Turn ignition on and inspect fuse. If fuse fails again, check and repair short to ground as necessary. See WIRING DIAGRAMS.

2) Turn ignition on. Measure voltage between ground and top terminal of METER fuse holder (Blue wire). If voltage is more than 10 volts, reinstall fuse and go to next step. If voltage is less than 10 volts, repair power feed for METER fuse. See WIRING DIAGRAMS.

3) Turn ignition off. Remove instrument cluster. See INSTRUMENT CLUSTER under REMOVAL & INSTALLATION. Disconnect all (3) instrument cluster electrical connectors. Measure voltage between ground and instrument cluster harness connector C254 terminal No. 10 (Black/Yellow wire). *See Fig. 5.* Measure voltage between ground and instrument cluster harness connector C252 terminals No. 4 and 8 (Black/Yellow wires). *See Fig. 6.* Measure voltage between ground and instrument cluster harness connector C253 terminals No. 1 and 8 (Black/Yellow wire). *See Fig. 8.* Voltage should be more than 10 volts at each Black/Yellow wire. If voltage is more than 10 volts, go to next step. If voltage is less than 10 volts, repair Black/Yellow wire(s) in question. See WIRING DIAGRAMS.

4) Turn ignition off. Measure resistance between ground and instrument cluster harness connector C254 terminal No. 5 (Black/Green wire). Measure resistance between ground and instrument cluster harness connector C252 terminal No. 7 (Blue wire). Measure resistance between ground and instrument cluster harness connector C253 terminal No. 11 (Black wire). Measure resistance between ground and instrument cluster harness connector C253 terminal No. 7 (Black/Green wire). Resistance should be less than 5 ohms. If resistance is less than 5 ohms on all wires, replace instrument cluster printed circuit and gauge contact clips. See PRINTED CIRCUIT under REMOVAL & INSTALLATION. If any resistance is more than 5 ohms, repair circuits in question. See WIRING DIAGRAMS.

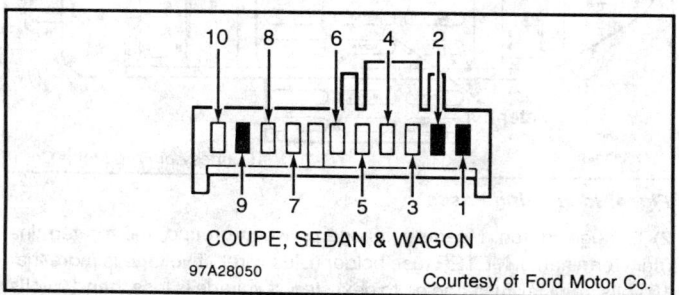

COUPE, SEDAN & WAGON

97A28050   Courtesy of Ford Motor Co.

Fig. 5: Identifying Instrument Cluster Harness Connector C254 Terminals

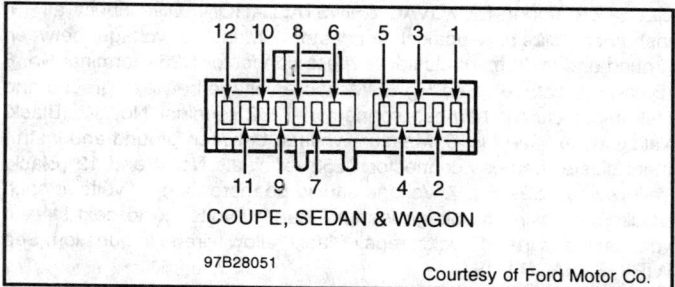

COUPE, SEDAN & WAGON

97B28051   Courtesy of Ford Motor Co.

Fig. 6: Identifying Instrument Cluster Harness Connector C252 Terminals

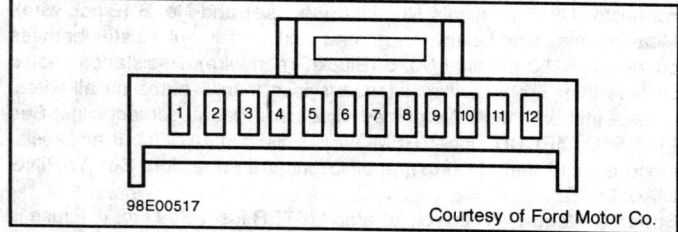

98E00517   Courtesy of Ford Motor Co.

Fig. 7: Identifying Instrument Cluster Harness Connector C253 Terminals (Coupe)

TEST B: FUEL GAUGE INACCURATE

1) Test fuel gauge. See FUEL GAUGE under COMPONENT TESTS. If fuel gauge is okay, go to next step. If fuel gauge tests bad, go to step 4).

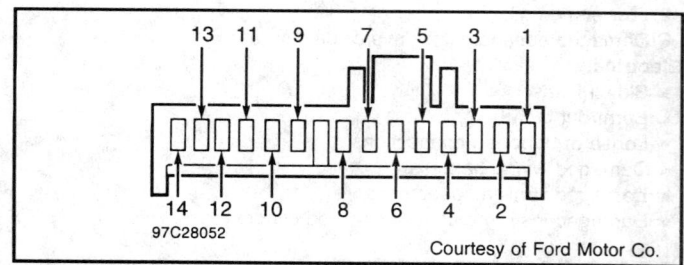

97C28052   Courtesy of Ford Motor Co.

Fig. 8: Identifying Instrument Cluster Harness Connector C253 Terminals (Sedan & Wagon)

2) Visually inspect fuel tank. Repair or replace as necessary. If fuel tank is okay, go to next step.

3) Visually inspect fuel level sensor/pump assembly and wiring harness. Repair or replace as necessary. If fuel level sensor/pump assembly and wiring harness are okay, replace fuel level sensor.

4) Turn ignition off. Disconnect fuel level sensor/pump connector. Measure resistance between ground and fuel level sensor and pump harness connector terminal No. 2 (Black wire). *See Fig. 9.* Resistance should be less than 5 ohms. If resistance is less than 5 ohms, go to next step. If resistance is more than 5 ohms, repair open in Black wire. See WIRING DIAGRAMS.

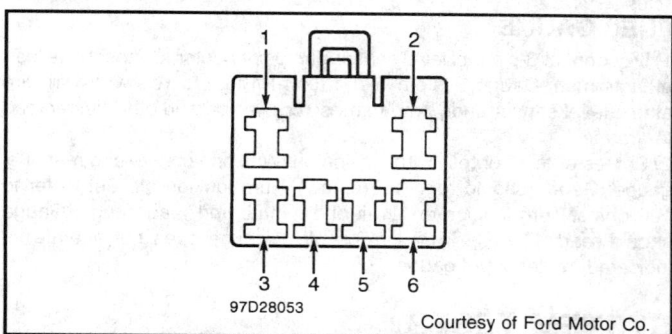

97D28053   Courtesy of Ford Motor Co.

Fig. 9: Identifying Fuel Level & Pump Harness Connector

5) Turn ignition off. Remove instrument cluster. See INSTRUMENT CLUSTER under REMOVAL & INSTALLATION. Disconnect instrument cluster harness connector C254. *See Fig. 5.* Measure resistance of Yellow/Brown wire between instrument cluster harness connector C254 terminal No. 4 and fuel level sensor/pump harness connector terminal No. 3. *See Figs. 5 and 9.* Resistance should be less than 5 ohms. Measure resistance between ground and instrument cluster harness connector C254 terminal No. 4 (Black/Yellow wire). Resistance should be more than 10 k/ohms. If resistance is as specified, go to next step. If resistance is not as specified, repair open or short to ground in Yellow/Brown wire. See WIRING DIAGRAMS.

6) Measure resistance between ground and instrument cluster harness connector C254 terminal No. 5 (Black/Green wire). Resistance should be less than 5 ohms. If resistance is less than 5 ohms, go to next step. If resistance is more than 5 ohms, repair open in Black/Green wire between instrument cluster harness connector and ground. See WIRING DIAGRAMS.

7) Visually inspect instrument cluster printed circuit for damage, cracks or hot spots. Replace as necessary. If instrument cluster printed circuit is okay, replace fuel gauge and retest system. If vehicle is equipped with fuel/temp gauge assembly, replace instrument cluster gauge amplifier. See INSTRUMENT CLUSTER GAUGE AMPLIFIER under REMOVAL & INSTALLATION.

TEST C: TEMPERATURE GAUGE INACCURATE

Coupe – 1) Test temperature gauge. See TEMPERATURE GAUGE under COMPONENT TESTS. If temperature gauge is okay, replace temperature indicator sender. If temperature gauge is not okay, go to next step.

2) Turn ignition off. Remove instrument cluster. See INSTRUMENT CLUSTER under REMOVAL & INSTALLATION. Disconnect 3 instrument cluster electrical connectors. Measure voltage between ground and instrument cluster harness connector C252 terminal No. 3 (Black/Orange wire). *See Fig. 6*. If resistance is less than 5 ohms, go to next step. If resistance is more than 5 ohms, repair open in Black/Orange wire or White/Light Blue wire between instrument cluster connector and temperature indicator sender connector.

NOTE: Black/Orange wire between instrument cluster connector and temperature indicator sender changes to White/Light Blue. See WIRING DIAGRAMS.

---

3) Measure resistance between ground and temperature indicator sender harness connector White/Light Blue wire. Resistance should be more than 10 k/ohms. If resistance is more than 10 k/ohms, go to next step. If resistance is not more than 10 k/ohms, repair White/Light Blue wire between temperature indicator sender harness connector and instrument cluster harness connector. See WIRING DIAGRAMS.

4) Turn ignition on. Measure voltage between ground and instrument cluster harness connector C254 terminal No. 6 (Black/Yellow wire). *See Fig. 5*. Voltage should be more than 10 volts. If voltage is more than 10 volts, go to next step. If voltage is less than 10 volts, repair Black/Yellow wire in question. See WIRING DIAGRAMS.

5) Turn ignition off. Measure resistance between ground and instrument cluster harness connector C254 terminal No. 5 (Black/Green wire). Resistance should be less than 5 ohms. If resistance is less than 5 ohms, go to next step. If resistance is more than 5 ohms, repair Black/Green wire in question. See WIRING DIAGRAMS.

6) Measure resistance between temperature gauge terminal "S" and temperature gauge terminal B+. Measure resistance between temperature gauge terminal "G" and temperature gauge terminal "S". Resistance should be 214-256 ohms between "S" and B+ terminals and 90-110 ohms between "G" and "S" terminals. If all resistance readings are as specified, replace instrument cluster printed circuit and gauge contact clips. See PRINTED CIRCUIT under REMOVAL & INSTALLATION. If resistance readings are not as specified, replace fuel gauge. If vehicle is equipped with a fuel/temp assembly, replace gauge amplifier. See INSTRUMENT CLUSTER GAUGE AMPLIFIER under REMOVAL & INSTALLATION.

Sedan & Wagon – 1) Test temperature gauge. See TEMPERATURE GAUGE under COMPONENT TESTS. If temperature gauge is okay, replace temperature indicator sender. If temperature gauge is not okay, go to next step.

2) Turn ignition off. Remove instrument cluster. See INSTRUMENT CLUSTER under REMOVAL & INSTALLATION. Disconnect 3 instrument cluster electrical connectors. Measure voltage between temperature indicator sender connector terminal (Red/White wire) and instrument cluster harness connector C253 terminal No. 5 (Black/Orange wire). *See Fig. 8*. If resistance is less than 5 ohms, go to next step. If resistance is more than 5 ohms, repair open in Black/Orange wire or Red/White wire between instrument cluster connector and temperature indicator sender connector.

NOTE: Black/Orange wire between instrument cluster connector and temperature indicator sender changes to Red/White. See WIRING DIAGRAMS.

---

3) Measure resistance between ground and temperature indicator sender harness connector Red/White wire. Resistance should be more than 10 k/ohms. If resistance is more than 10 k/ohms, go to next step. If resistance is not more than 10 k/ohms, repair Red/White wire between temperature indicator sender harness connector and instrument cluster harness connector. See WIRING DIAGRAMS.

4) Turn ignition on. Measure voltage between ground and instrument cluster harness connector C254 terminal No. 10 (Black/Yellow wire). *See Fig. 5*. Voltage should be more than 10 volts. If voltage is more than 10 volts, go to next step. If voltage is less than 10 volts, repair Black/Yellow wire in question. See WIRING DIAGRAMS.

5) Turn ignition off. Measure resistance between ground and instrument cluster harness connector C254 terminal No. 5 (Black/Green wire).

Resistance should be less than 5 ohms. If resistance is less than 5 ohms, go to next step. If resistance is more than 5 ohms, repair Black/Green wire in question. See WIRING DIAGRAMS.

6) Measure resistance between temperature gauge terminal "S" and temperature gauge terminal B+. Measure resistance between temperature gauge terminal "G" and temperature gauge terminal "S". Resistance should be 214-256 ohms between "S" and B+ terminals and 90-110 ohms between "G" and "S" terminals. If all resistance readings are as specified, replace instrument cluster printed circuit and gauge contact clips. See PRINTED CIRCUIT under REMOVAL & INSTALLATION. If resistance readings are not as specified, replace fuel gauge. If vehicle is equipped with a fuel/temp assembly, replace gauge amplifier. See INSTRUMENT CLUSTER GAUGE AMPLIFIER under REMOVAL & INSTALLATION.

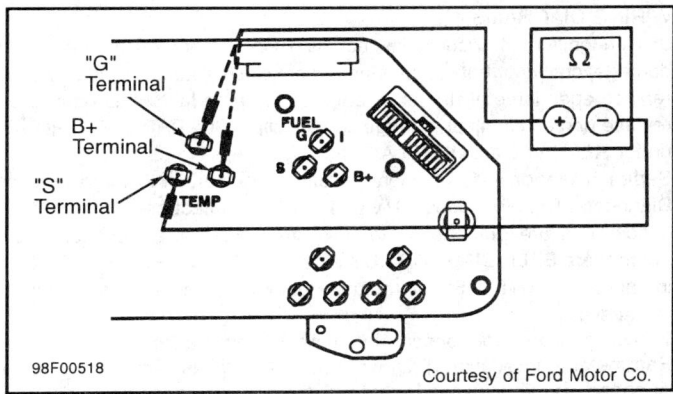

98F00518   Courtesy of Ford Motor Co.

Fig. 10: Checking Temperature Gauge Resistance

TEST D: SPEEDOMETER/ODOMETER INACCURATE

Coupe – 1) Turn ignition off. Connect scan tool and retrieve Diagnostic Trouble Codes (DTC) following manufacturer's instructions. If no DTCs are present, go to next step. If DTCs are present, see appropriate SELF-DIAGNOSTICS article in ENGINE PERFORMANCE in appropriate MITCHELL® manual. Repair DTCs as necessary, then retest system.

2) Using scan tool, observe Vehicle Speed Sensor (VSS) output Parameter Identification (PID) while assistant drives vehicle over range of speeds on various road surfaces. If VSS PID varies smoothly with vehicle speed, go to next step. If VSS PID does not vary or is erratic, see appropriate SELF-DIAGNOSTICS article in ENGINE PERFORMANCE in appropriate MITCHELL® manual to diagnose VSS.

3) Remove and check OBDII 10-amp fuse in engine compartment fuse box. If fuse is okay, reinstall fuse and go to step **5)**. If fuse is blown, go to next step.

4) Turn ignition off. Remove instrument cluster. See INSTRUMENT CLUSTER under REMOVAL & INSTALLATION. Disconnect instrument cluster electrical connectors. Measure resistance between ground and instrument cluster harness connector C253 terminal No. 1 (Green wire). *See Fig. 7*. Resistance should be more than 10 k/ohms. If resistance is more than 10 k/ohms, replace OBDII 10-amp fuse and go to next step. If resistance is less than 10 k/ohms, repair Green wire between instrument cluster harness connector and fuse. See WIRING DIAGRAMS.

5) Turn ignition off. Remove instrument cluster. See INSTRUMENT CLUSTER under REMOVAL & INSTALLATION. Disconnect instrument cluster electrical connectors. Measure voltage between ground and instrument cluster harness connector C253 terminal No. 1 (Green wire). *See Fig. 7*. Voltage should be more than 10 volts. If voltage is more than 10 volts, go to next step. If voltage is less than 10 volts, repair Green wire between instrument cluster harness connector and fuse. See WIRING DIAGRAMS.

6) Turn ignition off. Disconnect Vehicle Speed Sensor (VSS) harness connector. Measure resistance of Blue wire between VSS harness connector and instrument cluster harness connector C252 terminal No. 11. *See Fig. 6*. Measure resistance of White/Black wire between VSS harness connector and instrument cluster harness connector C252 terminal No. 1. Resistance in both tests should be less than 5 ohms. If resistances are as specified, go to next step. If resistances are not as specified, repair wire in question. See WIRING DIAGRAMS.

7) Measure resistance between ground and instrument cluster harness connector C252 terminal No. 1 (White/Black wire). Measured resistance should be more than 10 k/ohms. If resistance is more than 10 k/ohms, go to next step. If resistance is less than 10 k/ohms, repair short in White/Black wire.

8) Turn ignition on. Measure voltage between ground and instrument cluster harness connector C252 terminal No. 12 (Black/Yellow wire). *See Fig. 6.* Voltage should be more than 10 volts. If voltage is more than 10 volts, go to next step. If voltage is less than 10 volts, repair Black/Yellow wire between instrument cluster connector and fuse. See WIRING DIAGRAMS.

9) Turn ignition off. Visually inspect instrument cluster printed circuit for damage, cracks or hot spots. If instrument cluster printed circuit is okay, replace speedometer. If instrument cluster printed circuit is damaged, replace printed circuit and gauge contact clips. See PRINTED CIRCUIT under REMOVAL & INSTALLATION.

Sedan & Wagon – 1) Turn ignition off. Connect scan tool and retrieve Diagnostic Trouble Codes (DTC) following manufacturer's instructions. If no DTCs are present, go to next step. If DTCs are present, see appropriate SELF-DIAGNOSTICS article in ENGINE PERFORMANCE in appropriate MITCHELL® manual. Repair DTCs as necessary, then retest system.

2) Using scan tool, observe Vehicle Speed Sensor (VSS) output Parameter Identification (PID) while assistant drives vehicle over range of speeds on various road surfaces. If VSS PID varies smoothly with vehicle speed, go to next step. If VSS PID does not vary or is erratic, see appropriate SELF-DIAGNOSTICS article in ENGINE PERFORMANCE in appropriate MITCHELL® manual to diagnose VSS.

3) Remove and check OBDII 10-amp fuse in engine compartment fuse box. If fuse is okay, reinstall fuse and go to step **5)**. If fuse is blown, go to next step.

4) Turn ignition off. Remove instrument cluster. See INSTRUMENT CLUSTER under REMOVAL & INSTALLATION. Disconnect instrument cluster electrical connectors. Measure resistance between ground and instrument cluster harness connector C252 terminal No. 12 (Green wire). *See Fig. 6.* Measured resistance should be more than 10 k/ohms. If resistance is more than 10 k/ohms, replace OBDII 10-amp fuse and go to next step. If resistance is less than 10 k/ohms, repair Green wire between instrument cluster harness connector and fuse. See WIRING DIAGRAMS.

5) Turn ignition off. Remove instrument cluster. See INSTRUMENT CLUSTER under REMOVAL & INSTALLATION. Disconnect instrument cluster electrical connectors. Measure voltage between ground and instrument cluster harness connector C252 terminal No. 12 (Green wire). *See Fig. 6.* Voltage should be more than 10 volts. If voltage is more than 10 volts, go to next step. If voltage is less than 10 volts, repair Green wire between instrument cluster harness connector and fuse. See WIRING DIAGRAMS.

6) Turn ignition off. Disconnect Vehicle Speed Sensor (VSS) harness connector. Measure resistance of Blue wire between VSS harness connector and instrument cluster harness connector C252 terminal No. 7. *See Fig. 6.* Measure resistance of White/Black wire between VSS harness connector and instrument cluster harness connector C253 terminal No. 9. Resistance in both tests should be less than 5 ohms. If resistances are as specified, go to next step. If resistances are not as specified, repair wire in question. See WIRING DIAGRAMS.

7) Measure resistance between ground and instrument cluster harness connector C253 terminal No. 9 (White/Black wire). Resistance should be more than 10 k/ohms. If measured resistance is more than 10 k/ohms, go to next step. If resistance is less than 10 k/ohms, repair short in White/Black wire.

8) Turn ignition on. Measure voltage between ground and instrument cluster harness connector C252 terminals No. 8 and 4 (Black/Yellow wire). *See Fig. 6.* Voltage should be more than 10 volts. If voltage is

more than 10 volts, go to next step. If voltage is less than 10 volts, repair Black/Yellow wire between instrument cluster connector and fuse. See WIRING DIAGRAMS.

9) Turn ignition off. Visually inspect instrument cluster printed circuit for damage, cracks or hot spots. If instrument cluster printed circuit is okay, replace speedometer. If instrument cluster printed circuit is damaged, replace printed circuit and gauge contact clips. See PRINTED CIRCUIT under REMOVAL & INSTALLATION.

TEST E: TACHOMETER INACCURATE

Coupe – 1) Using scan tool, observe RPM output Parameter Identification (PID) over range of engine speeds. If RPM PID varies smoothly with vehicle RPM, vehicle is okay. If RPM PID does not vary or is erratic, see appropriate SELF-DIAGNOSTICS article in ENGINE PERFORMANCE in appropriate MITCHELL® manual to diagnose Clean Tach Output (CTO) circuit. If only tachometer is inaccurate or inoperative, go to next step.

2) Turn ignition off. Remove instrument cluster. See INSTRUMENT CLUSTER under REMOVAL & INSTALLATION. Disconnect instrument cluster electrical connector C253. *See Fig. 7.* Turn ignition on. Measure voltage between ground and instrument cluster harness connector C253 terminal No. 12 (Black/Yellow wire). Voltage should be more than 10 volts. If voltage is more than 10 volts, go to next step. If voltage is less than 10 volts, repair Black/Yellow wire between instrument cluster connector and fuse. See WIRING DIAGRAMS.

3) Turn ignition off. Measure resistance between ground and instrument cluster harness connector C253 terminal No. 6 (Black/Green wire). *See Fig. 7.* Resistance should be less than 5 ohms. If resistance is less than 5 ohms, go to next step. If resistance is more than 5 ohms, repair Black/Green wire between instrument cluster connector and ground. See WIRING DIAGRAMS.

4) Visually inspect instrument cluster printed circuit for damage, cracks or hot spots. If instrument cluster printed circuit is okay, go to next step. If instrument cluster printed circuit is damaged, replace printed circuit and gauge contact clips. See PRINTED CIRCUIT under REMOVAL & INSTALLATION.

5) Install EEC-V 104-pin Breakout Box (014-00950) following manufacturer's instructions. Measure resistance between breakout box terminal No. 48 and instrument cluster harness connector C253 terminal No. 5 (Light Green/Red wire). *See Fig. 7.* Resistance should be less than 5 ohms. Measure resistance between ground and instrument cluster harness connector C253 terminal No. 5 (Light Green/Red wire). Resistance should be more than 10 k/ohms. If both resistances are as specified, see appropriate SELF-DIAGNOSTICS article in ENGINE PERFORMANCE in appropriate MITCHELL® manual to diagnose Clean Tach Output (CTO) circuit. If resistances are not as specified, repair Light Green/Red wire. See WIRING DIAGRAMS.

Sedan & Wagon – 1) Using scan tool, observe RPM output Parameter Identification (PID) over range of engine speeds. If RPM PID varies smoothly with vehicle RPM, vehicle is okay. If RPM PID does not vary or is erratic, see appropriate SELF-DIAGNOSTICS article in ENGINE PERFORMANCE in appropriate MITCHELL® manual to diagnose Clean Tach Output (CTO) circuit. If only tachometer is inaccurate or inoperative, go to next step.

2) Turn ignition off. Remove instrument cluster. See INSTRUMENT CLUSTER under REMOVAL & INSTALLATION. Disconnect instrument cluster electrical connector C253. *See Fig. 7 or 8.* Turn ignition on. Measure voltage between ground and instrument cluster harness connector C253 terminal No. 8 (Black/Yellow wire). Voltage should be more than 10 volts. If voltage is more than 10 volts, go to next step. If voltage is less than 10 volts, repair Black/Yellow wire between instrument cluster connector and fuse. See WIRING DIAGRAMS.

3) Turn ignition off. Measure resistance between ground and instrument cluster harness connector C253 terminal No. 7 (Black/Green wire). *See Fig. 7 or 8.* Resistance should be less than 5 ohms. If resistance is less than 5 ohms, go to next step. If resistance is more than 5 ohms, repair Black Green wire between instrument cluster connector and ground. See WIRING DIAGRAMS.

4) Visually inspect instrument cluster printed circuit for damage, cracks or hot spots. If instrument cluster printed circuit is okay, go to next step. If instrument cluster printed circuit is damaged, replace printed circuit and gauge contact clips. See PRINTED CIRCUIT under REMOVAL & INSTALLATION.

5) Install EEC-V 104-pin Breakout Box (014-00950) following manufacturer's instructions. Measure resistance between breakout box terminal No. 48 and instrument cluster harness connector C253 terminal No. 6 (Light Green/Red wire). See Fig. 7 or 8. Resistance should be less than 5 ohms. Measure resistance between ground and instrument cluster harness connector C253 terminal No. 6 (Light Green/Red wire). Resistance should be more than 10 k/ohms. If both resistances are as specified, see appropriate SELF-DIAGNOSTICS article in ENGINE PERFORMANCE in appropriate MITCHELL® manual to diagnose Clean Tach Output (CTO) circuit. If resistances are not as specified, repair Light Green/Red wire. See WIRING DIAGRAMS.

TEST F: IMPROPER BRAKE WARNING OPERATION

Coupe – 1) Turn ignition off. Disconnect brake master cylinder fluid level sensor. Measure resistance between brake fluid level sensor terminals No. 1 and 3. See Fig. 11. With fluid level below MIN, resistance should be less than 5 ohms. With fluid level above MIN, resistance should be more than 10 k/ohms. If resistances are as specified, go to next step. If resistances are not as specified, replace brake fluid level sensor.

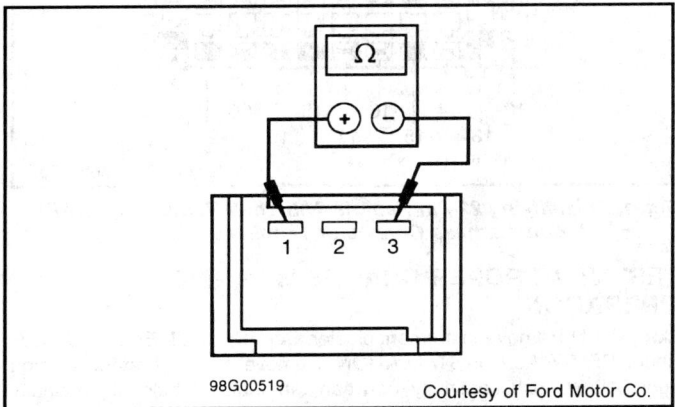

98G00519   Courtesy of Ford Motor Co.

Fig. 11: Checking Brake Fluid Level Sensor

2) Measure resistance between ground and brake master cylinder fluid level sensor harness connector terminal No. 1 (Black wire). Resistance should be less than 5 ohms. If resistance is less than 5 ohms, go to next step. If resistance is more than 5 ohms, repair Black wire between sensor harness connector and ground. See WIRING DIAGRAMS.

3) Turn ignition off. Remove instrument cluster. See INSTRUMENT CLUSTER under REMOVAL & INSTALLATION. Disconnect instrument cluster electrical connector C254. See Fig. 5. Turn ignition on. Measure voltage between ground and instrument cluster harness connector C254 terminal No. 6 (Black/Yellow wire). Voltage should be more than 10 volts. If voltage is more than 10 volts, go to next step. If voltage is less than 10 volts, repair Black/Yellow wire between instrument cluster connector and fuse. See WIRING DIAGRAMS.

4) Turn ignition off. Disconnect parking brake signal switch connector. Measure resistance between ground and parking brake signal switch connector terminal. With parking brake engaged, resistance should be less than 5 ohms. With parking brake disengaged, resistance should be more than 10 k/ohms. If resistances are as specified, go to next step. If resistances are not as specified, replace parking brake signal switch and bracket.

5) Remove instrument cluster. See INSTRUMENT CLUSTER under REMOVAL & INSTALLATION. Remove brake system warning light bulb. Check continuity between terminals of bulb. If continuity exists and concern is light never on, go to next step. If continuity exists and concern is light always on, go to step **7)**. If continuity does not exist, replace bulb.

6) Turn ignition off. Disconnect instrument cluster harness connectors. Disconnect Daytime Running Lights (DRL) control connector, if

equipped. Measure resistance between instrument cluster connector C253 terminal No. 9 (Green/Yellow wire) and brake master cylinder fluid level sensor connector Green/Yellow wire. See Fig. 6. Measure resistance between instrument cluster connector C253 terminal No. 9 (Green/Yellow wire) and parking brake signal switch Green/Yellow wire or DRL control connector (if equipped) Green/Yellow wire. Resistances in all tests should be less than 5 ohms. If resistance is less than 5 ohms, go to next step. If resistance is more than 5 ohms, repair Green/Yellow wire in question. See WIRING DIAGRAMS.

7) Measure resistance between ground and instrument cluster connector C253 terminal No. 9 (Green/Yellow wire). See Fig. 6. Resistance should be more than 10 k/ohms. If measured resistance is more than 10 k/ohms and vehicle is equipped with DRL, see appropriate DAYTIME RUNNING LIGHTS article. If resistance is more than 10 k/ohms and vehicle is not equipped with DRL, replace instrument cluster gauge amplifier. See INSTRUMENT CLUSTER GAUGE AMPLIFIER under REMOVAL & INSTALLATION. If resistance is less than 10 k/ohms, repair Green/Yellow wire. See WIRING DIAGRAMS.

Sedan & Wagon – 1) Turn ignition off. Disconnect brake master cylinder fluid level sensor. Measure resistance between brake fluid level sensor terminals No. 1 and 3. See Fig. 11. With fluid level below MIN, resistance should be less than 5 ohms. With fluid level above MIN, resistance should be more than 10 k/ohms. If resistances are as specified, go to next step. If resistances are not as specified, replace brake fluid level sensor.

2) Measure resistance between ground and brake master cylinder fluid level sensor harness connector Black wire. Resistance should be less than 5 ohms. If resistance is less than 5 ohms, go to next step. If resistance is more than 5 ohms, repair Black wire between sensor harness connector and ground. See WIRING DIAGRAMS.

3) Turn ignition off. Remove instrument cluster. See INSTRUMENT CLUSTER under REMOVAL & INSTALLATION. Disconnect instrument cluster electrical connector C254. See Fig. 5. Turn ignition on. Measure voltage between ground and instrument cluster harness connector C254 terminal No. 10 (Black/Yellow wire). Voltage should be more than 10 volts. If voltage is more than 10 volts, go to next step. If voltage is less than 10 volts, repair Black/Yellow wire between instrument cluster connector and fuse. See WIRING DIAGRAMS.

4) Turn ignition off. Disconnect parking brake signal switch connector. Measure resistance between ground and parking brake signal switch connector terminal. With parking brake engaged, resistance should be less than 5 ohms. With parking brake disengaged, resistance should be more than 10 k/ohms. If resistances are as specified, go to next step. If resistances are not as specified, replace parking brake signal switch and bracket.

5) Remove instrument cluster. See INSTRUMENT CLUSTER under REMOVAL & INSTALLATION. Remove brake system warning light bulb. Check continuity between terminals of bulb. If continuity exists and concern is light never on, go to next step. If continuity exists and concern is light always on, go to step **7)**. If continuity does not exist, replace bulb.

6) Turn ignition off. Disconnect instrument cluster harness connectors. Disconnect Daytime Running Lights (DRL) control connector, if equipped. Measure resistance between instrument cluster connector C252 terminal No. 3 (Green/Yellow wire) and brake master cylinder fluid level sensor connector Green/Yellow wire. See Fig. 6. Measure resistance between instrument cluster connector C252 terminal No. 3 (Green/Yellow wire) and parking brake signal switch Green/Yellow wire or DRL control connector (if equipped) Green/Yellow wire. Resistances in all tests should be less than 5 ohms. If resistance is less than 5 ohms, go to next step. If resistance is more than 5 ohms, repair Green/Yellow wire in question. See WIRING DIAGRAMS.

7) Measure resistance between ground and instrument cluster connector C252 terminal No. 3 (Green/Yellow wire). See Fig. 6. Resistance should be more than 10 k/ohms. If measured resistance is more than 10 k/ohms and vehicle is equipped with DRL, see appropriate DAYTIME RUNNING LIGHTS article. If resistance is more than 10 k/ohms and vehicle is not equipped with DRL, replace instrument cluster gauge amplifier. See INSTRUMENT CLUSTER GAUGE AMPLIFIER under

REMOVAL & INSTALLATION. If resistance is less than 10 k/ohms, repair Green/Yellow wire. See WIRING DIAGRAMS.

TEST G: IMPROPER LOW FUEL WARNING OPERATION

1) Remove instrument cluster. See INSTRUMENT CLUSTER under REMOVAL & INSTALLATION. Remove low fuel warning light bulb. Check continuity between terminals of bulb. If continuity exists, go to next step. If continuity does not exist, replace low fuel warning light bulb.
2) Visually inspect instrument cluster printed circuit for damage, cracks or hot spots. If instrument cluster printed circuit is okay, replace instrument cluster gauge amplifier. See INSTRUMENT CLUSTER GAUGE AMPLIFIER under REMOVAL & INSTALLATION. If instrument cluster printed circuit is damaged, replace printed circuit and gauge contact clips. See PRINTED CIRCUIT under REMOVAL & INSTALLATION.

TEST H: IMPROPER ANTI-THEFT WARNING OPERATION

Coupe – 1) Arm anti-theft system. If anti-theft system arms properly, go to next step. If anti-theft system does not arm properly, see ACTIVE ANTI-THEFT SYSTEMS – ESCORT & TRACER article.
2) Turn ignition off. Remove instrument cluster. See INSTRUMENT CLUSTER under REMOVAL & INSTALLATION. Disconnect instrument cluster harness connector C252. See Fig. 6. Disconnect 22-pin Remote Anti-Theft Personality (RAP) module harness connector located in luggage compartment. See Fig. 12. Measure resistance of Yellow/Purple wire between RAP module connector terminal No. 16 and instrument cluster harness connector C252 terminal No. 9. Resistance should be less than 5 ohms. Measure resistance between ground and instrument cluster harness connector C252 terminal No. 9 (Yellow/Purple wire). Resistance should be more than 10 k/ohms. If resistances are as specified, reconnect RAP module connector and go to next step. If resistances are not as specified, repair Yellow/Purple wire. See WIRING DIAGRAMS.
3) Turn ignition off. Connect scan tool to Data Link Connector (DLC). Turn ignition on. Monitor LEDFLASH PID. If LEDFLASH PID indicates ENABLED, go to next step. If LEDFLASH PID does not indicate ENABLED, go to active command menu and enable LED FLASH WHEN ARMED command. Retest system.
4) Visually inspect instrument cluster printed circuit for damage, cracks or hot spots. If instrument cluster printed circuit is okay, go to next step. If instrument cluster printed circuit is damaged, replace printed circuit and gauge contact clips. See PRINTED CIRCUIT under REMOVAL & INSTALLATION.
5) Arm anti-theft system. Measure voltage between ground and instrument cluster harness connector C252 terminal No. 9 (Yellow/Purple wire). Voltage should be about 2 volts. If voltage is about 2 volts and concern is indicator always on, see ACTIVE ANTI-THEFT SYSTEMS – ESCORT & TRACER article to perform RAP disarm procedure. If voltage is about 2 volts and concern is indicator always off, replace THEFT warning indicator LED. If voltage is not about 2 volts, replace RAP module.
Sedan & Wagon – 1) Arm anti-theft system. If anti-theft system arms properly, go to next step. If anti-theft system does not arm properly, see ACTIVE ANTI-THEFT SYSTEMS – ESCORT & TRACER article.
2) Turn ignition off. Remove instrument cluster. See INSTRUMENT CLUSTER under REMOVAL & INSTALLATION. Disconnect instrument cluster harness connector C253. See Fig. 7 or 8. Disconnect 22-pin Remote Anti-Theft Personality (RAP) module harness connector located in luggage compartment. See Fig. 12. Measure resistance of Yellow/Purple wire between RAP module connector terminal No. 16 and instrument cluster harness connector C253 terminal No. 9. Resistance should be less than 5 ohms. Measure resistance between ground and instrument cluster harness connector C253 terminal No. 9 (Yellow/Purple wire). Resistance should be more than 10 k/ohms. If resistances are as specified, reconnect RAP module connector and go to next step. If resistances are not as specified, repair Yellow/Purple wire. See WIRING DIAGRAMS.

3) Turn ignition off. Connect scan tool to Data Link Connector (DLC). Turn ignition on. Monitor LEDFLASH PID. If LEDFLASH PID indicates ENABLED, go to next step. If LEDFLASH PID does not indicate ENABLED, go to active command menu and enable LED FLASH WHEN ARMED command. Retest system.
4) Visually inspect instrument cluster printed circuit for damage, cracks or hot spots. If instrument cluster printed circuit is okay, go to next step. If instrument cluster printed circuit is damaged, replace printed circuit and gauge contact clips. See PRINTED CIRCUIT under REMOVAL & INSTALLATION.
5) Arm anti-theft system. Measure voltage between ground and instrument cluster harness connector C253 terminal No. 9 (Yellow/Purple wire). Voltage should be about 2 volts. If voltage is about 2 volts and concern is indicator always on, see ACTIVE ANTI-THEFT SYSTEMS – ESCORT & TRACER article to perform RAP disarm procedure. If voltage is about 2 volts and concern is indicator always off, replace THEFT warning indicator LED. If voltage is not about 2 volts, replace RAP module.

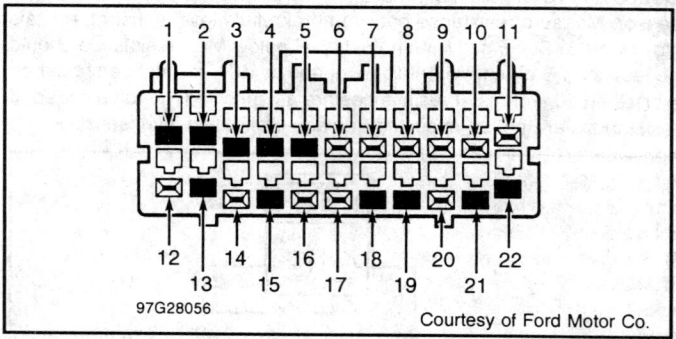

Fig. 12: Identifying 22-Pin Remote Anti-Theft Personality (RAP) Module Harness Connector Terminals

TEST J: IMPROPER CHARGE WARNING OPERATION

Coupe – 1) Remove instrument cluster. See INSTRUMENT CLUSTER under REMOVAL & INSTALLATION. Remove charge system warning light bulb. Check continuity between terminals of bulb. If continuity exists, go to next step. If continuity does not exist, replace charge system warning light bulb.
2) Disconnect instrument cluster harness connector C253. See Fig. 7. Disconnect generator voltage regulator 3-pin connector. Measure resistance between instrument cluster harness connector C253 terminal No. 11 (White/Blue wire) and voltage regulator harness connector White/Blue wire. Resistance should be less than 5 ohms. Measure resistance between ground and instrument cluster electrical harness connector C253 terminal No. 11 (White/Blue wire). Resistance should be more than 10 k/ohms. Measure resistance between ground and instrument cluster electrical harness connector C252 terminal No. 11 (White/Blue wire). See Fig. 6. Resistance should be more than 10 k/ohms. If resistances are as specified, go to next step. If resistances are not as specified, repair White/Blue wire between appropriate instrument cluster connector and generator voltage regulator connector. See WIRING DIAGRAMS.
3) Visually inspect instrument cluster printed circuit for damage, cracks or hot spots. If instrument cluster printed circuit is okay, check charging system. See appropriate GENERATORS article in STARTING & CHARGING SYSTEMS. If instrument cluster printed circuit is damaged, replace printed circuit and gauge contact clips. See PRINTED CIRCUIT under REMOVAL & INSTALLATION.
Sedan & Wagon – 1) Remove instrument cluster. See INSTRUMENT CLUSTER under REMOVAL & INSTALLATION. Remove charge system warning light bulb. Check continuity between terminals of bulb. If continuity exists, go to next step. If continuity does not exist, replace charge system warning light bulb.
2) Disconnect instrument cluster harness connector C252. See Fig. 6. Disconnect generator voltage regulator 3-pin connector. Measure resis-

tance between instrument cluster harness connector C252 terminal No. 11 (White/Blue wire) and voltage regulator harness connector White/Blue wire. Resistance should be less than 5 ohms. Measure resistance between ground and instrument cluster electrical harness connector C252 terminal No. 11 (White/Blue wire). Resistance should be more than 10 k/ohms. If resistances are as specified, go to next step. If resistances are not as specified, repair White/Blue wire between instrument cluster connector and generator voltage regulator connector. See WIRING DIAGRAMS.

3) Visually inspect instrument cluster printed circuit for damage, cracks or hot spots. If instrument cluster printed circuit is okay, check charging system. See appropriate GENERATORS article in STARTING & CHARGING SYSTEMS. If instrument cluster printed circuit is damaged, replace printed circuit and gauge contact clips. See PRINTED CIRCUIT under REMOVAL & INSTALLATION.

TEST K: IMPROPER OIL PRESSURE WARNING OPERATION

Coupe – 1) Using mechanical gauge at pressure sensor port, test engine oil pressure. Pressure should be 35-65 psi (2.4-4.5 kg/cm^2) @ 2000 RPM (hot). If oil pressure is as specified, go to next step. If oil pressure is not as specified, repair engine as necessary.

2) Disconnect oil pressure switch connector. Measure resistance between terminal of oil pressure switch and ground with engine off, and then with engine running. Resistance with engine running should be more than 10 k/ohms. Resistance with engine off should be less than 5 ohms. If resistances are as specified, go to next step. If resistances are not as specified, replace oil pressure switch.

3) Remove instrument cluster. See INSTRUMENT CLUSTER under REMOVAL & INSTALLATION. Remove low oil pressure warning light bulb. Check continuity between terminals of bulb. If continuity exists, go to next step. If continuity does not exist, replace low oil pressure warning light bulb.

4) Disconnect instrument cluster connector C253. *See Fig. 7 or 8.* Disconnect oil pressure switch connector. Measure resistance between instrument cluster harness connector C253 terminal No. 10 (Yellow/Red wire) and oil pressure switch connector. Resistance should be less than 5 ohms.

5) Measure resistance between ground and instrument cluster harness connector C253 terminal No. 10 (Yellow/Red wire). Resistance should be more than 10 k/ohms. If resistance in steps **4)** and **5)** is as specified, replace printed circuit and gauge contact clips. See PRINTED CIRCUIT under REMOVAL & INSTALLATION. If resistance is not as specified, repair Yellow/Red wire between instrument cluster connector and oil pressure switch connector. See WIRING DIAGRAMS.

Sedan & Wagon – 1) Using mechanical gauge at pressure sensor port, test engine oil pressure. Pressure should be 35-65 psi (2.4-4.5 kg/cm^2) @ 2000 RPM (hot). If oil pressure is as specified, go to next step. If oil pressure is not as specified, repair engine as necessary.

2) Disconnect oil pressure switch connector. Measure resistance between terminal of oil pressure switch and ground with engine off, and then with engine running. Resistance with engine running should be more than 10 k/ohms. Resistance with engine off should be less than 5 ohms. If resistances are as specified, go to next step. If resistances are not as specified, replace oil pressure switch.

3) Remove instrument cluster. See INSTRUMENT CLUSTER under REMOVAL & INSTALLATION. Remove low oil pressure warning light bulb. Check continuity between terminals of bulb. If continuity exists, go to next step. If continuity does not exist, replace low oil pressure warning light bulb.

4) Disconnect instrument cluster connector C253. *See Fig. 7 or 8.* Disconnect oil pressure switch connector. Measure resistance between instrument cluster harness connector C253 terminal No. 4 (Yellow/Red wire) and oil pressure switch connector. Resistance should be less than 5 ohms.

5) Measure resistance between ground and instrument cluster harness connector C253 terminal No. 4 (Yellow/Red wire). Resistance should be more than 10 k/ohms. If resistance in steps **4)** and **5)** is as specified, replace printed circuit and gauge contact clips. See PRINTED CIRCUIT

under REMOVAL & INSTALLATION. If resistance is not as specified, repair Yellow/Red wire between instrument cluster connector and oil pressure switch connector. See WIRING DIAGRAMS.

TEST L: IMPROPER AIR BAG WARNING OPERATION

Coupe – 1) Turn ignition off. Remove instrument cluster. See INSTRUMENT CLUSTER under REMOVAL & INSTALLATION. Disconnect instrument cluster electrical connector C254. *See Fig. 5.* Measure resistance between ground and instrument cluster harness connector C254 terminal No. 9 (Pink/Green wire). Resistance should be more than 10 k/ohms. If resistance is more than 10 k/ohms, go to next step. If resistance is less than 10 k/ohms, see AIR BAG RESTRAINT SYSTEMS – ESCORT & TRACER article to diagnose air bag system.

2) Visually inspect instrument cluster printed circuit for damage, cracks or hot spots. If instrument cluster printed circuit is okay, replace air bag warning indicator bulb. If instrument cluster printed circuit is damaged, replace printed circuit and gauge contact clips. See PRINTED CIRCUIT under REMOVAL & INSTALLATION.

Sedan & Wagon – 1) Turn ignition off. Remove instrument cluster. See INSTRUMENT CLUSTER under REMOVAL & INSTALLATION. Disconnect instrument cluster electrical connector C254. *See Fig. 5.* Measure resistance between ground and instrument cluster harness connector C254 terminal No. 8 (Pink/Green wire). Resistance should be more than 10 k/ohms. If resistance is more than 10 k/ohms, go to next step. If resistance is less than 10 k/ohms, see AIR BAG RESTRAINT SYSTEMS – ESCORT & TRACER article to diagnose air bag system.

2) Visually inspect instrument cluster printed circuit for damage, cracks or hot spots. If instrument cluster printed circuit is okay, replace air bag warning indicator bulb. If instrument cluster printed circuit is damaged, replace printed circuit and gauge contact clips. See PRINTED CIRCUIT under REMOVAL & INSTALLATION.

TEST M: IMPROPER ABS WARNING OPERATION

Coupe – 1) Turn ignition off. Remove instrument cluster. See INSTRUMENT CLUSTER under REMOVAL & INSTALLATION. Disconnect instrument cluster electrical connectors. Disconnect ABS control module connector. Measure resistance between ground and instrument cluster harness connector C253 terminal No. 2 (Yellow/Red wire). *See Fig. 7.* Resistance should be more than 10 k/ohms. If resistance is more than 10 k/ohms, go to next step. If resistance is less than 10 k/ohms, repair short in Yellow/Red wire between instrument cluster and ABS control module. ABS control module is mounted below passenger seat.

2) Install 60-pin Breakout Box (014-00322) following manufacturer's instructions. Measure resistance between breakout box terminal No. 17 and instrument cluster harness connector C253 terminal No. 2 (Yellow/Red wire). Resistance should be less than 5 ohms. If resistances are as specified, go to next step. If resistances are not as specified, repair open in Yellow/Red wire between instrument cluster and ABS control module.

3) Visually inspect instrument cluster printed circuit for damage, cracks or hot spots. If instrument cluster printed circuit is okay, go to next step. If instrument cluster printed circuit is damaged, replace printed circuit and gauge contact clips. See PRINTED CIRCUIT under REMOVAL & INSTALLATION.

4) Remove ABS warning indicator bulb. Check continuity between terminals of bulb. If continuity exists, see ANTI-LOCK article in BRAKES in appropriate MITCHELL® manual. If continuity does not exist, replace ABS warning indicator bulb.

Sedan & Wagon – 1) Turn ignition off. Remove instrument cluster. See INSTRUMENT CLUSTER under REMOVAL & INSTALLATION. Disconnect instrument cluster electrical connectors. Measure resistance between ground and instrument cluster harness connector C252 terminal No. 1 (Yellow/Red wire). *See Fig. 6.* Resistance should be more than 10 k/ohms. If resistance is more than 10 k/ohms, go to next step. If resistance is less than 10 k/ohms, repair short in Yellow/Red wire between instrument cluster and ABS control module. ABS control module is mounted below passenger seat.

2) Install 60-pin Breakout Box (014-00322) following manufacturer's instructions. Measure resistance between breakout box terminal No. 17

and instrument cluster harness connector C252 terminal No. 1 (Yellow/Red wire). Resistance should be less than 5 ohms. If resistances are as specified, go to next step. If resistances are not as specified, repair open in Yellow/Red wire between instrument cluster and ABS control module.

3) Visually inspect instrument cluster printed circuit for damage, cracks or hot spots. If instrument cluster printed circuit is okay, go to next step. If instrument cluster printed circuit is damaged, replace printed circuit and gauge contact clips. See PRINTED CIRCUIT under REMOVAL & INSTALLATION.

4) Remove ABS warning indicator bulb. Check continuity between terminals of bulb. If continuity exists, see appropriate ANTI-LOCK article in BRAKES in appropriate MITCHELL® manual. If continuity does not exist, replace ABS warning indicator bulb.

TEST N: TURN, HIGH BEAM & THEFT INDICATORS NEVER ON

Coupe – Turn ignition off. Remove instrument cluster. See INSTRUMENT CLUSTER under REMOVAL & INSTALLATION. Disconnect instrument cluster harness connectors. Measure resistance between ground and instrument cluster harness connector C252 terminal No. 8 (Black wire). *See Fig. 6.* Resistance should be less than 5 ohms. If resistance is more than 5 ohms, replace printed circuit and gauge contact clips. See PRINTED CIRCUIT under REMOVAL & INSTALLATION. If resistance is more than 5 ohms, repair Black wire between instrument cluster connector and ground. See WIRING DIAGRAMS.

Sedan & Wagon – Turn ignition off. Remove instrument cluster. See INSTRUMENT CLUSTER under REMOVAL & INSTALLATION. Disconnect instrument cluster harness connectors. Measure resistance between ground and instrument cluster harness connector C253 terminal No. 11 (Black wire). *See Fig. 8* . Resistance should be less than 5 ohms. If resistance is more than 5 ohms, replace printed circuit and gauge contact clips. See PRINTED CIRCUIT under REMOVAL & INSTALLATION. If resistance is more than 5 ohms, repair Black wire between instrument cluster connector and ground. See WIRING DIAGRAMS.

TEST P: IMPROPER LH TURN INDICATOR OPERATION

Coupe – **1)** Turn ignition on. Place turn signal switch in left turn position. If turn signal exterior lights operate properly, go to next step. If turn signal does not work properly, see appropriate wiring diagram in EXTERIOR LIGHTS article.

2) Turn ignition off. Remove instrument cluster. See INSTRUMENT CLUSTER under REMOVAL & INSTALLATION. Remove LH turn indicator light bulb. Check continuity between terminals of bulb. If continuity exists, go to next step. If continuity does not exist, replace LH turn indicator light bulb and retest system.

3) Disconnect instrument cluster harness connector C252. *See Fig. 6.* Disconnect indicator flasher. Measure resistance of Green/Black wire between indicator flasher connector terminal No. 5 and instrument cluster harness connector C252 terminal No. 7. *See Fig. 13.* Resistance should be less than 5 ohms. If resistance is less than 5 ohms, replace indicator flasher. If resistance is more than 5 ohms, repair Green/Black wire between instrument cluster connector and indicator flasher connector. See WIRING DIAGRAMS.

Sedan & Wagon – **1)** Turn ignition on. Place turn signal switch in left turn position. If turn signal exterior lights operate properly, go to next step. If turn signal does not work properly, see appropriate wiring diagram in EXTERIOR LIGHTS article.

2) Turn ignition off. Remove instrument cluster. See INSTRUMENT CLUSTER under REMOVAL & INSTALLATION. Remove LH turn indicator light bulb. Check continuity between terminals of bulb. If continuity exists, go to next step. If continuity does not exist, replace LH turn indicator light bulb and retest system.

3) Disconnect instrument cluster harness connector C253. *See Fig. 8.* Disconnect indicator flasher. Measure resistance of Green/Black wire between indicator flasher connector terminal No. 5 and instrument cluster harness connector C253 terminal No. 13. *See Fig. 13.* Resistance should be less than 5 ohms. If resistance is less than 5 ohms,

replace indicator flasher. If resistance is more than 5 ohms, repair Green/Black wire between instrument cluster connector and indicator flasher connector. See WIRING DIAGRAMS.

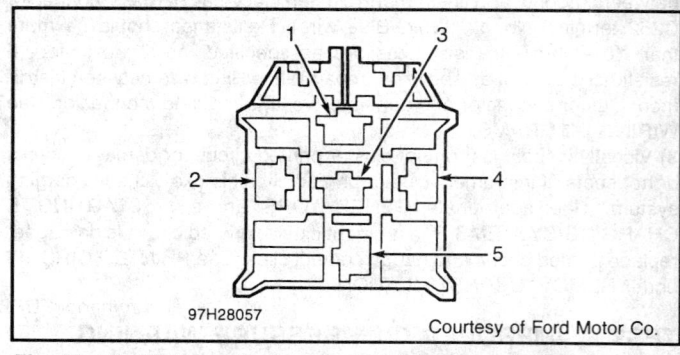

97H28057   Courtesy of Ford Motor Co.

Fig. 13: Identifying Indicator Flasher Connector Terminals

TEST Q: IMPROPER RH TURN INDICATOR OPERATION

Coupe – **1)** Turn ignition on. Place turn signal switch in right turn position. If turn signal operates properly, go to next step. If turn signal does not work properly, see appropriate wiring diagram in EXTERIOR LIGHTS article.

2) Remove instrument cluster. See INSTRUMENT CLUSTER under REMOVAL & INSTALLATION. Remove RH turn indicator light bulb. Check continuity between terminals of bulb. If continuity exists, go to next step. If continuity does not exist, replace RH turn indicator light bulb.

3) Disconnect instrument cluster harness connector C252. *See Fig. 6.* Disconnect indicator flasher. Measure resistance of Green/Black wire between indicator flasher connector terminal No. 1 and instrument cluster harness connector C252 terminal No. 10. *See Fig. 13.* Resistance should be less than 5 ohms. If resistance is less than 5 ohms, replace indicator flasher. If resistance is more than 5 ohms, repair Green/White wire between instrument cluster connector and indicator flasher connector. See WIRING DIAGRAMS.

Sedan & Wagon – **1)** Turn ignition on. Place turn signal switch in right turn position. If turn signal operates properly, go to next step. If turn signal does not work properly, see appropriate wiring diagram in EXTERIOR LIGHTS article.

2) Remove instrument cluster. See INSTRUMENT CLUSTER under REMOVAL & INSTALLATION. Remove RH turn indicator light bulb. Check continuity between terminals of bulb. If continuity exists, go to next step. If continuity does not exist, replace RH turn indicator light bulb.

3) Disconnect instrument cluster harness connector C253. *See Fig. 8.* Disconnect indicator flasher. Measure resistance of Green/Black wire between indicator flasher connector terminal No. 1 and instrument cluster harness connector C253 terminal No. 12. *See Fig. 13.* Resistance should be less than 5 ohms. If resistance is less than 5 ohms, replace indicator flasher. If resistance is more than 5 ohms, repair Green/White wire between instrument cluster connector and indicator flasher connector. See WIRING DIAGRAMS.

TEST R: IMPROPER HIGH BEAM INDICATOR OPERATION

Coupe – **1)** Turn headlights on. Operate high beams. If high beams operate properly, turn headlights off and go to next step. If high beams do not operate properly, see appropriate wiring diagram in EXTERIOR LIGHTS article.

2) Turn ignition off. Remove instrument cluster. See INSTRUMENT CLUSTER under REMOVAL & INSTALLATION. Remove high beam indicator light bulb. Check continuity between terminals of bulb. If continuity exists, go to next step. If continuity does not exist, replace high beam indicator light bulb.

3) Disconnect instrument cluster harness connector C252. *See Fig. 6.* Disconnect multifunction switch connector C1, or Daytime Running Lights (DRL) control connector, if equipped. *See Fig. 14.*

4) Measure resistance of Red/White wire between instrument cluster harness connector C252 terminal No. 6 and multifunction switch connector C1 terminal No. 1, or DRL control connector No. 3. *See Fig. 14.* Resistance should be less than 5 ohms. If resistance is less than 5 ohms, replace instrument cluster printed circuit and gauge contact clips. See PRINTED CIRCUIT under REMOVAL & INSTALLATION. If resistance is more than 5 ohms, repair Red/White wire. See WIRING DIAGRAMS.

Sedan & Wagon – 1) Turn headlights on. Operate high beams. If high beams operate properly, turn headlights of and go to next step. If high beams do not operate properly, see appropriate wiring diagram in EXTERIOR LIGHTS article.

2) Turn ignition off. Remove instrument cluster. See INSTRUMENT CLUSTER under REMOVAL & INSTALLATION. Remove high beam indicator light bulb. Check continuity between terminals of bulb. If continuity exists, go to next step. If continuity does not exist, replace high beam indicator light bulb.

3) Disconnect instrument cluster harness connector C253. *See Fig. 8.* Disconnect multifunction switch connector C1, or Daytime Running Lights (DRL) control connector, if equipped. *See Fig. 14.*

4) Measure resistance of Red/White wire between instrument cluster harness connector C253 terminal No. 10 and multifunction switch connector C1 terminal No. 1 or DRL control connector No. 3. *See Fig. 14.* Resistance should be less than 5 ohms. If resistance is less than 5 ohms, replace instrument cluster printed circuit and gauge contact clips. See PRINTED CIRCUIT under REMOVAL & INSTALLATION. If resistance is more than 5 ohms, repair Red/White wire. See WIRING DIAGRAMS.

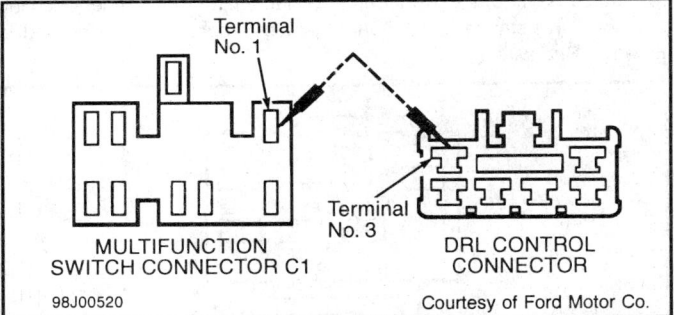

Fig. 14: Checking High Beam Indicator Circuit

TEST S: IMPROPER CHECK COOLANT INDICATOR OPERATION

Coupe – 1) Turn ignition off. Disconnect low coolant level warning sensor connector. Turn ignition on. Measure voltage between ground and low coolant level warning sensor connector Black/Yellow wire. Voltage should be more than 10 volts. If voltage is more than 10 volts, go to next step. If voltage is less than 10 volts, repair open or short in Black/Yellow wire. See WIRING DIAGRAMS.

2) Turn ignition off. Measure resistance between ground and low coolant level warning sensor connector Black wire. Resistance should be less than 5 ohms. If resistance is less than 5 ohms, go to next step. If resistance is more than 5 ohms, repair open in Black wire. See WIRING DIAGRAMS.

3) Turn ignition on. Measure voltage between ground and low coolant level warning sensor connector Yellow/Green wire. Voltage should be more than 10 volts. If voltage is more than 10 volts, replace low coolant level sensor. If voltage is less than 10 volts, go to next step.

4) Turn ignition off. Remove instrument cluster. See INSTRUMENT CLUSTER under REMOVAL & INSTALLATION. Remove CHECK COOLANT indicator light bulb. Check continuity between terminals of bulb. If continuity exists, go to next step. If continuity does not exist, replace CHECK COOLANT indicator light bulb and retest system.

5) Disconnect instrument cluster connectors. *See Fig. 5.* Measure resistance of Yellow/Green wire between low coolant sensor connector and instrument cluster harness connector C254 terminal No. 10. Resistance should be less than 5 ohms. Measure resistance between ground and instrument cluster harness connector C254 terminal No. 10 (Yellow/Green wire). Resistance should be more than 10 k/ohms. If resistances are as specified, replace instrument cluster printed circuit and gauge contact clips. See PRINTED CIRCUIT under REMOVAL & INSTALLATION. If resistances are not as specified, repair Yellow/Green wire. See WIRING DIAGRAMS.

Sedan & Wagon – 1) Turn ignition off. Disconnect low coolant level warning sensor connector. Turn ignition on. Measure voltage between ground and low coolant level warning sensor connector Black/Yellow wire. Voltage should be more than 10 volts. If voltage is more than 10 volts, go to next step. If voltage is less than 10 volts, repair open or short in Black/Yellow wire. See WIRING DIAGRAMS.

2) Turn ignition off. Measure resistance between ground and low coolant level warning sensor connector Black wire. Resistance should be less than 5 ohms. If resistance is less than 5 ohms, go to next step. If resistance is more than 5 ohms, repair open in Black wire. See WIRING DIAGRAMS.

3) Turn ignition on. Measure voltage between ground and low coolant level warning sensor connector Yellow/Green wire. Voltage should be more than 10 volts. If voltage is more than 10 volts, replace low coolant level sensor. If voltage is less than 10 volts, go to next step.

4) Turn ignition off. Remove instrument cluster. See INSTRUMENT CLUSTER under REMOVAL & INSTALLATION. Remove CHECK COOLANT indicator light bulb. Check continuity between terminals of bulb. If continuity exists, go to next step. If continuity does not exist, replace CHECK COOLANT indicator light bulb and retest system.

5) Disconnect instrument cluster connectors. *See Fig. 8.* Measure resistance of Yellow/Green wire between low coolant sensor connector and instrument cluster harness connector C253 terminal No. 3. Resistance should be less than 5 ohms. Measure resistance between ground and instrument cluster harness connector C253 terminal No. 3 (Yellow/Green wire). Resistance should be more than 10 k/ohms. If resistances are as specified, replace instrument cluster printed circuit and gauge contact clips. See PRINTED CIRCUIT under REMOVAL & INSTALLATION. If resistances are not as specified, repair Yellow/Green wire. See WIRING DIAGRAMS.

TEST T: SEAT BELT WARNING INDICATOR INOPERATIVE (CHIME OPERATIVE)

Coupe – 1) If safety belt warning chime works properly, go to next step. If warning chime is not okay, check warning chime and related circuits. See appropriate wiring diagram in WARNING SYSTEMS article.

2) Turn ignition off. Remove instrument cluster. See INSTRUMENT CLUSTER under REMOVAL & INSTALLATION. Remove safety belt warning indicator light bulb. Check continuity between terminals of bulb. If continuity exists, go to next step. If continuity does not exist, replace safety belt warning indicator light bulb.

3) Disconnect instrument cluster connectors. *See Fig. 6.* Disconnect interior fuse junction panel connector C230. *See Fig. 15.* Measure resistance of Pink/White wire between interior fuse junction panel connector C230 terminal No. 3 and instrument cluster harness connector C252 terminal No. 2. Resistance should be less than 5 ohms. Measure resistance between ground and instrument cluster harness connector C252 terminal No. 2 (Pink/White wire) . Resistance should be more than 10 k/ohms. If resistances are as specified, reconnect interior fuse junction panel connector C230 and go to next step. If resistances are not as specified, repair Pink/White wire between instrument cluster connector and junction panel connector. See WIRING DIAGRAMS.

4) Turn ignition on. Measure voltage between ground and instrument cluster harness connector C252 terminal No. 12 (Black/Yellow wire). *See Fig. 6.* Voltage should be more than 10 volts. If voltage is more than 10 volts, replace printed circuit and gauge contact clips. See PRINTED CIRCUIT under REMOVAL & INSTALLATION. If voltage is less than 10 volts, repair Black/Yellow wire. See WIRING DIAGRAMS.

Sedan & Wagon – 1) If safety belt warning chime works properly, go to next step. If warning chime is not okay, check warning chime and related circuits. See appropriate wiring diagram in WARNING SYSTEMS article.
2) Turn ignition off. Remove instrument cluster. See INSTRUMENT CLUSTER under REMOVAL & INSTALLATION. Remove safety belt warning indicator light bulb. Check continuity between terminals of bulb. If continuity exists, go to next step. If continuity does not exist, replace safety belt warning indicator light bulb.
3) Disconnect instrument cluster connectors. *See Fig. 5.* Disconnect interior fuse junction panel connector C230. *See Fig. 15.* Measure resistance of Pink/White wire between interior fuse junction panel connector C230 terminal No. 3 and instrument cluster harness connector C254 terminal No. 6. Resistance should be less than 5 ohms. Measure resistance between ground and instrument cluster harness connector C254 terminal No. 6 (Pink/White wire) . Resistance should be more than 10 k/ohms. If resistances are as specified, reconnect interior fuse junction panel connector C230 and go to next step. If resistances are not as specified, repair Pink/White wire between instrument cluster connector and junction panel connector. See WIRING DIAGRAMS.
4) Turn ignition on. Measure voltage between ground and instrument cluster harness connector C252 terminal No. 4 (Black/Yellow wire). *See Fig. 6.* Voltage should be more than 10 volts. If voltage is more than 10 volts, replace printed circuit and gauge contact clips. See PRINTED CIRCUIT under REMOVAL & INSTALLATION. If voltage is less than 10 volts, repair Black/Yellow wire. See WIRING DIAGRAMS.

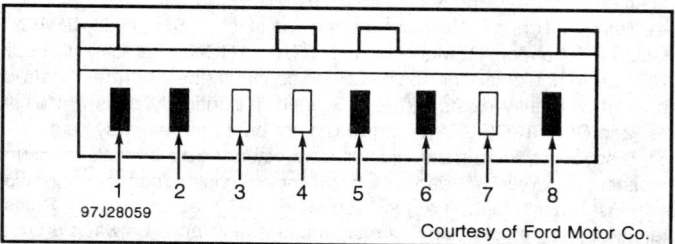

Fig. 15: Identifying Interior Fuse Junction Panel Connector C230

TEST U: IMPROPER UPSHIFT INDICATOR OPERATION

1) Turn ignition off. Remove instrument cluster. See INSTRUMENT CLUSTER under REMOVAL & INSTALLATION. Remove upshift indicator light bulb. Check continuity between terminals of bulb. If continuity exists, go to next step. If continuity does not exist, replace upshift indicator light bulb and retest system.
2) Visually inspect instrument cluster printed circuit for damage, cracks or hot spots. If instrument cluster printed circuit is okay, see appropriate SELF-DIAGNOSTICS article in ENGINE PERFORMANCE in appropriate MITCHELL® manual to diagnose upshift indicator circuit. If instrument cluster printed circuit is damaged, replace printed circuit and gauge contact clips. See PRINTED CIRCUIT under REMOVAL & INSTALLATION.

TEST V: IMPROPER LIFTGATE WARNING OPERATION (WAGON ONLY)

1) Turn ignition off. Disconnect liftgate latch switch connector. Measure resistance between ground and liftgate latch switch connector Orange/White wire. With liftgate open, resistance should be less than 5 ohms. With liftgate closed, resistance should be more than 10 k/ohms. If resistances are as specified, go to next step. If resistances are not as specified, replace liftgate latch.
2) Turn ignition off. Remove instrument cluster. See INSTRUMENT CLUSTER under REMOVAL & INSTALLATION. Remove liftgate ajar warning indicator light bulb. Check continuity between terminals of bulb. If continuity exists, go to next step. If continuity does not exist, replace liftgate ajar warning indicator light bulb.
3) Disconnect instrument cluster connector C253. *See Fig. 7 or 8.* Measure resistance between instrument cluster harness connector C253 terminal No. 1 (Orange/White wire) and liftgate switch harness connector Red/Yellow wire. Resistance should be less than 5 ohms.

Measure resistance between ground and instrument cluster harness connector C253 terminal No. 1 (Orange/White wire). Resistance should be more than 10 k/ohms. If resistances are as specified, go to next step. If resistances are not as specified, repair Orange/White and/or Red/Yellow wire between instrument cluster connector and liftgate harness connector. See WIRING DIAGRAMS.
4) Turn ignition on. Measure voltage between ground and instrument cluster harness connector C252 terminal No. 4 (Black/Yellow wire). *See Fig. 6.* Voltage should be more than 10 volts. If voltage is more than 10 volts, replace printed circuit and gauge contact clips. See PRINTED CIRCUIT under REMOVAL & INSTALLATION. If voltage is less than 10 volts, repair Black/Yellow wire. See WIRING DIAGRAMS.

TEST W: INSTRUMENT PANEL ILLUMINATION WILL NOT DIM

1) Turn ignition off. Disconnect instrument panel dimming module (dimmer switch) connector. Turn parking lights on. Measure voltage between ground and instrument panel dimming module connector terminal No. 4 (Red/Black wire). *See Fig. 16.* If voltage is more than 10 volts, turn parking lights off and go to next step. If voltage is less than 10 volts, repair Red/Yellow wire.
2) Measure resistance between ground and instrument panel dimming module connector terminal No. 2 (Black wire). If resistance is less than 5 ohms, go to next step. If resistance is more than 5 ohms, repair open in Black wire.
3) Disconnect transmission selector illumination harness connector. Disconnect instrument cluster connector C252. *See Fig. 6.* Disconnect Integrated Control Panel (ICP) connector (radio). *See Fig. 17.* Measure resistance between ground and instrument panel dimming module connector terminals No. 6 (Green wire) and No. 1 (Red wire). If resistance is more than 10 k/ohms, replace instrument panel dimming module. If resistance is 10 k/ohms or less, repair short to ground in green or Red wire.

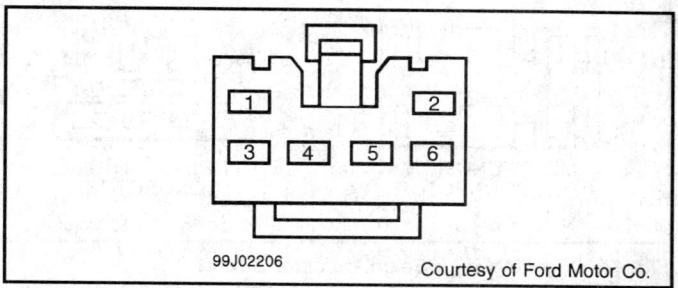

Fig. 16: Identifying Instrument Panel Dimming Module Connector C221 Terminals

TEST X: INSTRUMENT PANEL ILLUMINATION INOPERATIVE

1) Turn ignition off. Disconnect instrument cluster connector C252. *See Fig. 6.* Turn parking lights on. Measure voltage between ground and instrument cluster connector C252 terminal No. 5 (Red/Black wire). If voltage is more than 10 volts, go to next step. If voltage is less than 10 volts, repair open Red/Black wire.

NOTE: Ensure transmission selector illumination harness connector is connected or inaccurate results will occur.

2) Measure voltage between ground and instrument cluster connector C252 terminal No. 4 (Red wire) while rotating rheostat from left to right. If voltage range is .2-11 volts, replace instrument cluster printed circuit. See PRINTED CIRCUIT under REMOVAL & INSTALLATION. If voltage range is not .2-11 volts, repair Red wire.

TEST Y: CLIMATE CONTROL ILLUMINATION INOPERATIVE

1) Turn ignition off. Disconnect Integrated Control Panel (ICP) connector (radio). Turn parking lights on. Measure voltage between ground and ICP connector C274 terminal No. 5 (Red/Black wire). *See Fig. 17.* If voltage is more than 10 volts, go to next step. If voltage is less than 10 volts, repair open Red/Black wire.

2) Measure voltage between ground and ICP connector C274 terminal No. 7 (Green wire) while rotating rheostat from left to right. If voltage range is .2-11 volts, remove and repair ICP at authorized repair facility. If voltage range is not .2-11 volts, turn parking lights off and go to next step.

3) Turn ignition off. Disconnect instrument panel dimming module (dimmer switch) connector. Measure resistance of Green wire between ICP connector C274 terminal No. 7 and instrument panel dimming module connector terminal No. 6. *See Fig. 16.* If resistance is less than 5 ohms, replace instrument panel dimming module. If resistance is 5 ohms or more, repair open Green wire.

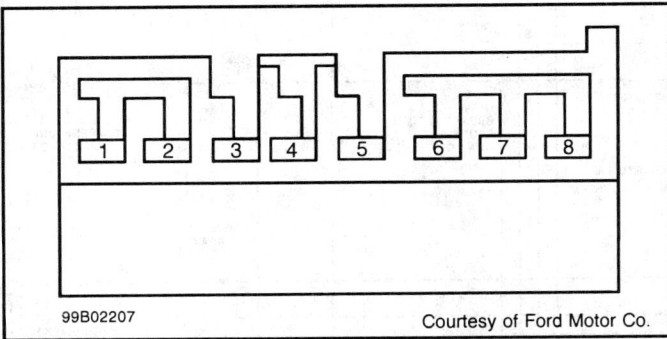

99B02207   Courtesy of Ford Motor Co.

Fig. 17: Identifying Integrated Control Panel (ICP) Connector C274 Terminals

TEST Z: TRANSMISSION SELECTOR ILLUMINATION INOPERATIVE

1) Turn ignition off. Remove transmission selector bulb. Check continuity between terminals of bulb. If continuity exists, go to next step. If continuity does not exist, replace transmission selector bulb.

2) Disconnect transmission selector illumination harness connector. Turn parking lights on. Measure voltage between ground and transmission selector illumination harness connector Red/Black wire. If voltage is more than 10 volts, go to next step. If voltage is less than 10 volts, repair open Red/Black wire.

NOTE: Ensure instrument cluster connector C252 is connected or inaccurate results will occur. See Fig. 6.

3) Measure voltage between ground and transmission selector illumination harness connector Red wire while rotating rheostat from left to right. If voltage range is .2-11 volts, repair or replace transmission selector illumination socket assembly. If voltage range is not .2-11 volts, repair Red wire.

REMOVAL & INSTALLATION

CAUTION: Electronic modules are sensitive to static electrical charges. Proper grounding of technician and workpiece is essential to prevent damage.

INSTRUMENT CLUSTER

Removal & Installation – Disconnect negative battery cable. Remove nut on back side of hood latch pull handle and remove handle. Remove screw from instrument panel steering column cover and panel and remove cover and panel. On Coupe, remove dimmer switch rheostat connector. On all models, remove 5 screws and instrument panel upper finish panel. On Coupe, disconnect power mirror switch connector. On all models, remove 4 instrument cluster mounting screws. Pull instrument cluster out and disconnect 3 electrical connectors. Remove instrument cluster. To install, reverse removal procedure.

INSTRUMENT CLUSTER GAUGE AMPLIFIER

Removal & Installation – Remove instrument cluster. See INSTRUMENT CLUSTER. Depress tang and remove instrument cluster gauge amplifier from rear of instrument cluster. *See Fig. 3.* To install, reverse removal procedure.

PRINTED CIRCUIT

Removal & Installation – 1) Remove instrument cluster. See INSTRUMENT CLUSTER. Remove 5 instrument cluster mask screws and remove mask and lens.

CAUTION: Handle gauges and components with care. Make no attempt to adjust indicator needles.

2) By pulling straight out, remove temperature gauge, fuel gauge, speedometer and tachometer (if equipped). Depress tang and remove instrument cluster gauge amplifier from rear of cluster.

3) Remove indicator and illumination bulbs from rear of instrument cluster. Remove gauge contact clips from rear of cluster by compressing clip ends together and pulling out. Discard clips. Carefully remove printed circuit from rear of instrument cluster. To install, reverse removal procedure using NEW gauge contact clips.

CAUTION: When removing gauge contact clips, DO NOT damage instrument cluster printed circuit.

FUEL GAUGE, TEMPERATURE GAUGE, SPEEDOMETER/ODOMETER & TACHOMETER INDICATORS/WARNING BULBS

Removal & Installation – Removal and installation for gauges, meters and bulbs is found in PRINTED CIRCUIT procedure.

WIRING DIAGRAMS

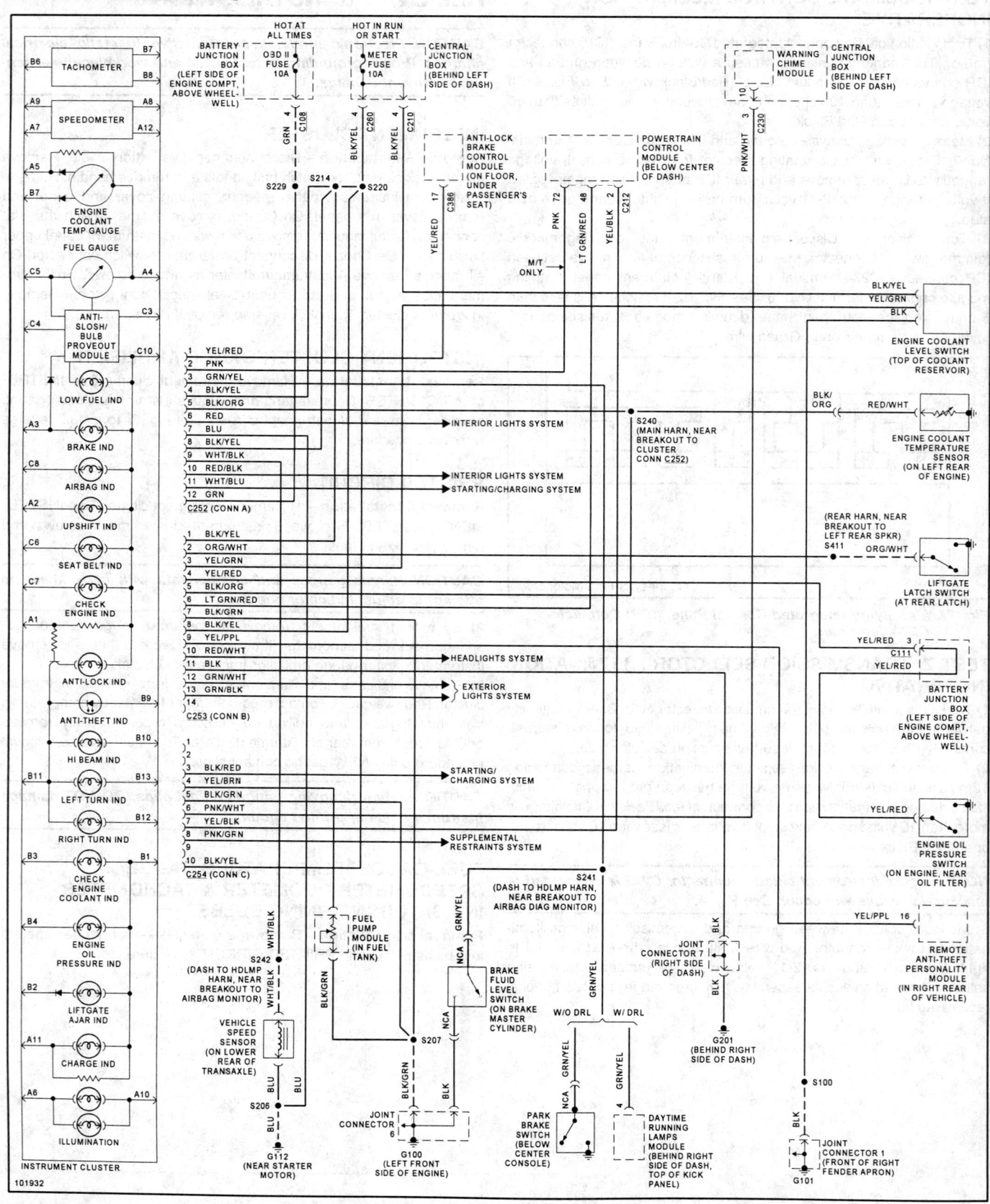

Fig. 18: Analog Instrument Panel Wiring Diagram (Escort & Tracer)

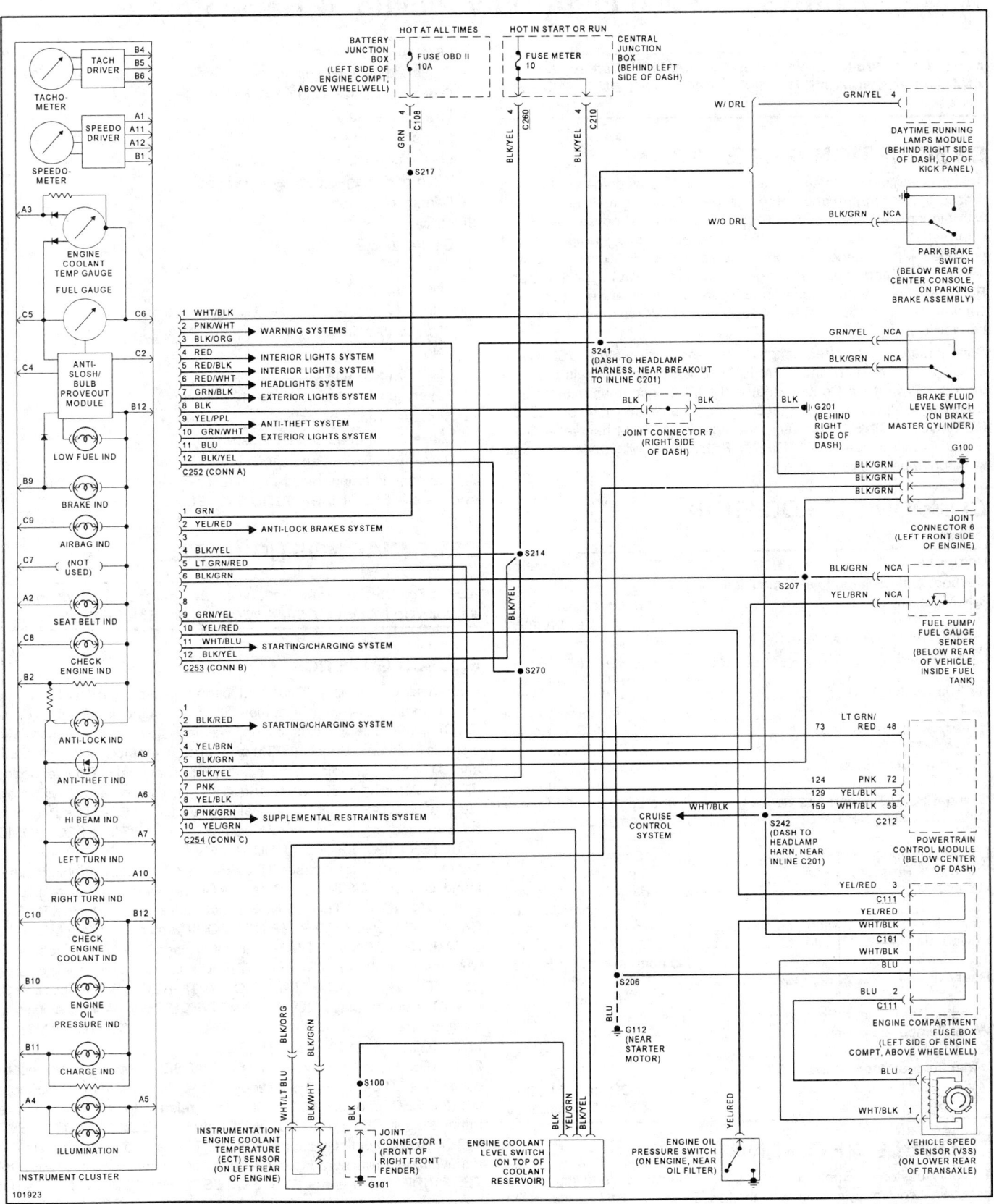

Fig. 19: Analog Instrument Panel Wiring Diagram (Escort ZX2)

1999 ACCESSORIES & EQUIPMENT
Analog Instrument Panels – Expedition, F150 & F250 Light-Duty Pickup, & Navigator

NOTE: For Natural Gas Vehicle (NGV) fuel indication system, see ANALOG INSTRUMENT PANELS – F250 LIGHT-DUTY PICKUP – CNG.

DESCRIPTION & OPERATION

Analog instrument cluster is equipped with speedometer, fuel, oil pressure, temperature and voltage gauges. Some models are equipped with tachometer. Instrument cluster is Electronic Hybrid Cluster (HEC) with self-diagnostic capability. All Expeditions and Navigators are equipped with Generic Electronic Module (GEM). F150 and F250 with 4-wheel drive and/or power windows are equipped with GEM. F150 and F250 2-wheel drive pickups without power windows are equipped with Central Timer Module (CTM). GEM and CTM have self-diagnostic capabilities.

Speedometer, odometer, engine coolant temperature, SERVICE ENGINE SOON lamp and LOW RANGE lamp input signals are sent from the Powertrain Control Module (PCM) to instrument cluster over Standard Corporate Protocol (SCP) communication network buses. SERVICE ENGINE SOON lamp will light when PCM has set a Diagnostic Trouble Code (DTC). FUEL RESET lamp will light when inertia switch has been tripped.

COMPONENT LOCATION

COMPONENT LOCATION

Component	Location
4-Wheel Anti-Lock Module (Expedition & Navigator)	Left Front Of Engine Compartment
4-Wheel Anti-Lock Module (F150 & F250 Pickup)	Behind Right Side Instrument Panel
Air Suspension Module	Behind Center Of Instrument Panel
Battery Junction Box	Left Side Engine Compartment
Central Junction Box	Under Left Side Of Instrument Panel
Cylinder Head Temperature Sensor	Top Left Front Of Engine
Data Link Connector (DLC)	Below Center Of Instrument Panel
Differential Speed Sensor	Center Of Rear Axle
Engine Oil Pressure Switch	Left Front Of Engine
GEM/CTM	Back Side Of Central Junction Box
Inertia Fuel Shutoff Switch	Behind Right Kick Panel
Powertrain Control Module	Right Side Engine Compartment Near Battery
Rear Wheel Anti-Lock Brake Module	Behind Right Side Of Instrument Panel
Transfer Case Speed Sensor	Left Rear Of Transmission
Water Temperature Sensor – 4.2L, 4.6L & 5.4L (2V)	Intake Manifold Near Thermostat Housing
Water Temperature Sensor – 5.4L (4V)	Front Of Intake Manifold Near Throttle Body

TROUBLE SHOOTING

1) Verify customer complaint by observing indicators and gauges to determine correct operation with ignition switch in RUN position with engine off, in START before ignition switch is released and in RUN with engine running.

2) Visually inspect following for obvious signs of damage:
Mechanical:
- Tripped inertia fuel switch.
- Low brake fluid level.
- Damaged engine oil filter.
- Damaged washer fluid reservoir.
- Low washer fluid.
- Low coolant level.
- Low engine oil.
- Worn or damaged generator drive belt.
- Damaged fuel tank.

Electrical:
- Central junction box fuses:
  - No. 2 (5-amp)
  - No. 6 (5-amp)
  - No. 8 (5-amp
  - No. 15 (5-amp)
  - No. 20 (5-amp)
  - No. 30 (30-amp)
- Battery junction box fuse No. 103 (50-amp).
- Damaged wiring harness.
- Loose or corroded connections.
- Damaged switches and sensors.

3) If damage is found, repair and retest system. If cause of fault is not evident, see SELF-DIAGNOSTIC SYSTEM.

SELF-DIAGNOSTIC SYSTEM

NOTE: For further information of self-diagnostic system, see appropriate MODULE COMMUNICATIONS NETWORK article.

SELF-DIAGNOSTICS

Instrument cluster is a Hybrid Electronic Cluster (HEC). HEC has self-diagnostic system which may store a Diagnostic Trouble Code (DTC) if a problem exists in the system. HEC communicates with Generic Electronic Module (GEM) or Central Timer Module (CTM). GEM and CTM have self-diagnostic capabilities. Diagnostic Trouble Codes (DTCs) stored in HEC, GEM and CTM may be obtained with New Generation STAR tester, or equivalent scan tool. HEC DTCs may also be displayed on the instrument cluster. See HYBRID ELECTRONIC CLUSTER (HEC) SELF-DIAGNOSTICS.

1) For preliminary testing, see TROUBLE SHOOTING. If problem is not found, connect NGS tester to Data Link Connector (DLC). Perform DATA LINK DIAGNOSTIC TEST. If NGS tester displays CKT914, CKT915 or CKT70 = ALL ECUS NO RESP/NOT EQUIP, see appropriate MODULE COMMUNICATIONS NETWORK article to diagnose network problem. If NGS tester displays NO RESP/NOT EQUIP for hybrid electronic cluster, go to TEST A: NO COMMUNICATION WITH HEC in SYSTEM TESTS. If NGS tester displays NO RESP/NOT EQUIP for generic electronic module/central timer module, go to TEST B: NO COMMUNICATION WITH GEM/CTM in SYSTEM TESTS.

2) If NGS tester displays SYSTEM PASSED, retrieve and record continuous DTCs. Erase continuous DTCs. Perform self-test diagnostics for HEC and GEM/CTM. If DTCs related to the concern are retrieved, see HEC DTC TEST INDEX table or GEM/CTM DTC TEST INDEX table to continue diagnosis. If no DTCs related to the concern are retrieved, perform appropriate test based on symptom. See SYMPTOM TEST INDEX table under SYSTEM TESTS. For GEM/CTM DTCs not covered in this article, see appropriate MODULE COMMUNICATIONS NETWORK article.

1999 ACCESSORIES & EQUIPMENT
Analog Instrument Panels – Expedition, F150 & F250 Light-Duty Pickup, & Navigator (Cont.)

FORD
4-759

HEC DTC TEST INDEX

DTC	Description	Test
B1202	Fuel Sender Open	C
B1204	Fuel Sender Short To Ground	C
B1213	Anti-Theft Number Of Programmed Keys Below Minimum	1
B1232	Antenna Not Connected Or Damaged Transceiver	1
B1317	Battery Voltage High	2
B1318	Battery Voltage Low	2
B1342	ECU Defective	3
B1356	Ignition RUN Circuit Open	4
B1364	Ignition START Circuit Open	4
B1600	PATS Ignition Key Transponder Signal Not Received	1
B1601	PATS Received Incorrect Key Code	1
B1602	PATS Received Invalid Key Code Format	1
B1681	PATS Transceiver Signal Not Received	1
B2103	Antenna Not Connected Or Defective Transceiver	1
B2139	PCM ID Mismatch Between PCM And HEC	1
B2141	NVM Configuration Failure	5
B2143	Odometer NVM Memory Failure	5
C1284	Oil Pressure Switch Failure	E
P1197	SELECT/RESET Switch Circuit Failure	5
U1011	SCP Invalid Or Missing Data For Engine Air Intake	6
U1027	SCP Invalid Or Missing Data For Engine RPM	6
U1041	SCP Invalid Or Missing Data For Vehicle Speed	6
U1073	SCP Invalid Or Missing Data For Engine Coolant	6
U1123	SCP Invalid Or Missing Data For Odometer	6
U1131	SCP Invalid Or Missing Data For Fuel System	1
U1147	SCP Invalid Or Missing Data For Vehicle Security For Vehicle Security	6
U1148	SCP Invalid Or Missing Data For Audio Control	7
U1262	Missing SCP Message	

1 – See appropriate PASSIVE ANTI-THEFT SYSTEMS article.
2 – See GENERATORS – ECONOLINE, EXPEDITION, EXPLORER (4.0L OHV), PICKUP (ALL GASOLINE), MOUNTAINEER (4.0L OHV), NAVIGATOR & RANGER article in STARTING & CHARGING SYSTEMS.
3 – Clear DTCs. Repeat self-test. If DTC B1342, replace instrument cluster. Clear DTCs and retest system.
4 – See appropriate STEERING COLUMN SWITCHES article and appropriate wiring diagram in POWER DISTRIBUTION article in WIRING DIAGRAMS.
5 – Replace instrument cluster. Clear DTCs and retest system.
6 – Carry out PCM self-test.
7 – For diagnosis, see appropriate MODULE COMMUNICATIONS NETWORK article.

GEM/CTM DTC TEST INDEX [1]

DTC	Description	Test
B1323	Door Ajar Circuit Failure (Lamp Never On)	J
B1323	Door Ajar Circuit Failure (Lamp Always On)	K
B1325	Door Ajar Lamp Circuit Short To Power	J
B1342	GEM Defective	2
B1426	Safety Belt Lamp Circuit Short To Power	H
B1428	Safety Belt Lamp Circuit Failure (Lamp Never On)	H
B1428	Safety Belt Lamp Circuit Failure (Lamp Always On)	I
P1804	4-Wheel Drive High Indicator Circuit Failure	N
P1806	4-Wheel Drive High Indicator Short To Power	N

1 – Codes listed in this table are only for testing covered in this article For complete GEM DTC listing, see appropriate MODULE COMMUNICATIONS NETWORK article.
2 – Replace GEM. See GENERIC ELECTRONIC MODULE/CENTRAL TIMER MODULE (GEM/CTM) under REMOVAL & INSTALLATION. Clear DTCs and repeat self-test.

HYBRID ELECTRONIC CLUSTER (HEC) SELF-DIAGNOSTICS

To enter HEC self-diagnostics, press instrument cluster SELECT/RESET button before turning ignition switch to RUN position. Within 5-8 seconds, odometer will display tESt to begin self-diagnostic mode. SELECT/RESET button must be released within 3 seconds of odometer displaying tESt. Repeatedly press SELECT/RESET button through odometer displays until dtc is displayed. When odometer displays dtc, press SELECT/RESET button again and any continuous DTCs will be displayed before odometer advances to next display. Other HEC diagnostic modes can be entered when self-diagnostic function is entered. See HEC SELF-DIAGNOSTIC MODES table.

HEC SELF-DIAGNOSTIC MODES [1] [2]

Odometer Display	Description
GAGE	Activates sweep of all gauges, then displays present gauge values. Does ROM and EE checksum tests. If gauge sweep is inoperative, replace instrument cluster.
All Segments Illuminated	Illuminates all odometer segments. If any odometer segment is inoperative, replace instrument cluster.
bulb	Illuminates all micro-controlled lamps and LEDs. Replace bulb or LED as necessary.

FORD
4-760

1999 ACCESSORIES & EQUIPMENT
Analog Instrument Panels – Expedition,
F150 & F250 Light-Duty Pickup, & Navigator (Cont.)

HEC SELF-DIAGNOSTIC MODES [1] [2] (Cont.)

Odometer Display	Description
r	Returns to normal operation all micro-controlled lamps and LEDs and displays hexadecimal values for ROM. If alternating flashes of FAIL and ROM level are displayed, replace instrument cluster.
EE	Hexadecimal value for EE level. If alternating flashes of FAIL and EE level are displayed, replace instrument cluster.
dtc	Displays continuous DTCs. Pressing SELECT/RESET button will display any DTCs stored before proceeding to next step.
enG	English value speed input.
m	Metric speed value input.
tAc	Tachometer value input.
FUEL	Fuel level input. Displays 255 for open circuit, about 232 for full stop, 215 for full tank, 178 for 3/4 full, 138 for 1/2 full, 93 for 1/4 full, 41 for empty mark, 0-20 circuit is shorted. Below 55 low fuel warning lamp should light.
OIL	Oil pressure input. Normal input reading will be 000-169. Below 6 psi or inoperative switch will be greater than 169.
dEGC	Last coolant temp input. About 49c, gauge should be at cold mark; 120c gauge should be at end of normal band. About 119c, temperature warning lamp should light. If -40c, input has not been received for more than 5 seconds.
br	Brake fluid level input.
bAtt	Battery voltage input.
Cr	RUN/START sense input. Shows -h with ignition switch in START or RUN position.

[1] – Modes only for use of the manufacturer have been deleted from this table.
[2] – Values displayed are instrument cluster input values, not gauge values.

SYSTEM TESTS

CAUTION: *Disconnect the battery before disconnecting Generic Electronic Module (GEM) or Central Timer Module (CTM) connectors. Failure to do so will result in GEM/CTM storing erroneous codes and may also result in erratic operation of GEM/CTM after reconnection.*

NOTE: *If concern is that indicator lamp never lights, check bulb before doing system testing. To test bulbs, enter instrument cluster self-diagnostics and advance to bulb mode. This will command all instrument cluster bulbs and LEDs to light. See HYBRID ELECTRONIC CLUSTER (HEC) SELF-DIAGNOSTICS.*

SYMPTOM TEST INDEX

Symptom	Test
No Communication With HEC	A
No Communication With GEM/CTM	B
A Single Gauge Does Not Return To Zero With Key Off	1
Fuel Gauge Inaccurate	C
LOW FUEL Lamp Never Or Always On	D
Voltmeter Inaccurate	2
Oil Pressure Gauge Inaccurate	E
Oil Gauge Reads Normal With Engine Off	1
Low Oil Warning Lamp Stays On & Temperature Gauge Reads Normally	E
Temperature Gauge Inaccurate	F
Temperature Warning Lamp Flickers, Temperature Gauge Reads Fully Hot	1

SYMPTOM TEST INDEX (Cont.)

Symptom	Test
Speedometer/Odometer Inoperative	G
Tachometer Inoperative	1
Tachometer Inaccurate	1
Low Oil Pressure Indicator Lamp Inoperative Or Always On	1
Safety Belt Indicator Lamp Inoperative (Chime Operative)	H
Safety Belt Indicator Lamp Does Not Operate Correctly (Chime Okay)	I
DOOR AJAR Lamp Inoperative (Chime Okay)	J
DOOR AJAR Lamp Does Not Operate Correctly (Chime Okay)	K
BRAKE Warning Lamp Inoperative Or Always On	L
Charging System Indicator Lamp Inoperative Or Always On	M
4X4 Indicator Lamp Inoperative Or Always On	N
LOW RANGE Lamp Inoperative Or Always On	3
High Beam Indicator Lamp Inoperative Or Always On	O
Air Bag Warning Lamp Inoperative Or Always On	4
ABS Warning Lamp Inoperative Or Always On	P
CK SUSP Lamp Inoperative Or Always On	Q
SERVICE ENGINE SOON Lamp Inoperative Or Always On	R
Turn/Hazard Indicator lamp Inoperative Or Always On	S
FUEL RESET Lamp Inoperative Or Always On	T
THEFT Indicator lamp Inoperative Or Always On	5
LOW WASHER Lamp Inoperative Or Always On	U
Integrated Circuit Display Inoperative Or Erratic	6

[1] – Replace instrument cluster. See INSTRUMENT CLUSTER under REMOVAL & INSTALLATION. Retest system.
[2] – See GENERATORS – ECONOLINE, EXPEDITION, EXPLORER (4.0L OHV), PICKUP, (ALL GASOLINE), MOUNTAINEER (4.0L OHV), NAVIGATOR & RANGER article in STARTING & CHARGING.
[3] – If gasoline engine, see TEST TG in SYSTEM TESTS in SELF-DIAGNOSTICS – EEC-V in ENGINE PERFORMANCE. If diesel engine, see TEST FH in SYSTEM TESTS in SELF-DIAGNOSTICS – DIESEL in ENGINE PERFORMANCE.
[4] – See appropriate AIR BAG RESTRAINT SYSTEMS article for diagnosis.
[5] – See appropriate PASSIVE ANTI-THEFT SYSTEMS article.
[6] – Perform HEC self-diagnostics.

TEST A: NO COMMUNICATION WITH HEC

NOTE: *After repair, clear DTCs and repeat self-test.*

1) Turn ignition off. Disconnect instrument cluster 20-pin connector C236. Measure voltage between instrument cluster connector C236 terminal No. 10 and ground. See Fig. 1. If voltage is more than 10 volts, go to next step. If voltage is 10 volts or less, repair Red/White wire.

2) Turn ignition switch to RUN position. Measure voltage between instrument cluster connector C236 terminal No. 11 and ground. If voltage is more than 10 volts, go to next step. If voltage is 10 volts or less, repair Gray/Yellow wire.

3) Turn ignition switch to RUN position. Measure voltage between instrument cluster connector C236 terminal No. 2 and ground. If voltage is more than 10 volts, go to next step. If voltage is 10 volts or less, repair Red/Light Green wire.

4) Turn ignition off. Measure resistance between instrument cluster connector C236 terminal No. 1 and ground. If resistance is less than 5 ohms, go to next step. If resistance is 5 ohms or more, repair open in Black ground wire. Ground point is located behind right kick panel.

5) Disconnect instrument cluster 22-pin connector C237. Measure resistance between instrument cluster connector C237 terminal No. 17 and ground. See Fig. 2. If resistance is less than 5 ohms, see appropriate MODULE COMMUNICATIONS NETWORK to diagnose concern. If resistance is 5 ohms or more, repair open in Pink/Orange ground wire. Ground point is located behind left kick panel.

1999 ACCESSORIES & EQUIPMENT
Analog Instrument Panels – Expedition, F150 & F250 Light-Duty Pickup, & Navigator (Cont.)

FORD
4-761

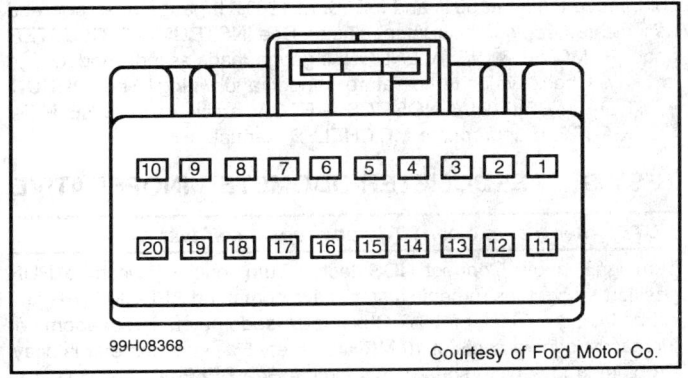

99H08368
Courtesy of Ford Motor Co.

Fig. 1: Identifying Instrument Cluster 20-Pin Connector C236 Terminals

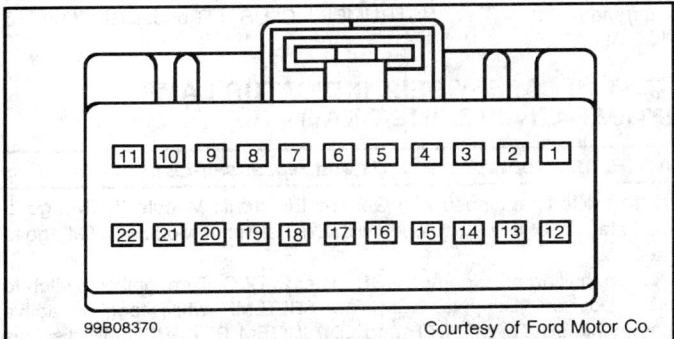

99B08370
Courtesy of Ford Motor Co.

Fig. 2: Identifying Instrument Cluster 22-Pin Connector C237 Terminals

TEST B: NO COMMUNICATION WITH GEM/CTM

NOTE: After repair, clear DTCs and repeat self-test.

1) Turn ignition off. Connect NGS tester to DLC. On manual transmission models, depress clutch pedal. Observe GEM/CTM PIDs IGN_A, IGN_S, IGN_O/L and IGN_R while turning ignition switch through all positions. If PID values agree with switch positions, go to next step. If PID values do not agree with switch positions, repair appropriate ignition switch circuit(s). See appropriate wiring diagram in POWER DISTRIBUTION article in WIRING DIAGRAMS.

2) Turn ignition off. Disconnect central junction box (interior fuse panel) 34-pin connector C243. Measure voltage between connector C243 terminal No. 11 and ground. *See Fig. 3.* If voltage is more than 10 volts, go to next step. If voltage is 10 volts or less, repair Tan/Black wire between battery junction box and central junction box.

3) Remove Generic Electronic Module/Central Timer Module (GEM/CTM) from central junction box 18-pin connector C267. See GENERIC ELECTRONIC MODULE/CENTRAL TIMER MODULE (GEM/CTM) under REMOVAL & INSTALLATION. Reconnect central junction box connector C243. Measure voltage between central junction box connector C267 terminal No. 4 (central junction box side) and ground. Also measure voltage between central junction box connector C267 terminal No. 16 (central junction box side) and ground. *See Fig. 3.* If each voltage is more than 10 volts, go to next step. If either voltage is 10 volts or less, replace central junction box.

4) Disconnect central junction box 34-pin connector C243. Measure internal resistance of central junction box between connector C243 terminal No. 11 (central junction box side) and connector C267 terminal No. 4 (central junction box side). Also measure internal resistance of central junction box between connector C243 terminal No. 11 (central junction box side) and connector C267 terminal No. 16 (central junction box side). *See Fig. 3.* If each resistance is less than 5 ohms, go to next step. If either resistance is 5 ohms or more, replace central junction box.

5) Disconnect GEM/CTM 26-pin connector C239. Measure resistance between GEM connector C239 terminal No. 26 and ground. *See Fig. 4.* If resistance is less than 5 ohms, go to next step. If resistance is 5 ohms or more, repair open in Black/Light Blue ground wire. Ground point is located behind left kick panel.

6) Measure resistance between GEM/CTM connector C239 terminal No. 14 and ground. If resistance is less than 5 ohms, problem is in module communications network. See appropriate MODULE COMMUNICATIONS NETWORK article. If resistance is 5 ohms or more, repair open in Black/Light Blue ground wire. Ground point is behind left kick panel.

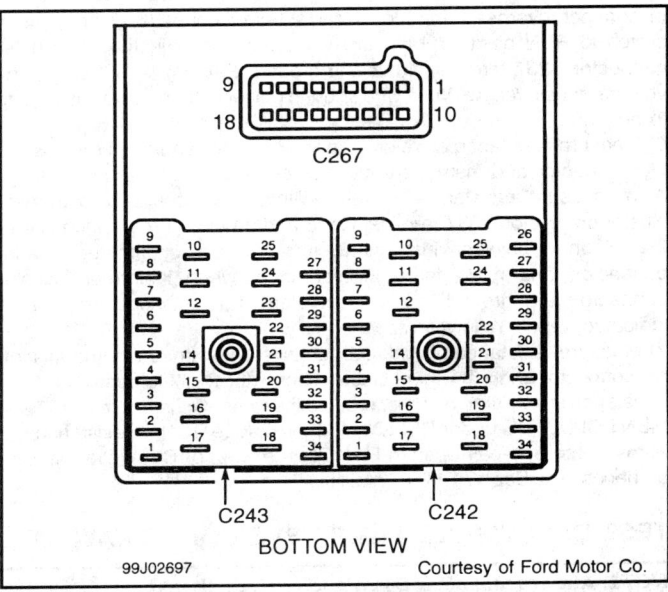

BOTTOM VIEW
99J02697
Courtesy of Ford Motor Co.

Fig. 3: Identifying Central Junction Box Connectors & Terminals

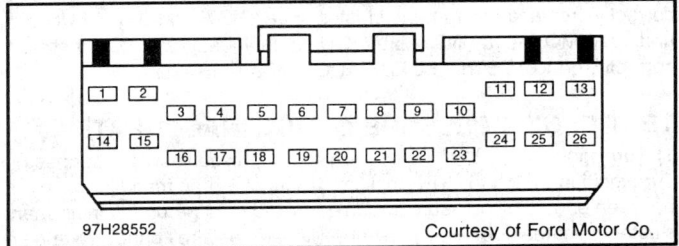

97H28552
Courtesy of Ford Motor Co.

Fig. 4: Identifying GEM/CTM 26-Pin Connector C239 Terminals

TEST C: FUEL GAUGE INACCURATE

NOTE: Fuel fills of less than 6 gallons require at least 12 minutes to update fuel gauge reading.

NOTE: After repair, clear DTCs and repeat self-test.

1) Turn ignition switch to RUN position. Select NGS tester instrument cluster FUEL LEVEL CONTROL active command. Trigger, observe and scroll FUELLEVEL at 0%, 54% and 100%. If fuel gauge displays below E with 0%, half with 54% and full stop with 100%, go to next step. If fuel gauge does not display as indicated, replace instrument cluster. See INSTRUMENT CLUSTER under REMOVAL & INSTALLATION.

2) Turn ignition off. Disconnect fuel pump assembly 4-pin connector located center of vehicle near fuel tank. Connect one lead of Instrument Gauge System Tester (014-R1063), or equivalent, to fuel pump assembly connector Yellow/White wire terminal and the other tester lead to fuel pump assembly connector Black/Orange wire terminal. Set Instrument Gauge System Tester to 15 ohms. Turn ignition switch to RUN position. Wait 5-10 minutes and read fuel gauge. Fuel gauge should read below

FORD
4-762

1999 ACCESSORIES & EQUIPMENT
Analog Instrument Panels – Expedition,
F150 & F250 Light-Duty Pickup, & Navigator (Cont.)

E. Turn ignition off. Set Instrument Gauge System Tester to 145 ohms. Turn ignition switch to RUN position. Wait 5-10 minutes and read fuel gauge. Fuel gauge should read F or above. If fuel gauge reads as indicated, to next step. If fuel gauge does not read as indicated, go to step 5).

3) Check fuel tank for any damage or deformation. If fuel tank is okay, go to next step. If fuel tank is damaged, replace fuel tank.

4) Check fuel pump assembly in-tank mounting, float, float rod, wiring and connection for damage or obstruction. If fuel pump and wiring are okay, replace fuel sender. If fuel pump assembly and/or wiring is damaged, repair or replace fuel pump as necessary. If fuel sender is damaged, repair or replace fuel pump as necessary.

5) Disconnect instrument cluster 22-pin connector C237. If equipped, disconnect overhead trip computer 20-pin connector. Turn ignition switch to RUN position. Measure voltage between instrument cluster connector C237 terminal No. 3 and ground. See Fig. 2. If there is any voltage, repair Yellow/White wire short to power. If there is no voltage, go to next step.

6) Measure resistance of Yellow/White wire between fuel pump assembly connector and instrument cluster connector C237 terminal No. 3. Also measure resistance of Yellow/White wire between instrument cluster connector C237 terminal No. 3 and ground. If resistance is less than 5 ohms between instrument cluster connector and fuel sender connector, and more than 10 k/ohms between instrument cluster connector and ground, go to next step. If resistances are not as indicated, repair Yellow/White wire.

7) Measure resistance of Pink/Orange wire between fuel pump assembly connector and instrument cluster connector C237 terminal No. 17. If resistance is less than 5 ohms, replace instrument cluster. See INSTRUMENT CLUSTER under REMOVAL & INSTALLATION. If resistance is 5 ohms or more, repair open in Pink/Orange wire, or Black/Orange wire, as necessary. See WIRING DIAGRAMS.

TEST D: LOW FUEL LAMP NEVER OR ALWAYS ON

NOTE: After repair, clear DTCs and repeat self-test.

Check fuel gauge for proper operation. If fuel gauge is operating correctly, replace instrument cluster. See INSTRUMENT CLUSTER under REMOVAL & INSTALLATION. If fuel gauge is not operating correctly, go to TEST C: FUEL GAUGE INACCURATE.

TEST E: OIL PRESSURE GAUGE INACCURATE

1) Turn ignition off. Disconnect engine oil pressure switch connector. Turn ignition switch to RUN position. Connect 5-amp fused jumper wire between engine oil pressure switch connector and ground. If instrument cluster indicates normal oil pressure with jumper wire connected and no oil pressure with jumper wire disconnected, replace engine oil pressure switch. If instrument cluster does not display as indicated, go to next step.

2) Turn ignition off. Disconnect instrument cluster 20-pin connector C236. Measure resistance of White/Red wire between engine oil pressure switch connector and instrument cluster connector C236 terminal No. 20. Also measure resistance of White/Red wire between instrument cluster connector C236 terminal No. 20 and ground. See Fig. 1. If resistance is less than 5 ohms between instrument cluster connector and oil pressure switch connector, and more than 10 k/ohms between instrument cluster connector and ground, replace instrument cluster. See INSTRUMENT CLUSTER under REMOVAL & INSTALLATION. If either resistance is not as indicated, repair White/Red wire.

TEST F: TEMPERATURE GAUGE INACCURATE

NOTE: After repair, clear DTCs and repeat self-test.

Connect NGS tester to DLC. Turn ignition switch to RUN position. Trigger instrument cluster active command ENGCOOLNT. Observe engine coolant temperature gauge while adjusting ENGCOOLNT active command to read 50% and 100%. Temperature gauge should start at

cold, move to half at 50% and full hot at 100%. If gauge does not read as indicated, replace instrument cluster. See INSTRUMENT CLUSTER under REMOVAL & INSTALLATION. If gauge reads as indicated, gauge is okay. Check water temperature sender and wiring. See CIRCUIT TEST DA in SELF-DIAGNOSTICS – EEC-V article in ENGINE PERFORMANCE in appropriate MITCHELL® manual.

TEST G: SPEEDOMETER/ODOMETER INOPERATIVE

NOTE: After repair, clear DTCs and repeat self-test.

Turn ignition off. Connect NGS tester. Turn ignition switch to RUN position. Trigger instrument cluster active command SPDOMETER and scroll in increments of 5%. Observe speedometer. If speedometer increases in increments of 10 MPH for every 5%, speedometer is okay. Problem is in vehicle speed input circuit. See SELF-DIAGNOSTICS – EEC-V article in ENGINE PERFORMANCE in appropriate MITCHELL® manual. If speedometer does not display as indicated, replace instrument cluster. See INSTRUMENT CLUSTER under REMOVAL & INSTALLATION.

TEST H: SAFETY BELT INDICATOR LAMP INOPERATIVE (CHIME OKAY)

NOTE: After repair, clear DTCs and repeat self-test.

1) If vehicle is equipped with Generic Electronic Module (GEM), go to next step. If vehicle is equipped with Central Timer Module (CTM), go to step 7).

2) Turn ignition off. Connect NGS tester to DLC. Turn ignition switch to RUN position. Observe GEM PID SBLTLMP while toggling active command SBLTLAMP OFF and ON. If GEM PID SBLTLMP displays OFF- - -, ON- - -, replace GEM. See GENERIC ELECTRONIC MODULE/CENTRAL TIMER MODULE (GEM/CTM) under REMOVAL & INSTALLATION. If PID displays OFFO-G, go to next step. If PID displays OFF-B-, go to step 5).

3) Turn ignition off. Disconnect GEM 26-pin connector C239. Connect 5-amp fused jumper wire between GEM connector C239 terminal No. 12 and ground. See Fig. 4. Turn ignition switch to RUN position. If seat belt indicator lamp lights, replace GEM. See GENERIC ELECTRONIC MODULE/CENTRAL TIMER MODULE (GEM/CTM) under REMOVAL & INSTALLATION. If seat belt indicator lamp does not light, go to next step.

4) Turn ignition off. Disconnect instrument cluster 22-pin connector C237. Measure resistance between instrument cluster connector C237 terminal No. 10 and GEM connector C239 terminal No. 12. See Figs. 2 and 4. If resistance is less than 5 ohms, replace instrument cluster. See INSTRUMENT CLUSTER under REMOVAL & INSTALLATION. If resistance is 5 ohms or more, repair open in Dark Green/Light Green wire.

5) Turn ignition off. Disconnect instrument cluster 22-pin connector C237. Turn ignition switch to RUN position. Observe GEM PID SBLTLMP while toggling active command SBLTLMP OFF and ON. If PID displays ON-B-, go to next step. If PID does not display as indicated, replace instrument cluster. See INSTRUMENT CLUSTER under REMOVAL & INSTALLATION.

6) Turn ignition off. Disconnect GEM 26-pin connector C239. Measure voltage between GEM connector C239 terminal No. 12 and ground. See Fig. 4. If there is any voltage, repair Dark Green/Light Green wire short to power. If there is no voltage, replace GEM. See GENERIC ELECTRONIC MODULE/CENTRAL TIMER MODULE (GEM/CTM) under REMOVAL & INSTALLATION.

7) Turn ignition off. Connect NGS tester. Turn ignition switch to RUN position. Observe CTM PID SBLTLMP while toggling active command SBLTLAMP OFF and ON. If PID displays OFF- - -, ON- - -, go to next step. If PID does not display as indicated, replace CTM. See GENERIC ELECTRONIC MODULE/CENTRAL TIMER MODULE (GEM/CTM) under REMOVAL & INSTALLATION.

8) Turn ignition off. Disconnect instrument cluster 22-pin connector C237 and 20-pin connector C236. Measure internal resistance of

1999 ACCESSORIES & EQUIPMENT
Analog Instrument Panels – Expedition,
F150 & F250 Light-Duty Pickup, & Navigator (Cont.)

FORD
4-763

instrument cluster between connector C237 terminal No. 10 (instrument cluster side) and connector C236 terminal No. 2 (instrument cluster side). *See Figs. 1 and 2.* If resistance is less than 5 ohms, go to next step. If resistance is 5 ohms or more, replace instrument cluster. See INSTRUMENT CLUSTER under REMOVAL & INSTALLATION.

9) Disconnect CTM 26-pin connector C239. Measure resistance between instrument cluster connector C237 terminal No. 10 and CTM connector C239 terminal No. 12. *See Figs. 2 and 4.* If resistance is less than 5 ohms, go to next step. If resistance is 5 ohms or more, repair open in Dark Green/Light Green wire.

10) Measure resistance between instrument cluster connector C237 terminal No. 10 and ground. If there is any voltage, repair Dark Green/Light Green wire short to power. If there is no voltage, replace CTM. See GENERIC ELECTRONIC MODULE/CENTRAL TIMER MODULE (GEM/CTM) under REMOVAL & INSTALLATION.

TEST I: SAFETY BELT INDICATOR LAMP DOES NOT OPERATE CORRECTLY (CHIME OKAY)

NOTE: After repair, clear DTCs and repeat self-test.

1) If vehicle is equipped with Generic Electronic Module (GEM), go to next step. If vehicle is equipped with Central Timer Module (CTM), go to step **5)**.

2) Turn ignition off. Connect NGS tester to DLC. Turn ignition switch to RUN position. Observe GEM PID SBLTLMP while toggling active command SBLTLAMP OFF and ON. If GEM PID SBLTLMP displays OFF- - -, ON- - -, replace GEM. See GENERIC ELECTRONIC MODULE/CENTRAL TIMER MODULE (GEM/CTM) under REMOVAL & INSTALLATION. If PID does not display as indicated, go to next step.

3) Turn ignition off. Disconnect GEM 26-pin connector C239. Turn ignition switch to RUN position. If safety belt indicator lamps stays on continuously, go to next step. If safety belt indicator lamp does not stay on, replace GEM. See GENERIC ELECTRONIC MODULE/CENTRAL TIMER MODULE (GEM/CTM) under REMOVAL & INSTALLATION.

4) Turn ignition off. Disconnect instrument cluster 22-pin connector C237. Measure resistance between GEM connector C239 terminal No. 12 and ground. *See Fig. 4.* If resistance is more than 10 k/ohms, replace GEM. See GENERIC ELECTRONIC MODULE/CENTRAL TIMER MODULE (GEM/CTM) under REMOVAL & INSTALLATION. If resistance is 10 k/ohms or less, repair Dark Green/Light Green wire short to ground.

5) Turn ignition off. Connect NGS tester to DLC. turn ignition switch to RUN position. Observe CTM PID SBLTLMP while toggling active command SBLTLAMP OFF and ON. If PID displays OFF- - -, ON- - -, go to next step. If PID does not display as indicated, replace CTM. See GENERIC ELECTRONIC MODULE/CENTRAL TIMER MODULE (GEM/CTM) under REMOVAL & INSTALLATION.

6) Turn ignition off. Disconnect CTM 26-pin connector C239. Turn ignition switch to RUN position. If safety belt indicator lamp stays on continuously, go to next step. If safety belt indicator lamp does not stay on, replace CTM. See GENERIC ELECTRONIC MODULE/CENTRAL TIMER MODULE (GEM/CTM) under REMOVAL & INSTALLATION.

7) Turn ignition off. Disconnect instrument cluster 22-pin connector C237. Measure resistance between CTM connector C239 terminal No. 12 and ground. *See Fig. 4.* If resistance is more than 10 k/ohms, replace instrument cluster. See INSTRUMENT CLUSTER under REMOVAL & INSTALLATION. If resistance is 10 k/ohms or less, repair Dark Green/Light Green wire short to ground.

TEST J: DOOR AJAR LAMP INOPERATIVE (CHIME OKAY)

NOTE: After repair, clear DTCs and repeat self-test.

1) If vehicle is equipped with Generic Electronic Module (GEM), go to next step. If vehicle is equipped with Central Timer Module (CTM), go to step **7)**.

2) Turn ignition off. Connect NGS tester to DLC. Turn ignition switch to RUN position. Observe GEM PID DRAJAR while toggling active command AJAR LAMP OFF and ON. If GEM PID DRAJAR displays OFF- - -, ON- - -, replace GEM. See GENERIC ELECTRONIC MODULE/CENTRAL TIMER MODULE (GEM/CTM) under REMOVAL & INSTALLATION. If PID displays OFFO-G, go to next step. If PID displays OFF-B, go to step **5)**.

3) Turn ignition off. Disconnect GEM 26-pin connector C239. Connect 5-amp fused jumper wire between GEM connector C239 terminal No. 9 and ground. *See Fig. 4.* Turn ignition switch to RUN position. If DOOR AJAR lamp lights, replace GEM. See GENERIC ELECTRONIC MODULE/CENTRAL TIMER MODULE (GEM/CTM) under REMOVAL & INSTALLATION. If DOOR AJAR lamp does not light, go to next step.

4) Turn ignition off. Disconnect instrument cluster 22-pin connector C237. Measure resistance between instrument cluster connector C237 terminal No. 5 and GEM connector C239 terminal No. 9. *See Figs. 2 and 4.* If resistance is less than 5 ohms, replace instrument cluster. See INSTRUMENT CLUSTER under REMOVAL & INSTALLATION. If resistance is 5 ohms or more, repair open in Dark Green/Orange wire.

5) Turn ignition off. Disconnect instrument cluster 22-pin connector C237. Turn ignition switch to RUN position. Observe GEM PID DRAJAR while toggling active command AJAR LAMP OFF and ON. If PID displays ON-B-, go to next step. If PID does not display as indicated, replace instrument cluster. See INSTRUMENT CLUSTER under REMOVAL & INSTALLATION.

6) Turn ignition off. Disconnect GEM 26-pin connector C239. Measure voltage between GEM connector C239 terminal No. 9 and ground. *See Fig. 4.* If there is any voltage, repair Dark Green/Orange wire short to power. If there is no voltage, replace GEM. See GENERIC ELECTRONIC MODULE/CENTRAL TIMER MODULE (GEM/CTM) under REMOVAL & INSTALLATION.

7) Turn ignition off. Connect NGS tester to DLC. Turn ignition switch to RUN position. Observe CTM PID DRAJAR while toggling active command AJAR LAMP OFF and ON. If PID displays OFF- - -, ON- - -, go to next step. If PID does not display as indicated, replace CTM. See GENERIC ELECTRONIC MODULE/CENTRAL TIMER MODULE (GEM/CTM) under REMOVAL & INSTALLATION.

8) Turn ignition off. Disconnect instrument cluster 22-pin connector C237 and 20-pin connector C236. Measure internal resistance of instrument cluster between connector C237 terminal No. 5 (instrument cluster side) and connector C236 terminal No. 11 (instrument cluster side). *See Figs. 1 and 2.* If resistance is less than 5 ohms, go to next step. If resistance is 5 ohms or more, replace instrument cluster. See INSTRUMENT CLUSTER under REMOVAL & INSTALLATION.

9) Disconnect CTM 26-pin connector C239. Measure resistance between instrument cluster connector C237 terminal No. 5 and CTM connector C239 terminal No. 9. *See Figs. 2 and 4.* If resistance is less than 5 ohms, go to next step. If resistance is 5 ohms or more, repair open in Dark Green/Orange wire.

10) Measure resistance between instrument cluster connector C237 terminal No. 5 and ground. If there is any voltage, repair Dark Green/Orange wire short to power. If there is no voltage, replace CTM. See GENERIC ELECTRONIC MODULE/CENTRAL TIMER MODULE (GEM/CTM) under REMOVAL & INSTALLATION.

TEST K: DOOR AJAR LAMP DOES NOT OPERATE CORRECTLY (CHIME OKAY)

NOTE: After repair, clear DTCs and repeat self-test.

1) If vehicle is equipped with Generic Electronic Module (GEM), go to next step. If vehicle is equipped with Central Timer Module (CTM), go to step **5)**.

2) Turn ignition off. Connect NGS tester to DLC. Turn ignition switch to RUN position. Observe GEM PID DRAJAR while toggling active command AJAR LAMP OFF and ON. If GEM PID DRAJAR displays OFF- - -, ON- - -, replace GEM. See GENERIC ELECTRONIC MODULE/

FORD
4-764

1999 ACCESSORIES & EQUIPMENT
Analog Instrument Panels – Expedition, F150 & F250 Light-Duty Pickup, & Navigator (Cont.)

CENTRAL TIMER MODULE (GEM/CTM) under REMOVAL & INSTAL-LATION. If PID does not display as indicated, go to next step.

3) Turn ignition off. Disconnect GEM 26-pin connector C239. Turn ignition switch to RUN position. If DOOR AJAR lamp stays on continuously, go to next step. If DOOR AJAR lamp does not stay on, replace GEM. See GENERIC ELECTRONIC MODULE/CENTRAL TIMER MODULE (GEM/CTM) under REMOVAL & INSTALLATION.

4) Turn ignition off. Disconnect instrument cluster 22-pin connector C237. Measure resistance between GEM connector C239 terminal No. 9 and ground. *See Fig. 4.* If resistance is more than 10 k/ohms, replace GEM. See GENERIC ELECTRONIC MODULE/CENTRAL TIMER MODULE (GEM/CTM) under REMOVAL & INSTALLATION. If resistance is 10 k/ohms or less, repair Dark Green/Orange wire short to ground.

5) Turn ignition off. Connect NGS tester to DLC. Turn ignition switch to RUN position. Observe CTM PID DRAJAR while toggling active command AJAR LAMP OFF and ON. If PID displays OFF- - -, ON- - -, go to next step. If PID does not display as indicated, replace CTM. See GENERIC ELECTRONIC MODULE/CENTRAL TIMER MODULE (GEM/CTM) under REMOVAL & INSTALLATION.

6) Turn ignition off. Disconnect CTM 26-pin connector C239. Turn ignition switch to RUN position. If DOOR AJAR lamp stays on continuously, go to next step. If DOOR AJAR lamp does not stay on, replace CTM. See GENERIC ELECTRONIC MODULE/CENTRAL TIMER MODULE (GEM/CTM) under REMOVAL & INSTALLATION.

7) Turn ignition off. Disconnect instrument cluster 22-pin connector C237. Measure resistance between CTM connector C239 terminal No. 9 and ground. *See Fig. 4.* If resistance is more than 10 k/ohms, replace instrument cluster. See INSTRUMENT CLUSTER under REMOVAL & INSTALLATION. If resistance is 10 k/ohms or less, repair Dark Green/Orange wire short to ground.

TEST L: BRAKE WARNING LAMP INOPERATIVE OR ALWAYS ON

NOTE: *After repair, clear DTCs and repeat self-test.*

1) Check the base brake system. If brakes are okay, go to next step. If brakes are faulty, repair problem. See appropriate ANTI-LOCK article in BRAKES in appropriate MITCHELL® manual.

2) Check parking brake control and brake fluid level. If parking brake control is fully disengaged and brake fluid at correct level, go to next step. If not as indicated, disengage parking brake and/or adjust fluid level.

3) Turn ignition off. Disconnect parking brake switch connector. Measure resistance between parking brake switch terminal and ground while engaging and fully disengaging parking brake control. If resistance is less than 5 ohms with parking brake engaged and greater than 10 k/ohms with parking brake fully disengaged, go to next step. If resistances are not as indicated, replace parking brake switch.

4) Turn ignition off. Disconnect instrument cluster 20-pin connector C236. Measure resistance of Light Green/Red wire between parking brake switch connector and instrument cluster connector C236 terminal No. 17. Also measure resistance of Light Green/Red wire between instrument cluster connector C236 terminal 17 and ground. *See Fig. 1.* If resistance is less than 5 ohms between instrument cluster connector and parking brake switch connector, and more than 10 k/ohms between instrument cluster connector and ground, go to next step. If either resistance is not as indicated, repair Light Green/Red wire.

5) Disconnect brake fluid level switch 3-pin connector. Measure resistances of brake fluid level switch between terminals No. 1 and 3; and between 2 and 3. *See Fig. 5.* If resistance is more than 10 k/ohms between fluid level switch terminals No. 1 and 3, and less than 5 ohms between 2 and 3, go to next step. If resistances are not as indicated, replace brake fluid level switch.

6) If vehicle is equipped with rear wheel anti-lock brakes, disconnect anti-lock brake control module 14-pin connector. Measure resistance of Dark Green/Yellow wire between instrument cluster connector C236

terminal No. 18 and ground. Also measure resistance of Tan/Light Green wire between terminal No. 19 and ground. *See Fig. 1.* If each resistance is more than 10 k/ohms, go to next step. If either resistance is 10 k/ohms or less, repair appropriate wire short to ground.

7) Measure resistance of Dark Green/Yellow wire between brake fluid level switch connector and instrument cluster connector C236 terminal No. 18. Also measure resistance of Tan/Light Green wire between brake fluid level switch connector and instrument cluster connector C236 terminal No. 19. If each resistance is less than 5 ohms, go to next step. If either resistance is 5 ohms or more, repair open in appropriate wire.

8) Measure resistance of Black wire between brake fluid level switch connector and ground. If resistance is less than 5 ohms and vehicle has rear anti-lock brakes, go to next step. If resistance is less than 5 ohms and vehicle has 4-wheel anti-lock brakes, replace instrument cluster. See INSTRUMENT CLUSTER under REMOVAL & INSTALLATION. If resistance is 5 ohms or more, repair open in Black ground wire. Ground point is located at left front radiator support.

9) Ensure rear anti-lock brake module is disconnected. Disconnect instrument cluster 20-pin connector C236. Disconnect parking brake switch 1-pin connector. Disconnect brake fluid level switch 3-pin connector. Turn ignition switch to RUN position. Observe red BRAKE lamp. If red BRAKE lamp lights, replace instrument cluster. See INSTRUMENT CLUSTER under REMOVAL & INSTALLATION. If red BRAKE lamp does not light, replace anti-lock brake module.

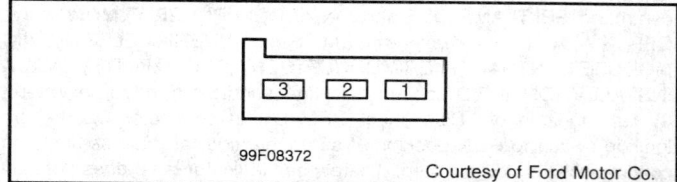

99F08372

Courtesy of Ford Motor Co.

Fig. 5: Identifying Brake Fluid Level Switch Terminals

TEST M: CHARGING SYSTEM INDICATOR LAMP INOPERATIVE OR ALWAYS ON

NOTE: *After repair, clear DTCs and repeat self-test.*

1) Check charging system operation. If charging system is operating properly, go to next step. If charging system is not operating properly, see GENERATORS – ECONOLINE, EXPEDITION, EXPLORER (4.0L OHV), PICKUP (ALL GASOLINE), MOUNTAINEER (4.0L OHV), NAVIGATOR & RANGER article in STARTING & CHARGING SYSTEMS.

2) Turn ignition switch to RUN position. If the charging system lamp lights, go to step **5)**. If charging system lamp does not light, go to next step.

3) Turn ignition off. Disconnect generator 3-pin connector. Connect 5-amp fused jumper wire between generator connector Light Green/Red wire terminal and ground. Turn ignition switch to RUN position. If charging system lamp lights, replace generator. If charging system lamp does not light, go to next step.

4) Turn ignition off. Disconnect instrument cluster 20-pin connector C236. Measure resistance of Light Green/Red wire between generator connector and instrument cluster connector C236 terminal No. 3. *See Fig. 1.* If resistance is less than 5 ohms, replace instrument cluster. See INSTRUMENT CLUSTER under REMOVAL & INSTALLATION. If resistance is 5 ohms or more, repair open in Light Green/Red wire.

5) Turn ignition off. Disconnect generator 3-pin connector. Turn ignition switch to RUN position. If charging system lamp lights, go to next step. If charging system lamp does not light, replace generator.

6) Turn ignition off. Measure resistance between generator connector Light Green/Red wire terminal and ground. If resistance is more than 10 k/ohms, replace instrument cluster. See INSTRUMENT CLUSTER under REMOVAL & INSTALLATION. If resistance is 10 k/ohms or less, repair Light Green/Red wire short to ground.

1999 ACCESSORIES & EQUIPMENT
Analog Instrument Panels – Expedition, F150 & F250 Light-Duty Pickup, & Navigator (Cont.)

FORD
4-765

TEST N: 4X4 INDICATOR LAMP INOPERATIVE OR ALWAYS ON

NOTE: After repair, clear DTCs and repeat self-test.

1) Turn ignition off. Connect NGS tester to DLC. On manual transmission models, depress clutch pedal. Observe GEM PIDs IGN_S, IGN_R, IGN_O/L and IGN_A while turning ignition switch through all positions. If PID values agree with switch positions, go to next step. If PID values do not agree with switch positions, repair ignition switch circuit(s) as necessary. See appropriate wiring diagram in POWER DISTRIBUTION article in WIRING DIAGRAMS.

2) Use GEM DTCs recorded from continuous and on-demand self-tests. If no DTCs, or DTC P1804 or P1806, are present, go to next step. If any other DTCs are present, see GEM DTC/CTM TEST INDEX table.

3) Turn ignition switch to RUN position. Observe GEM PID 4WDHIGH. Toggle GEM active command 4WDHIGH ON and OFF. 4X4 lamp should light, then go out. If 4X4 lamp operates as indicated, verify the symptom. See SYMPTOM TEST INDEX table to continue diagnosis. If 4X4 lamp does not operate as indicated and PID displays ON-B-, go to step **8)**. If 4X4 lamp stays on continuously and PID displays ONO-G, go to step **6)**. If 4X4 lamp does not light and PID displays ONO-G, go to next step.

4) Turn ignition off. Disconnect GEM 22-pin connector C241. Connect 5-amp fused jumper wire between GEM connector C241 terminal No. 9 (Light Blue wire terminal) and ground. *See Fig. 6.* Turn ignition switch to RUN position. If 4X4 lamp lights, replace GEM. See GENERIC ELECTRONIC MODULE/CENTRAL TIMER MODULE (GEM/CTM) under REMOVAL & INSTALLATION. If 4X4 lamp does not light, go to next step.

5) Turn ignition off. Disconnect instrument cluster 20-pin connector C236. Measure resistance between instrument cluster connector C236 terminal No. 4 and GEM connector C241 terminal No. 9. *See Figs. 1 and 6.* If resistance is less than 5 ohms, replace instrument cluster. See INSTRUMENT CLUSTER under REMOVAL & INSTALLATION. If resistance is 5 ohms or more, repair open in Light Blue wire.

6) Turn ignition off. Disconnect instrument cluster 20-pin connector C236. Disconnect GEM 22-pin connector C241. Measure resistance between instrument cluster connector C236 terminal No. 4 and ground. *See Fig. 1.* If resistance is more than 10 k/ohms, go to next step. If resistance is 10 k/ohms or less, repair Light Blue wire short to ground.

7) Turn ignition switch to RUN position. If 4X4 lamp is still lit, replace instrument cluster. See INSTRUMENT CLUSTER under REMOVAL & INSTALLATION. If 4X4 lamp goes out, replace GEM. See GENERIC ELECTRONIC MODULE/CENTRAL TIMER MODULE (GEM/CTM) under REMOVAL & INSTALLATION.

8) Turn ignition off. Disconnect GEM 22-pin connector C241. Disconnect instrument cluster 20-pin connector C236. Disconnect anti-lock brake control module connector (24-pin connector if 4-wheel anti-lock; 14-pin connector if rear wheel anti-lock). Turn ignition switch to RUN position. Measure voltage between GEM connector C241 terminal No. 9 and ground. *See Fig. 6.* If there is any voltage, repair Light Blue wire short to power. If there is no voltage, go to next step.

9) Using NGS tester, observe GEM PID 4WDHIGH. Toggle GEM active command HIGH LAMP to ON, then OFF. If PID displays ON-B-, replace GEM. See GENERIC ELECTRONIC MODULE/CENTRAL TIMER MODULE (GEM/CTM) under REMOVAL & INSTALLATION. If PID does not display as indicated, replace instrument cluster. See INSTRUMENT CLUSTER under REMOVAL & INSTALLATION.

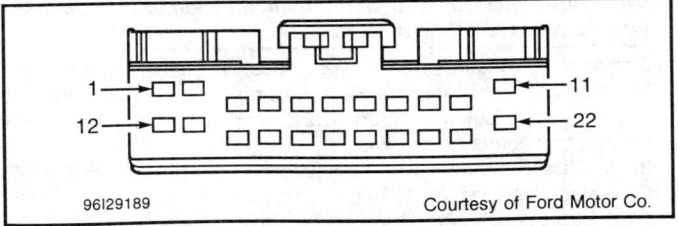

96129189   Courtesy of Ford Motor Co.

Fig. 6: Identifying GEM 22-Pin Connector C241 Terminals

TEST O: HIGH BEAM INDICATOR LAMP INOPERATIVE OR ALWAYS ON

NOTE: After repair, clear DTCs and repeat self-test.

1) Turn ignition switch to RUN position. Operate high beams. If high beams operate correctly, go to next step. If high beams do not operate correctly, see appropriate wiring diagram in EXTERIOR LIGHTS.

2) Turn ignition off. Disconnect instrument cluster 20-pin connector C236. Turn ignition switch to RUN position. Measure voltage between instrument cluster connector C236 terminal No. 12 and ground while turning high beams on and off. *See Fig. 1.* If voltage is 0 volts with high beams off and more than 10 volts with high beams on, replace instrument cluster. See INSTRUMENT CLUSTER under REMOVAL & INSTALLATION. If voltages are not as indicated, repair open in Gray/White wire.

TEST P: ABS WARNING LAMP INOPERATIVE OR ALWAYS ON

CAUTION: Use correct probe adapter(s) when testing at anti-lock brake module connector. Failure to do so may damage connector.

NOTE: After repair, clear DTCs and repeat self-test.

1) Turn ignition switch to RUN position. If ABS warning lamp is always on, see appropriate ANTI-LOCK BRAKES article in BRAKES in appropriate MITCHELL® manual for further diagnosis. If ABS warning lamp does not light, go to next step.

2) Turn ignition off. Disconnect anti-lock brake control module (24-pin connector if 4-wheel anti-lock; 14-pin connector if rear wheel anti-lock). Turn ignition switch to RUN position. If ABS lamp lights, replace anti-lock control module. See appropriate ANTI-LOCK BRAKES article in BRAKES in appropriate MITCHELL® manual. If ABS warning lamp does not light, go to next step.

3) Turn ignition off. Disconnect instrument cluster 20-pin connector C236. Measure resistance between instrument cluster connector C236 terminal No. 16 and ground. *See Fig. 1.* If resistance is more than 10 k/ohms, replace instrument cluster. See INSTRUMENT CLUSTER under REMOVAL & INSTALLATION. If resistance is 10 k/ohms or less, repair open in Dark Green wire.

TEST Q: CK SUSP LAMP INOPERATIVE OR ALWAYS ON

NOTE: After repair, clear DTCs and repeat self-test.

1) Turn ignition switch to RUN position. If CK SUSP lamp is always on, see appropriate ELECTRONIC – REAR AIR SUSPENSION, or ELECTRONIC SUSPENSION, article in SUSPENSION in appropriate MITCHELL® manual to continue diagnosis. If CK SUSP lamp does not light, go to next step.

2) Turn ignition off. Disconnect air suspension control module (Black 13-pin connector if pickup; 16-pin connector if Expedition or Navigator) connector. Connect 5-amp fused jumper wire between air suspension control module connector Dark Green/Light Green wire terminal and ground. Turn ignition switch to RUN position. If CK SUSP lamp lights, replace air suspension control module. See appropriate SUSPENSION – ELECTRONIC REAR AIR article in SUSPENSION in appropriate MITCHELL® manual. If CK SUSP lamp does not light, go to next step.

3) Turn ignition off. Disconnect instrument cluster 20-pin connector C236. Measure resistance of Dark Green/Light Green wire between air suspension control module connector and instrument cluster connector C236 terminal No. 5. *See Fig. 1.* If resistance is less than 5 ohms, replace instrument cluster. See INSTRUMENT CLUSTER under REMOVAL & INSTALLATION. If resistance is 5 ohms or more, repair open in Dark Green/Light Green wire.

FORD
4-766

1999 ACCESSORIES & EQUIPMENT
Analog Instrument Panels – Expedition,
F150 & F250 Light-Duty Pickup, & Navigator (Cont.)

TEST R: SERVICE ENGINE SOON LAMP INOPERATIVE OR ALWAYS ON

NOTE: After repair, clear DTCs and repeat self-test.

Turn ignition off. Connect NGS tester to DLC. Turn ignition switch to RUN position. Select instrument cluster INDICATOR LAMP CONTROL active command. Trigger active command MIL ON. If SERVICE ENGINE SOON lamp lights, see SELF-DIAGNOSTICS – EEC-V in ENGINE PERFORMANCE. If SERVICE ENGINE SOON lamp does not light, replace instrument cluster. See INSTRUMENT CLUSTER under REMOVAL & INSTALLATION.

TEST S: TURN/HAZARD INDICATOR LAMP INOPERATIVE OR ALWAYS ON

NOTE: After repair, clear DTCs and repeat self-test.

1) Turn ignition switch to RUN position. Operate both turn signals and hazard lamps. If turn signals and hazard lamps operate correctly, go to next step. If turn signals and hazard lamps do not operate correctly, see appropriate wiring diagram in EXTERIOR LIGHTS. For turn signal switch testing, see appropriate STEERING COLUMN SWITCHES article.

2) Turn ignition off. For right hand indicator, disconnect instrument cluster 20-pin connector C236. For left hand indicator, disconnect 22-pin connector C237. Turn ignition switch to RUN position. Measure voltage between instrument cluster connector C236 terminal No. 7 (White/Light Blue wire) and ground while multifunction switch is moved to right turn position; or between instrument cluster connector C237 terminal No. 4 (Light Green/White wire) and ground while multifunction switch is moved to left turn position. *See Figs. 1 and 2.* If voltage fluctuates between 0 volts with turn signal off and 12 volts with turn signal on, replace instrument cluster. See INSTRUMENT CLUSTER under REMOVAL & INSTALLATION. If voltage is not as indicated, repair White/Light Blue or Light Green/White wire as necessary. See appropriate wiring diagram in EXTERIOR LIGHTS.

TEST T: FUEL RESET LAMP INOPERATIVE OR ALWAYS ON

NOTE: After repair, clear DTCs and repeat self-test.

1) Check operation of FUEL RESET lamp by setting and resetting fuel inertia shutoff switch. If FUEL RESET lamp operates correctly, system is okay. If FUEL RESET lamp never lights, go to next step. If FUEL RESET lamp is always on, go to step **4)**.

2) Turn ignition off. Disconnect inertia fuel shutoff switch 3-pin connector. Connect 5-amp fused jumper wire between inertia fuel shutoff switch connector Gray/Orange wire terminal and ground. Turn ignition switch to RUN position. If FUEL RESET lamp lights, replace inertia fuel shutoff switch. If FUEL RESET lamp does not light, go to next step.

3) Turn ignition off. Disconnect instrument cluster 20-pin connector C236. Measure resistance of Gray/Orange wire between inertia fuel shutoff switch and instrument cluster connector C236 terminal No. 14. *See Fig. 1.* If resistance is less than 5 ohms, replace instrument cluster. See INSTRUMENT CLUSTER under REMOVAL & INSTALLATION. If resistance is 5 ohms or more, repair open in Gray/Orange wire.

4) Turn ignition off. Disconnect inertia fuel shutoff switch 3-pin connector. Turn ignition switch to RUN position. If FUEL RESET lamp lights, repair Gray/Orange wire short to ground. If FUEL RESET lamp does not light, replace inertia fuel shutoff switch.

TEST U: LOW WASHER LAMP INOPERATIVE OR ALWAYS ON

NOTE: After repair, clear DTCs and repeat self-test.

1) Use GEM DTCs recorded from continuous and on-demand self-tests. If B1454 is present, go to step **3)**. If B1456 is present, go to step **5)**. If no DTCs are present, go to next step.

2) Disconnect GEM 16-pin connector C240. Connect 5-amp fused jumper wire between GEM connector C240 terminal No. 14 and ground. *See Fig. 7.* Turn ignition switch to RUN position. If low washer fluid warning lamp lights, see TEST L in WIPER/WASHER SYSTEMS – EXPEDITION & NAVIGATOR article. If low washer warning lamp does not light, go to next step.

3) Turn ignition off. Disconnect GEM 16-pin connector C240. Disconnect instrument cluster 22-pin connector C237. Measure resistance between GEM connector C240 terminal No. 14 and instrument cluster connector C237 terminal No. 7. *See Figs. 2 and 7.* If resistance is less than 5 ohms, go to next step. If resistance is 5 ohms or more, repair open in Pink/Yellow wire.

4) Measure resistance between GEM connector C240 terminal No. 14 and ground. If resistance is more than 10 k/ohms, replace instrument cluster. See INSTRUMENT CLUSTER under REMOVAL & INSTALLATION. If resistance is 10 k/ohms or less, repair Pink/Yellow wire short to ground.

5) Disconnect GEM 16-pin connector C240. Disconnect instrument cluster 22-pin connector C237. Measure voltage between GEM connector C240 terminal No. 14 and ground. *See Fig. 7.* If there is any voltage, repair Pink/Yellow wire short to power. If there is no voltage, replace GEM. See GENERIC ELECTRONIC MODULE/CENTRAL TIMER MODULE (GEM/CTM) under REMOVAL & INSTALLATION.

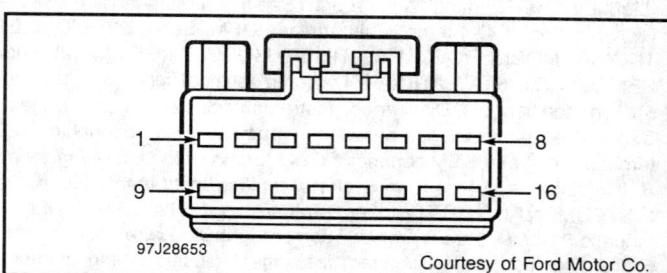

97J28653   Courtesy of Ford Motor Co.

Fig. 7: Identifying GEM 16-Pin Connector C240 Terminals

REMOVAL & INSTALLATION

CAUTION: When battery is disconnected, vehicle computer and memory systems may lose memory data. Driveability problems may exist until computer systems have completed a relearn cycle. See COMPUTER RELEARN PROCEDURES article in GENERAL INFORMATION before disconnecting battery.

GENERIC ELECTRONIC MODULE/CENTRAL TIMER MODULE (GEM/CTM)

CAUTION: Disconnect battery before disconnecting GEM or CTM connectors. Failure to do so will result in GEM/CTM storing erroneous codes and may also result in erratic operation of GEM/CTM after reconnection.

CAUTION: If replacing GEM/CTM, it is necessary to upload module configuration information to the New Generation STAR (NGS) tester. After installation this information needs to be downloaded into the new GEM/CTM module.

Removal & Installation – 1) Disconnect the battery ground cable. Remove the lower instrument panel steering column cover. Remove the bulkhead electrical connectors (C243 and C242) from the central junction box (interior fuse panel).

2) Unbolt and remove the central junction box. Disconnect the GEM/CTM electrical connectors. Remove screws and disconnect the GEM/CTM from the backside of the central junction box. To install, reverse removal procedure.

1999 ACCESSORIES & EQUIPMENT
Analog Instrument Panels – Expedition, F150 & F250 Light-Duty Pickup, & Navigator (Cont.)

FORD
4-767

HEADLAMP SWITCH

Removal & Installation – 1) Disconnect negative battery cable. Turn headlamp switch to ON position. Pull headlamp switch knob. Insert a thin tool to release headlamp switch knob and remove.

2) Reinstall headlamp switch knob 180 degrees from original position. Turn knob fully counterclockwise. Turn knob fully clockwise. Pull headlamp switch from instrument panel. Disconnect electrical connectors. To install, reverse removal procedure.

INSTRUMENT CLUSTER

CAUTION: Instrument cluster is a Hybrid Electronic Cluster (HEC). Passive anti-theft ignition key code is programmed into HEC. Car will not start without proper code. If replacing instrument cluster, it is necessary to upload HEC module configuration to NGS tester, or equivalent scan tool. Download configuration once new instrument cluster is installed.

Removal & Installation – 1) Disconnect negative battery cable. Remove headlamp switch. See HEADLAMP SWITCH. Carefully release 4 retaining clips and remove steering column opening cover.

2) Remove 7 instrument panel finish panel bolts. Remove instrument panel finish panel. Remove 4 instrument cluster bolts. Disconnect electrical connectors. Remove instrument cluster. If equipped, remove transmission range indicator. To install, reverse removal procedure.

1999 ACCESSORIES & EQUIPMENT
Analog Instrument Panels – Expedition,
F150 & F250 Light-Duty Pickup, & Navigator (Cont.)

WIRING DIAGRAMS

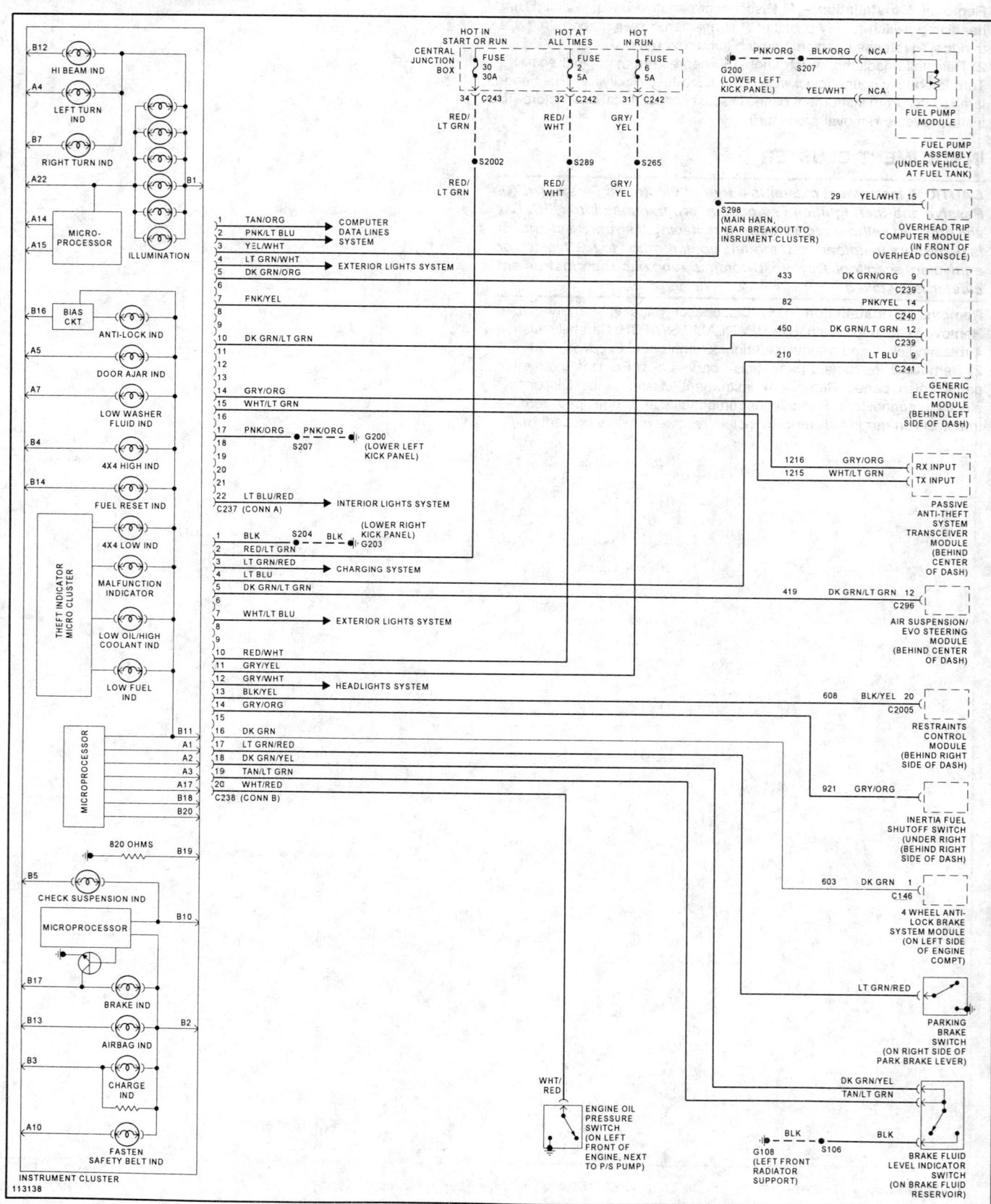

Fig. 8: Analog Instrument Panel Wiring Diagram (Expedition & Navigator)

1999 ACCESSORIES & EQUIPMENT
Analog Instrument Panels – Expedition, F150 & F250 Light-Duty Pickup, & Navigator (Cont.)

FORD
4-769

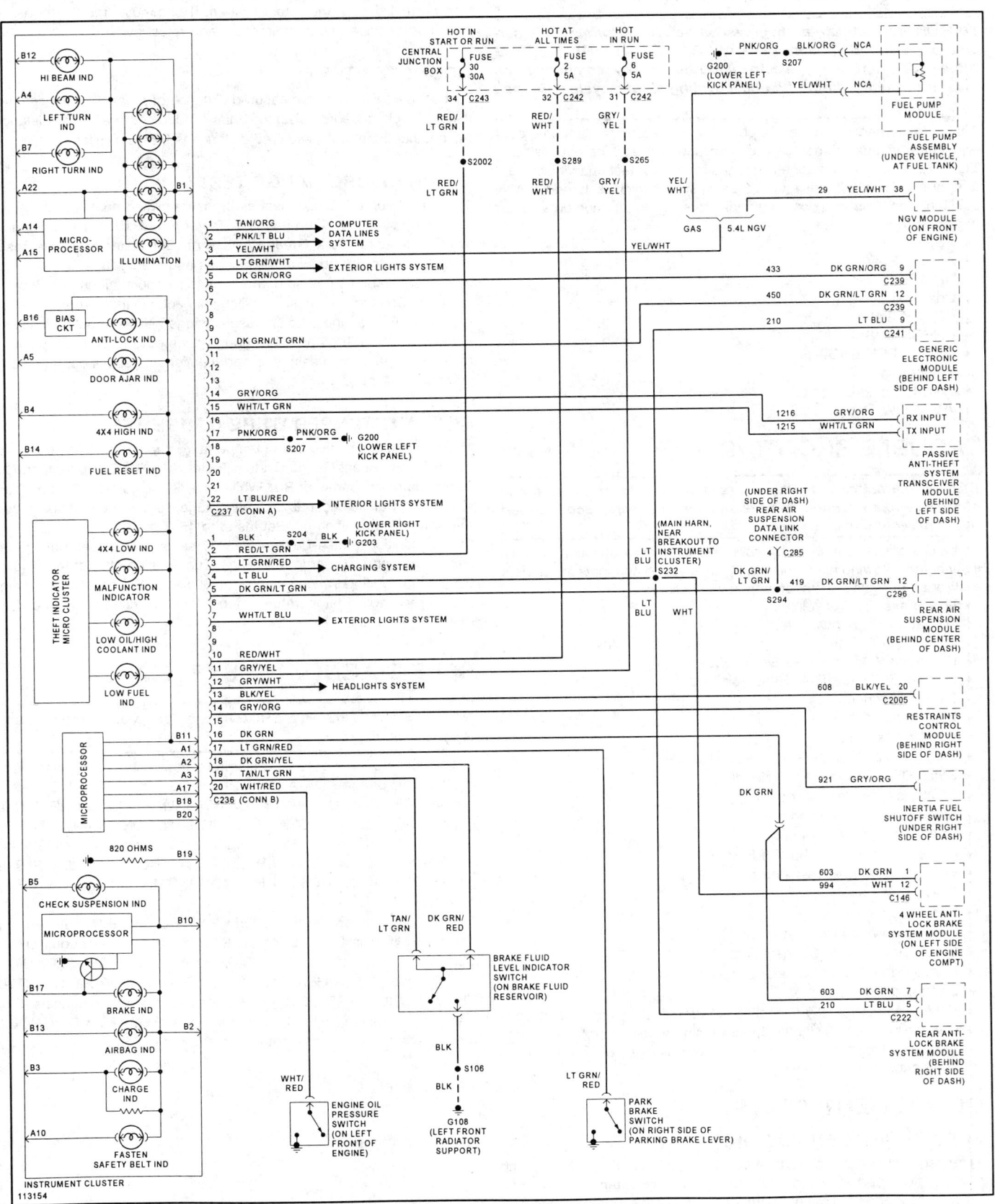

Fig. 9: Analog Instrument Panel Wiring Diagram (F150 & F250 Light-Duty Pickup)

DESCRIPTION & OPERATION

WARNING: Deactivate air bag system before performing any service operation. See appropriate AIR BAG RESTRAINT SYSTEMS article. DO NOT apply electrical power to any component on steering column without first deactivating air bag system. Air bag may deploy.

Analog instrument cluster is equipped with speedometer, tachometer (if equipped), voltmeter, fuel, oil pressure and temperature gauges. *See Fig. 1.* All models use magnetic gauges to monitor fuel quantity, coolant temperature and oil pressure. When ignition switch is turned to ON position, the following warning indicators will light momentarily for function proof:

- ABS
- Air Bag Readiness
- BRAKE
- Charging System
- CHECK GAGE
- CHECK SUS
- MIL (CHECK ENGINE)
- Safety Belt
- 4WD HIGH (if equipped)
- 4WD LOW (if equipped)

TROUBLE SHOOTING

CAUTION: Electronic modules are sensitive to static electrical charges. Proper grounding of technician and workpiece is essential to prevent damage.

Verify customers complaint by operating system in question. Visually inspect the following mechanical and electrical components for damage and repair or replace components as necessary:

- Low Brake Fluid Level
- Damaged Engine Oil Filter
- Damaged Oil Pump
- Damaged Vehicle Speed Sensor Gear
- Damaged Washer Fluid Reservoir
- Door Adjustment
- Low Engine Oil
- Low Washer Fluid
- Stuck Coolant Temperature Gauge Needle
- Stuck Oil Pressure Gauge Needle
- Stuck Voltage Gauge Needle
- Stuck Fuel Gauge Needle
- Stuck Speedometer Needle
- Tripped Inertia Fuel Shut Off Switch
- Worn Or Damaged Generator Drive Belt
- Blown Fuse(s)
- Damaged Miniature Bulbs
- Damaged Wiring Harness
- Loose Or Corroded Connections
- Damaged Instrument Cluster Printed Circuit
- Damaged Light Switches
- Verify charging system, cooling system, fuel system, safety belt warning chime, turn signals, headlights and theft control are working properly. Inspect wiring harness for obvious signs of shorts, opens, bad connections or damage.

COMPONENT TESTS

FUEL GAUGE SENDING UNIT TEST

1) Inspect fuel pump module, float and float rod for damage. If fuel pump module, float and float rod are okay, go to next step. If fuel pump module, float and float rod are damaged, replace fuel pump module and retest system.
2) Connect ohmmeter between ground and fuel pump module signal lead (Yellow/White wire). Slowly move float rod from full stop to empty

stop. If ohmmeter reading slowly decreases, check fuel gauge circuit or replace fuel gauge and retest system. If ohmmeter reading does not decrease, replace fuel pump module and retest system.

ODOMETER TEST

Test drive vehicle over a measured distance of at least 10 consecutive miles. Check measured distance against odometer measured distance. Acceptable odometer measured distance is 9.6-10.4 miles.

OIL PRESSURE GAUGE TEST

1) Turn ignition off. Disconnect oil pressure switch harness connector. Connect Instrument Gauge System Tester (014-R1063) to oil pressure switch connector Dark Green/White wire. Set tester to infinite resistance. Turn ignition on, wait 60 seconds and read gauge.
2) Center line on oil pressure gauge needle should fall on or below the "L" mark. Connect oil pressure switch connector Dark Green/White wire to ground. Center line on oil pressure gauge needle should fall slightly above mid-scale. If oil pressure gauge does not function as specified, replace gauge. If oil pressure gauge functions as specified, replace oil pressure switch.

COOLANT TEMPERATURE GAUGE TEST

1) Turn ignition off. Disconnect temperature sensor harness connector. Connect Instrument Gauge System Tester (014-R1063) to temperature sensor harness connector Red/White wire. Set tester at 300 ohms. Turn ignition on, wait 60 seconds and read gauge. Temperature gauge should read cold. Turn ignition off. Set tester to 45 ohms.
2) Turn ignition switch on and wait 60 seconds. Temperature gauge should read one quarter to mid range. Turn ignition off. Set tester to 18 ohms. Turn ignition switch on and wait 60 seconds. Temperature gauge should read hot. If temperature gauge does not function as specified, replace gauge.

SELF-DIAGNOSTIC SYSTEM

NOTE: Perform TROUBLE SHOOTING before proceeding with self-diagnostics.

1) Connect NGS tester to DLC located below instrument panel. Using NGS tester, perform DATA LINK DIAGNOSTIC TEST. If NGS tester displays CKT 914, CKT 915 or CKT 70=ALL ECUS NO RESP/NOT EQUIP, see MODULE COMMUNICATIONS NETWORK – EXPLORER & MOUNTAINEER article to diagnosis network concern. If NGS tester displays NO RESP/NOT EQUIP for Generic Electronic Module (GEM), go to TEST U: NO COMMUNICATION WITH GEM under SYSTEM TESTS.
2) If NGS tester displays SYSTEM PASSED for GEM, retrieve and record continuous DTCs using NGS tester. Erase continuous DTCs. Using NGS tester, perform GEM/CTM self-test. If any GEM/CTM DTCs are retrieved, see GENERIC ELECTRONIC MODULE/CENTRAL TIMER MODULE (GEM/CTM) DTCS table to continue diagnosis. If no DTCs are retrieved, repair by symptom. See SYMPTOM DIAGNOSIS table. Perform appropriate test under SYSTEM TESTS.

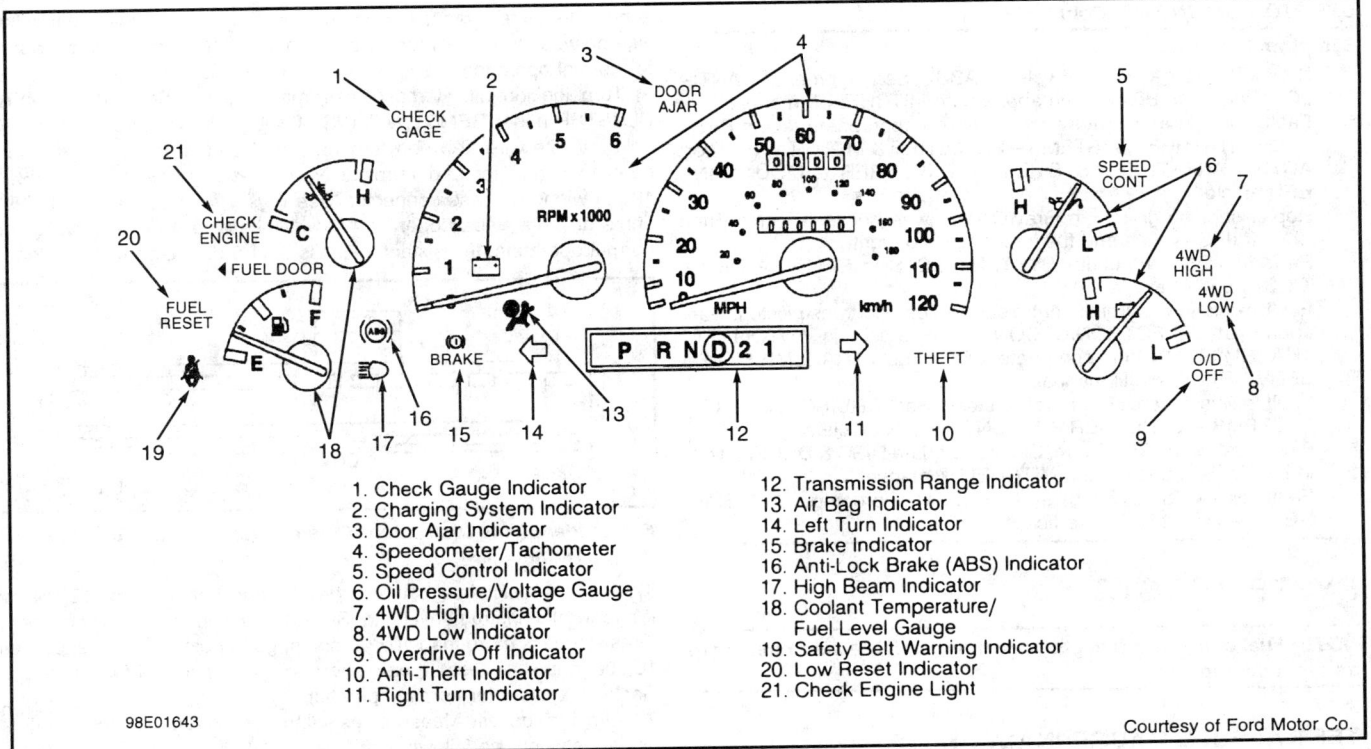

1. Check Gauge Indicator
2. Charging System Indicator
3. Door Ajar Indicator
4. Speedometer/Tachometer
5. Speed Control Indicator
6. Oil Pressure/Voltage Gauge
7. 4WD High Indicator
8. 4WD Low Indicator
9. Overdrive Off Indicator
10. Anti-Theft Indicator
11. Right Turn Indicator

12. Transmission Range Indicator
13. Air Bag Indicator
14. Left Turn Indicator
15. Brake Indicator
16. Anti-Lock Brake (ABS) Indicator
17. High Beam Indicator
18. Coolant Temperature/Fuel Level Gauge
19. Safety Belt Warning Indicator
20. Low Reset Indicator
21. Check Engine Light

98E01643

Courtesy of Ford Motor Co.

Fig. 1: Identifying Instrument Cluster Components

GENERIC ELECTRONIC MODULE/CENTRAL TIMER MODULE (GEM/CTM) DTCS

DTC [1]	Description	Test
B1323	Door Ajar Light Circuit Fault	V
B1325	Door Ajar Light Circuit Short To Voltage	V [2]
B1342	GEM/CTM Defective	
B1426	Seat Belt Light Circuit Short To Voltage	W
B1428	Seat Belt Light Circuit Fault	W
B1804	4WD High Indicator Light Circuit Fault	X
B1806	4WD High Indicator Light Circuit Short To Voltage	X
B1808	4WD Low Indicator Light Circuit Fault	X
B1810	4WD Low Indicator Light Circuit Short To Voltage	X

[1] – Codes listed in this table are only for testing covered in this article. For complete DTC listing, see MODULE COMMUNICATIONS NETWORK – EXPLORER & MOUNTAINEER article.

[2] – Using NGS tester, retrieve and document continuous DTCs. Clear all DTCs. Perform GEM/CTM self-test. If DTC B1342 is retrieved again, replace GEM/CTM.

SYMPTOM DIAGNOSIS

Symptom	Test
Fuel Gauge Inaccurate	A
Coolant Temperature Gauge Inaccurate	B
Oil Pressure Gauge Inaccurate	C [1]
Voltage Gauge Inaccurate	D
Speedometer Inaccurate	E
Speedometer/Odometer Inoperative	F
Tachometer Inoperative	G
Tachometer Inaccurate	H [1]
Charging System Warning Indicator Never/Always On	J [2]
Charging System Warning Indicator Always On	
Anti-Lock Brake Warning Indicator Inoperative	
Anti-Lock Brake Warning Indicator Always On	K [3]
Anti-Theft Indicator Inoperative	
Fuel Reset Indicator Inoperative	L [4]
Fuel Reset Indicator Always On	
High Beam Indicator Inoperative	M [5]
Check Engine/Malfunction Indicator Inoperative	
Check Engine/Malfunction Indicator Always On	N
Left Turn Signal Indicator Inoperative	P
Right Turn Signal Indicator Inoperative	

SYMPTOM DIAGNOSIS (Cont.)

Symptom	Test
Overdrive (O/D) Off Indicator Inoperative	Q [6]
Overdrive (O/D) Off Indicator Always On	[7]
Speed Control Indicator Always On	
Speed Control Indicator Never/Always On	R
Red Brake Warning Indicator Inoperative	S [8]
Red Brake Warning Indicator Always On	
Check Gauge Indicator Inoperative	T
No Communication With GEM	U
Door Ajar Indicator Does Not Operate Properly	V
Safety Belt Warning Indicator Does Not Operate Properly	W
4WD High Or 4WD Low Indicator Inoperative	X
Air Bag Indicator Inoperative	Y [9]
Air Bag Indicator Always On	Z
Check Suspension Indicator Inoperative	
Check Suspension Indicator Always On	AA

[1] – Check charging system and repair as necessary. If charging system is not functioning properly, repair as necessary. See appropriate GENERATORS article in STARTING & CHARGING SYSTEMS.

SYMPTOM DIAGNOSIS (Cont.)

Symptom **Test**

[2] – Repair Anti-Lock Brake System (ABS). See appropriate ANTI-LOCK article in BRAKES in appropriate MITCHELL® manual.

[3] – Fault exists in anti-theft system. Perform appropriate test in PASSIVE ANTI-THEFT SYSTEMS – EXPLORER & MOUNTAINEER or ACTIVE ANTI-THEFT SYSTEMS – EXPLORER & MOUNTAINEER article.

[4] – Repair short to ground in Gray/Orange wire between inertia Fuel Shutoff (IFS) switch and fuel reset indicator light.

[5] – Perform TEST NB under SYSTEM TESTS in SELF-DIAGNOSTICS – EEC-V article.

[6] – Fault exists in electronic controls for automatic transmission. See appropriate ELECTRONIC CONTROLS article in AUTOMATIC TRANSMISSIONS in appropriate MITCHELL® TRANSMISSION SERVICE & REPAIR manual.

[7] – Fault exists in cruise control system. See CRUISE CONTROL SYSTEMS – EXPLORER & MOUNTAINEER article.

[8] – Fault exists in brake system. See appropriate DISC & DRUM article in BRAKES in appropriate MITCHELL® manual.

[9] – Fault exists in air bag system. See appropriate AIR BAG RESTRAINT SYSTEMS article.

SYSTEM TESTS

NOTE: Fuel pump and fuel gauge sending unit are also referred to as fuel tank module.

TEST A: FUEL GAUGE INACCURATE

1) Turn ignition off. Disconnect fuel tank module 8-pin connector at fuel tank. *See Fig. 2.* Inspect connector for loose, damaged or corroded terminals. Repair connector as necessary. Connect one lead of Instrument Gauge System Tester (014-R1063) to terminal No. 5 (Yellow/White wire) at fuel tank module connector. Connect other tester lead to ground. Set tester to 160 ohms. Turn ignition on and wait one minute. Observe fuel gauge. Fuel gauge should read "F" (full) or higher. Turn ignition off. Set tester to 15 ohms. Turn ignition on and wait one minute. Observe fuel gauge. Fuel gauge should read "E" (full) or lower. If fuel gauge readings are as specified, go to next step. If fuel gauge reading are not as specified, go to step **4)**.

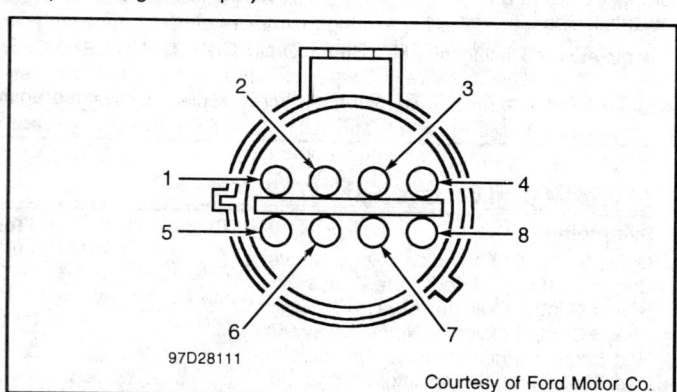

Fig. 2: Identifying Fuel Tank Module Wiring Harness Connector Terminals

2) Visually inspect fuel tank for any deformation and damage. Replace fuel tank as necessary and check system for normal operation. If fuel tank is okay, go to next step.

3) Remove fuel gauge sending unit from fuel tank. See FUEL GAUGE SENDING UNIT under REMOVAL & INSTALLATION. Inspect sending unit float and float rod for damage or obstruction. Repair float and/or float rod as necessary. Recheck system for normal operation. If float and float rod are okay, replace sending unit. Recheck system for normal operation.

4) Measure resistance between ground and terminal No. 8 (Black/Yellow wire) at fuel tank module connector. If resistance is less than 5 ohms, go

to next step. If resistance is 5 ohms or more, repair open in Black/Yellow wire between fuel tank module connector and ground. Recheck system for normal operation.

5) Turn ignition off. Remove instrument cluster. See INSTRUMENT CLUSTER under REMOVAL & INSTALLATION. Measure resistance of Yellow/White wire between terminal No. 5 at fuel tank module wiring harness connector and terminal No. 12 at instrument cluster Black 12-pin wiring harness connector. *See Figs. 2 and 3.* If resistance is 5 ohms or more, repair open in Yellow/White wire. Recheck system for normal operation. If resistance is less than 5 ohms, go to next step.

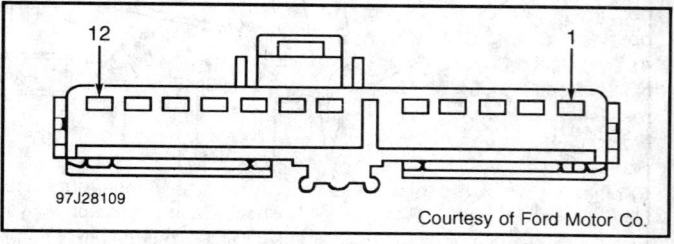

Fig. 3: Identifying Instrument Cluster Black 12-Pin Connector Terminals

6) Measure resistance between ground and terminal No. 12 (Yellow/White wire) at instrument cluster Black 12-pin wiring harness connector. If resistance is more than 10,000 ohms, go to next step. If resistance is 10,000 ohms or less, repair short to ground in Yellow/White wire. Recheck system for normal operation.

7) Turn ignition off. Measure resistance of instrument cluster printed circuit between the following:

- Fuel gauge "S" terminal and gauge amplifier terminal No. 3. Gauge amplifier is located on top left side of printed circuit board.
- Fuel gauge terminal "G" and instrument cluster printed circuit for terminal No. 2 of Black 12-pin connector.
- Fuel gauge terminal "B" and instrument cluster printed circuit for terminal No. 8 of Black 12-pin connector.
- Fuel gauge ground terminal and gauge amplifier terminal No. 5.
- Gauge amplifier and instrument cluster printed circuit terminals No. 2 and 12 of Black 12-pin connector.
- Gauge amplifier and instrument cluster printed circuit for terminal No. 1 of White 10-pin connector. *See Fig. 4.*

If all resistance readings are less than 5 ohms, replace fuel gauge and instrument cluster gauge amplifier. See GAUGES under REMOVAL & INSTALLATION. If any resistance reading is 5 ohms or more, replace instrument cluster printed circuit. See PRINTED CIRCUIT under REMOVAL & INSTALLATION. Recheck system for normal operation.

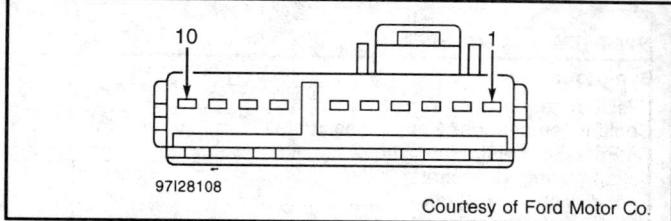

Fig. 4: Identifying Instrument Cluster White 10-Pin Connector Terminals

TEST B: COOLANT TEMPERATURE GAUGE INACCURATE

1) Perform COOLANT TEMPERATURE GAUGE TEST under COMPONENT TESTS. If temperature gauge performs properly, replace temperature gauge sender unit. Recheck system for normal operation. If temperature gauge does not perform properly, go to next step.

2) Turn ignition off. Disconnect temperature gauge sender unit 3-pin connector. Remove instrument cluster. See INSTRUMENT CLUSTER under REMOVAL & INSTALLATION. Measure resistance of Red/White wire between terminal No. 3 at instrument cluster Black 12-pin connector and temperature gauger sender wiring harness connector. *See Fig.*

3. Resistance should be less than 5 ohms. Measure resistance between ground and terminal No. 3 (Red/White wire) at instrument cluster Black 12-pin connector. Resistance should be more than 10,000 ohms. If resistance is as specified, go to next step. If resistance is not as specified, repair open or short in Red/White wire. Recheck system for normal operation.

3) Turn ignition on. Measure voltage between ground and terminal No. 1 (Red/Yellow wire) at instrument cluster White 10-pin connector. If voltage is more than 10 volts, go to next step. If voltage is 10 volts or less, repair open in Red/Yellow wire between instrument cluster connector and fuse No. 11 in interior fuse panel. Recheck system for normal operation.

4) Turn ignition off. Measure resistance between ground and terminal No. 2 (Black/White wire) at instrument cluster Black 12-pin connector. If resistance is less than 5 ohms, go to next step. If resistance is 5 ohms or more, repair open in Black/White wire between instrument cluster connector and ground. Recheck system for normal operation.

5) Measure resistance between instrument cluster temperature gauge clips "B" and "S". Resistance should be 214-256 ohms. Measure resistance between instrument cluster temperature gauge clips "G" and "S". Resistance should be 90-110 ohms. If resistance readings are as specified, replace instrument cluster printed circuit. Check system for normal operation. See PRINTED CIRCUIT under REMOVAL & INSTALLATION. If any resistance reading is not as specified, replace temperature gauge. Recheck system for normal operation. See GAUGES under REMOVAL & INSTALLATION.

TEST C: OIL PRESSURE GAUGE INACCURATE

NOTE: Ensure engine oil is at proper level and oil pressure switch connector is securely connected. Momentary drop in oil pressure is normal during hard breaking.

1) Start engine and observe oil pressure gauge. If oil pressure gauge indicates "L" (low) or below, go to step **5)**. If oil pressure gauge does not indicate "L" (low) or below, go to next step.
2) Turn ignition off. Turn ignition on and observe oil pressure gauge. If oil pressure gauge shows oil pressure, go to next step. If oil pressure gauge does not show oil pressure, system is okay.
3) Turn ignition off. Remove instrument cluster. See INSTRUMENT CLUSTER under REMOVAL & INSTALLATION. Turn ignition on. Measure resistance between ground and terminal No. 12 (Dark Green/White wire) at instrument cluster White 16-pin connector. *See Fig. 5.* If resistance is less than 5 ohms, go to next step. If resistance is 5 ohms or more, replace oil pressure gauge and recheck system operation. See GAUGES under REMOVAL & INSTALLATION.

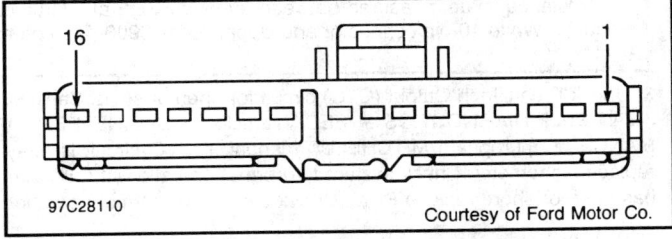

97C28110   Courtesy of Ford Motor Co.

Fig. 5: Identifying Instrument Cluster White 16-Pin Connector Terminals

4) Turn ignition off. Disconnect oil pressure switch connector. Measure resistance between ground and terminal No. 12 (Dark Green/White wire) at instrument cluster White 16-pin connector. If resistance is more than 10,000 ohms, replace oil pressure switch and recheck system operation. If resistance 10,000 ohms or less, repair short to ground in Dark Green/White wire between instrument cluster connector and oil pressure switch connector. Recheck system operation.
5) Turn ignition off. Disconnect oil pressure switch connector. Turn ignition on. Connect a fused jumper wire between ground and Dark Green/White wire at oil pressure switch wiring harness connector. Observe oil pressure gauge. If oil pressure gauge indicates in normal

range, replace oil pressure switch. Recheck system for normal operation. If oil pressure gauge does not indicate in normal range, go to next step.
6) Turn ignition off. Disconnect instrument cluster White 16-pin connector. *See Fig. 5.* Measure resistance of Dark Green/White wire between terminal No. 12 at instrument cluster White 16-pin connector and oil pressure switch wiring harness connector. If resistance is less than 5 ohms, go to next step. If resistance 5 ohms or more, repair open in Dark Green/White wire between instrument cluster connector and oil pressure switch harness connector. Recheck system for normal operation.
7) Measure resistance between instrument cluster printed circuit for terminal No. 12 of White 16-pin connector and oil pressure gauge terminal "S" clip. If resistance is less than 5 ohms, replace oil pressure gauge. Recheck system for normal operation. See GAUGES under REMOVAL & INSTALLATION. If resistance is 5 ohms or more, replace instrument cluster printed circuit. See PRINTED CIRCUIT under REMOVAL & INSTALLATION. Recheck system for normal operation.

TEST D: SPEEDOMETER INACCURATE

1) Ensure vehicle is equipped with correct size tires. If tires are correct size, go to next step. If tires are not correct size, replace with correct size tires and retest.
2) Perform ODOMETER TEST under COMPONENT TESTS. If odometer is operating and is accurate, go to SPEEDOMETER/ODOMETER INOPERATIVE test. If odometer is not operating or is not accurate, replace speedometer. See GAUGES under REMOVAL & INSTALLATION. Recheck system for normal operation.

TEST E: SPEEDOMETER/ODOMETER INOPERATIVE

1) Turn ignition off. Remove instrument cluster. See INSTRUMENT CLUSTER under REMOVAL & INSTALLATION. Measure voltage between ground and terminal No. 7 (White/Yellow wire) at instrument cluster White 10-pin connector . *See Fig. 4.* If voltage is more than 10 volts, go to next step. If voltage is 10 volts or less, repair open in White/Yellow wire between instrument cluster connector and fuse No. 25 located in interior fuse panel. Recheck system for normal operation.

NOTE: Measurements must be made at speedometer gauge pins inside instrument cluster printed circuit clips.

2) Measure resistance of printed circuit between speedometer pins (in center of clips) and corresponding instrument cluster connector terminal. See SPEEDOMETER PRINTED CIRCUIT CHECK table. *See Fig. 6.* If all resistance reading are less than one ohm, go to next step. If any resistance reading is one ohm or more, replace instrument cluster printed circuit. See PRINTED CIRCUIT under REMOVAL & INSTALLATION. Recheck system for normal operation.

SPEEDOMETER PRINTED CIRCUIT CHECK

Speedometer Pin	[1] Instrument Cluster Connector (Terminal No.)
Batt	White 10-Pin Connector (7)
"B"	White 16-Pin Connector (13)
"G"	Black 12-Pin Connector (2)
"S"	Black 12-Pin Connector (1)

[1] – See Figs. 3, 4 and 5.

3) Disconnect Anti-Lock Brake System (ABS) module 25-pin connector. ABS control module is located in left rear corner of engine compartment. Measure resistance of Gray/Black wire between terminal No. 1 at instrument cluster Black 12-pin connector and terminal No. 10 at ABS module connector. *See Fig. 7.* If resistance is less than 5 ohms, replace speedometer. If resistance is more than 5 ohms, repair open in Gray/Black wire between instrument cluster connector and ABS module. Recheck system for normal operation.

TEST F: TACHOMETER INOPERATIVE

1) Turn ignition off. Remove instrument cluster. See INSTRUMENT CLUSTER under REMOVAL & INSTALLATION. On 4.0L, measure resistance between ground and terminal No. 8 (Black/Yellow wire) at

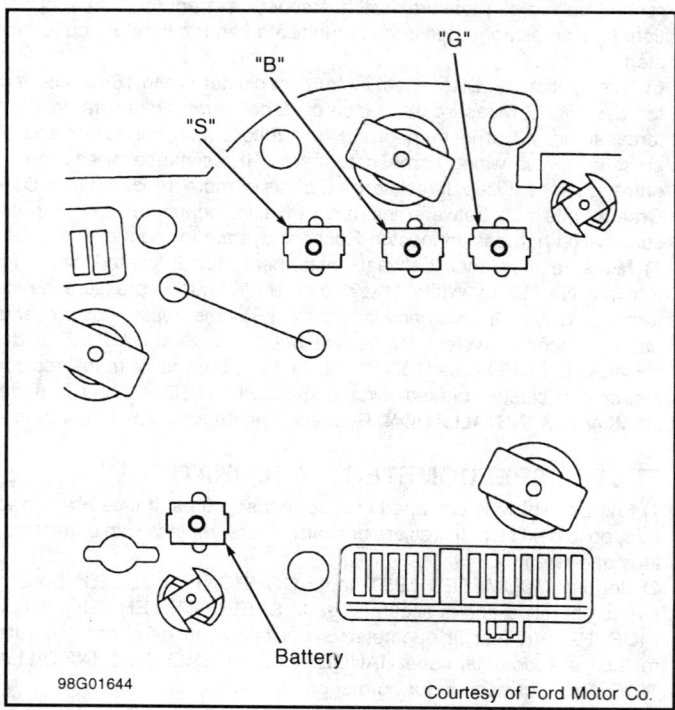

98G01644   Courtesy of Ford Motor Co.

Fig. 6: Identifying Instrument Cluster Speedometer Gauge Pins

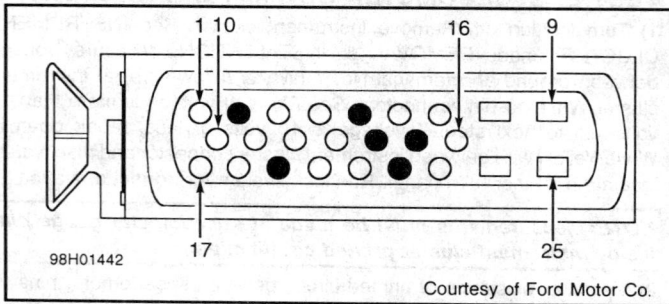

98H01442   Courtesy of Ford Motor Co.

Fig. 7: Identifying Anti-Lock Brake Module Connector Terminals

instrument cluster White 10-pin connector. *See Fig. 4.* On 5.0L, measure resistance between ground and terminal No. 16 (Black/White wire) at instrument cluster White 16-pin connector. *See Fig. 5.* On all models, if resistance is less than 5 ohms, go to next step. If resistance is 5 ohms or more, repair open in Black/White or Black/Yellow wire between instrument cluster connector and ground. Recheck system for normal operation.

2) Turn ignition off. Disconnect Powertrain Control Module (PCM). PCM is mounted on cowl in right rear of engine compartment. Install EEC-V 104-Pin Breakout Box (014-00950), leaving PCM disconnected. Measure resistance between terminal No. 15 (Tan/Yellow wire) at instrument cluster White 16-pin connector and test pin No. 48 at breakout box. If resistance is less than 5 ohms, remove breakout box. Reconnect PCM and go to next step. If resistance is 5 ohms or more, repair open in Tan/Yellow wire between instrument cluster connector and PCM. Recheck system for normal operation.

3) Start engine and allow to idle. Measure voltage between ground and terminal No. 15 (Tan/Yellow wire) at instrument cluster White 16-pin connector. If voltage is 5-8 volts, go to next step. If voltage is not 5-8 volts, replace PCM. Recheck system for normal operation.

4) Measure resistance of printed circuit between tachometer pins (in center of clips) and corresponding instrument cluster connector terminals. See TACHOMETER PRINTED CIRCUIT CHECK table. If all resistance readings are less than 5 ohms, replace tachometer. See GAUGES under REMOVAL & INSTALLATION. Recheck system for normal operation. If any resistance reading is 5 ohms or more, replace

instrument cluster printed circuit. See PRINTED CIRCUIT under REMOVAL & INSTALLATION. Recheck system for normal operation.

TACHOMETER PRINTED CIRCUIT CHECK

Tachometer Pin	[1] Instrument Cluster Connector (Terminal No.)
"B"	White 16-Pin Connector (13)
Lower "G"	Black 12-Pin Connector (2)
Upper "G"	White 10-Pin Connector (8)
4.0L	[2]
5.0L	White 16-Pin Connector (12)
"S"	White 16-Pin Connector (15)

[1] – *See Figs. 3, 4 and 5.*
[2] – Resistance value measured between terminal No. 8 at instrument cluster White 10-pin connector and Upper "G" is 3900-4700 ohms.

TEST G: TACHOMETER INACCURATE

1) Turn ignition off. Remove instrument cluster. See INSTRUMENT CLUSTER under REMOVAL & INSTALLATION. On 4.0L, measure resistance between ground and terminal No. 8 (Black/Yellow wire) instrument cluster White 10-pin connector. *See Fig. 4.* On 5.0L, measure resistance between ground and terminal No. 16 (Black/White wire) at instrument cluster White 16-pin connector. *See Fig. 5.* On all models, if resistance is less than 5 ohms, go to next step. If resistance is more than 5 ohms, repair open in Black/White or Black/Yellow wire between instrument cluster connector and ground. Recheck system for normal operation.

2) Measure resistance of printed circuit between tachometer pins (in center of clips) and corresponding instrument cluster connector terminals. See TACHOMETER PRINTED CIRCUIT CHECK table. If all resistance reading are less than 5 ohms, replace tachometer. See GAUGES under REMOVAL & INSTALLATION. Recheck system for normal operation. If any resistance reading is more than 5 ohms, replace instrument cluster printed circuit. See PRINTED CIRCUIT under REMOVAL & INSTALLATION. Recheck system for normal operation.

TACHOMETER PRINTED CIRCUIT CHECK

Tachometer Pin	[1] Instrument Cluster Connector (Terminal No.)
"B"	White 16-Pin Connector (13)
Lower "G"	Black 12-Pin Connector (2)
Upper "G"	White 10-Pin Connector (8)
4.0L	[2]
5.0L	White 16-Pin Connector (12)
"S"	White 16-Pin Connector (15)

[1] – *See Figs. 3, 4 and 5.*
[2] – Resistance value measured between terminal No. 8 at instrument cluster White 10-pin connector and Upper "G" is 3900-4700 ohms.

3) Check Clean Tach Output (CTO) circuit for open or short. See TEST JH in SELF-DIAGNOSTICS – EEC-V article in ENGINE PERFORMANCE in appropriate MITCHELL® manual. If CTO circuit is okay, replace tachometer. Check system for normal operation. If CTO circuit has open or short, replace PCM. Check system for normal operation.

TEST H: CHARGING SYSTEM WARNING INDICATOR NEVER/ALWAYS ON

1) Turn ignition off. Remove and inspect fuse No. 15 (7.5-amp) from interior fuse panel. If fuse is okay, go to next step. If fuse is blown, replace fuse and retest system. If fuse blows again, check for short to ground in Yellow wire between fuse and instrument cluster connector. Repair as necessary and recheck system for normal operation.

2) Disconnect generator voltage regulator 3-pin connector. Turn ignition on. Connect a fused jumper wire between ground and Light Green/Red wire at generator voltage regulator connector. Observe charging system warning indicator. If warning indicator is on, repair charging system as necessary. See appropriate GENERATORS article in CHARGING & STARTING SYSTEMS. If warning indicator is off, go to next step.

3) Turn ignition off. Remove instrument cluster. See INSTRUMENT CLUSTER under REMOVAL & INSTALLATION. Turn ignition on. Measure voltage between ground and terminal No. 2 (Yellow wire) at instrument cluster White 10-pin connector. See Fig. 4. If voltage is more than 10 volts, go to next step. If voltage is 10 volts or less, repair open in Yellow wire between instrument cluster connector and fuse panel. Recheck system for normal operation.

4) Turn ignition off. Measure resistance of Light Green/Red wire between terminal No. 3 at instrument cluster White 10-pin connector and generator voltage regulator connector. If resistance is less than 5 ohms, go to next step. If resistance is 5 ohms or more, repair open in Light Green/Red wire between instrument cluster connector and generator voltage regulator connector. Recheck system for normal operation.

5) Check continuity between terminals of charging system warning indicator bulb. If continuity exists, replace instrument cluster printed circuit. See PRINTED CIRCUIT under REMOVAL & INSTALLATION. Recheck system for normal operation. If continuity does not exist, replace bulb. Check system for normal operation.

TEST J: ANTI-LOCK BRAKE WARNING INDICATOR INOPERATIVE

1) Turn ignition off. Disconnect Anti-Lock Brake System (ABS) module. ABS module is located in left rear corner of engine compartment. Install 60-pin Breakout Box (014-00322), leaving ABS module disconnected. Turn ignition on. Connect a fused jumper wire between ground and test pin No. 16 at breakout box. If anti-lock brake warning indicator is on, repair anti-lock brake system as necessary and retest system. If anti-lock brake warning indicator is off, go to next step.

2) Check continuity between terminals of anti-lock brake warning indicator bulb. If continuity exists, go to next step. If continuity does not exist, replace bulb. Check system for normal operation.

3) Turn ignition off. Remove instrument cluster. See INSTRUMENT CLUSTER under REMOVAL & INSTALLATION. Measure resistance between terminal No. 6 (Dark Green wire) at instrument cluster White 10-pin connector and test pin No. 16 at breakout box. See Fig. 4. If resistance is less than 5 ohms, replace instrument cluster printed circuit. See PRINTED CIRCUIT under REMOVAL & INSTALLATION. Recheck system for normal operation. If resistance is more than 5 ohms, repair open in Dark Green wire between instrument cluster connector and ABS module connector. Recheck system for normal operation.

TEST K: FUEL RESET INDICATOR INOPERATIVE

1) Turn ignition off. Disconnect Inertia Fuel Shutoff (IFS) switch connector. Switch is located under instrument panel, below radio. Turn ignition on. Connect a fused jumper wire between ground and Gray/Orange wire at IFS switch connector Gray/Orange wire. If fuel reset indicator is on, IFS switch has been tripped (button up) or switch is defective. Check IFS switch. See ENGINE SENSORS & SWITCHES in SYSTEM & COMPONENT TESTING – EEC-V article. If fuel reset indicator does not illuminate, go to next step.

2) Turn ignition off. Remove instrument cluster. See INSTRUMENT CLUSTER under REMOVAL & INSTALLATION. Remove fuel reset indicator bulb. Check for continuity between fuel reset indicator bulb terminals. If continuity exists, bulb is okay. Go to next step. If continuity does not exist, bulb is defective. Replace bulb. Recheck system for normal operation.

3) Measure resistance of Gray/Orange wire between terminal No. 10 at instrument cluster Black 12-pin connector and IFS switch connector. See Fig. 3. If resistance is less than 5 ohms, replace instrument cluster printed circuit. See PRINTED CIRCUIT under REMOVAL & INSTALLATION. Recheck system for normal operation. If resistance is 5 ohms or more, repair open Gray/Orange wire between instrument cluster connector and IFS switch connector. Recheck system for normal operation.

TEST L: HIGH BEAM INDICATOR INOPERATIVE

1) Turn ignition off. Remove instrument cluster. See INSTRUMENT CLUSTER under REMOVAL & INSTALLATION. Turn ignition switch on. Turn headlight switch on. Set multifunction switch to high-beam. Mea-

sure voltage between ground and terminal No. 6 (Light Green/Black wire) at instrument cluster Black 12-pin connector. See Fig. 3. If voltage is more than 10 volts, go to next step. If voltage is 10 volts or less, repair open in Light Green/Black wire between instrument cluster connector and multifunction switch. See WIRING DIAGRAMS. Recheck system for normal operation.

2) Turn ignition off. Measure resistance between ground and terminal No. 7 (Black wire) at instrument cluster Black 12-pin connector. If resistance is less than 5 ohms, go to next step. If resistance 5 ohms or more, repair open in Black wire between instrument cluster connector and ground. Recheck system for normal operation.

3) Remove high beam indicator bulb. Check for continuity between high beam indicator bulb terminals. If continuity exists, replace printed circuit. See PRINTED CIRCUIT under REMOVAL & INSTALLATION. Recheck system for normal operation. If continuity does not exist, replace bulb and recheck system for normal operation.

TEST M: CHECK ENGINE/MALFUNCTION WARNING INDICATOR INOPERATIVE

1) Turn ignition off. Disconnect Powertrain Control Module (PCM) connector. PCM is mounted on cowl in right rear of engine compartment. Install EEC-V 104-Pin Breakout Box (014-00950), leaving PCM disconnected. Turn ignition on. Connect a fused jumper wire between test pins No. 2 and 24 at breakout box. If check engine warning indicator is on, check engine warning indicator circuits. See TEST NB, step 2) in SELF-DIAGNOSTICS – EEC-V article in ENGINE PERFORMANCE in appropriate MITCHELL® manual. If check engine warning indicator is off, go to next step.

2) Turn ignition off. Remove instrument cluster. See INSTRUMENT CLUSTER under REMOVAL & INSTALLATION. Remove check engine warning indicator bulb and check continuity between bulb terminals. If continuity exists, go to next step. If continuity does not exist, replace bulb. Recheck system for normal operation.

3) Measure resistance between test pin No. 2 and terminal No. 9 (Pink/Light Green wire) at instrument cluster Black 12-pin connector. See Fig. 3. If resistance is less than 5 ohms, replace instrument cluster printed circuit. See PRINTED CIRCUIT under REMOVAL & INSTALLATION. Recheck system for normal operation. If resistance is 5 ohms or more, repair open in Pink/Light Green wire between instrument cluster connector and PCM connector. See WIRING DIAGRAMS. Recheck system for normal operation.

TEST N: LEFT TURN SIGNAL INDICATOR INOPERATIVE

1) Turn ignition off. Remove instrument cluster. See INSTRUMENT CLUSTER under REMOVAL & INSTALLATION. Turn ignition on. Place multifunction switch in left turn position. Measure voltage between ground and terminal No. 5 (Light Green/White wire) at instrument cluster Black 12-pin connector. See Fig. 3. If voltage varies from zero volts to more than 10 volts, go to next step. If voltage does not vary from zero volts to more than 10 volts, repair open in Light Green/White wire between instrument cluster connector and multifunction switch. Recheck system for normal operation.

2) Turn ignition off. Measure resistance between ground and terminal No. 7 (Black wire) at instrument cluster Black 12-pin connector. If resistance is less than 5 ohms, go to next step. If resistance is 5 ohms or more, repair open in Black wire between instrument cluster connector and ground. Recheck system for normal operation.

3) Remove left turn indicator bulb and check for continuity between bulb terminals. If continuity exists, replace instrument cluster printed circuit. See PRINTED CIRCUIT under REMOVAL & INSTALLATION. Recheck system for normal operation. If continuity does not exist, replace bulb. Recheck system for normal operation.

TEST P: RIGHT TURN SIGNAL INDICATOR INOPERATIVE

1) Turn ignition off. Remove instrument cluster. See INSTRUMENT CLUSTER under REMOVAL & INSTALLATION. Turn ignition on. Place multifunction switch in right turn position. Measure voltage between ground and terminal No. 10 (White/Light Blue wire) at instrument cluster White 16-pin connector. *See Fig. 5.* If voltage varies from zero volts to more than 10 volts, go to next step. If voltage does not vary from zero to more than 10 volts, repair open in White/Light Blue wire between instrument cluster connector and multifunction switch. Recheck system for normal operation.

2) Turn ignition off. Measure resistance between ground and terminal No. 7 (Black wire) at instrument cluster Black 12-pin connector. *See Fig. 3.* If resistance is less than 5 ohms, go to next step. If resistance is 5 ohms or more, repair open in Black wire between instrument cluster connector and ground. Recheck system for normal operation.

3) Remove right turn indicator bulb and check for continuity between bulb terminals. If continuity exists, replace instrument cluster printed circuit. See PRINTED CIRCUIT under REMOVAL & INSTALLATION. Recheck system for normal operation. If continuity does not exist, replace bulb. Recheck system for normal operation.

TEST Q: OVERDRIVE (O/D) OFF INDICATOR INOPERATIVE

1) Road test vehicle to check overdrive operation. If overdrive operates properly, go to next step. If overdrive does not operate properly, go to appropriate ELECTRONIC CONTROLS article in AUTOMATIC TRANS-MISSIONS in appropriate MITCHELL® TRANSMISSION SERVICE & REPAIR manual to continue diagnosis.

2) Turn ignition off. Disconnect Powertrain Control Module (PCM) connector. PCM is mounted on cowl in right rear of engine compartment. Install EEC-V 104-Pin Breakout Box (014-00950), leaving PCM disconnected. Turn ignition on. Connect a fused jumper wire between test pins No. 24 and 79 at breakout box. Cycle headlight switch off then on. If O/D OFF indicator is on, go to appropriate ELECTRONIC CONTROLS article in AUTOMATIC TRANSMISSIONS in appropriate MITCHELL® TRANSMISSION SERVICE & REPAIR manual to continue diagnosis. If O/D OFF indicator is off with headlights on, go to next step. If O/D OFF indicator is off with headlights off, go to step **4)**. If O/D OFF indicator is off with headlights off or on, go to step **5)** .

3) Turn ignition off. Disconnect headlight switch connector located under left side of instrument panel. *See Fig. 8.* Turn ignition on. Rotate dimmer wheel to full bright position. Measure voltage between ground and terminal No. 9 (Red/Black wire) at headlight switch connector. If voltage is more than 10 volts, replace headlight switch. Recheck system for normal operation. If voltage is 10 volts or less, repair open in Red/Black wire between headlight switch and splice S264. S264 is located at take out in harness near instrument cluster.

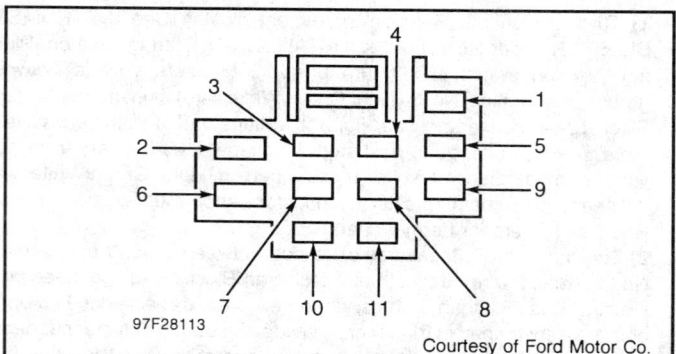

97F28113   Courtesy of Ford Motor Co.

Fig. 8: Identifying Headlight Switch Connector Terminals

4) Turn ignition off. Disconnect headlight switch connector located under left side of instrument panel. *See Fig. 8.* Turn ignition on. Measure voltage between ground and terminal No. 4 (Brown/White wire) at headlight switch connector. If voltage is more than 10 volts, replace headlight switch. Recheck system for normal operation. If voltage is 10 volts or less, repair open circuit between headlight switch and fuse No. 11 located in interior fuse panel. See WIRING DIAGRAMS. Recheck system for normal operation.

5) Turn ignition off. Disconnect headlight switch connector located under left side of instrument panel. *See Fig. 8.* Turn ignition on. Measure

voltage between ground and terminal No. 4 (Brown/White wire) at headlight switch connector. If voltage is more than 10 volts, reconnect headlight switch and go to next step. If voltage is 10 volts or less, repair open circuit between headlight switch and fuse No. 11 located in interior fuse panel. See WIRING DIAGRAMS. Recheck system for normal operation.

6) Turn ignition off. Remove instrument cluster. See INSTRUMENT CLUSTER under REMOVAL & INSTALLATION. Turn ignition on. Measure voltage between ground and terminal No. 5 (Orange/Black wire) at instrument cluster White 16-pin connector. *See Fig. 5.* If voltage is more than 10 volts, go to step **8)**. If voltage is 10 volts or less, go to next step.

7) Turn ignition off. Disconnect headlight switch connector. Measure resistance of Orange/Black wire between terminal No. 5 at instrument cluster White 16-pin connector and terminal No. 8 at headlight switch connector. *See Figs. 5 and 8.* If resistance is less than 5 ohms, replace headlight switch. Recheck system for normal operation. If resistance is 5 ohms or more, repair open in Orange/Black wire between instrument cluster connector and headlight switch connector. Recheck system for normal operation..

8) Ensure ignition is off. Disconnect Powertrain Control Module (PCM). PCM is mounted on cowl in right rear of engine compartment. Install EEC-V 104-Pin Breakout Box (014-00950), leaving PCM disconnected. Measure resistance between terminal No. 1 (White/Light Green wire) at instrument cluster White 16-pin connector and test pin No. 79 at breakout box. If resistance is less than 5 ohms, go to next step. If resistance is 5 ohms or more, repair open in White/Light Green wire between instrument cluster connector and PCM. Recheck system for normal operation.

9) Remove O/D OFF indicator bulb and check continuity between bulb terminals. If continuity exists, replace instrument cluster printed circuit. See PRINTED CIRCUIT under REMOVAL & INSTALLATION. Recheck system for normal operation. If continuity does not exist, replace bulb. Recheck system for normal operation.

TEST R: CRUISE CONTROL INDICATOR NEVER/ALWAYS ON

1) Road test vehicle to check cruise control operation. If cruise control is operating properly, go to next step. If cruise control is not operating properly, see CRUISE CONTROL SYSTEMS – EXPLORER & MOUNTAINEER article.

2) Turn ignition off. Disconnect cruise control servo connector located at right rear of engine compartment. *See Fig. 9.* Turn ignition on. Connect a fused jumper wire between ground and terminal No. 1 (Orange/Light Blue wire) cruise control connector. Cycle headlight switch off and back on. If cruise control indicator is on, replace cruise control servo. Recheck system for normal operation. If cruise control indicator is off in either headlight switch position, go to step **5)**. If cruise control indicator is off with headlight switch off, go to step **4)** . If cruise control indicator is off with headlight switch on, go to next step.

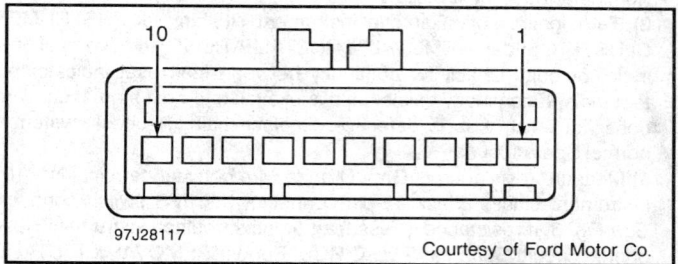

97J28117   Courtesy of Ford Motor Co.

Fig. 9: Identifying Cruise Control Servo Connector Terminals

3) Turn ignition off. Disconnect headlight switch connector located under left side of instrument panel. *See Fig. 8.* Turn ignition on. Measure voltage between ground and terminal No. 9 (Red/Black wire) at headlight switch connector. Recheck system for normal operation. If voltage is 10 volts or less, repair open in Red/Black wire between headlight switch and splice S264. S264 is located at take out in harness near instrument cluster.

4) Turn ignition off. Disconnect headlight switch connector located under left side of instrument panel. *See Fig. 8.* Turn ignition on. Measure voltage between ground and terminal No. 4 (Brown/White wire) at headlight switch connector. If voltage is more than 10 volts, replace headlight switch. Recheck system for normal operation. If voltage is 10 volts or less, repair open circuit between headlight switch and fuse No. 11 located in interior fuse panel. See WIRING DIAGRAMS. Recheck system for normal operation.

5) Turn ignition off. Disconnect headlight switch connector located under left side of instrument panel. *See Fig. 8.* Turn ignition on. Measure voltage between ground and terminal No. 4 (Brown/White wire) at headlight switch connector. If voltage is more than 10 volts, reconnect headlight switch and go to next step. If voltage is 10 volts or less, repair open circuit between headlight switch and fuse No. 11 located in interior fuse panel. See WIRING DIAGRAMS. Recheck system for normal operation.

6) Turn ignition off. Remove instrument cluster. See INSTRUMENT CLUSTER under REMOVAL & INSTALLATION. Turn ignition on. Measure voltage between ground and terminal No. 5 (Orange/Black wire) at instrument cluster White 16-pin connector. *See Fig. 5.* If voltage is more than 10 volts, go to step **8)**. If voltage is 10 volts or less, go to next step.

7) Turn ignition off. Disconnect headlight switch connector. Measure resistance of Orange/Black wire between terminal No. 5 at instrument cluster White 16-pin connector and terminal No. 8 at headlight switch connector. *See Figs. 5 and 8.* If resistance is less than 5 ohms, replace headlight switch. Recheck system for normal operation. If resistance is 5 ohms or more, repair open in Orange/Black wire between instrument cluster connector and headlight switch connector. Recheck system for normal operation..

8) Measure resistance of Orange/Light Blue wire between terminal No. 4 at instrument cluster White 16-pin connector and terminal No. 1 at cruise control servo connector. If resistance is less than 5 ohms, go to next step. If resistance is 5 ohms or more, repair open in Orange/Light Blue wire between instrument cluster connector and cruise control servo connector. Recheck system for normal operation.

9) Remove speed control indicator bulb and check for continuity between bulb terminals. If continuity exists, replace instrument cluster printed circuit. See PRINTED CIRCUIT under REMOVAL & INSTALLA-TION. Recheck system for normal operation. If continuity does not exist, replace bulb. Recheck system for normal operation.

TEST S: RED BRAKE WARNING INDICATOR INOPERATIVE

1) Turn ignition on. Apply parking brake. If Red brake warning indicator is off, go to step 5). If Red brake warning indicator is on, release parking brake and go to next step.

2) Turn ignition off. Disconnect brake fluid level switch connector (Gray 3-pin). Turn ignition on. Connect a fused jumper wire between ground and Purple/White wire at brake fluid level switch connector. If Red brake warning indicator is on, repair/replace brake fluid level switch. Recheck system for normal operation. If Red brake warning indicator is off, go to next step.

3) Turn ignition off. Remove instrument cluster. See INSTRUMENT CLUSTER under REMOVAL & INSTALLATION. Measure resistance of Purple/White wire between terminal No. 5 at instrument cluster White 10-pin connector and brake fluid level switch connector. *See Fig. 4.* If resistance is less than 5 ohms, go to next step. If resistance is 5 ohms or more, repair open in Purple/White wire between instrument cluster connector and brake fluid level switch connector. Recheck system for normal operation.

4) Remove Red brake warning indicator bulb and check for continuity between bulb terminals. If continuity exists, replace instrument cluster printed circuit. See PRINTED CIRCUIT under REMOVAL & INSTALLA-TION. Recheck system for normal operation. If continuity does not exist, replace bulb. Recheck system for normal operation.

5) Turn ignition off. Disconnect parking brake switch. Turn ignition on. Connect a fused jumper wire between ground and Light Green/Red wire at parking brake switch connector. If Red brake warning indicator is on,

replace parking brake switch. Recheck system for normal operation. If Red brake warning indicator is off, go to next step.

6) Turn ignition off. Remove instrument cluster. See INSTRUMENT CLUSTER under REMOVAL & INSTALLATION. Remove Red brake warning indicator bulb and check for continuity between bulb terminals. If continuity exists, go to next step. If continuity does not exist, replace bulb. Recheck system for normal operation.

7) Measure resistance between terminal No. 5 (Purple/White wire) at instrument cluster White 10-pin connector and Light Green/Red wire at parking brake switch connector. *See Fig. 4.* If resistance is less than 5 ohms, replace instrument cluster printed circuit. See PRINTED CIR-CUIT under REMOVAL & INSTALLATION. Recheck system for normal operation. If resistance is 5 ohms or more, repair open in Purple/White and/or Light Green/Red wire. See WIRING DIAGRAMS. Recheck system for normal operation.

TEST T: CHECK GAUGE INDICATOR INOPERATIVE

1) Start engine and observe gauges. If all gauges operate properly, go to next step. If any gauge does not operate properly, perform appropriate test for suspect gauge. Go to GENERIC ELECTRONIC MODULE/CENTRAL TIMER MODULE (GEM/CTM) DTCS.

2) Turn ignition off. Remove instrument cluster. See INSTRUMENT CLUSTER under REMOVAL & INSTALLATION. Remove gauge indicator bulb and check for continuity between bulb terminals. If continuity exists, go to next step. If continuity does not exist, replace bulb. Recheck system for normal operation.

3) Measure resistance of instrument cluster printed circuit between check gauge indicator bulb and terminal No. 8 at Black 12-pin connector. Also measure resistance of instrument cluster printed circuit between check gauge indicator bulb and at instrument cluster gauge amplifier terminal No. 2. If both resistance readings are less than 5 ohms, replace fuel gauge and instrument cluster gauge amplifier. See GAUGES under REMOVAL & INSTALLATION. Recheck system for normal operation. If any resistance reading is 5 ohms or more, replace instrument cluster printed circuit. See PRINTED CIRCUIT under REMOVAL & INSTALLA-TION. Recheck system for normal operation.

TEST U: NO COMMUNICATION WITH GEM

1) Using ohmmeter, check condition of maxi-fuse No. 1 (60-amp) in engine compartment Power Distribution Center (PDC). If fuse is okay, go to next step. If fuse is blown, replace fuse. Clear DTCs and recheck system operation. If fuse fails again, check for short to ground in Tan/Black wire between PDC and instrument panel fuse block. Repair circuit as necessary. Recheck system for normal operation.

2) Check instrument panel fuse block fuse No. 25 (7.5-amp). *See Fig. 10.* If fuse is okay, go to next step. If fuse is not okay, replace fuse. Clear DTCs and recheck system operation. If fuse fails again, check for short to ground in White/Yellow wire between instrument panel fuse block and GEM. Repair circuit as necessary. Recheck system for normal operation.

3) Measure voltage between ground and terminal No. 2 of fuse holder No. 25 at instrument panel fuse block. *See Fig. 10.* If voltage is more than 10 volts, go to next step. If voltage is 10 volts or less, repair Tan/Black wire. Clear DTCs and recheck system for normal operation.

4) Turn ignition off. Disconnect GEM 18-pin connector C283. GEM is located behind center of instrument panel. Measure voltage between ground and terminal No. 11 at GEM 18-pin connector C283 (White/Yellow wire). *See Fig. 11.* If voltage is more than 10 volts, go to next step. If voltage is 10 volts or less, repair White/Yellow wire between instrument panel fuse block and GEM. Clear DTCs and recheck system for normal operation.

5) Disconnect GEM 26-pin connector C280. Measure resistance between ground and terminal No. 14 (Black/White wire) at GEM 26-pin connector C280. *See Fig. 11.* If resistance is 5 ohms or more, repair open in Black/White wire between GEM connector and ground. Clear DTCs and recheck system for normal operation. If resistance is less than 5 ohms, repair module communication concern. See MODULE COMMUNICATIONS NETWORK – EXPLORER & MOUNTAINEER article.

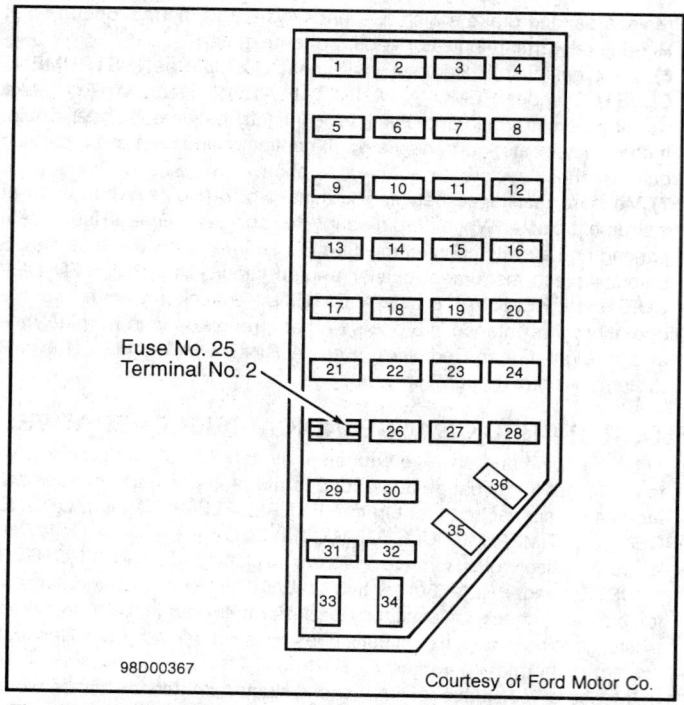

Fig. 10: Identifying Instrument Panel Fuse Block Fuse No. 25 Terminals

TEST V: DOOR AJAR INDICATOR DOES NOT OPERATE PROPERLY

1) Turn ignition off. Connect New Generation Star (NGS) tester to Data Link Connector (DLC). Using NGS tester, select GEM PID IGN_GEM from PID/DATA monitor menu. Monitor PID while turning ignition key to each position. On models with manual transmission, ensure clutch is depressed while turning ignition key to start. On all models, if PID values agree with key positions, go to next step. If PID values do not agree with key positions, repair power distribution circuit. See appropriate wiring diagram in POWER DISTRIBUTION article in WIRING DIAGRAMS.

2) Using NGS tester, perform GEM module self-test. If no DTCs are present, go to step **4)**. If DTC B1325 is present, go to step **9)**. If DTC B1323 is present, go to next step. If DTC B1342 is present, replace GEM. GEM is located behind center of instrument panel. Clear DTCs and recheck system for normal operation. If DTC B1322, B1330, B1334, B1338 or B1574 is present, check GEM/CTM PID values for suspect door ajar switch(es). See DTC IDENTIFICATION table for DTC description. See MODULE COMMUNICATIONS NETWORK – EXPLORER & MOUNTAINEER article for GEM/CTM PID list. Replace door ajar switch as necessary and recheck system operation. If PID values for door ajar switches is okay, check for short to ground in related door ajar switch circuits. See appropriate wiring diagram in ILLUMINATION/INTERIOR LIGHTS article. If switches and circuits are okay, replace GEM/CTM. Recheck system for normal operation.

DTC IDENTIFICATION

DTC	Description
B1322	Driver's Door Ajar Switch
B1330	Passenger's Door Ajar Switch
B1334	Liftgate Ajar Switch
B1338	Right Rear Door Ajar Switch
B1574	Left Rear Door Ajar Switch

3) Turn ignition on. Using NGS tester, select GEM PID DRAJR_L from PID/DATA monitor menu. Monitor PID value and toggle active command AJAR LAMP to ON then OFF. If PID value indicates ON when active command is ON and OFF when active command is OFF, replace GEM. GEM is located behind center of instrument panel. Clear DTCs and recheck system for normal operation. If PID value indicates OFF-B, go to step **9)**. If PID value indicates OFFO-G, go to next step.

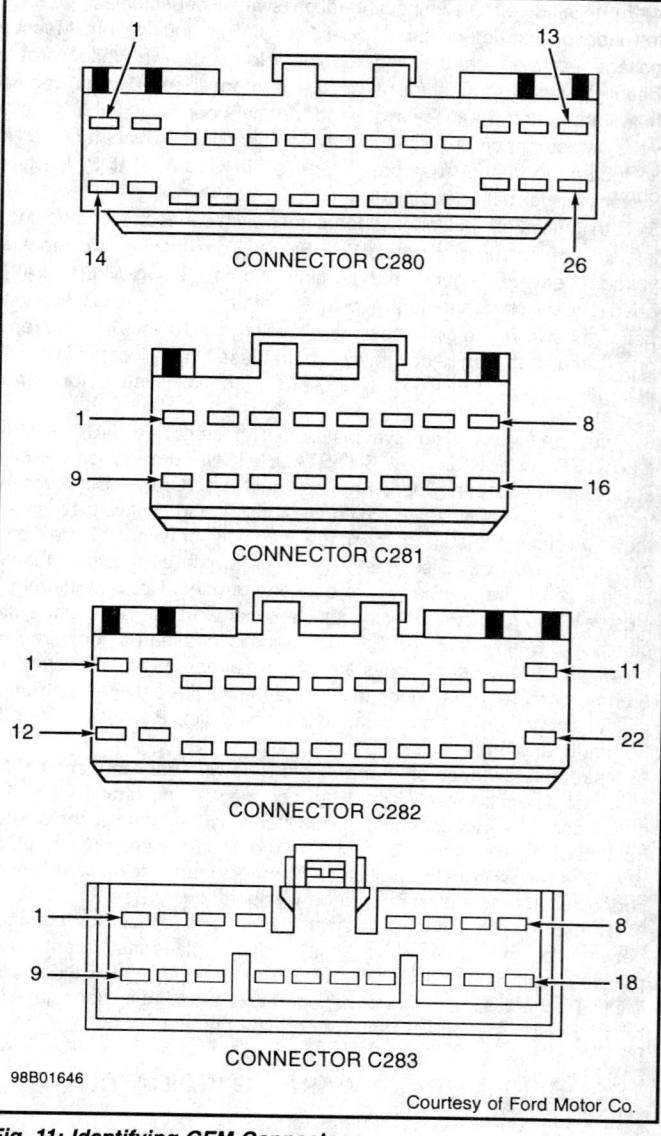

Fig. 11: Identifying GEM Connectors

4) Check oil pressure gauge and fuel gauge operation. If gauges operate properly, go to step **6)**. If gauges do not operate properly, go to next step.

5) Turn ignition off. Remove instrument cluster. See INSTRUMENT CLUSTER under REMOVAL & INSTALLATION. Turn ignition on. Measure voltage between ground and terminal No. 8 (Red/Yellow wire) at instrument cluster Black 12-pin connector. See Fig. 3. If voltage is more than 10 volts, go to next step. If voltage is 10 volts or less, repair open in Red/Yellow wire. See WIRING DIAGRAMS. Recheck system for normal operation.

6) Turn ignition off. Remove instrument cluster. See INSTRUMENT CLUSTER under REMOVAL & INSTALLATION. Measure resistance between instrument cluster printed circuit for terminal No. 11 at instrument cluster White 16-pin connector and terminal No. 8 at instrument cluster Black 12-pin connector. If resistance is less than 5 ohms, go to next step. If resistance is 5 ohms or more, check door ajar indicator bulb in instrument cluster. Replace bulb as necessary. If bulb is okay, replace instrument cluster printed circuit. See PRINTED CIRCUIT under REMOVAL & INSTALLATION. Clear DTCs and recheck system for normal operation.

7) Disconnect Generic Electronic Module (GEM) connector C280. GEM 26-pin connector C280 is located behind center of instrument cluster. Measure resistance of Black/Orange wire between terminal No. 9 at

GEM connector C280 and terminal No. 8 at instrument cluster Black 16-pin connector. *See Figs. 3 and 11.* If resistance is less than 5 ohms, go to next step. If resistance is 5 ohms or more, repair open in Black/Orange wire. Clear DTCs and recheck system for normal operation.

8) Measure resistance between ground and terminal No. 9 (Black/Orange wire) at GEM connector C280. If resistance is more than 10,000 ohms, replace GEM. Clear DTCs and recheck system for normal operation. If resistance is 10,000 ohms or less, repair short to ground in Black/Orange wire. Clear DTCs and recheck system for normal operation.

9) Turn ignition off. Remove instrument cluster. See INSTRUMENT CLUSTER under REMOVAL & INSTALLATION. Disconnect Generic Electronic Module (GEM) connector C280. GEM 26-pin connector C280 is located behind center of instrument cluster. Turn ignition on. Measure voltage between ground and terminal No. 9 (Black/Orange wire) at GEM connector C280 . If any voltage is present, repair short to voltage in Black/Orange wire. Clear DTCs and recheck system for normal operation. If no voltage is present, go to next step.

10) Using NGS tester, select GEM PID DRAJR_L from PID/DATA monitor menu. Monitor PID value and set active command ajar light OFF. If PID value indicates OFF---, replace instrument cluster printed circuit. See PRINTED CIRCUIT under REMOVAL & INSTALLATION. Clear DTCs and recheck system for normal operation. If PID value does not indicate OFF---, replace GEM. Clear DTCs and recheck system for normal operation.

TEST W: SEAT BELT WARNING INDICATOR DOES NOT OPERATE PROPERLY

1) Turn ignition off. Connect New Generation Star (NGS) tester to Data Link Connector (DLC). Using NGS tester, select GEM PID IGN_GEM from PID/DATA monitor menu. Monitor PID while turning ignition key to each position. On models with manual transmission, ensure clutch is depressed while turning ignition key to start. On all models, if PID values agree with key positions, go to next step. If PID values do not agree with key positions, repair power distribution circuit. See appropriate wiring diagram in POWER DISTRIBUTION article in WIRING DIAGRAMS.

2) Using NGS tester, perform GEM module self-test. If no DTCs are present, or DTC B1428 is present, go to next step. If DTC B1342 is present, replace GEM. GEM is located behind center of instrument panel. Clear DTCs and recheck system for normal operation. If DTC B1426 is present, go to step **9)**. If DTC B1462 is present, check for open or short in seat belt warning switch circuits. See appropriate wiring diagram in WARNING SYSTEMS article.

3) Turn ignition on. Check seat belt warning chime operation. Chime should sound for 4-8 seconds with seat belt unbuckled. If seat belt warning chime operates properly, turn ignition off and go to next step. If seat belt warning chime is not operating properly, check for open or short in seat belt warning switch circuits. See appropriate wiring diagram in WARNING SYSTEMS article.

4) Turn ignition on. Using NGS tester, select GEM PID SBLTLMP from PID/DATA monitor menu. Monitor PID and toggle active command SBLT LAMP to ON then OFF. If PID value indicates ON when active command is ON and OFF when active command is OFF, replace GEM. Clear DTCs and recheck system for normal operation. If PID value indicates ON-B, go to step **10)**. If PID value indicates OFFO-G, go to next step.

5) Check fuel gauge operation. If fuel gauge operates properly, go to step **7)**. If fuel gauge does not operate properly, go to next step.

6) Turn ignition off. Remove instrument cluster. See INSTRUMENT CLUSTER under REMOVAL & INSTALLATION. Turn ignition on. Measure voltage between ground and terminal No. 8 (Red/Yellow wire) at instrument cluster Black 12-pin connector. *See Fig. 3.* If voltage is more than 10 volts, go to next step. If voltage is 10 volts or less, repair open in Red/Yellow wire. Recheck system for normal operation.

7) Turn ignition off. Remove instrument cluster. See INSTRUMENT CLUSTER under REMOVAL & INSTALLATION. Measure resistance between printed circuit for terminal No. 10 of instrument cluster White 10-pin connector and terminal No. 8 of instrument cluster Black 12-pin connector. *See Figs. 3 and 4.* If resistance is less than 5 ohms, go to

next step. If resistance is 5 ohms or more, check seat belt warning indicator bulb in instrument cluster. Replace bulb as necessary and recheck system for normal operation.. If bulb is okay, replace instrument cluster printed circuit. See PRINTED CIRCUIT under REMOVAL & INSTALLATION. Clear DTCs and recheck system for normal operation.

8) Disconnect Generic Electronic Module (GEM) connector C280. GEM 26-pin connector C280 is located behind center of instrument cluster. Measure resistance of Yellow wire between terminal No. 12 at GEM connector C280 and terminal No. 10 at instrument cluster White 10-pin connector. *See Figs. 4 and 11.* If resistance is less than 5 ohms, go to next step. If resistance is 5 ohms or more, repair open in Yellow wire. Clear DTCs and recheck system for normal operation.

9) Measure resistance between ground and terminal No. 12 (Yellow wire) GEM connector C280. If resistance is more than 10,000 ohms, replace GEM. Clear DTCs and recheck system for normal operation. If resistance is 10,000 ohms or less, repair short to ground in Yellow wire. Clear DTCs and recheck system for normal operation.

10) Turn ignition off. Remove instrument cluster. See INSTRUMENT CLUSTER under REMOVAL & INSTALLATION. Disconnect Generic Electronic Module (GEM) connector C280. GEM 26-pin connector C280 is located behind center of instrument cluster. Turn ignition on. Measure voltage between ground and terminal No. 12 (Yellow wire) at GEM connector C280. If any voltage is present, repair short to voltage in Yellow wire. Clear DTCs and recheck system for normal operation. If no voltage is present, go to next step.

11) Using NGS tester, select GEM PID SBLTLMP from PID/DATA monitor menu. Monitor PID and set active command ajar light OFF. If PID value indicates OFFO-G, replace instrument cluster printed circuit. See PRINTED CIRCUIT under REMOVAL & INSTALLATION. Clear DTCs and recheck system for normal operation. If PID value does not indicate OFFO-G, replace GEM. Clear DTCs and recheck system for normal operation.

TEST X: 4WD HIGH OR 4WD LOW INDICATOR INOPERATIVE

1) Turn ignition off. Connect New Generation Star (NGS) tester to Data Link Connector (DLC). Using NGS tester, select GEM PID IGN_GEM from PID/DATA monitor menu. Monitor PID while turning ignition key to each position. On models with manual transmission, ensure clutch is depressed while turning ignition key to start. On all models, if PID values agree with key positions, go to next step. If PID values do not agree with key positions, repair power distribution circuit. See appropriate wiring diagram in POWER DISTRIBUTION article in WIRING DIAGRAMS.

2) Using NGS tester, perform GEM module self-test. If no DTCs or DTC P1804, P1806, P1808 or P1810 is present, go to next step. If DTC B1342 is present, replace GEM. GEM is located behind center of instrument panel. Clear DTCs and recheck system for normal operation.

3) If 4WD HIGH indicator is inoperative, go to step **7)**. If 4WD LOW indicator is inoperative, go to step **13)**. If 4WD HIGH and 4WD LOW indicators are inoperative, go to next step.

4) Turn ignition on. Verify O/D OFF indicator operation. O/D OFF indicator should be on when transmission control switch is depressed and ignition is on. If O/D OFF indicator operates properly, replace instrument cluster printed circuit. See PRINTED CIRCUIT under REMOVAL & INSTALLATION. Clear DTCs and recheck system for proper operation. If O/D OFF indicator does not operate properly, go to next step.

5) Turn ignition off. Remove instrument cluster. See INSTRUMENT CLUSTER under REMOVAL & INSTALLATION. Turn ignition on. Measure voltage between ground and terminal No. 5 (Orange/Black wire) at instrument cluster White 16-pin connector. *See Fig. 6.* If voltage is more than 10 volts, replace instrument cluster printed circuit. See PRINTED CIRCUIT under REMOVAL & INSTALLATION. Clear DTCs and recheck system for normal operation. If voltage is 10 volts or less, go to next step.

6) Turn ignition off. Disconnect headlight switch connector. Measure resistance of Orange/Black wire between terminal No. 5 at instrument cluster White 16-pin connector and terminal No. 8 at headlight switch connector terminal No. 8. *See Figs. 5 and 8.* Also, measure resistance between ground and terminal No. 5 (Orange/Black wire) at instrument cluster White 16-pin connector. If resistance is 5 ohms or more between instrument cluster and headlight switch or 10,000 ohms or less between ground and instrument cluster, repair open or short in Orange/Black wire. Recheck system for normal operation. If resistance is less than 5 ohms between instrument cluster and headlight switch and more than 10,000 ohms between ground and instrument cluster, fault exists between headlight switch and fuse No. 11 in interior fuse panel. Repair as necessary. See WIRING DIAGRAMS.

7) Turn ignition on. Using NGS tester, select GEM PID 4WDHIGH. Monitor PID and toggle active command HIGH LAMP to ON then OFF. If 4WD HIGH indicator should turn on then turn off. If 4WD HIGH indicator operates properly, go to appropriate TRANSFER CASES article in AUTOMATIC TRANSMISSIONS or MANUAL TRANSMISSIONS in appropriate MITCHELL® TRANSMISSION SERVICE & REPAIR manual to continue diagnosis. If 4WD HIGH indicator does not operate properly and PID 4WDHIGH indicates ON-B-, go to step **11)**. If 4WD HIGH indicator does not operate properly and PID 4WDHIGH indicates OFFO-G, go to next step.

8) Turn ignition off. Disconnect Generic Electronic Module (GEM) connector C282. GEM 22-pin connector C223 is located behind center of instrument cluster. Connect a fused jumper wire between ground and terminal No. 14 (Gray wire) at GEM connector C282. See Fig. 11. Turn ignition on. If 4WD HIGH indicator is on, replace GEM. Clear DTCs and recheck system for normal operation. If 4WD HIGH indicator is off, go to next step.

9) Remove instrument cluster. See INSTRUMENT CLUSTER under REMOVAL & INSTALLATION. Remove 4WD HIGH indicator bulb and check for continuity between bulb terminals. If continuity exists, go to next step. If continuity does not exist, replace bulb. Clear DTCs and recheck system for normal operation.

10) Remove instrument cluster. See INSTRUMENT CLUSTER under REMOVAL & INSTALLATION. Measure resistance of Gray wire between terminal No. 14 at GEM connector C282 and terminal No. 3 at instrument cluster White 16-pin connector. If resistance is less than 5 ohms, replace instrument cluster printed circuit. See PRINTED CIRCUIT under REMOVAL & INSTALLATION. Clear DTCs and recheck system for normal operation. If resistance is 5 ohms or more, repair open in Gray wire. Clear DTCs and recheck system for normal operation.

11) Turn ignition off. Remove instrument cluster. See INSTRUMENT CLUSTER under REMOVAL & INSTALLATION. Turn ignition on. Using NGS tester, monitor GEM PID 4WDHIGH. Toggle active command HIGH LAMP to ON then OFF. If PID value indicates ON-B-, go to next step. If PID value does not indicate ON-B-, replace instrument cluster printed circuit. See PRINTED CIRCUIT under REMOVAL & INSTALLATION. Clear DTCs and recheck system for normal operation.

12) Turn ignition off. Disconnect Generic Electronic Module (GEM) connector C282. GEM 22-pin connector C282 is located behind center of instrument cluster. Measure voltage between ground and terminal No. 14 (Gray wire) at GEM connector C282. If any voltage is indicated, repair short to voltage in Gray wire. Clear DTCs and recheck system for normal operation. If no voltage is indicated, replace GEM. Clear DTCs and recheck system for normal operation.

13) Turn ignition on. Using NGS tester, monitor GEM PID 4WDLOW. Toggle active command LOW LAMP to ON then OFF. If 4WD LOW indicator should turn on then turn off. If 4WD LOW indicator operates properly, go to appropriate TRANSFER CASES article in AUTOMATIC TRANSMISSIONS or MANUAL TRANSMISSIONS in appropriate MITCHELL® TRANSMISSION SERVICE & REPAIR manual to continue diagnosis. If 4WD LOW indicator does not operate properly and PID 4WDLOW indicates OFFO-G, go to next step. If 4WD LOW indicator does not operate properly and PID 4WDLOW indicates ON-B-, go to step **17)**.

14) Turn ignition off. Disconnect Generic Electronic Module (GEM) connector C282. GEM 22-pin connector C282 is located behind center of instrument cluster. Connect a fused jumper wire between ground and terminal No. 10 (Light Blue/Black wire) at GEM connector C282. See

Fig. 11. If 4WD LOW indicator is on, replace GEM. Clear DTCs and recheck system for normal operation. If 4WD LOW indicator is off, go to next step.

15) Remove instrument cluster. See INSTRUMENT CLUSTER under REMOVAL & INSTALLATION. Remove 4WD LOW indicator bulb and check for continuity between bulb terminals. If continuity exists, go to next step. If continuity does not exist, replace bulb. Clear DTCs and recheck system for normal operation.

16) Remove instrument cluster. See INSTRUMENT CLUSTER under REMOVAL & INSTALLATION. Measure resistance of Light Blue/Black wire between terminal No. 10 at GEM connector C282 and terminal No. 2 at instrument cluster White 16-pin connector. If resistance is less than 5 ohms, replace instrument cluster printed circuit. See PRINTED CIRCUIT under REMOVAL & INSTALLATION. Clear DTCs and recheck system for normal operation. If resistance is 5 ohms or more, repair open in Light Blue/Black wire. Clear DTCs and recheck system for normal operation.

17) Turn ignition off. Remove instrument cluster. See INSTRUMENT CLUSTER under REMOVAL & INSTALLATION. Turn ignition on. Using NGS tester, monitor GEM PID 4WDLOW. Toggle active command LOW LAMP to ON then OFF. If PID 4WDLOW indicates ON-B-, go to next step. If PID 4WDLOW does not indicate ON-B-, replace instrument cluster printed circuit. See PRINTED CIRCUIT under REMOVAL & INSTALLATION. Clear DTCs and recheck system for normal operation.

18) Turn ignition off. Disconnect Generic Electronic Module (GEM) connector C282. GEM 22-pin connector C282 is located behind center of instrument cluster. Measure voltage between ground and terminal No. 10 (Light Blue/Black wire) at GEM 22-pin connector C282. If any voltage is indicated, repair short to voltage in Light Blue/Black wire. Clear DTCs and recheck system for normal operation. If no voltage is indicated, replace GEM. Clear DTCs and recheck system for normal operation.

TEST Y: AIR BAG INDICATOR INOPERATIVE

1) Remove instrument cluster. See INSTRUMENT CLUSTER under REMOVAL & INSTALLATION. Remove air bag indicator bulb and check for continuity between bulb terminals. If continuity exists, go to next step. If continuity does not exist, replace bulb. Clear DTCs and recheck system for normal operation.

2) Visually inspect instrument cluster printed circuit for cracks, hot spots or other damage. Replace printed circuit as necessary. See PRINTED CIRCUIT under REMOVAL & INSTALLATION. Clear DTCs and recheck system for normal operation. If printed circuit is okay, check air bag system for open and short circuits. See appropriate AIR BAG RESTRAINT SYSTEMS article. Repair as necessary and recheck system for normal operation.

TEST Z: CHECK SUSPENSION INDICATOR INOPERATIVE

1) Turn ignition off. Disconnect air suspension control module Gray connector. Module is located behind left center of instrument panel. Connect a fused jumper wire between ground and terminal No. 12 at air suspension control module Gray connector. Turn ignition on. If CHECK SUSP indicator is off, go to next step. If CHECK SUSP indicator is on, repair air suspension concern. See appropriate ELECTRONIC article in SUSPENSION in appropriate MITCHELL® manual.

2) Turn ignition off. Remove instrument cluster. See INSTRUMENT CLUSTER under REMOVAL & INSTALLATION. Measure resistance of Dark Green/Light Green wire between terminal No. 12 at air suspension control module Gray connector and terminal No. 9 at instrument cluster White 10-pin connector. See Figs. 4 and 12. If resistance is less than 5 ohms, go to next step. If resistance is 5 ohms or more, repair open in Dark Green/Light Green wire. Recheck system for normal operation.

3) Turn ignition on. Measure voltage between terminal No. 13 (Red/Yellow wire) at instrument cluster White 16-pin connector. See Fig. 5. If voltage is more than 10 volts, replace printed circuit. See PRINTED CIRCUIT under REMOVAL & INSTALLATION. Recheck system for normal operation. If voltage is 10 volts or less, repair open in Red/Yellow wire. Recheck system for normal operation.

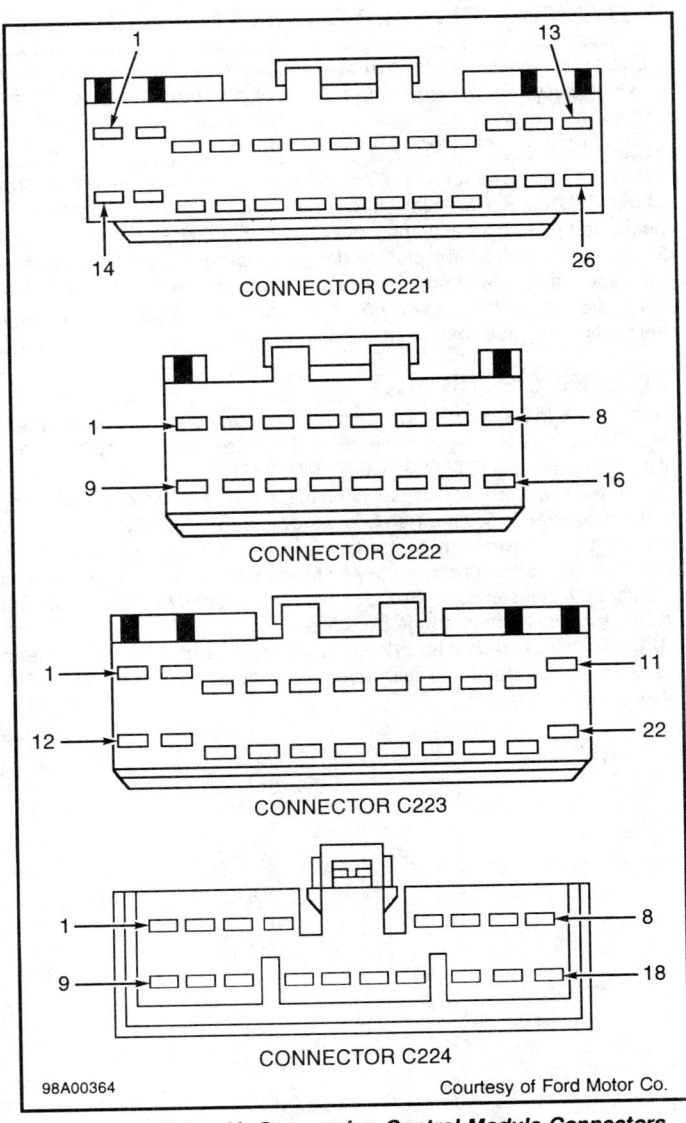

98A00364

Courtesy of Ford Motor Co.

Fig. 12: Identifying Air Suspension Control Module Connectors

TEST AA: CHECK SUSPENSION INDICATOR ALWAYS ON

Turn ignition off. Disconnect air suspension control module Gray connector. Module is located behind left center of instrument panel. Turn ignition on. If CHECK SUSP indicator is on, repair short to ground in Dark Green/Light Green wire between instrument cluster and air suspension control module. Recheck system for normal operation. If CHECK SUSP indicator is off, repair air suspension concern. See appropriate ELECTRONIC article in SUSPENSION in appropriate MITCHELL® manual.

REMOVAL & INSTALLATION

WARNING: Deactivate air bag system before performing any service operation. See appropriate AIR BAG RESTRAINT SYSTEMS article. DO NOT apply electrical power to any component on steering column without first deactivating air bag system. Air bag may deploy.

NOTE: When battery is disconnected and reconnected, some abnormal drive symptoms may occur while powertrain control module relearns its adaptive strategy. Vehicle may need to be driven 10 or more miles to relearn strategy.

FUEL SYSTEM PRESSURE RELEASE

With Fuel Pressure Gauge – Remove fuel tank cap to release fuel tank pressure. Connect Fuel Pressure Gauge (T80L-9974-B) to pressure relief valve (Schrader valve) located on fuel injection manifold rail. Using a suitable container, release fuel pressure.

Without Fuel Pressure Gauge – If fuel pressure gauge is not available, disconnect Inertia Fuel Shutoff (IFS) switch. IFS is located under instrument panel, below radio. Remove fuel cap to release fuel tank pressure. Crank engine for 15 seconds to release system pressure.

FUEL GAUGE SENDING UNIT

CAUTION: Before disconnecting any fuel line, release fuel pressure from fuel system to reduce possibility of injury or fire. See FUEL PRESSURE RELIEF. Use a rag as protection from fuel spray when disconnecting hoses. Plug hoses after disconnecting them.

Removal & Installation – 1) Turn ignition off. Disconnect battery cables. Raise vehicle on hoist. Drain fuel from tank. On 4WD models, remove skid plate from underneath fuel tank. On all models, support fuel tank with a jack. Remove fuel tank filler pipe and vent hose. Remove bolt from fuel tank support strap and remove strap.

2) Remove mounting bolts and push fuel tank back until lip on tank clears support bracket. Partially lower fuel tank to gain access to fuel lines. Disconnect fuel lines and vapor lines from fuel tank. Disconnect fuel pump/sending unit electrical connector near frame rail. Lower fuel tank from vehicle.

3) Place tank on bench. Clean dirt and debris from around fuel pump/sending unit assembly to prevent contamination of fuel. Remove fuel pump/sending mounting bolts. Remove fuel pump/sending unit assembly from fuel tank.

Installation – Clean fuel pump/sending unit mounting flange and mating surface on fuel tank. Position fuel pump/sending unit in fuel tank. Align arrow on fuel pump/sending unit flange with dimple on fuel tank. Install fuel pump/sending unit mounting bolts and tighten to 80 INCH lbs. (9 N.m). To complete installation, reverse removal procedure.

GAUGES

NOTE: Fuel gauge and instrument cluster gauge amplifier are calibrated together and cannot be serviced separately.

CAUTION: When removing gauges from instrument cluster, do not remove gauge pointers. Magnetic gauges cannot be recalibrated.

Removal & Installation – Remove instrument cluster. See INSTRUMENT CLUSTER. Remove instrument cluster gauge amplifier from top left side of instrument cluster. Remove 7 screws and instrument cluster lens and mask assembly from front of instrument cluster. Gently remove desired gauge block by grasping outside edges of gauge and lifting. Side gauge assemblies must be removed before removing center assembly. To install, reverse removal procedure. Do not reuse instrument gauge clips.

INSTRUMENT CLUSTER

CAUTION: When removing gauges from instrument cluster, do not remove gauge pointers. Magnetic gauges cannot be recalibrated.

Removal & Installation – 1) Disconnect negative battery cable. Remove rear wiper/washer switch knob. Remove center instrument panel finish panel screws. Disconnect electrical connectors and remove finish panel. Remove screws and parking brake release handle. Remove hood latch release handle from lower steering column cover. Remove screws and lower instrument panel steering column cover.

2) Remove 4 screws and instrument panel steering column opening cover reinforcement. Remove column gearshift lever and position aside (if equipped). Remove 5 screws and instrument cluster finish panel. Disconnect electrical connectors from panel.

3) Disconnect transmission range indicator (if equipped). Remove 4 instrument cluster screws. Pull instrument cluster forward and disconnect 3 connectors on back of instrument cluster. Remove instrument cluster from vehicle. To install, reverse removal procedure.

INSTRUMENT CLUSTER GAUGE AMPLIFIER

NOTE: Instrument cluster gauge amplifier is a printed circuit board assembly located in a pocket on back of instrument cluster. There are no provisions for calibration or adjustment. Amplifier and fuel gauge must be replaced as an assembly.

Removal & Installation – 1) Remove instrument cluster. See INSTRUMENT CLUSTER. Carefully depress retaining clip on component side of board and pull board assembly out of instrument cluster pocket.

2) To install instrument cluster gauge amplifier, insert into slots in instrument cluster and press home firmly with thumb on edge of board. An audible click will be heard as retaining clip engages. To complete installation, reverse removal procedure.

PRINTED CIRCUIT

Removal & Installation – 1) Remove instrument cluster. See INSTRUMENT CLUSTER. Remove instrument cluster gauge amplifier. See INSTRUMENT CLUSTER GAUGE AMPLIFIER.

2) Remove all instrument panel illumination and indicator bulbs by turning counterclockwise. Remove gauges. See GAUGES.

3) Remove 19 instrument gauge connector clips using long-nose pliers. Squeeze both sides of clip equally so locking ears pass through opening in instrument cluster case. Be careful not to overbend or distort clips. DO NOT reuse instrument gauge clips.

4) Ease instrument cluster printed circuit up and off locating pins and remove from case. To install, reverse removal procedure. Use NEW instrument gauge clips.

WIRING DIAGRAMS

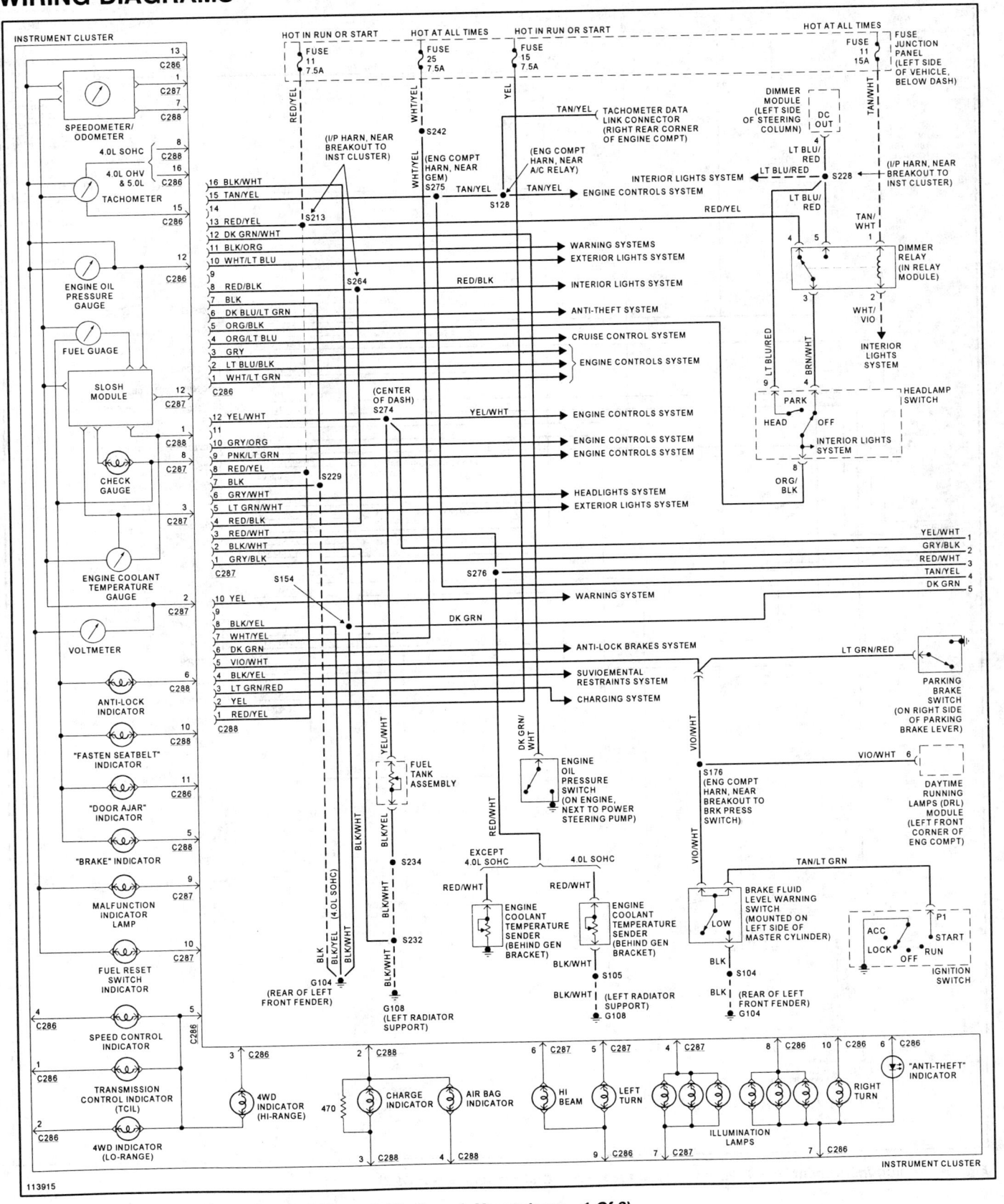

Fig. 13: Analog Instrument Panel Wiring Diagram (Explorer & Mountaineer – 1 Of 2)

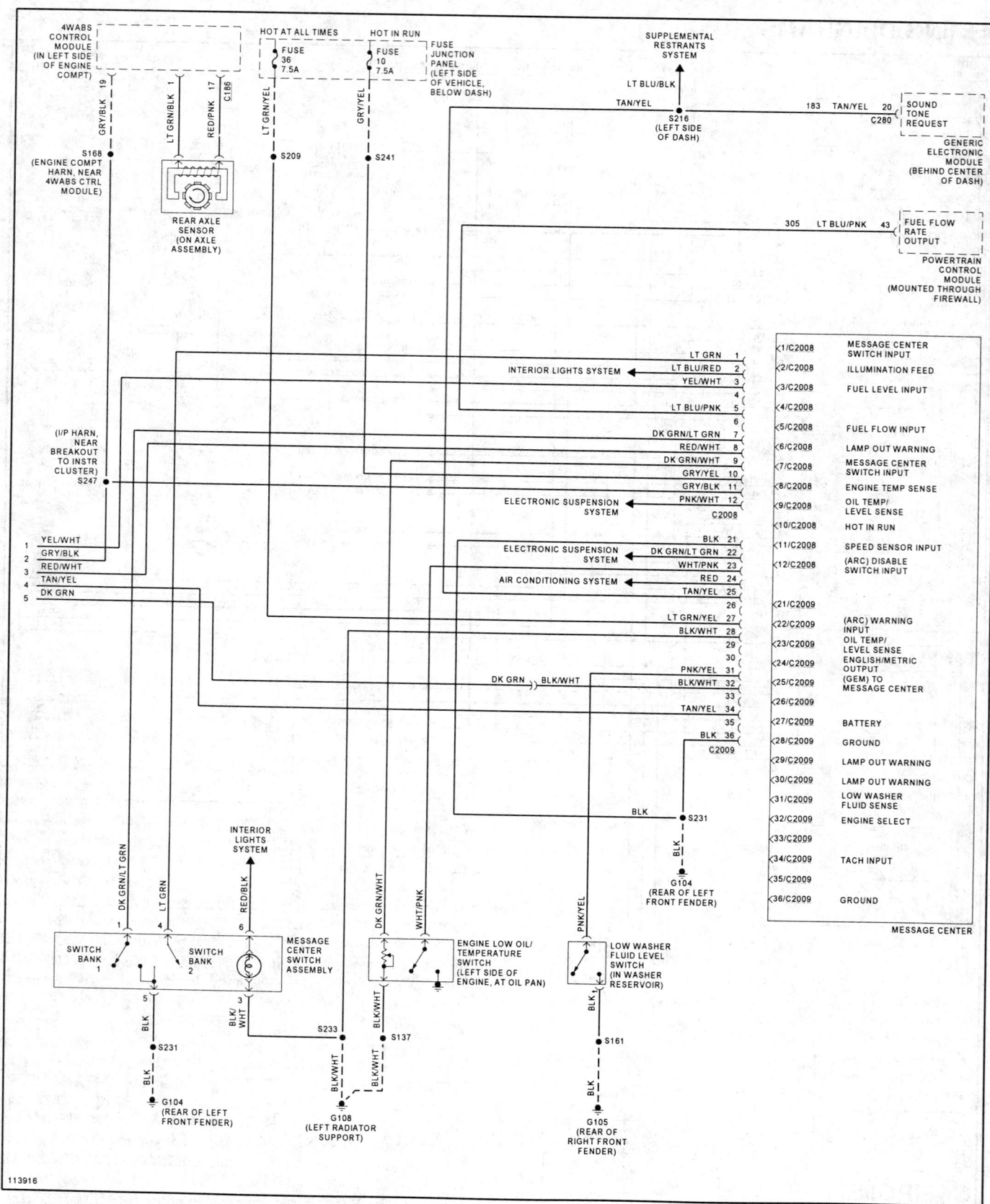

Fig. 14: Analog Instrument Panel Wiring Diagram (Explorer & Mountaineer – 2 Of 2)

DESCRIPTION & OPERATION

Instrument cluster contains a speedometer, tachometer, fuel gauge, temperature gauge, oil pressure gauge, voltmeter and odometer. Odometer/trip odometer are mounted at the bottom of speedometer. Warning lights are placed in line below speedometer and tachometer gauges. Turn signal and high beam indicators are mounted in top center of instrument cluster.

Instrument cluster gauges are not replaceable separately. Instrument cluster illumination light, warning indicators and instrument cluster lens are the only replaceable components. LOW FUEL light will illuminate when fuel level gets below 1/8 of a tank. SERVICE ENGINE SOON, AIR BAG, THEFT, O/D OFF, seat belt and traction control indicators will illuminate for 3 seconds after ignition switch is turned from LOCK to RUN position.

COMPONENT LOCATIONS

COMPONENT LOCATIONS

Component	Location
Air Bag System Module	Right Front Of Engine Compartment, Behind Radiator
Brake Fluid Level Sensor	On Brake Reservoir
Fuel Pump Assembly	Top Right Side Of Fuel Tank
Generic Electronic Module	Behind Left Side Of Instrument Panel, Left Of Steering Column
Oil Pressure Sensor	
3.8L	Above Oil Filter
4.6L (16 Valve)	Left Front Side Of Block
4.6L (32 Valve)	Left Front Of Cylinder Head
Parking Brake Switch	On Parking Brake Pedal Bracket
Restraint Control Module	Behind Instrument Panel, Right Of Steering Wheel

TROUBLE SHOOTING

Verify customer concern by observing indicators and gauges to determine correct operation with ignition switch in RUN position, in START position before ignition switch is released and in RUN position with engine running. Visually inspect components of instrument cluster. Inspect the following:

Mechanical:
- Low Washer Fluid Level
- Damaged Fuel Tank
- Low Engine Coolant Level
- Damaged Accessory Drive Belt
- Low Engine Oil Level
- Low Brake Fluid Level
- Damaged Parking Brake Switch

Electrical:
- Central Junction Box (CJB) Fuse(s):
  No. 5, 7, 11, 13, 29, 30, 32, 35, and 37 (all 15-amp)
  No. 21 and 29 (both 5-amp)
  No. 23 and 24 (both 10-amp)
  No. 34 and 38 (both 20-amp)
- Power Distribution Box Fuse No. 103 (50-amp)
- Damaged Circuitry
- Damaged Connectors
- Damaged Switches Or Sensors

If the inspection reveals obvious concern(s) that can be readily identified, repair as necessary. If concern remains after inspection, perform self-diagnostics. See SELF-DIAGNOSTIC SYSTEM.

COMPONENT TESTS

HEADLIGHT SWITCH

Remove headlight switch. Check continuity between appropriate terminals with headlight switch in appropriate position. See HEADLIGHT SWITCH RESISTANCE table. *See Fig. 1.* If continuity is not as specified, replace headlight switch.

HEADLIGHT SWITCH RESISTANCE

Switch Position	Between Terminals	Continuity
Headlight Circuit		
Off	B1 & H	No
Park	B1 & H	No
Head	B1 & H	Yes
Parking Light Circuit		
Off	B2 & R	No
Park	B2 & R	Yes
Head	B2 & R	Yes
Interior Light On		
Off	D1 & D2	No
On	D1 & D2	Yes
Dimmer Circuit	I & R	1

1 – Rotating thumbwheel from left to right should show a smoothly increasing resistance.

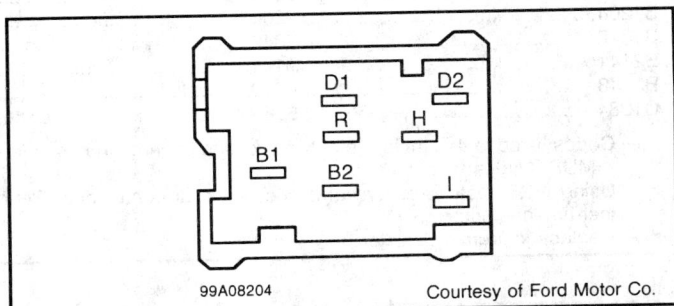

Fig. 1: Identifying Headlight Switch Terminals

SELF-DIAGNOSTIC SYSTEM

USING NEW GENERATION STAR (NGS) TESTER

NOTE: All diagnostic tests are written specifically for New Generation Star (NGS) tester. Most generic scan tools should be able to perform all test procedures.

Connect New Generation Star (NGS) tester to Data Link Connector (DLC), located beneath instrument panel. Using NGS tester, perform data link diagnostics test. See DATA LINK DIAGNOSTIC TEST under COMMUNICATION NETWORK DIAGNOSTICS in MODULE COMMUNICATIONS NETWORK – MUSTANG article. If NGS tester responds with CKT914, CKT915 or CKT70=ALL ECUS NO RESP/NOT EQUIP, repair module communications concern. See MODULE COMMUNICATIONS NETWORK – MUSTANG article. If NGS tester displays NO RESP/NOT EQUIP for Generic Electronic Module (GEM), perform TEST B: NO COMMUNICATION WITH GENERIC ELECTRONIC MODULE under SYSTEM TESTS. If NGS tester displays NO RESP/NOT EQUIP for instrument cluster, perform TEST A: NO COMMUNICATION WITH INSTRUMENT CLUSTER under SYSTEM TESTS.

If NGS tester responds with SYSTEM PASSED, retrieve and record continuous DTCs. Erase continuous DTCs. Using NGS tester, perform instrument cluster and GEM self-test. Perform appropriate test in accordance with DTC retrieved. See GENERIC ELECTRONIC MODULE DTC INDEX and/or INSTRUMENT CLUSTER DTC INDEX table. Codes listed in these tables are only for testing covered in this article. For complete DTC listing, see MODULE COMMUNICATIONS NETWORK – MUSTANG article. If no DTCs are retrieved, repair by symptom. See SYMPTOM CHART table under SYSTEM TESTS.

GENERIC ELECTRONIC MODULE DTC INDEX

DTC [1]	Description	Test
B1340	Chime Input Request Circuit Short To Ground	W
B1342	ECU Defective	[2]
B1353	Key-In-Ignition Circuit Open	V
B1426	Seat Belt Switch Circuit Short To Voltage	I
B1428	Seat Belt Indicator Circuit Failure	I
B1462	Seat Belt Switch Circuit Failure	Z
C1189	Brake Fluid Level Sensor Input Short To Voltage	L
C1223	Brake Light Warning Output Circuit Failure	L
C1225	Brake Light Warning Output Circuit Short To Voltage	L

[1] – Codes listed in this table are only for testing covered in this article. For complete DTC listing, see MODULE COMMUNICATIONS NETWORK – MUSTANG article.

[2] – Using NGS tester, retrieve and document all continuous. Perform Generic Electronic Module (GEM) self-test. If DTC B1342 is retrieved again, replace GEM.

INSTRUMENT CLUSTER DTC INDEX

Scan Tool DTC [1]	Dealer Test Mode DTC [1]	Description	Test
B1202	9202	Fuel Level Sensor Circuit Open	C
B1204	9204	Fuel Level Sensor Circuit Short To Ground	C
B1342	9342	ECU Defective	[2]
B2141	A141	NVM Configuration Failure	[3]
B2143	A143	NVM Memory Failure	[3]
C1284	5284	Oil Pressure Switch Failure	E

[1] – Codes listed in this table are only for testing covered in this article. For complete DTC listing, see MODULE COMMUNICATIONS NETWORK – MUSTANG article.

[2] – Using NGS tester, retrieve and document all continuous. Perform instrument cluster self-test. If DTC B1342 is retrieved again, replace instrument cluster.

[3] – Replace instrument cluster.

DEALER TEST MODE

1) Depress and hold instrument cluster trip odometer/reset button. Turn ignition switch to RUN position. Once "tESt" is displayed release trip odometer/reset button (approximately 5 seconds). Trip odometer/reset button MUST be released within 3 seconds of the odometer displaying "tESt" to begin the dealer test mode.

2) Depress trip odometer/reset button to advance through dealer test modes. See DEALER TEST MODE DISPLAYS. If problem exist during deal test mode, repair by symptom. See SYMPTOM CHART table under SYSTEM TESTS. If any DTCs exist, perform appropriate in accordance with DTC retrieved. See INSTRUMENT CLUSTER DTC INDEX table.

DEALER TEST MODE DISPLAYS

NOTE: Display modes are list in order of appearance.

"GAGE" – Activates gauge sweep of all gauges, then displays present gauge values. Also carries out the checksum tests on ROM and EE. If the gauge sweep is inoperative, replace instrument cluster.

All Segments Illuminated – Illuminates all odometer segments. If any odometer segment is inoperative, replace instrument cluster.

"bulb" – Illuminates all micro-controlled indicators and LEDs. If any bulb is inoperative, replace defective blub or LED as necessary.

"r" – All micro-controlled indicators and LEDs return to normal operation. If alternating flashes of FAIL and ROM level are displayed, replace instrument cluster.

"EE" – Displays hexadecimal value for EE level. If alternating flashes of FAIL and EE level are displayed, replace instrument cluster.

"dt" – Displays hexadecimal coding of final manufacturing test date.

"dtc" – Displays continuous DTCs in hexadecimal format. Pressing trip odometer/reset button again will display any stored DTCs before proceeding to next step. If any DTCs are stored, perform appropriate test in accordance with DTC(s) retrieved. See INSTRUMENT CLUSTER DTC INDEX table.

"enG" – Displays speed in MPH. Speedometer will indicate present speed within tolerance. Display will show 0 if input is not received, vehicle speed is zero, or input is invalid for one second or more.

"m" – Displays speed in KPH. Speedometer will indicate present speed within tolerance. Display will show 0 if input is not received, vehicle speed is zero, or input is invalid for one second or more.

"tAc" – Displays tachometer data received from PCM through module communication circuit (SCP bus circuit). Tachometer will indicate present engine RPM. Display will shows 0 if engine RPM is zero, input is not received or input received is invalid for one second or more.

"FUEL" – Displays a code (0–255) for fuel level sender input to instrument cluster. Fuel gauge will display a filtered fuel level value. See FUEL LEVEL VALUE. If the value displayed is 0–20 the circuit is shorted.

FUEL LEVEL VALUE

Gauge Reading	Display Value
Open Sending Unit [1]	255
Full Stop	232
Full Mark	205-225
3/4 Mark	170-186
1/2 Mark	131-145
1/4 Mark	88-98
Empty Mark	37-45
Low Fuel Indicator	Below 54
Short Circuit [1]	0-18

[1] – Circuit condition.

"OIL" – Displays code (0-250) for oil pressure switch input to instrument cluster. Oil pressure gauge will indicate present oil pressure. Normal oil pressure will display a value between 000-176. A low oil pressure or an inoperative engine oil pressure switch will display a value greater than 176.

"dEGC" – Displays engine temperature (°C) input from cylinder head temperature sensor. See TEMPERATURE VALUE.

TEMPERATURE VALUE

Gauge Reading	Display Value
Cold Mark	49C
Normal Band Start	60C
Normal Band End	120C
No Message for 5 seconds [1]	–40C

TEMPERATURE VALUE (Cont.)

Gauge Reading	Display Value
[1] – No message received thought module communications network (SCP bus circuit).	

"**bAtt**" – Displays a code (0–255) for battery voltage input to instrument cluster. Voltage gauge indicates present battery voltage. See BATTERY VOLTAGE table.

BATTERY VOLTAGE

Gauge Reading	Display Value
Low Voltage (6.9-9.1 Volts)	93-102
Normal Band Start (8.5-10.7 Volts)	115-124
Normal Band End (15.8-18 Volts)	215-225
High Voltage (16.9-19.1 Volts)	230-241

"**rhEo**" – Displays present rheostat dimming input (0-255).

"**rhi**", "**rhS**" & "**rho**" – Not used.

"**Cr**" – Displays present RUN/START sense input. Display will show "-h" for high input with ignition switch in START position and "-L" for low input with ignition switch in RUN position.

"**PA-PE7**" – Not used.

"**GAGE**" – Repeats test display cycle.

SYSTEM TESTS

CAUTION: *Electronic modules are sensitive to static electrical charges. Proper grounding of technician and component is essential to prevent damage.*

SYMPTOM CHART

Symptom	Test
AIR BAG Indicator Inoperative/Always On	[1]
THEFT Indicator Inoperative/Always On	[2]
Oil Gauge Reads Normal With Ignition Off	[3]
Single Gauge Does Not Return To Zero With Ignition Off	[3]
No Communication With Instrument Cluster	A
No Communication With Generic Electronic Module	B
Incorrect Fuel Gauge Indication	C
LOW FUEL Indicator Never/Always On	D
Incorrect Oil Pressure Gauge Indication	E
Incorrect Temperature Gauge Indication	F
Speedometer/Tachometer Is Inoperative	G
Odometer Inoperative	H
Safety Belt Indicator Is Inoperative (Chime Is Operative)/Does Not Operate Correctly	I
O/D OFF Indicator Is Never/Always On	J
Low Engine Coolant Indicator Never/Always On	K
BRAKE Indicator Never/Always On	L
Charge System Indicator Never/Always On	M
High Beam Indicator Is Never/Always On	N
ABS Indicator Is Inoperative/Always On	O
SERVICE ENGINE SOON Indicator Never/Always On	P
Turn Signal/Hazard Indicator Never/Always On	Q
Traction Control Indicator Is Never/Always On	R
Incorrect Voltage Gauge Indication	S
Incorrect Speedometer Indication	T
Incorrect Tachometer Indication	U
Key-In-Ignition Warning Chime Does Not Operate Properly	V
Air Bag Warning Chime Does Not Operate Properly	W
Door Ajar Warning Chime Does Not Operate Properly	X
Headlight Warning Chime Does Not Operate Properly	Y
Seat Belt Warning Chime Does Not Operate Properly	Z

[1] – See appropriate AIR BAG article in appropriate MITCHELL® AIR BAG SERVICE & REPAIR manual.

[2] – See PASSIVE ANTI-THEFT SYSTEMS – MUSTANG article.

[3] – Replace instrument cluster.

TEST A: NO COMMUNICATION WITH INSTRUMENT CLUSTER

1) Turn ignition switch to LOCK position. Disconnect instrument cluster harness connector C251. Measure voltage at terminal No. 10 (Red/White wire) at instrument cluster harness connector C251. *See Fig. 2.* If battery voltage exists, go to next step. If battery voltage does not exist, repair power distribution circuit. See appropriate wiring diagram in POWER DISTRIBUTION article in WIRING DIAGRAMS.

2) Turn ignition switch to RUN position. Measure voltage at terminal No. 11 (Pink/Black wire) at instrument cluster harness connector C251. If battery voltage exists, go to next step. If battery voltage does not exist, repair power distribution circuit. See appropriate wiring diagram in POWER DISTRIBUTION article in WIRING DIAGRAMS.

3) Measure voltage at terminal No. 12 (White/Light Blue wire) at instrument cluster harness connector C251. If battery voltage exists, go to next step. If battery voltage does not exist, repair power distribution circuit. See appropriate wiring diagram in POWER DISTRIBUTION article in WIRING DIAGRAMS.

4) Turn ignition switch to LOCK position. Measure resistance between ground and terminal No. 20 (Black/White wire) at instrument cluster harness connector C251. If resistance is 5 ohms or less, go to next step. If resistance is greater than 5 ohms, repair open in Black/White wire.

5) Measure resistance between ground and terminal No. 1 (Black wire) at instrument cluster harness connector C251. If resistance is 5 ohms or less, repair module communication concern. See MODULE COMMUNICATIONS NETWORK – MUSTANG ARTICLE. If resistance is greater than 5 ohms, repair open in Black wire.

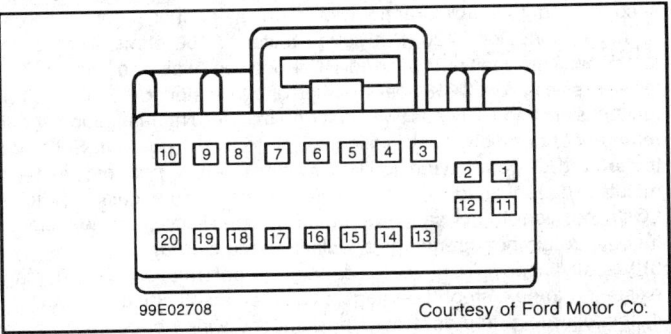

Fig. 2: Identifying Instrument Cluster Harness Connector C251 & GEM Harness Connector C292 Terminals

TEST B: NO COMMUNICATION WITH GENERIC ELECTRONIC MODULE

NOTE: *Before proceeding with this test ensure voltage exists at input side of fuse No. 39 (5-amp) in central junction box. Repair as necessary. See appropriate wiring diagram in POWER DISTRIBUTION article in WIRING DIAGRAMS.*

1) Turn ignition switch to LOCK position. Disconnect Generic Electronic Module (GEM) harness connector C291. Measure voltage at terminal No. 2 (White/Yellow wire) at GEM harness connector C291. *See Fig. 3.* If battery voltage exists, go to next step. If battery voltage does not exist, go to step **3)**.

2) Measure resistance between ground and terminal No. 4 (Black/White wire) at GEM harness connector C291. If resistance is 5 ohms or less, go to step **4)**. If resistance is greater than 5 ohms, repair open in Black/White wire. See WIRING DIAGRAMS.

3) Remove fuse No. 39 (5-amp) from central junction box. Measure resistance in White/Yellow wire between terminal No. 2 at GEM harness connector C291 and output side of fuse No. 39. If resistance is 5 ohms or less, power distribution circuit as necessary. See appropriate wiring diagram in POWER DISTRIBUTION article in WIRING DIAGRAMS. If resistance is greater than 5 ohms, repair open in White/Yellow wire.

4) Measure voltage at terminal No. 4 (Black/White wire) at GEM harness connector C291. If voltage exists, repair short to voltage in Black/White wire. If voltage does not exist, repair module communication concern. See MODULE COMMUNICATIONS NETWORK – MUSTANG article.

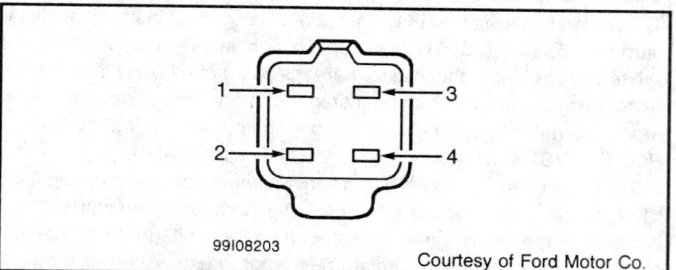

99108203   Courtesy of Ford Motor Co.

Fig. 3: Identifying GEM Harness Connector C291 Terminals

TEST C: INCORRECT FUEL GAUGE INDICATION

NOTE: Fuel gauge indication will require at least 10 minutes to updated if fuel tank has less than 2.5 gallons in it.

1) Connect New Generation Star (NGS) tester to Data Link Connector (DLC). Turn ignition switch to RUN position. Using NGS tester, select instrument cluster active command FUELLEVEL. Trigger, monitor and scroll FUELLEVEL at 0%, 50% and 100%. Fuel gauge should indicate empty at 0%, half at 50% and full at 100 %. If fuel gauge responds as specified, go to next step. If fuel gauge does not respond as specified, replace instrument cluster.
2) Turn ignition switch to LOCK position. Disconnect fuel pump assembly harness connector C420. Using Instrument Gauge System Tester (014–R1063), connect one lead to Yellow/White wire terminal and the second lead to Black/Orange wire terminal at fuel pump assembly harness connector C420. Set gauge tester to 160 ohms. Turn gauge tester on. Turn ignition switch to RUN position, wait one minute. Turn ignition switch to LOCK position. Set gauge tester to 15 ohms. Turn ignition switch to RUN position, wait one minute. The fuel gauge should read empty or below. Turn ignition switch to LOCK position. Set gauge tester to 160 ohms. Turn ignition switch to RUN position, wait one minute. The fuel gauge should read full or above. Turn ignition switch to LOCK position. If fuel gauge operated as specified, go to next step. If fuel gauge did not operate as specified, go to step **5)**.
3) Visually inspect fuel tank for damage or deformation. If no damage exists, go to next step. If damage exists, replace fuel tank.
4) Inspect fuel pump assembly for damaged wiring or connectors and float and float rod for damage or obstruction. If problem exists, repair as necessary. If problem does not exist, replace fuel level sender.
5) Disconnect instrument cluster harness connector C251. Turn ignition switch to RUN position. Measure voltage at terminal No. 19 (Yellow/White wire) at instrument cluster harness connector C251. *See Fig. 2.* If voltage does not exist, go to next step. If voltage exists, repair short to voltage in Yellow/White wire.
6) Measure resistance in Yellow/White wire between fuel pump assembly harness connector C420 and terminal No. 19 at instrument cluster harness connector C251. Resistance should be 5 ohms or less. Also, measure resistance between ground and terminal No. 19 (Yellow/White wire) at instrument cluster harness connector C251. Resistance should be greater than 10 k/ohms. If both resistance reading are as specified, go to next step. If either resistance reading is not as specified, repair open and/or short to ground in Yellow/White wire.
7) Measure resistance between ground and Black/Orange wire terminal at fuel pump assembly harness connector C420. Measure resistance between ground and terminal No. 20 (Black/White wire) at instrument cluster harness connector C251. If both resistance reading are 5 ohms or less, replace instrument cluster. If either resistance reading is greater than 5 ohms, repair open in appropriate wire.

TEST D: LOW FUEL INDICATOR NEVER/ALWAYS ON

Check fuel gauge operation. If fuel gauge operate properly, replace bulb or instrument cluster as necessary. If fuel gauge does not operate properly, perform TEST C: INCORRECT FUEL GAUGE INDICATION.

TEST E: INCORRECT OIL PRESSURE GAUGE INDICATION

1) Connect New Generation Star (NGS) tester to Data Link Connector (DLC). Turn ignition switch to RUN position. Using NGS tester, select instrument cluster active command OILGAUGE. Trigger, monitor and scroll OILGAUGE at 0%, 50% and 100%. Oil pressure gauge should indicate "L" at 0%, middle at 50% and "H" at 100 %. If oil pressure gauge responds as specified, go to next step. If oil pressure gauge does not respond as specified, replace instrument cluster.
2) Turn ignition switch to LOCK position. Disconnect oil pressure sensor harness connector C138. Disconnect instrument cluster harness connector C251. Measure resistance in White/Red wire between oil pressure sensor harness connector C138 and terminal No. 16 at instrument cluster harness connector C251. *See Fig. 2.* Resistance should be 5 ohms or less. Also, measure resistance between ground and terminal No. 16 (White/Red wire) at instrument cluster harness connector C251. Resistance should be greater than 10 k/ohms. If both resistance reading are as specified, replace oil pressure sensor. If either resistance reading is not as specified, repair open and/or short to ground in White/Red wire.

TEST F: INCORRECT TEMPERATURE GAUGE INDICATION

Connect New Generation Star (NGS) tester to Data Link Connector (DLC). Turn ignition switch to RUN position. Using NGS tester, select instrument cluster active command ENGCOOLNT. Trigger, monitor and scroll ENGCOOLNT at 0%, 50% and 100%. Temperature gauge should indicate cold at 0%, half at 50% and hot at 100 %. If temperature gauge responds as specified, repair engine coolant temperature sensor circuit. See appropriate SELF-DIAGNOSTICS article in ENGINE PERFORMANCE in appropriate MITCHELL® manual. If temperature gauge does not respond as specified, replace instrument cluster.

TEST G: SPEEDOMETER/TACHOMETER IS INOPERATIVE

NOTE: Instrument cluster received vehicle speed signal from PCM through the SCP bus circuit. PCM receives vehicle speed signal from output shaft sensor.

Perform dealer test mode. See DEALER TEST MODE under SELF-DIAGNOSTIC SYSTEM. If fuel gauge operated properly during "GAGE" portion of test, repair vehicle speed input from PCM (retrieve codes from PCM). See appropriate SELF-DIAGNOSTICS article in ENGINE PERFORMANCE in appropriate MITCHELL® manual. If fuel gauge did not operated properly during "GAGE" portion of test, replace instrument cluster.

TEST H: ODOMETER INOPERATIVE

NOTE: Instrument cluster received odometer signal from PCM through the SCP bus circuit. PCM receives vehicle speed signal from output· shaft sensor. If instrument cluster does not receive odometer rolling count status for two seconds, dashes will be displayed in odometer display.

Turn ignition switch to RUN position. If odometer displays all dashes, repair odometer input from PCM (retrieve codes from PCM). See appropriate SELF-DIAGNOSTICS article in ENGINE PERFORMANCE in appropriate MITCHELL® manual. If odometer does not display all dashes, replace instrument cluster.

TEST I: SAFETY BELT INDICATOR IS INOPERATIVE (CHIME IS OPERATIVE)/ DOES NOT OPERATE CORRECTLY

1) Connect New Generation Star (NGS) tester to Data Link Connector (DLC). Turn ignition switch to RUN position. Monitor Generic Electronic Module (GEM) PIDs IGN_KEY, IGN_S, IGN_R and IGN_A while cycling ignition switch through all position. If PIDs agree with ignition switch position, go to next step. If PIDs does not agree with ignition switch position, perform TEST V: KEY-IN-IGNITION WARNING CHIME DOES NOT OPERATE PROPERLY.

2) Using NGS tester, monitor GEM PID D_SBELT while buckling and unbuckling driver's seat belt. If PID agrees with seat belt position, go to next step. If PID does not agree with seat belt position, perform TEST Z: SEAT BELT WARNING CHIME DOES NOT OPERATE PROPERLY.

3) Ensure seat belt is unbuckled. Turn ignition switch to LOCK position. Turn ignition switch to RUN position. If seat belt indicator does not illuminate for 3 seconds then go out, go to next step. If seat belt indicator illuminates for 3 seconds then goes out, replace GEM.

4) Buckle driver's seat belt. If seat belt indicator is always illuminated, go to next step. If seat belt indicator is not always illuminated, go to step **7)**.

5) Turn ignition switch to LOCK position. Disconnect GEM harness connector C352. Turn ignition switch to RUN position. If seat belt indicator is always on, go to next step. If seat belt indicator goes out, replace GEM.

6) Turn ignition switch to LOCK position. Disconnect instrument cluster harness connector C250. Measure resistance between ground and terminal No. 26 (Dark Green/Light Green wire) at GEM harness connector C352. See Fig. 4. If resistance is greater than 10 k/ohms, replace instrument cluster. If resistance is 10 k/ohms or less, repair short to ground in Dark Green/Light Green wire.

7) Turn ignition switch to LOCK position. Disconnect instrument cluster harness connector C250. Disconnect GEM harness connector C352. Measure voltage at terminal No. 26 (Dark Green/Light Green wire) at GEM harness connector C352. See Fig. 4. If voltage does not exist, go to next step. If voltage exists, repair short to voltage in Dark Green/Light Green wire.

8) Connect instrument cluster harness connector C250. Using a fused jumper wire, ground terminal No. 26 (Dark Green/Light Green wire) at GEM harness connector C352. Turn ignition switch to RUN position. If seat belt indicator does not illuminate, go to next step. If seat belt indicator light illuminates, replace GEM.

9) Turn ignition switch to LOCK position. Disconnect instrument cluster harness connector C250. Measure resistance in Dark Green/Light Green wire between terminal No. 26 at GEM harness connector C352 and terminal No. 4 at instrument cluster harness connector C250. See Figs. 4 and 5. If resistance is 5 ohms or less, replace bulb or instrument cluster as necessary. If resistance is greater than 5 ohms, repair open in Dark Green/Light Green wire.

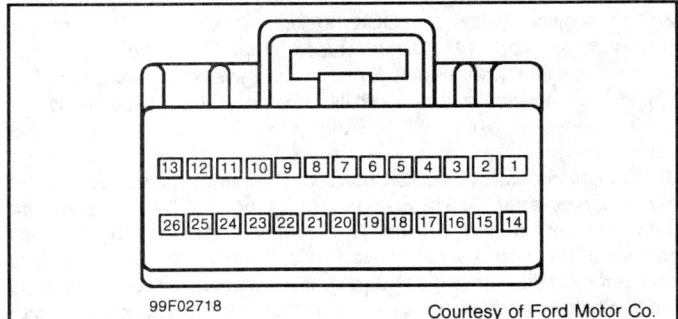

99F02718   Courtesy of Ford Motor Co.

Fig. 4: Identifying GEM Harness Connector C352 Terminals

TEST J: O/D OFF INDICATOR IS NEVER/ALWAYS ON

1) Turn ignition switch to RUN position. If O/D OFF indicator is always illuminated, go to next step. If O/D OFF indicator is not always illuminated, go to step **3)**.

2) Turn ignition switch to LOCK position. Disconnect instrument cluster harness connector C250. Turn ignition switch to RUN position. If O/D OFF indicator is not illuminated, repair transmission control switch circuit. See appropriate SELF-DIAGNOSTICS article in ENGINE PERFORMANCE in appropriate MITCHELL® manual. If O/D OFF indicator is illuminated, replace instrument cluster.

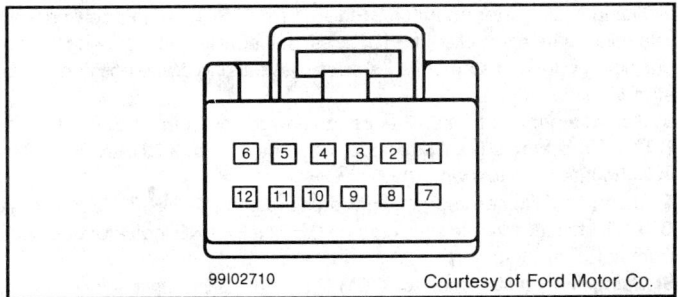

99102710   Courtesy of Ford Motor Co.

Fig. 5: Identifying Instrument Cluster Harness Connector C250 & GEM Harness Connector C293 Terminals

3) Perform dealer test mode. See DEALER TEST MODE under SELF-DIAGNOSTIC SYSTEM. If O/D OFF indicator operated properly during "bulb" portion of test, repair transmission control switch circuit. See appropriate SELF-DIAGNOSTICS article in ENGINE PERFORMANCE in appropriate MITCHELL® manual. If O/D OFF indicator did not operated properly during "bulb" portion of test, replace bulb or instrument cluster as necessary.

TEST K: LOW ENGINE COOLANT INDICATOR NEVER/ALWAYS ON

NOTE: Before testing, ensure coolant level is correct.

1) Turn ignition switch to RUN position. If low coolant indicator is not illuminated, go to next step. If low coolant indicator is illuminated, go to step **5)**.

2) Turn ignition switch to LOCK position. Connect New Generation Star (NGS) tester to Data Link Connector (DLC). Turn ignition switch to RUN position. Select instrument cluster active command CLNTLAMP. Trigger active command CLNTLAMP on. If low coolant indicator illuminates, go to next step. If low coolant indicator does not illuminate, replace bulb or instrument cluster as necessary.

3) Turn ignition switch to LOCK position. Disconnect low coolant sensor harness connector C137. Using a fused jumper wire, ground Light Blue wire terminal at low coolant sensor harness connector C137. Turn ignition switch to RUN position. If low coolant indicator illuminates, go to next step. If low coolant indicator does not illuminate, repair open in Light Blue wire.

4) Measure resistance between ground and Yellow/Red wire terminal at low coolant sensor harness connector C137. If resistance is 5 ohms or less, replace low coolant sensor. If resistance is greater than 5 ohms, repair open in Yellow/Red wire or Black/White wire between low coolant sensor and ground.

5) Turn ignition switch to LOCK position. Disconnect low coolant sensor harness connector C137. Turn ignition switch to RUN position. If low coolant indicator is illuminated, go to next step. If low coolant indicator is not illuminated, replace low coolant sensor.

6) Turn ignition switch to LOCK position. Disconnect instrument cluster harness connector C251. Measure resistance between ground and Light Blue wire terminal at low coolant sensor harness connector C137. If resistance is greater than 10 k/ohms, replace instrument cluster. If resistance is 10 k/ohms or less, repair short to ground in Light Blue wire.

TEST L: BRAKE INDICATOR NEVER/ALWAYS ON

NOTE: Before testing, ensure brake fluid level is correct.

1) Connect New Generation Star (NGS) tester to Data Link Connector (DLC). Turn ignition switch to RUN position. Monitor Generic Electronic Module (GEM) PIDs IGN_KEY, IGN_S, IGN_R and IGN_A while cycling ignition switch through all position. If PIDs agree with ignition switch position, go to next step. If PIDs does not agree with ignition switch position, perform TEST V: KEY-IN-IGNITION WARNING CHIME DOES NOT OPERATE PROPERLY.

2) Using NGS tester, monitor GEM PID PRK_BRK while applying and releasing parking brake. If PID does not agrees with parking brake position, go to next step. If PID agrees with parking brake position, go to step **5)**.

3) Release parking brake. Ensure ignition switch is in RUN position. If BRAKE indicator is not illuminated, go to next step. If BRAKE indicator is illuminated, go to step **10)**.

4) Using NGS tester, trigger GEM active command BKFLDLOW on. If BRAKE indicator illuminates, replace GEM. If BRAKE indicator does not illuminate, go to step **8)**.

5) Using NGS tester, monitor GEM PID PRK_BRK while applying and releasing parking brake. If PID does not always indicate ON, go to next step. If PID always indicates ON, go to step **7)**.

6) Turn ignition switch to LOCK position. Disconnect GEM harness connector C293. Disconnect parking brake switch harness connector C318. Measure resistance between Light Blue/Black wire terminal at parking brake switch harness connector C318 and terminal No. 4 (Violet/Yellow wire) at GEM harness connector C293. *See Fig. 5.* If resistance is 5 ohms or less, replace parking brake switch. If resistance is greater than 5 ohms, repair open in Violet/Yellow wire and/or Light Blue/Black wire.

7) Turn ignition switch to LOCK position. Disconnect GEM harness connector C293. Disconnect parking brake switch harness connector C318. Measure resistance between ground and terminal No. 4 (Violet/Yellow wire) at GEM harness connector C293. *See Fig. 5.* If resistance is greater than 10 k/ohms, replace parking brake switch. If resistance is 10 k/ohms or less, repair short to ground in Violet/Yellow wire.

8) Turn ignition switch to LOCK position. Disconnect GEM harness connector C352. Disconnect instrument cluster harness connector C251. Turn ignition switch to RUN position. Measure voltage at terminal No. 13 (Violet/Yellow wire) at GEM harness connector C352. *See Fig. 4.* If voltage does not exist, go to next step. If voltage exists, repair short to voltage in Violet/Yellow wire.

9) Turn ignition switch to LOCK position. Measure resistance in Violet/Yellow wire between terminal No. 13 at GEM harness connector C352 and terminal No. 14 at instrument cluster harness connector C251. *See Figs. 2 and 4.* If resistance is 5 ohms or less, replace bulb or instrument cluster as necessary. If resistance is greater than 5 ohms, repair open in Violet/Yellow wire.

10) Turn ignition switch to LOCK position. Disconnect brake fluid level sensor harness connector C164. Turn ignition switch to RUN position. Release parking brake. If BRAKE indicator is illuminated, go to next step. If BRAKE indicator is not illuminated, replace brake fluid level sensor.

11) Turn ignition switch to LOCK position. Disconnect GEM harness connector C352. Turn ignition switch to RUN position. If BRAKE indicator is illuminated, go to next step. If BRAKE indicator is not illuminated, replace GEM.

12) Turn ignition switch to LOCK position. Disconnect instrument cluster harness connector C251. Measure resistance between ground and terminal No. 13 (Violet/Yellow wire) at GEM harness connector C352. *See Fig. 4.* If resistance is greater than 10 k/ohms, replace instrument cluster, If resistance is 10 k/ohms or less, repair short to ground in Violet/Yellow wire.

TEST M: CHARGE SYSTEM INDICATOR NEVER/ALWAYS ON

1) Check charging system operation. See appropriate GENERATORS article in STARTING & CHARGING SYSTEMS. If charging system is operating correctly, go to next step. If charging system is not operating correctly, repair as necessary.

2) Turn ignition switch to RUN position. If charging indicator is not illuminated, go to next step. If charging indicator is illuminated, go to step **5)**.

3) Turn ignition switch to LOCK position. Disconnect generator harness connector C154. Using a fused jumper wire, ground Light Green/Red wire terminal at generator harness connector C154. Turn ignition switch to RUN position. If charging indicator is not illuminated, go to next step. If charging indicator is illuminated, repair or replace generator as necessary.

4) Turn ignition switch to LOCK position. Disconnect instrument cluster harness connector C250. Measure resistance in Light Green/Red wire between generator harness connector C154 and terminal No. 5 at instrument cluster harness connector C250. *See Fig. 5.* If resistance is 5 ohms or less, replace bulb or instrument cluster as necessary. If resistance is greater than 5 ohms, repair open in Light Green/Red wire.

5) Turn ignition switch to LOCK position. Disconnect generator harness connector C154. Turn ignition switch to RUN position. If charging indicator is illuminated, go to next step. If charging indicator is not illuminated, repair or replace generator as necessary.

6) Turn ignition switch to LOCK position. Disconnect instrument cluster harness connector C250. Measure resistance between ground and Light Green/Red wire terminal at generator harness connector C154. If resistance is greater than 10 k/ohms, replace instrument cluster. If resistance is 10 k/ohms or less, repair short to ground in Light Green/Red wire.

TEST N: HIGH BEAM INDICATOR IS NEVER/ALWAYS ON

1) Operate headlights in high beam position. If high beams operate, go to next step. If high beams do not operate, repair high beams as necessary. See appropriate wiring diagram in HEADLIGHT SYSTEMS article.

2) Turn ignition switch to LOCK position. Disconnect instrument cluster harness connector C251. Measure voltage at terminal No. 2 (Light Green/Black wire) at instrument cluster harness connector C251 while turning high beams on and off. *See Fig. 2.* Battery voltage should exists when high beams are on and zero volts should exist when high beams are off. If voltage is as specified, replace bulb or instrument cluster as necessary. If voltage is not as specified, repair open or short to voltage/ground in Light Green/Black wire.

TEST O: ABS INDICATOR IS INOPERATIVE/ALWAYS ON

1) Turn ignition switch to RUN position. If ABS indicator is never illuminated, go to next step. If ABS indicator is always illuminated, repair ABS system as necessary. See appropriate ANTI-LOCK article in BRAKES in appropriate MITCHELL® manual.

2) Turn ignition switch to LOCK position. Disconnect ABS module harness connector C141. Using a fused jumper wire, ground terminal No. 16 (Dark Green wire) at ABS module harness connector C141. *See Fig. 6.* Turn ignition switch to RUN position. If ABS indicator is not illuminated, go to next step. If ABS indicator is illuminated, replace ABS module.

3) Turn ignition switch to LOCK position. Disconnect instrument cluster harness connector C251. Measure resistance in Dark Green wire between terminal No. 16 (Dark Green wire) at ABS module harness connector C141 and terminal No. 15 at instrument cluster harness connector C251. *See Figs. 2 and 6.* If resistance is 5 ohms or less, replace bulb or instrument cluster as necessary. If resistance is greater than 5 ohms, repair open in Dark Green wire.

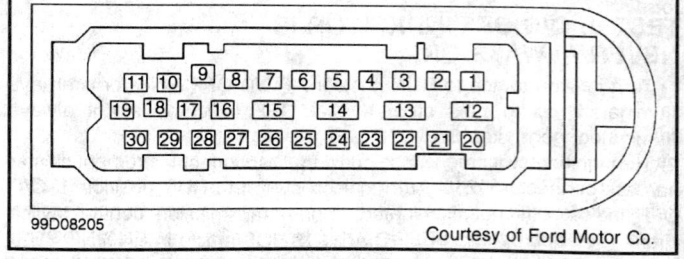

99D08205   Courtesy of Ford Motor Co.

Fig. 6: Identifying ABS Module Harness Connector C141 Terminals

TEST P: SERVICE ENGINE SOON INDICATOR NEVER/ALWAYS ON

Connect New Generation Star (NGS) tester to Data Link Connector (DLC). Turn ignition switch to RUN position. Using NGS tester, select instrument cluster active command MIL. Trigger MIL active command on. If SERVICE ENGINE SOON indicator illuminates, repair powertrain control concern. See appropriate SELF-DIAGNOSTICS article in ENGINE PERFORMANCE in appropriate MITCHELL® manual. If SERVICE ENGINE SOON indicator does not illuminate, replace bulb or instrument cluster as necessary.

TEST Q: TURN SIGNAL/HAZARD INDICATOR NEVER/ALWAYS ON

1) Turn ignition switch to RUN position. Operate left and right turn signals. If both turn signals operate, go to next step. If both turn signals do not operate, repair turn signals as necessary. See appropriate wiring diagram in EXTERIOR LIGHTS article.

2) Turn ignition switch to LOCK position. Disconnect instrument cluster harness connector C250 for right turn signal or C251 for left turn signal. Turn ignition switch to RUN position. Place multifunction switch in appropriate position. Measure voltage at terminal No. 3 (White/Light Blue wire for left turn signal; Light Green/White for right turn signal) at appropriate instrument cluster harness connector. See Fig. 2 or 5. Voltage should pulse between zero and battery voltage. If voltage is as specified, replace bulb or instrument cluster as necessary. If voltage is not as specified, repair open or short in appropriate wire.

TEST R: TRACTION CONTROL INDICATOR IS NEVER/ALWAYS ON

1) Turn ignition switch to RUN position. If traction control indicator is never illuminated, go to next step. If traction control indicator is always illuminated, repair traction control system as necessary. See appropriate ANTI-LOCK article in BRAKES in appropriate MITCHELL® manual.

2) Turn ignition switch to LOCK position. Connect New Generation Star (NGS) tester to Data Link Connector (DLC). Turn ignition switch to RUN position. Using NGS tester, select instrument cluster active command TRACOFF. Trigger TRACOFF active command on. If traction control indicator illuminates, repair traction control system as necessary. See appropriate ANTI-LOCK article in BRAKES in appropriate MITCHELL® manual. If traction control indicator does not illuminate, replace bulb or instrument cluster as necessary.

TEST S: INCORRECT VOLTAGE GAUGE INDICATION

1) Connect New Generation Star (NGS) tester to Data Link Connector (DLC). Turn ignition switch to RUN position. Using NGS tester, select instrument cluster active command BATTERY. Trigger, monitor and scroll BATTERY at 0%, 50% and 100%. Voltage gauge should indicate "L" at 0%, middle at 50% and "H" at 100 %. If voltage gauge responds as specified, go to next step. If voltage gauge does not respond as specified, replace instrument cluster.

2) Check charging system operation. See appropriate GENERATORS article in STARTING & CHARGING SYSTEMS. If charging system is operating correctly, go to next step. If charging system is not operating correctly, repair as necessary.

3) Turn ignition switch to LOCK position. Disconnect generator harness connector C154. Disconnect instrument cluster harness connector C250. Measure resistance in Light Green/Red wire between generator harness connector C154 and terminal No. 5 at instrument cluster harness connector C250. See Fig. 5. Resistance should be 5 ohms or less. Also, measure resistance between ground and terminal No. 5 (Light Green/Red wire) at instrument cluster harness connector C250. Resistance should be greater than 10 k/ohms. If both resistance reading are as specified, system is okay at this time. If either resistance reading is not as specified, repair open and/or short to ground in Light Green/ Red wire.

TEST T: INCORRECT SPEEDOMETER INDICATION

Connect New Generation Star (NGS) tester to Data Link Connector (DLC). Turn ignition switch to RUN position. Using NGS tester, select instrument cluster active command SPDOMETER. Trigger, monitor and scroll SPDOMETER at 0%, 50% and 100%. Speedometer should indicate 0 MPH at 0%, middle MPH at 50% and maximum MPH at 100 %. If speedometer responds as specified, repair vehicle speed input from PCM (retrieve codes from PCM). See appropriate SELF-DIAGNOSTICS article in ENGINE PERFORMANCE in appropriate MITCHELL® manual. If speedometer does not respond as specified, replace instrument cluster.

TEST U: INCORRECT TACHOMETER INDICATION

Connect New Generation Star (NGS) tester to Data Link Connector (DLC). Turn ignition switch to RUN position. Using NGS tester, select instrument cluster active command TCHOMETER. Trigger, monitor and scroll TCHOMETER at 0%, 50% and 100%. Tachometer should indicate 0 RPM at 0%, middle RPM at 50% and maximum RPM at 100 %. If tachometer responds as specified, repair vehicle speed input from PCM (retrieve codes from PCM). See appropriate SELF-DIAGNOSTICS article in ENGINE PERFORMANCE in appropriate MITCHELL® manual. If tachometer does not respond as specified, replace instrument cluster.

TEST V: KEY-IN-IGNITION WARNING CHIME DOES NOT OPERATE PROPERLY

1) Connect New Generation Star (NGS) tester to Data Link Connector (DLC). Turn ignition switch to RUN position. Monitor Generic Electronic Module (GEM) PIDs IGN_KEY, IGN_S, IGN_R and IGN_A while cycling ignition switch through all position. If PIDs agree with ignition switch position, go to next step. If PIDs does not agree with ignition switch position, go to step 4).

2) Using NGS tester, select GEM active command CHIME. Trigger CHIME active command ON and OFF. If chime operates properly, go to next step. If chime does not operate properly, replace GEM.

3) Using NGS tester, monitor GEM PID D_DR_SW while opening and closing driver's door. If PID agrees with door position, replace GEM. If PID does not agrees with door position, perform TEST X: DOOR AJAR WARNING CHIME DOES NOT OPERATE PROPERLY.

4) Remove fuse No. 28 (15-amp) from central junction box. Measure voltage at input side of fuse No. 28. Battery voltage should only exists when ignition switch is in RUN and START positions. If voltage is as specified, go to next step. If voltage is not as specified, repair power distribution circuit. See appropriate wiring diagram in POWER DISTRIBUTION article in WIRING DIAGRAMS.

5) Remove fuse No. 32 (15-amp) from central junction box. Measure voltage at input side of fuse No. 32. Battery voltage should only exists when ignition switch is in ACC and RUN positions. If voltage is as specified, go to next step. If voltage is not as specified, repair power distribution circuit. See appropriate wiring diagram in POWER DISTRIBUTION article in WIRING DIAGRAMS.

6) Turn ignition switch to LOCK position. Ensure fuse No. 28 is still removed. Disconnect GEM harness connector C352. Measure resistance in White/Light Green wire between output side of fuse No. 28 and terminal No. 8 at GEM harness connector C352. See Fig. 4. If resistance is 5 ohms or less, go to next step. If resistance is greater than 5 ohms, repair open in White/Light Green wire.

7) Ensure fuse No. 32 is still removed. Measure resistance in Black/Pink wire between output side of fuse No. 32 and terminal No. 22 at GEM harness connector C352. If resistance is 5 ohms or less, go to next step. If resistance is greater than 5 ohms, repair open in Black/Pink wire.

8) Measure resistance between ground and terminal No. 9 (Black/Pink wire) at GEM harness connector C352. With key in ignition switch, resistance should be 5 ohms or less. With key removed from ignition switch, resistance should be greater than 10 k/ohms. If resistance is as specified, go to next step. If resistance is not as specified, repair open or short in Black/Pink wire or replace key-in-ignition switch as necessary.

9) Turn ignition switch to LOCK position. Ensure fuses No. 28 and 32 are still removed and GEM harness connector C352 is disconnected.

Measure voltage at terminals No. 8 (White/Light Green) and No. 22 (Black/Pink wire) at GEM harness connector C352. If voltage does not exist at both terminals, go to next step. If voltage exists at either terminal, repair short to voltage in appropriate wire.

10) Measure resistance between ground and terminal No. 9 (Black/Pink wire) at GEM harness connector C352. If resistance is greater than 10 k/ohms, replace GEM. If resistance is 10 k/ohms or less, repair short to ground in Black/Pink wire.

TEST W: AIR BAG WARNING CHIME DOES NOT OPERATE PROPERLY

1) Connect New Generation Star (NGS) tester to Data Link Connector (DLC). Using NGS tester, perform Restraint Control Module (RCM) self-test. If no RCM DTCs exist, go to next step. If any RCM DTCs exist, repair air bag system as necessary. See MITCHELL® AIR BAG SERVICE & REPAIR MANUAL, DOMESTIC & IMPORTED MODELS.

2) Using NGS tester, monitor Generic Electronic Module (GEM) PIDs IGN_KEY, IGN_S, IGN_R and IGN_A while cycling ignition switch through all position. If PIDs agree with ignition switch position, go to next step. If PIDs does not agree with ignition switch position, perform TEST V: KEY-IN-IGNITION WARNING CHIME DOES NOT OPERATE PROPERLY.

3) Using NGS tester, select GEM active command CHIME. Trigger CHIME active command ON and OFF. If chime operates properly, go to next step. If chime does not operate properly, replace GEM.

4) Turn ignition switch to LOCK position. Disarm air bag system. See appropriate AIR BAG RESTRAINT SYSTEMS article. Disconnect RCM harness connector C276. Using NGS tester, monitor GEM PID ABCHIME. If PID indicates ON, go to next step. If PID does not indicate ON, go to step 6).

5) Turn ignition switch to LOCK position. Disconnect GEM module harness connector C352. Measure resistance between ground and terminal No. 10 (Light Blue/Black wire) at GEM harness connector C352. See Fig. 4. If resistance is greater than 10 k/ohms, replace GEM. If resistance is 10 k/ohms or less, repair short to ground in Light Blue/Black wire.

6) Turn ignition switch to LOCK position. Disconnect GEM module harness connector C352. Turn ignition switch to RUN position. Measure voltage at terminal No. 10 (Light Blue/Black wire) at GEM harness connector C352. See Fig. 4. If voltage does not exist, go to next step. If voltage exists, repair short to voltage in Light Blue/Black wire.

7) Turn ignition switch to LOCK position. Measure resistance in Light Blue/Black wire between terminal No. 26 at RCM harness connector C276 and terminal No. 10 at GEM harness connector C352. See Figs. 4 and 7. If resistance is 5 ohms or less, replace GEM. If resistance is greater than 5 ohms, repair open in Light Blue/Black wire.

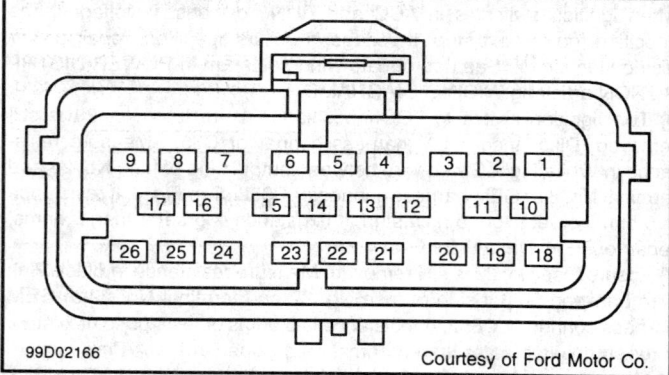

99D02166   Courtesy of Ford Motor Co.

Fig. 7: Identifying RCM Harness Connector C276 Terminals

TEST X: DOOR AJAR WARNING CHIME DOES NOT OPERATE PROPERLY

1) Connect New Generation Star (NGS) tester to Data Link Connector (DLC). Turn ignition switch to RUN position. Monitor Generic Electronic Module (GEM) PIDs IGN_KEY, IGN_S, IGN_R and IGN_A while cycling

ignition switch through all position. If PIDs agree with ignition switch position, go to next step. If PIDs does not agree with ignition switch position, perform TEST V: KEY-IN-IGNITION WARNING CHIME DOES NOT OPERATE PROPERLY.

2) Using NGS tester, select GEM active command CHIME. Trigger CHIME active command ON and OFF. If chime operates properly, go to next step. If chime does not operate properly, replace GEM.

3) Using NGS tester, monitor GEM PID D_DR_SW while opening and closing driver's door. If PID agrees with door position, go to next step. If PID does not agrees with door position, go to step 5).

4) Using NGS tester, monitor GEM PID P_DR_SW while opening and closing passenger's door. If PID agrees with door position, replace GEM. If PID does not agrees with door position, go to step 11).

5) Using NGS tester, monitor GEM PID D_DR_SW while opening and closing driver's door. If PID always indicates AJAR, go to next step. If PID does not always indicate AJAR, go to step 8).

6) Disconnect driver's door ajar switch harness connector C506. Using NGS tester, monitor GEM PID D_DR_SW. If PID still indicates AJAR, go to next step. If PID now indicates CLOSED, replace driver's door ajar switch.

7) Turn ignition switch to LOCK position. Disconnect GEM harness connector C292. Measure resistance between ground and terminal No. 13 (Yellow/Black wire) at GEM harness connector C292. See Fig. 2. If resistance is greater than 10 k/ohms, replace GEM. If resistance is 10 k/ohms or less, repair short to ground in Yellow/Black wire.

8) Disconnect driver's door ajar switch harness connector C506. Using a fused jumper wire, ground Yellow/Black wire terminal at driver's door ajar switch harness connector C506. Using NGS tester, monitor GEM PID D_DR_SW. If PID does not indicate AJAR, go to next step. If PID indicates AJAR, go to step 10).

9) Turn ignition switch to LOCK position. Disconnect GEM harness connector C292. Measure resistance in Yellow/Black wire between driver's door ajar switch harness connector C506 and terminal No. 13 at GEM harness connector C292. See Fig. 2. If resistance is 5 ohms or less, replace GEM. If resistance is greater than 5 ohms, repair open in Yellow/Black wire.

10) Measure resistance between ground and Black wire terminal at driver's door ajar switch harness connector C506. If resistance is 5 ohms or less, replace driver's door ajar switch. If resistance is greater than 5 ohms, repair open in Black wire.

11) Using NGS tester, monitor GEM PID P_DR_SW while opening and closing passenger's door. If PID always indicates AJAR, go to next step. If PID does not always indicates AJAR, go to step 14).

12) Disconnect passenger's door ajar switch harness connector C601. Using NGS tester, monitor GEM PID P_DR_SW. If PID still indicates AJAR, go to next step. If PID now indicates CLOSED, replace passenger' door ajar switch.

13) Turn ignition switch to LOCK position. Disconnect GEM harness connector C292. Measure resistance between ground and terminal No. 5 (Green/Red wire) at GEM harness connector C292. See Fig. 2. If resistance is greater than 10 k/ohms, replace GEM. If resistance is 10 k/ohms or less, repair short to ground in Green/Red wire.

14) Disconnect passenger's door ajar switch harness connector C601. Using a fused jumper wire, ground Green/Red wire terminal at passenger's door ajar switch harness connector C601. Using NGS tester, monitor GEM PID P_DR_SW. If PID does not indicate AJAR, go to next step. If PID indicates AJAR, go to step 16).

15) Turn ignition switch to LOCK position. Disconnect GEM harness connector C292. Measure resistance in Green/Red wire between passenger's door ajar switch harness connector C601 and terminal No. 5 at GEM harness connector C292. See Fig. 2. If resistance is 5 ohms or less, replace GEM. If resistance is greater than 5 ohms, repair open in Green/Red wire.

16) Measure resistance between ground and Black wire terminal at passenger's door ajar switch harness connector C601. If resistance is 5 ohms or less, replace passenger's door ajar switch. If resistance is greater than 5 ohms, repair open in Black wire.

TEST Y: HEADLIGHT WARNING CHIME DOES NOT OPERATE PROPERLY

1) Check headlights and exterior lights operation. If all exterior light operate properly, go to next step. If all exterior light do not operate properly, repair as necessary. See appropriate wiring diagrams in EXTERIOR LIGHTS and HEADLIGHT SYSTEMS articles.

2) Connect New Generation Star (NGS) tester to Data Link Connector (DLC). Turn ignition switch to RUN position. Monitor Generic Electronic Module (GEM) PIDs IGN_KEY, IGN_S, IGN_R and IGN_A while cycling ignition switch through all position. If PIDs agree with ignition switch position, go to next step. If PIDs does not agree with ignition switch position, perform TEST V: KEY-IN-IGNITION WARNING CHIME DOES NOT OPERATE PROPERLY.

3) Using NGS tester, select GEM active command CHIME. Trigger CHIME active command ON and OFF. If chime operates properly, go to next step. If chime does not operate properly, replace GEM.

4) Using NGS tester, monitor GEM PID D_DR_SW while opening and closing driver's door. If PID agrees with door position, go to next step. If PID does not agrees with door position, perform TEST X: DOOR AJAR WARNING CHIME DOES NOT OPERATE PROPERLY.

5) Using NGS tester, monitor GEM PID PARK_SW while turning headlight switch to PARK and OFF positions. If PID does not agree with switch position, go to next step. If PID agrees with switch position, replace GEM.

6) Using NGS tester, monitor GEM PID PARK_SW while turning headlight switch to PARK and OFF positions. If PID does not always indicates ON, go to next step. If PID always indicates ON, go to step **8)**.

7) Turn ignition switch to LOCK position. Disconnect GEM harness connector C352. Disconnect headlight switch harness connector C228. Measure resistance in Brown wire between terminal No. 7 at GEM harness connector C352 and terminal "R" at headlight switch harness connector C228. *See Figs. 4 and 8.* If resistance is 5 ohms or less, replace GEM. If resistance is greater than 5 ohms, repair open in Brown wire.

8) Turn ignition switch to LOCK position. Disconnect GEM harness connector C352. Ensure headlight switch is off. Turn ignition switch to RUN position. Measure voltage at terminal No. 7 (Brown wire) at GEM harness connector C352. *See Fig. 4.* If voltage does not exist, replace GEM. If voltage exists, repair short to voltage in Brown wire.

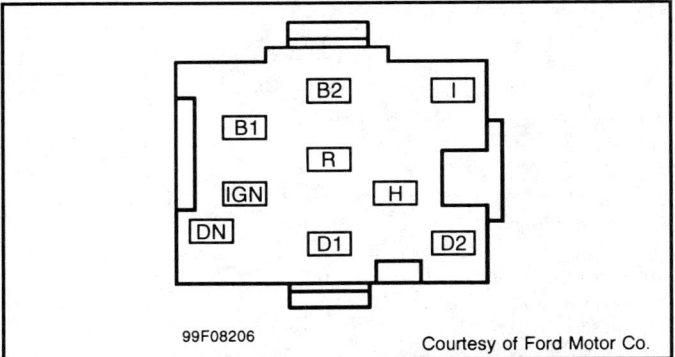

99F08206   Courtesy of Ford Motor Co.

Fig. 8: Identifying Headlight Switch Harness Connector C228 Terminals

TEST Z: SEAT BELT WARNING CHIME DOES NOT OPERATE PROPERLY

1) Connect New Generation Star (NGS) tester to Data Link Connector (DLC). Turn ignition switch to RUN position. Monitor Generic Electronic Module (GEM) PIDs IGN_KEY, IGN_S, IGN_R and IGN_A while cycling ignition switch through all position. If PIDs agree with ignition switch position, go to next step. If PIDs does not agree with ignition switch position, perform TEST V: KEY-IN-IGNITION WARNING CHIME DOES NOT OPERATE PROPERLY.

2) Using NGS tester, monitor GEM PID D_SBELT while buckling and unbuckling driver's seat belt. If PID agrees with seat belt position, go to next step. If PID does not agree with seat belt position, go to step **5)**.

3) Using NGS tester, select GEM active command CHIME. Trigger CHIME active command ON and OFF. If chime operates properly, go to next step. If chime does not operate properly, replace GEM.

4) Cycle ignition switch from LOCK to RUM position while monitoring seat belt indicator in instrument cluster. If seat belt indicator operates properly, replace GEM. If seat belt indicator does not operate properly, perform TEST I: SAFETY BELT INDICATOR IS INOPERATIVE (CHIME IS OPERATIVE)/ DOES NOT OPERATE CORRECTLY.

5) Using NGS tester, monitor GEM PID D_SBELT while buckling and unbuckling driver's seat belt. If PID always indicate OUT, go to next step. If PID does not always indicate OUT, go to step **8)**.

6) Turn ignition switch to LOCK position. Disconnect driver's seat belt switch harness connector C315. Using NGS tester, monitor GEM PID D_SBELT. If PID does not indicate IN, go to next step. If PID indicates IN, replace driver's seat belt switch.

7) Turn ignition switch to LOCK position. Disconnect GEM harness connector C293. Measure resistance between ground and terminal No. 8 (Brown/Light Blue wire) at GEM harness connector C293. *See Fig. 5.* If resistance is greater than 10 k/ohms, replace GEM. If resistance is 10 k/ohms or less, repair short to ground in Brown/Light Blue wire.

8) Disconnect driver's seat belt switch harness connector C315. Using a fused jumper wire, ground Brown/Light Blue wire terminal at driver's seat belt switch harness connector C315. Using NGS tester, monitor GEM PID D_SBELT. If PID does not indicate OUT, go to next step. If PID indicates OUT, go to step **10)**.

9) Disconnect GEM harness connector C293. Measure resistance in Brown/Light Blue wire between driver's seat belt switch harness connector C315 and terminal No. 8 at GEM harness connector C293. *See Fig. 5.* If resistance is 5 ohms or less, replace GEM. If resistance is greater than 5 ohms, repair open in Brown/Light Blue wire.

10) Measure resistance between ground and Black wire terminal at driver's seat belt switch harness connector C315. If resistance is 5 ohms or less, replace driver's seat belt switch. If resistance is greater than 5 ohms, repair open in Black wire.

REMOVAL & INSTALLATION

CAUTION: Electronic modules are sensitive to static electrical charges. Proper grounding of technician and workpiece is essential to prevent damage.

FUEL PRESSURE RELIEF

WARNING: Fuel supply lines on fuel injected engines remain pressurized for long periods of time after engine shutdown. System pressure MUST be relieved prior to fuel system service to prevent possible injury. A valve on fuel injector supply manifold is provided for this purpose.

CAUTION: Use a rag as protection from fuel spray when disconnecting hoses. Plug hoses after disconnection. Keep open flame away from any fuel related components.

Remove air cleaner. Unscrew and remove fuel pressure relief valve cap on fuel supply manifold. Connect Fuel Pressure Gauge (T80L-9974-B) to fuel pressure relief valve. Open manual valve on fuel pressure gauge to relieve fuel system pressure.

COOLANT TEMPERATURE SENDING UNIT

Removal & Installation – Sending unit is located in engine block or cylinder head, at left side of engine compartment. When installing, use thread sealant and tighten to 8-18 ft. lbs. (11-24 N.m).

FUEL PUMP ASSEMBLY

WARNING: Before disconnecting any fuel line, release fuel pressure from fuel system to reduce possibility of injury or fire. See FUEL PRESSURE RELIEF.

Removal & Installation – 1) Relieve fuel pressure. See FUEL PRESSURE RELIEF. Drain fuel with a siphon pump through fuel tank filler pipe.

2) Raise vehicle on hoist. Loosen fuel tank filler pipe and vent hose clamps at metal lines and disconnect hoses and tubes.

3) Disconnect electrical connector for fuel tank sensor. Place support under fuel tank and remove bolts from rear of fuel tank support straps. Swing support straps forward on hinges to clear tank. Remove tank from vehicle.

4) To prevent contamination of fuel and fuel tank, clean dirt and debris from around fuel pump module retaining flange. Using Fuel Tank Sender Wrench (D84P-9275-A), turn fuel pump locking retainer ring counterclockwise and remove locking retainer ring.

5) Pull fuel pump module out of tank. Remove "O" ring seal and discard. To install, reverse removal procedure using NEW "O" ring seal.

INDICATOR/WARNING BULBS

NOTE: All indicators/warning bulbs are removed and installed in same way.

Removal & Installation – Remove instrument cluster. See INSTRUMENT CLUSTER. Turn miniature bulb socket 1/4 turn counterclockwise to align tabs with slots in instrument cluster and pull bulb out of instrument cluster. To install, align tabs on miniature bulb with slots in instrument cluster and turn miniature bulb socket 1/4 turn clockwise until socket stops turning.

INSTRUMENT CLUSTER

NOTE: When battery is disconnected, vehicle computer and memory systems may lose memory data. Driveability problems may exist until computer systems have completed a relearn cycle. If replacing instrument cluster information MUST be uploaded to NGS tester to download into NEW module. See COMPUTER RELEARN PROCEDURES article in GENERAL INFORMATION before disconnecting battery.

Removal & Installation – 1) Disconnect negative battery cable. Remove light switch knob. Remove 2 upper retaining screws from instrument panel finish panel. Remove instrument panel finish panel.

2) Remove 4 retaining screws from instrument cluster. Pull cluster away from instrument panel. Disconnect instrument cluster harness connectors. Remove instrument cluster. To install, reverse removal procedure.

OIL PRESSURE SENSOR

Removal & Installation – Oil pressure sending unit is located in oil filter adapter at right front of engine compartment. When installing sending unit, use thread sealant.

WIRING DIAGRAMS

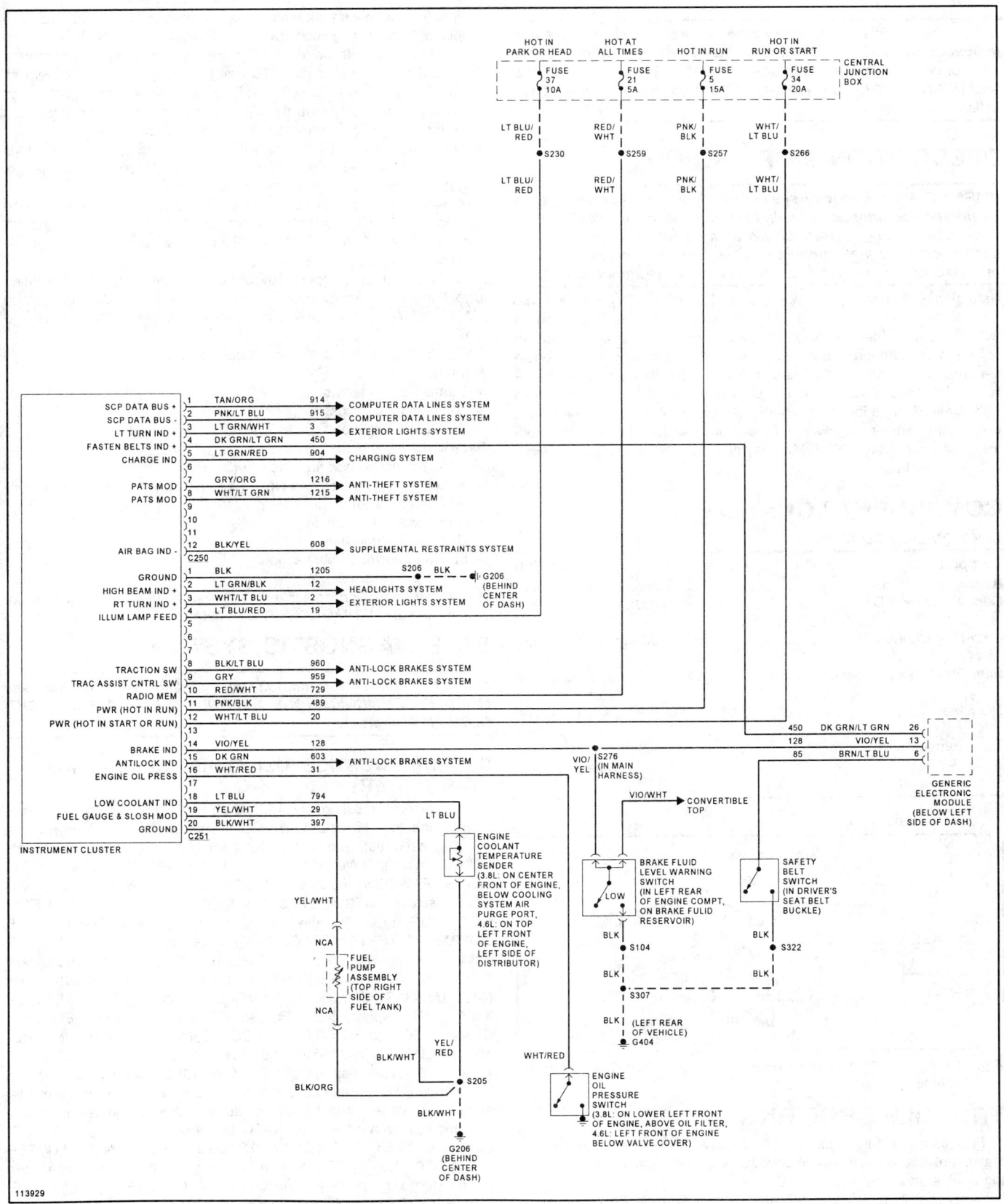

Fig. 9: Analog Instrument Panel Wiring Diagram (Mustang)

113929

NOTE: This article concerns unique features of natural gas fuel indication system. For instrument cluster functions and diagnostics not covered in this article, see ANALOG INSTRUMENT PANELS – EXPEDITION, F150 & F250 LIGHT-DUTY PICKUP, & NAVIGATOR article.

DESCRIPTION & OPERATION

WARNING: Do not modify system configuration or components. Do not replace components with parts not specifically designed for use with natural gas. Natural gas components and gasoline fuel components are not interchangeable. Use of improper parts or materials could result in fire, personal injury or engine damage.

Natural gas fuel system is optional on F250 light-duty 5.4L engine. Natural gas fuel indication system consists of Natural Gas Vehicle (NGV) module, fuel gauge in instrument cluster, fuel tank pressure sensor, tank temperature sensor and related circuitry. NGV module features injector drivers, fuel gauge driver and self-diagnostic capabilities. NGV module Diagnostic Trouble Codes (DTCs) may be retrieved with New Generation Star (NGS) tester, or equivalent scan tool. Instrument cluster is Hybrid Electronic Cluster (HEC) with self-diagnostic capability. HEC DTCs may be displayed on HEC or retrieved with NGS tester.

COMPONENT LOCATION

COMPONENT LOCATION

Component	Location
Battery Junction Box	Left Side Engine Compartment
Central Junction Box	Under Left Side Of Instrument Panel
Data Link Connector (DLC)	Below Center Of Instrument Panel
Fuel Tank Pressure Sensor	[1] In Rear Of In-Bed Fuel Tank Solenoid Valve
NGV Module	Center Radiator Support Behind Radiator Grille
Tank Temperature Sensor	[1] In Rear Of In-Bed Fuel Tank Solenoid Valve

[1] – See Fig. 1.

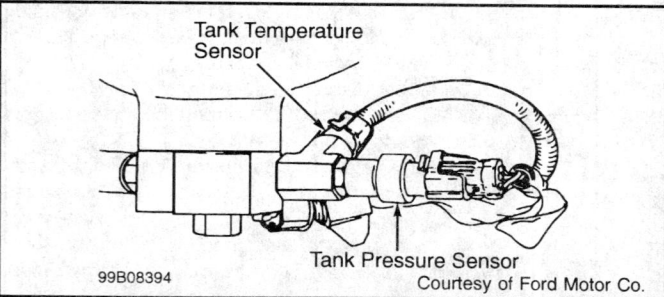

Tank Temperature Sensor

Tank Pressure Sensor

99B08394
Courtesy of Ford Motor Co.

Fig. 1: Locating Fuel Tank Pressure Sensor & Tank Temperature Sensor

TROUBLE SHOOTING

1) Fuel gauge accuracy can be affected by fast filling and fuel system leaks. Make sure the following conditions DO NOT exist before continuing trouble shooting:
- After fast fill, fuel gauge can drop up to 1/16 tank. This is normal.

- Fast filling causes tank temperature to drop to low temperatures. If this occurs with ignition switch in RUN position, NGV will store Diagnostic Trouble Codes (DTCs) in error. After temperature returns to normal operating range, DTCs will persist and need to be cleared.
- Fast filling with ignition switch in RUN position will cause fuel gauge to move very slowly toward full. This is normal and can be eliminated by turning ignition switch to LOCK position before filling.
- Fuel leaks will cause inaccurate fuel gauge readings. If leak exceeds instrument cluster and NGV module ability to update fuel gauge, gauge may read full when tanks are empty.
- After fuel system has been drained for repair, fuel gauge will read empty until ignition switch is turn from LOCK to RUN positions 4-5 times. After 4-5 times, system will build pressure and fuel gauge will display properly.

2) Verify customer complaint by observing fuel gauge to determine correct operation with ignition switch in RUN position with engine off, in START before ignition switch is released and in RUN with engine running.

3) Visually inspect following for obvious signs of damage.
Mechanical:
- Damaged fuel tank(s).
- Damaged solenoids.
- Damaged fuel line(s).

Electrical:
- Central junction box fuse No. 30 (30-amp).
- Battery junction box fuses No. 2 (3-amp), 18 (15-amp), 23 (15-amp) and 24 (15-amp).
- Damaged NGV module.
- Damaged wiring harness.
- Loose or corroded connections.
- Damaged sensors.

4) If damage is found, repair and test system. If cause of fault is not evident, see SELF-DIAGNOSTIC SYSTEM.

SELF-DIAGNOSTIC SYSTEM

NOTE: For further information on self-diagnostic system, see MODULE COMMUNICATIONS NETWORK – F150 & F250 LIGHT-DUTY PICKUP article.

SELF-DIAGNOSTICS (USING NEW GENERATION STAR TESTER)

1) For preliminary testing, see TROUBLE SHOOTING. If problem is not found, connect NGS tester to Data Link Connector (DLC). Perform data link diagnostic test. See DATA LINK DIAGNOSTIC TEST under COMMUNICATION NETWORK DIAGNOSTICS in MODULE COMMUNICATIONS NETWORK – F150 & F250 LIGHT-DUTY PICKUP article. If NGS tester displays CKT914, CKT915 or CKT70 = ALL ECUS NO RESP/ NOT EQUIP, repair module communications concern. See MODULE COMMUNICATIONS NETWORK – F150 & F250 LIGHT-DUTY PICKUP article. If NGS tester displays NO RESP/NOT EQUIP for Natural Gas Vehicle (NGV) module, go to TEST J: NO COMMUNICATION WITH NATURAL GAS VEHICLE (NGV) MODULE under SYSTEM TESTS. If NGS tester displays NO RESP/NOT EQUIP for Hybrid Electronic Cluster (HEC), go to TEST L: NO COMMUNICATION WITH INSTRUMENT CLUSTER in SYSTEM TESTS.

2) If NGS tester displays SYSTEM PASSED, retrieve and record continuous DTCs. Erase continuous DTCs. Perform instrument cluster and NGV module self-test. If DTCs related to the concern are retrieved, perform appropriate test. See NATURAL GAS VEHICLE (NGV) MODULE DTC TEST INDEX and/or HYBRID ELECTRONIC CLUSTER (HEC) DTC TEST INDEX table. If no DTCs related to the concern are retrieved, go to HYBRID ELECTRONIC CLUSTER (HEC) SELF-DIAGNOSTICS to continue diagnostics.

1999 ACCESSORIES & EQUIPMENT
Analog Instrument Panels
F250 Light-Duty Pickup – CNG (Cont.)

FORD
4-797

NATURAL GAS VEHICLE (NGV) MODULE DTC TEST INDEX

DTC	Description	Test
B1219	Fuel Tank Pressure Sensor Circuit Failure	A
B1220	Fuel Tank Pressure Sensor Circuit Short To Power	B
B1222	Tank Temperature Sensor Circuit Failure	C
B1223	Tank Temperature Sensor Circuit Open	D
B1224	Tank Temperature Sensor Circuit Short To Power	E
B1225	Tank Temperature Sensor Circuit Short To Ground	F
B1317	Battery Voltage High	G
B1318	Battery Voltage Low	H
B1342	ECU Defective	I

HYBRID ELECTRONIC CLUSTER (HEC) DTC TEST INDEX

DTC [1]	Description	Test
B1202	Fuel Sender Open	L
B1204	Fuel Sender Short To Ground	L

[1] – For HEC DTCs not listed here, see MODULE COMMUNICATIONS NETWORK – F150 & F250 LIGHT-DUTY PICKUP article.

HYBRID ELECTRONIC CLUSTER (HEC) SELF-DIAGNOSTICS

NOTE: Turning ignition switch to LOCK position will cause HEC to exit self-diagnostics.

Instrument cluster is a Hybrid Electronic Cluster (HEC). HEC has self-diagnostic system which may store a Diagnostic Trouble Code (DTC) if a problem exists in the system. HEC DTCs may be displayed on the instrument cluster or retrieved from Data Link Connector (DLC) with New Generation Star (NGS) tester.

Turn ignition switch to LOCK position. To enter HEC self-diagnostics, press and hold instrument cluster SELECT/RESET button. Turn ignition switch to RUN position. Within 5-8 seconds, odometer will display "tESt" to begin self-diagnostic mode. SELECT/RESET button must be released within 3 seconds of odometer displaying "tESt". Repeatedly press SELECT/RESET button through odometer displays until "dtc" is displayed. When odometer displays "dtc", press SELECT/RESET button again and any continuous DTCs will be displayed before odometer advances to next display. For other HEC diagnostic modes, see HYBRID ELECTRONIC CLUSTER (HEC) SELF-DIAGNOSTIC MODES.

If DTC is retrieved, see HYBRID ELECTRONIC CLUSTER (HEC) DTC TEST INDEX table under SELF-DIAGNOSTICS to continue diagnostics. If no DTCs related to the concern are retrieved, perform appropriate test based on symptom. See SYMPTOM TEST INDEX table under SYSTEM TESTS. For DTCs not covered in this article, see MODULE COMMUNICATIONS NETWORK – F150 & F250 LIGHT-DUTY PICKUP article.

HYBRID ELECTRONIC CLUSTER (HEC) SELF-DIAGNOSTIC MODES

NOTE: Values displayed are instrument cluster input values, not gauge values.

"GAGE" – Activates sweep of all gauges, then displays present gauge values. Does ROM and EE checksum tests. If gauge sweep is inoperative, replace instrument cluster.

All Segments Illuminated – Illuminates all odometer segments. If any odometer segment is inoperative, replace instrument cluster.

"bulb" – Illuminates all micro-controlled lamps and LEDs. Replace bulb or LED as necessary.

"r" – Returns to normal operation all micro-controlled lamps and LEDs and displays hexadecimal values for ROM. This is used when requesting assistance from Ford hotline. If alternating flashes of FAIL and ROM level are displayed, replace instrument cluster.

"EE" – Hexadecimal value for EE level. This is used when requesting assistance from Ford hotline. If alternating flashes of FAIL and EE level are displayed, replace instrument cluster.

"dt" – Displays hexadecimal coding of final manufacturing test date. This is used when requesting assistance from Ford hotline.

"dtc" – Displays continuous DTCs in 16-bit hexadecimal. Pressing SELECT/RESET button will display any DTCs stored before proceeding to next step.

"enG" – Displays English value speed input to instrument cluster. Speedometer will indicate present vehicle speed. Display will indicate zero if input is not received, if input is invalid for more than one second or if actual vehicle speed is zero.

"m" – Displays metric value speed input to instrument cluster. Speedometer will indicate present vehicle speed. Display will indicate zero if input is not received, if input is invalid for more than one second or if actual vehicle speed is zero.

"tAc" – Displays tachometer value input to instrument cluster. Tachometer will indicate present engine speed. Display will indicate zero if input is not received, if input is invalid for more than one second or if actual engine speed is zero.

"FUEL" – Displays fuel level input to instrument cluster. Fuel gauge will indicate present fuel level. Displays 255 for open circuit, about 232 for full stop, 215 for full tank, 178 for 3/4 tank, 138 for 1/2 tank, 93 for 1/4 tank, 41 for empty or 0-20 circuit is shorted. Below 55 low fuel warning lamp should light.

"OIL" – Displays last oil pressure reading input to instrument cluster. Oil pressure will indicate present oil pressure. If value displayed is more than 254, circuit is open.

"dEGC" – Displays last coolant temp input to instrument cluster. Coolant temperature gauge will indicate present coolant temperature. If value displayed is more than 254, circuit is open.

"br" – Displays brake fluid level input to instrument cluster.

"bAtt" – Displays battery voltage input to instrument cluster. Battery voltage gauge will indicate present battery voltage.

"rhEo" – Displays present hexadecimal value for instrument cluster backlight pulse width modulated input to instrument cluster. This is used when requesting assistance from Ford hotline.

"rhi" – Pulse width modulated input duty cycle to instrument cluster.

"rhS" – Standard Corporate Protocol (SCP) hexadecimal dimming step. This is used when requesting assistance from Ford hotline.

"rho" – Output driver counts in hexadecimal format. This is used when requesting assistance from Ford hotline.

"Cr" – Displays present RUN/START sense input to instrument cluster. Shows -h with ignition switch in START position and -L with ignition switch in RUN position.

"ALtF" – Displays 8-bit hexadecimal value for alternate fuel level. Shows -- if message not received and FF if message invalid. Go to TEST J: NO COMMUNICATION WITH NATURAL GAS VEHICLE (NGV) MODULE under SYSTEM TESTS.

"PA" – Displays 8-bit hexadecimal value for port "A". This is used when requesting assistance from Ford hotline.

FORD
4-798

1999 ACCESSORIES & EQUIPMENT
Analog Instrument Panels
F250 Light-Duty Pickup – CNG (Cont.)

"Pb" – Displays 8-bit hexadecimal value for port "B". This is used when requesting assistance from Ford hotline.

"PC" – Displays 8-bit hexadecimal value for port "C". This is used when requesting assistance from Ford hotline.

"Pd" – Displays 8-bit hexadecimal value for port "D". This is used when requesting assistance from Ford hotline.

"PE0" – Displays 8-bit hexadecimal value for port E0. This is used when requesting assistance from Ford hotline.

"PE1" – Displays 8-bit hexadecimal value for port E1. This is used when requesting assistance from Ford hotline.

"PE2" – Displays 8-bit hexadecimal value for port E2. This is used when requesting assistance from Ford hotline.

"PE3" – Displays 8-bit hexadecimal value for port E3. This is used when requesting assistance from Ford hotline.

"PE4" – Displays 8-bit hexadecimal value for port E4. This is used when requesting assistance from Ford hotline.

"PE5" – Displays 8-bit hexadecimal value for port E5. This is used when requesting assistance from Ford hotline.

"PE6" – Displays 8-bit hexadecimal value for port E6. This is used when requesting assistance from Ford hotline.

"PE7" – Displays 8-bit hexadecimal value for port E7. This is used when requesting assistance from Ford hotline.

"GAGE" – Repeats test display cycle.

SYSTEM TESTS

SYMPTOM TEST INDEX

Symptom	Test
No Communication With Natural Gas Vehicle (NGV) Module	J
Integrated Circuit Display Inoperative Or Erratic	K
No Communication With Instrument Cluster	L
Fuel Gauge Inaccurate	[1]

[1] – Using New Generation Star (NGS) tester, perform Natural Gas Vehicle (NGV) Module self-test. If DTCs are retrieved, perform appropriate test. See NATURAL GAS VEHICLE (NGV) MODULE DTC TEST INDEX under SELF-DIAGNOSTICS. If no DTCs are retrieved, go to TEST M: INCORRECT FUEL GAUGE INDICATION.

TEST A: FUEL TANK PRESSURE SENSOR CIRCUIT FAILURE (DTC B1219)

NOTE: After repair, clear DTCs and retest system.

1) Turn ignition switch to LOCK position. Connect New Generation Star (NGS) tester to Data Link Connector (DLC). Turn ignition switch to RUN position. Observe Natural Gas Vehicle (NGV) module PID TANKPR. If PID TANKPR displays zero (psi), go to next step. If PID TANKPR does not display zero, inspect connectors for loose, damaged or corroded terminals. Clear DTCs. Test system for normal operation. If DTC B1219 is retrieved again, replace NGV module. See NATURAL GAS VEHICLE (NGV) MODULE under REMOVAL & INSTALLATION.

2) Turn ignition switch to LOCK position. Disconnect NGV module 60-pin connector. Disconnect fuel tank pressure sensor 4-pin connector. Connect EEC-IV 60-Pin Breakout Box (418-005) to NGV module connector. Leave NGV module disconnected. Measure resistance between breakout box pins No. 7 and 46. If resistance is more than 10 k/ohms, go to next step. If resistance is 10 k/ohms or less, repair short between Dark Green/Orange wire and Brown wire.

3) Connect EEC-IV 60-Pin Breakout Box (418-005) to NGV module and NGV module connector. Turn ignition switch to RUN position. Measure voltage between fuel tank pressure sensor connector Brown wire terminal and Brown/White wire terminal. If voltage is 4.0-6.0 volts, go to next step. If voltage is not 4.0-6.0 volts, go to step **6)**.

4) Turn ignition switch to LOCK position. Connect jumper wire between fuel tank pressure sensor connector Dark Green/Orange wire terminal and Brown/White wire terminal. Turn ignition switch to RUN position.

Measure voltage between breakout box pins No. 7 and 26. If voltage is more than 4.61 volts, go to step **6)**. If voltage is less than 4.61 volts, go to next step.

5) Turn ignition switch to LOCK position. Disconnect NGV module from breakout box. Leave breakout box connected to NGV module connector. Measure resistance between breakout box pin No. 26 and fuel tank pressure sensor connector Brown/White wire terminal. If resistance is less than 5 ohms, repair open in Dark Green/Orange wire. If resistance is 5 ohms or more, repair open in Brown/White wire.

6) Turn ignition switch to LOCK position. Disconnect NGV module from breakout box. Leave breakout box connected to NGV module connector. Measure resistance between breakout box pin No. 46 and fuel tank pressure sensor connector Brown wire terminal. If resistance is less than 5 ohms, go to next step. If resistance is 5 ohms or more, repair open in Brown wire.

7) Measure resistance between breakout box pins No. 26 and 40 or 60. If resistance is more than 10 k/ohms, go to next step. If resistance is 10 k/ohms or less, repair short to ground in Brown/White wire.

8) Measure resistance between breakout box pins No. 46 and 40 or 60. If resistance is more than 10 k/ohms, go to next step. If resistance is 10 k/ohms or less, repair short to ground in Brown wire.

9) Measure resistance between breakout box pin No. 26 and fuel tank pressure sensor connector Brown/White wire terminal. If resistance is less than 5 ohms, go to next step. If resistance is 5 ohms or more, repair open in Brown/White wire.

10) Turn ignition switch to RUN position. Measure voltage between fuel tank pressor sensor connector Brown/White wire terminal and ground. If voltage is less than 0.5 volt, go to next step. If voltage is 0.5 volt or more, repair short to power in Brown/White wire.

11) Check fuel tank solenoid operation. See UNABLE TO VENT FUEL TANKS OR FUEL LINES (PICKUP) under FUEL SYSTEM (NATURAL GAS VEHICLES) in SYSTEM & COMPONENT TESTING – EEC-V article in ENGINE PERFORMANCE in appropriate MITCHELL® manual. If all fuel tank solenoids operate correctly, go to next step. If any fuel tank solenoids do not operate, repair as necessary.

12) Check fuel system for leaks. See LEAK TEST under FUEL SYSTEM (NATURAL GAS VEHICLES) in SYSTEM & COMPONENT TESTING – EEC-V article in ENGINE PERFORMANCE in appropriate MITCHELL® manual. If fuel system leaks, repair leaks as necessary. If fuel system does not leak, replace NGV module. See NATURAL GAS VEHICLE (NGV) MODULE under REMOVAL & INSTALLATION.

TEST B: FUEL TANK PRESSURE SENSOR CIRCUIT SHORT TO POWER (DTC B1220)

NOTE: After repair, clear DTCs and retest system.

1) Turn ignition switch to LOCK position. Connect New Generation Star (NGS) tester to Data Link Connector (DLC). Turn ignition switch to RUN position. Observe Natural Gas Vehicle (NGV) module PID TANKPR. If PID TANKPR displays zero (psi), go to next step. If PID TANKPR does not display zero, inspect connectors for loose, damaged or corroded terminals. Clear DTCs. Test system for normal operation. If DTC B1219 is retrieved again, replace NGV module. See NATURAL GAS VEHICLE (NGV) MODULE under REMOVAL & INSTALLATION.

2) Turn ignition switch to LOCK position. Disconnect NGV module 60-pin connector. Connect EEC-IV 60-Pin Breakout Box (418-005) to NGV module and NGV module connector. Disconnect fuel tank pressure sensor 4-pin connector. Turn ignition switch to RUN position. Measure voltage between breakout box pins No. 7 and 46. If voltage is less than 0.61 volt, replace fuel tank pressure sensor. See FUEL TANK PRESSURE SENSOR under REMOVAL & INSTALLATION. If voltage is 0.61 volt or more, go to next step.

3) Turn ignition switch to LOCK position. Measure resistance between breakout box pins No. 7 and 46. If resistance is more than 10 k/ohms, go to next step. If resistance is 10 k/ohms or less, repair short between Dark Green/Orange wire and Brown/White wire.

1999 ACCESSORIES & EQUIPMENT
Analog Instrument Panels
F250 Light-Duty Pickup – CNG (Cont.)

FORD
4-799

4) Measure resistance between breakout box pins No. 7 and 37 or 57. If resistance is more than 10 k/ohms, go to next step. If resistance is 10 k/ohms or less, repair short to power in Dark Green/Orange wire.

5) Check fuel tank solenoid operation. See UNABLE TO VENT FUEL TANKS OR FUEL LINES (PICKUP) under FUEL SYSTEM (NATURAL GAS VEHICLES) in SYSTEM & COMPONENT TESTING – EEC-V article in ENGINE PERFORMANCE in appropriate MITCHELL® manual. If all fuel tank solenoids operate correctly, go to next step. If any fuel tank solenoids do not operate correctly, repair as necessary.

6) Check fuel system for leaks. See LEAK TEST under FUEL SYSTEM (NATURAL GAS VEHICLES) in SYSTEM & COMPONENT TESTING – EEC-V article in ENGINE PERFORMANCE in appropriate MITCH-ELL® manual. If fuel system leaks, repair as necessary. If fuel system does not leak, replace NGV module. See NATURAL GAS VEHICLE (NGV) MODULE under REMOVAL & INSTALLATION.

TEST C: TANK TEMPERATURE SENSOR CIRCUIT FAILURE (DTC B1222)

NOTE: After repair, clear DTCs and retest system.

1) Turn ignition switch to LOCK position. Disconnect Natural Gas Vehicle (NGV) module 60-pin connector. Connect EEC-IV 60-Pin Breakout Box (418-005) to NGV module and NGV module connector. Turn ignition switch to RUN position. Measure voltage between breakout box pins No. 46 and 47. If voltage is more than 4.55 volts, go to next step. If voltage is 4.55 volts or less, go to step **6)**.

2) Turn ignition switch to LOCK position. Disconnect tank temperature sensor 2-pin connector. Connect jumper wire between tank temperature sensor connector terminals. Turn ignition switch to RUN position. Measure voltage between breakout box pins No. 46 and 47. If voltage is less than 0.12 volt, replace tank temperature sensor. See TANK TEMPERATURE SENSOR under REMOVAL & INSTALLATION. If voltage is more than 0.12 volt, go to next step.

3) Turn ignition switch to LOCK position. Disconnect NGV module from breakout box. Leave NGV module connector connected to breakout box. Measure resistance between breakout box pin No. 46 and tank temperature sensor connector Brown wire terminal. If resistance is less than 5 ohms, go to next step. If resistance is 5 ohms or more, repair open in Brown wire.

4) Measure voltage between breakout box pins No. 46 and 40 or 60. If voltage is 0.5 volt or less, go to next step. If voltage is more than 0.5 volt, repair short to power in Brown wire.

5) Turn ignition switch to RUN position. Measure voltage between breakout box pins No. 46 and 47. If voltage is more than 4.55 volts, replace tank temperature sensor. See TANK TEMPERATURE SENSOR under REMOVAL & INSTALLATION. If voltage is 4.55 volts or less, go to next step.

6) Turn ignition switch to LOCK position. If still connected, disconnect NGV module from breakout box. Leave NGV module connector connected to breakout box. Measure resistance between breakout box pins No. 40 and 46. If resistance is more than 10 k/ohms, go to next step. If resistance is 10 k/ohms or less, repair short to ground in Brown wire.

CAUTION: Use voltmeter function of NGS tester to monitor and record voltages in this step. Do not use standard voltmeter or inaccurate readings will be received, possibly leading to incorrect repairs.

7) Connect NGV module to breakout box. Connect tank temperature sensor connector. Assemble NGS tester accessory voltmeter leads. Connect NGS voltmeter positive lead to breakout box pin No. 47. Connect NGS voltmeter negative lead to breakout box pin No. 40 or 60. Turn ignition switch to RUN position. Access DIGITAL MEASUREMENT SYSTEM on NGS tester. Select VOLTMETER, then LINK. Select PID/DATA MONITOR AND RECORD, then NGV. Select TEMPS1, then START. Select REC, then push TRIGGER to capture data. Push TRIGGER to store data, then select VIEW to examine data. If voltage varies rapidly between 0.2-4.9 volts, inspect harness and connectors for

intermittent condition. Repair as necessary. If voltage does not vary rapidly between 0.2-4.9 volts, replace NGV module. See NATURAL GAS VEHICLE (NGV) MODULE under REMOVAL & INSTALLATION.

TEST D: TANK TEMPERATURE SENSOR CIRCUIT OPEN (DTC B1223)

NOTE: After repair, clear DTCs and retest system.

1) Turn ignition switch to LOCK position. Connect New Generation Star (NGS) tester to Data Link Connector (DLC). Turn ignition switch to RUN position. Access PID/DATA MONITOR AND RECORD. Select Natural Gas Vehicle (NGV) module PID TEMPS1. If temperature is 199°F, go to next step. If temperature is not 199°F, inspect for loose, damaged or corroded connectors and connector pins. Clear DTCs. Test system for normal operation. If DTC B1223 is retrieved again, replace NGV module. See NATURAL GAS VEHICLE (NGV) MODULE under REMOVAL & INSTALLATION.

2) Turn ignition switch to LOCK position. Disconnect NGV module 60-pin connector. Connect EEC-IV 60-Pin Breakout Box (418-005) to NGV module connector. Leave NGV module disconnected. Disconnect tank temperature sensor 2-pin connector. Measure resistance between breakout box pin No. 46 and tank temperature sensor connector Brown wire terminal. If resistance is less than 5 ohms, go to next step. If resistance is 5 ohms or more, repair open in Brown wire.

3) Measure resistance between breakout box pin No. 47 and tank temperature sensor Light Green/Red wire terminal. If resistance is less than 5 ohms, replace tank temperature sensor. See TANK TEMPERA-TURE SENSOR under REMOVAL & INSTALLATION. If resistance is 5 ohms or more, repair open in Light Green/Red wire.

TEST E: TANK TEMPERATURE SENSOR CIRCUIT SHORT TO POWER (DTC B1224)

NOTE: After repair, clear DTCs and retest system.

1) Turn ignition switch to LOCK position. Connect New Generation Star (NGS) tester to Data Link Connector (DLC). Turn ignition switch to RUN position. Access PID/DATA MONITOR AND RECORD. Select Natural Gas Vehicle (NGV) module PID TEMPS1. If temperature is 199°F, go to next step. If temperature is not 199°F, inspect for loose, damaged or corroded connectors and connector pins. Clear DTCs. Test system for normal operation. If DTC B1223 is retrieved again, replace NGV module. See NATURAL GAS VEHICLE (NGV) MODULE under REMOVAL & INSTALLATION.

2) Turn ignition switch to LOCK position. Disconnect NGV module 60-pin connector. Connect EEC-IV 60-Pin Breakout Box (418-005) to NGV module connector. Leave NGV module disconnected. Disconnect tank temperature sensor 2-pin connector. Turn ignition switch to RUN position. Measure voltage between breakout box pins No. 46 and 40 or 60. If voltage is less than 0.5 volt, go to next step. If voltage is 0.5 volt or more, repair short to power in Brown wire.

3) Measure voltage between breakout box pins No. 47 and 40 or 60. If voltage is less than 0.5 volt, replace NGV module. See NATURAL GAS VEHICLE (NGV) MODULE under REMOVAL & INSTALLATION. If voltage is 0.5 volt or more, repair short to power in Light Green/Red wire.

TEST F: TANK TEMPERATURE SENSOR CIRCUIT SHORT TO GROUND (DTC B1225)

NOTE: After repair, clear DTCs and retest system.

1) Turn ignition switch to LOCK position. Connect New Generation Star (NGS) tester to Data Link Connector (DLC). Turn ignition switch to RUN position. Access PID/DATA MONITOR AND RECORD. Select Natural Gas Vehicle (NGV) module PID TEMPS1. If temperature is 199°F, go to next step. If temperature is not 199°F, inspect for loose, damaged or corroded connectors and connector pins. Clear DTCs. Test system for

FORD
4-800

1999 ACCESSORIES & EQUIPMENT
Analog Instrument Panels
F250 Light-Duty Pickup – CNG (Cont.)

normal operation. If DTC B1223 is retrieved again, replace NGV module. See NATURAL GAS VEHICLE (NGV) MODULE under REMOVAL & INSTALLATION.

2) Turn ignition switch to LOCK position. Disconnect NGV module 60-pin connector. Connect EEC-IV 60-Pin Breakout Box (418-005) to NGV module connector. Leave NGV module disconnected. Disconnect tank temperature sensor 2-pin connector. Measure the resistance between breakout box pins No. 47 and 40 or 60. If resistance is less than 5 ohms, repair short to ground in Brown wire. If resistance is 5 ohms or more, go to next step.

3) Measure resistance between breakout box pins. No. 46 and 47. If resistance is less than 5 ohms, repair short between Light Green/Red wire and Brown wire. If resistance is 5 ohms or more, replace tank temperature sensor. See TANK TEMPERATURE SENSOR under REMOVAL & INSTALLATION.

TEST G: BATTERY VOLTAGE HIGH (DTC B1317)

NOTE: After repair, clear DTCs and retest system.

1) Turn ignition switch to LOCK position. Connect New Generation Star (NGS) tester to Data Link Connector (DLC). Retrieve and clear continuous DTCs. Connect voltmeter between battery terminals. Using NGS tester, perform Natural Gas Vehicle (NGV) module self-test and observe battery voltage. If battery voltage is 17 volts or below volts during self-test, go to next step. If battery voltage rises above 17 volts during self-test, repair charging system concern. See GENERATORS – ECONOLINE, EXPEDITION, EXPLORER (4.0L OHV), PICKUP (ALL GASOLINE), MOUNTAINEER (4.0L OHV), NAVIGATOR & RANGER article in STARTING & CHARGING SYSTEMS.

2) Start engine. Using NGS tester, perform NGV module self-test and observe battery voltage. If battery voltage is 17 volts or below during self-test, go to next step. If battery voltage rises above 17 volts during self-test, repair charging system concern. See GENERATORS – ECONOLINE, EXPEDITION, EXPLORER (4.0L OHV), PICKUP (ALL GASOLINE), MOUNTAINEER (4.0L OHV), NAVIGATOR & RANGER article in STARTING & CHARGING SYSTEMS.

NOTE: DTC B1317 will set if battery voltage rises above 17 volts for longer than 2 minutes.

3) Turn ignition switch to LOCK position. Clear continuous DTCs. Using NGS tester, perform NGV module self-test while observing battery voltage. If DTC B1317 is still present, replace NGV module. See NATURAL GAS VEHICLE (NGV) MODULE under REMOVAL & INSTALLATION. If DTC B1317 does not return, system is operating correctly.

TEST H: BATTERY VOLTAGE LOW (DTC B1318)

NOTE: After repair, clear DTCs and retest system.

1) Turn ignition switch to LOCK position. Connect New Generation Star (NGS) tester to Data Link Connector (DLC). Retrieve and clear continuous DTCs. Connect voltmeter between battery terminals. Using NGS tester, perform Natural Gas Vehicle (NGV) module self-test and observe battery voltage. If battery voltage stays above 8 volts during self-test, go to next step. If battery voltage drops to 8 volts or below during self-test, repair charging system concern. See GENERATORS – ECONOLINE, EXPEDITION, EXPLORER (4.0L OHV), PICKUP (ALL GASOLINE), MOUNTAINEER (4.0L OHV), NAVIGATOR & RANGER article in STARTING & CHARGING SYSTEMS.

2) Start engine. Using NGS tester, perform NGV module self-test and observe battery voltage. If battery voltage stays above 8 volts during self-test, go to next step. If battery voltage drops to 8 volts or below during self-test, repair charging system concern. See GENERATORS – ECONOLINE, EXPEDITION, EXPLORER (4.0L OHV), PICKUP (ALL

GASOLINE), MOUNTAINEER (4.0L OHV), NAVIGATOR & RANGER article in STARTING & CHARGING SYSTEMS.

NOTE: DTC B1317 will set if battery voltage drops to 8 volts or below for longer than 2 minutes.

3) Turn ignition switch to LOCK position. Clear continuous DTCs. Using NGS tester, perform NGV module self-test while observing battery voltage. If DTC B1317 is still present, replace NGV module. See NATURAL GAS VEHICLE (NGV) MODULE under REMOVAL & INSTALLATION. If DTC B1317 does not return, system is operating correctly.

TEST I: ECU DEFECTIVE (DTC B1342)

NOTE: After repair, clear DTCs and retest system.

1) Turn ignition switch to LOCK position. Disconnect Natural Gas Vehicle (NGV) module 60-pin connector. Check for loose, damaged or corroded NGV module pins and connector terminals. If any module or connector pins are damaged, repair module connector terminals and/or replace NGV module as necessary. See NATURAL GAS VEHICLE (NGV) MODULE under REMOVAL & INSTALLATION. If there is no damage, go to next step.

2) Connect EEC-IV 60-Pin Breakout Box (418-005) to NGV module connector. Leave NGV module disconnected. Measure voltage between breakout box pins No. 37 or 57 and 40 or 60. If voltage is more than 10.5 volts, replace NGV module. See NATURAL GAS VEHICLE (NGV) MODULE under REMOVAL & INSTALLATION. If voltage is 10.5 volts or less, go to next step.

3) Turn ignition switch to LOCK position. Measure resistance between breakout box pins No. 40 or 60 and ground. If resistance is less than 5 ohms, repair open in Red wire. If resistance is 5 ohms or more, repair open in Black/White wire.

TEST J: NO COMMUNICATION WITH NATURAL GAS VEHICLE (NGV) MODULE

NOTE: After repair, retest system.

1) Turn ignition switch to LOCK position. Disconnect Natural Gas Vehicle (NGV) module 60-pin connector. Measure voltage between NGV module connector terminal No. 1 (Red/White wire) and ground. *See Fig. 2.* If voltage is more than 10 volts, go to next step. If voltage is 10 volts or less, repair open or short in Red/White wire.

2) Turn ignition switch to RUN position. Measure voltage between NGV module connector terminal No. 37 (Red wire) and ground. Measure voltage between NGV module connector between terminal No. 57 (Red wire) and ground. *See Fig. 2.* If each reading is more than 10 volts, go to next step. If either reading is 10 volts or less, repair open in appropriate Red wire.

3) Turn ignition switch to LOCK position. Measure resistance between NGV module connector terminal No. 40 (Black/Yellow wire) and ground. Measure resistance between NGV module connector terminal No. 60 (Black wire) and ground. If each resistance is less than 5 ohms, repair module communication concern. See MODULE COMMUNICATIONS NETWORK – F150 & F250 LIGHT-DUTY PICKUP article. If either resistance is 5 ohms or more, repair open in appropriate wire(s).

TEST K: INTEGRATED CIRCUIT DISPLAY INOPERATIVE OR ERRATIC

NOTE: After repair, retest system.

1) Turn ignition switch to LOCK position. Disconnect Natural Gas Vehicle (NGV) module 60-pin connector. Connect EEC-IV 60-Pin Breakout Box (418-005) to NGV module connector. Leave NGV module disconnected. Measure voltage between breakout box pins No. 37 or 57 and 40 or 60. If voltage is more than 10 volts, go to step **5)**. If voltage is 10 volts or less, go to next step.

1999 ACCESSORIES & EQUIPMENT
Analog Instrument Panels
F250 Light-Duty Pickup – CNG (Cont.)

FORD
4-801

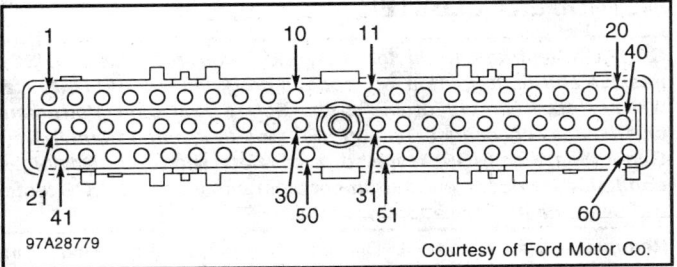

Fig. 2: Identifying Natural Gas Vehicle Module Connector Terminals

2) Turn ignition switch to LOCK position. Measure resistance between breakout box pins No. 26 and 37. If resistance is less than 5 ohms, repair short between Red wire and Brown/White wire. If resistance is 5 ohms or more, go to next step.

3) Measure resistance between breakout box pins No. 26 and 40 or 60. If resistance is less than 5 ohms, repair short to ground in Brown/White wire. If resistance is 5 ohms or more, go to next step.

4) Measure resistance between breakout box pins No. 40 or 60 and ground. If resistance is less than 5 ohms, repair open in Red wire. If resistance is 5 ohms or more, replace NGV module. See NATURAL GAS VEHICLE (NGV) MODULE under REMOVAL & INSTALLATION.

5) Disconnect instrument cluster White 22-pin connector C237. See INSTRUMENT CLUSTER under REMOVAL & INSTALLATION. Measure resistance between instrument cluster connector C237 terminal No. 17 (Pink/Orange wire) and ground. See Fig. 3. If resistance is less than 5 ohms, go to next step. If resistance is 5 ohms or more, repair open in Pink/Orange wire. Ground point is located behind left kick panel.

6) Measure resistance of Yellow/White wire between instrument cluster connector C237 terminal No. 3 and breakout box pin No. 38. See Fig. 3. If resistance is less than 5 ohms, repair or replace instrument cluster. If resistance is 5 ohms or more, repair open in Yellow/White wire.

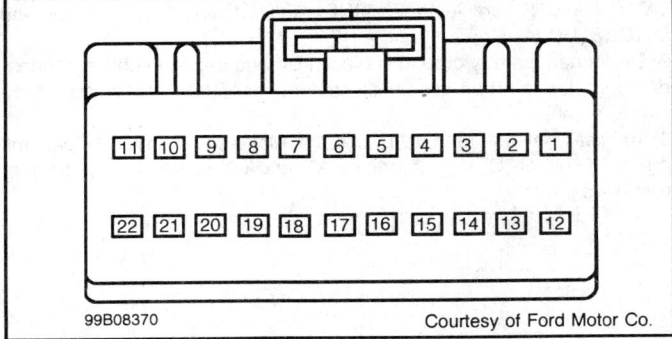

Fig. 3: Identifying Instrument Cluster 22-Pin Connector C237 Terminals

TEST L: NO COMMUNICATION WITH INSTRUMENT CLUSTER

NOTE: After repair, clear DTCs and repeat self-test.

1) Turn ignition switch to LOCK position. Disconnect instrument cluster Black 20-pin connector C236. Measure voltage between instrument cluster connector C236 terminal No. 10 (Red/White wire) and ground. See Fig. 4. If voltage is more than 10 volts, go to next step. If voltage is 10 volts or less, repair open or short in Red/White wire.

2) Turn ignition switch to RUN position. Measure voltage between instrument cluster connector C236 terminal No. 11 (Gray/Yellow wire) and ground. If voltage is more than 10 volts, go to next step. If voltage is 10 volts or less, repair open or short in Gray/Yellow wire.

3) Turn ignition switch to RUN position. Measure voltage between instrument cluster connector C236 terminal No. 2 (Red/Light Green

wire) and ground. See Fig. 4. If voltage is more than 10 volts, go to next step. If voltage is 10 volts or less, repair open or short in Red/Light Green wire.

4) Turn ignition switch to LOCK position. Measure resistance between instrument cluster connector C236 terminal No. 1 (Black wire) and ground. If resistance is less than 5 ohms, go to next step. If resistance is 5 ohms or more, repair open in Black wire. Ground point is located behind right kick panel.

5) Disconnect instrument cluster White 22-pin connector C237. Measure resistance between instrument cluster connector C237 terminal No. 17 (Pink/Orange wire) and ground. See Fig. 3. If resistance is less than 5 ohms, repair module communication concern. See MODULE COMMUNICATIONS NETWORK – F150 & F250 LIGHT-DUTY PICKUP article. If resistance is 5 ohms or more, repair open in Pink/Orange wire. Ground point is located behind left kick panel.

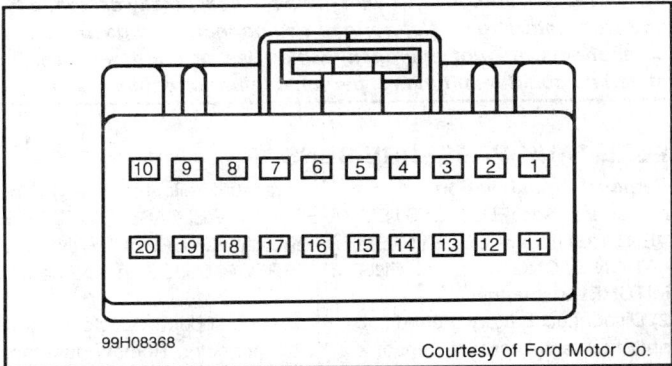

Fig. 4: Identifying Instrument Cluster 20-Pin Connector C236 Terminals

TEST M: INCORRECT FUEL GAUGE INDICATION

NOTE: Fuel fills of less than 6 gallons require at least 12 minutes to update fuel gauge reading.

NOTE: After repair, clear DTCs and repeat self-test.

1) Turn ignition switch to RUN position. Select NGS tester instrument cluster FUEL LEVEL CONTROL active command. Trigger, observe and scroll FUELLEVEL at 0%, 54% and 100%. Fuel gauge should display below empty at 0%, half at 54% and full stop at 100%. If fuel gauge displays as indicated, go to next step. If fuel gauge does not display as indicated, replace instrument cluster. See INSTRUMENT CLUSTER under REMOVAL & INSTALLATION.

2) Turn ignition switch to LOCK position. Disconnect Natural Gas Vehicle (NGV) module 60-pin connector. Connect EEC-IV 60-Pin Breakout Box (418-005) to NGV module connector. Leave NGV module disconnected. Connect one lead of Instrument Gauge System Tester (014-R1063), or equivalent, between breakout box pins No. 16 and 38. Set tester to 15 ohms. Turn ignition switch to RUN position. Wait 5-10 minutes and read fuel gauge. Fuel gauge should read below empty. Turn ignition switch to LOCK position. Set tester to 160 ohms. Turn ignition switch to RUN position. Wait 5-10 minutes and read fuel gauge. Fuel gauge should read full or above. If fuel gauge displays as indicated, replace NGV module. See NATURAL GAS VEHICLE (NGV) MODULE under REMOVAL & INSTALLATION. If fuel gauge does not display as indicated, disconnect tester and go to next step.

3) Disconnect instrument cluster White 22-pin connector C237. See INSTRUMENT CLUSTER under REMOVAL & INSTALLATION. Measure resistance of Yellow/White wire between instrument cluster connector C237 terminal No. 3 and breakout box pin No. 38. See Fig. 3. If resistance is less than 5 ohms, go to next step. If resistance is 5 ohms or more, repair open in Yellow/White wire.

FORD
4-802

1999 ACCESSORIES & EQUIPMENT
Analog Instrument Panels
F250 Light-Duty Pickup – CNG (Cont.)

4) Measure voltage between breakout box pins No. 38 and 40 or 60. If there is any voltage, repair short to power in Yellow/White wire. If there is no voltage, repair short to ground in Yellow/White wire.

REMOVAL & INSTALLATION

WARNING: Fuel in fuel system is under high pressure and highly flammable. Keep away from spark and flame. Properly vent fuel system pressure before removing components. See appropriate procedure under FUEL SYSTEM in REMOVAL, OVERHAUL & INSTALLATION – CNG article in ENGINE PERFORMANCE in appropriate MITCHELL® manual.

WARNING: Do not modify system configuration or components. Do not replace components with parts not specifically designed for use with natural gas. Natural gas components and gasoline fuel components are not interchangeable. Use of improper parts or materials could result in fire, personal injury or engine damage.

FUEL TANK PRESSURE SENSOR

Removal & Installation – 1) Perform pressure relief/fuel line venting procedure. See FUEL SYSTEM PRESSURE RELEASE (FUEL LINE VENTING) under FUEL SYSTEM in REMOVAL, OVERHAUL & INSTALLATION – CNG article in ENGINE PERFORMANCE in appropriate MITCHELL® manual.

2) Disconnect battery ground cable. Raise and support vehicle. Disconnect fuel tank pressure sensor electrical connector. Remove fuel tank pressure sensor.

3) To install, reverse removal procedure. Make sure to replace fuel tank pressure sensor "O" ring. Lubricate "O" ring with 5W30 engine oil prior to installation.

INSTRUMENT CLUSTER

CAUTION: Instrument cluster is Hybrid Electronic Cluster (HEC). Passive anti-theft ignition key code is programmed into HEC. Car will not start without proper code. Before replacing instrument cluster, it is necessary to upload HEC module configuration to New Generation Star (NGS) tester, or equivalent scan tool. Download configuration once new instrument cluster is installed. NGS tester will only retain information for 24 hours.

Removal & Installation – 1) Disconnect negative battery cable. Turn headlight switch to ON position. Pull headlight switch knob. Insert a thin tool to release headlight switch knob and remove. Reinstall headlight switch knob 180 degrees from original position. Turn knob fully counterclockwise. Turn knob fully clockwise. Pull headlight switch from instrument panel. Disconnect electrical connectors.

2) Carefully release 4 retaining clips and remove steering column opening cover. Remove 7 instrument panel finish panel bolts. Remove instrument panel finish panel. Remove 4 instrument cluster bolts. Disconnect electrical connectors. Remove instrument cluster. If equipped, remove transmission range indicator. To install, reverse removal procedure.

NATURAL GAS VEHICLE (NGV) MODULE

Removal & Installation – 1) Disconnect battery ground cable. Remove NGV module assembly lower retaining nut. Remove module harness connector plastic shroud. Loosen module assembly electrical connector retaining bolt. Disconnect electrical connector.

2) Remove module assembly upper retaining nuts and remove module assembly. Remove module from marine cover. To install, reverse removal procedure.

TANK TEMPERATURE SENSOR

Removal & Installation – 1) Perform pressure relief/fuel line venting procedure. See FUEL SYSTEM PRESSURE RELEASE (FUEL LINE VENTING) under FUEL SYSTEM in REMOVAL, OVERHAUL & INSTALLATION – CNG article in ENGINE PERFORMANCE in appropriate MITCHELL® manual.

2) Disconnect battery ground cable. Raise and support vehicle. Disconnect tank temperature sensor electrical connector. Remove tank temperature sensor.

3) To install, reverse removal procedure. Make sure to replace fuel tank pressure sensor "O" ring. Lubricate "O" ring with 5W30 engine oil prior to installation.

1999 ACCESSORIES & EQUIPMENT
Analog Instrument Panels
F250 Light-Duty Pickup – CNG (Cont.)

FORD
4-803

WIRING DIAGRAMS

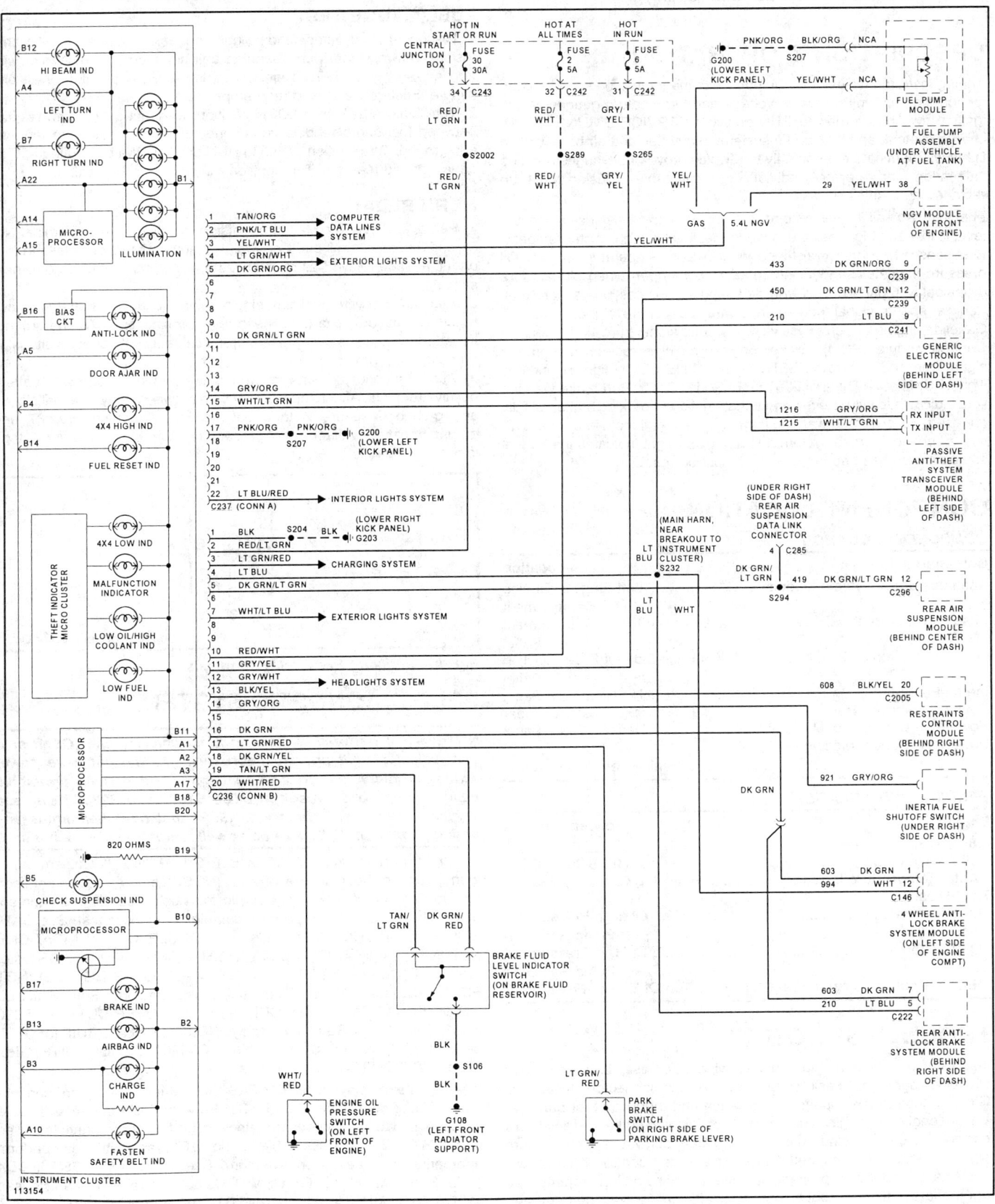

Fig. 5: Analog Instrument Panel Wiring Diagram (F150 & F250 Light-Duty Pickup)

1999 ACCESSORIES & EQUIPMENT
Analog Instrument Panels
F250 Super-Duty & F350 Pickup

NOTE: This article includes Cab & Chassis.

DESCRIPTION & OPERATION

Analog instrument cluster is equipped with magnetic type speedometer, tachometer, fuel, oil pressure, voltage and temperature gauges. When ignition switch is turned to RUN position, SERVICE ENGINE SOON, charge system, anti-lock brake system, safety belt and air bag warning lights will illuminate momentarily for display prove out. Gauges need no calibration and are not individually replaceable. Cluster must be replaced as a unit.

Fuel sending unit is a variable resistor that has low resistance when fuel level is low and high resistance when fuel level is high. Water temperature sensor has high resistance when water temperature is low. Oil pressure indicator sender unit contact points open when oil pressure drops below 6 psi (42 kPa). Vehicle speed sensor was deleted for 1999. Vehicle speed signal comes from anti-lock brake system module. Gasoline engine vehicles receive tachometer signal from the Powertrain Control Module (PCM). Diesel engine vehicles receive tachometer signal from the generator. SERVICE ENGINE SOON light illuminates when PCM sets a Diagnostic Trouble Code (DTC). Red brake warning light indicates low fluid level, brake malfunction or parking brake not fully released. Yellow brake warning light indicates malfunction, or deactivation, of anti-lock brake system. FUEL RESET light indicates inertia fuel shutoff switch has been tripped and must be reset.

COMPONENT LOCATION

COMPONENT LOCATION

Component	Location
Anti-Lock Brake System Module	Left Front Of Engine Compartment
Fuse Junction Panel	Lower Left Side Of Instrument Panel
Generic Electronic Module	On Back Side Of Fuse Junction Panel
Inertia Fuel Shutoff Switch	Behind Right Kick Panel
Power Distribution Box	Near Brake Master Cylinder
Powertrain Control Module	Near Left Kick Panel
Powertrain Control Module Connector	Behind Left Fender Apron

SENDING UNIT LOCATION

Engine	Sender Location
5.8L & 6.8L	
Oil Pressure	Lower Left Side Of Block
Water Temperature Indicator	Front Top Of Intake Manifold
7.5L (Diesel)	
Oil Pressure	Top Of High Pressure Oil Pump Reservoir
Oil Temperature	Side Of High Pressure Oil Pump Reservoir
Engine Coolant Temperature (ECT)	Top Of Engine Front Cover

TROUBLE SHOOTING

Inspect fuses, warning light bulbs, wiring harness, and instrument cluster for damage. Check for loose or corroded connectors. Inspect oil filter, oil pump, inertia fuel shut off switch and thermostat for damage. Ensure engine oil, engine coolant, washer fluid and brake fluid levels are correct. Ensure charging, fuel, cooling, safety belt warning chime, turn signals, headlights, anti-theft and vehicle speed control (if equipped) systems are operating properly. If system is not working properly, see appropriate article. If concern remains after inspection, perform self-diagnostics. See SELF-DIAGNOSTIC SYSTEM.

COMPONENT TESTS

FUEL GAUGE TEST

1) Disconnect fuel pump/sending unit connector. Connect a 22.4-ohm resistor between fuel pump/sending unit connector Yellow/White wire terminal and ground. Turn ignition switch to RUN position. Wait one minute. Fuel gauge should read empty.
2) Turn ignition switch to LOCK position. Connect a 145-ohm resistor between fuel pump/sending unit connector Yellow/White wire terminal and ground. Turn ignition switch to RUN position. Wait one minute. Fuel gauge should read full. Turn ignition switch to LOCK position.

HORN RELAY

1) Remove horn relay. Measure resistance between relay terminal No. 85 and all other terminals. See Fig. 1. If any resistances is less than 5 ohms, replace relay. If all resistances are 5 ohms or more, go to next step.
2) Attach jumper wire between relay terminal No. 30 and battery positive terminal. Measure voltage between relay terminal No. 87A and ground. If battery voltage is not present, replace relay. If battery voltage is present, go to next step.
3) Attach second jumper wire from relay terminal No. 86 to battery positive terminal. Attach third jumper wire between relay terminal No. 85 and ground. Measure voltage between relay terminal No. 87 and ground. If battery voltage is not present, replace relay. If battery voltage is present, relay is okay.

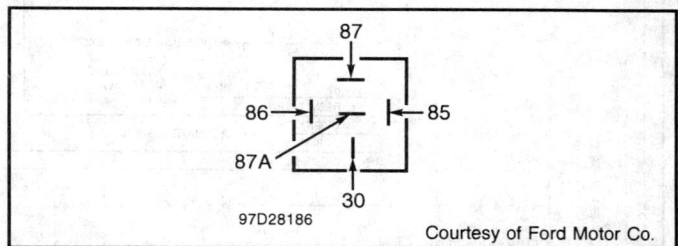

97D28186 — Courtesy of Ford Motor Co.

Fig. 1: Identifying Horn Relay Terminals

SELF-DIAGNOSTIC SYSTEM

NOTE: When performing Generic Electronic Module (GEM) self-test, vehicles built prior to February 5, 1998 must have power windows completely up and headlights and parking lights off. Failure to do so will result in DTCs B1577 and B2357 being set. Vehicles built after February 5, 1998 must have headlights and parking lights on. Failure to do so will result in B1575 being set.

For preliminary testing, see TROUBLE SHOOTING. If problem is not found, connect New Generation Star (NGS) tester, or equivalent scan tool, to Data Link Connector (DLC) located below center of instrument panel. Using NGS tester, perform data link diagnostic test. See DATA LINK DIAGNOSTIC TEST under in MODULE COMMUNICATIONS NETWORK – F250 SUPER-DUTY & F350 PICKUP article. If NGS tester displays CKT914, CKT915 or CKT70 = ALL ECUS NO RESP/NOT EQUIP, diagnose module communications concern. See MODULE COMMUNICATIONS NETWORK – F250 SUPER-DUTY & F350 PICKUP article. If NGS tester displays NO RESP/NOT EQUIP for GEM, perform TEST A: NO SCAN TOOL COMMUNICATION WITH GEM under SYSTEM TESTS.

If NGS tester displays SYSTEM PASSED, retrieve and record continuous DTCs. Erase continuous DTCs. Perform GEM self-test. If GEM DTCs related to the concern are retrieved, perform appropriate test. See GEM DTC TEST INDEX table. If no DTCs are retrieved, perform appropriate test based on symptom. See SYMPTOM TEST INDEX under SYSTEM TESTS. For GEM DTCs not covered in this article, see MODULE COMMUNICATIONS NETWORK – F250 SUPER-DUTY & F350 PICKUP article.

1999 ACCESSORIES & EQUIPMENT
Analog Instrument Panels
F250 Super-Duty & F350 Pickup (Cont.)

FORD
4-805

GEM DTC TEST INDEX

DTC [1]	Description	Test
B1323	Door Ajar Light Circuit Failure	V
B1325	Door Ajar Light Circuit Short To Power	V
B1342	ECU Defective	2
B1426	Seat Belt Warning Light Circuit Short To Power	W
B1428	Seat Belt Light Circuit Failure	W
B2141	NVM Configuration Failure	3
C1125	Brake Fluid Level Sensor Input Circuit Failure	M
C1189	Brake Fluid Level Sensor Input Circuit Short To Ground	M
C1223	Brake Light Warning Output Circuit Failure	M
C1225	Brake Light Warning Output Circuit Short To Power	M
C1230	Speed Wheel Sensor Rear Center Input Circuit Failure	H
C1446	Park Brake Switch Circuit Failure	M

[1] – Codes listed in this table are only for testing covered in this article. For complete DTC listing, see MODULE COMMUNICATIONS NETWORK – F250 SUPER-DUTY & F350 PICKUP article.

[2] – Using NGS tester, clear DTCs. Retrieve DTCs. If B1342 is retrieved again, replace GEM. See GENERIC ELECTRONIC MODULE (GEM) under REMOVAL & INSTALLATION.

[3] – Check GEM configuration. Refer to Ford Service Function (FSF) card to verify proper configuration. Clear DTCs. Retrieve DTCs. If B2141 is still present, replace GEM. See GENERIC ELECTRONIC MODULE (GEM) under REMOVAL & INSTALLATION.

SYSTEM TESTS

CAUTION: *When battery is disconnected, vehicle computer and memory systems may lose memory data. Driveability problems may exist until computer systems have completed a relearn cycle. See COMPUTER RELEARN PROCEDURES article in GENERAL INFORMATION before disconnecting battery.*

CAUTION: *Disconnect battery before disconnecting Generic Electronic Module (GEM) connectors. Failure to do so will result in GEM storing erroneous codes and may also result in erratic operation of GEM after reconnection.*

NOTE: *After making any repair, clear codes and perform data link diagnostic test. See DATA LINK DIAGNOSTIC TEST under in MODULE COMMUNICATIONS NETWORK – F250 SUPER-DUTY & F350 PICKUP article.*

SYMPTOM TEST INDEX

Symptom	Test
No Scan Tool Communication With GEM	A
Any Gauge(s) Inoperative	B
Fuel Gauge Reads Incorrectly	C
Low Fuel Warning Indicator Light Never On	D
Voltage Gauge Reads Incorrectly	E
Oil Pressure Gauge Reads Incorrectly	F
Temperature Gauge Reads Incorrectly	G
Speedometer Inoperative	H
Trip Odometer Inoperative, Speedometer Okay	1
Tachometer Reads Incorrectly	J
Speedometer Reads Incorrectly, Odometer Okay	K
Yellow Brake (ABS) Warning Indicator Light Never On	L
Yellow Brake (ABS) Warning Indicator Light Always On	2
Red BRAKE Warning Indicator Light Never On	M
Red BRAKE Warning Indicator Light Always On	3
FUEL RESET Warning Indicator Light Inoperative	N
FUEL RESET Warning Indicator Light Always On	4
SERVICE ENGINE SOON Warning Indicator Light Inoperative	P
SERVICE ENGINE SOON Warning Indicator Light Always On	5
Charge System Warning Indicator Light Inoperative	Q
Charge System Warning Indicator Light Always On	6
Air Bag Warning Indicator Light Inoperative Or Always On	R
High Beam Indicator Light Inoperative	S
Left Turn Signal Indicator Light Inoperative	T

SYMPTOM TEST INDEX (Cont.)

Symptom	Test
Right Turn Signal Indicator Light Inoperative	U
DOOR AJAR Warning Indicator Light Inoperative, Chime Okay	V
Safety Belt Warning Indicator Light Inoperative Or Does Not Operate Properly, Chime Okay	W
4X4 &/Or LOW RANGE Indicator Light Inoperative (Manual Shift)	X
4X4 &/Or LOW RANGE Indicator Light Always On (Manual Shift)	Y
4X4 &/Or LOW RANGE Indicator Light Inoperative (Automatic)	7
WAIT TO START Warning Indicator Light Inoperative (Diesel)	Z
WATER IN FUEL Warning Indicator Light Inoperative (Diesel)	AA

[1] – Verify trip odometer reset lever is not binding. If okay, repair instrument cluster.

[2] – Malfunction in anti-lock brakes system. See appropriate ANTI-LOCK article in BRAKES in appropriate MITCHELL® manual for diagnosis.

[3] – Problem with braking system, brake fluid level or parking brake switch/circuit. See WIRING DIAGRAMS.

[4] – Repair short to ground in Gray/Orange wire. See WIRING DIAGRAMS.

[5] – See appropriate SELF-DIAGNOSTICS article in ENGINE PERFORMANCE in appropriate MITCHELL® manual.

[6] – See appropriate GENERATORS article in CHARGING & STARTING SYSTEMS.

[7] – See appropriate article in TRANSFER CASES for electronic controls diagnostics.

TEST A: NO SCAN TOOL COMMUNICATION WITH GEM

1) Turn ignition switch to LOCK position. Check fuse junction panel fuse No. 15 (5-amp). If fuse is okay, install and go to next step. If fuse is blown, go to step **3)**.

2) Measure voltage between fuse junction panel fuse No. 15 (5-amp) and ground. If voltage is more than 10 volts, go to step **4)**. If voltage is 10 volts or less, go to step **5)**.

3) Remove fuse No. 15 (5-amp). Disconnect Generic Electronic Module (GEM) from fuse junction panel connector C241. *See Fig. 2.* See GENERIC ELECTRONIC MODULE (GEM) under REMOVAL & INSTALLATION. Measure resistance between fuse junction panel connector C241 terminal No. 4 (fuse junction panel side) and ground. Measure resistance between fuse junction panel connector C241 termi-

FORD
4-806

1999 ACCESSORIES & EQUIPMENT
Analog Instrument Panels
F250 Super-Duty & F350 Pickup (Cont.)

nal No. 16 (fuse junction panel side) and ground. If each resistance is more than 10 k/ohms, go to step **16**). If either resistance is 10 k/ohms or less, replace fuse junction panel.

4) Disconnect GEM 26-pin connector C239. Measure resistance between GEM connector C239 terminal No. 26 (Pink/Orange wire) and ground. *See Fig. 3*. If resistance is less than 5 ohms, go to step **7**). If resistance is 5 ohms or more, repair open in Pink/Orange wire.

5) Check power distribution box fuse No. 22 (50-amp). If fuse is okay, reinstall fuse and go to next step. If fuse is blown, repair short to ground in Tan/Black wire.

6) Measure voltage between power distribution box fuse No. 22 (50-amp) and ground. If voltage is more than 10 volts, repair open in Tan/Black wire. If voltage is 10 volts or less, repair or replace power distribution box.

7) Disconnect GEM 26-pin connector C239. Measure resistance of Light Blue/White wire between GEM connector C239 terminal No. 25 and Data Link Connector (DLC) terminal No. 7. *See Figs. 3 and 4*. If resistance is less than 5 ohms, go to next step. If resistance is 5 ohms or more, repair open in Light Blue/White wire.

8) Measure voltage between GEM connector C239 terminal No. 26 (Pink/Orange wire) and ground. *See Fig. 3*. If voltage is more than 10 volts, repair short to power in Pink/Orange wire and replace GEM. See GENERIC ELECTRONIC MODULE (GEM) under REMOVAL & INSTALLATION. If voltage is 10 volts or less and vehicle is equipped with 4WD mode selection switch, go to next step. If voltage is 10 volts or less and vehicle is not equipped with 4WD mode selection switch, go to step **11**).

9) Turn ignition switch to LOCK position. Disconnect GEM 22-pin connector C247. Turn ignition switch to RUN position. Measure voltage between GEM connector C247 terminal No. 4 (White/Light Blue wire) and ground. *See Fig. 5*. If voltage is more than 10 volts, go to next step. If voltage is 10 volts or less, go to step **11**).

10) Turn ignition switch to LOCK position. Disconnect 4WD mode switch 4-pin connector. Turn ignition switch to RUN position. Measure voltage between GEM connector C247 terminal No. 4 (White/Light Blue wire) and ground. *See Fig. 5*. If voltage is more than 10 volts, repair short to power in White/Light Blue wire and replace GEM. See GENERIC ELECTRONIC MODULE (GEM) under REMOVAL & INSTALLATION. If voltage is 10 volts or less, replace 4WD mode select switch and replace GEM.

11) Measure voltage between GEM connector C239 terminal No. 20 (Dark Blue wire) and ground. *See Fig. 3*. If voltage is more than 10 volts, go to next step. If voltage is 10 volts or less, go to step **13**).

12) Turn ignition switch to LOCK position. Disconnect multifunction switch 7-pin connector. Turn ignition switch to RUN position. Measure voltage between GEM connector C239 terminal No. 20 (Dark Blue wire) and ground. *See Fig. 3*. If voltage is more than 10 volts, repair short to power in Dark Blue wire and replace GEM. See GENERIC ELECTRONIC MODULE (GEM) under REMOVAL & INSTALLATION. If voltage is 10 volts or less, replace multifunction switch and replace GEM.

13) Measure voltage between GEM connector C239 terminal No. 23 (Pink/Yellow wire) and ground. *See Fig. 3*. If voltage is more than 10 volts, go to next step. If voltage is 10 volts or less and vehicle is equipped with rear wheel anti-lock brake system, go to step **15**). If voltage is 10 volts or less and vehicle is equipped with 4-wheel anti-lock brake system, replace GEM. See GENERIC ELECTRONIC MODULE (GEM) under REMOVAL & INSTALLATION.

14) Turn ignition switch to LOCK position. Disconnect multifunction switch 7-pin connector. Measure voltage between GEM connector C239 terminal No. 23 (Pink/Yellow wire) and ground. *See Fig. 3*. If voltage is more than 10 volts, repair short to power in Pink/Yellow wire and replace GEM. See GENERIC ELECTRONIC MODULE (GEM) under REMOVAL & INSTALLATION. If voltage is 10 volts or less, replace multifunction switch and replace GEM.

15) Turn ignition switch to LOCK position. Disconnect differential speed sensor connector located on center of rear axle. Turn ignition switch to RUN position. Measure voltage between GEM connector C239 terminal No. 9 (Light Green/Black wire) and ground. *See Fig. 3*. If voltage is more than 10 volts, repair short to power in Light Green/Black wire and replace GEM. See GENERIC ELECTRONIC MODULE (GEM) under REMOVAL & INSTALLATION. If voltage is 10 volts or less, replace GEM.

16) Check horn relay. See HORN RELAY under COMPONENT TESTS. If relay is okay, go to next step. If relay is faulty, replace relay.

17) Disconnect GEM from fuse junction panel 18-pin connector C241. See GENERIC ELECTRONIC MODULE (GEM) under REMOVAL & INSTALLATION. Disconnect GEM 22-pin connector C247. Disconnect Brake Position Pedal (BPP) switch 5-pin connector. Measure resistance between GEM connector C247 terminal No. 12 (Red/Light Green wire) and ground. *See Fig. 5*. If resistance is more than 10 k/ohms, go to next step. If resistance is 10 k/ohms or less, repair short to ground in Red/Light Green wire.

18) Disconnect fuse junction panel 34-pin connector C243. *See Fig. 2*. Measure resistance between BPP switch connector Light Blue/Black wire terminal and ground. If resistance is more than 10 k/ohms, replace BPP switch. If resistance is 10 k/ohms or less, repair short to ground in Light Blue/Black wire.

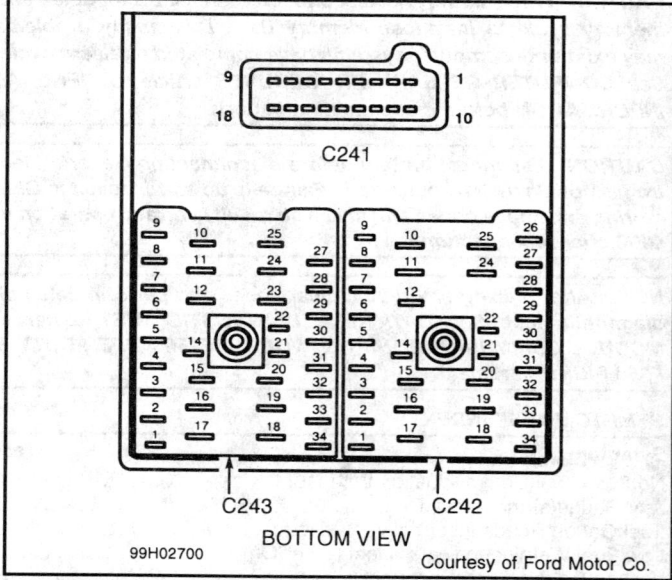

Fig. 2: Identifying Fuse Junction Panel Connectors & Terminals

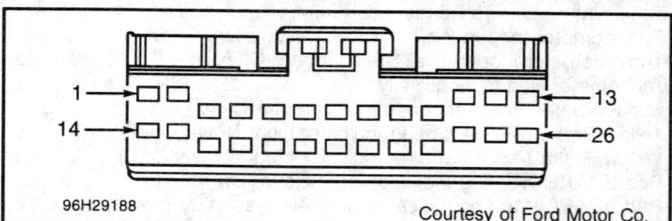

Fig. 3: Identifying GEM 26-Pin Connector C239 Terminals

TEST B: ANY GAUGE(S) INOPERATIVE

1) Turn ignition switch to RUN position. Observe instrument cluster warning indicator lights. Turn ignition switch to START position. If SERVICE ENGINE SOON, battery, seat belt, brake and anti-lock brake system lights prove out, go to step **3**). If all lights do not prove out, go to next step.

2) Turn ignition switch to LOCK position. Check fuse junction panel fuses No. 2 (5-amp), No. 19 (10-amp) and No. 29 (5-amp). If fuses are

1999 ACCESSORIES & EQUIPMENT
Analog Instrument Panels
F250 Super-Duty & F350 Pickup (Cont.)

FORD
4-807

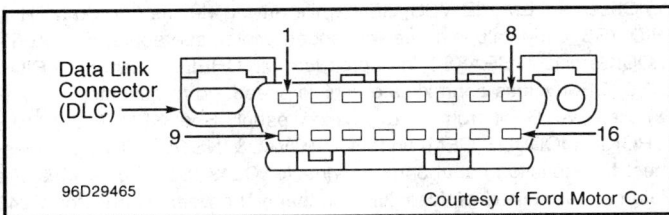

Fig. 4: Identifying Data Link Connector (DLC) Terminals

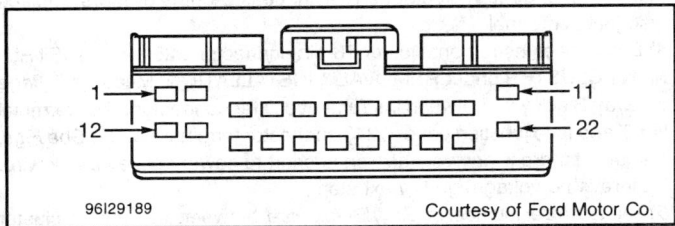

Fig. 5: Identifying GEM 22-Pin Connector C247 Terminals

okay, go to next step. If any fuse is blown, replace fuse. Test system operation. If fuse blows again, repair short to ground in appropriate wire. See WIRING DIAGRAMS.

3) Pull instrument cluster partially out and verify instrument cluster connectors are fully seated. See INSTRUMENT CLUSTER under REMOVAL & INSTALLATION. If connectors are properly seated, go to next step. If not properly seated, reconnect instrument cluster connectors.

4) Disconnect instrument cluster connectors. Turn ignition switch to RUN position. Reinstall fuse(s) in question. Check for voltage between specified instrument cluster connector terminals and ground. See INSTRUMENT CLUSTER TEST POINTS table. *See Figs. 6 and 7*. If each voltage is more than 10 volts, go to next step. If any voltage is 10 volts or less, repair open in appropriate wire(s). See WIRING DIAGRAMS.

INSTRUMENT CLUSTER TEST POINTS

Connector – Terminal	Wire Color
C250-7	White/Yellow
C250-12	Red/Yellow
C251-3	Red/White
C251-11	Red/Yellow

5) Measure resistance between instrument cluster connector C251 terminal No. 5 (Pink/Orange wire) and ground. *See Fig. 7*. If resistance is 5 ohms or more, repair open in Pink/Orange wire. If resistance is less than 5 ohms, verify instrument cluster printed circuit connector is fully locked. If fully locked, repair instrument cluster.

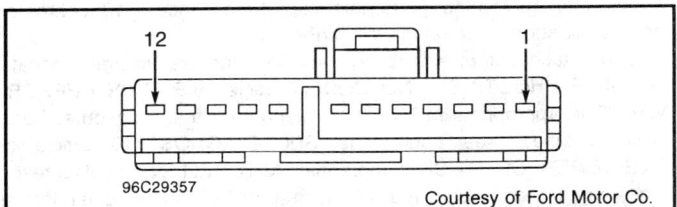

Fig. 6: Identifying Instrument Cluster 12-Pin Connector C250 Terminals

TEST C: FUEL GAUGE READS INCORRECTLY

1) Turn ignition switch to LOCK position. Turn ignition switch to RUN position. Observe fuel gauge. If fuel gauge reads correctly, system is okay. Remind customer that ignition switch must be turned to LOCK position while fueling. If fuel gauge does not read correctly, go to next step.

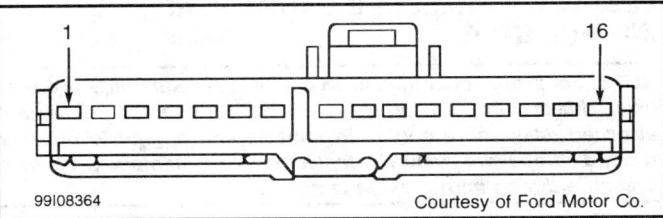

Fig. 7: Identifying Instrument Cluster 16-Pin Connector C251 Terminals

2) Test fuel gauge. See FUEL GAUGE TEST under COMPONENT TESTS. If gauge is okay, replace fuel level sensor and pump. If gauge fails test, go to next step.

3) Turn ignition switch to LOCK position. Partially remove instrument cluster and verify instrument cluster connectors are fully seated. See INSTRUMENT CLUSTER under REMOVAL & INSTALLATION. If connectors are properly seated, go to next step. If not properly seated, reconnect instrument cluster connectors.

4) Turn ignition switch to LOCK position. Disconnect fuel pump/sending unit 4-pin (8-pin, if California version) connector. Measure resistance between fuel pump/sending unit connector Black/Orange wire terminal and ground. If resistance is less than 5 ohms, go to next step. If resistance is 5 ohms or more, repair open in Black/Orange wire.

5) Disconnect instrument cluster connectors. Measure resistance of Yellow/White wire between fuel pump/sending unit connector and instrument cluster connector C251 terminal No. 10. *See Fig. 7*. Resistance should be less than 5 ohms. Measure resistance between instrument cluster connector C251 terminal No. 10 (Yellow/White wire) and ground. Resistance should be greater than 10 k/ohms. If resistances are as specified, repair instrument cluster. If resistances are not as specified, repair open and/or short to ground in Yellow/White wire.

TEST D: LOW FUEL WARNING INDICATOR LIGHT NEVER ON

1) Turn ignition switch to RUN position. Observe fuel gauge. If gauge reads correctly, go to next step. If gauge does not read correctly, go to TEST C: FUEL GAUGE READS INCORRECTLY.

2) Turn ignition switch to LOCK position. Remove instrument cluster. See INSTRUMENT CLUSTER under REMOVAL & INSTALLATION. Remove LOW FUEL warning light bulb. Test bulb for continuity. If bulb is okay, repair instrument cluster. If bulb is blown, replace bulb.

TEST E: VOLTAGE GAUGE READS INCORRECTLY

1) Check battery and charging system. See appropriate GENERATORS article in STARTING & CHARGING SYSTEMS. If battery and charging system is okay, go to next step. If battery and charging system are not okay, make appropriate repairs.

2) Turn ignition switch to RUN position. Observe voltage gauge. If gauge voltage is in proper range, go to step **5)** . If gauge voltage reads high, repair instrument cluster. If gauge voltage reads low, go to next step.

3) Turn ignition switch to LOCK position. Check fuse junction panel fuse No. 29 (5-amp). If fuse is okay, reinstall fuse and go to next step. If fuse is blown, replace fuse. Test system. If fuse blows again, repair short to ground in White/Yellow wire.

4) Remove instrument cluster. See INSTRUMENT CLUSTER under REMOVAL & INSTALLATION. Turn ignition switch to RUN position. Measure voltage between instrument cluster connector C250 terminal No. 7 (White/Yellow wire) and ground. *See Fig. 6*. If voltage is more than 10 volts, repair instrument cluster. If voltage is 10 volts or less, repair White/Yellow wire.

5) Turn ignition switch to START position. Observe voltage gauge. If gauge voltage reads in proper range, system is okay. If gauge voltage is not in proper range, check for poor engine to bulkhead or instrument panel ground connections. Repair as necessary.

FORD
4-808

1999 ACCESSORIES & EQUIPMENT
Analog Instrument Panels
F250 Super-Duty & F350 Pickup (Cont.)

TEST F: OIL PRESSURE GAUGE READS INCORRECTLY

NOTE: For proper operation of oil gauge, make sure oil is at correct level. Make sure oil pressure switch connector is securely attached. Make sure engine to chassis and engine to bulkhead ground straps are securely fastened. A momentary drop in oil pressure during hard braking is normal.

NOTE: After repair, retest system.

1) Turn ignition switch to START position. Check oil pressure gauge. If both oil pressure gauge and oil pressure warning light indicate low oil pressure, go to next step. If both oil pressure gauge and oil pressure warning light do not indicate low oil pressure, repair instrument cluster.
2) Turn ignition switch to LOCK position. Disconnect oil pressure switch connector. Connect jumper wire between oil pressure switch connector and ground. Turn ignition switch to RUN position. If oil pressure gauge reads normal pressure, check engine oil pressure. See appropriate article in ENGINES for oil pressure specifications. If pressure is within specification, replace oil pressure switch. If gauge does not read normal pressure, disconnect jumper wire and go to next step.
3) Disconnect instrument cluster 16-pin connector C251. Turn ignition switch to RUN position. Measure resistance of White/Red wire between oil pressure switch connector and instrument cluster connector C251 terminal No. 6. *See Fig. 7.* If resistance is less than 5 ohms, repair instrument cluster. If resistance is 5 ohms or more, repair open in White/Red wire.

TEST G: TEMPERATURE GAUGE READS INCORRECTLY

NOTE: Make sure engine coolant is at proper level. Make sure coolant temperature sender connector is securely attached.

1) Turn ignition switch to LOCK position. Disconnect coolant temperature sender connector. Turn ignition switch to RUN position. If temperature gauge reads in cold band, go to step **3)**. If gauge does not read in cold band, go to next step.
2) Turn ignition switch to LOCK position. Measure resistance between coolant temperature sender Red/White wire terminal and ground. If resistance is more than 10 k/ohms, go to step **4)**. If resistance is 10 k/ohms or less, repair short to ground in Red/White wire.
3) Connect jumper wire between both coolant temperature sender connector terminals. If temperature gauge does not read in hot band, go to next step. If temperature gauge reads in hot band, remove jumper wire. Reconnect coolant temperature sender. Start vehicle and allow engine to reach operating temperature. If gauge is not in normal range, replace coolant temperature sender.
4) Turn ignition switch to LOCK position. Measure resistance between coolant temperature sensor connector Yellow/Red wire terminal and ground. If resistance is less than 5 ohms, go to next step. If resistance is 5 ohms or more, repair open in Yellow/Red wire.
5) Turn ignition switch to LOCK position. Remove instrument cluster. See INSTRUMENT CLUSTER under REMOVAL & INSTALLATION. Measure resistance of Red/White wire between coolant temperature sensor connector and instrument cluster connector C251 terminal No. 9. *See Fig. 7.* If resistance is less than 5 ohms, repair instrument cluster. If resistance is 5 ohms or more, repair open in Red/White wire.

TEST H: SPEEDOMETER INOPERATIVE

NOTE: After repair, retest system.

1) Using NGS tester, observe GEM PID IGN_GEM while turning ignition switch through all positions. Depress clutch pedal when turning to START position (M/T). If PID values agree with ignition switch positions, go to next step. If PID values do not agree with ignition switch positions, repair appropriate ignition switch circuit. See appropriate wiring diagram in POWER DISTRIBUTION article in WIRING DIAGRAMS.

2) Observe GEM PID VSS_GEM while driving vehicle 0 to 55 MPH. If PID VSS_GEM values agree with speedometer, see appropriate ANTI-LOCK article in BRAKES in appropriate MITCHELL® manual. If PID VSS_GEM values approximate vehicle speed, go to next step.
3) Remove GEM from fuse junction panel. See GENERIC ELECTRONIC MODULE (GEM) under REMOVAL & INSTALLATION. Disconnect fuse junction panel 34-pin connector C243. *See Fig. 2.* Measure internal resistance of fuse junction panel between connector C243 terminals No. 21 and 22 (fuse junction panel side). If resistance is less than 5 ohms, go to next step. If resistance is 5 ohms or more, replace fuse junction panel.
4) Disconnect instrument cluster 16-pin connector C251. See INSTRUMENT CLUSTER under REMOVAL & INSTALLATION. Measure voltage on Gray/Black wire between instrument cluster connector C251 terminal No. 7 and fuse junction panel C243 connector terminal No. 22. *See Figs. 2 and 7.* If there is any voltage, repair short to power in Gray/Black wire. If there is no voltage, go to next step.
5) Measure resistance of Gray/Black wire between instrument cluster connector C251 terminal No. 7 and fuse junction panel C243 connector terminal No. 22. *See Figs. 2 and 7.* If resistance is less than 5 ohms, go to next step. If resistance is 5 ohms or more, repair open in Gray/Black wire.
6) Check resistance between instrument cluster connector C251 terminal No. 7 (Gray/Black wire) and ground. *See Fig. 7.* If resistance is less than 10 k/ohms, repair short to ground in Gray/Black wire. If resistance is 10 k/ohms or more, replace instrument cluster.

TEST J: TACHOMETER READS INCORRECTLY

NOTE: After repair, retest system.

1) Turn ignition switch to LOCK position. Remove instrument cluster. See INSTRUMENT CLUSTER under REMOVAL & INSTALLATION. Measure resistance between instrument cluster connector C251 terminal No. 8 (Black/White wire) and ground. Also measure resistance between instrument cluster connector C250 terminal No. 1 (Black/Yellow wire) and ground. *See Figs. 6 and 7.* If each resistance is less than 5 ohms, go to next step. If either resistance is 5 ohms or more, repair open in appropriate wire(s).
2) Disconnect Powertrain Control Module (PCM) 104-pin connector. Measure resistance of White/Pink wire between instrument cluster connector C251 terminal No. 12 and PCM connector terminal No. 48 (terminal No. 19 on vehicles equipped with diesel engine). *See Figs. 7 and 8.* If resistance is less than 5 ohms, go to next step. If resistance is 5 ohms or more, repair open in White/Pink wire.
3) Measure resistance between instrument cluster connector C251 terminal No. 12 (White/Pink wire) and ground. *See Fig. 7.* If resistance is more than 10 k/ohms, go to next step. If resistance is 10 k/ohms or less, repair short to ground in White/Pink wire.
4) Check tach output signal. For gasoline engines, see appropriate TROUBLE SHOOTING – NO CODES article in ENGINE PERFORMANCE in appropriate MITCHELL® manual for test procedure. For diesel engines, see appropriate SELF-DIAGNOSTICS article in ENGINE PERFORMANCE in appropriate MITCHELL® manual for test procedure. If tach output circuit is okay, repair instrument cluster. If tach output circuit is faulty, replace PCM.

1999 ACCESSORIES & EQUIPMENT
Analog Instrument Panels
F250 Super-Duty & F350 Pickup (Cont.)

FORD
4-809

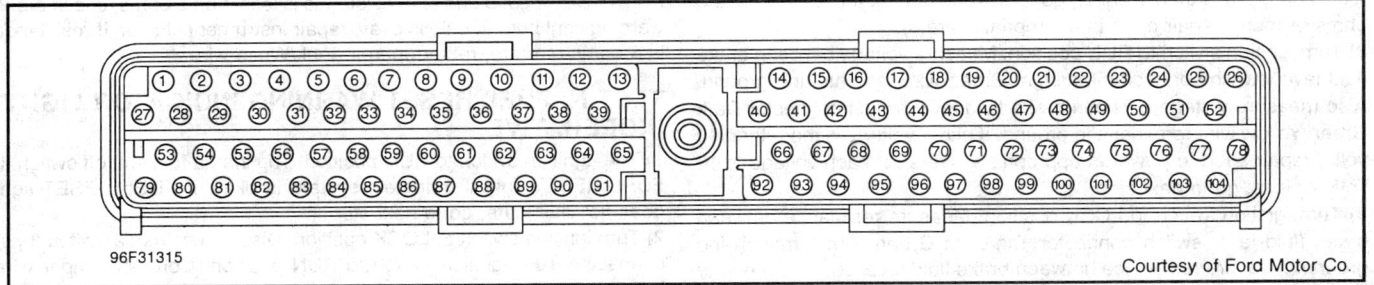

96F31315

Courtesy of Ford Motor Co.

Fig. 8: Identifying Powertrain Control Module (PCM) Connector Terminals

TEST K: SPEEDOMETER READS INCORRECTLY, ODOMETER OKAY

1) Using NGS tester, observe GEM PID VSS_GEM while driving vehicle at 30 MPH. When PID VSS_GEM indicates 30 MPH, hold speed steady (if equipped, set speed control). If speedometer reads 28-35 MPH, go to next step. If speedometer does not read 28-35 MPH, repair instrument cluster.

2) Using NGS tester, observe GEM PID VSS_GEM while driving vehicle at 60 MPH. When PID VSS_GEM indicates 60 MPH, hold speed steady (if equipped, set speed control). If speedometer reads 58-65 MPH, system is okay. If speedometer does not read 58-65 MPH, repair instrument cluster.

TEST L: YELLOW BRAKE (ABS) WARNING INDICATOR LIGHT NEVER ON

NOTE: After repair, retest system.

1) Turn ignition switch to LOCK position. Disconnect anti-lock brake system module 24-pin connector. Connect jumper wire between anti-lock brake system module connector terminal No. 1 (Dark Green wire) and ground. *See Fig. 9.* Turn ignition switch to RUN position. If anti-lock brake system warning light illuminates, see appropriate ANTI-LOCK article in BRAKES in appropriate MITCHELL® manual to diagnose anti-lock brake system. If anti-lock brake system warning light does not illuminate, go to next step.

2) Turn ignition switch to LOCK position. Remove Yellow anti-lock brake system warning light bulb. See INSTRUMENT CLUSTER under REMOVAL & INSTALLATION. Check bulb for continuity. If bulb is okay, go to next step. If bulb is blown, replace bulb.

3) Disconnect instrument cluster 12-pin connector C253. Measure resistance of Dark Green wire between instrument cluster connector C253 terminal No. 11 and anti-lock brake system module connector terminal No. 1. *See Figs. 9 and 10.* If resistance is less than 5 ohms, repair instrument cluster. If resistance is 5 ohms or more, repair open in Dark Green wire.

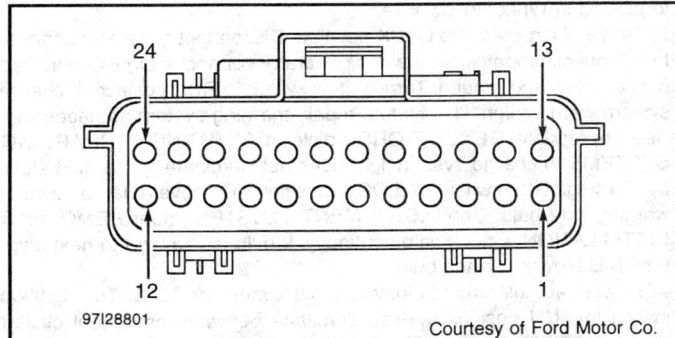

97I28801

Courtesy of Ford Motor Co.

Fig. 9: Identifying Anti-Lock Brake System Module Connector Terminals

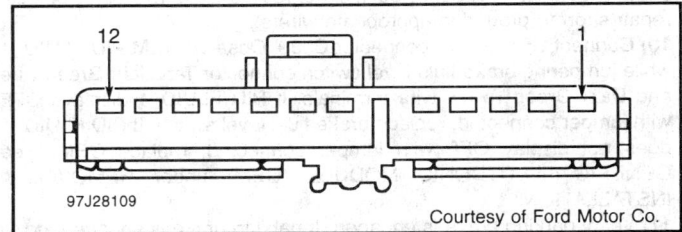

97J28109

Courtesy of Ford Motor Co.

Fig. 10: Identifying Instrument Cluster 12-Pin Connector C253 Terminals

TEST M: RED BRAKE WARNING INDICATOR LIGHT NEVER ON

1) Using NGS tester, perform Generic Electronic Module (GEM) self-test. If DTC C1125 is retrieved, go to step **7)**. If DTC C1189 is retrieved, go to step **9)**. If DTC C1223 or C1225 is retrieved, go to step **4)**. If DTC C1446 is retrieved, go to step **11)**. If DTC B1342 is retrieved, replace GEM. See GENERIC ELECTRONIC MODULE (GEM) under REMOVAL & INSTALLATION. If no DTCs are retrieved, go to next step.

2) Using NGS tester, observe GEM PID IGN_GEM while turning ignition switch through all positions. Depress clutch pedal when turning to START position (M/T). If PID values agree with ignition switch positions, go to next step. If PID values do not agree with ignition switch positions, repair appropriate ignition switch circuit. See appropriate wiring diagram in POWER DISTRIBUTION article in WIRING DIAGRAMS.

3) Turn ignition switch to RUN position. Observe GEM PID PARK_SW while engaging and disengaging parking brake. If PID PARK_SW displays OFF when disengaged and ON when engaged, go to next step. If PID always displays OFF, go to step **12)**. If PID always displays ON, go to step **14)**.

4) Ensure parking brake is not engaged. Using NGS tester, toggle GEM active command BRAKE LAMP to ON. Wait 5 minutes, then toggle BRAKE LAMP off. If the brake light illuminates for 5 seconds after OFF command is made, go to next step. If brake light does not illuminate, go to step **16)**. If brake light stays on at all times, go to step **18)**.

5) Turn ignition switch to LOCK position. Disconnect brake fluid level switch 3-pin connector. Measure resistance between brake fluid level switch connector Black wire terminal and ground. If resistance is less than 5 ohms, go to next step. If resistance is 5 ohms or more, repair open in Black wire.

6) Connect brake fluid level switch connector. Observe GEM PID FLUID_1 while disconnecting brake fluid level switch. If PID FLUID_1 changes from OFF to ON, replace brake fluid level switch. If PID FLUID_1 does not change from OFF to ON, replace GEM. See GENERIC ELECTRONIC MODULE (GEM) under REMOVAL & INSTALLATION.

7) Turn ignition switch to LOCK position. Disconnect brake fluid level switch 3-pin connector. Disconnect GEM 26-pin connector C239. Measure resistance of Tan/Light Green wire between brake fluid level switch connector and GEM connector C239 terminal No. 21. *See Fig. 3.* Measure resistance of Dark Green/Yellow wire between brake fluid level switch connector and GEM connector C239 terminal No. 24. If each

FORD
4-810

1999 ACCESSORIES & EQUIPMENT
Analog Instrument Panels
F250 Super-Duty & F350 Pickup (Cont.)

resistance is less than 5 ohms, go to next step. If either resistance is 5 ohms or more, repair open in appropriate wire(s).

8) Turn ignition switch to RUN position. Measure voltage between brake fluid level switch connector Tan/Light Green wire terminal and ground. Also measure voltage between brake fluid level switch connector Dark Green/Yellow wire terminal and ground. If either voltage is more than 10 volts, repair short to power in appropriate wire(s). If each voltage is 10 volts or less, go to next step.

9) Turn ignition switch to LOCK position. Measure resistance between brake fluid level switch connector Tan/Light Green wire terminal and ground. Measure resistance between brake fluid level switch connector Dark Green/Yellow wire terminal and ground. If each resistance is more than 10 k/ohms, go to next step. If either resistance is 10 k/ohms or less, repair short to ground in appropriate wire(s).

10) Connect GEM 26-pin connector C239. Observe GEM PID FLUID_1 while jumpering brake fluid level switch connector Tan/Light Green wire and Dark Green/Yellow wire terminals. If PID FLUID_1 displays OFF with jumper connected, replace brake fluid level switch. If PID FLUID_1 does not display OFF with jumper connected, replace GEM. See GENERIC ELECTRONIC MODULE (GEM) under REMOVAL & INSTALLATION.

11) Verify parking brake is engaged. If parking brake is engaged, go to next step. If parking brake is not engaged, engage parking brake and repeat GEM self-test.

12) Turn ignition switch to RUN position. Observe GEM PID PARK_SW while jumpering between parking brake switch 1-pin connector Light Green/Red wire terminal and ground. If PID PARK_SW displays ON with jumper connected, replace parking brake switch. If PID PARK_SW does not display ON with jumper connected, go to next step.

13) Disconnect GEM 26-pin connector C239. Disconnect parking brake switch 1-pin connector. Measure resistance of Light Green/Red wire between parking brake switch connector and GEM connector C239 terminal No. 7. See Fig. 3. If resistance is less than 5 ohms, replace GEM. See GENERIC ELECTRONIC MODULE (GEM) under REMOVAL & INSTALLATION. If resistance is 5 ohms or more, repair open in Light Green/Red wire.

14) Turn ignition switch to LOCK position. Observe GEM PID PARK_SW while disconnecting parking brake switch 1-pin connector. If PID PARK_SW displays OFF with switch disconnected, replace parking brake switch. If PID PARK_SW does not display OFF with switch disconnected, go to next step.

15) Turn ignition switch to LOCK position. Disconnect parking brake switch 1-pin connector. Disconnect GEM 26-pin connector C239. Measure resistance between parking brake switch connector Light Green/Red wire terminal and ground. If resistance is more than 10 k/ohms, replace GEM. See GENERIC ELECTRONIC MODULE (GEM) under REMOVAL & INSTALLATION. If resistance is 10 k/ohms or less, repair short to ground in Light Green/Red wire.

16) Turn ignition switch to LOCK position. Disconnect GEM 26-pin connector C239. Turn ignition switch to RUN position. Measure voltage between GEM connector C239 terminal No. 12 (Pink/White wire) and ground. See Fig. 3. If voltage is more than 10 volts, go to next step. If voltage is 10 volts or less, go to step **18)**.

17) Turn ignition switch to LOCK position. Disconnect instrument cluster 12-pin connector C250. Turn ignition switch to RUN position. Measure voltage between GEM connector C239 terminal No. 12 (Pink/White wire) and ground. See Fig. 3. If voltage is more than 10 volts, repair short to power in Pink/White wire. If voltage is 10 volts or less, replace GEM. See GENERIC ELECTRONIC MODULE (GEM) under REMOVAL & INSTALLATION.

18) Disconnect GEM 26-pin connector C239. Measure resistance between GEM connector C239 terminal No. 12 (Pink/White wire) and ground. See Fig. 3. If resistance is more than 10 k/ohms, go to next step. If resistance is 10 k/ohms or less, repair short to ground in Pink/White wire.

19) Measure resistance of Pink/White wire between GEM connector C239 terminal No. 12 and instrument cluster connector C250 terminal

No. 10. See Figs. 3 and 6. If resistance is less than 5 ohms, check brake warning light bulb. If bulb is okay, repair instrument cluster. If resistance is 5 ohms or more, repair open in Pink/White wire.

TEST N: FUEL RESET WARNING INDICATOR LIGHT INOPERATIVE

1) Turn ignition switch to RUN position. Trip inertia fuel shutoff switch. If FUEL RESET light illuminates, system is okay. If FUEL RESET light does not illuminate, go to next step.

2) Turn ignition switch to LOCK position. Disconnect inertia switch 3-pin connector. Turn ignition switch to RUN position. Connect jumper wire between inertia fuel shutoff switch connector Gray/Orange wire terminal and ground. If FUEL RESET light illuminates, replace inertia fuel shutoff switch. If FUEL RESET light does not illuminate, go to next step.

3) Turn ignition switch to LOCK position. Remove FUEL RESET light bulb. See INSTRUMENT CLUSTER under REMOVAL & INSTALLATION. Check bulb continuity. If bulb is okay, go to next step. If bulb is blown, replace bulb.

4) Disconnect instrument cluster 12-pin connector C253. Measure resistance of Gray/Orange wire between inertia fuel shutoff switch connector and instrument cluster connector C253 terminal No. 6. See Fig. 10. If resistance is less than 5 ohms, repair instrument cluster. If resistance is 5 ohms or more, repair open in Gray/Orange wire.

TEST P: SERVICE ENGINE SOON WARNING INDICATOR LIGHT INOPERATIVE

1) Turn ignition switch to LOCK position. Connect EEC-V 104-Pin Breakout Box (014-00950) to Powertrain Control Module (PCM) connector. Turn ignition switch to RUN position. Connect jumper wire between breakout box pin No. 2 (Pink/Light Green wire) and No. 24 (Black/White wire). If SERVICE ENGINE SOON warning light illuminates, retrieve DTCs from PCM. See appropriate SELF-DIAGNOSTICS article in ENGINE PERFORMANCE in appropriate MITCHELL® manual. If SERVICE ENGINE SOON warning light does not illuminate, go to next step.

2) Turn ignition switch to LOCK position. Remove SERVICE ENGINE SOON light bulb. See INSTRUMENT CLUSTER under REMOVAL & INSTALLATION. Check light bulb continuity. If bulb is okay, go to next step. If bulb is blown, replace bulb.

3) Disconnect instrument cluster 12-pin connector C253. Measure resistance of Pink/Light Green wire between breakout box pin No. 2 and instrument cluster C253 connector terminal No. 5. See Fig. 10. If resistance is less than 5 ohms, repair instrument cluster. If resistance is 5 ohms or more, repair open in Pink/Light Green wire.

TEST Q: CHARGE SYSTEM WARNING INDICATOR LIGHT INOPERATIVE

NOTE: After repair, retest system.

1) Check fuse junction panel fuse No. 29 (5-amp). If fuse is okay, go to next step. If fuse is blown, replace fuse. If fuse fails again, repair short to ground in White/Yellow wire.

2) Turn ignition switch to LOCK position. Disconnect generator connector. Connect jumper wire between generator connector Light Green/Red wire terminal and ground. Turn ignition switch to RUN position. If charge system warning light illuminates, repair charging system as necessary. See appropriate GENERATORS article in STARTING & CHARGING SYSTEMS. If charge system light does not illuminate, go to next step.

3) Turn ignition switch to LOCK position. Remove charge system warning light bulb. See INSTRUMENT CLUSTER under REMOVAL & INSTALLATION. Check bulb continuity. If bulb is okay, go to next step. If bulb is blown, replace bulb.

4) Disconnect instrument cluster 12-pin connector C250. Turn ignition switch to RUN position. Measure voltage between instrument cluster connector C250 terminal No. 7 (White/Yellow wire) and ground. See Fig. 6. If voltage is more than 10 volts, go to next step. If voltage is 10 volts or less, repair White/Yellow wire.

1999 ACCESSORIES & EQUIPMENT
Analog Instrument Panels
F250 Super-Duty & F350 Pickup (Cont.)

FORD
4-811

5) Turn ignition switch to LOCK position. Measure resistance of Light Green/Red wire between generator connector and instrument cluster connector C250 terminal No. 8. *See Fig. 6.* If resistance is less than 5 ohms, repair instrument cluster. If resistance is 5 ohms or more, repair open in Light Green/Red wire.

TEST R: AIR BAG WARNING INDICATOR LIGHT INOPERATIVE OR ALWAYS ON

WARNING: To avoid accidental deployment and possible personal injury, backup power supply must be depleted before repairing or replacing any air bag restraint system components. Disconnect battery and, if equipped, auxiliary power supplies. Wait one minute for backup power supply energy to deplete.

NOTE: Electronic Crash Sensor (ECS) module may also be referred to as air bag diagnostic module, air bag diagnostic monitor or Restraints Control Module (RCM).

1) Turn ignition switch to LOCK position. Turn ignition switch to RUN position while observing air bag light prove out. If air bag light prove out is normal, system is okay. If air bag light is always on, go to next step. If air bag light does not come on during prove out, go to step **3).**
2) Turn ignition switch to LOCK position. Disconnect battery ground cable and wait one minute. Disconnect air bag diagnostic monitor 28-pin connector. Disconnect Black/Orange wire at ground behind right kick panel. Measure resistance between instrument cluster connector C250 terminal No. 6 (Black/Yellow wire) and ground. *See Fig. 6.* If resistance is 10 k/ohms or less, repair Black/Yellow wire short to ground. If resistance is more than 10 k/ohms, problem is in air bag restraint system. See appropriate AIR BAG RESTRAINT SYSTEMS article for further diagnosis.
3) Check fuse junction panel fuse No. 29 (5-amp). If fuse is okay, go to next step. If fuse is blown, replace fuse. Test system operation. If fuse blows again, repair White/Yellow wire short to ground.
4) Verify instrument cluster connectors are fully seated. See INSTRUMENT CLUSTER under REMOVAL & INSTALLATION. If instrument cluster connectors are fully seated, go to next step. If instrument cluster connectors are not fully seated, properly seat connectors.
5) Check air bag light bulb continuity. If bulb is okay, go to next step. If bulb is blown, replace bulb.
6) Turn ignition switch to LOCK position. Disconnect instrument cluster 12-pin connector C250. Turn ignition switch to RUN position. Measure voltage between instrument cluster connector C250 terminal No. 7 (White/Yellow wire) and ground. *See Fig. 6.* If voltage is more than 10 volts, go to next step. If voltage is 10 volts or less, repair White/Yellow wire.
7) Turn ignition switch to LOCK position. Disconnect battery ground cable and wait one minute. Disconnect air bag diagnostic monitor 28-pin connector. Disconnect Black/Orange wire at ground behind right kick panel. Measure resistance of Black/Yellow wire between air bag diagnostic monitor connector and instrument cluster connector C250 terminal No. 6. *See Fig. 6.* If resistance is less than 5 ohms, go to next step. If resistance is 5 ohms or more, repair open in Black/Yellow wire.
8) Reconnect instrument cluster connector. Reconnect Black/Orange wire to ground behind right kick panel. Reconnect battery ground cable. Turn ignition switch to RUN position. If air bag light illuminates, replace air bag diagnostic monitor. See AIR BAG DIAGNOSTIC MONITOR under REMOVAL & INSTALLATION. If air bag light does not illuminate, repair instrument cluster.

TEST S: HIGH BEAM INDICATOR LIGHT INOPERATIVE

NOTE: After repair, retest system.

1) Turn ignition switch to LOCK position. Check high beam indicator bulb for continuity. See INSTRUMENT CLUSTER under REMOVAL & INSTALLATION. If bulb is okay, go to next step. If bulb is blown, replace bulb.
2) Disconnect instrument cluster 12-pin connector C253. Turn headlights on. Place multifunction switch in HIGH BEAM position. Measure voltage between instrument cluster connector C253 terminal No. 8 (Light Green/Black wire) and ground. *See Fig. 10.* If voltage is more than 10 volts, repair instrument cluster. If voltage is 10 volts or less, go to next step.
3) Verify high beam headlights operation. If high beams work properly, repair open in Light Green/Black wire. If high beams do not operate properly, repair high beam circuit. See appropriate wiring diagram in EXTERIOR LIGHTS article.

TEST T: LEFT TURN SIGNAL INDICATOR LIGHT INOPERATIVE

1) Turn ignition switch to LOCK position. Check left turn indicator bulb for continuity. See INSTRUMENT CLUSTER under REMOVAL & INSTALLATION. If bulb is okay, go to next step. If bulb is blown, replace bulb.
2) Disconnect instrument cluster 16-pin connector C251. Turn ignition switch to RUN position. Place multifunction switch in left hand turn signal position. Measure voltage between instrument cluster connector C251 terminal No. 16 (Light Green/White wire) and ground. *See Fig. 7.* If voltage fluctuates between 0-10 volts, go to next step. If voltage does not fluctuate 0-10 volts, repair open in Light Green/White wire.
3) Turn ignition switch to LOCK position. Disconnect instrument cluster 12-pin connector C253. Measure resistance between instrument cluster connector C253 terminal No. 12 (Black wire) and ground. *See Fig. 10.* If resistance is less than 5 ohms, repair instrument cluster. If resistance is 5 ohms or more, repair open in Black wire. Ground point is behind bottom of left hand cowl panel.

TEST U: RIGHT TURN SIGNAL INDICATOR LIGHT INOPERATIVE

NOTE: After repair, retest system.

1) Turn ignition switch to LOCK position. Check right turn indicator bulb for continuity. See INSTRUMENT CLUSTER under REMOVAL & INSTALLATION. If bulb is okay, go to next step. If bulb is blown, replace bulb.
2) Disconnect instrument cluster 16-pin connector C251. Turn ignition switch to RUN position. Place multifunction switch in right hand turn signal position. Measure voltage between instrument cluster connector C251 terminal No. 14 (White/Light Blue wire) and ground. *See Fig. 7.* If voltage fluctuates between 0-10 volts, go to next step. If voltage does not fluctuate 0-10 volts, repair open in White/Light Blue wire.
3) Turn ignition switch to LOCK position. Disconnect instrument cluster 12-pin connector C253. Measure resistance between instrument cluster connector C253 terminal No. 12 (Black wire) and ground. *See Fig. 10.* If resistance is less than 5 ohms, repair instrument cluster. If resistance is 5 ohms or more, repair open in Black wire. Ground point is behind bottom of left hand cowl panel.

TEST V: DOOR AJAR WARNING INDICATOR LIGHT INOPERATIVE, CHIME OKAY

1) Using NGS tester, perform Generic Electronic Module (GEM) self-tests. If DTC B1323 or B1325 is retrieved, go to step **3).** If DTC B1355 is retrieved, go to step **9).** If DTC B1342 is retrieved, replace GEM. See GENERIC ELECTRONIC MODULE (GEM) under REMOVAL & INSTALLATION. If no DTCs are retrieved, go to next step.

FORD
4-812

1999 ACCESSORIES & EQUIPMENT
Analog Instrument Panels
F250 Super-Duty & F350 Pickup (Cont.)

2) Using NGS tester, observe GEM PID IGN_GEM while turning ignition switch through all positions. Depress clutch pedal when turning to START position (M/T). If PID values agree with ignition switch positions, go to step **9)**. If PID values do not agree with ignition switch positions, repair appropriate ignition switch circuit. See appropriate wiring diagram in POWER DISTRIBUTION article in WIRING DIAGRAMS.

3) Open and close all doors while observing courtesy lights. If courtesy lights operate properly, go to next step. If courtesy lights do not operate properly, repair courtesy lights. See appropriate wiring diagram in ILLUMINATION/INTERIOR LIGHTS article.

4) Using NGS tester, select WARNING LAMP AND CHIME active command mode. Observe door ajar indicator light while triggering active command mode AJAR LAMP to ON and OFF. If door ajar light functions properly, replace GEM. See GENERIC ELECTRONIC MODULE (GEM) under REMOVAL & INSTALLATION. If door ajar light does not function properly, go to next step.

5) Turn ignition switch to LOCK position. Disconnect GEM 26-pin connector C239. Measure voltage between GEM connector C239 terminal No. 1 (Tan/Red wire) and ground. *See Fig. 3*. If voltage is more than 10 volts, go to next step. If voltage is 10 volts or less, go to step **7)**.

6) Turn ignition switch to LOCK position. Disconnect instrument cluster 12-pin connector C250. Turn ignition switch to RUN position. Measure voltage between GEM connector C239 terminal No. 11 (Dark Green/Orange wire) and ground. *See Fig. 3*. If voltage is more than 10 volts, repair short to power in Dark Green/Orange wire. If voltage is 10 volts or less, replace GEM. See GENERIC ELECTRONIC MODULE (GEM) under REMOVAL & INSTALLATION.

7) Turn ignition switch to LOCK position. Disconnect instrument cluster 12-pin connector C250. Measure resistance between GEM connector C239 terminal No. 11 (Dark Green/Orange wire) and ground. *See Fig. 3*. If resistance is more than 10 k/ohms, go to next step. If resistance is 10 k/ohms or less, repair short to ground in Dark Green/Orange wire.

8) Disconnect instrument cluster 12-pin connector C253. Measure resistance of Dark Green/Orange wire between GEM connector C239 terminal No. 11 and instrument cluster connector C253 terminal No. 2. *See Figs. 3 and 10*. If resistance is less than 5 ohms, check door ajar indicator bulb. If bulb is okay, repair instrument cluster. If resistance is 5 ohms or more, repair open in Dark Green/Orange wire.

9) Turn ignition switch to LOCK position. Check fuse junction panel fuse No. 19 (10-amp). If fuse is okay, go to step **12)**. If fuse is blown, go to next step.

10) Ensure fuse junction panel fuse No. 19 (10-amp) is removed. Disconnect GEM 26-pin connector C239. Measure resistance between GEM connector C239 terminal No. 18 (Red/Yellow wire) and ground. *See Fig. 3*. If resistance is more than 10 k/ohms, replace GEM. See GENERIC ELECTRONIC MODULE (GEM) under REMOVAL & INSTALLATION. If resistance is 10 k/ohms or less, go to next step.

11) Turn ignition switch to LOCK position. Disconnect fuse junction panel 34-pin connector C243. Measure resistance between GEM connector C239 terminal No. 18 (Red/Yellow wire) and ground. *See Fig. 3*. If resistance is less than 100 ohms, repair short to ground in Red/Yellow wire. If resistance is 100 ohms or more, repair or replace fuse junction panel.

12) Turn ignition switch to RUN position. Measure voltage between fuse function panel fuse No. 19 (10-amp) fuse holder (input side) and ground. If voltage is more than 10 volts, go to next step. If voltage is 10 volts or less, repair Red/Black wire between ignition switch and fuse junction panel.

13) Turn ignition switch to LOCK position. Disconnect GEM 26-pin connector C239. Turn ignition switch to RUN position. Measure voltage between GEM connector C239 terminal No. 18 (Red/Yellow wire) and ground. *See Fig. 3*. If voltage is more than 10 volts, replace GEM. See GENERIC ELECTRONIC MODULE (GEM) under REMOVAL & INSTALLATION. If voltage is 10 volts or less, repair Red/Yellow wire.

TEST W: SAFETY BELT WARNING INDICATOR LIGHT INOPERATIVE OR DOES NOT OPERATE PROPERLY, CHIME OKAY

1) Using NGS tester, perform Generic Electronic Module (GEM) self-test. If DTC B1426 or B1428 is retrieved, go to step **3)**. If DTC B1342 is retrieved, replace GEM. See GENERIC ELECTRONIC MODULE (GEM) under REMOVAL & INSTALLATION. If no DTCs are retrieved, go to next step.

2) Using NGS tester, observe GEM PID IGN_GEM while turning ignition switch through all positions. Depress clutch pedal when turning to START position (M/T). If PID values agree with ignition switch positions, go to next step. If PID values do not agree with ignition switch positions, repair appropriate ignition switch circuit. See appropriate wiring diagram in POWER DISTRIBUTION article in WIRING DIAGRAMS.

3) Observe GEM PID D_SBELT. Connect and disconnect driver's safety belt. If PID reads properly, go to next step. If PID does not read properly, repair driver's safety belt circuit as necessary.

4) Using NGS tester, observe and trigger SBLTLAMP active command ON and OFF. If safety belt warning light functions properly, replace GEM. See GENERIC ELECTRONIC MODULE (GEM) under REMOVAL & INSTALLATION. If safety belt warning light does not function properly, go to next step.

5) Turn ignition switch to LOCK position. Disconnect GEM 26-pin connector C239. Turn ignition switch to RUN position. Measure voltage between GEM connector C239 terminal No. 13 (Dark Green/Light Green wire) and ground. *See Fig. 3*. If voltage is more than 10 volts, go to next step. If voltage is 10 volts or less, go to step **7)**.

6) Turn ignition switch to LOCK position. Disconnect GEM 26-pin connector C239. Disconnect instrument cluster 12-pin connector C250. Turn ignition switch to RUN position. Measure voltage between GEM C239 connector terminal No. 13 (Dark Green/Light Green wire) and ground. *See Fig. 3*. If voltage is more than 10 volts, repair short to power in Dark Green/Light Green wire. If voltage is 10 volts or less, replace GEM. See GENERIC ELECTRONIC MODULE (GEM) under REMOVAL & INSTALLATION.

7) Turn ignition switch to LOCK position. Disconnect GEM 26-pin connector C239. Measure resistance between GEM connector C239 terminal No. 13 (Dark Green/Light Green wire) and ground. *See Fig. 3*. If resistance is more than 10 k/ohms, go to next step. If resistance is 10 k/ohms or more, repair short to ground in Dark Green/Light Green wire.

8) Turn ignition switch to LOCK position. Disconnect instrument cluster 12-pin connector C250. Measure resistance of Dark Green/Light Green wire between GEM connector C239 terminal No. 13 and instrument cluster connector C250 terminal No. 9. *See Figs. 3 and 6*. If resistance is less than 5 ohms, check safety belt warning light bulb. If bulb is okay, repair instrument cluster. If resistance is 5 ohms or more, repair open in Dark Green/Light Green wire.

TEST X: 4X4 &/OR LOW RANGE INDICATOR LIGHT INOPERATIVE (MANUAL SHIFT)

1) Disconnect 4x4 switch 2-pin connector located below center of vehicle near digital transmission range sensor. If 4x4 light is inoperative, connect jumper wire between 4x4 switch connector Light Blue wire terminal and ground. If LOW RANGE light is inoperative, connect jumper wire between 4x4 switch connector ight Blue/Black wire terminal and ground. If light illuminates, replace 4x4 switch. If light does not illuminate, go to next step.

2) Turn ignition switch to LOCK position. Check inoperative indicator bulb. See INSTRUMENT CLUSTER under REMOVAL & INSTALLATION. If bulb is okay, go to next step. If bulb is blown, replace bulb.

3) If 4x4 indicator light is inoperative, measure resistance of Light Blue wire between 4x4 switch connector and instrument cluster connector C253 terminal No. 4. *See Fig. 10*. If LOW RANGE indicator light is inoperative, measure resistance of Light Blue/Black wire between 4x4 switch connector and instrument cluster connector C253 terminal No. 10. If resistance is less than 5 ohms, repair instrument cluster. If resistance is 5 ohms or more, repair open in appropriate wire(s).

1999 ACCESSORIES & EQUIPMENT
Analog Instrument Panels
F250 Super-Duty & F350 Pickup (Cont.)

FORD
4-813

TEST Y: 4X4 &/OR LOW RANGE INDICATOR LIGHT ALWAYS ON (MANUAL SHIFT)

Disconnect 4x4 switch connector. Turn ignition switch to RUN position. If 4x4 indicator light illuminates, repair short to ground in Light Blue wire. If LOW RANGE indicator light illuminates, repair short to ground in Light Blue/Black wire. If neither light illuminates, replace 4x4 switch.

TEST Z: WAIT TO START WARNING INDICATOR LIGHT INOPERATIVE (DIESEL)

1) Turn ignition switch to LOCK position. Connect EEC-V 104-Pin Breakout Box (014-00950) to Powertrain Control Module (PCM) connector. Connect jumper wire between breakout box pin No. 70 (Black/Pink wire) and ground. Turn ignition switch to RUN position. If WAIT TO START light illuminates, see SELF-DIAGNOSTICS – DIESEL article in ENGINE PERFORMANCE in appropriate MITCHELL® manual for further diagnosis. If WAIT TO START light does not illuminate, go to next step.

2) Turn ignition switch to LOCK position. Disconnect instrument cluster 12-pin connector C253. See INSTRUMENT CLUSTER under REMOVAL & INSTALLATION. Measure resistance of Black/Pink wire between instrument cluster connector C253 terminal No. 1 and breakout box pin No. 70. *See Fig. 10.* If resistance is less than 5 ohms, go to next step. If resistance is 5 ohms or more, repair open in Black/Pink wire.

3) Check WAIT TO START bulb continuity. If bulb is okay, repair instrument cluster. If bulb is blown, replace bulb.

TEST AA: WATER IN FUEL WARNING INDICATOR LIGHT INOPERATIVE (DIESEL)

1) Disconnect water in fuel switch 2-pin connector located center of engine compartment on fuel heater. Connect jumper wire between water in fuel switch connector Gray/Red wire terminal and ground. Turn ignition switch to RUN position. If WATER IN FUEL light illuminates, replace water in fuel switch. If WATER IN FUEL light does not illuminate, go to next step.

2) Turn ignition switch to LOCK position. Connect EEC-V 104-Pin Breakout Box (014-00950) to Powertrain Control Module (PCM) connector. Measure resistance of Gray/Red wire between water in fuel switch connector and breakout box pin No. 36. If resistance is less than 5 ohms, go to next step. If resistance is 5 ohms or more, repair open in Gray/Red wire.

3) Connect jumper wire between breakout box pin No. 28 (Red wire) and ground. If WATER IN FUEL light illuminates, see SELF-DIAGNOS-TICS – DIESEL article in ENGINE PERFORMANCE in appropriate MITCHELL® manual for further diagnosis. If WATER IN FUEL light does not illuminate, go to next step.

4) Turn ignition switch to LOCK position. Disconnect instrument cluster 12-pin connector C250. See INSTRUMENT CLUSTER under REMOVAL & INSTALLATION. Measure resistance of Red wire between instrument cluster connector C250 terminal No. 11 and breakout box pin No. 28. *See Fig. 6.* If resistance is less than 5 ohms, go to next step. If resistance is 5 ohms or more, repair open in Red wire.

5) Check WATER IN FUEL bulb continuity. If bulb is okay, repair instrument cluster. If bulb is blown, replace bulb.

REMOVAL & INSTALLATION

CAUTION: When battery is disconnected, vehicle computer and memory systems may lose memory data. Driveability problems may exist until computer systems have completed a relearn cycle. See COMPUTER RELEARN PROCEDURES article in GENERAL INFORMATION before disconnecting battery.

AIR BAG DIAGNOSTIC MONITOR

WARNING: To avoid accidental deployment and possible personal injury, backup power supply must be depleted before repairing or replacing any air bag restraint system components. Disconnect battery and, if equipped, auxiliary power supplies. Wait one minute for backup power supply energy to deplete.

CAUTION: For proper operation, it is critical to tighten air bag diagnostic monitor bolts to specification.

NOTE: Electronic Crash Sensor (ECS) module may also be referred to as air bag diagnostic module, air bag diagnostic monitor or Restraints Control Module (RCM).

Removal & Installation – 1) Disconnect battery ground cable. If equipped, disconnect auxiliary power supplies. Wait one minute for backup power supply to be depleted before continuing.

2) Remove air bag diagnostic monitor cover. Disconnect air bag diagnostic monitor electrical connector locking clip and electrical connector. Remove air bag diagnostic monitor retaining screws. Remove air bag diagnostic monitor.

3) To install, reverse removal procedure. Tighten retaining bolts to 108 INCH lbs. (12 N.m).

GENERIC ELECTRONIC MODULE (GEM)

CAUTION: Disconnect battery before disconnecting Generic Electronic Module (GEM) connectors. Failure to do so will result in GEM storing erroneous codes and may also result in erratic operation of GEM after reconnection.

NOTE: GEM must be reconfigured upon replacement. Refer to NGS tester help screen on Ford Service Function (FSF) card to program tire size and axle ratio.

Removal & Installation – Remove instrument panel steering column cover. Disconnect bulkhead connector from fuse junction panel. Remove fuse junction panel nuts and bolts and position aside. Disconnect GEM electrical connectors and screws. Remove GEM. To install, reverse removal procedure.

INSTRUMENT CLUSTER

Removal & Installation – 1) Disconnect negative battery cable. Insert radio removing tool into radio face plate and release radio retaining clips. Pull outward on radio removing tool while pulling radio out from instrument panel.

2) Lower steering wheel. Remove bolts and pull back cluster finish panel. Disconnect electrical connectors and remove cluster finish panel.

3) Remove instrument panel screws. If automatic transmission, push in 2 clips and pull out transmission range indicator. Disconnect electrical connectors. Remove instrument cluster. To install, reverse removal procedure.

FORD
4-814

1999 ACCESSORIES & EQUIPMENT
Analog Instrument Panels
F250 Super-Duty & F350 Pickup (Cont.)

WIRING DIAGRAMS

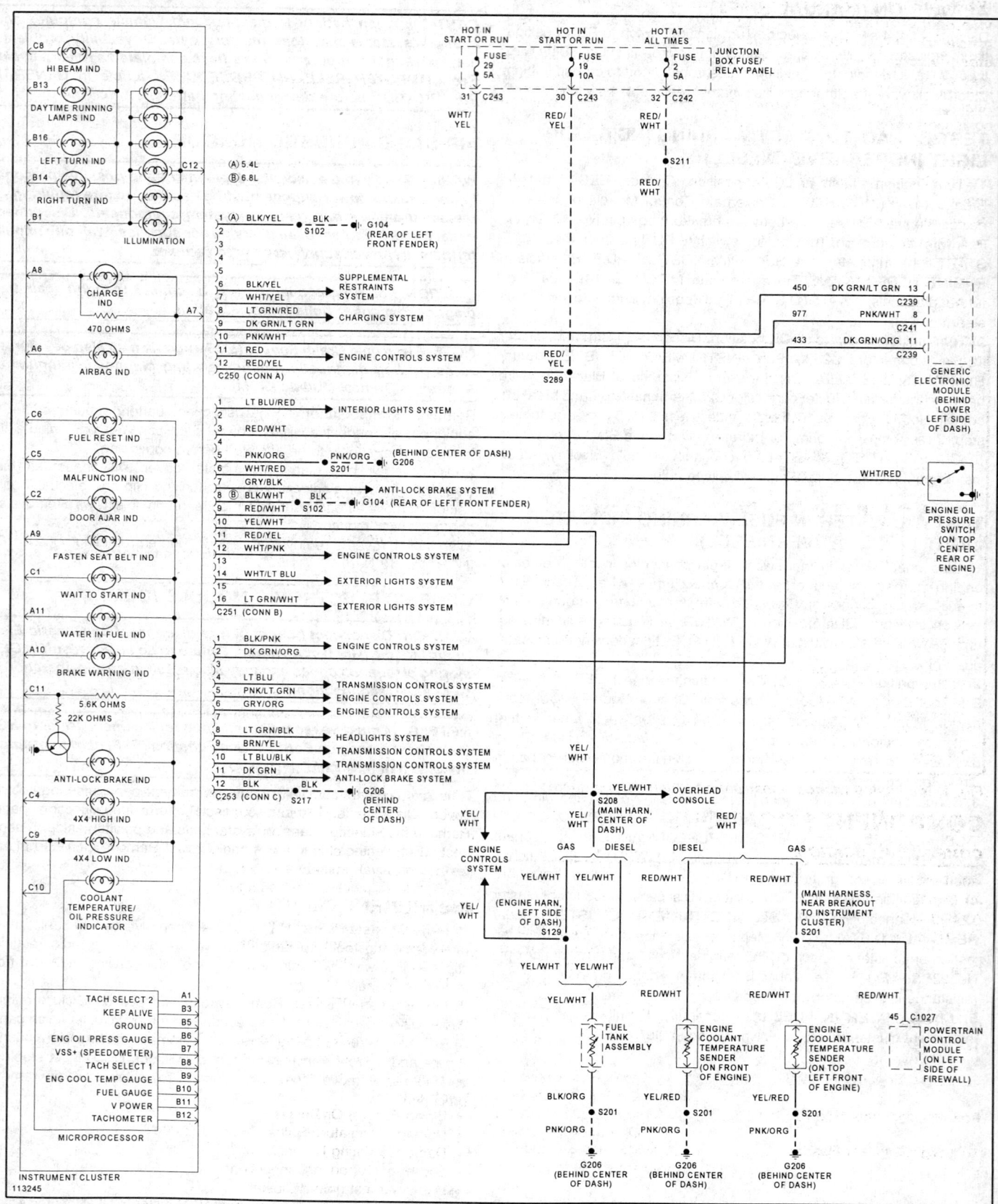

Fig. 11: Analog Instrument Panel Wiring Diagram (F250 Super-Duty & F350 Pickup)

DESCRIPTION & OPERATION

WARNING: Deactivate air bag system before performing any service operation. See AIR BAG RESTRAINT SYSTEMS – RANGER article. DO NOT apply electrical power to any component on steering column without first deactivating air bag system. Air bag may deploy.

Analog instrument cluster is equipped with speedometer, tachometer (if equipped), voltmeter, fuel, oil pressure and temperature gauges. *See Fig. 1.* All models use magnetic gauges to monitor fuel quantity, coolant temperature and oil pressure. When ignition switch is turned to ON position, the following warning indicators will light momentarily as a bulb check:

- Air Bag Readiness
- Charging System
- Check Gauges
- MIL (CHECK ENGINE)
- ABS
- Safety Belt

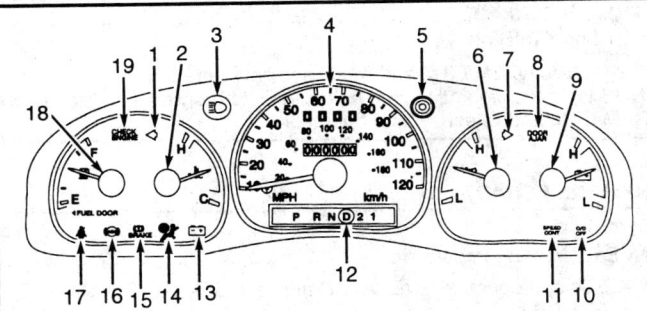

1. Left Turn Indicator	11. Speed Control Indicator
2. Coolant Temperature Gauge	12. Transmission Range Indicator
3. High Beam Indicator	13. Charge System Indicator
4. Speedometer	14. Air Bag Indicator
5. Trip Reset	15. Brake Indicator
6. Oil Pressure Gauge	16. Anti-Lock Brake (ABS) Indicator
7. Right Turn Indicator	17. Fasten Seat Belt Indicator
8. Door Ajar Indicator	18. Fuel Gauge
9. Battery Voltage Gauge	19. Check Engine Light
10. Overdrive Off Indicator	

98C00499

Courtesy of Ford Motor Co.

Fig. 1: Identifying Standard Instrument Cluster Components

COMPONENT LOCATIONS

COMPONENT LOCATIONS

Component	Location
Air Bag Diagnostic Monitor [1]	Behind Right Kick Panel
Air Bag Sliding Contact	Base Of Steering Column
Central Junction Box	Behind Left Side Of Instrument Panel
Data Link Connector (DLC)	Below Driver's Side Of Instrument Panel, To Right Of Steering Column
Generic Electronic Module/Central Timer Module (GEM/CTM)	Behind Center Of Instrument Panel
Fuel Level Sender Connector	Below Rear Center Of Vehicle On Top Of Fuel Tank
Powertrain Control Module (PCM)	Mounted Through Firewall, On Passenger's Side
Turn Signal/Hazard Flasher	Underdash Left Side Of Instrument Panel In Junction Box

[1] – Air bag diagnostic monitor may also be known as Electronic Crash Sensor (ECS) module.

COMPONENT TESTS

ODOMETER TEST

Test drive vehicle over a measured distance of at least 10 consecutive miles. Check measured distance against odometer measured distance. Acceptable odometer measured distance is 9.6-10.4 miles.

OIL PRESSURE GAUGE TEST

Disconnect oil pressure sensor harness connector. Connect instrument gauge system tester to oil pressure sensor harness connector wire. Turn ignition on. Set tester to infinity. Oil pressure gauge should read below "L" (low). Short oil pressure sensor harness connector wire to ground. Oil pressure gauge should read above mid scale. If oil pressure gauge functions as specified, replace oil pressure switch. If oil pressure gauge does not function as specified, replace oil pressure gauge.

TEMPERATURE GAUGE TEST

Turn ignition off. Disconnect temperature sender connector. Connect Instrument Gauge System Tester (014-R1063) to temperature sender harness connector Red/White wire. Set tester at 300 ohms. Turn ignition on, wait 60 seconds and read gauge. Temperature gauge should read "C" (cold). Set tester at 45 ohms. Turn ignition on, wait 60 seconds and read gauge. Temperature gauge should read within 1/4 and 1/2 range. Turn ignition off. Set tester to 18 ohms. Turn ignition on, wait 60 seconds. Temperature gauge should read "H" (hot). If temperature gauge does not function as specified, go to COOLANT TEMPERATURE READS INACCURATELY under SYSTEM TESTS.

TROUBLE SHOOTING

CAUTION: Electronic modules are sensitive to static electrical charges. Proper grounding of technician and workpiece is essential to prevent damage.

SELF-DIAGNOSTICS

The instrument cluster utilizes a self-diagnostic system which may store a Diagnostic Trouble Code (DTC) if a problem exists in the system. DTCs may be retrieved using New Generation Star (NGS) tester and Data Link Connector (DLC) for diagnosis of system. Before performing any testing, a preliminary procedure should be performed. See PRELIMINARY PROCEDURE.

PRELIMINARY PROCEDURE

1) Verify customers complaint by operating system in question. Visually inspect components. See following list. Repair or replace components as necessary. Verify charging system, cooling system, fuel system, safety belt warning chime, turn signals, headlights and theft control are working properly. Inspect wiring harness for obvious signs of shorts, opens, bad connections or damage.

Mechanical:
- Damaged Engine Oil Filter
- Damaged Coolant Thermostat
- Damaged Oil Pump
- Door Adjustment
- Low Engine Coolant
- Low Engine Oil
- Stuck Coolant Temperature Gauge Needle
- Stuck Oil Pressure Gauge Needle
- Tripped Inertia Switch

Electrical:
- Blown Fuse(s) Or Relays
- Damaged Miniature Bulbs
- Damaged Wiring Harness
- Loose Or Corroded Connections
- Damaged Instrument Cluster

2) If all components are okay, connect NGS tester to DLC located below instrument panel. Using NGS tester, perform DATA LINK DIAGNOSTIC

TEST. If NGS tester displays CKT 914, CKT 915 or CKT 70=ALL ECUS NO RESP/NOT EQUIP, see MODULE COMMUNICATIONS NETWORK – RANGER article to diagnosis network concern. If NGS tester displays NO RESP/NOT EQUIP for Generic Electronic Module (GEM), go to NO COMMUNICATION WITH GEM/CTM under SYSTEM TESTS.

3) If NGS tester displays SYSTEM PASSED for GEM, retrieve and record continuous DTCs using NGS tester. Erase continuous DTCs. Perform GEM/CTM self-test diagnostics using NGS tester. If any GEM/CTM DTCs are retrieved, perform appropriate system test. See GENERIC ELECTRONIC MODULE/CENTRAL TIMER MODULE (GEM/CTM) DTC DEFINITIONS table. Codes listed in this table are only for testing covered in this article. For complete DTC listing, see MODULE COMMUNICATIONS NETWORK – RANGER article. If no DTCs are retrieved, diagnose by symptom. See SYMPTOM CHART under SYSTEM TESTS.

GENERIC ELECTRONIC MODULE/CENTRAL TIMER MODULE (GEM/CTM) DTC DEFINITIONS

DTC	Description	Test
B1323	Driver Door Ajar Light Circuit Failure	W
B1325	Door Ajar Light Circuit Short To Battery	W
B1342	GEM/CTM Is Defective	1
B1426	Seat Belt Light Circuit Short To Battery	X
B1428	Seat Belt Light Circuit Failure	X
B2141	NVM Configuration Failure	2
C1751	VSS Output Short To Battery	E
C1752	VSS Output Short To Ground	E
P1804	4WD High Indicator Circuit Failure	Y
P1806	4WD High Indicator Circuit Short To Battery	Y
P1808	4WD Low Indicator Circuit Failure	Y
P1810	4WD Low Indicator Circuit Short To Battery	Y

1 – Using NGS tester, clear DTCs. Retrieve DTCs. If DTC B1342 is retrieved, replace GEM/CTM and retest system operation.
2 – Vehicle speed calibration data is not programmed into GEM/CTM. Use NGS tester configuration card help screen to program tire size and axle ratio. Retest system operation. If DTC B2141 is still present, replace GEM/CTM and retest system operation.

SYSTEM TESTS

CAUTION: When battery is disconnected or modules are replaced, vehicle computer and memory systems may lose memory data. Driveability problems may exist until computer systems have completed a relearn cycle. See COMPUTER RELEARN PROCEDURES article in GENERAL INFORMATION before disconnecting battery.

NOTE: Before beginning system tests, perform TROUBLE SHOOTING.

SYMPTOM CHART

Symptom	Test
Fuel Gauge Inaccurate	A
Temperature Gauge Inaccurate	B
Oil Pressure Gauge Inaccurate	C
Volt Gauge Inaccurate	1
Speedometer Inaccurate	D
Speedometer/Odometer Inoperative W/RABS	E
Speedometer/Odometer Inoperative W/4WABS	F
Tachometer Inoperative	G
Tachometer Inaccurate	H
Charge Warning Never/Always On	J
Anti-Lock Brake Warning Indicator Inoperative	K
Anti-Lock Brake Warning Always On	2
Anti-Theft Indicator Inoperative Or Always On	3
Fuel Reset Light Inoperative	L
Fuel Reset Light Always On	4
High Beam Warning Inoperative	M
CHECK ENGINE Light (MIL) Inoperative	N
CHECK ENGINE Light (MIL) Always On	5
Left Turn Indicator Inoperative	P
Right Turn Indicator Inoperative	Q
O/D Off Indicator Inoperative	R
Speed Control Indicator Never/Always On	S
Brake Warning Indicator Inoperative	T
CHECK GAGE Indicator Inoperative	U
No Communication With GEM/CTM	V
Door Ajar Chime Does Not Operate Properly	W
Seat Belt Warning Does Not Operate Properly	X
4X4 HIGH Or 4X4 LOW Indicator Inoperative	Y

SYMPTOM CHART (Cont.)

Symptom	Test
Air Bag Warning Imperative	Z

1 – See appropriate GENERATOR article in STARTING & CHARGING SYSTEM.
2 – See appropriate ANTI-LOCK article in BRAKES in appropriate MITCHELL® manual.
3 – See PASSIVE ANTI-THEFT SYSTEMS – RANGER article.
4 – Repair short to ground in Gray/Orange wire between inertia switch and instrument cluster.
5 – See appropriate SELF-DIAGNOSTICS article in ENGINE PERFORMANCE in appropriate MITCHELL® manual.

TEST A: FUEL GAUGE INACCURATE

1) Turn ignition off. Disconnect fuel gauge sending unit. Using Instrument Gauge System Tester (014-R-1063), connect one tester lead to fuel sending unit connector terminal No. 5 (Yellow/White wire). Connect second lead to ground. Set instrument gauge system tester to 160 ohms. Turn instrument gauge system tester on. Turn ignition on. Wait one minute and read fuel gauge. Fuel gauge should read "F" or above. Set tester to 15 ohms. Wait one minute and read fuel gauge. Fuel gauge should read "E" or below. If fuel gauge reads as specified, disconnect tester and go to next step. If fuel gauge does not read as specified, disconnect tester and go to step **4)**.

2) Visually inspect fuel tank for damage. If fuel tank is okay, go to next step. If fuel tank is damaged, repair or replace as necessary.

3) Visually inspect fuel pump assembly for damage or corroded connections. Inspect float and float rod. If fuel pump assembly is okay, replace fuel level sensor. If fuel pump assembly is damaged, replace assembly and retest system.

4) Turn ignition off. Remove instrument cluster. See INSTRUMENT CLUSTER under REMOVAL & INSTALLATION. Measure resistance of Yellow/White wire between instrument cluster connector C215 terminal No. 12 and fuel level sensor connector terminal No. 5. See Figs. 2 and 3. Resistance should be less than 5 ohms. Measure resistance between ground and instrument cluster connector C215 terminal No. 12 (Yellow/White wire). Resistance should be more than 10 k/ohms. If resistance is as specified, go to next step. If resistance is not as specified, repair open or short to ground in Yellow/White wire. See WIRING DIAGRAMS.

5) Measure resistance between ground and fuel level sensor connector C422 terminal No. 8 (Black/Orange wire). If resistance is less than 5 ohms, go to next step. If resistance is more than 5 ohms, repair open in Black/Orange wire. See WIRING DIAGRAMS.

6) Measure resistance of printed circuit. See FUEL GAUGE PRINTED CIRCUIT MEASUREMENTS table. If all resistance values are less than 5 ohms, replace fuel gauge and instrument cluster gauge amplifier. If resistance in any circuit measurement is 5 ohms or more, replace instrument cluster printed circuit.

FUEL GAUGE PRINTED CIRCUIT MEASUREMENTS

Connector/Terminal	Connector/Terminal
Fuel Gauge/S	Gauge Amplifier
Fuel Gauge/G	C215/2
Fuel Gauge/B	C215/8
Fuel Gauge/Ground	Gauge Amplifier
Gauge Amplifier	C215/2
Gauge Amplifier	C215/12
Gauge Amplifier	1 C216/1
Gauge Amplifier	1 2 C215/3

1 – Connector C216/1 is for optional cluster with tachometer and connector C215/3 is for standard cluster.

2 – Use illustration for connector C216 terminal identification. *See Fig. 4.*

97J28109
Courtesy of Ford Motor Co.

Fig. 2: Identifying Instrument Cluster Connector C215 Terminals

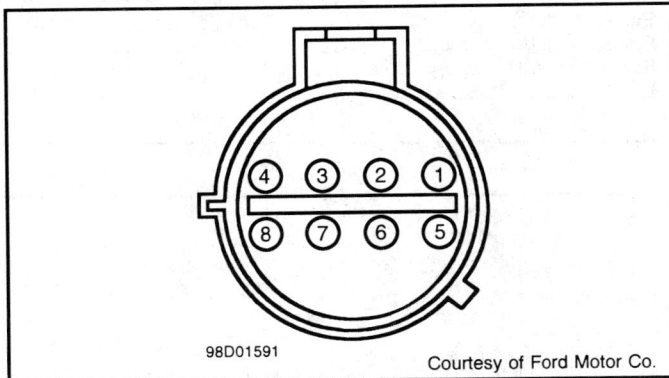

98D01591
Courtesy of Ford Motor Co.

Fig. 3: Identifying Fuel Gauge Sending Unit Connector C422 Terminals

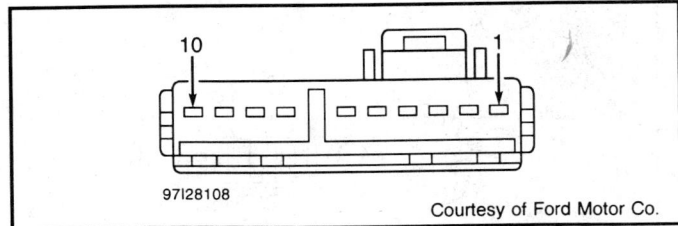

97I28108
Courtesy of Ford Motor Co.

Fig. 4: Identifying Instrument Cluster Connector C216 Terminals

TEST B: TEMPERATURE GAUGE INACCURATE

1) Perform TEMPERATURE GAUGE TEST under COMPONENT TESTS. If temperature gauge perform properly, replace temperature sender and retest system. If temperature gauge does not perform properly, go to next step.

2) Turn ignition off. Disconnect temperature sender harness connector. Remove instrument cluster. See INSTRUMENT CLUSTER under

REMOVAL & INSTALLATION. Disconnect instrument cluster connector C215. *See Fig. 2.* Measure resistance of Red/White wire between instrument cluster connector C215 terminal No. 3 and temperature sender harness connector. Resistance should be less than 5 ohms. Measure resistance between ground and instrument cluster connector C215 terminal No. 3 (Red/White wire). Resistance should be more than 10 k/ohms. If resistance is as specified, go to next step. If resistance is not as specified, repair open or short in Red/White wire and retest system.

3) Disconnect instrument cluster connector C216. Turn ignition on. Measure voltage between ground and optional instrument cluster (with tachometer) connector C216 terminal No. 1 (Red/Yellow wire) or standard instrument cluster (without tachometer) connector C215 terminal No. 8 (Red/Yellow wire). *See Fig. 2 or 4.* If voltage is more than 10 volts, go to next step. If voltage is less than 10 volts, repair open in Red/Yellow wire between instrument cluster connector and fuse No. 11 in interior fuse panel and retest system.

4) Turn ignition off. Measure resistance between ground and instrument cluster connector C215 terminal No. 2 (Black/White wire). If resistance is less than 5 ohms, go to next step. If resistance 5 ohms or more, repair open in Black/White wire between instrument cluster connector and ground and retest system.

5) Measure resistance between instrument cluster temperature gauge clips "B" and "S". Resistance should be 214-256 ohms. Measure resistance between instrument cluster temperature gauge clips "G" and "S". Resistance should be 90-110 ohms. If resistances are as specified, replace instrument cluster printed circuit and retest system. See PRINTED CIRCUIT under REMOVAL & INSTALLATION. If resistances are not as specified, replace temperature gauge and retest system. See GAUGES under REMOVAL & INSTALLATION.

TEST C: OIL PRESSURE GAUGE INACCURATE

NOTE: Ensure oil level is correct before proceeding and oil pressure switch connector is secure.

1) Start engine and allow to idle. If oil pressure gauge shows "L" or below, go to step 5). If oil pressure gauge does not show "L" or below, go to next step.

2) Turn engine off, key on. If oil pressure gauge shows oil pressure, go to next step. If oil pressure gauge does not show oil pressure, system is okay.

3) Turn ignition off. Remove instrument cluster connector C214. See INSTRUMENT CLUSTER under REMOVAL & INSTALLATION. Turn ignition on. Measure resistance between ground and instrument cluster connector C214 terminal No. 12 (Dark Green/White wire). *See Fig. 5.* If resistance is less than 5 ohms, go to next step. If resistance is 5 ohms or more, replace oil pressure gauge. See GAUGES under REMOVAL & INSTALLATION.

4) Turn ignition off. Disconnect oil pressure switch connector. Measure resistance between ground and instrument cluster connector C214 terminal No. 12 (Dark Green/White wire). If resistance is 10 k/ohms or less, repair short to ground in Dark Green/White wire. If resistance is more than 10 k/ohms, replace oil pressure switch.

5) Turn ignition off. Disconnect oil pressure switch connector. Turn ignition on. Connect fused jumper wire between oil pressure switch connector and ground. If oil pressure gauge shows normal range, replace oil pressure switch. If oil pressure gauge does not show normal range, go to next step.

6) Turn ignition off. Remove instrument cluster connector C214. See INSTRUMENT CLUSTER under REMOVAL & INSTALLATION. Measure resistance of Dark Green/White wire between ground and instrument cluster connector C214 terminal No. 12 and oil pressure switch connector. If resistance is less than 5 ohms, go to next step. If resistance is 5 ohms or more, repair open Dark Green/White wire.

7) Remove instrument cluster. See INSTRUMENT CLUSTER under REMOVAL & INSTALLATION. Measure resistance between instrument cluster connector C214 terminal No. 12 and oil pressure gauge contact clip terminal "S". If resistance is less than 5 ohms, replace oil pressure gauge. See GAUGES under REMOVAL & INSTALLATION. If resistance is 5 ohms or more, replace instrument cluster printed circuit and retest system. See PRINTED CIRCUIT under REMOVAL & INSTALLATION.

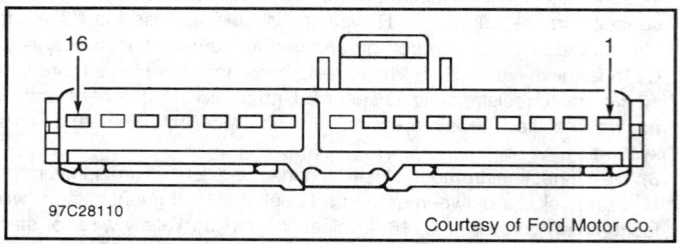

97C28110

Courtesy of Ford Motor Co.

Fig. 5: Identifying Instrument Cluster Connector C214 Terminals

TEST D: SPEEDOMETER INACCURATE

1) Ensure tires are proper size recommended by factory. If tires are proper size, go to next step. If tires are not proper size, replace tires and retest. .

2) Check accuracy of odometer. See ODOMETER TEST under COMPONENT TESTS. If odometer is accurate, go to appropriate SPEEDOMETER/ODOMETER INOPERATIVE test. If odometer is not accurate, replace speedometer.

TEST E: SPEEDOMETER/ODOMETER INOPERATIVE – WITH REAR ANTI-LOCK BRAKES (RABS)

1) Connect New Generation Star (NGS) tester to Data Link Connector (DLC). Monitor PID IGN_GEM while turning ignition switch through all positions. If PID values agree with switch positions, go to next step. If PID values do not agree with switch positions, check ignition switch. See STEERING COLUMN SWITCHES – RANGER article. Replace as necessary. If ignition switch is okay, check ignition switch circuits. See appropriate wiring diagram in POWER DISTRIBUTION article in WIRING DIAGRAMS.

2) Perform GEM/CTM SELF-TEST diagnostics. Retrieve DTCs. If DTC C1751 is present, go to step **9)**. If DTC C1752 is present, go to step **7)**. If DTC P0500 or no DTCs are present, go to next step.

3) Disconnect Generic Electronic Module (GEM) connector C224. GEM 20-pin connector C224 is located behind center of instrument cluster. Disconnect Rear Anti-lock Brake (RABS) module connector C238. RABS connector C238 is located behind center of dash, to left of ashtray assembly. Disconnect RABS sensor, located at center top of rear differential. Measure resistance between ground and GEM connector C224 terminal No. 9 (Red/Pink wire). *See Fig. 12.* Measure resistance between ground and GEM connector C224 terminal No. 18 (Light Green/Black wire). If either resistance is 10 k/ohms or less, repair short to ground in Red/Pink or Light Green/Black wire. If resistances are more than 10 k/ohms, go to next step.

4) Measure resistance of Red/Pink wire between RABS sensor connector and GEM connector terminal No. 9. Measure resistance of Light Green/Black wire between RABS sensor connector and GEM connector C224 terminal No. 18. If either resistance is 5 ohms or more, repair open in Red/Pink or Light Green/Black wire. If resistances are less than 5 ohms, go to next step.

5) Measure voltage between ground and GEM connector C224 terminal No. 9 (Red/Pink wire). Measure voltage between ground and GEM connector C224 terminal No. 18 (Light Green/Black wire). If voltage is present, repair short to battery voltage in appropriate Red/Pink or Light Green/Black wire. If voltage is not present, go to next step.

6) Using NGS tester, monitor PID VSS_GEM while driving 0-55 MPH. If PID VSS_GEM value is more than zero MPH, go to next step. If PID VSS_GEM value is zero MPH, check RABS sensor. See appropriate ANTI-LOCK article in BRAKES in appropriate MITCHELL® manual. If RABS sensor is okay, replace GEM.

7) Turn ignition off. Remove instrument cluster and disconnect connectors. See INSTRUMENT CLUSTER under REMOVAL & INSTALLATION. Disconnect Powertrain Control Module (PCM). PCM is located at right rear of engine compartment. Disconnect speed control servo. Disconnect Generic Electronic Module (GEM) connector C224. GEM

20-pin connector C224 is located behind center of instrument cluster. Measure resistance between ground and GEM connector C224 terminal No. 1 (Gray/Black wire). *See Fig. 12.* If resistance is 10 k/ohms or less, repair short to ground in Gray/Black wire. If resistance is more than 10 k/ohms, go to next step.

8) Measure resistance of Gray/Black wire between instrument cluster connector C215 terminal No. 1 and GEM connector C224 terminal No. 1. *See Figs. 2 and 12.* If resistance is 5 ohms or more, repair open in Gray/Black wire. If resistance is less than 5 ohms, go to next step.

9) Turn ignition off. Remove instrument cluster and disconnect connectors. See INSTRUMENT CLUSTER under REMOVAL & INSTALLATION. Disconnect Generic Electronic Module (GEM) connector C224. GEM 20-pin connector C224 is located behind center of instrument cluster. Turn ignition on. Measure voltage between ground and GEM connector C224 terminal No. 1 (Gray/Black wire). *See Fig. 12.* If voltage is more than 10 volts, repair short to voltage in Gray/Black wire. If voltage is 10 volts or less, go to next step.

10) Turn ignition off. Measure voltage between ground and instrument cluster connector C216 terminal No. 7 (White/Yellow wire). *See Fig. 4.* If voltage is more than 10 volts, go to next step. If voltage is 10 volts or less, repair open White/Yellow wire.

NOTE: Measurements must be made at speedometer gauge pins inside instrument cluster printed circuit clips.

---

11) Check resistance of printed circuit by making appropriate measurements. See SPEEDOMETER PRINTED CIRCUIT MEASUREMENTS table. If all resistance values are less than one ohm, replace speedometer. See GAUGES under REMOVAL & INSTALLATION. If resistance in any circuit measurement is one ohm or more, replace instrument cluster printed circuit. See PRINTED CIRCUIT under REMOVAL & INSTALLATION.

SPEEDOMETER PRINTED CIRCUIT MEASUREMENTS

Connector/Terminal [1]	Connector/Terminal
Speedometer/S	C215/1
Speedometer/G	C215/2
Speedometer/B	C214/13
Batt	C216/7

[1] – See Fig. 6.

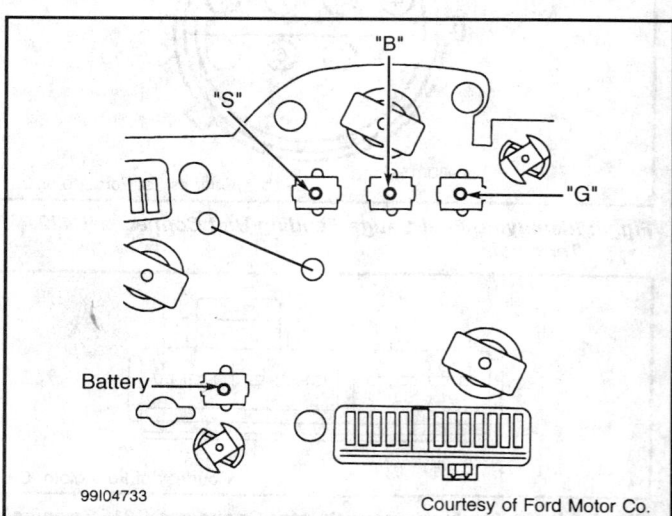

99I04733

Courtesy of Ford Motor Co.

Fig. 6: Identifying Speedometer Printed Circuit Terminals

TEST F: SPEEDOMETER/ODOMETER INOPERATIVE – WITH 4-WHEEL ANTI-LOCK BRAKES (4WABS)

1) Turn ignition off. Remove instrument cluster. See INSTRUMENT CLUSTER under REMOVAL & INSTALLATION. Disconnect instrument cluster connector C216. Measure voltage between ground and instrument cluster connector C216 terminal No. 7 (White/Yellow wire). *See Fig. 4.* If voltage is more than 10 volts, go to next step. If voltage is less than 10 volts, repair open in White/Yellow wire between instrument cluster connector and fuse No. 25 located in interior fuse panel and retest system.

NOTE: Measurements must be made at speedometer gauge pins inside instrument cluster printed circuit clips.

2) Measure resistance of printed circuit. See SPEEDOMETER PRINTED CIRCUIT MEASUREMENTS table. If all resistance values are less than one ohm, go to next step. If resistance in any circuit is one ohm or more, replace instrument cluster printed circuit.

3) Disconnect 4-Wheel Anti-lock Brakes (4WABS) 25-pin connector C154. 4WABS connector C154 is located in left rear corner of engine compartment. Measure resistance of Gray/Black wire between instrument cluster connector C215 terminal No. 1 and 4WABS connector C154 terminal No. 19. *See Figs. 2 and 7.* If resistance is less than 5 ohms, replace speedometer. If resistance is more than 5 ohms, repair open in Gray/Black wire between instrument cluster connector and 4WABS harness connector and retest system.

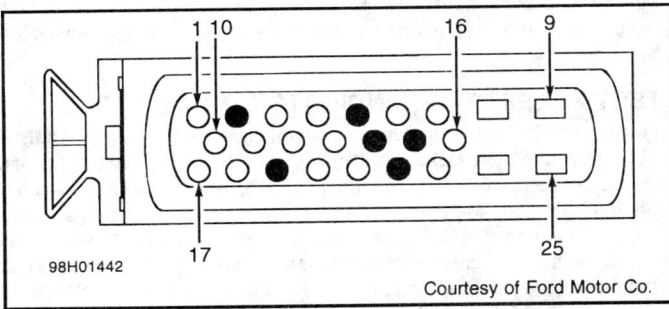

Fig. 7: Identifying 4WABS Connector C154 Terminals

98H01442 · Courtesy of Ford Motor Co.

TEST G: TACHOMETER INOPERATIVE

1) If vehicle is equipped with a 4-cylinder engine, go to next step. If vehicle is equipped with a V6 engine, turn ignition off. Remove instrument cluster. See appropriate INSTRUMENT CLUSTER under REMOVAL & INSTALLATION. Disconnect instrument cluster connector C216. Measure voltage between ground and instrument cluster connector C216 terminal No. 8 (Black/Yellow wire). *See Fig. 4.* If resistance is less than 5 ohms, go to next step. If resistance is more than 5 ohms, repair open in Black/Yellow wire between instrument cluster connector and ground. Retest system.

2) On all models, disconnect negative battery cable and Powertrain Control Module (PCM) connector. PCM is located at right rear of engine compartment. Install EEC-V 104-Pin Breakout Box (014-00950) following manufacturer's instructions. Measure resistance between instrument cluster connector C214 terminal No. 15 (Tan/Yellow wire) and breakout box test pin No. 48. *See Fig. 5.* If resistance is less than 5 ohms, remove breakout box. Reconnect PCM and negative battery cable and go to next step. If resistance is more than 5 ohms, repair open in Tan/Yellow wire between instrument cluster connector and PCM. Retest system.

3) Start engine and allow to idle. Measure voltage between ground and instrument cluster connector C214 terminal No. 15 (Tan/Yellow wire). If voltage is 5-8 volts, go to next step. If voltage is not 5-8 volts, replace PCM and retest system.

4) Measure resistance of printed circuit between tachometer pins (in center of clips) and corresponding instrument cluster connectors. See TACHOMETER PRINTED CIRCUIT MEASUREMENTS table. If all resistance values are less than 5 ohms, replace tachometer. See GAUGES under REMOVAL & INSTALLATION. If resistance in any circuit is 5 ohms or more, replace instrument cluster printed circuit. See PRINTED CIRCUIT under REMOVAL & INSTALLATION.

TACHOMETER PRINTED CIRCUIT MEASUREMENTS

Connector/Terminal	Connector/Terminal
Speedometer/S	C214/15

TACHOMETER PRINTED CIRCUIT MEASUREMENTS (Cont.)

Connector/Terminal	Connector/Terminal
Speedometer/G	C215/2
Speedometer/G (V6)	C216/8
Speedometer/B	C214/13

TEST H: TACHOMETER INACCURATE

NOTE: If equipped with 4-cylinder engine, start at step 2).

1) Turn ignition off. Remove instrument cluster. See INSTRUMENT CLUSTER under REMOVAL & INSTALLATION. Measure resistance between ground and instrument cluster connector C216 terminal No. 8 (Black/Yellow wire). *See Fig. 4.* If resistance is less than 5 ohms, go to next step. If resistance is more than 5 ohms, repair open in Black/Yellow wire between instrument cluster connector and ground and retest system.

2) Remove instrument cluster. See INSTRUMENT CLUSTER under REMOVAL & INSTALLATION. Measure resistance of printed circuit between tachometer pins (in center of clips) and corresponding instrument cluster connectors. See TACHOMETER PRINTED CIRCUIT MEASUREMENTS table. If all resistance values are less than 5 ohms, go to next step. If resistance in any circuit is 5 ohms or more, replace instrument cluster printed circuit. See PRINTED CIRCUIT under REMOVAL & INSTALLATION.

3) Disconnect negative battery cable and Powertrain Control Module (PCM). PCM is located at right rear of engine compartment. Install EEC-V 104-Pin Breakout Box (014-00950) following manufacturer's instructions. Measure resistance between instrument cluster connector C214 terminal No. 15 (Tan/Yellow wire) and breakout box test pin No. 48. *See Fig. 5.* Measure resistance between ground and breakout box test pin No. 48. If resistance is less than 5 ohms between ground and breakout box test pin No. 48 and between PCM and instrument cluster connector, replace tachometer. If resistance is 5 ohms or more between ground and breakout box test pin No. 48 or between PCM and instrument cluster connector, replace PCM.

TEST J: CHARGE INDICATOR ALWAYS/NEVER ON

1) Disconnect generator 3-pin connector. Turn ignition on. Connect a fused jumper wire between generator 3-pin connector Light Green/Red wire and ground. If charge indicator illuminates, see appropriate GENERATORS article in CHARGING & STARTING SYSTEMS. If charge indicator does not illuminate, go to next step.

2) Turn ignition off. Remove instrument cluster. See INSTRUMENT CLUSTER under REMOVAL & INSTALLATION. Disconnect instrument cluster connector C216. Measure voltage between ground and instrument cluster connector C216 terminal No. 2 (Yellow wire). *See Fig. 4.* If voltage is more than 10 volts, go to next step. If voltage is less than 10 volts, repair open in Yellow wire.

3) Turn ignition off. Measure resistance of Light Green/Red wire between instrument cluster connector C216 terminal No. 3 and generator 3-pin connector. If resistance is less than 5 ohms, go to next step. If resistance is 5 ohms or more, repair open Light Green/Red wire.

4) Check for continuity between charge indicator bulb terminals of printed circuit. See PRINTED CIRCUIT under REMOVAL & INSTALLATION. If continuity exists, replace printed circuit. If continuity does not exist, replace bulb.

TEST K: ANTI-LOCK BRAKE WARNING LIGHT INOPERATIVE

1) Cycle ignition off and on. If anti-lock brake warning light proves out (illuminates for 2 seconds and then turns off), system is functioning properly at this time. If anti-lock brake warning light does not prove out and vehicle is equipped with Rear Anti-lock Brake System (RABS), go to step **2)**. If anti-lock brake warning light does not prove out and vehicle is equipped with 4 Wheel Anti-lock Brake System (4WABS), go to step **4)**.

2) Turn ignition off. Disconnect RABS module connector. RABS connector is located behind center of dash, to left of ashtray assembly. Turn ignition on. Connect a fused jumper wire between ground and RABS module connector C238 terminal No. 7 (Dark Green wire). *See Fig. 8.* If anti-lock brake warning light illuminates, go to ANTI-LOCK – RABS II – RANGER article in BRAKES in appropriate MITCHELL® manual. If anti-lock brake warning light does not illuminate, go to next step.

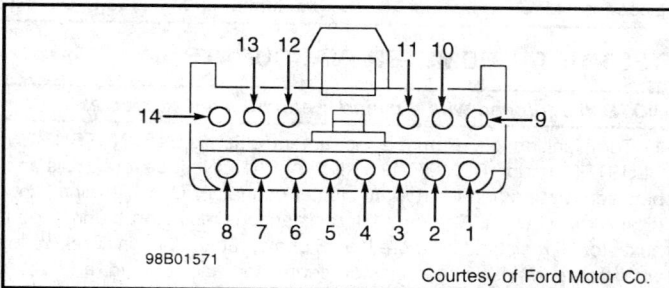

Fig. 8: Identifying RABS Module Connector C238 Terminals

3) Turn ignition off. Measure resistance of Dark Green wire between instrument cluster connector C216 terminal No. 6 and RABS module connector C238 terminal No. 7. *See Fig. 4.* If resistance is less than 5 ohms, check bulb. If bulb is okay, replace instrument cluster printed circuit. See PRINTED CIRCUIT under REMOVAL & INSTALLATION. If resistance is 5 ohms or more, repair open Dark Green wire.

4) Turn ignition off. Disconnect 4WABS module connector. 4WABS module connector C154 is located in left rear corner of engine compartment. Turn ignition on. Install EEC-IV 60-pin breakout box following manufacturer's instructions. Connect a fused jumper wire between ground and breakout box pin No. 16. If anti-lock brake warning light illuminates, go to ANTI-LOCK – 4WAL – RANGER article in BRAKES in appropriate MITCHELL® manual. If anti-lock brake warning light does not illuminate, go to next step.

5) Turn ignition off. Measure resistance of Dark Green wire between instrument cluster connector C216 terminal No. 6 and breakout box pin No. 16. If resistance is less than 5 ohms, check bulb. If bulb is okay, replace instrument cluster printed circuit. See PRINTED CIRCUIT under REMOVAL & INSTALLATION. If resistance is 5 ohms or more, repair open Dark Green wire.

TEST L: FUEL RESET LIGHT INOPERATIVE

1) Turn ignition off. Disconnect inertia main switch located on kick panel at right front passenger seat. Turn ignition on. Connect a fused jumper wire between ground and inertia switch connector terminal No. 1 (Gray/Orange wire). If fuel reset light illuminates, see appropriate SELF-DIAGNOSTICS article in ENGINE PERFORMANCE in appropriate MITCHELL® manual to check PCM grounds and DTCs. If fuel reset light does not illuminate, go to next step.

2) Turn ignition off. Remove instrument cluster. See INSTRUMENT CLUSTER under REMOVAL & INSTALLATION. Measure resistance of Gray/Orange wire between instrument cluster connector C215 terminal No. 10 and inertia switch connector terminal No. 1. If resistance is less than 5 ohms, check bulb. If bulb is okay, replace instrument cluster printed circuit. See PRINTED CIRCUIT under REMOVAL & INSTALLATION. If resistance is more than 5 ohms, repair open in Gray/Orange wire between instrument cluster connector and inertia switch connector and retest system.

TEST M: HIGH BEAM INDICATOR INOPERATIVE

1) Turn ignition off. Remove instrument cluster. See INSTRUMENT CLUSTER under REMOVAL & INSTALLATION. Disconnect instrument cluster connector C215. *See Fig. 2.* Turn ignition on. Turn multifunction switch to high beam position. Measure voltage between ground and instrument cluster connector C215 terminal No. 6 (Gray/White wire). If voltage is more than 10 volts, go to next step. If voltage is less than 10 volts, repair open in Gray/White wire.

2) Turn ignition off. Measure resistance between ground and instrument cluster connector C215 terminal No. 7 (Black wire). If resistance is less than 5 ohms, go to next step. If resistance is more than 5 ohms, repair open in Black wire between instrument cluster connector and ground.

3) Turn ignition off. Check for continuity across high beam indicator bulb. If continuity exists, check bulb. If bulb is okay, replace instrument cluster printed circuit. See PRINTED CIRCUIT under REMOVAL & INSTALLATION. If continuity does not exist, replace bulb.

TEST N: CHECK ENGINE LIGHT INOPERATIVE

NOTE: CHECK ENGINE light may also be referred to as Malfunction Indicator Light (MIL).

1) Cycle ignition off and on. Install EEC-V 104-pin Breakout Box (014-00950) following manufacturer's instructions. Connect a fused jumper wire between breakout box pins No. 2 and No. 24. If CHECK ENGINE (MIL) light illuminates, see appropriate SELF-DIAGNOSTICS article in ENGINE PERFORMANCE in appropriate MITCHELL® manual. If CHECK ENGINE (MIL) light does not illuminate, go to next step.

2) Turn ignition off. Remove instrument cluster. See INSTRUMENT CLUSTER under REMOVAL & INSTALLATION. Disconnect instrument cluster connector C215. *See Fig. 2.* Measure resistance between ground and instrument cluster connector C215 terminal No. 7 (Black wire). If resistance is less than 5 ohms, go to next step. If resistance is more than 5 ohms, repair open in Black wire between instrument cluster connector and ground.

TEST P: LEFT TURN INDICATOR INOPERATIVE

1) Turn ignition off. Remove instrument cluster. See INSTRUMENT CLUSTER under REMOVAL & INSTALLATION. Disconnect instrument cluster connector C215. Turn ignition on. Place multifunction switch in left turn position. Measure voltage between ground and instrument cluster connector C215 terminal No. 5 (Light Green/White wire). *See Fig. 2.* If voltage toggles between zero and more than 10 volts, go to next step. If voltage does not toggle between zero and more than 10 volts, repair open or short in Light Green/White wire between instrument cluster connector C215 and ground or voltage.

2) Turn ignition off. Measure resistance between ground and instrument cluster connector C215 terminal No. 7 (Black wire). If resistance is less than 5 ohms, go to next step. If resistance is 5 ohms or more, repair open Black wire between instrument cluster connector C215 and ground.

3) Check for continuity across left turn indicator bulb. If continuity exists, check bulb. If bulb is okay, replace instrument cluster printed circuit. See PRINTED CIRCUIT under REMOVAL & INSTALLATION. If continuity does not exist, replace bulb.

TEST Q: RIGHT TURN INDICATOR INOPERATIVE

1) Turn ignition off. Remove instrument cluster. See INSTRUMENT CLUSTER under REMOVAL & INSTALLATION. Disconnect instrument cluster connector C214. Turn ignition on. Place multifunction switch in right turn position. Measure voltage between ground and instrument cluster connector C214 terminal No. 10 (White/Light Blue wire). *See Fig. 5.* If voltage toggles between zero and more than 10 volts, go to next step. If voltage does not toggle between zero and more than 10 volts, repair open or short in White/Light Blue wire.

2) Turn ignition off. Measure resistance between ground and instrument cluster connector C215 terminal No. 7 (Black wire). *See Fig. 2.* If resistance is less than 5 ohms, go to next step. If resistance is 5 ohms or more, repair open Black wire between instrument cluster connector C215 and ground.

3) Check for continuity across right turn indicator bulb. If continuity exists, check bulb. If bulb is okay, replace instrument cluster printed circuit. See PRINTED CIRCUIT under REMOVAL & INSTALLATION. If continuity does not exist, replace bulb.

TEST R: OVERDRIVE (O/D) OFF INDICATOR INOPERATIVE

1) Test drive vehicle and verify O/D operation. If O/D operates properly, go to next step. If O/D does not operate properly, see appropriate article in AUTOMATIC TRANSMISSIONS in appropriate MITCHELL® TRANSMISSION SERVICE & REPAIR manual.

2) Turn ignition off. Install EEC-V 104-Pin Breakout Box (014-00950) following manufacturer's instructions. Turn ignition on. Connect a fused jumper wire between breakout box pins No. 24 and 79. Cycle headlight switch off and back on. If O/D off indicator illuminates, see appropriate ELECTRONIC CONTROLS article in AUTOMATIC TRANSMISSIONS in appropriate MITCHELL® TRANSMISSION SERVICE & REPAIR manual. If O/D off indicator does not illuminate with headlight switch in on or off position, go to step **5)**. If O/D off indicator does not illuminate with headlight switch in off position, go to step **4)**. If O/D off indicator does not illuminate, with headlight switch in on position, go to next step.

3) Turn ignition off. Disconnect headlight switch connector. Turn ignition on. Rotate headlight switch dimmer wheel to full bright position. Measure voltage between ground and headlight switch connector terminal No. 9 (Light Blue/Red wire). *See Fig. 9.* If voltage is more than 10 volts, replace headlight switch. If voltage is 10 volts or less, repair open in Light Blue/Red wire between headlight switch connector and fuse No. 11.

4) Turn ignition off. Disconnect headlight switch connector. Turn ignition on. Measure voltage between ground and headlight switch connector terminal No. 4 (Red/Yellow wire). If voltage is more than 10 volts, replace headlight switch. If voltage is 10 volts or less, repair open in Red/Yellow between headlight switch connector and instrument illumination dimming module near headlight switch.

5) Turn ignition off. Disconnect headlight switch connector. Turn ignition on. Measure voltage between ground and headlight switch connector terminal No. 4 (Red/Yellow wire). If voltage is more than 10 volts, reconnect headlight switch and go to next step. If voltage is 10 volts or less, repair open in Red/Yellow wire between headlight switch connector and instrument illumination dimming module near headlight switch.

6) Turn ignition off. Remove instrument cluster connector C214. See INSTRUMENT CLUSTER under REMOVAL & INSTALLATION. Measure voltage between ground and instrument cluster connector C214 terminal No. 5 (Orange/Black wire). *See Fig. 5.* If voltage is more than 10 volts, go to step **8)**. If voltage is 10 volts or less, go to next step.

7) Turn ignition off. Disconnect headlight switch connector. Measure resistance of Orange/Black wire between instrument cluster connector C214 terminal No. 5 and headlight switch connector terminal No. 8. If resistance is less than 5 ohms, replace headlight switch. If resistance is 5 ohms or more, repair open Orange/Black wire.

8) Disconnect Powertrain Control Module (PCM). PCM is located at right rear of engine compartment. Measure resistance between instrument cluster connector C214 terminal No. 1 (White/Light Green wire) and breakout box test pin No. 79. *See Fig. 5.* If resistance is less than 5 ohms, go to next step. If resistance is 5 ohms or more, repair open White/Light Green wire.

9) Check for continuity between O/D OFF indicator bulb terminals of printed circuit. If continuity exists, replace printed circuit. See PRINTED CIRCUIT under REMOVAL & INSTALLATION. If continuity does not exist, replace bulb.

2) Turn ignition off. Disconnect speed control servo connector. Speed control servo is located in right rear of engine compartment. Turn ignition on. Connect a fused jumper wire between ground and speed control servo connector terminal No. 1 (Orange/Light Blue wire). *See Fig. 10.* Cycle headlight switch off and back on. If speed control indicator illuminates, replace speed control servo. See CRUISE CONTROL SYSTEMS – RANGER article. If speed control indicator does not illuminate with headlight switch in on or off position, go to step **5)**. If speed control indicator does not illuminate with headlight switch in off position, go to step **4)**. If speed control indicator does not illuminate, with headlight switch in on position, go to next step.

3) Turn ignition off. Disconnect headlight switch connector. Turn ignition on. Rotate headlight switch dimmer wheel to full bright position. Measure voltage between ground and headlight switch connector terminal No. 9 (Light Blue/Red wire). *See Fig. 9.* If voltage is more than 10 volts, replace headlight switch. If voltage is 10 volts or less, repair open in Light Blue/Red wire between headlight switch connector and fuse No. 11.

4) Turn ignition off. Disconnect headlight switch connector. Turn ignition on. Measure voltage between ground and headlight switch connector terminal No. 4 (Red/Yellow wire). If voltage is more than 10 volts, replace headlight switch. If voltage is 10 volts or less, repair open in Red/Yellow between headlight switch connector and instrument illumination dimming module near headlight switch.

5) Turn ignition off. Disconnect headlight switch connector. Turn ignition on. Measure voltage between ground and headlight switch connector terminal No. 4 (Red/Yellow wire). If voltage is more than 10 volts, reconnect headlight switch and go to next step. If voltage is 10 volts or less, repair open in Red/Yellow between headlight switch connector and instrument illumination dimming module near headlight switch.

6) Turn ignition off. Remove instrument cluster connector C214. See INSTRUMENT CLUSTER under REMOVAL & INSTALLATION. Measure voltage between ground and instrument cluster connector C214 terminal No. 5 (Orange/Black wire). *See Fig. 5.* If voltage is more than 10 volts, go to step **8)**. If voltage is 10 volts or less, go to next step.

7) Turn ignition off. Disconnect headlight switch connector. Measure resistance of Orange/Black wire between instrument cluster connector C214 terminal No. 5 and headlight switch connector terminal No. 8. If resistance is less than 5 ohms, replace headlight switch. If resistance is 5 ohms or more, repair open Orange/Black wire.

8) Disconnect speed control servo connector. Measure resistance of Orange/Light Blue wire between instrument cluster connector C214 terminal No. 4 and speed control servo connector terminal No. 1. *See Figs. 5 and 10.* If resistance is less than 5 ohms, go to next step. If resistance is 5 ohms or more, repair open Orange/Light Blue wire.

9) Check for continuity between speed control indicator bulb terminals of printed circuit. See PRINTED CIRCUIT under REMOVAL & INSTALLATION. If continuity exists, replace printed circuit. If continuity does not exist, replace bulb.

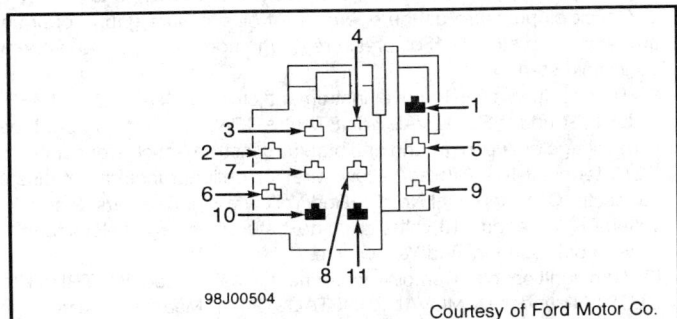

Fig. 9: Identifying Headlight Switch Connector Terminals

TEST S: SPEED CONTROL INDICATOR NEVER/ALWAYS ON

1) Test drive vehicle and operate speed control. If speed control operates properly, go to next step. If speed control does not operate properly, see CRUISE CONTROL SYSTEMS – RANGER article.

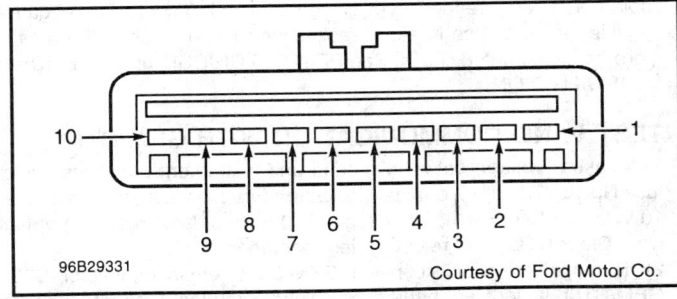

Fig. 10: Identifying Speed Control Servo Connector Terminals

TEST T: BRAKE WARNING LIGHT INOPERATIVE

1) Ensure brake fluid reservoir is full and parking brake is engaged. Turn ignition on. If brake warning light is on, release parking brake and go to next step. If brake warning light is not on, go to step **5)**.

2) Turn ignition off. Disconnect brake fluid level switch harness connector C137. Connect a fused jumper wire between ground and brake fluid level switch harness connector Dark Green/Yellow wire. Turn ignition on. If brake warning light is on, go to DISC & DRUM – TRUCKS – EXCEPT VILLAGER article in BRAKES in appropriate MITCHELL® manual. If warning light is not on and vehicle is equipped with 4 Wheel Anti-lock Brake System (4WABS), repair Violet/White wire or Dark Green/Yellow wire between brake fluid level switch and instrument cluster. If warning light is not on and vehicle is equipped with Rear Anti-lock Brake System (RABS), go to next step.

3) Turn ignition off. Disconnect instrument cluster harness connector C216. See INSTRUMENT CLUSTER under REMOVAL & INSTALLATION. Remove RABS diode from power distribution box. Measure resistance of Violet/White wire between instrument cluster harness connector C216 terminal No. 5 and power distribution box RABS diode. *See Fig. 4.* If resistance is less than 5 ohms, go to next step. If resistance is 5 ohms or more, repair open Violet/White wire.

4) Measure resistance of Dark Green/Yellow wire between brake fluid level switch harness connector C137 and power distribution box RABS diode. If resistance is less than 5 ohms, replace RABS diode. If resistance is 5 ohms or more, repair open Dark Green/Yellow wire.

5) Turn ignition off. Disconnect parking brake switch connector C202. Turn ignition on. Connect a fused jumper wire between ground and parking brake switch connector Light Green/Red wire. If brake warning light is on, replace parking brake switch. If brake warning light is not on, go to next step.

6) Turn ignition off. Disconnect instrument cluster harness connector C216. See INSTRUMENT CLUSTER under REMOVAL & INSTALLATION. Measure resistance between parking brake switch connector C202 Light Green/Red wire terminal and instrument cluster harness connector C216 terminal No. 5 (Violet/White wire). *See Fig. 4.* If resistance is 5 ohms or more, repair open in Violet/White wire between instrument cluster and brake fluid level switch and/or open in Light green/Red wire between parking brake switch and brake fluid level switch. If resistance is less than 5 ohms, check bulb. If bulb is okay, replace printed circuit. See PRINTED CIRCUIT under REMOVAL & INSTALLATION.

TEST U: CHECK GAGE INDICATOR INOPERATIVE

1) Start engine. If gauges are functioning properly, go to next step. If gauges are not functioning properly, go to appropriate gauge test. See SYMPTOM CHART table.

2) Check for continuity between check gauges indicator bulb terminals of printed circuit. If continuity exists, go to next step. If continuity does not exist, replace bulb.

3) Turn ignition off. Remove instrument cluster. See INSTRUMENT CLUSTER under REMOVAL & INSTALLATION. Measure resistance between check gauge indicator bulb and instrument cluster printed circuit connector C215 terminal No. 8. *See Fig. 2.* Measure resistance between check gauge indicator bulb and instrument cluster gauge amplifier. If both resistance measurements less than 5 ohms, replace coolant temperature/fuel level gauge and instrument cluster gauge amplifier. If resistance in either resistance measurement is 5 ohms or more, replace printed circuit. See PRINTED CIRCUIT under REMOVAL & INSTALLATION.

TEST V: NO COMMUNICATION WITH GEM/CTM

1) Measure voltage between ground and instrument panel fuse block fuse No. 25 (7.5-amp) terminal No. 2. *See Fig. 11.* If voltage is more than 10 volts, go to next step. If voltage is 10 volts or less, repair Tan/Black wire. Clear DTCs and retest system operation.

2) Turn ignition off. Disconnect GEM/CTM 18-pin connector C224. GEM/CTM is located behind center of instrument panel. Measure voltage between ground and GEM/CTM 18-pin connector C224 terminal No. 11 (White/Yellow wire). *See Fig. 12.* If voltage is more than 10 volts, go to next step. If voltage is 10 volts or less, repair White/Yellow wire between instrument panel fuse block and GEM/CTM. Clear DTCs and retest system operation.

3) Disconnect GEM/CTM 26-pin connector C221. Measure resistance between ground and GEM/CTM 26-pin connector C221 terminal No. 14 (Black/White wire). Measure resistance between ground and GEM/CTM

26-pin connector C221 terminal No. 26 (Black/White wire). If resistance is less than 5 ohms in both measurements, replace GEM/CTM. If resistance is 5 ohms or more in either measurement, repair appropriate open circuit. Clear DTCs and retest system operation.

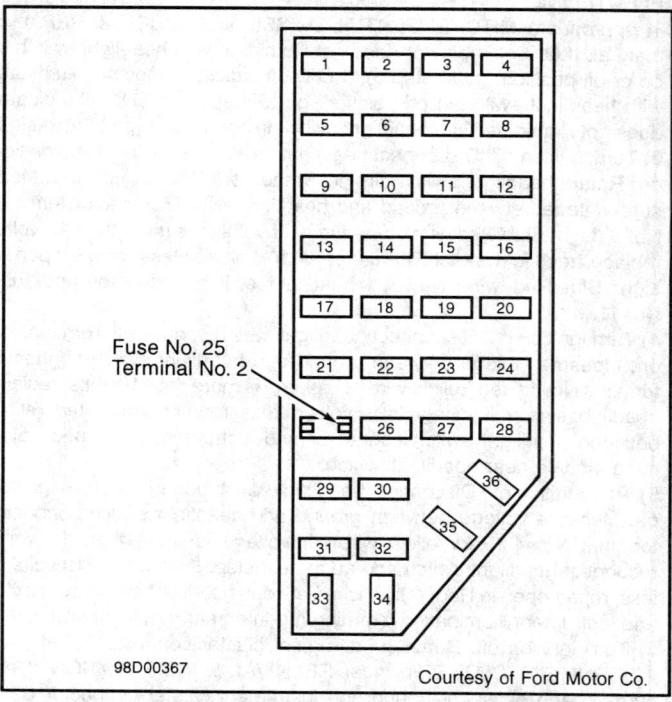

Fuse No. 25
Terminal No. 2

98D00367

Courtesy of Ford Motor Co.

Fig. 11: Identifying Instrument Panel Fuse Block Fuse No. 25 Terminals

TEST W: DOOR AJAR INDICATOR INOPERATIVE

1) Turn ignition off. Connect New Generation Star (NGS) tester to Data Link Connector (DLC). Monitor PID IGN_GEM while turning ignition switch through all positions. If PID values agree with ignition switch positions, go to next step. If PID values do not agree with ignition switch positions, see STEERING COLUMN SWITCHES – RANGER article.

2) Perform GEM/CTM SELF-TEST diagnostics. If no DTCs are present, go to step **4)**. If DTC B1322 or B1330 is present, see appropriate wiring diagram in ILLUMINATION/INTERIOR LIGHTS article. If DTC B1325 is present, go to step **9)**. If DTC B1323 is present, go to next step.

3) Turn ignition on. Using NGS tester, monitor PID DRAJR_L. Toggle active command AJAR LAMP ON and OFF. If PID DRAJR_L reads correct state, replace GEM. GEM is located behind center of instrument panel. Clear DTCs and retest system operation. If PID DRAJR_L reads OFF-B, go to step **9)**. If PID DRAJR_L reads OFFO-G, go to next step.

4) Check oil pressure gauge operation. If oil pressure gauge operates properly, go to step **6)**. If oil pressure gauge does not operate properly, go to next step.

5) Turn ignition off. Remove instrument cluster. See INSTRUMENT CLUSTER under REMOVAL & INSTALLATION. Turn ignition on. Measure voltage between ground and standard instrument cluster connector C215 terminal No. 8 (Red/Yellow wire) or optional instrument cluster connector C214 terminal No. 13 (Red/Yellow wire). *See Figs. 2 and 5.* If voltage is more than 10 volts, go to next step. If voltage is less than 10 volts, repair open in Red/Yellow wire.

6) Turn ignition off. Remove instrument cluster. See INSTRUMENT CLUSTER under REMOVAL & INSTALLATION. Measure resistance of standard instrument cluster connector C214 terminals No. 11 and No. 13 (component side). Measure resistance of optional instrument cluster connector C214 terminal No. 11 and instrument cluster connector C215 terminal No. 8 (component side). If resistance is less than 5 ohms, go to next step. If resistance is 5 ohms or more, check door ajar bulb in instrument cluster and replace as necessary. If bulb is okay, replace instrument cluster printed circuit. See PRINTED CIRCUIT under REMOVAL & INSTALLATION. Clear DTCs and retest system.

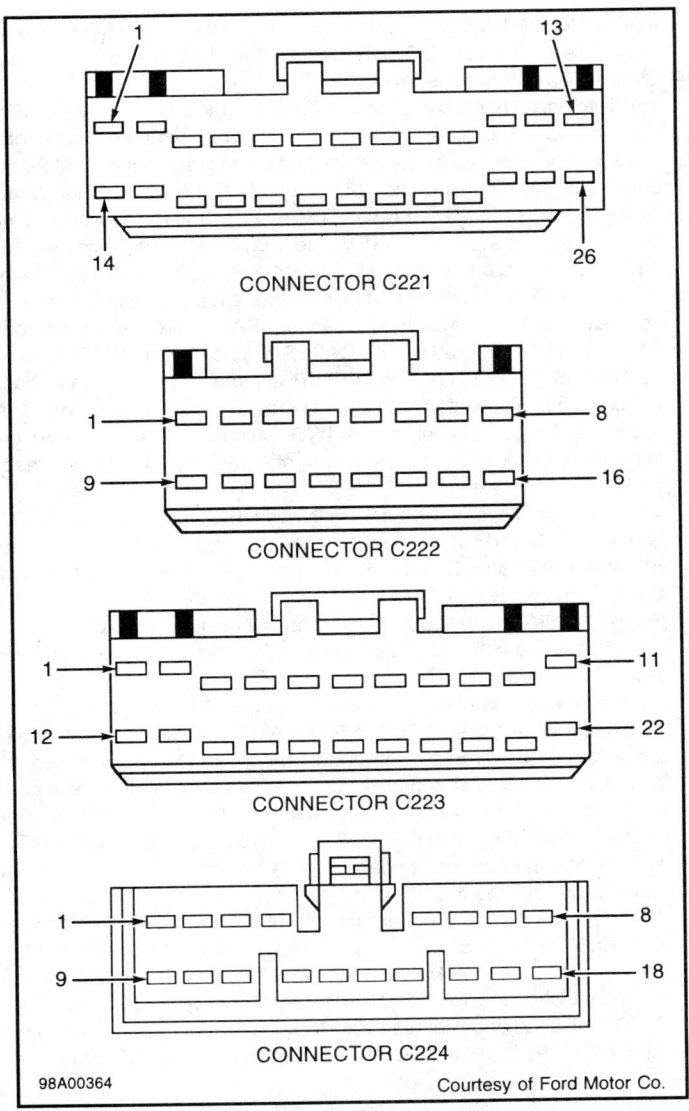

CONNECTOR C221

CONNECTOR C222

CONNECTOR C223

CONNECTOR C224

98A00364   Courtesy of Ford Motor Co.

Fig. 12: Identifying GEM Connector Terminals

7) Disconnect Generic Electronic Module (GEM) connector C221. GEM 26-pin connector C221 is located behind center of instrument cluster. Measure resistance of Black/Orange wire between GEM connector C221 terminal No. 9 and instrument cluster connector C214 terminal No. 11. *See Figs. 5 and 12.* If resistance is less than 5 ohms, go to next step. If resistance is 5 ohms or more, repair open in Black/Orange wire. Clear DTCs and retest system.

8) Measure resistance between ground and GEM connector C221 terminal No. 9 (Black/Orange wire). If resistance is more than 10 k/ohms, replace GEM. Clear DTCs and retest system. If resistance is 10 k/ohms or less, repair short to ground in Black/Orange wire. Clear DTCs and retest system.

9) Turn ignition off. Remove instrument cluster. See INSTRUMENT CLUSTER under REMOVAL & INSTALLATION. Disconnect Generic Electronic Module (GEM) connector C221. GEM 26-pin connector C221 is located behind center of instrument cluster. Turn ignition on. Measure voltage between ground and GEM connector C221 terminal No. 9 (Black/Orange wire). If voltage is present, repair short to voltage in Black/Orange wire. Clear DTCs and retest system. If no voltage is present, go to next step.

10) Using NGS tester, monitor PID DRAJR_L. Set active command ajar light off. If PID DRAJR_L reads OFF---?, replace instrument cluster printed circuit. See PRINTED CIRCUIT under REMOVAL & INSTALLA-

TION. Clear DTCs and retest system. If PID DRAJR_L does not read OFF---?, replace GEM. Clear DTCs and retest system.

TEST X: SEAT BELT WARNING INDICATOR INOPERATIVE

1) Turn ignition off. Connect New Generation Star (NGS) tester to Data Link Connector (DLC). Monitor PID IGN_GEM while turning ignition switch through all positions. If PID values agree with ignition switch positions, go to next step. If PID values do not agree with ignition switch positions, see STEERING COLUMN SWITCHES – RANGER article.

2) Perform GEM/CTM SELF-TEST diagnostics. If no DTCs or DTC B1428 is present, go to next step. If DTC B1342 is present, replace GEM. GEM is located behind center of instrument panel. If DTC B1426 is present, go to step 9). If DTC B1462 is present, repair seat belt warning chime.

3) Check seat belt warning chime operation. If seat belt warning chime operates properly, go to next step. If seat belt warning chime is not operating properly, repair warning chime as necessary.

4) Turn ignition on. Monitor PID SBLTLMP. Toggle active command SBLT light ON and OFF. If PID SBLTLMP reads correct state, replace GEM. Clear DTCs and retest system operation. If PID SBLTLMP reads ON-B, go to step 10). If PID SBLTLMP reads OFFO-G, go to next step.

5) Check oil pressure gauge operation. If oil pressure gauge operates properly, go to step 7). If oil pressure gauge does not operate properly, go to next step.

6) Turn ignition off. Remove instrument cluster. See INSTRUMENT CLUSTER under REMOVAL & INSTALLATION. Turn ignition on. Measure voltage between ground and instrument cluster connector C215 terminal No. 8 (Red/Yellow wire). *See Fig. 2.* If voltage is more than 10 volts, go to next step. If voltage is less than 10 volts, repair open in Red/Yellow wire.

7) Turn ignition off. Remove instrument cluster. See INSTRUMENT CLUSTER under REMOVAL & INSTALLATION. Measure resistance of standard instrument cluster connector C216 terminals No. 1 and No. 10 (component side). Measure resistance of optional instrument cluster connector C216 terminal No. 10 and instrument cluster connector C215 terminal No. 8 (component side). *See Figs. 2 and 4.* If resistance is less than 5 ohms, go to next step. If resistance is 5 ohms or more, check seat belt warning indicator bulb in cluster and replace as necessary. If bulb is okay, replace instrument cluster printed circuit. See PRINTED CIRCUIT under REMOVAL & INSTALLATION. Clear DTCs and retest system.

8) Disconnect Generic Electronic Module (GEM) connector C221. GEM 26-pin connector C221 is located behind center of instrument cluster. Measure resistance of Yellow wire between GEM connector C221 terminal No. 12 and instrument cluster connector C216 terminal No. 10. *See Figs. 4 and 12.* If resistance is less than 5 ohms, go to next step. If resistance is 5 ohms or more, repair open in Yellow wire. Clear DTCs and retest system.

9) Measure resistance between ground and GEM connector C221 terminal No. 12 (Yellow wire). If measured resistance is more than 10 k/ohms, replace GEM. Clear DTCs and retest system. If resistance is 10 k/ohms or less, repair short to ground in Yellow wire. Clear DTCs and retest system.

10) Turn ignition off. Remove instrument cluster. See INSTRUMENT CLUSTER under REMOVAL & INSTALLATION. Disconnect Generic Electronic Module (GEM) connector C221. GEM 26-pin connector C221 is located behind center of instrument cluster. Turn ignition on. Measure voltage between ground and GEM connector C221 terminal No. 12 (Yellow wire). If voltage is present, repair short to voltage in Yellow wire. Clear DTCs and retest system. If no voltage is present, go to next step.

11) Using NGS tester, monitor PID SBLTLMP. Set active command ajar light OFF. If PID SBLTLMP reads OFFO-G?, replace instrument cluster printed circuit. See PRINTED CIRCUIT under REMOVAL & INSTALLATION. Clear DTCs and retest system. If PID SBLTLMP does not read OFFO-G?, replace GEM. Clear DTCs and retest system.

TEST Y: 4X4 HIGH, 4X4 LOW INDICATOR INOPERATIVE

1) Turn ignition off. Connect New Generation Star (NGS) tester to Data Link Connector (DLC). Monitor PID IGN_GEM while turning ignition switch through all positions. If PID values agree with ignition switch positions, go to next step. If PID values do not agree with ignition switch positions, see STEERING COLUMN SWITCHES – RANGER article.

2) Perform GEM/CTM SELF-TEST diagnostics. If no DTCs or DTC P1804, P1806, P1808 or P1810 is present, go to next step. If DTC B1342 is present, replace GEM. GEM is located behind center of instrument panel.

3) If 4WD HIGH indicator is inoperative, go to step 7). If 4WD LOW indicator is inoperative, go to step 12). If 4WD HIGH and 4WD LOW indicator are inoperative, go to next step.

4) Turn ignition on. Verify O/D indicator light operation. If O/D off indicator light operates properly, replace instrument cluster printed circuit. See PRINTED CIRCUIT under REMOVAL & INSTALLATION. Clear DTCs and retest system operation. If O/D off indicator light does not operate properly, go to next step.

5) Turn ignition off. Remove instrument cluster. See INSTRUMENT CLUSTER under REMOVAL & INSTALLATION. Turn ignition on. Measure voltage between ground and instrument cluster connector C214 terminal No. 5 (Orange/Black wire). See Fig. 5. If voltage is more than 10 volts, check blub. Replace as necessary. If bulb is okay, replace instrument cluster printed circuit. See PRINTED CIRCUIT under REMOVAL & INSTALLATION. Clear DTCs and retest system operation. If voltage is less than 10 volts, go to next step.

6) Turn ignition off. Disconnect headlight switch connector. Measure resistance of Orange/Black wire between instrument cluster connector C214 terminal No. 5 and headlight switch connector terminal No. 8. Measure resistance between ground and instrument cluster connector C214 terminal No. 5 (Orange/Black wire). If resistance is less than 5 ohms between instrument cluster and headlight switch and more than 10 k/ohms between ground and instrument cluster, see appropriate wiring diagram in HEADLIGHT SYSTEMS article to diagnosis power to headlight switch. If resistance is 5 ohms or more between instrument cluster and headlight switch or 10 k/ohms or less between ground and instrument cluster, repair open or short in Orange/Black wire.

7) Turn ignition on. Monitor PID 4WDHIGH. Toggle active command HIGH light ON and OFF. If 4WD indicator proves out (illuminates for 2 seconds then turns off) see appropriate TRANSFER CASES article in AXLE SHAFTS & TRANSFER CASES in appropriate MITCHELL® TRANSMISSION SERVICE & REPAIR manual. If 4WD indicator does not prove out (illuminate for 2 seconds then turn off) and PID 4WDHIGH reads ON-B, go to step 10). If 4WD indicator does not prove out (illuminate for 2 seconds then turn off) and PID 4WDHIGH reads OFFO-G, go to next step.

8) Turn ignition off. Disconnect Generic Electronic Module (GEM) connector C223. GEM 22-pin connector C223 is located behind center of instrument cluster. Connect a fused jumper wire between ground and GEM connector C223 terminal No. 14 (Gray wire). See Fig. 12. Turn ignition on. If 4WD HIGH indicator illuminates, replace GEM. Clear DTCs and retest system. If 4WD HIGH indicator does not illuminate, go to next step.

9) Disconnect instrument cluster connector C214. See INSTRUMENT CLUSTER under REMOVAL & INSTALLATION. Measure resistance of Gray wire between GEM connector C223 terminal No. 14 and instrument cluster connector C214 terminal No. 3. If resistance is less than 5 ohms, replace instrument cluster printed circuit. See PRINTED CIRCUIT under REMOVAL & INSTALLATION. Clear DTCs and retest system. If resistance is 5 ohms or more, repair open in Gray wire. Clear DTCs and retest system.

10) Turn ignition off. Disconnect instrument cluster connector C214. See INSTRUMENT CLUSTER under REMOVAL & INSTALLATION. See Fig. 5. Turn ignition on. Monitor PID 4WDHIGH. Toggle active command HIGH light ON and OFF. If PID 4WDHIGH reads ON-B, go to next step.

If PID 4WDHIGH does not read ON-B, replace instrument cluster printed circuit. See PRINTED CIRCUIT under REMOVAL & INSTALLATION. Clear DTCs and retest system.

11) Turn ignition off. Disconnect Generic Electronic Module (GEM) connector C223. GEM 22-pin connector C223 is located behind center of instrument cluster. Measure voltage between ground and GEM 22-pin connector C223 terminal No. 14 (Gray wire). If voltage is indicated, repair short to voltage in Gray wire. Clear DTCs and retest system. If no voltage is indicated, replace GEM. Clear DTCs and retest system.

12) Turn ignition on. Monitor PID 4WDLOW. Toggle active command LOW light ON and OFF. If 4WD indicator proves out (illuminates for 2 seconds then turns off), see appropriate TRANSFER CASES article in AXLE SHAFTS & TRANSFER CASES in appropriate MITCHELL® TRANSMISSION SERVICE & REPAIR manual. If 4WD indicator does not prove out (illuminate for 2 seconds then turn off) and PID 4WDLOW reads ON-B, go to step 15). If 4WD indicator does not prove out (illuminate for 2 seconds then turn off) and PID 4WDLOW reads OFFO-G, go to next step.

13) Turn ignition off. Disconnect Generic Electronic Module (GEM) connector C223. GEM 22-pin connector C223 is located behind center of instrument cluster. Connect a fused jumper wire between ground and GEM connector C223 terminal No. 10 (Light Blue/Black wire). See Fig. 12. If 4WD LOW indicator illuminates, replace GEM. Clear DTCs and retest system. If 4WD LOW indicator does not illuminate, go to next step.

14) Disconnect instrument cluster connector C214. See INSTRUMENT CLUSTER under REMOVAL & INSTALLATION. Measure resistance of Light Blue/Black wire between GEM connector C223 terminal No. 10 and instrument cluster connector C214 terminal No. 2. If resistance is less than 5 ohms, replace instrument cluster printed circuit. See PRINTED CIRCUIT under REMOVAL & INSTALLATION. Clear DTCs and retest system. If resistance is 5 ohms or more, repair open in Light Blue/Black wire. Clear DTCs and retest system.

15) Turn ignition off. Disconnect instrument cluster connector C214. See INSTRUMENT CLUSTER under REMOVAL & INSTALLATION. See Fig. 5. Turn ignition on. Monitor PID 4WDLOW. Toggle active command LOW light ON and OFF. If PID 4WDLOW reads ON-B, go to next step. If PID 4WDLOW does not read ON-B, replace instrument cluster printed circuit. See PRINTED CIRCUIT under REMOVAL & INSTALLATION. Clear DTCs and retest system.

16) Turn ignition off. Disconnect Generic Electronic Module (GEM) connector C223. GEM 22-pin connector C223 is located behind center of instrument cluster. Measure voltage between ground and GEM 22-pin connector C223 terminal No. 10 (Light Blue/Black wire). If voltage is indicated, repair short to voltage in Light Blue/Black wire. Clear DTCs and retest system. If no voltage is indicated, replace GEM. Clear DTCs and retest system.

TEST Z: AIR BAG WARNING INDICATOR INOPERATIVE

Turn ignition off. Disconnect instrument cluster. See INSTRUMENT CLUSTER under REMOVAL & INSTALLATION. Visually inspect printed circuit for damage, hot spots or cracks, replace as necessary. If printed circuit is okay, see DIAGNOSIS & TESTING in MITCHELL® AIR BAG SERVICE & REPAIR MANUAL, DOMESTIC & IMPORTED MODELS.

REMOVAL & INSTALLATION

WARNING: Deactivate air bag system before performing any service operation. See AIR BAG RESTRAINT SYSTEMS – RANGER article. DO NOT apply electrical power to any component on steering column without first deactivating air bag system. Air bag may deploy.

NOTE: When battery is disconnected and reconnected, some abnormal drive symptoms may occur while powertrain control module relearns its adaptive strategy. Vehicle may need to be driven 10 or more miles to relearn strategy.

FUEL PRESSURE RELIEF

Disconnect inertia main switch located on kick panel at right front passenger seat. Crank engine 15-20 seconds to relieve pressure.

FUEL GAUGE SENDING UNIT

CAUTION: Before disconnecting any fuel line, release fuel pressure from fuel system to reduce possibility of injury or fire. Use a rag as protection from fuel spray when disconnecting hoses. Plug hoses after disconnection.

Removal & Installation – 1) Support tank during removal and installation. Drain fuel from tank. Loosen fuel tank filler pipe clamp. Remove fuel tank heat shield from vehicle. Remove bolt from rear fuel tank support strap. Remove rear fuel tank support strap.

2) Remove bolt from front fuel tank support strap. Remove front fuel tank support strap. Partially lower fuel tank to gain access and remove feed and return lines from sender ports. Remove electrical connector from sending unit. Remove fuel vapor hose from evaporative emission valve. Lower tank from vehicle. Place tank on bench, and clean dirt and debris from around fuel pump attaching flange to prevent contamination of tank contents.

3) Using Fuel Tank Lock Ring Wrench (T90T-9275-A), turn locking retainer ring counterclockwise to remove fuel tank sending unit locking retainer ring. Remove fuel pump and sending unit assembly. Remove and discard fuel pump mounting gasket. To install, reverse removal procedure. Use a NEW fuel pump mounting gasket lubricated with premium grade long-life grease to hold it in place during assembly.

GAUGES

NOTE: Fuel gauge and instrument cluster gauge amplifier are calibrated together and cannot be serviced separately.

Removal & Installation – Remove instrument cluster. See INSTRUMENT CLUSTER. Remove instrument cluster gauge amplifier from back of instrument cluster. Remove 7 screws and instrument cluster lens and mask assembly from instrument cluster. Outside gauge assemblies must be removed before center gauge assembly. Gently remove desired gauge block by grasping outside edges of gauge and lifting. To install, reverse removal procedure.

NOTE: When installing gauges, ensure gauge pins are correctly seated into backplate retaining clips.

INSTRUMENT CLUSTER

CAUTION: If gauges are being removed from cluster assembly, DO NOT remove gauge pointer. Magnetic gauges cannot be recalibrated.

Removal & Installation – 1) Disconnect negative battery cable. Remove radio. Remove 2 screws and center instrument panel finish panel. Disconnect electrical connectors. Remove hood latch control handle and cable from lower steering column cover.

2) Remove 2 screws and lower steering column cover. Remove 4 screws and steering column opening cover and reinforcement. Remove 3 screws and separate upper and lower steering column shrouds.

3) Remove 5 screws and instrument cluster finish panel. Disconnect electrical connectors. Disconnect transmission range indicator thumbwheel (if equipped). Remove 4 screws and instrument cluster. Disconnect electrical connectors. To install, reverse removal procedure.

INSTRUMENT CLUSTER GAUGE AMPLIFIER

NOTE: Instrument cluster amplifier is a printed circuit board assembly located in a pocket on back of instrument cluster. There are no provisions for calibration or adjustment. Amplifier and fuel gauge must be replaced as an assembly.

Removal & Installation – 1) Remove instrument cluster. See INSTRUMENT CLUSTER. Carefully depress retaining clip on component side of board and pull board assembly out of instrument cluster pocket.

2) To install cluster gauge amplifier, insert into slots in instrument cluster and press home firmly with thumb on edge of board. An audible click will be heard as retaining clip engages. To complete installation, reverse removal procedure.

PRINTED CIRCUIT

Removal & Installation – 1) Remove instrument cluster. See INSTRUMENT CLUSTER. Remove instrument cluster gauge amplifier. See INSTRUMENT CLUSTER GAUGE AMPLIFIER.

2) Remove all instrument panel illumination and indicator bulbs by turning counterclockwise. Remove gauges. See GAUGES.

3) Remove 19 instrument gauge connector clips using long-nose pliers. Squeeze both sides of clip equally so locking ears pass through opening in instrument cluster case. Be careful not to overbend or distort clips. DO NOT reuse instrument gauge clips.

4) Ease instrument cluster printed circuit up and off locating pins and remove from case. To install, reverse removal procedure using NEW instrument gauge clips.

WIRING DIAGRAMS

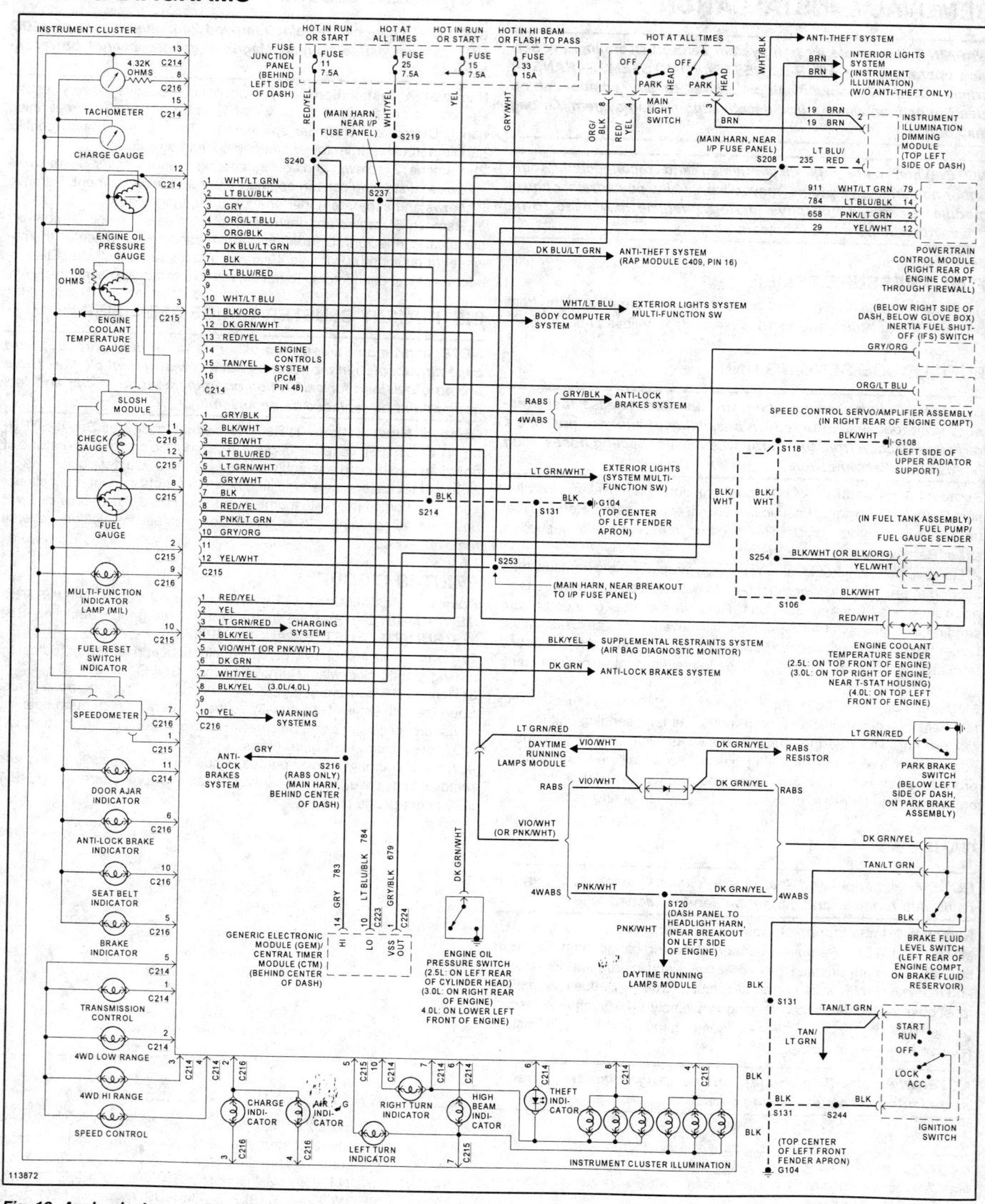

Fig. 13: Analog Instrument Panel Wiring Diagram (Ranger)

DESCRIPTION & OPERATION

Instrument cluster contains a printed circuit, speedometer/odometer, tachometer (if equipped), fuel gauge/temperature assembly and instrument cluster amplifier. Warning lights are placed in various locations around instrument cluster. Transmission range indicator is located below speedometer. Instrument cluster and panel will not illuminate when headlight switch is in OFF position.

Low fuel level warning/anti-slosh module is designed to light low fuel warning momentarily for function proof when ignition is turned on. Instrument cluster gauge amplifier is part of low fuel level warning/anti-slosh module and provides delay in fuel gauge to prevent fluctuation in fuel gauge pointer as a result of fuel movement in tank. The module is a small printed circuit board which latches into a pocket on back of instrument cluster. There are no provisions for calibration or adjustment of low fuel level warning/anti-slosh module.

When ignition switch is turned to ON position, the following warning indicators will light momentarily for function proof:

- ABS
- Air Bag
- Charging System
- Door Ajar
- Low Fuel
- Low Oil Pressure
- Anti-Lock Brake System
- SERVICE ENGINE SOON
- Safety Belt

COMPONENT LOCATIONS

COMPONENT LOCATIONS

Component	Location
Brake Fluid Level Switch	On Brake Reservoir
Coolant Temperature Sender	
Except SHO	Left Side Of Engine, Next To Thermostat
SHO	Rear Of Engine, Next To Thermostat
Daytime Running Lights Module	Behind Left Headlight
Engine Coolant Level Switch	On Coolant Reservoir
Flex Fuel Sensor Module	Behind Left Center Of Instrument Panel, Behind Integrated Control Panel
Fuel Pump/Fuel Gauge Sender	On Front Side Of Fuel Tank
Generic Electronic Module	Attached To Under Side Of Instrument Panel Fuse Box
Instrument Panel Fuse Box	Under Left Corner Of Instrument Panel
Oil Pressure Switch	
Except SHO	Left Rear Top Corner Of Engine
SHO	Above Starter
Passive Anti-Theft System Module	Behind Left Center Of Instrument Panel, Behind Integrated Control Panel
Powertrain Control Module	Right Rear Corner Of Engine Compartment
Remote Anti-Theft Personality Module	Above Accelerator Pedal
Speed Control Servo/Actuator	Next To Brake Master Cylinder
Vehicle Speed Sensor	On Transmission

TROUBLE SHOOTING

CAUTION: Electronic modules are sensitive to static electrical charges. Proper grounding of technician and workpiece is essential to prevent damage.

Verify charging system, turn signals, headlights and cruise control are working properly. Inspect wiring harness for obvious signs of shorts, opens, bad connections or damage. Verify customer concern by operating system in question. Attempt to duplicate condition with ignition switch in RUN position with engine off, in START position before ignition switch is released and in RUN position with engine running. Visually inspect the following components.

Mechanical:
- Damaged Fuel Tank
- Coolant Level
- Engine Oil Level
- Worn Or Damaged Accessory Drive Belt

Electrical:
- Blown Fuse(s)
- Damaged Wiring Harness
- Loose Or Corroded Connections
- Damaged Switches, Sensors Or Modules
- Damaged Instrument Cluster

If inspection reveals an obvious concern which can be easily serviced, repair as necessary. If inspection does not reveal an obvious concern which can be easily serviced, perform self-diagnostics. See SELF-DIAGNOSTIC SYSTEM.

COMPONENT TESTS

HEADLIGHT SWITCH

Remove headlight switch. Check continuity or resistance between appropriate terminals with switch in specified position. See HEADLIGHT SWITCH TEST table. *See Fig. 1.* If continuity or resistance is not as specified, replace headlight switch.

HEADLIGHT SWITCH TEST

Switch Position	Between Terminals	Continuity
Autolamp Feed Circuit		
Off	4 & 17	No
Park	4 & 17	No
Head	9 & 17	No
Autolamp On/Off Circuit		
Off	4 & 17	No [1]
Off	4 & 16	
On	4 & 17	Yes [2]
On	4 & 16	[3]
Instrument Cluster Illumination Circuit		
Dome Light Circuit		
Off	4 & 12	No
On	4 & 12	Yes
Headlight Circuit		
Off	6 & 7	No
Park	6 & 7	No
Head	6 & 7	Yes
Parking Lights Circuit		
Off	13 & 14	No
Park	13 & 14	Yes
Head	13 & 14	Yes
Warning Chime Circuit		
Off	10 & 11	No
Park	10 & 11	Yes
Head	10 & 11	Yes

[1] – Resistance should be 3.4-3.7 k/ohms.
[2] – Resistance should be 193-214 k/ohms.
[3] – Resistance should smoothly decrease as thumbwheel is rotated from up to down positions.

SELF-DIAGNOSTIC SYSTEM

Connect New Generation Star (NGS) tester to Data Link Connector (DLC), located beneath instrument panel. Using NGS tester, perform data link diagnostics test. See DATA LINK DIAGNOSTIC TEST under COMMUNICATION NETWORK DIAGNOSTICS in MODULE COMMUNICATIONS NETWORK – SABLE & TAURUS article. If NGS tester responds with CKT914, CKT915 or CKT70=ALL ECUS NO RESP/NOT EQUIP, repair module communications concern. See MODULE COMMUNICATIONS NETWORK – SABLE & TAURUS article. If NGS tester displays NO RESP/NOT EQUIP for Generic Electronic Module (GEM), perform TEST A: NO COMMUNICATION WITH GENERIC ELECTRONIC MODULE under SYSTEM TESTS.

If NGS tester responds with SYSTEM PASSED, retrieve and record continuous DTCs. Erase continuous DTCs. Using NGS tester, perform GEM self-test. Perform appropriate test in accordance with DTC retrieved. See GENERIC ELECTRONIC MODULE DTC INDEX table. Codes listed in this table are only for testing covered in this article. For complete DTC listing, see MODULE COMMUNICATIONS NETWORK – SABLE & TAURUS article. If no DTCs are retrieved, repair by symptom. See SYMPTOM CHART table under SYSTEM TESTS.

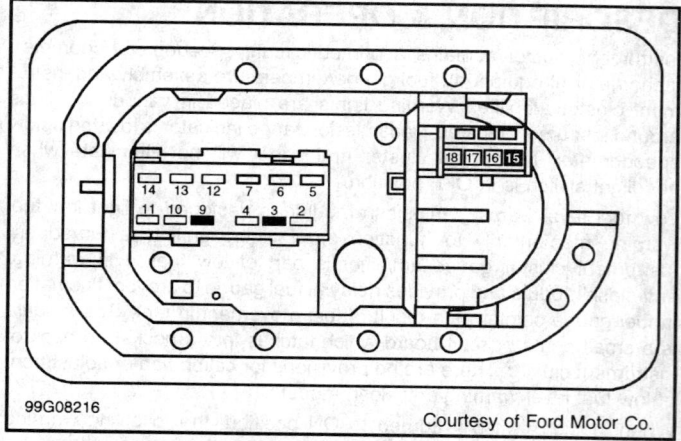

99G08216   Courtesy of Ford Motor Co.

Fig. 1: Identifying Headlight Switch Terminals

GENERIC ELECTRONIC MODULE DTC INDEX

DTC [1]	Description	Test
B1323	Door Ajar Indicator Circuit Failure	DTC B1323
B1325	Door Ajar Indicator Circuit Short To Voltage	DTC B1325
B1342	ECU Failure	[2]
B1352	Ignition Key-In Circuit Failure	T
B1354	Ignition Key-In Circuit Short To Ground	T
B1426	Seat Belt Indicator Circuit Short To Voltage	DTC B1426
B1428	Seat Belt Indicator Circuit Failure	DTC B1428
B1430	Seat Belt Switch Circuit Short To Ground	S
B1462	Seat Belt Switch Circuit Failure	S
B1575	Parking Light Input Circuit Failure	U
B1577	Parking Light Input Circuit Short To Voltage	U
P1881	Engine Coolant Level Switch Input Circuit Failure	DTC P1881
P1882	Engine Coolant Level Switch Circuit Short To Ground	DTC P1882
P1883	Engine Coolant Level Indicator Circuit Failure	DTC P1883
P1884	Engine Coolant Level Indicator Circuit Short To Voltage	DTC P1884

[1] – Codes listed in this table are only for testing covered in this article. For complete DTC listing, see MODULE COMMUNICATIONS NETWORK – SABLE & TAURUS article.

[2] – Using NGS tester, retrieve and document all continuous. Perform Generic Electronic Module (GEM) self-test. If DTC B1342 is retrieved again, replace GEM.

DIAGNOSTIC TESTS

DTC B1323: DOOR AJAR INDICATOR CIRCUIT FAILURE

1) Close all doors. Turn ignition switch to RUN position. If door ajar indicator is on at all times, go to next step. If door ajar indicator is not on at all times, go to step **4)**.

2) Turn ignition switch to LOCK position. Disconnect Generic Electronic Module (GEM) harness connector C236. Measure resistance between ground and terminal No. 2 (Black/Orange wire) at GEM harness connector C236. See Fig. 2. If resistance is 10 k/ohms or less, go to next step. If resistance is greater than 10 k/ohms, replace GEM.

3) Turn ignition switch to LOCK position. Disconnect instrument cluster harness connector C250. Measure resistance between ground and terminal No. 14 (Black/Orange wire) at instrument cluster harness connector C250. See Fig. 3. If resistance is 10 k/ohms or less, repair short to ground in Black/Orange wire. If resistance is greater than 10 k/ohms, replace instrument cluster printed circuit.

4) Turn ignition switch to LOCK position. Disconnect instrument cluster harness connector C250. Disconnect Generic Electronic Module (GEM) harness connector C236. Measure resistance in Black/Orange wire between terminal No. 14 at instrument cluster harness connector C250 and terminal No. 2 at GEM harness connector C236. See Figs. 2 and 3. If resistance is 5 ohms or less, go to next step. If resistance is greater than 5 ohms, repair open in Black/Orange wire.

5) Remove door ajar bulb from instrument cluster. Measure resistance of bulb. If resistance is greater than 5 ohms, replace bulb. If resistance is 5 ohms or less, replace instrument cluster printed circuit.

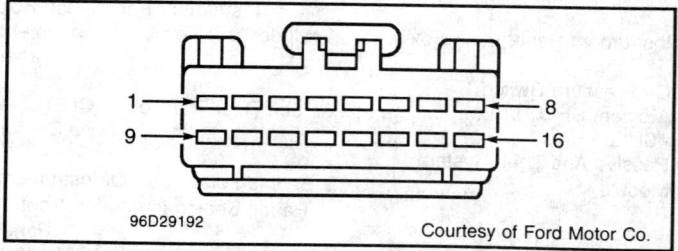

96D29192   Courtesy of Ford Motor Co.

Fig. 2: Identifying GEM Harness Connector C236 Terminals

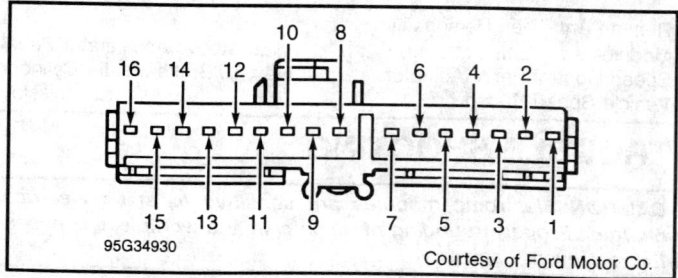

95G34930   Courtesy of Ford Motor Co.

Fig. 3: Identifying Instrument Cluster Harness Connector C250 Terminals

DTC B1325: DOOR AJAR INDICATOR CIRCUIT SHORT TO VOLTAGE

1) Turn ignition switch to LOCK position. Disconnect instrument cluster harness connector C250. Measure voltage at terminal No. 14 (Black/Orange wire) at instrument cluster harness connector C250. *See Fig. 3.* If voltage exists, go to next step. If no voltage exists, replace instrument cluster printed circuit.

2) Turn ignition switch to LOCK position. Disconnect GEM harness connector C236. Measure voltage at terminal No. 2 (Black/Orange wire) at GEM harness connector C236. *See Fig. 2.* If voltage exists, repair short to voltage in Black/Orange wire. If no voltage exists, replace GEM.

DTC B1426: SEAT BELT INDICATOR CIRCUIT SHORT TO VOLTAGE

1) Turn ignition switch to LOCK position. Disconnect instrument cluster harness connector C250. Measure voltage at terminal No. 13 (Yellow wire) at instrument cluster harness connector C250. *See Fig. 3.* If voltage exists, go to next step. If no voltage exists, replace instrument cluster printed circuit.

2) Turn ignition switch to LOCK position. Disconnect GEM harness connector C236. Measure voltage at terminal No. 1 (Yellow wire) at GEM harness connector C236. *See Fig. 2.* If voltage exists, repair short to voltage in Yellow wire. If no voltage exists, replace GEM.

DTC B1428: SEAT BELT INDICATOR CIRCUIT FAILURE

1) Turn ignition switch to RUN position. If seat belt indicator is on at all times, go to next step. If seat belt indicator is not on at all times, go to step **4)**.

2) Turn ignition switch to LOCK position. Disconnect GEM harness connector C236. Measure resistance between ground and terminal No. 1 (Yellow wire) at GEM harness connector C236. *See Fig. 2.* If resistance is 10 k/ohms or less, go to next step. If resistance is greater than 10 k/ohms, replace GEM.

3) Turn ignition switch to LOCK position. Disconnect instrument cluster harness connector C250. Measure resistance between ground and terminal No. 13 (Yellow wire) at instrument cluster harness connector C250. *See Fig. 3.* If resistance is 10 k/ohms or less, repair short to ground in Yellow wire. If resistance is greater than 10 k/ohms, replace instrument cluster printed circuit.

4) Turn ignition switch to LOCK position. Disconnect GEM harness connector C236. Turn ignition switch to RUN position. Measure voltage at terminal No. 1 (Yellow wire) at GEM harness connector C236. *See Fig. 2.* If battery voltage does not exist, go to next step. If battery voltage exists, replace GEM.

5) Turn ignition switch to LOCK position. Disconnect instrument cluster harness connector C250. Measure resistance in Yellow wire between terminal No. 13 at instrument cluster harness connector C250 and terminal No. 1 at GEM harness connector C236. *See Figs. 2 and 3.* If resistance is 5 ohms or less, go to next step. If resistance is greater than 5 ohms, repair open in Yellow wire.

6) Remove seat belt bulb from instrument cluster. Measure resistance of bulb. If resistance is greater than 5 ohms, replace bulb. If resistance is 5 ohms or less, replace instrument cluster printed circuit.

DTC P1881: ENGINE COOLANT LEVEL SWITCH INPUT CIRCUIT FAILURE
DTC P1882: ENGINE COOLANT LEVEL SWITCH SHORT TO GROUND

1) Ensure engine is cold. Check engine coolant level. If engine coolant level is low, go to next step. If coolant level is okay, go to step **3)**.

2) Fill engine coolant to COLD FILL mark. Start engine and observe LOW COOLANT indicator on instrument cluster. If LOW COOLANT indicator does not operate properly, go to next step. If LOW COOLANT indicator operates properly, system is okay at this time. Check for coolant leaks.

3) Turn ignition switch to LOCK position. Connect New Generation Star (NGS) tester to Data Link Connector (DLC). Using NGS tester, monitor

Generic Electronic Module (GEM) PID COOLANT. Disconnect engine coolant level switch harness connector C100. If PID did not change from NOTOK to OK, go to next step. If PID changed from NOTOK to OK, replace engine coolant level switch.

4) Turn ignition switch to LOCK position. Disconnect GEM harness connector C223. Measure resistance between ground and terminal No. 9 (White/Black wire) at GEM harness connector C223. *See Fig. 4.* If resistance is greater than 10 k/ohms, replace GEM. If resistance is 10 k/ohms or less, repair short to ground in White/Black wire.

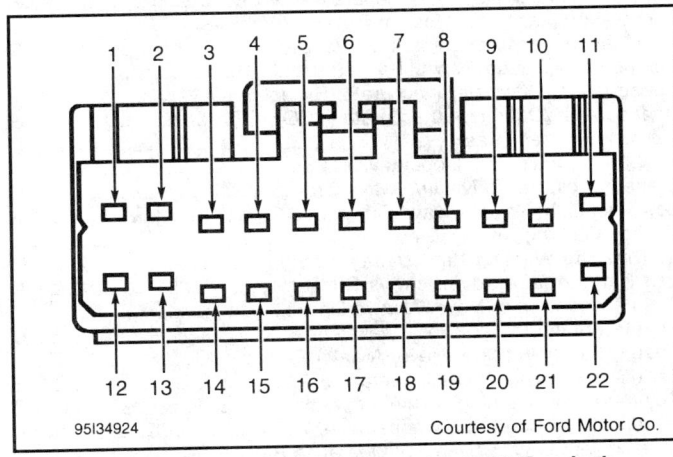

95I34924   Courtesy of Ford Motor Co.

Fig. 4: Identifying GEM Harness Connector C223 Terminals

DTC P1883: ENGINE COOLANT LEVEL INDICATOR CIRCUIT FAILURE

1) Turn ignition switch to RUN position. If engine coolant level indicator is on at all times, go to next step. If engine coolant level indicator is not on at all times, go to step **4)**.

2) Turn ignition switch to LOCK position. Disconnect Generic Electronic Module (GEM) harness connector C236. Measure resistance between ground and terminal No. 9 (Black/Pink wire) at GEM harness connector C236. *See Fig. 2.* If resistance is 10 k/ohms or less, go to next step. If resistance is greater than 10 k/ohms, replace GEM.

3) Turn ignition switch to LOCK position. Disconnect instrument cluster harness connector C250. Measure resistance between ground and terminal No. 12 (Black/Pink wire) at instrument cluster harness connector C250. *See Fig. 3.* If resistance is 10 k/ohms or less, repair short to ground in Black/Pink wire. If resistance is greater than 10 k/ohms, replace instrument cluster printed circuit.

4) Turn ignition switch to LOCK position. Disconnect GEM harness connector C236. Turn ignition switch to RUN position. Measure voltage at terminal No. 9 (Black/Pink wire) at GEM harness connector C236. *See Fig. 2.* If battery voltage does not exist, go to next step. If battery voltage exists, replace GEM.

5) Turn ignition switch to LOCK position. Disconnect instrument cluster harness connector C250. Measure resistance in Black/Pink wire between terminal No. 12 at instrument cluster harness connector C250 and terminal No. 1 at GEM harness connector C236. *See Figs. 2 and 3.* If resistance is 5 ohms or less, go to next step. If resistance is greater than 5 ohms, repair open Black/Pink wire.

6) Remove engine coolant level bulb from instrument cluster. Measure resistance of bulb. If resistance is greater than 5 ohms, replace bulb. If resistance is 5 ohms or less, replace instrument cluster printed circuit.

DTC P1884: ENGINE COOLANT LEVEL INDICATOR CIRCUIT SHORT TO VOLTAGE

1) Turn ignition switch to LOCK position. Disconnect instrument cluster harness connector C250. Measure voltage at terminal No. 12 (Black/Pink wire) at instrument cluster harness connector C250. *See Fig. 3.* If voltage exists, go to next step. If no voltage exists, replace instrument cluster printed circuit.

2) Turn ignition switch to LOCK position. Disconnect GEM harness connector C236. Measure voltage at terminal No. 9 (Black/Pink wire) at

GEM harness connector C236. *See Fig. 2.* If voltage exists, repair short to voltage in Black/Pink wire. If no voltage exists, replace GEM.

SYSTEM TESTS

SYMPTOM CHART

Symptom	Test
No Communication With Generic Electronic Module	A
Integrated Circuit Display(s) Inoperative Or Erratic	B
Fuel Gauge Inaccurate (Except Flex Fuel Vehicle)	C
Fuel Gauge Inaccurate (Flex Fuel Vehicle)	D
Temperature Gauge Inaccurate	E
Speedometer/Odometer Inaccurate (Except SHO)	F
Speedometer/Odometer Inaccurate (SHO)	G
Tachometer Inaccurate	H
All Warning Indicators Inoperative	I
Brake Warning Light Never/Always On	J
Low Fuel Light Never/Always On	K
Charge Warning Never/Always On	L
Oil Pressure Warning Never/Always On	M
Left Turn Indicator Never/Always On	N
Right Turn Indicator Never/Always On	P
High Beam Indicator Never/Always On	Q
Speed Control Indicator Never/Always On	R
Seat Belt Warning Chime Inoperative	S
Key-In-Ignition Warning Chime Inoperative	T
Headlight Warning Chime Inoperative	U
Low Coolant Level Chime Not Operating Properly	V

TEST A: NO COMMUNICATION WITH GENERIC ELECTRONIC MODULE

1) Remove fuse No. 23 from instrument panel fuse box. Measure resistance between ground and output side of fuse No. 23 in instrument panel fuse box. Resistance should start at greater than one m/ohm and drop steadily to less than 3 k/ohms. If resistance is not as specified, go to next step. If resistance is as specified, go to step **7**).

2) If resistance in step **1**) read greater than 10 ohms, go to next step. If resistance in step **1**) read 10 ohms or less, go to step **4**).

3) Remove Generic Electronic Module (GEM) from instrument panel fuse box. Disconnect and reconnect ohmmeter as in step **1**). If resistance is not greater than one m/ohm (may drop steadily to less than 3 k/ohms), go to next step. If resistance is greater than one m/ohm (may drop steadily to less than 3 k/ohms), replace GEM.

4) Disconnect instrument panel fuse box harness connector C247. Measure resistance between ground and output side of fuse No. 23. If resistance is 10 k/ohms or less, replace instrument panel fuse box. If resistance is greater than 10 k/ohms and equipped with anti-theft system, connect instrument panel fuse box harness connector C247 and go to next step. If resistance is greater than 10 k/ohms and not equipped with anti-theft system, connect instrument panel fuse box harness connector C247 and go to step **7**).

5) Disconnect Passive Anti-Theft System (PATS) module harness connector C242. Disconnect and reconnect ohmmeter as in step **1**). If resistance does not read greater than one m/ohm and drops steadily to less than 3 k/ohms, go to next step. If resistance reads greater than one m/ohm and drops steadily to less than 3 k/ohms, replace PATS module.

6) Disconnect Remote Anti-Theft Personality (RAP) module harness connector C254. Disconnect and reconnect ohmmeter as in step **1**). If resistance reads greater than one m/ohm, replace RAP module. If resistance reads one m/ohm or less, repair short to ground in White/Yellow wire between fuse No. 23 and RAP module.

7) Disconnect Generic Electronic Module (GEM) harness connector C248. Measure resistance between ground and terminals No. 14 and 25 (both Black wires) at GEM harness connector C248. *See Fig. 5.* If both resistance readings are 5 ohms or less, go to next step. If either resistance reading is greater than 5 ohms, repair open in appropriate wire(s).

8) Disconnect GEM harness connector C223. Measure resistance between ground and terminal No. 12 (Black/White wire) at GEM harness

connector C223. *See Fig. 4.* If resistance is 5 ohms or less, go to next step. If resistance is greater than 5 ohms, repair open in Black/White wire.

9) Disconnect GEM harness connector C236. Turn ignition switch to RUN position. Measure voltage at terminal No. 14 (Red/Yellow wire) at GEM harness connector C236. *See Fig. 2.* If battery voltage does not exist, go to next step. If battery voltage exists, go to step **11**).

10) Remove fuse No. 12 (5-amp) from instrument panel fuse box. Inspect fuse. If fuse tests okay, repair open in Red/Yellow wire between instrument panel fuse box and GEM. If fuse is blown, repair short to ground in Red/Yellow wire between instrument panel fuse box and GEM.

11) Measure resistance between ground and terminal No. 22 (Black/Light Green wire) at GEM harness connector C223. If resistance is 5 ohms or less, repair module communication concern. See MODULE COMMUNICATIONS NETWORK – SABLE & TAURUS article. If resistance is greater than 5 ohms, repair open in Black/Light Green wire.

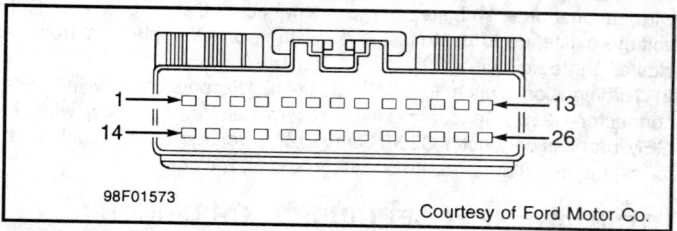

98F01573   Courtesy of Ford Motor Co.

Fig. 5: Identifying GEM Harness Connector C248 Terminals

TEST B: INTEGRATED CIRCUIT DISPLAY(S) INOPERATIVE OR ERRATIC

1) Disconnect negative battery cable. Disconnect instrument cluster harness connector C250. Remove fuse No. 12 (5-amp) from instrument panel fuse box. Measure resistance between ground and output side of fuse No. 12. If resistance is greater than 10 k/ohms, go to next step. If resistance is 10 k/ohms or less, repair short to ground in Red/Yellow wire.

2) Measure resistance in Red/Yellow wire between output side of fuse No. 12 and terminal No. 10 at instrument cluster harness connector C250. *See Fig. 3.* If resistance is one ohm or less, replace instrument cluster printed circuit. If resistance is greater than one ohm, repair open in Red/Yellow wire.

TEST C: FUEL GAUGE INACCURATE (EXCEPT FLEX FUEL VEHICLE)

1) Turn ignition switch to LOCK position. Disconnect fuel pump/fuel gauge sender harness connector C496. Connect Instrument Gauge System Tester (014-R1063) to Yellow/White wire terminal at fuel pump/fuel gauge sender harness connector C496. Set tester to 15 ohms. Turn ignition switch to RUN position, wait 60 seconds. Fuel gauge should read empty or below. Turn ignition switch to LOCK position. Set tester to 160 ohms. Turn ignition switch to RUN position, wait 60 seconds. Fuel gauge should read full or above. If fuel does not respond as specified, go to next step. If fuel gauge responds as specified, go to step **4**).

2) Remove fuel tank from vehicle. Inspect fuel tank for damage. If fuel tank is okay, go to next step. If fuel tank is damaged, repair or replace fuel tank as necessary.

3) Inspect fuel pump/fuel gauge sender assembly. Inspect fuel pump/fuel gauge sender wiring. If problem exists, repair as necessary. If problem does not exist, replace fuel level sender.

4) Turn ignition switch to LOCK position. Disconnect negative battery cable. Measure resistance in Yellow/White wire between fuel pump/fuel gauge sender harness connector C496 and terminal No. 7 at instrument cluster harness connector C250. *See Fig. 3.* Resistance should be 5 ohms or less. Also, measure resistance between ground and terminal No. 7 (Yellow/White wire) at instrument cluster harness connector C250. Resistance should be greater than 10 k/ohms. If both resistance readings are as specified, go to next step. If either resistance reading is not as specified, repair open and/or short to ground in Yellow/White wire.

5) Measure resistance between ground and Black/Yellow wire terminal at fuel pump/fuel gauge sender harness connector C496. If resistance is 5 ohms or less, go to next step. If resistance is greater than 5 ohms, repair open in Black/Yellow wire.

6) Disconnect negative battery cable. Disconnect instrument cluster harness connectors C250 and C251. Check continuity of instrument cluster printed circuit between terminals of printed circuit flex connection and terminals at gauge. See FUEL GAUGE CONTINUITY table. If there is continuity for each circuit, replace instrument cluster gauge amplifier and fuel gauge/temperature gauge. If there is no continuity, replace instrument cluster printed circuit.

FUEL GAUGE CONTINUITY

Terminal	Gauge Terminal
C250-10	B +
C250-8	GND
C250-7	SIG

TEST D: FUEL GAUGE INACCURATE (FLEX FUEL VEHICLE)

1) Turn ignition switch to LOCK position. Disconnect fuel pump/fuel gauge sender harness connector C496. Connect Instrument Gauge System Tester (014-R1063) to Yellow/White wire terminal at fuel pump/fuel gauge sender harness connector C496. Set tester to 11 ohms. Turn ignition switch to RUN position, wait 60 seconds. Fuel gauge should read empty or below. Turn ignition switch to LOCK position. Set tester to 115 ohms. Turn ignition switch to RUN position, wait 60 seconds. Fuel gauge should read full or above. If fuel does not respond as specified, disconnect tester and go to next step. If fuel gauge responds as specified, go to step **7)**.

2) Disconnect Flex Fuel Sensor Module (FFSM) harness connector C2040. Measure resistance in Black/Yellow wire between fuel pump/fuel gauge sender harness connector C496 and terminal No. 3 at FFSM harness connector C2040. See Fig. 6. If resistance is 5 ohms or less, go to next step. If resistance is greater than 5 ohms, repair open in Black/Yellow wire.

3) Measure resistance in Yellow/White wire between fuel pump/fuel gauge sender harness connector C496 and terminal No. 4 at FFSM harness connector C2040. Resistance should be 5 ohms or less. Also, measure resistance between ground and terminal No. 3 (Yellow/White wire) at FFSM harness connector C2040. Resistance should be greater than 10 k/ohms. If both resistance readings are as specified, go to next step. If either resistance reading is not as specified, repair open and/or short to ground in Yellow/White wire.

4) Connect Instrument Gauge System Tester (014-R1063) to terminal No. 6 (Orange/Light Green wire) at FFSM harness connector C2040. Set tester to 22 ohms. Turn ignition switch to RUN position, wait 60 seconds. Fuel gauge should read empty or below. Turn ignition switch to LOCK position. Set tester to 145 ohms. Turn ignition switch to RUN position, wait 60 seconds. Fuel gauge should read full or above. If fuel does not respond as specified, disconnect tester and go to next step. If fuel gauge responds as specified, replace FFSM.

5) Turn ignition switch to LOCK position. Disconnect instrument cluster harness connector C250. Measure resistance in Orange/Light Green wire between terminal No. 7 at instrument cluster harness connector C250 and terminal No. 6 at FFSM harness connector C2040. See Figs. 3 and 6. Resistance should be 5 ohms or less. Also, measure resistance between ground and terminal No. 6 (Orange/Light Green wire) at FFSM harness connector C2040. Resistance should be greater than 10 k/ohms. If both resistance readings are as specified, go to next step. If either resistance reading is not as specified, repair open and/or short to ground in Orange/Light Green wire.

6) Measure resistance in Brown wire between terminal No. 8 at instrument cluster harness connector C250 and terminal No. 2 at FFSM harness connector C2040. If resistance is 5 ohms or less, replace fuel gauge. If resistance is greater than 5 ohms, repair open in Brown wire.

7) Inspect fuel tank for damage. If fuel tank is okay, go to next step. If fuel tank is damaged, repair or replace fuel tank as necessary.

8) Inspect fuel pump/fuel gauge sender assembly. Inspect fuel pump/fuel gauge sender wiring. If problem exists, repair or replace as necessary. If problem does not exist, replace fuel level sender.

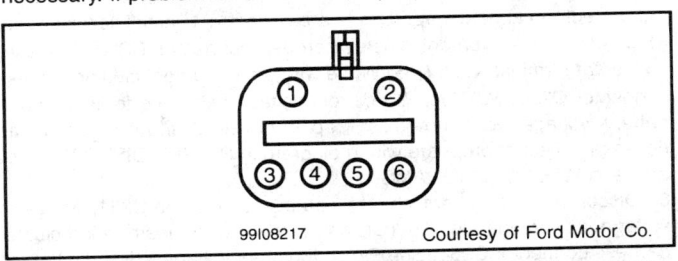

99108217   Courtesy of Ford Motor Co.

Fig. 6: Identifying Flex Fuel Sensor Module Harness Connector C2040 Terminals

TEST E: TEMPERATURE GAUGE INACCURATE

1) Turn ignition switch to LOCK position. Disconnect coolant temperature sender harness connector C182. Connect Instrument Gauge System Tester (014-R1063) to Red/White wire terminal at coolant temperature sender harness connector C182. Set tester at 275 ohms. Turn ignition switch to RUN position, wait 60 seconds. If gauge reads cold, go to next step. If gauge does not read cold, go to step **3)**.

2) Set tester to 18.3 ohms, wait 60 seconds and read gauge. If gauge does not read hot, go to next step. If gauge reads hot, replace coolant temperature sender.

3) Turn ignition switch to LOCK position. Disconnect instrument cluster harness connector C250. Measure resistance in Red/White wire between coolant temperature sender harness connector C182 and terminal No. 9 at instrument cluster harness connector C250. See Fig. 3. If resistance is 5 ohms or less, go to next step. If resistance is greater than 5 ohms, repair open in Red/White wire.

4) Turn ignition switch to LOCK position. Check continuity of instrument cluster printed circuit between terminals of printed circuit flex connection and terminals at gauge. See FLEX CONNECTOR C250 table. If there is continuity in each circuit, replace fuel gauge/temperature gauge. If continuity is not present on each flex circuit, replace instrument cluster printed circuit.

FLEX CONNECTOR C250

Pin	Gauge Terminal
10	B +
1	GND
9	SIG

TEST F: SPEEDOMETER/ODOMETER INACCURATE (EXCEPT SHO)

NOTE: Instrument cluster (speedometer) receives an input from the vehicle speed sensor to determine vehicle speed.

1) Connect NGS tester to Data Link Connector (DLC). Using NGS tester, monitor PCM PID VSS (+). Road test vehicle and monitor PID VSS (+). If the speedometer is operating and vehicle speed signal exists, go to next step. If speedometer is not operating and/or no vehicle speed signal exists, go to step **5)**.

2) Drive vehicle over a known, measured distance. If odometer is reading accurately, go to next step. If inaccurate, go to step **4)**.

3) Drive vehicle at a steady speed over a known measured distance and record time taken to travel that distance. If speedometer fails to meet speedometer calibration tolerance, go to next step. See SPEEDOMETER CALIBRATION TOLERANCE table. If speedometer meets speedometer calibration tolerance specifications, system is okay at this time.

SPEEDOMETER CALIBRATION TOLERANCE [1]

Actual Speed (MPH)	Allowable Range (MPH)
30	27.7-34.5
60	57.4-64.1

[1] – Odometer measured over actual 10 miles: 9.6-10.3 miles.

4) Check for correct driven gear on vehicle speed sensor. If driven or drive gear is suspect, refer to manufacturer's parts department for correct specifications in relation to final drive ratio and tire size. If parts are correct, go to next step. If parts are not correct, install correct parts.

5) Disconnect instrument cluster harness connector C250. Measure voltage at terminal No. 5 (Red/White wire) at instrument cluster harness connector C250. *See Fig. 3.* If battery voltage exists, go to next step. If battery voltage does not exist, repair power distribution circuit as necessary. See appropriate wiring diagram in POWER DISTRIBUTION article in WIRING DIAGRAMS.

6) Disconnect instrument cluster harness connector C251. Measure voltage at terminal No. 6 (Gray/Yellow wire) at instrument cluster harness connector C251. *See Fig. 7.* If battery voltage exists, go to next step. If battery voltage does not exist, repair power distribution circuit as necessary. See appropriate wiring diagram in POWER DISTRIBUTION article in WIRING DIAGRAMS.

7) Measure resistance between ground and terminal No. 13 (Black/Yellow wire, Brown wire on flex fuel vehicles) at instrument cluster harness connector C251. If resistance is 5 ohms or less, go to next step. If resistance is greater than 5 ohms, repair open in ground circuit. See appropriate wiring diagram in GROUND DISTRIBUTION article in WIRING DIAGRAMS.

8) Measure resistance between terminal No. 16 (Gray/Black wire) and No. 13 (Black/Yellow wire, Brown wire on flex fuel vehicles) at instrument panel harness connector C251. If resistance is not 200-300 ohms, go to next step. If resistance is 200-300 ohms, disconnect Vehicle Speed Sensor (VSS) harness connector C1043 and go to step **10)** .

9) Disconnect Vehicle Speed Sensor (VSS) harness connector C1043. Measure resistance between terminals at VSS (component side). If resistance is 200-300 ohms, go to next step. If resistance is not 200-300 ohms, replace VSS.

10) Measure resistance between ground and terminal No. 16 (Gray/Black wire) at cluster harness connector C251. If resistance is greater than 10 k/ohms, leave ohmmeter connected and go to next step. If resistance is 10 k/ohms or less, repair short to ground in Gray/Black wire.

11) Using a jumper wire connected to ground, connect other end to Gray/Black wire terminal at VSS harness connector C1043. If resistance is 5 ohms or less, go to next step. If resistance is greater than 5 ohms, repair open in Gray/Black wire.

12) Disconnect instrument cluster harness connectors C250 and C251. With an ohmmeter check speedometer for continuity from contact clips to printed circuit. If there is continuity at all clips, go to next step. If there is no continuity at any clip, replace contact clips.

13) Connect instrument cluster harness connectors. Check continuity from speedometer contact clips to cluster harness connector terminals. See PRINTED CIRCUIT CHECK table. If there is continuity in all circuits, replace speedometer assembly. If continuity is not present in all circuits, replace instrument cluster printed circuit.

PRINTED CIRCUIT CHECK

Connector/Terminal	Circuit No. (Wire Color)	Function
C251/6	1003 (GRY/YEL)	Power Input (RUN)
C250/5	729 (RED/WHT)	Power Input (Battery)
C251/13	[1]	Ground
C251/16	679 (GRY/BLK)	VSS Input Signal

[1] – Circuit No. 398 (Black/Yellow wire) on models without flex fuel. Circuit No. 564 (Brown wire) on models with flex fuel.

TEST G: SPEEDOMETER/ODOMETER INACCURATE (SHO)

NOTE: *Instrument cluster (speedometer) receives an input from ABS module to determine vehicle speed.*

1) Connect NGS tester to Data Link Connector (DLC). Using NGS tester, monitor PCM PID VSS (+). Road test vehicle and monitor PID VSS (+).

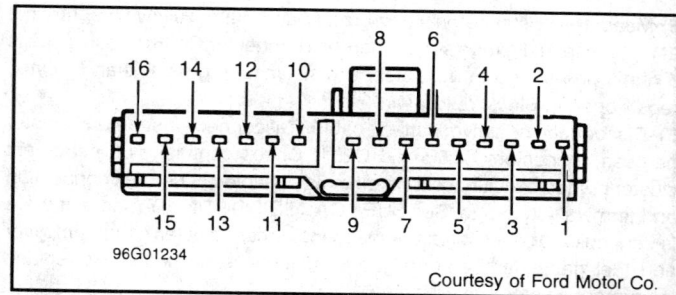

96G01234   Courtesy of Ford Motor Co.

Fig. 7: Identifying Instrument Cluster Harness Connector C251 Terminals

If the speedometer is operating and vehicle speed signal exists, go to next step. If speedometer is not operating and/or no vehicle speed signal exists, go to step **5)**.

2) Drive vehicle over a known, measured distance. If odometer is reading accurately, go to next step. If inaccurate, go to step **4)**.

3) Drive vehicle at a steady speed over a known measured distance and record time taken to travel that distance. If speedometer fails to meet speedometer calibration tolerance, go to next step. See SPEEDOMETER CALIBRATION TOLERANCE table. If speedometer meets speedometer calibration tolerance specifications, system is okay at this time.

SPEEDOMETER CALIBRATION TOLERANCE [1]

Actual Speed (MPH)	Allowable Range (MPH)
30	27.7-34.5
60	57.4-64.1

[1] – Odometer measured over actual 10 miles: 9.6-10.3 miles.

4) Using NGS tester, monitor Semi-Active Ride Control (SARC) PID VSS_SRC. Monitor vehicle speed on tester, while test driving vehicle. If vehicle speed shown on tester is approximate vehicle speed, go to next step. If vehicle speed shown on tester is not approximate vehicle speed, repair open in Gray/Black wire.

5) Measure resistance between ground and terminal No. 12 (Gray/Black wire) at ABS control module harness connector C1057. *See Fig. 8.* If resistance is 5 ohms or less, go to next step. If resistance is greater than 5 ohms, repair open in Gray/Black wire.

6) Measure resistance between ground and terminal No. 8 (Gray/Black wire) at instrument cluster harness connector C250. *See Fig. 3.* If resistance is 5 ohms or less, go to next step. If resistance is greater than 5 ohms, repair open in Gray/Black wire.

7) Disconnect instrument cluster harness connectors C250 and C251. With an ohmmeter check speedometer for continuity from contact clips to printed circuit. If there is continuity at all clips, go to next step. If there is no continuity, replace contact clips.

8) Reconnect cluster harness connectors. Check continuity from speedometer contact clips to cluster harness connector terminals. See PRINTED CIRCUIT CHECK table. If there is continuity in all circuits, replace speedometer assembly. If continuity is not present in all circuits, replace instrument cluster printed circuit.

PRINTED CIRCUIT CHECK

Connector/Terminal	Circuit No. (Wire Color)	Function
C251/10	1044 (WHT/YEL)	Power Input (RUN)
C250/1	57 (BLK)	GROUND
C251/16	679 (GRY/BLK)	VSS Input Signal

TEST H: TACHOMETER INACCURATE

NOTE: *Instrument cluster receives engine RPM signal from Powertrain Control Module (PCM).*

1) Disconnect instrument cluster harness connectors C250 and C251. Turn ignition switch to RUN position. Measure voltage at terminal No. 10 (Red/Yellow wire) at instrument cluster harness connector C250. *See*

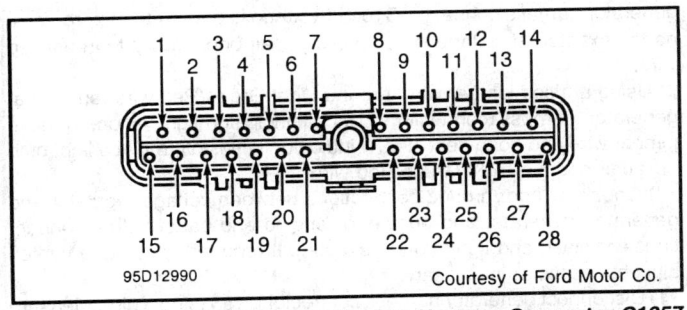

Fig. 8: Identifying ABS Control Module Harness Connector C1057 Terminals

Fig. 3. If battery voltage exists, go to next step. If battery voltage does not exist, repair power distribution circuit as necessary. See appropriate wiring diagram in POWER DISTRIBUTION article in WIRING DIAGRAMS.

2) Turn ignition switch to LOCK position. Measure resistance between ground and terminal No. 13 (Black/Yellow wire for non-flex fuel vehicles and Brown wire for flex fuel vehicles) at instrument cluster harness connector C251. *See Fig. 7.* Also, measure resistance between ground and terminal No. 8 (Black/Yellow wire for non-flex fuel vehicles and Brown wire for flex fuel vehicles) at instrument cluster harness connector C250. *See Fig. 3.* If both resistance readings are 3 ohms or less, go to next step. If either resistance reading is greater than 3 ohms, repair open in appropriate wire.

3) Disconnect negative battery cable. Disconnect Powertrain Control Module (PCM) harness connector C191. Measure resistance between ground and terminal No. 8 (Tan/Yellow wire) at instrument cluster harness connector C251. If resistance is greater than 10 k/ohms, go to next step. If resistance is 10 k/ohms or less, repair short to ground in Tan/Yellow wire.

4) Measure resistance in Tan/Yellow wire between terminal No. 8 at instrument cluster harness connector C251 and terminal No. 48 at PCM harness connector C191. *See Figs. 7 and 9.* If resistance is 5 ohms or less, go to next step. If resistance is greater than 5 ohms, repair open in Tan/Yellow wire.

5) Connect negative battery cable. Turn ignition switch to RUN position. Measure voltage at terminal No. 8 (Tan/Yellow wire) at instrument cluster harness connector C251. If voltage does not exist, go to next step. If voltage exists, repair short to voltage in Tan/Yellow wire.

6) Disconnect negative battery cable. Connect PCM harness connector C191. Connect negative battery cable. Start engine. Measure voltage at terminal No. 8 (Tan/Yellow wire) at instrument cluster harness connector C251. If voltage is 3-9 volts, replace tachometer. If voltage is not 3-9 volts, repair PCM concern. See appropriate SELF-DIAGNOSTICS article in ENGINE PERFORMANCE in appropriate MITCHELL® manual.

2) Remove fuse No. 12 from instrument panel fuse box. Inspect fuse. If fuse is okay, go to step. If fuse is blown, go to step **4)**.

3) Turn ignition switch to LOCK position. Install fuse No. 12. Disconnect instrument cluster harness connector C250. Turn ignition switch to RUN position. Measure voltage at terminal No. 10 (Red/Yellow wire) at instrument cluster harness connector C250. *See Fig. 3.* If battery voltage exists, replace instrument cluster printed circuit. If battery voltage does not exist, repair open in Red/Yellow wire.

4) Ensure fuse No. 12 is still removed. Measure resistance between ground and terminal No. 10 (Red/Yellow wire) at instrument cluster harness connector C250. *See Fig. 3.* If resistance is greater than 10 k/ohms, repair intermittent short to ground in Red/Yellow wire or short to ground in instrument cluster as necessary. If resistance is 10 k/ohms or less, repair short to ground in Red/Yellow wire.

TEST J: BRAKE WARNING LIGHT NEVER/ALWAYS ON

1) Turn ignition switch to RUN position. If brake warning indicator is always on, go to next step. If brake warning indicator is never on, go to step **6)**.

2) Ensure parking brake is completely released. Ensure brake fluid reservoir is full. If parking brake was released and brake fluid reservoir full, go to next step. If parking brake was not released and/or brake fluid reservoir was not full, correct the condition.

3) Turn ignition switch to LOCK position. Disconnect brake fluid level switch harness connector C177. Turn ignition switch to RUN position. If brake warning indicator does not illuminate, go to next step. If brake warning indicator is still on, repair short to ground in Light Green/Yellow wire between brake fluid level switch and ignition switch or instrument cluster. See WIRING DIAGRAMS.

4) Turn ignition switch to LOCK position. Measure resistance between brake fluid level switch terminals No. 1 (Light Green/Yellow wire terminal) and No. 3 (Black wire terminal) at component side. If resistance is greater than 10 k/ohms, go to next step. If resistance is 10 k/ohms or less, replace brake fluid level switch.

5) Disconnect parking brake switch harness connector C2010. Measure resistance between ground and Light Green wire terminal at brake fluid level switch harness connector. If resistance is 10 k/ohms or less, repair short to ground in Light Green wire. If resistance is greater than 10 k/ohms, replace parking brake switch.

6) Turn ignition switch to LOCK position. Measure continuity between terminals of brake warning indicator bulb. If continuity exists, install bulb and go to next step. If continuity does not exist, replace bulb.

7) Disconnect brake fluid level switch harness connector C177. Disconnect instrument cluster harness connector C251. Measure resistance in Light Green/Yellow wire between brake fluid level switch harness connector C177 and terminal No 4 at instrument cluster harness connector C251. *See Fig. 7.* If resistance is 5 ohms or less, go to next

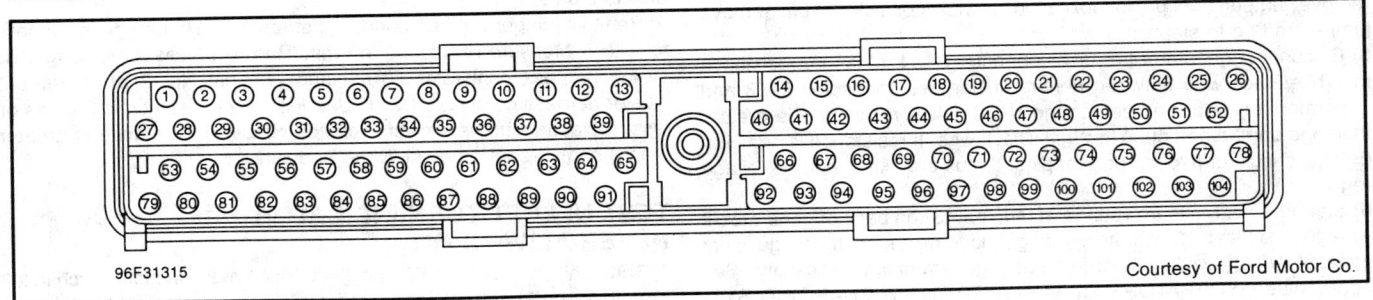

Fig. 9: Identifying PCM Harness Connector C191 Terminals

TEST I: ALL WARNING INDICATORS INOPERATIVE

1) Turn ignition switch to RUN position. Measure voltage at input side of fuse No. 12 (5-amp) in instrument panel fuse box. If battery voltage does not exist, repair power distribution circuit. See appropriate wiring diagram in POWER DISTRIBUTION article in WIRING DIAGRAMS. If battery voltage exists, go to next step.

step. If resistance is greater than 5 ohms, repair open Light Green/Yellow wire.

8) Measure resistance between brake fluid level switch terminals No. 1 (Light Green/Yellow wire terminal) and No. 2 (Light Green wire terminal) at component side. If resistance is 5 ohms or less, go to next step. If resistance is greater than 5 ohms, replace brake fluid level switch.

9) Disconnect parking brake switch harness connector C2010. Measure resistance in Light Green wire between parking brake switch harness connector C2010 and brake fluid level switch harness connector C177. If resistance is 5 ohms or less, go to next step. If resistance is greater than 5 ohms, repair open in Light Green wire.

10) Inspect instrument cluster printed circuit. If printed circuit is okay, replace parking brake switch. If printed circuit is not okay, replace instrument cluster printed circuit.

TEST K: LOW FUEL LIGHT NEVER/ALWAYS ON

1) Turn ignition switch to LOCK position. Connect Instrument Gauge System Tester (014-R1063) to terminal No. 7 (Yellow/White wire, Orange/Light Green wire on flex fuel vehicles) at instrument cluster harness connector C250 (with harness connector connected). Set tester to 56 ohms. Turn ignition switch to RUN position, wait 60 seconds. If low fuel warning light is not on, leave tester connected and go to next step. If low fuel warning light is on, replace low fuel level warning switch and fuel gauge.

2) Turn ignition switch to LOCK position. Change tester setting to 25 ohms. Turn ignition switch to RUN position, wait 60 seconds. If low fuel warning light is not on and fuel gauge does not read 16th of a tank, go to next step. If low fuel warning light is on and fuel gauge reads 16th of a tank, low fuel warning system is okay at this time.

3) Turn ignition switch to RUN position. Using a jumper wire, ground terminal No. 7 (Yellow/White wire, Orange/Light Green wire on flex fuel vehicles) at instrument cluster harness connector C250 (with harness connector connected). If low fuel level light is not on, go to next step. If low fuel level light is on, replace low fuel level warning switch and fuel gauge.

4) Turn ignition switch to LOCK position. Remove and inspect low fuel level indicator bulb. If bulb is okay, replace instrument cluster printed circuit. If bulb is not okay, replace bulb.

TEST L: CHARGE WARNING NEVER/ALWAYS ON

1) Check charging system warning indicator to determine if warning is always or never on. If warning is always on, go to next step. If warning is never on, go to step 8).

2) Measure voltage at terminal "A" (Orange/Light Blue wire) on voltage regulator. If battery voltage exists, go to next step. If battery voltage does not exist, repair power distribution circuit. See appropriate wiring diagram in POWER DISTRIBUTION article in WIRING DIAGRAMS.

3) Disconnect generator harness connectors C154. Turn ignition switch to RUN position. If indicator light is not on, go to next step. If indicator light is on, repair short to ground in Light Green/Yellow wire.

4) Connect generator harness connector C154. Disconnect generator harness connector C153 (single pin). Using a fused jumper wire, connect White/Black wire to positive battery post. If indicator light is on, remove jumper and go to next step. If indicator light is off, remove jumper and go to step 6).

5) Disconnect generator harness connector C154. Measure resistance in White/Black wire between generator harness connector C153 and generator regulator harness connector C154. If resistance is greater than one ohm, repair open in White/Black wire. If resistance is one ohm or less, check for a loose or bent pins. If pins are okay, replace voltage regulator.

6) Start engine. Measure voltage at terminal "S" on back of generator. If voltage is at least 1/2 of battery voltage, go to next step. If voltage is not at least 1/2 of battery voltage, repair generator as necessary. See appropriate GENERATORS article in STARTING & CHARGING SYSTEMS.

7) Measure voltage at B+ terminal on back of generator with engine running at 2000 RPM and all accessories off. If voltage is greater than 15.5 volts, repair charging system. See appropriate GENERATORS article in STARTING & CHARGING SYSTEMS. If voltage is 15.5 volts or less, repair or replace voltage regulator.

8) Disconnect generator harness connector C154. Turn ignition switch to RUN position. Measure voltage at Light Green/Red wire terminal at generator harness connector C154. If voltage is greater than zero volts, go to next step. If voltage is zero volts, repair open in Light Green/Red wire.

9) Using a fused jumper wire, ground Light Green/Red wire terminal at generator harness connector C154. If indicator light is on, remove jumper wire and go to next step. If indicator light is off, replace light bulb or repair open in Light Green/Red wire.

10) Check for poor ground connections between voltage regulator and generator, generator and engine, or engine and battery. If all connections are clean and tight, go to next step. If required, clean and tighten all connections as necessary.

11) Disconnect generator harness connector C153 (single pin). Measure voltage at White/Black wire terminal at generator harness connector C153. If voltage is zero volts, go to next step. If voltage is greater than zero volts, repair short to voltage in White/Black wire, which should be hot only when engine is running. Check for swapped wires in generator harness connector C154.

12) Measure voltage at terminal "S" on back of generator. If voltage is greater than one volt and warning light is on with "S" terminal harness connector disconnected, replace generator. If voltage is one volt or less, replace voltage regulator.

TEST M: OIL PRESSURE WARNING NEVER/ALWAYS ON

1) Start engine and determine if oil pressure warning is always or never on. If low oil pressure warning is always on, turn engine off and go to next step. If warning light is never on, go to step 4).

2) Turn ignition switch to RUN position. Disconnect oil pressure switch harness connector C1025. If warning light is illuminated, go to next step. If warning light is not illuminated, replace oil pressure switch.

3) Turn ignition switch to LOCK position. Disconnect instrument cluster harness connector C251. Measure resistance between ground and terminal No. 3 (White/Red wire) at instrument cluster harness connector C251. See Fig. 7 . If resistance is 10 k/ohms or less, repair short to ground in White/Red wire. If resistance is greater than 10 k/ohms, replace instrument cluster printed circuit.

4) Disconnect instrument cluster harness connectors C250 and C251. Turn ignition switch to RUN position. Measure voltage at terminal No. 10 (Red/Yellow wire) at instrument cluster harness connector C250. See Fig. 3. If battery voltage exists. If battery voltage does not exist, repair power distribution circuit. See appropriate wiring diagram in POWER DISTRIBUTION article in WIRING DIAGRAMS.

5) Connect instrument cluster harness connectors. Turn ignition switch to LOCK position. Disconnect oil pressure switch harness connector C1025. Using a fused jumper wire, ground White/Red wire terminal at oil pressure switch harness connector C1025. Turn ignition switch to RUN position. Observe oil pressure warning light. If warning light is not illuminated, go to next step. If warning light is illuminated, replace oil pressure switch.

6) Remove jumper wire. Disconnect instrument cluster connector C251. Measure resistance in White/Red wire between oil pressure switch harness connector C1025 and terminal No. 3 at instrument cluster harness connector C251. See Fig. 7. If resistance is 3 ohms or less, replace instrument cluster printed circuit. If resistance is greater than 3 ohms, repair open in White/Red wire.

TEST N: LEFT TURN INDICATOR NEVER/ALWAYS ON

1) Turn ignition switch to RUN position. Place multifunction switch in left turn position. If left turn signals operate properly, go to next step. If left turn signals do not operate properly, repair turn signals as necessary. See appropriate wiring diagram in EXTERIOR LIGHTS article.

2) Turn ignition switch to RUN position. If left turn indicator is on at all times, go to next step. If left turn indicator is not on at all time, go to step 5).

3) Turn ignition switch to LOCK position. Disconnect multifunction switch harness connector C269. Turn ignition switch to RUN position. Measure voltage at terminal No. 8 (Light Green/White wire) at multifunction switch

harness connector C269. *See Fig. 10*. If voltage is greater than 5 volts, go to next step. If voltage is 5 volts or less, replace multifunction switch.

4) Turn ignition switch to LOCK position. Disconnect instrument cluster harness connector C250. Turn ignition switch to RUN position. Measure voltage at terminal No. 8 (Light Green/White wire) at multifunction switch harness connector C269. If voltage is greater than 5 volts, repair short to voltage in Light Green/White wire. If voltage is 5 volts or less, replace instrument cluster printed circuit.

5) Turn ignition switch to LOCK position. Disconnect instrument cluster harness connector C250. Turn ignition switch to RUN position. Place multifunction switch in left turn position. Measure voltage at terminal No. 3 (Light Green/White wire) at instrument cluster harness connector C250. *See Fig. 3*. If voltage is greater than 10 volts, go to next step. If voltage is 10 volts or less, go to step **7)**.

6) Check continuity across left turn indicator bulb. If continuity exists, replace instrument cluster printed circuit. If continuity does not exist, replace bulb.

7) Disconnect multifunction switch harness connector C269. Measure resistance in Light Green/White wire between terminal No. 3 at instrument cluster harness connector C250 and terminal No. 8 at multifunction switch harness connector C269. *See Figs. 3 and 10*. If resistance is 3 ohms or less, replace multifunction switch. If resistance is greater than 3 ohms, repair open in Light Green/White wire.

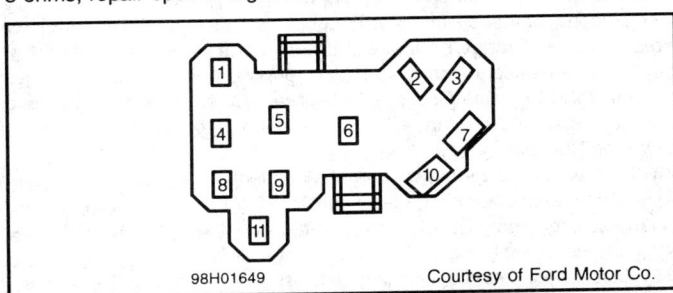

98H01649   Courtesy of Ford Motor Co.

Fig. 10: Identifying Multifunction Switch Harness Connector C269 Terminals

TEST P: RIGHT TURN INDICATOR NEVER/ALWAYS ON

1) Turn ignition switch to RUN position. Place multifunction switch in right turn position. If right turn signals operate properly, go to next step. If right turn signals do not operate properly, repair turn signals as necessary. See appropriate wiring diagram in EXTERIOR LIGHTS article.

2) Turn ignition switch to RUN position. If right turn indicator is on at all times, go to next step. If right turn indicator is not on at all time, go to step **5)**.

3) Turn ignition switch to LOCK position. Disconnect multifunction switch harness connector C269. Turn ignition switch to RUN position. Measure voltage at terminal No. 5 (White/Light Blue wire) at multifunction switch harness connector C269. *See Fig. 10*. If voltage is greater than 5 volts, go to next step. If voltage is 5 volts or less, replace multifunction switch.

4) Turn ignition switch to LOCK position. Disconnect instrument cluster harness connector C251. Turn ignition switch to RUN position. Measure voltage at terminal No. 5 (White/Light Blue wire) at multifunction switch harness connector C269. If voltage is greater than 5 volts, repair short to voltage in White/Light Blue wire. If voltage is 5 volts or less, replace instrument cluster printed circuit.

5) Turn ignition switch to LOCK position. Disconnect instrument cluster harness connector C251. Turn ignition switch to RUN position. Place multifunction switch in right turn position. Measure voltage at terminal No. 12 (White/Light Blue wire) at instrument cluster harness connector C251. *See Fig. 7*. If voltage is greater than 10 volts, go to next step. If voltage is 10 volts or less, go to step **7)**.

6) Check continuity across right turn indicator bulb. If continuity exists, replace instrument cluster printed circuit. If continuity does not exist, replace bulb.

7) Disconnect multifunction switch harness connector C269. Measure resistance in White/Light Blue wire between terminal No. 12 at instrument cluster harness connector C251 and terminal No. 5 at multifunction switch harness connector C269. *See Figs. 7 and 10*. If resistance is 3 ohms or less, replace multifunction switch. If resistance is greater than 3 ohms, repair open in White/Light Blue wire.

TEST Q: HIGH BEAM INDICATOR NEVER/ALWAYS ON

1) Turn ignition switch to RUN position. Turn headlights on. Place multifunction switch to high beam position. If high beams operate properly, go to next step. If high beams do not operate properly, repair headlights as necessary. See appropriate wiring diagram in HEADLIGHT SYSTEMS article.

2) Turn headlights off. Turn ignition switch to LOCK position. Disconnect instrument cluster harness connector C250. Turn ignition switch to RUN position. Measure voltage at terminal No. 2 (Gray/White wire) at instrument cluster harness connector C250. *See Fig. 3*. If voltage is 5 volts or less, go to step **4)**. If voltage is greater than 5 volts and vehicle is equipped with daytime running lights, go to next step. If voltage is greater than 5 volts and vehicle is not equipped with daytime running lights, repair short to voltage in Gray/White wire.

3) Turn ignition switch to LOCK position. Disconnect Daytime Running Lights (DRL) module harness connector C186. Turn ignition switch to RUN position. Measure voltage at terminal No. 2 (Gray/White wire) at instrument cluster harness connector C250. If voltage is greater than 5 volts, repair short to voltage in Gray/White wire. If voltage is 5 volts or less, replace DRL module.

4) Turn ignition switch to LOCK position. Disconnect instrument panel fuse box harness connector C235. Measure resistance in Gray/White wire between terminal No. 35 at instrument panel fuse box harness connector C235 and terminal No. 2 at instrument cluster harness connector C250. *See Figs. 11 and 13*. If resistance is less than 3 ohms, go to next step. If resistance is 3 ohms or more, repair open in Gray/White wire.

5) Disconnect both high beam headlight harness connectors. Measure resistance between ground and terminal No. 2 (Gary/White wire) at instrument cluster harness connector C250. If resistance is 10 k/ohms or less, repair short to ground in Gray/White wire. If resistance is greater than 10 k/ohms, go to next step.

6) Check for continuity between high beam indicator bulb terminal (component side). If continuity exists, replace instrument cluster printed circuit. If continuity does not exist, replace bulb.

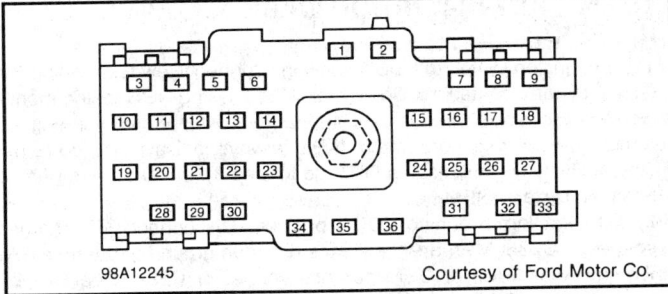

98A12245   Courtesy of Ford Motor Co.

Fig. 11: Identifying Fuse Panel Harness Connector C235 Terminals

TEST R: SPEED CONTROL INDICATOR NEVER/ALWAYS ON

1) Turn ignition switch to RUN position. If speed control indicator is always on, go to next step. If speed control indicator is never on, repair speed control concern. See CRUISE CONTROL SYSTEMS – SABLE & TAURUS article.

2) Turn ignition switch to LOCK position. Disconnect instrument cluster harness connector C251. Disconnect speed control servo/actuator harness connector C102. Measure resistance between ground and terminal No. 5 (Orange/Light Blue wire) at instrument cluster harness connector C251. *See Fig. 7*. If resistance is greater than 10 k/ohms, replace speed control servo. If resistance is 10 k/ohms or less, repair short to ground in Orange/Light Blue wire.

TEST S: SEAT BELT WARNING CHIME INOPERATIVE

1) Turn ignition switch to LOCK position. Connect New Generation Star (NGS) tester to Data Link Connector (DLC). Using NGS tester, monitor Generic Electronic Module (GEM) PID D_SBELT while buckling and unbuckling driver's seat belt. If PID always indicates FSTND, go to next step. If PID always indicates UNFSTD, go to step **3)**. If PID agrees with seat belt position, replace GEM.

2) Turn ignition switch to LOCK position. Disconnect GEM harness connector C248. Measure resistance between ground and terminal No. 5 (Brown/Light Blue wire) at GEM harness connector C248. *See Fig. 5.* If resistance is 10 k/ohms or less, go to step **6)**. If resistance is greater than 10 k/ohms, replace GEM.

3) Turn ignition switch to LOCK position. Disconnect GEM harness connector C248. Measure voltage at terminal No. 5 (Brown/Light Blue wire) at GEM harness connector C248. *See Fig. 5.* If voltage does not exist, go to next step. If voltage exists, repair short to voltage in Brown/Light Blue wire.

4) Disconnect driver's seat belt switch harness connector C302. Measure resistance between ground and Black wire terminal at driver's seat belt switch harness connector C302. If resistance is 5 ohms or less, go to next step. If resistance is greater than 5 ohms, repair open in Black wire.

5) Measure resistance in Brown/Light Blue wire between driver's seat belt switch harness connector C302 and terminal No. 5 at GEM harness connector C248. If resistance is 5 ohms or less, go to step **7)**. If resistance is greater than 5 ohms, repair open in Brown/Light Blue wire.

6) Measure resistance between terminals at driver's seat belt switch (component side) while buckling and unbuckling driver's seat belt. Resistance should be 5 ohms or less when seat belt is buckled and greater than 10 k/ohms when seat belt is unbuckled. If resistance is as specified, repair short to ground in Brown/Light Blue wire. If resistance is not as specified, replace driver's seat belt switch.

7) Measure resistance between terminals at driver's seat belt switch (component side) while buckling and unbuckling driver's seat belt. Resistance should be 5 ohms or less when seat belt is buckled and greater than 10 k/ohms when seat belt is unbuckled. If resistance is as specified, replace GEM. If resistance is not as specified, replace driver's seat belt switch.

TEST T: KEY-IN-IGNITION WARNING CHIME INOPERATIVE

1) Turn ignition switch to LOCK position. Connect New Generation Star (NGS) tester to Data Link Connector (DLC). Using NGS tester, monitor Generic Electronic Module (GEM) PID IGN_KEY while inserting and removing key in ignition switch. If PID always indicates IN, go to next step. If PID always indicates OUT, go to step **3)**. If PID agrees with key position, replace GEM.

2) Turn ignition switch to LOCK position. Disconnect GEM harness connector C236. Measure resistance between ground and terminal No. 7 (Black/Pink wire) at GEM harness connector C236. *See Fig. 2.* If resistance is 10 k/ohms or less, go to step **6)**. If resistance is greater than 10 k/ohms, replace GEM.

3) Turn ignition switch to LOCK position. Disconnect GEM harness connector C236. Measure voltage at terminal No. 7 (Black/Pink wire) at GEM harness connector C236. *See Fig. 2.* If voltage does not exist, go to next step. If voltage exists, repair short to voltage in Black/Pink wire.

4) Disconnect key warning switch harness connector C213. Measure resistance in Black/Pink wire between key warning switch harness connector C213 and terminal No. 7 (Black/Pink wire) at GEM harness connector C236. If resistance is 5 ohms or less, go to next step. If resistance is greater than 5 ohms, repair open in Black/Pink wire.

5) Measure resistance between terminals at key warning switch (component side) while inserting and removing key in ignition switch. Resistance should be 5 ohms or less when key is in ignition and greater than 10 k/ohms when key is out of ignition. If resistance is as specified, replace GEM. If resistance is not as specified, replace key warning switch.

6) Disconnect key warning switch harness connector C213. Measure resistance between terminals at key warning switch (component side) while inserting and removing key in ignition switch. Resistance should be 5 ohms or less when key is in ignition and greater than 10 k/ohms when key is out of ignition. If resistance is as specified, repair short to ground in Black/Pink wire. If resistance is not as specified, replace key warning switch.

TEST U: HEADLIGHT WARNING CHIME INOPERATIVE

1) Turn ignition switch to LOCK position. Connect New Generation Star (NGS) tester to Data Link Connector (DLC). Using NGS tester, monitor Generic Electronic Module (GEM) PID HDLMPSW while turning headlights on and off. If PID always indicates OFF, go to next step. If PID always indicates ON, go to step **5)**. If PID agrees with switch position, replace GEM.

2) Turn ignition switch to LOCK position. Disconnect GEM harness connector C236. Measure resistance between ground and terminal No. 15 (Orange/Red wire) at GEM harness connector C236. *See Fig. 2.* If resistance is greater than 10 k/ohms, go to next step. If resistance is 10 k/ohms or less, repair short to ground in Orange/Red wire.

3) Disconnect headlight switch harness connector C2031. Measure resistance in Orange/Red wire between terminal No. 10 at headlight switch harness connector C2031 and terminal No. 15 at GEM harness connector C236. *See Figs. 2 and 12.* If resistance is 5 ohms or less, go to next step. If resistance is greater than 5 ohms, repair open in Orange/Red wire.

4) Connect headlight switch harness connector C2031. Turn headlight switch on. Measure voltage terminal No. 15 (Orange/Red wire) at GEM harness connector C236. If battery voltage exist, replace GEM. If battery voltage does not exist, replace headlight switch.

5) Disconnect headlight switch harness connector C2031. Measure voltage at terminal No. 10 (Orange/Red wire) at headlight switch harness connector C2031. *See Fig. 12.* If voltage does not exist, go to next step. If voltage exists, repair short to voltage in Orange/Red wire. If voltage does not exist, go to next step.

6) Disconnect GEM harness connector C236. Ensure headlight switch is off. Connect headlight switch harness connector C2031. Measure voltage terminal No. 15 (Orange/Red wire) at GEM harness connector C236. *See Fig. 2.* If voltage exist, replace headlight switch. If voltage does not exist, replace GEM.

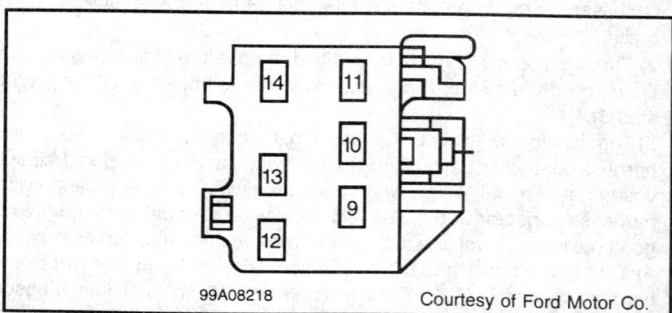

99A08218   Courtesy of Ford Motor Co.

Fig. 12: Identifying Headlight Switch Harness Connector C2031 Terminals

TEST V: LOW COOLANT LEVEL CHIME NOT OPERATING PROPERLY

1) Turn ignition switch to LOCK position. Connect New Generation Star (NGS) tester to Data Link Connector (DLC). Using NGS tester, perform Generic Electronic Module (GEM) self test. If no DTCs exist, go to next step. If any DTCs exist, repair them first.

2) Disconnect engine coolant level switch harness connector C100. Using a fused jumper wire, connect terminals at engine coolant level switch harness connector C100. Turn ignition switch to RUN position. If

LOW COOLANT indicator does not illuminate, go to next step. If LOW COOLANT indicator illuminates, replace engine coolant level switch.
3) Turn ignition switch to LOCK position. Disconnect jumper wire. Measure resistance between ground and Black wire terminal at engine coolant level switch harness connector C100. If resistance is 5 ohms or less, go to next step. If resistance is greater than 5 ohms, repair open in Black wire.
4) Measure voltage at White/Light Blue wire terminal at engine coolant level switch harness connector C100. If greater than 10 volts exist, system is okay at this time. If voltage is 10 volts or less, repair open in White/Light Blue wire.

REMOVAL & INSTALLATION

WARNING: Deactivate air bag system before performing any service operation. See appropriate AIR BAG RESTRAINT SYSTEMS article. DO NOT apply electrical power to any component on steering column without first deactivating air bag system. Air bag may deploy.

CAUTION: Electronic modules are sensitive to static electrical charges. Proper grounding of technician and workpiece is essential to prevent damage.

NOTE: When battery is disconnected, vehicle computer and memory systems may lose memory data. Driveability problems may exist until computer systems have completed a relearn cycle. See COMPUTER RELEARN PROCEDURES article in GENERAL INFORMATION before disconnecting battery.

FUEL PRESSURE RELIEF

WARNING: Contact with alcohol fuel (gasoline containing methanol or ethanol) on skin, in eyes or internally MUST be avoided. Permanent injury or death can result. Use protective clothing and equipment when handling fuel. Fuel supply lines on fuel injected engines remain pressurized for long periods of time after engine shutdown. System pressure MUST be relieved prior to fuel system service to prevent possible injury.

CAUTION: DO NOT use MFI Fuel Pressure Gauge Tool (T80L-9974-B) on flex fuel vehicles, or damage to gauge will occur.

Remove air cleaner. Unscrew and remove fuel pressure relief valve cap on fuel supply manifold. On gasoline vehicles, connect Fuel Pressure Gauge (T80L-9974-B) and on flex fuel vehicles, connect Rotunda Fuel (Methanol/Ethanol) Pressure Test Kit (134-R0087) to fuel pressure relief valve. Open manual valve on fuel pressure gauge or pressure test kit to relieve fuel system pressure.

FUEL GAUGE SENDING UNIT

CAUTION: Before disconnecting any fuel line, release fuel pressure from fuel system to reduce possibility of injury or fire. Use a rag as protection from fuel spray when disconnecting hoses. Plug hoses after disconnection.

Removal & Installation – 1) Relieve fuel pressure. See FUEL PRESSURE RELIEF. Drain fuel from non-flexible fuel vehicles with a siphon pump through fuel tank filler pipe. Flexible fuel vehicles have an anti-siphon screen in tank filler pipe. Drain fuel from flexible fuel vehicles using a siphon pump connected to fuel return tube at quick disconnect.
2) Raise vehicle on hoist. Loosen fuel tank filler pipe and vent hose clamps at metal lines and remove hoses.
3) Using Fuel Disconnect Tool Set (T90T-9550-S), disconnect push connect fittings for rear fuel supply return. Disconnect vapor tubes at fuel filter and steel line behind fuel filter.
4) Disconnect electrical harness connector for fuel tank wiring at left side of fuel filter. Disconnect White plastic push-connect fitting connecting line from evaporative emission tube shutoff valve to evaporative emissions canister.

5) Place support under fuel tank and remove bolts from rear of fuel tank support straps. Swing support straps forward on hinges to clear tank. Remove tank from vehicle. On flexible fuel vehicles, remove plastic shield with fuel tank.
6) On all vehicles, to prevent contamination of fuel and fuel tank, clean dirt and debris from around fuel pump module retaining flange. Using Fuel Tank Sender Wrench (D90P-9275-A), turn fuel pump locking retainer ring counterclockwise and remove locking retainer ring.
7) Pull fuel pump module sender plate up out of tank until locking tabs for module are accessible. Squeeze both locking tabs together and remove fuel pump module from fuel tank. Remove "O" ring seal and discard. For installation, reverse removal procedure, using NEW "O" ring.

FUEL GAUGE/TEMPERATURE GAUGE

NOTE: When installing fuel gauge/temperature gauge, ensure gauge pins are correctly seated into backplate retaining clips.

Removal & Installation – Remove instrument cluster. See INSTRUMENT CLUSTER. Remove instrument cluster main lens. Remove cluster mask and transmission range indicator from cluster. Carefully pull fuel gauge/temperature gauge out of instrument cluster. For installation, reverse removal procedure.

INDICATOR/WARNING BULBS

NOTE: All indicators/warning bulbs are removed and installed in same way.

Removal & Installation – Remove instrument cluster. See INSTRUMENT CLUSTER. Turn miniature bulb socket 1/4 turn counterclockwise to align tabs with slots in instrument cluster and pull bulb out of instrument cluster. To install, align tabs on miniature bulb with slots in instrument cluster and turn miniature bulb socket 1/4 turn clockwise until socket stops turning.

INSTRUMENT CLUSTER

NOTE: When battery is disconnected, vehicle computer and memory systems may lose memory data. Driveability problems may exist until computer systems have completed a relearn cycle. See COMPUTER RELEARN PROCEDURES article in GENERAL INFORMATION before disconnecting battery.

Removal & Installation (Floor Shift) – Disconnect negative battery cable. Tilt steering column to lowest position. Remove instrument cluster finish panel. Remove instrument cluster retaining screws. Pull top part of instrument cluster toward steering wheel. Disconnect instrument cluster harness connectors. Remove instrument cluster. To install, reverse removal procedure.

CAUTION: DO NOT use excessive force when installing radio removers. Excessive force will damage retaining clips and make control panel removal difficult.

Removal & Installation (Column Shift) – 1) Disconnect negative battery cable. Tilt steering column to lowest position. Remove upper and lower steering column covers. Remove instrument cluster finish panel. Using Radio Removing Tool (T87P-19061-A) into integrated control panel face plate. Push removers in about 1.5" to release retaining clips. Disconnect integrated control panel harness connectors and remove integrated control panel.
2) Remove instrument cluster retaining screws. Disconnect transmission range indicator cable from column selector tube. Pull top part of instrument cluster toward steering wheel. Disconnect instrument cluster harness connectors. Remove instrument cluster. To install, reverse removal procedure.

PRINTED CIRCUIT

Removal & Installation – 1) Remove instrument cluster. See INSTRUMENT CLUSTER. Remove miniature bulbs from instrument cluster. See INDICATOR/WARNING BULBS.

2) Remove 6 screws from instrument cluster main lens. Remove instrument cluster main lens.

3) Remove 2 screws from instrument cluster mask. Remove instrument cluster mask and transmission range indicator from instrument cluster.

4) Carefully remove speedometer, tachometer and fuel gauge/ temperature gauge. See SPEEDOMETER/ODOMETER, TACHOMETER and FUEL GAUGE/TEMPERATURE GAUGE.

5) Carefully depress retainer clip and remove low fuel level warning switch from instrument cluster. *See Fig. 13.*

6) Remove speedometer, tachometer and fuel gauge/temperature gauge retainer clips from instrument cluster. Carefully remove instrument cluster printed circuit from instrument cluster. *See Fig. 14.* For installation, reverse removal procedure.

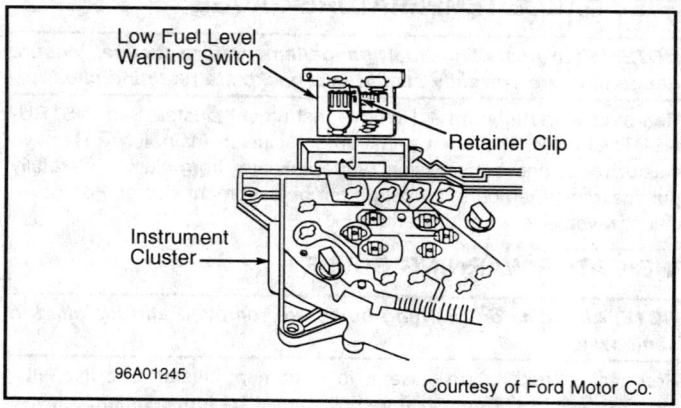

Fig. 13: Locating Low Fuel Level Warning Switch

SPEEDOMETER/ODOMETER

Removal & Installation – 1) Remove instrument cluster. See INSTRUMENT CLUSTER. Remove instrument cluster main lens, cluster mask and transmission range indicator. See PRINTED CIRCUIT.

2) Carefully pull speedometer/odometer out of instrument cluster. To install, reverse removal procedure.

TACHOMETER

Removal & Installation – 1) Remove instrument cluster. See INSTRUMENT CLUSTER. Remove instrument cluster main lens, cluster mask and transmission range indicator. See PRINTED CIRCUIT.

2) Carefully pull tachometer out of instrument cluster. To install, reverse removal procedure.

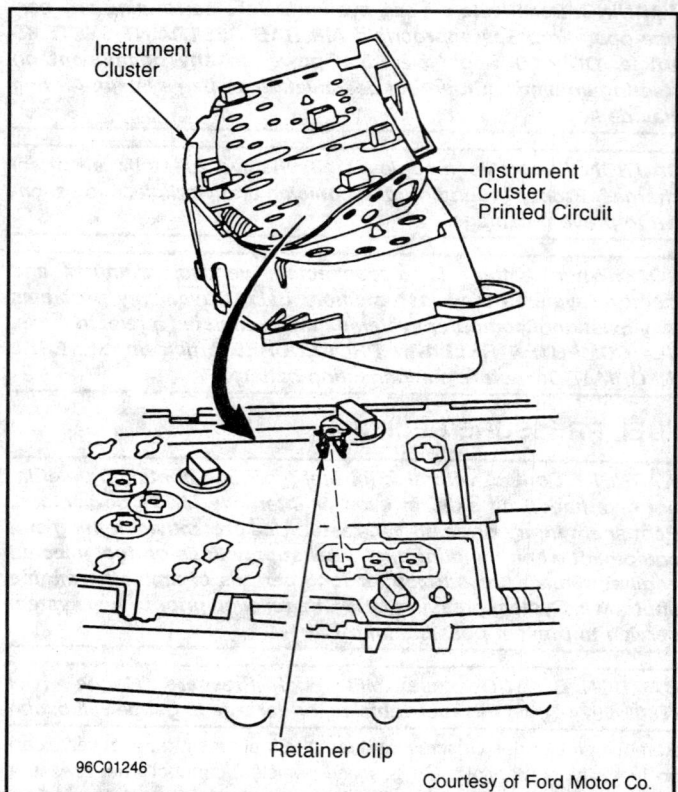

Fig. 14: Removing Instrument Cluster Printed Circuit

WIRING DIAGRAMS

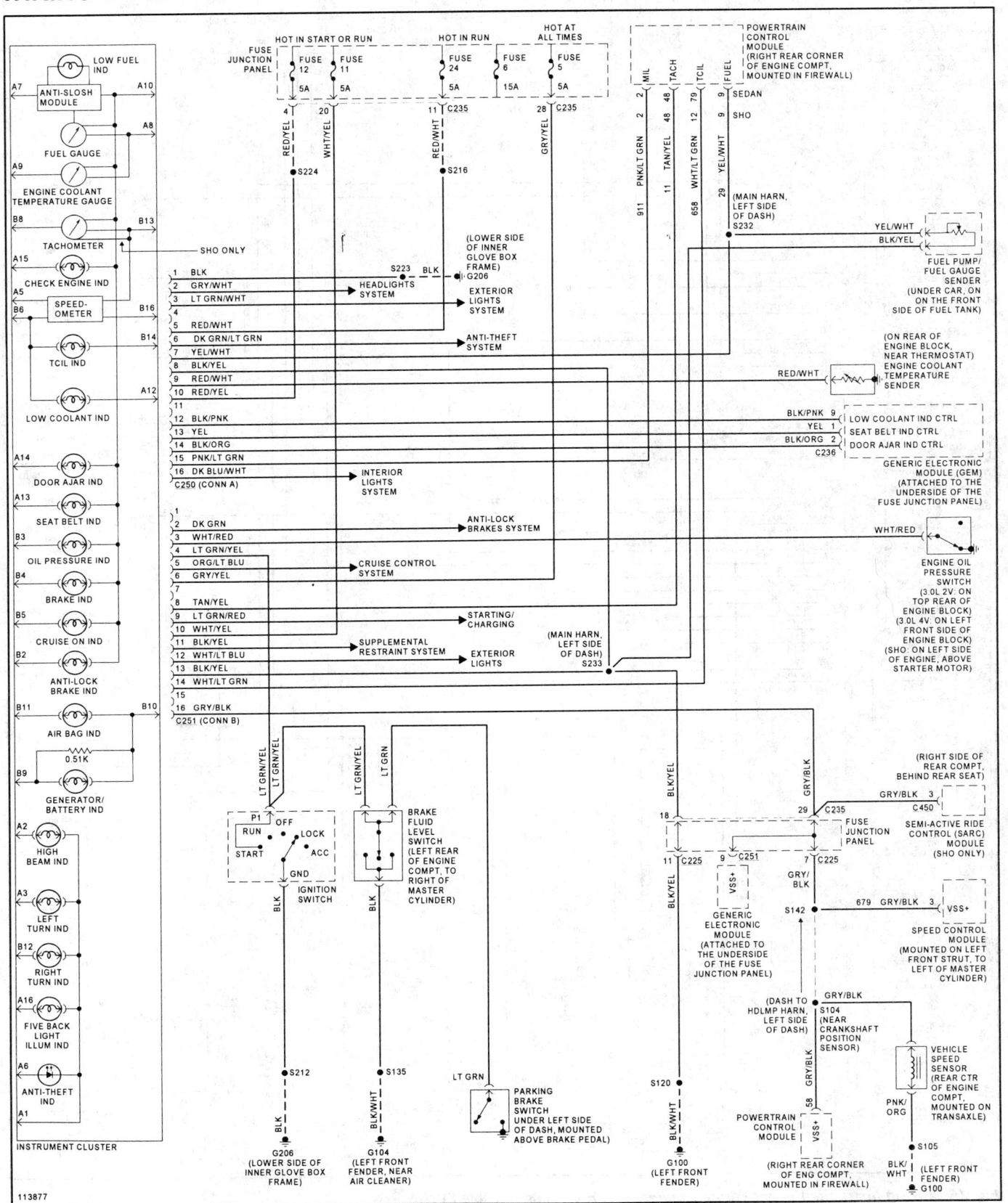

Fig. 15: Analog Instrument Panel Wiring Diagram (Sable & Taurus – Except 3.0L Flexible Fuel)

113877

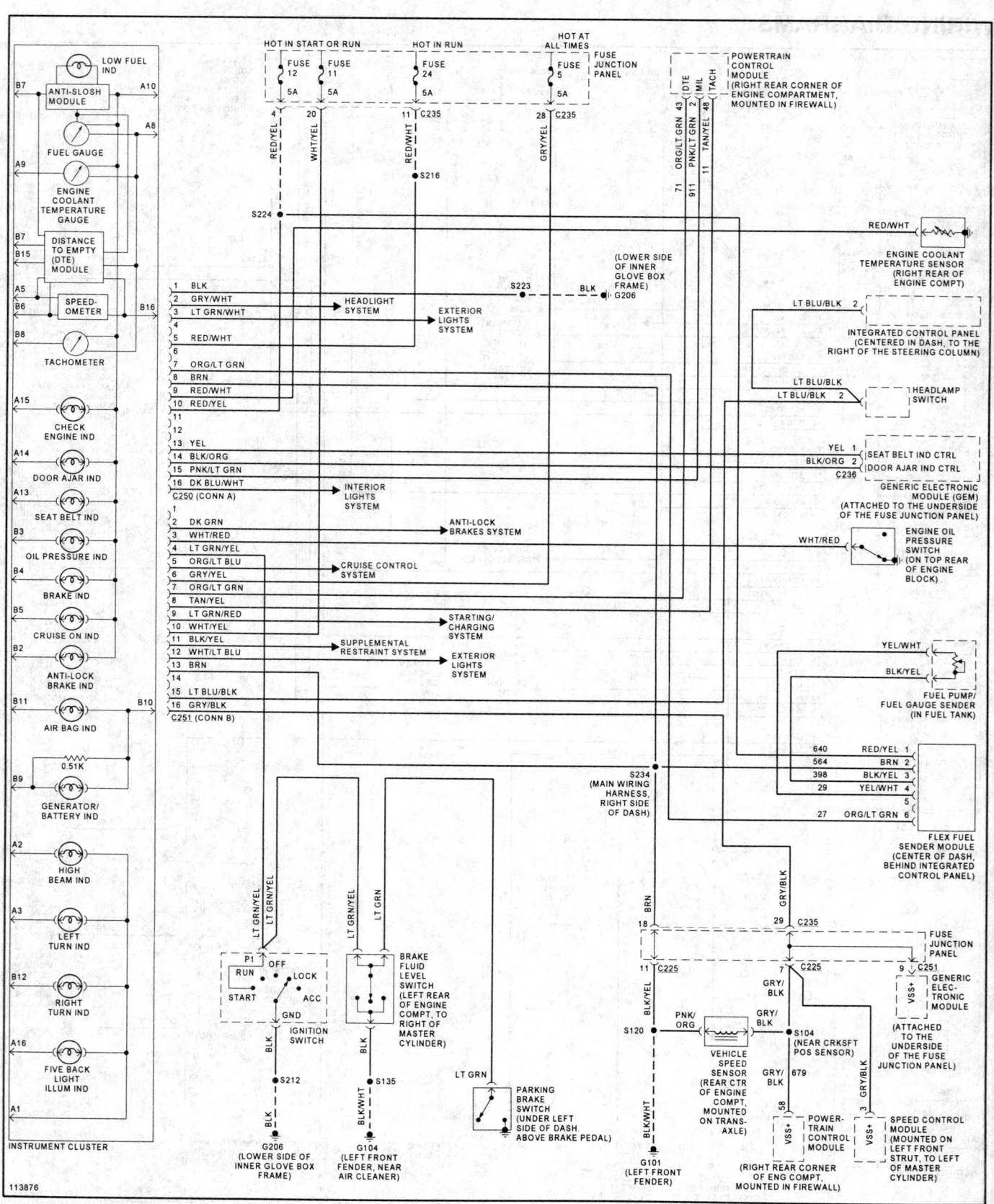

Fig. 16: Analog Instrument Panel Wiring Diagram (Taurus – 3.0L Flexible Fuel)

DESCRIPTION & OPERATION

WARNING: Deactivate air bag system before performing any service operation. See appropriate AIR BAG RESTRAINT SYSTEMS article. Do not apply electrical power to any component on steering column without first deactivating air bag system. Air bag may deploy.

Instrument cluster consists of an electronically driven analog speedometer and 2 message center displays. See Fig. 1. Also contained within the instrument cluster is a fuel gauge, temperature gauge, transmission range indicator and various warning and indicator lights.

Instrument cluster gauges, warning lights and message center displays are either controlled and driven directly by specific components or the information is requested and received through the Standard Corporate Protocol (SCP) network. The instrument cluster has self-diagnostic capabilities. One or more Diagnostic Trouble Codes (DTCs) will be stored in the event of malfunction. DTCs can be retrieved using a New Generation Star (NGS) Tester (007-00500). See SELF-DIAGNOSTIC SYSTEM.

The instrument cluster receives the following signals through the SCP network:

- Vehicle speed signal from ABS module.
- TRAC ACTIVE indicator signal (if equipped) from ABS module.
- High Beam Indicator signal from Lighting Control Module (LCM).
- SPEED CONTROL indicator signal from speed control amplifier.
- O/D OFF indicator signal from Powertrain Control Module (PCM).
- CHECK TRAC indicator signal from ABS module.
- AIR SUSPENSION indicator signal from air suspension/electronic variable orifice steering module.
- DOOR AJAR indicator signal from Driver's Door Module (DDM).
- TRUNK AJAR indicator signal from Driver's Door Module (DDM).
- ABS indicator signal from ABS module.
- SERVICE ENGINE SOON indicator signal from Powertrain Control Module (PCM).
- Fail-Safe cooling indicator and coolant temperature gauge signals from Powertrain Control Module (PCM).
- Seat belt indicator signal from Lighting Control Module (LCM).

COMPONENT LOCATIONS

COMPONENT LOCATIONS

Component	Location
Brake Fluid Level Switch	On Brake Fluid Reservoir
Compass Module	Center Of Windshield Header On Mirror
Data Link Connector	Under Instrument Panel, Right Of Steering Column
Dimmer Switch	Left Side Of Instrument Panel
Headlight Switch	Left Side Of Instrument Panel
Instrument Panel Fuse Box	Behind Instrument Panel, Left Of Steering Column
Lighting Control Module	Behind Center Of Instrument Panel
Power Distribution Box	Left Side Of Engine Compartment, In Front Of Wheelwell
Restraint Control Module (RCM)	Behind Left Front Of Instrument Panel

TROUBLE SHOOTING

Verify customer complaint. Check for low washer fluid level. Check for low engine coolant level. Check for low engine oil level. Check for low brake fluid level. Check for loose accessory drive belt. Check for loose or corroded connectors. Check for damaged wiring. Check for blown fuses. Check for faulty switches. If no problem is found, go to SELF-DIAGNOSTIC SYSTEM.

COMPONENT TESTS

HEADLIGHT SWITCH

Disconnect headlight switch harness connector. Continuity should be as specified between terminals with switch in specified position. See HEADLIGHT SWITCH TEST table. See Fig. 2. If continuity is not as specified, replace headlight switch.

HEADLIGHT SWITCH TEST

Switch Position	Between Terminals	Continuity
All	1 & 2	[1] Yes
Autolamp		
Off	4 & 7	No
On	4 & 7	Yes
Rheostat	9 & 7	[2]
Dome Light		
Off	6 & 7	No
On	6 & 7	Yes
Headlights		
Off	3 & 7; 7 & 8	No
Park	7 & 8	No
Park	3 & 7	Yes
On	3 & 7; 7 & 8	Yes

[1] – Backlighting illumination circuit.
[2] – Resistance should smoothly increase from 3000 to 200,000 ohms as headlight switch is rotated counterclockwise from OFF position toward AUTOLAMP position.

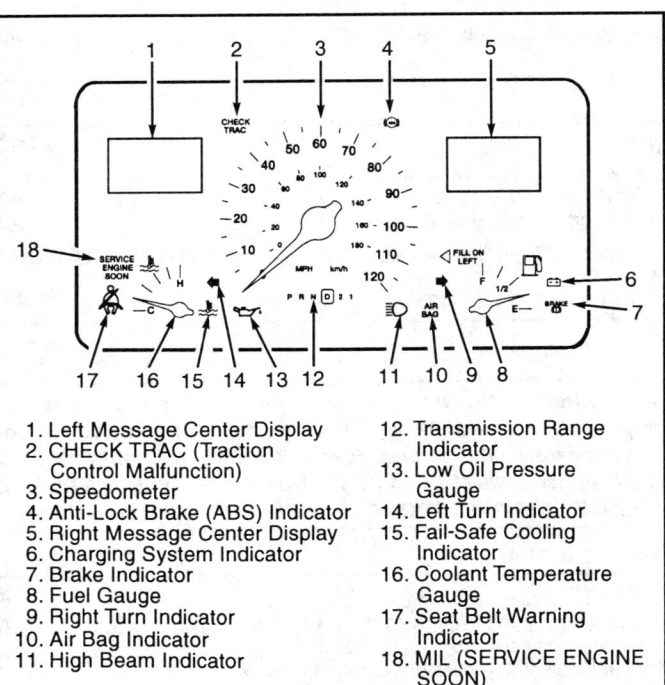

1. Left Message Center Display
2. CHECK TRAC (Traction Control Malfunction)
3. Speedometer
4. Anti-Lock Brake (ABS) Indicator
5. Right Message Center Display
6. Charging System Indicator
7. Brake Indicator
8. Fuel Gauge
9. Right Turn Indicator
10. Air Bag Indicator
11. High Beam Indicator
12. Transmission Range Indicator
13. Low Oil Pressure Gauge
14. Left Turn Indicator
15. Fail-Safe Cooling Indicator
16. Coolant Temperature Gauge
17. Seat Belt Warning Indicator
18. MIL (SERVICE ENGINE SOON)

98C01675

Courtesy of Ford Motor Co.

Fig. 1: Identifying Instrument Cluster Components

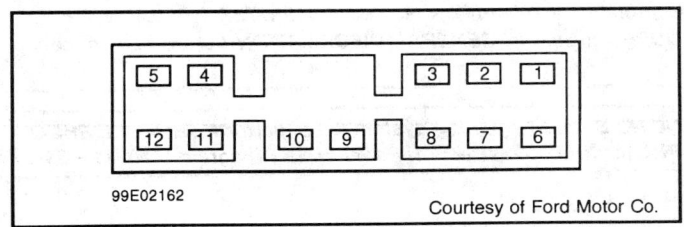

99E02162

Courtesy of Ford Motor Co.

Fig. 2: Identifying Headlight Switch Terminals

DIMMER SWITCH

Disconnect dimmer switch harness connector. Continuity should be as specified between terminals with switch in specified position. See DIMMER SWITCH TEST table. *See Fig. 3.* If continuity is not as specified, replace dimmer switch.

DIMMER SWITCH TEST

Switch Position	Between Terminals	Continuity
Dimmer		
Down	1 & 2	Yes
Neutral	1 & 2; 2 & 4	No
Up	2 & 4	Yes

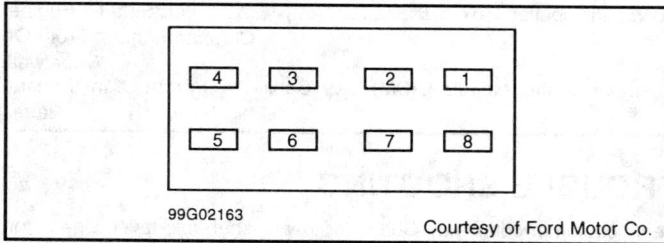

99G02163   Courtesy of Ford Motor Co.

Fig. 3: Identifying Dimmer Switch Terminals

SELF-DIAGNOSTIC SYSTEM

NOTE: Before beginning self-diagnostics, perform TROUBLE SHOOTING.

NOTE: A New Generation Star (NGS) tester is required to test the instrment cluster. If NGS tester does not communicate with vehicle, refer to NGS tester manual.

Connect New Generation Star (NGS) Tester (007-00500) to Data Link Connector (DLC) located below instrument panel. Using NGS tester, perform data link diagnostic test. If NGS tester displays CKT914, CKT915 or CKT70=ALL ECUS NO RESP/NOT EQUIP, repair communications concern. See MODULE COMMUNICATIONS NETWORK – TOWN CAR article. If NGS tester displays NO RESP/NOT EQUIP for instrument cluster, perform TEST A: NO COMMUNICATION WITH INSTRUMENT CLUSTER under SYSTEM TESTS. If NGS tester displays NO RESP/NOT EQUIP for Lighting Control Module (LCM), perform TEST X: NO COMMUNICATION WITH LIGHTING CONTROL MODULE (LCM) under SYSTEM TESTS. If NGS tester displays SYSTEM PASSED, retrieve and record DTCs from all modules. Erase DTCs from all modules. Perform instrument cluster and LCM self-test. Perform appropriate test in accordance with DTC retrieved. See INSTRUMENT CLUSTER DTC INDEX and/or LIGHTING CONTROL MODULE DTC INDEX table. Codes listed in these tables are only for testing covered in this article. For complete DTC listing, see MODULE COMMUNICATIONS NETWORK – TOWN CAR article. If self-test is passed and no DTCs are retrieved, repair by symptom. See SYMPTOM CHART under SYSTEM TESTS.

INSTRUMENT CLUSTER DTC INDEX

DTC [1]	Description	Test
B1201	Fuel Sender Circuit Failure	B
B1204	Fuel Sender Short To Ground	B
B1205	Instrument Cluster Switch 1 Assembly Circuit Failure (Open Or Short To Voltage)	AA
B1208	Instrument Cluster Switch 1 Assembly Circuit Short To Ground	AA
B1342	ECU Defective	[2]
B2143	NVM Memory Failure	V

[1] – Codes listed in this table are only for testing covered in this article. For complete DTC listing, see MODULE COMMUNICATIONS NETWORK – TOWN CAR article.

[2] – Using NGS tester, retrieve and record DTCs. Clear DTCs and perform instrument cluster Self-Test. If DTC B1342 still exists, replace instrument cluster.

LIGHTING CONTROL MODULE DTC INDEX

DTC [1]	Description	Test
B1342	ECU Defective	[2]
B1581	Panel Dim Increase Input Circuit Short To Voltage	AJ
B1585	Panel Dim Decrease Input Short To Voltage	AJ

[1] – Codes listed in this table are only for testing covered in this article. For complete DTC listing, see MODULE COMMUNICATIONS NETWORK – TOWN CAR article.

[2] – Using NGS tester, retrieve and document all continuous. Perform LCM self-test. If DTC B1342 is retrieved again, replace LCM.

SYSTEM TESTS

CAUTION: When battery is disconnected or modules are replaced, vehicle computer and memory systems may lose memory data. Driveability problems may exist until computer systems have completed a relearn cycle. See COMPUTER RELEARN PROCEDURES article in GENERAL INFORMATION before disconnecting battery.

NOTE: Before beginning system tests, perform TROUBLE SHOOTING.

NOTE: After repairs are complete, ensure all components are properly installed and all harness connectors are connected properly. Repeat data link diagnostic test. See DATA LINK DIAGNOSTIC TEST under COMMUNICATIONS NETWORK DIAGNOSTICS in MODULE COMMUNICATIONS NETWORK – TOWN CAR article.

SYMPTOM CHART

Symptom	Test
No Communication With Instrument Cluster	A
Fuel Gauge Inaccurate	B
Engine Coolant Temperature Gauge Inaccurate	C
Oil Pressure Indicator Never/Always On	D
Speedometer Inoperative	E

SYMPTOM CHART (Cont.)

Symptom	Test
Safety Belt Warning Indicator Inoperative Or Erratic (Chime Operative)	F
Door Ajar Indicator Inoperative Or Erratic (Chime Operative)	G
Charge System Warning Indicator Never/Always On	H
Brake Warning Never/Always On	J
High Beam Indicator Inoperative/Always On	K
Low Washer Display Inoperative/Always On	L
ABS Warning Indicator Inoperative/Always On	M
Traction Control Warning Display Inoperative/Always On	N
O/D OFF Warning Display Inoperative/Always On	P
Air Suspension Display Inoperative/Always On	Q
Speed Control Display Inoperative/Always On	R
Check TRAC Warning Indicator Inoperative/Always On	S
Service Engine Soon Indicator Inoperative/Always On	T
Turn/Hazard Indicator Inoperative/Always On	U
Odometer Inoperative	V
Fail-Safe Cooling Indicator Inoperative/Always On	W
No Communication With Lighting Control Module (LCM)	X
Clock Operation Erratic/Inoperative	Y
Message Center Not Operating Properly	Z
Message Center Switch Not Operating Properly	AA
Trunk Lid Ajar Indicator Not Operating Properly	AB
Seat Belt Warning Chime Not Operating Properly	AC
Key-In-Ignition Chime Not Operating Properly	AD
Door Ajar Chime Not Operating Properly	AE
Headlight Reminder Not Operating Properly	AF
Driver's Door Chime Sounds With Key Removed From Ignition & Headlights Off	AG
Air Bag Warning Chime Not Operating Properly	AH
Trunk Lid Ajar Chime Not Operating Properly	AI
Dash Dimming Control Inoperative	AJ
Single Dash Light Inoperative	AK

TEST A: NO COMMUNICATION WITH INSTRUMENT CLUSTER

1) Turn ignition switch to LOCK position. Disconnect instrument cluster harness connector C255. Turn ignition switch to RUN position. Measure voltage at terminal No. 9 (Gray/Yellow wire) at instrument cluster harness connector C255. See Fig. 4. If battery voltage exists, go to next step. If battery voltage does not exist, go to step **3)**.

2) Turn ignition switch to LOCK position. Measure resistance between ground and terminal No. 10 (Pink/Orange wire) at instrument cluster harness connector C255. If resistance is 5 ohms or less, diagnose network concern. See MODULE COMMUNICATIONS NETWORK – TOWN CAR article. If resistance is greater than 5 ohms, repair open in Pink/Orange wire.

3) Turn ignition switch to LOCK position. Remove fuse No. 4 (7.5-amp) from instrument panel fuse box. Inspect fuse. If fuse is okay, go to next step. If fuse is blown, go to step **5)**.

4) Turn ignition switch to RUN position. Measure voltage at input side of fuse No. 4 in instrument panel fuse box. If battery voltage exists, repair open in Gray/Yellow wire between instrument panel fuse box and instrument cluster. If battery voltage does not exist, repair open in Pink/Black wire between instrument panel fuse box and ignition switch.

5) Ensure fuse No. 4 is still removed. Turn ignition switch to LOCK position. Measure resistance between ground and terminal No. 9 (Gary/Yellow wire) at instrument cluster harness connector C255. If resistance is 10 k/ohms or less, repair short to ground in Gray/Yellow wire. If resistance is greater than 10 k/ohms, replace fuse No. 4 (7.5-amp) and retest system. If fuse blows again, repair or replace instrument cluster as necessary.

TEST B: FUEL GAUGE INACCURATE

1) Turn ignition switch to LOCK position. Connect NGS tester to Data Link Connector (DLC). Turn ignition switch to RUN position. Using NGS tester, retrieve and record continuous instrument cluster DTCs. Clear instrument cluster DTCs. Using NGS tester, perform instrument cluster self-test. If DTC B1201 or B1204 is not retrieved, go to next step. If DTC B1201 or B1204 are retrieved, go to step **5)**.

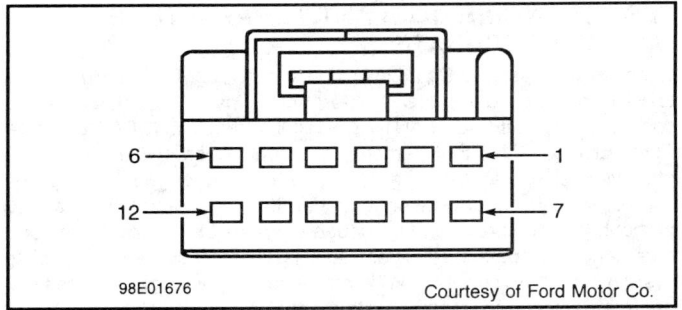

98E01676   Courtesy of Ford Motor Co.

Fig. 4: Identifying Instrument Cluster Harness Connector C255 Terminals

2) Using NGS tester, select instrument cluster active command FUEL LEVEL CONTROL. Trigger FUELLEVEL. Scroll FUEL LEVEL to 0 percent, 50 percent, then 100 percent while observing fuel gauge. Fuel gauge should display empty at 0 percent, half at 50 percent and full at 100 percent. If fuel gauge operates as described, go to next step. If fuel gauge does not operate as described, replace instrument cluster.

3) Turn ignition switch to LOCK position. Disconnect fuel pump/gauge sensor assembly harness connector C464. Connect one lead of Instrument Gauge System Tester (K26707-A) to ground and the other lead to terminal No. 8 (Yellow/White wire) at fuel pump/gauge sensor assembly harness connector C464. See Fig. 5. Set instrument gauge system tester to 15 ohms. Fuel gauge should read empty of below. Set instrument gauge system tester to 160 ohms. After one minute, fuel gauge should read full of greater. Set instrument gauge system tester to 15 ohms again. After one minute fuel gauge should read empty of below. If fuel gauge operates as described, go to next step. If fuel gauge does not operate as described, go to step **5)**.

4) Visually inspect fuel tank. If fuel tank is okay, inspect fuel pump/gauge sensor assembly and repair or replace as necessary. If fuel tank is damaged, repair or replace fuel tank as necessary.

5) Turn ignition switch to LOCK position. Disconnect fuel pump/gauge sensor harness connector C464. Disconnect instrument cluster harness connector C255. Measure resistance in Yellow/White wire between terminal No. 12 at instrument cluster harness connector C255 and terminal No. 8 at fuel pump/gauge sensor assembly harness connector C464. See Figs. 4 and 5. Resistance should be 5 ohms or less. Measure resistance between ground and terminal No. 12 (Yellow/White wire) at instrument cluster harness connector C255. Resistance should be greater than 10 k/ohms. If both resistance readings are as specified, go to next step. If either resistance reading is not as specified, repair open or short in Yellow/White wire as necessary.

6) Measure resistance between ground and terminal No. 5 (Pink/Orange wire) at fuel pump/gauge sensor harness connector C464. If resistance is 5 ohms or less, replace instrument cluster. If resistance is greater than 5 ohms, repair open in Pink/Orange wire.

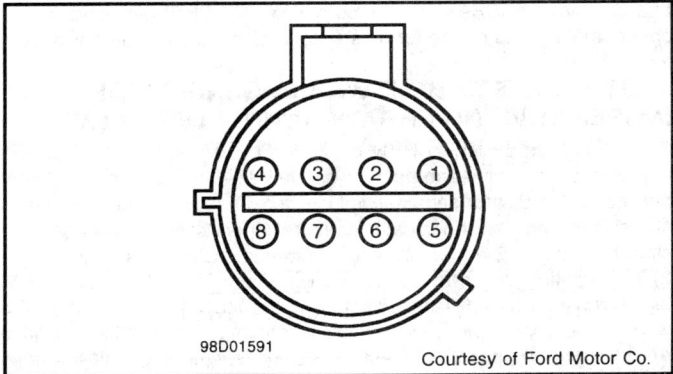

98D01591   Courtesy of Ford Motor Co.

Fig. 5: Identifying Fuel Pump/Gauge Sensor Assembly Harness Connector C464 Terminals

TEST C: ENGINE COOLANT TEMPERATURE GAUGE INACCURATE

Connect NGS tester to Data Link Connector (DLC). Turn ignition switch to RUN position. Using NGS tester, select instrument cluster active command ENGINE COOLANT CONTROL. Trigger ENGCOOLNT ON. Scroll ENGCOOLNT to 0 percent, 50 percent, then 100 percent while observing temperature gauge. Engine coolant temperature gauge should display cold at 0 percent, half at 50 percent and full hot at 100 percent. If coolant temperature gauge operates as specified, temperature gauge is operating properly at this time. Check engine cooling system for other possible problems. If temperature gauge does not operate as specified, replace instrument cluster.

TEST D: OIL PRESSURE INDICATOR NEVER/ALWAYS ON

1) Turn ignition switch to RUN position. Observe oil pressure indicator. Start engine and observe oil pressure indicator. If indicator operates properly, system is okay at this time. If indicator is inoperative, go to next step. If indicator is always on, go to step 3).

2) Turn ignition switch to LOCK position. Disconnect engine oil pressure switch harness connector. Turn ignition switch to RUN position. If oil pressure indicator is off, go to next step. If oil pressure indicator is on, replace engine oil pressure switch.

3) Turn ignition switch to LOCK position. Disconnect engine oil pressure switch harness connector. Turn ignition switch to RUN position. Connect jumper wire between ground and engine oil pressure switch harness connector. If oil pressure indicator is on, go to next step. If oil pressure indicator is off, go to step 6).

4) Turn ignition switch to LOCK position. Disconnect instrument cluster harness connector C255. Measure resistance between ground and terminal No. 2 (White/Red wire) at instrument cluster harness connector C255. See Fig. 4 . Resistance should be greater than 10 k/ohms. Measure resistance in White/Red wire between engine oil pressure switch harness connector and terminal No. 2 at instrument cluster harness connector C255. Resistance should be 5 ohms or less. If both resistance readings are as specified, go to next step. If either resistance reading is not as specified, repair open or short in White/Red wire.

5) Check continuity of oil pressure indicator bulb. If continuity exists, replace instrument cluster. If continuity does not exist, replace bulb.

6) Manually check engine oil pressure. If engine oil pressure is within specification, replace engine oil pressure switch. If engine oil pressure is not within specification, repair engine oiling system as necessary.

TEST E: SPEEDOMETER INOPERATIVE

Turn ignition switch to LOCK position. Connect NGS tester to Data Link Connector (DLC). Turn ignition switch to RUN position. Using NGS tester, select instrument cluster active command SPEEDOMETER COMMAND. Trigger SPDOMETER. Scroll in increments of 5 percent while monitoring speedometer. Speedometer indication should increase by 10 MPH for every 5 percent on NGS tester. If speedometer performs as specified, repair vehicle speed signal circuit. See appropriate ANTI-LOCK article in BRAKES in appropriate MITCHELL® manual. If speedometer does not perform as specified, replace instrument cluster.

TEST F: SAFETY BELT WARNING INDICATOR INOPERATIVE OR ERRATIC (CHIME OPERATIVE)

1) Turn ignition switch to RUN position. Observe safety belt warning indicator. Start engine and observe safety belt warning indicator. Safety belt warning indicator should illuminate for 60 seconds after vehicle is started then turn off. If indicator does not operate properly, go to next step. If indicator operates properly, system is okay at this time.

2) Turn ignition switch to LOCK position. Connect NGS tester to Data Link Connector (DLC). Turn ignition switch to RUN position. Using NGS tester, select instrument cluster active command WARNING LAMPS AND CHIME. Trigger SBLT LAMP. If safety belt warning indicator does not illuminate, go to next step. If safety belt warning indicator illuminates, perform TEST AC: SEAT BELT WARNING CHIME NOT OPERATING PROPERLY.

3) Turn ignition switch to LOCK position. Remove instrument cluster. Check continuity of safety belt warning indicator bulb. If continuity exists, replace instrument cluster. If continuity does not exist, replace bulb.

TEST G: DOOR AJAR INDICATOR INOPERATIVE OR ERRATIC (CHIME OPERATIVE)

1) Turn ignition switch to RUN position. Open driver door. If door ajar indicator illuminates and chime sounds, system is okay at this time. If chime operates and door ajar indicator is inoperative, go to next step. If chime is inoperative and door ajar indicator illuminates, perform TEST AE: DOOR AJAR CHIME NOT OPERATING PROPERLY.

2) Turn ignition switch to LOCK position. Connect NGS tester to Data Link Connector (DLC). Turn ignition switch to RUN position. Using NGS tester, select instrument cluster active command WARNING LAMPS AND CHIME. Trigger and monitor AJAR LAMP active command. If DOOR AJAR is displayed in left message center, go to next step. If DOOR AJAR is not displayed in left message center, replace instrument cluster.

3) A problem exists in door ajar circuit. Using NGS tester, check Parameter Identification (PID) for Driver's Door Module (DDM). Check SCP bus communications. See MODULE COMMUNICATIONS NETWORK – TOWN CAR article. Check door pin switches. Check wiring between door pin switches and DDM. See appropriate wiring diagram in ILLUMINATION/INTERIOR LIGHTS article.

TEST H: CHARGE SYSTEM WARNING INDICATOR NEVER/ALWAYS ON

1) Check charging system operation. If charging system is operating properly, go to next step. If charging system is not operating properly, repair charging system as necessary. See appropriate GENERATORS article in STARTING & CHARGING SYSTEMS.

2) Turn ignition switch to RUN position. Observe charge system warning indicator. If charge system warning indicator is off, go to next step. If charge system warning indicator is on, go to step 5).

3) Turn ignition switch to LOCK position. Disconnect instrument cluster harness connector C254. Disconnect generator/voltage regulator 3-terminal harness connector C154. Measure resistance in Light Green/Red wire between generator/voltage regulator 3-terminal harness connector C154 and terminal No. 15 at instrument cluster harness connector C254. See Fig. 6. If resistance is 5 ohms or less, go to next step. If resistance is greater than 5 ohms, repair open in Light Green/Red wire.

4) Check continuity of charge system warning indicator bulb. If continuity exists, replace instrument cluster. If continuity does not exist, replace bulb.

5) Turn ignition switch to LOCK position. Disconnect generator/voltage regulator 3-terminal harness connector C154. Measure resistance between ground and Light Green/Red wire at generator/voltage regulator 3-terminal harness connector C154. If resistance is greater than 10 k/ohms, replace instrument cluster. If resistance is 10 k/ohms or less, repair short to ground in Light Green/Red wire.

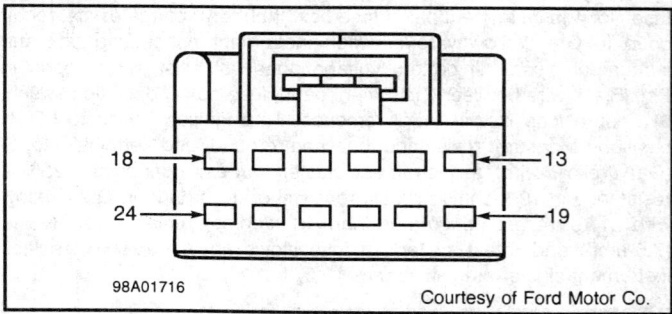

98A01716   Courtesy of Ford Motor Co.

Fig. 6: Identifying Instrument Cluster Harness Connector C254 Terminals

TEST J: BRAKE WARNING NEVER/ALWAYS ON

1) Ensure brake fluid is at proper level and parking brake is released. Start engine and operate brake system. If brake system operates properly, go to next step. If brake system does not operate properly,

repair brake system as necessary. See appropriate ANTI-LOCK article in BRAKES in appropriate MITCHELL® manual.

2) Turn ignition switch to RUN position. BRAKE warning indicator should illuminate. Start engine. BRAKE warning indicator should illuminate when ignition switch is in START position then go off after engine has been started. If BRAKE warning indicator operates as described, system is okay at this time. If BRAKE warning indicator is always on, go to next step. If BRAKE warning indicator is never on, go to step **8)**.

3) Turn ignition switch to LOCK position. Disconnect parking brake switch harness connector C296. Turn ignition switch to RUN position. If BRAKE warning indicator is on, go to next step. If BRAKE warning indicator is not on, replace parking brake switch.

4) Turn ignition switch to LOCK position. Disconnect brake fluid level switch harness connector C170. Turn ignition switch to RUN position. If BRAKE warning indicator is not on, go to next step. If BRAKE warning indicator is on, repair short to ground in Violet/White wire between brake fluid level switch and instrument cluster.

NOTE: Ensure brake fluid reservoir is full.

---

5) Measure resistance between terminals No. 1 (Black wire) and No. 3 (Violet wire) at brake fluid level switch (component side). Resistance should be greater than 10 k/ohms. Measure resistance between terminals No. 2 (Tan/Black wire) and No. 3 (Violet wire) at brake fluid level switch (component side). Resistance should be 5 ohms or less. If both resistance readings are as specified, go to next step. If either resistance reading is not as specified, replace brake fluid level switch.

6) Turn ignition switch to LOCK position. Measure resistance between ground and terminal No. 2 (Tan/Black wire) at brake fluid level switch harness connector C170. Resistance should be greater than 10 k/ohms. Turn ignition switch to START position while repeating resistance measurement. Resistance should be 5 ohms or less with ignition switch in START position. If either resistance reading is not as specified, go to next step. If both resistance readings are as specified, replace instrument cluster.

7) Turn ignition switch to LOCK position. Disconnect ignition switch harness connector C292. Measure resistance in Tan/Black wire between terminal No. 2 at brake fluid level switch harness connector and terminal No. P2 at ignition switch harness connector C292. *See Fig. 7.* If resistance is 5 ohms or less, test ignition switch. See IGNITION SWITCH under COMPONENT TEST in STEERING COLUMN SWITCHES – TOWN CAR article. If resistance is greater than 5 ohms, repair open in Tan/Black wire between ignition switch and brake fluid level switch.

8) Turn ignition switch to LOCK position. Remove instrument cluster. Check continuity of brake system warning indicator bulb. If continuity exists, go to next step. If no continuity exists, replace bulb.

9) Turn ignition switch to LOCK position. Disconnect brake fluid level switch harness connector C170. Measure resistance in Violet/White wire between terminal No. 2 at brake fluid level switch harness connector and terminal No. 14 at instrument cluster harness connector C254. *See Fig. 6.* If resistance is 5 ohms or less, go to step **5)** . If resistance is greater than 5 ohms, repair open in Violet/White wire.

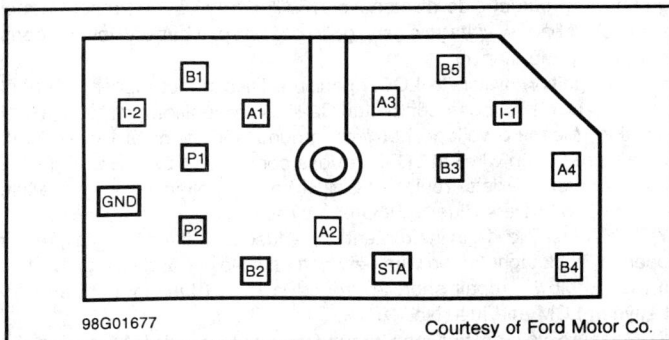

Fig. 7: Identifying Ignition Switch Harness Connector C292 Terminals

98G01677

Courtesy of Ford Motor Co.

TEST K: HIGH BEAM INDICATOR INOPERATIVE/ALWAYS ON

1) Turn ignition switch to RUN position. Turn headlights on. Place multifunction switch in high beam position. If high beams are on, go to next step. If high beams are not on, perform TEST C: HIGH BEAMS INOPERATIVE under SYSTEM TESTS in AUTOLAMP SYSTEMS – TOWN CAR article.

2) Connect NGS tester to Data Link Connector (DLC). Turn ignition switch to RUN position. Using NGS tester, select instrument cluster active command WARNING LAMPS AND CHIME. Trigger HIGH BEAM ON. If high beam indicator is not on, go to next step. If high beam indicator is on, perform TEST C: HIGH BEAMS INOPERATIVE under SYSTEM TESTS in AUTOLAMP SYSTEMS – TOWN CAR article.

3) Turn ignition switch to LOCK position. Remove instrument cluster. Check continuity of high beam indicator bulb. If continuity exists, replace instrument cluster. If continuity does not exist, replace bulb.

TEST L: LOW WASHER DISPLAY INOPERATIVE/ALWAYS ON

1) Turn ignition switch to LOCK position. Connect NGS tester to Data Link Connector (DLC). Turn ignition switch to RUN position. Using NGS tester, select instrument cluster active command FRONT WINDSHIELD WIPER. Trigger FLUID LOW active command. If WASHER is displayed, go to next step. If WASHER is not displayed, replace instrument cluster.

2) Turn ignition switch to LOCK position. Disconnect washer fluid level switch harness connector C1021. Turn ignition switch to RUN position. If WASHER is displayed, repair short to ground in Pink/Yellow wire between washer fluid level switch and instrument cluster. If WASHER is not displayed, replace washer fluid level switch.

TEST M: ABS WARNING INDICATOR INOPERATIVE/ALWAYS ON

1) Turn ignition switch to LOCK position. Connect NGS tester to Data Link Connector (DLC). Turn ignition switch to RUN position. Using NGS tester, select instrument cluster active command INDICATOR LAMP CONTROL. Trigger ABS LAMP active command. If ABS warning indicator is not illuminated, go to next step. If ABS warning indicator is illuminated, diagnosis anti-lock brake system concern. See appropriate ANTI-LOCK article in BRAKES in appropriate MITCHELL® manual.

2) Turn ignition switch to LOCK position. Remove instrument cluster. Check continuity of ABS warning indicator bulb. If continuity exists, replace instrument cluster. If continuity does not exist, replace bulb.

TEST N: TRACTION CONTROL WARNING DISPLAY INOPERATIVE/ALWAYS ON

Turn ignition switch to LOCK position. Connect NGS tester to Data Link Connector (DLC). Turn ignition switch to RUN position. Using NGS tester, select instrument cluster active command INDICATOR LAMP CONTROL. Trigger ACTIVELMP active command. Monitor left message center display for TRAC ACTIVE indicator. Select instrument cluster active command INDICATOR LAMP CONTROL II. Trigger TRAC OFF active command. Monitor left message center display for TRAC OFF. If left message center display is as described, repair traction control system concern. See appropriate ANTI-LOCK article in BRAKES in appropriate MITCHELL® manual for diagnosis of traction control system. If left message center display is not as described, replace instrument cluster.

TEST P: O/D OFF WARNING DISPLAY INOPERATIVE/ALWAYS ON

Turn ignition switch to LOCK position. Connect NGS tester to Data Link Connector (DLC). Turn ignition switch to RUN position. Using NGS tester, select instrument cluster active command INDICATOR LAMP CONTROL. Trigger O/DOFFLMP active command. Monitor left message center display. If left message center displays O/D OFF, repair overdrive system as necessary. See appropriate MITCHELL® TRANSMISSION SERVICE & REPAIR manual. If left message center does not display O/D OFF, replace instrument cluster.

TEST Q: AIR SUSPENSION DISPLAY INOPERATIVE/ALWAYS ON

Turn ignition switch to LOCK position. Connect NGS tester to Data Link Connector (DLC). Turn ignition switch to RUN position. Using NGS tester, select instrument cluster active command AIR SUSPENSION CONTROL. Trigger WARN MSG active command. Monitor left message center display. If AIR SUSPENSION is displayed, repair air suspension. See appropriate ELECTRONIC article in SUSPENSION in appropriate MITCHELL® manual. If left message center does not display AIR SUSPENSION, replace instrument cluster.

TEST R: SPEED CONTROL DISPLAY INOPERATIVE/ALWAYS ON

Turn ignition switch to LOCK position. Connect NGS tester to Data Link Connector (DLC). Turn ignition switch to RUN position. Using NGS tester, select instrument cluster active command INDICATOR LAMP CONTROL II. Trigger SC SET active command. Monitor left message center display. If SPEED CONTROL is displayed, repair cruise control system concern. See CRUISE CONTROL SYSTEMS – TOWN CAR article. If SPEED CONTROL is not displayed, replace instrument cluster.

TEST S: CHECK TRAC WARNING INDICATOR INOPERATIVE/ALWAYS ON

1) Turn ignition switch to LOCK position. Connect NGS tester to Data Link Connector (DLC). Turn ignition switch to RUN position. Using NGS tester, select instrument cluster active command INDICATOR LAMP CONTROL II. Trigger CHK TRAC active command. If CHECK TRAC warning indicator is not displayed, go to next step. If CHECK TRAC warning indicator is displayed, repair traction control concern. See appropriate ANTI-LOCK article in BRAKES in appropriate MITCH-ELL® manual.

2) Turn ignition switch to LOCK position. Remove instrument cluster. Check continuity of CHECK TRAC warning indicator bulb. If continuity exists, replace instrument cluster. If continuity does not exist, replace bulb.

TEST T: SERVICE ENGINE SOON INDICATOR INOPERATIVE/ALWAYS ON

1) Turn ignition switch to LOCK position. Connect NGS tester to Data Link Connector (DLC). Turn ignition switch to RUN position. Using NGS tester, select instrument cluster active command INDICATOR LAMP CONTROL. Trigger MIL active command. If SERVICE ENGINE SOON warning indicator is not displayed, go to next step. If SERVICE ENGINE SOON indicator is displayed, diagnosis engine control concern. See appropriate SELF-DIAGNOSTICS article in ENGINE PERFORMANCE in appropriate MITCHELL® manual.

2) Turn ignition switch to LOCK position. Remove instrument cluster. Check continuity of SERVICE ENGINE SOON warning indicator bulb. If continuity exists, replace instrument cluster. If continuity does not exist, replace bulb.

TEST U: TURN/HAZARD INDICATOR INOPERATIVE/ALWAYS ON

1) Turn ignition switch to RUN position. Operate turn signals in both directions. Operate hazard lights. If turn signal and hazard lights operate properly, go to next step. If turn signal and hazard lights do not operate properly, repair turn signal concern. See AUTOLAMP SYSTEM – TOWN CAR article.

2) Turn ignition switch to LOCK position. Remove instrument cluster. Check continuity of inoperative turn signal indicator bulb. If continuity exists, go to next step. If continuity does not exist, replace bulb.

3) Turn ignition switch to RUN position. With right turn signal on, measure voltage between ground and terminal No. 5 (White/Light Blue wire) at instrument cluster harness connector C255. See Fig. 4. With left turn signal on, measure voltage between ground and terminal No. 4 (Light Green/White wire) at instrument cluster harness connector C255. If voltage fluctuates from 0-12 volts, replace instrument cluster. If voltage does not fluctuate from 0-12 volts, repair open in appropriate circuit.

TEST V: ODOMETER INOPERATIVE

NOTE: If instrument cluster does not receive odometer rolling count status for 2 seconds, dashes will be displayed in odometer display and ABS warning indicator light will illuminate.

1) Turn ignition switch to LOCK position. Connect NGS tester to Data Link Connector (DLC). Turn ignition switch to RUN position. Using NGS tester, retrieve instrument cluster DTCs. If DTC B2143 is not present, go to next step. If DTC B2143 is present, see appropriate ANTI-LOCK article in BRAKES in appropriate MITCHELL® manual.

2) Using NGS tester, select instrument cluster ODOMETER READING function test. If NGS tester retrieves odometer reading, see appropriate ANTI-LOCK article in BRAKES in appropriate MITCHELL® manual. If NGS tester does not retrieve odometer reading, replace instrument cluster.

TEST W: FAIL-SAFE COOLING INDICATOR INOPERATIVE/ALWAYS ON

1) Turn ignition switch to RUN position. Fail-safe cooling indicator should illuminate for 3 seconds (prove-out cycle), then turn off. If indicator operates as specified, system is okay at this time. If indicator is never on, go to next step. If indicator is always on, see appropriate SELF-DIAGNOSTICS article in ENGINE PERFORMANCE in appropriate MITCHELL® manual.

2) Turn ignition switch to LOCK position. Remove instrument cluster. Check continuity of fail-safe cooling indicator bulb. If continuity exists, replace instrument cluster. If continuity does not exist, replace bulb.

TEST X: NO COMMUNICATION WITH LIGHTING CONTROL MODULE (LCM)

1) Turn ignition switch to LOCK position. Connect NGS tester to Data Link Connector (DLC). Turn ignition switch to RUN position. Using NGS tester, monitor LCM PID IGN_LC. If result is not UNABLE TO PERFORM TEST/FUNCTION, MODULE NOT RESPONDING: LCM, CHECK IGNITION STATUS/VERIFY CABLE REQUIREMENTS or CHECK CABLE CONNECTION, go to next step. If result is UNABLE TO PERFORM TEST/FUNCTION, MODULE NOT RESPONDING: LCM, CHECK IGNITION STATUS/VERIFY CABLE REQUIREMENTS or CHECK CABLE CONNECTION, go to step 8).

2) Using NGS tester, monitor LCM PID IGN_LC while cycling key through all positions except START. If PID does not show OFF in all positions, go to next step. If PID shows OFF in all positions, go to step 5).

3) Turn ignition switch to RUN position. Measure voltage between ground and output side of fuse No. 14 (7.5–amp) in instrument panel fuse box. If battery voltage does not exist, go to next step. If battery voltage exists, repair open Red/Yellow wire between LCM and fuse No. 14.

4) Check fuse No. 14 in instrument panel fuse box. If fuse is okay, repair open in White/Yellow wire between fuse No. 14 and ignition switch. If fuse is blown, repair short to ground in Red/Yellow wire between LCM and instrument panel fuse No. 14.

5) Turn ignition switch to RUN position. Measure voltage between ground and output side of fuse No. 18 (7.5–amp) in instrument panel fuse box. If battery voltage exists, go to next step. If battery voltage does not exist, go to step 7).

6) Turn ignition switch to LOCK position. Disconnect Lighting Control Module (LCM) harness connector C220. Turn ignition switch to RUN position. Measure voltage between ground and terminal No. 6 (Dark Blue/Light Green wire) at LCM harness connector C220. See Fig. 8. If battery voltage exists, replace LCM. If battery voltage does not exist, repair open in Dark Blue/Light Green wire.

7) Check fuse No. 18 in instrument panel fuse box. If fuse is okay, repair open in Black/Light Green wire between fuse No. 18 and ignition switch. If fuse is blown, repair short to ground in Dark Blue/Light Green wire between LCM and fuse No. 18.

8) Measure voltage between ground and output side of fuse No. 31 (7.5–amp) in instrument panel fuse box. If battery voltage does not exist, go to next step. If battery voltage exists, go to step 12).

9) Check fuse No. 31 in instrument panel fuse box. If fuse is blown, go to next step. If fuse is okay, repair open in Dark Blue/Orange wire between fuse No. 31 and power distribution box fuse No. 7.

10) Turn ignition switch to LOCK position. Disconnect headlight switch harness connector. Disconnect Lighting Control Module (LCM) harness connector C221. Measure resistance between ground and terminal No. 25 (Orange/White wire) at LCM harness connector C221. *See Fig. 9.* If resistance is greater than 10 k/ohms, go to next step. If resistance is 10 k/ohms or less, repair short to ground in Orange/White wire.

11) Connect headlight switch harness connector. Measure resistance between ground and terminal No. 25 (Orange/White wire) at LCM harness connector C221. If resistance is greater than 10 k/ohms, go to next step. If resistance is 10 k/ohms or less, replace headlight switch.

12) Disconnect Lighting Control Module (LCM) harness connector C221. Measure voltage between ground and terminal No. 25 (Orange/White wire) at LCM harness connector C221. *See Fig. 9.* If battery voltage exists, go to next step. If battery voltage does not exist, repair open in Orange/White wire.

13) Disconnect Lighting Control Module (LCM) harness connector C222. Measure resistance between ground and terminal No. 23 (Pink/Orange wire) at LCM harness connector C221. Measure resistance between ground and terminal No. 13 (Pink/Orange wire) at LCM harness connector C222. *See Fig. 10.* If both resistance readings are 5 ohms or less, diagnosis network concern. See MODULE COMMUNICATIONS NETWORK – TOWN CAR article. If either resistance reading is greater than 5 ohms, repair open in appropriate Pink/Orange wire.

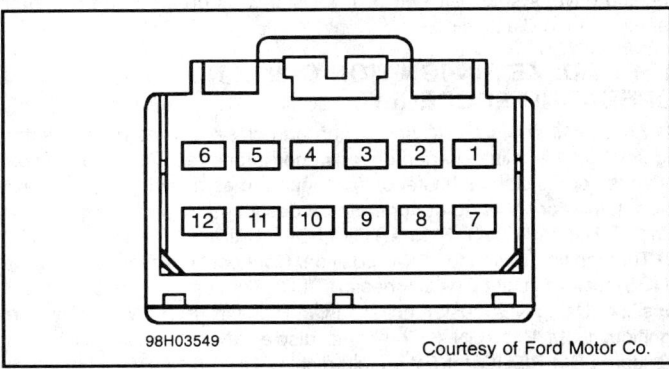

Fig. 8: Identifying Lighting Control Module Connector C220 Terminals

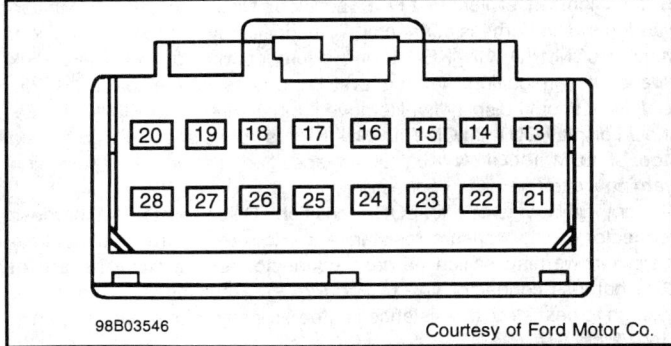

Fig. 9: Identifying Lighting Control Module Connector C221 Terminals

TEST Y: CLOCK OPERATION ERRATIC/INOPERATIVE

1) Turn ignition switch to LOCK position. Check fuse No. 19 (10-amp) in instrument panel fuse box. If fuse is okay, go to next step. If fuse is blown, repair short to ground in Red/White wire between fuse No. 19 and clock.

2) Turn ignition switch to ACC position. Disconnect clock harness connector C2009. Measure voltage at terminal No. 6 (Red/White wire) at

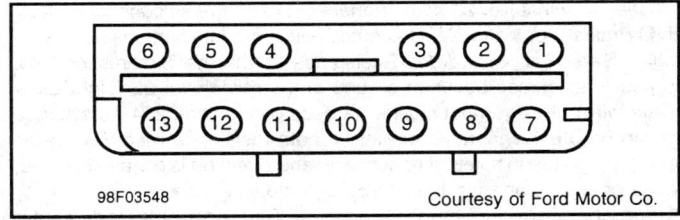

Fig. 10: Identifying Lighting Control Module Connector C222 Terminals

clock harness connector. *See Fig. 11.* If battery voltage exists, go to next step. If battery voltage does not exist, repair open in Red/White wire between fuse No. 19 and clock.

3) Turn ignition switch to LOCK position. Measure resistance between ground and terminal No. 5 (Black wire) at clock harness connector C2009. If resistance is 5 ohms or less, replace clock. If resistance is greater than 5 ohms, repair open in Black wire.

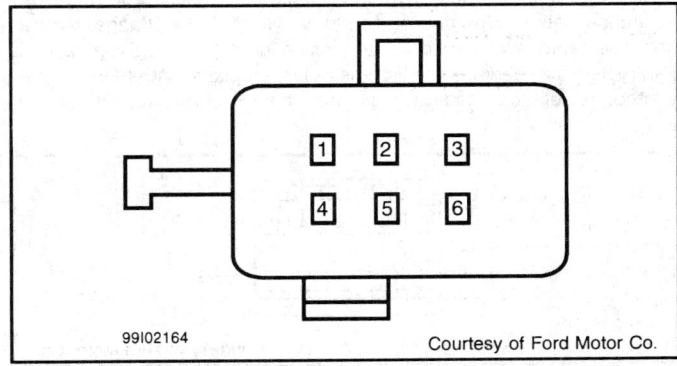

Fig. 11: Identifying Clock Harness Connector C2009 Terminals

TEST Z: MESSAGE CENTER NOT OPERATING PROPERLY

1) Turn ignition switch to LOCK position. Connect New Generation Star (NGS) tester to Data Link Connector (DLC). Turn ignition switch to RUN position. Using NGS tester, retrieve, record and clear all DTCs from all modules. Using NGS tester, perform instrument cluster self-test. If DTC B1205 or B1208 are not retrieved, go to next step. If DTC B1205 or B1208 is retrieved, perform TEST AA: MESSAGE CENTER SWITCH NOT OPERATING PROPERLY.

2) Turn ignition switch to RUN position. Observe fuel gauge operation. If fuel gauge is operating properly, go to next step. If fuel gauge does not operate properly, perform TEST B: FUEL GAUGE INACCURATE.

3) Check odometer operation. If odometer is operating properly, go to next step. If odometer does not operate properly, perform TEST V: ODOMETER INOPERATIVE.

4) Turn ignition switch to RUN position. Observe right message center display. All segments of right message center display should illuminate for approximately 6 seconds, then return to the last key ON selection setting. If right message center display responds as described, system is okay at this time. If SELECT or RESET buttons are inoperative, perform TEST AA: MESSAGE CENTER SWITCH NOT OPERATING PROPERLY. If right message center display does not respond as described, replace instrument cluster.

TEST AA: MESSAGE CENTER SWITCH NOT OPERATING PROPERLY

1) Connect New Generation Star (NGS) tester to Data Link Connector (DLC). Turn ignition switch to RUN position. Using NGS tester, retrieve, record and clear DTCs from all modules. Using NGS tester, perform instrument cluster self-test. If DTC B1205 or B1208 are not retrieved, go to next step. If DTC B1205 or B1208 is retrieved, go to step **3)**.

2) Turn ignition switch to LOCK position. Disconnect instrument cluster harness connector C254. Disconnect message center switch module harness connector C264. Measure resistance in Light Blue/White wire between terminal No. 22 at instrument cluster harness connector C254 and terminal No. 3 at message center switch module harness connector C264. *See Figs. 6 and 12.* Resistance should be 5 ohms or less. Measure resistance between ground and terminal No. 22 (Light Blue/White wire) at instrument cluster harness connector C254. Resistance should be greater than 10 k/ohms. If both resistance readings are as specified, go to next step. If either resistance reading is not as specified, repair open and/or short in Light Blue/White wire.

3) Turn ignition switch to LOCK position. Disconnect message center switch module harness connector C264. Measure resistance between terminals No. 1 and 3 at message center switch module (component side). *See Fig. 13.* With no buttons depressed, 3.3 k/ohms should exist. With SELECT button depressed, 1.25 k/ohms should exist. With RESET button depressed, .76 k/ohms should exist. With both SELECT and RESET buttons depressed, .55 k/ohms should exist. If all resistance readings are as specified, go to next step. If any resistance reading is not as specified, replace message center switch module.

4) Measure resistance between ground and terminal No. 6 (Black wire) at message center switch module harness connector C264. Measure resistance between ground and terminal No. 1 (Pink/Orange wire) at message center switch module harness connector C264. *See Fig. 12.* If both resistance readings are 5 ohms or less, replace instrument cluster. If either resistance reading is greater than 5 ohms, repair open in appropriate wire.

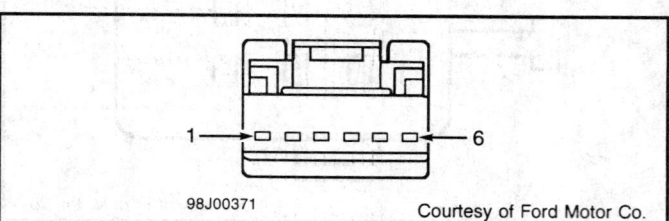

98J00371   Courtesy of Ford Motor Co.

Fig. 12: Identifying Message Center Switch Module Harness Connector C264 Terminals

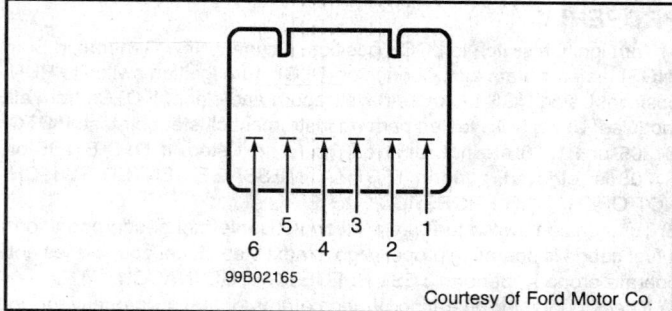

99B02165   Courtesy of Ford Motor Co.

Fig. 13: Identifying Message Center Switch Module Terminals

TEST AB: TRUNK LID AJAR INDICATOR NOT OPERATING PROPERLY

1) Turn ignition switch to RUN position. Operate trunk lid release switch. If trunk lid released, go to next step. If trunk lid did not release, repair trunk lid release. See appropriate wiring diagram in POWER DOOR LOCKS & TRUNK RELEASE article.

2) Turn ignition switch to LOCK position. Connect New Generation Star (NGS) tester to Data Link Connector (DLC). Using NGS tester, select LCM PID. Select LCM PID DECKLID. Monitor PID while opening and closing trunk lid. If PID agrees with trunk lid position and TRUNK AJAR is not displayed when trunk lid is open, replace instrument cluster. If PID does not agree with trunk lid position, repair trunk lid switch circuit. See appropriate wiring diagram in POWER DOOR LOCKS & TRUNK RELEASE article.

TEST AC: SEAT BELT WARNING CHIME NOT OPERATING PROPERLY

1) Using NGS tester, monitor Lighting Control Module (LCM) PID D_SBELT while buckling and unbuckling driver's seat belt. IN should be

displayed when seat belt is buckled and OUT should be displayed when seat belt is not buckled. If NGS tester only displays IN, go to next step. If NGS tester only displays IN, go to step4). If NGS tester responds as described, replace LCM.

2) Turn ignition switch to LOCK position. Disconnect driver's seat belt switch harness connector C304. Turn ignition switch to RUN position. Using NGS tester, monitor LCM PID D_SBELT. If OUT is displayed on NGS tester, go to next step. If OUT is not displayed on NGS tester, replace driver's seat belt switch.

3) Turn ignition switch to LOCK position. Disconnect LCM harness connector C221. Measure resistance between ground and terminal No. 14 (Brown/Light Blue wire) at LCM harness connector C221. *See Fig. 9.* If resistance is greater than 10 k/ohms, replace LCM. If resistance is 10 k/ohms or less, repair short to ground in Brown/Light Blue wire.

4) Turn ignition switch to LOCK position. Disconnect driver's seat belt switch harness connector C304. Turn ignition switch to RUN position. Using a jumper wire, ground Brown/Light Blue wire at driver's seat belt switch harness connector C304. Monitor LCM PID D_SBELT. If IN is displayed, go to next step. If IN is not displayed, go to step **6)**

5) Turn ignition switch to LOCK position. Disconnect LCM harness connector C221. Measure resistance in Brown/Light Blue wire between driver's seat belt switch harness connector C304 and terminal No. 14 at LCM harness connector C211. *See Fig. 9.* If resistance is 5 ohms or less, replace LCM. If resistance is greater than 5 ohms, repair open in Brown/Light Blue wire.

6) Measure resistance between ground and Black wire at driver's seat belt switch harness connector C304. If resistance is 5 ohms or less, replace driver's seat belt switch. If resistance is greater than 5 ohms, repair open in Black wire.

TEST AD: KEY-IN-IGNITION CHIME NOT OPERATING PROPERLY

1) Ensure all doors are closed. Open and close driver's door. Interior lights should illuminate when driver's door is opened and go out when driver's door is closed. If interior lights operate as described, go to next step. If interior lights do not operate as described, repair interior lights. See AUTOLAMP SYSTEMS – TOWN CAR article.

2) Turn ignition switch to LOCK position. Connect New Generation Star (NGS) tester to Data Link Connector (DLC). Turn ignition switch to RUN position. Using NGS tester, access LCM PID IGN_KEY. When key is in ignition, LCM PID IGN_KEY should display IN. When key is not in ignition, LCM PID IGN_KEY should display OUT. If NGS display is not as specified, go to next step. If NGS display is as specified, key-in-ignition inputs are okay at this time.

3) Turn ignition switch to LOCK position. Disconnect key-in-ignition warning switch harness connector. Turn ignition switch to RUN position. Monitor LCM PID IGN_KEY. Using a jumper wire, ground Black/Pink wire at key-in-ignition warning switch harness connector. LCM PID IGN_KEY should display IN. Remove jumper wire. LCM PID IGN_KEY should display OUT. If LCM PID IGN_KEY is not as specified, go to next step. If LCM PID IGN_KEY is as specified, replace key-in-ignition warning switch harness connector.

4) Turn ignition switch to LOCK position. Disconnect LCM harness connector C221. Measure resistance in Black/Pink wire between key-in-ignition warning switch harness connector and terminal No. 15 at LCM harness connector C221. *See Fig. 9.* If resistance is 5 ohms or less, go to next step. If resistance is greater than 5 ohms, repair open in Black/Pink wire.

5) Measure resistance between ground and terminal No. 15 (Black/Pink wire) at LCM harness connector C221. If resistance is greater than 10 k/ohms, replace LCM. If resistance is 10 k/ohms or less, repair short to ground in Black/Pink wire.

TEST AE: DOOR AJAR CHIME NOT OPERATING PROPERLY

1) Open and close driver's and passenger's doors one at a time while observing courtesy lights. If courtesy lights operate properly, go to next step. If courtesy lights do not operate properly, repair courtesy lights. See AUTOLAMP SYSTEMS – TOWN CAR article.

2) Turn ignition switch to LOCK position. Connect NGS tester to Data Link Module (DLC). Using NGS tester, monitor Lighting Control Module (LCM) PID IGN_LC. If RUN is displayed, replace LCM. If RUN is not displayed, repair Red/Yellow wire between LCM and fuse No. 14 (7.5–amp) in instrument panel fuse box.

TEST AF: HEADLIGHT REMINDER NOT OPERATING PROPERLY

1) Turn headlights on. If headlights and parking lights illuminate, go to next step. If headlights and parking lights do not illuminate, repair exterior lights. See AUTOLAMP SYSTEMS – TOWN CAR.

2) Ensure all doors are closed. Open and close driver's door while observing courtesy lights. If courtesy lights operate properly, replace LCM. If courtesy lights do not operate properly, repair courtesy lights. See AUTOLAMP SYSTEMS – TOWN CAR article.

TEST AG: DRIVER'S DOOR CHIME SOUNDS WITH KEY REMOVED FROM IGNITION & HEADLIGHTS OFF

1) Ensure headlights are off. Turn ignition switch to LOCK position. Remove key from ignition. Connect NGS tester to Data Link Connector (DLC). Using NGS tester, monitor Lighting Control Module (LCM) PID IGN_KEY. If LCM PID IGN_KEY indicates IN, go to next step. If LCM PID IGN_KEY does not display IN, replace LCM.

2) Ensure ignition switch is in LOCK position. Disconnect key-in-ignition warning switch harness connector. Measure resistance between ground and Black/Pink wire at key-in-ignition warning switch harness connector. If resistance is 10 k/ohms or less, go to next step. If resistance is greater than 10 k/ohms, replace key-in-ignition warning switch.

3) Ensure ignition switch is in LOCK position. Disconnect LCM harness connector C221. Measure resistance between ground and terminal No. 22 (Black/Pink wire) at LCM harness connector C221. *See Fig. 9.* If resistance is 10 k/ohms or less, repair short to ground in Black/Pink wire. If resistance is greater than 10 k/ohms, replace LCM.

TEST AH: AIR BAG WARNING CHIME NOT OPERATING PROPERLY

1) Turn ignition switch to LOCK position. Connect NGS tester to Data Link Connector (DLC). Using NGS tester, retrieve and record Restraint Control Module (RCM) DTCs. If no RCM DTCs exist, go to next step. If any RCM DTCs exist, repair air bag system. See MITCHELL® AIR BAG SERVICE & REPAIR MANUAL, DOMESTIC & IMPORTED MODELS.

2) Turn ignition switch to LOCK position. Disconnect Lighting Control Module (LCM) harness connector C221. Measure resistance between ground and terminal No. 16 (Tan/Yellow wire) at LCM harness connector C221. *See Fig. 9.* If resistance is greater than 10 k/ohms, go to next step. If resistance is 10 k/ohms or less, repair short to ground in Tan/Yellow wire.

3) Turn ignition switch to RUN position. Measure voltage at terminal No. 16 (Tan/Yellow wire) at LCM harness connector C221. If zero volts exists, go to next step. If any voltage exists, repair short to voltage in Tan/Yellow wire.

NOTE: Deactivate air bag system. See AIR BAG RESTRAINT SYSTEMS – TOWN CAR article.

---

4) Turn ignition switch to LOCK position. Disconnect RCM harness connector C276. Measure resistance in Tan/Yellow wire between terminal No. 15 at LCM harness connector C221 and terminal No. 26 at RCM harness connector C276. *See Figs. 9 and 14.* If resistance is 5 ohms or less, replace LCM. If resistance is greater than 5 ohms, repair open in Tan/Yellow wire.

TEST AI: TRUNK LID AJAR CHIME NOT OPERATING PROPERLY

1) Turn ignition switch to LOCK position. Connect NGS tester to Data Link Connector (DLC). Using NGS tester, monitor Lighting Control Module (LCM) PID DECKLID while opening and closing trunk lid. If PID

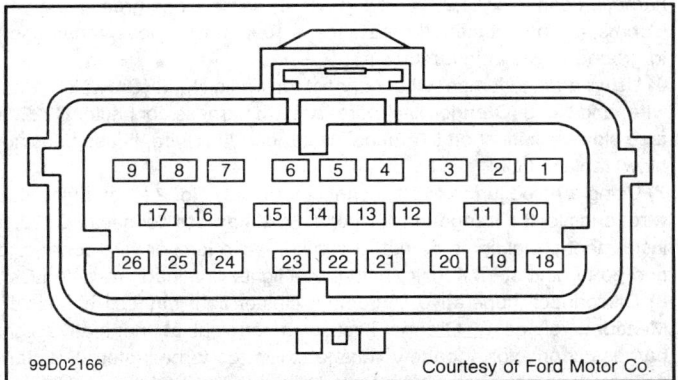

Fig. 14: Identifying RCM Harness Connector C276 Terminals

always indicates CLOSED, go to next step. If PID always indicates AJAR, go to step **5)**. If PID value agrees with trunk lid position, replace LCM.

2) Turn ignition switch to LOCK position. Disconnect trunk lid release solenoid/ajar switch harness connector C455. Measure resistance between Black and Brown/White wires at trunk lid release solenoid/ajar switch (component side). With trunk lid closed, resistance should be 5 ohms or less. If resistance is as specified, go to next step. If resistance is not as specified, replace trunk lid release solenoid/ajar switch.

3) Turn ignition switch to RUN position. Measure voltage at Brown/White wire at trunk lid release solenoid/ajar switch harness connector C455. If battery voltage exists, go to next step. If battery voltage does not exist, repair open in Brown/White wire.

4) Measure resistance between ground and Black wire at trunk lid release solenoid/ajar switch harness connector C455. If resistance is 5 ohms or less, replace LCM. If resistance is greater than 5 ohms, repair open in Black wire.

5) Turn ignition switch to LOCK position. Ensure trunk lid is open. Disconnect trunk lid release solenoid/ajar switch harness connector C455. Measure resistance between Black and Brown/White wires at trunk lid release solenoid/ajar switch (component side). With trunk lid open, resistance should be greater than 10 k/ohms. If resistance is as specified, go to next step. If resistance is not as specified, replace trunk lid release solenoid/ajar switch.

6) Disconnect LCM harness connector C220. Measure resistance between ground and terminal No. 4 (Brown/White wire) at LCM harness connector C220. *See Fig. 8.* If resistance is greater than 10 k/ohms, replace LCM. If resistance is 10 k/ohms or less, repair short to ground in Brown/White wire.

TEST AJ: DASH DIMMING CONTROL INOPERATIVE

1) Connect New Generation Star (NGS) tester to Data Link Connector (DLC). Using NGS tester, perform Lighting Control Module (LCM) self-test. If DTCs B1342, B1581 or B1585 are not retrieved, go to next step. If DTC B1581 is retrieved, go to step **10)**. If DTC B1585 is retrieved, go to step **12)**. If DTC B1342 is retrieved, clear DTC and repeat LCM self-test. If DTC B1342 is retrieved again, replace LCM.

2) Remove fuse No. 5 (7.5-amp) from instrument panel fuse box. Inspect fuse. If fuse is okay, go to next step. If fuse is blown, go to step **5)**.

3) Measure voltage at input side of fuse No. 5 in instrument panel fuse box. If battery voltage exists, install fuse and go to next step. If battery voltage does not exist, repair open in Dark Blue/Orange wire between power distribution box and instrument panel fuse box.

4) Turn ignition switch to LOCK position. Disconnect LCM harness connector C222. Measure voltage at terminal No. 2 (Gray/Light Blue wire) at LCM harness connector C222. *See Fig. 10.* If battery voltage exists, go to step **7)**. If battery voltage does not exist, repair open in Gray/Light Blue wire.

5) Ensure fuse No. 5 is still removed. Turn ignition switch to LOCK position. Disconnect LCM harness connector C222. Measure resistance between ground and terminal No. 2 (Gray/Light Blue wire) at LCM harness connector C222. *See Fig. 10.* If resistance is greater than 10 k/ohms, go to next step. If resistance is 10 k/ohms or less, repair short to ground in Gray/Light Blue wire.

6) Using a fused jumper wire, connect terminals No. 2 (Gray/Light Blue wire) and No. 3 (Orange/Black wire) at LCM harness connector C222. If fuse blows, repair short to ground in Orange/Black wire. If fuse does not blow, replace LCM.

7) Using a fused jumper wire, connect terminals No. 2 (Gray/Light Blue wire) and No. 3 (Orange/Black wire) at LCM harness connector C222. If instrument panel lights do not illuminate, leave jumper wire connected and go to next step. If instrument panel lights illuminate, replace LCM.

8) Disconnect inoperative instrument cluster light harness connector. Measure voltage at Orange/Black wire terminal at inoperative light harness connector. If battery voltage exists, go to next step. If battery voltage does not exist, repair open in Orange/Black wire.

9) Turn ignition switch to LOCK position. Measure resistance between ground and Black wire terminal at inoperative light harness connector. If resistance is 5 ohms or less, replace bulb. If resistance is greater than 5 ohms, repair open in Black wire.

10) Disconnect dimmer switch harness connector C235. Measure voltage at terminal No. 4 (Orange/Red wire) at dimmer switch harness connector C235. *See Fig. 15.* If battery voltage exists, go to next step. If battery voltage does not exist, replace dimmer switch.

11) Disconnect LCM harness connector C221. Measure voltage at terminal No. 4 (Orange/Red wire) at dimmer switch harness connector C235. If battery voltage exists, repair short to voltage in Orange/Red wire. If battery voltage does not exist, replace LCM.

12) Disconnect dimmer switch harness connector C235. Measure voltage at terminal No. 1 (Brown/White wire) at dimmer switch harness connector C235. *See Fig. 15.* If battery voltage exists, go to next step. If battery voltage does not exist, replace dimmer switch.

13) Disconnect LCM harness connector C221. Measure voltage at terminal No. 1 (Brown/White wire) at dimmer switch harness connector C235. If battery voltage exists, repair short to voltage in Brown/White wire. If battery voltage does not exist, replace LCM.

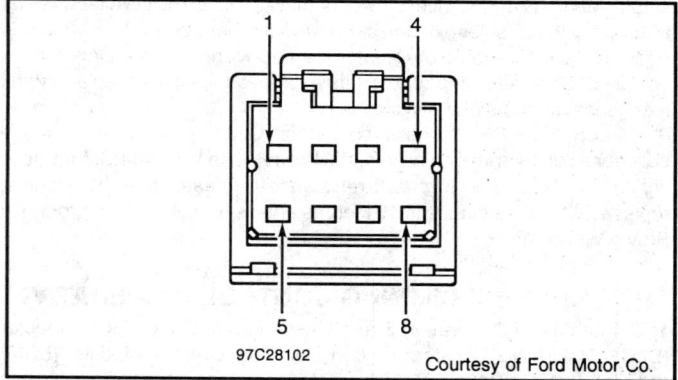

Fig. 15: Identifying Dimmer Switch Harness Connector C235 Terminals

TEST AK: SINGLE DASH LIGHT INOPERATIVE

1) Turn headlights on. Increase panel dimmer switch to maximum brightness. If any illumination source does not illuminate, go to next step. If all illumination sources illuminate, system is okay at this time.

2) Turn ignition switch to LOCK position. Disconnect inoperative light harness connector. Turn ignition switch to RUN position. Turn headlights on. Increase panel dimmer switch to maximum brightness. Measure voltage at Orange/Black wire terminal at inoperative light harness connector. If battery voltage exists, go to next step. If battery voltage does not exist, repair open in Orange/Black wire.

3) Turn ignition switch to LOCK position. Measure resistance between ground and Black wire terminal at inoperative light harness connector. If resistance is 5 ohms or less, replace bulb or component as necessary. If resistance is greater than 5 ohms, repair open in Black wire.

REMOVAL & INSTALLATION

CAUTION: When battery is disconnected or modules are replaced, vehicle computer and memory systems may lose memory data. Driveability problems may exist until computer systems have completed a relearn cycle. See COMPUTER RELEARN PROCEDURES article in GENERAL INFORMATION before disconnecting battery.

CAUTION: Electronic modules are sensitive to static electrical charges. Proper grounding of technician and workpiece is essential to prevent damage.

INSTRUMENT CLUSTER

Removal – 1) Disconnect negative battery cable. Remove radio, using Radio Removal Tool (T87P-19061-A). Remove cluster finish panel bolts inside radio opening.

2) Remove instrument cluster finish panel screws. *See Fig. 16.* Pull finish panel out at bottom and position aside. Disconnect clock harness connector from back of finish panel. Disconnect remaining harness connectors from back of finish panel and remove panel.

3) Remove lower steering column cover. Remove lower steering column metal reinforcement. Remove screw fastening transmission range indicator column bracket to steering column and position cable aside.

4) Remove 4 cluster retaining screws. Disconnect cluster harness connectors from instrument cluster back plate and remove instrument cluster.

Installation – 1) Position instrument cluster to instrument panel. Connect cluster harness connectors. Ensure transmission range cable is routed properly. Install 4 cluster retaining screws and tighten to 96-144 INCH lbs. (0.8-1.4 N.m).

2) Position transmission range indicator column bracket to steering column tube. Secure cable bracket with screw.

3) Reinstall lower steering column reinforcement. Position lower steering column shroud and install retaining screws. Connect negative battery cable and check operation of instruments.

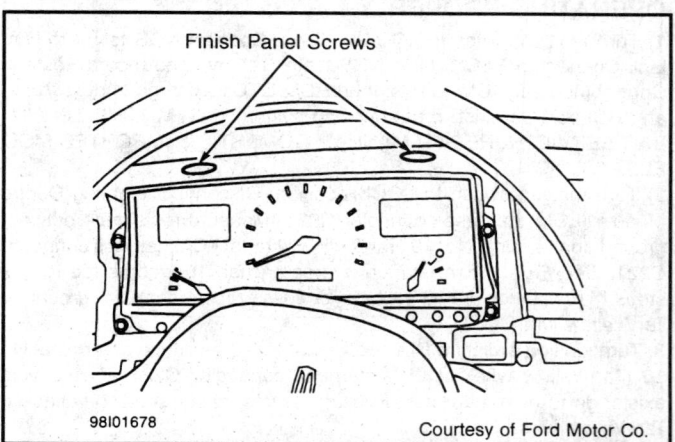

Fig. 16: Removing Instrument Panel Finish Panel Screws

WIRING DIAGRAMS

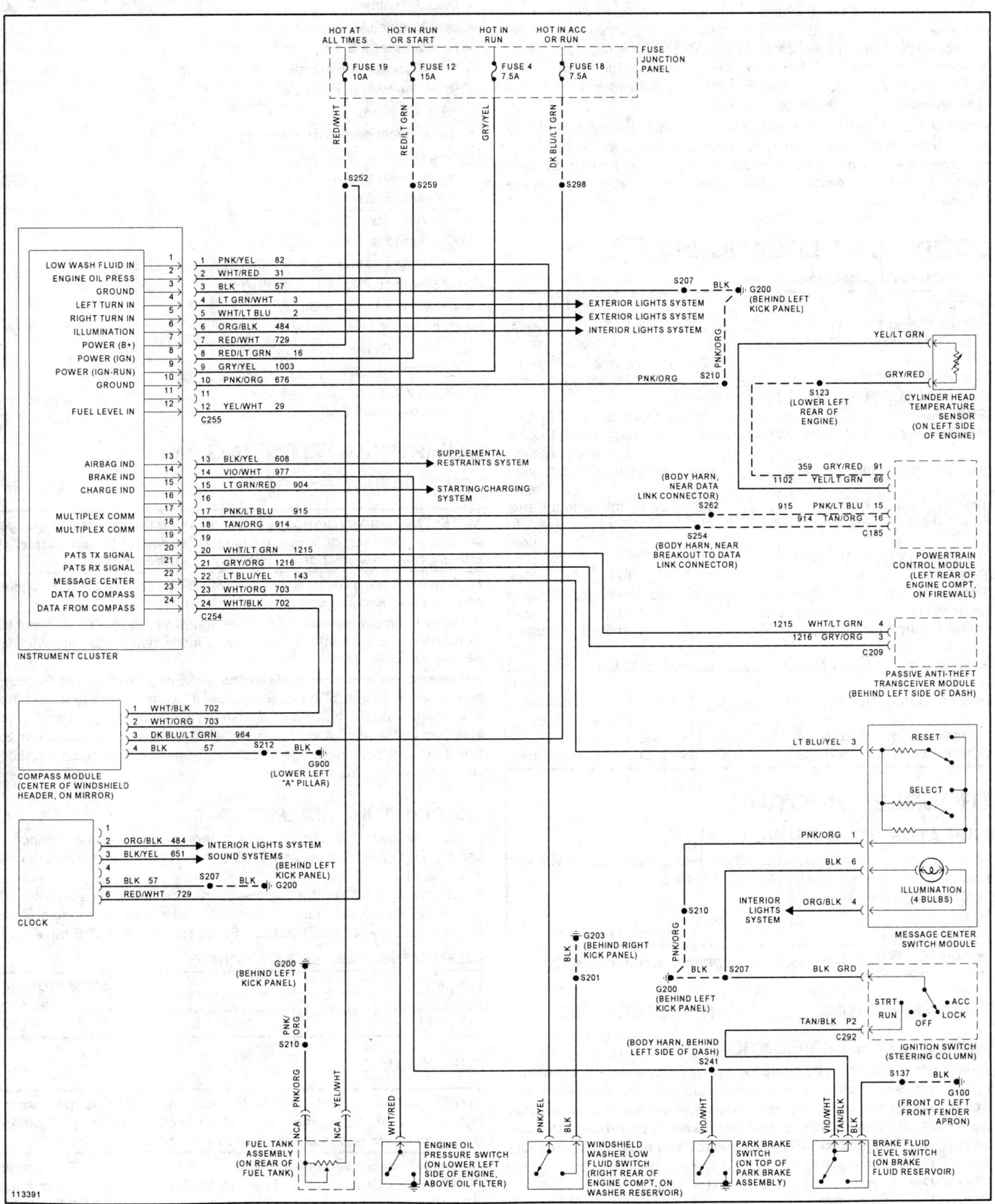

Fig. 17: Analog Instrument Panel Wiring Diagram (Town Car)

DESCRIPTION & OPERATION

Analog instrument cluster contains an analog speedometer and tachometer. Fuel gauge, temperature gauge, odometer, trip odometer and trip odometer reset button are located to right of centrally mounted speedometer. Warning/indicator lights and transmission range indicator are located in a row at bottom of cluster. Right and left turn signal indicators flank speedometer at cluster top. See Fig. 1.

Instrument cluster and instrument panel illumination is controlled by the autolamp/headlight switch rheostat resistor located on left side of instrument panel. Battery voltage to rheostat is supplied from tail light relay. Voltage from rheostat to bulbs ranges from 9.0 volts (brightest) to 0.2 volt (dimmest).

COMPONENT LOCATIONS

COMPONENT LOCATIONS

Component	Location
Air Bag Sliding Contact	In Steering Wheel
Data Link Connector (DLC)	Below Driver's Side Of Instrument Panel, To Right Of Steering Column
Engine Coolant Temperature (ECT) Sensor	Right Rear Side Of Engine
Engine Compartment Relay Box	Left Front Side Of Engine Compartment
Fuse Junction Panel	Below Left Side Of Instrument Panel
Headlight Switch Rheostat	Left Side Of Instrument Panel
Power Distribution Box	In Engine Compartment, Next To Battery
Powertrain Control Module (PCM)	Behind Glove Box
Smart Entry Control (SEC) Timer/Module	Behind Center Top Of Dash Panel
Speed Control Actuator	Left Side Of Engine Compartment
Speed Control Actuator Module	Below Left Side Of Instrument Panel
Lighting Control Module (LCM)	Bottom Of Center Console, Below Dash Panel
Transaxle Control Module (TCM)	Behind Instrument Cluster
Vehicle Speed Sensor (VSS)	Center Of Engine Compartment

TROUBLE SHOOTING

INDICATOR BULB PROVE-OUT

When ignition switch is turned to ON position, the following warning indicators will light momentarily for proof of function:

- Charging System
- Safety Belt
- Brake System
- Low Oil Pressure
- Anti-Lock Brake
- MIL (SERVICE ENGINE SOON)
- Overdrive (O/D) Off

INSPECTION & VERIFICATION

Verify customer concern by operating system in question. Verify charging system, safety belt warning chime, turn signals, headlights and cruise control are working properly. Inspect wiring harness for obvious signs of shorts, opens, bad connections or damage. If fault is not visible, go to SYMPTOM TESTS INDEX table and proceed to appropriate test under SYSTEM TESTING.

Mechanical:
- Low Brake Fluid Level
- Damaged Engine Oil Filter
- Damaged Oil Pump
- Damaged Vehicle Speed Sensor Gear

- Damaged Washer Fluid Reservoir
- Door Adjustment
- Low Engine Oil
- Low Washer Fluid
- Stuck Coolant Temperature Gauge Needle
- Stuck Tachometer Needle
- Worn Or Damaged Generator Drive Belt
- Stuck Speedometer Needle

Electrical:
- Blown Fuse(s):
  - 10-Amp Relays
  - 10-Amp Turn
  - 15-Amp Hazard
  - 15-Amp High/Low LH Headlights
  - 15-Amp High/Low RH Headlights
- Damaged Miniature Bulbs
- Damaged Wiring Harness
- Loose Or Corroded Connections
- Damaged Vehicle Speed Sensor
- Damaged Instrument Cluster
- Damaged Light Switches

COMPONENT TESTING

TEMPERATURE GAUGE

NOTE: The temperature gauge is part of fuel/temperature gauge assembly. Neither of these gauges is serviceable separately. If either gauge malfunctions, assembly must be replaced.

1) Remove instrument cluster. See INSTRUMENT CLUSTER under REMOVAL & INSTALLATION.
2) Using a jumper, connect coolant temperature gauge "B" terminal to battery voltage and the coolant temperature gauge "G" terminal to ground. See Fig. 2.
3) Connect one lead of Rotunda Instrument Gauge Tester (014-R1063), or equivalent, to the "S" terminal of coolant temperature gauge and the other lead to the "G" terminal of coolant temperature gauge. See Fig. 2.
4) Adjust instrument gauge tester to resistance values shown in Fig. 3. See Fig. 3. If coolant gauge does not indicate as specified, replace temperature/fuel gauge assembly.

TEMPERATURE SENDING UNIT

1) Allow engine to cool. Disconnect temperature sending unit connector. Using a DVOM, measure resistance between terminal of sending unit and ground.
2) Start engine. Measure sensor resistance as engine warms. If resistance values are not as specified, replace coolant temperature sending unit. See TEMPERATURE SENDER RESISTANCE table.

TEMPERATURE SENDER RESISTANCE

Temperature – °F (°C)	Resistance (Ohms)
167 (75)	179-219
212 (100)	60-72

FUEL GAUGE

NOTE: The fuel gauge is part of the fuel/temperature gauge assembly. Neither of these gauges is serviceable separately. If either gauge malfunctions, assembly must be replaced.

1) Remove instrument cluster. See INSTRUMENT CLUSTER under REMOVAL & INSTALLATION. Remove fuel indicator module from back of instrument cluster. See FUEL INDICATOR MODULE under REMOVAL & INSTALLATION.
2) Using a jumper, connect fuel gauge "B" terminal to battery voltage, and fuel gauge "G" terminal to ground. See Fig. 4.

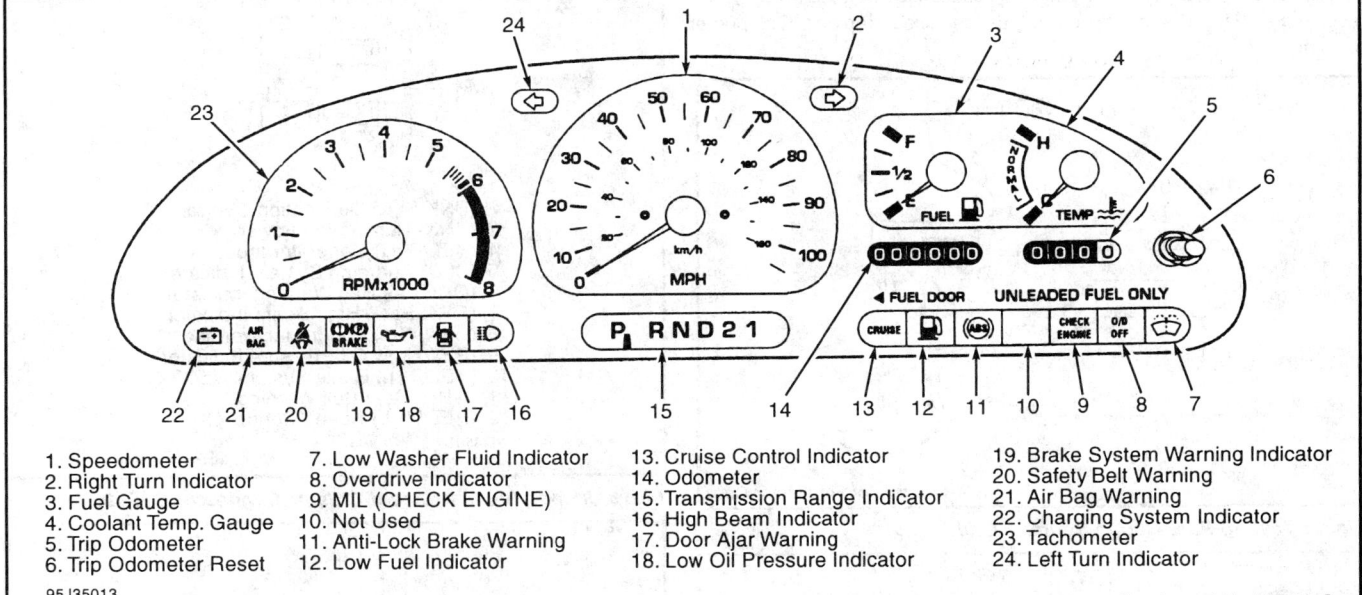

Fig. 1: Identifying Instrument Cluster Gauges & Indicators

1. Speedometer
2. Right Turn Indicator
3. Fuel Gauge
4. Coolant Temp. Gauge
5. Trip Odometer
6. Trip Odometer Reset
7. Low Washer Fluid Indicator
8. Overdrive Indicator
9. MIL (CHECK ENGINE)
10. Not Used
11. Anti-Lock Brake Warning
12. Low Fuel Indicator
13. Cruise Control Indicator
14. Odometer
15. Transmission Range Indicator
16. High Beam Indicator
17. Door Ajar Warning
18. Low Oil Pressure Indicator
19. Brake System Warning Indicator
20. Safety Belt Warning
21. Air Bag Warning
22. Charging System Indicator
23. Tachometer
24. Left Turn Indicator

95J35013

Courtesy of Ford Motor Co.

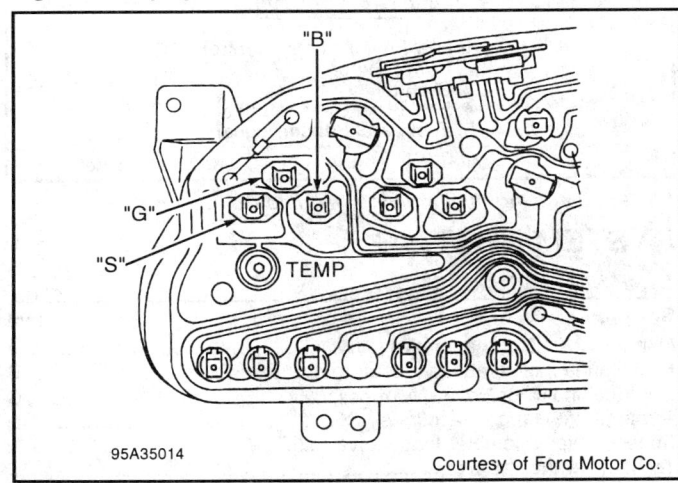

Fig. 2: Locating Temperature Gauge Terminals

95A35014

Courtesy of Ford Motor Co.

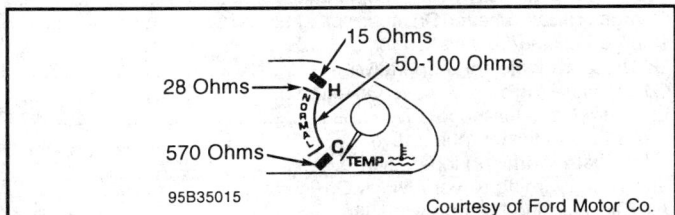

Fig. 3: Temperature Gauge Resistance Values

95B35015

Courtesy of Ford Motor Co.

3) Connect one lead of Rotunda Instrument Gauge System Tester (014-R1063), or equivalent, to "S" terminal of fuel gauge and other lead to "G" terminal of fuel gauge.

4) Adjust instrument gauge tester to resistances shown in FUEL GAUGE RESISTANCE table.

5) If fuel gauge does not operate as specified, replace fuel gauge. If fuel gauge is okay, test fuel gauge indicator module and fuel gauge sending unit.

FUEL GAUGE RESISTANCE

Fuel Gauge	Resistance (Ohms)
F	130-145

FUEL GAUGE RESISTANCE (Cont.)

Fuel Gauge	Resistance (Ohms)
3/4	95-110
1/2	65-75
1/4	50-55
E	10-15

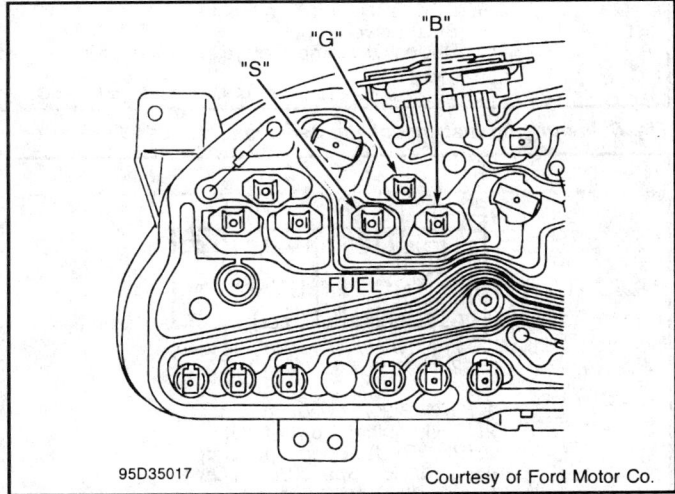

Fig. 4: Locating Fuel Gauge Terminals

95D35017

Courtesy of Ford Motor Co.

FUEL SENDING UNIT

1) Remove fuel pump/sending unit assembly. See FUEL GAUGE SENDING UNIT under REMOVAL & INSTALLATION.

2) Measure resistance between Blue/Red and Black wire terminals on fuel pump module while adjusting fuel tank float to positions as specified See Fig. 5. See FLOAT POSITION RESISTANCE table.

FLOAT POSITION RESISTANCE

Float Position – In. (mm)	Resistance (Ohms)
1 – (Empty) 5.94 (151)	15
2 – (1/2) 3.66 (93)	78
3 – (Full) 0.91 (23)	160

3) Gradually move float and monitor resistance for even change. If resistance change is erratic or not as specified, replace fuel pump sending unit.

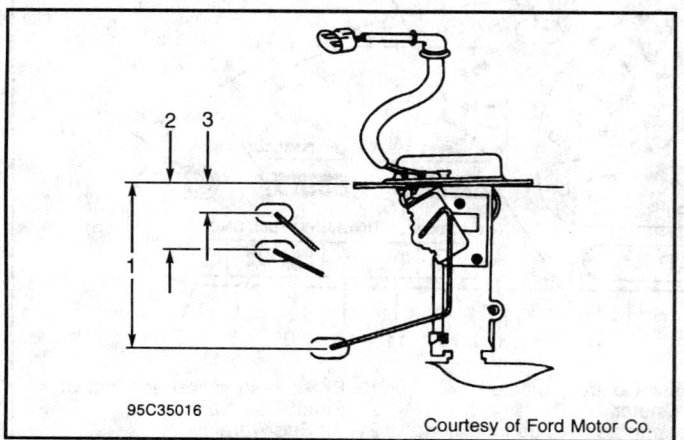

95C35016

Courtesy of Ford Motor Co.

Fig. 5: Testing Fuel Gauge Sending Unit

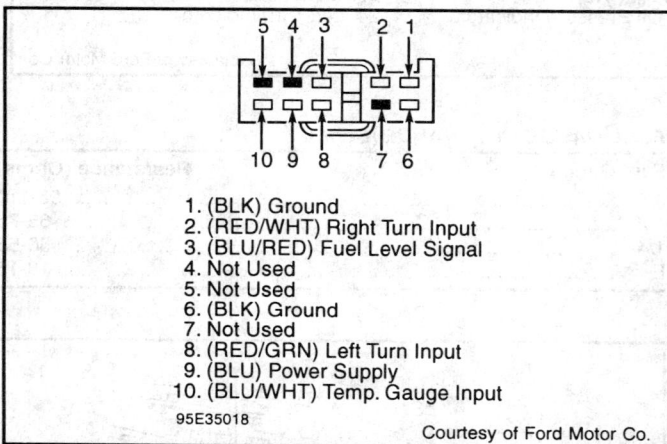

1. (BLK) Ground
2. (RED/WHT) Right Turn Input
3. (BLU/RED) Fuel Level Signal
4. Not Used
5. Not Used
6. (BLK) Ground
7. Not Used
8. (RED/GRN) Left Turn Input
9. (BLU) Power Supply
10. (BLU/WHT) Temp. Gauge Input

95E35018

Courtesy of Ford Motor Co.

Fig. 6: Identifying Instrument Cluster Connector C266A

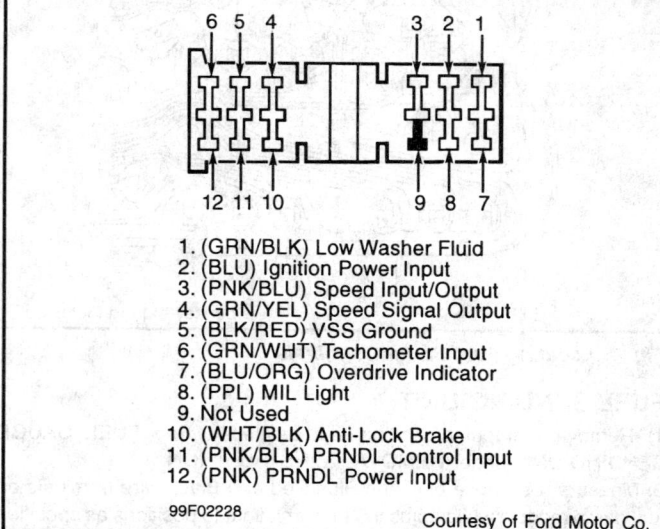

1. (GRN/BLK) Low Washer Fluid
2. (BLU) Ignition Power Input
3. (PNK/BLU) Speed Input/Output
4. (GRN/YEL) Speed Signal Output
5. (BLK/RED) VSS Ground
6. (GRN/WHT) Tachometer Input
7. (BLU/ORG) Overdrive Indicator
8. (PPL) MIL Light
9. Not Used
10. (WHT/BLK) Anti-Lock Brake
11. (PNK/BLK) PRNDL Control Input
12. (PNK) PRNDL Power Input

99F02228

Courtesy of Ford Motor Co.

Fig. 7: Identifying Instrument Cluster Connector C266B

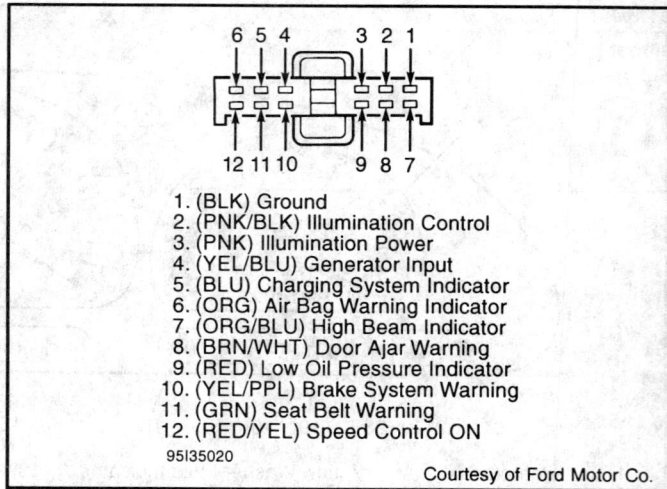

1. (BLK) Ground
2. (PNK/BLK) Illumination Control
3. (PNK) Illumination Power
4. (YEL/BLU) Generator Input
5. (BLU) Charging System Indicator
6. (ORG) Air Bag Warning Indicator
7. (ORG/BLU) High Beam Indicator
8. (BRN/WHT) Door Ajar Warning
9. (RED) Low Oil Pressure Indicator
10. (YEL/PPL) Brake System Warning
11. (GRN) Seat Belt Warning
12. (RED/YEL) Speed Control ON

95I35020

Courtesy of Ford Motor Co.

Fig. 8: Identifying Instrument Cluster Connector C266C

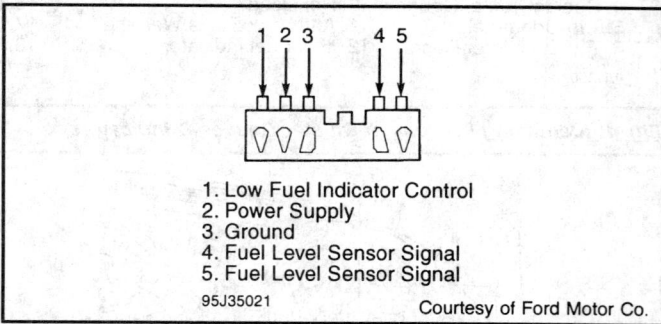

1. Low Fuel Indicator Control
2. Power Supply
3. Ground
4. Fuel Level Sensor Signal
5. Fuel Level Sensor Signal

95J35021

Courtesy of Ford Motor Co.

Fig. 9: Identifying Fuel Indicator Module Connector

SYSTEM TESTING

SYMPTOM TESTS INDEX

Symptom	Test
Instrument Cluster Inoperative	A
Fuel Gauge Inaccurate	B
Low Fuel Indicator Never/Always On	C
Temperature Gauge Inaccurate	D
Speedometer/Odometer Inoperative	E
Tachometer Inoperative	F
Brake Warning Never On	G
Brake Warning Always On	1
Charge Indicator Never On	H
Charge Indicator Always On	2
Oil Pressure Indicator Inoperative	I
Oil Pressure Indicator Always On	J
Left Turn Indicator Inoperative	K
Right Turn Indicator Inoperative	L
High Beam Warning Inoperative	M
Anti-Lock Warning Never/Always On	3
Air Bag Warning Never/Always On	4
MIL (SERVICE ENGINE SOON) Inoperative	N
MIL (SERVICE ENGINE SOON) Always On	5
Low Washer Fluid Indicator Inoperative	O
Safety Belt Warning Inoperative	P
Speed Control Indicator Never On	Q
Speed Control Indicator Always On	6
Door Ajar Indicator Inoperative	R
Overdrive Off Indicator Inoperative	S

[1] – See appropriate DISC & DRUM article in BRAKES in appropriate MITCHELL® manual.

[2] – See appropriate GENERATORS article in STARTING & CHARGING SYSTEMS.

[3] – See appropriate ANTI-LOCK article in BRAKES in appropriate MITCHELL® manual.

TEST A: INSTRUMENT CLUSTER INOPERATIVE

1) Turn ignition off. Disconnect negative battery cable. Remove instrument cluster. See INSTRUMENT CLUSTER under REMOVAL & INSTALLATION. Disconnect instrument cluster connectors. *See Figs. 6-8.* Reconnect negative battery cable and turn ignition on. Measure voltage between ground and instrument cluster connector C266A terminal No. 9 (Blue wire). Measure voltage between ground and instrument cluster connector C266B terminal No. 2 (Blue wire). Measure voltage between ground and instrument cluster connector C266C terminal No. 5 (Blue wire). If all voltage measurements are more than 10 volts, go to next step. If any voltage measurement is 10 volts or less, repair open or short to ground in Blue wire between interior fuse panel and instrument cluster.

2) Turn ignition off. Measure resistance between ground and instrument cluster connector C266A terminal No. 6 (Black wire) and connector C266B terminal No. 5 (Black/Red wire). If resistance in both measurements is less than 5 ohms, replace instrument cluster printed circuit and retest. See PRINTED CIRCUIT under REMOVAL & INSTALLATION. If resistance in either measurement is more than 5 ohms, repair open or high resistance in circuit(s) in question and retest system.

TEST B: FUEL GAUGE INACCURATE

1) Turn ignition off. Disconnect fuel sending unit connector. Connect Instrument Gauge Tester (014–R1063) test leads to fuel sending unit connector Blue/Red wire terminal and ground. Set tester to 160 ohms. Turn ignition on. Turn tester on and wait one minute. Fuel gauge should read full or above. Turn ignition off. Set tester to 15 ohms. Turn ignition on and wait one minute. Fuel gauge should read empty or below. If fuel gauge reads as specified, go to next step. If fuel gauge does not read as specified, go to step **4)**.

2) Visually inspect fuel tank for damage or deformation. Replace fuel tank as necessary. Retest system. If fuel tank is okay, go to next step.

3) Visually inspect fuel pump for damage or connector problems. Inspect float and float rod for damage or float rod obstruction. If fuel pump and wiring is okay, replace fuel sending unit. Retest system. If fuel pump and wiring is damaged, repair as necessary.

4) Turn ignition off. Measure resistance between ground and fuel sending unit connector Black wire. Resistance should be less than 5 ohms. If resistance is less than 5 ohms, go to next step. If resistance is more than 5 ohms, repair open in Black wire. Retest system.

5) Remove instrument cluster. See INSTRUMENT CLUSTER under REMOVAL & INSTALLATION. Disconnect instrument cluster connector C266A. Measure resistance of Blue/Red wire between instrument cluster connector C266A terminal No. 3 and fuel sending unit connector. *See Fig. 6.* Resistance should be less than 5 ohms. Measure resistance between ground and instrument cluster connector C266A terminal No. 3 (Blue/Red wire). Resistance should be more than 10 k/ohms. If resistance is as specified, go to next step. If resistance is not as specified, repair open or short to ground in Blue/Red wire. Retest system.

6) Visually inspect instrument cluster printed circuit for damage, cracks or hot spots. Replace instrument cluster printed circuit as necessary and retest system. See PRINTED CIRCUIT under REMOVAL & INSTALLATION. If printed circuit is okay, replace fuel gauge and fuel indicator module. See FUEL GAUGE and FUEL INDICATOR MODULE.

TEST C: LOW FUEL INDICATOR LIGHT NEVER/ALWAYS ON

Turn ignition on. Monitor fuel gauge operation. Start engine. Monitor fuel gauge operation. If fuel gauge operated properly, replace instrument cluster printed circuit. See PRINTED CIRCUIT under REMOVAL & INSTALLATION. If fuel gauge does not operate properly, go to TEST B: FUEL GAUGE INACCURATE test.

TEST D: TEMPERATURE GAUGE INACCURATE

1) Turn ignition off. Disconnect Engine Coolant Temperature (ECT) sensor connector. ECT sensor is located on right rear side of engine. Connect fused jumper between ECT sensor and ground. Turn ignition on. If temperature gauge indicates "H", replace ECT sensor. Retest system. If temperature gauge does not indicate "H", go to next step.

2) Test temperature gauge, see TEMPERATURE GAUGE under COMPONENT TESTING. If temperature gauge tests okay, go to next step. If temperature gauge is faulty, replace temperature/fuel gauge assembly. See TEMPERATURE GAUGE under REMOVAL & INSTALLATION. Retest system.

3) Turn ignition off. Disconnect instrument cluster connector C266A. Disconnect temperature sending unit connector. Measure resistance of Blue/White wire between ECT sensor connector terminal and instrument cluster connector C266A terminal No. 10. Resistance should be less than 5 ohms. *See Fig. 6.* Measure resistance between ground and instrument cluster connector C266A terminal No. 10 (Blue/White wire). Resistance should be more than 10 k/ohms. If resistance is as specified, replace instrument cluster printed circuit and retest. See PRINTED CIRCUIT under REMOVAL & INSTALLATION. If resistance is not as specified, repair open or short to ground in Blue/White wire. Retest system.

TEST E: SPEEDOMETER/ODOMETER INOPERATIVE

NOTE: Instrument cluster connector C266B must remain connected.

1) Remove instrument cluster. See INSTRUMENT CLUSTER under REMOVAL & INSTALLATION. With ignition switch in OFF position, connect a voltmeter between "S" terminal and "G" terminal on speedometer (back of instrument cluster). Place voltmeter in AC volts position. Drive vehicle and note speed to voltage readings. Compare noted readings to SPEED-TO-VOLTAGE COMPARISON table. If voltage readings are correct, replace speedometer. If readings are not correct, go to next step.

SPEED-TO-VOLTAGE COMPARISON

Speed – MPH (KM/H)	Approximate Voltage
0 (0)	0
5 (8)	0.5
10 (16)	1.0
15 (24)	1.6
20 (32)	2.0
25 (40)	2.4
30 (48)	2.8
35 (56)	3.1
40 (64)	3.4
45 (72)	3.6
50 (80)	3.9
55 (88)	4.2
60 (96)	4.4

2) With ignition switch in OFF position, ensure the 4 screws holding speedometer to instrument cluster printed circuit are securely fastened. Measure resistance between speedometer "S" terminal and instrument cluster connector C266B terminal No. 3 (Pink/Blue wire), speedometer "G" terminal and instrument cluster connector C266B terminal No. 5 (Black/Red wire), and speedometer "B" terminal and instrument cluster connector C266B terminal No. 2 (Blue wire). *See Fig. 7.* If resistances are less than 5 ohms, go to next step. If resistances are more than 5 ohms, replace instrument cluster printed circuit. See PRINTED CIRCUIT under REMOVAL & INSTALLATION.

3) With ignition switch in OFF position and instrument cluster still removed, disconnect instrument cluster connector C266B. Disconnect Vehicle Speed Sensor (VSS) connector. VSS is located in center of engine compartment. Measure resistance of Pink/Blue wire between VSS connector and instrument cluster connector C266B terminal No. 3. Measure resistance between ground and instrument cluster connector C266B terminal No. 3 (Pink/Blue wire). Measure resistance of Black/Red wire between VSS connector and instrument cluster connector C266B terminal No. 5. If resistances are less than 5 ohms between instrument cluster and VSS, and more than 10 k/ohms between Pink/Blue wire at instrument cluster and ground, replace VSS. If resistances are more than 5 ohms between instrument cluster and VSS, and less than 10 k/ohms between Pink/Blue wire at instrument cluster and ground, service wire(s) in question.

TEST F: TACHOMETER INACCURATE

1) With ignition in OFF position, verify instrument cluster connectors are secure. Remove instrument cluster and leave cluster connected. See INSTRUMENT CLUSTER under REMOVAL & INSTALLATION. With ignition ON and engine running, verify voltage on terminal No. 6 (Green/White wire) of instrument cluster connector C266B on back of instrument cluster at indicated engine speeds. *See Fig. 7.* See TACHOMETER SIGNAL VOLTAGES table. If voltages are correct, go to next step. If voltage readings are not correct, refer to appropriate SELF-DIAGNOSTICS article in ENGINE PERFORMANCE in appropriate MITCHELL® manual, for further information on diagnosing possible VSS or PCM concern.

TACHOMETER SIGNAL VOLTAGES

Engine Speed (RPM)	Voltage
1000	1.69
1500	2.64
2000	3.44
2500	4.50
3000	5.22

2) Turn ignition off. Remove instrument cluster and disconnect all cluster connectors. Measure resistance between tachometer terminals on back of instrument cluster and instrument cluster harness connector C266B as specified. See PRINTED CIRCUIT TESTING table. If all resistance measurements are less than 5 ohms, replace tachometer. If all resistance measurements are not less than 5 ohms, replace instrument cluster printed circuit. See PRINTED CIRCUIT under REMOVAL & INSTALLATION.

PRINTED CIRCUIT TESTING

Tachometer Terminal	Cluster C266B Terminal
"B"	2
"G"	5
"S"	6

TEST G: BRAKE WARNING LIGHT NEVER ON

1) Turn ignition switch off. Remove instrument cluster. See INSTRUMENT CLUSTER in REMOVAL & INSTALLATION. Remove brake warning light bulb and check continuity of bulb. If bulb is okay, go to next step. If bulb is bad, replace bulb and retest system.

2) Disconnect all instrument cluster connectors. Turn ignition on. Using voltmeter, measure voltage between instrument cluster connector C266C terminal No. 10 (Yellow/Purple wire) and instrument cluster connector C266B terminal No. 2 (Blue wire). *See Figs. 7 and 8.* If voltage is more than 10 volts, replace printed circuit. See PRINTED CIRCUIT under REMOVAL & INSTALLATION. If voltage is 10 volts or less, go to next step.

3) Turn ignition off. Disconnect brake fluid level switch 2-pin connector at brake fluid reservoir. Remove BULB CHECK relay from engine compartment fuse/relay panel. Remove joint connector located behind top right side of instrument cluster. Remove top shorting strip. Measure resistance of Yellow/Purple wire between instrument cluster connector C266C terminal No. 10 and joint connector C2011 terminal No. 10. *See Fig. 10.* Measure resistance of Yellow/Purple wire between BULB

CHECK relay connector and instrument cluster connector C266C terminal No. 10. Measure resistance of Yellow/Purple wire between brake fluid level switch connector and instrument cluster connector C266C terminal No. 10. If resistance in any measurement is more than 5 ohms, repair open in appropriate Yellow/Purple wire. Retest system. If resistance in all measurements are less than 5 ohms, go to next step.

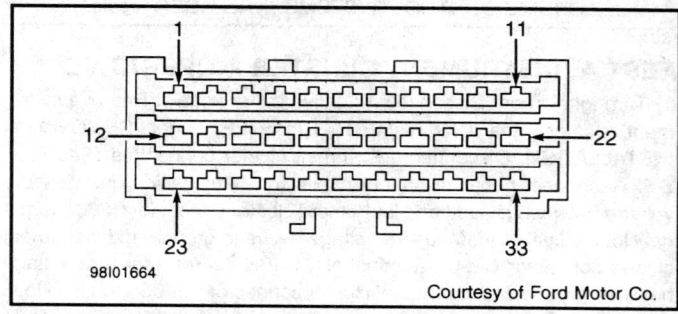

Fig. 10: Identifying Joint Connector C2011 Terminals

4) Ensure ignition is off. Connect jumper wire between battery voltage and BULB CHECK relay terminal No. 1. Measure resistances between BULB CHECK relay terminals No. 3 and No. 5. *See Fig. 11.* Ground BULB CHECK relay terminal No. 2. If resistance between BULB CHECK relay terminals No. 3 and No. 5 is less than 5 ohms with ground connected and more than 10 k/ohms with ground disconnected, go to next step. If resistance between BULB CHECK relay terminals No. 3 and 5 is 5 ohms or more with ground connected or 10 k/ohms or less with ground disconnected, replace BULB CHECK relay.

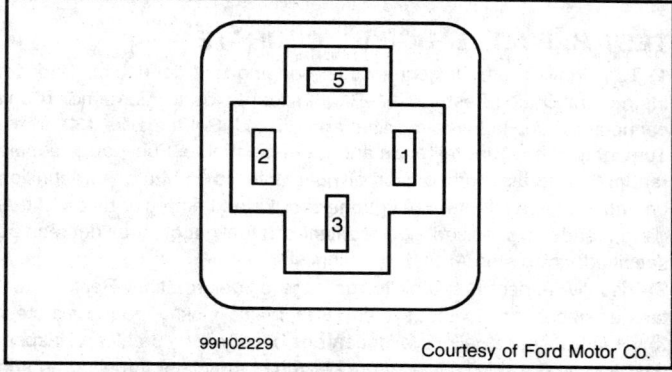

Fig. 11: Identifying BULB CHECK Relay Terminals

5) Turn ignition on. Measure voltage between ground and BULB CHECK relay connector terminal No. 1 (Blue wire). If voltage is more than 10 volts, go to next step. If voltage is 10 volts or less, repair open in Blue wire between BULB CHECK relay and interior fuse panel.

6) Turn ignition off. Measure resistance of Blue/Yellow wire between BULB CHECK relay connector terminal No. 2 and joint connector C2011 terminal No. 6. *See Figs. 10 and 11.* If resistance is more than 5 ohms, go to next step. If resistance is less than 5 ohms, repair open Blue/Yellow wire. Retest system.

7) Measure resistance between ground and brake fluid level switch connector Black wire. If resistance is less than 5 ohms, go to next step. If resistance is 5 ohms or more, repair open Black wire. Retest system.

8) Ensure ignition is off and brake fluid level switch 2-pin connector at brake fluid reservoir is disconnected. Remove screen inside brake fluid reservoir. Depress brake fluid reservoir float with a clean screwdriver. Measure resistance between brake fluid level switch terminals. If resistance is less than 5 ohms with float depressed and more than 10 k/ohms with float released, go to next step. If resistance is 5 ohms or more with float depressed or 10 k/ohms or less with float released, replace brake fluid level switch.

9) Ensure ignition is off. Disconnect parking brake switch connector. Measure resistance of Green/Black wire between parking brake switch connector and joint connector C2011 terminal No. 9. If resistance is less than 5 ohms, go to next step. If resistance is more than 5 ohms, repair open Green/Black wire. Retest system.

10) Ensure parking brake switch is disconnected. Set parking brake. Measure resistance between ground and parking brake switch terminal component side. If resistance is less than 5 ohms, go to next step. If resistance is 5 ohms or more, replace parking brake switch.

11) Measure resistance between joint connector C2011 (top shorting strip) terminals as follows (ensure polarity is correct; shorting strip is a diode shorting strip):

- Terminal No. 6 (+) and No. 5 (-).
- Terminal No. 2 (+) and No. 5 (-).
- Terminal No. 10 (+) and No. 9 (-).
- Terminal No. 10 (+) and No. 8 (-).

If resistance in all measurements is less than 5 ohms, go to TEST H: CHARGE INDICATOR NEVER ON. If resistance in any measurement is 5 ohms or more, replace top diode shorting strip on joint connector C2011. Retest system.

TEST H: CHARGE INDICATOR NEVER ON

1) Turn ignition off. Disconnect 2-pin generator harness connector. Using a jumper wire, ground Yellow/Black wire at generator harness connector. Turn ignition on and start engine. If charge warning indicator glows, repair charging system. See GENERATORS – VILLAGER article in STARTING & CHARGING SYSTEMS. If charge warning indicator does not glow, reconnect generator connector and go to next step.

2) Turn ignition off. Disconnect instrument cluster harness connector C266C. Measure voltage between instrument cluster harness connector C266C terminal No. 4 (Yellow/Blue wire) and No. 5 (Blue wire). *See Fig. 8.* If voltage is more than 10 volts, replace instrument cluster printed circuit. See PRINTED CIRCUIT under REMOVAL & INSTALLATION. If voltage is less than 10 volts, go to next step.

3) Turn ignition off. Remove joint connector C2011. Remove Black diode shorting strip from joint connector C2011. Measure resistance of Yellow/Blue wire between C266C terminal No. 4 and joint connector C2011 terminal No. 5. *See Figs. 8 and 10.* If resistance is less than 5 ohms, go to next step. If resistance is 5 ohms or more, repair Yellow/Black wire.

4) Disconnect 2-pin generator harness connector. Measure resistance of Yellow/Black wire between generator harness connector and diode junction box connector C2011 terminal No. 5. If resistance is less than 5 ohms, replace Black diode shorting strip. If resistance is 5 ohms or more, repair Yellow/Black wire.

TEST I: OIL PRESSURE INDICATOR INOPERATIVE

1) Turn ignition off. Disconnect oil pressure switch connector. Connect a fused jumper wire between ground and oil pressure switch connector. Turn ignition on. If oil pressure light illuminates, go to next step. If oil pressure light does not illuminate, go to step **3)**.

2) Manually check engine oil pressure. See appropriate article in ENGINES. If oil pressure is within specifications, replace oil pressure switch. If oil pressure is not within specifications, repair engine mechanical problem as necessary. See appropriate article in ENGINES.

3) Turn ignition off. Remove instrument cluster. See INSTRUMENT CLUSTER in REMOVAL & INSTALLATION. Disconnect instrument cluster connector C266C. Measure resistance of Red wire between oil pressure sensor connector and instrument cluster connector C266C terminal No. 9. *See Fig. 7.* If resistance is less than 5 ohms, replace instrument cluster printed circuit. See PRINTED CIRCUIT under REMOVAL & INSTALLATION. Retest system. If resistance is 5 ohms or more, repair Red wire. Retest system.

TEST J: OIL PRESSURE INDICATOR ALWAYS ON

1) Turn ignition off. Disconnect oil pressure switch connector. Turn ignition on. If oil pressure light does not illuminate, go to next step. If oil pressure light illuminates, go to step **3)**.

2) Manually check engine oil pressure. See appropriate article in ENGINES. If oil pressure is within specifications, replace oil pressure switch. If oil pressure is not within specifications, repair engine mechanical problem as necessary. See appropriate article in ENGINES.

3) Turn ignition off. Remove instrument cluster. See INSTRUMENT CLUSTER in REMOVAL & INSTALLATION. Disconnect instrument cluster connector C266C. Measure resistance between ground and instrument cluster connector C266 terminal No. 9 (Red wire). If resistance is more than 10 k/ohms, replace instrument cluster printed circuit. See PRINTED CIRCUIT under REMOVAL & INSTALLATION. Retest system. If resistance is 10 k/ohms or less, repair short to ground in Red wire. Retest system.

TEST K: LEFT TURN INDICATOR INOPERATIVE

1) Turn ignition on. Place multifunction switch in left turn position. If outside left turn signal operates, go to next step. If outside left turn signal does not operate properly, see appropriate wiring diagram in EXTERIOR LIGHTS article.

2) Turn ignition off. Remove instrument cluster. See INSTRUMENT CLUSTER in REMOVAL & INSTALLATION. Disconnect instrument cluster connector C266A. Turn ignition on. Place multifunction switch in left turn position. Measure voltage between ground and instrument cluster connector C266A terminal No. 8 (Red/Green wire). *See Fig. 6.* If voltage alternates between zero and 10 volts, replace instrument cluster printed circuit. See PRINTED CIRCUIT under REMOVAL & INSTALLATION. Retest system. If voltage does not alternate between zero and 10 volts, repair open or short in Red/Green wire. Retest system.

TEST L: RIGHT TURN INDICATOR INOPERATIVE

1) Turn ignition on. Place multifunction switch in right turn position. If outside right turn signal operates, go to next step. If outside right turn signal does not operate properly, see appropriate wiring diagram in EXTERIOR LIGHTS article.

2) Turn ignition off. Remove instrument cluster. See INSTRUMENT CLUSTER in REMOVAL & INSTALLATION. Disconnect instrument cluster connector C266A. Turn ignition on. Place multifunction switch in right turn position. Measure voltage between ground and instrument cluster connector C266A terminal No. 2 (Red/White wire). *See Fig. 6.* If voltage alternates between zero and 10 volts, replace instrument cluster printed circuit. See PRINTED CIRCUIT under REMOVAL & INSTALLATION. Retest system. If voltage does not alternate between zero and 10 volts, repair open or short in Red/White wire. Retest system.

TEST M: HIGH BEAM INDICATOR INOPERATIVE

1) Turn ignition on. Turn high beam headlights on. If high beam headlights operate properly, go to next step. If high beam headlights do not operate properly, see appropriate wiring diagram in HEADLIGHT SYSTEMS article.

2) Turn ignition off. Remove instrument cluster. See INSTRUMENT CLUSTER in REMOVAL & INSTALLATION. Disconnect instrument cluster connectors C266C. Measure voltage between ground and instrument cluster connectors C266C terminal No. 7 (Orange/Blue wire). *See Fig. 8.* If voltage is 10 volts or less, repair open or short to ground in Orange/Blue wire. Retest system. If voltage is 10 volts or more, go to next step.

3) Measure resistance between ground and instrument cluster connectors C266C terminal No. 1 (Black wire). If resistance is less than 5 ohms, replace instrument cluster printed circuit. See PRINTED CIRCUIT under REMOVAL & INSTALLATION. If resistance is 5 ohms or more, repair open in Black wire.

TEST N: SERVICE ENGINE SOON LIGHT INOPERATIVE

NOTE: SERVICE ENGINE SOON light may also be referred to as Malfunction Indicator Light (MIL).

1) Turn ignition off. Remove instrument cluster. See INSTRUMENT CLUSTER under REMOVAL & INSTALLATION. Disconnect instrument cluster connector C266B. *See Fig. 7.* Turn ignition on. Measure voltage between ground and instrument cluster connector C266B terminal No. 2 (Blue wire). If voltage is more than 10 volts, replace instrument cluster printed circuit. See PRINTED CIRCUIT under REMOVAL & INSTALLATION. Retest system. If voltage is 10 volts or less, go to next step.

2) Turn ignition off. Disconnect Powertrain Control Module (PCM) connector. PCM is located behind glove box. *See Fig. 12.* Measure resistance of Purple wire between PCM connector terminal No. 18 and instrument cluster connector C266B terminal No. 8. If resistance is less than 5 ohms, go to appropriate SELF-DIAGNOSTICS article in ENGINE PERFORMANCE in appropriate MITCHELL® manual. If resistance is 5 ohms or more, repair open Purple wire.

actuator module connector C247. Disconnect instrument cluster connector C266C. Measure resistance of Red/Yellow wire between instrument cluster connector C266C terminal No. 12 and speed control actuator module connector C247 terminal No. 4. *See Figs. 8 and 13.* Resistance should be less than 5 ohms. Measure resistance between ground and instrument cluster connector C266C terminal No. 12 (Red/Yellow wire). Resistance should be more than 10 k/ohms. If resistance measurements are as specified, replace instrument cluster printed circuit. See PRINTED CIRCUIT under REMOVAL & INSTALLATION.

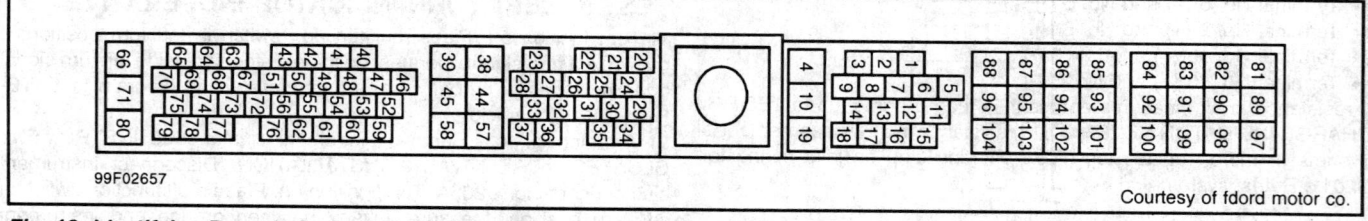

Courtesy of fdord motor co.

Fig. 12: Identifying Powertrain Control Module (PCM) Connector Terminals

TEST O: LOW WASHER FLUID INDICATOR INOPERATIVE

1) Turn ignition off. Disconnect washer fluid level switch 2-pin connector at washer fluid reservoir. Measure resistance between washer fluid level switch terminals. If resistance is less than 5 ohms with float depressed and more than 10 k/ohms with float released, go to next step. If resistance is 5 ohms or more with float depressed or 10 k/ohms or less with float released, replace washer fluid level switch.

2) Measure resistance between ground and washer fluid level switch Black wire. If resistance is less than 5 ohms, go to next step. If resistance is more than 5 ohms, repair open in Black wire.

3) Turn ignition switch off. Remove instrument cluster. See INSTRUMENT CLUSTER in REMOVAL & INSTALLATION. Disconnect instrument cluster connector C266B. Measure resistance of Green/Black wire between washer fluid level switch and instrument cluster connector C266C terminal No. 1. *See Fig. 8.* If resistance is less than 5 ohms, replace instrument cluster printed circuit. See PRINTED CIRCUIT under REMOVAL & INSTALLATION. Retest system. If resistance is 5 ohms or more, repair Green/Black wire. Retest system.

TEST P: SAFETY BELT WARNING INOPERATIVE (CHIME OPERATIVE)

1) Disconnect safety belt buckle switch 2-pin connector. Connect a fused jumper wire between ground and safety belt buckle switch 2-pin connector Green wire terminal. Turn ignition on. If safety belt light illuminates, go to next step. If safety belt light does not illuminate, go to step 3).

2) Turn ignition switch off. Remove instrument cluster. See INSTRUMENT CLUSTER in REMOVAL & INSTALLATION. Disconnect instrument cluster connector C266C. Measure resistance of Green wire between washer fluid level switch and instrument cluster connector C266C terminal No. 11. *See Fig. 8.* If resistance is less than 5 ohms, replace instrument cluster printed circuit. See PRINTED CIRCUIT under REMOVAL & INSTALLATION. Retest system. If resistance is 5 ohms or more, repair Green wire. Retest system.

3) Measure resistance between ground and safety belt buckle switch Black wire. If resistance is less than 5 ohms, replace safety belt buckle switch. If resistance is more than 5 ohms, repair open in Black wire.

TEST Q: CRUISE CONTROL INDICATOR NEVER ON

1) Turn ignition on and start engine. Road test vehicle and verify cruise control operation. If cruise control operates properly, go to next step. If cruise control does not operate properly, see CRUISE CONTROL SYSTEMS – VILLAGER article.

2) Turn ignition switch off. Remove instrument cluster. See INSTRUMENT CLUSTER in REMOVAL & INSTALLATION. Gain access to speed control actuator module. Speed control actuator module is located below left side of instrument panel. Disconnect speed control

Retest system. If resistance measurements are not as specified, repair Red/Yellow wire. Retest system.

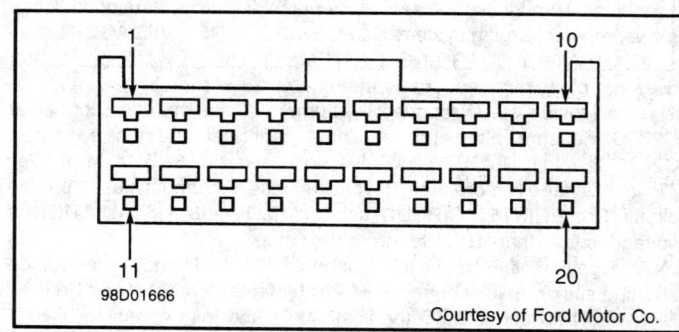

Courtesy of Ford Motor Co.

Fig. 13: Identifying Cruise Control Module Connector Terminals

TEST R: DOOR AJAR INDICATOR INOPERATIVE

1) Remove instrument cluster. See INSTRUMENT CLUSTER in REMOVAL & INSTALLATION. Disconnect instrument cluster connector C266C. Disconnect Smart Entry Control (SEC) timer/module connector C2032A. SEC timer/module is located in center console on left side. Measure resistance of Brown/White wire between instrument cluster connector C266C terminal No. 8 and SEC timer/module connector C2032A terminal No. 22. *See Figs. 8 and 14.* If resistance is less than 5 ohms, go to next step. If resistance is 5 ohms or more, repair open Brown/White wire.

2) Turn ignition on. Measure voltage between instrument cluster connector C266C terminal No. 8 (Brown/White wire) and instrument cluster connector C266B terminal No. 2 (Blue wire). If voltage is more than 10 volts with each door open, replace instrument cluster printed circuit. See PRINTED CIRCUIT under REMOVAL & INSTALLATION. Retest system. If voltage is not more than 10 volts with each door open, go to appropriate wiring diagram in ILLUMINATION INTERIOR LIGHTS – VILLAGER article.

TEST S: O/D OFF LIGHT INOPERATIVE

1) Turn ignition off. Connect New Generation Star (NGS) tester or equivalent scan tool to Data Link Connector (DLC). Turn ignition on. Access Transmission Control Module (TCM) PIDs. Monitor Overdrive Off Switch (ODS). Depress ODS. If O/D OFF light illuminates and ODS signal is present on NGS tester, replace TCM. See appropriate ELECTRONIC CONTROLS article in TRANSMISSIONS in appropriate MITCHELL® TRANSMISSION SERVICE & REPAIR manual. Retest system. If conditions are not as described, go to next step.

2) Turn ignition off. Disconnect TCM. TCM is located in bottom of center console. Remove instrument cluster. See INSTRUMENT CLUSTER in REMOVAL & INSTALLATION. Disconnect instrument cluster connector C266B. Using an ohmmeter, measure resistance of Blue/Orange wire

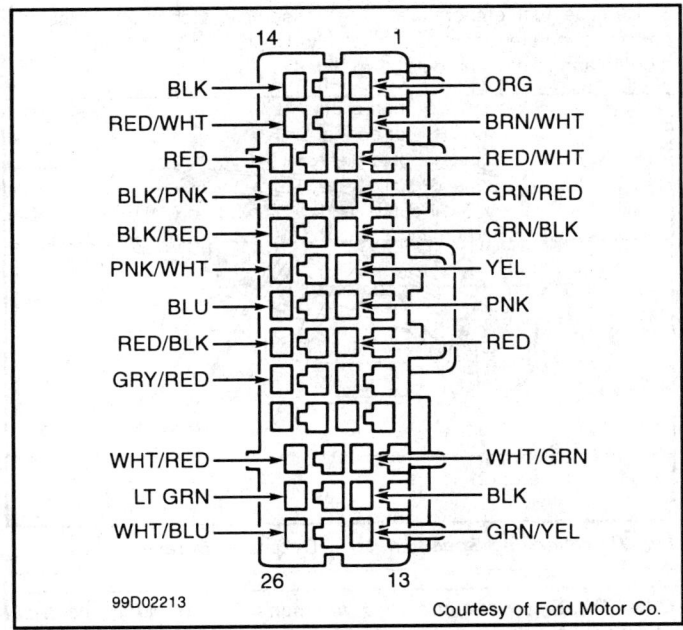

BLK — ORG
RED/WHT — BRN/WHT
RED — RED/WHT
BLK/PNK — GRN/RED
BLK/RED — GRN/BLK
PNK/WHT — YEL
BLU — PNK
RED/BLK — RED
GRY/RED —

WHT/RED — WHT/GRN
LT GRN — BLK
WHT/BLU — GRN/YEL

99D02213   Courtesy of Ford Motor Co.

Fig. 14: Identifying Smart Entry Control (SEC) Timer/Module Connector C2032A Terminals

between instrument cluster connector C266B terminal No. 7 and TCM connector C277A terminal No. 13. *See Figs. 7 and 15.* If resistance is less than 5 ohms, go to next step. If resistance is 5 ohms or more, repair open in Blue/Orange wire. Retest system.

3) Measure resistance between ground and TCM connector C277A terminal No. 22 (Green/Orange wire) while depressing O/D OFF switch to ON position. If resistance is less than 5 ohms, replace instrument cluster printed circuit. See PRINTED CIRCUIT under REMOVAL & INSTALLATION. Retest system. If resistance is 5 ohms or more, go to next step.

4) Disconnect overdrive off switch connector. Overdrive off switch is located at top of steering column near gear selector. Measure resistance between ground and overdrive off switch connector Black wire. If resistance is less than 5 ohms, go to next step. If resistance is 5 ohms or more, repair open in Black wire. Retest system.

5) Measure resistance of Green/Orange wire between TCM connector C277A terminal No. 22 and overdrive off switch connector. If resistance is less than 5 ohms, replace overdrive off switch. Retest system. If resistance is 5 ohms or more, repair Green/Orange wire. Retest system.

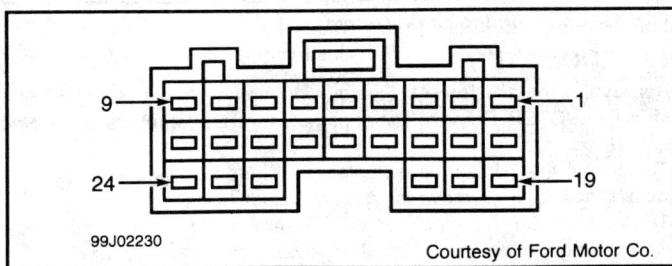

9 — 1
24 — 19

99J02230   Courtesy of Ford Motor Co.

Fig. 15: Identifying Transmission Control Module (TCM) Connector C277A Terminals

REMOVAL & INSTALLATION

CAUTION: Electronic modules are sensitive to static electrical charges. Proper grounding of technician and component is essential to prevent damage.

TEMPERATURE GAUGE

NOTE: The temperature gauge is part of fuel/temperature gauge assembly. Neither of these gauges is serviceable separately. If either gauge malfunctions, assembly must be replaced.

Removal & Installation – 1) Remove instrument cluster. See INSTRUMENT CLUSTER. Remove the 7 instrument cluster main lens screws and instrument cluster main lens. Remove instrument cluster mask.
2) Remove fuel/temperature gauge assembly. *See Fig. 16.* For installation, reverse removal procedure.

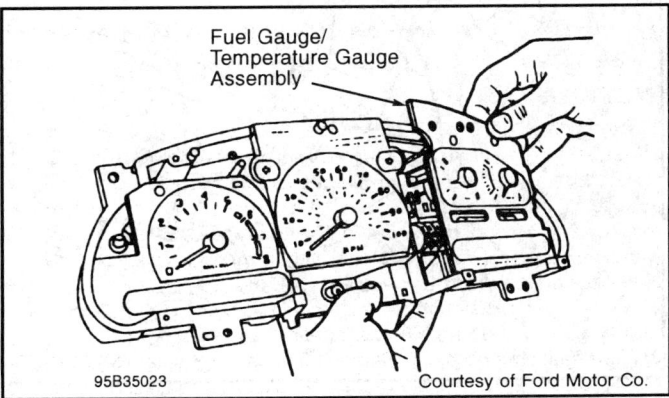

Fuel Gauge/
Temperature Gauge
Assembly

95B35023   Courtesy of Ford Motor Co.

Fig. 16: Removing Temperature/Fuel Gauge Assembly

TEMPERATURE GAUGE SENDING UNIT

Removal & Installation – Sending unit is located on top of water hose connection. When installing, use thread sealant.

FUEL GAUGE

NOTE: The fuel gauge is part of fuel/temperature gauge assembly. Neither of these gauges is serviceable separately. See TEMPERATURE GAUGE.

FUEL GAUGE SENDING UNIT

CAUTION: Before disconnecting any fuel line, release fuel pressure from fuel system to reduce possibility of injury or fire. Use a rag as protection from fuel spray when disconnection hoses. Plug hoses after disconnection.

Removal & Installation – 1) Remove LH engine compartment relay panel cover. Remove fuel pump relay from relay panel.
2) Start engine and run until it stalls. After stalling, crank engine 2 or 3 times to ensure all pressure has been released.
3) Turn ignition switch to OFF position, replace fuel pump relay and disconnect negative battery cable. Raise and support vehicle. Drain fuel from fuel tank.
4) Remove 2 pins from fuel tank front protector. Remove 3 fuel tank front protector bolts and remove fuel tank front protector.
5) Disconnect evaporative emission hose, fuel return hose and fuel supply hose. Disconnect fuel pump electrical connector. Separate fuel tank-to-filler pipe hose from fuel tank filler pipe.
6) Place jack under fuel tank for support when fuel tank support straps are removed. Remove the 2 tank support strap bolts and allow fuel tank support straps to hang down.
7) Remove spring clips from fuel tank support strap hinges. Remove fuel tank support strap hinges and remove fuel tank support straps. Lower tank from vehicle.

8) Remove 6 mounting screws from fuel pump/sender assembly. Remove fuel pump/gauge assembly from top of fuel tank.

9) Remove 2 fuel level sensor bolts and separate fuel level sensor from fuel pump. Remove and discard fuel level sensor gasket.

10) For installation, reverse removal procedure. Use a NEW "O" ring seal on installation of fuel pump/sender assembly. Tighten pump/gauge assembly mounting screws to 18-21 INCH lbs. (2.0-2.4 N.m).

FUEL INDICATOR MODULE

Removal & Installation – Remove instrument cluster. See INSTRUMENT CLUSTER. Depress clip on fuel indicator module and remove module. *See Fig. 17.* For installation, reverse removal procedure.

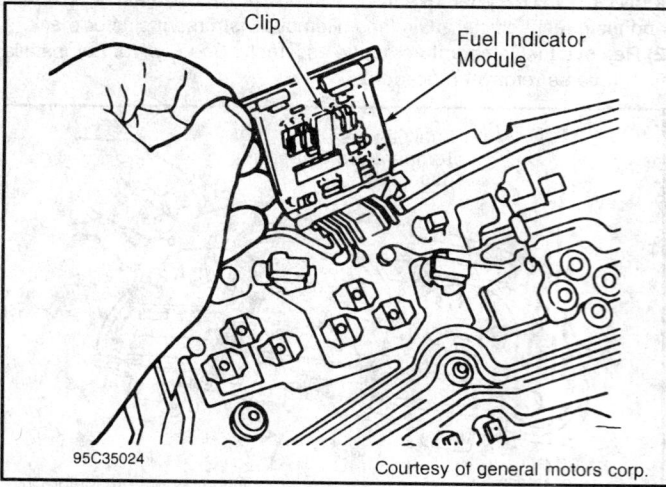

Fig. 17: Removing Fuel Indicator Module

INSTRUMENT CLUSTER

Removal & Installation – 1) Disconnect negative battery cable. Block wheels to prevent vehicle movement.

2) Ensure ignition switch is in OFF position. Shift transmission range selector to LOW (1). Tilt steering wheel to lowest position (if equipped).

3) Remove the 2 instrument panel finish panel screws. Removal instrument panel finish panel enough to access switch electrical connectors.

4) Disconnect rear windshield wiper/washer switch, heated rear window and light switch, emergency warning switch, SECURITY indicator light, cruise control ON/OFF switch, headlight switch connector and autolamp/light switch rheostat resistor connector. Remove instrument panel finish panel with switches attached.

5) Remove the 4 instrument cluster screws. Remove transmission range indicator from instrument cluster. Disconnect the 3 instrument cluster electrical connectors. Remove instrument cluster. For installation, reverse removal procedure.

OIL PRESSURE SENDING UNIT

Removal & Installation – Oil pressure sending unit is located in oil filter adapter at right front of engine compartment. When installing sending unit, use thread sealant.

PRINTED CIRCUIT

Removal & Installation – 1) Remove instrument cluster. See INSTRUMENT CLUSTER. Remove 4 speedometer and 2 odometer screws. *See Fig. 18 .*

2) Remove the 7 instrument cluster main lens screws and instrument cluster main lens. Remove instrument cluster mask.

3) Remove fuel/temperature gauge assembly, tachometer assembly and speedometer/odometer assembly. Depress clip on fuel indicator module and remove module. *See Fig. 17.*

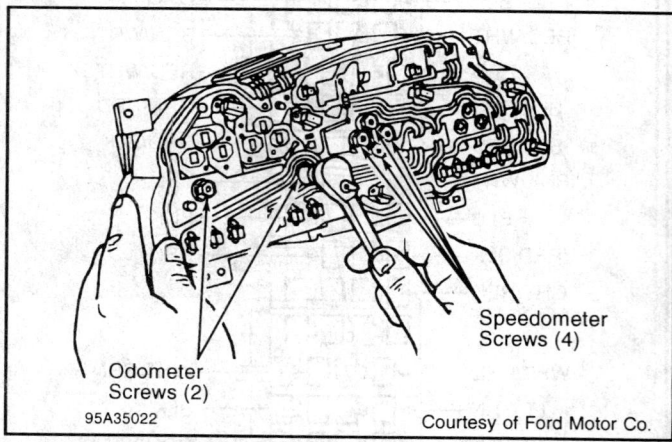

Fig. 18: Removing Speedometer & Odometer Screws

CAUTION: Electronic modules are sensitive to static electrical charges. Proper grounding of technician and component is essential to prevent damage.

---

4) Remove the 2 air bag warning LED assembly screws from air bag warning LED assembly leads. Turn air bag warning LED assembly counterclockwise and remove it from instrument cluster.

5) Turn the 5 illumination lights and 15 indicator lights counterclockwise and remove them from instrument cluster. Compress indicator terminals. *See Fig. 19.* Remove and discard the 9 indicator terminals from rear of instrument cluster back plate. *See Fig. 20.* Carefully remove instrument cluster printed circuit. *See Fig 15.* For installation, reverse removal procedure using NEW indicator terminals.

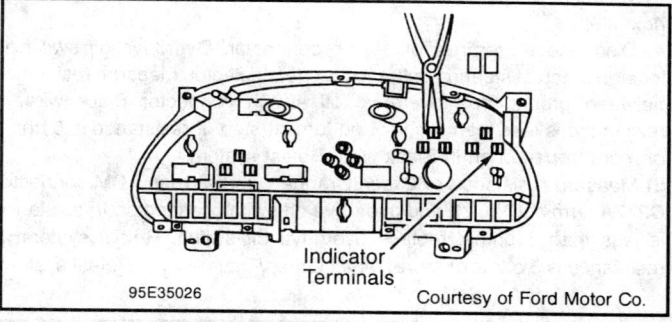

Fig. 19: Locating Indicator Terminals

SPEEDOMETER

Removal & Installation – 1) Remove instrument cluster. See INSTRUMENT CLUSTER. Remove 4 speedometer and 2 odometer screws. *See Fig. 18 .*

2) Remove the 7 instrument cluster main lens screws and instrument cluster main lens. Remove instrument cluster mask.

3) Remove speedometer/odometer assembly. Disconnect odometer electrical connector. For installation, reverse removal procedure.

TACHOMETER

Removal & Installation – Remove instrument cluster. See INSTRUMENT CLUSTER. Remove the 7 instrument cluster main lens screws and instrument cluster main lens. Remove instrument cluster mask. Remove tachometer assembly. For installation, reverse removal procedure.

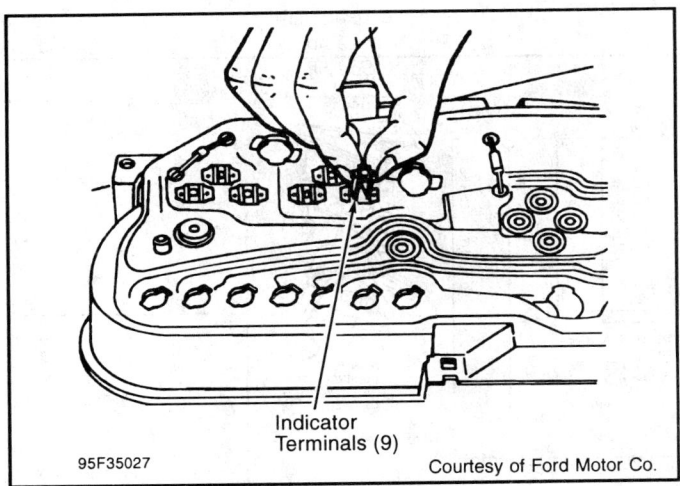

Fig. 20: Removing Indicator Terminals

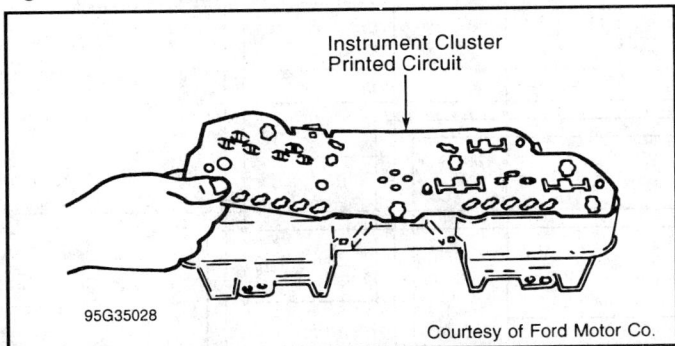

Fig. 21: Removing Instrument Cluster Printed Circuit

WIRING DIAGRAMS

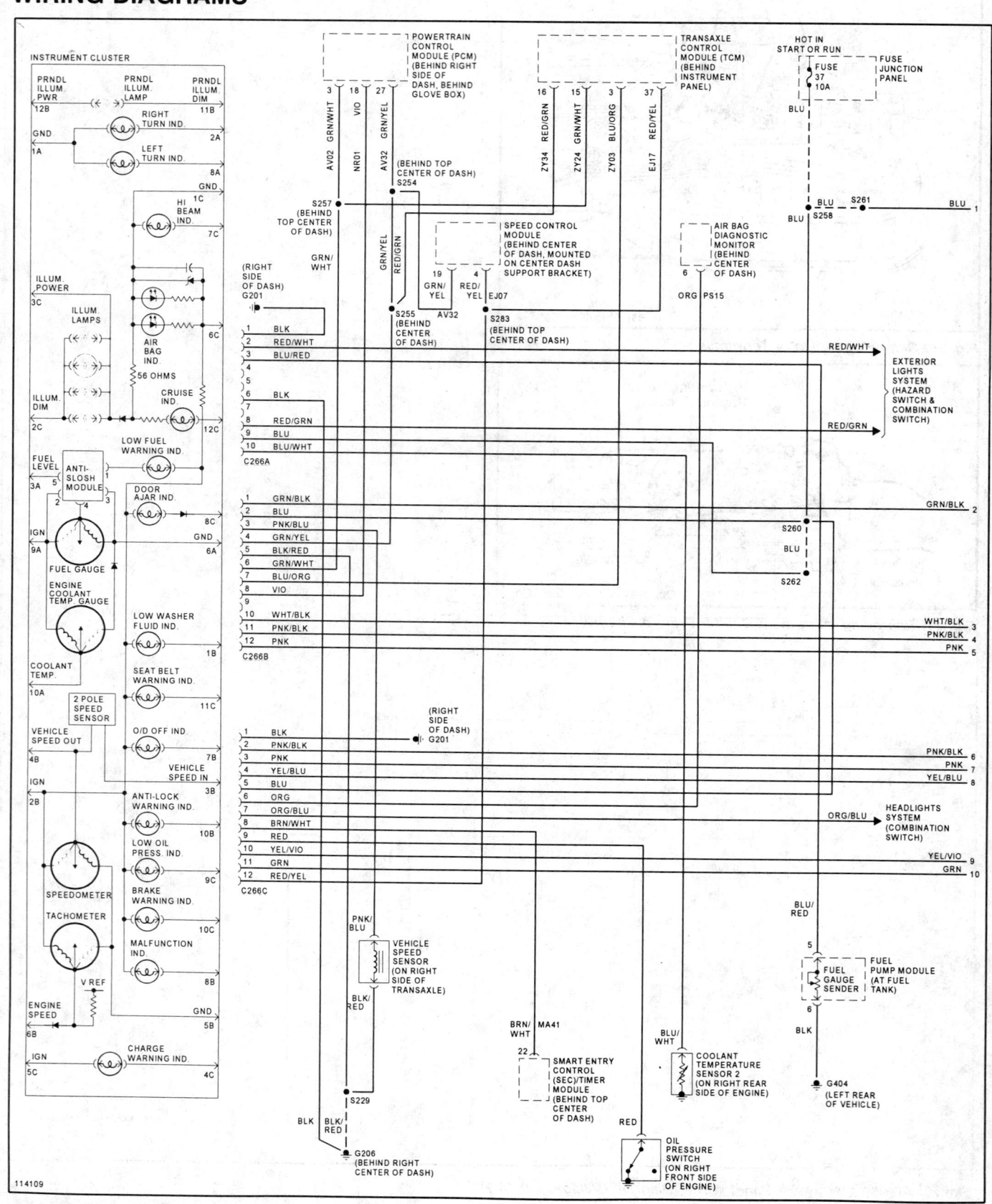

Fig. 22: Analog Instrument Panel Wiring Diagram (Villager – 1 Of 2)

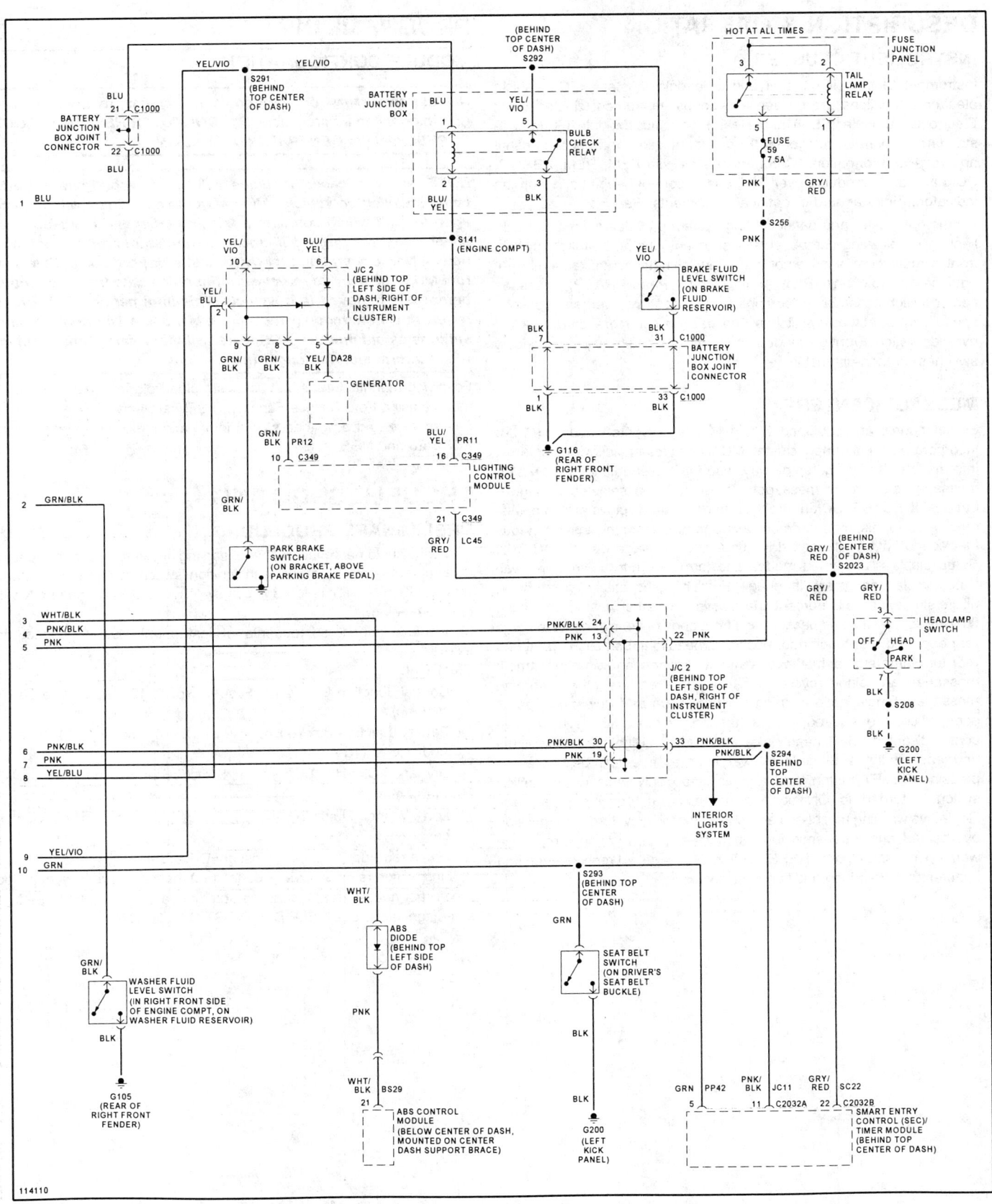

Fig. 23: Analog Instrument Panel Wiring Diagram (Villager – 2 Of 2)

114110

DESCRIPTION & OPERATION

INSTRUMENT CLUSTER

Instrument Cluster (IC) is a Hybrid Electronic Cluster (HEC). Vehicle electronic functions are divided into zones. Instrument cluster, Front Electronics Module (FEM) and Rear Electronics Module (REM) use standard corporate protocol (SCP) communication network to transmit and receive information. IC communicates with FEM, REM, ABS/TC, PCM and other modules over SCP bus to control gauges and warning indicators. For standard or optional IC contents. *See Fig. 1 or 2.*

Instrument cluster and panel lighting system provides dimmable backlighting to following components: instrument cluster, headlight switch, front climate control assembly, auxiliary climate control assembly (if equipped), audio unit, Rear Audio Control Panel (RACP), message center switch assembly (if equipped), front ashtray, overhead console, speed control actuator switches and traction control/reverse park aid override switch. Front power door lock switches and front power window switches are non-dimmable.

MESSAGE CENTER

Some models are equipped with a Message Center Module (MCM) incorporated in instrument cluster. MCM provides the following features: information displays, setup display, warning messages, temporary alert messages and status messages. These may be selected through 3 buttons: INFO, SETUP and RESET. Information displays are compass/ outside temp, distance to empty, average fuel economy, instantaneous fuel economy, trip elapsed drive time and message display ON/OFF. Setup displays are timed modes and terminate after a finite interval. Setup display modes are: language, English/metric units, system check, oil life status, oil life in percent charge system status, washer and brake fluid levels, driver's and passenger's front door, driver's and passenger's rear door and rear hatch door positions, headlight, brakelight, front and rear turn lamp status, fuel level status and distance to empty. Warning messages are single cycle, non rescuable and repetitive warning messages. Single cycle warning messages are as follows: change oil soon, oil change required, low washer and low brake fluid level, traction control disabled, check headlights, brakelights, tail lights, front turn lights and rear turn lights. Single cycle warning messages can be cleared by pressing RESET button, and are displayed only once when ignition switch is turned to ON position or when fault occurs in system. Repetitive warning messages are: check charging system, transmission overheated, check transmission and low fuel level. To remove repetitive warning message, press RESET button. Message will reoccur every ten minutes until warning condition is corrected.

PROGRAMMING

MODULE CONFIGURATION

NOTE: Powertrain Control Module (PCM) has to be flash programmed using a flash cable. See COMPUTER RELEARN PROCEDURES article in GENERAL INFORMATION.

NOTE: Newly released modules will require configuration after being installed on vehicle. All configurable modules will be packaged in a kit which contains a warning label and multi-language sheet reemphasizing requirements to configure replacement modules. A New Generation Star (NGS) tester or Ford compatible scan tool MUST be used to retrieve configuration data from old module before it is removed from vehicle. This information will be transferred into new module so that new module will contain same settings as old module. NGS tester will not retain stored configuration information for longer than 24 hours.

Following manufacturer's instructions, upload old information from old module using Ford Service Function (FSF) card and NGS tester. Install new module and download stored information into new module using FSF card and NGS tester.

TROUBLE SHOOTING

PRELIMINARY PROCEDURE

1) Verify customer concern by observing indicators and gauges to determine correct operation with ignition switch in ON position, with engine off, in START before ignition switch is released and in ON with engine running.

2) Visually inspect components of instrument cluster. Inspect the following:

Electrical:
- Central Junction Box (CJB) Fuse(s) No. 9, 10, 14, 16 And 28 (All 10-Amp)
- Battery Junction Box (BJB) Fuse No. 2 (10-amp), No. 13 (30-amp) And No. 23 (15-Amp)
- Damaged Circuitry, Connectors, Switches Or Sensors

Mechanical:
- Low Washer Fluid, Engine Oil, Brake Fluid And Engine Coolant Level
- Damaged Fuel Tank Or Accessory Drive Belt

3) If inspection reveals obvious concern(s) that can be readily identified, repair as necessary. If concern remains after inspection, perform self-diagnostics. See SELF-DIAGNOSTIC SYSTEM.

1999 ACCESSORIES & EQUIPMENT
Analog Instrument Panels – Windstar (Cont.)

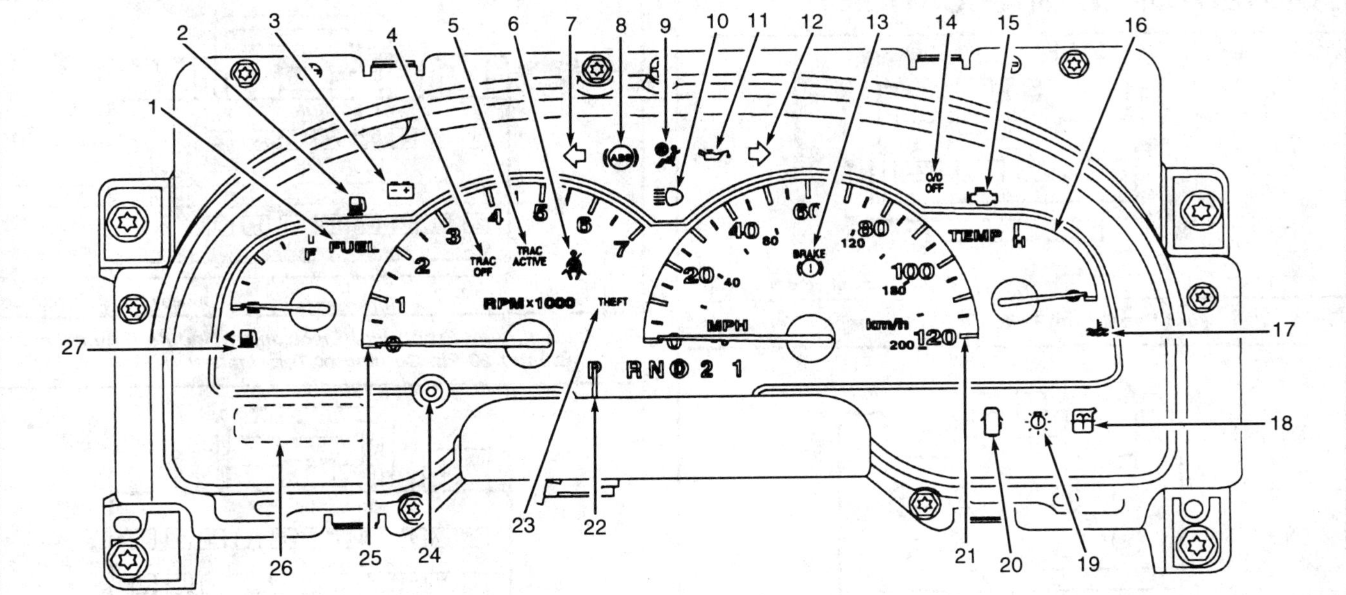

1. Fuel Gauge
2. Low Fuel Indicator
3. Charging System Indicator
4. TRAC OFF Indicator
5. TRAC ACTIVE Indicator
6. Safety Belt Indicator
7. Left Turn Signal Indicator
8. ABS Indicator
9. Air Bag Indicator
10. High Beam Indicator
11. Low Oil Pressure Indicator
12. Right Turn Signal Indicator
13. Brake System Indicator
14. O/D OFF Indicator
15. Service Engine Soon Indicator
16. Engine Coolant Temperature Gauge
17. Fail-Safe Cooling Indicator
18. Low Windshield Washer Solvent Indicator
19. Light Outage Indicator
20. Door Ajar Indicator
21. Speedometer
22. Transmission Range Indicator
23. Theft Indicator
24. Trip/Odometer Reset Button
25. RPM Gauge
26. Odometer/Trip Odometer Display
27. Fuel Fill Door Position

99I05006

Courtesy of Ford Motor Co.

Fig. 1: Identifying Analog Instrument Cluster (Standard)

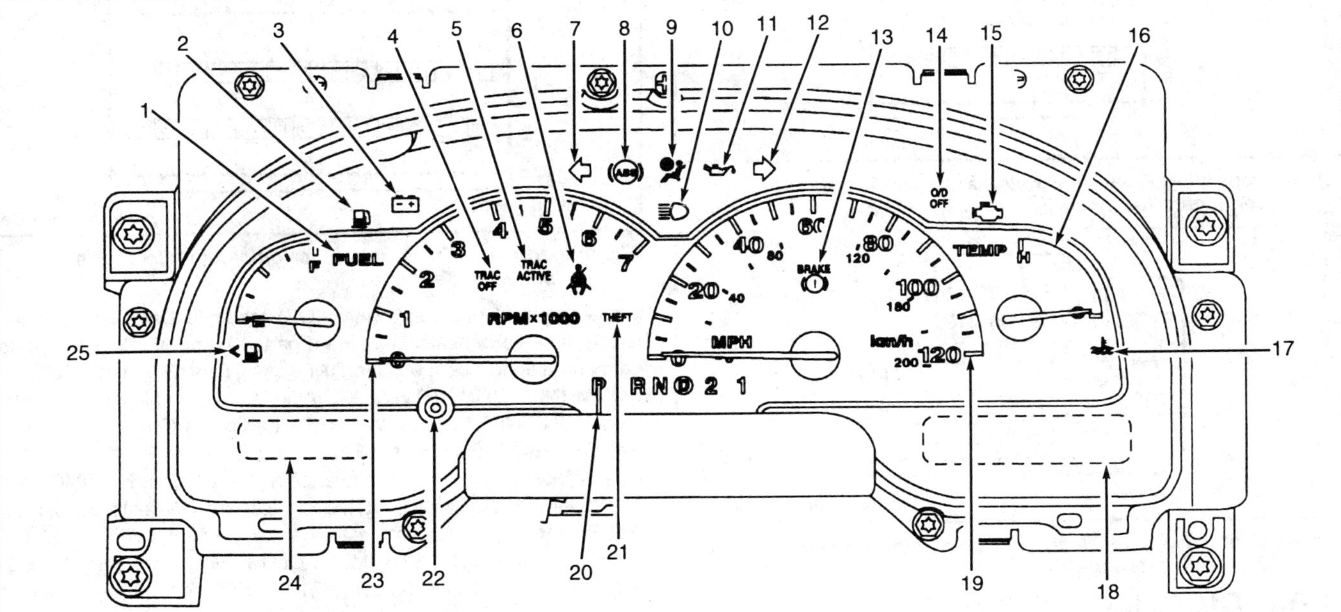

1. Fuel Gauge
2. Low Fuel Indicator
3. Charging System Indicator
4. TRAC OFF Indicator
5. TRAC ACTIVE Indicator
6. Safety Belt Indicator
7. Left Turn Signal Indicator
8. ABS Indicator
9. Air Bag Indicator
10. High Beam Indicator
11. Low Oil Pressure Indicator
12. Right Turn Signal Indicator
13. Brake System Indicator
14. O/D OFF Indicator
15. Service Engine Soon Indicator
16. Engine Coolant Temperature Gauge
17. Fail-Safe Cooling Indicator
18. Message Center Display
19. Speedometer
20. Transmission Range Indicator
21. Theft Indicator
22. Trip/Odometer Reset Button
23. RPM Gauge
24. Odometer/Trip Odometer Display
25. Fuel Fill Door Position

99A05007

Courtesy of Ford Motor Co.

Fig. 2: Identifying Analog Instrument Cluster (Optional)

CONNECTOR IDENTIFICATION

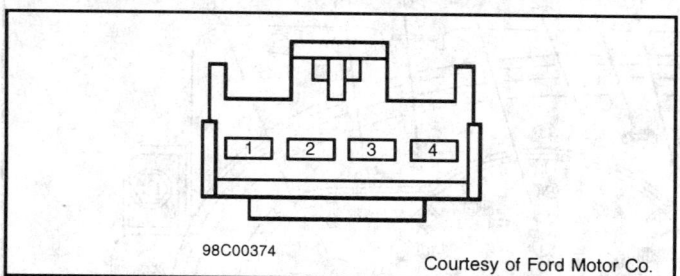

Fig. 3: Identifying Panel Dim Switch 4-Pin Connector Terminals

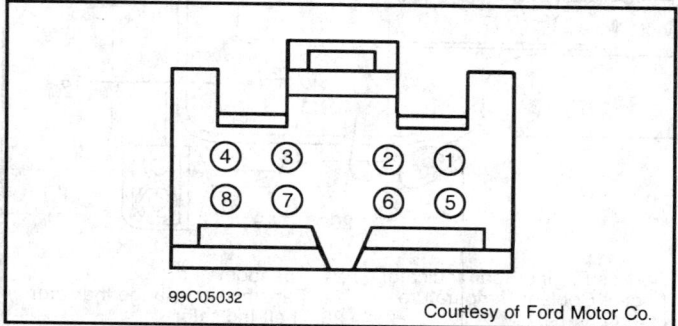

Fig. 4: Identifying Message Center Switch 8-Pin Connector Terminals

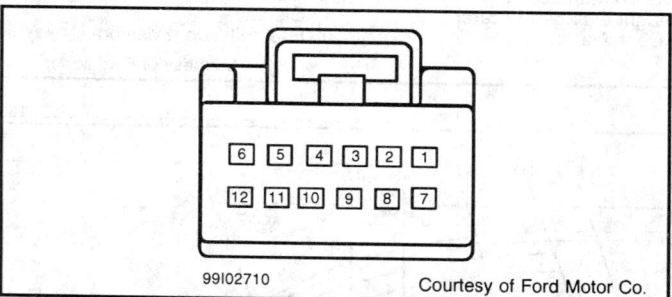

Fig. 5: Identifying Front/Rear Electronics Module 12-Pin Connector Terminals

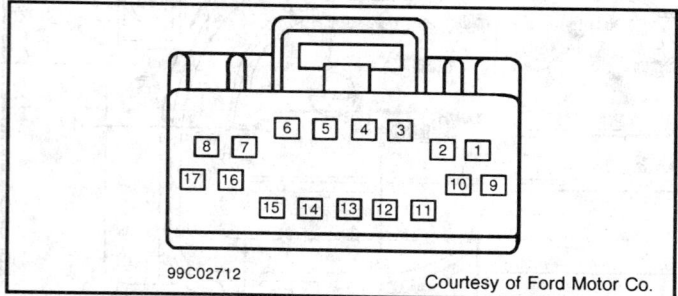

Fig. 6: Identifying Front/Rear Electronics Module 17-Pin Connector Terminals

SELF-DIAGNOSTIC SYSTEM

NOTE: *Many steps in the following tests refer to various connectors. These connectors are identified in illustrations. See Figs. 3-9 under CONNECTOR IDENTIFICATION.*

RETRIEVING CODES (SCAN TOOL)

NOTE: *All diagnostic tests are written specifically for New Generation Star (NGS) tester. Most generic scan tools should be able to perform all test procedures.*

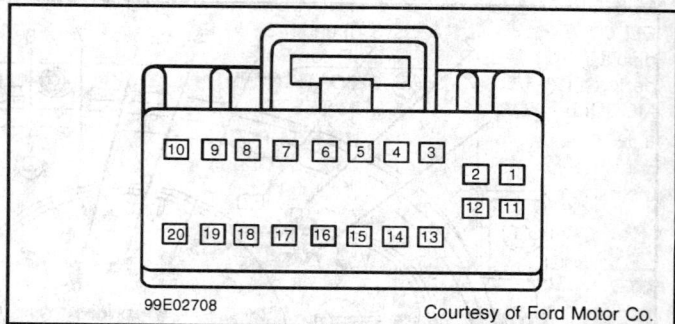

Fig. 7: Identifying Front/Rear Electronics Module & Instrument Cluster 20-Pin Connector Terminals

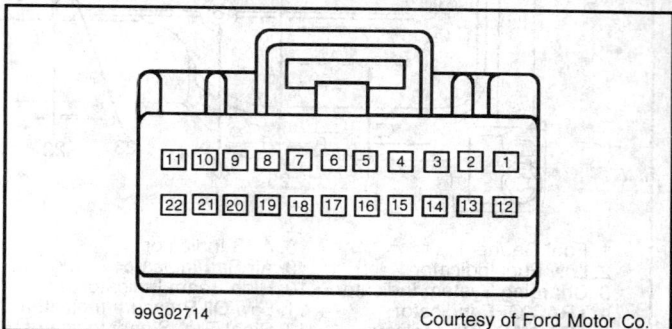

Fig. 8: Identifying Front/Rear Electronics Module & Instrument Cluster 22-Pin Connector Terminals

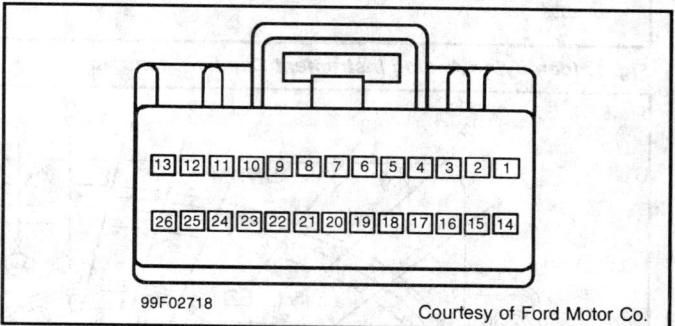

Fig. 9: Identifying Front/Rear Electronics Module 26-Pin Connector Terminals

Connect New Generation Star (NGS) tester to Data Link Connector (DLC), located beneath instrument panel. Using NGS tester, perform data link diagnostics test. See DATA LINK DIAGNOSTIC TEST under COMMUNICATION NETWORK DIAGNOSTICS in MODULE COMMUNICATIONS NETWORK – WINDSTAR article. If NGS tester responds with CKT914, CKT915 or CKT70 = ALL ECUS NO RESP/NOT EQUIP, repair module communications concern. See MODULE COMMUNICATIONS NETWORK – WINDSTAR article. If NGS tester displays NO RESP/NOT EQUIP for instrument cluster, perform TEST A: NO COMMUNICATION WITH INSTRUMENT CLUSTER under SYSTEM TESTS. If NGS tester displays NO RESP/NOT EQUIP for Front Electronics

Module (FEM), perform TEST B: NO COMMUNICATION WITH FRONT ELECTRONICS MODULE (FEM) under SYSTEM TESTS. If NGS tester displays NO RESP/NOT EQUIP for Rear Electronic Module (REM), perform TEST C: NO COMMUNICATION WITH REAR ELECTRONICS MODULE (REM) under SYSTEM TESTS.

If NGS tester responds with SYSTEM PASSED, retrieve and record continuous DTC. Erase continuous DTC. Using NGS tester, perform instrument cluster, FEM and REM self-test. Perform appropriate test in

accordance with DTC retrieved. See FRONT ELECTRONIC MODULE DTC INDEX, INSTRUMENT CLUSTER DTC INDEX, MESSAGE CENTER MODULE (MCM) DTC INDEX and/or REAR ELECTRONIC MODULE DTC INDEX table. Codes listed in these table are only for testing covered in this article. For complete DTC listing, see MODULE COMMUNICATIONS NETWORK – WINDSTAR article. If no DTC are retrieved, repair by symptom. See SYMPTOM CHART table under SYSTEM TESTS.

FRONT ELECTRONIC MODULE DTC INDEX

DTC [1]	Description	Test
B1254	Air Temperature External Sensor Circuit Failure	V
B1308	Oil Level Switch Circuit Short To Ground	F
B1342	ECU Defective	[2]
B1462	Seat Belt Switch Circuit Failure	H
B2479	Brake Park Switch Circuit Short To Ground	K
C1189	Brake Fluid Level Sensor Input Short Circuit To Ground	K

[1] – Codes listed in this table are only for testing covered in this article. For complete DTC listing, see MODULE COMMUNICATIONS NETWORK – WINDSTAR article.

[2] – Clear and document all DTC. Perform FEM self-test. If DTC B1342 is retrieved again, replace Front Electronic Module (FEM).

INSTRUMENT CLUSTER DTC INDEX

DTC [1]	Dealer Test Mode DTC	Description	Test
B1246	N/A	Dim Panel Potentiometer Switch Circuit Failure	AB
B1342	9342	ECU Defective	[2]
B1676	9676	Battery Voltage Out Of Range	A
B2167	A176	Overdrive Switch Circuit Short To Voltage	P
U1131	D131	Invalid Or Missing Data For Fuel System	[3] D
U2013	D013	Message Center Compass Inoperative	U

[1] – Codes listed in this table are only for testing covered in this article. For complete DTC listing, see MODULE COMMUNICATIONS NETWORK – WINDSTAR article.

[2] – Clear and document all DTC. Perform instrument cluster self-test. If DTC B1342 is retrieved again, replace instrument cluster.

[3] – Caused by Rear Electronic Module (REM).

MESSAGE CENTER MODULE DTC INDEX

DTC [1]	Description	Test
B1205	Message Center Compass Inoperative	U
B1342	ECU Defective	[2]
B1676	Battery Voltage Out Of Range	A
B2477	Module Configuration Failure	[3]
U2013	Message Center Compass Inoperative	U

[1] – Codes listed in this table are only for testing covered in this article. For complete DTC listing, see MODULE COMMUNICATIONS NETWORK – WINDSTAR article.

[2] – Clear and document all DTC. Perform message center self-test. If DTC B1342 is retrieved again, replace instrument cluster.

[3] – See MODULE COMMUNICATIONS NETWORK – WINDSTAR article for testing procedures.

REAR ELECTRONIC MODULE DTC INDEX

DTC [1]	Description	Test
B1201	Fuel Sender Circuit Failure	D
B1342	ECU Is Defective	[2]
B2570	Right Lamp Outage Signal Circuit Short To Ground	AA
B2571	Left Lamp Outage Signal Circuit Short To Ground	AA

[1] – Codes listed in this table are only for testing covered in this article. For complete DTC listing, see MODULE COMMUNICATIONS NETWORK – WINDSTAR article.

[2] – Clear and document all DTC. Perform REM self-test. If DTC B1342 is retrieved again, replace Rear Electronic Module (REM).

RETRIEVING CODES (DEALER TEST MODE)

Entering Dealer Test Mode – 1) Depress and hold instrument cluster trip odometer/reset button. Turn ignition switch to ON position. Continue pressing trip odometer/reset button until "tESt" is displayed in odometer.
2) Trip odometer/reset button must be released within 3 seconds of odometer displaying "tESt" to begin dealer test mode.
3) If no codes were displayed using scan tool, depress trip odometer/reset button to advance through following modes until "dtc" is displayed. Depressing trip odometer/reset button will display any continuous DTC stored. If any DTC are stored, perform appropriate test in accordance with

DTCs retrieved. See INSTRUMENT CLUSTER DTC INDEX table under RETRIEVING CODES (SCAN TOOL).
4) If no codes are stored, the following modes can be used to actuate instrument cluster displays. Depress trip odometer/reset button to advance through test modes. See DEALER TEST MODE DISPLAYS.
Exiting Dealer Test Mode – Turn ignition switch to OFF position, or press and hold trip odometer/reset button for 3 or more seconds, then release to exit instrument cluster dealer test mode. If no DTC are retrieved, repair by symptom. See SYMPTOM CHART table under SYSTEM TESTS.

DEALER TEST MODE DISPLAYS

All Segments Illuminated – Illuminates all odometer segments. If any odometer segment is inoperative, replace instrument cluster. See INSTRUMENT CLUSTER/MODULE (ICM) under REMOVAL & INSTALLATION.

"GAGE" – Activates gauge sweep of all gauges, then displays present gauge values. Also carries out checksum tests on ROM and EE. If gauge sweep is inoperative, replace instrument cluster. See INSTRUMENT CLUSTER/MODULE (ICM) under REMOVAL & INSTALLATION.

"bulb" – Illuminates all micro-controlled lamps and LEDs. If any bulb is inoperative, perform appropriate tests. See SYMPTOM CHART table under SYSTEM TESTS.

"r" – All micro-controlled lamps and LEDs return to normal operation. If alternating flashes of FAIL and ROM level are displayed, replace instrument cluster. See INSTRUMENT CLUSTER/MODULE (ICM) under REMOVAL & INSTALLATION.

"EE" – If alternating flashes of FAIL and EE level are displayed, replace instrument cluster. See INSTRUMENT CLUSTER/MODULE (ICM) under REMOVAL & INSTALLATION.

"dt" – Displays final manufacturing test date.

"dtc" – Displays instrument cluster DTCs. If any DTC are retrieved, perform appropriate test in accordance with DTCs retrieved. See INSTRUMENT CLUSTER DTC INDEX table under RETRIEVING CODES (SCAN TOOL).

"cFG0" – Displays software coding.

"cFG1" – Displays software coding.

"cFG2" – Displays software coding.

"cFG3" – Displays software coding.

"SPd xxx.x mi" – Displays speed in MPH. Speedometer will indicate present speed within tolerance. If display shows 0 and vehicle speed is more than 5MPH, input is not received, or input is invalid for one second or more. Perform TEST G: SPEEDOMETER INOPERATIVE under SYSTEM TESTS.

"SPd xxx.x kmi" – Displays speed in KM/H. Speedometer will indicate present speed within tolerance. If display shows 0 and vehicle speed is more than 10KM/H, input is not received, or input is invalid for one second or more. Perform TEST G: SPEEDOMETER INOPERATIVE under SYSTEM TESTS.

"tAc xxxx" – Displays tachometer data. Present RPM within tolerance. If display shows 0 and engine is running, if input is not received, or input received is invalid for one second or more. Perform TEST T: TACHOMETER INOPERATIVE under SYSTEM TESTS.

"FuEL" – Fuel gauge will display a filtered fuel level value. See FUEL LEVEL VALUE table. If value displayed is 0-20 circuit is shorted. Perform TEST D: INCORRECT FUEL GAUGE INDICATION under SYSTEM TESTS.

FUEL LEVEL VALUE

Gauge Reading	Value
Open Sending Unit [1]	255
Full Stop	222-242
Full Mark	205-225
3/4 Mark	170-186
1/2 mark	131-145
1/4 Mark	88-98
Empty Mark	37-45
Low Fuel Indicator	21-59
Short Circuit [1]	[2] 0-20

[1] – Circuit condition.
[2] – Perform TEST D: INCORRECT FUEL GAUGE INDICATION under SYSTEM TESTS.

"dEGC" – Displays engine temperature (°C). See TEMPERATURE VALUE table. If value displayed is -40C, engine temperature has not been received for more than 5 seconds. Perform TEST E: INCORRECT TEMPERATURE GAUGE INDICATION under SYSTEM TESTS.

TEMPERATURE VALUE

Temperature	Displayed Value
Cold Mark	49C
Normal Band Start	60C
Normal Band End	120C
No Message for 5 seconds	[1] -40C

[1] – Perform TEST E: INCORRECT TEMPERATURE GAUGE INDICATION under SYSTEM TESTS.

"bAtt" – Displays battery voltage input to HEC. Voltage gauge indicates present battery voltage. See BATTERY VOLTAGE table.

BATTERY VOLTAGE

Display Code	Voltage
93-102	6.9-9.1 (Low Voltage)
115-124	8.5-10.7 (Normal Band Start)
215-225	15.8-18 (Normal Band End)
230-241	16.9-19.1 (High Voltage)

"E0–E7" – Not used.

"PA–PH" – Not used.

"TEST" – Repeats test display cycle.

SYSTEM TESTS

NOTE: If module, sensor or other components requires replacement or removal, see REMOVAL & INSTALLATION. After any repairs to vehicle are made, always perform data link diagnostic test, see DATA LINK DIAGNOSTIC TEST under COMMUNICATION NETWORK DIAGNOSTICS in MODULE COMMUNICATIONS NETWORK – WINDSTAR article.

SYMPTOM CHART

Condition	Test
No Communication With Instrument Cluster	A
No Communication With Front Electronics Module (FEM)	B
No Communication With Rear Electronics Module (REM)	C
Incorrect Fuel Gauge Indication	D
Incorrect Temperature Gauge Indication	E
Low Oil Pressure Gauge Indicator Inoperative/Always ON	F
Speedometer Inoperative	G
Safety Belt Warning Indicator Inoperative (Chime Operative)/Does Not Operate Correctly	H
Door Ajar Indicator Inoperative (Chime Operative)/ Does Not Operate Correctly	I
Charge System Warning Indicator Never/Always On	J
Brake Warning Indicator Never/Always On	K
High Beam Indicator Inoperative/Always On	L
Low Washer Fluid Warning Indicator Inoperative/Always On	M
Air Bag Warning Indicator Inoperative/Always ON	[1]
ABS Warning Indicator Inoperative/Always On	N
Traction Control Warning Indicator Inoperative/Always On	O
O/D OFF Indicator Inoperative/Always On	P
SERVICE ENGINE SOON Indicator Always On	[2]
SERVICE ENGINE SOON Indicator Inoperative	Q
Turn/Hazard Indicator Inoperative/Always On	R
Odometer Inoperative	S
Tachometer Inoperative	T
Message Center Compass Inoperative	U
Message Center Not Operating Correctly	V
Message Center Switch Not Operating Correctly	W
Message Center Outside Temperature Display Operates Incorrectly	X
Message Center Low Fuel Level Display Not Operating Correctly	Y
Message Center Oil Life Status Inoperative	Z
Message Center Lamp Out Warning Indicator Inoperative	AA
Dim Panel Pontentiometer Switch Circuit Failure	AB
Message Center Display Is Blank	[3]
Anti-Theft Indicator Inoperative/Always On	[4]

SYMPTOM CHART (Cont.)

Condition	Test
1 – See DIAGNOSIS & TESTING article in MITCHELL® AIR BAG SERVICE & REPAIR MANUAL, DOMESTIC & IMPORTED MODELS.	
2 – See SELF-DIAGNOSTICS – EEC-V article in ENGINE PERFORMANCE in appropriate MITCHELL® manual.	
3 – Replace instrument cluster. Clear DTCs and repeat message center self-test.	
4 – See PASSIVE ANTI-THEFT SYSTEMS – WINDSTAR article.	

TEST A: NO COMMUNICATION WITH INSTRUMENT CLUSTER

CAUTION: Electronic modules are sensitive to static electrical charges. Proper grounding of technician and component is essential to prevent damage.

1) Turn ignition switch to OFF position. Disconnect instrument cluster 22-pin harness connector C239, and 20-pin harness connector C240. Turn ignition switch to ON position. Measure voltage between specified instrument cluster harness connector terminals and ground. See INSTRUMENT CLUSTER VOLTAGE table. If all readings are 10 volts or more, go to next step. If any reading is less than 10 volts, repair circuit.

INSTRUMENT CLUSTER VOLTAGE

Connector	Terminal	Circuit No.
C239	11	1001 (WHT/YEL)
C240	7	295 (LT BLU/PNK)
C240	8 & 9	1112 (WHT/LT BLU)

2) Turn ignition switch to OFF position. Measure resistance between instrument cluster harness connector C240 terminal No. 12 (Black wire) and ground. If resistance is less than 5 ohms, repair module communication concern. See MODULE COMMUNICATIONS NETWORK – WINDSTAR article. If resistance is 5 ohms or more, repair open or poor connection in Black wire to ground connector G304, located behind left kick panel.

TEST B: NO COMMUNICATION WITH FRONT ELECTRONICS MODULE (FEM)

1) Turn ignition switch to OFF position. Disconnect FEM harness connectors C190 (12-pin), C192 (17-pin), C346 (20-pin) and C348 (4-pin). Turn ignition switch to ON position. Measure voltage between FEM harness connector C346 terminal No. 1 (Light Blue/Red wire) and ground. Measure voltage between FEM harness connector C190 terminal No. 6 (Red wire) and ground. If voltage is more than 10 volts at both terminals, go to next step. If voltage is 10 volts or less at either terminal, repair open in Light Blue/Red wire or Red wire.

2) Turn ignition switch to OFF position. Measure resistance between FEM harness connector C190 terminal No. 12 (Black wire), FEM harness connector C192 terminals No. 11, 13, 14 and 15 (Black wires) and ground. If resistance is less than 5 ohms at every terminal, repair module communications concern. See MODULE COMMUNICATIONS NETWORK – WINDSTAR article. If resistance is 5 ohms or more at any terminal, repair open in Black wire.

TEST C: NO COMMUNICATION WITH REAR ELECTRONICS MODULE (REM)

NOTE: Turn ignition switch from OFF to ON position to enable system power feature.

1) Turn ignition switch to OFF position. Remove fuse No. 16 (10-amp) from Central Junction Block (CJB). Turn ignition switch to ON position. Measure voltage between CJB fuse No. 16 input terminal and ground. If voltage is more than 10 volts, install fuse No. 16 and go to next step. If voltage is 10 volts or less, repair (CJB) power supply circuit.

2) Turn ignition switch to OFF position. Disconnect REM 20-pin harness connector C343. Turn ignition switch to ON position. Measure voltage between REM harness connector C343 terminal No. 3 (White/Yellow

wire) and ground. If voltage is more than 10 volts, go to next step. If voltage is 10 volts or less, repair open in White/Yellow wire.

3) Turn ignition switch to OFF position. Disconnect REM harness connectors C341 (22-pin) and C342 (26-pin). Turn ignition switch to ON position. Measure resistance between appropriate REM harness connector terminals and ground. See REM VOLTAGE TERMINALS table. If resistance is less than 5 ohms at each terminal, repair module communications concern. See MODULE COMMUNICATIONS NETWORK – WINDSTAR article. If resistance is 5 ohms or more at any terminal, repair open in Black wire.

REM VOLTAGE TERMINALS

Connector	Terminal
C341	12
C342	11
C342	12
C342	25
C342	26

TEST D: INCORRECT FUEL GAUGE INDICATION

NOTE: Fuel gauge does not change indication unless there has been at LEAST 3 gallons of fuel added or deleted between ignition cycles.

1) Using NGS tester, perform Rear Electronic Module (REM) and instrument cluster self-tests. If no DTCs were retrieved, go to next step. If any DTCs were retrieved, go to step **6)**.

2) Turn ignition switch to ON position. Using NGS tester, select IC FUEL GAUGE CONTROL active command. Trigger FUELLEVEL active command. Monitor fuel gauge while adjusting FUELLEVEL active command to read 50% and 100%. If fuel gauge needle started at empty (E), moved to half at 50% and then moved to full (F) at 100%, go to next step. If fuel gauge needle does not started at empty (E), moved to half at 50% and then moved to full (F) at 100%, replace instrument cluster.

3) Turn ignition switch to OFF position. Disconnect fuel pump module 8-pin harness connector C412, located at top of fuel tank. Connect one lead of Instrument Gauge System Tester (014–R1063) or equivalent to fuel pump module harness connector C412 terminal No. 5 (Light Blue/Yellow wire). Connect second lead from Instrument Gauge System Tester (IGST) to fuel pump module harness connector C412 terminal No. 8 (Light Green/Violet wire). Turn IGST power switch to ON position and set IGST to 15 ohms. Turn ignition switch to ON position, wait one minute. Turn ignition switch to OFF position. Set IGST to 160 ohms. Turn ignition switch to ON position, wait one minute. Fuel gauge should read full or above. Turn ignition switch to OFF position. Set IGST to 15 ohms. Turn ignition switch to ON position, wait one minute. Fuel gauge should read empty or below. Turn ignition switch to OFF position. If fuel gauge operated correctly, go to next step. If fuel gauge does not operate correctly, go to step **6)**.

4) Visually inspect fuel tank for damage or deformation. If there is no damage or deformity, go to next step. If there is damage or deformity, replace fuel tank.

5) Inspect fuel pump assembly for damaged wiring, connectors, float and float rod or obstruction. If fuel pump or wiring is damaged, repair as necessary. If fuel pump and wiring are okay, replace fuel level sender.

6) Disconnect Rear Electronic Module (REM) harness connectors. Measure resistance between REM harness connector C343 terminal No. 15 (Light Green/Violet wire) and ground. Measure resistance between REM harness connector C342 terminal No. 23 (Light Blue/Yellow wire) and ground. If resistance is less than 10 k/ohms at both terminals, go to next step. If resistance is 10 k/ohms or more at both terminals, go to step **8)**.

7) Disconnect fuel pump module 8-pin harness connector C412. Measure resistance between REM harness connector C343 terminal No. 15 (Light Green/Violet wire) and ground. Measure resistance between REM harness connector C342 terminal No. 23 (Light Blue/Yellow wire) and ground. If resistance is less than 10 k/ohms at either terminal, repair short to ground in Light Green/Violet wire or Light Blue/Yellow wire. If resistance is 10 k/ohms or more at both terminals, repair fuel sender circuit.

8) Turn ignition switch to OFF position. Disconnect REM harness connectors. Disconnect fuel pump module 8-pin harness connector C412. Measure resistance between REM harness connector C343 terminal No. 15 (Light Green/Violet wire) and fuel pump module harness connector C412 terminal No. 8 (Light Green/Violet wire). Measure resistance between REM harness connector C342 terminal No. 23 (Light Blue/Yellow wire) and fuel pump module harness connector C412 terminal No. 5 (Light Blue/Yellow wire). If both resistances are less than 5 ohms, go to next step. If either resistance is 5 ohms or more, repair open in Light Green/Violet wire and/or Light Blue/Yellow wire.

9) Measure resistance between fuel pump module terminals No. 8 and 5 (component side). If resistance is 15-160 ohms, go to next step. If resistance is not 15-160 ohms, repair or replace fuel pump module as necessary.

10) Turn ignition switch to ON position. Measure voltage between REM harness connector C343 terminal No. 15 (Light Green/Violet wire) and ground. Measure voltage between REM harness connector C342 terminal No. 23 (Light Blue/Yellow wire and ground. If voltage is not present, go to next step. If voltage is present, repair short to voltage in Light Green/Violet wire and/or Light Blue/Yellow wire.

11) Measure voltage between fuel pump module harness connector C412 terminals No. 8 (Light Green/Violet wire) and No. 5 (Light Blue/Yellow wire) and ground. If voltage is present, repair short to voltage. If voltage is not present, replace REM. Test system for normal operation. If incorrect fuel gauge indication is still present, replace instrument cluster.

TEST E: INCORRECT TEMPERATURE GAUGE INDICATION

1) Using NGS tester, perform instrument cluster self-test. If no DTCs were retrieved, go to next step. If DTC U1073 was retrieved, repair coolant temperature sensor input circuit. See SELF-DIAGNOSTICS – EEC-V article in ENGINE PERFORMANCE in appropriate MITCHELL® manual. For all other instrument cluster DTC, perform appropriate test in accordance with DTC retrieved. See INSTRUMENT CLUSTER DTC INDEX table under SELF-DIAGNOSTIC SYSTEM.

2) Turn ignition switch to ON position. Using NGS tester, select instrument cluster ENGINE COOLANT CONTROL active command. Trigger ENGCOOLANT active command. Monitor engine coolant temperature gauge while adjusting ENGCOOLANT active command to read 50% and 100%. If engine coolant temperature gauge needle started at cold, moved to half at 50% and then moved to full hot at 100%, repair coolant temperature sensor input circuit. See SELF–DIAGNOSTICS – EEC-V article in ENGINE PERFORMANCE in appropriate MITCHELL® manual. If gauge did not perform correctly, replace instrument cluster.

TEST F: LOW OIL PRESSURE INDICATOR INOPERATIVE

1) Using NGS tester, perform FEM self-test. If DTC B1308 is retrieved, go to next step. If no DTC was retrieved , go to step **4)**. If any other DTC were retrieved, perform appropriate test in accordance with DTC retrieved. See INSTRUMENT CLUSTER DTC INDEX table under SELF-DIAGNOSTIC SYSTEM.

2) Turn ignition switch to ON position. Using NGS tester, select and monitor FEM PID OIL_LVL. If PID reads OK, go to next step. If PID reads NOTOK, replace FEM.

3) Disconnect oil pressure switch harness connector C169. Monitor FEM PID OIL_LVL. If PID reads OK, replace oil pressure switch. If PID reads NOTOK, repair short to ground in Brown/Orange wire.

4) Turn ignition switch to ON position. Monitor FEM PID OIL_LVL. Turn ignition switch to START position. Monitor FEM PID OIL_LVL. If PID does not read OK, go to next step, If PID reads NOTOK and changes to OK, go to step **8)**.

5) Turn ignition switch to OFF position. Monitor FEM PID OIL_LVL. Disconnect oil pressure switch harness connector C169. Connect fused jumper wire between oil pressure switch harness connector C169 (Brown/Orange wire) and ground. If FEM PID does not read NOTOK, remove jumper wire, EXIT FEM PID and go to next step. If FEM PID reads NOTOK replace oil pressure switch. If fused jumper wire blows, remove jumper and go to step **7)**.

6) Turn ignition switch to OFF position. Disconnect FEM 12-pin harness connector C190. Measure resistance between FEM harness connector C190 terminal No. 9 (Brown/Orange wire) and oil pressure switch harness connector C169 (Brown/Orange wire). If resistance is less than 5 ohms, go to next step. If resistance is 5 ohms or more, repair open in Brown/Orange wire.

7) Measure voltage between FEM harness connector C190 terminal No. 9 (Brown/Orange wire) and ground. If no voltage is present, replace FEM. If voltage is present, repair short to voltage.

8) Turn ignition switch to ON position. Monitor low oil pressure indicator. Indicator should illuminate. Turn ignition switch to START position. Monitor low oil pressure indicator. Indicator should remain illuminated for about 3 seconds after engine is started, then turn off. If oil pressure indicator is okay, replace FEM. If oil pressure indicator does not prove out, replace instrument cluster.

TEST G: SPEEDOMETER IS INOPERATIVE

1) Using NGS tester, perform instrument cluster self-test. If no DTCs were retrieved, go to next step. If DTC U1041 was retrieved, see SELF-DIAGNOSTICS – EEC-V article in ENGINE PERFORMANCE in appropriate MITCHELL® manual. If any other DTCs were retrieved, perform appropriate test in accordance with DTC retrieved. See INSTRUMENT CLUSTER DTC INDEX table under SELF-DIAGNOSTIC SYSTEM.

2) Turn ignition switch to ON position. Using NGS tester, select instrument cluster SPEEDOMETER COMMAND active command. Trigger SPDOMETER, and scroll in increments of 5%. Monitor speedometer gauge. Speedometer should increase in increments of 10 MPH for every 5%. If speedometer increases within specification, see SELF-DIAGNOSTICS – EEC-V article in ENGINE PERFORMANCE in appropriate MITCHELL® manual. If speedometer does not increase within specification, replace instrument cluster.

TEST H: SAFETY BELT WARNING INDICATOR IS INOPERATIVE (CHIME IS OPERATIVE)/ DOES NOT OPERATE CORRECTLY

1) Using NGS tester, perform Front Electronic Module (FEM) self-test. If DTC B1462 was retrieved, go to next step. If any other DTCs were retrieved, perform appropriate test in accordance with DTC retrieved. See INSTRUMENT CLUSTER DTC INDEX table under SELF-DIAGNOSTIC SYSTEM. If no DTCs were retrieved, go to step **8)**.

2) Verify that safety belt is unbuckled. Clear DTCs and repeat FEM self-test. If DTC B1462 is retrieved, go to next step. If DTC B1462 is not retrieved, go to step **8)**.

3) Verify safety belt is unbuckled. Using NGS tester, select and monitor FEM PID D_SBELT. If PID reads IN, go to next step. If PID does not read IN, replace FEM.

4) Turn ignition switch to OFF position. Disconnect safety belt switch 2-pin harness connector C304. Turn ignition switch to ON position. Connect a fused jumper wire between safety belt switch harness connector C304 terminal No. 1 (Orange wire) and ground. Select and monitor FEM PID D_SBELT. If PID reads OUT, go to next step. If PID does not read OUT, remove jumper wire and go to step **6)**. If fused jumper blows, remove jumper wire and go to step **7)**.

5) Measure resistance between safety belt switch harness connector C304 terminal No. 2 (Black wire) and ground. If resistance is less than 5 ohms, replace safety belt switch (part of buckle end). If resistance is 5 ohms or more, repair open in Black wire.

6) Turn ignition switch to OFF position. Disconnect FEM 20-pin harness connector C346. Measure resistance between FEM harness connector C346 terminal No. 10 (Orange wire) and safety belt switch harness connector C304 terminal No. 1 (Orange wire). If resistance is less than 5 ohms, go to next step. If resistance is 5 ohms or more, repair open in Orange wire.

7) Measure voltage between FEM harness connector C346 terminal No. 10 (Orange wire) and ground. If voltage is present, repair short to voltage in Orange wire. If voltage is not present, replace FEM.

8) Using NGS tester, select and monitor FEM PID D_SBELT while fastening and unfastening safety belt. If PID does not read IN, go to next step. If PID reads IN, replace instrument cluster.

9) Turn ignition switch to OFF position. Disconnect safety belt switch 2-pin harness connector C304. Turn ignition switch to ON position. Select and monitor FEM PID D_SBELT. If PID does not read IN, go to next step. If PID reads IN, replace safety belt switch (part of buckle end).

10) Turn ignition switch to OFF position. Disconnect FEM 20-pin harness connector C346. Measure resistance between FEM harness connector C346 terminal No. 10 (Orange wire) and safety belt harness connector C304 terminal No. 1 (Orange wire). If resistance is less than 5 ohms, replace FEM. If resistance is 5 ohms or more, repair open in Orange wire.

TEST I: DOOR AJAR INDICATOR IS INOPERATIVE (CHIME IS OPERATIVE)/ DOES NOT OPERATE CORRECTLY

1) Using NGS tester, perform FEM self-test. If no DTCs were retrieved, go to next step. If any DTCs were retrieved, perform appropriate test in accordance with DTC retrieved. See FRONT ELECTRONIC MODULE table under DIAGNOSTIC TROUBLE CODE (DTC) DEFINITIONS in MODULE COMMUNICATIONS NETWORK – WINDSTAR article.

2) Select and monitor FEM PID D_DOOR. Open driver's door. If PID reads CLOSED, go to next step. If PID does not read CLOSED, go to step **5)**.

3) Disconnect driver's door ajar switch harness connector C500. Monitor FEM PID D_DOOR. If PID reads CLOSED, go to next step. If PID does not read CLOSED, replace driver's door ajar switch.

4) Turn ignition switch to OFF position. Disconnect FEM 20-pin harness connector C346. Measure resistance between FEM harness connector C346 terminal No. 8 (Light Green/Black wire) and ground. If resistance is more than 10 k/ohms, replace FEM. If resistance is 10 k/ohms or less, repair short to ground in Light Green/Black wire.

5) Select and monitor FEM PID P_DOOR. Open passenger's door. If PID reads CLOSED, go to next step. If PID does not read CLOSED, go to step **8)**.

6) Disconnect front passenger's door ajar switch harness connector C300. Monitor FEM PID P_DOOR. If PID reads CLOSED, go to next step. If PID does not read CLOSED, replace front passenger's door ajar switch.

7) Turn ignition switch to OFF position. Disconnect FEM 26-pin harness connector C347. Measure resistance between FEM harness connector C347 terminal No. 15 (Yellow/Light Green wire) and ground. If resistance is more than 10 k/ohms, replace FEM. If resistance is 10 k/ohms or less, repair short to ground in Yellow/Light Green wire.

8) Using NGS tester, select instrument cluster WARNING LAMPS AND CHIME active command. Trigger ALL LAMPS active command. Observe door ajar warning indicator. If door ajar warning indicator illuminates, system is okay. Repeat FEM and instrument cluster self-tests. If door ajar warning indicator does not illuminate, replace instrument cluster.

TEST J: CHARGE SYSTEM WARNING INDICATOR NEVER/ALWAYS ON

1) Check charging system operation. See appropriate GENERATORS article in STARTING & CHARGING SYSTEMS. If charging system is operating correctly, go to next step. If charging system is not operating correctly, make needed repairs before proceeding.

2) Turn ignition switch to ON position. Observe charge system warning indicator. Turn ignition switch to START position. Observe charge system warning indicator. If charge system warning indicator illuminates for 3 seconds, then turns off, repair charging system as necessary. See appropriate GENERATORS article in STARTING & CHARGING SYSTEMS. If charge system warning indicator does not illuminate for 3 seconds, then turn off, replace instrument cluster.

TEST K: BRAKE WARNING INDICATOR NEVER/ALWAYS ON

NOTE: Before testing, ensure brake fluid level is correct.

1) Turn ignition switch to ON position. Observe brake warning indicator. Turn ignition switch to START position. Observe brake warning indicator. If brake warning indicator does not illuminate for 3 seconds, then turn off, go to next step. If brake warning indicator illuminates for 3 seconds, then turns off, system is okay. Repeat FEM and instrument cluster self-test.

2) Using NGS tester, perform FEM self-test. If DTC C1189 is retrieved, go to next step. If DTC B2479 is retrieved, go to step **10)**. If no DTCs are retrieved, go to step **5)**.

3) Using NGS tester, select FEM PID BRK_LVL. If PID reads NOTOK, go to next step. If PID does not read NOTOK, replace FEM.

4) Disconnect brake fluid warning switch 3-pin harness connector C139. Monitor FEM PID BRK_LVL. If PID reads NO, replace brake fluid warning switch. If PID does not read NO, repair short to ground in Dark Blue wire.

5) Turn ignition switch to OFF position. Disconnect brake fluid warning switch 3-pin harness connector C139. Monitor FEM PID BRK_LVL. Connect a 10-amp fused jumper wire between brake fluid warning switch harness connector C139 terminal No. 1 (Dark Blue wire) and ground. Turn ignition switch to ON position. Monitor FEM PID BRK_LVL. If PID does not read OK and then NOTOK, remove jumper wire and go to next step. If PID reads OK then NOTOK, go to step **8)**. If fused jumper wire blows, remove jumper wire and go to step **7)**.

6) Turn ignition switch to OFF position. Disconnect FEM 12-pin harness connector C190. Measure resistance between FEM harness connector C190 terminal No. 11 (Dark Blue wire) and brake fluid warning switch harness connector C139 terminal No. 1 (Dark Blue wire). If resistance is less than 5 ohms, go to next step. If resistance is 5 ohms or more, repair open in Dark Blue wire.

7) Measure voltage between FEM harness connector C190 terminal No. 11 (Dark Blue wire) and ground. If voltage is present, repair short to voltage in Dark Blue wire. If voltage is not present, replace FEM.

8) Measure resistance between brake fluid warning switch harness connector C139 terminal No. 3 (Black wire) and ground. If resistance is less than 5 ohms, go to next step. If resistance is 5 ohms or more, repair open in Black wire.

9) Measure resistance between brake fluid warning switch terminals No. 1 and 3 (component side) with fluid level empty then full. Resistance should be less than 5 ohms when empty and more than 10 k/ohms when full. If resistance is as specified, go to next step. If resistance is not as specified, replace brake fluid warning switch.

NOTE: Ensure parking brake control is fully released during FEM self-test

10) Using NGS tester, clear DTC and repeat FEM self-test. If DTC B1279 is retrieved, go to next step. If DTC B1279 is not retrieved, go to step **13)**.

11) Select and monitor FEM PID PRK_BRK. If PID reads ON, go to next step. If PID does not read ON, replace FEM.

12) Disconnect park brake switch single-pin harness connector C321. Monitor FEM PID PRK_BRK. If PID reads ON, repair short to ground in Red/Yellow wire. If PID does not read ON, replace park brake switch.

13) Select and monitor FEM PID PRK_BRK with parking brake control disengaged and engaged. If PID reading does not agree with park brake position, go to next step. If PID reading agrees with park brake position, replace instrument cluster.

14) Turn ignition switch to OFF position. Disconnect park brake switch harness connector C321. Connect 10-amp fused jumper between park brake switch harness connector C321 (Red/Yellow wire) and ground. Monitor FEM PID PRK_BRK. If PID does not read ON, go to next step. If PID reads ON, replace park brake switch. If fused jumper wire blows, remove jumper wire and go to step **16)**.

15) Turn ignition switch to OFF position. Disconnect FEM 20-pin harness connector C346. Measure resistance between FEM harness connector C346 terminal No. 19 (Red/Yellow wire) and park brake switch harness connector (Red/Yellow wire). If resistance is less than 5 ohms, go to step **7**). If resistance is 5 ohms or more, repair open in Red/Yellow wire.

16) Measure voltage between FEM harness connector C346 terminal No. 19 (Red/Yellow wire) and ground. If voltage is present, repair short to voltage in Red/Yellow wire. If voltage is not present, replace FEM.

TEST L: HIGH BEAM INDICATOR IS INOPERATIVE/ALWAYS ON

1) Using NGS tester, perform instrument cluster self-test. If no DTCs were retrieved, go to next step. If DTC B2586 is retrieved, see AUTOLAMP SYSTEMS – WINDSTAR article for testing procedure.

2) Turn ignition switch to ACC position. Place headlight switch in ON position. Ensure multifunction switch is in high beam position. Select and monitor instrument cluster PID LSWMODE. If PID reads HIGH_B, go to next step. If PID does not read HIGH_B, repair high beam circuit. See AUTOLAMP SYSTEMS – WINDSTAR article.

3) Select instrument cluster WARNING LAMPS AND CHIME active command. Trigger ALL LAMPS active command. If high beam indicator turns on, system is okay. If high beam indicator does not turn on, replace instrument cluster.

TEST M: LOW WASHER FLUID WARNING DISPLAY IS INOPERATIVE/ALWAYS ON

1) Using NGS tester, perform FEM self-test. If DTC B1482 is retrieved, go to next step. If no DTCs were retrieved, go to step **4**).

2) Select and monitor FEM PID WFLUID. If PID reads LOW, go to next step. If PID does not read LOW, replace FEM.

3) Disconnect washer fluid level switch 2-pin harness connector C117. Monitor FEM PID WFLUID. If PID reads OK, replace washer fluid level switch. If PID does not read OK, repair short to ground in Gray wire.

4) Disconnect washer fluid level switch 2-pin harness connector C117. Monitor FEM PID WFLUID. Connect a 10-amp fused jumper wire between washer fluid level switch harness connector C117 terminal No. 1 (Gray wire) and ground. Monitor FEM PID WFLUID. If PID does not read OK and change to LOW, remove jumper, exit PID and go to next step. If fused jumper wire blows, remove jumper and go to step **6**). If PID changes from OK to LOW, go to step **7**).

5) Turn ignition switch to OFF position. Disconnect FEM 22-pin harness connector C191. Measure resistance between FEM harness connector C191 terminal No. 15 (Gray wire) and washer fluid level switch harness connector C117 terminal No. 1 (Gray wire). If resistance is less than 5 ohms, go to next step. If resistance is 5 ohms or more, repair open in Gray wire.

6) Turn ignition switch to OFF position. Disconnect FEM 22-pin harness connector C191. Measure voltage between FEM harness connector C191 terminal No. 15 (Gray wire) and ground. If voltage is present, repair short to voltage in Gray wire. If no voltage present, replace FEM.

7) Measure resistance between washer fluid level switch connector C117 terminal No. 2 (Black wire) and ground. If resistance is less than 5 ohms, go to next step. If resistance is 5 ohms or more, repair open in Black wire.

8) Measure resistance between washer fluid level switch terminals No. 1 and 2 (component side), while reservoir is empty and then full. Resistance should be less than 5 ohms when empty and more than 10 k/ohms when full. If resistance is as specified, replace instrument cluster. If resistance is not as specified, replace washer fluid level switch.

TEST N: ABS WARNING INDICATOR IS INOPERATIVE/ALWAYS ON

Select instrument cluster WARNING LAMPS AND CHIME active command. Trigger ALL LAMPS active command. Observe ABS warning indicator. If ABS warning indicator illuminates, repair ABS system concern. See appropriate ANTI-LOCK article in BRAKES in appropriate MITCHELL® manual. If ABS warning indicator does not illuminate, replace instrument cluster. See INSTRUMENT CLUSTER/MODULE (ICM) under REMOVAL & INSTALLATION.

TEST O: TRACTION CONTROL INDICATOR IS INOPERATIVE/ALWAYS ON

1) Using NGS tester, perform instrument cluster self-test. If no DTCs were retrieved, go to next step. If DTC U1043 is retrieved, see appropriate ANTI-LOCK article in BRAKES in appropriate MITCHELL® manual for testing procedure. If any other DTCs were retrieved, perform appropriate test in accordance with DTC retrieved. See INSTRUMENT CLUSTER DTC INDEX table under SELF-DIAGNOSTIC SYSTEM.

2) Select instrument cluster WARNING LAMPS AND CHIME active command. Trigger ALL LAMPS active command. Observe TRAC ACTIVE and TRAC OFF indicators. If both indicators are illuminated, go to next step. If TRAC ACTIVE indicator is always on, repair traction control system. See appropriate ANTI-LOCK article in BRAKES in appropriate MITCHELL® manual for testing procedure. If both indicators are not illuminated, replace instrument cluster.

3) Select and monitor instrument cluster PID TRAC_SW with traction off switch in OFF and ON positions. If PID agrees with switch position, go to next step. If PID does not agree switch position, replace instrument cluster.

4) Disconnect traction off switch 6-pin harness connector C257. Connect a 10-amp fused jumper wire between traction off switch harness connector C257 terminal No. 3 (White/Pink wire) and ground. Turn ignition switch to ON position. If TRAC OFF indicator illuminates, go to next step. If TRAC OFF indicator does not illuminate, repair open in White/Pink wire. See WIRING DIAGRAMS.

5) Measure resistance between traction off switch harness connector C257 terminal No. 4 (Black wire) and ground. If resistance is less than 5 ohms, replace traction off switch. If resistance is 5 ohms or more, repair open in Black wire.

TEST P: O/D INDICATOR IS INOPERATIVE/ALWAYS ON

1) Ensure operation of overdrive function. If overdrive functions correctly, go to next step. If overdrive does not function correctly, repair overdrive system as necessary. See appropriate article in appropriate MITCHELL® TRANSMISSION SERVICE & REPAIR manual.

2) Turn ignition switch to ON position. Using NGS tester, select instrument cluster WARNING LAMPS AND CHIME active command. Trigger ALL LAMPS active command. Observe O/D OFF indicator light. If O/D OFF indicator light does not illuminate, replace instrument cluster. If O/D OFF indicator light does illuminate, repair overdrive system as necessary. See appropriate article in appropriate MITCHELL® TRANSMISSION SERVICE & REPAIR manual.

TEST Q: SERVICE ENGINE SOON INDICATOR IS INOPERATIVE

Turn ignition switch to ON position. Using NGS tester, select instrument cluster WARNING LAMPS AND CHIME active command. Trigger ALL LAMPS active command. Observe SERVICE ENGINE SOON warning indicator. If SERVICE ENGINE SOON warning indicator illuminates, repair engine performance concern. See SELF-DIAGNOSTICS – EEC-V article in ENGINE PERFORMANCE in appropriate MITCHELL® manual. If SERVICE ENGINE SOON warning indicator does not illuminate, replace instrument cluster.

TEST R: TURN/HAZARD INDICATOR IS INOPERATIVE/ALWAYS ON

1) Turn ignition switch to ON position. Operate turn signals. Operate hazard lights. If turn signals and hazard lights operate correctly, go to next step. If turn signals and hazard lamps do not operate correctly, repair as necessary. See appropriate wiring diagram in EXTERIOR LIGHTS article

2) Turn ignition switch to RUN position. Using NGS tester, select instrument cluster WARNING LAMPS AND CHIME active command. Trigger ALL LAMPS active command. Observe left and right turn signal indicators. If indicators illuminate, check communication between FEM,

REM and instrument cluster. See MODULE COMMUNICATIONS NETWORK – WINDSTAR article. If indicators do not illuminate, replace instrument cluster.

TEST S: ODOMETER INOPERATIVE

NOTE: If instrument cluster does not receive odometer rolling count status for 2 seconds, dashes will be displayed in odometer display and ABS warning light will be on.

1) Using NGS tester, perform instrument cluster self-test. If no DTCs were retrieved, go to next step. If DTC U1123 is retrieved, see appropriate ANTI-LOCK article in BRAKES in appropriate MITCHELL® manual. If any other DTCs were retrieved, perform appropriate test in accordance with DTC retrieved. See INSTRUMENT CLUSTER DTC INDEX table under SELF-DIAGNOSTIC SYSTEM.

2) Using NGS tester, select ODOMETER READING function test. Vehicle odometer reading should be retrieved in miles and kilometers. If odometer reading is retrieved, go to next step. If odometer readings are not retrieved, replace instrument cluster.

3) Turn ignition switch to ON position. Press trip odometer button. Display should change odometer to trip odometer. If display changes from odometer to trip odometer, system is okay. If display does not change from odometer to trip odometer, replace instrument cluster.

TEST T: TACHOMETER INOPERATIVE

Turn ignition switch to ON position. Using NGS tester, select instrument cluster TACHOMETER CONTROL active command. Trigger TCHOMETER active command. Adjust scroll knob until TCHMETER reads 50%. Observe tachometer gauge reading. Adjust scroll knob until TCHMETER reads 100%. Observe change in tachometer gauge reading. Tachometer gauge needle should start at 0 RPM, move to 3500 RPM at 50% and 7000 RPM at 100%. If tachometer operates as specified, check communication between PCM and instrument cluster. See MODULE COMMUNICATIONS NETWORK – WINDSTAR article. If tachometer does not operate as specified, replace instrument cluster.

TEST U: MESSAGE CENTER COMPASS INOPERATIVE

1) Using NGS tester, perform Message Center Module (MCM) self-test. If DTC B2013 is retrieved, go to next step. If any other DTCs were retrieved, perform appropriate test in accordance with DTCs retrieved. See MESSAGE CENTER MODULE (MCM) DTC INDEX table under SELF-DIAGNOSTIC SYSTEM. If no DTCs were retrieved, go to step **8)**.

2) Turn ignition switch to OFF position. Disconnect compass sensor module 4-pin harness connector C918. Turn ignition switch to ON position. Measure voltage between compass sensor module harness connector C918 terminal No. 2 (Red/Yellow wire) and ground. If voltage is more then 10 volts, go to next step. If voltage is 10 volts or less, repair open in Red/Yellow wire.

3) Measure resistance between compass sensor module harness connector C918 terminal No. 1 (Black wire) and ground. If resistance is less than 5 ohms, go to next step. If resistance is 5 ohms or more, repair open in Black wire.

4) Remove instrument cluster and disconnect instrument cluster 22-pin harness connector C239. Measure resistance between compass sensor module harness connector C918 terminal No. 3 (White/Orange wire) and instrument cluster harness connector C239 terminal No. 13 (White/Orange wire). If resistance is less than 5 ohms, go to next step. If resistance is more than 5 ohms, repair open in White/Orange wire.

5) Measure resistance between compass sensor module harness connector C918 terminal No. 3 (White/Orange wire) and ground. If resistance is more than 10 k/ohms, go to next step. If resistance is 10 k/ohms or less, repair short to ground in White/Orange wire.

6) Measure resistance between compass sensor module harness connector C918 terminal No. 4 (White/Black wire) and instrument cluster harness connector C239 terminal No. 12 (White/Black wire). If resistance is less than 5 ohms, go to next step. If resistance is more than 5 ohms, repair open in White/Black wire.

7) Measure resistance between compass sensor module harness connector C918 terminal No. 4 (White/Black wire) and ground. If resistance is more than 10 k/ohms, reconnect instrument cluster and go to next step. If resistance is 10 k/ohms or less, repair short to ground in White/Black wire.

8) Turn ignition switch to ON position. Select compass/outside temperature display. Observe message center display. If outside temperature display is not operating correctly, perform TEST X: MESSAGE CENTER OUTSIDE TEMPERATURE DISPLAY OPERATES INCORRECTLY. If outside temperature display is operating correctly, replace compass sensor module.

TEST V: MESSAGE CENTER NOT OPERATING CORRECTLY

1) Turn ignition switch to ON position. Observe odometer display in instrument cluster. If odometer is displayed, go to next step. If odometer is not displayed, perform TEST S: ODOMETER INOPERATIVE.

2) With ignition switch still in ON position, use NGS tester and select MCM MESSAGE CENTER DISPLAY CHARACTER active command. Trigger SEGMENTS active command ON. Observe right digital message center display. If message center display illuminates all segments, system is okay. If SELECT or RESET buttons are inoperative, perform TEST W: MESSAGE CENTER SWITCH NOT OPERATING CORRECTLY. If message center display does not illuminate all segments, replace instrument cluster.

TEST W: MESSAGE CENTER SWITCH NOT OPERATING CORRECTLY

1) Using NGS tester, perform Message Center Module (MCM) self-test. If no DTCs were retrieved, go to next step. If DTC B1205 is retrieved, go to step 3). If any other DTCs were retrieved, perform appropriate test in accordance with DTC retrieved. See MESSAGE CENTER MODULE (MCM) DTC INDEX table under SELF-DIAGNOSTIC SYSTEM.

2) Using NGS, select and monitor MCM PID RESETSW, INFOSW and SETUPSW while pressing each message center button (INFO, SETUP and RESET). If PID does not agree with button position, go to next step. If PID agrees with button position, replace instrument cluster.

3) Turn ignition switch to OFF position. Remove instrument cluster. Disconnect instrument cluster 22-pin harness connector C239 and message center switch harness connector C280. Measure resistance between instrument cluster harness connector C239 terminal No. 7 (Gray/Orange wire) and message center switch harness connector C280 terminal No. 1 (Gray/Orange wire). If resistance is less than 5 ohms, go to next step. If resistance is 5 ohms or more, repair open in Gray/Orange wire.

4) Measure resistance between instrument cluster harness connector C239 terminal No. 7 (Gray/Orange wire) and ground. If resistance is more than 10 k/ohms, go to next step. If resistance is 10 k/ohms or less, repair short to ground in Gray/Orange wire.

5) Measure resistance between instrument cluster harness connector C239 terminal No. 4 (Tan/Orange wire) and message center harness connector C280 terminal No. 5 (Tan/Orange wire). If resistance is less than 5 ohms, go to next step. If resistance is 5 ohms or more, repair open in Tan/Orange wire.

6) Measure resistance between instrument cluster harness connector C239 terminal No. 4 (Tan/Orange wire) and ground. If resistance is more than 10 k/ohms, replace message center switch. If resistance is 10 k/ohms or less, repair short to ground in Tan/Orange wire.

TEST X: MESSAGE CENTER OUTSIDE TEMPERATURE DISPLAY OPERATES INCORRECTLY

1) Using NGS tester, perform Powertrain Control Module (PCM) and Anti-lock Brake System (ABS) self-tests. If no DTCs were retrieved, go to next step. If DTC U1041, U1073 or U1123 were retrieved, or NO RESP/NOT EQUIP is displayed, repair module communications concern. See MODULE COMMUNICATIONS NETWORK – WINDSTAR article.

2) Using NGS tester, perform Front Electronics Module (FEM) self-test. If DTC B1254 is retrieved, go to next step. If any other DTCs were retrieved, perform appropriate test in accordance with DTC retrieved. See FRONT ELECTRONIC MODULE DTC INDEX table under SELF-DIAGNOSTIC SYSTEM. If no DTCs were retrieved, go to step 6).

3) Disconnect ambient temperature sensor 2-pin harness connector C182 and FEM 22-pin harness connector C191. Measure resistance between FEM harness connector C191 terminal No. 2 (Red/Light Blue wire) and ambient temperature sensor harness connector terminal No. 2 (Red/Light Blue wire). If resistance is less than 5 ohms, go to next step. If resistance is 5 ohms or more, repair open in Red/Light Blue wire.

4) Measure resistance between FEM harness connector C191 terminal No. 9 (Light Blue/Orange wire) and ambient temperature sensor harness connector C182 terminal No. 1 (Light Blue/Orange wire). If resistance is less than 5 ohms, go to next step. If resistance is 5 ohms or more, repair open in Light Blue/Orange wire.

5) Measure voltage between FEM harness connector C191 terminals No. 9 (Light Blue/Orange wire) and No. 2 (Red/Light Blue wire) and ground. If voltage is present at either terminal, repair short to voltage in Light Blue/Orange wire and/or Red/Light Blue wire. If voltage is not present at both terminals, replace ambient temperature sensor.

6) Measure resistance between FEM harness connector C191 terminal No. 2 (Red/Light Blue wire) and ambient temperature sensor harness connector C182 terminal No. 2 (Red/Light Blue wire). If resistance is less than 5 ohms, go to next step. If resistance is 5 ohms or more, repair open in Red/Light Blue wire.

7) Measure resistance between FEM harness connector C191 terminal No. 9 (Light Blue/Orange wire) and ambient temperature sensor harness connector C182 terminal No. 1 (Light Blue/Orange wire). If resistance is less than 5 ohms, go to next step. If resistance is 5 ohms or more, repair open in Light Blue/Orange wire

8) Measure resistance between FEM harness connector C191 terminal No. 2 (Red/Light Blue wire) and ground. If resistance is more than 10 k/ohms go to next step. If resistance is 10 k/ohms or less, repair short to ground in Red/Light Blue wire.

9) Measure voltage between FEM harness connector C191 terminal No. 2 (Red/Light Blue wire) and ground. If voltage is not present, reconnect FEM and ambient temperature sensor and go to next step. If voltage is present, repair short to voltage in Red/Light Blue wire.

10) Using NGS tester, select and monitor FEM PID EXTTEMP. If FEM PID EXTTEMP agrees with outside air temperature, replace FEM. If FEM PID EXTTEMP does not agree with outside air temperature, replace ambient temperature sensor.

TEST Y: MESSAGE CENTER LOW FUEL LEVEL DISPLAY NOT OPERATING CORRECTLY

Turn ignition switch to ON position. Observe fuel gauge operation. If fuel gauge operates correctly, replace instrument cluster. If fuel gauge does not operate correctly, perform TEST D: INCORRECT FUEL GAUGE INDICATION.

TEST Z: MESSAGE CENTER OIL LIFE STATUS INOPERATIVE

1) Observe odometer operation. If odometer operates correctly, go to next step. If odometer does not operate correctly, perform TEST S: ODOMETER INOPERATIVE.

2) Turn ignition switch to ON position. Observe low oil pressure indicator. Turn ignition switch to START position, while observing low oil pressure indicator. If low oil pressure indicator operates correctly, replace instrument cluster. If low oil pressure indicator does not operate correctly, perform TEST F: LOW OIL PRESSURE INDICATOR INOPERATIVE.

TEST AA: MESSAGE CENTER LAMP OUT WARNING INDICATOR INOPERATIVE

NOTE: Ensure Front Electronics Module (FEM) and Rear Electronics Module (REM) operate correctly and communicate with instrument cluster and message center.

Operate each exterior light and observe operation. If all exterior lights operate correctly, replace instrument cluster. If any exterior lights do not operate correctly, repair appropriate light as necessary. See AUTO-LAMP SYSTEMS – WINDSTAR article.

TEST AB: DIM PANEL POTENTIOMETER SWITCH CIRCUIT FAILURE

1) Using NGS tester, perform instrument cluster self-test. If no DTCs were retrieved, go to next step. If DTC B1246 is retrieved, go to step 3). If any other DTCs were retrieved, perform appropriate test in accordance with DTC retrieved. See INSTRUMENT CLUSTER DTC INDEX table under SELF-DIAGNOSTIC SYSTEM.

2) Place headlight switch in ON position. Using NGS tester, monitor panel dimmer switch input status PID while turning panel dim switch from lowest position to highest position. If PID does not agree with panel dim switch position, go to next step. If PID agrees with panel dim switch position, replace instrument cluster.

3) Turn ignition switch to OFF position. Disconnect instrument cluster harness connectors and panel dim switch 4-pin harness connector C259. Measure resistance between panel dim switch harness connector C259 terminal No. 4 (Black/White wire) and instrument cluster harness connector C239 terminal No. 2 (Black/White wire). If resistance is less than 5 ohms, go to next step. If resistance is 5 ohms or more, repair open in Black/White wire.

4) Measure resistance between panel dim switch harness connector C259 terminal No. 4 (Black/White wire) and ground. If resistance is more than 10 k/ohms, go to next step. If resistance is 10 k/ohms or less, repair short to ground in Black/White wire.

5) Measure resistance between panel dim switch harness connector C259 terminal No. 3 (Yellow wire) and instrument cluster harness connector C239 terminal No. 1 (Yellow wire). If resistance is less than 5 ohms, go to next step. If resistance is 5 ohms or more, repair open in Yellow wire.

6) Measure resistance between panel dim switch harness connector C259 terminal No. 3 (Yellow wire) and ground. If resistance is more than 10 k/ohms, go to next step. If resistance is 10 k/ohms or less, repair short to ground in Yellow wire.

7) Measure resistance between panel dim switch harness connector C259 terminal No. 2 (Light Blue/Black wire) and instrument cluster harness connector C239 terminal No. 3 (Light Blue/Black wire). If resistance is less than 5 ohms, go to next step. If resistance is 5 ohms or more, repair open in Light Blue/Black wire.

8) Measure resistance between panel dim switch harness connector C259 terminal No. 2 (Light Blue/Black wire) and ground. If resistance is more than 10 k/ohms, replace panel dim switch. If resistance is 10 k/ohms or less, repair short to ground in Light Blue/Black wire.

REMOVAL & INSTALLATION
FUEL LEVEL SENDER

CAUTION: Before disconnecting any fuel line, release fuel pressure from fuel system to reduce possibility of injury or fire. Use a rag as protection from fuel spray when disconnecting hoses. Plug hoses after disconnecting.

Removal & Installation – 1) Place vehicle on hoist but do not raise. Remove air cleaner assembly. Connect Multiport Fuel Injection (MFI) Fuel Pressure Gauge (T80L-9974-B) to fuel pressure relief valve on fuel supply manifold.

2) Open manual valve on pressure gauge to relieve fuel system pressure. Drain fuel from tank. Raise and support vehicle. Disconnect and remove fuel tank filler pipe. Support fuel tank and remove fuel tank

support straps. Lower fuel tank and remove fuel lines, electrical connectors and vent tubes from tank. Remove fuel tank.

3) Clean dirt and debris from around fuel pump module retaining flange to prevent contamination during removal and installation. Using Fuel Tank Sender Wrench (D84P-9275-A) or equivalent, turn fuel pump locking retainer ring counterclockwise and remove. Remove fuel pump module. Remove seal gasket and discard. To install, reverse removal procedure using NEW seal gasket.

FRONT ELECTRONICS MODULE (FEM)

CAUTION: Electronic modules are sensitive to static electrical charges. Proper grounding of technician and workplace is essential to prevent damage.

CAUTION: Prior to removal of module, it is necessary to upload module configuration information to New Generation Star (NGS) tester. This information needs to be downloaded into new module once installed. See PROGRAMMING.

NOTE: When battery is disconnected and reconnected, some abnormal drive symptoms may occur while vehicle relearns it's adaptive strategy. Vehicle may need to be driven 10 miles or more to learn strategy.

Removal & Installation – 1) Disconnect battery ground cable. Remove 2 bolts holding instrument panel lower steering column opening cover. Remove cover. Remove 3 bolts holding instrument panel opening cover reinforcement. Remove reinforcement. Disconnect six electrical connectors to FEM, remove 3 bolts holding FEM and remove FEM.

2) To install FEM, reverse removal procedures.

INSTRUMENT CLUSTER/MODULE (ICM)

CAUTION: Electronic modules are sensitive to static electrical charges. Proper grounding of technician and workplace is essential to prevent damage.

CAUTION: Prior to removal of module, it is necessary to upload module configuration information to New Generation Star (NGS) tester. This information needs to be downloaded into new module once installed. See PROGRAMMING.

NOTE: After instrument cluster replacement, see PASSIVE ANTI-THEFT SYSTEMS – WINDSTAR article in ACCESSORIES & EQUIPMENT for anti-theft system programming.

Removal & Installation – 1) Disconnect negative battery cable. Remove 2 screws and remove instrument panel steering column cover ("D") from below steering column. *See Fig. 10.*

2) Remove 4 nuts and remove instrument panel steering column cover reinforcement from below steering column. Loosen 4 bolts retaining steering column. Lower steering column. Remove lower steering column shroud from steering column. Using a punch, push button below ignition lock cylinder and pull ignition switch lock cylinder out.

3) Remove upper steering column shroud from steering column. Remove light switch knob and gently pry instrument panel finish panel ("E") away from instrument panel ("A") . *See Fig. 11.* Disconnect headlight switch miniature bulb socket from instrument panel finish panel.

4) Remove 2 retaining screws at bottom of cluster opening panel and gently pry from instrument panel. *See Fig. 11.* Disconnect electrical connectors. Remove 2 retaining screws and gently pry instrument panel finish panel ("F") from instrument panel. *See Fig. 12.* Disconnect transaxle range indicator cable from column by removing retaining screw and cable loop.

5) Remove 4 screws retaining instrument cluster. Pull instrument cluster forward to gain access to electrical connectors. Disconnect electrical connectors. Remove instrument cluster. To install, reverse removal procedure. Tighten instrument cluster retaining screws to 18-26 INCH

lbs. (2-3 N.m). Tighten instrument panel steering column cover reinforcement retaining screws to 106 INCH lbs. (12 N.m).

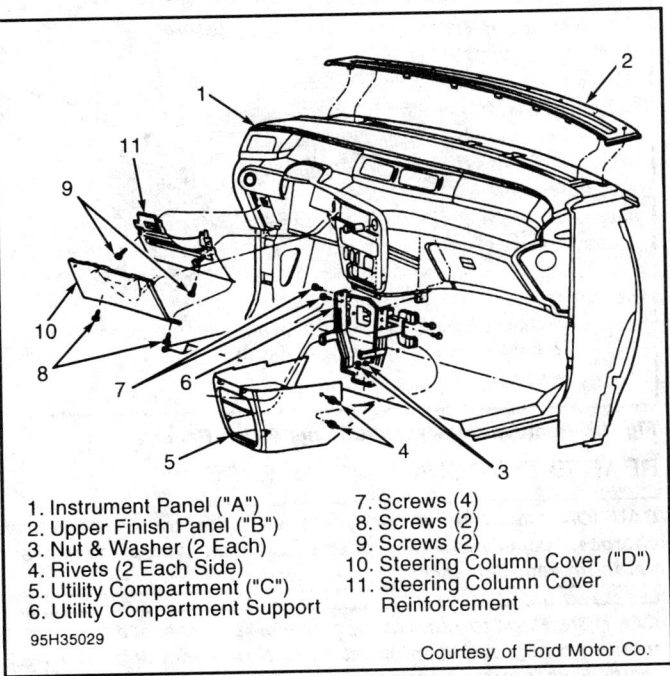

1. Instrument Panel ("A")
2. Upper Finish Panel ("B")
3. Nut & Washer (2 Each)
4. Rivets (2 Each Side)
5. Utility Compartment ("C")
6. Utility Compartment Support
7. Screws (4)
8. Screws (2)
9. Screws (2)
10. Steering Column Cover ("D")
11. Steering Column Cover Reinforcement

95H35029

Courtesy of Ford Motor Co.

Fig. 10: Exploded View Of Instrument Panel

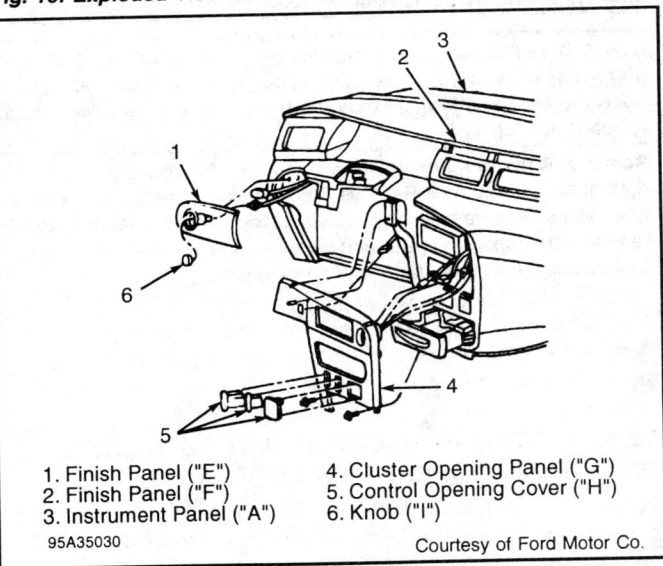

1. Finish Panel ("E")
2. Finish Panel ("F")
3. Instrument Panel ("A")
4. Cluster Opening Panel ("G")
5. Control Opening Cover ("H")
6. Knob ("I")

95A35030

Courtesy of Ford Motor Co.

Fig. 11: Removing Cluster Opening Panel

MESSAGE CENTER SWITCH

Removal & Installation – Remove instrument panel cluster finish panel. See INSTRUMENT CLUSTER/MODULE (ICM). Remove 2 screws retaining message center switch and remove message center switch. To install, reverse removal procedure.

OIL PRESSURE SWITCH

Removal & Installation – On 3.0L, oil pressure sending unit is located on upper rear of engine block, behind right cylinder head. On 3.8L, oil pressure sending unit is located in oil filter adapter at right front of engine compartment. Tighten oil pressure sending unit to 12-16 ft. lbs. (16-22 N.m).

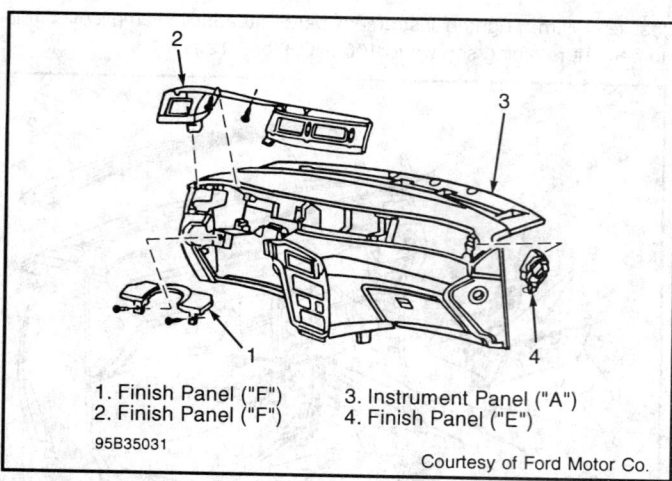

1. Finish Panel ("F")   3. Instrument Panel ("A")
2. Finish Panel ("F")   4. Finish Panel ("E")
95B35031

Courtesy of Ford Motor Co.

Fig. 12: Removing Instrument Panel Finish Panel

REAR ELECTRONICS MODULE (REM)

CAUTION: *Electronic modules are sensitive to static electrical charges. Proper grounding of technician and workplace is essential to prevent damage.*

CAUTION: *Prior to removal of module, it is necessary to upload module configuration information to New Generation Star (NGS) tester. This information needs to be downloaded into new module once installed. See PROGRAMMING.*

NOTE: *When battery is disconnected and reconnected, some abnormal drive symptoms may occur while vehicle relearns it's adaptive strategy. Vehicle may need to be driven 10 miles or more to learn strategy.*

Removal & Installation – 1) Disconnect battery ground cable. Remove right quarter trim panel. Remove 3 bolts holding service jack mounting bracket and remove bracket. Disconnect 5 electrical connectors to REM, remove 3 nuts holding REM and remove REM.
2) To install REM, reverse removal procedure.

WIRING DIAGRAMS

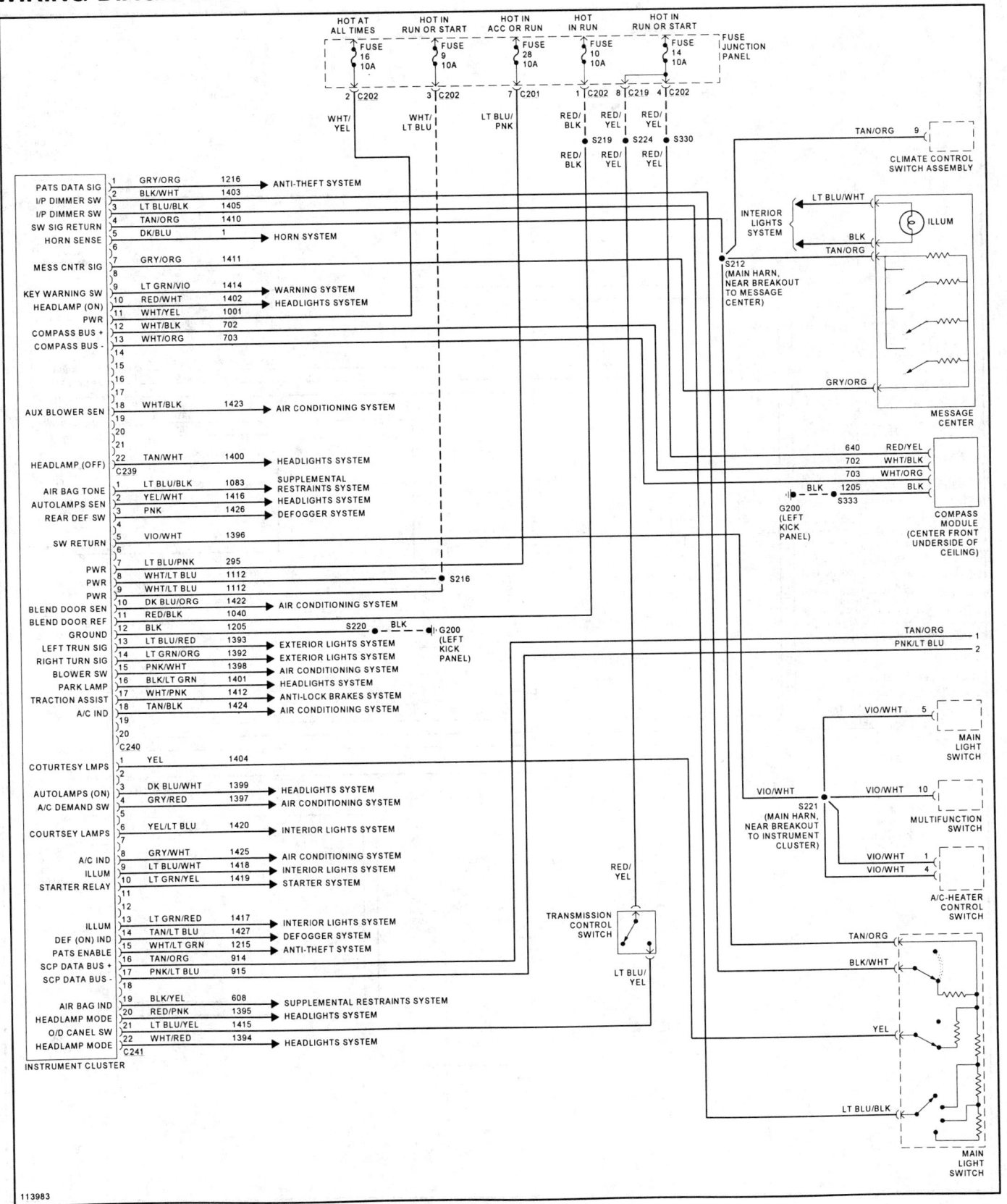

Fig. 13: Analog Instrument Panel Wiring Diagram (Windstar – 1 Of 2)

113983

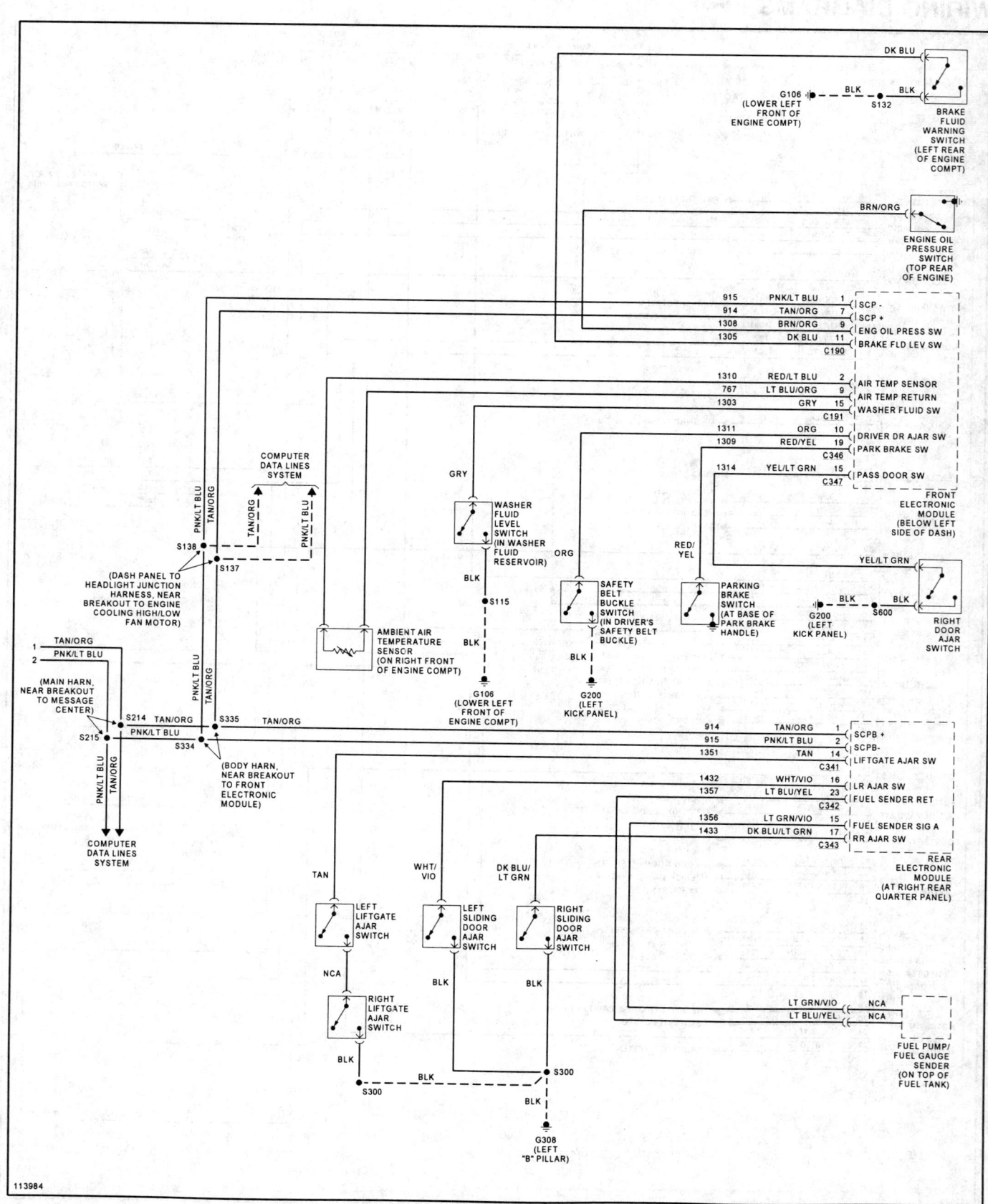

Fig. 14: Analog Instrument Panel Wiring Diagram (Windstar – 2 Of 2)

113984

DESCRIPTION

WARNING: Deactivate air bag system before performing any service operation. See appropriate AIR BAG RESTRAINT SYSTEMS article. DO NOT apply electrical power to any component on steering column without first deactivating air bag system. Air bag may deploy.

The electronic instrument cluster consists of a display panel and a microcomputer. It is operational only when ignition is on. Major components are a speedometer, odometer, fuel gauge, coolant temperature gauge, message center, and warning indicators. *See Fig. 1.* The warning indicators include:

Left Section:
- AIR BAG
- Charging System
- MIL (CHECK ENGINE)
- Safety Belt
- Oil Pressure
- Fail Safe Cooling
- Low Fuel

Center Section:
- SPEED CONTROL
- High Beam
- Left And Right Turn Signals

Right Section:
- CHECK AIR SUSPENSION
- OVERDRIVE OFF
- DOOR AJAR
- TRUNK AJAR
- LOW WASHER FLUID

OPERATION

PROVE-OUT MODE

When ignition is turned on, all electronic displays come on momentarily, go off momentarily, and then return to normal operation. Safety belt, MIL (CHECK ENGINE), AIR BAG, charging and oil pressure warning lights will remain on while other lights go out during prove-out mode. These lights will go off at beginning of normal display.

MESSAGE CENTER CONTROL BUTTONS

Control buttons are located to the right of the instrument cluster, just below the message center, in the message center switch module. Control button functions are as follows:

- **E/M Button** – Changes odometer or speedometer display from English to Metric or from Metric to English.
- **RESET Button** – Resets or clears information on message center.
- **SELECT Button** – Selects and displays TRIP DISTANCE – TRIP "A" and TRIP "B", FUEL REMAINING, INSTANTANEOUS FUEL ECONOMY, AVERAGE FUEL ECONOMY, or DISTANCE TO EMPTY.

A tone will sound when each button is pressed.

GAUGES

Coolant Temperature Gauge – This gauge displays coolant temperature. If the engine overheats, 255°F (124°C), a thermometer symbol will flash, a tone will sound every 5 seconds for one minute to alert the driver, the MIL (CHECK ENGINE) will light and PCM will disable 4 fuel injectors. If engine continues to overheat and reaches 331°F (166°C) the PCM will shut down the remaining 4 injectors. A bad signal or defective sending unit is indicated when only top 2 and bottom 2 bars of gauge appear.

NOTE: A display of CO indicates circuit open. A display of CS indicates circuit shorted.

Fuel Gauge – This gauge displays amount of fuel remaining in tank. Bad signal or defective sending unit is indicated when only top 2 and bottom 2 bars of gauge appear. A CO or CS will appear if FUEL REMAINING or DISTANCE TO EMPTY is selected on message center and an open or short exists in fuel tank sending unit circuit. When fuel level is more than 18 gallons, the letter "F" is displayed. When fuel level is less than one gallon, the letter "E" is displayed. A low fuel alert will be indicated by a flashing fuel pump symbol whenever remaining fuel is 1/8 tank or less.

MESSAGE CENTER/FUEL COMPUTER DISPLAY

The message center is located on the right side of the instrument cluster. The SELECT button can be pressed to set the desired function. The following can be displayed on the message center:

Average Fuel Economy – Average fuel economy is determined by a Vehicle Speed Sensor (VSS) signal (distance traveled) and the fuel flow signal from the Powertrain Control Module (PCM). Average fuel economy can be reset with the RESET button.

Distance To Empty – Distance to empty is calculated by using average fuel economy over the last 500 miles, and current amount of fuel remaining in tank. When distance to empty is less than 50 miles, the fuel computer overrides the current display function and flashes distance to empty display for 5 seconds. The display repeats at 25 and 10 miles. Distance to empty cannot be reset.

Instantaneous Fuel Economy – Fuel economy is determined by a Vehicle Speed Sensor (VSS) signal (distance traveled) and the fuel flow signal from the Powertrain Control Module (PCM). If vehicle is running but not moving, the display will show 0 miles per gallon or 99 liters/100 kilometers. Instantaneous fuel economy cannot be reset.

Fuel Remaining – Fuel remaining in the tank is displayed based on input from fuel tank sending unit. If fuel tank sending unit resistance is out of range, or if defective circuitry exists, a CO or CS will appear if FUEL REMAINING or DISTANCE TO EMPTY is selected.

Trip Distance – Elapsed distance since last reset is displayed and can be used as a trip odometer. Trip distance can be reset by pressing RESET button. TRIP "A" and TRIP "B" work independently.

SPEEDOMETER/ODOMETER

The speedometer displays vehicle speed, based on input signals from the transmission-mounted speed sensor. If the odometer has been serviced, an "S" will appear whenever the instrument cluster is turned on, except in the off-period of prove-out mode. If the odometer cannot read a valid odometer mileage from memory, it will flash the word ERROR as a service alert.

WARNING INDICATORS

NOTE: Seat belt warning indicator will come on for 4 to 8 seconds after ignition is turned on, and a tone will occur. This tone is independent of instrument cluster.

Various warning indicators are displayed on the instrument cluster. The instrument cluster contains warning indicators for air bag, anti-lock, brake, charging system, check engine, safety belt, oil pressure, air suspension, washer fluid, and door ajar. Warning indicators operate as follows:

AIR SUSPENSION, DOOR AJAR, TRUNK AJAR & LOW WASHER FLUID – Warning indicator flashes for 5 seconds, remains on, and a tone sounds. The indicator will remain on until the condition is resolved. The warning indicator will operate after prove-out mode. See PROVE-OUT MODE. Warning indicators cannot be dimmed.

AIR BAG, Charging System, CHECK ENGINE & Oil Pressure – Warning indicators remain on whenever ignition is on until the condition is resolved. Warning indicators operate during prove-out. See PROVE-OUT MODE. Warning indicators cannot be dimmed.

1999 ACCESSORIES & EQUIPMENT
Electronic Instrument Panels
Crown Victoria & Grand Marquis (Cont.)

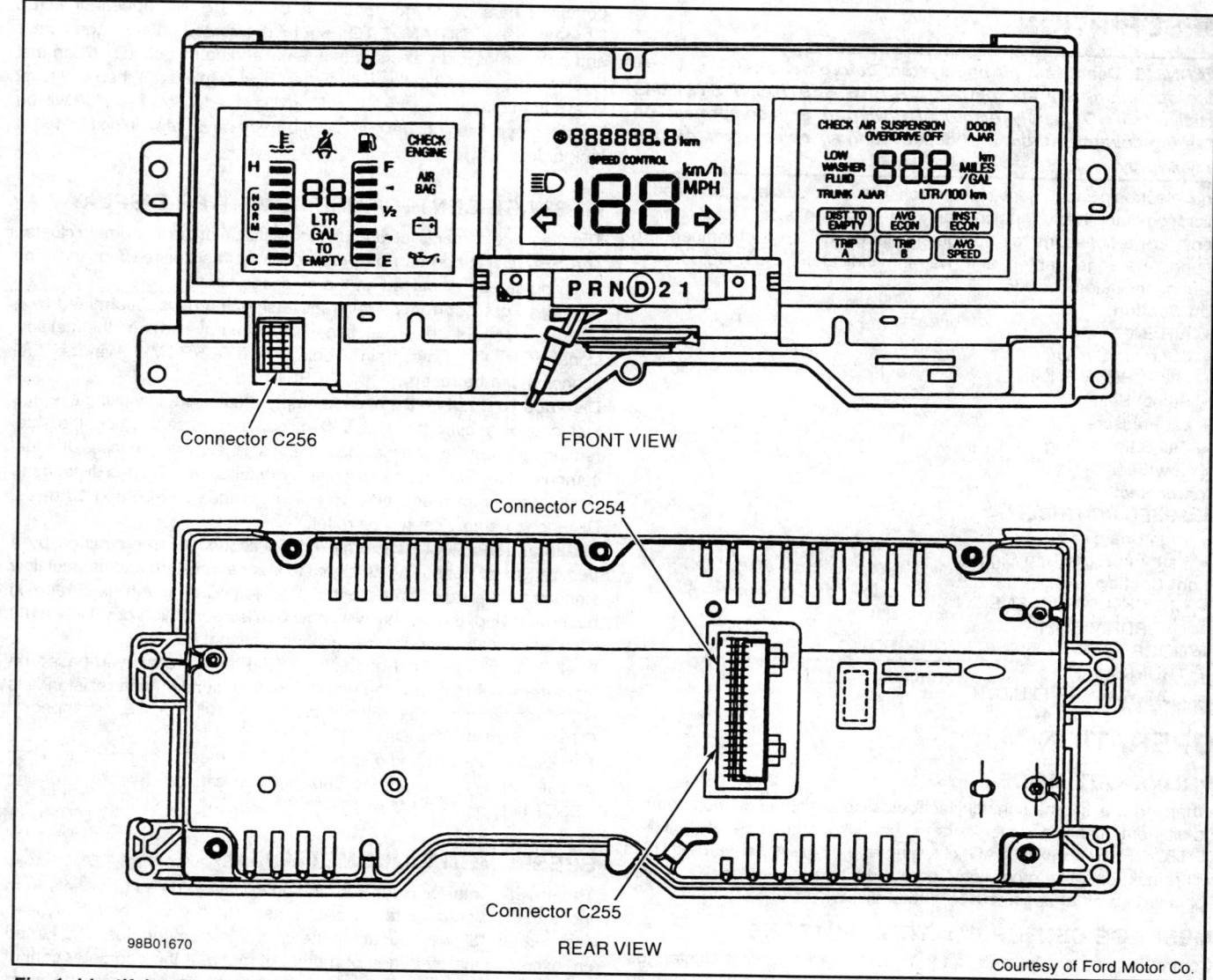

Fig. 1: Identifying Electronic Instrument Cluster Components & Connector Locations

COMPONENT LOCATIONS

COMPONENT LOCATIONS

Component	Location
Air Suspension Control Module	Behind Instrument Panel, Above Glove Box
Anti-Lock Brake System Module	Left Front Of Vehicle, On Radiator Support
Data Link Connector	Behind Left Side Of Instrument Panel
Daytime Running Light Module	Front Center Of Radiator Support
Engine Coolant Temperature Sender	Top Front Right Of Engine
Fuel Pump Module	On Rear Of Fuel Tank
Headlight Switch	Left Side Of Instrument Panel
Ignition Switch	On Steering Column
Instrument Panel Fuse Box	Behind Left Side Of Instrument Panel
Lighting Control Module	Behind Instrument Panel, Right Of Steering Column
Natural Gas Vehicle Module	On Front Radiator Support

COMPONENT LOCATIONS (Cont.)

Component	Location
Powertrain Control Module	Left Rear Corner Of Engine Compartment, In Firewall
Vehicle Speed Sensor	Located At Left Rear Of Transmission

TROUBLE SHOOTING

Verify customer concern by operating system in question. Attempt to duplicate condition with ignition switch in RUN position, in START position before ignition switch is released, and in RUN position with engine running. Visually inspect components. If inspection reveals an obvious concern which can be easily serviced, correct malfunction before continuing.

Mechanical Inspection:
- Damaged Fuel Tank
- Damaged Oil Filter
- Damaged Oil Pump
- Low Engine Coolant Level
- Low Engine Oil Level
- Worn Or Damaged Accessory Drive Belt

1999 ACCESSORIES & EQUIPMENT
Electronic Instrument Panels
Crown Victoria & Grand Marquis (Cont.)

FORD
4-881

Electrical Inspection:

- Blown Fuses
- Damaged Indicator Bulbs
- Damaged Wiring Harness
- Loose Or Corroded Connections
- Damaged Switches, Sensors Or Modules
- Damaged VSS
- Damaged Instrument Cluster

Verify charging system, fuel system, cooling system, safety belt warning chime, turn signals, headlights, anti-lock brake system and cruise control are working properly. Inspect wiring harness for obvious signs of shorts, opens, bad connections or damage. If inspection reveals obvious concerns that can be readily identified, repair as necessary and retest system. If all components are okay, perform self-diagnostics. See SELF-DIAGNOSTIC SYSTEM.

COMPONENT TESTS

HEADLIGHT SWITCH

Disconnect headlight switch harness connectors. Check resistance between indicated terminal with switch in specified position. See HEADLIGHT SWITCH CONTINUITY TEST table. *See Fig. 2.* If resistance is not as specified, replace headlight switch.

HEADLIGHT SWITCH CONTINUITY TEST

Switch Position	Terminals	Resistance
Headlight Circuit		
Off	7 & 8	1
Park	7 & 8	1
Head	7 & 8	2
Parking Light Circuit		
Off	7 & 3	1
Park	7 & 3	2
Head	7 & 3	2
Dome Light Circuit		
Off	6 & 7	1
On	6 & 7	2
Autolamp Circuit		
Off	4 & 7	1
On	4 & 7	2
Rheostat	7 & 9	3

1 – Resistance should be greater than 10 k/ohms.
2 – Resistance should be 5 ohms or less.
3 – Rotate dial clockwise from off to max. Resistance should increase smoothly from 3 k/ohms to 200 k/ohms.

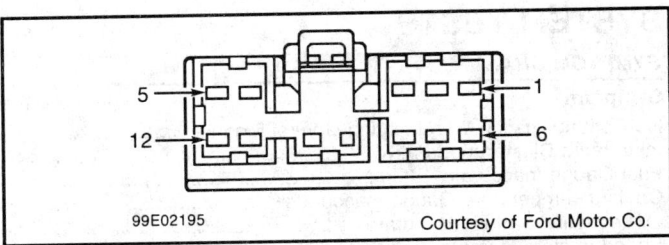

Fig. 2: Identifying Headlight Switch Terminals

SELF-DIAGNOSTIC SYSTEM

NOTE: *Enter self-diagnostic mode to determine if a problem exists in sending unit circuits or display.*

1) Turn ignition switch to LOCK position. Simultaneously press and hold E/M and <SELECT buttons on message center. While holding buttons, turn ignition switch to RUN position. If instrument cluster flashes on and off continuously, replace instrument cluster. If instrument cluster displays upper 2 and lower 2 bars or just bottom bar is displayed in temperature gauge, diagnose temperature gauge system. If instrument cluster displays upper 2 and lower 2 bars in fuel gauge, diagnose fuel gauge system.

2) CO (circuit open) or CS (circuit short) will be displayed if FUEL REMAINING or DISTANCE TO EMPTY is selected on message center and an open or short exists in fuel tank sending unit circuitry. If ERROR is displayed in odometer display, diagnose speedometer/odometer circuitry.

3) If problem remains, connect New Generation Star (NGS) tester (007-00500) to Data Link Connector (DLC). Perform data link diagnostics test. See DATA LINK DIAGNOSTIC TEST under COMMUNICATION NETWORK DIAGNOSTICS in MODULE COMMUNICATIONS NETWORK – CROWN VICTORIA & GRAND MARQUIS article. If NGS tester responds with CKT914, CKT915 or CKT70=ALL ECUS NO RESP/NOT EQUIP, repair module communications concern. See MODULE COMMUNICATIONS NETWORK – CROWN VICTORIA & GRAND MARQUIS article. If NGS responds with NO RESPONSE/NOT EQUIPPED for Lighting Control Module (LCM), perform TEST A: NO COMMUNICATION WITH LIGHTING CONTROL MODULE under SYSTEM TESTS.

4) If NGS tester responds with SYSTEM PASSED, retrieve and record continuous DTCs. Erase continuous DTCs. Using NGS tester, perform LCM self-test. Perform appropriate test in accordance with DTC retrieved. See LIGHTING CONTROL MODULE DTC INDEX table. Codes listed in this table are only for testing covered in this article. For complete DTC listing, see MODULE COMMUNICATIONS NETWORK – CROWN VICTORIA & GRAND MARQUIS article. If no DTCs are retrieved, repair by symptom. See SYMPTOM CHART table under SYSTEM TESTS.

LIGHTING CONTROL MODULE DTC INDEX

DTC [1]	Description	Test [2]
B1342	ECU Defective	
B1579	Panel Dim Increase Circuit Failure	AH
B1581	Panel Dim Increase Circuit Short To Voltage	AI
B1583	Panel Dim Decrease Input Circuit Failure	AJ
B1585	Panel Dim Decrease Input Short To Voltage	AK

1 – Codes listed in this table are only for testing covered in this article. For complete DTC listing, see MODULE COMMUNICATIONS NETWORK – CROWN VICTORIA & GRAND MARQUIS article.
2 – Using NGS tester, clear and document continuous DTCs. Perform Driver's Door Module (DDM) self-test. If DTC B1342 is retrieved again, replace DDM.

FORD
4-882

1999 ACCESSORIES & EQUIPMENT
Electronic Instrument Panels
Crown Victoria & Grand Marquis (Cont.)

SYSTEM TESTS

SYMPTOM CHART

Symptom	Test
No Communication With Lighting Control Module	A
Instrument Cluster Inoperative	B
Fuel Gauge Inaccurate	C
Coolant Temperature Gauge Inaccurate	D
Oil Pressure Gauge Inaccurate	E
Speedometer/Odometer Inoperative	F
Low Fuel Warning Light Never/Always On	G
Charge Warning Light Never On	H
Brake Warning Light Never On	I
Check Engine Light Inoperative	J
Seat Beat Warning Light Inoperative (Chime Operative)	K
Air Suspension Warning Light Never/Always On	L
Left Turn Indicator Never/Always On	M
Right Turn Indicator Never/Always On	N
High Beam Warning Never/Always On	O
Traction Control Indicator Inoperative	P
Overdrive Off Indicator Inoperative	Q
ABS Indicator Inoperative	R
Fail-Safe Cooling Indicator Inoperative	S
Door Ajar Indicator Inoperative	T
Trunk Ajar Indicator Inoperative	U
Low Washer Fluid Indicator Inoperative	V
Hazard Indicator Inoperative	W
Panel Illumination Control Inoperative	AB
Instrument Cluster Illumination Inoperative	AC
Instrument Panel Illumination Does Not Dim	AD
Message Center Inoperative	AE

TEST A: NO COMMUNICATION WITH LIGHTING CONTROL MODULE

1) Turn ignition switch to RUN position. Using NGS tester, monitor Lighting Control Module (LCM) PID IGN_LC. If NGS tester does not indicate UNABLE TO PERFORM TEST FUNCTION, MODULE NOT RESPONDING, CHECK IGNITION STATUS/VERIFY CABLE REQUIREMENTS, OR CHECK CABLE CONNECTIONS, go to next step. If NGS tester indicates UNABLE TO PERFORM TEST FUNC-TION, MODULE NOT RESPONDING, CHECK IGNITION STATUS/ VERIFY CABLE REQUIREMENTS, OR CHECK CABLE CONNEC-TIONS, go to step 11).

2) Turn ignition switch to RUN position. Using NGS tester, monitor LCM PID IGN_LC while rotating ignition switch through ACCY, OFF and RUN positions. If PID indicates START while ignition switch is in RUN position, go to next step. If PID indicates RUN while ignition switch is in RUN position, go to step 12). If PID indicates ACCY while ignition switch is in RUN position, go to step 7).

3) Turn ignition switch to LOCK position. Remove fuse No. 6 (15-amp) from instrument panel fuse box. Check fuse. If fuse is okay, go to next step. If fuse is blown, go to step 6).

4) Turn ignition switch to RUN position. Measure voltage at input side of fuse No. 6 in instrument panel fuse box. If battery voltage exists, go to next step. If battery voltage does not exist, repair power supply to fuse No. 6. See appropriate wiring diagram in POWER DISTRIBUTION article in WIRING DIAGRAMS.

5) Turn ignition switch to LOCK position. Install fuse No. 6. Disconnect LCM harness connector C2027. Turn ignition switch to RUN position. Measure voltage at terminal No. 1 (White/Violet wire) at LCM harness connector C2027. See Fig. 3. If battery voltage exists, replace LCM. If battery voltage does not exist, repair open in White/Violet wire.

6) Turn ignition switch to LOCK position. Disconnect Lighting Control Module (LCM) harness connector C2027. Measure resistance between ground and terminal No. 1 (White/Violet wire) at LCM harness connector C2027. See Fig. 3 . If resistance is greater than 10 k/ohms, replace LCM. If resistance is 10 k/ohms or less, repair short to ground in White/Violet wire.

7) Turn ignition switch to LOCK position. Remove fuse No. 13 (15-amp) from instrument panel fuse box. Check fuse. If fuse is okay, go to next step. If fuse is blown, go to step 10).

8) Turn ignition switch to RUN position. Measure voltage at input side of fuse No. 13 in instrument panel fuse box. If battery voltage exists, go to next step. If battery voltage does not exist, repair power supply to fuse No. 13. See appropriate wiring diagram in POWER DISTRIBUTION article in WIRING DIAGRAMS.

9) Turn ignition switch to LOCK position. Install fuse No. 13 (15-amp). Disconnect LCM harness connector C2027. Turn ignition switch to RUN position. Measure voltage at terminal No. 9 (Red/Yellow wire) at LCM harness connector C2027. See Fig. 3. If battery voltage exists, replace LCM. If battery voltage does not exist, repair open in Red/Yellow wire.

10) Turn ignition switch to LOCK position. Disconnect LCM harness connector C2027. Measure resistance between ground and terminal No. 9 (Red/Yellow wire) at LCM harness connector C2027. See Fig. 3. If resistance is greater than 10 k/ohms, replace LCM. If resistance is 10 k/ohms or less, repair short to ground in Red/Yellow wire.

11) Turn ignition switch to LOCK position. Disconnect LCM harness connector C2029. Measure resistance between ground and terminals No. 4 and 9 (both Black wire) at LCM harness connector C2029. See Fig. 4. If either resistance reading is greater than 5 ohms, repair open in appropriate Black wire(s). If both resistance readings are 5 ohms or less, repair module communication concern. See MODULE COMMUNICA-TIONS NETWORK – CROWN VICTORIA & GRAND MARQUIS article.

12) Turn ignition switch to LOCK position. Disconnect LCM harness connector C2029. Measure voltage at terminal No. 6 (Tan/White wire) at LCM harness connector C2029. See Fig. 4. If battery voltage does not exist, go to next step. If battery voltage exists, go to step 16).

13) Remove fuse No. 4 (15-amp) from instrument panel fuse box. Measure resistance between ground and terminal No. 6 (Tan/White wire) at LCM harness connector C2029. If resistance is greater than 10 k/ohms, go to next step. If resistance is 10 k/ohms or less, repair short to ground in Tan/White wire and replace fuse.

14) Measure voltage at input side of fuse No. 4 in instrument panel fuse box. If battery voltage exists, go to next step. If battery voltage does not exist, repair power distribution circuit. See appropriate wiring diagram in POWER DISTRIBUTION article in WIRING DIAGRAMS.

15) Measure resistance in Tan/White wire between output side of fuse No. 4 and terminal No. 6 at LCM harness connector C2029. If resistance is 5 ohms or less, system is okay at this time. If resistance is greater than 5 ohms, repair open in Tan/White wire.

16) Measure voltage at terminal No. 11 (Light Green/Yellow wire) at LCM harness connector C2029. If battery voltage does not exist, go to next step. If battery voltage exists, go to step 20).

17) Remove fuse No. 8 (15-amp) from instrument panel fuse box. Measure resistance between ground and terminal No. 11 (Light Green/Yellow wire) at LCM harness connector C2029. If resistance is greater than 10 k/ohms, go to next step. If resistance is 10 k/ohms or less, repair short to ground in Light Green/Yellow wire and replace fuse.

18) Measure voltage at input side of fuse No. 8. If battery voltage exists, go to next step. If battery voltage does not exist, repair power distribution circuit. See appropriate wiring diagram in POWER DISTRIBUTION article in WIRING DIAGRAMS.

19) Measure resistance in Light Green/Yellow wire between output side of fuse No. 8 and terminal No. 11 at LCM harness connector C2029. If resistance is 5 ohms or less, system is okay at this time. If resistance is greater than 5 ohms, repair open in Light Green/Yellow wire.

20) Measure resistance between ground and terminal No. 9 (Black wire) at LCM harness connector C2029. If resistance is 5 ohms or less, repair module communication concern. See MODULE COMMUNICATIONS NETWORK – CROWN VICTORIA & GRAND MARQUIS article. If resistance is greater than 5 ohms, repair open in Black wire.

1999 ACCESSORIES & EQUIPMENT
Electronic Instrument Panels
Crown Victoria & Grand Marquis (Cont.)

FORD
4-883

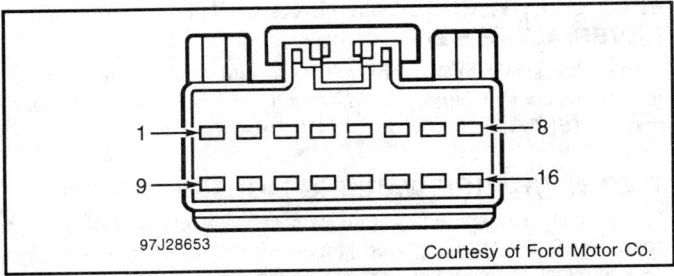

Fig. 3: Identifying Lighting Control Module Harness Connector C2027 Terminals

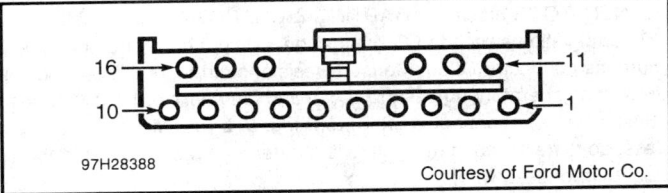

Fig. 4: Identifying Lighting Control Module Harness Connector C2029 Terminals

TEST B: INSTRUMENT CLUSTER INOPERATIVE

1) Turn ignition switch to LOCK position. Disconnect instrument cluster harness connectors. Measure voltage at terminal No. 9 (Black/White wire) at instrument cluster harness connector C255. *See Fig. 5.* Measure voltage at terminals No. 2 and 7 (both Black/White wires) at instrument cluster harness connector C256. *See Fig. 6.* If battery voltage exists at all terminals, go to next step. If battery voltage does not exist at all terminals, repair appropriate power distribution circuit. See appropriate wiring diagram in POWER DISTRIBUTION article in WIRING DIAGRAMS.

2) Turn ignition switch to LOCK position. Measure resistance between ground and terminal No. 8 (Pink/Orange wire) at instrument cluster harness connector C255. Measure resistance between ground and terminal No. 1 (Pink/Orange wire) at instrument cluster harness connector C256. If both resistance readings are 5 ohms or less, replace instrument cluster. If either resistance reading is greater than 5 ohms, repair open in appropriate Pink/Orange wire. See appropriate wiring diagram in GROUND DISTRIBUTION article in WIRING DIAGRAMS.

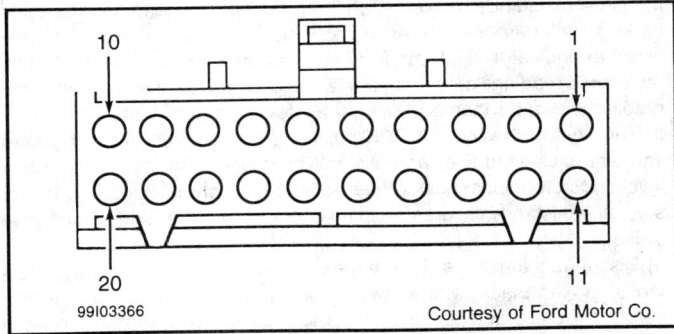

Fig. 5: Identifying Instrument Cluster Harness Connector C255 Terminals

TEST C: FUEL GAUGE INACCURATE

1) Turn ignition switch to LOCK position. Press and hold E/M and <SELECT button on instrument cluster while turning ignition switch to RUN position. If CS or CO is displayed next to fuel gauge, go to next step. If CS or CO is not displayed next to fuel gauge, replace instrument cluster.

2) Turn ignition switch to LOCK position. Disconnect fuel pump module harness connector C464. Connect Instrument Gauge System Tester (014-R1063) to ground and terminal No. 8 (Yellow/White wire) at fuel

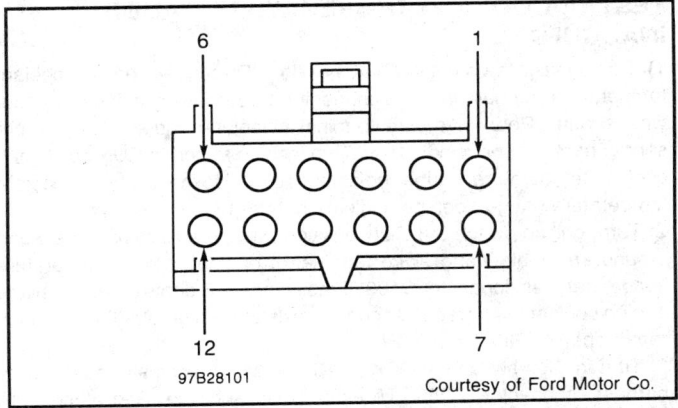

Fig. 6: Identifying Instrument Cluster Harness Connector C256 Terminals

pump module harness connector C464. *See Fig. 7.* Set tester to 160 ohms. Turn ignition switch to RUN position. Turn tester on. Wait one minute. Fuel gauge should indicate full or above. Turn ignition switch to LOCK position. Set tester to 15 ohms. Turn ignition switch to RUN position. Wait one minute. Fuel gauge should indicate empty or below. Turn ignition switch to LOCK position. If fuel gauge responded as specified, go to next step. If fuel gauge did not respond as specified, go to step **5)**.

3) Inspect fuel tank for damage or distortion. If there is no damage, go to next step. If there is damage or distortion, replace fuel tank.

4) Visually inspect fuel pump assembly and wiring for damage. If damage exists, repair or replace as necessary. If damage does not exist, replace fuel level sensor.

5) Turn ignition switch to LOCK position. Disconnect instrument cluster harness connector C256. Measure resistance in Yellow/White wire between terminal No. 6 at instrument cluster harness connector C256 and terminal No. 8 at fuel pump module harness connector C464. *See Figs. 6 and 7.* Resistance should be 5 ohms or less. Measure resistance between ground and terminal No. 8 (Yellow/White wire) at fuel pump module harness connector C464. Resistance should be greater than 10 k/ohms. If both resistance readings are as specified, go to next step. If either resistance readings is not as specified, repair open or short to ground in Yellow/White wire.

6) Measure resistance between ground and terminal No. 5 (Pink/Orange wire) at fuel pump module harness connector C464. If resistance is 5 ohms or less, replace instrument cluster. If resistance is greater than 5 ohms, repair open in Pink/Orange wire.

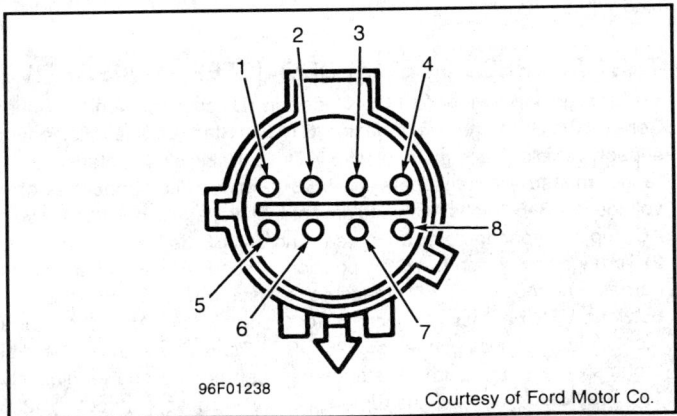

Fig. 7: Identifying Fuel Pump Module Harness Connector C464 Terminals

FORD
4-884

1999 ACCESSORIES & EQUIPMENT
Electronic Instrument Panels
Crown Victoria & Grand Marquis (Cont.)

TEST D: COOLANT TEMPERATURE GAUGE INACCURATE

1) Turn ignition switch to LOCK position. Disconnect engine coolant temperature sender harness connector C189. Using a fused jumper wire, ground Red/White wire terminal at engine coolant temperature sender harness connector C189. Turn ignition switch to RUN position. If coolant temperature gauge indicates hot, go to next step. If coolant temperature gauge does not indicate hot, go to step **3)**.

2) Turn ignition switch to LOCK position. Measure resistance between ground and Pink/Orange wire terminal at engine coolant temperature sender harness connector C189. If resistance is 5 ohms or less, replace engine coolant temperature sender. If resistance is greater than 5 ohms, repair open in Pink/Orange wire.

3) Turn ignition switch to LOCK position. Disconnect instrument cluster harness connector C255. Measure resistance in Red/White wire between engine coolant temperature sender harness connector C189 and terminal No. 4 at instrument cluster harness connector C255. *See Fig. 5.* Resistance should be 5 ohms or less. Measure resistance between ground and terminal No. 4 (Red/White wire) at instrument cluster harness connector C255. Resistance should be greater than 10 k/ohms. If both resistance readings are as specified, replace coolant temperature gauge. If either resistance readings is not as specified, repair open or short to ground in Red/White wire.

TEST E: OIL PRESSURE GAUGE INACCURATE

1) Turn ignition switch to LOCK position. Disconnect oil pressure sender harness connector C1014. Using a fused jumper wire, ground White/Red wire terminal at oil pressure sender harness connector C1014. Turn ignition switch to RUN position. If oil pressure gauge indicates normal, go to next step. If oil pressure gauge does not indicate normal, go to step **3)**.

2) Using a mechanical oil pressure gauge, check engine oil pressure. If oil pressure is 40-70 psi at normal operating temperature, replace oil pressure sender. If oil pressure is not 40-70 psi at normal operating temperature, repair engine oiling system as necessary.

3) Turn ignition switch to LOCK position. Disconnect instrument cluster harness connector C256. Measure resistance in White/Red wire between oil pressure sender harness connector C1014 and terminal No. 8 at instrument cluster harness connector C256. *See Fig. 6.* Resistance should be 5 ohms or less. Measure resistance between ground and terminal No. 8 (White/Red wire) at instrument cluster harness connector C256. Resistance should be greater than 10 k/ohms. If both resistance readings are as specified, replace oil pressure gauge. If either resistance readings is not as specified, repair open or short to ground in Red/White wire.

TEST F: SPEEDOMETER/ODOMETER INOPERATIVE

1) Turn ignition switch to LOCK position. Disconnect Vehicle Speed Sensor (VSS) harness connector C1020. Start engine. Raise and support vehicle. Place gear selector in Drive. Using a voltmeter set to AC range, measure voltage between VSS terminals (component side). If voltage is 1.3–6.1 volts AC, go to next step. If voltage is not 1.3–1.6 volts AC, replace speedometer drive gear and/or VSS as necessary.

2) Turn ignition switch to LOCK position. Disconnect instrument cluster harness connector C255. Measure resistance in Gray/Black wire between VSS harness connector C1020 and terminal No. 12 at instrument cluster harness connector C255. *See Fig. 5.* Resistance should be 5 ohms or less. Measure resistance between ground and terminal No. 12 (Gray/Black wire) at instrument cluster harness connector C255. Resistance should be greater than 10 k/ohms. If both resistance readings are as specified, replace instrument cluster. If either resistance readings is not as specified, repair open or short to ground in Gray/Black wire.

TEST G: LOW FUEL WARNING LIGHT NEVER/ALWAYS ON

Turn ignition switch to RUN position. If fuel gauge is operating properly, replace instrument cluster. If fuel gauge is not operating properly, perform TEST C: FUEL GAUGE INACCURATE.

TEST H: CHARGE WARNING LIGHT NEVER ON

1) Turn ignition switch to LOCK position. Disconnect generator harness connector C154. Using a fused jumper wire, ground Light Green/Red wire terminal at generator harness connector C154. Start engine. If charge warning light does not illuminate, go to next step. If charging warning light illuminates, repair charging system. See appropriate GENERATORS article in STARTING & CHARGING SYSTEMS.

2) Turn ignition switch to LOCK position. Disconnect instrument cluster harness connector C256. Measure resistance in Light Green/Red wire between generator harness connector and terminal No. 10 at instrument cluster harness connector C256. *See Fig. 6.* If resistance is 5 ohms or less, go to next step. If resistance is greater than 5 ohms, repair open in Light Green/Red wire.

3) Turn ignition switch to RUN position. Measure voltage at terminal No. 7 (Black/White wire) at instrument cluster harness connector C256. If battery voltage exists, replace bulb or instrument cluster as necessary. If battery voltage does not exist, repair power distribution circuit. See appropriate wiring diagram in POWER DISTRIBUTION article in WIRING DIAGRAMS.

TEST I: BRAKE WARNING LIGHT NEVER ON

NOTE: Ensure brake fluid is at correct level in reservoir.

1) Turn ignition switch to LOCK position. Disconnect brake fluid level switch harness connector C170. Using a fused jumper wire, ground Violet/White terminal at brake fluid level switch harness connector C170. Turn ignition switch to RUN. If brake warning light does not illuminate, go to next step. If brake warning light illuminates, go to step **3)**.

2) Turn ignition switch to LOCK position. Disconnect indicator light module harness connector C2004. Disconnect parking brake switch harness connector C296. Measure resistance in Violet/White wire between brake fluid level switch harness connector C170 and terminal No. 3 at indicator light module harness connector C2004. *See Fig. 8.* Measure resistance between Tan/Light Green wire terminal at parking brake switch harness connector C296 and terminal No. 3 (Violet/White wire) at indicator light module harness connector C2004. If both resistance readings are 5 ohms or less, go to step **6)**. If either resistance reading is greater than 5 ohms, repair open in appropriate wire.

3) Turn ignition switch to LOCK position. Measure resistance between Tan/Black wire terminal and Violet/White wire terminal at brake fluid level switch (component side). If resistance is 5 ohms or less, go to next step. If resistance is greater than 5 ohms, replace brake fluid level switch.

4) Disconnect ignition switch harness connector C292. Measure resistance in Tan/Black wire between brake fluid level switch harness connector C170 and terminal P2 at ignition switch harness connector C292. *See Fig. 9.* If resistance is 5 ohms or less, go to next step. If resistance is greater than 5 ohms, replace open in Tan/Black wire.

5) Measure resistance between ground and terminal GND (Black wire) at ignition switch harness connector C292. If resistance is 5 ohms or less, replace ignition switch. If resistance is greater than 5 ohms, replace open in Black wire.

6) Measure resistance between Tan/Light Green wire terminal at parking brake switch (component side). Resistance should be 5 ohms or less with parking brake applied. Resistance should be greater than 10 k/ohms with parking brake released. If resistance is as specified, replace bulb or indicator light module as necessary. If resistance is not as specified, replace parking brake switch.

Electronic Instrument Panels
Crown Victoria & Grand Marquis (Cont.)

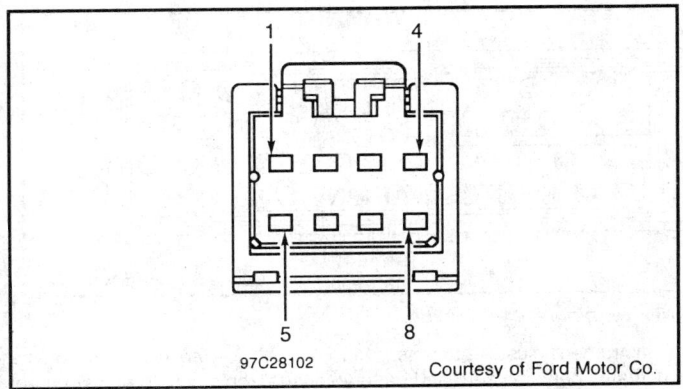

Fig. 8: Identifying Indicator Light Module Harness Connector C2004, Headlight Switch Harness Connector C249 & Message Center Switch Harness Connector C264 Terminals

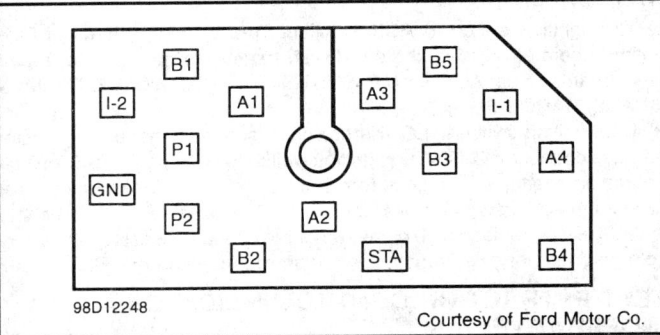

Fig. 9: Identifying Ignition Switch Harness Connector C292 Terminals

TEST J: CHECK ENGINE LIGHT INOPERATIVE

Turn ignition switch to LOCK position. Disconnect Powertrain Control Module (PCM) harness connector C185. Disconnect instrument cluster harness connector C256. Measure resistance is Pink/Light Green wire between terminal No. 2 at PCM harness connector C185 and terminal No. 9 at instrument cluster harness connector C256. *See Figs. 6 and 10.* If resistance is 5 ohms or less, repair powertrain concern. See appropriate SELF-DIAGNOSTICS article in ENGINE PERFORMANCE in appropriate MITCHELL® manual. If resistance is greater than 5 ohms, repair open in Pink/Light Green wire.

TEST K: SEAT BEAT WARNING LIGHT INOPERATIVE (CHIME OPERATIVE)

1) Turn ignition switch to LOCK position. Disconnect instrument cluster harness connector C256. Turn ignition switch to RUN position. Measure voltage at terminal No. 11 (Dark Green/Light Green wire) at instrument cluster harness connector C256. *See Fig. 6.* If battery voltage does not exist, go to next step. If battery voltage exists, replace bulb or instrument cluster as necessary.

2) Turn ignition switch to LOCK position. Disconnect Lighting Control Module (LCM) harness connector C2029. Measure resistance in Dark Green/Light Green wire between terminal No. 11 at instrument cluster harness connector C256 and terminal No. 8 at LCM harness connector C2029. *See Figs. 4 and 6.* Resistance should be 5 ohms or less. Measure resistance between ground and terminal No. 11 (Dark Green/Light Green wire) at instrument cluster harness connector C256. Resistance should be greater than 10 k/ohms. If both resistance readings are as specified, replace LCM. If either resistance reading is not as specified, repair open or short to ground in Dark Green/Light Green wire.

TEST L: AIR SUSPENSION WARNING LIGHT NEVER/ALWAYS ON

1) Start engine. If air suspension warning light is always on, go to next step. If air suspension warning light is not always on, go to step **5)**.

2) Check air suspension service switch. Air suspension service switch is located on right side in trunk. If air suspension service switch is on, go to next step. If air suspension service switch is off turn air suspension service switch to ON position.

3) Turn ignition switch to LOCK position. Disconnect air suspension control module harness connector C215. Turn ignition switch to ACC position. If air suspension warning light is always on, go to next step. If air suspension warning light is not always on, replace air suspension module.

4) Disconnect instrument cluster harness connector C254. Measure resistance in Dark Green/Light Green wire between terminal No. 11 at instrument cluster harness connector C254 and terminal No. 11 at air suspension control module harness connector C215. *See Figs. 11 and 12.* Resistance should be 5 ohms or less. Measure resistance between ground and terminal No. 11 (Dark Green/Light Green wire) at instrument cluster harness connector C254. Resistance should be greater than 10 k/ohms. If both resistance readings are as specified, replace instrument cluster. If either resistance readings is not as specified, repair open or short to ground in Dark Green/Light Green wire.

5) Turn ignition switch to LOCK position. Disconnect air suspension control module harness connector C215. Turn ignition switch to RUN position. Using a fused jumper wire, ground terminal No. 11 (Dark Green/Light Green wire) at air suspension control module harness connector C215. *See Fig. 11.* If air suspension warning light does not illuminate, go to next step. If air suspension warning light illuminates, replace air suspension control module.

6) Turn ignition switch to LOCK position. Disconnect instrument cluster harness connector C254. Measure resistance in Dark Green/Light Green wire between terminal No. 25 at instrument cluster harness connector C254 and terminal No. 11 at air suspension control module harness connector C215. *See Figs. 11 and 12.* If resistance is 5 ohms or less, replace instrument cluster. If resistance is greater than 5 ohms, repair open in Dark Green/Light Green wire.

FORD
4-886

1999 ACCESSORIES & EQUIPMENT
Electronic Instrument Panels
Crown Victoria & Grand Marquis (Cont.)

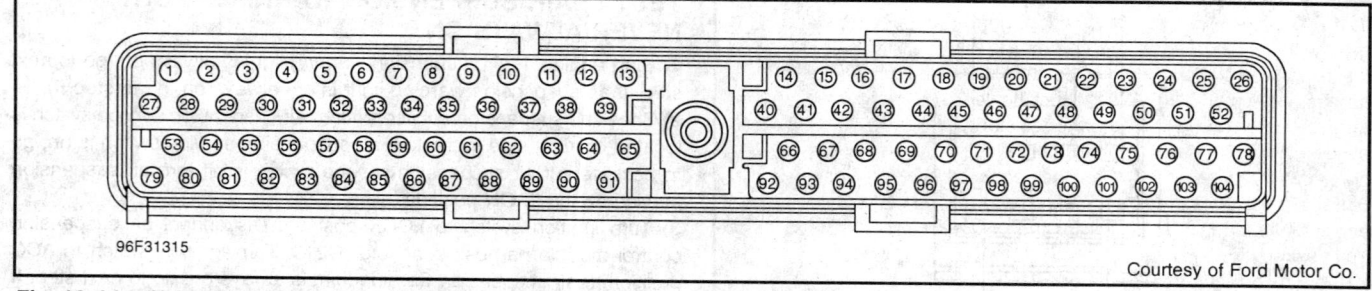

Fig. 10: Identifying Powertrain Control Module Harness Connector C185 Terminals

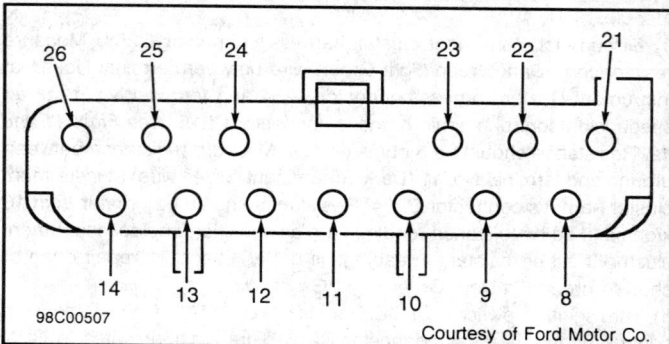

Fig. 11: Identifying Air Suspension Control Module Harness Connector C215 Terminals

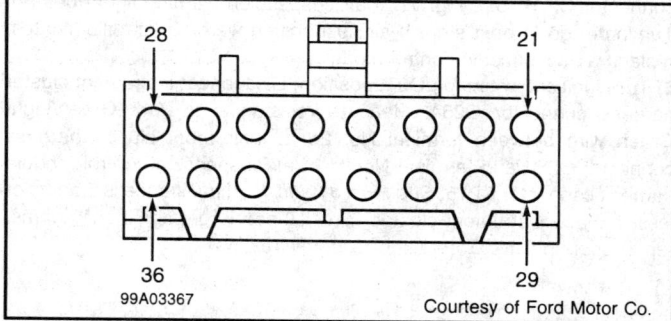

Fig. 12: Identifying Instrument Cluster Harness Connector C254 Terminals

TEST M: LEFT TURN INDICATOR NEVER/ALWAYS ON

1) Turn ignition switch to RUN position. Operate turn signals. If turn signals operate, go to next step. If turn signals do not operate, repair turn signals. See AUTOLAMP SYSTEMS – CROWN VICTORIA & GRAND MARQUIS article.

2) Turn ignition switch to LOCK position. Disconnect instrument cluster harness connector C256. Turn ignition switch to RUN position. Turn left turn signal on. Measure voltage at terminal No. 6 (Light Green/White wire) at instrument cluster harness connector C256. See Fig. 6. If voltage fluctuates between zero and battery voltage, replace bulb or instrument cluster as necessary. If voltage does not fluctuate between zero and battery voltage, repair open or short in Light Green/White wire.

TEST N: RIGHT TURN INDICATOR NEVER/ALWAYS ON

1) Turn ignition switch to RUN position. Operate turn signals. If turn signals operate, go to next step. If turn signals do not operate, repair turn signals. See AUTOLAMP SYSTEMS – CROWN VICTORIA & GRAND MARQUIS article.

2) Turn ignition switch to LOCK position. Disconnect instrument cluster harness connector C256. Turn ignition switch to RUN position. Turn right turn signal on. Measure voltage at terminal No. 5 (White/Light Blue wire) at instrument cluster harness connector C256. See Fig. 6. If voltage fluctuates between zero and battery voltage, replace bulb or instrument cluster as necessary. If voltage does not fluctuate between zero and battery voltage, repair open or short in White/Light Blue wire.

TEST O: HIGH BEAM WARNING NEVER/ALWAYS ON

1) Turn ignition switch to RUN position. Turn on high beams. If high beams operate, go to next step. If high beams do not operate, repair high beams. See AUTOLAMP SYSTEMS – CROWN VICTORIA & GRAND MARQUIS article.

2) Turn ignition switch to LOCK position. Disconnect instrument cluster harness connector C256. Turn ignition switch to RUN position. Turn high beams on. Measure voltage at terminal No. 14 (Light Green/Black wire) at instrument cluster harness connector C256. See Fig. 6. If battery voltage exists, replace bulb or instrument cluster as necessary. If battery voltage does not exist, repair open or short in Light Green/Black wire.

TEST P: TRACTION CONTROL INDICATOR INOPERATIVE

1) Turn ignition switch to LOCK position. Disconnect Anti-Lock Brake System (ABS) control module harness connector C162. Turn ignition switch to RUN position. Using a fused jumper wire, ground terminal No. 15 (Violet wire) at ABS control module harness connector C162. See Fig. 13. If traction control indicator does not illuminate, go to next step. If traction control indicator illuminates, repair ABS concern. See appropriate ANTI-LOCK article in BRAKES in appropriate MITCHELL® manual.

2) Turn ignition switch to LOCK position. Disconnect indicator light module harness connector C2004. Measure resistance in Violet wire between terminal No. 1 at indicator light module harness connector C2004 and terminal No. 15 at anti-lock brake control module harness connector C162. See Figs. 8 and 13. Resistance should be 5 ohms or less. Measure resistance between ground and terminal No. 1 (Violet wire) at indicator light module harness connector C2004. Resistance should be greater than 10 k/ohms. If both resistance readings are as specified, replace indicator light module. If either resistance readings is not as specified, repair open or short to ground in Violet wire.

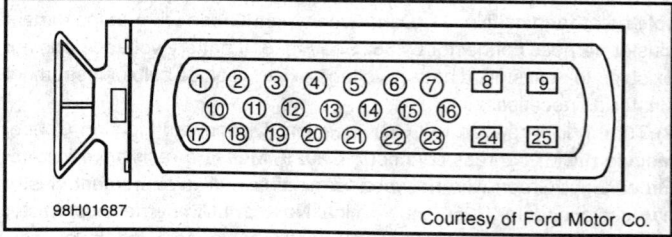

Fig. 13: Identifying Anti-Lock Brake Control Module Harness Connector C162 Terminals

TEST Q: OVERDRIVE OFF INDICATOR INOPERATIVE

1) Turn ignition switch to LOCK position. Connect NGS tester to Data Link Connector (DLC). Turn ignition switch to RUN position. Using NGS

1999 ACCESSORIES & EQUIPMENT
Electronic Instrument Panels
Crown Victoria & Grand Marquis (Cont.)

FORD
4-887

tester, monitor PCM PID TCIL while pressing overdrive switch on and off. If PID agrees with switch position, go to next step. If PID does not agree with switch position, go to step **3**).

2) Turn ignition switch to LOCK position. Disconnect instrument cluster harness connector C255. Disconnect Powertrain Control Module (PCM) harness connector C185. Measure resistance in White/Light Green wire between terminal No. 14 at instrument cluster harness connector C255 and terminal No. 12 at PCM harness connector C185. *See Figs. 5 and 10.* If resistance is 5 ohms or less, replace bulb or instrument cluster as necessary. If resistance is greater than 5 ohms, repair open in White/Light Green wire.

3) Turn ignition switch to LOCK position. Disconnect Powertrain Control Module (PCM) harness connector C185. Turn ignition switch to RUN position. Turn overdrive switch on. Measure voltage at terminal No. 29 (Tan/White wire) at PCM harness connector C185. *See Fig. 10.* If battery voltage does not exist, go to next step. If battery voltage exists, replace PCM.

4) Turn ignition switch to LOCK position. Disconnect overdrive switch harness connector C202. Turn ignition switch to RUN position. Measure voltage at Red/Yellow wire terminal at overdrive switch harness connector C202. If battery voltage exists, go to next step. If battery voltage does not exist, repair power distribution circuit. See appropriate wiring diagram in POWER DISTRIBUTION article in WIRING DIAGRAMS.

5) Turn ignition switch to LOCK position. Measure resistance in Tan/White wire between overdrive switch harness connector C202 and terminal No. 29 at PCM harness connector C185. Resistance should be 5 ohms or less. Measure resistance between ground and terminal No. 29 (Tan/White wire) at PCM harness connector C185. Resistance should be greater than 10 k/ohms. If both resistance readings are as specified, replace overdrive switch. If either resistance readings is not as specified, repair open or short to ground in Tan/White wire.

TEST R: ABS INDICATOR INOPERATIVE

1) Turn ignition switch to LOCK position. Disconnect Anti-Lock Brake System (ABS) control module harness connector C162. Turn ignition switch to RUN position. Using a fused jumper wire, ground terminal No. 16 (Dark Green wire) at ABS control module harness connector C162. *See Fig. 13.* If ABS indicator does not illuminate, go to next step. If ABS indicator illuminates, repair ABS concern. See appropriate ANTI-LOCK article in BRAKES in appropriate MITCHELL® manual.

2) Turn ignition switch to LOCK position. Disconnect indicator light module harness connector C2004. Measure resistance in Dark Green wire between terminal No. 2 at indicator light module harness connector C2004 and terminal No. 16 at anti-lock brake control module harness connector C162. *See Figs. 8 and 13.* Resistance should be 5 ohms or less. Measure resistance between ground and terminal No. 2 (Dark Green wire) at indicator light module harness connector C2004. Resistance should be greater than 10 k/ohms. If both resistance readings are as specified, replace indicator light module. If either resistance readings is not as specified, repair open or short to ground in Violet wire.

TEST S: FAIL-SAFE COOLING INDICATOR INOPERATIVE

1) Turn ignition switch to LOCK position. Disconnect Powertrain Control Module (PCM) harness connector C185. Turn ignition switch to RUN position. Using a fused jumper wire, ground terminal No. 45 (Orange/Red wire) at PCM harness connector C185. *See Fig. 10.* If fail-safe cooling indicator does not illuminate, go to next step. If fail-safe cooling indicator illuminates, repair powertrain concern. See appropriate SELF-DIAGNOSTICS article in ENGINE PERFORMANCE in appropriate MITCHELL® manual.

2) Turn ignition switch to LOCK position. Disconnect instrument cluster harness connector C255. Measure resistance in Black/Yellow wire between terminal No. 18 at instrument cluster harness connector C255 and terminal No. 45 at PCM harness connector C185. *See Figs. 5 and 10.* Resistance should be 5 ohms or less. Measure resistance between ground and terminal No. 18 (Black/Yellow wire) at instrument cluster

harness connector C255. Resistance should be greater than 10 k/ohms. If both resistance readings are as specified, replace instrument cluster. If either resistance readings is not as specified, repair open or short to ground in Black/Yellow wire.

TEST T: DOOR AJAR INDICATOR INOPERATIVE

1) Turn ignition switch to LOCK position. Disconnect Driver's Door Module (DDM) harness connector C518. Turn ignition switch to RUN position. Using a fused jumper wire, ground terminal No. 9 (Black/Yellow wire) at DDM harness connector C518. *See Fig. 14.* If door ajar indicator does not illuminate, go to next step. If door ajar indicator illuminates, replace DDM.

2) Turn ignition switch to LOCK position. Disconnect instrument cluster harness connector C255. Measure resistance in Black/Yellow wire between terminal No. 17 at instrument cluster harness connector C255 and terminal No. 9 at DDM harness connector C518. *See Figs. 5 and 14.* Resistance should be 5 ohms or less. Measure resistance between ground and terminal No. 17 (Black/Yellow wire) at instrument cluster harness connector C255. Resistance should be greater than 10 k/ohms. If both resistance readings are as specified, replace instrument cluster. If either resistance readings is not as specified, repair open or short to ground in Black/Yellow wire.

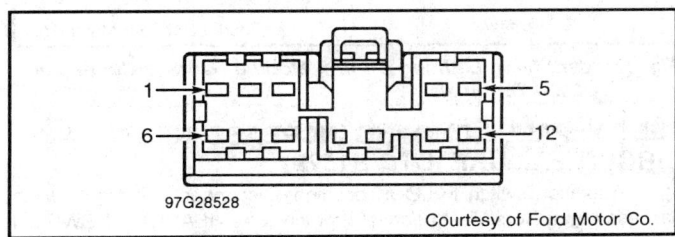

Fig. 14: Identifying Driver's Door Module Harness Connector C518 Terminals

TEST U: TRUNK AJAR INDICATOR INOPERATIVE

1) Operate remote trunk release. If remote trunk release operates, go to next step. If remote trunk release does not operate, repair remote trunk release. See appropriate wiring diagram in POWER DOOR LOCKS & TRUNK RELEASE article.

2) Turn ignition switch to LOCK position. Disconnect trunk release solenoid harness connector C478. Disconnect instrument cluster harness connector C254. Measure resistance in Brown/White wire between trunk release solenoid harness connector C478 and terminal No. 27 at instrument cluster harness connector C254. *See Fig. 12.* If resistance is 5 ohms or less, replace instrument cluster. If resistance is greater than 5 ohms, repair open in Brown/White wire.

TEST V: LOW WASHER FLUID INDICATOR INOPERATIVE

1) Turn ignition switch to LOCK position. Disconnect washer fluid level switch harness connector C1021. Turn ignition switch to RUN position. Using a fused jumper wire, ground Pink/Yellow wire terminal at washer fluid level switch harness connector C1021. If low washer fluid indicator illuminates, go to next step. If low washer fluid indicator does not illuminate, go to step **3**).

2) Turn ignition switch to LOCK position. Measure resistance between ground and Black wire terminal at washer fluid level switch harness connector C1021. If resistance is 5 ohms or less, replace washer fluid level switch. If resistance is greater than 5 ohms, repair open in Black wire.

3) Turn ignition switch to LOCK position. Disconnect instrument cluster harness connector C255. Measure resistance in Pink/Yellow wire between washer fluid level switch harness connector C1021 and terminal No. 10 at instrument cluster harness connector C255. *See Fig. 5.* If resistance is 5 ohms or less, replace instrument cluster. If resistance is greater than 5 ohms, repair open in Pink/Yellow wire.

FORD
4-888

1999 ACCESSORIES & EQUIPMENT
Electronic Instrument Panels
Crown Victoria & Grand Marquis (Cont.)

TEST W: HAZARD INDICATOR INOPERATIVE

1) Turn ignition switch to LOCK position. Disconnect Lighting Control Module (LCM) harness connector C2026. Turn ignition switch to RUN position. Using a fused jumper wire, ground terminal No. 9 (Red/White wire) at LCM harness connector C2026. *See Fig. 15*. If hazard indicator does not illuminate, go to next step. If hazard indicator does not illuminate, repair hazards. See AUTOLAMP SYSTEMS – CROWN VICTORIA & GRAND MARQUIS article.

2) Turn ignition switch to LOCK position. Disconnect indicator light module harness connector C2004. Measure resistance in Red/White wire between indicator light module harness connector C2004 and terminal No. 9 at LCM harness connector C2026. *See Figs. 8 and 15*. If resistance is 5 ohms or less, replace indicator light module. If resistance is greater than 5 ohms, repair open in Red/White wire.

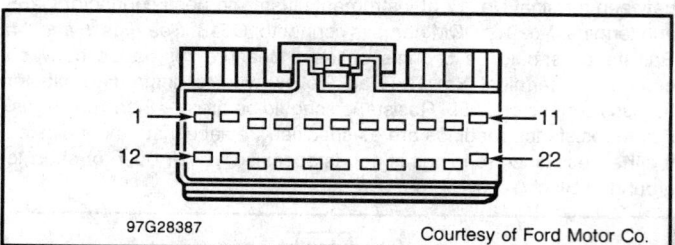

97G28387   Courtesy of Ford Motor Co.

Fig. 15: Identifying Lighting Control Module Harness Connector C2026 Terminals

TEST X: PANEL DIMMING INCREASE INPUT CIRCUIT FAILURE (DTC B1579)

1) Turn ignition switch to LOCK position. Disconnect headlight switch harness connectors. Test headlight switch. See HEADLIGHT SWITCH under COMPONENT TESTS. If headlight switch is okay, go to next step. If headlight switch is defective, replace headlight switch.

2) Disconnect Lighting Control Module (LCM) harness connector C2026. Measure resistance in Orange/Red wire between terminal No. 4 at headlight switch harness connector C249 and terminal No. 16 at LCM harness connector C2026. *See Figs. 8 and 15*. Resistance should be 5 ohms or less. Measure resistance between ground and terminal No. 16 (Orange/Red wire) at LCM harness connector C2026. Resistance should be greater than 10 k/ohms. If both resistance readings are as specified, replace LCM. If either resistance reading is not as specified, repair open or short to ground in Orange/Red wire.

TEST Y: PANEL DIMMING INCREASE INPUT CIRCUIT SHORT TO VOLTAGE (DTC B1581)

1) Turn ignition switch to LOCK position. Disconnect headlight switch harness connector C249. Turn ignition switch to RUN position. Measure voltage at terminal No. 4 (Orange/Red wire) at headlight switch harness connector C249. *See Fig. 8*. If any voltage exists, go to next step. If zero volts exists, replace headlight switch.

2) Turn ignition switch to LOCK position. Disconnect Lighting Control Module (LCM) harness connector C2026. Turn ignition switch to RUN position. Measure voltage at terminal No. 4 (Orange/Red wire) at headlight switch harness connector C249. If zero volts exists, replace LCM. If any voltage exists, repair short to voltage in Orange/Red wire.

TEST Z: PANEL DIMMING DECREASE INPUT CIRCUIT FAILURE (DTC B1583)

1) Turn ignition switch to LOCK position. Disconnect headlight switch harness connectors. Test headlight switch. See HEADLIGHT SWITCH under COMPONENT TESTS. If headlight switch is okay, go to next step. If headlight switch is defective, replace headlight switch.

2) Disconnect Lighting Control Module (LCM) harness connector C2026. Measure resistance in Brown/White wire between terminal No. 1 at headlight switch harness connector C249 and terminal No. 15 at LCM harness connector C2026. *See Figs. 8 and 15*. Resistance should be 5

ohms or less. Measure resistance between ground and terminal No. 15 (Brown/White wire) at LCM harness connector C2026. Resistance should be greater than 10 k/ohms. If both resistance readings are as specified, replace LCM. If either resistance reading is not as specified, repair open or short to ground in Brown/White wire.

TEST AA: PANEL DIMMING DECREASE INPUT CIRCUIT SHORT TO VOLTAGE (DTC B1585)

1) Turn ignition switch to LOCK position. Disconnect headlight switch harness connector C249. Turn ignition switch to RUN position. Measure voltage at terminal No. 1 (Brown/White wire) at headlight switch harness connector C249. *See Fig. 8*. If any voltage exists, go to next step. If zero volts exists, replace headlight switch.

2) Turn ignition switch to LOCK position. Disconnect Lighting Control Module (LCM) harness connector C2026. Turn ignition switch to RUN position. Measure voltage at terminal No. 1 (Brown/White wire) at headlight switch harness connector C249. If zero volts exists, replace LCM. If any voltage exists, repair short to voltage in Brown/White wire.

TEST AB: PANEL ILLUMINATION CONTROL INOPERATIVE

1) Using NGS tester, perform Lighting Control Module (LCM) self-test. If not DTC are retrieved, go to next step. If any DTC are retrieved, perform appropriate test. See LIGHTING CONTROL MODULE DTC INDEX table under SELF-DIAGNOSTIC SYSTEM.

2) Turn ignition switch to RUN position. Turn parking lights on. If parking lights illuminate, go to next step. If parking lights do not illuminate, perform TEST Q: PARKING LIGHTS INOPERATIVE under SYSTEM TESTS in AUTOLAMP SYSTEM – CROWN VICTORIA & GRAND MARQUIS article.

3) Turn ignition switch to LOCK position. Disconnect LCM harness connector C2029. Using a fused jumper wire, connect terminals No. 2 (Light Blue/Red wire) and No. 6 (Tan/White wire) at LCM harness connector C2029. *See Fig. 4*. Turn ignition switch to RUN position. If instrument cluster panel lights do not illuminate, remove jumper wire and go to next step. If instrument cluster panel lights illuminate, replace LCM.

4) Ensure ignition switch is in RUN position. Measure voltage at terminal No. 6 (Tan/White wire) at LCM harness connector C2029. If battery voltage exists, repair open in Light Blue/Red wire. If battery voltage does not exist, repair power distribution circuit. See appropriate wiring diagram in POWER DISTRIBUTION article in WIRING DIAGRAMS.

TEST AC: INSTRUMENT CLUSTER ILLUMINATION INOPERATIVE

Turn ignition switch to LOCK position. Disconnect instrument cluster harness connectors. Measure voltage at terminal No. 3 (Orange/Black wire) at instrument cluster harness connector C256. *See Fig. 6*. Measure voltage at terminal No. 13 (Light Blue/Red wire) at instrument cluster harness connector C255. *See Fig. 5*. If battery voltage exists at both terminals, replace instrument cluster. If battery voltage does not exist at either terminal, repair appropriate power distribution circuit. See appropriate wiring diagram in POWER DISTRIBUTION article in WIRING DIAGRAMS.

TEST AD: INSTRUMENT PANEL ILLUMINATION DOES NOT DIM

1) Turn ignition switch to RUN position. Turn headlights on. Using NGS tester, monitor Lighting Control Module (LCM) PID DIM_DEC while holding dim switch down. If PID indicates ON, go to next step. If PID does not indicate ON, go to step **3)**.

2) Turn ignition switch to LOCK position. Disconnect LCM harness connector C2026. Disconnect headlight switch harness connector C249. Measure resistance in Brown/White wire between terminal No. 15 at LCM harness connector C2026 and terminal No. 1 at headlight switch

1999 ACCESSORIES & EQUIPMENT
Electronic Instrument Panels
Crown Victoria & Grand Marquis (Cont.)

FORD
4-889

harness connector C249. *See Figs. 8 and 15.* If resistance is 5 ohms or less, go to next step. If resistance is greater than repair open in Brown/White wire.

3) Using NGS tester, monitor LCM PID DIM_INC while holding dim switch up. If PID does not indicate ON, go to next step. If PID indicates ON, replace LCM.

4) Turn ignition switch to LOCK position. Disconnect LCM harness connector C2026. Disconnect headlight switch harness connector C249. Measure resistance in Orange/Red wire between terminal No. 16 at LCM harness connector C2026 and terminal No. 4 at headlight switch harness connector C249. *See Figs. 8 and 15.* If resistance is 5 ohms or less, go to next step. If resistance is greater than repair open in Orange/Red wire.

5) Measure resistance between ground and terminal No. 2 (Tan/White wire) at headlight switch harness connector C249. If resistance is greater than 10 k/ohms, go to next step. If resistance is 10 k/ohms or less, repair short to ground in Tan/White wire.

6) Test headlight switch. See HEADLIGHT SWITCH under COMPONENT TESTS. If headlight switch is okay, replace LCM. If headlight switch is defective, replace headlight switch.

TEST AE: MESSAGE CENTER INOPERATIVE

1) Turn ignition switch to RUN position while observing instrument cluster. All instrument cluster segment should illuminate for several seconds then turn off. If instrument cluster operates as specified, go to next step. If instrument cluster does not operate as specified, repair instrument cluster. See SELF-DIAGNOSTIC SYSTEM.

2) Press E/M and SELECT (back) buttons simultaneously. OA should be displayed in left 2 digits of odometer display. Press SELECT (forward) button twice quickly. 1B should be displayed in 2 left digits of odometer display. Press SELECT (forward) button until 5F is displayed in left 2 digits of odometer display. Depress accelerator pedal. If 0000 is no displayed in right 4 digits of odometer display, go to next step. If 0000 is displayed in right 4 digits of odometer display, go to step 7).

3) Turn ignition switch to LOCK position. Disconnect message center switch harness connector C264. Turn ignition switch to RUN position. Measure voltage at terminal No. 4 (Pink/Orange wire) at message center switch harness connector C264. *See Fig. 8.* If battery voltage exists, go to next step. If battery voltage does not exists, repair power distribution circuit. See appropriate wiring diagram in POWER DISTRIBUTION article in WIRING DIAGRAMS.

4) Turn ignition switch to LOCK position. Disconnect instrument cluster harness connectors C254 and C255. Measure resistance in Light Blue/White wire between terminal No. 23 at instrument cluster harness connector C254 and terminal No. 6 at message center switch harness connector C264. *See Figs. 8 and 12.* Measure resistance in Light Blue/Yellow wire between terminal No. 3 at instrument cluster harness connector C255 and terminal No. 5 at message center switch harness connector C264. *See Figs. 5 and 8.* If both resistance readings are 5 ohms or less, go to next step. If either resistance reading is greater than 5 ohms, repair open in appropriate wire.

5) Measure resistance between ground and terminal No. 3 (Light Blue/Yellow wire) at instrument cluster harness connector C255. Measure resistance between ground and terminal No. 23 (Light Blue/White wire) at instrument cluster harness connector C254. If both resistance readings are greater than 10 k/ohms, go to next step. If either resistance reading is 10 k/ohms or less, repair short to ground in appropriate wire.

6) Measure resistance between appropriate terminal at message center switch (component side) with switch in specified position. See MESSAGE CENTER SWITCH RESISTANCE table. *See Fig. 16.* If resistance is as specified, replace instrument cluster. If resistance is not as specified, replace message center switch.

7) Turn ignition switch to LOCK position. Disconnect PCM harness connector C185. Measure resistance in Dark Green/Light Green wire between terminal No. 11 at instrument cluster harness connector C255 and terminal No. 43 at PCM harness connector C185. *See Figs. 5 and 10.* Resistance should be 5 ohms or less. Measure resistance between

ground and terminal No. 11 (Black/Yellow wire) at instrument cluster harness connector C255. Resistance should be greater than 10 k/ohms. If either resistance readings is not as specified, repair open or short to ground in Dark Green/Light Green wire. If both resistance readings are as specified, repair powertrain control concern. See appropriate SELF-DIAGNOSTICS article ENGINE PERFORMANCE.

MESSAGE CENTER SWITCH RESISTANCE

Switch Position	Between Terminals	Resistance
E/M	4 & 6	7.32
RESET	4 & 6	2.67
SELECT	4 & 5	7.32
SELECT	4 & 6	2.67

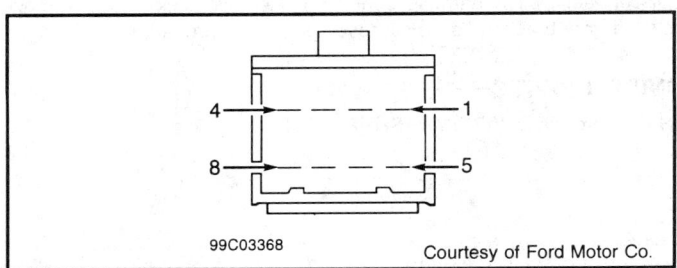

99C03368   Courtesy of Ford Motor Co.

Fig. 16: Identifying Message Center Switch Terminals

REMOVAL & INSTALLATION

WARNING: Deactivate air bag system before performing any service operation. See appropriate AIR BAG RESTRAINT SYSTEMS article. DO NOT apply electrical power to any component on steering column without first deactivating air bag system. Air bag may deploy.

CAUTION: When battery is disconnected, vehicle computer and memory systems may lose memory data. Driveability problems may exist until computer systems have completed a relearn cycle. See COMPUTER RELEARN PROCEDURES article in GENERAL INFORMATION before disconnecting battery.

ELECTRONIC INSTRUMENT CLUSTER (EIC)

Removal & Installation – 1) Disconnect negative battery cable. Apply parking brake. Unsnap center moldings on both sides of instrument cluster. Pull center panel switches forward (if equipped) far enough to unplug connectors, then remove. Remove steering column cover.

2) Remove 4 steering column nuts. Lower steering column. Remove headlight switch knob. Move finish panel outward. Set transmission range selector to Low (1) position. Disconnect connectors from message center control assembly and message center switch module. Remove finish panel, taking care not to scratch it.

3) Disconnect connector from front of instrument cluster. Disconnect shift indicator by bending bottom tab downward and pulling shift indicator assembly forward.

4) Pull instrument cluster outward. Disconnect remaining electrical connectors. Remove instrument cluster. To install, reverse removal procedure.

MESSAGE CENTER SWITCH MODULE

Removal & Installation – 1) Disconnect negative battery cable. Apply parking brake. Unsnap center moldings on both sides of instrument cluster. Remove steering column cover and shroud.

2) Remove knobs for autodimmer and autolamp (if equipped). Remove instrument panel screws. Pull instrument panel outward.

FORD
4-890

1999 ACCESSORIES & EQUIPMENT
Electronic Instrument Panels
Crown Victoria & Grand Marquis (Cont.)

3) Disconnect electrical connections as necessary. Remove instrument panel from front of instrument cluster. Remove retaining screws and switch module from rear of instrument panel. To install, reverse removal procedure.

HEADLIGHT SWITCH

Removal & Installation – 1) Disconnect negative battery cable. Insert hooked tool into slot at base of headlight switch knob to release retaining spring clip. Pull knob from shaft. Remove dimmer knob/trim bezel from shaft.

2) Remove left and right instrument panel horizontal trim moldings. Remove all cluster finish panel retaining screws. Remove panel. Remove headlight switch bracket screws. Remove switch from panel. Disconnect switch harness connector. Remove lock nut to remove switch from bracket. To install, reverse removal procedure.

WIPER SWITCH

See appropriate WIPER/WASHER SYSTEMS article.

WIRING DIAGRAMS

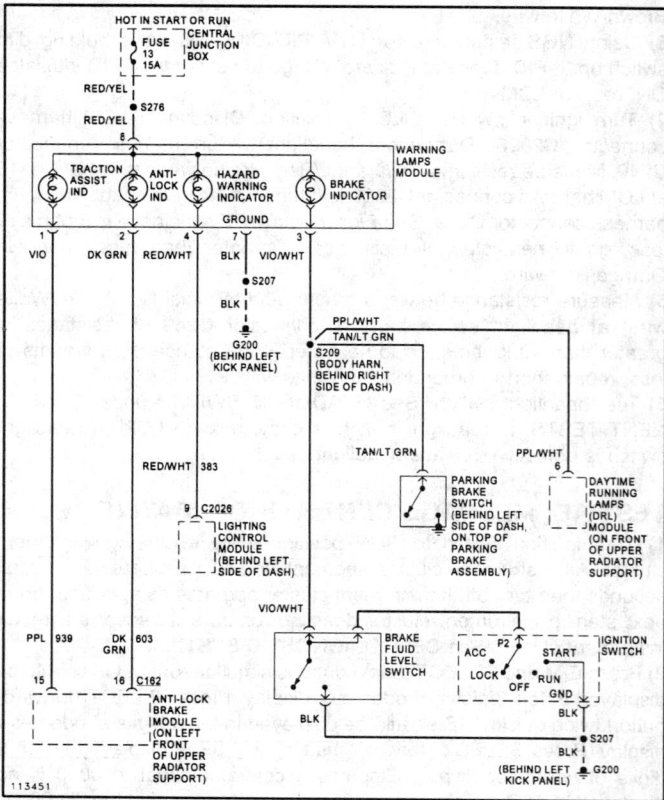

Fig. 17: Electronic Instrument Panel Warning Lights Wiring Diagram (Crown Victoria & Grand Marquis)

1999 ACCESSORIES & EQUIPMENT
Electronic Instrument Panels
Crown Victoria & Grand Marquis (Cont.)

FORD
4-891

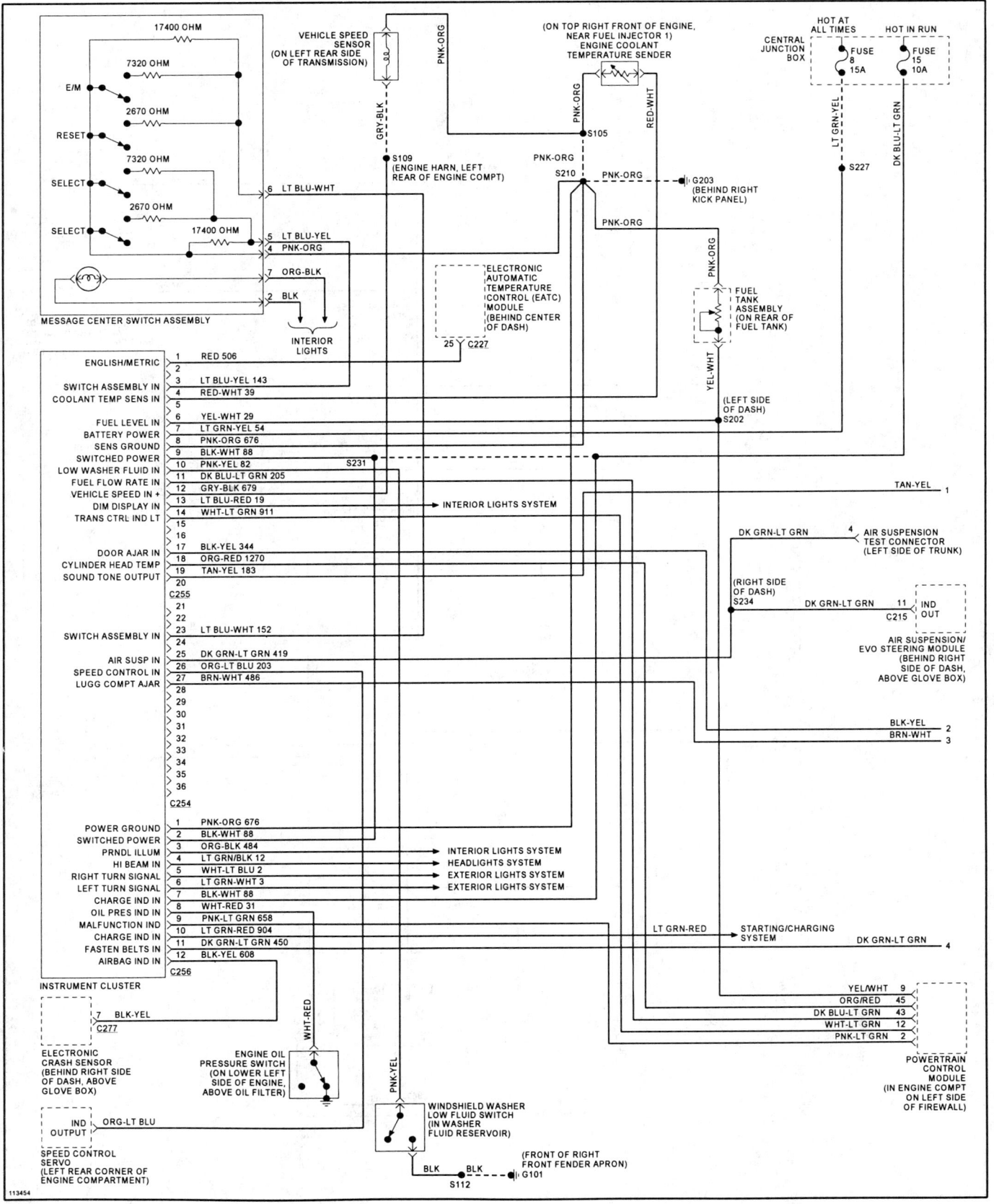

Fig. 18: Electronic Instrument Panel Wiring Diagram (Crown Victoria & Grand Marquis – 1 Of 2)

FORD
4-892

1999 ACCESSORIES & EQUIPMENT
Electronic Instrument Panels
Crown Victoria & Grand Marquis (Cont.)

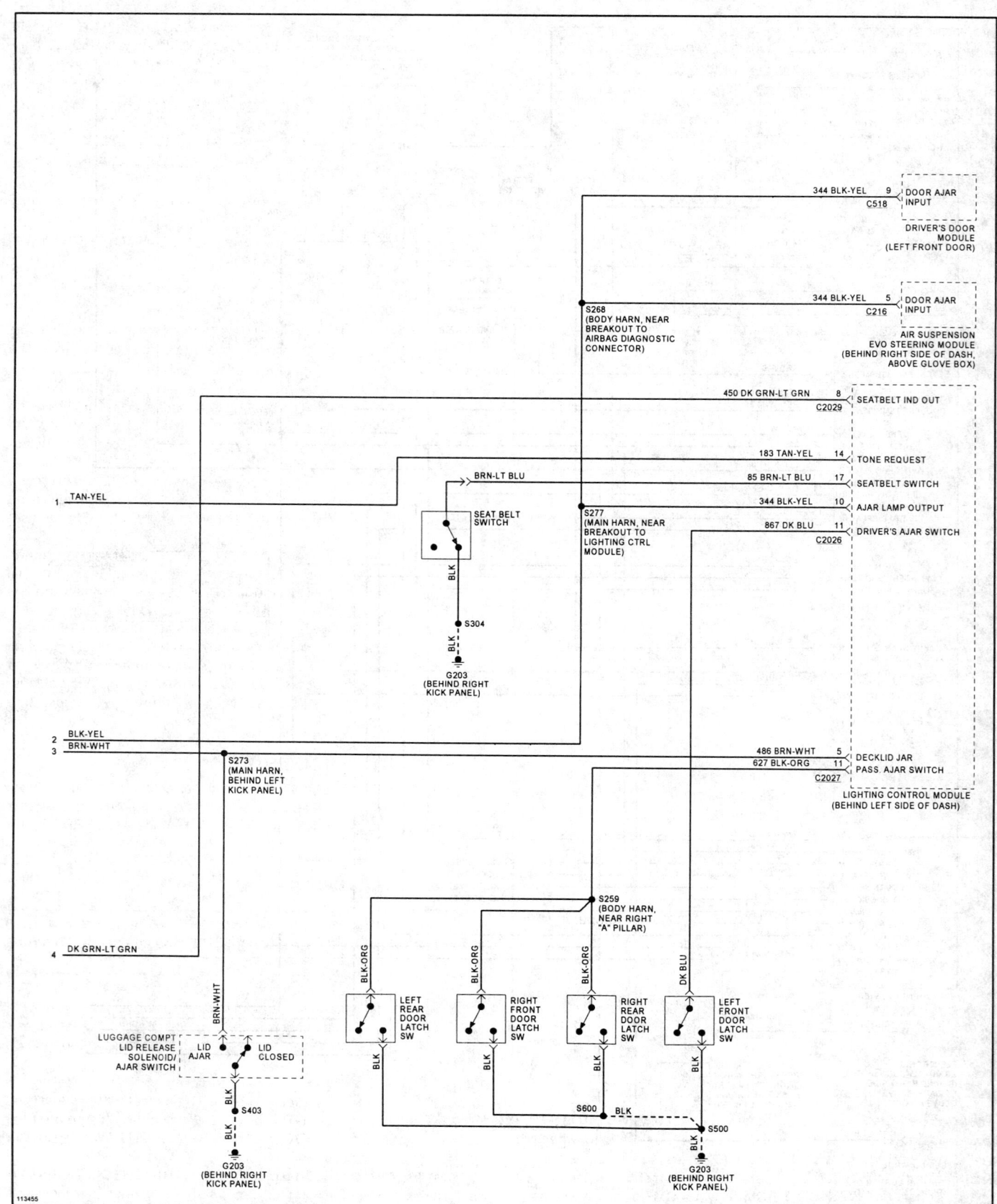

Fig. 19: Electronic Instrument Panel Wiring Diagram (Crown Victoria & Grand Marquis – 2 Of 2)

DESCRIPTION

WARNING: Deactivate air bag system before performing any service operation. See AIR BAG RESTRAINT SYSTEMS – VILLAGER article. DO NOT apply electrical power to any component on steering column without first deactivating air bag system. Air bag may deploy.

The electronic instrument cluster consists of a display panel and a microcomputer. It is operational only when ignition is on. Major components are a speedometer, odometer, fuel gauge, coolant temperature gauge, message center, and warning indicators. *See Fig. 1.*

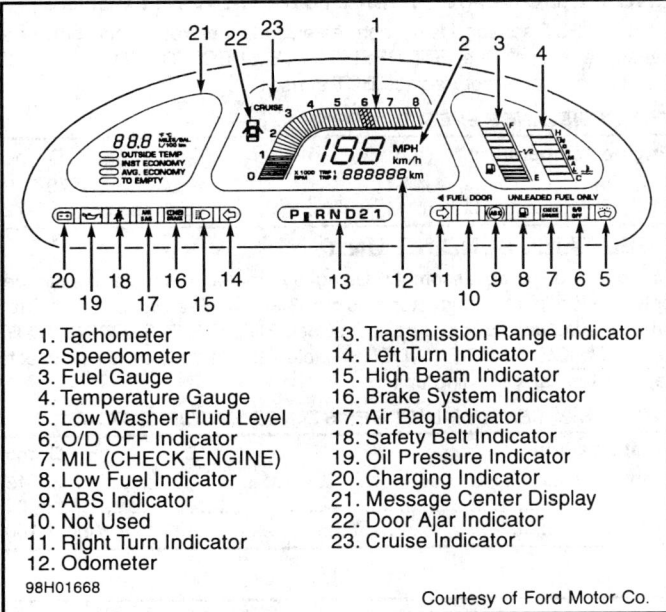

1. Tachometer
2. Speedometer
3. Fuel Gauge
4. Temperature Gauge
5. Low Washer Fluid Level
6. O/D OFF Indicator
7. MIL (CHECK ENGINE)
8. Low Fuel Indicator
9. ABS Indicator
10. Not Used
11. Right Turn Indicator
12. Odometer
13. Transmission Range Indicator
14. Left Turn Indicator
15. High Beam Indicator
16. Brake System Indicator
17. Air Bag Indicator
18. Safety Belt Indicator
19. Oil Pressure Indicator
20. Charging Indicator
21. Message Center Display
22. Door Ajar Indicator
23. Cruise Indicator

98H01668

Courtesy of Ford Motor Co.

Fig. 1: Identifying Electronic Instrument Cluster Components

OPERATION

GAUGES

Coolant Temperature Gauge – This gauge displays coolant temperature. Coolant temperature gauge is calibrated by segments. Each segment has a specific temperature value. *See Fig. 2.*

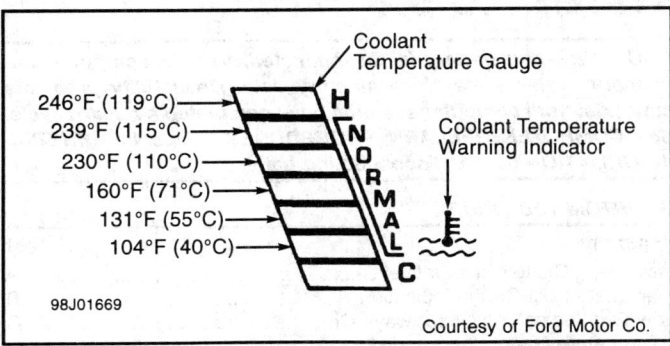

246°F (119°C)
239°F (115°C)
230°F (110°C)
160°F (71°C)
131°F (55°C)
104°F (40°C)

Coolant Temperature Gauge

Coolant Temperature Warning Indicator

98J01669

Courtesy of Ford Motor Co.

Fig. 2: Identifying Coolant Temperature Gauge Calibration

Fuel Gauge – This gauge displays amount of fuel remaining in tank. A low fuel alert will be indicated by a flashing fuel pump symbol whenever fuel remaining is less than 2.5 gallons (9.5 liters).

Tachometer – The tachometer operates on a Camshaft Position (CMP) sensor signal sent to PCM. The PCM converts CMP sine wave signal to a digital signal and sends to tachometer in electronic instrument cluster. Engine RPM is indicated by the number of bars lit. Each bar represents 200 RPM.

MESSAGE CENTER CONTROL BUTTONS

Control buttons are located to the left of the instrument cluster, just below the message center in the message center switch module. Control button functions are as follows: A tone will sound when each button is pressed.

SELECT – Selects and displays TRIP DISTANCE, FUEL REMAINING, INSTANTANEOUS FUEL ECONOMY, AVERAGE FUEL ECONOMY, or DISTANCE TO EMPTY.

RESET – Resets or clears information on message center.

ENG/MET Button – Changes odometer or speedometer display from English to Metric or from Metric to English.

TRIP/RST Button – Clears trip distance displayed on TRIP1 or TRIP2 displays.

OD/TRIP Button – Switches odometer display between TRIP1, TRIP2 or odometer displays.

MESSAGE CENTER

The message center is located on the left side of the instrument cluster. The SELECT button can be pressed to set the desired function. The following can be displayed on the message center:

Instantaneous Fuel Economy – Fuel economy is determined by a speed sensor signal (distance traveled) and the fuel flow signal from the powertrain control module. If vehicle is running but not moving, the display will show 0 miles per gallon or 99 liters/100 kilometers. Instantaneous fuel economy cannot be reset.

Average Fuel Economy – Average fuel economy is determined by a speed sensor signal (distance traveled) and the fuel flow signal from the powertrain control module. Average fuel economy display can be reset with the RESET button.

Distance To Empty – Distance to empty is calculated by using average fuel economy over the last 200-300 miles, and current amount of fuel remaining in tank. When distance to empty is less than 50 miles, the fuel computer overrides the current display function and flashes distance to empty display for 5 seconds. The display repeats at 25 and 10 miles.

Outside Temperature – Outside air temperature will be displayed. If an abrupt change occurs in temperature, temperature display will be inaccurate until vehicle has been driven at 30 MPH for a period of time. The period of time will be longer for larger amount of temperature change.

SPEEDOMETER/ODOMETER

The speedometer displays vehicle speed, based on input signals from the transmission-mounted speed sensor. If the odometer cannot read a valid odometer mileage from memory, it will flash the word ERROR as a service alert.

WARNING INDICATORS

NOTE: Safety belt warning indicator will come on for 4 to 8 seconds after ignition is turned on, and a tone will occur. This tone is independent of instrument cluster.

Various warning indicators are displayed on the instrument cluster. The instrument cluster contains warning indicators for air bag, anti-lock, brake, charging system, check engine, safety belt, oil pressure, air suspension, washer fluid, and door ajar. Warning indicators operate as follows:

ABS, Door Ajar & Washer Fluid – Warning indicators flash for 5 seconds, remain on, and a tone sounds. The indicators will remain on until the condition is resolved. The warning indicators will operate after prove-out mode. See INDICATOR BULB PROVE-OUT. Warning indicators cannot be dimmed.

Air Bag, Brake System, Charging System, MIL (CHECK ENGINE) & Low Oil Pressure – Warning indicators remain on whenever ignition is on until the condition is resolved. Warning indicators operate during prove-out. See INDICATOR BULB PROVE-OUT. Warning indicators cannot be dimmed.

COMPONENT LOCATIONS

COMPONENT LOCATIONS

Component	Location
Air Bag Sliding Contact	In Steering Wheel
Data Link Connector (DLC)	Below Driver's Side Of Instrument Panel, To Right Of Steering Column
Engine Coolant Temperature (ECT) Sensor	Right Rear Side Of Engine
Engine Compartment Relay Box	Left Front Side Of Engine Compartment
Headlight Switch Rheostat	Left Side Of Instrument Panel
Interior Fuse Junction Panel	Below Left Side Of Instrument Panel
Power Distribution Box	In Engine Compartment, Next To Battery
Powertrain Control Module (PCM)	Behind Glove Box
Smart Entry Control (SEC) Timer/Module	Behind Center Top Of Dash Panel
Speed Control Actuator Module	Below Left Side Of Instrument Panel
Lighting Control Module (LCM)	Bottom Of Center Console, Below Dash Panel
Transaxle Control Module (TCM)	Behind Instrument Cluster
Vehicle Speed Sensor (VSS)	Center Of Engine Compartment

TROUBLE SHOOTING

INDICATOR BULB PROVE-OUT

When ignition is turned on, all electronic displays come on momentarily, go off momentarily, and then return to normal operation. Prove-out for the following warning indicators will also occur:

- Charging System
- Safety Belt
- Air Bag
- Brake System
- Low Oil Pressure
- Anti-Lock Brake System (ABS)
- MIL (SERVICE ENGINE SOON)
- Overdrive (O/D) Off

INSPECTION & VERIFICATION

Verify customer concern by operating system in question. Verify charging system, safety belt warning chime, turn signals, headlights and cruise control are working properly. Inspect wiring harness for obvious signs of shorts, opens, bad connections or damage. If fault is not visible, go to SYMPTOM TESTS INDEX table and proceed to appropriate test under SYSTEM TESTS.

Mechanical:
- Low Brake Fluid Level
- Damaged Engine Oil Filter
- Damaged Oil Pump
- Damaged Vehicle Speed Sensor Gear
- Door Adjustment
- Low Engine Oil
- Low Washer Fluid
- Low Coolant Level
- Worn Or Damaged Generator Drive Belt
- Damaged Coolant Thermostat

Electrical:
- Blown Interior Fuse Panel Fuse(s):
  - 7.5-Amp F59
  - 10-Amp F37
  - 10-Amp F41
  - 10-Amp F49
  - 10-Amp F58
- Blown Main Fuse Panel Fuse(s):
  - 15-Amp F12
  - 15-Amp F15
- Damaged Miniature Bulbs
- Damaged Wiring Harness
- Loose Or Corroded Connections
- Damaged Vehicle Speed Sensor
- Damaged Instrument Cluster
- Damaged Message Center

COMPONENT TESTS

ENGINE COOLANT TEMPERATURE (ECT) SENSOR

Remove ECT sensor. Using ohmmeter, measure resistance between sensor terminals. See ECT RESISTANCE SPECIFICATIONS table. If resistance is incorrect, replace ECT sensor.

ECT RESISTANCE SPECIFICATIONS

Engine Temperature °F (°C)	Ohms
167 (75)	179-219
212 (100)	60-72

FUEL TANK SENDING UNIT

Remove fuel pump assembly. Using ohmmeter, measure resistance between fuel pump connector pins No. 3 and 4. *See Fig. 3.* Adjust fuel tank sending unit float to 3 positions. See FUEL TANK SENDING UNIT RESISTANCE SPECIFICATIONS table. If resistance is incorrect, replace fuel tank sending unit.

FUEL TANK SENDING UNIT RESISTANCE SPECIFICATIONS

Float Position	Ohms
Empty	15
1/2	84
Full	About 160

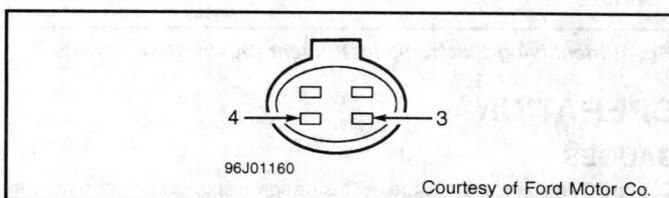

96J01160

Courtesy of Ford Motor Co.

Fig. 3: Identifying Fuel Pump Connector C343 Terminals

SYSTEM TESTS

CAUTION: When battery is disconnected, vehicle computer and memory systems may lose memory data. Driveability problems may exist until computer systems have completed a relearn cycle. See COMPUTER RELEARN PROCEDURES article in GENERAL INFORMATION before disconnecting battery.

SYMPTOM TEST INDEX

Symptom	Test
Instrument Cluster Inoperative	A
Inaccurate Fuel Gauge Indication	B
Low Fuel Indicator Never/Always On	C
Temperature Gauge Inaccurate	D
Speedometer/Odometer Inoperative	E
Tachometer Inoperative	F
Brake Warning Never On	G
Brake Warning Always On	1
Charge Indicator Never On	H
Charge Indicator Always On	2
Oil Pressure Indicator Inoperative	I
Oil Pressure Indicator Always On	J
Both Right & Left Turn Indicator Inoperative	3
Left Turn Indicator Inoperative	K

SYMPTOM TEST INDEX (Cont.)

1 – See appropriate DISC & DRUM article in BRAKES in appropriate MITCHELL® manual.

2 – See GENERATORS – VILLAGER article in STARTING & CHARGING SYSTEMS.

3 – Repair Black wire between electronic instrument cluster connector C267C terminal No. 19 and ground.

4 – See appropriate ANTI-LOCK article in BRAKES in appropriate MITCHELL® manual.

5 – See AIR BAG RESTRAINT SYSTEMS – VILLAGER article.

6 – Check indicator bulb, printed circuit and PCM. See appropriate SELF-DIAGNOSTICS article in ENGINE PERFORMANCE in appropriate MITCHELL® manual.

7 – See CRUISE CONTROL SYSTEMS – VILLAGER article.

TEST A: INSTRUMENT CLUSTER INOPERATIVE

1) Turn ignition off. Disconnect negative battery cable. Remove instrument cluster. See ELECTRONIC INSTRUMENT CLUSTER (EIC) under REMOVAL & INSTALLATION. Disconnect instrument cluster connectors. Reconnect negative battery cable and turn ignition on. Measure voltage between ground and instrument cluster connector C267B terminal No. 3 (Blue wire). Measure voltage between ground and instrument cluster connector C267A terminal No. 5 (Violet wire). Measure voltage between ground and instrument cluster connector C267C terminal No. 20 (Blue wire). *See Figs. 4 - 6.* If all voltage measurements are more than 10 volts, go to next step. If any voltage measurement is 10 volts or less, repair open or short to ground in Blue or Violet wire between interior fuse panel and instrument cluster.

2) Turn ignition off. Measure resistance between ground and instrument cluster connector C267B terminals No. 4 (Black/Red wire) and No. 6 (Black wire). Measure resistance between ground and instrument cluster connector C267C terminal No. 19 (Black wire). If resistance in all measurements is less than 5 ohms, replace instrument cluster and retest. See ELECTRONIC INSTRUMENT CLUSTER (EIC) under REMOVAL & INSTALLATION. If resistance in any measurement is more than 5 ohms, repair open or high resistance in circuit(s) in question and retest system.

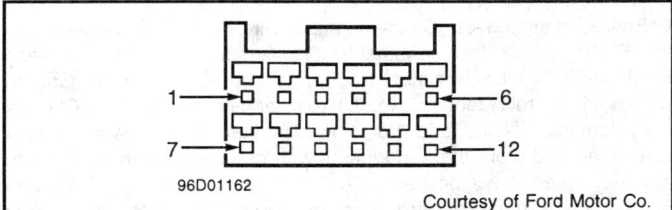

96D01162

Courtesy of Ford Motor Co.

Fig. 4: Identifying Electronic Instrument Cluster (EIC) Connector C267B Terminals

TEST B: FUEL GAUGE INACCURATE

1) Turn ignition off. Disconnect fuel sending unit connector. Connect Instrument Gauge Tester (014–R1063) test leads to fuel sending unit connector Blue/Red wire terminal and ground. Set tester to 160 ohms. Turn ignition on. Turn tester on and wait one minute. Fuel gauge should read full or above. Turn ignition off. Set tester to 15 ohms. Turn ignition

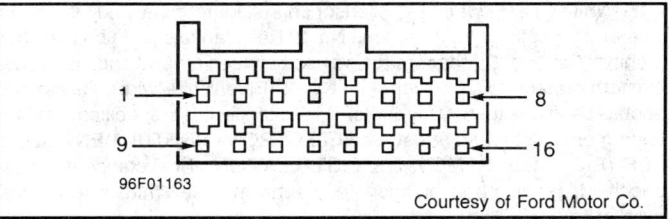

96F01163

Courtesy of Ford Motor Co.

Fig. 5: Identifying Electronic Instrument Cluster (EIC) Connector C267A Terminals

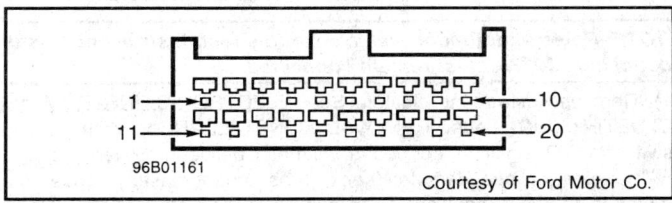

96B01161

Courtesy of Ford Motor Co.

Fig. 6: Identifying Electronic Instrument Cluster (EIC) Connector C267C Terminals & Speed Control Actuator Module Connector C247 Terminals

on and wait one minute. Fuel gauge should read empty or below. If fuel gauge reads as specified, go to next step. If fuel gauge does not read as specified, go to step **4)**.

2) Visually inspect fuel tank for damage or deformation. Replace fuel tank as necessary. Retest system. If fuel tank is okay, go to next step.

3) Visually inspect fuel pump for damage or connector problems. Inspect float and float rod for damage or float rod obstruction. If fuel pump and wiring is okay, replace fuel sending unit. Retest system. If fuel pump and wiring is damaged, repair as necessary.

4) Turn ignition off. Measure resistance between ground and fuel sending unit connector Black wire. Resistance should be less than 5 ohms. If resistance is less than 5 ohms, go to next step. If resistance is more than 5 ohms, repair open in Black wire. Retest system.

5) Remove instrument cluster. See ELECTRONIC INSTRUMENT CLUSTER (EIC) under REMOVAL & INSTALLATION. Disconnect instrument cluster connector C267A. Measure resistance of Blue/Red wire between instrument cluster connector C267A terminal No. 1 and fuel sending unit connector. *See Fig. 5.* Resistance should be less than 5 ohms. Measure resistance between ground and instrument cluster connector C267A terminal No. 1 (Blue/Red wire). Resistance should be more than 10 k/ohms. If resistance is as specified, replace instrument cluster as necessary and retest system. See ELECTRONIC INSTRUMENT CLUSTER (EIC) under REMOVAL & INSTALLATION. If resistance is not as specified, repair open or short to ground in Blue/Red wire. Retest system.

TEST C: LOW FUEL INDICATOR LIGHT NEVER/ALWAYS ON

Turn ignition off. Disconnect instrument cluster. See ELECTRONIC INSTRUMENT CLUSTER (EIC) under REMOVAL & INSTALLATION. Measure resistance of Violet/White wire between instrument cluster connector C267C terminal No. 15 and connector C267B terminal No. 8. *See Fig. 6.* Resistance should be less than 5 ohms. Measure resistance between ground and instrument cluster connector C267C terminal No. 15 (Violet/White wire). Resistance should be 10 k/ohms or more. If resistance in both measurements is as specified, replace instrument cluster. See INSTRUMENT CLUSTER under REMOVAL & INSTALLATION. If resistance is not as specified, repair short in Violet/White wire.

TEST D: TEMPERATURE GAUGE INACCURATE

1) Turn ignition off. Disconnect Engine Coolant Temperature (ECT) sensor connector. ECT sensor is located on right rear side of engine. Connect fused jumper between ECT sensor and ground. Turn ignition on. If temperature gauge indicates "H", replace ECT sensor. Retest system. If temperature gauge does not indicate "H", go to next step.

2) Turn ignition off. Disconnect instrument cluster connector C267A. Disconnect temperature sending unit connector. Measure resistance of

Blue/White wire between ECT sensor connector terminal and instrument cluster connector C267A terminal No. 2. Resistance should be less than 5 ohms. *See Fig. 5.* Measure resistance between ground and instrument cluster connector C267A terminal No. 2 (Blue/White wire). Resistance should be more than 10 k/ohms. If resistance is as specified, replace instrument cluster and retest. See ELECTRONIC INSTRUMENT CLUSTER (EIC) under REMOVAL & INSTALLATION. If resistance is not as specified, repair open or short to ground in Blue/White wire. Retest system.

TEST E: SPEEDOMETER/ODOMETER INOPERATIVE

NOTE: Raise and support vehicle for this test. Instrument cluster connector C267A must remain connected.

1) Remove instrument cluster. See ELECTRONIC INSTRUMENT CLUSTER (EIC) under REMOVAL & INSTALLATION. With ignition switch in OFF position, connect a voltmeter between "S" terminal and "G" terminal on speedometer (back of instrument cluster). Place voltmeter in AC volts position. Turn ignition on and start engine. Raise vehicle speed and note speed to voltage readings. Compare noted readings to SPEED-TO-VOLTAGE COMPARISON table. If voltage readings are correct, replace speedometer. If readings are not correct, go to next step.

SPEED-TO-VOLTAGE COMPARISON

Speed – MPH (KM/H)	Approximate Voltage
0 (0)	0
5 (8)	0.5
10 (16)	1.0
15 (24)	1.6
20 (32)	2.0
25 (40)	2.4
30 (48)	2.8
35 (56)	3.1
40 (64)	3.4
45 (72)	3.6
50 (80)	3.9
55 (88)	4.2
60 (96)	4.4

2) With ignition switch in OFF position and instrument cluster still removed, disconnect instrument cluster connector C267A. Disconnect Vehicle Speed Sensor (VSS) connector. VSS is located in center of engine compartment. Measure resistance of Pink/Blue wire between VSS connector and instrument cluster connector C267A terminal No. 3. Measure resistance between ground and instrument cluster connector C267A terminal No. 3 (Pink/Blue wire). *See Fig. 5.* If resistances are less than 5 ohms between instrument cluster and VSS, and more than 10 k/ohms between Pink/Blue wire at instrument cluster and ground, go to next step. If resistances are more than 5 ohms between instrument cluster and VSS, and less than 10 k/ohms between Pink/Blue wire at instrument cluster and ground, repair open or short to ground in Pink/Blue wire.

3) Measure resistance of Black/Red wire between VSS connector and instrument cluster connector C267A terminal No. 5. If resistance is less than 5 ohms, replace VSS. If resistance is 5 ohms or more, repair open Black/Red wire.

TEST F: TACHOMETER INACCURATE

With ignition in OFF position, verify instrument cluster connectors are secure. Remove instrument cluster and leave cluster connected. See ELECTRONIC INSTRUMENT CLUSTER (EIC) under REMOVAL & INSTALLATION. With ignition ON and engine running, backprobe instrument cluster connector C267A, verifying voltage on terminal No. 4 (Green/White wire) at indicated engine speeds. See TACHOMETER SIGNAL VOLTAGES table. If voltages are correct, replace instrument cluster. See ELECTRONIC INSTRUMENT CLUSTER (EIC) under REMOVAL & INSTALLATION. If voltage readings are not correct, refer to appropriate SELF-DIAGNOSTICS article in ENGINE PERFORMANCE in appropriate MITCHELL® manual, for further information on diagnosing possible VSS or PCM concern.

TACHOMETER SIGNAL VOLTAGES

Engine Speed (RPM)	Voltage
1000	1.69
1500	2.64
2000	3.44
2500	4.50
3000	5.22

TEST G: BRAKE WARNING LIGHT NEVER ON

1) Turn ignition switch off. Remove instrument cluster. See ELECTRONIC INSTRUMENT CLUSTER (EIC) in REMOVAL & INSTALLATION. Remove brake warning light bulb and check continuity of bulb. If bulb is okay, go to next step. If bulb is bad, replace bulb and retest system.

2) Disconnect all instrument cluster connectors. Turn ignition on. Using voltmeter, measure voltage between instrument cluster connector C267C terminal No. 16 (Yellow/Violet wire) and terminal No. 20 (Blue wire). *See Fig. 6.* If voltage is more than 10 volts, replace instrument cluster. See ELECTRONIC INSTRUMENT CLUSTER (EIC) under REMOVAL & INSTALLATION. If voltage is 10 volts or less, go to next step.

3) Turn ignition off. Disconnect brake fluid level switch 2-pin connector at brake fluid reservoir. Remove BULB CHECK relay from engine compartment fuse/relay panel. Remove joint connector located behind top right side of instrument cluster. Remove top shorting strip. Measure resistance of Yellow/Purple wire between instrument cluster connector C267C terminal No. 16 and joint connector C2011 terminal No. 10. *See Fig. 7.* Measure resistance of Yellow/Purple wire between BULB CHECK relay connector and instrument cluster connector C267C terminal No. 16. Measure resistance of Yellow/Purple wire between brake fluid level switch connector and instrument cluster connector C267C terminal No. 16. If resistance in any measurement is more than 5 ohms, repair open in appropriate Yellow/Purple wire. Retest system. If resistance in all measurements are less than 5 ohms, go to next step.

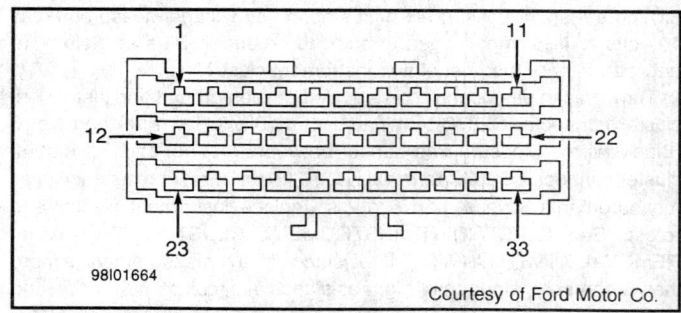

98I01664

Courtesy of Ford Motor Co.

Fig. 7: Identifying Joint Connector C2011 Terminals

4) Ensure ignition is off. Connect jumper wire between battery voltage and BULB CHECK relay terminal No. 1. Measure resistances between BULB CHECK relay terminals No. 3 and No. 5. *See Fig. 8.* Ground BULB CHECK relay terminal No. 2. If resistance between BULB CHECK relay terminals No. 3 and No. 5 is less than 5 ohms with ground connected and more than 10 k/ohms with ground disconnected, go to next step. If resistance between BULB CHECK relay terminals No. 3 and 5 is 5 ohms or more with ground connected or 10 k/ohms or less with ground disconnected, replace BULB CHECK relay.

5) Turn ignition on. Measure voltage between ground and BULB CHECK relay connector terminal No. 1 (Blue wire). If voltage is more than 10 volts, go to next step. If voltage is 10 volts or less, repair open in Blue wire between BULB CHECK relay and interior fuse panel.

6) Turn ignition off. Measure resistance of Blue/Yellow wire between BULB CHECK relay connector terminal No. 2 and joint connector C2011 terminal No. 6. *See Figs. 7 and 8.* If resistance is more than 5 ohms, go to next step. If resistance is less than 5 ohms, repair open Blue/Yellow wire. Retest system.

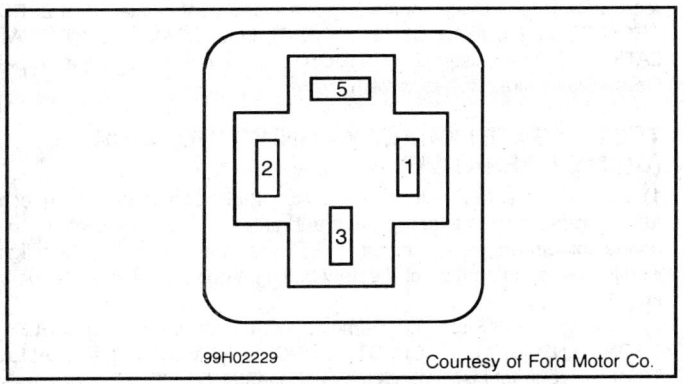

99H02229   Courtesy of Ford Motor Co.

Fig. 8: Identifying BULB CHECK Relay Terminals

7) Measure resistance between ground and brake fluid level switch connector Black wire. If resistance is less than 5 ohms, go to next step. If resistance is 5 ohms or more, repair open Black wire. Retest system.

8) Ensure ignition is off and brake fluid level switch 2-pin connector at brake fluid reservoir is disconnected. Remove screen inside brake fluid reservoir. Depress brake fluid reservoir float with a clean screwdriver. Measure resistance between brake fluid level switch terminals. If resistance is less than 5 ohms with float depressed and more than 10 k/ohms with float released, go to next step. If resistance is 5 ohms or more with float depressed or 10 k/ohms or less with float released, replace brake fluid level switch.

9) Ensure ignition is off. Disconnect parking brake switch connector. Measure resistance of Green/Black wire between parking brake switch connector and joint connector C2011 terminal No. 9. If resistance is less than 5 ohms, go to next step. If resistance is more than 5 ohms, repair open Green/Black wire. Retest system.

10) Ensure parking brake switch is disconnected. Set parking brake. Measure resistance between ground and parking brake switch terminal component side. If resistance is less than 5 ohms, go to next step. If resistance is 5 ohms or more, replace parking brake switch.

11) Measure resistance between joint connector C2011 (top shorting strip) terminals as follows (ensure polarity is correct; shorting strip is a diode shorting strip):

- Terminal No. 6 (+) and No. 5 (-).
- Terminal No. 2 (+) and No. 5 (-).
- Terminal No. 10 (+) and No. 9 (-).
- Terminal No. 10 (+) and No. 8 (-).

If resistance in all measurements is less than 5 ohms, go to TEST H: CHARGE INDICATOR NEVER ON. If resistance in any measurement is 5 ohms or more, replace top diode shorting strip on joint connector C2011. Retest system.

TEST H: CHARGE INDICATOR NEVER ON

1) Turn ignition off. Disconnect 2-pin generator harness connector. Using a jumper wire, ground Yellow/Black wire at generator harness connector. Turn ignition on and start engine. If charge warning indicator glows, repair charging system. See GENERATORS – VILLAGER article in STARTING & CHARGING SYSTEMS. If charge warning indicator does not glow, reconnect generator connector and go to next step.

2) Turn ignition off. Disconnect instrument cluster harness connector C267C. Measure voltage between instrument cluster harness connector C267C terminal No. 8 (Yellow/Blue wire) and No. 7 (Blue wire). See Fig. 6. If voltage is more than 10 volts, replace instrument cluster. See ELECTRONIC INSTRUMENT CLUSTER (EIC) under REMOVAL & INSTALLATION. If voltage is less than 10 volts, go to next step.

3) Turn ignition off. Remove joint connector C2011. Remove Black diode shorting strip from joint connector C2011. Measure resistance of Yellow/Blue wire between C267C terminal No. 8 and joint connector C2011 terminal No. 5. See Figs. 6 and 7. If resistance is less than 5 ohms, go to next step. If resistance is 5 ohms or more, repair Yellow/Black wire.

4) Disconnect 2-pin generator harness connector. Measure resistance of Yellow/Black wire between generator harness connector and diode

junction box connector C2011 terminal No. 5. If resistance is less than 5 ohms, replace Black diode shorting strip. If resistance is 5 ohms or more, repair Yellow/Black wire.

TEST I: OIL PRESSURE INDICATOR INOPERATIVE

1) Turn ignition off. Disconnect oil pressure switch connector. Connect a fused jumper wire between ground and oil pressure switch connector. Turn ignition on. If oil pressure light illuminates, go to next step. If oil pressure light does not illuminate, go to step **3)**.

2) Manually check engine oil pressure. See appropriate article in ENGINES. If oil pressure is within specifications, replace oil pressure switch. If oil pressure is not within specifications, repair engine mechanical problem as necessary. See appropriate article in ENGINES.

3) Turn ignition off. Remove instrument cluster. See ELECTRONIC INSTRUMENT CLUSTER (EIC) in REMOVAL & INSTALLATION. Disconnect instrument cluster connector C267C. Measure resistance of Red wire between oil pressure sensor connector and instrument cluster connector C267C terminal No. 17. See Fig. 6. If resistance is less than 5 ohms, replace instrument cluster. See ELECTRONIC INSTRUMENT CLUSTER (EIC) under REMOVAL & INSTALLATION. Retest system. If resistance is 5 ohms or more, repair Red wire. Retest system.

TEST J: OIL PRESSURE INDICATOR ALWAYS ON

1) Turn ignition off. Disconnect oil pressure switch connector. Turn ignition on. If oil pressure light does not illuminate, go to next step. If oil pressure light illuminates, go to step **3)**.

2) Manually check engine oil pressure. See appropriate article in ENGINES. If oil pressure is within specifications, replace oil pressure switch. If oil pressure is not within specifications, repair engine mechanical problem as necessary. See appropriate article in ENGINES.

3) Turn ignition off. Remove instrument cluster. See ELECTRONIC INSTRUMENT CLUSTER (EIC) in REMOVAL & INSTALLATION. Disconnect instrument cluster connector C267C. Measure resistance between ground and instrument cluster connector C266 terminal No. 17 (Red wire). If resistance is more than 10 k/ohms, replace instrument cluster. See ELECTRONIC INSTRUMENT CLUSTER (EIC) under REMOVAL & INSTALLATION. Retest system. If resistance is 10 k/ohms or less, repair short to ground in Red wire. Retest system.

TEST K: LEFT TURN INDICATOR INOPERATIVE

1) Turn ignition on. Place multifunction switch in left turn position. If outside left turn signal operates, go to next step. If outside left turn signal does not operate properly, see appropriate wiring diagram in EXTERIOR LIGHTS article.

2) Turn ignition off. Remove instrument cluster. See ELECTRONIC INSTRUMENT CLUSTER (EIC) in REMOVAL & INSTALLATION. Disconnect instrument cluster connector C267C. Turn ignition on. Place multifunction switch in left turn position. Measure voltage between ground and instrument cluster connector C267C terminal No. 6 (Red/Green wire). See Fig. 6. If voltage alternates between zero and 10 volts, replace instrument cluster. See ELECTRONIC INSTRUMENT CLUSTER (EIC) under REMOVAL & INSTALLATION. Retest system. If voltage does not alternate between zero and 10 volts, repair open or short in Red/Green wire. Retest system.

TEST L: RIGHT TURN INDICATOR INOPERATIVE

1) Turn ignition on. Place multifunction switch in right turn position. If outside right turn signal operates, go to next step. If outside right turn signal does not operate properly, see appropriate wiring diagram in EXTERIOR LIGHTS article.

2) Turn ignition off. Remove instrument cluster. See ELECTRONIC INSTRUMENT CLUSTER (EIC) in REMOVAL & INSTALLATION. Disconnect instrument cluster connector C267C. Turn ignition on. Place multifunction switch in right turn position. Measure voltage between ground and instrument cluster connector C267C terminal No. 3 (Red/White wire). See Fig. 6. If voltage alternates between zero and 10 volts, replace instrument cluster. See ELECTRONIC INSTRUMENT CLUSTER (EIC) under REMOVAL & INSTALLATION. Retest system. If voltage does not alternate between zero and 10 volts, repair open or short in Red/White wire. Retest system.

TEST M: HIGH BEAM INDICATOR INOPERATIVE

1) Turn ignition on. Turn high beam headlights on. If high beam headlights operate properly, go to next step. If high beam headlights do not operate properly, see appropriate wiring diagram in HEADLIGHT SYSTEMS article.

2) Turn ignition off. Remove instrument cluster. See ELECTRONIC INSTRUMENT CLUSTER (EIC) in REMOVAL & INSTALLATION. Disconnect instrument cluster connectors C267C. Measure voltage between ground and instrument cluster connectors C267C terminal No. 18 (Orange/Blue wire). See Fig. 6. If voltage is 10 volts or less, repair open or short to ground in Orange/Blue wire. Retest system. If voltage is 10 volts or more, go to next step.

3) Measure resistance between ground and instrument cluster connectors C267C terminal No. 19 (Black wire). If resistance is less than 5 ohms, replace instrument cluster. See ELECTRONIC INSTRUMENT CLUSTER (EIC) under REMOVAL & INSTALLATION. If resistance is 5 ohms or more, repair open in Black wire.

TEST N: SERVICE ENGINE SOON LIGHT INOPERATIVE

NOTE: SERVICE ENGINE SOON light may also be referred to as Malfunction Indicator Light (MIL).

1) Turn ignition off. Remove instrument cluster. See ELECTRONIC INSTRUMENT CLUSTER (EIC) under REMOVAL & INSTALLATION. Disconnect instrument cluster connector C267C. See Fig. 6. Turn ignition on. Measure voltage between instrument cluster connector C267C terminal No. 2 (Blue wire) and No. 1 (Violet wire). If voltage is more than 10 volts, replace instrument cluster. See ELECTRONIC INSTRUMENT CLUSTER (EIC) under REMOVAL & INSTALLATION. Retest system. If voltage is 10 volts or less, go to next step.

2) Turn ignition off. Disconnect Powertrain Control Module (PCM) connector. PCM is located behind glove box. See Fig. 9. Measure resistance of Violet wire between PCM connector terminal No. 18 and instrument cluster connector C267C terminal No. 1. If resistance is less than 5 ohms, go to appropriate SELF-DIAGNOSTICS article in ENGINE PERFORMANCE in appropriate MITCHELL® manual. If resistance is 5 ohms or more, repair open Violet wire.

resistance is less than 5 ohms, replace instrument cluster. See ELECTRONIC INSTRUMENT CLUSTER (EIC) under REMOVAL & INSTALLATION. Retest system. If resistance is 5 ohms or more, repair Green/Black wire. Retest system.

TEST P: SAFETY BELT WARNING INOPERATIVE (CHIME OPERATIVE)

1) Disconnect safety belt buckle switch 2-pin connector. Connect a fused jumper wire between ground and safety belt buckle switch 2-pin connector Green wire terminal. Turn ignition on. If safety belt light illuminates, go to next step. If safety belt light does not illuminate, go to step 3).

2) Turn ignition switch off. Remove instrument cluster. See ELECTRONIC INSTRUMENT CLUSTER (EIC) in REMOVAL & INSTALLATION. Disconnect instrument cluster connector C267C. Measure resistance of Green wire between washer fluid level switch and instrument cluster connector C267C terminal No. 9. See Fig. 6. If resistance is less than 5 ohms, replace instrument cluster. See ELECTRONIC INSTRUMENT CLUSTER (EIC) under REMOVAL & INSTALLATION. Retest system. If resistance is 5 ohms or more, repair Green wire. Retest system.

3) Measure resistance between ground and safety belt buckle switch Black wire. If resistance is less than 5 ohms, replace safety belt buckle switch. If resistance is more than 5 ohms, repair open in Black wire.

TEST Q: CRUISE CONTROL INDICATOR NEVER ON

1) Turn ignition on and start engine. Road test vehicle and verify cruise control operation. If cruise control operates properly, go to next step. If cruise control does not operate properly, see CRUISE CONTROL SYSTEMS – VILLAGER article.

2) Turn ignition switch off. Remove instrument cluster. See ELECTRONIC INSTRUMENT CLUSTER (EIC) in REMOVAL & INSTALLATION. Gain access to speed control actuator module. Speed control actuator module is located below left side of instrument panel. Disconnect speed control actuator module connector C247. Disconnect instrument cluster connector C267B. Measure resistance of Red/Yellow wire between instrument cluster connector C267B terminal No. 10 and speed control actuator module connector C247 terminal No. 4. See Figs. 4 and 6. Resistance should be less than 5 ohms. Measure resistance between ground and instrument cluster connector C267B terminal No. 10 (Red/Yellow wire). Resistance should be more than 10 k/ohms. If resistance

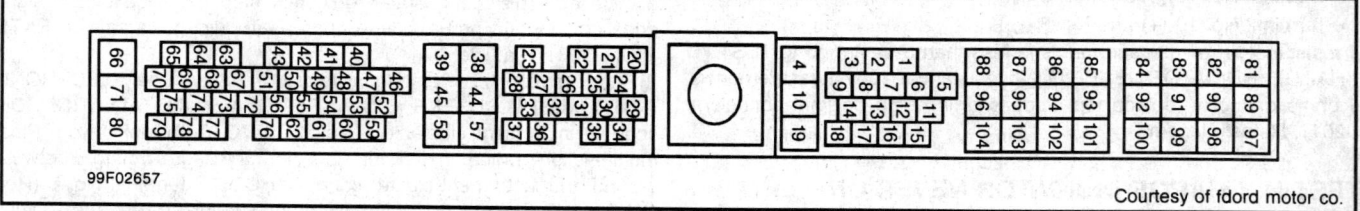

Fig. 9: Identifying Powertrain Control Module (PCM) Connector Terminals

TEST O: LOW WASHER FLUID INDICATOR INOPERATIVE

1) Turn ignition off. Disconnect washer fluid level switch 2-pin connector at washer fluid reservoir. Measure resistance between washer fluid level switch terminals. If resistance is less than 5 ohms with float depressed and more than 10 k/ohms with float released, go to next step. If resistance is 5 ohms or more with float depressed or 10 k/ohms or less with float released, replace washer fluid level switch.

2) Measure resistance between ground and washer fluid level switch Black wire. If resistance is less than 5 ohms, go to next step. If resistance is more than 5 ohms, repair open in Black wire.

3) Turn ignition switch off. Remove instrument cluster. See ELECTRONIC INSTRUMENT CLUSTER (EIC) in REMOVAL & INSTALLATION. Disconnect instrument cluster connector C267A. Measure resistance of Green/Black wire between washer fluid level switch and instrument cluster connector C267C terminal No. 2. See Fig. 6. If

measurements are as specified, replace instrument cluster. See ELECTRONIC INSTRUMENT CLUSTER (EIC) under REMOVAL & INSTALLATION. Retest system. If resistance measurements are not as specified, repair Red/Yellow wire. Retest system.

TEST R: DOOR AJAR INDICATOR INOPERATIVE

1) Remove instrument cluster. See ELECTRONIC INSTRUMENT CLUSTER (EIC) in REMOVAL & INSTALLATION. Disconnect instrument cluster connector C267B. Disconnect Smart Entry Control (SEC) timer/module connector C2032A. SEC timer/module is located in center console on left side. Measure resistance of Brown/White wire between instrument cluster connector C267B terminal No. 11 and SEC timer/module connector C2032A terminal No. 22. See Figs. 4 and 10. If resistance is less than 5 ohms, go to next step. If resistance is 5 ohms or more, repair open Brown/White wire.

2) Turn ignition on. Measure voltage between instrument cluster connector C267B terminal No. 11 (Brown/White wire) and instrument cluster

connector C267C terminal No. 20 (Blue wire). *See Fig. 6.* If voltage is more than 10 volts with each door open, replace instrument cluster. See ELECTRONIC INSTRUMENT CLUSTER (EIC) under REMOVAL & INSTALLATION. Retest system. If voltage is not more than 10 volts with each door open, go to appropriate wiring diagram in ILLUMINATION INTERIOR LIGHTS – VILLAGER article.

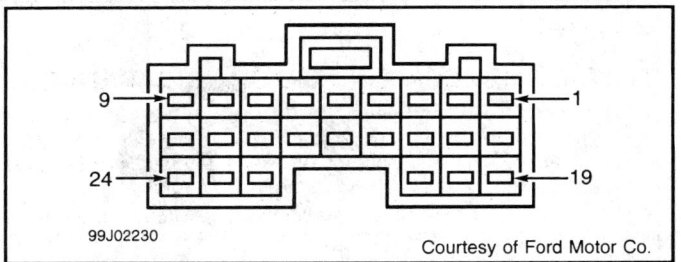

Courtesy of Ford Motor Co.

Fig. 11: Identifying Transmission Control Module (TCM) Connector C277A Terminals

REMOVAL & INSTALLATION

WARNING: Deactivate air bag system before performing any service operation. See AIR BAG RESTRAINT SYSTEMS – VILLAGER article. DO NOT apply electrical power to any component on steering column without first deactivating air bag system. Air bag may deploy.

CAUTION: When battery is disconnected, vehicle computer and memory systems may lose memory data. Driveability problems may exist until computer systems have completed a relearn cycle. See COMPUTER RELEARN PROCEDURES article in GENERAL INFORMATION before disconnecting battery.

ELECTRONIC INSTRUMENT CLUSTER (EIC)

Removal & Installation – Apply parking brake. Disconnect negative battery cable. Remove instrument center finish panel retaining screws. Remove 4 instrument cluster retaining screws. Remove transaxle gear range indicator. *See Fig. 12.* Disconnect 3 electrical connectors. *See Fig. 13.* Remove instrument cluster. To install, reverse removal procedure.

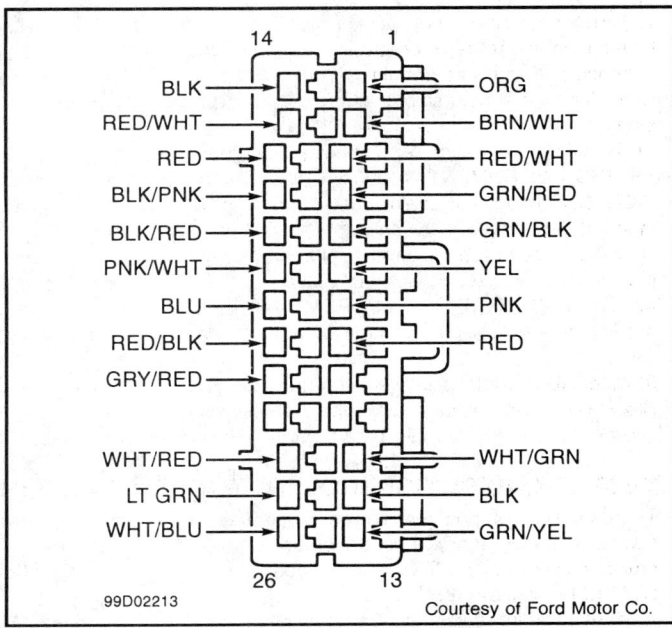

Fig. 10: Identifying Smart Entry Control (SEC) Timer/Module Connector C2032A Terminals

TEST S: O/D OFF LIGHT INOPERATIVE

1) Turn ignition off. Connect New Generation Star (NGS) tester or equivalent scan tool to Data Link Connector (DLC). Turn ignition on. Access Transmission Control Module (TCM) PIDs. Monitor Overdrive Off Switch (ODS). Depress ODS. If O/D OFF light illuminates and ODS signal is present on NGS tester, replace TCM. See appropriate ELECTRONIC CONTROLS article in TRANSMISSIONS in appropriate MITCHELL® TRANSMISSION SERVICE & REPAIR manual. Retest system. If conditions are not as described, go to next step.

2) Turn ignition off. Disconnect TCM. TCM is located in bottom of center console. Remove instrument cluster. See ELECTRONIC INSTRUMENT CLUSTER (EIC) in REMOVAL & INSTALLATION. Disconnect instrument cluster connector C267C. Using an ohmmeter, measure resistance of Blue/Orange wire between instrument cluster connector C267C terminal No. 4 and TCM connector C277A terminal No. 13. *See Figs. 6 and 11.* If resistance is less than 5 ohms, go to next step. If resistance is 5 ohms or more, repair open in Blue/Orange wire. Retest system.

3) Measure resistance between ground and TCM connector C277A terminal No. 22 (Green/Orange wire) while depressing O/D OFF switch to ON position. If resistance is less than 5 ohms, replace instrument cluster. See ELECTRONIC INSTRUMENT CLUSTER (EIC) under REMOVAL & INSTALLATION. Retest system. If resistance is 5 ohms or more, go to next step.

4) Disconnect overdrive off switch connector. Overdrive off switch is located at top of steering column near gear selector. Measure resistance between ground and overdrive off switch connector Black wire. If resistance is less than 5 ohms, go to next step. If resistance is 5 ohms or more, repair open in Black wire. Retest system.

5) Measure resistance of Green/Orange wire between TCM connector C277A terminal No. 22 and overdrive off switch connector. If resistance is less than 5 ohms, replace overdrive off switch. Retest system. If resistance is 5 ohms or more, repair Green/Orange wire. Retest system.

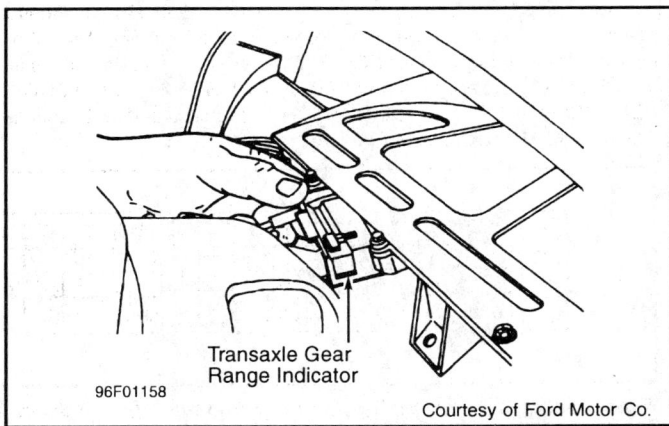

Transaxle Gear Range Indicator

96F01158

Courtesy of Ford Motor Co.

Fig. 12: Removing Transaxle Gear Range Indicator

MESSAGE CENTER SWITCH MODULE

Removal & Installation – Apply parking brake. Disconnect negative battery cable. Remove upper instrument panel finish panel. Remove retaining screws and switch module from rear of instrument panel. To install, reverse removal procedure.

WIPER SWITCH

See WIPER/WASHER SYSTEMS – VILLAGER article.

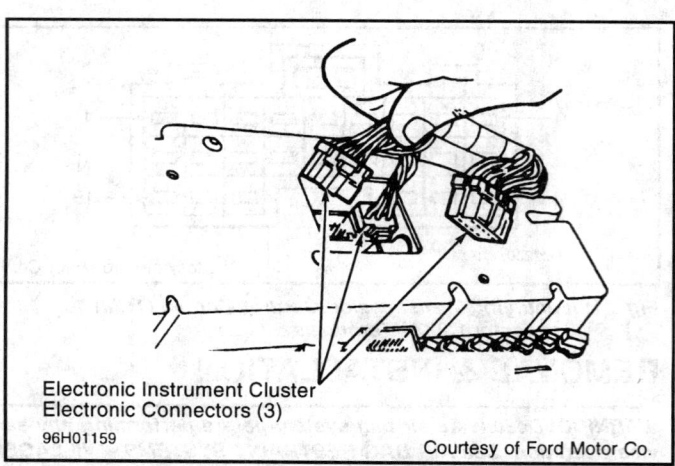

Electronic Instrument Cluster
Electronic Connectors (3)

96H01159

Courtesy of Ford Motor Co.

Fig. 13: Removing Electronic Instrument Cluster Electrical Connectors

WIRING DIAGRAMS

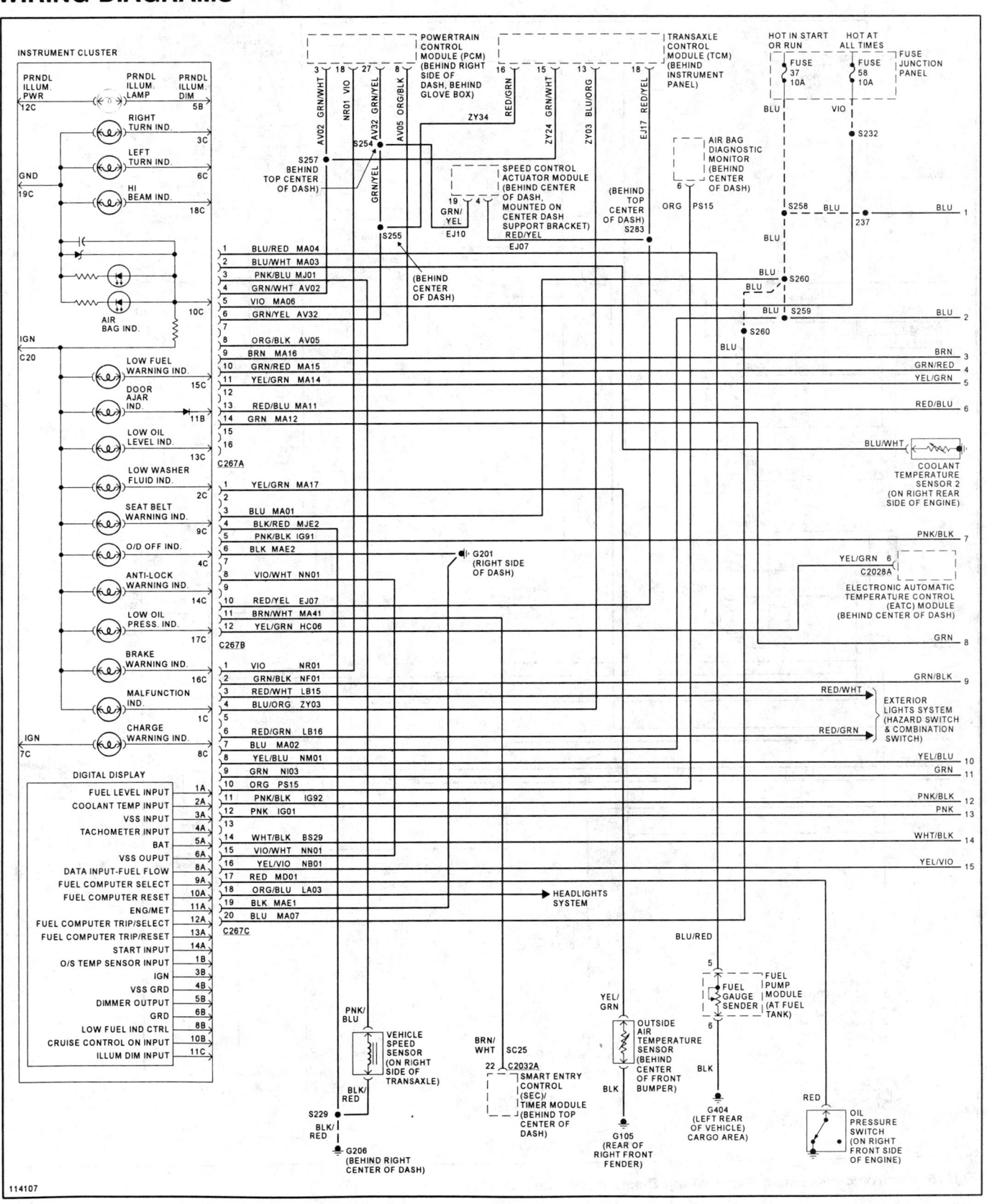

Fig. 14: Electronic Instrument Panel Wiring Diagram (Villager – 1 Of 2)

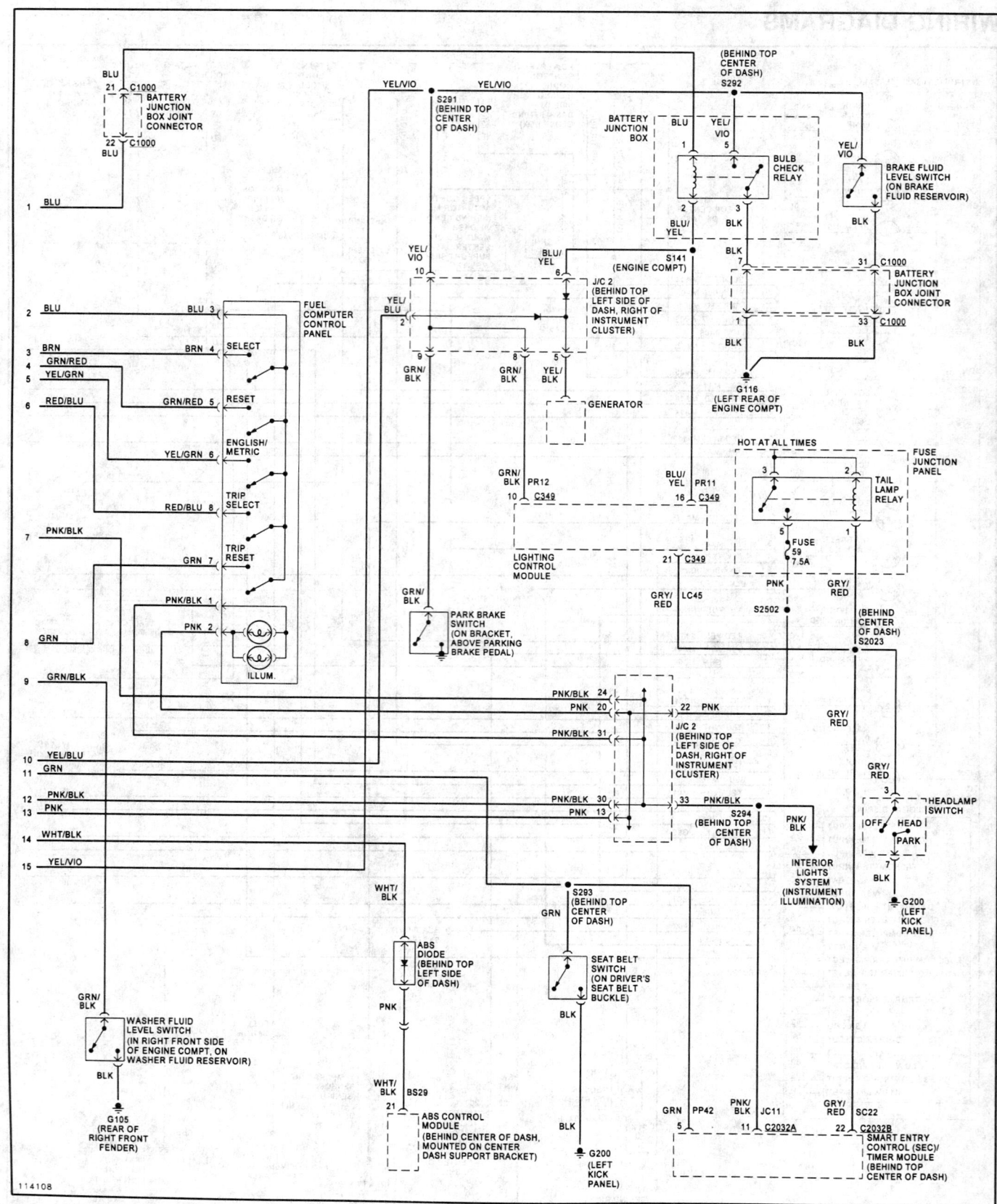

Fig. 15: Electronic Instrument Panel Wiring Diagram (Villager – 2 Of 2)

WIRING DIAGRAMS

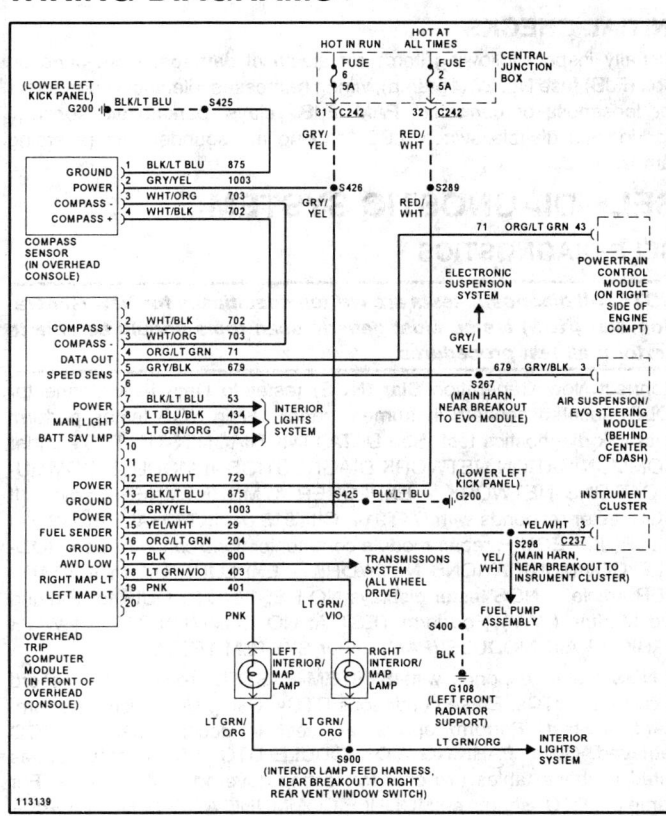

Fig. 1: Overhead Console Wiring Diagram (Expedition & Navigator)

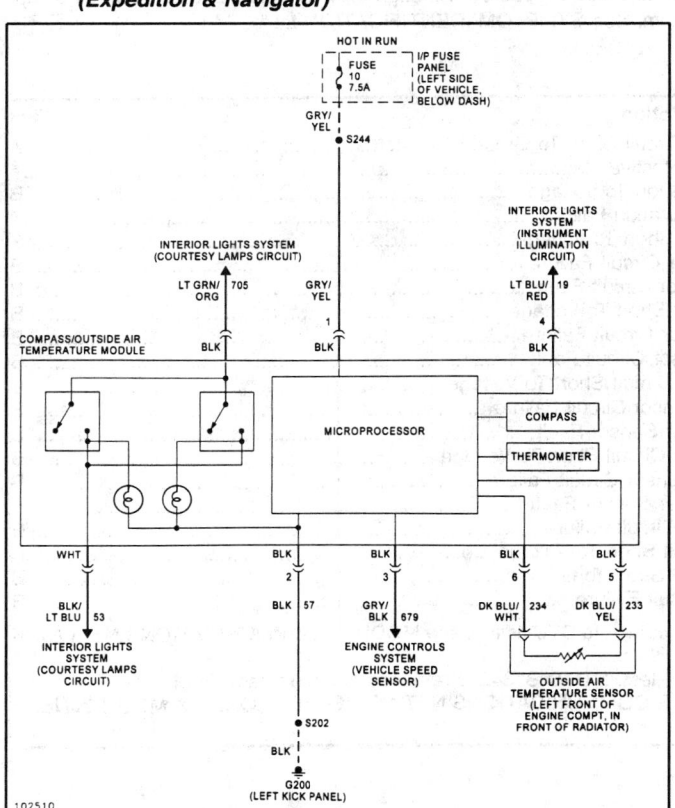

Fig. 2: Overhead Console Wiring Diagram (Explorer & Mountaineer)

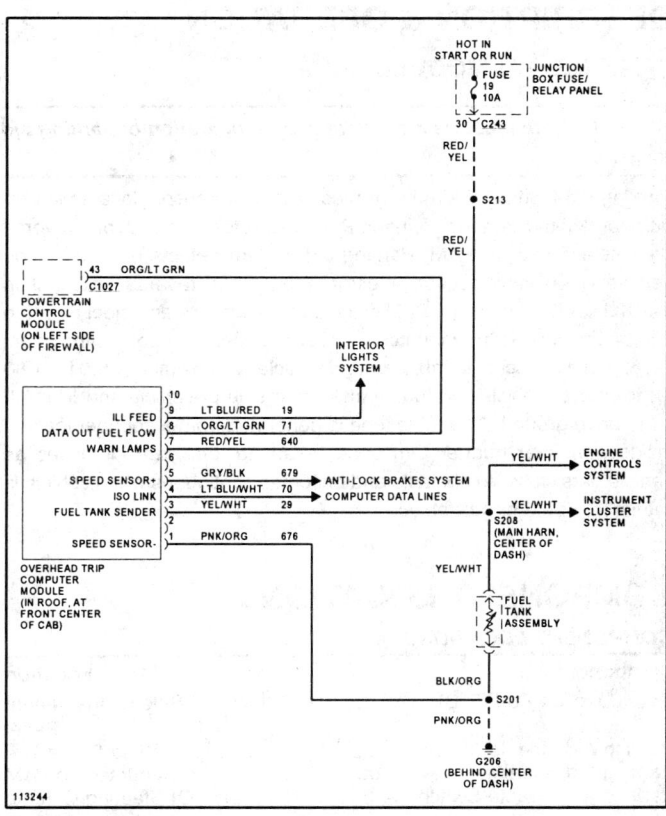

Fig. 3: Overhead Console Wiring Diagram (F250 Super-Duty & F350 Pickup)

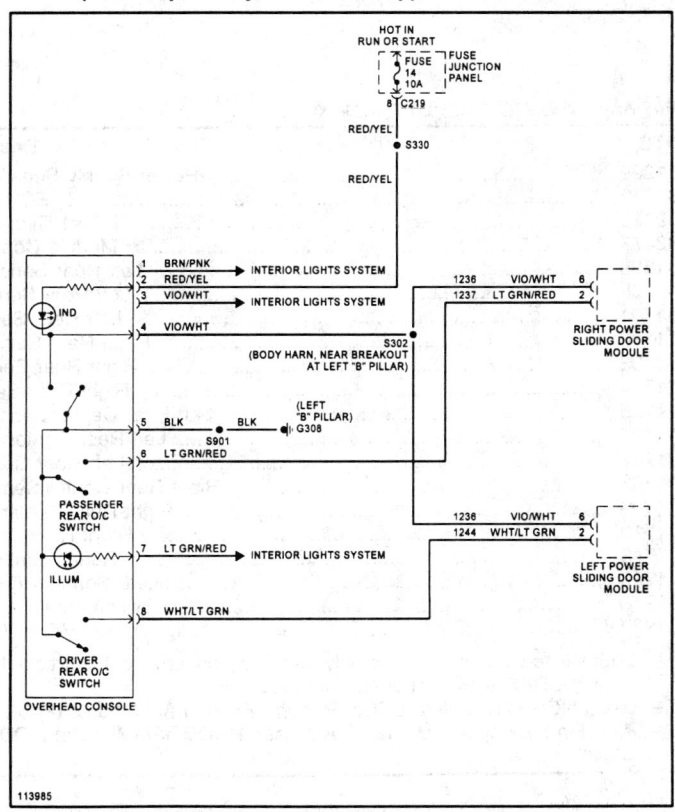

Fig. 4: Overhead Console Wiring Diagram (Windstar)

DESCRIPTION & OPERATION

PARKING AID MODULE (PAM)

NOTE: Liftgate must be closed for proper operation of parking aid system.

Parking Aid Module (PAM) system consists of 4 sensors located in rear bumper, an audible tone sounder, PAM, PAM disable switch and reverse gear select input to PAM. Parking aid system detects objects behind vehicle when vehicle gear selector is placed in reverse and ignition switch is in RUN position. PAM calculates distance to an object by using 4 ultrasonic sensors mounted in rear bumper. Sensors can detect objects in a semicircular area around vehicle, approximately 5.9 ft. (1.80 m) to rear of vehicle 18″ (50.0 cm) to rear side of vehicle and 6″ (16.0 cm) above ground. A variable tone is generated from a sounder located inside right rear quarter trim panel. Warning tone rate increases as vehicle gets closer to obstacle and becomes continuous when vehicle is within 10″ (25.0 cm) of object.

COMPONENT LOCATION

COMPONENT LOCATIONS

Component	Location
Fuse Junction Box (FJB)	Below Left Side Of Instrument Panel
Parking Aid Module (PAM)	Behind Spare Tire
Parking Aid Sounder	Mounted To PAM
Parking Aid Disable Switch	Right Side Of Steering Column On Instrument Panel

TROUBLE SHOOTING

INITIAL CHECKS

Visually inspect following items for electrical damage: Fuse Junction Box (FJB) fuse No. 27 (15-amp), wiring harnesses, electrical connectors for looseness or corrosion, PAM, FJB, relays, parking aid sensors, parking aid disable switch, LED, parking aid sounder and reversing lamps.

SELF-DIAGNOSTIC SYSTEM

SELF-DIAGNOSTICS

NOTE: All diagnostic tests are written specifically for New Generation Star (NGS) tester. Most generic scan tools should be able to perform all test procedures.

Connect New Generation Star (NGS) tester to Data Link Connector (DLC), located beneath instrument panel. Using NGS tester, perform data link diagnostics test. See DATA LINK DIAGNOSTIC TEST under COMMUNICATION NETWORK DIAGNOSTICS in MODULE COMMUNICATIONS NETWORK – EXPLORER & MOUNTAINEER article. If NGS tester responds with CKT914, CKT915 or CKT70=ALL ECUS NO RESP/NOT EQUIP, repair module communications concern. See MODULE COMMUNICATIONS NETWORK – EXPLORER & MOUNTAINEER article. If NGS tester displays NO RESP/NOT EQUIP for Parking Aid Module (PAM) , perform TEST A: NO COMMUNICATION WITH PARKING AID MODULE (PAM) under SYSTEM TESTS.

If NGS tester responds with SYSTEM PASSED, retrieve and record continuous DTCs. Erase continuous DTCs. Using NGS tester, perform PAM self-test. Perform appropriate test in accordance with DTC retrieved. Go to PARKING AID MODULE DTC INDEX table. Codes listed in these tables are only for testing covered in this article. For complete DTC listing, see MODULE COMMUNICATIONS NETWORK – EXPLORER & MOUNTAINEER article.

If no DTCs are retrieved though PAM self-diagnostics, repair by symptom. See SYMPTOM IDENTIFICATION table.

PARKING AID MODULE DTC INDEX

DTC [1]	Description	Test
B1299	Power Supply Sensor Circuit Short To Ground	A
B1342	ECU Defective	[2]
B2373	LED #1 Circuit Short To Voltage	B
B2477	Module Configuration Failure	[3]
C1699	Left Rear Sensor Short To Voltage	B
C1700	Left Rear Sensor Circuit Failure	B
C1701	Left Rear Sensor Circuit Fault	B
C1702	Right Rear Sensor Short To Voltage	B
C1703	Right Rear Sensor Circuit Failure	B
C1704	Right Rear Sensor Circuit Fault	B
C1705	Left Rear Center Sensor Circuit Short To Voltage	B
C1706	Left Rear Center Sensor Circuit Failure	B
C1707	Left Rear Center Sensor Fault	B
C1708	Right Rear Center Sensor Circuit Short To Voltage	B
C1709	Right Rear Center Sensor Circuit Failure	B
C1710	Right Rear Center Sensor Fault	B
C1742	Rear Sounder Circuit Failure	B
C1743	Rear Sounder Circuit Short To Voltage	B
C1748	Switch Input Circuit Short To Ground	B
C1920	LED #1 Circuit Failure	B

[1] – Codes listed in this table are only for testing covered in this article. For complete DTC listing, see MODULE COMMUNICATIONS NETWORK – EXPLORER & MOUNTAINEER article.

[2] – Using NGS tester, clear DTCs. Perform Parking Aid Module (PAM) self-test. If DTC B1342 is retrieved again, replace PAM.

[3] – Program Parking Aid Module (PAM), see PROGRAMMING in MODULE COMMUNICATIONS NETWORK – EXPLORER & MOUNTAINEER article.

SYMPTOM IDENTIFICATION

Condition	Test
No Communication With Parking Aid Module (PAM)	A
Parking Aid Is Inoperative	B
Continuous Or Intermittent Tone When No Obstacles Or Fault Codes Are Present	1

1 – Ensure rear bumper and sensors are clean, parking aid sensors and sensor holders are locked correctly into position and perform azimuth and elevation checks. See AZIMUTH SYSTEM CHECK or ELEVATION SYSTEM CHECK under VERIFICATION TESTS.

SYSTEM TESTS

NOTE: For module, switch or sensor replacement procedure, see REMOVAL & INSTALLATION. For help with wiring diagnosis or repairs, see WIRING DIAGRAMS. After any repairs are made to vehicle always perform data link diagnostic test. See DATA LINK DIAGNOSTIC TEST in MODULE COMMUNICATIONS NETWORK – EXPLORER & MOUNTAINEER article.

CAUTION: Be careful when probing Fuse Junction Box (FJB), power distribution box or any connectors. Damage will result to connector receptacle if probe or terminal being used is too large. Electronic modules are sensitive to static electrical charges. If exposed to these charges, damage may result.

TEST A: NO COMMUNICATION WITH PARKING AID MODULE (PAM)

1) Using New Generation Star (NGS) tester, perform Parking Aid Module (PAM) self-test. If no DTCs are retrieved, go to next step. If DTC B1299 is retrieved, go to step 4).

2) Turn ignition switch to OFF position. Disconnect PAM 26-pin connector C440. Turn ignition switch to RUN position. Measure voltage between PAM harness connector C440 terminal No. 1 (Violet/Orange wire) and ground. If voltage is more than 10 volts, go to next step. If voltage is 10 volts or less, repair open in Violet/Orange wire between PAM and Fuse Junction Box (FJB).

3) Turn ignition switch to OFF position. Measure resistance between PAM harness connector C440 terminal No. 3 (Black wire) and ground. If resistance is less than 5 ohms, see MODULE COMMUNICATIONS NETWORK – EXPLORER & MOUNTAINEER article. If resistance is 5 ohms or more, repair open in Black wire between PAM and ground.

4) Turn ignition switch to OFF position. Disconnect PAM 26-pin connector C440. Measure resistance between PAM harness connector C440 terminal No. 1 (Violet/Orange wire) and ground. If resistance is more than 10 k/ohms, go to step 2). If resistance is 10 k/ohms or less, repair short to ground in Violet/Orange wire.

TEST B: PARKING AID INOPERATIVE

1) Turn ignition switch to OFF position. Using New Generation Star (NGS) tester, perform Parking Aid Module (PAM) self-test. If no DTCs are retrieved, go to step 24). Use following table for code to step procedures:

PARKING AID DTC TEST STEPS

DTC	Step
C1700, C1701, C1703, C1704, C1706, C1707, C1709 & C1710	2)
CC1699, 1702, C1705 & C1708	8)
C1742	11)
C1743	17)
C1748	27)
C1920	19)
B2373	23)

2) Disconnect appropriate parking aid sensor and PAM 26-pin connector C440. Measure resistance between PAM harness connector C440 terminal No. 16 (Dark Green/Yellow wire) and ground. If resistance is more than 10 k/ohms, go to next step. If resistance is 10 k/ohms or less, repair short to ground in Dark Green/Yellow wire.

3) Measure resistance between PAM harness connector C440 terminal No. 15 (Brown/Pink wire) and ground. If resistance is more than 10 k/ohms, go to next step. If resistance is 10 k/ohms or less, repair short to ground in Brown/Pink wire.

4) Using PAM TERMINAL IDENTIFICATION table to measure resistances between PAM harness connector C440 and ground. If resistances are more than 10 k/ohms on all circuits, go to next step. If resistance on any circuit is 10 k/ohms or less, repair short to ground in affected circuit.

PAM TERMINAL IDENTIFICATION

PAM Terminal	PAM Sensor	Sensor Terminal No. 2 Wire Color
10	Left Inner	DK GRN/WHT
11	Left Outer	WHT/LT GRN
23	Right Inner	WHT/LT BLU
24	Right Outer	DK BLU/YEL

5) Measure resistance between PAM harness connector C440 terminal No. 16 (Dark Green/Yellow wire) and appropriate parking aid sensor harness connector terminal No. 1 (Dark Green/Yellow wire). See Fig. 1. If resistance is less than 5 ohms, go to next step. If resistance is 5 ohms or more, repair open in Dark Green/Yellow wire.

6) Measure resistance between PAM harness connector C440 terminal No. 15 (Brown/Pink wire) and appropriate parking aid sensor harness connector terminal No. 3 (Brown/Pink wire). See Fig. 1. If resistance is less than 5 ohms, go to next step. If resistance is 5 ohms or more, repair open in Brown/Pink wire.

7) Using PAM TERMINAL IDENTIFICATION table to measure resistances between appropriate PAM harness connector C440 terminal and appropriate parking aid sensor harness connector terminal No. 2. See Fig. 1. If resistances are less than 5 ohms on all circuits and all 4 sensors set DTCs, replace PAM. If resistances are less than 5 ohms on all circuits and all 4 sensors did not set DTCs, replace appropriate sensor. If resistance on any circuit is 5 ohms or more, repair open in affected circuit.

8) Disconnect appropriate parking aid sensor 3-pin connector and PAM 26-pin connector C440. Turn ignition switch to RUN position. Measure voltage between PAM harness connector C440 terminal No. 16 (Dark Green/Yellow wire) and ground. If voltage is not present, go to next step. If voltage is present, repair short to voltage in Dark Green/Yellow wire.

9) Measure voltage between PAM harness connector C440 terminal No. 15 (Brown/Pink wire) and ground. If voltage is not present, go to next step. If voltage is present, repair short to voltage in Brown/Pink wire.

10) Using PAM TERMINAL IDENTIFICATION table to measure voltages between appropriate PAM harness connector C440 terminals and ground. If voltage is present on any circuits, repair short to voltage in affected circuit. If voltage is not present on any circuit and all 4 parking aid sensors set DTCs, replace PAM. If voltage is not present on any circuit and less than 4 parking aid sensor DTCs are retrieved, replace appropriate parking aid sensor(s).

11) Disconnect PAM 26-pin connector C440. Measure resistance between PAM harness connector C440 terminals No. 14 (Black/Pink wire) and No. 17 (Dark Green wire). If resistance is more than 60 ohms, go to next step. If resistance is 60 ohms or less, go to step 14).

12) Disconnect parking aid sounder 2-pin connector C441. Measure resistance between PAM harness connector C440 terminal No. 14 (Black/Pink wire) and parking aid sounder harness connector C441 terminal No. 1 (Black/Pink wire). If resistance is less than 5 ohms, go to next step. If resistance is 5 ohms or more, repair open in Black/Pink wire.

13) Measure resistance between PAM harness connector C440 terminal No. 17 (Dark Green wire) and parking aid sounder harness connector C441 terminal No. 2 (Dark Green wire). If resistance is less than 5 ohms, replace parking aid sounder. If resistance is 5 ohms or more, repair open in Dark Green wire.

14) Disconnect parking aid sounder 2-pin connector C441. Measure resistance between PAM harness connector C440 terminal No. 14

(Black/Pink wire) and ground. If resistance is more than 10 k/ohms, go to next step. If resistance is 10 k/ohms or less, repair short to ground in Black/Pink wire.

15) Measure resistance between PAM harness connector C440 terminal No. 17 (Dark Green wire) and ground. If resistance is more than 10 k/ohms, go to next step. If resistance is 10 k/ohms or less, repair short to ground in Dark Green wire.

16) Measure resistance between parking aid sounder component connector C441 terminal No. 1 and ground. If resistance is more than 10 k/ohms, replace PAM. If resistance is 10 k/ohms or less, replace parking aid sounder.

17) Disconnect PAM 26-pin connector C440. Turn ignition switch to RUN position. Measure voltage between PAM harness connector C440 terminal No. 14 (Black/Pink wire) and ground. If voltage is more than 10 volts, go to next step. If voltage is 10 volts or less, replace PAM.

18) Turn ignition switch to OFF position. Disconnect parking aid sounder. Turn ignition switch to RUN position. Measure voltage between PAM harness connector C440 terminal No. 14 (Black/Pink wire) and ground. If voltage is more than 10 volts, repair short to voltage in Black/Pink wire. If voltage is 10 volts or less, repair short to voltage in Dark Green wire.

19) Disconnect PAM 26-pin connector C440. Measure resistance between PAM harness connector C440 terminal No. 19 (Violet/Orange wire) and ground. If resistance is more than 10 k/ohms, go to next step. If resistance is 10 k/ohms or less, repair short to ground in Violet/Orange wire.

20) Disconnect parking aid disable switch 6-pin connector C2015. Measure resistance between PAM harness connector C440 terminal No. 19 (Violet/Orange wire) and parking aid disable switch harness connector C2015 terminal No. 2 (Violet/Orange wire). *See Fig. 2.* If resistance is less than 5 ohms, go to next step. If resistance is 5 ohms or more, repair open in Violet/Orange wire.

21) Measure resistance between parking aid disable switch harness connector C2015 terminal No. 5 (Black wire) and ground. *See Fig. 2.* If resistance is less than 5 ohms, go to next step. If resistance is 5 ohms or more, repair open in Black wire.

22) Check parking aid disabled indicator diode. If parking aid disabled indicator is okay, replace PAM. If parking aid disabled indicator is not okay, replace parking aid disable switch.

23) Disconnect PAM 26-pin connector C440. Turn ignition switch to RUN position. If parking aid disabled indicator illuminates, repair short to voltage in Violet/Orange wire between PAM and parking aid disable switch. If parking aid disabled indicator does not illuminate, replace PAM.

NOTE: *If vehicle has been in an accident, parking aid sensors may not be aligned properly.*

---

24) Inspect bumper for proper alignment. Also, inspect parking aid sensors and holders for proper alignment. See AZIMUTH SYSTEM CHECK or ELEVATION SYSTEM CHECK under VERIFICATION TESTS. If bumper and parking aid sensors are properly aligned, go to next step. If bumper or parking aid sensors are not properly aligned, realign sensors or replace bumper. If vehicle has been in an accident, further body work may be necessary to bring parking aid sensors into correct alignment.

25) Turn ignition switch to RUN position. Set parking brake, and place transmission shift lever in Reverse. If right hand reversing lamp illuminates, go to next step. If right hand reversing lamp does not illuminate, see AUTOLAMPS SYSTEMS – EXPLORER & MOUNTAINEER article for testing procedures.

26) Turn ignition switch to OFF position. Disconnect PAM 26-pin connector C440. Turn ignition switch to RUN position. Measure voltage between PAM harness connector C440 terminal No. 9 (Black/Pink wire) and ground. If voltage is more than 10 volts, go to next step. If voltage is 10 volts or less, repair open in Black/Pink wire.

27) Measure resistance between PAM harness connector C440 terminal No. 7 (Dark Green/Violet wire) and ground. If resistance is 10 k/ohms or less, go to next step. If resistance is more than 10 k/ohms, go to step **29)**.

28) Turn ignition switch to OFF position. Disconnect parking aid disable switch 6-pin connector C2015. Measure resistance between PAM harness connector C440 terminal No. 7 (Dark Green/Violet wire) and ground. If resistance is more than 10 k/ohms, replace parking aid disable switch. If resistance is 10 k/ohms or less, repair short to ground in Dark Green/Violet wire.

29) While depressing parking aid disable switch, measure resistance between PAM harness connector C440 terminal No. 7 (Dark Green/Violet wire) and ground. If resistance is less than 5 ohms, replace PAM. If resistance is 5 ohms or more, go to next step.

30) Disconnect parking aid disable switch 6-pin connector C2015. Measure resistance between PAM harness connector C440 terminal No. 4 (Black wire) and ground. If resistance is less than 5 ohms, go to next step. If resistance is 5 ohms or more, repair open in Black wire.

31) Using PARKING AID DISABLE SWITCH RESISTANCE table, measure resistance between parking aid disable switch component terminals No. 4 and No. 6. *See Fig. 2.* If resistance readings are not correct for switch position, replace parking aid disable switch. If resistance readings are correct for switch position, replace PAM.

PARKING AID DISABLE SWITCH RESISTANCE

Between Terminals	Reading With Switch Pressed	Reading With Switch Released
4 & 6	Less Than 35 Ohms	More Than 10 K/Ohms

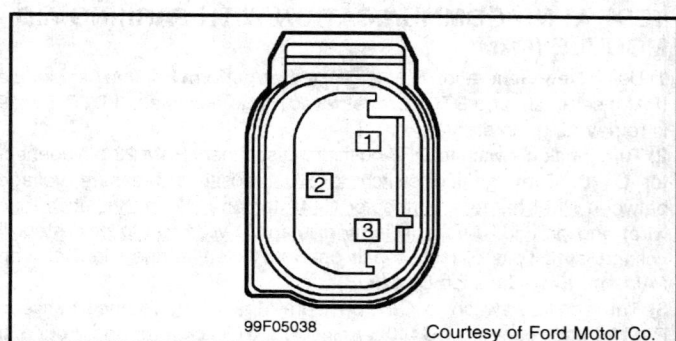

99F05038   Courtesy of Ford Motor Co.

Fig. 1: Identifying Parking Aid Sensor 3-Pin Connector Terminals

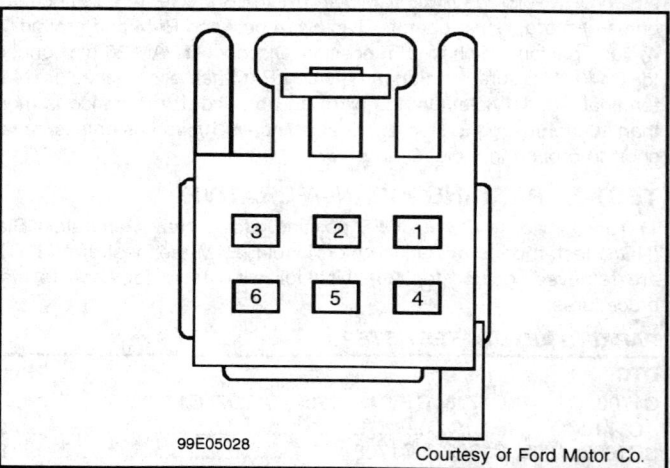

99E05028   Courtesy of Ford Motor Co.

Fig. 2: Identifying Parking Aid Disable Switch 6-Pin Connector Terminals

VERIFICATION TESTS

AZIMUTH SYSTEM CHECK

NOTE: Object used in this system check can be fabricated from 3″ diameter pipe 39″ (99.1 cm) in length. Azimuth system check should be performed with vehicle on a level surface. Parking Aid Module (PAM) will default to ON when ignition key is turned from OFF to RUN position.

Turn ignition switch to RUN position with engine off. Set parking brake and place shift lever in Reverse. Ensure PAM detects objects within appropriate distances. See MINIMUM DETECTABLE OBJECT DISTANCES table. For 5 specified object locations, *see Fig. 3.*

MINIMUM DETECTABLE OBJECT DISTANCES

Detectable Object Location	Distances In. (cm)
P1 & P5	35 (90)
P2 & P4	63 (160)
P3	63 (160)

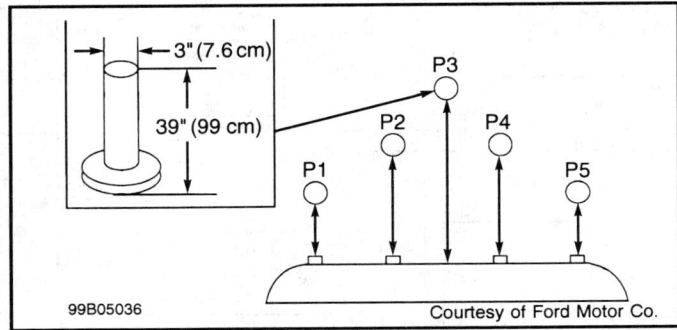

Fig. 3: Minimum Detectable Object Distances – Azimuth System Check

ELEVATION SYSTEM CHECK

1) Parking aid system must be inspected to ensure system does not receive signals from ground reflections. Perform system check with vehicle on 10 x 15 foot smooth concrete surface. Area should be free of obstacles and noise from fans and pneumatic equipment.

2) Turn ignition switch to RUN position, with engine off. Set parking brake and place shift lever in Reverse. No audible alerts should be heard. If audible alerts are heard, ensure bumper is properly installed and is not tilting downward so sensors are pointing at ground. If no audible alerts are heard, system is operating correctly.

REMOVAL & INSTALLATION

PARKING AID MODULE (PAM) & SOUNDER

Removal & Installation – Remove jack storage panel. Disconnect electrical connector. Remove 2 module retaining nuts and remove Parking Aid Module (PAM). To install, reverse removal procedure.

PARKING AID SENSOR

Removal & Installation – Remove rear bumper assembly. Disconnect electrical connector. Disconnect Parking Aid Module (PAM) sensor electrical connector, release locking tabs on sides of sensor and remove PAM sensor. To install, reverse removal procedure.

WIRING DIAGRAMS

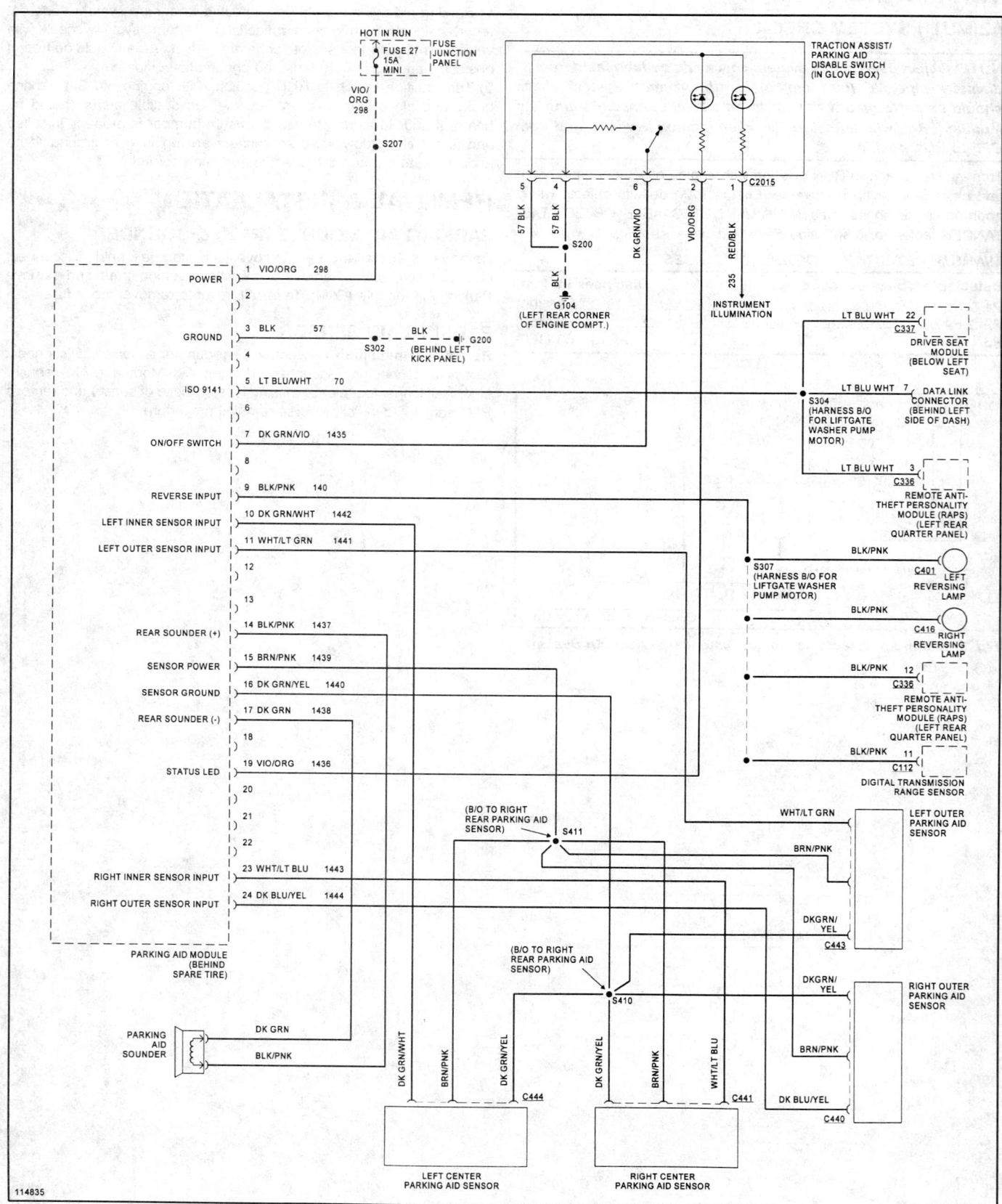

Fig. 4: Parking Aid Module Wiring Diagram (Explorer & Mountaineer)

DESCRIPTION & OPERATION

PARKING AID MODULE (PAM)

NOTE: Liftgate must be closed for proper operation of parking aid system.

Parking aid system consists of 4 sensors located in rear bumper, an audible tone sounder, Parking Aid Module (PAM), parking aid disable/traction assist switch and reverse gear select input to PAM. Parking aid system detects objects behind vehicle when vehicle gear selector is placed in Reverse and ignition switch is in RUN position. PAM calculates distance to an object by using 4 ultrasonic sensors mounted in rear bumper. Sensors can detect objects in a semicircular area around vehicle, approximately 5.9 ft. (1.80 m) to rear of vehicle, 18″ (50.0 cm) to rear side of vehicle and 6″ (16.0 cm) above ground. A variable tone is generated from a sounder located inside right rear quarter trim panel. Warning tone rate increases as vehicle gets closer to obstacle and becomes continuous when vehicle is within 10″ (25.0 cm) of object.

SWITCHED SYSTEM POWER (SSP) RELAYS

SSP is invoked by Front Electronic Module (FEM) and Rear Electronic Module (REM), and removes power function from relays that provides power to exterior lights, interior lights and power door locks. This is only accomplished when FEM and REM are in sleep mode. FEM and REM are in sleep mode when ignition switch is in OFF position and no wake up (inputs) occur for 30 minutes. Modules will not sleep if parking or hazard lights are active. SSP1, SSP2, SSP3 and SSP4 relays are controlled by SSP function. SSP relays will be energized when FEM or REM are not in sleep mode, and each relay will supply power to multiple features/functions.

COMPONENT LOCATIONS

COMPONENT LOCATIONS

Component	Location
Fuse Junction Box (FJB)	Behind Left Side Of Instrument Panel
Left Power Sliding Door Module (LPSDM)	Behind Left Rear Quarter Panel
Parking Aid Module (PAM)	Behind Left Rear Quarter Panel
Parking Aid Sounder	Behind Left Rear Quarter Panel
Parking Aid Disable/Traction Assist Switch	Center Of Instrument Panel
Rear Electronic Module (REM)	Behind Right Rear Quarter Panel
Restraint Control Module (RCM)	Lower Left Side Of Instrument Panel
Right Power Sliding Door Module (RPSDM)	Behind Right Rear Quarter Panel

TROUBLE SHOOTING

INITIAL CHECKS

Visually inspect following items for electrical damage: Fuse Junction Box (FJB) fuses No. 10 (10-amp) and No. 16 (10-amp), wiring harnesses, electrical connectors for looseness or corrosion, Parking Aid Module (PAM), FJB, Switched System Power (SSP) relays, parking aid sensors, parking aid disable/traction assist switch, LED, Rear Electronic Module (REM), parking aid sounder and reverse lights.

SELF-DIAGNOSTIC SYSTEM

SELF-DIAGNOSTICS

NOTE: All diagnostic tests are written specifically for New Generation Star (NGS) tester. Most generic scan tools should be able to perform all test procedures.

Connect New Generation Star (NGS) tester to Data Link Connector (DLC), located beneath instrument panel. Using NGS tester, perform data link diagnostics test. See DATA LINK DIAGNOSTIC TEST under COMMUNICATION NETWORK DIAGNOSTICS in MODULE COMMUNICATIONS NETWORK – WINDSTAR article. If NGS tester responds with CKT914, CKT915 or CKT70=ALL ECUS NO RESP/NOT EQUIP, repair module communications concern. See MODULE COMMUNICATIONS NETWORK – WINDSTAR article. If NGS tester displays NO RESP/NOT EQUIP for Parking Aid Module (PAM) , perform TEST A: NO COMMUNICATION WITH PARKING AID MODULE (PAM) under SYSTEM TESTS. If NGS tester displays NO RESP/NOT EQUIP for Rear Electronic Module (REM), perform TEST B: NO COMMUNICATION WITH REAR ELECTRONIC MODULE (REM) under SYSTEM TESTS.

If NGS tester responds with SYSTEM PASSED, retrieve and record continuous DTCs. Erase continuous DTCs. Using NGS tester, perform PAM and REM self-test. Perform appropriate test in accordance with DTC retrieved. See PARKING AID MODULE DTC INDEX and/or REAR ELECTRONIC MODULE DTC INDEX table. Codes listed in these tables are only for testing covered in this article. For complete DTC listing, see MODULE COMMUNICATIONS NETWORK – WINDSTAR article. If no DTCs are retrieved though PAM or REM self-diagnostics, repair by symptom. See SYMPTOM CHART table.

PARKING AID MODULE DTC INDEX

DTC [1]	Description	Test
B1299	Power Supply Sensor Circuit Short To Ground	A [2]
B1342	ECU Defective	C
B2373	LED #1 Circuit Short To Voltage	C [3]
B2477	Module Configuration Failure	C
C1699	Left Rear Sensor Short To Voltage	C
C1700	Left Rear Sensor Circuit Failure	C
C1701	Left Rear Sensor Circuit Fault	C
C1702	Right Rear Sensor Short To Voltage	C
C1703	Right Rear Sensor Circuit Failure	C
C1704	Right Rear Sensor Circuit Fault	C
C1705	Left Rear Center Sensor Circuit Short To Voltage	C
C1706	Left Rear Center Sensor Circuit Failure	C
C1707	Left Rear Center Sensor Fault	C
C1708	Right Rear Center Sensor Circuit Short To Voltage	C
C1709	Right Rear Center Sensor Circuit Failure	C
C1710	Right Rear Center Sensor Fault	C
C1742	Rear Sounder Circuit Failure	C

PARKING AID MODULE DTC INDEX (Cont.)

DTC [1]	Description	Test
C1743	Rear Sounder Circuit Short To Voltage	C
C1748	Switch Input Circuit Short To Ground	C
C1920	LED #1 Circuit Failure	C

[1] – Codes listed in this table are only for testing covered in this article. For complete DTC listing, see MODULE COMMUNICATIONS NETWORK – WINDSTAR article.

[2] – Using NGS tester, clear DTCs. Perform Parking Aid Module (PAM) self-test. If DTC B1342 is retrieved again, replace PAM.

[3] – Program Parking Aid Module (PAM), see PROGRAMMING in MODULE COMMUNICATIONS NETWORK – WINDSTAR article.

REAR ELECTRONIC MODULE DTC INDEX

DTC [1]	Description	Test
B1342	ECU Defective	2

[1] – Codes listed in this table are only for testing covered in this article. For complete DTC listing, see MODULE COMMUNICATIONS NETWORK – WINDSTAR article.

[2] – Clear DTCs. Perform Rear Electronic Module (REM) self-test. If DTC B1342 is retrieved again, replace REM.

SYMPTOM CHART

Condition	Test
No Communication With Parking Aid Module (PAM)	A
No Communication With Rear Electronics Module (REM)	B
Parking Aid System Inoperative	C
Continuous Or Intermittent Tone When No Obstacles Or Fault Codes Are Present	1

[1] – Ensure rear bumper and sensors are clean, parking aid sensors and sensor holders are locked correctly into position and perform azimuth and elevation checks. See AZIMUTH SYSTEM CHECK and ELEVATION SYSTEM CHECK under VERIFICATION TESTS.

SYSTEM TESTS

NOTE: For module, switch or sensor replacement procedure, see REMOVAL & INSTALLATION. For help with wiring diagnosis or repairs, see WIRING DIAGRAMS. After any repairs are made to vehicle always perform data link diagnostic test. See DATA LINK DIAGNOSTIC TEST under COMMUNICATION NETWORK DIAGNOSTICS in MODULE COMMUNICATIONS NETWORK – WINDSTAR article.

CAUTION: Be careful when probing Fuse Junction Box (FJB), power distribution box or any connectors. Damage will result to connector receptacle if probe or terminal being used is too large. Electronic modules are sensitive to static electrical charges. If exposed to these charges, damage may result.

TEST A: NO COMMUNICATION WITH PARKING AID MODULE (PAM)

1) Using New Generation Star (NGS) tester, perform Parking Aid Module (PAM) self-test. If no DTCs are retrieved, go to next step. If DTC B1299 is retrieved, go to step **4)**.

2) Turn ignition switch to OFF position. Disconnect PAM 26-pin harness connector C445. Turn ignition switch to RUN position. Measure voltage between PAM harness connector C445 terminal No. 1 (Red/Black wire) and ground. If voltage is more than 10 volts, go to next step. If voltage is 10 volts or less, repair open in Red/Black wire between PAM and Fuse Junction Box (FJB).

3) Turn ignition switch to OFF position. Measure resistance between PAM harness connector C445 terminal No. 3 (Black wire) and ground. If resistance is less than 5 ohms, repair module communication concern. See MODULE COMMUNICATIONS NETWORK – WINDSTAR article. If resistance is 5 ohms or more, repair open in Black wire between PAM and ground.

4) Turn ignition switch to OFF position. Disconnect PAM 26-pin harness connector C445. Measure resistance between PAM harness connector C445 terminal No. 1 (Red/Black wire) and ground. If resistance is more than 10 k/ohms, go to step **2)**. If resistance is 10 k/ohms or less, repair short to ground in Red/Black wire.

TEST B: NO COMMUNICATION WITH REAR ELECTRONIC MODULE (REM)

NOTE: Turn ignition switch from OFF to RUN position to enable system power feature.

1) Turn ignition switch to OFF position. Remove fuse No. 16 (10-amp) from Fuse Junction Box (FJB). Turn ignition switch to RUN position. Measure voltage between FJB fuse No. 16 input terminal and ground. If voltage is more than 10 volts, install fuse No. 16 and go to next step. If voltage is 10 volts or less, repair open in Dark Blue wire between Battery Junction Box (BJB) and FJB.

2) Turn ignition switch to OFF position. Disconnect REM 20-pin harness connector C343. Measure voltage between REM harness connector C343 terminal No. 3 (White/Yellow wire) and ground. See Fig. 1. If voltage is more than 10 volts, go to next step. If voltage is 10 volts or less, repair White/Yellow wire.

3) Turn ignition switch to OFF position. Disconnect REM 22-pin harness connectors C341 and 26-pin harness connector C342. Measure resistances between REM harness connector C341 terminal No. 12 (Black wire), REM harness connector C342 terminals No. 11, 12, 25 and 26 (Black wires) and ground. See Figs. 2 and 3. If all resistances are less than 5 ohms, repair module communication concern. See MODULE COMMUNICATIONS NETWORK – WINDSTAR article. If any resistance is 5 ohms or more, repair open in appropriate Black wire(s).

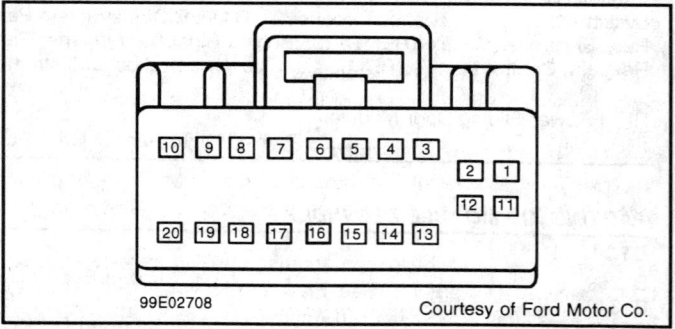

99E02708   Courtesy of Ford Motor Co.

Fig. 1: Identifying Rear Electronics Module 20-Pin Harness Connector C343 Terminals

TEST C: PARKING AID SYSTEM INOPERATIVE

NOTE: Manufacturer does not provide PAM 26-pin harness connector C445 illustration. Identify terminals by wire color. See WIRING DIAGRAMS.

1) Turn ignition switch to OFF position. Using New Generation Star (NGS) tester, perform Parking Aid Module (PAM) self-test. If no DTCs are retrieved, go to step **24)**. If any DTCs are retrieved, go to appropriate step. See PARKING AID DTC TEST STEPS table.

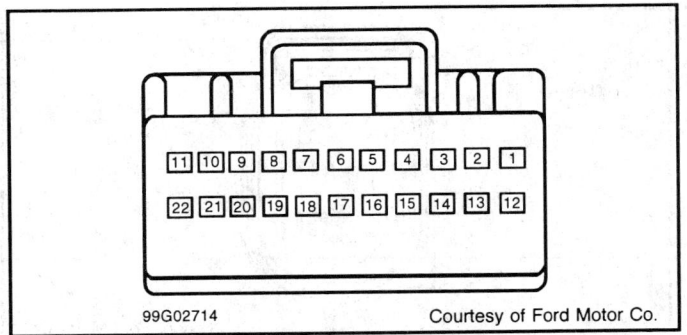

Fig. 2: Identifying Rear Electronics Module 22-Pin Harness Connector C341 Terminals

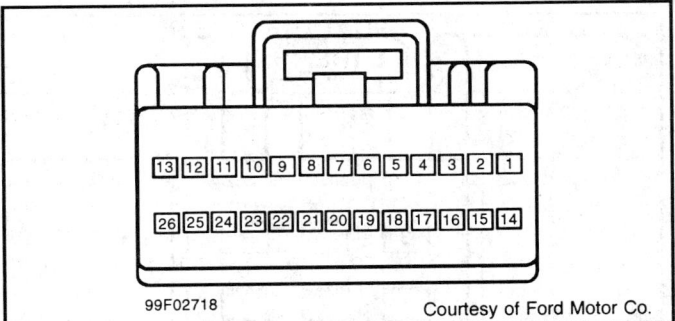

Fig. 3: Identifying Rear Electronics Module 26-Pin Harness Connector C342 Terminals

PARKING AID DTC TEST STEPS

DTC	Step
C1700, C1701, C1703, C1704, C1706, C1707, C1709 & C1710	2)
C1699, C1702, C1705 & C1708	8)
C1742	11)
C1743	17)
C1748	27)
C1920	19)
B2373	23)

2) Disconnect appropriate parking aid sensor harness connector. Disconnect PAM 26-pin harness connector C445. Measure resistance between PAM harness connector C445 terminal No. 16 (Dark Green/Yellow wire) and ground. If resistance is more than 10 k/ohms, go to next step. If resistance is 10 k/ohms or less, repair short to ground in Dark Green/Yellow wire.

3) Measure resistance between PAM harness connector C445 terminal No. 15 (Brown/Pink wire) and ground. If resistance is more than 10 k/ohms, go to next step. If resistance is 10 k/ohms or less, repair short to ground in Brown/Pink wire.

4) Measure resistances between appropriate PAM harness connector C445 terminal and ground. See PAM TERMINAL IDENTIFICATION table. If resistance is more than 10 k/ohms, go to next step. If resistance is 10 k/ohms or less, repair short to ground in appropriate wire.

PAM TERMINAL IDENTIFICATION

PAM Terminal	PAM Sensor	Wire Color
10	Left Inner	DK GRN/WHT
11	Left Outer	WHT/LT GRN
23	Right Inner	WHT/LT BLU
24	Right Outer	DK BLU/YEL

5) Measure resistance between PAM harness connector C445 terminal No. 16 (Dark Green/Yellow wire) and appropriate parking aid sensor harness connector terminal No. 1 (Dark Green/Yellow wire). See Fig. 4. If resistance is less than 5 ohms, go to next step. If resistance is 5 ohms or more, repair open in Dark Green/Yellow wire.

6) Measure resistance between PAM harness connector C445 terminal No. 15 (Brown/Pink wire) and appropriate parking aid sensor harness connector terminal No. 3 (Brown/Pink wire). If resistance is less than 5 ohms, go to next step. If resistance is 5 ohms or more, repair open in Brown/Pink wire.

7) Measure resistances between appropriate PAM harness connector C445 terminal(s) and appropriate parking aid sensor harness connector terminal No. 2. See PAM TERMINAL IDENTIFICATION table. If resistance is more than 10 k/ohms, go to next step. If resistance is 10 k/ohms or less, repair short to ground in appropriate wire.

8) Disconnect appropriate parking aid sensor 3-pin harness connector. Disconnect PAM 26-pin harness connector C445. Turn ignition switch to RUN position. Measure voltage between PAM harness connector C445 terminal No. 16 (Dark Green/Yellow wire) and ground. If voltage is not present, go to next step. If voltage is present, repair short to voltage in Dark Green/Yellow wire.

9) Measure voltage between PAM harness connector C445 terminal No. 15 (Brown/Pink wire) and ground. If voltage is not present, go to next step. If voltage is present, repair short to voltage in Brown/Pink wire.

10) Measure voltage between appropriate PAM harness connector C445 terminal(s) and ground. See PAM TERMINAL IDENTIFICATION table. If voltage is present, repair short to voltage in appropriate wire. If voltage is not present and all 4 parking aid sensors recorded DTCs, replace PAM. If voltage is not present and less than 4 parking aid sensor DTCs are retrieved, replace appropriate parking aid sensor(s).

11) Turn ignition switch to OFF position. Disconnect PAM 26-pin harness connector C445. Measure resistance between PAM harness connector C445 terminals No. 14 (Black/Pink wire) and No. 17 (Dark Green wire). If resistance is more than 60 ohms, go to next step. If resistance is 60 ohms or less, go to step **14)**.

12) Disconnect parking aid sounder 2-pin harness connector C439. Measure resistance between PAM harness connector C445 terminal No. 14 (Black/Pink wire) and parking aid sounder harness connector C439 terminal No. 1 (Black/Pink wire). If resistance is less than 5 ohms, go to next step. If resistance is 5 ohms or more, repair open in Black/Pink wire.

13) Measure resistance between PAM harness connector C445 terminal No. 17 (Dark Green wire) and parking aid sounder harness connector C439 terminal No. 2 (Dark Green wire). If resistance is less than 5 ohms, replace parking aid sounder. If resistance is 5 ohms or more, repair open in Dark Green wire.

14) Disconnect parking aid sounder 2-pin harness connector C439. Measure resistance between PAM harness connector C445 terminal No. 14 (Black/Pink wire) and ground. If resistance is more than 10 k/ohms, go to next step. If resistance is 10 k/ohms or less, repair short to ground in Black/Pink wire.

15) Measure resistance between PAM harness connector C445 terminal No. 17 (Dark Green wire) and ground. If resistance is more than 10 k/ohms, go to next step. If resistance is 10 k/ohms or less, repair short to ground in Dark Green wire.

16) Measure resistance between parking aid sounder terminal No. 1 (component side) and ground. If resistance is more than 10 k/ohms, replace PAM. If resistance is 10 k/ohms or less, replace parking aid sounder.

17) Disconnect PAM 26-pin harness connector C445. Turn ignition switch to RUN position. Measure voltage between PAM harness connector C445 terminal No. 14 (Black/Pink wire) and ground. If voltage is more than 10 volts, go to next step. If voltage is 10 volts or less, replace PAM.

18) Turn ignition switch to OFF position. Disconnect parking aid sounder harness connector. Turn ignition switch to RUN position. Measure voltage between PAM harness connector C445 terminal No. 14 (Black/Pink wire) and ground. If voltage is more than 10 volts, repair short to voltage in Black/Pink wire. If voltage is 10 volts or less, repair short to voltage in Dark Green wire.

19) Disconnect PAM 26-pin harness connector C445. Measure resistance between PAM harness connector C445 terminal No. 19 (Violet/

Orange wire) and ground. If resistance is more than 10 k/ohms, go to next step. If resistance is 10 k/ohms or less, repair short to ground in Violet/Orange wire.

20) Disconnect parking aid disable/traction assist switch 6-pin harness connector C257. Measure resistance between PAM harness connector C445 terminal No. 19 (Violet/Orange wire) and parking aid disable/traction assist switch harness connector C257 terminal No. 2 (Violet/Orange wire). *See Fig. 5.* If resistance is 5 ohms or more, go to next step. If resistance is less than 5 ohms, repair open in Violet/Orange wire.

21) Measure resistance between parking aid disable/traction assist switch harness connector C257 terminal No. 5 (Black wire) and ground. If resistance is less than 5 ohms, go to next step. If resistance is 5 ohms or more, repair open in Black wire.

22) Check parking aid disabled indicator diode. If parking aid disabled indicator is okay, replace PAM. If parking aid disabled indicator is not okay, replace parking aid disable/traction assist switch.

23) Disconnect PAM 26-pin harness connector C445. Turn ignition switch to RUN position. If parking aid disabled indicator illuminates, repair short to voltage in Violet/Orange wire between PAM and parking aid disable/traction assist switch. If parking aid disabled indicator does not illuminate, replace PAM.

NOTE: If vehicle has been in an accident, parking aid sensors may not be aligned properly.

24) Inspect bumper for proper alignment. Also, inspect parking aid sensors and holders for proper alignment. See AZIMUTH SYSTEM CHECK and ELEVATION SYSTEM CHECK under VERIFICATION TESTS. If bumper and parking aid sensors are properly aligned, go to next step. If bumper or parking aid sensors are not properly aligned, realign sensors or replace bumper. If vehicle has been in an accident, further body work may be necessary to bring parking aid sensors into correct alignment.

25) Turn ignition switch to RUN position. Set parking brake. Place transmission shift lever in Reverse. If right hand reverse lights illuminates, go to next step. If right hand reverse light does not illuminate, repair reverse lights as necessary. See AUTOLAMPS SYSTEMS – WINDSTAR article for testing procedures.

26) Turn ignition switch to OFF position. Disconnect PAM 26-pin harness connector C445. Turn ignition switch to RUN position. Measure voltage between PAM harness connector C445 terminal No. 9 (White/Yellow wire) and ground. If voltage is more than 10 volts, go to next step. If voltage is 10 volts or less, repair White/Yellow wire.

27) Measure resistance between PAM harness connector C445 terminal No. 7 (Dark Green/Violet wire) and ground. If resistance is 10 k/ohms or less, go to next step. If resistance is more than 10 k/ohms, go to step **29)**.

28) Turn ignition switch to OFF position. Disconnect parking aid disable/traction assist switch 6-pin harness connector C257. Measure resistance between PAM harness connector C445 terminal No. 7 (Dark Green/Violet wire) and ground. If resistance is more than 10 k/ohms, replace parking aid disable/traction assist switch. If resistance is 10 k/ohms or less, repair short to ground in Dark Green/Violet wire.

29) While depressing parking aid disable/traction assist switch, measure resistance between PAM harness connector C445 terminal No. 7 (Dark Green/Violet wire) and ground. If resistance is 5 ohms or more, go to next step. If resistance is less than 5 ohms, replace PAM.

30) Disconnect parking aid disable/traction assist switch 6-pin harness connector C257. Measure resistance between parking aid disable/traction assist switch harness connector C257 terminal No. 4 (Black wire) and ground. *See Fig. 5.* If resistance is less than 5 ohms, go to next step. If resistance is 5 ohms or more, repair open in Black wire.

31) Measure resistance between parking aid disable/traction assist switch terminals No. 4 and 6 (component side). *See Fig. 5.* Resistance should be less than 25 ohms when switch is pressed and 10 k/ohms or more when switch is released. If resistance is not as specified, replace parking aid disable/traction assist switch. If resistance is as specified, replace PAM.

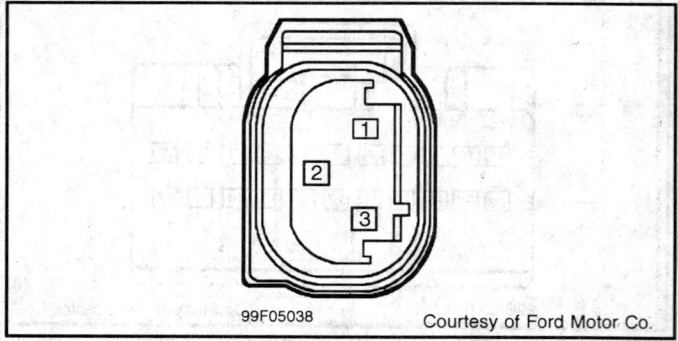

99F05038   Courtesy of Ford Motor Co.

Fig. 4: Identifying Parking Aid Sensor 3-Pin Harness Connector Terminals

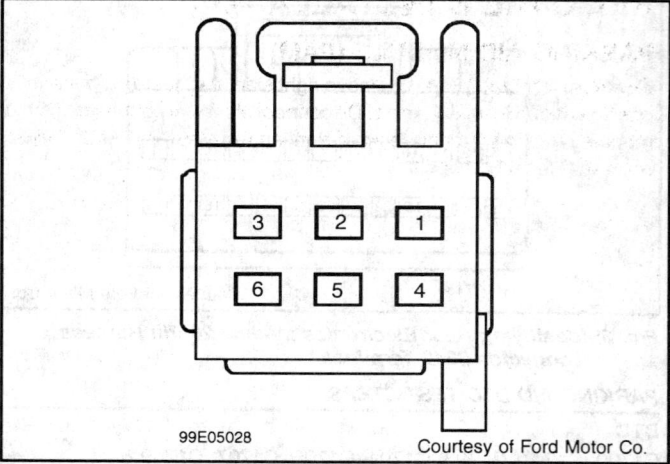

99E05028   Courtesy of Ford Motor Co.

Fig. 5: Identifying Parking Aid Disable/Traction Assist Switch 6-Pin Harness Connector Terminals

VERIFICATION TESTS
AZIMUTH SYSTEM CHECK

NOTE: Object used in this system check can be fabricated from 3″ diameter pipe 39″ (99.1 cm) in length. Azimuth system check should be performed with vehicle on a level surface. Parking Aid Module (PAM) will default to ON when ignition key is turned from OFF to RUN position.

Turn ignition switch to RUN position. Set parking brake and place shift lever in Reverse. Ensure PAM detects objects within appropriate distances. See MINIMUM DETECTABLE OBJECT DISTANCES table. For object locations, *see Fig. 6.*

MINIMUM DETECTABLE OBJECT DISTANCES

Object Location	In. (cm)
P1 & P5	12 (30.4)
P2 & P4	36 (91.4)
P3	60 (152.4)

ELEVATION SYSTEM CHECK

1) Parking aid system must be inspected to ensure system does not receive signals from ground reflections. Perform system check with vehicle on 10 x 15 foot smooth concrete surface. Area should be free of obstacles and noise from fans and pneumatic equipment.

2) Turn ignition switch to RUN position. Set parking brake and place shift lever in Reverse. No audible alerts should be heard. If audible alerts are heard, ensure bumper is properly installed and is not tilting downward so sensors are pointing at ground. If no audible alerts are heard, system is operating correctly.

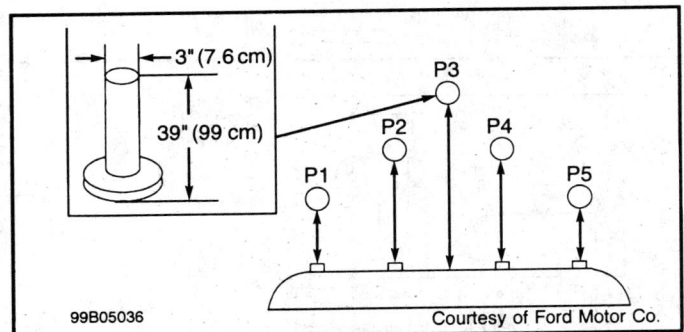

99B05036   Courtesy of Ford Motor Co.

Fig. 6: Minimum Detectable Object Distances (Azimuth System Check)

REMOVAL & INSTALLATION

PARKING AID MODULE (PAM)

Removal & Installation – Remove right side rear quarter trim panel and position sound insulator aside. Disconnect electrical connector. Remove module retaining nut and remove Parking Aid Module (PAM). To install, reverse removal procedure.

PARKING AID SOUNDER

CAUTION: Be careful when positioning aside right rear corner of headliner, when removing Parking Aid Module (PAM) sounder bracket.

Removal & Installation – Lift safety belt guide cover and remove safety belt guide bolt. Remove pin-type retainer and remove upper "D" pillar trim panel. Remove headliner pin-type retainers and remove bolt retaining PAM sounder bracket. Disconnect electrical connector and remove bracket. To install, reverse removal procedures

PARKING AID SENSOR

Removal & Installation – Remove 3 pin-type retainers on underside of rear bumper cover and remove 3 screws from each side of bumper cover, inside rear wheel well area. Disconnect electrical connector. Remove 5 screws from rear bumper cover at bottom of liftgate area and remove bumper cover. Disconnect parking aid sensor electrical connector, release locking tabs on sides of sensor and remove parking aid sensor.

WIRING DIAGRAMS

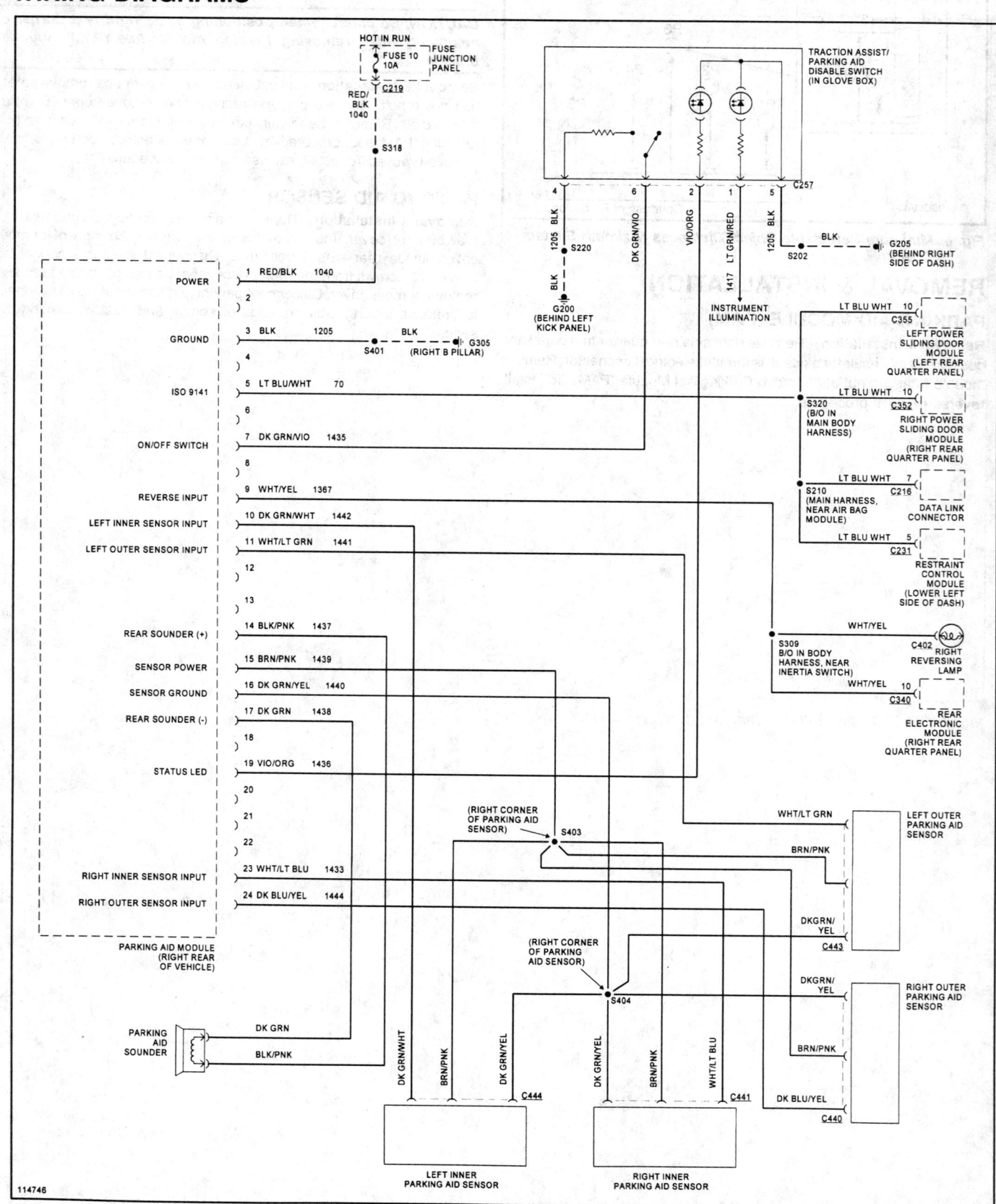

Fig. 7: Parking Aid Module Wiring Diagram (Windstar)

1999 ACCESSORIES & EQUIPMENT
Power Antennas

WIRING DIAGRAMS

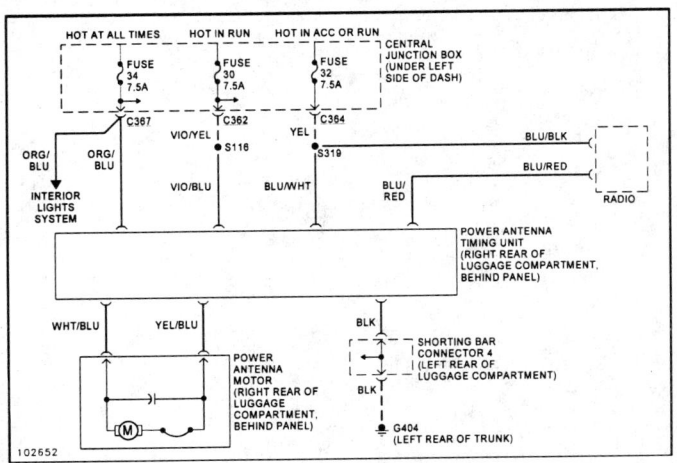

Fig. 1: Power Antenna Wiring Diagram (Contour & Mystique)

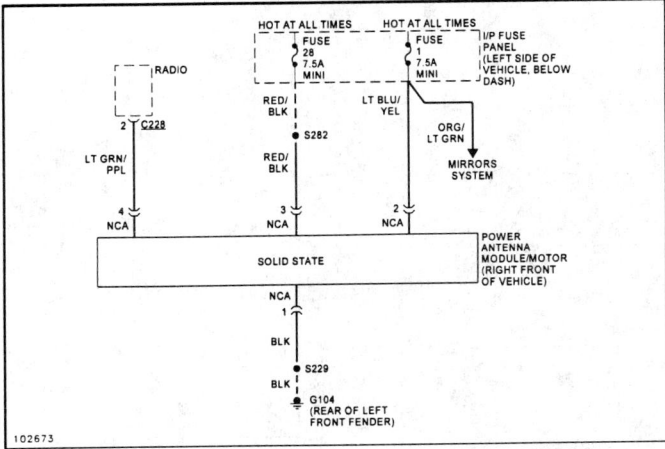

Fig. 2: Power Antenna Wiring Diagram (Explorer & Mountaineer)

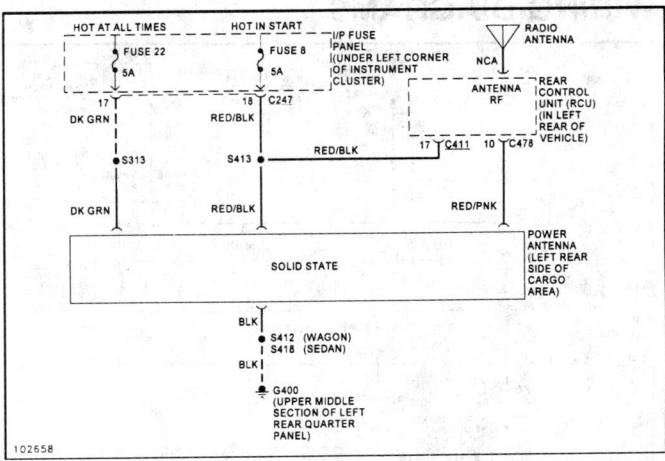

Fig. 3: Power Antenna Wiring Diagram (Sable & Taurus)

WIRING DIAGRAMS

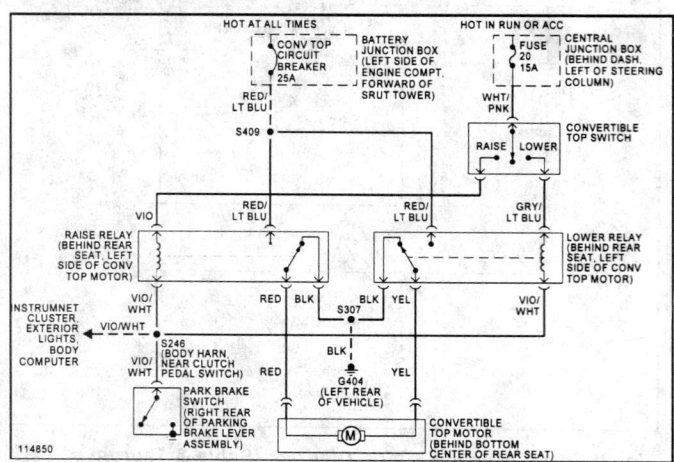

Fig. 1: Power Convertible Top Wiring Diagram (Mustang)

WIRING DIAGRAMS

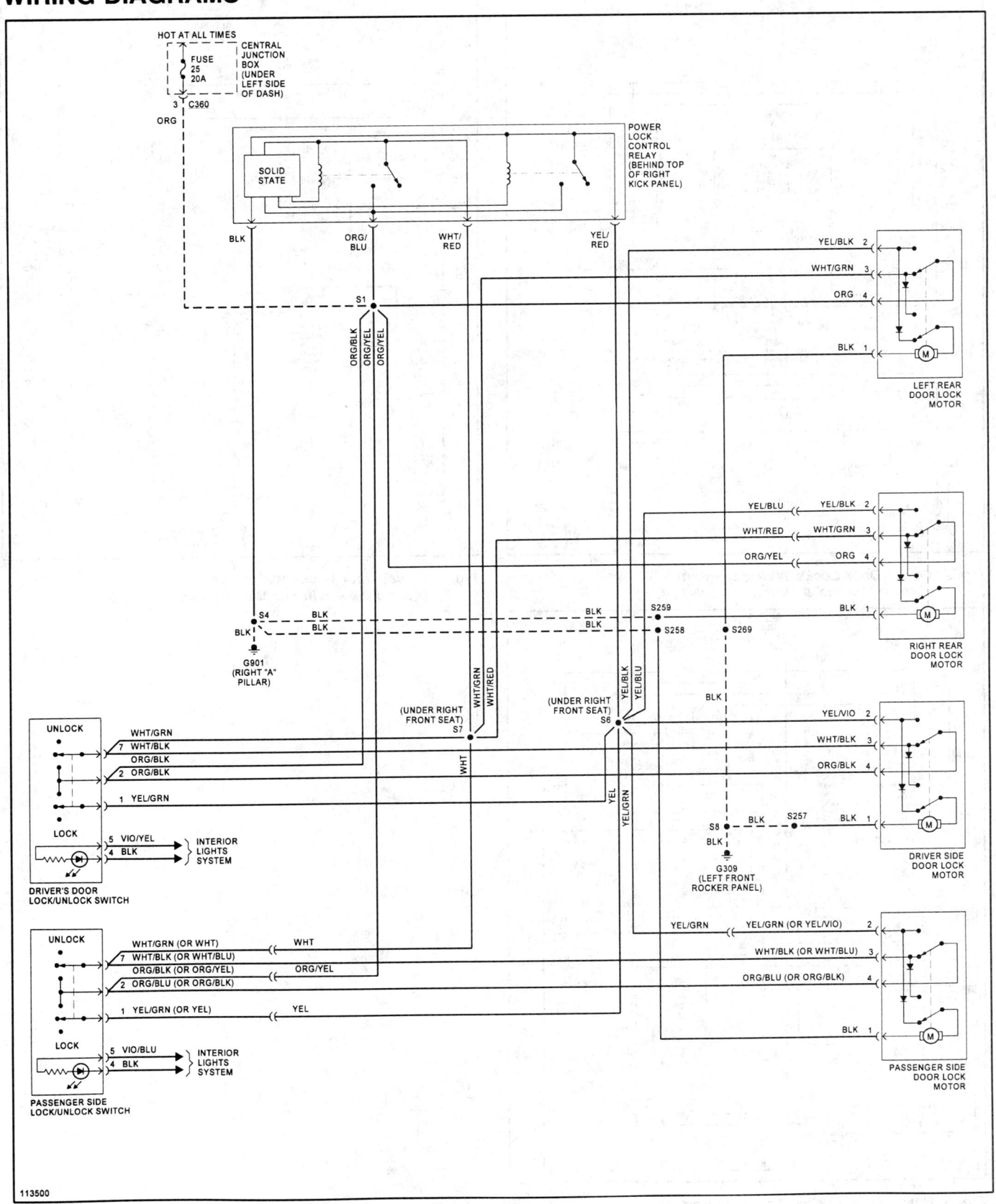

Fig. 1: Power Door Locks Wiring Diagram (Contour & Mystique)

113500

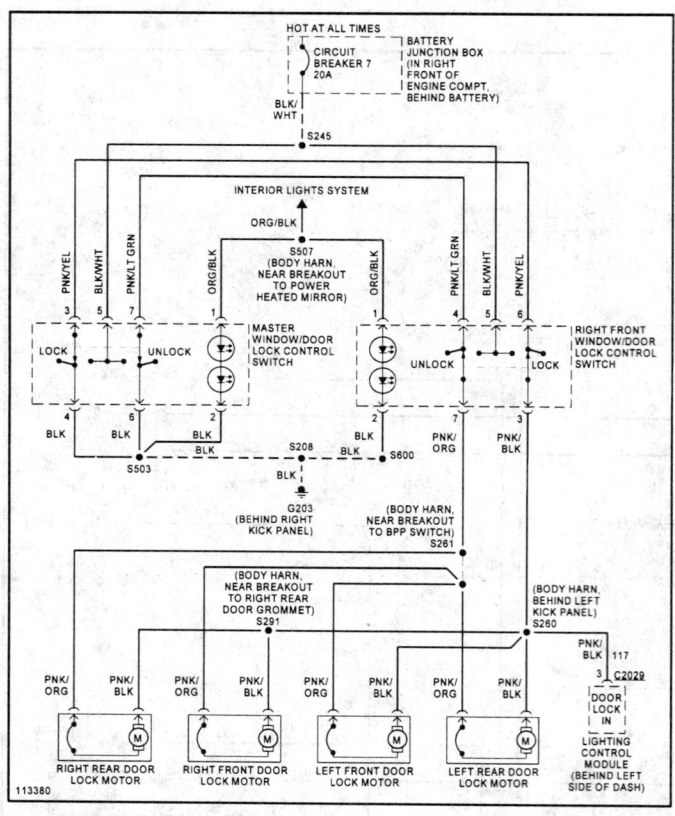

**Fig. 2: Power Door Locks Wiring Diagram
(Crown Victoria & Grand Marquis)**

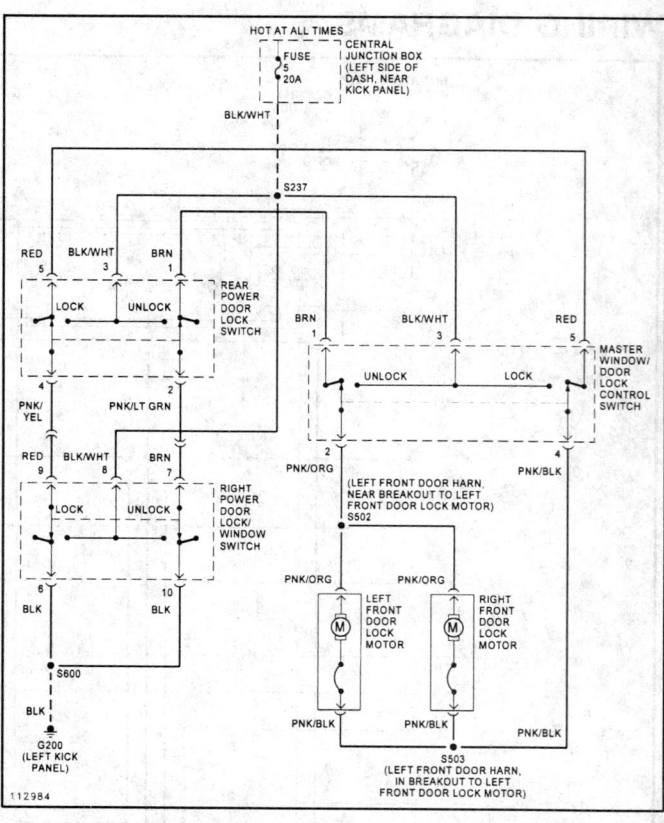

**Fig. 4: Power Door Locks Wiring Diagram
(Econoline – Without Memory Locks)**

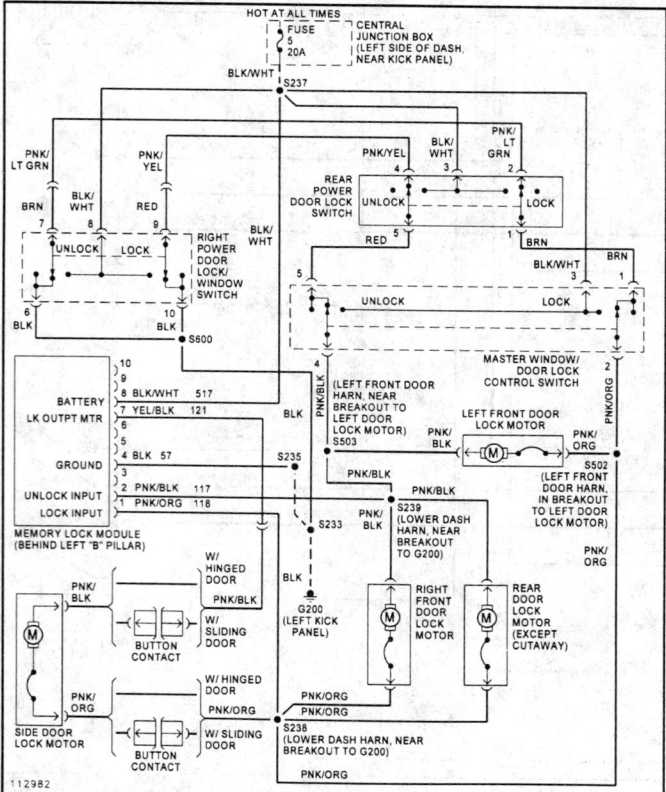

**Fig. 3: Power Door Locks Wiring Diagram
(Econoline – With Memory Locks)**

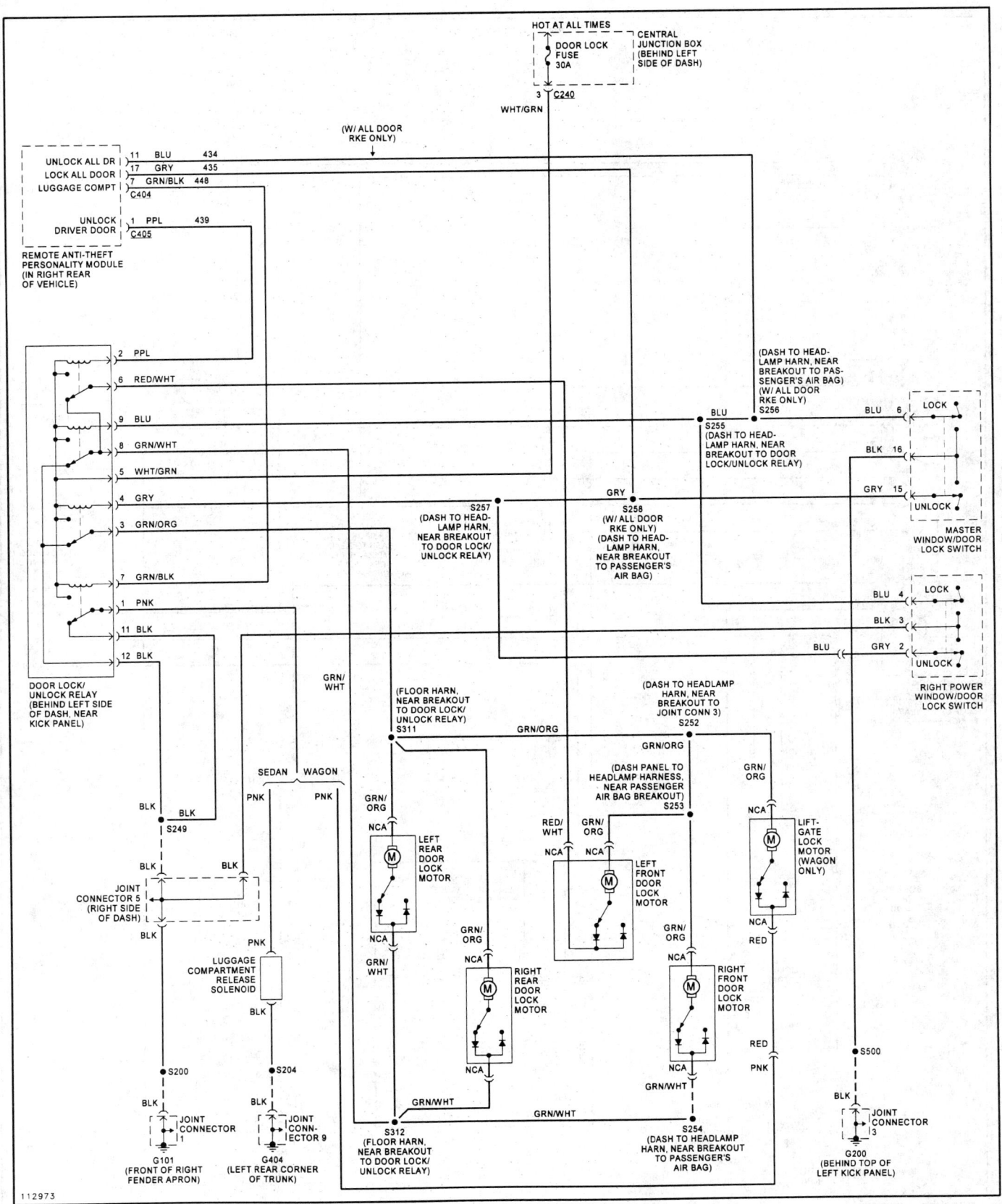

Fig. 5: Power Door Locks Wiring Diagram (Escort & Tracer)

112973

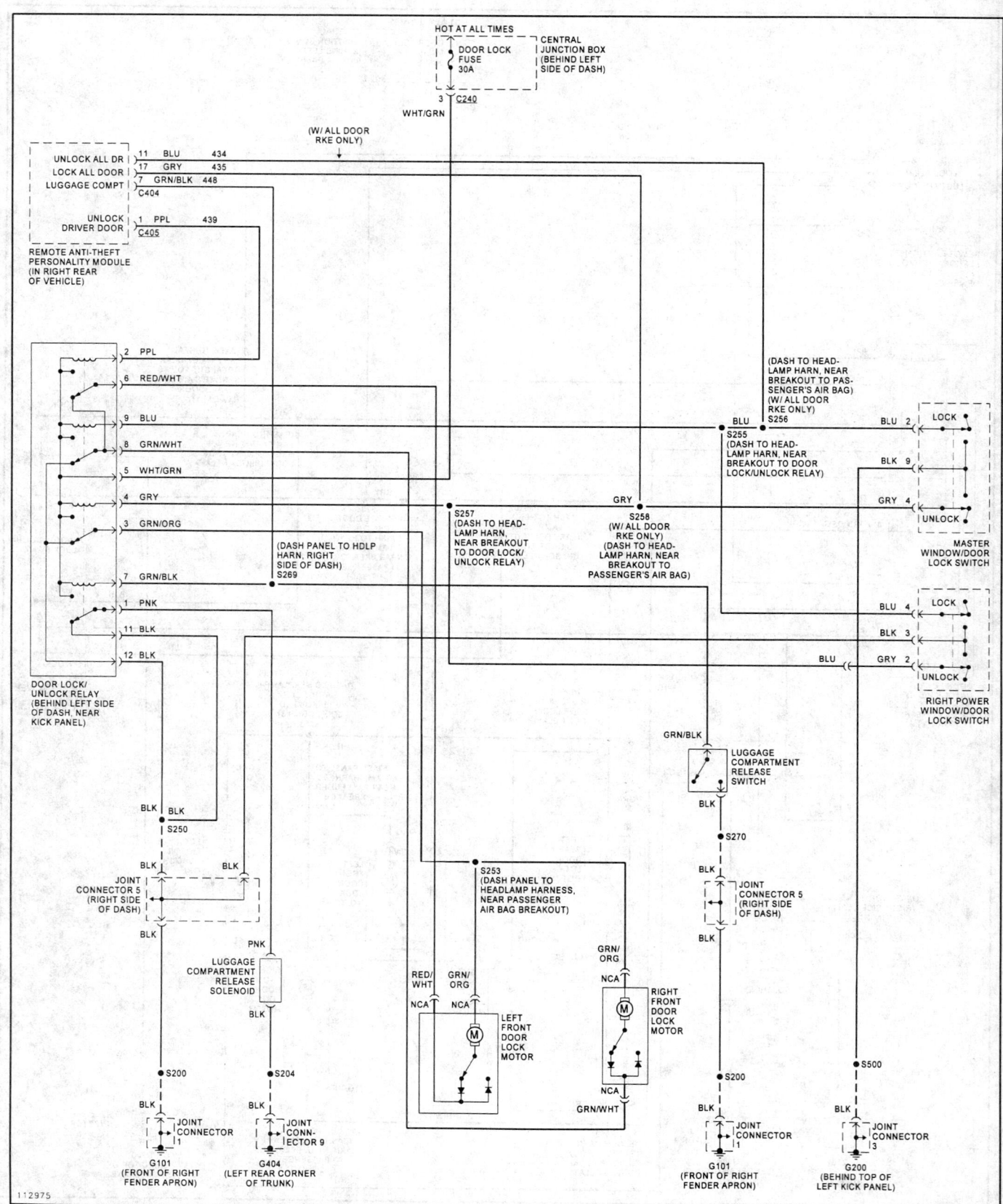

Fig. 6: Power Door Locks Wiring Diagram (Escort ZX2)

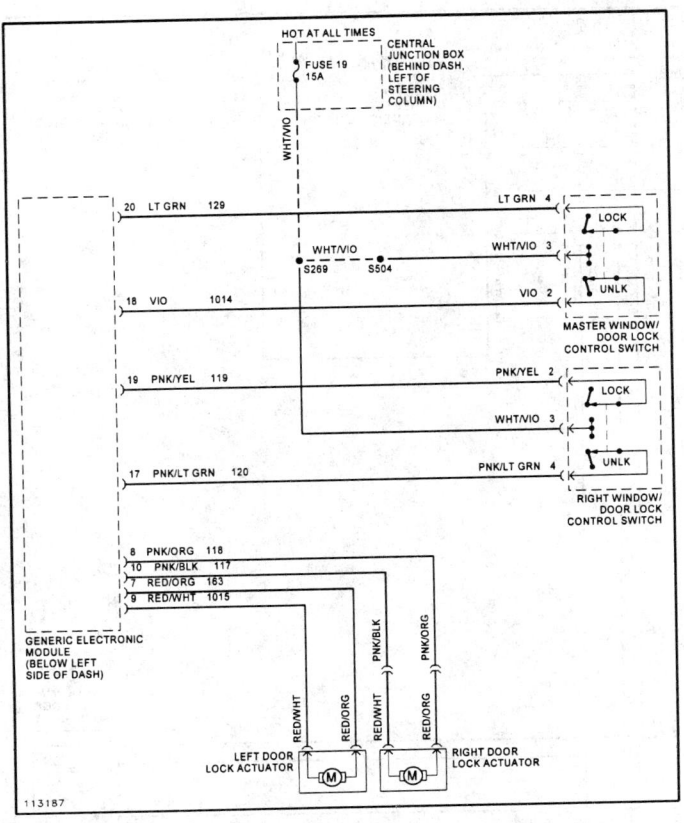

Fig. 7: Power Door Locks Wiring Diagram (Mustang)

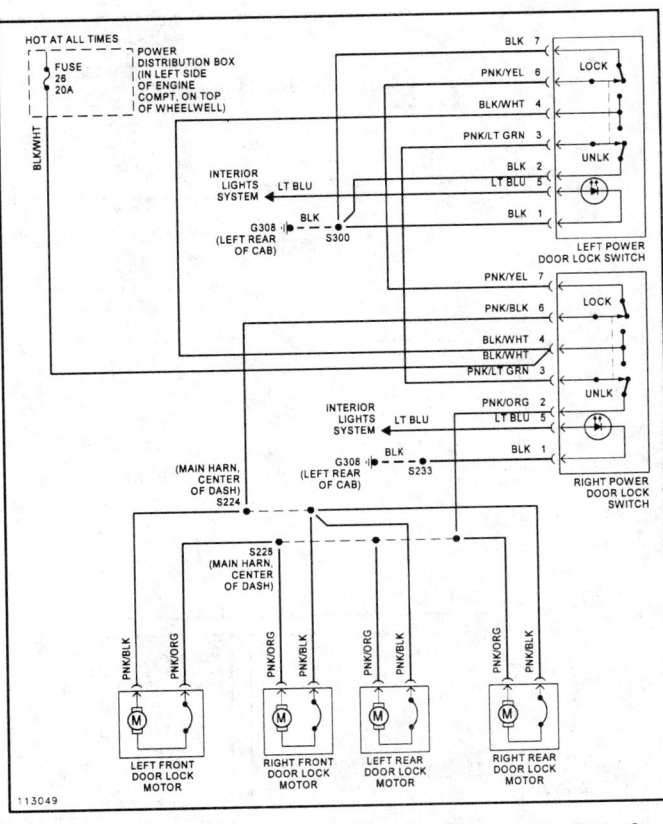

Fig. 9: Power Door Locks Wiring Diagram (F250 Super-Duty & F350 Pickup – Crew Cab – Without Remote Keyless Entry)

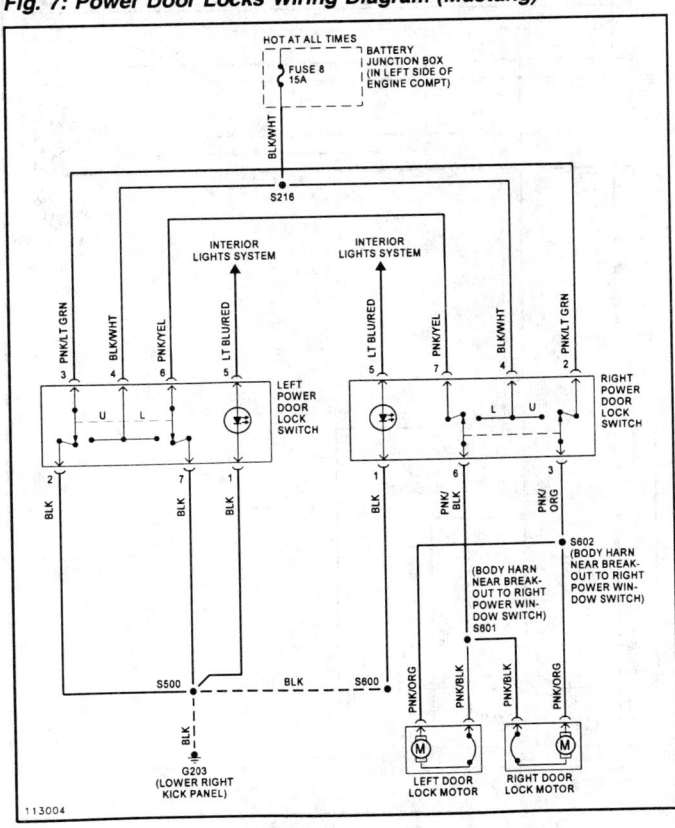

Fig. 8: Power Door Locks Wiring Diagram (F150 & F250 Light-Duty Pickup)

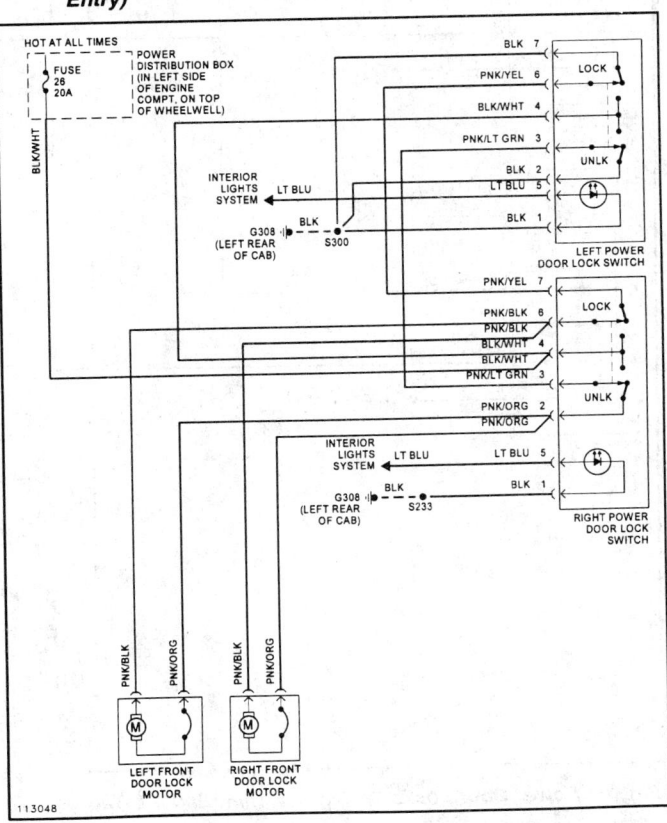

Fig. 10: Power Door Locks Wiring Diagram (F250 Super-Duty & F350 Pickup – Except Crew Cab – Without Remote Keyless Entry)

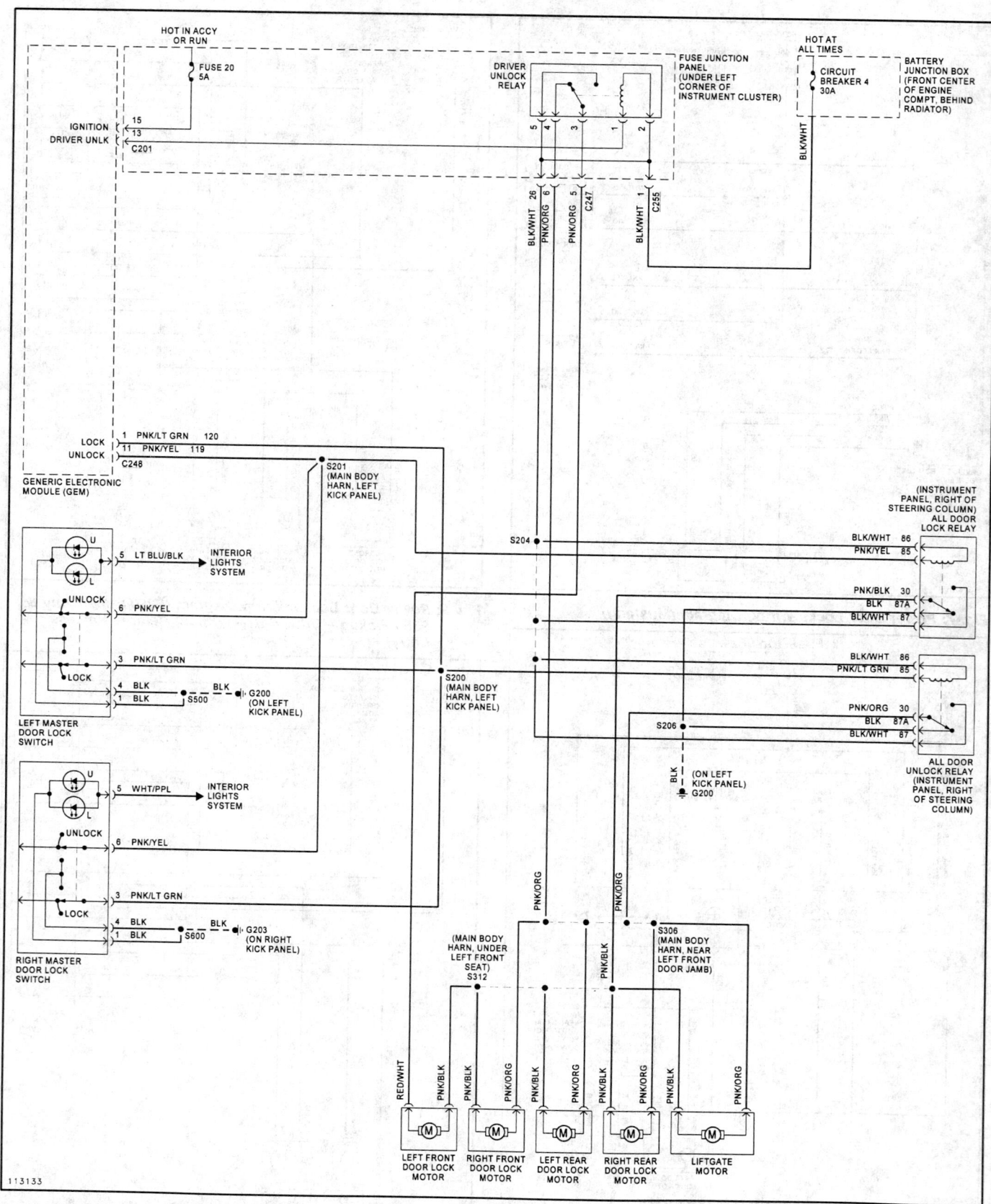

Fig. 11: Power Door Locks Wiring Diagram (Sable & Taurus – Without Remote Keyless Entry)

WIRING DIAGRAMS

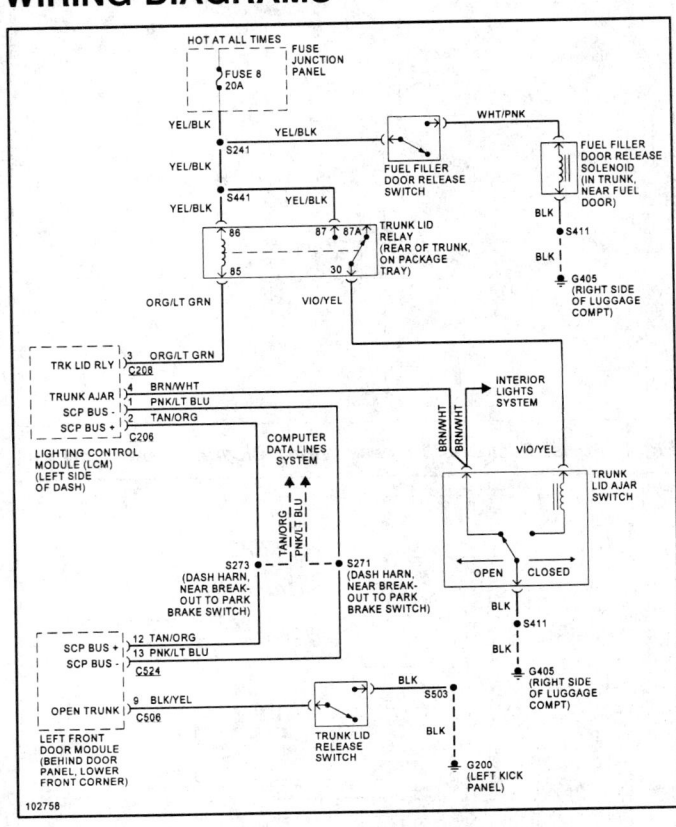

Fig. 1: Power Trunk & Fuel Door Release Wiring Diagram (Continental)

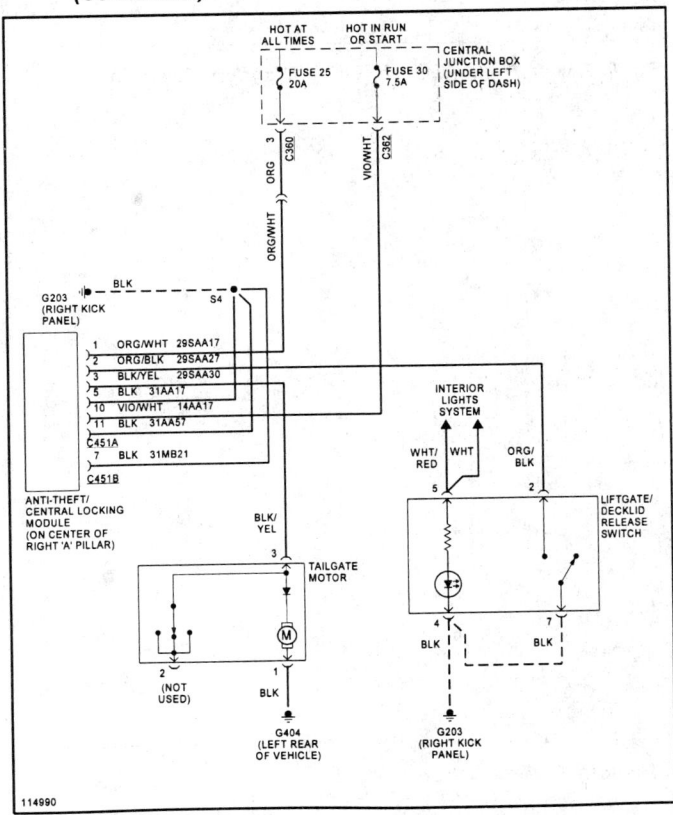

Fig. 2: Power Trunk Release Wiring Diagram (Cougar)

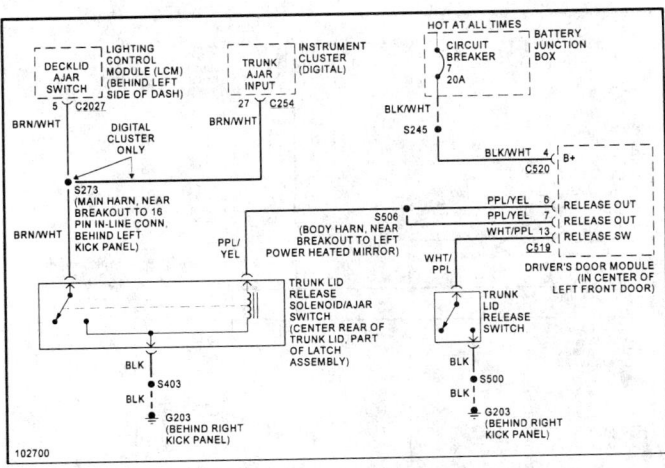

Fig. 3: Power Trunk Release Wiring Diagram (Crown Victoria & Grand Marquis – With Keyless Entry)

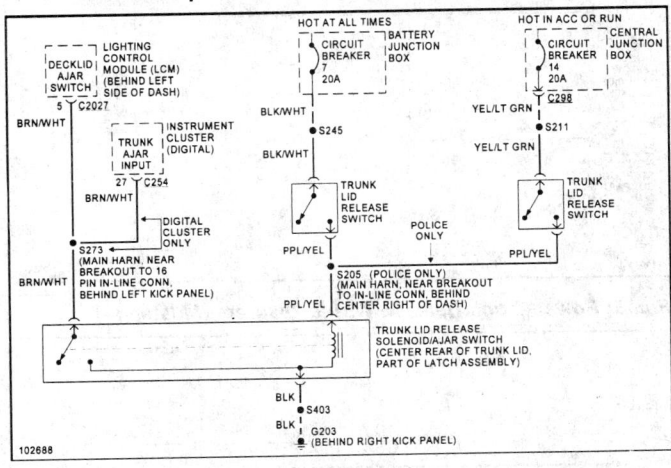

Fig. 4: Power Trunk Release Wiring Diagram (Crown Victoria & Grand Marquis – Without Keyless Entry)

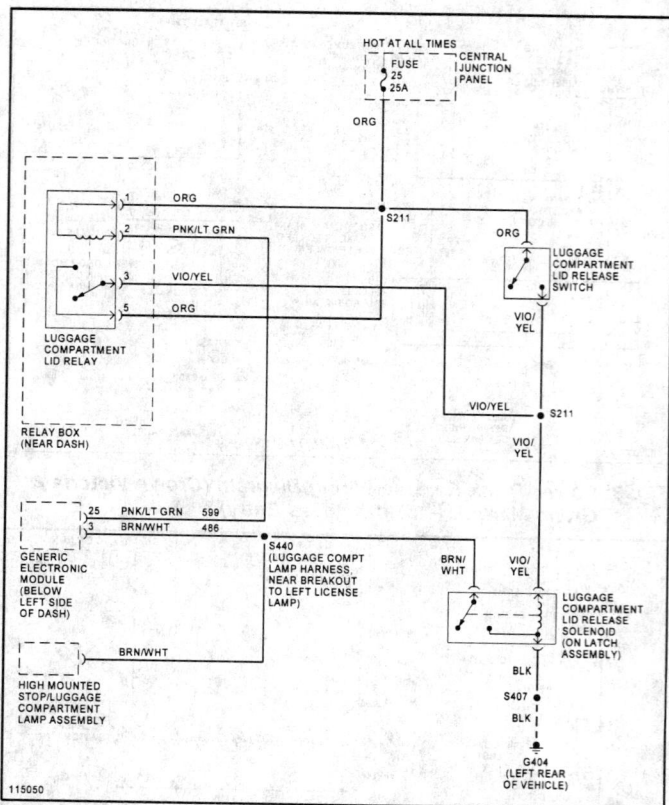

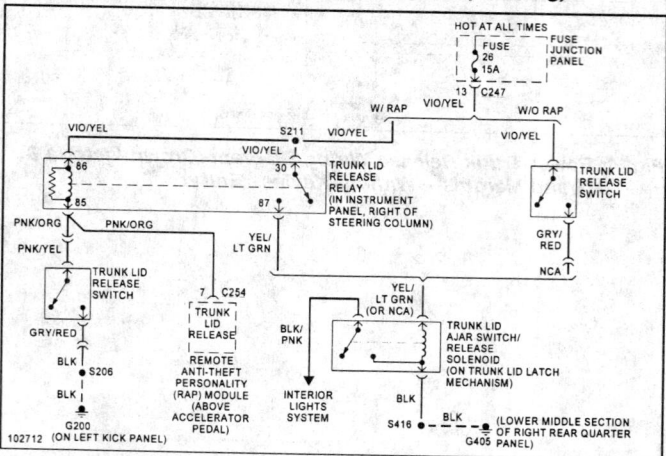

Fig. 5: Power Trunk Release Wiring Diagram (Mustang)

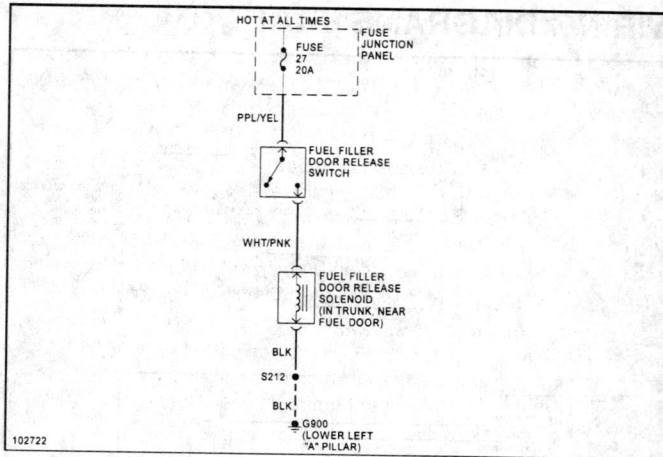

Fig. 7: Power Fuel Door Release Wiring Diagram (Town Car)

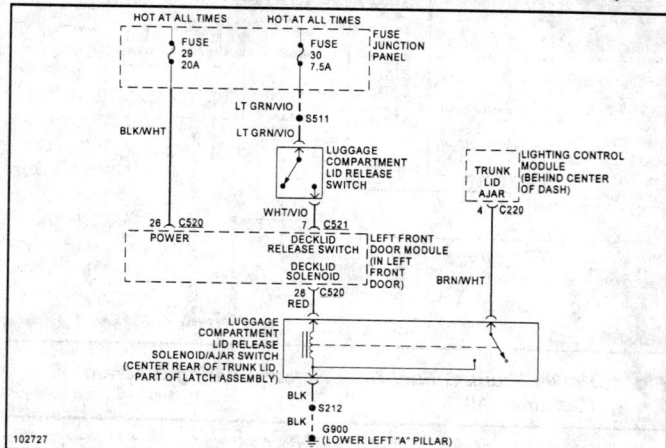

Fig. 8: Power Trunk Release Wiring Diagram (Town Car)

Fig. 6: Power Trunk Release Wiring Diagram (Sable & Taurus)

DESCRIPTION & OPERATION

The power memory seat/mirror system allows 2 seat/mirror positions into memory. Seat and outside mirrors will automatically move to preset position(s) by pressing button 1 or 2. The mirrors and seat will not operate unless transmission is in Park or Neutral.

The optional inside electronic dimming rear view mirror is controlled by 2 light-sensitive photocells. Outside light level is measured by a sensor on backside of mirror housing. A second sensor, located on reflective side of mirror, detects approaching rear lights. The mirror switches to normal state whenever transmission gear selector is placed in Reverse position. The driver's side outside rear view mirror is available with a similar glare reduction system as an option.

Power side view mirror system consists of mirror head with integral servo motor assembly. Memory mirror is controlled by Driver's Door Module (DDM) and Driver's Seat Module (DSM). Both glass and servo can be replaced separately.

COMPONENT LOCATIONS

COMPONENT LOCATIONS

Component	Location
Data Link Connector	Under Instrument Panel, Right Of Steering Column
Door Lock Switch	Appropriate Door Panel Arm Rest
Driver Door Module (DDM)	Behind Driver Door Panel, Lower Front Corner
Instrument Panel Fuse Box	Below Left Instrument Panel
Keyless Entry Keypad	Drivers Door Below Exterior Door Handle
Message Center Switches	On Instrument Panel, Right Of Instrument Cluster
Power Distribution Box	Left Side Of Engine Compartment, Above Wheel Well
Power Mirror Switch	Driver Door Panel Arm Rest

TROUBLE SHOOTING

Before performing individual component tests and system test, check the following for possible cause of system malfunction. Repair any problems as necessary and operate mirrors to see if malfunction is repaired. If malfunction still exists, go to SELF-DIAGNOSTIC SYSTEM.

- Blown fuses or faulty circuit breakers.
- Loose or corroded connectors.
- Damaged wiring.
- Damaged mirror assembly.
- Faulty switches.

COMPONENT TESTS

DOOR LOCK SWITCH

Using an ohmmeter, check for continuity between indicated switch terminals when switch is activated as specified. See POWER DOOR LOCK SWITCH CONTINUITY TEST table. *See Fig. 1.* Replace switch if it does not test as specified.

POWER DOOR LOCK SWITCH CONTINUITY TEST

Switch Position	Continuity Between Pins
Lock	1 & 6
Unlock	5 & 6

MIRROR CONTROL SWITCH

Using an ohmmeter, check for continuity between indicated switch connector terminals when switch is activated as specified. See POWER MIRROR SWITCH CONTINUITY TEST table. *See Fig. 1.* Replace switch if it does not test as specified.

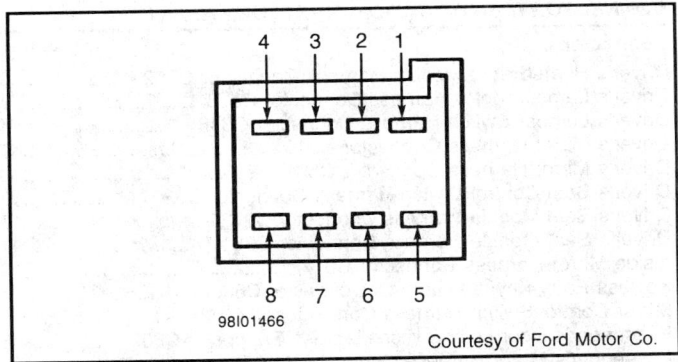

Fig. 1: Identifying Power Door Lock Switch & Power Mirror Control Switch Terminals

POWER MIRROR SWITCH CONTINUITY TEST

Switch Position	Continuity Between Pins
Left Mirror	
Up	2 & 3; 4 & 7
Down	2 & 4; 7 & 8
Left	1 & 8; 4 & 7
Right	1 & 4; 5 & 7
Right Mirror	
Up	3 & 6; 4 & 7
Down	4 & 6; 5 & 7
Left	4 & 7; 5 & 8
Right	4 & 5; 7 & 8

SEAT CONTROL SWITCH

Remove seat control switch. Check resistance between terminals. See SEAT CONTROL SWITCH RESISTANCE table. *See Fig. 2.* If resistances are not as specified, replace seat control switch.

SEAT CONTROL SWITCH RESISTANCE

Switch Position	Between Terminals	Resistance In Ohms
Front Up	4 & 6	Less Than 5
Front Down	6 & 9	Less Than 5
Rear Up	3 & 6	Less Than 5
Rear Down	6 & 8	Less Than 5
Seat FWD	2 & 6	Less Than 5
Seat RWD	6 & 7	Less Than 5
Seat Up	3 & 6; 4 & 6	Less Than 5
Seat Down	6 & 9; 6 & 8	Less Than 5
Recline FWD	5 & 6	Less Than 5
Recline RWD	6 & 10	Less Than 5

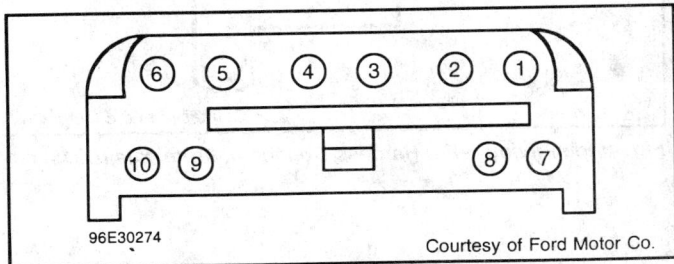

Fig. 2: Identifying Seat Control Switch Terminals

CONNECTOR IDENTIFICATION

CONNECTOR IDENTIFICATION DIRECTORY

Connector	See Fig.
Driver's Door Lock Switch Harness Connector C505	5
Driver's Door Module Harness Connector C506	10
Driver's Door Module Harness Connector C523	12
Driver's Door Module Harness Connector C524	9

CONNECTOR IDENTIFICATION DIRECTORY (Cont.)

Connector	See Fig.
Driver's Heated Seat Module Harness Connector C352	9
Driver's Lumbar Motor Harness Connector C315	1
Driver's Lumbar Switch Harness Connector C348	4
Driver's Mirror Harness Connector C515	7
Driver's Mirror Harness Connector C521	3
Driver's Seat Control Switch Harness Connector C520	8
Driver's Seat Module Harness Connector C342	13
Driver's Seat Module Harness Connector C361	11
Inside Mirror Harness Connector C917	6
Keyless Entry Keypad Harness Connector C525	7
Mirror Control Switch Harness Connector C550	5
Passenger's Door Lock Switch Harness Connector C602	5
Passenger's Mirror Harness Connector C605	3
Passenger's Mirror Harness Connector C606	7
Powerfold Mirror Switch Harness Connector C213	2

1 – Driver's Lumbar Motor Harness Connector C315 is a Black 4-pin connector. Identify by wire colors. See WIRING DIAGRAMS.

2 – Connector illustration is not avaliable from manufacturer.

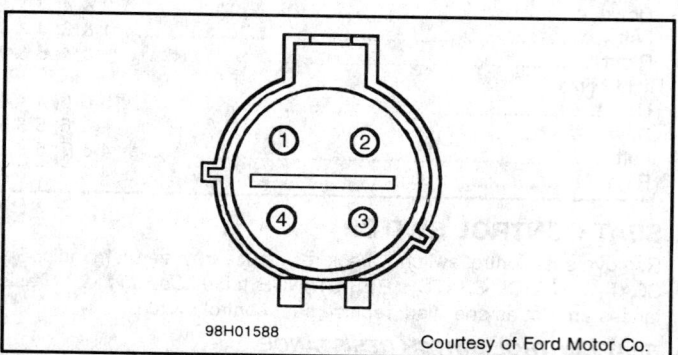

Fig. 3: Identifying 4-Pin Harness Connector Terminals (C521 & C605)

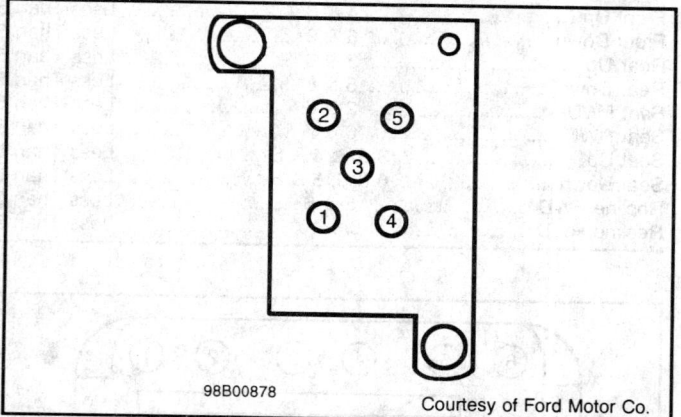

Fig. 4: Identifying 5-Pin Harness Connector Terminals (C348)

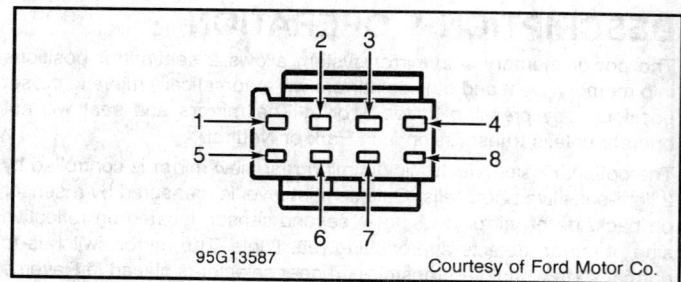

Fig. 5: Identifying 8-Pin Harness Connector Terminals (C505, C550 & C602)

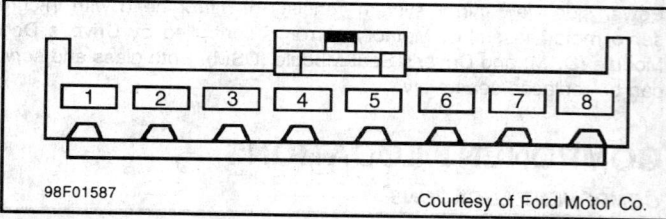

Fig. 6: Identifying 8-Pin Harness Connector Terminals (C917)

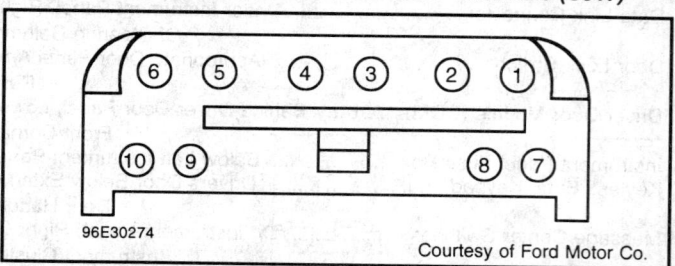

Fig. 7: Identifying 10-Pin Harness Connector Terminals (C515, C525 & C606)

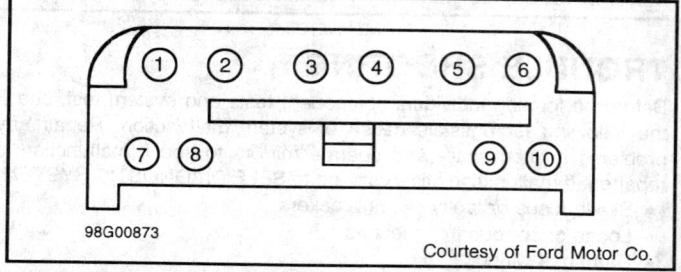

Fig. 8: Identifying 10-Pin Harness Connector Terminals (C520)

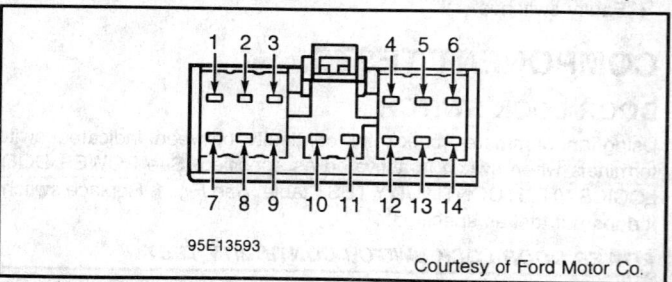

Fig. 9: Identifying 14-Pin Harness Connector Terminals (C524 & C352)

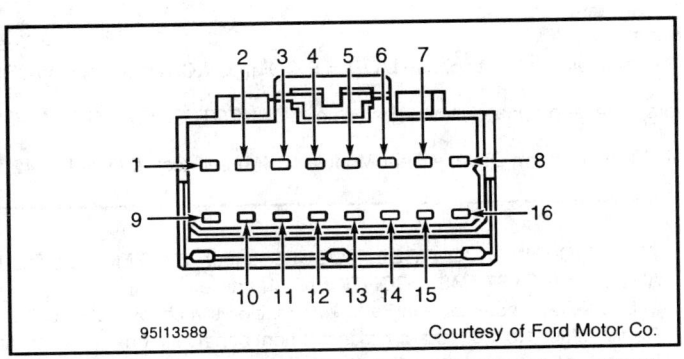

Fig. 10: Identifying 16-Pin Harness Connector Terminals (C506)

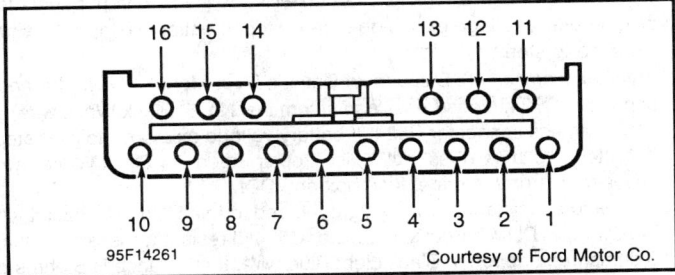

Fig. 11: Identifying 16-Pin Harness Connector Terminals (C361)

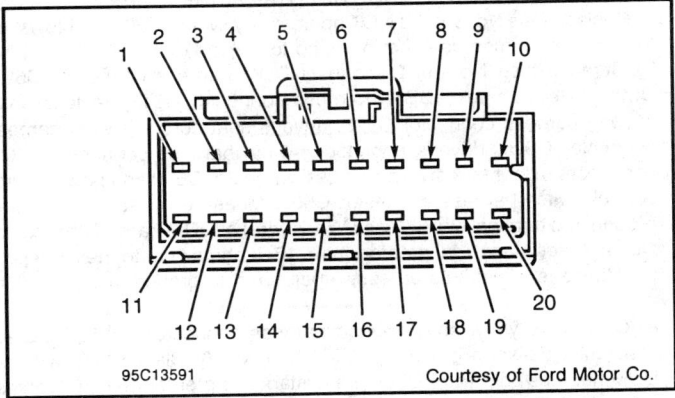

Fig. 12: Identifying 20-Pin Harness Connector Terminals (C523)

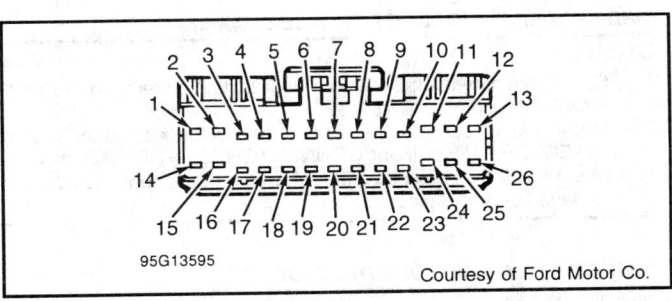

Fig. 13: Identifying 26-Pin Harness Connector Terminals (C342)

SELF-DIAGNOSTIC SYSTEM

NOTE: *Before beginning self-diagnostics, perform TROUBLE SHOOTING.*

NOTE: *Many test steps refer to various connectors. To identify connectors, use appropriate illustration. See CONNECTOR IDENTIFICATION DIRECTORY table under CONNECTOR IDENTIFICATION.*

NOTE: *After any repairs are complete, ensure all component are properly installed and all harness connectors are connected properly and repeat data link diagnostic test.*

Verify customers complaint. Check for loose or corroded connectors and damaged wiring harness. Repair or replace components as necessary.

If all components are okay, connect New Generation Star (NGS) tester to Data Link Connector (DLC), located beneath instrument panel. Using NGS tester, perform data link diagnostics test. See DATA LINK DIAGNOSTIC TEST under COMMUNICATION NETWORK DIAGNOSTICS in MODULE COMMUNICATIONS NETWORK – CONTINENTAL article. If NGS tester responds with CKT914, CKT915 or CKT70=ALL ECUS NO RESP/NOT EQUIP, repair module communications concern. See MODULE COMMUNICATIONS NETWORK – CONTINENTAL article. If NGS tester displays NO RESP/NOT EQUIP for Driver's Door Module, perform TEST A: NO COMMUNICATION WITH DRIVER'S DOOR MODULE under SYSTEM TESTS. If NGS tester displays NO RESP/NOT EQUIP for Driver's Seat Module (DSM), perform TEST B: NO COMMUNICATION WITH DRIVER'S SEAT MODULE under SYSTEM TESTS.

If NGS tester responds with SYSTEM PASSED, retrieve and record continuous DTCs. Erase continuous DTCs. Using NGS tester, perform DDM and DSM self-test. Perform appropriate test in accordance with DTC retrieved. See DRIVER'S DOOR MODULE DTC INDEX and/or DRIVER'S SEAT MODULE DTC INDEX table. Codes listed in these tables are only for testing covered in this article. For complete DTC listing, see MODULE COMMUNICATIONS NETWORK – CONTINENTAL article. If no DTCs are retrieved, repair by symptom. See SYMPTOM CHART table under SYSTEM TESTS.

DRIVER'S SEAT MODULE DTC INDEX

DTC [1]	Description	Test [2]
B1342	ECU Defective	[3]
B1667	Driver Mirror Up/Down Circuit Failure	C
B1668	Driver Mirror Right/Left Circuit Failure	C
B1669	Passenger Mirror Up/Down Circuit Failure	C
B1670	Passenger Mirror Right/Left Circuit Failure	C
B2312	Passenger Mirror Horizontal Feedback Potentiometer – Circuit Failure	D
B2315	Passenger Mirror Horizontal Feedback Potentiometer – Short To Ground	D
B2316	Passenger Mirror Vertical Feedback Potentiometer – Circuit Failure	D
B2319	Passenger Mirror Vertical Feedback Potentiometer – Short To Ground	D
B2320	Driver Mirror Horizontal Feedback Potentiometer – Circuit Failure	D
B2323	Driver Mirror Horizontal Feedback Potentiometer – Short To Ground	D
B2324	Driver Mirror Vertical Feedback Potentiometer – Circuit Failure	D
B2327	Driver Mirror Vertical Feedback Potentiometer – Short To Ground	D

DRIVER'S SEAT MODULE DTC INDEX (Cont.)

DTC [1]	Description	[2] Test

[1] – Codes listed in this table are only for testing covered in this article. For complete DTC listing, see MODULE COMMUNICATIONS NETWORK – CONTINENTAL article.

[2] – Many test steps refer to various connectors. To identify connectors, use appropriate illustration. See CONNECTOR IDENTIFICATION DIRECTORY table under CONNECTOR IDENTIFICATION.

[3] – Using NGS tester, retrieve and document continuous DTCs. Clear all DTCs. Perform Driver's Seat Module (DSM) self-test. If DTC B1342 is retrieved again, replace DSM.

DRIVER'S DOOR MODULE DTC INDEX

DTC [1]	Description	[2] Test
B1342	DDM Defective	3
B1541	Driver Mirror Short To Voltage	C

[1] – Codes listed in this table are only for testing covered in this article. For complete DTC listing, see MODULE COMMUNICATIONS NETWORK – CONTINENTAL article.

[2] – Many test steps refer to various connectors. To identify connectors, use appropriate illustration. See CONNECTOR IDENTIFICATION DIRECTORY table under CONNECTOR IDENTIFICATION.

[3] – Using NGS tester, retrieve and document continuous DTCs. Clear all DTCs. Perform Driver's Door Module (DDM) self-test. If DTC B1342 is retrieved again, replace DDM.

SYSTEM TESTS

CAUTION: When battery is disconnected or modules are replaced, vehicle computer and memory systems may lose memory data. Driveability problems may exist until computer systems have completed a relearn cycle. See COMPUTER RELEARN PROCEDURES article in GENERAL INFORMATION before disconnecting battery.

NOTE: Many test steps refer to various connectors. To identify connectors, use appropriate illustration. See CONNECTOR IDENTIFICATION DIRECTORY table under CONNECTOR IDENTIFICATION.

NOTE: After any repairs are complete, ensure all component are properly installed and all harness connectors are connected properly and repeat data link diagnostic test.

SYMPTOM CHART

Symptom	[1] Test
No Communication With Driver's Door Module	A
No Communication With Driver's Seat Module	B
Single Mirror Inoperative	C
Mirror Operates In One Second Intervals	D
Reverse Tilt Feature Inoperative	E
Memory Mirror Inoperative	F
Automatic Dimming Function Inoperative	G
Heated Mirrors Inoperative	H
Powerfold Mirror(s) Inoperative	J

[1] – Many test steps refer to various connectors. To identify connectors, use appropriate illustration. See CONNECTOR IDENTIFICATION DIRECTORY table under CONNECTOR IDENTIFICATION.

TEST A: NO COMMUNICATION WITH DRIVER'S DOOR MODULE

1) Connect NGS tester to Data Link Connector (DLC). Turn ignition switch to RUN position. Using NGS tester, monitor Driver's Door Module (DDM) PIDs SFWD_SW, SREARSW, SFNT_SW and SRCL_SW while activating power seat control switch. If UNABLE TO PERFORM TEST FUCTION MODULE NOT RESPONDING: DDM CHECK IGNITION STATUS/VERIFY CABLE REQUIREMENTS CHEK CABLE CONNECTIONS? is not displayed, go to next step. If UNABLE TO PERFORM TEST FUCTION MODULE NOT RESPONDING: DDM CHECK IGNITION STATUS/VERIFY CABLE REQUIREMENTS CHEK CABLE CONNECTIONS? is displayed, perform TEST B: NO COMMUNICATION

WITH LIGHTING CONTROL MODULE under SYSTEM TESTS in AUTOLAMP SYSTEMS – CONTINENTAL article.

2) Ensure gear selector is in Park. Turn ignition switch to LOCK position. Remove fuse No. 39 (10-amp) in instrument panel fuse box. Check fuse. If fuse is okay, go to next step. If fuse is blown, go to step 6).

3) Measure voltage at input side of fuse No. 39 in instrument panel fuse box. If battery voltage exists, go to next step. If battery voltage does not exist, go to step 24).

4) Install fuse No. 39. Disconnect Driver's Door Module (DDM) harness connector C524. Measure voltage at terminal No. 6 (Black/White wire) at DDM harness connector C524. If battery voltage exists, go to next step. If battery voltage does not exist, repair open in Black/White wire between instrument panel fuse box and DDM.

5) Measure resistance between ground and terminal No. 14 (Black/Light Blue wire) at DDM harness connector C524. If resistance is greater than 5 ohms, repair open in Black/Light Blue wire. If resistance is 5 ohms or less, repair module communication concern. See MODULE COMMUNICATIONS NETWORK – CONTINENTAL article.

6) Replace fuse No. 39. DO NOT operate any switches. If fuse blows, go to next step. If fuse does not blow, go to step 14).

7) Remove fuse No. 39. Disconnect DDM harness connector C524, Driver's Seat Module (DSM) harness connector C342, keyless entry keypad harness connector C525, driver's seat control switch harness connector C520, driver's door lock switch harness connector C505, passenger's door lock switch harness connector C602 and power mirror control switch harness connector C550. Measure resistance between ground and terminal No. 6 (Black/White wire) at DDM harness connector C524. If resistance is greater than 10 k/ohms, go to next step. If resistance is 10 k/ohms or less, repair short to ground in Black/White wire.

8) Connect keyless entry keypad harness connector C525. Measure resistance between ground and terminal No. 6 (Black/White wire) at DDM harness connector C524. If resistance is greater than 10 k/ohms, go to next step. If resistance is 10 k/ohms or less, replace keyless entry keypad.

9) Connect driver's seat control switch harness connector C520. Measure resistance between ground and terminal No. 6 (Black/White wire) at DDM harness connector C524. If resistance is greater than 10 k/ohms, go to next step. If resistance is 10 k/ohms or less, replace driver's seat control switch.

10) Connect DSM harness connector C342. Measure resistance between ground and terminal No. 6 (Black/White wire) at DDM harness connector C524. If resistance is greater than 10 k/ohms, go to next step. If resistance is 10 k/ohms or less, replace driver's seat module.

11) Connect DDM harness connector C524. Measure resistance between ground and terminal No. 6 (Black/White wire) at driver's door lock switch harness connector C505. If resistance is greater than 10 k/ohms, go to next step. If resistance is 10 k/ohms or less, replace driver's door switch.

12) Connect passenger's door lock switch harness connector C602. Measure resistance between ground and terminal No. 6 (Black/White wire) at driver's door lock switch harness connector C505. If resistance is greater than 10 k/ohms, go to next step. If resistance is 10 k/ohms or less, replace passenger's door lock switch.

13) Connect power mirror control switch harness connector C550. Measure resistance between ground and terminal No. 6 (Black/White wire) at driver's door lock switch harness connector C505. If resistance is greater than 10 k/ohms, replace driver's door lock switch. If resistance is 10 k/ohms or less, replace power mirror control switch.

14) Lock and unlock doors at all door lock switches. If fuse No. 39 blows, go to next step. If fuse No. 39 does not blow, go to step 17).

15) Remove driver's and passenger's door lock switches. Test both door lock switches. See DOOR LOCK SWITCH under COMPONENT TESTS. If both door lock switches are okay, go to next step. If either door lock switch is defective, replace appropriate door lock switch.

16) Disconnect Driver's Door Module (DDM) harness connector C506. Measure resistance between ground and terminal No. 1 (Pink/Yellow wire) at driver's door lock switch harness connector C505. Also, measure resistance between ground and terminal No. 5 (Pink/Light Green wire) at driver's door lock switch harness connector C505. If either resistance reading is 10 k/ohms or less, repair short to ground in appropriate wire(s). If both resistance readings are greater than 10 k/ohms, replace driver's door module.

17) Press each number on keyless entry pad one at a time. If fuse No. 39 blows, go to next step. If fuse No. 39 does not blow, go to step 19).

18) Disconnect Driver's Door Module (DDM) harness connector C523. Disconnect keyless entry keypad harness connector C525. Measure resistance between ground and appropriate terminals at remote keyless entry keypad harness connector C525. See REMOTE KEYLESS ENTRY TERMINAL IDENTIFICATION table. If all resistance readings are greater than 10 k/ohms, replace driver's door module. If any resistance readings are 10 k/ohms or less, repair short to ground in appropriate wire.

REMOTE KEYLESS ENTRY TERMINAL IDENTIFICATION

Terminal	Wire Color
1	Red
2	Yellow
3	Yellow/Black
4	Light Green/Red
5	Light Blue/Yellow
9	Light Blue

19) Activate mirrors in all directions. If fuse No. 39 blows, go to next step. If fuse No. 39 does not blow, go to step 22).

20) Remove mirror control switch. Test mirror control switch. See MIRROR CONTROL SWITCH under COMPONENT TESTS. If mirror control switch is okay, go to next step. If mirror control switch is defective, replace mirror control switch.

21) Disconnect Driver's Door Module (DDM) harness connector C506. Disconnect mirror control switch harness connector C550. Measure resistance between ground and appropriate terminals at mirror control switch harness connector C550. See MIRROR CONTROL SWITCH TERMINAL IDENTIFICATION table. If all resistance readings are greater than 10 k/ohms, replace driver's door module. If any resistance reading are 10 k/ohms or less, repair short to ground in appropriate wire.

MIRROR CONTROL SWITCH TERMINAL IDENTIFICATION

Terminal	Wire Color
3	Dark Blue/Orange
4	Red/Orange
6	Yellow/Black
7	Violet/Orange
8	Dark Green/Orange

22) Activate driver's seat control switch in all directions. If fuse No. 39 blows, go to next step. If fuse No. 39 does not blow, system is operating properly at this time.

23) Disconnect Driver's Door Module (DDM) harness connector C506. Disconnect driver's seat control switch harness connector C520. Measure resistance between ground and appropriate terminals at driver's seat control switch harness connector C520. See DRIVER'S SEAT CONTROL SWITCH TERMINAL IDENTIFICATION table. If all resistance readings are greater than 10 k/ohms, replace driver's door module. If any resistance readings are 10 k/ohms or less, repair short to ground in appropriate wire.

DRIVER'S SEAT CONTROL SWITCH TERMINAL IDENTIFICATION

Terminal	Wire Color
2	Red/White
3	Red/Light Green
4	Red/Light Blue
5	Gray
7	Yellow/White
8	Yellow/Light Green
9	Yellow/Light Blue
10	Gray/Black

24) Turn ignition switch to LOCK position. Remove maxi-fuse No. 1 (30-amp) in power distribution box. Check fuse. If fuse is okay, go to next step. If fuse is blown, go to step 26).

25) Measure voltage at input side of maxi-fuse No. 1 in power distribution box. If battery voltage exists, repair open in Red wire between power distribution box and instrument panel fuse box. If battery voltage does not exist, repair or replace power distribution box as necessary.

26) Ensure maxi-fuse No. 1 in power distribution box is still removed. Disconnect Driver's Seat Module (DSM) harness connector C362. Disconnect driver's heated seat module harness connector C352. Disconnect driver's lumbar switch harness connector C348. Measure resistance between ground and terminal No. 1 (Red wire) at DSM harness connector C362. If resistance is greater than 10 k/ohms, go to next step. If resistance is 10 k/ohms or less, repair short to ground in Red wire.

27) Connect DSM harness connector C362. Measure resistance between ground and output side of maxi-fuse No. 1 in power distribution box. If resistance is greater than 10 k/ohms, go to next step. If resistance is 10 k/ohms or less, replace driver's seat module.

28) Replace maxi-fuse No. 1 (30-amp) in power distribution box. Connect driver's lumbar switch harness connector C348. Operate driver's lumbar switch in both directions. If maxi-fuse No. 1 blows, go to next step. If maxi-fuse No. 1 does not blow, go to step 32).

29) Remove maxi-fuse No. 1 (30-amp) from power distribution box. Measure resistance between ground and output side of maxi-fuse No. 1 in power distribution box. If resistance is greater than 10 k/ohms, go to next step. If resistance is 10 k/ohms or less, replace driver's lumbar switch.

30) Disconnect driver's lumbar switch harness connector C348. Measure resistance between ground and terminal No. 4 (Pink wire) at driver's lumbar switch harness connector C348. Also, measure resistance between ground and terminal No. 2 (Brown wire) at driver's lumbar switch harness connector C348. If both resistance readings are greater than 10 k/ohms, go to next step. If either resistance reading is 10 k/ohms or less, replace driver's lumbar switch.

31) Disconnect driver's lumbar motor harness connector C315. Measure resistance between ground and terminal No. 4 (Pink wire) at driver's lumbar switch harness connector C348. Also, measure resistance between ground and terminal No. 2 (Brown wire) at driver's lumbar switch harness connector C348. If both resistance readings are greater than 10 k/ohms, replace power lumbar motor. If either resistance reading is 10 k/ohms or less, repair short to ground in appropriate wire.

32) Disconnect driver's heated seat module harness connector C352. Measure resistance between ground and appropriate terminals at driver's heated seat module harness connector C352. See HEATED SEAT MODULE CONNECTOR TERMINAL IDENTIFICATION table. If all resistance readings are greater than 10 k/ohms, replace driver's heated seat module. If any resistance readings are 10 k/ohms or less, repair short to ground in appropriate wire.

HEATED SEAT MODULE CONNECTOR TERMINAL IDENTIFICATION

Terminal	Wire Color
5	Black/Light Blue
6	Brown/Light Blue
8	Yellow/Light Blue
9	Gray/Light Blue
10	Red/Light Blue

HEATED SEAT MODULE CONNECTOR TERMINAL IDENTIFICATION (Cont.)

Terminal	Wire Color
11	Orange/Light Blue
12	Violet/Light Blue
13	White/Light Blue

TEST B: NO COMMUNICATION WITH DRIVER'S SEAT MODULE

1) Check fuse No. 39 (10-amp) in instrument panel fuse box. If fuse is okay, go to next step. If fuse is blown, perform TEST A: NO COMMUNICATION WITH DRIVER'S DOOR MODULE.

2) Measure voltage at input side of fuse No. 39 in instrument panel fuse box. If battery voltage exist, go to next step. If battery voltage does not exist, perform TEST A: NO COMMUNICATION WITH DRIVER'S DOOR MODULE.

3) Install fuse No. 39. Disconnect Driver's Seat Module (DSM) harness connector C342. Measure voltage at terminal No. 14 (Black/White wire) at DSM harness connector C342. If battery voltage exists, go to next step. If battery voltage does not exist, repair open in Black/White wire.

4) Measure resistance between ground and terminal No. 1 (Black/Light Green wire) at DSM harness connector C342. If resistance is 5 ohms or less, diagnose network concern. See MODULE COMMUNICATIONS NETWORK – CONTINENTAL article. If resistance is greater than 5 ohms, repair open in Black/Light Green wire.

TEST C: SINGLE MIRROR INOPERATIVE

1) Connect New Generation Star (NGS) tester to Data Link Connector (DLC). Using NGS tester, perform Driver's Door Module (DDM) self-test. If DTC B1541 does not exist, go to next step. If DTC B1541 exists, go to step **4)**.

2) Using NGS tester, perform Driver's Seat Module (DSM) self-test. If no DTCs exist, go to next step. If any DTCs exist, perform appropriate test or appropriate step. See DTC TEST PROCEDURE table.

DTC TEST PROCEDURE

DTC [1]	Perform
B1667	step 10)
B1667 & B1668	TEST D
B1667 & B2324	TEST D
B1667 & B2327	TEST D
B1668	step 10)
B1668 & B2320	TEST D
B1668 & B2323	TEST D
B1669	step 14)
B1669 & B1670	TEST D
B1669 & B2316	TEST D
B1669 & B2319	TEST D
B1670	step 14)
B1670 & B2312	TEST D
B1670 & B2315	TEST D
B1667, B1668, B1669 & B1670	TEST D

[1] – DTCs B1663, B1664, B1665 and B1666 may also be present.

3) Using NGS tester, monitor DDM PIDs MIR_SEL, MIRV_SW and MIRH_SW. Select appropriate mirror on mirror control switch. Move mirror control switch through all positions. If PID does not agree with mirror control switch position, go to next step. If PID agrees with mirror control switch position, go to step **9)**.

4) Disconnect mirror control switch harness connector C550. Measure voltage at terminal No. 1 (Black/White wire) at mirror control switch harness connector C550. If battery voltage exists, go to next step. If battery voltage does not exist, repair open in Black/White wire.

5) Turn ignition switch to LOCK position. Measure resistance between ground and terminal No. 5 (Black/Light Blue wire) at mirror control switch harness connector C550. If resistance is 5 ohms or less, go to next step. If resistance is greater than 5 ohms, repair open in Black/Light Blue wire.

6) Disconnect DDM harness connector C506. Measure resistance in wires between mirror control switch harness connector C550 and DDM harness connector C506. See MIRROR CONTROL RESISTANCE

table. If all resistance readings are 5 ohms or less, go to next step. If any resistance reading is greater than 5 ohms, repair open in appropriate wire.

MIRROR CONTROL RESISTANCE

DDM Terminal	Switch Terminal	Wire Color
12	6	Yellow/Black
13	8	Dark Green/Orange
14	4	Red/Orange
15	7	Violet/Orange
16	3	Dark Blue/Orange

7) Turn ignition switch is in RUN position. Measure voltage at appropriate terminals at driver's mirror control switch harness connector C550. See MIRROR SWITCH CIRCUIT table. If voltage does not exist at any terminal, go to next step. If voltage exists at any terminal, repair short to voltage in appropriate wire.

MIRROR SWITCH CIRCUIT

Terminal	Wire Color
3	Dark Blue/Orange
4	Red/Orange
6	Yellow/Black
7	Violet/Orange
8	Dark Green/Orange

8) Test mirror control switch. See MIRROR CONTROL SWITCH under COMPONENT TESTS. If mirror control switch is okay, replace DDM. If mirror control switch is defective, replace mirror control switch.

9) Place transmission in Park. Using NGS tester, select DSM active command POWER MIRROR CONTROL. Using NGS tester, operate both mirrors in all directions. If both mirrors respond correctly, system is okay at this time. If driver's mirror did not respond correctly, go to next step. If passenger's mirror did not respond correctly, go to step **14)**.

10) Disconnect driver's mirror harness connector C515. Measure voltage at terminals No. 3 (Red wire), No. 4 (Yellow/Red wire), No. 5 (Yellow/Light Blue wire) and No. 6 (Dark Blue wire) at driver's mirror harness connector C515. If voltage does not exist at any terminal, go to next step. If voltage exists at any terminal, go to step **13)**.

11) Disconnect DSM harness connector C342. Measure resistance between ground and terminals No. 3 (Red wire), No. 4 (Yellow/Red wire), No. 5 (Yellow/Light Blue wire) and No. 6 (Dark Blue wire) at driver's mirror harness connector C515. If all resistance readings are greater than 10 k/ohms, go to next step. If any resistance reading is 10 k/ohms or less, repair short to ground in appropriate wire.

12) Measure resistance in wires between driver's mirror harness connector C515 and DSM harness connector C342. See MIRROR DRIVER'S RESISTANCE table. If all resistance readings are 5 ohms or less, go to step **18)**. If any resistance reading is greater than 5 ohms, repair open in appropriate wire.

MIRROR DRIVER'S RESISTANCE

DSM Terminal	Mirror Terminal	Wire Color
2	3	Red
3	6	Dark Blue
4	5	Yellow/Light Blue
16	4	Yellow/Red

13) Disconnect DSM harness connector C342. Measure voltage at terminals No. 3 (Red wire), No. 4 (Yellow/Red wire), No. 5 (Yellow/Light Blue wire) and No. 6 (Dark Blue wire) at driver's mirror harness connector C515. If voltage does not exist at any terminal, replace DSM. If voltage exists at any terminal, repair short to voltage in appropriate wire.

14) Disconnect passenger's mirror harness connector C606. Measure voltage at terminals No. 3 (White/Light Green wire), No. 4 (Dark Green wire), No. 5 (White/Violet wire) and No. 6 (Violet wire) at passenger's mirror harness connector C606. If voltage does not exist at any terminal, go to next step. If voltage exists at any terminal, go to step **17)**.

15) Disconnect DSM harness connector C342. Measure resistance between ground and terminals No. 3 (White/Light Green wire), No. 4

(Dark Green wire), No. 5 (White/Violet wire) and No. 6 (Violet wire) at passenger's mirror harness connector C606. If resistance is greater than 10 k/ohms, go to next step. If resistance is 10 k/ohms or less, repair short to ground in appropriate wire.

16) Measure resistance in wires between passenger's mirror harness connector C606 and DSM harness connector C342. See PASSENGER'S MIRROR RESISTANCE table. If all resistance readings are 5 ohms or less, go to step 21). If any resistance reading is greater than 5 ohms, repair open in appropriate wire.

PASSENGER'S MIRROR RESISTANCE

DSM Terminal	Mirror Terminal	Wire Color
5	6	Violet
6	5	White/Violet
7	3	White/Light Green
8	4	Dark Green

17) Disconnect DSM harness connector C342. Measure voltage at terminals No. 3 (White/Light Green wire), No. 4 (Dark Green wire), No. 5 (White/Violet wire) and No. 6 (Violet wire) at passenger's mirror harness connector C606. If voltage does not exist at any terminal, replace DSM. If voltage exists at any terminal, repair short to voltage in appropriate wire.

18) Disconnect driver's mirror harness connector C515. Measure resistance between terminal No. 5 (Yellow/Light Blue wire) and No. 4 (Yellow/Red wire) at driver's mirror harness connector C515. Also, measure resistance between terminals No. 3 (Red wire) and No. 6 (Dark Blue wire) at driver's mirror connector C515. If resistance readings are 10 k/ohms or less, go to next step. If resistance readings are greater than 10 k/ohms, go to step 24).

19) Measure voltage at terminals No. 3 (Red wire), No. 4 (Yellow/Red wire), No. 5 (Yellow/Light Blue wire) and No. 6 (Dark Blue wire) at driver's mirror harness connector C515. If voltage does not exist at any terminal, go to next step. If voltage exists at any terminal, go to step 24).

20) Measure resistance between ground and terminals No. 3 (Red wire), No. 4 (Yellow/Red wire), No. 5 (Yellow/Light Blue wire) and No. 6 (Dark Blue wire) at driver's mirror harness connector C515. If all resistance readings are greater than 10 k/ohms, replace DSM. If any resistance reading is 10 k/ohms or less, go to step 24).

21) Disconnect passenger's mirror harness connector C606. Measure resistance between terminal No. 6 (Violet wire) and No. 5 (White/Violet wire) at passenger's mirror connector. Also, measure resistance between terminals No. 3 (White/Light Green wire) and No. 4 (Dark Green wire) at passenger's mirror connector C606. If resistance readings are 10 k/ohms or less, go to next step. If resistance readings are greater than 10 k/ohms, go to step 25).

22) Measure voltage at terminals No. 3 (White/Light Green wire), No. 4 (Dark Green wire), No. 5 (White/Violet wire) and No. 6 (Violet wire) at passenger's mirror harness connector C606. If voltage does not exist at any terminal, go to next step. If voltage exists at any terminal, go to step 25).

23) Measure resistance between ground and terminals No. 3 (White/Light Green wire), No. 4 (Dark Green wire), No. 5 (White/Violet wire) and No. 6 (Violet wire) at passenger's mirror harness connector C606. If all resistance readings are greater than 10 k/ohms, replace DSM. If any resistance reading is 10 k/ohms or less, go to step 25).

24) Remove driver's mirror assembly. Inspect mirror wiring. If wiring is damaged, repair as necessary. If wiring is okay, replace driver's mirror assembly.

25) Remove passenger's mirror assembly. Inspect mirror wiring. If wiring is damaged, repair as necessary. If wiring is okay, replace passenger's mirror assembly.

TEST D: MIRROR OPERATES IN ONE SECOND INTERVALS

1) Ensure transmission is in Park. Operate both mirrors in all directions. If both mirrors move in all directions, go to next step. If either mirror does not operate in any direction, repair as necessary. See SYMPTOM CHART table.

2) Connect New Generation Star (NGS) tester to Data Link Connector (DLC). Using NGS tester, perform Driver's Door Module (DDM) self-test. If no DTCs exist, go to next step. If any DTCs exists, perform appropriate test. See DRIVER'S DOOR MODULE DTC INDEX table under SELF-DIAGNOSTIC SYSTEM.

3) Using NGS tester, perform Driver's Seat Module (DSM) self-test. If no DTCs exist, go to next step. If any DTCs exist, perform appropriate test or appropriate step. See DTC TEST PROCEDURE table.

DTC TEST PROCEDURE

DTC	Go To
B1667, B1668, B1669 & B1670	Step 4)
B1667, B1668, B1669, B1670, B1663, B1664, B1665 & B1666	Step 11)
B1667 & B1668	Step 6)
B1667 & B2324	Step 5)
B1667 & B2327	Step 6)
B1668 & B2320	Step 5)
B1668 & B2323	Step 6)
B1669 & B1670	Step 9)
B1669 & B2316	Step 9)
B1669 & B2319	Step 8)
B1670 & B2312	Step 9)
B1670 & B2315	Step 8)

4) Ensure transmission is in Park. Position driver's and passenger's mirrors in center position. Operate both mirrors through complete travel in all directions. If both mirror move smoothly and completely, replace DSM. If driver's mirror does not operate properly, go to next step. If passenger's mirror does not operate properly, go to step 8). If both mirrors do not operate properly, go to step 11).

5) Disconnect driver's mirror harness connector C521. Disconnect DSM harness connector C342. Measure resistance between ground and terminals No. 3 (Red/White wire) and No. 1 (Dark Blue/White wire) at driver's mirror harness connector C521. If both resistance readings are greater than 10 k/ohms, go to next step. If either resistance reading is 10 k/ohms or less, repair short to ground in appropriate wire.

6) Measure resistance in wires between DSM harness connector C342 and driver's mirror harness connector C521. See DRIVER'S POTENTIOMETER CIRCUIT TEST table. If all resistance readings are 5 ohms or less, go to next step. If any resistance reading is greater than 5 ohms, repair open in appropriate wire.

DRIVER'S POTENTIOMETER CIRCUIT TEST

DSM Terminal	Mirror Terminal	Wire Color
9	3	Red/White
10	1	Dark Blue/White
13	4	Gray
15	2	Gray/Red

7) Measure voltage at terminal No. 1 (Dark Blue/White wire), No. 2 (Gray/Red wire), No. 3 (Red/White wire) and No. 4 (Gray wire) at driver's mirror harness connector C521. If voltage does not exist at any terminal, go to step 14) . If voltage exists at any terminal, repair short to voltage in appropriate wire.

8) Disconnect passenger's mirror harness connector C605. Disconnect DSM harness connector C342. Measure resistance between ground and terminals No. 1 (Violet/White wire) and No. 3 (Dark Green/White wire) at passenger's mirror harness connector C605. If both resistance readings are greater than 10 k/ohms, go to next step. If either resistance reading is 10 k/ohms or less, repair short to ground in appropriate wire.

9) Measure resistance in wires between DSM harness connector C342 and passenger's mirror harness connector C605. See PASSENGER'S POTENTIOMETER CIRCUIT TEST table. If all resistance readings are 5 ohms or less, go to next step. If any resistance reading is greater than 5 ohms, repair open in appropriate wire.

PASSENGER'S POTENTIOMETER CIRCUIT TEST

DSM Terminal	Mirror Terminal	Wire Color
11	3	Dark Green/White
12	1	Violet/White

PASSENGER'S POTENTIOMETER CIRCUIT TEST (Cont.)

DSM Terminal	Mirror Terminal	Wire Color
13	4	Gray
15	2	Gray/Red

10) Measure voltage at terminal No. 1 (Violet/White wire), No. 2 (Gray/Red wire), No. 3 (Dark Green/White wire) and No. 4 (Gray wire) at passenger's mirror harness connector C605. If voltage does not exist at any terminal, go to step **16**). If voltage exists at any terminal, repair short to voltage in appropriate wire.

11) Disconnect DSM harness connector C342, driver's mirror harness connector C521 and passenger's mirror harness connector C605. Measure resistance in Gary/Red wire between terminal No. 15 at DSM harness connector C342 and terminal No. 2 at both mirror harness connectors. Also measure resistance in Gray wire between terminal No. 13 at DSM harness connector C342 and terminal No. 4 at both mirror harness connectors. If all resistance readings are 5 ohms or less, go to next step. If any resistance reading is greater than 5 ohms, repair open in appropriate wire.

12) Measure resistance between ground and terminal No. 2 (Gray/Red wire) at both mirror harness connectors. If resistance is greater than 10 k/ohms, go to next step. If resistance is 10 k/ohms or less, repair short to ground in Gray/Red wire.

13) Measure voltage at terminal No. 2 (Gray/Red wire) at both mirror harness connectors. If voltage does not exist, go to step **18**). If voltage exists, repair short to voltage in Gray/Red wire.

14) Connect DSM harness connector C342. Measure voltage at terminals No. 1 (Dark Blue/White wire), No. 2 (Gray/Red wire) and No. 3 (Red/White wire) at driver's mirror harness connector C521. If voltage exists, go to next step. If voltage does not exist, replace DSM.

15) Measure resistance between ground and terminal No. 4 (Gray wire) at driver's mirror harness connector C521. If resistance is greater than 10 k/ohms, replace DSM. If resistance is 10 k/ohms or less, go to step **20**).

16) Connect DSM harness connector C342. Measure voltage at terminals No. 1 (Violet/White wire), No. 2 (Gray/Red wire) and No. 3 (Dark Green/White wire) at passenger's mirror harness connector C605. If voltage exists, go to next step. If voltage does not exist, replace DSM.

17) Measure resistance between ground and terminal No. 4 (Gray wire) at passenger's mirror harness connector C605. If resistance is greater than 10 k/ohms, replace DSM. If resistance is 10 k/ohms or less, go to step **21**).

18) Disconnect driver's mirror harness connector C521 and passenger's mirror harness connector C605. Measure voltage at terminal No. 2 (Gray/Red wire) at driver's and passenger's mirror harness connectors. If voltage does not exist, go to next step. If voltage exists at driver's mirror harness connector, go to step **20**). If voltage exists at passenger's mirror, go to step **21**).

19) Measure resistance between ground and terminal No. 2 (Gray/Red wire) at driver's and passenger's mirror harness connectors. If both resistance reading are greater than 10 k/ohms, go to step **22**). If resistance is 10 k/ohms or less at driver's mirror harness connector, go to next step. If resistance is 10 k/ohms or less at passenger's mirror harness connector, go to step **21**).

20) Remove driver's mirror assembly. Inspect mirror wiring. If wiring is damaged, repair as necessary. If wiring is okay, replace driver's mirror assembly.

21) Remove passenger's mirror assembly. Inspect mirror wiring. If wiring is damaged, repair as necessary. If wiring is okay, replace passenger's mirror assembly.

22) Connect all disconnected components. Using NGS tester, perform DSM self-test. If DTCs B1663, B1664, B1665 and B1666 do not exist, replace DSM. If DTCs B1663, B1664, B1665 and B1666 exist, preform appropriate test. See POWER SEATS – CONTINENTAL article.

TEST E: REVERSE TILT FEATURE INOPERATIVE

1) Operate both mirror through all positions. If both mirrors operate properly, go to next step. If both mirrors do not operate properly, repair mirrors as necessary. See SYMPTOM CHART table.

2) Turn ignition switch to RUN position. Select REVERSE MIRRORS feature on message center. If REVERSE MIRROR feature is enabled, go to next step. If REVERSE MIRROR feature is not enabled, enable feature and inform customer of proper operation.

3) Turn ignition switch to RUN position. Set parking brake. Place gear selector in Reverse. Wait 15 seconds then place transmission in Park. If mirrors do not move down when in Reverse and return to pervious position when returned to Park, go to next step. If mirrors move down when in Reverse and return to pervious position when returned to Park, system is okay at this time.

4) Connect New Generation Star (NGS) tester to Data Link Connector (DLC). Using NGS tester, perform Driver's Seat Module (DSM) self-test. If no DTCs exist, replace DSM. If any DTCs exist, perform appropriate test. See REVERSE TILT FEATURE TEST table.

REVERSE TILT FEATURE TEST

DTC	Perform
B1667 & B2324	TEST D
B1667 & B2327	TEST D
B1669 & B2316	TEST D
B1669 & B2319	TEST D
U1059	[1]

[1] – See DRIVER'S SEAT MODULE DTC INDEX table under SELF-DIAGNOSTIC SYSTEM.

TEST F: MEMORY MIRROR INOPERATIVE

1) Operate both mirror through all positions. If both mirrors operate properly, go to next step. If both mirrors do not operate properly, repair mirrors as necessary. See SYMPTOM CHART table.

2) Activate both mirror memory positions from instrument panel message center (DRIVER ID button). If both memory positions operate at message center, go to next step. If both memory position do not operate at message center, perform TEST D: MIRROR OPERATES IN ONE SECOND INTERVALS.

3) Enter keyless entry code on keyless entry keypad and within one second press the 1/2 button for memory position one or the 3/4 button for memory position 2 on keyless entry keypad. If both memory positions operate from keypad, go to next step. If either memory position does not operate from keypad, repair remote keyless entry system. See appropriate wiring diagram in REMOTE KEYLESS ENTRY SYSTEMS article.

NOTE: Only 2 remote transmitters can be programmed for memory feature. Depending which transmitter is used will determine which memory position should be obtained.

4) Unlock vehicle with both remote transmitter that have memory programed in them. If both memory positions operate from transmitters, system is okay at this time. If either memory position does not operate from transmitter, repair remote keyless entry system. See appropriate wiring diagram in REMOTE KEYLESS ENTRY SYSTEMS article.

TEST G: AUTOMATIC DIMMING FUNCTION INOPERATIVE

1) Place transmission in Park. Turn ignition switch to RUN position. Set inside rear view mirror dimming control to HIGH position. Cover light sensor on rear of inside mirror. Shine bright light on inside mirror. If inside mirror does not darken, go to next step. If inside mirror darkens and driver's mirror does not darken, go to step **7**). If both mirrors darken, system is operating properly at this time.

2) Turn ignition switch to LOCK position. Disconnect inside mirror harness connector C917. Turn ignition switch to RUN position. Measure voltage at terminal No. 8 (Black/Pink wire) at inside mirror harness connector C917. If battery voltage does not exist, go to next step. If battery voltage exists, go to step **5**).

3) Turn ignition switch to LOCK position. Remove fuse No. 4 (10-amp) in instrument panel fuse box. If fuse is blown, go to next step. If fuse is okay, repair open in Black/Pink wire.

4) Measure resistance between ground and terminal No. 8 (Black/Pink wire) at inside mirror harness connector C917. If resistance is 10 k/ohms or less, repair short to ground in Black/Pink wire. If resistance is greater than 10 k/ohms, replace inside mirror.

5) Measure resistance between ground and terminal No. 7 (Black wire) at inside mirror harness connector C917. If resistance is 5 ohms or less, go to next step. If resistance is greater than 5 ohms, repair open in Black wire.

6) Turn ignition switch to RUN position. Place gear selector in Reverse. Measure voltage at terminal No. 6 (Black/Pink wire) at inside mirror harness connector C917. If battery voltage exists, replace inside mirror. If battery voltage does not exist, repair open in Black/Pink wire or reverse light circuit as necessary.

7) Turn ignition switch to LOCK position. Test driver's mirror dimming by connecting positive voltage to terminal No. 5 (Violet wire) and ground terminal No. 4 (Light Blue/White wire) at inside mirror harness connector C917. If driver's mirror darkens, go to next step. If driver's mirror does not darken, repair wiring between mirror or replace driver's mirror glass as necessary.

8) Turn ignition switch to LOCK position. Disconnect driver's mirror harness connector C515. Connect inside mirror harness connector C917. Measure voltage at terminal No. 9 (Light Blue/White wire) at driver's mirror harness connector C515. If battery voltage exists, go to next step. If battery voltage does not exist, go to step **10)**.

9) Disconnect inside mirror harness connector C917. Measure voltage at terminal No. 9 (Light Blue/White wire) at driver's mirror harness connector C515. If battery voltage exists, repair short to voltage in Light Blue/White wire. If battery voltage does not exist, replace inside mirror.

10) Measure voltage at terminal No. 10 (Violet wire) at driver's mirror harness connector C515. If battery voltage exists, go to next step. If battery voltage does not exist, go to step **12)**.

11) Disconnect inside mirror harness connector C917. Measure voltage at terminal No. 10 (Violet wire) at driver's mirror harness connector C515. If battery voltage exists, repair short to voltage in Violet wire. If battery voltage does not exist, replace inside mirror.

12) Measure resistance between ground and terminal No. 9 (Light Blue/White wire) at driver's mirror harness connector C515. If resistance is 10 k/ohms or less, go to next step. If resistance is greater than 10 k/ohms, go to step **14)**.

13) Disconnect inside mirror harness connector C917. Measure resistance between ground and terminal No. 9 (Light Blue/White wire) at driver's mirror harness connector C515. If resistance is 10 k/ohms or less, repair short to ground in Light Blue/White wire. If resistance is greater than 10 k/ohms, replace inside mirror and retest.

14) Measure resistance between ground and terminal No. 10 (Violet wire) at driver's mirror harness connector C515. If resistance is 10 k/ohms or less, go to next step. If resistance is greater than 10 k/ohms, go to step **16)**.

15) Disconnect inside mirror harness connector C917. Measure resistance between ground and terminal No. 10 (Violet wire) at driver's mirror harness connector C515. If resistance is 10 k/ohms or less, repair short to ground in Violet wire. If resistance is greater than 10 k/ohms, replace inside mirror.

16) Disconnect inside mirror harness connector C917. Measure resistance in Light Blue/White wire between terminal No. 4 at inside mirror harness connector C917 and terminal No. 9 at driver's mirror harness connector C515. If resistance is 5 ohms or less, go to next step. If resistance is greater than 5 ohms, repair open in Light Blue/White wire.

17) Measure resistance in Violet wire between terminal No. 5 at inside mirror harness connector C917 and terminal No. 10 at driver's mirror harness connector C515. If resistance is 5 ohms or less, replace inside mirror. If resistance is greater than 5 ohms, repair open in Violet wire.

TEST H: HEATED MIRRORS INOPERATIVE

1) Turn ignition switch to RUN position. Turn defogger on. If rear window defogger works, go to next step. If rear window defogger does not work, repair rear window defogger. See appropriate REAR WINDOW DEFOGGERS article.

2) Turn ignition switch to LOCK position. Remove fuse No. 30 (10-amp) in instrument panel fuse box. Check fuse. If fuse is blown, go to next step. If fuse is okay, go to step **6)**.

3) Measure resistance between ground and output side of fuse No. 30. If resistance is 10 k/ohms or less, go to next step. If resistance is greater than 10 k/ohms, replace fuse.

4) Disconnect driver's mirror harness connector C515. Measure resistance between ground and output side of fuse No. 30. If resistance is 10 k/ohms or less, go to next step. If resistance is greater than 10 k/ohms, replace driver's mirror glass.

5) Disconnect passenger's mirror harness connector C606. Measure resistance between ground and output side of fuse No. 30. If resistance is 10 k/ohms or less, repair short to ground in Dark Green/Violet wire. If resistance is greater than 10 k/ohms, replace passenger's mirror glass.

6) Ensure fuse No. 30 is still removed. Turn ignition switch to RUN position. Turn defogger on. Measure voltage at input side of fuse No. 30. If battery voltage exists, go to next step. If battery voltage does not exist, repair open in Brown/Light Blue wire.

7) Turn ignition switch to LOCK position. Disconnect driver's mirror harness connector C515. Measure resistance in Dark Green/Violet wire between output side of fuse No. 30 and terminal No. 2 at driver's mirror harness connector C515. If resistance is 5 ohms or less, go to next step. If resistance is greater than 5 ohms, repair open in Dark Green/Violet wire.

8) Turn ignition switch to LOCK position. Disconnect passenger's mirror harness connector C606. Measure resistance Dark Green/Violet wire between output side of fuse No. 30 and terminal No. 2 at passenger's mirror harness connector C606. If resistance is greater than 5 ohms, repair open in Dark Green/Violet wire. If resistance is 5 ohms or less, go to next step if driver's mirror does not defrost or go to step **10)** if passenger's mirror does not defrost.

9) Measure resistance between ground and terminal No. 1 (Black wire) at driver's mirror harness connector C515. If resistance is 5 ohms or less, replace driver's mirror glass. If resistance is greater than 5 ohms, repair open in Black wire.

10) Measure resistance between ground and terminal No. 1 (Black wire) at passenger's mirror harness connector C606. If resistance is 5 ohms or less, replace passenger's mirror glass. If resistance is greater than 5 ohms, repair open in Black wire.

TEST J: POWERFOLD MIRROR(S) INOPERATIVE

1) Operate powerfold mirrors. If both powerfold mirrors are inoperative, go to next step. If one powerfold mirror is inoperative, go to step **5)**.

2) Disconnect powerfold mirror switch harness connector C213. Measure voltage at terminal No. 1 (Light Blue/White wire) at powerfold mirror switch harness connector C213. If battery voltage exists, go to next step. If battery voltage does not exist, go to step **4)**.

3) Measure resistance between ground and terminal No. 3 (Black wire) at powerfold mirror switch harness connector C213. If resistance is 5 ohms or less, go to step. **5)**. If resistance is greater than 5 ohms, repair open in Black wire.

4) Remove fuse No. 35 (10-amp) in instrument panel fuse box. Measure resistance in Light Blue/White wire between output side of fuse No. 35 and terminal No. 1 at powerfold mirror switch harness connector C213. If resistance is 5 ohms or less, go to next step. If resistance is greater than 5 ohms, repair open in Light Blue/White wire.

5) Disconnect driver's mirror harness connector C515 and passenger's side mirror harness connector C606. Measure resistance in Violet/Light Green wire between terminal No. 4 at powerfold mirror switch harness connector C213 and terminal No. 7 at driver's mirror harness connector C515. Measure resistance in Violet/Light Green wire between terminal No. 4 at powerfold mirror switch harness connector C213 and terminal No. 7 at passenger's mirror harness connector C606. If both resistance readings are 5 ohms or less, go to next step. If either resistance reading is greater than 5 ohms, repair open in Violet/Light Green wire.

6) Measure resistance in Pink/Yellow wire between terminal No. 2 at powerfold mirror switch harness connector C213 and terminal No. 8 at driver's mirror harness connector C515. Measure resistance in Pink/Yellow wire between terminal No. 2 at powerfold mirror switch harness connector C213 and terminal No. 8 at passenger's **mirror harness**

connector C606. If both resistance readings are 5 ohms or less, go to next step. If either resistance reading is greater than 5 ohms, repair open in Pink/Yellow wire.

7) Test powerfold mirror switch. If switch is okay, replace inoperative powerfold mirror. If switch is defective, replace powerfold mirror switch.

REMOVAL & INSTALLATION

CAUTION: When battery is disconnected or modules are replaced, vehicle computer and memory systems may lose memory data. Driveability problems may exist until computer systems have completed a relearn cycle. See COMPUTER RELEARN PROCEDURES article in GENERAL INFORMATION before disconnecting battery.

ELECTRONIC INSIDE MIRROR

Removal & Installation – Unplug harness connectors at rear of mirror. Grasp mirror firmly, insert Mirror Remover (T91T-17700-A) or screwdriver into slot and press retaining spring. Slide mirror upward and away from mounting bracket. To install, reverse removal procedure.

SIDE MIRROR ASSEMBLY

Removal & Installation – Disconnect negative battery cable. Remove door trim panel. Disconnect mirror harness connector. Remove mirror attaching screws. Remove mirror assembly while guiding wiring and connector through hole in door. To install, reverse removal procedure.

SIDE MIRROR GLASS & MOTOR

WARNING: To prevent personal injury, place shop towel between mirror glass and hand when removing glass from mirror shell.

Removal – 1) Rotate mirror glass to maximum upward travel. Insert flat blade screwdriver between mirror shell and glass on bottom edge about 1" from lower inside corner of glass. *See Fig. 14.* Place hand and shop towel over mirror glass, to keep it from falling out.

2) Gently pry downward on screwdriver until snap is hear and mirror glass loosens from mirror motor. If glass does not come loose, move screwdriver to lower outside corner of mirror about 1" from outside corner. Gently pry downward. Glass will snap out without being damaged. Remove motor attaching screws. Disconnect motor connector, and remove motor.

Installation – Connect motor harness connector. Place motor in mirror shell and install mounting screws. Align mirror glass locating tabs with slots in mirror motor. Place shop towel over glass. Press inward with the palm of the hand until glass locks in place.

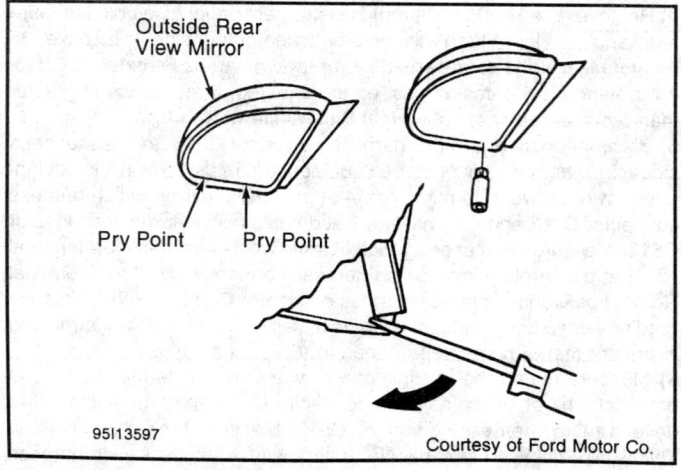

95I13597   Courtesy of Ford Motor Co.

Fig. 14: Removing Side Mirror Glass

MIRROR CONTROL SWITCH

Removal & Installation – Disconnect negative battery cable. Remove screw retaining power window switch bezel. Lift bezel to expose harness connector. Unplug harness connector. Remove switch. To install, reverse removal procedure.

WIRING DIAGRAMS

NOTE: See REAR WINDOW DEFOGGERS article for heated mirror wiring diagram.

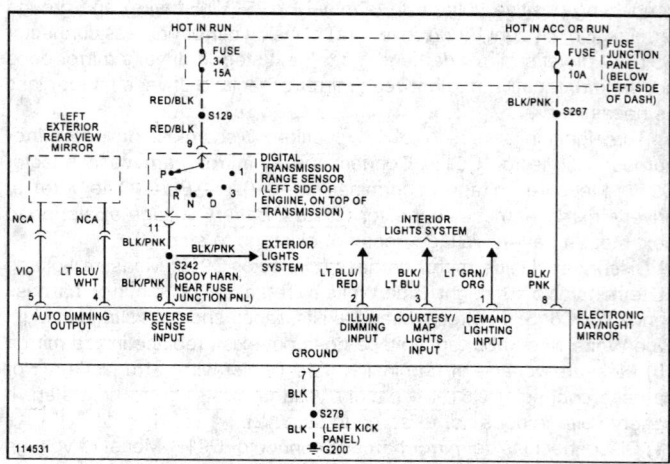

Fig. 15: Automatic Day/Night Mirror System Wiring Diagram (Continental)

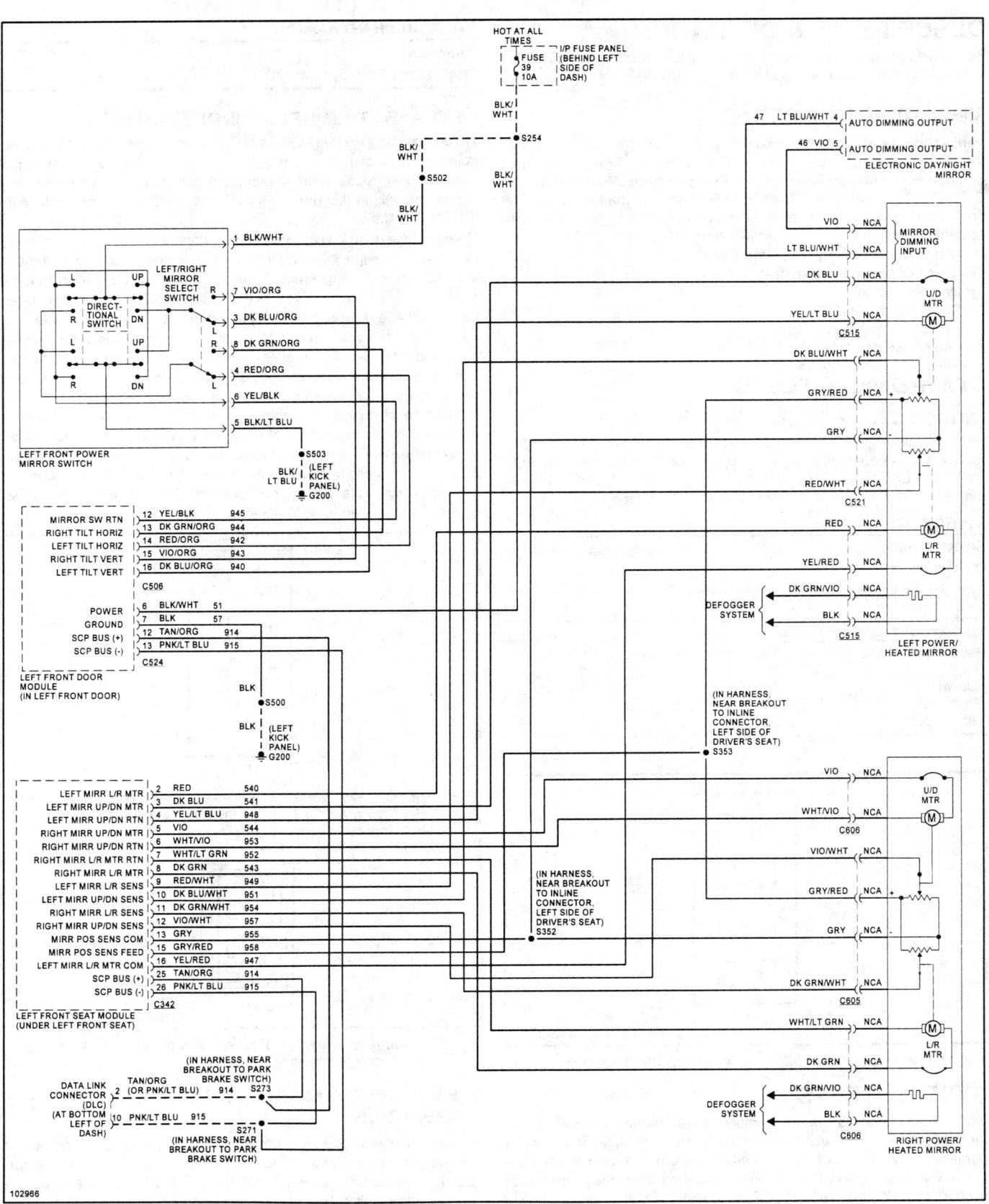

Fig. 16: Power Memory System Wiring Diagram (Continental)

102966

DESCRIPTION & OPERATION

Power side mirror system consists of control switch and mirror assembly with replaceable motor and glass.

TROUBLE SHOOTING

Verify customer complaint by operating power mirrors. Visually inspect for obvious sign of mechanical and electrical damage. If no visual damage is evident, perform appropriate system test. See SYMPTOM CHART table under SYSTEM TESTS. Before performing individual component tests or system tests, check the following for possible cause of system malfunction and repair as necessary:

- Blown fuses or faulty circuit breaker.
- Loose or corroded connectors.
- Damaged wiring.
- Damaged motors.
- Damaged mirror assemblies.
- Faulty switches.

COMPONENT TESTS

MIRROR CONTROL SWITCH

Remove mirror control switch. Measure resistance between specified terminals while operating switch in appropriate direction. See MIRROR SWITCH TEST table. See Fig. 1. Resistance in all tests should be less than 5 ohms. If switch fails any portion of test, replace switch.

MIRROR SWITCH TEST

Switch Position	Continuity Between Terminals
Driver's Mirror	
Up	1 & 6; 3 & 4
Down	1 & 4; 3 & 6
Left	3 & 6; 7 & 4
Right	3 & 4; 7 & 6
Passenger's Mirror	
Up	2 & 6; 3 & 4
Down	2 & 4; 3 & 6
Left	3 & 6; 4 & 5
Right	3 & 4; 5 & 6

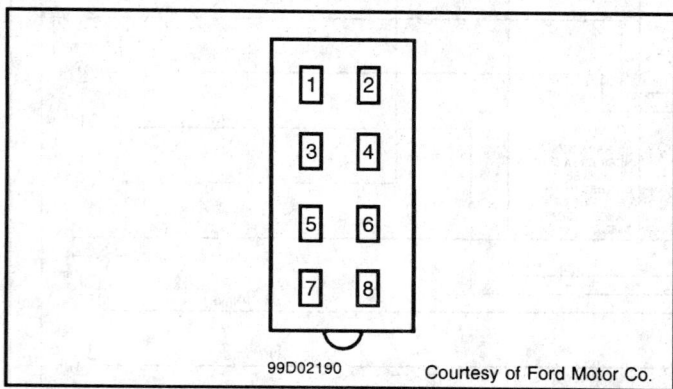

Fig. 1: Identifying Power Mirror Control Switch Terminals

SYSTEM TESTS

Verify customer complaint by operating power mirrors. Visually inspect for obvious sign of mechanical and electrical damage. If no visual damage is evident, perform appropriate system test. See SYMPTOM CHART table. A digital volt-ohmmeter is required to test the power mirror system. See WIRING DIAGRAMS for terminal identification.

SYMPTOM CHART

Symptom	Test
Both Mirrors Inoperative	A
Single Mirror Completely Inoperative	B

SYMPTOM CHART (Cont.)

Symptom	Test
Single Mirror Partially Inoperative	C

TEST A: BOTH MIRRORS INOPERATIVE

1) Turn ignition switch to LOCK position. Remove fuse No. 34 (7.5-amp) from central junction box. Check fuse. If fuse is okay, go to next step. If fuse is blown, repair short to ground in power distribution circuit. See appropriate wiring diagram in POWER DISTRIBUTION article in WIRING DIAGRAMS.

2) Install fuse no. 34. Disconnect mirror control switch harness connector C740. Turn ignition switch to RUN position. Measure voltage at terminal No. 6 (Orange/Yellow wire) at mirror control switch harness connector C740. See Fig. 2. If battery voltage exists, go to next step. If battery voltage does not exist, repair open in Orange/Yellow wire.

3) Turn ignition switch to LOCK position. Measure resistance between ground and terminal No. 4 (Black wire) at mirror control switch harness connector C740. If resistance is 5 ohms or less, go to next step. If resistance is greater than 5 ohms, repair open in Black wire.

4) Disconnect driver's side mirror harness connector C807. Measure resistance between terminal No. 3 (Yellow/Red wire) at mirror control switch harness connector and terminal No. 2 (Yellow wire) at driver's side mirror harness connector C807. See Figs. 2 and 3. If resistance is 5 ohms or less, replace mirror control switch. If resistance is greater than 5 ohms, repair open in Yellow/Red wire.

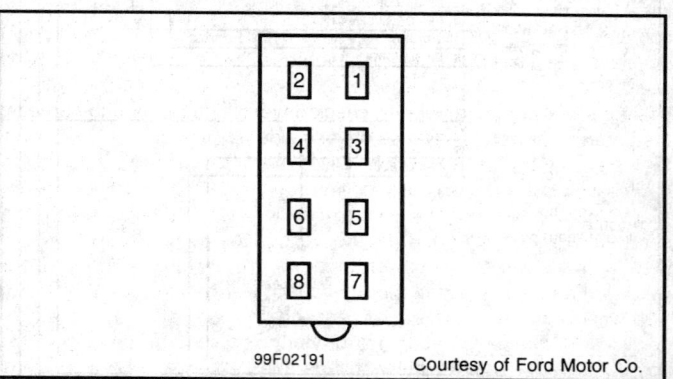

Fig. 2: Identifying Mirror Control Switch Harness Connector C740 Terminals

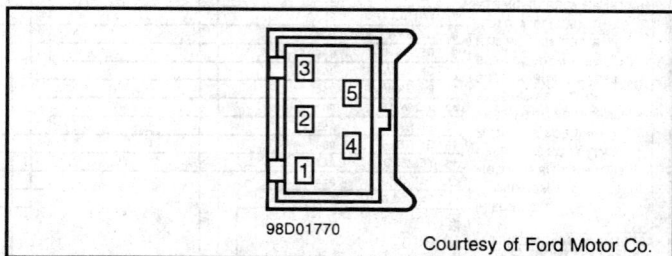

Fig. 3: Identifying Driver's & Passenger's Side Mirror Harness Connector Terminals

TEST B: SINGLE MIRROR COMPLETELY INOPERATIVE

Turn ignition switch to LOCK position. Disconnect mirror control switch harness connector C740. Disconnect inoperative mirror harness connector. Measure resistance between terminal No. 3 (Yellow/Red wire) at mirror control switch harness connector C740 and terminal No. 2 at inoperative mirror harness connector. See Figs. 2 and 3. If resistance is greater than 5 ohms, repair open in appropriate circuit. See WIRING DIAGRAMS. If resistance is 5 ohms or less, replace mirror control switch.

TEST C: SINGLE MIRROR PARTIALLY INOPERATIVE

NOTE: Control circuit between terminal No. 3 (Yellow/Red wire) at mirror control switch harness connector C740 and driver's and passenger's side mirrors changes color at soldered joint S3 depending on options. Soldered joint S3 is located at bottom of pillar "A". Also, control circuits between mirror control switch and passenger's side mirror all change color if vehicle is not equipped with power windows. See WIRING DIAGRAMS.

1) Remove mirror control switch. Test mirror control switch. See MIRROR CONTROL SWITCH under COMPONENT TESTS. If switch is okay, go to appropriate step. See TEST STEP table. If switch is defective, replace mirror control switch.

TEST STEP

Malfunction	Perform Step
Driver's Mirror	
Up/Down	2)
Right/Left	4)
Passenger's Mirror	
Up/Down	3)
Right/Left	5)

2) Install mirror control switch. Disconnect driver's side mirror harness connector C807. Turn ignition switch to RUN position. Ensure rear window defogger is off. Place mirror control switch in driver's side adjustment position. Measure voltage between terminals No. 2 (Yellow wire) and No. 4 (White/Red wire) at driver's side mirror harness connector C807 while operating mirror control switch to up and down positions. *See Fig. 3.* If battery voltage does not exist in both positions with opposite polarity, go to step 6). If battery voltage exists in both positions with opposite polarity, check driver's side mirror sub-harness. If sub-harness is okay, replace driver's side mirror.

3) Install mirror control switch. Disconnect passenger's side mirror harness connector C71. Turn ignition switch to RUN position. Ensure rear window defogger is off. Place mirror control switch in passenger's side adjustment position. Measure voltage between terminals No. 2 (Yellow/Green wire with power windows; Yellow wire without power windows) and No. 4 (White/Black wire with power windows; White/Red wire without power windows) at passenger's side mirror harness connector C71 while operating mirror control switch to up and down positions. *See Fig. 3.* If battery voltage does not exist in both positions with opposite polarity, go to step 7). If battery voltage exists in both positions with opposite polarity, check passenger's side mirror sub-harness. If sub-harness is okay, replace passenger's side mirror.

4) Install mirror control switch. Disconnect driver's side mirror harness connector C807. Turn ignition switch to RUN position. Ensure rear window defogger is off. Place mirror control switch in driver's side adjustment position. Measure voltage between terminals No. 2 (Yellow wire) and No. 5 (White/Blue wire) at driver's side mirror harness connector C807 while operating mirror control switch to right and left positions. *See Fig. 3.* If battery voltage does not exist in both positions with opposite polarity, go to step 8). If battery voltage exists in both positions with opposite polarity, check driver's side mirror sub-harness. If sub-harness is okay, replace driver's side mirror.

5) Install mirror control switch. Disconnect passenger's side mirror harness connector C71. Turn ignition switch to RUN position. Ensure rear window defogger is off. Place mirror control switch in passenger's side adjustment position. Measure voltage between terminals No. 2 (Yellow/Green wire with power windows; Yellow wire without power windows) and No. 5 (White/Violet wire with power windows; White/Blue wire without power windows) at passenger's side mirror harness connector C71 while operating mirror control switch to right and left positions. *See Fig. 3.* If battery voltage does not exist in both positions with opposite polarity, go to step 9). If battery voltage exists in both positions with opposite polarity, check passenger's side mirror sub-harness. If sub-harness is okay, replace passenger's side mirror.

6) Turn ignition switch to LOCK position. Disconnect mirror control switch harness connector C740. Measure resistance in White/Red wire between terminal No. 1 at mirror control switch harness connector C740 and terminal No. 4 at driver's side mirror harness connector C807. Also, measure resistance between terminal No. 3 (Yellow/Red wire) at mirror control switch harness connector C740 and terminal No. 2 (Yellow wire) at driver's side mirror harness connector C807. If both resistance readings are 5 ohms or less, replace mirror control switch. If either resistance reading is greater than 5 ohms, repair open in appropriate wire.

7) Turn ignition switch to LOCK position. Disconnect mirror control switch harness connector C740. Measure resistance between terminal No. 2 (White/Black wire) at mirror control switch harness connector C740 and terminal No. 4 (White/Black wire with power windows; White/Red wire without power windows) at passenger's side mirror harness connector C71. Also, measure resistance between terminal No. 3 (Yellow/Red wire) at mirror control switch harness connector C740 and terminal No. 2 (Yellow/Green wire with power windows; Yellow wire without power windows) at passenger's side mirror harness connector C71. If both resistance readings are 5 ohms or less, replace mirror control switch. If either resistance reading is greater than 5 ohms, repair open in appropriate wire.

8) Turn ignition switch to LOCK position. Disconnect mirror control switch harness connector C740. Measure resistance in White/Blue wire between terminal No. 7 at mirror control switch harness connector C740 and terminal No. 5 at driver's side mirror harness connector C807. Also, measure resistance between terminal No. 3 (Yellow/Red wire) at mirror control switch harness connector C740 and terminal No. 2 (Yellow wire) at driver's side mirror harness connector C807. If both resistance readings are 5 ohms or less, replace mirror control switch. If either resistance reading is greater than 5 ohms, repair open in appropriate wire.

9) Turn ignition switch to LOCK position. Disconnect mirror control switch harness connector C740. Measure resistance between terminal No. 5 (White/Violet wire) at mirror control switch harness connector C740 and terminal No. 5 (White/Violet wire with power windows; White/Blue wire without power windows) at passenger's side mirror harness connector C71. Also, measure resistance between terminal No. 3 (Yellow/Red wire) at mirror control switch harness connector C740 and terminal No. 2 (Yellow/Green wire with power windows; Yellow wire without power windows) at passenger's side mirror harness connector C71. If both resistance readings are 5 ohms or less, replace mirror control switch. If either resistance reading is greater than 5 ohms, repair open in appropriate wire.

REMOVAL & INSTALLATION

SIDE MIRROR ASSEMBLY

Removal & Installation – Remove screw retaining mirror mounting hole cover, and remove cover. Disconnect mirror assembly wiring connector. Remove mirror attaching screws. Remove mirror assembly. To install, reverse removal procedure.

SIDE MIRROR GLASS & MOTOR

Removal & Installation – Push mirror glass as far inboard as possible to allow finger clearance at outboard edge of mirror. Insert fingers into clearance, and pull mirror glass. Glass will snap out without being damaged. Remove motor attaching screws. Disconnect motor connector, and remove motor. To install, reverse removal procedure.

SIDE MIRROR SWITCH

Removal & Installation – Carefully pry side mirror control switch from instrument panel trim panel. Unplug harness connector and remove switch. To install, reverse removal procedure.

WIRING DIAGRAMS

NOTE: For heated mirror wiring diagram, see appropriate wiring diagram in REAR WINDOW DEFOGGERS article.

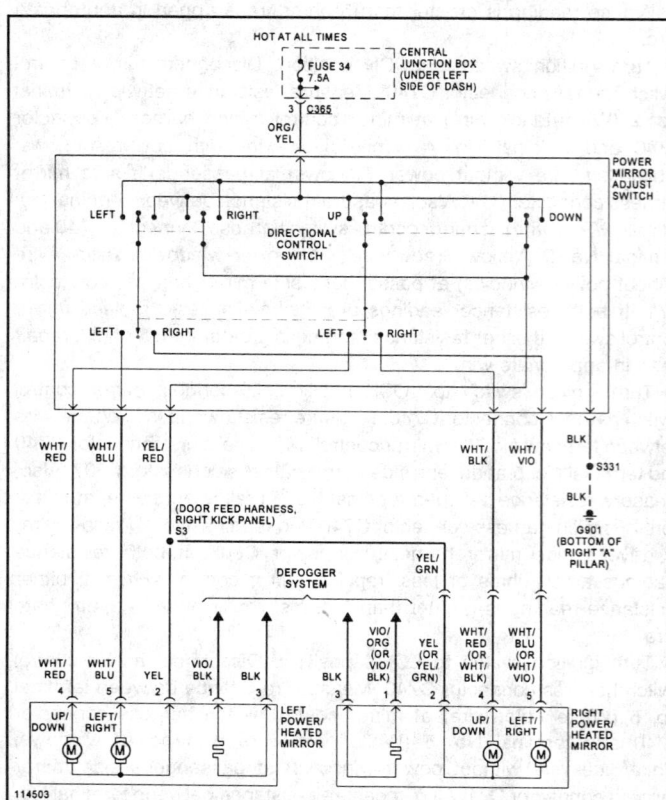

Fig. 4: Power Mirror System Wiring Diagram (Contour & Mystique)

DESCRIPTION & OPERATION

Power side mirror system consists of control switch and mirror assembly with replaceable motor and glass.

TROUBLE SHOOTING

Verify customer complaint by operating power mirrors. Visually inspect for obvious sign of mechanical and electrical damage. If no visual damage is evident, perform appropriate system test. See SYMPTOM CHART table under SYSTEM TESTS. Before performing individual component tests or system tests, check the following for possible cause of system malfunction and repair as necessary:

- Blown fuses or faulty circuit breaker.
- Loose or corroded connectors.
- Damaged wiring.
- Damaged motors.
- Damaged mirror assemblies.
- Faulty switches.

COMPONENT TESTS

MIRROR CONTROL SWITCH

Disconnect mirror control switch harness connector (remove mirror control switch if necessary). Check continuity between mirror control switch terminals with switch in appropriate position. See MIRROR CONTROL SWITCH CONTINUITY table. See Fig. 1. If continuity is not as specified, replace mirror control switch.

MIRROR CONTROL SWITCH CONTINUITY

Switch Position	Continuity Between Terminals
Driver's Side Mirror	
Down	2 & 6; 3 & 4
Left	3 & 4; 5 & 6
Up	2 & 4; 3 & 6
Right	3 & 6; 4 & 5
Passenger's Side Mirror	
Down	1 & 6; 3 & 4
Left	3 & 4; 6 & 7
Up	1 & 4; 3 & 6
Right	3 & 6; 4 & 7

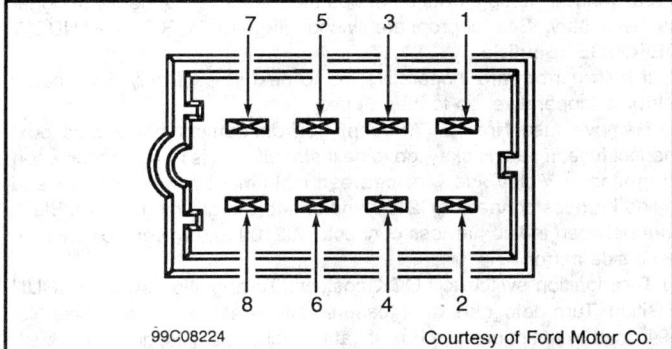

Fig. 1: Identifying Mirror Control Switch Terminals

SYSTEM TESTS

Verify customer complaint by operating power mirrors. Visually inspect for obvious sign of mechanical and electrical damage. If no visual damage is evident, perform appropriate system test. See SYMPTOM CHART table. A digital volt-ohmmeter is required to test the power mirror system.

SYMPTOM CHART

Symptom	Test
Both Mirrors Inoperative	A
Single Mirror Completely Inoperative	B

SYMPTOM CHART (Cont.)

Symptom	Test
Single Mirror Partially Inoperative	C
One Or Both Heated Mirrors Inoperative	D

TEST A: BOTH MIRRORS INOPERATIVE

1) Turn ignition switch to LOCK position. Remove fuse No. 34 (7.5-amp) from instrument panel fuse box. Inspect fuse. If fuse is okay, go to next step. If fuse is blown, repair short to ground in power distribution circuit. See appropriate wiring diagram in POWER DISTRIBUTION article in WIRING DIAGRAMS.

2) Install fuse no. 34. Disconnect mirror control switch harness connector C740. Measure voltage at terminal No. 4 (Orange/Yellow wire) at mirror control switch harness connector C740. See Fig. 2. If battery voltage exists, go to next step. If battery voltage does not exist, repair open in Orange/Yellow wire.

3) Turn ignition switch to LOCK position. Measure resistance between ground and terminal No. 6 (Black wire) at mirror control switch harness connector C740. If resistance is 5 ohms or less, go to next step. If resistance is greater than 5 ohms, repair open in Black wire.

4) Disconnect driver's side mirror harness connector C807. Measure resistance between terminal No. 3 (Yellow/Red wire) at mirror control switch harness connector and terminal No. 2 (Yellow wire) at driver's side mirror harness connector C807. See Figs. 2 and 3. If resistance is 5 ohms or less, replace mirror control switch. If resistance is greater than 5 ohms, repair open in Yellow/Red wire.

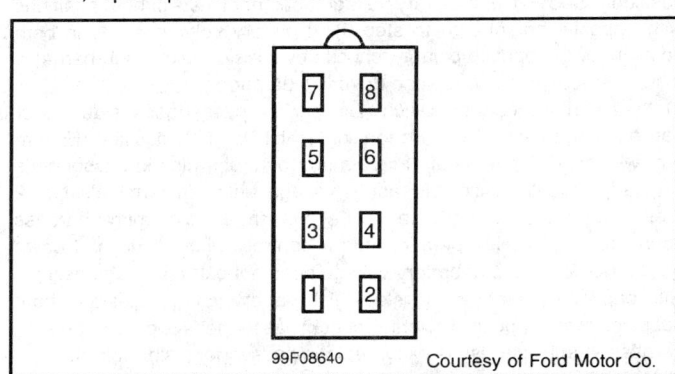

Fig. 2: Identifying Mirror Control Switch Harness Connector C740 Terminals

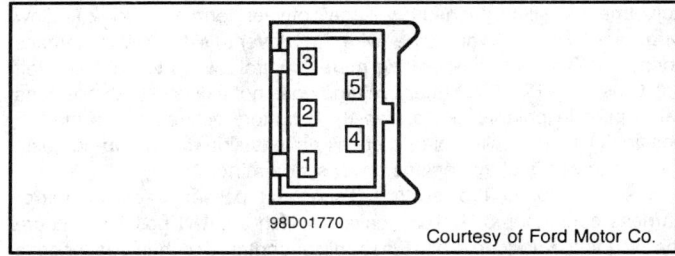

Fig. 3: Identifying Driver's & Passenger's Side Mirror Harness Connector Terminals

TEST B: SINGLE MIRROR COMPLETELY INOPERATIVE

Turn ignition switch to LOCK position. Disconnect mirror control switch harness connector C740. Disconnect inoperative mirror harness connector. Measure resistance between terminal No. 3 (Yellow/Red wire) at mirror control switch harness connector C740 and terminal No. 2 at inoperative mirror harness connector. See Figs. 2 and 3. If resistance is greater than 5 ohms, repair open in appropriate circuit. See WIRING DIAGRAMS. If resistance is 5 ohms or less, replace mirror control switch.

TEST C: SINGLE MIRROR PARTIALLY INOPERATIVE

NOTE: Control circuit between terminal No. 3 (Yellow/Red wire) at mirror control switch harness connector C740 and driver's and passenger's side mirrors changes color at soldered joint S3. Also control circuits between mirror control switch and passenger's side mirror all change color. See WIRING DIAGRAMS.

1) Remove mirror control switch. Test mirror control switch. See MIRROR CONTROL SWITCH under COMPONENT TESTS. If switch is okay, go to appropriate step. See TEST STEP table. If switch is defective, replace mirror control switch.

TEST STEP

Malfunction	Perform Step
Driver's Mirror	
Up/Down	2)
Right/Left	4)
Passenger's Mirror	
Up/Down	3)
Right/Left	5)

2) Install mirror control switch. Disconnect driver's side mirror harness connector C807. Turn ignition switch to RUN position. Ensure rear window defogger is off. Place mirror control switch in driver's side adjustment position. Measure voltage between terminals No. 2 (Yellow wire) and No. 4 (White/Red wire) at driver's side mirror harness connector C807 while operating mirror control switch to up and down positions. *See Fig. 3.* If battery voltage does not exists in both positions with opposite polarity, go to step **6)**. If battery voltage exists in both positions with opposite polarity, check driver's side mirror sub-harness. If sub-harness is okay, replace driver's side mirror.

3) Install mirror control switch. Disconnect passenger's side mirror harness connector C71. Turn ignition switch to RUN position. Ensure rear window defogger is off. Place mirror control switch in passenger's side adjustment position. Measure voltage between terminals No. 2 (Yellow wire) and No. 4 (White wire) at passenger's side mirror harness connector C71 while operating mirror control switch to up and down positions. *See Fig. 3.* If battery voltage does not exists in both positions with opposite polarity, go to step **7)**. If battery voltage exists in both positions with opposite polarity, check passenger's side mirror sub-harness. If sub-harness is okay, replace passenger's side mirror.

4) Install mirror control switch. Disconnect driver's side mirror harness connector C807. Turn ignition switch to RUN position. Ensure rear window defogger is off. Place mirror control switch in driver's side adjustment position. Measure voltage between terminals No. 2 (Yellow wire) and No. 5 (White/Blue wire) at driver's side mirror harness connector C807 while operating mirror control switch to right and left positions. *See Fig. 3.* If battery voltage does not exists in both positions with opposite polarity, go to step **8)**. If battery voltage exists in both positions with opposite polarity, check driver's side mirror sub-harness. If sub-harness is okay, replace driver's side mirror.

5) Install mirror control switch. Disconnect passenger's side mirror harness connector C71. Turn ignition switch to RUN position. Ensure rear window defogger is off. Place mirror control switch in passenger's side adjustment position. Measure voltage between terminals No. 2 (Yellow wire) and No. 5 (White/Red wire) at passenger's side mirror harness connector C71 while operating mirror control switch to right and left positions. *See Fig. 3.* If battery voltage does not exists in both positions with opposite polarity, go to step **9)**. If battery voltage exists in both positions with opposite polarity, check passenger's side mirror sub-harness. If sub-harness is okay, replace passenger's side mirror.

6) Turn ignition switch to LOCK position. Disconnect mirror control switch harness connector C740. Measure resistance in White/Red wire between terminal No. 2 at mirror control switch harness connector C740 and terminal No. 4 at driver's side mirror harness connector C807. Also, measure resistance between terminal No. 3 (Yellow/Red wire) at mirror control switch harness connector C740 and terminal No. 2 (Yellow wire) at driver's side mirror harness connector C807. If both resistance

readings are 5 ohms or less, replace mirror control switch. If either resistance reading is greater than 5 ohms, repair open in appropriate wire.

7) Turn ignition switch to LOCK position. Disconnect mirror control switch harness connector C740. Measure resistance between terminal No. 2 (White/Black wire) at mirror control switch harness connector C740 and terminal No. 4 (White wire) at passenger's side mirror harness connector C71. Also, measure resistance between terminal No. 3 (Yellow/Red wire) at mirror control switch harness connector C740 and terminal No. 2 (Yellow wire) at passenger's side mirror harness connector C71. If both resistance readings are 5 ohms or less, replace mirror control switch. If either resistance reading is greater than 5 ohms, repair open in appropriate wire.

8) Turn ignition switch to LOCK position. Disconnect mirror control switch harness connector C740. Measure resistance in White/Blue wire between terminal No. 5 at mirror control switch harness connector C740 and terminal No. 5 at driver's side mirror harness connector C807. Also, measure resistance between terminal No. 3 (Yellow/Red wire) at mirror control switch harness connector C740 and terminal No. 2 (Yellow wire) at driver's side mirror harness connector C807. If both resistance readings are 5 ohms or less, replace mirror control switch. If either resistance reading is greater than 5 ohms, repair open in appropriate wire.

9) Turn ignition switch to LOCK position. Disconnect mirror control switch harness connector C740. Measure resistance between terminal No. 7 (White/Violet wire) at mirror control switch harness connector C740 and terminal No. 5 (White/Red wire) at passenger's side mirror harness connector C71. Also, measure resistance between terminal No. 3 (Yellow/Red wire) at mirror control switch harness connector C740 and terminal No. 2 (Yellow wire) at passenger's side mirror harness connector C71. If both resistance readings are 5 ohms or less, replace mirror control switch. If either resistance reading is greater than 5 ohms, repair open in appropriate wire.

TEST D: ONE OR BOTH HEATED MIRRORS INOPERATIVE

NOTE: In-line harness connector C2109 in located at bottom of pillar "A" on passenger's side of vehicle.

1) Operate defogger. If rear window defogger operates, go to next step. If rear window defogger does not operate, repair rear window defogger as necessary. See appropriate wiring diagram in REAR WINDOW DEFOGGERS article.

2) If both mirrors are inoperative, go to next step. If only one heated mirror is inoperative, go to step **7)**.

3) Remove fuse No. 19 (7.5-amp) from instrument panel fuse box. Inspect fuse. If fuse is okay, go to next step. If fuse is blown, repair short to ground in Violet/Blue wire between instrument panel fuse box and in-line harness connector C2109 and/or short to ground in Violet/Black wire between in-line harness connector C2109 and driver's or passenger's side mirror.

4) Turn ignition switch to LOCK position. Turn ignition switch to RUN position. Turn defoggers on. Measure voltage at input side of fuse No. 19 in instrument panel fuse box. If battery voltage exists, go to next step. If battery voltage does not exist, repair or replace instrument panel fuse box as necessary.

5) Install fuse No. 19 in instrument panel fuse box. Disconnect driver's side mirror harness connector C807. Turn ignition switch to LOCK position. Turn ignition switch to RUN position. Turn defoggers on. Measure voltage at terminal No. 1 (Violet/Black wire) at driver's side mirror harness connector C807. *See Fig. 3.* If battery voltage exists, go to next step. If battery voltage does not exist, repair open in Violet/Blue wire between instrument panel fuse box and in-line harness connector C2109.

6) Verify with customer that both mirrors stopped working at the same time. If both mirrors did not stop working at the same time, go to next step. If both mirrors stopped working at the same time, check for intermittent open in Violet/Black wire.

7) Disconnect inoperative mirror harness connector. Measure resistance between ground and terminal No. 3 (Black wire) at inoperative mirror harness connector. *See Fig. 3.* If resistance is 5 ohms or less, go to next step. If resistance is greater than 5 ohms, repair open in Black wire.

8) Turn ignition switch to LOCK position. Turn ignition switch to RUN position. Turn defoggers on. Measure voltage at terminal No. 1 (Violet/Black wire) at inoperative mirror harness connector. If battery voltage exists, replace inoperative mirror glass. If battery voltage does not exist, repair open in Violet/Black wire.

REMOVAL & INSTALLATION

SIDE MIRROR ASSEMBLY

Removal & Installation – Remove appropriate door panel. Remove bezel. Remove window inner weather stripping. Detach rubber cover. Disconnect mirror assembly harness connector. Remove mirror attaching screws. Remove mirror assembly. To install, reverse removal procedure.

SIDE MIRROR GLASS

Removal & Installation – Push mirror glass as far down as possible to expose rear of mirror glass. Using a thin flat-bladed screwdriver, release each retaining tang and tilt mirror glass down. Disconnect heated mirror electrical connectors (if equipped). Remove mirror glass. To install, reverse removal procedure.

WIRING DIAGRAMS

NOTE: For heated mirror wiring diagram, see appropriate wiring diagram REAR WINDOW DEFOGGERS article.

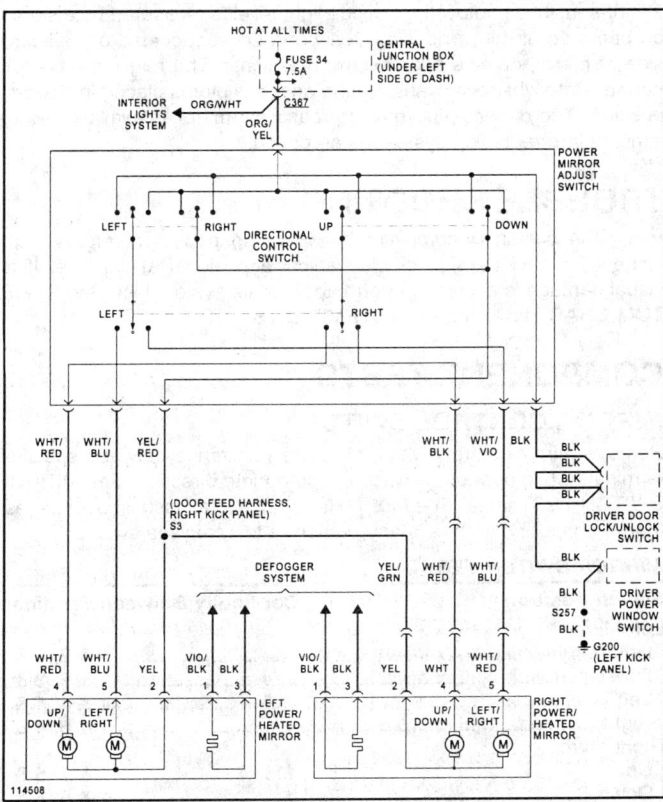

Fig. 4: Power Mirror System Wiring Diagram (Cougar)

1999 ACCESSORIES & EQUIPMENT
Power Mirrors – Crown Victoria & Grand Marquis

DESCRIPTION & OPERATION

Power side view mirror system consists of mirror head with integral reversible servomotor assembly and mirror control switch. Some models are equipped with an electronic dimming rear view mirror.

The optional inside electronic dimming rear view mirror is controlled by 2 light-sensitive photocells. Outside light level is measured by a sensor on backside of mirror housing. A second sensor, located on reflective side of mirror, detects approaching rear lights. The mirror switches to normal state whenever transmission gear selector is placed in Reverse position. The driver's side outside rear view mirror is available with a similar glare reduction system as an option.

TROUBLE SHOOTING

Verify the customer complaint by operating power mirrors. Visually inspect for obvious sign of mechanical and electrical damage. If no visual damage is evident, perform appropriate system test. See SYMPTOM CHART table under SYSTEM TESTS.

COMPONENT TESTS

MIRROR CONTROL SWITCH

Remove mirror control switch. Measure resistance between specified terminals while operating switch in appropriate direction. See MIRROR SWITCH TEST table. *See Fig. 1*. Resistance in all tests should be less than 5 ohms. If switch fails any portion of test, replace switch.

MIRROR SWITCH TEST

Switch Position	Continuity Between Terminals
Left Mirror	
Up	1 & 3; 5 & 6
Down	1 & 6; 3 & 5
Left	1 & 4; 5 & 6
Right	1 & 6; 4 & 5
Right Mirror	
Up	1 & 7; 5 & 6
Down	1 & 6; 5 & 7
Left	1 & 8; 5 & 6
Right	1 & 6; 5 & 8

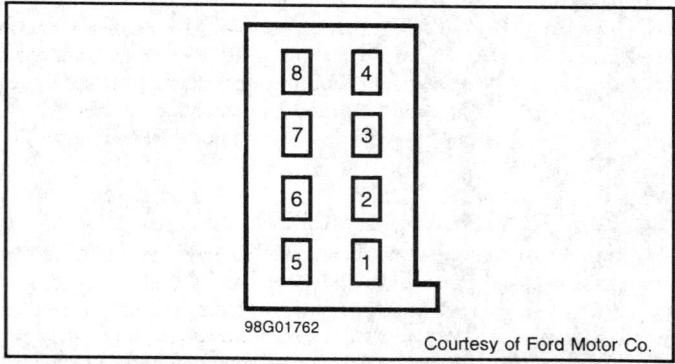

98G01762   Courtesy of Ford Motor Co.

Fig. 1: Identifying Power Mirror Control Switch Terminals

SYSTEM TESTS

SYMPTOM CHART

Symptom	Test
Both Mirrors Inoperative	A
Single Mirror Inoperative	B
Switch Logic Malfunction	C
Auto Dimming Feature Malfunctioning	D

TEST A: BOTH MIRRORS INOPERATIVE

1) Remove mirror control switch and disconnect mirror control switch harness connector C550. Measure voltage at terminal No. 1 (Light Green/Yellow wire) at mirror control switch harness connector C550. *See Fig. 2*. If battery voltage does not exist, go to next step. If battery voltage exists, go to step **5**).

2) Remove fuse No. 8 (15-amp) in instrument panel fuse box. Check fuse. If fuse is blown, go to next step. If fuse is okay, repair open in Light Green/Yellow wire.

3) Measure resistance between ground and terminal No. 1 (Light Green/Yellow wire) at mirror control switch harness connector C550. If resistance is greater than 10 k/ohms, go to next step. If resistance is 10 k/ohms or less, repair short to ground in Light Green/Yellow wire.

NOTE: Yellow wire changes to White wire between mirror control switch and passenger side mirror harness connectors.

4) Measure resistance between ground and terminals No. 3 (Dark Blue wire), No. 4 (Red wire), No. 6 (Yellow wire), No. 7 (Violet wire) and No. 8 (Dark Green wire) at mirror control switch harness connector C550. If all resistance readings are greater than 10 k/ohms, replace mirror control switch. If any resistance readings are 10 k/ohms or less, repair short to ground in appropriate wire or internal short in driver's or passenger's mirror motor.

5) Measure resistance between ground and terminal No. 5 (Black wire) at mirror control switch harness connector C550. If resistance is 5 ohms or less, replace mirror control switch. If resistance is greater than 5 ohms, repair open in Black wire.

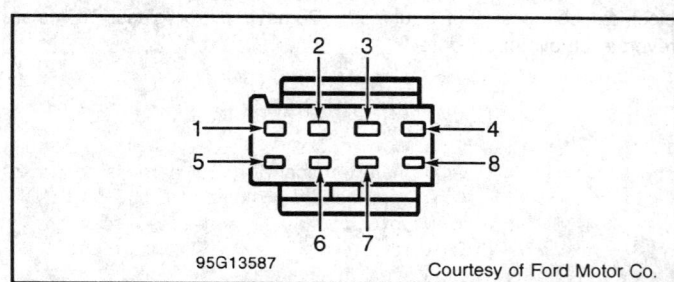

95G13587   Courtesy of Ford Motor Co.

Fig. 2: Identifying Mirror Control Switch Harness Connector C550 Terminals

TEST B: SINGLE MIRROR INOPERATIVE

1) Disconnect inoperative mirror harness connector. Measure voltage at terminal No. 2 (Yellow wire on driver's side; White wire on passenger's side) at mirror harness connector. *See Fig. 3*. Select appropriate mirror on mirror control switch. Operate mirror control switch to the down and right positions. If battery voltage does not exist in either position, go to next step. If battery voltage exists in both positions, go to step **3**).

2) Disconnect mirror control switch harness connector C550. Measure resistance between terminal No. 2 (Yellow wire on driver's side; White wire on passenger's side) at mirror harness connector and terminal No. 6 at mirror control switch harness connector C550. *See Figs. 2 and 3*. If resistance is 5 ohms or less, replace mirror control switch. If resistance is greater than 5 ohms, repair open in appropriate wire.

3) Measure voltage at terminal No. 1 (Dark Blue wire on driver's side; Violet wire on passenger's side) at mirror harness connector. Operate mirror control switch to the up position. If battery voltage does not exist, go to next step for driver's mirror or step **5**) for passenger's mirror. If battery voltage exist, go to step **6**).

4) Disconnect mirror control switch harness connector C550. Measure resistance in Dark Blue wire between terminal No. 1 at mirror harness connector and terminal No. 3 at mirror control switch harness connector C550. *See Figs. 2 and 3*. If resistance is 5 ohms or less, replace mirror control switch. If resistance is greater than 5 ohms, repair open in Dark Blue wire.

5) Disconnect mirror control switch harness connector C550. Measure resistance in Violet wire between terminal No. 1 at mirror harness connector and terminal No. 7 at mirror control switch harness connector C550. *See Figs. 2 and 3*. If resistance is 5 ohms or less, replace mirror control switch. If resistance is greater than 5 ohms, repair open in Violet wire.

1999 ACCESSORIES & EQUIPMENT
Power Mirrors – Crown Victoria & Grand Marquis (Cont.)

FORD
4-943

6) Measure voltage at terminal No. 3 (Red wire on driver's side; Dark Green wire on passenger's side) at mirror harness connector. Operate mirror control switch to the left position. If battery voltage does not exist, go to next step for driver's mirror or step **8)** for passenger's mirror. If battery voltage exist, replace appropriate mirror motor.

7) Disconnect mirror control switch harness connector C550. Measure resistance in Red wire between terminal No. 3 at mirror harness connector and terminal No. 4 at mirror control switch harness connector C550. *See Figs. 2 and 3.* If resistance is 5 ohms or less, replace mirror control switch. If resistance is greater than 5 ohms, repair open in Red wire.

8) Disconnect mirror control switch harness connector C550. Measure resistance in Dark Green wire between terminal No. 3 at mirror harness connector and terminal No. 8 at mirror control switch harness connector C550. *See Figs. 2 and 3.* If resistance is 5 ohms or less, replace mirror control switch. If resistance is greater than 5 ohms, repair open in Dark Green wire.

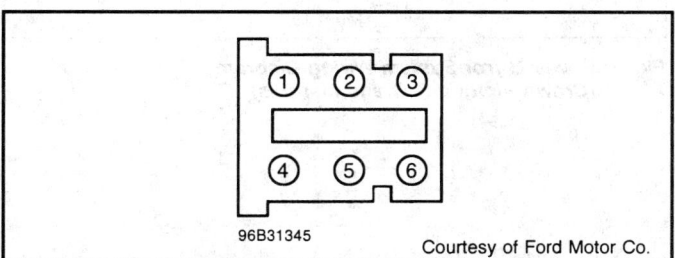

96B31345   Courtesy of Ford Motor Co.

Fig. 3: Identifying Mirror Harness Connector Terminals

TEST C: SWITCH LOGIC MALFUNCTION

1) Disconnect malfunctioning mirror harness connector. Measure voltage or resistance at appropriate terminal at mirror harness connector with mirror control switch in appropriate position. See MIRROR CONTROL CIRCUIT table. *See Fig. 3.* If voltage and resistance readings are not as specified, go to next step. If voltage and resistance readings are as specified, replace appropriate mirror motor.

MIRROR CONTROL CIRCUIT

Terminal	Switch Position	Value
Driver's Mirror		
3	Driver's Mirror Left	Battery Voltage
3	Driver's Mirror Right	5 Ohms Or Less
1	Driver's Mirror Up	Battery Voltage
1	Driver's Mirror Down	5 Ohms Or Less
2	Driver's Mirror Left Or Up	5 Ohms Or Less
2	Driver's Mirror Right Or Down	Battery Voltage
Passenger's Mirror		
3	Passenger's Mirror Left	Battery Voltage
3	Passenger's Mirror Right	5 Ohms Or Less
1	Passenger's Mirror Up	Battery Voltage
1	Passenger's Mirror Down	5 Ohms Or Less
2	Passenger's Mirror Left Or Up	5 Ohms Or Less
2	Passenger's Mirror Right Or Down	Battery Voltage

2) Test mirror control switch. See MIRROR CONTROL SWITCH under COMPONENT TESTS. If mirror control switch is defective, replace mirror control switch. If mirror control switch is okay, repair appropriate circuit(s) between mirror control switch and appropriate mirror.

TEST D: AUTO DIMMING FEATURE MALFUNCTION

1) Turn ignition switch to RUN position. Place gear selector in Reverse. If reverse lights operate, go to next step. If reverse lights do not operate, repair reverse lights as necessary. See appropriate wiring diagram in BACK-UP LIGHTS article.

2) Turn ignition switch to LOCK position. Disconnect inside rear view mirror harness connector C900. Turn ignition switch to RUN position. Measure voltage at terminal No. 7 (Violet/Orange wire) at inside rear view mirror harness connector C900. *See Fig. 4.* If battery voltage exists, go to next step. If battery voltage does not exists, repair open in Violet/Orange wire.

3) Turn ignition switch to LOCK position. Measure resistance between ground and terminal No. 6 (Black wire) at inside mirror harness connector. If resistance is 5 ohms or less, go to next step. If resistance is greater than 5 ohms, repair open in Black wire.

4) Turn ignition switch to RUN position. Measure voltage at terminal No. 5 (Black/Pink wire) at inside mirror harness connector C900. Battery voltage should exists when transmission is in Reverse and battery voltage should not exist with transmission in any other gear. If voltage is as specified, replace inside rear view mirror. If voltage is not as specified, repair open in Black/Pink wire.

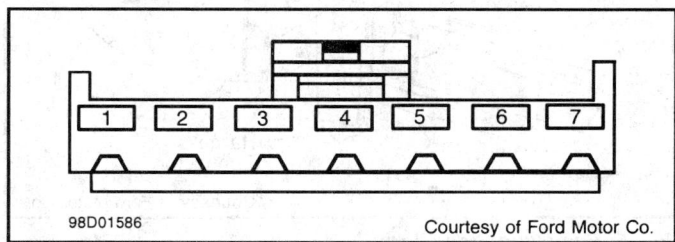

98D01586   Courtesy of Ford Motor Co.

Fig. 4: Identifying Inside Mirror Harness Connector C900 Terminals

REMOVAL & INSTALLATION

WARNING: When battery is disconnected, vehicle computer and memory systems may lose memory data. Driveability problems may exist until computer systems have completed a relearn cycle. See COMPUTER RELEARN PROCEDURES article in GENERAL INFORMATION before disconnecting battery.

INSIDE MIRROR ASSEMBLY

Removal & Installation – Disconnect negative battery cable. Disconnect harness connector (if equipped). Insert small flat-blade screwdriver in slot on bottom of mirror, between mirror bracket and mirror base. Pull screwdriver rearward until mirror snaps off mirror bracket. To install, slide mirror downward onto mirror bracket until it snaps into place.

SIDE MIRROR ASSEMBLY

Removal & Installation – Disconnect negative battery cable. Remove door panel. Remove mirror mounting hole cover. *See Fig. 5.* Disconnect mirror wiring harness connector. Remove mirror attaching nuts. Remove mirror assembly while guiding wiring and connector through hole in door. To install, reverse removal procedure. Tighten nuts to 71-88 INCH lbs. (8-10 N.m).

SIDE MIRROR GLASS & MOTOR

Removal & Installation – Point mirror glass as far inward as possible to allow clearance between glass and mirror housing at outer edge of mirror. Insert fingers into clearance, and pull mirror glass. If fingers will not fit between glass and housing, use a screwdriver and cloth to pry mirror glass out. Glass will unsnap without being damaged. Disconnect heater wires (if equipped). Remove motor attaching screws. Unplug motor connector, and remove motor. To install, reverse removal procedure. Ensure mirror glass locking tabs align before snapping in glass.

MIRROR CONTROL SWITCH

Removal & Installation – Pry out regulator switch plate assembly from armrest. Disconnect mirror control switch harness connector. Depress retaining clips on switch housing. Push switch out of regulator switch plate. Remove switch. To install, reverse removal procedure.

FORD
4-944

1999 ACCESSORIES & EQUIPMENT
Power Mirrors – Crown Victoria & Grand Marquis (Cont.)

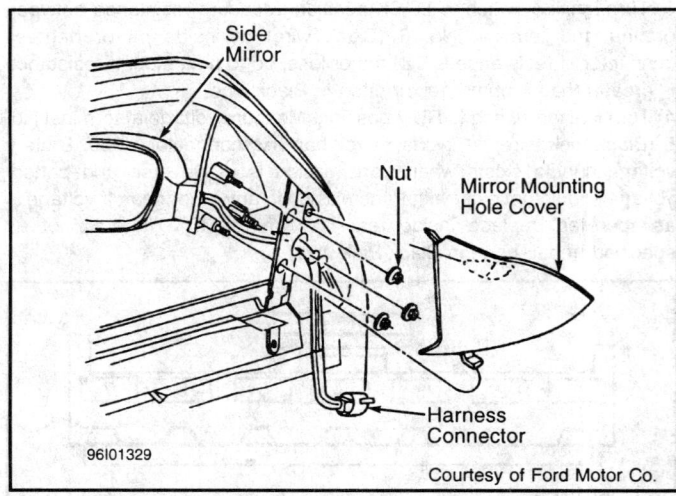

Fig. 5: Removing Side Mirror

WIRING DIAGRAMS

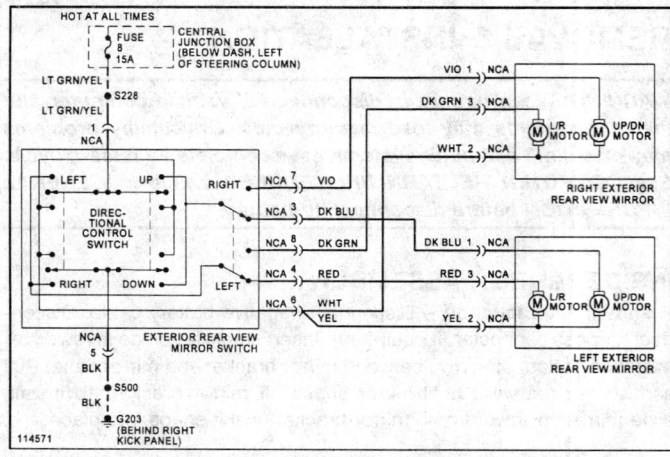

Fig. 6: Automatic Day/Night Mirror System Wiring Diagram (Crown Victoria & Grand Marquis)

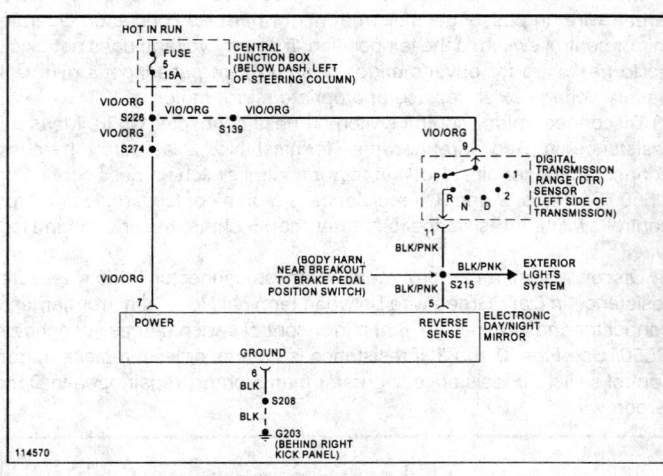

Fig. 7: Power Mirror System Wiring Diagram (Crown Victoria & Grand Marquis)

NOTE: This article includes Cutaway and RV Cutaway.

DESCRIPTION

Power side view mirror system consists of mirror head with integral reversible servomotor assembly and mirror control switch.

TROUBLE SHOOTING

Before performing individual component tests or system tests, check the following for possible cause of system malfunction and repair as necessary:

- Blown fuses.
- Loose or corroded connectors.
- Damaged wiring.
- Damaged motors.
- Damaged mirror assemblies.
- Faulty switches.

COMPONENT TESTS

MIRROR CONTROL SWITCH

Remove mirror control switch. Check for continuity between specified terminals while operating switch in appropriate direction. See appropriate MIRROR SWITCH TEST table. *See Fig. 1 or 2.* Continuity should exist between specified terminals. If continuity does not exist as specified, replace switch.

MIRROR SWITCH TEST (WITH DOOR TRIM)

Switch Position	Continuity Between Terminals
Driver Mirror	
Up	1 & 7; 5 & 6
Down	1 & 6; 5 & 7
Left	1 & 4; 5 & 6
Right	1 & 6; 4 & 5
Passenger Mirror	
Up	1 & 8; 5 & 6
Down	1 & 6; 5 & 8
Left	1 & 3; 5 & 6
Right	1 & 6; 3 & 5

MIRROR SWITCH TEST (WITHOUT DOOR TRIM)

Switch Position	Continuity Between Terminals
Driver Mirror	
Up	1 & 5; 2 & 4
Down	1 & 4; 2 & 5
Left	1 & 5; 2 & 8
Right	1 & 8; 2 & 5
Passenger Mirror	
Up	1 & 5; 2 & 3
Down	1 & 3; 2 & 5
Left	1 & 5; 2 & 7
Right	1 & 7; 2 & 5

SYSTEM TESTS

Verify customer complaint by operating power mirrors. Visually inspect for obvious sign of mechanical and electrical damage. If no visual damage is evident, perform appropriate system test. See SYMPTOM CHART table. A digital volt-ohmmeter is required to test power mirror system.

SYMPTOM CHART

Symptom	Test
Both Mirrors Inoperative	A
One Mirror Inoperative	B

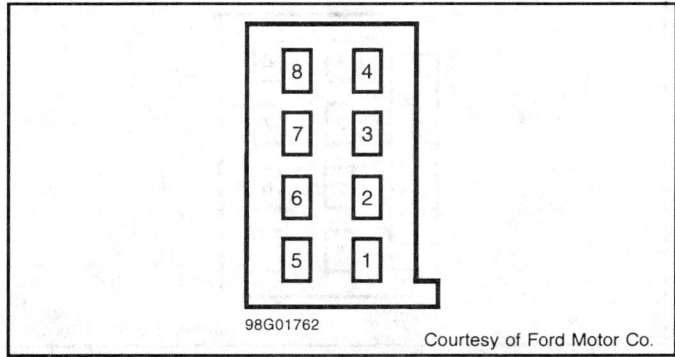

98G01762   Courtesy of Ford Motor Co.

Fig. 1: Identifying Power Mirror Control Switch Terminals (With Door Trim)

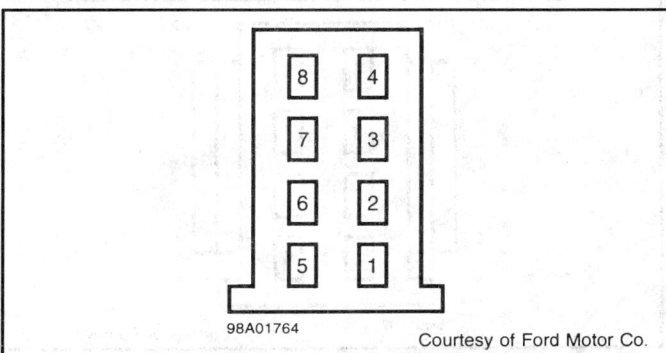

98A01764   Courtesy of Ford Motor Co.

Fig. 2: Identifying Power Mirror Control Switch Terminals (Without Door Trim)

TEST A: BOTH SIDE MIRRORS INOPERATIVE

1) Remove mirror control switch and disconnect harness connector. Test mirror control switch. See MIRROR CONTROL SWITCH under COMPONENT TESTS. If switch is okay, go to next step. If switch is defective, replace mirror control switch.

2) Measure voltage between ground and Light Green/Yellow wire at mirror control switch harness connector. If battery voltage exists, go to next step. If battery voltage does not exist, repair Light Green/Yellow wire.

3) Measure resistance between ground and Black wire at mirror control switch harness connector. If resistance is 5 ohms or less, repair Yellow wire between mirrors and mirror control switch. If resistance is greater than 5 ohms, repair open Black wire.

TEST B: ONE SIDE MIRROR INOPERATIVE

1) Test mirror control switch. See MIRROR CONTROL SWITCH under COMPONENT TESTS. If switch is okay and left mirror is inoperative, go to next step. If switch is okay and right mirror is inoperative go to step **3)**. If switch is defective, replace mirror control switch.

2) Measure resistance of 3 wires between mirror control switch harness connector and driver mirror harness connector. See WIRING DIAGRAMS table. *See Figs. 3 and 4.* If any resistance reading is greater than 5 ohms, repair open in appropriate wire. If all resistance readings are 5 ohms or less, replace driver mirror assembly.

3) Measure resistance of 3 wires between mirror control switch harness connector and passenger mirror harness connector. See WIRING DIAGRAMS table. If any resistance reading is greater than 5 ohms, repair open in appropriate wire. If all resistance readings are 5 ohms or less, replace passenger mirror assembly.

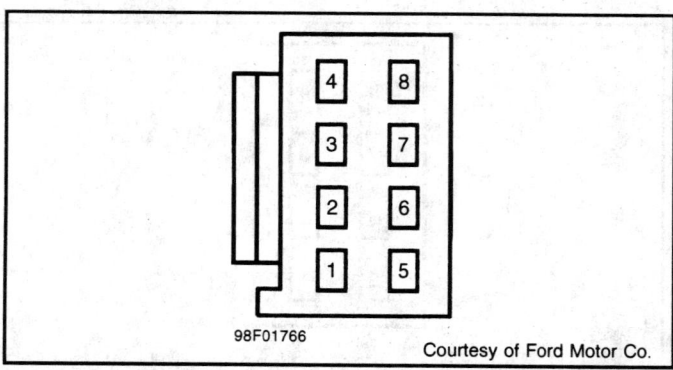

Fig. 3: Identifying Mirror Control Switch Harness Connector Terminals (With Door Trim)

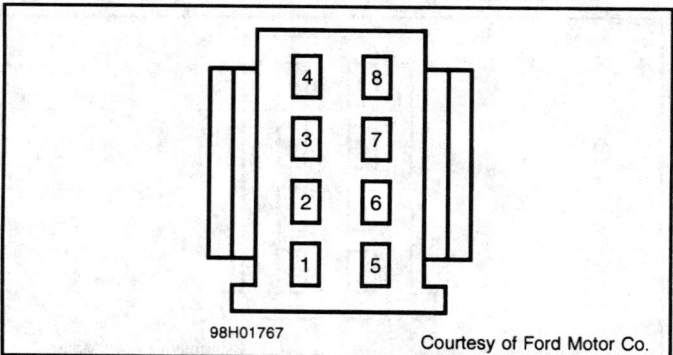

Fig. 4: Identifying Mirror Control Switch Harness Connector Terminals (Without Door Trim)

REMOVAL & INSTALLATION

WARNING: When battery is disconnected, vehicle computer and memory systems may lose memory data. Driveability problems may exist until computer systems have completed a relearn cycle. See COMPUTER RELEARN PROCEDURES article in GENERAL INFORMATION before disconnecting battery.

SIDE MIRROR ASSEMBLY

Removal & Installation – Disconnect negative battery cable. Remove mirror mounting hole cover. *See Fig. 5.* Remove door panel. Remove and disconnect speaker. Disconnect mirror wiring harness connector. Remove mirror attaching nuts. Remove mirror assembly while guiding wiring and connector through hole in door. To install, reverse removal procedure. Tighten nuts to approximately 53 INCH lbs. (6 N.m).

MIRROR CONTROL SWITCH

Removal & Installation – Pry control switch assembly from driver arm rest. Disconnect mirror harness connector. Depress retaining clips on switch housing. Push base of switch out of switch assembly plate. Remove switch. To install, reverse removal procedure.

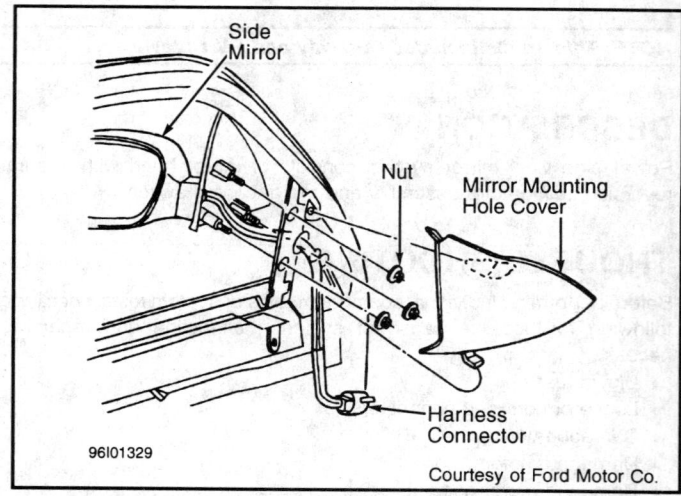

Fig. 5: Removing Side Mirror

WIRING DIAGRAMS

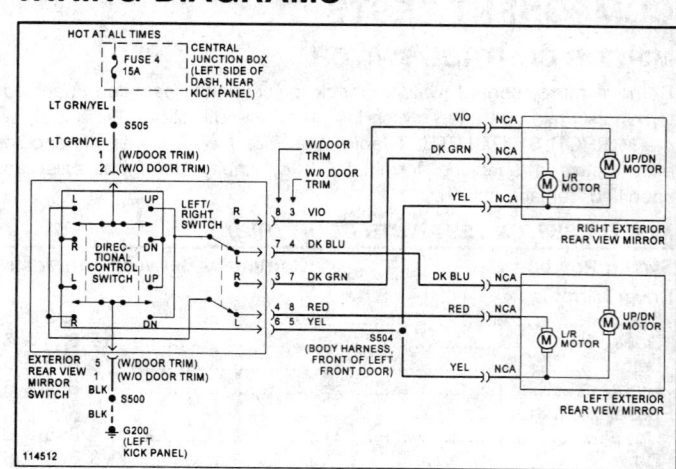

Fig. 6: Power Mirror System Wiring Diagram (Econoline)

DESCRIPTION & OPERATION

Power side view mirror system consists of mirror head with integral servo motor assembly and mirror control switch. Operating mirror control switch moves mirror up, down, left and right.

COMPONENT LOCATIONS

COMPONENT LOCATIONS

Component	Location
Data Link Connector (DLC)	Below Driver's Side Of Instrument Panel, To Right Of Steering Column
Mirror Switch	In Driver's Door Panel Arm Rest
Central Junction Box	Below Left Side Of Instrument Panel
Power Distribution Box	Left Side Of Engine Compartment, Above Wheelwell
Powertrain Control Module (PCM)	In Center Console Below Shifter

TROUBLE SHOOTING

Verify customer concern by operating power mirrors. Ensure battery is fully charged. Visually inspect the following components for physical or electrical damage.

Mechanical:
- Mirror Control Switch
- Mirror Assembly

Electrical:
- RADIO Fuse (5-Amp) On Coupe
- MIRR Fuse (5-Amp) On Sedan And Wagon
- Mirror Control Switch
- Mirror Assembly
- Loose Or Corroded Connections
- Inspect wiring harness for obvious signs of shorts, opens, bad connections or damage.

If inspection reveals an obvious problem which can be easily serviced, correct malfunction before continuing inspection and verification. If problem is not visually evident, go to SYSTEM TESTS to continue diagnosis.

COMPONENT TESTS

MIRROR CONTROL SWITCH

Remove mirror control switch. See MIRROR CONTROL SWITCH under REMOVAL & INSTALLATION. Measure resistance between specified terminals while operating switch in appropriate direction. See MIRROR SWITCH TEST table. Resistance in all tests should be less than 5 ohms. If switch fails any portion of test, replace switch. *See Fig. 1.*

MIRROR SWITCH TEST

Switch Position	Continuity Between Terminals
Left Mirror	
Up	1 & 6; 5 & 7
Down	1 & 7; 5 & 6
Left	1 & 7; 4 & 5
Right	1 & 4; 5 & 7
Right Mirror	
Up	1 & 6; 5 & 8
Down	1 & 8; 5 & 6
Left	1 & 8; 3 & 5
Right	1 & 3; 5 & 8

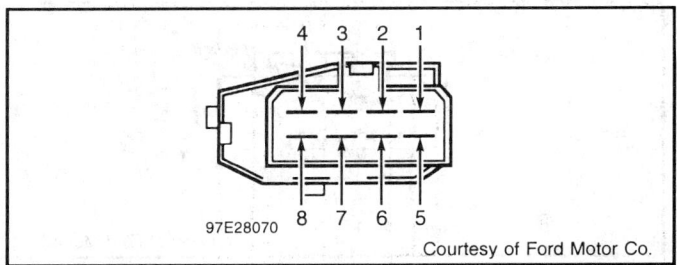

97E28070

Courtesy of Ford Motor Co.

Fig. 1: Identifying Power Mirror Control Switch Terminals

SYSTEM TESTS

CAUTION: When battery is disconnected or modules are replaced, vehicle computer and memory systems may lose memory data. Driveability problems may exist until computer systems have completed a relearn cycle. See COMPUTER RELEARN PROCEDURES article in GENERAL INFORMATION before disconnecting battery.

NOTE: Before beginning system tests, perform TROUBLE SHOOTING.

NOTE: After repairs are complete, ensure all component are properly installed and all harness connectors are connected properly and repeat data link diagnostic test. See DATA LINK DIAGNOSTIC TEST under COMMUNICATIONS NETWORK DIAGNOSTICS in MODULE COMMUNICATIONS NETWORK – ESCORT & TRACER article.

Verify the customer complaint by operating power mirror. Visually inspect for obvious sign of mechanical and electrical damage. If no visual damage is evident, perform appropriate system test. See SYSTEM TEST INDEX table. A Digital Volt-Ohmmeter (DVOM) is required to test the power mirror system. See WIRING DIAGRAMS for terminal numbers.

SYSTEM TEST INDEX

Symptom	Go To
Both Mirrors Inoperative	TEST A
Single Mirror Inoperative	TEST B
Single Mirror Inoperative With Switch Logic	TEST C

TEST A: BOTH MIRRORS INOPERATIVE

1) Turn ignition off. Check MIRR fuse (5-amp) on sedan and wagon or RADIO fuse (5-amp) on coupe, located in central junction box. If fuse is good, go to next step. If fuse is blown, repair short to ground in Blue/Black wire between central junction box and mirror switch.

2) Ensure fuse is installed. Disconnect mirror switch harness connector. Turn ignition switch to RUN position. Measure voltage between ground and mirror switch harness connector terminal No. 1 (Blue/Black wire). *See Fig. 2.* If battery voltage exists, go to next step. If battery voltage does not exist, repair open in Blue/Black wire between central junction box and mirror switch.

3) Measure resistance between ground and mirror switch harness connector terminal No. 5 (Black wire). If resistance is 5 ohms or less, replace mirror switch. If resistance is greater than 5 ohms, repair open in Black wire.

TEST B: SINGLE MIRROR INOPERATIVE

1) Remove mirror switch. Test mirror switch. See MIRROR CONTROL SWITCH under COMPONENT TESTS. If switch is okay, go to next step for driver mirror or step **3)** for passenger mirror. If switch is defective, replace mirror switch.

2) Turn ignition off. Disconnect mirror switch harness connector. Disconnect driver mirror harness connector. Measure resistance between mirror switch harness connector terminal No. 7 (Light Green wire) and driver mirror harness connector Yellow wire. If resistance reading is 5

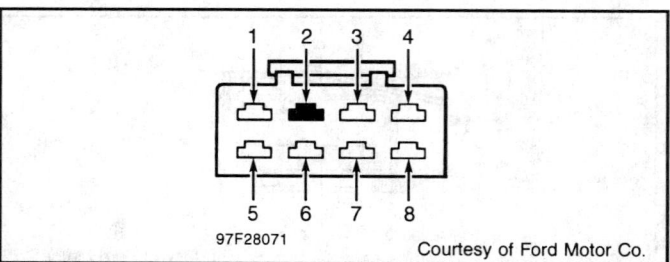

Fig. 2: Identifying Power Mirror Control Switch Harness Connector Terminals

ohms or less, replace driver mirror assembly. See SIDE MIRROR ASSEMBLY under REMOVAL & INSTALLATION. If resistance reading is greater than 5 ohms, repair open in appropriate wire.

3) Turn ignition off. Disconnect mirror switch harness connector. Disconnect passenger mirror harness connector. Measure resistance between mirror switch harness connector terminal No. 8 (Light Green/Black wire) and passenger mirror harness connector Yellow wire. If resistance reading is 5 ohms or less, replace passenger mirror assembly. See SIDE MIRROR ASSEMBLY under REMOVAL & INSTALLATION. If resistance reading is greater than 5 ohms, repair open in appropriate wire.

TEST C: SINGLE MIRROR INOPERATIVE WITH SWITCH LOGIC

1) Turn ignition off. Disconnect mirror switch harness connector. Test mirror switch. See MIRROR CONTROL SWITCH under COMPONENT TESTS. If switch is okay, go to next step for driver mirror or step **3)** for passenger mirror. If switch is defective, replace mirror switch.

2) Turn ignition off. Disconnect mirror switch harness connector. Disconnect driver mirror harness connector. Measure resistance of Brown wire between mirror switch harness connector terminal No. 6 and driver mirror harness connector. Measure resistance of Brown/Yellow wire between mirror switch harness connector terminal No. 4 and driver mirror harness connector. If all resistance readings are 5 ohms or less, replace driver mirror assembly. See SIDE MIRROR ASSEMBLY under REMOVAL & INSTALLATION. If any resistance reading is greater than 5 ohms, repair open in appropriate wire.

3) Turn ignition off. Disconnect mirror switch harness connector. Disconnect passenger mirror harness connector. Measure resistance between mirror switch harness connector terminal No. 3 (Brown/Black wire) and passenger mirror harness connector Black wire. Measure resistance of Brown wire between mirror switch harness connector terminal No. 6 and passenger mirror harness connector. If all resistance readings are 5 ohms or less, replace passenger mirror assembly. See SIDE MIRROR ASSEMBLY under REMOVAL & INSTALLATION. If any resistance reading is greater than 5 ohms, repair open in appropriate wire.

REMOVAL & INSTALLATION

CAUTION: When battery is disconnected, vehicle computer and memory systems may lose memory data. Driveability problems may exist until computer systems have completed a relearn cycle. See COMPUTER RELEARN PROCEDURES article in GENERAL INFORMATION before disconnecting battery.

SIDE MIRROR ASSEMBLY

Removal & Installation – 1) Disconnect negative battery cable. Remove mirror mounting hole trim from inside vehicle. Remove door pull cup retaining screw. Remove screw cap and screw from inside door handle and disconnect door latch remote control link.

2) Remove 2 push pins from front door trim panel. Push inboard, then upward to remove front door trim panel. Remove water shield. Disconnect power mirror electrical connector. Remove 3 mirror assembly retaining screws. Remove mirror assembly. To install, reverse removal procedure. Tighten mirror assembly retaining screws to 30-40 INCH lbs. (3.4-4.6 N.m).

SIDE MIRROR GLASS & MOTOR

Removal & Installation – Mirror glass and motor must be replaced as an assembly. See SIDE MIRROR ASSEMBLY.

MIRROR CONTROL SWITCH

Removal & Installation – Mirror control switch is located on instrument panel, left of steering column. Removal and installation procedure is not available from manufacturer.

WIRING DIAGRAMS

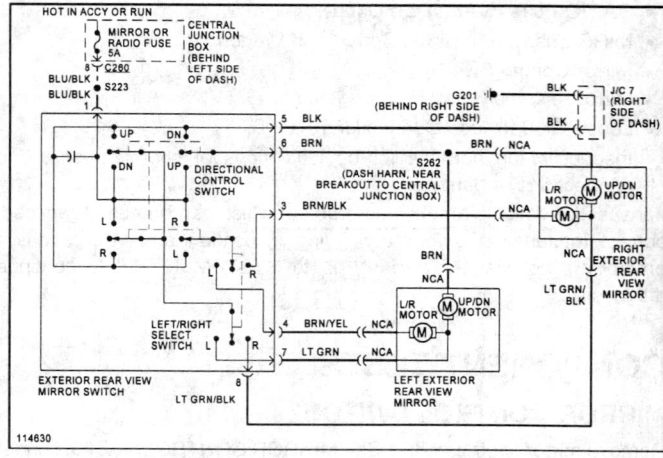

Fig. 3: Power Mirror System Wiring Diagram (Escort & Tracer)

DESCRIPTION & OPERATION

Power side view mirror system consists of mirror head with integral reversible servomotor assembly and mirror control switch.

TROUBLE SHOOTING

Before performing individual component tests or diagnostic tests, check the following for possible cause of system malfunction and repair as necessary:

- Blown fuses or faulty circuit breaker.
- Loose or corroded connectors.
- Damaged wiring.
- Damaged motors.
- Damaged mirror assemblies.
- Faulty switches.

SYSTEM TESTS

Verify the customer complaint by operating power mirrors. Visually inspect for obvious sign of mechanical and electrical damage. If no visual damage is evident, perform appropriate diagnostic test. See SYMPTOM CHART table. A digital volt-ohmmeter is required to test the power mirror system.

SYMPTOM CHART

Symptom	Test
Both Mirrors Inoperative	A
Single Mirror Inoperative	B
Single Mirror Malfunction With Switch Logic	C

TEST A: BOTH MIRRORS INOPERATIVE

1) Remove mirror control switch and disconnect harness connector. Measure voltage between ground and mirror control switch harness connector terminal No. 1 (Orange/Light Green wire). *See Fig. 1.* If battery voltage exists, go to next step. If battery voltage does not exist, repair Orange/Light Green wire, connectors or central junction fox fuse No. 4 (15-amp). See WIRING DIAGRAMS. Check system for normal operation.

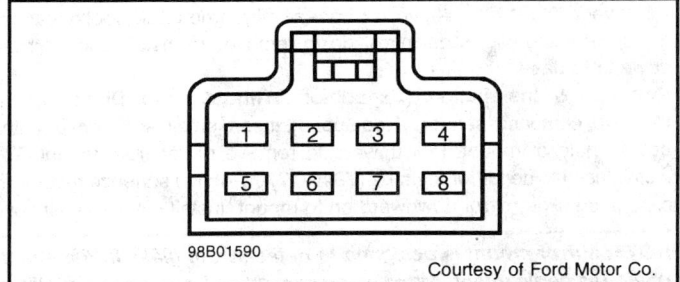

Fig. 1: Identifying Mirror Control Switch Harness Connector Terminals

2) Measure resistance between ground and mirror control switch harness connector terminal No. 5 (Black wire). *See Fig. 1.* If resistance less than 5 ohms, go to next step. If resistance is 5 ohms or greater, repair open in Black wire or ground connection. See WIRING DIAGRAMS. Check system for normal operation.

3) Turn ignition switch to Run position. Measure voltage between ground and mirror control switch harness connector terminal No. 6. *See Fig. 1.* If no voltage is present, go to next step. If any voltage is present, repair short to power in Yellow wire. See WIRING DIAGRAMS. Check system for normal operation.

4) Turn ignition off. Measure resistance between ground and mirror control switch harness connector terminal No. 6. *See Fig. 1.* If resistance is greater than 10 k/ohms, go to next step. If resistance is 10 k/ohms or less, repair short to ground in Yellow wire. See WIRING DIAGRAMS. Check system for normal operation.

5) Disconnect driver side mirror harness connector. Measure resistance of Yellow wire between driver side mirror harness connector terminal No. 2 and mirror control switch harness connector terminal No. 6. *See Figs. 1 and 2.* If resistance is less than 5 ohms, install new mirror control switch. If resistance is 5 ohms or greater, repair open or high resistance in Yellow wire. See WIRING DIAGRAMS. Check system for normal operation.

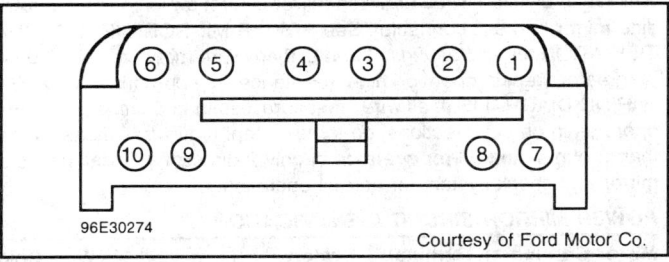

Fig. 2: Identifying Driver & Passenger Mirror Harness Connector Terminals

TEST B: SINGLE MIRROR INOPERATIVE

1) Attempt to operate mirrors from switch. If passenger side mirror is inoperative, go to next step. If driver side mirror is inoperative, go to step **4)**.

2) Turn ignition off. Disconnect passenger side mirror harness connector. Remove mirror control switch and disconnect harness connector. Measure resistance of Yellow wire between passenger side mirror harness connector terminal No. 2 and mirror control switch harness connector terminal No. 6. *See Figs. 1 and 2.* If resistance is less than 5 ohms, go to next step. If resistance is 5 ohms or greater, repair open or high resistance in Yellow wire. See WIRING DIAGRAMS. Check system for normal operation.

3) Place mirror control switch in right mirror position. Measure resistance between mirror control switch terminals No. 1 and 8 while holding control switch in UP position. *See Fig. 3.* If resistance is less than 5 ohms, install new passenger side mirror. If resistance is 5 ohms or greater, install new mirror control switch. Check system for normal operation.

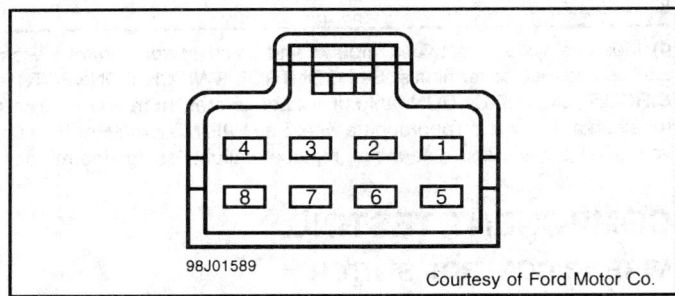

Fig. 3: Identifying Power Mirror Control Switch Terminals

4) Turn ignition off. Disconnect driver side mirror harness connector. Remove mirror control switch and disconnect harness connector. Measure resistance of Yellow wire between driver side mirror harness connector terminal No. 2 and mirror control switch harness connector terminal No. 6. *See Figs. 1 and 2.* If resistance is less than 5 ohms, go to next step. If resistance is 5 ohms or greater, repair open or high resistance in Yellow wire. See WIRING DIAGRAMS. Check system for normal operation.

5) Place mirror control switch in left mirror position. Measure resistance between mirror control switch terminals No. 1 and 7 while holding control switch in UP position. *See Fig. 3.* If resistance is less than 5 ohms, install new driver side mirror. If resistance is 5 ohms or greater, install new mirror control switch. Check system for normal operation.

FORD
4-950

1999 ACCESSORIES & EQUIPMENT
Power Mirrors
Expedition, & F150 & F250 Light-Duty Pickup (Cont.)

TEST C: SINGLE MIRROR MALFUNCTION WITH SWITCH LOGIC

1) Turn ignition off. Remove mirror control switch and disconnect harness connector. Test switch. See MIRROR CONTROL SWITCH under COMPONENT TESTING. Replace as necessary. If control switch is okay, go to next step.

2) Disconnect inoperative side mirror harness connector. Measure resistance of listed wires between mirror control switch and inoperative side mirror harness connector. See POWER MIRROR CIRCUIT IDENTIFICATION table. *See Figs. 1 and 2.* If any wire measures are 5 ohms or greater, repair open or high resistance in appropriate wire. See WIRING DIAGRAMS. If all wires measure less than 5 ohms, and mirror operates in only 3 directions, go to next step. If all wires measure less than 5 ohms, and mirror operates in only 2 directions, install new side mirror and check system for normal operation.

POWER MIRROR CIRCUIT IDENTIFICATION

Mirror Connector Terminal	Switch Terminal	Wire Color
Driver Side Mirror		
1	4	Red
4	7	Dark Blue
2	6	Yellow
Passenger Side Mirror		
2	6	Yellow
1	3	Dark Green
4	8	Purple

3) Turn ignition off. Measure resistance between ground and listed mirror control switch harness connector terminals. See CONTROL SWITCH CONNECTOR CIRCUIT IDENTIFICATION table. If resistance in all circuits is greater than 10 k/ohms, go to next step. If resistance in any circuit is 10 k/ohms or less, repair short to ground in appropriate wire. See WIRING DIAGRAMS.

CONTROL SWITCH CONNECTOR CIRCUIT IDENTIFICATION

Terminal	Wire Color
3	Dark Green
4	Red
7	Dark Blue
8	Purple

4) Measure voltage between ground and listed mirror control switch harness connector terminals. See CONTROL SWITCH CONNECTOR CIRCUIT IDENTIFICATION table. If voltage is present at any terminal, repair short to power in appropriate wire. See WIRING DIAGRAMS. If no voltage is present at any terminal, replace malfunctioning side mirror.

COMPONENT TESTING

MIRROR CONTROL SWITCH

Remove mirror control switch. Measure resistance between specified terminals while operating switch in appropriate direction. See MIRROR SWITCH TEST table. *See Fig. 3.* Resistance in all tests should be less than 5 ohms. If switch fails any portion of test, replace switch.

MIRROR SWITCH TEST

Switch Position	Continuity Between Terminals
Driver Mirror Position	
Up	1 & 7; 5 & 6
Down	1 & 6; 5 & 7
Left	1 & 4; 5 & 6
Right	1 & 6; 4 & 5
Passenger Mirror Position	
Up	1 & 8; 5 & 6
Down	1 & 6; 5 & 8
Left	1 & 3; 5 & 6
Right	1 & 6; 3 & 5

REMOVAL & INSTALLATION

WARNING: When battery is disconnected, vehicle computer and memory systems may lose memory data. Driveability problems may exist until computer systems have completed a relearn cycle. See COMPUTER RELEARN PROCEDURES article in GENERAL INFORMATION before disconnecting battery.

SIDE MIRROR ASSEMBLY

Removal & Installation – Disconnect negative battery cable. Remove appropriate door panel. Disconnect mirror harness connectors. Disengage wiring clips. Remove 3 mirror retaining nuts. Remove mirror. To install, reverse removal procedure. Tighten retaining nuts to 53-71 INCH lbs. (6-8 N.m).

SIDE MIRROR GLASS

Removal – Position mirror in position to obtain gap between lower inside edge and housing. Disengage power side mirror motor jack screws from the mirror backing plate. Carefully pry glass from mirror assembly by pulling on outboard edge. Disconnect mirror heater harness connector, if equipped. Disconnect motor assembly harness connector. Remove friction pins from mirror backing plate.

Installation – Using a heat gun, warm mirror backing plate sockets at top and outboard edges. Install friction pins. Rotate power side mirror jackscrews in housing with locator tabs facing center of housing. Push power side mirror jackscrews into mirror housing until they bottom out. Using heat gun, warm remaining backing plate sockets. Connect harness connector, if equipped. Install mirror glass by applying sufficient force to the mirror glass until mirror backing plate snaps into center pivot of mirror housing. Apply sufficient force at lower and inboard edges of mirror to snap jackscrews into backing plate. Check mirror for normal operation.

INTERIOR REAR VIEW MIRROR

Removal & Installation (Pickup) – Insert Interior Rear View Mirror Remover (T91T-17700-A), up into base of mirror mount. As tool releases mirror retaining clip, slide mirror up to remove. To install, slide mirror down onto base.

Removal & Installation (Expedition Without Auto Dimming) – Remove compass sensor, if equipped. Insert small screwdriver into bottom hole of mount. Pull upward to remove mirror from mount. To install, use Inside Mirror Installer (T94P-17700-AH) to squeeze retaining clips, then slide mirror downward on to mount. Install compass sensor.

NOTE: Mirror mount is designed to detach from glass in the event of air bag deployment. Avoid using excessive force when installing mirror.

Removal & Installation (Expedition With Auto Dimming) – Remove compass sensor, if equipped. Disconnect mirror electrical connector. Rotate mirror counterclockwise until the tube assembly bottoms out and the spring releases from the mounting button. To install, position mirror on the mounting button. While keeping mirror parallel to windshield surface, install mirror downward onto the rear view mirror bracket. Use Inside Mirror Installer (T94P-17700-AH) to squeeze retaining clips, then slide mirror downward on to mount. Install compass sensor.

1999 ACCESSORIES & EQUIPMENT
Power Mirrors
Expedition, & F150 & F250 Light-Duty Pickup (Cont.)

FORD
4-951

WIRING DIAGRAMS

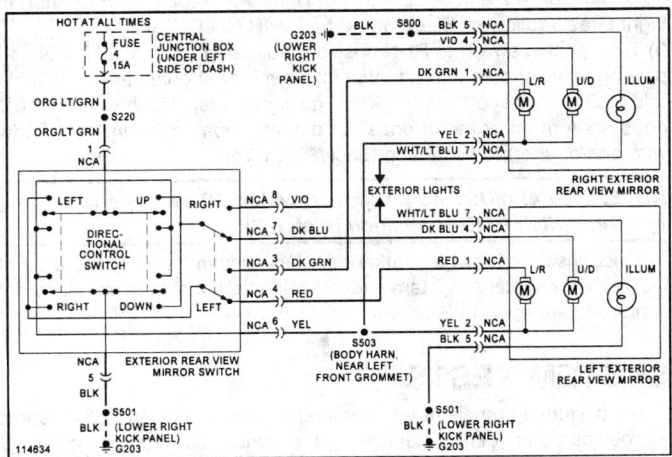

**Fig. 4: Power Mirror System Wiring Diagram
(Expedition & Navigator)**

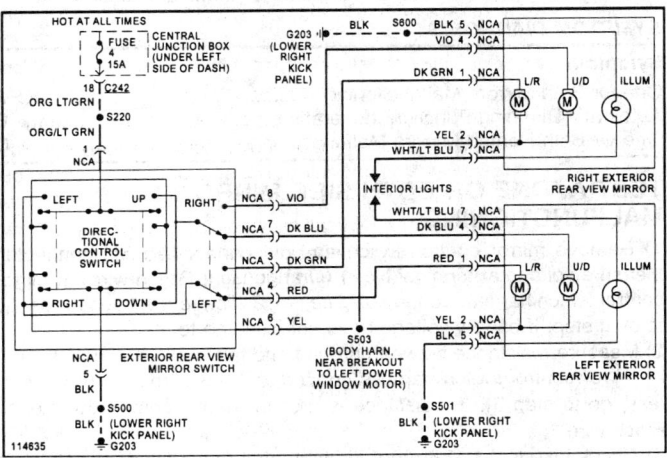

**Fig. 5: Power Mirror System Wiring Diagram
(F150 & F250 Light-Duty Pickup)**

1999 ACCESSORIES & EQUIPMENT
Power Mirrors – Explorer & Mountaineer

DESCRIPTION & OPERATION

Power side view mirror system consists of mirror head with integral reversible servomotor assembly and mirror control switch. Some models are equipped with an electronic dimming rear view mirror and/or a heating element in outside mirror glass.

The optional inside electronic dimming rear view mirror is controlled by 2 light-sensitive photocells. Outside light level is measured by a sensor on backside of mirror housing. A second sensor, located on reflective side of mirror, detects approaching rear lights. The mirror switches to normal state whenever transmission gear selector is placed in Reverse. The driver's side outside rear view mirror is available with a similar glare reduction system as an option.

TROUBLE SHOOTING

Before performing individual component tests or diagnostic tests, visually check the following for possible cause of system malfunction and repair as necessary:

- Blown fuses or faulty circuit breaker.
- Loose or corroded connectors.
- Damaged wiring.
- Damaged motors.
- Damaged mirror assemblies.
- Faulty switches.

COMPONENT TESTS

MIRROR CONTROL SWITCH

Remove mirror control switch. Measure resistance between specified terminals while operating switch in appropriate direction. See MIRROR SWITCH TEST table. *See Fig. 1.* Resistance in all tests should be less than 5 ohms. If switch fails any portion of test, replace switch.

MIRROR SWITCH TEST

Switch Position	Continuity Between Terminals
Driver Mirror	
Up	1 & 7; 5 & 6
Down	1 & 6; 5 & 7
Left	1 & 4; 5 & 6
Right	1 & 6; 4 & 5
Passenger Mirror	
Up	1 & 8; 5 & 6
Down	1 & 6; 5 & 8
Left	1 & 3; 5 & 6
Right	1 & 6; 3 & 5

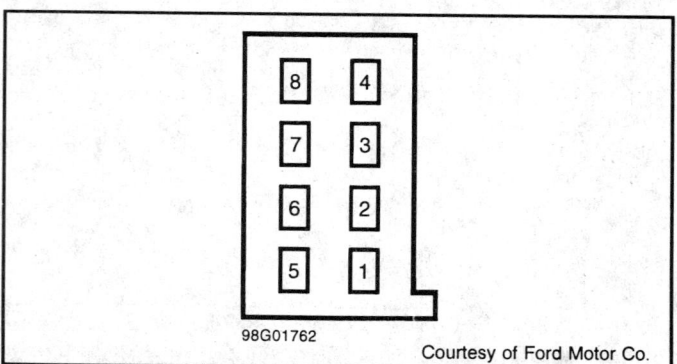

98G01762

Courtesy of Ford Motor Co.

Fig. 1: Identifying Power Mirror Control Switch Terminals

INSIDE MIRROR SELF-TEST

1) Turn ignition switch to LOCK position. Place autolamp in OFF position. Using a paper clip, press and hold mode switch located on bottom of inside mirror. After 3 seconds, autolamp LED, head lights and parking lights should illuminate. If lights illuminate, go to next step. If lights do not illuminate, repair open or short in White/Purple wire or replace defective parking light relay. See WIRING DIAGRAMS.

2) Release mode switch. If headlights and LED illuminate, go to next step. If headlights and/or LED do not illuminate, repair open or short in Light Green/Yellow or Black wires. See WIRING DIAGRAMS.

3) Turn ignition switch to RUN position. Autolamp LED, head lights and parking lights should turn off. Also inside mirror should darken. If lights and LED turn off and mirror darkens, go to next step. If lights and/or LED does not turn off or mirror does not darken, repair open in Red/Yellow wire and/or short to voltage in Black/Pink wire.

NOTE: Step 4) MUST be performed within 10 seconds of turning ignition switch to RUN position in step 3).

---

4) Once inside mirror has darkened, place transmission in Reverse. If inside mirror lightens, system passed self-test. If inside mirror does not lighten, repair open in Black/Pink wire.

SYSTEM TESTS

Verify customer complaint by operating power mirrors. Visually inspect for obvious sign of mechanical and electrical damage. If no visual damage is evident, perform appropriate system test. See SYMPTOM DIAGNOSIS table. A digital volt-ohmmeter is required to test the power mirror system. See WIRING DIAGRAMS for terminal identification.

SYMPTOM DIAGNOSIS

Symptom	Test
One Or Both Mirrors Malfunctioning	A
Automatic Dimming Function Inoperative	B
One Or Both Heated Mirrors Malfunctioning	C

TEST A: ONE OR BOTH SIDE MIRRORS MALFUNCTIONING

1) Remove mirror control switch and disconnect harness connector. Measure voltage at terminal No. 1 (Orange/Light Green wire) at mirror control switch harness connector. *See Fig. 2.* If battery voltage exists, go to next step. If battery voltage does not exist, go to step 3).

2) Measure resistance between ground and terminal No. 5 (Black wire) at mirror control switch harness connector. If resistance is 5 ohms or less, go to step 5). If resistance is greater than 5 ohms, repair open Black wire.

3) Check fuse No. 1 (7.5-amp) in instrument panel fuse box. If fuse is okay, go to next step. If fuse is blown, repair short to ground in Orange/Light Green wire or power distribution circuit. See appropriate wiring diagram in POWER DISTRIBUTION article in WIRING DIAGRAMS.

4) Measure voltage at input side of fuse No. 1. If battery voltage exists, repair open in Orange/Light Green wire. If battery voltage does not exist, repair power distribution. See appropriate wiring diagram in POWER DISTRIBUTION article in WIRING DIAGRAMS.

5) Test mirror control switch. See MIRROR CONTROL SWITCH under COMPONENT TESTS. If switch is okay, go to next step. If switch is defective, replace mirror control switch.

6) Disconnect driver and passenger mirror harness connectors. Turn ignition switch to RUN position. Measure voltage at terminals at mirror control switch harness connector. See TERMINAL IDENTIFICATION table. If voltage does not exist at any terminal, go to next step. If voltage exists at any terminal, repair short to voltage in appropriate wire.

TERMINAL IDENTIFICATION

Terminal	Wire Color
3	Dark Green
4	Red
6	Yellow
7	Dark Blue
8	Purple

7) Ignition off. Measure resistance between ground and terminals at mirror control switch harness connector. See TERMINAL IDENTIFICATION table in previous step. If all resistance readings are greater than

10,000 ohms, go to next step. If any resistance reading is 10,000 ohms or less, repair short to ground in appropriate wire.

8) Measure resistance in wires between mirror control switch harness connector and mirror harness connector. See CIRCUIT RESISTANCE TERMINAL IDENTIFICATION table. *See Figs. 2 and 3*. If any resistance reading is greater than 5 ohms, repair open in appropriate wire. If all resistance readings are 5 ohms or less, replace appropriate mirror assembly.

CIRCUIT RESISTANCE TERMINAL IDENTIFICATION

Mirror Terminal	Switch Terminal	Wire Color
Driver Side		
1	7	Dark Blue
2	4	Red
5	6	Yellow
Passenger Side		
1	8	Purple
2	3	Dark Green
5	6	Yellow

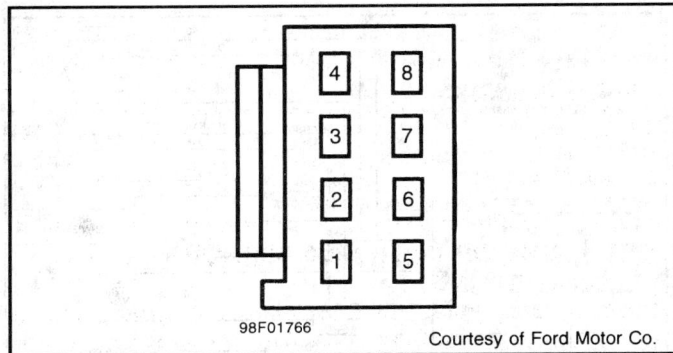

Fig. 2: Identifying Mirror Control Switch Harness Connector Terminals

98F01766   Courtesy of Ford Motor Co.

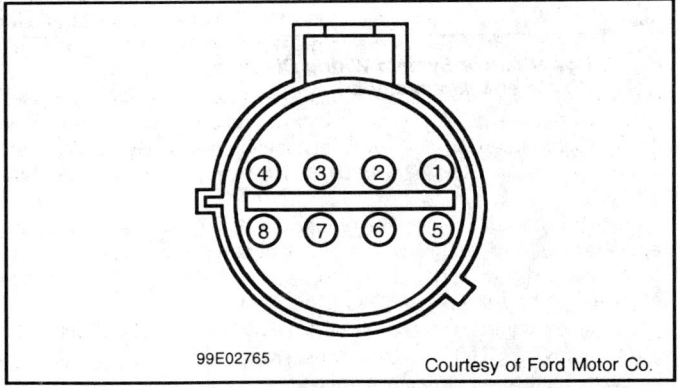

Fig. 3: Identifying Driver & Passenger Mirror Harness Connector Terminals

99E02765   Courtesy of Ford Motor Co.

TEST B: AUTO DIMMING FEATURE MALFUNCTIONING

NOTE: Preform inside mirror self-test before proceeding with this procedure. See INSIDE MIRROR SELF-TEST under COMPONENT TESTING.

1) Ensure transmission is in Park. Turn ignition switch to RUN position. Cover light sensor on back of inside mirror. Using a flashlight, shine light into light sensor on front of inside mirror. If mirror does not darken, go to next step. If mirror darkens, system is okay at this time.

2) Turn ignition switch to LOCK position. Disconnect inside mirror harness connector. Turn ignition switch to RUN position. Measure voltage between terminals No. 6 (Red/Yellow wire) and No. 4 (Black

wire) at inside mirror harness connector. *See Fig. 4*. If battery voltage exists, go to step **6)**. If battery voltage does not exist, go to next step.

3) Measure voltage at terminal No. 6 (Red/Yellow wire) at inside mirror harness connector. If battery voltage does not exist, go to next step. If battery voltage exists, repair open in Black wire.

4) Remove fuse No. 11 (7.5-amp) from instrument panel fuse box. If fuse is okay, go to next step. If fuse is blown, repair short to ground in Red/Yellow wire or power distribution circuit. See appropriate wiring diagram in POWER DISTRIBUTION article in WIRING DIAGRAMS.

5) Measure voltage at input side of fuse No. 11. If battery voltage exists, repair open in Red/Yellow wire. If battery voltage does not exist, repair power distribution. See appropriate wiring diagram in POWER DISTRIBUTION article in WIRING DIAGRAMS.

6) Ensure ignition switch is in RUN position. Measure voltage at terminal No. 3 (Black/Pink wire) at inside mirror harness connector. Battery voltage should exists only when transmission is in Reverse. If battery voltage only exists when transmission is in Reverse, replace inside mirror assembly. If battery voltage exists in any other gear or does not exists when transmission is in Reverse, repair back-up light system as necessary. See appropriate wiring diagrams in BACK-UP LIGHTS article.

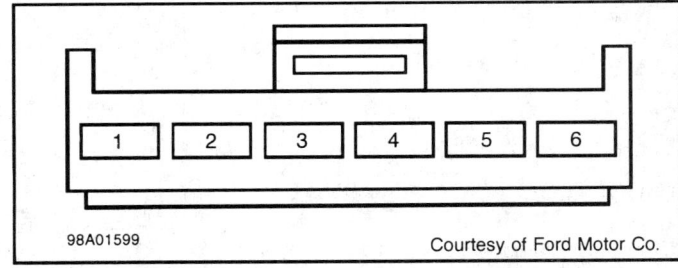

98A01599   Courtesy of Ford Motor Co.

Fig. 4: Identifying Inside Mirror Harness Connector Terminals

TEST C: ONE OR BOTH HEATED MIRRORS MALFUNCTIONING

1) Operate rear window defogger. If rear window defogger operates, go to next step. If rear window defogger does not operate, repair rear window defogger. See appropriate wiring diagram in REAR WINDOW DEFOGGERS article.

2) Remove fuse No. 32 (10-amp) from instrument panel fuse box. If fuse is blown, repair short to ground in Dark Green/Purple wire. If fuse is okay, go to next step.

3) Turn ignition switch to RUN position. Turn rear window defogger on. Measure voltage at input side of fuse No. 32. If battery voltage exists, go to next step. If battery voltage does not exist, open in Brown/Light Blue wire.

4) Turn ignition switch to LOCK position. Install fuse No. 32. Disconnect inoperative mirror harness. Turn ignition switch to RUN position. Turn rear window defogger on. Measure voltage at terminal No. 8 (Dark Green/Purple wire) at mirror harness connector. If battery voltage exists, go to next step. If battery voltage does not exist, repair open in Dark Green/Purple wire.

5) Measure resistance between ground and terminal No. 3 (Black wire) at mirror harness connector. If resistance is 5 ohms or less, replace mirror glass. If resistance is greater than 5 ohms, repair open in Black wire.

REMOVAL & INSTALLATION

WARNING: When battery is disconnected, vehicle computer and memory systems may lose memory data. Driveability problems may exist until computer systems have completed a relearn cycle. See COMPUTER RELEARN PROCEDURES article in GENERAL INFORMATION before disconnecting battery.

INSIDE MIRROR ASSEMBLY

Removal & Installation – Disconnect negative battery cable. Disconnect inside mirror harness connector. Rotate mirror counterclockwise. Discon-

until vertical. Twist mirror assembly horizontally until tube assembly bottoms out and spring releases off mounting button. To install, reverse removal procedure.

SIDE MIRROR ASSEMBLY

Removal & Installation – Disconnect negative battery cable. Remove door panel. Remove speaker and disconnect speaker harness connector. Remove mirror mounting hole cover. Disconnect mirror wiring harness connector. Remove mirror attaching nuts. Remove mirror assembly while guiding wiring and connector through hole in door. To install, reverse removal procedure. Tighten nuts to approximately 54-71 INCH lbs. (6-8 N.m).

MIRROR CONTROL SWITCH

Removal & Installation – Removal and installation procedures are not available from manufacturer.

WIRING DIAGRAMS

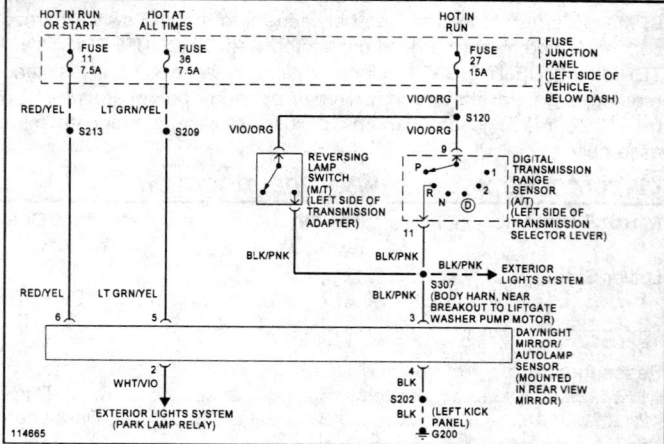

Fig. 5: Automatic Day/Night Mirror System Wiring Diagram (Explorer & Mountaineer)

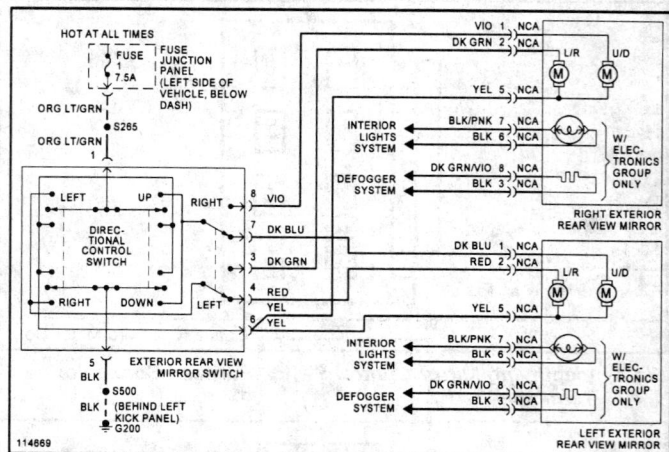

Fig. 6: Power Mirror System Wiring Diagram (Explorer & Mountaineer)

DESCRIPTION & OPERATION

Power side view mirror system consists of mirror head with integral reversible servomotor assembly and mirror control switch.

TROUBLE SHOOTING

Verify the customer complaint by operating power mirrors. Visually inspect for obvious sign of mechanical and electrical damage. If no visual damage is evident, perform appropriate system test. See SYMPTOM CHART table under SYSTEM TESTS.

COMPONENT TESTS

MIRROR CONTROL SWITCH

Remove mirror control switch. Measure resistance between specified terminals while operating switch in appropriate direction. See MIRROR SWITCH TEST table. *See Fig. 1.* Resistance in all tests should be less than 5 ohms. If switch fails any portion of test, replace switch.

MIRROR SWITCH TEST

Switch Position	Continuity Between Terminals
Left Mirror	
Up	1 & 3; 5 & 6
Down	1 & 6; 3 & 5
Left	1 & 4; 5 & 6
Right	1 & 6; 4 & 5
Right Mirror	
Up	1 & 7; 5 & 6
Down	1 & 6; 5 & 7
Left	1 & 8; 5 & 6
Right	1 & 6; 5 & 8

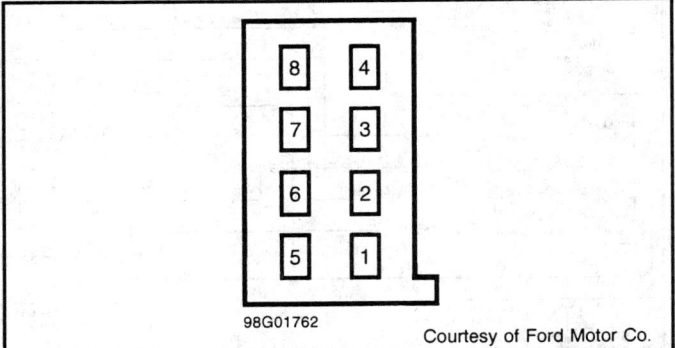

98G01762   Courtesy of Ford Motor Co.

Fig. 1: Identifying Power Mirror Control Switch Terminals

SYSTEM TESTS

SYMPTOM CHART

Symptom	Test
Both Mirrors Inoperative	A
Single Mirror Inoperative	B
Switch Logic Malfunction	C

TEST A: BOTH MIRRORS INOPERATIVE

1) Remove mirror control switch and disconnect mirror control switch harness connector C501. Measure voltage at terminal No. 1 (White/Violet wire) at mirror control switch harness connector C501. *See Fig. 2.* If battery voltage exists, go to next step. If battery voltage does not exist, repair power distribution circuit. See appropriate wiring diagram in POWER DISTRIBUTION article in WIRING DIAGRAMS.

2) Measure resistance between ground and terminal No. 5 (Black wire) at mirror control switch harness connector C501. If resistance is 5 ohms or less, go to next step. If resistance is greater than 5 ohms, repair open in Black wire.

3) Disconnect passenger's mirror harness connector C610. Measure resistance in Yellow wire between passenger's mirror harness connector C610 and terminal No. 6 at mirror control switch harness connector C501. If resistance is 5 ohms or less, replace mirror control switch. If resistance is greater than 5 ohms, repair open in Yellow wire.

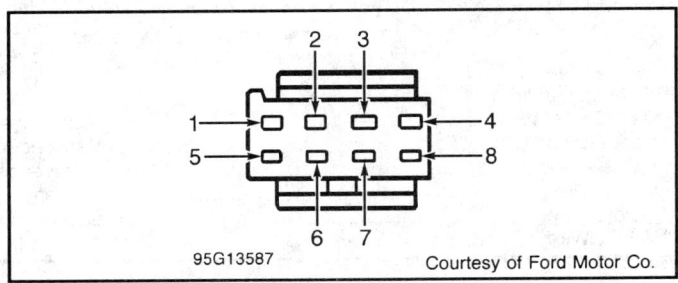

95G13587   Courtesy of Ford Motor Co.

Fig. 2: Identifying Mirror Control Switch Harness Connector C501 Terminals

TEST B: SINGLE MIRROR INOPERATIVE

1) Disconnect inoperative mirror harness connector. Measure voltage at Yellow wire terminal at mirror harness connector. Select appropriate mirror on mirror control switch. Operate mirror control switch to the down and right positions. If battery voltage exists in both positions, go to next step. If battery voltage does not exist in both positions, go to step **3)**.

2) Disconnect mirror control switch harness connector C501. Measure resistance in Yellow wire between mirror harness connector and terminal No. 6 at mirror control switch harness connector C501. *See Fig. 2.* If resistance is 5 ohms or less, replace mirror control switch. If resistance is greater than 5 ohms, repair open in appropriate wire.

3) Measure voltage at Dark Blue/Yellow wire terminal (Violet wire terminal on passenger's side) at mirror harness connector. Operate mirror control switch to the up position. If battery voltage does not exist, go to next step for driver's mirror or step **5)** for passenger's mirror. If battery voltage exist, go to step **6)**.

4) Disconnect mirror control switch harness connector C501. Measure resistance in Dark Blue/Yellow wire between mirror harness connector and terminal No. 3 at mirror control switch harness connector C501. *See Fig. 2.* If resistance is 5 ohms or less, replace mirror control switch. If resistance is greater than 5 ohms, repair open in Dark Blue/Yellow wire.

5) Disconnect mirror control switch harness connector C501. Measure resistance in Violet wire between mirror harness connector and terminal No. 7 at mirror control switch harness connector C501. *See Fig. 2.* If resistance is 5 ohms or less, replace mirror control switch. If resistance is greater than 5 ohms, repair open in Violet wire.

6) Measure voltage at Red wire terminal (Dark Green wire terminal on passenger's side) at mirror harness connector. Operate mirror control switch to the left position. If battery voltage does not exist, go to next step for driver's mirror or step **8)** for passenger's mirror. If battery voltage exist, replace appropriate mirror motor.

7) Disconnect mirror control switch harness connector C501. Measure resistance in Red wire between mirror harness connector and terminal No. 4 at mirror control switch harness connector C501. *See Fig. 2.* If resistance is 5 ohms or less, replace mirror control switch. If resistance is greater than 5 ohms, repair open in Red wire.

8) Disconnect mirror control switch harness connector C501. Measure resistance in Dark Green wire between mirror harness connector and terminal No. 8 at mirror control switch harness connector C501. *See Fig. 2.* If resistance is 5 ohms or less, replace mirror control switch. If resistance is greater than 5 ohms, repair open in Dark Green wire.

TEST C: SWITCH LOGIC MALFUNCTION

1) Disconnect malfunctioning mirror harness connector. Measure voltage or resistance at appropriate terminal at mirror harness connector with mirror control switch in appropriate position. See MIRROR CONTROL CIRCUIT table. If voltage and resistance readings are not as specified, go to next step. If voltage and resistance readings are as specified, replace appropriate mirror motor.

MIRROR CONTROL CIRCUIT

Terminal	Switch Position	Value
Driver's Mirror		
Red Wire	Driver's Mirror Left	Battery Voltage
Red Wire	Driver's Mirror Right	5 Ohms Or Less
Dark Blue/Yellow Wire	Driver's Mirror Up	Battery Voltage
Dark Blue/Yellow Wire	Driver's Mirror Down	5 Ohms Or Less
Yellow Wire	Driver's Mirror Left Or Up	5 Ohms Or Less
Yellow Wire	Driver's Mirror Right Or Down	Battery Voltage
Passenger's Mirror		
Dark Green Wire	Passenger's Mirror Left	Battery Voltage
Dark Green Wire	Passenger's Mirror Right	5 Ohms Or Less
Violet Wire	Passenger's Mirror Up	Battery Voltage
Violet Wire	Passenger's Mirror Down	5 Ohms Or Less
Yellow Wire	Passenger's Mirror Left Or Up	5 Ohms Or Less
Yellow Wire	Passenger's Mirror Right Or Down	Battery Voltage

2) Test mirror control switch. See MIRROR CONTROL SWITCH under COMPONENT TESTS. If mirror control switch is defective, replace mirror control switch. If mirror control switch is okay, repair appropriate circuit(s) between mirror control switch and appropriate mirror.

REMOVAL & INSTALLATION

WARNING: When battery is disconnected, vehicle computer and memory systems may lose memory data. Driveability problems may exist until computer systems have completed a relearn cycle. See COMPUTER RELEARN PROCEDURES article in GENERAL INFORMATION before disconnecting battery.

INSIDE MIRROR ASSEMBLY

Removal & Installation – Disconnect negative battery cable. Disconnect harness connector (if equipped). Insert small flat-blade screwdriver in slot on bottom of mirror, between mirror bracket and mirror base. Pull screwdriver rearward until mirror snaps off mirror bracket. To install, slide mirror downward onto mirror bracket until it snaps into place.

SIDE MIRROR ASSEMBLY

Removal & Installation – Disconnect negative battery cable. Remove door panel. Remove mirror mounting hole cover. *See Fig. 3.* Disconnect mirror wiring harness connector. Remove mirror attaching nuts. Remove mirror assembly while guiding wiring and connector through hole in door. To install, reverse removal procedure. Tighten nuts to 98-115 INCH lbs. (11-13 N.m).

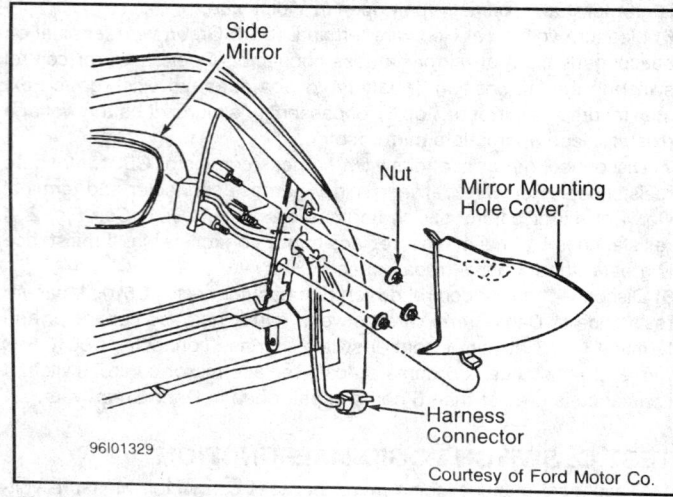

Fig. 3: Removing Side Mirror

SIDE MIRROR GLASS & MOTOR

Removal & Installation – Point mirror glass as far inward as possible to allow clearance between glass and mirror housing at outer edge of mirror. Insert fingers into clearance, and pull mirror glass. If fingers will not fit between glass and housing, use a screwdriver and cloth to pry mirror glass out. Glass will unsnap without being damaged. Disconnect heater wires (if equipped). Remove motor attaching screws. Unplug motor connector, and remove motor. To install, reverse removal procedure. Ensure mirror glass locking tabs align before snapping in glass.

MIRROR CONTROL SWITCH

Removal & Installation – Pry out regulator switch plate assembly from armrest. Disconnect mirror control switch harness connector. Depress retaining clips on switch housing. Push switch out of regulator switch plate. Remove switch. To install, reverse removal procedure.

WIRING DIAGRAMS

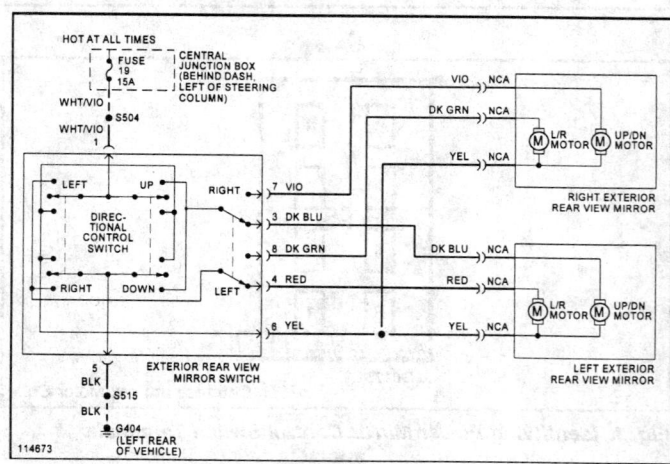

Fig. 4: Power Mirror System Wiring Diagram (Mustang)

DESCRIPTION & OPERATION

The power memory seat/mirror system allows storage of 3 seat/mirror positions into memory. Seat and outside mirrors will automatically move to preset position(s) by pressing button No. 1, 2 or both simultaneously. Memory recall will not operate unless transmission is in Park or Neutral.

The optional interior electronic dimming rear view mirror is controlled by 2 light-sensitive photocells. Outside light level is measured by a sensor on backside of mirror housing. A second sensor, located on reflective side of mirror, detects approaching rear lights. The mirror switches to normal state whenever transmission gear selector is placed in Reverse position.

Power side view mirror system consists of mirror head with integral servomotor assembly. Memory mirror is controlled by Driver Seat Module (DSM).

COMPONENT LOCATIONS

COMPONENT LOCATIONS

Component	Location
Central Junction Box	Below Left Side Of Instrument Panel
Data Link Connector	Under Instrument Panel, Right Of Steering Column
Driver Seat Module	Under Driver Seat
Power Mirror Switch	Driver Door Panel Arm Rest

TROUBLE SHOOTING

Before performing individual component tests and system test, check the following for possible cause of system malfunction:

- Blown fuses or faulty circuit breakers.
- Loose or corroded connectors.
- Damaged wiring.
- Damaged mirror assembly.
- Faulty switches.

COMPONENT TESTS

MEMORY SET SWITCH

Remove memory set switch and disconnect harness connector. Measure resistance between listed memory switch terminals with switch in each position. See MEMORY SET SWITCH RESISTANCE table. See Fig. 1. If resistance is not as specified, replace memory switch.

MEMORY SET SWITCH RESISTANCE

Switch Position	Terminals	Resistance (Ohms)
SET	1 & 6	Less Than 5
MEM 1	6 & 3	Less Than 5
MEM 2	6 & 4	Less Than 5

1 – Between terminals No. 8 and 9, resistance should be infinite. When ohmmeter leads are reversed, resistance should be low.

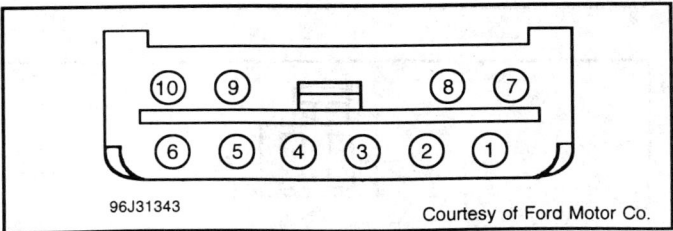

96J31343   Courtesy of Ford Motor Co.

Fig. 1: Identifying Memory Set Switch Terminals

MIRROR CONTROL SWITCH

Remove mirror control switch and disconnect harness connector. Ensure that there is continuity between mirror control switch terminals with switch in listed positions. See POWER MIRROR SWITCH TERMINAL IDENTIFICATION table. See Fig. 2. If continuity is not as specified, replace mirror control switch.

POWER MIRROR SWITCH TERMINAL IDENTIFICATION

Switch Position	Check Between Terminals
Left Mirror	
Up	1 & 7; 5 & 6
Down	1 & 6; 5 & 7
Left	1 & 4; 5 & 6
Right	1 & 6; 4 & 5
Right Mirror	
Up	1 & 8; 5 & 6
Down	1 & 6; 5 & 8
Left	1 & 3; 5 & 6
Right	1 & 6; 3 & 5

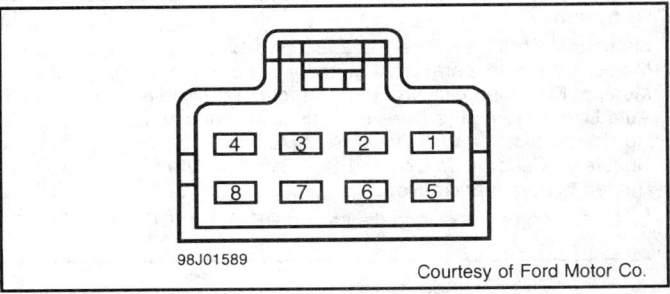

98J01589   Courtesy of Ford Motor Co.

Fig. 2: Identifying Power Mirror Control Switch Terminals

SELF-DIAGNOSTIC SYSTEM

NOTE: Before beginning system testing, perform TROUBLE SHOOTING.

NOTE: A New Generation Star (NGS) tester is required to test the power mirror system. If NGS tester does not communicate with vehicle, refer to NGS tester manual.

Connect New Generation Star (NGS) tester to data link connector. Perform DATA LINK DIAGNOSTIC TEST. See appropriate MODULE COMMUNICATIONS NETWORK article. If NGS tester responds with CKT 914, CKT 915 or CKT 70=ALL ECUS NO RESP/NOT EQUIP, diagnose network concern. See appropriate MODULE COMMUNICATIONS NETWORK article. If NGS tester responds with, NO RESPONSE/NOT EQUIPPED for Driver Seat Module (DSM), go to TEST E: NO COMMUNICATION WITH DRIVER SEAT MODULE under SYSTEM TESTS.

If NGS tester responds with SYSTEM PASSED for all modules, retrieve DTCs for DSM modules. If any DTCs exist, perform appropriate test. See DSM DTC DEFINITIONS table. If no DTCs were retrieved, repair system by symptom. See SYMPTOM CHART table and perform appropriate test under SYSTEM TESTS.

DSM DTC DEFINITIONS

DTC	Description	Test
B1342	ECU Defective	Replace DSM
B1529	Memory Set Switch Short To Power	B
B1533	Memory 1 Switch Short To Power	B
B1537	Memory 2 Switch Short To Power	B
B1667	Driver Mirror Up/Down Motor Stalled	A Or B
B1668	Driver Mirror Right/Left Motor Stalled	A Or B
B1669	Passenger Mirror Up/Down Motor Stalled	A Or B
B1670	Passenger Mirror Right/Left Motor Stalled	A Or B
B1676	Battery Voltage Out Or Range	[1]
B1697	Driver/Passenger Mirror Switch Circuit Short To Voltage	A
B1735	Driver Mirror Vertical Switch Circuit Short To Voltage	A
B1739	Driver Mirror Horizontal Switch Circuit Short To Voltage	A
B1743	Passenger Mirror Vertical Switch Circuit Short To Voltage	A
B1747	Passenger Mirror Horizontal Switch Circuit Short To Voltage	A

[1] – Check charging system and repair as necessary. See appropriate GENERATORS article in STARTING & CHARGING SYSTEMS. If charging system is okay, repair wiring as necessary. See WIRING DIAGRAMS.

SYMPTOM CHART

Symptom	Test
Memory Mirror Inoperative	A
Memory Mirror Inoperative At Memory Set Switch	B
Memory Mirror Inoperative From Remote Transmitter	C
Auto Dimming Feature Does Not Function Properly	D
No Communication With Driver Seat Module	E
Unable To Perform On-Demand Self Test With DSM	E
Heated Mirrors Inoperative	[1]

[1] – See appropriate wiring diagram in REAR WINDOW DEFOGGERS article.

SYSTEM TESTS

TEST A: MEMORY MIRROR INOPERATIVE

1) Place transmission in Park. Turn ignition switch off. Connect New Generation Star (NGS) tester to data link connector. Retrieve and record continuous DTCs. Clear continuous DTCs. Perform Driver Seat Module (DSM) on-demand self-test. If no DSM DTCs were retrieved, go to next step. If any DSM DTCs were retrieved, go to appropriate step. See DTC TO TEST STEP table.

DTC TO TEST STEP

DTC	Go To
B1342	[1]
B1667	Step **10)**
B1668	Step **10)**
B1669	Step **14)**
B1670	Step **14)**
B1697	Step **3)**
B1735	Step **3)**
B1739	Step **3)**
B1743	Step **3)**
B1747	Step **3)**

[1] – Replace Driver Seat Module (DSM).

2) Monitor DSM PIDs MIR_SEL, MIRV_SW and MIRH_SW, while operating mirror control switch through all positions. If PID values correspond to switch position, go to step **9)**. If PID values do not correspond to switch position and fuse No. 4 (in central junction box in engine compartment) blows while operating mirror control switch, go to step **7)**. If PID values do not correspond to switch position and fuse No. 4 does not blow while operating mirror control switch, go to next step.
3) Turn ignition switch to LOCK position. Remove mirror control switch. Test mirror control switch. See MIRROR CONTROL SWITCH under COMPONENT TESTS. If mirror control switch is okay, go to next step. If mirror control switch is defective, replace mirror control switch and check system for normal operation..
4) Measure voltage between ground and mirror control switch harness connector terminal No. 1 (Orange/Light Green wire). *See Fig. 3.* If

battery voltage exists, go to next step. If battery voltage does not exist, repair open in Orange/Light Green wire and check system for normal operation. See WIRING DIAGRAMS.

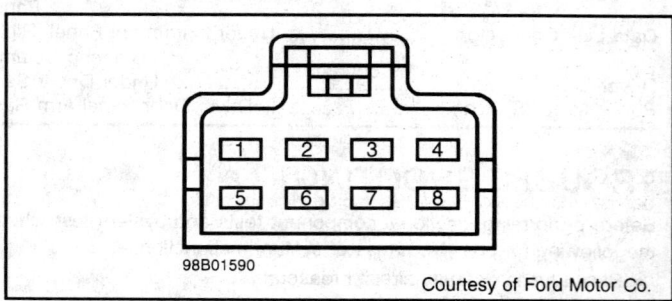

Courtesy of Ford Motor Co.

Fig. 3: Identifying Power Mirror Control Switch Harness Connector Terminals

5) Measure resistance between ground and mirror control switch harness connector terminal No. 5 (Black/Light Blue wire). If resistance is 5 ohms or less, go to next step. If resistance is greater than 5 ohms, repair open in Black/Light Blue wire and check system for normal operation. See WIRING DIAGRAMS.
6) Disconnect Driver Seat Module (DSM) 16-pin harness connector. Turn ignition switch to RUN position. Measure voltage between ground and each listed mirror control switch harness connector terminal. See SWITCH CONNECTOR TERMINAL IDENTIFICATION table. If voltage does not exist at any terminal, go to next step. If voltage exists at any terminal, repair short to voltage in appropriate wire and check system for normal operation. See WIRING DIAGRAMS.

SWITCH CONNECTOR TERMINAL IDENTIFICATION

Terminal	Wire Color
3	Dark Green/Orange
4	Red/Orange
6	Yellow/Black
7	Dark Blue/Orange
8	Violet/Orange

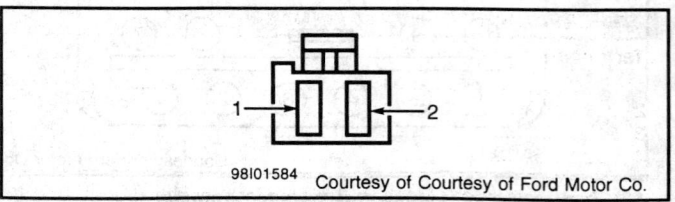

98I01584   Courtesy of Courtesy of Ford Motor Co.

Fig. 4: Identifying Driver Seat Module (DSM) 16-Pin Harness Connector Terminals

7) Turn ignition off. Measure resistance between ground and listed terminals at mirror control switch harness connector. See SWITCH CONNECTOR TERMINAL IDENTIFICATION table. If all resistance readings are greater than 10 k/ohms, go to next step. If any resistance reading is 10 k/ohms or less, repair short to ground in appropriate wire and check system for normal operation. See WIRING DIAGRAMS.

8) Measure resistance in listed wires between mirror control switch harness connector and DSM 16-pin harness connector. See CIRCUIT IDENTIFICATION table. If all resistance readings are 5 ohms or less, replace DSM. If any resistance reading is greater than 5 ohms, repair open in appropriate wire and check system for normal operation. See WIRING DIAGRAMS.

CIRCUIT IDENTIFICATION

DSM Connector Terminal	Connector Terminal	Wire Color
4	8	Violet/Orange
5	4	Red/Orange
6	6	Yellow/Black
7	3	Dark Green/Orange
8	7	Dark Blue/Orange

9) Using NGS tester, operate both mirrors through all positions with by toggling DSM active commands on and off. Active commands are DR_UP, DR_DOWN, DR_LEFT, DR_RIGHT, PR_UP, PR_DOWN, PR_LEFT and PR_RIGHT. If driver mirror does not operate properly, go to next step. If passenger mirror does not operate properly, go to step **14)**.

10) Turn ignition switch off. Disconnect driver side mirror harness connector. Turn ignition switch to RUN position. Measure voltage between terminals No. 4 (Dark Blue wire) and No. 2 (Yellow/Light Blue wire) at driver mirror harness connector. See Fig. 5. Using NGS tester, operate driver mirror up and down. Battery voltage should exists in both directions with opposite polarity. Measure voltage between driver side mirror harness connector terminals No. 1 (Yellow/Red wire) and No. 3 (Red wire). Using NGS tester, operate driver mirror right and left. Battery voltage should exists in both directions with opposite polarity. If voltage is as specified, replace driver mirror assembly. If voltage is not as specified, go to next step.

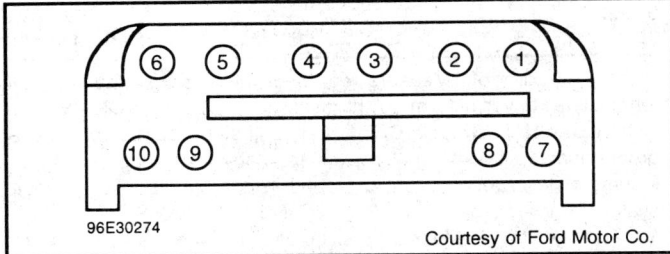

Fig. 5: Identifying Driver Side Mirror, Passenger Side Mirror & Memory Set Switch Harness Connector Terminals

11) Turn ignition switch off. Disconnect DSM 22-pin harness connector. Turn ignition switch to RUN position. Measure voltage between ground and listed driver mirror harness connector terminals. See DRIVER MIRROR TERMINAL IDENTIFICATION table. See Fig. 5. If voltage does not exist at any terminal, go to next step. If voltage exists at any terminal, repair short to voltage in appropriate wire and check system for normal operation. See WIRING DIAGRAMS.

DRIVER MIRROR TERMINAL IDENTIFICATION

Terminal	Wire Color
1	Yellow/Red
2	Yellow/Light Blue
3	Red
4	Dark Blue

12) Turn ignition off. Measure resistance between ground and listed terminals at driver mirror harness connector. See DRIVER MIRROR TERMINAL IDENTIFICATION table. See Fig. 5. If all resistance read-

ings are greater than 10 k/ohms, go to next step. If any resistance reading is 10 k/ohms or less, repair short to ground in appropriate wire and check system for normal operation. See WIRING DIAGRAMS.

13) Measure resistance in wires between driver mirror harness connector and DSM 22-pin harness connector. See DRIVER MIRROR CIRCUIT IDENTIFICATION table. See Figs. 5 and 6. If all resistance readings are 5 ohms or less, replace DSM. If any resistance reading is greater than 5 ohms, repair open in appropriate wire and check system for normal operation. See WIRING DIAGRAMS.

DRIVER MIRROR CIRCUIT IDENTIFICATION

DSM Connector Terminal	Connector Terminal	Wire Color
6	1	Yellow/Red
7	3	Red
9	4	Dark Blue
10	2	Yellow/Light Blue

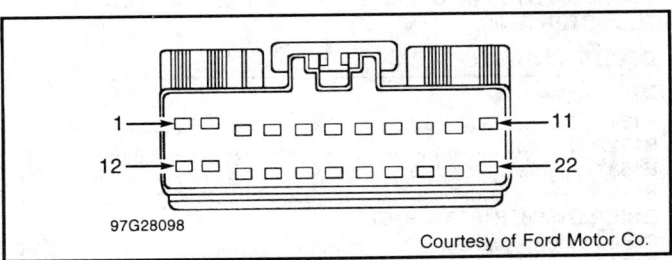

Fig. 6: Identifying Driver Seat Module And RAP Module 22-Pin Harness Connector Terminals

14) Place transmission in PARK position. Turn ignition off. Disconnect passenger side mirror harness connector. Turn ignition switch to RUN position. Measure voltage between passenger side mirror terminals No. 4 (White/Violet wire) and No. 2 (Violet wire). See Fig. 5. Using NGS tester, operate passenger mirror up and down. Battery voltage should exists in both directions with opposite polarity. Measure voltage between terminals No. 1 (White/Light Green wire) and No. 3 (Dark Green wire) at passenger mirror harness connector. Using NGS tester, operate passenger mirror right and left. Battery voltage should exists in both directions with opposite polarity. If voltage is as specified, replace passenger mirror assembly. If voltage is not as specified, go to next step.

15) Turn ignition switch off. Disconnect DSM 22-pin harness connector. Turn ignition switch to RUN position. Measure voltage between ground and listed passenger side mirror harness connector terminals. See PASSENGER MIRROR TERMINAL IDENTIFICATION table. If voltage does not exist at any terminal, go to next step. If voltage exists at any terminal, repair short to voltage in appropriate wire and check system for normal operation. See WIRING DIAGRAMS.

PASSENGER MIRROR TERMINAL IDENTIFICATION

Terminal	Wire Color
1	White/Light Green
2	Violet
3	Dark Green
7	White/Violet

16) Turn ignition off. Measure resistance between ground and listed terminals at passenger side mirror harness connector. See PASSENGER MIRROR TERMINAL IDENTIFICATION table. If all resistance readings are greater than 10 k/ohms, go to next step. If any resistance reading is 10 k/ohms or less, repair short to ground in appropriate wire and check system for normal operation. See WIRING DIAGRAMS.

17) Measure resistance in wires between passenger side mirror harness connector and DSM 22-pin harness connector. See PASSENGER MIRROR CIRCUIT IDENTIFICATION table. See Figs. 5 and 6. If all resistance readings are less than 5 ohms, replace DSM. If any resistance reading is 5 ohms or greater, repair open or high resistance in appropriate wire and check system for normal operation. See WIRING DIAGRAMS.

PASSENGER MIRROR CIRCUIT IDENTIFICATION

DSM Connector Terminal	Connector Terminal	Wire Color
1	1	White/Light Green
2	3	Dark Green
4	2	Violet
5	4	White/Violet

TEST B: MEMORY MIRROR INOPERATIVE AT MEMORY SET SWITCH

1) Place transmission in Park. Turn ignition off. Connect New Generation Star (NGS) tester to data link connector. Retrieve and record DTCs. Clear continuous DTCs. Perform Driver Seat Module (DSM) on-demand self-test. If memory set switch LED does not illuminate during DSM self-test, go to step 5). If no DSM DTCs were retrieved, go to next step. If any DSM DTCs were retrieved, go to appropriate step. See DTC TO TEST STEP table.

DTC TO TEST STEP

DTC	Go To
B1342	1
B1529	Step 3)
B1533	Step 3)
B1537	Step 3)
B1667, B1668, B1669 & B1670 Concurrently	Step 9)
B1667	Step 10)
B1668	Step 10)
B1669	Step 13)
B1670	Step 13)

1 – Replace Driver Seat Module (DSM).

2) Monitor DSM PIDs MEM1_SW, MEM2_SW and MEM_SW, while operating memory set and recall switches. If PID values correspond to switch position, go to step 9). If PID values do not correspond to switch position and central junction box fuse No. 4 (15-amp) blows while operating switch, go to step 7). If PID values do not correspond to switch position and fuse No. 4 does not blow while operating switch, go to next step.
3) Turn ignition off. Test memory set switch. See MEMORY SET SWITCH under COMPONENT TESTS. If switch is okay, go to next step. If switch is defective, install new switch and check system for normal operation.
4) Measure voltage between ground and memory switch harness connector terminal No. 1 (Orange/Light Green wire). See Fig. 5. If battery voltage exists, go to next step. If battery voltage does not exist, repair open in Orange/Light Green wire and check system for normal operation. See WIRING DIAGRAMS.
5) Turn ignition off. Measure resistance between ground and memory switch harness connector terminal No. 8 (Black/Light Blue wire). If resistance is 5 ohms or less, go to next step. If resistance is greater than 5 ohms, repair open in Black/Light Blue wire and check system for normal operation. See WIRING DIAGRAMS.
6) Disconnect DSM 22-pin harness connector. Turn ignition switch to RUN position. Measure voltage between ground and listed memory switch harness connector terminals. See MEMORY SET SWITCH TERMINAL IDENTIFICATION table. If voltage does not exist at any terminal, go to next step. If voltage exists at any terminal, repair short to voltage in appropriate wire and check system for normal operation. See WIRING DIAGRAMS.

MEMORY SET SWITCH TERMINAL IDENTIFICATION

Terminal	Wire Color
3	Brown/Light Green
4	Black/Orange
6	Brown/Orange
9	White/Orange

7) Turn ignition off. Measure resistance between ground and listed terminals at memory switch harness connector. See MEMORY SET SWITCH TERMINAL IDENTIFICATION table. If all resistance readings are greater than 10 k/ohms, go to next step. If any resistance reading is 10 k/ohms or less, repair short to ground in appropriate wire and check system for normal operation. See WIRING DIAGRAMS.
8) Turn ignition off. Measure resistance in listed wires between memory switch harness connector and DSM 22-pin harness connector. See MEMORY SET SWITCH CIRCUIT IDENTIFICATION table. See Figs. 5 and 6. If all resistance readings are 5 ohms or less, replace DSM. If any resistance reading is greater than 5 ohms, repair open in appropriate wire and check system for normal operation. See WIRING DIAGRAMS.

MEMORY SET SWITCH CIRCUIT IDENTIFICATION

DSM Connector Terminal	Connector Terminal	Wire Color
3	6	Brown/Orange
13	9	White/Orange
15	4	Black/Orange
16	3	Brown/Light Green

9) Monitor PIDs DMIR_R, DMIR_UP, PMIR_R and PMIR_UP, while using NGS tester to operate both side mirrors through all positions. If PID values agree with mirror actual positions, replace DSM. If PID values do not agree with driver side mirror actual positions, go to next step. If PID values do not agree with passenger side mirror actual positions, go to step 13).
10) Turn ignition off. Disconnect DSM 22-pin harness connector. Disconnect driver side mirror harness connector. Turn ignition switch to RUN position. Measure voltage between ground and listed terminals at driver side mirror harness connector. See DRIVER MIRROR TERMINAL IDENTIFICATION table. See Fig. 5. If voltage does not exist at any terminal, go to next step. If voltage exists at any terminal, repair short to voltage in appropriate wire and check system for normal operation. See WIRING DIAGRAMS.

DRIVER MIRROR TERMINAL IDENTIFICATION

Terminal	Wire Color
7	Gray
8	Red/White
9	Gray/Red
10	Dark Blue/White

11) Turn ignition off. Measure resistance between ground and listed terminals at driver side mirror harness connector. See DRIVER MIRROR TERMINAL IDENTIFICATION table. If all resistance readings are greater than 10 k/ohms, go to next step. If any resistance reading is 10 k/ohms or less, repair short to ground in appropriate wire and check system for normal operation. See WIRING DIAGRAMS.
12) Turn ignition off. Measure resistance in listed wires between driver side mirror harness connector and DSM 22-pin harness connector. See DRIVER MIRROR CIRCUIT IDENTIFICATION table. See Figs. 5 and 6. If all resistance readings are 5 ohms or less, replace driver mirror assembly. If any resistance reading is greater than 5 ohms, repair open in appropriate wire and check system for normal operation. See WIRING DIAGRAMS.

DRIVER MIRROR CIRCUIT IDENTIFICATION

DSM Connector Terminal	Connector Terminal	Wire Color
8	8	Red/White
14	9	Gray/Red
19	10	Dark Blue/White
21	7	Gray

13) Turn ignition off. Disconnect DSM 22-pin harness connector. Disconnect passenger side mirror harness connector. Turn ignition switch to RUN position. Measure voltage between ground and listed passenger side mirror harness connector terminals. See Fig. 5. See PASSENGER MIRROR TERMINAL IDENTIFICATION table. If voltage does not exist at any terminal, go to next step. If voltage exists at any terminal, repair

short to voltage in appropriate wire and check system for normal operation. See WIRING DIAGRAMS.

PASSENGER MIRROR TERMINAL IDENTIFICATION

Terminal	Wire Color
7	Gray
8	Dark Green/White
9	Gray/Red
10	Violet/White

14) Turn ignition off. Measure resistance between ground and listed passenger side mirror harness connector terminals. See PASSENGER MIRROR TERMINAL IDENTIFICATION table. If all resistance readings are greater than 10 k/ohms, go to next step. If any resistance reading is 10 k/ohms or less, repair short to ground in appropriate wire and check system for normal operation. See WIRING DIAGRAMS.

15) Measure resistance in listed wires between passenger side mirror harness connector and DSM 22-pin harness connector. See PASSENGER MIRROR CIRCUIT IDENTIFICATION table. *See Figs. 5 and 6.* If all resistance readings are 5 ohms or less, replace passenger side mirror assembly. If any resistance reading is greater than 5 ohms, repair open or high resistance in appropriate wire and check system for normal operation. See WIRING DIAGRAMS.

PASSENGER MIRROR CIRCUIT IDENTIFICATION

DSM Connector Terminal	Connector Terminal	Wire Color
14	9	Gray/Red
17	10	Violet/White
18	8	Dark Green/White
21	7	Gray

TEST C: MEMORY MIRROR INOPERATIVE FROM REMOTE TRANSMITTER

1) Place transmission in Park. Turn ignition switch off. Connect New Generation Star (NGS) tester to data link connector. Retrieve and record DTCs. Clear continuous DTCs. Perform Driver Seat Module (DSM) on-demand self-test. If no DSM DTCs were retrieved during self-test, go to next step. If any DSM DTCs were retrieved during self-test, perform appropriate test. See DSM DTC DEFINITIONS table under SYSTEM TESTS.

2) Turn ignition off. Disconnect Remote Anti-Theft Personality (RAP) module 22-pin harness connector. Disconnect memory switch harness connector. Measure resistance in Brown/Light Green wire between RAP module 22-pin harness connector terminal No. 6 and memory switch harness connector terminal No. 3. *See Figs. 5 and 6.* Also, measure resistance in Black/Orange wire between RAP module 22-pin harness connector terminal No. 18 and memory switch harness connector terminal No. 4. If either resistance reading is greater than 5 ohms, repair open or high resistance in appropriate wire. If both resistance readings are 5 ohms or less, diagnose remote keyless entry system concern. See appropriate wiring diagram in REMOTE KEYLESS ENTRY SYSTEMS article.

TEST D: AUTO DIMMING FEATURE DOES NOT FUNCTION PROPERLY

1) Turn ignition switch to RUN position. Move gear selector through all positions while observing reverse lights. If reverse lights only operate when gear selector is in Reverse, go to next step. If reverse lights do not operate or operate in any other position other than Reverse, repair reverse lights. See appropriate wiring diagram in BACK-UP LIGHTS article.

2) Cover light sensor on back of inside mirror. Use a flashlight to shine light into light sensor on front of inside mirror. With gear selector in Park, inside mirror should darken. With gear selector in Reverse, inside mirror should undarken. If inside mirror operates as described, system is okay at this time. If inside mirror only darkens, go to next step. If inside mirror will not undarken in Reverse, go to step **7)**.

3) Turn ignition off. Place gear selector in Park. Check fuse No. 23 (10-amp) in instrument panel fuse box. If fuse is okay, go to next step.

If fuse is blown, replace fuse and check system for normal operation. If fuse blows again, repair short to ground in White/Light Blue wire and check system for normal operation. See WIRING DIAGRAMS.

4) Disconnect inside mirror harness connector. Turn ignition switch to RUN position. Measure voltage between ground and inside mirror harness connector terminal No. 7 (White/Light Blue wire). *See Fig. 7.* If battery voltage does not exist, go to next step. If battery voltage exists, go to step **6)**.

5) Turn ignition off. Disconnect central junction box 26-pin harness connector (central junction box is located under left side of instrument panel). Measure resistance in White/Light Blue wire between inside mirror harness connector terminal No. 7 and central junction box harness connector terminal No. 1. If resistance is 5 ohms or less, replace instrument panel fuse box. If resistance is greater than 5 ohms, repair open in White/Light Blue wire and check system for normal operation. See WIRING DIAGRAMS.

6) Turn ignition off. Measure resistance between ground and inside mirror harness connector terminal No. 6 (Black wire). If resistance is 5 ohms or less, replace inside mirror assembly. If resistance is greater than 5 ohms, repair open or high resistance in Black wire and check system for normal operation. See WIRING DIAGRAMS.

7) Place gear selector in Reverse. Measure voltage between ground and inside mirror harness connector terminal No. 5 (Black/Pink wire). If battery voltage exists, replace inside mirror assembly. If battery voltage does not exist, repair open in Black/Pink wire and check system for normal operation. See WIRING DIAGRAMS.

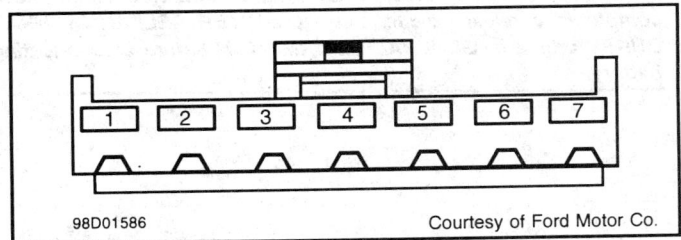

98D01586   Courtesy of Ford Motor Co.

Fig. 7: Identifying Inside Mirror Harness Connector Terminals

TEST E: NO COMMUNICATION WITH DRIVER SEAT MODULE

1) Connect scan tool to data link connector. Ensure transmission is in Park. Turn ignition switch to RUN position. Monitor DSM PID P/N_SW on scan tool. If scan tool displays UNABLE TO PERFORM TEST/FUNCTION – MODULE NOT RESPONDING; DSM – CHECK IGNITION STATUS – VERIFY CABLE REQUIREMENTS or CHECK CABLE CONNECTIONS, go to next step. If scan tool does not display any of the above messages, go to step **7)**.

2) Turn ignition off. Remove fuse No. 4 (15-amp) from central junction box. If fuse is okay, go to next step. If fuse is blown, go to step **4)**.

3) Turn ignition switch to RUN position. Measure voltage between ground and input side of fuse No. 4 cavity in central junction box. If battery voltage exists, go to step **5)**. If battery voltage does not exist, check power distribution wiring to central junction box. See appropriate wiring diagram in POWER DISTRIBUTION article in WIRING DIAGRAMS. If power distribution wiring is okay, replace instrument panel fuse box.

4) Turn ignition off. Ensure that fuse No. 4 is still removed. Disconnect Driver Seat Module (DSM) 22-pin harness connector. Measure resistance between ground and DSM 22-pin harness connector terminal No. 12 (Orange/Light Green wire). *See Fig. 6.* If resistance is greater than 10 k/ohms, install new fuse and check system for normal operation. If resistance is 10 k/ohms or less, repair short to ground in Orange/Light Green wire. See WIRING DIAGRAMS.

5) Install fuse No. 4. Turn ignition off. Disconnect DSM 22-pin harness connector. Turn ignition switch to RUN position. Measure voltage between DSM 22-pin harness connector terminal No. 12 (Orange/Light Green wire) and ground. *See Fig. 6.* If battery voltage exists, go to next step. If battery voltage does not exist, repair open in Orange/Light Green wire. See WIRING DIAGRAMS.

6) Measure resistance between ground and DSM 22-pin harness connector terminal No. 11 (Black/Light Blue wire). *See Fig. 6.* If resistance is less than 5 ohms or less, repair network concern. See appropriate MODULE COMMUNICATIONS NETWORK article. If resistance is 5 ohms or greater, repair open in Black/Light Blue wire. See WIRING DIAGRAMS.

7) Monitor DSM PID P/N_SW on scan tool while moving transmission through entire range. If PID value does not agree with transmission position, go to next step. If PID value agrees with transmission position, replace driver seat module.

8) Remove fuse No. 20 (5-amp) from central junction box. Measure resistance of Red/Black wire between output side of fuse No. 20 cavity in central junction box and DSM 22-pin harness connector terminal No. 20. *See Fig. 6.* If resistance is 5 ohms or less, diagnose transmission range sensor circuit. See appropriate ELECTRONIC CONTROLS article in AUTOMATIC TRANSMISSIONS in appropriate MITCHELL® TRANSMISSION SERVICE & REPAIR manual. If resistance is greater than 5 ohms, repair open in Red/Black wire. See WIRING DIAGRAMS.

REMOVAL & INSTALLATION

CAUTION: When battery is disconnected or modules are replaced, vehicle computer and memory systems may lose memory data. Driveability problems may exist until computer systems have completed a relearn cycle. See COMPUTER RELEARN PROCEDURES article in GENERAL INFORMATION before disconnecting battery.

INSIDE MIRROR

NOTE: Mirror mount is designed to detach from glass in the event of air bag deployment. Avoid using excessive force when installing mirror.

Removal & Installation (With Auto Dimming) – Remove compass sensor, if equipped. Disconnect mirror electrical connector. Rotate mirror counterclockwise until the tube assembly bottoms out and the spring releases from the mounting button. To install, position mirror on the mounting button. While keeping mirror parallel to windshield surface, install mirror downward onto the rear view mirror bracket. Use Inside Mirror Installer (T94P-17700-AH) to squeeze retaining clips, then slide mirror downward on to mount. Install compass sensor.

Removal & Installation (Without Auto Dimming) – Remove compass sensor, if equipped. Insert small screwdriver into bottom hole of mount. Pull upward to remove mirror from mount. To install, use Inside Mirror Installer (T94P-17700-AH) to squeeze retaining clips, then slide mirror downward on to mount. Install compass sensor.

DRIVER & PASSENGER MIRROR

Removal & Installation – Disconnect negative battery cable. Remove appropriate door panel. Disconnect mirror harness connectors. Disengage wiring clips. Remove 3 mirror retaining nuts. Remove mirror. To install, reverse removal procedure. Tighten retaining nuts to 53-71 INCH lbs. (6-8 N.m).

DRIVER & PASSENGER MIRROR GLASS

WARNING: During removal and installation, place shop towel between glass and hand to avoid injury from possible glass breakage.

Removal & Installation – Position mirror in position to obtain gap between outside edge and housing. Pry mirror from housing by pulling on outside edge. Disconnect mirror heater harness connector. During installation, transfer insulator from old mirror to new mirror. To complete installation, reverse removal procedure.

1999 ACCESSORIES & EQUIPMENT
Power Memory Mirrors – Navigator (Cont.)

WIRING DIAGRAMS

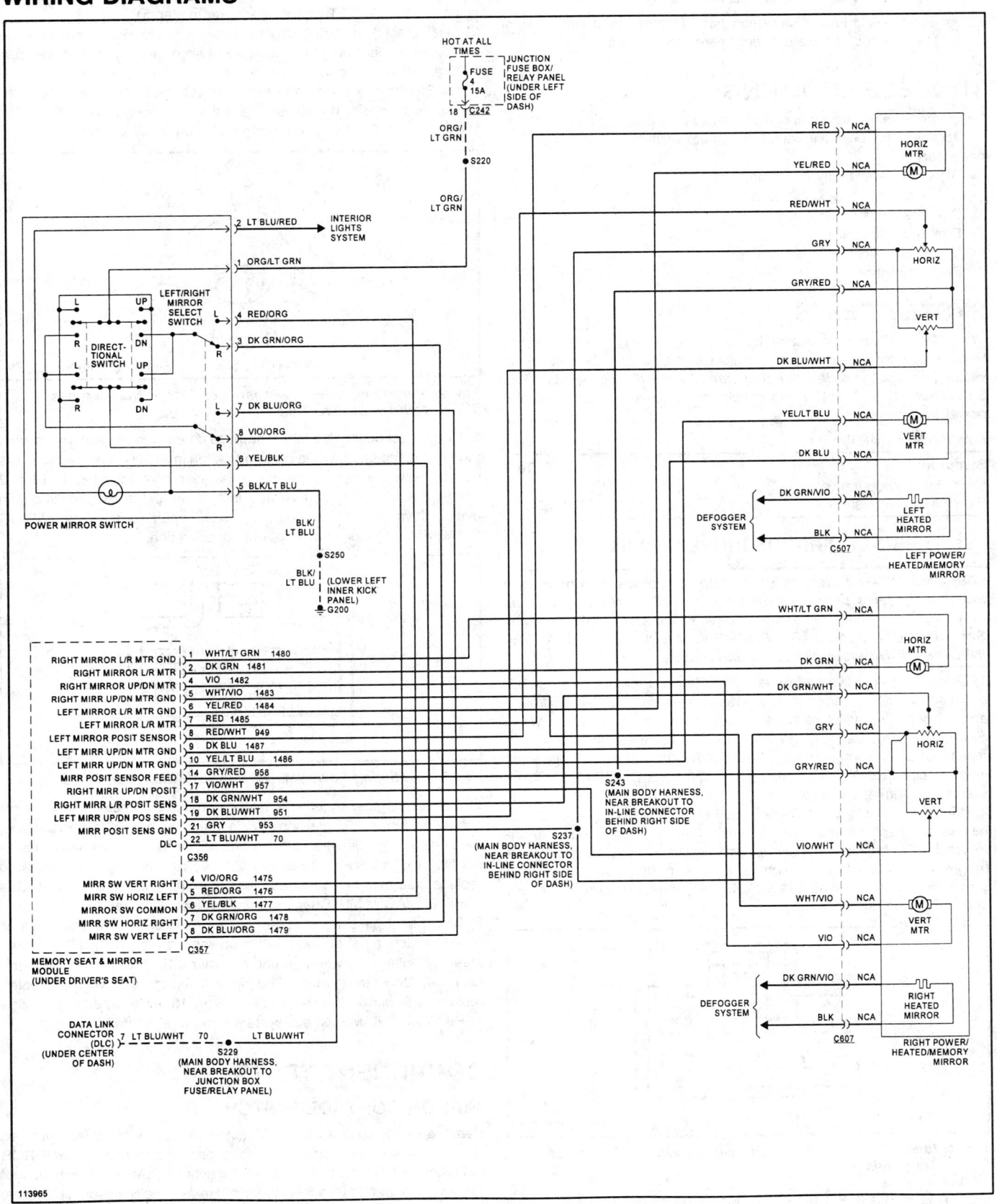

Fig. 8: Power Memory Mirror System Wiring Diagram (Navigator)

113965

DESCRIPTION & OPERATION

Power side view mirror system consists of mirror head with integral reversible servomotor assembly and mirror control switch.

TROUBLE SHOOTING

Before performing individual component tests or diagnostic tests, check the following for possible cause of system malfunction and repair as necessary:

- Blown fuses or faulty circuit breaker.
- Loose or corroded connectors.
- Damaged wiring.
- Damaged motors.
- Damaged mirror assemblies.
- Faulty switches.

SYSTEM TESTS

Verify the customer complaint by operating power mirrors. Visually inspect for obvious sign of mechanical and electrical damage. If no visual damage is evident, perform appropriate diagnostic test. See SYMPTOM CHART table. A digital volt-ohmmeter is required to test the power mirror system.

SYMPTOM CHART

Symptom	Test
Both Mirrors Inoperative	A
Single Mirror Inoperative	B

TEST A: BOTH MIRRORS INOPERATIVE

WARNING: When battery is disconnected, vehicle computer and memory systems may lose memory data. Driveability problems may exist until computer systems have completed a relearn cycle. See COMPUTER RELEARN PROCEDURES article in GENERAL INFORMATION before disconnecting battery.

1) Disconnect negative battery terminal. Remove mirror control switch and disconnect harness connector. Measure resistance between ground and mirror control switch harness connector terminal No. 6 (Yellow wire). *See Fig. 1.* If resistance is greater than 10 k/ohms, go to next step. If resistance is 10 k/ohms or less, repair Yellow wire, connectors or central junction box fuse No. 4 (15-amp). See WIRING DIAGRAMS. Check system for normal operation.

2) Measure resistance between ground and mirror control switch harness connector terminal No. 5 (Black wire). *See Fig. 1.* If resistance is less than 5 ohms, replace mirror control switch. If resistance is 5 ohms or greater, repair open or high resistance in Black wire or ground connection. See WIRING DIAGRAMS. Reconnect battery and check system for normal operation.

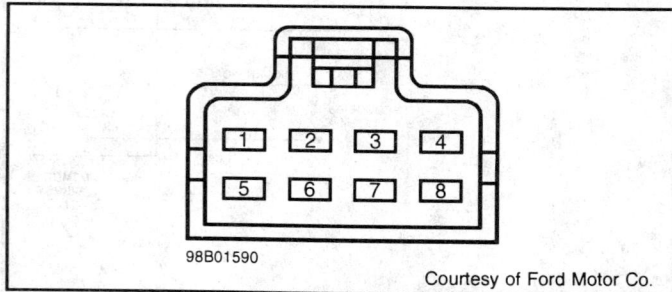

Fig. 1: Identifying Mirror Control Switch Harness Connector Terminals

TEST B: SINGLE MIRROR INOPERATIVE

1) Attempt to operate mirrors from switch. If driver side mirror is inoperative in UP/DOWN mode, go to next step. If driver side mirror is inoperative in LEFT/RIGHT mode, go to step 3). If passenger side mirror is inoperative in UP/DOWN mode, go to step 4). If passenger side mirror is inoperative in LEFT/RIGHT mode, go to step 5).

2) Disconnect driver side mirror harness connector. Place mirror control switch in "L" position. While pressing switch in UP position, measure voltage between ground and mirror harness connector terminal No. 4 (Dark Blue/Yellow wire). *See Fig. 2.* If voltage is 10 volts or greater, replace side mirror. If voltage is less than 10 volts, repair circuit. See WIRING DIAGRAMS. Check system for normal operation.

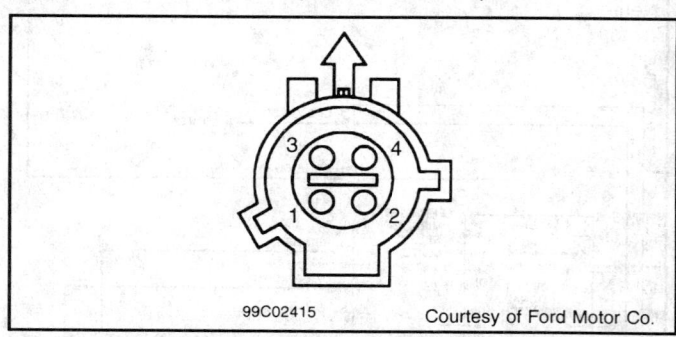

Fig. 2: Identifying Driver & Passenger Side Mirror Harness Connector Terminals

3) Disconnect driver side mirror harness connector. Place mirror control switch in "L" position. While pressing switch in RIGHT position, measure voltage between ground and mirror harness connector terminal No. 2 (Red wire). *See Fig. 2.* If voltage is 10 volts or greater, replace side mirror. If voltage is less than 10 volts, repair circuit. See WIRING DIAGRAMS. Check system for normal operation.

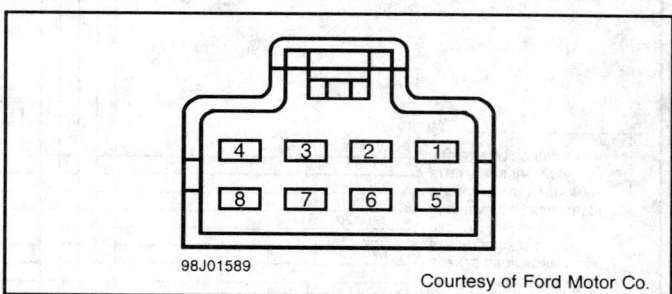

Fig. 3: Identifying Power Mirror Control Switch Terminals

4) Disconnect passenger side mirror harness connector. Place mirror control switch in "R" position. While pressing switch in UP position, measure voltage between ground and mirror harness connector terminal No. 4 (Purple wire). *See Fig. 2.* If voltage is 10 volts or greater, replace side mirror. If voltage is less than 10 volts, repair circuit. See WIRING DIAGRAMS. Check system for normal operation.

5) Disconnect passenger side mirror harness connector. Place mirror control switch in "R" position. While pressing switch in RIGHT position, measure voltage between ground and mirror harness connector terminal No. 2 (Dark Green wire) . *See Fig. 2.* If voltage is 10 volts or greater, replace side mirror. If voltage is less than 10 volts, repair circuit. See WIRING DIAGRAMS. Check system for normal operation.

COMPONENT TESTS

MIRROR CONTROL SWITCH

Remove mirror control switch. Measure resistance between specified terminals while operating switch in appropriate direction. See MIRROR SWITCH TEST table. *See Fig. 3.* Resistance between each pair of terminals should be less than 5 ohms. Resistance between all terminal pairs and conditions not listed in table should be greater than 10 k/ohms. If switch fails any portion of test, replace switch.

1999 ACCESSORIES & EQUIPMENT
Power Mirrors – F250 Super-Duty & F350 Pickup (Cont.)

FORD
4-965

MIRROR SWITCH TEST

Switch Position	Continuity Between Terminals
Driver Mirror Position	
Up	1 & 7; 1 & 8; 2 & 3; 2 & 4; 4 & 6; 7 & 8
Down	1 & 4; 1 & 7; 1 & 8; 2 & 3; 2 & 4; 6 & 8
Left	1 & 4; 1 & 8; 2 & 3; 2 & 4; 6 & 7; 6 & 8; 7 & 8
Right	1 & 8; 2 & 3; 2 & 4; 4 & 6; 6 & 7
Neutral	1 & 6; 1 & 7; 1 & 8; 2 & 3; 2 & 4; 6 & 7; 6 & 8; 7 & 8
Passenger Mirror Position	
Up	4 & 5; 7 & 8
Down	4 & 7; 5 & 8
Left	5 & 7; 5 & 8; 7 & 8
Right	4 & 5; 4 & 7; 5 & 7
Neutral	5 & 7; 5 & 8; 7 & 8

REMOVAL & INSTALLATION

WARNING: When battery is disconnected, vehicle computer and memory systems may lose memory data. Driveability problems may exist until computer systems have completed a relearn cycle. See COMPUTER RELEARN PROCEDURES article in GENERAL INFORMATION before disconnecting battery.

SIDE MIRROR ASSEMBLY

Removal & Installation – Disconnect negative battery cable. Remove appropriate door panel and watershield. Remove interior trim cover to access retaining nuts. Disconnect mirror harness connectors. Disengage wiring clips. Remove 3 mirror retaining nuts. Remove mirror. To install, reverse removal procedure. Tighten retaining nuts to 62 INCH lbs. (7 N.m).

MIRROR CONTROL SWITCH

Removal & Installation – Disconnect negative battery cable. Push door command center forward while pulling up on leading edge. Disconnect harness connectors. Remove door command center from vehicle. Disengage mirror switch retaining clips from door command center, and remove switch. To install, reverse removal procedure.

INTERIOR REAR VIEW MIRROR

Removal & Installation – Insert Interior Rear View Mirror Remover (T91T-17700-A), up into base of mirror mount. As tool releases mirror retaining clip, slide mirror up to remove. To install, slide mirror down onto base.

WIRING DIAGRAMS

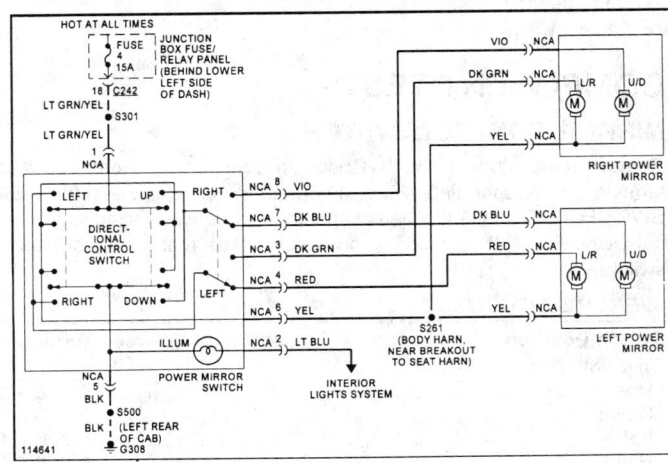

Fig. 4: Power Mirror System Wiring Diagram (F250 Super-Duty & F350 Pickup)

DESCRIPTION

Power side view mirror system consists of mirror head with integral reversible servomotor assembly and mirror control switch.

TROUBLE SHOOTING

Before performing individual component tests or system tests, check the following for possible cause of system malfunction and repair as necessary:

- Blown fuses.
- Loose or corroded connectors.
- Damaged wiring.
- Damaged mirror motors.
- Damaged mirror assemblies.
- Faulty switch.

COMPONENT TESTS

MIRROR CONTROL SWITCH

Remove mirror control switch. Check for continuity between specified terminals while operating switch in appropriate direction. See MIRROR SWITCH TEST table. Continuity should exist between specified terminals. *See Fig. 1.* If continuity is not as specified, replace mirror control switch.

MIRROR SWITCH TEST

Switch Position	Continuity Between Terminals
Driver Mirror	
Up	4 & 7; 6 & 8
Down	4 & 8; 6 & 7
Left	1 & 7; 6 & 8
Right	1 & 8; 6 & 7
Passenger Mirror	
Up	2 & 7; 6 & 8
Down	2 & 8; 6 & 7
Left	3 & 7; 6 & 8
Right	3 & 8; 6 & 7

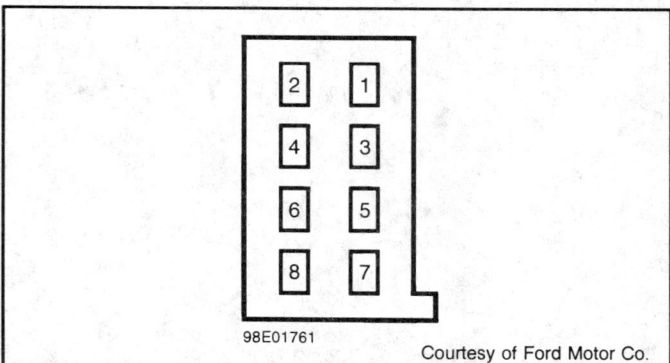

98E01761   Courtesy of Ford Motor Co.

Fig. 1: Identifying Power Mirror Control Switch Terminals

SYSTEM TESTS

Verify customer complaint by operating power mirrors. Visually inspect for obvious sign of mechanical and electrical damage. If no visual damage is evident, perform appropriate system test. See SYMPTOM CHART table. A digital volt-ohmmeter is required to test power mirror system.

SYMPTOM CHART

Symptom	Test
Both Mirrors Inoperative	A
Single Mirror Inoperative	B
Single Mirror Inoperative With Switch Logic	C

TEST A: BOTH MIRRORS INOPERATIVE

1) Check fuse No. 1 (7.5-amp) in instrument panel fuse box. If fuse is okay, go to next step. If fuse is blown, check for short to ground in Orange/Light Green wire. Repair as necessary.
2) Remove mirror control switch and disconnect harness connector. Measure voltage between ground and mirror control switch terminal No. 7 (Orange/Light Green wire) at mirror control switch harness connector. *See Fig. 2.* If battery voltage exists, go to next step. If battery voltage does not exist, repair Orange/Light Green wire.

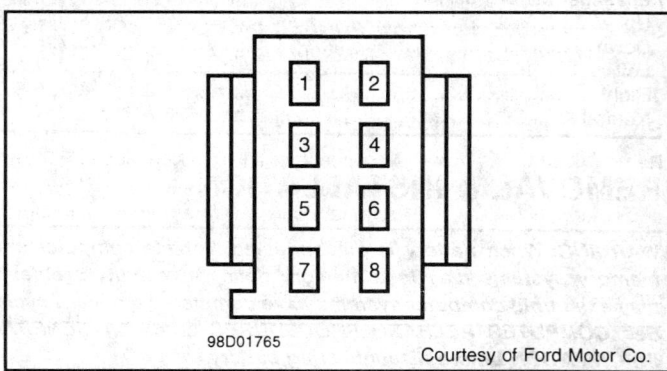

98D01765   Courtesy of Ford Motor Co.

Fig. 2: Identifying Mirror Control Switch Harness Connector Terminals

3) Measure resistance between ground and mirror control switch harness connector terminal No. 1 (Black wire). If resistance is 5 ohms or less, go to next step. If resistance is more than 5 ohms, repair open Black wire.
4) Disconnect driver and passenger mirror harness connectors. Measure resistance of Yellow wire between mirror control switch harness connector terminal No. 3 and left outside mirror connector. If resistance is less than 5 ohms, replace mirror control switch. If resistance is 5 ohms or more, repair open Yellow wire.

TEST B: SINGLE MIRROR INOPERATIVE

1) Disconnect inoperative mirror harness connector. Measure resistance of Yellow wire between mirror control switch harness connector terminal No. 3 and appropriate outside mirror connector. If resistance is less than 5 ohms, go to next step. If resistance is 5 ohms or more, repair open Yellow wire.
2) Test mirror control switch. See MIRROR CONTROL SWITCH under COMPONENT TESTS. If switch is okay, replace appropriate mirror assembly. If switch is defective, replace mirror control switch.

TEST C: SINGLE MIRROR INOPERATIVE WITH SWITCH LOGIC

1) Operate mirrors in left and right direction. If mirrors move left and right, go to next step. If mirrors do not move left and right, go to step **3)**.
2) Operate mirrors in up and down direction. If mirrors move up and down, system is functioning properly at this time. If mirrors do not move up and down, go to step **5)**.
3) Turn ignition off. Disconnect inoperative mirror connector. Measure voltage between ground inoperative mirror connector Dark Green wire (left mirror) or Red wire (right mirror). If voltage is 10 volts or less, go to next step. If voltage is more than 10 volts, replace inoperative mirror.
4) Remove mirror control switch and disconnect harness connector. Test mirror control switch. See MIRROR CONTROL SWITCH under COMPONENT TESTS. If switch is okay, repair Red and/or Dark Green wires between inoperative mirror motor and mirror control switch. If switch is defective, replace mirror control switch.
5) Turn ignition off. Disconnect inoperative mirror connector. Measure voltage between ground inoperative mirror connector Dark Blue wire (left mirror) or Violet wire (right mirror). If voltage is 10 volts or less, go to next step. If voltage is more than 10 volts, replace inoperative mirror.
6) Remove mirror control switch and disconnect harness connector. Test mirror control switch. See MIRROR CONTROL SWITCH under COM-

PONENT TESTS. If switch is okay, repair Violet and/or Dark Blue wires between inoperative mirror motor and mirror control switch. If switch is defective, replace mirror control switch.

REMOVAL & INSTALLATION

WARNING: When battery is disconnected, vehicle computer and memory systems may lose memory data. Driveability problems may exist until computer systems have completed a relearn cycle. See COMPUTER RELEARN PROCEDURES article in GENERAL INFORMATION before disconnecting battery.

SIDE MIRROR ASSEMBLY

Removal & Installation – Disconnect negative battery cable. Remove door panel. Remove mirror mounting hole cover. *See Fig. 3.* Remove and disconnect speaker. Disconnect mirror wiring harness connector. Remove mirror attaching nuts. Remove mirror assembly while guiding wiring and connector through hole in door. To install, reverse removal procedure. Tighten nuts to approximately 53 INCH lbs. (6 N.m).

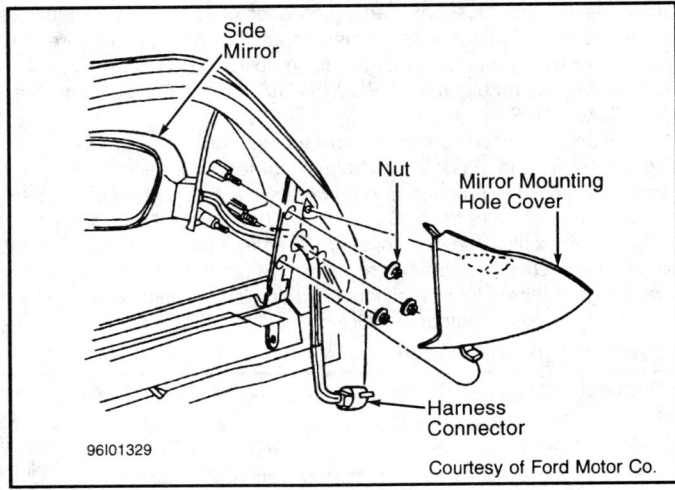

Fig. 3: Removing Side Mirror

MIRROR CONTROL SWITCH

Removal & Installation – Remove driver-side door panel. Depress retaining clips on switch housing. Push base of switch out of door panel. Disconnect mirror harness connector. Remove switch. To install, reverse removal procedure.

WIRING DIAGRAMS

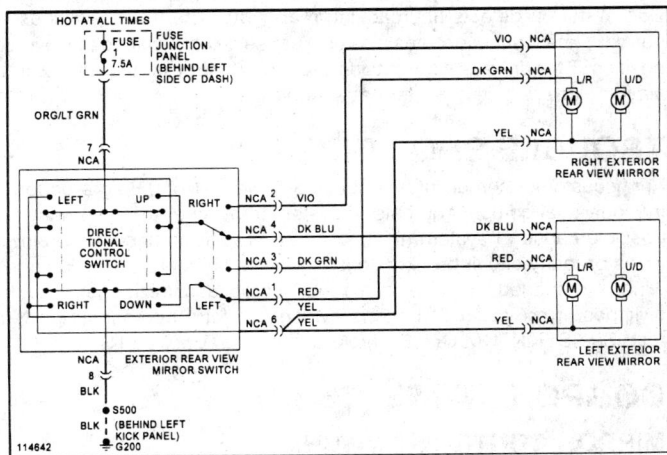

Fig. 4: Power Mirror System Wiring Diagram (Ranger)

DESCRIPTION & OPERATION

Power side view mirror system consists of mirror head with integral reversible servomotor assembly and mirror control switch. Some models are equipped with an electronic dimming rear view mirror.

The optional inside electronic dimming rear view mirror is controlled by 2 light-sensitive photocells. Outside light level is measured by a sensor on backside of mirror housing. A second sensor, located on reflective side of mirror, detects approaching rear lights. The mirror switches to normal state whenever transmission gear selector is placed in Reverse position. The driver's side outside rear view mirror is available with a similar glare reduction system as an option.

TROUBLE SHOOTING

Verify customer complaint by operating power mirrors. Before performing individual component tests or system tests, check the following for possible cause of system malfunction and repair as necessary: blown fuses or faulty circuit breaker, loose or corroded connectors, damaged wiring, damaged motors, damaged mirror assemblies and faulty switches. If no visual damage is evident, perform appropriate system test. See SYMPTOM CHART table under SYSTEM TESTS.

COMPONENT TESTS

MIRROR CONTROL SWITCH

Remove mirror control switch. Measure resistance between specified terminals while operating switch in appropriate position. See MIRROR SWITCH TEST table. See Fig. 1. Resistance in all tests should be less than 5 ohms. If switch fails any portion of test, replace switch.

MIRROR SWITCH TEST

Switch Position	Continuity Between Terminals
Left Mirror	
Up	1 & 6; 5 & 8
Down	1 & 8; 5 & 6
Left	1 & 6; 3 & 5
Right	1 & 3; 5 & 6
Right Mirror	
Up	1 & 6; 7 & 5
Down	1 & 7; 5 & 6
Left	1 & 6; 4 & 5
Right	1 & 4; 5 & 6

harness connector C518. See Fig. 2. If battery voltage exists, go to next step. If battery voltage does not exist, go to step 3).

2) Measure resistance between ground and terminal No. 5 (Black wire) at mirror control switch harness connector C518. If resistance is 5 ohms or less, go to step 1). If resistance is greater than 5 ohms, repair open in Black wire.

3) Remove fuse No. 22 (5-amp) in instrument panel fuse box. Inspect fuse. If fuse is blown, go to next step. If fuse is okay, repair power distribution circuit. See appropriate wiring diagram in POWER DISTRIBUTION article in WIRING DIAGRAMS.

4) Connect mirror control switch harness connector C518. Disconnect instrument panel fuse box harness connector C247. Measure resistance between ground and terminal No. 17 (Dark Green wire) at instrument panel fuse box harness connector C247. See Fig. 3. If resistance is 10 k/ohms or less, go to next step. If resistance is greater than 10 k/ohms, go to step 6).

NOTE: *Power antenna, light sensor/amplifier and luggage compartment light (anti-theft disarm switch on wagon) also receive power from fuse No. 22.*

5) Disconnect mirror control switch harness connector C518. Measure resistance between ground and terminal No. 17 (Dark Green wire) at instrument panel fuse box harness connector C247. If resistance is greater than 10 k/ohms, replace mirror control switch. If resistance is 10 k/ohms or less, repair short to ground in power distribution circuit. See appropriate wiring diagram in POWER DISTRIBUTION article in WIRING DIAGRAMS.

6) Disconnect mirror control switch harness connector C518. Disconnect driver's and passenger's mirror harness connectors. Measure resistance between ground and appropriate terminals at mirror control switch harness connector C518. See TERMINAL IDENTIFICATION table. If all resistance readings are greater than 10 k/ohms, repair intermittent short to ground or short to ground in driver's and/or passenger's mirror. If any resistance reading is 10 k/ohms or less, repair short to ground in appropriate wire.

TERMINAL IDENTIFICATION

Terminal	Wire Color
3	Red
4	White
6	Yellow
7	Violet
8	Dark Blue

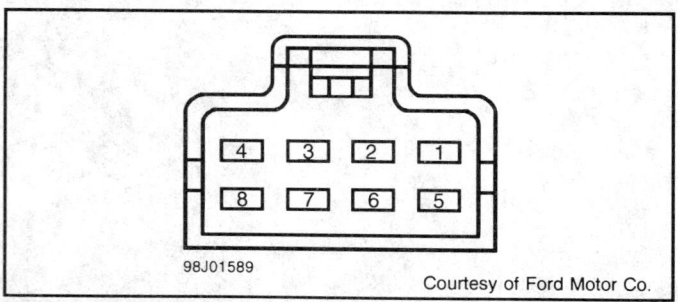

98J01589   Courtesy of Ford Motor Co.

Fig. 1: Identifying Mirror Control Switch Terminals

SYSTEM TESTS

SYMPTOM CHART

Symptom	Test
Both Mirrors Inoperative	A
Single Mirror Inoperative	B
Single Mirror Does Not Operate With Switch Logic	C
One Or Both Heated Mirrors Inoperative	D

TEST A: BOTH MIRRORS INOPERATIVE

1) Disconnect mirror control switch harness connector C518. Measure voltage at terminal No. 1 (Dark Green wire) at mirror control switch

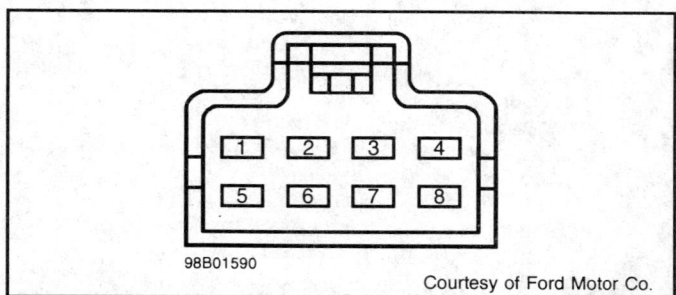

98B01590   Courtesy of Ford Motor Co.

Fig. 2: Identifying Mirror Control Switch Harness Connector C518 Terminals

TEST B: SINGLE MIRROR INOPERATIVE

1) Disconnect inoperative outside mirror harness connector. Measure voltage at terminal No. 5 (Yellow wire) at inoperative outside mirror harness connector while operating mirror control switch to UP, then LEFT position for that mirror. See Fig. 4. If battery voltage does not exist in both readings, go to next step. If battery voltage exists in both readings, go to step 3).

2) Disconnect mirror control switch harness connector C518. Measure resistance in Yellow wire between terminal No. 5 at inoperative mirror harness connector and terminal No. 6 at mirror control switch harness

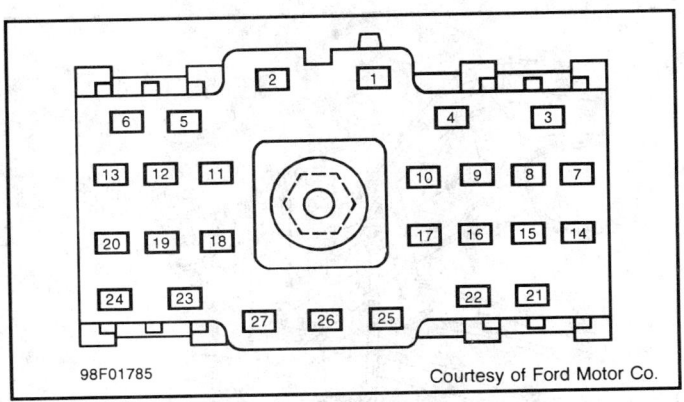

Fig. 3: Identifying Instrument Panel Fuse Box Harness Connector C247 Terminals

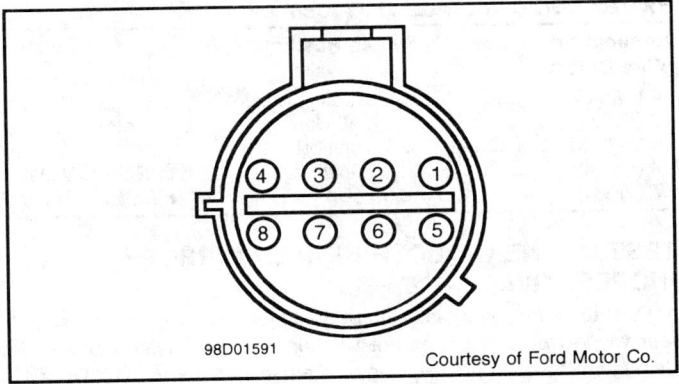

Fig. 4: Identifying Driver's & Passenger's Side Mirror Harness Connector Terminals

connector C518. *See Figs. 2 and 4.* If resistance is 5 ohms or less, replace mirror control switch. If resistance is greater than 5 ohms, repair open in Yellow wire.

3) Measure voltage at terminal No. 6 (Dark Blue wire on driver's side; Violet wire on passenger's side) at inoperative mirror harness connector while operating mirror control switch to DOWN position for that mirror. If battery voltage does not exist, go to next step. If battery voltage exists, go to step **5)**.

4) Disconnect mirror control switch harness connector C518. Measure resistance in appropriate wire between inoperative mirror harness connector and mirror control switch harness connector C518. See CIRCUIT IDENTIFICATION table. *See Figs. 2 and 4.* If resistance is 5 ohms or less, replace mirror control switch. If resistance is greater than 5 ohms, repair open in appropriate wire.

CIRCUIT IDENTIFICATION

Mirror Terminal	Switch Terminal	Wire Color
Driver's Side		
7	3	Red
5	6	Yellow
6	8	Dark Blue
Passenger's Side		
6	7	Violet
5	6	Yellow
7	4	White

5) Measure voltage at terminal No. 7 (Red wire on driver's side; White wire on passenger's side) at inoperative mirror harness connector while operating mirror control switch to RIGHT position for that mirror. If battery voltage does not exist, go to next step. If battery voltage exists, replace appropriate outside mirror.

6) Disconnect mirror control switch harness connector C518. Measure resistance in appropriate wire between inoperative mirror harness connector and mirror control switch harness connector C518. See IRCUIT IDENTIFICATION table. *See Figs. 2 and 4.* If resistance is 5 ohms or less, replace mirror control switch. If resistance is greater than 5 ohms, repair open in appropriate wire.

TEST C: SINGLE MIRROR DOES NOT OPERATE WITH SWITCH LOGIC

1) Turn ignition switch to LOCK position. Disconnect malfunctioning outside mirror harness connector. Inspect wiring. Ensure wires are connected to proper terminals. See WIRE/TERMINAL IDENTIFICATION table. *See Fig. 4.* If wires are not damaged and properly connected, go to next step. If wires are damaged and/or connected improperly, repair as necessary.

WIRE/TERMINAL IDENTIFICATION

Mirror Terminal	Wire Color
Driver's Side	
7	Red

WIRE/TERMINAL IDENTIFICATION (Cont.)

Mirror Terminal	Wire Color
5	Yellow
6	Dark Blue
Passenger's Side	
6	Violet
5	Yellow
7	White

2) Measure voltage/resistance at appropriate terminal at malfunctioning outside mirror harness connector while operating mirror control switch to appropriate position. See MIRROR LOGIC VOLTAGE TEST table. If voltage/resistance readings are not as specified, go to next step. If voltage/resistance readings are as specified, replace appropriate outside mirror.

MIRROR LOGIC VOLTAGE TEST

Terminal No. (Wire Color)	Switch Position	Value
Driver's Side		
5 (Yellow)	Left/Up	Battery Voltage
5 (Yellow)	Down/Right	Ground
6 (Dark Blue)	Down	Battery Voltage
6 (Dark Blue)	Up	Ground
7 (Red)	Right	Battery Voltage
7 (Red)	Left	Ground
Passenger's Side		
5 (Yellow)	Left/Up	Battery Voltage
5 (Yellow)	Down/Right	Ground
6 (Violet)	Down	Battery Voltage
6 (Violet)	Up	Ground
7 (White)	Right	Battery Voltage
7 (White)	Left	Ground

3) Remove mirror control switch leaving harness connected. Using a DVOM, backprobe at appropriate terminal at mirror control switch harness connector C518 while operating switch in appropriate position. See SWITCH LOGIC VOLTAGE TEST table. If voltage/resistance readings are as specified, repair crossed wires. If voltage/resistance readings are not as specified, replace mirror control switch.

SWITCH LOGIC VOLTAGE TEST

Terminal No. (Wire Color)	Switch Position	Value
Driver's Side		
3 (Red)	Right	Battery Voltage
3 (Red)	Left	Ground
6 (Yellow)	Left/Up	Battery Voltage
6 (Yellow)	Down/Right	Ground
8 (Dark Blue)	Down	Battery Voltage
8 (Dark Blue)	Up	Ground
Passenger's Side		
4 (White)	Right	Battery Voltage

SWITCH LOGIC VOLTAGE TEST (Cont.)

Terminal No. (Wire Color)	Switch Position	Value
4 (White)	Left	Ground
6 (Yellow)	Left/Up	Battery Voltage
6 (Yellow)	Down/Right	Ground
7 (Violet)	Down	Battery Voltage
7 (Violet)	Up	Ground

TEST D: ONE OR BOTH HEATED MIRRORS INOPERATIVE

1) Operate defogger. If rear window defogger is okay, go to next step. If rear window defogger does not function properly, repair rear window defogger. See appropriate wiring diagram in REAR WINDOW DEFOGGERS article.

2) Check fuse No. 32 (10-amp) in instrument panel fuse box. If fuse is okay, go to next step. If fuse is blown, repair short to ground in Dark Green/Violet wire or power distribution circuit. See appropriate wiring diagram in POWER DISTRIBUTION article in WIRING DIAGRAMS.

3) Turn rear defoggers on. Measure voltage at input side of fuse No. 32 in instrument panel fuse box. If battery voltage exists, go to next step. If battery voltage does not exist, repair or replace instrument panel fuse box as necessary.

4) Ensure fuse No. 32 is installed. Disconnect inoperative mirror harness connector. Turn ignition switch to RUN position. Turn rear window defogger on. Measure voltage at terminal No. 2 (Dark Green/Violet wire) at appropriate mirror harness connector. *See Fig. 4.* If battery voltage exists, go to next step. If battery voltage does not exist, repair open in Dark Green/Violet wire.

5) Turn ignition switch to LOCK position. Measure resistance between ground and terminal No. 1 (Black wire) at appropriate mirror harness connector. If resistance is 5 ohms or less, replace appropriate mirror glass. If resistance is greater than 5 ohms, repair open in Black wire.

REMOVAL & INSTALLATION

WARNING: *When battery is disconnected, vehicle computer and memory systems may lose memory data. Driveability problems may exist until computer systems have completed a relearn cycle. See COMPUTER RELEARN PROCEDURES article in GENERAL INFORMATION before disconnecting battery.*

SIDE MIRROR ASSEMBLY

Removal & Installation – Remove door panel. Remove mirror mounting hole cover. *See Fig. 5.* Disconnect mirror wiring harness connector. Remove mirror attaching nuts. Remove mirror assembly while guiding wiring and connector through hole in door. To install, reverse removal procedure. Tighten nuts to approximately 53 INCH lbs. (6 N.m).

SIDE MIRROR GLASS & MOTOR

Removal & Installation – Point mirror glass as far inward as possible to allow clearance between glass and mirror housing at outer edge of mirror. Insert fingers into clearance, and pull mirror glass. If fingers will not fit between glass and housing, use a screwdriver and cloth to pry mirror glass out. Glass will snap out without being damaged. Disconnect heater wires (if equipped). Remove motor attaching screws. Unplug motor connector, and remove motor. To install, reverse removal procedure. Ensure mirror glass locking tabs align before snapping in glass.

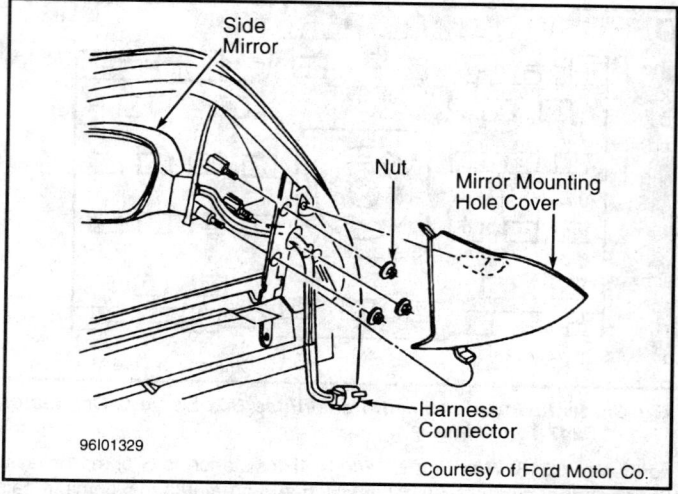

96I01329

Courtesy of Ford Motor Co.

Fig. 5: Removing Side Mirror

MIRROR CONTROL SWITCH

Removal & Installation – Remove driver-side door panel. Depress retaining clips on switch housing. Push base of switch out of door panel. Unplug wiring connector. Remove switch. To install, reverse removal procedure.

WIRING DIAGRAMS

NOTE: For heated mirror wiring diagram, see REAR WINDOW DEFOGGERS article.

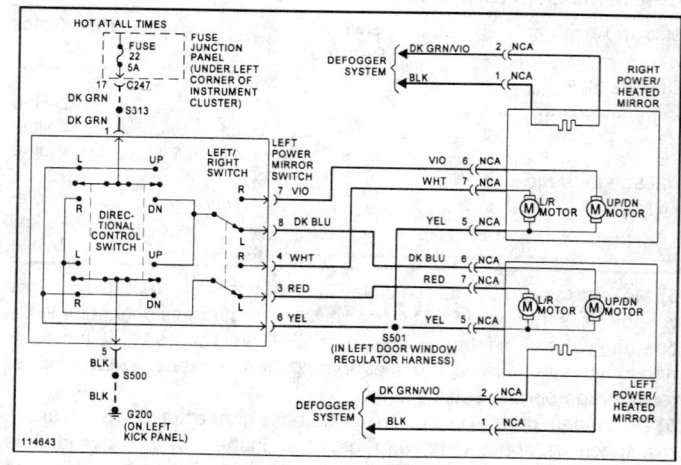

Fig. 6: Power Mirror System Wiring Diagram (Sable & Taurus)

Power Mirrors – Town Car

DESCRIPTION & OPERATION

The power memory seat/mirror system allows storing 2 seat/mirror positions into memory. Seat and outside mirrors will automatically move to preset position(s) by pressing button 1 or 2. The mirror and seat memory will not operate unless transmission is in Park or Neutral.

The optional automatic dimming rear view mirror is controlled by 2 light-sensitive photocells. Outside light level is measured by a sensor on backside of mirror housing. A second sensor, located on reflective side of mirror, detects approaching rear lights. The mirror photochromically dims when glare is detected from rear of vehicle. Mirror switches to normal state whenever transmission gear selector is placed in Reverse. The driver's side outside rear view mirror is also available with auto-dimming function.

Power side-view mirror system consists of mirror head with integral servomotor assembly. Memory mirror is controlled by Driver's Door Module (DDM) and Driver's Seat Module (DSM). Side mirror glass and motor can be replaced separately. Side mirrors are equipped with heating elements. The rear window defogger switch controls operation.

COMPONENT LOCATIONS

COMPONENT LOCATIONS

Component	Location
Data Link Connector	Under Instrument Panel, Right Of Steering Column
Door Lock Switch	Appropriate Door Panel Arm Rest
Driver's Door Module (DDM)	Behind Driver's Door Panel, Lower Front Corner
Driver's Heated Seat Module	Under Driver's Seat
Front Seat Track Assembly	[1] Under Appropriate Seat
Heated Seat Switch	Driver's Door Trim Panel
Instrument Panel Fuse Box	Below Left Instrument Panel
Keyless Entry Keypad	Driver's Door Below Exterior Door Handle
Lumbar Switch	Side Of Seat Cushion
Power Distribution Box	Left Side Of Engine Compartment, Above Wheelwell
Power Mirror Switch	Driver's Door Panel Arm Rest

[1] – Front seat track and adjustment motors are a complete assembly.

TROUBLE SHOOTING

Verify customer complaint. Check for blown fuses or faulty circuit breaker. Check for loose or corroded connectors. Check for damaged wiring. Check for damaged motors. Check for damaged mirror assemblies. Check for faulty switches. If no problem was found, go to SELF-DIAGNOSTIC SYSTEM.

COMPONENT TESTS

DOOR LOCK SWITCH

Remove door lock switch. Using an ohmmeter, check for continuity between indicated switch terminals with switch in appropriate position. See POWER DOOR LOCK SWITCH TERMINAL IDENTIFICATION table. See Fig. 1. Replace door lock switch if it does not test as specified.

POWER DOOR LOCK SWITCH TERMINAL IDENTIFICATION

Switch Position	Continuity Between Terminals
Driver's Side	
Lock	2 & 4
Unlock	4 & 6
Passenger's Side	
Lock	4 & 6
Unlock	2 & 4

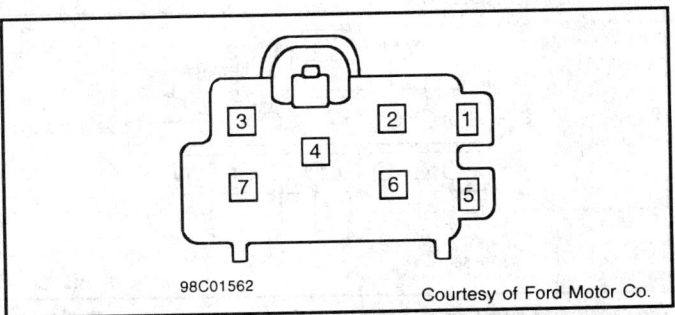

Fig. 1: Identifying Power Door Lock Switch Terminals

MIRROR CONTROL SWITCH

Remove mirror control switch. Using an ohmmeter, check for continuity between indicated switch terminals with switch in appropriate position. See MIRROR CONTROL SWITCH TERMINAL IDENTIFICATION table. See Fig. 2. Replace mirror control switch if it does not test as specified.

MIRROR CONTROL SWITCH TERMINAL IDENTIFICATION

Switch Position	Continuity Between Terminals
Left Mirror	
Up	3 & 9; 4 & 7
Down	3 & 4; 7 & 9
Left	1 & 3; 4 & 7
Right	1 & 7; 3 & 4
Right Mirror	
Up	3 & 8; 4 & 7
Down	3 & 4; 7 & 8
Left	2 & 3; 4 & 7
Right	2 & 7; 3 & 4

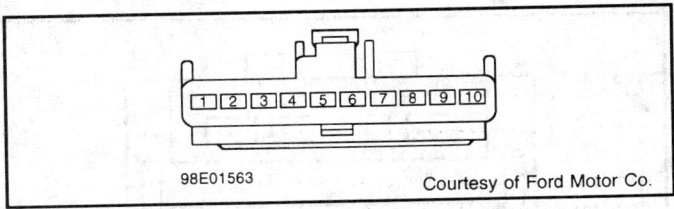

Fig. 2: Identifying Mirror Control Switch Terminals

DRIVER'S SEAT CONTROL SWITCH (WITH MEMORY)

Remove driver's seat control switch. Using an ohmmeter, check for continuity between indicated switch terminals with switch in appropriate position. See DRIVER'S SEAT CONTROL SWITCH RESISTANCE (WITH MEMORY) table. See Fig. 3. Replace driver's seat control switch if it does not test as specified.

DRIVER'S SEAT CONTROL SWITCH RESISTANCE (WITH MEMORY)

Switch Position	Continuity Between Terminals
Front Up	2 & 10
Front Down	3 & 10
Rear Up	10 & 12
Rear Down	10 & 11
Seat FWD	9 & 10
Seat RWD	1 & 10
Recline FWD	10 & 13
Recline RWD	10 & 14
Memory Set	5 & 10
Memory "1"	6 & 10
Memory "2"	7 & 10

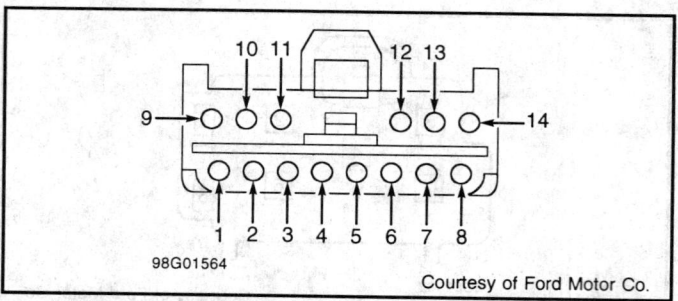

Fig. 3: Identifying Driver's Seat Control Switch Terminals (With Memory)

DRIVER'S SEAT CONTROL SWITCH (WITHOUT MEMORY)

Remove driver's seat control switch. Using an ohmmeter, check for continuity between indicated switch terminals with switch in appropriate position. See DRIVER'S SEAT CONTROL SWITCH RESISTANCE (WITHOUT MEMORY) table. See Fig. 4. Replace appropriate seat control switch if it does not test as specified.

DRIVER'S SEAT CONTROL SWITCH RESISTANCE (WITHOUT MEMORY)

Switch Position	Continuity Between Terminals
Neutral	1 & All Except 3
Front Up	3 & 7
Front Down	3 & 5
Rear Up	3 & 4
Rear Down	3 & 6
Seat FWD	2 & 3
Seat RWD	3 & 8

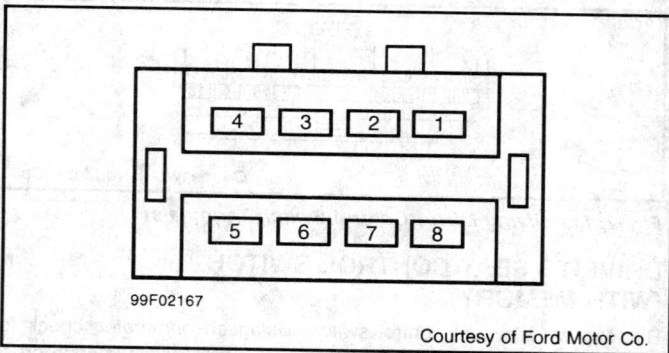

Fig. 4: Identifying Driver's Seat Control Switch Terminals (Without Memory) & Passenger's Seat Control Switch (Executive Model)

PASSENGER'S SEAT CONTROL SWITCH

Remove passenger's seat control switch. Using an ohmmeter, check for continuity between indicated switch terminals with switch in appropriate position. See SEAT CONTROL SWITCH RESISTANCE (PASSENGER'S SEAT) table. See Fig. 4 or 5. Replace appropriate seat control switch if it does not test as specified.

SEAT CONTROL SWITCH RESISTANCE (PASSENGER'S SEAT)

Switch Position	Continuity Between Terminals
Neutral	
Except Executive Model	7 & All Except 12
Executive Model	5 & All Except 8
Front Up	
Except Executive Model	1 & 7
Executive Model	2 & 8
Front Down	
Except Executive Model	2 & 7

SEAT CONTROL SWITCH RESISTANCE (PASSENGER'S SEAT) (Cont.)

Switch Position	Continuity Between Terminals
Executive Model	3 & 8
Rear Up	
Except Executive Model	7 & 11
Executive Model	4 & 8
Rear Down	
Except Executive Model	6 & 7
Executive Model	1 & 8
Seat FWD	
Except Executive Model	7 & 8
Executive Model	6 & 8
Seat RWD	
Except Executive Model	7 & 10
Executive Model	7 & 8
Seat Recline FWD [1]	5 & 7
Seat Recline RWD [1]	4 & 7

[1] – Does not apply to executive model.

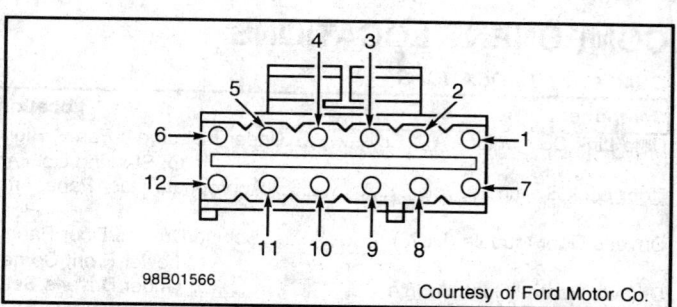

Fig. 5: Identifying Passenger's Seat Control Switch (Except Executive Model)

REMOTE TRUNK RELEASE SWITCH

Remove remote trunk release switch. Using an ohmmeter, check continuity between switch terminals. With switch depressed, continuity should exist. With switch not depressed, continuity should not exist. Replace switch if continuity is not as specified.

CONNECTOR IDENTIFICATION

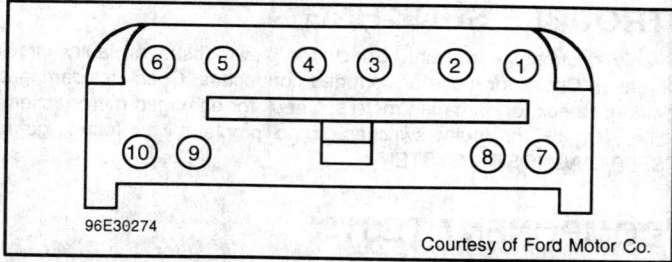

Fig. 6: Identifying Driver's & Passenger's Mirror Harness Connector Terminals

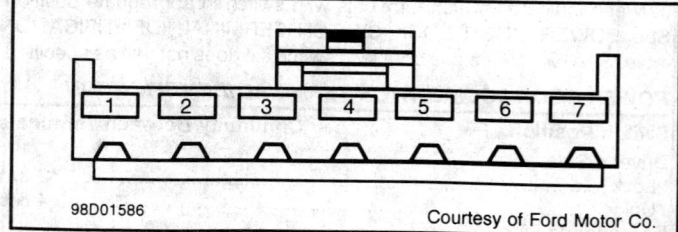

Fig. 7: Identifying Inside Mirror Harness Connector C902 Terminals

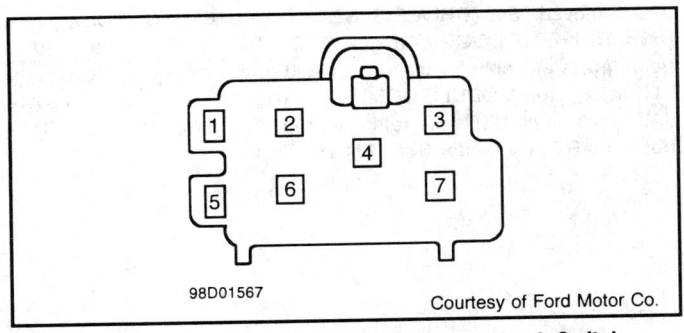

Fig. 8: Identifying Driver's & Passenger's Door Lock Switch Harness Connector Terminals

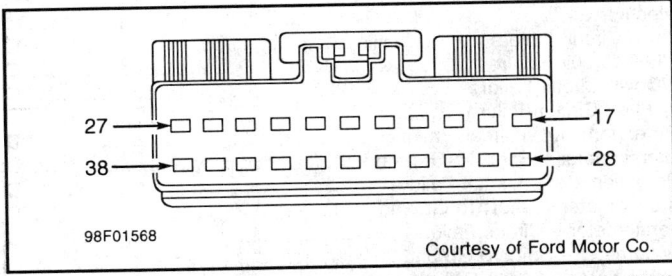

Fig. 9: Identifying Driver's Door Module Harness Connector C520 Terminals

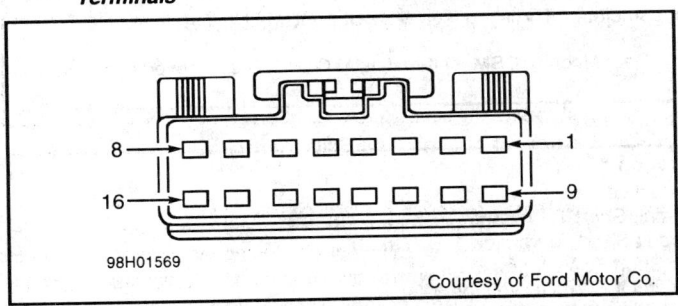

Fig. 10: Identifying Driver's Door Module Harness Connector C521 Terminals

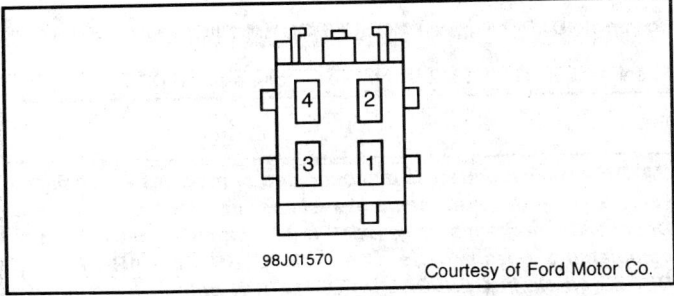

Fig. 11: Identifying Driver's Door Module Harness Connector C522 Terminals

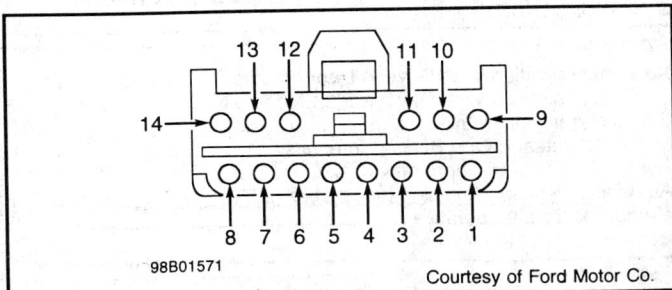

Fig. 12: Identifying Driver's Seat Control Switch Harness Connector C509 Terminals

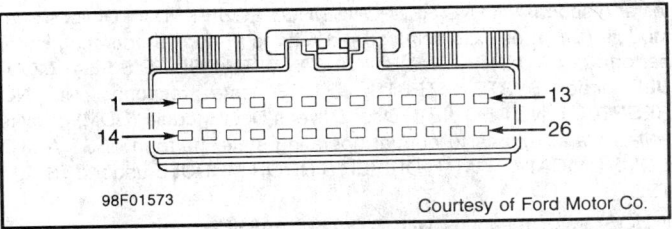

Fig. 13: Identifying Driver's Seat Module Harness Connector C313 Terminals

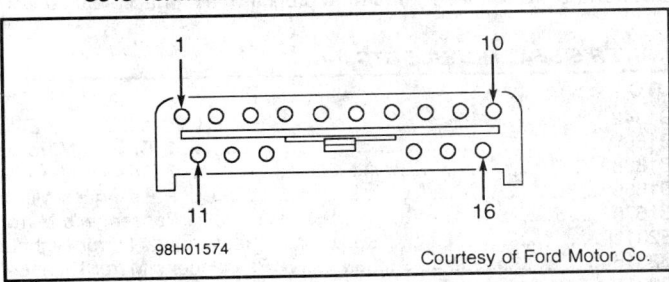

Fig. 14: Identifying Driver's Seat Module Harness Connector C338 Terminals

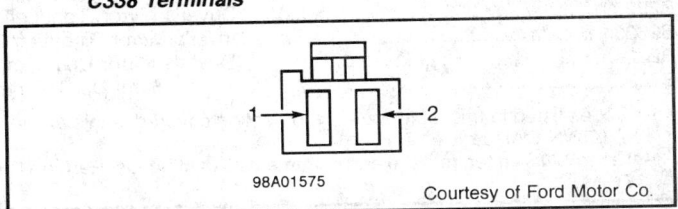

Fig. 15: Identifying Driver's Seat Module Harness Connector C337 Terminals

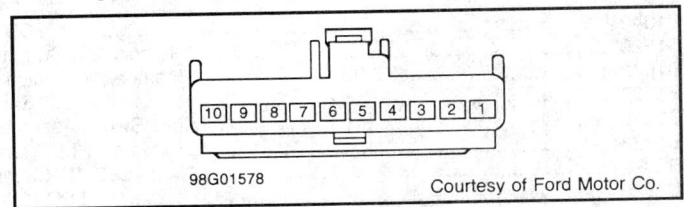

Fig. 16: Identifying Mirror Control Switch Harness Connector

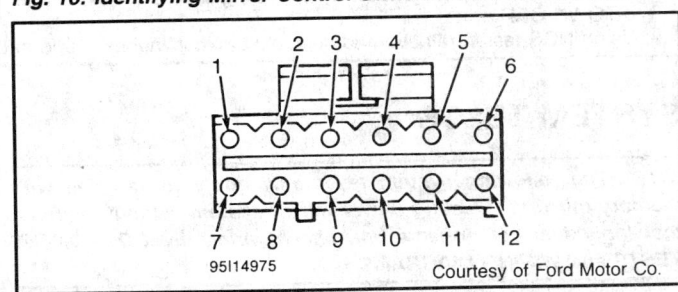

Fig. 17: Identifying Passenger's Seat Control Switch Harness Connector (C609)

SELF-DIAGNOSTIC SYSTEM

NOTE: Before beginning system testing, perform TROUBLE SHOOTING.

Connect New Generation Star (NGS) tester to Data Link Connector (DLC). Perform data link diagnostic test. See DATA LINK DIAGNOSTIC TEST under COMMUNICATION NETWORK DIAGNOSTICS in MODULE COMMUNICATIONS NETWORK – TOWN CAR article. If NGS tester responds with CKT 914 or CKT 915=ALL MODULES NO RESPONSE/NOT EQUIPPED, diagnose network concern. See MODULE COMMUNICATIONS NETWORK – TOWN CAR article. If NGS tester responds with NO RESPONSE/NOT EQUIPPED for Driver's Seat Module (DSM) or exits self-test and returns to normal operating state, perform TEST B: NO COMMUNICATION WITH DRIVER'S SEAT MODULE under SYSTEM TESTS. If NGS tester responds with NO RESPONSE/NOT EQUIPPED for Driver's Door Module (DDM) or exits self-test and returns to normal operating state, perform TEST A: NO COMMUNICATION WITH DRIVER'S DOOR MODULE under SYSTEM TESTS.

If NGS tester responds with SYSTEM PASSED, retrieve and record continuous DTCs. Erase continuous DTCs. Using NGS tester, perform DDM and DSM self-test. Perform appropriate test in accordance with

DTC retrieved. See DRIVER'S SEAT MODULE DTC INDEX table and/or DRIVER'S DOOR MODULE DTC INDEX table. Codes listed in these tables are only for testing covered in this article. For complete DTC listing, see MODULE COMMUNICATIONS NETWORK – TOWN CAR article. If no DTCs are retrieved, repair by symptom. See SYMPTOM CHART table under SYSTEM TESTS.

DRIVER'S SEAT MODULE DTC INDEX

DTC [1]	Description	Test
B1342	ECU Defective	2
B1667	Driver's Mirror Up/Down Circuit Failure	C
B1668	Driver's Mirror Right/Left Circuit Failure	C
B1669	Passenger's Mirror Up/Down Circuit Failure	C
B1670	Passenger's Mirror Right/Left Circuit Failure	C
B2312	Passenger's Mirror Right/Left Potentiometer – Circuit Failure	D
B2315	Passenger's Mirror Right/Left Potentiometer – Short To Ground	D
B2316	Passenger's Mirror Up/Down Potentiometer – Circuit Failure	D
B2319	Passenger's Mirror Up/Down Potentiometer – Short To Ground	D
B2320	Driver's Mirror Right/Left Potentiometer – Circuit Failure	D
B2323	Driver's Mirror Right/Left Potentiometer – Shirt To Ground	D
B2324	Driver's Mirror Up/Down Potentiometer – Circuit Failure	D
B2327	Driver's Mirror Up/Down Potentiometer – Short To Ground	D

[1] – Codes listed in this table are only for testing covered in this article. For complete DTC listing, see MODULE COMMUNICATIONS NETWORK – TOWN CAR article.

[2] – Using NGS tester, retrieve and document all continuous. Perform Driver's Seat Module (DSM) self-test. If DTC B1342 is retrieved again, replace DSM.

DRIVER'S DOOR MODULE DTC INDEX

DTC [1]	Description	Test
B1342	ECU Defective	2
B1529	Memory Set Switch Circuit Short To Voltage	D
B1533	Memory "1" Switch Circuit Short To Voltage	D
B1537	Memory "2" Switch Short To Voltage	D
B2338	Mirror Switch Assembly Circuit Short To Voltage	C
B2368	Memory LED Output Short To Voltage	D
B2373	LED "1" Circuit Short To Voltage	G
C1920	LED "1" Circuit Failure	D

[1] – Codes listed in this table are only for testing covered in this article. For complete DTC listing, see MODULE COMMUNICATIONS NETWORK – TOWN CAR article.

[2] – Using NGS tester, retrieve and document all continuous. Perform DDM self-test. If DTC B1342 is retrieved again, replace DDM.

SYSTEM TESTS

NOTE: The following system tests only apply to vehicles with memory mirrors. If testing power mirror system without memory, test individual components and check wiring. See COMPONENT TESTS and WIRING DIAGRAMS.

NOTE: Many steps in the following tests refer to various connectors. These connectors are identified in illustrations under CONNECTOR IDENTIFICATION. See Figs. 6-17.

NOTE: After repairs are complete, ensure all component are properly installed and all harness connectors are connected properly and repeat data link diagnostic test. See DATA LINK DIAGNOSTIC TEST under COMMUNICATIONS NETWORK DIAGNOSTICS in MODULE COMMUNICATIONS NETWORK – TOWN CAR article.

CAUTION: When battery is disconnected or modules are replaced, vehicle computer and memory systems may lose memory data. Driveability problems may exist until computer systems have completed a relearn cycle. See COMPUTER RELEARN PROCEDURES article in GENERAL INFORMATION before disconnecting battery.

SYMPTOM CHART

Symptom	Test
No Communication With Driver's Door Module	A
No Communication With Driver's Seat Module	B
Single Mirror Inoperative	C
Mirror Operates In One Second Intervals	D
Reverse Tilt Feature Inoperative	E
Automatic Dimming Function Inoperative	F
Memory Mirrors Inoperative	G
Heated Mirrors Inoperative	H

TEST A: NO COMMUNICATION WITH DRIVER'S DOOR MODULE

1) Ensure transmission is in Park. Turn ignition switch to LOCK position. Check fuse No. 30 (7.5-amp) in instrument panel fuse box. If fuse is okay, go to next step. If fuse is blown, go to step **5**).

2) Measure voltage at input side of fuse No. 30. If battery voltage exists, go to next step. If battery voltage does not exist, go to step **20**).

3) Ensure fuse No. 30 is removed from instrument panel fuse box. Disconnect Driver's Door Module (DDM) harness connector C520. Measure resistance in Light Green/Violet wire between terminal No. 29 at DDM harness connector C520 and output side of fuse No. 30. If resistance is 5 ohms or less, go to next step. If resistance is greater than 5 ohms, repair open in Light Green/Violet wire between instrument panel fuse box and DDM.

4) Measure resistance between ground and terminal No. 23 (Pink/Orange wire) at DDM harness connector C520. If resistance is greater than 5 ohms, repair open in Pink/Orange wire. If resistance is 5 ohms or less, replace driver's door module.

5) Replace fuse No. 30. DO NOT operate any switches. If fuse blows, go to next step. If fuse does not blow, go to step **9**).

6) Remove fuse No. 30. Disconnect Driver's Door Module (DDM) harness connector C520 and Driver's Seat Module (DSM) harness connector C313. Measure resistance between ground and terminal No. 29 (Light Green/Violet wire) at DDM harness connector C520. If resistance is 10 k/ohms or less, go to next step. If resistance is greater than 10 k/ohms, go to step **8**).

7) Test door lock switches, remote trunk release switch, mirror control switch and seat control switches. See appropriate test under COMPONENT TESTS. If no switch is defective, repair short to ground in Light Green/Violet wire. If any switch is defective, replace appropriate switch.

8) Connect DSM harness connector C313. Measure resistance between ground and terminal No. 29 (Light Green/Violet wire) at DDM harness connector C520. If resistance is greater than 10 k/ohms, replace driver's door module. If resistance is 10 k/ohms or less, replace driver's seat module.

9) Lock and unlock doors at all door lock switches. If fuse No. 30 blows, go to next step. If fuse No. 30 does not blow, go to step **12**).

10) Remove door lock switches. Test all door lock switches. See DOOR LOCK SWITCH under COMPONENT TESTING. If all door lock switches are okay, go to next step. If any door lock switch is defective, replace appropriate door lock switch.

11) Disconnect Driver's Door Module (DDM) harness connector C520. Disconnect driver's door lock switch harness connector C503. Disconnect passenger's door lock switch harness connector C603. Measure resistance between ground and terminal No. 2 (Pink/Yellow wire) at driver's door lock switch harness connector C503. Also, measure resistance between ground and terminal No. 6 (Pink/Light Green wire) at driver's door lock switch harness connector C503. If either or both resistance reading are 10 k/ohms or less, repair short to ground in appropriate wire(s). If both resistance readings are greater than 10 k/ohms, replace driver's door module.

12) Activate mirrors in all directions. If fuse No. 30 blows, go to next step. If fuse No. 30 does not blow, go to step **15**).

13) Remove mirror control switch. Test mirror control switch. See MIRROR CONTROL SWITCH under COMPONENT TESTS. If mirror control switch is okay, go to next step. If mirror control switch is defective, replace mirror control switch.

14) Disconnect Driver's Door Module (DDM) harness connector C520. Disconnect mirror control switch harness connector C550. Measure resistance between ground and appropriate terminals at DDM harness connector C520. See MIRROR CONTROL SWITCH CIRCUIT IDENTIFICATION table. If all resistance readings are greater than 10 k/ohms, replace driver's door module. If any resistance reading are 10 k/ohms or less, repair short to ground in appropriate wire.

MIRROR CONTROL SWITCH CIRCUIT IDENTIFICATION

Terminal	Wire Color
18	Yellow/Black
19	Dark Blue/Orange
30	Red/Orange
31	Violet/Orange
32	Dark Green/Orange

15) Activate memory switch through all positions. If fuse No. 30 blows, go to next step. If fuse No. 30 does not blow, go to step **18**).

16) Remove driver's seat control switch. Test memory portion of driver's seat control switch. See DRIVER'S SEAT CONTROL SWITCH (WITH MEMORY) under COMPONENT TESTS. If memory switch is okay, go to next step. If memory switch is defective, replace driver's seat control switch.

17) Disconnect Driver's Door Module (DDM) harness connectors C520 and C521. Measure resistance between ground and appropriate terminals at driver's seat control switch harness connector C509. See SEAT SWITCH CIRCUIT TERMINAL IDENTIFICATION table. If all resistance readings are greater than 10 k/ohms, replace driver's door module. If any resistance readings are 10 k/ohms or less, repair short to ground in appropriate wire.

SEAT SWITCH CIRCUIT TERMINAL IDENTIFICATION

Terminal	Wire Color
4	White/Orange
5	Brown/Orange
6	Brown/Light Green
7	Black/Orange

18) Activate driver's seat control switch in all directions. If fuse No. 30 blows, go to next step. If fuse No. 30 does not blow, system is operating properly at this time.

19) Disconnect Driver's Door Module (DDM) harness connector C521. Disconnect driver's seat control switch harness connector C509. Measure resistance between ground and appropriate terminals at driver's seat control switch harness connector C509. See DRIVER'S SEAT CONTROL SWITCH TERMINAL IDENTIFICATION table. If all resistance readings are greater than 10 k/ohms, replace driver's door module. If any resistance readings are 10 k/ohms or less, repair short to ground in appropriate wire.

DRIVER'S SEAT CONTROL SWITCH TERMINAL IDENTIFICATION

Terminal	Wire Color
1	Yellow/White
2	Red/Light Blue
3	Yellow/Light Blue
9	Red/White
11	Yellow/Light Green
12	Red/Light Green
13	Gray
14	Gray/Black

20) Turn ignition switch to LOCK position. Remove maxi-fuse No. 8 (30-amp) from power distribution box. Measure voltage at input side of maxi-fuse No. 8 at power distribution box. If battery voltage exists, go to next step. If battery voltage does not exist, repair power supply to maxi-fuse No. 8.

21) Ensure maxi-fuse No. 8 is still removed. Remove fuse No. 30 (7.5-amp) from instrument panel fuse box. Disconnect Driver's Seat Module (DSM) harness connector C337. Measure resistance in Red wire between output side of maxi-fuse No. 8 and input side of fuse No. 30. If resistance is 5 ohms or less, go to next step. If resistance is greater than 5 ohms, repair open in Red wire.

22) Measure resistance between ground and output side of maxi-fuse No. 8 at power distribution box. If resistance is greater than 10 k/ohms, replace driver's door module. If resistance is 10 k/ohms or less, repair short to ground in Red wire.

TEST B: NO COMMUNICATION WITH DRIVER'S SEAT MODULE

1) Remove fuse No. 30 (7.5–amp) from instrument panel fuse box. Check fuse No. 30. If fuse is okay, go to next step. If fuse is blown, perform TEST A: NO COMMUNICATION WITH DRIVER'S DOOR MODULE.

2) Measure voltage at input cavity of fuse No. 30 at instrument panel fuse box. If battery voltage exist, go to next step. If battery voltage does not exist, perform TEST A: NO COMMUNICATION WITH DRIVER'S DOOR MODULE.

3) Install fuse No. 30. Disconnect Driver's Seat Module (DSM) harness connector C313. Measure voltage at terminal No. 14 (Light Green/Violet wire) at DSM harness connector C313. If battery voltage exists, go to next step. If battery voltage does not exist, repair open in Light Green/Violet wire.

4) Measure resistance between ground and terminal No. 1 (Pink/Orange wire) at DSM harness connector C313. If resistance is 5 ohms or less, diagnosis network concern. See appropriate MODULE COMMUNICATIONS NETWORK article. If resistance is greater than 5 ohms, repair open in Pink/Orange wire.

TEST C: SINGLE MIRROR INOPERATIVE

1) Connect New Generation Star (NGS) tester to Data Link Connector (DLC). Using NGS tester, perform Driver's Door Module (DDM) self-test. If DTC B2338 does not exist, go to next step. If DTC B2338 exists, go to step **4)**.

2) Using NGS tester, perform Driver's Seat Module (DSM) self-test. If no DTCs exist, go to next step. If any DTCs exist, perform appropriate test or appropriate step. See DTC TEST PROCEDURE table.

DTC TEST PROCEDURE

DTC [1]	Go To
B1667	Step 10)
B1667 & B1668	TEST D
B1667 & B2324	TEST D
B1667 & B2327	TEST D
B1668	Step 10)
B1668 & B2320	TEST D
B1668 & B2323	TEST D
B1669	Step 14)
B1669 & B1670	TEST D
B1669 & B2316	TEST D
B1669 & B2319	TEST D
B1670	Step 14)
B1670 & B2312	TEST D
B1670 & B2315	TEST D
B1667, B1668, B1669 & B1670	TEST D

[1] – DTCs B1663, B1664, B1665 and B1666 may also be present.

3) Using NGS tester, monitor DDM PIDs MIRV_SW and MIRH_SW. Select appropriate mirror on mirror control switch. Move mirror control switch through all positions. If PID values do not agree with mirror control switch position, go to next step. If PID values agrees with mirror control switch position, go to step **9)**.

4) Disconnect mirror control switch harness connector C550. Turn ignition switch to RUN position. Measure voltage at terminal No. 3 (Light Green/Violet wire) wire at mirror control switch harness connector C550. If battery voltage exists, go to next step. If battery voltage does not exist, repair open in Light Green/Violet wire.

5) Turn ignition switch to LOCK position. Measure resistance between ground and terminal No. 5 (Black wire) at mirror control switch connector C550. Also, measure resistance between ground and terminal No. 7 (Black wire) at mirror control switch harness connector C550. If both resistance readings are 5 ohms or less, go to next step. If either resistance reading is more than 5 ohms, repair open in appropriate Black wire.

6) Disconnect DDM harness connector C520. Measure resistance in wires between mirror control switch harness connector C550 and DDM harness connector C520. See MIRROR CONTROL CIRCUIT IDENTIFICATION table. If all resistance readings are 5 ohms or less, go to next

step. If any resistance reading is more than 5 ohms, repair open in appropriate wire.

MIRROR CONTROL CIRCUIT IDENTIFICATION

DDM Terminal	Switch Terminal	Wire Color
18	4	Yellow/Black
19	9	Dark Blue/Orange
30	1	Red/Orange
31	8	Violet/Orange
32	2	Dark Green/Orange

7) Ensure ignition switch is in RUN position. Measure voltage at appropriate terminals at mirror control switch harness connector C550. See MIRROR SWITCH TERMINAL IDENTIFICATION table. If voltage does not exist at any terminal, go to next step. If voltage exists at any terminal, repair short to voltage in appropriate wire.

MIRROR SWITCH TERMINAL IDENTIFICATION

Terminal	Wire Color
1	Red/Orange
2	Dark Green/Orange
4	Yellow/Black
8	Violet/Orange
9	Dark Blue/Orange

8) Test mirror control switch. See MIRROR CONTROL SWITCH under COMPONENT TESTS. If mirror control switch is okay, replace DDM. If mirror control switch is defective, replace mirror control switch.

9) Place transmission in Park. Using NGS tester, select ACTIVE COMMAND POWER MIRROR CONTROL. Using NGS tester, operate both mirrors in all directions. If both mirrors respond correctly, system is okay at this time. If driver's mirror did not respond correctly, go to next step. If passenger's mirror did not respond correctly, go to step **14)**.

10) Disconnect driver's mirror harness connector C508. Measure voltage at terminals No. 3 (Red wire), No. 4 (Yellow/Red wire), No. 5 (Yellow/Light Blue wire) and No. 6 (Dark Blue wire) at driver's mirror harness connector C508. If voltage does not exist at any terminal, go to next step. If voltage exists, go to step **13)**.

11) Disconnect DSM harness connector C313. Measure resistance between ground and terminals No. 3 (Red wire), No. 4 (Yellow/Red wire), No. 5 (Yellow/Light Blue wire) and No. 6 (Dark Blue wire) at driver's mirror harness connector C508. If all resistance readings are more than 10 k/ohms, go to next step. If any resistance reading is 10 k/ohms or less, repair short to ground in appropriate wire.

12) Measure resistance in wires between driver's mirror harness connector C508 and DSM harness connector C313. See DRIVER'S MIRROR TERMINAL IDENTIFICATION table. If all resistance readings are 5 ohms or less, go to step **18)** . If any resistance reading is more than 5 ohms, repair open in appropriate wire.

DRIVER'S MIRROR TERMINAL IDENTIFICATION

DSM Terminal	Mirror Terminal	Wire Color
2	3	Red
3	6	Dark Blue
4	5	Yellow/Light Blue
16	4	Yellow/Red

13) Disconnect DSM harness connector C313. Measure voltage at terminals No. 3 (Red wire), No. 4 (Yellow/Red wire), No. 5 (Yellow/Light Blue wire) and No. 6 (Dark Blue wire) at driver's mirror harness connector C508. If voltage does not exist at any terminal, replace DSM. If voltage exists at any terminal, repair short to voltage in appropriate wire.

14) Disconnect passenger's mirror harness connector C608. Measure voltage at terminals No. 1 (White/Light Green wire), No. 2 (Violet wire), No. 3 (Dark Green wire) and No. 5 (White/Violet wire) at passenger's mirror harness connector C608. If voltage does not exist at any terminal, go to next step. If voltage exists at any terminal, go to step **17)**.

15) Disconnect DSM harness connector C313. Measure resistance between ground and terminals No. 1 (White/Light Green wire), No. 2 (Violet wire), No. 3 (Dark Green wire) and No. 5 (White/Violet wire) at passenger's mirror harness connector C608. If resistance is more than 10 k/ohms, go to next step. If resistance is 10 k/ohms or less, repair short to ground in appropriate wire.

16) Measure resistance in wires between passenger's mirror harness connector C608 and DSM harness connector C313. See PASSENGER'S MIRROR TERMINAL IDENTIFICATION table. If all resistance readings are 5 ohms or less, go to step **21)**. If any resistance reading is more than 5 ohms, repair open in appropriate wire.

PASSENGER'S MIRROR TERMINAL IDENTIFICATION

DSM Terminal	Mirror Terminal	Wire Color
5	2	Violet
6	5	White/Violet
7	1	White/Light Green
8	3	Dark Green

17) Disconnect DSM harness connector C313. Measure voltage at terminals No. 1 (White/Light Green wire), No. 2 (Violet wire), No. 3 (Dark Green wire) and No. 5 (White/Violet wire) at passenger's mirror harness connector C608. If voltage does not exist at any terminal, replace DSM. If voltage exists at any terminal, repair short to voltage in appropriate wire.

18) Disconnect driver's mirror harness connector C508. Measure resistance between terminal No. 5 (Yellow/Light Blue wire) and No. 6 (Dark Blue wire) at driver's mirror harness connector C508. Also, measure resistance between terminals No. 3 (Red wire) and No. 4 (Yellow/Red wire) at driver's mirror harness connector C508. If resistance readings are 10,000 or less, go to next step. If resistance readings are more than 10 k/ohms, go to step **24)**.

19) Measure voltage at terminals No. 3 (Red wire), No. 4 (Yellow/Red wire), No. 5 (Yellow/Light Blue wire) and No. 6 (Dark Blue wire) at driver's mirror harness connector C508. If voltage does not exist at any terminal, go to next step. If voltage exists at any terminal, go to step **24)**.

20) Measure resistance between ground and terminals No. 3 (Red wire), No. 4 (Yellow/Red wire), No. 5 (Yellow/Light Blue wire) and No. 6 (Dark Blue wire) at driver's mirror harness connector C508. If all resistance readings are more than 10 k/ohms, replace DSM. If any resistance reading is 10 k/ohms or less, go to step **24)**.

21) Disconnect passenger's mirror harness connector C608. Measure resistance between terminal No. 2 (Violet wire) and No. 5 (White/Violet wire) at passenger's mirror harness connector C608. Also, measure resistance between terminals No. 1 (White/Light Green wire) and No. 3 (Dark Green wire) at passenger's mirror harness connector C508. If resistance readings are 10,000 or less, go to next step. If resistance readings are more than 10 k/ohms, go to step **25)**.

22) Measure voltage at terminals No. 1 (White/Light Green wire), No. 2 (Violet wire), No. 3 (Dark Green wire) and No. 5 (White/Violet wire) at passenger's mirror harness connector C608. If voltage does not exist at any terminal, go to next step. If voltage exists at any terminal, go to step **25)**.

23) Measure resistance between ground and terminals No. 1 (White/Light Green wire), No. 2 (Violet wire), No. 3 (Dark Green wire) and No. 5 (White/Violet wire) at passenger's mirror harness connector C608. If all resistance readings are more than 10 k/ohms, replace DSM. If any resistance reading is 10 k/ohms or less, go to step **25)**.

24) Remove driver's mirror assembly. Inspect mirror wiring. If wiring is damaged, repair as necessary. If wiring is okay, replace driver's mirror assembly.

25) Remove passenger's mirror assembly. Inspect mirror wiring. If wiring is damaged, repair as necessary. If wiring is okay, replace passenger's mirror assembly.

TEST D: MIRROR OPERATES IN ONE SECOND INTERVALS

1) Ensure transmission is in Park. Operate both mirrors in all directions. If both mirrors move in all directions, go to next step. If either mirror does not operate in any direction, repair as necessary. See SYMPTOM CHART table.

2) Connect New Generation Star (NGS) tester to Data Link Connector (DLC). Using NGS tester, perform Driver's Door Module (DDM) self-test. If no DDM DTCs exist, go to next step. If any DDM DTCs exists, perform appropriate test. See DRIVER'S DOOR MODULE DTC INDEX table under SELF-DIAGNOSTIC SYSTEM.

3) Perform Driver's Seat Module (DSM) self-test. If no DSM DTCs exist, go to next step. If any DSM DTCs exist, perform appropriate test or appropriate step. See DTC TEST PROCEDURE table.

DTC TEST PROCEDURE

DTC	Go To
B1667, B1668, B1669 & B1670	Step 4)
B1667, B1668, B1669, B1670, B1663, B1664, B1665 & B1666	Step 11)
B1667 & B1668	Step 6)
B1667 & B2324	Step 6)
B1667 & B2327	Step 5)
B1668 & B2320	Step 6)
B1668 & B2323	Step 5)
B1669 & B1670	Step 9)
B1669 & B2316	Step 9)
B1669 & B2319	Step 8)
B1670 & B2312	Step 9)
B1670 & B2315	Step 8)

4) Ensure transmission is in Park. Position driver's and passenger's mirrors in center position. Operate both mirrors through complete travel in all directions. If both mirror move smoothly and completely, replace DSM. If driver's mirror does not operate properly, go to next step. If passenger's mirror does not operate properly, go to step **8)**. If both mirrors do not operate properly, go to step **11)**.

5) Disconnect driver's mirror harness connector C523. Disconnect DSM harness connector C313. Measure resistance between ground and terminals No. 4 (Red/White wire) and No. 1 (Dark Blue/White wire) at driver's mirror harness connector C523. If both resistance readings are more than 10 k/ohms, go to next step. If either resistance reading is 10 k/ohms or less, repair short to ground in appropriate wire.

6) Measure resistance in wires between DSM harness connector C313 and driver's mirror harness connector C523. See DRIVER'S POTENTIOMETER CIRCUIT IDENTIFICATION table. If all resistance readings are 5 ohms or less, go to next step. If any resistance reading is more than 5 ohms, repair open in appropriate wire.

DRIVER'S POTENTIOMETER CIRCUIT IDENTIFICATION

DSM Terminal	Mirror Terminal	Wire Color
9	4	Red/White
10	1	Dark Blue/White
13	3	Gray
15	2	Gray/Red

7) Measure voltage at terminal No. 1 (Dark Blue/White wire), No. 2 (Gray/Red wire), No. 3 (Gray wire) and No. 4 (Red/White wire) at driver's mirror harness connector C523. If voltage does not exist at any terminal, go to step **14)**. If voltage exists at any terminal, repair short to voltage in appropriate wire.

8) Disconnect passenger's mirror harness connector C615. Disconnect DSM harness connector C313. Measure resistance between ground and terminals No. 1 (Violet/White wire) and No. 4 (Dark Green/White wire) at passenger's mirror harness connector C615. If both resistance readings are more than 10 k/ohms, go to next step. If either resistance reading is 10 k/ohms or less, repair short to ground in appropriate wire.

9) Measure resistance in wires between DSM harness connector C313 and passenger's mirror harness connector C615. See PASSENGER'S POTENTIOMETER CIRCUIT IDENTIFICATION table. If all resistance readings are 5 ohms or less, go to next step. If any resistance reading is more than 5 ohms, repair open in appropriate wire.

PASSENGER'S POTENTIOMETER CIRCUIT IDENTIFICATION

DSM Terminal	Mirror Terminal	Wire Color
11	4	Dark Green/White
12	1	Violet/White
13	3	Gray
15	2	Gray/Red

10) Measure voltage at terminal No. 1 (Violet/White wire), No. 2 (Gray/Red wire), No. 3 (Gray wire) and No. 4 (Dark Green/White wire) at passenger's mirror harness connector C615. If voltage does not exist at any terminal, go to step 16). If voltage exists at any terminal, repair short to voltage in appropriate wire.

11) Disconnect DSM harness connector C313, driver's mirror harness connector C523 and passenger's mirror harness connector C615. Measure resistance in Gary/Red wire between terminal No. 15 at DSM and terminal No. 2 at both mirror harness connectors. Also measure resistance in Gray wire between terminal No. 13 at DSM harness connector C313 and terminal No. 3 at both mirror harness connectors. If all resistance readings are 5 ohms or less, go to next step. If any resistance reading is more than 5 ohms, repair open in appropriate wire.

12) Measure resistance between ground and terminal No. 2 (Gray/Red wire) at both mirror harness connectors. If both resistance readings are more than 10 k/ohms, go to next step. If either resistance is 10 k/ohms or less, repair short to ground in Gray/Red wire.

13) Measure voltage at terminal No. 2 (Gray/Red wire) at both mirror harness connectors. If voltage does not exist, go to step 18). If voltage exists, repair short to voltage in Gray/Red wire.

14) Connect DSM harness connector C313. Measure voltage at terminals No. 1 (Dark Blue/White wire), No. 2 (Gray/Red wire) and No. 4 (Red/White wire) at driver's mirror harness connector C523. If voltage exists, go to next step. If voltage does not exist, replace DSM.

15) Measure resistance between ground and terminal No. 3 (Gray wire) at driver's mirror harness connector C523. If resistance is more than 10 k/ohms, replace DSM. If resistance is 10 k/ohms or less, go to step 20).

16) Connect DSM harness connector C313. Measure voltage at terminals No. 1 (Violet/White wire), No. 2 (Gray/Red wire) and No. 4 (Dark Green/White wire) at passenger's mirror harness connector C615. If voltage exists, go to next step. If voltage does not exist, replace DSM.

17) Measure resistance between ground and terminal No. 3 (Gray wire) at passenger's mirror harness connector C615. If resistance is more than 10 k/ohms, replace DSM. If resistance is 10 k/ohms or less, go to step 21).

18) Disconnect driver's mirror harness connector C523 and passenger's mirror harness connector C615. Measure voltage at terminal No. 2 (Gray/Red wire) at driver's and passenger's mirror harness connectors. If voltage does not exist, go to next step. If voltage exists at driver's mirror harness connector, go to step 20). If voltage exists at passenger's mirror, go to step 21).

19) Measure resistance between ground and terminal No. 2 (Gray/Red wire) at driver's and passenger's mirror harness connectors. If both resistance reading are more than 10 k/ohms, go to step 22). If resistance is 10 k/ohms or less at driver's mirror harness connector, go to next step. If resistance is 10 k/ohms or less at passenger's mirror harness connector, go to step 21).

20) Remove driver's mirror assembly. Inspect mirror wiring. If wiring is damaged, repair as necessary. If wiring is okay, replace driver's mirror assembly.

21) Remove passenger's mirror assembly. Inspect mirror wiring. If wiring is damaged, repair as necessary. If wiring is okay, replace passenger's mirror assembly.

22) Connect all disconnected components. Perform DSM self-test. If DTCs B1663, B1664, B1665 and B1666 do not exist, replace DSM. If DTCs B1663, B1664, B1665 and B1666 exist, preform appropriate test. See POWER SEATS – TOWN CAR article.

TEST E: REVERSE TILT FEATURE INOPERATIVE

1) Operate both mirror through all positions. If both mirrors operate properly, go to next step. If both mirrors do not operate properly, repair mirrors as necessary. See SYMPTOM CHART table.

2) Turn ignition switch to RUN position. Select REVERSE MIRRORS feature on message center. If REVERSE MIRROR feature is enabled, go to next step. If REVERSE MIRROR feature is not enabled, enable feature and inform customer of proper operation.

3) Turn ignition switch to RUN position. Set parking brake. Place transmission in Reverse. Wait 15 seconds then place transmission in Park. If mirrors do not move down when transmission is in Reverse and return to pervious position when transmission is returned to Park, go to next step. If mirrors move down when transmission is in Reverse and return to pervious position when transmission is returned to Park, system is okay at this time.

4) Connect New Generation Star (NGS) tester to Data Link Connector (DLC). Using NGS tester, perform Driver's Seat Module (DSM) self-test. If no DSM DTCs exist, replace DSM. If any DSM DTCs exist, perform appropriate test. See TILT FEATURE TEST table.

TILT FEATURE TEST

DTC	Go To
B1667 & B2324	TEST D
B1667 & B2327	TEST D
B1669 & B2327	TEST D
B1669 & B2319	TEST D
U1059	1

[1] – See DRIVER'S SEAT MODULE DTC INDEX table under SELF-DIAGNOSTIC SYSTEM.

TEST F: AUTOMATIC DIMMING FUNCTION INOPERATIVE

1) Place transmission in Park. Turn ignition switch to RUN position. Cover light sensor on back side of inside mirror. Shine bright light into front of inside mirror. If inside mirror does not darken, go to next step. If inside mirror darkens and driver's mirror does not darken, go to step 7). If both mirrors darken, system is operating properly at this time.

2) Turn ignition switch to LOCK position. Disconnect inside mirror harness connector C902. Turn ignition switch to RUN position. Measure voltage at terminal No. 7 (Dark Blue/Light Green wire) at inside mirror harness connector C902. If battery voltage exists, go to step 5). If battery voltage does not exist, go to next step.

3) Turn ignition switch to LOCK position. Remove fuse No. 18 (7.5-amp) from instrument panel fuse box. If fuse is okay, repair open in Dark Blue/Light Green wire. If fuse is blown, go to next step.

4) Ensure fuse No. 18 is still removed. Measure resistance between ground and terminal No. 7 (Dark Blue/Light Green wire) at inside mirror harness connector C902. If resistance is 10 k/ohms or less, repair short to ground in Dark Blue/Light Green wire. If resistance is more than 10 k/ohms, replace inside mirror.

5) Measure resistance between ground and terminal No. 6 (Black wire) at inside mirror harness connector C902. If resistance is more than 5 ohms, repair open in Black wire and retest. If resistance is 5 ohms or less, go to next step.

6) Turn ignition switch to RUN position. Ensure transmission is in Reverse. Measure voltage at terminal No. 5 (Black/Pink wire) at inside mirror harness connector C902. If battery voltage exists, replace inside mirror. If battery voltage does not exist, repair open in Black/Pink wire.

7) Turn ignition switch to LOCK position. Test driver's mirror dimming by connecting a D-size battery (1.5 volts or less), positive to terminal No. 4 (Violet wire) and negative to terminal No. 3 (Light Blue/White wire) at inside mirror harness connector C902. If driver's mirror darkens, go to next step. If driver's mirror does not darken, replace driver's mirror glass.

8) Turn ignition switch to LOCK position. Disconnect driver's mirror harness connector C508. Connect inside mirror harness connector C902. Measure voltage at terminal No. 9 (Light Blue/White wire) at driver's mirror harness connector C508. If battery voltage exists, go to next step. If battery voltage does not exist, go to step 10).

9) Disconnect inside mirror harness connector C902. Measure voltage at terminal No. 9 (Light Blue/White wire) at driver's mirror harness connector C508. If battery voltage exists, repair short to voltage in Light Blue/White wire. If battery voltage does not exist, replace inside mirror.

10) Measure voltage at terminal No. 10 (Violet wire) at driver's mirror harness connector C508. If battery voltage exists, go to next step. If battery voltage does not exist, go to step **12**).

11) Disconnect inside mirror harness connector C902. Measure voltage at terminal No. 10 (Violet wire) at driver's mirror harness connector C508. If battery voltage exists, repair short to voltage in Violet wire. If battery voltage does not exist, replace inside mirror.

12) Measure resistance between ground and terminal No. 9 (Light Blue/White wire) at driver's mirror harness connector C508. If resistance is 10 k/ohms or less, go to next step. If resistance is more than 10 k/ohms, go to step **14**) .

13) Disconnect inside mirror harness connector C902. Measure resistance between ground and terminal No. 9 (Light Blue/White wire) at driver's mirror harness connector C508. If resistance is 10 k/ohms or less, repair short to ground in Light Blue/White wire. If resistance is more than 10 k/ohms, replace inside mirror.

14) Measure resistance between ground and terminal No. 10 (Violet wire) at driver's mirror harness connector C508. If resistance is 10 k/ohms or less, go to next step. If resistance is more than 10 k/ohms, go to step **16**).

15) Disconnect inside mirror harness connector C902. Measure resistance between ground and terminal No. 10 (Violet wire) at driver's mirror harness connector C508. If resistance is 10 k/ohms or less, repair short to ground in Violet wire. If resistance is more than 10 k/ohms, replace inside mirror.

16) Disconnect inside mirror harness connector C902. Measure resistance in Light Blue/White wire between terminal No. 3 at inside mirror harness connector C902 and terminal No. 9 at driver's mirror harness connector C508. If resistance is 5 ohms or less, go to next step. If resistance is more than 5 ohms, repair open in Light Blue/White wire.

17) Measure resistance in Violet wire between terminal No. 4 at inside mirror harness connector C902 and terminal No. 10 at driver's mirror harness connector C508. If resistance is 5 ohms or less, replace inside mirror. If resistance is more than 5 ohms, repair open in Violet wire.

TEST G: MEMORY MIRRORS INOPERATIVE

1) Connect New Generation Star (NGS) tester to Data Link Connector (DLC). Perform Driver's Door Module (DDM) self-test. If no DDM DTCs exist, go to next step. If any DDM DTCs exist, perform appropriate test or step. See DTC TEST table.

DTC TEST

DTC	Go To
B1529	Step 11)
B1533	Step 16)
B1537	Step 18)
B2373	Step 20)
U1180	[1]

[1] – See DRIVER'S DOOR MODULE DTC INDEX under SELF-DIAGNOSTIC SYSTEM.

2) Perform Driver's Seat Module (DSM) self-test. If no DSM DTCs exist, go to next step. If any DSM DTCs exist, perform appropriate test. See DRIVER'S SEAT MODULE DTC INDEX table under SELF-DIAGNOSTIC SYSTEM.

3) Operate both mirror through all positions. If both mirrors operate through all positions, go to next step. If either mirror does not operate through all positions, repair by symptom. See SYMPTOM CHART.

4) Activate memory feature at memory switch to both memory position. If memory feature operates properly, go to next step. If memory feature does not operate properly, go to step **6**).

5) Activate memory feature at remote transmitter to both memory position. If memory feature operates properly, memory feature is okay at this time. If memory feature does not operate properly, repair keyless entry system. See REMOTE KEYLESS ENTRY SYSTEMS article.

6) Turn ignition switch to RUN position. If memory switch LED is not always illuminated, go to next step. If memory switch LED is always illuminated, go to step **23**).

7) Using NGS tester, observe DDM PID MEMS_SW. Press memory set switch. If NGS tester displays OFF when switch is pressed and ON when released, go to next step. If NGS tester does not display OFF when switch is pressed and ON when released, go to step **11**).

8) Press and release memory set switch. If memory switch LED remains on for 5 seconds, go to next step. If memory switch LED does not remain on for 5 seconds, go to step **14**).

9) Observer DDM PID MEM1_SW on NGS tester. Press memory switch position No. 1 button. If NGS tester displays ON when switch is pressed and OFF when released, go to next step. If NGS tester does not display ON when switch is pressed and OFF when released, go to step **13**).

10) Observer DDM PID MEM2_SW on NGS tester. Press memory switch position No. 2 button. If NGS tester displays ON when switch is pressed and OFF when released, replace DSM. If NGS tester does not display ON when switch is pressed and OFF when released, go to step **13**).

11) Disconnect DDM harness connector C520. Measure voltage at terminal No. 20 (Brown/Orange wire) at DDM harness connector C520. If voltage exists, go to next step. If voltage does not exist, replace DDM.

12) Disconnect DDM harness connector C520 and driver's seat control switch harness connector C509. Measure voltage at terminal No. 20 (Brown/Orange wire) at DDM harness connector C520. If voltage exists, repair short to voltage in Brown/Orange wire. If voltage does not exist, replace seat control switch.

13) Disconnect DDM harness connector C520. Measure resistance between ground and terminals No. 20 (Brown/Orange wire), No. 21 (Brown/Light Green wire) and No. 33 (Black/Orange wire) at DDM harness connector C520. If any resistance reading is 10 k/ohms or less, go to next step. If all resistance readings are more than 10 k/ohms, go to step **15**).

14) Disconnect driver's seat control switch harness connector C509. Measure resistance between ground and terminals No. 20 (Brown/Orange wire), No. 21 (Brown/Light Green wire) and No. 33 (Black/Orange wire) at DDM harness connector C520. If any resistance reading is 10 k/ohms or less, repair short to ground in appropriate wire. If all resistance readings are more than 10 k/ohms, replace driver's seat switch.

15) Disconnect driver's seat control switch harness connector C509. Measure resistance in Brown/Orange wire between terminal No. 20 at DDM harness connector C520 and terminal No. 5 at driver's seat control switch harness connector C509. Also, measure resistance in Brown/Light Green wire between terminal No. 21 at DDM harness connector C520 and terminal No. 6 at driver's seat control switch harness connector C509. Also, measure resistance in Black/Orange wire between terminal No. 33 at DDM harness connector C520 and terminal No. 7 at driver's seat control switch harness connector C509. If all resistance readings are 5 ohms or less, go to next step. If any resistance reading is more than 5 ohms, repair open in appropriate wire.

16) Disconnect DDM harness connector C520. Measure voltage at terminal No. 21 (Brown/Light Green wire) at DDM harness connector C520. If voltage exists, go to next step. If voltage does not exist, replace DDM.

17) Disconnect driver's seat control switch harness connector C509. Measure voltage at terminal No. 21 (Brown/Light Green wire) at DDM harness connector C520. If voltage exists, repair short to voltage in Brown/Light Green wire. If voltage does not exist, replace driver's seat switch.

18) Disconnect DDM harness connector C520. Measure voltage at terminal No. 33 (Black/Orange wire) at DDM harness connector C520. If voltage exists, go to next step. If voltage does not exist, replace DDM.

19) Disconnect driver's seat control switch harness connector C509. Measure voltage at terminal No. 33 (Black/Orange wire) at DDM harness connector C520. If voltage exists, repair short to voltage in Black/Orange wire. If voltage does not exist, replace driver's seat switch.

20) Disconnect DDM harness connector C521. Measure voltage at terminal No. 14 (White/Orange wire) at DDM harness connector C521. If voltage exists, go to next step. If voltage does not exist, replace DDM.

21) Disconnect driver's seat control switch harness connector C509. Measure voltage at terminal No. 14 (White/Orange wire) at DDM harness connector C521. If voltage exists, repair short to voltage in White/Orange wire. If voltage does not exist, replace driver's seat switch.

22) Disconnect driver's seat control switch harness connector C509. Disconnect DDM harness connector C521. Measure resistance in White/Orange wire between terminal No. 14 at DDM harness connector C521 and terminal No. 4 at driver's seat control switch harness connector C509. If resistance is 5 ohms or less, go to step **24)**. If resistance is more than 5 ohms, repair open in White/Orange wire.

23) Disconnect driver's seat control switch harness connector C509. Disconnect DDM harness connector C521. Measure resistance between ground and terminal No. 14 at DDM harness connector C521. If resistance is more than 10 k/ohms, replace driver's seat switch. If resistance is 10 k/ohms or less, repair short to ground in White/Orange wire.

24) Test driver's seat switch. See DRIVER'S SEAT CONTROL SWITCH (WITH MEMORY) under COMPONENT TESTS article. If driver's seat switch is okay, replace DDM. If driver's seat switch is defective, replace driver's seat switch.

TEST H: HEATED MIRRORS INOPERATIVE

1) Turn ignition switch to RUN position. Turn rear window defogger on. If rear window defogger works, go to next step. If rear window defogger does not work, repair rear window defoggers. See appropriate REAR WINDOW DEFOGGERS article.

2) Turn ignition switch to LOCK position. Remove and check fuse No. 28 (10-amp). If fuse is okay, go to step **6)** . If fuse is blown, go to next step.

3) Measure resistance between ground and output side of fuse No. 28. If resistance is 10 k/ohms or less, go to next step. If resistance is more than 10 k/ohms, replace fuse.

4) Disconnect driver's mirror harness connector C508. Measure resistance between ground and output side of fuse No. 28. If resistance is 10 k/ohms or less, go to next step. If resistance is more than 10 k/ohms, replace driver's mirror glass.

5) Disconnect passenger's mirror harness connector C608. Measure resistance between ground and output side of fuse No. 28. If resistance is 10 k/ohms or less, repair short to ground in Dark Green/Violet wire and retest. If resistance is more than 10 k/ohms, replace passenger's mirror glass.

6) Remove fuse No. 28. Turn ignition switch to RUN position. Turn rear window defogger on. Measure voltage at input side of fuse No. 28. If battery voltage exists, go to next step. If battery voltage does not exist, repair open in Brown/Light Blue wire.

7) Turn ignition switch to LOCK position. Disconnect driver's mirror harness connector C508. Measure resistance in Dark Green/Violet wire between terminal No. 2 at driver's mirror harness connector C508 and output side of fuse No. 28. If resistance is 5 ohms or less, go to next step. If resistance is more than 5 ohms, repair open in Dark Green/Violet wire.

8) Turn ignition switch to LOCK position. Disconnect passenger's mirror harness connector C608. Measure resistance Dark Green/Violet wire between terminal No. 6 at passenger's mirror harness connector C608 and output side of fuse No. 28. If resistance is more than 5 ohms, repair open in Dark Green/Violet wire. If resistance is 5 ohms or less, check both mirrors for heat. If driver's mirror does not heat, go to next step. If passenger's mirror does not heat, go to step **10)**.

9) Measure resistance between ground and terminal No. 1 (Black wire) at driver's mirror harness connector C508. If resistance is 5 ohms or less, replace driver's mirror glass. If resistance is more than 5 ohms, repair open in Black wire.

10) Measure resistance between ground and terminal No. 4 (Black wire) at passenger's mirror harness connector C608. If resistance is 5 ohms or less, replace passenger's mirror glass. If resistance is more than 5 ohms, repair open in Black wire.

REMOVAL & INSTALLATION

CAUTION: When battery is disconnected or modules are replaced, vehicle computer and memory systems may lose memory data. Driveability problems may exist until computer systems have completed a relearn cycle. See COMPUTER RELEARN PROCEDURES article in GENERAL INFORMATION before disconnecting battery.

INSIDE MIRROR

Removal & Installation – Unplug harness connectors at rear of mirror. Grasp mirror firmly, insert small, flat-bladed screwdriver into slot and pry mirror off mount. To install, using Mirror Replacer (T91P-17700-AH) slide mirror onto mounting bracket. Reconnect wiring.

SIDE MIRROR ASSEMBLY

Removal & Installation – Disconnect negative battery cable. Remove door trim panel. Disconnect mirror wiring connector. Pivot mirror assembly inward to expose mounting bolt. Unscrew bolt while holding nut inside door. Remove mirror assembly while guiding wiring and connector through hole in door. To install, reverse removal procedure. Tighten bolt to 71-88 INCH lbs. (8-10 N.m).

SIDE MIRROR GLASS & MOTOR

WARNING: To prevent personal injury, place shop towel between mirror glass and hand when removing glass from mirror shell.

Removal & Installation – Rotate mirror glass to maximum upward travel. Insert flat-bladed screwdriver between mirror shell and glass on bottom edge to unlatch and release glass. *See Fig. 18*. Place hand and shop towel over mirror glass to keep it from falling out. Remove mirror motor screws. Remove wiring. To install, align retainer tabs and snap glass into mirror housing.

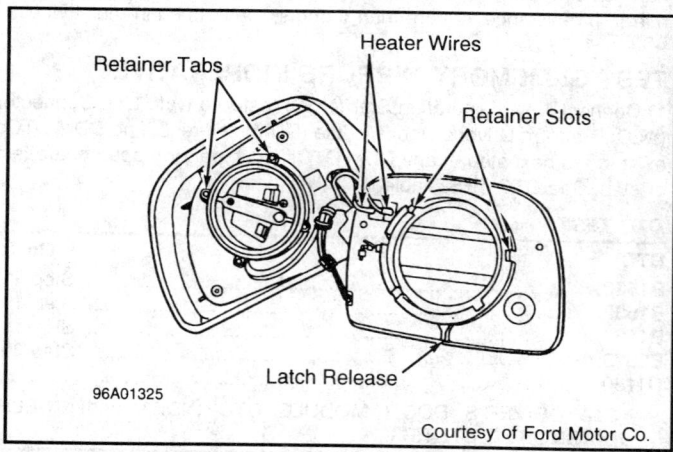

Fig. 18: Removing Side Mirror Glass

SIDE MIRROR SWITCH

Removal & Installation – Disconnect negative battery cable. Remove door panel. Push switch out of door panel and disconnect harness connector. To install, reverse removal procedure.

WIRING DIAGRAMS

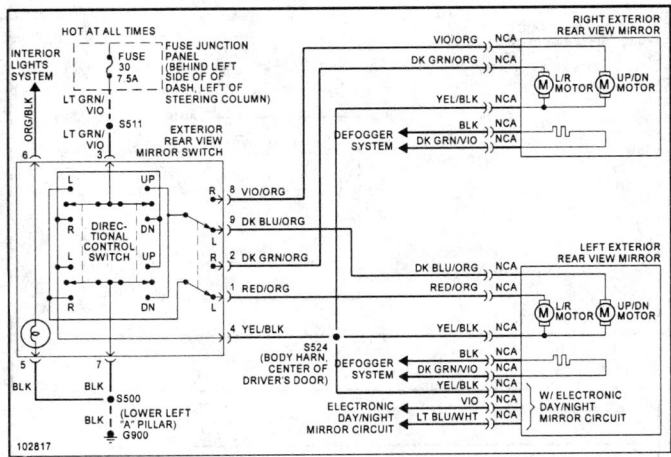

Fig. 19: Power Mirror System Wiring Diagram (Town Car)

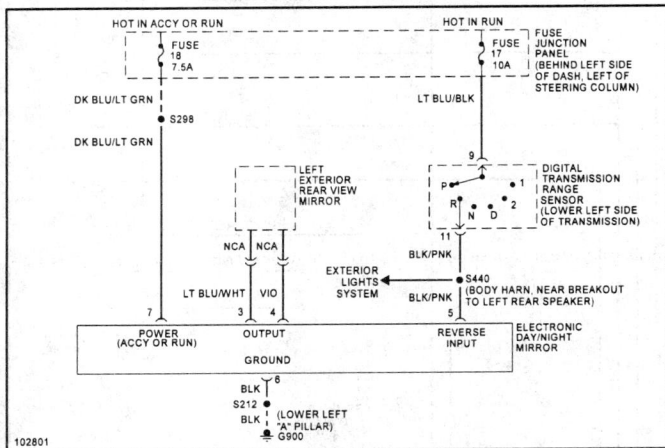

Fig. 20: Electronic Day/Night Mirror System Wiring Diagram
(Town Car)

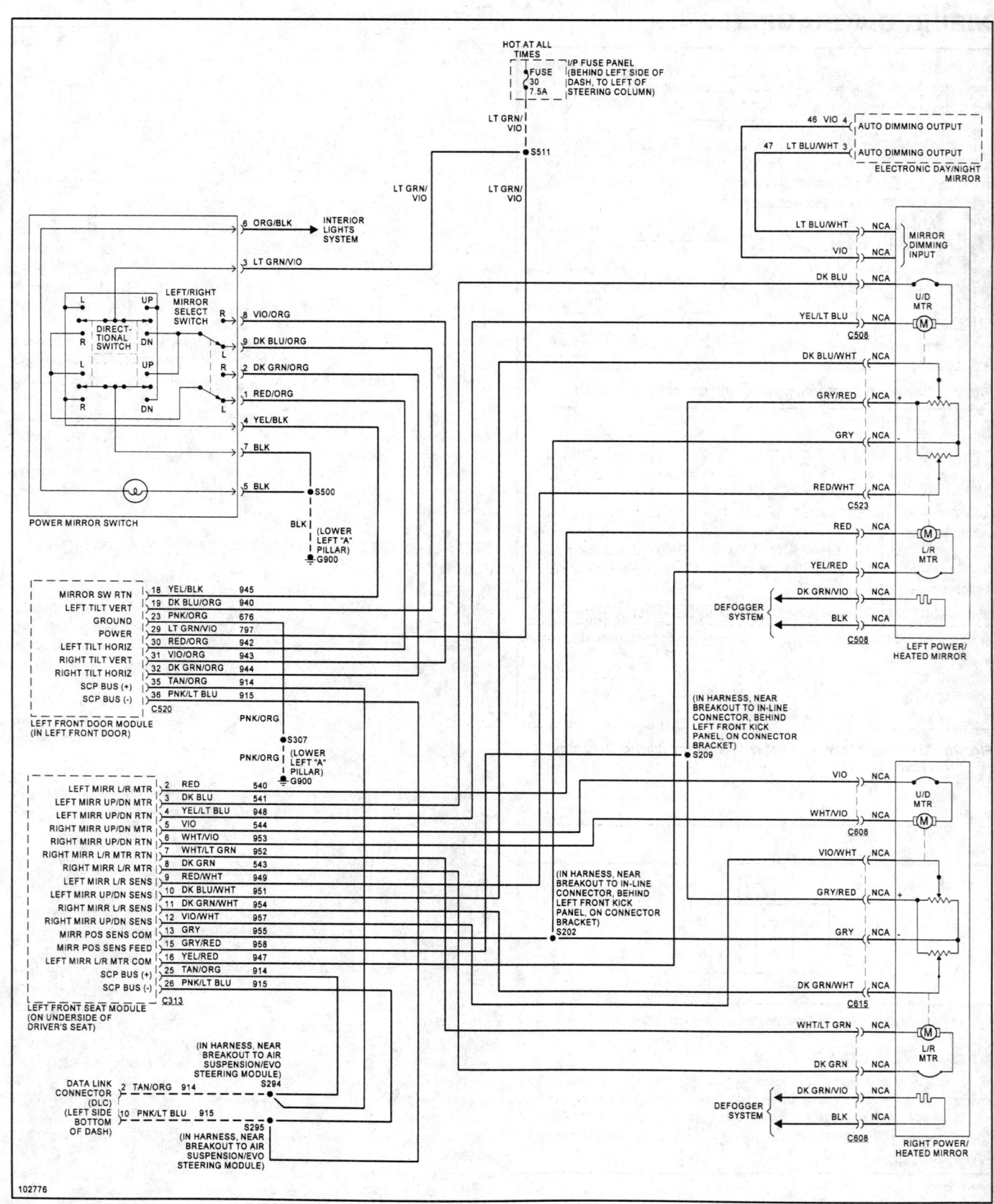

Fig. 21: Memory Mirror System Wiring Diagram (Town Car)

102776

DESCRIPTION & OPERATION

Power rear side view mirror system consists of mirror head with integral reversible servomotor assembly and mirror control switch. Some models are equipped with an heating element in outside mirror glass operated when rear window defogger (heated back window) is used.

The optional memory rear side view mirrors are controlled by Driver's Seat Module (DSM). Mirrors can be programmed with up to 3 personalized positions using memory switch or remote transmitter. Once the mirror is located in preferred position, driver must press SET switch within 5 seconds or operation is aborted.

TROUBLE SHOOTING

Before performing individual component tests or diagnostic tests, check the following for possible cause of system malfunction and repair as necessary:

- Blown fuses or faulty circuit breaker.
- Loose or corroded connectors.
- Damaged wiring.
- Damaged motors.
- Damaged mirror assemblies.
- Faulty switches.

COMPONENT TESTS

MIRROR CONTROL SWITCH

Remove mirror control switch. Measure resistance between specified terminals while operating switch in appropriate direction. See MIRROR CONTROL SWITCH TERMINAL IDENTIFICATION table. *See Fig. 1.* Resistance in all tests should be less than 5 ohms. If switch fails any portion of test, replace switch.

MIRROR CONTROL SWITCH TERMINAL IDENTIFICATION

Switch Position	Continuity Between Terminals
Driver's Mirror	
Up	1 & 2; 5 & 6
Down	1 & 6; 2 & 5
Left	1 & 4; 2 & 5
Right	1 & 2; 4 & 5
Passenger's Mirror	
Up	1 & 2; 5 & 7
Down	1 & 7; 2 & 5
Left	1 & 8; 2 & 5
Right	1 & 2; 5 & 8

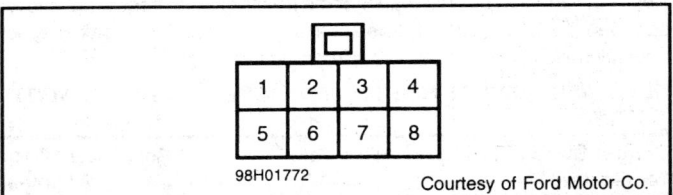

98H01772   Courtesy of Ford Motor Co.

Fig. 1: Identifying Mirror Control Switch Terminals

SYSTEM TESTS

Verify customer complaint by operating power mirror. Visually inspect for obvious sign of mechanical and electrical damage. If no visual damage is evident, perform appropriate diagnostic test. See SYMPTOM CHART table. A digital volt-ohmmeter is required to test power mirror system.

SYMPTOM CHART

Symptom	Test
Mirrors Are Inoperative	A
Mirrors Are Inoperative – Memory Function	B
Driver's Or Passenger's Mirror Is Inoperative	C
Driver's Or Passenger's Mirror Is Inoperative – Memory Function	D

SYMPTOM CHART (Cont.)

Symptom	Test
Driver's Or Passenger's Mirror Is Inoperative With Switch Logic	E
Driver's Or Passenger's Mirror Is Inoperative With Switch Logic – Memory Function	F
Memory Mirror Position Function Is Inoperative	G
Memory Mirror Inoperative With Remote Transmitter	H
Rear View Mirror Heated Function Is Inoperative	I

TEST A: MIRRORS ARE INOPERATIVE

1) Ensure ignition is off. Disconnect mirror control switch. See REMOVAL & INSTALLATION. Turn ignition on. Using voltmeter, measure voltage between ground and terminal No. 1 (Light Green/Red wire) on mirror control switch harness connector. *See Fig. 1.* If voltage is greater than 10 volts, go to next step. If voltage is 10 volts or less, repair open Light Green/Red wire.

2) Turn ignition off. Using ohmmeter, measure resistance between ground and terminal No. 5 (Black wire) on mirror control switch harness connector. If resistance is less than 5 ohms, go to next step. If resistance is 5 ohms or greater, repair open Black wire.

3) Disconnect driver's rear view mirror connector. Measure resistance of Yellow/Green wire between terminal No. 2 on mirror control switch harness connector and terminal No. 3 (center terminal) on driver's rear view mirror harness connector. If resistance is less than 5 ohms, replace power mirror switch. If resistance is 5 ohms or greater, repair open Yellow/Green wire.

TEST B: MIRRORS ARE INOPERATIVE – MEMORY FUNCTION

1) Ensure ignition is off. Disconnect mirror control switch. See REMOVAL & INSTALLATION. Turn ignition on. Using voltmeter, measure voltage between ground and terminal No. 1 (Light Green/Red wire) on mirror control switch harness connector. *See Fig. 1.* If voltage is greater than 10 volts, go to next step. If voltage is 10 volts or less, repair open Light Green/Red wire.

2) Turn ignition off. Using ohmmeter, measure resistance between ground and terminal No. 5 (Black wire) on mirror control switch harness connector. If resistance is less than 5 ohms, go to next step. If resistance is 5 ohms or greater, repair open Black wire.

3) Inspect mirror control switch. See MIRROR CONTROL SWITCH under COMPONENT TESTS. Replace switch as needed. If switch is okay, replace Driver's Seat Module (DSM). See REMOVAL & INSTALLATION.

TEST C: DRIVER'S OR PASSENGER'S MIRROR IS INOPERATIVE

1) Operate each rear view mirror. If driver's rear view mirror operates correctly, go to next step. If driver's rear view mirror does not operate correctly, go to step **4)**.

2) Ensure ignition is off. Disconnect mirror control switch. See REMOVAL & INSTALLATION. Disconnect passenger's rear view mirror connector. Measure resistance of Yellow/Green wire between terminal No. 2 on mirror control switch harness connector and terminal No. 3 (center terminal) on passenger's rear view mirror harness connector. If resistance is less than 5 ohms, go to next step. If resistance is 5 ohms or greater, repair open Yellow/Green wire.

3) Inspect mirror control switch. See MIRROR CONTROL SWITCH under COMPONENT TESTS. Replace switch as needed. If switch is okay, replace passenger's rear view mirror. See REMOVAL & INSTALLATION.

4) Ensure ignition is off. Disconnect mirror control switch. See REMOVAL & INSTALLATION. Disconnect driver's rear view mirror connector. Measure resistance of Yellow/Green wire between terminal No. 2 on mirror control switch harness connector and terminal No. 3 (center terminal) on driver's rear view mirror harness connector. If resistance is less than 5 ohms, go to next step. If resistance is 5 ohms or greater, repair open Yellow/Green wire.

5) Inspect mirror control switch. See MIRROR CONTROL SWITCH under COMPONENT TESTS. Replace switch as needed. If switch is okay, replace driver's rear view mirror. See REMOVAL & INSTALLATION.

TEST D: DRIVER'S OR PASSENGER'S MIRROR IS INOPERATIVE – MEMORY FUNCTION

1) Operate each rear view mirror. If driver's rear view mirror operates correctly, go to next step. If driver's rear view mirror does not operate correctly, go to step **4)**.

2) Ensure ignition is off. Disconnect mirror control switch. See REMOVAL & INSTALLATION. Inspect mirror control switch. See MIRROR CONTROL SWITCH under COMPONENT TESTS. Replace switch as needed. If switch is okay, go to next step.

3) Ensure ignition is off. Disconnect Driver's Seat Module (DSM) connectors. See REMOVAL & INSTALLATION. Disconnect passenger's rear view mirror connector. Measure resistance of Yellow/Green wire between terminal No. 7 on DSM C2046a harness connector and terminal No. 3 (center terminal) on passenger's rear view mirror harness connector. See Fig. 2. Resistance should be less than 5 ohms. Measure resistance between ground and terminal No. 3 (center terminal) on passenger's rear view mirror harness connector. Resistance should be greater than 10,000 ohms. If resistance is as specified, replace DSM. If resistance is not as specified, repair open Yellow/Green wire if resistance is 5 ohms or greater. If resistance is less than 10,000 ohms, repair Yellow/Green wire for short to ground.

4) Ensure ignition is off. Disconnect mirror control switch. See REMOVAL & INSTALLATION. Inspect mirror control switch. See MIRROR CONTROL SWITCH under COMPONENT TESTS. Replace switch as needed. If switch is okay, go to next step.

5) Ensure ignition is off. Disconnect Driver's Seat Module (DSM) connectors. See REMOVAL & INSTALLATION. Disconnect driver's rear view mirror connector. Measure resistance of Yellow/Green wire between terminal No. 8 on DSM C2046a harness connector and terminal No. 3 (center terminal) on passenger's rear view mirror harness connector. See Fig. 2. Resistance should be less than 5 ohms. Measure resistance between ground and terminal No. 3 (center terminal) on passenger's rear view mirror harness connector. Resistance should be greater than 10,000 ohms. If resistance is as specified, replace DSM. If resistance is not as specified, repair open Yellow/Green wire if resistance is 5 ohms or greater. If resistance is less than 10,000 ohms, repair Yellow/Green wire for short to ground.

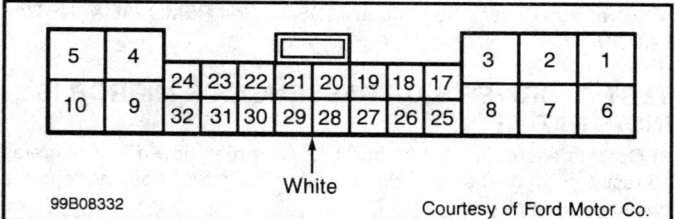

99B08332   Courtesy of Ford Motor Co.

Fig. 2: Identifying Driver's Seat Module C2046a Harness Connector Or Smart Entry Control (SEC) /Timer Module Harness Connector Terminals

TEST E: DRIVER'S OR PASSENGER'S MIRROR IS INOPERATIVE WITH SWITCH LOGIC

1) Ensure ignition is off. Disconnect mirror control switch. See REMOVAL & INSTALLATION. Inspect mirror control switch. See MIRROR CONTROL SWITCH under COMPONENT TESTS. Replace switch as needed. If switch is okay, go to next step.

2) Disconnect suspect rear view mirror connector. Measure resistance of specified circuits between rear view mirror arness connector and mirror control switch harness connector. See MIRROR CONTROL SWITCH-TO-REAR VIEW MIRROR CIRCUIT CONTINUITY TESTING table. See Figs. 1 and 3. Resistance should be less than 5 ohms for all circuits. If resistance is as specified and mirror only operates in 3 out of 4 directions, go to next step. If resistance is as specified and mirror only operates in 2 out of 4 directions, replace rear view mirror. If resistance

is not as specified, repair suspect open circuit.

MIRROR CONTROL SWITCH-TO-REAR VIEW MIRROR CIRCUIT CONTINUITY TESTING

Control Switch Terminal	Wire Color	Rear View Mirror Terminal
Driver's Rear View Mirror		
4	Yellow/Black	4
6	Orange	5
2	Yellow/Green	3
Passenger's Rear View Mirror		
2	Yellow/Green	3
8	Yellow/Red	4
7	Orange/Black	5

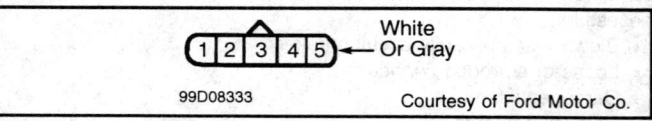

99D08333   Courtesy of Ford Motor Co.

Fig. 3: Identifying Rear View Mirror Harness Connector Terminals

3) Ensure ignition off. Measure resistance between ground and terminals No. 4, 6, 7 and 8 on mirror control switch harness connector. See Fig. 1. Resistance for each circuit should be greater than 10,000 ohms. If resistance is as specified, go to next step. If resistance is not as specified, repair suspect circuit for short to ground.

4) Turn ignition on. Measure voltage between ground and terminals No. 4, 6, 7 and 8 on mirror control switch harness connector. See Fig. 1. No voltage should be present on any circuit. If voltage is as specified, replace suspect rear view mirror. If voltage is not as specified, repair suspect circuit for short to voltage.

TEST F: DRIVER'S OR PASSENGER'S MIRROR IS INOPERATIVE WITH SWITCH LOGIC – MEMORY FUNCTION

1) Ensure ignition is off. Disconnect mirror control switch. See REMOVAL & INSTALLATION. Inspect mirror control switch. See MIRROR CONTROL SWITCH under COMPONENT TESTS. Replace switch as needed. If switch is okay, go to next step.

2) Disconnect suspect rear view mirror connector. Measure resistance of specified circuits between rear view mirror harness connector and mirror control switch harness connector. See REAR VIEW MEMORY MIRROR CIRCUIT CONTINUITY TESTING table. See Figs. 1 and 3. Resistance should be less than 5 ohms for all circuits. If resistance is as specified, go to next step. If resistance is not as specified, repair suspect open circuit.

REAR VIEW MEMORY MIRROR CONTROL CIRCUIT CONTINUITY TESTING

Control Switch Terminal	Wire Color	Rear View Mirror Terminal
Driver's Rear View Mirror		
4	Yellow/Black	4
6	Orange	5
Passenger's Rear View Mirror		
8	Yellow/Red	4
7	Orange/Black	5

3) Ensure ignition is off. Measure resistance of specified circuits between Driver's Seat Module (DSM) 2046a harness connector and mirror control switch harness connector. See MIRROR CONTROL SWITCH-TO-DSM CIRCUIT CONTINUITY TESTING table. See Figs. 1 and 2. Resistance should be less than 5 ohms for all circuits. If resistance is as specified, go to next step. If resistance is not as specified, repair suspect open circuit.

MIRROR CONTROL SWITCH-TO-DSM CIRCUIT CONTINUITY TESTING

Mirror Control Switch Terminal	Wire Color	Driver's Seat Module Terminal
2	Blue	29
4	Yellow/Black	3
6	Orange	18
8	Yellow/Red	26
7	Orange/Black	25

4) Ensure ignition off. Measure resistance between ground and terminals No. 2, 4, 6, 7 and 8 on mirror control switch harness connector. *See Fig. 1.* Resistance for each circuit should be greater than 10,000 ohms. If resistance is as specified, go to next step. If resistance is not as specified, repair suspect circuit for short to ground.

5) Turn ignition on. Measure voltage between ground and terminals No. 2, 4, 6, 7 and 8 on mirror control switch harness connector. *See Fig. 1.* No voltage should be present on any circuit. If voltage is as specified, go to next step. If voltage is not as specified, repair suspect circuit for short to voltage.

6) Turn ignition off. Measure resistance of specified circuits between Driver's Seat Module (DSM) 2046a harness connector and each rear view mirror harness connector. See REAR VIEW MIRROR-TO-DSM CIRCUIT CONTINUITY TESTING table. *See Figs. 2 and 3.* Resistance should be less than 5 ohms for all circuits. If resistance is as specified, go to next step. If resistance is not as specified, repair suspect open circuit.

REAR VIEW MIRROR-TO-DSM CIRCUIT CONTINUITY TESTING

Driver's Seat Module Terminal	Wire Color	Rear View Mirror Terminal
Driver's Rear View Mirror		
8	Yellow/Green	3
Passenger's Rear View Mirror		
7	Yellow/Green	3

7) Measure resistance between ground and terminals No. 7 and 8 (Yellow/Green wires) on DSM harness connector. *See Fig. 2.* If resistance is greater than 10,000 ohms for both circuits, go to next step. If resistance is 10,000 ohms or less for either circuit, repair Yellow/Green wire for short to ground.

8) Turn ignition on. Measure voltage between ground and terminals No. 7 and 8 (Yellow/Green wires) on DSM harness connector. *See Fig. 2.* If no voltage is present on either circuit, go to next step. If voltage is present on either circuit, repair Yellow/Green wire for short to voltage.

9) To test Up/Down mirror function, connect fused 10-amp jumper wire between battery voltage and terminal No. 5 on rear view mirror White component connector. *See Fig. 3.* Connect second jumper wire between ground and terminal No. 3 on rear view mirror White component connector. Mirror should move in one direction. Reverse jumper wires and mirror should move in opposite direction. To test Right/Left mirror function, connect fused 10-amp jumper wire between battery voltage and terminal No. 4 on rear view mirror White component connector. Connect second jumper wire between ground and terminal No. 5 on rear view mirror Gray component connector. Mirror should move in one direction. Reverse jumper wires and mirror should move in opposite direction. If mirror operates as specified, replace Driver's Seat Module (DSM). See REMOVAL & INSTALLATION. If mirror does not operate as specified, replace inoperative mirror.

TEST G: MEMORY MIRROR POSITION FUNCTION IS INOPERATIVE

1) Press memory position buttons No. 1 and 2 at the same time. If memory seat moves, go to next step. If memory seat does not move, repair memory seat system as necessary. See POWER MEMORY SEAT SYSTEM wiring diagram in POWER SEATS – VILLAGER article.
2) Operate rear view mirrors using memory function. If driver's rear view mirror operates correctly, go to step **10)**. If driver's rear view mirror does not operate correctly, go to next step. If both rear view mirrors do not operate correctly, go to step **7)**.

3) Turn ignition off. Disconnect Driver's Seat Module (DSM) C2046a connector. Disconnect driver's rear view mirror Gray connector. Measure resistance of specified circuits between DSM 2046a harness connector and rear view mirror Gray harness connector. See DRIVER'S MIRROR-TO-DSM CIRCUIT CONTINUITY TESTING table. *See Figs. 2 and 3.* Resistance should be less than 5 ohms for all circuits. If resistance is as specified, go to next step. If resistance is not as specified, repair suspect open circuit.

DRIVER'S MIRROR-TO-DSM CIRCUIT CONTINUITY TESTING

Driver's Mirror Terminal	Wire Color	Driver's Seat Module Terminal
1	White	2
2	Blue/White	21
3	Gray/Red	22
4	Black/Blue	17

4) Turn ignition on. Using voltmeter, measure voltage between ground and terminals No. 2, 17, 21 and 22 on DSM (C2046a) harness connector. If any voltage is present, repair suspect circuit for short to voltage. If no voltage is present on any circuit, go to next step.

5) Turn ignition off. Using ohmmeter, measure resistance between ground and terminals No. 2, 17, 21 and 22 on DSM C2046a harness connector. If resistance on any circuit is 10,000 ohms or less, repair suspect circuit for short to ground. If resistance is greater than 10,000 ohms on all circuits, go to next step.

6) With DSM C2046a connector disconnected, remove terminals No. 21 (Blue/White wire) and 22 (Gray/Red wire) from connector block using appropriate tool. Plug connector into module. Turn ignition on. Measure voltage between ground and terminal No. 21. *See Fig. 4.* Operate mirror control switch in all directions for driver's side rear view mirror. Move voltmeter lead to terminal No. 22 and repeat mirror control switch operation. If voltage varies between zero and about 4 volts for both circuits while operating mirror control switch, replace DSM. See REMOVAL & INSTALLATION. If voltage does not vary between zero and about 4 volts for both circuits while operating mirror control switch, replace driver's rear view mirror.

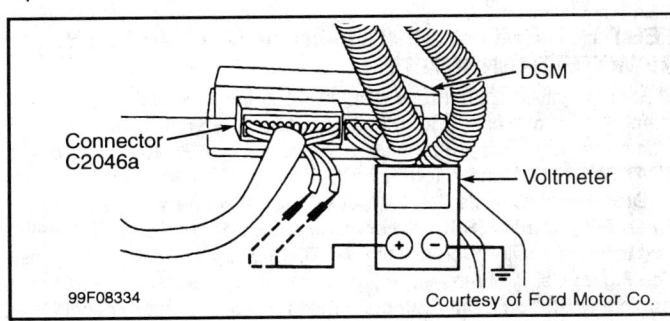

99F08334   Courtesy of Ford Motor Co.

Fig. 4: Measuring Rear View Mirror Feedback Voltage

7) Turn ignition off. Disconnect driver's rear view mirror and Driver's Seat Module (DSM) connectors. Using ohmmeter, measure resistance of White wire between terminal No. 2 on DSM C2046a harness connector and terminal No. 1 on driver's rear view mirror Gray harness connector. *See Figs. 2 and 3.* Resistance should be less than 5 ohms. Measure resistance of Black/Blue wire between terminal No. 17 on DSM C2046a harness connector and terminal No. 4 on driver's rear view mirror Gray harness connector. Resistance should be less than 5 ohms. If resistance for both circuits is as specified, go to next step. If resistance is not as specified for either circuit, repair suspect open circuit.

8) Turn ignition on. Measure voltage between ground and terminals No. 2 and 17 on DSM C2046a harness connector. If any voltage is present, repair suspect circuit for short to voltage. If no voltage is present on either circuit, go to next step.

9) Turn ignition off. Using ohmmeter, measure resistance between ground and terminals No. 2 and 17 on DSM C2046a harness connector. If resistance on either circuit is 10,000 ohms or less, repair suspect circuit for short to ground. If resistance is greater than 10,000 ohms on both circuits, replace DSM. See REMOVAL & INSTALLATION.

10) Turn ignition off. Disconnect Driver's Seat Module (DSM) C2046a connector. Disconnect driver's rear view mirror Gray connector. Measure resistance of specified circuits between DSM 2046a harness connector and rear view mirror Gray harness connector. See PASSENGER'S MIRROR-TO-DSM CIRCUIT CONTINUITY TESTING table. See Figs. 2 and 3. Resistance should be less than 5 ohms for all circuits. If resistance is as specified, go to next step. If resistance is not as specified, repair suspect open circuit.

PASSENGER'S MIRROR-TO-DSM CIRCUIT CONTINUITY TESTING

Passenger's Mirror Terminal	Wire Color	Driver's Seat Module Terminal
1	White	2
2	Blue/Yellow	30
3	Blue/Red	31
4	Black/Blue	17

11) Turn ignition on. Using voltmeter, measure voltage between ground and terminals No. 2, 17, 30 and 31 on DSM 2046a harness connector. If any voltage is present, repair suspect circuit for short to voltage. If no voltage is present on any circuit, go to next step.

12) Turn ignition off. Using ohmmeter, measure resistance between ground and terminals No. 2, 17, 30 and 31 on DSM C2046a harness connector. If resistance on any circuit is 10,000 ohms or less, repair suspect circuit for short to ground. If resistance is greater than 10,000 ohms on all circuits, go to next step.

13) With DSM C2046a connector disconnected, remove terminals No. 30 (Blue/Yellow wire) and No. 31 (Blue/Red wire) from connector block using appropriate tool. Plug connector into module. Turn ignition on. Measure voltage between ground and terminal No. 30. See Fig. 4. Operate mirror control switch in all directions for passenger's side rear view mirror. Move voltmeter lead to terminal No. 31 and repeat mirror control switch operation. If voltage varies between zero and about 4 volts for both circuits while operating mirror control switch, replace DSM. See REMOVAL & INSTALLATION. If voltage does not vary between zero and about 4 volts for both circuits while operating mirror control switch, replace passenger's rear view mirror.

TEST H: MEMORY MIRROR INOPERATIVE WITH REMOTE TRANSMITTER

1) Ensure ignition is off. Press UNLOCK button on remote transmitter. If memory seat moves, go to next step. If memory seat does not move, repair memory seat system as necessary. See POWER MEMORY SEAT SYSTEM wiring diagram in POWER SEATS – VILLAGER article.

2) Disconnect Driver's Seat Module (DSM) connectors. Disconnect Smart Entry Control (SEC)/Timer module. SEC/Timer module is located next to Transmission Control Module (TCM) under center of dash panel. See Fig. 5. Using ohmmeter, measure resistance of Pink wire between terminal No. 24 on DSM C2046a harness connector and terminal No. 7 on SEC/Timer module harness connector. See Fig. 2. Resistance should be 5 ohms. Measure resistance between ground and terminal No. 24 (Pink wire) on DSM (C2046a) harness connector. Resistance should be greater than 10,000 ohms. If resistance is as specified, go to next step. If resistance is not as specified, repair open Pink wire is resistance is 5 ohms or greater. Repair Pink wire for short to ground if resistance 10,000 ohms or less.

3) Turn ignition on. Measure voltage between ground and terminal No. 24 (Pink wire) on DSM C2046a harness connector. If any voltage is present, repair Pink wire for short to voltage. If no voltage is present, go to next step.

4) Install known-good Smart Entry Control (SEC)/Timer module. Connect Driver's Seat Module (DSM) connectors. Press memory position buttons No. 1 and 2 at the same time. If memory mirror moves, replace SEC/Timer module. If memory mirror does not move, replace DSM. See REMOVAL & INSTALLATION.

TEST I: REAR VIEW MIRROR HEATED FUNCTION IS INOPERATIVE

1) Ensure shift selector is Park position. Start engine. Press heated back window (rear window defroster) switch to ON position. If heated back

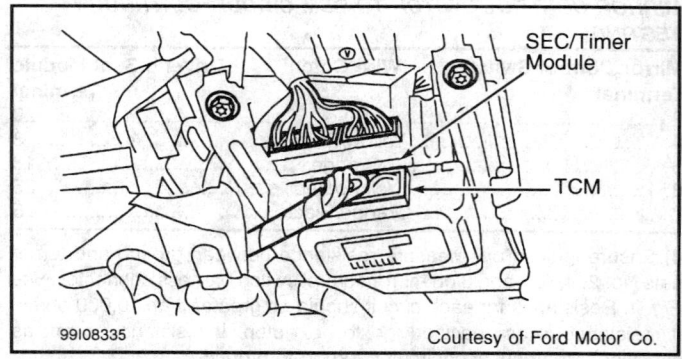

99I08335   Courtesy of Ford Motor Co.

Fig. 5: Locating Smart Entry Control (SEC)/Timer Module

window operates correctly, go to next step. If heated rear window does operate correctly, repair heated back window as necessary. See appropriate wiring diagram in REAR WINDOW DEFOGGERS article in WIRING DIAGRAMS.

2) Inspect rear view mirrors for correct heating element operation. If heating element is operating, go to next step. If heating elements for both mirrors are not operating, inspect and repair Green wire between HEATED MIRROR fuse (10-amp) and terminal No. 2 on rear view mirror harness White connector. If heating element for either rear view mirror is not operating, go to next step.

3) Turn ignition off. Disconnect suspect mirror connector. Turn ignition on. Measure voltage between ground and terminal No. 2 (Green wire) on mirror harness White connector. See Fig. 3. If voltage is greater than 10 volts, go to next step. If voltage is 10 volts or less, repair open Green wire.

4) Turn ignition off. Measure resistance between ground and terminal No. 1 (Black wire) on suspect mirror harness White connector. See Fig. 3. If resistance is less than 5 ohms, replace suspect rear view mirror. If resistance is 5 ohms or greater, repair open Black wire.

REMOVAL & INSTALLATION

WARNING: When battery is disconnected, vehicle computer and memory systems may lose memory data. Driveability problems may exist until computer systems have completed a relearn cycle. See COMPUTER RELEARN PROCEDURES article in GENERAL INFORMATION before disconnecting battery.

DRIVER'S SEAT MODULE (DSM)

Disconnect negative battery cable. Remove outer trim panel from driver's bucket seat. Remove rear bracket and side bracket mounting screws. Disconnect electrical connectors and remove module. To install, reverse removal procedure.

REAR VIEW MIRROR ASSEMBLY

Removal & Installation – Remove door panel. Remove upper speaker. Remove mirror mounting hole cover. See Fig. 6. Disconnect mirror wiring harness connector. Remove mirror attaching nuts. Remove mirror assembly while guiding wiring and connector through hole in door. To install, reverse removal procedure. Tighten nuts to approximately 27-35 INCH lbs. (3-4 N.m).

MIRROR CONTROL SWITCH

Removal & Installation – Using a small flat-blade screwdriver, pry mirror control switch from instrument panel. Disconnect mirror control switch harness connector. Remove switch. To install, reverse removal procedure.

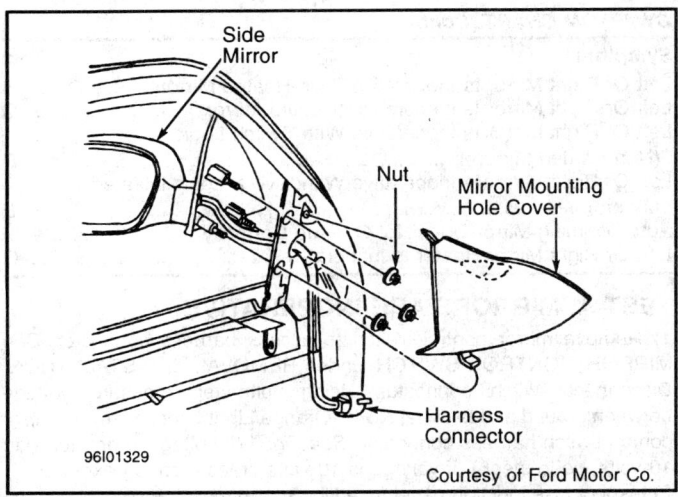

Fig. 6: Removing Rear View Mirror

WIRING DIAGRAMS

NOTE: For heated mirror wiring diagram, see appropriate wiring diagram in REAR WINDOW DEFOGGERS article in WIRING DIAGRAMS.

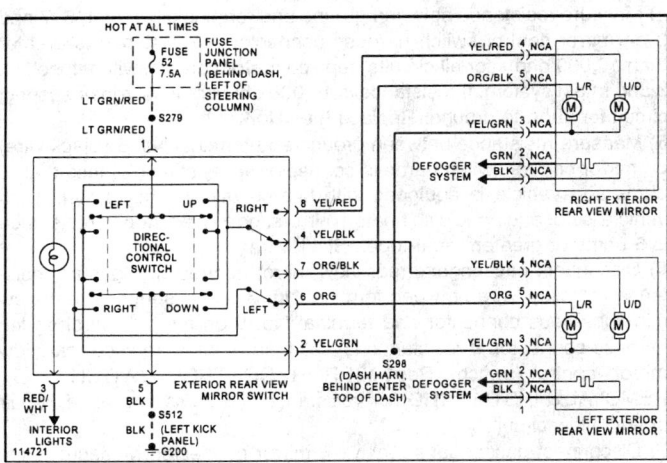

Fig. 7: Power Mirror System Wiring Diagram (Villager)

DESCRIPTION & OPERATION

Power side view mirror system consists of mirror head with integral reversible servomotor assembly and mirror control switch. Some models are equipped with an electronic dimming rear view mirror and heating element in outside mirror glass.

The optional inside electronic dimming rear view mirror is controlled by 2 light-sensitive photocells. Outside light level is measured by a sensor on backside of mirror housing. A second sensor, located on reflective side of mirror, detects approaching rear lights. The mirror switches to normal state whenever transmission gear selector is placed in Reverse.

TROUBLE SHOOTING

Before performing individual component tests or system tests, check the following for possible cause of system malfunction and repair as necessary:

- Blown fuses or faulty circuit breaker.
- Loose or corroded connectors.
- Damaged wiring.
- Damaged motors.
- Damaged mirror assemblies.
- Faulty switches.

COMPONENT TESTS

MIRROR CONTROL SWITCH

Remove mirror control switch. Measure resistance between specified terminals while operating switch in appropriate direction. See MIRROR SWITCH TERMINAL IDENTIFICATION table. See Fig. 1. Resistance in all tests should be less than 5 ohms. If switch fails any portion of test, replace switch.

MIRROR SWITCH TERMINAL IDENTIFICATION

Switch Position	Continuity Between Terminals
Driver's Mirror	
Up	1 & 7; 5 & 6
Down	1 & 6; 3 & 5
Left	1 & 4; 5 & 6
Right	1 & 6; 4 & 5
Passenger's Mirror	
Up	1 & 8; 5 & 6
Down	1 & 6; 5 & 8
Left	1 & 3; 5 & 6
Right	1 & 6; 3 & 5

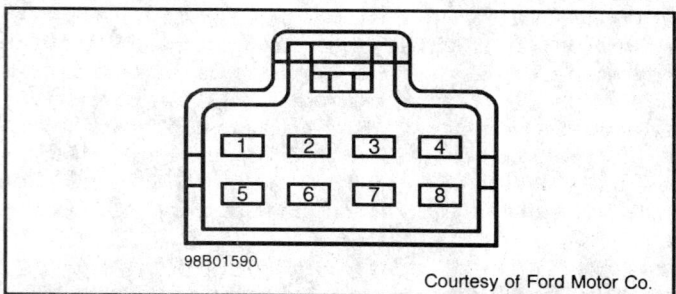

98B01590

Courtesy of Ford Motor Co.

Fig. 1: Identifying Power Mirror Control Switch Terminals

SYSTEM TESTS

Verify customer complaint by operating power mirror. Visually inspect for obvious sign of mechanical and electrical damage. If no visual damage is evident, perform appropriate diagnostic test. See SYMPTOM CHART table. A digital volt-ohmmeter is required to test power mirror system.

SYMPTOM CHART

Symptom	Test
Mirrors Are Inoperative	A

SYMPTOM CHART (Cont.)

Symptom	Test
Left Or Right Mirror Is Inoperative (Non-Heated Mirrors)	B
Left Or Right Mirror Is Inoperative (Heated Mirrors)	C
Left Or Right Mirror Is Inoperative With Switch Logic (Non-Heated Mirrors)	D
Left Or Right Mirror Is Inoperative With Switch Logic (Heated Mirrors)	E
Auto Dimming Mirror Does Not Operate Correctly	F
Left Or Right Mirror Heater Is Inoperative	G

TEST A: MIRRORS ARE INOPERATIVE

1) Remove mirror control switch to access harness connector. See MIRROR CONTROL SWITCH under REMOVAL & INSTALLATION. Disconnect switch connector. Using voltmeter, measure voltage between ground and terminal No. 1 (Orange/Light Green wire) on mirror control switch harness connector. See Fig. 1. If voltage is greater than 10 volts, go to step5). If voltage is 10 volts or less, go to next step.

2) Inspect fuse junction panel fuse No. 3 (10-amp). If fuse is blown, go to next step. If fuse is okay, inspect and repair Orange/Light Green wire between fuse No. 3 and mirror control switch.

3) Ensure fuse junction panel fuse No. 3 (10-amp) is removed. Using ohmmeter, measure resistance between ground and terminal No. 1 (Orange/Light Green wire) on mirror control switch harness connector. If resistance is greater than 10, 000 ohms, go to next step. If resistance is 10,000 ohms or less, repair Orange/Light Green wire. Replace fuse No. 3.

4) Measure resistance between ground and terminals No. 3, 4, 6, 7 and 8 on mirror control switch harness connector. If resistance is greater than 10,000 ohms for all circuits, replace mirror control switch, fuse No. 3 and retest system. If resistance is 10,000 ohms or less, repair suspect circuit for short to ground. Replace fuse No. 3.

5) Measure resistance between ground and terminal No. 5 (Black wire) on mirror control switch harness connector. If resistance is less than 5 ohms and vehicle is equipped with heated mirrors, go to step7) . If vehicle is not equipped with heated mirrors, go to next step. If resistance is 5 ohms or greater, repair open Black wire.

6) Disconnect passenger's rear view mirror connector. Measure resistance of Yellow wire between terminal No. 3 on passenger's rear view mirror harness connector and terminal No. 6 on mirror control switch harness connector. If resistance is less than 5 ohms, replace rear view mirror control switch. See MIRROR CONTROL SWITCH under REMOVAL & INSTALLATION. If resistance is 5 ohms or greater, repair open Yellow circuit.

7) Disconnect passenger's rear view mirror connector. Measure resistance of Yellow wire between terminal No. 2 on passenger's rear view mirror connector and terminal No. 6 on mirror control switch harness connector. See Fig. 2. If resistance is less than 5 ohms, replace rear view mirror control switch. See MIRROR CONTROL SWITCH under REMOVAL & INSTALLATION. If resistance is 5 ohms or greater, repair open Yellow circuit.

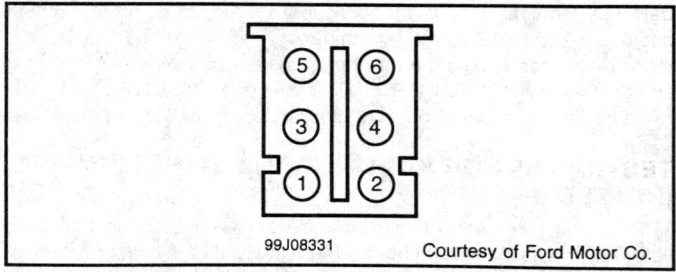

99J08331

Courtesy of Ford Motor Co.

Fig. 2: Identifying Heated Side Rear View Harness Connector

TEST B: LEFT OR RIGHT MIRROR IS INOPERATIVE (NON-HEATED MIRRORS)

1) Disconnect inoperative rear view mirror connector. Using voltmeter, measure voltage between ground and terminal No. 3 (Yellow wire) on suspect rear view mirror harness connector. Using mirror control switch,

actuate mirror in down, then right position. If voltage is greater than 10 volts in both positions, go to step **3**). If voltage is 10 volts or less in either position, go to next step.

2) Remove mirror control switch to access harness connector. See MIRROR CONTROL SWITCH under REMOVAL & INSTALLATION. Disconnect switch connector. Measure resistance of Yellow wire between terminal No. 3 on suspect rear view mirror harness connector and terminal No. 6 on mirror control switch harness connector. If resistance is less than 5 ohms, replace rear view mirror control switch. See MIRROR CONTROL SWITCH under REMOVAL & INSTALLATION. If resistance is 5 ohms or greater, repair open Yellow wire.

3) Measure voltage between ground and terminal No. 2 (Dark Blue/ Yellow wire or Violet wire) on suspect rear view mirror harness connector. Using mirror control switch, actuate mirror in up position. If voltage is greater than 10 volts, go to step **6**). If voltage is 10 volts or less, go to next step if driver's side mirror is inoperative. Go to step **5**) if passenger's mirror is inoperative.

4) Remove mirror control switch to access harness connector. See MIRROR CONTROL SWITCH under REMOVAL & INSTALLATION. Disconnect switch connector. Measure resistance of Dark Blue/Yellow wire between terminal No. 2 on driver's rear view mirror harness connector and terminal No. 7 on mirror control switch harness connector. If resistance is less than 5 ohms, replace rear view mirror control switch. See MIRROR CONTROL SWITCH under REMOVAL & INSTALLATION. If resistance is 5 ohms or greater, repair open Dark Blue/Yellow wire.

5) Remove mirror control switch to access harness connector. See MIRROR CONTROL SWITCH under REMOVAL & INSTALLATION. Disconnect switch connector. Measure resistance of Violet wire between terminal No. 2 on passenger's rear view mirror harness connector and terminal No. 8 on mirror control switch harness connector. If resistance is less than 5 ohms, replace rear view mirror control switch. See MIRROR CONTROL SWITCH under REMOVAL & INSTALLATION. If resistance is 5 ohms or greater, repair open Violet wire.

6) Measure voltage between ground and terminal No. 1 (Red wire or dark Green wire) on suspect rear view mirror harness connector. Using mirror control switch, actuate mirror in left position. If voltage is greater than 10 volts, replace mirror motor in suspect mirror. See SIDE REAR VIEW MIRROR ASSEMBLY under REMOVAL & INSTALLATION. If voltage is 10 volts or less, go to next step if driver's side mirror is inoperative. Go to step **8**) if passenger's mirror is inoperative.

7) Remove mirror control switch to access harness connector. See MIRROR CONTROL SWITCH under REMOVAL & INSTALLATION. Disconnect switch connector. Measure resistance of Red wire between terminal No. 1 on passenger's rear view mirror harness connector and terminal No. 4 on mirror control switch harness connector. If resistance is less than 5 ohms, replace rear view mirror control switch. See MIRROR CONTROL SWITCH under REMOVAL & INSTALLATION. If resistance is 5 ohms or greater, repair open Red wire.

8) Remove mirror control switch to access harness connector. See MIRROR CONTROL SWITCH under REMOVAL & INSTALLATION. Disconnect switch connector. Measure resistance of Dark Green wire between terminal No. 1 on passenger's rear view mirror harness connector and terminal No. 3 on mirror control switch harness connector. If resistance is less than 5 ohms, replace rear view mirror control switch. See MIRROR CONTROL SWITCH under REMOVAL & INSTALLATION. If resistance is 5 ohms or greater, repair open Dark Green wire.

TEST C: LEFT OR RIGHT MIRROR IS INOPERATIVE (HEATED MIRRORS)

1) Disconnect inoperative rear view mirror harness connector. Using voltmeter, measure voltage between ground and terminal No. 2 (Yellow wire) on suspect rear view mirror harness connector. See Fig. 2. Using mirror control switch, actuate inoperative mirror in down, then right position. If voltage is 10 volts in both positions, go to step **3**). If voltage is 10 volts or less in either position, go to next step.

2) Remove mirror control switch to access harness connector. See MIRROR CONTROL SWITCH under REMOVAL & INSTALLATION. Disconnect switch connector. Measure resistance of Yellow wire

between terminal No. 2 on suspect rear view mirror harness connector and terminal No. 6 on mirror control switch harness connector. See Figs. 1 and 2. If resistance is less than 5 ohms, replace rear view mirror control switch. See MIRROR CONTROL SWITCH under REMOVAL & INSTALLATION. If resistance is 5 ohms or greater, repair open Yellow wire.

3) Measure voltage between ground and terminal No. 4 (Dark Blue/ Yellow wire or Violet wire) on suspect rear view mirror harness connector. Using mirror control switch, actuate mirror in up position. If voltage is greater than 10 volts, go to step **6**). If voltage is 10 volts or less, go to next step if driver's side mirror is inoperative or go to step **5**) if passenger's mirror is inoperative.

4) Remove mirror control switch to access harness connector. See MIRROR CONTROL SWITCH under REMOVAL & INSTALLATION. Disconnect switch connector. Measure resistance of Dark Blue/Yellow wire between terminal No. 4 on driver's rear view mirror harness connector and terminal No. 7 on mirror control switch harness connector. If resistance is less than 5 ohms, replace rear view mirror control switch. See MIRROR CONTROL SWITCH under REMOVAL & INSTALLATION. If resistance is 5 ohms or greater, repair open Dark Blue/Yellow wire.

5) Remove mirror control switch to access harness connector. See MIRROR CONTROL SWITCH under REMOVAL & INSTALLATION. Disconnect switch connector. Measure resistance of Violet wire between terminal No. 4 on passenger's rear view mirror harness connector and terminal No. 8 on mirror control switch harness connector. If resistance is less than 5 ohms, replace rear view mirror control switch. See MIRROR CONTROL SWITCH under REMOVAL & INSTALLATION. If resistance is 5 ohms or greater, repair open Violet wire.

6) Measure voltage between ground and terminal No. 6 (Red wire or dark Green wire) on suspect rear view mirror harness connector. Using mirror control switch, actuate mirror in left position. If voltage is greater than 10 volts, replace mirror motor in suspect mirror. See SIDE REAR VIEW MIRROR ASSEMBLY under REMOVAL & INSTALLATION. If voltage is 10 volts or less, go to next step if driver's side mirror is inoperative. Go to step **8**) if passenger's mirror is inoperative.

7) Remove mirror control switch to access harness connector. See MIRROR CONTROL SWITCH under REMOVAL & INSTALLATION. Disconnect switch connector. Measure resistance of Red wire between terminal No. 6 on passenger's rear view mirror harness connector and terminal No. 4 on mirror control switch harness connector. If resistance is less than 5 ohms, replace rear view mirror control switch. See MIRROR CONTROL SWITCH under REMOVAL & INSTALLATION. If resistance is 5 ohms or greater, repair open Red wire.

8) Remove mirror control switch to access harness connector. See MIRROR CONTROL SWITCH under REMOVAL & INSTALLATION. Disconnect switch connector. Measure resistance of Dark Green wire between terminal No. 6 on passenger's rear view mirror harness connector and terminal No. 3 on mirror control switch harness connector. If resistance is less than 5 ohms, replace rear view mirror control switch. See MIRROR CONTROL SWITCH under REMOVAL & INSTALLATION. If resistance is 5 ohms or greater, repair open Dark Green wire.

TEST D: LEFT OR RIGHT MIRROR IS INOPERATIVE WITH SWITCH LOGIC (NON-HEATED MIRRORS)

1) Disconnect suspect rear view mirror harness connector. Using DVOM, measure voltage or resistance between ground and specified terminal on rear view mirror harness connector while moving mirror control switch to specified position. See REAR VIEW MIRROR CIRCUIT LOGIC TESTING table. If all resistance and voltage measurements are as specified, replace suspect mirror motor. See REMOVAL & INSTALLATION. If any resistance or voltage measurement is not as specified, go to next step.

REAR VIEW MIRROR CIRCUIT LOGIC TESTING (NON-HEATED MIRROR)

Switch Position	Wire Color	Terminal	Result
Driver's Rear View Mirror			
Left	Red	1	1
Right	Red	1	2
Up	Dark Blue/Yellow	2	1
Down	Dark Blue/Yellow	2	2
Left/Up	Yellow	3	2
Right/Down	Yellow	3	1
Passenger's Rear View Mirror			

REAR VIEW MIRROR CIRCUIT LOGIC TESTING (NON-HEATED MIRROR) (Cont.)

Switch Position	Wire Color	Terminal	Result
Left	Dark Green	1	1
Right	Dark Green	1	2
Up	Violet	2	1
Down	Violet	2	2
Left/Up	Left/Up	3	2
Right/Down	Right/Down	3	1

[1] – Voltage should be greater than 10 volts.
[2] – Resistance should be less than 5 ohms.

REAR VIEW MIRROR CONTROL CIRCUIT LOGIC TESTING

Switch Position	Terminal	Wire Color	Result
Left/Up	6	Yellow	2
Right/Down	6	Yellow	1
Driver's Side Selected			
Left	4	Red	1
Right	4	Red	2
Up	7	Dark Blue/Yellow	1
Down	7	Dark Blue/Yellow	2
Passenger's Side Selected			
Left	3	Dark Green	1
Right	3	Dark Green	2
Up	8	Violet	1
Down	8	Violet	2

[1] – Voltage should be greater than 10 volts.
[2] – Resistance should be less than 5 ohms.

REAR VIEW MIRROR CIRCUIT LOGIC TESTING (HEATED MIRROR)

Switch Position	Terminal	Wire Color	Result
Driver's Rear View Mirror			
Left	6	Red	1
Right	6	Red	2
Up	4	Dark Blue/Yellow	1
Down	4	Dark Blue/Yellow	2
Left/Up	2	Yellow	2
Right/Down	2	Yellow	1
Passenger's Rear View Mirror			
Left	6	Dark Green	1
Right	6	Dark Green	2
Up	4	Violet	1
Down	4	Violet	2
Left/Up	2	Left/Up	2
Right/Down	2	Right/Down	1

[1] – Voltage should be greater than 10 volts.
[2] – Resistance should be less than 5 ohms.

2) Remove mirror control switch to access harness connector. See MIRROR CONTROL SWITCH under REMOVAL & INSTALLATION. Do not disconnect switch connector. Backprobing connector, measure voltage or resistance between ground and specified terminal on mirror control switch connector while moving switch to specified position. See REAR VIEW MIRROR CONTROL CIRCUIT LOGIC TESTING table. If all resistance and voltage measurements are as specified, repair suspect circuit found in step 1). If any resistance or voltage measurement is not as specified, replace suspect mirror control switch. See MIRROR CONTROL SWITCH under REMOVAL & INSTALLATION.

TEST E: LEFT OR RIGHT MIRROR IS INOPERATIVE WITH SWITCH LOGIC (HEATED MIRRORS)

1) Disconnect suspect rear view mirror harness connector. Using DVOM, measure voltage or resistance between ground and specified terminal on rear view mirror harness connector while moving mirror control switch to specified position. See REAR VIEW MIRROR CIRCUIT LOGIC TESTING table. If all resistance and voltage measurements are as specified, replace suspect mirror motor. See REMOVAL & INSTALLATION. If any resistance or voltage measurement is not as specified, go to next step.

2) Remove mirror control switch to access harness connector. See MIRROR CONTROL SWITCH under REMOVAL & INSTALLATION. Do not disconnect switch connector. Backprobing connector, measure voltage or resistance between ground and specified terminal on mirror control switch connector while moving switch to specified position. See REAR VIEW MIRROR CONTROL CIRCUIT LOGIC TESTING table. If all resistance and voltage measurements are as specified, repair suspect circuit found in step 1). If any resistance or voltage measurement is not as specified, replace suspect mirror control switch. See MIRROR CONTROL SWITCH under REMOVAL & INSTALLATION.

REAR VIEW MIRROR CONTROL CIRCUIT LOGIC TESTING

Switch Position	Terminal	Wire Color	Result
Left/Up	6	Yellow	2
Right/Down	6	Yellow	1
Driver's Side Selected			
Left	4	Red	1
Right	4	Red	2
Up	7	Dark Blue/Yellow	1
Down	7	Dark Blue/Yellow	2
Passenger's Side Selected			
Left	3	Dark Green	1
Right	3	Dark Green	2
Up	8	Violet	1
Down	8	Violet	2

1 – Voltage should be greater than 10 volts.
2 – Resistance should be less than 5 ohms.

TEST F: AUTO DIMMING MIRROR DOES NOT OPERATE CORRECTLY

1) Using New Generation Star (NGS) tester, perform Rear Electronic Module (REM) self-test. If any DTCs are present, see MODULE COMMUNICATIONS NETWORK – WINDSTAR article. If no DTCs are present, go to next step.

2) Remove fuse No. 14 (10-amp) from junction panel fuse block. Turn ignition on. Using voltmeter, measure voltage between ground and input terminal (left terminal) on fuse No. 14 socket. If voltage is greater than 10 volts, go to next step. If voltage is 10 volts or less, repair open power supply circuit to fuse No.14.

3) Turn ignition off. Install fuse No. 14 in junction panel fuse block. Disconnect interior mirror harness connector. Turn ignition on. Measure voltage between ground and terminal No. 7 (Red/Yellow wire) on interior mirror harness connector. If voltage is greater than 10 volts, go to next step. If voltage is 10 volts or less, repair open Red/Yellow wire.

4) Turn ignition off. Measure resistance between ground and terminal No. 6 (Black wire) on interior mirror harness connector. If resistance is less than 5 ohms, go to next step. If resistance is 5 ohms or greater, repair open Black wire.

5) Turn ignition on. Ensure engine is not running. Measure voltage between ground and terminal No. 5 (Black/Pink wire) on interior mirror harness connector. If voltage is greater than 10 volts, go to step **8)**. If voltage is 10 volts or less, go to next step.

6) Ensure shift selector is Park position. Turn ignition off. Disconnect REM 22-pin C341 connector. REM is located in jack storage area. *See Fig. 4.* Using ohmmeter, measure resistance of Black/Pink wire between terminal No. 5 on interior mirror harness connector and terminal No. 4 on REM 22-pin harness connector. If resistance is less than 5 ohms, go to next step. If resistance is 5 ohms or greater, repair open Black/Pink wire.

7) Measure resistance between ground and terminal No. 4 (Black/Pink wire) on REM 22-pin harness connector. If resistance is greater than 10,000 ohms, go to next step. If resistance is 10,000 ohms or less, repair Black/Pink wire for short to ground.

NOTE: Prior to replacement of REM module, it is necessary to upload module configuration information using NGS tester. See COMPUTER RELEARN PROCEDURES article in GENERAL INFORMATION.

8) Turn ignition on. Using voltmeter, measure voltage between ground and terminal No. 4 (Black/Pink wire) on REM 22-pin harness connector. If voltage is greater than 10 volts, repair Black/Pink wire for short to voltage. If voltage is 10 volts or less, replace interior mirror. See INTERIOR MIRROR ASSEMBLY under REMOVAL & INSTALLATION. Test system for correct operation. If auto dimming mirror continues not to function, replace REM. Download module configuration information into new REM. Test system for correct operation.

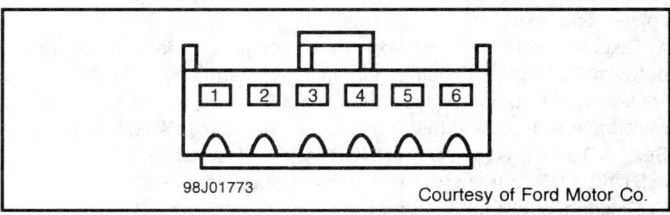

Fig. 3: Identifying Interior Mirror Harness Connector Terminals

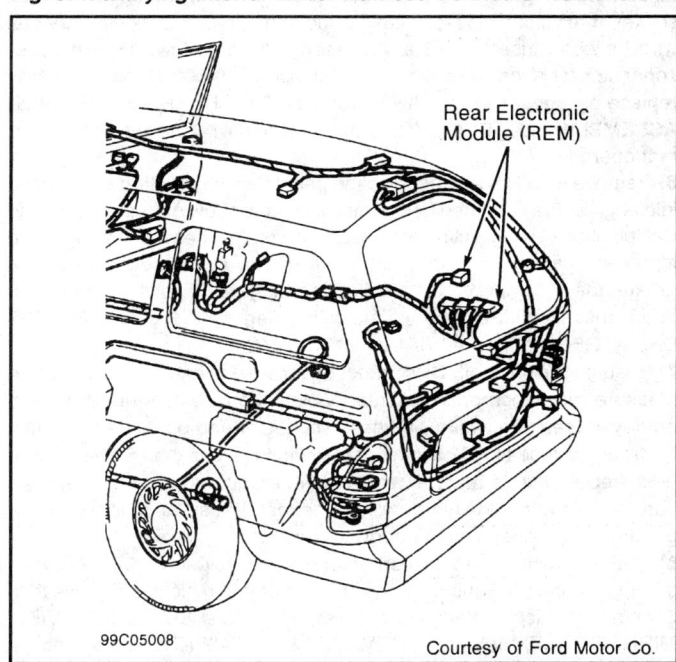

Fig. 4: Locating Rear Electronic Module (REM)

TEST G: LEFT OR RIGHT MIRROR HEATER IS INOPERATIVE

1) Ensure shift selector is Park position. Start engine. Press heated back window (rear window defroster) switch to ON position. If heated back window operates correctly, go to next step. If heated rear window does operate correctly, repair as necessary. See appropriate wiring diagram in REAR WINDOWS DEFOGGERS article in WIRING DIAGRAMS.

2) Inspect fuse No. 22 (10-amp) in junction panel fuse block. If fuse okay, go to step **6)**. If fuse is blown, go to next step.

3) Ensure fuse No. 22 (10-amp) is removed from junction panel fuse block. Ensure ignition is off. Using ohmmeter, measure resistance between ground and output terminal (left terminal) on fuse No. 22

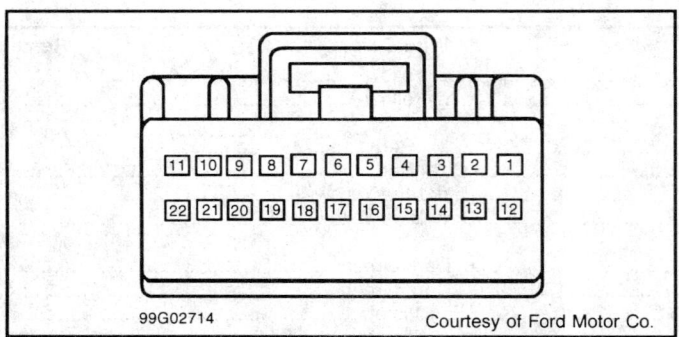

99G02714   Courtesy of Ford Motor Co.

Fig. 5: Identifying REM 22-Pin C341 Harness Connector Terminals

socket. If resistance is less than 10,000 ohms, go to next step. If resistance is 10,000 ohms or greater, install new fuse. Test system for correct operation.

4) Disconnect driver's rear view mirror connector. Measure resistance between ground and output terminal (left terminal) on fuse No. 22 socket. If resistance is less than 10,000 ohms, go to next step. If resistance is 10,000 ohms or greater, replace driver's rear view mirror. See SIDE REAR VIEW MIRROR ASSEMBLY under REMOVAL & INSTALLATION. Test system for correct operation.

5) Disconnect passenger's rear view mirror connector. Measure resistance between ground and output terminal (left terminal) on fuse No. 22 socket. If resistance is less than 10,000 ohms, repair Dark Green/Violet wire between fuse No. 22 and passenger's rear view mirror harness connector for short to ground. If resistance is 10,000 ohms or greater, replace passenger's rear view mirror. See SIDE REAR VIEW MIRROR ASSEMBLY under REMOVAL & INSTALLATION. Test system for correct operation.

6) Remove fuse No. 22 from junction panel fuse block. Start vehicle and idle engine. Press heated back window (rear window defroster) switch to ON position. Using voltmeter, measure voltage between ground and input terminal on (right terminal) on fuse No. 22 socket. If voltage is greater than 10 volts, go to next step. If voltage is 10 volts or less, repair open input circuit. See appropriate wiring diagram in REAR WINDOWS DEFOGGERS article in WIRING DIAGRAMS.

7) Ensure ignition is off. Disconnect driver's rear view mirror connector. Measure resistance of Dark Green/Violet wire between terminal No. 5 on driver's rear view mirror harness connector and output terminal (left terminal) on fuse No. 22 socket. If resistance is less than 5 ohms, go to next step if driver's rear view mirror will not defrost or go to step **9)** if passenger's rear view mirror will not defrost. If resistance is 5 ohms or greater, repair open Dark Green/Violet wire.

8) Measure resistance between ground and terminal No. 3 (Black wire) on driver's rear view mirror harness connector. If resistance is less than 5 ohms, replace driver's rear view mirror. See SIDE REAR VIEW MIRROR ASSEMBLY under REMOVAL & INSTALLATION. If resistance is 5 ohms or greater, repair open Black wire. Test system for correct operation.

9) Measure resistance between ground and terminal No. 3 (Black wire) on passenger's rear view mirror harness connector. If resistance is less than 5 ohms, replace passenger's rear view mirror. See SIDE REAR VIEW MIRROR ASSEMBLY under REMOVAL & INSTALLATION. If resistance is 5 ohms or greater, repair open Black wire. Test system for correct operation.

REMOVAL & INSTALLATION

WARNING: When battery is disconnected, vehicle computer and memory systems may lose memory data. Driveability problems may exist until computer systems have completed a relearn cycle. See COMPUTER RELEARN PROCEDURES article in GENERAL INFORMATION before disconnecting battery.

INTERIOR MIRROR ASSEMBLY

Removal & Installation – Disconnect inside mirror harness connector. Rotate inside mirror counterclockwise until top of mirror is facing driver door. Twist mirror horizontally toward passenger door using screwdriver until mirror bottoms out and retaining clip releases. Remove inside mirror. To install, slide inside mirror assembly onto mount until spring clip snaps in place. Connect harness connector.

SIDE REAR VIEW MIRROR ASSEMBLY

Removal & Installation – Remove door panel. Remove mirror mounting hole cover. *See Fig. 6.* Disconnect mirror wiring harness connector. Remove mirror attaching nuts. Remove mirror assembly while guiding wiring and connector through hole in door. To install, reverse removal procedure. Tighten nuts to approximately 53-70 INCH lbs. (6-8 N.m).

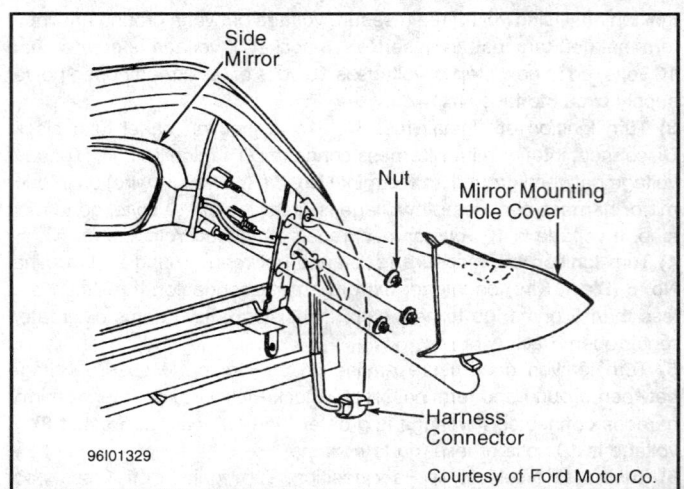

96I01329   Courtesy of Ford Motor Co.

Fig. 6: Removing Side Mirror

SIDE REAR VIEW MIRROR GLASS & MOTOR

Removal & Installation – Remove rear view mirror. Push in upper edge of mirror glass to its maximum travel and pull outward until mirror glass is released. Remove motor attaching screws. Remove mirror motor back cover plate. Slide rubber boot off mirror motor. Ensure electrical connector locations are record before motor removal. Remove mirror motor. To install, reverse removal procedure. Ensure rubber boot is correctly installed on motor before snapping in glass.

MIRROR CONTROL SWITCH

Removal & Installation – Remove window switch bezel. Depress retaining clips on switch housing. Push base of switch out of switch bezel. Unplug harness connector. Remove switch. To install, reverse removal procedure.

WIRING DIAGRAMS

NOTE: For heated mirror wiring diagram, see appropriate wiring diagram in REAR WINDOW DEFOGGERS article in WIRING DIAGRAMS.

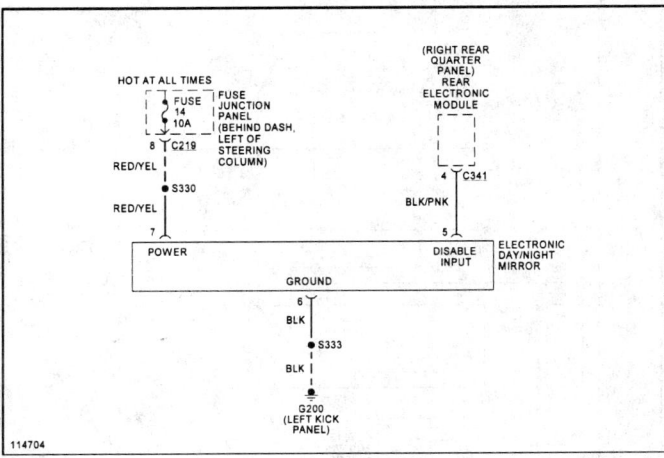

Fig. 7: Automatic Day/Night Mirror System Wiring Diagram (Windstar)

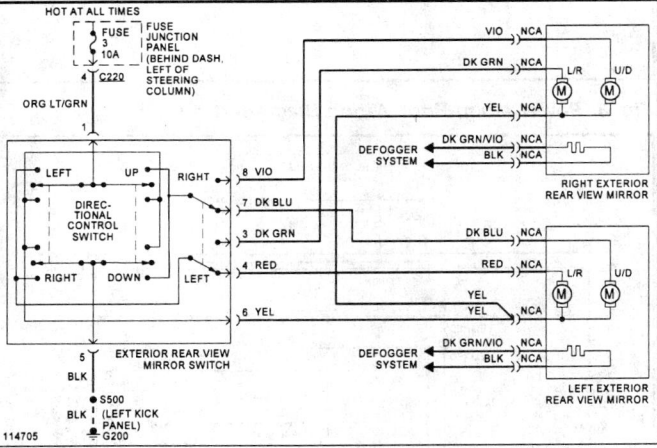

Fig. 8: Power Mirror System Wiring Diagram (Windstar)

WIRING DIAGRAMS

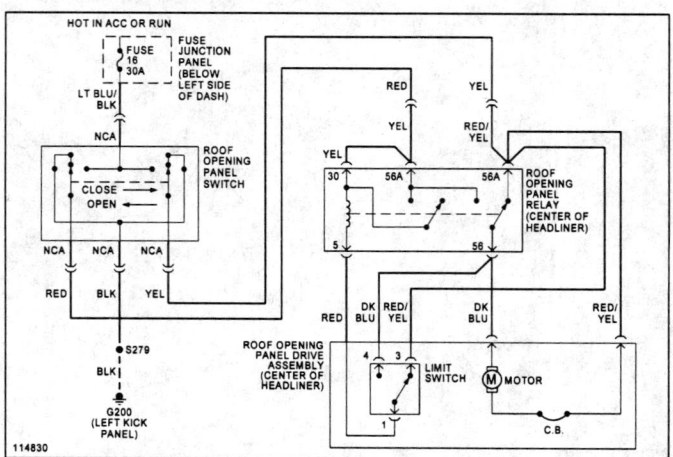

Fig. 1: Power Moon Roof Wiring Diagram (Continental)

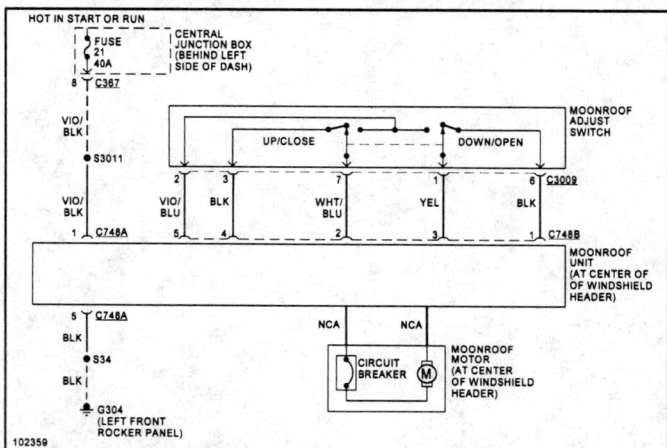

Fig. 2: Power Moon Roof Wiring Diagram (Contour & Mystique)

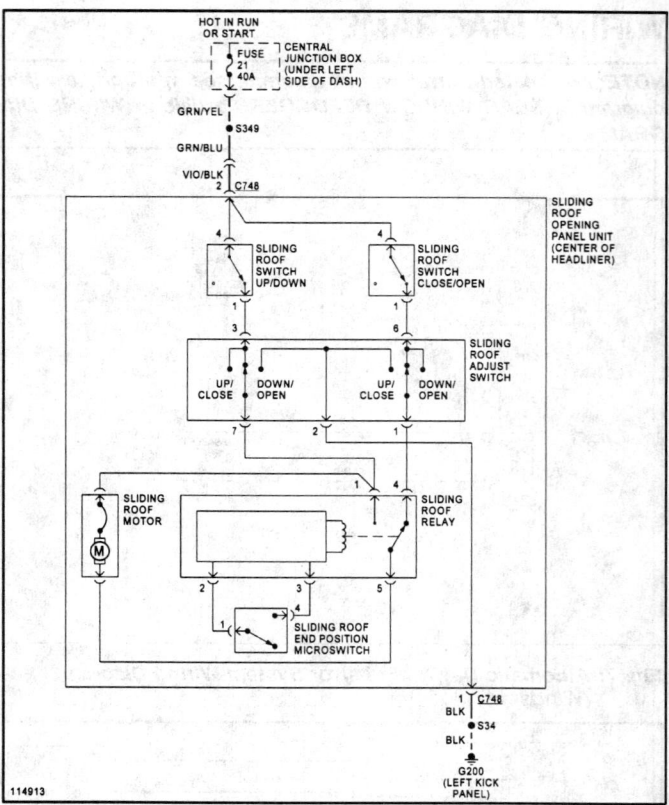

Fig. 3: Power Moon Roof Wiring Diagram (Cougar)

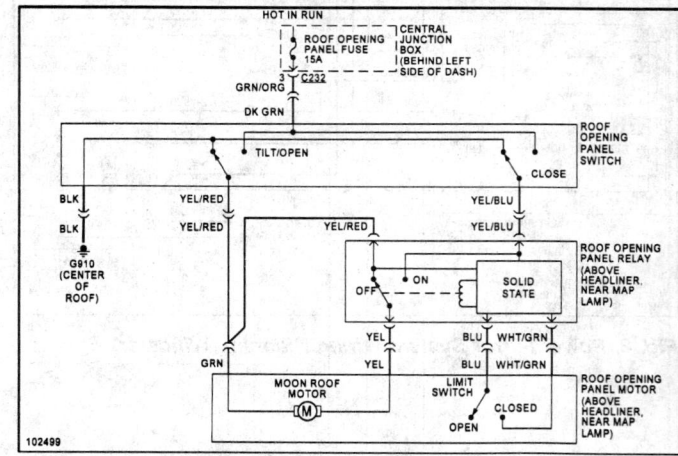

Fig. 4: Power Moon Roof Wiring Diagram (Escort ZX2)

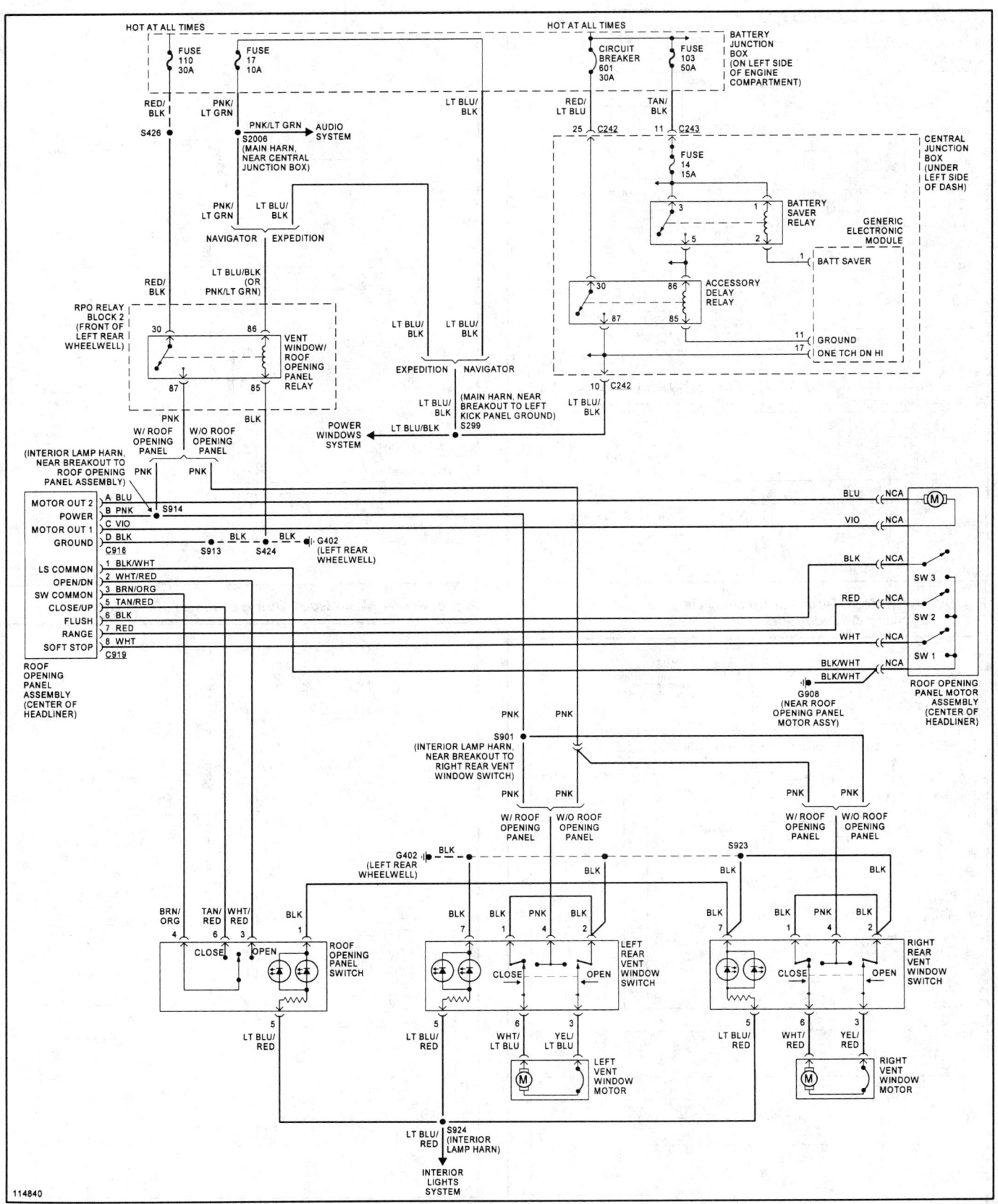

Fig. 5: Power Moon Roof Wiring Diagram (Expedition & Navigator)

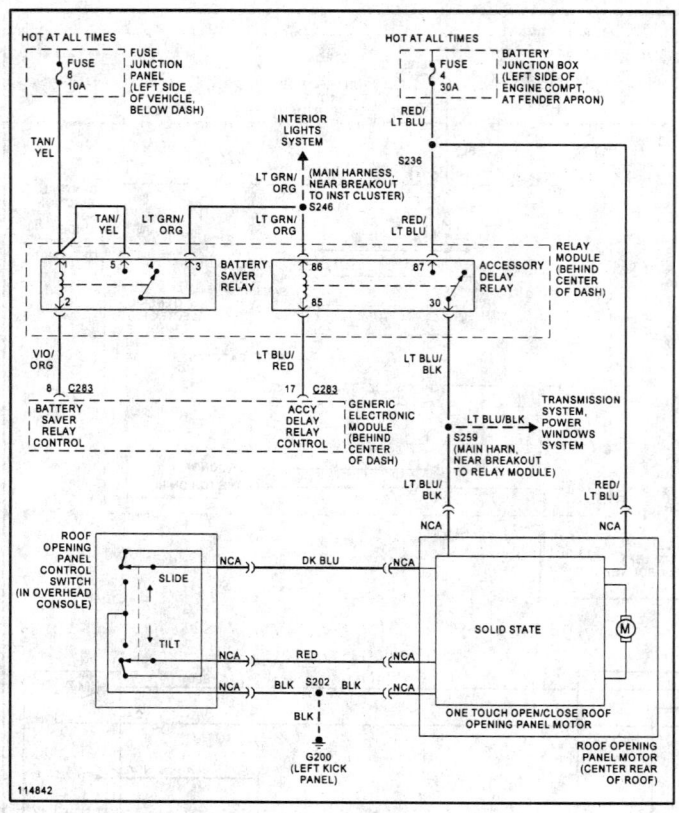

Fig. 6: Power Moon Roof Wiring Diagram (Explorer & Mountaineer)

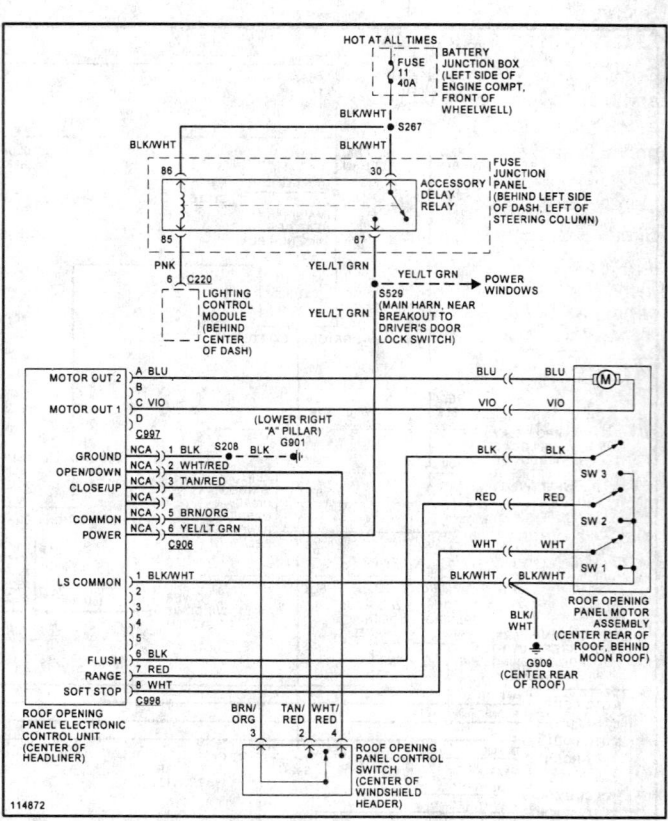

Fig. 8: Power Moon Roof Wiring Diagram (Town Car)

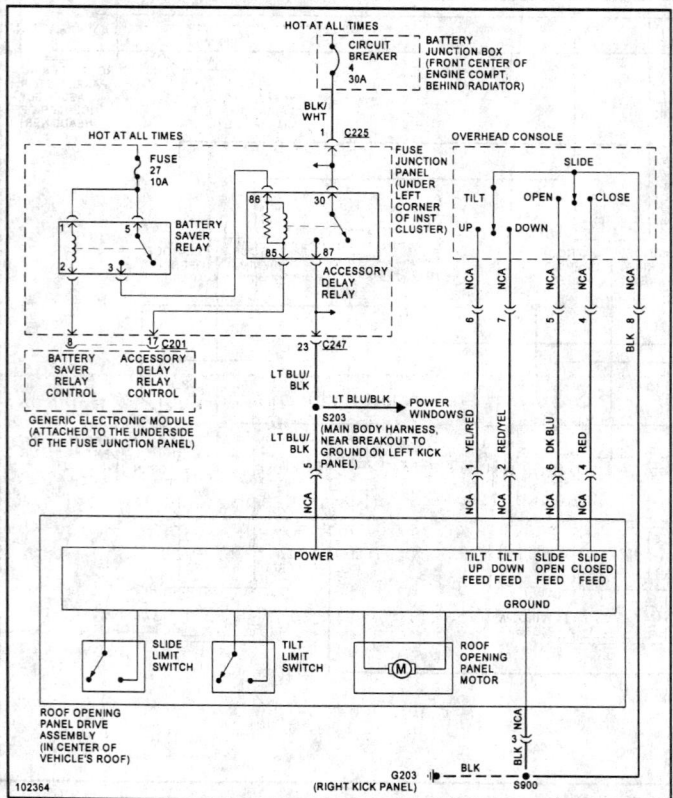

Fig. 7: Power Moon Roof Wiring Diagram (Sable & Taurus)

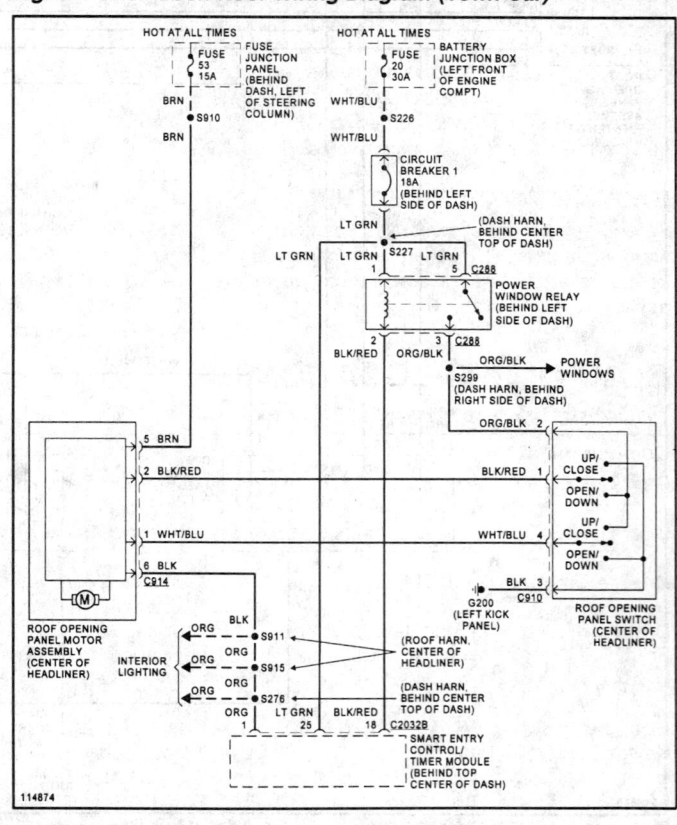

Fig. 9: Power Moon Roof Wiring Diagram (Villager)

DESCRIPTION

Continental is equipped with a 6-way power seat with memory function and heated seat cushions as an option. Seat movement is provided by a tri-motor assembly located under seat bottom. A recliner motor provides seat back movement. Seat function is controlled by the Driver's Door Module (DDM) and Driver's Seat Module (DSM), with outputs to Lighting Control Module (LCM).

Circuit protection is provided by maxi-fuses No. 1 and 2 (30-amp) in power distribution box and fuse No. 39 (10-amp) in interior fuse panel. System ground points are located just ahead of left and right front doors, beneath kick panels.

OPERATION

MESSAGE CENTER

Message center is only operational with ignition switch in RUN position. Message center is used to display driver's profile messages and warnings and program many driver's profile system features. Press the following controls for desired programing:

- MENU control will display options for the express window, auto door locks, horn chirp, easy entry/exit seat access and reverse mirror features which can be set by using SELECT control.
- VEHICLE HANDLING control will display options for adjusting vehicle handling features.
- DRIVER ID control will display the option for selecting DRIVER 1, DRIVER 2 or OFF.

For further information on message center, see appropriate INSTRUMENT PANELS article.

HEATED SEATS

Heated seat controls are located in center of instrument panel, below heater control. To heat only seat back, slide control to BACK position, then adjust thumbwheel to select desired heat setting (zero to 5). To heat both seat back and seat cushion, slide control to BOTH position, then adjust thumbwheel to select desired heat setting (zero to 5). If heated seat switch is not turned to OFF position, seat will heat up to selected temperature each time vehicle is started.

EASY ENTRY/EXIT FEATURE

When easy entry/exit feature is enabled, driver's seat will move rearward approximately 2" when key is removed from ignition switch. When key is inserted into ignition switch, driver's seat will move forward approximately 2".

COMPONENT LOCATIONS

COMPONENT LOCATIONS

Component	Location
Data Link Connector	Under Instrument Panel, Right Of Steering Column
Door Lock Switch	Appropriate Door Panel Arm Rest
Driver's Door Module (DDM)	Behind Driver's Door Panel, Lower Front Corner
Driver's Heated Seat Module	Under Driver's Seat
Front Seat Track Assembly	[1] Under Appropriate Seat
Heated Seat Switch	Center Of Instrument Panel, Under Heater Controls
Instrument Panel Fuse Box	Below Left Instrument Panel
Keyless Entry Keypad	Driver's Door Below Exterior Door Handle
Lumbar Switch	Side Of Seat Cushion
Message Center Switches	On Instrument Panel, Right Of Instrument Cluster
Power Distribution Box	Left Side Of Engine Compartment, Above Wheelwell
Power Mirror Switch	Driver's Door Panel Arm Rest

COMPONENT LOCATIONS (Cont.)

Component	Location

[1] – Front seat track and adjustment motors are a complete assembly.

TROUBLE SHOOTING

Before performing individual component tests and system test, check the following for possible cause of system malfunction. Repair any problems as necessary and operate seat to see if malfunction is repaired. If malfunction still exists, go to SELF-DIAGNOSTIC SYSTEM.

- Blown fuses or faulty circuit breakers.
- Obstructed seat track.
- Loose or corroded connectors.
- Damaged wiring.
- Damaged motors.
- Faulty switches.
- Damaged lumbar support bladder.
- Damaged or kinked air hoses.

COMPONENT TESTS

DOOR LOCK SWITCH

Using an ohmmeter, check for continuity between indicated switch connector terminals when switch is operated as specified. See POWER DOOR LOCK SWITCH CONTINUITY TEST table. *See Fig. 1.* Replace switch if it does not test as specified.

POWER DOOR LOCK SWITCH CONTINUITY TEST

Switch Position	Continuity Between Pins
Lock	1 & 6
Unlock	5 & 6

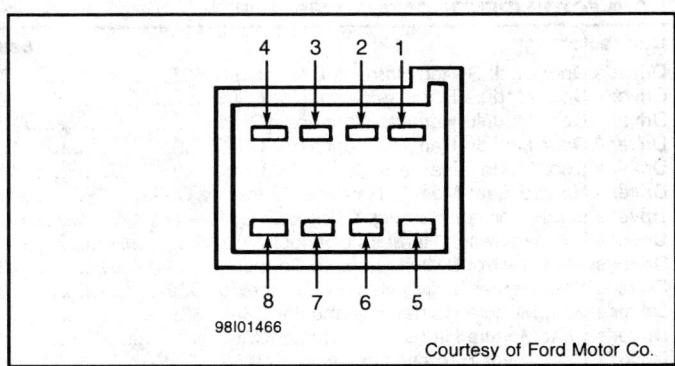

Fig. 1: Identifying Power Door Lock Switch Connector & Mirror Control Switch Connector Terminals

MIRROR CONTROL SWITCH

Using an ohmmeter, check for continuity between indicated switch connector terminals when switch is activated as specified. See POWER MIRROR SWITCH CONTINUITY TEST table. *See Fig. 1.* Replace switch if it does not test as specified.

POWER MIRROR SWITCH CONTINUITY TEST

Switch Position	Continuity Between Pins
Left Mirror	
Up	2 & 3; 4 & 7
Down	2 & 4; 7 & 8
Left	1 & 8; 4 & 7
Right	1 & 4; 5 & 7
Right Mirror	
Up	3 & 6; 4 & 7
Down	4 & 6; 5 & 7
Left	4 & 7; 5 & 8
Right	4 & 5; 7 & 8

SEAT CONTROL SWITCH

Remove seat control switch. Check resistance between terminals. See SEAT CONTROL SWITCH RESISTANCE table. *See Fig. 2*. If resistances are not as specified, replace seat control switch.

SEAT CONTROL SWITCH RESISTANCE

Switch Position	Between Terminals	Resistance In Ohms
Front Up	4 & 6	Less Than 5
Front Down	6 & 9	Less Than 5
Rear Up	3 & 6	Less Than 5
Rear Down	6 & 8	Less Than 5
Seat FWD	2 & 6	Less Than 5
Seat RWD	6 & 7	Less Than 5
Seat Up	3 & 6; 4 & 6	Less Than 5
Seat Down	6 & 9; 6 & 8	Less Than 5
Recline FWD	5 & 6	Less Than 5
Recline RWD	6 & 10	Less Than 5

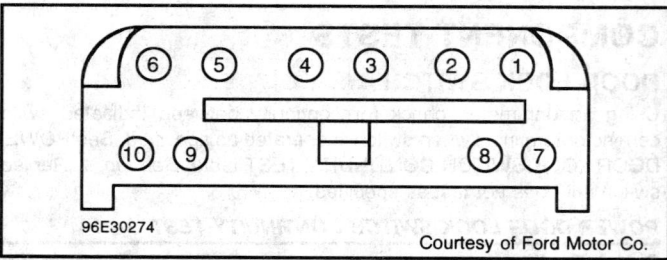

Fig. 2: Identifying Seat Control Switch Terminals

CONNECTOR IDENTIFICATION

CONNECTOR IDENTIFICATION DIRECTORY

Connector	See
Driver's Door Lock Switch Harness Connector C505	7
Driver's Door Module Harness Connector C506	12
Driver's Door Module Harness Connector C522	3
Driver's Door Module Harness Connector C523	13
Driver's Door Module Harness Connector C524	11
Driver's Heated Seat Module Harness Connector C352	11
Driver's Lumbar Motor Harness Connector C315	1
Driver's Lumbar Switch Harness Connector C348	4
Driver's Seat Control Switch Harness Connector C520	9
Driver's Seat Heater Switch Harness Connector C222	8
Driver's Seat Module Harness Connector C342	14
Driver's Seat Module Harness Connector C362	2
Driver's Seat Motor Harness Connector C316	5
Front Height Motor Potentiometer Harness Connector C358	3
Horizontal Motor Potentiometer Harness Connector C359	3
Keyless Entry Keypad Harness Connector C525	10
Passenger's Door Lock Switch Harness Connector C602	7
Passenger's Heated Seat Module Harness Connector C356	11
Passenger's Lumbar Motor Harness Connector C314	1
Passenger's Seat Control Switch Harness Connector C612	9
Passenger's Seat Heater Switch Harness Connector C221	6
Passenger's Seat Lumbar Switch Harness Connector C350	4
Passenger's Seat Motor Harness Connector C302	5
Power Mirror Control Switch Harness Connector C550	7
Rear Height Motor Potentiometer Harness Connector C357	3
Recline Motor Harness Connector C331	2
Recline Motor Potentiometer Harness Connector C349	4

[1] – Driver's lumbar motor harness connector C315 and passenger's lumbar motor harness connector C314 is a Black 4-pin connector. Identify by wire colors. See WIRING DIAGRAMS.

[2] – Driver's seat module harness connector C362 and recline motor harness connector C331 is a 2-pin connector. Identify by wire colors. See WIRING DIAGRAMS.

CONNECTOR IDENTIFICATION DIRECTORY (Cont.)

Connector	See

[3] – Rear height motor potentiometer harness connector C357, front height motor potentiometer harness connector C358 and horizontal motor potentiometer harness connector C359 are Brown 3-pin connector. Identify by wire colors. See WIRING DIAGRAMS.

[4] – Recline motor potentiometer harness connector C349 is a 3-pin connector. Identify by wire colors. See WIRING DIAGRAMS.

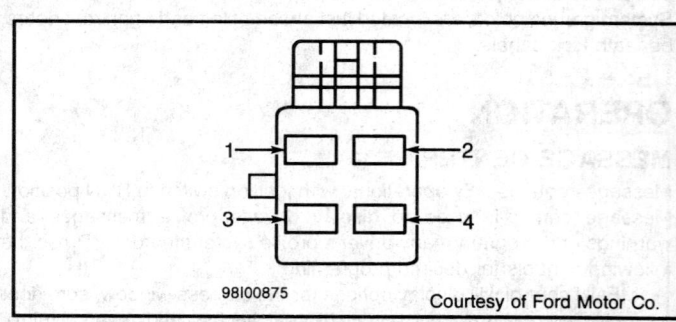

Fig. 3: Identifying 4-Pin Harness Connector Terminals (C522)

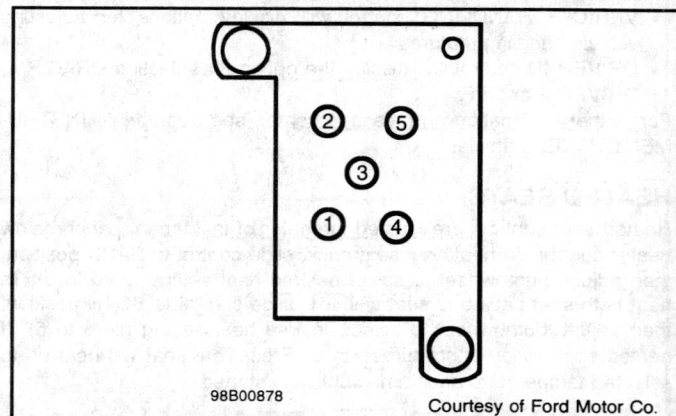

Fig. 4: Identifying 5-Pin Harness Connector Terminals (C348 & C350)

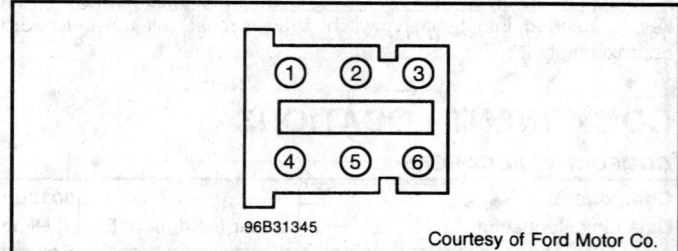

Fig. 5: Identifying 6-Pin Harness Connector Terminals (C316 & C302)

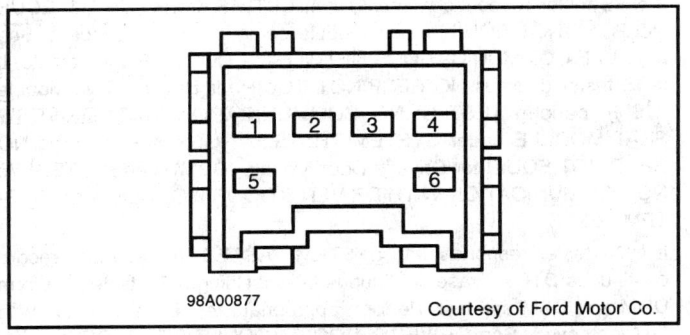

98A00877   Courtesy of Ford Motor Co.

Fig. 6: Identifying 6-Pin Harness Connector Terminals (C221)

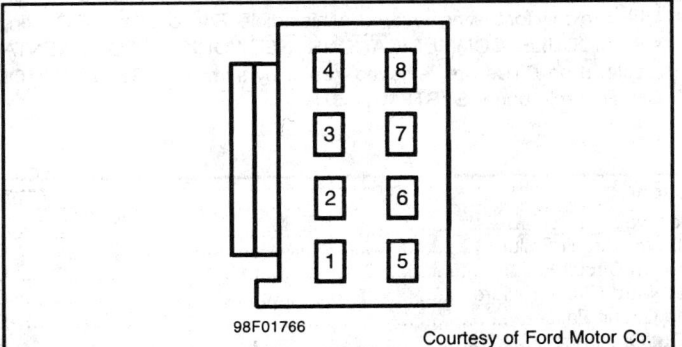

98F01766   Courtesy of Ford Motor Co.

Fig. 7: Identifying 8-Pin Harness Connector Terminals (C505, C550 & C602)

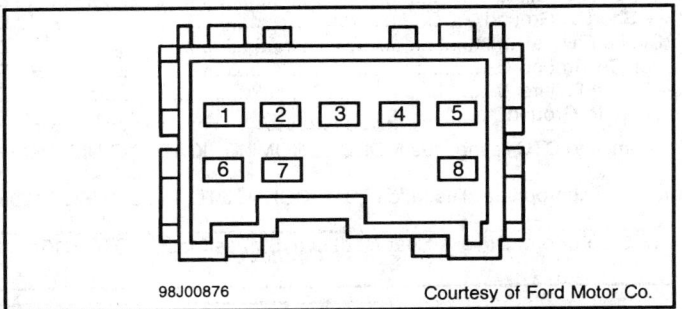

98J00876   Courtesy of Ford Motor Co.

Fig. 8: Identifying 8-Pin Harness Connector Terminals (C222)

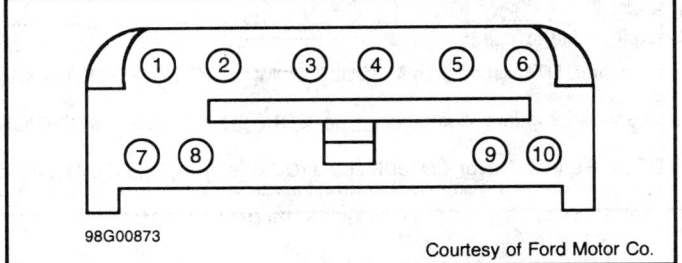

98G00873   Courtesy of Ford Motor Co.

Fig. 9: Identifying 10-Pin Harness Connector Terminals (C520 & C612)

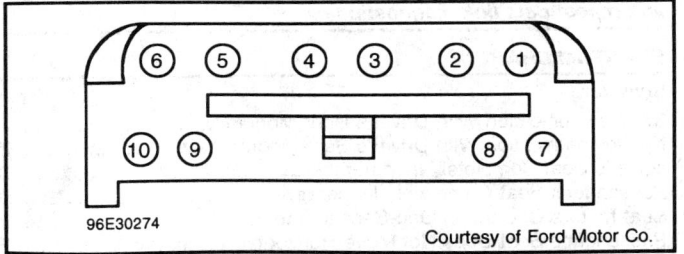

96E30274   Courtesy of Ford Motor Co.

Fig. 10: Identifying 10-Pin Harness Connector Terminals (C525)

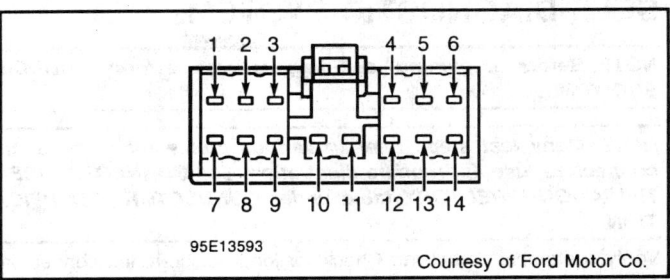

95E13593   Courtesy of Ford Motor Co.

Fig. 11: Identifying 14-Pin Harness Connector Terminals (C352, C356 & C524)

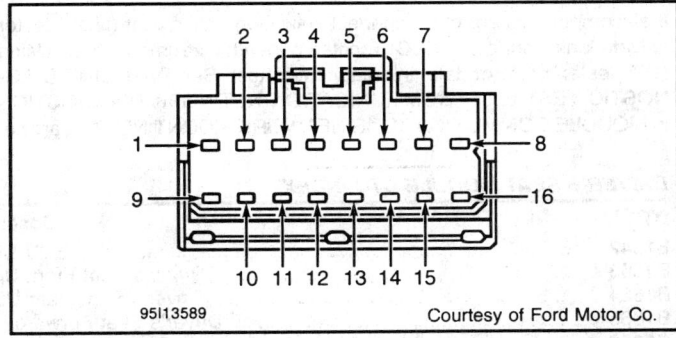

95I13589   Courtesy of Ford Motor Co.

Fig. 12: Identifying 16-Pin Harness Connector Terminals (C506)

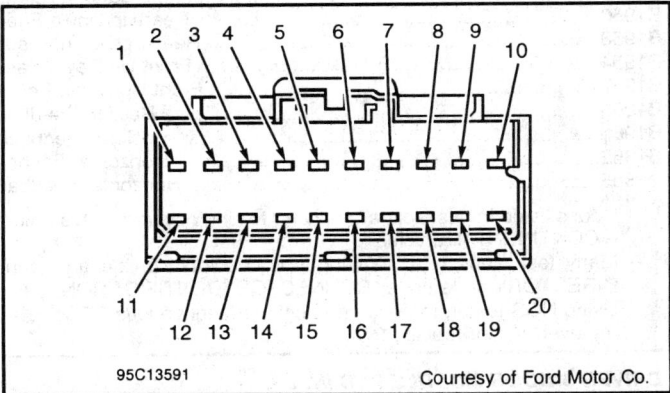

95C13591   Courtesy of Ford Motor Co.

Fig. 13: Identifying 20-Pin Harness Connector Terminals (C523)

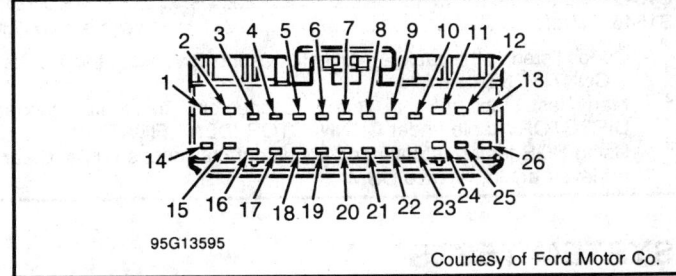

95G13595   Courtesy of Ford Motor Co.

Fig. 14: Identifying 26-Pin Harness Connector Terminals (C342)

SELF-DIAGNOSTIC SYSTEM

NOTE: Before beginning self-diagnostics, perform TROUBLE SHOOTING.

NOTE: Many test steps refer to various connectors. To identify connectors, use appropriate illustration. See CONNECTOR IDENTIFICATION DIRECTORY table under CONNECTOR IDENTIFICATION.

Verify customers complaint. Check for loose or corroded connectors, blown fuses and damaged wiring harness. Check for obstructed seat tracks and damaged motors. Repair or replace components as necessary.

If all components are okay, connect New Generation Star (NGS) tester to Data Link Connector (DLC), located beneath instrument panel. Using NGS tester, perform data link diagnostics test. See DATA LINK DIAGNOSTIC TEST under COMMUNICATION NETWORK DIAGNOSTICS in MODULE COMMUNICATIONS NETWORK – CONTINENTAL article.

If NGS tester responds with CKT914, CKT915 or CKT70=ALL ECUS NO RESP/NOT EQUIP, repair module communications concern. See MODULE COMMUNICATIONS NETWORK – CONTINENTAL article. If NGS tester displays NO RESP/NOT EQUIP for Driver's Seat Module (DSM), perform TEST B: NO COMMUNICATION WITH DRIVER'S SEAT MODULE under SYSTEM TESTS. If NGS tester displays NO RESP/NOT EQUIP for Driver's Door Module (DDM), perform TEST A: NO COMMUNICATION WITH DRIVER'S DOOR MODULE under SYSTEM TESTS.

If NGS tester responds with SYSTEM PASSED, retrieve and record continuous DTCs. Erase continuous DTCs. Using NGS tester, perform DDM and DSM self-test. Perform appropriate test in accordance with DTC retrieved. See DRIVER'S DOOR MODULE DTC INDEX and/or DRIVER'S SEAT MODULE DTC INDEX table. Codes listed in these table are only for testing covered in this article. For complete DTC listing, see MODULE COMMUNICATIONS NETWORK – CONTINENTAL article. If no DTCs are retrieved, repair by symptom. See SYMPTOM CHART table under SYSTEM TESTS.

DRIVER'S SEAT MODULE DTC INDEX

DTC [1]	Description	[2] Test
B1342	ECU Defective	[3]
B1663	Driver's Seat Front Up/Down Circuit Failure	C
B1664	Driver's Seat Rear Up/Down Circuit Failure	C
B1665	Driver's Seat Forward/Backward Circuit Failure	C
B1666	Driver's Seat Recline Circuit Failure	C
B1676	Battery Voltage Out Of Range	R
B1950	Rear Up/Down Feedback – Circuit Failure	D
B1953	Rear Up/Down Feedback – Short to Ground	D
B1954	Front Up/Down Feedback – Circuit Failure	D
B1957	Front Up/Down Feedback – Short to Ground	D
B1958	Recline Feedback – Circuit Failure	D
B1961	Recline Feedback – Short To Ground	D
B1962	Horizontal Feedback – Circuit Failure	D
B1965	Horizontal Feedback – Short To Ground	D

[1] – Codes listed in this table are only for testing covered in this article. For complete DTC listing, see MODULE COMMUNICATIONS NETWORK – CONTINENTAL article.

[2] – Many test steps refer to various connectors. To identify connectors, use appropriate illustration. See CONNECTOR IDENTIFICATION DIRECTORY table under CONNECTOR IDENTIFICATION.

[3] – Using NGS tester, retrieve and document continuous DTCs. Clear all DTCs. Perform Driver's Seat Module (DSM) self-test. If DTC B1342 is retrieved again, replace DSM.

DRIVER'S DOOR MODULE DTC INDEX

DTC [1]	Description	[2] Test
B1342	ECU Defective	[3]
B1545	Power Seat Switch Short To Voltage	C

[1] – Codes listed in this table are only for testing covered in this article. For complete DTC listing, see MODULE COMMUNICATIONS NETWORK – CONTINENTAL article.

[2] – Many test steps refer to various connectors. To identify connectors, use appropriate illustration. See CONNECTOR IDENTIFICATION DIRECTORY table under CONNECTOR IDENTIFICATION.

[3] – Using NGS tester, retrieve and document continuous DTCs. Clear all DTCs. Perform Driver's Door Module (DDM) self-test. If DTC B1342 is retrieved again, replace DDM.

SYSTEM TESTS

CAUTION: When battery is disconnected or modules are replaced, vehicle computer and memory systems may lose memory data. Driveability problems may exist until computer systems have completed a relearn cycle. See COMPUTER RELEARN PROCEDURES article in GENERAL INFORMATION before disconnecting battery.

NOTE: Many test steps refer to various connectors. To identify connectors, use appropriate illustration. See CONNECTOR IDENTIFICATION DIRECTORY table under CONNECTOR IDENTIFICATION.

NOTE: After any repairs are complete, ensure all components are properly installed, all harness connectors are connected properly and repeat data link diagnostic test.

SYMPTOM CHART

Symptom	[1] Test
No Communication With Driver's Door Module	A
No Communication With Driver's Seat Module	B
Driver's Seat Completely Inoperative	C
Passenger's Seat Completely Inoperative	D
Seat Motors Operate In One-Second Intervals	E
Passenger's Seat Does Not Move Horizontally/Vertically	F
Memory Seat Inoperative	G

SYMPTOM CHART (Cont.)

Symptom	[1] Test
Easy Exit/Entry Feature Inoperative	H
Driver's Seat Heater Inoperative	J
Driver's Heated Seat Cushion Inoperative	K
Passenger's Seat Heater Inoperative	L
Passenger's Heated Seat Cushion Inoperative	M
Both Heated Seats Inoperative	N
Driver's Lumbar Inoperative	P
Passenger's Lumbar Inoperative	Q
Battery Voltage Out Of Range (DTC B1676)	R

[1] – Many test steps refer to various connectors. To identify connectors, use appropriate illustration. See CONNECTOR IDENTIFICATION DIRECTORY table under CONNECTOR IDENTIFICATION.

TEST A: NO COMMUNICATION WITH DRIVER'S DOOR MODULE

1) Connect NGS tester to Data Link Connector (DLC). Turn ignition switch to RUN position. Using NGS tester, monitor Driver's Door Module (DDM) PIDs SFWD_SW, SREARSW, SFNT_SW and SRCL_SW while activating power seat control switch. If UNABLE TO PERFORM TEST FUCTION MODULE NOT RESPONDING: DDM CHECK IGNITION STATUS/VERIFY CABLE REQUIREMENTS CHEK CABLE CONNECTIONS? is not displayed, go to next step. If UNABLE TO PERFORM TEST FUCTION MODULE NOT RESPONDING: DDM CHECK IGNITION STATUS/VERIFY CABLE REQUIREMENTS CHEK CABLE CONNECTIONS? is displayed, perform TEST B: NO COMMUNICATION WITH LIGHTING CONTROL MODULE under SYSTEM TESTS in AUTOLAMP SYSTEMS – CONTINENTAL article.

2) Ensure gear selector is in Park. Turn ignition switch to LOCK position. Remove fuse No. 39 (10-amp) in instrument panel fuse box. Check fuse. If fuse is okay, go to next step. If fuse is blown, go to step **6)**.

3) Measure voltage at input side of fuse No. 39 in instrument panel fuse box. If battery voltage exists, go to next step. If battery voltage does not exist, go to step **24)**.

4) Install fuse No. 39. Disconnect Driver's Door Module (DDM) harness connector C524. Measure voltage at terminal No. 6 (Black/White wire) at DDM harness connector C524. If battery voltage exists, go to next step. If battery voltage does not exist, repair open in Black/White wire between instrument panel fuse box and DDM.

5) Measure resistance between ground and terminal No. 14 (Black/Light Blue wire) at DDM harness connector C524. If resistance is greater than 5 ohms, repair open in Black/Light Blue wire. If resistance is 5 ohms or less, repair module communication concern. See MODULE COMMUNICATIONS NETWORK – CONTINENTAL article.

6) Replace fuse No. 39. DO NOT operate any switches. If fuse blows, go to next step. If fuse does not blow, go to step **14)**.

7) Remove fuse No. 39. Disconnect DDM harness connector C524, Driver's Seat Module (DSM) harness connector C342, keyless entry keypad harness connector C525, driver's seat control switch harness connector C520, driver's door lock switch harness connector C505, passenger's door lock switch harness connector C602 and power mirror control switch harness connector C550. Measure resistance between ground and terminal No. 6 (Black/White wire) at DDM harness connector C524. If resistance is greater than 10 k/ohms, go to next step. If resistance is 10 k/ohms or less, repair short to ground in Black/White wire.

8) Connect keyless entry keypad harness connector C525. Measure resistance between ground and terminal No. 6 (Black/White wire) at DDM harness connector C524. If resistance is greater than 10 k/ohms, go to next step. If resistance is 10 k/ohms or less, replace keyless entry keypad.

9) Connect driver's seat control switch harness connector C520. Measure resistance between ground and terminal No. 6 (Black/White wire) at DDM harness connector C524. If resistance is greater than 10 k/ohms, go to next step. If resistance is 10 k/ohms or less, replace driver's seat control switch.

10) Connect DSM harness connector C342. Measure resistance between ground and terminal No. 6 (Black/White wire) at DDM harness connector C524. If resistance is greater than 10 k/ohms, go to next step. If resistance is 10 k/ohms or less, replace driver's seat module.

11) Connect DDM harness connector C524. Measure resistance between ground and terminal No. 6 (Black/White wire) at driver's door lock switch harness connector C505. If resistance is greater than 10 k/ohms, go to next step. If resistance is 10 k/ohms or less, replace driver's door module.

12) Connect passenger's door lock switch harness connector C602. Measure resistance between ground and terminal No. 6 (Black/White wire) at driver's door lock switch harness connector C505. If resistance is greater than 10 k/ohms, go to next step. If resistance is 10 k/ohms or less, replace passenger's door lock switch.

13) Connect power mirror control switch harness connector C550. Measure resistance between ground and terminal No. 6 (Black/White wire) at driver's door lock switch harness connector C505. If resistance is greater than 10 k/ohms, replace driver's door lock switch. If resistance is 10 k/ohms or less, replace power mirror control switch.

14) Lock and unlock doors at all door lock switches. If fuse No. 39 blows, go to next step. If fuse No. 39 does not blow, go to step **17)**.

15) Remove driver's and passenger's door lock switches. Test both door lock switches. See DOOR LOCK SWITCH under COMPONENT TESTS. If both door lock switches are okay, go to next step. If either door lock switch is defective, replace appropriate door lock switch.

16) Disconnect Driver's Door Module (DDM) harness connector C506. Measure resistance between ground and terminal No. 1 (Pink/Yellow wire) at driver's door lock switch harness connector C505. Also, measure resistance between ground and terminal No. 5 (Pink/Light Green wire) at driver's door lock switch harness connector C505. If either resistance reading is 10 k/ohms or less, repair short to ground in appropriate wire(s). If both resistance readings are greater than 10 k/ohms, replace driver's door module.

17) Press each number on keyless entry pad one at a time. If fuse No. 39 blows, go to next step. If fuse No. 39 does not blow, go to step **19)**.

18) Disconnect Driver's Door Module (DDM) harness connector C523. Disconnect keyless entry keypad harness connector C525. Measure resistance between ground and appropriate terminals at remote keyless entry keypad harness connector C525. See REMOTE KEYLESS ENTRY TERMINAL IDENTIFICATION table. If all resistance readings are greater than 10 k/ohms, replace driver's door module. If any resistance readings are 10 k/ohms or less, repair short to ground in appropriate wire.

REMOTE KEYLESS ENTRY TERMINAL IDENTIFICATION

Terminal	Wire Color
1	Red
2	Yellow
3	Yellow/Black
4	Light Green/Red
5	Light Blue/Yellow
9	Light Blue

19) Activate mirrors in all directions. If fuse No. 39 blows, go to next step. If fuse No. 39 does not blow, go to step **22)**.

20) Remove mirror control switch. Test mirror control switch. See MIRROR CONTROL SWITCH under COMPONENT TESTS. If mirror control switch is okay, go to next step. If mirror control switch is defective, replace mirror control switch.

21) Disconnect Driver's Door Module (DDM) harness connector C506. Disconnect mirror control switch harness connector C550. Measure resistance between ground and appropriate terminals at mirror control switch harness connector C550. See MIRROR CONTROL SWITCH TERMINAL IDENTIFICATION table. If all resistance readings are greater than 10 k/ohms, replace driver's door module. If any resistance reading are 10 k/ohms or less, repair short to ground in appropriate wire.

MIRROR CONTROL SWITCH TERMINAL IDENTIFICATION

Terminal	Wire Color
3	Dark Blue/Orange
4	Red/Orange

MIRROR CONTROL SWITCH TERMINAL IDENTIFICATION (Cont.)

Terminal	Wire Color
6	Yellow/Black
7	Violet/Orange
8	Dark Green/Orange

22) Activate driver's seat control switch in all directions. If fuse No. 39 blows, go to next step. If fuse No. 39 does not blow, system is operating properly at this time.

23) Disconnect Driver's Door Module (DDM) harness connector C506. Disconnect driver's seat control switch harness connector C520. Measure resistance between ground and appropriate terminals at driver's seat control switch harness connector C520. See DRIVER'S SEAT CONTROL SWITCH TERMINAL IDENTIFICATION table. If all resistance readings are greater than 10 k/ohms, replace driver's door module. If any resistance readings are 10 k/ohms or less, repair short to ground in appropriate wire.

DRIVER'S SEAT CONTROL SWITCH TERMINAL IDENTIFICATION

Terminal	Wire Color
2	Red/White
3	Red/Light Green
4	Red/Light Blue
5	Gray
7	Yellow/White
8	Yellow/Light Green
9	Yellow/Light Blue
10	Gray/Black

24) Turn ignition switch to LOCK position. Remove maxi-fuse No. 1 (30-amp) in power distribution box. Check fuse. If fuse is okay, go to next step. If fuse is blown, go to step 26).

25) Measure voltage at input side of maxi-fuse No. 1 in power distribution box. If battery voltage exists, repair open in Red wire between power distribution box and instrument panel fuse box. If battery voltage does not exist, repair or replace power distribution box as necessary.

26) Ensure maxi-fuse No. 1 in power distribution box is still removed. Disconnect Driver's Seat Module (DSM) harness connector C362. Disconnect driver's heated seat module harness connector C352. Disconnect driver's lumbar switch harness connector C348. Measure resistance between ground and terminal No. 1 (Red wire) at DSM harness connector C362. If resistance is greater than 10 k/ohms, go to next step. If resistance is 10 k/ohms or less, repair short to ground in Red wire.

27) Connect DSM harness connector C362. Measure resistance between ground and output side of maxi-fuse No. 1 in power distribution box. If resistance is greater than 10 k/ohms, go to next step. If resistance is 10 k/ohms or less, replace driver's seat module.

28) Replace maxi-fuse No. 1 (30-amp) in power distribution box. Connect driver's lumbar switch harness connector C348. Operate driver's lumbar switch in both directions. If maxi-fuse No. 1 blows, go to next step. If maxi-fuse No. 1 does not blow, go to step 32).

29) Remove maxi-fuse No. 1 (30-amp) from power distribution box. Measure resistance between ground and output side of maxi-fuse No. 1 in power distribution box. If resistance is greater than 10 k/ohms, go to next step. If resistance is 10 k/ohms or less, replace driver's lumbar switch.

30) Disconnect driver's lumbar switch harness connector C348. Measure resistance between ground and terminal No. 4 (Pink wire) at driver's lumbar switch harness connector C348. Also, measure resistance between ground and terminal No. 2 (Brown wire) at driver's lumbar switch harness connector C348. If both resistance readings are greater than 10 k/ohms, go to next step. If either resistance reading is 10 k/ohms or less, replace driver's lumbar switch.

31) Disconnect driver's lumbar motor harness connector C315. Measure resistance between ground and terminal No. 4 (Pink wire) at driver's lumbar switch harness connector C348. Also, measure resistance between ground and terminal No. 2 (Brown wire) at driver's lumbar switch harness connector C348. If both resistance readings are greater than 10 k/ohms, replace power lumbar motor. If either resistance reading is 10 k/ohms or less, repair short to ground in appropriate wire.

32) Disconnect driver's heated seat module harness connector C352. Measure resistance between ground and appropriate terminals at driver's heated seat module harness connector C352. See HEATED SEAT MODULE CONNECTOR TERMINAL IDENTIFICATION table. If all resistance readings are greater than 10 k/ohms, replace driver's heated seat module. If any resistance readings are 10 k/ohms or less, repair short to ground in appropriate wire.

HEATED SEAT MODULE CONNECTOR TERMINAL IDENTIFICATION

Terminal	Wire Color
5	Black/Light Blue
6	Brown/Light Blue
8	Yellow/Light Blue
9	Gray/Light Blue
10	Red/Light Blue
11	Orange/Light Blue
12	Violet/Light Blue
13	White/Light Blue

TEST B: NO COMMUNICATION WITH DRIVER'S SEAT MODULE

1) Check fuse No. 39 (10-amp) in instrument panel fuse box. If fuse is okay, go to next step. If fuse is blown, perform TEST A: NO COMMUNICATION WITH DRIVER'S DOOR MODULE.

2) Measure voltage at input side of fuse No. 39 at instrument panel fuse box. If battery voltage exists, go to next step. If battery voltage does not exist, perform TEST A: NO COMMUNICATION WITH DRIVER'S DOOR MODULE.

3) Install fuse No. 39. Disconnect DSM harness connector C342. Measure voltage at terminal No. 14 (Black/White wire) at DSM harness connector C342. If battery voltage exists, go to next step. If battery voltage does not exist, repair open in Black/White wire.

4) Measure resistance between ground and terminal No. 1 (Black/Light Green wire) at DSM harness connector C342. If resistance is 5 ohms or less, diagnosis network concern. See appropriate MODULE COMMUNICATIONS NETWORK – CONTINENTAL article. If resistance is greater than 5 ohms, repair open in Black/Light Green wire.

TEST C: DRIVER'S SEAT COMPLETELY INOPERATIVE

1) Using NGS tester, perform Driver's Door Module (DDM) self-test. If DTC B1545 was not retrieved, go to next step. If DTC B1545 is retrieved, go to step 4).

2) Using NGS tester, perform Driver's Seat Module (DSM) self-test. If no DTCs were retrieved, go to next step. If any DTCs were retrieved, perform appropriate test or go to appropriate step. See DSM DTC TEST table.

DSM DTC TEST

DTC	Perform
B1663	Step 16)
B1663 & B1957	TEST E
B1663 & B1954	TEST E
B1664	Step 18)
B1664 & B1953	TEST E
B1664 & B1950	TEST E
B1665	Step 20)
B1665 & B1965	TEST E
B1665 & B1962	TEST E
B1666	Step 22)
B1666 & B1961	TEST E
B1666 & B1958	TEST E
B1663, B1664, B1665 & B1666	Step 8)
B1663, B1664, B1665, B1666 & B1670	TEST E

3) Using NGS tester, monitor DDM PIDs SFWD_SW, SREARSW, SFNT_SW and SRCL_SW while activating driver's seat control switch in

all directions. If PIDs does not agree with driver's seat control switch position, go to next step. If PIDs agree with driver's seat control switch position, go to step **8**).

4) Remove driver's seat control switch. Test driver's seat control switch. See SEAT CONTROL SWITCH under COMPONENT TESTS. If switch is okay, go to next step. If switch is defective, replace driver's seat control switch.

5) Measure voltage at terminal No. 6 (Black/White wire) at driver's seat control switch harness connector C520. If battery voltage exists, go to next step. If battery voltage does not exist, repair open in Black/White wire.

6) Disconnect DDM harness connector C506. Measure voltage at appropriate terminals at DDM harness connector C506. See DDM HARNESS CONNECTOR C506 TERMINAL IDENTIFICATION table. If voltage does not exist at any terminal, go to next step. If voltage exists at any terminal, repair short to voltage in appropriate wire.

DDM HARNESS CONNECTOR C506 TERMINAL IDENTIFICATION

Terminal	Wire Color
2	Red/White
3	Red/Light Green
4	Red/Light Blue
5	Gray
7	Yellow/White
8	Yellow/Light Green
9	Yellow/Light Blue
10	Gray/Black

7) Ensure DDM harness connector C506 and driver's seat control switch harness connector C520 are still disconnected. Measure resistance in wire between appropriate terminals at DDM harness connector C506 and driver's seat control switch harness connector C520. See DDM CIRCUIT RESISTANCE table. If all resistance readings are 5 ohms or less, replace driver's door module. If any resistance readings are greater than 5 ohms, repair open in appropriate wire.

DDM CIRCUIT RESISTANCE

DDM Terminal	Switch Terminal	Wire Color
1	3	Red/Light Green
2	8	Yellow/Light Green
3	5	Gray
4	10	Gray/Black
5	4	Red/Light Blue
6	9	Yellow/Light Blue
7	2	Red/White
8	7	Yellow/White

8) Operate driver's seat in all directions. If driver's seat does not move in one-second intervals, go to next step. If driver's seat moves in one-second intervals, perform TEST E: MOTORS OPERATE IN ONE-SECOND INTERVALS.

9) Place transmission in Park. Using NGS tester, select DSM active command DRIVER SEAT CONTROL. Using NGS tester, operate driver's seat in all directions. If driver's seat responds correctly, replace driver's seat module. If driver's seat does not respond correctly, go to appropriate step. See DRIVER'S SEAT MALFUNCTION table.

DRIVER'S SEAT MALFUNCTION

Malfunction	Perform Step
No Seat Movement	10)
No Front Motor Movement	16)
No Rear Motor Movement	18)
No Horizontal Motor Movement	20)
No Recline Motor Movement	22)

10) Disconnect DSM harness connector C362. Measure voltage at terminal No. 1 (Red wire) at DSM harness connector C362. If battery voltage exists, go to next step. If battery voltage does not exist, repair open in Red wire.

11) Measure resistance between ground and terminal No. 2 (Black wire) at DSM harness connector C362. If resistance is 10 k/ohms or less, go to next step. If resistance is greater than 10 k/ohms, repair open in Black wire.

12) Remove DSM internal fuse (30-amp). If fuse is blown, go to next step. If fuse is okay, replace driver's seat module.

13) Ensure transmission is in Park. Disconnect DSM harness connector C361 and driver's seat motor harness connector C316. Measure resistance between ground and appropriate terminals at DSM harness connector C361. See DSM CIRCUIT RESISTANCE table. If all resistance readings are greater than 10 k/ohms, go to next step. If any resistance reading is 10 k/ohms or less, repair short to ground in appropriate wire(s).

DSM CIRCUIT RESISTANCE

Terminal	Wire Color
4	Yellow/White
5	Yellow/Light Green
6	Yellow/Light Blue
11	Red/Light Blue
13	Red/Light Green
14	Red/White

14) Disconnect recline motor harness connector C331. Measure resistance between ground and terminal No. 7 (Gray/Black wire), then between ground and terminal No. 16 (Gray wire) at DSM harness connector C361. If both resistance readings are greater than 10 k/ohms, go to next step. If either resistance reading is 10 k/ohms or less, repair short to ground in appropriate wire(s).

15) Connect driver's recline motor harness connector C331. Connect DSM harness connector C361. Ensure all other driver's seat motors are still disconnected. Replace DSM internal fuse. Using power seat control switch, recline driver's seat back completely backward and forward. If DSM internal fuse does not blow, replace driver's seat track assembly. If DSM internal fuse blows, replace recline motor.

16) Disconnect driver's motor harness connector C316. Using NGS tester, select DSM active command DRIVER SEAT CONTROL. Measure voltage between terminals No. 5 (Red/Light Blue wire) and No. 6 (Yellow/Light Blue wire) at driver's seat motor harness connector C316. Using NGS tester, operate driver's seat front height motor up and down. If voltage does not exist when motor is commanded on, go to next step. If voltage exists only when motor is commanded on, replace driver's front seat track assembly.

17) Disconnect DSM harness connector C361. Measure resistance in Red/Light Blue wire between terminal No. 11 at DSM harness connector C361 and terminal No. 6 at driver's seat motor harness connector C316. Also, measure resistance in Yellow/Light Blue wire between terminal No. 6 at DSM harness connector C361 and terminal No. 5 at driver's seat motor harness connector C316. If both resistance readings are 5 ohms or less, replace driver's seat module. If either resistance reading is greater than 5 ohms, repair open in appropriate wire(s).

18) Disconnect driver's seat motor harness connector C316. Using NGS tester, select DSM active command DRIVER SEAT CONTROL. Measure voltage between terminals No. 2 (Red/Light Green wire) and No. 3 (Yellow/Light Green wire) at driver's seat motor harness connector C316. Using NGS tester, operate driver's seat rear height motor up and down. If voltage does not exist when motor is commanded on, go to next step. If voltage exists only when motor is commanded on, replace driver's front seat track assembly.

19) Disconnect DSM harness connector C361. Measure resistance in Red/Light Green wire between terminal No. 13 at DSM harness connector C316. Also, measure resistance in Yellow/Light Green wire between terminal No. 5 at DSM harness connector C361 and terminal No. 3 at driver's seat motor harness connector C316. If both resistance reading are 5 ohms or less, replace driver's seat module. If either resistance reading is greater than 5 ohms, repair open in appropriate wire(s).

20) Disconnect driver's seat motor harness connector C316. Using NGS tester, select DSM active command DRIVER SEAT CONTROL. Measure voltage between terminals No. 4 (Red/White wire) and No. 1

(Yellow/White wire) at driver's seat motor harness connector C316. Using NGS tester, operate driver's seat horizontal motor forward and backward. If voltage does not exist when motor is commanded on, go to next step. If voltage exists only when motor is commanded on, replace driver's front seat track assembly.

21) Disconnect DSM harness connector C361. Measure resistance in Red/White wire between terminal No. 14 at DSM harness connector C361 and terminal No. 4 at driver's seat motor harness connector C316. Also, measure resistance in Yellow/White wire between terminal No. 4 at DSM harness connector C361 and terminal No. 1 at driver's seat motor harness connector C316. If both resistance readings are 5 ohms or less, replace driver's seat module. If either resistance reading is greater than 5 ohms, repair open in appropriate wire(s).

22) Disconnect drive seat recline motor harness connector C331. Using NGS tester, select DSM active command DRIVER SEAT CONTROL. Measure voltage between terminals No. 1 (Gray wire) and No. 2 (Gray/Black wire) at driver's seat recline motor harness connector C331. Using NGS tester, operate driver's seat recline motor forward and backward. If voltage does not exist when motor is commanded on, go to next step. If voltage exists only when motor is commanded on, replace driver's front seat track assembly.

23) Disconnect DSM harness connector C361. Measure resistance in Gray wire between terminal No. 16 at DSM harness connector C361 and terminal No. 1 at driver's seat recline motor harness connector C331. Also, measure resistance in Gray/Black wire between terminal No. 7 at DSM harness connector C361 and terminal No. 2 at driver's seat recline motor harness connector C331. If both resistance readings are 5 ohms or less, replace driver's seat module. If either resistance reading is greater than 5 ohms, repair open in appropriate wire(s).

TEST D: PASSENGER'S SEAT COMPLETELY INOPERATIVE

1) Disconnect passenger's seat motor harness connector C302. Measure voltage between terminal No. 6 (Red/Light Blue wire) and No. 5 (Yellow/Light Blue wire) at passenger's seat motor harness connector C345. Using passenger's seat control switch, operate passenger's seat front up and down. If battery voltage does not exist when switch is operated, go to next step. If battery voltage exists when switch is operated, replace passenger's front seat track assembly.

2) Disconnect passenger's seat control switch harness connector C612. Measure resistance between ground and terminal No. 6 (Black wire) at passenger's seat control switch harness connector C612. If resistance is 5 ohms or less, go to next step. If resistance is greater than 5 ohms, repair open in Black wire.

3) Measure voltage at terminal No. 1 (Dark Green wire) at passenger's seat control switch harness connector C612. If battery voltage does not exist, go to next step. If battery voltage exists, check wiring between passenger's seat control switch and motor. If wiring is okay, replace passenger's seat control switch. If wiring is damaged, repair wiring as necessary.

4) Check maxi-fuse No. 2 (30-amp) in power distribution box. If fuse is blown, go to next step. If fuse is okay, check for voltage to fuse. If voltage exists, repair open in Dark Green wire. If voltage does not exist, repair voltage supply as necessary.

5) Ensure maxi-fuse No. 2 is still removed and passenger's seat control switch harness connector C612 is still disconnected. Measure resistance between ground and terminal No. 1 (Dark Green wire) at passenger's seat control switch harness connector C612. If resistance is less than 100 ohms, go to next step. If resistance is 100 ohms or greater, go to step 9).

6) Measure resistance between ground and output side of maxi-fuse No. 2 (Dark Green wire) at power distribution box. If resistance is 100 ohms or greater, replace passenger's seat control switch. If resistance is less than 100 ohms, go to next step.

7) Disconnect passenger's seat lumbar switch harness connector C350. Measure resistance between ground and output side of fuse No. 2 (Dark Green wire) at power distribution box. If resistance is 100 ohms or greater, replace passenger's seat lumber control switch. If resistance is less than 100 ohms, go to next step if equipped with heated seat. Otherwise repair short to ground in Dark Green wire.

8) Disconnect passenger's heated seat module harness connector C356. Measure resistance between ground and output side of fuse No. 2 (Dark Green wire) at power distribution box. If resistance is 100 ohms or greater, replace passenger's heated seat module. If resistance is less than 100 ohms, repair short to ground in Dark Green wire.

9) Replace maxi-fuse No. 2. Operate passenger's seat through all positions. If fuse blows, go to next step. If fuse does not blow, go to step 11).

10) Disconnect passenger's seat control switch harness connector C612. Measure resistance between ground and appropriate terminals at passenger's seat control switch harness connector C612. See PASSENGER'S SEAT CONTROL SWITCH CIRCUIT RESISTANCE table. If all resistance readings are greater than 10 k/ohms, replace passenger's seat control switch. If any resistance reading is 10 k/ohms or less, repair short to ground in appropriate wire(s).

PASSENGER'S SEAT CONTROL SWITCH CIRCUIT RESISTANCE

Terminal	Wire Color
2	Gray
3	Red/Light Blue
4	Red/Light Green
5	Red/White
7	Gray/Black
8	Yellow/Light Blue
9	Yellow/Light Green
10	Yellow/White

11) Operate passenger's seat lumbar through all positions. If maxi-fuse No. 2 blows, go to next step. If fuse No. 2 does not blow, go to step 13) if equipped with heated seats. Otherwise, repair intermittent short to ground in Dark Green wire.

12) Disconnect passenger's lumbar switch harness connector C350. Measure resistance between ground and terminal No. 4 (Pink wire) at passenger's lumbar switch harness connector C350. Also measure resistance between ground and terminal No. 2 (Brown wire) at passenger's lumbar switch harness connector C350. If both resistance readings are greater than 10 k/ohms, replace passenger's lumbar switch. If either resistance reading is 10 k/ohms or less, repair short to ground in appropriate wire(s).

13) Operate passenger's seat heater through all heat ranges. If maxi-fuse No. 2 blows, go to next step. If maxi-fuse No. 2 does not blow, repair intermittent short to ground in Dark Green wire.

14) Disconnect passenger's heated seat control module harness connector C356. Measure resistance between ground and appropriate terminals at passenger's heated seat control module harness connector C356. See PASSENGER'S SEAT HEATER CIRCUIT RESISTANCE table. If all resistance readings are greater than 10 k/ohms, replace passenger's heated seat module. If any resistance reading is 10 k/ohms or less, repair short to ground in appropriate wire(s).

PASSENGER'S SEAT HEATER CIRCUIT RESISTANCE

Terminal	Wire Color
8	Yellow/Light Blue
9	Gray/Light Blue
12	Violet/Light Blue
13	White/Light Blue

TEST E: SEAT MOTORS OPERATE IN ONE-SECOND INTERVALS

1) Ensure transmission is in Park. Operate driver's seat in all directions. If seat moves in all directions, go to next step. If seat does not move in some or any direction, refer to SYMPTOM CHART table.

2) Using NGS tester, perform Driver's Door Module (DDM) self test. If DTC U1181 was not retrieved, go to next step. If DTC U1181 was retrieved, go to INSTRUMENT PANELS – CONTINENTAL article.

3) Using NGS tester, perform Driver's Seat Module (DSM) self test. If no DTCs were retrieved, go to next step. If any DTCs were retrieved, go to appropriate step. See DTC STEP CHART table.

DTC STEP CHART

DTCs	Perform Step
B1663 & B1957	5)
B1663 & B1954	6)
B1664 & B1953	8)
B1664 & B1950	9)
B1665 & B1965	11)
B1665 & B1962	12)
B1666 & B1961	14)
B1666 & B1958	15)
B1663, B1664, B1665 & B1666	4)
B1663, B1664, B1665, B1666, B1667, B1668, B1669 & B1670	17)

4) Ensure transmission is in Park. Using driver's seat control switch, place seat in center position. Using driver's seat control switch, move each seat motor through complete travel. If all motors move through complete travel smoothly without stopping, replace driver's seat module. If any motor(s) do not move through complete travel smoothly without stopping, go to appropriate step. See MOTOR STEP CHART table.

MOTOR STEP CHART

Inoperative Motor	Perform Step
All	17)
Front Height	5)
Horizontal	11)
Rear Height	8)
Recline	14)

5) Disconnect DSM harness connector C361. Disconnect front height motor potentiometer harness connector C358. Measure resistance between ground and terminal No. 2 (Light Green/Red wire) at front height motor potentiometer harness connector C358. If resistance is greater than 10 k/ohms, go to next step. If resistance is 10 k/ohms or less, repair short to ground in Light Green/Red wire.

6) Measure resistance between front height motor potentiometer harness connector C358 and driver's seat module harness connector C361. See FRONT HEIGHT MOTOR POTENTIOMETER CIRCUIT RESISTANCE table. If all resistance readings are 5 ohms or less, go to next step. If any resistance reading is greater than 5 ohms, repair open in appropriate wire(s).

FRONT HEIGHT MOTOR POTENTIOMETER CIRCUIT RESISTANCE

DSM Terminal	Terminal	Wire Color
1	1	Orange/Red
3	3	Orange/White
9	2	Light Green/Red

7) Measure voltage at terminals No. 2 (Light Green/Red wire), No. 3 (Orange/White wire) and No. 1 (Orange/Red wire) at front height motor potentiometer harness connector C358. If voltage does not exist at any terminal, go to step 21). If voltage exists at any terminal, repair short to voltage in appropriate wire(s).

8) Disconnect DSM harness connector C361. Disconnect rear height motor potentiometer harness connector C357. Measure resistance between ground and terminal No. 2 (Light Green/Black wire) at rear height motor potentiometer harness connector C357. If resistance is greater than 10 k/ohms, go to next step. If resistance is 10 k/ohms or less, repair short to ground in Light Green/Black wire.

9) Measure resistance between rear height motor potentiometer harness connector C357 and driver's seat module harness connector C361. See REAR HEIGHT MOTOR POTENTIOMETER CIRCUIT RESISTANCE table. If all resistance readings are 5 ohms or less, go to next step. If any resistance readings are greater than 5 ohms, repair open in appropriate wire(s).

REAR HEIGHT MOTOR POTENTIOMETER CIRCUIT RESISTANCE

DSM Terminal	Motor Terminal	Wire Color
1	1	Orange/Red

REAR HEIGHT MOTOR POTENTIOMETER CIRCUIT RESISTANCE (Cont.)

DSM Terminal	Motor Terminal	Wire Color
3	3	Orange/White
8	2	Light Green/Black

10) Measure voltage at terminals No. 2 (Light Green/Black wire), No. 3 (Orange/White wire) and No. 1 (Orange/Red wire) at rear height motor potentiometer harness connector C357. If voltage does not exist at any terminal, go to step 23). If voltage exists at any terminal, repair short to voltage in appropriate wire(s).

11) Disconnect DSM harness connector C361. Disconnect horizontal motor potentiometer harness connector C359. Measure resistance between ground and terminal No. 2 (Light Green/Orange wire) at horizontal motor potentiometer harness connector C359. If resistance is greater than 10 k/ohms, go to next step. If resistance is 10 k/ohms or less, repair short to ground in Light Green/Orange wire.

12) Measure resistance between horizontal motor potentiometer harness connector C359 and driver's seat module harness connector C361. See HORIZONTAL MOTOR POTENTIOMETER CIRCUIT RESISTANCE table. If all resistance readings are 5 ohms or less, go to next step. If any resistance readings are greater than 5 ohms, repair open in appropriate wire(s).

HORIZONTAL MOTOR POTENTIOMETER CIRCUIT RESISTANCE

DSM Terminal	Motor Terminal	Wire Color
1	1	Orange/Red
3	3	Orange/White
10	2	Light Green/Orange

13) Measure voltage at terminals No. 2 (Light Green/Orange wire), No. 3 (Orange/White wire) and No. 1 (Orange/Red wire) at horizontal motor potentiometer harness connector C359. If voltage does not exist at any terminal, go to step 25). If voltage exists at any terminal, repair short to voltage in appropriate wire(s).

14) Disconnect DSM harness connector C361. Disconnect recline motor potentiometer harness connector C349. Measure resistance between ground and terminal No. 2 (Orange/Light Blue wire) at recline motor potentiometer harness connector C349. If resistance is greater than 10 k/ohms, go to next step. If resistance is 10 k/ohms or less, repair short to ground in Orange/Light Blue wire.

15) Measure resistance between recline motor potentiometer harness connector C349 and driver's seat module harness connector C361. See RECLINE MOTOR POTENTIOMETER CIRCUIT RESISTANCE table. If all resistance readings are 5 ohms or less, go to next step. If any resistance readings are greater than 5 ohms, repair open in appropriate wire(s).

RECLINE MOTOR POTENTIOMETER CIRCUIT RESISTANCE

DSM Terminal	Motor Terminal	Wire Color
1	1	Orange/Red
3	3	Orange/White
15	2	Orange/Light Blue

16) Measure voltage at terminals No. 2 (Orange/Light Blue wire), No. 3 (Orange/White wire) and No. 1 (Orange/Red wire) at recline motor potentiometer harness connector C349. If voltage does not exist at any terminal, go to step 27) . If voltage exists at any terminal, repair short to voltage in appropriate wire(s).

17) Disconnect DSM harness connector C361, front height motor potentiometer harness connector C358, rear height motor potentiometer harness connector C357, horizontal motor potentiometer harness connector C359 and recline motor potentiometer harness connector C349. Measure resistance in Orange/White wire between terminal No. 3 at DSM harness connector C361 and terminal No. 3 at each motor potentiometer harness connector. If all resistance readings are 5 ohms or less, go to next step. If any resistance reading is greater than 5 ohms, repair open in appropriate wire(s).

18) Measure resistance in Orange/Red wire between terminal No. 1 at DSM harness connector C361 and terminal No. 1 at each motor potentiometer harness connector. If all resistance readings are 5 ohms or less, go to next step. If any resistance reading is greater than 5 ohms, repair open in appropriate wire(s).

19) Measure resistance between ground and terminal No. 3 (Orange/White wire) at each motor potentiometer harness connector. If all resistance readings are greater than 10 k/ohms, go to next step. If any resistance reading is 10 k/ohms or less, repair short to ground in appropriate wire(s).

20) Measure voltage between ground and terminal No. 3 (Orange/White wire) at each motor potentiometer harness connector. If voltage does not exist at any terminal, go to step **29)**. If voltage exists at any terminal, repair short to voltage in appropriate wire(s).

21) Connect DSM harness connector C361. Measure voltage at terminals No. 3 (Orange/White wire) and No. 2 (Light Green/Red wire) at front height motor potentiometer harness connector C358. If voltage exists, go to next step. If voltage does not exist, replace driver's seat module.

22) Measure resistance between ground and terminal No. 1 (Orange/Red wire) at front height motor potentiometer harness connector C358. If resistance is greater than 10 k/ohms, replace driver's seat module. If resistance is 10 k/ohms or less, replace front seat track assembly.

23) Connect DSM harness connector C361. Measure voltage at terminals No. 3 (Orange/White wire) and No. 2 (Light Green/Black wire) at rear height motor potentiometer harness connector C357. If voltage exists, go to next step. If voltage does not exist, replace driver's seat module.

24) Measure resistance between ground and terminal No. 1 (Orange/Red wire) at rear height motor potentiometer harness connector C357. If resistance is greater than 10 k/ohms, replace driver's seat module. If resistance is 10 k/ohms or less, replace front seat track assembly.

25) Connect DSM harness connector C361. Measure voltage at terminals No. 3 (Orange/White wire) and No. 2 (Light Green/Orange wire) at horizontal motor potentiometer harness connector C359. If voltage exists, go to next step. If voltage does not exist, replace driver's seat module.

26) Measure resistance between ground and terminal No. 1 (Orange/Red wire) at horizontal motor potentiometer harness connector C359. If resistance is greater than 10 k/ohms, replace driver's seat module. If resistance is 10 k/ohms or less, replace front seat track assembly.

27) Connect DSM harness connector C361. Measure voltage at terminals No. 3 (Orange/White wire) and No. 2 (Orange/Light Blue wire) at recline motor potentiometer harness connector C349. If voltage exists, go to next step. If voltage does not exist, replace driver's seat module.

28) Measure resistance between ground and terminal No. 1 (Orange/Red wire) at recline motor potentiometer harness connector C349. If resistance is greater than 10 k/ohms, replace driver's seat module. If resistance is 10 k/ohms or less, replace front seat track assembly.

29) Using NGS tester, perform DSM self-test. If DTCs B1667, B1668 and B1670 were not also retrieved, replace driver's seat module. If DTCs B1667, B1668 and B1670 were also retrieved, repair power mirror system. See POWER MEMORY MIRRORS – CONTINENTAL article.

TEST F: PASSENGER'S SEAT DOES NOT MOVE HORIZONTALLY/VERTICALLY

1) Disconnect suspect motor harness connector. Measure voltage between appropriate motor harness connector terminals. See CONNECTOR IDENTIFICATION table. Operate seat control switch in both directions for suspected motor. If voltage does not exist in both directions, go to next step. If voltage exists in both directions, replace front seat track assembly.

CONNECTOR IDENTIFICATION

Motor	Connector	Between Terminals
Front Height	C302	5 & 6

CONNECTOR IDENTIFICATION (Cont.)

Motor	Connector	Between Terminals
Rear Height	C302	2 & 3
Horizontal	C302	1 & 4
Recline	C330	1 & 2

2) Turn ignition switch to RUN position. Using a voltmeter, backprobe at appropriate terminal at passenger's seat control switch. See PASSENGER'S SEAT CONTROL SWITCH CIRCUIT TEST table. If voltage does not exist, go to next step. If voltage exists, repair short to voltage in appropriate wire between seat control switch and motor.

PASSENGER'S SEAT CONTROL SWITCH CIRCUIT TEST

Motor	Terminals	Wire Color
Rear Down	4	Red/Light Green
Rear Up	9	Yellow/Light Green
Recline FWD	2	Gray
Recline RWD	7	Gray/Black
Front Down	3	Red/Light Blue
Front Up	8	Yellow/Light Blue
Forward	10	Yellow/White
Rearward	5	Red/White

3) Disconnect passenger's seat control switch harness connector C612. Measure resistance between ground and appropriate passenger's seat control switch terminals. See SEAT CONTROL SWITCH CIRCUIT TEST table. If all resistance readings are greater than 10 k/ohms, go to next step. If any resistance reading is 10 k/ohms or less, repair short to ground in appropriate wire(s).

SEAT CONTROL SWITCH CIRCUIT TEST

Terminal	Wire Color
2	Gray
3	Red/Light Blue
4	Red/Light Green
5	Red/White
7	Gray/Black
8	Yellow/Light Blue
9	Yellow/Light Green
10	Yellow/White

4) Turn ignition switch to LOCK position. Measure resistance in wires between passenger's seat control switch harness connector C612 terminal and suspected motor harness connector terminal. See PASSENGER'S SEAT CONTROL SWITCH CIRCUIT TEST table in step **2)**. If all resistance reading are 5 ohms or less, replace passenger's seat control switch. If any resistance reading is greater than 5 ohms, repair open in appropriate wire(s).

TEST G: MEMORY SEAT INOPERATIVE

1) Ensure transmission is in Park. Using driver's seat control switch, operate seat in all directions. If driver's seat operates properly in all directions, go to next step. If driver's seat does not operate properly, repair seat by symptom. See SYMPTOM CHART table.

2) Activate memory recall positions No. 1 and 2 from instrument panel message center. If memory recall feature operates properly, go to next step. If memory recall feature does not operate properly, perform TEST E: MOTORS OPERATE IN ONE-SECOND INTERVALS.

3) Activate memory recall positions No. 1 and 2 from keyless entry keypad. If memory recall feature operates properly, go to next step. If memory recall feature does not operate properly, repair keyless entry system. See appropriate wiring diagram in REMOTE KEYLESS ENTRY SYSTEMS article.

4) Activate memory recall positions No. 1 and 2 from remote transmitter. If memory recall feature operates properly, memory seats system is okay at this time. If memory recall feature does not operate properly, repair keyless entry system. See appropriate wiring diagram in REMOTE KEYLESS ENTRY SYSTEMS article.

TEST H: EASY EXIT/ENTRY FEATURE INOPERATIVE

1) Ensure transmission is in Park. Using driver's seat control switch, operate seat in all directions. If seat operates properly in all directions, go to next step. If seat does not operate properly, repair seat by symptom. See SYMPTOM CHART table.

2) Select easy entry/exit feature on instrument cluster message center. See MESSAGE CENTER under OPERATION. If easy exit/entry feature is enabled, go to next step. If easy exit/entry feature is not enabled, enable feature and recheck system. If feature operates properly, inform customer on proper operation. If feature is still inoperative, go to next step.

3) Turn ignition switch to RUN position. Position seat in center of travel. Remove key from ignition. If seat does not move rearward approximately 2 inches, go to next step. If seat moves rearward approximately 2 inches, go to step **6)**.

4) Turn ignition switch to RUN position. Turn ignition switch to LOCK position, leaving key in ignition. Using NGS tester, monitor Lighting Control Module (LCM) PID IGN_KEY. Remove key while observing LCM PID IGN_KEY. If PID indicates OUT when key is removed, go to next step. If PID does not indicate OUT when key is removed, perform TEST AA: KEY-IN-IGNITION CHIME DOES NOT OPERATE PROPERLY under SYSTEM TEST in ANALOG INSTRUMENT PANELS – CONTINENTAL article.

NOTE: DSM DTC U1135 is caused because DSM is not receiving ignition switch signal from Lighting Control Module (LCM) over BUS communication circuit.

---

5) Using NGS tester, perform DSM self-test. If no DTCs are retrieved, replace driver's seat module. If DTC U1135 is retrieved, repair Lighting Control Module (LCM) DTC related malfunction. See INSTRUMENT PANELS – CONTINENTAL article.

6) Insert key into ignition. If driver's seat does not move forward approximately 2 inches, go to next step. If driver's seat moves forward approximately 2 inches, system is okay at this time.

7) Retrieve and record LCM related DTCs. Clear LCM DTCs. Perform LCM self-test. If any LCM related DTC exists, diagnosis DTC as necessary. See MODULE COMMUNICATIONS NETWORK – CONTINENTAL article. If no LCM related DTCs exist, replace DSM.

TEST J: DRIVER'S SEAT HEATER INOPERATIVE

1) Operate passenger's seat heater. If passenger's seat heater is operational, go to next step. If passenger's seat heater is inoperative, perform TEST N: BOTH HEATED SEATS INOPERATIVE.

2) Turn ignition switch to LOCK position. Disconnect driver's seat heater switch harness connector C222. Turn ignition switch to RUN position. Measure voltage at terminal No. 7 (Light Green/Violet wire) at driver's seat heater seat switch harness connector C222. If battery voltage exists, go to next step. If battery voltage does not exist, repair open in Light Green/Violet wire.

3) Turn ignition switch to LOCK position. Connect driver's seat heater switch harness connector C222. Disconnect driver's heated seat module harness connector C352. Measure voltage at terminal No. 7 (Red wire) at driver's heated seat module harness connector C352. If battery voltage exists, go to next step. If battery voltage does not exist, repair open in Red wire.

4) Measure resistance between ground and terminal No. 14 (Black wire) at driver's heated seat module harness connector C352. If resistance is 5 ohms or less, go to next step. If resistance is greater than 5 ohms, repair open in Black wire.

5) Ensure ignition switch is in LOCK position. Measure resistance between terminal No. 3 (Light Green/Orange wire) and No. 4 (Tan/Light Blue wire) at driver's heated seat module harness connector C352. Turn driver's seat heater switch to position No. 1. If resistance is not 2000-2750 ohms, go to next step. If resistance is 2000-2750 ohms, go to step **12)**.

6) Turn driver's seat heater switch off. Measure resistance between ground and terminal No. 3 (Light Green/Orange wire) at driver's heated seat module harness connector C352. If resistance is 10 k/ohms or less, go to next step. If resistance is greater than 10 k/ohms, go to step **8)**.

7) Disconnect driver's seat heater switch harness connector C222. Measure resistance between ground and terminal No. 3 (Light Green/Orange wire) at driver's heated seat module harness connector C352. If resistance is 10 k/ohms or less, repair short to ground in Light Green/Orange wire. If resistance is greater than 10 k/ohms, replace driver's seat heater switch.

8) Ensure ignition switch is in LOCK position. Measure resistance between ground and terminal No. 4 (Tan/Light Blue wire) at driver's heated seat module harness connector C352. If resistance is 10 k/ohms or less, go to next step. If resistance is greater than 10 k/ohms, go to step **10)**.

9) Disconnect driver's seat heater switch harness connector C222. Measure resistance between ground and terminal No. 4 (Tan/Light Blue wire) at driver's heated seat module harness connector C352. If resistance is 10 k/ohms or less, repair short to ground in Tan/Light Blue wire. If resistance is greater than 10 k/ohms, replace driver's seat heater switch.

10) Disconnect driver's seat heater switch harness connector C222. Measure resistance in Tan/Light Blue wire between ground and terminal No. 4 at driver's heated seat module harness connector C352 and terminal No. 5 at driver's seat heater switch harness connector C222. If resistance is 5 ohms or less, go to next step. If resistance is greater than 5 ohms, repair open in Tan/Light Blue wire.

11) Measure resistance in Light Green/Orange wire between terminal No. 3 at driver's heated seat module harness connector C352 and terminal No. 4 at driver's seat heater switch harness connector C222. If resistance is 5 ohms or less, replace driver's seat heater switch. If resistance is greater than 5 ohms, repair open in Light Green/Orange wire.

12) Measure resistance between terminals No. 9 (Gray/Light Blue wire) and No. 12 (Violet/Light Blue wire) at driver's heated seat module harness connector C352. If resistance is 2.5-10.0 ohms, replace driver's heated seat module. If resistance is not 2.5-10.0 ohms, repair wire and/or replace seat back cushion as necessary.

TEST K: DRIVER'S HEATED SEAT CUSHION INOPERATIVE

1) Turn ignition switch to LOCK position. Disconnect driver's heated seat module harness connector C352. Turn ignition switch to RUN position. Turn driver's seat heater switch to No. 1 position. Push seat cushion enable button. Measure voltage at terminal No. 1 (Dark Green/Violet wire) at driver's heated seat module harness connector C352. If battery voltage does not exist, go to next step. If battery voltage exists, go to step **3)**.

2) Disconnect driver's seat heater switch harness connector C222. Measure resistance in Dark Green/Violet wire between terminal No. 1 at driver's heated seat module harness connector C352 and terminal No. 2 at driver's seat heater switch harness connector C222. If resistance is 5 ohms or less, replace driver's seat heater switch. If resistance is greater than 5 ohms, repair open in Dark Green/Violet wire.

3) Measure resistance between terminals No. 8 (Yellow/Light Blue wire) and No. 13 (White/Light Blue wire) at driver's heated seat module harness connector C352. If resistance is 2.5-10.0 ohms, replace driver's heated seat module. If resistance is not 2.5-10.0 ohms, repair wire and/or replace driver's seat cushion as necessary.

TEST L: PASSENGER'S SEAT HEATER INOPERATIVE

1) Operate driver's seat heater. If driver's seat heater is operational, go to next step. If driver's seat heater is inoperative, perform TEST N: BOTH HEATED SEATS INOPERATIVE.

2) Turn ignition switch to LOCK position. Disconnect passenger's seat heater switch harness connector C221. Turn ignition switch to RUN position. Measure voltage at terminal No. 5 (Light Green/Violet wire) at passenger's seat heater switch harness connector C221. If battery voltage exists, go to next step. If battery voltage does not exist, repair open in Light Green/Violet wire.

3) Turn ignition switch to LOCK position. Connect passenger's seat heater switch harness connector C221. Disconnect passenger's heated seat module harness connector C356. Measure voltage at terminal No. 7 (Dark Green wire) at passenger's heated seat module harness connector C356. If battery voltage exists, go to next step. If battery voltage does not exist, repair open in Dark Green wire.

4) Measure resistance between ground and terminal No. 14 (Black wire) at passenger's heated seat module harness connector C356. If resistance is 5 ohms or less, go to next step. If resistance is greater than 5 ohms, repair open in Black wire.

5) Ensure ignition switch is in LOCK position. Measure resistance between terminal No. 3 (Black/Orange wire) and No. 4 (Brown wire) at passenger's heated seat module harness connector C356. Turn passenger's seat heater switch to position No. 1. If resistance is not 2000-2750 ohms, go to next step. If resistance is 2000-2750 ohms, go to step **12**) .

6) Turn passenger's seat heater switch off. Measure resistance between ground and terminal No. 3 (Black/Orange wire) at driver's heated seat module harness connector C356. If resistance is 10 k/ohms or less, go to next step. If resistance is greater than 10 k/ohms, go to step **8**).

7) Disconnect passenger's seat heater switch harness connector C221. Measure resistance between ground and terminal No. 3 (Black/Orange wire) at passenger's heated seat module harness connector C356. If resistance is 10 k/ohms or less, repair short to ground in Black/Orange wire. If resistance is greater than 10 k/ohms, replace passenger's seat heater switch.

8) Ensure ignition switch is in LOCK position. Measure resistance between ground and terminal No. 4 (Brown wire) at passenger's heated seat module harness connector C356. If resistance is 10 k/ohms or less, go to next step. If resistance is greater than 10 k/ohms, go to step **10**).

9) Disconnect passenger's seat heater switch harness connector C221. Measure resistance between ground and terminal No. 4 (Brown wire) at passenger's heated seat module harness connector C356. If resistance is 10 k/ohms or less, repair short to ground in Brown wire. If resistance is greater than 10 k/ohms, replace passenger's seat heater switch.

10) Disconnect passenger's seat heater switch harness connector C221. Measure resistance in Brown wire between ground and terminal No. 4 at passenger's heated seat module harness connector C356 and terminal No. 4 at passenger's seat heater switch harness connector C221. If resistance is 5 ohms or less, go to next step. If resistance is greater than 5 ohms, repair open in Brown wire.

11) Measure resistance in Black/Orange wire between terminal No. 3 at passenger's heated seat module harness connector C356 and terminal No. 4 at passenger's seat heater switch harness connector C221. If resistance is 5 ohms or less, replace passenger's seat heater switch. If resistance is greater than 5 ohms, repair open in Black/Orange wire.

12) Measure resistance between terminals No. 9 (Gray/Light Blue wire) and No. 12 (Violet/Light Blue wire) at passenger's heated seat module harness connector C356. If resistance is 2.5-10.0 ohms, replace passenger's heated seat module. If resistance is not 2.5-10.0 ohms, repair wiring and/or replace seat back cushion as necessary.

TEST M: PASSENGER'S HEATED SEAT CUSHION INOPERATIVE

1) Turn ignition switch to LOCK position. Disconnect passenger's heated seat module harness connector C356. Turn ignition switch to RUN position. Turn passenger's seat heater switch to No. 1 position. Push seat cushion enable button. Measure voltage at terminal No. 1 (Red wire) at passenger's heated seat module harness connector C356. If battery voltage does not exist, go to next step. If battery voltage exists, go to step **3**).

2) Disconnect passenger's seat heater switch harness connector C221. Measure resistance in Red wire between terminal No. 1 at passenger's heated seat module harness connector C356 and terminal No. 1 at passenger's seat heater switch harness connector C221. If resistance is 5 ohms or less, replace passenger's seat heater switch. If resistance is greater than 5 ohms, repair open in Red wire.

3) Measure resistance between terminals No. 8 (Yellow/Light Blue wire) and No. 13 (White/Light Blue wire) at passenger's heated seat module harness connector C356. If resistance is 2.5-10 ohms, replace passen-

ger's heated seat module. If resistance is not 2.5-10 ohms, repair wiring and/or replace passenger's seat cushion as necessary.

TEST N: BOTH HEATED SEATS INOPERATIVE

1) Turn ignition switch to LOCK position. Disconnect driver's seat heater switch harness connector C222. Turn ignition switch to RUN position. Measure voltage at terminal No. 7 (Light Green/Violet wire) at driver's seat heater switch harness connector C222. If battery voltage does not exist, go to next step. If battery voltage exists, replace driver's seat heater switch.

2) Turn ignition switch to LOCK position. Check fuse No. 28 (10-amp) in instrument panel fuse box. If fuse is blown, go to next step. If fuse is okay, check voltage to fuse No. 28. If battery voltage does not exist, repair voltage supply as necessary. If battery voltage exists, repair open in Light Green/Violet wire.

3) Connect driver's seat heater switch harness connector C222. Measure resistance between ground and output side of fuse No. 28 at instrument panel fuse box. If resistance is 10 k/ohms or less, go to next step. If resistance is greater than 10 k/ohms, repair intermittent short in Light Green/Violet wire.

4) Disconnect driver's seat heater switch harness connector C222. Measure resistance between ground and output side of fuse No. 28 at instrument panel fuse box. If resistance is 10 k/ohms or less, go to next step. If resistance is greater than 10 k/ohms, replace driver's seat heater switch.

5) Disconnect passenger's seat heater switch harness connector C221. Measure resistance between ground and output side of fuse No. 28 at instrument panel fuse box. If resistance is 10 k/ohms or less, repair short to ground in Light Green/Violet wire. If resistance is greater than 10 k/ohms, replace passenger's seat heater switch.

TEST P: DRIVER'S LUMBAR INOPERATIVE

1) Turn ignition switch to LOCK position. Disconnect driver's lumbar switch harness connector C348. Turn ignition switch to RUN position. Measure voltage at terminal No. 3 (Red wire) at driver's lumbar switch harness connector C348. If battery voltage exists, go to next step. If battery voltage does not exist, repair open in Red wire.

2) Measure resistance between ground and terminals No. 1 (Black wire) and No. 5 (Black wire) at driver's lumbar switch harness connector C348. If resistance is 5 ohms or less, go to next step. If resistance is greater than 5 ohms, repair open in appropriate Black wire.

3) Connect driver's lumbar switch harness connector C348. Disconnect driver's lumbar motor harness connector C315. Measure voltage between terminals No. 1 (Pink wire) and No. 2 (Brown wire) at driver's lumbar motor harness connector C315. Operate lumbar switch to OUT position. If battery voltage does not exist, go to next step. If battery voltage exists, replace driver's lumbar motor.

4) Measure resistance between ground and terminal No. 2 (Brown wire) at driver's lumbar motor harness connector C315. If resistance is 5 ohms or less, go to next step. If resistance is greater than 5 ohms, repair open in Brown wire.

5) Ensure driver's lumbar switch is in neutral position. Measure resistance between ground and terminal No. 1 (Pink wire) at driver's lumbar motor harness connector C315. If resistance is 5 ohms or less, replace driver's lumbar switch. If resistance is greater than 5 ohms, repair open in Pink wire.

TEST Q: PASSENGER'S LUMBAR INOPERATIVE

1) Turn ignition switch to LOCK position. Disconnect passenger's lumbar switch harness connector C350. Turn ignition switch to RUN position. Measure voltage at terminal No. 3 (Dark Green wire) at passenger's lumbar switch harness connector C350. If battery voltage exists, go to next step. If battery voltage does not exist, repair open in Dark Green wire.

2) Measure resistance between ground and terminals No. 1 (Black wire) and No. 5 (Black wire) at driver's lumbar switch harness connector C350. If resistance is 5 ohms or less, go to next step. If resistance is greater than 5 ohms, repair open in appropriate Black wire.

3) Connect passenger's lumbar switch harness connector C350. Disconnect passenger's lumbar motor harness connector C314. Measure voltage between terminals No. 1 (Pink wire) and No. 2 (Brown wire) at passenger's lumbar motor harness connector C314. Operate lumbar switch to OUT position. If battery voltage does not exist, go to next step. If battery voltage exists, replace passenger's lumbar motor.

4) Measure resistance between ground and terminal No. 2 (Brown wire) at passenger's lumbar motor harness connector C314. If resistance is 5 ohms or less, go to next step. If resistance is greater than 5 ohms, repair open in Brown wire.

5) Ensure passenger's lumbar switch is in neutral position. Measure resistance between ground and terminal No. 1 (Pink wire) at passenger's lumbar motor harness connector C314. If resistance is 5 ohms or less, replace passenger's lumbar switch. If resistance is greater than 5 ohms, repair open in Pink wire.

TEST R: BATTERY VOLTAGE OUT OF RANGE (DTC B1676)

1) Clear Driver's Seat Module (DSM) DTCs. Using NGS tester, perform DSM self-test. If DTC B2316 was not retrieved, go to next step. If DTC B2316 was retrieved, repair power mirror concern. See POWER MEMORY MIRRORS – CONTINENTAL article.

2) Turn ignition switch to LOCK position. Disconnect DSM harness connector C362. Turn ignition switch to RUN position. Measure voltage at terminal No. 1 (Red wire) at DSM harness connector C362. If 11.5-12.6 volts does not exist, repair charging system as necessary. See appropriate GENERATORS article in STARTING & CHARGING SYSTEMS. If 11.5-12.6 volts exists, repeat DSM self-test. If DTC B1676 is retrieved, replace driver's seat module.

REMOVAL & INSTALLATION

> **WARNING: Vehicle is equipped with an air bag system. To prevent air bag deployment, system must be disabled before working near steering column and instrument cluster. See appropriate AIR BAG RESTRAINT SYSTEMS article.**

> **CAUTION: When battery is disconnected or modules are replaced, vehicle computer and memory systems may lose memory data. Driveability problems may exist until computer systems have completed a relearn cycle. See COMPUTER RELEARN PROCEDURES article in GENERAL INFORMATION before disconnecting battery.**

CONTROL SWITCH

Removal & Installation – 1) Disconnect negative battery cable. Remove screw cover from armrest and remove 2 screws. Using a trim panel removal tool, release trim panel retainers.

2) Pull door trim panel outward. Disconnect wires as necessary. Remove 2 screws retaining seat control switch to door panel. Remove switch. To install, reverse removal procedure.

DRIVER'S DOOR MODULE

Removal & Installation – Remove driver's door trim panel. See CONTROL SWITCH. Disconnect all connectors from module. Remove module from door. To install, reverse removal procedure.

DRIVER'S SEAT MODULE

Removal & Installation – Remove driver's seat. See FRONT SEATS. Remove driver's seat module mounting screws. Disconnect all wiring harnesses from control module. To install, reverse removal procedure.

FRONT SEATS

Removal & Installation – Remove plastic appearance covers from seat track mounting nuts. Remove mounting nuts and washers. Lift seat high enough to disconnect harness connectors. Remove seat. To install, reverse removal procedure.

WIRING DIAGRAMS

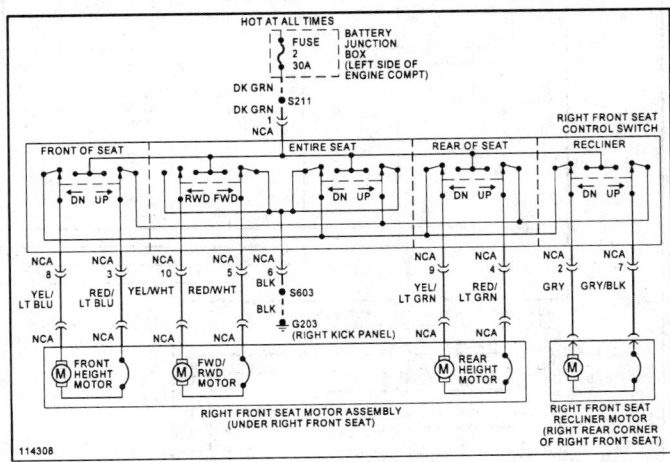

Fig. 15: Passenger's Power Seat System Wiring Diagram (Continental)

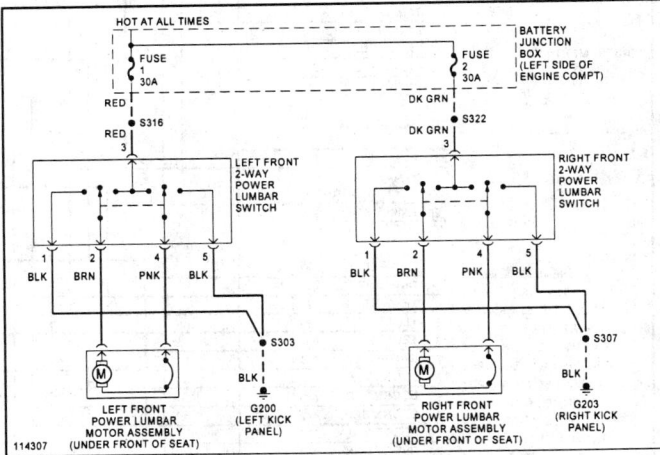

Fig. 16: Power Lumbar Seat System Wiring Diagram (Continental)

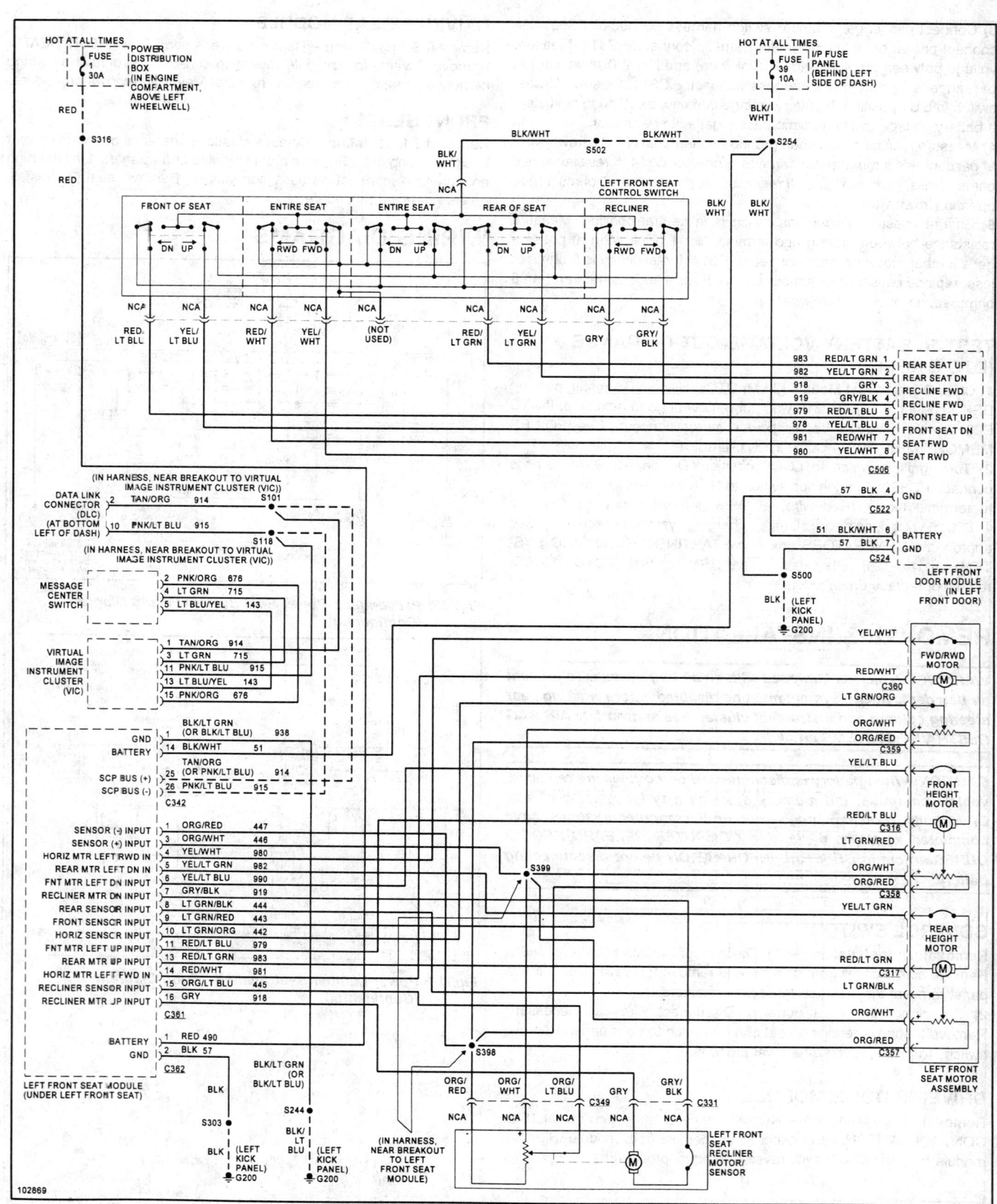

Fig. 17: Power Memory Seat System Wiring Diagram (Continental)

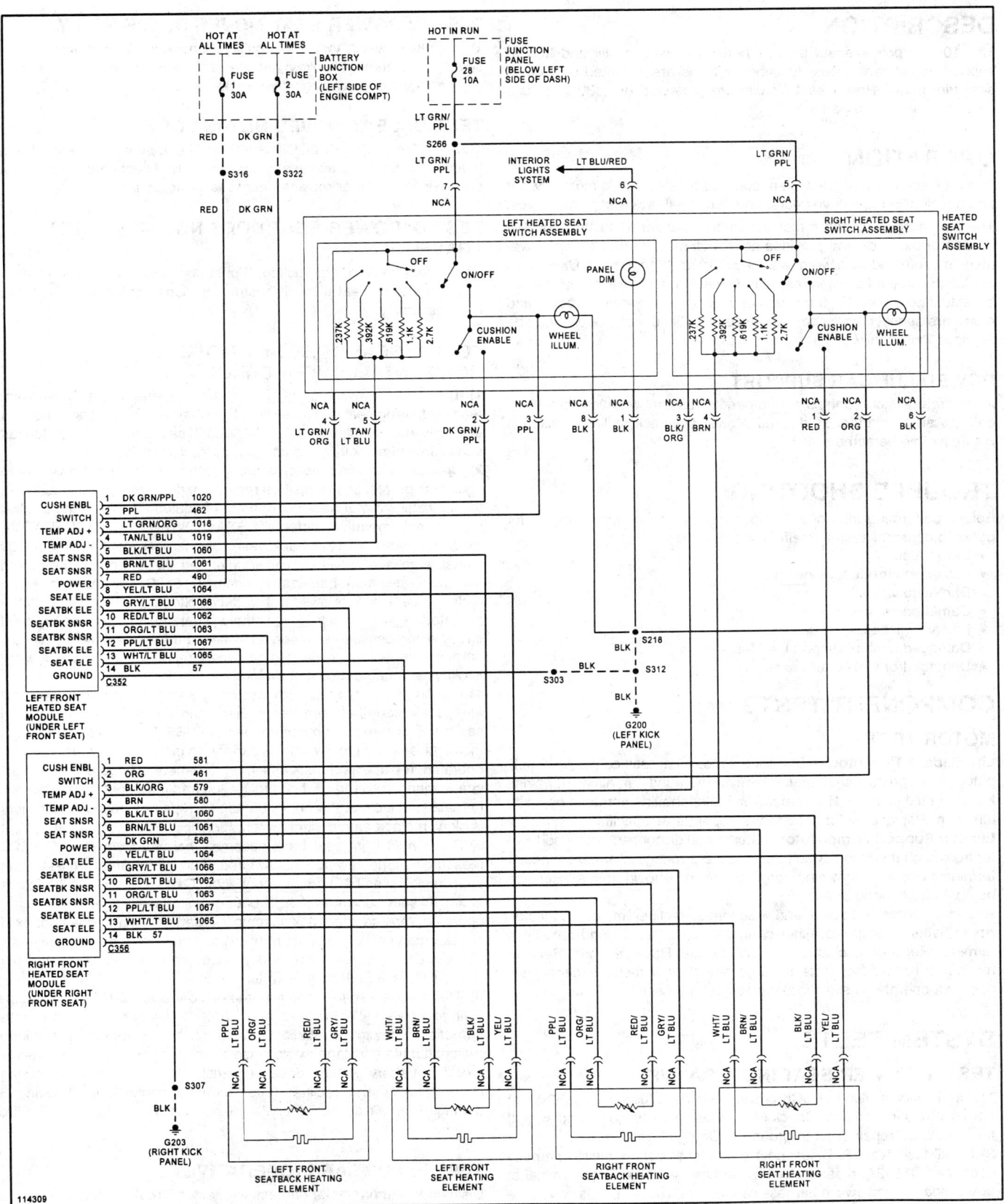

Fig. 18: Heated Seat System Wiring Diagram (Continental)

1999 ACCESSORIES & EQUIPMENT
Power Seats – Contour & Mystique

DESCRIPTION

The 10-way power seats provide horizontal, vertical, tilt and lumbar support adjustments. Seat function switches are mounted on side of seat trim panel. Power seat circuits are protected by a 30-amp fuse located in dash fuse panel.

OPERATION

The rack and pinion drive system consists of a reversible motor, switch and housing, vertical drive gears, and horizontal rack and pinion drives.

The pinion housing and motor assembly is attached to the movable section of the track and provides horizontal movement. Vertical movement is controlled by a worm and sector gear arrangement. Drive units are located at the front and rear of the seat. The tilt function is controlled by actuating either the front or rear sector gear. Pinion housing and motor are serviced as a complete assembly. Other components can be serviced individually.

POWER LUMBAR SUPPORT

A separate switch controls a pump/motor assembly which inflates or deflates an air bladder as desired. Power seatback recline function is controlled by the same switch.

TROUBLE SHOOTING

Before performing individual component test, check the following for possible cause of system malfunction:
- Blown fuse.
- Loose or corroded connectors.
- Damaged wiring.
- Damaged motors.
- Faulty switches.
- Damaged lumbar support bladder.
- Damaged or kinked air hoses.

COMPONENT TESTS

MOTOR TEST

Lift, Slide & Tilt Motors – Disconnect motor harness connector. Apply battery voltage to either motor terminal. Ground remaining terminal. Motor should operate. Reverse leads. Motor should operate in opposite direction. Replace motor if it does not operate as specified.
Lumbar Support Pump/Motor – Locate and disconnect motor connector from lumbar support switch. Apply battery voltage to either connector terminal. Ground remaining terminal. Motor should rotate. Replace pump/motor if inoperative.
Recliner Motor – Locate and disconnect recliner motor connector. Apply battery voltage to either connector terminal. Ground remaining terminal. Recliner mechanism should operate. Reverse leads. Recliner mechanism should operate in other direction. If recliner mechanism does not operate as specified, replace as an assembly.

SYSTEM TESTS

TEST A: POWER SEAT INOPERATIVE

1) Turn ignition switch to LOCK position. Remove fuse No. 28 (30-amp) from central junction box. Check fuse. If fuse is okay, go to next step. If fuse is blown, repair short to ground in Orange/Yellow wire.
2) Install fuse No. 28. Disconnect power seat control switch harness connector C1852A. Measure voltage at Orange/Yellow wire terminal at power seat control switch harness connector C1852A. If battery voltage exists, go to next step. If battery voltage does not exist, repair open in Orange/Yellow wire.
3) Measure resistance between ground and Black wire terminal at power seat control switch harness connector C1852A. If resistance is 5 ohms or less, replace power seat control switch. If resistance is greater than 5 ohms, repair open in Black wire.

TEST B: POWER SEAT MOVES BUT IS NOISY

Turn ignition switch to LOCK position. Check seat track alignment. If seat track alignment is okay, replace seat track assembly. If seat track alignment is not okay, align seat track.

TEST C: SEAT MOVES BUT IS LOOSE

Turn ignition switch to LOCK position. Check seat hardware. If seat hardware is tight, replace seat track assembly. If seat hardware is loose or missing, tighten or replace hardware as necessary.

TEST D: POWER SEAT DOES NOT MAKE FULL TRAVEL

Check seat track for obstruction. If obstruction exists, remove obstruction and grease seat track. If obstruction does not exist, replace seat track assembly.

TEST E: SEAT DOES NOT MOVE HORIZONTALLY/VERTICALLY

1) Turn ignition switch to LOCK position. Operate seat forward and rearward, using seat control switch. If seat moves forward and rearward smoothly and completely, go to next step. If seat does not move forward and rearward smoothly and completely, go to step **5)**.
2) Operate seat tilting movement at seat control switch. If front motor does not operate, go to step **4)**. If rear motor does not operate, go to next step. If recline motor does not operate (if equipped), go to step **6)** . If all motors are inoperative, perform TEST A: POWER SEAT INOPERATIVE.
3) Disconnect front seat track assembly harness connector C1852D. Measure voltage between Yellow/Violet and White/Violet wires at front seat track assembly harness connector C1852D. Operate rear height motor at seat control switch. If battery voltage exists when switch is operated, replace seat track assembly. If battery voltage does not exist, check wiring between seat control switch and front seat track assembly harness connectors. If wiring is damaged, repair as necessary. If wiring is okay, replace seat control switch.
4) Disconnect front seat track assembly harness connector C1852D. Measure voltage between Yellow/Black and White/Black wires at front seat track assembly harness connector C1852D. Operate front height motor at seat control switch. If battery voltage exists when switch is operated, replace seat track assembly. If battery voltage does not exist, check wiring between seat control switch and front seat track assembly harness connectors. If wiring is damaged, repair as necessary. If wiring is okay, replace seat control switch.
5) Disconnect front seat track assembly harness connector C1852D. Measure voltage between Yellow/Green and White/Green wires at front seat track assembly harness connector C1852D. Operate horizontal motor at seat control switch. If battery voltage exists when switch is operated, replace seat track assembly. If battery voltage does not exist, check wiring between seat control switch and front seat track assembly harness connectors. If wiring is damaged, repair as necessary. If wiring is okay, replace seat control switch.
6) Disconnect recline motor harness connector C1852B. Measure voltage between Yellow/Red and White/Red wires at recline motor harness connector C1852B. Operate recline motor at seat control switch. If battery voltage exists when switch is operated, replace recline motor. If battery voltage does not exist, check wiring between seat control switch and recline motor harness connectors. If wiring is damaged, repair as necessary. If wiring is okay, replace seat control switch.

TEST F: LUMBAR INOPERATIVE

Disconnect lumbar motor harness connector C1852C. Measure voltage between Yellow/Blue and White/Blue wires at lumbar motor harness connector C1852C. Operate lumbar motor at seat control switch. If battery voltage exists when switch is operated, replace lumbar motor. If battery voltage does not exist, check wiring between seat control switch and lumbar motor harness connectors. If wiring is damaged, repair as necessary. If wiring is okay, replace seat control switch.

REMOVAL & INSTALLATION

CAUTION: When battery is disconnected, vehicle computer and memory systems may lose memory data. Driveability problems may exist until computer systems have completed a relearn cycle. See COMPUTER RELEARN PROCEDURES article in GENERAL INFORMATION before disconnecting battery.

POWER SEAT SWITCH

Removal & Installation – Disconnect negative battery cable. Remove seat cushion side shield. Unplug switch harness connector and lumbar support hoses. Remove 2 screws securing power seat switch. Remove switch. *See Fig. 1.* To install, reverse removal procedure.

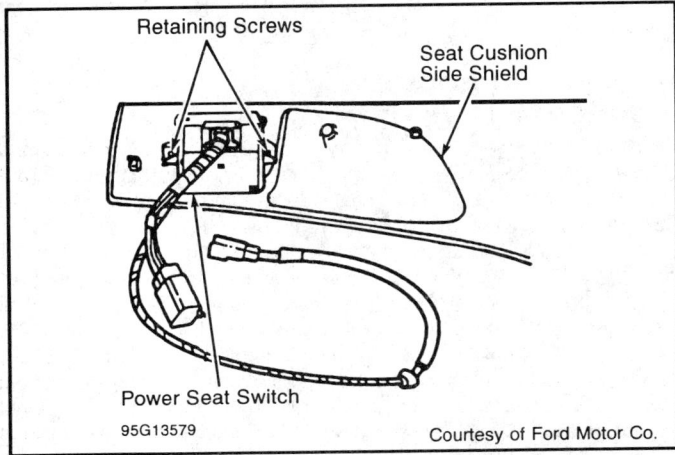

95G13579   Courtesy of Ford Motor Co.

Fig. 1: Removing Power Seat Switch

SEAT ASSEMBLY

Removal & Installation – 1) Disconnect negative battery cable. Remove seat side shields. Remove bolt securing seat belt retractor and tongue to seat frame. Slide seat belt upward from behind seat. Position seat fully forward.

2) Remove screws retaining seat track rear shields. Remove rear seat track shields. Remove 4 bolts retaining seat tracks to floorpan.

3) Position seat fully rearward. Remove 2 bolts retaining seat tracks to floorpan. Lift seat slightly and disconnect harness connectors. Remove seat assembly. To install, reverse removal procedure.

SEAT CUSHION

Removal & Installation – 1) Remove seat and track assembly. See SEAT ASSEMBLY. Remove screws from left-side shield. Carefully disconnect and tag air hoses from lumbar support switch. Disconnect switch-to-motor connector. Remove left-side shield. Remove remaining shields.

2) Remove hog rings securing lower portion of seatback cover. Slide seatback cover up enough to remove seatback frame bolts. Remove seatback. Disconnect air line from lumbar bladder. Remove hog rings securing cover rods to seat frame. Remove cover and cushion. To install, reverse removal procedure.

POWER SEAT MOTOR

Removal & Installation – Seat motor removal and installation procedures are not available from manufacturer.

RECLINER MOTOR

Removal & Installation – Disconnect negative battery cable. Remove seat assembly. See SEAT ASSEMBLY. Remove hog rings. Pull back seat cushion cover and pad. Remove screws retaining front seatback cover and pad. Remove recliner motor. *See Fig. 2.* To install, reverse removal procedure.

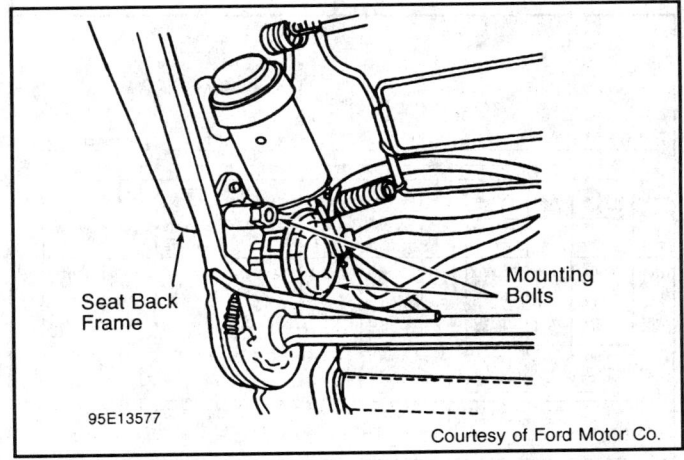

95E13577   Courtesy of Ford Motor Co.

Fig. 2: Removing Recliner Motor

LUMBAR SUPPORT PUMP/MOTOR ASSEMBLY

Removal & Installation – Disconnect negative battery cable. Remove seat and track assembly. See SEAT ASSEMBLY. Remove seat cushion. See SEAT CUSHION. Remove pump/motor mounting screws. Disconnect electrical connector and inflation tube. Remove pump/motor assembly. To install, reverse removal procedure.

LUMBAR SUPPORT AIR BLADDER

Removal & Installation – Remove seat and track assembly. See SEAT ASSEMBLY. Remove seat cushion. See SEAT CUSHION. Remove lumbar support bladder inflation tube. Remove seatback trim cover and pad. Remove 2 hog rings retaining lumbar support bladder to seatback frame. Remove bladder from seatback frame. To install, reverse removal procedure.

WIRING DIAGRAMS

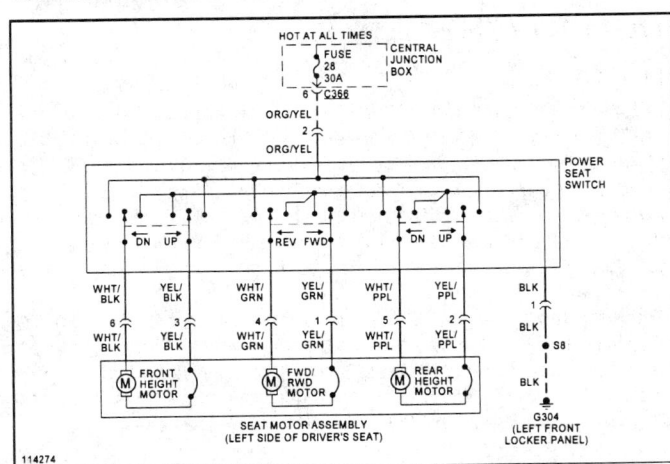

Fig. 3: 6-Way Power Seat System Wiring Diagram (Contour & Mystique)

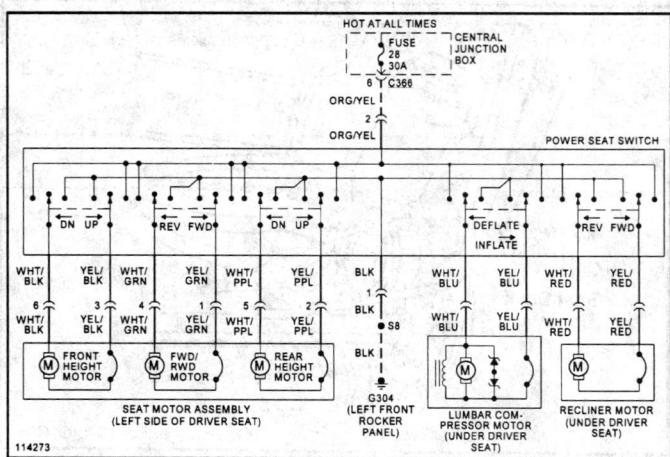

**Fig. 4: 10-Way Power Seat System Wiring Diagram
(Contour & Mystique)**

DESCRIPTION & OPERATION

Vehicle may be equipped with seat that manually adjust forward/rearward with an electrical height adjustment or equipped with 8-way power seats. 8-way power seats provide horizontal, vertical, backrest and lumbar support adjustments. Seat function switches are mounted on front side of seat trim panel. Power seat circuits are protected by fuse No. 28 (30-amp) in instrument panel fuse box.

TROUBLE SHOOTING

Verify customer complaint by operating power seat system. Visually inspect for blown fuse, loose or corroded connectors, damaged wiring, damaged motors, faulty switches, damaged lumbar support bladder and damaged or kinked air hoses. If problem exists, repair as necessary. If no problem is found, repair by symptom, see SYMPTOM CHART under SYSTEM TESTS.

COMPONENT TESTS

POWER SEAT CONTROL SWITCH

8-Way Power Seat Control Switch – Disconnect power seat control switch harness connector (remove power seat control switch if necessary). Check continuity between power seat control switch terminals with switch in appropriate position. See 8-WAY POWER SEAT CONTROL SWITCH CONTINUITY table. *See Fig. 1.* If continuity is not as specified, replace power seat control switch.

8-WAY POWER SEAT CONTROL SWITCH CONTINUITY

Switch Position	Continuity Between Terminals
Backrest	
Forward	A & C; B & D
Neutral	B, C & D
Rearward	A & B; C & D
Lumbar	
Deflate	A & F; E & D
Inflate	A & E; D & F
Neutral	D, E & F
Forward/Rearward	
Forward	A & H; D & G
Neutral	d, g & h
Rearward	A & G; D & H
Front Height	
Front Down	A & I; D & K
Front Up	A & K; D & I
Neutral	D, I & K

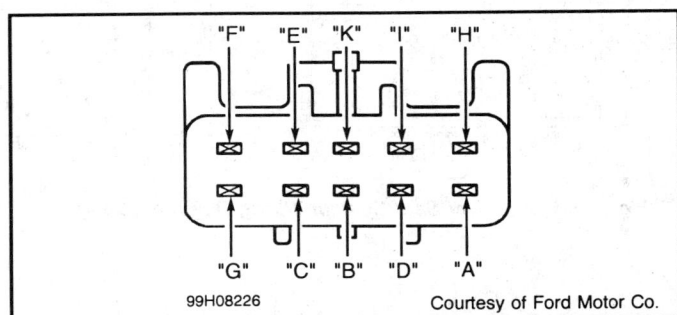

Fig. 1: Identifying 8-Way Power Seat Control Switch Terminals

99H08226   Courtesy of Ford Motor Co.

2-Way Power Seat Control Switch – Disconnect power seat control switch harness connector (remove power seat control switch if necessary). Check continuity between power seat control switch terminals with switch in appropriate position. See 2-WAY POWER SEAT CONTROL SWITCH CONTINUITY table. *See Fig. 2.* If continuity is not as specified, replace power seat control switch.

2-WAY POWER SEAT CONTROL SWITCH CONTINUITY

Switch Position	Continuity Between Terminals
Down	1 & 6; 2 & 7
Neutral	1 & 6; 3 & 7
Up	1 & 2; 3 & 7

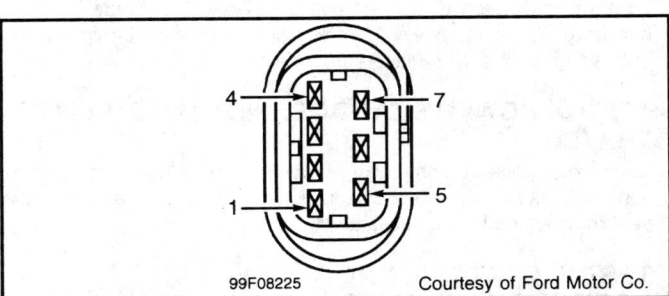

99F08225   Courtesy of Ford Motor Co.

Fig. 2: Identifying 2-Way Power Seat Control Switch Terminals

SYSTEM TESTS

SYMPTOM CHART

Symptom	Test
Power Seat Inoperative	A
Power Seat Moves But Is Noisy	B
Seat Moves But Is Loose	C
Power Seat Does Not Make Full Travel	D
Seat Does Not Move Horizontally/Vertically [1]	E

[1] – Test only applies to vehicles with 8-way power seats.

TEST A: POWER SEAT INOPERATIVE

1) Turn ignition switch to LOCK position. Remove fuse No. 28 (30-amp) from instrument panel fuse box. Inspect fuse. If fuse is okay, go to next step. If fuse is blown, repair short to ground in Orange/Yellow wire.

2) Measure voltage at input side of fuse No. 28 in instrument panel fuse box. If battery voltage exists, go to next step. If battery voltage does not exist, repair power distribution circuit as necessary. See appropriate wiring diagram in POWER DISTRIBUTION article in WIRING DIAGRAMS.

3) Install fuse No. 28. Disconnect power seat control switch harness connector. Measure voltage at Orange/Yellow wire terminal at power seat control switch harness connector. If battery voltage exists, go to next step. If battery voltage does not exist, repair open in Orange/Yellow wire.

4) Measure resistance between ground and Black wire terminal(s) at power seat control switch harness connector. If resistance is 5 ohms or less and vehicle is equipped with 2-way power seats, go to next step. If resistance is 5 ohms or less and vehicle is equipped with 8-way power seats, replace power seat control switch. If resistance is greater than 5 ohms, repair open in Black wire.

5) Connect power seat control switch harness connector. Disconnect power seat motor harness connector. Measure voltage between Yellow/Black wire and White/Black wire terminals at power seat motor harness connector while operating power seat control switch to UP and DOWN positions. If battery voltage does not exist with opposite polarity, go to next step. If battery voltage exists with opposite polarity, replace power seat motor.

6) Disconnect power seat control switch harness connector. Measure resistance in Yellow/Black wire between power seat control switch harness connector and power seat motor harness connector. Also, measure resistance in White/Black wire between power seat control switch harness connector and power seat motor harness connector. If both resistance readings are 5 ohms or less, replace power seat control switch. If either resistance reading is greater than 5 ohms, repair open in appropriate wire.

TEST B: POWER SEAT MOVES BUT IS NOISY

Turn ignition switch to LOCK position. Check seat track alignment. If seat track alignment is okay, replace seat track assembly. If seat track alignment is not okay, align seat track.

TEST C: SEAT MOVES BUT IS LOOSE

Turn ignition switch to LOCK position. Check seat hardware. If seat hardware is tight, replace seat track assembly. If seat hardware is loose or missing, tighten or replace hardware as necessary.

TEST D: POWER SEAT DOES NOT MAKE FULL TRAVEL

Check seat track for obstruction. If obstruction exists, remove obstruction and grease seat track. If obstruction does not exist, repair or replace seat track assembly as necessary.

TEST E: SEAT DOES NOT MOVE HORIZONTALLY/VERTICALLY

NOTE: This test only applies to vehicles with 8-way power seats.

1) Turn ignition switch to LOCK position. Operate seat forward and rearward, using power seat control switch. If seat moves forward and rearward smoothly and completely, go to next step. If seat does not move forward and rearward smoothly and completely, go to step **5)**.

2) Operate backrest movement using power seat control switch. If backrest moves forward and rearward smoothly and completely, go to next step. If backrest does not move forward and rearward smoothly and completely, go to step **7)**.

3) Disconnect seat height motor harness connector. Measure voltage between Yellow/Black wire and White/Black wire terminals at seat height motor harness connector while operating power seat control switch to seat UP and DOWN positions. If battery voltage does not exist with opposite polarity, go to next step. If battery voltage exists with opposite polarity, replace seat height motor assembly.

4) Disconnect power seat control switch harness connector. Measure resistance in Yellow/Black wire between power seat control switch harness connector and seat height motor harness connector. Also, measure resistance in White/Black wire between power seat control switch harness connector and seat height motor harness connector. If both resistance readings are 5 ohms or less, replace power seat control switch. If either resistance reading is greater than 5 ohms, repair open in appropriate wire.

5) Disconnect forward/rearward motor harness connector. Measure voltage between Yellow/Green wire and White/Green wire terminals at forward/rearward motor harness connector while operating power seat control switch to seat FORWARD and REARWARD positions. If battery voltage does not exist with opposite polarity, go to next step. If battery voltage exists with opposite polarity, replace seat forward/rearward motor assembly.

6) Disconnect power seat control switch harness connector. Measure resistance in Yellow/Green wire between power seat control switch harness connector and seat forward/rearward motor harness connector. Also, measure resistance in White/Black wire between power seat control switch harness connector and seat forward/rearward motor harness connector. If both resistance readings are 5 ohms or less, replace power seat control switch. If either resistance reading is greater than 5 ohms, repair open in appropriate wire.

7) Disconnect backrest motor harness connector. Measure voltage between Yellow/Red wire and White/Red wire terminals at backrest motor harness connector while operating power seat control switch to backrest FORWARD and REARWARD positions. If battery voltage does not exist with opposite polarity, go to next step. If battery voltage exists with opposite polarity, replace seat backrest motor assembly.

8) Disconnect power seat control switch harness connector. Measure resistance in Yellow/Red wire between power seat control switch harness connector and seat backrest motor harness connector. Also, measure resistance in White/Red wire between power seat control switch harness connector and seat backrest motor harness connector. If

both resistance readings are 5 ohms or less, replace power seat control switch. If either resistance reading is greater than 5 ohms, repair open in appropriate wire.

TEST F: LUMBAR INOPERATIVE

1) Disconnect lumbar motor harness connector. Measure voltage between Yellow/Blue wire and White/Blue wire terminals at lumbar motor harness connector while operating power seat control switch to lumbar INFLATE and DEFLATE positions. If battery voltage does not exist with opposite polarity, go to next step. If battery voltage exists with opposite polarity, replace seat lumbar assembly.

2) Disconnect power seat control switch harness connector. Measure resistance in Yellow/Blue wire between power seat control switch harness connector and seat lumbar motor harness connector. Also, measure resistance in White/Blue wire between power seat control switch harness connector and seat lumbar motor harness connector. If both resistance readings are 5 ohms or less, replace power seat control switch. If either resistance reading is greater than 5 ohms, repair open in appropriate wire.

REMOVAL & INSTALLATION

CAUTION: When battery is disconnected, vehicle computer and memory systems may lose memory data. Driveability problems may exist until computer systems have completed a relearn cycle. See COMPUTER RELEARN PROCEDURES article in GENERAL INFORMATION before disconnecting battery.

POWER SEAT CONTROL SWITCH

Removal & Installation – Disconnect negative battery cable. Remove front seat assembly. Remove seat cushion side shield. Disconnect power seat control switch harness connector. Using trim tool, remove control knobs. Remove 2 screws securing power seat control switch. Remove switch. To install, reverse removal procedure.

WIRING DIAGRAMS

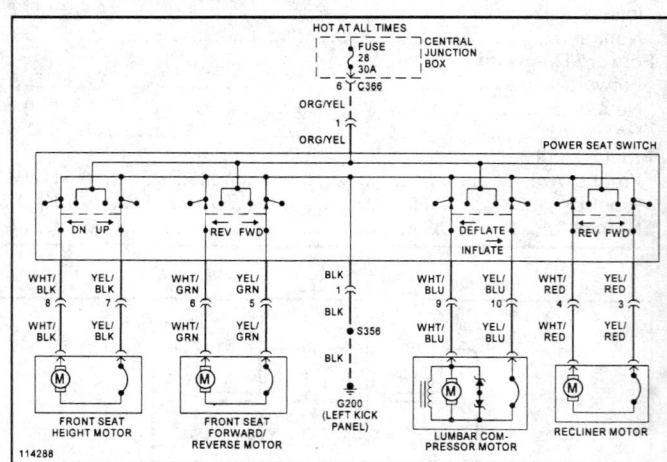

Fig. 3: 8-Way Power Seat System Wiring Diagram (Cougar)

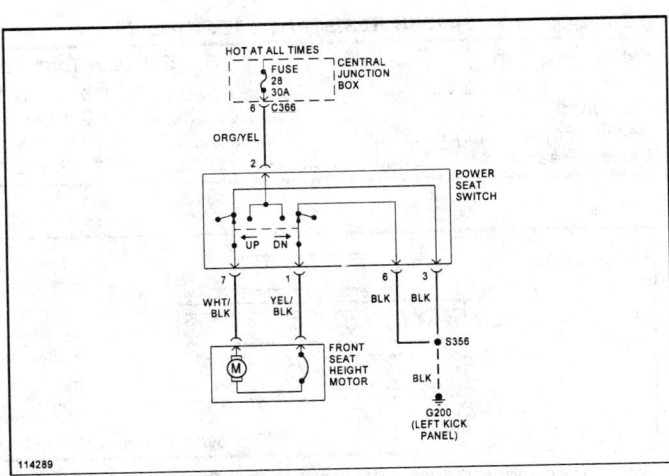

Fig. 4: Seat Height Adjuster System Wiring Diagram (Cougar)

1999 ACCESSORIES & EQUIPMENT
Power Seats – Crown Victoria & Grand Marquis

DESCRIPTION & OPERATION

The power seats provide horizontal, vertical, recline and tilt adjustments. Seat control switches are mounted on the side of the seat trim panel. Power seat circuits are protected by a circuit breaker. A lumbar support pad can be inflated by a separate pump, controlled by a switch.

Major components of the power seat system are the motor and drive assembly, control switches, lumbar support bladder and lumbar compressor. A separate motor and drive mechanism provides recline adjustment. Seat motors and associated drive mechanisms are serviced as a complete assembly.

TROUBLE SHOOTING

Verify the customer complaint by operating power seat. Visually inspect for obvious sign of mechanical and electrical damage. Check for blown fuses or faulty circuit breakers, loose or corroded connectors, damaged wiring, damaged motors, faulty switches, damaged lumbar support bladder and damaged or kinked air hoses. If no visual damage is evident, perform appropriate system test. See SYMPTOM CHART table under SYSTEM TESTS.

COMPONENT TESTS

SEAT CONTROL SWITCH

Driver's (Without Power Passenger's Seat) – Remove seat control switch. Measure resistance between appropriate seat control switch terminals with seat control switch in appropriate position. See DRIVER'S SEAT CONTROL SWITCH RESISTANCE TEST table. *See Fig. 1.* If any resistance reading is greater than 5 ohms, replace seat control switch.

DRIVER'S SEAT CONTROL SWITCH RESISTANCE TEST

Switch Position	Between Terminals
Neutral	1 & All Other Except 3
Front Down	1 & 7; 3 & 5
Front Up	1 & 5; 3 & 7
Rear Down	1 & 4; 3 & 6
Rear Up	1 & 6; 3 & 4
Forward	1 & 8; 2 & 3
Rearward	1 & 2; 3 & 8

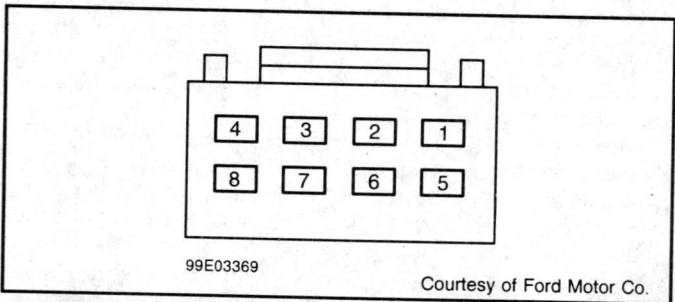

99E03369

Courtesy of Ford Motor Co.

Fig. 1: Identifying Driver's Seat Control Switch Terminal (Without Power Passenger's Seat)

Driver's (With Power Passenger's Seat) & Passenger's – Remove seat control switch. Measure resistance between appropriate seat control switch terminals with seat control switch in appropriate position. See SEAT CONTROL SWITCH RESISTANCE TEST table. *See Fig. 2.* If any resistance reading is greater than 5 ohms, replace seat control switch.

SEAT CONTROL SWITCH RESISTANCE TEST

Switch Position	Between Terminals
Neutral	12 & All Other Except 6
Front Down	3 & 12; 6 & 9
Front Up	3 & 6; 9 & 12
Rear Down	2 & 12; 6 & 8
Rear Up	2 & 6; 8 & 12

SEAT CONTROL SWITCH RESISTANCE TEST (Cont.)

Switch Position	Between Terminals
Forward	1 & 6; 7 & 12
Rearward	1 & 12; 6 & 7
Recline Forward	5 & 6; 11 & 12
Recline Rearward	5 & 12; 6 & 11

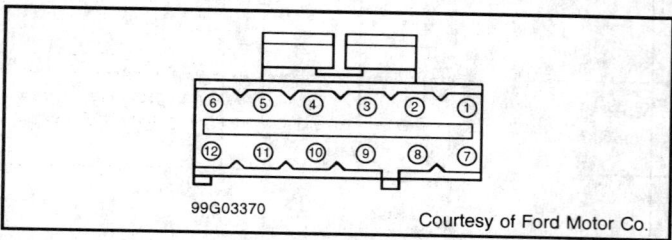

99G03370

Courtesy of Ford Motor Co.

Fig. 2: Identifying Driver's (Without Power Passenger's Seat) & Passenger's Seat Control Switch Terminal

SYSTEM TESTS

SYMPTOM CHART

Symptom	Test
Power Seat Completely Inoperative	A
Driver's Seat Forward/Rearward Function Does Not Work Properly (Without Power Passenger's Seat)	B
Driver's Seat Forward/Rearward Function Does Not Work Properly (With Power Passenger's Seat)	C
Passenger's Seat Forward/Rearward Function Does Not Work Properly	D
Driver's Seat Does Not Recline	E
Passenger's Seat Does Not Recline	F
Lumbar Support Function Does Not Work Properly	G

TEST A: POWER SEAT COMPLETELY INOPERATIVE

1) Operate inoperative power seat in all directions. If power seat moves in at least one direction, repair seat by symptom. See SYMPTOM CHART table. If power seat is completely inoperative, go to next step if not equipped with power passenger's seat or go to step 3) if equipped with power passenger's seat.

2) Disconnect driver's power seat control switch harness connector C327. Measure voltage at terminal No. 8 (Black/White wire) at driver's power seat control switch harness connector C327. *See Fig. 3.* If battery voltage does not exist, go to step 4). If battery voltage exists, go to step 6).

3) Disconnect appropriate power seat control switch harness connector. Measure voltage at terminal No. 6 (Black/Wire wire) at power seat control switch harness connector. *See Fig. 4.* If battery voltage does not exist, go to next step. If battery voltage exists, go to step 7).

4) Operate power door locks. If power door locks do not operate, go to next step. If power door locks operate, repair open in Black/White wire.

5) Remove circuit breaker No. 7 (20-amp) from power distribution box. Measure voltage at input side of circuit breaker No. 7 in power distribution box. If battery voltage exists, repair open in Black/White wire. If battery voltage does not exist, repair power distribution circuit. See appropriate wiring diagram in POWER DISTRIBUTION article in WIRING DIAGRAMS.

6) Measure resistance between ground and terminal No. 5 (Black wire) at driver's power seat control switch harness connector C327. If resistance is 5 ohms or less, go to step 8). If resistance is greater than 5 ohms, repair open in Black wire.

7) Measure resistance between ground and terminal No. 12 (Black wire) at power seat control switch harness connector. If resistance is 5 ohms or less, go to step 8). If resistance is greater than 5 ohms, repair open in Black wire.

8) Inspect seat track for damage or obstructions. If seat track is okay, replace appropriate seat control switch. If seat track is damage or obstructed, repair or replace seat track assembly as necessary.

1999 ACCESSORIES & EQUIPMENT
Power Seats – Crown Victoria & Grand Marquis (Cont.)

FORD
4-1019

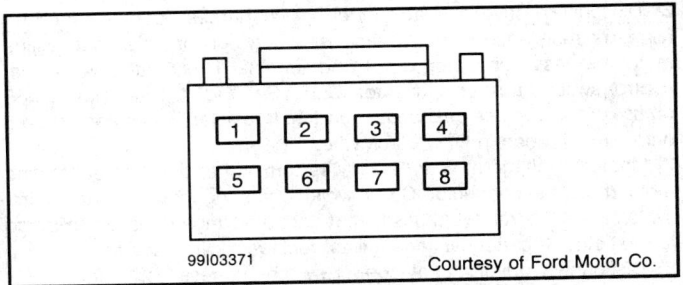

Fig. 3: Identifying Driver's Power Seat Control Switch Harness Connector C327 Terminals (Without Passenger's Power Seat)

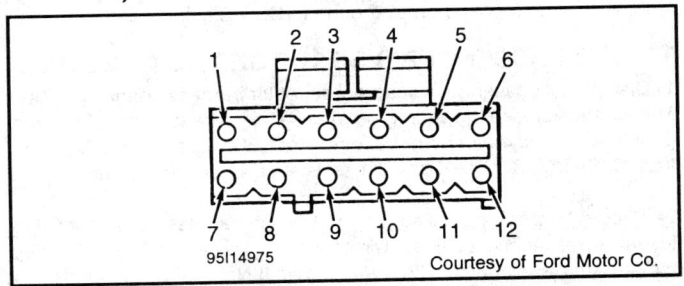

Fig. 4: Identifying Driver's & Passenger's Power Seat Control Switch Harness Connector Terminals (With Passenger's Power Seat)

TEST B: DRIVER'S SEAT FORWARD/REARWARD FUNCTION DOES NOT WORK PROPERLY (WITHOUT POWER PASSENGER'S SEAT)

1) Disconnect driver's seat motor harness connector C325. Measure voltage at appropriate terminal at driver's seat motor harness connector C325 while operating driver's power seat switch in appropriate direction. See SEAT MOTOR VOLTAGE SUPPLY table. *See Fig. 5.* If battery voltage exists at all terminals, go to next step. If battery voltage does not exist at all terminals, go to step 3).

SEAT MOTOR VOLTAGE SUPPLY

Terminal No. (Wire Color)	Switch Position
1 (Red/Light Green)	Rearward
2 (Red/Light Blue)	Rear Up
3 (Yellow/White)	Rear Down
4 (Red/White)	Forward
5 (Yellow/Light Green)	Front Down
6 (Yellow/Light Blue)	Front Up

2) Measure resistance between ground and all terminals at driver's seat motor harness connector C325. If all resistance readings are 5 ohms or less, replace seat track assembly. If any resistance reading is greater than 5 ohms, replace seat control switch.
3) Disconnect driver's seat control switch harness connector C327. Measure resistance between ground and all terminals at driver's seat motor harness connector C325. If all resistance readings are greater than 10 k/ohms, go to next step. If any resistance reading is 10 k/ohms or less, repair short to ground in appropriate wire.
4) Measure resistance in all wires between driver's seat control switch harness connector C327 and driver's seat motor harness connector C325. See DRIVER'S SEAT CIRCUIT RESISTANCE table. *See Figs. 3 and 5.* If all resistance readings are 5 ohms or less, replace seat control switch. If any resistance reading is greater than 5 ohms, repair open in appropriate wire.

DRIVER'S SEAT CIRCUIT RESISTANCE

Motor Terminal (Wire Color)	Switch Terminal	Switch Position
1 (Red/Light Green)	2	Rearward
2 (Red/Light Blue)	4	Rear Up

DRIVER'S SEAT CIRCUIT RESISTANCE (Cont.)

Motor Terminal (Wire Color)	Switch Terminal	Switch Position
3 (Yellow/White)	6	Rear Down
4 (Red/White)	8	Forward
5 (Yellow/Light Green)	5	Front Down
6 (Yellow/Light Blue)	7	Front Up

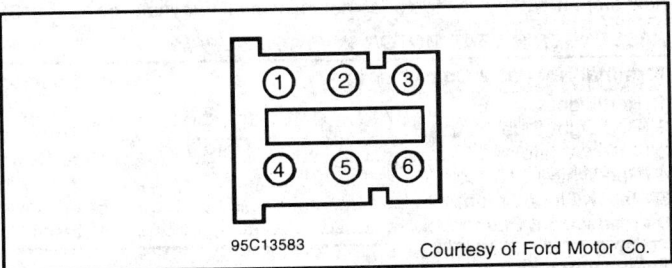

Fig. 5: Identifying Power Seat Motor Harness Connector Terminals

TEST C: DRIVER'S SEAT FORWARD/REARWARD FUNCTION DOES NOT WORK PROPERLY (WITH POWER PASSENGER'S SEAT)

1) Disconnect driver's seat motor harness connector C325. Measure voltage at appropriate terminal at driver's seat motor harness connector C325 while operating driver's power seat switch in appropriate direction. See DRIVER'S SEAT MOTOR VOLTAGE SUPPLY table. *See Fig. 5.* If battery voltage exists at all terminals, go to next step. If battery voltage does not exist at all terminals, go to step 3).

DRIVER'S SEAT MOTOR VOLTAGE SUPPLY

Terminal No. (Wire Color)	Switch Position
1 (Yellow/White)	Rearward
2 (Red/Light Green)	Rear Up
3 (Yellow/Light Green)	Rear Down
4 (Red/White)	Forward
5 (Yellow/Light Blue)	Front Down
6 (Red/Light Blue)	Front Up

2) Measure resistance between ground and all terminals at driver's seat motor harness connector C325. If all resistance readings are 5 ohms or less, replace seat track assembly. If any resistance reading is greater than 5 ohms, replace seat control switch.
3) Disconnect driver's seat control switch harness connector C516. Measure resistance between ground and all terminals at driver's seat motor harness connector C325. If all resistance readings are greater than 10 k/ohms, go to next step. If any resistance reading is 10 k/ohms or less, repair short to ground in appropriate wire.
4) Measure resistance in all wires between driver's seat control switch harness connector C516 and driver's seat motor harness connector C325. See DRIVER'S SEAT CIRCUIT RESISTANCE table. *See Figs. 4 and 5.* If all resistance readings are 5 ohms or less, replace seat control switch. If any resistance reading is greater than 5 ohms, repair open in appropriate wire.

DRIVER'S SEAT CIRCUIT RESISTANCE

Motor Terminal No. (Wire Color)	Switch Terminal	Switch Position
1 (Yellow/White)	7	Rearward
2 (Red/Light Green)	2	Rear Up
3 (Yellow/Light Green)	8	Rear Down
4 (Red/White)	1	Forward
5 (Yellow/Light Blue)	9	Front Down
6 (Red/Light Blue)	3	Front Up

FORD
4-1020

1999 ACCESSORIES & EQUIPMENT
Power Seats – Crown Victoria & Grand Marquis (Cont.)

TEST D: PASSENGER'S SEAT FORWARD/REARWARD FUNCTION DOES NOT WORK PROPERLY

1) Disconnect passenger's seat motor harness connector C326. Measure voltage at appropriate terminal at passenger's seat motor harness connector C326 while operating passenger's power seat switch in appropriate direction. See PASSENGER'S SEAT MOTOR VOLTAGE SUPPLY table. *See Fig. 5.* If battery voltage exists at all terminals, go to next step. If battery voltage does not exist at all terminals, go to step 3).

PASSENGER'S SEAT MOTOR VOLTAGE SUPPLY

Terminal No. (Wire Color)	Switch Position
1 (Red/Light Green)	Rearward
2 (Red/Light Blue)	Rear Up
3 (Yellow/White)	Rear Down
4 (Red/White)	Forward
5 (Yellow/Light Green)	Front Down
6 (Yellow/Light Blue)	Front Up

2) Measure resistance between ground and all terminals at passenger's seat motor harness connector C326. If all resistance readings are 5 ohms or less, replace seat track assembly. If any resistance reading is greater than 5 ohms, replace seat control switch.

3) Disconnect passenger's seat control switch harness connector C616. Measure resistance between ground and all terminals at passenger's seat motor harness connector C326. If all resistance readings are greater than 10 k/ohms, go to next step. If any resistance reading is 10 k/ohms or less, repair short to ground in appropriate wire.

4) Measure resistance in all wires between passenger's seat control switch harness connector C616 and passenger's seat motor harness connector C326. See PASSENGER'S SEAT CIRCUIT RESISTANCE table. *See Figs. 3 and 5.* If all resistance readings are 5 ohms or less, replace seat control switch. If any resistance reading is greater than 5 ohms, repair open in appropriate wire.

PASSENGER'S SEAT CIRCUIT RESISTANCE

Motor Terminal No. (Wire Color)	Switch Terminal	Switch Position
1 (Red/Light Green)	2	Rearward
2 (Red/Light Blue)	4	Rear Up
3 (Yellow/White)	6	Rear Down
4 (Red/White)	8	Forward
5 (Yellow/Light Green)	5	Front Down
6 (Yellow/Light Blue)	7	Front Up

TEST E: DRIVER'S SEAT DOES NOT RECLINE

1) Disconnect driver's seat recline motor harness connector C329. Measure resistance between ground and Gray wire terminal at driver's seat recline motor harness connector C329. If resistance is greater than 5 ohms, go to next step. If resistance is 5 ohms or less, go to step 3).

2) Disconnect driver's seat control switch harness connector C516. Measure resistance in Gray wire between driver's seat recline motor harness connector C329 and terminal No. 5 at driver's seat control switch harness connector C516. *See Fig. 4.* If resistance is 5 ohms or less, replace seat control switch. If resistance is greater than 5 ohms, repair open in Gray wire.

3) Measure voltage at Gray wire terminal at driver's seat recline motor harness connector C329 while operating power seat control switch to recline forward position. If battery voltage does not exist, go to next step. If battery voltage exists, go to step 5).

4) Disconnect driver's seat control switch harness connector C516. Measure resistance between ground and Gray wire terminal at driver's seat recline motor harness connector C329. If resistance is greater than 10 k/ohms, replace seat control switch. If resistance is 10 k/ohms or less, repair short to ground in Gray wire.

5) Measure resistance between ground and Gray/Black wire terminal at driver's seat recline motor harness connector C329. If resistance is greater than 5 ohms, go to next step. If resistance is 5 ohms or less, go to step 7).

6) Disconnect driver's seat control switch harness connector C516. Measure resistance in Gray/Black wire between driver's seat recline motor harness connector C329 and terminal No. 5 at driver's seat control switch harness connector C516. *See Fig. 4.* If resistance is 5 ohms or less, replace seat control switch. If resistance is greater than 5 ohms, repair open in Gray/Black wire.

7) Measure voltage at Gray/Black wire terminal at driver's seat recline motor harness connector C329 while operating power seat control switch to recline rearward position. If battery voltage does not exist, go to next step. If battery voltage exists, replace recline motor.

8) Disconnect driver's seat control switch harness connector C516. Measure resistance between ground and Gray/Black wire terminal at driver's seat recline motor harness connector C329. If resistance is greater than 10 k/ohms, replace seat control switch. If resistance is 10 k/ohms or less, repair short to ground in Gray/Black wire.

TEST F: PASSENGER'S SEAT DOES NOT RECLINE

1) Disconnect passenger's seat recline motor harness connector C300. Measure resistance between ground and Gray wire terminal at passenger's seat recline motor harness connector C300. If resistance is greater than 5 ohms, go to next step. If resistance is 5 ohms or less, go to step 3).

2) Disconnect passenger's seat control switch harness connector C616. Measure resistance in Gray wire between passenger's seat recline motor harness connector C300 and terminal No. 5 at passenger's seat control switch harness connector C616. *See Fig. 4.* If resistance is 5 ohms or less, replace seat control switch. If resistance is greater than 5 ohms, repair open in Gray wire.

3) Measure voltage at Gray wire terminal at passenger's seat recline motor harness connector C300 while operating power seat control switch to recline forward position. If battery voltage does not exist, go to next step. If battery voltage exists, go to step 5).

4) Disconnect passenger's seat control switch harness connector C616. Measure resistance between ground and Gray wire terminal at passenger's seat recline motor harness connector C300. If resistance is greater than 10 k/ohms, replace seat control switch. If resistance is 10 k/ohms or less, repair short to ground in Gray wire.

5) Measure resistance between ground and Gray/Black wire terminal at passenger's seat recline motor harness connector C300. If resistance is greater than 5 ohms, go to next step. If resistance is 5 ohms or less, go to step 7) .

6) Disconnect passenger's seat control switch harness connector C616. Measure resistance in Gray/Black wire between passenger's seat recline motor harness connector C300 and terminal No. 5 at passenger's seat control switch harness connector C616. *See Fig. 4.* If resistance is 5 ohms or less, replace seat control switch. If resistance is greater than 5 ohms, repair open in Gray/Black wire.

7) Measure voltage at Gray/Black wire terminal at passenger's seat recline motor harness connector C300 while operating power seat control switch to recline rearward position. If battery voltage does not exist, go to next step. If battery voltage exists, replace recline motor.

8) Disconnect passenger's seat control switch harness connector C616. Measure resistance between ground and Gray/Black wire terminal at passenger's seat recline motor harness connector C300. If resistance is greater than 10 k/ohms, replace seat control switch. If resistance is 10 k/ohms or less, repair short to ground in Gray/Black wire.

TEST G: LUMBAR SUPPORT FUNCTION DOES NOT WORK PROPERLY

1) Operate lumbar seat control switch to inflate position. If lumbar support compressor does not run, go to next step. If lumbar support compressor runs, go to step 8).

2) Operate power seat. If power seat operates, go to next step. If power seat does not operate, perform TEST A: POWER SEAT COMPLETELY INOPERATIVE.

3) Disconnect appropriate lumbar seat control switch harness connector. Measure voltage at Black/White wire terminal at lumbar seat control switch harness connector. If battery voltage exists, go to next step. If battery voltage does not exist, repair open in Black/White wire.

1999 ACCESSORIES & EQUIPMENT
Power Seats – Crown Victoria & Grand Marquis (Cont.)

FORD
4-1021

4) Disconnect appropriate lumbar support compressor harness connector. Measure resistance between ground and Black wire terminal at lumbar support compressor harness connector. If resistance is 5 ohms or less, go to next step. If resistance is greater than 5 ohms, repair open in Black wire.

5) Connect lumbar seat control switch harness connector. Measure voltage at Red wire terminal at lumbar support compressor harness connector while operating lumbar seat control switch to inflate position. If battery voltage does not exist, go to next step. If battery voltage exists, replace lumbar support compressor.

6) Measure resistance between ground and Red wire terminal at lumbar support compressor harness connector. If resistance is greater than 10 k/ohms, go to next step. If resistance is 10 k/ohms or less, repair short to ground in Red wire.

7) Disconnect appropriate lumbar seat control switch harness connector. Measure resistance in Red wire between lumbar seat control switch harness connector and lumbar support compressor harness connector. If resistance is 5 ohms or less, replace lumbar seat control switch. If resistance is greater than 5 ohms, repair open in Red wire.

8) Operate lumbar seat control switch to inflate position while observing seat back. If seat back bladder does not inflate, go to next step. If seat back bladder inflates, go to step **12)**.

9) Visually inspect lumbar support bladder. If bladder is okay, go to next step. If bladder is damaged, replace bladder.

10) Disconnect inflate hose from lumbar support compressor. Operate lumbar seat control switch to inflate position. If air is felt from inflate port on lumbar support compressor, go to next step. If air is not felt from inflate port on lumbar support compressor, replace lumbar support compressor.

11) Connect inflate hose to lumbar support compressor. Disconnect lumbar support bladder hose at lumbar seat control switch. Operate lumbar seat control switch to inflate position. If air is felt from inflate port at lumbar seat control switch, go to next step. If air is not felt from inflate port at lumbar seat control switch, replace inflate hose or lumbar switch as necessary.

12) Connect lumbar support bladder hose at lumbar seat control switch (if disconnected). Disconnect inflate hose at lumbar support bladder. Connect a pressure gauge to disconnect hose. Operate lumbar seat control switch to inflate position until pressure gauge reads 5 psi (0.35 kg/cm²). System should hold pressure for at least 3 hours. If pressure reading is greater than 4.7 psi (0.32 kg/cm²) after 3 hours, go to next step. If pressure reading is 4.7 psi (0.32 kg/cm²) or less after 3 hours, replace leaking switch, compressor or hose as necessary.

13) Using a hand pump, inflate lumbar support bladder to 5 psi (0.35 kg/cm²). Bladder should hold pressure for at least 3 hours. If pressure reading is greater than 4.7 psi (0.32 kg/cm²) after 3 hours, system is okay at this time. If pressure reading is 4.7 psi (0.32 kg/cm²) or less after 3 hours, replace lumbar support bladder.

REMOVAL & INSTALLATION

CAUTION: When battery is disconnected, vehicle computer and memory systems may lose memory data. Driveability problems may exist until computer systems have completed a relearn cycle. See COMPUTER RELEARN PROCEDURES article in GENERAL INFORMATION before disconnecting battery.

SEAT ASSEMBLY

Removal & Installation – Remove insulators covering mounting nuts and bolts. Remove mounting nuts, bolts, and washers. Lift seat slightly and unplug harness connectors. Remove seat. To install, reverse removal procedure.

RECLINER MOTOR

Removal & Installation – Remove seat assembly. See SEAT ASSEMBLY. Remove trim cover. Disconnect lumbar air hose. Remove screws retaining front seatback cover and pad. Remove seatback assembly. Remove recliner motor. To install, reverse removal procedure.

LUMBAR SUPPORT PUMP

Removal & Installation – Remove seat and track. See SEAT ASSEMBLY. Remove pump mounting rivets. Disconnect wiring harness connector. Disconnect inflation tube. Remove pump. To install, reverse removal procedure.

LUMBAR SUPPORT PAD

Removal & Installation – Remove seat and track assembly. See SEAT ASSEMBLY. Remove seat cushion. Disconnect inflation tube. Remove seatback trim cover and pad. Pry pad retaining tabs outward. Remove pad. To install, reverse removal procedure.

WIRING DIAGRAMS

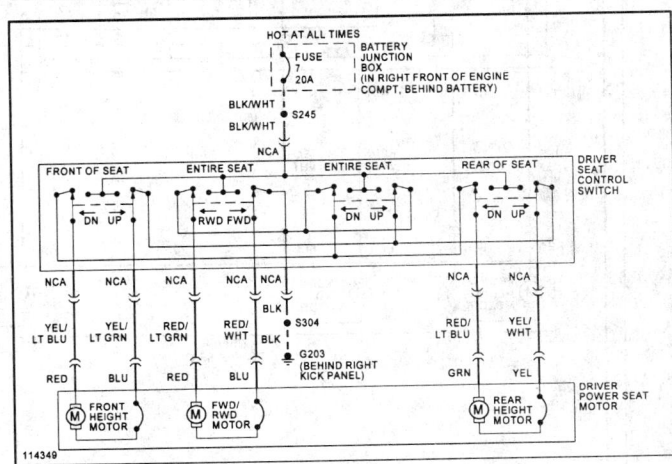

Fig. 6: Driver Power Seat System Wiring Diagram (Crown Victoria & Grand Marquis)

FORD
4-1022

1999 ACCESSORIES & EQUIPMENT
Power Seats – Crown Victoria & Grand Marquis (Cont.)

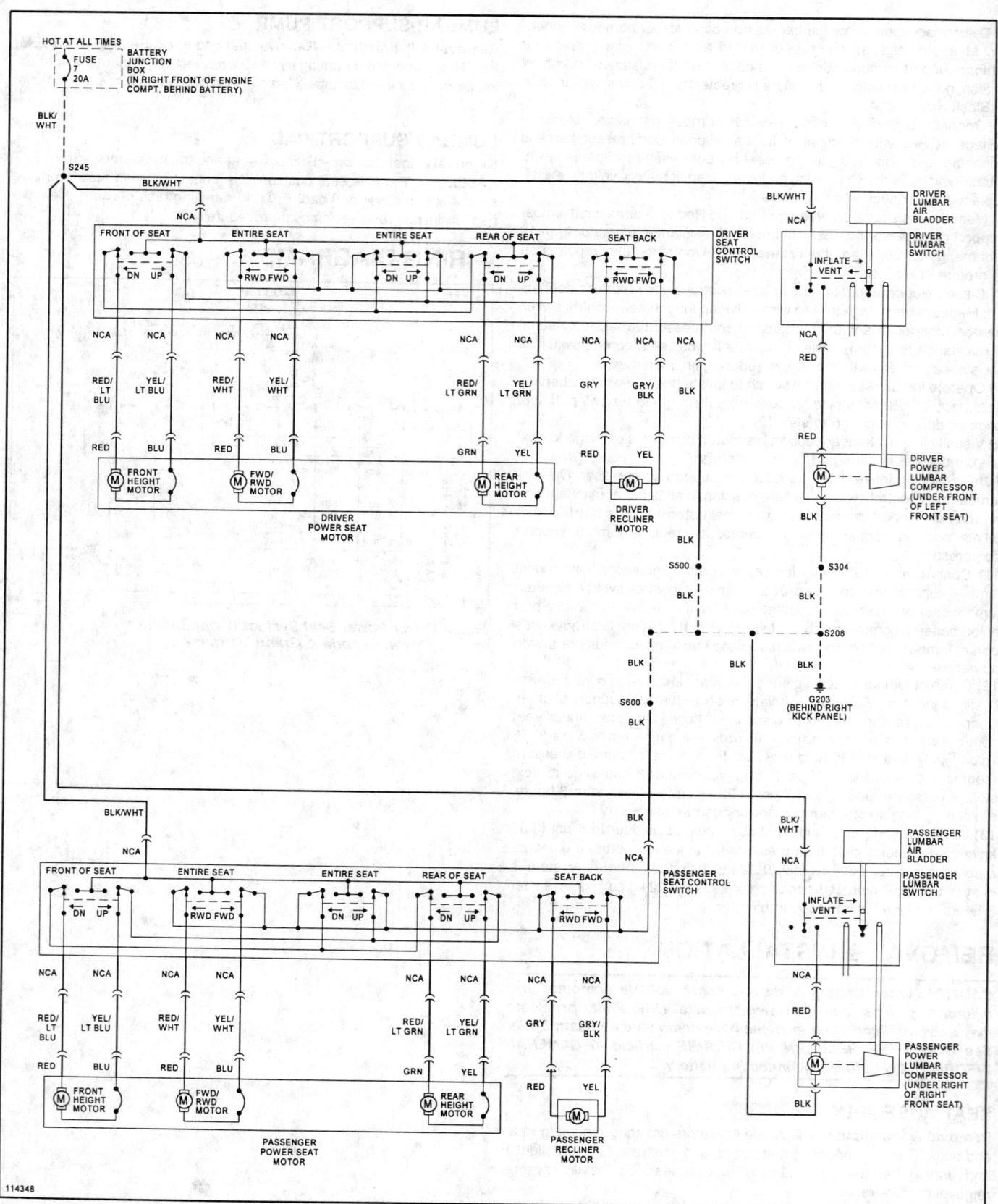

Fig. 7: Power Lumbar, Reclining & 6-Way Power Seats System Wiring Diagram (Crown Victoria & Grand Marquis)

NOTE: This article includes Cutaway and RV Cutaway.

DESCRIPTION & OPERATION

The 6-way power seats provide horizontal, vertical and tilt adjustments. System consists of control switch, seat regulator motor, vertical and horizontal screw drives and gear mechanism, housing assembly and necessary wiring. Seat function switches are mounted on side of seat trim panel. Power seat circuits are protected by fuses and/or circuit breakers located in fuse panel and power distribution box.

Horizontal movement is controlled by a transmission, lead screw and motor attached to the movable section of the track. Vertical drive unit is located on left side of the movable track. Vertical operation energizes center and rear armatures and vertical drive units move seat up or down. In tilt operation, armatures move front or rear vertical drive screws to adjust seat. The motor unit is serviced as an assembly.

COMPONENT LOCATIONS

COMPONENT LOCATIONS

Component	Location
Air Bag Diagnostic Monitor [1]	Behind Right Kick Panel
Air Bag Sliding Contact	Top Of Steering Column
Data Link Connector	Below Driver's Side Of Instrument Panel, To Right Of Steering Column
Forward/Reverse Seat Motor	Front Motor In Seat Track Assembly
Powertrain Control Module	Left Rear Of Engine Compartment, Near Brake Master Cylinder
Seat Control Switch	Outside Seat Trim Panel

[1] – Air bag diagnostic monitor may also be referred to as Electronic Crash Sensor (ECS) module.

TROUBLE SHOOTING

Before performing individual component tests or system tests, check the following for possible cause of system malfunction:

- Blown fuse.
- Loose or corroded connectors.
- Damaged wiring.
- Damaged motors.
- Faulty switches.

COMPONENT TESTS

NOTE: Some individual component testing is not available from manufacturer. See SYMPTOM CHART table under SYSTEM TESTS.

SEAT CONTROL SWITCH

Remove seat control switch and disconnect harness connector. Measure resistance between seat control switch terminals with switch in appropriate position. See SEAT CONTROL SWITCH RESISTANCE table. *See Fig. 1.* If resistance is not as specified, replace seat control switch.

SEAT CONTROL SWITCH RESISTANCE

Switch Position	Between Terminals	Ohms
Neutral [1]	1 & 3	More Than 5
Entire Seat Down	1, 7 & 8; 3, 4 & 6	Less Than 5
Entire Seat Up	1, 4 & 6; 3, 7 & 8	Less Than 5
Forward	1 & 2; 3 & 5	Less Than 5
Rearward	1 & 5; 2 & 3	Less Than 5
Front Down	1 & 8; 3 & 6	Less Than 5
Front Up	1 & 6; 3 & 8	Less Than 5
Rear Down	1 & 7; 3 & 4	Less Than 5
Rear Up	1 & 4; 3 & 7	Less Than 5

SEAT CONTROL SWITCH RESISTANCE (Cont.)

Switch Position	Between Terminals	Ohms
[1] – Resistance between terminal No. 1 and all other terminals (except terminal No. 3) should be less than 5 ohms.		

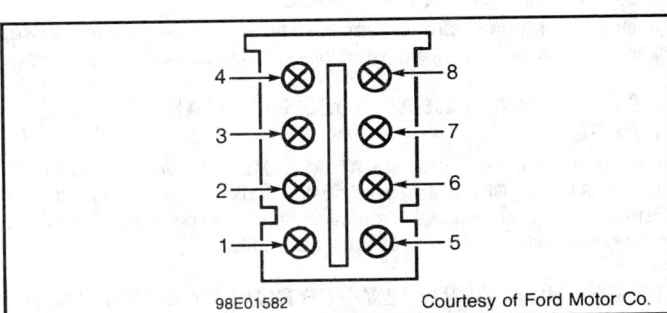

Fig. 1: Identifying Seat Control Switch Terminals

98E01582   Courtesy of Ford Motor Co.

SYSTEM TESTS

NOTE: Before beginning system testing, perform TROUBLE SHOOTING.

Verify customer complaint by operating power seat. Visually inspect for obvious sign of mechanical and electrical damage. If no visual damage is evident, perform appropriate diagnostic test. See SYMPTOM CHART table. A digital volt-ohmmeter is required to test the power seat system. See WIRING DIAGRAMS for terminal numbers.

SYMPTOM CHART

Symptom	Test
Power Seat Inoperative	A
Power Seat Noisy	B
Power Seat Loose	C
Power Seat Does Not Make Full Travel	D
Horizontal/Vertical Operation Inoperative	E

TEST A: POWER SEAT INOPERATIVE

NOTE: Before beginning this test, ensure seat and seat track are free from all obstructions.

1) Disconnect seat control switch harness connector. Measure voltage between ground and seat control switch harness connector terminal No. 3 (Black/White wire). *See Fig. 2.* If battery voltage exists, go to next step. If battery voltage does not exist, repair open or short to ground in Black/White wire.

2) Measure resistance between ground and seat control switch harness connector terminal No. 1 (Black wire). If resistance is less than 5 ohms, replace seat control switch. If resistance 5 ohms or more, repair open in Black wire.

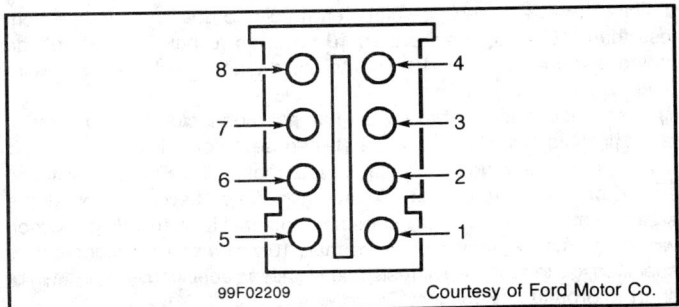

99F02209   Courtesy of Ford Motor Co.

Fig. 2: Identifying Seat Control Switch Harness Connector Terminals

TEST B: POWER SEAT NOISY

Ensure ignition is off. Check alignment of seat track to floor and seat bottom. If seat track is out of alignment, align seat track. If seat track is not out of alignment, replace seat track assembly.

TEST C: POWER SEAT LOOSE

Check fastening hardware for proper installation. If hardware is loose, tighten hardware. If hardware is not loose, replace seat track assembly.

TEST D: POWER SEAT DOES NOT MAKE FULL TRAVEL

Remove driver's seat. See SEAT ASSEMBLY under REMOVAL & INSTALLATION. Check for any obstructions in seat track. If any obstructions exist, remove obstructions and grease seat track. If no obstructions exist, replace seat track assembly.

TEST E: HORIZONTALLY/VERTICALLY OPERATION IMPROPER

NOTE: Before beginning this test, ensure seat and seat track are free from all obstructions.

1) Operate seat in all directions. If seat does not move horizontally, go to next step. If seat does not move vertically, go to step 5).
2) Disconnect forward/reverse seat motor harness connector. Forward/reverse seat motor is first motor from front of seat. Measure voltage between forward/reverse seat motor harness connector Yellow/White and Red/White wires. Operate seat control switch in both horizontal directions, while observing voltmeter. If voltage does not change from less than -10 volts to more than 10 volts, go to next step. If voltage changes from less than -10 volts to more than 10 volts, replace seat track assembly.
3) Disconnect seat control switch harness connector. Measure resistance in Yellow/White wire between seat control switch harness connector terminal No. 5 and forward/reverse seat motor harness connector. See Fig. 2. Resistance should be less than 5 ohms. Measure resistance between ground and seat control switch harness connector terminal No. 5 (Yellow/White wire). Resistance should be more than 10 k/ohms. If resistance is as specified, go to next step. If resistance is not as specified, repair open or short to ground in Yellow/White wire.
4) Measure resistance in Red/White wire between seat control switch harness connector terminal No. 2 and forward/reverse seat motor harness connector. Resistance should be less than 5 ohms. Measure resistance between ground and seat control switch harness connector terminal No. 2 (Red/White wire). Resistance should be more than 10 k/ohms. If resistance is as specified, replace seat control switch. If resistance is not as specified, repair open or short to ground in Red/White wire.
5) Operate tilting functions. If only forward tilting function works, go to next step. If only rear tilting function works, go to step 9). If no tilting functions work, replace seat control switch.
6) Disconnect rear tilt seat motor harness connector. Measure voltage between rear tilt seat motor harness connector Red/Light Green and Yellow/Light Green wires. Operate seat control switch in both rear tilting directions, while observing voltmeter. If voltage does not change from less than -10 volts to more than 10 volts, go to next step. If voltage changes from less than -10 volts to more than 10 volts, replace seat track assembly.
7) Disconnect seat control switch harness connector. Measure resistance in Red/Light Green wire between seat control switch harness connector terminal No. 4 and rear tilt seat motor. See Fig. 2. Resistance should be less than 5 ohms. Measure resistance between ground and seat control switch harness connector terminal No. 4 (Red/Light Green wire). Resistance should be more than 10 k/ohms. If resistance is as specified, go to next step. If resistance is not as specified, repair open or short to ground in Red/Light Green wire.
8) Measure resistance in Yellow/Light Green wire between seat control switch harness connector terminal No. 7 and rear tilt seat motor harness connector. Resistance should be less than 5 ohms. Measure resistance

between ground and seat control switch harness connector terminal No. 7 (Yellow/Light Green wire). Resistance should be more than 10 k/ohms. If resistance is as specified, replace seat control switch. If resistance is not as specified, repair open or short to ground in Yellow/Light Green wire.
9) Disconnect front tilt seat motor harness connector. Measure voltage between front tilt seat motor harness connector Red/Light Blue and Yellow/Light Blue wires. Operate seat control switch in both front tilting directions, while observing voltmeter. If voltage does not change from less than -10 volts to more than 10 volts, go to next step. If voltage changes from less than -10 volts to more than 10 volts, replace seat track assembly.
10) Disconnect seat control switch harness connector. Measure resistance in Red/Light Blue wire between seat control switch harness connector terminal No. 6 and front tilt seat motor. See Fig. 2. Resistance should be less than 5 ohms. Measure resistance between ground and seat control switch harness connector terminal No. 6 (Red/Light Blue wire). Resistance should be more than 10 k/ohms. If resistance is as specified, go to next step. If resistance is not as specified, repair open or short to ground in Red/Light Blue wire.
11) Measure resistance in Yellow/Light Blue wire between seat control switch harness connector terminal No. 8 and front tilt seat motor harness connector. Resistance should be less than 5 ohms. Measure resistance between ground and seat control switch harness connector terminal No. 7 (Yellow/Light Blue wire). Resistance should be more than 10 k/ohms. If resistance is as specified, replace seat control switch. If resistance is not as specified, repair open or short to ground in Yellow/Light Blue wire.

REMOVAL & INSTALLATION

CAUTION: When battery is disconnected, vehicle computer and memory systems may lose memory data. Driveability problems may exist until computer systems have completed a relearn cycle. See COMPUTER RELEARN PROCEDURES article in GENERAL INFORMATION before disconnecting battery.

WARNING: On vehicle with automatic seat belt tensioner, the back-up power supply MUST BE depleted before repairs are performed.

SEAT ASSEMBLY

Removal & Installation – Disconnect negative battery cable and wait one minute before proceeding with removal. Remove seat track lower shield, if equipped. Remove insulators covering mounting nuts and/or bolts. Remove mounting nuts, bolts and washers. Lift seat slightly and disconnect harness connectors. Remove seat assembly. To install, reverse removal procedure.

SEAT CUSHION

NOTE: Procedure may vary slightly depending on seat size and power options.

Removal & Installation – 1) Remove seat and track assembly. See SEAT ASSEMBLY. Remove screws from left side shield. Carefully disconnect and tag air hoses from lumbar/bolster support switches, if equipped. Disconnect switch-to-motor connectors. Remove left side shield. Remove remaining shields.
2) Remove hog rings securing lower portion of seatback cover. Slide seatback cover up enough to remove seatback frame bolts. Remove seatback. Disconnect air line from lumbar and bolster bladders, if equipped. Remove hog rings securing cover rods to seat frame. Remove cover and cushion. To install, reverse removal procedure.

POWER SEAT MOTOR

NOTE: Power seat motors are not serviceable. If power seat motor is defective, entire seat track assembly must be replaced. See SEAT ASSEMBLY.

SEAT CONTROL SWITCH

Removal & Installation – Disconnect negative battery cable an wait one minute before proceeding with removal. Remove side shield retaining screws. Remove side shield. Remove 2 switch retaining screws. Remove switch and housing. Disconnect electrical connector. Remove control switch. To install, reverse removal procedure.

WIRING DIAGRAMS

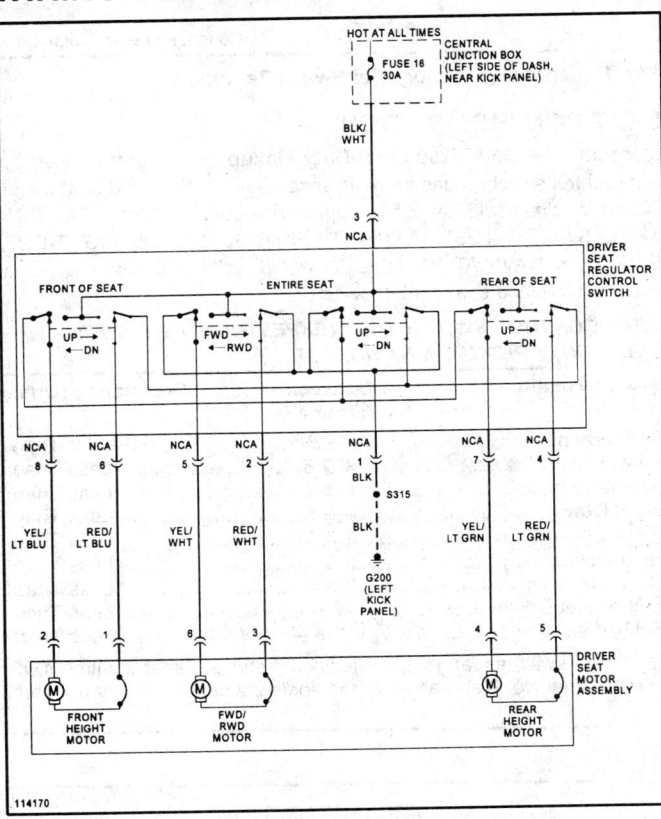

Fig. 3: Power Seats System Wiring Diagram (Econoline)

1999 ACCESSORIES & EQUIPMENT
Power Seats – Expedition, Pickup & Navigator

DESCRIPTION & OPERATION

The 6-way power seats provide horizontal, vertical and tilt adjustments. System consists of seat control switches, seat motor/track assembly and necessary wiring. Seat control switches are mounted on side of seat trim panel. Horizontal movement is controlled by a transmission, lead screw and motor attached to movable section of track. Vertical operation energizes center and rear armatures and vertical drive units move seat up or down. In tilt operation, armatures move front or rear vertical drive screws to adjust seat. Motor unit is serviced as an assembly.

Navigator has driver memory seat. Memory system automatically positions driver's seat, outside rear view mirrors and adjustable pedals (if equipped) to one of three programmable positions. Positions can be recalled by memory set switch located on driver's door or remote entry transmitter. Power driver's seat and power outside rear view mirrors are controlled by Driver's Seat Module (DSM).

PROGRAMMING

PROGRAMMING SEAT POSITIONS

Move driver's seat to desired position using driver's seat switches. Press memory SET switch which activates set switch light emitting diode (LED). Within 5 seconds (before LED goes out) select memory position. To select position 1, press memory switch button 1. To select position 2, press memory switch button 2. To select position 3, press memory switch buttons 1 and 2 simultaneously.

RECALLING PROGRAMMED SEAT POSITIONS

To initiate memory recall, vehicle must be in Park, or Neutral, and ignition switch MUST NOT be in START position. Memory seat recall can be initiated from driver's door memory switch or remote entry transmitter. Seat positions 1 and 2 can be initiated by pressing respective buttons on memory switch. Seat position 3 is initiated by simultaneously pressing buttons 1 and 2 on memory switch.

Remote entry transmitters are assigned personality numbers 1, 2 or 3 at manufacturer. Personality designation is marked on back of remote transmitter. When UNLOCK switch on remote transmitter is pressed first time, seat memory position corresponding to transmitter personality number will be initiated.

TROUBLE SHOOTING

Verify customer complaint by operating power or memory seat. Check for blown fuses, loose or corroded connectors, damaged wiring, damaged motors, faulty switches, damaged seat track and damaged driver's seat module (Navigator with memory seat). If damage is found, repair as necessary and retest system. If cause of fault is not evident and vehicles does not have memory seats, repair by symptom. See SYMPTOM TEST INDEX table under SYSTEM TESTS. If cause of fault is not evident and vehicle has memory seat, perform self-diagnostics. See SELF-DIAGNOSTIC SYSTEM.

COMPONENT TESTS

MEMORY SET SWITCH

Remove memory set switch. Measure resistance between indicated switch terminals with switch in appropriate position. See MEMORY SET SWITCH TEST table. See Fig. 1 If resistance is 5 ohms or more between any test terminals, replace switch.

To test memory set switch LED, connect positive DVOM lead to memory set switch terminal No. 8. Connect negative lead to memory set switch terminal No. 9. Resistance should read more than 0.3 ohms. Reverse leads. Resistance should be 10 k/ohms or more. If resistances are not as indicated, replace switch.

MEMORY SET SWITCH TEST

Switch Position	Between Terminals
1	4 & 6
2	3 & 6
Set	1 & 6

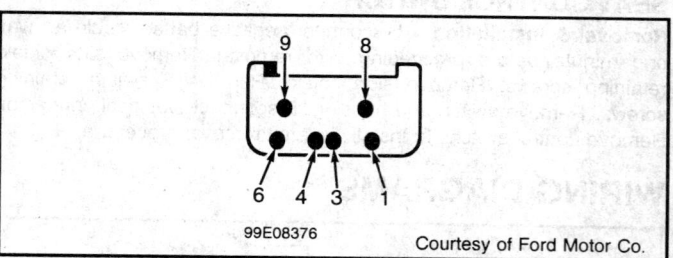

99E08376 Courtesy of Ford Motor Co.

Fig. 1: Identifying Memory Set Switch Terminals

SEAT CONTROL SWITCH

Expedition, F150 & F250 Light-Duty Pickup, & Navigator – Remove seat control switch. Measure resistance between indicated seat control switch terminals with switch in appropriate position. See SEAT CONTROL SWITCH TEST (EXPEDITION, F150 & F250 LIGHT-DUTY PICKUP, & NAVIGATOR) table. See Fig. 2. If resistance is not as specified, replace seat control switch.

SEAT CONTROL SWITCH TEST (EXPEDITION, F150 & F250 LIGHT-DUTY PICKUP, & NAVIGATOR)

Switch Position	Between Terminals	Resistance (Ohms)
All Positions	4 & 8 [1]	Greater Than 5
Forward	4 & 6	Less Than 5
Rearward	4 & 7	Less Than 5
Front Down	4 & 5	Less Than 5
Front Up	1 & 4	Less Than 5
Rear Down	2 & 4	Less Than 5
Rear Up	3 & 4	Less Than 5
Entire Seat Down	4, 2 & 5	Less Than 5
Entire Seat Up	1, 3 & 4	Less Than 5

[1] – With switches at rest, resistance between seat control switch terminal No. 8 and all other terminals should be less than 5 ohms.

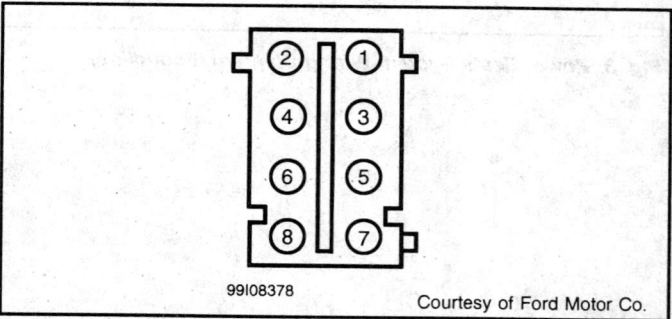

99I08378 Courtesy of Ford Motor Co.

Fig. 2: Identifying Seat Control Switch Terminals (Expedition, F150 & F250 Light-Duty Pickup, & Navigator)

F250 Super-Duty & F350 Pickup – Remove seat control switch. Measure resistance between indicated seat control switch terminals with switch in appropriate position. See SEAT CONTROL SWITCH TEST (F250 SUPER-DUTY & F350 PICKUP) table. See Fig. 3. If resistance is not as specified, replace seat control switch.

SEAT CONTROL SWITCH TEST (F250 SUPER-DUTY & F350 PICKUP)

Switch Position	Between Terminals	Resistance (Ohms)
All Positions	1 & 3 [1]	Greater Than 5
Forward	3 & 5	Less Than 5
Rearward	2 & 3	Less Than 5
Front Down	3 & 6	Less Than 5
Front Up	3 & 8	Less Than 5
Rear Down	3 & 4	Less Than 5
Rear Up	3 & 7	Less Than 5
Entire Seat Down	3, 4 & 6	Less Than 5
Entire Seat Up	3, 7 & 8	Less Than 5

[1] – With switches at rest, resistance between seat control switch terminal No. 1 and all other terminals should be less than 5 ohms.

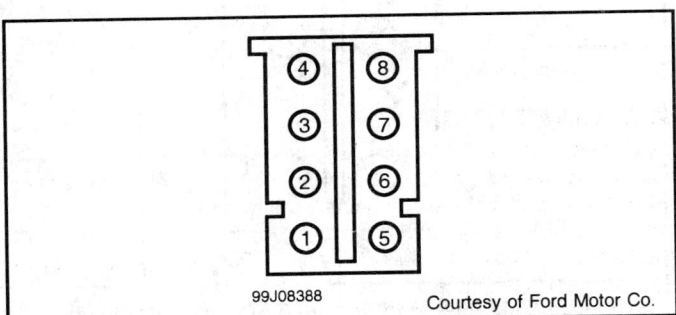

99J08388   Courtesy of Ford Motor Co.

Fig. 3: Identifying Seat Control Switch Terminals (F250 Super-Duty & F350 Pickup)

SELF-DIAGNOSTIC SYSTEM

NOTE: Self-diagnostics is available only on Navigator with memory seat option.

For preliminary testing, see TROUBLE SHOOTING. If problem is not found, connect New Generation Star (NGS) tester to Data Link Connector (DLC) located below center of instrument panel. Perform data link diagnostic test. See DATA LINK DIAGNOSTIC TEST under COMMUNICATION NETWORK DIAGNOSTICS in appropriate MODULE COMMUNICATIONS NETWORK article. If NGS tester displays CKT914, CKT915 or CKT70 = ALL ECUS NO RESP/NOT EQUIP, repair module communication concern. See appropriate MODULE COMMUNICATIONS NETWORK article. If NGS tester displays NO RESP/NOT EQUIP for Driver's Door Module (DSM), perform TEST J: NO COMMUNICATION WITH DSM OR UNABLE TO PERFORM DSM ON-DEMAND SELF-TEST (NAVIGATOR ONLY) under SYSTEM TESTS.

If NGS tester displays SYSTEM PASSED for DSM, retrieve and record continuous Diagnostic Trouble Codes (DTCs). Erase continuous DTCs. Perform DSM self-test. If DTCs related to the concern are retrieved, perform appropriate test. See DSM DTC TEST INDEX table. If no DTCs related to the concern are retrieved, perform appropriate test based on symptom. See SYMPTOM TEST INDEX table under SYSTEM TESTS. For DTCs not covered in this article, see appropriate MODULE COMMUNICATIONS NETWORK article.

DSM DTC TEST INDEX

DTC [1]	Description	Test [2]
B1342	ECU Defective	
B1529	Memory Set Switch Circuit Short To Power	G
B1533	Memory 1 Switch Circuit Short To Power	G
B1537	Memory 2 Switch Circuit Short To Power	G
B1663	Driver's Seat Front Up/Down Motor Stalled	F Or G
B1664	Driver's Seat Rear Up/Down Motor Stalled	F Or G
B1665	Driver's Seat Forward/Backward Motor Stalled	F Or G
B1711	Driver's Seat Front Up Switch Circuit Short To Power	F
B1715	Driver's Seat Front Down Switch Circuit Short To Power	F
B1719	Driver's Seat Forward Switch Circuit Short To Power	F
B1723	Driver's Seat Rearward Switch Circuit Short To Power	F
B1727	Driver's Seat Rear Up Switch Circuit Short To Power	F
B1731	Driver's Seat Rear Down Switch Circuit Short To Power	F
B1751	Park/Neutral Switch Circuit Short To Power	J
B1950	Seat Rear Up/Down Potentiometer Feedback Circuit Failure	G
B1952	Seat Rear Up/Down Potentiometer Feedback Circuit Short To Power	G
B1954	Seat Front Up/Down Potentiometer Feedback Circuit Failure	G
B1956	Seat Front Up/Down Potentiometer Feedback Circuit Short To Power	G
B1962	Seat Horizontal Forward/Rearward Potentiometer Feedback Circuit Failure	G
B1964	Seat Horizontal Forward/Rearward Potentiometer Feedback Circuit Short To Power	G

[1] – Codes listed in this table are only for testing covered in this article. For complete DTC listing, see appropriate MODULE COMMUNICATIONS NETWORK article.

[2] – Using NGS tester, retrieve and document all continuous. Perform Driver's Seat Module (DSM) self-test. If DTC B1342 is retrieved again, replace DSM.

SYSTEM TESTS

NOTE: Before beginning system testing, perform TROUBLE SHOOTING.

SYMPTOM TEST INDEX

Symptom	Test
Power Seat Inoperative	A
Power Seat Moves But Is Noisy	B
Power Seat Moves But Is Loose	C
Power Seat Does Not Make Full Travel	D
Power Seat Does Not Move Horizontally/Vertically	E
Memory Seat Inoperative (Navigator Only)	F
Memory Seat Only Moves In 1 Second Intervals (Navigator Only)	G
Memory Seat Does Not Operate Using Memory Switch (Navigator Only)	G
Memory Seat Does Not Operate Using Remote Transmitter (Navigator Only)	H
No Communication With DSM Or Unable To Perform DSM Self-Test (Navigator Only)	J
Heated Seat Inoperative	K
Heated Seat Switch Lights When Pressed But Seat Does Not Heat	L
Seat Heats But Heated Seat Switch Does Not Light When Pressed	M
Seat Cushion Does Not Heat But Seat Back Heats And Heated Seat Switch Lights	1
Heated Seat Switch Lights When Switch Is Off	2

1 – Check for short between Yellow/Light Blue and Gray/Light Blue wires. Repair as necessary.
2 – Check for short between Orange wire and ground. Repair as necessary.

TEST A: POWER SEAT INOPERATIVE

NOTE: For Navigator driver's seat, see TEST F: MEMORY SEAT INOPERATIVE.

Expedition, F150 & F250 Light-Duty Pickup, & Navigator – 1) Disconnect seat control switch 8-pin connector. Measure voltage between seat control switch terminal No. 4 (Dark Green wire on driver's seat without memory; Orange/Light Green wire on driver's seat with memory; Black/White wire on passenger's seat) and ground. *See Fig. 4.* If voltage is more than 10 volts, go to next step. If voltage is 10 volts or less, repair appropriate wire.
2) Measure resistance between seat control switch connector terminal No. 8 (Black wire) and ground. If resistance is less than 5 ohms, replace seat control switch. See SEAT CONTROL SWITCH under REMOVAL & INSTALLATION. If resistance is 5 ohms or more, repair open in Black wire.

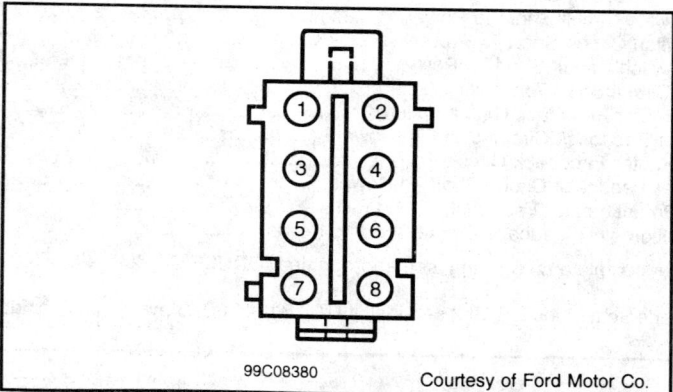

Fig. 4: Identifying Seat Control Switch Connector Terminals (Expedition, F150 & F250 Light-Duty Pickup, & Navigator)

F250 Super-Duty & F350 Pickup – 1) Disconnect seat control switch 8-pin connector. Measure voltage between seat control switch terminal No. 3 (Dark Green wire on driver's seat; Black/White wire on passenger's seat) and ground. *See Fig. 5.* If voltage is more than 10 volts, go to next step. If voltage is 10 volts or less, repair appropriate wire.
2) Measure resistance between seat control switch connector terminal No. 1 (Black wire) and ground. If resistance is less than 5 ohms, replace seat control switch. See SEAT CONTROL SWITCH under REMOVAL & INSTALLATION. If resistance is 5 ohms or more, repair open in Black wire.

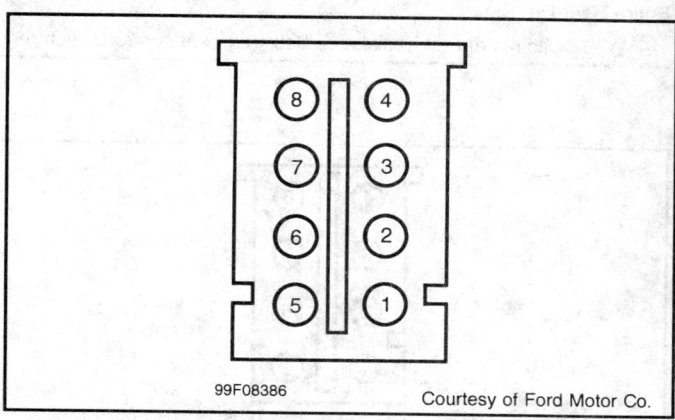

Fig. 5: Identifying Seat Control Switch Connector Terminals (F250 Super-Duty & F350 Pickup)

TEST B: POWER SEAT MOVES BUT IS NOISY

Turn ignition switch to LOCK position. Check alignment of seat track to floor and seat bottom. If seat track is out of alignment, align track. If seat track is not out of alignment, replace track assembly. See SEAT TRACK under REMOVAL & INSTALLATION.

TEST C: POWER SEAT MOVES BUT IS LOOSE

Turn ignition switch to LOCK position. Check fastening hardware for proper installation. If hardware is loose, tighten hardware. If hardware is not loose, replace seat track assembly. See SEAT TRACK under REMOVAL & INSTALLATION.

TEST D: POWER SEAT DOES NOT MAKE FULL TRAVEL

Turn ignition switch to LOCK position. Remove seat and check for obstructions in the track. See SEAT ASSEMBLY under REMOVAL & INSTALLATION. If there are obstructions, remove and grease track. If there are no obstructions, replace seat track. See SEAT TRACK under REMOVAL & INSTALLATION.

TEST E: POWER SEAT DOES NOT MOVE HORIZONTALLY/VERTICALLY

NOTE: For Navigator driver's seat, see TEST F: MEMORY SEAT INOPERATIVE.

Expedition & Navigator – 1) If driver's power seat operates correctly, go to step **13)**. If problem is with driver's power seat, go to next step.
2) Operate driver's seat forward and rearward. If the track will move horizontally, go to step **6)**. If track will not move horizontally, go to next step.
3) Disconnect driver's seat motor assembly 6-pin connector. Measure voltage between seat motor assembly connector terminals No. 1 (Yellow/White wire) and No. 2 (Red/White wire) while pushing forward/reverse switch forward and backward. *See Fig. 6.* Voltage should be more than 10 volts when forward/reverse switch is pushed forward, zero volts when switch is in rest position and more than 10 volts with opposite polarity when switch is pushed backward. If voltage is as specified, replace seat motor assembly. See SEAT MOTOR ASSEMBLY under REMOVAL & INSTALLATION. If voltage is not as specified, go to next step.

4) Disconnect seat control switch 8-pin connector. Measure resistance of Yellow/White wire between seat control switch connector terminal No. 7 and seat motor assembly connector terminal No. 2. *See Figs. 4 and 6.* Resistance should be less than 5 ohms. Measure resistance between seat control switch connector terminal No. 7 and ground. Resistance should be 10 k/ohms or more. If resistances are as specified, go to next step. If resistances are not as specified, repair Yellow/White wire.

5) Measure resistance of Red/White wire between seat control switch connector terminal No. 6 and seat motor assembly connector terminal No. 1. Resistance should be less than 5 ohms. Measure resistance between seat control switch connector terminal No. 6 and ground. Resistance should be 10 k/ohms or more, If resistances are as specified, replace seat control switch. See SEAT CONTROL SWITCH under REMOVAL & INSTALLATION. If resistances are not as specified, repair Red/White wire.

6) Determine seat tilting failure. If only forward tilting operates, go to next step. If only rear tilting operates, go to step **10)**. If seat cannot be tilted either way, replace seat control switch. See SEAT CONTROL SWITCH under REMOVAL & INSTALLATION.

7) Disconnect seat motor assembly 6-pin connector. Measure voltage between seat motor assembly connector terminals No. 4 (Red/Light Green wire) and No. 6 (Yellow/Light Green wire) while pressing rear tilt switch up and down. *See Fig. 6.* Voltage should be more than 10 volts when rear tilt switch is pressed up, zero volts when switch is in rest position and more than 10 volts with opposite polarity when rear tilt switch is pressed down. If voltage is as specified, replace seat motor assembly. See SEAT MOTOR ASSEMBLY under REMOVAL & INSTAL-LATION. If voltage is not as specified, go to next step.

8) Disconnect seat control switch 8-pin connector. Measure resistance of Red/Light Green wire between seat control switch connector terminal No. 2 and seat motor assembly connector terminal No. 4. *See Figs. 4 and 6.* Resistance should be less than 5 ohms. Measure resistance between seat control switch connector terminal No. 2 and ground. Resistance should be 10 k/ohms or more. If resistances are as specified, go to next step. If resistances are not as specified, repair Red/Light Green wire.

9) Measure resistance of Yellow/Light Green wire between seat control switch connector terminal No. 3 and seat motor assembly connector terminal No. 6. Resistance should be less than 5 ohms. Measure resistance between seat control switch connector terminal No. 3 and ground. Resistance should be 10 k/ohms or more. If resistances are as specified, replace seat control switch. See SEAT CONTROL SWITCH under REMOVAL & INSTALLATION. If resistances are not as specified, repair Yellow/Light Green wire.

10) Disconnect seat motor assembly 6-pin connector. Measure voltage between seat motor assembly connector terminals No. 5 (Red/Light Blue wire) and No. 3 (Yellow/Light Blue wire) while pressing front tilting switch up and down. *See Fig. 6.* Voltage should be more than 10 volts when front tilt switch is pressed up, zero volts when switch is in rest position and more than 10 volts with opposite polarity when front tilt switch is pressed down. If voltage is as specified, replace seat motor assembly. See SEAT MOTOR ASSEMBLY under REMOVAL & INSTAL-LATION. If voltage is not as specified, go to next step.

11) Disconnect seat control switch 8-pin connector. Measure resistance of Red/Light Blue wire between seat control switch connector terminal No. 5 and seat motor assembly connector terminal No. 5. *See Figs. 4 and 6.* Resistance should be less than 5 ohms. Measure resistance between seat control switch connector terminal No. 5 and ground. Resistance should be 10 k/ohms or more. If resistances are as specified, go to next step. If resistances are not as specified, repair Red/Light Blue wire.

12) Measure resistance of Yellow/Light Blue wire between seat control switch connector terminal No. 1 and seat motor assembly connector terminal No. 3. Resistance should be less than 5 ohms. Measure resistance between seat control switch connector terminal No. 1 and ground. Resistance should be 10 k/ohms or more. If resistances are as specified, replace seat control switch. See SEAT CONTROL SWITCH under REMOVAL & INSTALLATION. If resistances are not as specified, repair Yellow/Light Blue wire.

13) Operate passenger's seat forward and rearward. If track will move horizontally, go to step **17)**. If track will not move horizontally, go to next step.

14) Disconnect passenger's seat motor assembly 6-pin connector. Measure voltage between passenger's seat motor assembly connector terminals No. 1 (Yellow/White wire) and No. 2 (Red/White wire) while pushing forward/reverse switch forward and backward. *See Fig. 6.* Voltage should be more than 10 volts when forward/reverse switch is pushed forward, zero volts when switch is in rest position and more than 10 volts with opposite polarity when switch is pushed backward. If voltages are as specified, replace seat motor assembly. See SEAT MOTOR ASSEMBLY under REMOVAL & INSTALLATION. If voltages are not as specified, go to next step.

15) Disconnect seat control switch 8-pin connector. Measure resistance of Yellow/White wire between seat control switch connector terminal No. 6 and seat motor assembly connector terminal No. 1. *See Figs. 4 and 6.* Resistance should be less than 5 ohms. Measure resistance between seat control switch connector terminal No. 6 and ground. Resistance should be 10 k/ohms or more. If resistances are as specified, go to next step. If resistances are not as specified, repair Yellow/White wire.

16) Measure resistance of Red/White wire between seat control switch connector terminal No. 7 and seat motor assembly connector terminal No. 2. Resistance should be less than 5 ohms. Measure resistance between seat control switch connector terminal No. 7 and ground. Resistance should be 10 k/ohms or more. If resistances are as specified, replace seat control switch. See SEAT CONTROL SWITCH under REMOVAL & INSTALLATION. If resistances are not as specified, repair Red/White wire.

17) Determine seat tilting failure. If only forward tilting operates, go to next step. If only rear tilting operates, go to step **21)**. If seat cannot be tilted either way, replace seat control switch. See SEAT CONTROL SWITCH under REMOVAL & INSTALLATION.

18) Disconnect seat motor assembly 6-pin connector. Measure voltage between seat motor assembly connector terminals No. 5 (Red/Light Green wire) and No. 3 (Yellow/Light Green wire) while pressing rear tilt switch up and down. *See Fig. 6.* Voltage should be more than 10 volts when rear tilt switch is pressed up, zero volts when switch is in rest position and more than 10 volts with opposite polarity when rear tilt switch is pressed down. If voltages are as specified, replace seat motor assembly. See SEAT MOTOR ASSEMBLY under REMOVAL & INSTAL-LATION. If voltages are not as specified, go to next step.

19) Disconnect seat control switch 8-pin connector. Measure resistance of Red/Light Green wire between seat control switch connector terminal No. 2 and seat motor assembly connector terminal No. 5. *See Figs. 4 and 6.* Resistance should be less than 5 ohms. Measure resistance between seat control switch connector terminal No. 2 and ground. Resistance should be 10 k/ohms or more. If resistances are as specified, go to next step. If resistances are not as specified, repair Red/Light Green wire.

20) Measure resistance of Yellow/Light Green wire between seat control switch connector terminal No. 3 and seat motor assembly connector terminal No. 3. Resistance should be less than 5 ohms. Measure resistance between seat control switch connector terminal No. 3 and ground. Resistance should be 10 k/ohms or more. If resistances are as specified, replace seat control switch. See SEAT CONTROL SWITCH under REMOVAL & INSTALLATION. If resistances are not as specified, repair Yellow/Light Green wire.

21) Disconnect seat motor assembly 6-pin connector. Measure voltage between seat motor assembly connector terminals No. 4 (Red/Light Blue wire) and No. 6 (Yellow/Light Blue wire) while pressing front tilting switch up and down. *See Fig. 6.* Voltage should be more than 10 volts when front tilt switch is pressed up, zero volts when switch is in rest position and more than 10 volts with opposite polarity when front tilt switch is pressed down. If voltages are as specified, replace seat motor assembly. See SEAT MOTOR ASSEMBLY under REMOVAL & INSTAL-LATION. If voltages are not as specified, go to next step.

22) Disconnect seat control switch 8-pin connector. Measure resistance of Red/Light Blue wire between seat control switch connector terminal No. 5 and seat motor assembly connector terminal No. 4. *See Figs. 4* *and* 6. Resistance should be less than 5 ohms. Measure resistance between seat control switch connector terminal No. 5 and ground. Resistance should be 10 k/ohms or more. If resistances are as specified, go to next step. If resistances are not as specified, repair Red/Light Blue wire.

23) Measure resistance of Yellow/Light Blue wire between seat control switch connector terminal No. 1 and seat motor assembly connector terminal No. 6. Resistance should be less than 5 ohms. Measure resistance between seat control switch connector terminal No. 1 and ground. Resistance should be 10 k/ohms or more. If resistances are as specified, replace seat control switch. See SEAT CONTROL SWITCH under REMOVAL & INSTALLATION. If resistances are not as specified, repair Yellow/Light Blue wire.

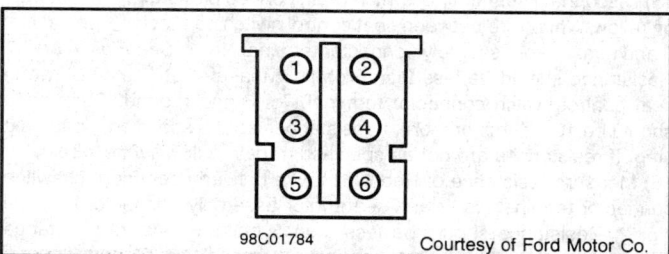

Fig. 6: Identifying Seat Motor Assembly Connector Terminals (Expedition & Navigator)

F150 & F250 Light-Duty Pickup – 1) Turn ignition switch to LOCK position. Operate seat control switch forward and reverse switch. If seat will move horizontally, go to step **5)**. If seat does not operate horizontally, go to next step.

2) Disconnect seat motor assembly 6-pin connector. Measure voltage between seat motor assembly connector terminals No. 6 (Yellow/White wire) and No. 5 (Red/White wire) while pressing froward/reverse switch forward and backward. *See Fig. 7.* Voltage should be more than 10 volts when forward/reverse switch is pushed forward, zero volts when switch is in rest position and more than 10 volts with opposite polarity when switch is pushed backward. If voltages are as specified, replace seat motor assembly. See SEAT MOTOR ASSEMBLY under REMOVAL & INSTALLATION. If voltages are not as specified, go to next step.

3) Disconnect seat control switch 8-pin connector. Measure resistance of Yellow/White wire between seat control switch connector terminal No. 7 and seat motor assembly connector terminal No. 6. *See Figs. 4 and 7.* Resistance should be less than 5 ohms. Measure resistance between seat control switch connector terminal No. 7 and ground. Resistance should be 10 k/ohms or more. If resistances are as specified, go to next step. If resistances are not as specified, repair Yellow/White wire.

4) Measure resistance of Red/White wire between seat control switch connector terminal No. 6 and seat motor assembly connector terminal No. 5. Resistance should be less than 5 ohms. Measure resistance between seat control switch connector terminal No. 6 and ground. Resistance should be 10 k/ohms or more. If resistances are as specified, replace seat control switch. See SEAT CONTROL SWITCH under REMOVAL & INSTALLATION. If resistances are not as specified, repair Red/White wire.

5) Operate seat tilt switches up and down. If only forward tilting works, go to next step. If only rear tilting works, go to step **9)**. If neither tilting works, replace seat control switch. See SEAT CONTROL SWITCH under REMOVAL & INSTALLATION.

6) Disconnect seat motor assembly 6-pin connector. Measure voltage between seat motor assembly connector terminals No. 4 (Red/Light Green wire) and No. 2 (Yellow/Light Green wire) while pressing rear tilting switch up and down. *See Fig. 7.* Voltage should be more than 10 volts when rear tilt switch is pressed up, zero volts when switch is in rest position and more than 10 volts with opposite polarity when rear tilt switch is pressed down. If voltages are as specified, replace seat motor assembly. See SEAT MOTOR ASSEMBLY under REMOVAL & INSTALLATION. If voltages are not as specified, go to next step.

7) Disconnect seat control switch 8-pin connector. Measure resistance of Red/Light Green wire between seat control switch connector terminal

No. 2 and seat motor assembly connector terminal No. 4. *See Figs. 4 and 7.* Resistance should be less than 5 ohms. Measure resistance between seat control switch connector terminal No. 2 and ground. Resistance should be 10 k/ohms or more. If resistances are as specified, go to next step. If resistances are not as specified, repair Red/Light Green wire.

8) Measure resistance of Yellow/Light Green wire between seat control switch connector terminal No. 3 and seat motor assembly connector terminal No. 2. Resistance should be less than 5 ohms. Measure resistance between seat control switch connector terminal No. 3 and ground. Resistance should be 10 k/ohms or more. If resistances are as specified, replace seat control switch. See SEAT CONTROL SWITCH under REMOVAL & INSTALLATION. If resistances are not as specified, repair Yellow/Light Green wire.

9) Disconnect seat motor assembly 6-pin connector. Measure voltage between seat motor assembly connector terminals No. 1 (Red/Light Blue wire) and No. 3 (Yellow/Light Blue wire) while pressing front tilting switch up and down. *See Fig. 7.* Voltage should be more than 10 volts when front tilt switch is pressed up, zero volts when switch is in rest position and more than 10 volts with opposite polarity when front tilt switch is pressed down. If voltage is as specified, replace seat motor assembly. See SEAT MOTOR ASSEMBLY under REMOVAL & INSTALLATION. If voltages are not as indicated, go to next step.

10) Disconnect seat control switch 8-pin connector. Measure resistance of Red/Light Blue wire between seat control switch connector terminal No. 5 and seat motor assembly connector terminal No. 1. *See Figs. 4 and 7.* Resistance should be less than 5 ohms. Measure resistance between seat control switch connector terminal No. 5 and ground. Resistance should be 10 k/ohms or more. If resistances are as specified, go to next step. If resistances are not as specified, repair Red/Light Blue wire.

11) Measure resistance of Yellow/Light Blue wire between seat control switch connector terminal No. 1 and seat motor assembly connector terminal No. 3. Resistance should be less than 5 ohms. Measure resistance between seat control switch connector terminal No. 1 and ground. Resistance should be 10 k/ohms or more. If resistances are as specified, replace seat control switch. See SEAT CONTROL SWITCH under REMOVAL & INSTALLATION. If resistances are not as specified, repair Yellow/Light Blue wire.

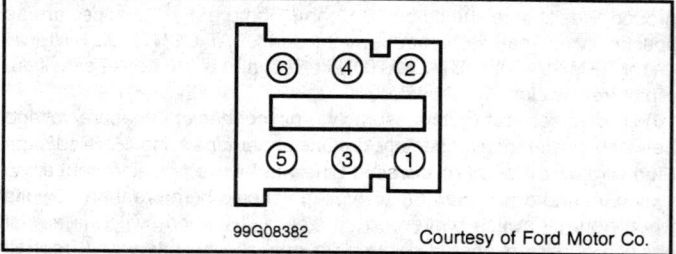

Fig. 7: Identifying Seat Motor Assembly Connector Terminals (F150 & F250 Light-Duty Pickup)

F250 Super-Duty & F350 Pickup – 1) Turn ignition switch to LOCK position. Operate seat control switch forward and reverse switch. If seat will move horizontally, go to step **5)**. If seat does not operate horizontally, go to next step.

2) Disconnect seat motor assembly 6-pin connector. Measure voltage between seat motor assembly connector terminals No. 6 (Yellow/White wire) and No. 3 (Red/White wire) while pressing froward/reverse switch forward and backward. *See Fig. 8.* Voltage should be more than 10 volts when forward/reverse switch is pushed forward, zero volts when switch is in rest position and more than 10 volts with opposite polarity when switch is pushed backward. If voltages are as specified, replace seat motor assembly. See SEAT MOTOR ASSEMBLY under REMOVAL & INSTALLATION. If voltages are not as specified, go to next step.

3) Disconnect seat control switch 8-pin connector. Measure resistance of Yellow/White wire between seat control switch connector terminal No. 5 and seat motor assembly connector terminal No. 6. *See Figs. 5 and 8.* Resistance should be less than 5 ohms. Measure resistance between seat control switch connector terminal No. 5 and ground. Resistance should be 10 k/ohms or more. If resistances are as specified, go to next step. If resistances are not as specified, repair Yellow/White wire.

4) Measure resistance of Red/White wire between seat control switch connector terminal No. 2 and seat motor assembly connector terminal No. 3. Resistance should be less than 5 ohms. Measure resistance between seat control switch connector terminal No. 2 and ground. Resistance should be 10 k/ohms or more. If resistances are as specified, replace seat control switch. See SEAT CONTROL SWITCH under REMOVAL & INSTALLATION. If resistances are not as specified, repair Red/White wire.

5) Operate seat tilt switches up and down. If only forward tilting works, go to next step. If only rear tilting works, go to step **9)**. If neither tilting works, replace seat control switch. See SEAT CONTROL SWITCH under REMOVAL & INSTALLATION.

6) Disconnect seat motor assembly 6-pin connector. Measure voltage between seat motor assembly connector terminals No. 5 (Red/Light Green wire) and No. 4 (Yellow/Light Green wire) while pressing rear tilting switch up and down. *See Fig. 8.* Voltage should be more than 10 volts when rear tilt switch is pressed up, zero volts when switch is in rest position and more than 10 volts with opposite polarity when rear tilt switch is pressed down. If voltages are as specified, replace seat motor assembly. See SEAT MOTOR ASSEMBLY under REMOVAL & INSTALLATION. If voltages are not as specified, go to next step.

7) Disconnect seat control switch 8-pin connector. Measure resistance of Red/Light Green wire between seat control switch connector terminal No. 4 and seat motor assembly connector terminal No. 5. *See Figs. 5 and 8.* Resistance should be less than 5 ohms. Measure resistance between seat control switch connector terminal No. 4 and ground. Resistance should be 10 k/ohms or more. If resistances are as specified, go to next step. If resistances are not as specified, repair Red/Light Green wire.

8) Measure resistance of Yellow/Light Green wire between seat control switch connector terminal No. 7 and seat motor assembly connector terminal No. 4. Resistance should be less than 5 ohms. Measure resistance between seat control switch connector terminal No. 7 and ground. Resistance should be 10 k/ohms or more. If resistances are as specified, replace seat control switch. See SEAT CONTROL SWITCH under REMOVAL & INSTALLATION. If resistances are not as indicated, repair Yellow/Light Green wire.

9) Disconnect seat motor assembly 6-pin connector. Measure voltage between seat motor assembly connector terminals No. 1 (Red/Light Blue wire) and No. 2 (Yellow/Light Blue wire) while pressing front tilting switch up and down. *See Fig. 8.* Voltage should be more than 10 volts when front tilt switch is pressed up, zero volts when switch is in rest position and more than 10 volts with opposite polarity when front tilt switch is pressed down. If voltage is as specified, replace seat motor assembly. See SEAT MOTOR ASSEMBLY under REMOVAL & INSTALLATION. If voltages are not as indicated, go to next step.

10) Disconnect seat control switch 8-pin connector. Measure resistance of Red/Light Blue wire between seat control switch connector terminal No. 6 and seat motor assembly connector terminal No. 1. *See Figs. 5 and 8.* Resistance should be less than 5 ohms. Measure resistance between seat control switch connector terminal No. 6 and ground. Resistance should be 10 k/ohms or more. If resistances are as specified, go to next step. If resistances are not as indicated, repair Red/Light Blue wire.

11) Measure resistance of Yellow/Light Blue wire between seat control switch connector terminal No. 8 and seat motor assembly connector terminal No. 2. Resistance should be less than 5 ohms. Measure resistance between seat control switch connector terminal No. 8 and ground. Resistance should be 10 k/ohms or more. If resistances are as specified, replace seat control switch. See SEAT CONTROL SWITCH under REMOVAL & INSTALLATION. If resistances are not as indicated, repair Yellow/Light Blue wire.

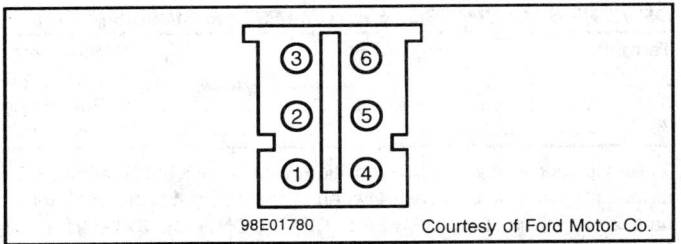

Fig. 8: Identifying Seat Motor Assembly Connector Terminals (F250 Super-Duty & F350 Pickup)

TEST F: MEMORY SEAT INOPERATIVE (NAVIGATOR ONLY)

1) Ensure vehicle is in Park. Turn ignition switch to LOCK position. Connect New Generation Star (NGS) tester, or equivalent scan tool, to Data Link Connector (DLC) located below center of instrument panel. Retrieve and note continuous DTCs. Clear continuous DTCs. Using NGS tester, perform Driver's Seat Module (DSM) self-test. If any DTCs are retrieved, go to appropriate step. See TEST F DTC TEST INDEX table. If no DTCs are retrieved, go to next step.

TEST F DTC TEST INDEX

DTC	Step
B1342	1
B1663, B1664 & B1665	10)
B1663	22)
B1664	25)
B1665	28)
B1711	3)
B1715	3)
B1719	3)
B1723	3)
B1727	3)
B1731	3)

[1] – Replace DSM. See DRIVER'S SEAT MODULE under REMOVAL & INSTALLATION. Clear DTCs and retest system.

2) Observe DSM PIDs SFNT_SW, SREARSW and SFWD_SW while activating seat switch. If PID values agree with switch positions, go to step **9)**. If PID values do not agree with switch position and central junction box fuse No. 4 (15-amp) fails while operating seat control switch, go to step **7)**. If PID values do not agree with switch position and central junction box fuse No. 4 (15-amp) is okay, go to next step.

3) Turn ignition switch to LOCK position. Check driver's seat control switch. See SEAT CONTROL SWITCH under COMPONENT TESTS. If switch is okay, go to next step. If switch is faulty, replace seat control switch. See SEAT CONTROL SWITCH under REMOVAL & INSTALLATION.

4) Measure voltage between driver's seat control switch connector terminal No. 4 (Orange/Light Green wire) and ground. *See Fig. 4.* If voltage is more than 10 volts, go to next step. If voltage is 10 volts or less, repair Orange/Light Green wire.

5) Measure resistance between driver's seat control switch connector terminal No. 8 (Black/Light Blue wire) and ground. If resistance is less than 5 ohms, go to next step. If resistance is 5 ohms or more, repair open in Black/Light Blue wire.

6) Disconnect DSM 16-pin connector. Turn ignition switch to RUN position. With driver's seat control switch at rest, measure voltages between indicated switch connector terminals and ground. See DRIVER'S SEAT CONTROL SWITCH TEST TERMINALS table. *See Fig. 4.* If there is any voltage, repair short to voltage in appropriate wire(s). If there are no voltages, go to next step.

DRIVER'S SEAT CONTROL SWITCH TEST TERMINALS

Terminal	Wire Color
1	Yellow
2	Gray/Light Blue
3	Gray/Yellow

DRIVER'S SEAT CONTROL SWITCH TEST TERMINALS (Cont.)

Terminal	Wire Color
5	Red/Yellow
6	Gray/White
7	Gray/Orange

7) Turn ignition switch to LOCK position. With driver's seat control switch at rest, measure resistances between indicated switch connector terminals and ground. See DRIVER'S SEAT CONTROL SWITCH TEST TERMINALS table. If any resistance is less than 10 k/ohms, repair short to ground in appropriate wire(s). If each resistance is 10 k/ohms or more, go to next step.

8) Measure resistances between indicated driver's seat control switch connector terminals and DSM connector C357 terminals. See DSM & SEAT CONTROL SWITCH TEST TERMINALS table. *See Figs. 4 and 9.* If each resistance is less than 5 ohms, replace DSM. See DRIVER'S SEAT MODULE under REMOVAL & INSTALLATION. If any resistance is 5 ohms or more, repair open in appropriate wire(s).

DSM & SEAT CONTROL SWITCH TEST TERMINALS

DSM Connector C357 Terminal	Wire Color	Seat Control Switch Connector Terminal
11	Red/Yellow	 5
12	Yellow	 1
13	Gray/White	 6
14	Gray/Orange	 7
15	Gray/Light Blue	 2
16	Gray/Yellow	 3

9) Connect NGS tester. Toggle the following DSM active commands to ON and OFF: FRONT UP, FRONT DWN, REAR UP, REAR DOWN, HORZ FWD and HORZ RWD. If driver's seat operates properly, replace DSM. See DRIVER'S SEAT MODULE under REMOVAL & INSTALLATION. If there is no seat movement, go to next step. If there is no front vertical seat movement, go to step **22)**. If there is no rear vertical seat movement, go to step **25)**. If there is no horizontal seat movement, go to step **28)**.

10) Turn ignition switch to LOCK position. Disconnect DSM 2-pin connector C307. Measure voltage between DSM connector C307 Dark Green wire terminal and ground. If voltage is more than 10 volts, go to step **14)**. If voltage is 10 volts or less, go to next step.

11) Check battery junction box fuse No. 112 (30-amp). If fuse is okay, go to step **13)**. If fuse is blown, go to next step.

12) Remove battery junction box fuse No. 112 (30-amp). Measure resistance between DSM connector C307 Dark Green wire terminal and ground. If resistance is more than 10 k/ohms, repair battery junction box. If resistance is 10 k/ohms or less, repair short to ground in Dark Green wire.

13) Remove battery junction box fuse No. 112 (30-amp). Measure resistance of Dark Green wire between DSM connector C307 and battery junction box fuse No. 112 fuse holder (output side). If resistance is less than 5 ohms, go to next step. If resistance is 5 ohms or more, repair open in Dark Green wire.

14) Measure resistance between DSM 2-pin connector C307 Black wire terminal and ground. If resistance is less than 5 ohms, go to next step. If resistance is 5 ohms or more, repair open in Black wire.

15) Check DSM internal fuse (30-amp). If fuse is okay, go to step **22)**. If fuse is blown, go to next step.

16) Disconnect DSM 16-pin connector C351. *See Fig. 10.* Measure resistance between DSM connector C351 terminal No. 11 (Red/Light Blue wire) and ground. Measure resistance between DSM connector C351 terminal No. 6 (Yellow/Light Blue wire) and ground. If each resistance is more than 10 k/ohms, go to step **18)**. If either resistance is 10 k/ohms or less, go to next step.

17) Disconnect DSM 22-pin connector C356. Disconnect seat motor assembly 6-pin connector. Measure resistance between DSM connector C351 terminal No. 11 (Red/Light Blue wire) and ground. Measure resistance between terminal No. 6 (Yellow/Light Blue wire) and ground. *See Fig. 10.* If each resistance is more than 10 k/ohms, replace seat

track. See SEAT TRACK under REMOVAL & INSTALLATION. If either resistance is 10 k/ohms or less, repair short to ground in appropriate wire(s).

18) Connect seat motor assembly 6-pin connector. Measure resistance between DSM connector C351 terminal No. 13 (Red/Light Green wire) and ground. Measure resistance between terminal No. 5 (Yellow/Light Green wire) and ground. *See Fig. 10.* If each resistance is more than 10 k/ohms, go to step **20)**. If either resistance is 10 k/ohms or less, go to next step.

19) Disconnect seat motor assembly 6-pin connector. Measure resistance between DSM connector C351 terminal No. 13 (Red/Light Green wire) and ground. Measure resistance between terminal No. 5 (Yellow/Light Green wire) and ground. If each resistance is more than 10 k/ohms, replace seat motor assembly. See SEAT MOTOR ASSEMBLY under REMOVAL & INSTALLATION. If either resistance is 10 k/ohms or less, repair short to ground in appropriate wire(s).

20) Connect seat motor assembly 6-pin connector. Measure resistance between DSM connector C351 terminal No. 4 (Yellow/White wire) and ground. Measure resistance between terminal No. 14 (Red/White wire) and ground. If each resistance is more than 10 k/ohms, replace DSM. See DRIVER'S SEAT MODULE under REMOVAL & INSTALLATION. If either resistance is 10 k/ohms or more, go to next step.

21) Disconnect seat motor assembly 6-pin connector. Measure resistance between DSM connector C351 terminal No. 4 (Yellow/White wire) and ground. Measure resistance between terminal No. 14 (Red/White wire) and ground. If each resistance is more than 10 k/ohms, replace seat motor assembly. See SEAT MOTOR ASSEMBLY under REMOVAL & INSTALLATION. If either resistance is 10 k/ohms or less, repair short to ground in appropriate wire(s).

22) Turn ignition switch to LOCK position. Ensure vehicle is in Park. Disconnect seat motor assembly 6-pin connector. Turn ignition switch to RUN position. Measure voltage between seat motor assembly connector terminals No. 5 (Red/Light Blue wire) and No. 3 (Yellow/Light Blue wire) while toggling DSM active commands FRONT UP and FRONT DOWN to ON and OFF. If voltage changes from zero volts, replace seat motor assembly. See SEAT MOTOR ASSEMBLY under REMOVAL & INSTALLATION. If voltage stays at zero volts, go to next step.

23) Turn ignition switch to LOCK position. Disconnect DSM 16-pin connector C351. Turn ignition switch to RUN position. Measure voltage between DSM connector C351 terminal No. 11 (Red/Light Blue wire) and ground. Measure voltage between DSM connector C351 terminal No. 6 (Yellow/Light Blue wire) and ground. *See Fig. 10.* If there is any voltage, repair short to power in appropriate wire(s). If there is no voltage, go to next step.

24) Turn ignition switch to LOCK position. Measure resistance of Red/Light Blue wire between DSM connector C351 terminal No. 11 and seat motor assembly connector terminal No. 5. Measure resistance of Yellow/Light Blue wire between DSM connector C351 terminal No. 6 and seat motor assembly connector terminal No. 3. *See Figs. 6 and 10.* If each resistance is less than 5 ohms, replace DSM. See DRIVER'S SEAT MODULE under REMOVAL & INSTALLATION. If either resistance is 5 ohms or more, repair open in appropriate wire(s).

25) Turn ignition switch to LOCK position. Ensure vehicle is in Park. Disconnect seat motor assembly 6-pin connector. Turn ignition switch to RUN position. Measure voltage between seat motor assembly connector terminals No. 4 (Red/Light Green wire) and No. 6 (Yellow/Light Green wire) while toggling active commands REAR UP and REAR DOWN to ON and OFF. *See Fig. 6.* If voltage changes from zero volts, replace seat motor assembly. See SEAT MOTOR ASSEMBLY under REMOVAL & INSTALLATION. If voltage stays at zero volts, go to next step.

26) Turn ignition switch to LOCK position. Disconnect DSM 16-pin connector C351. Turn ignition switch to RUN position. Measure voltage between DSM connector C351 terminal No. 13 (Red/Light Green wire) and ground. Measure voltage between DSM connector C351 terminal No. 5 (Yellow/Light Green wire) and ground. *See Fig. 10.* If there is any voltage, repair short to power in appropriate wire(s). If there is no voltage, go to next step.

27) Turn ignition switch to LOCK position. Measure resistance of Red/Light Green wire between DSM connector C351 terminal No. 13 and seat motor assembly connector terminal No. 4. Measure resistance of Yellow/Light Green wire between DSM connector C351 terminal No. 5 and seat motor assembly connector terminal No. 6. If each resistance is less than 5 ohms, replace DSM. See DRIVER'S SEAT MODULE under REMOVAL & INSTALLATION. If either resistance is 5 ohms or more, repair open in appropriate wire(s).

28) Turn ignition switch to LOCK position. Ensure vehicle is in Park. Disconnect seat motor assembly 6-pin connector. Turn ignition switch to RUN position. Measure voltage between seat motor assembly connector terminals No. 1 (Red/White wire) and No. 2 (Yellow/White wire) while toggling DSM active commands HORZ FWD and HORZ RWD to ON and OFF. *See Fig. 6.* If voltage changes from zero volts, replace seat motor assembly. See SEAT MOTOR ASSEMBLY under REMOVAL & INSTALLATION. If voltage stays at zero volts, go to next step.

29) Turn ignition switch to LOCK position. Disconnect DSM 16-pin connector C351. Turn ignition switch to RUN position. Measure voltage between DSM connector C351 terminal No. 4 (Yellow/White wire) and ground. Measure voltage between DSM connector C351 terminal No. 14 (Red/White wire) and ground. *See Fig. 10.* If there is any voltage, repair short to power in appropriate wire(s). If there is no voltage, go to next step.

30) Turn ignition switch to LOCK position. Measure resistance of Yellow/White wire between DSM connector C351 terminal No. 4 and seat motor assembly connector terminal No. 2. Measure resistance of Red/White wire between DSM connector C351 terminal No. 14 and seat motor assembly connector terminal No. 1. If each resistance is less than 5 ohms, replace DSM. See DRIVER'S SEAT MODULE under REMOVAL & INSTALLATION. If either resistance is 5 ohms or more, repair open in appropriate wire(s).

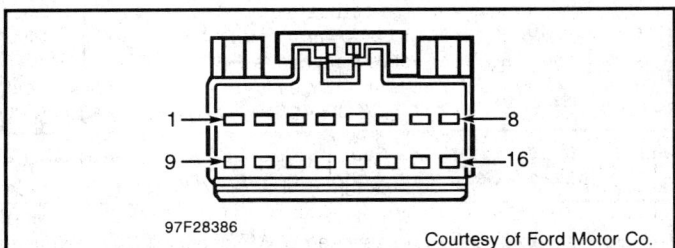

97F28386   Courtesy of Ford Motor Co.

Fig. 9: Identifying Driver's Seat Module (DSM) Connector C357 Terminals (Navigator With Memory Seat)

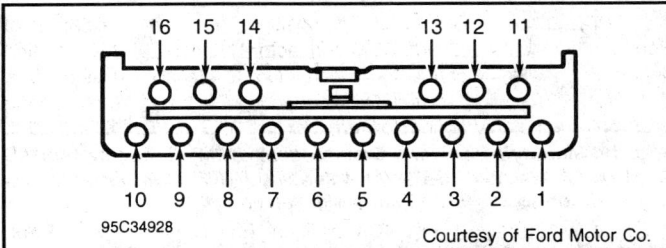

95C34928   Courtesy of Ford Motor Co.

Fig. 10: Identifying Driver's Seat Module (DSM) Connector C351 Terminals (Navigator With Memory Seat)

TEST G: MEMORY SEAT DOES NOT OPERATE FROM MEMORY SWITCH (NAVIGATOR ONLY)

1) Ensure vehicle is in Park. Turn ignition switch to LOCK position. Connect New Generation Star (NGS) tester, or equivalent scan tool to Data Link Connector (DLC) located below center of instrument panel. Retrieve and note continuous DTCs. Clear continuous DTCs. Using NGS tester, perform Driver's Seat Module (DSM) self-test. During self-test note when memory set LED lights and turns off. If any DTCs are retrieved, perform appropriate test. See TEST G DTC TEST INDEX table. If no DTCs are retrieved, go to next step. If memory set LED fails to light during self-test, go to step **5)**.

TEST G DTC TEST INDEX

DTC	Step
B1342	1
B1529	3)
B1533	3)
B1537	3)
B1663	10)
B1664	13)
B1665	16)
B1950	13)
B1950, B1954 & B1962	9)
B1952	13)
B1954	10)
B1956	10)
B1962	16)
B1964	16)

[1] – Replace DSM. See DRIVER'S SEAT MODULE under REMOVAL & INSTALLATION. Clear DTCs and retest system.

2) Observe DSM PIDs MEM1_SW, MEM2_SW and MEMS_SW while activating seat switch. If PID values agree with switch positions, go to step **9)**. If PID values do not agree with switch positions and central junction box fuse No. 4 (15-amp) blows while operating memory set switch, go to step **7)**. If PID values do not agree with switch positions and central junction box fuse No. 4 is okay, go to next step.

3) Turn ignition switch to LOCK position. Check memory set switch. See MEMORY SET SWITCH under COMPONENT TESTS. If switch is okay, go to next step. If switch is faulty, replace memory set switch.

4) Turn ignition switch to RUN position. Measure voltage between memory set switch connector terminal No. 1 (Orange/Light Green wire) and ground. *See Fig. 11.* If voltage is more than 10 volts, go to next step. If voltage is 10 volts or less, repair Orange/Light Green wire.

5) Turn ignition switch to LOCK position. Measure resistance between memory set switch connector terminal No. 8 (Black/Light Blue wire) and ground. *See Fig. 1.* If resistance is less than 5 ohms, go to next step. If resistance is 5 ohms or more, repair open in Black/Light Blue wire.

6) Disconnect DSM 22-pin connector C356. Disconnect Remote Anti-Theft Personality (RAP) module 22-pin connector located behind left side of instrument panel. Turn ignition switch to RUN position. Measure voltage between indicated memory set switch connector terminals and ground. See MEMORY SET SWITCH TEST TERMINALS table. *See Fig. 11.* If there is any voltage, repair short to power in appropriate wire(s). If there is no voltage, go to next step.

MEMORY SET SWITCH TEST TERMINALS

Memory Set Switch Connector Terminal	Wire Color
3	Brown/Light Green
4	Black/Orange
6	Brown/Orange
9	White/Orange

7) Turn ignition switch to LOCK position. Measure resistance between indicated memory set switch connector terminals and ground. See MEMORY SET SWITCH TEST TERMINALS table. *See Fig. 11.* If each resistance is more than 10 k/ohms, go to next step. If any resistance is 10 k/ohms or less, repair short to ground in appropriate wire(s).

8) Measure resistance between indicated memory set switch connector terminals and indicated DSM connector C356 terminals. See MEMORY SET SWITCH & DSM TEST TERMINALS table. *See Figs. 11 and 12.* If each resistance is less than 5 ohms, replace DSM. See DRIVER'S SEAT MODULE under REMOVAL & INSTALLATION. If any resistance is 5 ohms or more, repair open in appropriate wire(s).

MEMORY SET SWITCH & DSM TEST TERMINALS

Memory Set Switch Connector Terminal	Wire Color	DSM Connector Terminal
3	Brown/Light Green	16
4	Black/Orange	15
6	Brown/Orange	3

MEMORY SET SWITCH & DSM TEST TERMINALS (Cont.)

Memory Set Switch Connector Terminal	Wire Color	DSM Connector Terminal
9	White/Orange	13

9) Using seat control switch, place seat in central position. Observe DSM PIDs SFWD_P while operating seat control forward/rearward switch, SFNT_P while operating seat control front up/down switch and SREAR_P while operating seat control rear up/down switch. If PID values (position percentage of travel) increase with forward/down movement and decrease with rearward/up movement throughout entire travel, replace DSM. See DRIVER'S SEAT MODULE under REMOVAL & INSTALLATION. If PID SFWD_P values do not increase or decrease, go to step **16)**. If PID SFNT_P values do not increase or decrease, go to next step. If PID SREAR_P values do not increase or decrease, go to step **13)**.

10) Turn ignition switch to LOCK position. Disconnect DSM 16-pin connector C351. Disconnect front height position sensor 3-pin connector located under driver's seat. Turn ignition switch to RUN position. Measure voltage between front height position sensor connector Light Green/Red wire terminal and ground. Measure voltage between front height position sensor connector Orange/Red wire terminal and ground. Measure voltage between front height position sensor connector Orange/White wire terminal and ground. If there is any voltage, repair short to power in appropriate wire(s) . If there is no voltage on each wire, go to next step.

11) Turn ignition switch to LOCK position. Measure resistance between front height position sensor connector Light Green/Red wire terminal and ground. Measure resistance between front height position sensor connector Orange/Red wire terminal and ground. Measure resistance between front height position sensor connector Orange/White wire terminal and ground. If each resistance is more than 10 k/ohms, go to next step. If any resistance is 10 k/ohms or less, repair short to ground in appropriate wire(s).

12) Measure resistance of Light Green/Red wire between front height position sensor connector and DSM connector C351 terminal No. 9. Measure resistance of Orange/Red wire between front height position sensor connector and DSM connector C351 terminal No. 1. Measure resistance of Orange/White wire between front height position sensor connector and DSM connector C351 terminal No. 3. See Fig. 10. If each resistance is less than 5 ohms, replace seat motor assembly. See SEAT MOTOR ASSEMBLY under REMOVAL & INSTALLATION. If any resistance is 5 ohms or more, repair open in appropriate wire(s).

13) Turn ignition switch to LOCK position. Disconnect DSM 16-pin connector C351. Disconnect rear height position sensor 3-pin connector. Measure voltage between rear height position sensor connector Light Green/Black wire terminal and ground. Measure voltage between rear height position sensor connector Orange/Red wire terminal and ground. Measure voltage between rear height position sensor connector Orange/White wire terminal and ground. If there is any voltage, repair short to power in appropriate wire(s). If there is no voltage, go to next step.

14) Turn ignition switch to LOCK position. Measure resistance between rear height position sensor connector Light Green/Black wire terminal and ground. Measure resistance between rear height position sensor connector Orange/Red wire terminal and ground. Measure resistance between rear height position sensor connector Orange/White wire terminal and ground. If each resistance is more than 10 k/ohms, go to next step. If any resistance is 10 k/ohms or less, repair short to ground in appropriate wire(s).

15) Measure resistance of Light Green/Black wire between rear height position sensor connector and DSM connector C351 terminal No. 8. Measure resistance of Orange/Red wire between rear height position sensor connector and DSM connector C351 terminal No. 1. Measure resistance of Orange/White wire between rear height position sensor connector and DSM connector C351 terminal No. 3. See Fig. 10. If each resistance is less than 5 ohms, replace seat motor assembly. See SEAT MOTOR ASSEMBLY under REMOVAL & INSTALLATION. If any resistance is 5 ohms or more, repair open in appropriate wire(s).

16) Turn ignition switch to LOCK position. Disconnect DSM 16-pin connector C351. Disconnect forward/rearward position sensor 3-pin connector. Measure voltage between forward/rearward position sensor connector Light Green/Orange wire terminal and ground. Measure voltage between forward/rearward position sensor connector Orange/Red wire terminal and ground. Measure voltage between forward/rearward position sensor connector Orange/White wire terminal and ground. If there is any voltage, repair short to power in appropriate wire(s). If there is no voltage, go to next step.

17) Turn ignition switch to LOCK position. Measure resistance between forward/rearward position sensor connector Light Green/Orange wire terminal and ground. Measure resistance between forward/rearward position sensor connector Orange/Red wire terminal and ground. Measure resistance between forward/rearward position sensor connector Orange/White wire terminal and ground. If each resistance is more than 10 k/ohms, go to next step. If any resistance is 10 k/ohms or less, repair short to ground in appropriate wire(s).

18) Measure resistance of Light Green/Orange wire between forward/rearward position sensor connector and DSM connector C351 terminal No. 10. Measure resistance of Orange/Red wire between forward/rearward position sensor connector and DSM connector C351 terminal No. 1. Measure resistance of Orange/White wire between forward/rearward position sensor connector and DSM connector C351 terminal No. 3. See Fig. 10. If each resistance is less than 5 ohms, replace seat motor assembly. See SEAT MOTOR ASSEMBLY under REMOVAL & INSTALLATION. If any resistance is 5 ohms or more, repair open in appropriate wire(s).

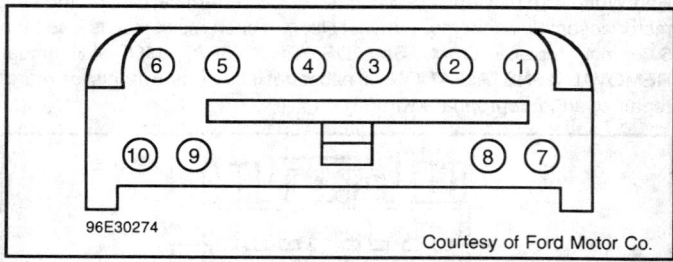

96E30274

Courtesy of Ford Motor Co.

Fig. 11: Identifying Driver's Seat Module (DSM) Connector C351 & Memory Set Switch Connector Terminals

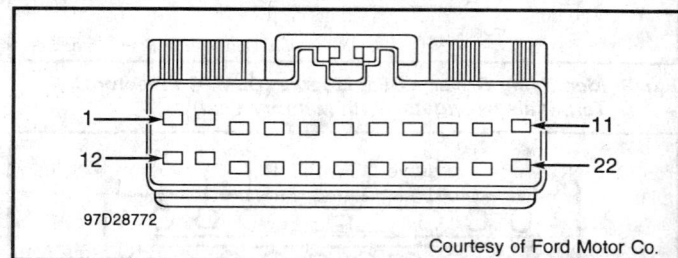

97D28772

Courtesy of Ford Motor Co.

Fig. 12: Identifying Driver's Seat Module (DSM) Connector C356 & Remote Anti-Theft Personality (RAP) Module Connector C257 Terminals

TEST H: MEMORY SEAT DOES NOT OPERATE FROM REMOTE TRANSMITTER (NAVIGATOR ONLY)

1) Ensure vehicle is in Park. Turn ignition switch to LOCK position. Connect New Generation Star (NGS) tester, or equivalent scan tool, to Data Link Connector (DLC) located below center of instrument panel. Retrieve and note continuous DTCs. Clear continuous DTCs. Using NGS tester, perform Driver's Seat Module (DSM) self-test. If any DTCs are retrieved, perform appropriate test. See DSM DTC TEST INDEX table under SELF-DIAGNOSTIC SYSTEM. If there are no DTCs retrieved, go to next step.

2) Turn ignition switch to LOCK position. Disconnect memory set switch 10-pin connector. Disconnect Remote Anti-Theft Personality (RAP) module 22-pin connector. RAP is located behind left side of instrument panel. Measure resistance of Brown/Light Green wire between memory set switch connector terminal No. 3 and RAP module connector terminal

No. 6. Measure resistance of Black/Orange wire between memory set switch connector terminal No. 4 and RAP module connector terminal No. 18. *See Fig. 12.* If each resistance is less than 5 ohms, problem is in keyless entry system. See appropriate wiring diagram in REMOTE KEYLESS ENTRY SYSTEMS article. If any resistance is 5 ohms or more, repair open in appropriate wire(s).

TEST J: NO COMMUNICATION WITH DSM OR UNABLE TO PERFORM DSM SELF-TEST (NAVIGATOR ONLY)

1) Verify vehicle has memory seat/mirror option. If vehicle has memory seat/mirror option, go to next step. If vehicle does not have memory seat/mirror option, system is okay.

2) Ensure vehicle is in Park. Turn ignition switch to RUN position. Using NGS tester, observe DSM PID P/N_SW. If NGS tester displays UNABLE TO PERFORM TEST/FUNCTION – MODULE NOT RESPONDING: DSM – CHECK IGNITION STATUS – VERIFY CABLE REQUIRE- MENTS – CHECK CABLE CONNECTIONS, go to next step. If NGS tester does not display UNABLE TO PERFORM TEST/FUNCTION – MODULE NOT RESPONDING: DSM – CHECK IGNITION STATUS – VERIFY CABLE REQUIREMENTS – CHECK CABLE CONNECTIONS, go to step **8)**.

3) Check central junction box fuse No. 4 (15-amp). If fuse is okay, go to next step. If fuse is blown, go to step **5)**.

4) Turn ignition switch to RUN position. Measure voltage between central junction box fuse No. 4 (15-amp) input side and ground. If voltage is more than 10 volts, go to step **6)**. If voltage is 10 volts or less, repair central junction box.

5) Turn ignition switch to LOCK position. Remove central junction box fuse No. 4 (15-amp). Disconnect Driver's Seat Module (DSM) 22-pin connector C356. Measure resistance between DSM connector C356 terminal No. 12 (Orange/Light Green wire) and ground. *See Fig. 12.* If resistance is more than 10 k/ohms, connect DSM connector, replace fuse No. 4 and retest system. If resistance is 10 k/ohms or less, repair short to ground in Orange/Light Green wire.

6) Turn ignition switch to LOCK position. Disconnect DSM 22-pin connector C356. Turn ignition switch to RUN position. Measure voltage between DSM connector C356 terminal No. 12 (Orange/Light Green wire) and ground. *See Fig. 12.* If voltage is more than 10 volts, go to next step. If voltage is 10 volts or less, repair Orange/Light Green wire.

7) Turn ignition switch to LOCK position. Measure resistance between DSM connector C356 terminal No. 11 (Black/Light Blue wire) and ground. If resistance is less than 5 ohms, problem is in module communications network. See appropriate MODULE COMMUNICA- TIONS NETWORK article. If resistance is 5 ohms or more, repair open in Black/Light Blue wire.

8) Using NGS tester, observe DSM PID P/N_SW while moving trans- mission gearshift lever through entire range. If PID values agree with gearshift lever positions, replace DSM. See DRIVER'S SEAT MODULE under REMOVAL & INSTALLATION. If PID values do not agree with gearshift lever positions, go to next step.

9) Remove central junction box fuse No. 20 (5-amp). Measure resis- tance between DSM connector C356 terminal No. 20 (Red/Black wire) and central junction box fuse No. 20 fuse holder (output side). If resistance is less than 5 ohms, check transmission range sensor. See appropriate ELECTRONIC CONTROLS article in AUTOMATIC TRANS- MISSIONS in appropriate MITCHELL® TRANSMISSION SERVICE & REPAIR manual. If resistance is 5 ohms or more, repair open in Red/Black wire.

TEST K: HEATED SEAT INOPERATIVE

1) Disconnect inoperative heated seat module 10-pin connector. Mea- sure voltage between heated seat module connector terminal No. 4 (Red/Black wire) and ground. *See Fig. 13.* If voltage is more than 10 volts, go to next step. If voltage is 10 volts or less, repair Red/Black wire.

2) Turn ignition switch to LOCK position. Disconnect inoperative heated seat switch 8-pin connector. Turn ignition switch to RUN position. Measure voltage between heated seat switch connector White/Light Blue wire terminal and ground. Measure voltage between heated seat

module connector terminal No. 6 (White/Light Blue wire) and ground. *See Fig. 13.* If each voltage is more than 10 volts, go to next step. If either voltage is 10 volts or less, repair White/Light Blue wire.

3) Measure resistance between heated seat module connector terminal No. 8 (Black wire) and ground. If resistance is less than 5 ohms, go to next step. If resistance is 5 ohms or more, repair open in Black wire. Ground is located near fuel tank.

4) Turn ignition switch to RUN position. Measure voltage between heated seat module connector terminal No. 6 (White/Light Blue wire) and ground. If voltage is more than 10 volts, go to next step. If voltage is 10 volts or less, repair White/Light Blue wire.

5) Turn ignition switch to LOCK position. Connect heated seat switch connector. Measure resistance between heated seat module connector terminal No. 2 (Dark Green/Violet wire) and ground while pressing and holding heated seat switch. *See Fig. 13.* If resistance is less than 500 ohms, go to step **8)**. If resistance is 500 ohms or more, go to next step.

6) Turn ignition switch to LOCK position. Disconnect inoperative heated seat switch 8-pin connector. Turn ignition switch to RUN position. Measure voltage between heated seat switch connector White/Light Blue wire terminal and ground. Measure voltage between heated seat module connector terminal No. 6 (White/Light Blue wire) and ground. *See Fig. 13.* If each voltage is more than 10 volts, go to next step. If either voltage is 10 volts or less, repair White/Light Blue wire.

7) Turn ignition switch to LOCK position. Measure resistance of Dark Green/Violet wire between heated seat module connector terminal No. 2 and heated seat switch connector terminal No 2. If resistance is less than 5 ohms, replace heated seat switch. If resistance is 5 ohms or more, repair open in Dark Green/Violet wire.

8) Turn ignition switch to LOCK position. Disconnect inoperative heated seat module 10-pin connector. Measure resistance between heated seat module connector terminals No. 3 (Yellow/Light Blue wire) and No. 5 (Violet/Light Blue wire). *See Fig. 13.* Resistance should be less than 5 ohms. Measure resistance between heated seat module connector terminal No. 3 (Yellow/Light Blue wire) and ground. Resistance should be more than 10 k/ohms. If resistances are as specified, replace appropriate heated seat module. See HEATED SEAT MODULE under REMOVAL & INSTALLATION. If resistances are not as specified, go to next step.

9) Disconnect inoperative seat heater and temperature sensor 4-pin connector located under seat. Measure resistance of Yellow/Light Blue wire between heated seat module connector terminal No. 3 and seat heater and temperature sensor connector. Resistance should be less than 5 ohms. Measure resistance between heated seat module connec- tor terminal No. 3 and ground. Resistance should be more than 10 k/ohms. If resistances are as specified, go to next step. If resistances are not as specified, repair Yellow/Light Blue wire.

10) Disconnect inoperative seat back heater 2-pin connector located under seat. Measure resistance of Violet/Light Blue wire between seat back heater connector and heated seat module connector terminal No. 5. If resistance is less than 5 ohms, go to next step. If resistance is 5 ohms or more, repair open in Violet/Light Blue wire.

11) Measure resistance of Gray/Light Blue wire between seat back heater connector and seat heater and temperature sensor connector. If resistance is less than 5 ohms, go to next step. If resistance is 5 ohms or more, repair open in Gray/Light Blue wire.

12) Turn ignition switch to LOCK position. Measure resistance between heated seat module connector terminals No. 1 (Brown/Light Blue wire) and No. 7 (Black/Light Blue wire). *See Fig. 13.* If resistance is 50-300,000 ohms, replace heated seat module. See HEATED SEAT MODULE under REMOVAL & INSTALLATION. If resistance is not 50-300,000 ohms, go to next step.

13) Disconnect inoperative seat heater and temperature sensor 4-pin connector located under seat. Measure resistance of Black/Light Blue wire between heated seat module connector terminal No. 7 and seat heater and temperature sensor connector. Resistance should be less than 5 ohms. Measure resistance between heated seat module connec- tor terminal No. 7 and ground. Resistance should be more than 10 k/ohms. If resistances are as specified, go to next step. If resistances are not as specified, repair Black/Light Blue wire.

14) Measure resistance of Brown/Light Blue wire between heated seat module connector terminal No. 1 and seat heater and temperature sensor connector. Resistance should be less than 5 ohms. Measure resistance between heated seat module connector terminal No. 1 and ground. Resistance should be more than 10 k/ohms. If resistances are as specified, replace seat heater and temperature sensor. If resistances are not as specified, repair Brown/Light Blue wire.

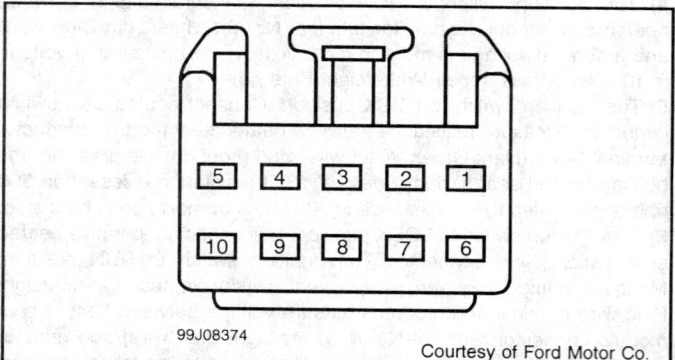

99J08374

Courtesy of Ford Motor Co.

Fig. 13: Identifying Heated Seat Module Connector Terminals

TEST L: HEATED SEAT SWITCH LIGHTS WHEN PRESSED BUT SEAT DOES NOT HEAT

1) Turn ignition switch to LOCK position. Disconnect inoperative heated seat module 10-pin connector. Measure resistance between heated seat module connector terminals No. 3 (Yellow/Light Blue wire) and No. 5 (Violet/Light Blue wire). *See Fig. 13.* Resistance should be 1.5-4.0 ohms. Measure resistance between heated seat module connector terminal No. 3 (Yellow/Light Blue wire) and ground. Resistance should be more than 10 k/ohms. If resistances are as specified, replace appropriate heated seat module. See HEATED SEAT MODULE under REMOVAL & INSTALLATION. If resistances are not as specified, go to next step.

2) Disconnect inoperative seat heater and temperature sensor 4-pin connector located under driver's seat. Measure resistance of Yellow/Light Blue wire between heated seat module connector terminal No. 3 and seat heater and temperature sensor connector. Resistance should be less than 5 ohms. Measure resistance between heated seat module connector terminal No. 3 and ground. Resistance should be more than 10 k/ohms. If resistances are as specified, go to next step. If resistances are not as specified, repair Yellow/Light Blue wire.

3) Disconnect inoperative seat back heater 2-pin connector located under seat. Measure resistance of Violet/Light Blue wire between seat back heater connector and heated seat module connector terminal No. 5. *See Fig. 13.* If resistance is less than 5 ohms, go to next step. If resistance is 5 ohms or more, repair open in Violet/Light Blue wire.

4) Measure resistance of Gray/Light Blue wire between seat back heater connector and seat heater and temperature sensor connector. Resistance should be less than 5 ohms. Measure resistance between seat back heater connector Gray/Light Blue wire terminal and ground. Resistance should be more than 10 k/ohms. If resistances are as specified, go to next step. If resistances are not as specified, repair Gray/Light Blue wire.

5) Turn ignition switch to LOCK position. Measure resistance between heated seat module connector terminals No. 1 (Brown/Light Blue wire) and No. 7 (Black/Light Blue wire). If resistance is less than 10 ohms, replace heated seat module. See HEATED SEAT MODULE under REMOVAL & INSTALLATION. If resistance is 10 ohms or more, go to next step.

6) Disconnect inoperative seat heater and temperature sensor 4-pin connector. Measure resistance of Black/Light Blue wire between heated seat module connector terminal No. 7 and seat heater and temperature sensor connector. Resistance should be less than 5 ohms. Measure resistance between heated seat module connector terminal No. 7 and

ground. Resistance should be more than 10 k/ohms. If resistances are as specified, go to next step. If resistances are not as specified, repair Black/Light Blue wire.

7) Measure resistance of Brown/Light Blue wire between heated seat module connector terminal No. 1 and seat heater and temperature sensor connector. Resistance should be less than 5 ohms. Measure resistance between heated seat module connector terminal No. 1 and ground. Resistance should be more than 10 k/ohms. If resistances are as specified, replace heated seat module. See HEATED SEAT MODULE under REMOVAL & INSTALLATION. If resistances are not as specified, repair Brown/Light Blue wire.

TEST M: SEAT HEATS BUT HEATED SEAT SWITCH DOES NOT LIGHT WHEN PRESSED

1) Turn ignition switch to LOCK position. Disconnect inoperative heated seat module 10-pin connector. Turn ignition switch to RUN position. Measure voltage between heated seat module connector terminal No. 10 (Orange wire) and ground. *See Fig. 13.* If voltage is more than 10 volts, replace heated seat module. See HEATED SEAT MODULE under REMOVAL & INSTALLATION. If voltage is 10 volts or less, go to next step.

2) Turn ignition switch to LOCK position. Disconnect inoperative heated seat switch 8-pin connector. Turn ignition switch to RUN position. Measure voltage between heated seat switch connector White/Light Blue wire terminal and ground. If voltage is more than 10 volts, go to next step. If voltage is 10 volts or less, repair White/Light Blue wire.

3) Turn ignition switch to LOCK position. Measure resistance of Orange wire between heated seat switch connector and heated seat module connector terminal No. 10. If resistance is less than 5 ohms, replace heated seat switch. If resistance is 5 ohms or more, repair open in Orange wire.

REMOVAL & INSTALLATION

CAUTION: When battery is disconnected, vehicle computer and memory systems may lose memory data. Driveability problems may exist until computer systems have completed a relearn cycle. See COMPUTER RELEARN PROCEDURES article in GENERAL INFORMATION before disconnecting battery.

DRIVER'S SEAT MODULE

Removal & Installation – Remove driver's seat. See SEAT ASSEMBLY. Remove seat track. See SEAT TRACK. Disconnect Driver's Seat Module (DSM) electrical connectors. Remove screws and DSM retainers from module bracket. Remove module. To install, reverse removal procedure.

HEATED SEAT MODULE

Removal & Installation – Remove driver's seat. See SEAT ASSEMBLY. Remove seat track. See SEAT TRACK. Disconnect electrical connectors. Release clip and remove heated seat module. To install, reverse removal procedure.

SEAT ASSEMBLY

Removal & Installation – Disconnect battery negative cable. Remove 3 bolts. Disconnect electrical connectors. Remove nut. Remove seat from vehicle. To install, reverse removal procedure.

SEAT CONTROL SWITCH

Removal & Installation – **1)** Disconnect negative battery cable. Remove front seat back adjusting handle. Pull to remove seat lumbar support handle. Remove front seat track shield screws. Remove pin-type retainer on back of front seat track shield. Remove screws on bottom of front seat track shield.

2) If equipped with heated seats, disconnect switch. Remove 2 switch retaining screws. Disconnect seat control switch. Disconnect seat control switch electrical connector. Remove seat control switch. To install, reverse removal procedure.

SEAT MOTOR ASSEMBLY

NOTE: Power seat motors are not serviceable. If power seat motor is defective, entire seat track must be replaced. See SEAT TRACK.

SEAT TRACK

Removal & Installation – Remove seat. See SEAT ASSEMBLY. Remove 4 seat track to seat cushion bolts. Disconnect electrical connectors. Remove seat track. To install, reverse removal procedure.

WIRING DIAGRAMS

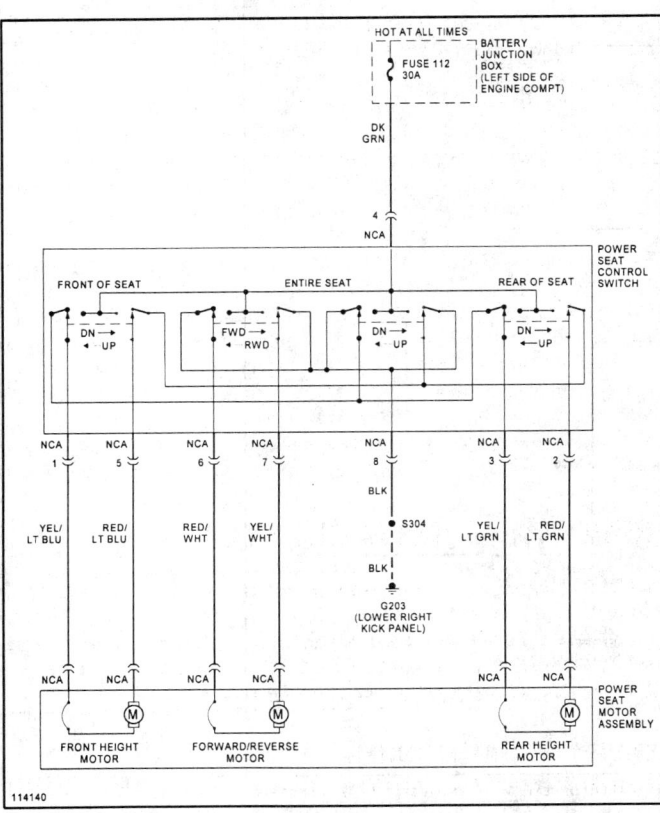

**Fig. 14: Power Seats System Wiring Diagram
(F150 & F250 Light-Duty Pickup)**

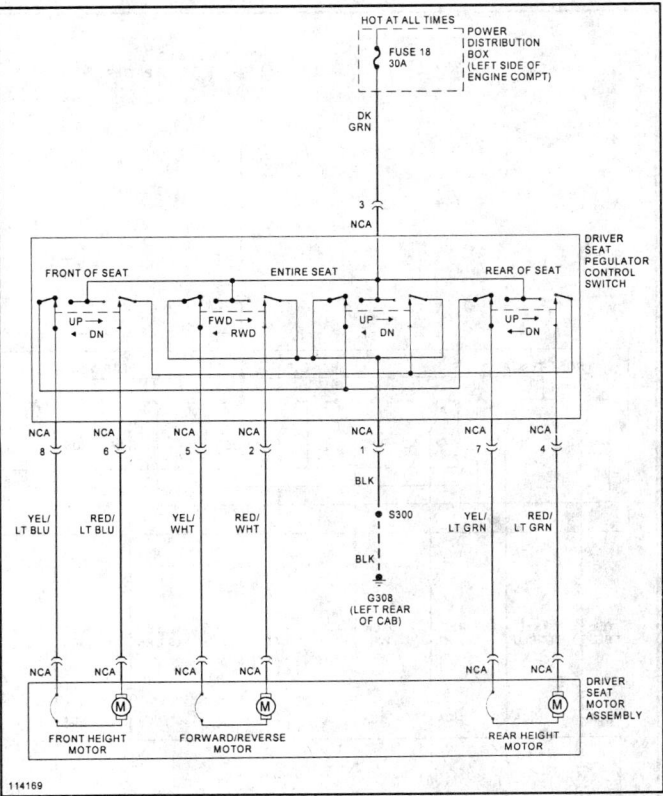

**Fig. 15: Power Seats System Wiring Diagram
(F250 Super-Duty & F350 Pickup)**

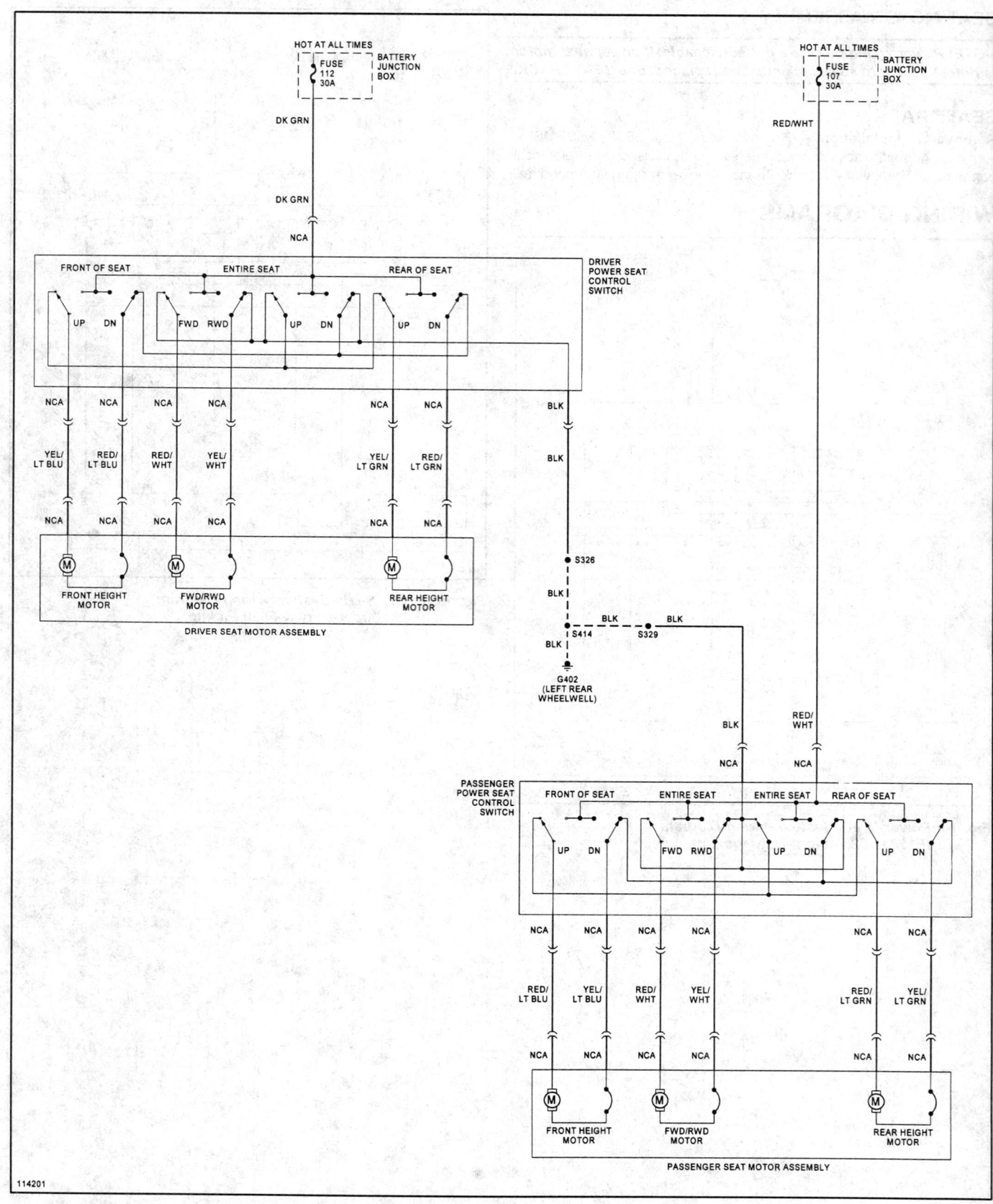

Fig. 16: Power Seats System Wiring Diagram (Expedition & Navigator)

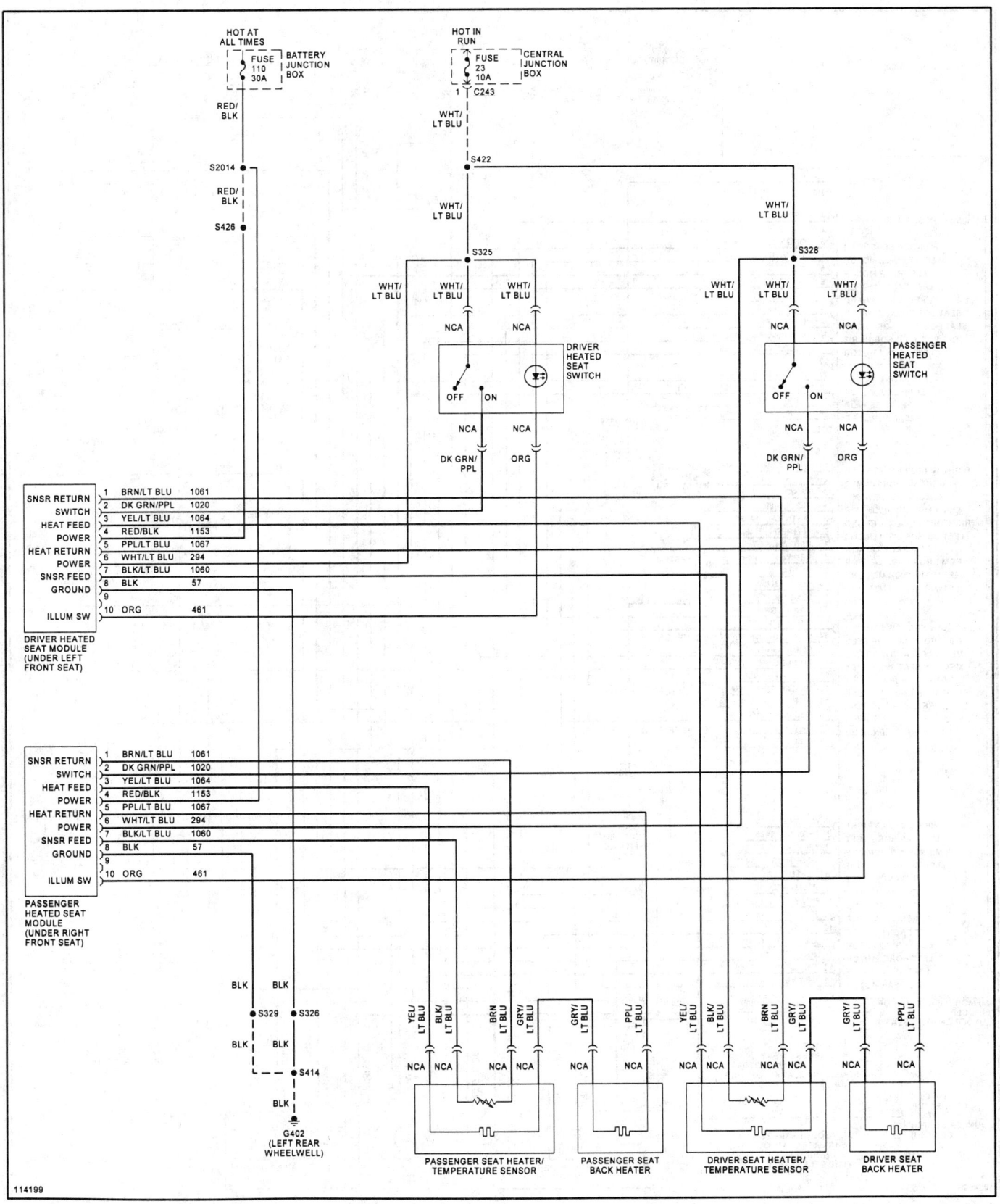

Fig. 17: Power Heated Seats System Wiring Diagram (Expedition & Navigator)

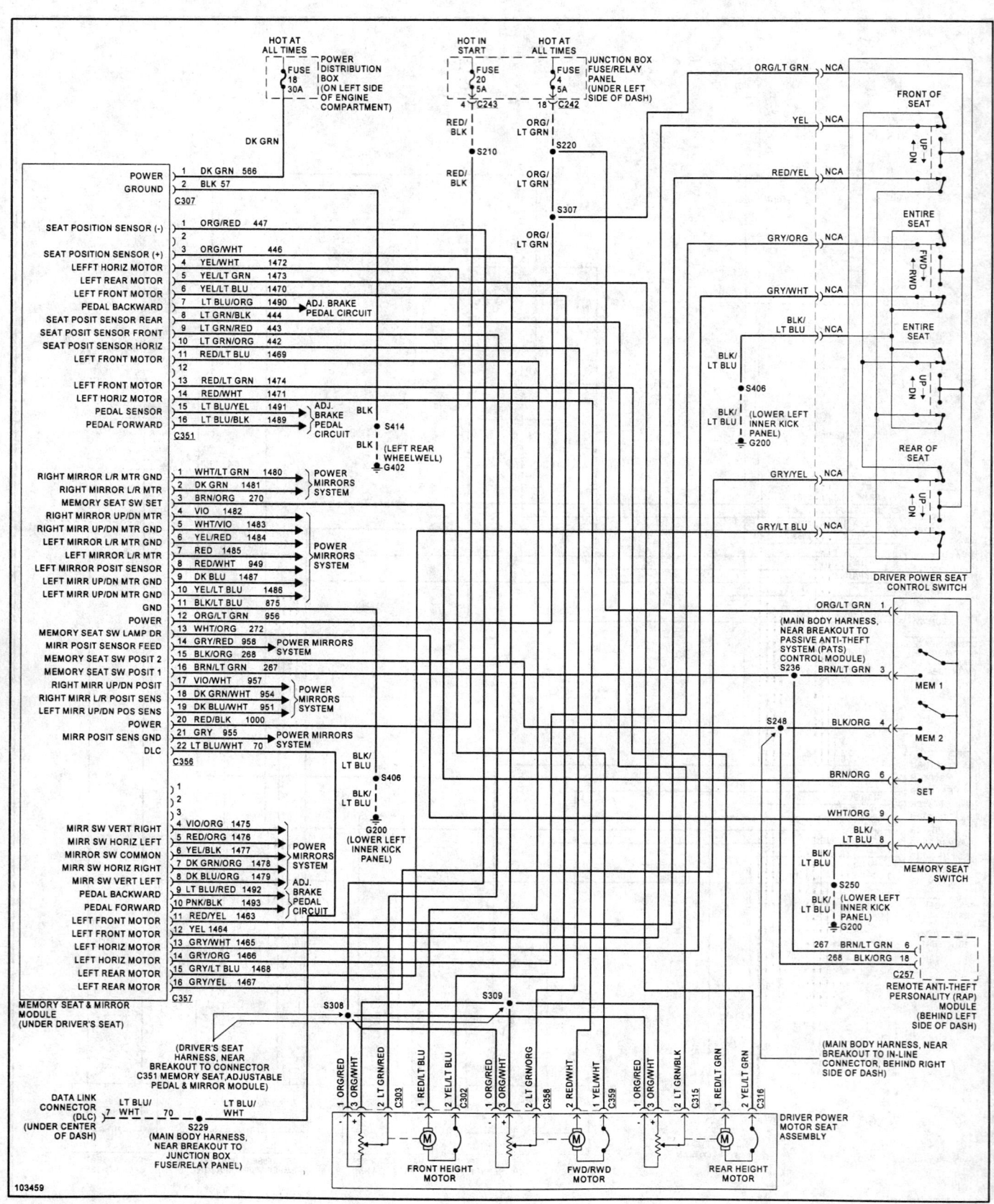

Fig. 18: Power Memory Seats System Wiring Diagram (Navigator)

103459

DESCRIPTION & OPERATION

The 6-way power seats provide horizontal, vertical and tilt adjustments. System consists of control switch, seat regulator motor, vertical and horizontal screw drives and gear mechanism, housing assembly and necessary wiring. Seat function switches are mounted on side of seat trim panel. Power seat circuits are protected by fuses and/or circuit breakers located in fuse panel and power distribution box. Some models are equipped with memory function for driver's seat and a lumbar support system.

Horizontal movement is controlled by a transmission, lead screw and motor attached to the movable section of the track. Vertical drive unit is located on left side of the movable track. Vertical operation energizes center and rear armatures and vertical drive units move seat up or down. In tilt operation, armatures move front or rear vertical drive screws to adjust seat. The motor unit is serviced as an assembly.

TROUBLE SHOOTING

Verify customers complaint by operating power seat(s). Visually inspect the following mechanical and electrical components for damage and repair or replace components as necessary:

- Blown fuses or faulty circuit breaker.
- Loose or corroded connectors.
- Damaged wiring.
- Damaged motors.
- Faulty switches.
- Damaged lumbar/bolster support bladders.
- Damaged or kinked air hoses.

COMPONENT TESTS

MEMORY SWITCH

Remove memory switch and disconnect harness connector. Measure resistance between appropriate memory switch terminals with switch in specified position. See MEMORY SWITCH RESISTANCE table. *See Fig. 1.* If resistance is not as specified, replace memory switch.

MEMORY SWITCH RESISTANCE

Switch Position	Terminals	Ohms
Neutral [1]	1 & 6	More Than 10,000
SET	1 & 6	Less Than 5
MEM 1	4 & 6	Less Than 5
MEM 2	3 & 6	Less Than 5

[1] – Terminals No. 8 and 9 are for the switch LED, which has a diode. Resistance between terminals No. 8 and 9 should be infinite. When ohmmeter leads are reversed, resistance should be low resistance.

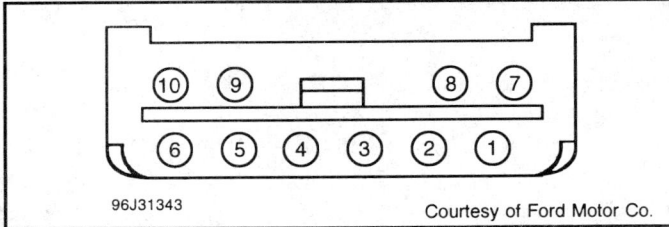

96J31343   Courtesy of Ford Motor Co.

Fig. 1: Identifying Memory Switch Terminals

SEAT CONTROL SWITCH

Remove seat control switch and disconnect harness connector. Measure resistance between seat control switch terminals with switch in appropriate position. See SEAT CONTROL SWITCH RESISTANCE table. *See Fig. 2.* If resistance is not as specified, replace seat control switch.

SEAT CONTROL SWITCH RESISTANCE

Switch Position	Between Terminals	Ohms
Entire Seat Down	1, 4 & 8; 2, 3 & 7	Less Than 5
Entire Seat Up	1, 2 & 8; 3, 4 & 7	Less Than 5
Forward	2 & 5; 4 & 6	Less Than 5
Rearward	2 & 6; 4 & 5	Less Than 5
Front Down	2 & 7; 1 & 4	Less Than 5
Front Up	1 & 2; 4 & 7	Less Than 5
Rear Down	2 & 3; 4 & 8	Less Than 5
Rear Up	2 & 8; 3 & 4	Less Than 5

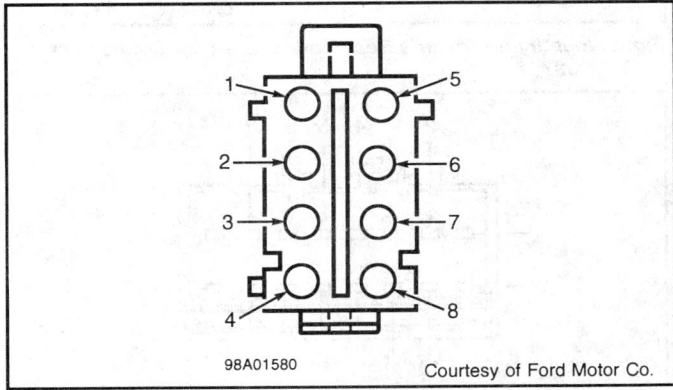

98A01580   Courtesy of Ford Motor Co.

Fig. 2: Identifying Seat Control Switch Terminals

CONNECTOR IDENTIFICATION

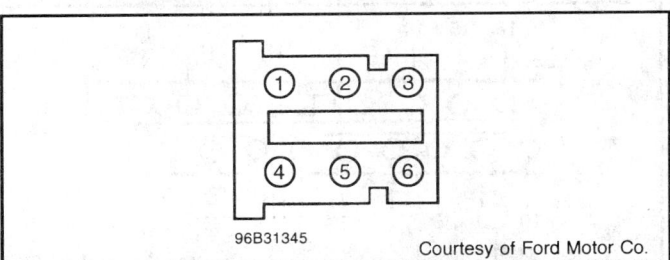

96B31345   Courtesy of Ford Motor Co.

Fig. 3: Identifying Driver's Seat Motor Assembly Harness Connectors (With Memory Seat)

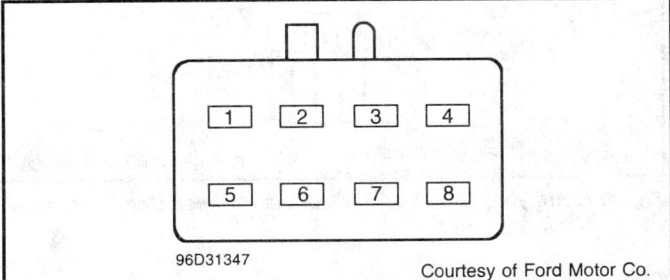

96D31347   Courtesy of Ford Motor Co.

Fig. 4: Position Sensor Connector C359

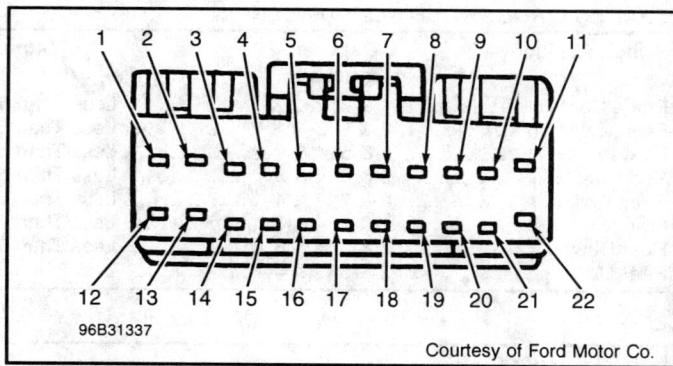

Fig. 5: Identifying Driver's Seat Module Harness Connectors C337

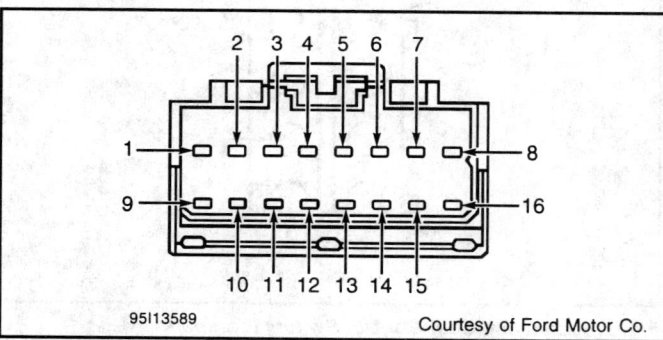

Fig. 6: Identifying Driver's Seat Module Harness Connectors C335

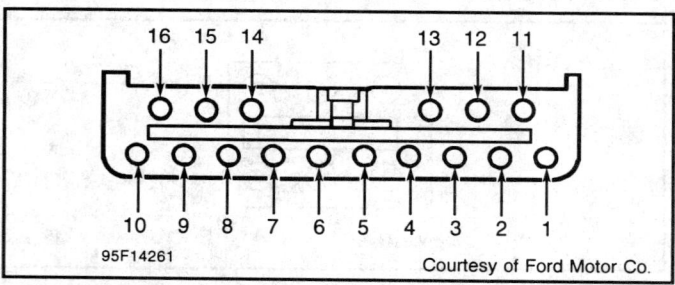

Fig. 7: Identifying Driver's Seat Module Harness Connector C351

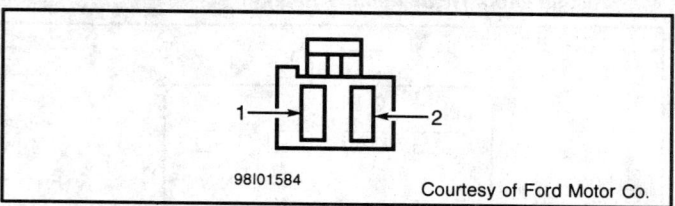

Fig. 8: Identifying Driver's Seat Module Harness Connectors C350

SELF-DIAGNOSTIC SYSTEM

NOTE: Perform TROUBLE SHOOTING before proceeding with self-diagnostics.

DRIVER'S SEATS (WITHOUT MEMORY) & PASSENGER'S SEATS

Verify customer complaint by operating power seat. Visually inspect for obvious signs of mechanical and electrical damage. If no visual damage is evident, repair by symptom. See SYMPTOM DIAGNOSIS table and perform appropriate system test. A digital volt-ohmmeter is required to test power seat system. See WIRING DIAGRAMS for circuit identification.

DRIVER'S SEATS WITH MEMORY

1) Connect NGS tester to DLC located below instrument panel. Using NGS tester, perform DATA LINK DIAGNOSTIC TEST. If NGS tester displays CKT 914, CKT 915 or CKT 70=ALL ECUS NO RESP/NOT EQUIP, see MODULE COMMUNICATIONS NETWORK – EXPLORER & MOUNTAINEER article to diagnosis network concern. If NGS tester displays NO RESP/NOT EQUIP for Driver's Seat Module (DSM), go to TEST K: NO COMMUNICATION WITH DRIVER SEAT MODULE (DSM) under SYSTEM TESTS.

2) If NGS tester displays SYSTEM PASSED for DSM, retrieve and record continuous DTCs using NGS tester. Erase continuous DTCs. Using NGS tester, perform DSM self-test. If any DSM DTCs are retrieved, see DRIVER'S SEAT MODULE (DSM) DTCS table to continue diagnosis. If no DTCs are retrieved, repair by symptom. See SYMPTOM DIAGNOSIS table. Perform appropriate test under SYSTEM TESTS.

DRIVER'S SEAT MODULE (DSM) DTCS

DTC [1]	Description	Test
B1342	ECU Defective	[2]
B1529	Memory Set Switch Short To Power	H
B1533	Memory 1 Switch Short To Power	H
B1537	Memory 2 Switch Short To Power	H
B1663	Seat Front Up/Down Motor Stalled	[3]
B1664	Seat Rear Up/Down Motor Stalled	[3]
B1665	Seat Horizontal Motor Stalled	[3]
B1676	Battery Voltage Out Or Range	[4]
B1711	Driver's Seat Front Up Circuit Short To Voltage	G
B1715	Driver's Seat Front Down Circuit Short To Voltage	G
B1719	Driver's Seat Forward Circuit Short To Voltage	G
B1723	Driver's Seat Rearward Circuit Short To Voltage	G
B1727	Driver's Seat Rear Up Circuit Short To Voltage	G
B1731	Driver's Seat Rear Down Circuit Short To Voltage	G
B1950	Driver's Seat Rear Up/Down Feedback Circuit Failure	H
B1952	Driver's Seat Rear Up/Down Feedback Circuit Short To Voltage	H
B1954	Driver's Seat Front Up/Down Feedback Circuit Failure	H
B1956	Driver's Seat Front Up/Down Feedback Circuit Short To Voltage	H
B1962	Driver's Seat Horizontal Feedback Circuit Failure	H
B1964	Driver's Seat Horizontal Feedback Circuit Short To Voltage	H

[1] – Codes listed in this table are only for testing covered in this article. For complete DTC listing, see MODULE COMMUNICATIONS NETWORK – EXPLORER & MOUNTAINEER article.

[2] – Using NGS tester, retrieve and document continuous DTCs. Clear all DTCs. Perform GEM/CTM self-test. If DTC B1342 is retrieved again, replace GEM/CTM.

[3] – Refer to SYMPTOM DIAGNOSIS table for customer concern, then perform TEST G or TEST H.

[4] – Check charging system and repair as necessary. See appropriate GENERATORS article in STARTING & CHARGING SYSTEMS. If charging system is okay, repair wiring as necessary. See appropriate wiring diagram in POWER DISTRIBUTION article in WIRING DIAGRAMS.

SYMPTOM DIAGNOSIS

Symptom	Test
Power Seat Completely Inoperative	[1]
Power Seat Moves But Is Noisy	B
Power Seat Moves But Is Loose	C
Power Seat Does Not Make Full Travel	D
Power Seat Does Not Move Horizontal/Vertical	[2]
Power Lumbar Inoperative	F
Memory Seat Inoperative	G
Memory Seat Inoperative Using Memory Set Switch	H
Memory Seat Does Not Operate Properly – Seat Moves In One Second Intervals	H
Memory Seat Does Not Operate Properly – Seat Does Not Move To Correct Memory Position	H
Heated Seat Is Inoperative	I
Memory Seat Inoperative Using Remote Transmitter	J
No Communication With Driver's Seat Module	K
Heated Seat Does Not Function Properly – Seat Does Not Heat, But Heated Switch Illuminates When Pressed	L
Heated Seat Does Not Function Properly – Seat Heats, But Heated Switch Does Not Illuminate When Pressed	M
Heated Seat Does Not Function Properly – Seatback Heats, Heated Switch Illuminates, But Seat Cushion Does Not Heat	[3]
Heated Seat Does Not Function Properly – Heated Switch Illuminates When Heated Seat Function Is Not Selected	[4]

[1] – If not equipped with memory seats, go to TEST A: POWER SEAT COMPLETELY INOPERATIVE under SYSTEM TESTS. If equipped with memory seats, go to TEST G: MEMORY SEAT INOPERATIVE under SYSTEM TESTS.

[2] – If not equipped with memory seats, go to TEST E: POWER SEAT DOES NOT MOVE HORIZONTAL//VERTICAL under SYSTEM TESTS. If equipped with memory seats, go to TEST G: MEMORY SEAT INOPERATIVE under SYSTEM TESTS.

[3] – Check if Yellow/Light Blue wire at appropriate front heated seat module and Gray/Light Blue wire at appropriate front seat heater switch are shorted together. See WIRING DIAGRAMS. Repair as necessary.

SYMPTOM DIAGNOSIS (Cont.)

Symptom	Test

[4] – Check for short to ground in Orange wire between appropriate front heated seat module and appropriate front heated seat switch. See WIRING DIAGRAMS. Repair as necessary.

SYSTEM TESTS

TEST A: POWER SEAT COMPLETELY INOPERATIVE

NOTE: Before beginning this test, ensure seat and seat track are free from all obstructions. This test applies to passenger's seat and driver's seat (without memory). For driver's seat (with memory), perform TEST G: MEMORY SEAT INOPERATIVE. For connector identification, see CONNECTOR IDENTIFICATION.

1) Turn ignition off. Remove fuse No. 18 (25-amp) from instrument panel fuse box. Check fuse. If fuse is not blown, install fuse and go to next step. If fuse is blown, check for short to ground in Black/White wire. Repair as necessary and replace fuse.

2) Disconnect inoperative seat control switch connector. For driver's seat, connector is located on left side of seat. For passenger's seat, connector is located underneath seat. On all models, measure voltage between ground and terminal No. 2 (Black/White wire) at seat control switch harness connector. *See Fig. 2.* If battery voltage exists, go to next step. If battery voltage does not exist, repair open in Black/White wire.

3) Measure resistance between ground and terminal No. 4 (Black wire) at seat control switch harness connector. If resistance is less than 5 ohms, replace seat control switch. If resistance is 5 ohms or more, repair open in Black wire.

TEST B: POWER SEAT MOVES BUT IS NOISY

NOTE: For connector identification, see CONNECTOR IDENTIFICATION.

Turn ignition off. Check alignment of seat track to floor and seat bottom. If seat track is out of alignment, align seat track. Recheck seat operation. If seat track is not out of alignment, replace seat track assembly.

TEST C: POWER SEAT MOVES BUT IS LOOSE

Check fastening hardware for proper installation. If hardware is loose, tighten hardware. Recheck seat operation. If hardware is not loose, replace seat track assembly.

TEST D: POWER SEAT DOES NOT MAKE FULL TRAVEL

Check seat track for obstructions. If any obstructions exists, repair as necessary. Recheck seat operation. If no obstructions exist, replace seat track assembly.

TEST E: POWER SEAT DOES NOT MOVE HORIZONTAL//VERTICAL

NOTE: Before beginning this test, ensure seat and seat track are free from all obstructions. Test applies to passenger's seat and driver's seat (without memory). For driver's seat (with memory), perform TEST G: MEMORY SEAT INOPERATIVE. For connector identification, see CONNECTOR IDENTIFICATION.

1) Turn ignition off. Operate inoperative seat in forward and rearward directions. If seat moves horizontally, go to next step. If seat does not move horizontally, go to step **9)**.

2) Operate inoperative seat in both tilting directions. If rear height motor does not operate, go to next step. If front height motor does not operate, go to step **6)**. If both front and rear height motors do not operate, replace seat control switch.

3) Disconnect inoperative seat motor assembly harness connector. Measure voltage between Yellow/Light Green and Red/Light Green wires at seat motor assembly harness connector. Operate switch in rear up and rear down directions, while observing voltmeter. If voltage does not change from less than -10 volts to more than 10 volts, go to next step. If voltage changes from less than -10 volts to more than 10 volts, check seat track for smooth operation. If seat track is okay, replace rear height motor.

4) Disconnect suspect seat control switch harness connector. Measure resistance of Red/Light Green wire between seat control switch harness connector and seat motor harness connector. If resistance is 5 ohms or less, go to next step. If resistance is more than 5 ohms, repair open in Red/Light Green wire.

5) Measure resistance of Yellow/Light Green wire between seat control switch harness connector and seat motor harness connector. If resistance is less than 5 ohms, replace seat control switch. If resistance is 5 ohms or more, repair open in Yellow/Light Green wire.

6) Disconnect inoperative seat motor assembly harness connector. If driver's seat is inoperative, measure voltage between Red/Light Blue and Yellow/Light Blue wires at seat motor assembly harness connector. If passenger's seat is inoperative, measure voltage between Yellow/White and Red/White wires at seat motor assembly harness connector. On all applications, operate switch in front up and front down directions, while observing voltmeter. If voltage does not change from less than -10 volts to more than 10 volts, go to next step. If voltage changes from less than -10 volts to more than 10 volts, check seat track for smooth operation. If seat track is okay, replace front height motor.

7) Disconnect suspect seat control switch harness connector. If driver's seat is inoperative, measure resistance of Yellow/Light Blue wire between seat control switch harness connector and seat motor harness connector. If passenger's seat is inoperative, measure resistance of Red/White wire between seat control switch harness connector and seat motor harness connector. On all applications, if resistance is 5 ohms or less, go to next step. If resistance is more than 5 ohms, repair open in Yellow/Light Blue wire or Red/White wire.

8) If driver's seat is inoperative, measure resistance of Red/Light Blue wire between seat control switch harness connector and seat motor harness connector. If passenger's seat is inoperative, measure resistance of Yellow/White wire between seat control switch harness connector and seat motor harness connector. On all applications, if resistance is 5 ohms or less, go to next step. If resistance is 5 ohms or more, repair open in Red/Light Blue wire or Yellow/White wire.

9) Disconnect inoperative seat motor assembly harness connector. If driver's seat is inoperative, measure voltage between Yellow/White and Red/White wires at seat motor assembly harness connector. If passenger's seat is inoperative, measure voltage between Red/Light Blue and Yellow/White Blue wires at seat motor assembly harness connector. On all applications, operate switch in front up and front down directions, while observing voltmeter. If voltage does not change from less than -10 volts to more than 10 volts, go to next step. If voltage changes from less than -10 volts to more than 10 volts, check seat track for smooth operation. If seat track is okay, replace horizontal motor.

10) Disconnect suspect seat control switch harness connector. If driver's seat is inoperative, measure resistance of Yellow/White wire between seat control switch harness connector and seat motor harness connector. If passenger's seat is inoperative, measure resistance of Red/Light Blue wire between seat control switch harness connector and seat motor harness connector. On all applications, if resistance is 5 ohms or less, go to next step. If resistance is more than 5 ohms, repair open in Yellow/White wire or Red/Light Blue wire.

11) If driver's seat is inoperative, measure resistance of Red/White wire between seat control switch harness connector and seat motor harness connector. If passenger's seat is inoperative, measure resistance of Yellow/Light Blue wire between seat control switch harness connector and seat motor harness connector. On all applications, if resistance is less than 5 ohms, replace seat control switch. If resistance is 5 ohms or more, repair open in Red/White wire or Yellow/Light Blue wire.

TEST F: POWER LUMBAR INOPERATIVE

NOTE: For connector identification, see CONNECTOR IDENTIFICATION.

1) Turn ignition off. Operate lumbar switch to inflate position. If adjusting pump does not run, go to next step. If adjusting pump runs, go to step **7)**.

2) Operate power seat. If power seat operates, go to next step. If power seat does not operate, go to TEST A: POWER SEAT COMPLETELY INOPERATIVE if not equipped with power memory seats or go to TEST G: MEMORY SEAT INOPERATIVE if equipped with power memory seats.

3) Disconnect lumbar switch Gray 2-pin connector. Measure voltage at Black/White wire (Red/Light Blue if equipped with memory seats) at lumbar switch harness connector. If battery voltage exists, go to next step. If battery voltage does not exist, repair open in Black/White wire (Red/Light Blue if equipped with memory seats).

4) Remove lumbar switch. Measure resistance between lumbar switch terminals. Resistance should be less than 5 ohms with switch in inflate position and more than 10,000 ohms with switch in any other position. If resistance is as specified, install lumbar switch and go to next step. If resistance is not as specified, replace lumbar switch.

NOTE: Adjusting pump may also be referred to as power lumbar motor.

5) Disconnect adjusting pump harness connector. Measure voltage between ground and Red wire at adjusting pump harness connector. Press lumbar switch to inflate position. If battery voltage exists, go to next step. If battery voltage does not exist, repair open in Red wire.

6) Measure resistance between ground and Black wire at adjusting pump harness connector. If resistance is less than 5 ohms, replace adjusting pump. If resistance is 5 ohms or more, repair open in Black wire.

7) Activate lumbar switch to inflate position. Observe seatback pad. If seatback does not inflate, go to next step. If seatback inflates, go to step **13)**.

8) Gain access to suspect support bladder. Visually inspect support bladder. If no damage is visible, go to next step. If any damage is visible, replace support bladder.

9) Remove support bladder hose from adjusting pump. Activate lumbar switch to inflate position. If air is felt coming from adjusting pump, go to next step. If no air is felt coming from adjusting pump, replace adjusting pump.

10) Connect support bladder hose to adjusting pump. Disconnect hose coming from adjusting pump from lumbar switch. Activate lumbar switch to inflate position. If air is felt at open hose, go to next step. If no air is felt at open hose, replace hose.

11) Connect hose to lumbar switch. Disconnect hose going to support bladder from lumbar switch. Activate lumbar switch to inflate position. If air is felt at lumbar switch port, go to next step. If no air is felt at lumbar switch port, replace lumbar switch.

12) Connect hose to lumbar switch. Disconnect hose from support bladder. Activate lumbar switch to inflate position. If air is felt at hose, go to next step. If no air is felt at hose, replace hose.

13) Connect hose at support bladder. Disconnect hose from adjusting pump. Connect hand pump to disconnected hose. Pressurize system to 5 psi (0.35 kg/cm^2). Wait 3 hours. Observe pressure. If pressure does not hold, go to next step. If pressure holds, system is okay.

14) Disconnect hose from lumbar support bladder. Using hand pump, inflate pad to 5 psi (0.35 kg/cm^2). Wait 3 hours. Observe pressure. If pressure does not hold, replace lumbar support bladder. If pressure holds, replace lumbar switch.

TEST G: MEMORY SEAT INOPERATIVE

NOTE: Before beginning this test, ensure seat and seat track are free from all obstructions. For connector identification, see CONNECTOR IDENTIFICATION.

1) Ensure transmission is in Park. Turn ignition switch to LOCK position. Connect New Generation Star (NGS) tester to data link connector. Retrieved and record continuous DTCs. Clear continuous DTCs. Perform Driver's Seat Module (DSM) self-test. If no DTCs were retrieved during self-test, go to next step. If any DTCs were retrieved during self-test, perform appropriate test. See DIAGNOSTIC TROUBLE CODES table.

DIAGNOSTIC TROUBLE CODES

DTC	Go To
B1342	1
B1529	Test H
B1533	Test H
B1537	Test H
B1663, B1664 & B1665	Test G, step 10)
B1663	Test G, step 22)
B1664	Test G, step 25)
B1665	Test G, step 28)
B1711	Test G, step 3)
B1715	Test G, step 3)
B1719	Test G, step 3)
B1723	Test G, step 3)
B1727	Test G, step 3)
B1731	Test G, step 3)
B1952	TEST J
B1954	TEST J
B1956	TEST J
B1962	TEST J
B1964	TEST J

[1] – Replace driver's seat module.

2) Using NGS tester, monitor DSM PIDs SFNT_SW, SREARSW and SFWS_SW while activating seat control switch in all directions. If PID values do not agree with seat control switch positions and fuse No. 9 (7.5-amp) is blown, go to step 7). If PID value does not agree with seat control switch position and fuse No. 18 (25-amp) is okay, go to next step. If PID value agrees with seat control switch position, go to step 9).

3) Turn ignition off. Remove seat control switch. Test seat control switch. See SEAT CONTROL SWITCH under COMPONENT TESTS. Replace seat control switch as necessary. If seat control switch is okay, go to next step.

4) Ensure seat control switch harness connector is still disconnected. Measure voltage at Light Green/Yellow wire at seat control switch harness connector. If battery voltage exists, go to next step. If battery voltage does not exist, repair open in Light Green/Yellow wire.

5) Measure resistance between ground and Black wire at seat control switch harness connector. If resistance is less than 5 ohms, go to next step. If resistance is 5 ohms or more, repair open in Black wire.

6) Disconnect DSM 18-pin harness connector C335. DSM is located underneath driver's seat. Turn ignition on. Measure voltage at Yellow/Light Blue, Red/Light Green, Yellow/Light Green, Red/Light Blue, Red/White and Yellow/White wires at seat control switch harness connector. If voltage does not exists at any wire, go to next step. If voltage exists at any wire, repair short to voltage in appropriate wire(s).

7) Turn ignition off. Measure resistance between ground and Yellow/Light Blue, Red/Light Green, Yellow/Light Green, Red/Light Blue, Red/White and Yellow/White wires at seat control switch harness connector. If all resistance reading are more than 10,000 ohms, go to next step. If any resistance reading is 10,000 ohms or less, repair short to ground in appropriate wire(s).

8) Measure resistance in Yellow/Light Blue, Red/Light Green, Yellow/Light Green, Red/Light Blue, Red/White and Yellow/White wires between DSM harness connector C335 and seat control switch harness connector. If all resistance readings are less than 5 ohms, replace driver's seat module. If any resistance reading is 5 ohms or more, repair open in appropriate wire(s).

9) Using NGS tester, operate seat in all directions. If seat operates as commanded, replace driver's seat module. If seat does not operate as commanded, go to appropriate step. See TEST STEP table.

TEST STEP

Malfunction	Step
No Seat Movement	10)
No Front Height Movement	22)
No Rear Height Movement	25)
No Horizontal Movement	28)

10) Ensure ignition is off. Disconnect DSM 2-pin Gray connector C350. Measure voltage between ground and Red/Light Blue wire at DSM harness connector C350. If battery voltage does not exist, go to next step. If battery voltage exists, go to step 14).

11) Remove fuse No. 18 (25-amp) from instrument panel fuse box. If fuse is blown, go to next step. If fuse is okay, go to step 13).

12) Measure resistance between ground and Red/Light Blue wire at DSM harness connector C350. If resistance is more than 10,000 ohms, repair or replace instrument panel fuse box. If resistance 10,000 ohms or less, repair short to ground in Red/Light Blue wire.

13) Ensure fuse No. 18 is still removed. Measure resistance of Red/Light Blue wire between output side of fuse No. 18 and DSM harness connector C350. If resistance is less than 5 ohms, go to next step. If resistance is 5 ohms or more, repair open in Red/Light Blue wire.

14) Measure resistance between ground and Black wire at DSM harness connector C350. If resistance is less than 5 ohms, go to next step. If resistance is 5 ohms or more, repair open in Black wire.

15) Remove and inspect DSM internal fuse. If fuse is okay, go to next step. If fuse is blown, replace driver's seat module.

16) Disconnect DSM Black 16-pin harness connector C351. Measure resistance between ground and Red/Light Blue and Yellow/Light Blue wires at DSM harness connector C351. If any resistance reading is 10,000 ohms or less, go to next step. If both resistance readings are more than 10,000 ohms, go to step 18).

17) Disconnect front height motor harness connector. Disconnect DSM Brown 6-pin harness connector C353. Measure resistance between ground and Red/Light Blue and Yellow/Light Blue wires at DSM harness connector C351. If any resistance reading is 10,000 or less, repair short to ground in appropriate wire. If both resistance readings are more than 10,000 ohms, replace front seat track assembly.

18) Measure resistance between ground and Red/Light Green and Yellow/Light Green wires at DSM harness connector C351. If any resistance reading is 10,000 ohms or less, go to next step. If both resistance readings are more than 10,000 ohms, go to step 20).

19) Disconnect rear height motor harness connector. Measure resistance between ground and Red/Light Green and Yellow/Light Green wires at DSM harness connector C351. If any resistance reading is

10,000 ohms or less, repair short to ground in appropriate wire. If both resistance readings are more than 10,000 ohms, replace front seat track assembly.

20) Measure resistance between ground and Red/White and Yellow/White wires at DSM harness connector C351. If any resistance reading is 10,000 ohms or less, go to next step. If both resistance readings are more than 10,000 ohms, replace driver's seat module.

21) Disconnect horizontal motor harness connector. Measure resistance between ground and Red/White and Yellow/White wires at DSM harness connector C351. If any resistance reading is 10,000 ohms or less, repair short to ground in appropriate wire. If both resistance readings are more than 10,000 ohms, replace front seat track assembly.

22) Turn ignition off. Ensure transmission is in Park. Disconnect front height motor Brown 6-pin harness connector. Turn ignition on. Measure voltage between Red/Light Blue and Yellow/Light Blue wires at front height motor harness connector. Using NGS tester, trigger front height motor up and down. If voltage does not exist when front height motor is triggered both up and down, go to next step. If voltage exists when front height motor is triggered both up and down, replace front seat track assembly.

23) Turn ignition off. Disconnect DSM Black 16-pin harness connector C351. Turn ignition on. Measure voltage between ground and Red/Light Blue and Yellow/Light Blue wires at DSM harness connector C351. If voltage does not exist at both wires, go to next step. If voltage exists at either wire, repair short to voltage in appropriate wire.

24) Turn ignition off. Measure resistance of Red/Light Blue and Yellow/Light Blue wires between front height motor harness connector and DSM harness connector C351. If both resistance readings are less than 5 ohms, replace driver's seat module. If any resistance reading is 5 ohms or more, repair open in appropriate wire.

25) Turn ignition off. Ensure transmission is in Park. Disconnect rear height motor Brown 6-pin harness connector. Turn ignition on. Measure voltage between Red/Light Green and Yellow/Light Green wires at rear height motor harness connector. Using NGS tester, trigger rear height motor up and down. If voltage does not exist when rear height motor is triggered both up and down, go to next step. If voltage exists when rear height motor is triggered both up and down, replace front seat track assembly.

26) Turn ignition off. Disconnect DSM Black 16-pin harness connector C351. Turn ignition on. Measure voltage at Red/Light Green and Yellow/Light Green wires at DSM harness connector C351. If voltage does not exist at both wires, go to next step. If voltage exists at either wire, repair short to voltage in appropriate wire.

27) Turn ignition off. Measure resistance of Red/Light Green and Yellow/Light Green wires between rear height motor harness connector and DSM harness connector C351. If both resistance readings are 5 ohms or less, replace driver's seat module. If any resistance reading is more than 5 ohms, repair open in appropriate wire.

28) Turn ignition off. Ensure transmission is in Park. Disconnect horizontal motor harness connector. Turn ignition on. Measure voltage between Red/White and Yellow/White wires at horizontal motor harness connector. Using NGS tester, trigger horizontal motor up and down. If voltage does not exist when horizontal motor is triggered both up and down, go to next step. If voltage exists when horizontal motor is triggered both up and down, replace front seat track assembly.

29) Turn ignition off. Disconnect DSM Black 16-pin harness connector C351. Turn ignition on. Measure voltage at Red/White and Yellow/White wires at DSM harness connector C351. If voltage does not exist at both wires, go to next step. If voltage exists at either wire, repair short to voltage in appropriate wire.

30) Turn ignition off. Measure resistance of Red/White and Yellow/White wires between horizontal motor harness connector and DSM harness connector C351. If both resistance readings are 5 ohms or less, replace driver's seat module. If any resistance reading is more than 5 ohms, repair open in appropriate wire.

TEST H: MEMORY SEAT INOPERATIVE USING MEMORY SET SWITCH

NOTE: Before beginning this test, ensure seat and seat track are free from all obstructions. For connector identification, see CONNECTOR IDENTIFICATION.

1) Ensure transmission is in Park. Turn ignition off. Connect New Generation Star (NGS) tester to data link connector. Retrieved and record continuous DTCs. Clear continuous DTCs. Perform Driver's Seat Module (DSM) self-test. If no DTCs were retrieved during self-test, go to next step. If any DTCs were retrieved and memory switch LED fails to illuminate during self-test, go to step 5). If any DTCs were retrieved and memory switch LED illuminates during self-test, go to appropriate test step. See DTC TEST STEP table.

DTC TEST STEP

DTC	Step
B1342	[1]
B1950, B1954 & B1962	9
B1529	3
B1533	3
B1537	3
B1663	10
B1664	13
B1665	16
B1950	13
B1952	13
B1954	10
B1956	10
B1962	16
B1964	16

[1] – Replace driver's seat module.

2) Using NGS tester, monitor DSM PIDs MEM1_SW, MEM2_SW and MEMS_SW on while activating memory switch in all positions. If PID value does not agree with switch position and fuse No. 1 is blown, go to step 7). If PID value does not agree with switch position and fuse No. 1 is okay, go to step 3). If PID value agrees with seat control switch position, go to step 9).

3) Remove memory switch. Test memory switch. See MEMORY SWITCH under COMPONENT TESTS. Replace memory switch as necessary. If memory switch is okay, go to next step.

4) Ensure memory switch harness connector is still disconnected. Turn ignition on. Measure voltage between ground and Orange/Light Green wire at memory switch harness connector. If battery voltage exists, go to next step. If battery voltage does not exist, repair open in Orange/Light Green wire.

5) Turn ignition off. Measure resistance between ground and Black wire at memory switch harness connector. If resistance is less than 5 ohms, go to next step. If resistance is 5 ohms or more, repair open in Black wire.

6) Disconnect DSM 22-pin harness connector C337. DSM is located underneath driver's seat. Disconnect Remote Anti-Theft Personality (RAP) module Gray 22-pin harness connector C338. RAP module is located behind left rear quarter panel. Turn ignition on. Measure voltage between ground and Brown/Light Green, Black/Orange, Brown/Orange and White/Orange wires at memory switch harness connector. If voltage does not exists at any wire, go to next step. If voltage exists at any wire, repair short to voltage in appropriate wire(s).

7) Turn ignition off. Measure resistance between ground and Brown/Light Green, Black/Orange, Brown/Orange and White/Orange wires at memory switch harness connector. If all resistance readings are 10,000 ohms or more, go to next step. If any resistance reading is less than 10,000 ohms, repair short to ground in appropriate wire(s).

8) Measure resistance of Brown/Light Green, Black/Orange, Brown/Orange and White/Orange wires between DSM harness connector C337 and memory switch harness connector. If all resistance readings are 5 ohms or less, replace driver's seat module. If any resistance reading is more than 5 ohms, repair open in appropriate wire(s).

9) Place seat in center position using seat control switch. Using NGS tester, monitor PIDs SFWD_P, SFNT_P and SREAR_P while moving seat through all positions. PID valves should increased during forward and upward movement and decreased during rearward and downward movement. If PID valves changed as specified, replace driver's seat module. If PID valves did not change as specified, go to appropriate step. See TEST STEP table.

TEST STEP

Malfunction	Step
Improper PID SFNT_P Value	Next Step
Improper PID SREAR_P Value	13)
Improper PID SFWD_P Value	16)

10) Turn ignition off. Disconnect DSM Black 16-pin harness connector C351. Disconnect memory seat position sensor 8-pin harness connector. Turn ignition on. Measure voltage between ground and Light Green/Red, Orange/Red and Orange/White wires at memory seat position sensor harness connector. If voltage does not exist, go to next step. If voltage exists, repair short to voltage in appropriate wire.

11) Turn ignition off. Measure resistance between ground and Light Green/Red, Orange/Red and Orange/White wire at memory seat position sensor harness connector. If all resistance readings are more than 10,000 ohms, go to next step. If any resistance reading is 10,000 ohms or less, repair short to ground in appropriate wire.

12) Measure resistance of Light Green/Red, Orange/Red and Orange/White wires between memory seat position sensor harness connector and DSM harness connector C351. If all resistance readings are less than 5 ohms, replace front seat track assembly. If any resistance reading is 5 ohms or more, repair open in appropriate wire.

13) Turn ignition off. Disconnect DSM Black 16-pin harness connector C351. Disconnect memory seat position sensor harness connector. Turn ignition on. Measure voltage between ground and Light Green/Black, Orange/Red and Orange/White wires at DSM harness connector C351. If voltage does not exist at any wire, go to next step. If voltage exists at any wire, repair short to voltage in appropriate wire(s).

14) Turn ignition off. Measure resistance between ground and Light Green/Black, Orange/Red and Orange/White wires at DSM harness connector C351. If all resistance readings are 10,000 ohms or more, go to next step. If any resistance reading is less than 10,000 ohms, repair short to ground in appropriate wire.

15) Measure resistance of Light Green/Black, Orange/Red and Orange/White wires between memory seat position sensor harness connector and DSM harness connector C351. If all resistance readings are less than 5 ohms, replace front seat track assembly. If any resistance reading is 5 ohms or more, repair open in appropriate wire(s).

16) Turn ignition off. Disconnect DSM Black 16-pin harness connector C351. Disconnect memory seat position sensor harness connector. Turn ignition on. Measure voltage between ground and Light Green/Orange, Orange/Red and Orange/White wires at memory seat position harness connector. If voltage does not exist at any wire, go to next step. If voltage exists at any wire, repair short to voltage in appropriate wire.

17) Turn ignition off. Measure resistance between ground and Light Green/Orange, Orange/Red and Orange/White wires at memory seat position sensor harness connector. If all resistance readings are more than 10,000 ohms or more, go to next step. If any resistance reading is 10,000 ohms or less, repair short to ground in appropriate wire.

18) Measure resistance of Light Green/Orange, Orange/Red and Orange/White wires between memory seat position sensor harness connector and DSM harness connector C351. If all resistance readings are less than 5 ohms, replace front seat track assembly. If any resistance reading is 5 ohms or more, repair open in appropriate wire.

TEST I: HEATED SEAT IS INOPERATIVE

NOTE: For connector identification, see CONNECTOR IDENTIFICATION.

1) Turn ignition off. Remove and inspect fuse No. 2 (30-amp) from power distribution box in engine compartment. Also remove and inspect fuse No. 10 (7.5-amp) from instrument panel fuse box. If both fuses are okay, go to next step. If any fuse is blown, install NEW fuse and recheck system operation. If fuse blows again, check for short to ground in appropriate circuit. See WIRING DIAGRAMS.

2) Disconnect inoperative heated seat module 10-pin connector located underneath seat. Measure voltage between ground and Light Blue/White wire at heated seat module harness connector. If voltage is more than 10 volts, go to next step. If voltage is 10 volts or less, repair Light Blue/White wire.

3) Disconnect inoperative heated seat switch 8-pin connector. Turn ignition on. Measure voltage between ground and Gray/Yellow wire at heated seat switch harness connector. If voltage is more than 10 volts, reconnect heated seat switch and go to next step. If voltage is 10 volts or less, repair Gray/Yellow wire.

4) Turn ignition off. Measure resistance between ground and Black wire at heated seat module harness connector. If resistance is less than 5 ohms, go to next step. If resistance is 5 ohms or more, repair open in Black wire.

5) Turn ignition on. Measure voltage between ground and Gray/Yellow wire at heated seat module harness connector. If voltage is more than 10 volts, go to next step. If voltage is 10 volts or less, repair Gray/Yellow wire.

6) While pressing heated seat switch, measure voltage between ground and Dark Green/Violet at heated seat module harness connector. If voltage is more than 10 volts, go to step 8). If voltage is 10 volts or less, go to next step.

7) Turn ignition off. Measure resistance of Dark Green wire between heated seat module harness connector and heated seat switch harness connector. If resistance is less than 5 ohms, replace heated seat switch. If resistance is 5 ohms or more, repair open Dark Green wire.

8) Measure resistance between Yellow/Light Blue and Violet/Light Blue wires at heated seat module harness connector. Also measure resistance between ground and Yellow/Light Blue wire at heated seat module harness connector. If resistance is less than 5 ohms between Yellow/Light Blue and Violet/Light Blue wires and more than 10,000 ohms between ground and Yellow/Light Blue wire, replace heated seat module. If resistance is not as specified, go to next step.

9) Disconnect inoperative seat heater/temperature sensor 4-pin connector. Measure resistance of Yellow/Light Blue wire between heated seat module harness connector and seat heater/temperature sensor harness connector. Also measure resistance between ground and Yellow/Light Blue wire at heated seat module harness connector. If resistance of Yellow/Light Blue wire between connectors is less than 5 ohms, and more than 10,000 ohms between ground and Yellow/Light Blue wire, go to next step. If resistance is not as specified, repair open or short to ground in Yellow/Light Blue wire.

10) Disconnect inoperative seat heater 2-pin connector. Measure resistance of Violet/Light Blue wire between heated seat module harness connector and seat heater harness connector. If resistance is less than 5 ohms, go to next step. If resistance is 5 ohms or more, repair open Violet/Light Blue wire.

11) Measure resistance of Gray/Light Blue wire between seat heater harness connector and seat heater/temperature sensor harness connector. If resistance is less than 5 ohms, go to next step. If resistance is 5 ohms or more, repair open Gray/Light Blue wire.

12) Reconnect seat heater/temperature sensor harness connector. Measure resistance between Black/Light Blue and Brown/Light Blue wires at heated seat module harness connector. If resistance is 50-300,000 ohms, replace heated seat module. If resistance is not 50-300,000 ohms, go to next step.

13) Ensure inoperative seat heater/temperature sensor 4-pin is disconnected. Measure resistance of Black/Light Blue wire between heated seat module harness connector and seat heater/temperature sensor harness connector. Also measure resistance between ground and Black/Light Blue wire at heated seat module harness connector. If resistance of Black/Light Blue wire between connectors is less than 5 ohms, and more than 10,000 ohms between ground and Black/Light Blue wire, go to next step. If resistance is not as specified, repair open or short to ground in Black/Light Blue wire.

14) Measure resistance of Brown/Light Blue wire between heated seat module harness connector and seat heater/temperature sensor harness connector. Also measure resistance between ground and Brown/Light Blue wire at heated seat module harness connector. If resistance of Brown/Light Blue wire between connectors is less than 5 ohms, and more than 10,000 ohms between ground and Brown/Light Blue wire, go to next step. If resistance is not as specified, repair open or short to ground in Brown/Light Blue wire.

TEST J: MEMORY SEAT INOPERATIVE USING REMOTE TRANSMITTER

NOTE: Before beginning this test, ensure seat and seat track are free from all obstructions. For connector identification, see CONNECTOR IDENTIFICATION.

1) Ensure transmission is in Park. Turn ignition off. Connect New Generation Star (NGS) tester to data link connector. Retrieved and record continuous DTCs. Clear continuous DTCs. Perform Driver's Seat Module (DSM) self-test. If no DTCs were retrieved during self-test, go to next step. If any DTCs were retrieved during self-test, perform appropriate test. See DRIVER'S SEAT MODULE DTC INDEX table under SELF-DIAGNOSTIC SYSTEM.

2) Disconnect memory switch harness connector. Disconnect Remote Anti-Theft Personality (RAP) module harness connector. RAP module is located behind left rear quarter panel. Disconnect Driver's Seat Module (DSM) harness connector. DSM is located underneath driver's seat. Measure resistance of Brown/Light Green and Black/Orange wires between memory switch harness connector and RAP module harness connector. If any resistance reading is 5 ohms or more, repair open in appropriate wire. If both resistance readings are less than 5 ohms, check for opens and shorts in remote keyless entry system. See appropriate wiring diagram in REMOTE KEYLESS ENTRY SYSTEMS article.

TEST K: NO COMMUNICATION WITH DRIVER'S SEAT MODULE

NOTE: Before beginning this test, ensure seat and seat track are free from all obstructions. For connector identification, see CONNECTOR IDENTIFICATION.

1) If vehicle is equipped with memory seat/mirror feature, go to next step. If vehicle is not equipped with memory seat/memory feature, test power seats for proper operation. If seats do not operate properly, repair by symptom, see SYMPTOM DIAGNOSIS table under SYSTEM TESTS.

2) Connect NGS tester to data link connector. Ensure transmission is in Park. Turn ignition switch on. Using NGS tester, monitor DSM PID P/N_SW. If NGS tester displays UNABLE TO PERFORM TEST/ FUNCTION, MODULE NOT RESPONDING: DSM, CHECK IGNITION STATUS, VERIFY CABLE REQUIREMENTS or CHECK CABLE CONNECTIONS, go to next step. If NGS tester does not display UNABLE TO PERFORM TEST/FUNCTION, MODULE NOT RESPONDING: DSM, CHECK IGNITION STATUS, VERIFY CABLE REQUIREMENTS or CHECK CABLE CONNECTIONS, go to step 8).

3) Turn ignition off. Remove fuse No. 36 (7-5-amp) from instrument panel fuse box. If fuse is okay, go to next step. If fuse is blown, go to step 5).

4) Turn ignition on. Measure voltage at input side of fuse No. 36. If battery voltage exists, go to step 6). If battery voltage does not exist, check power distribution from fuse No. 1 in power distribution box in engine compartment. See appropriate wiring diagram in POWER DISTRIBUTION article in WIRING DIAGRAMS. If power distribution is okay, replace instrument panel fuse box. If power distribution is not okay, repair as necessary.

5) Turn ignition off. Ensure fuse No. 36 is still removed. Disconnect DSM 22-pin harness connector C337. DSM is located underneath driver's seat. Measure resistance between ground and Light Green/Yellow wire at DSM harness connector C337. If resistance is more than 10,000

ohms, system is okay at this time. Replace fuse and recheck system operation. If resistance is 10,000 ohms or less, repair short to ground in Light Green/Yellow wire.

6) Turn ignition off. Disconnect DSM 22-pin harness connector C337. DSM is located underneath driver's seat. Turn ignition on. Measure voltage between ground and Light Green/Yellow wire at DSM harness connector C337. If battery voltage exists, go to next step. If battery voltage does not exist, repair open in Light Green/Yellow wire.

7) Measure resistance between ground and Black/White wire at DSM harness connector C337. If resistance is less than 5 ohms, repair network concern. See MODULE COMMUNICATIONS NETWORK – EXPLORER & MOUNTAINEER article. If resistance is 5 ohms or more, repair open in Black/White wire.

8) Using NGS tester, monitor DSM PID P/N_SW while moving transmission through entire range. If PID value does not agree with transmission position, go to next step. If PID value agrees with transmission position, replace driver's seat module.

9) Remove fuse No. 28 (7.5-amp) from instrument panel fuse box. Measure resistance of Red/Black wire between output side of fuse No. 28 and DSM harness connector C337. If resistance is 5 ohms or less, repair transmission range sensor circuit. If resistance is more than 5 ohms, repair open in Red/Black wire.

TEST L: HEATED SEAT DOES NOT FUNCTION PROPERLY – SEAT DOES NOT HEAT, BUT HEATED SWITCH ILLUMINATES WHEN PRESSED

NOTE: For connector identification, see CONNECTOR IDENTIFICATION.

1) Turn ignition off. Disconnect inoperative heated seat module 10-pin connector located underneath seat. Measure resistance between Yellow/Light Blue and Violet/Light Blue wires at heated seat module harness connector. Also measure resistance between ground and Yellow/Light Blue wire at heated seat module harness connector. If resistance is less than 5 ohms between Yellow/Light Blue and Violet/ Light Blue wires and more than 10,000 ohms between ground and Yellow/Light Blue wire, replace heated seat module. If resistance is not as specified, go to next step.

2) Disconnect inoperative seat heater/temperature sensor 4-pin connector. Measure resistance of Yellow/Light Blue wire between heated seat module harness connector and seat heater/temperature sensor harness connector. Also measure resistance between ground and Yellow/Light Blue wire at heated seat module harness connector. If resistance of Yellow/Light Blue wire between connectors is less than 5 ohms, and more than 10,000 ohms between ground and Yellow/Light Blue wire, go to next step. If resistance is not as specified, repair open or short to ground in Yellow/Light Blue wire.

3) Disconnect inoperative seat heater 2-pin connector. Measure resistance of Violet/Light Blue wire between heated seat module harness connector and seat heater harness connector. If resistance is less than 5 ohms, go to next step. If resistance is 5 ohms or more, repair open Violet/Light Blue wire.

4) Measure resistance of Gray/Light Blue wire between seat heater harness connector and seat heater/temperature sensor harness connector. Also measure resistance between ground and Gray/Light Blue wire at seat heater/temperature sensor harness connector. If resistance of Gray/Light Blue wire between connectors is less than 5 ohms, and more than 10,000 ohms between ground and Gray/Light Blue wire, go to next step. If resistance is not as specified, repair open or short to ground in Gray/Light Blue wire.

5) Reconnect seat heater/temperature sensor harness connector. Measure resistance between Black/Light Blue and Brown/Light Blue wires at heated seat module harness connector. If resistance is 50-300,000 ohms, replace heated seat module. If resistance is not 50-300,000 ohms, go to next step.

6) Ensure inoperative seat heater/temperature sensor 4-pin is disconnected. Measure resistance of Black/Light Blue wire between heated seat module harness connector and seat heater/temperature sensor harness connector. Also measure resistance between ground and

Black/Light Blue wire at heated seat module harness connector. If resistance of Black/Light Blue wire between connectors is less than 5 ohms, and more than 10,000 ohms between ground and Black/Light Blue wire, go to next step. If resistance is not as specified, repair open or short to ground in Black/Light Blue wire.

7) Measure resistance of Brown/Light Blue wire between heated seat module harness connector and seat heater/temperature sensor harness connector. Also measure resistance between ground and Brown/Light Blue wire at heated seat module harness connector. If resistance of Brown/Light Blue wire between connectors is less than 5 ohms, and more than 10,000 ohms between ground and Brown/Light Blue wire, replace seat heater/temperature sensor. If resistance is not as specified, repair open or short to ground in Brown/Light Blue wire.

TEST M: HEATED SEAT DOES NOT FUNCTION PROPERLY – SEAT HEATS, BUT HEATED SWITCH DOES NOT ILLUMINATE WHEN PRESSED

NOTE: For connector identification, see CONNECTOR IDENTIFICATION.

1) Turn ignition off. Disconnect inoperative heated seat module 10-pin connector located underneath seat. Turn ignition on. Measure voltage between ground and Orange wire at heated seat module harness connector. If battery voltage exists, replace heated seat module. If battery voltage does not exist, go to next step.

2) Turn ignition off. Disconnect inoperative heated seat switch connector. Turn ignition on. Measure voltage between ground and Gray/Yellow wire at heated seat switch harness connector. If battery voltage exists, go to next step. If battery voltage does not exist, repair open Gray/Yellow wire.

3) Turn ignition off. Measure resistance of Orange wire between heated seat module 10-pin harness connector and heated switch harness connector. If resistance is less than 5 ohms, replace heated seat switch. If resistance is 5 ohms or more, repair open Orange wire.

REMOVAL & INSTALLATION

CAUTION: When battery is disconnected, vehicle computer and memory systems may lose memory data. Driveability problems may exist until computer systems have completed a relearn cycle. See COMPUTER RELEARN PROCEDURES article in GENERAL INFORMATION before disconnecting battery.

SEAT ASSEMBLY

Removal & Installation – Position seat in full up position. Disconnect negative battery cable and wait one minute. Remove caps from seat retaining nuts. Remove 2 nuts and 2 bolts retaining seat track to floorpan. Disconnect wiring harness connectors and remove seat from vehicle. To install, reverse removal procedure.

SEAT CUSHION

NOTE: Procedure may vary slightly depending on seat size and power options.

Removal & Installation – **1)** Remove seat and track assembly. See SEAT ASSEMBLY. Remove screws from left side shield. Carefully disconnect and tag air hoses from lumbar/bolster support switches, if equipped. Disconnect switch-to-motor connectors. Remove left side shield. Remove remaining shields.

2) Remove hog rings securing lower portion of seatback cover. Slide seatback cover up enough to remove seatback frame bolts. Remove seatback. Disconnect air line from lumbar and bolster bladders, if equipped. Remove hog rings securing cover rods to seat frame. Remove cover and cushion. To install, reverse removal procedure.

POWER SEAT MOTOR

NOTE: Power seat motors are not serviceable. If power seat motor is defective, entire seat track must be replaced.

LUMBAR SUPPORT BACK PAD ADJUSTER

Removal & Installation – Remove seat and track assembly. See SEAT ASSEMBLY. Remove seatback cover. Disconnect seatback adjusting hose. Using a screwdriver, bend adjuster-to-seatback frame retaining tabs inward. Remove adjuster from seatback frame. To install, reverse removal procedure.

SEAT CONTROL SWITCH

Removal & Installation – Disconnect negative battery cable and wait one minute. Remove side shield retaining screws. Remove side shield. Remove 2 switch retaining screws. Remove switch and housing. Disconnect electrical connector. Remove control switch. To install, reverse removal procedure.

SEAT BACK CONTROL SWITCH

Removal & Installation – Disconnect negative battery cable and wait one minute. Remove seat cushion frame and spring assembly. Remove regulator control processor sensor. Remove control switch and housing attaching screws. Disconnect adjusting hose and electrical connector from switch. Remove switch. To install, reverse removal procedure.

MEMORY CONTROL SWITCH

Removal & Installation – Using screwdriver, disengage retaining stud at rear edge of bezel from door panel and remove trim panel. Gently snap switch from bezel. Disconnect electrical connector and remove switch. To install, reverse removal procedure.

DRIVER'S SEAT MODULE

Removal & Installation – Remove driver's seat and track assembly. See SEAT ASSEMBLY. Place seat upside-down on clean surface. Remove 2 nuts and screw attaching module to seat track. Remove module. To install, reverse removal procedure.

WIRING DIAGRAMS

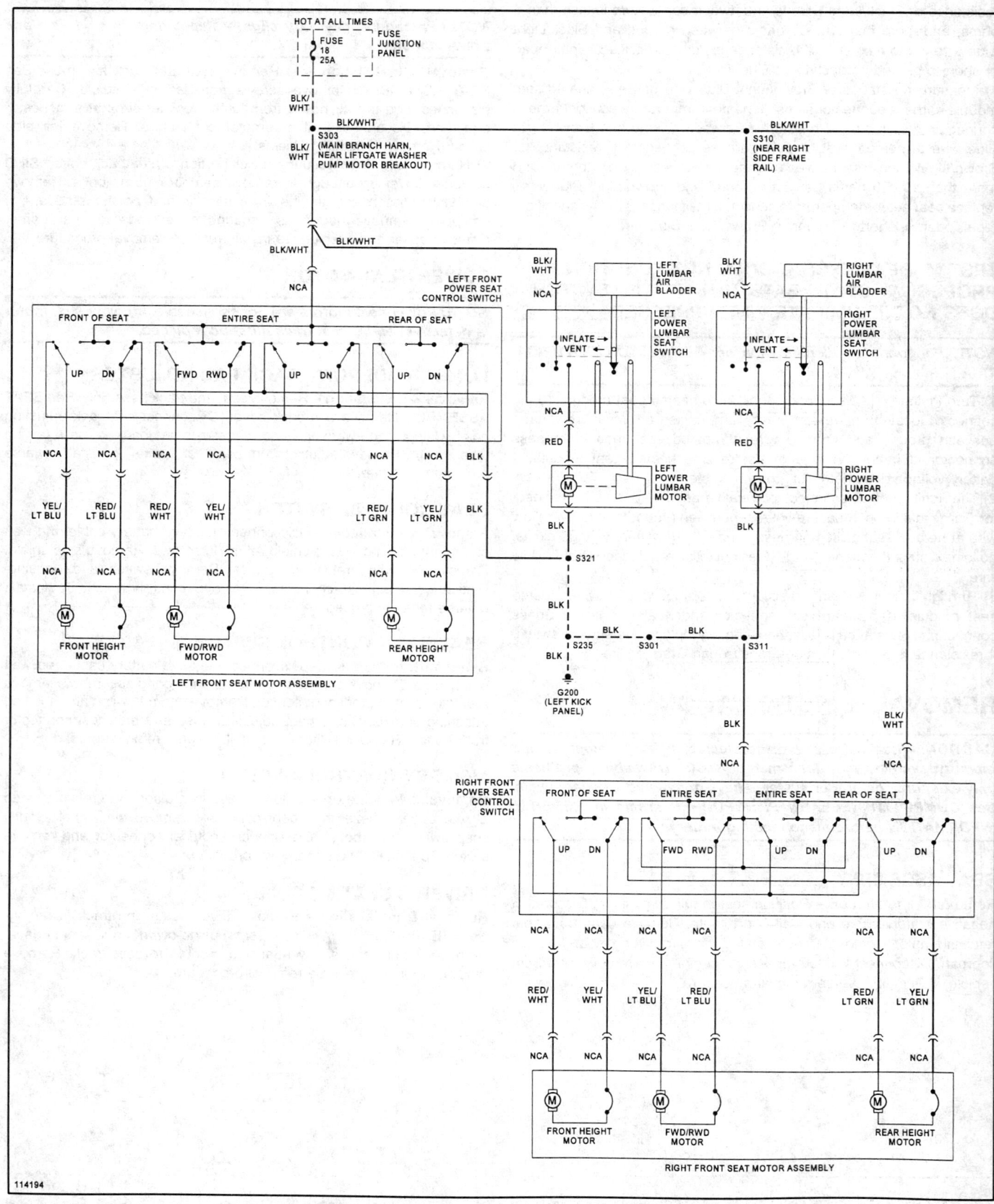

Fig. 9: *Power Lumbar & Power Seats System Wiring Diagram (Explorer & Mountaineer)*

114194

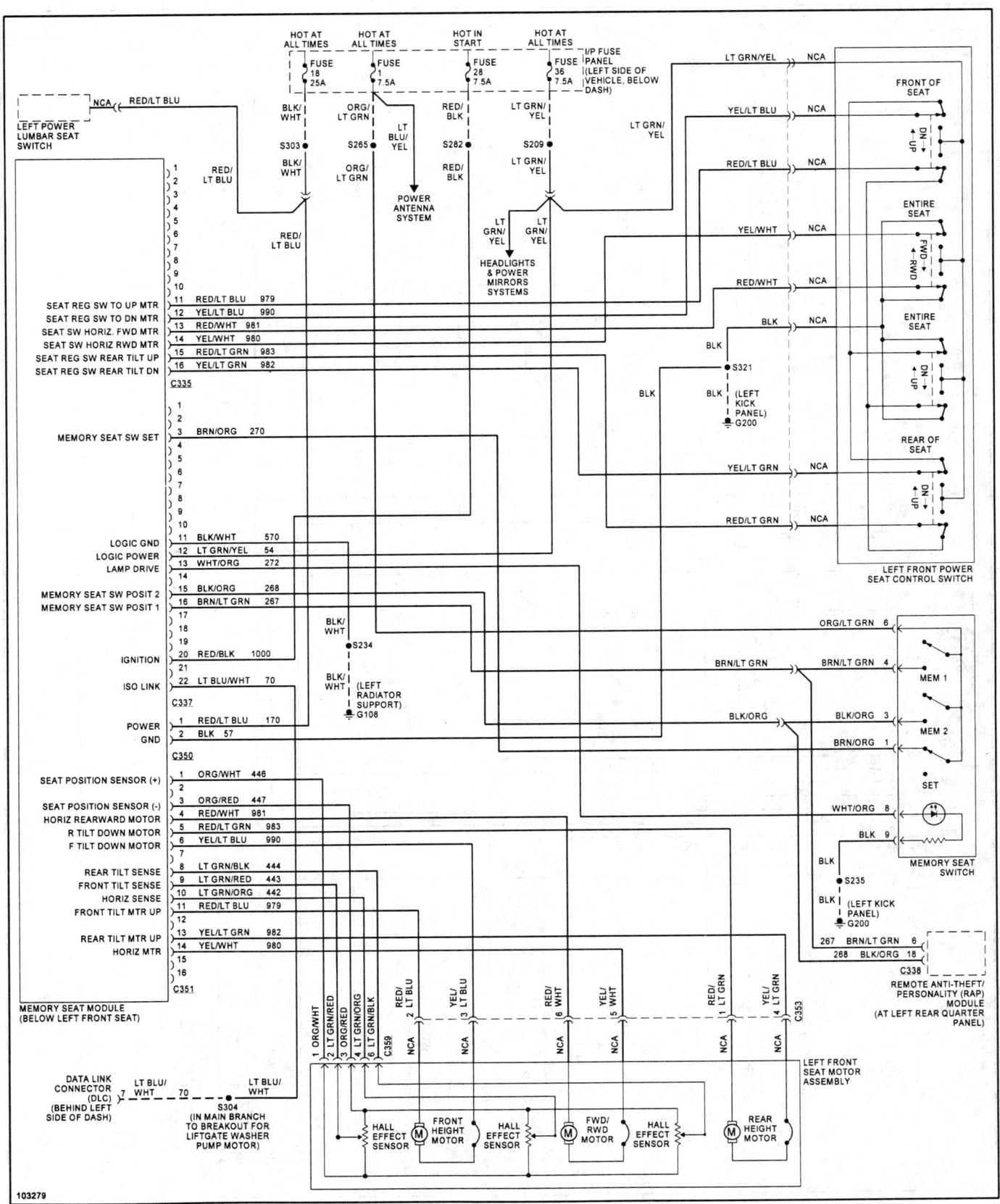

Fig. 10: Power Seats System Wiring Diagram (Explorer & Mountaineer – With Memory Seat)

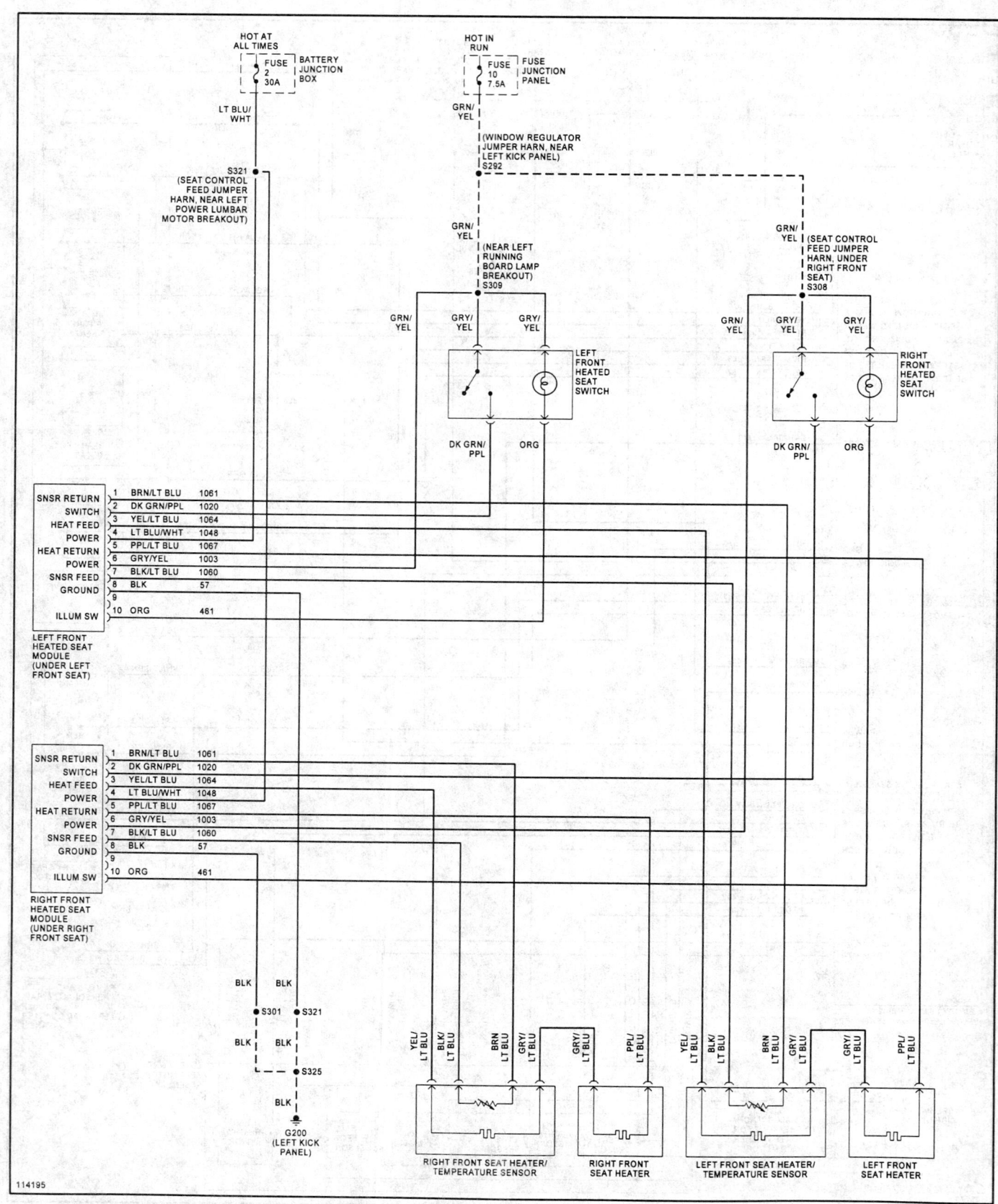

Fig. 11: Heated Seat System Wiring Diagram (Explorer & Mountaineer)

DESCRIPTION & OPERATION

The 6-way power seats provide horizontal, vertical and tilt adjustments and an optional lumbar support adjustment. Seat function switches are mounted on side of seat trim panel. Power seat circuits are protected by circuit breakers and/or fuses. All models have a circuit breaker mounted on each motor armature and use an additional fuse in the engine compartment fuse box.

TROUBLE SHOOTING

Before performing individual component test, check the following for possible cause of system malfunction:

- Blown fuses or faulty circuit breakers.
- Loose or corroded connectors.
- Damaged wiring.
- Damaged motors.
- Faulty switches.
- Damaged lumbar support bladder.
- Damaged or kinked air hoses.

COMPONENT TESTS

SEAT CONTROL SWITCH

Remove seat control switch. Check resistance between appropriate terminals with seat control switch in appropriate position. See SEAT CONTROL SWITCH RESISTANCE table. See Fig. 1. If resistances are not as specified, replace seat control switch.

SEAT CONTROL SWITCH RESISTANCE

Switch Position	Terminals	Resistance (Ohms)
Neutral	4 & All Except 2	Less Than 5
Front Up	2 & 7	Less Than 5
Front Down	2 & 5	Less Than 5
Rear Up	1 & 2	Less Than 5
Rear Down	2 & 6	Less Than 5
Seat FWD	2 & 3	Less Than 5
Seat RWD	2 & 8	Less Than 5

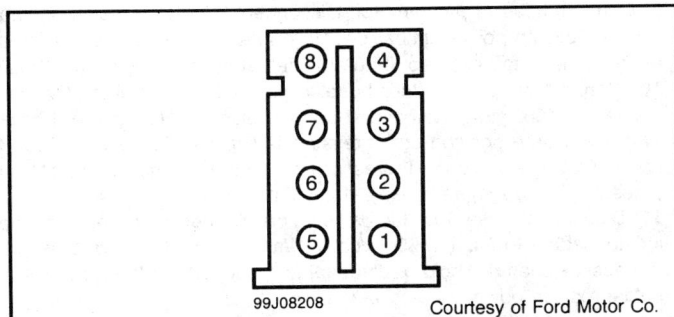

99J08208   Courtesy of Ford Motor Co.

Fig. 1: Identifying Seat Control Switch Terminals

SYSTEM TESTS

NOTE: To determine correct test, see SYMPTOM CHART table. Unless otherwise directed, perform tests in order listed.

CAUTION: When battery is disconnected, vehicle computer and memory systems may lose memory data. Driveability problems may exist until computer systems have completed a relearn cycle. See COMPUTER RELEARN PROCEDURES article in GENERAL INFORMATION before disconnecting battery.

SYMPTOM CHART

Symptom	Test
Power Seat Completely Inoperative	A
Front Height Movement Inoperative	B
Rear Height Movement Inoperative	C
Horizontal Movement Inoperative	D
Power Lumbar Support Inoperative	E

TEST A: POWER SEAT COMPLETELY INOPERATIVE

1) Disconnect seat control switch harness connector C312. Measure voltage at terminal No. 2 (Dark Green wire) at seat control switch harness connector C312. See Fig. 2. If battery voltage exists, go to next step. If battery voltage does not exist, repair power distribution circuit as necessary. See WIRING DIAGRAMS.

2) Measure resistance between ground and terminal No. 4 (Black wire) at seat control switch harness connector C312. If resistance is 5 ohms or less, go to next step. If resistance is greater than 5 ohms, repair open in Black wire.

3) Test seat control switch. See SEAT CONTROL SWITCH under COMPONENT TESTS. If switch is defective, replace seat control switch. If switch is okay, repair or replace seat track assembly as necessary.

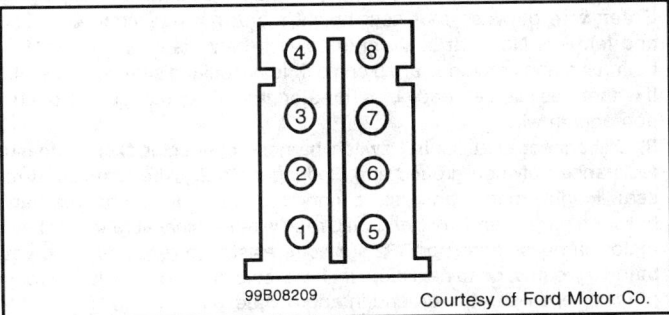

99B08209   Courtesy of Ford Motor Co.

Fig. 2: Identifying Seat Control Switch Harness Connector C312 Terminals

TEST B: FRONT HEIGHT MOVEMENT INOPERATIVE

1) Disconnect front seat height motor harness connector C328. Measure resistance between ground and Red/Light Blue wire terminal at front seat height motor harness connector C328. Measure resistance between ground and Yellow/Light Blue wire terminal at front seat height motor harness connector C328. If either resistance reading is greater than 5 ohms, go to next step. If both resistance reading are 5 ohms or less, go to step **3)**.

2) Disconnect seat control switch harness connector C312. Measure resistance in Red/Light Blue wire between front seat height motor harness connector C328 and terminal No. 7 at seat control switch harness connector C312. See Fig. 2. Measure resistance in Yellow/Light Blue wire between front seat height motor harness connector C328 and terminal No. 5 at seat control switch harness connector C312. If both resistance readings are 5 ohms or less, replace seat control switch. If either resistance reading is greater than 5 ohms, repair open in appropriate wire.

3) Disconnect seat control switch harness connector C312. Measure resistance between ground and Red/Light Blue wire terminal at front seat height motor harness connector C328. Measure resistance between ground and Yellow/Light Blue wire terminal at front seat height motor harness connector C328. If both resistance readings are greater than 10 k/ohms, go to next step. If either resistance reading is 10 k/ohms or less, repair short to ground in appropriate wire.

4) Connect seat control switch harness connector C312. Measure voltage at Red/Light Blue wire terminal at front seat height motor harness connector C328 while pressing seat control switch to front up position. If battery voltage exists, go to next step. If battery voltage does not exist, replace seat control switch.

5) Measure voltage at Yellow/Light Blue wire terminal at front seat height motor harness connector C328 while pressing seat control switch to front down position. If battery voltage exists, replace seat track assembly. If battery voltage does not exist, replace seat control switch.

TEST C: REAR HEIGHT MOVEMENT INOPERATIVE

1) Disconnect rear seat height motor harness connector C329. Measure resistance between ground and Red/Light Green wire terminal at rear seat height motor harness connector C329. Measure resistance between ground and Yellow/Light Green wire terminal at rear seat height motor harness connector C329. If either resistance reading is greater than 5 ohms, go to next step. If both resistance reading are 5 ohms or less, go to step **3)**.

2) Disconnect seat control switch harness connector C312. Measure resistance in Red/Light Green wire between rear seat height motor harness connector C329 and terminal No. 6 at seat control switch harness connector C312. *See Fig. 2.* Measure resistance in Yellow/Light Green wire between rear seat height motor harness connector C329 and terminal No. 1 at seat control switch harness connector C312. If both resistance readings are 5 ohms or less, replace seat control switch. If either resistance reading is greater than 5 ohms, repair open in appropriate wire.

3) Disconnect seat control switch harness connector C312. Measure resistance between ground and Red/Light Green wire terminal at rear seat height motor harness connector C329. Measure resistance between ground and Yellow/Light Green wire terminal at rear seat height motor harness connector C329. If both resistance readings are greater than 10 k/ohms, go to next step. If either resistance reading is 10 k/ohms or less, repair short to ground in appropriate wire.

4) Connect seat control switch harness connector C312. Measure voltage at Red/Light Green wire terminal at rear seat height motor harness connector C329 while pressing seat control switch to rear up position. If battery voltage exists, go to next step. If battery voltage does not exist, replace seat control switch.

5) Measure voltage at Yellow/Light Green wire terminal at rear seat height motor harness connector C329 while pressing seat control switch to rear down position. If battery voltage exists, replace seat track assembly. If battery voltage does not exist, replace seat control switch.

TEST D: HORIZONTAL MOVEMENT INOPERATIVE

1) Disconnect horizontal seat height motor harness connector C311. Measure resistance between ground and Yellow/White wire terminal at horizontal seat height motor harness connector C311. Measure resistance between ground and Red/White wire terminal at horizontal seat height motor harness connector C311. If either resistance reading is greater than 5 ohms, go to next step. If both resistance reading are 5 ohms or less, go to step **3)**.

2) Disconnect seat control switch harness connector C312. Measure resistance in Red/White wire between horizontal seat height motor harness connector C311 and terminal No. 3 at seat control switch harness connector C312. *See Fig. 2.* Measure resistance in Yellow/White wire between horizontal seat height motor harness connector C311 and terminal No. 8 at seat control switch harness connector C312. If both resistance readings are 5 ohms or less, replace seat control switch. If either resistance reading is greater than 5 ohms, repair open in appropriate wire.

3) Disconnect seat control switch harness connector C312. Measure resistance between ground and Red/White wire terminal at horizontal seat height motor harness connector C311. Measure resistance between ground and Yellow/White wire terminal at horizontal seat height motor harness connector C311. If both resistance readings are greater than 10 k/ohms, go to next step. If either resistance reading is 10 k/ohms or less, repair short to ground in appropriate wire.

4) Connect seat control switch harness connector C312. Measure voltage at Red/White wire terminal at horizontal seat height motor harness connector C311 while pressing seat control switch to rearward position. If battery voltage exists, go to next step. If battery voltage does not exist, replace seat control switch.

5) Measure voltage at Yellow/White wire terminal at horizontal seat height motor harness connector C311 while pressing seat control switch to forward position. If battery voltage exists, replace seat track assembly. If battery voltage does not exist, replace seat control switch.

TEST E: POWER LUMBAR SUPPORT INOPERATIVE

1) Operate seat back cushion to INFLATE position. If pump does not run, go to next step. If pump runs, go to step **6)**.

2) Disconnect power lumbar switch harness connector C313. Measure voltage at Dark Green wire terminal at power lumbar switch harness connector C313. If battery voltage exists, go to next step. If battery voltage does not exist, repair power distribution circuit. See WIRING DIAGRAMS.

3) Disconnect lumbar motor harness connector C308. Measure resistance between ground and Black wire terminal at power lumbar motor harness connector C308. If resistance is 5 ohms or less, go to next step. If resistance is greater than 5 ohms, repair open in Black wire.

4) Connect power lumbar switch harness connector C313. Measure voltage at Black/White wire terminal at power lumbar motor harness connector C308 while operating lumbar switch to inflate position. If battery voltage does not exist, go to next step. If battery voltage exists, replace power lumbar motor.

5) Disconnect power lumbar switch harness connector C313. Measure resistance in Black/White wire between power lumbar switch harness connector C313 and power lumbar motor harness connector C308. If resistance is 5 ohms or less, replace power lumbar switch. If resistance is greater than 5 ohms, repair open in Black/White wire.

6) Operate seat back cushion to INFLATE position. If seat back does not inflate, go to next step. If seat back inflates, go to step **10)**.

7) Inspect backrest adjusting bladder. If bladder is okay, go to next step. If bladder is damaged, replace bladder.

8) Disconnect hose from power lumbar motor. Operate seat back cushion to INFLATE position. If air is felt from port on power lumbar motor, go to next step. If air is not felt from port on power lumbar motor, replace power lumbar motor.

9) Connect hose to pump/motor. Disconnect hose from power lumbar switch. Activate power lumbar switch to inflate position. If air is felt at open hose, go to next step. If no air is felt at open hose, replace hose.

10) Connect support bladder hose to power lumbar switch. Connect in-line pressure gauge to hose at support bladder. Hold power lumbar switch in inflate position until pressure is 5 psi (0.35 kg/cm^2). Wait 3 hours. Observe pressure. If pressure does not hold, go to next step. If pressure holds, system is okay at this time.

11) Disconnect hose from lumbar support bladder. Using hand pump, inflate bladder to 5 psi (0.35 kg/cm^2). Wait 3 hours. Observe pressure. If pressure does not hold, replace lumbar support bladder. If pressure holds, replace power lumbar switch.

REMOVAL & INSTALLATION

CAUTION: When battery is disconnected, vehicle computer and memory systems may lose memory data. Driveability problems may exist until computer systems have completed a relearn cycle. See COMPUTER RELEARN PROCEDURES article in GENERAL INFORMATION before disconnecting battery.

SEAT ASSEMBLY

Removal & Installation – Disconnect negative battery cable. Remove insulators covering mounting nuts and/or bolts. Remove mounting nuts, bolts and washers. Lift seat slightly and disconnect harness connectors. Remove seat assembly. To install, reverse removal procedure.

WIRING DIAGRAMS

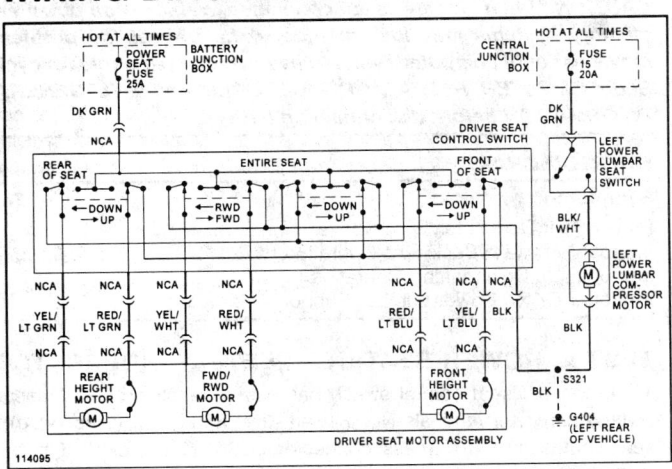

Fig. 3: Power Lumbar & Power Seats System Wiring Diagram (Mustang)

1999 ACCESSORIES & EQUIPMENT
Power Seats – Sable & Taurus

DESCRIPTION & OPERATION

The 6-way power seats provide horizontal, vertical and tilt adjustments with optional power lumbar adjustment. Seat function switches are mounted on side of seat trim panel. Power seat circuits are protected by circuit breakers and/or fuses. All models have a circuit breaker mounted on each motor armature and use an additional fuse in the engine compartment fuse box.

TROUBLE SHOOTING

Before performing individual component test, check the following for possible cause of system malfunction:

- Blown fuses or faulty circuit breakers.
- Loose or corroded connectors.
- Damaged wiring.
- Damaged motors.
- Faulty switches.
- Damaged lumbar support bladder.
- Damaged or kinked air hoses.

COMPONENT TESTS

SEAT CONTROL SWITCH

Remove seat control switch. Check resistance between terminals with seat control switch in appropriate position. See SEAT CONTROL SWITCH RESISTANCE table. See Fig. 1. If resistances are not as specified, replace seat control switch.

SEAT CONTROL SWITCH RESISTANCE

Switch Position	Between Terminals	Ohms
Neutral	8 & All Except 4	Less Than 5
Entire Seat		
Down	2 & 4; 4 & 5	Less Than 5
Up	1 & 4; 3 & 4	Less Than 5
Front Up	1 & 4	Less Than 5
Front Down	4 & 5	Less Than 5
Rear Up	3 & 4	Less Than 5
Rear Down	2 & 4	Less Than 5
Seat FWD	4 & 7	Less Than 5
Seat RWD	4 & 6	Less Than 5

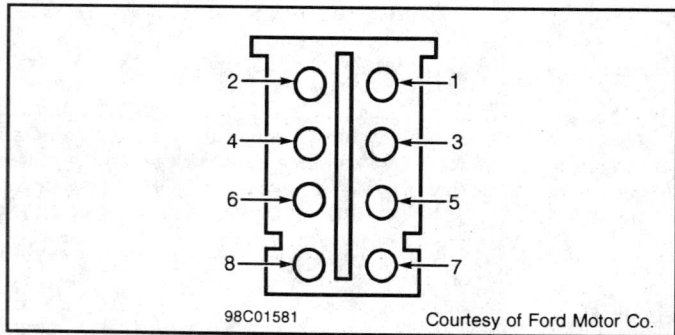

Fig. 1: Identifying Seat Control Switch Terminals

98C01581   Courtesy of Ford Motor Co.

SYSTEM TESTS

NOTE: To determine correct test, see SYMPTOM CHART table. Unless otherwise directed, perform tests in order listed.

CAUTION: When battery is disconnected, vehicle computer and memory systems may lose memory data. Driveability problems may exist until computer systems have completed a relearn cycle. See COMPUTER RELEARN PROCEDURES article in GENERAL INFORMATION before disconnecting battery.

SYMPTOM CHART

Symptom	Test
Power Seat Completely Inoperative	A
Improper Forward/Backward Operation	B
Improper Up/Down Lifting Operation	C
Improper Or No Power Lumbar Support Operation	D

TEST A: POWER SEAT COMPLETELY INOPERATIVE

1) Disconnect seat control switch harness connector C334. Measure voltage between terminals No. 4 (Red wire) and No. 8 (Black wire) at seat control switch harness connector C334. See Fig. 2. If battery voltage does not exist, go to next step. If battery voltage exists, go to step 6).

2) Measure resistance between ground and terminal No. 8 (Black wire) at seat control switch harness connector. If resistance is 5 ohms or less, go to next step. If resistance is greater than 5 ohms, repair open in Black wire.

3) Remove fuse No. 4 (30-amp) in power distribution box in engine compartment. Connect seat control switch harness connector C334. Measure resistance between ground and output side of fuse No. 4. If resistance is 10 k/ohms or less, go to next step. If resistance is greater than 10 k/ohms, go to step 5).

4) Disconnect seat control switch harness connector. Measure resistance between ground and output side of fuse No. 4. If resistance is 10 k/ohms or less, repair short to ground in power distribution circuit (Red wire). See appropriate wiring diagram in POWER DISTRIBUTION article in WIRING DIAGRAMS. If resistance is greater than 10 k/ohms, replace seat control switch.

5) Disconnect seat control switch harness connector C334. Measure resistance in Red wire between terminal No. 4 at seat control switch harness connector C334 and output side of fuse No. 4. If resistance is 5 ohms or less, replace fuse and go to next step. If resistance is greater than 5 ohms, repair open in Red wire.

6) Using jumper wires, connect one jumper wire to Red wire at power seat control switch harness connector C334. Connect other jumper wire to ground. Connect other ends of jumper wires to appropriate terminals at seat control switch harness connector. See SEAT MOTOR OPERATION table. Observe motor operation. If motor does not operate as specified, go to next step. If motor operates correctly, replace seat control switch.

SEAT MOTOR OPERATION

Positive Voltage	Negative Voltage	Seat Response
Yellow/Light Green	Red/Light Green	Rear Down
Yellow/Light Blue	Red/Light Blue	Front Down
Red/Light Green	Yellow/Light Green	Rear Up
Red/Light Blue	Yellow/Light Blue	Front Up
Yellow/White	Red/White	Rearward
Red/White	Yellow/White	Forward

7) Measure resistance between ground and appropriate wires at seat control switch harness connector C334. See SEAT MOTOR CIRCUIT IDENTIFICATION table. If all resistance readings are greater than 10 k/ohms, go to next step. If any resistance reading is 10 k/ohms or less, repair short in appropriate wire(s).

SEAT MOTOR CIRCUIT IDENTIFICATION

Terminal	Wire Color
1	Yellow/Light Blue
2	Red/Light Green
3	Yellow/Light Green
5	Red/Light Blue

SEAT MOTOR CIRCUIT IDENTIFICATION (Cont.)

Terminal	Wire Color
6	Red/White
7	Yellow/White

8) Measure resistance in wires between seat control switch harness connector C334 and seat motor harness connector. See SEAT MOTOR CIRCUIT IDENTIFICATION table. If all resistance readings are 5 ohms or less, system okay at this time. If any resistance reading is greater than 5 ohms, repair open in appropriate wire(s).

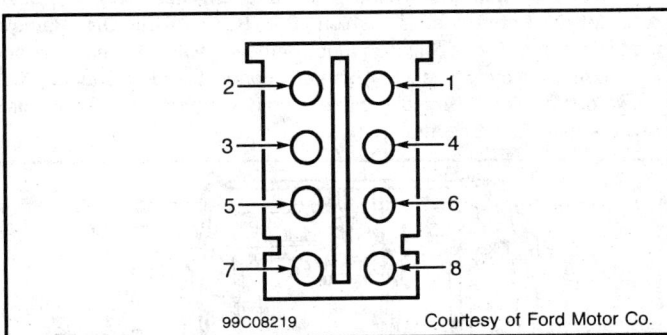

99C08219   Courtesy of Ford Motor Co.

Fig. 2: Identifying Seat Control Switch Harness Connector C334 Terminals

TEST B: IMPROPER FORWARD/BACKWARD OPERATION

1) Disconnect seat motor harness connector. Connect fused jumper wire to positive battery voltage. Connect a second jumper wire to ground. Connect jumper leads to Red/White wire and Yellow/White wire terminals at seat motor (component side). Observe motor operation. Reverse leads. Motor should operate in both directions. If motor operates correctly, go to next step. If motor does not operate as specified, replace driver seat motor assembly.

2) Disconnect seat switch harness connector C334. Measure resistance in Yellow/White and Red/White wires between seat control switch harness connector C334 and seat motor harness connector. If both resistance readings are less than 5 ohms, go to next step. If either resistance is 5 ohms or greater, repair open in appropriate wire.

3) Measure resistance between ground and Yellow/White and Red/White wires at seat control switch harness connector C334. If both resistance readings are greater than 10 k/ohms, replace seat motor assembly. If either resistance reading is 10 k/ohms or less, repair short to ground in appropriate wire.

TEST C: IMPROPER UP/DOWN LIFTING OPERATION

1) Disconnect seat motor harness connector. Connect fused jumper wire to positive battery voltage. Connect a second jumper wire to ground. Connect jumper leads to appropriate wires at seat motor harness connector terminals. See MOTOR OPERATION table. Observe motor operation. If motors operates correctly, go to next step. If motor does not operate as specified, replace seat motor assembly.

MOTOR OPERATION

Positive Voltage	Negative Voltage	Motor Response
Yellow/Light Blue	Red/Light Blue	Front Up
Red/Light Blue	Yellow/Light Blue	Front Down
Yellow/Light Green	Red/Light Green	Rear Up
Red/Light Green	Yellow/Light Green	Rear Down

2) Disconnect seat control switch harness connector C334. Measure resistance in Yellow/Light Blue, Yellow/Light Green, Red/Light Blue and Red/Light Green wires between seat control switch harness connector C334 and seat motor harness connector. If all resistance readings are 5 ohms or less, go to next step. If any resistance is greater than 5 ohms, repair open in appropriate wire.

3) Measure resistance between ground and Yellow/Light Blue, Yellow/Light Green, Red/Light Blue and Red/Light Green wires at seat control

switch harness connector C334. If all resistance readings are greater than 10 k/ohms, replace seat motor assembly. If any resistance reading is 10 k/ohms or less, repair short to ground in appropriate wire.

TEST D: IMPROPER OR NO POWER LUMBAR SUPPORT OPERATION

1) Operate power seat. If power seat operates, go to next step. If power seat does not operate, perform TEST A: POWER SEAT COMPLETELY INOPERATIVE.

2) Disconnect lumbar switch harness connector C336. Measure voltage at Red wire terminal at lumbar switch harness connector C336. If battery voltage exists, go to next step. If battery voltage does not exist, repair open in Red wire.

3) Connect lumbar switch harness connector C336. Using voltmeter, backprobe at Pink wire terminal at power lumbar switch while activating power lumbar switch to INFLATE position. If battery voltage exists, go to next step. If battery voltage does not exist, replace power lumbar switch.

4) Activate power lumbar switch to INFLATE position. If pump/motor does not run, go to next step. If pump/motor runs, go to step 7).

5) Disconnect pump/motor harness connector C335. Measure voltage between Black and Pink wire terminals at pump/motor harness connector C335. Activate power lumbar switch to INFLATE position. If battery voltage does not exist, go to next step. If battery voltage exists, replace pump/motor.

6) Measure voltage at Pink wire terminal at pump/motor harness connector C336. Activate power lumbar switch to INFLATE position. If battery voltage exists, repair open in Black wire. If battery voltage does not exist, repair open in Pink wire.

7) Connect pump/motor harness connector C336. Activate power lumbar switch to INFLATE position. Observe seatback. If seatback does not inflate, go to next step. If seatback inflates, go to step 9).

8) Disconnect support bladder hose from pump/motor. Activate power lumbar switch to inflate position. If air is felt coming from pump/motor, go to next step. If air is not felt coming from pump/motor, replace pump/motor.

9) Connect support bladder hose to pump/motor. Disconnect hose from power lumbar switch. Activate power lumbar switch to inflate position. If air is felt coming from open hose, go to next step. If air is not felt coming from open hose, replace hose.

10) Connect support bladder hose to power lumbar switch. Connect in-line pressure gauge to hose. Hold power lumbar switch in inflate position until pressure is 5 psi (0.35 kg/cm^2). Wait 3 hours. Observe pressure. If pressure does not hold, go to next step. If pressure holds, system is okay at this time.

11) Disconnect hose from lumbar support bladder. Using hand pump, inflate support bladder to 5 psi (0.35 kg/cm^2). Wait 3 hours. Observe pressure. If pressure does not hold, replace lumbar support bladder. If pressure holds, replace power lumbar switch.

REMOVAL & INSTALLATION

CAUTION: When battery is disconnected, vehicle computer and memory systems may lose memory data. Driveability problems may exist until computer systems have completed a relearn cycle. See COMPUTER RELEARN PROCEDURES article in GENERAL INFORMATION before disconnecting battery.

SEAT ASSEMBLY

Removal & Installation – Disconnect negative battery cable. Remove insulators covering mounting nuts and/or bolts. Remove mounting nuts, bolts and washers. Lift seat slightly and disconnect harness connectors. Remove seat assembly. To install, reverse removal procedure.

SEAT CUSHION

NOTE: Procedure may vary slightly depending on seat size and power options.

Removal & Installation – 1) Disconnect negative battery cable. Remove seat and track assembly. See SEAT ASSEMBLY. Remove screws from left side shield. Carefully disconnect and tag air hoses from lumbar support switch (if equipped). Disconnect switch-to-motor connectors. Remove left side shield. Remove remaining shields.

2) Remove hog rings securing lower portion of seatback cover. Slide seatback cover up enough to remove seatback frame bolts. Remove seatback. Disconnect air line from lumbar bladder (if equipped). Remove hog rings securing cover rods to seat frame. Remove cover and cushion. To install, reverse removal procedure.

POWER SEAT MOTOR

NOTE: Seat motors and track assemblies are serviced as a complete unit.

Removal & Installation – Disconnect negative battery cable. Remove seat from vehicle. See SEAT ASSEMBLY. Disconnect power seat control switch from seat track assembly at connectors. *See Fig. 3.* Disconnect air bladder hoses (if equipped). Remove seat cushion side shields (if equipped). Remove bolt retaining safety belt to seat track. Remove 4 seat track-to-seat cushion bolts. To install, reverse removal procedure.

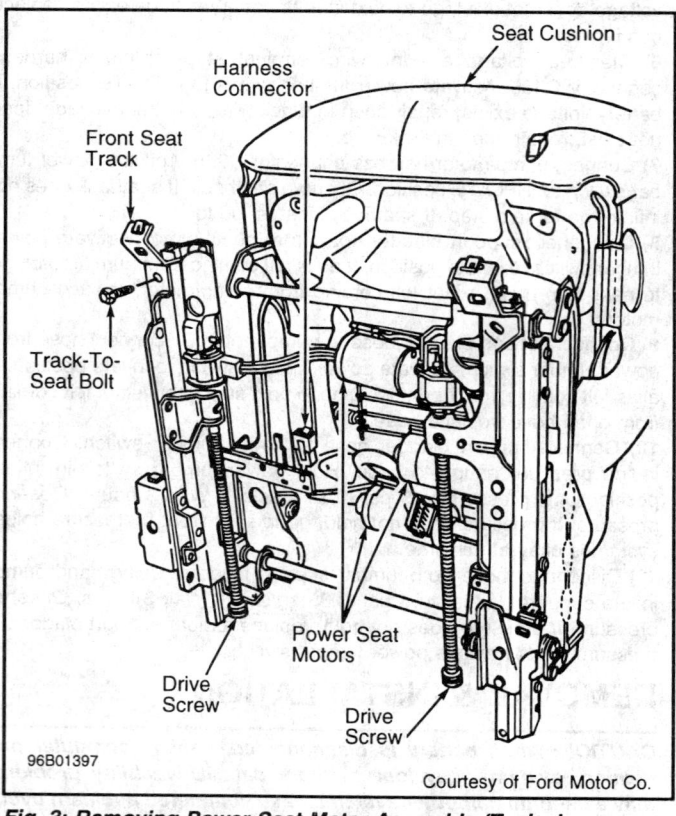

Fig. 3: Removing Power Seat Motor Assembly (Typical Screw-Type Drive)

LUMBAR SUPPORT PUMP/MOTOR ASSEMBLY

Removal & Installation – Remove seat and track assembly. See SEAT ASSEMBLY. Remove seat cushion. See SEAT CUSHION. Remove pump/motor assembly mounting screws. Disconnect electrical connector and inflation tube. Remove pump/motor assembly. To install, reverse removal procedure.

LUMBAR SUPPORT AIR BLADDER

Removal & Installation – Remove seat and track assembly. See SEAT ASSEMBLY. Remove seat cushion. See SEAT CUSHION. Remove lumbar support bladder inflation tube. Remove seatback trim cover and pad. Using a screwdriver, pry lumbar support bladder retaining tabs outward. *See Fig. 4.* Remove bladder from seatback frame. To install, reverse removal procedure.

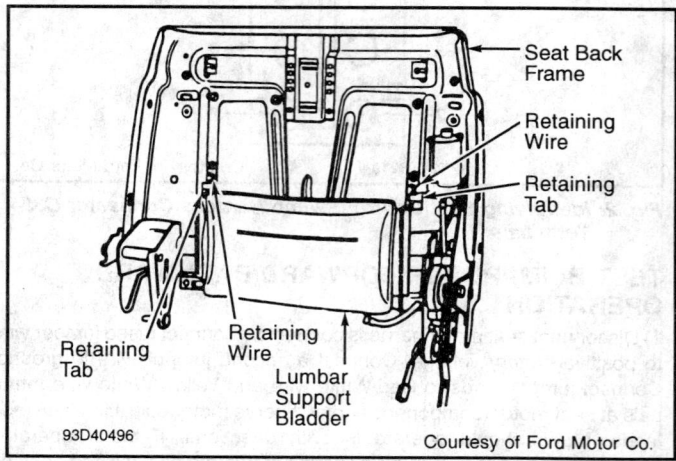

Fig. 4: Removing Lumbar Support Bladder (Typical)

WIRING DIAGRAMS

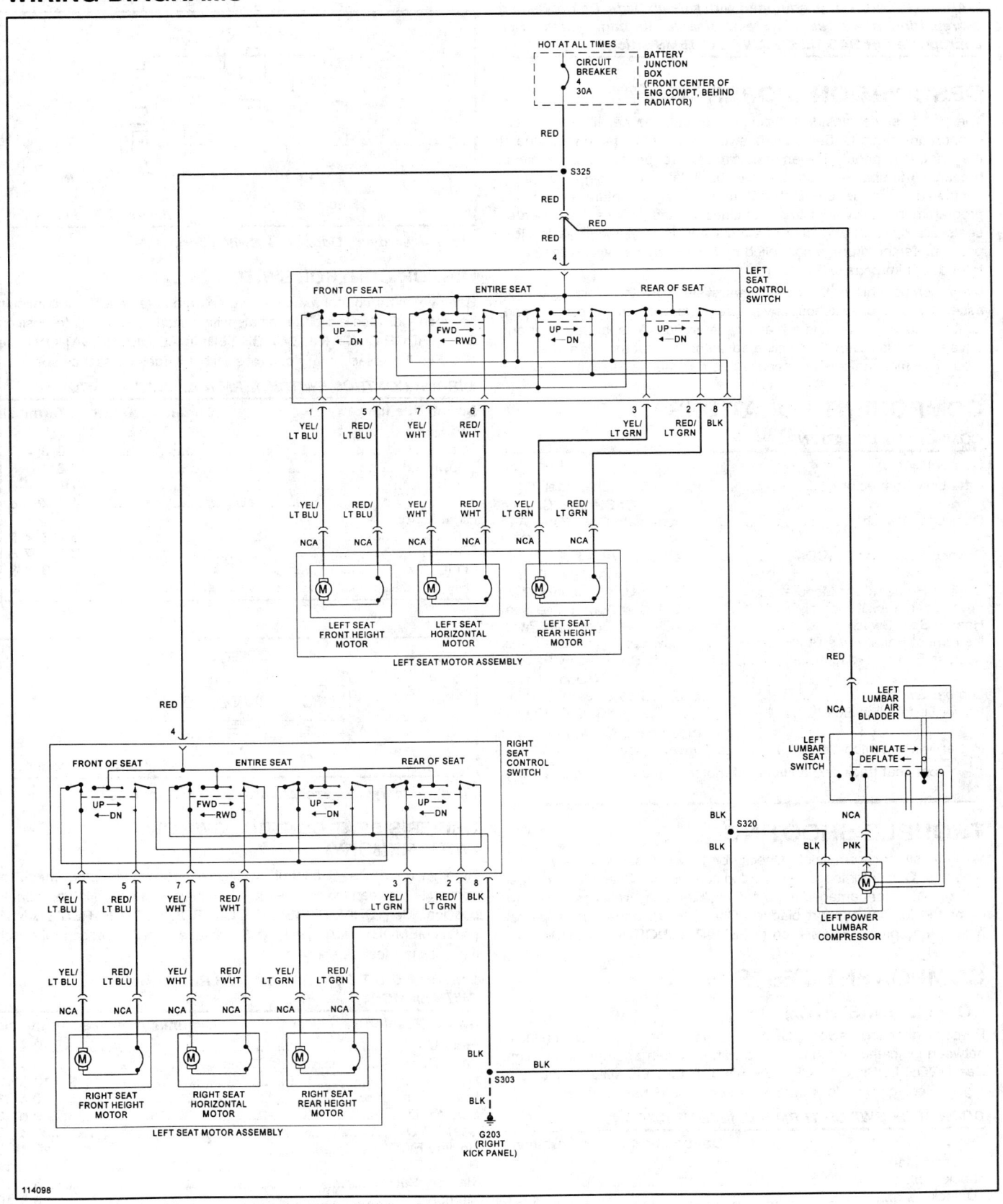

Fig. 5: Power Lumbar & Power Seats System Wiring Diagram (Sable & Taurus)

WARNING: *Town Car is equipped with side air bags. Before testing or repairing power seat system, disable air bag system. See appropriate AIR BAG RESTRAINT SYSTEMS article.*

DESCRIPTION & OPERATION

The power seats provide horizontal, vertical, recline, tilt and lumbar support adjustments. Seat control switches are mounted on the side of the seat trim panel. Power seat circuits are protected by a circuit breaker. A lumbar support pad can be inflated by a separate pump controlled by a switch. Optional memory seat feature provides 2 programmable seat adjustment settings for the driver's seat. Heated seats are optional and only operate when ignition switch is in RUN position. Temperature is controlled by an adjustable switch located on front door trim panels.

Major components of the power seat system are the motor and drive assembly, control switches, driver's seat module, lumbar support pad, lumbar support pump and a memory set switch. A separate motor and drive mechanism provides recline adjustment. Seat motors and associated drive mechanisms are serviced as a complete assembly.

COMPONENT LOCATIONS

COMPONENT LOCATIONS

Component	Location
Data Link Connector	Under Instrument Panel, Right Of Steering Column
Door Lock Switch	Appropriate Door Panel Arm Rest
Driver's Door Module (DDM)	Behind Driver's Door Panel, Lower Front Corner
Driver's Heated Seat Module	Under Driver's Seat
Front Seat Track Assembly	[1] Under Appropriate Seat
Heated Seat Switch	Driver's Door Trim Panel
Instrument Panel Fuse Box	Below Left Instrument Panel
Keyless Entry Keypad	On Driver's Door, Below Exterior Door Handle
Lumbar Switch	Side Of Seat Cushion
Power Distribution Box	Left Side Of Engine Compartment, Above Wheelwell
Power Mirror Switch	Driver's Door Panel Arm Rest

[1] – Front seat track and adjustment motors are a complete assembly.

TROUBLE SHOOTING

Verify customer complaint. Check for blown fuses or faulty circuit breakers. Check for loose or corroded connectors. Check for damaged wiring. Check for damaged motors. Check for faulty switches. Check for damaged lumbar support bladder. Check for damaged or kinked air hoses. If no problem exists, go to SELF-DIAGNOSTIC SYSTEM.

COMPONENT TESTS

DOOR LOCK SWITCH

Remove door lock switch. Using an ohmmeter, check for continuity between indicated switch terminals with switch in appropriate position. See DOOR LOCK SWITCH TERMINAL IDENTIFICATION table. See Fig. 1. Replace door lock switch if it does not test as specified.

DOOR LOCK SWITCH TERMINAL IDENTIFICATION

Switch Position	Continuity Between Terminals
Driver's Side	
Lock	2 & 4
Unlock	4 & 6
Passenger's Side	
Lock	4 & 6
Unlock	2 & 4

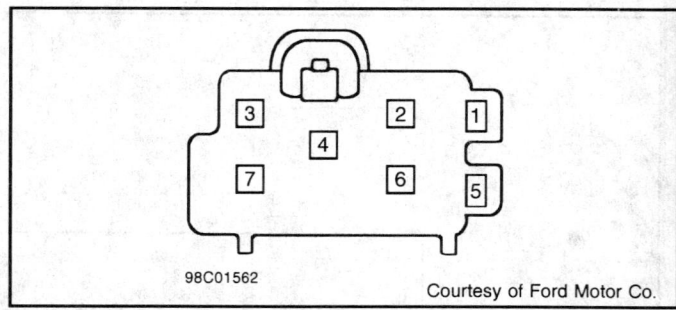

98C01562   Courtesy of Ford Motor Co.

Fig. 1: Identifying Door Lock Switch Terminals

MIRROR CONTROL SWITCH

Remove mirror control switch. Using an ohmmeter, check for continuity between indicated switch terminals with switch in appropriate position. See MIRROR CONTROL SWITCH TERMINAL IDENTIFICATION table. See Fig. 2. Replace mirror control switch if it does not test as specified.

MIRROR CONTROL SWITCH TERMINAL IDENTIFICATION

Switch Position	Continuity Between Terminals
Left Mirror	
Up	3 & 9; 4 & 7
Down	3 & 4; 7 & 9
Left	1 & 3; 4 & 7
Right	1 & 7; 3 & 4
Right Mirror	
Up	3 & 8; 4 & 7
Down	3 & 4; 7 & 8
Left	2 & 3; 4 & 7
Right	2 & 7; 3 & 4

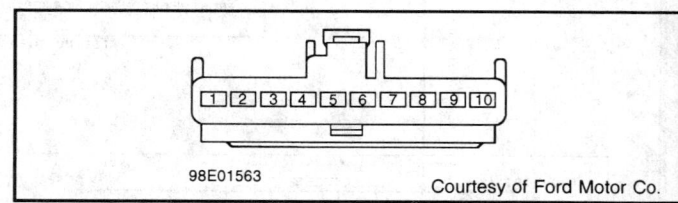

98E01563   Courtesy of Ford Motor Co.

Fig. 2: Identifying Mirror Control Switch Terminals

DRIVER'S SEAT CONTROL SWITCH (WITH MEMORY)

Remove driver's seat control switch. Using an ohmmeter, check for continuity between indicated switch terminals with switch in appropriate position. See DRIVER'S SEAT CONTROL SWITCH RESISTANCE (WITH MEMORY) table. See Fig. 3. Replace driver's seat control switch if it does not test as specified.

DRIVER'S SEAT CONTROL SWITCH RESISTANCE (WITH MEMORY)

Switch Position	Continuity Between Terminals
Front Up	2 & 10
Front Down	3 & 10
Rear Up	10 & 12
Rear Down	10 & 11
Seat FWD	9 & 10
Seat RWD	1 & 10
Recline FWD	10 & 13
Recline RWD	10 & 14
Memory Set	5 & 10
Memory "1"	6 & 10
Memory "2"	7 & 10

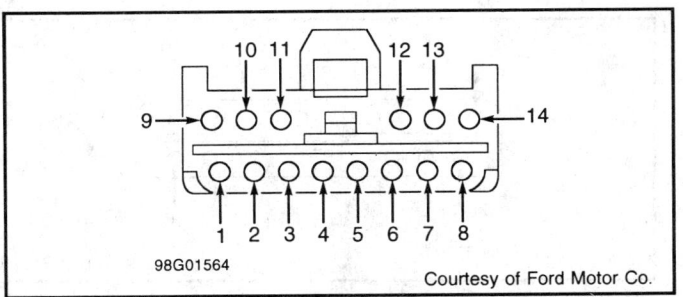

Fig. 3: Identifying Driver's Seat Control Switch Terminals (With Memory)

DRIVER'S SEAT CONTROL SWITCH (WITHOUT MEMORY)

Remove driver's seat control switch. Using an ohmmeter, check for continuity between indicated switch terminals with switch in appropriate position. See DRIVER'S SEAT CONTROL SWITCH RESISTANCE (WITHOUT MEMORY) table. *See Fig. 4.* Replace driver's seat control switch if it does not test as specified.

DRIVER'S SEAT CONTROL SWITCH RESISTANCE (WITHOUT MEMORY)

Switch Position	Continuity Between Terminals
Neutral	1 & All Except 3
Front Up	3 & 7
Front Down	3 & 5
Rear Up	3 & 4
Rear Down	3 & 6
Seat FWD	2 & 3
Seat RWD	3 & 8

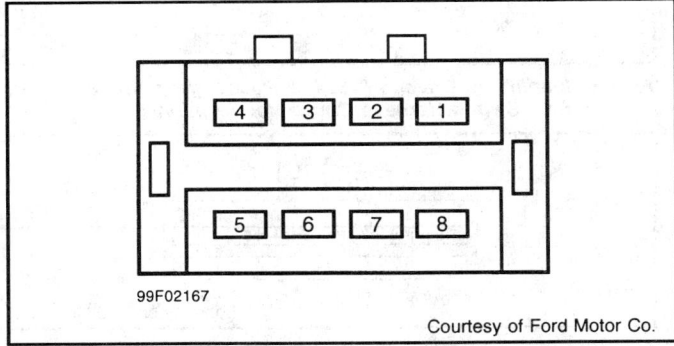

Fig. 4: Identifying Driver's Seat Control Switch Terminals (Without Memory) & Passenger's Seat Control Switch (Executive Model)

PASSENGER'S SEAT CONTROL SWITCH

Remove passenger seat control switch. Using an ohmmeter, check for continuity between indicated switch terminals with switch in appropriate position. See SEAT CONTROL SWITCH RESISTANCE (PASSENGER'S SEAT) table. *See Fig. 4 or 5.* Replace passenger's seat control switch if it does not test as specified.

SEAT CONTROL SWITCH RESISTANCE (PASSENGER'S SEAT)

Switch Position	Continuity Between Terminals
Neutral	
Except Executive Model	7 & All Except 12
Executive Model	5 & All Except 8
Front Up	
Except Executive Model	1 & 7
Executive Model	2 & 8
Front Down	
Except Executive Model	2 & 7

SEAT CONTROL SWITCH RESISTANCE (PASSENGER'S SEAT) (Cont.)

Switch Position	Continuity Between Terminals
Executive Model	3 & 8
Rear Up	
Except Executive Model	7 & 11
Executive Model	4 & 8
Rear Down	
Except Executive Model	6 & 7
Executive Model	1 & 8
Seat FWD	
Except Executive Model	7 & 8
Executive Model	6 & 8
Seat RWD	
Except Executive Model	7 & 10
Executive Model	7 & 8
Seat Recline FWD [1]	5 & 7
Seat Recline RWD [1]	4 & 7

[1] – Does not apply to executive model.

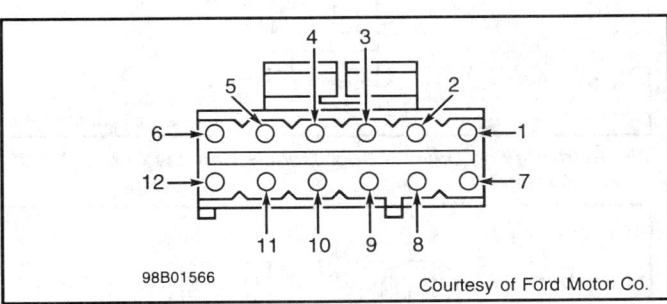

Fig. 5: Identifying Passenger's Seat Control Switch (Except Executive Model)

REMOTE TRUNK RELEASE SWITCH

Remove remote trunk release switch. Using an ohmmeter, check continuity between switch terminals. With switch depressed, continuity should exist. With switch not depressed, continuity should not exist. Replace remote trunk release switch if continuity is not as specified.

CONNECTOR IDENTIFICATION

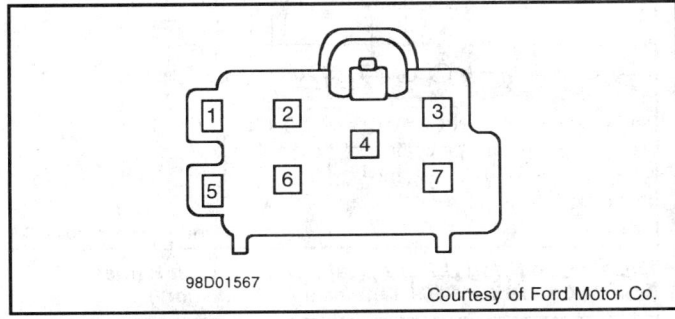

Fig. 6: Identifying Driver's Door Lock (C503) & Passenger's Door Lock (C603) Switch Harness Connector Terminals

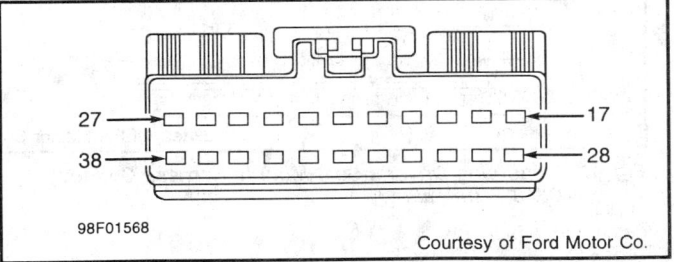

Fig. 7: Identifying Driver's Door Module Harness Connector C520 Terminals

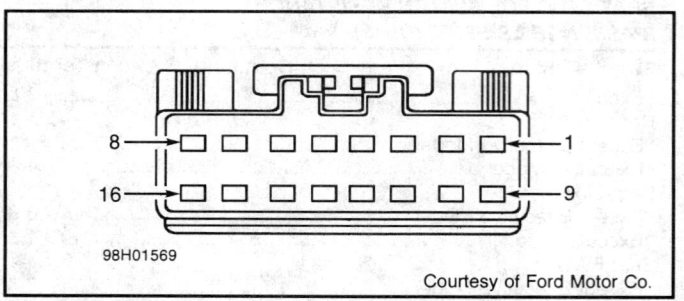

Fig. 8: Identifying Driver's Door Module Harness Connector C521 Terminals

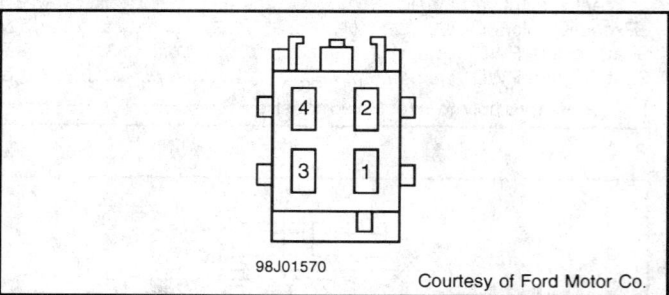

Fig. 9: Identifying Driver's Door Module Harness Connector C522 Terminals

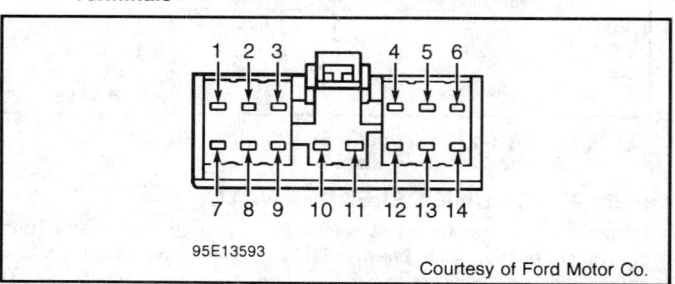

Fig. 10: Identifying Driver's (C347) & Passenger's (C344) Heated Seat Control Module Harness Connector Terminals

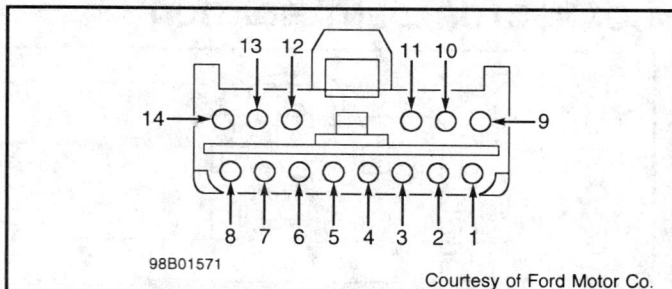

Fig. 11: Identifying Driver's Seat Control Switch Harness Connector C509 Terminals (With Memory)

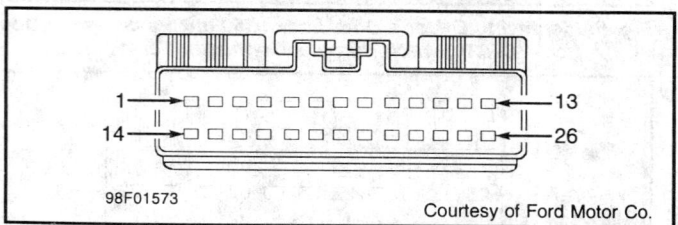

Fig. 12: Identifying Driver's Seat Module Harness Connector C313 Terminals

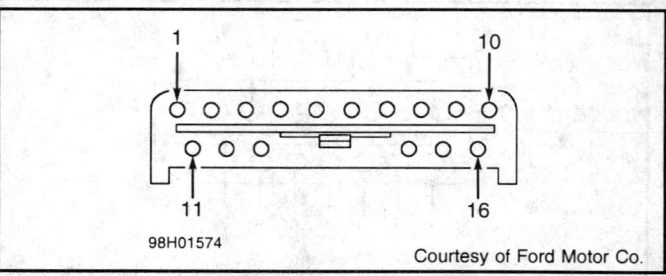

Fig. 13: Identifying Driver's Seat Module Harness Connector C338 Terminals

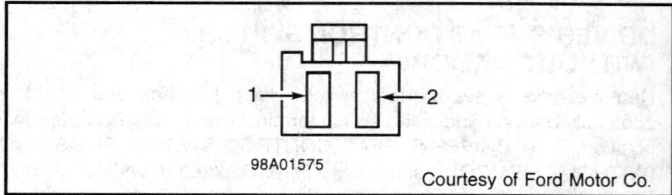

Fig. 14: Identifying Driver's Seat Module Harness Connector C337 Terminals

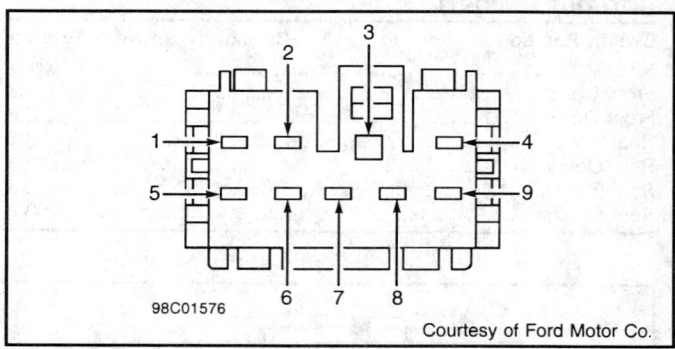

Fig. 15: Identifying Driver's (C524) & Passenger's (C616) Heated Seat Switch Harness Connector Terminals

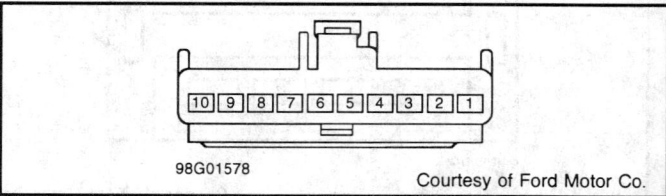

Fig. 16: Identifying Mirror Control Switch Harness Connector C550 Terminals

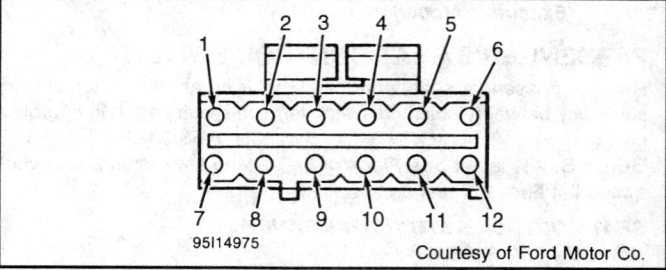

Fig. 17: Identifying Passenger's Seat Control Switch Harness Connector C609 Terminals (Except Executive Model)

SELF-DIAGNOSTIC SYSTEM

NOTE: Many steps in the following tests refer to various connectors. These connectors are identified in illustrations under CONNECTOR IDENTIFICATION. See Figs. 6-17.

WITH MEMORY SEATS

A New Generation Star (NGS) tester is required to test the power seat system. Connect NGS tester to Data Link Connector (DLC), located beneath instrument panel. Using NGS tester, perform data link diagnostics test. See DATA LINK DIAGNOSTIC TEST under COMMUNICATION NETWORK DIAGNOSTICS in MODULE COMMUNICATIONS NETWORK – TOWN CAR article. If NGS tester responds with CKT194 or CKT915=ALL MODULE NO RESP/NOTEQUIP, repair module communications concern. See MODULE COMMUNICATIONS NETWORK –

TOWN CAR article. If NGS responds with NO RESPONSE/NOT EQUIPPED for driver's seat module, perform TEST B: NO COMMUNICATION WITH DRIVER'S SEAT MODULE under SYSTEM TESTS. If NGS responds with NO RESPONSE/NOT EQUIPPED for driver's door module, perform TEST A: NO COMMUNICATION WITH DRIVER'S DOOR MODULE under SYSTEM TESTS.

If NGS tester responds with SYSTEM PASSED, retrieve and record continuous DTCs. Erase continuous DTCs. Using NGS tester, perform DDM and DSM self-test. Perform appropriate test in accordance with DTC retrieved. See DRIVER'S SEAT MODULE DTC INDEX and/or DRIVER'S DOOR MODULE DTC INDEX table. Codes listed in these tables are only for testing covered in this article. For complete DTC listing, see MODULE COMMUNICATIONS NETWORK – TOWN CAR article. If no DTCs are retrieved, repair by symptom. See SYMPTOM CHART table under SYSTEM TESTS.

DRIVER'S SEAT MODULE DTC INDEX

DTC [1]	Description	Test
B1342	ECU Defective	2
B1663	Driver's Seat Front Up/Down Circuit Failure	C
B1664	Driver's Seat Rear Up/Down Circuit Failure	C
B1665	Driver's Seat Forward/Backward Circuit Failure	C
B1666	Driver's Seat Recline Circuit Failure	C
B1676	Battery Voltage Out Of Range	P
B1950	Driver's Seat Rear Up/Down Potentiometer – Circuit Failure	E
B1953	Driver's Seat Rear Up/Down Potentiometer – Short to Ground	E
B1954	Driver's Seat Front Up/Down Potentiometer – Circuit Failure	E
B1957	Driver's Seat Front Up/Down Potentiometer – Short to Ground	E
B1958	Driver's Seat Recline Potentiometer – Circuit Failure	E
B1961	Driver's Seat Recline Potentiometer – Short To Ground	E
B1962	Driver's Seat Horizontal Potentiometer – Circuit Failure	E
B1965	Driver's Seat Horizontal Potentiometer – Short To Ground	E

[1] – Codes listed in this table are only for testing covered in this article. For complete DTC listing, see MODULE COMMUNICATIONS NETWORK – TOWN CAR article.
[2] – Using NGS tester, retrieve and document all continuous. Perform DSM self-test. If DTC B1342 is retrieved again, replace DSM.

DRIVER'S DOOR MODULE DTC INDEX

DTC [1]	Description	Test
B1342	ECU Defective	2
B1545	Power Seat Switch Short To Voltage	C

[1] – Codes listed in this table are only for testing covered in this article. For complete DTC listing, see MODULE COMMUNICATIONS NETWORK – TOWN CAR article.
[2] – Using NGS tester, retrieve and document all continuous. Perform DDM self-test. If DTC B1342 is retrieved again, replace DDM.

WITHOUT MEMORY SEATS

No self-diagnostic system is available on vehicles without driver's side memory seat. If testing power seat system without memory, test individual components and check wiring. See COMPONENT TESTS and WIRING DIAGRAMS.

SYSTEM TESTS

CAUTION: When battery is disconnected or modules are replaced, vehicle computer and memory systems may lose memory data. Driveability problems may exist until computer systems have completed a relearn cycle. See COMPUTER RELEARN PROCEDURES article in GENERAL INFORMATION before disconnecting battery.

NOTE: The following system tests only apply to vehicle with memory seats. If testing power seat system without memory, test individual components and check wiring. See COMPONENT TESTS and WIRING DIAGRAMS.

NOTE: Many steps in the following tests refer to various connectors. These connectors are identified in illustrations under CONNECTOR IDENTIFICATION. See Figs. 6-17.

SYMPTOM CHART

Symptom	Test
No Communication with Driver's Door Module	A
No Communication With Driver's Seat Module	B
Driver's Seat Completely Inoperative (With Memory)	C
Passenger's Seat Completely Inoperative	D
Seat Motors Operate In One Second Intervals	E
Passenger's Seat Does Not Move Horizontally/Vertically	F
Memory Seat Inoperative	G
Easy Entry/Exit Feature Inoperative	H
Driver's Heated Seat Inoperative	I
Driver's Heated Seat Cushion Inoperative	J
Passenger's Heated Seat Inoperative	K
Passenger's Heated Seat Cushion Inoperative	L
Both Heated Seats Inoperative	M
Driver's Lumbar Support Inoperative	N
Passenger's Lumbar Support Inoperative	O
Battery Voltage Out Of Range (DTC B1676)	P

TEST A: NO COMMUNICATION WITH DRIVER'S DOOR MODULE

NOTE: After repairs are complete, ensure all component are properly installed and all harness connectors are connected properly and repeat data link diagnostic test. See DATA LINK DIAGNOSTIC TEST under COMMUNICATIONS NETWORK DIAGNOSTICS in appropriate MODULE COMMUNICATIONS NETWORK – TOWN CAR article.

1) Ensure transmission is in Park. Turn ignition switch to LOCK position. Check fuse No. 30 (7.5-amp) in instrument panel fuse box. If fuse is okay, go to next step. If fuse is blown, go to step 5).

2) Measure voltage at input side of fuse No. 30. If battery voltage exists, go to next step. If battery voltage does not exist, go to step 20).

3) Ensure ignition switch is in LOCK position. Remove fuse No. 30 (7.5-amp) in instrument panel fuse box. Disconnect Driver's Door Module (DDM) harness connector C520. Measure resistance in Light Green/Violet wire between terminal No. 29 at DDM harness connector C520 and output side of fuse No. 30. If resistance is 5 ohms or less, go to next step. If resistance is greater than 5 ohms, repair open in Light Green/Violet wire between instrument panel fuse box and DDM.

4) Measure resistance between ground and terminal No. 23 (Pink/Orange wire) at DDM harness connector C520. If resistance is greater than 5 ohms, repair open in Pink/Orange wire. If resistance is 5 ohms or less, replace driver's door module.

5) Replace fuse No. 30. DO NOT operate power seat switch. If fuse blows, go to next step. If fuse does not blow, go to step 9).

6) Ensure ignition switch is in LOCK position. Remove fuse No. 30 from instrument panel fuse box. Disconnect DDM harness connector C520 and Driver's Seat Module (DSM) harness connector C313. Measure resistance between ground and terminal No. 29 (Light Green/Violet wire) at DDM harness connector C520. If resistance is 10 k/ohms or less, go to next step. If resistance is greater than 10 k/ohms, go to step 8).

7) Test driver's and passenger's door lock switches. Test remote trunk lock switch. Test mirror control switch. Test seat control switches. See appropriate test under COMPONENT TESTS. If no switch is defective, repair short to ground in Light Green/Violet wire. If any switch is defective, replace appropriate switch.

8) Ensure ignition switch is in LOCK position. Connect DSM harness connector C313. Measure resistance between ground and terminal No. 29 (Light Green/Violet wire) at DDM harness connector C520. If resistance is greater than 10 k/ohms, replace driver's door module. If resistance is 10 k/ohms or less, replace driver's seat module.

9) Lock and unlock doors at all door lock switches. If fuse No. 30 blows, go to next step. If fuse No. 30 does not blow, go to step 12).

10) Remove door lock switches. Test all door lock switches. See DOOR LOCK SWITCH under COMPONENT TESTS. If all door lock switches are okay, go to next step. If any door lock switch is defective, replace appropriate door lock switch.

11) Ensure ignition switch is in LOCK position. Disconnect Driver's Door Module (DDM) harness connector C520. Disconnect driver's door lock switch harness connector C503. Disconnect passenger's door lock switch harness connector C603. Measure resistance between ground and terminal No. 2 (Pink/Yellow wire) at driver's door lock switch harness connector C503. Also, measure resistance between ground and terminal No. 6 (Pink/Light Green wire) at driver's door lock switch harness connector C503. If either or both resistance reading are 10 k/ohms or less, repair short to ground in appropriate wire(s). If both resistance readings are greater than 10 k/ohms, replace driver's door module.

12) Activate mirrors in all directions. If fuse No. 30 blows, go to next step. If fuse No. 30 does not blow, go to step 15).

13) Remove mirror control switch. Test mirror control switch. See MIRROR CONTROL SWITCH under COMPONENT TESTS. If mirror control switch is okay, go to next step. If mirror control switch is defective, replace mirror control switch.

14) Ensure ignition switch is in LOCK position. Disconnect Driver's Door Module (DDM) harness connector C520. Disconnect mirror control switch harness connector C550. Measure resistance between ground and appropriate terminals at mirror control switch harness connector C550. See MIRROR CONTROL SWITCH TERMINAL IDENTIFICATION table. If all resistance readings are greater than 10 k/ohms, replace driver's door module. If any resistance reading is 10 k/ohms or less, repair short to ground in appropriate wire.

MIRROR CONTROL SWITCH TERMINAL IDENTIFICATION

Terminal	Wire Color
1	Red/Orange
2	Dark Green/Orange
4	Yellow/Black
8	Violet/Orange
9	Dark Blue/Orange

15) Activate memory switch through all positions. If fuse No. 30 blows, go to next step. If fuse No. 30 does not blow, go to step 18).

16) Remove driver's seat control switch. Test memory portion of driver's seat control switch. See DRIVER'S SEAT CONTROL SWITCH (WITH MEMORY) under COMPONENT TESTS. If memory switch is okay, go to next step. If memory switch is defective, replace driver's seat control switch.

17) Ensure ignition switch is in LOCK position. Disconnect Driver's Door Module (DDM) harness connectors C520 and C521. Measure resistance between ground and appropriate terminals at driver's seat control switch harness connector C509. See SEAT SWITCH CIRCUIT IDENTIFICATION table. If all resistance readings are greater than 10 k/ohms, replace driver's door module. If any resistance readings are 10 k/ohms or less, repair short to ground in appropriate wire.

SEAT SWITCH CIRCUIT IDENTIFICATION

Terminal	Wire Color
4	White/Orange
5	Brown/Orange
6	Brown/Light Green
7	Black/Orange

18) Activate driver's seat control switch in all directions. If fuse No. 30 blows, go to next step. If fuse No. 30 does not blow, system is operating properly at this time.

19) Ensure ignition switch is in LOCK position. Disconnect Driver's Door Module (DDM) harness connector C521. Disconnect driver's seat control switch harness connector C509. Measure resistance between ground and appropriate terminals at driver's seat control switch harness connector C509. See DRIVER'S SEAT CONTROL SWITCH TERMINAL IDENTIFICATION table. If all resistance readings are greater than 10 k/ohms, replace driver's door module. If any resistance readings are 10 k/ohms or less, repair short to ground in appropriate wire.

DRIVER'S SEAT CONTROL SWITCH TERMINAL IDENTIFICATION

Terminal	Wire Color
1	Yellow/White
2	Red/Light Blue
3	Yellow/Light Blue
9	Red/White
11	Yellow/Light Green
12	Red/Light Green
13	Gray
14	Gray/Black

20) Remove maxi-fuse No. 8 (30-amp) from power distribution box. Measure voltage at input side of maxi-fuse No. 8 at power distribution box. If battery voltage exists, go to next step. If battery voltage does not exist, repair power supply to maxi-fuse No. 8. See appropriate wiring diagram in POWER DISTRIBUTION article in WIRING DIAGRAMS.

21) Ensure ignition switch is in LOCK position. Ensure maxi-fuse No. 8 is still removed. Remove fuse No. 30 (7.5-amp) from instrument panel fuse box. Disconnect Driver's Seat Module (DSM) harness connector C337. Measure resistance in Red wire between output side of maxi-fuse

No. 8 and input side of fuse No. 30. If resistance is 5 ohms or less, go to next step. If resistance is greater than 5 ohms, repair open in Red wire.

22) Measure resistance between ground and output side of maxi-fuse No. 8 at power distribution box. If resistance is greater than 10 k/ohms, go to next step. If resistance is 10 k/ohms or less, repair short to ground in Red wire.

23) Ensure ignition switch is in LOCK position. Install maxi-fuse No. 8 in power distribution box. Install fuse No. 30 in instrument panel fuse box. Connect DSM harness connector C337. Operate driver's power seat in all directions. If driver's power seat operates properly in all directions, go to next step. If driver's power seat does not operate properly in all directions, replace driver's seat module.

24) Inspect DSM for water damage. If water damage does not exist, go to next step. If water damage exists, replace driver's seat module.

25) Turn ignition switch to RUN position. Operate driver's power window, power mirror and door lock switches in all directions. If maxi-fuse No. 8 blows, replace driver's door module. If maxi-fuse No. 8 does not blow, verify symptom and repair as necessary. See SYMPTOM CHART table.

TEST B: NO COMMUNICATION WITH DRIVER'S SEAT MODULE

NOTE: After repairs are complete, ensure all component are properly installed and all harness connectors are connected properly and repeat data link diagnostic test. See DATA LINK DIAGNOSTIC TEST under COMMUNICATIONS NETWORK DIAGNOSTICS in appropriate MODULE COMMUNICATIONS NETWORK – TOWN CAR article.

1) Check fuse No. 30 (7.5-amp) in instrument panel fuse box. If fuse is okay, go to next step. If fuse is blown, perform TEST A: NO COMMUNICATION WITH DRIVER'S DOOR MODULE.

2) Measure voltage at input cavity of fuse No. 30 at instrument panel fuse box. If battery voltage exist, go to next step. If battery voltage does not exist, perform TEST A: NO COMMUNICATION WITH DRIVER'S DOOR MODULE.

3) Ensure ignition switch is in LOCK position. Install fuse No. 30 in instrument panel fuse box. Disconnect Driver's Seat Module (DSM) harness connector C313. Measure voltage at terminal No. 14 (Light Green/Violet wire) at DSM harness connector C313. If battery voltage exists, go to next step. If battery voltage does not exist, repair open in Light Green/Violet wire.

4) Measure resistance between ground and terminal No. 1 (Pink/Orange wire) at DSM harness connector C313. If resistance is 5 ohms or less, diagnosis network concern. See MODULE COMMUNICATIONS NETWORK – TOWN CAR article. If resistance is greater than 5 ohms, repair open in Pink/Orange wire.

TEST C: DRIVER'S SEAT COMPLETELY INOPERATIVE (WITH MEMORY)

NOTE: After any repairs are complete, ensure all component are properly installed and all harness connectors are connected properly and repeat data link diagnostic test. See DATA LINK DIAGNOSTIC TEST under COMMUNICATIONS NETWORK DIAGNOSTICS in appropriate MODULE COMMUNICATIONS NETWORK – TOWN CAR article.

NOTE: Connector C332 is a 6-terminal connector. Manufacturer does not provide connector view. Identify connector by wire color. Connector C307 is a 2-terminal connector. Identify connector by wire color. See WIRING DIAGRAMS.

1) Using NGS tester, perform Driver's Door Module (DDM) self-test. If DTC B1545 was not retrieved, go to next step. If DTC B1545 is retrieved, go to step **4)**.

2) Using NGS tester, perform Driver's Seat Module (DSM) self-test. If no DSM DTCs were retrieved, go to next step. If any DSM DTCs were retrieved, perform appropriate test or go to appropriate step. See DSM DTC TEST table.

DSM DTC TEST

DTC	Perform
B1663	Step **16)**
B1663 & B1957	TEST E
B1663 & B1954	TEST E
B1664	Step **18)**
B1664 & B1953	TEST E
B1664 & B1950	TEST E
B1665	Step **20)**
B1665 & B1965	TEST E
B1665 & B1952	TEST E
B1666	Step **22)**
B1666 & B1961	TEST E
B1666 & B1958	TEST E
B1663, B1664, B1665 & B1666	Step **8)**
B1667, B1668, B1669 & B1670	TEST E

3) Turn ignition switch to RUN position. Using NGS tester, monitor DDM PIDs SFWD_SW, SREARSW, SPNT_SW and SRCL_SW while activating driver's seat control switch in all directions. If DDM PID values do not agree with driver's seat control switch positions, go to next step. If DDM PID values agree with driver's seat control switch positions, go to step **8)**.

4) Remove driver's seat control switch. Test driver's seat control switch. See DRIVER'S SEAT CONTROL SWITCH (WITH MEMORY) under COMPONENT TESTS. If switch is okay, go to next step. If switch is defective, replace driver's seat control switch.

5) Measure voltage at terminal No. 10 (Light Green/Violet wire) at driver's seat control switch harness connector C509. If battery voltage exist, go to next step. If battery voltage does not exist, repair open in Light Green/Violet wire.

6) Disconnect DDM harness connector C521. Measure for voltage between ground and appropriate terminals at driver's seat control switch harness connector C509. See DRIVER'S SEAT CONTROL SWITCH TERMINAL IDENTIFICATION table. If voltage does not exist at any terminal, go to next step. If voltage exists at any terminal, repair short to voltage in appropriate wire.

DRIVER'S SEAT CONTROL SWITCH TERMINAL IDENTIFICATION

Terminal	Wire Color
1	Yellow/White
2	Red/Light Blue
3	Yellow/Light Blue
9	Red/White
11	Yellow/Light Green
12	Red/Light Green
13	Gray
14	Gray/Black

7) Ensure DDM harness connector C521 and driver's seat control switch harness connector C509 are still disconnected. Measure resistance between appropriate DDM and driver's seat control switch harness connector terminals. See DDM CIRCUIT IDENTIFICATION table. If all resistance reading are 5 ohms or less, replace driver's door module. If any resistance readings are greater than 5 ohms, repair open in appropriate wire.

DDM CIRCUIT IDENTIFICATION

DDM Terminal	Switch Terminal	Wire Color
1	3	Yellow/Light Blue
2	2	Red/Light Blue
3	12	Red/Light Green
4	11	Yellow/Light Green
9	1	Yellow/White
10	9	Red/White
11	14	Gray/Black
12	13	Gray

8) Operate driver's seat in all directions. If driver's seat does not move in one second intervals, go to next step. If driver's seat moves in one second intervals, perform TEST E: SEAT MOTORS OPERATE IN ONE SECOND INTERVALS.

9) Ensure transmission is in Park. Using NGS tester, select DSM active command DRIVER SEAT CONTROL. Using NGS tester, operate driver's seat in all directions. If driver's seat responds correctly, replace driver's seat module. If driver's seat does not respond correctly, go to appropriate step. See DRIVER'S SEAT MALFUNCTION table.

DRIVER'S SEAT MALFUNCTION

Malfunction	Go To
No Seat Movement	Next Step
No Front Motor Movement	Step 16)
No Rear Motor Movement	Step 18)
No Horizontal Motor Movement	Step 20)
No Recline Motor Movement	Step 22)

10) Ensure ignition switch is in LOCK position. Disconnect DSM harness connector C337. Measure voltage at terminal No. 1 (Red wire) at DSM harness connector C337. If battery voltage exists, go to next step. If battery voltage does not exist, repair open in Red wire.

11) Measure resistance between ground and terminal No. 2 (Black wire) at DSM harness connector C337. If resistance is 10 k/ohms or less, go to next step. If resistance is greater than 10 k/ohms, repair open in Black wire.

12) Remove DSM internal fuse (30-amp). If fuse is blown, go to next step. If fuse is okay, replace driver's seat module.

13) Ensure ignition switch is in LOCK position. Ensure transmission is in Park. Disconnect DSM harness connector C338 and driver's front seat track motor assembly harness connectors. Measure resistance between ground and appropriate terminals at DSM harness connector C338. See DSM CIRCUIT IDENTIFICATION table. If all resistance readings are greater than 10 k/ohms, go to next step. If any resistance reading is 10 k/ohms or less, repair short to ground in appropriate wire(s).

DSM CIRCUIT IDENTIFICATION

Terminal	Wire Color
4	Yellow/White
5	Yellow/Light Green
6	Yellow/Light Blue
11	Red/Light Blue
13	Red/Light Green
14	Red/White

14) Disconnect driver's recline motor harness connector C307. Measure resistance between ground and terminal No. 7 (Gray/Black wire), then between ground and terminal No. 16 (Gray wire) at DSM harness connector C338. If both resistance readings are greater than 10 k/ohms, go to next step. If either resistance reading is 10 k/ohms or less, repair short to ground in appropriate wire(s).

15) Connect driver's recline motor harness connector C307. Connect DSM harness connector C338. Ensure driver's front seat track assembly harness connector C332 is still disconnected. Replace DSM internal fuse. Using driver's seat control switch, recline driver's seat-back completely backward and forward. If DSM internal fuse does not blow, replace driver's front seat track assembly. If DSM internal fuse blows, replace recline motor.

16) Disconnect driver's front seat track assembly harness connector C332. Using NGS tester, select DSM active command DRIVER SEAT CONTROL. Measure voltage between Red/Light Blue wire and Yellow/Light Blue wire at driver's front seat track assembly harness connector C332. Using NGS tester, operate driver's seat front height motor up and down. If voltage does not exist when motor is commanded on, go to next step. If voltage exists only when motor is commanded on, replace driver's front seat track assembly.

17) Disconnect DSM harness connector C338. Measure resistance in Red/Light Blue wire between terminal No. 11 at DSM harness connector C338 and driver's front seat track assembly harness connector C332. Also, measure resistance in Yellow/Light Blue wire between terminal No. 6 at DSM harness connector C338 and driver's front seat track assembly harness connector C332. If both resistance readings are 5 ohms or less, replace driver's seat module. If either resistance reading is greater than 5 ohms, repair open in appropriate wire(s).

18) Disconnect driver's front seat track assembly harness connector C332. Using NGS tester, select DSM active command DRIVER SEAT CONTROL. Measure voltage between Red/Light Green wire and Yellow/Light Green wire of driver's front seat track assembly harness connector C332. Using NGS tester, operate driver's seat rear height motor up and down. If voltage exists only when motor is commanded on, replace driver's front seat track assembly. If voltage does not exist when motor is commanded on, go to next step.

19) Disconnect DSM harness connector C338. Measure resistance in Red/Light Green wire between terminal No. 13 at DSM harness connector C338 and driver's front seat track assembly harness connector C332. Also, measure resistance in Yellow/Light Green wire between terminal No. 5 at DSM harness connector C338 and driver's front seat track assembly harness connector C332. If both resistance reading are 5 ohms or less, replace driver's seat module. If either resistance reading is greater than 5 ohms, repair open in appropriate wire(s).

20) Disconnect driver's front seat track assembly harness connector C332. Using NGS tester, select DSM active command DRIVER SEAT CONTROL. Measure voltage between Red/White wire and Yellow/White wire of driver's front seat track assembly harness connector C332. Using NGS tester, operate driver's seat horizontal motor forward and backward. If voltage exists only when motor is commanded on, replace driver's front seat track assembly. If voltage does not exist when motor is commanded on, go to next step.

21) Disconnect DSM harness connector C338. Measure resistance in Red/White wire between terminal No. 14 at DSM harness connector C338 and driver's front seat track assembly harness connector C332. Also, measure resistance in Yellow/White wire between terminal No. 4 at DSM harness connector C338 and driver's front seat track assembly harness connector C332. If both resistance readings are 5 ohms or less, replace driver's seat module. If either resistance reading is greater than 5 ohms, repair open in appropriate wire(s).

22) Disconnect drive seat recline motor harness connector C307. Using NGS tester, select DSM active command DRIVER SEAT CONTROL. Measure voltage between Gray wire and Gray/Black wire at driver's seat recline motor harness connector C307. Using NGS tester, operate driver's seat recline motor forward and backward. If voltage exists only when motor is commanded on, replace driver's front seat track assembly. If voltage does not exist when motor is commanded on, go to next step.

23) Disconnect DSM harness connector C338. Measure resistance in Gray wire between terminal No. 16 at DSM harness connector C338 and driver's seat recline motor harness connector C307. Also, measure resistance in Gray/Black wire between terminal No. 7 at DSM harness connector C338 and driver's seat recline motor harness connector C307. If both resistance readings are 5 ohms or less, replace driver's seat module. If either resistance reading is greater than 5 ohms, repair open in appropriate wire(s).

TEST D: PASSENGER'S SEAT COMPLETELY INOPERATIVE

NOTE: After any repairs are complete, ensure all component are properly installed and all harness connectors are connected properly and repeat data link diagnostic test. See DATA LINK DIAGNOSTIC TEST under COMMUNICATIONS NETWORK DIAGNOSTICS in appropriate MODULE COMMUNICATIONS NETWORK – TOWN CAR article.

NOTE: Connector C306 is a 6-terminal connector. Manufacturer does not provide connector view. Identify connector by wire color. Connectors C302 and C318 are 2-terminal connectors. Identify connectors by wire color. See WIRING DIAGRAM.

1) Disconnect passenger's front seat track assembly harness connector C306. Measure voltage between Red/Light Blue wire and Yellow/Light Blue wire of passenger's front seat track assembly harness connector

C306. Using passenger's seat control switch, operate seat front up and down. If battery voltage does not exist when switch is operated, go to next step. If battery voltage exists when switch is operated, replace passenger's front seat track assembly.

2) Disconnect passenger's seat control switch harness connector C609. Measure resistance between ground and terminal No. 12 (Black wire) at passenger's seat control switch harness connector C609. If resistance is 5 ohms or less, go to next step. If resistance is greater than 5 ohms, repair open in Black wire.

3) Measure voltage at terminal No. 7 (Dark Green wire) at passenger's seat control switch harness connector C609. If battery voltage does not exist, go to next step. If battery voltage exists, check wiring between passenger's seat control switch and motor. If wiring is okay, replace passenger's seat control switch. If wiring is damaged, repair wiring as necessary.

4) Check maxi-fuse No. 25 (30-amp) in power distribution box. If fuse is blown, go to next step. If fuse is okay, check for voltage to fuse. If voltage exists, repair open in Dark Green wire. If voltage does not exist, repair voltage supply as necessary.

5) Ensure fuse No. 25 is still removed and passenger's seat control switch harness connector C609 is still disconnected. Measure resistance between ground and output cavity of maxi-fuse No. 25 (Dark Green wire) at power distribution box. If resistance is 100 ohms or less, go to next step. If resistance is greater than 100 ohms, go to step **8)**.

6) Disconnect passenger's seat control switch harness connector C609. Measure resistance between ground and output cavity of maxi-fuse No. 25 (Dark Green wire) at power distribution box. If resistance is 100 ohms or less, go to next step. If resistance is greater than 100 ohms, replace passenger's seat control switch.

7) Disconnect passenger's seat lumbar switch harness connector C318. Measure resistance between ground and output side of maxi-fuse No. 25 (Dark Green wire) at power distribution box. If resistance is greater than 100 ohms, replace passenger's seat lumber control switch. If resistance is 100 ohms or less, repair short to ground in Dark Green wire.

8) Replace maxi-fuse No. 25. Connect passenger's seat control switch harness connector C609. Operate passenger's seat through all positions. If fuse blows, go to next step. If fuse does not blow, go to step **10)**.

9) Disconnect passenger's seat control switch harness connector C609. Measure resistance between ground and terminals at passenger's seat control switch harness connector C609. See PASSENGER'S SEAT SWITCH CIRCUIT IDENTIFICATION table. If all resistance readings are greater than 10 k/ohms, replace passenger's seat control switch. If any resistance reading is 10 k/ohms or less, repair short to ground in appropriate wire(s).

PASSENGER'S SEAT SWITCH CIRCUIT IDENTIFICATION

Terminal	Wire Color
1	Yellow/Light Green
2	Red/Light Green
4	Gray/Black
5	Gray
6	Red/Light Blue
8	Red/White
10	Yellow/White
11	Yellow/Light Blue

10) Operate passenger's seat lumbar switch through all positions. If maxi-fuse No. 25 blows, go to next step. If maxi-fuse No. 25 does not blow, repair intermittent short to ground in Dark Green wire.

11) Disconnect passenger's lumbar switch harness connector C318. Disconnect passenger's lumbar motor harness connector C302. Measure resistance between ground and Red wire at passenger's lumbar switch harness connector C318. If resistance is greater than 10 k/ohms, replace passenger's lumbar switch. If resistance is 10 k/ohms or less, repair short to ground in Red wire.

TEST E: SEAT MOTORS OPERATE IN ONE SECOND INTERVALS

NOTE: After any repairs are complete, ensure all component are properly installed and all harness connectors are connected properly and repeat data link diagnostic test. See DATA LINK DIAGNOSTIC TEST under COMMUNICATIONS NETWORK DIAGNOSTICS in appropriate MODULE COMMUNICATIONS NETWORK – TOWN CAR article.

NOTE: Connector C334, C335, C336 and C341 are 3-terminal connectors. Identify connectors by wire color. See WIRING DIAGRAMS.

1) Ensure transmission is in Park. Operate driver's seat in all directions. If seat moves in all directions, go to next step. If seat does not move in some or any direction, refer to SYMPTOM CHART table to diagnosis problem.

2) Using NGS tester, perform Driver's Door Module (DDM) self-test. If any DTCs were retrieved, perform appropriate test. See DRIVER'S DOOR MODULE DTC INDEX table under SELF-DIAGNOSTIC SYSTEM. If no DTCs were retrieved, go to next step.

3) Using NGS tester, perform Driver's Seat Module (DSM) self-test. If no DTCs were retrieved during DSM self-test, go to next step. If any DTC were retrieved during DSM self-test, go to appropriate step. See DTC STEP CHART table.

DTC STEP CHART

DTCs	Perform Step
B1663 & B1957	5)
B1663 & B1954	6)
B1664 & B1953	8)
B1664 & B1950	9)
B1665 & B1965	11)
B1665 & B1962	12)
B1666 & B1961	14)
B1666 & B1958	15)
B1663, B1664, B1665 & B1666	4)
B1663, B1664, B1665, B1666, B1667, B1668, B1669 & B1670	17)

4) Ensure transmission is in Park. Using driver's seat control switch, place seat in center position. Using driver's seat control switch, move each seat motor through complete travel. If all motors move through complete travel smoothly with out stopping, replace driver's seat module. If all motors do not move through complete travel smoothly without stopping, go to appropriate step. See MOTOR STEP CHART table.

MOTOR STEP CHART

Inoperative Motor	Perform Step
All	17)
Front Height	Next Step
Horizontal	11)
Rear Height	8)
Recline	14)

5) Ensure ignition switch is in LOCK position. Disconnect DSM harness connector C338. Disconnect front height motor potentiometer harness connector C336. Measure resistance between ground and terminal No. 6 (Light Green/Red wire) at front height motor potentiometer harness connector C336. If resistance is greater than 10 k/ohms, go to next step. If resistance is 10 k/ohms or less, repair short to ground in Light Green/Red wire.

6) Measure resistance between front height motor potentiometer harness connector C336 and driver's seat module harness connector C338. See FRONT HEIGHT MOTOR POTENTIOMETER CIRCUIT IDENTIFICATION table. If all resistance readings are 5 ohms or less, go to next step. If any resistance reading is greater than 5 ohms, repair open in appropriate wire(s).

FRONT HEIGHT MOTOR POTENTIOMETER CIRCUIT IDENTIFICATION

DSM Terminal	Terminal	Wire Color
1	3	Orange/Red
3	1	Orange/White
9	2	Light Green/Red

7) Measure voltage at terminals No. 2 (Light Green/Red wire), No. 1 (Orange/White wire) and No. 3 (Orange/Red wire) at front height motor potentiometer harness connector C336. If voltage does not exist at any terminal, go to step 21). If voltage exists at any terminal, repair short to voltage in appropriate wire(s).

8) Ensure ignition switch is in LOCK position. Disconnect DSM harness connector C338. Disconnect rear height motor potentiometer harness connector C334. Measure resistance between ground and terminal No. 2 (Light Green/Black wire) at rear height motor potentiometer harness connector C334. If resistance is greater than 10 k/ohms, go to next step. If resistance is 10 k/ohms or less, repair short to ground in Light Green/Black wire.

9) Measure resistance between rear height motor potentiometer harness connector C334 and driver's seat module harness connector C338. See REAR HEIGHT POTENTIOMETER MOTOR CIRCUIT IDENTIFICATION table. If all resistance readings are 5 ohms or less, go to next step. If any resistance readings are greater than 5 ohms, repair open in appropriate wire(s).

REAR HEIGHT POTENTIOMETER MOTOR CIRCUIT IDENTIFICATION

DSM Terminal	Motor Terminal	Wire Color
1	3	Orange/Red
3	1	Orange/White
8	2	Light Green/Black

10) Measure voltage at terminals No. 2 (Light Green/Black wire), No. 1 (Orange/White wire) and No. 3 (Orange/Red wire) at rear height motor potentiometer harness connector C334. If voltage exists at any terminal, repair short to voltage in appropriate wire(s). If voltage does not exist at any terminal, go to step 23).

11) Ensure ignition switch is in LOCK position. Disconnect DSM harness connector C338. Disconnect horizontal motor potentiometer harness connector C335. Measure resistance between ground and terminal No. 2 (Light Green/Orange wire) at horizontal motor potentiometer harness connector C335. If resistance is greater than 10 k/ohms, go to next step. If resistance is 10 k/ohms or less, repair short to ground in Light Green/Orange wire.

12) Measure resistance between horizontal motor potentiometer harness connector C335 and driver's seat module harness connector C338. See HORIZONTAL MOTOR POTENTIOMETER CIRCUIT IDENTIFICATION table. If all resistance readings are 5 ohms or less, go to next step. If any resistance readings are greater than 5 ohms, repair open in appropriate wire(s).

HORIZONTAL MOTOR POTENTIOMETER CIRCUIT IDENTIFICATION

DSM Terminal	Motor Terminal	Wire Color
1	3	Orange/Red
3	1	Orange/White
10	2	Light Green/Orange

13) Measure voltage at terminals No. 2 (Light Green/Orange wire), No. 1 (Orange/White wire) and No. 3 (Orange/Red wire) at horizontal motor potentiometer harness connector C335. If voltage does not exist at any terminal, go to step 25). If voltage exists at any terminal, repair short to voltage in appropriate wire(s).

14) Ensure ignition switch is in LOCK position. Disconnect DSM harness connector C338. Disconnect recline motor potentiometer harness connector C341. Measure resistance between ground and terminal No. 2 (Orange/Light Blue wire) at recline motor potentiometer harness connector C341. If resistance is greater than 10 k/ohms, go to next step. If resistance is 10 k/ohms or less, repair short to ground in Orange/Light Blue wire.

15) Measure resistance between recline height motor potentiometer harness connector C341 and driver's seat module harness connector C338. See RECLINE MOTOR POTENTIOMETER CIRCUIT IDENTIFICATION table. If all resistance readings are 5 ohms or less, go to next step. If any resistance readings are greater than 5 ohms, repair open in appropriate wire(s).

RECLINE MOTOR POTENTIOMETER CIRCUIT IDENTIFICATION

DSM Terminal	Motor Terminal	Wire Color
1	3	Orange/Red
3	1	Orange/White
15	2	Orange/Light Blue

16) Measure voltage at terminals No. 2 (Orange/Light Blue wire), No. 1 (Orange/White wire) and No. 3 (Orange/Red wire) at recline motor potentiometer harness connector C341. If voltage does not exist at any terminal, go to step 27). If voltage exists at any terminal, repair short to voltage in appropriate wire(s).

17) Ensure ignition switch is in LOCK position. Disconnect DSM harness connector C338, front height motor potentiometer harness connector C336, rear height motor potentiometer harness connector C334, horizontal motor potentiometer harness connector C335 and recline motor potentiometer harness connector C341. Measure resistance in Orange/White wire between terminal No. 3 at DSM harness connector C338 and terminal No. 1 at each motor potentiometer harness connector. If all resistance readings are 5 ohms or less, go to next step. If any resistance reading is greater than 5 ohms, repair open in appropriate wire(s).

18) Measure resistance in Orange/Red wire between terminal No. 1 at DSM harness connector C338 and terminal No. 3 at each motor potentiometer harness connector. If all resistance readings are 5 ohms or less, go to next step. If any resistance reading is greater than 5 ohms, repair open in appropriate wire(s).

19) Measure resistance between ground and terminal No. 1 (Orange/White wire) at each motor potentiometer harness connector. If all resistance readings are greater than 10 k/ohms, go to next step. If any resistance reading is 10 k/ohms or less, repair short to ground in appropriate wire(s).

20) Measure voltage between ground and terminal No. 1 (Orange/White wire) at each motor potentiometer harness connector. If voltage does not exist at any terminal, go to step 29). If voltage exists at any terminal, repair short to voltage in Orange/White wire.

21) Ensure ignition switch is in LOCK position. Connect DSM harness connector C338. Measure voltage at terminals No. 1 (Orange/White wire) and No. 2 (Light Green/Red wire) at front height motor potentiometer harness connector C336. If voltage exists, go to next step. If voltage does not exist, replace driver's seat module.

22) Measure resistance between ground and terminal No. 3 (Orange/Red wire) at front height motor potentiometer harness connector C336. If resistance is greater than 10 k/ohms, replace driver's seat module. If resistance is 10 k/ohms or less, replace driver's front seat track assembly.

23) Ensure ignition switch is in LOCK position. Connect DSM harness connector C338. Measure voltage at terminals No. 1 (Orange/White wire) and No. 2 (Light Green/Black wire) at rear height motor potentiometer harness connector C334. If voltage exists, go to next step. If voltage does not exist, replace driver's seat module.

24) Measure resistance between ground and terminal No. 3 (Orange/Red wire) at rear height motor potentiometer harness connector C334. If resistance is greater than 10 k/ohms, replace driver's seat module. If resistance is 10 k/ohms or less, replace driver's front seat track assembly.

25) Ensure ignition switch is in LOCK position. Connect DSM harness connector C338. Measure voltage at terminals No. 1 (Orange/White wire) and No. 2 (Light Green/Orange wire) at horizontal motor potenti-

ometer harness connector C335. If voltage exists, go to next step. If voltage does not exist, replace driver's seat module.

26) Measure resistance between ground and terminal No. 3 (Orange/Red wire) at horizontal motor potentiometer harness connector C335. If resistance is greater than 10 k/ohms, replace driver's seat module. If resistance is 10 k/ohms or less, replace driver's front seat track assembly.

27) Ensure ignition switch is in LOCK position. Connect DSM harness connector C338. Measure voltage at terminals No. 3 (Orange/White wire) and No. 2 (Orange/Light Blue wire) at recline motor potentiometer harness connector C341. If voltage exists, go to next step. If voltage does not exist, replace driver's seat module.

28) Measure resistance between ground and terminal No. 3 (Orange/Red wire) at recline motor potentiometer harness connector C341. If resistance is greater than 10 k/ohms, replace driver's seat module. If resistance is 10 k/ohms or less, replace driver's front seat track assembly.

29) Using NGS tester, perform DSM self-test. If DTCs B1667, B1667, B1668 and B1670 were not also retrieved, replace driver's seat module. If DTCs B1667, B1667, B1668 and B1670 were also retrieved, repair memory mirror system. See appropriate POWER MEMORY MIRRORS article.

TEST F: PASSENGER'S SEAT DOES NOT MOVE HORIZONTALLY/VERTICALLY

NOTE: After repairs are complete, ensure all component are properly installed and all harness connectors are connected properly and repeat data link diagnostic test. See DATA LINK DIAGNOSTIC TEST under COMMUNICATIONS NETWORK DIAGNOSTICS in appropriate MODULE COMMUNICATIONS NETWORK – TOWN CAR article.

1) Disconnected suspected motor harness connector. Measure voltage between appropriate motor harness connector terminals. Operate seat control switch in both direction for suspected motor. If voltage does not exists in either direction, go to next step. If voltage exists in both directions, replace front seat track assembly.

2) Turn ignition switch to RUN position. Using a voltmeter, backprobe at appropriate terminal at passenger's seat control switch. See PASSENGER'S SEAT CONTROL SWITCH CIRCUIT IDENTIFICATION table. If voltage does not exist, go to next step. If voltage exists, repair short to voltage in appropriate wire between passenger's seat control switch and motor harness connectors.

PASSENGER'S SEAT CONTROL SWITCH CIRCUIT IDENTIFICATION

Motor	Terminal	Wire Color
Front Down	6	Red/Light Blue
Front Up	11	Yellow/Light Blue
Rear Down	2	Red/Light Green
Rear Up	1	Yellow/Light Green
Recline FWD	5	Gray
Recline RWD	4	Gray/Black
Forward	10	Yellow/White
Rearward	8	Red/White

3) Disconnect passenger's seat control switch harness connector C609. Measure resistance between ground and appropriate seat control switch harness connector terminals. See SEAT CONTROL SWITCH CIRCUIT IDENTIFICATION. If all resistance readings are greater than 10 k/ohms, go to next step. If any resistance reading is 10 k/ohms or less, repair short to ground in appropriate wire(s).

SEAT CONTROL SWITCH CIRCUIT IDENTIFICATION

Terminal	Wire Color
1	Yellow/Light Green
2	Red/Light Green
4	Gray/Black
5	Gray

SEAT CONTROL SWITCH CIRCUIT IDENTIFICATION (Cont.)

Terminal	Wire Color
6	Red/Light Blue
8	Red/White
10	Yellow/White
11	Yellow/Light Blue

4) Measure resistance in wires between passenger's seat control switch harness connector C609 terminal and suspected motor harness connector terminal. See PASSENGER'S SEAT CONTROL SWITCH CIRCUIT IDENTIFICATION table. If all resistance reading are 5 ohms or less, replace passenger's seat control switch. If any resistance reading is greater than 5 ohms, repair open in appropriate wire(s).

TEST G: MEMORY SEAT INOPERATIVE

NOTE: After any repairs are complete, ensure all component are properly installed and all harness connectors are connected properly and repeat data link diagnostic test. See DATA LINK DIAGNOSTIC TEST under COMMUNICATIONS NETWORK DIAGNOSTICS in appropriate MODULE COMMUNICATIONS NETWORK – TOWN CAR article.

1) Using NGS tester, perform Driver's Door Module (DDM) self-test. If any DTCs were retrieved, perform appropriate test. If no DTCs were retrieved, go to next step. See DRIVER'S DOOR MODULE DTC INDEX table under SELF-DIAGNOSTIC SYSTEM.

2) Using NGS tester, perform Driver's Seat Module (DSM) self-test. If no DTCs were retrieved, go to next step. If any DTCs were retrieved, perform appropriate test. See DRIVER'S SEAT MODULE DTC INDEX under SELF-DIAGNOSTIC SYSTEM.

3) Ensure transmission is in Park. Using seat control switch, operate seat in all directions. If seat operates properly in all directions, go to next step. If seat does not operate properly, repair seat by symptom. See SYMPTOM CHART table.

4) Activate memory recall positions No. 1 and 2 at memory switch. If memory recall feature operates properly, go to next step. If memory recall feature does not operate properly, go to step **6)**.

5) Activate memory recall position No. 1 and 2 from remote transmitter. If memory recall feature operates properly, memory seats system is okay at this time. If memory recall feature does not operate properly, repair keyless entry system. See appropriate REMOTE KEYLESS ENTRY SYSTEMS article.

6) If memory switch LED is not always on, go to next step. If memory switch LED is always on, go to step **15)**.

7) Using NGS tester, access DDM PID MEMS_SW. Press and release memory set switch. OFF should be displayed when button is depressed and ON should be displayed when button is not depressed. If display responds as described, go to next step. If display does not respond as described, go to step **11)**.

8) Press and release memory set switch. If LED remains on for 5 seconds, go to next step. If LED does not remain on for 5 seconds, go to step **14)**.

9) Using NGS tester, access DDM PID MEM1_SW. Press and release memory "1" switch. ON should be displayed when button is depressed and OFF should be displayed when button is not depressed. If display responds as described, go to next step. If display does not respond as described, go to step **11)**.

10) Using NGS tester, access DDM PID MEM2_SW. Press and release memory "2" switch. ON should be displayed when button is depressed and OFF should be displayed when button is not depressed. If display responds as described, replace driver's seat module. If display does not respond as described, go to next step.

11) Disconnect driver's door module harness connector C520. Measure resistance between ground and terminal No. 20 (Brown/Orange wire) at DDM harness connector C520. Also, measure resistance between ground and terminal No. 21 (Brown/Light Green wire). Also, measure resistance between ground and terminal No. 33 (Black/Orange wire). If any resistance reading is 10 k/ohms or less, go to next step. If all resistance readings are greater than 10 k/ohms, go to step **13)**.

12) Disconnect driver's seat control switch harness connector C509. Measure resistance between ground and terminal No. 20 (Brown/Orange wire) at DDM harness connector C520. Also, measure resistance between ground and terminal No. 21 (Brown/Light Green wire). Also, measure resistance between ground and terminal No. 33 (Black/Orange wire). If any resistance reading is 10 k/ohms or less, repair short in appropriate wire. If all resistance reading are greater than 10 k/ohms, replace driver's seat control switch.

13) Disconnect DDM harness connector C520 and driver's seat control switch harness connector C509. Measure resistance in Brown/Orange wire between terminal No. 20 at DDM harness connector C521 and terminal No. 5 at driver's seat control switch harness connector C509. Also, measure resistance in Brown/Light Green wire between terminal No. 21 at DDM harness connector C520 and terminal No. 6 at driver's seat control switch harness connector C509. Also, measure resistance in Black/Orange wire between terminal No. 33 at DDM harness connector C520 and terminal No. 7 at driver's seat control switch harness connector C509. If all resistance reading are 5 ohms or less, go to step **16)**. If any resistance reading is greater than 5 ohms, repair open in appropriate wire(s).

14) Disconnect DDM harness connector C521 and driver's seat control switch harness connector C509. Measure resistance in White/Orange wire between terminal No. 14 at DDM harness connector C521 and terminal No. 4 at driver's seat control switch harness connector C509. If resistance is 5 ohms or less, go to step **16)**. If resistance is greater than 5 ohms, repair open in White/Orange wire.

15) Disconnect DDM harness connector C521 and driver's seat control switch harness connector C509. Measure resistance between ground and terminal No. 14 (White/Orange wire) at DDM harness connector C521. If resistance is 10 k/ohms or less, repair short to ground in White/Orange wire. If resistance is greater than 10 k/ohms, replace driver's seat control switch.

16) Test memory switch portion of driver's seat control switch. See DRIVER'S SEAT CONTROL SWITCH (WITH MEMORY) under COMPONENT TESTS. If switch is okay, replace driver's door module. If switch is defective, replace driver's seat control switch.

TEST H: EASY EXIT/ENTRY FEATURE INOPERATIVE

NOTE: After any repairs are complete, ensure all component are properly installed and all harness connectors are connected properly and repeat data link diagnostic test. See DATA LINK DIAGNOSTIC TEST under COMMUNICATIONS NETWORK DIAGNOSTICS in appropriate MODULE COMMUNICATIONS NETWORK – TOWN CAR article.

1) Ensure transmission is in Park. Using driver's seat control switch, operate driver's seat in all directions. If seat operates properly in all directions, go to next step. If seat does not operate properly, repair seat by symptom. See SYMPTOM CHART table.

2) Turn ignition switch to RUN position. Position seat in center of travel. Remove key from ignition. If seat does not move rearward approximately 2 inches, go to next step. If seat moves rearward approximately 2 inches, go to step **5)**.

3) Connect NGS tester to Data Link Connector (DLC). Access LCM on scan tool. Select LCM PIP IGN_KEY and IGN_LC. Starting with key in LOCK position, turn key one position at a time while monitoring scan tool display. Remove key while observing LCM PIP IGN_KEY. If scan tool display corresponds to switch position, go to next step. If scan tool display does not correspond to switch position, repair ignition switch concern. See appropriate STEERING COLUMN SWITCHES article.

4) Using NGS tester, perform Driver's Seat Module (DSM) self-test. If no DTCs are retrieved, replace driver's seat module. If DTC B1665, B1962 or B1965 are retrieved, perform TEST E: SEAT MOTORS OPERATE IN ONE SECOND INTERVALS. If any other DTCs are retrieved, perform appropriate test. See DRIVER'S SEAT MODULE DTC INDEX table under SELF-DIAGNOSTIC SYSTEM.

5) Remove key and exit vehicle. Ensure all doors are closed completely. After 10 seconds, enter vehicle and close door. Insert key into ignition switch. If driver's seat does not move forward approximately 2 inches, go to next step. If driver's seat move forward approximately 2 inches, system is okay at this time.

6) Using NGS tester, retrieve and record Lighting Control Module (LCM) DTCs. Clear LCM DTCs. Using NGS tester, perform LCM self-test. If any LCM DTCs exist, diagnosis DTCs as necessary. See MODULE COMMUNICATIONS NETWORK – TOWN CAR article. If no LCM DTCs exist, go to next step.

7) Using NGS tester, retrieve Driver's Seat Module (DSM) DTCs. If DSM DTCs exist, perform appropriate test. See DRIVER'S SEAT MODULE DTC INDEX table under SELF-DIAGNOSTIC SYSTEM. If DSM DTCs do not exist, replace driver's seat module.

TEST I: DRIVER'S HEATED SEAT INOPERATIVE

NOTE: After any repairs are complete, ensure all component are properly installed and all harness connectors are connected properly and repeat data link diagnostic test. See DATA LINK DIAGNOSTIC TEST under COMMUNICATIONS NETWORK DIAGNOSTICS in appropriate MODULE COMMUNICATIONS NETWORK – TOWN CAR article.

1) Operate passenger's seat heater. If passenger's seat heater is operational, go to next step. If passenger's seat heater is inoperative, perform TEST M: BOTH HEATED SEATS INOPERATIVE.

2) Turn ignition switch to LOCK position. Disconnect driver's seat heater switch harness connector C524. Turn ignition switch to RUN position. Measure voltage at terminal No. 2 (Red/Black wire) at driver's seat heater seat switch harness connector C524. If battery voltage exists, go to next step. If battery voltage does not exist, repair open in Red/Black wire.

3) Turn ignition switch to LOCK position. Connect driver's seat heater switch harness connector C524. Disconnect driver's heated seat module harness connector C347. Measure voltage at terminal No. 7 (Light Blue/White wire) at driver's heated seat module harness connector C347. If battery voltage exists, go to next step. If battery voltage does not exist, repair open in Light Blue/White wire.

4) Measure resistance between ground and terminal No. 14 (Black wire) at driver's heated seat module harness connector C347. If resistance is 5 ohms or less, go to next step. If resistance is greater than 5 ohms, repair open in Black wire.

5) Ensure ignition switch is in LOCK position. Measure resistance between terminals No. 3 (Light Green/Orange wire) and No. 4 (Tan/Light Blue wire) at driver's heated seat module harness connector C347. Turn driver's seat heater switch to position No. 1. If resistance is not 2000-2750 ohms, go to next step. If resistance is 2000-2750 ohms, go to step **12)**.

6) Turn driver's seat heater switch off. Measure resistance between ground and terminal No. 3 (Light Green/Orange wire) at driver's heated seat module harness connector C347. If resistance is less then 10 k/ohms, go to next step. If resistance is greater than 10 k/ohms, go to step **8)**.

7) Disconnect driver's seat heater switch harness connector C524. Measure resistance between ground and terminal No. 3 (Light Green/Orange wire) at driver's heated seat module harness connector C347. If resistance is less then 10 k/ohms, repair short to ground in Light Green/Orange wire. If resistance is greater than 10 k/ohms, replace driver's seat heater switch.

8) Ensure ignition switch is in LOCK position. Measure resistance between ground and terminal No. 4 (Tan/Light Blue wire) at driver's heated seat module harness connector C347. If resistance is less then 10 k/ohms, go to next step. If resistance is greater than 10 k/ohms, go to step **10)**.

9) Disconnect driver's seat heater switch harness connector C524. Measure resistance between ground and terminal No. 4 (Tan/Light Blue wire) at driver's heated seat module harness connector C347. If resistance is 10 k/ohms or less, repair short to ground in Tan/Light Blue wire. If resistance is greater than 10 k/ohms, replace driver's seat heater switch.

10) Disconnect driver's seat heater switch harness connector C524. Measure resistance in Tan/Light Blue wire between ground and terminal No. 4 at driver's heated seat module harness connector C347 and terminal No. 9 at driver's seat heater switch harness connector C524. If resistance is 5 ohms or less, go to next step. If resistance is greater than 5 ohms, repair open in Tan/Light Blue wire.

11) Measure resistance in Light Green/Orange wire between terminal No. 3 at driver's heated seat module harness connector C347 and terminal No. 8 at driver's seat heater switch harness connector C524. If resistance is 5 ohms or less, replace driver's seat heater switch. If resistance is greater than 5 ohms, repair open in Light Green/Orange wire.

12) Measure resistance between terminals No. 9 (Gray/Light Blue wire) and No. 12 (Violet/Light Blue wire) at driver's heated seat module harness connector C347. If resistance is 2.5-10.0 ohms, replace driver's heated seat module. If resistance in not 2.5-10.0 ohms, repair wire and/or replace seat back cushion as necessary.

TEST J: DRIVER'S HEATED SEAT CUSHION INOPERATIVE

NOTE: *After any repairs are complete, ensure all component are properly installed and all harness connectors are connected properly and repeat data link diagnostic test. See DATA LINK DIAGNOSTIC TEST under COMMUNICATIONS NETWORK DIAGNOSTICS in appropriate MODULE COMMUNICATIONS NETWORK – TOWN CAR article.*

1) Turn ignition switch to LOCK position. Disconnect driver's heated seat module harness connector C347. Turn ignition switch to RUN position. Turn heated seat cushion on. Measure voltage at terminal No. 1 (Dark Green/Violet wire) at driver's heated seat module harness connector C347. If battery voltage does not exist, go to next step. If battery voltage exists, go to step 3).

2) Disconnect driver's seat heater switch harness connector C524. Measure resistance in Dark Green/Violet wire between terminal No. 1 at driver's heated seat module harness connector C347 and terminal No. 6 at driver's seat heater switch harness connector C524. If resistance is 5 ohms or less, replace driver's seat heater switch. If resistance is greater than 5 ohms, repair open in Dark Green/Violet wire.

3) Measure resistance between terminals No. 8 (Yellow/Light Blue wire) and No. 13 (White/Light Blue wire) at driver's heated seat module harness connector C347. If resistance is 2.5-10.0 ohms, replace driver's heated seat module. If resistance in not 2.5-10.0 ohms, repair wire and/or replace driver's seat cushion as necessary.

TEST K: PASSENGER'S HEATED SEAT INOPERATIVE

NOTE: *After any repairs are complete, ensure all component are properly installed and all harness connectors are connected properly and repeat data link diagnostic test. See DATA LINK DIAGNOSTIC TEST under COMMUNICATIONS NETWORK DIAGNOSTICS in appropriate MODULE COMMUNICATIONS NETWORK – TOWN CAR article.*

1) Operate driver's seat heater. If driver's seat heater is operational, go to next step. If driver's seat heater is inoperative, perform TEST M: BOTH HEATED SEATS INOPERATIVE.

2) Turn ignition switch to LOCK position. Disconnect passenger's seat heater switch harness connector C616. Turn ignition switch to RUN position. Measure voltage at terminal No. 2 (Red/Black wire) at passenger's seat heater switch harness connector C616. If battery voltage exists, go to next step. If battery voltage does not exist, repair open in Red/Black wire.

3) Turn ignition switch to LOCK position. Connect passenger's seat heater switch harness connector C616. Disconnect passenger's heated seat module harness connector C344. Measure voltage at terminal No. 7 (Light Blue/White wire) at passenger's heated seat module harness connector C344. If battery voltage exists, go to next step. If battery voltage does not exist, repair open in Light Blue/White wire.

4) Measure resistance between ground and terminal No. 14 (Black wire) at passenger's heated seat module harness connector C344. If resistance is 5 ohms or less, go to next step. If resistance is greater than 5 ohms, repair open in Black wire.

5) Ensure ignition switch is in LOCK position. Measure resistance between terminals No. 3 (Black/Orange wire) and No. 4 (Brown wire) at passenger's heated seat module harness connector C344. Turn passenger's seat heater switch to position No. 1. If resistance is not 2000-2750 ohms, go to next step. If resistance is 2000-2750 ohms, go to step 12) .

6) Turn passenger's seat heater switch off. Measure resistance between ground and terminal No. 3 (Black/Orange wire) at driver's heated seat module harness connector C344. If resistance is less then 10 k/ohms, go to next step. If resistance is greater than 10 k/ohms, go to step 8).

7) Disconnect passenger's seat heater switch harness connector C616. Measure resistance between ground and terminal No. 3 (Black/Orange wire) at passenger's heated seat module harness connector C344. If resistance is 10 k/ohms or less, repair short to ground in Black/Orange wire. If resistance is greater than 10 k/ohms, replace passenger's seat heater switch.

8) Ensure ignition switch is in LOCK position. Measure resistance between ground and terminal No. 4 (Brown wire) at passenger's heated seat module harness connector C344. If resistance is less then 10 k/ohms, go to next step. If resistance is greater than 10 k/ohms, go to step 10).

9) Disconnect passenger's seat heater switch harness connector C616. Measure resistance between ground and terminal No. 4 (Brow wire) at passenger's heated seat module harness connector C344. If resistance is 10 k/ohms or less, repair short to ground in Brown wire. If resistance is greater than 10 k/ohms, replace passenger's seat heater switch.

10) Disconnect passenger's seat heater switch harness connector C616. Measure resistance in Brown wire between ground and terminal No. 4 at passenger's heated seat module harness connector C344 and terminal No. 9 at driver's seat heater switch harness connector C616. If resistance is 5 ohms or less, go to next step. If resistance is greater than 5 ohms, repair open in Brown wire.

11) Measure resistance in Black/Orange wire between terminal No. 3 at passenger's heated seat module harness connector C344 and terminal No. 8 at passenger's seat heater switch harness connector C616. If resistance is 5 ohms or less, replace passenger's seat heater switch. If resistance is greater than 5 ohms, repair open in Black/Orange wire.

12) Measure resistance between terminals No. 9 (Red/Light Blue wire) and No. 12 (Violet/Light Blue wire) at passenger's heated seat module harness connector C344. If resistance is 2.5-10.0 ohms, replace passenger's heated seat module. If resistance in not 2.5-10.0 ohms, repair wiring and/or replace seat back cushion as necessary.

TEST L: PASSENGER'S HEATED SEAT CUSHION INOPERATIVE

NOTE: *After any repairs are complete, ensure all component are properly installed and all harness connectors are connected properly and repeat data link diagnostic test. See DATA LINK DIAGNOSTIC TEST under COMMUNICATIONS NETWORK DIAGNOSTICS in appropriate MODULE COMMUNICATIONS NETWORK – TOWN CAR article.*

1) Turn ignition switch to LOCK position. Disconnect passenger's heated seat module harness connector C344. Turn ignition switch to RUN position. Turn passenger's seat heater on. Measure voltage at terminal No. 1 (Red wire) at passenger's heated seat module harness connector C344. If battery voltage does not exist, go to next step. If battery voltage exists, go to step 3).

2) Disconnect passenger's seat heater switch harness connector C616. Measure resistance in Red wire between terminal No. 1 at passenger's heated seat module harness connector C344 and terminal No. 6 at passenger's seat heater switch harness connector C616. If resistance is 5 ohms or less, replace passenger's seat heater switch. If resistance is greater than 5 ohms, repair open in Red wire.

3) Measure resistance between terminals No. 8 (Yellow/Light Blue wire) and No. 13 (White/Light Blue wire) at passenger's heated seat module harness connector C344. If resistance is 2.5-10.0 ohms, replace passenger's heated seat module. If resistance in not 2.5-10.0 ohms, repair wiring and/or replace passenger's seat cushion as necessary.

TEST M: BOTH HEATED SEATS INOPERATIVE

NOTE: After any repairs are complete, ensure all component are properly installed and all harness connectors are connected properly and repeat data link diagnostic test. See DATA LINK DIAGNOSTIC TEST under COMMUNICATIONS NETWORK DIAGNOSTICS in appropriate MODULE COMMUNICATIONS NETWORK – TOWN CAR article.

1) Turn ignition switch to LOCK position. Disconnect driver's seat heater switch harness connector C524. Turn ignition switch to RUN position. Measure voltage at terminal No. 2 (Red/Black wire) at driver's seat heater switch harness connector C524. If battery voltage does not exist, go to next step. If battery voltage exists, replace driver's seat heater switch.

2) Turn ignition switch to LOCK position. Remove fuse No. 6 (15-amp) from instrument panel fuse box. If fuse is blown, go to next step. If fuse is okay, check voltage to fuse No. 6. If battery voltage does not exist, repair voltage supply as necessary. If battery voltage exists, repair open in Red/Black wire.

3) Ensure fuse NO. 6 is still removed. Connect driver's seat heater switch harness connector C524. Measure resistance between ground and output cavity of fuse No. 6 at instrument panel fuse box. If resistance is 10 k/ohms or less, go to next step. If resistance is greater than 10 k/ohms, repair intermittent short in Red/Black wire or replace driver's heated seat switch as necessary.

4) Disconnect driver's seat heater switch harness connector C524. Measure resistance between ground and output cavity of fuse No. 6 at instrument panel fuse box. If resistance is 10 k/ohms or less, go to next step. If resistance is greater than 10 k/ohms, replace driver's seat heater switch.

5) Disconnect passenger's seat heater switch harness connector C616. Measure resistance between ground and output cavity of fuse No. 6 at instrument panel fuse box. If resistance is 10 k/ohms or less, short to ground in Red/Black wire. If resistance is greater than 10 k/ohms, replace passenger's seat heater switch.

TEST N: DRIVER'S LUMBAR SUPPORT INOPERATIVE

NOTE: After any repairs are complete, ensure all component are properly installed and all harness connectors are connected properly and repeat data link diagnostic test. See DATA LINK DIAGNOSTIC TEST under COMMUNICATIONS NETWORK DIAGNOSTICS in appropriate MODULE COMMUNICATIONS NETWORK – TOWN CAR article.

NOTE: Connector C303 is a 2-terminal connector. Identify connector by wire color. See WIRING DIAGRAMS.

1) Turn ignition switch to LOCK position. Disconnect driver's lumbar switch harness connector C319. Measure voltage at terminal No. 6 (Red wire) at driver's lumbar switch harness connector C319. If battery voltage exists, go to next step. If battery voltage does not exist, repair open or short in Red wire.

2) Measure resistance between ground and terminals 2 and 5 (both Black wires) at driver's lumbar switch harness connector C319. If both resistance readings are 5 ohms or less, go to next step. If either resistance reading is greater than 5 ohms, repair open in Black(s) wire.

3) Disconnect driver's lumbar motor harness connector C303. Connect driver's lumbar switch harness connector C319. Measure voltage between terminals No. 1 (Pink wire) and No. 2 (Brown wire) at driver's lumbar motor harness connector C303 while operating lumbar switch in both directions. If battery voltage does not exist, go to next step. If battery voltage exists, replace driver's lumbar motor.

4) Disconnect driver's lumbar switch harness connector C319. Measure resistance in Pink wire between terminal No. 7 at driver's lumbar switch harness connector C319 and terminal No. 1 at driver's lumbar motor harness connector C303. If resistance is 5 ohms or less, go to next step. If resistance is greater than 5 ohms, repair open in Pink wire.

5) Measure resistance in Brown wire between terminal No. 1 at driver's lumbar switch harness connector C319 and terminal No. 2 at driver's lumbar motor harness connector C303. If resistance is 5 ohms or less, replace driver's lumbar switch. If resistance is greater than 5 ohms, repair open in Brown wire.

TEST O: PASSENGER'S LUMBAR SUPPORT INOPERATIVE

NOTE: After any repairs are complete, ensure all component are properly installed and all harness connectors are connected properly and repeat data link diagnostic test. See DATA LINK DIAGNOSTIC TEST under COMMUNICATIONS NETWORK DIAGNOSTICS in appropriate MODULE COMMUNICATIONS NETWORK – TOWN CAR article.

NOTE: Connectors C302 is a 2-terminal connector. Identify connector by wire color. See WIRING DIAGRAMS.

1) Turn ignition switch to LOCK position. Disconnect passenger's lumbar switch harness connector C318. Measure voltage at terminal No. 6 (Dark Green wire) at passenger's lumbar switch harness connector C318. If battery voltage exists, go to next step. If battery voltage does not exist, repair open or short in Dark Green wire.

2) Measure resistance between ground and terminals No. 2 and 5 (both Black wires) at driver's lumbar motor harness connector C318. If resistance is 5 ohms or less, go to next step. If resistance is greater than 5 ohms, repair open in Black wire(s).

3) Disconnect passenger's lumbar motor harness connector C302. Connect passenger's lumbar switch harness connector C318. Measure voltage between terminals No. 1 (Pink wire) and terminal No. 2 (Brown wire) at passenger's lumbar motor harness connector C302 while operating lumbar switch in both directions. If battery voltage does not exist, go to next step. If battery voltage exists, replace passenger's lumbar motor.

4) Disconnect passenger's lumbar switch harness connector C318. Measure resistance in Pink wire between terminal No. 7 at passenger's lumbar switch harness connector C318 and terminal No. 1 at passenger's lumbar motor harness connector C302. If resistance is 5 ohms or less, go to next step. If resistance is greater than 5 ohms, repair open in Pink wire.

5) Measure resistance in Brown wire between terminal No. 1 at passenger's lumbar switch harness connector C318 and terminal No. 2 at passenger's lumbar motor harness connector C303. If resistance is 5 ohms or less, replace passenger's lumbar switch. If resistance is greater than 5 ohms, repair open in Brown wire.

TEST P: BATTERY VOLTAGE OUT OF RANGE (DTC B1676)

NOTE: After any repairs are complete, ensure all component are properly installed and all harness connectors are connected properly and repeat data link diagnostic test. See DATA LINK DIAGNOSTIC TEST under COMMUNICATIONS NETWORK DIAGNOSTICS in appropriate MODULE COMMUNICATIONS NETWORK – TOWN CAR article.

1) Using NGS tester, clear Driver's Seat Module (DSM) DTCs. Perform DSM self-test. If DTC B2316 was not retrieved, go to next step. If DTC B2316 was retrieved, repair power mirror concern. See appropriate POWER MEMORY MIRRORS article.

2) Turn ignition switch to LOCK position. Disconnect DSM harness connector C337. Turn ignition switch to RUN position. Measure voltage at terminal No. 1 (Red wire) at DSM harness connector C337. If battery voltage does not exist, repair open in Red wire, blown fuse No. 8

(30–amp) in power distribution box or replace charge system as necessary. If battery voltage exists, repeat DSM self-test. If DTC B1676 is retrieved, replace driver's seat module.

REMOVAL & INSTALLATION

CAUTION: When battery is disconnected or modules are replaced, vehicle computer and memory systems may lose memory data. Driveability problems may exist until computer systems have completed a relearn cycle. See COMPUTER RELEARN PROCEDURES article in GENERAL INFORMATION before disconnecting battery.

WARNING: Town Car is equipped with side air bags. Before testing or repairing power seat system, disable air bag system. See appropriate AIR BAG RESTRAINT SYSTEMS article.

DRIVER'S SEAT MODULE

Removal & Installation – See FRONT SEAT TRACK.

FRONT SEAT ASSEMBLY

Removal & Installation – Move seat forward. Remove rear seat track covers. Remove rear seat retaining nuts. Move seat all the way back. Disconnect negative battery cable and wait at least one minute. Remove front seat track covers. Remove front seat track retaining bolts. Disconnect necessary harness connectors. Remove seat from vehicle. To install, reverse removal procedure. Tighten nuts and bolt to specification. See TORQUE SPECIFICATIONS. Check air bag system for proper operation. See appropriate AIR BAG RESTRAINT SYSTEMS article.

FRONT SEATBACK

Removal & Installation – Remove seat and track assembly. See FRONT SEAT ASSEMBLY. Remove seatback trim panel. Release seatback j-retainers. Pull seat back cover. Remove seatback retaining bolts. Disconnect necessary harness connectors. Remove seatback. To install, reverse removal procedure. Tighten nuts and bolt to specification. See TORQUE SPECIFICATIONS. Check air bag system for proper operation. See appropriate AIR BAG RESTRAINT SYSTEMS article.

SIDE AIR BAG

Removal & Installation – Remove front seatback. SeeFRONT SEATBACK. Remove headrest from seatback. Unzip side air bag deployment chute. Remove side air bag retaining nuts. Separate side air bag from seat back frame. Disconnect side air bag harness connector. Remove side air bag. To install, reverse removal procedure. Tighten nuts and bolt to specification. See TORQUE SPECIFICATIONS. Check air bag system for proper operation. See appropriate AIR BAG RESTRAINT SYSTEMS article.

FRONT SEAT TRACK

Removal & Installation – Remove seat and track assembly. See FRONT SEAT ASSEMBLY. Remove front seat belt retaining nut. Disconnect seat belt harness connector (driver's side only). Remove both J-retainers. Remove seat back. See FRONT SEAT BACK. Remove seat track covers. Remove seat track retaining bolts. Disconnect necessary harness connectors. Remove driver's seat module (if equipped). To install, reverse removal procedure. Tighten nuts and bolt to specification. See TORQUE SPECIFICATIONS. Check air bag system for proper operation. See appropriate AIR BAG RESTRAINT SYSTEMS article.

RECLINE MOTOR

Removal & Installation – Remove seat and track assembly. See FRONT SEAT ASSEMBLY. Remove J-retainers. Pull back seat cushion cover and pad. Disconnect recline motor harness connector. Remove seatback trim panel. Release seat back j-retainers. Pull seat back cover. Remove recline motor retaining bolts. Remove recliner motor. To install, reverse removal procedure. Tighten nuts and bolt to specification. See TORQUE SPECIFICATIONS. Check air bag system for proper operation. See appropriate AIR BAG RESTRAINT SYSTEMS article.

TORQUE SPECIFICATIONS

TORQUE SPECIFICATIONS

Application	Ft. Lbs. (N.m)
Front Seat Assembly	
Rear Nuts	
Inner	59 (80)
Outer	20 (27)
Front Bolts	17-20 (23-27)
Front Seat Belt Retaining Nut	26-33 (35-45)
Seat Track Retaining Bolts	15 (20)
Seat Back Retaining Bolt	35 (47)
Recline Motor Retaining Bolt	
On Seat-Back	17-22 (23-30)
On Seat Cushion	41 (55)
	INCH Lbs.
Side Air Bag Retaining Nut	62 (7)

WIRING DIAGRAMS

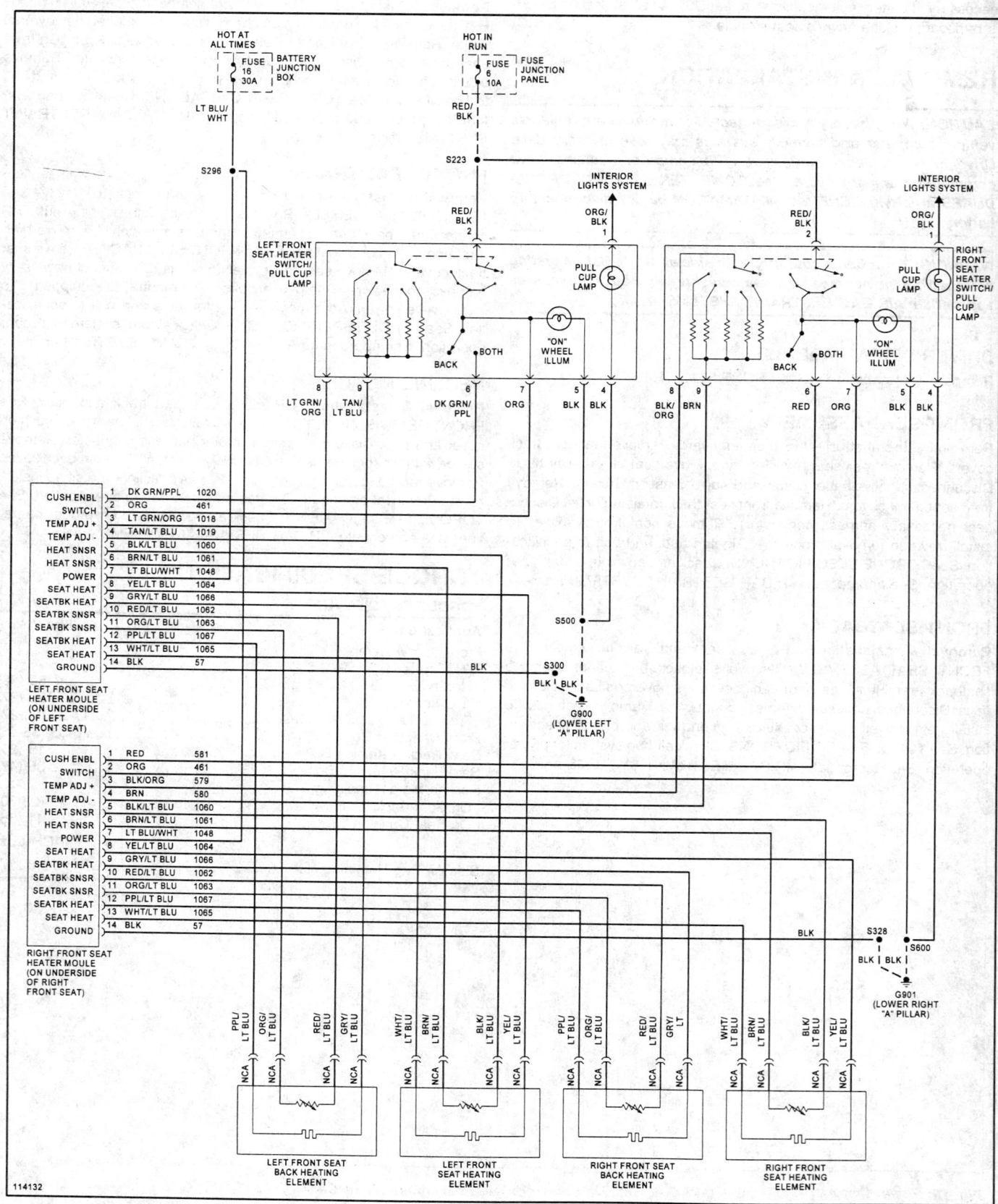

Fig. 18: Power Heated Seats System Wiring Diagram (Town Car)

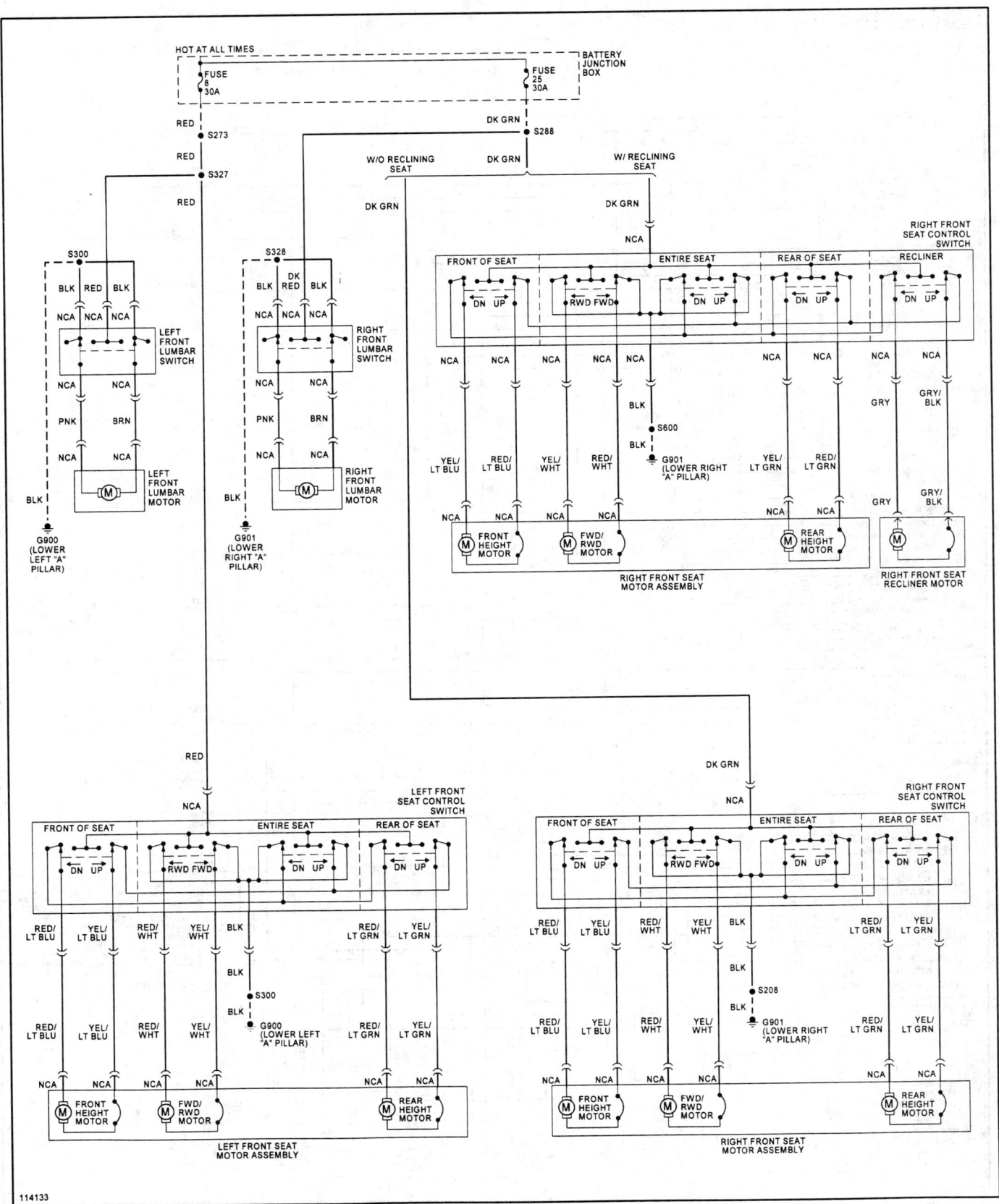

Fig. 19: Power Lumbar, Reclining & 6-Way Power Seats System Wiring Diagram (Town Car)

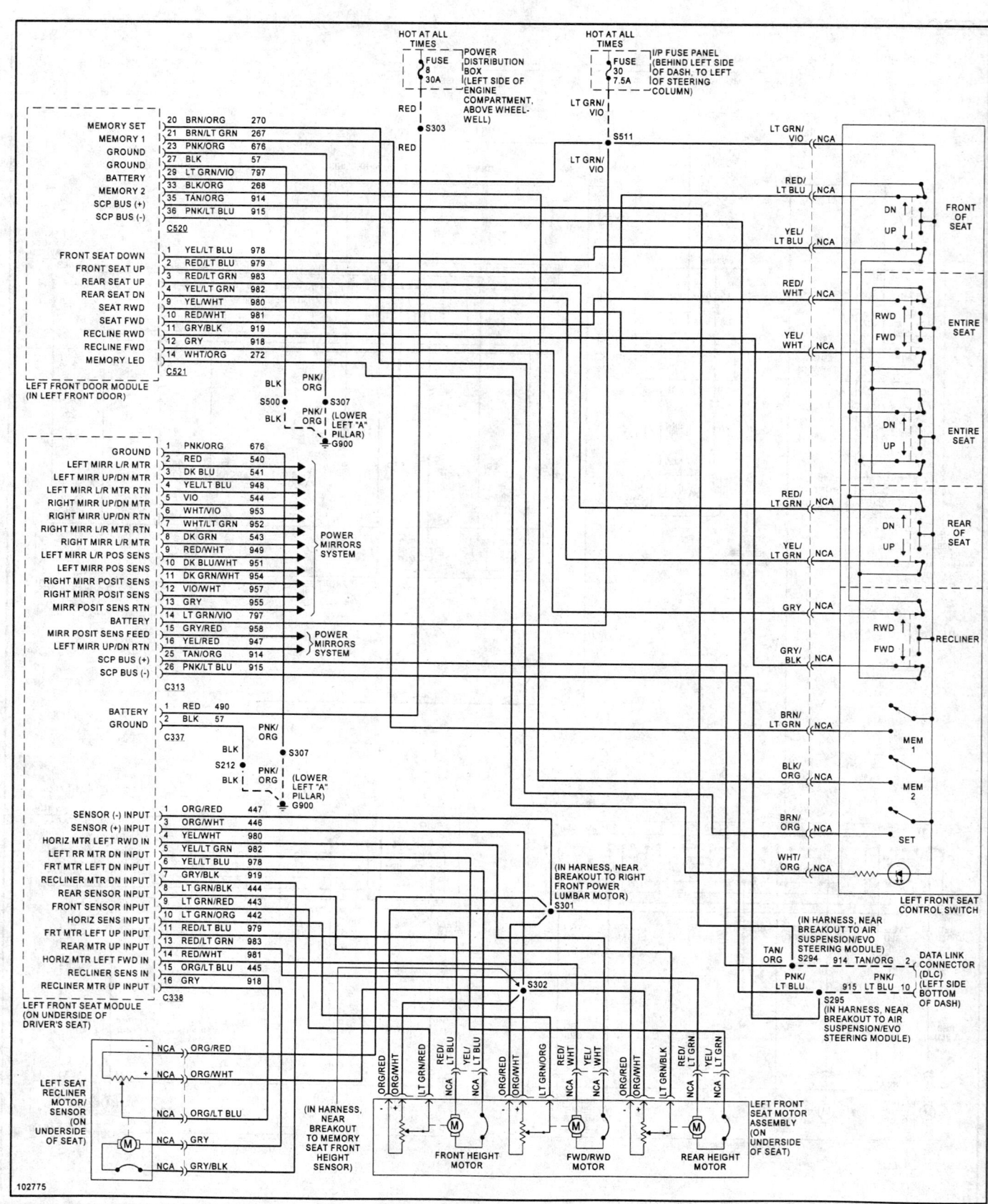

Fig. 20: Power Memory Seats System Wiring Diagram (Town Car)

102775

DESCRIPTION & OPERATION

The 6-way power driver seats provide horizontal, vertical and reclining adjustments. System consists of a control switch, 3 armature seat regulator motor assembly (tri-motor), vertical and horizontal screw drives and gear mechanism, recliner knuckle/hinge assembly, housing assembly and necessary wiring. Seat function switches are mounted on side of seat trim panel.

Horizontal movement is controlled by a transmission, lead screw and motor attached to the movable section of the track. Vertical drive unit is located on left side of the movable track. Vertical operation energizes center and rear armature and vertical drive units move seat up or down. In reclining operation, recliner armature operates a transmission knuckle/hinge assembly on front of seat back frame to achieve desired seat position. The motor unit is serviced as an assembly. The flexible shafts can be serviced individually.

Driver's seat is available with optional memory system. Memory system only works with gear selector in Park or Neutral position. Driver can set seat to desired position from power seat switch and recall from memory switches or remote transmitter.

The 4-way passenger's seat is only capable of horizontal and reclining adjustment. Power seat circuit protection is provided by a 30-amp F20 fuse located in engine compartment fuse box and an in-line circuit breaker located behind left side of instrument panel.

COMPONENT LOCATIONS

COMPONENT LOCATIONS

Component	Location
Air Bag Sliding Contact	In Steering Wheel
Battery Junction Box	In Engine Compartment, Next To Battery
Data Link Connector (DLC)	Below Driver's Side Of Instrument Panel, To Right Of Steering Column
Driver Seat Module (DSM)	Under Driver Seat
Engine Coolant Temperature (ECT) Sensor	Right Rear Side Of Engine
Engine Compartment Relay Box	Left Front Side Of Engine Compartment
Interior Fuse Junction Panel	Below Left Side Of Instrument Panel
Powertrain Control Module (PCM)	Behind Glove Box
Power Seat Switch	In Outside Trim Panel Of Seat
Smart Entry Control (SEC) Timer/Module	Behind Center Top Of Dash Panel
Lighting Control Module (LCM)	Bottom Of Center Console, Below Dash Panel
Transaxle Control Module (TCM)	Behind Instrument Cluster
Transaxle Range (TR) Sensor	Left Side Of Engine Compartment On Front Of Transaxle

TROUBLE SHOOTING

Before performing individual component test, check the following for possible cause of system malfunction:

- Blown Fuse Or Faulty Circuit Breaker
- Loose Or Corroded Connectors
- Damaged Wiring
- Damaged Motors
- Damaged Position Sensor
- Faulty Switches
- Damaged Lumbar Support Cable
- Damaged Driver Seat Module (DSM)

COMPONENT TESTS

NOTE: See SYSTEM TESTS for testing of components not covered in COMPONENT TESTS.

LEFT POWER SEAT SWITCH

Remove left power seat switch. Using ohmmeter, measure resistance between indicated switch terminals when switch is activated as specified. See LEFT POWER SEAT SWITCH RESISTANCE table. *See Fig. 1.* Replace switch if it does not test as specified.

LEFT POWER SEAT SWITCH RESISTANCE

Switch Position	Wire Terminals	Ohms
Sliding Switch		
Forward	3 & 2; 6 & 1	Less Than 5
Neutral	All	Open
Reverse	3 & 1; 6 & 2	Less Than 5
Lifting Switch		
Up	3 & 4; 5 & 6	Less Than 5
Neutral	All	Open
Down	3 & 5; 4 & 6	Less Than 5
Reclining		
Up	3 & 8; 6 & 7	Less Than 5
Neutral	All	Open
Down	3 & 7; 6 & 8	Less Than 5

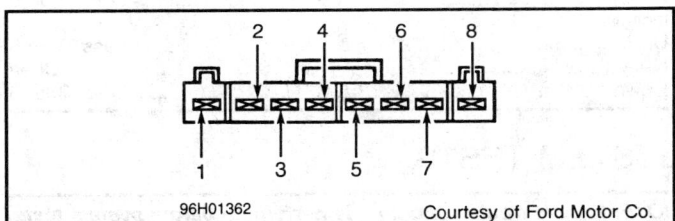

96H01362   Courtesy of Ford Motor Co.

Fig. 1: Identifying Left Power Seat Switch Terminals

RIGHT POWER SEAT SWITCH

Remove right power seat switch. Using ohmmeter, measure resistance between indicated switch terminals when switch is activated as specified. See RIGHT POWER SEAT SWITCH RESISTANCE table. *See Fig. 2.* Replace switch if it does not test as specified.

RIGHT POWER SEAT SWITCH RESISTANCE

Switch Position	Wire Terminals	Ohms
Sliding Switch		
Forward	1 & 6; 2 & 7	Less Than 5
Neutral	All	Open
Reverse	2 & 3; 1 & 6	Less Than 5
Reclining Switch		
Up	4 & 11; 5 & 12	Less Than 5
Neutral	All	Open
Down	5 & 11; 4 & 12	Less Than 5

MEMORY POWER SEAT SWITCH

Remove memory power seat switch. Using ohmmeter, measure resistance between indicated switch terminals when switch is activated as specified. See MEMORY POWER SEAT SWITCH RESISTANCE table. *See Fig. 2.* Replace switch if it does not test as specified.

MEMORY POWER SEAT SWITCH RESISTANCE

Switch Position	Wire Terminals	Ohms
Sliding Switch		
Forward	1 & 7	Less Than 5

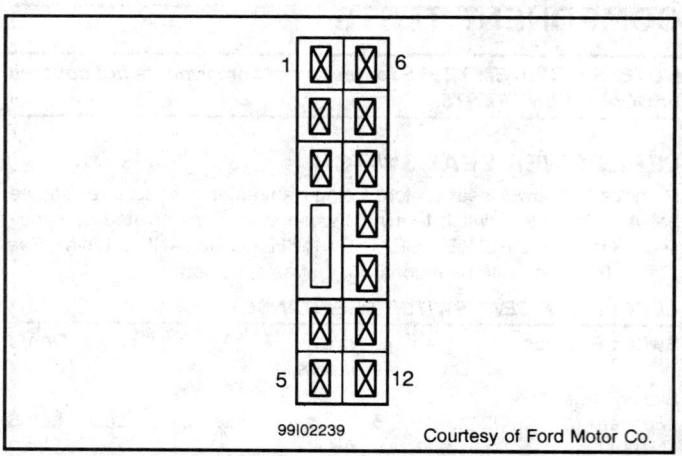

Fig. 2: Identifying Right & Memory Power Seat Switch Terminals

MEMORY POWER SEAT SWITCH RESISTANCE (Cont.)

Switch Position	Wire Terminals	Ohms
Neutral	All	Open
Reverse	1 & 6	Less Than 5
Lifting Switch		
Up	5 & 12	Less Than 5
Neutral	All	Open
Down	4 & 5	Less Than 5
Reclining		
Up	5 & 8	Less Than 5
Neutral	All	Open
Down	3 & 5	Less Than 5

SYSTEM TESTS

NOTE: Ensure trouble shooting is performed before system tests. See TROUBLE SHOOTING. To determine correct system test, see SYMPTOM CHART table. Unless otherwise directed, perform testing in order listed.

CAUTION: When battery is disconnected, vehicle computer and memory systems may lose memory data. Driveability problems may exist until computer systems have completed a relearn cycle. See COMPUTER RELEARN PROCEDURES article in GENERAL INFORMATION before disconnecting battery.

SYMPTOM CHART

Symptom	Test
Power Seats Inoperative	A
Power Seat Inoperative – Memory	B
Power Seat Noisy	C
Power Seat Loose	D
Power Seat Does Not Make Full Travel	E
Power Seat Does Not Move Horizontal/Vertical	F
Power Seat Does Not Move Horizontal/Vertical – Memory	G
Power Seat Does Not Recline	H
Power Seat Does Not Recline – Memory	I
Memory Seat Inoperative – Does Not Operate Correctly	J
Memory Seat Switch Indicator Inoperative/Always On	K
Memory Seat Inoperative From Remote Transmitter	L
Memory Seat Changes Position From Memory Switch While Driving	M

TEST A: POWER SEATS COMPLETELY INOPERATIVE

1) If both left and right power seats are inoperative, go to next step. If either left or right power seat is inoperative, go to **3)**.
2) Remove circuit breaker 2 from interior fuse junction panel. Measure voltage between ground and circuit breaker 2 socket White/Blue wire

terminal. If voltage is more than 10 volts, repair White/Red wire between circuit breaker 2 and power seat switch. If voltage is 10 volts or less, repair open White/Blue wire between circuit breaker 2 and battery junction box.
3) Disconnect inoperative power seat switch connector. Measure voltage between ground and left power seat switch connector C359 terminal No. 6 (White/Red wire) or right power seat switch connector C360 terminal No. 1 (White/Red wire). *See Fig. 3 or 4.* If voltage is more than 10 volts, go to next step. If voltage is 10 volts or less, repair open or short to ground in White/Red wire.
4) Ensure ignition is off. Measure resistance between ground and left power seat switch connector C359 terminal No. 3 (Black wire) or right power seat switch connector C360 terminal No. 7 (Black wire). If resistance is less than 5 ohms, replace related switch. If resistance is more than 5 ohms, repair open Black wire between ground and power seat switch connector.

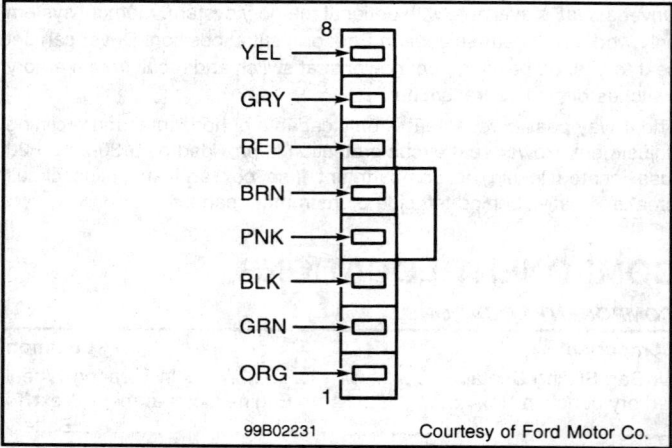

Fig. 3: Identifying Left Power Seat Switch Connector C359 Terminals

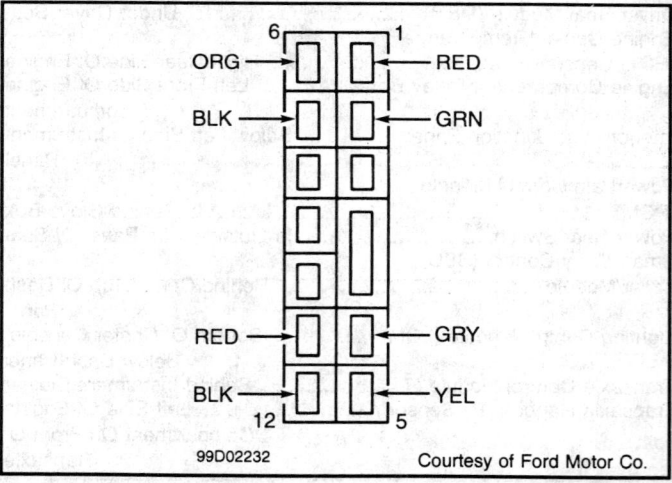

Fig. 4: Identifying Right Power Seat Switch Connector C360 Terminals

TEST B: POWER SEAT INOPERATIVE – MEMORY

1) Remove circuit breaker 2 from interior fuse junction panel. Measure voltage between ground and circuit breaker 2 socket White/Blue wire terminal. If voltage is more than 10 volts, go to next step. If voltage is 10 volts or less, repair open White/Blue wire between circuit breaker No. 2 and battery junction box.
2) Turn ignition off. Disconnect Driver Seat Module (DSM) connectors. DSM is located under driver's seat. Replace circuit breaker No. 2 in interior fuse junction panel. Turn ignition on. Measure voltage between ground and DSM connector C2046A power circuits. See POWER CIRCUITS TO DSM table. *See Fig. 5.* If all voltage measurements are

more than 10 volts, go to next step. If any voltage measurement is 10 volts or less, repair appropriate circuit.

POWER CIRCUITS TO DSM

DSM Connector Terminal	Wire Color
1	White/Red
4	Brown
6	White/Red
32	Light Green/Red

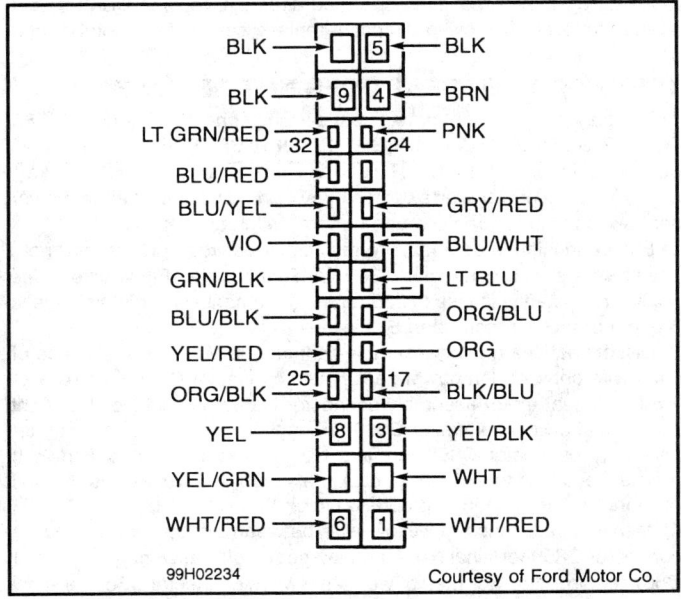

Fig. 5: Identifying Driver Seat Module (DSM) Connector C2046A Terminals

3) Turn ignition off. Measure resistance between ground and DSM connector C2046A ground circuits. See GROUND CIRCUITS TO DSM table. If all resistance measurements are less than 5 ohms, go to next step. If any resistance measurement is 5 ohms or more, repair open in appropriate ground circuit.

GROUND CIRCUITS TO DSM

DSM Connector Terminal	Wire Color
5	Black
9	Black
10	Black

4) Disconnect memory power seat switch connector C389. Perform memory power seat switch component test. See MEMORY POWER SEAT SWITCH test under COMPONENT TESTS. Replace switch as necessary. If memory power seat switch is okay, go to next step.
5) Measure resistance of Brown/White wire between memory power seat switch connector C389 terminal No. 1 and DSM connector C2046B terminal No. 38. *See Figs. 6 and 7.* If resistance is less than 5 ohms, replace DSM. If resistance is 5 ohms or more, repair open Brown/White wire.

TEST C: POWER SEAT NOISY

Ensure ignition is off. Check for obstructions and alignment of seat track to floor and seat bottom. Clear obstructions as necessary. If seat track is out of alignment, align seat track. If no obstructions are present and seat track is not out of alignment, replace seat track assembly.

TEST D: POWER SEAT LOOSE

Check fastening hardware for proper installation. If hardware is loose, tighten hardware. If hardware is not loose, replace seat track assembly.

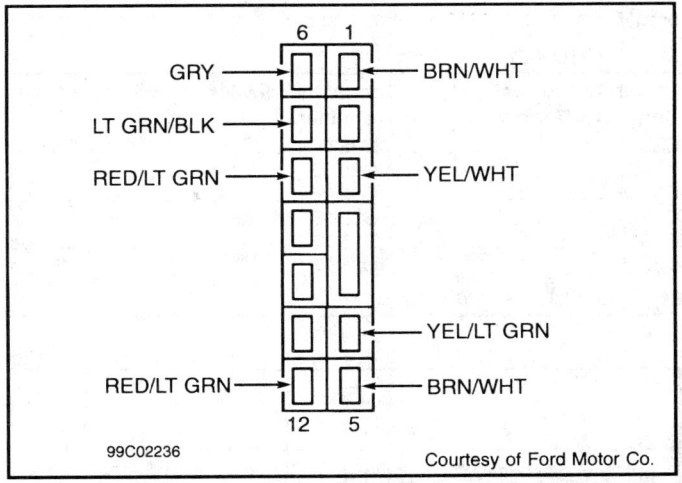

Fig. 6: Identifying Power Seat Switch Connector C389 Terminals

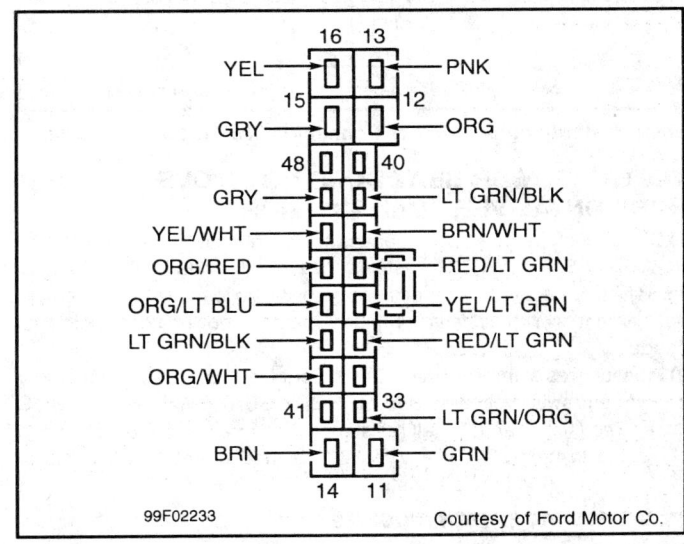

Fig. 7: Identifying Driver Seat Module (DSM) Connector C2046B Terminals

TEST E: POWER SEAT DOES NOT MAKE FULL TRAVEL

Ensure ignition is off. Check for obstructions of seat track. Clear obstructions as necessary and lubricate seat track. If no obstructions are present, replace seat track assembly.

TEST F: POWER SEAT DOES NOT MOVE HORIZONTAL/VERTICAL

1) Perform LEFT POWER SEAT SWITCH or RIGHT POWER SEAT SWITCH tests as described under COMPONENT TESTS. If left power seat switch is okay, go to step **4)**. If right power seat switch is okay, go to next step. If either power seat switch is faulty, replace appropriate switch as needed.
2) Measure voltage between ground and right power seat switch connector C360 terminal No. 1 (White/Red wire). *See Fig. 4.* If voltage is more than 10 volts, go to next step. If voltage is 10 volts or less, repair open White/Red wire.
3) Ensure ignition is off. Measure resistance between ground and right power seat switch connector C360 terminal No. 7 (Black wire). If resistance is less than 5 ohms, go to next step. If resistance is 5 ohms or more, repair open Black wire.
4) Disconnect appropriate seat motor connector. Measure resistance between seat motor and seat switch power circuits. See SEAT MOTOR CIRCUITS table. If all resistance measurements are less than 5 ohms, replace seat motor assembly. If any resistance measurement is 5 ohms

or more, repair open in appropriate circuit.

SEAT MOTOR CIRCUITS [1]

Power Seat Switch Connector/Terminal	Connector/ Terminal	Wire Color
C359/1	C357/2	Orange
C359/2	C357/3	Green
C359/5	C357/6	Brown
C359/4	C357/5	Pink
C360/6	C358/5	Orange
C360/2	C358/6	Green

[1] – See Figs. 3, 4 and 8.

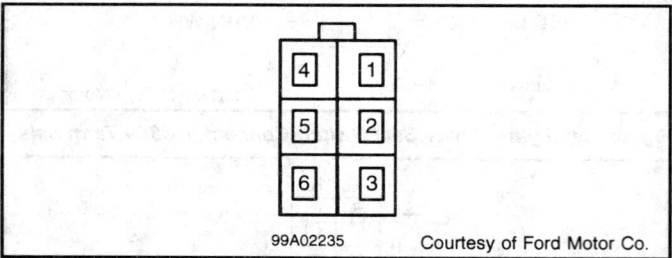

99A02235   Courtesy of Ford Motor Co.

Fig. 8: Identifying Seat Motor Connector C357 & C358 Terminals

TEST G: POWER SEAT DOES NOT MOVE HORIZONTAL/VERTICAL – MEMORY

1) Disconnect memory power seat switch connector. Perform MEMORY POWER SEAT SWITCH test as described under COMPONENT TESTS. If memory power seat switch is okay, go to next step. If memory power seat switch is faulty, replace memory power seat switch as needed.

2) Measure resistance between Driver Seat Module (DSM) and memory power seat switch circuits. See MEMORY SEAT SWITCH CIRCUITS table. *See Figs. 6 and 7.* If all resistance measurements are less than 5 ohms, go to next step. If any resistance measurement is 5 ohms or more, repair open in appropriate circuit.

MEMORY SEAT SWITCH CIRCUITS

Memory Power Seat Switch Connector/Terminal	DSM Connector/Terminal	Wire Color
C389/3	C2046B/46	Yellow/White
C389/8	C2046B/35	Red/Light Green
C389/4	C2046B/36	Yellow/Light Green
C389/12	C2046B/37	Red/Light Green
C389/5	C2046B/38	Brown/White

3) Measure resistance between ground and memory power seat switch connector C389 at specified terminals. See MEMORY SEAT SWITCH CIRCUITS table. *See Fig. 6.* If all resistance measurements are more than 10 k/ohms, go to next step. If any resistance measurement is 10 k/ohms or less, repair short to ground in appropriate circuit.

4) Disconnect seat motor assembly C357. Measure resistance between DSM and seat motor connector C357 circuits. See SEAT MOTOR CIRCUITS table. *See Figs. 7 and 8.* If all resistance measurements are less than 5 ohms, go to next step. If any resistance measurement is 5 ohms or more, repair open in appropriate circuit.

SEAT MOTOR CIRCUITS

Seat Motor Connector/Terminal	DSM Connector/Terminal	Wire Color
C357/5	C2046B/12	Orange
C357/4	C2046B/15	Gray
C357/1	C2046B/11	Green
C357/2	C2046B/16	Yellow

5) Measure resistance between ground and seat motor connector C357 at specified terminals. See SEAT MOTOR CIRCUITS table. *See Fig. 7.* If all resistance measurements are more than 10 k/ohms, go to next step. If any resistance measurement is 10 k/ohms or less, repair short to ground in appropriate circuit.

6) Using a 30-amp fused jumper wire apply power and ground to specified seat motor pins. Apply voltage to pin No. 5 and ground to pin No. 4. Seat should move forward. Reverse jumper wires and seat should move in reverse direction. Apply voltage to pin No. 1 and ground to pin No. 2. Seat should move up. Reverse jumper wires and seat should move down. If seat moves in specified direction, replace DSM. If seat does not move in specified direction, replace seat track assembly.

TEST H: POWER SEAT DOES NOT RECLINE

1) Disconnect left or right power seat switch connectors. Perform LEFT POWER SEAT SWITCH or RIGHT POWER SEAT SWITCH tests as described under COMPONENT TESTS. If left power seat switch is okay, go to **3)**. If right power seat switch is okay, go to next step. If either power seat switch is faulty, replace appropriate switch as needed.

2) Ensure ignition is off. Measure resistance between ground and right power seat switch connector C360 terminal No. 12 (Black wire). *See Fig. 4.* If resistance is less than 5 ohms, go to next step. If resistance is 5 ohms or more, repair open Black wire.

3) Disconnect seat motor assembly connectors. Measure resistance of Gray wire between left power seat switch connector C359 terminal No. 7 and left seat motor assembly connector C357 terminal No. 1 or right power seat switch connector C360 terminal No. 4 and right seat motor assembly connector C358 terminal No. 4. *See Figs. 3, 4 and 8.* If resistance is less than 5 ohms, go to next step. If resistance is 5 ohms or more, repair open in appropriate circuit.

4) Measure resistance of Yellow wire between left power seat switch connector C359 terminal No. 8 and left seat motor assembly connector C357 terminal No. 4 or right power seat switch connector C360 terminal No. 5 and right seat motor assembly connector C358 terminal No. 1. If resistance is less than 5 ohms, replace seat track assembly. If resistance is 5 ohms or more, repair open in appropriate circuit.

TEST I: POWER SEAT DOES NOT RECLINE – MEMORY

1) Disconnect memory power seat switch connector. Perform MEMORY POWER SEAT SWITCH test as described under COMPONENT TESTS. If memory power seat switch is okay, go to next step. If memory power seat switch is faulty, replace memory power seat switch as needed.

2) Measure resistance of Gray wire between Driver Seat Module (DSM) connector C2046B terminal No. 47 and memory power seat switch connector C389 terminal No. 6. *See Figs. 6 and 7.* Measure resistance of Light Green/Black wire between DSM connector C2046B terminal No. 39 and memory power seat switch connector C389 terminal No. 7. If all resistance measurements are less than 5 ohms, go to next step. If any resistance measurement is 5 ohms or more, repair open in appropriate circuit.

3) Measure resistance between ground and memory power seat switch connector C389 terminal No. 6 (Gray wire). Measure resistance between ground and memory power seat switch connector C389 terminal No. 7 (Light Green/Black wire). If all resistance measurements are more than 10 k/ohms, go to next step. If any resistance measurement is 10 k/ohms or less, repair short to ground in appropriate circuit.

4) Disconnect seat motor assembly C357. Measure resistance of Brown wire between DSM connector C2046B terminal No. 14 and seat motor connector C357 terminal No. 3. *See Figs. 7 and 8.* Measure resistance of Pink wire between DSM connector C2046B terminal No. 13 and seat motor connector C357 terminal No. 6. If all resistance measurements are less than 5 ohms, go to next step. If any resistance measurement is 5 ohms or more, repair open in appropriate circuit.

5) Measure resistance between ground and seat motor connector C357 terminal No. 3 (Brown wire). Measure resistance between ground and seat motor connector C357 terminal No. 6 (Pink wire). If all resistance measurements are more than 10 k/ohms, go to next step. If any resistance measurement is 10 k/ohms or less, repair short to ground in appropriate circuit.

6) Using a 30-amp fused jumper wire apply power to pin No. 3 and ground to pin No. 6. Seat should move up. Reverse jumper wires and seat should move down. If seat moves in specified direction, replace DSM. If seat does not move in specified direction, replace seat track assembly.

TEST J: MEMORY SEAT INOPERATIVE – DOES NOT OPERATE CORRECTLY

1) Turn ignition off. Disconnect memory set switch. Measure resistance between memory set switch pins No. 1 and 2 (component side) while pressing and releasing "1" button. *See Fig. 9.* Measure resistance between memory set switch pins No. 1 and 3 (component side) while pressing and releasing "2" button. Resistance should be less than 5 ohms with switch button pressed and more than 10 k/ohms with switch button released. If resistance is as specified in all measurements, go to next step. If resistance is not as specified in any measurement, replace memory set switch.

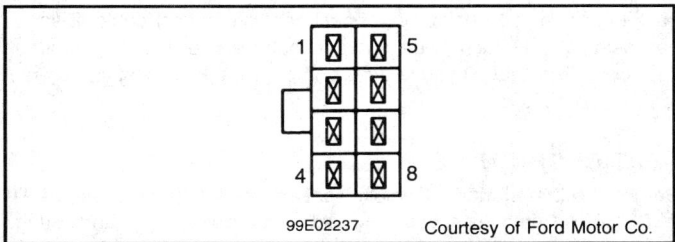

Fig. 9: Identifying Memory Set Switch Component Pins

2) Disconnect Driver Seat Module (DSM) connectors. DSM is located below driver's seat. Measure voltage between ground and memory set switch connector C521 terminal No. 2 (Green/Black wire). *See Fig. 10.* Measure voltage between ground and memory set switch connector C521 terminal No. 3 (Light Blue wire). If any voltage is present in either measurement, repair short to voltage in appropriate wire. If voltage is not present in any measurement, go to next step.

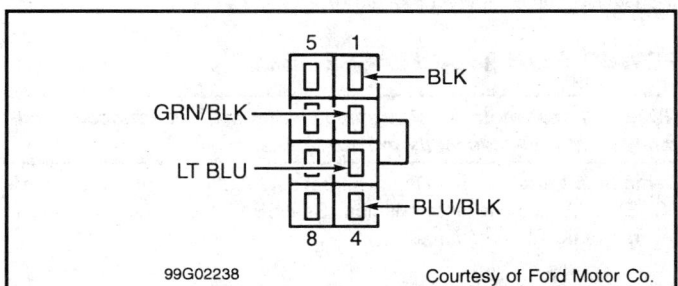

Fig. 10: Identifying Memory Set Switch Connector C521 Terminals

3) Measure resistance of Green/Black wire between memory set switch connector C521 terminal No. 2 and DSM connector C2046A terminal No. 20. Measure resistance between ground and memory set switch connector C521 terminal No. 2 (Green/Black wire). Resistance should be less than 5 ohms between memory set switch and DSM and more than 10 k/ohms between memory set switch and ground. If resistance is as specified, go to next step. If resistance is not as specified, repair open or short in Green/Black wire.

4) Measure resistance of Light Blue wire between memory set switch connector C521 terminal No. 3 and DSM connector C2046A terminal No. 28. Measure resistance between ground and memory set switch connector C521 terminal No. 3 (Light Blue wire). Resistance should be less than 5 ohms between memory set switch and DSM and more than 10 k/ohms between memory set switch and ground. If resistance is as specified, go to next step. If resistance is not as specified, repair open or short in Light Blue wire.

5) Measure resistance between ground and memory set switch connector C521 terminal No. 1 (Black wire). If resistance is less than 5 ohms, go to next step. If resistance is 5 ohms or more, repair open Black wire.

6) Disconnect 3-pin seat track sliding (C380), lifting (C381) and reclining (C382) position sensor connectors. Measure voltage between ground and DSM connector C2046B position sensor circuits. See DSM POSITION SENSOR CIRCUITS table. *See Fig. 7.* If no voltage is present in all measurements, go to next step. If voltage is present in any measurement, repair short to voltage in appropriate position sensor circuit.

DSM POSITION SENSOR CIRCUITS

DSM Connector Terminal	Position Sensor Connector/Terminal	Wire Color
41	C380/1, C381/1 & C382/1	Orange/White
33	C380/2	Light Green/Orange
42	C381/2	Light Green/Black
43	C382/2	Orange/Light Blue
44	C380/3, C381/3 & C382/3	Orange/Red

7) Measure resistance between DSM connector C2046B and appropriate seat track position sensor connectors. See DSM POSITION SENSOR CIRCUITS table. If all resistance measurements are less than 5 ohms, go to next step. If any resistance measurement is 5 ohms or more, repair open in appropriate circuit.

8) Measure resistance between ground and DSM connector C2046B position sensor circuits. See DSM POSITION SENSOR CIRCUITS table. If all resistance measurements are more than 10 k/ohms, go to next step. If any resistance measurement is 10 k/ohms or less, repair short to ground in appropriate position sensor circuit.

9) Reconnect DSM connector. Measure voltage between seat track sliding position sensor connector terminal No. 1 (Orange/White wire) and No. 3 (Orange/Red wire). Move seat fully forward and fully reverse. If voltage is about 4 volts, go to next step. If voltage is not about 4 volts, replace DSM.

10) Turn ignition off. Reconnect 3-pin seat track sliding (C380), lifting (C381) and reclining (C382) position sensor connectors. Disconnect DSM connector C2046B. Remove DSM connector 2046B terminal No. 33 (Light Green/Orange wire) from connector. Reconnect DSM connector. Turn ignition on. Measure voltage between ground and DSM connector 2046B terminal No. 33 (Light Green/Orange wire) that was removed from connector. Move seat fully forward and fully reverse. If voltage varies between 0-2.5 volts, go to next step. If voltage does not vary between 0-2.5 volts, replace seat track assembly.

11) Turn ignition off. Disconnect DSM connector C2046B. Replace terminal No. 33 (Light Green/Orange wire) into DSM connector 2046B. Remove terminal No. 42 (Light Green/Black wire) from connector. Reconnect DSM connector. Turn ignition on. Measure voltage between ground and DSM connector 2046B terminal No. 42 (Light Green/Black wire) that was removed from connector. Move seat fully forward and fully reverse. If voltage varies between 0-2.5 volts, go to next step. If voltage does not vary between 0-2.5 volts, replace seat track assembly.

12) Turn ignition off. Disconnect DSM connector C2046B. Replace terminal No. 42 (Light Green/Black wire) into DSM connector 2046B. Remove terminal No. 43 (Orange/Light Blue wire) from connector. Reconnect DSM connector. Turn ignition on. Measure voltage between ground and DSM connector 2046B terminal No. 43 (Orange/Light Blue wire) that was removed from connector. Move seat fully forward and fully reverse. If voltage varies between 02.5 volts, replace DSM. If voltage does not vary between 0-2.5 volts, replace seat track assembly.

TEST K: MEMORY SEAT SWITCH INDICATOR INOPERATIVE/ALWAYS ON

1) Turn ignition off. Disconnect memory set switch connector. Using DVOM in diode check position, measure resistance between memory set switch pins No. 1 and 4. *See Fig. 9.* Switch leads and measure resistance again. If resistance is low in one direction and infinite in other, go to next step. If resistance is not low in one direction and infinite in other, replace memory set switch.

2) Measure resistance between ground and memory set switch connector C521 terminal No. 1 (Black wire). *See Fig. 10.* If resistance is less than 5 ohms, go to next step. If resistance is 5 ohms or more, repair open Black wire.

3) Disconnect Driver Seat Module (DSM) connectors. DSM is located below driver's seat. Turn ignition on. Measure voltage between ground and memory set switch connector C521 terminal No. 4 (Blue/Black wire). If voltage is present, go to next step. If no voltage is present, repair short to voltage in Blue/Black wire.

4) Turn ignition off. Measure resistance of Blue/Black wire between DSM connector C2046A terminal No. 27 and memory set switch connector C521 terminal No. 4. *See Fig. 5.* Resistance should be less than 5 ohms. Measure resistance between ground and memory set switch connector C521 terminal No. 4 (Blue/Black wire). Resistance should be more than 10 k/ohms. If resistance is as specified, replace DSM. If resistance is not as specified, repair open or short to ground in Blue/Black wire.

TEST L: MEMORY SEAT INOPERATIVE FROM REMOTE TRANSMITTER

1) Turn ignition off. Disconnect Driver Seat Module (DSM) connectors. DSM is located below driver's seat. Disconnect Smart Entry Control (SEC) timer/module. SEC timer/module is located behind center top of dash panel. Measure resistance of Pink wire between DSM connector C2046A terminal No. 24 and SEC timer/module connector C2032B terminal No. 7. *See Figs. 5 and 11.* Resistance should be less than 5 ohms. Measure resistance between ground and DSM connector C2046A terminal No. 24 (Pink wire). Resistance should be more than 10 k/ohms. If resistance is as specified, go to next step. If resistance is not as specified, repair open or short to ground in Pink wire.

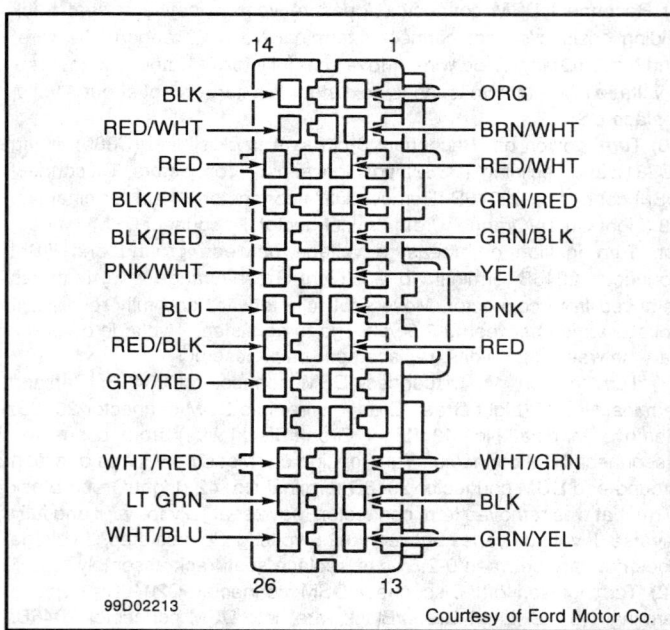

14	1
BLK	ORG
RED/WHT	BRN/WHT
RED	RED/WHT
BLK/PNK	GRN/RED
BLK/RED	GRN/BLK
PNK/WHT	YEL
BLU	PNK
RED/BLK	RED
GRY/RED	
WHT/RED	WHT/GRN
LT GRN	BLK
WHT/BLU	GRN/YEL
26	13

99D02213   Courtesy of Ford Motor Co.

Fig. 11: Identifying SEC Timer/Module Connector C2032B Terminals

2) Turn ignition on. Measure voltage between ground and DSM connector C2046A terminal No. 24 (Pink wire). If any voltage is present, repair short to voltage in Pink wire. If no voltage is present, go to next step.

3) Reconnect DSM connector. Install a known good SEC timer/module. Press memory set switch buttons No. 1 and 2 at same time. Using remote transmitter, press unlock button. If memory mirror moves, install NEW SEC timer/module. If memory mirror does not move, replace DSM.

TEST M: MEMORY SEAT CHANGES POSITION FROM MEMORY SWITCH WHILE DRIVING

Turn ignition off. Disconnect Driver Seat Module (DSM) connectors. DSM is located below driver's seat. Disconnect transmission range switch connector. Turn ignition on. Measure voltage between ground

and DSM connector C2046A terminal No. 19 (Orange/Blue wire). *See Fig. 5.* If voltage is present, repair short to voltage in Orange/Blue wire. If no voltage is present, replace DSM.

REMOVAL & INSTALLATION

CAUTION: When battery is disconnected, vehicle computer and memory systems may lose memory data. Driveability problems may exist until computer systems have completed a relearn cycle. See COMPUTER RELEARN PROCEDURES article in GENERAL INFORMATION before disconnecting battery.

NOTE: All seat motors and transmissions are not serviced separately, seat track assembly must be replaced.

SEAT ASSEMBLY

Removal & Installation – Move seat fully forward. Remove 2 rear seat track-to-seat support bolts. Move seat fully rearward. Remove 2 seat track-to-seat support bolts. Disconnect negative battery cable. Disconnect seat control switch. Slide front seat belt retractor and tongue out of cushion side shield. Remove seat and seat track. To install, reverse removal procedure.

SEAT CUSHION

Removal & Installation – Remove seat and track assembly. See SEAT ASSEMBLY. Remove seat cushion pad from cushion frame and spring. Cut hog rings attaching cushion cover to cushion pad. Remove cushion cover from cushion pad. To install, reverse removal procedure.

POWER SEAT SWITCH

Removal & Installation – Disconnect negative battery cable. Slide front seat belt through seat side shield. Remove side shield retaining screws. Remove side shield. Remove 2 switch retaining screws. Remove switch and housing. Disconnect electrical connector. Remove control switch. To install, reverse removal procedure.

POWER SEAT TRACK ASSEMBLY

NOTE: All seat motors and transmissions are not serviced separately, seat track assembly must be replaced.

Removal & Installation – Remove front seat and seat track. See SEAT ASSEMBLY. Remove seat cushion. See SEAT CUSHION. To install, reverse removal procedure.

WIRING DIAGRAMS

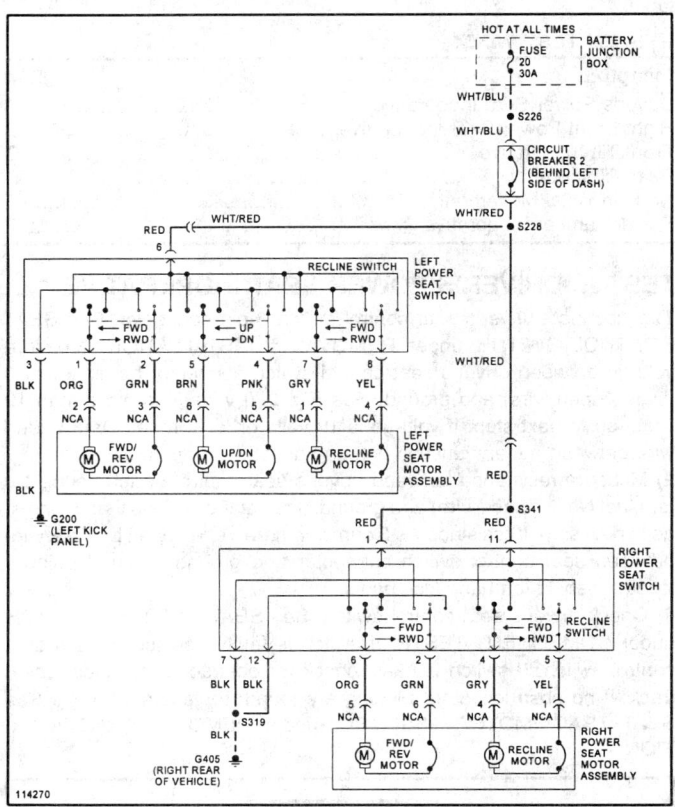

Fig. 12: Power Seats System Wiring Diagram (Villager)

DESCRIPTION & OPERATION

The 6-way power seats provide horizontal and tilt adjustments. System consists of seat control switch, seat regulator motor, vertical and horizontal screw drives and gear mechanism, housing assembly and related wiring. Seat function switches are mounted on side of seat trim panel. Power seat circuits are protected by fuses located in battery junction box and circuit breakers located in seat track/motor assembly. Some models are equipped with front seat lumbar support system.

Horizontal movement is controlled by a transmission, lead screw and motor attached to the movable section of the track. In tilt operation, armatures move front or rear vertical drive screws to adjust seat. The seat track/motor assembly is serviced as a unit.

TROUBLE SHOOTING

Verify customer complaint by operating power seat. Before performing individual component tests or system tests, check for blown battery junction box fuses No. 104 (40-amp) and 122 (40-amp). Check for loose or corroded connectors, damaged motors, faulty switches, binding seat track assembly, damaged wiring, damaged lumbar adjusting pad and damaged or kinked air hoses. If no damage is evident, perform appropriate system test. See SYSTEM TEST INDEX table under SYSTEM TESTS.

COMPONENT TESTS

NOTE: Some individual component testing is not available from manufacturer. See appropriate symptom test in SYSTEM TEST INDEX table under SYSTEM TESTS.

SEAT CONTROL SWITCH

Remove seat control switch. See SEAT CONTROL SWITCH under REMOVAL & INSTALLATION. Measure resistance between appropriate seat control switch terminals with switch in appropriate position. See SEAT CONTROL SWITCH RESISTANCE table. *See Fig. 1.* If resistance is not as specified, replace seat control switch.

SEAT CONTROL SWITCH RESISTANCE

Switch Position	Between Terminals	Resistance (Ohms)
Neutral	8 & 5	More Than 5
	5 & All Others Except 8	Less Than 5
Forward	8 & 6	Less Than 5
Rearward	8 & 7	Less Than 5
Front Down	8 & 1	Less Than 5
Front Up	8 & 4	Less Than 5
Rear Down	8 & 3	Less Than 5
Rear Up	8 & 2	Less Than 5

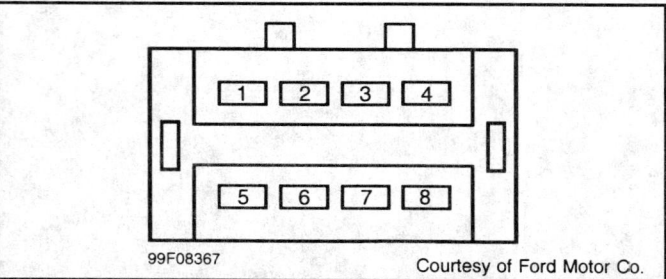
99F08367   Courtesy of Ford Motor Co.

Fig. 1: Identifying Seat Control Switch Terminals (Switch Side)

SYSTEM TESTS

NOTE: After making any repairs, test system for normal operation.

Verify customer complaint by operating power seat. Visually inspect for obvious sign of mechanical and electrical damage. If no visual damage is evident, perform appropriate system test. See SYSTEM TEST INDEX table.

SYSTEM TEST INDEX

Symptom	Test
Driver's Power Seat Inoperative	A
Right Front Power Seat Inoperative	B
Front Tilt Inoperative	C
Rear Tilt Inoperative	D
No Horizontal Movement	E
Power Lumbar Inoperative	F

TEST A: DRIVER'S POWER SEAT INOPERATIVE

1) Disconnect driver's seat control switch 8-pin connector. See SEAT CONTROL SWITCH under REMOVAL & INSTALLATION. Measure voltage between driver's seat control switch connector terminal No. 8 (Dark Green wire) and ground. *See Fig. 2.* If voltage is more than 10 volts, go to next step. If voltage is 10 volts or less, repair Dark Green wire between battery junction box and driver's seat control switch.

2) Measure resistance between driver's seat control switch connector terminal No. 5 (Black wire) and ground. If resistance is less than 5 ohms, go to next step. If resistance is 5 ohms or more, repair open in Black wire between seat control switch connector and ground. Ground point is located behind left hand kick panel.

3) Check driver's seat control switch. See SEAT CONTROL SWITCH under COMPONENT TESTS. If switch is faulty, replace driver's seat control switch. If switch is okay, check for obstructed or binding seat track. If no obstructions or binding are found, replace seat track. See SEAT TRACK/MOTOR ASSEMBLY under REMOVAL & INSTALLATION.

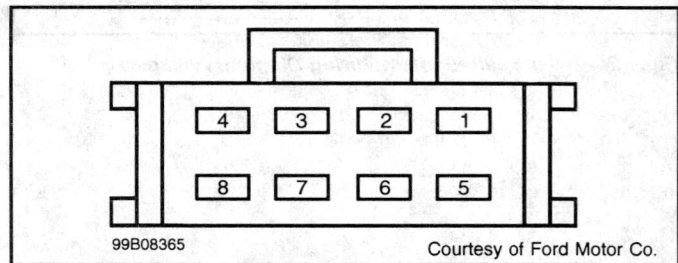
99B08365   Courtesy of Ford Motor Co.

Fig. 2: Identifying Seat Control Switch Connector Terminals (Harness Side)

TEST B: RIGHT FRONT POWER SEAT INOPERATIVE

1) Disconnect right front seat control switch 8-pin connector. See SEAT CONTROL SWITCH under REMOVAL & INSTALLATION. Measure voltage between right front seat control switch connector terminal No. 8 (Black/White wire) and ground. *See Fig. 2.* If voltage is more than 10 volts, go to next step. If voltage is 10 volts or less, repair Black/White wire between battery junction box and right front seat control switch.

2) Measure resistance between right front seat control switch connector terminal No. 5 (Black wire) and ground. If resistance is less than 5 ohms, go to next step. If resistance is 5 ohms or more, repair open in Black wire between seat control switch connector and ground. Ground point is behind left hand kick panel.

3) Check right front seat control switch. See SEAT CONTROL SWITCH under COMPONENT TESTS. If switch is faulty, replace right front seat control switch. If switch is okay, check for obstructed or binding seat track. If no obstructions or binding are found, replace seat track. See SEAT TRACK/MOTOR ASSEMBLY under REMOVAL & INSTALLATION.

TEST C: FRONT TILT INOPERATIVE

1) Disconnect inoperative seat's front height motor 2-pin connector. Measure resistance between front height motor connector Red/Light Blue wire terminal and ground. Also measure resistance between front height motor connector Yellow/Light Blue wire terminal and ground. If each resistance is less than 5 ohms, go to step 4). If testing driver's seat and any resistance is 5 ohms or more, go to next step. If testing right front seat and any resistance is 5 ohms or more, go to step 3).

2) Disconnect driver's seat control switch 8-pin connector. Measure resistance of Red/Light Blue wire between driver's seat front height motor connector and driver's seat control switch connector terminal No. 1. See Fig. 2. Also measure resistance of Yellow/Light Blue wire between driver's seat front height motor connector and driver's seat control switch connector terminal No. 4. If each resistance is less than 5 ohms, replace driver's seat control switch. See SEAT CONTROL SWITCH under REMOVAL & INSTALLATION. If any resistance is 5 ohms or more, repair open in appropriate wire(s) between front height motor connector and seat control switch connector.

3) Disconnect right front seat control switch 8-pin connector. Measure resistance of Red/Light Blue wire between right front seat front height motor connector and right front seat control switch connector terminal No. 3. See Fig. 2. Also measure resistance of Yellow/Light Blue wire between right front seat front height motor connector and right front seat control switch connector terminal No. 2. If each resistance is less than 5 ohms, replace right front seat control switch. If any resistance is 5 ohms or more, repair open in appropriate wire(s) between seat front height motor connector and right front seat control switch connector.

4) Press and hold inoperative seat's seat control switch in FRONT UP position. Measure voltage between front height motor connector Red/Light Blue wire terminal and ground. If voltage is more than 10 volts, go to next step. If voltage is 10 volts or less, replace seat control switch. See SEAT CONTROL SWITCH under REMOVAL & INSTALLATION.

5) Press and hold inoperative seat's control switch in FRONT DOWN position. Measure voltage between seat front height motor connector Yellow/Light Blue wire terminal and ground. If voltage is more than 10 volts, replace seat track assembly. See SEAT TRACK/MOTOR ASSEMBLY under REMOVAL & INSTALLATION. If voltage is 10 volts or less, replace seat control switch. See SEAT CONTROL SWITCH under REMOVAL & INSTALLATION.

TEST D: REAR TILT INOPERATIVE

1) Disconnect inoperative seat's rear height motor 2-pin connector. Measure resistance between rear height motor connector Red/Light Green wire terminal and ground. Also measure resistance between rear height motor connector Yellow/Light Green wire terminal and ground. If each resistance is less than 5 ohms, go to step 4). If testing driver's seat and any resistance is 5 ohms or more, go to next step. If testing right front seat and any resistance is 5 ohms or more, go to step 3).

2) Disconnect driver's seat control switch 8-pin connector. Measure resistance of Red/Light Green wire between driver's seat rear height motor connector and driver's seat control switch connector terminal No. 3. See Fig. 2. Also measure resistance of Yellow/Light Green wire between driver's seat rear height motor connector and driver's seat control switch connector terminal No. 2. If each resistance is less than 5 ohms, replace driver's seat control switch. See SEAT CONTROL SWITCH under REMOVAL & INSTALLATION. If any resistance is 5 ohms or more, repair open in appropriate wire(s) between seat rear height motor connector and seat control switch connector.

3) Disconnect right front seat control switch 8-pin connector. Measure resistance of Red/Light Green wire between right front seat rear height motor connector and right front seat control switch connector terminal No. 1. See Fig. 2. Also measure resistance of Yellow/Light Green wire between right front seat rear height motor connector and right front seat control switch connector terminal No. 4. If each resistance is less than 5 ohms, replace right front seat control switch. See REMOVAL & INSTALLATION. If any resistance is 5 ohms or more, repair open in appropriate wire(s) between seat rear height motor connector and seat control switch connector.

4) Press and hold inoperative seat's control switch in REAR UP position. Measure voltage between rear height motor connector Red/Light Green wire terminal and ground. If voltage is more than 10 volts, go to next step. If voltage is 10 volts or less, replace seat control switch. See SEAT CONTROL SWITCH under REMOVAL & INSTALLATION.

5) Press and hold inoperative seat's control switch in REAR DOWN position. Measure voltage between appropriate seat rear height motor connector Yellow/Light Green wire terminal and ground. If voltage is more than 10 volts, replace seat track assembly. See SEAT TRACK/MOTOR ASSEMBLY under REMOVAL & INSTALLATION. If voltage is 10 volts or less, replace seat control switch. See SEAT CONTROL SWITCH under REMOVAL & INSTALLATION.

TEST E: NO HORIZONTAL MOVEMENT

1) Disconnect inoperative seat's horizontal motor 2-pin connector. Measure resistance between horizontal motor connector Red/White wire terminal and ground. Also measure resistance between horizontal motor connector Yellow/White wire terminal and ground. If each resistance is less than 5 ohms, go to step 4). If testing driver's seat and any resistance is 5 ohms or more, go to next step. If testing right front seat and any resistance is 5 ohms or more, go to step 3).

2) Disconnect driver's seat control switch 8-pin connector. Measure resistance of Red/White wire between horizontal motor connector and driver's seat control switch connector terminal No. 6. See Fig. 2. Also measure resistance of Yellow/White wire between horizontal motor connector and driver's seat control switch connector terminal No. 7. If each resistance is less than 5 ohms, replace seat control switch. See SEAT CONTROL SWITCH under REMOVAL & INSTALLATION. If any resistance is 5 ohms or more, repair open in appropriate wire(s) between horizontal motor conductor and seat control switch connector.

3) Disconnect right front seat control switch 8-pin connector. Measure resistance of Red/White wire between horizontal motor connector and right front seat control switch connector terminal No. 7. See Fig. 2. Also measure resistance of Yellow/White wire between horizontal motor connector and right front seat control switch connector terminal No. 6. If each resistance is less than 5 ohms, replace seat control switch. See SEAT CONTROL SWITCH under REMOVAL & INSTALLATION. If any resistance is 5 ohms or more, repair open in appropriate wire(s) between horizontal motor connector and seat control switch connector.

4) Press and hold inoperative seat's control switch in REARWARD position. Measure voltage between appropriate seat horizontal motor connector Red/White wire terminal and ground. If voltage is more than 10 volts, go to next step. If voltage is 10 volts or less, replace seat control switch. See SEAT CONTROL SWITCH under REMOVAL & INSTALLATION.

5) Press and hold inoperative seat's control switch in FORWARD position. Measure voltage between appropriate seat horizontal motor connector Yellow/White wire terminal and ground. If voltage is more than 10 volts, replace seat track/motor assembly. See SEAT TRACK/MOTOR ASSEMBLY under REMOVAL & INSTALLATION. If voltage is 10 volts or less, replace seat control switch. See SEAT CONTROL SWITCH under REMOVAL & INSTALLATION.

TEST F: POWER LUMBAR INOPERATIVE

1) Press inoperative seat's lumbar seat control switch to INFLATE position. If lumbar compressor runs, go to step 7). If lumbar compressor does not run, go to next step.

2) Operate power seat controls on seat with inoperative power lumbar system. If power seat operates, go to next step. If driver's power seat does not operate, go to TEST A: DRIVER'S POWER SEAT INOPERATIVE. If right front power seat does not operate, go to TEST B: RIGHT FRONT POWER SEAT INOPERATIVE.

3) Disconnect inoperative seat's lumbar seat control switch 2-pin connector. Measure voltage between lumbar seat control switch connector Dark Green wire terminal (Black/White wire terminal on right front seat) and ground. If voltage is more than 10 volts, go to next step. If voltage is 10 volts or less, repair open in appropriate wire between lumbar seat control switch connector and battery junction box.

4) Disconnect lumbar motor 2-pin connector. Measure resistance between lumbar motor connector Black wire terminal and ground. If resistance is less than 5 ohms, go to next step. If resistance is 5 ohms or more, repair open in Black wire between lumbar motor connector and ground. Ground point is located behind left hand kick panel.

5) Connect lumbar seat control switch connector. Press and hold inoperative seat's lumbar seat control switch in INFLATE position. Measure voltage between lumbar motor Red wire terminal and ground. If voltage is more than 10 volts, replace lumbar motor. See LUMBAR MOTOR under REMOVAL & INSTALLATION. If voltage is 10 volts or less, go to next step.

6) Disconnect inoperative seat's lumbar seat control switch. Measure resistance of Red wire between lumbar seat control switch connector and lumbar motor connector. If resistance is less than 5 ohms, replace lumbar seat control switch. See LUMBAR SEAT CONTROL SWITCH under REMOVAL & INSTALLATION. If resistance is 5 ohms or less, repair open in Red wire between lumbar seat control switch connector and lumbar motor connector.

7) Press lumbar seat control switch to INFLATE position and observe seat back lumbar adjusting pad. If lumbar adjusting pad inflates, go to step 11). If lumbar adjusting pad does not inflate, go to next step.

8) Visually inspect lumbar adjusting pad. If lumbar adjusting pad is damaged, replace lumbar adjusting pad. See LUMBAR ADJUSTING PAD under REMOVAL & INSTALLATION. If lumbar adjusting pad is not damaged, go to next step.

9) Disconnect lumbar adjusting hose from the lumbar motor. Press lumbar seat control switch to INFLATE position while feeling for air at motor hose connection. If air is felt at lumbar motor hose connection, go to next step. If air is not felt at lumbar motor hose connection, replace lumbar motor. See LUMBAR MOTOR under REMOVAL & INSTALLATION.

10) Connect hose to lumbar motor. Disconnect lumbar adjusting hose from lumbar seat control switch. Press lumbar seat control switch to INFLATE position. If air can be felt at lumbar adjusting hose, go to next step. If air can not be felt at lumbar adjusting hose, replace lumbar adjusting hose.

11) Reconnect hose at lumbar seat control switch. Disconnect lumbar adjusting hose at lumbar adjusting pad. Install in-line pressure gauge on lumbar adjusting hose. Press and hold lumbar seat control switch at INFLATE position until gauge reads 5 psi (34.47 kPa). Wait 3 hours, then read gauge. If pressure reading is 4.7 psi (32.41 kPa) or more, system is operating correctly. If pressure reading is less than 4.7 psi (32.41 kPa), go to next step.

12) Remove in-line pressure gauge. Use hand pump and inflate lumbar adjusting pad to 5 psi (34.47 kPa). Wait 3 hours, then read gauge. If pressure reading is 4.7 psi (34.47 kPa) or more, replace lumbar seat control switch. See LUMBAR SEAT CONTROL SWITCH under REMOVAL & INSTALLATION. If pressure reading is less than 4.7 psi (34.47 kPa), replace lumbar adjusting pad. See LUMBAR ADJUSTING PAD under REMOVAL & INSTALLATION.

REMOVAL & INSTALLATION

CAUTION: When battery is disconnected, vehicle computer and memory systems may lose memory data. Driveability problems may exist until computer systems have completed a relearn cycle. See COMPUTER RELEARN PROCEDURES article in GENERAL INFORMATION before disconnecting battery.

LUMBAR ADJUSTING PAD

CAUTION: If seat has optional side air bag, deactivate air bag system before removing or disassembling seat. Disconnect battery negative cable. If equipped, disconnect auxiliary battery and power supplies. Wait at least one minute for air bag backup power supply to deplete before proceeding.

Removal & Installation – 1) Disconnect battery ground cable and wait at least one minute before proceeding. Remove seat. See SEAT ASSEMBLY under REMOVAL & INSTALLATION.

2) Remove trim cover screw and trim cover. Raise armrest to upright position and remove armrest. Remove armrest stud. Release seat backrest cover "J" retainers.

3) If equipped with side air bag, release side air bag wiring harness pin-type retainers. Guide side air bag harness through seat cushion.

4) Disconnect lumbar air hose connector. Pull up seat backrest cover enough to access and remove 3 bolts. Remove headrest. Remove 2 screw covers and screws. Using 12 mm socket and extension, remove headrest guide rod sleeve.

5) If equipped with side air bag, remove side air bag harness pin-type retainer. Remove screws and side air bag module. Remove seat backrest frame. Remove seat backrest cover clips. Separate trim cover from pad. To install, reverse removal procedure.

LUMBAR MOTOR

Removal & Installation – 1) Disconnect battery negative cable and wait at least one minute before proceeding. Remove seat. See SEAT ASSEMBLY.

2) Release seat cover "J" retainer. Disconnect electrical connector. Disconnect lumbar air hose connector. Remove lumbar motor.

3) To install, reverse removal procedure. Check restraint system for proper operation. Prove out air bag system.

LUMBAR SEAT CONTROL SWITCH

Removal & Installation – Disconnect negative battery cable and wait one minute before proceeding. Remove seat. See SEAT ASSEMBLY. Disconnect lumbar switch electrical connector. Remove trim cover screw. Disconnect hoses and remove trim cover. Remove lumbar seat control switch. To install, reverse removal procedure.

SEAT ASSEMBLY

CAUTION: If seat has optional side air bag, deactivate air bag system before removing or disassembling seat. Disconnect battery negative cable. If equipped, disconnect auxiliary battery and power supplies. Wait at least one minute for air bag backup power supply to deplete before proceeding.

Removal & Installation – Disconnect negative battery cable and wait at least one minute. Remove seat retaining nuts. Disconnect electrical connectors and remove seat from vehicle. To install, reverse removal procedure. Check restraint system for proper operation. Prove out air bag system.

SEAT CONTROL SWITCH

Removal & Installation – Disconnect negative battery cable and wait one minute before proceeding with removal. Remove recliner handle. Remove seat trim cover screw. Remove seat trim cover. Disconnect electrical connector. Remove 2 screws and seat control switch. To install, reverse removal procedure.

SEAT TRACK/MOTOR ASSEMBLY

Removal & Installation – 1) Disconnect battery negative cable and wait at least one minute. Remove seat. See SEAT ASSEMBLY.

2) Remove trim cover screws. Remove lumbar switch. Disconnect air hoses. Remove pin-type retainers on each side of trim cover. Remove 2 recliner bolts. On other side, remove single bolt. Release christmas tree clips.

3) If equipped with side air bag, remove pin-type retainers holding side air bag wire harness to seat cushion. Guide wire harness through seat cushion.

4) On all models, remove 2 seat track screws. Remove seat track bolt. Disconnect electrical connectors. Remove wiring harness and seat track. Remove safety belt buckle bolt and safety belt buckle.

5) To install, reverse removal procedure. Tighten seat track bolt, 2 seat track screws and single bolt to 17 ft. lbs. (23 N.m). Tighten 2 recliner bolts to 33 ft. lbs. (45 N.m). Check restraint system for proper operation. Prove out air bag system.

WIRING DIAGRAMS

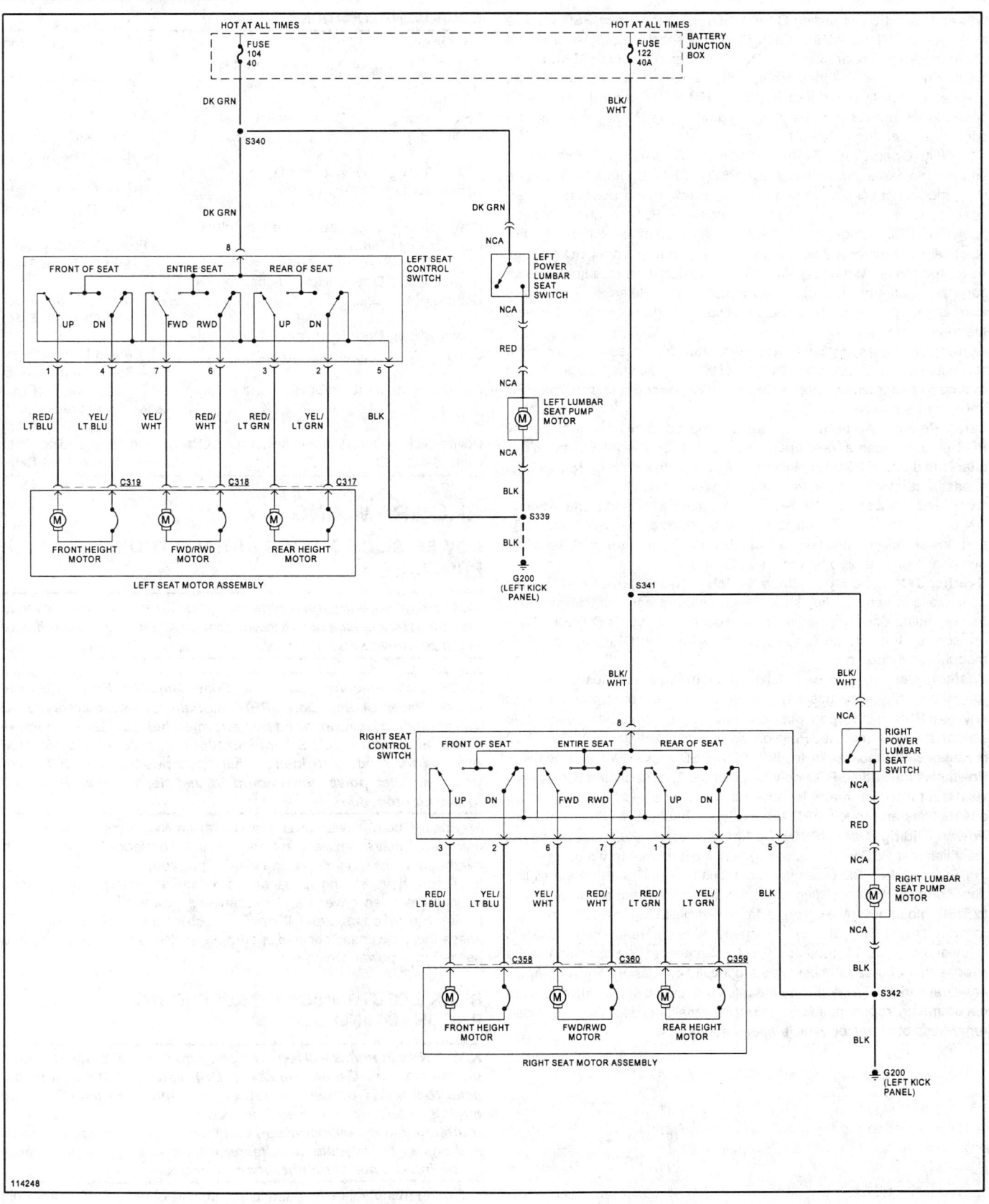

Fig. 3: Power Seats System Wiring Diagram (Windstar)

114248

DESCRIPTION & OPERATION

Left and right Power Sliding Door (PSD) have their own PSD module and operate independently. Each PSD has specific outputs to control appropriate PSD operation. The Rear Electronic Module (REM) signal inputs and control switches are specific for each PSD module, except overhead console on/off switch input, REM PARK input, REM vehicle speed input and fused battery logic circuit. Power sliding door system components and their operation follow:

"B" Pillar Open/Close Switch – Pressing "B" pillar open/close switch sends a momentary ground signal to PSD module. Upon receiving input, PSD module checks overhead console on/off switch position. If overhead console on/off switch is in ON position, PSD module will send power to PSD motor. If overhead console on/off switch is in OFF position, PSD motor will not be supplied with power from PSD module.

Actuator Drive Assembly Clutch – Actuator drive assembly clutch separates actuator drive assembly motor from cable spool. This allows for manual opening and closing of power sliding doors without driving the motor.

Actuator Drive Assembly Motor – Actuator drive assembly motor is a reversible motor. Upon valid activation, PSD module supplies power and ground to motor circuits depending on PSD position and direction PSD needs to be moved.

Latch Release Actuator – Power is supplied to release actuator by PSD module when a valid open command is received. PSD module is unable to detect if PSD is unlocked. If PSD is activated with PSD locked, release actuator will operate, but PSD will not open.

Overhead Console On/Off Switch – Supplies a ground signal when in ON position to enable or disable "B" pillar open/close switch activation and power assist activation of PSD. Both functions are enabled when overhead console on/off switch is in ON position.

Overhead Console Open/Close Switch – Pressing overhead console open/close switch supplies a momentary ground signal to PSD module. Power sliding door module will power open or close PSD if conditions are correct. If overhead console on/off switch is in OFF position, PSD module will ignore input.

Position Sensor – Power sliding door module supplies a five volt reference voltage to position sensor on a valid open command or anytime PSD is in open position. Ground is constantly supplied to sensor by PSD module. Position sensor has 2 data lines that PSD module reads and tracks to determine PSD movement and position. Position is tracked so PSD may be powered in correct direction when a valid operation command is received. Velocity is monitored to identify obstructions and reverse PSD operation if required.

Power Sliding Door (PSD) Detent Switch – PSD detent switch identifies rear PSD latch position by sending a momentary ground signal to PSD module. PSD detent switch circuit is connected through sliding door contacts. Power sliding doors will operate so long as REM circuits to PSD modules are at ground from vehicle being in PARK position (provided by PCM) and wheel speed sensors read below 6 MPH (provided by ABS/TC module). REM will prevent PSD operation in the event either of these 2 messages are invalid or missing. These 2 inputs have network DTCs and if they are retrieved and power sliding doors are not operating, repair these DTCs first. Power sliding doors can be closed regardless of PARK or vehicle speed status.

COMPONENT LOCATIONS

COMPONENT LOCATIONS

Component	Location
Power Sliding Door Ajar Switch (Left Or Right Side)	At Left Or Right "C" Pillar
Power Sliding Door Detent Switch (Left Or Right Side)	Lower Rear Of Sliding Door (Left Or Right Side)
Power Sliding Door Actuator Drive Assembly (Left Or Right Side)	Behind Left Or Right Rear Quarter Panel
Power Sliding Door Latch Release Actuator (Left Or Right Side)	Front Of Sliding Door (Left Or Right Side)
Power Sliding Door Lock Actuator (Left Or Right Side)	Front Of Sliding Door (Left Or Right Side)
Power Sliding Door Module (Left Or Right Side)	Behind Left Or Right Rear Quarter Panel
Position Sensors (Left Or Right Side)	Located On Drive Assembly Actuators (Left Or Right Side)
Power Sliding Door Detent Switch (Left Or Right Side)	On Rear Sliding Door Latch (Left Or Right Side)

PROGRAMMING

POWER SLIDING DOOR INITIALIZATION PROCEDURE

NOTE: Keyless entry transmitter or "B" pillar open/close switches may be used in place of overhead console Open/Close switches to initialize power sliding doors.

NOTE: Disconnecting battery or Fuse Junction Box (FJB) will cause Power Sliding Door (PSD) module to lose memory. PSD initialization procedure must be performed before PSD will operate under all conditions. PSD initialization procedure is a learning process for module to identify full open position and full close position. After power is restored to vehicle, initialize PSD with following procedure:

1) Ensure both power sliding doors are fully closed, latched and unlocked. Ensure vehicle is in Park and fuel filler door is closed. Switch overhead console on/off switch is in ON position.

2) Press driver's and passenger's overhead console open/close switches to open driver's and passenger's power sliding doors. After power sliding doors are full open and stopped, press driver's and passenger's overhead console open/close switches to close driver's and passenger's power sliding doors.

REAR ELECTRONICS MODULE (REM) PROGRAMMING

NOTE: New modules will require configuration after being installed on vehicle. New Generation Star (NGS) tester or Ford compatible scan tool MUST be used to retrieve configuration data from old module before it is removed from vehicle. This information will be transferred into new module so that new module will contain same settings as old module. NGS tester will not retain stored configuration information for longer than 24 hours.

Following manufacturer's instructions, upload old information from old module using Ford Service Function (FSF) card and NGS tester. Install new module and download stored information into new module using FSF card and NGS tester.

ADJUSTMENTS

POWER SLIDING DOOR ADJUSTMENT

CAUTION: For correct sliding door operation, it is critical that door adjuster wedge and striker on "B" pillar fit smoothly into wedge pocket and latch in power sliding door. If any adjustments are made to power sliding door, realignment of wedge may be necessary.

NOTE: Never use wedge or strikers to adjust or fit sliding door. Using a wedge to force door to move will cause wedges to squeak and eventually break. It will also cause power sliding door to reverse prior to full closure or not close completely. Using striker to force door to move, will cause a rattle or affect door opening or closing efforts. If upper and lower wedges are not loosened during door adjustment, they will pull power sliding door into same position door was in before adjustment.

Sliding Door Flushness Adjustment – 1) Power sliding door flushness is inset or outset of panels to each other. Inspect sliding door and measure door flushness. See SLIDING DOOR FLUSHNESS SPECIFICATIONS table. If flushness is not within specification, go to next step. If flushness is within specification, no adjustment is needed at this time.

2) Loosen upper and lower sliding door 4 wedge screws on appropriate "B" or "C" pillar. Center wire striker in appropriate catch or latch assembly opening. Do not use "B" or "C" pillar strikers to position door. Inspect alignment of "B" pillar wire striker in catch, and "C" pillar wire striker in latch. If they are not aligned, mark edges of appropriate wire striker and slightly loosen 2 screws on striker. Tap striker into correct position, tighten 2 striker screws to 18 ft. lbs. (25 N.m) and go to next step.

3) Inspect upper and lower power sliding door to front door flushness specification. If lower portion of power sliding door does not meet loosen lower check bracket bolt. Move bracket until lower portion of power sliding door is flush with lower portion of front door and tighten lower check bracket bolt to 108 INCH lbs. (12 N.m). If upper portion of power sliding door does not meet power sliding door to front door flushness specification, mark forward and rearward edges of bracket. Loosen 2 upper guide roller assembly bolts, move power sliding door to gain flushness specification and tighten 2 upper guide roller assembly bolts to 120 INCH lbs. (14 N.m). The "B" and "C" pillar wire strikers should be centered after this step is completed. For further adjustment, repeat step **2)**.

SLIDING DOOR FLUSHNESS SPECIFICATIONS

Location	In. (mm)
Front Door-To-Fender	-.08-.08 (-2.0-2.0)
Manual Sliding Door-To-Front Door	-.12-.12 (-3.0-3.0)
Power Sliding Door-To-Front Door	-.04-.12 (-1.0-3.0)
Manual Sliding Door-To-Quarter Panel	-.12-.12 (-3.0-3.0)
Power Sliding Door-To-Quarter Panel	-.04-.12 (-1.0-3.0)

NOTE: Lower roller bracket and guide assembly bolts should be loosened enough to allow assembly to move, but not so loose that assembly cannot hold position when moved.

Sliding Door Margin Adjustment – 1) Margin is air gap between 2 adjoining panels. Inspect power sliding door and measure margins of power sliding door. See SLIDING DOOR MARGIN SPECIFICATIONS table. *See Fig. 1.* If margin in not within specifiecation, go to next step. If margin is within specification, no adjustment is needed at this time.

2) If sliding door to front door margin does not meet specification or if door requires horizontal or vertical adjustment at "B" pillar, go to next step. If sliding door to quarter panel does not meet specifications or if door requires horizontal or vertical adjustment at "C" pillar, go to step **4)**.

3) Remove bolt plug cover from lower corner of sliding door trim panel. Mark door around lower roller bracket to measure adjustment increments and loosen 3 lower guide roller assembly bolts. Using a nylon hammer, adjust hinge up or down. Ensure front door margin is equal and within specification at top and bottom. Close sliding door and inspect for correct fit. Adjust if necessary. Tighten 3 lower guide roller assembly bolts to 15 Ft lbs. (20.0 N.m) and install bolt plug cover

NOTE: Do not swing door open more than 25 degrees, or damage to other hinges may occur.

4) Remove center roller hinge nut and lift rear of door to separate center roller hinge bracket from center roller hinge mount bracket. Swing door open and support if necessary. Mark edges of center roller hinge mount bracket and slightly loosen 2 mount bracket bolts. Reattach center roller hinge bracket and tap center roller hinge into correct position. Separate center roller hinge bracket from center roller hinge mount bracket and tighten 2 mount bracket bolts to 15 ft. lbs. (20.0 N.m). Reattach center roller hinge bracket to center roller hinge mount bracket, install center roller hinge nut and tighten to 15 ft lbs. (20.0 N.m). Close door and inspect alignment. If "B" and/or "C" Pillar wire strikers are not aligned after these steps, go to step **2)** under SLIDING DOOR MARGIN ADJUSTMENT.

SLIDING DOOR MARGIN SPECIFICATIONS

Location (No.) [1]	In. (mm)
Sliding Door-To-Roof (1)	.15-.24 (4.0-6.0)
Sliding Door-To-Quarter Panel (2)	.12-.27 (3.0-7.0)
Sliding Door-To-Front Door (3)	.16-.39 (4.0-10.0)
Sliding Door-To-Rocker Panel (4)	.15-.24 (4.0-6.0)
Front Door-To-Rocker Panel (5)	.15-.24 (4.0-6.0)
Front Door-To-Fender (6)	.12-.22 (3.0-5.6)
Front Door-To-"A" Pillar (7)	.15-.24 (4.0-6.0)
Front Door-To-Roof (8)	.15-.24 (4.0-6.0)

[1] – Numbers refer to locations in illustration. *See Fig. 1.*

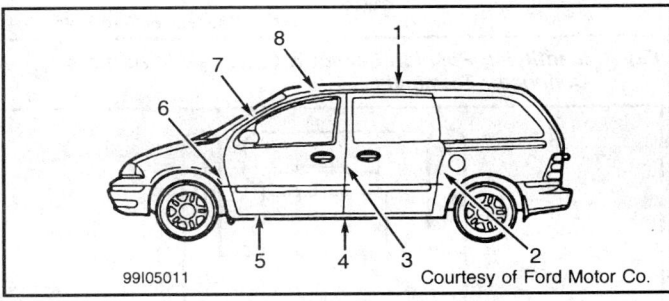

99I05011   Courtesy of Ford Motor Co.

Fig. 1: Sliding Door Margin Measurement Locations

TROUBLE SHOOTING

INSPECTION & VERIFICATION

Electrical – Ensure customer concern. Check all fuses for appropriate system. Check following electrical items:

- Fuse Junction Box (FJB) fuses No. 10 (10-amp), No. 14 (10-amp) and No. 6 (15-amp).
- Battery Junction Box (BJB) fuses No. 110 and 118 (both 50-amp).
- Overhead console on/off switch, overhead console open/close switches and "B" pillar open/close switches.
- Sliding door contact alignment and fuel filler door switch (left power sliding door only).
- Check for damaged wiring harness and/or loose, corroded connections.

Mechanical – Check for damage to following items:

- Power sliding door wedges and strikers misaligned.
- Actuator drive assembly cables disconnected or damaged.
- Sliding door tracks and rollers binding or obstructed.
- Fuel filler door interlock mechanism binding or damaged (left power sliding door only).

If an obvious cause for an observed or reported concern are found, correct cause if possible before proceeding to SELF-DIAGNOSTIC SYSTEM.

CONNECTOR IDENTIFICATION

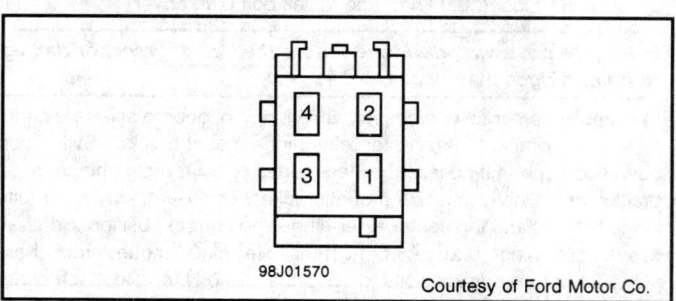

Fig. 2: Identifying LPSDM & RPSDM 4-Pin Harness Connector Terminals (C354 & C351)

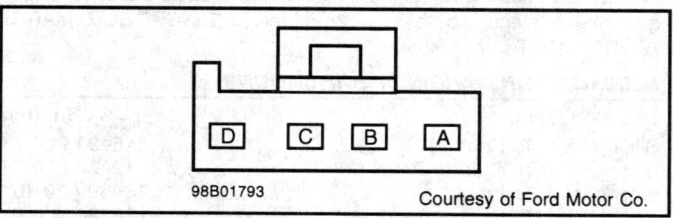

Fig. 3: Identifying LPSDM Motor & RPSDM Motor 4-Pin Harness Connector Terminals

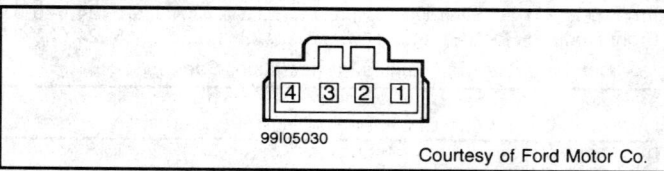

Fig. 4: Identifying Position Sensor & Clutch 4-Pin Harness Connector Terminals

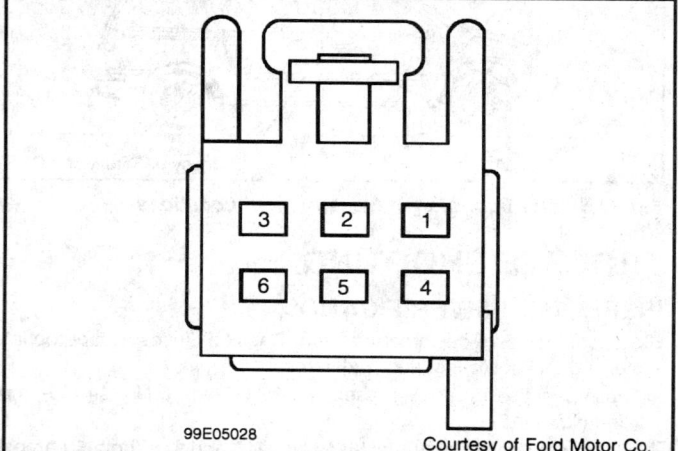

Fig. 5: Identifying Left & Right "B" Pillar Switch 6-Pin Connector Terminals (C942 & C941)

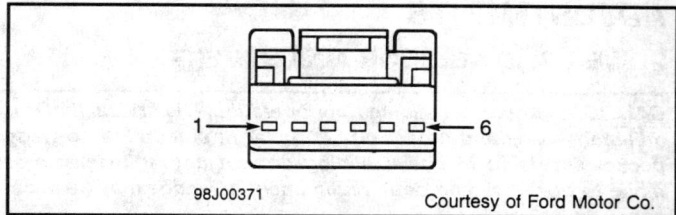

Fig. 6: Identifying Overhead Console 8-Pin Harness Connector Terminals (C915)

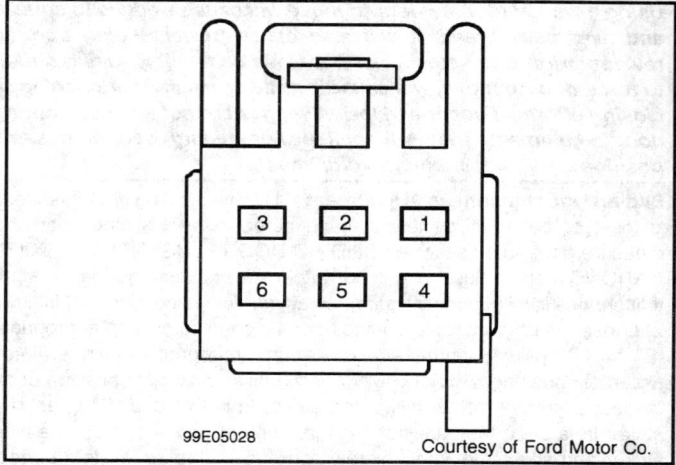

Fig. 7: Identifying LPSDM, RPSDM , Left & Right Sliding Door Contact 8-Pin Harness Connector Terminals (C337, C338, C700 & C800)

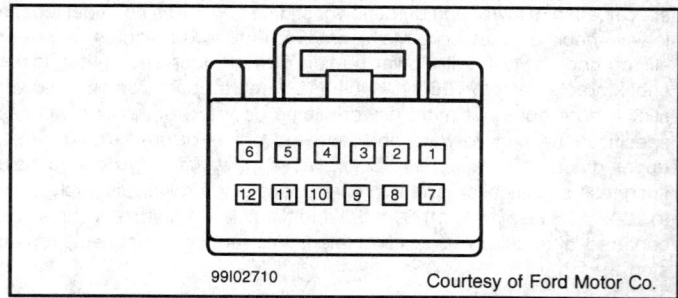

Fig. 8: Identifying LPSDM, RPSDM & REM 12-Pin Harness Connector Terminals (C355, C352 & C344)

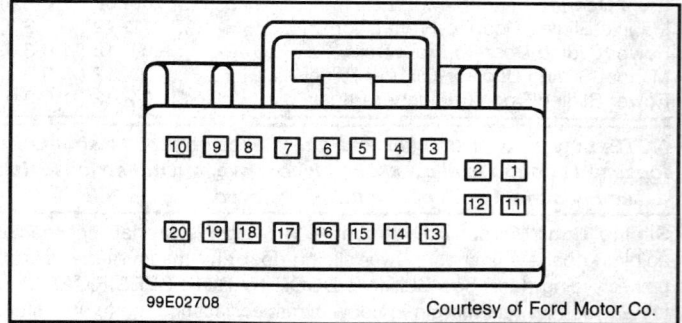

Fig. 9: Identifying REM 20-Pin Harness Connector Terminals (C343)

SELF-DIAGNOSTIC SYSTEM

WARNING: During Power Sliding Door (PSD) module self-test, PSD module will attempt to fully open and close PSD. PSD module self-test does not require PARK or VSS signal to open door. DO NOT carry out PSD self-test with vehicle in motion.

NOTE: All diagnostic tests are written specifically for New Generation Star (NGS) tester. Most generic scan tools should be able to perform all test procedures.

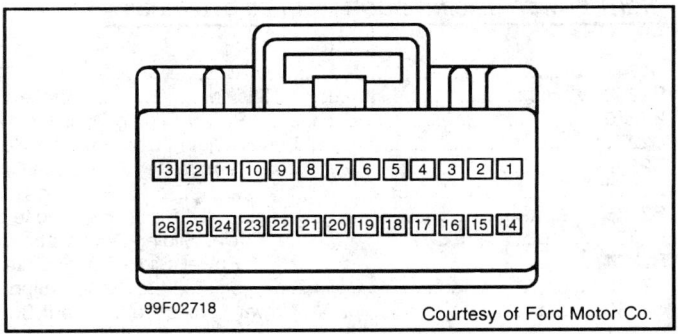

99F02718   Courtesy of Ford Motor Co.

Fig. 11: Identifying REM 26-Pin Harness Connector Terminals (C342)

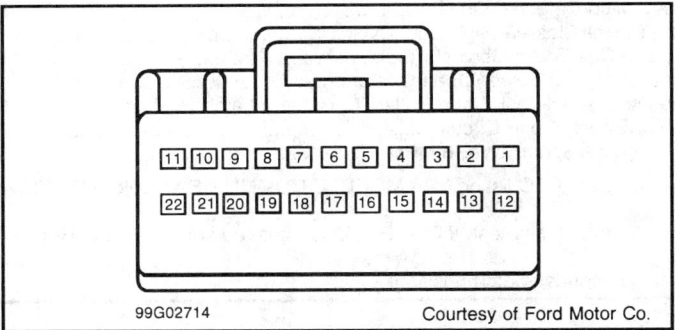

99G02714   Courtesy of Ford Motor Co.

Fig. 10: Identifying REM 22-Pin Harness Connector Terminals (C341)

NOTE: To carry out power sliding door module self-tests, overhead console on/off switch must be in ON position, door must be completely closed, unlocked, vehicle must be in Park, ignition switch in RUN position and for left power sliding door only, fuel filler door must be completely closed.

Connect New Generation Star (NGS) tester to Data Link Connector (DLC), located beneath instrument panel. Using NGS tester, perform data link diagnostics test. See DATA LINK DIAGNOSTIC TEST under COMMUNICATION NETWORK DIAGNOSTICS in MODULE COMMU-

NICATIONS NETWORK – WINDSTAR article. If NGS tester responds with CKT914, CKT915 or CKT70=ALL ECUS NO RESP/NOT EQUIP, repair module communications concern. See MODULE COMMUNICA-TIONS NETWORK – WINDSTAR article. If NGS tester displays NO RESP/NOT EQUIP for Left Power Sliding Door Module (LPSDM), perform TEST A: NO COMMUNICATION WITH LEFT POWER SLIDING DOOR MODULE (LPSDM) under SYSTEM TESTS. If NGS tester displays NO RESP/NOT EQUIP for Right Power Sliding Door Module (RPSDM), perform TEST B: NO COMMUNICATION WITH RIGHT POWER SLIDING DOOR MODULE (RPSDM) under SYSTEM TESTS. If NGS tester displays NO RESP/NOT EQUIP for Rear Electronic Module (REM), perform TEST C: NO COMMUNICATION WITH REAR ELECTRONICS MODULE (REM) under SYSTEM TESTS.

If NGS tester responds with SYSTEM PASSED, retrieve and record continuous DTCs. Erase continuous DTCs. Using NGS tester, perform LPSDM, RPSDM and REM self-test. Perform appropriate test in accordance with DTC retrieved. See LEFT POWER SLIDING DOOR MODULE DTC INDEX, RIGHT POWER SLIDING DOOR MODULE DTC INDEX and/or REAR ELECTRONICS MODULE DTC INDEX table. Codes listed in these tables are only for testing covered in this article. For complete DTC listing, see MODULE COMMUNICATIONS NETWORK – WINDSTAR article. If no DTCs are retrieved, repair by symptom. See SYMPTOM CHART table.

LEFT POWER SLIDING DOOR MODULE DTC INDEX

DTC [1]	Description	Test
B1342	ECU Defective	[2]
B2238	Broken Cable Detected	D
B2270 [3]	Power Sliding Door Exceeded Time Allowed To Cinch Door [4]	E
B2271 [3]	Power Sliding Door Did Not Reach Full Open Position During Self-Test	F
B2362	Remote Key Fob Open/Close Signal Circuit Short To Ground	X
B2363	Position Sensor System Failure	G
B2364	Fuel Filler Door Open Circuit	H
B2365	"B" Pillar Open/Close Switch Circuit Short To Ground	I
B2366	Power Sliding Door Open/Close Switch Circuit Short To Ground	J
B2374	Power Sliding Door Detent Switch Circuit Short To Ground	K
B2483	Enable Signal Open Circuit (Park)	L
B2589	No Power Sliding Door Detent Switch Detected On Closing & Door Reversed	M
B2591	No Power Sliding Door Detent Switch Detected On Unlatch	N
B2592	Door Not Pulled Into Primary During Power Close & High Duty Cycles	O
B2593 [3]	Door Reversed While Closing Due To An Obstacle	P
B2594	No Movement Detected After An Unlatch During Power Open Operation	Q
B2603	Power Sliding Door Not Fully Closed During Power Close During Self-Test When Pulled To Primary Latch Position	R
B2604	Power Sliding Door On/Off Switch Open Circuit	S
B2605	Disable Signal Open Circuit – Vehicle Speed Over 6 MPH	T

[1] – DTCs listed in this table are only for testing covered in this article. For complete DTC listing, see MODULE COMMUNICATIONS NETWORK – WINDSTAR article.

[2] – Clear and document all DTC. Perform Left Power Sliding Door Module (LPSDM) self-test. If DTC B1342 is retrieved again, replace LPSDM.

[3] – Repair all other DTCs before proceeding with this test.

[4] – Exceeded the time allowed to reach primary latch position after reaching secondary latch position.

RIGHT POWER SLIDING DOOR MODULE DTC INDEX

DTC [1]	Description	Test
B1342	ECU Defective	2
B2238	Broken Cable Detected	D
B2270 [3]	Power Sliding Door Exceeded Time Allowed To Cinch Door [4]	E
B2271 [3]	Power Sliding Door Did Not Reach Full Open Position During Self-Test	F
B2362	Remote Key Fob Open/Close Signal Circuit Short To Ground	X
B2363	Position Sensor System Failure	G
B2365	"B" Pillar Open/Close Switch Circuit Short To Ground	I
B2366	Power Sliding Door Open/Close Switch Circuit Short To Ground	J
B2374	Power Sliding Door Detent Switch Circuit Short To Ground	K
B2483	Enable Signal Open Circuit (Park)	L
B2589	No Power Sliding Door Detent Switch Detected On Closing & Door Reversed	M
B2591	No Power Sliding Door Detent Switch Detected On Unlatch	N
B2592 [3]	Door Not Pulled Into Primary During Power Close & High Duty Cycles	O
B2593 [3]	Door Reversed While Closing Due To An Obstacle	P
B2594	No Movement Detected After An Unlatch During Power Open Operation	Q
B2603	Power Sliding Door Not Fully Closed During Power Close During Self-Test When Pulled To Primary Latch Position	R
B2604	Power Sliding Door On/Off Switch Open Circuit	S
B2605	Disable Signal Open Circuit – Vehicle Speed Over 6 MPH	T

[1] – DTCs listed in this table are only for testing covered in this article. For complete DTC listing, see MODULE COMMUNICATIONS NETWORK – WINDSTAR article.

[2] – Clear and document all DTC. Perform Right Power Sliding Door Module (RPSDM) self-test. If DTC B1342 is retrieved again, replace RPSDM.

[3] – Repair all other DTCs before proceeding with this test.

[4] – Exceeded the time allowed to reach primary latch position after reaching secondary latch position.

REAR ELECTRONIC MODULE DTC INDEX

DTC [1]	Description	Test
B1342	ECU Defective	2
B2553	Disable Signal Output Circuit Short To Battery	3
B2556	Enable Signal Circuit Short To Battery	3
B2557	Left Power Sliding Door Open/Close Output Circuit Short To Battery	X
B2558	Right Power Sliding Door Open/Close Output Circuit Short To Battery	X

[1] – DTCs listed in this table are only for testing covered in this article. For complete DTC listing, see MODULE COMMUNICATIONS NETWORK – WINDSTAR article.

[2] – Clear and document all DTC. Perform REM self-test. If DTC B1342 is retrieved again, replace Rear Electronic Module (REM).

[3] – Repair other DTCs or refer to SYMPTOM CHART.

SYMPTOM CHART

Symptom	Test
No Communication With Left Power Sliding Door Module (LPSDM)	A
No Communication With Right Power Sliding Door Module (RPSDM)	B
No Communication With Rear Electronic Module (REM)	C
Right Power Sliding Door Inoperative – No DTCs	U
Left Power Sliding Door Inoperative – No DTCs	V
Power Sliding Door Inoperative From One Switch – No DTCs	W
Power Sliding Door Inoperative From Remote Keyless Entry Transmitter	X
Left Power Door Operates With Fuel Door Open	Y
Power Sliding Door Operates From "B" Pillar Open/Close Switch With Overhead Console Switch In Off Position	Z
Power Sliding Door Will Not Power Open From An Interior Door Handle Release	1

[1] – Check child safety lock operation, interior door handle operation and remote control assembly or retrieve DTCs from Left Power Sliding Door Module (LPSDM) or Right Power Sliding Door Module (RPSDM).

SYSTEM TESTS

NOTE: Many steps in the following tests refer to various harness connectors. These connectors are identified in illustrations. See Figs. 2-11. After any repairs have been made on vehicle, always perform self-test on affected system to check for normal operation of power sliding doors.

NOTE: Anytime battery or Fuse Junction Box (FJB) fuse No. 6 (15-amp) is disconnected, power sliding doors must be initialized before they will operate correctly. If Left Power Sliding Door Module (LPSDM) harness connector C355 or Right Power Sliding Door Module (RPSDM) harness connector C352 is disconnected, only single power sliding door must be initialized. If any module, switch or sensor is replaced or wire repaired, power sliding doors must be initialized. See POWER SLIDING DOOR INITIALIZATION PROCEDURE under PROGRAMMING. For module, switch or sensor replacement procedure, see REMOVAL & INSTALLATION.

TEST A: NO COMMUNICATION WITH LEFT POWER SLIDING DOOR MODULE (LPSDM)

1) Disconnect LPSDM 12-pin harness connector C355. Measure voltage between LPSDM harness connector C355 terminal No. 1 (Red/White wire) and ground. If voltage is 10 volts or less, go to next step. If voltage is more than 10 volts, go to step 6).

2) Check Fuse Junction Box (FJB) fuse No. 6 (15-amp). If fuse is not okay, go to next step. If fuse is okay, repair open in Red/White wire between LPSDM and FJB.

3) Disconnect Right Power Sliding Door Module (RPSDM) 12-pin harness connector C352. Measure resistance between LPSDM harness

connector C355 terminal No. 1 (Red/White wire) and ground. If resistance is more than 10 k/ohms, go to next step. If resistance is 10 k/ohms or less, repair short to ground in Red/White wire between LPSDM and FJB.

4) Connect RPSDM 12-pin harness connector C352. Install a NEW fuse No. 6 (15-amp) into FJB. Carry out power sliding door initialization procedure on right power sliding door. If fuse is okay, go to next step. If fuse is not okay, replace RPSDM.

5) Connect LPSDM 12-pin harness connector C355. Carry out power sliding door initialization procedure on left power sliding door. If fuse No. 6 is okay, system is operating correctly at this time. Check Red/White wire for intermittent short to ground. If fuse No. 6 is not okay, replace LPSDM.

6) Turn ignition switch to RUN position. Measure voltage between LPSDM harness connector C355 terminal No. 11 (Red/Black wire) and ground. If voltage is 10 volts or less, go to next step. If voltage is more than 10 volts, go to step .11)

7) Check Fuse Junction Box (FJB) fuse No. 10 (10-amp). If fuse is not okay, go to next step. If fuse is okay, repair open in Red/Black wire between LPSDM and FJB.

8) Turn ignition switch to OFF position. Disconnect Right Power Sliding Door Module (RPSDM) 12-pin harness connector C352. Measure resistance between LPSDM harness connector C355 terminal No. 11 (Red/Black wire) and ground. If resistance is more than 10 k/ohms, go to next step. If resistance is 10 k/ohms or less, repair short to ground in Red/Black wire between LPSDM and FJB.

9) Connect RPSDM 12-pin harness connector C352. Install a NEW fuse No. 10 (10-amp) into FJB. Carry out power sliding door initialization procedure on right power sliding door. If fuse No. 10 is okay, go to next step. If fuse No. 10 is not okay, replace RPSDM.

10) Connect LPSDM 12-pin harness connector C355. Carry out power sliding door initialization procedure on left power sliding door. If fuse No. 10 is okay, system is operating correctly at this time. Check Red/Black wire for intermittent short to ground. If fuse No. 10 is not okay, replace LPSDM.

11) Turn ignition switch to OFF position. Disconnect LPSDM 4-pin harness connector C354. Measure resistance between LPSDM harness connector C354 terminal No. 3 (Black wire) and ground. If resistance is less than 5 ohms, go to next step. If resistance is 5 ohms or more, repair open in Black wire (ground circuit).

12) Disconnect left position sensor harness connector. Measure resistance between left position sensor harness connector terminal No. 3 (White wire) and ground. If resistance is more than 10 k/ohms, repair module communication concern. See MODULE COMMUNICATIONS NETWORK – WINDSTAR article. If resistance is 10 k/ohms or less, replace left position sensor.

TEST B: NO COMMUNICATION WITH RIGHT POWER SLIDING DOOR MODULE (RPSDM)

1) Disconnect RPSDM 12-pin harness connector C352. Measure voltage between RPSDM harness connector C352 terminal No. 1 (Red/White wire) and ground. If voltage is 10 volts or less, go to next step. If voltage is more than 10 volts, go to step 6).

2) Check Fuse Junction Box (FJB) fuse No. 6 (15-amp). If fuse is not okay, go to next step. If fuse is okay, repair open in Red/White wire between RPSDM and FJB.

3) Disconnect Left Power Sliding Door Module (LPSDM) 12-pin harness connector C355. Measure resistance between RPSDM harness connector C352 terminal No. 1 (Red/White wire) and ground. If resistance is more than 10 k/ohms, go to next step. If resistance is 10 k/ohms or less, repair short to ground in Red/White wire between RPSDM and FJB.

4) Connect LPSDM 12-pin harness connector C355. Install a NEW fuse No. 6 (15-amp) into FJB. Carry out power sliding door initialization procedure on left power sliding door. If fuse No. 6 is okay, go to next step. If fuse No. 6 is not okay, replace LPSDM.

5) Connect RPSDM 12-pin harness connector C352. Carry out power sliding door initialization procedure on right power sliding door. If fuse No. 6 is okay, system is operating correctly at this time. Check Red/White wire for intermittent short to ground. If fuse No. 6 is not okay, replace RPSDM.

6) Turn ignition switch to RUN position. Measure voltage between RPSDM harness connector C352 terminal No. 11 (Red/Black wire) and ground. If voltage is 10 volts or less, go to next step. If voltage is more than 10 volts, go to step 11).

7) Check Fuse Junction Box (FJB) fuse No. 10 (10-amp). If fuse is not okay, go to next step. If fuse is okay, repair open in Red/Black wire between RPSDM and FJB.

8) Turn ignition switch to OFF position. Disconnect Left Power Sliding Door Module (LPSDM) 12-pin harness connector C355. Measure resistance between LPSDM harness connector C355 terminal No. 11 (Red/Black wire) and ground. If resistance is more than 10 k/ohms, go to next step. If resistance is 10 k/ohms or less, repair short to ground in Red/Black wire between RPSDM and FJB.

9) Connect LPSDM 12-pin harness connector C355. Install a NEW fuse No. 10 (10-amp) into FJB. Carry out power sliding door initialization procedure on left power sliding door. If fuse No. 10 is okay, go to next step. If fuse No. 10 is not okay, replace LPSDM.

10) Connect RPSDM 12-pin harness connector C352. Carry out power sliding door initialization procedure on right power sliding door. If fuse No. 10 is okay, system is operating correctly at this time. Check Red/Black wire for intermittent short to ground. If fuse No. 10 is not okay, replace RPSDM.

11) Turn ignition switch to OFF position. Disconnect RPSDM 4-pin harness connector C351. Measure resistance between RPSDM harness connector C351 terminal No. 3 (Black wire) and ground. If resistance is less than 5 ohms, go to next step. If resistance is 5 ohms or more, repair open in Black wire (ground circuit).

12) Disconnect right position sensor harness connector. Measure resistance between right position sensor harness connector terminal No. 3 (Black wire) and ground. If resistance is more than 10 k/ohms, repair module communications concern. See MODULE COMMUNICATIONS NETWORK – WINDSTAR article. If resistance is 10 k/ohms or less, replace right position sensor.

TEST C: NO COMMUNICATION WITH REAR ELECTRONICS MODULE (REM)

NOTE: Turn ignition switch from OFF to RUN position to enable switched system power feature. Switched system power will remain active for 30 minutes after ignition switch is turned to OFF position.

1) Turn ignition switch to OFF position. Remove fuse No. 16 (10-amp) from Fuse Junction Box (FJB). Turn ignition switch to RUN position. Measure voltage between FJB fuse No. 16 input terminal and ground. If voltage is more than 10 volts, install fuse No. 16 and go to next step. If voltage is 10 volts or less, repair FJB power supply circuit. See appropriate wiring diagram in POWER DISTRIBUTION article in WIRING DIAGRAMS.

2) Turn ignition switch to OFF position. Disconnect REM 20-pin harness connector C343. Measure voltage between REM harness connector C343 terminal No. 3 (White/Yellow wire) and ground. Turn ignition switch to RUN position. If voltage is more than 10 volts, go to next step. If voltage is 10 volts or less, repair open in White/Yellow wire.

3) Turn ignition switch to OFF position. Disconnect REM harness connectors C341 (22-pin) and C342 (26-pin). Measure resistances between REM harness connector C341 terminal No. 12 (Black wire), REM harness connector C342 terminals No. 11,12, 25 and 26 (all Black wires) and ground. If all resistances are less than 5 ohms, repair module communications concern. See MODULE COMMUNICATIONS NETWORK – WINDSTAR article. If any resistance is 5 ohms or more, repair open in appropriate ground circuit(s).

TEST D: BROKEN CABLE DETECTED

1) Turn overhead console on/off switch to OFF position. Inspect cable attachment on power sliding door center roller hinge. Check for missing clip. Check that clip eyelet is seated over hinge pin and tab is seated behind pin. If cable attachments are okay, go to next step. If cable attachments are not okay, repair cable attachment. If retaining clip is missing, install a new retaining clip. If cable is damaged or broken, replace power sliding door actuator drive assembly.

2) Manually open and close power sliding door while observing cable movement. If cable retracts into assembly actuator and tension remains consistent, go to next step. If cable does not retract into assembly actuator and tension does not remain consistent, replace power sliding door actuator drive assembly.

3) Remove Fuse Junction Box (FJB) fuse No. 6 (15-amp). Wait 30 seconds and install fuse No. 6. Close power sliding door and press overhead console on/off switch to ON position. Using New Generation Star (NGS) tester, perform Left Power Sliding Door Module (LPSDM) or Right Power Sliding Door Module (RPSDM) self-test. If power sliding door cycled open and closed during self-test and DTC B2338 was retrieved, replace appropriate power sliding door module. If DTC B2338 was not retrieved, system is operating correctly. Initialize power sliding doors. If power sliding door did not cycle correctly and DTCs B2363, B2364, B2483, B2591 or B2605 are retrieved, perform appropriate test in accordance with DTC retrieved. See LEFT POWER SLIDING DOOR MODULE DTC INDEX and/or REAR ELECTRONIC MODULE (REM) DTC INDEX table under SELF-DIAGNOSTIC SYSTEM. If power sliding door did not cycle correctly and DTCs B2363, B2364, B2483, B2591 or B2605 are not retrieved, replace appropriate power sliding door actuator drive assembly.

TEST E: EXCEEDED TIME ALLOWED TO CINCH DOOR

NOTE: Repair all other DTCs before proceeding with this test.

1) Press overhead console on/off switch to OFF position. Manually open and close power sliding door while inspecting wedge alignment, front and rear striker alignment, sliding door roller hinges, door tracks and runs, weather-strips and manual operating effort. If power sliding door operates correctly manually, go to next step. If power sliding door does not operate correctly manually, repair sliding door mechanical system as necessary.

2) Check power sliding door alignment and adjustment. If power sliding door alignment and adjustment is correct, go to next step for left power sliding door, or go to step 4) for right power sliding door. If alignment and/or adjustment are not correct, repair or adjust sliding door. See POWER SLIDING DOOR ADJUSTMENT under ADJUSTMENTS.

3) Turn ignition switch to RUN position. Using a voltmeter, backprobe between Left Power Sliding Door Module (LPSDM) 4-pin harness connector C354 terminal No. 4 (Red wire) and ground. Press left "B" pillar open/close switch to operate power sliding door to full open then full close positions while monitoring voltage readings. If voltage is always greater than 10.5 volts, repair or adjust power sliding door as necessary. Initialize power sliding doors. If voltage is lower than 10.5 volts, check charging system to diagnose low system voltage. See appropriate GENERATORS article in STARTING & CHARGING SYSTEMS and/or see appropriate wiring diagram in POWER DISTRIBUTION article in WIRING DIAGRAMS. Initialize power sliding doors.

4) Turn ignition switch to RUN position. Using a voltmeter, backprobe between Right Power Sliding Door Module (RPSDM) 4-pin harness connector C351 terminal No. 4 (Red wire) and ground. Press right "B" pillar open/close switch to operate power sliding door to full open then full close positions while monitoring voltage readings. If voltage is always greater than 10.5 volts, repair or adjust power sliding door as necessary. Initialize power sliding doors. If voltage is lower than 10.5 volts, check charging system to diagnose low system voltage. See appropriate GENERATORS article in STARTING & CHARGING SYSTEMS and/or see appropriate wiring diagram in POWER DISTRIBUTION article in WIRING DIAGRAMS.

TEST F: POWER SLIDING DOOR DID NOT REACH FULL OPEN POSITION DURING SELF-TEST

NOTE: Repair all other DTCs before proceeding with this test.

1) Using New Generation Star (NGS) tester, perform Left Power Sliding Door Module (LPSDM) and Right Power Sliding Door Module (RPSDM) self-tests. If DTC B2363 is not retrieved, go to next step. If DTC B2363 is retrieved, perform TEST G: POSITION SENSOR SYSTEM FAILURE.

2) Press overhead console on/off switch to OFF position. Manually open power sliding door while observing front and rear latches for sticking or binding. Make sure latches fully release without increased effort. If power sliding doors release correctly, go to next step. If power sliding doors do not release correctly, repair latches as necessary.

3) Press overhead console on/off switch to OFF position. Manually open and close power sliding door while inspecting wedge alignment, front and rear striker alignment, sliding door roller hinges, door tracks and runs, weather-strips and manual operating effort. If power sliding door does not operate correctly manually, go to next step. If power sliding door operates correctly manually, clear all DTCs and repeat appropriate self-test. See appropriate DTC index or SYMPTOM CHART table under SELF-DIAGNOSTIC SYSTEM to continue diagnosis.

4) Disconnect front and rear cables from center roller hinge. Manually open and close power sliding door. If power sliding door operates correctly manually, replace appropriate power sliding door actuator drive assembly. Initialize power sliding doors. If power sliding door does not operate correctly manually, repair sliding door mechanical system as necessary.

TEST G: POSITION SENSOR SYSTEM FAILURE

1) Using New Generation Star (NGS) tester, perform Left Power Sliding Door Module (LPSDM) and Right Power Sliding Door Module (RPSDM) self-tests. If DTC B2363 is retrieved from LPSDM, go to next step. If DTC B2363 is retrieved from RPSDM, go to step 7).

2) Access position sensor on left actuator drive assembly. If position sensor is installed and seated correctly, go to next step. If it is not installed or seated correctly, install correctly. Repeat LPSDM self-test. If DTC B2363 is retrieved, go to next step. If DTC B2363 is not retrieved, test system for normal operation.

3) Remove Fuse Junction Box (FJB) fuse No. 6 (15-amp). Wait 30 seconds and reinstall fuse. Carry out power sliding door initializing procedure. If power sliding door does not open and close completely, go to next step. If power sliding door opens and closes completely, repeat LPSDM self-test. Repair any remaining DTCs. See LEFT POWER SLIDING DOOR MODULE DTC INDEX table under SELF-DIAGNOSTIC SYSTEM.

4) Close power sliding door. Turn ignition switch to RUN position. Verify overhead console on/off switch is in ON position. Using a voltmeter, backprobe between left position sensor 4-pin harness connector terminal No. 3 (White wire) and ground. Press left "B" pillar open/close switch. If voltage is approximately 5 volts, go to next step. If voltage is not approximately 5 volts, replace LPSDM. Initialize power sliding doors.

5) Close power sliding door. Using an ohmmeter, backprobe left position sensor 4-pin harness connector terminal No. 4 (White wire) and ground. Press left "B" pillar open/close switch. If resistance is less than 5 ohms, go to next step. If resistance is 5 ohms or more, replace LPSDM. Initialize power sliding doors.

6) Remove FJB fuse No. 6 (15-amp). Install a new left position sensor. Install FJB fuse No. 6. Close power sliding door completely. Perform LPSDM self-test. If DTC B2363 is retrieved, remove new position switch, install previous position sensor and replace LPSDM. If any other DTC is retrieved, perform appropriate test in accordance with DTC retrieved. See LEFT POWER SLIDING DOOR MODULE DTC INDEX table under SELF-DIAGNOSTIC SYSTEM. If no DTCs are retrieved, system is operating correctly.

7) Access right position sensor on right actuator drive assembly. If right position sensor is installed and seated correctly, go to next step. If right position sensor is not installed or seated correctly, install correctly. Repeat RPSDM self-test. If DTC B2363 is retrieved, go to next step. If DTC B2363 is not retrieved, test system for normal operation.

8) Remove Fuse Junction Box (FJB) fuse No. 6 (15-amp). Wait 30 seconds and install fuse. Carry out power sliding door initializing procedure. If power sliding door does not open and close completely, go to next step. If power sliding door opens and closes completely, repeat RPSDM self-test. Repair any remaining DTCs. See RIGHT POWER SLIDING DOOR MODULE DTC INDEX table under SELF-DIAGNOSTIC SYSTEM.

9) Close power sliding door. Turn ignition switch to RUN position. Verify overhead console on/off switch is in ON position. Using a voltmeter, backprobe between right position sensor 4-pin harness connector terminal No. 3 (Black wire) and ground. Press right "B" pillar open/close switch. If voltage is approximately 5 volts, go to next step. If voltage is not approximately 5 volts, replace RPSDM.

10) Close power sliding door. Using an ohmmeter, backprobe between right position sensor 4-pin harness connector terminal No. 4 (Black wire) and ground. Press right "B" pillar open/close switch. If resistance is less than 5 ohms, go to next step. If resistance is 5 ohms or more, replace RPSDM.

11) Remove FJB fuse No. 6 (15-amp). Install a new right position sensor. Install FJB fuse No. 6. Close power sliding door completely. Perform RPSDM self-test. If DTC B2363 is retrieved, remove new position switch, install previous position sensor and replace RPSDM. Perform RPSDM self-test. If any other DTC is retrieved, perform appropriate test in accordance with DTC retrieved. See RIGHT POWER SLIDING DOOR MODULE DTC INDEX table under SELF-DIAGNOSTIC SYSTEM. If no DTCs are retrieved, system is operating correctly.

TEST H: FUEL FILLER DOOR OPEN CIRCUIT

1) Ensure fuel filler door magnet is correctly attached and aligned. Ensure fuel filler door switch is correctly seated. If fuel door is correctly aligned, go to next step. If fuel door is not correctly aligned, repair fuel filler door as necessary.

2) Turn ignition switch to RUN position. Using New Generation Star (NGS) tester, monitor Left Power Sliding Door (LPSDM) PID FUEL_DR. Ensure fuel filler door is completely closed. If PID reads NOTACT, go to next step. If PID reads ACTIVE, go to step 4).

3) Using NGS tester, monitor LPSDM PID FUEL_DR. Open and close fuel filler door while observing PID. If PID does not read NOTACT when door is closed and ACTIVE when door is open, go to next step. If PID reads NOTACT when door is closed and ACTIVE when door is open, clear LPSDM DTCs and repeat LPSDM self-test. If DTC B2364 is retrieved, replace LPSDM.

4) Disconnect fuel door switch 2-pin harness connector C314. Measure resistance between fuel door switch harness connector C314 terminal No. 1 (Black wire) and ground. If resistance is less than 5 ohms, go to next step. If resistance is 5 ohms or more, repair open in Black wire.

5) Connect a jumper wire between fuel filler door switch harness connector C314 terminals (Black wire and Gray/Black wire). Using NGS tester, monitor LPSDM PID FUEL_DR. If PID FUEL_DR reads ACTIVE, go to next step. If PID FUEL_DR reads NOTACT, replace fuel filler switch.

6) Disconnect LPSDM 12-pin harness connector C355. Measure resistance between LPSDM harness connector C355 terminal No. 9 (Gray/Black wire) and fuel filler switch harness connector C314 Gray/Black wire terminal. If resistance is less than 5 ohms, replace LPSDM. If resistance is 5 ohms or more, repair open in Gray/Black wire.

TEST I: "B" PILLAR OPEN/CLOSE SWITCH CIRCUIT SHORT TO GROUND

1) Using New Generation Star (NGS) tester, perform Left Power Sliding Door Module (LPSDM) and Right Power Sliding Door Module (RPSDM) self-tests. If DTC B2365 is retrieved from LPSDM, go to next step. If DTC B2365 is retrieved from RPSDM, go to step 5).

2) Turn ignition switch to RUN position. Using NGS tester, monitor LPSDM PID SD_B_SW. Ensure left "B" pillar open/close switch is not pressed. If PID reads ACTIVE, go to next step. If PID reads NOTACT, clear LPSDM DTCs and repeat LPSDM self-test. If DTC B2365 is retrieved, replace LPSDM.

3) Disconnect left "B" pillar open/close switch 6-pin harness connector C942. Using NGS tester, monitor LPSDM PID SD_B_SW. If PID still reads ACTIVE, go to next step. If PID reads NOTACT, replace left "B" pillar open/close switch.

4) Disconnect LPSDM 12-pin harness connector C355. Measure resistance between LPSDM harness connector C355 terminal No. 3 (Tan/Light Blue wire) and ground. If resistance is more than 10 k/ohms, replace LPSDM. If resistance is 10 k/ohms or less, repair short to ground in Tan/Light Blue wire.

5) Turn ignition switch to RUN position. Using NGS tester, monitor RPSDM PID SD_B_SW. Ensure right "B" pillar open/close switch is not pressed. If PID reads ACTIVE, go to next step. If PID reads NOTACT, clear RPSDM DTCs and repeat RPSDM self-test. If DTC B2365 is retrieved, replace RPSDM.

6) Disconnect right "B" pillar open/close switch 6-pin harness connector C941. Using NGS tester, monitor RPSDM PID SD_B_SW. If PID still reads ACTIVE, go to next step. If PID reads NOTACT, replace right "B" pillar open/close switch.

7) Disconnect RPSDM 12-pin harness connector C352. Measure resistance between RPSDM harness connector C352 terminal No. 3 (Tan/Light Blue wire) and ground. If resistance is more than 10 k/ohms, replace RPSDM. If resistance is 10 k/ohms or less, repair short to ground in Tan/Light Blue wire.

TEST J: POWER SLIDING DOOR OPEN/CLOSE SWITCH CIRCUIT SHORT TO GROUND

1) Using New Generation Star (NGS) tester, perform Left Power Sliding Door Module (LPSDM) and Right Power Sliding Door Module (RPSDM) self-tests. If DTC B2366 is retrieved from LPSDM, go to next step. If DTC B2366 is retrieved from RPSDM, go to step 5).

2) Turn ignition switch to RUN position. Using NGS tester, monitor LPSDM PID SD_OPSW. Ensure overhead console open/close switch is not pressed. If PID reads ACTIVE, go to next step. If PID reads NOTACT, clear LPSDM DTCs and repeat LPSDM self-test. If DTC B2366 is retrieved, replace LPSDM.

3) Disconnect overhead console switch 8-pin harness connector C915. Using NGS tester, monitor LPSDM PID SD_OPSW. If PID reads ACTIVE, go to next step. If PID reads NOTACT, replace overhead console switch assembly.

4) Disconnect LPSDM 12-pin harness connector C355. Measure resistance between LPSDM harness connector C355 terminal No. 2 (White/Light Green wire) and ground. If resistance is more than 10 k/ohms, replace LPSDM. If resistance is 10 k/ohms or less, repair short to ground in White/Light Green wire.

5) Turn ignition switch to RUN position. Using NGS tester, monitor RPSDM PID SD_OPSW. Ensure overhead console open/close switch is not pressed. If PID reads ACTIVE, go to next step. If PID reads NOTACT, clear RPSDM DTCs and repeat RPSDM self-test. If DTC B2366 is retrieved, replace RPSDM.

6) Disconnect overhead console switch 8-pin harness connector C915. Using NGS tester, monitor RPSDM PID SD_OPSW. If PID still reads ACTIVE, go to next step. If PID reads NOTACT, replace overhead console switch assembly.

7) Disconnect RPSDM 12-pin harness connector C352. Measure resistance between RPSDM harness connector C352 terminal No. 2 (Light Green/Red wire) and ground. If resistance is more than 10 k/ohms, replace RPSDM. If resistance is 10 k/ohms or less, repair short to ground in Light Green/Red wire.

TEST K: POWER SLIDING DOOR DETENT SWITCH CIRCUIT SHORT TO GROUND

1) Using New Generation Star (NGS) tester, perform Left Power Sliding Door Module (LPSDM) and Right Power Sliding Door Module (RPSDM) self-tests. If DTC B2374 is retrieved from LPSDM, go to next step. If DTC B2374 is retrieved from RPSDM, go to step 10).

2) Ensure power sliding door is completely closed and latched. Turn ignition switch to RUN position. Using NGS tester, monitor LPSDM PID LATCHSW. If PID reads NOTACT, go to next step. If PID reads ACTIVE, go to step 5).

3) Ensure power sliding door is closed. Press overhead console on/off switch to OFF position. Monitor LPSDM PID LATCHSW. Using interior door handle, slowly open power sliding door while monitoring PID LATCHSW for states listed below:

NOTACT – with door completely closed and latched.

ACTIVE – as interior handle is activated to release latch.

NOTACT – as handle is released, latch is fully released and power sliding door contacts are still touching.

NOTACT – as door is opened and power sliding door contacts separate. Slowly close power sliding door while monitoring PID LATCHSW for states listed below:

NOTACT – as door is closing.

NOTACT – as power sliding door contacts touch.

ACTIVE – as latch reaches first latch position (door partially latched).

NOTACT – as door is moved to completely closed and latched position. If PID states do not change as described, go to next step. If PID states change as described, repeat LPSDM self-test If DTC B2374 is retrieved, replace LPSDM. If other DTCs are retrieved, perform appropriate test in accordance with DTC retrieved. See LEFT POWER SLIDING DOOR MODULE DTC INDEX table under SELF-DIAGNOSTIC SYSTEM.

4) Ensure power sliding door is completely closed and latched. Perform LPSDM self-test. If DTC B2374 is only DTC retrieved, there may be an intermittent concern. DTC B2374 can also be set in error to system conditions when self-test was initiated. Check door adjustment, power sliding door latch for sticking or binding and interior and exterior handle operation for sticking or binding, but do not repair any condition unless it is identified. If any other DTCs are retrieved, perform appropriate test in accordance with DTC retrieved. See LEFT POWER SLIDING DOOR MODULE DTC INDEX table under SELF-DIAGNOSTIC SYSTEM. If no DTCs are retrieved, system is operating correctly.

5) Ensure power sliding door is completely closed and latched. Disconnect LPSDM 12-pin harness connector C355. Measure resistance between LPSDM harness connector C355 terminal No. 5 (White wire) and ground. If resistance is 10 k/ohms or less, go to next step. If resistance is more than 10 k/ohms, repeat LPSDM self-test. If DTC B2374 is retrieved, replace LPSDM.

6) Ensure power sliding door is completely closed and latched. Disconnect LPSDM 4-pin harness connector C354. Measure resistance between LPSDM harness connector C355 terminal No. 5 (White wire) and ground. If resistance is more than 10 k/ohms, go to next step. If resistance is 10 k/ohms or less, go to step **8**).

7) Ensure power sliding door is completely closed and latched. Disconnect power sliding door detent switch 2-pin harness connector C704. Measure resistance between LPSDM harness connector C355 terminal No. 5 (White wire) and LPSDM harness connector C354 terminal No. 2 (Yellow/Red wire). If resistance is more than 10 k/ohms, replace PSD detent switch. If resistance is 10 k/ohms or less, repair possible short between White wire and Yellow/Red wire or damaged PSD contacts.

8) Disconnect left power sliding door contact 8-pin harness connector C338. See WIRING DIAGRAMS for wire colors to ensure correct 8-pin harness connector is disconnected. Measure resistance between LPSDM harness connector C355 terminal No. 5 (White wire) and ground. If resistance is more than 10 k/ohms, go to next step. If resistance is 10 k/ohms or less, repair short to ground in White wire.

9) Disconnect left power sliding door contact 8-pin harness connector C700. See WIRING DIAGRAMS for wire colors to ensure correct 8-pin harness connector is disconnected. Measure resistance between left sliding door contact harness connector C700 terminal No. 7 (White wire) and ground. If resistance is more than 10 k/ohms, check left sliding door contact alignment. If alignment is correct, replace left sliding door contact. If resistance is 10 k/ohms or less, repair short to ground in White wire.

10) Ensure power sliding door is completely closed and latched. Turn ignition switch to RUN position. Using NGS tester, monitor RPSDM PID LATCHSW. If PID reads NOTACT, go to next step. If PID reads ACTIVE, go to step **13**).

11) Ensure power sliding door is closed. Press overhead console on/off switch to OFF position. Monitor RPSDM PID LATCHSW. Using interior door handle, slowly open power sliding door while monitoring PID LATCHSW for states listed below:

NOTACT – with door completely closed and latched.

ACTIVE – as interior handle is activated to release latch.

NOTACT – as handle is released, latch is fully released and power sliding door contacts are still touching.

NOTACT – as door is opened and power sliding door contacts separate. Slowly close power sliding door while monitoring PID LATCHSW for states listed below:

NOTACT – as door is closing.

NOTACT – as power sliding door contacts touch.

ACTIVE – as latch reaches first latch position (door partially latched).

NOTACT – as door is moved to completely closed and latched position. If PID states do not change as described, go to next step. If PID states change as described, repeat RPSDM self-test. If DTC B2374 is retrieved, replace RPSDM. If other DTCs are retrieved, perform appropriate test in accordance with DTC retrieved, See RIGHT POWER SLIDING DOOR MODULE DTC INDEX table under SELF-DIAGNOSTIC SYSTEM.

12) Ensure power sliding door is completely closed and latched. Perform RPSDM self-test. If DTC B2374 is only DTC retrieved, there may be an intermittent concern. DTC B2374 can also be set in error to system conditions when self-test was initiated. Check door adjustment, power sliding door latch for sticking or binding and interior and exterior handle operation for sticking or binding, but do not repair any condition unless it is identified. If any other DTCs are retrieved, perform appropriate test in accordance with DTC retrieved, See RIGHT POWER SLIDING DOOR MODULE DTC INDEX table under SELF-DIAGNOSTIC SYSTEM. If no DTCs are retrieved, system is operating correctly.

13) Ensure power sliding door is completely closed and latched. Disconnect RPSDM 12-pin harness connector C352. Measure resistance between RPSDM harness connector C352 terminal No. 5 (White wire) and ground. If resistance is 10 k/ohms or less, go to next step. If resistance is more than 10 k/ohms, repeat RPSDM self-test. If DTC B2374 is retrieved, replace RPSDM.

14) Ensure power sliding door is completely closed and latched. Disconnect RPSDM 4-pin harness connector C351. Measure resistance between RPSDM harness connector C352 terminal No. 5 (White wire) and ground. If resistance is more than 10 k/ohms, go to next step. If resistance is 10 k/ohms or less, go to step **16**)

15) Ensure power sliding door is completely closed and latched. Disconnect power sliding door detent switch 2-pin harness connector C804. Measure resistance between RPSDM harness connector C352 terminal No. 5 (White wire) and RPSDM harness connector C351 terminal No. 2 (Yellow/Red wire). If resistance is more than 10 k/ohms, replace power sliding door detent switch. If resistance is 10 k/ohms or less, replace PSD contacts.

16) Disconnect right power sliding door contact 8-pin harness connector C337. See WIRING DIAGRAMS for wire colors to ensure correct 8-pin harness connector is disconnected. Measure resistance between RPSDM harness connector C352 terminal No. 5 (White wire) and ground. If resistance is more than 10 k/ohms, go to next step. If resistance is 10 k/ohms or less, repair short to ground in White wire.

17) Disconnect right power sliding door contact 8-pin harness connector C800. See WIRING DIAGRAMS for wire colors to ensure correct 8-pin harness connector is disconnected. Measure resistance between right sliding door contact harness connector C800 terminal No. 7 (White wire) and ground. If resistance is more than 10 k/ohms, check sliding door contact alignment. If alignment is correct, replace right sliding door contact. If resistance is 10 k/ohms or less, repair short to ground in White wire.

TEST L: PARK ENABLE SIGNAL OPEN CIRCUIT

1) Using New Generation Star (NGS) tester, perform Rear Electronic Module (REM) self-test. If no other DTC is retrieved, go to next step. If DTC U1059 is retrieved, perform PCM self-test.

2) Check vehicle for left and right power sliding doors. If vehicle is equipped with left and right power sliding doors, go to next step. If vehicle only has right side power sliding door, go to step 7).

3) Using NGS tester, perform Left Power Sliding Door Module (LPSDM) and Right Power Sliding Door Module (RPSDM) self-tests. If DTC B2483 is retrieved from both modules, go to next step. If DTC B2483 is retrieved from RPSDM only, go to step 7). If DTC B2483 is retrieved from LPSDM only, go to step 9).

4) Disconnect RPSDM 12-pin harness connector C352. Measure voltage between RPSDM harness connector C352 terminal No. 7 (Light Blue/Pink wire) and ground. If voltage is more than 10 volts, go to next step. If voltage is 10 volts or less, go to step 6).

5) Disconnect REM 22-pin harness connector C341. Measure voltage between RPSDM harness connector C352 terminal No. 7 (Light Blue/Pink wire) and ground. If voltage is more than 10 volts, repair short to voltage. If voltage is 10 volts or less, replace REM.

6) Turn ignition switch to OFF position. Disconnect REM 22-pin harness connector C341. Measure resistance between RPSDM harness connector C352 terminal No. 7 (Light Blue/Pink wire) and REM harness connector C341 terminal No. 9 (Light Blue wire). If resistance is less than 5 ohms, replace REM. If resistance is 5 ohms or more, repair open in Light Blue/Pink wire.

7) Disconnect RPSDM 12-pin harness connector C352. Turn ignition switch to RUN position. Place vehicle shifter handle in Park position. Measure resistance between RPSDM harness connector C352 terminal No. 7 (Light Blue/Pink wire) and ground. If resistance is 5 ohms or more, go to next step. If resistance is less than 5 ohms, clear RPSDM DTCs and repeat RPSDM self-test. If DTC B2483 is retrieved, replace RPSDM.

8) Turn ignition switch to OFF position. Disconnect REM 22-pin harness connector C341. Measure resistance between RPSDM harness connector C352 terminal No. 7 (Light Blue/Pink wire) and REM harness connector C341 terminal No. 9 (Light Blue/Pink wire). If resistance is less than 5 ohms, replace REM. If resistance is 5 ohms or more, repair open in Light Blue/Pink wire.

9) Disconnect LPSDM 12-pin harness connector C355. Turn ignition switch to RUN position. Place vehicle shifter handle in Park position. Measure resistance between LPSDM harness connector C355 terminal No. 7 (Light Blue/Pink wire) and ground. If resistance is 5 ohms or more, go to next step. If resistance is less than 5 ohms, clear LPSDM DTCs and repeat LPSDM self-test. If DTC B2483 is retrieved, replace LPSDM.

10) Turn ignition switch to OFF position. Disconnect REM 22-pin harness connector C341. Measure resistance between LPSDM harness connector C355 terminal No. 7 (Light Blue/Pink wire) and REM harness connector C341 terminal No. 9 (Light Blue/Pink wire). If resistance is less than 5 ohms, replace REM. If resistance is 5 ohms or more, repair open in Light Blue/Pink wire.

TEST M: NO POWER SLIDING DOOR DETENT SWITCH DETECTED ON CLOSING & DOOR REVERSED

1) Ensure power sliding door is completely closed and latched. Manually open and close power sliding door. Check wedge alignment and front and rear striker alignment. If power sliding door adjustment and alignment is correct, go to next step. If power sliding door adjustment and alignment is incorrect, adjust strikers and wedges. See POWER SLIDING DOOR ADJUSTMENT under ADJUSTMENTS.

2) Using New Generation Star (NGS) tester, perform Left Power Sliding Door Module (LPSDM) and Right Power Sliding Door Module (RPSDM) self-tests. If DTC B2589 is retrieved from LPSDM, go to next step. If DTC B2589 is retrieved from RPSDM, go to step 12).

3) If DTC B2374 is not also retrieved, go to next step. If DTC B2374 is also retrieved, perform TEST K: POWER SLIDING DOOR DETENT SWITCH CIRCUIT SHORT TO GROUND.

4) Ensure fuel filler door is completely closed. Open left power sliding door. Inspect fuel filler interlock catch located toward bottom of "C" pillar opening. Ensure catch moves freely, and when catch is rotated it returns to open position without binding or sticking. If fuel filler interlock catch

operates correctly, go to next step. If fuel filler interlock catch does not operate correctly, replace fuel filler interlock catch.

5) Disconnect left power sliding door contact 8-pin harness connector C338. See WIRING DIAGRAMS for wire colors to ensure correct 8-pin harness connector is disconnected. Turn ignition switch to RUN position. Measure voltage between left power sliding door contact harness connector C338 terminal No. 4 (Gray/Red wire) and ground. If voltage is present, go to next step. If voltage is not present, go to step 7).

6) Turn ignition switch to OFF position. Disconnect LPSDM 4-pin harness connector C354. Turn ignition switch to RUN position. Measure voltage between left power sliding door contact harness connector C338 terminal No. 4 (Gray/Red wire) and ground. If voltage is present, repair short to voltage in Gray/Red wire. If voltage is not present, replace LPSDM.

7) Connect left power sliding door contact 8-pin harness connector C338. Remove sliding door trim panel. Using NGS tester, trigger LPSDM active command RELEASE ON and OFF while observing release actuator operation. If release actuator does not return to retracted state after 10 seconds, go to next step. If release actuator returns to retracted state after 10 seconds, go to step 9).

8) Remove remote control release assembly. Disconnect latch release actuator from remote control release assembly. Operate remote control release assembly and inspect for damage or binding. If remote control release assembly operates correctly, replace latch release actuator. If remote control release assembly does not operate correctly, replace remote control release assembly.

9) Ensure power sliding door is closed. Press overhead console on/off switch to OFF position. Using NGS tester, monitor LPSDM PID LATCHSW. Using interior door handle, slowly open power sliding door while monitoring PID LATCHSW for states listed below:

NOTACT – with door completely closed and latched.

ACTIVE – as interior handle is activated to release latch.

NOTACT – as handle is released, latch is fully released and power sliding door contacts are still touching.

NOTACT – as door is opened and power sliding door contacts separate. Slowly close power sliding door while monitoring PID LATCHSW for states listed below:

NOTACT – as door is closing.

NOTACT – as power sliding door contacts touch.

ACTIVE – as latch reaches first latch position (door partially latched).

NOTACT – as door is moved to completely closed and latched position. If PID states do not change as described, go to next step. If PID states change as described, go to step 11).

10) Disconnect left power sliding door contact 8-pin harness connector C700. See WIRING DIAGRAMS for wire colors to ensure correct 8-pin harness connector is disconnected. Measure resistance between left power sliding door contact harness connector terminals No. 4 (Yellow/Red wire) and No. 7 (White wire). With power sliding door open, slowly operate rear power sliding door latch to first latch position and then to second latch position. Resistance should be momentarily less than 5 ohms in first latch position, then open circuit and then momentarily less than 5 ohms in second latch position then open circuit again. Using interior or exterior door handle, release rear power sliding door latch. If resistance is correct when latch is operated, check sliding door contact alignment. If alignment is correct, replace left power sliding door contact. Initialize power sliding doors. If resistance is not correct when latch is operated, replace left power sliding door detent switch.

11) Disconnect negative battery cable. Wait 30 seconds and then connect negative battery cable. Turn ignition switch to RUN position. Perform LPSDM self-test. If power sliding door opened and closed during self-test and DTC B2589 was only DTC retrieved, replace LPSDM. If power sliding door did not open and close completely during self-test and DTC B2589 is only DTC retrieved, repair power sliding door alignment or adjustment. See POWER SLIDING DOOR ADJUSTMENT under ADJUSTMENTS. Initialize power sliding doors. If power sliding doors do or do not open and close completely during self-test and other DTCs are retrieved, perform appropriate test in accordance with DTC retrieved. See LEFT POWER SLIDING DOOR MODULE DTC INDEX table under SELF-DIAGNOSTIC SYSTEM.

12) Using NGS tester, perform RPSDM self-test. If DTC B2589 is only DTC retrieved, go to next step. If DTC B2374 is also retrieved, perform TEST K: POWER SLIDING DOOR DETENT SWITCH CIRCUIT SHORT TO GROUND.

13) Disconnect right power sliding door contact 8-pin harness connector C337. See WIRING DIAGRAMS for wire colors to ensure correct 8-pin harness connector is disconnected. Turn ignition switch to RUN position. Measure voltage between right power sliding door contact harness connector C337 terminal No. 4 (Gray/Red wire) and ground. If voltage is present, go to next step. If voltage is not present, go to step **15)**

14) Turn ignition switch to OFF position. Disconnect RPSDM 4-pin harness connector C351. Turn ignition switch to RUN position. Measure voltage between right power sliding door contact harness connector C337 terminal No. 4 (Gray/Red wire) and ground. If voltage is present, repair short to voltage in Gray/Red wire. If voltage is not present, replace RPSDM.

15) Connect right power sliding door contact 8-pin harness connector C337. Remove sliding door trim panel. Using NGS tester, trigger RPSDM active command RELEASE ON and OFF while observing release actuator operation. If release actuator does not return to retracted state after 10 seconds, go to next step. If release actuator returns to retracted state after 10 seconds, go to step **17)**.

16) Remove remote control release assembly. Disconnect latch release actuator from remote control release assembly. Operate remote control release assembly and inspect for damage or binding. If remote control release assembly operates correctly, replace latch release actuator. If remote control release assembly does not operate correctly, replace remote control release assembly.

17) Ensure power sliding door is closed. Press overhead console on/off switch to OFF position. Using NGS tester, monitor RPSDM PID LATCHSW. Using interior door handle, slowly open power sliding door while monitoring PID LATCHSW for states listed below:
NOTACT – with door completely closed and latched.
ACTIVE – as interior handle is activated to release latch.
NOTACT – as handle is released, latch is fully released and power sliding door contacts are still touching.
NOTACT – as door is opened and power sliding door contacts separate. Slowly close power sliding door while monitoring PID LATCHSW for states listed below:
NOTACT – as door is closing.
NOTACT – as power sliding door contacts touch.
ACTIVE – as latch reaches first latch position (door partially latched).
NOTACT – as door is moved to completely closed and latched position. If PID states do not change as described, go to next step. If PID states change as described, go to step **19)**.

18) Disconnect right power sliding door contact 8-pin harness connector C800. See WIRING DIAGRAMS for wire colors to ensure correct 8-pin harness connector is disconnected. Measure resistance between right power sliding door contact harness connector terminals No. 4 (Yellow/Red wire) and No. 7 (White wire). With power sliding door open, slowly operate rear power sliding door latch to first latch position and then to second latch position. Resistance should be momentarily less than 5 ohms in first latch position, then open circuit and then momentarily less than 5 ohms in second latch position then open circuit again. Using interior or exterior door handle, release rear power sliding door latch. If resistance is correct when latch is operated, check sliding door contact alignment. If alignment is correct, replace right power sliding door contact. If resistance is not correct when latch is operated, replace right power sliding door detent switch.

19) Disconnect negative battery cable. Wait 30 seconds and then connect negative. Turn ignition switch to RUN position. Perform RPSDM self-test. If power sliding door opened and closed during self-test and DTC B2589 was only DTC retrieved, replace RPSDM. If power sliding door did not open and close completely during self-test and DTC B2589 is only DTC retrieved, repair power sliding door alignment or adjustment. See POWER SLIDING DOOR ADJUSTMENT under ADJUSTMENTS. Initialize power sliding doors. If power sliding doors do or do not open and close completely during self-test and other DTCs are retrieved,

perform appropriate test in accordance with DTC retrieved. See RIGHT POWER SLIDING DOOR MODULE DTC INDEX table under SELF-DIAGNOSTIC SYSTEM.

TEST N: NO POWER SLIDING DOOR DETENT SWITCH DETECTED ON UNLATCH

1) Using New Generation Star (NGS) tester, perform Left Power Sliding Door Module (LPSDM) and Right Power Sliding Door Module (RPSDM) self-tests. If DTC B2591 is retrieved from LPSDM, go to next step. If DTC B2591 is retrieved from RPSDM, go to step **18)**.

2) Ensure power sliding door is closed. Press overhead console on/off switch to OFF position. Using NGS tester, monitor LPSDM PID LATCHSW. Using interior door handle, slowly open power sliding door while monitoring PID LATCHSW for states listed below:
NOTACT – with door completely closed and latched.
ACTIVE – as interior handle is activated to release latch.
NOTACT – as handle is released, latch is fully released and power sliding door contacts are still touching.
NOTACT – as door is opened and power sliding door contacts separate. Slowly close power sliding door while monitoring PID LATCHSW for states listed below:
NOTACT – as door is closing.
NOTACT – as power sliding door contacts touch.
ACTIVE – as latch reaches first latch position (door partially latched).
NOTACT – as door is moved to completely closed and latched position. If PID states do not change as described, go to next step. If PID states change as described, go to step **11)**.

3) Ensure sliding door is completely closed and latched. Turn ignition switch to OFF position. Disconnect left power sliding door detent switch 2-pin harness connector C704. Measure resistance between left power sliding door detent switch harness connector C704 terminal No. 1 (Yellow/Red wire) and ground. If resistance is 5 ohms or more, go to next step. If resistance is less than 5 ohms, go to step **7)**.

4) Disconnect left power sliding door contact 8-pin harness connector C338. Measure resistance between left power sliding door contact harness connector C338 terminal No. 1 (Yellow/Red wire) and ground. If resistance is 5 ohms or more, go to next step. If resistance is less than 5 ohms, go to step **6)**.

5) Disconnect LPSDM 4-pin harness connector C354. Measure resistance between LPSDM harness connector C354 terminal No. 2 (Yellow/Red wire) and left power sliding door contact harness connector C338 terminal No. 1 (Yellow/Red wire). If resistance is less than 5 ohms, replace LPSDM. If resistance is 5 ohms or more, repair open in Yellow/Red wire between LPSDM and left power sliding door contact.

6) Disconnect left power sliding door contact 8-pin harness connector C700. Measure resistance between left power sliding door contact harness connector C700 terminal No. 4 (Yellow/Red wire) and left power sliding door detent switch harness connector C704 terminal No. 1 (Yellow/Red wire). If resistance is less than 5 ohms, check left power sliding door contact alignment. Repair if possible, otherwise replace left power sliding door contact. If resistance is 5 ohms or more, repair open in Yellow/Red wire between left power sliding door contact and left power sliding door detent switch.

NOTE: *Power sliding door may open during this test step.*

---

7) Turn ignition switch to RUN position. Using NGS tester, monitor LPSDM PID LATCHSW while connecting a jumper wire between left power sliding door detent switch harness terminals No. 1 (Yellow/Red wire) and No. 2 (White wire). If PID LATCHSW reads NOTACT, go to next step. If PID LATCHSW reads ACTIVE, replace left power sliding door detent switch.

8) Disconnect Left power sliding door contact 8-pin harness connector C700. Measure resistance between left power sliding door contact harness connector C700 terminal No. 7 (White wire) and left power sliding door detent switch harness connector C704 terminal No. 2 (White wire). If resistance is less than 5 ohms, go to next step. If resistance is 5 ohms or more, repair open in White wire between left power sliding door contact and left power sliding door detent switch.

9) Disconnect left power sliding door contact 8-pin harness connector C338. Turn ignition switch to RUN position. Monitor LPSDM PID LATCHSW while connecting a jumper wire between left power sliding door contact harness connector C338 terminals No. 1 (Yellow/Red wire) and No. 3 (White wire). If PID LATCHSW read NOTACT, go to next step. If PID LATCHSW reads ACTIVE, check left power sliding door contact alignment. Repair if possible, otherwise replace left power sliding door contact.

10) Disconnect LPSDM 12-pin harness connector C355. Measure resistance between LPSDM harness connector C355 terminal No. 5 (White wire) and left power sliding door contact harness connector C338 terminal No. 3 (White wire). If resistance is less than 5 ohms, replace LPSDM. If resistance is 5 ohms or more, repair open in White wire between LPSDM and left power sliding door contact.

11) Disconnect LPSDM 4-pin harness connector C354. Measure voltage between LPSDM harness connector C354 terminal No. 4 (Red/Black wire) and ground. If voltage is more than 10 volts, go to next step. If voltage is 10 volts or less, perform TEST V: LEFT POWER SLIDING DOOR INOPERATIVE – NO DTCS.

12) Ensure power sliding door is completely closed and latched. Disconnect left power sliding door latch release actuator 2-pin harness connector C703. Measure resistance between left power sliding door latch release actuator harness connector C703 terminal No. 1 (Yellow/Red wire) and ground. If resistance is less than 5 ohms, go to next step. If resistance is 5 ohms or more, repair open in Yellow/Red wire (ground circuit).

13) Ensure power sliding door is completely closed and latched. Measure voltage between left power sliding door latch release actuator harness connector C703 terminal No. 2 (Gray/Red wire) and ground. Using NGS tester, select active command POWER SLIDING DOOR CONTROL. Trigger RELEASE ON. If voltage is 10 volts or less, go to next step. If voltage is more than 10 volts, replace left power sliding door latch release actuator.

14) Ensure power sliding door is completely closed and latched. Disconnect LPSDM 4-pin harness connector C354. Measure resistance between left power sliding door latch release actuator harness connector C703 terminal No. 2 (Gray/Red wire) and ground. If resistance is more than 10 k/ohms, go to next step. If resistance is 10 k/ohms or less, repair short to ground in Gray/Red wire.

15) Disconnect left power sliding door contact 8-pin harness connector C338. Measure resistance between LPSDM harness connector C354 terminal No. 1 (Gray/Red wire) and left power sliding door contact harness connector C338 terminal No. 4 (Gray/Red wire). If resistance is less than 5 ohms, go to next step. If resistance is 5 ohms or more, repair open in Gray/Red wire between LPSDM and left power sliding door contact.

16) Disconnect left power sliding door contact 8-pin harness connector C700. Measure resistance between left power sliding door latch release actuator harness connector C703 terminal No. 2 (Gray/Red wire) and left power sliding door contact harness connector C700 terminal No. 8 (Gray/Red wire). If resistance is less than 5 ohms, go to next step. If resistance is 5 ohms or more, repair open in Gray/Red wire between left power sliding door contact and left power sliding door latch release.

17) Ensure power sliding door is completely closed and latched. Disconnect LPSDM 4-pin harness connector C354. Measure resistance between LPSDM harness connector C354 terminal No. 1 (Gray/Red wire) and left power sliding door release actuator harness connector C703 terminal No. 2 (Gray/Red wire). If resistance is less than 5 ohms, replace LPSDM. If resistance is 5 ohms or more, check left power sliding door contact alignment. Repair if possible, otherwise replace left power sliding door contact.

18) Ensure power sliding door is closed. Press overhead console on/off switch to OFF position. Monitor RPSDM PID LATCHSW. Using interior door handle, slowly open power sliding door while monitoring PID LATCHSW for states listed below:
NOTACT – with door completely closed and latched.
ACTIVE – as interior handle is activated to release latch.
NOTACT – as handle is released, latch is fully released and power sliding door contacts are still touching.

NOTACT – as door is opened and power sliding door contacts separate. Slowly close power sliding door while monitoring PID LATCHSW for states listed below:
NOTACT – as door is closing.
NOTACT – as power sliding door contacts touch.
ACTIVE – as latch reaches first latch position (door partially latched).
NOTACT – as door is moved to completely closed and latched position. If PID states do not change as described, go to next step. If PID states change as described, go to step 27).

19) Ensure power sliding door is completely closed and latched. Turn ignition switch to OFF position. Disconnect right power sliding door detent switch 2-pin harness connector C804. Measure resistance between right power sliding door detent switch harness connector C804 terminal No. 1 (Yellow/Red wire) and ground. If resistance is 5 ohms or more, go to next step. If resistance is less than 5 ohms, go to step 23).

20) Disconnect right power sliding door contact 8-pin harness connector C337. Measure resistance between right power sliding door contact harness connector C337 terminal No. 1 (Yellow/Red wire) and ground. If resistance is 5 ohms or more, go to next step. If resistance is less than 5 ohms, go to step 22).

21) Disconnect RPSDM 4-pin harness connector C351. Measure resistance between RPSDM harness connector C351 terminal No. 2 (Yellow/Red wire) and right power sliding door contact harness connector C337 terminal No. 1 (Yellow/Red wire). If resistance is less than 5 ohms, replace RPSDM. If resistance is 5 ohms or more, repair open in Yellow/Red wire between RPSDM and right power sliding door contact.

22) Disconnect right power sliding door contact 8-pin harness connector C800. Measure resistance between right power sliding door contact harness connector C800 terminal No. 4 (Yellow/Red wire) and right power sliding door detent switch harness connector C804 terminal No. 1 (Yellow/Red wire). If resistance is less than 5 ohms, check right power sliding door contact alignment. Repair if possible, otherwise replace right power sliding door contact. If resistance is 5 ohms or more, repair open in Yellow/Red wire between right power sliding door contact and right power sliding door detent switch.

NOTE: Power sliding door may open during this test step.

23) Turn ignition switch to RUN position. Using NGS tester, monitor RPSDM PID LATCHSW while connecting a jumper wire between right power sliding door detent switch harness terminals No. 1 (Yellow/Red wire) and No. 2 (White wire). If PID LATCHSW reads NOTACT, go to next step. If PID LATCHSW reads ACTIVE, replace right power sliding door detent switch.

24) Disconnect right power sliding door contact 8-pin harness connector C800. Measure resistance between right power sliding door contact harness connector C800 terminal No. 7 (White wire) and right power sliding door detent switch harness connector C804 terminal No. 2 (White wire). If resistance is less than 5 ohms, go to next step. If resistance is 5 ohms or more, repair open in White wire between right power sliding door contact and right power sliding door detent switch.

25) Disconnect right power sliding door contact 8-pin harness connector C337. Turn ignition switch to RUN position. Monitor RPSDM PID LATCHSW while connecting a jumper wire between right power sliding door contact harness connector C337 terminals No. 1 (Yellow/Red wire) and No. 3 (White wire). If PID LATCHSW reads NOTACT, go to next step. If PID LATCHSW reads ACTIVE, check right power sliding door contact alignment. Repair if possible, otherwise replace right power sliding door contact.

26) Disconnect RPSDM 12-pin harness connector C352. Measure resistance between RPSDM harness connector C352 terminal No. 5 (White wire) and right power sliding door contact harness connector C337 terminal No. 3 (White wire). If resistance is less than 5 ohms, replace RPSDM. If resistance is 5 ohms or more, repair open in White wire between RPSDM and right power sliding door contact.

27) Disconnect RPSDM 4-pin harness connector C351. Measure voltage between RPSDM harness connector C351 terminal No. 4 (Light Green/Red wire) and ground. If voltage is more than 10 volts, go to next step. If voltage is 10 volts or less, perform TEST U: RIGHT POWER SLIDING DOOR INOPERATIVE – NO DTCS.

28) Ensure power sliding door is completely closed and latched. Disconnect right power sliding door latch release actuator 2-pin harness connector C803. Measure resistance between right power sliding door latch release actuator harness connector C803 terminal No. 1 (Yellow/Red wire) and ground. If resistance is less than 5 ohms, go to next step. If resistance is 5 ohms or more, repair open in Yellow/Red wire (ground circuit).

29) Ensure power sliding door is completely closed and latched. Measure voltage between right power sliding door latch release actuator harness connector C803 terminal No. 2 (Gray/Red wire) and ground. Using NGS tester, select active command POWER SLIDING DOOR CONTROL. Trigger RELEASE ON. If voltage is 10 volts or less, go to next step. If voltage is more than 10 volts, replace right power sliding door latch release actuator.

30) Ensure power sliding door is completely closed and latched. Disconnect RPSDM 4-pin harness connector C351. Measure resistance between right power sliding door latch release actuator harness connector C803 terminal No. 2 (Gray/Red wire) and ground. If resistance is more than 10 k/ohms, go to next step. If resistance is 10 k/ohms or less, repair short to ground in Gray/Red wire.

31) Disconnect right power sliding door contact 8-pin harness connector C337. Measure resistance between RPSDM harness connector C351 terminal No. 1 (Gray/Red wire) and right power sliding door contact harness connector C337 terminal No. 4 (Gray/Red wire). If resistance is less than 5 ohms, go to next step. If resistance is 5 ohms or more, repair open in Gray/Red wire between RPSDM and right power sliding door contact.

32) Disconnect right power sliding door contact 8-pin harness connector C800. Measure resistance between right power sliding door latch release actuator harness connector C803 terminal No. 2 (Gray/Red wire) and right power sliding door contact harness connector C800 terminal No. 8 (Gray/Red wire). If resistance is less than 5 ohms, go to next step. If resistance is 5 ohms or more, repair open in Gray/Red wire between right power sliding door latch release actuator and right power sliding door contact.

33) Ensure power sliding door is completely closed and latched. Disconnect RPSDM 4-pin harness connector C351. Measure resistance between RPSDM harness connector C351 terminal No. 1 (Gray/Red wire) and right power sliding door release actuator harness connector C803 terminal No. 2 (Gray/Red wire). If resistance is less than 5 ohms, replace RPSDM. If resistance is 5 ohms or more, check right power sliding door contact alignment. Repair if possible, otherwise replace right power sliding door contact.

TEST O: DOOR NOT PULLED TO PRIMARY DURING POWER CLOSE & HIGH DUTY CYCLES

NOTE: DTC B2592 can be set as a continuous DTC due to extreme temperature variations or low battery voltage.

Using New Generation Star (NGS) tester, perform Left Power Sliding Door Module (LPSDM) and Right Power Sliding Door Module (RPSDM) self-tests. If DTC B2603 is retrieved, perform TEST R: POWER SLIDING DOOR NOT FULLY CLOSED DURING SELF-TEST. If DTC B2603 is not retrieved, system is not currently detecting conditions that would cause DTC B2592.

TEST P: DOOR REVERSED WHILE CLOSING DUE TO AN OBSTACLE

NOTE: Repair all other retrieved DTCs before proceeding with this test.

1) Press overhead console on/off switch to OFF position. Manually open and close power sliding door while inspecting wedge alignment, front and rear striker alignment, sliding door roller hinges, door tracks and runs, weather-strips and manual operating effort. If power sliding door operates correctly manually, go to next step. If power sliding door does not operate correctly manually, repair sliding door mechanical system.
2) Check sliding door alignment and adjustment. See POWER SLIDING DOOR ADJUSTMENT under ADJUSTMENTS. If sliding door adjust-

ment and alignment are correct, go to next step for left PSD and to step 5) for right PSD. If alignment or adjustment is incorrect, repair or adjust PSD.

3) Using a voltmeter, backprobe between Left Power Sliding Door Module (LPSDM) 4-pin harness connector C354 terminal No. 4 (Red wire) and ground. Press left "B" pillar open/close switch to operate power sliding door to full open then to full close positions while monitoring voltage reading. If voltage is always more than 10 volts, repeat LPSDM self-test. If DTC B2593 is retrieved and sliding door did reverse, go to next step. If DTC B2593 is retrieved and door did not reverse, replace LPSDM. If voltage is not always more than 10 volts, check charging system to diagnose low system voltage. See appropriate GENERATORS article in STARTING & CHARGING SYSTEMS and/or see appropriate wiring diagram in POWER DISTRIBUTION article in WIRING DIAGRAMS. Initialize power sliding doors.

4) Check track and rollers for an obstruction at point door reversed during self-test. If there is damage or an obstruction at point of reversal, repair damage and remove obstruction. Initialize power sliding doors. If there is no damage or an obstruction at point of reversal, replace left actuator drive assembly. Initialize power sliding doors.

5) Using a voltmeter, backprobe between Right Power Sliding Door Module (RPSDM) 4-pin harness connector C351 terminal No. 4 (Red wire) and ground. Press right "B" pillar open/close switch to operate power sliding door to full open then to full close positions while monitoring voltage reading. If voltage is always more than 10 volts, repeat RPSDM self-test. If DTC B2593 is retrieved and sliding door did reverse, go to next step. If DTC B2593 is retrieved and door did not reverse, replace RPSDM. If voltage is not always more than 10 volts, check charging system to diagnose low system voltage. See appropriate GENERATORS article in STARTING & CHARGING SYSTEMS and/or see appropriate wiring diagram in POWER DISTRIBUTION article in WIRING DIAGRAMS. Initialize power sliding doors.

6) Check track and rollers for an obstruction at point door reversed during self-test. If there is damage or an obstruction at point of reversal, repair damage and remove obstruction. Initialize power sliding doors. If there is no damage or an obstruction at point of reversal, replace right actuator drive assembly. Initialize power sliding doors.

TEST Q: NO MOVEMENT DETECTED AFTER AN UNLATCH DURING POWER OPEN

1) Using New Generation Star (NGS) tester, perform Left Power Sliding Door Module (LPSDM) and Right Power Sliding Door Module (RPSDM) self-tests. If DTC B2594 is only DTC retrieved from LPSDM, go to next step. If DTC B2594 is only DTC retrieved from RPSDM, go to step 7). If DTC B2363 is also retrieved from LPSDM self-test, perform TEST G: POSITION SENSOR SYSTEM FAILURE.

NOTE: Active command PSD_OPEN is only active for one second. Observe meter reading as command is triggered ON.

2) Ensure fuel filler door is completely closed. Turn ignition switch to RUN position. Using NGS tester, monitor LPSDM active command PSD_OPEN. Using a voltmeter, backprobe between actuator drive assembly motor 4-pin harness connector terminal "A" (Red wire) and ground. Trigger LPSDM PSD_OPEN ON. If voltage is 10 volts or less, go to next step. If voltage is more than 10 volts, go to step 4).

3) Disconnect LPSDM 4-pin harness connector C354. Measure voltage between LPSDM harness connector C354 terminal No. 4 (Red/Black wire) and ground. If voltage is 10 volts or less, perform TEST V: LEFT POWER SLIDING DOOR INOPERATIVE – NO DTCS. If voltage is more than 10 volts, replace LPSDM.

4) Using an ohmmeter, backprobe between actuator drive assembly motor 4-pin harness connector terminal "B" (Yellow wire) and ground. If resistance is less than 5 ohms, go to next step. If resistance is 5 ohms or more, replace LPSDM.

5) Ensure fuel filler door is completely closed and latched. Turn ignition switch to RUN position. Using NGS tester, monitor LPSDM active command M_CLUTCH. Using a voltmeter, backprobe between actuator drive assembly clutch 4-pin harness connector terminal No. 3 (Yellow

wire) and ground. Trigger LPSDM M_CLUTCH ON. If voltage is more than 10 volts, go to next step. If voltage is 10 volts or less, replace LPSDM

6) Using an ohmmeter, backprobe between actuator drive assembly clutch 4-pin harness connector terminal No. 4 (Yellow wire) and ground. If resistance is less than 5 ohms, replace left actuator drive assembly. If resistance is 5 ohms or more, replace LPSDM.

NOTE: Active command PSD_OPEN is only active for one second. Observe meter reading as command is triggered ON.

---

7) Turn ignition switch to RUN position. Using NGS tester, monitor RPSDM active command PSD_OPEN. Using a voltmeter, backprobing between actuator drive assembly motor 4-pin harness connector terminal "A" (Red wire) and ground. Trigger RPSDM PSD_OPEN ON. If voltage is 10 volts or less, go to next step. If voltage is more than 10 volts, go to step **9)**.

8) Disconnect RPSDM 4-pin harness connector C351. Measure voltage between RPSDM harness connector C351 terminal No. 4 (Light Green/Red wire) and ground. If voltage is 10 volts or less, perform TEST U: RIGHT POWER SLIDING DOOR INOPERATIVE – NO DTCS. If voltage is more than 10 volts, replace RPSDM.

9) Using an ohmmeter, backprobe between actuator drive assembly motor 4-pin harness connector terminal "B" (Black wire) and ground. If resistance is less than 5 ohms, go to next step. If resistance is 5 ohms or more, replace RPSDM.

10) Turn ignition switch to RUN position. Using NGS tester, monitor RPSDM active command M_CLUTCH. Using a voltmeter, backprobe between actuator drive assembly clutch 4-pin component connector terminal No. 3 (Black wire) and ground. Trigger RPSDM M_CLUTCH ON. If voltage is more than 10 volts, go to next step. If voltage is 10 volts or less, replace RPSDM.

11) Using an ohmmeter, backprobe between actuator drive assembly clutch 4-pin component connector terminal No. 4 (Black wire) and ground. If resistance is less than 5 ohms, replace right actuator drive assembly. If resistance is 5 ohms or more, replace RPSDM.

TEST R: POWER SLIDING DOOR NOT FULLY CLOSED DURING SELF-TEST

1) Using New Generation Star (NGS) tester, perform Left Power Sliding Door Module (LPSDM) self-test. Visually inspect power sliding door as it closes during self-test. If power sliding door does not fully close and latch, go to next step. If power sliding door fully closes and latches, go to step **6)**.

2) Press overhead console on/off switch to OFF position. Manually open and close power sliding door while inspecting wedge alignment, front and rear striker alignment, sliding door roller hinges, door tracks and runs, weather-strips and manual operating effort. If power sliding door operates correctly manually, go to next step. If power sliding door does not operate correctly manually, repair sliding door mechanical system.

3) Using a voltmeter, backprobe between LPSDM harness connector C354 terminal No. 4 (Red wire) and ground. Press left "B" pillar open/close switch to operate power sliding door to full open position then to full close positions while monitoring voltage. If voltage is always more than 10 volts, go to next step. If voltage is 10 volts or less, check charging system to diagnose low system voltage. See appropriate GENERATORS article in STARTING & CHARGING SYSTEMS and/or see appropriate wiring diagram in POWER DISTRIBUTION article in WIRING DIAGRAMS.

4) Using an ohmmeter, backprobe between LPSDM harness connector C354 terminal No. 3 (Black wire) and ground. If resistance is less than 5 ohms, go to next step. If resistance is 5 ohms or more, repair open in Black wire.

5) Adjust power sliding door to outer most limits of specification. See POWER SLIDING DOOR ADJUSTMENT under ADJUSTMENTS. If power sliding door completely closed and latched, power sliding door is operating correctly. If power sliding door did not close and latch correctly, replace left actuator drive assembly.

6) Using NGS tester, perform Left Power Sliding Door Module (LPSDM) and Right Power Sliding Door Module (RPSDM) self-tests. If DTC B2603 is retrieved from LPSDM, go to next step. If DTC B2603 is retrieved from RPSDM, go to step **10)**.

7) Disconnect left power sliding door contact 8-pin harness connector C700. Measure resistance between left power sliding door contact harness connector C700 terminals No. 4 (Yellow/Red wire) and No. 7 (White wire). With power sliding door open, manually operate rear power sliding door latch to first position. Resistance should be momentarily less than 5 ohms in first latch position, then open circuit and momentarily less than 5 ohms in second position then open circuit again. If resistance readings are correct as latch is operated, go to next step. If resistance readings are incorrect as latch is operated, replace left power sliding door detent switch.

8) Turn ignition switch to OFF position. Disconnect LPSDM 12-pin harness connector C355, left power sliding door contact 8-pin harness connector C700 and left power sliding door detent switch 2-pin harness connector C704. Close power sliding door. Measure resistance between LPSDM harness connector C355 terminal No. 5 (White wire) and left power sliding door detent switch harness connector C704 terminal No. 2 (White wire). Open and close power sliding door while observing meter. Resistance should stay at 5 ohms or less when sliding door contacts are touching while door is opening and closing. If resistance readings are correct, go to next step. If resistance readings are incorrect, replace left power sliding door contact.

9) Disconnect LPSDM 4-pin harness connector C354. Close power sliding door. Measure resistance between LPSDM harness connector C354 terminal No. 2 (Yellow/Red wire) and left power sliding door detent switch harness connector C704 terminal No. 1 (Yellow/Red wire). Open and close power sliding door while observing meter. Resistance should stay at 5 ohms or less when sliding door contacts are touching while door is opening and closing. If resistance readings are correct, replace LPSDM. If resistance readings are incorrect, replace left PSD contact.

10) Disconnect right power sliding door contact 8-pin harness connector C800. Measure resistance between right power sliding door contact harness connector C800 terminals No. 4 (Yellow/Red wire) and No. 7 (White wire). With power sliding door open, manually operate rear power sliding door latch to first position. Resistance should be momentarily less than 5 ohms in first latch position, then open circuit and momentarily less than 5 ohms in second position then open circuit again. If resistance readings are correct as latch is operated, go to next step. If resistance readings are incorrect as latch is operated, replace right power sliding door detent switch.

11) Turn ignition switch to OFF position. Disconnect RPSDM 12-pin harness connector C352, right power sliding door contact 8-pin harness connector C800 and right power sliding door detent switch 2-pin harness connector C804. Close power sliding door. Measure resistance between RPSDM harness connector C352 terminal No. 5 (White wire) and right power sliding door detent switch harness connector C804 terminal No. 2 (White wire). Open and close power sliding door while observing meter. Resistance should stay at 5 ohms or less when sliding door contacts are touching while door is opening and closing. If resistance readings are correct, go to next step. If resistance readings are incorrect, replace right power sliding door contact.

12) Disconnect RPSDM 4-pin harness connector C351. Close power sliding door. Measure resistance between RPSDM harness connector C351 terminal No. 2 (Yellow/Red wire) and right power sliding door detent switch harness connector C804 terminal No. 1 (Yellow/Red wire). Open and close power sliding door while observing meter. Resistance should stay at 5 ohms or less when sliding door contacts are touching while door is opening and closing. If resistance readings are correct, replace RPSDM. If resistance readings are incorrect , replace right power sliding door contact.

TEST S: POWER SLIDING DOOR ON/OFF SWITCH OPEN CIRCUIT

1) Turn ignition switch to RUN position. Ensure power sliding door is completely closed and latched. Press overhead console on/off switch to ON position. Using New Generation Star (NGS) tester, perform Left Power Siding Door Module (LPSDM) or Right Power Siding Door Module (RPSDM) self-tests. If DTC B2604 is retrieved, go to next step.

If DTC B2604 is not retrieved, conditions were not correct for self-test. Repair any remaining DTCs. See LEFT POWER SLIDING DOOR MODULE DTC INDEX or RIGHT POWER SLIDING DOOR MODULE DTC INDEX table under SELF-DIAGNOSTIC SYSTEM.

2) Using NGS tester, perform RPSDM self-test. If DTC B2604 is not retrieved, go to next step. If DTC B2604 is retrieved, go to step 4).

3) Disconnect overhead console switch 8-pin harness connector C915 and LPSDM 12-pin harness connector C355. Measure resistance between LPSDM harness connector C355 terminal No. 6 (Violet/White wire) and overhead console switch harness connector C915 terminal No. 4 (Violet/White wire). If resistance is less than 5 ohms, clear LPSDM DTCs and repeat LPSDM self-test. If DTC B2604 is retrieved, replace LPSDM. If resistance is 5 ohms or more, repair open in Violet/White wire.

4) Open and close right power sliding door from overhead console open/close switch. If door does not operate correctly, go to next step. If door operates correctly, go to step 6).

5) Disconnect overhead console switch 8-pin harness connector C915. Measure resistance between overhead console switch harness connector C915 terminal No. 6 (Black wire) and ground. If resistance is less than 5 ohms, replace overhead console switch assembly. If resistance is 5 ohms or more, repair open in Black wire.

6) Turn ignition switch to RUN position. Measure voltage between overhead console switch harness connector C915 terminal No. 4 (Violet/White wire) and ground. If voltage is 10 volts or less, go to next step. If voltage is more than 10 volts, repair short to voltage in Violet/White wire.

7) Disconnect overhead console switch 8-pin harness connector C915 and RPSDM 12-pin harness connector C352. Measure resistance between RPSDM harness connector C352 terminal No. 6 (Violet/White wire) and overhead console switch harness connector C915 terminal No. 4 (Violet/White wire). If resistance is less than 5 ohms, clear RPSDM DTCs and repeat RPSDM self-test. If DTC B2604 is retrieved, replace RPSDM. If resistance is 5 ohms or more, repair open in Violet/White wire.

TEST T: DISABLE SIGNAL OPEN CIRCUIT (VSS MORE THAN 6 MPH)

1) Using New Generation Star (NGS) tester, perform Rear Electronic Module (REM) self-test. If DTC B2605 is only DTC retrieved, go to next step. If DTC U1041 is retrieved, perform ABS self-test to diagnose missing speed signal.

2) If vehicle is equipped with left and right power sliding doors, go to next step. If vehicle is equipped with only a right side power sliding door, go to step 6).

3) Using NGS tester, perform Left Power Sliding Door Module (LPSDM) and Right Power Sliding Door Module (RPSDM) self-tests. If DTC B2605 is retrieved from both modules, go to next step. If DTC B2605 is retrieved from RPSDM only, go to step 7). If DTC B2605 is retrieved from LPSDM only, go to step 9).

4) Disconnect RPSDM 12-pin harness connector C352. Measure voltage between RPSDM harness connector C352 terminal No. 8 (Pink/Black wire) and ground. If voltage is more than 10 volts, go to next step. If voltage is 10 volts or less, go to step 6).

5) Disconnect REM 22-pin harness connector C341. Measure voltage between RPSDM harness connector C352 terminal No. 8 (Pink/Black wire) and ground. If voltage is more than 10 volts, repair short to voltage in Pink/Black wire. If voltage is 10 volts or less, replace REM.

6) Turn ignition switch to OFF position. Disconnect REM 22-pin harness connector C341. Measure resistance between RPSDM harness connector C352 terminal No. 8 (Pink/Black wire) and REM harness connector C341 terminal No. 8 (Pink/Black wire). If resistance is less than 5 ohms, replace REM. If resistance is 5 ohms or more, repair open in Pink/Black wire.

7) Disconnect RPSDM 12-pin harness connector C352. Measure resistance between RPSDM harness connector C352 terminal No. 8 (Pink/Black wire) and ground. If resistance is 5 ohms or more, go to next step. If resistance is less than 5 ohms, clear RPSDM DTCs and repeat RPSDM self-test. If DTC B2605 is retrieved, replace RPSDM.

8) Turn ignition switch to OFF position. Disconnect REM 22-pin harness connector C341. Measure resistance between RPSDM harness connector C352 terminal No. 8 (Pink/Black wire) and REM harness connector C341 terminal No. 8 (Pink/Black wire). If resistance is less than 5 ohms, replace REM. If resistance is 5 ohms or more, repair open in Pink/Black wire.

9) Disconnect LPSDM 12-pin harness connector C355. Turn ignition switch to RUN position. Measure resistance between LPSDM harness connector C355 terminal No. 8 (Pink/Black wire) and ground. If resistance is 5 ohms or more, go to next step. If resistance is less than 5 ohms, clear LPSDM DTCs and repeat LPSDM self-test. If DTC B2605 is retrieved again, replace LPSDM.

10) Turn ignition switch to OFF position. Disconnect REM 22-pin harness connector C341. Measure resistance between LPSDM harness connector C355 terminal No. 8 (Pink/Black wire) and REM harness connector C341 terminal No. 8 (Pink/Black wire). If resistance is less than 5 ohms, replace REM. If resistance is 5 ohms or more, repair open in Pink/Black wire.

TEST U: RIGHT POWER SLIDING DOOR INOPERATIVE – NO DTCS

1) Disconnect Right Power Sliding Door Module (RPSDM) 4-pin harness connector C351. Measure voltage between RPSDM harness connector C351 terminal No. 4 (Light Green/Red wire) and ground. If voltage is 10 volts or less, go to next step. If voltage is more than 10 volts, go to step 5).

2) Remove Battery Junction Box (BJB) fuse No. 110 (50-amp). Inspect fuse. If fuse is not okay, go to next step. If fuse is okay, repair open in Light Green/Red wire.

3) Measure resistance between RPSDM harness connector C351 terminal No. 4 (Light Green/Red wire) and ground. If resistance is more than 10 k/ohms, go to next step. If resistance is 10 k/ohms or less, repair short to ground in Light Green/Red wire.

4) Disconnect actuator drive assembly motor 4-pin harness connector. Measure resistance between actuator drive assembly motor harness connector terminal "A" (Red wire) and ground. If resistance is more than 10 k/ohms, replace 50-amp BJB fuse No. 110. If fuse opens again, replace RPSDM. If resistance is 10 k/ohms or less, replace right actuator drive assembly.

5) Turn ignition switch to RUN position. Measure voltage between RPSDM harness connector C351 terminal No. 2 (Yellow/Red wire) and ground. If voltage is 10 volts or less, go to next step. If voltage is more than 10 volts, repair short to voltage in Yellow/Red wire.

6) Ensure power sliding door is completely closed and unlocked. Turn ignition switch to OFF position. Connect RPSDM 4-pin harness connector C351. Turn ignition switch to RUN position. Press overhead console on/off switch to ON position. Using a voltmeter, backprobe between RPSDM harness connector C351 terminal No. 1 (Gray/Red wire) and ground. Press right "B" pillar open/close switch. If voltage is more than 10 volts, go to next step. If voltage is 10 volts or less, replace RPSDM.

7) Using an ohmmeter, backprobe between RPSDM harness connector C351 terminal No. 2 (Yellow/Red wire) and ground. If resistance is less than 5 ohms, go to next step. If resistance is 5 ohms or more, replace RPSDM.

8) Turn ignition switch to RUN position. Ensure overhead console on/off switch is in OFF position. Manually operate power sliding door. Using NGS tester, monitor RPSDM PID LATCHSW as door opens to first (primary) latch position and when closing at first (primary) latch position. PID should reads NOTACT closed, ACTIVE in first (primary) latch position and NOTACT when opening. Then NOTACT closing, ACTIVE in first (primary) latch position and NOTACT closed. If PID read as specified, go to next step. If PID did not read as specified, perform TEST K: POWER SLIDING DOOR DETENT SWITCH CIRCUIT SHORT TO GROUND.

9) Close power sliding door. Ensure overhead console on/off switch is in ON position. Using a voltmeter, backprobe between actuator drive assembly motor harness connector terminals "A" (Red wire) and "B" (Black wire). Press right "B" pillar open/close switch. If voltage is more than 10 volts, go to next step. If voltage is 10 volts or less, go to step 11).

10) Close power sliding door. Ensure overhead console on/off switch is in ON position. Using a voltmeter, backprobe between actuator drive assembly clutch harness connector terminals No. 3 (Black wire) and No. 4 (Black wire). Press right "B" pillar open/close switch. If voltage is 10 volts or less, go to next step. If voltage is more than 10 volts, replace right actuator drive assembly.

11) Remove Fuse Junction Box (FJB) fuse No. 6 (15-amp). Wait 30 seconds and install fuse. Close power sliding door. Ensure overhead on/off switch is in ON position. Press right "B" pillar open/close switch to open power sliding door, then press to close power sliding door. If power sliding door operated correctly, initialize power sliding doors. If power sliding door does not operate correctly, repeat RPSDM self-test. If no DTCs are retrieved, replace RPSDM.

TEST V: LEFT POWER SLIDING DOOR INOPERATIVE – NO DTCS

1) Disconnect Left Power Sliding Door Module (LPSDM) 4-pin harness connector C354. Measure voltage between LPSDM harness connector C354 terminal No. 4 (Red/Black wire) and ground. If voltage is 10 volts or less, go to next step. If voltage is more than 10 volts, go to step **5)**.

2) Remove Battery Junction Box (BJB) fuse No. 118 (50-amp). Inspect fuse. If fuse is not okay, go to next step. If fuse is okay, repair open in Red/Black wire.

3) Measure resistance between LPSDM harness connector C354 terminal No. 4 (Red/Black wire) and ground. If resistance is more than 10 k/ohms, go to next step. If resistance is 10 k/ohms or less, repair short to ground in Red/Black wire.

4) Disconnect actuator drive assembly motor 4-pin harness connector. Measure resistance between actuator drive assembly motor harness connector terminal "A" (Red wire) and ground. If resistance is more than 10 k/ohms, replace BJB fuse No. 118 (50-amp). Initialize power sliding doors. If fuse opens, replace LPSDM. If resistance is 10 k/ohms or less, replace left actuator drive assembly.

5) Turn ignition switch to RUN position. Measure voltage between LPSDM harness connector C354 terminal No. 2 (Yellow/Red wire) and ground. If voltage is 10 volts or less, go to next step. If voltage is more than 10 volts, repair short to voltage in Yellow/Red wire.

6) Ensure power sliding door is completely closed and unlocked. Turn ignition switch to OFF position. Connect LPSDM 4-pin harness connector C354. Turn ignition switch to RUN position. Press overhead console on/off switch to ON position. Using a voltmeter, backprobe between LPSDM harness connector C354 terminal No. 1 (Gray/Red wire) and ground. Press left "B" pillar open/close switch. If voltage is more than 10 volts, go to next step. If voltage is 10 volts or less, replace LPSDM.

7) Using an ohmmeter, backprobe between LPSDM harness connector C354 terminal No. 2 (Yellow/Red wire) and ground. If resistance is less than 5 ohms, go to next step. If resistance is 5 ohms or more, replace LPSDM.

8) Turn ignition switch to RUN position. Ensure overhead console on/off switch is in OFF position. Manually operate power sliding door. Using New Generation Star (NGS) tester, monitor LPSDM PID LATCHSW as door opens to first (primary) latch position and when closing at first (primary) latch position. PID should reads NOTACT closed, ACTIVE in first (primary) latch position and NOTACT when opening. Then NOTACT closing, ACTIVE in first (primary) latch position and NOTACT closed. Is PID READ as specified, go to next step. If PID did not read as specified, perform TEST K: POWER SLIDING DOOR DETENT SWITCH CIRCUIT SHORT TO GROUND.

9) Close power sliding door. Ensure overhead console on/off switch is in ON position. Using a voltmeter, backprobe between actuator drive assembly motor harness connector terminals "A" (Red wire) and "B" (Yellow wire). Press left "B" pillar open/close switch. If voltage is more than 10 volts, go to next step. If voltage is 10 volts or less, go to step **11)**.

10) Close power sliding door. Ensure overhead console on/off switch is in ON position. Using a voltmeter, backprobe between actuator drive assembly clutch harness connector terminals No. 3 (Yellow wire) and No. 4 (Yellow wire). Press left "B" pillar open/close switch. If voltage is 10 volts or less, go to next step. If voltage is more than 10 volts, replace left actuator drive assembly.

11) Remove Fuse Junction Box (FJB) fuse No. 6 (15-amp). Wait 30 seconds and install fuse. Close power sliding door. Ensure overhead on/off switch is in ON position. Press left "B" pillar open/close switch to open power sliding door, then press to close power sliding door. If power sliding door operated correctly, initialize power sliding doors. If power sliding door does not operate correctly, repeat LPSDM self-test. If no DTCs are retrieved, replace LPSDM.

TEST W: POWER SLIDING DOOR INOPERATIVE FROM ONE SWITCH – NO DTCS

1) Open and close power sliding door from overhead console open/close switch. If left power sliding door operates correctly, go to next step. If right power sliding door operates correctly, go to step **5)**. If left power sliding door does not operate correctly, go to step **8)**. If right power sliding door does not operate correctly, go to step **10)**.

2) Disconnect left "B" pillar open/close switch 6-pin harness connector C942. Measure resistance between left "B" pillar open/close switch harness connector C942 terminal No. 4 (Black wire) and ground. If resistance is less than 5 ohms, go to next step. If resistance is 5 ohms or more, repair open in Black wire.

3) Turn ignition switch to RUN position. Using New Generation Star (NGS) tester, monitor Left Power Sliding Door Module (LPSDM) PID SD_B_SW. Connect a fused jumper wire between left "B" pillar open/close switch harness connector C942 terminals No. 3 (Tan/Light Blue wire) and No. 4 (Black wire). If PID SD_B_SW reads NOTACT, go to next step. If PID SD_B_SW reads ACTIVE, replace left "B" pillar open/close switch.

4) Turn ignition switch to OFF position. Disconnect LPSDM 12-pin harness connector C355. Measure resistance between LPSDM harness connector C355 terminal No. 3 (Tan/Light Blue wire) and left "B" pillar open/close switch harness connector C942 terminal No. 3 (Tan/Light Blue wire). If resistance is less than 5 ohms, replace LPSDM. Initialize power sliding doors. If resistance is 5 ohms or more, repair open in Tan/Light Blue wire. Initialize power sliding doors.

5) Disconnect right "B" pillar open/close switch 6-pin harness connector C941. Measure resistance between right "B" pillar open/close switch harness connector C942 terminal No. 4 (Black wire) and ground. If resistance is less than 5 ohms, go to next step. If resistance is 5 ohms or more, repair open in Black wire.

6) Turn ignition switch to RUN position. Using NGS tester, monitor Right Power Sliding Door Module (RPSDM) PID SD_B_SW. Connect a fused jumper wire between right "B" pillar open/close switch harness connector C942 terminals No. 3 (Tan/Light Blue wire) and No. 4 (Black wire). If PID SD_B_SW reads NOTACT, go to next step. If PID SD_B_SW reads ACTIVE, replace right "B" pillar open/close switch.

7) Turn ignition switch to OFF position. Disconnect RPSDM 12-pin harness connector C352. Measure resistance between RPSDM harness connector C352 terminal No. 3 (Tan/Light Blue wire) and right "B" pillar open/close switch harness connector C941 terminal No. 3 (Tan/Light Blue wire). If resistance is less than 5 ohms, replace RPSDM. Initialize power sliding doors. If resistance is 5 ohms or more, repair open in Tan/Light Blue wire. Initialize power sliding doors.

8) Disconnect overhead console switch 8-pin harness connector C915. Monitor Left Power Sliding Door Module (LPSDM) PID SD_OPSW. Connect fused jumper wire between overhead console switch harness connector C915 terminals No. 5 (Black wire) and No. 8 (White/Light Green wire). If LPSDM PID SD_OPSW reads NOTACT, go to next step. If LPSDM PID SD_OPSW reads ACTIVE, replace overhead console switch assembly.

9) Disconnect LPSDM 12-pin harness connector C355. Measure resistance between LPSDM harness connector C355 terminal No. 2 (White/Light Green wire) and overhead console switch harness connector C915 terminal No. 8 (White/Light Green wire). If resistance is less than 5 ohms, replace LPSDM. Initialize power sliding doors. If resistance is 5 ohms or more, repair open in White/Light Green wire. Initialize power sliding doors.

10) Disconnect overhead console switch 8-pin harness connector C915. Monitor Right Power Sliding Door Module (RPSDM) PID SD_OPSW. Connect fused jumper wire between overhead console switch harness connector C915 terminals No. 5 (Black wire) and No. 6 (Light Green/Red wire). If RPSDM PID SD_OPSW reads NOTACT, go to next step. If RPSDM PID SD_OPSW reads ACTIVE, replace overhead console switch.

11) Disconnect RPSDM 12-pin harness connector C352. Measure resistance between RPSDM harness connector C352 terminal No. 2 (Light Green/Red wire) and overhead console switch harness connector C915 terminal No. 6 (Light Green/Red wire). If resistance is less than 5 ohms, replace RPSDM. If resistance is 5 ohms or more, repair open in Light Green/Red wire.

TEST X: POWER SLIDING DOOR INOPERATIVE FROM REMOTE KEYLESS ENTRY TRANSMITTER

1) Using New Generation Star (NGS) tester, perform Rear Electronic Module (REM) self-test. If DTC B2557 is retrieved, go to next step. If DTC B2558 is retrieved, go to step **4)**. If DTCs B2557 and B2558 are not retrieved, go to step **6)**.

2) Turn ignition switch to OFF position. Disconnect Left Power Sliding Door Module (LPSDM) 12-pin harness connector C355. Turn ignition switch to RUN position. Measure voltage between LPSDM harness connector C355 terminal No. 4 (Gray/Yellow wire) and ground. If voltage is more than 10 volts, go to next step. If voltage is 10 volts or less, replace LPSDM.

3) Disconnect REM 22-pin harness connector C341. Turn ignition switch to RUN position. Measure voltage between LPSDM harness connector C355 terminal No. 4 (Gray/Yellow wire) and ground. If voltage is more than 10 volts, repair short to voltage in Gray/Red wire. If voltage is 10 volts or less, replace REM.

4) Turn ignition switch to OFF position. Disconnect Right Power Sliding Door Module (RPSDM) 12-pin harness connector C352. Turn ignition switch to RUN position. Measure voltage between RPSDM harness connector C352 terminal No. 4 (Tan/Red wire) and ground. If voltage is more than 10 volts, go to next step. If voltage is 10 volts or less, replace RPSDM.

5) Disconnect REM 22-pin harness connector C341. Turn ignition switch to RUN position. Measure voltage between RPSDM harness connector C352 terminal No. 4 (Tan/Red wire) and ground. If voltage is more than 10 volts, repair short to voltage in Tan/Red wire. If voltage is 10 volts or less, replace REM.

6) Using NGS tester, perform Left Power Sliding Door Module (LPSDM) and Right Power Sliding Door Module (RPSDM) self-tests. If DTC B2362 is retrieved from LPSDM, go to next step. If DTC B2362 is retrieved from RPSDM, go to step **9)**. If DTC B2362 is not retrieved from either LPSDM or RPSDM, go to step **11)**.

7) Disconnect LPSDM 12-pin harness connector C355. Measure resistance between LPSDM harness connector C355 terminal No. 4 (Gray/Yellow wire) and ground. If resistance is 10 k/ohms or less, go to next step. If resistance is more than 10 k/ohms, clear LPSDM DTCs and repeat LPSDM self-test. If DTC B2362 is retrieved, replace LPSDM.

8) Disconnect REM 22-pin harness connector C341. Measure resistance between LPSDM harness connector C355 terminal No. 4 (Gray/Yellow wire) and ground. If resistance is more than 10 k/ohms, replace REM. If resistance is 10 k/ohms or less, repair short to ground in Gray/Yellow wire.

9) Disconnect RPSDM 12-pin harness connector C352. Measure resistance between RPSDM harness connector C352 terminal No. 4 (Tan/Red wire) and ground. If resistance is 10 k/ohms or less, go to next step. If resistance is more than 10 k/ohms, clear RPSDM DTCs and repeat RPSDM self-test. If DTC B2362 is retrieved, replace RPSDM.

10) Disconnect REM 22-pin harness connector C341. Measure resistance between RPSDM harness connector C352 terminal No. 4 (Tan/Red wire) and ground. If resistance is more than 10 k/ohms, replace REM. If resistance is 10 k/ohms or less, repair short to ground in Tan/Red wire.

11) Press LOCK and UNLOCK buttons on remote keyless entry transmitter. If left power sliding door locked and unlocked, go to next step. If right power sliding door locked and unlocked, go to step **13)**. If left or right power sliding door did not lock and unlock, repair remote keyless entry system. See appropriate wiring diagram in REMOTE KEYLESS ENTRY SYSTEMS article.

12) Disconnect REM 22-pin harness connector C341. Measure resistance between LPSDM harness connector C355 terminal No. 4 (Gray/Yellow wire) and REM harness connector C341 terminal No. 10 (Gray/Yellow wire). If resistance is less than 5 ohms, replace REM. If resistance is 5 ohms or more, repair open in Gray/Yellow wire.

13) Disconnect REM 22-pin harness connector C341. Measure resistance between LPSDM harness connector C352 terminal No. 4 (Tan/Red wire) and REM harness connector C341 terminal No. 11 (Tan/Red wire). If resistance is less than 5 ohms, replace REM. If resistance is 5 ohms or more, repair open in Tan/Red wire.

TEST Y: LEFT POWER DOOR OPERATES WITH FUEL DOOR OPEN

1) Turn ignition switch to RUN position. Using New Generation Star (NGS) tester, monitor Left Power Sliding Door Module (LPSDM) PID FUEL_DR while opening and closing fuel filler door. If LPSDM PID FUEL_DR does not agree with fuel filler door positions, go to next step. If LPSDM PID FUEL_DR agrees with fuel filler door positions, verify symptom. If power sliding door still operates with fuel filler door open, replace LPSDM.

2) Turn ignition switch to OFF position. Disconnect LPSDM 12-pin harness connector C355. Measure resistance between LPSDM harness connector C355 terminal No. 9 (Gray/Black wire) and ground. Open fuel filler door. If resistance is 10 k/ohms or less, go to next step. If resistance is more than 10 k/ohms, replace LPSDM.

3) Disconnect fuel filler door switch 2-pin harness connector C314. Measure resistance between LPSDM harness connector C355 terminal No. 9 (Gray/Black wire) and ground. If resistance is more than 10 k/ohms, replace fuel filler door switch. If resistance is 10 k/ohms or less, repair short to ground in Gray/Black wire.

TEST Z: POWER SLIDING DOOR OPERATES FROM "B" PILLAR OPEN/CLOSE SWITCH WITH OVERHEAD CONSOLE SWITCH IN OFF POSITION

1) If vehicle is not equipped with left power sliding door, go to next step. If vehicle is equipped with left and right power sliding doors, go to step **5)**.

2) Turn ignition switch to RUN position. Using New Generation Star (NGS) tester, monitor Right Power Sliding Door Module (RPSDM) PID SD_ONSW while pressing overhead console on/off switch to ON position, then to OFF position. If RPSDM PID SD_ONSW did not agree with on/off switch positions, go to next step. If RPSDM PID SD_ONSW agrees with on/off switch positions, verify symptom. If right power sliding door still operates from right "B" pillar open/close switch or by manual activation with on/off switch in OFF position, replace RPSDM.

3) Disconnect overhead console switch 8-pin harness connector C915. Measure resistance between overhead console switch harness connector C915 terminal No. 4 (Violet/White wire) and ground. If resistance is 10 k/ohms or less, go to next step. If resistance is more than 10 k/ohms, replace overhead console switch.

4) Disconnect RPSDM 12-pin harness connector C352 Measure resistance between overhead console switch harness connector C915 terminal No. 4 (Violet/White wire) and ground. If resistance is more than 10 k/ohms, replace RPSDM. If resistance is 10 k/ohms or less, repair short to ground in Violet/White wire

5) Turn ignition switch to RUN position. Using NGS tester, monitor Left Power Sliding Door Module (LPSDM) PID SD_ONSW while pressing overhead console on/off switch to ON position then to OFF position. If LPSDM PID SD_ONSW did not agree with on/off switch positions, go to next step. If LPSDM PID SD_ONSW agrees with on/off switch positions, verify symptom. If right power sliding door still operates from right "B" pillar open/close switch or by manual activation with on/off switch in OFF position, replace RPSDM. If left power sliding door still operates from left "B" pillar open/close switch or by manual activation with on/off switch in OFF position, replace LPSDM.

6) Disconnect overhead console switch 8-pin harness connector C915. Measure resistance between overhead console switch harness connector C915 terminal No. 4 (Violet/White wire) and ground. If resistance is 10 k/ohms or less, go to next step. If resistance is more than 10 k/ohms, replace overhead console switch.

7) Disconnect RPSDM 12-pin harness connector C352. Measure resistance between overhead console switch harness connector C915 terminal No. 4 (Violet/White wire) and ground. If resistance is 10 k/ohms or less, go to next step. If resistance is more than 10 k/ohms, replace RPSDM.

8) Disconnect LPSDM 12-pin harness connector C355. Measure resistance between overhead console switch harness connector C915 terminal No. 4 (Violet/White wire) and ground. If resistance is 10 k/ohms or less, repair short to ground in Violet/White wire. If resistance is more than 10 k/ohms, replace LPSDM.

REMOVAL & INSTALLATION

NOTE: Anytime actuator drive assembly, Left Power Sliding Door Module (LPSDM), Right Power Sliding Door Module (RPSDM), Rear Electronic Module (REM) or Fuse Junction Box (FJB) fuse No. 6 (15-amp). are replaced or removed, power sliding doors must be initialized. See POWER SLIDING DOOR INITIALIZATION PROCEDURE under PROGRAMMING.

FUEL FILLER INTERLOCK CATCH

Removal & Installation – Remove left rear tire and wheel assembly. Remove left rear inner fender splash shield and remove electrical connector from interlock catch. Loosen lower roller bolt on power sliding door and move power sliding door up slightly. Block and support power sliding door. Remove 3 rivets holding interlock catch and remove fuel filler interlock catch as an assembly. To install, reverse removal procedure.

POWER SLIDING DOOR LATCH RELEASE ACTUATOR

Removal & Installation – Remove power sliding door trim panel and remove 3 latch screws retaining latch inside door assembly. Remove 3 screws retaining remote control assembly. Disconnect exterior door handle linkage, position remote control assembly outside of door assembly, and disconnect electrical connector to release actuator. Remove cap on linkage arm and remove 2 bolts retaining latch release actuator and remove latch release actuator.

LEFT ACTUATOR DRIVE ASSEMBLY

NOTE: When removing or replacing actuator drive assembly, cable eyelet retaining clip can not be reused. Always replace clip.

Removal & Installation – 1) Open left power sliding door and left rear quarter window. Remove Fuse Junction Box (FJB) fuse No. 6 (15-amp). Remove left upper and lower rear quarter trim panel, upper and lower air conditioning ducts and power sliding door center track molding. Manually close power sliding door to within approximately 4 in. (100 mm) from "B" pillar, remove cable eyelet clip and remove front cable from door. Remove 2 bolts retaining rear cable housing and feed through body to interior of vehicle.

2) Remove 3 bolts retaining front cable housing and feed through to interior of vehicle. Remove all connectors from Right Power Sliding Door Module (RPSDM) and remove screw retaining module to actuator drive assembly. Unsnap control module off actuator drive assembly, remove 2 bolts retaining actuator and remove actuator drive assembly. To install, reverse removal procedure.

LEFT POSITION SENSOR

Removal & Installation – Remove Fuse Junction Box (FJB) fuse No. 6 (15-amp). Remove rear seat assembly and upper and lower rear quarter trim panel. Remove upper and lower air conditioning ducts. Release left position sensor from actuator drive assembly. Disconnect electrical connector from left position sensor, release sensor wiring from harness and remove left position sensor.

POWER SLIDING DOOR (PSD) DETENT SWITCH

Removal & Installation – Remove power sliding door trim panel and remove 3 rear latch screws. Disconnect power sliding door detent switch connector. Remove screw retaining PSD detent switch and remove PSD detent switch assembly. To install, reverse removal procedure.

POWER SLIDING DOOR MODULES (LPSDM/RPSDM)

CAUTION: Electronic modules are sensitive to static electrical charges. Proper grounding of technician and workplace is essential to prevent damage.

Removal & Installation (Left Power Sliding Door Module (LPSDM)) – Remove Fuse Junction Box (FJB) fuse No. 6 (15-amp). Remove left upper and lower quarter trim panel. Remove upper and lower air conditioning ducts. Disconnect all connectors to LPSDM and remove screw retaining LPSDM to actuator drive assembly. Unsnap control module hinge from actuator drive assembly and remove LPSDM. To install, reverse removal procedure.

Removal & Installation (Right Power Sliding Door Module (RPSDM)) – Remove Fuse Junction Box (FJB) fuse No. 6 (15-amp). Remove right rear quarter trim panel Disconnect all connectors to RPSDM and remove screw retaining RPSDM to actuator drive assembly. Slide control module off actuator drive assembly and remove RPSDM.

REAR ELECTRONICS MODULE (REM)

CAUTION: Electronic modules are sensitive to static electrical charges. Proper grounding of technician and workplace is essential to prevent damage.

CAUTION: Prior to removal of Module, it is necessary to upload module configuration information to New Generation Star (NGS) tester. This information needs to be downloaded into new module once installed. See REAR ELECTRONICS MODULE (REM) PROGRAMMING under PROGRAMMING.

NOTE: When battery is disconnected and connected, some abnormal drive symptoms may occur while vehicle relearns it's adaptive strategy. Vehicle may need to be driven 10 miles or more to learn strategy.

Removal & Installation – Disconnect battery ground cable. Remove right quarter trim panel. Remove 3 bolts holding service jack mounting bracket and remove bracket. Disconnect five electrical connectors to REM, remove 3 nuts holding REM and remove REM. To install REM, reverse removal procedure.

REMOTE CONTROL LATCH RELEASE ASSEMBLY

Removal & Installation – 1) Remove sliding door trim panel and remove 3 screws retaining latch release assembly. Release cable housing on latch release assembly and remove cable. Release clip on remote control latch release assembly arm. Remove 3 screws retaining latch release assembly, slide door latch push button rod through strap and remove remote control latch release assembly.

2) Disconnect all electrical connectors to assembly and remove 3 screws on rear door lock actuator at rear of sliding door. Disconnect electrical connector to detent switch, remove screw retaining switch to assembly and remove switch. Remove screw retaining actuator to latch release assembly and remove rods from assembly. To install, reverse removal procedure.

RIGHT ACTUATOR DRIVE ASSEMBLY

NOTE: When removing or replacing actuator drive assembly, cable eyelet retaining clip can not be reused. Always replace clip.

Removal & Installation – 1) Open right power sliding door and right rear quarter window. Remove Fuse Junction Box (FJB) fuse No. 6

(15-amp). Remove right rear quarter trim panel and power sliding door center track molding. Close power sliding door to within approximately 4 in. (100 mm) from "B" pillar, remove cable eyelet clip and remove front cable from door. Remove 2 bolts retaining rear cable housing and feed through body to interior of vehicle.

2) Remove 3 bolts retaining front cable housing and feed through to interior of vehicle. Remove all connectors from Right Power Sliding Door Module (RPSDM) and remove screw retaining module to actuator drive assembly. Slide control module off actuator drive assembly, remove 4 bolts retaining actuator and remove actuator drive assembly. To install, reverse removal procedure.

RIGHT POSITION SENSOR

Removal & Installation – Remove Fuse Junction Box (FJB) fuse No. 6 (15-amp). Remove right rear quarter trim panel. Disconnect all connectors on Right Power Sliding Door Module (RPSDM) and remove bolt retaining RPSDM to actuator drive assembly. Slide module off actuator drive assembly. Remove 4 bolts retaining actuator drive assembly, position assembly forward and remove position sensor from back of actuator drive assembly.

WIRING DIAGRAMS

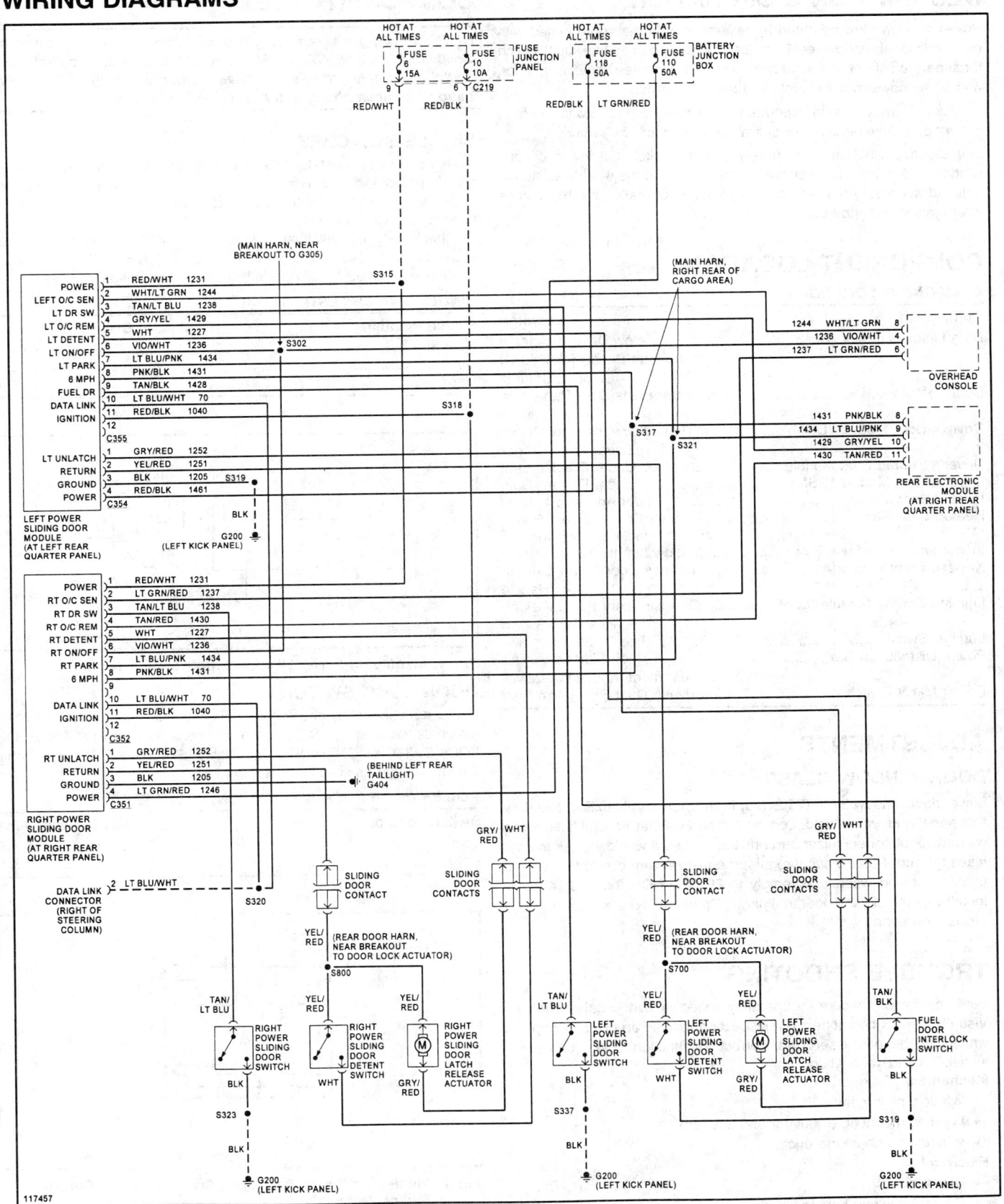

Fig. 12: Power Sliding Door System Wiring Diagram (Windstar)

DESCRIPTION & OPERATION

Power windows are operated by reversible type motors mounted with each individual window regulator. Each window has an individual switch for separate control. A master control switch is located on left front door, and all windows may be controlled from this switch.

A lock-out switch is incorporated in master control switch. When actuated, it prevents window operation from individual switches.

One-touch down feature in master control switch will lower driver's window to full down position with a brief touch on the window switch. A delayed accessory feature will allow window operation for 10 minutes after ignition is turned off.

COMPONENT LOCATIONS

COMPONENT LOCATIONS

Component	Location
Data Link Connector (DLC)	Below Driver's Side Of Instrument Panel, To Right Of Steering Column
Door Lock Switch	Appropriate Door Panel Arm Rest
Driver's Door Module (DDM)	Behind Driver's Door Panel, Lower Front Corner
Driver's Heated Seat Module	Under Driver's Seat
Driver's Seat Module (DSM)	Under Driver's Seat
Heated Seat Module	Under Appropriate Seat
Heated Seat Switch	Center Of Instrument Panel, Under Heater Controls
Instrument Panel Fuse Box	Below Left Instrument Panel
Keyless Entry Keypad	Driver's Door Below Exterior Door Handle
Lighting Control Module (LCM)	On Instrument Panel, Behind Headlight Switch
Lumbar Switch	Side Of Seat Cushion
Power Distribution Box	Left Side Of Engine Compartment, Above Wheelwell
Power Mirror Switch	Driver's Door Panel Arm Rest

ADJUSTMENTS

DOOR WINDOW GLASS

Lower door window 3.00" (76.2 mm) from full up position. Remove door trim panel and watershield. Loosen nut and washer assembly securing window regulator equalizer arm bracket. Seat the window glass to door glass top run. Push window regulator equalizer arm bracket down and tighten nut and washer assembly to 89-124 INCH lbs. (10-14 N.m). Install watershield and door trim panel. Open and close window to verify proper operation.

TROUBLE SHOOTING

Verify customer concern by operating windows to duplicate condition. Visually inspect components. If inspection reveals an obvious concern which can be easily serviced, correct malfunction before continuing inspection and verification.

Mechanical:
- Window alignment.
- Window mounting (regulator and bracket).
- Window frame interference.

Electrical:
- Blown fuse(s).
- Damaged wiring harness.
- Loose or corroded connections.
- Damaged switches.
- Damaged window motor.

COMPONENT TESTS

NOTE: In wiring diagram, single switch connectors are labeled as C600, C601, C709, C711, C809, and C811. In single switch test, switch terminals are referred to as connector C1 and C2. Identification has been changed for test references only.

SINGLE SWITCHES

1) Remove switch from door. Each single switch contains a relay. To test switch, power and ground must be applied to switch relay. Using jumper wires, apply battery voltage to switch terminal C1-2 and ground to terminal C2-1. *See Fig. 1.*
2) Check continuity between indicated terminals with switch in appropriate position. *See Fig. 1.* See SINGLE SWITCH TESTING table. If continuity is not as specified, replace power window switch(es).

SINGLE SWITCH TESTING

Switch Position	Continuity Between Terminals
Neutral	C2-1, C2-2 & C2-3
Up	C2-3 & C2-4
Down	C2-2 & C2-4

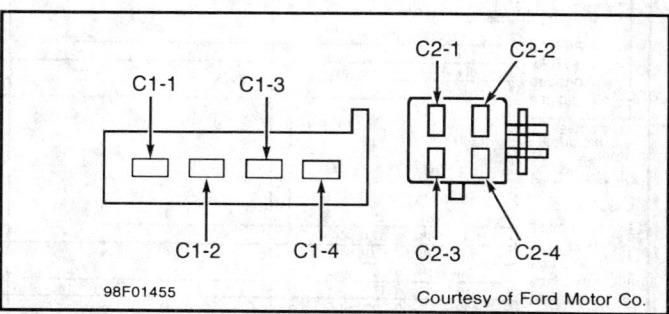

98F01455   Courtesy of Ford Motor Co.

Fig. 1: Identifying Power Window Single Switch Terminals

DOOR LOCK SWITCH

Using an ohmmeter, check for continuity between indicated switch terminals when switch is operated as specified. See POWER DOOR LOCK SWITCH CONTINUITY TEST table. *See Fig. 2.* Replace switch if it does not test as specified.

POWER DOOR LOCK SWITCH CONTINUITY TEST

Switch Position	Continuity Between Pins
Lock	1 & 6
Unlock	5 & 6

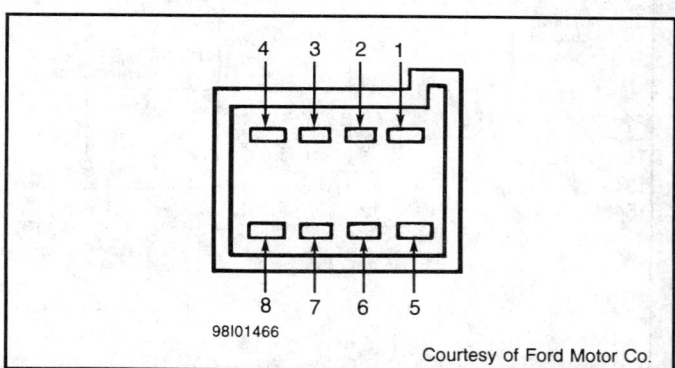

98I01466   Courtesy of Ford Motor Co.

Fig. 2: Identifying Power Door Lock Switch & Mirror Control Switch Terminals

MIRROR CONTROL SWITCH

Using an ohmmeter, check for continuity between indicated switch terminals when switch is activated as specified. See POWER MIRROR

SWITCH CONTINUITY TEST table. *See Fig. 2.* Replace switch if it does not test as specified.

POWER MIRROR SWITCH CONTINUITY TEST

Switch Position	Continuity Between Pins
Left Mirror	
Up	1 & 6; 3 & 5
Down	1 & 3; 5 & 6
Left	1 & 6; 4 & 5
Right	1 & 4; 5 & 6
Right Mirror	
Up	1 & 6; 5 & 7
Down	1 & 7; 5 & 6
Left	1 & 6; 5 & 8
Right	1 & 8; 5 & 6

WINDOW MOTOR

Remove window motor from vehicle. Using fused jumper wires, connect a fully charged battery to motor terminals. Observe motor. Motor should operate smoothly. Reverse leads. Motor should operate smoothly in reverse direction. Replace window motor if it does not operate as specified.

SELF-DIAGNOSTIC SYSTEM

Verify customer's complaint by operating power windows. Check window alignment and window mounting. Check for window frame interference or damaged switches. Check for blown fuse(s), loose or corroded connectors, or damaged wiring harness. Repair or replace components as necessary.

If all components are okay, connect New Generation Star (NGS) tester to Data Link Connector (DLC), located beneath instrument panel. Using NGS tester, perform data link diagnostics test. See DATA LINK DIAGNOSTIC TEST under COMMUNICATION NETWORK DIAGNOSTICS in MODULE COMMUNICATIONS NETWORK – CONTINENTAL article. If NGS tester responds with CKT914, CKT915 or CKT70=ALL ECUS NO RESP/NOT EQUIP, repair module communications concern. See MODULE COMMUNICATIONS NETWORK – CONTINENTAL article. If NGS tester displays NO RESP/NOT EQUIP for Driver's Door Module (DDM), perform TEST A: NO COMMUNICATION WITH DRIVER'S DOOR MODULE under SYSTEM TESTS. If NGS tester displays NO RESP/NOT EQUIP for Lighting Control Module (LCM), perform TEST B: NO COMMUNICATION WITH LIGHTING CONTROL MODULE under SYSTEM TESTS.

If NGS tester responds with SYSTEM PASSED, retrieve and record continuous DTCs. Erase continuous DTCs. Using NGS tester, perform DDM and LCM self-test. Perform appropriate test in accordance with DTC retrieved. See DRIVER'S DOOR MODULE DTC INDEX and/or LIGHTING CONTROL MODULE DTC INDEX table. Codes listed in these tables are only for testing covered in this article. For complete DTC listing, see MODULE COMMUNICATIONS NETWORK – CONTINENTAL article. If no DTCs are retrieved, repair by symptom. See SYMPTOM CHART table under SYSTEM TESTS.

DRIVER'S DOOR MODULE DTC INDEX

DTC [1]	Description	Test
B1342	ECU Defective	[2]
B1549	Power Window Master Switch Short To Voltage	C

[1] – Codes listed in this table are only for testing covered in this article. For complete DTC listing, see MODULE COMMUNICATIONS NETWORK – CONTINENTAL article.

[2] – Using NGS tester, retrieve and document all continuous. Perform Driver's Door Module (DDM) self-test. If DTC B1342 is retrieved again, replace DDM.

LIGHTING CONTROL MODULE DTC INDEX

DTC [1]	Description	Test
B1342	ECU Defective	[2]

LIGHTING CONTROL MODULE DTC INDEX (Cont.)

DTC [1]	Description	Test

[1] – Codes listed in this table are only for testing covered in this article. For complete DTC listing, see MODULE COMMUNICATIONS NETWORK – CONTINENTAL article.

[2] – Using NGS tester, retrieve and document continuous DTCs. Clear all DTCs. Perform Lighting Control Module (LCM) self-test. If DTC B1342 is retrieved again, replace LCM.

SYSTEM TESTS

SYMPTOM CHART

Symptom	Test
No Communication With Driver's Door Module	A
No Communication With Lighting Control Module	B
All Windows Are Inoperative	C
Left Front Window Is Inoperative	D
Left Rear Window Is Inoperative	E
Right Front Window Is Inoperative	F
Right Rear Window Is Inoperative	G
Left Front & Left Rear Windows Are Inoperative	H
Right Front, Right Rear & Left Rear Windows Are Inoperative	J
Window Lock-Out Feature Does Not Operate Properly	K
One-Touch Down Feature Does Not Operate Properly	L

TEST A: NO COMMUNICATION WITH DRIVER'S DOOR MODULE

NOTE: After any repairs are complete, ensure all component are properly installed and all harness connectors are connected properly and repeat data link diagnostic test.

1) Connect NGS tester to Data Link Connector (DLC). Turn ignition switch to RUN position. Monitor Driver's Door Module (DDM) PIDs SFWD_SW, SREAR_SW, SFNT_SW and SRCL_SW while activating power seat control switch. If UNABLE TO PERFORM TEST FUCTION MODULE NOT RESPONDING: DDM CHECK IGNITION STATUS/ VERIFY CABLE REQUIREMENTS CHEK CABLE CONNECTIONS? is not displayed, go to next step. If UNABLE TO PERFORM TEST FUCTION MODULE NOT RESPONDING: DDM CHECK IGNITION STATUS/VERIFY CABLE REQUIREMENTS CHEK CABLE CONNECTIONS? is displayed, perform TEST B: NO COMMUNICATION WITH LIGHTING CONTROL MODULE.

2) Turn ignition switch to LOCK position. Remove fuse No. 39 (10-amp) in instrument panel fuse box. Check fuse. If fuse is okay, go to next step. If fuse is blown, go to step 6).

3) Measure voltage at input side of fuse No. 39 in instrument panel fuse box. If battery voltage exists, go to next step. If battery voltage does not exist, go to step 24).

4) Install fuse No. 39. Disconnect Driver's Door Module (DDM) harness connector C524. Measure voltage at terminal No. 6 (Black/White wire) at DDM harness connector C524. *See Fig. 3.* If battery voltage exists, go to next step. If battery voltage does not exist, repair open in Black/White wire between instrument panel fuse box and DDM.

5) Measure resistance between ground and terminal No. 14 (Black/Light Blue wire) at DDM harness connector C524. If resistance is greater than 5 ohms, repair open in Black/Light Blue wire. If resistance is 5 ohms or less, repair module communication concern. See MODULE COMMUNICATIONS NETWORK – CONTINENTAL article.

6) Replace fuse No. 39. DO NOT operate any switches. If fuse blows, go to next step. If fuse does not blow, go to step 14).

7) Remove fuse No. 39. Disconnect DDM harness connector C524, Driver's Seat Module (DSM) harness connector C342, keyless entry keypad harness connector C525, driver's seat control switch harness connector C520, driver's door lock switch harness connector C505, passenger's door lock switch harness connector C602 and power mirror control switch harness connector C550. Measure resistance between ground and terminal No. 6 (Black/White wire) at DDM harness connector C524. If resistance is greater than 10 k/ohms, go to next step. If resistance is 10 k/ohms or less, repair short to ground in Black/White wire.

8) Connect keyless entry keypad harness connector C525. Measure resistance between ground and terminal No. 6 (Black/White wire) at DDM harness connector C524. If resistance is greater than 10 k/ohms, go to next step. If resistance is 10 k/ohms or less, replace keyless enter keypad.

9) Connect driver's seat control switch harness connector C520. Measure resistance between ground and terminal No. 6 (Black/White wire) at DDM harness connector C524. If resistance is greater than 10 k/ohms, go to next step. If resistance is 10 k/ohms or less, replace driver's seat control switch.

10) Connect DSM harness connector C342. Measure resistance between ground and terminal No. 6 (Black/White wire) at DDM harness connector C524. If resistance is greater than 10 k/ohms, go to next step. If resistance is 10 k/ohms or less, replace driver's seat module.

11) Connect DDM harness connector C524. Measure resistance between ground and terminal No. 6 (Black/White wire) at driver's door lock switch harness connector C505. See Fig. 4. If resistance is greater than 10 k/ohms, go to next step. If resistance is 10 k/ohms or less, replace driver's door module.

12) Connect passenger's door lock switch harness connector C602. Measure resistance between ground and terminal No. 6 (Black/White wire) at driver's door lock switch harness connector C505. If resistance is greater than 10 k/ohms, go to next step. If resistance is 10 k/ohms or less, replace passenger's door lock switch.

13) Connect power mirror control switch harness connector C550. Measure resistance between ground and terminal No. 6 (Black/White wire) at driver's door lock switch harness connector C505. If resistance is greater than 10 k/ohms, replace driver's door lock switch. If resistance is 10 k/ohms or less, replace power mirror control switch.

14) Lock and unlock doors at all door lock switches. If fuse No. 39 blows, go to next step. If fuse No. 39 does not blow, go to step **17)**.

15) Remove driver's and passenger's door lock switches. Test both door lock switches. See DOOR LOCK SWITCH under COMPONENT TESTS. If both door lock switches are okay, go to next step. If either door lock switch is defective, replace appropriate door lock switch.

16) Disconnect Driver's Door Module (DDM) harness connector C506. Measure resistance between ground and terminal No. 1 (Pink/Yellow wire) at driver's door lock switch harness connector C505. Also, measure resistance between ground and terminal No. 5 (Pink/Light Green wire) at driver's door lock switch harness connector C505. See Fig. 4. If either resistance reading is 10 k/ohms or less, repair short to ground in appropriate wire(s). If both resistance readings are greater than 10 k/ohms, replace driver's door module.

17) Press each number on keyless entry pad one at a time. If fuse No. 39 blows, go to next step. If fuse No. 39 does not blow, go to step **19)**.

18) Disconnect Driver's Door Module (DDM) harness connector C523. Disconnect keyless entry keypad harness connector C525. Measure resistance between ground and appropriate terminals at remote keyless entry keypad harness connector C525. See REMOTE KEYLESS ENTRY TERMINAL IDENTIFICATION table. See Fig. 5. If all resistance readings are greater than 10 k/ohms, replace driver's door module. If any resistance readings are 10 k/ohms or less, repair short to ground in appropriate wire.

REMOTE KEYLESS ENTRY TERMINAL IDENTIFICATION

Terminal	Wire Color
1	Red
2	Yellow
3	Yellow/Black
4	Light Green/Red
5	Light Blue/Yellow
9	Light Blue

19) Activate mirrors in all directions. If fuse No. 39 blows, go to next step. If fuse No. 39 does not blow, go to step **22)**.

20) Remove mirror control switch. Test mirror control switch. See MIRROR CONTROL SWITCH under COMPONENT TESTS. If mirror control switch is okay, go to next step. If mirror control switch is defective, replace mirror control switch.

21) Disconnect Driver's Door Module (DDM) harness connector C506. Disconnect mirror control switch harness connector C550. Measure resistance between ground and appropriate terminals at mirror control switch harness connector C550. See MIRROR CONTROL SWITCH TERMINAL IDENTIFICATION table. See Fig. 4. If all resistance readings are greater than 10 k/ohms, replace driver's door module. If any resistance reading are 10 k/ohms or less, repair short to ground in appropriate wire.

MIRROR CONTROL SWITCH TERMINAL IDENTIFICATION

Terminal	Wire Color
3	Dark Blue/Orange
4	Red/Orange
6	Yellow/Black
7	Violet/Orange
8	Dark Green/Orange

22) Activate driver's seat control switch in all directions. If fuse No. 39 blows, go to next step. If fuse No. 39 does not blow, system is operating properly at this time.

23) Disconnect Driver's Door Module (DDM) harness connector C506. Disconnect driver's seat control switch harness connector C520. Measure resistance between ground and appropriate terminals at driver's seat control switch harness connector C520. See DRIVER'S SEAT CONTROL SWITCH TERMINAL IDENTIFICATION table. See Fig. 6. If all resistance readings are greater than 10 k/ohms, replace driver's door module. If any resistance readings are 10 k/ohms or less, repair short to ground in appropriate wire.

DRIVER'S SEAT CONTROL SWITCH TERMINAL IDENTIFICATION

Terminal	Wire Color
2	Red/White
3	Red/Light Green
4	Red/Light Blue
5	Gray
7	Yellow/White
8	Yellow/Light Green
9	Yellow/Light Blue
10	Gray/Black

24) Turn ignition switch to LOCK position. Remove fuse No. 1 (30-amp) in power distribution box. Check fuse. If fuse is okay, go to next step. If fuse is blown, go to step **26)**.

25) Measure voltage at input side of fuse No. 1 in power distribution box. If battery voltage exists, repair open in Red wire between power distribution box and instrument panel fuse box. If battery voltage does not exist, repair or replace power distribution box as necessary.

26) Ensure fuse No. 1 in power distribution box is still removed. Disconnect Driver's Seat Module (DSM) harness connector C362. Disconnect driver's heated seat module harness connector C352. Disconnect driver's lumbar switch harness connector C348. Measure resistance between ground and terminal No. 1 (Red wire) at DSM harness connector C362. If resistance is greater than 10 k/ohms, go to next step. If resistance is 10 k/ohms or less, repair short to ground in Red wire.

27) Connect DSM harness connector C362. Measure resistance between ground and output side of fuse No. 1 in power distribution box. If resistance is greater than 10 k/ohms, go to next step. If resistance is 10 k/ohms or less, replace driver's seat module.

28) Replace fuse No. 1 (30-amp) in power distribution box. Connect driver's lumbar switch harness connector C348. Operate driver's lumbar switch in both directions. If fuse No. 1 blows, go to next step. If fuse No. 1 does not blow, go to step **32)**.

29) Remove fuse No. 1 (30-amp) from power distribution box. Measure resistance between ground and output side of fuse No. 1 in power distribution box. If resistance is greater than 10 k/ohms, go to next step. If resistance is 10 k/ohms or less, replace driver's lumbar switch.

30) Disconnect driver's lumbar switch harness connector C348. Measure resistance between ground and terminal No. 4 (Pink wire) at driver's lumbar switch harness connector C348. Also, measure resistance between ground and terminal No. 2 (Brown wire) at driver's lumbar switch harness connector C348. *See Fig. 7*. If both resistance readings are greater than 10 k/ohms, go to next step. If either resistance reading is 10 k/ohms or less, replace driver's lumbar switch.

31) Disconnect driver's lumbar motor harness connector C315. Measure resistance between ground and terminal No. 4 (Pink wire) at driver's lumbar switch harness connector C348. Also, measure resistance between ground and terminal No. 2 (Brown wire) at driver's lumbar switch harness connector C348. If both resistance readings are greater than 10 k/ohms, replace power lumbar motor. If either resistance reading is 10 k/ohms or less, repair short to ground in appropriate wire.

32) Disconnect driver's heated seat module harness connector C352. Measure resistance between ground and appropriate terminals at driver's heated seat module harness connector C352. See HEATED SEAT MODULE CONNECTOR TERMINAL IDENTIFICATION table. *See Fig. 3*. If all resistance readings are greater than 10 k/ohms, replace driver's heated seat module. If any resistance readings are 10 k/ohms or less, repair short to ground in appropriate wire.

HEATED SEAT MODULE CONNECTOR TERMINAL IDENTIFICATION

Terminal	Wire Color
5	Black/Light Blue
6	Brown/Light Blue
8	Yellow/Light Blue
9	Gray/Light Blue
10	Red/Light Blue
11	Orange/Light Blue
12	Violet/Light Blue
13	White/Light Blue

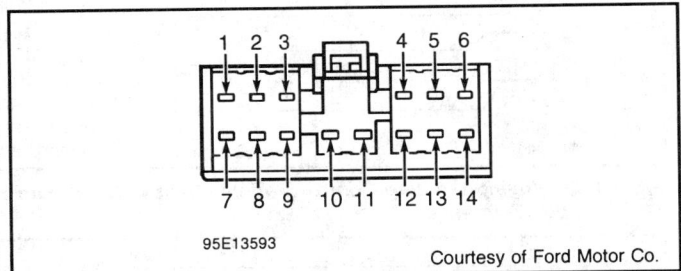

95E13593   Courtesy of Ford Motor Co.

Fig. 3: Identifying Driver's Door Module Harness Connector C524 & Driver's Heated Seat Module Harness Connector C352 Terminals

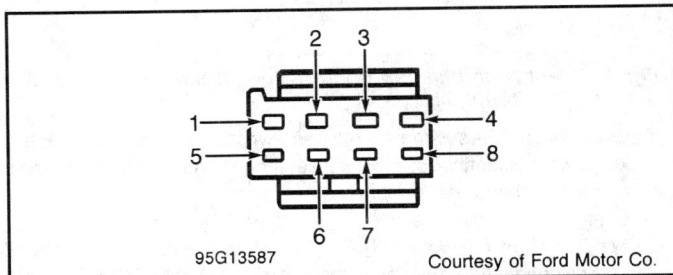

95G13587   Courtesy of Ford Motor Co.

Fig. 4: Identifying Driver's Door Lock Switch Harness Connector C505 & Mirror Control Switch Harness Connector C550 Terminals

TEST B: NO COMMUNICATION WITH LIGHTING CONTROL MODULE

1) Turn ignition switch to LOCK position. Connect New Generation Star (NGS) tester to Data Link Connector (DLC). Monitor Lighting Control Module (LCM) PID IGN_LC. If NGS tester does not display UNABLE TO PERFORM TEST/FUNCTION or MODULE NOT RESPONDING: LCM or CHECK IGNITION STATUS/VERIFY CABLE REQUIREMENTS or CHECK CABLE CONNECTIONS, go to next step. If NGS tester displays UNABLE TO PERFORM TEST/FUNCTION or MODULE NOT

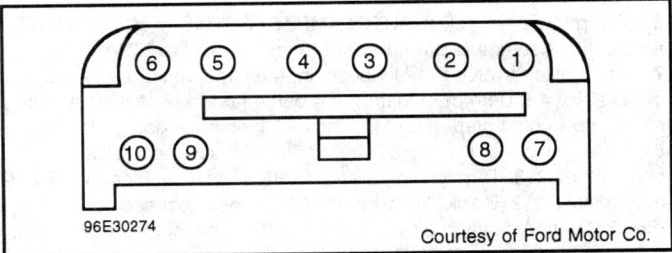

96E30274   Courtesy of Ford Motor Co.

Fig. 5: Identifying Remote Keyless Entry Keypad Harness Connector C525 Terminals

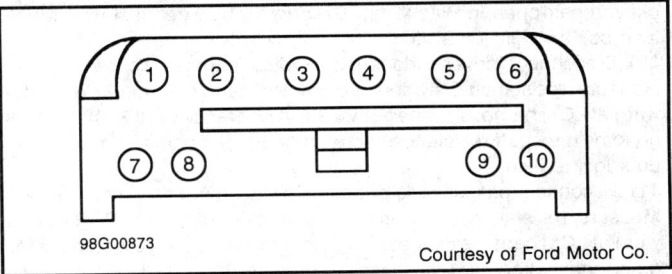

98G00873   Courtesy of Ford Motor Co.

Fig. 6: Identifying Driver's Seat Control Switch Harness Connector C520 Terminals

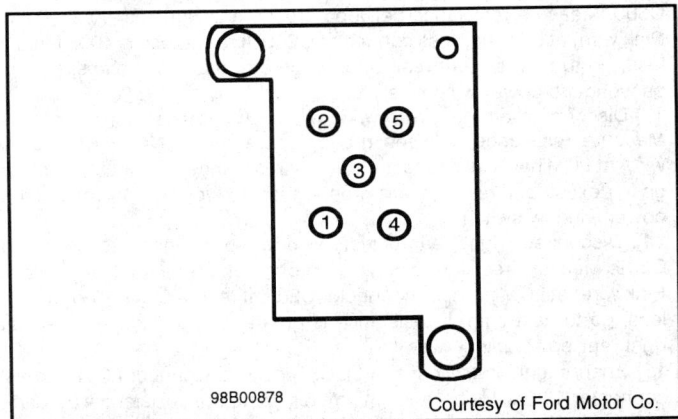

98B00878   Courtesy of Ford Motor Co.

Fig. 7: Identifying Driver's Lumbar Switch Harness Connector C348 Terminals

RESPONDING: LCM or CHECK IGNITION STATUS/VERIFY CABLE REQUIREMENTS or CHECK CABLE CONNECTIONS, go to step **16**).

2) Turn ignition switch to RUN position. Monitor LCM PID IGN_LC while turning key to each position. If PID IGN_LC indicates ACCY while in ACCESSORY position and OFF in all other positions, replace LCM. If PID IGN_LC indicates ACCY while in RUN position, go to next step. If PID IGN_LC indicates OFF in all positions, go to step **7**).

3) Turn ignition switch to RUN position. Measure voltage at output side of fuse No. 5 (10-amp) in instrument panel fuse box. If battery voltage does not exist, go to next step. If battery voltage exists, repair open in Red/Yellow wire between instrument panel fuse box and LCM.

4) Check fuse No. 5 in instrument panel fuse box. If fuse is blown, go to next step. If fuse is okay, repair open in Brown/Pink wire between instrument panel fuse box and ignition switch.

5) Turn ignition switch to LOCK position. Disconnect LCM harness connector C206. Disconnect light sensor amplifier harness connector C243. Measure resistance between ground and terminal No. 17 (Red/Yellow wire) at LCM harness connector C206. *See Fig. 8*. If resistance is 20 ohms or less, go to next step. If resistance is greater than 20 ohms, repair short to ground in Red/Yellow wire.

6) Turn ignition switch to LOCK position. Connect LCM harness connector C206. Remove fuse No. 5 (10-amp) in instrument panel fuse box. Measure resistance between ground and output side of fuse No. 5 in instrument panel fuse box. If resistance is 20 ohms or less, repair autolamp concern. See AUTOLAMP SYSTEMS – CONTINENTAL article. If resistance is greater than 20 ohms, replace LCM.

7) Turn ignition switch to RUN position. Measure voltage at output side of fuse No. 4 (10-amp) in instrument panel fuse box. If battery voltage exists, go to next step. If battery voltage does not exist, go to step **9)**.

8) Turn ignition switch to LOCK position. Disconnect LCM harness connector C208. Turn ignition switch to RUN position. Measure voltage at terminal No. 2 (Black/Pink wire) at LCM harness connector C208. See Fig. 9. If battery voltage exists, replace LCM. If battery voltage does not exist, repair open in Black/Pink wire.

9) Turn ignition switch to LOCK position. Check fuse No. 4 (10-amp) in instrument panel fuse box. If fuse is blown, go to next step. If fuse is okay, repair open in Black/Light Green wire between instrument panel fuse box and ignition switch.

10) Disconnect driver's door lock switch harness connector C505. Measure resistance between ground and terminal No. 2 (Black/Pink wire) at LCM harness connector C208. If resistance is 10 k/ohms or less, go to next step. If resistance is greater than 10 k/ohms, replace driver's door lock switch.

11) Disconnect passenger's door lock switch harness connector C602. Measure resistance between ground and terminal No. 2 (Black/Pink wire) at LCM harness connector C208. If resistance is 10 k/ohms or less, go to next step. If resistance is greater than 10 k/ohms, replace passenger's door lock switch.

12) Disconnect passenger's power window switch harness connector C600. Measure resistance between ground and terminal No. 2 (Black/Pink wire) at LCM harness connector C208. If resistance is 10 k/ohms or less, go to next step. If resistance is greater than 10 k/ohms, replace passenger's power window switch.

13) Disconnect left rear power window switch harness connector C709. Measure resistance between ground and terminal No. 2 (Black/Pink wire) at LCM harness connector C208. If resistance is 10 k/ohms or less, go to next step. If resistance is greater than 10 k/ohms, replace left rear power window switch.

14) Disconnect right rear power window switch harness connector C809. Measure resistance between ground and terminal No. 2 (Black/Pink wire) at LCM harness connector C208. If resistance is 10 k/ohms or less, go to next step. If resistance is greater than 10 k/ohms, replace right rear power window switch.

15) Ensure ignition switch is in LOCK position. Connect LCM harness connector C208. Using and ohmmeter, measure resistance by back-probing between ground and terminal No. 2 (Black/Pink wire) at LCM harness connector C208. If resistance is greater than 2 k/ohms, replace LCM. If resistance is 2 k/ohms or less, repair Black/Pink wire.

16) Turn ignition switch to LOCK position. Disconnect LCM harness connectors. Measure resistance between ground and terminal No. 13 (Black wire) at LCM harness connector C206. See Fig. 8. Measure resistance between ground and terminal No. 1 (Black wire) at LCM harness connector C207. See Fig. 10. Measure resistance between ground and terminal No. 9 (Black wire) at LCM harness connector C211. See Fig. 11. If all resistance readings are 5 ohms or less, go to next step. If any resistance reading is greater than 5 ohms, repair appropriate Black wire.

17) Measure resistance between ground and terminal No. 15 (Black/Light Blue wire) at LCM harness connector C207. If resistance is 5 ohms or less, repair module communication concern. See MODULE COMMUNICATIONS NETWORK – CONTINENTAL article. If resistance is greater than 5 ohms, repair open in Black/Light Blue wire.

TEST C: ALL WINDOWS ARE INOPERATIVE

1) Ensure all window switches are not pressed. Using NGS tester, clear Driver's Door Module (DDM) DTCs and perform DDM self-test. If DTC B1549 is not retrieved, go to next step. If DTC B1549 is retrieved, go to step **3)**.

2) Using NGS tester, select and monitor DDM PIDs, RRPW_SW, LRPW_SW, P_PW_SW, and D_PW_SW. Press and release each driver's door window control switches several times. If each PID does not indicate that the button releases within one second from when switch is released, go to next step. If each PID indicates that the button

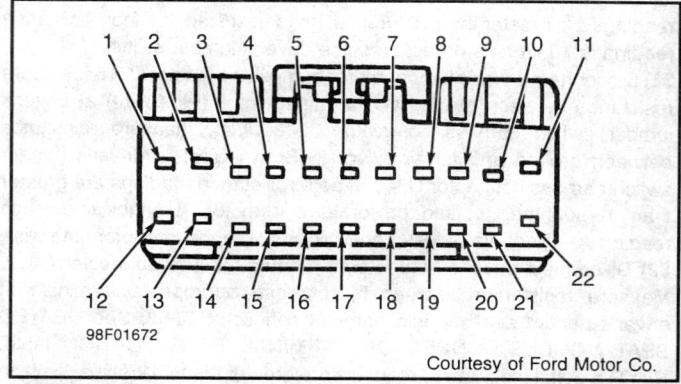

Fig. 8: Identifying Lighting Control Module Harness Connector C206 Terminals

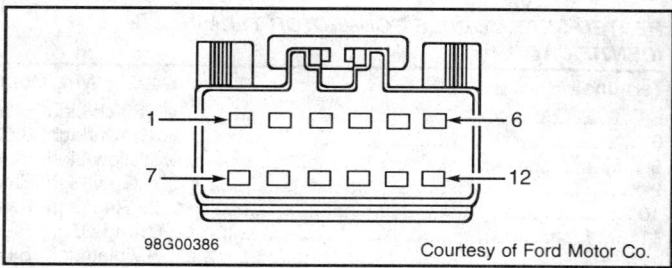

Fig. 9: Identifying Lighting Control Module Harness Connector C208 Terminals

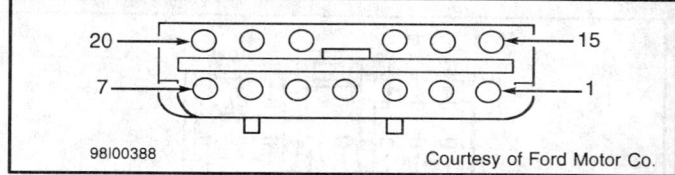

Fig. 10: Identifying Lighting Control Module Harness Connector C207 Terminals

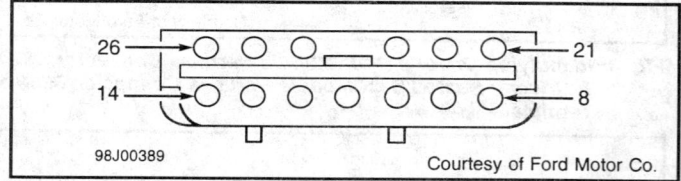

Fig. 11: Identifying Lighting Control Module Harness Connector C211 Terminals

releases within one second from when switch is released, check for a sticking switch. Continuous fault will set if any window switch is held for greater than 2 minutes.

3) Using NGS tester, select and monitor DDM PIDs, RRPW_SW, LRPW_SW, P_PW_SW, and D_PW_SW. Remove driver's door module without disconnecting any connectors. If the PID still indicates a stuck window control switch, replace driver's door module. If the PID does not indicate a stuck window control switch anymore, replace driver's door window control switch bezel.

TEST D: LEFT FRONT WINDOW IS INOPERATIVE

1) Using NGS tester, select and monitor Driver's Door Module (DDM) PID D_PW_SW. Press and release driver's door window control switch in the UP and DOWN position several times. If PID agrees with the switch position, go to next step. If PID does not agree with the switch position, replace driver's door module.

2) Turn ignition switch to LOCK position. Disconnect DDM harness connector C522. Measure voltage at terminal No. 3 (Yellow/Light Green wire) at DDM harness connector C522. *See Fig. 12.* If battery voltage exists, go to next step. If battery voltage does not exist, repair open in Yellow/Light Green wire.

3) Measure resistance between ground and terminal No. 4 (Black wire) at DDM harness connector C522. If resistance is 5 ohms or less, go to next step. If resistance is greater than 5 ohms, repair open in Black wire.

4) Connect DDM harness connector C522. Disconnect left front window motor harness connector C514. Turn ignition switch to RUN position. Measure voltage at Red/Yellow wire terminal at left front window motor harness connector C514 while pressing left front window control switch to UP position. Measure voltage at Pink/Yellow wire terminal at left front window motor harness connector C514 while pressing left front window control switch to DOWN position. If voltage does not cycle from zero volts to battery voltage when switches are pressed, go to next step. If voltage cycles from zero volts to battery voltage when switches are pressed, go to step **6)**.

5) Turn ignition switch to LOCK position. Disconnect DDM harness connector C522. Measure resistance in Pink/Yellow wire between terminal No. 1 at DDM harness connector C522 and left front window motor harness connector C514. Measure resistance in Red/Yellow wire between terminal No. 2 at DDM harness connector C522 and left front window motor harness connector C514. If either resistance reading is greater than 5 ohms, repair open in Pink/Yellow or Red/Yellow wire(s). If both resistance readings are 5 ohms or less, replace driver's door module.

6) Measure resistance between ground and each terminal at left front window motor (component side). If both resistance readings are greater than 10 k/ohms, go to next step. If either resistance reading is 10 k/ohms or less, replace shorted window motor.

7) Test left front window motor. See WINDOW MOTOR under COMPONENT TESTS. If motor is defective, replace left front window motor. If motor is okay, repair binding window regulator.

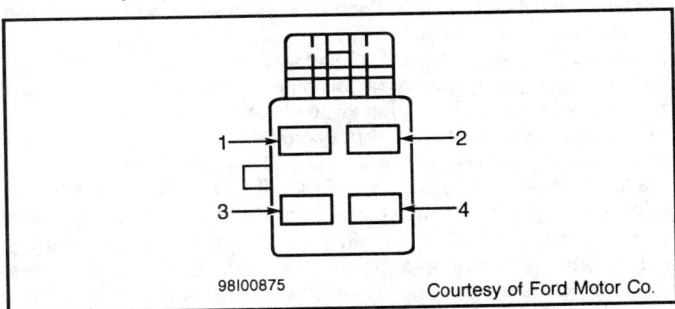

98I00875 Courtesy of Ford Motor Co.

Fig. 12: Identifying Driver's Door Module Harness Connector C522 Terminals

TEST E: LEFT REAR WINDOW IS INOPERATIVE

NOTE: Left rear window control switch harness connector C711 is a flat 4-pin connector. Left rear window control switch harness connector C709 is a square 4-pin connector.

1) Turn ignition switch to RUN position. Using NGS tester, select and monitor Driver's Door Module (DDM) PID LRPW_SW. Press and release driver's door window control switch left rear window switch in the UP and DOWN position several times. If PID agrees with the switch position, go to next step. If PID does not agree with the switch position, replace driver's door module.

2) Attempt to operate left rear window from master window control switch. If left rear window does not operate properly, go to next step. If left rear window operates properly, go to step **9)**.

3) Turn ignition switch to LOCK position. Disconnect left rear window control switch harness connector C711. Turn ignition switch to RUN position. Measure voltage at Yellow/Light Blue wire terminal at left rear window control switch harness connector C711 while pressing master window control switch left rear window to UP position. Measure voltage at Gray/Orange wire terminal at left rear window control switch harness connector C711 while pressing master window control switch left rear window to DOWN position. If voltage cycles from zero volts to battery

voltage when switches are pressed, go to next step. If voltage does not cycle from zero volts to battery voltage when switches are pressed, go to step **7)**.

4) Disconnect left rear window control switch harness connector C709. Measure voltage at Yellow/Light Green wire terminal at left rear window control switch harness connector C709. If battery voltage exists, go to next step. If battery voltage does not exist, repair open in Yellow/Light Green wire.

5) Turn ignition switch to LOCK position. Measure resistance between ground and Black wire terminal at left rear window control switch harness connector C709. If resistance is 5 ohms or less, go to next step. If resistance is greater than 5 ohms, repair open in Black wire.

6) Test left rear window control switch. See SINGLE SWITCHES under COMPONENT TESTS. If left rear window control switch is okay, go to step **8)**. If left rear window control switch is defective, replace switch.

7) Disconnect DDM harness connector C523. Measure resistance in Yellow/Light Blue wire between terminal No. 1 at DDM harness connector C523 and left rear window control switch harness connector C711. *See Fig. 13.* Measure resistance in Gray/Orange wire between terminal No. 2 at DDM harness connector C523 and left rear window control switch harness connector C711. If either resistance reading is greater than 5 ohms, repair open in Yellow/Light Blue and/or Gray/Orange wire. If both resistance readings are 5 ohms or less, replace driver's door module.

8) Disconnect left rear window motor harness connector C710. Measure resistance in Yellow/Black wire between left rear window control switch harness connector C711 and left rear window motor harness connector C710. Measure resistance in Yellow/Light Blue wire between left rear window control switch harness connector C711 and left rear window motor harness connector C710. If either resistance reading is greater than 5 ohms, repair open in Yellow/Black and/or Yellow/Light Blue wire. If both resistance readings are 5 ohms or less, replace left rear window motor.

9) Disconnect left rear window control switch harness connector C711. Turn ignition switch to RUN position. Measure voltage at Red/Light Blue wire terminal at left rear window control switch harness connector C711. If battery voltage exists, replace left rear window control switch. If battery voltage does not exist, repair open in Red/Light Blue wire.

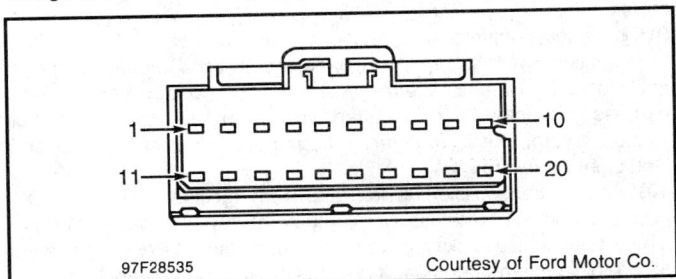

97F28535 Courtesy of Ford Motor Co.

Fig. 13: Identifying Driver's Door Module Harness Connector C523 Terminals

TEST F: RIGHT FRONT WINDOW IS INOPERATIVE

NOTE: Right front window control switch harness connector C600 is a flat 4-pin connector. Right front window control switch harness connector C601 is a square 4-pin connector.

1) Turn ignition switch to RUN position. Using NGS tester, select and monitor Driver's Door Module (DDM) PID P_PW_SW. Press and release master window control switch right front window switch in the UP and DOWN position several times. If PID agrees with the switch position, go to next step. If PID does not agree with the switch position, replace driver's door module.

2) Attempt to operate right front window from master window control switch. If right front window does not operate properly, go to next step. If right front window operates properly, go to step **9)**.

3) Turn ignition switch to LOCK position. Disconnect right front window control switch harness connector C600. Turn ignition switch to RUN position. Measure voltage at Tan/Light Blue wire terminal at right front window control switch harness connector C600 while pressing master window control switch right front window to UP position. Measure voltage at White/Yellow wire terminal at right front window control switch harness connector C600 while pressing master window control switch right front window to DOWN position. If voltage cycles from zero volts to battery voltage when switch is pressed, go to next step. If voltage does not cycle from zero volts to battery voltage when switch is pressed, go to step **7**).

4) Disconnect right front window control switch harness connector C601. Turn ignition switch to RUN position. Measure voltage at Pink wire terminal at right front window control switch harness connector C601. If battery voltage exists, go to next step. If battery voltage does not exist, go to step **10**).

5) Turn ignition switch to LOCK position. Measure resistance between ground and Black wire terminal at right front window control switch harness connector C601. If resistance is 5 ohms or less, go to next step. If resistance is greater than 5 ohms, repair open in Black wire.

6) Test right front window control switch. See SINGLE SWITCHES under COMPONENT TESTS. If right front window control switch is okay, go to step **8**). If right front window control switch is defective, replace switch.

7) Disconnect DDM harness connector C523. Measure resistance in White/Yellow wire between terminal No. 6 at DDM harness connector C523 and right front window control switch harness connector C600. *See Fig. 13.* Measure resistance in Tan/Light Blue wire between terminal No. 5 at DDM harness connector C523 and right front window control switch harness connector C600. If either resistance reading is greater than 5 ohms, repair open in White/Yellow and/or Tan/Light Blue wire. If both resistance readings are 5 ohms or less, replace driver's door module.

8) Disconnect right front window motor harness connector C614. Measure resistance in Yellow wire between right front window control switch harness connector C601 and right front window motor harness connector C614. Measure resistance in White/Black wire between right front window control switch harness connector C601 and right front window motor harness connector C614. If either resistance reading is greater than 5 ohms, repair open in Yellow and/or White/Black wire. If both resistance readings are 5 ohms or less, replace right front window motor.

9) Disconnect right front window control switch harness connector C600. Turn ignition switch to RUN position. Measure voltage between ground and Red/Light Blue wire terminal at right front window control switch harness connector C600. If battery voltage exists, replace right front window control switch. If battery voltage does not exist, repair open in Red/Light Blue wire.

10) Ensure transmission is in Park. Turn ignition switch to LOCK position. Remove mini-fuse No. 8 (30-amp) in power distribution box. Check fuse. If fuse is okay, go to next step. If fuse is blown, replace fuse and retest system operation. If new fuse blows, go to step **12**).

11) Measure voltage between ground and input side of mini-fuse No. 8 (30-amp) in power distribution box. If battery voltage exists, repair open in Pink wire. If battery voltage does not exist, replace power distribution box.

12) Disconnect right front window control switch harness connector C601. Measure resistance between ground and output side of mini-fuse No. 8 (30-amp) in power distribution box. If resistance is greater than 10 k/ohms, go to next step. If resistance is 10 k/ohms or less, repair short to ground in Pink wire.

13) Test right front window control switch. See SINGLE SWITCHES under COMPONENT TESTS. If right front window control switch is okay, go to next step. If right front window control switch is defective, replace switch.

14) Disconnect DDM harness connector C523. Measure voltage at White/Yellow wire terminal at right front window control switch harness connector C600. Measure voltage at Tan/Light Blue wire terminal right front window control switch harness connector C600. If voltage does not exist at both terminals, go to next step. If voltage exists at either terminal, repair short to voltage in White/Yellow and/or Tan/Light Blue wire.

15) Measure resistance between ground and White/Yellow wire terminal at right front window control switch harness connector C600. Measure resistance between ground and Tan/Light Blue wire terminal at right front window control switch harness connector C600. If both resistance readings are greater than 10 k/ohms, go to next step. If either resistance reading is 10 k/ohms or less, repair short to ground in White/Yellow and/or Tan/Light Blue wire.

16) Connect DDM harness connector C523. Disconnect right front window control switch harness connector C601. Measure voltage at White/Black wire terminal at right front window control switch harness connector C601. Measure voltage at Yellow wire terminal at right front window control switch harness connector C601. If voltage does not exist at either terminal, go to next step. If voltage exists are either terminal , repair short to voltage in White/Black and/or Yellow wire.

17) Disconnect right front window motor harness connector C614. Measure resistance between ground and White/Black wire terminal at right front window control switch harness connector C601. Measure resistance between ground and Yellow wire terminal at right front window control switch harness connector C601. If both resistance readings are greater than 10 k/ohms, replace right front window motor. If either resistance reading is 10 k/ohms or less, repair short to ground in White/Black and/or Yellow wire.

TEST G: RIGHT REAR WINDOW IS INOPERATIVE

NOTE: Right rear window control switch harness connector C809 is a flat 4-pin connector. Right rear window control switch harness connector C811 is a square 4-pin connector.

1) Turn ignition switch to RUN position. Using NGS tester, select and monitor Driver's Door Module (DDM) PID RRPW_SW. Press and release master window control switch right rear window switch in the UP and DOWN position several times. If PID agrees with the switch position, go to next step. If PID does not agree with the switch position, replace driver's door module.

2) Attempt to operate right rear window from master window control switch. If right rear window does not operate properly, go to next step. If right rear window operates properly, go to step **9**).

3) Turn ignition switch to LOCK position. Disconnect right rear window control switch harness connector C809. Turn ignition switch to RUN position. Measure voltage at Yellow/Black wire terminal at right rear window control switch harness connector C809 while pressing master window control switch right rear window to UP position. Measure voltage at Red/Black wire terminal at right rear window control switch harness connector C809 while pressing master window control switch right rear window to DOWN position. If voltage cycles from zero volts to battery voltage when switch is pressed, go to next step. If voltage does not cycle from zero volts to battery voltage when switch is pressed, go to step **7**).

4) Disconnect right rear window control switch harness connector C811. Turn ignition switch to RUN position. Measure voltage at Gray/Light Blue wire terminal at right rear window control switch harness connector C811. If battery voltage exists, go to next step. If battery voltage does not exist, go to step **10**).

5) Turn ignition switch to LOCK position. Measure resistance between ground and Black wire terminal at right rear window control switch harness connector C811. If resistance is 5 ohms or less, go to next step. If resistance is greater than 5 ohms, repair open in Black wire.

6) Test right rear window control switch. See SINGLE SWITCHES under COMPONENT TESTS. If right rear window control switch is okay, go to step **8**). If right rear window control switch is defective, replace switch.

7) Disconnect DDM harness connector C523. Measure resistance in Yellow/Black wire between terminal No. 8 at DDM harness connector C523 and right rear window control switch harness connector C809. *See Fig. 13.* Measure resistance in Red/Black wire between terminal No. 7 at DDM harness connector C523 and right rear window control switch harness connector C809. If either resistance reading is greater than 5 ohms, repair open in Yellow/Black and/or Red/Black wire. If both resistance readings are 5 ohms or less, replace driver's door module.

8) Disconnect right rear window motor harness connector C810. Measure resistance in Brown/Yellow wire between right rear window control switch harness connector C811 and right rear window motor harness connector C810. Measure resistance in Brown wire between right rear window control switch harness connector C811 and right rear window motor harness connector C810. If either resistance reading is greater than 5 ohms, repair open in Brown/Yellow and/or Brown wire. If both resistance readings are 5 ohms or less, replace right rear window motor.

9) Disconnect right rear window control switch harness connector C809. Turn ignition switch to RUN position. Measure voltage at Red/Light Blue wire terminal at right rear window control switch harness connector C809. If battery voltage exists, replace right rear window control switch. If battery voltage does not exist, repair open in Red/Light Blue wire.

10) Ensure transmission is in Park. Turn ignition switch to LOCK position. Remove mini-fuse No. 3 (30-amp) in power distribution box. Check fuse. If fuse is okay, go to next step. If fuse is blown, replace fuse and retest system operation. If new fuse blows, go to step 12).

11) Measure voltage at input side of mini-fuse No. 3 (30-amp) in power distribution box. If battery voltage exists, repair open in Gray/Light Blue wire. If battery voltage does not exist, replace power distribution box.

12) Disconnect right rear window control switch harness connector C811. Measure resistance between ground and output side of mini-fuse No. 3 (30-amp) in power distribution box. If resistance is greater than 10 k/ohms, go to next step. If resistance is 10 k/ohms or less, repair short to ground in Gray/Light Blue wire.

13) Test right rear window control switch. See SINGLE SWITCHES under COMPONENT TESTS. If right rear window control switch is okay, go to next step. If right rear window control switch is defective, replace switch.

14) Disconnect DDM harness connector C523. Measure voltage at Yellow/Black wire terminal at right rear window control switch harness connector C809. Measure voltage at Red/Black wire terminal at right rear window control switch harness connector C809. If voltage does not exist at both terminals, go to next step. If voltage exists at either terminal, repair short to voltage in Yellow/Black and/or Red/Black wire.

15) Measure resistance between ground and Yellow/Black wire terminal at right rear window control switch harness connector C809. Measure resistance between ground and Red/Black wire terminal at right rear window control switch harness connector C809. If both resistance readings are greater than 10 k/ohms, go to next step. If either resistance reading is 10 k/ohms or less, repair short to ground in Yellow/Black and/or Red/Black wire.

16) Connect DDM harness connector C523. Disconnect right rear window control switch harness connector C811. Measure voltage at Brown wire terminal at right rear window control switch harness connector C811. Measure voltage at Brown/Yellow wire terminal at right rear window control switch harness connector C811. If voltage does not exists at both terminals, go to next step. If voltage exists at either terminal, repair short to voltage in Brown and/or Brown/Yellow wire.

17) Disconnect right rear window motor harness connector C810. Measure resistance between ground and Brown wire terminal at right rear window control switch harness connector C811. Measure resistance between ground and Brown/Yellow wire terminal at right rear window control switch harness connector C811. If both resistance readings are greater than 10 k/ohms, replace right rear window motor. If either resistance reading is 10 k/ohms or less, repair short to ground in Brown and/or Brown/Yellow wire.

TEST H: LEFT FRONT & LEFT REAR WINDOWS ARE INOPERATIVE

NOTE: Left rear window control switch harness connector C711 is a flat 4-pin connector. Left rear window control switch harness connector C709 is a square 4-pin connector.

1) Turn ignition switch to RUN position. Using NGS tester, select and monitor Driver's Door Module (DDM) PIDs D_PW_SW and LRPW_SW. Press and release master window control switch left front and left rear window switch in the UP and DOWN position several times. If PID agrees with the switch position, go to next step. If PID does not agree with the switch position, replace driver's door module.

2) Ensure transmission is in Park. Turn ignition switch to LOCK position. Remove maxi-fuse No. 5 (40-amp) in power distribution box. Check fuse. If fuse is okay, go to next step. If fuse is blown, replace fuse and retest system operation. If new fuse blows, go to step 4).

3) Measure voltage at input side of maxi-fuse No. 5 (40-amp) in power distribution box. If battery voltage exists, repair open in Yellow/Light Green wire. If battery voltage does not exist, replace power distribution box.

4) Remove fuse No. 9 (40-amp) in power distribution box. Remove fuse No. 41 (20-amp) in instrument panel fuse box. Disconnect left rear window control switch harness connector C709. Measure resistance between ground and output side of maxi-fuse No. 5 (40-amp) in power distribution box. If resistance is greater than 10 k/ohms, go to next step. If resistance is 10 k/ohms or less, repair short to ground in Yellow/Light Green wire.

5) Test left rear window control switch. See SINGLE SWITCHES under COMPONENT TESTS. If left rear window control switch is okay, go to next step. If left rear window control switch is defective, replace switch.

6) Measure at Yellow/Light Blue wire terminal at left rear window control switch harness connector C711. Measure voltage at Gray/Orange wire terminal at left rear window control switch harness connector C711. If voltage does not exist at both terminals, go to next step. If voltage exists at either terminal, repair short to voltage in Yellow/Light Blue and/or Gray/Orange wire.

7) Disconnect DDM harness connector C523. Measure resistance between ground and Yellow/Light Blue wire terminal at left rear window control switch harness connector C711. Measure resistance between ground and Gray/Orange wire terminal at left rear window control switch harness connector C711. If both resistance readings are greater than 10 k/ohms, go to next step. If either resistance reading is 10 k/ohms or less, repair short to ground in Yellow/Light Blue and/or Gray/Orange wire.

8) Measure voltage at Yellow/Black wire terminal at left rear window control switch harness connector C709. Measure voltage at Yellow/Light Blue wire terminal at left rear window control switch harness connector C709. If voltage exists at either terminal, go to next step. If voltage does not exist at both terminals, go to step 10).

9) Disconnect left rear window motor harness connector C710. Measure voltage between ground and Yellow/Black wire terminal at left rear window control switch harness connector C709. If voltage exists, repair short to voltage in Yellow/Black wire. If voltage does not exist, repair short to voltage in Yellow/Light Blue wire.

10) Measure resistance between ground and Yellow/Black wire terminal at left rear window control switch harness connector C709. Measure resistance between ground and Yellow/Light Blue wire terminal at left rear window control switch harness connector C709. If both resistance readings are 10 k/ohms or less, go to next step. If both resistance readings are greater than 10 k/ohms, go to step 12).

11) Disconnect left rear window motor harness connector C710. Measure resistance between ground and Yellow/Black wire terminal at left rear window control switch harness connector C709. Measure resistance between ground and Yellow/Light Blue wire terminal at left rear window control switch harness connector C709. If both resistance readings are greater than 10 k/ohms, replace left rear window motor. If either resistance reading is 10 k/ohms or less, repair short to ground in Yellow/Black and/or Yellow/Light Blue wire.

12) Disconnect DDM harness connector C522. Measure voltage at terminal No. 1 (Pink/Yellow wire) at DDM harness connector C522. Measure voltage at terminal No. 2 (Red/Yellow wire) at DDM harness connector C522. *See Fig. 12.* If voltage exist at either terminal, go to next step. If voltage does not exist at both terminals, go to step 14) .

13) Disconnect left front window motor harness connector C514. Measure voltage at terminal No. 1 (Pink/Yellow wire) at DDM harness connector C522. If voltage exists, repair short to voltage in Pink/Yellow wire. If voltage does not exist, repair short to voltage in Red/Yellow wire.

14) Measure resistance between ground and terminal No. 1 (Pink/Yellow wire) at DDM harness connector C522. Measure resistance between ground and terminal No. 2 (Red/Yellow wire) at DDM harness connector

C522. If either resistance reading is 10 k/ohms or less, go to next step. If both resistance readings are greater than 10 k/ohms, replace driver's door module.

15) Disconnect left front window motor harness connector C514. Measure resistance between ground and terminal No. 1 (Pink/Yellow wire) at DDM harness connector C522. Measure resistance between ground and terminal No. 2 (Red/Yellow wire) at DDM harness connector C522. If both resistance readings are greater than 10 k/ohms, replace left front window motor. If either resistance reading is 10 k/ohms or less, repair short to ground in Pink/Yellow and/or Red/Yellow wire.

TEST J: RIGHT FRONT, RIGHT REAR & LEFT REAR WINDOWS ARE INOPERATIVE

NOTE: Right rear window control switch harness connector C809, left rear window control switch harness connector C711 and right front window control switch harness connector C600 are flat 4-pin connector.

1) Turn ignition switch to RUN position. Activate all windows from master window control switch. If all windows operate properly from master control switch, go to next step. If all windows do not operate properly from master window control switch, go to step 3).

2) Disconnect Driver's Door Module (DDM) harness connector C523. Using a fused jumper wire, apply battery voltage to terminal No. 10 (Red/Light Blue wire) at DDM harness connector C523. *See Fig. 13.* Activate each passenger's door window switch. If all passenger's windows operate, replace driver's door module. If each passenger's window does not operate, repair open in Red/Light Blue wire.

3) Measure resistance between ground and terminal No. 10 (Red/Light Blue wire) at DDM harness connector C523. If resistance is 10 k/ohms or less, go to next step. If resistance is greater than 10 k/ohms, replace driver's door module.

4) Disconnect left rear window control switch harness connector C711. Measure resistance between ground and terminal No. 10 (Red/Light Blue wire) at DDM harness connector C523. *See Fig. 13.* If resistance is 10 k/ohms or less, go to next step. If resistance is greater than 10 k/ohms, replace left rear window control switch.

5) Disconnect right front window control switch harness connector C600. Measure resistance between ground and terminal No. 10 (Red/Light Blue wire) at DDM harness connector C523. If resistance is 10 k/ohms or less, go to next step. If resistance is greater than 10 k/ohms, replace right front window control switch.

6) Disconnect right rear window control switch harness connector C809. Measure resistance between ground and terminal No. 10 (Red/Light Blue wire) at DDM harness connector C523. If resistance is 10 k/ohms or less, repair short to ground in Red/Light Blue wire. If resistance is greater than 10 k/ohms, replace right rear window control switch.

TEST K: WINDOW LOCK-OUT FEATURE DOES NOT OPERATE PROPERLY

NOTE: Right rear window control switch harness connector C809, left rear window control switch harness connector C711 and right front window control switch harness connector C600 are flat 4-pin connector.

1) Turn ignition switch to RUN position. Ensure window lock-out switch is not engaged (switch is up). Activate each passenger's door window switch. Engage window lock-out switch (switch is down). Activate each passenger's door window switch. If window lock-out feature does not operate properly, go to next step. If window lock-out feature operates properly, system is okay at this time.

2) Disconnect Driver's Door Module (DDM) harness connector C523. Measure voltage at terminal No. 10 (Red/Light Blue wire) at DDM harness connector C523. *See Fig. 13.* If battery voltage exists, go to next step. If battery voltage does not exist, repair open in Red/Light Blue wire.

3) Disconnect left rear window control switch harness connector C711. Measure voltage at terminal No. 10 (Red/Light Blue wire) at DDM harness connector C523. If battery voltage exists, go to next step. If battery voltage does not exist, replace left rear window control switch.

4) Disconnect right rear window control switch harness connector C809. Measure voltage at terminal No. 10 (Red/Light Blue wire) at DDM harness connector C523. If battery voltage exists, go to next step. If battery voltage does not exist, replace right rear window control switch.

5) Disconnect right front window control switch harness connector C600. Measure voltage at terminal No. 10 (Red/Light Blue wire) at DDM harness connector C523. If battery voltage exists, replace driver's door module. If battery voltage does not exist, replace right front window control switch.

TEST L: ONE-TOUCH DOWN FEATURE DOES NOT OPERATE PROPERLY

1) Turn ignition switch to RUN position. Lightly press master control switch to driver's door window switch DOWN position. If driver's door window does not go all the way down, go to next step. If driver's door window goes all the way down, go to step 3).

2) Press message center MENU switch until message center reads EXPRESS WINDOW. If one-touch down feature is ON, go to next step. If one-touch down feature is not ON, press SELECT switch to turn one-touch down feature on.

3) Operate driver's door window several times while observing window operation. If window operates smoothly without any sticking or binding, go to next step. If window does not operate smoothly without any sticking or binding, repair window mechanism as necessary.

4) Operate driver's door window to full UP position. Press master window control switch to driver's window switch DOWN position. While window is in motion, press master window control switch to driver's window UP position. If driver's door window stops, system is okay at this time. If driver's door window does not stop, replace driver's door module.

REMOVAL & INSTALLATION

NOTE: Component removal & installation information is not available from manufacturer.

WIRING DIAGRAMS

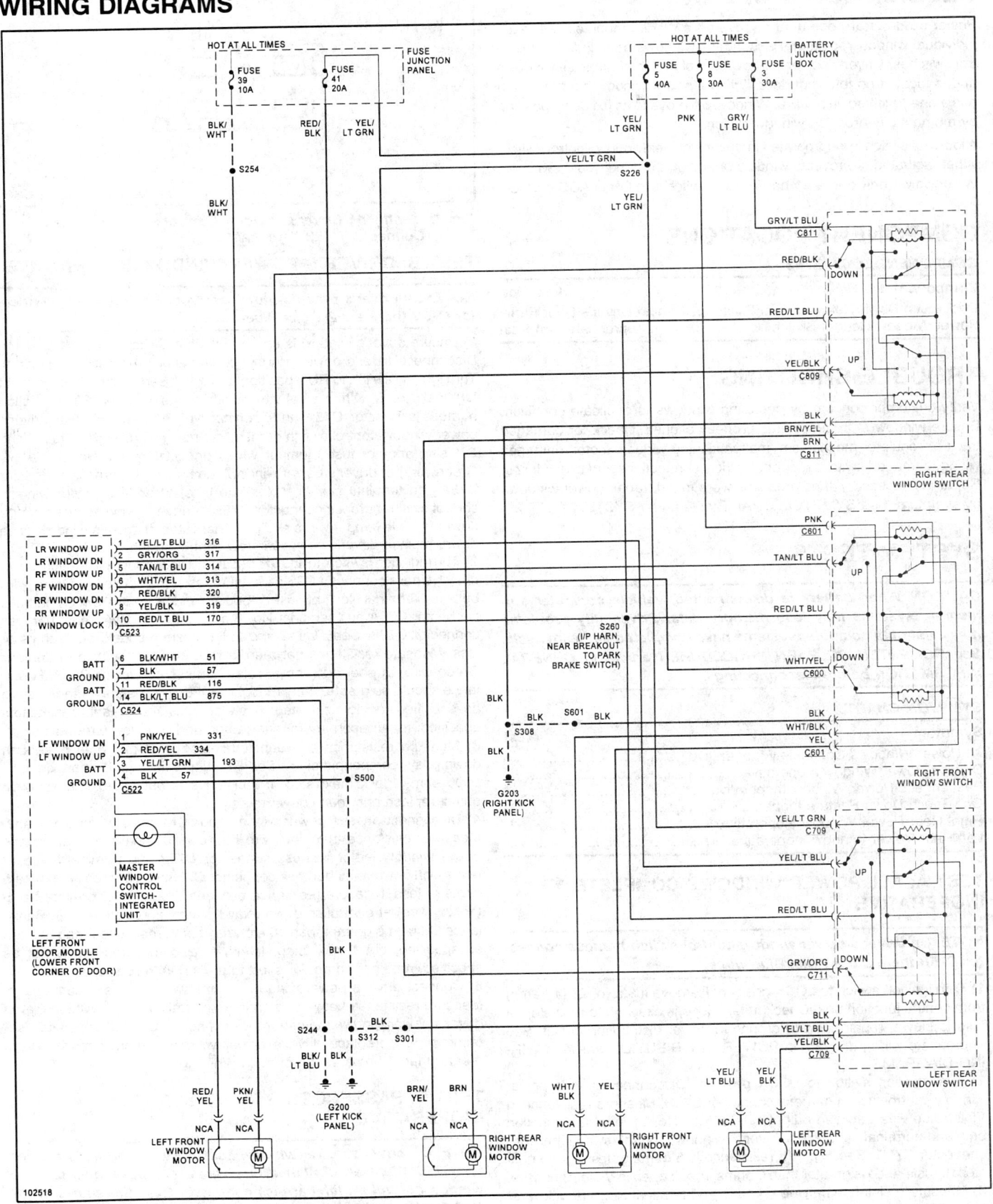

Fig. 14: Power Window System Wiring Diagram (Continental)

1999 ACCESSORIES & EQUIPMENT
Power Windows – Contour & Mystique

DESCRIPTION & OPERATION

Power windows are operated by reversible motors mounted with each individual window regulator. Passenger's windows have individual control switches. Driver's power window control switch controls all windows and is located on left front door. Driver's power window control switch has a one-touch down feature. Window will move to its full down position by momentarily pressing window switch.

A lock-out switch is incorporated in driver's power window control switch. When actuated, it prevents window operation from individual switches. Windows will only operate when ignition switch is in ON or ACC position.

COMPONENT LOCATIONS

COMPONENT LOCATIONS

Component	Location
One-Touch Down Relay	Behind Driver's Door Panel
Power Window Control Switch	On Appropriate Arm Rest

TROUBLE SHOOTING

Verify customer concern by operating windows to duplicate condition. Ensure window(s) in question is properly aligned. Check for damaged track or regulator mechanism, malfunctioning window motor, damaged wiring, damaged switches, poor electrical connections and blown fuses. Repair as necessary. If no problems were found, repair power windows by symptom. See SYMPTOM CHART table under SYSTEM TESTS.

SYSTEM TESTS

CAUTION: When battery is disconnected, vehicle computer and memory systems may lose memory data. Driveability problems may exist until computer systems have completed a relearn cycle. See COMPUTER RELEARN PROCEDURES article in GENERAL INFORMATION before disconnecting battery.

SYMPTOM CHART

Symptom	Test
All Power Windows Completely Inoperative	A
Driver's Power Window Inoperative	B
Passenger's Power Window Inoperative	C
One-Touch Down Feature Inoperative	D
Right Rear Power Window Inoperative	E
Left Rear Power Window Inoperative	F

TEST A: ALL POWER WINDOWS COMPLETELY INOPERATIVE

NOTE: On driver's power window control switch harness connector C75B there are 2 Violet/Blue wires.

1) Turn ignition switch to LOCK position. Remove fuse No. 21 (40-amp) from central junction box. Check fuse. If fuse is okay, go to next step. If fuse is blown, repair short to ground in power distribution circuit. See appropriate wiring diagram in POWER DISTRIBUTION article in WIRING DIAGRAMS.

2) Turn ignition switch to LOCK position. Disconnect driver's power window control switch harness connector C75B. Measure resistance in Violet/Blue wire between output side of fuse No. 21 in central junction box and terminal No. 2 at driver's window control switch harness connector C75B. *See Fig. 1.* If resistance is 5 ohms or less, go to next step. If resistance is greater than 5 ohms, repair open in Violet/Blue wire.

3) Measure resistance between ground and terminal No. 3 (Black wire) at driver's power window control switch harness connector C75B. If resistance is 5 ohms or less, replace driver's power window control switch. If resistance is greater than 5 ohms, repair open in Black wire.

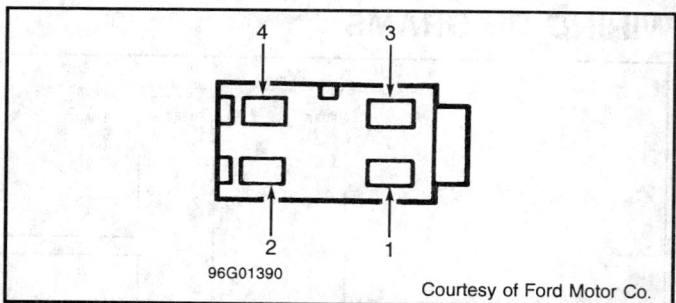

Fig. 1: Identifying Driver's Window Control Switch Harness Connector C75B Terminals

TEST B: DRIVER'S POWER WINDOW INOPERATIVE

NOTE: On driver's power window control switch harness connector C75B there are 2 Violet/Blue wires.

1) Ensure driver's window is up. Turn ignition switch to LOCK position. Disconnect driver's power window control switch harness connectors. Turn ignition switch to RUN position. Using a fused jumper wire, connect terminal No. 6 (White wire) at driver's power window control switch harness connector C75A and terminal No. 3 (Black wire) at driver's power window control switch harness connector C75B. *See Figs. 1 and 2.* Using another fused jumper wire, connect terminal No. 7 (Yellow/Green wire) at driver's power window control switch harness connector C75A and terminal No. 2 (Violet/Blue wire) at driver's power window control switch harness connector C75B. If driver's window does not go down, remove jumper wires and go to next step. If driver's window goes down, replace driver's power window control switch.

2) Turn ignition switch to LOCK position. Disconnect one-touch down relay harness connector C738. Measure resistance in Yellow/Green wire between terminal No. 7 at driver's power window control switch harness connector C75A and one-touch down relay harness connector C738. *See Figs. 2 and 3.* Resistance should be 5 ohms or less. Measure resistance between ground and terminal No. 3 (Yellow/Green wire) at one-touch down relay harness connector C738. Resistance should be greater than 10 k/ohms. If both resistance readings are as specified, go to next step. If either resistance reading is not as specified, repair open and/or short to ground in Yellow/Green wire.

3) Measure resistance between terminals No. 3 and 5 at one-touch down relay (component side). *See Fig. 4.* If resistance is approximately 1000 ohms, go to next step. If resistance is not approximately 1000 ohms, replace one-touch down relay.

4) Disconnect driver's power window motor harness connector C782. Measure resistance in Yellow wire between terminal No. 1 at driver's power window motor harness connector C782 and terminal No. 5 at one-touch down relay harness connector C738. Resistance should be 5 ohms or less. Measure resistance between ground and terminal No. 5 (Yellow wire) at one-touch down relay harness connector C738. Resistance should be greater than 10 k/ohms. If both resistance readings are as specified, go to next step. If either resistance reading is not as specified, repair open and/or short to ground in Yellow wire.

5) Connect driver's power window control switch harness connectors. Measure resistance between ground and terminal No. 2 (White wire) at driver's power window motor harness connector C782. If resistance is 5 ohms or less, replace driver's power window motor. If resistance is greater than 5 ohms, repair open in White wire.

TEST C: PASSENGER'S POWER WINDOW INOPERATIVE

NOTE: On driver's power window control switch harness connector C75B there are 2 Violet/Blue wires. On passenger's power window control switch harness connector C489 there are 2 White/Violet wires and 2 Yellow/Violet wires.

1) Ensure passenger's window is up. Turn ignition switch to LOCK position. Disconnect driver's power window control switch harness

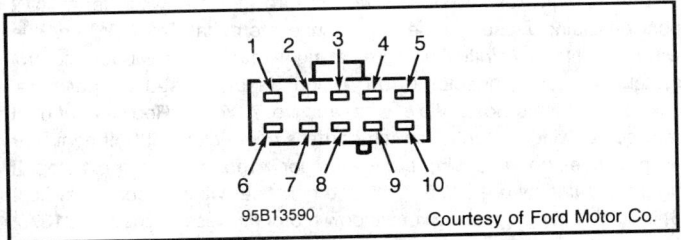

Fig. 2: Identifying Driver's Power Window Control Switch Harness Connector C75A Terminals

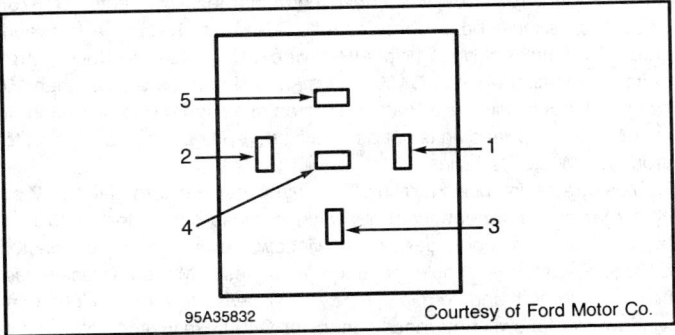

Fig. 3: Identifying One-Touch Down Relay Harness Connector C738 Terminals

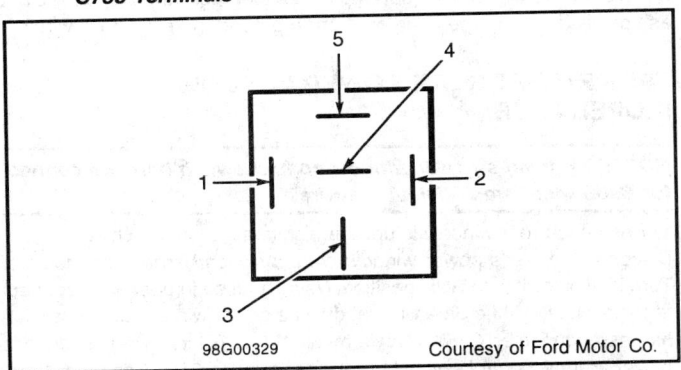

Fig. 4: Identifying One-Touch Down Relay Terminals

connectors. Turn ignition switch to RUN position. Using a fused jumper wire, connect terminal No. 1 (White/Violet wire) at driver's power window control switch harness connector C75A and terminal No. 3 (Black wire) at driver's power window control switch harness connector C75B. See Figs. 1 and 2. Using another fused jumper wire, connect terminal No. 2 (Yellow/Violet wire) at driver's power window control switch harness connector C75A and terminal No. 2 (Violet/Blue wire) at driver's power window control switch harness connector C75B. If passenger's window does not go down, remove jumper wires and go to next step. If passenger's window goes down, replace driver's power window control switch.

2) Turn ignition switch to LOCK position. Disconnect passenger's power window control switch harness connector C489. Measure resistance in White/Violet wire between terminal No. 6 at passenger's power window control switch harness connector C489 and terminal No. 1 at driver's power window control switch harness connector C75A. See Figs. 2 and 5. Resistance should be 5 ohms or less. Measure resistance between ground and terminal No. 6 (White/Violet wire) at passenger's power window control switch harness connector C489. Resistance should be greater than 10 k/ohms. If both resistance readings are as specified, go to next step. If either resistance reading is not as specified, repair open and/or short to ground in White/Violet wire.

3) Measure resistance in Yellow/Violet wire between terminal No. 3 at passenger's power window control switch harness connector C489 and terminal No. 2 at driver's power window control switch harness connector C75A. Resistance should be 5 ohms or less. Measure resistance

between ground and terminal No. 3 (Yellow/Violet wire) at passenger's power window control switch harness connector C489. Resistance should be greater than 10 k/ohms. If both resistance readings are as specified, go to next step. If either resistance reading is not as specified, repair open and/or short to ground in Yellow/Violet wire.

4) Turn ignition switch to RUN position. Measure voltage at terminal No. 2 (Violet/White wire) at passenger's window control switch harness connector C489. If battery voltage exists, go to next step. If battery voltage does not exist, repair open in Violet/White wire.

5) Ensure passenger's window is up. Turn ignition switch to LOCK position. Connect driver's power window switch harness connectors. Turn ignition switch to RUN position. Using a fused jumper wire, connect terminals No. 6 (White/Violet wire) and No. 1 (White/Violet wire) at passenger's power window control switch harness connector C489. Using another fused jumper wire, connect terminals No. 2 (Violet/White wire) and No. 7 (Yellow/Violet wire) at passenger's power window control switch harness connector C489. If passenger's window does not go down, remove jumper wires and go to next step. If passenger's window goes down, replace passenger's window control switch.

6) Disconnect passenger's power window motor harness connector C1869. Measure resistance in White/Violet wire between terminal No. 1 at passenger's power window control switch harness connector C489 and terminal No. 2 at passenger's power window motor harness connector C1869. Resistance should be 5 ohms or less. Measure resistance between ground and terminal No. 1 (White/Violet wire) at passenger's window control switch harness connector C489. Resistance should be greater than 10 k/ohms. If both resistance readings are as specified, go to next step. If either resistance reading is not as specified, repair open and/or short to ground in White/Violet wire.

7) Measure resistance in Yellow/Violet wire between terminal No. 7 at passenger's power window control switch harness connector C489 and terminal No. 1 at passenger's power window motor harness connector C1869. Resistance should be 5 ohms or less. Measure resistance between ground and terminal No. 7 (Yellow/Violet wire) at passenger's window control switch harness connector C489. Resistance should be greater than 10 k/ohms. If both resistance readings are as specified, replace passenger's power window motor. If either resistance reading is not as specified, repair open and/or short to ground in Yellow/Violet wire.

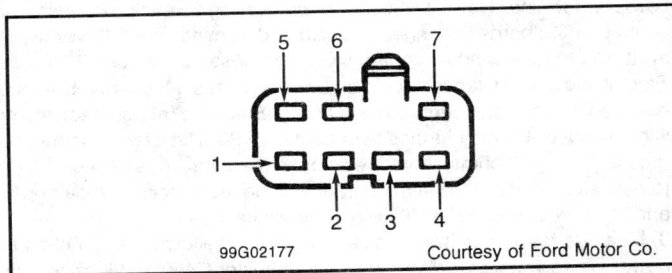

Fig. 5: Identifying Passenger's, Right Rear & Left Rear Power Window Control Switch Harness Connector Terminals

TEST D: ONE-TOUCH DOWN FEATURE INOPERATIVE

NOTE: On driver's power window control switch harness connector C75B there are 2 Violet/Blue wires.

1) Ensure driver's window is up. Turn ignition switch to LOCK position. Disconnect driver's power window control switch harness connectors. Turn ignition switch to RUN position. Using a fused jumper wire, connect terminal No. 6 (White wire) at driver's power window control switch harness connector C75A and terminal No. 3 (Black wire) at driver's power window control switch harness connector C75B. See Figs. 1 and 2. Using another fused jumper wire, connect terminal No. 7 (Yellow/Green wire) at driver's power window control switch harness connector C75A and terminal No. 2 (Violet/Blue wire) at driver's power window control switch harness connector C75B. If driver's window does not go down, remove jumper wires and go to next step. If driver's window goes down, replace driver's power window control switch.

2) Turn ignition switch to LOCK position. Disconnect one-touch down relay harness connector C738. Measure resistance in Yellow/Green wire between terminal No. 7 at driver's power window control switch harness connector C75A and terminal No. 3 at one-touch down relay harness connector C738. *See Figs. 2 and 3.*Resistance should be 5 ohms or less. Measure resistance between ground and terminal No. 3 (Yellow/Green wire) at one-touch down relay harness connector C738. Resistance should be greater than 10 k/ohms. If both resistance readings are as specified, go to next step. If either resistance reading is not as specified, repair open and/or short to ground in Yellow/Green wire.

3) Measure voltage at terminal No. 2 (Violet/Orange wire) at one-touch down relay harness connector C738. If battery voltage exists, go to next step. If battery voltage does not exist, repair open in Violet/Orange wire.

4) Measure resistance between ground and terminal No. 1 (Black wire) at one-touch down relay harness connector C738. If resistance is 5 ohms or less, replace one-touch down relay. If resistance is greater than 5 ohms, repair open in Black wire.

TEST E: RIGHT REAR POWER WINDOW INOPERATIVE

NOTE: On driver's power window control switch harness connector C75B there are 2 Violet/Blue wires.

---

1) Ensure right rear window is up. Turn ignition switch to LOCK position. Disconnect driver's power window control switch harness connectors. Turn ignition switch to RUN position. Using a fused jumper wire, connect terminal No. 3 (White wire) at driver's power window control switch harness connector C75A and terminal No. 3 (Black wire) at driver's power window control switch harness connector C75B. *See Figs. 1 and 2.* Using another fused jumper wire, connect terminal No. 4 (Yellow wire) at driver's power window control switch harness connector C75A and terminal No. 2 (Violet/Blue wire) at driver's power window control switch harness connector C75B. If right rear window does not go down, remove jumper wires and go to next step. If right rear window goes down, replace driver's power window control switch.

2) Turn ignition switch to LOCK position. Disconnect right rear power window control switch harness connector C490. Measure resistance between terminal No. 6 (White/Blue wire) at right rear power window control switch harness connector C490 and terminal No. 3 (White wire) at driver's power window control switch harness connector C75A. *See Figs. 2 and 5.* Resistance should be 5 ohms or less. Measure resistance between ground and terminal No. 6 (White/Blue wire) at right rear power window control switch harness connector C490. Resistance should be greater than 10 k/ohms. If both resistance readings are as specified, go to next step. If either resistance reading is not as specified, repair open and/or short to ground in White/Blue or White wire.

3) Measure resistance between terminal No. 3 (Yellow/Blue) at right rear power window control switch harness connector C490 and terminal No. 4 (Yellow wire) at driver's power window control switch harness connector C75A. Resistance should be 5 ohms or less. Measure resistance between ground and terminal No. 3 (Yellow wire) at right rear power window control switch harness connector C490. Resistance should be greater than 10 k/ohms. If both resistance readings are as specified, go to next step. If either resistance reading is not as specified, repair open and/or short to ground in Yellow/Blue or Yellow wire.

NOTE: Right rear power window switch power wire changes color 3 times between driver's power window control switch and right rear power window control switch.

---

4) Turn ignition switch to LOCK position. Connect driver's power window control switch harness connector. Ensure driver's power window switch lockout switch is not in LOCK position. Turn ignition switch to RUN position. Measure voltage at terminal No. 2 (Violet wire) at right rear window control switch harness connector C490. If battery voltage exists, go to next step. If battery voltage does not exist, repair open in Violet or Violet/Yellow wire.

5) Ensure right rear window is up. Ensure ignition switch is in RUN position. Using a fused jumper wire, connect terminals No. 6 (White/Blue wire) and No. 1 (White/Red wire) at right rear power window control switch harness connector C490. Using another fused jumper wire, connect terminals No. 2 (Violet wire) and No. 7 (Yellow/Red wire) at right rear power window control switch harness connector C490. If right rear window does not go down, remove jumper wires and go to next step. If right rear window goes down, replace right rear window control switch.

6) Disconnect right rear power window motor harness connector C1876. Measure resistance in White/Red wire between terminal No. 1 at right rear power window control switch harness connector C490 and terminal No. 2 at right rear power window motor harness connector C1876. Resistance should be 5 ohms or less. Measure resistance between ground and terminal No. 1 (White/Red wire) at right rear window control switch harness connector C490. Resistance should be greater than 10 k/ohms. If both resistance readings are as specified, go to next step. If either resistance reading is not as specified, repair open and/or short to ground in White/Red wire.

7) Measure resistance in Yellow/Red wire between terminal No. 7 at right rear power window control switch harness connector C490 and terminal No. 1 at right rear power window motor harness connector C1876. Resistance should be 5 ohms or less. Measure resistance between ground and terminal No. 7 (Yellow/Red wire) at right rear window control switch harness connector C490. Resistance should be greater than 10 k/ohms. If both resistance readings are as specified, replace right rear power window motor. If either resistance reading is not as specified, repair open and/or short to ground in Yellow/Red wire.

TEST F: LEFT REAR POWER WINDOW INOPERATIVE

NOTE: On driver's power window control switch harness connector C75B there are 2 Violet/Blue wires.

---

1) Ensure left rear window is up. Turn ignition switch to LOCK position. Disconnect driver's power window control switch harness connectors. Turn ignition switch to RUN position. Using a fused jumper wire, connect terminal No. 8 (White/Blue wire) at driver's power window control switch harness connector C75A and terminal No. 3 (Black wire) at driver's power window control switch harness connector C75B. *See Figs. 1 and 2.* Using another fused jumper wire, connect terminal No. 9 (Yellow/Blue wire) at driver's power window control switch harness connector C75A and terminal No. 2 (Violet/Blue wire) at driver's power window control switch harness connector C75B. If left rear window does not go down, remove jumper wires and go to next step. If left rear window goes down, replace driver's power window control switch.

2) Turn ignition switch to LOCK position. Disconnect left rear power window control switch harness connector C1854. Measure resistance between terminal No. 6 (White/Blue wire) at left rear power window control switch harness connector C1854 and terminal No. 8 (White/Blue wire) at driver's power window control switch harness connector C75A. *See Figs. 2 and 5.* Resistance should be 5 ohms or less. Measure resistance between ground and terminal No. 6 (White/Blue wire) at left rear power window control switch harness connector C1854. Resistance should be greater than 10 k/ohms. If both resistance readings are as specified, go to next step. If either resistance reading is not as specified, repair open and/or short to ground in White/Blue wire.

3) Measure resistance between terminal No. 3 (Yellow/Blue) at left rear power window control switch harness connector C1854 and terminal No. 9 (Yellow/Blue wire) at driver's power window control switch harness connector C75A. Resistance should be 5 ohms or less. Measure resistance between ground and terminal No. 3 (Yellow/Blue wire) at left rear power window control switch harness connector C1854. Resistance should be greater than 10 k/ohms. If both resistance readings are as specified, go to next step. If either resistance reading is not as specified, repair open and/or short to ground in Yellow/Blue or wire.

NOTE: Left rear power window switch power wire changes color 2 times between driver's power window control switch and left rear power window control switch.

---

4) Turn ignition switch to LOCK position. Connect driver's power window control switch harness connector. Ensure driver's power window switch lockout switch is not in LOCK position. Turn ignition switch to RUN position. Measure voltage at terminal No. 2 (Violet wire) at left rear window control switch harness connector C1854. If battery voltage exists, go to next step. If battery voltage does not exist, repair open in Violet or Violet/Blue wire.

5) Ensure left rear window is up. Ensure ignition switch is in RUN position. Using a fused jumper wire, connect terminals No. 6 (White/Blue wire) and No. 1 (White/Red wire) at left rear power window control switch harness connector C1854. Using another fused jumper wire, connect terminals No. 2 (Violet wire) and No. 7 (Yellow/Red wire) at left rear power window control switch harness connector C1854. If left rear window does not go down, remove jumper wires and go to next step. If left rear window goes down, replace left rear window control switch.

6) Disconnect left rear power window motor harness connector C801. Measure resistance in White/Red wire between terminal No. 1 at left rear power window control switch harness connector C1854 and terminal No. 2 at left rear power window motor harness connector C801. Resistance should be 5 ohms or less. Measure resistance between ground and terminal No. 1 (White/Red wire) at left rear window control switch harness connector C1854. Resistance should be greater than 10 k/ohms. If both resistance readings are as specified, go to next step. If either resistance reading is not as specified, repair open and/or short to ground in White/Red wire.

7) Measure resistance in Yellow/Red wire between terminal No. 7 at left rear power window control switch harness connector C1854 and terminal No. 1 at left rear power window motor harness connector C801. Resistance should be 5 ohms or less. Measure resistance between ground and terminal No. 7 (Yellow/Red wire) at left rear window control switch harness connector C1854. Resistance should be greater than 10 k/ohms. If both resistance readings are as specified, replace left rear power window motor. If either resistance reading is not as specified, repair open and/or short to ground in Yellow/Red wire.

REMOVAL & INSTALLATION

CAUTION: When battery is disconnected, vehicle computer and memory systems may lose memory data. Driveability problems may exist until computer systems have completed a relearn cycle. See COMPUTER RELEARN PROCEDURES article in GENERAL INFORMATION before disconnecting battery.

POWER WINDOW MOTOR

Removal & Installation – 1) Remove door trim panel and trim shield. Remove side view mirror. Reinstall window control switch and lower window to align window regulator-to-window glass retaining bolts with access holes in door.

2) Disconnect negative battery cable. Unplug wire connector from window control switch. Remove 2 bolts retaining window regulator to window glass. While holding window glass, carefully pry regulator from glass. Pull belt line outside weatherstrip from door.

3) Raise rear of window glass and carefully remove from door. Loosen 3 regulator-to-door retaining bolts. Remove 3 window motor bolts. Slide window regulator bolts from slots in door and disconnect wire harness from window motor. Remove window regulator.

4) Remove screws retaining window motor to window regulator. To install, reverse removal procedure. Tighten window regulator-to-window glass retaining bolts to 71 INCH lbs. (8 N.m).

POWER WINDOW SWITCH

Removal & Installation – Disconnect negative battery cable. Remove inside door handle cup. Push window switch retaining tab and pull switch from door trim panel. Disconnect wiring harness and remove switch. To install, reverse removal procedure.

ONE-TOUCH WINDOW DOWN RELAY

Removal & Installation – Disconnect negative battery cable. Remove left-side door trim panel. Remove 2 screws retaining relay to door. Disconnect wiring harness and remove relay. To install, reverse removal procedure.

WIRING DIAGRAMS

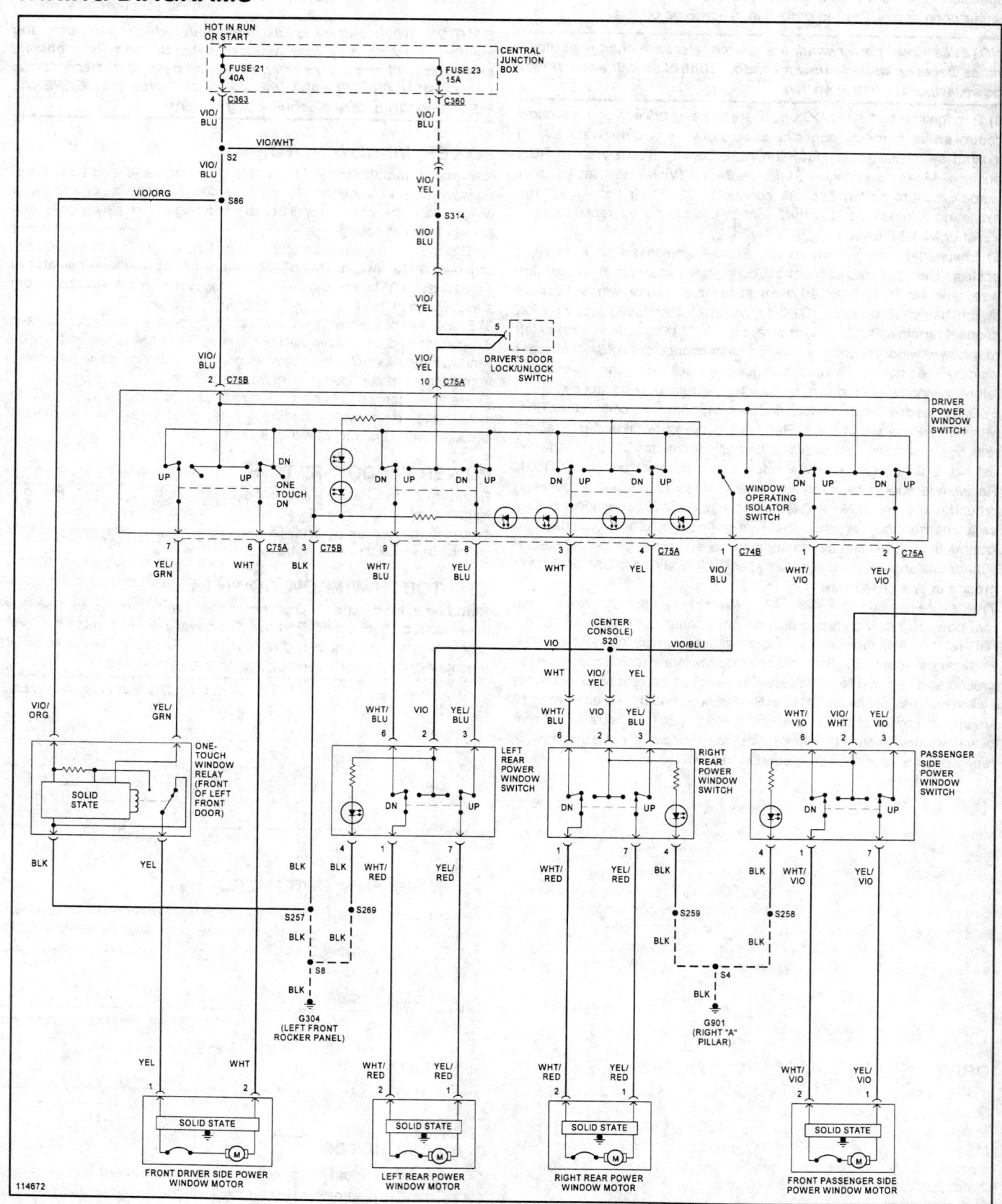

Fig. 6: Power Window System Wiring Diagram (Contour & Mystique)

DESCRIPTION & OPERATION

Power windows are operated by reversible type motors mounted with each window regulator. Each passenger's window has an individual switch for separate control. A master switch is located on driver's door and all windows may be controlled from this switch.

One-touch down feature allows the driver's to lower the left front window fully by momentarily actuating the driver's window down switch at the master power window switch. The driver's window may be stopped in mid-travel by momentarily pressing the driver's window up switch. The one-touch down feature can only be actuated at the master switch.

A lock-out switch is incorporated in master switch. When actuated, switch prevents window operation from individual switches.

COMPONENT LOCATIONS

COMPONENT LOCATIONS

Component	Location
Data Link Connector	Behind Left Side Of Instrument Panel
Driver's Door Module	Behind Driver's Door Panel
Instrument Panel Fuse Box	Behind Left Side Of Instrument Panel
Lighting Control Module	Behind Instrument Panel, Right Of Steering Column
One Touch Down Module	Behind Driver's Door Panel
Power Distribution Box	Right Front Of Engine Compartment Next To Battery
Powertrain Control Module	Left Rear Corner Of Engine Compartment, In Firewall

ADJUSTMENTS

DOOR WINDOW GLASS

Remove door trim panel and watershield. Loosen upper regulator retaining nuts. Raise window glass to full up position and tighten upper regulator retaining nuts to 89-124 INCH lbs. (10-14 N.m). Lower window glass to full down position and tighten retainer bolt to 89-124 INCH lbs. (10-14 N.m). Install watershield and door trim panel. Open and close window to verify proper operation.

TROUBLE SHOOTING

Verify customer concern by operating windows to duplicate condition. Visually inspect components. Check for the following: proper window alignment, window mounting (regulator and bracket), window frame interference, blown fuse(s), damaged wiring harness, loose or corroded connections, damaged switches and damaged window motor. If inspection reveals an obvious concern which can be easily serviced, repair as necessary. If inspection does not reveal an obvious concern which can be easily serviced, perform self-diagnostics. See SELF-DIAGNOSTIC SYSTEM.

COMPONENT TESTS

DRIVER'S DOOR MASTER WINDOW SWITCH

1) Remove driver's door master window switch. With all switches in NEUTRAL position and lock-out switch in OFF position, continuity should exist between terminals No. 19 and 20. See Fig. 1. Continuity should also exist between terminal No. 13 and all other terminals except terminal No. 19. If continuity is as specified, go to next step. If continuity is not as specified, replace driver's door master window switch.

2) Check continuity between specified switch terminals with switch in appropriate position. See DRIVER'S DOOR MASTER WINDOW SWITCH TEST table. If continuity is not as specified, replace driver's door master window switch.

DRIVER'S DOOR MASTER WINDOW SWITCH TEST

Switch Position	Continuity Between Terminals
Left Front Window	
Down	8 & 13; 10 & 19
Up	8 & 19; 10 & 13
Left Rear Window	
Down	13 & 17; 15 & 19
Up	13 & 15; 17 & 19
Right Front Window	
Down	9 & 13; 11 & 19
Up	9 & 19; 11 & 13
Right Rear Window	
Down	13 & 18; 16 & 19
Up	13 & 16; 18 & 19

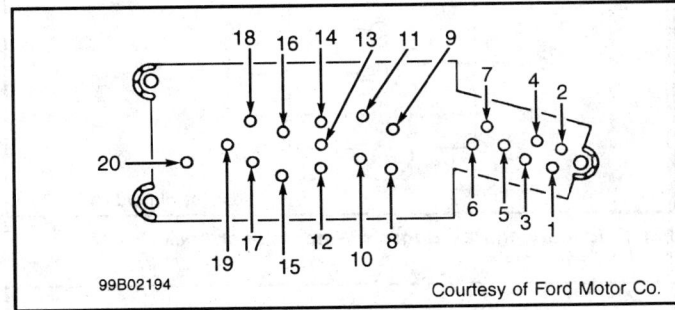

Fig. 1: Identifying Driver's Door Master Switch Terminals

PASSENGER'S WINDOW/DOOR LOCK SWITCH

Remove passenger's window/door lock switch. Check continuity between specified switch terminals with switch in appropriate position. See PASSENGER'S WINDOW/DOOR LOCK SWITCH TEST table. If continuity is not as specified, replace passenger's window/door lock switch.

PASSENGER'S WINDOW/DOOR LOCK SWITCH TEST

Switch Position	Continuity Between Terminals
Neutral	
Window Circuit	8 & 9; 11 & 12
Door Lock Circuit	3 & 5; 4 & 7
Down	8 & 9; 10 & 12
Up	8 & 10; 11 & 12
Lock	3 & 5; 6 & 7
Unlock	3 & 6; 4 & 7

REAR WINDOW SWITCHES

Remove switch to be tested. Check continuity between specified switch terminals with switch in appropriate position. See REAR WINDOW SWITCH TEST table. If continuity is not as specified, replace rear window switch.

REAR WINDOW SWITCH TEST

Switch Position	Continuity Between Terminals
Neutral	1 & 4; 2 & 5
Down	1 & 4; 3 & 5
Up	1 & 3; 2 & 5

WINDOW MOTOR

Remove window motor from vehicle. Using fused jumper wires, connect a fully charged battery to motor terminals. Observe motor. Motor should operate smoothly. Reverse leads. Motor should operate in reverse direction. Replace window motor if it does not operate as specified.

FORD
4-1122

1999 ACCESSORIES & EQUIPMENT
Power Windows – Crown Victoria & Grand Marquis (Cont.)

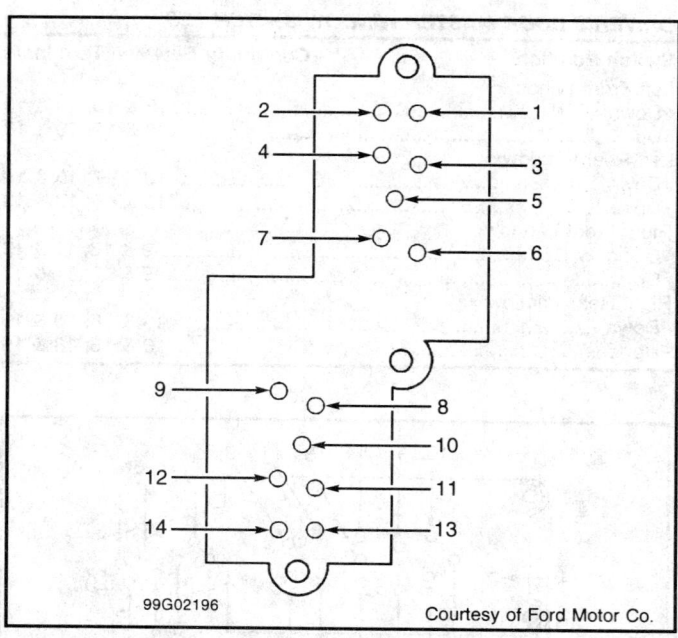

Fig. 2: Identifying Passenger's Window/Door Lock Switch Terminals

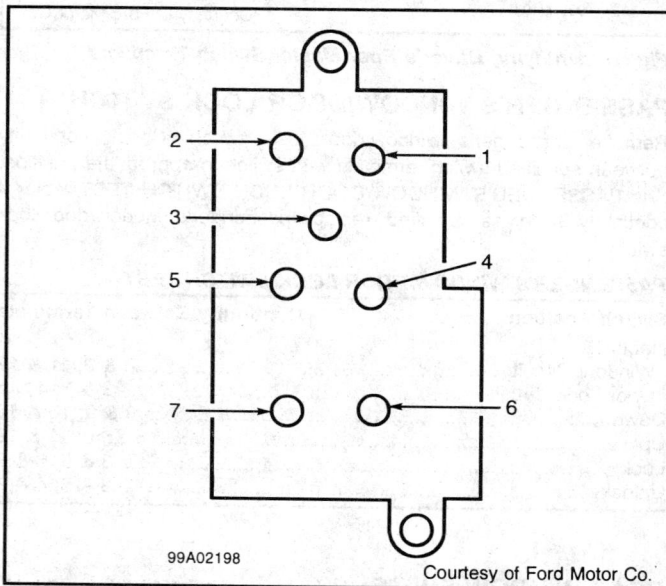

Fig. 3: Identifying Rear Window Switch Terminals

SELF-DIAGNOSTIC SYSTEM

NOTE: Only vehicles equipped with keyless entry system have a Driver's Door Module (DDM).

Connect New Generation Star (NGS) tester to Data Link Connector (DLC), located beneath instrument panel. Using NGS tester, perform data link diagnostics test. See DATA LINK DIAGNOSTIC TEST under COMMUNICATION NETWORK DIAGNOSTICS in MODULE COMMUNICATIONS NETWORK – CROWN VICTORIA & GRAND MARQUIS article. If NGS tester responds with CKT914, CKT915 or CKT70=ALL ECUS NO RESP/NOT EQUIP, repair module communications concern. See MODULE COMMUNICATIONS NETWORK – CROWN VICTORIA & GRAND MARQUIS article. If NGS tester displays NO RESP/NOT EQUIP for Driver's Door Module (DDM), perform TEST A: NO COMMUNICATION WITH DRIVER'S DOOR MODULE under SYSTEM TESTS.

If NGS tester displays NO RESP/NOT EQUIP for Lighting Control Module (LCM), perform TEST B: NO COMMUNICATION WITH LIGHTING CONTROL MODULE under SYSTEM TESTS.

If NGS tester responds with SYSTEM PASSED, retrieve and record continuous DTCs. Erase continuous DTCs. Using NGS tester, perform DDM and LCM self-test. Perform appropriate test in accordance with DTC retrieved. See DRIVER'S DOOR MODULE DTC INDEX and/or LIGHTING CONTROL MODULE DTC INDEX table. Codes listed in these table are only for testing covered in this article. For complete DTC listing, see MODULE COMMUNICATIONS NETWORK – CROWN VICTORIA & GRAND MARQUIS article. If no DTCs are retrieved, repair by symptom. See SYMPTOM CHART table under SYSTEM TESTS.

DRIVER'S DOOR MODULE DTC INDEX

DTC [1]	Description	Test
B1342	ECU Defective	[2]
B1549	Master Window Switch Circuit Short To Voltage	D

[1] – Codes listed in this table are only for testing covered in this article. For complete DTC listing, see MODULE COMMUNICATIONS NETWORK – CROWN VICTORIA & GRAND MARQUIS article.

[2] – Using NGS tester, retrieve and document all continuous DTCs. Perform Driver's Door Module (DDM) self-test. If DTC B1342 is retrieved again, replace DDM.

LIGHTING CONTROL MODULE DTC INDEX

DTC [1]	Description	Test
B1342	ECU Defective	[2]

[1] – Codes listed in this table are only for testing covered in this article. For complete DTC listing, see MODULE COMMUNICATIONS NETWORK – CROWN VICTORIA & GRAND MARQUIS article.

[2] – Using NGS tester, retrieve and document all continuous DTCs. Perform Lighting Control Module (LCM) self-test. If DTC B1342 is retrieved again, replace LCM.

SYSTEM TESTS

SYMPTOM CHART

Symptom	Test
No Communication With Driver's Door Module	A
No Communication With Lighting Control Module	B
Both Windows Completely Inoperative	C
Driver's Window Is Inoperative	D
Passenger's Window Is Inoperative	E
Rear Window Is Inoperative	F
One Touch Down Feature Inoperative	G

TEST A: NO COMMUNICATION WITH DRIVER'S DOOR MODULE

NOTE: Only vehicles equipped with keyless entry system have a Driver's Door Module (DDM).

1) Turn ignition switch to LOCK position. Disconnect Driver's Door Module (DDM) harness connector C520. Measure voltage at terminal No. 4 (Black/White wire) at DDM harness connector C520. *See Fig. 4.* If battery voltage does not exist, go to next step. If battery voltage exists, go to step **4)**.

2) Remove circuit breaker No. 7 (20-amp) from power distribution box. Measure resistance between ground at terminal No. 4 (Black/White wire) at DDM harness C520. If resistance is greater than 10 k/ohms, go to next step. If resistance is 10 k/ohms or less, repair short to ground in Black/White wire.

3) Measure voltage between ground and input side circuit breaker No. 7 in power distribution box. If battery voltage exists, repair open in Black/White wire. If battery voltage does not exist, repair open in power supply to power distribution box. See appropriate wiring diagram in POWER DISTRIBUTION article in WIRING DIAGRAMS.

4) Measure voltage at terminal No. 3 (Yellow/Light Green wire) at DDM harness connector C520. If battery voltage does not exist, go to next step. If battery voltage exists, go to step **7)**.

1999 ACCESSORIES & EQUIPMENT
Power Windows – Crown Victoria & Grand Marquis (Cont.)

FORD
4-1123

5) Remove circuit breaker No. 14 (20-amp) from instrument panel fuse box. Measure resistance between ground and terminal No. 3 (Yellow/Light Green wire) at DDM harness connector C520. If resistance is greater than 10 k/ohms, go to next step. If resistance is 10 k/ohms or less, repair short to ground in Yellow/Light Green wire.

6) Measure voltage at input side circuit breaker No. 14 in instrument panel fuse box. If battery voltage exists, repair open in Yellow/Light Green wire. If battery voltage does not exist, repair open in power supply to power distribution box. See appropriate wiring diagram in POWER DISTRIBUTION article in WIRING DIAGRAMS.

7) Disconnect DDM harness connector C519. Measure resistance between ground and terminals No. 4 (Pink/Orange wire) and No. 15 (Black wire) at DDM harness connector C519. *See Fig. 5.* If either resistance reading is greater than 5 ohms, repair open in appropriate wire. If both resistance readings are 5 ohms or less, repair module communications concern. See MODULE COMMUNICATIONS NETWORK – CROWN VICTORIA & GRAND MARQUIS article.

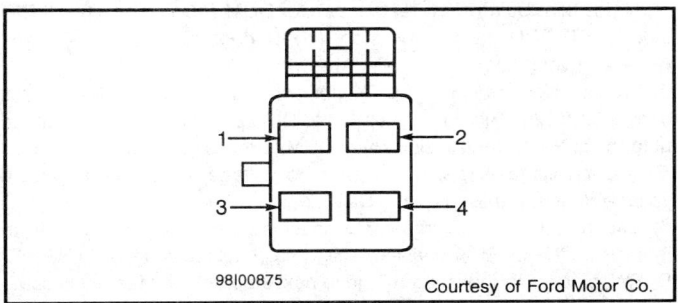

Fig. 4: Identifying Driver's Door Module Harness Connector C520 Terminals

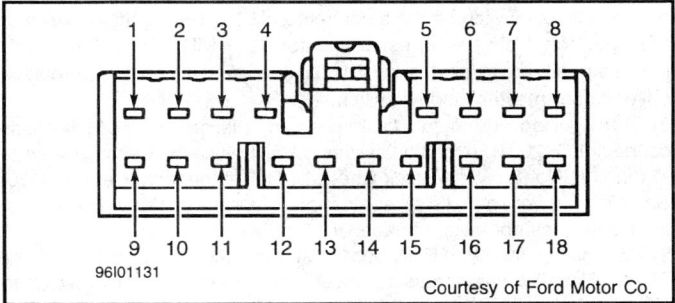

Fig. 5: Identifying Driver's Door Module Harness Connector C519 Terminals

TEST B: NO COMMUNICATION WITH LIGHTING CONTROL MODULE

1) Turn ignition switch to RUN position. Using NGS tester, monitor Lighting Control Module (LCM) PID IGN_LC. If NGS tester does not indicate UNABLE TO PERFORM TEST FUNCTION, MODULE NOT RESPONDING, CHECK IGNITION STATUS/VERIFY CABLE REQUIREMENTS, OR CHECK CABLE CONNECTIONS, go to next step. If NGS tester indicates UNABLE TO PERFORM TEST FUNCTION, MODULE NOT RESPONDING, CHECK IGNITION STATUS/VERIFY CABLE REQUIREMENTS, OR CHECK CABLE CONNECTIONS, go to step **11)**.

2) Turn ignition switch to RUN position. Using NGS tester, monitor LCM PID IGN_LC while rotating ignition switch through ACCY, OFF and RUN positions. If PID indicates START while ignition switch is in RUN position, go to next step. If PID indicates RUN while ignition switch is in RUN position, go to step **12)**. If PID indicates ACCY while ignition switch is in RUN position, go to step **7)**.

3) Turn ignition switch to LOCK position. Remove fuse No. 6 (15-amp) from instrument panel fuse box. Check fuse. If fuse is okay, go to next step. If fuse is blown, go to step **6)**.

4) Turn ignition switch to RUN position. Measure voltage at input side of fuse No. 6 in instrument panel fuse box. If battery voltage exists, go to

next step. If battery voltage does not exist, repair power supply to fuse No. 6. See appropriate wiring diagram in POWER DISTRIBUTION article in WIRING DIAGRAMS.

5) Turn ignition switch to LOCK position. Install fuse No. 6. Disconnect LCM harness connector C2027. Turn ignition switch to RUN position. Measure voltage at terminal No. 1 (White/Violet wire) at LCM harness connector C2027. *See Fig. 6.* If battery voltage exists, replace LCM. If battery voltage does not exist, repair open in White/Violet wire.

6) Turn ignition switch to LOCK position. Disconnect Lighting Control Module (LCM) harness connector C2027. Measure resistance between ground and terminal No. 1 (White/Violet wire) at LCM harness connector C2027. *See Fig. 6 .* If resistance is greater than 10 k/ohms, replace LCM. If resistance is 10 k/ohms or less, repair short to ground in White/Violet wire.

7) Turn ignition switch to LOCK position. Remove fuse No. 13 (15-amp) from instrument panel fuse box. Check fuse. If fuse is okay, go to next step. If fuse is blown, go to step **10)**.

8) Turn ignition switch to RUN position. Measure voltage at input side of fuse No. 13 in instrument panel fuse box. If battery voltage exists, go to next step. If battery voltage does not exist, repair power supply to fuse No. 13. See appropriate wiring diagram in POWER DISTRIBUTION article in WIRING DIAGRAMS.

9) Turn ignition switch to LOCK position. Install fuse No. 13 (15-amp). Disconnect LCM harness connector C2027. Turn ignition switch to RUN position. Measure voltage at terminal No. 9 (Red/Yellow wire) at LCM 16-pin connector C2027. *See Fig. 6.* If battery voltage exists, replace LCM. If battery voltage does not exist, repair open in Red/Yellow wire.

10) Turn ignition switch to LOCK position. Disconnect LCM harness connector C2027. Measure resistance between ground and terminal No. 9 (Red/Yellow wire) at LCM harness connector C2027. *See Fig. 6.* If resistance is greater than 10 k/ohms, replace LCM. If resistance is 10 k/ohms or less, repair short to ground in Red/Yellow wire.

11) Turn ignition switch to LOCK position. Disconnect LCM harness connector C2029. Measure resistance between ground and terminals No. 4 and 9 (both Black wire) at LCM harness connector C2029. *See Fig. 7.* If either resistance reading is greater than 5 ohms, repair open in appropriate Black wire(s). If both resistance readings are 5 ohms or less, repair module communication concern. See MODULE COMMUNICATIONS NETWORK – CROWN VICTORIA & GRAND MARQUIS article.

12) Turn ignition switch to LOCK position. Disconnect LCM harness connector C2029. Measure voltage at terminal No. 6 (Tan/White wire) at LCM harness connector C2029. *See Fig. 7.* If battery voltage does not exist, go to next step. If battery voltage exists, go to step **16)**.

13) Remove fuse No. 4 (15-amp) from instrument panel fuse box. Measure resistance between ground and terminal No. 6 (Tan/White wire) at LCM harness connector C2029. If resistance is greater than 10 k/ohms, go to next step. If resistance is 10 k/ohms or less, repair short to ground in Tan/White wire and replace fuse.

14) Measure voltage at input side of fuse No. 4 in instrument panel fuse box. If battery voltage exists, go to next step. If battery voltage does not exist, repair power distribution circuit. See appropriate wiring diagram in POWER DISTRIBUTION article in WIRING DIAGRAMS.

15) Measure resistance in Tan/White wire between output side of fuse No. 4 and terminal No. 6 at LCM harness connector C2029. If resistance is 5 ohms or less, system is okay at this time. If resistance is greater than 5 ohms, repair open in Tan/White wire.

16) Measure voltage at terminal No. 11 (Light Green/Yellow wire) at LCM harness connector C2029. If battery voltage does not exist, go to next step. If battery voltage exists, go to step **20)**.

17) Remove fuse No. 8 (15-amp) from instrument panel fuse box. Measure resistance between ground and terminal No. 11 (Light Green/Yellow wire) at LCM harness connector C2029. If resistance is greater than 10 k/ohms, go to next step. If resistance is 10 k/ohms or less, repair short to ground in Light Green/Yellow wire and replace fuse.

18) Measure voltage at input side of fuse No. 8. If battery voltage exists, go to next step. If battery voltage does not exist, repair power distribution circuit. See appropriate wiring diagram in POWER DISTRIBUTION article in WIRING DIAGRAMS.

FORD
4-1124

1999 ACCESSORIES & EQUIPMENT
Power Windows – Crown Victoria & Grand Marquis (Cont.)

19) Measure resistance in Light Green/Yellow wire between output side of fuse No. 8 and terminal No. 11 at LCM harness connector C2029. If resistance is 5 ohms or less, system is okay at this time. If resistance is greater than 5 ohms, repair open in Light Green/Yellow wire.

20) Measure resistance between ground and terminal No. 9 (Black wire) at LCM harness connector C2029. If resistance is 5 ohms or less, repair communication concern. See MODULE COMMUNICATIONS NETWORK – CROWN VICTORIA & GRAND MARQUIS article. If resistance is greater than 5 ohms, repair open in Black wire.

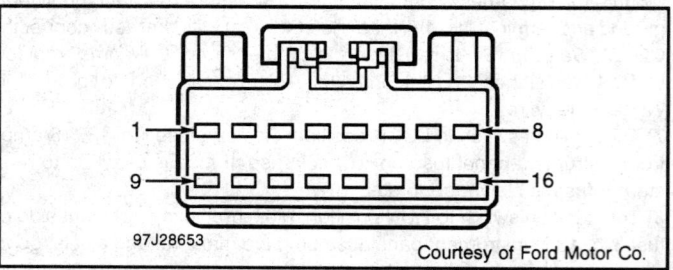

97J28653   Courtesy of Ford Motor Co.

Fig. 6: Identifying Lighting Control Module Harness Connector C2027 Terminals

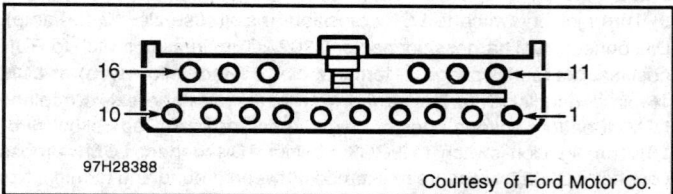

97H28388   Courtesy of Ford Motor Co.

Fig. 7: Identifying Lighting Control Module Harness Connector C2029 Terminals

TEST C: BOTH WINDOWS COMPLETELY INOPERATIVE

1) Remove and disconnect driver's door master window switch harness connector C503. Measure voltage at terminal No. 19 (Yellow/Light Green wire) at driver's door master switch harness connector C503. See Fig. 8. If battery voltage does not exist, go to next step. If battery voltage exists, go to step **3)**.

2) Remove circuit breaker No. 14 (20-amp) from instrument panel fuse box. Measure resistance between ground and terminal No. 19 (Yellow/Light Green wire) at driver's door master switch harness connector C503. If resistance is greater than 10 k/ohms, repair open in Yellow/Light Green wire. If resistance is 10 k/ohms or less, repair short to ground in Yellow/Light Green wire.

3) Measure resistance between ground and terminal No. 13 (Black wire) at driver's door master window switch connector C503. If resistance is 5 ohms or less, replace driver's door master window switch. If resistance is greater than 5 ohms, repair open in Black wire.

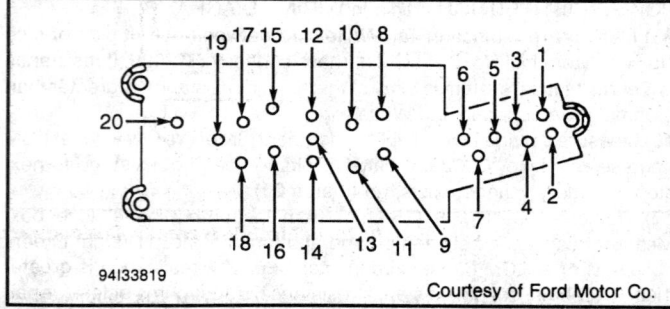

94I33819   Courtesy of Ford Motor Co.

Fig. 8: Identifying Driver's Door Master Switch Harness Connector C503 Terminals

TEST D: DRIVER'S WINDOW IS INOPERATIVE

NOTE: Only vehicles equipped with keyless entry system have a Driver's Door Module (DDM).

1) If vehicle is equipped with a Driver's Door Module (DDM), go to next step. If vehicle is not equipped with a Driver's Door Module (DDM), go to step **24)**.

2) Connect NGS tester to Data Link Connector (DLC). Using NGS tester, perform DDM self-test. If DTC B1549 is retrieved, go to next step. If DTC B1549 is not retrieved, go to step **9)**.

3) Ensure driver's door master window switch is not pressed. Turn ignition switch to RUN position. Using NGS tester, monitor DDM PID D_PW_SW. If PID indicates DOWN, go to next step. If PID does not indicate DOWN, go to step **6)** .

4) Turn ignition switch to LOCK position. Disconnect driver's door master window switch harness connector C503. Turn ignition switch to RUN position. Using NGS tester, monitor DDM PID D_PW_SW. If PID indicates DOWN, go to next step. If PID does not indicate DOWN, replace driver's door master window switch.

5) Turn ignition switch to LOCK position. Disconnect DDM harness connector C520. Turn ignition switch to RUN position. Measure voltage at terminal No. 1 (Tan/Black wire) at DDM harness connector C520. See Fig. 4. If voltage exists, repair short to voltage in Tan/Black wire. If voltage does not exist, replace DDM.

6) Ensure driver's door master window switch is not pressed. Turn ignition switch to RUN position. Using NGS tester, monitor DDM PID D_PW_SW. If PID indicates UP, go to next step. If PID does not indicate UP, clear DTCs. Repeat DDM self-test. If DTC B1549 is retrieved again, replace DDM.

7) Turn ignition switch to LOCK position. Disconnect driver's door master window switch harness connector C503. Turn ignition switch to RUN position. Using NGS tester, monitor DDM PID D_PW_SW. If PID indicates UP, go to next step. If PID does not indicate UP, replace driver's door master window switch.

8) Turn ignition switch to LOCK position. Disconnect DDM harness connector C520. Turn ignition switch to RUN position. Measure voltage at terminal No. 2 (White/Black wire) at DDM harness connector C520. See Fig. 4. If voltage exists, repair short to voltage in White/Black wire. If voltage does not exist, replace DDM.

9) Turn ignition switch to RUN position. Using NGS tester, monitor DDM PID D_PW_SW while pressing driver's door master window switch to driver's window UP position. If PID does not indicate UP, go to next step. If PID indicates UP, go to step **14)**.

10) Turn ignition switch to LOCK position. Disconnect DDM harness connector C518. Measure resistance between ground and terminal No. 2 (White/Black wire) at DDM harness connector C518. See Fig. 9. If resistance is 10 k/ohms or less, go to next step. If resistance is greater than 10 k/ohms, go to step **13)**.

11) Disconnect driver's door master window switch harness connector C503. Measure resistance between ground and terminal No. 2 (White/Black wire) at DDM harness connector C518. If resistance is greater than 10 k/ohms, go to next step. If resistance is 10 k/ohms or less, repair short to ground in White/Black wire.

12) Connect driver's door master window switch harness connector C503. Turn ignition switch to RUN position. Measure voltage at terminal No. 2 (White/Black wire) at DDM harness connector C518 while pressing driver's door master window switch to driver's window UP position. If battery voltage exists, replace DDM. If battery voltage does not exist, replace driver's door master window switch.

13) Disconnect driver's door master window switch harness connector C503. Measure resistance in White/Black wire between terminal No. 2 at DDM harness connector C518 and terminal No. 8 at driver's door master window switch harness connector C503. See Figs. 8 and 9. If resistance is 5 ohms or less, replace driver's door master window switch. If resistance is greater than 5 ohms, repair open in White/Black wire.

14) Turn ignition switch to RUN position. Using NGS tester, monitor DDM PID D_PW_SW while pressing driver's door master window switch

1999 ACCESSORIES & EQUIPMENT
Power Windows – Crown Victoria & Grand Marquis (Cont.)

FORD
4-1125

to driver's window DOWN position. If PID does not indicate DOWN, go to next step. If PID indicates DOWN, go to step **19**).

15) Turn ignition switch to LOCK position. Disconnect DDM harness connector C520. Measure resistance between ground and terminal No. 1 (Tan/Black wire) at DDM harness connector C520. *See Fig. 4.* If resistance is 10 k/ohms or less, go to next step. If resistance is greater than 10 k/ohms, go to step **18**).

16) Disconnect driver's door master window switch harness connector C503. Measure resistance between ground and terminal No. 1 (Tan/Black wire) at DDM harness connector C520. If resistance is greater than 10 k/ohms, go to next step. If resistance is 10 k/ohms or less, repair short to ground in Tan/Black wire.

17) Connect driver's door master window switch harness connector C503. Turn ignition switch to RUN position. Measure voltage at terminal No. 1 (Tan/Black wire) at DDM harness connector C520 while pressing driver's door master window switch to driver's window DOWN position. If battery voltage exists, replace DDM. If battery voltage does not exist, replace driver's door master window switch.

18) Disconnect driver's door master window switch harness connector C503. Measure resistance in Tan/Black wire between terminal No. 1 at DDM harness connector C520 and terminal No. 10 at driver's door master window switch harness connector C503. *See Figs. 4 and 8.* If resistance is 5 ohms or less, replace driver's door master window switch. If resistance is greater than 5 ohms, repair open in Tan/Black wire.

19) Disconnect driver's window motor harness connector C510. Turn ignition switch to RUN position. Measure voltage at Yellow wire terminal at driver's window motor harness connector C510 while pressing driver's door master window switch to driver's window DOWN position. If battery voltage exists, go to next step. If battery voltage does not exist, go to step **22**).

20) Measure resistance between ground and White/Black wire at driver's window motor harness connector C510. If resistance is greater than 5ohms, go to next step. If resistance is 5 ohms or less, replace driver's door master window switch.

21) Disconnect driver's door master window switch harness connector C503. Measure resistance in White/Black wire between driver's window motor harness connector C510 and terminal No. 8 driver's door master window switch harness connector C503. *See Fig. 8.* If resistance is 5 ohms or less, replace driver's door master window switch. If resistance greater than 5 ohms, repair open in White/Black wire.

22) Turn ignition switch to LOCK position. Disconnect DDM harness connector C520. Measure resistance between ground and terminal No. 2 (Yellow wire) at DDM harness connector C520. *See Fig. 4.* If resistance is greater than 10 k/ohms, go to next step. If resistance is 10 k/ohms or less, repair short to ground in Yellow wire.

23) Measure resistance in Yellow wire between driver's window motor harness connector C510 and terminal No. 2 at DDM harness connector C520. If resistance is 5 ohms or less, replace DDM. If resistance is greater than 5 ohms, repair open in Yellow wire.

24) Disconnect driver's window motor harness connector C510. Turn ignition switch to RUN position. Measure voltage at Yellow wire terminal at driver's window motor harness connector C510 while pressing driver's door master window switch to driver's window DOWN position. If battery voltage does not exist, go to next step. If battery voltage exists, go to step **30**).

25) Turn ignition switch to LOCK position. Disconnect one touch down module harness connector C507. Turn ignition switch to RUN position. Measure voltage at terminal No. 2 (Tan/Black wire) at one touch down module harness connector C507 while pressing driver's door master window switch to driver's window DOWN position. *See Fig. 10.* If battery voltage does not exist, go to next step. If battery voltage exists, go to step **28**).

26) Turn ignition switch to LOCK position. Disconnect driver's door master window switch harness connector C503. Measure resistance between ground and terminal No. 2 (Tan/Black wire) at one touch down module harness connector C507. If resistance is greater than 10 k/ohms, go to next step. If resistance is 10 k/ohms or less, repair short to ground in Tan/Black wire.

27) Measure resistance in Tan/Black wire between terminal No. 2 at one touch down module harness connector C507 and terminal No. 10 at driver's door master window switch harness connector C503. *See Figs. 8 and 10.* If resistance is 5 ohms or less, driver's door master window switch. If resistance is greater than 5 ohms, repair open in Tan/Black wire.

28) Measure resistance between ground and Yellow wire terminal at driver's window motor harness connector C510. If resistance is greater than 10 k/ohms, go to next step. If resistance is 10 k/ohms or less, repair short to ground in Yellow wire.

29) Measure resistance in Yellow wire between terminal No. 1 at one touch down module harness connector C507 and driver's window motor harness connector C510. If resistance is 5 ohms or less, replace one touch down module. If resistance is greater than 5 ohms, repair open in Yellow wire.

30) Measure resistance between ground and White/Black wire terminal at driver's window motor harness connector C510. If resistance is greater than 5 ohms, go to next step. If resistance is 5 ohms or less, go to step **32**).

31) Disconnect driver's door master window switch harness connector C503. Measure resistance in White/Black wire between driver's window motor harness connector C510 and terminal No. 8 driver's door master window switch harness connector C503. *See Fig. 8.* If resistance is 5 ohms or less, replace driver's door master window switch. If resistance greater than 5 ohms, repair open in White/Black wire.

32) Disconnect driver's door master window switch harness connector C503. Measure resistance between ground and White/Black wire terminal at driver's window motor harness connector C510. If resistance is greater than 10 k/ohms, go to next step. If resistance is 10 k/ohms or less, repair short to ground in White/Black wire.

33) Connect driver's door master window switch harness connector C503. Turn ignition switch to RUN position. Measure voltage at White/Black wire terminal at driver's window motor harness connector C510 while pressing driver's door master window switch to driver's window UP position. If battery voltage does not exist, replace driver's door master window switch. If battery voltage exists, replace driver's window motor.

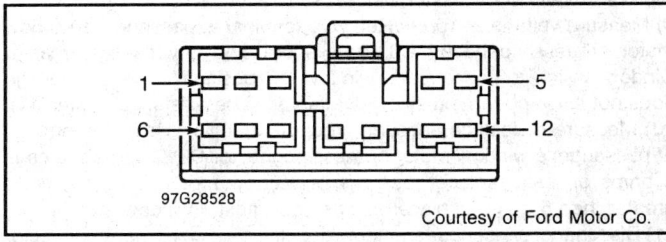

97G28528

Courtesy of Ford Motor Co.

Fig. 9: Identifying Driver's Door Module Harness Connector C518 Terminals

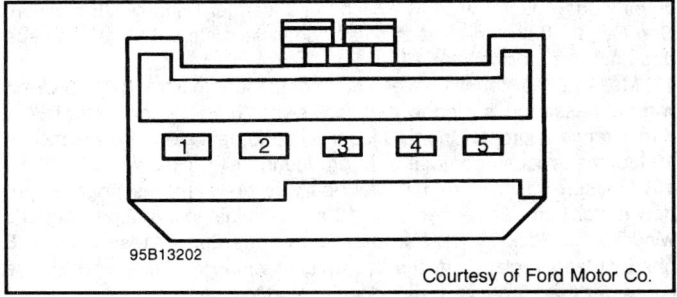

95B13202

Courtesy of Ford Motor Co.

Fig. 10: Identifying One Touch Down Module Harness Connector C507 Terminals

TEST E: PASSENGER'S WINDOW IS INOPERATIVE

1) Turn ignition switch to RUN position. Operate passenger's window from driver's door master window switch. If passenger's window does not operate, go to next step. If passenger's window operates, go to step **16**).

FORD
4-1126

1999 ACCESSORIES & EQUIPMENT
Power Windows – Crown Victoria & Grand Marquis (Cont.)

2) Turn ignition switch to LOCK position. Disconnect passenger's window motor harness connector C610. Turn ignition switch to RUN position. Measure voltage at Red/Yellow wire terminal at passenger's window motor harness connector C610 while pressing driver's door master window switch to passenger's window DOWN position. If battery voltage does not exist, go to next step. If battery voltage exists, go to step **8**).

3) Disconnect passenger's window/door lock switch harness connector C606. Measure voltage at terminal No. 11 (Tan/Light Blue wire) at passenger's window/door lock switch harness connector C606 while pressing driver's door master window switch to passenger' window DOWN position. *See Fig. 11*. If battery voltage does not exist, go to next step. If battery voltage exists, go to step **6**).

4) Turn ignition switch to LOCK position. Disconnect driver's door master window switch harness connector C503. Measure resistance between ground and terminal No. 11 (Tan/Light Blue wire) at passenger's window/door lock switch harness connector C606. If resistance is greater than 10 k/ohms, go to next step. If resistance is 10 k/ohms or less, repair short to ground in Tan/Light Blue wire.

5) Measure resistance in Tan/Light Blue wire between terminal No. 11 at passenger's window/door lock switch harness connector C606 and terminal No. 11 at driver's door master window switch harness connector C503. *See Figs. 8 and 11*. If resistance is 5 ohms or less, replace driver's door master window switch. If resistance is greater than 5 ohms, repair open in Tan/Light Blue wire.

6) Measure resistance between ground and Red/Yellow wire terminal at passenger's window motor harness connector C610. If resistance is greater than 10 k/ohms, go to next step. If resistance is 10 k/ohms or less, repair short to ground in Red/Yellow wire.

7) Measure resistance in Red/Yellow wire between passenger's window motor harness connector C610 and terminal No. 12 at passenger's window/door lock switch harness connector C606. If resistance is 5 ohms or less, replace driver's door master window switch. If resistance is greater than 5 ohms, repair open in Red/Yellow wire.

8) Measure resistance between ground and Red/Yellow wire terminal at passenger's window motor harness connector C610. If resistance is 5 ohms or less, go to next step. If resistance is greater than 5 ohms, replace driver's door master window switch.

9) Measure voltage at Yellow/Red wire terminal at passenger's window motor harness connector C610 while pressing driver's door master window switch to passenger's window UP position. If battery voltage does not exist, go to next step. If battery voltage exists, go to step **11**).

10) Measure resistance between ground and Yellow/Red wire terminal at passenger's window motor harness connector C610. If resistance is 5 ohms or less, replace passenger's window motor. If resistance is greater than 5 ohms, replace driver's door master window switch.

11) Disconnect passenger's window/door lock switch harness connector C606. Measure voltage at terminal No. 9 (White/Yellow wire) at passenger's window/door lock switch harness connector C606 while pressing driver's door master window switch to passenger' window UP position. *See Fig. 11*. If battery voltage exists, go to next step. If battery voltage does not exist, go to step **14**).

12) Measure resistance between ground and terminal No. 8 (Yellow/Red wire) at passenger's window/door lock switch harness connector C606. If resistance is greater than 10 k/ohms, go to next step. If resistance is 10 k/ohms or less, repair short to ground in Yellow/Red wire.

13) Measure resistance in Yellow/Red wire between passenger's window motor harness connector C610 and terminal No. 8 at passenger's window/door lock switch harness connector C606. If resistance is 5 ohms or less, replace driver's door master window switch. If resistance is greater than 5 ohms, repair open in Red/Yellow wire.

14) Disconnect driver's door master window switch harness connector C503. Measure resistance between ground and terminal No. 9 (White/Yellow wire) at passenger's window/door lock switch harness connector C606. If resistance is greater than 10 k/ohms, go to next step. If resistance is 10 k/ohms or less, repair short to ground in White/Yellow wire.

15) Measure resistance in White/Yellow wire between terminal No. 9 at passenger's window/door lock switch harness connector C606 and terminal No. 9 at driver's door master window switch harness connector C503. *See Figs. 8 and 11*. If resistance is 5 ohms or less, replace driver's door master window switch. If resistance is greater than 5 ohms, repair open in White/Yellow wire wire.

16) Operate rear power window from individual window control switches. If rear windows operate, go to next step. If rear windows do not operate, go to step **18**).

17) Disconnect passenger's window/door lock switch harness connector C606. Turn ignition switch to RUN position. Measure voltage at terminal No. 10 (Red/Light Blue wire) at passenger's window/door lock switch harness connector C606. *See Fig. 11*. If battery voltage exists, replace passenger's window/door lock switch. If battery voltage does not exist, repair open in Red/Light Blue wire.

18) Disconnect passenger's window/door lock switch harness connector C606. Disconnect driver's door master window switch harness connector C503. Measure resistance in Red/Light Blue wire between terminal No. 10 at passenger's window/door lock switch harness connector C606 and terminal No. 20 at driver's door master window switch harness connector C503. *See Figs. 8 and 11*. If resistance is 5 ohms or less, go to next step. If resistance is greater than 5 ohms, repair open in Red/Light Blue wire.

19) Measure resistance between ground and terminal No. 10 (Red/Light Blue wire) at passenger's window/door lock switch harness connector C606. If resistance is greater than 10 k/ohms, replace driver's door master window switch. If resistance is 10 k/ohms or less, repair short to ground in Red/Light Blue wire.

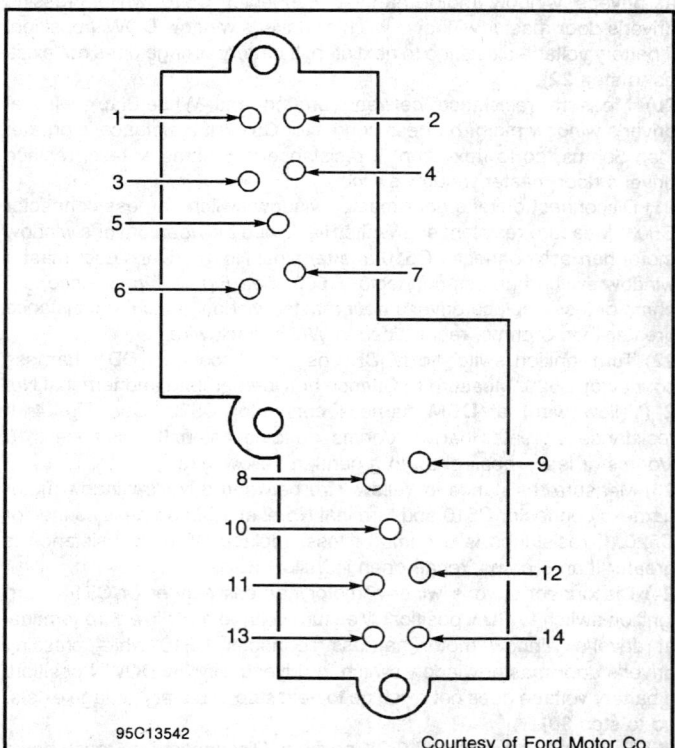

95C13542   Courtesy of Ford Motor Co.

Fig. 11: Identifying Passenger's Window/Door Lock Switch Harness Connector C606 Terminals

TEST F: REAR WINDOW IS INOPERATIVE

1) Turn ignition switch to RUN position. Operate inoperative window from driver's door master window switch. If window does not operate, go to next step. If window operates, go to step **26**).

2) Turn ignition switch to LOCK position. Disconnect inoperative window motor harness connector. Turn ignition switch to RUN position. Measure voltage at Yellow/Red wire terminal at inoperative window motor harness connector while pressing driver's door master window switch to appropriate window DOWN position. If battery voltage does not exist, go

to next step for left rear window or go to step **8)** for right rear window. If battery voltage exists, go to step **13)**.

3) Disconnect left rear window switch harness connector C706. Turn ignition switch to RUN position. Measure voltage at terminal No. 2 (Yellow/Light Blue wire) at left rear window switch harness connector C706 while pressing driver's door master window switch to left rear window DOWN position. *See Fig. 12.* If battery voltage does not exist, go to next step. If battery voltage exists, go to step **6)**.

4) Disconnect driver's door master window switch harness connector C503. Measure resistance between ground and terminal No. 2 (Yellow/Light Blue wire) at left rear window switch harness connector C706. If resistance is greater than 10 k/ohms, go to next step. If resistance is 10 k/ohms or less, repair short to ground in Yellow/Light Blue wire.

5) Measure resistance in Yellow/Light Blue wire between terminal No. 2 at left rear window switch harness connector C706 and terminal No. 15 at driver's door master window switch harness connector C503. *See Figs. 8 and 12.* If resistance is 5 ohms or less, replace driver's door master window switch. If resistance is greater than 5 ohms, repair open in Yellow/Light Blue wire.

6) Measure resistance between ground and Yellow/Red wire terminal at left rear window motor harness connector. If resistance is greater than 10 k/ohms, go to next step. If resistance is 10 k/ohms or less, repair short to ground in Yellow/Red wire.

7) Measure resistance in Yellow/Red wire between left rear window motor harness connector and terminal No. 5 at left rear window switch harness connector C706. *See Fig. 12.* If resistance is 5 ohms or less, replace left rear window switch. If resistance is greater than 5 ohms, repair open in Yellow/Red wire.

8) Disconnect right rear window switch harness connector C806. Turn ignition switch to RUN position. Measure voltage at terminal No. 2 (Yellow/Black wire) at right rear window switch harness connector C706 while pressing driver's door master window switch to right rear window DOWN position. *See Fig. 12.* If battery voltage does not exist, go to next step. If battery voltage exists, go to step **11)**.

9) Disconnect driver's door master window switch harness connector C503. Measure resistance between ground and terminal No. 2 (Yellow/Black wire) at right rear window switch harness connector C706. If resistance is greater than 10 k/ohms, go to next step. If resistance is 10 k/ohms or less, repair short to ground in Yellow/Black wire.

10) Measure resistance in Yellow/Black wire between terminal No. 2 at right rear window switch harness connector C706 and terminal No. 15 at driver's door master window switch harness connector C503. *See Figs. 8 and 12.* If resistance is 5 ohms or less, replace driver's door master window switch. If resistance is greater than 5 ohms, repair open in Yellow/Light Blue wire.

11) Measure resistance between ground and Yellow/Red wire terminal at right rear window motor harness connector. If resistance is greater than 10 k/ohms, go to next step. If resistance is 10 k/ohms or less, repair short to ground in Yellow/Red wire.

12) Measure resistance in Yellow/Red wire between right rear window motor harness connector and terminal No. 5 at right rear window switch harness connector C806. *See Fig. 12.* If resistance is 5 ohms or less, replace right rear window switch. If resistance is greater than 5 ohms, repair open in Yellow/Red wire.

13) Measure resistance between ground and Yellow/Red wire terminal at inoperative window motor harness connector. If resistance is 5 ohms or less, go to next step. If resistance is greater than 5 ohms, replace driver's door master window switch.

14) Measure voltage at Red/Yellow wire terminal at inoperative window motor harness connector while pressing driver's door master window switch to appropriate window UP position. If battery voltage does not exist, go to next step for left rear window or go to step **20)** for right rear window. If battery voltage exists, go to step **25)** .

15) Disconnect left rear window switch harness connector C706. Turn ignition switch to RUN position. Measure voltage at terminal No. 4 (Gray/Orange wire) at left rear window switch harness connector C706 while pressing driver's door master window switch to left rear window UP position. *See Fig. 12.* If battery voltage does not exist, go to next step. If battery voltage exists, go to step **18)**.

16) Disconnect driver's door master window switch harness connector C503. Measure resistance between ground and terminal No. 4 (Gray/Orange wire) at left rear window switch harness connector C706. If resistance is greater than 10 k/ohms, go to next step. If resistance is 10 k/ohms or less, repair short to ground in Gray/Orange wire.

17) Measure resistance in Gray/Orange wire between terminal No. 4 at left rear window switch harness connector C706 and terminal No. 17 at driver's door master window switch harness connector C503. *See Figs. 8 and 12.* If resistance is 5 ohms or less, replace driver's door master window switch. If resistance is greater than 5 ohms, repair open in Gray/Orange wire.

18) Measure resistance between ground and Red/Yellow wire terminal at left rear window motor harness connector. If resistance is greater than 10 k/ohms, go to next step. If resistance is 10 k/ohms or less, repair short to ground in Red/Yellow wire.

19) Measure resistance in Red/Yellow wire between left rear window motor harness connector and terminal No. 1 at left rear window switch harness connector C706. *See Fig. 12.* If resistance is 5 ohms or less, replace left rear window switch. If resistance is greater than 5 ohms, repair open in Red/Yellow wire.

20) Disconnect right rear window switch harness connector C806. Turn ignition switch to RUN position. Measure voltage at terminal No. 4 (Red/Black wire) at right rear window switch harness connector C806 while pressing driver's door master window switch to right rear window UP position. *See Fig. 12.* If battery voltage does not exist, go to next step. If battery voltage exists, go to step **23)**.

21) Disconnect driver's door master window switch harness connector C503. Measure resistance between ground and terminal No. 4 (Red/Black wire) at right rear window switch harness connector C806. If resistance is greater than 10 k/ohms, go to next step. If resistance is 10 k/ohms or less, repair short to ground in Red/Black wire.

22) Measure resistance in Red/Black wire between terminal No. 4 at right rear window switch harness connector C806 and terminal No. 18 at driver's door master window switch harness connector C503. *See Figs. 8 and 12.* If resistance is 5 ohms or less, replace driver's door master window switch. If resistance is greater than 5 ohms, repair open in Red/Black wire.

23) Measure resistance between ground and Red/Yellow wire terminal at right rear window motor harness connector. If resistance is greater than 10 k/ohms, go to next step. If resistance is 10 k/ohms or less, repair short to ground in Red/Yellow wire.

24) Measure resistance in Red/Yellow wire between right rear window motor harness connector and terminal No. 1 at right rear window switch harness connector C806. *See Fig. 12.* If resistance is 5 ohms or less, replace right rear window switch. If resistance is greater than 5 ohms, repair open in Red/Yellow wire.

25) Measure resistance between ground and Red/Yellow wire terminal at inoperative window motor harness connector. If resistance is 5 ohms or less, replace appropriate window motor. If resistance is greater than 5 ohms, replace driver's door master window switch.

26) Operate passenger's window from passenger's window/door lock switch. If passenger's window operates, go to next step. If passenger's window does not operate, perform TEST E: PASSENGER'S WINDOW IS INOPERATIVE.

27) Turn ignition switch to LOCK position. Disconnect inoperative window switch harness connector. Turn ignition switch to RUN position. Measure voltage at terminal No. 3 (Red/Light Blue wire) at inoperative window switch harness connector. *See Fig. 12.* If battery voltage exists, replace appropriate rear window control switch. If battery voltage does not exist, repair open in Red/Light Blue wire

FORD
4-1128

1999 ACCESSORIES & EQUIPMENT
Power Windows – Crown Victoria & Grand Marquis (Cont.)

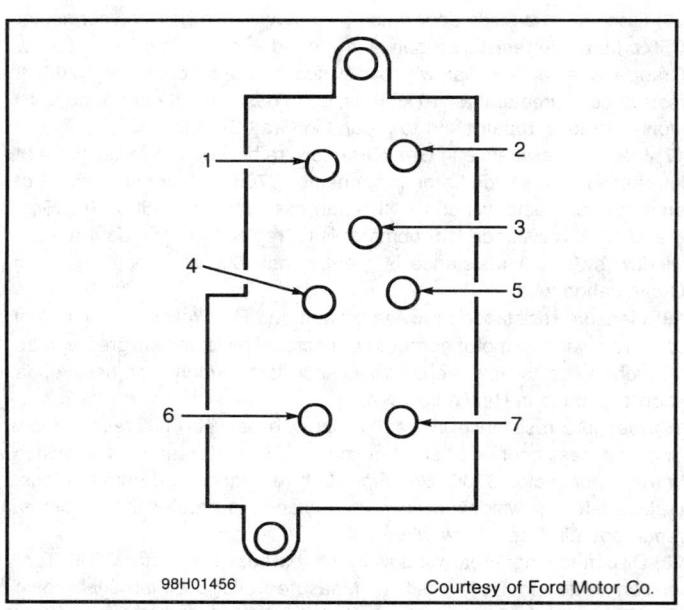

98H01456   Courtesy of Ford Motor Co.

Fig. 12: Identifying Right & Left Rear Window Switch Harness Connector Terminals

TEST G: ONE TOUCH DOWN FEATURE INOPERATIVE

NOTE: Vehicles with keyless entry system incorporate one-touch down feature in Driver's Door Module (DDM) located in left front door. Vehicles without keyless entry system have a separate one-touch down module located in left front door.

1) Turn ignition switch to RUN position. Operate driver's window. If driver's window operates, go to next step. In driver's window does not operate, perform TEST D: DRIVER'S WINDOW IS INOPERATIVE.

2) Operate driver's window. If window operates smoothly and completely, go to next step. If window does not operate smoothly and completely, repair mechanical failure.

3) Close driver's window. Momentarily press driver's door master window switch to driver's window DOWN position. If one touch down feature operated, go to step 8). If one touch down feature did not operate, go to next step if equipped with remote keyless entry or go to step 5) if not equipped with remote keyless entry.

4) Turn ignition switch to RUN position. Using NGS tester, monitor Driver's Door Module (DDM) PID D_PW_SW while pressing then releasing driver's door master window switch to driver's window DOWN position. If PID indicates ACTIVE when switch is depressed and NOTACTIVE when switch is released, replace DDM. If PID does not indicate ACTIVE when switch is depressed and NOTACTIVE when switch is released, replace driver's door master window switch.

5) Turn ignition switch to LOCK position. Disconnect one touch down module harness connector C507. Turn ignition switch to RUN position. Measure voltage at terminal No. 3 (Yellow/Light Green wire) at one touch down module harness connector C507. *See Fig. 10.* If battery voltage exists, go to next step. If battery voltage does not exist, repair open in Yellow/Light Green wire.

6) Measure resistance between ground and terminal No. 5 (Black wire) at one touch down module harness connector C507. If resistance is 5 ohms or less, go to next step. If resistance is greater than 5 ohms, repair open in Black wire.

7) Measure voltage at terminal No. 2 (Tan/Black wire) at one touch down module harness connector C507 while pressing and releasing driver's door master window switch to driver's window DOWN position. Battery voltage should exist when switch is pressed and zero volts should exist when switch is released. If voltage is as specified, replace one touch down module. If voltage is not as specified, replace driver's door master window switch.

8) Turn ignition switch to RUN position. Close driver's window. Operate one touch down feature. While window is going down, press driver's door master window switch to driver's window UP position. If window stops, one touch down feature is operating properly at this time. If window does not stop, go to next step if not equipped with remote keyless entry or go to step 10) if equipped with remote keyless entry.

9) Turn ignition switch to LOCK position. Disconnect one touch down module harness connector C507. Turn ignition switch to RUN position. Measure voltage at terminal No. 4 (White/Black wire) at one touch down module harness connector C507 while pressing driver's door master window switch to driver's window UP position. *See Fig. 10.* If battery voltage exists, replace one touch down module. If battery voltage does not exist, repair open in White/Black wire.

10) Using NGS tester, monitor Driver's Door Module (DDM) PID D_PW_SW while pressing driver's door master window switch to driver's window UP position. If PID does not indicate UP, go to next step. If PID indicates UP, replace DDM.

11) Turn ignition switch to LOCK position. Disconnect DDM harness connector C518. Measure voltage at terminal No. 2 (White/Black wire) at DDM harness connector C518 while pressing driver's door master window switch to driver's window UP position. *See Fig. 9.* If battery voltage exists, replace DDM. If battery voltage does not exist, repair open in White/Black wire.

REMOVAL & INSTALLATION

DRIVER'S DOOR MODULE (DDM)

Removal & Installation – Disconnect negative battery cable. Remove driver's door trim panel. Disconnect Driver's Door Module (DDM) harness connectors. Remove mounting screws. Remove module through access hole in door. To install, reverse removal procedure.

WINDOW MOTOR

Removal & Installation (Front Door) – 1) Remove door trim panel and protective shield. Place window glass in full up position and tape window in place. Disconnect negative battery cable. Disconnect window motor harness connector.

2) Using a 1/4" drill, remove 3 window regulator motor bracket rivets from door. Move motor, with drive cables attached, so motor retaining screws can be accessed. Remove window motor Torx retaining screws.

3) Separate window motor from window regulator. Remove window motor through access hole in door. To install, reverse removal procedure. Tighten motor-to-regulator bolts to 53 INCH lbs. (6 N.m).

Removal & Installation (Rear Door) – 1) Remove door trim panel and protective shield. Disconnect negative battery cable. Disconnect window motor harness connector.

CAUTION: When drilling out rivets, do not enlarge holes in door.

2) Using a 1/4" drill, remove 3 window regulator motor bracket rivets from door. Move motor with drive cables attached, so motor retaining screws can be accessed. Remove power window motor Torx retaining screws.

3) Separate window motor from window regulator. Remove window motor through access hole in door. To install, reverse removal procedure. Tighten motor-to-regulator bolts to 53 INCH lbs. (6 N.m).

POWER WINDOW SWITCH

Removal & Installation – Disconnect negative battery cable. Remove screw(s) from inner edge of armrest. Pry up front portion of switch housing. Unhook rear edge of housing and remove from armrest. Remove screw(s) from harness connector. Pry switch from connector with small screwdriver's. To install, reverse removal procedure.

1999 ACCESSORIES & EQUIPMENT
Power Windows – Crown Victoria & Grand Marquis (Cont.)

FORD
4-1129

WIRING DIAGRAMS

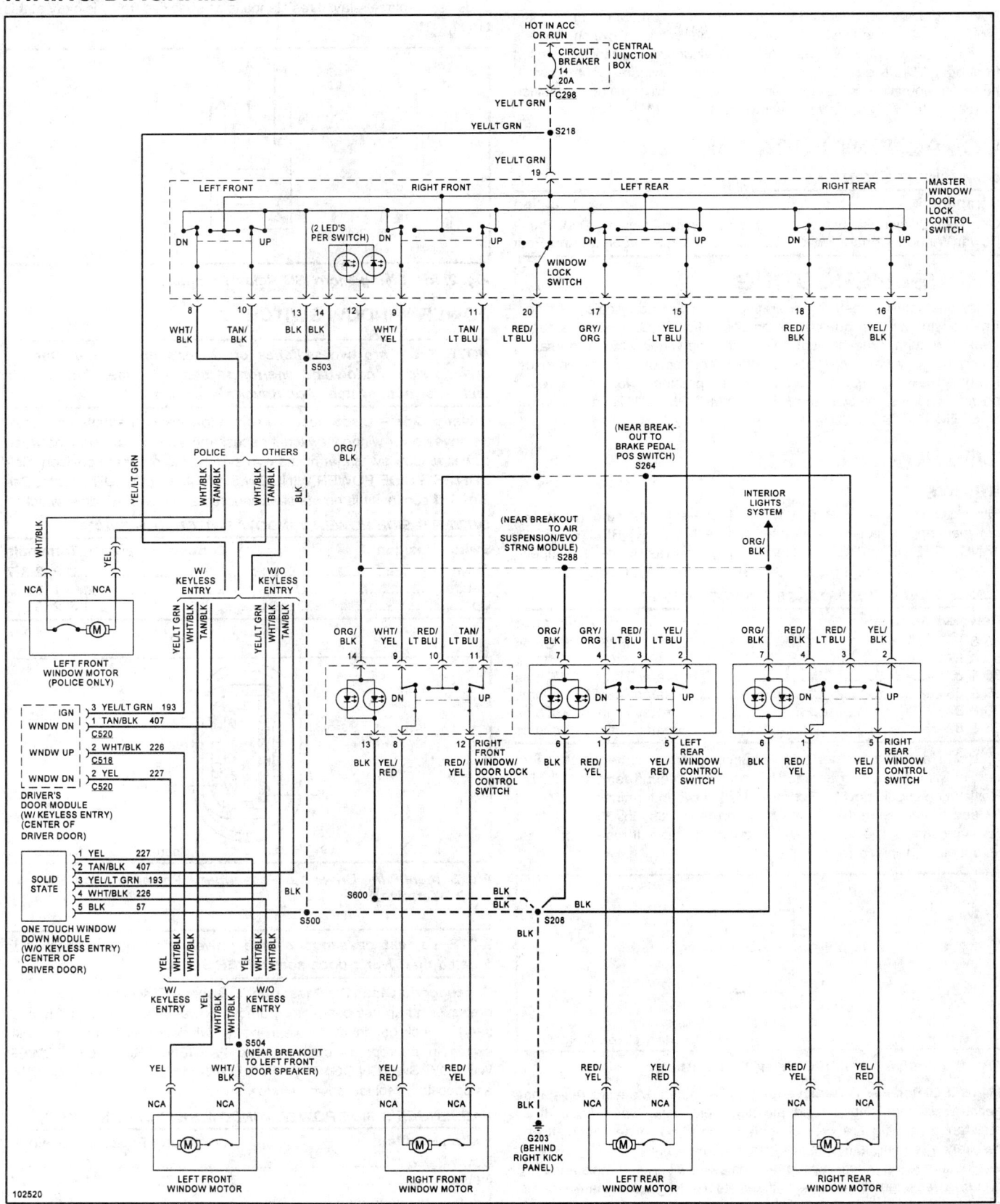

Fig. 13: Power Window System Wiring Diagram (Crown Victoria & Grand Marquis)

102520

DESCRIPTION & OPERATION

Power windows are operated by reversible motors mounted on window regulator. Passenger's window has an individual control switch. Driver's power window control switches control all windows and is located on left front door (2 individual switches). Driver's power window control switch has a one-touch down feature. Window will move to its full down position by momentarily pressing window switch.

COMPONENT LOCATIONS

COMPONENT LOCATIONS

Component	Location
One-Touch Down Relay	Behind Driver's Door Panel
Power Window Control Switch	On Appropriate Arm Rest

TROUBLE SHOOTING

Verify customer concern by operating windows to duplicate condition. Ensure window(s) in question is properly aligned. Check for damaged track or regulator mechanism, malfunctioning window motor, damaged wiring, damaged switches, poor electrical connections and blown fuses. If problem exists, repair as necessary. If no problems were found, repair power windows by symptom. See SYMPTOM CHART table under SYSTEM TESTS.

COMPONENT TESTS

RELAYS

Mini ISO Relay – 1) Remove mini ISO relay. Measure resistance between appropriate relay terminals. See MINI ISO RELAY RESISTANCE SPECIFICATIONS table. *See Fig. 1.* If resistance is as specified, go to next step. If resistance is not as specified, replace relay.

MINI ISO RELAY RESISTANCE SPECIFICATIONS

Between Terminals	Resistance
85 & 86	50-100 Ohms
30 & 87a	5 Ohms Or Less
30 & 87	Greater Than 10 K/Ohms
30 & 86	Greater Than 10 K/Ohms
86 & 87a	Greater Than 10 K/Ohms
86 & 87	Greater Than 10 K/Ohms

2) Using a fused jumper wire, connect positive battery voltage to terminal No. 85. Using another jumper wire, ground terminal No. 86. Resistance should now be 5 ohms or less between terminals No. 30 and 87 and greater than 10 k/ohms between terminals No. 30 and 87a. If resistance is as specified, relay is okay at this time. If resistance is not as specified, replace relay.

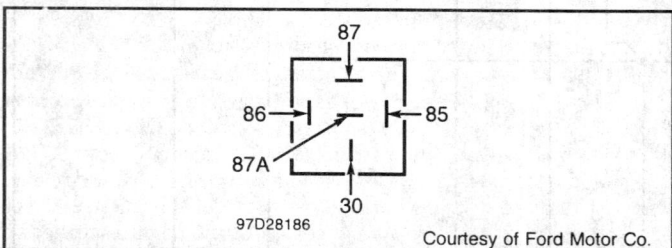

Fig. 1: Identifying Mini ISO Relay Terminals

Micro ISO Relay – 1) Remove relay to be tested. Measure resistance between terminal No. 5 and all other terminals. *See Fig. 2.* If all resistance reading are greater than 5 ohms, go to next step. If any resistance reading is 5 ohms or less, replace relay.
2) Measure resistance between terminals No. 3 and 4. If resistance is 5 ohms or less, go to next step. If resistance is greater than 5 ohms, replace relay.
3) Apply battery voltage and ground between terminals No. 1 and 2. Measure resistance between terminals No. 3 and 5. Resistance should be 5 ohms or less. Measure resistance between terminals No. 3 and 4.

Resistance should be greater than 10 k/ohms. If resistance is not as specified, replace relay. If resistance is as specified, relay is okay at this time.

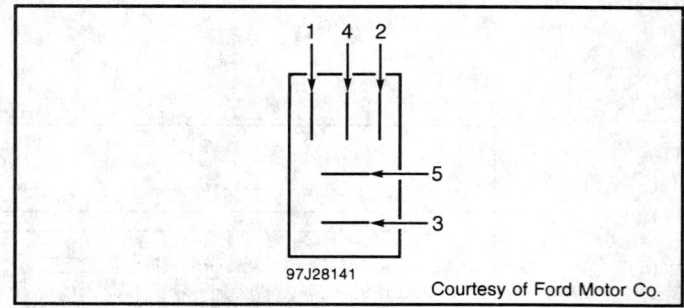

Fig. 2: Identifying Micro ISO Relay Terminals

POWER WINDOW SWITCH

NOTE: There are two switches on driver's door panel. One for driver's side window and one for passenger's side window. This test is for both switches on driver's door panel.

Driver's Side – Disconnect power window switch harness connector (remove power window switch if necessary). Check continuity between power window switch terminals with switch in appropriate position. See DRIVER'S SIDE POWER WINDOW SWITCH CONTINUITY table. *See Fig. 3.* If continuity is not as specified, replace power window switch.

DRIVER'S SIDE POWER WINDOW SWITCH CONTINUITY

Switch Position	Continuity Between Terminals
Down	1 & 3; 2 & 7
Neutral	1, 3 & 7
Up	1 & 2; 3 & 7

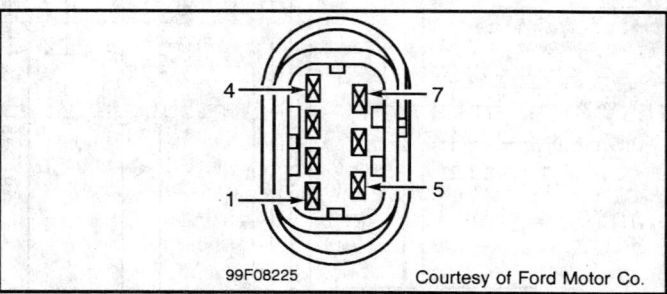

Fig. 3: Identifying Driver's & Passenger's Power Window Switch Terminals

NOTE: To test passenger's side power window switch that is located on driver's door, see DRIVER'S SIDE.

Passenger's Side (On Passenger's Door) – Disconnect power window switch harness connector (remove power window switch if necessary). Check continuity between power window switch terminals with switch in appropriate position. See PASSENGER'S SIDE POWER WINDOW SWITCH CONTINUITY table. *See Fig. 3.* If continuity is not as specified, replace power window switch.

PASSENGER'S SIDE POWER WINDOW SWITCH CONTINUITY

Switch Position	Continuity Between Terminals
Down	1 & 6; 2 & 7
Neutral	1 & 6; 3 & 7
Up	1 & 2; 3 & 7

SYSTEM TESTS

SYMPTOM CHART

Symptom	Test
All Power Windows Completely Inoperative	A
Driver's Power Window Inoperative	B
Passenger's Power Window Inoperative	C
One-Touch Down Feature Inoperative	D

TEST A: ALL POWER WINDOWS COMPLETELY INOPERATIVE

1) Turn ignition switch to LOCK position. Remove fuse No. 21 (40-amp) from instrument panel fuse box. Inspect fuse. If fuse is okay, go to next step. If fuse is blown, repair short to ground in power distribution circuit. See appropriate wiring diagram in POWER DISTRIBUTION article in WIRING DIAGRAMS.

2) Turn ignition switch to LOCK position. Disconnect driver's power window control switch harness connector C74. Measure resistance in Violet/Blue wire between output side of fuse No. 21 in instrument panel fuse box and terminal No. 2 at driver's window control switch harness connector C74. *See Fig. 4.* If resistance is 5 ohms or less, go to next step. If resistance is greater than 5 ohms, repair open in Violet/Blue wire.

3) Measure resistance between ground and terminal No. 3 (Black wire) at driver's power window control switch harness connector C74. If resistance is 5 ohms or less, replace driver's power window control switch. If resistance is greater than 5 ohms, repair open in Black wire.

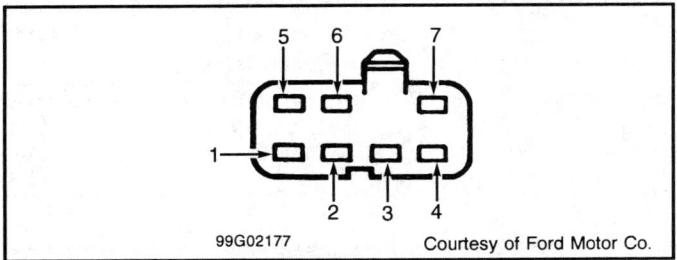

99G02177   Courtesy of Ford Motor Co.

Fig. 4: Identifying Driver's & Passenger's Window Control Switch Harness Connector Terminals

TEST B: DRIVER'S POWER WINDOW INOPERATIVE

1) Ensure driver's window is up. Turn ignition switch to LOCK position. Disconnect driver's power window control switch harness connector C74. Test driver's power window switch. See POWER WINDOW SWITCH under COMPONENT TESTS. If switch is okay, go to next step. If switch is defective, replace driver's power window switch.

2) Turn ignition switch to LOCK position. Disconnect one-touch down relay harness connector C738. Measure resistance in Yellow/Green wire between terminal No. 7 at driver's power window control switch harness connector C74 and terminal No. 3 at one-touch down relay harness connector C738. *See Figs. 4 and 5.* Resistance should be 5 ohms or less. Measure resistance between ground and terminal No. 3 (Yellow/Green wire) at one-touch down relay harness connector C738. Resistance should be greater than 10 k/ohms. If both resistance readings are as specified, go to next step. If either resistance reading is not as specified, repair open and/or short to ground in Yellow/Green wire.

3) Measure resistance between terminals No. 3 and 5 at one-touch down relay (component side). *See Fig. 6.* If resistance is 5 ohms or less, go to next step. If resistance is greater than 5 ohms, replace one-touch down relay.

4) Disconnect driver's power window motor harness connector C782. Measure resistance in Yellow wire between terminal No. 1 at driver's power window motor harness connector C782 and terminal No. 5 at one-touch down relay harness connector C738. Resistance should be 5 ohms or less. Measure resistance between ground and terminal No. 5 (Yellow wire) at one-touch down relay harness connector C738. Resistance should be greater than 10 k/ohms. If both resistance readings are as specified, go to next step. If either resistance reading is not as specified, repair open and/or short to ground in Yellow wire.

5) Connect driver's power window control switch harness connector C74. Measure resistance between ground and White wire terminal at driver's power window motor harness connector C782. If resistance is 5 ohms or less, replace driver's power window motor. If resistance is greater than 5 ohms, repair open in White wire.

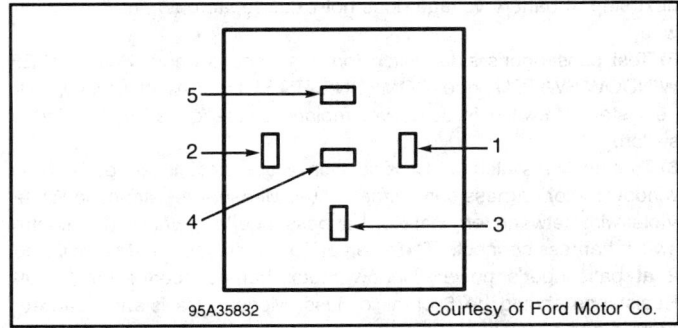

95A35832   Courtesy of Ford Motor Co.

Fig. 5: Identifying One-Touch Down Relay Harness Connector C738 Terminals

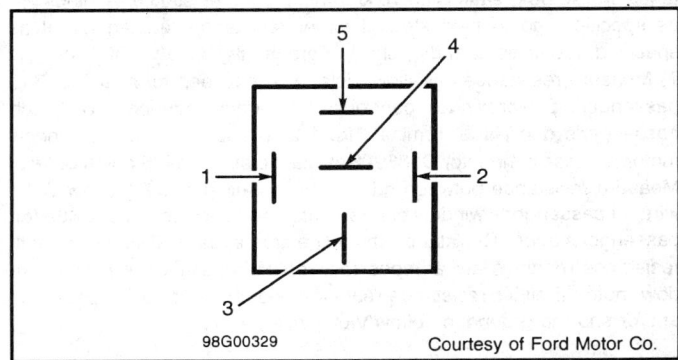

98G00329   Courtesy of Ford Motor Co.

Fig. 6: Identifying One-Touch Down Relay Terminals

TEST C: PASSENGER'S POWER WINDOW INOPERATIVE

NOTE: On passenger's power window control switch harness connector C489 there are 2 White/Violet wires and 2 Yellow/Violet wires.

1) Turn ignition switch to LOCK position. Disconnect passenger's power window control switch harness connector C2125 (the one on driver's door). Test switch. See POWER WINDOW SWITCH under COMPONENT TESTS. If switch is okay, go to next step. If switch is defective, replace driver's power window switch.

2) Disconnect passenger's power window control switch harness connector C489 (on passenger's door). Measure resistance in White/Violet wire between terminal No. 6 at passenger's power window control switch harness connector C489 (on passenger's door) and terminal No. 1 at passenger's power window control switch harness connector C2125 (on driver's door). *See Fig. 4.* Resistance should be 5 ohms or less. Measure resistance between ground and terminal No. 6 (White/Violet wire) at passenger's power window control switch harness connector C489 (on passenger's door). Resistance should be greater than 10 k/ohms. If both resistance readings are as specified, go to next step. If either resistance reading is not as specified, repair open and/or short to ground in White/Violet wire.

3) Measure resistance in Yellow/Violet wire between terminal No. 3 at passenger's power window control switch harness connector C489 (on passenger's door) and terminal No. 2 at passenger's power window control switch harness connector C2125 (on driver's door). Resistance should be 5 ohms or less. Measure resistance between ground and terminal No. 3 (Yellow/Violet wire) at passenger's power window control switch harness connector C489 (on passenger's door). Resistance should be greater than 10 k/ohms. If both resistance readings are as specified, go to next step. If either resistance reading is not as specified, repair open and/or short to ground in Yellow/Violet wire.

4) Turn ignition switch to RUN position. Measure voltage at terminal No. 2 (Violet/White wire) at passenger's window control switch harness connector C489 (on passenger's door). If battery voltage exists, go to next step. If battery voltage does not exist, repair open in Violet/White wire.

5) Test passenger's side switch (on passenger's door). See POWER WINDOW SWITCH under COMPONENT TESTS. If switch is okay, go to next step. If switch is defective, replace passenger's power window switch.

6) Turn ignition switch to LOCK position. Disconnect passenger's power window motor harness connector C1869. Measure resistance in White/Violet wire between terminal No. 1 at passenger's power window control switch harness connector C489 (on passenger's door) and terminal No. 2 at passenger's power window motor harness connector C1869. Resistance should be 5 ohms or less. Measure resistance between ground and terminal No. 1 (White/Violet wire) at passenger's window control switch harness connector C489 (on passenger's door). Resistance should be greater than 10 k/ohms. If both resistance readings are as specified, go to next step. If either resistance reading is not as specified, repair open and/or short to ground in White/Violet wire.

7) Measure resistance in Yellow/Violet wire between terminal No. 7 at passenger's power window control switch harness connector C489 (on passenger's door) and terminal No. 1 at passenger's power window motor harness connector C1869. Resistance should be 5 ohms or less. Measure resistance between ground and terminal No. 7 (Yellow/Violet wire) at passenger's window control switch harness connector C489 (on passenger's door). Resistance should be greater than 10 k/ohms. If both resistance readings are as specified, replace passenger's power window motor. If either resistance reading is not as specified, repair open and/or short to ground in Yellow/Violet wire.

TEST D: ONE-TOUCH DOWN FEATURE INOPERATIVE

1) Turn ignition switch to LOCK position. Disconnect one-touch down relay harness connector C738. Turn ignition switch to RUN position. Measure voltage at terminal No. 2 (Violet/Orange wire) at one-touch down relay harness connector C738. *See Fig. 5.* If battery voltage exists, go to next step. If battery voltage does not exist, repair open in Violet/Orange wire.

2) Measure resistance between ground and terminal No. 1 (Black wire) at one-touch down relay harness connector C738. If resistance is 5 ohms or less, replace one-touch down relay. If resistance is greater than 5 ohms, repair open in Black wire.

REMOVAL & INSTALLATION

CAUTION: When battery is disconnected, vehicle computer and memory systems may lose memory data. Driveability problems may exist until computer systems have completed a relearn cycle. See COMPUTER RELEARN PROCEDURES article in GENERAL INFORMATION before disconnecting battery.

ONE-TOUCH WINDOW DOWN RELAY

Removal & Installation – Disconnect negative battery cable. Remove driver's side door trim panel. Remove 2 screws retaining relay to door. Disconnect harness connector and remove relay. To install, reverse removal procedure.

WIRING DIAGRAMS

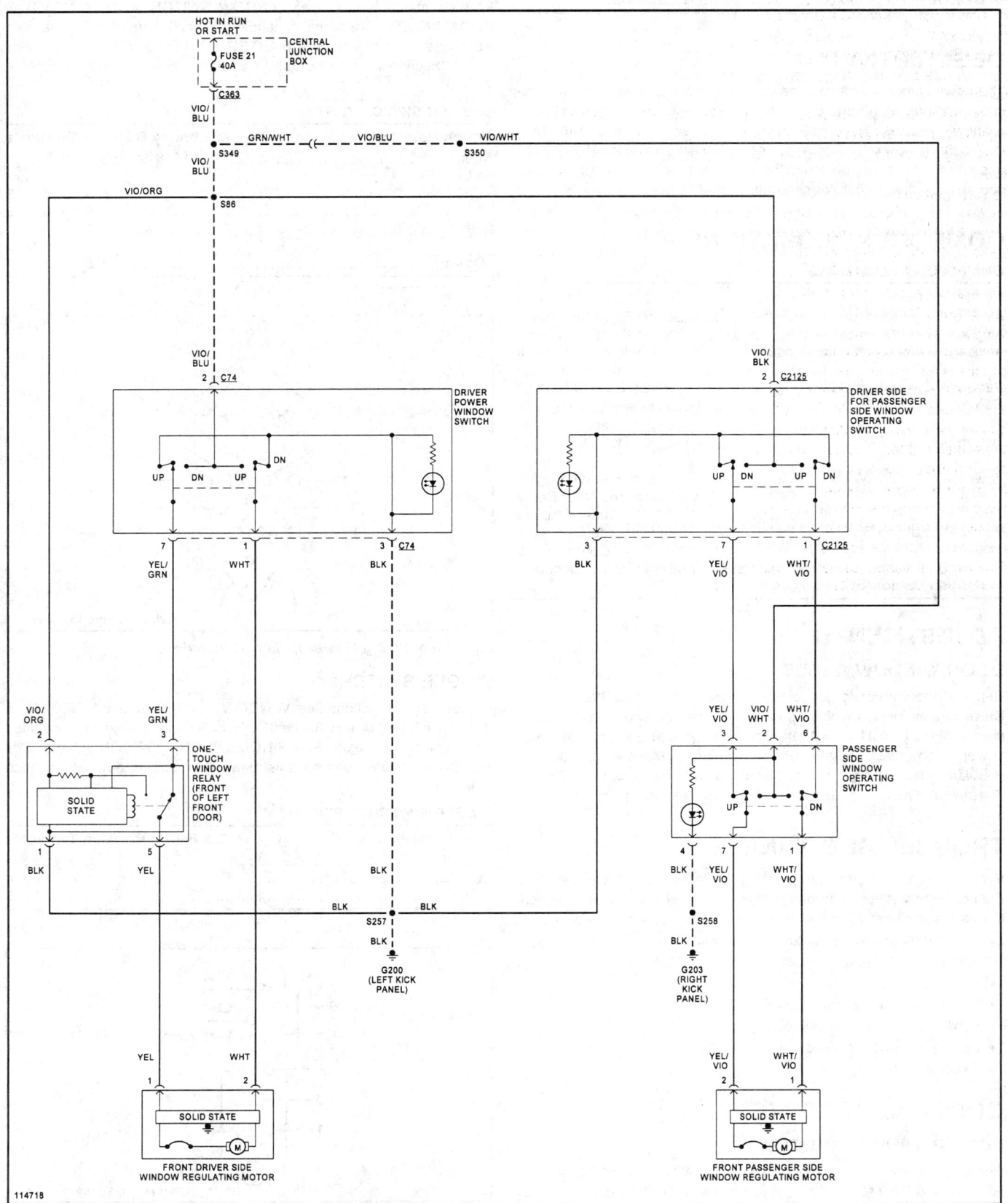

Fig. 7: Power Window System Wiring Diagram (Cougar)

114718

1999 ACCESSORIES & EQUIPMENT
Power Windows – Econoline

NOTE: *This article includes Cutaway and RV Cutaway.*

DESCRIPTION

The power window system consists of window switches, window regulators, motors, wiring and connectors. Power windows are operated by window switches. Reversible type motors are mounted with each individual window regulator. A master control switch is located on the left door. All windows may be controlled from this switch. Passenger window has an individual switch for separate control.

COMPONENT LOCATIONS

COMPONENT LOCATIONS

Component	Location
Air Bag Diagnostic Monitor [1]	Behind Right Kick Panel
Air Bag Sliding Contact	Top Of Steering Column
Auxiliary Powertrain Control Module	Below Left Side Of Instrument Panel
Data Link Connector	Below Driver's Side Of Instrument Panel, To Right Of Steering Column
Instrument Fuse Panel	Lower Left Side Of Steering Column
Powertrain Control Module	Left Rear Of Engine Compartment, Near Brake Master Cylinder
Power Distribution Box	Left Front Side Of Engine Compartment

[1] – Air bag diagnostic monitor may also be referred to as Electronic Crash Sensor (ECS) module.

ADJUSTMENTS

DOOR WINDOW GLASS

Remove door trim panel. Loosen upper window regulator bracket nuts. Raise window glass to full up position. Tighten upper regulator bracket nuts to 89-124 INCH lbs. (10-14 N.m). Loosen rear glass channel bolt. Lower window glass partially, to allow adjustment. Move window glass to rearward position. Tighten rear glass channel bolt to 62-89 INCH lbs. (7-10 N.m). Open and close window to verify proper operation.

TROUBLE SHOOTING

Verify customer concern by operating windows to duplicate condition. Ensure battery is fully charged. Ensure windows are properly aligned. Check the following for possible cause of malfunction:

- Window mounting (regulator and bracket).
- Window frame interference.
- Faulty fuse.
- Open or shorted supply circuit.
- Loose or corroded connectors.
- Poor ground connections.
- Faulty switch.

COMPONENT TESTS

POWER WINDOW MOTOR

Remove window motor from vehicle. See WINDOW MOTOR under REMOVAL & INSTALLATION. Using fused jumper wires, connect a fully charged battery to motor terminals. Observe motor. Motor should operate smoothly. Reverse leads. Motor should operate in reverse direction. Replace window motor if it does not operate as specified.

MASTER SWITCH

Remove master switch. See WINDOW SWITCH under REMOVAL & INSTALLATION. Check for continuity between terminals as specified while operating switch. See MASTER SWITCH TESTING table. *See Fig. 1.* If continuity does not exist between specified terminals, replace switch.

MASTER SWITCH TESTING

Switch Position	Continuity Between Terminals
Neutral	9 & 15; 8 & 14; 6 & 12; 7 & 13
Left	
Up	6 & 10; 7 & 13
Down	10 & 13; 6 & 12
Right	
Up	8 & 11; 9 & 15
Down	11 & 15; 8 & 14

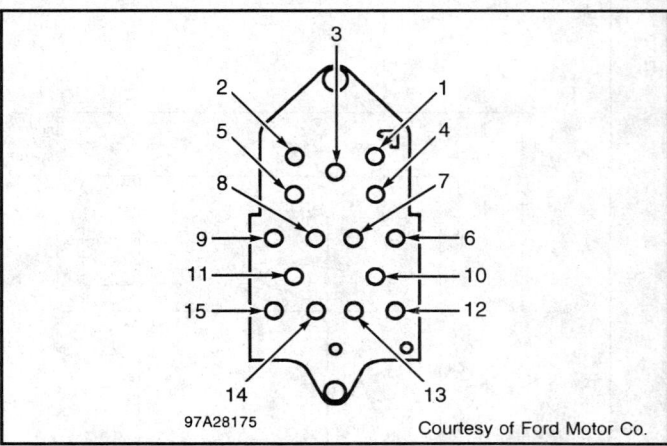

97A28175   Courtesy of Ford Motor Co.

Fig. 1: Identifying Master Switch Terminals

SINGLE SWITCH

Remove single switch. See WINDOW SWITCH under REMOVAL & INSTALLATION. Check for continuity between terminals as specified while operating switch. See SINGLE SWITCH TESTING table. *See Fig. 2.* If continuity does not exist between specified terminals, replace switch.

SINGLE SWITCH TESTING

Switch Position	Continuity Between Terminals
Neutral	1 & 4; 2 & 5
Up	3 & 5; 1 & 4
Down	1 & 3; 2 & 5

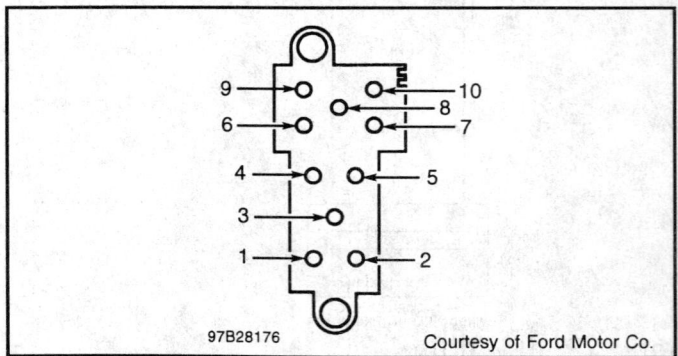

97B28176   Courtesy of Ford Motor Co.

Fig. 2: Identifying Single Switch Terminals

SYSTEM TESTS

CAUTION: When battery is disconnected, vehicle computer and memory systems may lose memory data. Driveability problems may exist until computer systems have completed a relearn cycle. See COMPUTER RELEARN PROCEDURES article in GENERAL INFORMATION before disconnecting battery.

NOTE: Before beginning system tests, perform TROUBLE SHOOTING.

SYSTEM TEST INDEX

TEST A: ALL POWER WINDOWS INOPERATIVE

1) Remove fuse No. 21 (30-amp) from instrument panel fuse block located on lower left side of steering column. Turn ignition switch to RUN position. Using a voltmeter, check voltage between ground and fuse No. 21 input terminal (left terminal) on fuse block. *See Fig. 3.* If voltage is more than 10 volts, go to next step. If voltage is 10 volts or less, repair Black/Light Green wire between instrument panel fuse block and ignition switch. Retest system operation.

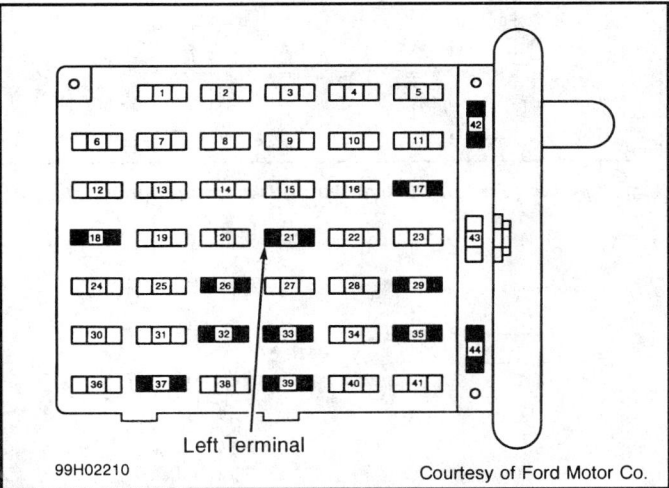

Fig. 3: Identifying Fuse No. 21 Left Terminal

2) Turn ignition off. Remove driver door master switch assembly. See WINDOW SWITCH under REMOVAL & INSTALLATION. Using an ohmmeter, check resistance between ground and all Black (4) wires of driver door master switch connector. If all resistance measurements are less than 5 ohms, repair open in Red/Light Blue wire between instrument panel fuse block fuse No. 21 (30-amp) and driver door master window switch connector C500 terminal No. 10. *See Fig. 4.* Retest system operation. If any resistance measurement is 5 ohms or more, repair open in Black wire(s) between ground and driver door master window switch connector. Retest system operation.

TEST B: DRIVER POWER WINDOW INOPERATIVE

1) Remove and disconnect driver door master window switch. See WINDOW SWITCH under REMOVAL & INSTALLATION. Turn ignition switch to RUN position. Using a voltmeter, check voltage between ground and driver door master window switch connector C500 terminal No. 10 (Red/Light Blue wire). *See Fig. 4.* If voltage is more than 10 volts, go to next step. If voltage is 10 volts or less, repair open in Red/Light Blue wire between driver door master window switch and instrument panel fuse block fuse No. 21. Retest system operation.

2) Turn ignition off. Using an ohmmeter, check resistance between ground and driver door master window switch connector terminals No. 7

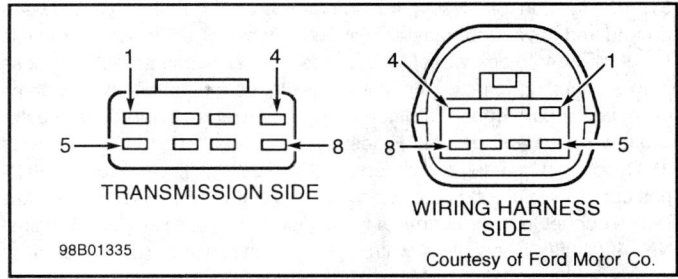

Fig. 4: Identifying Master Switch Harness Connector C500 Terminals

and 12 (Black wires). If both resistance measurements are less than 5 ohms, go to next step. If any resistance measurement is 5 ohms or more, repair open in Black wire(s) between driver door master window switch and ground. Retest system operation.

3) Reconnect driver door master window switch connector. Disconnect driver door window motor connector. Turn ignition switch to RUN position. Using a voltmeter, check voltage between driver door window motor connector White/Black wire and Yellow wire terminals with left window switch (on driver door master window switch) held in UP position. Check voltage with left window switch held in DOWN position. If voltage is 10 volts or less in both measurements, check for open or short to ground in White/Black or Yellow wire between driver door master window switch and driver door window motor. If wires are okay, replace driver door window motor and retest system operation. If voltage is more than 10 volts in both measurements, replace driver door window motor and retest system operation.

TEST C: PASSENGER POWER WINDOW INOPERATIVE

1) Remove and disconnect passenger door window switch. See WINDOW SWITCH under REMOVAL & INSTALLATION. Turn ignition switch to RUN position. Using a voltmeter, check voltage between ground and passenger door window switch connector C600 terminal No. 3 (Red/Light Blue wire). *See Fig. 5.* If voltage is more than 10 volts, go to next step. If voltage is 10 volts or less, repair open in Red/Light Blue wire between passenger door window switch and instrument panel fuse block. Retest system operation.

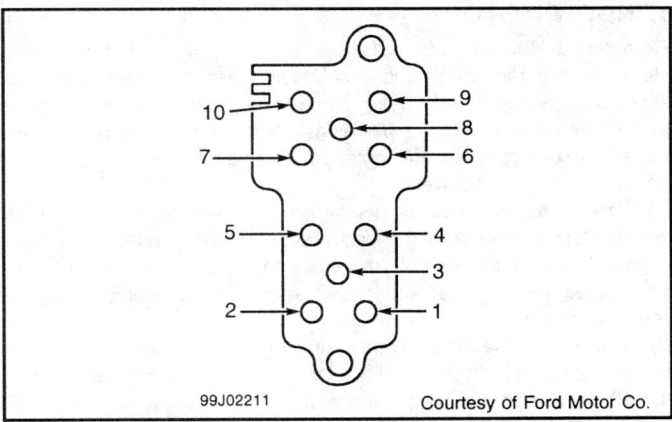

Fig. 5: Identifying Passenger Switch Harness Connector C600 Terminals

2) Turn ignition off. Remove and disconnect driver door master window switch. See WINDOW SWITCH under REMOVAL & INSTALLATION. Turn ignition switch to RUN position. Using a voltmeter, check voltage between ground and driver door master window switch connector C500 terminal No. 11 (Red/Light Blue wire). If voltage is more than 10 volts, go to next step. If voltage is 10 volts or less, repair open in Red/Light Blue wire between driver door master window switch and instrument panel fuse block. Retest system operation.

3) Turn ignition off. Using an ohmmeter, check resistance between ground and driver door master window switch connector C500 terminals No. 9 and 14 (Black wires). If both resistance measurements are less than 5 ohms, go to next step. If any resistance measurement is 5 ohms or more, repair open in Black wire(s) between driver door master window switch and ground. Retest system operation.

4) Reconnect master switch connector. Turn ignition switch to RUN position. Using a voltmeter, check voltage between passenger window switch connector C600 terminal No. 2 (Tan/Light Blue wire) and terminal No. 4 (White/Yellow wire) with right window switch (on driver door master window switch) held in UP position. Check voltage with right window switch (on driver door master window switch) held in DOWN position. If voltage in both measurements are 10 volts or less, check for open or short to ground in Tan/Light Blue or White/Yellow wire between driver door master window switch and passenger door window switch. If wires are okay, replace driver door master window switch. Retest system operation. If voltage is more than 10 volts in both measurements, go to next step.

5) Turn ignition off. Reconnect passenger door window switch. Disconnect passenger door window motor connector. Turn ignition switch to RUN position. Using a voltmeter, check voltage between passenger door motor connector Red/Yellow wire and Yellow/Red wire terminal with passenger door window switch in UP position. Check voltage with passenger door window switch in DOWN position. If voltage is 10 volts or less at both circuits, check for open or short to ground in Red/Yellow or Yellow/Red wire between passenger door window switch and passenger door window motor. If wires are okay, replace passenger door window motor and retest system operation. If voltage is more than 10 volts at both circuits, replace passenger door window motor and retest system operation.

REMOVAL & INSTALLATION

CAUTION: When battery is disconnected, vehicle computer and memory systems may lose memory data. Driveability problems may exist until computer systems have completed relearn cycle. See COMPUTER RELEARN PROCEDURES article in GENERAL INFORMATION before disconnecting battery.

WINDOW MOTOR

Removal & Installation – 1) Disconnect negative battery cable. Remove door trim panel and watershield. Disconnect window motor wiring and window switch. Using care not to enlarge sheet metal holes in door inner panel, remove 1/4" rivets attaching motor bracket to inner panel. Use drift to knock out center pins from each rivet. Using 1/4" drill bit, drill out remaining rivet.

2) Working through access hole, remove motor bracket from inner panel. Rotate bracket to gain access to 3 screws retaining window regulator and motor. Remove screws and separate window regulator and motor from bracket and cable drum housing. Remove window regulator and motor.

3) To install, reverse removal procedure. Tighten motor mounting screws to 53-62 INCH lbs. (6-7 N.m). Install motor bracket to inner panel using 1/4-20 X 1/2" bolts, nuts and washers.

WINDOW SWITCH

Removal & Installation – Disconnect negative battery cable. Gently pry up on rear of switch plate to remove switch housing from door trim panel. Remove 2 screws securing connector. Using thin-blade screwdriver, pry connector from switch plate. To install, reverse removal procedure.

WIRING DIAGRAMS

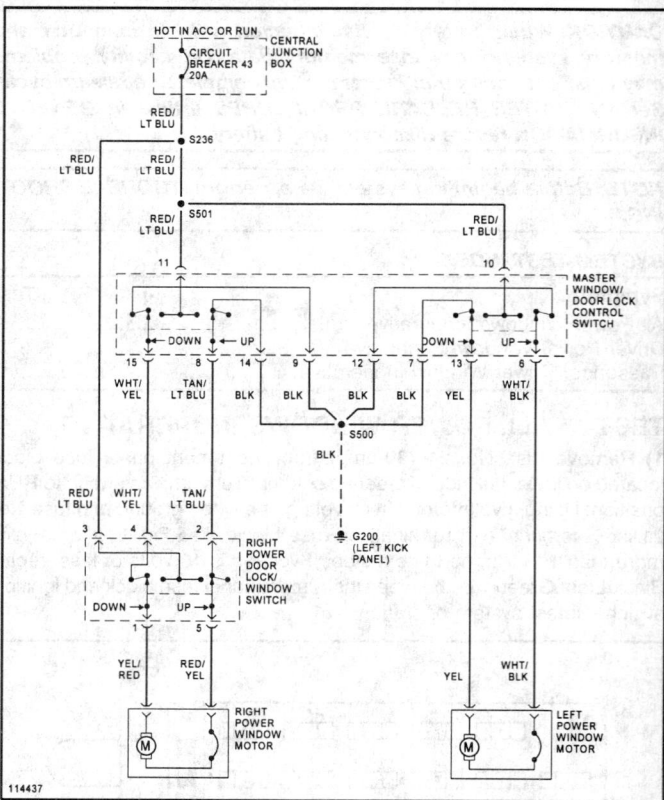

Fig. 6: Power Window System Wiring Diagram (Econoline)

DESCRIPTION & OPERATION

Power windows are operated by reversible type motors mounted to individual window regulators. Each window has an individual switch for separate control. A master switch is located on left front door and all windows may be controlled from this switch.

One-touch down feature will lower driver window to full down position with a brief touch on the window switch. On sedan and wagon models, a lock-out switch is incorporated in master switch. When actuated, lock-out switch prevents window operation from remaining individual switches.

COMPONENT LOCATIONS

COMPONENT LOCATIONS

Component	Location
Data Link Connector (DLC)	Below Driver's Side Of Instrument Panel, To Right Of Steering olumn
Master Window/Door Lock Switch	Driver's Door Panel Arm Rest
Instrument Cluster [1]	Behind Left Side Of Instrument Panel
Central Junction Box	Below Left Side Of Instrument Panel
Power Distribution Box	Left Side Of Engine Compartment, Above Wheelwell
Powertrain Control Module (PCM)	In Center Console Below Shifter

[1] – Instrument cluster may also be referred to as Virtual Instrument Cluster (VIC).

TROUBLE SHOOTING

INSPECTION & VERIFICATION

Verify customer concern by operating windows to duplicate condition. Visually inspect components. If inspection reveals an obvious problem which can be easily serviced, correct malfunction before continuing inspection and verification.

Mechanical:
- Window alignment.
- Window mounting (regulator and bracket).
- Window frame interference.

Electrical:
- Blown fuse(s).
- Faulty circuit breaker.
- Damaged wiring harness.
- Loose or corroded connections.
- Damaged switches.
- Damaged window motor.

COMPONENT TESTS

POWER WINDOW MOTOR

With motor and drive assembly removed from vehicle, connect battery leads to motor terminals. Motor should operate smoothly. Reverse battery connections. Motor should reverse rotation. If motor does not operate as specified, replace motor.

MASTER WINDOW SWITCH

Remove driver door master window switch from vehicle. Using an ohmmeter, check resistance between specified terminals while operating switch. See appropriate MASTER WINDOW SWITCH TESTING table. *See Fig. 1 or 2.* Replace switch if resistance between specified terminals is 5 ohms or more. DO NOT check resistance between terminals not specified.

MASTER WINDOW SWITCH TESTING (COUPE)

Switch Position	Continuity Between Terminals
Left	
Up	10 & 13; 6 & 12
Down	6 & 10; 7 & 13
Right	
Up	11 & 15; 8 & 14
Down	8 & 11; 9 & 15

MASTER WINDOW SWITCH TESTING (SEDAN & WAGON)

Switch Position	Continuity Between Terminals
Lock-Out	8 & 9
Left Front	
Up	4 & 9; 1 & 5
Down	5 & 9; 4 & 1
Right Front	
Up	9 & 13; 1 & 12
Down	9 & 12; 1 & 13
Left Rear	
Up	3 & 9; 1 & 2
Down	2 & 9; 1 & 3
Right Rear	
Up	9 & 11; 1 & 10
Down	9 & 10; 1 & 11

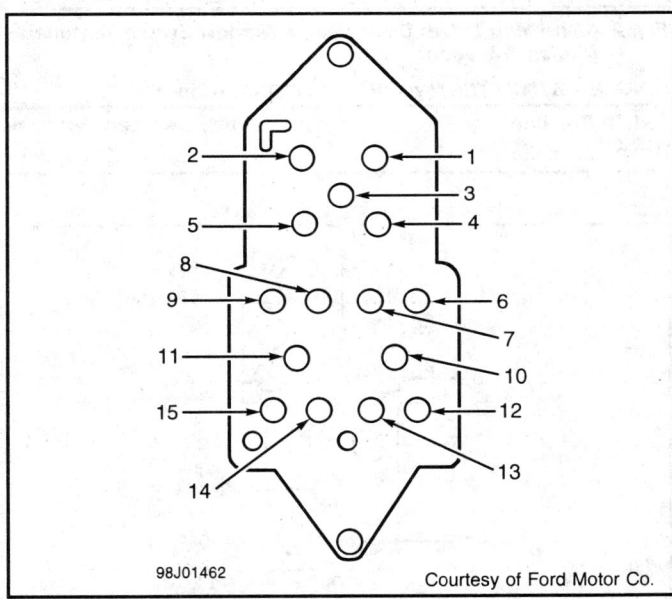

98J01462   Courtesy of Ford Motor Co.

Fig. 1: Identifying Driver Door Master Window Switch Terminals (Coupe)

SINGLE SWITCH

Remove appropriate single switch from vehicle. Using an ohmmeter, check resistance between specified terminals while operating switch. See appropriate SINGLE SWITCH TESTING table. *See Fig. 3 or 4.* Replace switch if resistance between specified terminals is 5 ohms or more. DO NOT check resistance between terminals not specified.

SINGLE SWITCH TESTING (RIGHT FRONT DOOR)

Switch Position	Continuity Between Terminals
Neutral	6 & 9; 7 & 10
Up	8 & 10; 6 & 9
Down	6 & 8; 7 & 10

SINGLE SWITCH TESTING (REAR DOORS)

Switch Position	Continuity Between Terminals
Neutral	1 & 4; 2 & 5
Up	3 & 5; 1 & 4

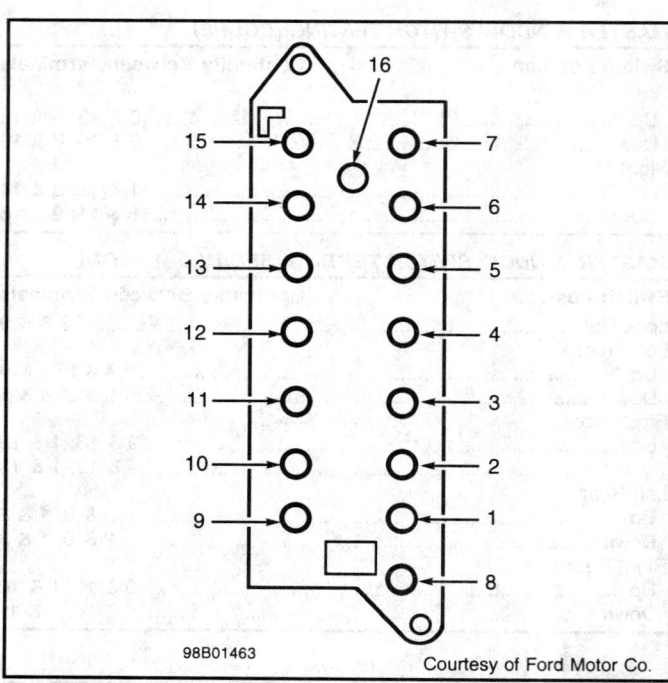

98B01463

Courtesy of Ford Motor Co.

Fig. 2: Identifying Driver Door Master Window Switch Terminals (Sedan & Wagon)

SINGLE SWITCH TESTING (REAR DOORS) (Cont.)

Switch Position	Continuity Between Terminals
Down	1 & 3; 2 & 5

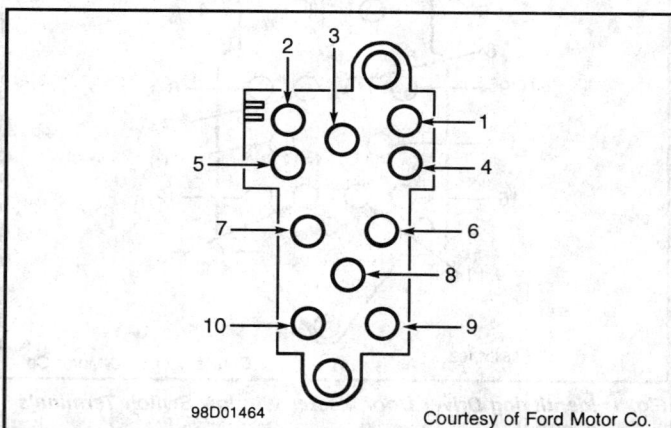

98D01464

Courtesy of Ford Motor Co.

Fig. 3: Identifying Right Front Door Window Switch Terminals

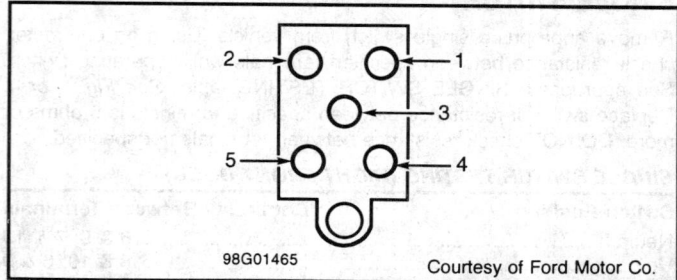

98G01465

Courtesy of Ford Motor Co.

Fig. 4: Identifying Rear Door Window Switch Terminals

SYSTEM TESTS

CAUTION: When battery is disconnected or modules are replaced, vehicle computer and memory systems may lose memory data. Driveability problems may exist until computer systems have completed a relearn cycle. See COMPUTER RELEARN PROCEDURES article in GENERAL INFORMATION before disconnecting battery.

NOTE: Before beginning system tests, perform TROUBLE SHOOTING.

NOTE: After repairs are complete, ensure all components are properly installed and all harness connectors are connected properly. Repeat data link diagnostic test. See DATA LINK DIAGNOSTIC TEST under COMMUNICATIONS NETWORK DIAGNOSTICS in MODULE COMMUNICATIONS NETWORK – ESCORT & TRACER article.

Verify the customer complaint by operating appropriate window. Visually inspect for obvious sign of mechanical and electrical damage. If no visual damage is evident, perform appropriate system test. See SYSTEM TEST INDEX table. A digital volt-ohmmeter is required to test the power mirror system. See WIRING DIAGRAMS for terminal numbers.

SYSTEM TEST INDEX

Symptom	Go To
All Power Windows Inoperative (Coupe)	TEST A
Single Power Window Inoperative (Coupe)	TEST B
One Touch Down Feature Inoperative (Coupe)	TEST C
All Power Windows Inoperative (Sedan & Wagon)	TEST D
Single Power Window Inoperative (Sedan & Wagon)	TEST E
One Touch Down Feature Inoperative (Sedan & Wagon)	TEST F

TEST A: ALL POWER WINDOWS INOPERATIVE (COUPE)

1) Turn ignition off. Check POWER WIND (30-amp) circuit breaker (located in central junction box). If breaker is okay, go to next step. If breaker is tripped, replace circuit breaker and retest system. If circuit breaker trips again, repair short to ground in Black/White wire between central junction box and master window switch or relay box.

2) Turn ignition off. Disconnect 15-pin driver door master window switch connector C509. Turn ignition switch to RUN position. Using a voltmeter, check voltage between ground and driver door master window switch connector C509 terminal No. 10 (Black/White wire). If voltage is more than 10 volts, go to next step. If voltage is 10 volts or less, repair Black/White wire and retest system operation.

3) Ensure ignition is off. Using an ohmmeter, check resistance between ground and driver door master window switch connector C509 terminal No. 9 (Black wire). If resistance is less than 5 ohms, replace driver door master window switch and retest system operation. If resistance is 5 ohms or more, repair open in Black wire and retest system operation.

TEST B: SINGLE POWER WINDOW INOPERATIVE (COUPE)

1) Turn ignition switch to RUN position. Attempt to operate right door window. If right door window operates, go to next step. If right door window does not operate, go to step **10)**.

2) Turn ignition off. Check position of driver door window. If driver door window is not closed, go to next step. If driver door window is closed, go to step **4)**.

3) Disconnect 15-pin driver door master window switch connector C509. Momentarily touch a jumper wire between positive battery terminal and driver door master window switch connector C509 terminal No. 13 (Red/Black wire). Connect another jumper wire between ground and driver door master window switch connector C509 terminal No. 6 (Green wire). If driver door window does not go up, go to step **5)**. If driver door window goes up, go to step **8)**.

4) Disconnect 15-pin driver door master window switch connector C509. Momentarily touch a jumper wire between positive battery terminal and driver door master window switch connector C509 terminal No. 6 (Green wire). Connect another jumper wire between ground and driver door master window switch connector C509 terminal No. 13 (Red/Black wire). If driver door window does not go down, go to next step. If driver door window goes down, go to step 8).

5) Using an ohmmeter, check resistance of Green wire between driver door master window switch connector C509 terminal No. 6 and back-probe the one-touch down control unit connector C205 terminal No. 2 (located behind left side of instrument panel). If resistance is less than 5 ohms, go to next step. If resistance is 5 ohms or more, repair open in Green wire. Retest system operation.

6) Check resistance of Red/Green wire between driver door power window motor connector C504 and backprobe the one-touch down control unit connector C205 terminal No. 1. If resistance is less than 5 ohms, go to next step. If resistance is 5 ohms or more, repair open in Red/Green wire. Retest system operation.

7) Check resistance of Red/Black wire between driver door power window motor connector C504 and driver door master window switch connector C509 terminal No. 13. If resistance is less than 5 ohms, replace driver door power window motor and retest system operation. If resistance is 5 ohms or more, repair open in Red/Black wire. Retest system operation.

8) Turn ignition switch to RUN position. Using a voltmeter, check voltage between ground and driver door master window switch connector C509 terminal No. 10 (Black/White wire). If voltage is more than 10 volts, go to next step. If voltage is 10 volts or less, repair Black/White wire and retest system operation.

9) Turn ignition off. Using an ohmmeter, check resistance between ground and driver door master window switch connector C509 terminals No. 7 and 12 (Black wires). If resistance is less than 5 ohms in both measurements, replace driver door master window switch and retest system operation. If either resistance reading is 5 ohms or more, repair open in appropriate Black wire(s). Retest system operation.

10) Turn ignition off. Disconnect 15-pin driver door master window switch connector C509. Disconnect right door window switch connector C609. Turn ignition switch to RUN position. Using a voltmeter, check voltage between ground and driver door master window switch connector C509 terminal No. 11 (Black/White wire). Check Voltage between ground and right door window switch connector C609 terminal No. 8 (Black/White wire). If both voltage readings are more than 10 volts, go to next step. If either voltage reading is 10 volts or less, repair appropriate Black/White wire(s) and retest system operation.

11) Turn ignition off. Using an ohmmeter, check resistance between ground and driver door master window switch connector C509 terminals No. 7, 9, 12, and 14 (Black wires). If all resistance readings are less than 5 ohms, reconnect both window switch connectors and go to next step. If any resistance is 5 ohms or more, repair open in appropriate Black wire(s). Retest system operation.

12) Turn ignition switch to RUN position. Operate right door window from driver door master window switch controls. Operate right door window switch. If driver door master window switch is inoperative in both directions and right door window switch operates in only one direction, go to step 18). If driver door master window switch operates in one direction and right door window switch does not operate in only one direction, go to next step.

13) Operate right door window from driver door master window switch controls. Operate right door window switch. If driver door master window switch is inoperative in both directions and right door window switch operates properly, replace driver door master window switch and retest system operation. If driver door master window switch operates properly and right door window switch does not operate properly, go to next step.

14) Operate right door window from driver door master window switch controls. Operate right door window switch. If driver door master window switch operates properly and right door window switch is inoperative, replace right door window switch and retest system operation. If driver door master window switch does not operate properly and right door window switch is not inoperative, go to next step.

15) Perform power window motor test. See POWER WINDOW MOTOR under COMPONENT TESTS. If right front power window motor is faulty, replace right front power window motor and retest system operation. If right front power window motor is okay, go to next step.

16) Turn ignition off. Disconnect right door power window motor connector C607. Disconnect right door window switch connector C609. Using an ohmmeter, check resistance in Red wire between right door window switch connector C609 terminal No. 10 and right door power window motor connector C607. If resistance is less than 5 ohms, go to next step. If resistance is 5 ohms or more, repair open in Red wire and retest system operation.

17) Using an ohmmeter, check resistance in White wire between right door window switch connector C609 terminal No. 6 and right door power window motor connector C607. If resistance is less than 5 ohms, replace right door window switch and retest system operation. If resistance is 5 ohms or more, repair open in White wire and retest system operation.

18) Turn ignition off. Disconnect 15-pin driver door master window switch connector C509. Disconnect right door window switch connector C609. Using an ohmmeter, check resistance in Green/Black wire between driver door master window switch connector C509 terminal No. 15 and right door window switch connector C609 terminal No. 7. If resistance is less than 5 ohms, repair Light Green/Red wire and retest system operation. If resistance is 5 ohms or more, repair Green/Black wire and retest system operation.

TEST C: ONE-TOUCH DOWN FEATURE INOPERATIVE (COUPE)

1) Turn ignition off. Using a voltmeter, check voltage between ground and backprobe one-touch down control unit (located behind left side of instrument panel) 5-pin connector C205 terminal No. 3 (Black/White wire). If voltage is more than 10 volts, go to next step. If voltage is 10 volts or less, repair Black/White wire and retest system operation.

2) Using an ohmmeter, check resistance between ground and backprobe one-touch down control unit 5-pin connector C205 terminal No. 5 (Black wire). If resistance is less than 5 ohms, go to next step. If resistance is 5 ohms or more, repair open in Black wire between one-touch down control unit 5-pin connector and ground. Retest system operation.

3) Disconnect 15-pin driver door master window switch connector C509. Using an ohmmeter, check resistance in Red/Black wire between driver door master window switch connector C509 terminal No. 13 and backprobe one-touch down control unit connector C205 terminal No. 4. If resistance is less than 5 ohms, replace one-touch down control unit and retest system operation. If resistance is 5 ohms or more, repair open in Red/Black wire and retest system operation.

TEST D: ALL POWER WINDOWS INOPERATIVE (SEDAN & WAGON)

1) Turn ignition off. Check POWER WIND (30-amp) circuit breaker (located in central junction box). If breaker is tripped, replace circuit breaker and retest system. If circuit breaker trips again, repair short to ground in Black/White wire between central junction box and master window switch or relay box. If fuse is okay, go to next step.

2) Turn ignition off. Disconnect 16-pin driver door master window switch connector C509. Turn ignition switch to RUN position. Using a voltmeter, check voltage between ground and driver door master window switch connector C509 terminal No. 9 (Black/White wire). If voltage is more than 10 volts, go to next step. If voltage is 10 volts or less, repair Black/White wire and retest system operation.

3) Perform driver door master window switch test. See MASTER WINDOW SWITCH under COMPONENT TESTS. If driver door master window switch is okay, repair Black wire between driver door master window switch and ground. Retest system operation. If master switch is faulty, replace switch and retest system operation.

TEST E: SINGLE POWER WINDOW INOPERATIVE (SEDAN & WAGON)

1) Turn ignition switch to RUN position. Operate all windows from driver door master window switch. If all windows open and close properly,

verify lock-out switch is not engaged and go to step **3)**. If all windows do not operate from driver door master window switch, go to next step.

2) Perform driver door master window switch test. See MASTER WINDOW SWITCH under COMPONENT TESTS. If driver door master window switch is faulty, replace driver door master window switch and retest system operation. If driver door master window switch is okay and left front window is inoperative, see TEST F: ONE-TOUCH DOWN FEATURE INOPERATIVE (SEDAN & WAGON) test. If driver door master window switch is okay and any other window is inoperative, go to next step.

3) Turn ignition off. Reconnect driver door master window switch connector. Turn ignition switch to RUN position. Press lock-out switch to ON position (located on driver door master window switch assembly). Operate all passenger windows from the individual (not master) switches. If all windows operate, advise customer of lock-out switch. If right/front window does not operate, go to next step. If either rear window does not operate, go to step **7)**.

4) Turn ignition off. Unplug right front window switch connector C609. Turn ignition switch to RUN position. While operating right front window from driver door master window switch to UP position, check voltage between ground and right front window switch connector C609 terminal No. 7 (Green/Black wire). While operating right front window from driver door master window switch to DOWN position, check voltage between ground and right front window switch connector C609 terminal No. 9 (Light Green/Red wire). If voltages are more than 10 volts, go to next step. If either voltage reading is 10 volts or less, repair Green/Black and/or Light Green/Red wire(s). Retest system operation.

5) Turn ignition off. Using an ohmmeter, check resistance between right front window switch connector C609 terminal No. 6 (White wire) and terminal No. 10 (Red wire). Resistance should be less than 5 ohms. Check resistance between ground and right front window switch connector C609 terminals No. 6 (White wire) and No. 10 (Red wire) individually. Resistances should be more than 10 k/ohms. If all resistances are as specified, replace right front window switch and retest system operation. If resistances are not as specified, go to next step.

6) Perform power window motor test. See POWER WINDOW MOTOR under COMPONENT TESTS. If right front power window motor is faulty, replace right front power window motor. If right front power window motor is okay, repair circuit(s) between right front window switch and right front power window motor. Retest system operation.

7) Perform single switch test. See SINGLE SWITCH under COMPONENT TESTS. If rear window switch is faulty, replace rear window switch and retest system operation. If rear window switch is okay, go to next step.

8) Turn ignition off. Unplug appropriate rear window switch connector. Turn ignition switch to RUN position. While operating appropriate rear window from driver door master window switch to UP position, check voltage between ground and appropriate rear window switch connector terminal No. 2 (Blue/White wire). While operating appropriate rear window from driver door master window switch to DOWN position, check voltage between ground and rear window switch connector terminal No. 4 (Yellow/Green wire). If voltages are more than 10 volts, go to next step. If either voltage reading is 10 volts or less, repair Blue/White and/or Yellow/Green wire(s). Retest system operation.

9) Perform power window motor test. See POWER WINDOW MOTOR under COMPONENT TESTS. If rear power window motor is faulty, replace rear power window motor and retest system operation. If rear power window motor is okay, repair Red and/or Green wire(s) between rear power window switch and rear power window motor. Retest system operation.

TEST F: ONE-TOUCH DOWN FEATURE INOPERATIVE (SEDAN & WAGON)

1) Turn ignition off. Disconnect 16-pin driver door master window switch connector C509. Disconnect 5-pin one-touch down control unit connector C205 (located behind left side of instrument panel). Using an ohmmeter, check resistance of Green, Red/Black and Black/White wires between driver door master window switch connector C509 and one-touch down control unit connector C205. If all resistances are less than

5 ohms, go to next step. If resistance of any wire is 5 ohms or more, repair open in appropriate wire(s). Retest system operation.

2) Using an ohmmeter, check resistance between ground and one-touch down control unit 5-pin connector C205 terminal No. 5 (Black wire). If resistance is less than 5 ohms, go to next step. If resistance is 5 ohms or more, repair open in Black wire between one-touch down control unit 5-pin connector and ground. Retest system operation.

3) Perform power window motor test. See POWER WINDOW MOTOR under COMPONENT TESTS. If left front power window motor is faulty, replace left front power window motor and retest system operation. If left front power window motor is okay, go to next step.

4) Disconnect left front power window motor connector C504. Using an ohmmeter, check resistance of Red/Green and Red/Black wires between one-touch down control unit 5-pin connector C205 and left front power window motor connector C504. If both resistances are less than 5 ohms, replace one-touch down control unit and retest system operation. If resistance of either wire is 5 ohms or more, repair open in Red/Green and/or Red/Black wire(s). Retest system operation.

REMOVAL & INSTALLATION

DOOR GLASS

Removal & Installation (Front & Rear) – Open window fully. Remove door panel. Remove door armrest bracket. Remove watershield. Remove 3 screws and access cover (front door only). Remove one glass retaining bolt and 2 glass retaining nuts from bottom of door. Lift glass out of door. To install, reverse removal procedure.

POWER WINDOW MOTOR & REGULATOR

NOTE: Window motor and regulator are serviced as an assembly.

NOTE: Manufacturer does not give procedure for removal and installation of rear power window motor and regulator assembly.

Removal & Installation (Front) – Disconnect negative battery cable. Remove door glass. See DOOR GLASS under REMOVAL & INSTALLATION. Unplug motor harness connector. Remove fasteners securing regulator. Remove regulator through large opening in door. To install, reverse removal procedure.

POWER WINDOW SWITCH

NOTE: Manufacturer does not give procedure for removal and installation of rear power window switch on sedan and wagon models.

Removal & Installation (Coupe) – Remove door pull handle screw covers. Remove door pull handle screws and pushpin. Remove door pull handle assembly. Disconnect window switch connector. Remove 2 screws and power window switch. To install, reverse removal procedure.

Removal & Installation (Sedan & Wagon) – Disconnect negative battery cable. Remove door trim panel. Squeeze tabs to remove power window switch housing. Disconnect window switch connector. Remove 2 screws and power window switch. To install, reverse removal procedure.

WIRING DIAGRAMS

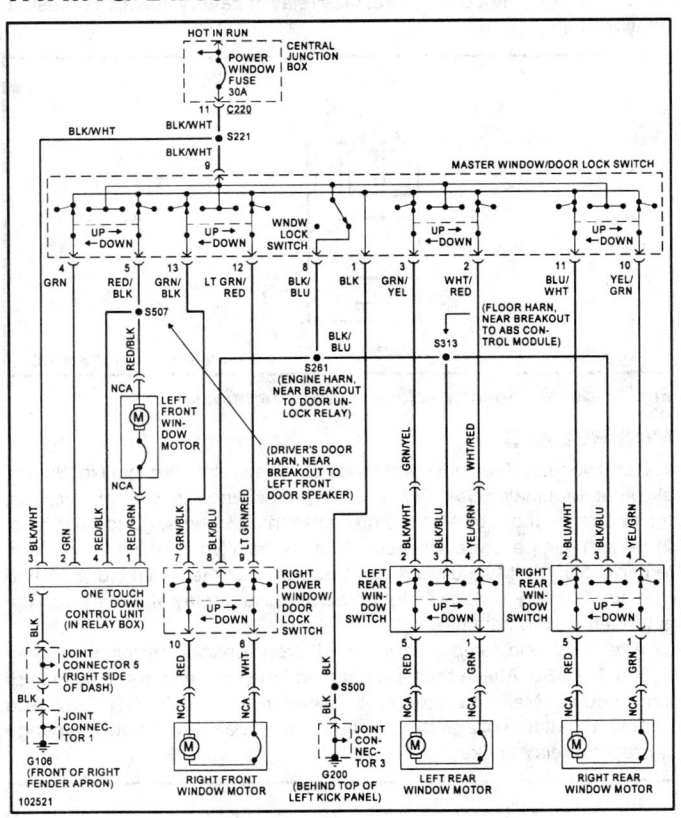

Fig. 5: Power Window System Wiring Diagram (Escort & Tracer)

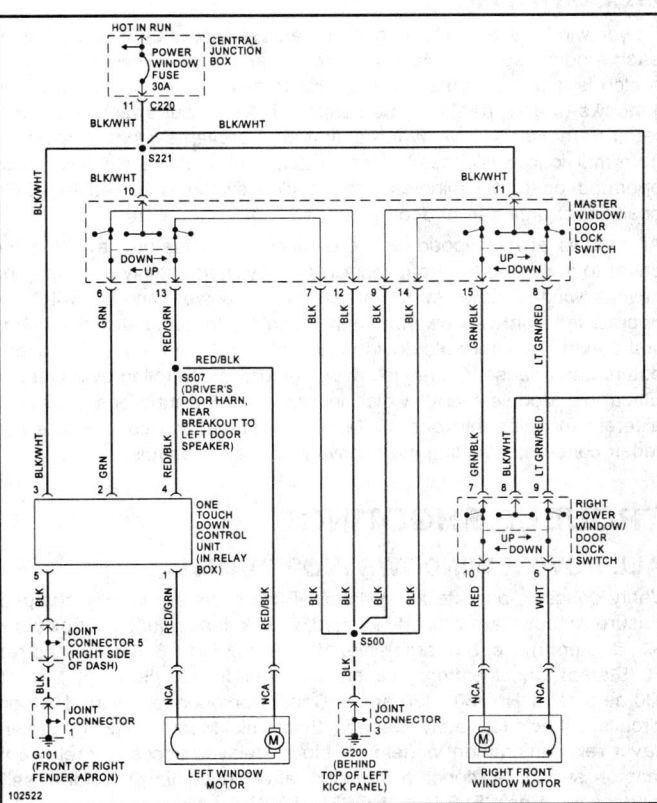

Fig. 6: Power Window System Wiring Diagram (Escort ZX2)

1999 ACCESSORIES & EQUIPMENT
Power Windows – Expedition & Navigator

DESCRIPTION

Power windows are operated by reversible type motors mounted on each window regulator. Each window has an individual switch. A master switch is located on the driver's door from which both front and rear windows (if equipped) may be controlled. A lock-out switch is incorporated in master switch. When actuated, it prevents window operation from individual switches. Accessory delay relay allows windows to be operated up to 10 minutes after ignition switch is turned to LOCK position, or until a front door is opened.

All models are equipped with one-touch down feature, allowing the driver to lower the left front window fully by momentarily actuating the driver's window down switch at the master power window switch. To operate left front window in manual down mode, press down switch to first detent. To enter auto down mode, press left front switch to second detent and release. One-touch down feature is controlled by a Generic Electronic Module (GEM) which incorporates the functions of several different modules into one. GEM offers self-diagnostics to locate and repair concerns affecting the subsystems that it controls.

TROUBLE SHOOTING

ALL POWER WINDOWS INOPERATIVE

Verify concern, operate all switches. Ensure battery is fully charged. Ensure windows are properly aligned. Check central junction box fuses No. 6 (5-amp), No. 8 (5-amp), No. 15 (5-amp), No. 18 (5-amp) and No. 20 (5-amp). Check battery junction box fuses No. 103 (50-amp), No. 110 (30-amp) and No. 601 (30-amp). Check for open or shorted supply circuits. Check for faulty Generic Electronic Module (GEM), battery saver relay, instrument panel fuse block, delayed accessory relay and master switch. If concern remains after inspection, perform self-diagnostics. See SELF-DIAGNOSTIC SYSTEM.

ONE POWER WINDOW INOPERATIVE

Verify concern. Ensure battery is fully charged. Ensure window in question is properly aligned. Check for damaged guide or regulator mechanism. Check window motor. See POWER WINDOW MOTOR under COMPONENT TESTS. Check for open or shorted circuit. Check for faulty one-touch down relay, master window switch, passenger window switch, battery saver relay, instrument panel fuse block, and Generic Electronic Module (GEM). If concern remains after inspection, perform self-diagnostics. See SELF-DIAGNOSTIC SYSTEM.

ONE-TOUCH DOWN FEATURE INOPERATIVE

Verify concern. Check for open or shorted circuit. Check for faulty one-touch down relay, master window switch, Generic Electronic Module (GEM), and instrument panel fuse block. If concern remains after inspection, perform self-diagnostics. See SELF-DIAGNOSTIC SYSTEM.

WINDOW STUCK OR BINDING

Verify concern. Check for damaged window tracks, window regulator and window motor. If concern remains after inspection, perform self-diagnostics. See SELF-DIAGNOSTIC SYSTEM.

COMPONENT TESTS

MICRO RELAYS

1) Remove relay. Measure resistance between relay terminal No. 2 and all other terminals. *See Fig. 1*. If any resistance is 5 ohms or less, replace relay. If all resistances are 5 ohms or more, go to next step.
2) Attach jumper wire between battery positive terminal and relay terminal No. 3. Measure voltage between relay terminal No. 4 and ground. If battery voltage is not present, replace relay. If battery voltage is present, go to next step.
3) Attach second jumper wire from battery positive terminal to relay terminal No. 1. Attach third jumper wire between relay terminal No. 2 and

ground. Measure voltage between relay terminal No. 5 and ground. If battery voltage is not present, replace relay. If battery voltage is present, relay is okay

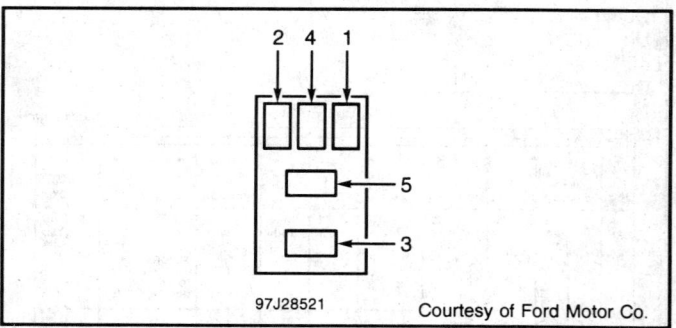

97J28521   Courtesy of Ford Motor Co.

Fig. 1: Identifying Micro Relay Socket Terminals

MINI RELAYS

1) Remove relay. Measure resistance between relay terminal No. 85 and all other terminals. *See Fig. 2*. If any resistance is 5 ohms or less, replace relay. If all resistances are more than 5 ohms, go to next step.
2) Attach jumper wire between battery positive terminal and relay terminal No. 30. Measure voltage between relay terminal No. 87A and ground. If battery voltage is not present, replace relay. If battery voltage is present, go to next step.
3) Attach second jumper wire from battery positive terminal to relay terminal No. 86. Attach third jumper wire between relay terminal No. 85 and ground. Measure voltage between relay terminal No. 87 and ground. If battery voltage is not present, replace relay. If battery voltage is present, relay is okay.

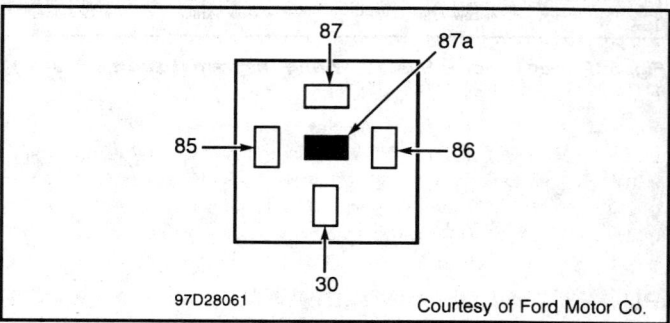

97D28061   Courtesy of Ford Motor Co.

Fig. 2: Identifying Mini Relay Socket Terminals

POWER WINDOW MASTER SWITCH

1) Remove master switch. See POWER WINDOW SWITCH under REMOVAL & INSTALLATION. Check continuity between master window switch connector C509 terminals No. 1 and 2 in all switch positions. *See Fig. 3*. If there is continuity in any position, replace switch. If there is no continuity, go to next step.
2) With master window switch at rest, check continuity between master window switch connector C509 terminals No. 1, 3, 4, 6 and 7. Check continuity between master window switch connector C510 terminals No. 4, 5, 6 and 7. If there is no continuity between any specified terminals, replace switch. If there is continuity between all specified terminals, go to next step.
3) Check continuity between appropriate master window switch connector and terminals with switch in appropriate position. See MASTER SWITCH TESTING table. If continuity is not as specified, replace switch.

MASTER SWITCH TESTING

Switch Position	Connector	Continuity Between Terminals
Left Front		
Down	C509	2 & 6
Up	C509	2 & 7
Right Front		

MASTER SWITCH TESTING (Cont.)

Switch Position	Connector	Continuity Between Terminals
Down	C509	2 & 4
Up	C509	2 & 3
Left Rear		
Down	C510	2 & 6
Up	C510	2 & 7
Right Rear		
Down	C510	2 & 4
Up	C510	2 & 5

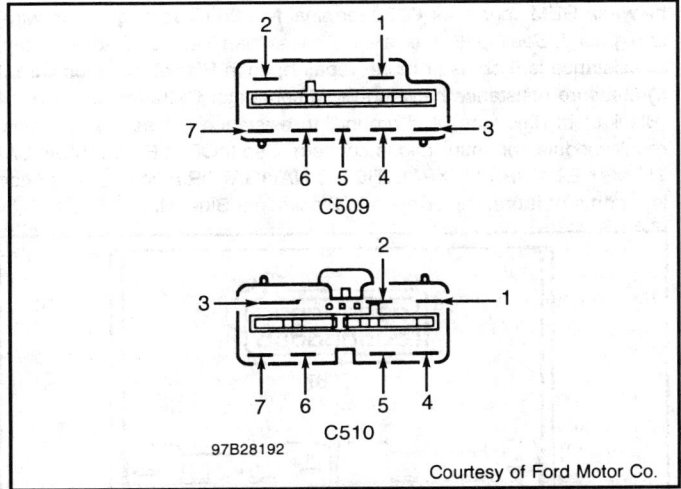

Fig. 3: Identifying Power Window Master Switch Terminals

POWER WINDOW MOTOR

Remove window motor from vehicle. See POWER WINDOW MOTOR under REMOVAL & INSTALLATION. Using fused jumper wires, connect a fully charged battery to motor terminals. Observe motor. Motor should operate smoothly. Reverse leads. Motor should operate in reverse direction. Replace window motor if it does not operate as specified.

POWER WINDOW SINGLE SWITCH

Remove suspect window switch. See POWER WINDOW SWITCH under REMOVAL & INSTALLATION. Check continuity between appropriate terminals with switch in appropriate position. See SINGLE SWITCH TESTING table. See Fig. 4. If continuity is not as specified, replace switch.

SINGLE SWITCH TESTING

Switch Position	Continuity Between Terminals
Right Front & Left Rear	
Rest	2 & 6; 7 & 3
Down	4 & 6
Up	4 & 3
Right Rear	
Rest	2 & 3; 7 & 6
Down	4 & 3

SINGLE SWITCH TESTING (Cont.)

Switch Position	Continuity Between Terminals
Up	4 & 6

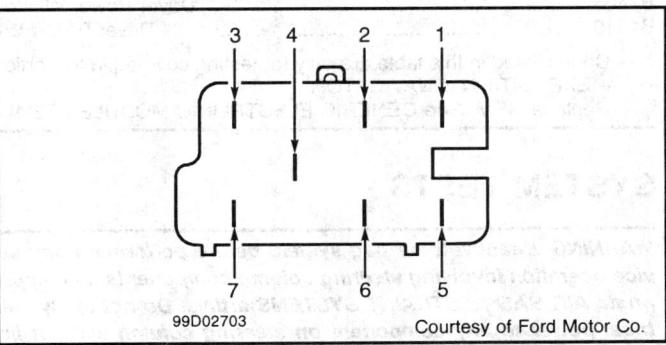

Fig. 4: Identifying Single Switch & Vent Window Switch Terminals

POWER VENT WINDOW SWITCH

Remove suspect vent window switch. Check continuity between appropriate switch terminals with switch in appropriate position. See VENT WINDOW SWITCH TESTING table. See Fig. 4. If continuity is not as specified, replace switch.

VENT WINDOW SWITCH TESTING

Switch Position	Continuity Between Terminals
Rest	1 & 6; 2 & 3
Down	3 & 4; 1 & 6
Up	4 & 6; 2 & 3

SELF-DIAGNOSTIC SYSTEM

SELF-DIAGNOSTICS

NOTE: The power window system utilizes a self-diagnostic system which may store a Diagnostic Trouble Code (DTC) if a problem exists in system. DTCs may be retrieved using New Generation Star (NGS) tester, or equivalent scan tool, connected to Data Link Connector (DLC).

Connect New Generation Star (NGS) tester to Data Link Connector (DLC) located below center of instrument panel. Using NGS tester, perform data link diagnostic test. See DATA LINK DIAGNOSTIC TEST under COMMUNICATION NETWORK DIAGNOSTICS in MODULE COMMUNICATIONS NETWORK – EXPEDITION & NAVIGATOR article. If NGS tester displays CKT914, CKT915 or CKT70 = ALL ECUS NO RESP/NOT EQUIP, repair module communication concern. See MODULE COMMUNICATIONS NETWORK – EXPEDITION & NAVIGATOR article. If NGS tester displays NO RESP/NOT EQUIP for Generic Electronic Module (GEM), perform TEST A: NO SCAN TOOL COMMUNICATION WITH GEM under SYSTEM TESTS.

If NGS tester displays SYSTEM PASSED, retrieve and record continuous DTCs. Erase continuous DTCs. Using NGS tester, perform GEM self-test. If GEM DTCs related to the concern are retrieved, perform appropriate test. See GEM DTC TEST INDEX table. If no DTCs related to the concern are retrieved, perform appropriate test based on symptom. See SYMPTOM TEST INDEX under SYSTEM TESTS. For GEM DTCs not covered in this article, see MODULE COMMUNICATIONS NETWORK – EXPEDITION & NAVIGATOR article.

GEM DTC TEST INDEX

DTC [1]	Description	Test
B1302	Accessory Delay Relay Coil Circuit Failure	B
B1304	Accessory Delay Relay Coil Circuit Short To Power	B
B1313	Battery Saver Relay Coil Circuit Failure	B
B1315	Battery Saver Relay Coil Circuit Short To Power	B

GEM DTC TEST INDEX (Cont.)

DTC[1]	Description	Test
B1342	ECU Defective	2
B1398	Driver Window One-Touch Window Relay Circuit Failure	D
B1400	Driver Power Window One-Touch Window Relay Circuit Short To Power	D
B1405	Driver Power Window Down Circuit Short To Power	C
B1410	Driver Power Window Motor Circuit Failure	C

[1] – Codes listed in this table are only for testing covered in this article. For complete DTC listing, see MODULE COMMUNICATIONS NETWORK – EXPEDITION & NAVIGATOR.

[2] – Replace GEM. See GENERIC ELECTRONIC MODULE (GEM) under REMOVAL & INSTALLATION.

SYSTEM TESTS

WARNING: Deactivate air bag system before performing any service operation involving steering column components. See appropriate AIR BAG RESTRAINT SYSTEMS article. Do not apply electrical power to any component on steering column without first deactivating air bag system. Air bag may deploy.

CAUTION: When battery is disconnected, vehicle computer and memory systems may lose memory data. Driveability problems may exist until computer systems have completed a relearn cycle. See COMPUTER RELEARN PROCEDURES article in GENERAL INFORMATION before disconnecting battery.

CAUTION: Disconnect battery before disconnecting Generic Electronic Module (GEM). Failure to do so will result in GEM storing erroneous codes and may also result in erratic operation of GEM after reconnection.

NOTE: Complete entire system test related to the symptom before installing GEM.

SYMPTOM TEST INDEX

Symptom	Test
No Scan Tool Communication With GEM	A
All Power Windows Inoperative	B
Single Window Inoperative (All Other Windows Operate)	C
One-Touch Down Feature Inoperative	D
Vent Window Inoperative	E

TEST A: NO SCAN TOOL COMMUNICATION WITH GEM

NOTE: After repair, clear DTCs and retest system.

1) Turn ignition switch to LOCK position. Connect New Generation Star (NGS) tester to Data Link Connector (DLC). DLC is located below center of instrument panel. Using NGS tester, observe Generic Electronic Module (GEM) PIDs IGN_A, IGN_R, IGN_S and IGN_O/L while turning ignition switch through all positions. If PID values agree with ignition switch positions, go to next step. If PID values do not agree with ignition switch positions, repair appropriate ignition switch circuit(s). See appropriate wiring diagram in POWER DISTRIBUTION article in WIRING DIAGRAMS.

2) Turn ignition switch to LOCK position. Disconnect central junction box 34-pin connector C243. Measure voltage between connector C243 terminal No. 11 (Tan/Black wire) and ground. See Fig. 5. If voltage is more than 10 volts, go to next step. If voltage is 10 volts or less, repair Tan/Black wire.

3) Disconnect GEM from central junction box 18-pin connector C267. Connect central junction box connector C243. Measure voltage between central junction box connector C267 terminal No. 4 (central junction box side) and ground. Measure voltage between connector C267 terminal No. 16 (central junction box side) and ground. See Fig. 5. If voltages are more than 10 volts, go to next step. If voltages are 10 volts or less, replace central junction box.

4) Disconnect GEM 26-pin connector C239. Measure resistance between GEM connector C239 terminal No. 26 (Black/Light Blue wire) and ground. See Fig. 6. If resistance is less than 5 ohms, go to next step. If resistance is 5 ohms or more, repair open in Black/Light Blue wire.

5) Measure resistance between GEM connector C239 terminal No. 14 (Black/Light Blue wire) and ground. If resistance is less than 5 ohms, repair module communications concern. See MODULE COMMUNICATIONS NETWORK – EXPEDITION & NAVIGATOR article. If resistance is 5 ohms or more, repair open in Black/Light Blue wire.

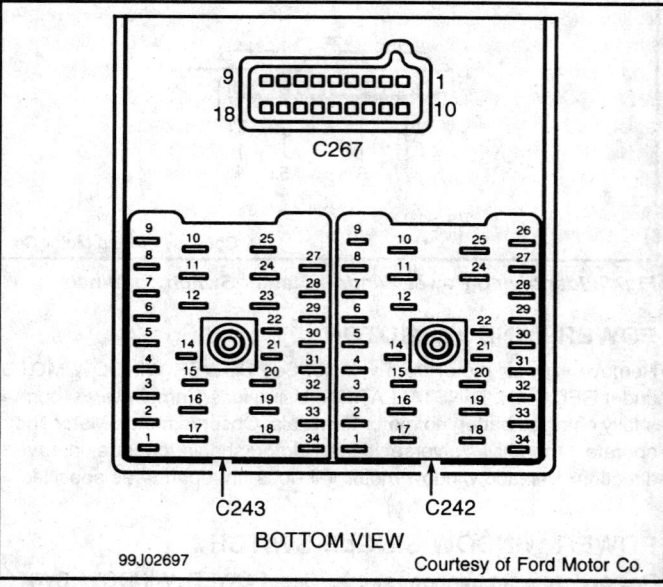

99J02697   Courtesy of Ford Motor Co.

Fig. 5: Identifying Central Junction Box Connectors & Terminals

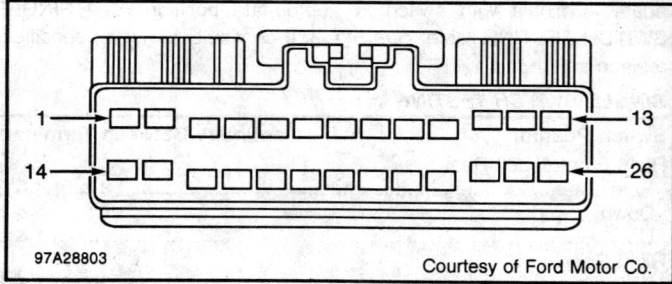

97A28803   Courtesy of Ford Motor Co.

Fig. 6: Identifying GEM 26-Pin Connector C239 Terminals

TEST B: ALL POWER WINDOWS INOPERATIVE

NOTE: After repair, clear DTCs and retest system.

1) Turn ignition switch to LOCK position. Connect New Generation Star (NGS) tester to Data Link Connector (DLC). DLC is located below center of instrument panel. Using NGS tester, observe Generic Electronic Module (GEM) PIDs IGN_A, IGN_R, IGN_S and IGN_O/L while turning ignition switch through all positions. If PID values agree with ignition switch positions, go to next step. If PID values do not agree with ignition switch positions, repair appropriate ignition switch circuit(s). See appropriate wiring diagram in POWER DISTRIBUTION article in WIRING DIAGRAMS.

2) Using NGS tester, perform GEM self-tests. If no DTCs, DTC B1313 or DTC B1315 are present, go to next step. If DTC B1302 or B1304 is present, go to step **9)**.

3) Turn ignition switch to RUN position. Using NGS tester, observe GEM PID BATSAV while triggering GEM active command BATTSAVR to ON and OFF. If PID value agrees with command mode, go to step **9)**. If PID value does not agree with command mode and displays OFFO-G, go to next step. If PID value does not agree with command mode and displays ON-B-, go to step **7)**.

4) Turn ignition switch to LOCK position. Disconnect battery saver relay, located in central junction box. Measure voltage between battery saver relay socket terminal No. 1 and ground. *See Fig. 1.* If voltage is more than 10 volts, go to next step. If voltage is less than 10 volts, replace central junction box.

5) Check battery saver relay. See MICRO RELAYS under COMPONENT TESTS. If battery saver relay is okay, go to next step. If battery saver relay is faulty, replace relay.

6) Disconnect GEM from central junction box 18-pin connector C267. Measure resistance between central junction box connector C267 terminal No. 1 and battery saver relay socket terminal No. 2. *See Figs. 1 and 5.* If resistance is less than 5 ohms, replace GEM. See GENERIC ELECTRONIC MODULE (GEM) under REMOVAL & INSTALLATION. If resistance is 5 ohms or more, replace central junction box.

7) Turn ignition switch to LOCK position. Check battery saver relay. See MICRO RELAYS under COMPONENT TESTS. If battery saver relay is okay, go to next step. If battery saver relay is faulty, replace relay.

8) Disconnect GEM from central junction box 18-pin connector C267. Turn ignition switch to RUN position. Measure voltage between battery saver relay socket terminal No. 2 and ground. *See Fig. 1.* If any voltage is present, replace central junction box. If no voltage is present, replace GEM. See GENERIC ELECTRONIC MODULE (GEM) under REMOVAL & INSTALLATION.

9) Using NGS tester, observe GEM PID ACCDLY while triggering GEM active command ACCY RLY to ON and OFF. If PID value agrees with command mode, go to step **16)**. If PID value does not agree with command mode and displays OFFO-G, go to next step. If PID value does not agree with command mode and displays ON-B-, go to step **14)**.

10) Turn ignition switch to LOCK position. Remove accessory delay relay from central junction box. Turn ignition switch to RUN position. Measure voltage between accessory delay relay socket terminal No. 86 and ground. *See Fig. 2.* If voltage is more than 10 volts, go to step **12)**. If voltage is 10 volts or less, go to next step.

11) Remove battery saver relay. Measure resistance between battery saver relay socket terminal No. 5 and accessory delay relay socket terminal No. 86. *See Figs. 2 and 5.* If resistance is less than 5 ohms, replace battery saver relay. If resistance is 5 ohms or more, replace central junction box.

12) Check accessory delay relay. See MINI RELAYS under COMPONENT TESTS. If accessory delay relay is okay, go to next step. If accessory delay relay is faulty, replace relay.

13) Disconnect GEM from central junction box 18-pin connector C267. Measure internal resistance of central junction box between connector C267 terminal No. 11 and accessory delay relay socket terminal No. 85. *See Figs. 2 and 5.* If resistance is less than 5 ohms, replace GEM. See GENERIC ELECTRONIC MODULE (GEM) under REMOVAL & INSTALLATION. If resistance is 5 ohms or more, replace central junction box.

14) Turn ignition switch to LOCK position. Check accessory delay relay. See MINI RELAYS under COMPONENT TESTS. If accessory delay relay is okay, go to next step. If accessory delay relay is faulty, replace relay.

15) Disconnect GEM from central junction box 18-pin connector C267. Turn ignition switch to RUN position. Measure voltage between accessory delay relay socket terminal No. 85 and ground. *See Fig. 2.* If

voltage is present, replace central junction box. If voltage is not present, replace GEM. See GENERIC ELECTRONIC MODULE (GEM) under REMOVAL & INSTALLATION.

16) Turn ignition switch to LOCK position. Remove one-touch down relay from central junction box. Turn ignition switch to RUN position. Using NGS tester, trigger GEM active command ACCY RLY to ON. Measure voltage between one-touch down relay socket terminal No. 85 and ground. *See Fig. 2.* If voltage is more than 10 volts, install one-touch down relay and go to step **20)**. If voltage is 10 volts or less, go to next step.

17) Turn ignition switch to LOCK position. Remove accessory delay relay from central junction box. Measure voltage between accessory delay relay socket terminal No. 30 and ground. *See Fig. 2.* If voltage is 10 volts or less, go to next step. If voltage is more than 10 volts, go to step **19)**.

18) Disconnect central junction box 34-pin connector C242. Measure voltage between central junction box connector C242 terminal No. 25 (Red/Light Blue wire) and ground. *See Fig. 5.* If voltage is more than 10 volts, replace central junction box. If voltage is 10 volts or less, repair open in Red/Light Blue wire.

19) Check accessory delay relay. See MINI RELAYS under COMPONENT TESTS. If accessory delay relay is okay, replace central junction box. If accessory delay relay is faulty, replace relay.

20) Turn ignition switch to LOCK position. Disconnect master window switch 7-pin connector C509. Turn ignition switch to RUN position. Using NGS tester, trigger GEM active command mode ACCY RLY to ON. Measure voltage between master window switch connector C509 terminal No. 2 (Light Blue/Black wire) and ground. *See Fig. 7.* If voltage is 10 volts or less, go to next step. If voltage is more than 10 volts, go to step **22)**.

21) Turn ignition switch to LOCK position. Disconnect central junction box 34-pin connector C242. Measure resistance in Light Blue/Black wire between central junction box connector C242 terminal No. 10 and master window switch connector C509 terminal No. 2. *See Figs. 5 and 7.* If resistance is less than 5 ohms, replace central junction box. If resistance is 5 ohms or more, repair open in Light Blue/Black wire.

22) Turn ignition switch to LOCK position. Disconnect master window switch 7-pin connector C509. Measure resistance between master window switch connector C509 terminal No. 1 (Black wire) and ground. *See Fig. 7.* If resistance is less than 5 ohms, replace master window switch. If resistance is 5 ohms or more, repair open in Black wire.

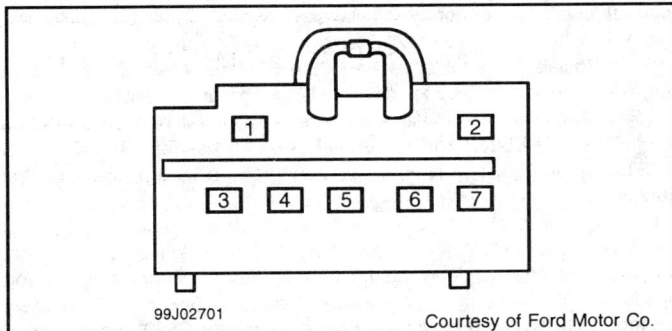

99J02701   Courtesy of Ford Motor Co.

Fig. 7: Identifying Master Window Switch Connector C509 Terminals

TEST C: SINGLE WINDOW INOPERATIVE (ALL OTHER WINDOWS OPERATE)

NOTE: After repair, clear DTCs and retest system.

1) Operate power windows from each power window switch. If all windows operate properly, system is okay. If left front window does not operate, go to next step. If any other window does not operate, go to step **17)**.

2) Turn ignition switch to LOCK position. Using New Generation Star (NGS) tester, observe Generic Electronic Module (GEM) PIDs D_DN_SW, D_UP_SW and OTD_SW while pressing master window switch driver's window through UP, DOWN and AUTO positions. If PID values agree with switch position, go to step **8)**. If PID values do not agree with switch position, go to next step.

3) Turn ignition switch to LOCK position. Disconnect master window switch 7-pin connector C509. *See Fig. 7*. Using NGS tester, observe GEM PIDs D_DN_SW, D_UP_SW and OTD_SW. Connect 10-amp fused jumper wire between master switch connector C509 terminal No. 2 (Light Blue/Black wire) and No. 5 (Gray wire), then between terminals No. 2 (Light Blue/Black wire) and No. 7 (White/Black wire) and then between terminals No. 2 (Light Blue/Black wire) and No. 6 (Tan/Light Blue wire). If PIDs D_DN_SW and OTD_SW indicate DOWN, and PID D_UP_SW indicates UP when jumper is connected, replace master switch. If PIDs do not indicate DOWN or UP as specified, go to next step. If any PID constantly indicates DOWN or UP, go to step **6)**.

4) Turn ignition switch to LOCK position. Disconnect central junction box 34-pin connector C243. Measure resistance in Tan/Light Blue wire between master switch connector C509 terminal No. 6 and central junction box connector C243 terminal No. 10. *See Figs. 5 and 7*. Resistance should be less than 5 ohms. Measure resistance between master switch connector C509 terminal No. 6 (Tan/Light Blue wire) and ground. Resistance should be 10 k/ohms or more. Measure resistance in White/Black wire between master switch connector C509 terminal No. 7 and central junction box connector C243 terminal No. 9. Resistance should be less than 5 ohms. Measure resistance between master switch connector C509 terminal No. 7 (White/Black wire) and ground. Resistance should be 10 k/ohms or more. Measure resistance in Gray wire between master switch connector C509 terminal No. 5 and central junction box connector C243 terminal No. 28. Resistance should be less than 5 ohms. Measure resistance between master switch connector C509 terminal No. 5 (Gray wire) and ground. Resistance should be 10 k/ohms or more. If resistances are as specified, go to next step. If any resistance is not as specified, repair appropriate wire(s).

5) Disconnect GEM from central junction box 18-pin connector C267. Measure central junction box internal resistance between connector C243 terminal No. 10 and connector C267 terminal No. 8 (down switch input). *See Fig. 5*. Resistance should be less than 5 ohms. Measure resistance between connector C267 terminal No. 8 and ground. Resistance should be 10 k/ohms or more. Measure central junction box internal resistance between connector C243 terminal No. 9 and connector C267 terminal No. 6 (up switch input). Resistance should be less than 5 ohms. Measure resistance between connector C267 terminal No. 6 and ground. Resistance should be 10 k/ohms or more. Measure central junction box internal resistance between connector C243 terminal No. 28 and connector C267 terminal No. 9 (one-touch down switch input). Resistance should be less than 5 ohms. Measure resistance between connector C267 terminal No. 9 and ground. Resistance should be 10 k/ohms or more. If resistances are as specified, replace GEM. See GENERIC ELECTRONIC MODULE (GEM) under REMOVAL & INSTALLATION. If any resistance is not as specified, replace central junction box.

6) Turn ignition switch to LOCK position. Disconnect central junction box 34-pin connector C243. *See Fig. 5*. Turn ignition switch to RUN position. Measure voltage between master window switch connector C509 terminal No. 6 (Tan/Light Blue wire) and ground. *See Fig. 7*. Measure voltage between master window switch connector C509 terminal No. 7 (White/Black wire) and ground. Measure voltage between master window switch connector C509 terminal No. 5 (Gray wire) and ground. If any voltage is present, repair short to power in appropriate wire. See WIRING DIAGRAMS. If there is no voltage present, connect central junction box and go to next step.

7) Turn ignition switch to LOCK position. Disconnect GEM from central junction box 18-pin connector C267. Turn ignition switch to RUN position. Measure voltage between central junction box connector C267 terminal No. 8 and ground. *See Fig. 5*. Measure voltage between central junction box connector C267 terminal No. 6 and ground. Measure voltage between connector C267 terminal No. 9 and ground. If each voltage reading is more than 10 volts, replace GEM. See GENERIC ELECTRONIC MODULE (GEM) under REMOVAL & INSTALLATION. If any voltage is 10 volts or less, replace central junction box.

8) Turn ignition switch to LOCK position. Disconnect left front window motor 2-pin connector. Turn ignition switch to RUN position. Using NGS tester, trigger GEM active command ONE TOUCH to ON. Measure voltage between window motor connector Orange/White wire terminal and ground. If voltage is more than 10 volts, go to step **12)**. If voltage is 10 volts or less, exit GEM active command mode and go to next step.

9) Turn ignition switch to LOCK position. Remove one-touch down relay. Measure resistance of Orange/White wire between left front window motor connector and one-touch down relay socket terminal No. 30. *See Fig. 2*. If resistance is less than 5 ohms, go to step **11)**. If resistance is 5 ohms or more, go to next step.

10) Disconnect central junction box 34-pin connector C242. Measure resistance of Orange/White wire between left front window motor connector and central junction box connector C242 terminal No. 24. *See Fig. 5*. If resistance is less than 5 ohms, replace central junction box. If resistance is 5 ohms or more, repair open in Orange/White wire.

11) Remove accessory delay relay from central junction box. Measure resistance between one-touch down relay socket terminal No. 87 and accessory delay relay socket terminal 87. *See Fig. 2*. If resistance is less than 5 ohms, replace one-touch down relay. If resistance is 5 ohms or more, replace central junction box.

12) Trigger GEM active command ONE TOUCH to OFF. Turn ignition switch to LOCK position. Measure resistance of Orange/White wire between left front window motor connector and ground. If resistance is less than 5 ohms, go to step **15)**. If resistance is 5 ohms or more, go to next step.

13) Remove one-touch down relay. Measure resistance between one-touch down relay socket terminal No. 87A and ground. *See Fig. 2*. If resistance is less than 5 ohms, replace one-touch down relay. If resistance is 5 ohms or more, go to next step.

14) Disconnect central junction box 34-pin connector C243. Measure resistance between central junction box connector C243 terminal No. 24 (Black wire) and ground. *See Fig. 5*. If resistance is less than 5 ohms, replace central junction box. If resistance is 5 ohms or more, repair open in Black wire. Ground point is at lower right inner cowl panel.

15) Turn ignition switch to RUN position. While pressing master window switch to UP position, measure voltage at between left front window motor White/Black wire terminal and ground. If voltage is more than 10 volts, go to next step. If voltage is 10 volts or less, repair White/Black wire.

16) Turn ignition switch to LOCK position. Disconnect master window switch 7-pin connector C509. Measure resistance of White/Black wire between left front window motor connector and ground. If resistance is less than 5 ohms, replace left front window motor. See POWER WINDOW MOTOR under REMOVAL & INSTALLATION. If resistance is 5 ohms or more, replace master window switch. See POWER WINDOW SWITCH under REMOVAL & INSTALLATION.

17) Turn ignition switch to LOCK position. Disconnect inoperative power window switch connector. Turn ignition switch to RUN position. Place master window switch remote lock-out feature in UNLOCK position. Measure voltage between power window switch connector terminal No. 4 (Yellow/Light Green wire) and ground. *See Fig. 8*. If voltage is more than 10 volts, go to next step. If voltage is 10 volts or less, go to step **19)**.

18) Turn ignition switch to LOCK position. Measure resistance between power window switch connector terminal No. 2 and ground. Measure resistance between terminal No. 7 and ground. *See Fig. 8*. If each resistance is less than 5 ohms, go to step **21)**. If any resistance is 5 ohms or more, go to step **20)**.

19) Turn ignition switch to LOCK position. Remove inoperative power window switch. See POWER WINDOW SWITCH under REMOVAL & INSTALLATION. Ensure master window switch remote lock-out feature is in UNLOCK position. Measure resistance between master window switch connector C509 terminal No. 2 (component side) and connector C510 terminal No. 3 (component side) . *See Fig. 3*. If resistance is less than 5 ohms, repair open in Yellow/Light Green wire. If resistance is 5 ohms or more, replace master window switch. See POWER WINDOW SWITCH under REMOVAL & INSTALLATION.

20) Turn ignition switch to LOCK position. Remove and disconnect master window switch connectors. See POWER WINDOW SWITCH

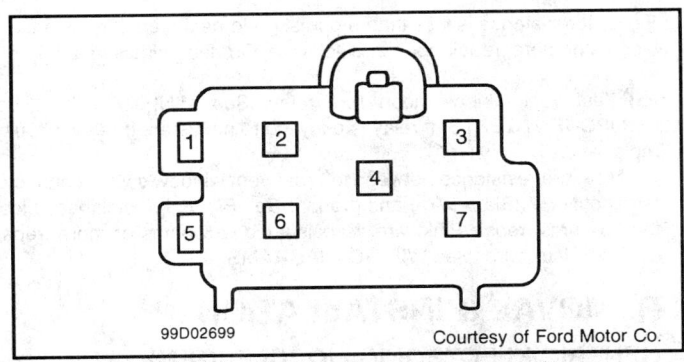

99D02699
Courtesy of Ford Motor Co.

Fig. 8: Identifying Vent Window & Single Switch Connector Terminals

under REMOVAL & INSTALLATION. Measure resistance in appropriate wires between master window switch connectors and inoperative window switch connector. See WINDOW CONTROL CIRCUITS table. If all resistances are less than 5 ohms, replace master window switch. If any resistance is 5 ohms or more, repair open in appropriate wire.

WINDOW CONTROL CIRCUITS

Inoperative Window	Wire Colors
Right Front	Tan/Light Blue & White/Yellow
Left Rear	Gray/Orange & Yellow/Light Blue
Right Rear	Red/Black & Yellow/Black

21) Connect 10-amp fused jumper wire between positive battery voltage and appropriate wire terminal at inoperative window switch connector. Using another jumper wire, ground appropriate terminal at inoperative window switch connector. If window motor operates correctly, go to step 23). If window motor does not operate correctly, go to next step.

WINDOW OPERATION TEST

Window Operation	Positive Voltage	Ground
Up		
Right Front	Red/Yellow Wire	Yellow/Red Wire
Right Rear	Brown/Yellow Wire	Brown Wire
Left Rear	Yellow/Light Blue Wire	Yellow/Black Wire
Down		
Right Front	Yellow/Red Wire	Red/Yellow Wire
Right Rear	Brown Wire	Brown/Yellow Wire
Left Rear	Yellow/Black Wire	Yellow/Light Blue Wire

22) Turn ignition switch to LOCK position. Disconnect inoperative window motor connector. Measure resistance in circuits between inoperative window switch connector and window motor connector. See WIRING DIAGRAMS. If resistances are less than 5 ohms, replace inoperative power window motor. See POWER WINDOW MOTOR under REMOVAL & INSTALLATION. If resistances are 5 ohms or more, repair open in appropriate wire(s).

23) Test inoperative window switch. See POWER WINDOW SINGLE SWITCH under COMPONENT TESTS. If switch is faulty, replace switch. If switch is okay, replace master window switch.

TEST D: ONE-TOUCH DOWN FEATURE INOPERATIVE

NOTE: After repair, clear DTCs and retest system.

1) Using New Generation Star (NGS) tester, perform Generic Electronic Module (GEM) self-test. If no DTCs, DTC B1398 or DTC B1400 are present, go to next step. If DTCs B1405 or B1410 are present, go to TEST C: SINGLE WINDOW INOPERATIVE (ALL OTHER WINDOWS OPERATE). If DTC B1342 is present, replace GEM. See GENERIC ELECTRONIC MODULE (GEM) under REMOVAL & INSTALLATION.

2) Turn ignition switch to RUN position. Using NGS tester, trigger GEM active command ACCY RLY to ON. Observe GEM PID D_PWRLY while triggering GEM active command ONE TOUCH to ON and OFF. If PID

value agrees with command mode, go to TEST C: SINGLE WINDOW INOPERATIVE (ALL OTHER WINDOWS OPERATE). If PID does not agree with command mode and displays OFFO-G, go to next step. If PID does not agree with command mode and displays ON-B-, go to step 6).

3) Turn ignition switch to LOCK position. Check one-touch down relay. See MINI RELAYS under COMPONENT TESTS. If one-touch down relay is okay, go to next step. If one-touch down relay is faulty, replace relay.

4) Remove accessory delay relay from central junction box. Measure resistance between accessory delay relay socket terminal No. 87 and one-touch down relay socket terminal No. 85. *See Fig. 2.* If resistance is less than 5 ohms, go to next step. If resistance is 5 ohms or more, replace central junction box.

5) Disconnect GEM from central junction box 18-pin connector C267. Measure resistance internal resistance of central junction box between one-touch down relay socket terminal No. 86 and central junction box connector C267 terminal No. 2. *See Figs. 2 and 5.* Resistance should be less than 5 ohms. Measure resistance between central junction box connector C267 terminal No. 2 (central junction box side) and ground. Resistance should be 10 k/ohms or more. If resistances are as specified, replace GEM. See GENERIC ELECTRONIC MODULE (GEM) under REMOVAL & INSTALLATION. If resistances are not as specified, replace central junction box.

6) Turn ignition switch to LOCK position. Check one-touch down relay. See MINI RELAYS under COMPONENT TESTS. If one-touch down relay is okay, go to next step. If one-touch down relay is faulty, replace relay.

7) Disconnect GEM from central junction box 18-pin connector C267. Turn ignition switch to RUN position. Measure voltage between one-touch down relay socket terminal No. 86 and ground. *See Fig. 2.* If voltage is present, replace central junction box. If voltage is not present, replace GEM. See GENERIC ELECTRONIC MODULE (GEM) under REMOVAL & INSTALLATION.

TEST E: VENT WINDOW INOPERATIVE

NOTE: After repair, clear DTCs and retest system.

1) If vehicle is equipped with moon roof, go to next step. If vehicle is not equipped with moon roof, go to step 3).

2) Turn ignition switch to RUN position. Verify moon roof operation. If moon roof operates properly, go to step 4). If moon roof does not operate properly, repair moon roof as necessary. See appropriate wiring diagram in POWER MOON ROOFS article.

3) Verify vent windows operation. If both vent windows operate, go to step 13). If both vent windows do not operate, go to step 20). If only left rear vent window does not operate, go to step 6).

4) Verify vent windows operation. If both vent windows operate, go to step 13). If both vent windows do not operate, go to next step. If left vent window does not operate, go to step 6).

5) Turn ignition switch to LOCK position. Disconnect left rear vent window switch connector. Measure resistance between left vent window switch connector terminal No. 7 (Black wire) and ground. *See Fig. 8.* If resistance is less than 5 ohms, repair Pink wire. See WIRING DIAGRAMS. If resistance is 5 ohms or more, repair open in Black wire.

6) Turn ignition switch to LOCK position. Disconnect left rear vent window switch connector. Turn ignition switch to RUN position. Measure voltage between left rear vent window switch connector terminal No. 4 (Pink wire) and ground. *See Fig. 8.* If voltage is more than 10 volts, go to next step. If voltage is 10 volts or less, repair Pink wire. See WIRING DIAGRAMS.

7) Turn ignition switch to LOCK position. Measure resistance between left rear vent window switch connector terminal No. 1 (Black wire) and ground. *See Fig. 8.* Measure resistance between left rear vent window switch connector terminal No. 2 (Black wire) and ground. If each resistance is less than 5 ohms, go to next step. If any resistance is 5 ohms or more, repair open in appropriate Black wire(s).

8) Test left rear vent window switch. See POWER VENT WINDOW SWITCH under COMPONENT TESTS. If switch is okay, go to next step. If switch is faulty, replace left rear vent window switch.

9) Disconnect left rear vent window motor connector. Connector is located at left rear corner panel. Measure resistance of Yellow/Light Blue wire between window motor connector and left rear vent window switch connector terminal No. 3. *See Fig. 8.* If resistance is less than 5 ohms, go to next step. If resistance is 5 ohms or more, replace repair open in Yellow/Light Blue wire.

10) Measure resistance between left rear vent window switch connector terminal No. 3 (Yellow/Light Blue wire) and ground. *See Fig. 8.* If resistance is more than 10 k/ohms, go to next step. If resistance is 10 k/ohms or less, repair short to ground in Yellow/Light Blue wire.

11) Measure resistance of White/Light Blue wire between left rear vent window motor connector and left rear vent window switch connector terminal No. 6. *See Fig. 8.* If resistance is less than 5 ohms, go to next step. If resistance is 5 ohms or more, repair open in White/Light Blue wire.

12) Measure resistance between left rear vent window switch connector terminal No. 6 (White/Light Blue wire) and ground. *See Fig. 8.* If resistance is more than 10 k/ohms, replace left rear vent window motor. If resistance is 10 k/ohms or less, repair short to ground in White/Light Blue wire.

13) Turn ignition switch to LOCK position. Disconnect right rear vent window switch connector. Turn ignition switch to RUN position. Measure voltage between right rear vent window switch connector terminal No. 4 (Pink wire) and ground. *See Fig. 8.* If voltage is more than 10 volts, go to next step. If voltage is 10 volts or less, repair Pink wire.

14) Turn ignition switch to LOCK position. Measure resistance between right rear vent window switch connector terminal No. 1 (Black wire) and ground. Measure resistance between right rear vent window switch connector terminal No. 2 (Black wire) and ground. *See Fig. 8.* If each resistance is less than 5 ohms, go to next step. If either resistance is 5 ohms or more, repair open in appropriate Black wire(s). See WIRING DIAGRAMS.

15) Test right rear vent window switch. See POWER VENT WINDOW SWITCH under COMPONENT TESTS. If switch is okay, go to next step. If switch is faulty, replace vent window switch.

16) Disconnect right rear vent window motor connector. Connector is located at right rear corner panel. Measure resistance of Yellow/Red wire between right rear vent window motor connector and right rear vent window switch connector terminal No. 3. *See Fig. 8.* If resistance is less than 5 ohms, go to next step. If resistance is 5 ohms or more, repair open in Yellow/Red wire.

17) Measure resistance between right rear vent window switch connector terminal No. 3 (Yellow/Red wire) and ground. *See Fig. 8.* If resistance is more than 10 k/ohms, go to next step. If resistance is 10 k/ohms or less, repair short to ground in Yellow/Red wire.

18) Measure resistance of White/Red wire between right rear vent window motor connector and right rear vent window switch connector terminal No. 6. *See Fig. 8.* If resistance is less than 5 ohms, go to next step. If resistance is 5 ohms or more, repair open in White/Red wire.

19) Measure resistance between right rear vent window switch connector terminal No. 6 (White/Red wire) and ground. *See Fig. 8.* If resistance is more than 10 k/ohms, replace right rear vent window motor. If resistance is 10 k/ohms or less, repair short to ground in White/Red wire.

20) Remove vent window/moon roof relay from RPO relay block No. 2. RPO relay block No. 2 is located left front of rear wheelwell. Turn ignition switch to RUN position. Measure voltage between vent window/moon roof relay socket terminal No. 30 and ground. *See Fig. 2.* If voltage is more than 10 volts, go to next step. If voltage is 10 volts or less, repair Red/Black wire. See WIRING DIAGRAMS.

21) Measure voltage between vent window/moon roof relay socket terminal No. 86 and ground. *See Fig. 2.* If voltage is more than 10 volts, go to next step. If voltage is 10 volts or less, go to TEST D: ONE-TOUCH DOWN FEATURE INOPERATIVE.

22) Turn ignition switch to LOCK position. Measure resistance between vent window/moon roof relay socket terminal No. 85 and ground. See

Fig. 2. If resistance is less than 5 ohms, go to next step. If resistance is 5 ohms or more, repair open in Black wire. Ground point is near left rear wheelwell.

23) Test vent window/moon roof relay. See MINI RELAYS under COMPONENT TESTS. If relay is okay, go to next step. If relay is faulty, replace relay.

24) Measure resistance between left rear vent window switch connector terminal No. 7 (Black wire) and ground. *See Fig. 8.* If resistance is less than 5 ohms, repair Pink wire. If resistance is 5 ohms or more, repair open in Black wire. See WIRING DIAGRAMS.

REMOVAL & INSTALLATION
GENERIC ELECTRONIC MODULE (GEM)

CAUTION: Prior to replacing GEM, it is necessary to upload module configuration information to New Generation STAR (NGS) tester. After installation this information needs to be downloaded into new GEM.

Removal & Installation – 1) Disconnect battery ground cable. Remove steering column opening cover. Remove fuse door. Disconnect hood latch release handle and parking brake release handle from instrument panel steering column cover.

2) Remove lower instrument panel steering column cover. Remove bulkhead connectors (C242 and C243) from central junction box.

3) Remove central junction box bolts and remove interior fuse junction panel nuts. Disconnect GEM electrical connectors. Remove GEM. To install, reverse removal procedure.

POWER WINDOW MOTOR

WARNING: Failure to ensure regulator arms are in fixed position before removing window motor from regulator could result in personal injury.

Removal & Installation (Doors) – 1) Remove door trim panel and watershield. Raise and support glass in full up position. Disconnect motor electrical connector. Remove window glass to regulator nuts.

2) Drill out rivets that attach motor and window regulator assembly to door. Remove motor and window regulator assembly.

3) Ensure regulator arms are in fixed position to prevent counterbalance spring unwind when motor is removed. Remove motor from regulator assembly.

4) To install, reverse removal procedure. Use Heavy Duty Riveter to install new rivets. Cycle door glass to ensure gear engagement.

Removal & Installation (Vent) – Remove quarter trim panel. Unclip vent window regulator from vent window. Disconnect vent window motor electrical connector. Remove nuts and vent window motor. To install, reverse removal procedure.

POWER WINDOW SWITCH

Removal & Installation – Disconnect negative battery cable. Carefully pry up front and rear of switch plate. Using thin-blade screwdriver, pry connector from switch. Remove window switch by carefully prying up with a flat-bladed tool on switch plate. To install, reverse removal procedure.

WIRING DIAGRAMS

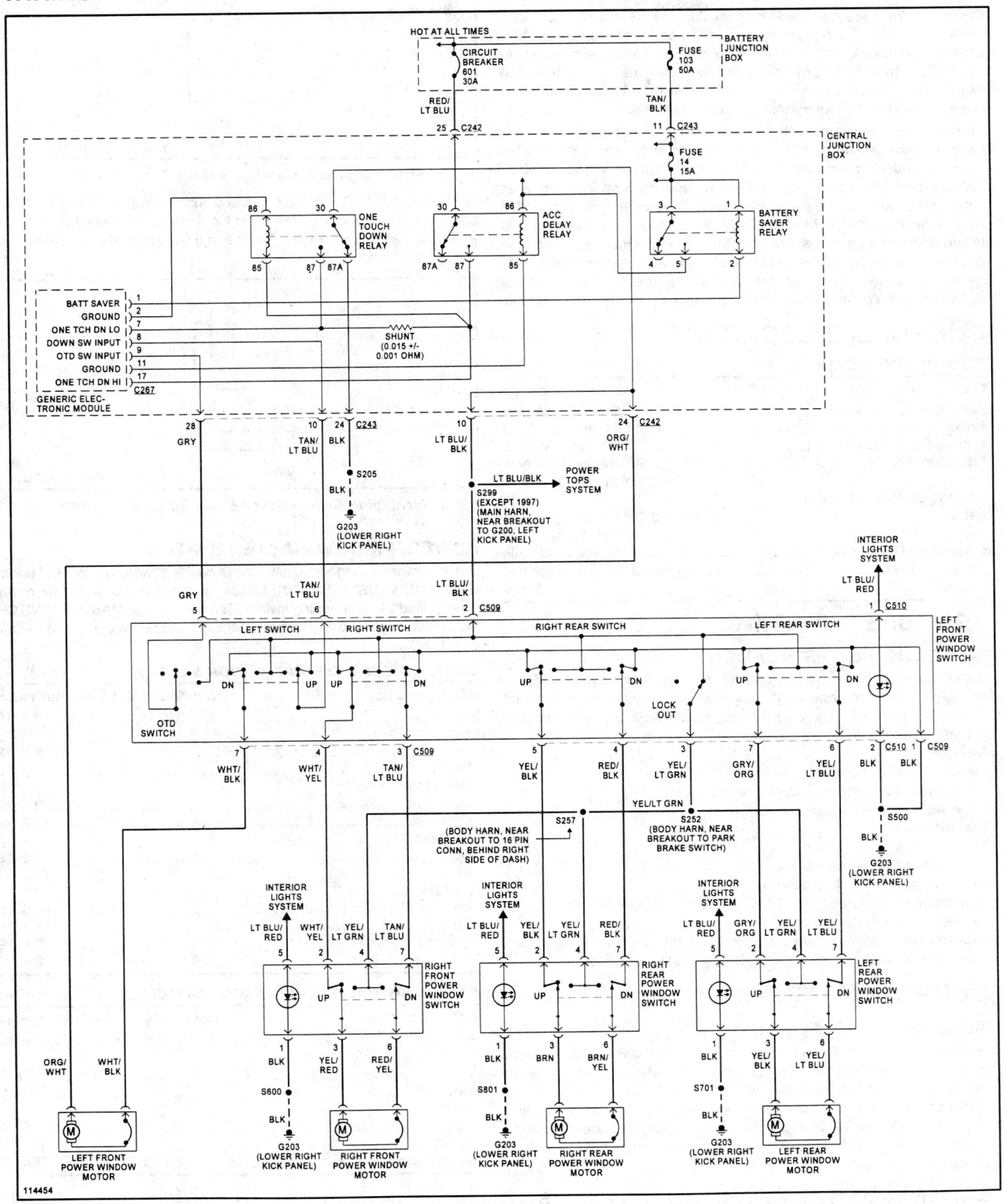

Fig. 9: Power Window System Wiring Diagram (Expedition & Navigator)

114454

DESCRIPTION

Power windows are operated by reversible motors mounted on each window regulator. Each passenger window has an individual switch for separate control. A master switch is located on the driver's door from which both front and rear (if equipped) windows may be controlled. A lock-out switch is incorporated in master switch. When actuated, it prevents window operation from individual switches.

All models are equipped with a one-touch down feature, allowing the driver to lower the left front window fully by momentarily actuating the driver's window down switch at the master power window switch. Holding the switch down longer allows the driver to stop the window as soon as the switch is released. The one-touch down feature is controlled by a Generic Electronic Module (GEM). The GEM offers diagnostics to locate and repair concerns affecting the subsystem that it controls. The one-touch down feature can only be actuated at the master switch. After ignition is turned off, delayed accessory feature will allow window operation until a passenger door is opened, or 10 minutes have passed.

COMPONENT LOCATION

COMPONENT LOCATIONS

Component	Location
Accessory Delay Relay	On Relay Module
Battery Junction Box	Left Of Master Cylinder
Battery Saver Relay	On Relay Module
Fuse Junction Panel	Left Side Of Instrument Panel Facing Driver's Door
Generic Electronic Module (GEM)	Behind Center Of Instrument Panel Finish Panel
One-Touch Down Relay	On Relay Module
Relay Module	Behind Center Of Instrument Panel

TROUBLE SHOOTING

INSPECTION & VERIFICATION

Verify customer concern by operating windows to duplicate condition. Visually inspect components. If inspection reveals an obvious concern which can be easily serviced, correct malfunction before continuing inspection and verification.

Mechanical:
- Window alignment.
- Window mounting (regulator and bracket).
- Window frame interference.

Electrical:
- Blown fuse(s).
- Damaged wiring harness.
- Loose or corroded connections.
- Damaged switches.
- Damaged window motor.

If problem is not found, check for Diagnostic Trouble Codes (DTCs). See SELF-DIAGNOSTICS under SELF-DIAGNOSTIC SYSTEM.

COMPONENT TESTS

ACCESSORY DELAY RELAY

Remove accessory delay relay from relay module. Using an ohmmeter, check relay continuity. Continuity should exist between relay terminals No. 85 and 86, and also between terminals No. 30 and 87A. See Fig. 1. Connect 2 fused jumper wires between battery positive terminal and relay terminals No. 85 and 86. Continuity should now exist between relay terminals No. 30 and 87. Replace relay if continuity is not as specified.

BATTERY SAVER & ONE-TOUCH DOWN RELAYS

Remove battery saver relay or one-touch down relay from relay module. Using an ohmmeter, check relay continuity. Continuity should exist between relay terminals No. 1 and 2, and also between terminals No. 3

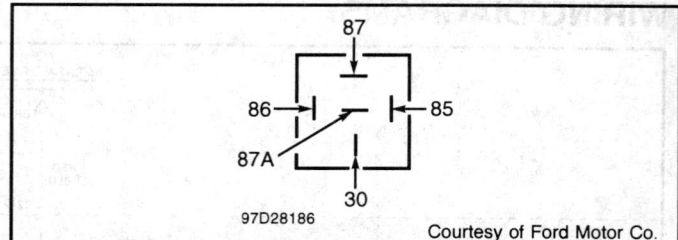

Fig. 1: Identifying Accessory Delay Relay Terminals

and 4. See Fig. 2. Connect 2 fused jumper wires between battery positive terminal and relay terminals No. 1 and 2. Continuity should now exist between relay terminals No. 3 and 5. Replace relay if continuity is not as specified.

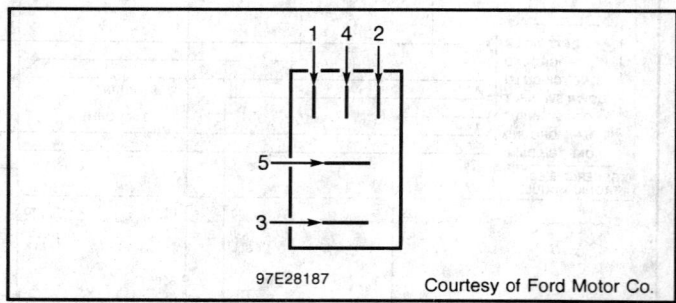

Fig. 2: Identifying Battery Saver & One-Touch Down Relay Terminals

POWER WINDOW MASTER SWITCH

Remove master window switch. See POWER WINDOW SWITCH under REMOVAL & INSTALLATION. Check for continuity between terminals as specified while operating switch. See appropriate MASTER SWITCH TESTING table. If continuity does not exist as specified, replace switch. See Fig. 3 or 8.

MASTER SWITCH TESTING (4-DOOR MODELS)

Switch Position	Continuity Between Terminals
Neutral	8, 9, 10, 11, 13, 15, 16, 17 & 18
Left Front	
Up	8 & 19
Down	10 & 19
Right Front	
Up	9 & 19
Down	11 & 19
Left Rear	
Up	15 & 19
Down	17 & 19
Right Rear	
Up	16 & 19
Down	18 & 19
Lockout Unlocked	20 & 19
Switch Illumination	1 & 5; 12 & 14

MASTER SWITCH TESTING (2-DOOR MODELS)

Switch Position	Continuity Between Terminals
Neutral	1, 5, 9 & 11; 2, 4, 8 & 12
Left	
Up	3 & 5
Down	1 & 3
Right	
Up	10 & 12
Down	8 & 10
Switch Illumination	6 & 7; 13 & 14

POWER WINDOW MOTOR

Remove window motor from vehicle, see POWER WINDOW MOTOR under REMOVAL & INSTALLATION. Using 2 fused jumper wires,

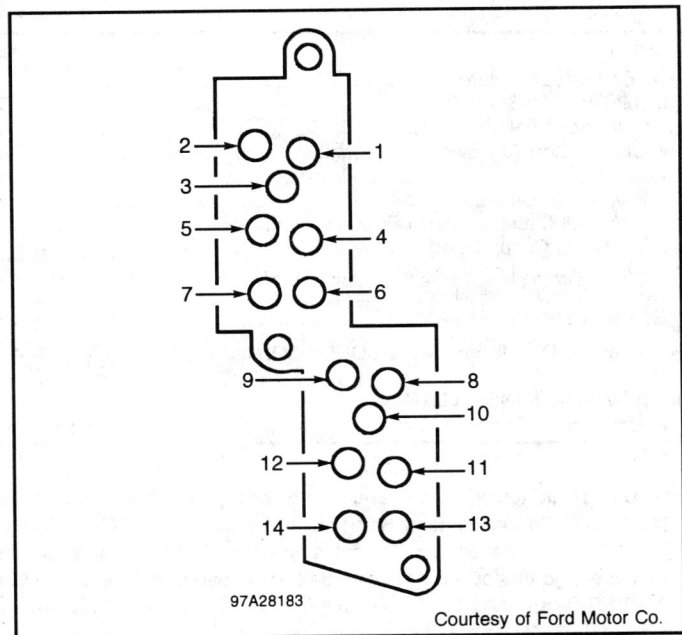

Fig. 3: Identifying Driver's Window Control Switch Terminals (2-Door Models)

connect a fully charged battery to motor terminals. Observe motor. Motor should operate smoothly. Reverse leads. Motor should operate in reverse direction. Replace window motor if it does not operate as specified.

POWER WINDOW SINGLE SWITCH

Remove suspect window switch. See POWER WINDOW SWITCH under REMOVAL & INSTALLATION. Check for continuity between terminals as specified while operating switch. See appropriate SWITCH TESTING table. If continuity does not exist as specified, replace switch. See Fig. 4 or 5.

RIGHT FRONT & RIGHT REAR SWITCH TESTING

Switch Position	Continuity Between Terminals
Neutral	1 & 2; 5 & 6
Up	2 & 4
Down	4 & 5
Switch Illumination	3 & 7

LEFT REAR PASSENGER SWITCH TESTING

Switch Position	Continuity Between Terminals
Neutral	1 & 5; 2 & 6
Up	4 & 5
Down	2 & 4
Switch Illumination	3 & 7

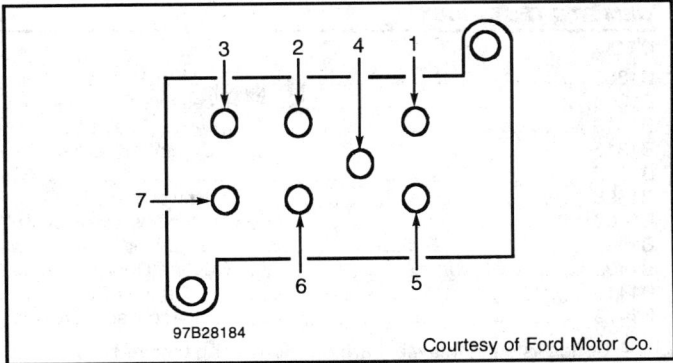

Fig. 4: Identifying Right Front & Left Rear Window Switch Terminals

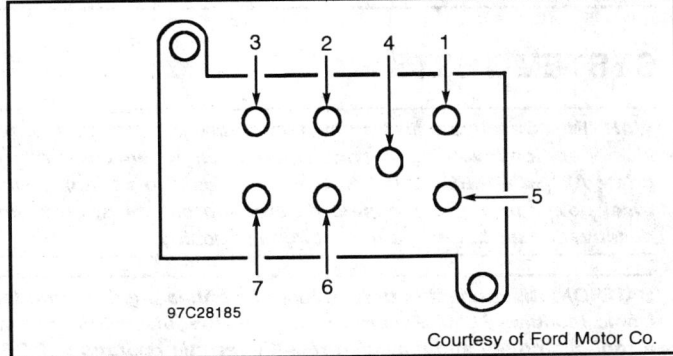

Fig. 5: Identifying Right Rear Window Switch Terminals

SELF-DIAGNOSTIC SYSTEM

NOTE: For further information of self-diagnostic system, see MODULE COMMUNICATIONS NETWORK – EXPLORER & MOUNTAINEER article.

SELF-DIAGNOSTICS

1) For preliminary testing, see TROUBLE SHOOTING. If problem is not found, check Generic Electronic Module (GEM) for Diagnostic Trouble Codes (DTCs). Connect New Generation STAR (NGS) tester, or equivalent scan tool, to Data Link Connector (DLC) located below center of instrument panel. Using NGS tester, perform DATA LINK DIAGNOSTIC TEST. If NGS tester displays CKT914, CKT915 or CKT70 = ALL ECUS NO RESP/NOT EQUIP, see MODULE COMMUNICATIONS NETWORK – EXPLORER & MOUNTAINEER article to diagnosis network concern. If NGS tester displays NO RESP/NOT EQUIP for GEM, perform TEST J: NO SCAN TOOL COMMUNICATION WITH GEM under SYSTEM TESTS.

2) If NGS tester displays SYSTEM PASSED, retrieve and record continuous DTCs. Erase continuous DTCs. Using NGS tester, perform On-Demand Self-Test for GEM. If GEM DTCs related to the concern are retrieved, see GEM DTC TEST INDEX table to continue diagnosis. If no DTCs related to the concern are retrieved, perform appropriate test based on symptom. See SYMPTOM TEST INDEX under SYSTEM TESTS. For GEM DTCs not covered in this article, see MODULE COMMUNICATIONS NETWORK – EXPLORER & MOUNTAINEER.

GEM DTC TEST INDEX [1]

DTC	Description	Test
B1302	Accessory Delay Relay Coil Circuit Failure	A
B1304	Accessory Delay Relay Coil Circuit Open Or Short To Power	A
B1313	Battery Saver Relay Coil Circuit Failure	A
B1315	Battery Saver Relay Coil Circuit Short To Power	A
B1342	GEM Is Defective	2
B1398	Power Window One-Touch Down Relay Circuit Failure	3
B1400	Power Window One-Touch Down Relay Coil Circuit Short To Power	3
B1404	Driver's Door Power Window Down Circuit Open	3
B1405	Driver's Door Power Window Down Circuit Short To Power	3
B1410	Driver's Door Power Window Motor Circuit Failure	3
B1475	Accessory Delay Relay Contacts Short To Power	3

[1] – Codes listed in this table are only for testing covered in this article. For complete DTC listing, see MODULE COMMUNICATIONS NETWORK – EXPLORER & MOUNTAINEER article.

[2] – Replace GEM. See GENERIC ELECTRONIC MODULE (GEM) under REMOVAL & INSTALLATION.

[3] – Go to SYMPTOM TEST INDEX under SYSTEM TESTS.

SYSTEM TESTS

WARNING: Deactivate air bag system before performing any service operation involving steering column components. See appropriate AIR BAG RESTRAINT SYSTEMS article. Do not apply electrical power to any component on steering column without first deactivating air bag system. Air bag may deploy.

CAUTION: Disconnect battery before disconnecting Generic Electronic Module (GEM). Failure to do so will result in GEM storing erroneous codes and may also result in erratic operation of GEM after reconnection. When battery is disconnected, vehicle computer and memory systems may lose memory data. Driveability problems may exist until computer systems have completed a relearn cycle. See COMPUTER RELEARN PROCEDURES article in GENERAL INFORMATION before disconnecting battery.

NOTE: Complete entire system test related to the symptom before replacing GEM.

SYMPTOM TEST INDEX

Symptom	Test
All Power Windows Inoperative (2-Door & 4-Door)	A
Driver's Door Power Window Inoperative (4-Door)	B
Driver's Door Power Window Inoperative (2-Door)	C
Right Front Power Window Inoperative (4-Door)	D
Right Front Power Window Inoperative (2-Door)	E
Left Rear Power Window Inoperative	F
Right Rear Power Window Inoperative	G
One-Touch Down Feature Inoperative	H
No Scan Tool Communication With GEM	J
All Windows Operate When Ignition Off	1

[1] – Check accessory delay relay. See ACCESSORY DELAY RELAY under COMPONENT TESTS. If okay, repair Light Blue/Black wire. If faulty, replace relay. Retest system operation.

TEST A: ALL POWER WINDOWS INOPERATIVE

NOTE: After all repairs, clear DTCs and retest system.

1) Using NGS tester, observe GEM PID IGN_GEM while turning ignition switch through all positions. If PID IGN_GEM values agree with ignition switch positions, go to next step. If PID IGN_GEM values do not agree with ignition switch positions, check battery saver and accessory delay relays. See ACCESSORY DELAY RELAY and BATTERY SAVER & ONE-TOUCH DOWN RELAYS under COMPONENT TESTS. Check ignition switch and ignition circuits. See STEERING COLUMN SWITCHES – EXPLORER & MOUNTAINEER article. Also see appropriate wiring diagram in POWER DISTRIBUTION article in WIRING DIAGRAMS.

2) Using NGS tester, retrieve and record continuous DTCs. Clear DTCs. Perform GEM On-Demand Self-Test. If no DTCs, or DTCs B1313 or B1315, are retrieved, go to next step. If DTC B1302 or B1304 is retrieved, go to step **4)**. If DTC B1342 is retrieved, replace GEM. See GENERIC ELECTRONIC MODULE (GEM) under REMOVAL & INSTALLATION.

3) Turn ignition switch to RUN position. Using NGS tester, observe GEM PID BATSAV while triggering GEM active command BATT SAVR on and off. If GEM PID BATSAV value agrees with command mode, go to next step. If GEM PID BATSAV value does not agree with command mode and displays OFFO-G or ON-B-, check battery saver relay and circuits. See BATTERY SAVER & ONE-TOUCH DOWN RELAYS under COMPONENT TESTS and WIRING DIAGRAMS.

4) Using NGS tester, observe GEM PID ACCDLY while triggering GEM active command ACCY RLY on and off. If PID ACCDLY value agrees with command mode and vehicle is a 2-door, go to step **11)**. If PID ACCDLY value agrees with command mode and vehicle is a 4-door, go to step **10)**. If PID ACCDLY value does not agree with command mode and displays ON-B-, go to step **8)**. If PID ACCDLY value does not agree with command mode and displays OFFO-G, go to next step.

5) Turn ignition off. Remove accessory delay relay. Measure voltage between accessory delay relay socket terminal No. 86 and ground. *See Fig. 6.* If voltage is more than 10 volts, go to next step. If voltage is 10 volts or less, repair Light Green/Orange wire.

6) Check accessory delay relay. See ACCESSORY DELAY RELAY under COMPONENT TESTS. Replace relay as necessary. If accessory delay relay is okay, go to next step.

7) Disconnect GEM 18-pin connector C283. Measure resistance between accessory delay relay socket terminal No. 85 and GEM connector C283 terminal No. 17. *See Figs. 6 and 7.* If resistance is less than 5 ohms, replace GEM. See GENERIC ELECTRONIC MODULE (GEM) under REMOVAL & INSTALLATION. If resistance is 5 ohms or more, repair open in Light Blue/Red wire.

8) Turn ignition off. Check accessory delay relay. See ACCESSORY DELAY RELAY under COMPONENT TESTS. Replace relay as necessary. If accessory delay relay is okay, go to next step.

9) Disconnect GEM 18-pin connector C283. Turn ignition switch to RUN position. Measure voltage between accessory delay relay socket terminal No. 85 and ground. *See Fig. 6.* If there is any voltage, repair Light Blue/Red wire short to power. If there is no voltage, replace GEM. See GENERIC ELECTRONIC MODULE (GEM) under REMOVAL & INSTALLATION.

10) Turn ignition off. Disconnect driver's door master window/door lock switch 20-pin connector. See POWER WINDOW SWITCH under REMOVAL & INSTALLATION. Turn ignition switch to RUN position. Using NGS tester, trigger ACCY RLY on. Measure voltage between master window/door lock switch connector Light Blue/Black wire terminal and ground. If voltage is more than 10 volts, go to step **14)**. If voltage is 10 volts or less, go to next step.

11) Turn ignition off. Remove maxi-fuse No. 4 (30-amp) from battery junction box. If fuse is okay, go to next step. If fuse is blown, replace fuse and retest system operation. If fuse fails again, repair Red/Light Blue wire short to ground. See WIRING DIAGRAMS.

12) Remove accessory delay relay. Measure voltage between accessory delay relay socket terminal No. 87 and ground. *See Fig. 6.* If voltage is more than 10 volts, go to next step. If voltage is 10 volts or less, repair Red/Light Blue wire.

13) Check accessory delay relay. See ACCESSORY DELAY RELAY under COMPONENT TESTS. Replace relay as necessary. If accessory delay relay is okay, repair Light Blue/Black wire. See WIRING DIAGRAMS.

14) Turn ignition off. Measure resistance of Black wire between master window/door lock switch connector terminal No. 13 and ground. *See Fig. 8.* If resistance is less than 5 ohms, replace master window/door lock switch. If resistance is 5 ohms or more, repair open in Black wire between master window/door lock switch connector and ground. Ground point is behind driver's kick panel. After repair, clear DTCs and retest system.

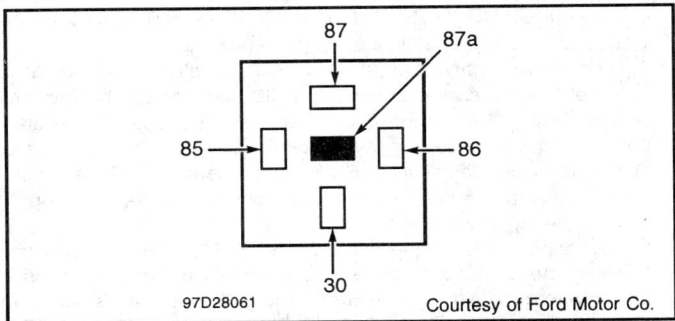

Fig. 6: Identifying Accessory Delay Relay Socket Terminals

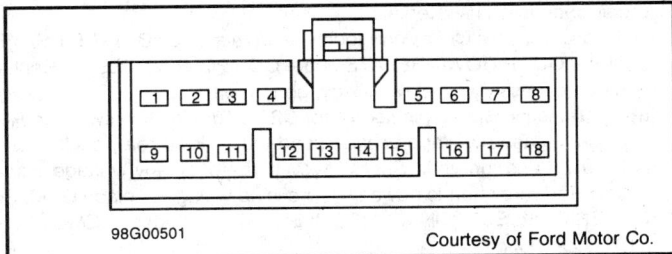

Fig. 7: Identifying GEM 18-Pin Connector C283 Terminals

TEST B: DRIVER'S DOOR POWER WINDOW INOPERATIVE (4-DOOR)

NOTE: After all repairs, clear DTCs and retest system.

1) Using NGS tester, observe GEM PID IGN_GEM while turning ignition switch through all positions. If PID IGN_GEM values agree with ignition switch positions, go to next step. If PID IGN_GEM values do not agree with ignition switch positions, check battery saver and accessory delay relays. See ACCESSORY DELAY RELAY and BATTERY SAVER & ONE-TOUCH DOWN RELAYS under COMPONENT TESTS. Check ignition switch and ignition circuits. See STEERING COLUMN SWITCHES – EXPLORER & MOUNTAINEER article. Also see appropriate wiring diagram in POWER DISTRIBUTION article in WIRING DIAGRAMS.

2) Using NGS tester, retrieve and record continuous DTCs. Clear continuous DTCs. Perform GEM On-Demand Self-Test. If no DTCs are present, go to step **13)**. If DTC B1398 or B1400 is retrieved, go to next step. If DTC B1404 or B1410 is retrieved, go to step **9)**. If DTC B1405 is retrieved, go to step **12)**. If DTC B1342 is retrieved, replace GEM. See GENERIC ELECTRONIC MODULE (GEM) under REMOVAL & INSTALLATION.

3) Turn ignition switch to RUN position. Using NGS tester, trigger GEM active command ACCY RLY on. Observe GEM PID D_PWRLY while

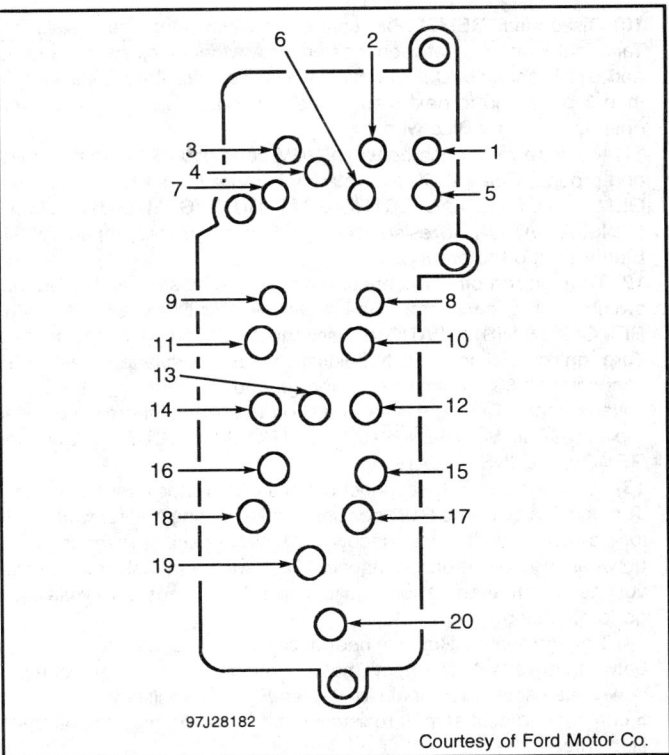

Fig. 8: Identifying Master Window/Door Lock Switch Terminals (4-Door Models)

triggering active command ONE TOUCH on and off. If PID D_PWRLY value agrees with command mode, go to step **9)**. If PID D_PWRLY value does not agree with command mode and displays OFFO-G, go to next step. If PID D_PWRLY value does not agree with command mode and displays ON-B-, go to step **7)**.

4) Turn ignition off. Check one-touch down relay. See BATTERY SAVER & ONE-TOUCH DOWN RELAYS under COMPONENT TESTS. Replace relay as necessary. If one-touch down relay is okay, go to next step.

5) Remove accessory delay relay. Measure resistance between accessory delay relay socket terminal No. 30 and one-touch down relay socket terminal No. 2. *See Figs. 6 and 9.* If resistance is less than 5 ohms, go to next step. If resistance is 5 ohms or more, repair open in appropriate Light Blue/Black wire.

6) Disconnect GEM 18-pin connector C283. Measure resistance between one-touch down relay socket terminal No. 1 and GEM connector C283 terminal No. 7. *See Figs. 7 and 9.* If resistance is less than 5 ohms, replace GEM. See GENERIC ELECTRONIC MODULE (GEM) under REMOVAL & INSTALLATION. If resistance is 5 ohms or more, repair open in Yellow/Red wire.

7) Turn ignition off. Check one-touch down relay. See BATTERY SAVER & ONE-TOUCH DOWN RELAYS under COMPONENT TESTS. Replace relay as necessary. If one-touch down relay is okay, go to next step.

8) Disconnect GEM 18-pin connector C283. Turn ignition switch to RUN position. Measure voltage between one-touch down relay socket terminal No. 1 and ground. *See Fig. 9.* If there is any voltage, repair Yellow/Red wire short to power. If there is no voltage, replace GEM. See GENERIC ELECTRONIC MODULE (GEM) under REMOVAL & INSTALLATION.

9) Turn ignition off. Disconnect driver's door master window/door lock switch 20-pin connector. See POWER WINDOW SWITCH under REMOVAL & INSTALLATION. Connect a jumper wire between master window/door lock switch connector Red/Yellow wire terminal and ground. Connect second jumper wire between Tan/Light Blue wire terminal and battery positive terminal. Turn ignition switch to RUN position. If driver's door window does not go down, remove jumper wires and go to next step. If driver's door window goes down, replace master window/door lock switch.

10) Disconnect GEM 18-pin connector C283. Measure resistance of Tan/Light Blue wire between master window/door lock switch connector and GEM connector C283 terminal No. 3. *See Fig. 7.* If resistance is less than 5 ohms, go to next step. If resistance is 5 ohms or more, repair open in Tan/Light Blue wire.

11) Measure resistance between GEM connector C283 terminal No. 3 and ground. *See Fig. 7.* If resistance is more than 10 k/ohms, replace GEM. See GENERIC ELECTRONIC MODULE (GEM) under REMOVAL & INSTALLATION. If resistance is 10 k/ohms or less, repair Tan/Light Blue wire short to ground.

12) Turn ignition off. Disconnect driver's door master window/door lock switch 20-pin connector. See POWER WINDOW SWITCH under REMOVAL & INSTALLATION. Disconnect GEM 18-pin connector C283. Turn ignition switch to RUN position. Measure voltage between GEM connector C283 terminal No. 3 and ground. *See Fig. 7.* If there is any voltage, repair Tan/Light Blue wire short to power. If there is no voltage, replace GEM. See GENERIC ELECTRONIC MODULE (GEM) under REMOVAL & INSTALLATION.

13) Turn ignition off. Disconnect driver's door window motor connector. Turn ignition switch to RUN position. While holding master window/door lock switch driver's door window in DOWN position, measure voltage between window motor connector Red wire terminal and ground. If voltage is more than 10 volts, go to step **15)**. If voltage is 10 volts or less, go to next step.

14) Turn ignition off. Remove one-touch down relay. Measure resistance between driver's door window motor connector Red wire and one-touch down relay socket terminal No. 3. *See Fig. 9.* If resistance is less than 5 ohms, go to next step. If resistance is 5 ohms or more, repair open in Red wire.

15) Remove one-touch down relay. Disconnect master window/door lock switch 20-pin connector. See POWER WINDOW SWITCH under REMOVAL & INSTALLATION. Measure resistance between master window/door lock switch Tan/Light Blue wire terminal and one-touch down relay socket terminal No. 4. *See Fig. 9.* If resistance is less than 5 ohms, replace one-touch down relay. If resistance is 5 ohms or more, repair open in Tan/Light Blue wire.

16) While holding master window/door lock switch driver's door window in UP position, measure voltage between driver's door window motor connector White/Black wire terminal and ground. If voltage is more than 10 volts, replace driver's door window motor. See POWER WINDOW MOTOR under REMOVAL & INSTALLATION. If voltage is 10 volts or less, repair White/Black wire. After repair, clear DTCs and retest system.

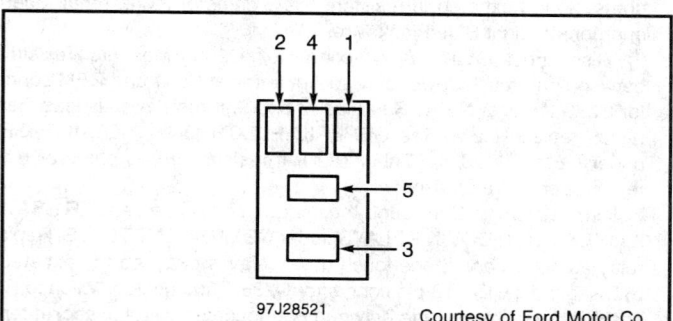

Fig. 9: Identifying Battery Saver & One-Touch Down Relay Socket Terminals

97J28521   Courtesy of Ford Motor Co.

Fig. 9: Identifying Battery Saver & One-Touch Down Relay Socket Terminals

TEST C: DRIVER'S DOOR POWER WINDOW INOPERATIVE (2 DOOR)

NOTE: *After all repairs, clear DTCs and retest system.*

1) Using NGS tester, observe GEM PID IGN_GEM while turning ignition switch through all positions. If PID IGN_GEM values agree with ignition switch positions, go to next step. If PID IGN_GEM values do not agree with ignition switch positions, check battery saver and accessory delay relays. See ACCESSORY DELAY RELAY and BATTERY SAVER & ONE-TOUCH DOWN RELAYS under COMPONENT TESTS. Check

ignition switch and ignition circuits. See STEERING COLUMN SWITCHES – EXPLORER & MOUNTAINEER article. Also see appropriate wiring diagram in POWER DISTRIBUTION article in WIRING DIAGRAMS.

2) Using NGS tester, retrieve and record continuous DTCs. Clear continuous DTCs. Perform GEM On-Demand Self-Test. If no DTCs are present, go to step **13)**. If DTC B1398 or B1400 is retrieved, go to next step. If DTC B1404 or B1410 is retrieved, go to step **9)**. If DTC B1405 is retrieved, go to step **12)**. If DTC B1342 is retrieved, replace GEM. See GENERIC ELECTRONIC MODULE (GEM) under REMOVAL & INSTALLATION. Clear DTCs and retest system.

3) Turn ignition switch to RUN position. Using NGS tester, trigger GEM active command ACCY RLY on. Observe GEM PID D_PWRLY while triggering active command ONE TOUCH on and off. If PID D_PWRLY value agrees with command mode, go to step **9)**. If PID D_PWRLY value does not agree with command mode and displays OFFO-G, go to next step. If PID D_PWRLY value does not agree with command mode and displays ON-B-, go to step **7)**.

4) Turn ignition off. Check one-touch down relay. See BATTERY SAVER & ONE-TOUCH DOWN RELAYS under COMPONENT TESTS. Replace relay as necessary. If relay is okay, go to next step.

5) Remove accessory delay relay. Measure resistance between accessory delay relay socket terminal No. 30 and one-touch down relay socket terminal No. 2. *See Figs. 6 and 9.* Also measure resistance between accessory delay relay socket terminal No. 30 and one-touch down relay socket terminal No. 5. If each resistance is less than 5 ohms, go to next step. If either resistance is 5 ohms or more, repair open in appropriate Light Blue/Black wire(s).

6) Disconnect GEM 18-pin connector C283. Measure resistance between one-touch down relay socket terminal No. 1 and GEM connector C283 terminal No. 7. *See Figs. 7 and 9.* If resistance is less than 5 ohms, replace GEM. See GENERIC ELECTRONIC MODULE (GEM) under REMOVAL & INSTALLATION. If resistance is 5 ohms or more, repair open in Yellow/Red wire.

7) Turn ignition off. Check one-touch down relay. See BATTERY SAVER & ONE-TOUCH DOWN RELAYS under COMPONENT TESTS. Replace relay as necessary. If relay is okay, go to next step.

8) Disconnect GEM 18-pin connector C283. Turn ignition switch to RUN position. Measure voltage between one-touch down relay socket terminal No. 1 and ground. *See Fig. 9.* If there is any voltage, repair Yellow/Red wire short to power. If there is no voltage, replace GEM. See GENERIC ELECTRONIC MODULE (GEM) under REMOVAL & INSTALLATION.

9) Turn ignition off. Disconnect driver's window control switch 14-pin connector. Connect jumper wire between driver's window control switch connector Tan/Light Blue wire terminal and battery positive terminal. Connect second jumper wire between driver's window control switch connector White/Black wire terminal and ground. If window goes down, replace window regulator control switch. Clear DTCs and retest system. If window does not go down, remove jumper wires and go to next step.

10) Disconnect GEM 18-pin connector C283. Measure resistance of Tan/Light Blue wire between driver's window control switch connector and GEM connector C283 terminal No. 3. *See Fig. 7.* If resistance is less than 5 ohms, go to next step. If resistance is 5 ohms or more, repair open in Tan/Light Blue wire.

11) Measure resistance between GEM connector C283 terminal No. 3 and ground. *See Fig. 7.* If resistance is more than 10 k/ohms, replace GEM. See GENERIC ELECTRONIC MODULE (GEM) under REMOVAL & INSTALLATION. If resistance is 10 k/ohms or less, repair Tan/Light Blue short to ground.

12) Turn ignition off. Disconnect driver's window control switch 14-pin connector. Disconnect GEM 18-pin connector C283. Turn ignition switch to RUN position. Measure voltage between GEM connector C283 terminal No. 3 and ground. *See Fig. 7.* If there is any voltage, repair Tan/Light Blue wire short to power. If there is no voltage, replace GEM. See GENERIC ELECTRONIC MODULE (GEM) under REMOVAL & INSTALLATION.

13) Turn ignition off. Disconnect driver's window motor connector. Turn ignition switch to RUN position. While holding driver's window control switch in DOWN position, measure voltage between driver's window motor connector Red wire terminal and ground. If voltage is more than 10 volts, go to step **16)**. If voltage is 10 volts or less, go to next step.

14) Turn ignition off. Remove one-touch down relay. Measure resistance between driver's window motor connector Red wire terminal and one-touch down relay socket terminal No. 3. *See Fig. 9.* If resistance is less than 5 ohms, go to next step. If resistance is 5 ohms or more, repair open in Red wire.

15) Disconnect driver's window control switch 14-pin connector. Measure resistance of Tan/Light Blue wire between driver's window control switch connector and one-touch down relay socket terminal No. 4. *See Fig. 9.* If resistance is less than 5 ohms, replace one-touch down relay. If resistance is 5 ohms or more, repair open in Tan/Light Blue wire.

16) While holding driver's window control switch in UP position, measure voltage between driver's window motor connector White/Black wire terminal and ground. If voltage is more than 10 volts, replace driver's window motor. See POWER WINDOW MOTOR under REMOVAL & INSTALLATION. If voltage is 10 volts or less, repair White/Black wire.

TEST D: RIGHT FRONT POWER WINDOW INOPERATIVE (4-DOOR)

NOTE: After all repairs, clear DTCs and retest system.

1) Turn ignition off. Disconnect right front window switch 7-pin connector. Ensure window lock-out switch on driver's door master window/door lock switch is in OFF position. Turn ignition switch to RUN position. Measure voltage between right front window switch connector Red/Light Blue wire terminal and ground. If voltage is more than 10 volts, go to next step. If voltage is 10 volts or less, go to step **3)**.

2) Turn ignition off. Measure resistance between right front switch connector White/Yellow wire terminal and ground. Also measure resistance between Tan/Light Blue wire terminal and ground. If each resistance is less than 14 ohms, go to step **5)**. If either resistance is 14 ohms or more, go to step **4)**.

3) Turn ignition off. Remove driver's door master window/door lock switch. Ensure window lock switch is in UNLOCK position. Measure resistance between master window/door lock switch terminals No. 19 and 20. *See Fig. 8.* If resistance is 5 ohms or more, replace master window/door lock switch. If resistance is less than 5 ohms, repair appropriate Red/Light Blue wire(s). See WIRING DIAGRAMS.

4) Turn ignition off. Remove master window/door lock switch. Measure resistance of White/Yellow wire between master window/door lock switch connector and right front window switch connector. Also measure resistance of Tan/Light Blue wire between master window/door lock switch connector and right front window switch connector. If each resistance is less than 5 ohms, replace master window/door lock switch. If either resistance is 5 ohms or more, repair appropriate wire(s).

5) Connect jumper wire between right front window switch connector White/Yellow wire and Yellow/Red wire terminals. Connect second jumper between right front window switch connector Red/Light Blue wire and Red/Yellow wire terminals. Turn ignition switch to RUN position. If right front window does not operate in downward direction, remove jumper wires and go to next step. If right front window operates in downward direction, but does not operate with right front window switch, replace right front window switch. If right front window operates in downward direction and operates with right front window switch, but not with master window/door lock switch, replace master window/door lock switch.

6) Turn ignition off. Connect jumper wire between right front window switch connector Red/Yellow wire and Tan/Light Blue wire terminals. Connect second jumper wire between right front window switch connector Yellow/Red wire and Red/Light Blue wire terminals. If right front window does not operate in upward direction, disconnect jumper wires and go to next step. If right front window operates in upward direction, but does not operate with right front window switch, replace right front window switch. If right front window operates in upward direction and operates with right front window switch, but not with master window/door lock switch, replace master window/door lock switch. After repair, clear DTCs and retest system.

7) Turn ignition off. Disconnect window motor connector. Measure resistance of Yellow/Red wire between right front window switch connector and window motor connector. If resistance is less than 5 ohms, go to next step. If resistance is 5 ohms or more, repair open in Yellow/Red wire. Clear DTCs and retest system.

8) Measure resistance of Red/Yellow wire between right front window switch connector and right front window motor connector. If resistance is less than 5 ohms, replace right front window motor. See POWER WINDOW MOTOR under REMOVAL & INSTALLATION. If resistance is 5 ohms or more, repair open in Red/Yellow wire.

TEST E: RIGHT FRONT POWER WINDOW INOPERATIVE (2-DOOR)

NOTE: After all repairs, clear DTCs and retest system.

1) Turn ignition off. Disconnect right front window switch 7-pin connector. See POWER WINDOW SWITCH under REMOVAL & INSTALLATION. Turn ignition switch to RUN position. Measure voltage between right front window switch connector Light Blue/Black wire terminal and ground. If voltage is more than 10 volts, go to next step. If voltage is 10 volts or less, repair Light Blue/Black wire. See WIRING DIAGRAMS.

2) Turn ignition off. Measure resistance between right front switch connector White/Yellow wire terminal and ground. Also measure resistance between Tan/Light Blue wire terminal and ground. If each resistance is less than 14 ohms, go to step **4)**. If either resistance is 14 ohms or more, go to next step.

3) Disconnect driver's window control switch 14-pin connector. Measure resistance of White/Yellow wire between driver's window control switch connector and right front window switch connector. Also measure resistance of Tan/Light Blue wire between driver's window control switch connector and right front window switch connector. If each resistance is less than 5 ohms, replace right front window switch. If either resistance is 5 ohms or more, repair open in appropriate wire(s).

4) Connect jumper wire between right front window switch connector White/Yellow wire and Yellow/Red wire terminals. Connect second jumper wire between right front window switch connector Light Blue/Black wire and Red/Yellow wire terminals. Turn ignition switch to RUN position. If right front window does not operate in downward direction, remove jumper wires and go to next step. If right front window operates in downward direction and does not operate with right front window switch, replace right front window switch. If right front window operates in downward direction and operates with right front window switch, but not with driver's window control switch, replace driver's window control switch.

5) Turn ignition off. Connect jumper wire between right front window switch connector Red/Yellow wire and Tan/Light Blue wire terminals. Connect second jumper wire between right front window switch connector Yellow/Red wire and Light Blue/Black wire terminals. Turn ignition switch to RUN position. If right front window does not operate in upward direction, remove jumper wires and go to next step. If right front window operates in upward direction, but does not operate from right front window switch, replace right front window switch. If right front window operates in upward direction and operates from right front window switch, but not driver's window control switch, replace driver's window control switch.

6) Turn ignition off. Disconnect right front window motor connector. Measure resistance of Yellow/Red wire between right front window motor connector and right front window switch connector. If resistance is less than 5 ohms, go to next step. If resistance is 5 ohms or more, repair open in Yellow/Red wire.

7) Measure resistance of Red/Yellow wire between right front window motor connector and right front window switch connector. If resistance is less than 5 ohms, replace right front window motor. See POWER WINDOW MOTOR under REMOVAL & INSTALLATION. If resistance is 5 ohms or more, repair open in Red/Yellow wire.

TEST F: LEFT REAR POWER WINDOW INOPERATIVE

NOTE: After all repairs, clear DTCs and retest system.

1) Turn ignition off. Disconnect left rear window switch 7-pin connector. See POWER WINDOW SWITCH under REMOVAL & INSTALLATION. Ensure window lock-out switch on driver's door master window/door lock switch is in OFF position. Turn ignition switch to RUN position. Measure voltage between left rear window switch connector Red/Light Blue wire terminal and ground. If voltage is more than 10 volts, go to next step. If voltage is 10 volts or less, go to step **3**).

2) Turn ignition off. Measure resistance between left rear window switch connector Gray/Orange wire terminal and ground. Also measure resistance between Yellow/Light Blue wire terminal and ground. If each resistance is less than 5 ohms, go to step **6**). If either resistance is 5 ohms or more, go to step **4**).

3) Disconnect driver's door master window/door lock switch 20-pin connector. Measure resistance between master window/door lock switch terminals No. 19 and 20. *See Fig. 8.* If resistance is 5 ohms or more, replace master window/door lock switch. If resistance is less than 5 ohms, repair Red/Light Blue wire. See WIRING DIAGRAMS.

4) Disconnect driver's door master window/door lock switch 20-pin connector. Measure resistance of Yellow/Light Blue wire between master window/door lock switch connector and left rear window switch connector. If resistance is less than 5 ohms, go to next step. If resistance is 5 ohms or more, repair open in Yellow/Light Blue wire.

5) Measure resistance of Gray/Orange wire between master window/door lock switch connector and left rear window switch connector. If resistance is less than 5 ohms, replace master window/door lock switch. If resistance is 5 ohms or more, repair open in Gray/Orange wire.

6) Connect jumper wire between left rear window switch connector Gray/Orange wire and Yellow/Black wire terminals. Connect second jumper wire between left rear window switch connector Yellow/Light Blue wire and Red/Light Blue wire terminals. Turn ignition switch to RUN position. If left rear window does not operate in downward direction, remove jumper wires and go to next step. If left rear window operates in downward direction, but does not operate with left rear window switch, replace left rear window switch. If left rear window operates in downward direction and operates with left rear window switch, but does not operate with master window/door lock switch, replace master window/door lock switch.

7) Turn ignition off. Connect jumper wire between left rear window switch connector Yellow/Light Blue wire terminals. Connect second jumper wire between left rear window switch connector Red/Light blue wire and Yellow/Black wire terminals. If window does not operate in upward direction, remove jumper wires and go to next step. If window operates in upward direction, but does not operate from left rear window switch, replace left rear window switch. If window operates in upward direction and operates from left rear window switch, but does not operate from master window/door lock switch, replace master window/door lock switch.

8) Turn ignition off. Disconnect left rear window motor connector. Measure resistance of Yellow/Black wire between left rear switch connector and window motor connector. If resistance is less than 5 ohms, go to next step. If resistance is 5 ohms or more, repair open in Yellow/Black wire.

9) Measure resistance of Yellow/Light Blue wire between left rear window switch connector and window motor connector. If resistance is less than 5 ohms, replace window motor. See POWER WINDOW MOTOR under REMOVAL & INSTALLATION. If resistance is 5 ohms or more, repair open in Yellow/Light Blue wire.

TEST G: RIGHT REAR POWER WINDOW INOPERATIVE

NOTE: After all repairs, clear DTCs and retest system.

1) Turn ignition off. Disconnect right rear window switch 7-pin connector. Ensure window lock-out switch on driver's door master window/door lock switch is in OFF position. Turn ignition switch to RUN position. Measure voltage between right rear window switch connector Red/Light Blue wire terminal and ground. If voltage is more than 10 volts, go to next step. If voltage is 10 volts or less, go to step **3**).

2) Turn ignition off. Measure resistance between right rear window switch connector Red/Black wire terminal and ground. Also measure resistance between Yellow/Black wire terminal and ground. If each resistance is less than 5 ohms, go to step **6**). If either resistance is 5 ohms or more, go to step **4**).

3) Disconnect master window/door lock switch 20-pin connector. Measure resistance between master window/door lock switch terminals No. 19 and 20. *See Fig. 8.* If resistance is 5 ohms or more, replace master window/door lock switch. If resistance is less than 5 ohms, repair Red/Light Blue wire(s). See WIRING DIAGRAMS.

4) Turn ignition off. Disconnect master window/door lock switch 20-pin connector. Measure resistance of Yellow/Black wire between master window/door lock switch connector and right rear window switch connector. If resistance is less than 5 ohms, go to next step. If resistance is 5 ohms or more, repair open in Yellow/Black wire.

5) Measure resistance of Red/Black wire between master window/door lock switch connector and right rear window switch connector. If resistance is less than 5 ohms, replace master window/door lock switch. If resistance is 5 ohms or more, repair open in Red/Black wire.

6) Connect jumper wire between right rear window switch connector Yellow/Black wire and Brown wire terminals. Connect second jumper wire between right rear window switch connector Red/Light Blue wire and Brown/Yellow wire terminals. If window does not operate in downward direction, remove jumper wires and go to next step. If window operates in downward direction, but does not operate from right rear window switch, replace right rear window switch. If window operates in downward direction and operates from right rear window switch, but does not operate from master window/door lock switch, replace master window/door lock switch.

7) Turn ignition off. Connect jumper wire between right rear window switch connector Brown/Yellow wire and Red/Black wire terminals. Connect second jumper wire between right rear window switch connector Brown wire and Red/Light Blue wire terminals. If window does not operate in upward direction, remove jumper wires and go to next step. If window operates in upward direction, but does not operate with right rear window switch, replace right rear window switch. If window operates in upward direction and operates with right rear window switch, but not with master window/door lock switch, replace master window/door lock switch.

8) Turn ignition off. Disconnect right rear window motor connector. Measure resistance of Brown wire between right rear window switch connector and right rear window motor connector. If resistance is less than 5 ohms, go to next step. If resistance is 5 ohms or more, repair open in Brown wire.

9) Measure resistance of Brown/Yellow wire between right rear window switch connector and right rear window motor connector. If resistance is less than 5 ohms, replace right rear window motor. If resistance is 5 ohms or more, repair open in Brown/Yellow wire.

TEST H: ONE-TOUCH DOWN FEATURE INOPERATIVE

NOTE: After all repairs, clear DTCs and retest system.

1) Using NGS tester, observe GEM PID IGN_GEM while turning ignition switch through all positions. If PID IGN_GEM values agree with ignition switch positions, go to next step. If PID IGN_GEM values do not agree with ignition switch positions, check battery saver and accessory delay relays. See ACCESSORY DELAY RELAY and BATTERY SAVER & ONE-TOUCH DOWN RELAYS under COMPONENT TESTS. Check ignition switch and ignition circuits. See STEERING COLUMN SWITCHES – EXPLORER & MOUNTAINEER article. Also see appropriate wiring diagram in POWER DISTRIBUTION article in WIRING DIAGRAMS.

2) Using NGS tester, retrieve and record continuous DTCs. Clear continuous DTCs. Perform GEM On-Demand Self-Test. If no DTCs, or

DTCs B1398 or B1400, are retrieved, go to next step. If DTC B1342 is retrieved, replace GEM. See GENERIC ELECTRONIC MODULE (GEM) under REMOVAL & INSTALLATION.

3) Turn ignition switch to RUN position. Using NGS tester, trigger GEM active command ACCY RLY on. Observe GEM PID D_PWRLY while triggering active command ONE TOUCH on and off. If PID D_PWRLY value agrees with command mode, go to step **9)**. If PID D_PWRLY value does not agree with command mode and displays OFFO-G, go to next step. If PID D_PWRLY value does not agree with command mode and displays ON-B-, go to step **7)**.

4) Turn ignition off. Check one-touch down relay. See BATTERY SAVER & ONE-TOUCH DOWN RELAYS under COMPONENT TESTS. Replace relay as necessary. If relay is okay, go to next step.

5) Remove accessory delay relay. Measure resistance between one-touch down relay socket terminal No. 2 and accessory delay relay socket terminal No. 30. *See Figs. 6 and 9.* If resistance is less than 5 ohms, go to next step. If resistance is 5 ohms or more, repair open in Light Blue/Black wire.

6) Disconnect GEM 18-pin connector C283. Measure resistance between one-touch down relay socket terminal No. 1 and GEM connector C283 terminal No. 7. *See Figs. 7 and 9.* If resistance is less than 5 ohms, replace GEM. See GENERIC ELECTRONIC MODULE (GEM) under REMOVAL & INSTALLATION. If resistance is 5 ohms or more, repair open in Yellow/Red wire.

7) Turn ignition off. Check one-touch down relay. See BATTERY SAVER & ONE-TOUCH DOWN RELAYS under COMPONENT TESTS. Replace relay as necessary. If relay is okay, go to next step.

8) Disconnect GEM 18-pin connector C283. Turn ignition switch to RUN position. Measure voltage between one-touch down relay socket terminal No. 1 and ground. *See Fig. 9.* If there is any voltage, repair Yellow/Red wire short to power. If there is no voltage, replace GEM. See GENERIC ELECTRONIC MODULE (GEM) under REMOVAL & INSTALLATION.

9) Turn ignition off. Check one-touch down relay. See BATTERY SAVER & ONE-TOUCH DOWN RELAYS under COMPONENT TESTS. Replace relay as necessary. If relay is okay, go to next step.

10) Turn ignition switch to RUN position. Measure voltage between one-touch down relay socket terminal No. 5 and ground. Also measure resistance between one-touch down relay socket terminal No. 2 and ground. *See Fig. 9.* If each voltage is more than 10 volts, go to next step. If either voltage is 10 volts or less, repair appropriate Light Blue/Black wire(s). See WIRING DIAGRAMS.

11) Turn ignition off. Disconnect GEM 18-pin connector C283. Measure resistance between left front window motor connector Red wire terminal and GEM connector C283 terminal No. 10 (Gray wire). *See Fig. 7.* If resistance is less than 5 ohms, go to next step. If resistance is 5 ohms or more, repair open in Gray wire.

12) Measure resistance between left front window motor connector Red wire terminal and GEM connector C283 terminal No. 2. *See Fig. 7.* If resistance is less than 5 ohms, replace GEM. See GENERIC ELECTRONIC MODULE (GEM) under REMOVAL & INSTALLATION. If resistance is 5 ohms or more, repair open in Orange/White wire.

TEST J: NO SCAN TOOL COMMUNICATION WITH GEM

NOTE: After all repairs, clear DTCs and retest system.

1) Check battery junction box maxi-fuse No. 1 (50-amp). If fuse is okay, go to next step. If fuse is not okay, replace fuse. Clear DTCs and retest system. If fuse fails again, check Tan/Black wire between battery junction box and fuse junction panel for short to ground. Repair circuit as necessary.

2) Check fuse junction panel fuse No. 25 (7.5-amp). If fuse is okay, go to next step. If fuse is not okay, replace fuse. Clear DTCs and retest system operation. If fuse fails again, check White/Yellow wire between fuse junction panel and GEM for short to ground. Repair circuit as necessary.

3) Measure voltage between fuse junction panel fuse No. 25 (7.5-amp) fuse holder (input side) and ground. If voltage is more than 10 volts, go to next step. If voltage is 10 volts or less, repair Tan/Black wire. See appropriate wiring diagram in POWER DISTRIBUTION article in WIRING DIAGRAMS.

4) Turn ignition off. Disconnect GEM 18-pin connector C283. Measure voltage between GEM connector C283 terminal No. 11 and ground. *See Fig. 7.* If voltage is more than 10 volts, go to next step. If voltage is 10 volts or less, repair White/Yellow wire between fuse junction panel and GEM.

5) Disconnect GEM 26-pin connector C280. Measure resistance between GEM connector C280 terminal No. 14 and ground. *See Fig. 10.* Also measure resistance between terminal No. 26 and ground. If each resistance is less than 5 ohms, go to next step. If either resistance is 5 ohms or more, repair open in appropriate Black/White wire(s) between GEM connector C280 and ground. Ground point is located left front engine compartment near radiator.

6) Measure resistance between GEM 18-pin connector C283 terminal No. 18 and ground. *See Fig. 7.* If resistance is less than 5 ohms, problem is in module communications network. See MODULE COMMUNICATIONS NETWORK – EXPLORER & MOUNTAINEER article. If resistance is 5 ohms or more, repair open in Black wire.

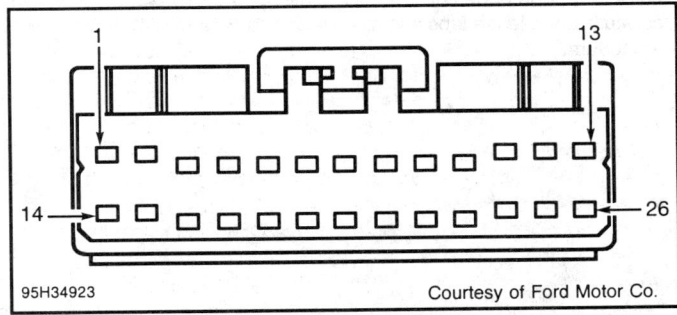

95H34923   Courtesy of Ford Motor Co.

Fig. 10: Identifying GEM 26-Pin Connector C280 Terminals

REMOVAL & INSTALLATION

GENERIC ELECTRONIC MODULE (GEM)

CAUTION: Disconnect negative battery cable before disconnecting GEM. Failure to do so will result in GEM storing erroneous codes and may also result in erratic operation of GEM after reconnection. When battery is disconnected, vehicle computer and memory systems may lose memory data. Driveability problems may exist until computer systems have completed a relearn cycle. See COMPUTER RELEARN PROCEDURES article in GENERAL INFORMATION before disconnecting battery.

CAUTION: If replacing GEM, it is necessary to upload module configuration information to New Generation STAR (NGS) tester. After installation, download saved module configuration information to new GEM.

Removal & Installation – Disconnect negative battery cable. Insert radio removing tool into radio face plate and release retaining clips. Pull outward on tool to remove radio from instrument panel. Remove 2 screws and remove center instrument panel finish panel. Remove GEM. To install, reverse removal procedure.

POWER WINDOW MOTOR

Removal & Installation (Front) – 1) Lower glass to full down position. Remove door trim panel. Raise glass to full up position and support glass. Disconnect negative battery cable. Disconnect inside front door handle and rod. Disconnect window motor connector. If equipped, remove equalizer bracket nuts.

2) Drill out 3 rivets holding regulator/motor assembly. Remove nut and remove regulator/motor assembly. Ensure regulator arm is in fixed position to prevent counterbalance spring from unwinding. Remove motor from regulator/motor assembly. To install, reverse procedure. Cycle window to ensure engagement of drive mechanism.

Removal & Installation (Rear) – 1) Lower glass to full down position. Remove rear door trim panel. Remove rear inside door handle. Remove speaker and watershield. Raise and support glass in full up position. Disconnect negative battery cable. Disconnect window motor electrical connector.

2) Drill out 3 window regulator rivets. Slide regulator arms off window glass track and remove regulator/motor assembly. Ensure regulator arm is in fixed position to prevent counterbalance spring from unwinding. Remove motor from regulator/motor assembly. To install, reverse procedure. Cycle window to ensure engagement of drive mechanism.

POWER WINDOW SWITCH

Removal & Installation (Front) – Disconnect negative battery cable. Remove door trim panel. Remove 4 screws holding wiring connector to switch plate. Using thin-blade screwdriver, carefully pry connector from switch. Remove window switch by carefully prying on release tabs. To install, reverse removal procedure.

Removal & Installation (Rear) – Disconnect negative battery cable. Remove 2 screws securing switch plate to door trim. Remove screws holding wiring connector to switch plate. Using thin-blade screwdriver, carefully pry release tabs and remove switch. To install, reverse removal procedure.

WIRING DIAGRAMS

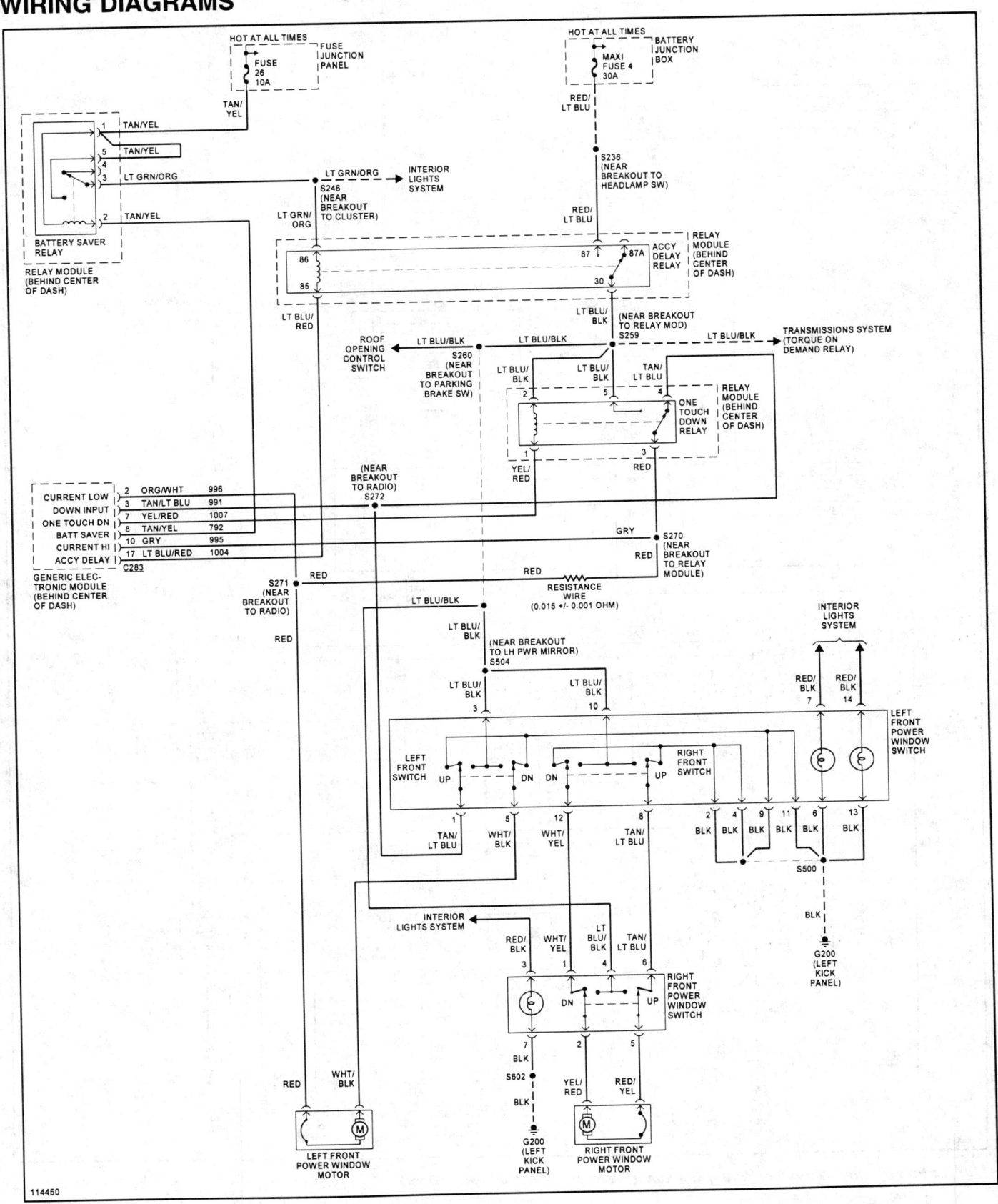

Fig. 11: Power Window System Wiring Diagram (Explorer 2-Door)

114450

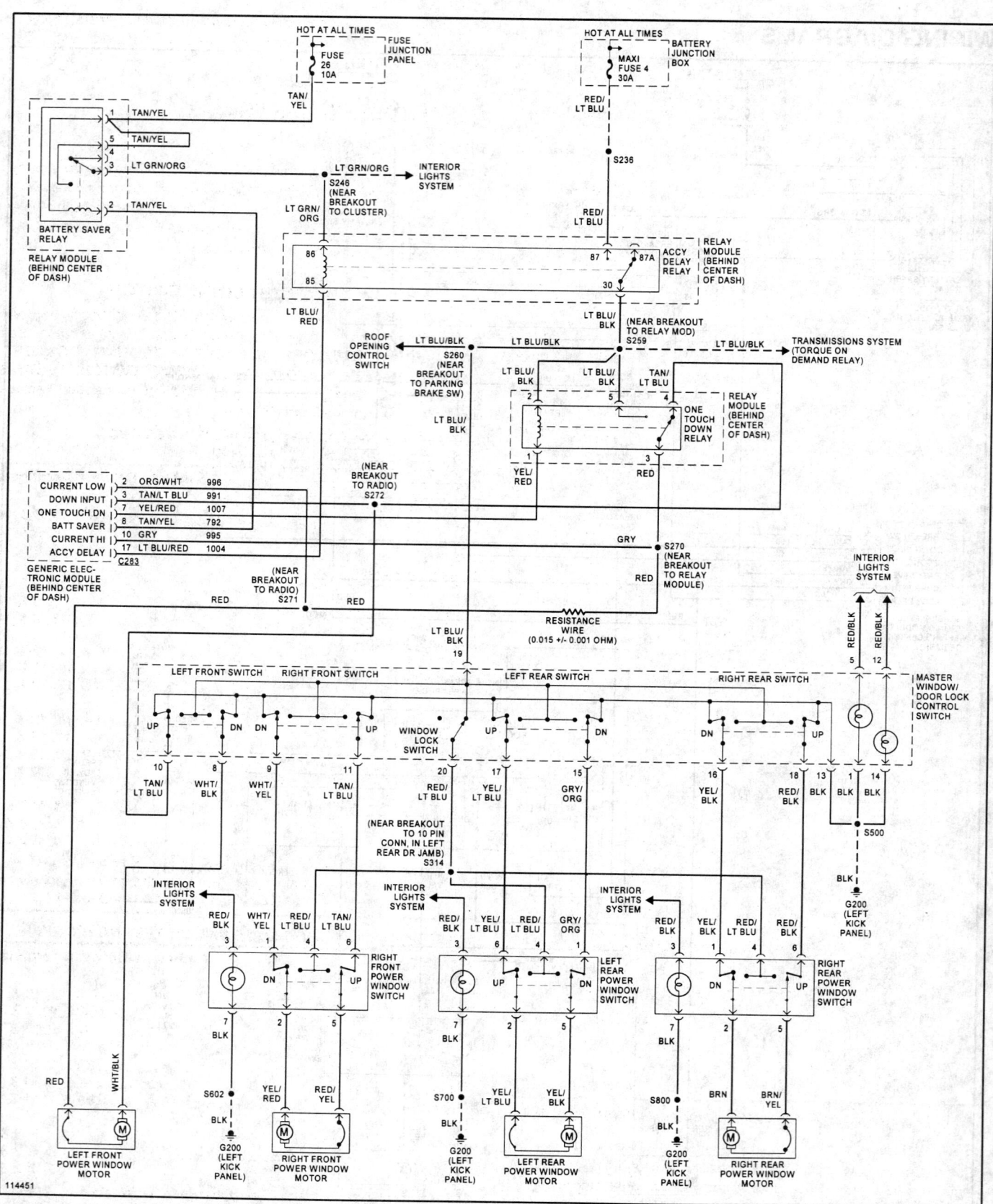

Fig. 12: Power Window System Wiring Diagram (Explorer & Mountaineer 4-Door)

DESCRIPTION & OPERATION

Power windows are operated by reversible type motors mounted with each individual window regulator. Passenger's door window have individual switches for separate control. A master control switch, which controls all windows, is located on left front door. Driver door window is equipped with a one-touch down feature which will lower driver door window to full down position by briefly touching driver door window switch in down position.

On convertible models, a lock-out switch is incorporated in master switch. When actuated, it prevents window operation from individual switches. Windows will only operate when ignition switch is in ON or ACC position.

COMPONENT LOCATIONS

COMPONENT LOCATIONS

Component	Locations
Generic Electronic Module	Behind Left Side Of Instrument Panel, Left Of Steering Column

ADJUSTMENTS

DOOR WINDOW HEIGHT STOP ADJUSTMENT

Close door. Loosen door window stop bracket nuts. Raise door window glass to necessary height. Tighten door window stop bracket nuts to 89-124 INCH lbs. (10-14 N.m).

REAR QUARTER GLASS (CONVERTIBLE)

Rear quarter glass has 6 adjustment points. Adjustments that can be made are: fore/aft adjustment, regulator plate tilt, glass-to-regulator tilt, front high/low up stop, rear high/low/tilt channel stop, and inboard/outboard tip. Refer to illustration for proper adjustment points. *See Fig. 1.*

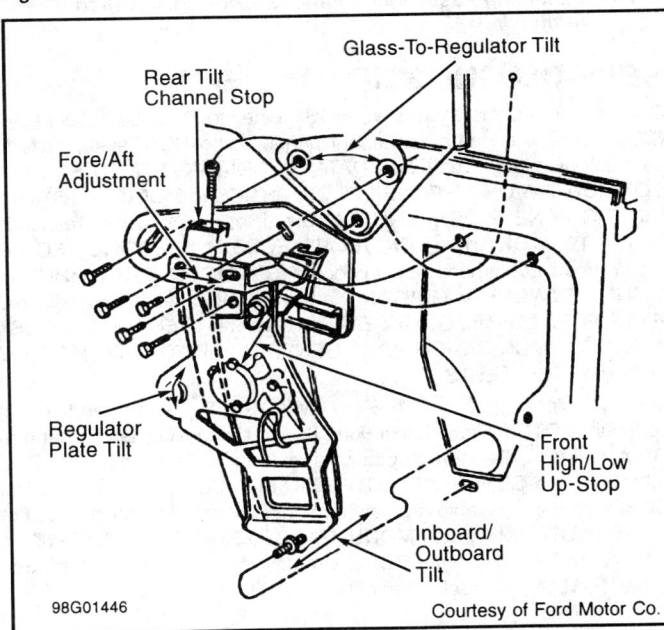

Fig. 1: Rear Quarter Window Glass Adjusting Points (Convertible)

STABILIZER

Raise door window glass to full up position. Loosen door window glass inner stabilizer nuts. Push door window glass inner stabilizers firmly against door window glass and tighten nuts to 89-124 INCH lbs. (10-14 N.m).

TROUBLE SHOOTING

Verify customer concern by operating power window system. Check for, blown fuses, damaged/corroded connectors, damaged switches, damaged motors and binding window regulator. If problem exists, repair as necessary. If problem does not exist, perform self-diagnostics. See SELF-DIAGNOSTIC SYSTEM.

COMPONENT TESTS

WINDOW MOTOR

Disconnect window motor harness connector for inoperative window. Using fused jumper wires, connect battery power and ground to window motor harness connector terminals. To reverse motor direction, reverse polarity of jumper wires. Motor should operate rapidly and smoothly in both directions. Replace motor if necessary.

MASTER WINDOW/DOOR LOCK SWITCH

Remove master window/door lock switch. Check continuity between appropriate switch terminals with switch in appropriate position. See MASTER WINDOW/DOOR LOCK SWITCH TESTING (CONVERTIBLE) or MASTER WINDOW/DOOR LOCK SWITCH TESTING (COUPE) table. *See Fig. 2 or 3.* If continuity is not as specified, replace master window/door lock switch.

MASTER WINDOW/DOOR LOCK SWITCH TESTING (CONVERTIBLE)

Switch Position	[1] Continuity Between Terminals
Driver's Window	
Down	6 & 15; 8 & 14
Neutral	6, 8 & 14
Up	8 & 15; 6 & 14
Passenger's Window	
Down	7 & 14; 9 & 15
Neutral	7, 9 & 14
Up	7 & 15; 9 & 14
Left Rear Window	
Down	10 & 14; 12 & 15
Neutral	10, 12 & 14
Up	10 & 15; 12 & 14
Right Rear Window	
Down	11 & 14; 13 & 15
Neutral	11, 13 & 14
Up	11 & 15; 13 & 14
Window Lock-Out Switch Locked	15 & 16
Door Lock Switch	
Lock	2 & 5; 3 & 4
Neutral	[2] 1 & 4; 2 & 5
Unlock	1 & 4; 2 & 3

[1] – Continuity should never exist between terminals No. 14 and 15.
[2] – With door lock switches at rest, continuity should not exist between terminals No. 2 and 3 or between terminals No. 3 and 4.

MASTER WINDOW/DOOR LOCK SWITCH TESTING (COUPE)

Switch Position	[1] Continuity Between Terminals
Driver's Window	
Down	6 & 12; 10 & 13
Neutral	6 & 12; 7 & 13
Up	6 & 10; 7 & 13
Passenger's Window	
Down	8 & 11; 14 & 15
Neutral	8 & 9; 14 & 15
Up	8 & 9; 11 & 15
Door Lock Switch	
Lock	2 & 5; 3 & 4
Neutral	[2] 1 & 4; 2 & 5
Unlock	1 & 4; 2 & 3

[1] – Continuity should never exist between terminals No. 9 and 11, between terminals No. 11 and 14, between terminals No. 7 and 10 or between terminals No. 10 and 12.
[2] – With door lock switches at rest, continuity should not exist between terminals No. 2 and 3 or between terminals No. 3 and 4.

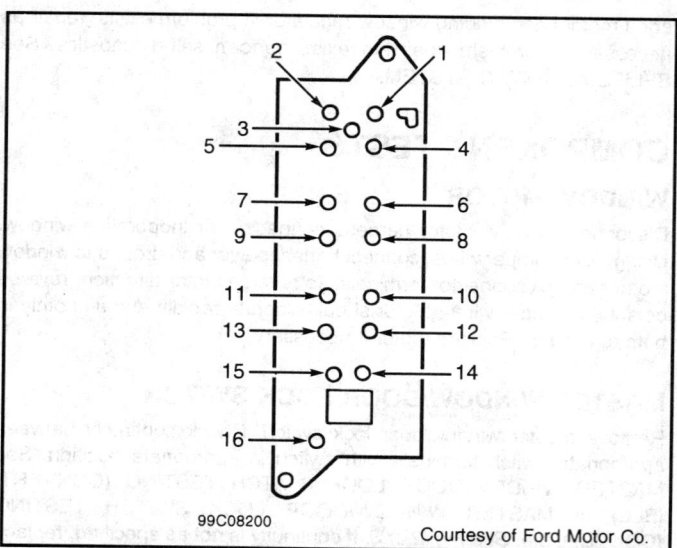

Fig. 2: Identifying Master Window/Door Lock Switch Terminals (Convertible)

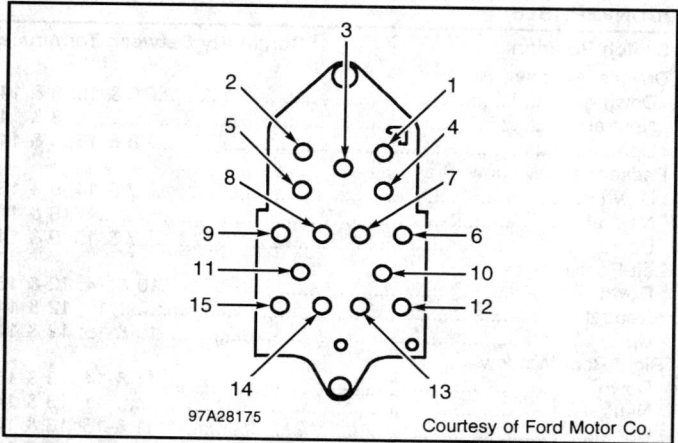

Fig. 3: Identifying Master Window/Door Lock Switch Terminals (Coupe)

PASSENGER'S WINDOW/DOOR LOCK SWITCH

Remove passenger's window/door lock switch. Check continuity between appropriate switch terminals with switch in appropriate position. See PASSENGER'S WINDOW/DOOR LOCK SWITCH TESTING table. See Fig. 4. If continuity is not as specified, replace passenger's window/door lock switch.

PASSENGER'S WINDOW/DOOR LOCK SWITCH TESTING

Switch Position	[1] Continuity Between Terminals
Window	
Down	6 & 8; 7 & 10
Neutral	6 & 9; 7 & 10
Up	6 & 9; 8 & 10

PASSENGER'S WINDOW/DOOR LOCK SWITCH TESTING (Cont.)

Switch Position	[1] Continuity Between Terminals
Lock	2 & 3; 4 & 5
Neutral	[2] 1 & 2; 4 & 5
Unlock	1 & 2; 3 & 4

[1] – Continuity should never exist between terminals No. 7 and 8 or between 8 and 9.

[2] – With door lock switches at rest, continuity should not exist between terminals No. 1 and 3 or between terminals No. 3 and 5.

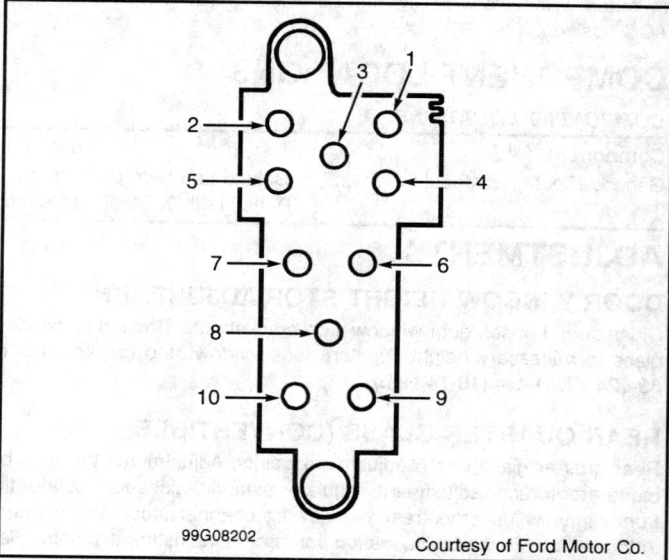

Fig. 4: Identifying Passenger's Window/Door Lock Switch Terminals

SELF-DIAGNOSTIC SYSTEM

Connect New Generation Star (NGS) tester to Data Link Connector (DLC), located beneath instrument panel. Using NGS tester, perform data link diagnostics test. See DATA LINK DIAGNOSTIC TEST under COMMUNICATION NETWORK DIAGNOSTICS in MODULE COMMUNICATIONS NETWORK – MUSTANG article. If NGS tester responds with CKT914, CKT915 or CKT70=ALL ECUS NO RESP/NOT EQUIP, repair module communications concern. See MODULE COMMUNICATIONS NETWORK – MUSTANG article. If NGS tester displays NO RESP/NOT EQUIP for Generic Electronic Module (GEM), perform TEST A: NO COMMUNICATION WITH GENERIC ELECTRONIC MODULE under SYSTEM TESTS.

If NGS tester responds with SYSTEM PASSED, retrieve and record continuous DTCs. Erase continuous DTCs. Using NGS tester, perform GEM self-test. Perform appropriate test in accordance with DTC retrieved. See GENERIC ELECTRONIC MODULE DTC INDEX table. Codes listed in this table are only for testing covered in this article. For complete DTC listing, see MODULE COMMUNICATIONS NETWORK – MUSTANG article. If no DTCs are retrieved, repair by symptom. See SYMPTOM CHART table under SYSTEM TESTS.

GENERIC ELECTRONIC MODULE DTC INDEX

DTC	Description	Test
B1342	ECU Defective	1
B1405	Driver's Window Down Circuit Short To Voltage	2
B1408	Driver's Window Up Circuit Short To Voltage	2
B1410	Driver's Window Motor Circuit Failure	2

[1] – Using NGS tester, retrieve and document all continuous. Perform Generic Electronic Module (GEM) self-test. If DTC B1342 is retrieved again, replace GEM.

[2] – Perform TEST D: DRIVER'S POWER WINDOW INOPERATIVE (CONVERTIBLE) on convertible or TEST E: DRIVER'S POWER WINDOW INOPERATIVE (COUPE) on coupe.

SYSTEM TESTS

SYMPTOM CHART

Symptom	Test
No Communication With Generic Electronic Module	A
Power Windows Completely Inoperative (Convertible)	B
Power Windows Completely Inoperative (Coupe)	C
Driver's Power Window Inoperative (Convertible)	D
Driver's Power Window Inoperative (Coupe)	E
Passenger's Power Window Inoperative	F
Rear Power Window Inoperative (Convertible)	G
One-Touch Down Feature Inoperative	[1]

[1] – Perform TEST D: DRIVER'S POWER WINDOW INOPERATIVE (CONVERTIBLE) on convertible or TEST E: DRIVER'S POWER WINDOW INOPERATIVE (COUPE) on coupe.

TEST A: NO COMMUNICATION WITH GENERIC ELECTRONIC MODULE

NOTE: Before proceeding with this test ensure voltage exists at input side of fuse No. 39 (5-amp) in central junction box. Repair as necessary.

1) Turn ignition switch to LOCK position. Disconnect Generic Electronic Module (GEM) harness connector C291. Measure voltage at terminal No. 2 (White/Yellow wire) at GEM harness connector C291. *See Fig. 5.* If battery voltage exists, go to next step. If battery voltage does not exist, go to step **3)**.

2) Measure resistance between ground and terminal No. 4 (Black/White wire) at GEM harness connector C291. If resistance is 5 ohms or less, go to step **4)**. If resistance is greater than 5 ohms, repair open in Black/White wire.

3) Remove fuse No. 39 (5-amp) from central junction box. Measure resistance in White/Yellow wire between terminal No. 2 at GEM harness connector C291 and output side of fuse No. 39. If resistance is 5 ohms or less, repair central junction box as necessary. If resistance is greater than 5 ohms, repair open in White/Yellow wire.

4) Measure voltage at terminal No. 4 (Black/White wire) at GEM harness connector C291. If any voltage exists, repair short to voltage in Black/White wire. If no voltage exists, repair module communication concern. See MODULE COMMUNICATIONS NETWORK – MUSTANG article.

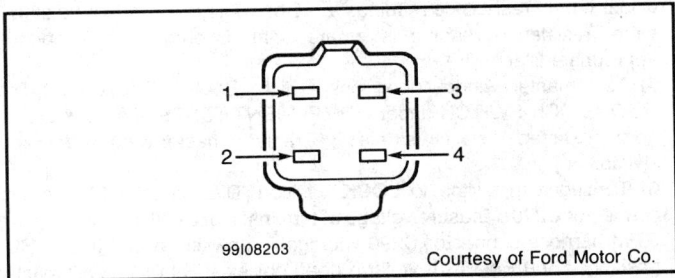

Fig. 5: Identifying GEM Harness Connector C290 & C291 Terminals

TEST B: POWER WINDOWS COMPLETELY INOPERATIVE (CONVERTIBLE)

1) Disconnect master window/door lock switch harness connector C505. Turn ignition switch to RUN position. Measure voltage at terminal No. 15 (Light Blue/Black wire) at master window/door lock switch harness connector C505. *See Fig. 6.* If battery voltage exists, go to next step. If battery voltage does not exist, repair power distribution circuit. See WIRING DIAGRAMS.

2) Turn ignition switch to LOCK position. Measure resistance between ground and terminal No. 14 (Black wire) at master window/door lock switch harness connector C505. If resistance is 5 ohms or less, replace master window/door lock switch. If resistance is greater than 5 ohms, repair open in Black wire.

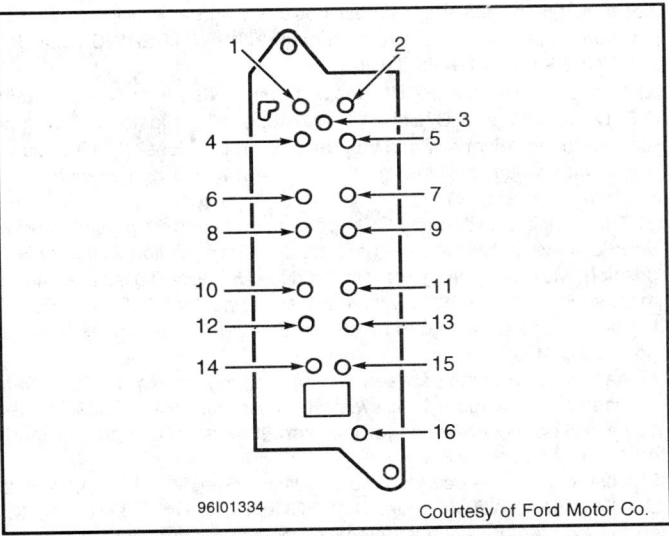

Fig. 6: Identifying Master Window/Door Lock Switch Harness Connector C505 Terminals (Convertible)

TEST C: POWER WINDOWS COMPLETELY INOPERATIVE (COUPE)

1) Disconnect master window/door lock switch harness connector C502. Turn ignition switch to RUN position. Measure voltage at terminal No. 10 (Light Blue/Black wire) at master window/door lock switch harness connector C502. *See Fig. 7.* If battery voltage exists, go to next step. If battery voltage does not exist, repair power distribution circuit. See WIRING DIAGRAMS.

2) Turn ignition switch to LOCK position. Measure resistance between ground and terminals No. 7, 9, 12 and 14 (all Black wires) at master window/door lock switch harness connector C502. If all resistance readings are 5 ohms or less, replace master window/door lock switch. If any resistance reading is greater than 5 ohms, repair open in Black wire.

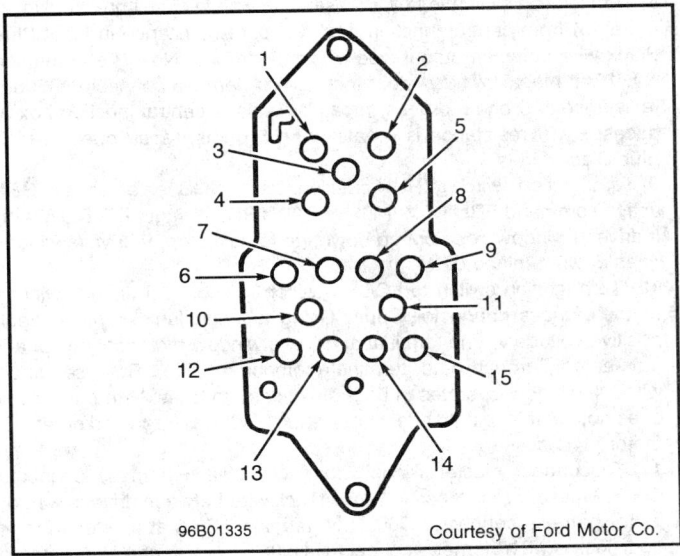

Fig. 7: Identifying Master Window/Door Lock Switch Harness Connector C502 Terminals (Sedan)

TEST D: DRIVER'S POWER WINDOW INOPERATIVE (CONVERTIBLE)

1) Connect New Generation Star (NGS) tester to Data Link Connector (DLC). Using NGS tester, monitor Generic Electronic Module (GEM) PID IGN_A, IGN_R, IGN_S and IGN_KEY. Insert key into ignition switch and turn ignition switch to each position. If PID agrees with ignition switch position, go to next step. If PID does not agree with ignition switch position, repair ignition switch concern. See STEERING COLUMN SWITCHES – MUSTANG article.

2) Turn ignition switch to RUN position. Using NGS tester, monitor GEM PID D_UP_SW and D_DN_SW while operating master window/door lock switch to driver's window up and down positions. If PID does not agree with switch position, go to next step. If PID agrees with switch position, go to step **9**).

3) Turn ignition switch to LOCK position. Disconnect master window/door lock switch harness connector C505. Turn ignition switch to RUN position. Measure voltage at terminal No. 15 (Light Blue/Black wire) at master window/door lock switch harness connector C505. See Fig. 6. If battery voltage exists, go to next step. If battery voltage does not exist, go to step **8**).

4) Measure resistance between ground and terminal No. 14 (Black wire) at master window/door lock switch harness connector C505. If resistance is 5 ohms or less, go to next step. If resistance is greater than 5 ohms, repair open in Black wire.

5) Test master window/door lock switch. See MASTER WINDOW/DOOR LOCK SWITCH under COMPONENT TESTS. If switch is okay, go to next step. If switch is defective, replace master window/door lock switch.

6) Turn ignition switch to LOCK position. Disconnect GEM harness connector C290. Measure voltage at terminal No. 2 (White/Black wire) at GEM harness connector C290 with ignition switch in LOCK and RUN positions. See Fig. 5 . If voltage does not exist with ignition switch in either position, go to next step. If voltage exists with ignition switch in either position, repair short to voltage in White/Black wire.

7) Turn ignition switch to LOCK position. Disconnect GEM harness connector C292. Measure resistance in Tan/Light Blue wire between terminal No. 3 at GEM harness connector C290 and terminal No. 8 at master window door lock switch harness connector C505. See Figs. 5 and 6. Also measure resistance in White/Black wire between terminal No. 14 at GEM harness connector C292 and terminal No. 6 at master window door lock switch harness connector C505. See Figs. 6 and 8. If both resistance readings are 5 ohms or less, replace GEM. If either resistance reading is greater than 5 ohms, repair open in appropriate wire.

8) Turn ignition switch to LOCK position. Remove circuit breaker No. 43 (20-amp) from central junction box. Measure resistance in Light Blue/Black wire between output side of circuit breaker No. 43 and terminal No. 15 at master window/door lock switch harness connector C505. If resistance is 5 ohms or less, repair or replace central junction box as necessary. If resistance is greater than 5 ohms, repair open in Light Blue/Black wire.

9) Turn ignition switch to RUN position. Using NGS tester, access GEM active command FRONT WINDOW CONTROL. Trigger DR DOWN on. If driver's window does not go down, go to next step. If driver's window goes down, replace GEM.

10) Turn ignition switch to LOCK position. Disconnect driver's window motor harness connector C504. Using a fused jumper wires, apply positive voltage to one terminal at driver's window motor connector and momentarily ground other terminal (component side). Reverse jumper wires. If window operates in both directions, go to next step. If window does not operate in both directions, repair binding linkage and/or replace motor as necessary.

11) Disconnect master window/door lock switch harness connector C505. Measure resistance in White/Black wire between driver's window motor harness connector C504 and terminal No. 6 at master window/door lock switch harness connector C505. If resistance is 5 ohms or less, go to next step. If resistance is greater than 5 ohms, repair open in White/Black wire.

12) Disconnect GEM harness connector C290. Measure resistance in White/Black wire between driver's window motor harness connector C504 and terminal No. 2 at GEM harness connector C290. See Fig. 5. If resistance is 5 ohms or less, go to next step. If resistance is greater than 5 ohms, repair open in White/Black wire.

13) Turn ignition switch to LOCK position. Remove circuit breaker No. 43 (20-amp) from central junction box. Measure resistance in Light Blue/

Black wire between output side of circuit breaker No. 43 and terminal No. 4 at GEM harness connector C290. If resistance is 5 ohms or less, replace GEM. If resistance is greater than 5 ohms, repair open in Light Blue/Black wire.

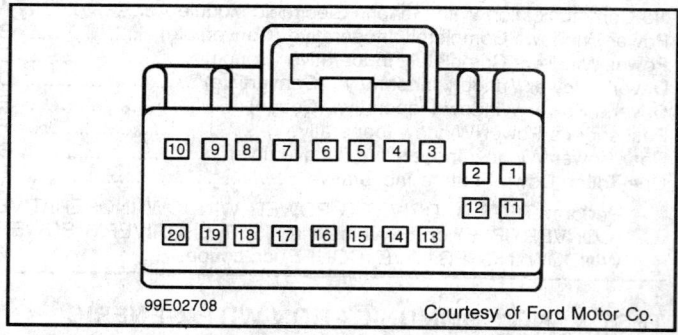

99E02708   Courtesy of Ford Motor Co.

Fig. 8: Identifying GEM Harness Connector C292 Terminals

TEST E: DRIVER'S POWER WINDOW INOPERATIVE (COUPE)

1) Connect New Generation Star (NGS) tester to Data Link Connector (DLC). Using NGS tester, monitor Generic Electronic Module (GEM) PID IGN_A, IGN_R, IGN_S and IGN_KEY. Insert key into ignition switch and turn ignition switch to each position. If PID agrees with ignition switch position, go to next step. If PID does not agree with ignition switch position, repair ignition switch concern. See STEERING COLUMN SWITCHES – MUSTANG article.

2) Turn ignition switch to RUN position. Using NGS tester, monitor GEM PID D_UP_SW and D_DN_SW while operating master window/door lock switch to driver's window up and down positions. If PID does not agree with switch position, go to next step. If PID agrees with switch position, go to step **9**).

3) Turn ignition switch to LOCK position. Disconnect master window/door lock switch harness connector C502. Turn ignition switch to RUN position. Measure voltage at terminal No. 10 (Light Blue/Black wire) at master window/door lock switch harness connector C502. See Fig. 7. If battery voltage exists, go to next step. If battery voltage does not exist, go to step **8**).

4) Measure resistance between ground and terminals No. 7 and 14 (both Black wires) at master window/door lock switch harness connector C502. If both resistance readings are 5 ohms or less, go to next step. If either resistance reading is greater than 5 ohms, repair open in appropriate Black wire.

5) Test master window/door lock switch. See MASTER WINDOW/DOOR LOCK SWITCH under COMPONENT TESTS. If switch is okay, go to next step. If switch is defective, replace master window/door lock switch.

6) Turn ignition switch to LOCK position. Disconnect GEM harness connector C290. Measure voltage at terminal No. 2 (White/Black wire) at GEM harness connector C290 with ignition switch in LOCK and RUN positions. See Fig. 5 . If voltage does not exist with ignition switch in either position, go to next step. If voltage exists with ignition switch in either position, repair short to voltage in White/Black wire.

7) Turn ignition switch to LOCK position. Disconnect GEM harness connector C292. Measure resistance in Tan/Light Blue wire between terminal No. 3 at GEM harness connector C290 and terminal No. 8 at master window door lock switch harness connector C502. See Figs. 7 and 5. Also measure resistance in White/Black wire between terminal No. 14 at GEM harness connector C292 and terminal No. 13 at master window door lock switch harness connector C502. See Figs. 7 and 8. If both resistance readings are 5 ohms or less, replace GEM. If either resistance reading is greater than 5 ohms, repair open in appropriate wire.

8) Turn ignition switch to LOCK position. Remove circuit breaker No. 43 (20-amp) from central junction box. Measure resistance in Light Blue/Black wire between output side of circuit breaker No. 43 and terminal No. 10 at master window/door lock switch harness connector C505. If resistance is 5 ohms or less, repair or replace central junction box as necessary. If resistance is greater than 5 ohms, repair open in Light Blue/Black wire.

9) Turn ignition switch to RUN position. Using NGS tester, access GEM active command FRONT WINDOW CONTROL. Trigger DR DOWN on. If driver's window does not go down, go to next step. If driver's window goes down, replace GEM.

10) Turn ignition switch to LOCK position. Disconnect driver's window motor harness connector C504. Using a fused jumper wires, apply positive voltage to one terminal at driver's window motor connector and momentarily ground other terminal (component side). Reverse jumper wires. If window operates in both directions, go to next step. If window does not operate in both directions, repair binding linkage and/or replace motor as necessary.

11) Disconnect master window/door lock switch harness connector C502. Measure resistance in White/Black wire between driver's window motor harness connector C504 and terminal No. 13 at master window/door lock switch harness connector C502. If resistance is 5 ohms or less, go to next step. If resistance is greater than 5 ohms, repair open in White/Black wire.

12) Disconnect GEM harness connector C290. Measure resistance in White/Black wire between driver's window motor harness connector C504 and terminal No. 2 at GEM harness connector C290. *See Fig. 5.* If resistance is 5 ohms or less, go to next step. If resistance is greater than 5 ohms, repair open in White/Black wire.

13) Turn ignition switch to LOCK position. Remove circuit breaker No. 43 (20-amp) from central junction box. Measure resistance in Light Blue/Black wire between output side of circuit breaker No. 43 and terminal No. 4 at GEM harness connector C290. If resistance is 5 ohms or less, replace GEM. If resistance is greater than 5 ohms, repair open in Light Blue/Black wire.

TEST F: PASSENGER'S POWER WINDOW INOPERATIVE

1) Turn ignition switch to RUN position. Operate passenger's window from master window/door lock switch. If passenger's window does not operate, go to next step. If passenger's window operates, go to step **15)**.

2) Turn ignition switch to LOCK position. Disconnect passenger's window motor harness connector C604. Measure resistance between ground and Red/Yellow wire terminal at passenger's window motor harness connector C604. If resistance is greater than 5 ohms, go to next step. If resistance is 5 ohms or less, go to step **8)**.

3) Disconnect passenger's window/door lock switch harness connector C602. Measure resistance between ground and terminal No. 9 (Tan/Light Blue wire) at passenger's window/door lock switch harness connector C602. *See Fig. 9.* If resistance is greater than 5 ohms, go to next step for convertible or step **5)** for coupe. If resistance is 5 ohms or less, go to step **7)**.

4) Disconnect master window/door lock switch harness connector C505. Measure resistance in Tan/Light Blue wire between terminal No. 9 at master window/door lock switch harness connector C505 and terminal No. 9 at passenger's window/door lock switch harness connector C602. *See Figs. 6 and 9.* If resistance is 5 ohms or less, replace master window/door lock switch. If resistance is greater than 5 ohms, repair open in Tan/Light Blue wire.

5) Disconnect master window/door lock switch harness connector C502. Measure resistance in Tan/Light Blue wire between terminal No. 8 at master window/door lock switch harness connector C502 and terminal No. 9 at passenger's window/door lock switch harness connector C602. *See Figs. 7 and 9.* If resistance is 5 ohms or less, go to next step. If resistance is greater than 5 ohms, repair open in Tan/Light Blue wire.

6) Measure resistance between ground and terminal No. 9 (Black wire) at master window/door lock switch harness connector C502. If resistance is 5 ohms or less, replace master window/door lock switch. If resistance is greater than 5 ohms, repair open in Black wire.

7) Measure resistance in Red/Yellow wire between passenger's window motor harness connector C604 and terminal No. 6 at passenger's window/door lock switch harness connector C602. If resistance is 5

ohms or less, replace passenger's window/door lock switch. If resistance is greater than 5 ohms, repair open in Red/Yellow wire.

8) Measure resistance between ground and Yellow/Red wire terminal at passenger's window motor harness connector C604. If resistance is greater than 5 ohms, go to next step. If resistance is 5 ohms or less, go to step **14)**.

9) Disconnect passenger's window/door lock switch harness connector C602. Measure resistance between ground and terminal No. 7 (White/Yellow wire) at passenger's window/door lock switch harness connector C602. *See Fig. 9.* If resistance is greater than 5 ohms, go to next step for convertible or step **11)** for coupe. If resistance is 5 ohms or less, go to step **13)**.

10) Disconnect master window/door lock switch harness connector C505. Measure resistance in White/Yellow wire between terminal No. 7 at master window/door lock switch harness connector C505 and terminal No. 7 at passenger's window/door lock switch harness connector C602. *See Figs. 6 and 9.* If resistance is 5 ohms or less, replace master window/door lock switch. If resistance is greater than 5 ohms, repair open in White/Yellow wire.

11) Disconnect master window/door lock switch harness connector C502. Measure resistance in White/Yellow wire between terminal No. 15 at master window/door lock switch harness connector C502 and terminal No. 7 at passenger's window/door lock switch harness connector C602. *See Figs. 7 and 9.* If resistance is 5 ohms or less, go to next step. If resistance is greater than 5 ohms, repair open in White/Yellow wire.

12) Measure resistance between ground and terminal No. 14 (Black wire) at master window/door lock switch harness connector C502. If resistance is 5 ohms or less, replace master window/door lock switch. If resistance is greater than 5 ohms, repair open in Black wire.

13) Measure resistance in Yellow/Red wire between passenger's window motor harness connector C604 and terminal No. 10 at passenger's window/door lock switch harness connector C602. If resistance is 5 ohms or less, replace passenger's window/door lock switch. If resistance is greater than 5 ohms, repair open in Yellow/Red wire.

14) Test master window/door lock switch. See MASTER WINDOW/DOOR LOCK SWITCH under COMPONENT TESTS. If switch is okay, replace passenger's window/door lock switch. If switch is defective, replace master window/door lock switch.

15) Turn ignition switch to LOCK position. Disconnect passenger's window/door lock switch harness connector C602. Turn ignition switch to RUN position. Measure voltage at terminal No. 8 (Pink wire) at passenger's window/door lock switch harness connector C602. *See Fig. 9.* If battery voltage exists, replace passenger's window/door lock switch. If battery voltage does exist, go to next step for convertible or repair open in Pink wire for coupe.

16) Turn ignition switch to LOCK position. Disconnect master window/door lock switch harness connector C505. Measure resistance in Pink wire between terminal No. 16 at master window/door lock switch harness connector C505 and terminal No. 8 at passenger's window/door lock switch harness connector C602. *See Figs. 6 and 9.* If resistance is 5 ohms or less, replace master window/door lock switch. If resistance is greater than 5 ohms, repair open in Pink wire.

TEST G: REAR POWER WINDOW INOPERATIVE (CONVERTIBLE)

1) If left rear window is in operative, go to next step. If right rear window is inoperative, go to step **7)**.

2) Disconnect left rear window motor harness connector C322. Measure resistance between ground and Yellow/Light Blue wire terminal at left rear window motor harness connector C322. If resistance is greater than 5 ohms, go to next step. If resistance is 5 ohms or less, go to step **4)**.

3) Disconnect master window/door lock switch harness connector C505. Measure resistance in Yellow/Light Blue wire between left rear window motor harness connector C322 at terminal No. 12 at master window/door lock switch harness connector C505. *See Fig. 6.* If resistance is 5 ohms or less, replace master window/door lock switch. If resistance is greater than 5 ohms, repair open in Yellow/Light Blue wire.

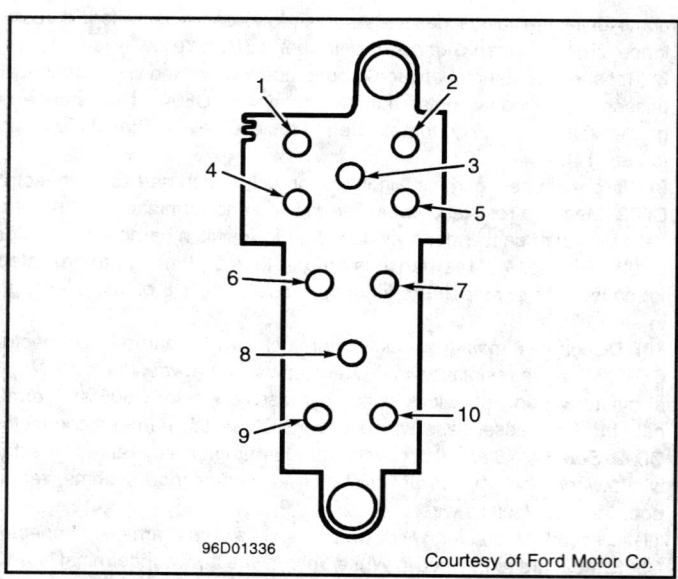

Fig. 9: Identifying Passenger's Window/Door Lock Switch Harness Connector C602 Terminals

96D01336

Courtesy of Ford Motor Co.

4) Measure resistance between ground and Gray/Orange wire terminal at left rear window motor harness connector C322. If resistance is greater than 5 ohms, go to next step. If resistance is 5 ohms or less, go to step **6**).

5) Disconnect master window/door lock switch harness connector C505. Measure resistance in Gray/Orange wire between left rear window motor harness connector C322 at terminal No. 10 at master window/door lock switch harness connector C505. *See Fig. 6*. If resistance is 5 ohms or less, replace master window/door lock switch. If resistance is greater than 5 ohms, repair open in Gray/Orange wire.

6) Test master window/door lock switch. See MASTER WINDOW/DOOR LOCK SWITCH under COMPONENT TESTS. If switch is okay, replace left rear window motor. If switch is defective, replace master window/door lock switch.

7) Disconnect right rear window motor harness connector C321. Measure resistance between ground and Yellow/Black wire terminal at right rear window motor harness connector C321. If resistance is greater than 5 ohms, go to next step. If resistance is 5 ohms or less, go to step **9**).

8) Disconnect master window/door lock switch harness connector C505. Measure resistance in Yellow/Black wire between right rear window motor harness connector C321 at terminal No. 13 at master window/door lock switch harness connector C505. *See Fig. 6*. If resistance is 5 ohms or less, replace master window/door lock switch. If resistance is greater than 5 ohms, repair open in Yellow/Black wire.

9) Measure resistance between ground and Red/Black wire terminal at right rear window motor harness connector C321. If resistance is greater than 5 ohms, go to next step. If resistance is 5 ohms or less, go to step **11**).

10) Disconnect master window/door lock switch harness connector C505. Measure resistance in Red/Black wire between right rear window motor harness connector C321 at terminal No. 11 at master window/door lock switch harness connector C505. *See Fig. 6*. If resistance is 5 ohms or less, replace master window/door lock switch. If resistance is greater than 5 ohms, repair open in Red/Black wire.

11) Test master window/door lock switch. See MASTER WINDOW/DOOR LOCK SWITCH under COMPONENT TESTS. If switch is okay, replace right rear window motor. If switch is defective, replace master window/door lock switch.

REMOVAL & INSTALLATION

WINDOW MOTOR

Removal & Installation – If possible, raise window to full up position and tape in place to prevent movement. Disconnect negative battery cable. Remove door trim panel and protective liner. Unplug motor harness connector. Remove 3 electric motor mounting screws and motor. To install, reverse removal procedure. Tighten motor mounting screws to 53-89 INCH lbs. (6-10 N.m).

MASTER WINDOW/DOOR LOCK SWITCH

Removal & Installation – Carefully pull power window switch plate from door. Remove 2 connector attaching screws from bottom of switch plate. Using a small screwdriver, pry connector from switch. To install, reverse removal procedure.

WIRING DIAGRAMS

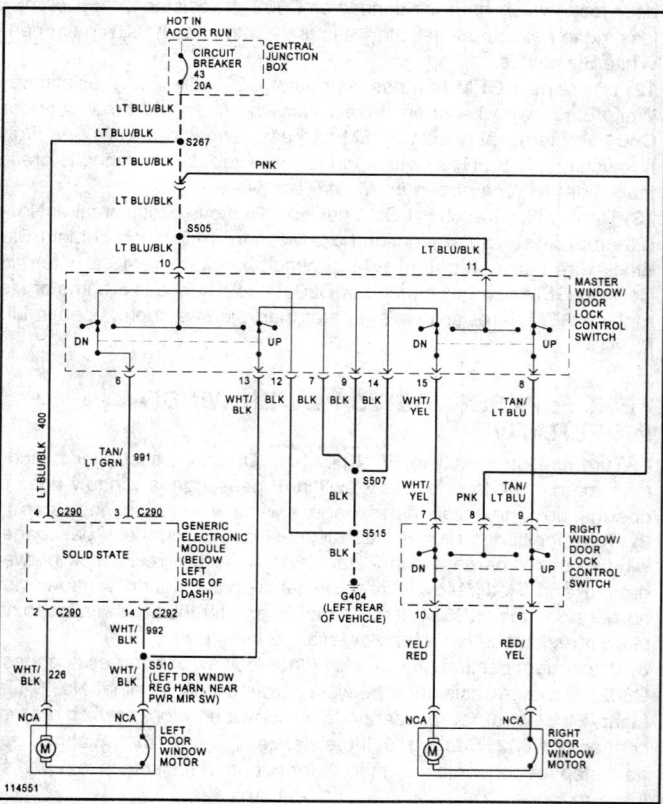

Fig. 10: Power Window System Wiring Diagram (Mustang Coupe)

114551

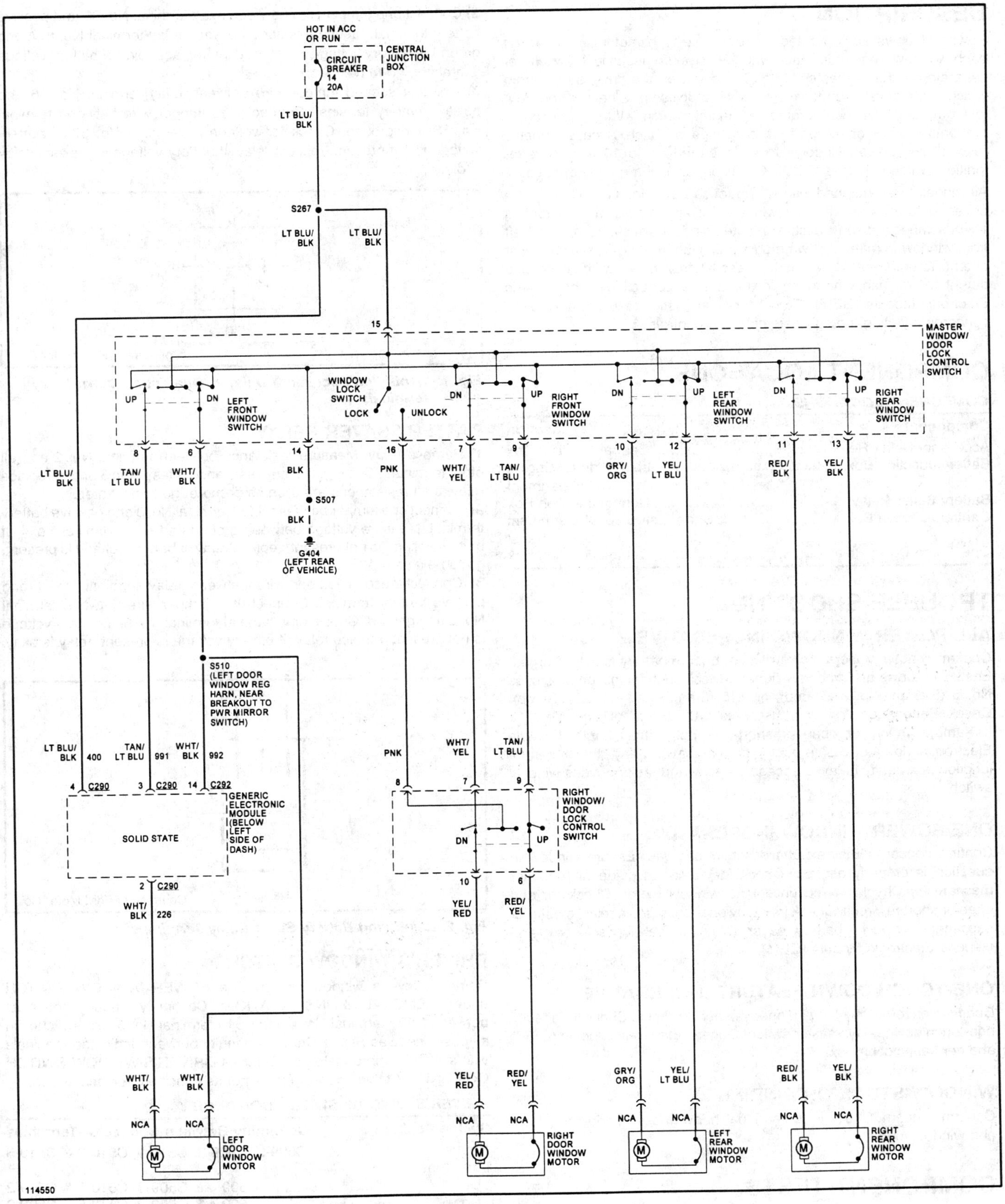

Fig. 11: Power Window System Wiring Diagram (Mustang Convertible)

114550

1999 ACCESSORIES & EQUIPMENT
Power Windows -- F150 & F250 Light-Duty Pickup

DESCRIPTION

Power windows are operated by reversible type motors mounted on each window regulator. Each window has an individual switch for separate control. A master switch is located on the driver's door from which both driver's and passenger's windows may be controlled. A lock-out switch is incorporated in master switch. When actuated, it prevents window operation from passenger's switch. Accessory delay relay allows power windows to be operated up to 10 minutes after ignition switch is turned to LOCK position, or until a door is opened.

All models are equipped with a one-touch down feature, allowing the driver to lower the left front window fully by momentarily actuating driver's window down switch at master window switch. To operate left front window in manual down mode, press left front down switch to first detent. To enter auto down mode, press left front down switch to second detent and release. One-touch down feature is controlled by the Generic Electronic Module (GEM). GEM offers diagnostics to locate and repair concerns affecting the subsystems that it controls.

COMPONENT LOCATIONS

COMPONENT LOCATIONS

Component	Location
Accessory Delay Relay	Central Junction Box
Battery Junction Box	Left Side Of Engine Compartment
Battery Saver Relay	Central Junction Box
Central Junction Box	Under Left Side Of Instrument Panel
One-Touch Down Relay	Central Junction Box

TROUBLE SHOOTING

ALL POWER WINDOWS INOPERATIVE

Confirm concern. Operate all switches. Ensure battery is fully charged. Ensure windows are properly aligned. Check central junction box fuses No. 6 (5-amp), No. 8 (5-amp), No. 15 (5-amp) and No. 20 (5-amp). Check Battery junction box fuses No. 103 (50-amp) and No. 110 (30-amp). Check for open or shorted supply circuit, faulty Generic Electronic Module (GEM), faulty battery saver relay, faulty central junction box, faulty delayed accessory relay and faulty driver's window switch.

ONE POWER WINDOW INOPERATIVE

Confirm concern. Ensure battery is fully charged. Ensure window in question is properly aligned. Check for damaged guide or regulator mechanism. Check for malfunctioning window motor. Check for and open or shorted circuit. Check for faulty one-touch down relay, master or passenger's switch, battery saver relay, central junction box and Generic Electronic Module (GEM).

ONE-TOUCH DOWN FEATURE INOPERATIVE

Confirm concern. Check for an open or shorted circuit. Check for a faulty one-touch down relay, master switch, Generic Electronic Module (GEM) and central junction box.

WINDOW STUCK OR BINDING

Confirm concern. Check for damaged window tracks, window regulator and window motor.

COMPONENT TESTS

ACCESSORY DELAY & ONE-TOUCH DOWN RELAYS

1) Remove relay. Measure resistance between relay terminal No. 85 and all other terminals. *See Fig. 1.* If any resistance is less than 5 ohms, replace relay. If all resistances are 5 ohms or more, go to next step.

2) Connect one jumper wire between relay terminal No. 30 and positive battery terminal. Measure voltage between relay terminal No. 87A and ground. If battery voltage is not present, replace relay. If battery voltage is present, go to next step.

3) Connect second jumper wire between relay terminal No. 86 and positive battery terminal. Connect third jumper wire between terminal No. 85 and ground. Check for voltage at terminal No. 87. If battery voltage is not present, replace relay, If battery voltage is present, relay is okay.

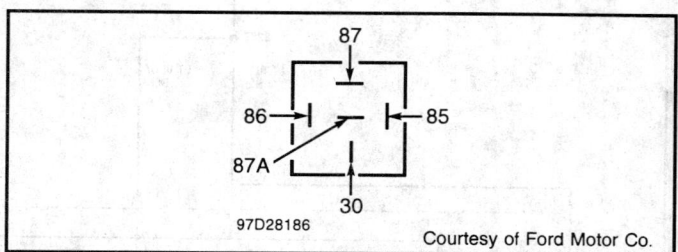

Fig. 1: Identifying Accessory Delay & One-Touch Down Relay Terminals

BATTERY SAVER RELAY

1) Remove relay. Measure resistance between terminal No. 2 and all other terminals. *See Fig. 2.* If any resistance is less than 5 ohms, replace relay. If all resistances are 5 ohms or more, go to next step.

2) Connect one jumper between relay terminal No. 3 and positive battery terminal. Measure voltage between ground and relay terminal No. 4. If battery voltage is not present, replace relay. If battery voltage is present, go to next step.

3) Connect second jumper wire between relay terminal No. 1 and positive battery terminal. Connect third jumper wire between terminal No. 2 and ground. Check for voltage at terminal No. 5. If battery voltage is not present, replace relay. If battery voltage is present, relay is okay.

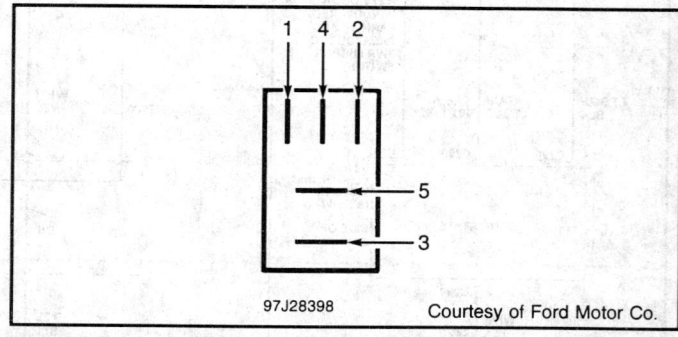

Fig. 2: Identifying Battery Saver Relay Terminals

DRIVER'S WINDOW SWITCH

Remove driver's window switch. See POWER WINDOW SWITCH under REMOVAL & INSTALLATION. Continuity should not exist between C509 terminal No. 4 and C510 terminal No. 5 with switches in all positions. *See Fig. 3.* Check continuity between indicated terminals with switch in appropriate position. See DRIVER'S WINDOW SWITCH CONTINUITY table. If continuity is not as specified, replace switch.

DRIVER'S WINDOW SWITCH CONTINUITY

Switch Position	Continuity Between Connector-Terminals
Neutral	C509-2, C509-3, C510-1, C510-2 & C510-5
Left Front	
Up	C509-4 & C509-3; C510-5 & C509-2
Down	C509-4 & C509-2; C510-5 & C509-3
Right Front	
Up	C509-4 & C510-1; C510-5 & C510-2
Down	C509-4 & C510-2; C510-5 & C510-1

1999 ACCESSORIES & EQUIPMENT
Power Windows – F150 & F250 Light-Duty Pickup (Cont.)

FORD
4-1169

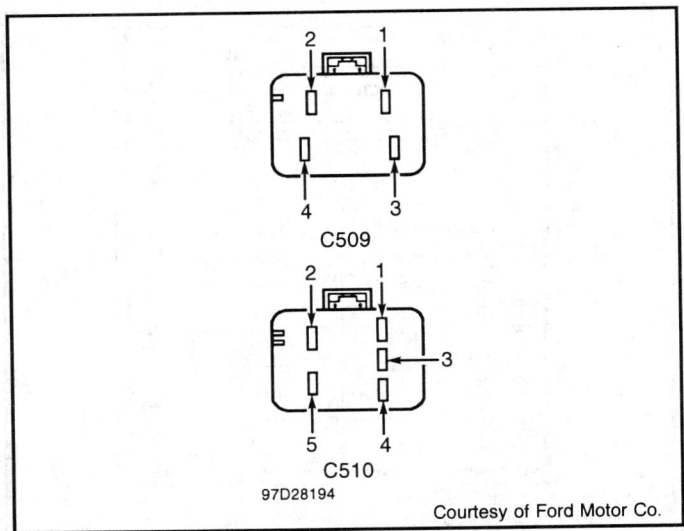

C509

C510

97D28194

Courtesy of Ford Motor Co.

Fig. 3: Identifying Driver's Window Switch Terminals

PASSENGER'S WINDOW SWITCH

Remove passenger's window switch. See POWER WINDOW SWITCH under REMOVAL & INSTALLATION. With switch at rest, there should not be continuity between terminal No. 4 and terminals No. 2, 3, 6 or 7. *See Fig. 4.* Check continuity between indicated terminals with switch in appropriate position. See PASSENGER'S WINDOW SWITCH CONTINUITY table. If continuity is not as specified, replace switch.

PASSENGER'S WINDOW SWITCH CONTINUITY

Switch Position	Continuity Between Terminals
Neutral	2 & 3; 6 & 7
Up	4 & 3; 7 & 6
Down	4 & 6; 2 & 3

POWER WINDOW MOTOR

Remove window motor from vehicle, see POWER WINDOW MOTOR under REMOVAL & INSTALLATION. Using fused jumper wires, connect a fully charged battery to motor terminals. Observe motor. Motor should operate smoothly. Reverse leads. Motor should operate in reverse direction. Replace window motor if it does not operate as specified.

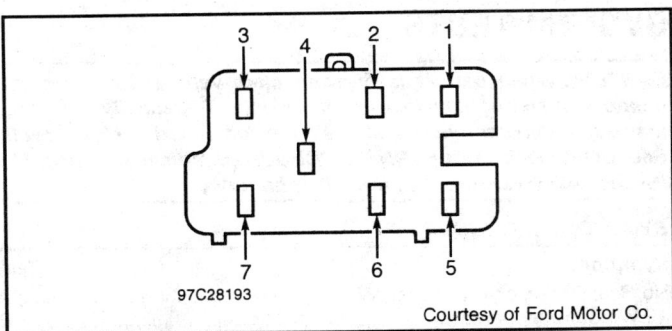

97C28193

Courtesy of Ford Motor Co.

Fig. 4: Identifying Passenger's Window Switch Terminals

SELF-DIAGNOSTIC SYSTEM

NOTE: The power window system utilizes a self-diagnostic system which may store a Diagnostic Trouble Code (DTC) if a problem exists in the system. DTCs may be retrieved using New Generation STAR (NGS) tester, or equivalent scan tool, when connected to Data Link Connector (DLC). For preliminary testing, see TROUBLE SHOOTING.

Connect New Generation Star (NGS) tester to Data Link Connector (DLC) located below center of instrument panel. Using NGS tester, perform data link diagnostic test. See DATA LINK DIAGNOSTIC TEST under COMMUNICATION NETWORK DIAGNOSTICS in MODULE COMMUNICATIONS NETWORK – F150 & F250 LIGHT-DUTY PICKUP article.

If NGS tester displays CKT914, CKT915 or CKT70 = ALL ECUS NO RESP/NOT EQUIP, repair module communication concern. See MODULE COMMUNICATIONS NETWORK – F150 & F250 LIGHT-DUTY PICKUP article to diagnosis network concern. If NGS tester displays NO RESP/NOT EQUIP for GEM, perform TEST A: NO SCAN TOOL COMMUNICATION WITH GEM under SYSTEM TESTS.

If NGS tester displays SYSTEM PASSED, retrieve and record continuous DTCs. Erase continuous DTCs. Using NGS tester, perform GEM self-test. If GEM DTCs related to concern are retrieved, perform appropriate test. See GEM DTC TEST INDEX table. If no DTCs related to the concern are retrieved, perform appropriate test based on symptom. See SYMPTOM TEST INDEX under SYSTEM TESTS. For GEM DTCs not covered in this article, see MODULE COMMUNICATIONS NETWORK – F150 & F250 LIGHT-DUTY PICKUP article.

GEM DTC TEST INDEX

DTC [1]	Description	Test
B1302	Accessory Delay Relay Coil Circuit Failure	B
B1304	Accessory Delay Relay Coil Circuit Short To Power	B
B1342	ECU Defective	[2]
B1398	Driver's Door One-Touch Down Relay Coil Circuit Failure	C
B1400	Driver's Door One-Touch Down Relay Coil Circuit Short To Power	C
B1405	Driver's Door Power Window Down Circuit Short To Power	C
B1408	Driver's Door Power Window Switch Up Circuit Short To Power	C
B1410	Driver's Door Power Window Motor Excessive Current Draw	C

[1] – Codes listed in this table are only for testing covered in this article. For complete DTC listing, see MODULE COMMUNICATIONS NETWORK – F150 & F250 LIGHT-DUTY PICKUP article.

[2] – Clear DTCs. Retrieve DTCs. If DTC B1342 retrieved again, replace GEM. See GENERIC ELECTRONIC MODULE (GEM) under REMOVAL & INSTALLATION.

FORD
4-1170

1999 ACCESSORIES & EQUIPMENT
Power Windows – F150 & F250 Light-Duty Pickup (Cont.)

SYSTEM TESTS

CAUTION: When battery is disconnected, vehicle computer and memory systems may lose memory data. Driveability problems may exist until computer systems have completed a relearn cycle. See COMPUTER RELEARN PROCEDURES article in GENERAL INFORMATION before disconnecting battery.

SYMPTOM TEST INDEX

TEST A: NO SCAN TOOL COMMUNICATION WITH GEM

NOTE: After repair, clear DTCs and retest system.

1) Using New Generation Star (NGS) tester, observe Generic Electronic Module (GEM) PID IGN_GEM while turning ignition switch through all positions. Depress clutch pedal when turning to START position (M/T). If PID values agree with ignition switch positions, go to next step. If PID values do not agree with ignition switch positions, repair appropriate ignition switch circuit as necessary. See appropriate wiring diagram in POWER DISTRIBUTION article in WIRING DIAGRAMS.
2) Turn ignition switch to LOCK position. Disconnect central junction box 34-pin connector C243. See Fig. 5. Measure voltage between central junction box connector C243 terminal No. 11 (Tan/Black wire) and ground. If voltage is more than 10 volts, go to next step. If voltage is 10 volts or less, repair Tan/Black wire.
3) Disconnect GEM from central junction box 18-pin connector C267. Connect central junction box connector C243 . Measure voltage between central junction box connector C267 terminal No. 4 (central junction box side) and ground. Measure voltage between connector C267 terminal No. 16 (central junction box side) and ground. See Fig. 5. If each voltage is more than 10 volts, go to next step. If either voltage is 10 volts or less, replace central junction box.
4) Disconnect central junction box 34-pin connector C243 . Measure internal resistance of central junction box between C243 terminal No. 11 (central junction box side) and connector C267 terminal No. 4 (central junction box side). Measure internal resistance of central junction box between connector C243 terminal No. 11 (central junction box side) and connector C267 terminal No. 16 (central junction box side). See Fig. 5. If each resistance is less than 5 ohms, go to next step. If either resistance is 5 ohms or more, replace central junction box.
5) Disconnect GEM 26-pin connector C239. Measure resistance between GEM connector C239 terminal No. 26 (Black/Light Blue wire) and ground. See Fig. 6. If resistance is less than 5 ohms, go to next step. If resistance is 5 ohms or more, repair open in Black/Light Blue wire. Ground point is at lower left inner cowl panel.
6) Measure resistance between GEM connector C239 terminal No. 14 (Black/Light Blue wire) and ground. See Fig. 6. If resistance is less than 5 ohms, repair module communications concern. See MODULE COMMUNICATIONS NETWORK – F150 & F250 LIGHT-DUTY PICKUP article. If resistance is 5 ohms or more, repair open in Black/Light Blue wire. Ground point is at lower left inner cowl panel.

TEST B: ALL WINDOWS INOPERATIVE

NOTE: After repair, clear DTCs and retest system.

1) Using New Generation Star (NGS) tester, observe Generic Electronic Module (GEM) PID IGN_GEM while turning ignition switch through all positions. Depress clutch pedal when turning to START position (M/T).

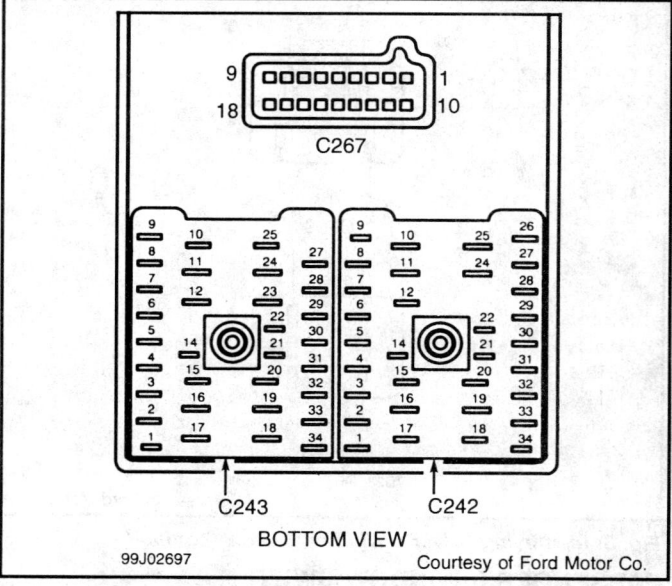

Fig. 5: Identifying Central Junction Box Connectors & Terminals

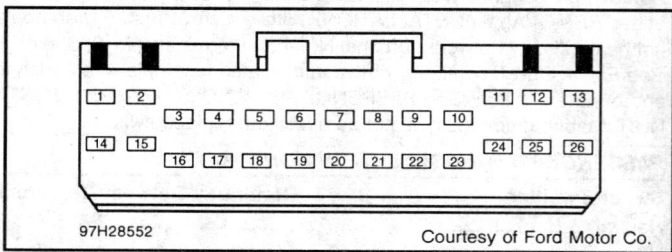

Fig. 6: Identifying GEM 26-Pin Connector C239 Terminals

If PID values agree with ignition switch positions, go to next step. If PID values do not agree with ignition switch positions, repair appropriate ignition switch circuit. See appropriate wiring diagram in POWER DISTRIBUTION article in WIRING DIAGRAMS.
2) Using NGS tester, perform GEM self-test. If there are no DTCs, or DTC B1313 or B1315 is present, go to next step. If DTC B1302 or B1304 is present, go to step 9). If DTC B1342 is present, replace GEM. See GENERIC ELECTRONIC MODULE (GEM) under REMOVAL & INSTALLATION.
3) Turn ignition switch to RUN position. Observe GEM PID BATSAV while triggering GEM active command BATTERY SAVER to ON and OFF. If PID value agrees with command mode, go to step 12). If PID value does not agree with command mode and displays OFFO-G, go to next step. If PID value does not agree with command mode and displays ON-B-, go to step 7).
4) Turn ignition switch to LOCK position. Remove battery saver relay. Measure voltage between battery saver relay socket terminal No. 1 and ground. See Fig. 7. If voltage is more than 10 volts, go to next step. If voltage is 10 volts or less, replace central junction box.

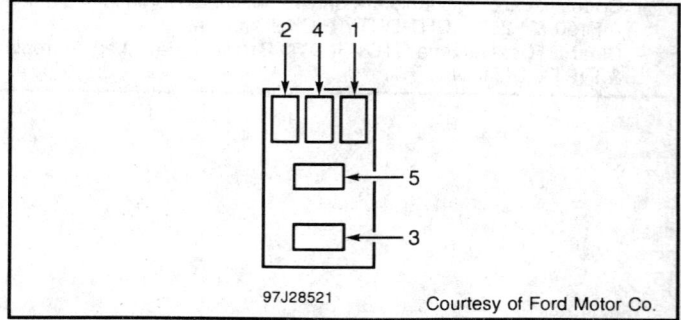

Fig. 7: Identifying Battery Saver Relay Socket Terminals

1999 ACCESSORIES & EQUIPMENT
Power Windows – F150 & F250 Light-Duty Pickup (Cont.)

FORD
4-1171

5) Check battery saver relay. See BATTERY SAVER RELAY under COMPONENT TESTS. If relay is okay, go to next step. If relay is faulty, replace relay.

6) Disconnect GEM from central junction box connector C267. See GENERIC ELECTRONIC MODULE (GEM) under REMOVAL & INSTALLATION. Measure resistance between battery saver relay socket terminal No. 2 and central junction box connector C267 terminal No. 1 (central junction box side). See Figs. 5 and 7. If resistance is less than 5 ohms, replace GEM. If resistance is 5 ohms or more, replace central junction box.

7) Turn ignition switch to LOCK position. Check battery saver relay. See BATTERY SAVER RELAY under COMPONENT TESTS. If relay is okay, go to next step. If relay is faulty, replace relay.

8) Remove GEM from central junction box connector C267. See GENERIC ELECTRONIC MODULE (GEM) under REMOVAL & INSTALLATION. Turn ignition switch to RUN position. Measure voltage between battery saver relay socket terminal No. 2 and ground. See Fig. 7. If voltage is present, replace central junction box. If voltage is not present, replace GEM.

9) Using NGS tester, observe GEM PID ACCDLY while triggering GEM active command DELAYED ACCESSORY to ON and Off. If PID value agrees with command mode, go to step **15)**. If PID value does not agree with command mode and displays OFFO-G, go to next step. If PID value does not agree with command mode and displays ON-B-, go to step **13)**.

10) Turn ignition switch to LOCK position. Remove accessory delay relay. Turn ignition switch to RUN position. Measure voltage between accessory delay relay socket terminal No. 86 and ground. See Fig. 8. If voltage is more than 10 volts, go to next step. If voltage is 10 volts or less, go to step **22)**.

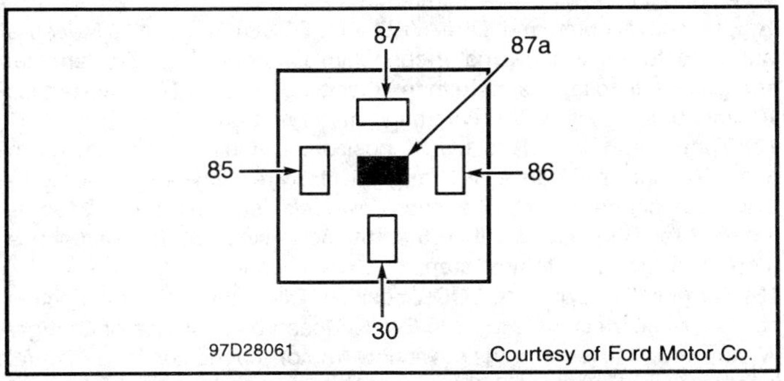

Fig. 8: Identifying Accessory Delay & One-Touch Down Relay Socket Terminals

11) Turn ignition switch to LOCK position. Check accessory delay relay. See ACCESSORY DELAY & ONE-TOUCH DOWN RELAYS under COMPONENT TESTS. If relay is okay, go to next step. If relay is faulty, replace relay.

12) Remove GEM from central junction box 18-pin connector C267. See GENERIC ELECTRONIC MODULE (GEM) under REMOVAL & INSTALLATION. Measure internal resistance of central junction box between connector C267 terminal No. 11 (central junction box side) and accessory delay relay socket terminal No. 85. See Figs. 5 and 8. If resistance is less than 5 ohms, replace GEM. If resistance is 5 ohms or more, replace central junction box.

13) Turn ignition switch to LOCK position. Check accessory delay relay. See ACCESSORY DELAY & ONE-TOUCH DOWN RELAYS under COMPONENT TESTS. If relay is okay, go to next step. If relay is faulty, replace relay.

14) Disconnect GEM from central junction box 18-pin connector C267. See GENERIC ELECTRONIC MODULE (GEM) under REMOVAL & INSTALLATION. Turn ignition switch to RUN position. Measure voltage between accessory delay relay socket terminal No. 85 and ground. See Fig. 8. If voltage is present, replace central junction box. If voltage is not present, replace GEM.

15) Turn ignition switch to LOCK position. Remove one-touch down relay. Turn ignition switch to RUN position. Using NGS tester, trigger GEM active command DELAYED ACCESSORY to ON. Measure volt-age between one-touch down relay socket terminal No. 85 and ground. See Fig. 8. If voltage is more than 10 volts, connect one-touch down relay and go to step **19)**. If voltage is 10 volts or less, go to next step.

16) Turn ignition switch to LOCK position. Remove accessory delay relay. Measure voltage between accessory delay relay socket terminal No. 30 and ground. See Fig. 8. If voltage is more than 10 volts, go to step **18)**. If voltage is 10 volts or less, go to next step.

17) Turn ignition switch to LOCK position. Disconnect central junction box 34-pin connector C242. Measure voltage between central junction box connector C242 terminal No. 25 (Red/Light Blue wire) and ground. See Fig. 5. If voltage is more than 10 volts, replace central junction box. If voltage is 10 volts or less, repair Red/Light Blue wire.

18) Check accessory delay relay. See ACCESSORY DELAY & ONE-TOUCH DOWN RELAY under COMPONENT TESTS. If relay is okay, replace central junction box. If relay is faulty, replace relay.

19) Turn ignition switch to LOCK position. Disconnect driver's window switch 4-pin connector C509. Turn ignition switch to RUN position. Using NGS tester, trigger GEM active command DELAYED ACCESSORY to ON. Measure voltage between driver's window switch connector C509 Light Blue/Black wire terminal and ground. If voltage is more than 10 volts, go to step **21)**. If voltage is 10 volts or less, go to next step.

20) Turn ignition switch to LOCK position. Disconnect central junction box 34-pin connector C242. See Fig. 5. Measure resistance in Light Blue/Black wire terminal between driver's window switch connector C509 and central junction box connector C242 terminal No. 10. If resistance is less than 5 ohms, replace central junction box. If resistance is 5 ohms or more, repair open in Light Blue/Black wire.

21) Turn ignition switch to LOCK position. Disconnect driver's window switch 5-pin connector C510. Measure resistance between driver's window switch connector C510 terminal No. 5 (Black wire) and ground. See Fig. 3. If resistance is less than 5 ohms, replace driver's window switch. If resistance is 5 ohms or more, repair Black wire. Ground point is at lower right inner cowl panel.

22) Turn ignition switch to LOCK position. Check battery saver relay. See BATTERY SAVER RELAY under COMPONENT TESTS. If relay is okay, replace central junction box. If relay is faulty, replace relay.

TEST C: DRIVER'S WINDOW INOPERATIVE

NOTE: After repair, clear DTCs and retest system.

1) Using New Generation Star (NGS) tester, perform Generic Electronic Module self-test. If there are no DTCs, DTC B1398 or B1400 is present, go to next step. If DTC B1405 is present, go to step **8)**. If DTC B1342 is present, replace GEM. See GENERIC ELECTRONIC MODULE (GEM) under REMOVAL & INSTALLATION.

2) Turn ignition switch to ACC position. Using NGS tester, trigger GEM active command DELAYED ACCESSORY to ON. Observe GEM PID D_PWRLY while triggering GEM active command ONE TOUCH DOWN to ON and OFF. If PID value agrees with command mode, go to step **8)**. If PID value does not agree with command mode and displays OFFO-G, go to next step. If PID value does not agree with command mode and displays ON-B-, go to step **6)**.

3) Turn ignition switch to LOCK position. Check one-touch down relay. See ACCESSORY DELAY & ONE-TOUCH DOWN RELAYS under COMPONENT TESTS. If relay is okay, go to next step. If relay is faulty, replace relay.

4) Remove accessory delay relay. Measure resistance between accessory delay relay socket terminal No. 87 and one-touch down relay socket terminal No. 85. See Fig. 8. If resistance is less than 5 ohms, go to next step. If resistance is 5 ohms or more, replace central junction box.

5) Disconnect GEM from central junction box 18-pin connector C267. Measure internal resistance of central junction box between connector C267 terminal No. 2 (central junction box side) and one-touch down relay socket terminal No. 86. See Figs. 5 and 8. Resistance should be less than 5 ohms. Measure resistance between one-touch down relay socket terminal No. 86 and ground. Resistance should be more than 10 k/ohms. If resistances are as specified, replace GEM. See GENERIC

FORD
4-1172

1999 ACCESSORIES & EQUIPMENT
Power Windows – F150 & F250 Light-Duty Pickup (Cont.)

ELECTRONIC MODULE (GEM) under REMOVAL & INSTALLATION. If either resistance is not as specified, replace central junction box.

6) Turn ignition switch to LOCK position. Check one-touch down relay. See ACCESSORY DELAY & ONE-TOUCH DOWN RELAYS under COMPONENT TESTS. If relay is okay, go to next step. If relay is faulty, replace relay.

7) Disconnect GEM from central junction box 18-pin connector C267. See GENERIC ELECTRONIC MODULE (GEM) under REMOVAL & INSTALLATION. Turn ignition switch to RUN position. Measure voltage between one-touch down relay socket terminal No. 86 and ground. *See Fig. 8.* If voltage is present, replace central junction box. If voltage is not present, replace GEM.

8) Turn ignition switch to RUN position. Observe GEM PIDs D_UP_SW, D_DN_SW and OTD_SW while pressing driver's window switch through all positions. See DRIVER'S WINDOW SWITCH INPUTS table. If PIDs agree with switch positions, go to step **16)**. If PIDs do not agree with switch positions, go to next step.

DRIVER'S WINDOW SWITCH INPUTS

Switch Position	PID	NGS Tester Expected Response
OFF	D_UP_SW	OFF
	D_DN_SW	OFF
	OTD_SW	OFF
UP	D_UP_SW	UP
	D_DN_SW	OFF
	OTD_SW	OFF
DOWN	D_UP_SW	OFF
	D_DN_SW	DOWN
	OTD_SW	OFF
AUTO	D_UP_SW	OFF
	D_DN_SW	DOWN
	OTD_SW	DOWN

9) Turn ignition switch to LOCK position. Disconnect driver's window switch 4-pin connector C509. Turn ignition switch to RUN position. Using NGS tester, trigger GEM active command DELAYED ACCESSORY to ON. Measure voltage between driver's window switch connector C509 Light Blue/Black wire terminal and ground. If voltage is more than 10 volts, go to next step. If voltage is 10 volts or less, repair Light Blue/Black wire.

10) Observe GEM PIDs D_DN_SW and OTD_SW. Connect 10-amp fused jumper wire between driver's window switch connector Light Blue/Black wire and Gray wire terminals. PID D_DN_SW and OTD_SW should display DOWN. Disconnect jumper and attach between Light Blue/Black wire and Tan/Light Blue wire terminals. PID D_DN_SW should display DOWN and PID OTD_SW should display OFF. If PIDs display as specified, replace driver's window switch. If PIDs do not display as specified and PID D_DN_SW or OTD_SW displayed OFF when UP or DOWN was expected in step **8)**, go to next step. If PIDs do not display as specified and PID D_DN_SW or OTD_SW displayed UP or DOWN when OFF was expected in step **8)**, go to step **12)**.

11) Turn ignition switch to LOCK position. Disconnect central junction box 34-pin connector C243. *See Fig. 5.* Measure resistance of Tan/Light Blue wire between driver's window switch 4-pin connector C509 and central junction box connector C243 terminal No. 10. Resistance should be less than 5 ohms. Measure resistance between driver's window switch connector C509 Tan/Light Blue wire terminal and ground. Resistance should be more than 10 k/ohms. Measure resistance of Gray wire between driver's window switch connector C509 and central junction box connector C243 terminal No. 28. Resistance should be less than 5 ohms. Measure resistance between driver's window switch connector C509 Gray wire terminal and ground. Resistance should be more than 10 k/ohms. If resistances are as specified, go to step **13)**. If resistances are not as specified, repair appropriate wire(s).

12) Turn ignition switch to LOCK position. Disconnect central junction box 34-pin connector C243. Turn ignition switch to RUN position. Measure voltage between driver's window switch connector C509 Tan/Light Blue wire terminal and ground. Measure voltage between driver's window switch connector C509 Gray wire terminal and ground.

If either wire shows voltage, repair appropriate wire(s). If voltage is not present on either wire, go to step **15)**.

13) Disconnect GEM from central junction box 18-pin connector C267. See GENERIC ELECTRONIC MODULE (GEM) under REMOVAL & INSTALLATION. Measure internal resistance of central junction box between connector C243 terminal No. 10 (central junction box side) and connector C267 terminal No. 8 (central junction box side). Measure internal resistance of central junction box between connector C243 terminal No. 28 (central junction box side) and connector C267 terminal No. 9 (central junction box side). *See Fig. 5.* If each resistance is 5 ohms or less, go to next step. If either resistance is 5 ohms or more, replace central junction box.

14) Measure resistance between central junction box connector C267 terminal No. 8 (central junction box side) and ground. Measure resistance between central junction box connector C267 terminal No. 9 (central junction box side) and ground. *See Fig. 5.* If each resistance is more than 10 k/ohms, replace GEM. See GENERIC ELECTRONIC MODULE (GEM) under REMOVAL & INSTALLATION. If either resistance is 10 k/ohms or less, replace central junction box.

15) Turn ignition switch to RUN position. Measure voltage between central junction box connector C267 terminal No. 8 (central junction box side) and ground. Measure voltage between central junction box connector C267 terminal No. 9 (central junction box side) and ground. *See Fig. 5.* If voltage is present, replace central junction box. If voltage is not present, replace GEM. See GENERIC ELECTRONIC MODULE (GEM) under REMOVAL & INSTALLATION.

16) Turn ignition switch to LOCK position. Disconnect driver's window motor 2-pin connector. Turn ignition switch to RUN position. Using NGS tester, trigger GEM active command ONE TOUCH DOWN to ON. Trigger active command DELAYED ACCESSORY to ON. Measure voltage between window motor connector Orange/White wire terminal and ground. If voltage is more than 10 volts, go to step **20)**. If voltage is 10 volts or less, exit active command mode and go to next step.

17) Turn ignition switch to LOCK position. Remove one-touch down relay. Measure resistance of Orange/White wire between driver's window motor connector and one-touch down relay socket terminal 30. *See Fig. 8.* If resistance is less than 5 ohms, go to step **19)**. If resistance is 5 ohms or more, go to next step.

18) Turn ignition switch to LOCK position. Disconnect central junction box 34-pin connector C242. *See Fig. 5.* Measure resistance of Orange/White wire between driver's window motor connector and central junction box connector C242 terminal No. 24. If resistance is less than 5 ohms, replace central junction box. If resistance is 5 ohms or more, repair open in Orange/White wire.

19) Remove accessory delay relay. Measure resistance between one-touch down relay socket terminal No. 87 and accessory delay relay socket terminal No. 87. *See Fig. 8.* If resistance is less than 5 ohms, replace one-touch down relay. If resistance is 5 ohms or more, replace central junction box.

20) Trigger GEM active command ONE TOUCH DOWN to OFF. Turn ignition switch to LOCK position. Measure resistance between driver's window motor connector Orange/White wire terminal and ground. If resistance is less than 5 ohms, go to step **23)**. If resistance is 5 ohms or more, go to next step.

21) Turn ignition switch to LOCK position. Remove one-touch down relay. Measure resistance between one-touch down relay socket terminal No. 87A and ground. *See Fig. 8.* If resistance is less than 5 ohms, replace relay. If resistance is 5 ohms or more, go to next step.

22) Disconnect central junction box 34-pin connector C243. *See Fig. 5.* Measure resistance between central junction box connector C243 terminal No. 24 and ground. If resistance is less than 5 ohms, replace central junction box. If resistance is 5 ohms or more, repair open in Black wire. Ground point is at lower right inner cowl panel.

23) Turn ignition switch to RUN position. While pressing driver's window switch to UP position, measure voltage between driver's window motor connector White/Black wire terminal and ground. If voltage is more than 10 volts, go to next step. If voltage is 10 volts or less, repair White/Black or Red/Yellow wire. See WIRING DIAGRAMS.

1999 ACCESSORIES & EQUIPMENT
Power Windows – F150 & F250 Light-Duty Pickup (Cont.)

FORD
4-1173

24) Turn ignition switch to LOCK position. Measure resistance between driver's window motor connector White/Black wire terminal and ground. If resistance is less than 5 ohms, replace driver's window motor. See POWER WINDOW MOTOR under REMOVAL & INSTALLATION. If resistance is 5 ohms or more, replace driver's window switch. See DRIVER'S WINDOW SWITCH under REMOVAL & INSTALLATION.

TEST D: PASSENGER'S WINDOW INOPERATIVE

NOTE: After repair, clear DTCs and retest system.

1) Turn ignition switch to RUN position. Operate passenger's window from both switches. If passenger's window operates both directions from passenger's window switch, but not from driver's window switch, replace driver's window switch. If passenger's window operates in both directions from driver's window switch, but is inoperative in one direction from passenger's window switch, replace passenger's window switch. If passenger's window operates in both directions from driver's window switch, but is inoperative in both directions from passenger's window switch, go to next step. If passenger's window operates in only one direction from passenger's window switch and is inoperative in both directions from driver's window switch, go to step **3)**. If passenger's window is inoperative from both window switches, go to step **5)**. If unable to confirm operation of passenger's window, go to step **4)**.

2) Turn ignition switch to LOCK position. Disconnect passenger's window switch 7-pin connector. Turn ignition switch to RUN position. Measure voltage between passenger's window switch connector Light Blue/Black wire terminal and ground. If voltage is more than 10 volts, replace passenger's window switch. See POWER WINDOW SWITCH under REMOVAL & INSTALLATION. If voltage is 10 volts or less, repair Light Blue/Black wire. See WIRING DIAGRAMS.

3) Turn ignition switch to LOCK position. Disconnect driver's window switch 5-pin connector C510. Measure resistance of White/Yellow wire between driver's window switch connector C510 and passenger's window switch connector. Measure resistance of Tan/Light Blue wire between driver's window switch connector C510 and passenger's window switch connector. If each resistance is less than 5 ohms, replace driver's window switch. See POWER WINDOW SWITCH under REMOVAL & INSTALLATION. If either resistance is 5 ohms or more, repair open in appropriate wire(s).

4) Turn ignition switch to LOCK position. Disconnect driver's window switch 5-pin connector C510. Measure resistance of White/Yellow wire between driver's window switch connector C510 and passenger's window switch connector. Measure resistance of Tan/Light Blue wire between driver's window switch connector C510 and passenger's window switch connector. If each resistance is less than 5 ohms, go to next step. If either resistance is 5 ohms or more, repair appropriate wire(s).

5) Turn ignition switch to LOCK position. Disconnect passenger's window motor connector. Measure resistance of Red/Yellow wire between passenger's window switch connector and window motor connector. Measure resistance of Yellow/Red wire between passenger's window switch connector and window motor connector. If each resistance is less than 5 ohms, replace passenger's window motor. See POWER WINDOW MOTOR under REMOVAL & INSTALLATION. If either resistance is 5 ohms or more, repair open in appropriate wire(s).

TEST E: DELAYED ACCESSORY DOES NOT TURN OFF

NOTE: After repair, clear DTCs and retest system.

1) Turn ignition switch to LOCK position. Remove accessory delay relay. Turn ignition switch to RUN position. Measure voltage between accessory delay relay socket terminal No. 87 and ground. *See Fig. 8.* If voltage is present, go to next step. If voltage is not present, go to TEST B: ALL WINDOWS INOPERATIVE.

2) Turn ignition switch to LOCK position. Disconnect central junction box 34-pin connector C242. Turn ignition switch to RUN position. Measure voltage between accessory delay relay socket terminal No. 87 and ground. *See Fig. 8.* If voltage is present, go to next step. If voltage is not present, repair Light Blue/Black wire between central junction box and window switches. See WIRING DIAGRAMS.

3) Turn ignition switch to LOCK position. Disconnect GEM from central junction box 18-pin connector C267. See GENERIC ELECTRONIC MODULE (GEM) under REMOVAL & INSTALLATION. Turn ignition switch to RUN position. Measure voltage between accessory delay relay socket terminal No. 87 and ground. *See Fig. 8.* If voltage is present, replace central junction box. If voltage is not present, replace GEM.

REMOVAL & INSTALLATION

CAUTION: When battery is disconnected, vehicle computer and memory systems may lose memory data. Driveability problems may exist until computer systems have completed a relearn cycle. See COMPUTER RELEARN PROCEDURES article in GENERAL INFORMATION before disconnecting battery.

GENERIC ELECTRONIC MODULE (GEM)

CAUTION: Disconnect battery before disconnecting Generic Electronic Module (GEM) connectors. Failure to do so will result in GEM storing erroneous codes and may also result in erratic operation of GEM after reconnection.

CAUTION: If replacing GEM, it is necessary to upload module configuration information to the New Generation Star (NGS) tester. After installation this information needs to be downloaded into the new GEM module.

Removal & Installation – 1) Disconnect the battery ground cable. Remove the lower instrument panel steering column cover. Remove the bulkhead electrical connectors (C243 and C242) from the central junction box (interior fuse panel).

2) Unbolt and remove the central junction box. Disconnect the GEM electrical connectors. Remove screws and disconnect the GEM from the backside of the central junction box. To install, reverse removal procedure.

POWER WINDOW MOTOR

Removal & Installation – 1) Raise glass to full up position. Remove door trim panel and peel back watershield. Disconnect motor wiring connector, and position wiring out of way. Using a 3/4" hole saw with a 1/4" pilot, drill out existing 2 dimples in door to expose motor mounting bolts.

2) Prior to motor removal, ensure regulator arm is in a fixed position to prevent counterbalance spring from unwinding. Remove bolts. Disengage motor from regulator. To install, reverse removal procedure. Cycle motor to make sure gears engage.

POWER WINDOW SWITCH

Removal & Installation – Disconnect negative battery cable. Carefully pry up front and rear of switch plate. Using thin-blade screwdriver, pry connector from switch. Remove window switch from backside of switch plate. To install, reverse removal procedure.

FORD
4-1174

1999 ACCESSORIES & EQUIPMENT
Power Windows – F150 & F250 Light-Duty Pickup (Cont.)

WIRING DIAGRAMS

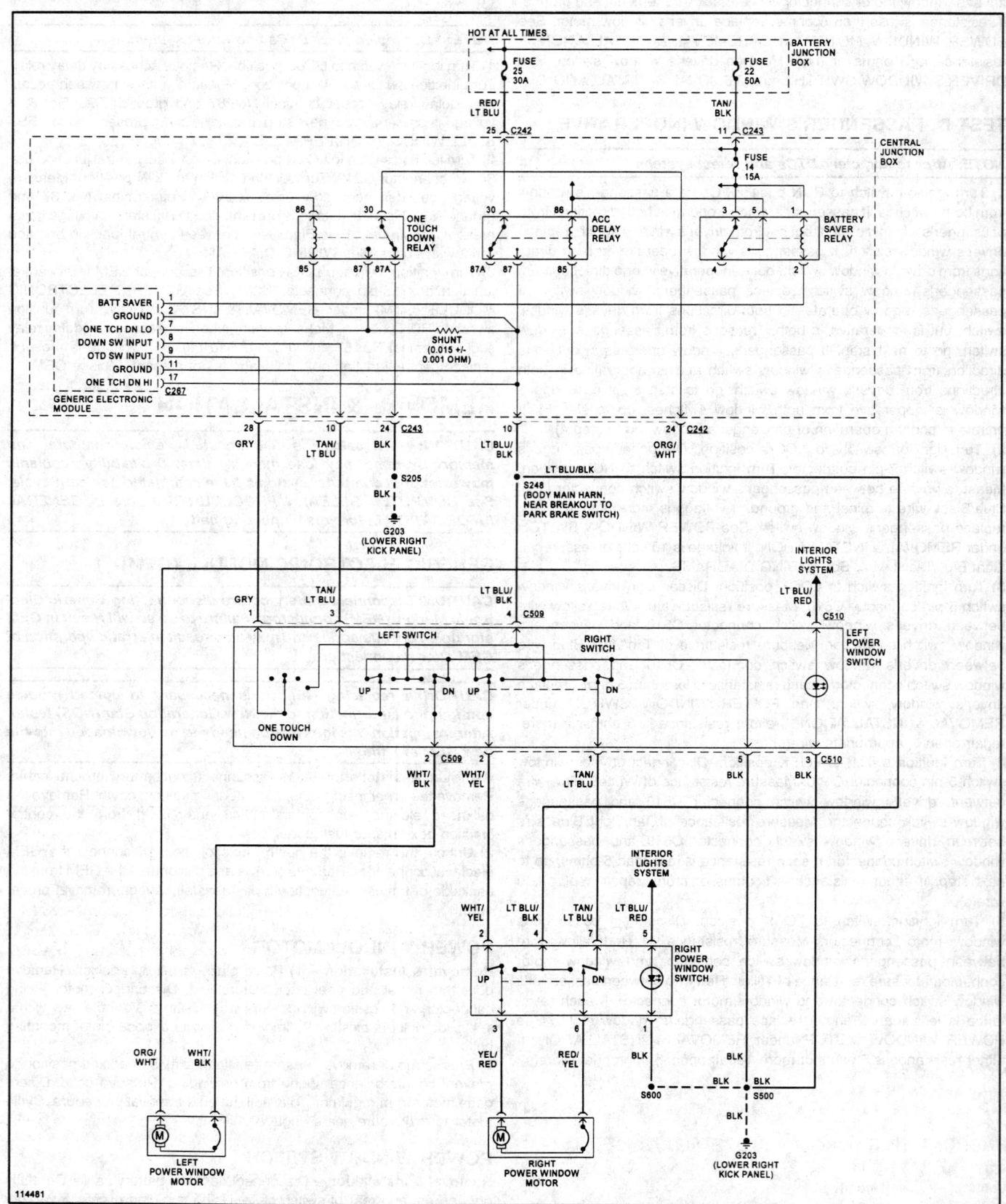

Fig. 9: Power Window System Wiring Diagram (F150 & F250 Light-Duty Pickup)

NOTE: This article includes Cab & Chassis.

DESCRIPTION

Power windows are operated by reversible motors mounted on each window regulator. Each passenger's window has an individual switch for separate control. A master window switch is located on the driver's door from which all windows may be controlled. A lock-out switch is incorporated in master window switch (crew cab only). When actuated, it prevents window operation from passenger's door switch(es). Accessory delay feature allows power windows to be operated up to 10 minutes after ignition is turned to LOCK position, or until a front door is opened.

All models are equipped with a one-touch down feature allowing driver to fully lower left front window by momentarily actuating driver's window down switch at the master window switch. To operate driver's window in manual down mode, press driver's window down switch to first detent. To enter auto down mode, press driver's window down switch to second detent and release. The one-touch down feature is controlled by the Generic Electronic Module (GEM). GEM offers diagnostics to locate and repair concerns affecting the subsystems it controls.

COMPONENT LOCATION

COMPONENT LOCATION

Component	Location
Accessory Delay Relay	Fuse Junction Panel
One-Touch Down Relay	Fuse Junction Panel
Fuse Junction Panel	Lower Left Hand Side Of Instrument Panel
Power Distribution Box	Near Brake Master Cylinder

TROUBLE SHOOTING

ALL POWER WINDOWS INOPERATIVE

Verify customer concern by operating windows to duplicate condition. Ensure battery is fully charged. Ensure windows are properly aligned. Check for faulty circuit breaker No. 25 (30-amp) in power distribution box. Check for open or shorted supply circuit. Check for loose or corroded connectors. Check for poor ground connections. If problem is not found, perform self-diagnostics. See SELF-DIAGNOSTIC SYSTEM.

DRIVER'S WINDOW INOPERATIVE

Verify customer concern by operating window to duplicate condition. Ensure battery is fully charged. Ensure driver's power window is properly aligned. Check for faulty master window switch. See MASTER WINDOW SWITCH under COMPONENT TESTS. Check for open or shorted circuit(s). Check for faulty power window motor. See POWER WINDOW MOTOR under COMPONENT TESTS. If problem is not found, perform self-diagnostics. See SELF-DIAGNOSTIC SYSTEM.

PASSENGER'S WINDOW INOPERATIVE FROM BOTH SWITCHES

Verify customer concern by operating window to duplicate condition. Ensure battery is fully charged. Ensure window in question is properly aligned. Check for faulty master window switch. See MASTER WINDOW SWITCH under COMPONENT TESTS. Check for open or shorted circuit(s). Check for faulty power window motor. See POWER WINDOW MOTOR under COMPONENT TESTS. Check for faulty single switch. See SINGLE SWITCH under COMPONENT TESTS. If problem is not found, perform self-diagnostics. See SELF-DIAGNOSTIC SYSTEM.

PASSENGER'S WINDOW INOPERATIVE FROM SINGLE SWITCH

Verify customer concern by operating window to duplicate condition. Check for faulty single switch. See SINGLE SWITCH under COMPONENT TESTS. Check for open or shorted power supply circuit. If problem is not found, perform self-diagnostics. See SELF-DIAGNOSTIC SYSTEM.

COMPONENT TESTS

MASTER WINDOW SWITCH

Remove master window switch. See WINDOW SWITCH under REMOVAL & INSTALLATION. Check continuity between appropriate terminals at appropriate connector with switch in specified position. See appropriate MASTER WINDOW SWITCH TESTING table. *See Fig. 1 or 2.* If continuity does not exist as specified, replace switch.

MASTER WINDOW SWITCH TESTING (REGULAR & SUPER CAB)

Switch Position	[1] Continuity Between Connector-Terminals
Neutral	C510-4, C510-2, C510-3, C511-1 & C511-2
Left	
Up	C510-4 & C510-2
Down	C510-4 & C510-3
Right	
Up	C510-4 & C511-2
Down	C510-4 & C511-1
One-Touch Down	
Engaged	C510-4 & C510-1

[1] – There should be an open circuit with switch in all positions between C510-4 and C511-3.

MASTER WINDOW SWITCH TESTING (CREW CAB)

Switch Position	[1] Continuity Between Connector-Terminals
Neutral	C510-3, C510-4, C510-6, C510-7, C511-2, C511-4, C511-5, C511-6 & C511-7
Left Front	
Up	C510-2 & C510-6
Down	C510-2 & C510-7
Right Front	
Up	C510-2 & C510-3
Down	C510-2 & C510-4
Left Rear	
Up	C510-2 & C511-7
Down	C510-2 & C511-6
Right Rear	
Up	C510-2 & C511-5
Down	C510-2 & C511-4
Lock-Out	
Unlocked	C510-2 & C511-3
One-Touch Down	
Engaged	C510-2 & C510-5

[1] – There should be an open circuit in all switch positions between C510-2 and C511-2.

POWER WINDOW MOTOR

Remove window motor from vehicle. See WINDOW MOTOR under REMOVAL & INSTALLATION. Using fused jumper wires, connect a fully charged battery to motor terminals. Observe motor. Motor should operate smoothly. Reverse leads. Motor should operate in reverse direction. Replace window motor if it does not operate as specified.

RELAYS

1) Remove relay. Measure resistance between relay terminal No. 85 and all other terminals. *See Fig. 3.* If any resistance is 5 ohms or less, replace relay. If all resistances are more than 5 ohms, go to next step.
2) Attach jumper wire between battery positive terminal and relay terminal No. 30. Measure voltage between relay terminal No. 87A and ground. If battery voltage is not present, replace relay. If battery voltage is present, go to next step.
3) Attach second jumper wire from battery positive terminal to relay terminal No. 86. Attach third jumper wire between relay terminal No. 85 and ground. Measure voltage between relay terminal No. 87 and ground. If battery voltage is not present, replace relay. If battery voltage is present, relay is okay.

FORD
4-1176

1999 ACCESSORIES & EQUIPMENT
Power Windows – F250 Super-Duty & F350 Pickup (Cont.)

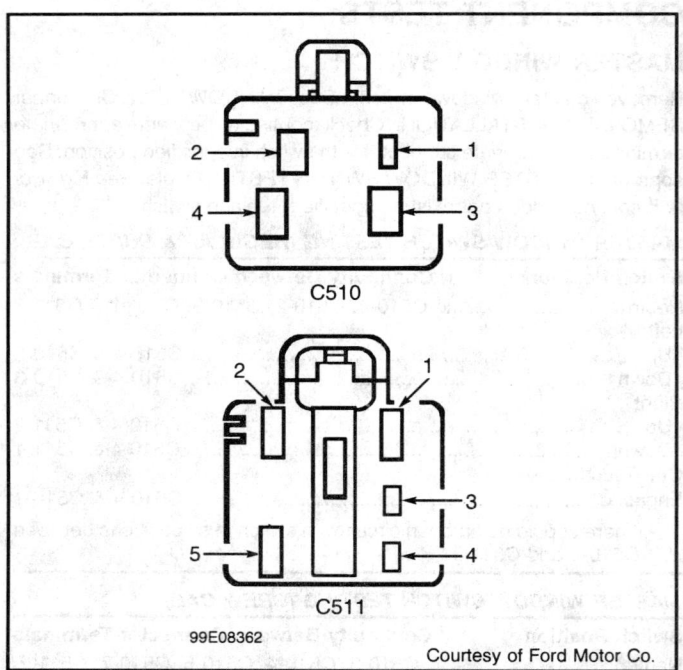

Fig. 1: Identifying Master Window Switch Terminals (Regular & Super Cab)

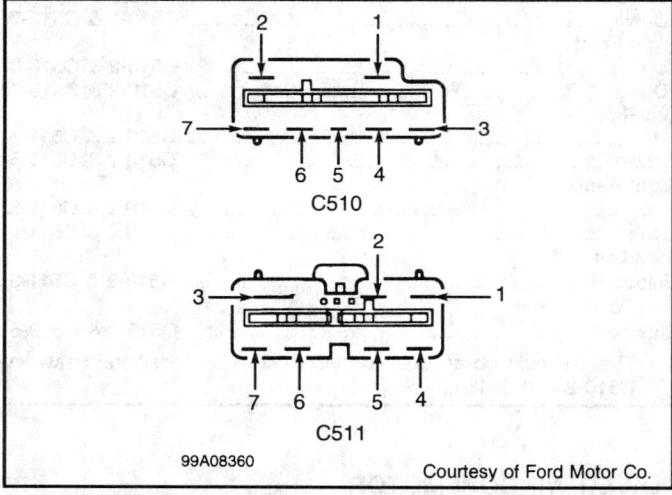

Fig. 2: Identifying Master Window Switch Terminals (Crew Cab)

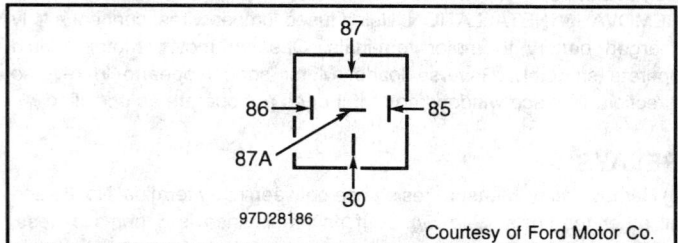

Fig. 3: Identifying Relay Terminals

SINGLE SWITCH

Remove suspect window switch. See WINDOW SWITCH under REMOVAL & INSTALLATION. Check continuity between appropriate terminals with switch in specified position. See appropriate SWITCH

TESTING table. *See Fig. 4.* Replace switch if continuity does not exist as specified.

SWITCH TESTING (RIGHT FRONT)

Switch Position	Continuity Between Terminals
Up	4 & 6; 2 & 3
Down	4 & 3; 7 & 6

SWITCH TESTING (REAR – CREW CAB)

Switch Position	Continuity Between Terminals
Up	4 & 3; 7 & 6
Down	4 & 6; 2 & 3

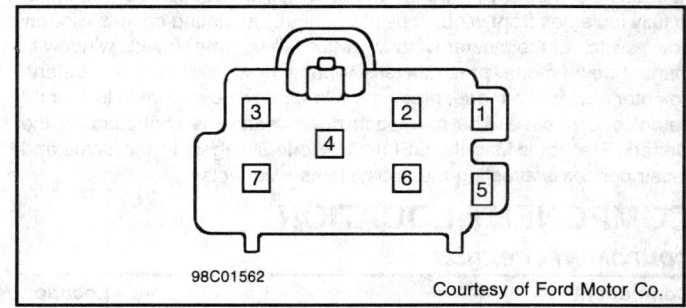

Fig. 4: Identifying Single Switch Terminals

SELF-DIAGNOSTIC SYSTEM

NOTE: When performing Generic Electronic Module (GEM) self-test, vehicles built prior to February 5, 1998 must have power windows completely up and headlights and parking lights off. Failure to do so will result in DTCs B1577 and B2357 being set. Vehicles built after February 5, 1998 must have headlights and parking lights on. Failure to do so will result in B1575 being set.

For preliminary testing, see TROUBLE SHOOTING. If problem is not found, connect New Generation STAR (NGS) tester, or equivalent scan tool, to Data Link Connector (DLC) located below center of instrument panel. Using NGS tester, perform data link diagnostic test. See DATA LINK DIAGNOSTIC TEST under COMMUNICATION NETWORK DIAGNOSTICS in MODULE COMMUNICATIONS NETWORK – F250 SUPER-DUTY & F350 PICKUP article. If NGS tester displays CKT914, CKT915 or CKT70 = ALL ECUS NO RESP/NOT EQUIP, repair module communications concern. See MODULE COMMUNICATIONS NETWORK – F250 SUPER-DUTY & F350 PICKUP article. If NGS tester displays NO RESP/NOT EQUIP for GEM, perform TEST A: NO SCAN TOOL COMMUNICATION WITH GEM under SYSTEM TESTS.

If NGS tester displays SYSTEM PASSED, retrieve and record continuous Diagnostic Trouble Codes (DTCs). Erase continuous DTCs. Perform GEM self-test. If GEM DTCs related to the concern are retrieved, perform appropriate test. See GEM DTC TEST INDEX table. If no DTCs related to the concern are retrieved, perform appropriate test based on symptom. See SYMPTOM TEST INDEX under SYSTEM TESTS. For GEM DTCs not covered in this article, see MODULE COMMUNICATIONS NETWORK – F250 SUPER-DUTY & F350 PICKUP article.

1999 ACCESSORIES & EQUIPMENT
Power Windows – F250 Super-Duty & F350 Pickup (Cont.)

FORD
4-1177

GEM DTC TEST INDEX

DTC [1]	Description	Test
B1243	One-Touch Down Switch Circuit Short To Power	G
B1302	Accessory Delay Relay Coil Circuit Failure	B
B1304	Accessory Delay Relay Coil Circuit Short To Power	B
B1342	ECU Defective	[2]
B1398	One-Touch Down Relay Circuit Failure	C
B1400	One-Touch Down Relay Short To Power	C
B1405	Driver's Window Down Circuit Short To Power	C
B1410	Driver's Window Motor Circuit Failure	G
B1475	Accessory Delay Relay Contact Short To Power	H
B2357	Driver's Window Down Current Sense Failure	C

[1] – Codes listed in this table are only for testing covered in this article. For complete DTC listing, see MODULE COMMUNICATIONS NETWORK – F250 SUPER-DUTY & F350 PICKUP article.

[2] – Replace GEM. See GENERIC ELECTRONIC MODULE (GEM) under REMOVAL & INSTALLATION.

SYSTEM TESTS

CAUTION: When battery is disconnected, vehicle computer and memory systems may lose memory data. Driveability problems may exist until computer systems have completed a relearn cycle. See COMPUTER RELEARN PROCEDURES article in GENERAL INFORMATION before disconnecting battery.

CAUTION: Disconnect battery before disconnecting Generic Electronic Module (GEM) connectors. Failure to do so will result in GEM storing erroneous codes and may also result in erratic operation of GEM after reconnection.

SYMPTOM TEST INDEX

Symptom	Test
No Scan Tool Communication With GEM	A
All Windows Inoperative	B
Driver's Window Inoperative	C
Right Front Window Inoperative	D
Left Rear Window Inoperative	E
Right Rear Window Inoperative	F
One-Touch Down Feature Inoperative	G
Delayed Accessory Feature Does Not Turn Off	H

TEST A: NO SCAN TOOL COMMUNICATION WITH GEM

1) Turn ignition switch to LOCK position. Check fuse junction panel fuse No. 15 (5-amp). If fuse is okay, go to next step. If fuse is blown, go to step **3)**.

2) Measure voltage between fuse junction panel fuse No. 15 (5-amp) input side and ground. If voltage is more than 10 volts, go to step **4)**. If voltage is 10 volts or less, go to step **5)**.

3) Disconnect Generic Electronic Module (GEM) from fuse junction panel connector C241. See GENERIC ELECTRONIC MODULE (GEM) under REMOVAL & INSTALLATION. Remove horn relay from fuse junction panel. Measure resistance between fuse junction panel connector C241 terminal No. 4 (fuse junction panel side) and ground. Measure resistance between fuse junction panel connector C241 terminal No. 12 (fuse junction panel side) and ground. Measure resistance between fuse junction panel connector between terminal No. 16 (fuse junction panel side) and ground. If all resistances are greater than 10 k/ohms, go to step **16)**. If any resistance is less than 10 k/ohms, replace fuse junction panel.

4) Disconnect GEM 26-pin connector C239. Measure resistance between GEM connector C239 terminal No. 26 (Pink/Orange wire) and ground. *See Fig. 5.* If resistance is less than 5 ohms, go to next step. If resistance is 5 ohms or more, repair open in Pink/Orange wire.

5) Check power distribution box fuse No. 22 (50-amp). If fuse is okay, go to next step. If fuse is blown, repair short to ground in Tan/Black wire.

6) Measure voltage between power distribution box fuse No. 22 fuse holder (input side) and ground. If voltage is more than 10 volts, repair

Tan/Black wire between power distribution box and fuse junction panel. If voltage is 10 volts or less, repair or replace power distribution box.

7) Measure resistance of Light Blue/White wire between GEM connector C239 terminal No. 25 and DLC terminal No. 7. *See Figs. 5 and 6.* If resistance is less than 5 ohms, go to next step. If resistance is 5 ohms or more, repair open in Light Blue/White wire.

8) Turn ignition switch to RUN position. Measure voltage between GEM connector C239 terminal No. 26 (Pink/Orange wire) and ground. *See Fig. 5.* If voltage is more than 10 volts, repair short to power in Pink/Orange wire. If voltage is 10 volts or less and vehicle is equipped with electronic shift transfer case, go to next step. If voltage is 10 volts or less and vehicle is not equipped with electronic shift transfer case, go to step **11)**.

9) Turn ignition switch to LOCK position. Disconnect GEM 22-pin connector C247. Turn ignition switch to RUN position. Measure voltage between GEM connector C247 terminal No. 4 (White/Light Blue wire) and ground. *See Fig. 7.* If voltage is more than 10 volts, go to next step. If voltage is 10 volts or less, go to step **11)**.

10) Turn ignition switch to LOCK position. Disconnect 4-wheel drive mode switch 4-pin connector located at center of instrument panel. Turn ignition switch to RUN position. Measure voltage between GEM connector C247 terminal No. 4 (White/Light Blue wire) and ground. *See Fig. 7.* If voltage is more than 10 volts, repair short to power in White/Light Blue wire and replace GEM. If voltage is 10 volts or less, replace 4-wheel drive mode switch and replace GEM. See GENERIC ELECTRONIC MODULE (GEM) under REMOVAL & INSTALLATION.

11) Measure voltage between GEM connector C239 terminal No. 20 (Dark Blue wire) and ground. *See Fig. 5.* If voltage is more than 10 volts, go to next step. If voltage is 10 volts or less, go to step **13)**.

12) Turn ignition switch to LOCK position. Disconnect multifunction switch 7-pin connector. Turn ignition switch to RUN position. Measure voltage between GEM connector C239 terminal No. 20 (Dark Blue wire) and ground. *See Fig. 5.* If voltage is more than 10 volts, repair short to power in Dark Blue wire and replace GEM. If voltage is 10 volts or less, replace multifunction switch and replace GEM. See GENERIC ELECTRONIC MODULE (GEM) under REMOVAL & INSTALLATION.

13) Measure voltage between GEM connector C239 terminal No. 23 (Pink/Yellow wire) and ground. *See Fig. 5.* If voltage is more than 10 volts, go to next step. If voltage is 10 volts or less and vehicle is not equipped with anti-lock brakes, go to step **15)**. If voltage is 10 volts or less and vehicle is equipped with anti-lock brakes, replace GEM. See GENERIC ELECTRONIC MODULE (GEM) under REMOVAL & INSTALLATION.

14) Turn ignition switch to LOCK position. Disconnect multifunction switch 7-pin connector. Turn ignition switch to RUN position. Measure voltage between GEM connector C239 terminal No. 23 (Pink/Yellow wire) and ground. *See Fig. 5.* If voltage is more than 10 volts, repair short to power in Pink/Yellow wire and replace GEM. If voltage is 10 volts or less, replace multifunction switch and replace GEM. See GENERIC ELECTRONIC MODULE (GEM) under REMOVAL & INSTALLATION.

15) Turn ignition switch to LOCK position. Disconnect differential speed sensor connector located on center of rear axle. Turn ignition switch to

FORD
4-1178

1999 ACCESSORIES & EQUIPMENT
Power Windows – F250 Super-Duty & F350 Pickup (Cont.)

RUN position. Measure voltage between GEM connector C239 terminal No. 9 (Light Green/Black wire) and ground. *See Fig. 5*. If voltage is more than 10 volts, repair Light Green/Black wire. If voltage is 10 volts or less, replace GEM. See GENERIC ELECTRONIC MODULE (GEM) under REMOVAL & INSTALLATION.

16) Turn ignition switch to LOCK position. Remove horn relay from fuse junction panel. Check horn relay. See RELAYS under COMPONENT TESTS. If relay is okay, go to next step. If relay is faulty, replace relay.

17) Remove GEM from fuse junction panel. See GENERIC ELECTRONIC MODULE (GEM) under REMOVAL & INSTALLATION. Disconnect GEM 22-pin connector C247. Disconnect Brake Pedal Position (BPP) switch 5-pin connector. Measure resistance between GEM connector C247 terminal No. 12 (Red/Light Green wire) and ground. *See Fig. 7*. If resistance is more than 10 k/ohms, go to next step. If resistance is 10 k/ohms or less, repair short to ground in Red/Light Green wire.

18) Disconnect fuse junction panel 34-pin connector C243. *See Fig. 8*. Measure resistance between BPP switch connector Light Blue/Black wire terminal and ground. If resistance is more than 10 k/ohms, replace BPP switch. If resistance is 10 k/ohms or less, repair short to ground in Light Blue/Black wire.

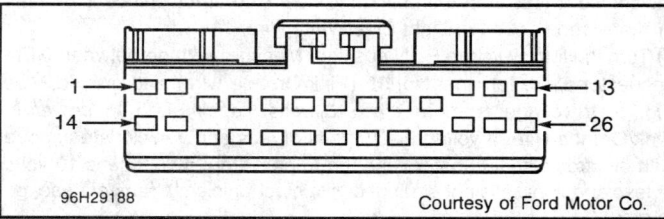

Courtesy of Ford Motor Co.

Fig. 5: Identifying GEM 26-Pin Connector C239 Terminals

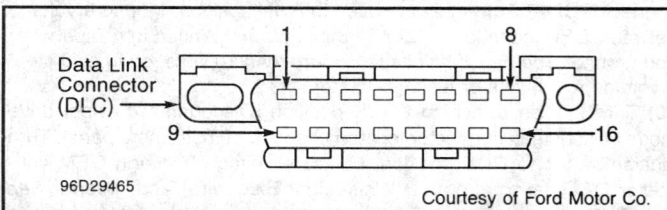

Courtesy of Ford Motor Co.

Fig. 6: Identifying Data Link Connector (DLC) Terminals

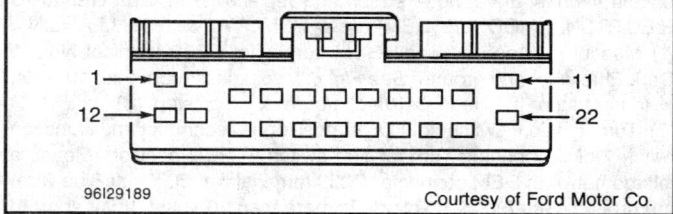

Courtesy of Ford Motor Co.

Fig. 7: Identifying GEM 22-Pin Connector C247 Terminals

TEST B: ALL WINDOWS INOPERATIVE

1) Using NGS tester, perform Generic Electronic Module (GEM) self-test. If DTC B1302 was retrieved, go to step **9)**. If DTC B1304 was retrieved, go to step **13)**. If DTC B1398 or no DTCs were retrieved, go to next step.

2) Turn ignition switch to LOCK position. Remove accessory delay relay. Measure voltage between accessory delay relay socket terminal No. 30 and ground. *See Fig. 9*. If voltage is more than 10 volts, go to step **4)**. If voltage is 10 volts or less, go to next step.

3) Disconnect fuse junction panel 34-pin connector C242. *See Fig. 8*. Measure voltage between fuse junction panel connector C242 terminal No. 25 (Red/Light Blue wire) and ground. If voltage is more than 10 volts, replace fuse junction panel. If voltage is 10 volts or less, repair Red/Light Blue wire.

4) Install accessory delay relay. Remove one-touch down relay. Turn ignition switch to RUN position. Measure voltage between one-touch

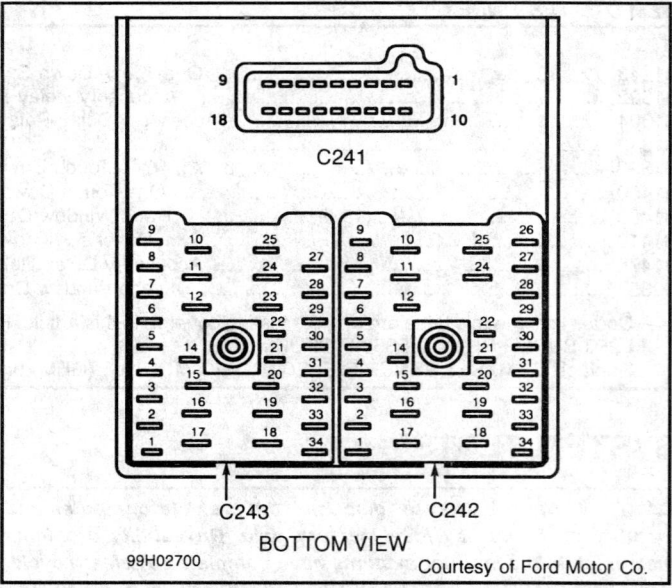

Fig. 8: Identifying Fuse Junction Panel Connectors & Terminals

down relay socket terminal No. 86 and ground. *See Fig. 9*. If voltage is more than 10 volts, go to next step. If voltage is 10 volts or less, go to step **8)**.

5) Turn ignition switch to LOCK position. Disconnect master window switch connector. Turn ignition switch to RUN position. Measure voltage between master window switch connector Light Blue/Black wire terminal and ground. If voltage is more than 10 volts, go to step **7)**. If voltage is 10 volts or less, go to next step.

6) Turn ignition switch to LOCK position. Disconnect fuse junction panel 34-pin connector C242. *See Fig. 8*. Turn ignition switch to RUN position. Measure resistance of Light Blue/Black wire between master window switch and fuse junction panel connector C242 terminal No. 10. If resistance is less than 5 ohms, replace fuse junction panel. If resistance is 5 ohms or more, repair open in Light Blue/Black wire.

7) Turn ignition switch to LOCK position. Measure resistance between each master window switch connector Black wire terminal and ground. If each resistance is less than 10 ohms, replace master window switch. If any resistance is 10 ohms or more, repair open in appropriate Black wire(s). Ground point is at left rear of cab.

8) Check accessory delay relay. See RELAYS under COMPONENT TESTS. If relay is okay, replace master window switch. If relay is faulty, replace relay.

9) Turn ignition switch to LOCK position. Remove accessory delay relay. Measure voltage between accessory delay relay socket terminal No. 86 and ground. *See Fig. 9*. If voltage is more than 10 volts, go to step **11)**. If voltage is 10 volts or less, go to next step.

10) Open driver's door. If interior lights operate, replace fuse junction panel. If interior lights do not operate, see appropriate wiring diagram in ILLUMINATION/INTERIOR LIGHTS article.

11) Check accessory delay relay. See RELAYS under COMPONENT TESTS. If relay is okay, go to next step. If relay is faulty, replace relay.

12) Remove GEM from fuse junction panel. See GENERIC ELECTRONIC MODULE (GEM) under REMOVAL & INSTALLATION. Measure internal resistance of fuse junction panel between connector C241 terminal No. 11 (fuse junction panel side) and accessory delay relay socket terminal No. 85. *See Figs. 8 and 9*. If resistance is less than 5 ohms, replace GEM. If resistance is 5 ohms or more, replace fuse junction panel.

13) Turn ignition switch to LOCK position. Check accessory delay relay. See RELAYS under COMPONENT TESTS. If relay is okay, go to next step. If relay is faulty, replace relay.

14) Remove GEM from fuse junction panel. See GENERIC ELECTRONIC MODULE (GEM) under REMOVAL & INSTALLATION. Turn ignition switch to RUN position. Measure voltage between accessory

1999 ACCESSORIES & EQUIPMENT
Power Windows – F250 Super-Duty & F350 Pickup (Cont.)

FORD
4-1179

delay relay socket terminal No. 85 and ground. *See Fig. 9*. If voltage is more than 10 volts, replace fuse junction panel. If voltage is 10 volts or less, replace GEM.

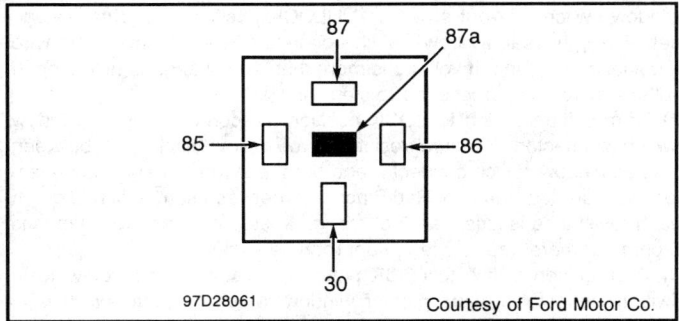

Fig. 9: Identifying Relay Socket Terminals

TEST C: DRIVER'S WINDOW INOPERATIVE

1) Using NGS tester, perform Generic Electronic Module (GEM) self-test. If DTC B1398 was retrieved, go to next step. If DTC B1400 was retrieved, go to step **6**). If DTC B1405 was retrieved, go to step **22**). If DTC B2357 was retrieved, go to step **8**). If no DTCs were retrieved, go to step **8**).

2) Turn ignition switch to LOCK position. Check one-touch down relay. See RELAYS under COMPONENT TESTS. If relay is okay, go to next step. If relay is faulty, replace relay.

3) Turn ignition switch to RUN position. Measure voltage between one-touch down relay socket terminal No. 86 and ground. *See Fig. 9*. If voltage is more than 10 volts, go to next step. If voltage is 10 volts or less, replace fuse junction panel.

4) Turn ignition switch to LOCK position. Remove GEM from fuse junction panel. See GENERIC ELECTRONIC MODULE (GEM) under REMOVAL & INSTALLATION. Measure internal resistance of fuse junction panel between connector C241 terminal No. 2 (fuse junction panel side) and one-touch down relay socket terminal No. 86. *See Figs. 8 and 9*. If resistance is less than 5 ohms, go to next step. If resistance is 5 ohms or more, replace fuse junction panel.

5) Measure resistance between one-touch down relay socket terminal No. 86 and ground. *See Fig. 9*. If resistance is more than 10 k/ohms, replace GEM. If resistance is 10 k/ohms or less, replace fuse junction panel.

6) Turn ignition switch to LOCK position. Check one-touch down relay. See RELAYS under COMPONENT TESTS. If relay is okay, go to next step. If relay is faulty, replace relay.

7) Remove GEM from fuse junction panel. See GENERIC ELECTRONIC MODULE (GEM) under REMOVAL & INSTALLATION. Turn ignition switch to RUN position. Measure voltage between one-touch down relay socket terminal No. 85 and ground. *See Fig. 9*. If voltage is more than 10 volts, replace fuse junction panel. If voltage is 10 volts or less, replace GEM.

8) Turn ignition switch to RUN position. Using NGS tester, observe GEM PID D_DN_SW while pressing on master window switch to driver's window DOWN position. If PID value agrees with switch position, go to next step. If PID value does not agree with switch position, go to step **14**).

9) Turn ignition switch to LOCK position. Check one-touch down relay. See RELAYS under COMPONENT TESTS. If relay is okay, go to next step. If relay is faulty, replace relay.

10) Turn ignition switch to LOCK position. Disconnect master window switch connector. Turn ignition switch to RUN position. Using NGS tester, trigger GEM active command ONE TOUCH DOWN to ON. Connect fused jumper wire between master window switch connector White/Black wire terminal and ground. Disconnect jumper. Trigger active command ONE TOUCH DOWN to OFF. Connect fused jumper wire between master window switch connector White/Black wire terminal and Light Blue/Black wire terminal. Connect master window switch connector. If window moves up and down, replace master window switch. If window does not move up and down, go to next step.

11) Turn ignition switch to LOCK position. Disconnect driver's window motor 2-pin connector. Turn ignition switch to RUN position. Trigger GEM active command ONE TOUCH DOWN to ON. Measure voltage between driver's window motor connector Orange/White wire terminal and ground. If voltage is more than 10 volts, go to next step. If voltage is 10 volts or less, go to step **19**).

12) Turn ignition switch to LOCK position. Measure resistance between driver's window motor connector Orange/White wire terminal and ground. If resistance is less than 5 ohms, go to next step. If resistance is 5 ohms or more, go to step **21**).

13) Disconnect master window switch connector. Measure resistance of White/Black wire between master window switch connector and window motor connector. If resistance is less than 5 ohms, replace driver's window motor. See WINDOW MOTOR under REMOVAL & INSTALLATION. If resistance is 5 ohms or more, repair open in White/Black wire.

14) Turn ignition switch to LOCK position. Disconnect master window switch connector. Turn ignition switch to RUN position. Using NGS tester, observe GEM PID D_DN_SW. Connect fused jumper wire between master window switch connector Tan/Light Blue wire terminal and Light Blue/Black wire terminal. If PID reads DOWN when jumper wire is connected and OFF when disconnected, replace master window switch. If fuse in the jumper wire blows or there is no change in PID value, go to next step.

15) Turn ignition switch to LOCK position. Disconnect fuse junction panel 34-pin connector C243. *See Fig. 8*. Measure resistance of Tan/Light Blue wire between master window switch connector and fuse junction panel connector C243 terminal No. 10. If resistance is less than 5 ohms, go to next step. If resistance is 5 ohms or more, repair open in Tan/Light Blue wire.

16) Measure resistance between master window switch connector Tan/Light Blue wire terminal and ground. If resistance is more than 10 k/ohms, go to next step. If resistance is 10 k/ohms or less, repair short to ground in Tan/Light Blue wire.

17) Remove GEM from fuse junction panel. See GENERIC ELECTRONIC MODULE (GEM) under REMOVAL & INSTALLATION. Measure internal resistance of fuse junction panel between connector C241 terminal No. 8 (fuse junction panel side) and connector C243 terminal No. 10 (fuse junction panel side). *See Fig. 8*. If resistance is less than 5 ohms, go to next step. If resistance is 5 ohms or more, replace fuse junction panel.

18) Measure resistance between fuse junction panel connector C243 terminal No. 10 (fuse junction panel side) and ground. *See Fig. 8*. If resistance is more than 10 k/ohms, replace GEM. If resistance is 10 k/ohms or less, replace fuse junction panel.

19) Remove one-touch down relay. Turn ignition switch to RUN position. Measure voltage between one-touch down relay socket terminal No. 30 and ground. *See Fig. 9*. If voltage is more than 10 volts, go to next step. If voltage is 10 volts or less, replace fuse junction panel.

20) Turn ignition switch to LOCK position. Disconnect driver's window motor 2-pin connector. Disconnect fuse junction panel 34-pin connector C242. Measure resistance of Orange/White wire between window motor connector and fuse junction panel connector C242 terminal No. 24. *See Fig. 8*. If resistance is less than 5 ohms, replace fuse junction panel. If resistance is 5 ohms or more, repair open in Orange/White wire.

21) Disconnect fuse junction panel 34-pin connector C243. Measure resistance between connector C243 terminal No. 24 (Black wire) and ground. *See Fig. 8*. If resistance is less than 5 ohms, replace fuse junction panel. If resistance is 5 ohms or more, repair open in Black wire.

22) Turn ignition switch to LOCK position. Disconnect master window switch connector. Measure voltage between master window switch connector Tan/Light Blue wire terminal and ground. If voltage is more than 10 volts, go to next step. If voltage is 10 volts or less, replace master window switch.

23) Remove GEM from fuse junction panel. See GENERIC ELECTRONIC MODULE (GEM) under REMOVAL & INSTALLATION. Measure voltage between fuse junction panel connector C241 terminal No. 9 (fuse junction panel side) and ground. *See Fig. 8*. If voltage is more than 10 volts, go to next step. If voltage is 10 volts or less, replace GEM.

FORD
4-1180

1999 ACCESSORIES & EQUIPMENT
Power Windows – F250 Super-Duty & F350 Pickup (Cont.)

24) Disconnect fuse junction panel 34-pin connector C243. Measure voltage between connector C243 terminal No. 10 (Tan/Light Blue wire) and ground. *See Fig. 8*. If voltage is more than 10 volts, repair short to power in Tan/Light Blue wire. If voltage is 10 volts or less, replace fuse junction panel.

TEST D: RIGHT FRONT WINDOW INOPERATIVE

1) Turn ignition switch to LOCK position. Disconnect right front window switch connector. Turn ignition switch to RUN position. Put master window switch lock-out switch in UNLOCK position (crew cab). Measure voltage between right front window connector Light Blue/Black wire (Yellow/Light Green wire on crew cab) terminal and ground. If voltage is more than 10 volts, go to next step. If voltage is 10 volts or less and vehicle is not a crew cab, repair Light Blue/Black wire. If voltage is 10 volts or less and vehicle is a crew cab, go to step **3)**.

2) Turn ignition switch to LOCK position. Disconnect master window switch connector. Measure resistance of White/Yellow wire between master window switch connector and right front window switch connector. Measure resistance of Tan/Light Blue wire between same connectors. If each resistance is less than 5 ohms, go to step **4)**. If any resistance is 5 ohms or more, repair open in appropriate wire(s).

3) Turn ignition switch to LOCK position. Disconnect master window switch connector. Ensure master window switch lock-out switch is in UNLOCK position. Measure resistance between master window switch connector C510 terminal No. 2 (switch side) and master window switch connector C511 terminal No. 3 (switch side). *See Fig. 2*. If resistance is less than 5 ohms, repair Yellow/Light Green wire. See WIRING DIAGRAMS. If resistance is 5 ohms or more, replace master window switch.

4) Test right front window switch. See SINGLE SWITCH under COMPONENT TESTS. If switch is okay, go to next step. If switch is faulty, replace switch.

5) Disconnect right front window motor 2-pin connector. Measure resistance of Yellow/Red wire between right front window switch connector and right front window motor connector. Measure resistance of Red/Yellow wire between same connectors. If each resistance is less than 5 ohms, replace right front window motor. See WINDOW MOTOR under REMOVAL & INSTALLATION. If either resistance is 5 ohms or more, repair open in appropriate wire(s).

TEST E: LEFT REAR WINDOW INOPERATIVE

1) Turn ignition switch to LOCK position. Disconnect left rear window switch connector. Turn ignition switch to RUN position. Put master window switch lock-out switch in UNLOCK position. Measure voltage between left rear window switch connector Yellow/Light Green wire terminal and ground. If voltage is more than 10 volts, go to next step. If voltage is 10 volts or less, go to step **3)**.

2) Turn ignition switch to LOCK position. Disconnect master window switch connector. Measure resistance of Yellow/Light Blue wire between master window switch connector and left rear window switch connector. Measure resistance of Gray/Orange wire between same connectors. If each resistance is less than 5 ohms, go to step **4)**. If any resistance is 5 ohms or more, repair open in appropriate wire(s).

3) Turn ignition switch to LOCK position. Disconnect master window switch connector. Ensure master window switch lock-out switch is in UNLOCK position. Measure resistance between master window switch connector C510 terminal No. 2 (switch side) and master window switch connector C511 terminal No. 3 (switch side). *See Fig. 2*. If resistance is less than 5 ohms, repair Yellow/Light Green wire. If resistance is 5 ohms or more, replace master window switch.

4) Test left rear window switch. See SINGLE SWITCH under COMPONENT TESTS. If switch is okay, go to next step. If switch is faulty, replace left rear window switch.

5) Disconnect left rear window motor 2-pin connector. Measure resistance of Yellow/Black wire between left rear window switch connector and window motor connector. Measure resistance of Yellow/Light Blue wire between same connectors. If each resistance is less than 5 ohms, replace window motor. See WINDOW MOTOR under REMOVAL & INSTALLATION. If either resistance is 5 ohms or more, repair appropriate wire(s).

TEST F: RIGHT REAR WINDOW INOPERATIVE

1) Turn ignition switch to LOCK position. Disconnect right rear window switch connector. Turn ignition switch to RUN position. Put master window switch lock-out switch in UNLOCK position. Measure voltage between right rear window switch connector Yellow/Light Green wire terminal and ground. If voltage is more than 10 volts, go to next step. If voltage is 10 volts or less, go to step **3)**.

2) Turn ignition switch to LOCK position. Disconnect master window switch connector. Measure resistance of Yellow/Black wire between master window switch connector and right rear window switch connector. Measure resistance of Red/Black wire between same connectors. If each resistance is less than 5 ohms, go to step **4)**. If any resistance is 5 ohms or more, repair open in appropriate wire(s).

3) Turn ignition switch to LOCK position. Disconnect master window switch connector. Ensure master window switch lock-out switch is in UNLOCK position. Measure resistance between master window switch connector C510 terminal No. 2 (switch side) and master window switch connector C511 terminal No. 3 (switch side). *See Fig. 2*. If resistance is less than 5 ohms, repair Yellow/Light Green wire. See WIRING DIAGRAMS. If resistance is 5 ohms or more, replace master window switch.

4) Test right rear window switch. See SINGLE SWITCH under REMOVAL & INSTALLATION. If switch is okay, go to next step. If switch is faulty, replace switch.

5) Disconnect right rear window motor connector. Measure resistance of Brown wire between right rear window switch connector and window motor connector. Measure resistance of Brown/Yellow wire between same connectors. If each resistance is less than 5 ohms, replace window motor. See WINDOW MOTOR under REMOVAL & INSTALLATION. If any resistance is 5 ohms or more, repair open in appropriate wire(s).

TEST G: ONE-TOUCH DOWN FEATURE INOPERATIVE

1) Using NGS tester, perform Generic Electronic Module (GEM) self-test. If DTC B1243 was retrieved, go to step **3)**. If DTC B1410 or B2357, was retrieved, go to step **10)**. If other DTCs were retrieved with B2357, service other DTCs first. If DTC B1342 is retrieved, replace GEM. See GENERIC ELECTRONIC MODULE (GEM) under REMOVAL & INSTALLATION. If no DTCs were retrieved, go to next step.

2) Turn ignition switch to RUN position. Observe GEM PID OTD_SW while depressing master window switch driver's window down button. If PID value agrees with switch positions, go to step **10)**. If PID values does not agree with switch positions, go to next step.

3) Turn ignition switch to LOCK position. Disconnect master window switch connector. Turn ignition switch to RUN position. Observe GEM PID OTD_SW while connecting fused jumper wire between master window switch connector Light Blue/Black wire terminal and Gray wire terminal. If PID displays DOWN when fused jumper is connected and OFF when disconnected, replace master window switch. IF PID only displays OFF or fused jumper blows, go to next step. If PID only displays DOWN, go to step **8)**.

4) Turn ignition switch to LOCK position. Disconnect fuse junction panel 34-pin connector C243. *See Fig. 8*. Measure resistance of Gray wire between master window switch connector and fuse junction panel connector C243 terminal No. 28. If resistance is less than 5 ohms, go to next step. If resistance is 5 ohms or more, repair open in Gray wire.

5) Measure resistance between master window switch connector Gray wire terminal and ground. If resistance is more than 10 k/ohms, go to next step. If resistance is 10 k/ohms or less, repair short to ground in Gray wire.

6) Remove GEM from fuse junction panel. See GENERIC ELECTRONIC MODULE (GEM) under REMOVAL & INSTALLATION. Measure internal resistance of fuse junction panel between connector C243 terminal No. 28 (fuse junction panel side) and connector C241 terminal No. 9 (fuse junction panel side). *See Fig. 8*. If resistance is less than 5 ohms, go to next step. If resistance is 5 ohms or more, replace fuse junction panel.

7) Measure resistance between fuse junction panel connector C243 terminal No. 28 (fuse junction panel side) and ground. *See Fig. 8*. If

1999 ACCESSORIES & EQUIPMENT
Power Windows – F250 Super-Duty & F350 Pickup (Cont.)

FORD
4-1181

resistance is more than 10 k/ohms, replace GEM. If resistance is 10 k/ohms or less, replace fuse junction panel.

8) Measure voltage between master window switch connector Gray wire terminal and ground. If voltage is more than 10 volts, repair short to power in Gray wire. If voltage is 10 volts or less, go to next step.

9) Measure voltage between fuse junction panel connector C243 terminal No. 28 (fuse junction panel side) and ground. *See Fig. 8*. If voltage is more than 10 volts, replace fuse junction panel. If voltage is 10 volts or less, replace GEM. See GENERIC ELECTRONIC MODULE (GEM) under REMOVAL & INSTALLATION.

10) Turn ignition switch to RUN position. Toggle master window switch up and down. If window operates properly except for one-touch down, go to next step. If window does not operate properly, repair other window problem. See SYMPTOM TEST INDEX table.

11) Turn ignition switch to LOCK position. Remove one-touch down relay. Measure internal resistance of fuse junction panel between connector C241 terminal No. 7 (fuse junction panel side) and one-touch down relay socket terminal No. 87. *See Figs. 8 and 9*. Measure internal resistance of fuse junction panel resistance between connector C241 terminal No. 17 (fuse junction panel side) and one-touch down relay socket terminal No. 87. If each resistance is less than 5 ohms, go to next step. If either resistance is 5 ohms or more, replace fuse junction panel.

12) Measure voltage between fuse junction panel connector C241 terminal No. 7 (fuse junction panel side) and ground. *See Fig. 8*. If voltage is more than 10 volts, replace fuse junction panel. If voltage is 10 volts or less, replace GEM.

TEST H: DELAYED ACCESSORY DOES NOT TURN OFF

1) Using NGS tester, perform Generic Electronic Module (GEM) self-test. If DTC B1302 was retrieved, go to step **7)** . If DTC B1475 was retrieved, go to step **4)**. If DTC B1342 was retrieved, replace GEM. See GENERIC ELECTRONIC MODULE (GEM) under REMOVAL & INSTALLATION. If no DTCs were retrieved, go to next step.

2) Using NGS tester, observe GEM PID IGN_GEM while turning ignition switch through all positions. Depress clutch pedal (M/T). If PID values agree with switch positions, go to next step. If PID values do not agree with switch positions, repair appropriate ignition switch circuit. See appropriate wiring diagram in POWER DISTRIBUTION article in WIRING DIAGRAMS.

3) Turn ignition switch to RUN position. Observe PID ACCDLY while toggling active command ACC RLY to ON and OFF. If PID value agrees with active command mode, go to next step. If PID does not agree with active command mode, go to step **7)**.

4) Turn ignition switch to LOCK position. Check accessory delay relay. See RELAYS under COMPONENT TESTS. If relay is okay, go to next step. If relay is faulty, replace relay.

5) Turn ignition switch to LOCK position. Disconnect fuse junction panel 34-pin connector C243. *See Fig. 8*. Disconnect master window switch connector. Measure voltage between master window switch connector Light Blue/Black wire terminal and ground. If voltage is more than 10 volts, repair short to power in Light Blue/Black wire. If voltage is 10 volts or less, go to next step.

6) Remove GEM from fuse junction panel. See GENERIC ELECTRONIC MODULE (GEM) under REMOVAL & INSTALLATION. Turn ignition switch to RUN position. Measure voltage between fuse junction panel connector C241 terminal No. 17 (fuse junction panel side) and ground. *See Fig. 8*. If voltage is more than 10 volts, replace fuse junction panel. If voltage is 10 volts or less, replace GEM.

7) Turn ignition switch to LOCK position. Check accessory delay relay. See RELAYS under COMPONENT TESTS. If relay is okay, go to next step. If relay is faulty, replace relay.

8) Turn ignition switch to LOCK position. Remove GEM from fuse junction panel. See GENERIC ELECTRONIC MODULE (GEM) under REMOVAL & INSTALLATION. Remove accessory delay relay. Measure resistance between fuse junction panel connector C241 terminal No. 11 (fuse junction panel side) and ground. *See Fig. 8*. If resistance is more than 10 k/ohms, replace GEM. If resistance is 10 k/ohms or less, replace fuse junction panel.

REMOVAL & INSTALLATION

CAUTION: When battery is disconnected, vehicle computer and memory systems may lose memory data. Driveability problems may exist until computer systems have completed relearn cycle. See COMPUTER RELEARN PROCEDURES article in GENERAL INFORMATION before disconnecting battery.

GENERIC ELECTRONIC MODULE (GEM)

CAUTION: Disconnect battery before disconnecting Generic Electronic Module (GEM) connectors. Failure to do so will result in GEM storing erroneous codes and may also result in erratic operation of GEM after reconnection.

NOTE: GEM must be reconfigured upon replacement. Refer to NGS tester help screen on Ford Service Function (FSF) card to program tire size and axle ratio.

Removal & Installation – Remove instrument panel steering column cover. Disconnect bulkhead connectors from fuse junction panel. Remove fuse junction panel nuts and bolts and position aside. Disconnect GEM electrical connectors and screws. Remove GEM. To install, reverse removal procedure.

WINDOW MOTOR

Removal & Installation – Remove window switch, door panel and watershield. Tape window in full up position. Disconnect window motor electrical connector. On rear door position electrical connector inside door. Remove 3 window motor mounting screws, or bolts, and remove motor. To install, reverse removal procedure.

WINDOW SWITCH

Removal & Installation – Disconnect battery ground cable. Remove switch by pushing forward and lifting up on front of trim plate that contains switch. Disconnect electrical connectors. Remove retaining clips and remove switch. To install, reverse removal procedure.

FORD
4-1182

1999 ACCESSORIES & EQUIPMENT
Power Windows – F250 Super-Duty & F350 Pickup (Cont.)

WIRING DIAGRAMS

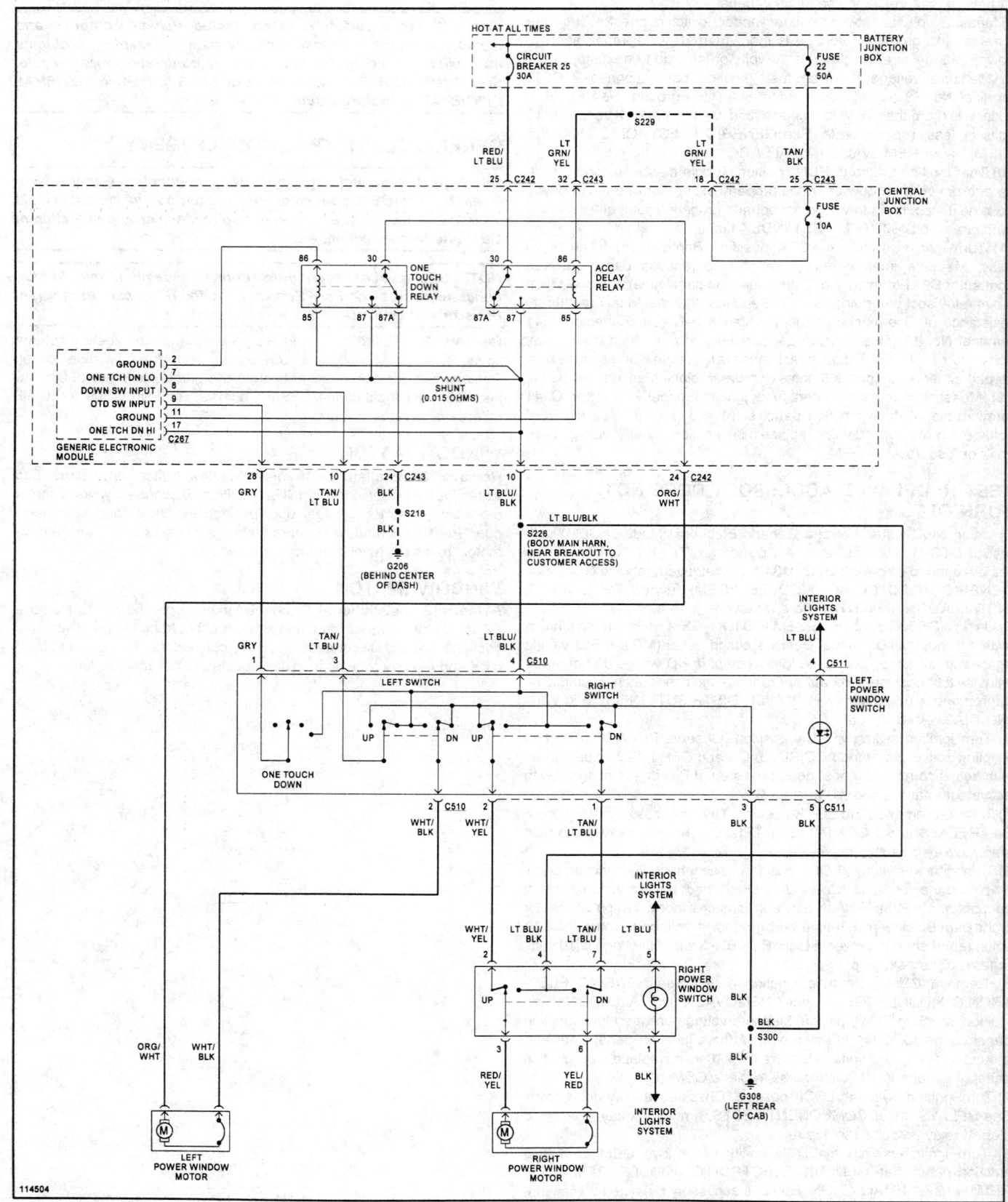

Fig. 10: Power Window System Wiring Diagram (F250 Super-Duty & F350 Pickup – Except Crew Cab)

114504

1999 ACCESSORIES & EQUIPMENT
Power Windows – F250 Super-Duty & F350 Pickup (Cont.)

FORD
4-1183

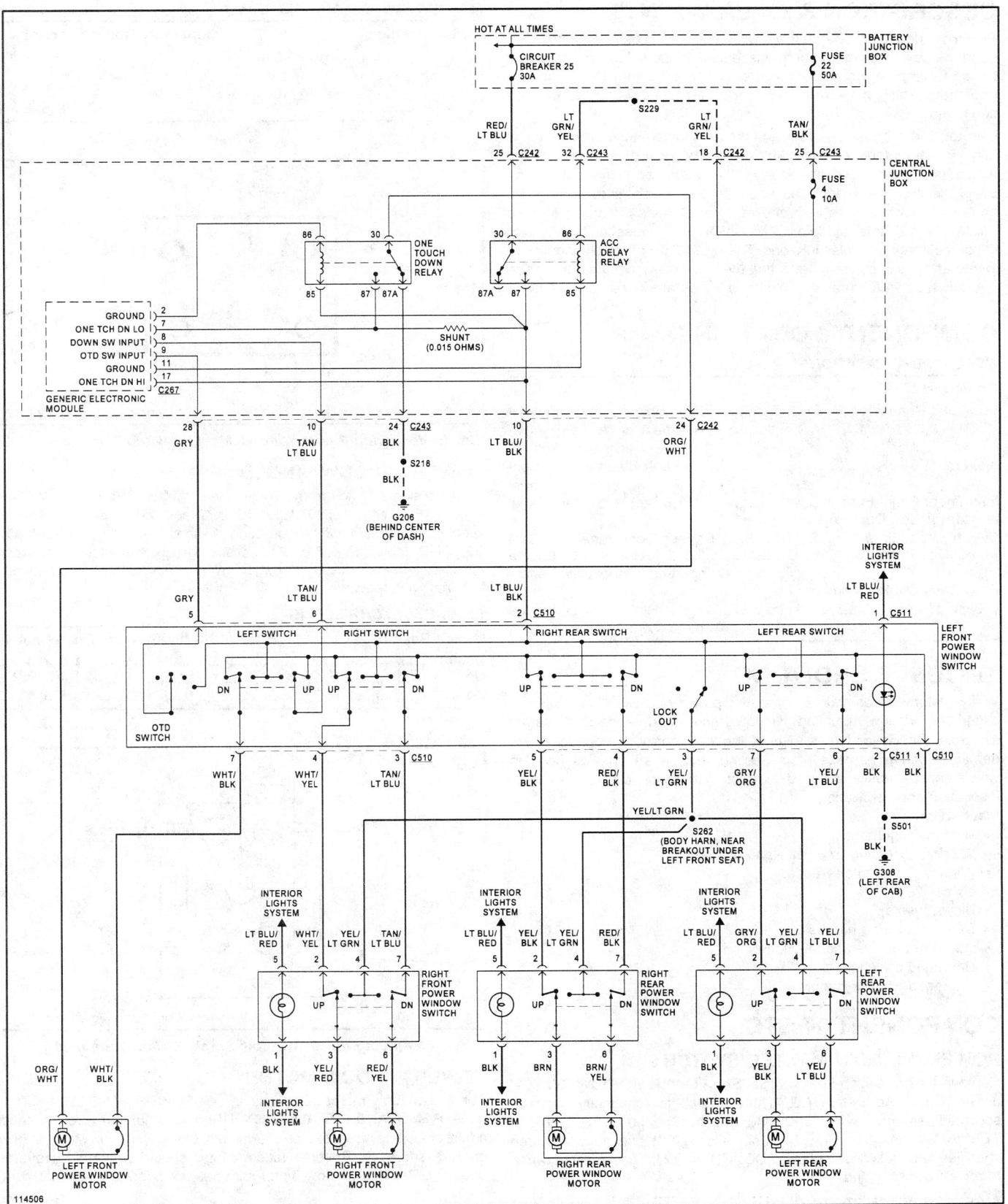

Fig. 11: Power Window System Wiring Diagram (F250 Super-Duty & F350 Pickup – Crew Cab)

114506

DESCRIPTION & OPERATION

Power windows are operated by reversible type motors mounted with each window regulator. Each passenger window has an individual switch for separate control. A master switch is located on the driver's door from which both front and rear (if equipped) windows may be controlled.

One-touch down feature allows the driver to lower the left front window fully by momentarily actuating the driver's window down switch at the master power window switch. Holding the switch down longer allows the driver to stop the window as soon as the switch is released. The one-touch down feature is controlled by a Generic Electronic Module (GEM)/Central Timer Module (CTM) which incorporates the functions of several different modules into one. The GEM/CTM offers diagnostics to locate and repair concerns affecting the subsystem that it controls. The one-touch down feature can only be actuated at the master switch.

COMPONENT LOCATIONS

COMPONENT LOCATIONS

Component	Location
Data Link Connector (DLC)	Below Driver's Side Of Instrument Panel, To Right Of Steering Column
Instrument Cluster	Behind Left Side Of Instrument Panel
Instrument Panel Fuse Block	Below Left Instrument Panel
Master Window/Door Lock Switch	Driver's Door Panel Arm Rest
Power Distribution Box	Left Side Of Engine Compartment, Above Wheelwell
Powertrain Control Module (PCM)	Right Rear Of Engine Compartment Through Firewall

TROUBLE SHOOTING

Verify customers complaint by operating power windows. Check window alignment, window mounting, window frame interference or damaged switches. Check for blown fuse(s), loose or corroded connectors, or damaged wiring harness. If inspection reveals an obvious concern which can be easily serviced, correct malfunction before continuing inspection and verification.

Mechanical:
- Window alignment.
- Window mounting (regulator and bracket).
- Window frame interference.

Electrical:
- Blown fuse(s).
- Damaged wiring harness.
- Loose or corroded connections.
- Damaged switches.
- Damaged window motor.

COMPONENT TESTS

POWER WINDOW MASTER SWITCH

Remove master switch from vehicle. See POWER WINDOW SWITCH under REMOVAL & INSTALLATION. Check for continuity between specified terminals while operating switch. See MASTER SWITCH TESTING table. *See Fig. 1.* Replace switch if continuity between specified terminals does not exist. DO NOT check for continuity between terminals not specified.

MASTER SWITCH TESTING

Switch Position	Continuity Between Terminals
Neutral	1, 2, 3, 4 & 6
Left	
Up	3 & 5; 2 & 6

Switch Position	Continuity Between Terminals
Down	5 & 6; 2 & 3
Right	
Up	4 & 5; 1 & 2
Down	1 & 5; 2 & 4

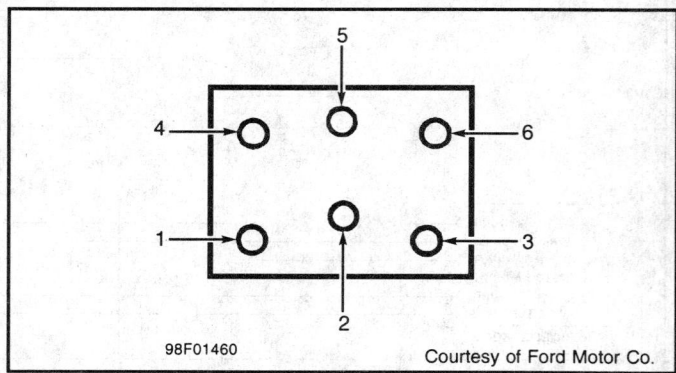

Fig. 1: Identifying Power Window Master Switch Terminals

POWER WINDOW SINGLE SWITCH

Remove single switch from vehicle. See POWER WINDOW SWITCH under REMOVAL & INSTALLATION. Check for continuity between specified terminals while operating switch. See SINGLE SWITCH TESTING table. *See Fig. 2.* Replace switch if continuity between specified terminals does not exist. DO NOT check for continuity between terminals not specified.

SINGLE SWITCH TESTING

Switch Position	Continuity Between Terminals
Neutral	1 & 2; 4 & 5
Up	1 & 3; 4 & 5
Down	3 & 5; 1 & 2

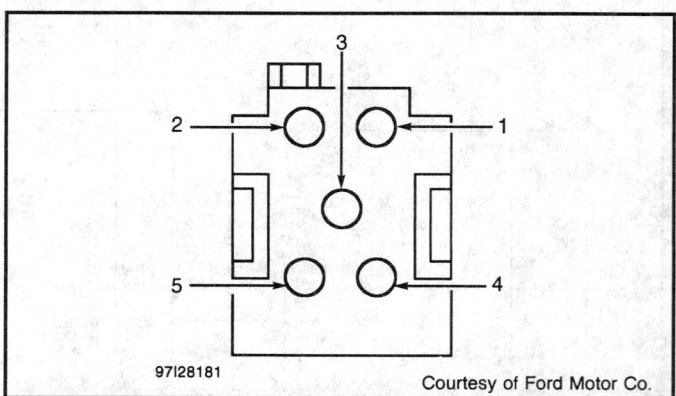

Fig. 2: Identifying Power Window Single Switch Terminals

POWER WINDOW MOTOR

Remove window motor from vehicle, see POWER WINDOW MOTOR under REMOVAL & INSTALLATION. Using fused jumper wires, connect a fully charged battery to motor terminals. Observe motor. Motor should operate smoothly. Reverse leads. Motor should operate in reverse direction. Replace window motor if it does not operate as specified.

DELAYED ACCESSORY RELAY

Remove delayed accessory relay (located under instrument panel, behind glove box). Using an ohmmeter, check continuity between relay terminals No. 85 and 86. *See Fig. 3.* Continuity should always exist. Check continuity between relay terminals No. 30 and 87a. Continuity should exist. Apply battery voltage and ground to relay terminals No. 85 and 86. Continuity should now exist between relay terminals No. 30 and 87. Replace relay if it does not test as specified. *See Fig. 3.*

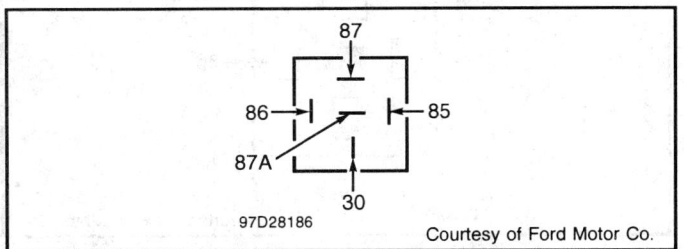

Fig. 3: Identifying Delayed Accessory Relay Terminals

ONE-TOUCH DOWN RELAY

Remove one-touch down relay (located in relay module, on left side of glove box). Using an ohmmeter, check continuity between relay terminals No. 1 and 2. *See Fig. 4.* Continuity should always exist. Check continuity between relay terminals No. 3 and 4. Continuity should exist. Apply battery voltage and ground to relay terminals No. 1 and 2. Continuity should now exist between relay terminals No. 3 and 5. Replace relay if it does not test as specified.

SELF-DIAGNOSTIC SYSTEM

1) Connect New Generation Star (NGS) tester to Data Link Connector (DLC) located below instrument panel. Using NGS tester, perform DATA LINK DIAGNOSTIC TEST. If NGS tester displays CKT 914, CKT 915 or

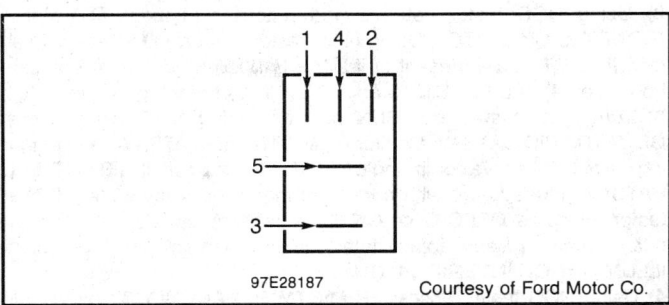

Fig. 4: Identifying One-Touch Down Relay Terminals

CKT 70=ALL ECUS NO RESP/NOT EQUIP, see MODULE COMMUNICATIONS NETWORK – RANGER article to diagnosis network concern. If NGS tester displays NO RESP/NOT EQUIP for Generic Electronic Module (GEM)/Central Timer Module (CTM), go to TEST E: NO COMMUNICATION WITH GEM/CTM under SYSTEM TESTS.

2) If NGS tester displays SYSTEM PASSED for GEM/CTM, retrieve and record continuous DTCs using NGS tester. Erase continuous DTCs. Perform GEM/CTM On-Demand SELF-TEST using NGS tester. If any DTCs are present, see GENERIC ELECTRONIC MODULE/CENTRAL TIMER MODULE (GEM/CTM) DTC DEFINITIONS table. If no DTCs are retrieved, perform appropriate system test. See SYMPTOM INDEX table under SYSTEM TESTS.

GENERIC ELECTRONIC MODULE/CENTRAL TIMER MODULE (GEM/CTM) DTC DEFINITIONS

DTC [1]	Description	Test
B1302	Accessory Delay Relay Coil Circuit Failure	A
B1304	Accessory Delay Relay Coil Circuit Short To Battery	A
B1313	Battery Saver Relay Coil Circuit Failure	A
B1315	Battery Saver Relay Coil Circuit Short To Battery	A
B1342	GEM/CTM Is Defective	[2]
B1398	Driver Door One-Touch Window Relay Circuit Failure	B Or D
B1400	Driver Door One-Touch Window Relay Coil Circuit Short To Battery	B Or D
B1404	Driver Door Window Down Switch Input Circuit Open	B
B1405	Driver Door Window Down Switch Input Circuit Short To Battery	B
B1410	Driver Door Window Motor Circuit Failure	B [3]
B1475	Delayed Accessory Relay Contacts Short To Battery	A
B2141	NVM Configuration Failure	[4]

[1] – Codes listed in this table are for testing covered in this article. For complete DTC listing, see MODULE COMMUNICATIONS NETWORK – RANGER article.

[2] – Using NGS tester, clear DTCs. Retrieve DTCs. If DTC B1342 is retrieved, replace GEM/CTM and retest system operation.

[3] – This DTC may also be present from GEM/CTM wiggle test.

[4] – Vehicle speed calibration data is not programmed into GEM/CTM. Use NGS tester configuration card help screen to program tire size and axle ratio. Retest system operation. If DTC B2141 is still present, replace GEM/CTM and retest system operation.

SYSTEM TESTS

CAUTION: When battery is disconnected or modules are replaced, vehicle computer and memory systems may lose memory data. Driveability problems may exist until computer systems have completed a relearn cycle. See COMPUTER RELEARN PROCEDURES article in GENERAL INFORMATION before disconnecting battery.

NOTE: Before beginning system tests, perform TROUBLE SHOOTING.

SYMPTOM INDEX

Symptom	Test
Power Windows Are Inoperative	A
Driver Power Window Inoperative	B

SYMPTOM INDEX (Cont.)

Symptom	Test
Passenger Power Window Inoperative	C
One Touch Down Feature Inoperative	D
No Communication With GEM/CTM	E
All Windows Operate With Ignition Off	F

TEST A: ALL POWER WINDOWS ARE INOPERATIVE

1) Turn ignition off. Using NGS tester, access GEM/CTM PID IGN_GEM/CTM. Monitor GEM/CTM PID IGN_GEM/CTM while rotating ignition switch through START, RUN, OFF and ACC positions. If PID values agree with ignition switch positions, go to next step. If PID values do not agree with ignition switch positions, check ignition switch and retest system operation. See STEERING COLUMN SWITCHES – RANGER article. Replace switch as necessary. If switch is okay, check ignition switch circuits. See appropriate wiring diagram in POWER DISTRIBUTION article in WIRING DIAGRAMS.

2) Using NGS tester, retrieve and record continuous DTCs from GEM/CTM. Clear DTCs. Using NGS tester, perform On-Demand self-test. If no DTCs are present or if DTCs B1302 and B1304 are present, go to step **4)**. If DTCs B1313 and B1315 are present, go to next step.

3) Turn ignition switch to RUN position. Using NGS tester, access GEM/CTM PID BATSAV. Monitor GEM/CTM PID BATSAV while triggering GEM/CTM active command BATTSAVR on and off. If GEM/CTM PID BATSAV values agree with command mode, go to next step. If NGS tester indicates OFFO-G or ON-B-, repair appropriate battery saver relay circuit. See appropriate wiring diagram in appropriate ILLUMINATION/INTERIOR LIGHTS article.

4) Using NGS tester, access GEM/CTM PID ACCDLY. Monitor GEM/CTM PID ACCDLY while triggering GEM/CTM active command ACCY RLY on and off. If NGS tester indicates OFFO-G, go to next step. If NGS tester indicates ON-B-, go to step **8)**. If GEM/CTM PID ACCDLY values agree with command mode, go to step **10)**.

5) Turn ignition off. Remove delayed accessory relay (located under right side of instrument panel, behind glove box). Using a voltmeter, check voltage between ground and delayed accessory relay connector terminal No. 86 (Light Green/Orange wire). See Fig. 5. If voltage is more than 10 volts, go to next step. If voltage is 10 volts or less, repair Light Green/Orange wire and retest system operation.

6) Check delayed accessory relay. See DELAYED ACCESSORY RELAY under COMPONENT TESTS. If delayed accessory relay is okay, go to next step. If delayed accessory relay does not test as specified, replace delayed accessory relay. Clear DTCs and retest system operation.

7) Disconnect 18-pin GEM/CTM connector C224 (located behind center of instrument panel). Using an ohmmeter, check resistance in Light Blue/Red wire between DELAYED ACCESSORY RELAY connector terminal No. 85 and 18-pin GEM/CTM connector C224 terminal No. 17. See Figs. 5 and 6. If resistance is less than 5 ohms, replace GEM/CTM. Clear DTCs and retest system operation. If resistance is 5 ohms or more, repair open in Light Blue/Red wire. Clear DTCs and retest system operation.

8) Check delayed accessory relay. See DELAYED ACCESSORY RELAY under COMPONENT TESTS. If delayed accessory relay is okay, go to next step. If delayed accessory relay does not test as specified, replace delayed accessory relay. Clear DTCs and retest system operation.

9) Disconnect 18-pin GEM/CTM connector C224 (located behind center of instrument panel). Turn ignition switch to RUN position. Using a voltmeter, check voltage between ground and delayed accessory relay connector terminal No. 85 (Light Blue/Red wire). See Fig. 5. If any voltage is present, repair short to power in Light Blue/Red wire. Clear DTCs and retest system operation. If no voltage is present, replace GEM/CTM. Clear DTCs and retest system operation.

10) Remove maxi-fuse No. 4 (20-amp) from engine compartment fuse box. If fuse is okay, go to next step. If fuse is blown, replace fuse. Clear DTCs and retest system operation. If fuse fails again, repair short to ground in Light Green/Orange wire. Clear DTCs and retest system operation.

11) Remove delayed accessory relay (located under right side of instrument panel, behind glove box). Using a voltmeter, check voltage between ground and delayed accessory relay connector terminal No. 87 (Red/Light Blue wire). See Fig. 5. If voltage is more than 10 volts, go to next step. If voltage is 10 volts or less, repair Red/Light Blue wire. Clear DTCs and retest system operation.

12) Check delayed accessory relay. See DELAYED ACCESSORY RELAY under COMPONENT TESTS. If delayed accessory relay is okay, repair Light Blue/Black wire. Clear DTCs and retest system operation. If delayed accessory relay does not test as specified, replace delayed accessory relay. Clear DTCs and retest system operation.

TEST B: DRIVER WINDOW DOES NOT OPERATE (PASSENGER WINDOW OPERATES)

1) Turn ignition off. Using NGS tester, access GEM/CTM PID IGN_GEM/CTM. Monitor GEM/CTM PID IGN_GEM/CTM while rotating ignition switch through START, RUN, OFF and ACC positions. If PID values

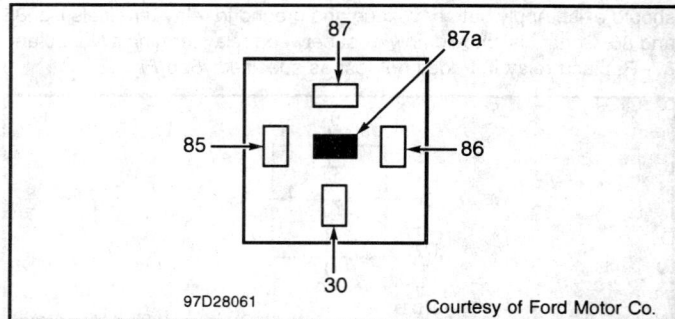

Fig. 5: Identifying Delayed Accessory Relay Connector Terminals

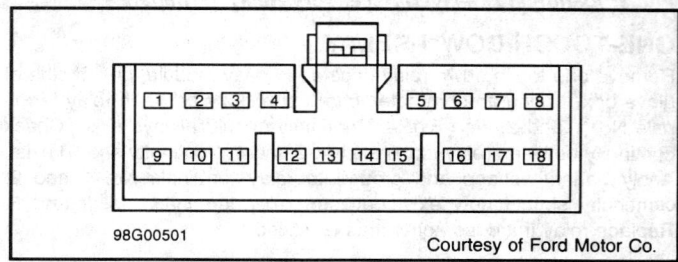

Fig. 6: Identifying GEM/CTM Connector C224 Terminals

agree with ignition switch positions, go to next step. If PID values do not agree with ignition switch positions, check ignition switch and retest system operation. See STEERING COLUMN SWITCHES – RANGER article. Replace switch as necessary. If switch is okay, check ignition switch circuits. See appropriate wiring diagram in POWER DISTRIBUTION article in WIRING DIAGRAMS.

2) Using NGS tester, retrieve and record continuous DTCs from GEM/CTM. Using NGS tester, clear continuous DTCs and perform GEM/CTM On-Demand Self-Test. If DTCs B1398 and/or B1400 are recorded, go to next step. If DTCs B1404 and/or B1410 are recorded, go to step **9)**. If DTC B1405 is recorded, go to step **12)**. If no DTCs are recorded, go to step **13)**. If DTC B1342 is recorded, replace GEM/CTM. Clear DTCs and retest system operation.

3) Turn ignition switch to RUN position. Using NGS tester, trigger GEM/CTM active command ACCY RLY on. Monitor GEM/CTM PID D_PWRLY while triggering GEM/CTM active command ONE TOUCH on and off. If GEM/CTM PID D_PWRLY value agrees with command mode, go to step **9)**. If NGS tester indicates OFFO-G, go to next step. If NGS tester indicates ON-B-, go to step **7)**.

4) Turn ignition off. Check one-touch down relay. See ONE-TOUCH DOWN RELAY under COMPONENT TESTS. If one-touch down relay is okay, go to next step. If one-touch down relay does not test as specified, replace one-touch down relay. Clear DTCs and retest system operation.

5) Remove delayed accessory relay (located under right side of instrument panel, behind glove box). Using an ohmmeter, check resistance in Light Blue/Black wire between delayed accessory relay connector terminal No. 30 and one-touch down relay connector terminal No. 1. See Figs. 5 and 7. Check resistance in Light Blue/Black wire between delayed accessory relay connector terminal No. 30 and one-touch down relay connector terminal No. 5. If resistances are less than 5 ohms, go to next step. If either resistance is 5 ohms or more, repair open in appropriate Light Blue/Black wire. Clear DTCs and retest system operation.

6) Disconnect 18-pin GEM/CTM connector C224 (located behind center of instrument panel). Using an ohmmeter, check resistance in Yellow/Red wire between one-touch down relay connector terminal No. 2 and 18-pin GEM/CTM connector C224 terminal No. 7. See Figs. 6 and 7. If resistance is less than 5 ohms, replace GEM/CTM. Clear DTCs and retest system operation. If resistance is 5 ohms or more, repair open in Yellow/Red wire. Clear DTCs and retest system operation.

7) Turn ignition off. Check one-touch down relay. See ONE-TOUCH DOWN RELAY under COMPONENT TESTS. If one-touch down relay is okay, go to next step. If one-touch down relay does not test as specified, replace one-touch down relay. Clear DTCs and retest system operation.

8) Disconnect 18-pin GEM/CTM connector C224 (located behind center of instrument panel). Turn ignition switch to RUN position. Using a voltmeter, check voltage between ground and one-touch down relay connector terminal No. 2 (Yellow/Red wire). *See Fig. 7.* If any voltage is present, repair short to power in Yellow/Red wire. Clear DTCs and retest system operation. If voltage is not present, replace GEM/CTM. Clear DTCs and retest system operation.

9) Turn ignition off. Remove and disconnect master window switch connector C502. See POWER WINDOW SWITCH under REMOVAL & INSTALLATION. Using NGS tester, access GEM/CTM PID D_PW_SW. Connect a jumper wire between ground and master window switch connector C502 terminal No. 6 (White/Black wire). Connect another jumper wire between battery voltage and master window switch connector C502 terminal No. 3 (Tan/Light Blue wire). Turn ignition switch to RUN position. If NGS tester does not indicate DOWN, remove jumper wires and go to next step. If NGS tester indicates DOWN, replace master window switch. Clear DTCs and retest system operation.

10) Disconnect 18-pin GEM/CTM connector C224 (located behind center of instrument panel). Using an ohmmeter, check resistance in Tan/Light Blue wire between 18-pin GEM/CTM connector C224 terminal No. 3 and master window switch connector C502 terminal No. 3. If resistance is less than 5 ohms, go to next step. If resistance is 5 ohms or more, repair open in Tan/Light Blue wire. Clear DTCs and retest system operation.

11) Using an ohmmeter, check resistance between ground and 18-pin GEM/CTM connector C224 terminal No. 3 (Tan/Light Blue wire). If resistance is more than 10 k/ohms, replace GEM/CTM and retest system operation. If resistance is 10 k/ohms or less, repair short to ground in Tan/Light Blue wire. Clear DTCs and retest system operation.

12) Turn ignition off. Remove and disconnect master window switch connector C502. See POWER WINDOW SWITCH under REMOVAL & INSTALLATION. Disconnect 18-pin GEM/CTM connector C224. Turn ignition switch to RUN position. Using a voltmeter, check voltage between ground and 18-pin GEM/CTM connector terminal No. 3 (Tan/Light Blue wire). If any voltage is present, repair short to voltage in Tan/Light Blue wire. Clear DTCs and retest system operation. If voltage is not present, replace GEM/CTM and retest system operation.

13) Turn ignition off. Disconnect driver door window motor connector C504. See POWER WINDOW MOTOR under REMOVAL & INSTALLATION. Turn ignition switch to RUN position. Using a voltmeter, check voltage between ground and driver door window motor connector C504 Red wire terminal while holding master window switch driver door window in DOWN position. If voltage is more than 10 volts, go to step **16**. If voltage is 10 volts or less, go to next step.

14) Turn ignition off. Remove one-touch down relay (located in relay module, on left side of glove box). Using an ohmmeter, check resistance in Red wire between one-touch down relay connector terminal No. 3 and driver door window motor connector. If resistance is less than 5 ohms, go to next step. If resistance is 5 ohms or more, repair open in Red wire. Clear DTCs and retest system operation.

15) Remove and disconnect master window switch connector C502. See POWER WINDOW SWITCH under REMOVAL & INSTALLATION. Using an ohmmeter, check resistance in Tan/Light Blue wire between master window switch connector C502 terminal No. 3 and one-touch down relay connector terminal No. 4. If resistance is less than 5 ohms, replace one-touch down relay. Clear DTCs and retest system operation. If resistance is 5 ohms or more, repair open in Tan/Light Blue wire. Clear DTCs and retest system operation.

16) Using a voltmeter, check voltage between ground and driver door window motor connector C504 White/Black wire terminal while holding master window switch driver door window in UP position. If voltage is more than 10 volts, replace driver door window motor. Clear DTCs and retest system operation. If voltage is 10 volts or less, repair White/Black wire. Clear DTCs and retest system operation.

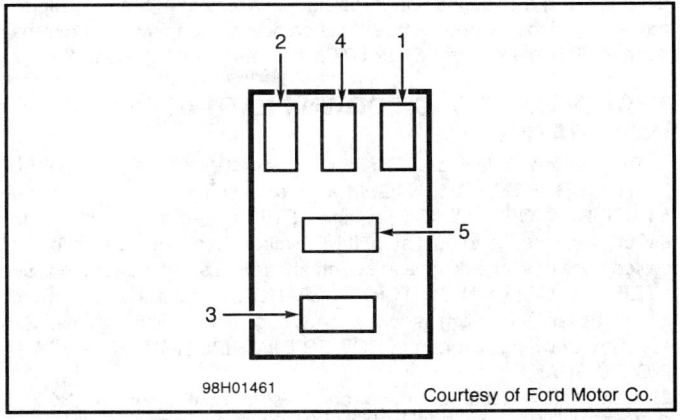

98H01461   Courtesy of Ford Motor Co.

Fig. 7: Identifying One-Touch Down Relay Connector Terminals

TEST C: PASSENGER WINDOW DOES NOT OPERATE (ALL OTHER WINDOWS OPERATE)

1) Turn ignition off. Remove and disconnect passenger window switch connector C602. See POWER WINDOW SWITCH under REMOVAL & INSTALLATION. Turn ignition switch to RUN position. Using a voltmeter, check voltage between ground and passenger window switch connector C602 terminal No. 3 (Light Blue/Black wire). If voltage is more than 10 volts, go to next step. If voltage is 10 volts or less, repair Light Blue/Black wire. Clear DTCs and retest system operation.

2) Turn ignition off. Using an ohmmeter, check resistance between ground and passenger window switch connector C602 terminal No. 4 (White/Yellow wire). Check resistance between ground and passenger window switch connector C602 terminal No. 2 (Tan/Light Blue wire). If either resistance is 14 ohms or more, go to next step. If resistances are less than 14 ohms, go to step **4)**.

3) Turn ignition switch off. Remove and disconnect master window switch. See POWER WINDOW SWITCH under REMOVAL & INSTALLATION. Using an ohmmeter, check resistance in White/Yellow wire between master window switch connector C502 terminal No. 4 and passenger window switch connector C602 terminal No. 4. Check resistance in Tan/Light Blue wire between master window switch connector C502 terminal No. 1 and passenger window switch connector C602 terminal No. 2. If either resistance is less than 5 ohms, replace master window switch. Clear DTCs and retest system operation. If resistances are 5 ohms or more, repair open in White/Yellow or Tan/Light Blue wire(s). Clear DTCs and retest system operation.

4) Connect jumper wire between passenger window switch connector C602 terminals No. 4 (White/Yellow wire) and No. 1 (Yellow/Red wire). Connect another jumper wire between passenger window switch connector C602 terminals No. 3 (Light Blue/Black wire) and No. 5 (Red/Yellow wire). Turn ignition switch to RUN position. If passenger window operates in DOWN direction, replace inoperative window switch. Clear DTCs and retest system operation. If passenger window does not operate in DOWN direction, remove jumper wires and go to next step.

5) Turn ignition off. Connect jumper wire between passenger window switch connector C602 terminals No. 5 (Red/Yellow wire) and No. 2 (Tan/Light Blue wire). Connect another jumper wire between passenger window switch connector C602 terminals No. 1 (Yellow/Red wire) and No. 3 (Light Blue/Black wire). Turn ignition switch to RUN position. If passenger window operates in UP direction, replace inoperative window switch. Clear DTCs and retest system operation. If passenger window does not operate in UP direction, remove jumper wires and go to next step.

6) Turn ignition off. Disconnect passenger door window motor connector C604. Using an ohmmeter, check resistance in Yellow/Red wire between passenger window switch connector C602 terminal No. 1 and passenger door window motor connector. If resistance is less than 5 ohms, go to next step. If resistance is 5 ohms or more, repair open in Yellow/Red wire. Clear DTCs and retest system operation.

7) Using an ohmmeter, check resistance in Red/Yellow wire between passenger window switch connector C602 terminal No. 5 and passenger window motor connector. If resistance is less than 5 ohms, replace passenger door window motor. If resistance is 5 ohms or more, repair open in Red/Yellow wire. Clear DTCs and retest system operation.

TEST D: ONE-TOUCH DOWN FEATURE IS INOPERATIVE

1) Turn ignition off. Using NGS tester, access GEM/CTM PID IGN_GEM. Monitor GEM/CTM PID IGN_GEM while rotating ignition switch through START, RUN, OFF and ACC positions. If PID values agree with ignition switch positions, go to next step. If PID values do not agree with ignition switch positions, check ignition switch and retest system operation. See STEERING COLUMN SWITCHES – RANGER article. Replace switch as necessary. If switch is okay, check ignition switch circuits. See appropriate wiring diagram in POWER DISTRIBUTION article in WIRING DIAGRAMS.

2) Using NGS tester, retrieve and record continuous DTCs from GEM/CTM. Using NGS tester, clear continuous DTCs and perform GEM/CTM On-Demand Self-Test. If no DTCs are recorded, go to next step. If DTCs B1398 and/or B1400 are recorded, go to next step.

3) Turn ignition switch to RUN position. Using NGS tester, trigger GEM/CTM active command ACCY RLY on. Monitor GEM/CTM PID D_PWRLY while triggering GEM/CTM active command ONE TOUCH on and off. If GEM/CTM PID D_PWRLY value agrees with command mode, go to step **10)**. If NGS tester indicates OFFO-G, go to next step. If NGS tester indicates ON-B-, go to step **7)**.

4) Turn ignition off. Check one-touch down relay. See ONE-TOUCH DOWN RELAY under COMPONENT TESTS. If one-touch down relay is okay, go to next step. If one-touch down relay does not test as specified, replace one-touch down relay. Clear DTCs and retest system operation.

5) Remove delayed accessory relay (located under right side of instrument panel, behind glove box). Using an ohmmeter, check resistance in Light Blue/Black wire between delayed accessory relay connector terminal No. 30 and one-touch down relay connector terminal No. 1. *See Figs. 5 and 7.* If resistance is less than 5 ohms, go to next step. If resistance is 5 ohms or more, repair open in appropriate Light Blue/Black wire. Clear DTCs and retest system operation.

6) Disconnect 18-pin GEM/CTM connector C224 (located behind center of instrument panel). Using an ohmmeter, check resistance in Yellow/Red wire between one-touch down relay connector terminal No. 2 and 18-pin GEM/CTM connector C224 terminal No. 7. *See Figs. 6 and 7.* If resistance is less than 5 ohms, replace GEM/CTM. Clear DTCs and retest system operation. If resistance is 5 ohms or more, repair open in Yellow/Red wire. Clear DTCs and retest system operation.

7) Turn ignition off. Check one-touch down relay. See ONE-TOUCH DOWN RELAY under COMPONENT TESTS. If one-touch down relay is okay, go to next step. If one-touch down relay does not test as specified, replace one-touch down relay. Clear DTCs and retest system operation.

8) Disconnect 18-pin GEM/CTM connector C224 (located behind center of instrument panel). Turn ignition switch to RUN position. Using a voltmeter, check voltage between ground and one-touch down relay connector terminal No. 2 (Yellow/Red wire). *See Fig. 7.* If any voltage is present, repair short to power in Yellow/Red wire. Clear DTCs and retest system operation. If voltage is not present, replace GEM/CTM. Clear DTCs and retest system operation.

9) Turn ignition off. Check one-touch down relay. See ONE-TOUCH DOWN RELAY under COMPONENT TESTS. If one-touch down relay is okay, go to next step. If one-touch down relay does not test as specified, replace one-touch down relay. Clear DTCs and retest system operation.

10) Turn ignition switch to RUN position. Using a voltmeter, check voltage between ground and one-touch down relay connector terminal No. 1 (Light Blue/Black wire). *See Fig. 7.* Check voltage between ground and one-touch down relay connector terminal No. 5 (Light Blue/Black wire). If voltages are more than 10 volts, go to next step. If either voltage is 10 volts or less, repair appropriate Light Blue/Black wire(s). Clear DTCs and retest system operation.

11) Turn ignition off. Disconnect driver door window motor connector C504. See POWER WINDOW MOTOR under REMOVAL & INSTALLATION. Disconnect 18-pin GEM/CTM connector C224 (located behind center of instrument panel). Using an ohmmeter, check resistance

between 18-pin GEM/CTM connector C224 terminal No. 10 (Gray wire) and driver door window motor connector C504 Red wire terminal. If resistance is less than 5 ohms, go to next step. If resistance is 5 ohms or more, repair open in Gray wire. Clear DTCs and retest system operation.

12) Using an ohmmeter, check resistance between 18-pin GEM/CTM connector C224 terminal No. 2 (Orange/White wire) and driver door window motor connector Red wire terminal. If resistance is less than 5 ohms, replace GEM/CTM. Clear DTCs and retest system operation. If resistance is 5 ohms or more, repair open in Orange/White wire. Clear DTCs and retest system operation.

TEST E: NO COMMUNICATION WITH GEM/CTM

1) Using ohmmeter, check condition of maxi-fuse No. 1 (50-amp) in engine compartment fuse/relay box. If fuse is okay, go to next step. If fuse is not okay, replace fuse. Clear DTCs and retest system operation. If fuse fails again, check Tan/Black wire between engine compartment fuse/relay box and instrument panel fuse block for short to ground. Repair circuit as necessary.

2) Using ohmmeter, check condition of instrument panel fuse block fuse No. 25 (7.5-amp). If fuse is okay, go to next step. If fuse is not okay, replace fuse. Clear DTCs and retest system operation. If fuse fails again, check White/Yellow wire between instrument panel fuse block and GEM/CTM for short to ground. Repair circuit as necessary.

3) Using a voltmeter, check voltage between ground and instrument panel fuse block fuse No. 25 (7.5-amp) terminal No. 2. *See Fig. 8.* If voltage is more than 10 volts, go to next step. If voltage is 10 volts or less, repair Tan/Black wire. Clear DTCs and retest system operation.

4) Turn ignition off. Disconnect 18-pin GEM/CTM connector C224 (located behind center of instrument panel). Using a voltmeter, check voltage between ground and 18-pin GEM/CTM connector C224 terminal No. 11 (White/Yellow wire). *See Fig. 6.* If voltage is more than 10 volts, go to next step. If voltage is 10 volts or less, repair White/Yellow wire between instrument panel fuse block and GEM/CTM. Clear DTCs and retest system operation.

5) Disconnect 26-pin GEM/CTM connector C221 (located behind center of instrument panel). Using an ohmmeter, check resistance between ground and 26-pin GEM/CTM connector C221 terminal No. 14 (Black/White wire). *See Fig. 9.* Check resistance between ground and 26-pin GEM/CTM connector C221 terminal No. 26 (Black/White wire). If both resistance readings are less than 5 ohms, go to next step. If either resistance reading is 5 ohms or more, repair open in appropriate Black/White wire(s). Clear DTCs and retest system operation.

6) Using an ohmmeter, check resistance between ground and 18-pin GEM/CTM connector C224 terminal No. 18 (Light Green/Black or Black wire). *See Fig. 6.* If resistance is less than 5 ohms, replace GEM/CTM. Clear DTCs and retest system operation. If resistance is 5 ohms or more, repair open in Light Green/Black or Black wire. Clear DTCs and retest system operation.

TEST F: ALL WINDOWS OPERATE WITH IGNITION OFF

Turn ignition off. Check delayed accessory relay. See DELAYED ACCESSORY RELAY under COMPONENT TESTS. If relay is okay, repair Light Blue/Black wire. Clear DTCs and retest system operation. If delayed accessory relay does not test as specified, replace delayed accessory relay. Clear DTCs and retest system operation.

REMOVAL & INSTALLATION

POWER WINDOW MOTOR

Removal & Installation – 1) Disconnect negative battery cable. Remove door trim panel and watershield. Raise window glass fully and tape in place. Disconnect motor wiring connector. Remove top and bottom center door glass run retainer nuts to loosen center door glass run retainer.

CAUTION: When drilling out rivets, do not enlarge holes in door.

2) Using a punch, drive pin from center of all 4 window regulator assembly retaining rivets. Ensure wiring is not in line with window

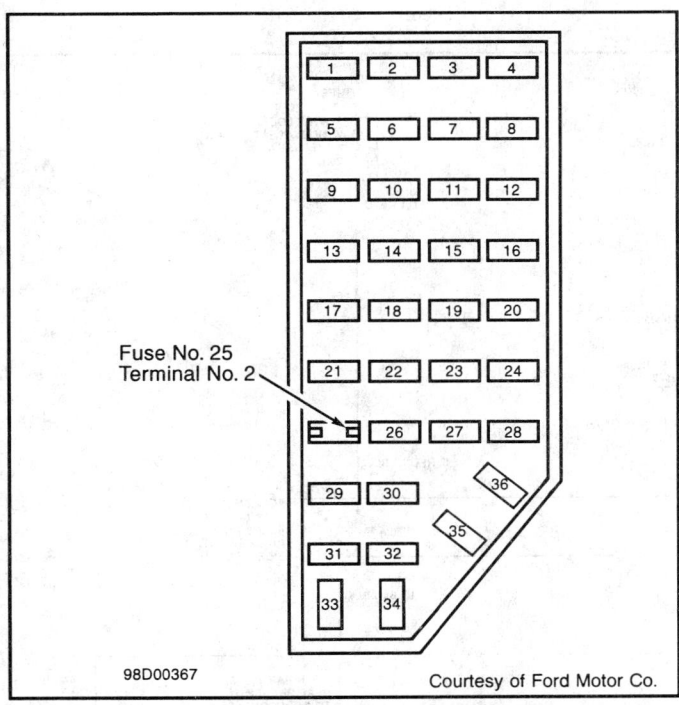

Fig. 8: Identifying Instrument Panel Fuse Block Fuse No. 25 Terminals

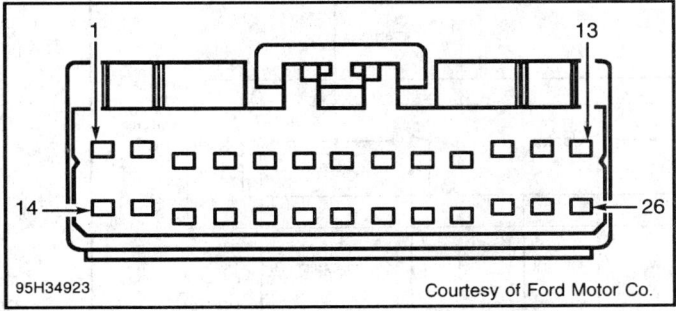

Fig. 9: Identifying GEM/CTM Connector C221 Terminals

regulator retaining rivets. Using 1/4" (6.35 mm) drill bit, drill out remainder of each rivet. Remove window regulator assembly.

3) Remove bolts and separate window motor from regulator. To install, reverse removal procedure. Tighten window motor retaining bolts to 53-80 INCH lbs. (6-9 N.m).

POWER WINDOW SWITCH

Removal & Installation – Remove door trim panel finish panel screws. Remove window switch by carefully prying up with a thin-blade screwdriver under switch plate finish panel located on door trim panel. Remove screws attaching wiring connector to switch plate. Carefully pry connector from switch. To install, reverse removal procedure.

WIRING DIAGRAMS

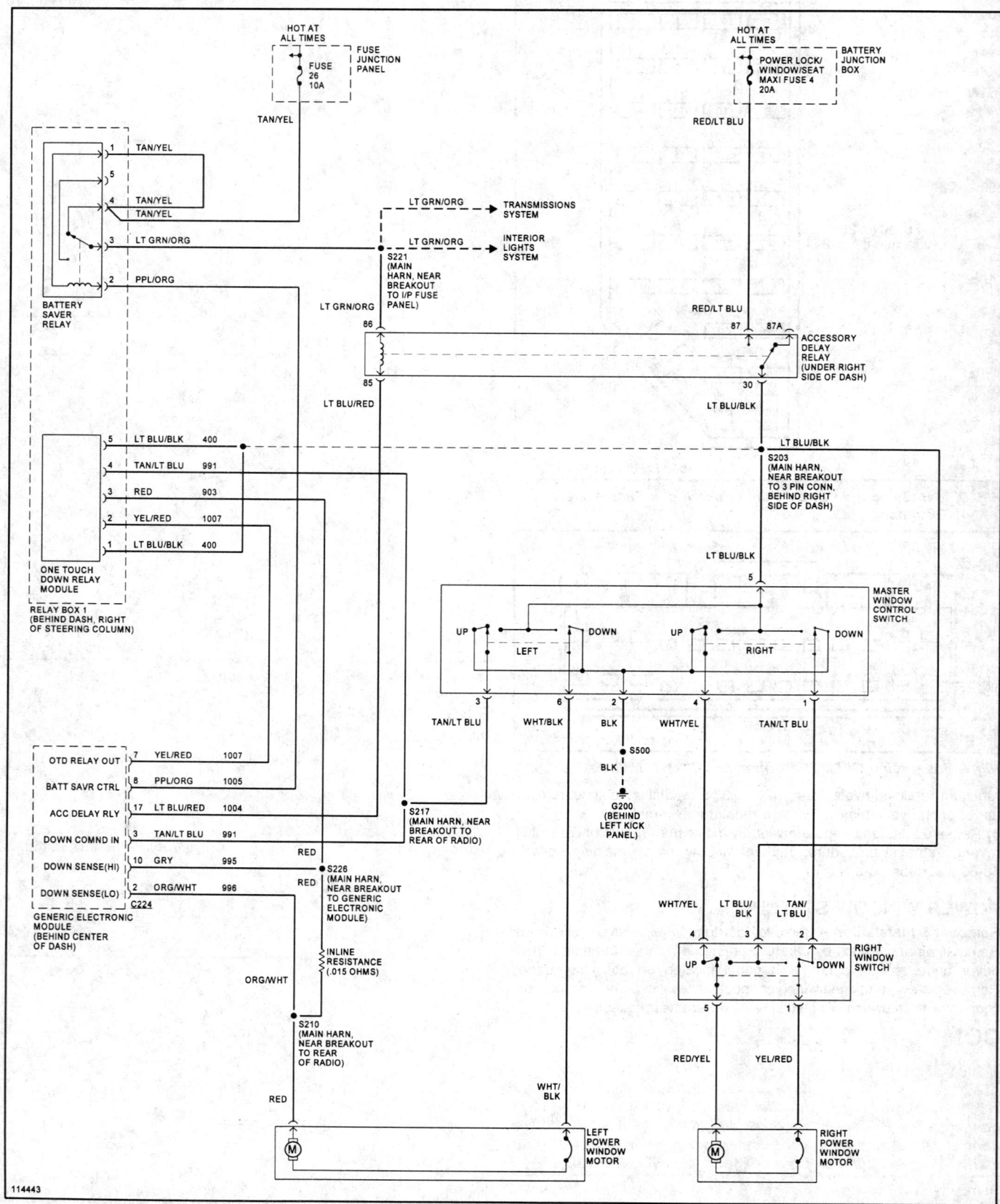

Fig. 10: Power Window System Wiring Diagram (Ranger)

DESCRIPTION & OPERATION

Power windows are operated by reversible type motors mounted with each window regulator. A master control switch located on driver's door can operate all windows. Single switches in each passenger door can be locked out from the master switch.

One-touch down feature will lower driver's window to full down position with a brief touch on the window switch. A delayed accessory feature will allow window operation for 45 seconds after ignition is turned off. One-touch down and delayed accessory functions are controlled by the Generic Electronic Module (GEM). The GEM has the ability to store and output Diagnostic Trouble Codes (DTCs) and Parameter Identification (PID) values.

ADJUSTMENTS

FRONT DOOR WINDOW GLASS

Lower door window 3.00″ (76.2 mm) from full up position. Remove door trim panel and watershield. Loosen nut and washer assembly securing window glass inner stabilizer. With front door open, place hands on each side of front door window glass and pull front door window glass fully into front door window glass top run. Set door window glass inner stabilizer so that it is slightly touching window glass. Tighten nut and washer assembly to 62-89 INCH lbs. (7-10 N.m) . Install watershield and door trim panel. Open and close window to verify proper operation.

REAR DOOR WINDOW GLASS IN & OUT

Remove rear door trim panel and watershield. Loosen 2 screws securing window stabilizer. Position window glass in or out as needed. Tighten window stabilizer retaining screws. Install watershield and rear door trim panel.

REAR DOOR WINDOW GLASS FORE/AFT

Remove rear door trim panel and watershield. Loosen window glass front run and bracket retaining screw and washer assembly. Adjust window glass fore or aft as needed. Tighten screw and washer assembly. Install watershield and rear door trim panel.

TROUBLE SHOOTING

Verify customer concern by operating windows to duplicate condition. Ensure battery is fully charged. Ensure windows are properly aligned. Check the following for possible cause of malfunction:

- Blown fuses.
- Faulty relays.
- Open or shorted supply circuit.
- Loose or corroded connectors.
- Poor ground connections.
- Faulty Generic Electronic Module (GEM).
- Faulty motor.
- Binding tracks or regulator mechanism.
- Faulty master switch. See MASTER WINDOW CONTROL SWITCH under COMPONENT TESTS.

COMPONENT TESTS

MASTER WINDOW CONTROL SWITCH

NOTE: In wiring diagram, master window control switch harness connectors are labeled as C501 and C509. In master window control switch test, terminal numbers have been changed to for clarity. Identification has been changed for test references only.

Remove master window control switch from vehicle. Check continuity between specified terminals while operating switch to specified position. See MASTER WINDOW CONTROL SWITCH TESTING table. *See Fig. 1.* Replace master window control switch if continuity between specified terminals is not as specified.

MASTER WINDOW CONTROL SWITCH TESTING

Switch Position	Terminals	Continuity
Any	8 & 9	No
Neutral	4, 5, 6, 7, 8, 10, 11, 12 & 13	Yes
Lock-Out Circuit		
Locked	3 & 9	No
Unlocked	3 & 9	Yes
Driver's Side		
Up	8 & 11; 9 & 10	Yes
Down	8 & 10; 9 & 11	Yes
Passenger's Side		
Up	8 & 12; 9 & 13	Yes
Down	8 & 13; 9 & 12	Yes
Left Rear		
Up	6 & 9; 7 & 8	Yes
Down	6 & 8; 7 & 9	Yes
Right Rear		
Up	4 & 9; 5 & 8	Yes
Down	4 & 8; 5 & 9	Yes

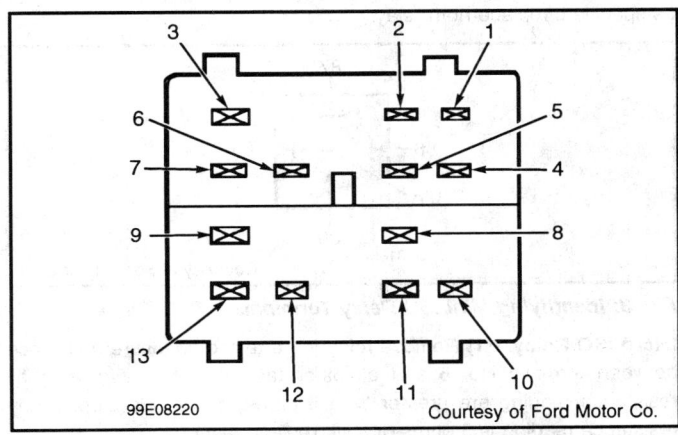

99E08220　　Courtesy of Ford Motor Co.

Fig. 1: Identifying Power Window Master Switch Terminals

SINGLE SWITCH

Remove single switch from vehicle. Check continuity between specified terminals while operating switch to specified position. See SINGLE SWITCH TESTING table. *See Fig. 2.* Replace switch if continuity between specified terminals is not specified.

SINGLE SWITCH TESTING

Switch Position	Continuity Between Terminals
Neutral	2 & 3; 6 & 7
Up	2 & 3; 4 & 6
Down	3 & 4; 6 & 7

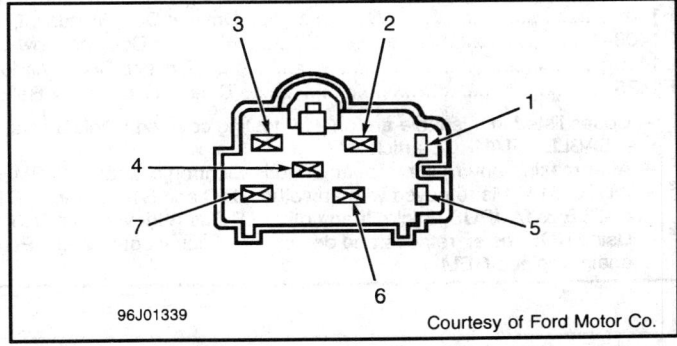

96J01339　　Courtesy of Ford Motor Co.

Fig. 2: Identifying Power Window Single Switch Terminals

RELAYS

Mini ISO Relay – 1) Remove mini ISO relay. Measure resistance between appropriate relay terminals. See MINI ISO RELAY RESISTANCE SPECIFICATIONS table. *See Fig. 3*. If resistance is as specified, go to next step. If resistance is not as specified, replace relay.

MINI ISO RELAY RESISTANCE SPECIFICATIONS

Between Terminals	Resistance
85 & 86	50-100 Ohms
30 & 87a	5 Ohms Or Less
30 & 87	Greater Than 10 K/Ohms
30 & 86	Greater Than 10 K/Ohms
86 & 87a	Greater Than 10 K/Ohms
86 & 87	Greater Than 10 K/Ohms

2) Using a fused jumper wire, connect positive battery voltage to terminal No. 85. Using another jumper wire, ground terminal No. 86. Resistance should now be 5 ohms or less between terminals No. 30 and 87 and greater than 10 k/ohms between terminals 30 and 87a. If resistance is as specified, relay is okay at this time. If resistance is not as specified, replace horn relay.

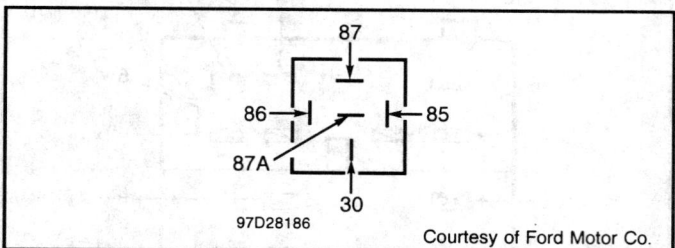

97D28186   Courtesy of Ford Motor Co.

Fig. 3: Identifying Mini ISO Relay Terminals

Micro ISO Relay – 1) Remove relay to be tested. Measure resistance between terminal No. 5 and all other terminals. *See Fig. 4*. If all resistance reading are greater than 5 ohms, go to next step. If any resistance reading is 5 ohms or less, replace relay.

2) Measure resistance between terminals No. 3 and 4. If resistance is 5 ohms or less, go to next step. If resistance is greater than 5 ohms, replace relay.

3) Apply battery voltage and ground between terminals No. 1 and 2. Measure resistance between terminals No. 3 and 5. Resistance should be 5 ohms or less. Measure resistance between terminals No. 3 and 4.

Resistance should be greater than 5 ohms. If resistance is not as specified, replace relay. If resistance is as specified, relay is okay at this time.

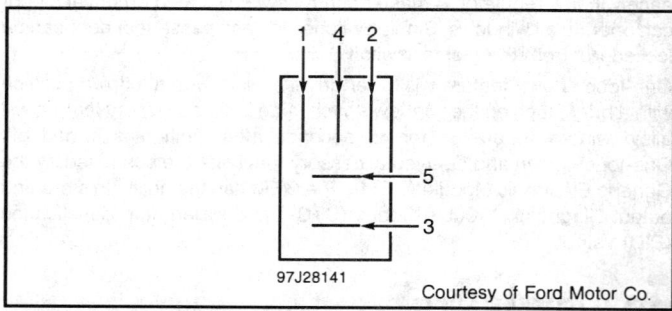

97J28141   Courtesy of Ford Motor Co.

Fig. 4: Identifying Micro ISO Relay Terminals

WINDOW MOTOR

Disconnect window motor harness connector for inoperative window. Using jumper wires, connect battery power and ground to window motor connector terminals. To reverse motor direction, reverse polarity of jumper wires. Motor should operate rapidly in both directions. Replace motor if necessary.

SELF-DIAGNOSTIC SYSTEM

Connect New Generation Star (NGS) tester to Data Link Connector (DLC), located beneath instrument panel. Using NGS tester, perform data link diagnostics test. See DATA LINK DIAGNOSTIC TEST under COMMUNICATION NETWORK DIAGNOSTICS in MODULE COMMUNICATIONS NETWORK – SABLE & TAURUS article. If NGS tester responds with CKT914, CKT915 or CKT70=ALL ECUS NO RESP/NOT EQUIP, repair module communications concern. See MODULE COMMUNICATIONS NETWORK – SABLE & TAURUS article. If NGS tester displays NO RESP/NOT EQUIP for Generic Electronic Module (GEM), perform TEST A: NO COMMUNICATION WITH GENERIC ELECTRONIC MODULE under SYSTEM TESTS.

If NGS tester responds with SYSTEM PASSED, retrieve and record continuous DTCs. Erase continuous DTCs. Using NGS tester, perform GEM self-test. Perform appropriate test in accordance with DTC retrieved. See GENERIC ELECTRONIC MODULE DTC INDEX table. Codes listed in this table are only for testing covered in this article. For complete DTC listing, see MODULE COMMUNICATIONS NETWORK – SABLE & TAURUS article. If no DTCs are retrieved, repair by symptom. See SYMPTOM CHART table under SYSTEM TESTS.

GENERIC ELECTRONIC MODULE DTC INDEX

DTC [1]	Description	[2] Test
B1302	Delayed Accessory Relay Coil Circuit Failure	DTC B1302
B1304	Delayed Accessory Relay Coil Circuit Short To Voltage	DTC B1304
B1342	ECU Defective	[4]
B1398	Driver's Door Window One-Touch Relay Circuit Failure	DTC B1398
B1400	Driver's Door Window One-Touch Relay Circuit Short To Voltage	DTC B1400
B1405	Driver's Door Window Down Circuit Short To Voltage	DTC 1405/B1408
B1408	Driver's Door Window Up Circuit Short To Voltage	DTC 1405/B1408
B1410 [3]	Driver's Door Window Motor Circuit Failure	DTC B1410
B1475	Delayed Accessory Relay Contact Short To Voltage	DTC B1475

[1] – Codes listed in this table are only for testing covered in this article. For complete DTC listing, see MODULE COMMUNICATIONS NETWORK – SABLE & TAURUS article.
[2] – After making any repair, repeat Generic Electronic Module (GEM) self-test using NGS tester.
[3] – If DTC B1474 is retrieved with any other DTC and B1410, repair DTC B1474 first before repairing DTC B1410. See AUTOLAMP SYSTEMS – SABLE & TAURUS article. If any other DTC is retrieved with B1410, repair those first.
[4] – Using NGS tester, retrieve and document all continuous DTCs. Perform Generic Electronic Module (GEM) self-test. If DTC B1342 is retrieved again, replace GEM.

DIAGNOSTIC TESTS

DTC B1302: DELAYED ACCESSORY RELAY COIL CIRCUIT FAILURE

NOTE: After making any repair, repeat Generic Electronic Module (GEM) self-test using NGS tester.

1) Turn ignition switch to RUN position. Operate power windows. If power windows do not operate, go to next step. If power windows operate, go to step **5)**.

2) Turn ignition switch to LOCK position. Remove accessory delay relay from instrument panel fuse box. Using NGS tester, access GEM active commands. Select ACCY RLY, and trigger relay on. Measure resistance between ground and terminal No. 85 at accessory delay relay socket. *See Fig. 5.* If resistance is 5 ohms or less, go to next step. If resistance is greater than 5 ohms, go to step **4)**.

3) Disconnect Generic Electronic Module (GEM) from instrument panel fuse box (connector C201). Measure resistance between terminal No. 85 at accessory delay relay socket and terminal No. 17 at GEM connector C201 (on fuse box). *See Figs. 5 and 6.* If resistance is 5 ohms or less, replace GEM. If resistance is greater than 5 ohms, replace instrument panel fuse box.

4) Disconnect GEM harness connector C204. Remove battery saver relay from instrument panel fuse box. Measure resistance between terminal No. 3 at battery saver relay socket and terminal No. 86 at accessory delay relay socket. *See Figs. 5 and 7.* If resistance is 5 ohms or less, go to next step. If resistance is greater than 5 ohms, replace instrument panel fuse box.

5) Turn ignition switch to LOCK position. Open driver's door. Remove accessory delay relay from instrument panel fuse box. Measure resistance between ground and terminal No. 85 at accessory delay relay socket. *See Fig. 5.* If resistance is 10 k/ohms or less, go to next step. If resistance is greater than 10 k/ohms, replace accessory delay relay.

6) Disconnect GEM from instrument panel fuse box (connector C201). Measure resistance between ground and terminal No. 85 at accessory delay relay socket. If resistance is 10 k/ohms or less, replace instrument panel fuse box. If resistance is greater than 10 k/ohms, replace GEM.

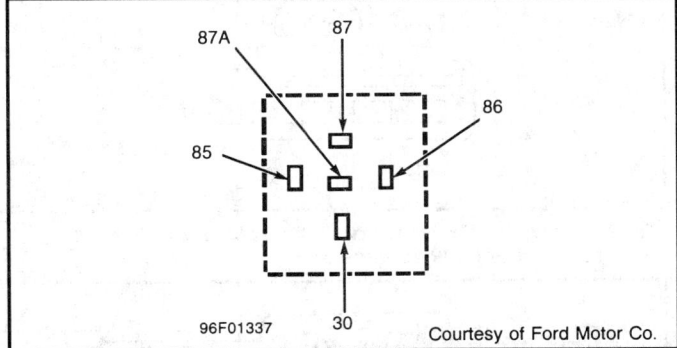

Fig. 5: Identifying Accessory Delay & One-Touch Window Down Relay Socket Terminals

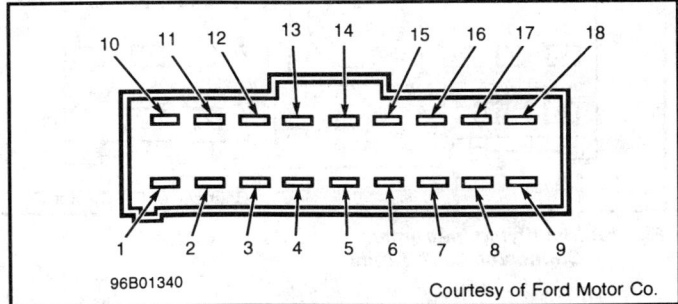

Fig. 6: Identifying GEM Connector C201 Terminals (On Fuse Box)

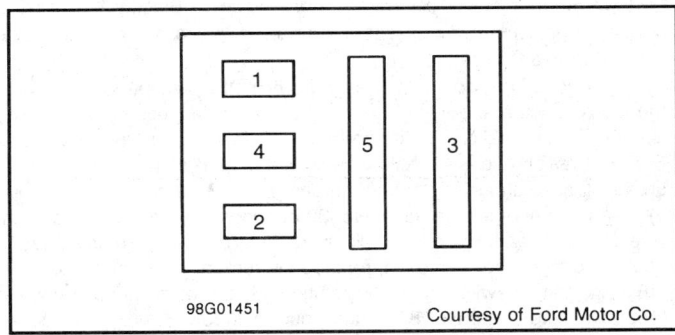

Fig. 7: Identifying Battery Saver Relay Socket Terminals

DTC B1304: DELAYED ACCESSORY RELAY COIL CIRCUIT SHORT TO VOLTAGE

NOTE: After making any repair, repeat Generic Electronic Module (GEM) self-test using NGS tester.

1) Using NGS tester, monitor GEM PID ACCDLY. Remove accessory delay relay from instrument panel fuse box. Turn ignition switch to RUN position. If PID indicates SHORTVBAT, go to next step. If PID does not indicate SHORTVBAT, replace accessory delay relay.

2) Turn ignition switch to LOCK position. Disconnect Generic Electronic Module (GEM) from instrument panel fuse box (connector C201). Turn ignition switch to RUN position. Measure voltage at terminal No. 85 at accessory delay relay socket. *See Fig. 5.* If battery voltage exists, replace instrument panel fuse box. If battery voltage does not exist, replace GEM.

DTC B1398: DRIVER'S WINDOW ONE-TOUCH RELAY CIRCUIT FAILURE

NOTE: After making any repair, repeat Generic Electronic Module (GEM) self-test using NGS tester.

1) Turn ignition switch to RUN position. Press driver's window up switch. If window goes up, go to next step. If window does not go up, go to step **4)**.

2) Turn ignition switch to LOCK position. Remove one-touch window down relay from instrument panel fuse box. Using NGS tester, access GEM active commands. Select ONE TOUCH WINDOW DOWN and ACCY DELAY. Trigger ONE TOUCH to ON. Measure resistance between ground and terminal No. 85 at one-touch window down relay socket. *See Fig. 5.* If resistance is greater than 5 ohms, go to next step. If resistance is 5 ohms or less, replace one-touch window down relay.

3) Turn ignition switch to LOCK position. Disconnect Generic Electronic Module (GEM) from instrument panel fuse box (connector C201). Measure resistance between terminal No. 7 at GEM connector C201 (on fuse box) and terminal No. 85 at one-touch window down relay socket. *See Figs. 5 and 6.* If resistance is 5 ohms or less, replace GEM. If resistance is greater than 5 ohms, replace instrument panel fuse box.

4) Turn ignition switch to LOCK position. Remove one-touch window down relay from instrument panel fuse box. Turn ignition switch to RUN position. Measure voltage at terminals No. 86 and 87 at one-touch window down relay socket. If battery voltage does not exist at both terminals, go to next step. If battery voltage exists at both terminals, go to step **10)**.

5) Operate power door locks. If power door locks do not operate, go to next step. If power door locks operate, go to step **8)**.

6) Disconnect instrument panel fuse box harness connector C225. Measure voltage at terminal No. 1 (Black/White wire) instrument panel fuse box harness connector C225. *See Fig. 8.* If battery voltage does not exist, go to next step. If battery voltage exists, replace instrument panel fuse box.

7) Remove fuse No. 4 (30-amp) from engine compartment fuse box. Measure resistance between ground and terminal No. 1 (Black/White wire) at instrument panel fuse box harness connector C225. If resistance is greater than 10 k/ohms, repair open in Black/White wire. If resistance is 10 k/ohms or less, repair short to ground in Black/White wire and replace fuse.

8) Remove accessory delay relay from instrument panel fuse box. Measure resistance between terminal No. 87 at accessory delay relay socket and terminal No. 87 at one-touch window down relay socket. *See Fig. 5.* If resistance is 5 ohms or less, go to next step. If resistance is greater than 5 ohms, replace instrument panel fuse box.

9) Measure voltage at terminal No. 30 at accessory delay relay socket. *See Fig. 5.* If battery voltage exists, replace accessory delay relay. If battery voltage does not exist, replace instrument panel fuse box.

10) Turn ignition switch to LOCK position. Measure resistance between ground and terminal No. 85 at one-touch window down relay socket. *See Fig. 5.* If resistance is 10 k/ohms or less, go to next step. If resistance is greater than 10 k/ohms, replace one-touch window down relay.

11) Disconnect GEM from instrument panel fuse box (connector C201). Measure resistance between ground and terminal No. 85 at one-touch window down relay socket. If resistance is 10 k/ohms or less, replace instrument panel fuse box. If resistance is greater than 10 k/ohms, replace GEM.

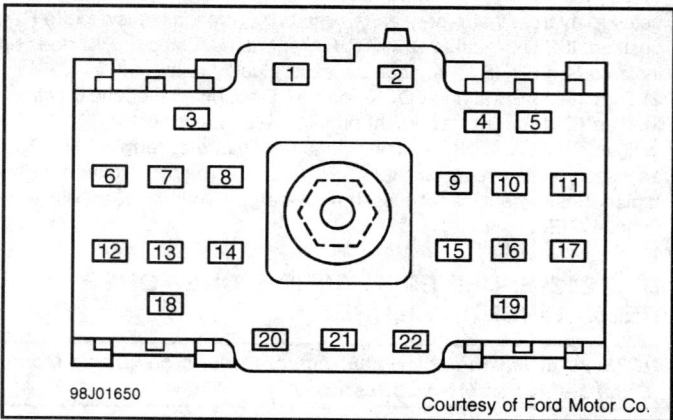

Fig. 8: Identifying Instrument Panel Fuse Box Harness Connector C225 Terminals

DTC B1400: DRIVER'S WINDOW ONE-TOUCH RELAY CIRCUIT SHORT TO VOLTAGE

NOTE: After making any repair, repeat Generic Electronic Module (GEM) self-test using NGS tester.

1) Turn ignition switch to RUN position. Using NGS tester, monitor Generic Electronic Module (GEM) PID D_PWRLY. If PID indicates SHORTVBAT, go to next step. If PID does not indicate SHORTVBAT, inspect one-touch window down relay and GEM terminals for corrosion or damage and repair as necessary.

2) With GEM PID D_PWRLY still accessed, remove one-touch window down relay from instrument panel fuse box. If PID still indicates SHORTVBAT, go to next step. If PID no longer indicates SHORTVBAT, replace one-touch window down relay.

3) Turn ignition switch to LOCK position. Disconnect GEM from instrument panel fuse box (connector C201). Turn ignition switch to RUN position. Measure voltage at terminal No. 85 at one-touch window down relay socket. *See Fig. 5.* If battery voltage exists, replace instrument panel fuse box. If battery voltage does not exist, replace GEM.

DTC B1405/B1408: DRIVER'S WINDOW CIRCUIT SHORT TO VOLTAGE

NOTE: After making any repair, repeat Generic Electronic Module (GEM) self-test using NGS tester.

1) Remove one-touch window down relay from instrument panel fuse box. Turn ignition switch to RUN position. Measure voltage at terminal

No. 87A at one-touch window down relay socket. *See Fig. 5.* If battery voltage does not exist, go to next step. If battery voltage exists, go to step **3)**.

2) Measure voltage at terminal No. 30 at one-touch window down relay socket. If battery voltage exists, go to step **5)**. If battery voltage does not exist, replace one-touch window down relay.

3) Disconnect master window control switch harness connector C509. Measure voltage at terminal No. 87A at one-touch window down relay socket. If battery voltage does not exist, go to next step. If battery voltage exists, go to step **8)**.

4) Measure voltage at terminal No. 7 (White/Black wire) at master window control switch harness connector C509. *See Fig. 9.* If battery voltage exists, go to next step. If battery voltage does not exist, replace master window control switch.

5) Disconnect Generic Electronic Module (GEM) from instrument panel fuse box (connector C201). Measure voltage at terminal No. 30 at one-touch window down relay socket. *See Fig. 5.* If battery voltage exists, go to next step. If battery voltage does not exist, replace GEM.

6) Disconnect instrument panel fuse box harness connector C247. Measure voltage at terminal No. 25 (Orange/White wire) at instrument panel fuse box harness connector C247. *See Fig. 10.* If battery voltage exists, go to next step. If battery voltage does not exist, replace instrument panel fuse box.

7) Disconnect driver's door window motor harness connector C503. Measure voltage at terminal No. 25 (Orange/White wire) at instrument panel fuse box harness connector C247. If battery voltage exists, repair short to voltage in Orange/White wire. If battery voltage does not exist, repair short to voltage in White/Black wire.

8) Disconnect instrument panel fuse box harness connector C247. Measure voltage at terminal No. 87A at one-touch window down relay socket. *See Fig. 5.* If battery voltage exists, go to next step. If battery voltage does not exist, repair short to voltage in Tan/Light Blue wire.

9) Disconnect GEM from instrument panel fuse box (connector C201). Measure voltage at terminal No. 87A at one-touch window down relay socket. If battery voltage exists, replace instrument panel fuse box. If battery voltage does not exist, replace GEM.

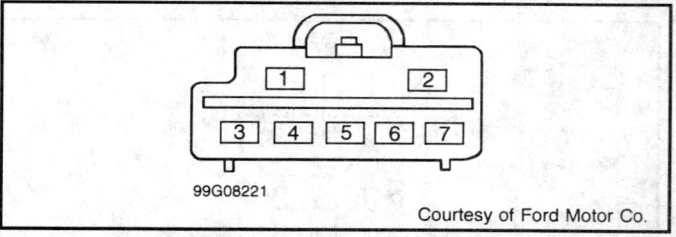

Fig. 9: Identifying Master Window Control Switch Harness Connector C509 Terminals

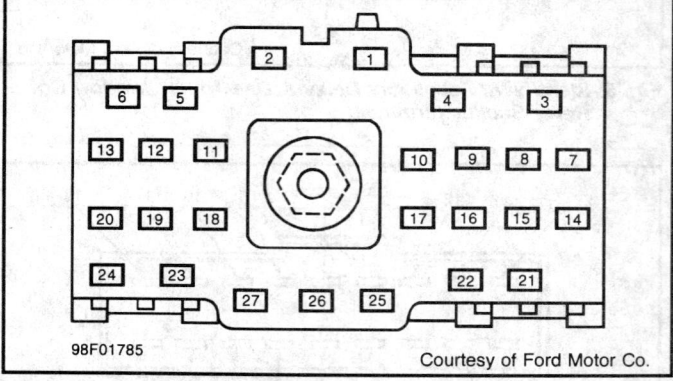

Fig. 10: Identifying Instrument Panel Fuse Box Harness Connector C247 Terminals

DTC B1410: DRIVER'S WINDOW MOTOR CIRCUIT FAILURE

NOTE: After making any repair, repeat Generic Electronic Module (GEM) self-test using NGS tester.

NOTE: If DTC B1474 is retrieved with any other DTC and B1410, repair DTC B1474 first before repairing DTC B1410. See MODULE COMMUNICATIONS NETWORK – SABLE & TAURUS article for description of code. If any other DTC is retrieved with B1410, repair those first.

1) Using NGS tester, monitor GEM PID D_PWAMP. Press driver's window switch up. If PID indicates zero amps, go to next step. If PID does not indicate zero amps, go to step **6**).

2) Disconnect instrument panel fuse box harness connector C247. Measure resistance between terminals No. 1 and 25 at instrument panel fuse box connector C247 (fuse box side). If resistance is 5 ohms or less, go to next step. If resistance is greater than 5 ohms, go to step **4**).

3) Disconnect GEM from instrument panel fuse box (connector C201). Measure resistance between terminal No. 2 at GEM connector C201 (on fuse box) and terminal No. 25 at instrument panel fuse box connector C247 (on fuse box). *See Figs. 6 and 10.* If resistance is 5 ohms or less, replace GEM. If resistance is greater than 5 ohms, replace instrument panel fuse box.

4) Disconnect driver's door window motor harness connector C503. Measure resistance between terminal No. 25 at instrument panel fuse box harness connector C247 and Orange/White wire terminal at driver's door window motor harness connector C503. *See Fig. 10.* If resistance is 5 ohms or less, go to next step. If resistance is greater than 5 ohms, repair open in Orange/White wire.

5) Measure resistance between terminal No. 1 at instrument panel box harness connector C247 and White/Black wire terminal at driver's door window motor harness connector. If resistance is 5 ohms or less, replace driver's door window motor. Using NGS tester, repeat GEM self-test. If resistance is greater than 5 ohms, repair open in White/Black wire. Using NGS tester, repeat GEM self-test.

6) Disconnect instrument panel fuse box harness connector C247. Measure resistance between ground and terminal No. 25 at instrument panel fuse box harness connector C247. *See Fig. 10.* If resistance is 10 k/ohms or less, go to next step. If resistance is greater than 10 k/ohms, go to step **8**).

7) Disconnect driver's door window motor harness connector. Measure resistance between ground and terminal No. 25 (Orange/White wire) at instrument panel fuse box harness connector C247. If resistance is greater than 10 k/ohms, replace driver's door window motor. If resistance is 10 k/ohms or less, repair short to ground in Orange/White wire.

8) Disconnect GEM from instrument panel fuse box (connector C201). Measure resistance between ground and terminal No. 2 (Tan/Light Blue wire) at instrument panel fuse box harness connector C247. *See Fig. 10.* If resistance is 10 k/ohms or less, replace instrument panel fuse box. If resistance is greater than 10 k/ohms, replace GEM.

DTC B1475: DELAYED ACCESSORY RELAY CONTACT SHORT TO VOLTAGE

NOTE: After making any repair, repeat Generic Electronic Module (GEM) self-test using NGS tester.

1) Remove accessory delay relay from instrument panel fuse box. Measure voltage at terminal No. 87 at accessory delay relay socket. *See Fig. 5.* If battery voltage exists, go to next step. If battery voltage does not exist, replace accessory delay relay.

2) Disconnect instrument panel fuse box harness connector C247. Measure voltage at terminal No. 87 at accessory delay relay socket. If battery voltage does not exist, go to next step. If battery voltage exists, replace instrument panel fuse box.

3) Measure voltage at terminal No. 7 (White/Violet wire) at instrument panel fuse box harness connector C247. *See Fig. 10.* If battery voltage exists, go to next step. If battery voltage does not exist, go to step **8**).

4) Disconnect driver's door window switch harness connector C501. Measure voltage at terminal No. 7 (White/Violet wire) at instrument panel fuse box harness connector C247. If battery voltage exists, go to next step. If battery voltage does not exist, replace driver's door window switch.

5) Disconnect passenger's door window switch harness connector C609. Measure voltage at terminal No. 7 (White/Violet wire) at instrument panel fuse box harness connector C247. If battery voltage exists, go to next step. If battery voltage does not exist, replace passenger's door window switch.

6) Disconnect right rear door window switch harness connector C809. Measure voltage at terminal No. 7 (White/Violet wire) at instrument panel fuse box harness connector C247. If battery voltage exists, go to next step. If battery voltage does not exist, replace right rear door window switch.

7) Disconnect left rear door window switch harness connector C709. Measure voltage at terminal No. 7 (White/Violet wire) at instrument panel fuse box harness connector C247. If battery voltage exists, repair short to voltage in White/Violet wire. If battery voltage does not exist, replace left rear door window switch.

8) Disconnect master window control switch harness connector C509. Measure voltage at terminal No. 23 (Light Blue/Black wire) at instrument panel fuse box harness connector C247. *See Fig. 10.* If battery voltage exists, repair short to voltage in Light Blue/Black wire. If battery voltage does not exist, replace master window control switch.

SYSTEM TESTS

SYMPTOM CHART

Symptom	[1] Test
No Communication With Generic Electronic Module	A
Power Windows Completely Inoperative	B
One Power Window Inoperative	C
Window Stuck/Binding	D

[1] – After making any repair, repeat Generic Electronic Module (GEM) self-test using NGS tester.

TEST A: NO COMMUNICATION WITH GENERIC ELECTRONIC MODULE

NOTE: After making any repair, repeat Generic Electronic Module (GEM) self-test using NGS tester.

1) Remove fuse No. 23 (5-amp) from instrument panel fuse box. Measure resistance between ground and output side of fuse No. 23. Resistance should start at greater than one megohm and steadily drop to less than 3 k/ohms. If resistance does not drop as described, go to next step. If resistance drops as described, go to step **7**).

2) With ohmmeter connected as specified in step **1**), check resistance. If resistance is greater than 10 ohms, go to next step. If resistance is 10 ohms or less, go to step **4**).

3) Disconnect Generic Electronic Module (GEM) from instrument panel fuse box (connector C201). Disconnect, then reconnect ohmmeter as specified in step **1**). If resistance is not one megohm or less, go to next step. If resistance is greater than one megohm (resistance may drop steadily to less than 3 k/ohms), replace GEM.

4) Disconnect instrument panel fuse box harness connectors C247 and C235. Measure resistance between ground and terminal No. 5 at GEM connector C201 (on fuse box). *See Fig. 6.* If resistance is 10 k/ohms or less, replace instrument panel fuse box. If resistance is greater than 10 k/ohms and vehicle is equipped with Passive Anti-Theft System (PATS)/ Remote Anti-Theft Personality (RAP), go to next step. If resistance is greater than 10 k/ohms and vehicle is not equipped with PATS/RAP, go to step **7**).

5) Connect instrument panel fuse box harness connectors C235 and C247. Disconnect PATS module harness connector C242. Disconnect, then reconnect ohmmeter as specified in step **1**). Observe ohmmeter reading. Resistance should start at greater than one megohm and steadily drop to 3 k/ohms or less. If resistance drops as described,

replace PATS module. If resistance does not drop as described and vehicle is equipped with RAP module, go to next step. If resistance does not drop as described and vehicle is not equipped with RAP module, repair short to ground in White/Yellow wire.

6) Disconnect RAP module harness connector C254. Disconnect, then reconnect ohmmeter as specified in step **1)**. If resistance is greater than one megohm, replace RAP module. If resistance is one megohm or less, repair short to ground in White/Yellow wire.

7) Disconnect GEM harness connector C248. Measure resistance between ground and terminals No. 14 (Black wire) and No. 25 (Black wire) at GEM harness connector C248. See Fig. 11. If both resistance readings are 5 ohms or less, go to next step. If either resistance reading is greater than 5 ohms, repair open in appropriate Black wire(s).

8) Disconnect GEM harness connector C223. Measure resistance between ground and terminal No. 12 (Black/White wire) at GEM harness connector C223. See Fig. 12. If resistance is 5 ohms or less, go to next step. If resistance is greater than 5 ohms, repair open in Black/White wire.

9) Disconnect GEM harness connector C236. Turn ignition switch to RUN position. Measure voltage at terminal No. 14 (Red/Yellow wire) at GEM harness connector C236. See Fig. 13. If battery voltage exists, go to next step. If battery voltage does not exist, repair open in Red/Yellow wire.

10) Measure resistance between ground and terminal No. 22 (Black/Light Green wire) at GEM harness connector C223. See Fig. 12. If resistance is 5 ohms or less, repair module communication concern. See MODULE COMMUNICATIONS NETWORK – SABLE & TAURUS article. If resistance is greater than 5 ohms, repair open in Black/Light Green wire.

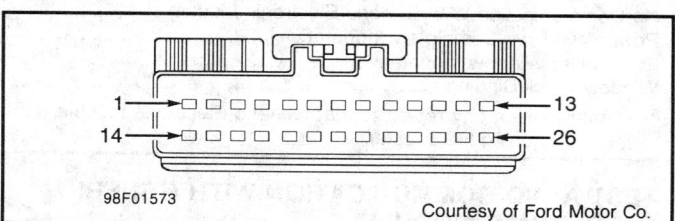

98F01573

Courtesy of Ford Motor Co.

Fig. 11: Identifying GEM Harness Connector C248 Terminals

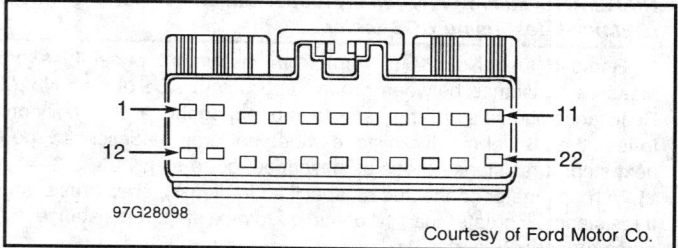

97G28098

Courtesy of Ford Motor Co.

Fig. 12: Identifying GEM Harness Connector C223 Terminals

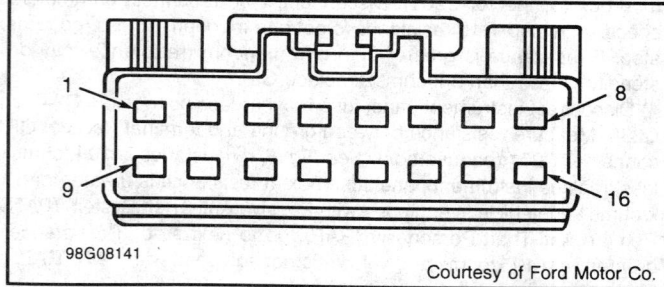

98G08141

Courtesy of Ford Motor Co.

Fig. 13: Identifying GEM Harness Connector C236 Terminals

TEST B: POWER WINDOWS COMPLETELY INOPERATIVE

NOTE: After making any repair, repeat Generic Electronic Module (GEM) self-test using NGS tester.

1) Operate passenger's windows from driver's master power window switch. If windows do not operate, go to next step. If windows operate, perform TEST C: SINGLE POWER WINDOW INOPERATIVE.

2) Disconnect master window control switch harness connector C509. Turn ignition switch to RUN position. Measure voltage at terminal No. 2 (Light Blue/Black wire) at master window control switch harness connector C509. See Fig. 9. If battery voltage does not exist, go to next step. If battery voltage exists, go to step **4)**.

3) Disconnect instrument panel fuse box harness connector C247. Measure resistance between ground and terminal No. 23 (Light Blue/Black wire) at instrument panel fuse box harness connector C247. See Fig. 10. If resistance is 10 k/ohms or less, repair short to ground in Light Blue/Black wire. If resistance is greater than 10 k/ohms, repair open in Light Blue/Black wire.

4) Measure resistance between ground and terminal No. 1 (Black wire) at driver's door window switch harness connector C509. If resistance is 5 ohms or less, replace master window control switch. If resistance is greater than 5 ohms, repair open in Black wire.

TEST C: ONE POWER WINDOW INOPERATIVE

NOTE: After making any repair, repeat Generic Electronic Module (GEM) self-test using NGS tester.

1) Determine inoperative window. Test master window control switch and inoperative window switch. See MASTER WINDOW CONTROL SWITCH and SINGLE SWITCH under COMPONENT TESTS. If both switches are okay, reinstall switches and go to next step. If switch is defective, replace appropriate switch.

2) Disconnect inoperative window motor harness connector. Connect a test light or voltmeter between suspect window motor harness connector terminals. Turn ignition switch to RUN position and operate master window control switch up and down for inoperative window. If battery voltage does not exist, go to next step. If battery voltage exists, ensure window tracks and mechanisms are not causing window to bind and repair if necessary. If window is not binding, replace window motor.

3) Remove single window switch for inoperative window. Check resistance of circuits between inoperative window motor and single switch. For wire color identification, see WIRING DIAGRAMS. If resistance is 5 ohms or less, go to next step. If resistance is greater than 5 ohms, repair open in appropriate circuit.

4) Remove master window control switch. Check resistance of circuits between single switch for inoperative window and master window control switch. For wire color identification, see WIRING DIAGRAMS. If resistance is 5 ohms or less, replace single switch. If resistance is greater than 5 ohms, repair open in appropriate circuit.

TEST D: WINDOW STUCK/BINDING

NOTE: After making any repair, repeat Generic Electronic Module (GEM) self-test using NGS tester.

1) Remove front door trim at suspect window. Actuate window in DOWN position. Check window glass runs. If there is an obstruction in glass run, remove obstruction, clean and lubricate glass, and retest system operation. If no obstruction is present, go to next step.

2) Actuate window to UP position and observe window regulator operation. If window regulator skips or binds, go to next step. If window regulator does not skip or bind, adjust regulator and guides, and retest system operation.

3) Remove appropriate motor. Carefully inspect motor and regulator gears. If there is damage to regulator gears, replace regulator and retest system operation. If there is no gear damage, replace window motor.

REMOVAL & INSTALLATION

CAUTION: When battery is disconnected, vehicle computer and memory systems may lose memory data. Driveability problems may exist until computer systems have completed a relearn cycle. See COMPUTER RELEARN PROCEDURES article in GENERAL INFORMATION before disconnecting battery.

POWER WINDOW MOTOR

Removal – 1) Raise window to full up position (if possible) and tape window in place. If window will not go up, support glass so it will not fall into door when motor is removed. Disconnect battery ground cable. Remove inner door trim panel and watershield.

2) Support regulator arm in fixed position to prevent counterbalance spring from unwinding when motor is removed. Remove 3 motor mounting screws and motor.

Installation – 1) Assemble window drive motor to regulator assembly. Tighten motor-to-regulator bolts until snug (DO NOT fully tighten) . Connect wiring to motor.

2) Connect negative battery cable. Operate window to ensure proper gear engagement. Tighten motor-to-regulator bolts to 53-89 INCH lbs. (6-10 N.m). Install watershield and door trim panel.

POWER WINDOW SWITCH

Removal & Installation – Disconnect negative battery cable. Remove door trim panel. Carefully spread retaining clips and pull switch from switch plate. To install, reverse removal procedure.

WIRING DIAGRAMS

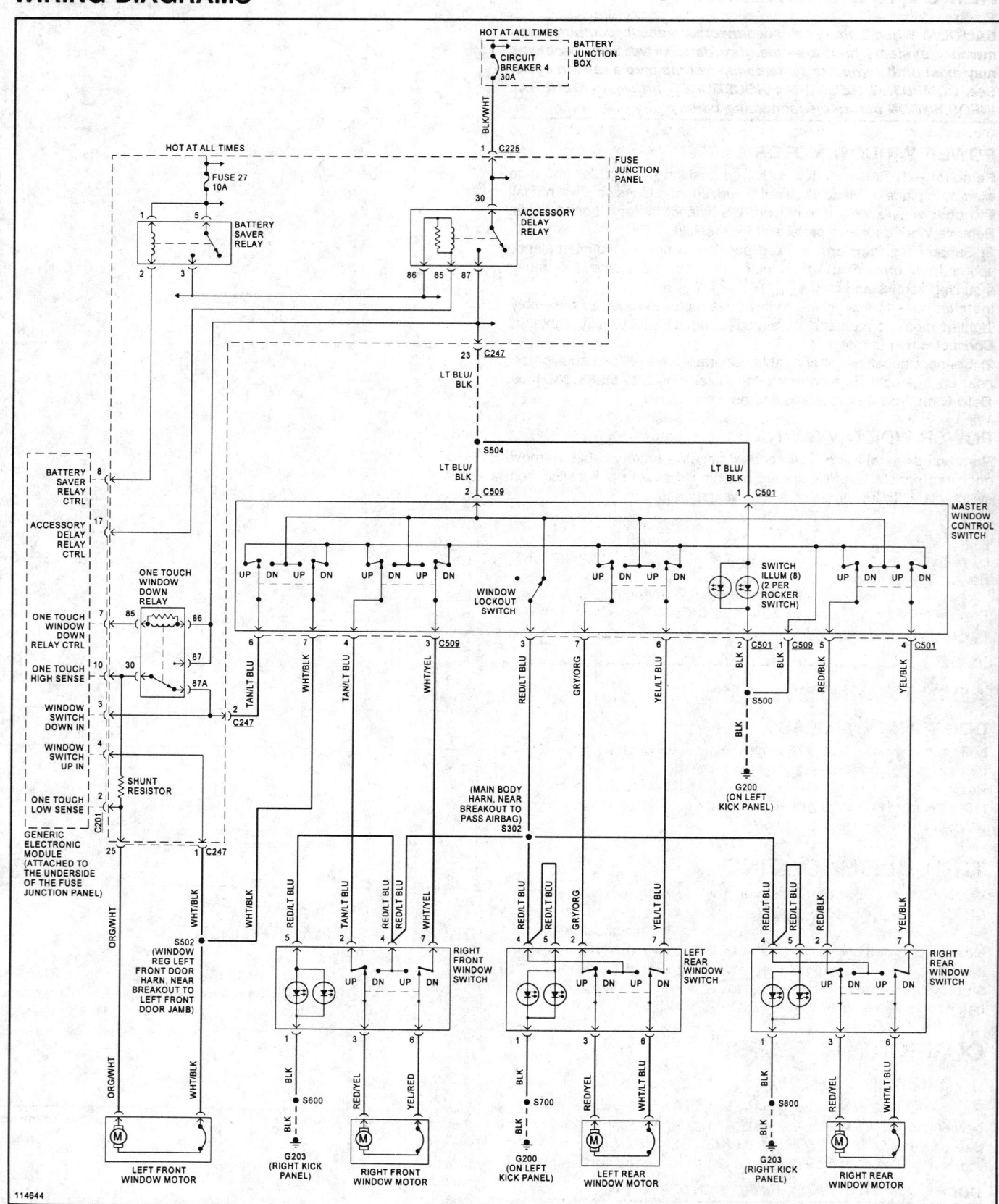

Fig. 14: Power Window System Wiring Diagram (Sable & Taurus)

DESCRIPTION & OPERATION

Power windows are operated by reversible type motors mounted with each window regulator. Each passenger's window has an individual switch for separate control. A master switch is located on driver's door, and all windows may be controlled from this switch.

One-touch down feature allows the driver to lower the left front window fully by momentarily actuating the driver's window down switch at the master power window switch. The driver's window may be stopped in mid-travel by momentarily pressing the driver's window up switch. The one-touch down feature can only be actuated at the master switch.

A lock-out switch is incorporated in master switch. When actuated, it prevents window operation from individual switches. A delayed accessory feature will allow window operation for 10 minutes after ignition is turned off.

COMPONENT LOCATIONS

COMPONENT LOCATIONS [1]

Component	Location
Data Link Connector	Under Instrument Panel, Right Of Steering Column
Delayed Accessory Relay/Power Window Relay	In Instrument Panel Fuse Box
Door Lock Switch	Appropriate Door Panel Arm Rest
Driver's Door Module (DDM)	Behind Driver's Door Panel, Lower Front Corner
Driver's Heated Seat Module	Under Driver's Seat
Heated Seat Switch	Driver's Door Trim Panel
Instrument Panel Fuse Box	Below Left Instrument Panel
Lumbar Switch	Side Of Seat Cushion
Power Distribution Box	Left Side Of Engine Compartment, Above Wheelwell
Power Mirror Switch	Driver's Door Panel Arm Rest

[1] – Front seat track and adjustment motors are a complete assembly.

ADJUSTMENTS

DOOR WINDOW GLASS

Lower door window 3.00" (76.2 mm) from full up position. Remove door trim panel and watershield. Loosen nuts securing window regulator. Raise door window to full up position. Tighten nuts to 89-124 INCH lbs. (10-14 N.m). Install watershield and door trim panel. Open and close window to verify proper operation.

TROUBLE SHOOTING

Verify customer concern by operating windows to duplicate condition. Check for mechanical faults such as window alignment, window mounting and window frame interference. Check for electrical faults such as blown fuses, damaged wiring harness, loose or corroded connections, damaged switches and/or damaged window motor. If inspection reveals an obvious concern which can be easily serviced, correct malfunction before proceeding to SELF-DIAGNOSTIC SYSTEM.

COMPONENT TESTS

DOOR LOCK SWITCH

Remove door lock switch. Using an ohmmeter, check for continuity between indicated switch terminals with switch in appropriate position. See DOOR LOCK SWITCH TERMINAL IDENTIFICATION table. See Fig. 1. Replace door lock switch if it does not test as specified.

DOOR LOCK SWITCH TERMINAL IDENTIFICATION

Switch Position	Continuity Between Terminals
Driver's Side	
Lock	2 & 4

DOOR LOCK SWITCH TERMINAL IDENTIFICATION (Cont.)

Switch Position	Continuity Between Terminals
Unlock	4 & 6
Passenger's Side	
Lock	4 & 6
Unlock	2 & 4

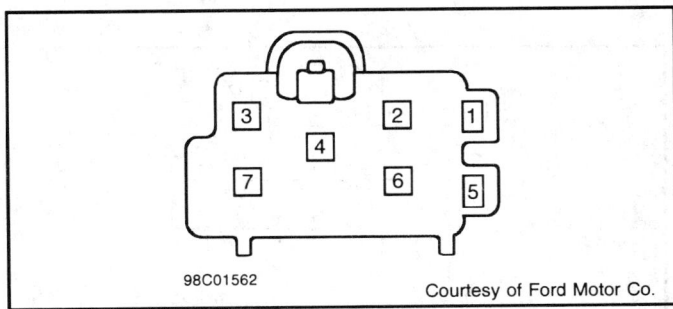

98C01562   Courtesy of Ford Motor Co.

Fig. 1: Identifying Door Lock Switch Terminals

MIRROR CONTROL SWITCH

Remove mirror control switch. Using an ohmmeter, check for continuity between indicated switch terminals with switch in appropriate position. See MIRROR CONTROL SWITCH TERMINAL IDENTIFICATION table. See Fig. 2. Replace mirror control switch if it does not test as specified.

MIRROR CONTROL SWITCH TERMINAL IDENTIFICATION

Switch Position	Continuity Between Terminals
Left Mirror	
Up	3 & 9; 4 & 7
Down	3 & 4; 7 & 9
Left	1 & 3; 4 & 7
Right	1 & 7; 3 & 4
Right Mirror	
Up	3 & 8; 4 & 7
Down	3 & 4; 7 & 8
Left	2 & 3; 4 & 7
Right	2 & 7; 3 & 4

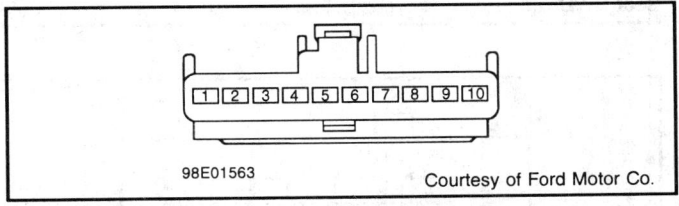

98E01563   Courtesy of Ford Motor Co.

Fig. 2: Identifying Mirror Control Switch Terminals

DRIVER'S SEAT CONTROL SWITCH (WITH MEMORY)

Remove driver's seat control switch. Using an ohmmeter, check for continuity between indicated switch terminals with switch in appropriate position. See DRIVER'S SEAT CONTROL SWITCH RESISTANCE (WITH MEMORY) table. See Fig. 3. Replace driver's seat control switch if it does not test as specified.

DRIVER'S SEAT CONTROL SWITCH RESISTANCE (WITH MEMORY)

Switch Position	Continuity Between Terminals
Front Up	2 & 10
Front Down	3 & 10
Rear Up	10 & 12
Rear Down	10 & 11
Seat FWD	9 & 10
Seat RWD	1 & 10
Recline FWD	10 & 13

DRIVER'S SEAT CONTROL SWITCH RESISTANCE (WITH MEMORY) (Cont.)

Switch Position	Continuity Between Terminals
Recline RWD	10 & 14
Memory Set	5 & 10
Memory "1"	6 & 10
Memory "2"	7 & 10

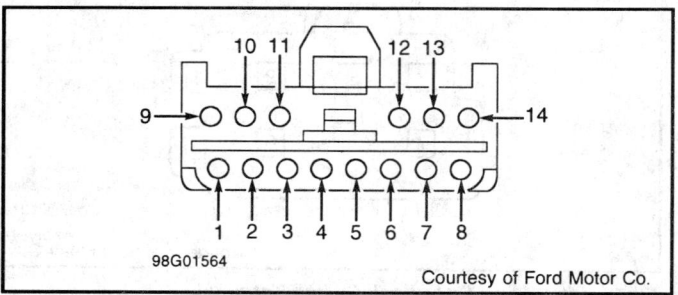

98G01564

Courtesy of Ford Motor Co.

Fig. 3: Identifying Driver's Seat Control Switch Terminals (With Memory)

DRIVER'S SEAT CONTROL SWITCH (WITHOUT MEMORY)

Remove driver's seat control switch. Using an ohmmeter, check for continuity between indicated switch terminals with switch in appropriate position. See DRIVER'S SEAT CONTROL SWITCH RESISTANCE (WITHOUT MEMORY) table. *See Fig. 4.* Replace driver's seat control switch if it does not test as specified.

DRIVER'S SEAT CONTROL SWITCH RESISTANCE (WITHOUT MEMORY)

Switch Position	Continuity Between Terminals
Neutral	1 & All, Except 3
Front Up	3 & 7
Front Down	3 & 5
Rear Up	3 & 4
Rear Down	3 & 6
Seat FWD	2 & 3
Seat RWD	3 & 8

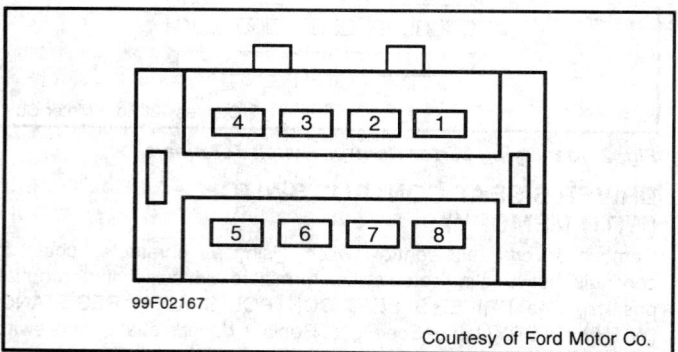

99F02167

Courtesy of Ford Motor Co.

Fig. 4: Identifying Driver's Seat Control Switch Terminals (Without Memory) & Passenger's Seat Control Switch (Executive Model)

PASSENGER'S SEAT CONTROL SWITCH

Remove passenger's seat control switch. Using an ohmmeter, check for continuity between indicated switch terminals with switch in appropriate position. See SEAT CONTROL SWITCH RESISTANCE (PASSENGER'S SEAT) table. *See Fig. 4 or 5.* Replace passenger's seat control switch if it does not test as specified.

SEAT CONTROL SWITCH RESISTANCE (PASSENGER'S SEAT)

Switch Position	Continuity Between Terminals
Neutral	
Except Executive Model	7 & All Except 12
Executive Model	5 & All Except 8
Front Up	
Except Executive Model	1 & 7
Executive Model	2 & 8
Front Down	
Except Executive Model	2 & 7
Executive Model	3 & 8
Rear Up	
Except Executive Model	7 & 11
Executive Model	4 & 8
Rear Down	
Except Executive Model	6 & 7
Executive Model	1 & 8
Seat FWD	
Except Executive Model	7 & 8
Executive Model	6 & 8
Seat RWD	
Except Executive Model	7 & 10
Executive Model	7 & 8
Seat Recline FWD [1]	5 & 7
Seat Recline RWD [1]	4 & 7

[1] – Does not apply to executive model.

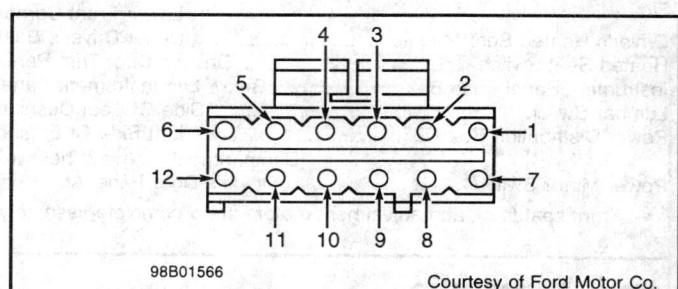

98B01566

Courtesy of Ford Motor Co.

Fig. 5: Identifying Passenger's Seat Control Switch (Except Executive Model)

REMOTE TRUNK RELEASE SWITCH

Remove remote trunk release switch. Using an ohmmeter, check continuity between switch terminals. With switch depressed, continuity should exist. With switch not depressed, continuity should not exist. Replace remote trunk release switch if continuity is not as specified.

WINDOW MOTOR

Remove window motor from vehicle. Using fused jumper wires, connect a fully charged battery to motor terminals. Observe motor. Motor should operate smoothly. Reverse leads. Motor should operate in reverse direction. Replace window motor if it does not operate as specified.

DRIVER'S DOOR MASTER WINDOW SWITCH

NOTE: In wiring diagram, driver's door master window switch connectors are labeled as C506 and C511. In driver's door master window switch test, connector C506 is referred to as connector C1, and connector C511 is referred to as connector C2. Identification has been changed for test references only.

Remove driver's door master window switch from vehicle. See POWER WINDOW SWITCH under REMOVAL & INSTALLATION. Using ohmmeter, check for continuity between switch terminals in specified switch positions. See DRIVER'S DOOR MASTER WINDOW SWITCH TEST table. *See Figs. 6 and 7.* Replace driver's door master window switch if it does not test as specified.

DRIVER'S DOOR MASTER WINDOW SWITCH TEST

Switch Position	Between Terminals
Neutral	C1-1, C1-3, C1-4, C1-5, C1-6, C2-1, C2-2, C2-4, C2-5, C2-6 & C2-7
Left Front Up	C1-2 & C2-4; C1-1 & C2-5
Left Front Down	C1-2 & C2-5; C1-1 & C2-4
Right Front Up	C1-2 & C2-6; C1-1 & C2-7
Right Front Down	C1-2 & C2-7; C1-1 & C2-6
Left Rear Up	C1-2 & C1-4; C1-1 & C1-3
Left Rear Down	C1-2 & C1-3; C1-1 & C1-4
Right Rear Up	C1-2 & C1-5; C1-1 & C1-6
Right Rear Down	C1-2 & C1-6; C1-1 & C1-5
Lock-Out Off	C1-2 & C2-3

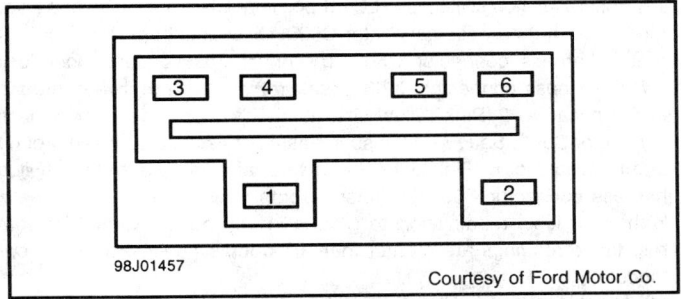

Fig. 6: Identifying Master Power Window Switch Terminals (Connector C1)

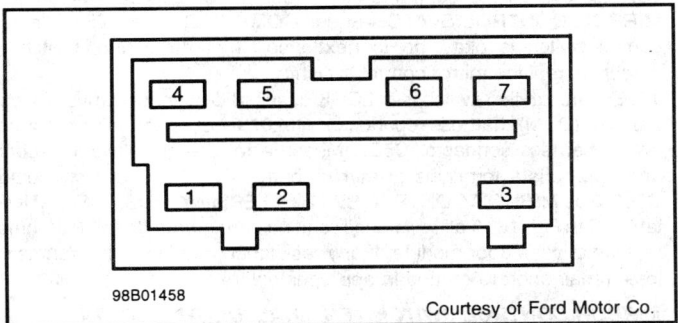

Fig. 7: Identifying Master Power Window Switch Terminals (Connector C2)

PASSENGER'S DOOR WINDOW SWITCH

Remove passenger's door window switch from vehicle. See POWER WINDOW SWITCH under REMOVAL & INSTALLATION. Using ohmmeter, check for continuity between switch terminals in specified switch positions. See appropriate PASSENGER'S DOOR WINDOW SWITCH TEST table. See Fig. 8. Replace passenger's door window switch if it does not test as specified.

PASSENGER'S DOOR WINDOW SWITCH TEST (RIGHT FRONT)

Switch Position	Between Terminals
Neutral	2 & 3; 6 & 7
Up	2 & 4; 6 & 7
Down	2 & 3; 4 & 6

PASSENGER'S DOOR WINDOW SWITCH TEST (REAR)

Switch Position	Between Terminals
Neutral	2 & 7; 3 & 6
Up	2 & 7; 4 & 6
Down	2 & 4; 3 & 6

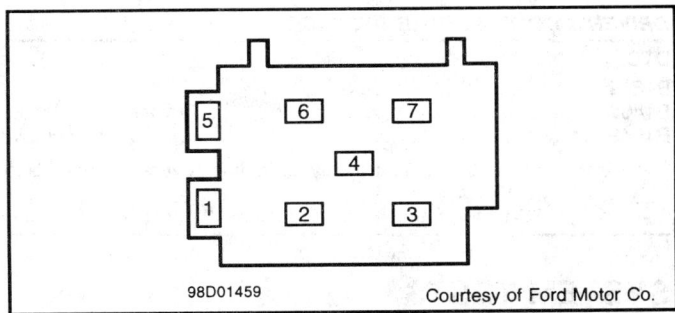

Fig. 8: Identifying Passenger's Door Window Switch Terminals

DELAYED ACCESSORY RELAY/POWER WINDOW RELAY

NOTE: Delayed accessory relay is used on LTS, Signature, and Cartier models. Power window relay is used on Executive models.

Remove delayed accessory relay/power window relay from instrument panel fuse box. Using an ohmmeter, check continuity between relay terminals No. 85 and 86. See Fig. 9. Continuity should always exist. Check continuity between relay terminals No. 30 and 87a. Continuity should exist. Apply battery voltage and ground between relay terminals No. 85 and 86. Continuity should now exist between relay terminals No. 30 and 87. Replace relay if it does not test as specified.

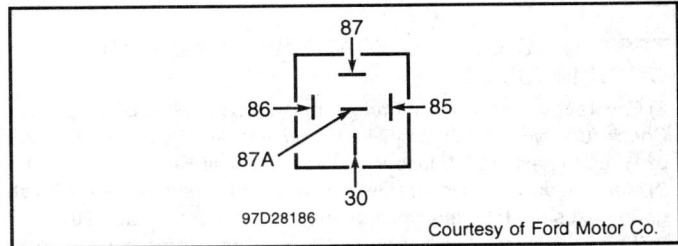

Fig. 9: Identifying Delayed Accessory Relay/Power Window Relay Terminals

SELF-DIAGNOSTIC SYSTEM

Verify customers complaint. Check for blown fuses. Check for loose or corroded connectors and damaged wiring harness. Repair or replace components as necessary.

If all components are okay, connect New Generation Star (NGS) tester to Data Link Connector (DLC), located beneath instrument panel. Using NGS tester, preform data link diagnostics test. See DATA LINK DIAGNOSTIC TEST under COMMUNICATION NETWORK DIAGNOSTICS in MODULE COMMUNICATIONS NETWORK – TOWN CAR article. If NGS tester responds with CKT914 or CKT915=ALL ECUS NO RESP/ NOT EQUIP, repair module communications concern. See MODULE COMMUNICATIONS NETWORK – TOWN CAR article. If NGS tester displays NO RESP/NOT EQUIP for Driver's Door Module (DDM), perform TEST A: NO COMMUNICATION WITH DRIVER'S DOOR MODULE under SYSTEM TESTS.

If NGS tester responds with SYSTEM PASSED, retrieve and record continuous DTCs. Erase continuous DTCs. Using NGS tester, perform DDM self-test. Perform appropriate test in accordance with DTC retrieved. See DRIVER'S DOOR MODULE DTC INDEX table. Codes listed in this table are only for testing covered in this article. For complete DTC listing, see MODULE COMMUNICATIONS NETWORK – TOWN CAR article. If no DTCs are retrieved, repair by symptom. See SYMPTOM CHART table under SYSTEM TESTS.

DRIVER'S DOOR MODULE DTC INDEX

DTC [1]	Description	Test
B1342	ECU Defective	[2]
B1402	Driver's Door Window Switch Down Circuit Open	B
B1549	Power Window Switch Short To Voltage	B

[1] – Codes listed in this table are only for testing covered in this article. For complete DTC listing, see MODULE COMMUNICATIONS NETWORK – TOWN CAR article.

[2] – Using NGS tester, retrieve and document all continuous DTCs. Perform DDM self-test. If DTC B1342 is retrieved again, replace DDM.

SYSTEM TESTS

NOTE: *After repairs are complete, ensure all component are properly installed and all harness connectors are connected properly and repeat data link diagnostic test. See DATA LINK DIAGNOSTIC TEST under COMMUNICATIONS NETWORK DIAGNOSTICS in appropriate MODULE COMMUNICATIONS NETWORK – TOWN CAR article.*

SYMPTOM CHART

Symptom	Test
No Communication With Driver's Door Module	A
Single Window Is Inoperative	B
One-Touch Down Feature Is Inoperative	C
Delayed Accessory Feature Does Not Turn Off	D
Delayed Accessory Feature Does Not Operate Properly	E

TEST A: NO COMMUNICATION WITH DRIVER'S DOOR MODULE

1) Ensure transmission is in Park. Turn ignition switch to LOCK position. Check fuse No. 30 (7.5-amp) in instrument panel fuse box. If fuse is okay, go to next step. If fuse is blown, go to step **5**).

2) Measure voltage at input side of fuse No. 30. If battery voltage exists, go to next step. If battery voltage does not exist, go to step **20**).

3) Ensure ignition switch is in LOCK position. Remove fuse No. 30 (7.5–amp) in instrument panel fuse box. Disconnect Driver's Door Module (DDM) harness connector C520. Measure resistance in Light Green/Violet wire between output side of fuse No. 30 and terminal No. 29 at DDM harness connector C520. *See Fig. 10.* If resistance is 5 ohms or less, go to next step. If resistance is greater than 5 ohms, repair open in Light Green/Violet wire between instrument panel fuse box and DDM.

4) Measure resistance between ground and terminal No. 23 (Pink/Orange wire) at DDM harness connector C520. If resistance is greater than 5 ohms, repair open in Pink/Orange wire. If resistance is 5 ohms or less, replace driver's door module.

5) Replace fuse No. 30. DO NOT operate power seat switch. If fuse blows, go to next step. If fuse does not blow, go to step **9**).

6) Ensure ignition switch is in LOCK position. Remove fuse No. 30 from instrument panel fuse box. Disconnect DDM harness connector C520 and Driver's Seat Module (DSM) harness connector C313. Measure resistance between ground and terminal No. 29 (Light Green/Violet wire) at DDM harness connector C520. *See Fig. 10.* If resistance is 10 k/ohms or less, go to next step. If resistance is greater than 10 k/ohms, go to step **8**).

7) Test driver's and passenger's door lock switches. Test remote trunk lock switch. Test mirror control switch. Test seat control switches. See appropriate test under COMPONENT TESTS. If no switch is defective, repair short to ground in Light Green/Violet wire. If any switch is defective, replace appropriate switch.

8) Ensure ignition switch is in LOCK position. Connect DSM harness connector C313. Measure resistance between ground and terminal No. 29 (Light Green/Violet wire) at DDM harness connector C520. If resistance is greater than 10 k/ohms, replace driver's door module. If resistance is 10 k/ohms or less, replace driver's seat module.

9) Lock and unlock doors at all door lock switches. If fuse No. 30 blows, go to next step. If fuse No. 30 does not blow, go to step **12**).

10) Remove door lock switches. Test all door lock switches. See DOOR LOCK SWITCH under COMPONENT TESTS. If all door lock switches are okay, go to next step. If any door lock switch is defective, replace appropriate door lock switch.

11) Ensure ignition switch is in LOCK position. Disconnect Driver's Door Module (DDM) harness connector C520. Disconnect driver's door lock switch harness connector C503. Disconnect passenger's door lock switch harness connector C603. Measure resistance between ground and terminal No. 2 (Pink/Yellow wire) at driver's door lock switch harness connector C503. *See Fig. 11.* Also, measure resistance between ground and terminal No. 6 (Pink/Light Green wire) at driver's door lock switch harness connector C503. If either or both resistance reading are 10 k/ohms or less, repair short to ground in appropriate wire(s). If both resistance readings are greater than 10 k/ohms, replace driver's door module.

12) Activate mirrors in all directions. If fuse No. 30 blows, go to next step. If fuse No. 30 does not blow, go to step **15**).

13) Remove mirror control switch. Test mirror control switch. See MIRROR CONTROL SWITCH under COMPONENT TESTS. If mirror control switch is okay, go to next step. If mirror control switch is defective, replace mirror control switch.

14) Ensure ignition switch is in LOCK position. Disconnect Driver's Door Module (DDM) harness connector C520. Disconnect mirror control switch harness connector C550. Measure resistance between ground and appropriate terminals at mirror control switch harness connector C550. See MIRROR CONTROL SWITCH TERMINAL IDENTIFICATION table. *See Fig. 12 .* If all resistance readings are greater than 10 k/ohms, replace driver's door module. If any resistance reading is 10 k/ohms or less, repair short to ground in appropriate wire.

MIRROR CONTROL SWITCH TERMINAL IDENTIFICATION

Terminal	Wire Color
1	Red/Orange
2	Dark Green/Orange
4	Yellow/Black
8	Violet/Orange
9	Dark Blue/Orange

15) Activate memory switch through all positions. If fuse No. 30 blows, go to next step. If fuse No. 30 does not blow, go to step **18**).

16) Remove driver's seat control switch. Test memory portion of driver's seat control switch. See DRIVER'S SEAT CONTROL SWITCH (WITH MEMORY) under COMPONENT TESTS. If memory switch is okay, go to next step. If memory switch is defective, replace driver's seat control switch.

17) Ensure ignition switch is in LOCK position. Disconnect Driver's Door Module (DDM) harness connectors C520 and C521. Measure resistance between ground and appropriate terminals at driver's seat control switch harness connector C509. See SEAT SWITCH CIRCUIT IDENTIFICATION table. *See Fig. 13.* If all resistance readings are greater than 10 k/ohms, replace driver's door module. If any resistance readings are 10 k/ohms or less, repair short to ground in appropriate wire.

SEAT SWITCH CIRCUIT IDENTIFICATION

Terminal	Wire Color
4	White/Orange
5	Brown/Orange
6	Brown/Light Green
7	Black/Orange

18) Activate driver's seat control switch in all directions. If fuse No. 30 blows, go to next step. If fuse No. 30 does not blow, system is okay at this time.

19) Ensure ignition switch is in LOCK position. Disconnect Driver's Door Module (DDM) harness connector C521. Disconnect driver's seat control switch harness connector C509. Measure resistance between ground and appropriate terminals at driver's seat control switch harness connector C509. See DRIVER'S SEAT CONTROL SWITCH TERMINAL IDENTIFICATION table. See Fig. 13. If all resistance readings are greater than 10 k/ohms, replace driver's door module. If any resistance readings are 10 k/ohms or less, repair short to ground in appropriate wire.

DRIVER'S SEAT CONTROL SWITCH TERMINAL IDENTIFICATION

Terminal	Wire Color
1	Yellow/White
2	Red/Light Blue
3	Yellow/Light Blue
9	Red/White
11	Yellow/Light Green
12	Red/Light Green
13	Gray
14	Gray/Black

20) Remove maxi-fuse No. 8 (30-amp) from power distribution box. Measure voltage at input side of maxi-fuse No. 8 at power distribution box. If battery voltage exists, go to next step. If battery voltage does not exist, repair power supply to maxi-fuse No. 8. See appropriate wiring diagram in POWER DISTRIBUTION article in WIRING DIAGRAMS.

21) Ensure ignition switch is in LOCK position. Ensure maxi-fuse No. 8 is still removed. Remove fuse No. 30 (7.5-amp) from instrument panel fuse box. Disconnect Driver's Seat Module (DSM) harness connector C337. Measure resistance in Red wire between output side of maxi-fuse No. 8 and input side of fuse No. 30. If resistance is 5 ohms or less, go to next step. If resistance is greater than 5 ohms, repair open in Red wire.

22) Measure resistance between ground and output side of maxi-fuse No. 8 at power distribution box. If resistance is greater than 10 k/ohms, go to next step. If resistance is 10 k/ohms or less, repair short to ground in Red wire.

23) Ensure ignition switch is in LOCK position. Install maxi-fuse No. 8 in power distribution box. Install fuse No. 30 in instrument panel fuse box. Connect DSM harness connector C337. Operate driver's power seat in all directions. If driver's power seat operates properly in all directions, go to next step. If driver's power seat does not operate properly in all directions, replace driver's seat module.

24) Inspect DSM for water damage. If water damage does not exist, go to next step. If water damage exists, replace driver's seat module.

25) Turn ignition switch to RUN position. Operate driver's power window, power mirror and door lock switches in all directions. If maxi-fuse No. 8 blows, replace driver's door module. If maxi-fuse No. 8 does not blow, verify symptom and repair as necessary. See SYMPTOM CHART table.

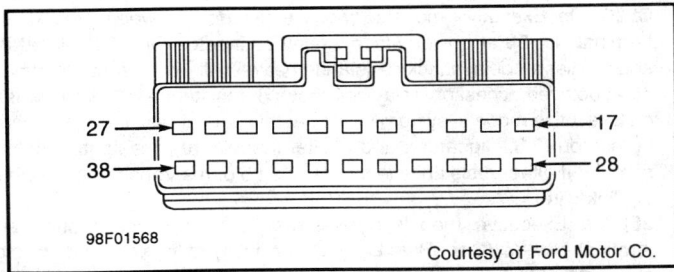

Fig. 10: Identifying Driver's Door Module Harness Connector C520 Terminals

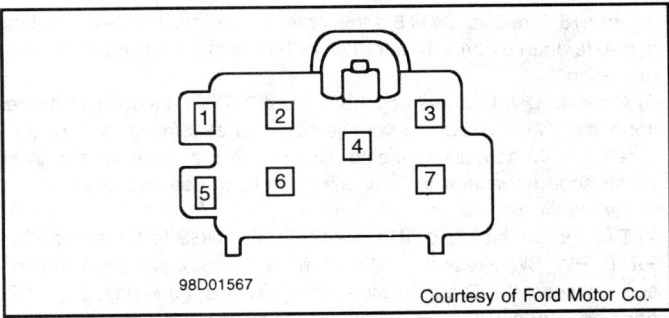

Fig. 11: Identifying Driver's Door Lock Switch Harness Connector C503 Terminals

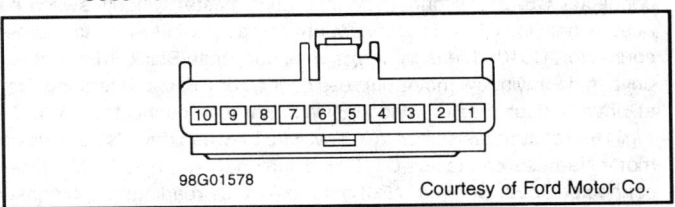

Fig. 12: Identifying Mirror Control Switch Harness Connector C550 Terminals

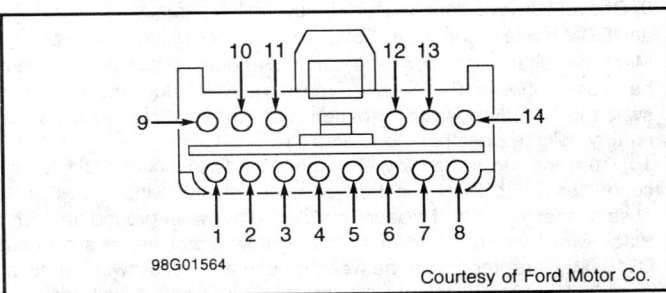

Fig. 13: Identifying Driver's Seat Control Switch Harness Connector C509 Terminals

TEST B: SINGLE WINDOW IS INOPERATIVE

1) Use recorded results from Driver's Door Module (DDM) self-test performed in self-diagnostics. If DTC B1549 was retrieved, go to next step. If DTC B1402 was retrieved, go to step **4)**. If no DDM DTCs were retrieved and all windows do not operate, go to step **7)**. If no DDM DTCs were retrieved and passenger's windows do not operate, go to step **28)**.

2) Disconnect DDM harness connectors C521 and C522. Measure voltage at terminal No. 15 (Gray wire) at DDM harness connector C521. See Fig. 14. Measure voltage at terminals No. 2 (Tan/Black wire) and No. 4 (White/Black wire) at DDM harness connector C522. See Fig. 15. If all voltage readings are greater than 5 volts, go to next step. If all voltage reading are 5 volts or less, replace driver's door module and retest system operation.

3) Disconnect driver's door master window switch harness connector C511. Measure voltage at terminals No. 2 (Tan/Black wire) and No. 4 (White/Black wire) at DDM harness connector C522. Measure voltage at terminal No. 15 (Gray wire) at DDM harness connector C521. If any voltage reading is greater than 5 volts, repair short to voltage in appropriate wire. If all voltage readings are 5 volts or less, replace driver's door master window switch.

4) Test driver's door master window switch. See DRIVER'S DOOR MASTER WINDOW SWITCH under COMPONENT TESTS. If switch is okay, go to next step. If switch is defective, replace switch.

5) Turn ignition switch to LOCK position. Disconnect DDM harness connector C522. Disconnect driver's door master window switch harness connector C511. Measure resistance in Tan/Black wire between terminal No. 2 at DDM harness connector C522 and terminal No. 5 at driver's door master window switch harness connector C511. See Figs.

15 and 16. If resistance is 5 ohms or less, go to next step. If resistance is greater than 5 ohms, repair open in Tan/Black wire and retest system operation.

6) Connect DDM harness connector C522. Disconnect DDM harness connector C521. Measure voltage between at terminal No. 15 (Gray wire) at DDM harness connector C521. *See Fig. 14*. If voltage exists, repair short to voltage in Gray wire. If voltage does not exist, replace driver's door module.

7) Turn ignition switch to RUN position. Using NGS tester, access DDM PID D_PW_SW. Press driver's door master window switch up and down several times. If PID agree with switch positions, go to next step. If PID does not agree with switch positions, go to step 12).

8) Turn ignition switch to LOCK position. Disconnect DDM harness connector C522. Disconnect driver's door master window switch harness connector C511. Disconnect driver's door window motor harness connector C510. Measure resistance in White/Black wire between driver's door window motor harness connector C510 and terminal No. 4 at driver's door master window switch harness connector C511. *See Fig. 16*. Measure resistance in Yellow wire between driver's door window motor harness connector C510 and terminal No. 1 at DDM harness connector C522. *See Fig. 15*. If both resistance readings are 5 ohms or less, go to next step. If either resistance reading is greater than 5 ohms, repair open in White/Black and/or Yellow wire.

9) Connect driver's door master window switch harness connector C511 and DDM harness connector C522. Turn ignition switch to RUN position. Measure voltage at Yellow wire terminal at driver's door window motor harness connector C510 while pressing driver's door master window switch in DOWN position. If battery voltage exist, go to next step. If battery voltage does not, go to step 11).

10) Turn ignition switch to LOCK position. Disconnect DDM harness connector C522. Disconnect driver's door master window switch harness connector C511. Measure resistance between ground and White/Black wire terminal at driver's door window motor harness connector C510. Measure resistance between ground and Yellow wire terminal at driver's door window motor harness connector C510. If both resistance readings are greater than 10 k/ohms, replace driver's door window motor. If either resistance reading is 10 k/ohms or less, repair short to ground in White/Black and/or Yellow wire.

11) Turn ignition switch to LOCK position. Disconnect DDM harness connector C522. Measure voltage at Yellow wire terminal at driver's door window motor harness connector C510. If voltage does not exist, go to step 47). If voltage is exists, repair short to voltage in Yellow wire.

12) Turn ignition switch to LOCK position. Disconnect DDM harness connector C522. Disconnect driver's door master window switch harness connector C511. Measure resistance in White/Black wire between terminal No. 4 at DDM harness connector C522 and terminal No. 4 at driver's door master window switch harness connector C511. Measure resistance in Tan/Black wire between terminal No. 2 at DDM harness connector C522 and terminal No. 5 at driver's door master window switch harness connector C511. *See Figs. 15 and 16*. If both resistance readings are 5 ohms or less, go to next step. If either resistance reading is greater than 5 ohms, repair open in White/Black and/or Tan/Black wire.

13) Measure resistance between ground and terminal No. 4 (White/Black wire) at DDM harness connector C522. Measure resistance between ground and terminal No. 2 (Tan/Black wire) at DDM harness connector C522. If both resistance readings are greater than 10 k/ohms, go to next step. If either resistance reading is 10 k/ohms or less, repair short to ground in White/Black and/or Tan/Black wire.

14) Ensure driver's door master window switch harness connector C511 is disconnected. Disconnect DDM harness connector C521. Measure voltage at terminal No. 15 (Gray wire) at DDM harness connector C521. *See Fig. 14*. If voltage does not exist, go to next step. If voltage exists, repair short to voltage in Gray wire.

15) Ensure DDM harness connector C522 is disconnected. Disconnect driver's door master window switch harness connector C506. Turn ignition switch to RUN position. Measure voltage at terminal No. 2 (Yellow/Light Green wire) at driver's door master window switch harness

connector C506. *See Fig. 17*. If battery voltage exists, go to next step. If battery voltage does not exist, go to step 17).

16) Test driver's door master window switch. See DRIVER'S DOOR MASTER WINDOW SWITCH under COMPONENT TESTS. If switch is okay, repair open in Black wire. If switch is defective, replace switch.

17) Ensure DDM harness connector C522 and driver's door master window switch harness connector C506 are disconnected. Measure resistance in Yellow/Light Green wire between terminal No. 3 at DDM harness connector C522 and terminal No. 2 at driver's door master window switch harness connector C506. If resistance is 5 ohms or less, go to next step. If resistance is greater than 5 ohms, repair open in Yellow/Light Green wire.

18) Measure resistance between ground and terminal No. 3 (Yellow/Light Green wire) at DDM harness connector C522. If resistance is greater than 10 k/ohms, go to next step. If resistance is 10 k/ohms or less, repair short to ground in Yellow/Light Green wire.

19) Test delayed accessory relay/power window relay. See DELAYED ACCESSORY RELAY/POWER WINDOW RELAY under COMPONENT TESTS. If relay is okay, go to next step. If relay is defective, replace relay.

20) Ensure DDM harness connector C522 is disconnected. Remove delayed accessory relay/power window relay from instrument panel fuse box. Measure resistance in Yellow/Light Green wire between terminal No. 3 at DDM harness connector C522 and terminal No. 87 at delayed accessory relay/power window relay harness connector. *See Fig. 18*. If resistance is 5 ohms or less, go to next step. If resistance is greater than 5 ohms, repair open in Yellow/Light Green wire.

21) Remove maxi-fuse No. 11 (40-amp) in power distribution box. Check fuse. If fuse is okay, go to next step. If fuse is blown, replace fuse and retest system operation. If fuse opens again, go to step 26).

22) Measure voltage at input side of maxi-fuse No. 11 (Black/Orange wire) in power distribution box. If battery voltage exists and vehicle is an Executive model, go to next step. If battery voltage exists and vehicle is a LTS, Signature, or Cartier model, go to step 24). If battery voltage does not exist, repair open in Black/Orange wire.

23) Ensure ignition switch is in LOCK position. Remove power window relay from instrument panel fuse box. Remove fuse No. 18 (7.5-amp) in instrument panel fuse box. Measure resistance in Black/White wire between output side of maxi-fuse No. 11 (40-amp) and terminal No. 30 at power window relay harness connector. Measure resistance in Dark Blue/Light Green wire between output side of fuse No. 18 (7.5-amp) in instrument panel fuse box and terminal No. 85 at power window relay harness connector. If both resistance readings are 5 ohms or less, go to step 25). If either resistance reading is greater than 5 ohms, repair open in Black/White and/or Dark Blue/Light Green wire.

24) Remove delayed accessory relay from instrument panel fuse box. Measure resistance in Black/White wire between output side of maxi-fuse No. 11 (40-amp) and terminal No. 30 at delayed accessory relay harness connector. Measure resistance in Black/White wire between output side maxi-fuse No. 11 (40-amp) and terminal No. 85 at delayed accessory relay harness connector. If both resistance readings are 5 ohms or less, go to next step. If either resistance reading is greater than 5 ohms, repair open in Black/White wire(s).

25) Disconnect Lighting Control Module (LCM) harness connector C220. On Executive models, check resistance between ground and terminal No. 86 at power window relay connector. On LTS, Signature, and Cartier models, check resistance between ground and terminal No. 86 at delayed accessory relay connector. If resistance is 5 ohms or less on Executive models, system is okay at this time. If resistance is 5 ohms or less on LTS, Signature, and Cartier models, replace lighting control module. If either resistance is greater than 5 ohms, repair open in Black or Pink wire.

26) On Executive models, check resistance between ground and terminal No. 85 (Dark Blue/Light Green wire) at power window relay connector. On LTS, Signature, and Cartier models, check resistance between ground and terminal No. 85 (Black/White wire) at delayed accessory relay connector. On all models, if resistance is greater than 10 k/ohms, go to next step. If resistance is 10 k/ohms or less, repair short to ground in Dark Blue/Light Green or Black/White wire.

27) Ensure DDM harness connector C522 is disconnected. Ensure delayed accessory relay/power window relay is removed from instrument panel fuse box. Measure resistance between ground and DDM harness connector C522 terminal No. 3 (Yellow/Light Green wire). If resistance is more than 10 k/ohms, replace driver's door master window switch and retest system operation. If resistance is 10 k/ohms or less, repair short to ground in Yellow/Light Green wire and retest system operation.

28) Ensure driver's door master switch lock-out is not engaged. Operate each passenger's door window. If a passenger's door window still does not operate, go to next step. If all passenger's door windows operate, system is okay at this time.

29) Test driver's door master window switch. See DRIVER'S DOOR MASTER WINDOW SWITCH under COMPONENT TESTS. If switch is okay, go to next step. If switch is defective, replace switch and retest system operation.

30) Operate all passenger's door windows. If all passenger's door windows do not operate, go to next step. If left rear passenger's door window does not operate, go to step **32)**. If right front passenger's door does not operate, go to step **37)**. If right rear passenger's door window does not operate, go to step **42)**.

31) Disconnect driver's door master window switch harness connector C511. Measure resistance between ground and terminal No. 3 (Red/Light Blue wire) at driver's door master window switch harness connector C511. If resistance is greater than 10 k/ohms, repair open in Red/Light Blue wire. If resistance is 10 k/ohms or less, repair short to ground in Red/Light Blue wire.

32) Disconnect driver's door master window switch harness connector C506. Disconnect left rear passenger's door window switch harness connector C706. Measure resistance in Yellow/Light Blue wire between terminal No. 4 at driver's door master window switch harness connector C506 and terminal No. 3 at left rear passenger's door window switch harness connector C706. Measure resistance in Gray/Orange wire between terminal No. 3 at driver's door master window switch harness connector C506 and terminal No. 7 at left rear passenger's door window switch harness connector C706. If both resistance readings are 5 ohms or less, go to next step. If either resistance reading is greater than 5 ohms, repair open in Yellow/Light Blue and/or Gray/Orange wire.

33) Measure resistance between ground and terminal No. 4 (Yellow/Light Blue wire) at driver's door master window switch harness connector C506. Measure resistance between ground and terminal No. 3 (Gray/Orange wire) at driver's door master window switch harness connector C506. If both resistance readings are greater than 10 k/ohms, go to next step. If either resistance reading is 10 k/ohms or less, repair short to ground in Yellow/Light Blue and/or Gray/Orange wire.

34) Disconnect left rear passenger's door window motor harness connector C710. Measure resistance in Yellow/Red wire between left rear passenger's door window motor harness connector C710 and terminal No. 2 at left rear passenger's door window switch harness connector C706. Measure resistance in Red/Yellow wire between left rear passenger's door window motor harness connector C710 and terminal No. 6 at left rear passenger's door window switch harness connector C706. If both resistance readings are 5 ohms or less, go to next step. If either resistance reading is greater than 5 ohms, repair open in Yellow/Red and/or Red/Yellow wire.

35) Measure resistance between ground and terminal No. 2 (Yellow/Red wire) at left rear passenger's door window switch harness connector C706. Measure resistance between ground and terminal No. 6 (Red/Yellow wire) at left rear passenger's door window switch harness connector C706. If both resistance readings are greater than 10 k/ohms, go to next step. If either resistance reading is 10 k/ohms or less, repair short to ground in Yellow/Red and/or Red/Yellow wire.

36) Test left rear passenger's door window switch. See PASSENGER'S DOOR WINDOW SWITCH under COMPONENT TESTS. If switch is okay, replace left rear passenger's door window motor. If switch is defective, replace switch.

37) Disconnect driver's door master window switch harness connector C511. Disconnect right front passenger's door window switch harness connector C606. Measure resistance in White/Yellow wire between terminal No. 7 at driver's door master window switch harness connector C511 and terminal No. 7 at right front passenger's door window switch harness connector C606. Measure resistance in Tan/Light Blue wire between terminal No. 6 at driver's door master window switch harness connector C511 and terminal No. 3 at right front passenger's door window switch harness connector C606. If both resistance readings are 5 ohms or less, go to next step. If either resistance reading is greater than 5 ohms, repair open in White/Yellow and/or Tan/Light Blue wire.

38) Measure resistance between ground and terminal No. 7 (White/Yellow wire) at driver's door master window switch harness connector C511. Check resistance between ground and terminal No. 6 (Tan/Light Blue wire) at driver's door master window switch harness connector C511. If both resistance readings are greater than 10 k/ohms, go to next step. If either resistance reading is 10 k/ohms or less, repair short to ground in White/Yellow and/or Tan/Light Blue wire.

39) Disconnect right front passenger's door window motor harness connector C610. Measure resistance in Yellow/Red wire between right front passenger's door window motor harness connector C610 and terminal No. 2 at right front passenger's door window switch harness connector C606. Measure resistance in Red/Yellow wire between right front passenger's door window motor harness connector C610 and terminal No. 6 at right front passenger's door window switch harness connector C606. If both resistance readings are 5 ohms or less, go to next step. If either resistance reading is greater than 5 ohms, repair open in Yellow/Red and/or Red/Yellow wire.

40) Measure resistance between ground and terminal No. 2 (Yellow/Red wire) at right front passenger's door window switch harness connector C606. Check resistance between ground and terminal No. 6 (Red/Yellow wire) at right front passenger's door window switch harness connector C606. If both resistance readings are greater than 10 k/ohms, go to next step. If either resistance reading is 10 k/ohms or less, repair short to ground in Yellow/Red and/or Red/Yellow wire.

41) Test right front passenger's door window switch. See PASSENGER'S DOOR WINDOW SWITCH under COMPONENT TESTS. If switch is okay, replace right front passenger's door window motor. If switch is defective, replace switch.

42) Disconnect driver's door master window switch harness connector C506. Disconnect right rear passenger's door window switch harness connector C806. Measure resistance in Yellow/Black wire between terminal No. 6 at driver's door master window switch harness connector C506 and terminal No. 7 at right rear passenger's door window switch harness connector C806. Measure resistance in Red/Black wire between terminal No. 5 at driver's door master window switch harness connector C506 and terminal No. 3 at right rear passenger's door window switch harness connector C806. If both resistance readings are 5 ohms or less, go to next step. If either resistance reading is greater than 5 ohms, repair open in Yellow/Black and/or Red/Black wire.

43) Measure resistance between ground and terminal No. 6 (Yellow/Black wire) at driver's door master window switch harness connector C506. Measure resistance between ground and terminal No. 5 (Red/Black wire) at driver's door master window switch harness connector C506. If both resistance readings are greater than 10 k/ohms, go to next step. If either resistance reading is 10 k/ohms or less, repair short to ground in Yellow/Black and/or Red/Black wire.

44) Disconnect right rear passenger's door window motor harness connector C810. Measure resistance in Yellow/Red wire between right rear passenger's door window motor harness connector C810 and terminal No. 2 at right rear passenger's door window switch harness connector C806. Measure resistance in Red/Yellow wire between right rear passenger's door window motor harness connector C810 and terminal No. 6 at right rear passenger's door window switch harness connector C806. If both resistance readings are 5 ohms or less, go to next step. If either resistance reading is greater than 5 ohms, repair open in Yellow/Red and/or Red/Yellow wire.

45) Measure resistance between ground and terminal No. 2 (Yellow/Red wire) at right rear passenger's door window switch harness connector C806. Measure resistance between ground and terminal No. 6 (Red/Yellow wire) at right rear passenger's door window switch harness connector C806. If both resistance readings are greater than 10 k/ohms, go to next step. If either resistance reading is 10 k/ohms or less, repair short to ground in Yellow/Red and/or Red/Yellow wire.

46) Check right rear passenger's door window switch. See PASSENGER'S DOOR WINDOW SWITCH under COMPONENT TESTS. If switch is okay, replace right rear passenger's door window motor. If switch is defective, replace switch.

47) Disconnect DDM harness connector C522. Disconnect driver's door window motor harness connector C510. Measure resistance in Yellow wire between terminal No. 1 at DDM harness connector C522 and driver's door window motor connector C510. If resistance is 5 ohms or less, replace driver's door module. If resistance is greater than 5 ohms, repair open in Yellow wire.

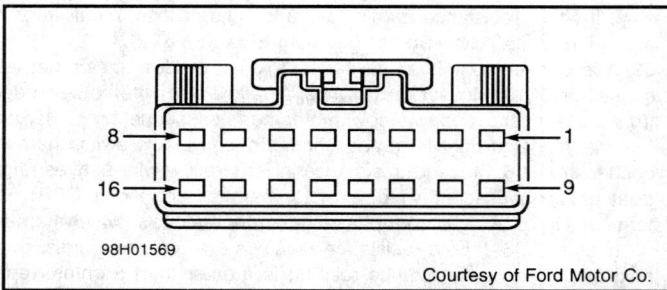

98H01569

Courtesy of Ford Motor Co.

Fig. 14: Identifying Driver's Door Module Harness Connector C521 Terminals

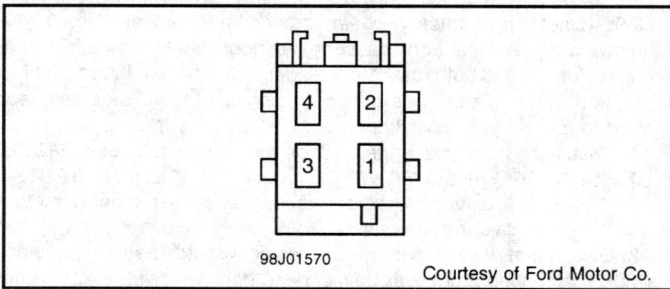

98J01570

Courtesy of Ford Motor Co.

Fig. 15: Identifying Driver's Door Module Harness Connector C522 Terminals

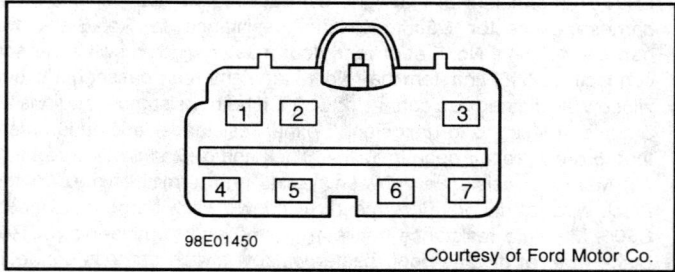

98E01450

Courtesy of Ford Motor Co.

Fig. 16: Identifying Driver's Door Master Window Switch Harness Connector C511 Terminals

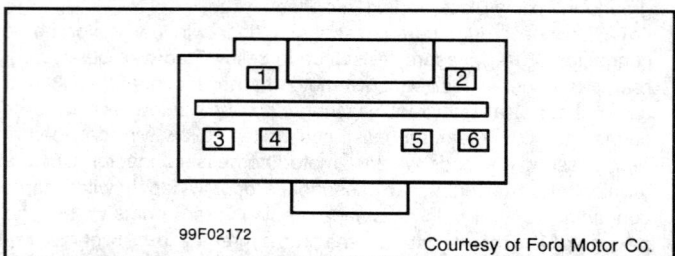

99F02172

Courtesy of Ford Motor Co.

Fig. 17: Identifying Driver's Door Master Window Switch Harness Connector C506 Terminals

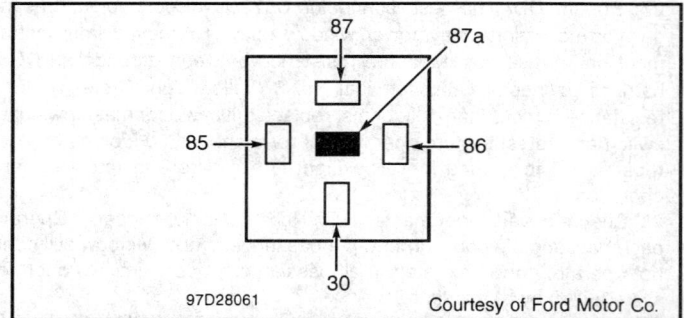

97D28061

Courtesy of Ford Motor Co.

Fig. 18: Identifying Delayed Accessory Relay/Power Window Relay Connector Terminals

TEST C: ONE-TOUCH DOWN FEATURE IS INOPERATIVE

1) Test driver's door master window switch. See DRIVER'S DOOR MASTER WINDOW SWITCH under COMPONENT TESTS. If switch is okay, go to next step. If switch is defective, replace switch.

2) Disconnect DDM harness connector C521. Measure resistance in Gray wire between terminal No. 15 at DDM harness connector C521 and terminal No. 1 at driver's door master window switch harness connector C511. See Figs. 14 and 16. If resistance is 5 ohms or less, go to next step. If resistance is greater than 5 ohms, repair short to ground in Gray wire.

3) Measure resistance between ground and terminal No. 15 (Gray wire) at DDM harness connector C521. If resistance is greater than 10 k/ohms, go to next step. If resistance is 10 k/ohms or less, repair short to ground in Gray wire.

4) Measure voltage between ground and terminal No. 15 (Gray wire) at DDM harness connector C521. If voltage does not exist, go to next step. If voltage exists, repair short to voltage in Gray wire.

5) Connect DDM harness connector C521. Disconnect DDM harness connector C522. Remove delayed accessory relay/power window relay from instrument panel fuse box. Measure resistance in Yellow/Light Green wire between terminal No. 3 at DDM harness connector C522 and terminal No. 87 at delayed accessory relay/power window relay connector. See Fig. 18. If resistance is 5 ohms or less, go to next step. If resistance is greater than 5 ohms, repair open in Yellow/Light Green wire.

6) Measure resistance between ground and terminal No. 3 (Yellow/Light Green wire) at DDM harness connector C522. If resistance is greater than 10 k/ohms, go to next step. If resistance is 10 k/ohms or less, repair short to ground in Yellow/Light Green wire.

7) Connect all disconnected harness connectors. Turn ignition switch to RUN position. Operate driver's door window up and down several times while observing window operation. If window operates without jerking or sticking, replace driver's door module. If window does not operate without jerking or sticking, repair as necessary.

TEST D: DELAYED ACCESSORY FEATURE DOES NOT TURN OFF

1) Using NGS tester, monitor DDM PIDs D_DR_DD and P_DR_DD. Open and close doors several times. If PIDs agree with door positions, go to next step. If PIDs do not agree with door positions, go to step **9)**.

2) Test delayed accessory relay. See DELAYED ACCESSORY RELAY/ POWER WINDOW RELAY under COMPONENT TESTS. If relay is okay, go to next step. If relay is defective, replace relay.

3) Measure resistance between ground and terminal No. 86 (Pink wire) at delayed accessory relay harness connector. See Fig. 18. Wait 10 minutes. If resistance is greater than 10 k/ohms after 10 minutes, go to next step. If resistance is 10 k/ohms or less after 10 minutes, go to step **6)**.

4) Measure resistance between ground and terminal No. 86 (Pink wire) at delayed accessory relay harness connector. Open driver's door. If resistance is greater than 10 k/ohms after opening driver's door, go to next step. If resistance is 10 k/ohms or less after opening driver's door, go to step **8**).

5) Disconnect DDM harness connector C522. Measure voltage between ground and terminal No. 3 (Yellow/Light Green wire) at DDM harness connector C522. If voltage exists, repair short to voltage in Yellow/Light Green wire. If voltage does not exist, replace driver's door module.

6) Using NGS tester, perform LCM self-test. Retrieve and record LCM continuous DTCs. If no LCM DTCs are retrieved, go to next step. If any LCM DTCs are retrieved, perform appropriate test. See LIGHTING CONTROL MODULE DTC INDEX table under DIAGNOSTIC TROUBLE CODE (DTC) DEFINITIONS in MODULE COMMUNICATIONS NETWORK – TOWN CAR article.

7) Remove delayed accessory relay from instrument panel fuse box. Disconnect Lighting Control Module (LCM) harness connector C220. Measure resistance between ground and terminal No. 86 (Pink wire) at delayed accessory relay harness connector. *See Fig. 18.* If resistance is greater than 10 k/ohms, go to next step. If resistance is 10 k/ohms or less, repair short to ground in Pink wire.

8) Connect LCM harness connector C220 and delayed accessory relay. Using NGS tester, access LCM PID IGN_LCM. If PID indicates OFF, replace driver's door module. If PID does not indicate OFF, replace lighting control module.

9) Use results from DDM self-test performed in self-diagnostics. If no DDM DTCs were retrieved, go to next step. If any DDM DTCs are retrieved, perform appropriate test. See DRIVER'S DOOR MODULE DTC INDEX table under DIAGNOSTIC TROUBLE CODE (DTC) DEFINITIONS in MODULE COMMUNICATIONS NETWORK – TOWN CAR article.

10) Remove passenger's and driver's door ajar switches. Measure resistance between door ajar switch terminals with switch in open and closed positions. Resistance should be greater than 10 k/ohms with switch in closed position and 5 ohms or less with switch in open position. If resistance is as specified, go to next step. If resistance is not as specified, replace appropriate door ajar switch.

11) Turn ignition switch to LOCK position. Disconnect driver's door ajar switch harness connector C500. Disconnect DDM harness connector C521. Measure resistance in Dark Blue wire between terminal No. 5 at DDM harness connector C521 and door ajar switch harness connector C500. *See Fig. 14.* If resistance is 5 ohms or less, go to next step. If resistance is greater than 5 ohms, repair open in Dark Blue wire.

12) Measure voltage at terminal No. 5 (Dark Blue wire) at DDM harness connector C521. If voltage does not exist, go to next step. If voltage exists, repair short to voltage in Dark Blue wire.

13) Turn ignition switch to LOCK position. Disconnect passenger's door ajar switches. Disconnect DDM harness connector C521. Measure resistance in Black/Orange wire between terminal No. 6 at DDM harness connector C521 and each passenger's door ajar switch harness connector. If resistance is 5 ohms or less, go to next step. If resistance is greater than 5 ohms, repair open in Black/Orange wire.

14) Measure voltage at terminal No. 6 (Black/Orange wire) at DDM harness connector C521. If voltage does not exist, go to next step. If voltage exists, repair short to voltage in Black/Orange wire.

15) Measure resistance between ground and Black wire terminal at each door ajar switch harness connector. If resistances are 5 ohms or less, replace driver's door module. If any resistance is greater than 5 ohms, repair open in appropriate Black wire.

TEST E: DELAYED ACCESSORY FEATURE DOES NOT OPERATE PROPERLY

1) Using NGS tester, monitor DDM PIDs D_DR_DD and P_DR_DD. Open and close doors several times. If PIDs agree with door positions, go to next step. If PIDs do not agree with door positions, go to step **5**).

2) Test delayed accessory relay. See DELAYED ACCESSORY RELAY/ POWER WINDOW RELAY under COMPONENT TESTS. If relay is okay, go to next step. If relay is defective, replace relay.

3) Using NGS tester, perform LCM self-test. Retrieve and record LCM continuous DTCs. If no LCM DTCs are retrieved, go to next step. If any LCM DTCs are retrieved, perform appropriate test. See LIGHTING CONTROL MODULE DTC INDEX table under DIAGNOSTIC TROUBLE CODE (DTC) DEFINITIONS in MODULE COMMUNICATIONS NETWORK – TOWN CAR article.

4) Disconnect DDM harness connector C522. Remove delayed accessory relay from instrument panel fuse box. Measure resistance between ground and terminal No. 86 (Pink wire) at delayed accessory relay harness connector. *See Fig. 18.* Wait 10 minutes. If resistance is greater than 10 k/ohms after 10 minutes, replace driver's door module. If resistance is 10 k/ohms or less after 10 minutes, replace lighting control module.

5) Remove passenger's and driver's door ajar switches. Measure resistance between door ajar switch terminals with switch in open and closed positions. Resistance should be greater than 10 k/ohms with switch in closed position and 5 ohms or less with switch in open position. If resistance is as specified, replace driver's door module. If resistance is not as specified, replace appropriate door ajar switch.

REMOVAL & INSTALLATION

CAUTION: When battery is disconnected, vehicle computer and memory systems may lose memory data. Driveability problems may exist until computer systems have completed a relearn cycle. See COMPUTER RELEARN PROCEDURES article in GENERAL INFORMATION before disconnecting battery.

DRIVER'S DOOR MODULE (DDM)

Removal & Installation – Disconnect negative battery cable. Remove driver's door trim panel. Unplug module wiring connectors. Remove mounting screws. Remove module through access hole in door. To install, reverse removal procedure.

WINDOW MOTOR

Removal & Installation – Remove door trim panel and watershield. Disconnect negative battery cable. Unplug power window motor wiring connector. Remove 3 window motor retaining Torx screws. Remove window motor from door. To install, reverse removal procedure.

POWER WINDOW SWITCH

Removal & Installation – Disconnect negative battery cable. Carefully pry up switch housing. Remove electrical connectors. To install, reverse removal procedure.

WIRING DIAGRAMS

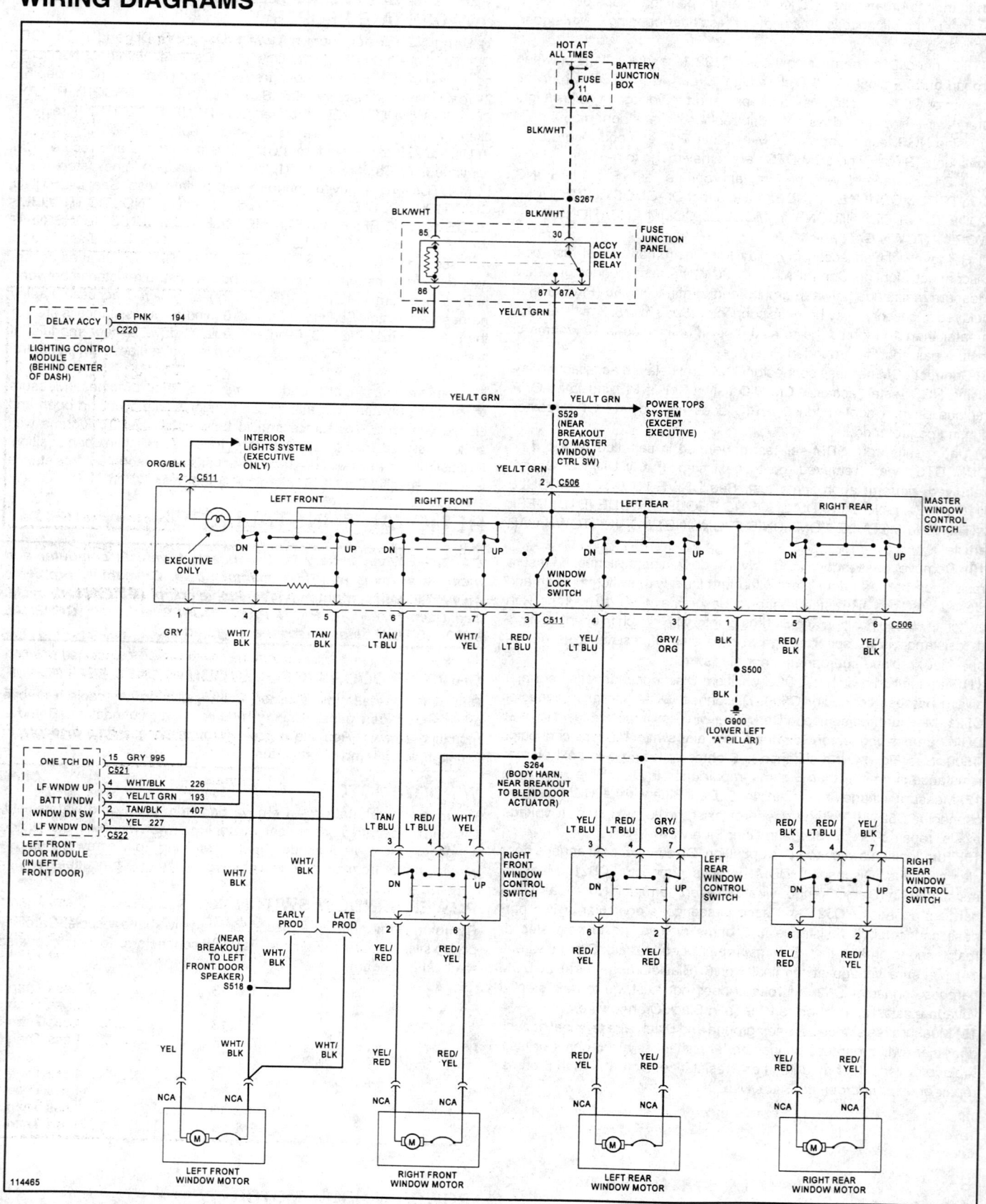

Fig. 19: Power Window System Wiring Diagram (Town Car)

DESCRIPTION

Power windows are operated by reversible motors mounted with each window regulator. Each passenger window has an individual switch for separate control. A master switch is located on the driver door from which both front windows may be controlled.

One-touch down feature allows the driver to fully lower the left front window by momentarily actuating the driver window down switch at the master power window switch. The driver window may be stopped in mid-travel by momentarily pressing the driver window up switch. The one-touch down feature can only be actuated at the master switch. A lock-out switch is incorporated in master switch. When actuated, lock-out switch prevents window operation from individual switches.

Power rear quarter window are operated remotely from a control panel located on the roof mounted overhead console.

COMPONENT LOCATIONS

COMPONENT LOCATIONS

Component	Location
Data Link Connector (DLC)	Below Driver's Side Of Instrument Panel, To Right Of Steering Column
Engine Compartment Relay Box	Left Front Side Of Engine Compartment
Interior Fuse Junction Panel	Below Left Side Of Instrument Panel
Lighting Control Module (LCM)	Bottom Of Center Console, Below Dash Panel
Powertrain Control Module (PCM)	Behind Glove Box
Power Distribution Box	In Engine Compartment, Next To Battery
Power Window Master Switch	In Driver's Door Panel
Transaxle Control Module (TCM)	Behind Instrument Cluster

TROUBLE SHOOTING

INSPECTION & VERIFICATION

Verify customer concern by operating windows to duplicate condition. Visually inspect components. If inspection reveals an obvious problem which can be easily serviced, correct malfunction before continuing inspection and verification.

Mechanical:
- Window alignment.
- Window mounting (regulator and bracket).
- Window frame interference.

Electrical:
- Blown fuse(s).
- Damaged wiring harness.
- Loose or corroded connections.
- Damaged switches.
- Faulty relay.
- Damaged window motor.

COMPONENT TESTS

POWER REAR QUARTER GLASS POWER LATCH MOTOR

Disconnect quarter glass power latch connector. Using jumper wires, connect battery to motor 2-pin connector. Latch should turn in one direction (open or close). Reverse battery connections. Motor should reverse rotation. If latch motor does not operate as specified, replace latch motor assembly.

POWER WINDOW MASTER SWITCH (FRONT POWER)

Disconnect power window master switch. Using an ohmmeter, measure resistance between indicated terminals with switch in specified position. See POWER WINDOW MASTER SWITCH RESISTANCE table. *See*

Fig. 1. If switch resistance is not as specified, replace power window master switch.

POWER WINDOW MASTER SWITCH RESISTANCE

Switch & Position	Terminals	Ohms
Left Window Switch		
UP	1 & 2	Less Than 5
	6 & 7	Less Than 5
DOWN	1 & 7	Less Than 5
	2 & 6	Less Than 5
Right Window Switch		
UP	6 & 11	Less Than 5
	1 & 12	Less Than 5
DOWN	6 & 12	Less Than 5
	1 & 12	Less Than 5

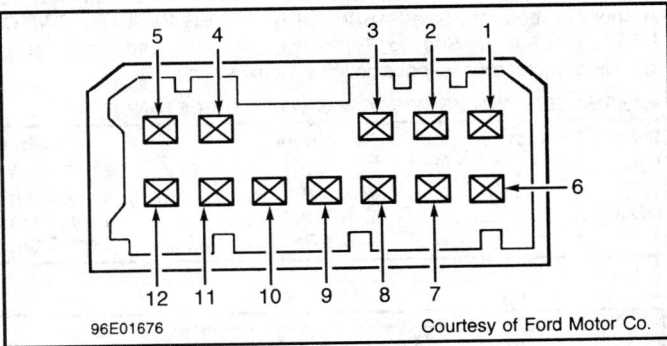

Fig. 1: Identifying Power Window Master Switch (Front Power) Terminals

POWER WINDOW MASTER SWITCH (FRONT & REAR POWER)

Disconnect power window master switch. Using an ohmmeter, measure resistance between indicated terminals with switch in specified position. See POWER WINDOW MASTER SWITCH (FRONT & REAR POWER) RESISTANCE table. *See Fig. 2.* If switch resistance is not as specified, replace power window master switch.

POWER WINDOW MASTER SWITCH (FRONT & REAR POWER) RESISTANCE

Switch & Position	Terminals	Ohms
Left Front Window Switch		
UP	13 & 15	Less Than 5
	8 & 16	Less Than 5
DOWN	8 & 13	Less Than 5
	15 & 16	Less Than 5
Right Front Window Switch		
UP	10 & 13	Less Than 5
	9 & 16	Less Than 5
DOWN	9 & 13	Less Than 5
	10 & 16	Less Than 5
Left Rear Window Switch		
OPEN	7 & 13	Less Than 5
	5 & 16	Less Than 5
CLOSED	5 & 13	Less Than 5
	7 & 16	Less Than 5
Right Rear Window Switch		
OPEN	2 & 13	Less Than 5
	1 & 16	Less Than 5
CLOSED	1 & 13	Less Than 5
	2 & 16	Less Than 5

POWER WINDOW MOTOR

Disconnect window motor harness connector. See POWER WINDOW MOTOR under REMOVAL & INSTALLATION. Using jumper wires, connect battery to motor 2-pin connector. Window will move in one

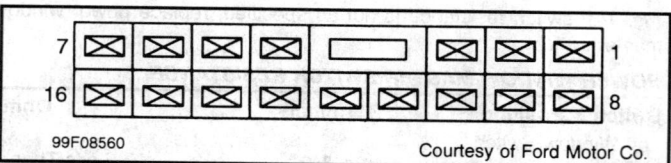

Fig. 2: Identifying Power Window Master Switch (Front & Rear Power) Terminals

direction (down or up). Reverse battery connections. Motor should reverse rotation. If window motor does not operate as specified, replace window motor.

PASSENGER POWER WINDOW SWITCH

Remove passenger power window switch from door pull cup. Using an ohmmeter, measure resistance between indicated terminals with switch in specified position. See PASSENGER POWER WINDOW SWITCH RESISTANCE table. *See Fig. 3 .* If switch resistance readings are not as specified, replace passenger power window switch.

PASSENGER POWER WINDOW SWITCH RESISTANCE

Switch Position	Terminals	Ohms
UP	2 & 3	Less Than 5
	7 & 8	Less Than 5
DOWN	2 & 3	Less Than 5
	6 & 7	Less Than 5

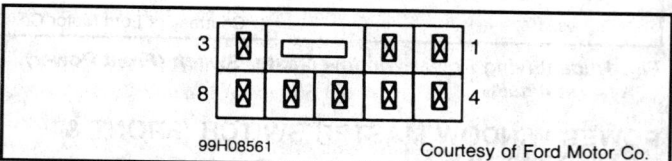

Fig. 3: Identifying Passenger Power Window Master Switch Terminals

SYSTEM TESTS

NOTE: Ensure trouble shooting is performed before system tests. See TROUBLE SHOOTING. To determine correct system test, see SYMPTOM CHART table. Unless otherwise directed, perform testing in order listed.

CAUTION: When battery is disconnected, vehicle computer and memory systems may lose memory data. Driveability problems may exist until computer systems have completed a relearn cycle. See COMPUTER RELEARN PROCEDURES article in GENERAL INFORMATION before disconnecting battery.

SYMPTOM CHART

Symptom	Test
All Power Windows Inoperative	A
Single Power Window Inoperative	B
Power Vent Window Inoperative – Rear Quarter Glass	C
One Touch Down Feature Inoperative	D

TEST A: ALL POWER WINDOWS INOPERATIVE

1) Turn ignition off. Disconnect driver door master window switch connector. See POWER WINDOW MASTER SWITCH under REMOVAL & INSTALLATION. Turn ignition on. Using a voltmeter, check voltage between ground and Orange/Black wire at driver door master window switch connector C509 terminal No. 6 or C508 terminal No. 13, if equipped with quarter glass power latches. *See Fig. 4 or 5.* If voltage is more than 10 volts, go to next step. If voltage is 10 volts or less, repair appropriate Orange/Black wire(s). Retest system operation.
2) Check driver door master window switch. See appropriate test under COMPONENT TESTS. If driver door master window switch is defective

replace switch and retest system operation. If driver door master window switch is okay, repair Black wire between driver door master window switch and ground. Retest system operation.

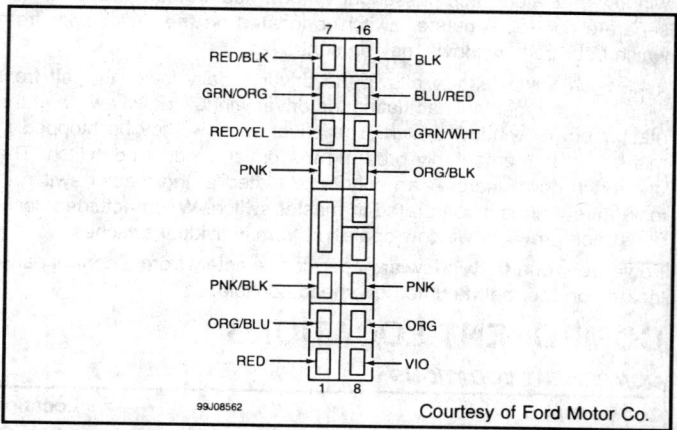

Fig. 4: Identifying Power Window Master Switch Connector C509 (Front Power) Terminals

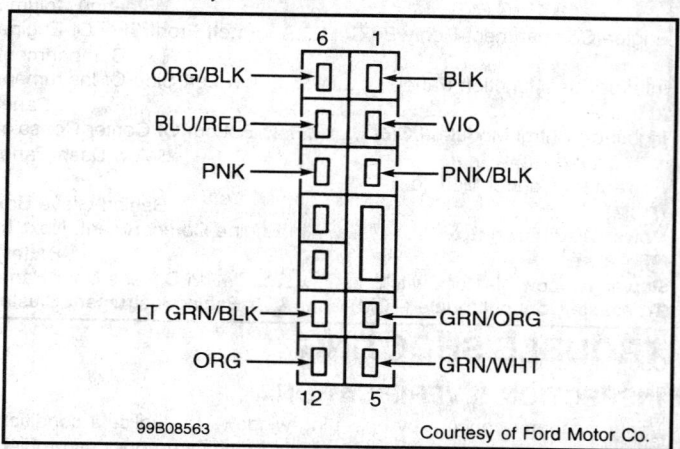

Fig. 5: Identifying Power Window Master Switch Connector C508 (Front & Rear Power) Terminals

TEST B: SINGLE POWER WINDOW INOPERATIVE

1) Turn ignition off. Disconnect driver door master window switch connector. Check driver door master window switch. See appropriate test under COMPONENT TESTS. If driver door master window switch is defective replace switch. Retest system operation. If driver door master window switch is okay, go to next step.
2) Check operation of power window motor in question. See POWER WINDOW MOTOR under COMPONENT TESTS. If power window motor is defective, replace motor and retest system operation. If power window motor is okay, go to next step.
3) Turn ignition off. Disconnect driver door master window switch connector C509 or C508. See POWER WINDOW MASTER SWITCH under REMOVAL & INSTALLATION. Using an ohmmeter, check resistance between ground and Black wire at driver door master window switch connector C509 terminal No. 1 or C508 terminal No. 16, if equipped with quarter glass power latches. *See Fig. 4 or 5.* If resistance is less than 5 ohms and problem is with left door window, go to next step. If resistance is less than 5 ohms and problem is with right door window, go to step **5).** If resistance is 5 ohms or more, repair open in Black wire. Retest system operation.
4) Turn ignition off. Using an ohmmeter, check resistance between ground and Blue/Red wire at driver door master window switch connector C509 terminal No. 7 or C508 terminal No. 15, if equipped with quarter glass power latches. Resistance should be more than 10 k/ohms. Check resistance of Blue/Red wire between driver door master window switch connector C509 terminal No. 7 or C508 terminal No. 15, if equipped with quarter glass power latches and left door window motor connector.

Resistance should be less than 5 ohms. If resistances are as specified, repair open or short to ground in Violet wire between left door window motor and driver door master window switch. If resistances are not as specified, repair open or short to ground in Blue/Red wire. Retest system operation.

5) Turn ignition off. Disconnect right door window switch connector C608. See SINGLE POWER WINDOW SWITCH under REMOVAL & INSTALLATION. Turn ignition on. Using a voltmeter, check voltage between ground and right door window switch connector C608 terminal No. 8 (Orange/Black wire). *See Fig. 6.* If voltage is more than 10 volts, go to next step. If voltage is 10 volts or less, repair open in Orange/Black wire and retest system operation.

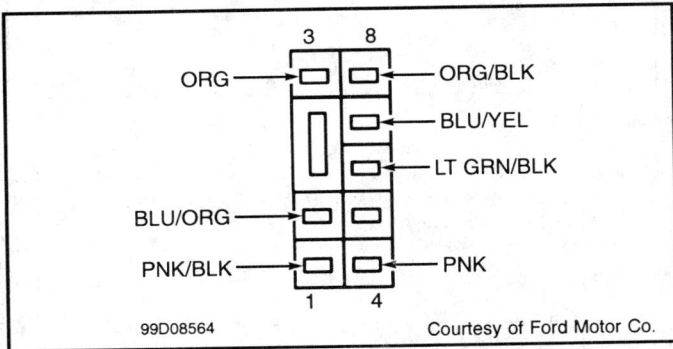

Fig. 6: Identifying Passenger Power Window Switch Connector C608 Terminals

6) Check right door window switch operation. See SINGLE POWER WINDOW SWITCH under COMPONENT TESTS. If switch is defective, replace switch and retest system operation. If switch is okay, go to next step.

7) Turn ignition off. Using an ohmmeter, check resistance of Light Green/Black wire between driver door master window switch connector C509 terminal No. 11 or C508 terminal No. 10, if equipped with quarter glass power latches and right door window switch connector C608 terminal No. 6. Resistance should be less than 5 ohms. Check resistance at Light Green/Black wire between ground and driver door master window switch connector C509 terminal No. 11 or C508 terminal No. 10, if equipped with quarter glass power latches. Resistance should be more than 10 k/ohms. If resistances are as specified, go to next step. If resistances are not as specified, repair open or short to ground in Light Green/Black wire. Retest system operation.

8) Using an ohmmeter, check resistance of Orange wire driver door master window switch connector C509 terminal No. 12 or C508 terminal No. 9, if equipped with quarter glass power latches and right door window switch connector C608 terminal No. 3. Resistance should be less than 5 ohms. Check resistance at Orange wire between ground and driver door master window switch connector C509 terminal No. 12 or C508 terminal No. 9, if equipped with quarter glass power latches. Resistance should be more than 10 k/ohms. If resistances are as specified, go to next step. If resistances are not as specified, repair open or short to ground in Orange wire. Retest system operation.

9) Disconnect right door window motor connector. Using an ohmmeter, check resistance of Blue/Yellow wire between right door window switch connector C608 terminal No. 7 and right door window motor connector. Resistance should be less than 5 ohms. Check resistance between ground and right door window switch connector C608 terminal No. 7 (Blue/Yellow wire). Resistance should be more than 10 k/ohms. If resistances are as specified, go to next step. If resistances are not as specified, repair open or short to ground in Blue/Yellow wire. Retest system operation.

10) Check resistance of Blue/Orange wire between right door window switch connector C608 terminal No. 2 and right door window motor connector. Resistance should be less than 5 ohms. Check resistance between ground and right door window switch connector C608 terminal No. 2 (Blue/Orange wire). Resistance should be more than 10 k/ohms. If resistances are as specified, replace right door window motor and

retest system operation. If resistances are not as specified, repair open or short to ground in Blue/Orange wire. Retest system operation.

TEST C: POWER VENT WINDOW INOPERATIVE – REAR QUARTER GLASS

1) Turn ignition off. Disconnect inoperative quarter glass power latch connector. Perform rear quarter glass motor component test. See POWER REAR QUARTER GLASS POWER LATCH MOTOR under COMPONENT TESTS. If rear quarter glass motor operated as specified, go to next step. If rear quarter glass motor does not operate as specified, replace quarter glass power latch motor assembly.

2) Disconnect driver door master window switch connector C508. See POWER WINDOW MASTER SWITCH under REMOVAL & INSTALLATION. Check driver door master window switch. See POWER WINDOW MASTER SWITCH (FRONT & REAR POWER) under COMPONENT TESTS. If driver door master window switch is defective, replace switch. Retest system operation. If driver door master window switch is okay and inoperative quarter glass power latch is right side, go to step **4)**. If driver door master window switch is okay and inoperative quarter glass power latch is left side, go to next step.

3) Reconnect driver door master window switch connector C508. Turn ignition on. Measure voltage between ground and left quarter glass power latch connector Red/Black wire. If voltage is more than 10 volts with left vent window switch held in OPEN position, repair open Red/Yellow wire between driver door master window switch and quarter glass power latch connector. If voltage is 10 volts or less with left vent window switch held in OPEN position, repair open Red/Black wire.

4) Reconnect driver door master window switch connector C508. Turn ignition on. Measure voltage between ground and right quarter glass power latch connector Orange/Blue wire. If voltage is more than 10 volts with right vent window switch held in OPEN position, repair open Red wire between driver door master window switch and quarter glass power latch connector. If voltage is 10 volts or less with right vent window switch held in OPEN position, repair open Orange/Blue wire.

TEST D: ONE-TOUCH DOWN FEATURE INOPERATIVE

NOTE: Replace master window switch and retest system. See POWER WINDOW MASTER SWITCH under REMOVAL & INSTALLATION.

REMOVAL & INSTALLATION
POWER WINDOW MASTER SWITCH

Removal & Installation – Remove driver door pull cup. Disconnect power window master switch electrical connector. Remove power window master switch assembly from door pull cup. To install, reverse removal procedure.

POWER WINDOW MOTOR

Removal & Installation – **1)** Disconnect negative battery cable. Using 1/4" flat-blade screwdriver, carefully pry off front door inside handle escutcheon and trim plate. Remove 2 cover caps and door panel screws. Slide flat-blade screwdriver behind each door trim panel retainer and twist to disengage. Disconnect electrical connectors.

2) Remove 2 front door trim panel bracket bolts and bracket. Remove weatherseal from door frame. Lower door glass to access regulator-to-bottom channel bolts. Remove window glass from door.

3) Remove 2 door brace bolts and brace. Disconnect window motor electrical connector. Remove 4 window regulator track bolts (2 at top and 2 at bottom). Remove 3 window motor attaching bolts. Remove window regulator and motor as an assembly. To install, reverse removal procedure.

SINGLE POWER WINDOW SWITCH

Removal & Installation – Remove passenger door pull cup. Disconnect power window switch electrical connector. Remove power window switch assembly from door pull cup. To install, reverse removal procedure.

WIRING DIAGRAMS

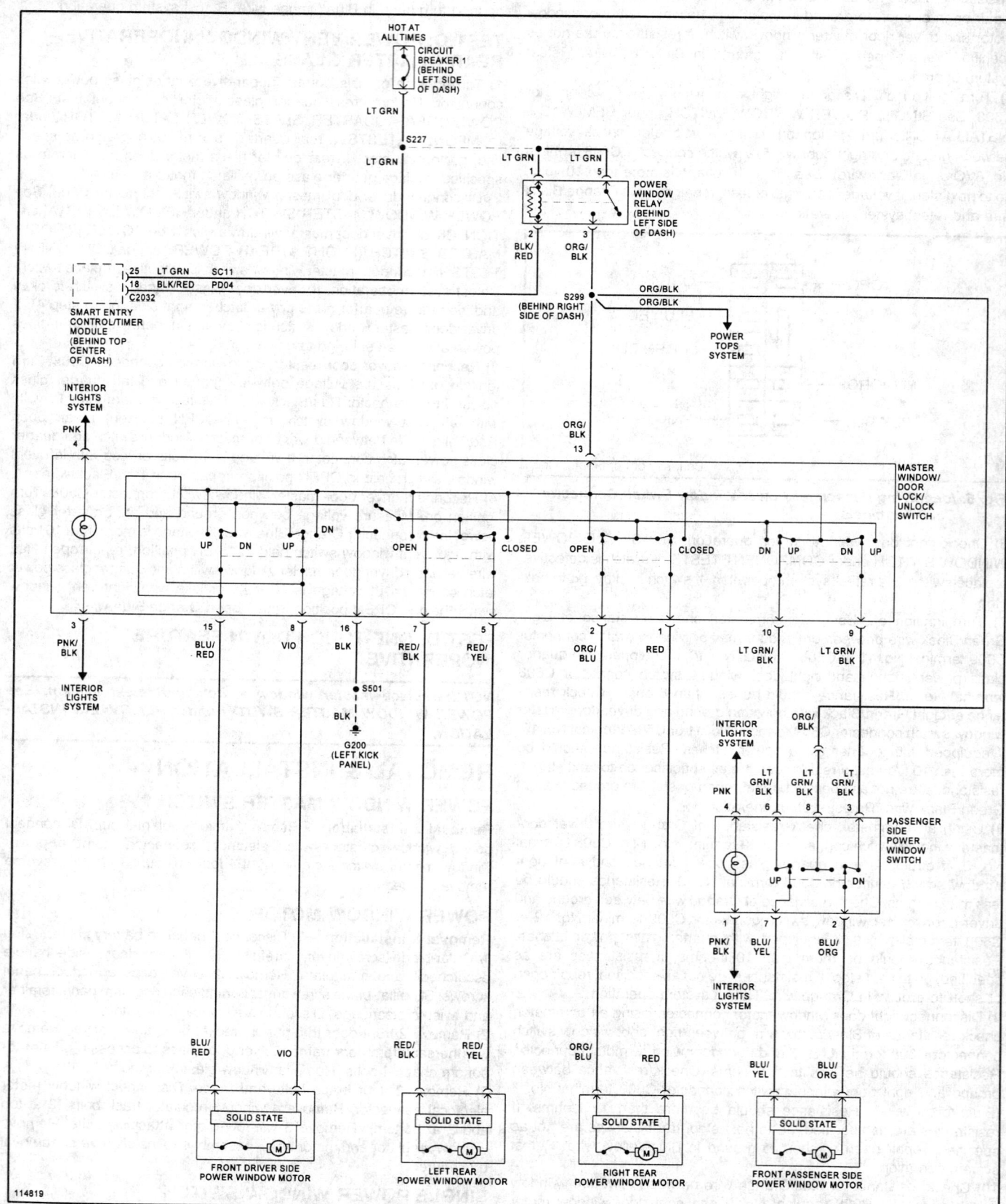

Fig. 7: Power Window System Wiring Diagram (Villager)

DESCRIPTION & OPERATION

Window Regulator Control Switch – Driver's side window regulator control switch controls actuation of left and right side front door power window regulators and left and right side rear quarter-glass flip-out actuators (if equipped). First detent position of driver's window regulator control switch will cause front door window glass to move downward until window regulator control switch is released. Second detent position will express-open front door window glass. Passenger's side window regulator control switch controls actuation of passenger front door window regulator.

One Touch Down Window Operation – One touch down driver's window feature is controlled by Front Electronic Module (FEM). When driver's window regulator control switch is actuated to express down position, FEM powers window regulator until window regulator control switch is actuated to a different position or FEM detects front door window glass is in full down position.

Rear Quarter Window Glass – Left and right side rear quarter glass are an optional power flip-open design which is operated by driver utilizing master window regulator control switch.

Heated Back Window Glass – Heated back window is controlled by Rear Electronic Module (REM), PCM and instrument cluster. System consists of REM, heated back window relay and heated back window switch (part of climate control assembly). Heated back window switch is a push button, spring-loaded to neutral position which turns system on or off. REM controls heated back window relay, which will turn off after approximately 10 minutes of operation or when button is pressed to OFF position.

Delayed Accessory – Delayed accessory operation allows power windows and radio to operate for up to 10 minutes after ignition switch is turned to OFF position. Delayed accessory function is controlled by FEM. When ignition switch is turned from RUN to OFF position, FEM will begin timing sequence. If a door is opened or ignition switch is activated to another position, FEM will cancel delayed accessory operation.

COMPONENT LOCATIONS

COMPONENT LOCATIONS

Component	Location
Accessory Delay Relay	In Fuse Junction Box (FJB)
Front Electronic Module (FEM)	[1] Below Left Side Of Instrument Panel
Rear Electronic Module (REM)	[2] Behind Right Side Rear Quarter Panel

[1] – See Fig. 1.
[2] – See Fig. 2.

PROGRAMMING

MODULE CONFIGURATION

NOTE: Powertrain Control Module (PCM) has to be flash programmed using a flash cable. See COMPUTER RELEARN PROCEDURES article in GENERAL INFORMATION.

NOTE: Newly released modules will require configuration after being installed on vehicle. All configurable modules will be packaged in a kit which contains a warning label and multi-language sheet reemphasizing requirements to configure replacement modules. A New Generation Star (NGS) tester or Ford compatible scan tool MUST be used to retrieve configuration data from old module before it is removed from vehicle. This information will be transferred into new module so that new module will contain same settings as old module. NGS tester will not retain stored configuration information for longer than 24 hours.

Following manufacturer's instructions, upload old information from old module using Ford Service Function (FSF) card and NGS tester. Install new module and download stored information into new module using FSF card and NGS tester.

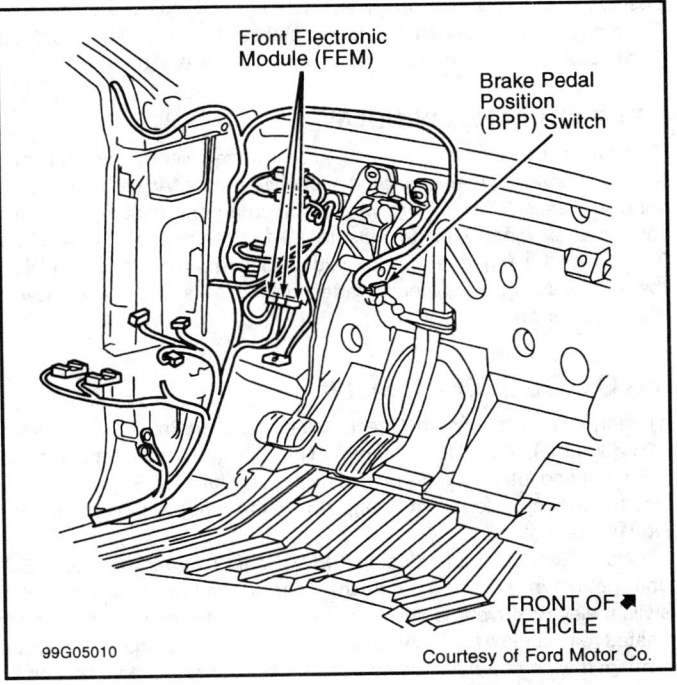

99G05010   Courtesy of Ford Motor Co.

Fig. 1: Locating Front Electronic Module (FEM)

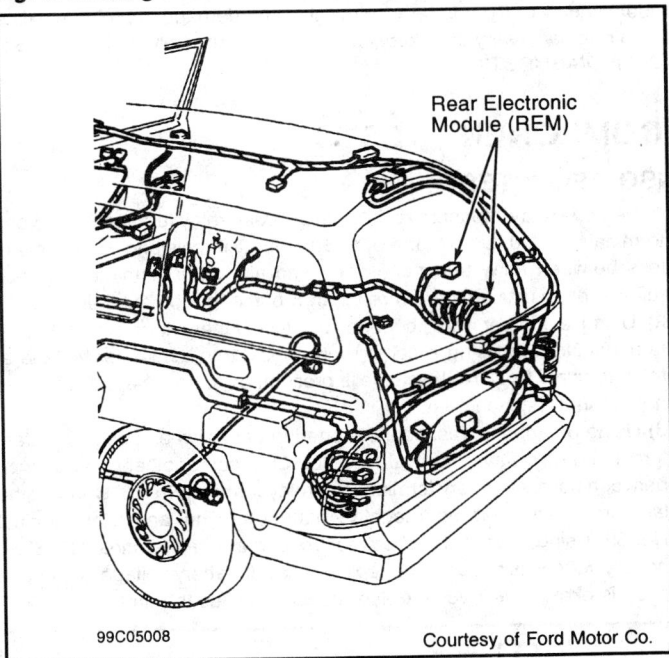

99C05008   Courtesy of Ford Motor Co.

Fig. 2: Locating Rear Electronic Module (REM)

ADJUSTMENTS

DOOR WINDOW HEIGHT STOP ADJUSTMENT

1) Remove front door trim panel and front door inside panel sound insulator. Lower door window 3.00″ (76.2 mm) from full up position. Loosen nut and washer assemblies securing window regulator equalizer arm bracket to front door inner panel.

2) With front door open, place hands on each side of glass and pull glass fully rearward into door glass top runner. Tighten nut and washer assembly securing the front of the window regulator equalizer arm bracket.

3) Apply downward pressure on window regulator equalizer arm bracket. If the hole is a vertical slotted hole, ensure the nut and washer securing the rear of the window regulator equalizer arm bracket is positioned at the bottom of the slot as you apply downward pressure. Tighten remaining nut and washer assemblies to 62-89 INCH lbs. (7-10 N.m). Open and close window to verify proper operation.

REAR QUARTER WINDOW

Remove rear quarter trim. Loosen 4 rear quarter window latch retaining screws. Loosen 2 rear quarter window hinge nuts. Adjust rear quarter window glass. While holding window, have an assistant tighten the 2 rear quarter window hinge nuts to 89-124 INCH lbs. (10-14 N.m). Tighten the 4 rear quarter window latch retaining screws to 89-124 INCH lbs. (10-14 N.m). Install rear quarter trim. Open and close window to verify proper operation.

TROUBLE SHOOTING

1) Verify customer concern. Check Battery Junction Box (BJB) fuses No. 106 (30-amp), No. 113 (30-amp), No. 116 (30-amp), fuse No. 23 (15-amp) and fuse No. 2 (5-amp). Check Fuse Junction Box (FJB) fuses No. 10 (10-amp), No. 14 (10-amp), No. 18 (10-amp), No. 9 (5-amp) and No. 16 (5-amp).
2) Check Front Electronic Module (FEM), Rear Electronic Module (REM) and instrument cluster for damage. Check window regulator control switch, electric drive and flip quarter window motor for damage. Check heated rear window relay, switch and window grid for damage. Check for damaged wiring harness, bulbs and/or loose, corroded connections.
3) Check power window regulator or switch, window run weatherstrip, door window or flip quarter window glass for damage. If problem exists, repair as necessary. If no problem exists, perform self-diagnostics. See SELF-DIAGNOSTIC SYSTEM.

COMPONENT TESTS

ISO RELAY TEST

1) Remove relay. Measure resistance between relay terminal No. 85 and terminals No. 30, 86, 87, and 87a. *See Fig. 3.* If resistance is 5 ohms or less between relay terminal No. 85 and any other terminals, replace relay. If all resistances are more than 5 ohms, go to next step.
2) Using a jumper wire, connect positive battery terminal and relay terminal No. 30. Using a self-powered test lamp, check for voltage at relay terminal No. 87a. If voltage is present, go to next step. If voltage is not present, replace relay.
3) Using 3 jumper wires, connect one jumper between positive battery terminal and relay terminal No. 30. Connect another jumper wire between positive battery terminal and relay terminal No. 86. Connect the last jumper wire between negative battery terminal and relay terminal No. 85. Using a test light, check for voltage at relay terminal No. 87. If battery voltage is not present, replace relay. If battery voltage is present, relay is okay. Check voltage and ground supplies to relay.

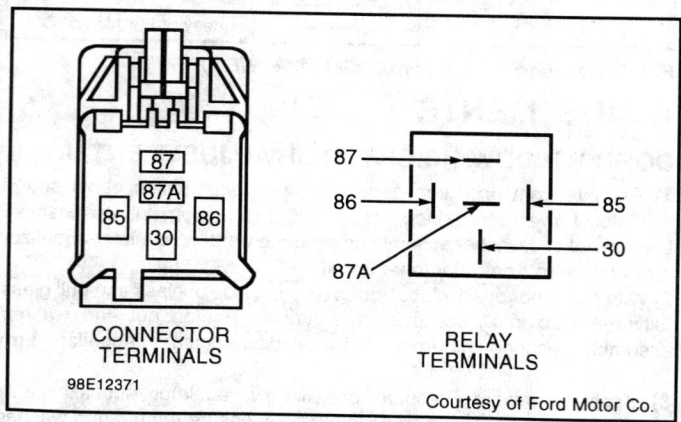

Fig. 3: Identifying ISO Relay Terminals

HEATED REAR WINDOW GRID

1) Using a bright light in vehicle, inspect wire grid from exterior. A broken grid wire will appear as a brown spot. Run engine at idle. Set heated rear window switch in ON position, indicator should illuminate. Working inside vehicle with voltmeter, contact broad red-brown stripes of rear glass window positive lead to battery side and negative lead to ground side. Meter should read 10-13 volts. A lower reading indicates a loose ground connection.
2) Contact a good ground point with negative lead of meter. Voltage reading should remain the same. With negative lead of meter grounded, touch each grid line of heated rear window glass at its midpoint with positive lead. A reading of approximately 6 volts indicates that line is okay. A reading of zero volts indicates that line is broken between midpoint and positive side of grid line. A reading of 12 volts indicates that circuit is broken between midpoint of grid line and ground.

MASTER WINDOW REGULATOR CONTROL SWITCH

Disconnect master window regulator control switch. Check continuity between specified master window regulator control switch terminals with switch in appropriate position. See MASTER WINDOW REGULATOR CONTROL SWITCH table. *See Figs. 4 and 5.* If continuity is not as specified, replace master window regulator control switch.

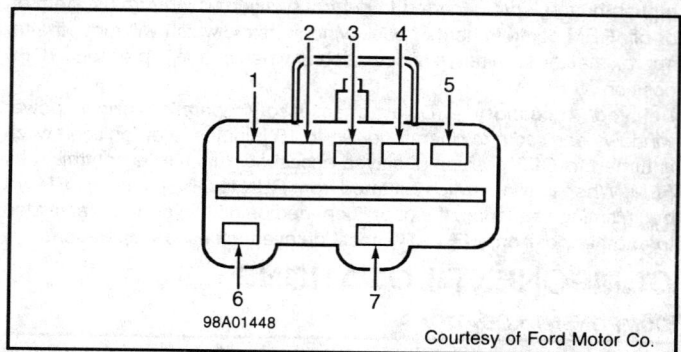

Fig. 4: Identifying Master Window Regulator Control Connector C501 Terminals

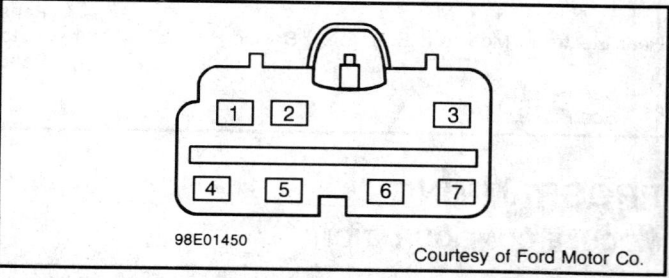

Fig. 5: Master Window Regulator Control Switch Connector C514 Terminals

MASTER WINDOW REGULATOR CONTROL SWITCH

Connector (Terminals No.)	Switch Position	Specification
One-Touch Down Circuit		
C501 (6 & 2)	Down	480 ohms
Power/Ground Checks Before Other Tests		
C501 (6 & 7)	Both Front Switches (All Positions)	No
C501 (7 & All others, Except 6 & 2)	Both Front Switches (At Rest)	Yes
Left Front Window Circuit		
C501 (6 & 3)	Up	Yes
C501 (6 & 1)	Down	Yes
Right Front Window Switch		
C501 (6 & 4)	Up	Yes
C501 (6 & 5)	Down	Yes
Left Flip Window Switch		
C514 (1 & 5)	Up	Yes
C514 (1 & 4)	Down	Yes
Right Flip Window Switch		
C514 (1 & 7)	Up	Yes
C514 (1 & 6)	Down	Yes

PASSENGER'S WINDOW REGULATOR CONTROL SWITCH

Disconnect passenger's window regulator control switch. Check continuity between specified passenger's window regulator control switch terminals with switch in appropriate position. See PASSENGER'S WINDOW REGULATOR CONTROL SWITCH table. *See Fig. 6.* If continuity is not as specified, replace passenger's window regulator control switch.

PASSENGER'S WINDOW REGULATOR CONTROL SWITCH

Switch Position	Continuity Between Terminals
Up	4 & 3; 6 & 7
Down	4 & 6; 3 & 2
At Rest	2 & 3; 7 & 6

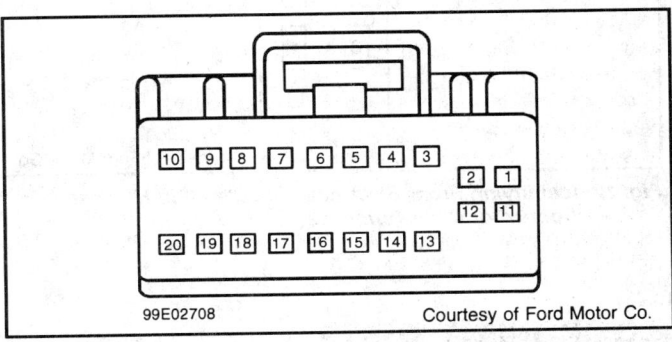

Fig. 8: Identifying Front/Rear Electronic Module & Instrument Cluster 20-Pin Harness Connector Terminals

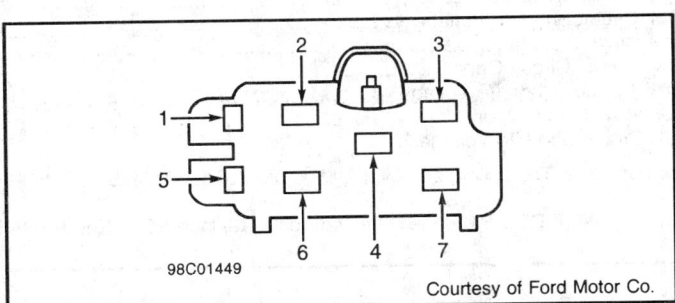

Fig. 6: Identifying Passenger's Window Regulator Control Switch Connector C600 Terminals

CONNECTOR IDENTIFICATION

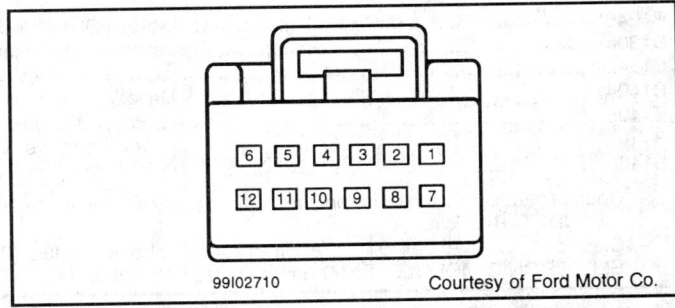

Fig. 9: Identifying Front/Rear Electronic Module & Climate Control 12-Pin Harness Connector Terminals

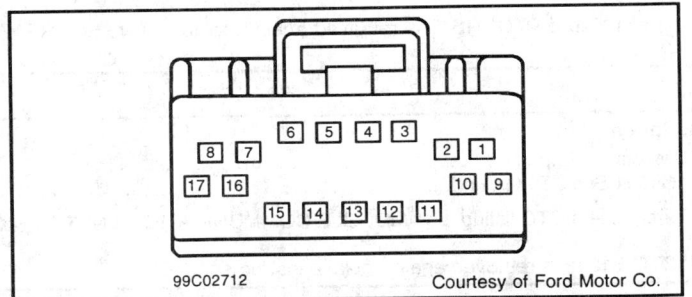

Fig. 7: Identifying Front/Rear Electronic Module 17-Pin Harness Connector Terminals

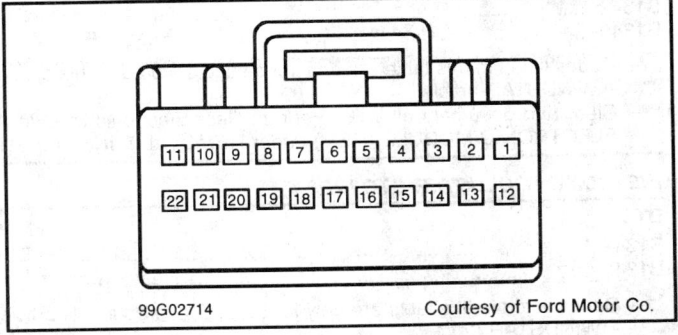

Fig. 10: Identifying Front/Rear Electronic Module & Instrument Cluster 22-Pin Harness Connector Terminals

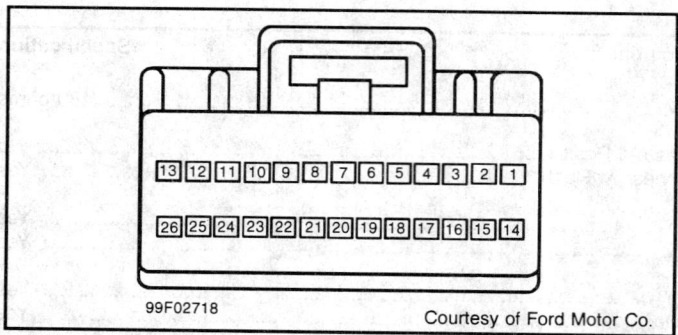

99F02718

Courtesy of Ford Motor Co.

Fig. 11: Identifying Front/Rear Electronic Module 26-Pin Harness Connector Terminals

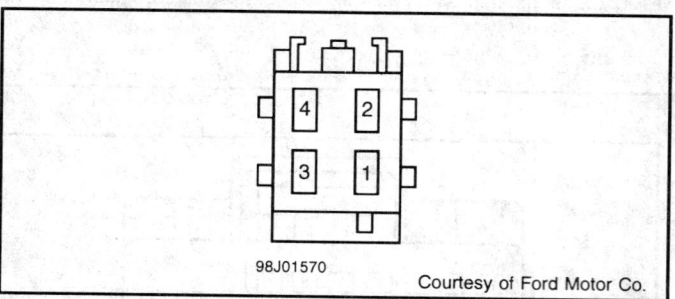

98J01570

Courtesy of Ford Motor Co.

Fig. 12: Identifying Front Electronic Module 4-Pin Harness Connector C348 Terminals

SELF-DIAGNOSTIC SYSTEM

NOTE: All diagnostic tests are written specifically for New Generation Star (NGS) tester. Most generic scan tools should be able to perform all test procedures.

Connect New Generation Star (NGS) tester to Data Link Connector (DLC), located beneath instrument panel. Using NGS tester, perform data link diagnostics test. See DATA LINK DIAGNOSTIC TEST under COMMUNICATION NETWORK DIAGNOSTICS in MODULE COMMUNICATIONS NETWORK – WINDSTAR article. If NGS tester responds with CKT914, CKT915 or CKT70=ALL ECUS NO RESP/NOT EQUIP, repair module communications concern. See MODULE COMMUNICATIONS NETWORK – WINDSTAR article. If NGS tester displays NO RESP/NOT EQUIP for Front Electronic Module (FEM), perform TEST A: NO COMMUNICATION WITH FRONT ELECTRONIC MODULE (FEM) under SYSTEM TESTS. If NGS tester displays NO RESP/NOT EQUIP for Rear Electronic Module (REM), perform TEST B: NO COMMUNICATION WITH REAR ELECTRONIC MODULE (REM) under SYSTEM TESTS. If NGS tester displays NO RESP/NOT EQUIP for instrument cluster, perform TEST C: NO COMMUNICATION WITH INSTRUMENT CLUSTER under SYSTEM TESTS.

If NGS tester responds with SYSTEM PASSED, retrieve and record continuous DTCs. Erase continuous DTCs. Using NGS tester, perform instrument cluster, FEM and REM self-tests. Perform appropriate test in accordance with DTC retrieved. See FRONT ELECTRONIC MODULE (FEM) DTC INDEX, REAR ELECTRONIC MODULE (REM) DTC INDEX and/or INSTRUMENT CLUSTER DTC INDEX table. Codes listed in these tables are only for testing covered in this article. For complete DTC listing, see MODULE COMMUNICATIONS NETWORK – WINDSTAR article. If no DTCs are retrieved, repair by symptom. See SYMPTOM CHART table.

FRONT ELECTRONIC MODULE (FEM) DTC INDEX

DTC [1]	Description	Test
B1243	Express Down Switch Circuit Short To Voltage	H
B1304	Accessory Delay Relay Coil Circuit Short To Voltage	D
B1342	ECU Defective	[2]
B1404	Driver's Power Window DOWN Circuit Open	E
B1405	Driver's Power Window DOWN Circuit Short To Voltage	E
B1407	Driver's Power Window UP Circuit Open	E
B1408	Driver's Power Window UP Circuit Short To Voltage	E

[1] – Codes listed in this table are only for testing covered in this article. For complete DTC listing, see MODULE COMMUNICATIONS NETWORK – WINDSTAR article.

[2] – Clear and document all DTC. Perform Front Electronic Module (FEM) self-test. If DTC B1342 is retrieved again, replace FEM. See FRONT ELECTRONIC MODULE (FEM) under REMOVAL & INSTALLATION.

REAR ELECTRONIC MODULE (REM) DTC INDEX

DTC [1]	Description	Test
B1342	ECU Defective	[2]
B1349	Heated Rear Window Relay Short To Voltage	I

[1] – Codes listed in this table are only for testing covered in this article. For complete DTC listing, see MODULE COMMUNICATIONS NETWORK – WINDSTAR article.

[2] – Clear and document all DTC. Perform Rear Electronic Module (REM) self-test. If DTC B1342 is retrieved again, replace REM. See REAR ELECTRONIC MODULE (REM) under REMOVAL & INSTALLATION.

INSTRUMENT CLUSTER DTC INDEX

DTC [1]	Description	Test
B1342	ECU Defective	[2]
B1345	Heated Backlite Input Circuit Short To Ground	I

[1] – Codes listed in this table are only for testing covered in this article. For complete DTC listing, see MODULE COMMUNICATIONS NETWORK – WINDSTAR article.

[2] – Clear and document all DTC. Perform instrument cluster self-test. If DTC B1342 is retrieved again, replace instrument cluster.

SYMPTOM CHART

Condition	Test
No Communication With Front Electronic Module (FEM)	A
No Communication With Rear Electronic Module (REM)	B
No Communication With Instrument Cluster	C
All Power Windows Inoperative	D
Driver's Front Power Window Inoperative	E
Passenger's Front Power Window Inoperative	F
Vent Power Window(s) Inoperative	G
One Touch Down Feature Inoperative	H
Rear Window Will Not Defrost	I
Rear Window Defroster Will Not Shut Off Automatically	J
Delayed Accessory Does Not Turn Off	K

SYSTEM TESTS

NOTE: *Many steps in the following tests refer to various connectors. These connectors are identified in illustrations. See Figs. 3-7 under CONNECTOR IDENTIFICATION.*

TEST A: NO COMMUNICATION WITH FRONT ELECTRONIC MODULE (FEM)

NOTE: *Turn ignition switch from OFF to ON position to enable system power feature.*

1) Turn ignition switch to OFF position. Remove fuses No. 2 (10-amp) and No. 23 (15-amp) from Battery Junction Box (BJB) . Inspect fuses. If either or both fuse(s) are blown, repair short as necessary. If fuses are okay, go to next step.

2) Turn ignition switch to ON position. Measure voltage between fuses No. 2 input side and No. 23 input side and ground. If voltages are more than 10 volts, install fuses and go to next step. If voltages are 10 volts or less, repair power supply circuit(s). See WIRING DIAGRAMS.

3) Turn ignition switch to OFF position. Disconnect FEM harness connectors. Measure voltage between FEM harness connectors C346 terminal No. 1 (Light Blue/Red wire) and ground. Measure voltage between FEM harness connector C190 terminal No. 6 (Red wire) and ground. If voltages are more than 10 volts, go to next step. If voltages are 10 volts or less, repair power supply circuit(s). See WIRING DIAGRAMS.

4) Turn ignition switch to OFF position. Measure resistance between FEM harness connector C190 terminal No. 12 (Black wire), FEM harness connector C192 terminals No. 11, 13, 14 and 15 (Black wires) and ground. If all resistances are less than 5 ohms, repair module communication concern. See MODULE COMMUNICATIONS NETWORK – WINDSTAR article. If any resistance is 5 ohms or more, repair open in appropriate Black wire. See WIRING DIAGRAMS.

TEST B: NO COMMUNICATION WITH REAR ELECTRONIC MODULE (REM)

NOTE: *Turn ignition switch from OFF to ON position to enable system power feature.*

1) Turn ignition switch to OFF position. Remove fuse No. 16 (10-amp) from Fuse Junction Box (FJB). Turn ignition switch to ON position. Measure voltage between fuse No. 16 input terminal and ground. If voltage is more than 10 volts, install fuse and go to next step. If voltage is 10 volts or less, repair FJB power supply circuit. See WIRING DIAGRAMS.

2) Turn ignition switch to OFF position. Disconnect REM harness connectors. Turn ignition switch to ON position. Measure voltage between REM harness connector C343 terminal No. 3 (White/Yellow wire) and ground. If voltage is more than 10 volts, go to next step. If voltage is 10 volts or less, repair power supply circuit. See WIRING DIAGRAMS.

3) Turn ignition switch to OFF position. Measure resistances between REM harness connector C341 terminal No. 12 (Black wire), REM harness connector C342 terminals No. 11, 12, 25 and 26 (Black wires) and ground. If all resistances are less than 5 ohms, repair module communications concern. See MODULE COMMUNICATIONS NETWORK – WINDSTAR article. If any resistance is 5 ohms or more, repair open in appropriate Black wire. See WIRING DIAGRAMS.

TEST C: NO COMMUNICATION WITH INSTRUMENT CLUSTER

NOTE: *Turn ignition switch from OFF to ON position to enable system power feature.*

1) Turn ignition switch to OFF position. Disconnect instrument cluster 22-pin harness connector C239, and 20-pin harness connector C240. Turn ignition switch to ON position. Measure voltage between specified harness connector terminals and ground. See INSTRUMENT CLUSTER VOLTAGE table. If all readings are 10 volts or more, go to next step. If any reading is less than 10 volts, repair power supply circuit(s).

INSTRUMENT CLUSTER VOLTAGE

Connector	Terminal	Circuit No. (Wire Color)
C239	11	1001 (WHT/YEL)
C240	7	295 (LT BLU/PNK)
C240	8	1112 (WHT/LT BLU)
C240	9	1112 (WHT/LT BLU)

2) Turn ignition switch to OFF position. Measure resistance between instrument cluster harness connector C240 terminal No. 12 (Black wire) and ground. If resistance is less than 5 ohms, repair module communications concern. See MODULE COMMUNICATIONS NETWORK – WINDSTAR article. If resistance is 5 ohms or more, repair open in Black wire. See WIRING DIAGRAMS.

TEST D: ALL POWER WINDOWS INOPERATIVE

1) Using New Generation Star (NGS) tester, perform Front Electronic Module (FEM) self-test. If DTC B1304 is retrieved, go to next step. If no DTCs are retrieved, go to step **4)**. If any other DTCs are retrieved, perform appropriate test in accordance with DTC retrieved. See FRONT ELECTRONIC MODULE (FEM) DTC INDEX table under SELF-DIAGNOSTIC SYSTEM.

2) Disconnect FEM 22-pin harness connector C191. Turn ignition switch to ON position. Measure voltage between FEM harness connector C191 terminal No. 6 (Light Blue wire) and ground. If voltage is more than 10 volts, go to next step. If voltage is 10 volts or less, replace FEM. See FRONT ELECTRONIC MODULE (FEM) under REMOVAL & INSTALLATION.

3) Turn ignition switch to OFF position. Remove accessory delay relay. Turn ignition switch to ON position. Measure voltage between FEM harness connector C191 terminal No. 6 (Light Blue wire) and ground. If voltage is more than 10 volts, repair short to voltage in Light Blue wire. See WIRING DIAGRAMS. If voltage is 10 volts or less, replace accessory delay relay.

4) Remove fuse No. 106 (30-amp) from Battery Junction Box (BJB). Measure voltage between fuse No. 106 input side and ground. If voltage is more than 10 volts, go to next step. If voltage is 10 volts or less, repair power supply circuit. See WIRING DIAGRAMS.

5) Remove fuse No. 106 (30-amp) from Battery Junction Box (BJB). Remove accessory delay relay. Measure voltage between accessory delay relay harness connector terminals No. 86 and No. 30 and ground. *See Fig. 3.* If voltage is more than 10 volts, go to next step. If voltage is 10 volts or less, repair power supply circuit. See WIRING DIAGRAMS.

6) Test accessory delay relay. See ISO RELAY TEST under COMPONENT TESTS. If accessory delay relay is okay, go to next step. If accessory delay relay is not okay, replace accessory delay relay.

7) Using NGS tester, access FEM active command ONE TOUCH WINDOW DOWN AND ACCY DELAY. Trigger ACCY RLY ON and OFF while measuring resistance between accessory delay relay harness connector terminal No. 85 (Light Blue wire) and ground. If resistance is 5 ohms or more when ON and 10 k/ohms or less when OFF, go to next step. If resistance is less than 5 ohms when ON and more than 10 k/ohms when OFF, go to step **10)**.

8) Turn ignition switch to OFF position. Disconnect FEM 22-pin harness connector C191. Measure resistance between accessory delay relay harness connector terminal No. 85 (Light Blue wire) and ground. If resistance is more than 10 k/ohms, go to next step. If resistance is 10 k/ohms or less, repair short to ground in Light Blue wire. See WIRING DIAGRAMS.

9) Measure resistance between FEM harness connector C191 terminal No. 6 (Light Blue wire) and accessory delay relay harness connector terminal No. 85 (Light Blue wire). If resistance is less than 5 ohms, replace FEM. See FRONT ELECTRONIC MODULE (FEM) under REMOVAL & INSTALLATION. If resistance is 5 ohms or more, repair open in Light Blue wire. See WIRING DIAGRAMS.

10) Remove master window regulator control switch. Test master window regulator control switch. See MASTER WINDOW REGULATOR CONTROL SWITCH under COMPONENT TESTS. If master window regulator control switch is okay, go to next step. If master window regulator control switch is not okay, replace master window regulator control switch.

11) With accessory delay relay removed, measure resistance between master window regulator control switch harness connector C501 terminal No. 6 (Light Blue/Black wire) and ground. *See Fig. 4.* If resistance is more than 10 k/ohms, go to next step. If resistance is 10 k/ohms or less, repair short to ground in Light Blue/Black wire. See WIRING DIAGRAMS.

12) Measure resistance between accessory delay relay harness connector terminal No. 87 (Light Blue/Black wire) and master window regulator control switch harness connector C501 terminal No. 6 (Light Blue/Black wire). If resistance is less than 5 ohms, go to next step. If resistance is 5 ohms or more, repair open in Light Blue/Black wire. See WIRING DIAGRAMS.

13) Turn ignition switch to ON position. Measure voltage between master window regulator control switch harness connector C501 terminal No. 6 (Light Blue/Black wire) and ground. If voltage is more than 10 volts, repair short to voltage in Light Blue/Black wire. See WIRING DIAGRAMS. If voltage is 10 volts or less, replace FEM. See FRONT ELECTRONIC MODULE (FEM) under REMOVAL & INSTALLATION.

TEST E: DRIVER'S FRONT POWER WINDOW INOPERATIVE

NOTE: Turn ignition switch from OFF to ON position to enable system power feature.

1) Using New Generation Star (NGS) tester, perform Front Electronic Module (FEM) self-test. If DTC B1404 or B1407 is retrieved, go to next step. If DTC B1405 is retrieved, go to step **4)**. If DTC B1408 is retrieved, go to step **6)**. If no DTCs are retrieved, go to step **8)**.

2) Using NGS tester, access FEM active command FRONT WINDOW CONTROL. Trigger DR DOWN to ON and DR UP to ON. If driver's window motion did not agreed with command, go to next step. If driver's window motion agrees with command, replace FEM. See FRONT ELECTRONIC MODULE (FEM) under REMOVAL & INSTALLATION.

3) Disconnect driver's window motor 2-pin harness connector C512. Measure voltage between driver's window motor harness connector C512 terminal No. 2 (Black/Yellow wire) and ground. Trigger DR UP to ON and record reading. Measure voltage between driver's window motor harness connector C512 terminal No. 1 (Orange/Yellow wire) and ground. Trigger DR DOWN to ON and record reading. If voltage is 10 volts or less on either circuit, go to step **20)**. If voltage is more than 10 volts on each circuit, replace driver's window motor. See FRONT DOOR WINDOW REGULATOR MOTOR under REMOVAL & INSTALLATION.

4) Disconnect FEM 26-pin harness connector C347. Measure voltage between FEM harness connector C347 terminal No. 10 (Brown/Yellow wire) and ground. If voltage is more than 10 volts, go to next step. If voltage is 10 volts or less, replace FEM. See FRONT ELECTRONIC MODULE (FEM) under REMOVAL & INSTALLATION.

5) Disconnect master window regulator control switch C501. Measure voltage between FEM harness connector C347 terminal No. 10 (Brown/Yellow wire) and ground. If voltage is more than 10 volts, repair short to voltage in Brown/Yellow wire. See WIRING DIAGRAMS. If voltage is 10

volts or less, replace master window regulator control switch. See WINDOW REGULATOR CONTROL SWITCH under REMOVAL & INSTALLATION.

6) Disconnect FEM 26-pin harness connector C347. Measure voltage between FEM harness connector C347 terminal No. 25 (Black/Orange wire) and ground. If voltage is more than 10 volts, go to next step. If voltage is 10 volts or less, replace FEM. See FRONT ELECTRONIC MODULE (FEM) under REMOVAL & INSTALLATION.

7) Disconnect master window regulator control switch harness connector C501. Measure voltage between FEM harness connector C347 terminal No. 25 (Black/Orange wire) and ground. If voltage is more than 10 volts, repair short to voltage in Black/Orange wire. See WIRING DIAGRAMS. If voltage is 10 volts or less, replace master window regulator control switch. See WINDOW REGULATOR CONTROL SWITCH under REMOVAL & INSTALLATION.

8) Remove fuse No.113 (30-amp) from Battery Junction Box (BJB). Measure voltage between fuse No. 113 input side and ground. If voltage is more than 10 volts, go to next step. If voltage is 10 volts or less, repair power supply circuit. See WIRING DIAGRAMS.

9) Remove fuse No. 113 (30-amp) from Battery Junction Box (BJB). Disconnect FEM 4-pin harness connector C348. Measure voltage between FEM harness connector C348 terminal No. 3 (Yellow/Light Green wire) and ground. *See Fig. 12 .* If voltage is more than 10 volts, go to next step. If voltage is 10 volts or less, repair power supply circuit. See WIRING DIAGRAMS.

10) Measure resistance between FEM harness connector C348 terminal No. 4 (Black wire) and ground. If resistance is more than 5 ohms, go to next step. If resistance is 5 ohms or less, repair open in Black wire. See WIRING DIAGRAMS.

11) Measure voltage between FEM harness connector C348 terminal No. 4 (Black wire) and ground. If voltage is 10 volts or less, go to next step. If voltage is more than 10 volts, repair short to voltage in Black wire. See WIRING DIAGRAMS.

12) Using NGS tester, monitor FEM PIDs D_UP_SW and D_DN_SW. Actuate master window regulator control switch to driver's window UP and DOWN positions. If PIDs do not agree with window movement, go to next step. If PIDs agree with window movement, go to step **16)**.

13) Remove master window regulator control switch. Test master window regulator control switch. See MASTER WINDOW REGULATOR CONTROL SWITCH under COMPONENT TESTS. If master window regulator control switch is okay, go to next step. If master window regulator control switch is not okay, replace master window regulator control switch. See WINDOW REGULATOR CONTROL SWITCH under REMOVAL & INSTALLATION.

14) Disconnect FEM 26-pin harness connector C347. Measure resistance between master window regulator control switch harness connector C501 terminal No. 1 (Black/Orange wire) and ground. Measure resistance between master window regulator control switch harness connector C501 terminal No. 2 (Brown/Yellow wire) and ground. If resistances are more than 10 k/ohms, go to next step. If either resistance is 10 k/ohms or less, repair short to ground in appropriate wire. See WIRING DIAGRAMS.

15) Measure resistance between master window regulator control switch harness connector C501 terminal No. 1 (Black/Orange wire) and FEM harness connector C347 terminal No. 27 (Black/Orange wire). Measure resistance between master window regulator control switch harness connector C501 terminal No. 2 (Brown/Yellow wire) and FEM harness connector C347 terminal No. 10 (Brown/Yellow wire). If resistances are 5 ohms or less, replace FEM. See FRONT ELECTRONIC MODULE (FEM) under REMOVAL & INSTALLATION. If either resistance is more than 5 ohms, repair open in appropriate wire. See WIRING DIAGRAMS.

16) Using NGS tester, monitor FEM PID IGN_R while cycling ignition switch from OFF to ON position. If PID IGN_R agrees with ignition switch position, go to next step. If PID did not agree with ignition switch position, repair ignition switch circuits as necessary. See STEERING COLUMN SWITCHES – WINDSTAR article.

17) Using NGS tester, access FEM active command FRONT WINDOW CONTROL. Trigger FEM DR UP to ON and DR DOWN to ON. If window does not move to up then down, go to next step. If window moves to up then down, replace FEM. See FRONT ELECTRONIC MODULE (FEM) under REMOVAL & INSTALLATION.

18) Disconnect driver's window motor 2-pin harness connector C512 and FEM 4-pin harness connector C348. Measure resistance between driver's window motor harness connector C512 terminal No. 1 (Orange/Yellow wire) and ground. Measure resistance between driver's window motor harness connector C512 terminal No. 2 (Black/Yellow wire) and ground. If resistances are more than 10 k/ohms, go to next step. If either resistance is 10 k/ohms or less, repair short to ground in appropriate wire. See WIRING DIAGRAMS.

19) Measure voltage between driver's window motor harness connector C512 terminal No. 1 (Orange/Yellow wire) and ground. Measure voltage between driver's window motor harness connector C512 terminal No.2 (Black/Yellow wire) and ground. If either voltage is more than 10 volts, repair short to voltage in appropriate wire. See WIRING DIAGRAMS. If voltages are 10 volts or less, replace driver's window motor. See FRONT DOOR WINDOW REGULATOR MOTOR under REMOVAL & INSTALLATION.

20) Measure resistance between FEM harness connector C348 terminal No. 1 (Black/Yellow wire) and driver's window motor harness connector C512 terminal No. 2 (Black/Yellow wire). Measure resistance between FEM harness connector C348 terminal No. 2 (Orange/Yellow wire) and driver's window motor harness connector C512 terminal No. 1 (Orange/Yellow wire). If resistances are less than 5 ohms, replace FEM. See FRONT ELECTRONIC MODULE (FEM) under REMOVAL & INSTALLATION. If either resistance is 5 ohms or more, repair open in appropriate wire. See WIRING DIAGRAMS.

TEST F: PASSENGER'S FRONT POWER WINDOW INOPERATIVE

1) Turn ignition switch to ON position. Operate passenger's window from master window regulator control switch. If passenger's window is inoperative from master window regulator control switch, go to next step. If passenger's window is operative from master window regulator control switch, go to step **12)**.

2) Turn ignition switch to OFF position. Disconnect passenger's window motor 2-pin harness connector C608. Measure resistance between passenger's window motor harness connector C608 terminal No. 1 (Red/White wire) and ground. If resistance is 5 ohms or more, go to next step. If resistance is less than 5 ohms, go to step **6)**.

3) Disconnect passenger's window regulator control switch 7-pin harness connector C600. Measure resistance between passenger's window regulator control switch harness connector C600 terminal No. 7 (White/Yellow wire) and ground. *See Fig. 6.* If resistance is 5 ohms or more, go to next step. If resistance is less than 5 ohms, go to step **5)**.

4) Disconnect master window regulator control switch harness connector C501. Measure resistance between master window regulator control switch harness connector C501 terminal No. 5 (White/Yellow wire) and passenger's window regulator control switch harness connector C600 terminal No. 7 (White/Yellow wire). If resistance is less than 5 ohms, replace master window regulator control switch. See WINDOW REGULATOR CONTROL SWITCH under REMOVAL & INSTALLATION. If resistance is 5 ohms or more, repair open in White/Yellow wire. See WIRING DIAGRAMS.

5) Measure resistance between passenger's window regulator control switch harness connector C600 terminal No. 6 (Red/White wire) and passenger's window motor harness connector C608 terminal No. 1 (Red/White wire). If resistance is less than 5 ohms, replace passenger's window regulator control switch. If resistance is 5 ohms or more, repair circuit. See WIRING DIAGRAMS.

6) Disconnect master window regulator control switch harness connector C501. Measure resistance between passenger's window motor harness connector C608 terminal No. 1 (Red/White wire) and ground. If resistance is more than 10 k/ohms, go to next step. If resistance is 10 k/ohms or less, repair short to ground in Red/White wire. See WIRING DIAGRAMS.

7) Disconnect master window regulator control switch harness connector C501. Measure resistance between passenger's window motor

harness connector C608 terminal No. 2 (Yellow/Red wire) and ground. If resistance is 5 ohms or more, go to next step. If resistance is less than 5 ohms, go to step **11)**.

8) Disconnect passenger's window regulator control switch 7-pin harness connector C600. Measure resistance between passenger's window regulator control switch harness connector C600 terminal No. 2 (Tan/Light Blue wire) and ground. If resistance is 5 ohms or more, go to next step. If resistance is less than 5 ohms, go to step **10)**.

9) Disconnect master window regulator control switch harness connector C501. Measure resistance between passenger's window regulator control switch harness connector C600 terminal No. 2 (Tan/Light Blue wire) and master window regulator control switch harness connector C501 terminal No. 4 (Tan/Light Blue wire). If resistance is less than 5 ohms, replace master window regulator control switch. See WINDOW REGULATOR CONTROL SWITCH under REMOVAL & INSTALLATION. If resistance is 5 ohms or more, repair open in Tan/Light Blue wire. See WIRING DIAGRAMS.

10) Measure resistance between passenger's window regulator control switch harness connector C600 terminal No. 3 (Yellow/Red wire) and passenger's window motor harness connector C608 terminal No. 2 (Yellow/Red wire). If resistance is less than 5 ohms, replace passenger's window regulator control switch. If resistance is 5 ohms or more, repair open in Yellow/Red wire. See WIRING DIAGRAMS.

11) Disconnect master window regulator control switch harness connector C501. Measure resistance between passenger's window motor harness connector C608 terminal No. 2 (Yellow/Red wire) and ground. If resistance is more than 10 k/ohms, replace passenger's window motor. See FRONT DOOR WINDOW REGULATOR MOTOR under REMOVAL & INSTALLATION. If resistance is 10 k/ohms or less, repair short to ground in Yellow/Red wire. See WIRING DIAGRAMS.

12) Turn ignition switch to OFF position. Disconnect passenger's window regulator control switch 7-pin harness connector C600. Turn ignition switch to ON position. Measure voltage between passenger's window regulator control switch harness connector C600 terminal No. 4 (Light Blue/Black wire) and ground. If voltage is more than 10 volts, replace passenger's window regulator control switch. If voltage is 10 volts or less, repair power supply circuit. See WIRING DIAGRAMS.

TEST G: VENT POWER WINDOW(S) INOPERATIVE

1) Disconnect left and right rear quarter flip window motor 2-pin harness connectors C418 and C419. Measure resistance between left rear quarter flip window motor harness connector C418 terminal No. 1 (Brown/Yellow wire) and ground, or right rear quarter flip window motor harness connector C419 terminal No. 1 (Yellow/Black wire) and ground. If resistance is 5 ohms or more, go to next step. If resistance is less than 5 ohms, go to step **3)**.

2) Disconnect master window regulator control switch 7-pin harness connector C514. Measure resistance between left rear quarter flip window motor harness connector C418 terminal No. 1 (Brown/Yellow wire) and master window regulator control switch harness connector C514 terminal No. 4 (Brown/Yellow wire), or between right rear quarter flip window motor harness connector C419 terminal No. 1 (Yellow/Black wire) and master window regulator control switch harness connector C514 terminal No. 7 (Yellow/Black wire). If resistance is less than 5 ohms, replace master window regulator control switch. See WINDOW REGULATOR CONTROL SWITCH under REMOVAL & INSTALLATION. If resistance is 5 ohms or more, repair open in appropriate wire. See WIRING DIAGRAMS.

3) Disconnect master window regulator control switch 7-pin harness connector C514. Measure resistance between left rear quarter flip window motor harness connector C418 terminal No. 1 (Brown/Yellow wire) and ground, or between right rear quarter flip window motor harness connector C419 terminal No. 1 (Yellow/Black wire) and ground. If resistance is more than 10 k/ohms, go to next step. If resistance is 10 k/ohms or less, repair short to ground in appropriate wire. See WIRING DIAGRAMS.

4) Disconnect master window regulator control switch 7-pin harness connector C514. Measure resistance between left rear quarter flip window motor harness connector C418 terminal No. 2 (Brown wire) and ground, or between right rear quarter flip window motor harness connector C419 terminal No. 2 (Yellow/Light Blue wire) and ground. If resistance is 5 ohms or more, go to next step. If resistance is less than 5 ohms, go to step **6**).

5) Disconnect master window regulator control switch 7-pin harness connector C514. Measure resistance between left rear quarter flip window motor harness connector C418 terminal No. 2 (Brown wire) and master window regulator control switch harness connector C514 terminal No. 5 (Brown wire), or between right rear quarter flip window motor harness connector C419 terminal No. 2 (Yellow/Light Blue wire) and master window regulator control switch harness connector C514 terminal No. 6 (Yellow/Light Blue wire). If resistance is less than 5 ohms, replace master window regulator control switch. See WINDOW REGULATOR CONTROL SWITCH under REMOVAL & INSTALLATION. If resistance is 5 ohms or more, repair open in appropriate wire. See WIRING DIAGRAMS.

6) Disconnect master window regulator control switch 7-pin harness connector C514. Measure resistance between left rear quarter flip window motor harness connector C418 terminal No. 2 (Brown wire) and ground, or between right rear quarter flip window motor harness connector C419 terminal No. 2 (Yellow/Light Blue wire) and ground. If resistance is more than 10 k/ohms, replace rear quarter flip window motor. See REAR QUARTER FLIP WINDOW MOTOR under REMOVAL & INSTALLATION. If resistance is 10 k/ohms or less, repair short to ground in appropriate wire. See WIRING DIAGRAMS.

TEST H: ONE-TOUCH DOWN FEATURE INOPERATIVE

1) Using New Generation Star (NGS) tester, perform Front Electronic Module (FEM) self-test. If DTC B1243 was retrieved, go to next step. If DTC B1243 was not retrieved, go to step **4**).

2) Disconnect FEM 26-pin harness connector C347. Measure voltage between FEM harness connector C347 terminal No. 19 (Red/Light Green wire) and ground. If voltage is more than 10 volts, go to next step. If voltage is 10 volts or less, replace FEM. See FRONT ELECTRONIC MODULE (FEM) under REMOVAL & INSTALLATION.

3) Disconnect master window regulator control switch 7-pin harness connector C501. Measure voltage between FEM harness connector C347 terminal No. 19 (Red/Light Green wire) and ground. If voltage is more than 10 volts, repair short to voltage in Red/Light Green wire. See WIRING DIAGRAMS. If voltage is 10 volts or less, replace master window regulator control switch. See WINDOW REGULATOR CONTROL SWITCH under REMOVAL & INSTALLATION.

NOTE: Excessive drag caused by window runs, tracks or regulators may cause one-touch down feature to cancel.

4) Turn ignition switch to ON position. Observe driver's power window movement while operating driver's power window. If glass does not bind, drag or tilt while operating, go to next step. If glass binds, drags or tilts while operating, repair door glass runs, weather-strips or regulator as necessary.

5) Remove master window regulator control switch. Test master window regulator control switch. See MASTER WINDOW REGULATOR CONTROL SWITCH under COMPONENT TESTS. If master window regulator control switch is okay, go to next step. If master window regulator control switch is not okay, replace master window regulator control switch. See WINDOW REGULATOR CONTROL SWITCH under REMOVAL & INSTALLATION.

6) Disconnect FEM 26-pin harness connector C347. Measure resistance between FEM harness connector C347 terminal No. 19 (Red/Light Green wire) and ground. If resistance is more than 10 k/ohms, go to next step. If resistance is 10 k/ohms or less, repair short to ground in Red/Light Green wire. See WIRING DIAGRAMS.

7) Measure resistance between FEM harness connector C347 terminal No. 19 (Red/Light Green wire) and master window regulator control switch harness connector C501 terminal No. 3 (Red/Light Green wire). If resistance is less than 5 ohms, replace FEM. See FRONT ELEC-

TRONIC MODULE (FEM) under REMOVAL & INSTALLATION. If resistance is 5 ohms or more, repair open in Red/Light Green wire. See WIRING DIAGRAMS.

TEST I: REAR WINDOW WILL NOT DEFROST

1) Using New Generation Star (NGS) tester, perform Rear Electronic Module (REM) self-test. If no DTCs are retrieved, go to next step. If DTCs are retrieved, go to step **13**).

2) Using NGS tester, perform instrument cluster self-test. If no DTCs are retrieved, go to next step. If any DTCs are retrieved, go to step **11**).

NOTE: Engine speed must be above 400 RPM before heated rear window system will operate.

3) Start engine and allow to idle. Press heated rear window switch. If heated rear window switch indicator is not ON, go to next step. If heated rear window switch indicator is ON, go to step **13**).

4) Turn ignition switch to ON position. Using NGS tester, monitor instrument cluster PID RFOG_SW and press heated rear window switch to ON position. If PID RFOG_SW does not read ON, go to next step. If PID RFOG_SW reads ON, go to step **8**).

5) Turn ignition switch to OFF position. Disconnect instrument cluster 20-pin harness connector C240. Measure resistance between instrument cluster harness connector C240 terminal No. 3 (Pink wire) and ground. Press heated rear window switch to ON position. If resistance is 5 ohms or more, go to next step. If resistance is less than 5 ohms, replace instrument cluster. See ANALOG INSTRUMENT PANELS – WINDSTAR article.

6) Disconnect climate control 12-pin harness connector C244. Located in center of instrument panel on climate control assembly. Measure voltage between instrument cluster harness connector C240 terminal No. 3 (Pink wire) and ground. If voltage is 10 volts or less, go to next step. If voltage is more than 10 volts, repair short to voltage in Pink wire. See WIRING DIAGRAMS.

7) Measure resistance between instrument cluster harness connector C240 terminal No. 3 (Pink wire) and climate control harness connector C244 terminal No. 10 (Pink wire). If resistance is less than 5 ohms, replace instrument cluster. See ANALOG INSTRUMENT PANELS – WINDSTAR article. If resistance is 5 ohms or more, repair open in Pink wire. See WIRING DIAGRAMS.

8) Disconnect climate control 12-pin harness connector C244. Located in center of instrument panel on climate control assembly. Turn ignition switch to ON position. Measure voltage between climate control harness connector C244 terminal No. 11 (Tan/Light Blue wire) and ground. Using NGS tester, select instrument cluster active command INDICATOR LAMP CONTROL. Trigger R DEF LMP to ON and record voltage. If no voltage is present, go to next step. If voltage is present, replace climate control assembly. See CLIMATE CONTROL ASSEMBLY under REMOVAL & INSTALLATION.

9) Turn ignition switch to OFF position. Disconnect instrument cluster 22-pin harness connector C241. Measure resistance between instrument cluster harness connector C241 terminal No. 14 (Tan/Light Blue wire) and ground. If resistance is more than 10 k/ohms, go to next step. If resistance is 10 k/ohms or less, repair short to ground in Tan/Light Blue wire. See WIRING DIAGRAMS.

10) Measure resistance between instrument cluster harness connector C241 terminal No. 14 (Tan/Light Blue wire) and climate control harness connector C244 terminal No. 11 (Tan/Light Blue wire). If resistance is less than 5 ohms, replace instrument cluster. See ANALOG INSTRUMENT PANELS – WINDSTAR article. If resistance is 5 ohms or more, repair open in Tan/Light Blue wire. See WIRING DIAGRAMS.

11) Disconnect instrument cluster 20-pin harness connector C240. Measure resistance between instrument cluster harness connector C240 terminal No. 3 (Pink wire) and ground. If resistance is 10 k/ohms or less, go to next step. If resistance is more than 10 k/ohms, replace instrument cluster. See ANALOG INSTRUMENT PANELS – WINDSTAR article.

12) Disconnect climate control 12-pin harness connector C244. Located in center of instrument panel on climate control assembly. Measure resistance between instrument cluster harness connector C240 terminal

No. 3 (Pink wire) and ground. If resistance is 10 k/ohms or less, repair short to ground in Pink wire. See WIRING DIAGRAMS. If resistance is more than 10 k/ohms, replace climate control assembly. See CLIMATE CONTROL ASSEMBLY under REMOVAL & INSTALLATION.

13) Using NGS tester, monitor REM PID RDEFRLY. Start engine and allow to idle. Press heated rear window switch to ON position. If PID RDEFRLY states differently with switch in ON position, leave engine idling and go to next step. If PID reads correctly, replace REM. See REAR ELECTRONIC MODULE (REM) under REMOVAL & INSTALLATION.

14) Disconnect heated rear window single pin harness connector C914. Measure voltage between heated rear window harness connector C914 Brown/Light Blue wire terminal and ground. Using NGS tester, select active command REM EXTERIOR LAMP CONTROL. Trigger R DEF RLY to ON. If voltage is more than 10 volts, go to next step. If voltage is 10 volts or less, go to step **16)**.

15) Turn ignition switch to OFF position. Disconnect heated rear window ground side harness connector. Measure resistance between heated rear window ground harness connector Black wire terminal and ground. If resistance is less than 5 ohms, test heated rear window grid. See HEATED REAR WINDOW GRID under COMPONENT TESTS. If resistance is 5 ohms or more, repair open in Black wire. See WIRING DIAGRAMS.

16) Remove heated rear window relay from Fuse Junction Box (FJB). Start engine and allow to idle. Measure voltage between heated rear window relay harness connector terminal No. 86 and ground, then between heated rear window relay harness connector terminal No. 30 (Black wire) and ground. If voltages are more than 10 volts, go to next step. If either voltage is 10 volts or less, repair power supply circuit. See WIRING DIAGRAMS.

17) Test heated rear window relay. See ISO RELAY TEST under COMPONENT TESTS. If heated rear window relay is okay, go to next step. If heated rear window relay is not okay, replace relay.

18) Disconnect REM 22-pin harness connector C341. Measure resistance between heated rear window relay harness connector terminal No. 85 (White wire) and REM harness connector C341 terminal No. 7 (White wire). If resistance is less than 5 ohms, go to next step. If resistance is 5 ohms or more, repair open in White wire. See WIRING DIAGRAMS.

19) Measure voltage between REM harness connector C341 terminal No. 7 (White wire) and ground. If voltage is more than 10 volts, repair short to voltage in White wire. See WIRING DIAGRAMS. If voltage is 10 volts or less, replace REM. See REAR ELECTRONIC MODULE (REM) under REMOVAL & INSTALLATION.

TEST J: REAR WINDOW DEFROSTER WILL NOT SHUT OFF AUTOMATICALLY

1) Using New Generation Star (NGS) tester, perform Rear Electronic Module (REM) and instrument cluster self-tests. If no DTCs are retrieved, go to next step. If any DTCs are retrieved, perform appropriate test in accordance with DTC retrieved. See REAR ELECTRONIC MODULE (REM) DTC INDEX and/or INSTRUMENT CLUSTER DTC INDEX table under SELF-DIAGNOSTIC SYSTEM.

2) Remove heated rear window relay. Test relay. See ISO RELAY TEST under COMPONENT TESTS. If heated rear window relay is okay, go to next step. If heated rear window relay is not okay, replace relay.

3) Turn ignition switch to ON position. Measure voltage between heated rear window relay harness connector terminal No. 87 (Brown/Light Blue wire) and ground. If voltage is not present, go to next step. If voltage is present, repair short to voltage in Brown/Light Blue wire. See WIRING DIAGRAMS.

4) Disconnect REM 22-pin harness connector C341. Measure resistance between REM harness connector C341 terminal No. 7 (White wire) and ground. If resistance is more than 10 k/ohms, replace REM. See REAR ELECTRONIC MODULE (REM) under REMOVAL & INSTALLATION. If resistance is 10 k/ohms or less, repair short to ground in White wire. See WIRING DIAGRAMS.

TEST K: DELAYED ACCESSORY DOES NOT TURN OFF

NOTE: Turn ignition switch from OFF to ON position to enable system power feature.

1) Using New Generation Star (NGS) tester, perform Front Electronic Module (FEM) self-test. If no DTCs are retrieved, go to next step. If any DTCs are retrieved, perform appropriate test in accordance with DTC retrieved. See FRONT ELECTRONIC MODULE (FEM) DTC INDEX table under SELF-DIAGNOSTIC SYSTEM.

2) Remove accessory delay relay located in Fuse Junction Box (FJB). Operate driver's and passenger's front power windows. If both windows are inoperative, go to next step. If both windows are operative, go to step **5)**.

3) Test accessory delay relay. See ISO RELAY TEST under COMPONENT TESTS. If accessory delay relay is okay, go to next step. If accessory delay relay is not okay, replace relay.

4) Disconnect FEM 22-pin harness connector C191. Measure resistance between FEM harness connector C191 terminal No. 6 (Light Blue wire) and ground. If resistance is more than 10 k/ohms, replace FEM. See FRONT ELECTRONIC MODULE (FEM) under REMOVAL & INSTALLATION. If resistance is 10 k/ohms or less, repair short to ground in Light Blue wire. See WIRING DIAGRAMS.

5) Measure resistance between accessory delay relay harness connector terminal No. 87 (Light Blue/Black wire) and ground. Record reading. Disconnect master window regulator control switch 7-pin harness connector C501. Take resistance reading again. If resistance went to 10 k/ohms or less when master window regulator control switch was disconnected, go to next step. If resistance went to more than 10 k/ohms when master window regulator control switch was disconnected, replace master window regulator control switch. See WINDOW REGULATOR CONTROL SWITCH under REMOVAL & INSTALLATION.

6) Measure resistance between accessory delay relay harness connector terminal No. 87 (Light Blue/Black wire) and ground. Record reading. Disconnect passenger's window regulator control switch 7-pin harness connector C600. Take resistance reading again. If resistance went to 10 k/ohms or less when passenger's window regulator control switch was disconnected, repair short to ground in Light Blue/Black wire. See WIRING DIAGRAMS. If resistance went to more than 10 k/ohms when passenger's window regulator control switch was disconnected, replace passenger's window regulator control switch.

REMOVAL & INSTALLATION

CAUTION: Electronic modules are sensitive to static electrical charges. Proper grounding of technician and workplace is essential to prevent damage.

NOTE: When battery is disconnected and reconnected, some abnormal drive symptoms may occur while vehicle relearns it's adaptive strategy. Vehicle may need to be driven 10 miles or more to learn strategy.

CLIMATE CONTROL ASSEMBLY

CAUTION: Slider knobs are illuminated using LEDs. Use care not to damage them when removing slider knobs.

Removal & Installation – Disconnect battery ground cable. Remove ashtray. Remove audio unit using Radio Removing Tool (T87P-19061-A). Remove 4 screws retaining finish panel and unsnap finish panel. Disconnect harness connectors from backside of finish panel. Remove 4 screws from control assembly and remove control assembly from instrument panel. To install, reverse removal procedure.

FRONT DOOR WINDOW REGULATOR MOTOR

NOTE: Check interior of door, ensure front window regulator wiring is not in line with holes to be drilled into door inner panel.

WARNING: Window regulator motor has counterbalanced spring. Window must be in UP position to remove motor or blocked to prevent window from suddenly raising. Failure to follow these instructions may result in personal injury.

Removal & Installation – Remove front door trim panel and water shield. Disconnect window regulator motor harness connector. Using 1/2-inch drill bit, drill out drill dimples located opposite of unexposed window regulator motor retaining screws. *See Fig. 13.* Remove 3 bolts retaining window regulator motor to regulator and remove motor. To install, reverse removal procedure.

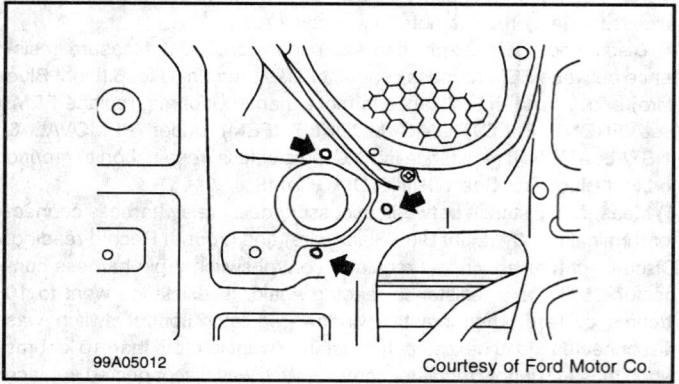

99A05012   Courtesy of Ford Motor Co.

Fig. 13: Front Door Window Regulator Motor Drill Locations

FRONT ELECTRONIC MODULE (FEM)

CAUTION: Prior to removal of module, it is necessary to upload module configuration information to New Generation Star (NGS) tester. This information needs to be downloaded into new module once installed. See PROGRAMMING.

Removal & Installation – 1) Disconnect battery ground cable. Remove 2 bolts retaining instrument panel lower steering column opening cover. Remove cover. Remove 3 bolts retaining instrument panel opening cover reinforcement.
2) Remove reinforcement. Disconnect 6 FEM harness connectors, remove 3 bolts retaining FEM and remove FEM. To install, reverse removal procedures.

REAR ELECTRONIC MODULE (REM)

CAUTION: Prior to removal of module, it is necessary to upload module configuration information to New Generation Star (NGS) tester. This information needs to be downloaded into new module once installed. See PROGRAMMING.

Removal & Installation – Disconnect battery ground cable. Remove right quarter trim panel. Remove 3 bolts retaining service jack mounting bracket and remove bracket. Disconnect 5 REM harness connectors. Remove 3 nuts retaining REM and remove REM. To install, reverse removal procedure.

REAR QUARTER FLIP WINDOW MOTOR

Removal & Installation – Remove quarter trim panel and disconnect rear quarter flip window motor harness connector. Remove 3 screws retaining rear quarter flip window motor and remove rear quarter flip window motor. To install, reverse removal procedure.

WINDOW REGULATOR CONTROL SWITCH

CAUTION: Use shop towel or similar material between tool and front door trim panel or damage to front door trim panel may occur.

Removal & Installation – Disengage window regulator control switch from panel and disconnect harness connectors. Release clips and remove window regulator control switch. To install, reverse removal procedures

WIRING DIAGRAMS

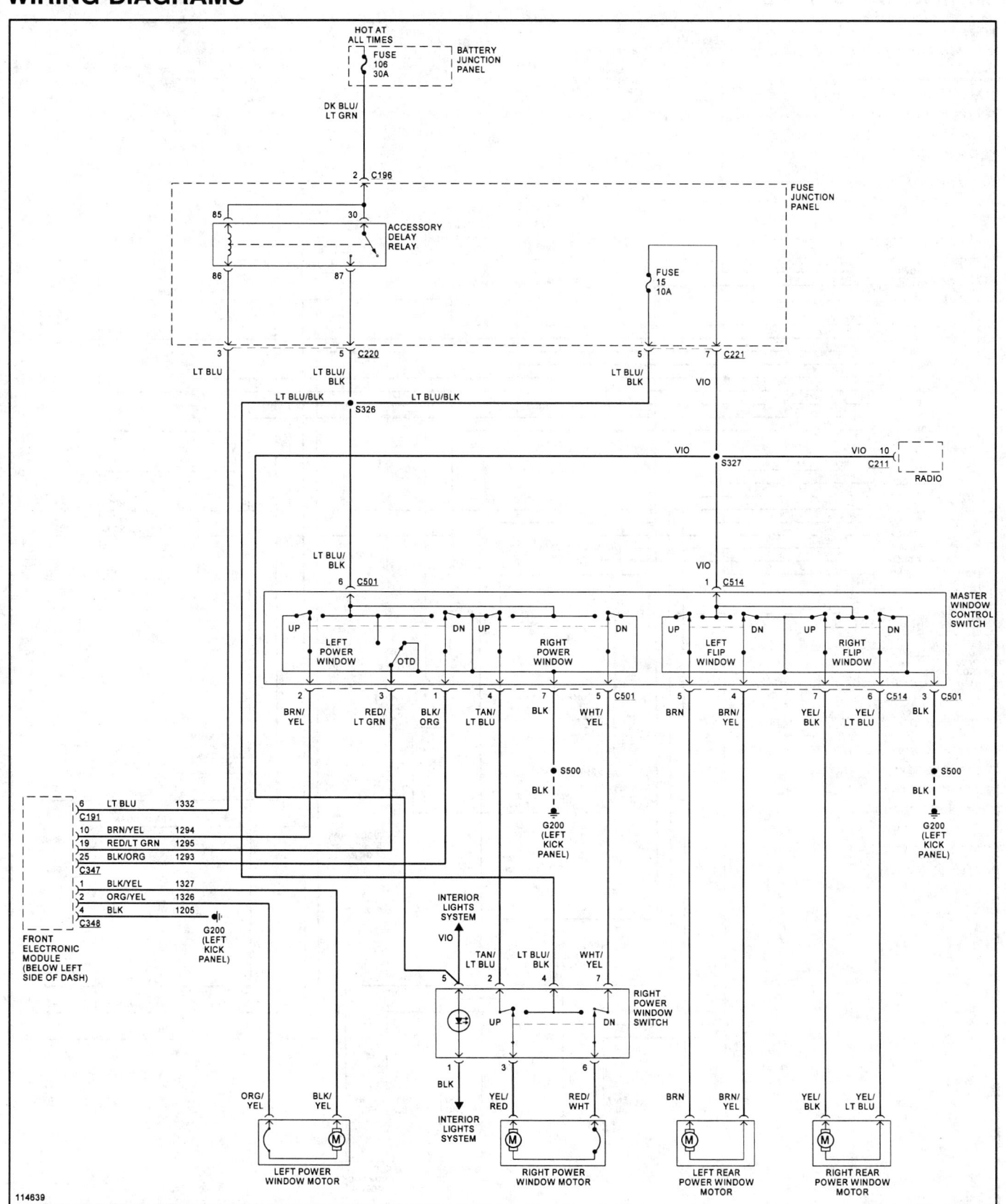

Fig. 14: Power Window System Wiring Diagram (Windstar)

114639

WIRING DIAGRAMS

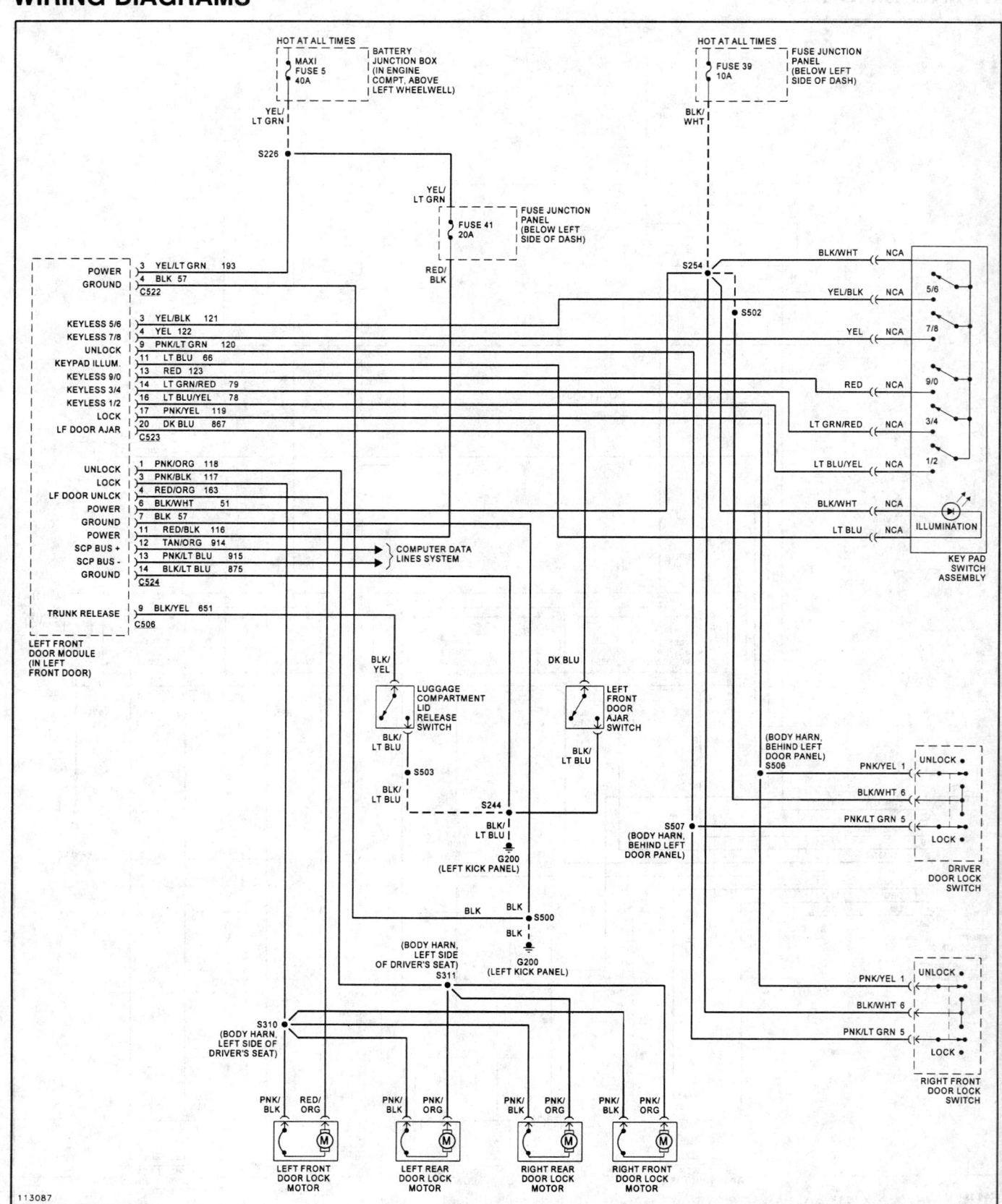

Fig. 1: Remote Keyless Entry System Wiring Diagram (Continental)

113087

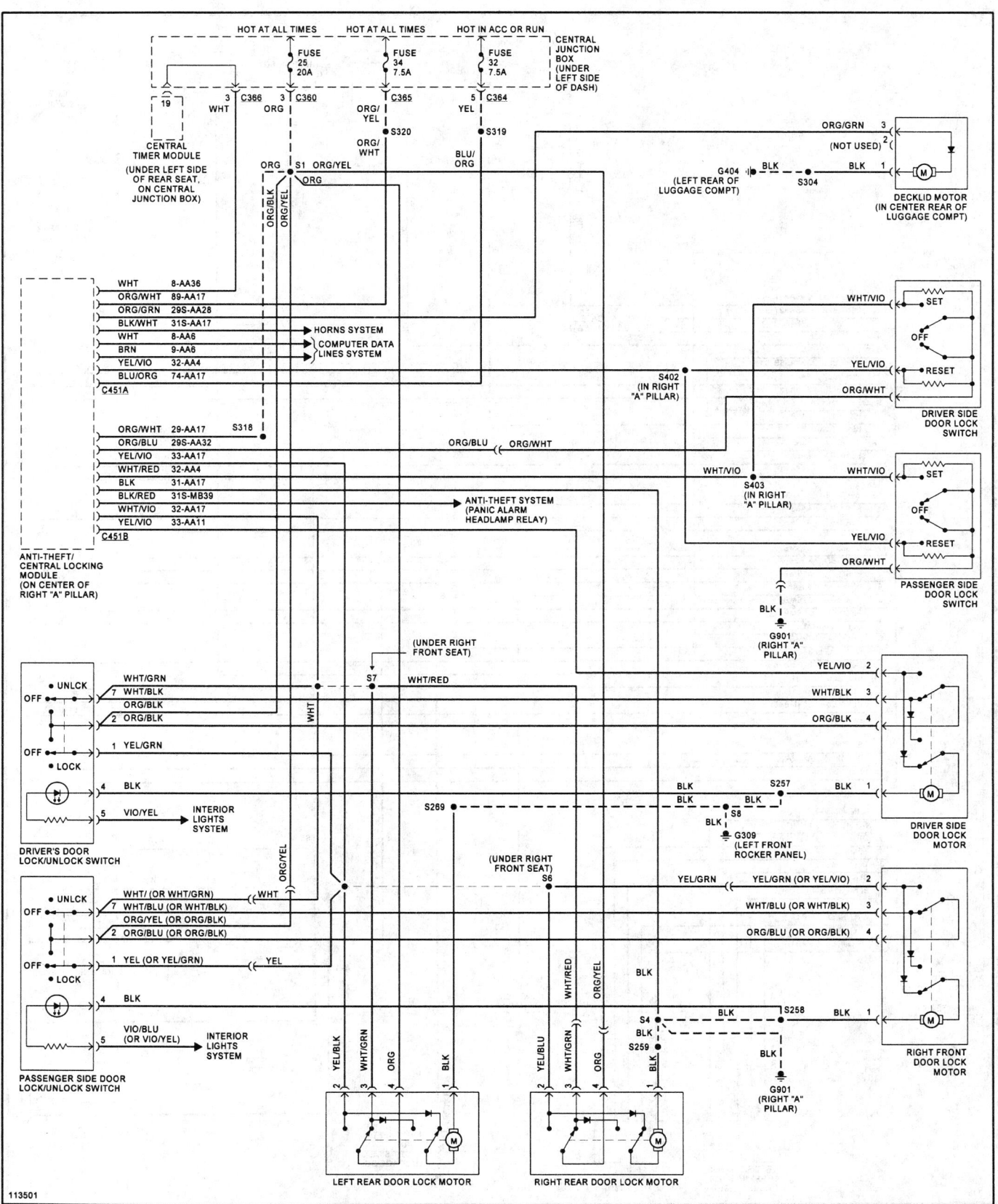

Fig. 2: Remote Keyless Entry System Wiring Diagram (Contour & Mystique)

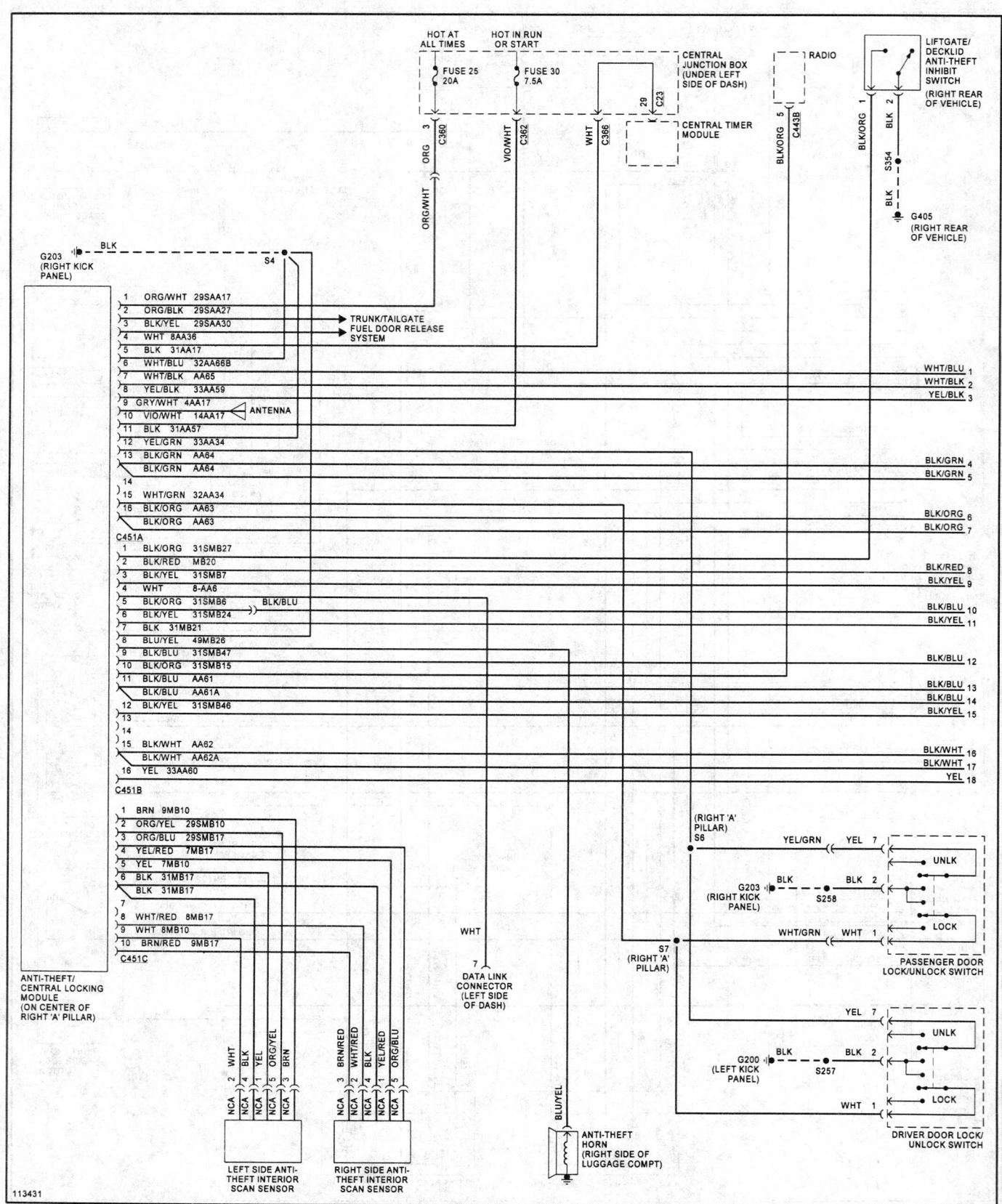

Fig. 3: Remote Keyless Entry System Wiring Diagram (Cougar – 1 Of 2)

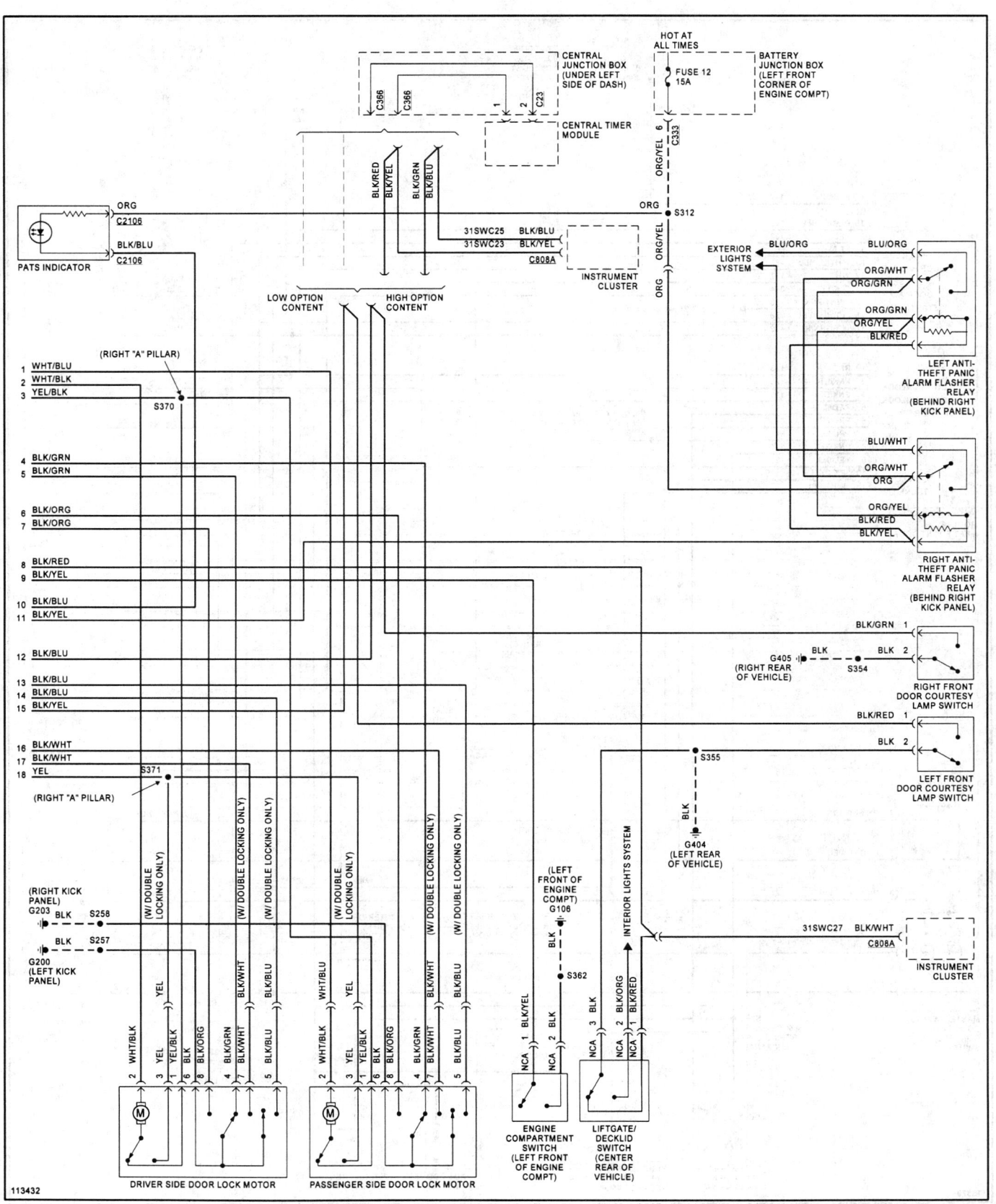

Fig. 4: Remote Keyless Entry System Wiring Diagram (Cougar – 2 Of 2)

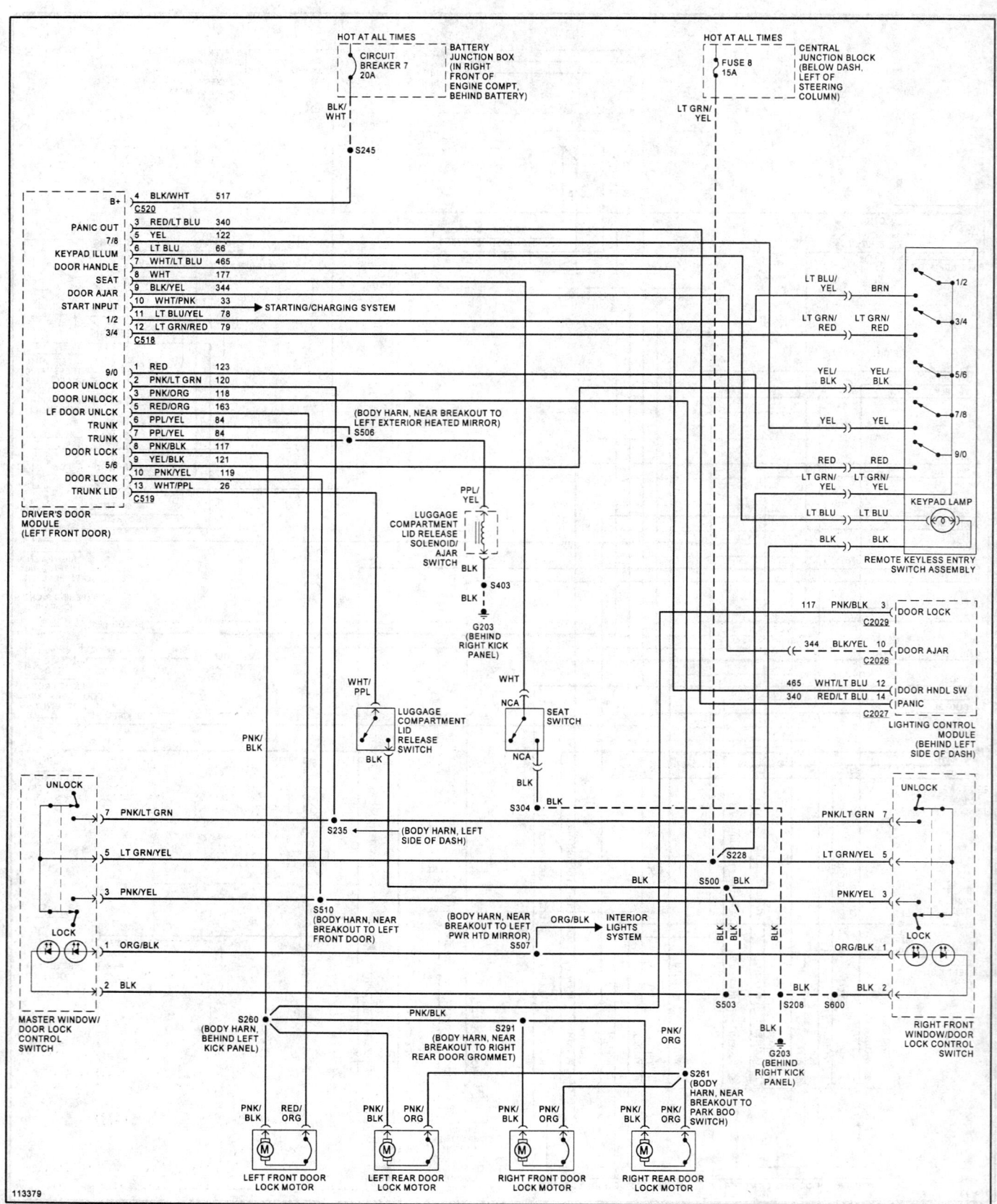

Fig. 5: Remote Keyless Entry System Wiring Diagram (Crown Victoria & Grand Marquis)

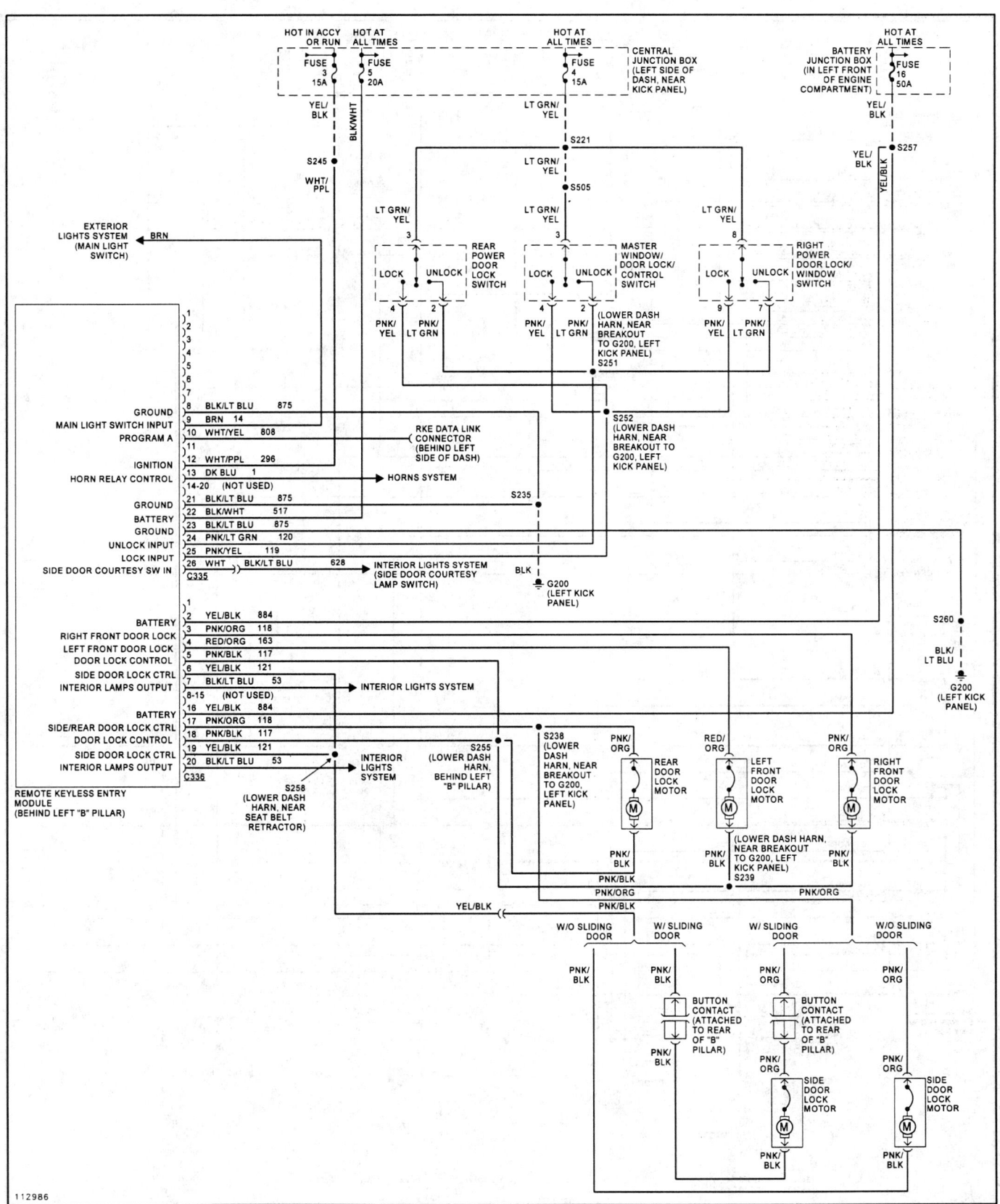

Fig. 6: Remote Keyless Entry System Wiring Diagram (Econoline)

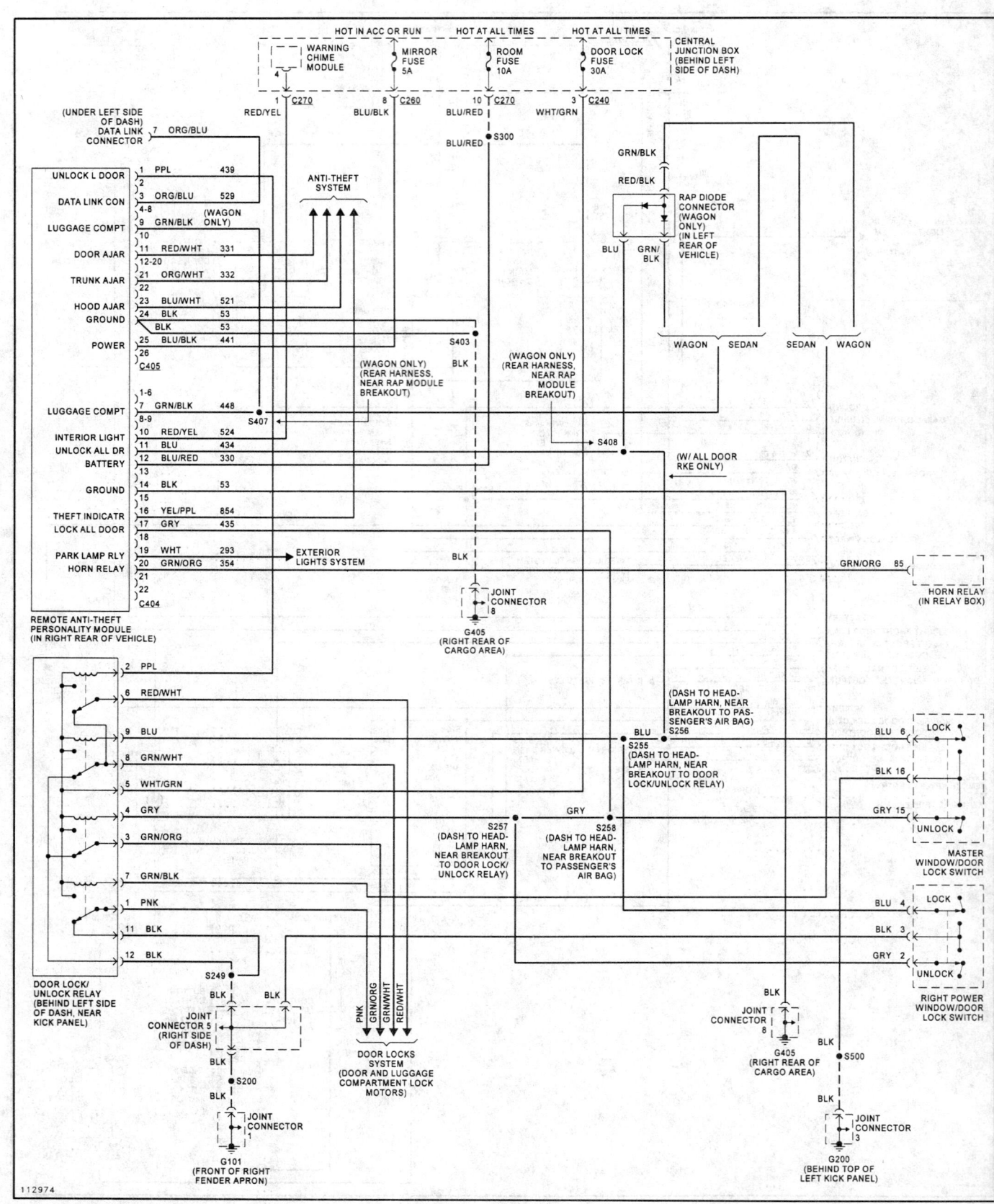

Fig. 7: Remote Keyless Entry System Wiring Diagram (Escort & Tracer)

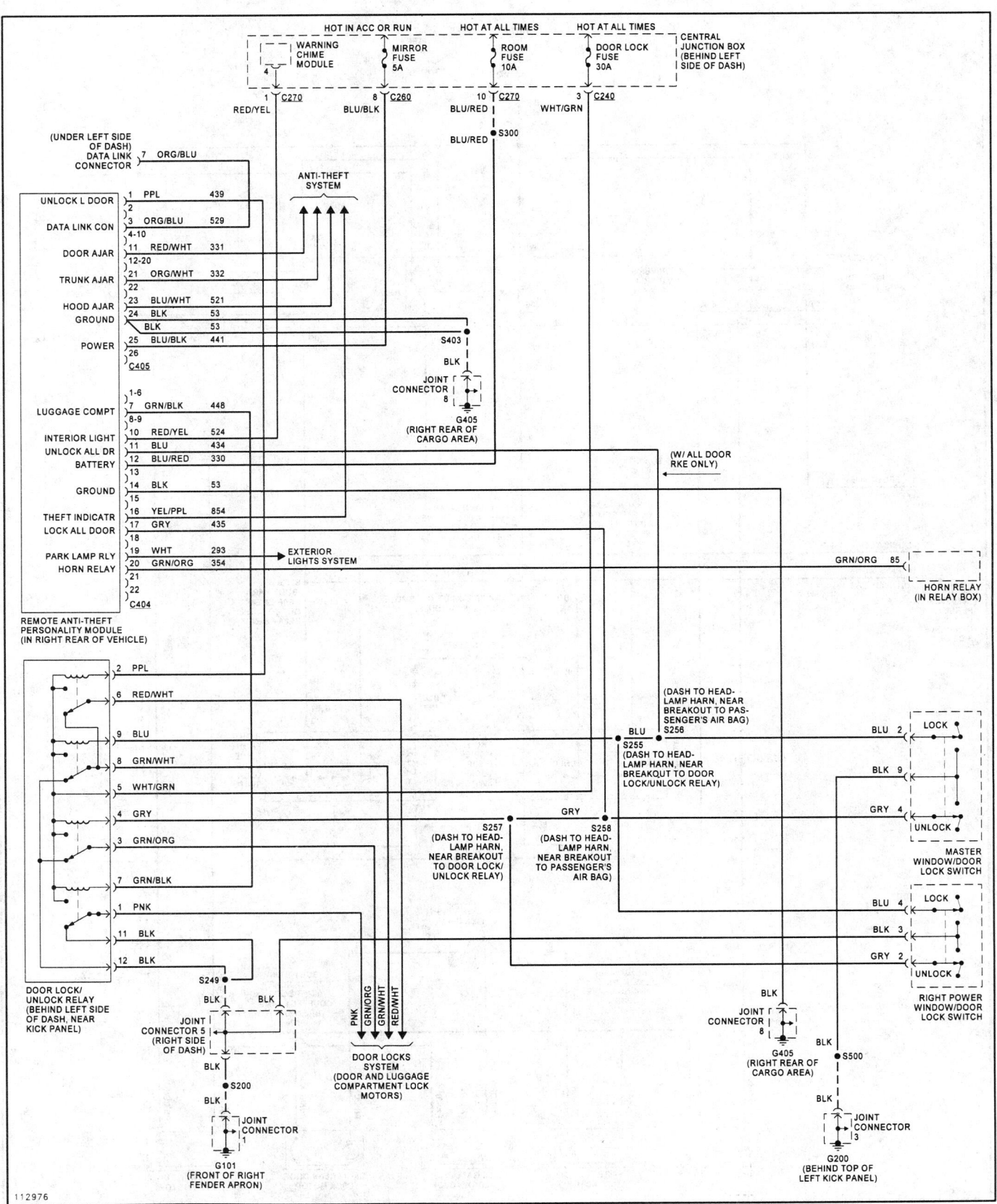

Fig. 8: Remote Keyless Entry System Wiring Diagram (Escort ZX2)

112976

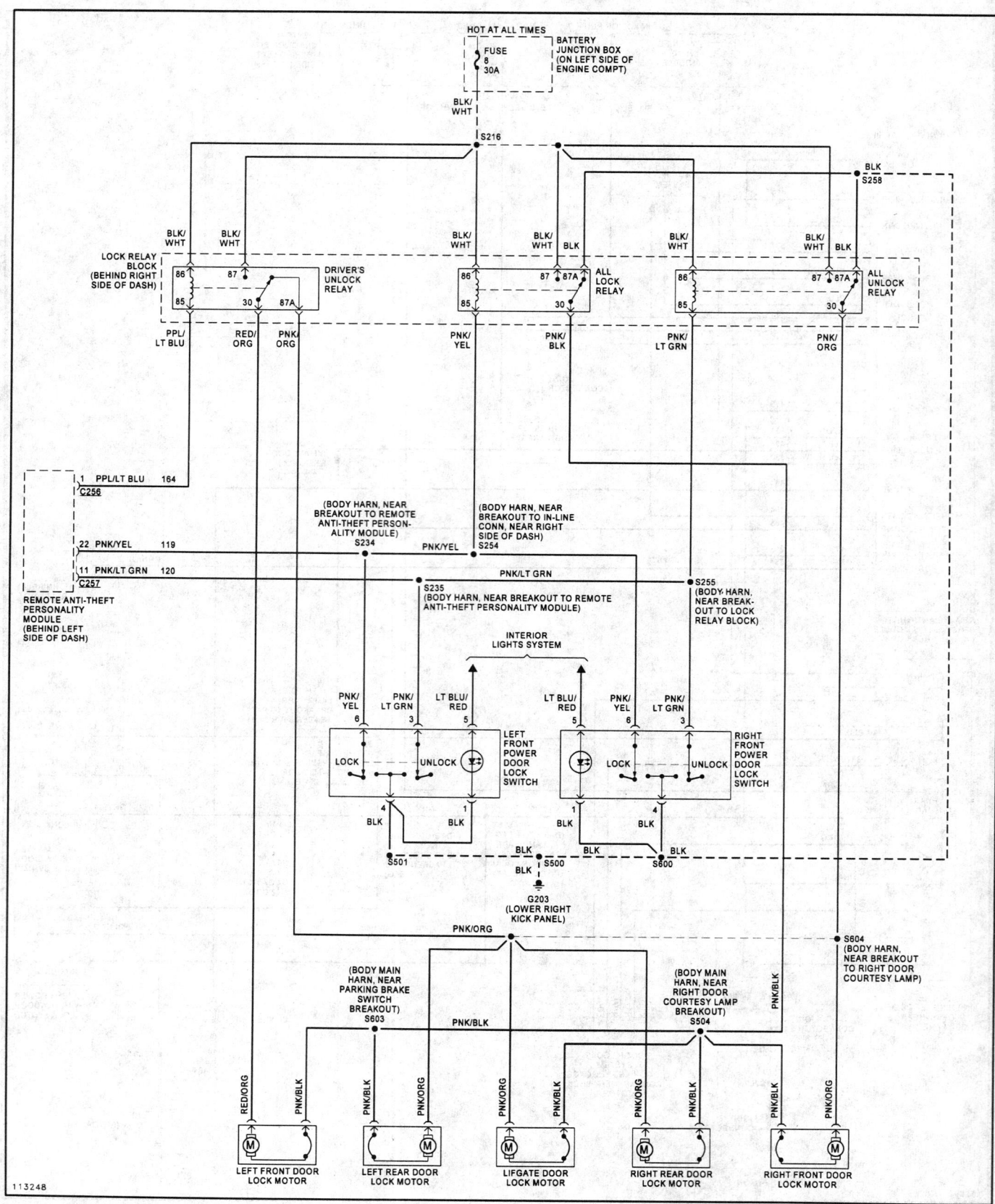

Fig. 9: Remote Keyless Entry System Wiring Diagram (Expedition & Navigator)

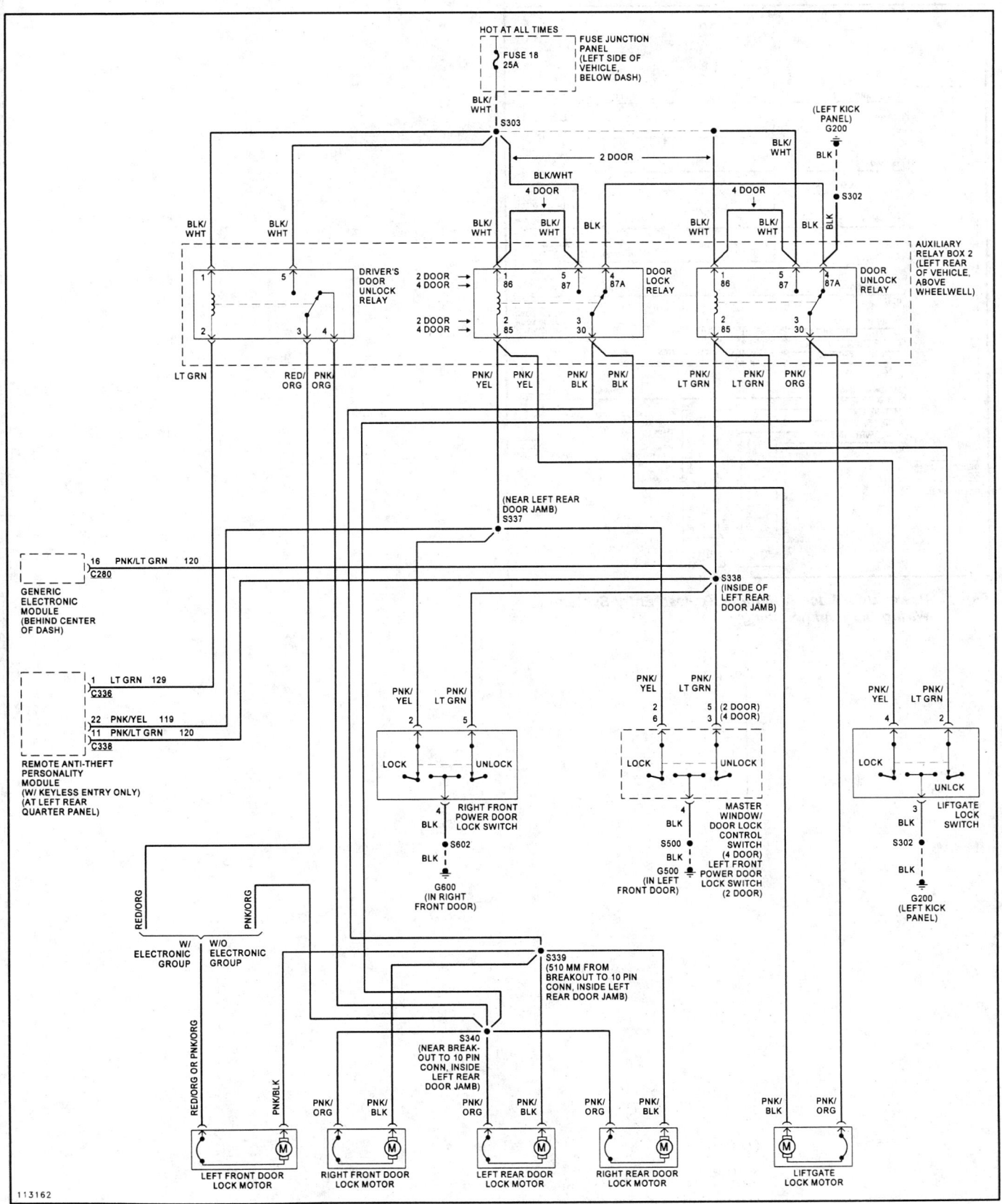

Fig. 10: Remote Keyless Entry System Wiring Diagram (Explorer & Mountaineer)

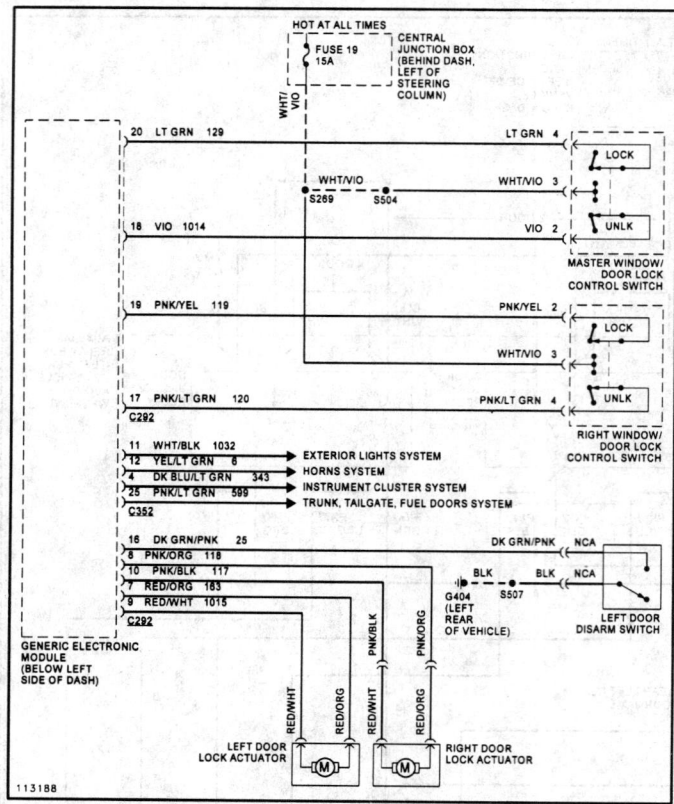

**Fig. 11: Power Door Lock & Remote Keyless Entry System
Wiring Diagram (Mustang)**

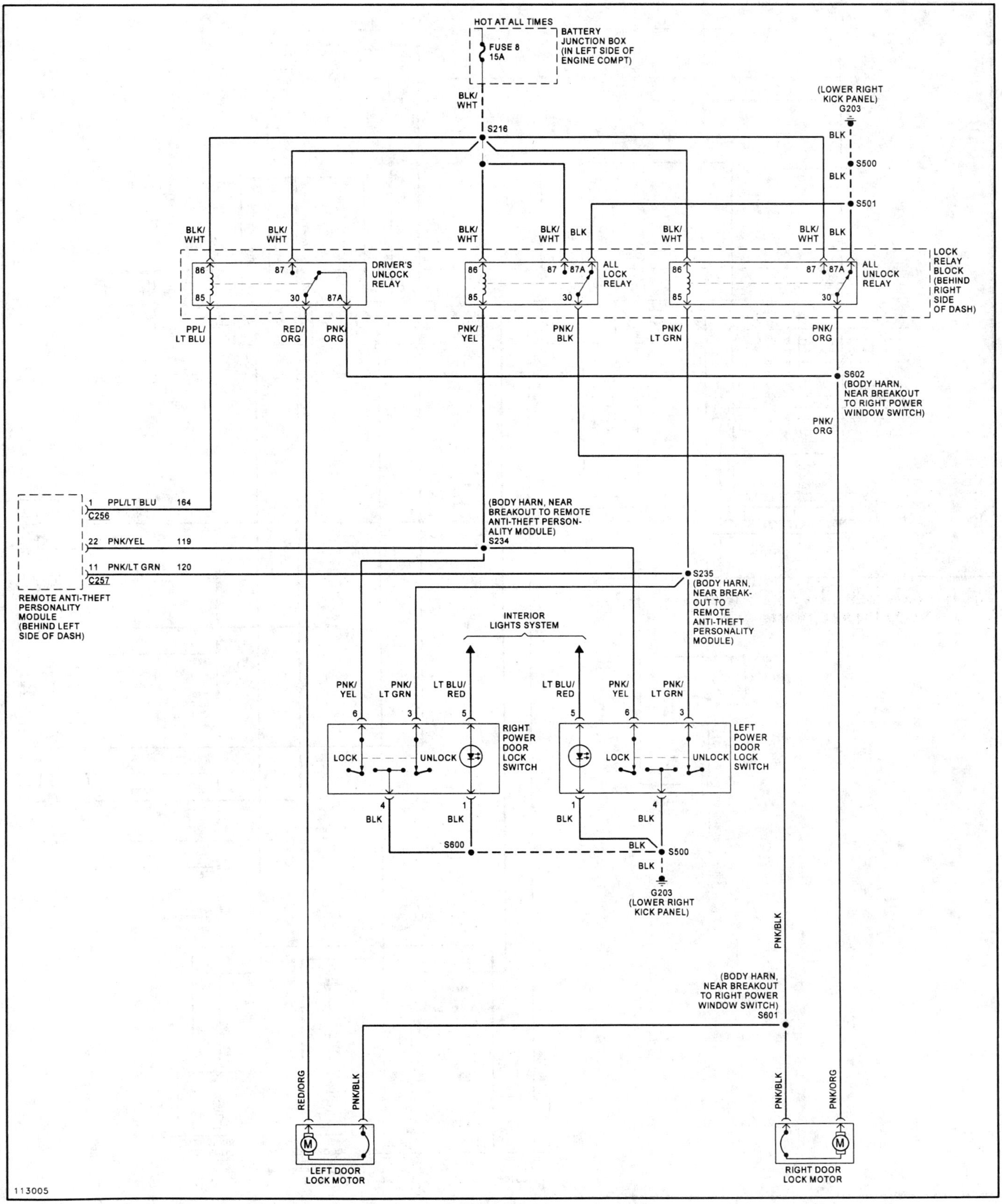

Fig. 12: Remote Keyless Entry System Wiring Diagram (F150 & F250 Light-Duty Pickup)

113005

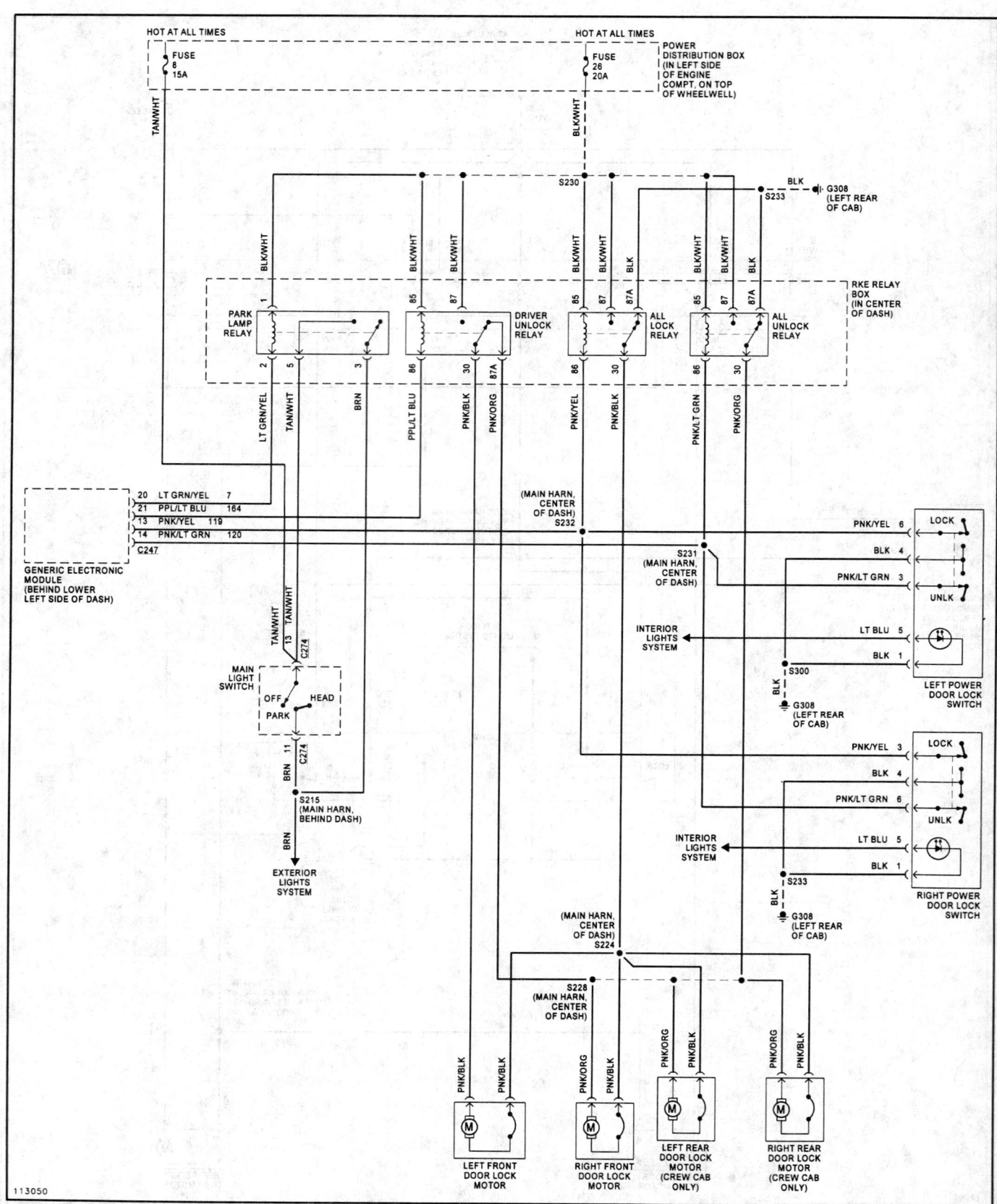

Fig. 13: Remote Keyless Entry System Wiring Diagram (F250 Super-Duty & F350 Pickup)

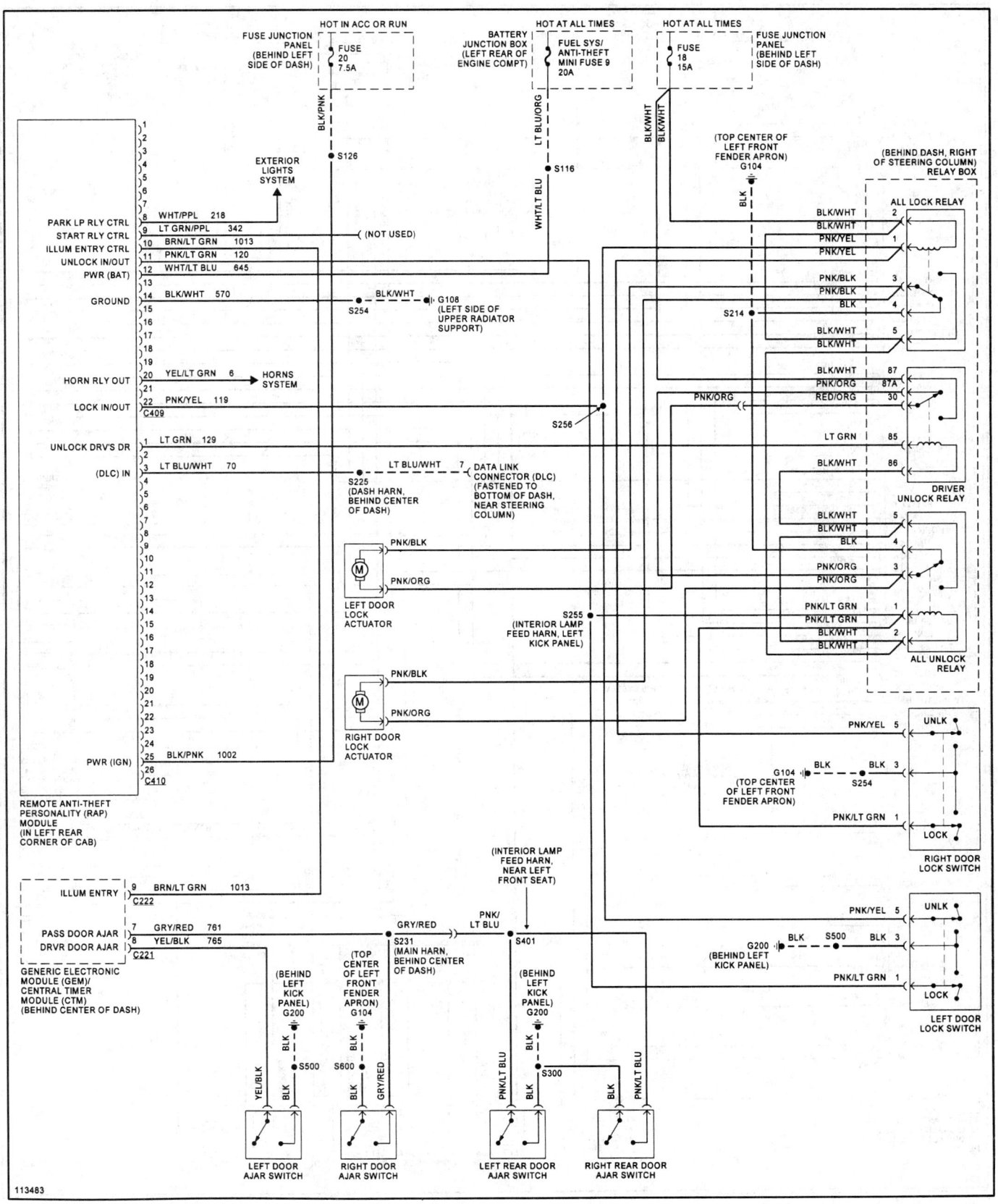

Fig. 14: Remote Keyless Entry System Wiring Diagram (Ranger)

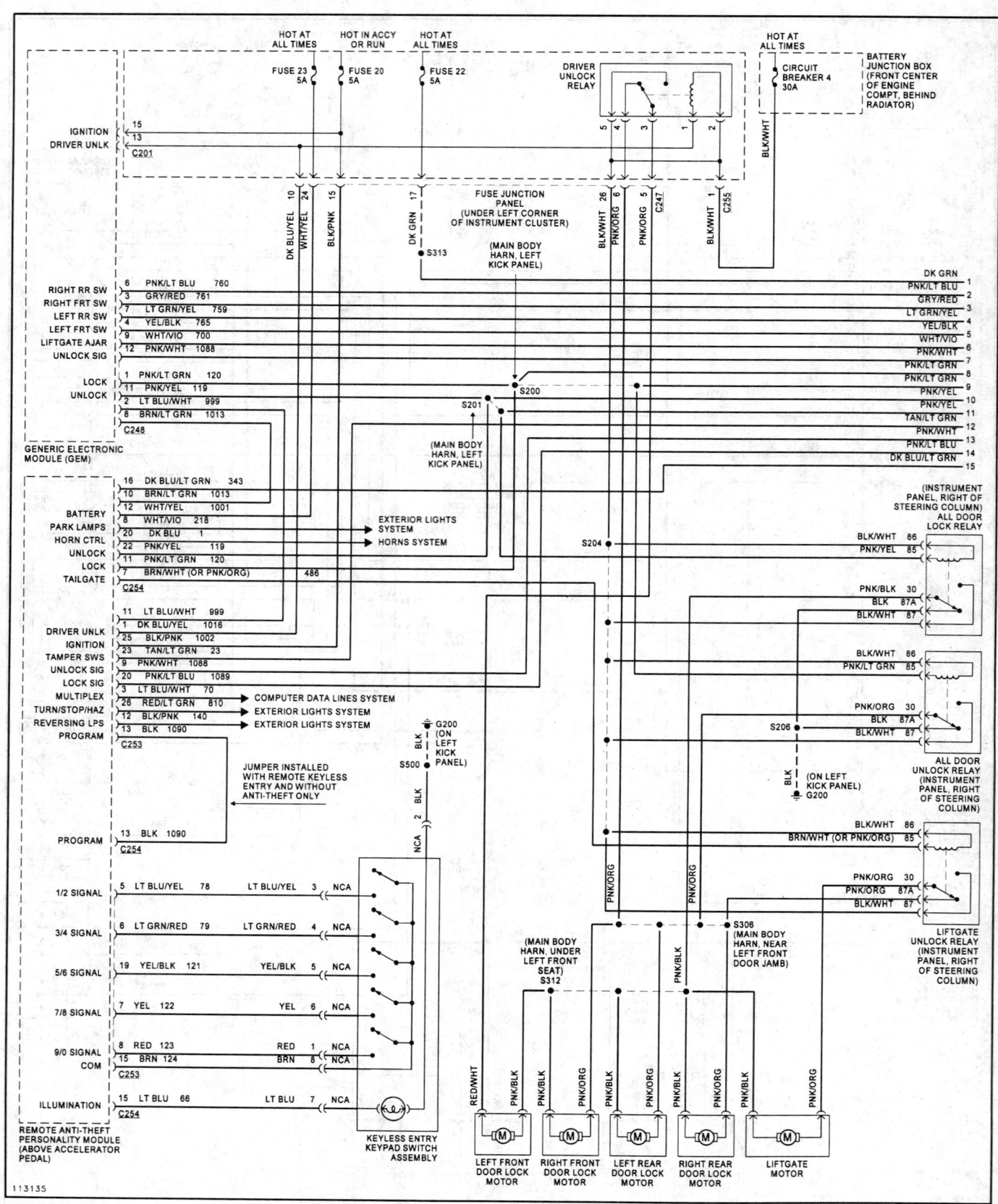

Fig. 15: Remote Keyless Entry System Wiring Diagram (Sable & Taurus – 1 Of 2)

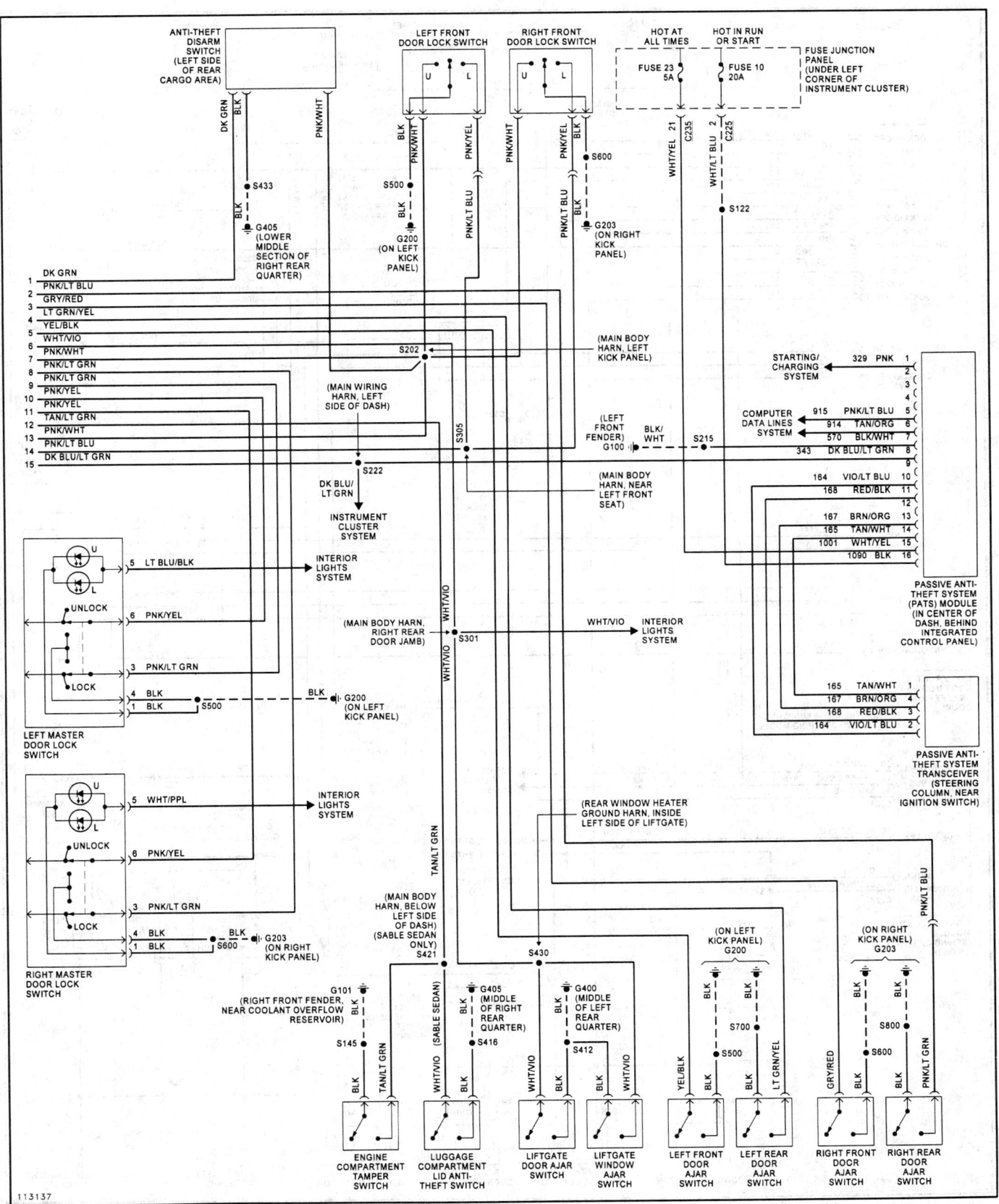

Fig. 16: Remote Keyless Entry System Wiring Diagram (Sable & Taurus – 2 Of 2)

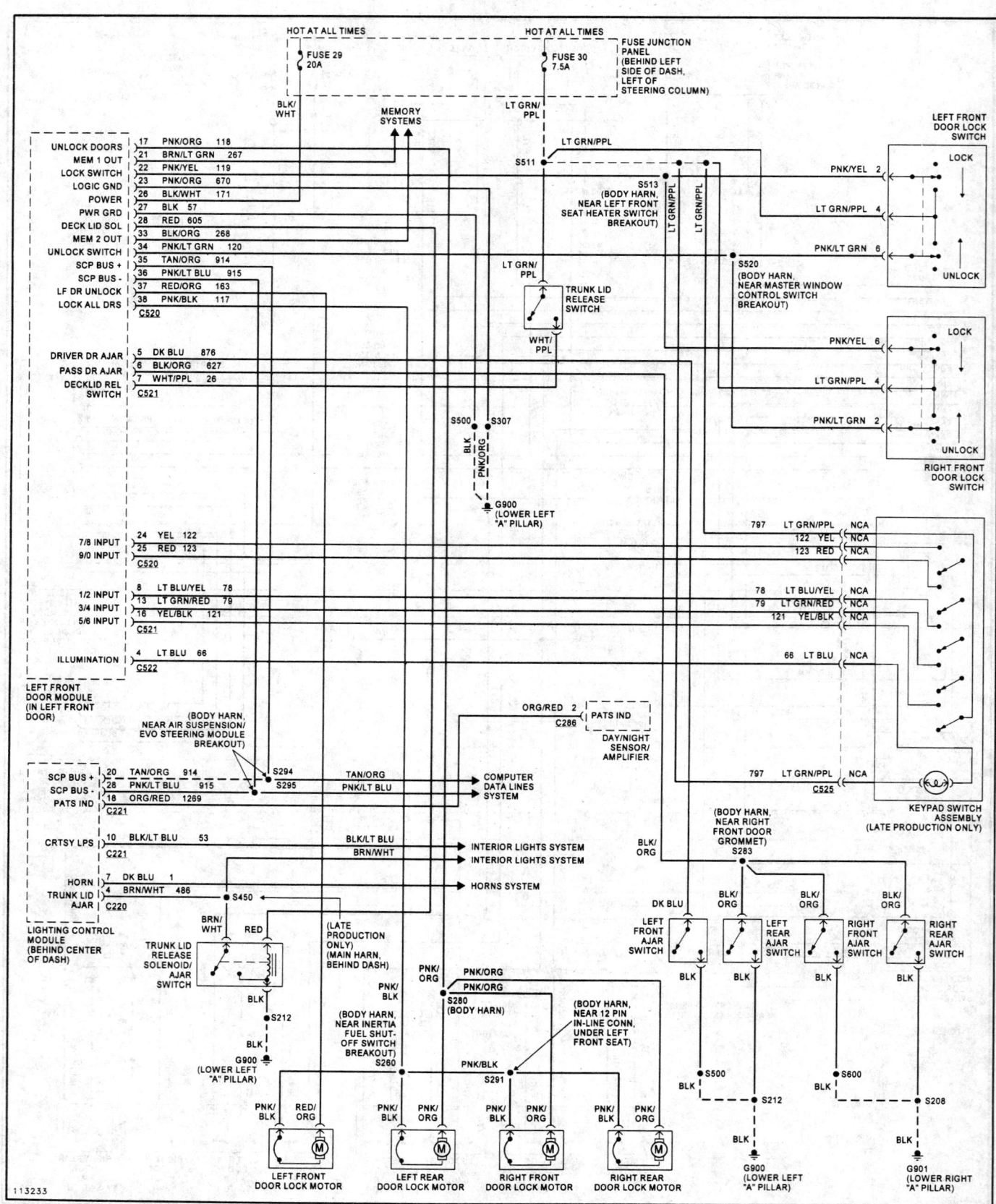

Fig. 17: Remote Keyless Entry System Wiring Diagram (Town Car)

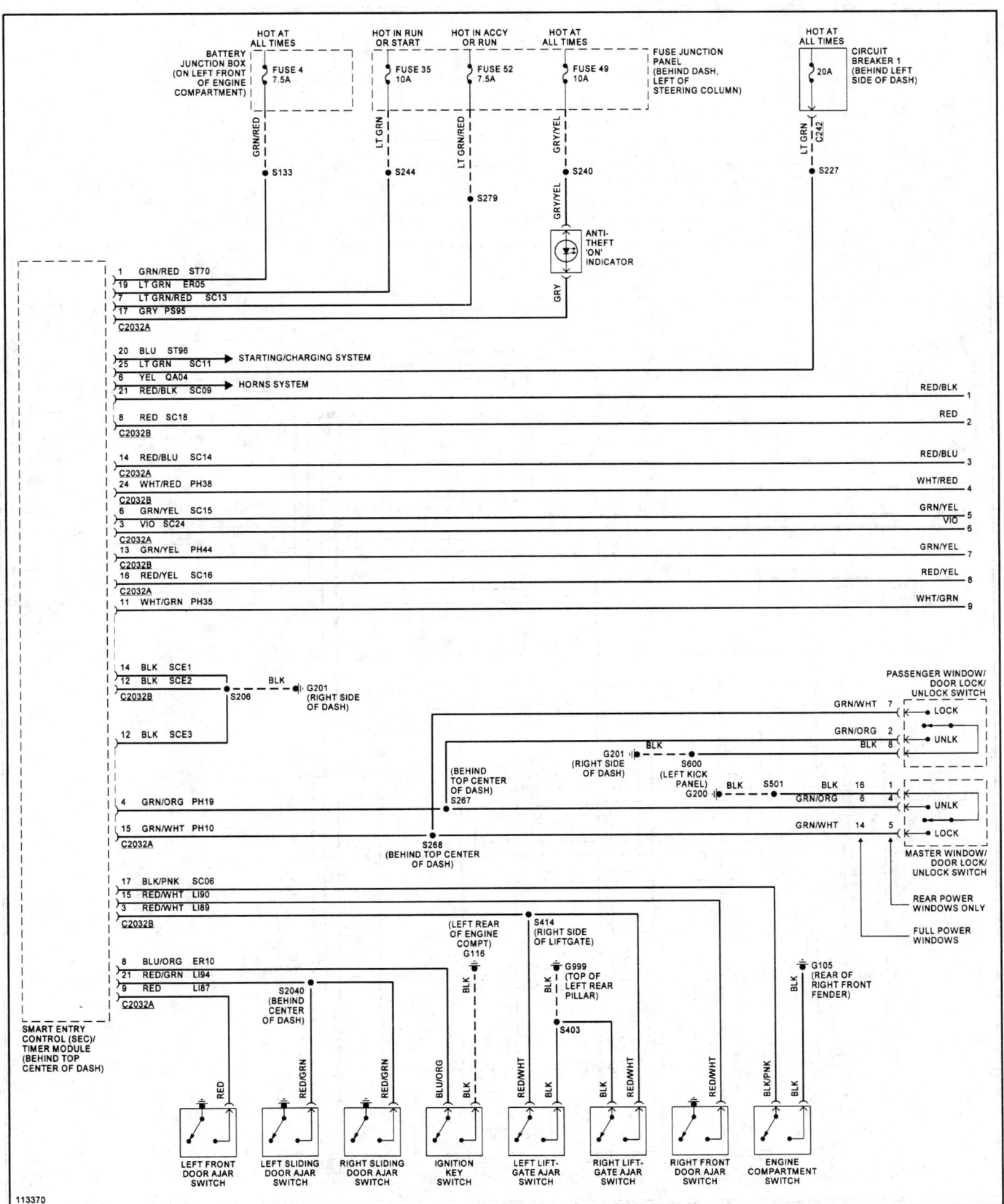

Fig. 18: Remote Keyless Entry System Wiring Diagram (Villager – 1 Of 2)

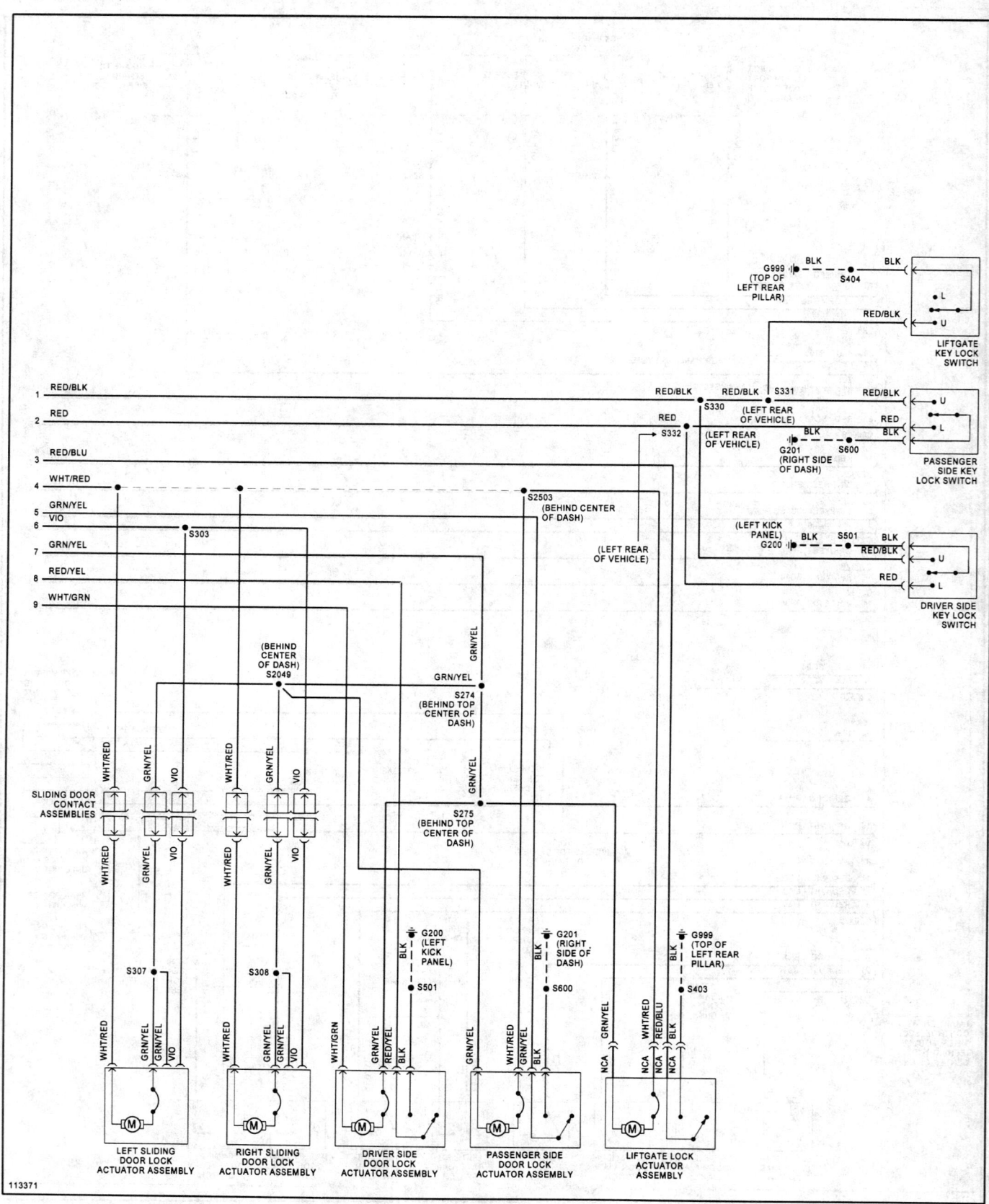

Fig. 19: Remote Keyless Entry System Wiring Diagram (Villager – 2 Of 2)

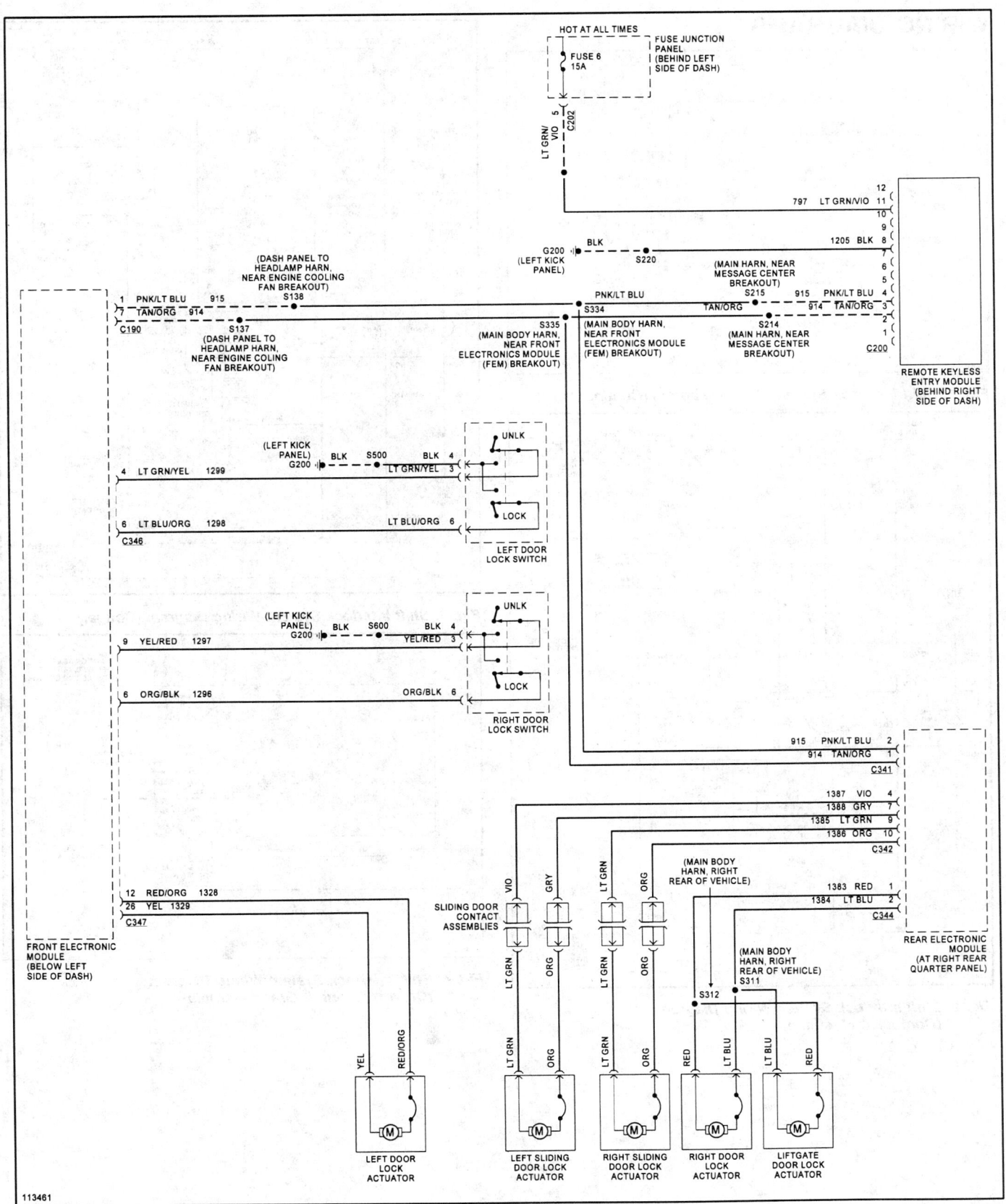

Fig. 20: Remote Keyless Entry System Wiring Diagram (Windstar)

WIRING DIAGRAMS

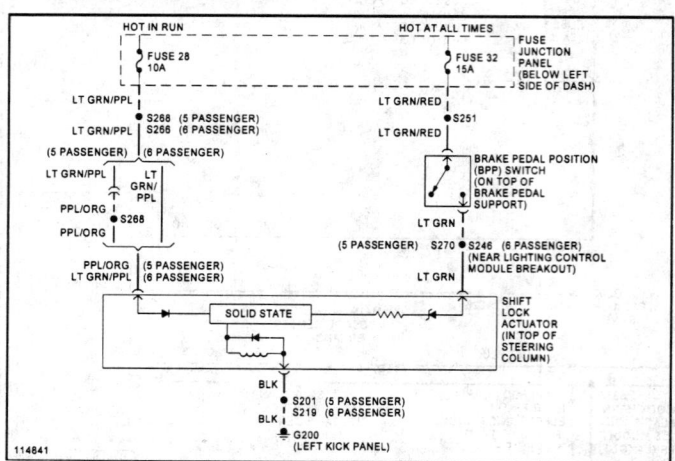

Fig. 1: Shift Interlock System Wiring Diagram (Continental)

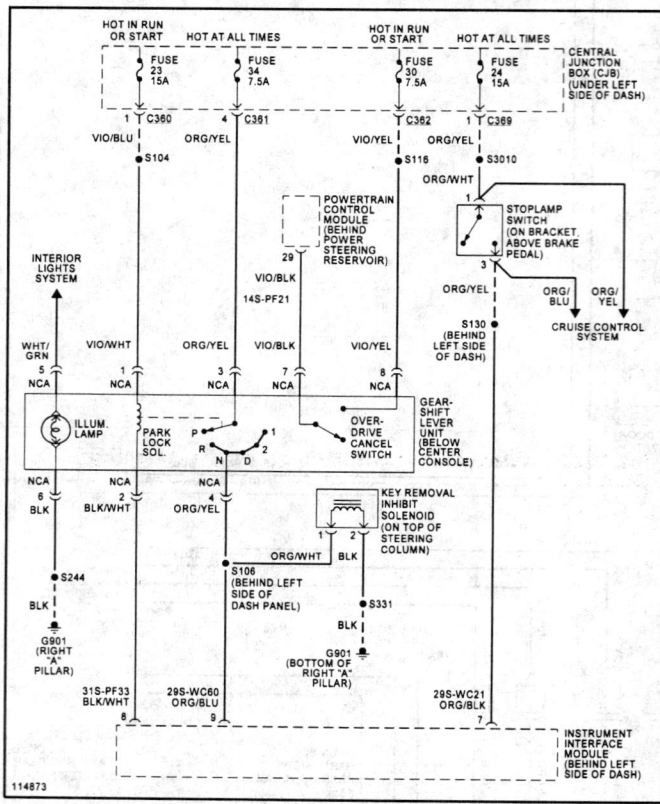

Fig. 2: Shift Interlock System Wiring Diagram
(Contour & Mystique)

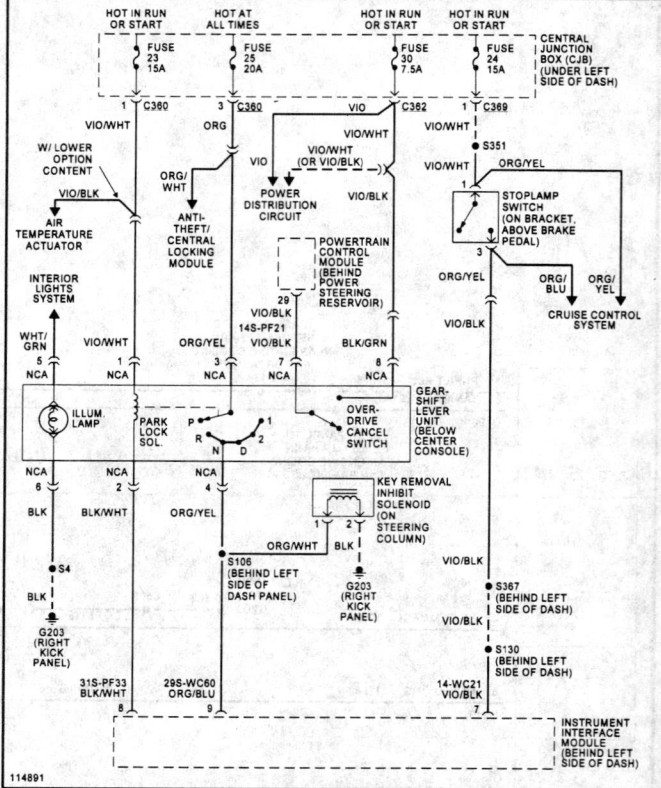

Fig. 3: Shift Interlock System Wiring Diagram (Cougar)

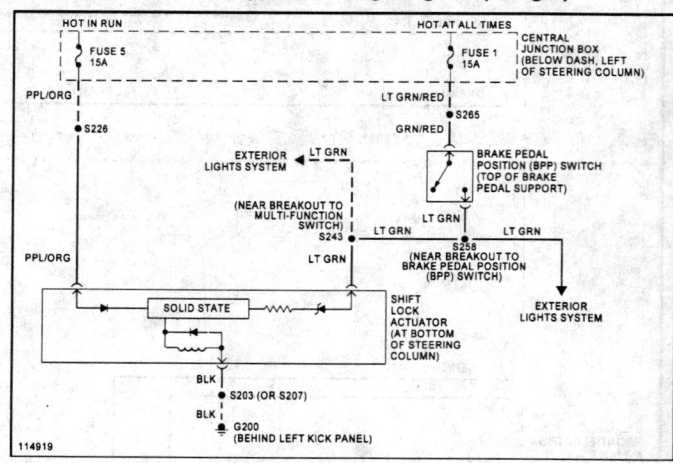

Fig. 4: Shift Interlock System Wiring Diagram
(Crown Victoria & Grand Marquis)

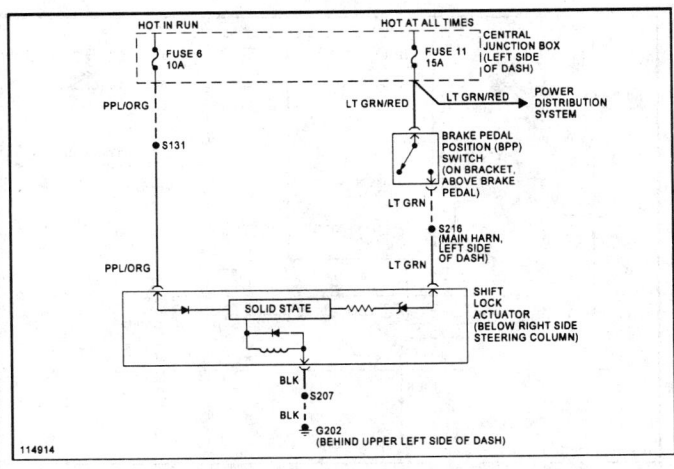

Fig. 5: Shift Interlock System Wiring Diagram (Econoline)

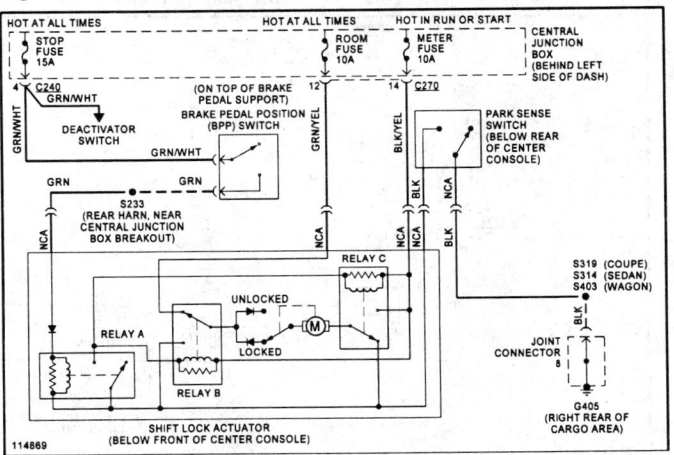

Fig. 6: Shift Interlock System Wiring Diagram (Escort & Tracer)

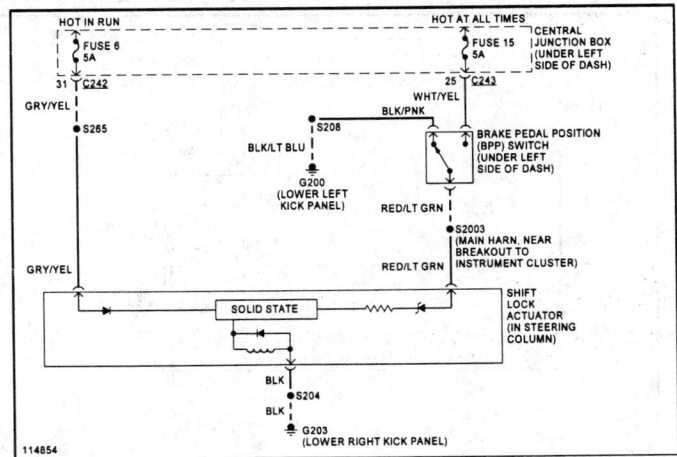

Fig. 7: Shift Interlock System Wiring Diagram (Expedition & Navigator)

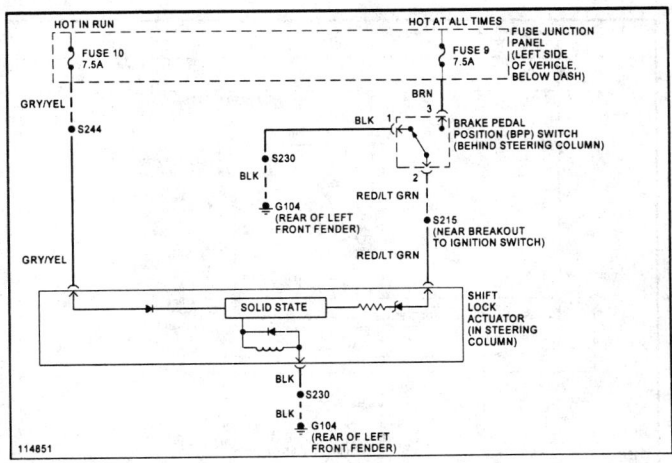

Fig. 8: Shift Interlock System Wiring Diagram (Explorer & Mountaineer)

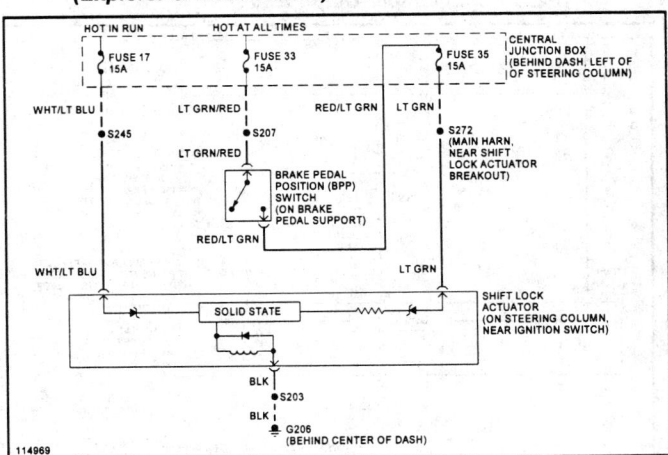

Fig. 9: Shift Interlock System Wiring Diagram (Mustang)

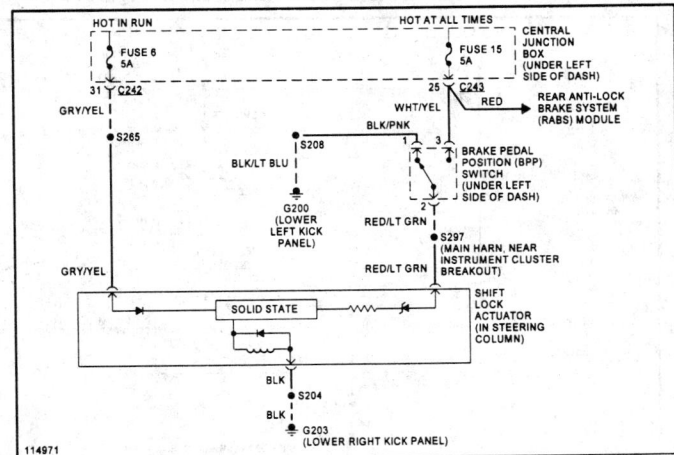

Fig. 10: Shift Interlock System Wiring Diagram (F150 & F250 Light-Duty Pickup)

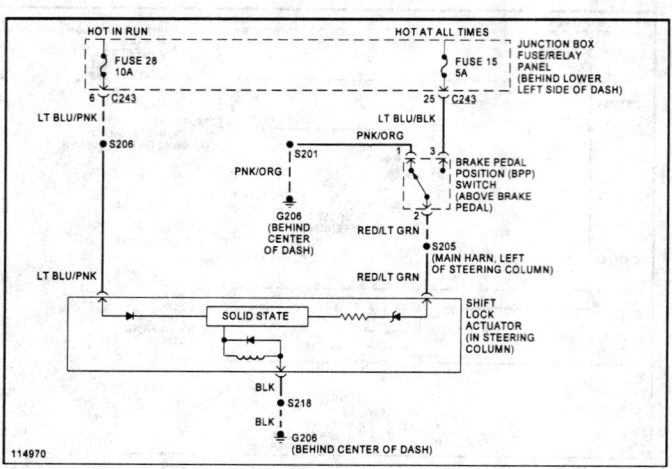

Fig. 11: Shift Interlock System Wiring Diagram
(F250 & F350 Super-Duty Pickup)

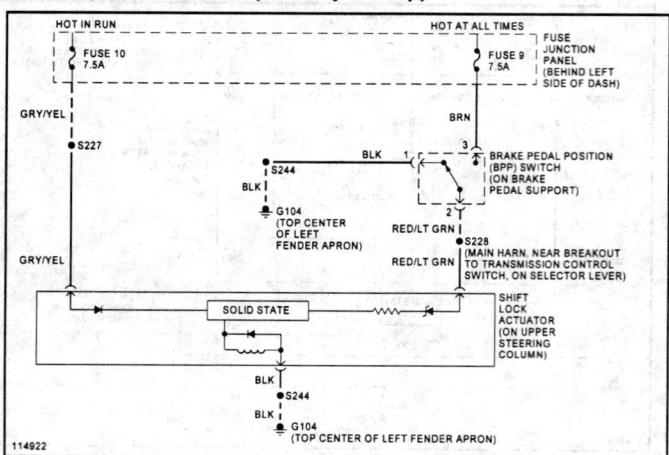

Fig. 12: Shift Interlock System Wiring Diagram (Ranger)

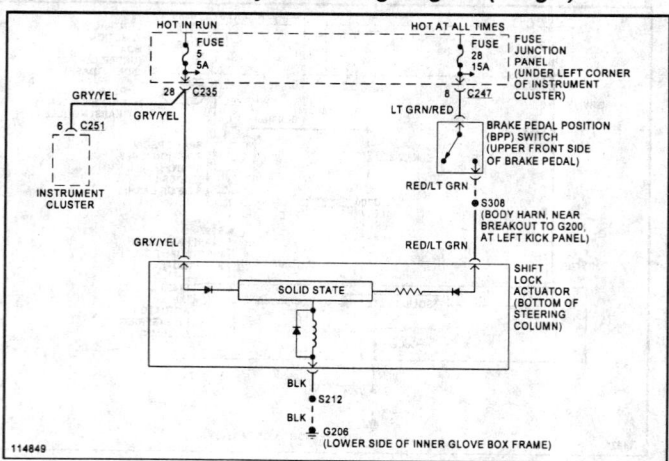

Fig. 13: Shift Interlock System Wiring Diagram (Sable & Taurus)

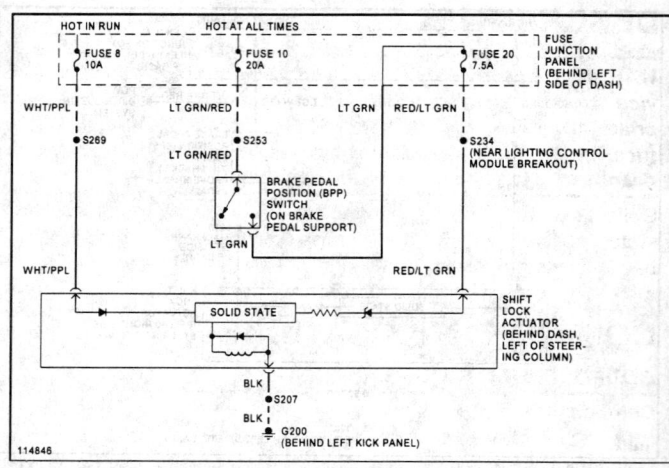

Fig. 14: Shift Interlock System Wiring Diagram (Town Car)

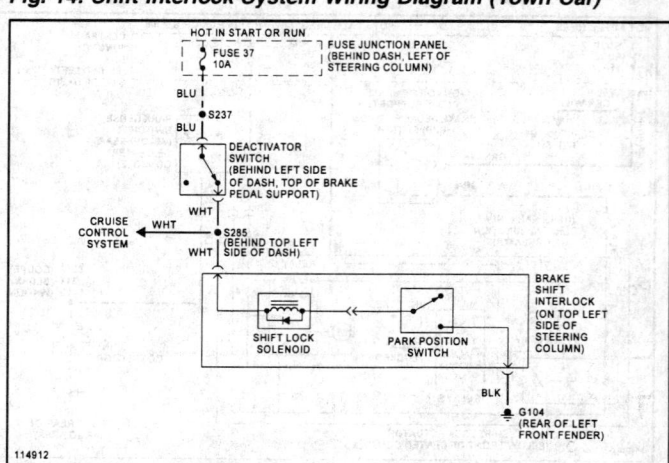

Fig. 15: Shift Interlock System Wiring Diagram (Villager)

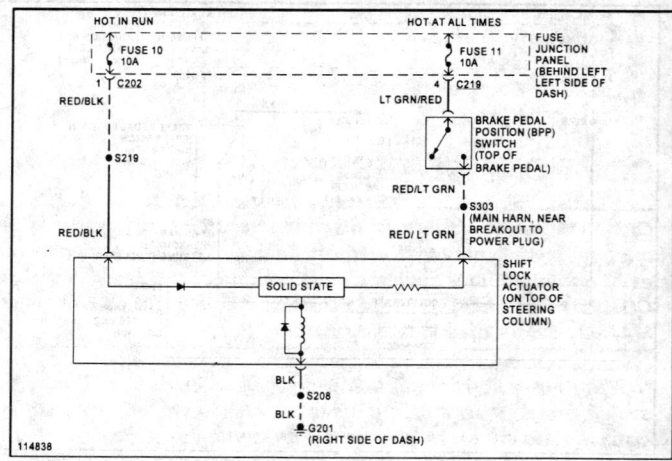

Fig. 16: Shift Interlock System Connector Wiring Diagram
(Windstar)

DESCRIPTION

WARNING: Deactivate air bag system before performing any service operation involving steering column components. See appropriate AIR BAG RESTRAINT SYSTEMS article. Do not apply electrical power to any component on steering column without first deactivating air bag system. Air bag may deploy.

Switches mounted on the steering column are the ignition switch, horn switch, multifunction switch and cruise control switches. Driver's side air bag is located on center of steering wheel.

COMPONENT LOCATIONS

COMPONENT LOCATIONS

Component	Location
Cruise Control Switches	On Steering Wheel
Data Link Connector	Under Instrument Panel, Right Of Steering Column
Door Lock Switch	Appropriate Door Panel Arm Rest
Ignition Switch	On Steering Column
Instrument Panel Fuse Box	Below Left Instrument Panel
Headlight Switch	Left Side Of Instrument Panel
High Beam Relay	In Power Distribution Box
Light Switch	Left Side Of Instrument Panel
Lighting Control Module (LCM)	Left Side Of Instrument Panel, Above Parking Brake Pedal Assembly
Multifunction Switch	On Steering Column
Power Distribution Box	Left Side Of Engine Compartment, Above Wheelwell
Wiper Switch	Part Of Multifunction Switch

TROUBLE SHOOTING

Before performing individual component tests, system testing and/or individual diagnostic tests, inspect for the following possible causes of system malfunction. Correct any obvious defects before proceeding.

- Mechanical Failure
- Low Battery Charge
- Faulty Fuses
- Loose Or Corroded Connectors
- Damaged Wiring

COMPONENT TESTS

CAUTION: When battery is disconnected, vehicle computer and memory system may lose memory data. Driveability problems may exist until computer systems have completed a relearn cycle. See COMPUTER RELEARN PROCEDURES article in GENERAL INFORMATION before disconnecting battery.

NOTE: Before performing following tests, ensure all multifunction switch grounds, wiring, and fuses are okay. Also, ensure all circuit connections are clean and tight. For ignition switch circuit identification, see appropriate wiring diagram in POWER DISTRIBUTION article in WIRING DIAGRAMS. For multifunction switch circuit identification, see appropriate wiring diagram in EXTERIOR LIGHTS article.

MULTIFUNCTION SWITCH

Disconnect multifunction switch harness connectors. Set hazard flasher switch to OFF position unless specified otherwise. Measure resistance between specified circuits at multifunction switch with switch in appropriate position. See MULTIFUNCTION SWITCH RESISTANCE table. *See Fig. 1.* If resistance is not as specified, or is poor in any switch position, replace multifunction switch.

MULTIFUNCTION SWITCH RESISTANCE

Switch Position	Circuit No.	Resistance (Ohms)
Flash-To-Pass On	196 & 383; 164 & 296	[1]
Hazard Switch		
On	44, 52, 64, 104 & 105; 383 & 1039	[1]
Off	8 & 1039; [2] 44, 104 & 105	[1]
High Beams On	196 & 296	[1]
Low Beams On	164 & 296	[1]
Turn Signals [3]		
Left Turn	8 & 1039; 44, 52 & 105	[1]
Right Turn	8 & 1039; 44, 64 & 104	[1]
Cornering Lights [3]		
Left Turn	296 & 380	[1]
Right Turn	296 & 379	[1]
Washer		
On	590 & 993	[1]
Off	590 & 993	[4] 103,300
Wipers		
Off	589 & 993	[4] 47,600
Low Speed	589 & 993	[4] 4080
High Speed	589 & 993	[1]
Interval	589 & 993	[4] 11,330
Interval Delay [5][6]		
MAX	590 & 993	[4] 103,300
MIN	590 & 993	[4] 3300

[1] – Resistance should be less than 5 ohms.
[2] – Brake light trough circuit.
[3] – Hazard switch MUST be off.
[4] – Resistance may vary by as much as 5 percent.
[5] – Resistance should vary smoothly between specified limits as knob is rotated between MIN and MAX positions.
[6] – These values are with wiper switch in OFF position. If wiper switch is in LOW or HIGH position, resistance between terminals No. 590 and 993 should be within 10 percent of 3300 ohms.

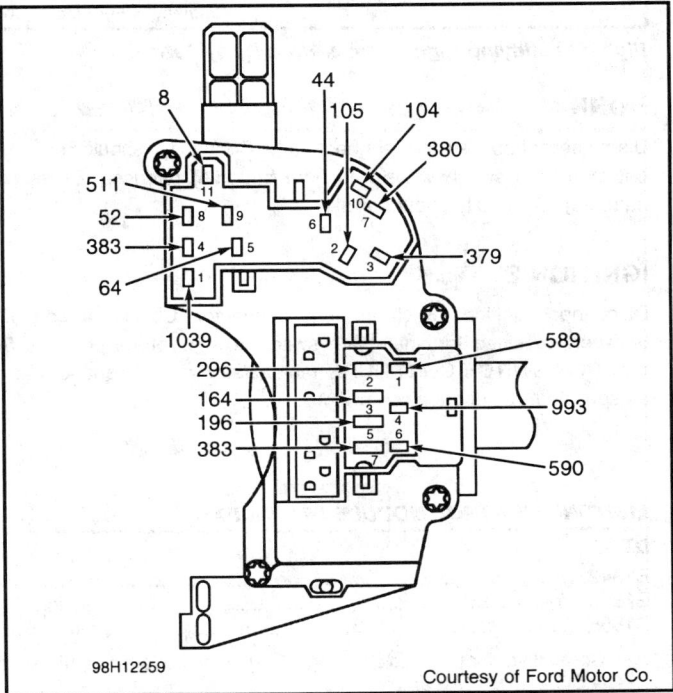

Fig. 1: Identifying Multifunction Switch Circuit Terminals

HEADLIGHT SWITCH

Headlight switch is an integral part of the lighting control module. For testing of the headlight system, see AUTOLAMP SYSTEMS – CONTINENTAL article.

HIGH BEAM & HORN RELAY

1) Remove high beam relay from power distribution box in engine compartment. Measure resistance between terminal No. 2 and all other terminals of high beam relay. *See Fig. 2.* If resistance is greater than 5 ohms between terminal No. 2 and all other terminals, go to next step. If resistance is 5 ohms or less between terminal No. 2 and any other terminal, replace high beam relay.

2) Using 2 fused jumper wires, apply battery voltage to terminals No. 1 and 3 of high beam relay. Measure voltage at terminal No. 4 of high beam relay. If battery voltage exists, leave jumper wires connected and go to next step. If battery voltage does not exist, replace high beam relay.

3) Ground terminal No. 2 of high beam relay. Measure voltage at terminal No. 5 of high beam relay. If battery voltage exists, relay is okay at this time. If battery voltage does not exist, replace high beam relay.

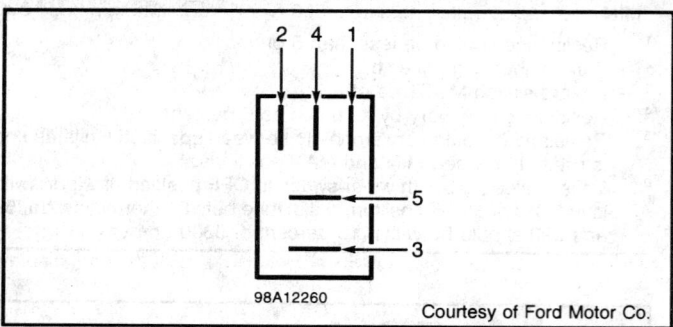

98A12260

Courtesy of Ford Motor Co.

Fig. 2: Identifying High Beam & Horn Relay Terminals

HORN

Disconnect horn switch connector(s). Continuity should not exist between horn switch wires with horn button(s) released. Press horn button(s). Continuity should exist.

IGNITION SWITCH

Disconnect ignition switch harness connector. Check for continuity between specified terminals with switch in appropriate position. See IGNITION SWITCH CONTINUITY table. *See Fig. 3.* If continuity is not as specified, replace ignition switch.

Switch Position	Continuity Between Terminals
Accessory	A1 & B3
Run	A1 & B1; A3 & B3; A4 & B4; B5 & I1
Start	B4 & STA; B5 & I1; P1 & GND

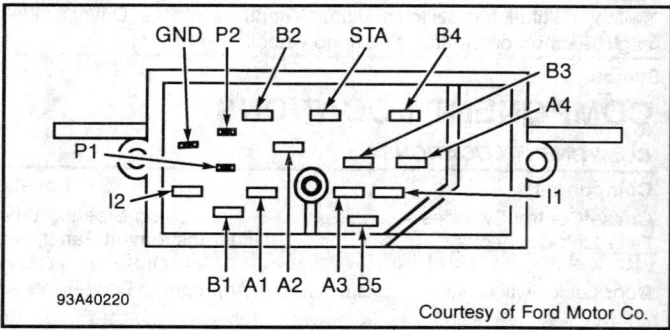

93A40220

Courtesy of Ford Motor Co.

Fig. 3: Identifying Ignition Switch Terminals

SELF-DIAGNOSTIC SYSTEM

NOTE: Before beginning self-diagnostics, perform TROUBLE SHOOTING. A New Generation Star (NGS) tester is required to test system. If NGS tester does not communicate with vehicle, refer to NGS tester manual.

Verify customers complaint. Check for damaged ignition lock cylinder switch or open fuses. Check for loose or corroded connectors, damaged wiring harness or damaged ignition switch. Repair or replace components as necessary.

If all components are okay, connect New Generation Star (NGS) tester to Data Link Connector (DLC), located beneath instrument panel. Using NGS tester, perform data link diagnostics test. See DATA LINK DIAGNOSTIC TEST under COMMUNICATION NETWORK DIAGNOSTICS in MODULE COMMUNICATIONS NETWORK – CONTINENTAL article. If NGS tester responds with CKT914, CKT915 or CKT70=ALL ECUS NO RESP/NOT EQUIP, repair module communications concern. See MODULE COMMUNICATIONS NETWORK – CONTINENTAL article. If NGS tester displays NO RESP/NOT EQUIP for Lighting Control Module (LCM), perform TEST E: NO COMMUNICATION WITH LIGHTING CONTROL MODULE under SYSTEM TESTS.

If NGS tester responds with SYSTEM PASSED, retrieve and record continuous DTCs. Erase continuous DTCs. Using NGS tester, perform LCM self-test. Perform appropriate test in accordance with DTC retrieved. See LIGHTING CONTROL MODULE DTC INDEX table. Codes listed in this table are only for testing covered in this article. For complete DTC listing, see MODULE COMMUNICATIONS NETWORK – CONTINENTAL article. If no DTCs are retrieved, repair by symptom. See SYMPTOM CHART table under SYSTEM TESTS.

LIGHTING CONTROL MODULE DTC INDEX

DTC [1]	Description	Test
B1342	ECU Defective	[2]
B1359	Ignition RUN/ACC Circuit Failure	B
B1555	Ignition RUN/START Circuit Failure	D

[1] – Codes listed in this table are only for testing covered in this article. For complete DTC listing, see MODULE COMMUNICATIONS NETWORK – CONTINENTAL article.

[2] – Using NGS tester, retrieve and document continuous DTCs. Clear all DTCs. Perform Lighting Control Module (LCM) self-test. If DTC B1342 is retrieved again, replace LCM.

SYSTEM TESTS

CAUTION: When battery is disconnected or modules are replaced, vehicle computer and memory systems may lose memory data. Driveability problems may exist until computer systems have completed a relearn cycle. See COMPUTER RELEARN PROCEDURES article in GENERAL INFORMATION before disconnecting battery.

SYMPTOM CHART

Symptom	Test
Ignition Switch Inoperative	A
No Power In ACC Position	B
No Power In RUN Position	C
No Power In START Position	D
No Communication With Lighting Control Module	E

TEST A: IGNITION SWITCH INOPERATIVE

1) Turn ignition switch to LOCK position. Remove maxi-fuses No. 3 (40-amp) and No. 4 (40-amp) in power distribution box. Check fuses. If either fuse is blown, go to next step. If both fuses are okay, go to step **3)**.
2) Ensure maxi-fuses No. 3 and 4 are still removed. Disconnect ignition switch harness connector C236. Measure resistance between ground and terminals B1, B3, B4 and B5 (all Black/Orange wires) at ignition switch harness connector C236. *See Fig. 4.* If any resistance reading is 10 k/ohms or less, repair short to ground in appropriate wire. If all resistance readings are greater than 10 k/ohms, test ignition switch and replace if defective. See IGNITION SWITCH under COMPONENT TESTS.
3) Disconnect ignition switch harness connector C236. Install maxi-fuses No. 3 and 4. Measure voltage at terminals B1, B3, B4 and B5 (all Black/Orange wires) at ignition switch harness connector C236. *See Fig. 4.* If battery voltage exists at all terminals, go to next step. If battery voltage does not exist at any terminal, repair open in appropriate Black/Orange wire between ignition switch and power distribution box.
4) Test ignition switch. See IGNITION SWITCH under COMPONENT TESTS. If ignition switch is okay, check for intermittent short to ground and/or poor connections and repair as necessary. If ignition switch is defective, replace ignition switch.

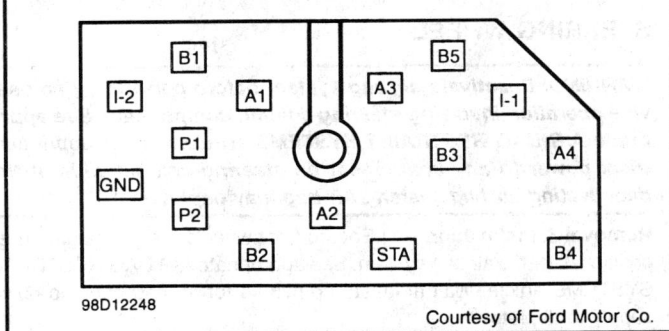

98D12248   Courtesy of Ford Motor Co.

Fig. 4: Identifying Ignition Switch Harness Connector C236 Terminals

TEST B: NO POWER IN ACC POSITION

1) Disconnect ignition switch harness connector C236. Measure voltage at terminal B3 (Black/Orange wire) at ignition switch harness connector C236. *See Fig. 4.* If battery voltage exists, go to next step. If battery voltage does not exist, repair open in Black/Orange wire between ignition switch and maxi-fuse No. 3 in power distribution box.
2) Turn ignition switch to ACC position. Measure resistance between terminals A1 and B3 at ignition switch (component side). *See Fig. 3.* If resistance is 5 ohms or less, system is okay at this time. If resistance is greater than 5 ohms, replace ignition switch.

TEST C: NO POWER IN RUN POSITION

1) Disconnect ignition switch harness connector C236. Measure voltage at terminals B1, B3, B4 and B5 (all Black/Orange wires) at ignition switch harness connector C236. *See Fig. 4.* If battery voltage exists at all terminals, go to next step. If battery voltage does not exist at any terminal, repair open in appropriate Black/Orange wire between ignition switch and power distribution box.
2) Turn ignition switch to RUN position. Measure resistance between terminals B5 and I1 at ignition switch (component side). *See Fig. 3.* Turn ignition switch to START position. Measure resistance between terminals B5 and I1 at ignition switch (component side). If resistances are 5 ohms or less, system is operating properly. If resistances are greater than 5 ohms, replace ignition switch.

TEST D: NO POWER IN START POSITION

1) Disconnect ignition switch harness connector C236. Measure voltage at terminals B4 and B5 (both Black/Orange wires) at ignition switch harness connector C236. *See Fig. 4.* If battery voltage exists at both terminals, go to next step. If battery voltage does not exist at both terminals, repair open in Black/Orange wire between ignition switch and maxi-fuse No. 4 in power distribution box.
2) Test ignition switch. See IGNITION SWITCH under COMPONENT TESTS. If ignition switch is defective, replace ignition switch. If ignition switch is okay, repair starting system. See appropriate STARTERS article in STARTING & CHARGING SYSTEMS.

TEST E: NO COMMUNICATION WITH LIGHTING CONTROL MODULE

1) Turn ignition switch to LOCK position. Connect New Generation Star (NGS) tester to Data Link Connector (DLC). Monitor Lighting Control Module (LCM) PID IGN_LC. If NGS tester does not display UNABLE TO PERFORM TEST/FUNCTION or MODULE NOT RESPONDING: LCM or CHECK IGNITION STATUS/VERIFY CABLE REQUIREMENTS or CHECK CABLE CONNECTIONS, go to next step. If NGS tester displays UNABLE TO PERFORM TEST/FUNCTION or MODULE NOT RESPONDING: LCM or CHECK IGNITION STATUS/VERIFY CABLE REQUIREMENTS or CHECK CABLE CONNECTIONS, go to step **16)**.
2) Turn ignition switch to RUN position. Monitor LCM PID IGN_LC while turning key to each position. If PID IGN_LC indicates ACCY while in ACCESSORY position and OFF in all other positions, replace LCM. If PID IGN_LC indicates ACCY while in RUN position, go to next step. If PID IGN_LC indicates OFF in all positions, go to step **7)**.
3) Turn ignition switch to RUN position. Measure voltage at output side of fuse No. 5 (10-amp) in instrument panel fuse box. If battery voltage does not exist, go to next step. If battery voltage exists, repair open in Red/Yellow wire between instrument panel fuse box and LCM.
4) Check fuse No. 5 in instrument panel fuse box. If fuse is blown, go to next step. If fuse is okay, repair open in Brown/Pink wire between instrument panel fuse box and ignition switch.
5) Turn ignition switch to LOCK position. Disconnect LCM harness connector C206. Disconnect light sensor amplifier harness connector C243. Measure resistance between ground and terminal No. 17 (Red/Yellow wire) at LCM harness connector C206. *See Fig. 5.* If resistance is 20 ohms or less, go to next step. If resistance is greater than 20 ohms, repair short to ground in Red/Yellow wire.
6) Turn ignition switch to LOCK position. Connect LCM harness connector C206. Remove fuse No. 5 (10-amp) in instrument panel fuse box. Measure resistance between ground and output side of fuse No. 5 in instrument panel fuse box. If resistance is 20 ohms or less, repair autolamp concern. See AUTOLAMP SYSTEMS – CONTINENTAL article. If resistance is greater than 20 ohms, replace LCM.
7) Turn ignition switch to RUN position. Measure voltage at output side of fuse No. 4 (10-amp) in instrument panel fuse box. If battery voltage exists, go to next step. If battery voltage does not exist, go to step **9)**.
8) Turn ignition switch to LOCK position. Disconnect LCM harness connector C208. Turn ignition switch to RUN position. Measure voltage at terminal No. 2 (Black/Pink wire) at LCM harness connector C208. *See Fig. 6.* If battery voltage exists, replace LCM. If battery voltage does not exist, repair open in Black/Pink wire.

9) Turn ignition switch to LOCK position. Check fuse No. 4 (10-amp) in instrument panel fuse box. If fuse is blown, go to next step. If fuse is okay, repair open in Black/Light Green wire between instrument panel fuse box and ignition switch.

10) Disconnect driver's door lock switch harness connector C505. Measure resistance between ground and terminal No. 2 (Black/Pink wire) at LCM harness connector C208. If resistance is 10 k/ohms or less, go to next step. If resistance is greater than 10 k/ohms, replace driver's door lock switch.

11) Disconnect passenger's door lock switch harness connector C602. Measure resistance between ground and terminal No. 2 (Black/Pink wire) at LCM harness connector C208. If resistance is 10 k/ohms or less, go to next step. If resistance is greater than 10 k/ohms, replace passenger's door lock switch.

12) Disconnect passenger's power window switch harness connector C600. Measure resistance between ground and terminal No. 2 (Black/Pink wire) at LCM harness connector C208. If resistance is 10 k/ohms or less, go to next step. If resistance is greater than 10 k/ohms, replace passenger's power window switch.

13) Disconnect left rear power window switch harness connector C709. Measure resistance between ground and terminal No. 2 (Black/Pink wire) at LCM harness connector C208. If resistance is 10 k/ohms or less, go to next step. If resistance is greater than 10 k/ohms, replace left rear power window switch.

14) Disconnect right rear power window switch harness connector C809. Measure resistance between ground and terminal No. 2 (Black/Pink wire) at LCM harness connector C208. If resistance is 10 k/ohms or less, go to next step. If resistance is greater than 10 k/ohms, replace right rear power window switch.

15) Ensure ignition switch is in LOCK position. Connect LCM harness connector C208. Using and ohmmeter, measure resistance by back-probing between ground and terminal No. 2 (Black/Pink wire) at LCM harness connector C208. If resistance is greater than 2 k/ohms, replace LCM. If resistance is 2 k/ohms or less, repair Black/Pink wire.

16) Turn ignition switch to LOCK position. Disconnect LCM harness connectors. Measure resistance between ground and terminal No. 13 (Black wire) at LCM harness connector C206. *See Fig. 5.* Measure resistance between ground and terminal No. 1 (Black wire) at LCM harness connector C207. *See Fig. 7.* Measure resistance between ground and terminal No. 9 (Black wire) at LCM harness connector C211. *See Fig. 8.* If all resistance readings are 5 ohms or less, go to next step. If any resistance reading is greater than 5 ohms, repair appropriate Black wire.

17) Measure resistance between ground and terminal No. 15 (Black/Light Blue wire) at LCM harness connector C207. If resistance is 5 ohms or less, repair module communication concern. See MODULE COMMUNICATIONS NETWORK – CONTINENTAL article. If resistance is greater than 5 ohms, repair open in Black/Light Blue wire.

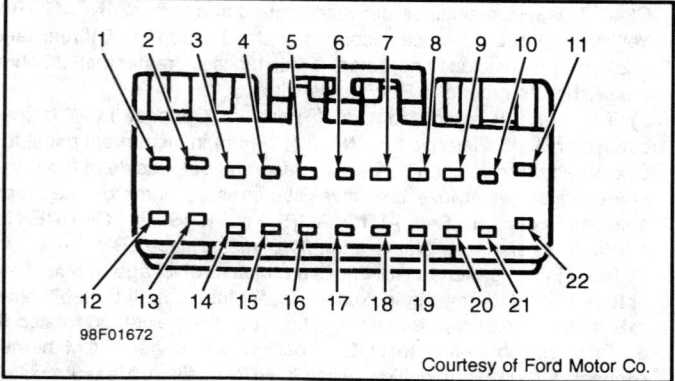

Fig. 5: Identifying Lighting Control Module Harness Connector C206 Terminals

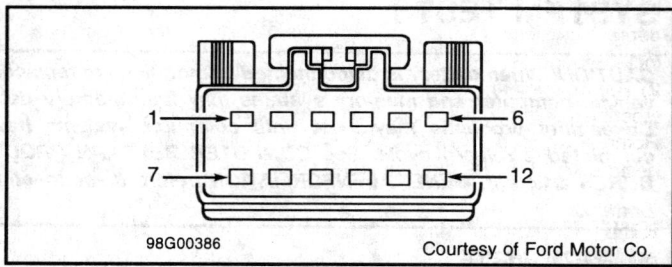

Fig. 6: Identifying Lighting Control Module Harness Connector C208 Terminals

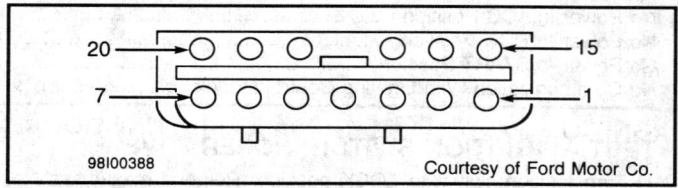

Fig. 7: Identifying Lighting Control Module Harness Connector C207 Terminals

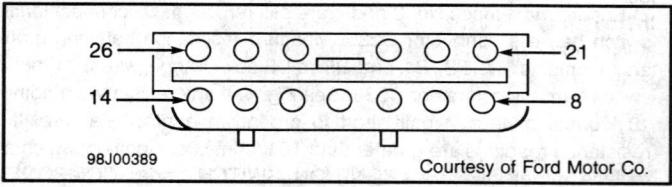

Fig. 8: Identifying Lighting Control Module Harness Connector C211 Terminals

REMOVAL & INSTALLATION

CAUTION: When battery is disconnected or modules are replaced, vehicle computer and memory systems may lose memory data. Driveability problems may exist until computer systems have completed a relearn cycle. See COMPUTER RELEARN PROCEDURES article in GENERAL INFORMATION before disconnecting battery.

STEERING WHEEL

WARNING: Deactivate air bag system before performing any service operation involving steering column components. See appropriate AIR BAG RESTRAINT SYSTEMS article. Do not apply electrical power to any component on steering column without first deactivating air bag system. Air bag may deploy.

Removal & Installation – 1) Ensure front wheels are in straight-ahead position. Disable air bag system. See appropriate AIR BAG RESTRAINT SYSTEMS article. Wait at least one minute for air bag back-up power supply to deplete.

2) Remove air bag module retaining nuts/screws. Lift air bag module from steering wheel. Disconnect air bag wiring harness from module. Disconnect cruise control switch connector (if equipped). Remove and discard steering wheel bolt.

3) Remove steering wheel. While removing steering wheel, guide wiring harnesses through steering wheel. To install, reverse removal procedure. Install NEW steering wheel bolt and tighten to specification. See TORQUE SPECIFICATIONS. Check AIR BAG light to verify proper system operation.

MULTIFUNCTION SWITCH

Removal & Installation – 1) Disconnect negative battery cable. On models with tilt wheel, adjust steering wheel to lowest position, then remove tilt lever. On all models, turn ignition switch to RUN position.

Insert punch into access hole in lower steering column cover and depress ignition switch lock cylinder release tab. Remove ignition switch lock cylinder.

2) Remove lower instrument panel cover. Remove upper and lower steering column covers. Remove multifunction switch from housing. Remove wiring harness retainer. Disconnect multifunction switch connectors. To install, reverse removal procedure.

IGNITION SWITCH (ELECTRICAL PORTION)

Removal & Installation – Disconnect negative battery cable. Remove lower instrument panel cover. Unbolt hood release latch and position aside. Unbolt parking brake release handle and position aside. Remove lower instrument panel reinforcement. Disconnect ignition switch harness connector. Remove retaining screws and ignition switch. To install, reverse removal procedure.

IGNITION SWITCH LOCK CYLINDER (FUNCTIONAL)

Removal – Disconnect negative battery cable. Turn lock cylinder to RUN position. Locate hole in lower steering column cover. Insert a 1/8" drill bit or punch into hole. Press lock cylinder retaining pin while pulling lock cylinder from housing.

Installation – Turn lock cylinder to RUN position. Press retaining pin inward and insert lock cylinder into housing. Ensure lock cylinder is fully seated and aligned with interlocking washer.

IGNITION SWITCH LOCK CYLINDER (NON-FUNCTIONAL)

NOTE: If lock cylinder is functional (key is available and lock cylinder turns freely), see IGNITION SWITCH LOCK CYLINDER (FUNCTIONAL) under REMOVAL & INSTALLATION.

Removal & Installation – 1) Disconnect negative battery cable. Disable air bag system. See appropriate AIR BAG RESTRAINT SYSTEMS article. Remove steering wheel. See STEERING WHEEL. Using a 1/8" bit, drill out retaining pin located below lock cylinder on housing. DO NOT drill deeper than 1/2".

2) Using channel lock pliers, twist lock cylinder cap until it separates from lock cylinder. Using a 3/8" drill bit, drill down center of ignition lock key slot about 1 3/4" until lock cylinder breaks loose from its base.

3) Remove retainer, washer, and lock cylinder gear from housing. Remove metal shavings from lock cylinder bore. Replace housing if damaged. To install, reverse removal procedure. Connect negative battery cable. Check AIR BAG light for proper system operation.

TORQUE SPECIFICATIONS

TORQUE SPECIFICATIONS

Application	Ft. Lbs. (N.m)
Steering Wheel Bolt [1]	23-35
	(31-48)

[1] – Use NEW bolt when installing steering wheel.

WIRING DIAGRAMS

NOTE: For additional wiring information on steering column switches, see appropriate wiring diagram(s) in EXTERIOR LIGHTS and HEADLIGHT SYSTEMS articles. Also see appropriate wiring diagram in POWER DISTRIBUTION article in WIRING DIAGRAMS.

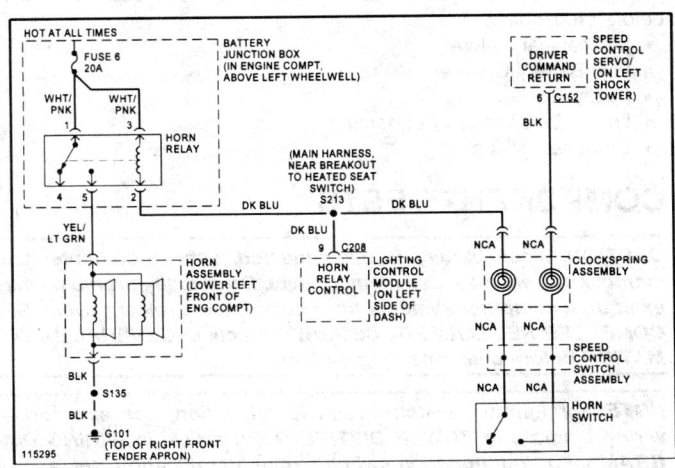

Fig. 9: Horn System Wiring Diagram (Continental)

1999 ACCESSORIES & EQUIPMENT
Steering Column Switches – Contour & Mystique

DESCRIPTION

WARNING: Deactivate air bag system before performing any service operation involving steering column components. See appropriate AIR BAG RESTRAINT SYSTEMS article. DO NOT apply electrical power to any component on steering column without first deactivating air bag system. Air bag may deploy.

Steering column switch consist of a multifunction switch, ignition switch and wiper/washer switch. The multifunction switch controls hazards, turn signals head light high beams and flash-to-pass feature.

TROUBLE SHOOTING

Before performing individual component tests, inspect for the following possible causes of system malfunction. Correct any obvious defects before proceeding:
- Mechanical Failure
- Low Battery Charge
- Faulty Fuses
- Loose Or Corroded Connectors
- Damaged Wiring

COMPONENT TESTS

CAUTION: When battery is disconnected, vehicle computer and memory system may lose memory data. Driveability problems may exist until computer systems have completed a relearn cycle. See COMPUTER RELEARN PROCEDURES article in GENERAL INFORMATION before disconnecting battery.

NOTE: For ignition switch circuit identification, see appropriate wiring diagram in POWER DISTRIBUTION article in WIRING DIAGRAMS. For multifunction switch circuit identification, see appropriate wiring diagram in EXTERIOR LIGHTS article.

MULTIFUNCTION SWITCH

Disconnect multifunction switch harness connectors. Set hazard flasher switch in OFF position unless specified otherwise. Continuity between terminals should be as specified with switch in specified position. See MULTIFUNCTION SWITCH CONTINUITY table. *See Fig. 1.* If resistance is not as specified, or is poor in any switch position, replace multifunction switch.

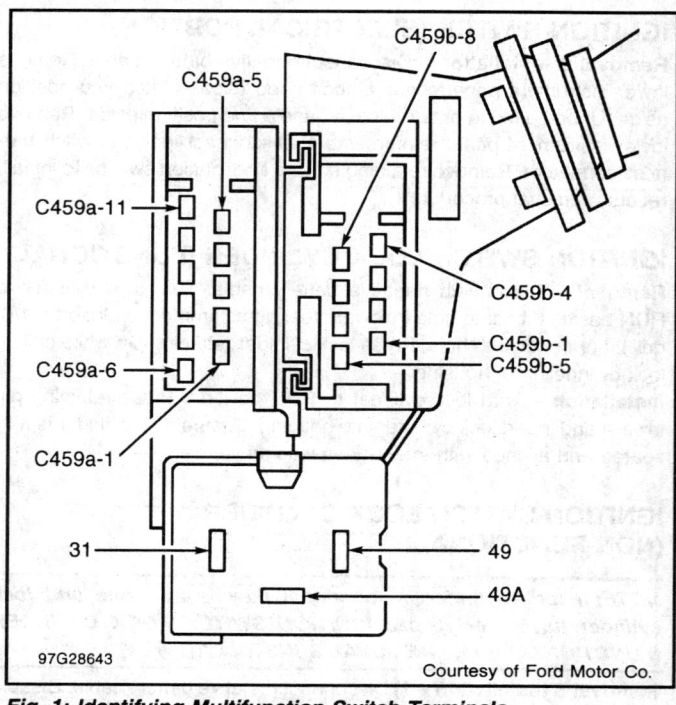

97G28643
Courtesy of Ford Motor Co.

Fig. 1: Identifying Multifunction Switch Terminals

MULTIFUNCTION SWITCH CONTINUITY

Terminals	Switch Position	[1] Normal Condition
Flash-To-Pass		
C459a-2 & C459a-4	High	No Continuity
C459a-2 & C459a-4	Low	No Continuity
C459a-2 & C459a-4	Pass	Continuity
High Beams		
C459a-2 & C459a-5	High	Continuity
C459a-2 & C459a-5	Low	No Continuity
C459a-2 & C459a-5	Pass	No Continuity
Low Beams		
C459a-3 & C459a-5	High	No Continuity
C459a-3 & C459a-5	Low	Continuity
C459a-3 & C459a-5	Pass	Continuity
Left Turn		
C459b-3 & C459a-8	Left Turn	Continuity
C459b-3 & C459a-8	Neutral	No Continuity
C459b-3 & C459a-8	Right Turn	No Continuity
Right Turn		
C459b-1 & C459a-9	Left Turn	No Continuity
C459b-1 & C459a-9	Neutral	No Continuity
C459b-1 & C459a-9	Right Turn	Continuity
Hazard Warning		
C459b-1, C459b-3, C459a-8, C459a-9 & C459a-10	On	Continuity
C459b-1, C459b-3, C459a-8, C459a-9 & C459a-10	Off	No Continuity
C459a-11 & 49	On	No Continuity
C459a-11 & 49	Off	Continuity

[1] – Continuity should always exist between terminals No. 31 and C459a-7/

HEADLIGHT SWITCH

See appropriate INSTRUMENT PANELS article.

HORN

Disconnect horn switch connector(s). Continuity should not exist between horn switch wires with horn button(s) released. Press horn button(s). Continuity should exist.

IGNITION SWITCH

Check resistance between specified terminals with switch in each position. See IGNITION SWITCH RESISTANCE table. *See Fig. 2.* If resistance is not as specified, replace ignition switch.

IGNITION SWITCH RESISTANCE

Switch Position	Between Terminals	Ohms
Off		
Key Out .... 1 & All Other Terminals .... [1]		
Key In .... 1 & 3 .... [2]		
Accessory .... 1 & 8 .... [2]		
Run .... 1 & 4; 1 & 8 .... [2]		
Start .... 1 & 4; 1 & 5; 6 & 7 .... [2]		

[1] – Resistance should be greater than 10,000 ohms.
[2] – Resistance should be less than 5 ohms.

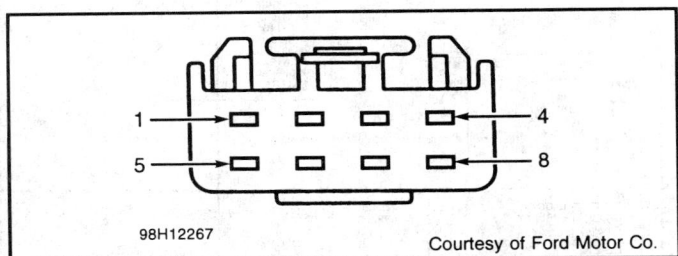

Fig. 2: Identifying Ignition Switch Terminals

RELAYS

High Beam & Low Beam Relays – 1) Remove relay to be tested. Check continuity between terminals No. 3 and 5 of relay. *See Fig. 3.* If continuity does not exist, go to next step. If continuity exists, replace relay.
2) Apply battery voltage between terminals No. 1 and 2 of relay. With battery voltage applied continuity should now exist between terminals No. 3 and 5. If continuity is as specified, relay is okay at this time. If continuity is not as specified, replace relay.
Ignition & Starter Relays – 1) Remove relay to be tested. Measure resistance between terminal No. 1 and all other terminals of relay. *See Fig. 4.* If resistance is greater than 5 ohms between terminal No. 2 any all other terminal, go to next step. If resistance is 5 ohms or less between terminal No. 2 any other terminal, replace relay.
2) Using 2 fused jumper wires, apply battery voltage to terminals No. 2 and 3 of relay. Measure voltage at terminal No. 4 of beam relay. If battery voltage exists, leave jumper wires connected and go to next step. If battery voltage does not exist, replace relay.
3) Ground terminal No. 1 of relay. Measure voltage at terminal No. 5 of relay. If battery voltage exists, relay is okay at this time. If battery voltage does not exist, replace relay.

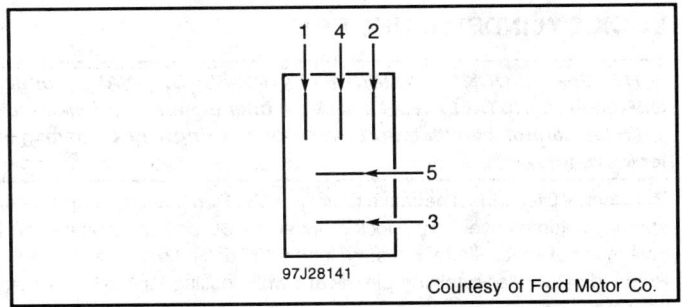

Fig. 3: Identifying High Beam & Low Beam Relay Terminals

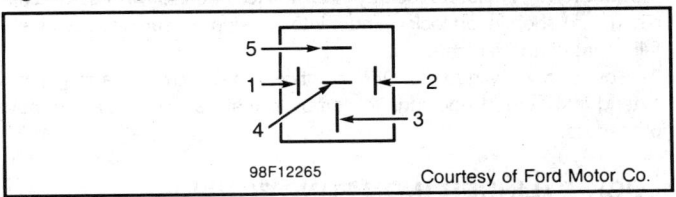

Fig. 4: Identifying Ignition & Starter Relay Terminals

REMOVAL & INSTALLATION

CAUTION: When battery is disconnected, vehicle computer and memory system may lose memory data. Driveability problems may exist until computer systems have completed a relearn cycle. See COMPUTER RELEARN PROCEDURES article in GENERAL INFORMATION before disconnecting battery.

STEERING WHEEL

WARNING: Deactivate air bag system before performing any service operation involving steering column components. See appropriate AIR BAG RESTRAINT SYSTEMS article. DO NOT apply electrical power to any component on steering column without first deactivating air bag system. Air bag may deploy.

Removal & Installation – 1) Ensure front wheels are in straight-ahead position. Disable air bag system. See appropriate AIR BAG RESTRAINT SYSTEMS article. Wait at least one minute for air bag back-up power supply to deplete.
2) Remove air bag module retaining nuts/screws. Lift air bag module from steering wheel. Disconnect air bag wiring harness from module. Disconnect cruise control switch connector (if equipped). Remove and discard steering wheel bolt.
3) Remove steering wheel. While removing steering wheel, guide wiring harnesses through steering wheel. To install, reverse removal procedure. Install NEW steering wheel bolt and tighten to specification. Check AIR BAG light to verify proper system operation.

MULTIFUNCTION SWITCH

Removal & Installation – Disconnect negative battery cable. Remove upper steering column cover. Depress switch locking tab. Slide switch outward from steering column. Disconnect connectors. Remove switch from housing. To install, reverse removal procedure.

IGNITION SWITCH

Removal & Installation – Disconnect negative battery cable. Remove upper and lower steering column covers. Disconnect ignition switch harness connector. Remove ignition switch retaining screws. Remove ignition switch. To install, reverse removal procedure.

LOCK CYLINDER (FUNCTIONAL)

NOTE: See LOCK CYLINDER (NON-FUNCTIONAL) under REMOVAL & INSTALLATION if lock cylinder is non-functional (lock cylinder cannot be rotated because of missing key or damaged lock cylinder).

Removal – Disconnect negative battery cable. Remove upper and lower steering column covers. Turn lock cylinder to ACC position. Locate small hole in top of lock cylinder housing. Insert 1/8" drill bit or punch into hole. Press lock cylinder retaining pin inward while pulling lock cylinder from housing.

Installation – **1)** Rotate lock cylinder to ACC position. Press retaining pin inward, then insert lock cylinder into housing. Ensure lock cylinder is fully seated and aligned.

2) Rotate lock cylinder to OFF position. This allows retaining pin to extend into hole in housing. To complete installation, reverse removal procedure.

LOCK CYLINDER (NON-FUNCTIONAL)

NOTE: If lock cylinder is functional (key is available and lock cylinder turns freely), see LOCK CYLINDER (FUNCTIONAL) under REMOVAL & INSTALLATION.

Removal – Disconnect negative battery cable. Remove upper and lower steering column covers. Using a 1/8" bit, drill out retaining pin located on top of lock cylinder housing. DO NOT drill deeper than 1/2". Remove lock cylinder from lock cylinder housing. Remove metal shavings from cylinder housing. Replace housing if damaged.

Installation – **1)** Rotate lock cylinder to ACC position. Press retaining pin inward, then insert lock cylinder into housing. Ensure lock cylinder is fully seated and aligned.

2) Rotate lock cylinder to OFF position. This allows retaining pin to extend into hole in housing. To complete installation, reverse removal procedure.

TORQUE SPECIFICATIONS

TORQUE SPECIFICATIONS

Application	Ft. Lbs. (N.m)
Steering Wheel Bolt [1]	37 (50)

[1] – Use NEW bolt when installing steering wheel.

WIRING DIAGRAMS

NOTE: For ignition switch circuit identification, see appropriate wiring diagram in POWER DISTRIBUTION article in WIRING DIAGRAMS. For multifunction switch circuit identification, see appropriate wiring diagram in EXTERIOR LIGHTS article.

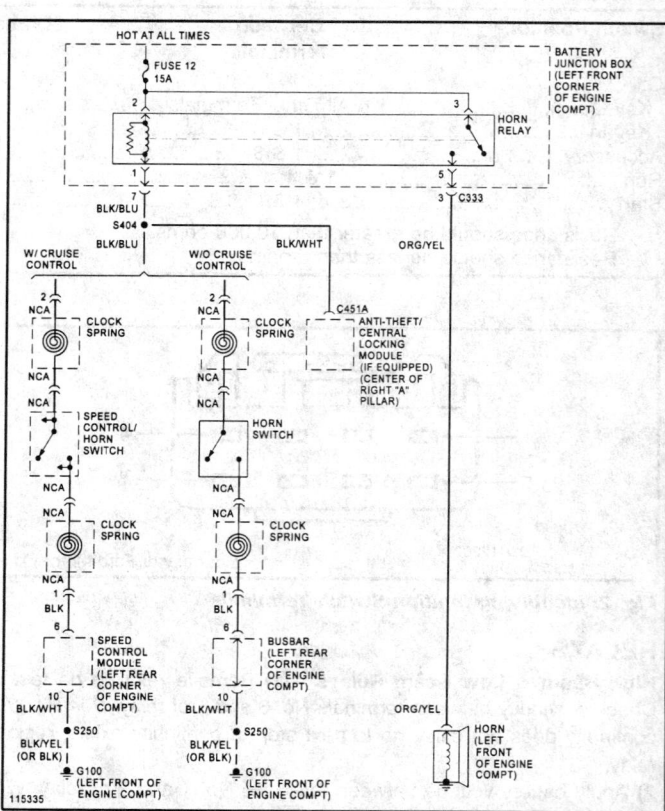

Fig. 5: Horn System Wiring Diagram (Contour & Mystique)

DESCRIPTION

WARNING: Deactivate air bag system before performing any service operation involving steering column components. See appropriate AIR BAG RESTRAINT SYSTEMS article. DO NOT apply electrical power to any component on steering column unless instructed to do so. Air bag may deploy.

Steering column switch consists of a multifunction switch, ignition switch and wiper/washer switch. The multifunction switch controls hazards, turn signals head light high beams and flash-to-pass feature.

TROUBLE SHOOTING

Before performing individual component tests, inspect for the following possible causes of system malfunction. Correct any obvious defects before proceeding:

- Mechanical Failure
- Low Battery Charge
- Faulty Fuses
- Loose Or Corroded Connectors
- Damaged Wiring

COMPONENT TESTS

CAUTION: When battery is disconnected, vehicle computer and memory system may lose memory data. Driveability problems may exist until computer systems have completed a relearn cycle. See COMPUTER RELEARN PROCEDURES article in GENERAL INFORMATION before disconnecting battery.

NOTE: For ignition switch circuit identification, see appropriate wiring diagram in POWER DISTRIBUTION article in WIRING DIAGRAMS. For multifunction switch circuit identification, see appropriate wiring diagram in EXTERIOR LIGHTS article.

MULTIFUNCTION SWITCH

Turn Signal Switch – Disconnect turn signal switch harness connector (remove turn signal switch if necessary). Remove turn signal relay. Check continuity between turn signal switch terminals with switch in appropriate position. See TURN SIGNAL SWITCH CONTINUITY table. *See Fig. 1.* If continuity is not as specified, replace turn signal switch.

TURN SIGNAL SWITCH CONTINUITY

Switch Position	Continuity Between Terminals
All Positions	7 & 31
Off	3 & 5; 7 & 31; 11 & 49
Right Turn	1, 9 & 49a
Left Turn	3, 8 & 49a
High Beam	2 & 5
Flash-To-Pass	2 & 4; 3 & 5
Hazard	8, 9 & 49a; 10 & 49

Wiper Switch – Disconnect wiper switch harness connector (remove wiper switch if necessary). Check continuity between wiper switch terminals with switch in appropriate position. See WIPER SWITCH CONTINUITY table. *See Fig. 2.* If continuity is not as specified, replace wiper switch.

WIPER SWITCH CONTINUITY

Switch Position	Continuity Between Terminals
Front Wiper	
Off	A & D
Single Wipe	A & H
Low	A & H
High	B & H
Intermittent	[1] A & D; E & H
Rear Wiper	
Off	G & I

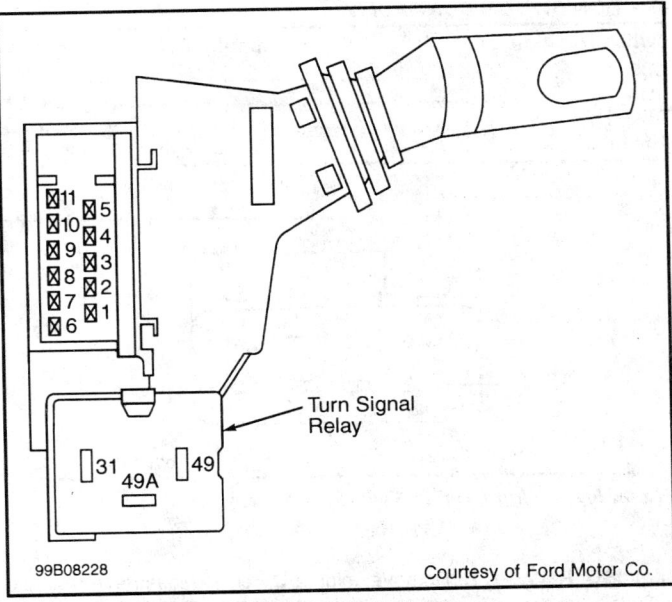

Fig. 1: Identifying Turn Signal Switch Terminals

WIPER SWITCH CONTINUITY (Cont.)

Switch Position	Continuity Between Terminals
On	G & H
Washer	
Off	H, I & K
Front	H & K; I & J
Rear	H & I; J & K

[1] – Resistance between terminals "E" and "F" should be one k/ohms at detent one, 10 k/ohms at detent 2, 20 k/ohms at detent 3, 30 k/ohms at detent 4, 40 k/ohms at detent 5, 47 k/ohms at detent 6.

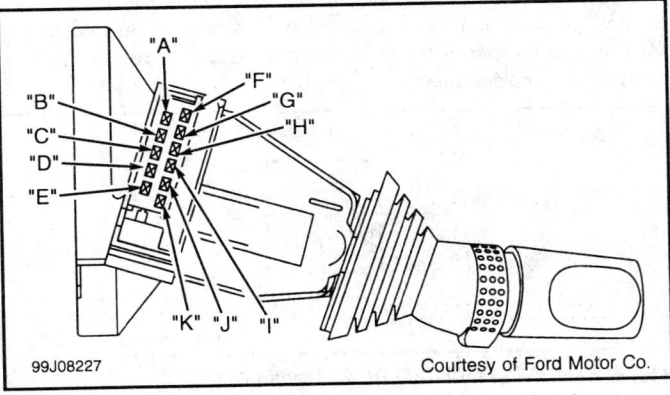

Fig. 2: Identifying Wiper Switch Terminals

HORN

Disconnect horn switch connector(s). Continuity should not exist between horn switch wires with horn button(s) released. Press horn button(s). Continuity should exist.

IGNITION SWITCH

Disconnect ignition switch harness connector (remove ignition switch if necessary). Check continuity between ignition switch terminals with switch in appropriate position. See IGNITION SWITCH CONTINUITY table. *See Fig. 3.* If continuity is not as specified, replace ignition switch.

IGNITION SWITCH CONTINUITY

Switch Position	Continuity Between Terminals
ACC	1 & 8
RUN	1, 4 & 8
START	1, 4 & 5; 6 & 7
Key In	1 & 3

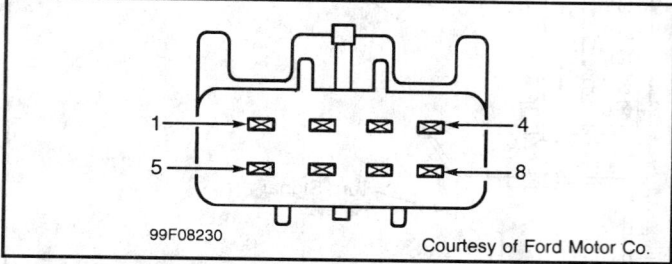

99F08230   Courtesy of Ford Motor Co.

Fig. 3: Identifying Ignition Switch Terminals

RELAYS

Mini ISO Relay – 1) Remove mini ISO relay. Measure resistance between appropriate relay terminals. See MINI ISO RELAY RESISTANCE SPECIFICATIONS table. *See Fig. 4.* If resistance is as specified, go to next step. If resistance is not as specified, replace relay.

MINI ISO RELAY RESISTANCE SPECIFICATIONS

Between Terminals	Resistance
85 & 86	50-100 Ohms
30 & 87a	5 Ohms Or Less
30 & 87	Greater Than 10 K/Ohms
30 & 86	Greater Than 10 K/Ohms
86 & 87a	Greater Than 10 K/Ohms
86 & 87	Greater Than 10 K/Ohms

2) Using a fused jumper wire, connect positive battery voltage to terminal No. 85. Using another jumper wire, ground terminal No. 86. Resistance should now be 5 ohms or less between terminals No. 30 and 87 and greater than 10 k/ohms between terminals 30 and 87a. If resistance is as specified, relay is okay at this time. If resistance is not as specified, replace relay.

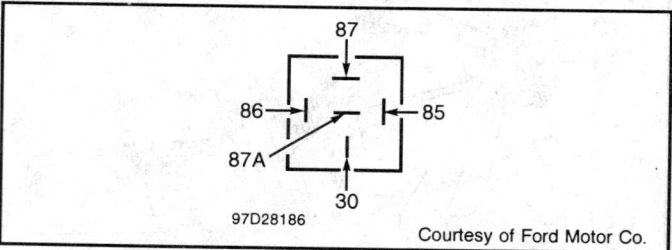

97D28186   Courtesy of Ford Motor Co.

Fig. 4: Identifying Mini ISO Relay Terminals

Micro ISO Relay – 1) Remove relay to be tested. Measure resistance between terminal No. 5 and all other terminals. *See Fig. 5.* If all resistance reading are greater than 5 ohms, go to next step. If any resistance reading is 5 ohms or less, replace relay.
2) Measure resistance between terminals No. 3 and 4. If resistance is 5 ohms or less, go to next step. If resistance is greater than 5 ohms, replace relay.
3) Apply battery voltage and ground between terminals No. 1 and 2. Measure resistance between terminals No. 3 and 5. Resistance should be 5 ohms or less. Measure resistance between terminals No. 3 and 4. Resistance should be greater than 5 ohms. If resistance is not as specified, replace relay. If resistance is as specified, relay is okay at this time.

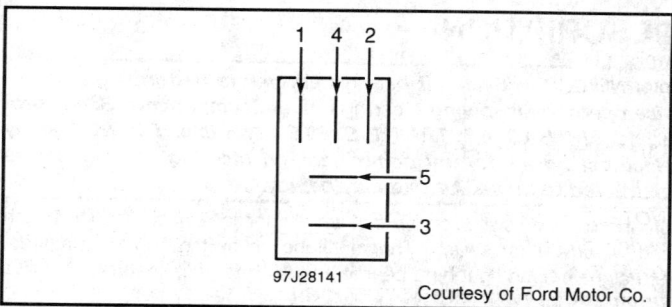

97J28141   Courtesy of Ford Motor Co.

Fig. 5: Identifying Micro ISO Relay Terminals

REMOVAL & INSTALLATION

WARNING: Deactivate air bag system before performing any service operation involving steering column components. See appropriate AIR BAG RESTRAINT SYSTEMS article. DO NOT apply electrical power to any component on steering column unless instructed to do so. Air bag may deploy.

CAUTION: When battery is disconnected, vehicle computer and memory system may lose memory data. Driveability problems may exist until computer systems have completed a relearn cycle. See COMPUTER RELEARN PROCEDURES article in GENERAL INFORMATION before disconnecting battery.

STEERING WHEEL

Removal & Installation – 1) Ensure front wheels are in straight-ahead position. Disconnect battery cables. Wait at least 2 minutes for air bag back-up power supply to deplete.
2) Remove air bag module retaining nuts/screws. Lift air bag module from steering wheel. Disconnect air bag harness connector from module. Disconnect cruise control switch harness connector (if equipped). Remove steering wheel bolt.
3) Remove steering wheel. To install, reverse removal procedure. Tighten steering wheel bolt to 37 Ft. Lbs. (50 N.m). Check AIR BAG light to verify proper system operation.

MULTIFUNCTION SWITCH

Turn Signal Switch (Removal & Installation) – Disconnect negative battery cable. Wait at least 2 minutes for air bag back-up power supply to deplete. Remove upper and lower steering column covers. Depress switch locking tab. Slide switch outward from steering column. Disconnect harness connector. Remove switch from housing. To install, reverse removal procedure.
Wiper Switch (Removal & Installation) – Disconnect negative battery cable. Wait at least 2 minutes for air bag back-up power supply to deplete. Remove upper and lower steering column covers. Depress switch locking tab. Slide switch outward from steering column. Disconnect harness connector. Remove switch from housing. To install, reverse removal procedure.

IGNITION SWITCH

Removal & Installation – Disconnect negative battery cable. Wait at least 2 minutes for air bag back-up power supply to deplete. Remove lower steering column cover. Disconnect ignition switch harness connector. Remove ignition switch retaining screws. Remove ignition switch. To install, reverse removal procedure.

LOCK CYLINDER

Removal & Installation – Disconnect negative battery cable. Remove upper and lower steering column covers. Disconnect Passive Anti-Theft System (PATS) transceiver harness connector. Remove PATS transceiver retaining screws. Remove PATS transceiver. Turn ignition switch to ACC position. Locate small hole in top of lock cylinder housing. Insert

1/8" drill bit or punch into hole. Press lock cylinder retaining pin inward while pulling lock cylinder from housing. To install, reverse removal procedure.

WIRING DIAGRAMS

NOTE: For ignition switch circuit identification, see appropriate wiring diagram in POWER DISTRIBUTION article in WIRING DIAGRAMS. For multifunction switch circuit identification, see appropriate wiring diagram in EXTERIOR LIGHTS article.

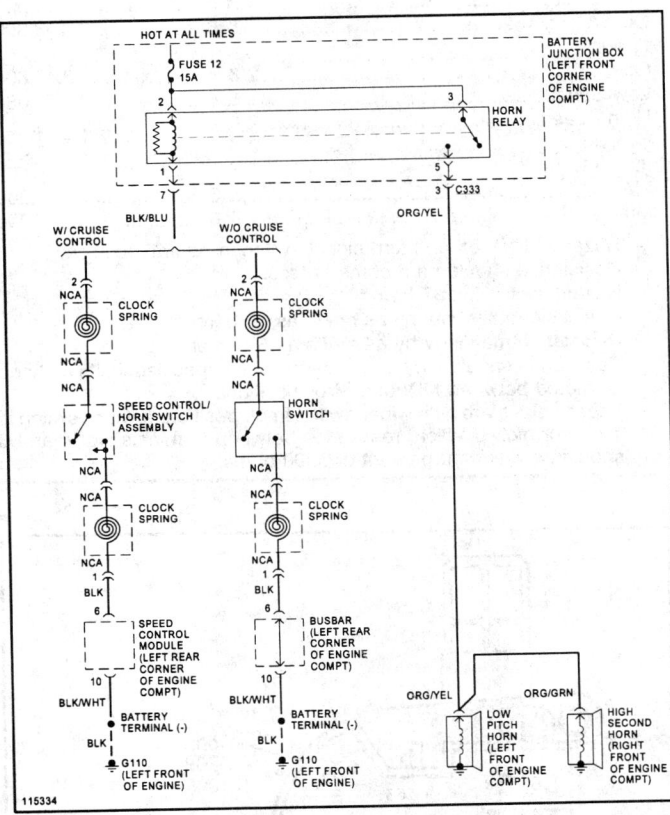

Fig. 6: Horn System Wiring Diagram (Cougar)

1999 ACCESSORIES & EQUIPMENT
Steering Column Switches
Crown Victoria & Grand Marquis

DESCRIPTION & OPERATION

WARNING: Deactivate air bag system before performing any service operation involving steering column components. See appropriate AIR BAG RESTRAINT SYSTEMS article. DO NOT apply electrical power to any component on steering column without first deactivating air bag system. Air bag may deploy.

Switches mounted on the steering column are the ignition switch, horn switch, multifunction switch and cruise control switches. Driver's side air bag is located on center of steering wheel.

COMPONENT LOCATIONS

COMPONENT LOCATIONS

Component	Location
Data Link Connector	Behind Left Side Of Instrument Panel
Lighting Control Module	Behind Instrument Panel, Right Of Steering Column
Power Distribution Box	Right Front Of Engine Compartment Next To Battery
Powertrain Control Module	Left Rear Corner Of Engine Compartment, In Firewall

TROUBLE SHOOTING

Before performing individual component tests and/or system tests, inspect fuses No. 1, 4, 7, 13 and 15 in instrument panel fuse box. Inspect fuses No. 2, 9 and 10 in power distribution box. Check for mechanical failure, low battery charge, faulty circuit breaker No. 14, loose or corroded connectors and damaged wiring. If no problem exists, perform self-diagnostics. See SELF-DIAGNOSTIC SYSTEM.

COMPONENT TESTS

CAUTION: When battery is disconnected, vehicle computer and memory system may lose memory data. Driveability problems may exist until computer systems have completed a relearn cycle. See COMPUTER RELEARN PROCEDURES article in GENERAL INFORMATION before disconnecting battery.

NOTE: Before performing following tests, ensure all multifunction switch grounds, wiring, and fuses are okay. Also, ensure all circuit connections are clean and tight. For ignition switch circuit identification, see appropriate wiring diagram in POWER DISTRIBUTION article in WIRING DIAGRAMS. For multifunction switch circuit identification, see appropriate wiring diagram in EXTERIOR LIGHTS article.

MULTIFUNCTION SWITCH

Disconnect multifunction switch harness connectors. Set hazard flasher switch to OFF position unless specified otherwise. Measure resistance between terminals with switch in specified position. See MULTIFUNCTION SWITCH RESISTANCE table. *See Fig. 1.* If resistance is not as specified, or is poor in any switch position, replace multifunction switch.

MULTIFUNCTION SWITCH RESISTANCE

Switch Position	Terminals	Ohms
Brakelight Feed		
Through [1]	2, 9 &10	[2]
Flash-To-Pass On	1 & 3; 5 & 7	[2]
Hazard Switch		
Off	1 & 11	[2]
On	4 & 11; 2, 5, 6 & 10	[2]

MULTIFUNCTION SWITCH RESISTANCE (Cont.)

Switch Position	Terminals	Ohms
Headlight Dimmer		
High Beam	1 & 5	[2]
Low Beam	1 & 3	[2]
Turn Signals [3]		
Left Turn	6, 8 & 10	[2]
Left Cornering Light	1 & 7	[2]
Right Turn	2, 5 & 6	[2]
Right Cornering Light	1 & 3	[2]
Washer		
On	4 & 6	[2]
Off	4 & 6	[4] 103,300
Wipers		
Off	2 & 4	[5] 47,600
Low Speed	2 & 4	[5] 4080
High Speed	2 & 4	[5]
Interval	2 & 4	[5] 11,330
Interval Delay [6] [7]		
MAX	4 & 6	[4] 103,300
MIN	4 & 6	[4] 3300

[1] – Hazard switch off and turn signal switch in neutral position.
[2] – Resistance should be 5 ohms or less.
[3] – Hazard switch MUST be off.
[4] – Resistance may vary by as much as 10 percent.
[5] – Resistance may vary by as much as 5 percent.
[6] – Resistance should vary smoothly between specified limits as knob is rotated between MIN and MAX positions.
[7] – These values are with wiper switch in off position. If wiper switch is in low or high position, resistance between terminals No. 4 and 6 should be within 10 percent of 3300 ohms.

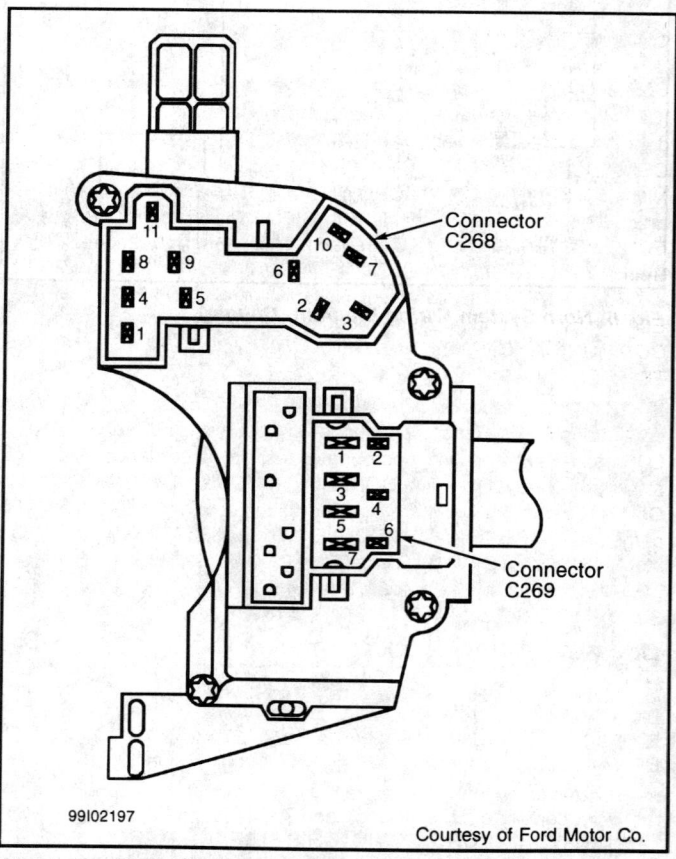

99I02197

Courtesy of Ford Motor Co.

Fig. 1: Identifying Multifunction Switch Circuit Terminals

1999 ACCESSORIES & EQUIPMENT
Steering Column Switches
Crown Victoria & Grand Marquis (Cont.)

FORD
4-1259

HEADLIGHT SWITCH

See appropriate INSTRUMENT PANELS article.

IGNITION SWITCH

Disconnect ignition switch harness connector. Check for continuity between specified terminals with switch in each position. See IGNITION SWITCH CONTINUITY table. *See Fig. 2.* If continuity is not as specified, replace ignition switch.

IGNITION SWITCH CONTINUITY

Switch Position	Continuity Between Terminals
Accessory	A1 & B5
Run	A1 & B1; A2 & B2; A3 & B3; A4 & B4; B5 & I1
Start	B5 & I1; B4 & STA; P2 & GND

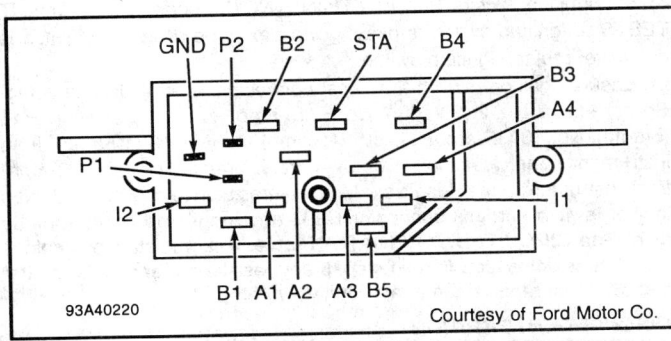

93A40220   Courtesy of Ford Motor Co.

Fig. 2: Identifying Ignition Switch Terminals

SELF-DIAGNOSTIC SYSTEM

Connect New Generation Star (NGS) tester to Data Link Connector (DLC), located beneath instrument panel. Using NGS tester, perform data link diagnostics test. See DATA LINK DIAGNOSTIC TEST under COMMUNICATION NETWORK DIAGNOSTICS in MODULE COMMUNICATIONS NETWORK – CROWN VICTORIA & GRAND MARQUIS article. If NGS tester responds with CKT914, CKT915 or CKT70=ALL ECUS NO RESP/NOT EQUIP, repair module communications concern. See MODULE COMMUNICATIONS NETWORK – CROWN VICTORIA & GRAND MARQUIS article. If NGS tester displays NO RESP/NOT EQUIP for Lighting Control Module (LCM), perform TEST A: NO COMMUNICATION WITH LIGHTING CONTROL MODULE under SYSTEM TESTS.

If NGS tester responds with SYSTEM PASSED, retrieve and record continuous DTCs. Erase continuous DTCs. Using NGS tester, perform LCM self-test. Perform appropriate test in accordance with DTC retrieved. See LIGHTING CONTROL MODULE DTC INDEX table. Codes listed in this table are only for testing covered in this article. For complete DTC listing, see MODULE COMMUNICATIONS NETWORK – CROWN VICTORIA & GRAND MARQUIS article. If no DTCs are retrieved, repair by symptom. See SYMPTOM CHART table under SYSTEM TESTS.

LIGHTING CONTROL MODULE DTC INDEX

DTC [1]	Description	Test
B1342	ECU Defective	[2]
B1359	Ignition RUN/ACC Input Circuit Failure	F
B1555	Ignition RUN/START Circuit Failure	G

[1] – Codes listed in this table are only for testing covered in this article. For complete DTC listing, see MODULE COMMUNICATIONS NETWORK – CROWN VICTORIA & GRAND MARQUIS article.

[2] – Using NGS tester, retrieve and document all continuous DTCs. Perform Lighting Control Module (LCM) self-test. If DTC B1342 is retrieved again, replace LCM.

SYSTEM TESTS

SYMPTOM CHART

Symptom	Test
No Communication With Lighting Control Module	A
Ignition Switch Inoperative	B
No Power In ACC Position	C
No Power In RUN Position	D
No Power In START Position	E
Ignition RUN/ACC Circuit Failure (DTC B1359)	F
Ignition RUN/START Circuit Failure (DTC B1555)	G
Automatic Parking Brake Release Inoperative	H

TEST A: NO COMMUNICATION WITH LIGHTING CONTROL MODULE

1) Turn ignition switch to RUN position. Using NGS tester, monitor Lighting Control Module (LCM) PID IGN_LC. If NGS tester does not indicate UNABLE TO PERFORM TEST FUNCTION, MODULE NOT RESPONDING, CHECK IGNITION STATUS/VERIFY CABLE REQUIREMENTS, OR CHECK CABLE CONNECTIONS, go to next step. If NGS tester indicates UNABLE TO PERFORM TEST FUNCTION, MODULE NOT RESPONDING, CHECK IGNITION STATUS/ VERIFY CABLE REQUIREMENTS, OR CHECK CABLE CONNECTIONS, go to step **11**).

2) Turn ignition switch to RUN position. Using NGS tester, monitor LCM PID IGN_LC while rotating ignition switch through ACCY, OFF and RUN positions. If PID indicates START while ignition switch is in RUN position, go to next step. If PID indicates RUN while ignition switch is in RUN position, go to step **12**). If PID indicates ACCY while ignition switch is in RUN position, go to step **7**).

3) Turn ignition switch to LOCK position. Remove fuse No. 6 (15-amp) from instrument panel fuse box. Check fuse. If fuse is okay, go to next step. If fuse is blown, go to step **6**).

4) Turn ignition switch to RUN position. Measure voltage at input side of fuse No. 6 in instrument panel fuse box. If battery voltage exists, go to next step. If battery voltage does not exist, repair power supply to fuse No. 6. See appropriate wiring diagram in POWER DISTRIBUTION article in WIRING DIAGRAMS.

5) Turn ignition switch to LOCK position. Install fuse No. 6. Disconnect LCM harness connector C2027. Turn ignition switch to RUN position. Measure voltage at terminal No. 1 (White/Violet wire) at LCM harness connector C2027. *See Fig. 3.* If battery voltage exists, replace LCM. If battery voltage does not exist, repair open in White/Violet wire.

6) Turn ignition switch to LOCK position. Disconnect Lighting Control Module (LCM) harness connector C2027. Measure resistance between ground and terminal No. 1 (White/Violet wire) at LCM harness connector C2027. *See Fig. 3 .* If resistance is greater than 10 k/ohms, replace LCM. If resistance is 10 k/ohms or less, repair short to ground in White/Violet wire.

7) Turn ignition switch to LOCK position. Remove fuse No. 13 (15-amp) from instrument panel fuse box. Check fuse. If fuse is okay, go to next step. If fuse is blown, go to step **10**).

8) Turn ignition switch to RUN position. Measure voltage at input side of fuse No. 13 in instrument panel fuse box. If battery voltage exists, go to next step. If battery voltage does not exist, repair power supply to fuse No. 13. See appropriate wiring diagram in POWER DISTRIBUTION article in WIRING DIAGRAMS.

9) Turn ignition switch to LOCK position. Install fuse No. 13 (15-amp). Disconnect LCM harness connector C2027. Turn ignition switch to RUN position. Measure voltage at terminal No. 9 (Red/Yellow wire) at LCM 16-pin connector C2027. *See Fig. 3.* If battery voltage exists, replace LCM. If battery voltage does not exist, repair open in Red/Yellow wire.

10) Turn ignition switch to LOCK position. Disconnect LCM harness connector C2027. Measure resistance between ground and terminal No. 9 (Red/Yellow wire) at LCM harness connector C2027. *See Fig. 3.* If resistance is greater than 10 k/ohms, replace LCM. If resistance is 10 k/ohms or less, repair short to ground in Red/Yellow wire.

FORD
4-1260

1999 ACCESSORIES & EQUIPMENT
Steering Column Switches
Crown Victoria & Grand Marquis (Cont.)

11) Turn ignition switch to LOCK position. Disconnect LCM harness connector C2029. Measure resistance between ground and terminals No. 4 and 9 (both Black wire) at LCM harness connector C2029. See Fig. 4. If either resistance reading is greater than 5 ohms, repair open in appropriate Black wire(s). If both resistance readings are 5 ohms or less, repair module communication concern. See MODULE COMMUNICATIONS NETWORK – CROWN VICTORIA & GRAND MARQUIS article.

12) Turn ignition switch to LOCK position. Disconnect LCM harness connector C2029. Measure voltage at terminal No. 6 (Tan/White wire) at LCM harness connector C2029. See Fig. 4. If battery voltage does not exist, go to next step. If battery voltage exists, go to step **16**).

13) Remove fuse No. 4 (15-amp) from instrument panel fuse box. Measure resistance between ground and terminal No. 6 (Tan/White wire) at LCM harness connector C2029. If resistance is greater than 10 k/ohms, go to next step. If resistance is 10 k/ohms or less, repair short to ground in Tan/White wire and replace fuse.

14) Measure voltage at input side of fuse No. 4 in instrument panel fuse box. If battery voltage exists, go to next step. If battery voltage does not exist, repair power distribution circuit. See appropriate wiring diagram in POWER DISTRIBUTION article in WIRING DIAGRAMS.

15) Measure resistance in Tan/White wire between output side of fuse No. 4 and terminal No. 6 at LCM harness connector C2029. If resistance is 5 ohms or less, system is okay at this time. If resistance is greater than 5 ohms, repair open in Tan/White wire.

16) Measure voltage at terminal No. 11 (Light Green/Yellow wire) at LCM harness connector C2029. If battery voltage does not exist, go to next step. If battery voltage exists, go to step **20**).

17) Remove fuse No. 8 (15-amp) from instrument panel fuse box. Measure resistance between ground and terminal No. 11 (Light Green/Yellow wire) at LCM harness connector C2029. If resistance is greater than 10 k/ohms, go to next step. If resistance is 10 k/ohms or less, repair short to ground in Light Green/Yellow wire and replace fuse.

18) Measure voltage at input side of fuse No. 8. If battery voltage exists, go to next step. If battery voltage does not exist, repair power distribution circuit. See appropriate wiring diagram in POWER DISTRIBUTION article in WIRING DIAGRAMS.

19) Measure resistance in Light Green/Yellow wire between output side of fuse No. 8 and terminal No. 11 at LCM harness connector C2029. If resistance is 5 ohms or less, system is okay at this time. If resistance is greater than 5 ohms, repair open in Light Green/Yellow wire.

20) Measure resistance between ground and terminal No. 9 (Black wire) at LCM harness connector C2029. If resistance is 5 ohms or less, repair communication concern. See MODULE COMMUNICATIONS NETWORK – CROWN VICTORIA & GRAND MARQUIS article. If resistance is greater than 5 ohms, repair open in Black wire.

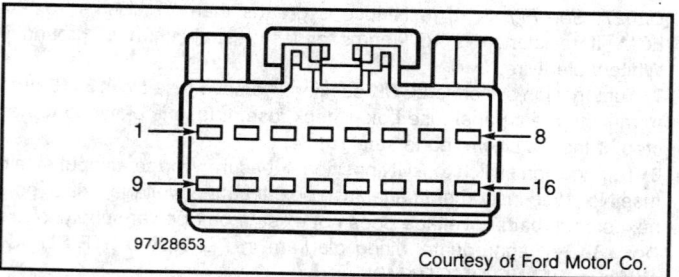

Fig. 3: Identifying Lighting Control Module Harness Connector C2027 Terminals

TEST B: IGNITION SWITCH INOPERATIVE

1) Turn ignition switch to LOCK position. Disconnect ignition switch harness connector C292. Measure voltage at terminals B1 (Brown wire), B2 (Light Green wire), B3 (Light Green wire), B4 (Yellow wire) and B5 (Brown wire) at ignition switch harness connector. See Fig. 5. If battery voltage does not exist at any terminal, go to next step. If battery voltage exists at all terminals, go to step .

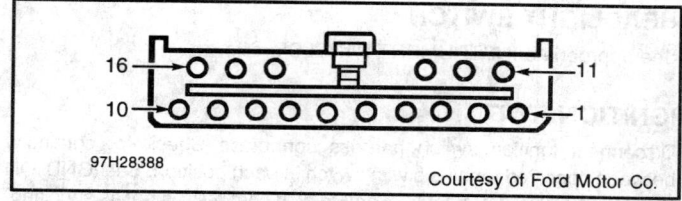

Courtesy of Ford Motor Co.

Fig. 4: Identifying Lighting Control Module Harness Connector C2029 Terminals

2) Remove maxi fuses No. 9 (50-amp) and No. 10 (50-amp) from power distribution box. Measure resistance between ground and output side of maxi fuses No. 9 and 10. If both resistance readings are greater than 10 k/ohms, go to next step. If either resistance reading is 10 k/ohms or less, repair short to ground in appropriate wire. See appropriate wiring diagram in POWER DISTRIBUTION article in WIRING DIAGRAMS.

3) Test ignition switch. See IGNITION SWITCH under COMPONENT TESTS. If ignition switch is okay, go to next step. If ignition switch is defective, replace ignition switch.

4) Ensure ignition switch harness connector is still disconnected. Remove fuses No. 2 (30-amp), No. 6 (15-amp), No. 7 (25-amp), No. 11 (5-amp), No. 13 (15-amp), No. 15 (10-amp) and No. 18 (10-amp), from instrument panel fuse box. Remove circuit breaker No. 14 (20-amp) from instrument panel fuse box. Measure resistance in wires between ignition switch harness connector C292 and input side of appropriate fuse. See CIRCUIT IDENTIFICATION table. If all resistance readings are 5 ohms or less, go to next step. If any resistance reading is greater than 5 ohms, repair open in appropriate wire(s).

CIRCUIT IDENTIFICATION

Switch Terminal	Wire Color	Fuse No.
A1	Black/Light Green	1
A4	Black/Pink	15 & 18
I1	Black/Pink	7 & 13

1 – Fuses No. 2, 6 and 11 and circuit breaker No. 14.

5) Measure resistance between ground and terminal at ignition switch harness connector. See CIRCUIT IDENTIFICATION table. If any resistance reading is 10 k/ohms or less, repair short to ground in appropriate wire. If all resistance readings are greater than 10 k/ohms, system is okay at this time. Check for poor connections and/or intermittent shorts/opens.

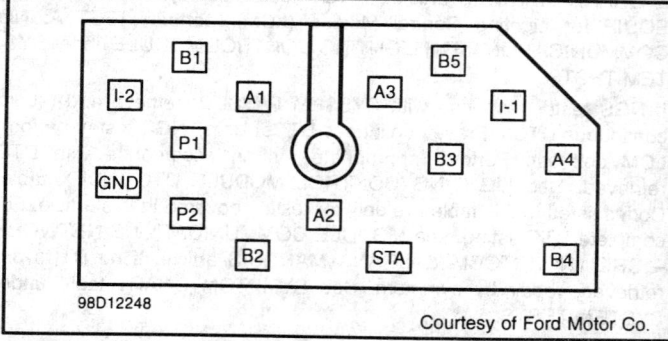

Courtesy of Ford Motor Co.

Fig. 5: Identifying Ignition Switch Harness Connector C292 Terminals

TEST C: NO POWER IN ACC POSITION

1) Test ignition switch. See IGNITION SWITCH under COMPONENT TESTS. If ignition switch is okay, go to next step. If ignition switch is defective, replace ignition switch.

2) Ensure ignition switch is installed and harness connector is connected. Remove fuses No. 2 (30-amp), No. 6 (15-amp) and No. 11 (5-amp) from instrument panel fuse box. Remove circuit breaker No. 14 (20-amp) from instrument panel fuse box. Turn ignition switch to RUN

1999 ACCESSORIES & EQUIPMENT
Steering Column Switches
Crown Victoria & Grand Marquis (Cont.)

FORD
4-1261

position. Measure voltage at input side of fuses just removed. If battery voltage exists to all fuses, replace appropriate fuse(s). If battery voltage does not exist, repair open in appropriate wire(s).

TEST D: NO POWER IN RUN POSITION

1) Test ignition switch. See IGNITION SWITCH under COMPONENT TESTS. If ignition switch is okay, go to next step. If ignition switch is defective, replace ignition switch.

2) Ensure ignition switch is installed and harness connector is connected. Remove fuses No. 2 (30-amp), No. 5 (15-amp), No. 6 (15-amp), No. 7 (25-amp), No. 11 (5-amp), No. 13 (15-amp), No. 9 (30-amp), No. 15 (10-amp) and No. 18 (10-amp) in instrument panel fuse box. Remove circuit breaker No. 14 (20-amp) from instrument panel fuse box. Turn ignition switch to RUN position. Measure voltage at input side of fuses just removed. If battery voltage exists to all fuses, replace appropriate fuse(s). If battery voltage does not exist, repair open in appropriate wire(s).

TEST E: NO POWER IN START POSITION

Test ignition switch. See IGNITION SWITCH under COMPONENT TESTS. If ignition switch is okay, repair open in White/Pink wire. If ignition switch is defective, replace ignition switch.

TEST F: IGNITION RUN/ACC CIRCUIT FAILURE (DTC B1359)

1) Connect New Generation Star (NGS) tester to Data Link Connector (DLC). Access Lighting Control Module (LCM) PID IGN_LCM. Monitor NGS display while turning ignition switch to all positions. If PID does not agree with ignition switch position, go to next step. If PID agrees with ignition switch position, replace LCM.

2) Turn ignition switch to LOCK position. Disconnect LCM harness connector C2027. Measure resistance between ground and terminal No. 1 (White/Pink wire) at LCM harness connector C2027. *See Fig. 3.* If resistance is greater than 10 k/ohms, repair open in White/Pink wire. If resistance is 10 k/ohms or less, repair short to ground in White/Pink wire and replace fuse No. 6 (15-amp) in instrument panel fuse box.

TEST G: IGNITION RUN/START CIRCUIT FAILURE (DTC B1555)

1) Connect New Generation Star (NGS) tester to Data Link Connector (DLC). Access Lighting Control Module (LCM) PID IGN_LCM. Monitor NGS display while turning ignition switch to all positions. If PID does not agree with ignition switch position, go to next step. If PID agrees with ignition switch position, replace LCM.

2) Turn ignition switch to LOCK position. Disconnect LCM harness connector C2027. Measure resistance between ground and terminal No. 9 (Red/Yellow wire) at LCM harness connector C2027. *See Fig. 3.* If resistance is greater than 10 k/ohms, repair open in Red/Yellow wire. If resistance is 10 k/ohms or less, repair short to ground in Red/Yellow wire and replace fuse No. 13 (15-amp) in instrument panel fuse box.

TEST H: AUTOMATIC PARKING BRAKE RELEASE INOPERATIVE

NOTE: Parking brake release vacuum switch is attached to top of steering column. Manufacturer says switch is adjustable but does not supply adjusting procedures.

1) Apply parking brake. Check for disconnected vacuum lines. Check vacuum hoses for leaks and cracks. If problem does not exist, go to next step. If problem exists, repair as necessary.

2) Disconnect vacuum source hose at right side of steering column. *See Fig. 6.* Connect vacuum gauge to disconnected vacuum source hose. Start engine. If vacuum exists, go to next step. If vacuum does not exist, repair vacuum supply as necessary.

3) Connect vacuum source hose. Turn ignition switch to LOCK position. Disconnect vacuum hose from release actuator on parking brake pedal

bracket. Connect vacuum gauge to disconnected vacuum source hose. Start engine. Shift transmission into Drive. If vacuum exists, replace release actuator. If vacuum does not exist, adjust and/or replace parking brake release vacuum switch as necessary.

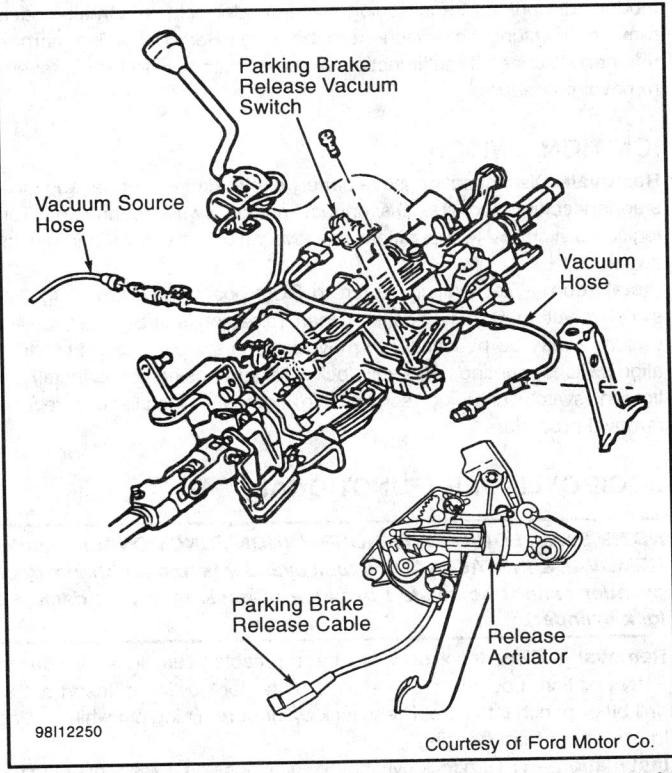

Fig. 6: Identifying Automatic Parking Brake Release Components

REMOVAL & INSTALLATION

CAUTION: When battery is disconnected, vehicle computer and memory system may lose memory data. Driveability problems may exist until computer systems have completed a relearn cycle. See COMPUTER RELEARN PROCEDURES article in GENERAL INFORMATION before disconnecting battery.

STEERING WHEEL

WARNING: Deactivate air bag system before performing any service operation involving steering column components. See appropriate AIR BAG RESTRAINT SYSTEMS article. DO NOT apply electrical power to any component on steering column without first deactivating air bag system. Air bag may deploy.

Removal & Installation – 1) Ensure front wheels are in straight-ahead position. Disable air bag system. See appropriate AIR BAG RESTRAINT SYSTEMS article. Wait at least one minute for air bag back-up power supply to deplete.

2) Remove air bag module retaining nuts/screws. Lift air bag module from steering wheel. Disconnect air bag wiring harness from module. Disconnect cruise control switch connector (if equipped). Remove and discard steering wheel bolt.

3) Remove steering wheel. While removing steering wheel, guide wiring harnesses through steering wheel. To install, reverse removal procedure. Install NEW steering wheel bolt and tighten to specification. Check AIR BAG light to verify proper system operation.

MULTIFUNCTION SWITCH

Removal & Installation – 1) Disconnect negative battery cable. On models with tilt wheel, adjust steering wheel to lowest position, then

FORD
4-1262

1999 ACCESSORIES & EQUIPMENT
Steering Column Switches
Crown Victoria & Grand Marquis (Cont.)

remove tilt lever. On all models, remove lock cylinder. See LOCK CYLINDER (FUNCTIONAL) or LOCK CYLINDER (NON-FUNCTIONAL).

2) Remove upper and lower steering column covers. On column shift models, disconnect transmission shift indicator column. On all models, remove multifunction switch from housing. Remove wiring harness retainer. Disconnect multifunction switch connectors. To install, reverse removal procedure.

IGNITION SWITCH

Removal – Disconnect negative battery cable. Remove upper and lower steering column covers. Disconnect ignition switch connector. Turn ignition switch to RUN position. Remove retaining screws and ignition switch.

Installation – Set ignition switch to RUN position by turning ignition switch shaft to START position, then releasing shaft. Install ignition switch. It may be necessary to move ignition switch back and forth to align switch mounting holes with lock cylinder housing holes. Install and tighten switch retaining screws. To complete installation, reverse removal procedure.

LOCK CYLINDER (FUNCTIONAL)

NOTE: See LOCK CYLINDER (NON-FUNCTIONAL) under REMOVAL & INSTALLATION if lock cylinder is non-functional (lock cylinder cannot be rotated because of missing key or damaged lock cylinder).

Removal – Disconnect negative battery cable. Turn lock cylinder to RUN position. Locate hole in shroud under lock cylinder. Insert a 1/8" drill bit or punch into hole. Press lock cylinder retaining pin while pulling lock cylinder from housing.

Installation – 1) Turn lock cylinder to RUN position. Press retaining pin inward and insert lock cylinder into housing. Ensure lock cylinder is fully seated and aligned with interlocking washer.

2) Rotate lock cylinder to OFF position. This allows retaining pin to extend into hole in housing. To install remaining components, reverse removal procedure.

LOCK CYLINDER (NON-FUNCTIONAL)

NOTE: If lock cylinder is functional (key is available and lock cylinder turns freely), see LOCK CYLINDER (FUNCTIONAL) under REMOVAL & INSTALLATION.

Removal & Installation – 1) Disconnect negative battery cable. Disable air bag system. See appropriate AIR BAG RESTRAINT SYSTEMS article. Remove steering wheel. See STEERING WHEEL. Using a 1/8" bit, drill out retaining pin located below lock cylinder on housing. DO NOT drill deeper than 1/2".

2) Using channel lock pliers, twist lock cylinder cap until it separates from lock cylinder. Using a 3/8" drill bit, drill down center of ignition lock key slot about 1 3/4" until lock cylinder breaks loose from its base.

3) Remove retainer, washer, and lock cylinder gear from housing. Remove metal shavings from lock cylinder bore. Replace housing if damaged. To install, reverse removal procedure. Connect negative battery cable. Check AIR BAG light for proper system operation.

TORQUE SPECIFICATIONS

TORQUE SPECIFICATIONS

Application	Ft. Lbs. (N.m)
Steering Wheel Bolt [1]	23-33 (31-45)

[1] – Use NEW bolt when installing steering wheel.

WIRING DIAGRAMS

NOTE: For ignition switch circuit identification, see appropriate wiring diagram in POWER DISTRIBUTION article in WIRING DIAGRAMS. For multifunction switch circuit identification, see appropriate wiring diagram in EXTERIOR LIGHTS article.

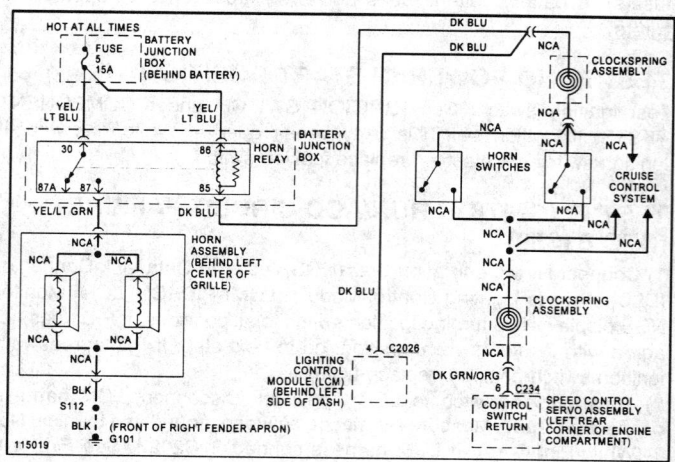

Fig. 7: Horn System Wiring Diagram (Crown Victoria & Grand Marquis)

NOTE: This article includes Cutaway and RV Cutaway.

DESCRIPTION

The multifunction switch, located on the steering column, includes headlight dimmer, flash-to-pass and front windshield wiper/washer switches. The ignition switch and lock cylinder are also mounted on the steering column.

WARNING: Deactivate air bag system before performing any service operation involving steering column components. See AIR BAG RESTRAINT SYSTEMS – ECONOLINE article. Do not apply electrical power to any component on steering column without first deactivating air bag system. Air bag may deploy.

COMPONENT LOCATIONS

COMPONENT LOCATIONS

Component	Location
Air Bag Diagnostic Monitor [1]	Behind Right Kick Panel
Air Bag Sliding Contact	Top Of Steering Column
Auxiliary Powertrain Control Module	Below Left Side Of Instrument Panel
Chime Module	Behind Center Of Instrument Cluster
Data Link Connector	Below Driver's Side Of Instrument Panel, To Right Of Steering Column
Ignition Switch	On Bottom Side At Base Of Steering Column
Multifunction Switch	Left Side At Top Of Steering Column
Powertrain Control Module	Left Rear Of Engine Compartment, Near Brake Master Cylinder

[1] – Air bag diagnostic monitor may also be referred to as Electronic Crash Sensor (ECS) module.

TROUBLE SHOOTING

Check the following items before proceeding with SYSTEM TESTING:
- Fuse No. 4 (15-amp), No. 9 (30-amp) and No. 10 (20-amp) in instrument panel fuse panel.
- Fuse No. 15 (40-amp) in engine compartment Power Distribution Center (PDC).
- Loose or damaged harness connectors.
- Damaged ignition switch.
- Damaged multifunction switch.

COMPONENT TESTS

DIMMER, FLASH-TO-PASS, TURN SIGNAL & HAZARD SWITCH

Remove and disconnect multifunction switch. See MULTIFUNCTION SWITCH under REMOVAL & INSTALLATION. Check continuity between specified circuits while operating multifunction switch lever to positions as specified. *See Fig. 1.* See DIMMER & TURN SIGNAL SWITCH TESTING table. If continuity is not as specified, replace multifunction switch.

DIMMER & TURN SIGNAL SWITCH TESTING

Switch Position	Check For Continuity Between Circuits No.
Left Turn Signal On & Hazard Switch Off	3, 9, & 44
Right Turn Signal On & Hazard Switch Off	2, 5 & 44
Hazard Switch On	2, 3, 5, 9 & 44
Turn Signal Neutral (Off) & Hazard Switch Off	5, 9 & 511
Flash-To-Pass On	12 & 196

DIMMER & TURN SIGNAL SWITCH TESTING (Cont.)

Switch Position	Check For Continuity Between Circuits No.
Headlight Dimmer	
On High Beam	12 & 15
On Low Beam	13 & 15

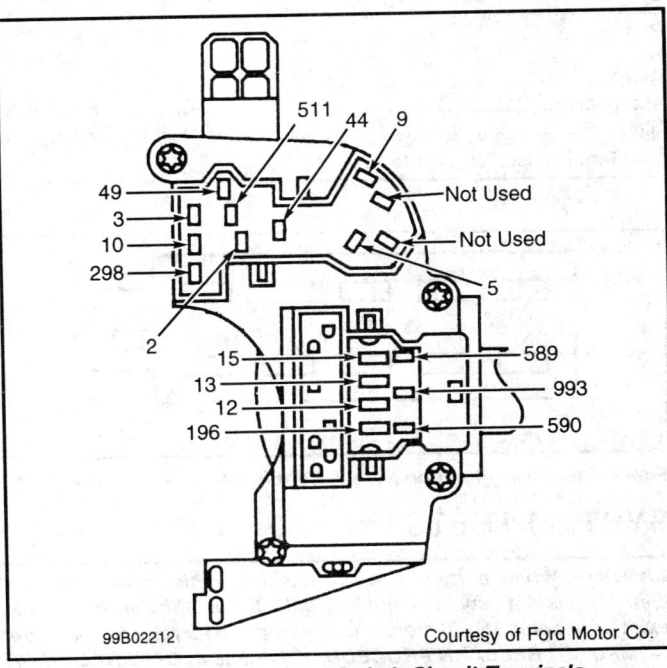

Fig. 1: Identifying Multifunction Switch Circuit Terminals

WIPER/WASHER SWITCH

Remove and disconnect multifunction switch. See MULTIFUNCTION SWITCH under REMOVAL & INSTALLATION. Measure resistance between specified circuits while operating multifunction switch lever to positions as specified. *See Fig. 1.* See WIPER/WASHER SWITCH TESTING table. If continuity is not as specified, replace multifunction switch.

WIPER/WASHER SWITCH TESTING

Switch Position	Circuits No.	[1] Ohms
Wiper Switch		
Off	589 & 993	47,600
Int	589 & 993	11,330
Lo	589 & 993	4080
Hi	589 & 993	0-4
Washer Switch On	590 & 993	0-4
Wiper Intermittent	590 & 993	[2]

[1] – Specification can vary by as much as 10 percent.
[2] – Rotate control from maximum delay to minimum delay. Resistance should gradually decrease from approximately 103 k/ohms to 3.3 k/ohms.

IGNITION SWITCH

1) To inspect ignition switch for mechanical operation, rotate lock cylinder through all switch positions. Lock cylinder should not bind, and should return from START to RUN position without assistance.
2) If binding or incorrect modes occur, lock cylinder should either be disassembled and inspected for damage, or ignition switch should be replaced.
3) To test electrical function of ignition switch, disconnect ignition switch connector. Test switch continuity using a self-powered test light or

ohmmeter. See IGNITION SWITCH CONTINUITY TEST table. If continuity is not as specified, replace ignition switch. *See Fig. 2* for switch terminal identification.

IGNITION SWITCH CONTINUITY TEST

Switch Position	Continuity Between Terminals
All	BATT & BATT
All	A2 & A2
Start	BATT & ST
Run	[1] ATT & A2
Run	BATT & I1
Start	BATT & I2
Accessory	BATT & A1
Start	P1, P2 & Switch Case

[1] – Terminal located next to P2.

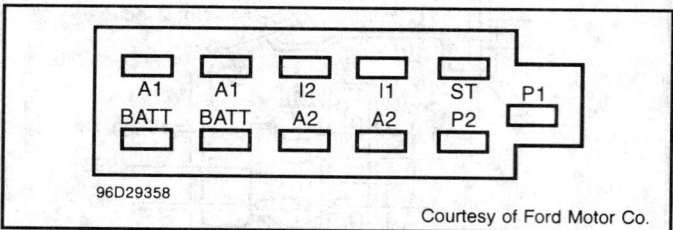

Fig. 2: Identifying Ignition Switch Terminals

SYSTEM TESTS

CAUTION: When battery is disconnected, vehicle computer and memory system may lose memory data. Driveability problems may exist until computer systems have completed a relearn cycle. See COMPUTER RELEARN PROCEDURES article in GENERAL INFORMATION before disconnecting battery.

NOTE: Before performing following tests, ensure all multifunction switch grounds, wiring, and fuses are okay. Also, ensure all circuit connections are clean and tight. For ignition switch circuit identification, see appropriate wiring diagram in POWER DISTRIBUTION article in WIRING DIAGRAMS. For multifunction switch circuit identification, see appropriate wiring diagram in EXTERIOR LIGHTS article.

SYMPTOM CHART

Symptom	Test
Ignition Switch Inoperative	A
No Power In ACC Position	B
No Power In RUN Position	C
No Power In START Position	D
No Communication With GEM/CTM	E
Multifunction Switch Does Not Operate Properly	[1]

[1] – Perform appropriate test under COMPONENT TESTS.

TEST A: IGNITION SWITCH INOPERATIVE

1) Check fuse No. 23 (60-amp) located in engine compartment Power Distribution Center (PDC), if fuse is okay, go to step **4**). If fuse is blown, go to next step.
2) Replace blown fuse. If fuse fails again, go to next step. If fuse does not fail again, go to step **4**).
3) Remove blown fuse No. 23 from fuse panel. Measure resistance between load side of fuse panel cavity No. 23 and chassis ground. If resistance is greater than 10 k/ohms go to next step. If resistance is less than 10 k/ohms, repair short to ground in Yellow wire between fuse panel and ignition switch or replace shorted ignition switch.
4) Turn ignition off. Disconnect ignition switch. Measure voltage between ground and both BATT terminals (Yellow wires) at ignition switch harness connector. If battery voltage exists, replace ignition switch. If battery voltage does not xist, repair open circuit in Yellow wire.

TEST B: NO POWER IN ACC POSITION

Turn ignition on. Check radio operation. If radio operates, replace ignition switch. See IGNITION SWITCH under REMOVAL & INSTALLATION. If radio does not operate, go to TEST C: NO POWER IN RUN POSITION.

TEST C: NO POWER IN RUN POSITION

NOTE: Testing is performed at ignition switch CONNECTOR terminals, illustration is a view of ignition switch. Ensure proper terminal on connector is being tested.

1) Check ignition switch continuity. See IGNITION SWITCH under COMPONENT TESTS. If switch tests okay, go to next step. If ignition switch does not test okay, replace ignition switch. See IGNITION SWITCH under REMOVAL & INSTALLATION.
2) Turn ignition on. Measure voltage between fuses No. 2 (Red/Light Green wire), No. 6 (Gray/Yellow wire), No. 7 (Gray/Yellow wire) and No. 34 (White/Pink wire) and ground. *See Fig. 3.* If all voltages are greater than 10 volts, system is okay. If any voltage is 10 volts or less, repair open circuit in wiring.

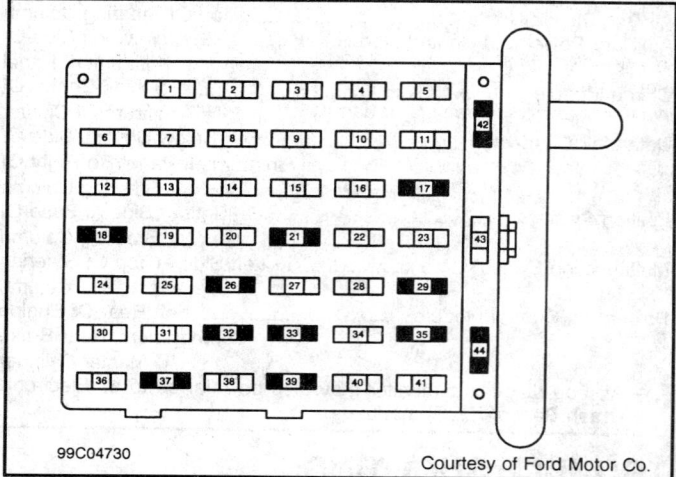

Fig. 3: Identifying Fuses

TEST D: NO POWER IN START POSITION

NOTE: Testing is performed at ignition switch CONNECTOR terminals, illustration is a view of ignition switch. Ensure proper terminal on connector is being tested.

1) Check ignition switch continuity. See IGNITION SWITCH under COMPONENT TESTS. If switch tests okay, go to next step. If ignition switch does not test okay, replace ignition switch. See IGNITION SWITCH under REMOVAL & INSTALLATION.
2) Reconnect ignition switch connector. Turn ignition switch to START position. If starter engages, repair open circuit in Red/Light Green wire. If starter does not engage, repair open circuit in White/Pink wire.

REMOVAL & INSTALLATION

WARNING: Deactivate air bag system before performing any service operation involving steering column components. See AIR BAG RESTRAINT SYSTEMS – ECONOLINE article. Do not apply electrical power to any component on steering column without first deactivating air bag system. Air bag may deploy.

MULTIFUNCTION SWITCH

Removal & Installation – Disconnect negative battery cable. Remove steering column covers. Remove retaining screws. Disconnect multifunction switch connectors. Remove switch. To install, reverse removal procedure.

IGNITION SWITCH

Removal & Installation – Disconnect negative battery cable. Remove steering column covers. Disconnect ignition switch connector. Remove ignition switch retaining screws. Remove ignition switch. To install, reverse removal procedure.

LOCK CYLINDER

Removal & Installation (With Key) – Disconnect negative battery cable. Set ignition switch to RUN position. Using a 1/8" drill bit, press retaining pin inward and pull out lock cylinder. To install, lubricate lock cylinder. Turn lock cylinder to RUN position. Press retaining pin inward and insert lock cylinder into housing. To install remaining components, reverse removal procedure.

Removal (Without Key) – **1)** Use this procedure to remove ignition lock cylinder if key is missing or cylinder is frozen. Disconnect negative battery cable. Remove steering wheel. Using pliers, twist cap until it separates from ignition switch lock cylinder.

2) Using a 1/8" drill bit, drill out lock cylinder retaining pin. Using a 3/8" drill bit, drill down middle of ignition lock key slot until ignition switch lock cylinder breaks loose. Remove ignition switch lock cylinder and drill shavings from lock cylinder housing.

3) Remove bearing retainer, bearing and gear. Thoroughly clean all metal shavings and other foreign material from housing. Carefully inspect housing for damage. If damage is apparent, replace housing.

Installation – Install gear, bearing, and retainer. Lubricate cylinder cavity. Rotate lock cylinder to RUN position. Press retaining pin inward and insert new lock cylinder into lock cylinder housing. Before rotating key to OFF position, ensure cylinder is fully seated and aligned. Use key to rotate cylinder to ensure mechanical operation is okay in all positions.

WIRING DIAGRAMS

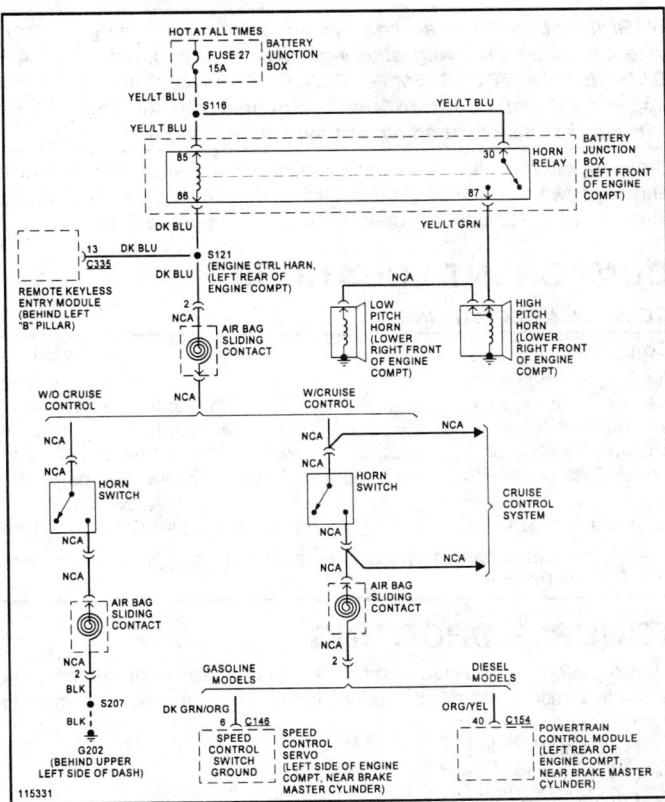

Fig. 4: Horn System Wiring Diagram (Econoline)

DESCRIPTION

WARNING: Deactivate air bag system before performing any service operation involving steering column components. See AIR BAG RESTRAINT SYSTEMS – ESCORT & TRACER article. Do not apply electrical power to any component on steering column without first deactivating air bag system. Air bag may deploy.

Steering column switch consists of a multifunction switch, ignition switch and wiper/washer switch. The multifunction switch controls hazards, turn signals, headlight high beams and flash-to-pass feature.

COMPONENT LOCATIONS

COMPONENT LOCATIONS

Component	Location
Air Bag Sliding Contact	Below Steering Wheel
Central Junction Box	Below Left Side Of Instrument Panel
Instrument Cluster [1]	Behind Left Side Of Instrument Panel
Multifunction Switch	Part Of Upper Steering Column
Power Distribution Box	Left Side Of Engine Compartment, Above Wheelwell
Turn Signal/Hazard Flasher	Underdash, Near Left Cowl Side Trim

[1] – Instrument cluster may also be referred to as Virtual Instrument Cluster (VIC).

TROUBLE SHOOTING

Before performing individual component tests, inspect for the following possible causes of system malfunction. Correct any obvious defects before proceeding.

- Mechanical Failure
- Low Battery Charge
- Faulty Fuses
- Loose Or Corroded Connectors
- Damaged Wiring

COMPONENT TESTS

CAUTION: When battery is disconnected, vehicle computer and memory system may lose memory data. Driveability problems may exist until computer systems have completed a relearn cycle. See COMPUTER RELEARN PROCEDURES article in GENERAL INFORMATION before disconnecting battery.

NOTE: Before performing following tests, ensure all multifunction switch grounds, wiring, and fuses are okay. Also, ensure all circuit connections are clean and tight. For ignition switch circuit identification, see appropriate wiring diagram in POWER DISTRIBUTION article in WIRING DIAGRAMS. For multifunction switch circuit identification, see appropriate wiring diagram in EXTERIOR LIGHTS article.

MULTIFUNCTION SWITCH

1) Disconnect multifunction switch connectors. Set hazard flasher switch to OFF position unless specified otherwise. Continuity should exist between terminals with switch in specified position. See MULTIFUNCTION SWITCH CONTINUITY table. *See Fig. 1.*

2) If continuity is not as specified, or is poor in any switch position, replace multifunction switch. To test windshield wiper/washer switch, see WIPER/WASHER SYSTEMS – ESCORT & TRACER article.

MULTIFUNCTION SWITCH CONTINUITY

Switch Position	Between Terminals
Left Turn Signal On	12 & 15
Right Turn Signal On	11 & 12
Fog Light Switch On	1 & 13
Hazard Switch On	2 & 3
Headlight Switch Flash-To-Pass On	5 & 6; 8 & 9

MULTIFUNCTION SWITCH CONTINUITY (Cont.)

Switch Position	Between Terminals
Headlight Dimmer On High Beam	5 & 6; 8 & 9
Headlight Dimmer On Low Beam	4 & 6; 7 & 9
Headlights On	13 & 14; 13 & 15
Parking Lights On	13 & 14
Flash-To-Pass Switch On	13 & 15

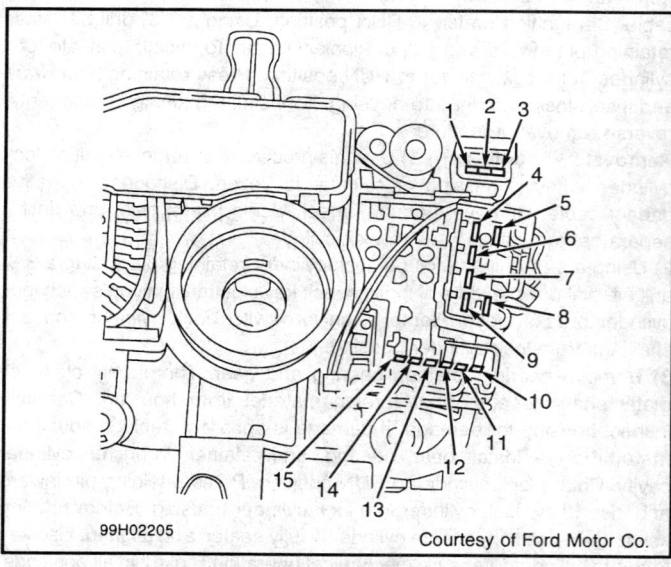

99H02205   Courtesy of Ford Motor Co.

Fig. 1: Identifying Multifunction Switch Terminals

HEADLIGHT SWITCH

See MULTIFUNCTION SWITCH.

HORN

Disconnect horn switch connector(s). Continuity should not exist between horn switch wires with horn button(s) released. Press horn button(s). Continuity should exist.

IGNITION SWITCH

Check for continuity between specified terminals with switch in each position. See appropriate IGNITION SWITCH CONTINUITY table. *See Fig. 2.* If continuity is not as specified, replace ignition switch.

IGNITION SWITCH CONTINUITY

Switch Position	Between Connector-Terminal
Lock	No Continuity
Accessory	C281-1, C281-2 & C283-2
Run	C281-1, C281-2 & C283-1; C281-1, C281-2 & C283-2; C281-1, C281-2 & C283-2
Start	C281-1, C281-2 & C283-1; C281-1, C281-2 & C283-4

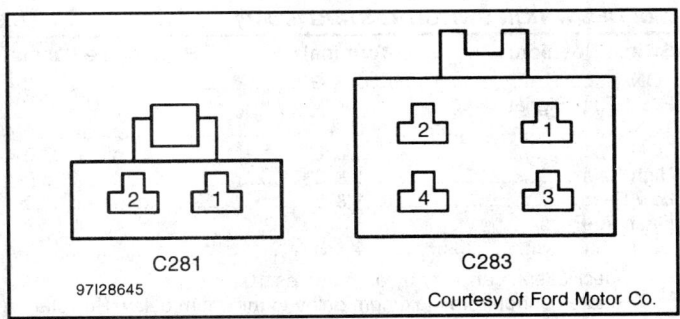

Fig. 2: Identifying Ignition Switch Terminals

C281
97128645

C283
Courtesy of Ford Motor Co.

REMOVAL & INSTALLATION

CAUTION: When battery is disconnected, vehicle computer and memory system may lose memory data. Driveability problems may exist until computer systems have completed a relearn cycle. See COMPUTER RELEARN PROCEDURES article in GENERAL INFORMATION before disconnecting battery.

STEERING WHEEL

WARNING: Deactivate air bag system before performing any service operation involving steering column components. See appropriate AIR BAG RESTRAINT SYSTEMS article. Do not apply electrical power to any component on steering column without first deactivating air bag system. Air bag may deploy.

Removal & Installation – 1) Ensure front wheels are in straight-ahead position. Disable air bag system. See AIR BAG RESTRAINT SYSTEMS – ESCORT & TRACER article. Wait at least one minute for air bag back-up power supply to deplete.

2) Remove air bag module retaining nuts/screws. Lift air bag module from steering wheel. Disconnect air bag wiring harness from module. Disconnect cruise control switch connector (if equipped). Remove and discard steering wheel bolt.

3) Remove steering wheel. While removing steering wheel, guide wiring harnesses through steering wheel. To install, reverse removal procedure. Install NEW steering wheel bolt and tighten to specification. Check AIR BAG light to verify proper system operation.

MULTIFUNCTION SWITCH

Removal & Installation – Disconnect negative battery cable. Wait at least one minute for air bag back-up power supply to deplete. Remove upper and lower steering column covers. Remove covers. Remove switch retaining screws. Disconnect connectors. Remove switch. To install, reverse removal procedure.

IGNITION SWITCH

Removal & Installation – Disconnect negative battery cable. Wait at least one minute for air bag back-up power supply to deplete. Remove upper and lower steering column covers. Remove ignition switch connector cover. Disconnect ignition switch connector. Remove mounting screws and ignition switch. To install, reverse removal procedure.

LOCK CYLINDER

Removal & Installation – 1) Disconnect negative battery cable. Wait at least one minute for air bag back-up power supply to deplete. Remove steering wheel. See STEERING WHEEL. Remove multifunction switch. See MULTIFUNCTION SWITCH. Disconnect ignition switch connector. Remove shift lock cable mount bracket.

2) Remove steering column upper mounting bolts. Lower steering column. Use chisel to make groove on heads of lock cylinder bolts. Remove and discard mounting bolts. Remove lock cylinder and bracket. To install, reverse removal procedure. Tighten mounting bolts until heads break off.

TORQUE SPECIFICATIONS

TORQUE SPECIFICATIONS

Application	Ft. Lbs. (N.m)
Steering Wheel Bolt [1]	34-47 (46-63)

[1] – Use NEW bolt when installing steering wheel.

WIRING DIAGRAMS

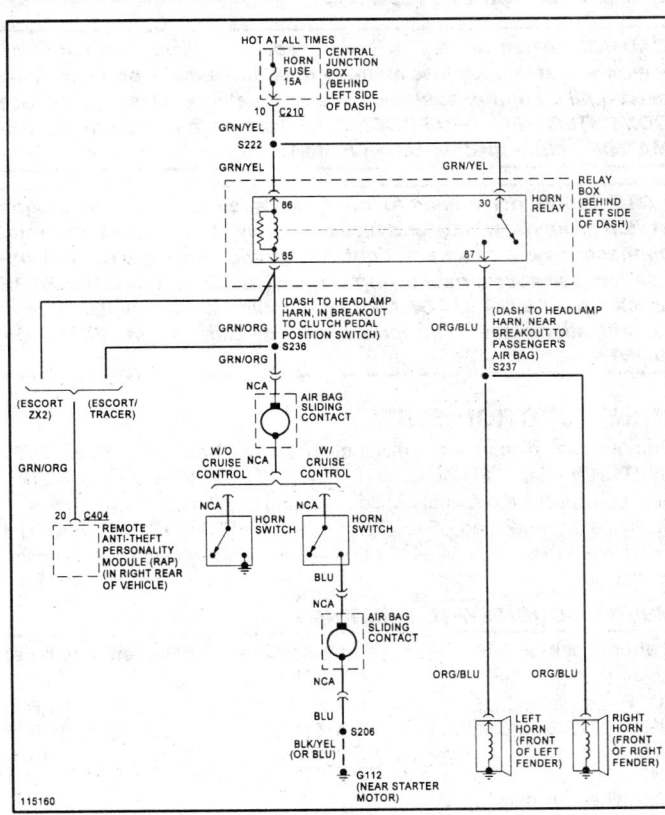

Fig. 3: Horn System Wiring Diagram (Escort & Tracer)

DESCRIPTION

The multifunction switch, located on the steering column, includes headlight dimmer, flash-to-pass and front windshield wiper/washer switches. The ignition switch and lock cylinder are also mounted on the steering column.

WARNING: Deactivate air bag system before performing any service operation involving steering column components. See appropriate AIR BAG RESTRAINT SYSTEMS article. Do not apply electrical power to any component on steering column without first deactivating air bag system. Air bag may deploy.

TROUBLE SHOOTING

Verify customers complaint by operating multifunction switch or headlight switch. Check for obvious signs of mechanical or electrical damage. Check for blown fuse(s), loose or corroded connectors, or damaged wiring harness. Check for damaged ignition switch or ignition key. Repair or replace components as necessary.

COMPONENT TESTS

CAUTION: When battery is disconnected, vehicle computer and memory system may lose memory data. Driveability problems may exist until computer systems have completed a relearn cycle. See COMPUTER RELEARN PROCEDURES article in GENERAL INFORMATION before disconnecting battery.

NOTE: Before performing following tests, ensure all multifunction switch grounds, wiring, and fuses are okay. Also, ensure all circuit connections are clean and tight. For ignition switch circuit identification, see appropriate wiring diagram in POWER DISTRIBUTION article in WIRING DIAGRAMS. For multifunction switch circuit identification, see appropriate wiring diagram in EXTERIOR LIGHTS article.

MULTIFUNCTION SWITCH

Remove and disconnect multifunction switch. See MULTIFUNCTION SWITCH under REMOVAL & INSTALLATION. Measure resistance between specified terminals while operating multifunction switch lever to positions as specified. *See Fig. 1.* See MULTIFUNCTION SWITCH TESTING table. If continuity is not as specified, replace multifunction switch.

MULTIFUNCTION SWITCH TESTING

Switch Position	Terminals	[1] Resistance (Ohms)
Wiper Switch		
OFF	5 & 6	47,600
INT	5 & 6	11,330
LO	5 & 6	4080
HI	5 & 6	0-4
Intermittent Wipers		
INT & OFF	6 & 7	[2]
LO & HI	6 & 7	3300
Washer Switch		
OFF	6 & 7	103,300
ON	6 & 7	0-4
Rear Wiper Switch		
OFF	H & 6	2900
INT 1	H & 6	11,000
INT 2	H & 6	330
Rear Washer Switch	H & 6	0-4
Hazard Switch		
ON	B & I	0-4
ON	B & A	0-4
ON	B & G	0-4
ON	B & E	0-4
Left Turn Signal		
ON	C & A	0-4

MULTIFUNCTION SWITCH TESTING (Cont.)

Switch Position	Terminals	[1] Resistance (Ohms)
ON	C & G	0-4
Right Turn Signal		
ON	C & I	0-4
ON	C & E	0-4
High Beam	1 & 3	0-4
Low Beam	1 & 2	0-4
Flash-To-Pass		
ON	4 & 3	0-4

[1] – Specification can vary by as much as 10 percent.

[2] – Rotate control from maximum delay to minimum delay. Resistance should gradually decrease from approximately 103,000 to 3300 ohms.

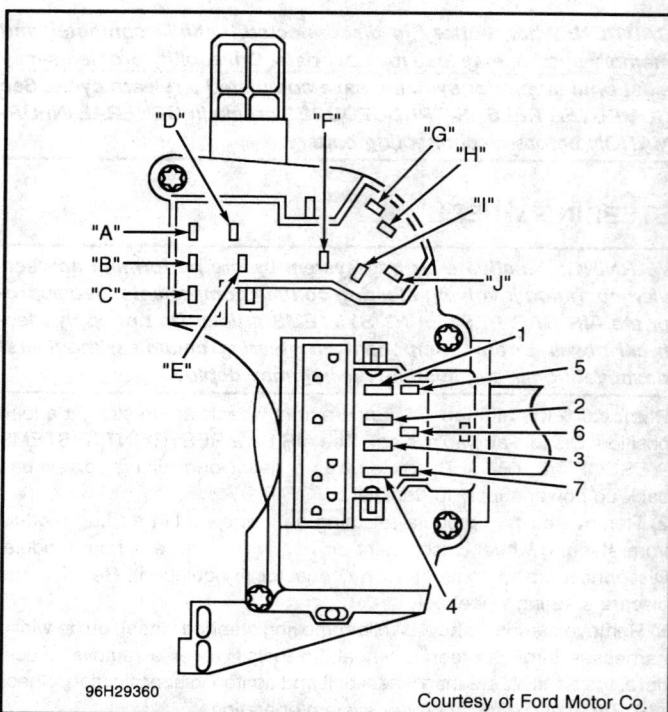

96H29360   Courtesy of Ford Motor Co.

Fig. 1: Identifying Multifunction Switch Terminals

IGNITION SWITCH

1) To inspect ignition switch for mechanical operation, rotate lock cylinder through all switch positions. Lock cylinder should not bind, and should return from START to RUN position without assistance.

2) To test electrical function of ignition switch, disconnect ignition switch connector. Check continuity between specified switch terminals using a self-powered test light or ohmmeter. *See Fig. 2.* See IGNITION SWITCH CONTINUITY table. If resistance is not as specified, replace ignition switch.

IGNITION SWITCH CONTINUITY

Switch Position	Continuity Between Terminals
Start	STA & B4
Run	B5 & I1; B1 & A1; B2 & A2; B3 & A3; B4 & A4
ACC	B5 & A1

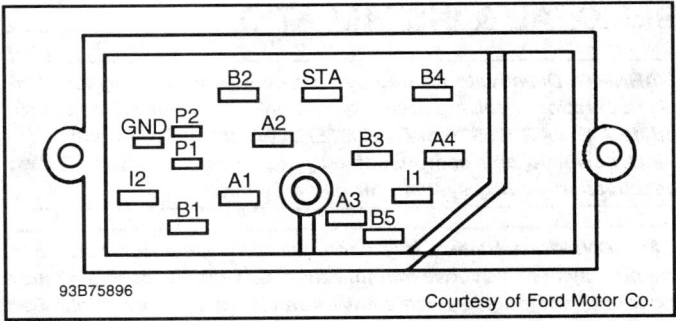

Fig. 2: Identifying Ignition Switch Harness Connector Terminals

SELF-DIAGNOSTIC SYSTEM

NOTE: Before beginning self-diagnostics, perform TROUBLE SHOOTING.

Connect New Generation Star (NGS) tester to Data Link Connector (DLC) located below instrument panel. Using NGS tester, perform DATA LINK DIAGNOSTIC TEST. If NGS tester displays CKT 914, CKT 915 or CKT 70=ALL ECUS NO RESP/NOT EQUIP, see appropriate MODULE COMMUNICATIONS NETWORK article to diagnosis network concern. If NGS tester displays NO RESP/NOT EQUIP for Generic Electronic Module (GEM), perform TEST A: NO COMMUNICATION WITH GENERIC ELECTRONIC MODULE (GEM) under SYSTEM TESTS.

If NGS tester displays SYSTEM PASSED, retrieve and record continuous DTCs. Erase continuous DTCs. Perform self-test diagnostics for GEM using NGS tester. If GEM DTCs are retrieved, see GENERIC ELECTRONIC MODULE (GEM) DTC DEFINITIONS table to continue diagnosis. If no DTCs were retrieved, repair system by symptom. See SYMPTOM CHART table and perform appropriate test under SYSTEM TESTS.

GENERIC ELECTRONIC MODULE (GEM) DTC DEFINITIONS

DTC [1]	Description	Test
B1342	GEM Is Defective	2
B1355	Ignition Run Circuit Failure	E
B1359	Ignition RUN/ACC Circuit Failure	E
B1365	Ignition START Circuit Failure	F

[1] – Codes listed in this table are only for testing covered in this article. For complete DTC listing, see appropriate MODULE COMMUNICATIONS NETWORK article.

2 – Clear DTCs. Retrieve DTCs. If DTC B1342 is retrieved, replace GEM and retest system operation.

SYMPTOM CHART

Symptom	Test
No Communication With Generic Electronic Module (GEM)	A
Unable To Enter Self-Test	B
Ignition Switch Inoperative	C
No Power In ACC Position	D
No Power In RUN Position	E
No Power In START Position	F

SYSTEM TESTS

CAUTION: When battery is disconnected, vehicle computer and memory system may lose memory data. Driveability problems may exist until computer systems have completed a relearn cycle. See COMPUTER RELEARN PROCEDURES article in GENERAL INFORMATION before disconnecting battery.

TEST A: NO COMMUNICATION WITH GENERIC ELECTRONIC MODULE (GEM)

1) Turn ignition off. Connect New Generation Star (NGS) tester to Data Link Connector (DLC). Depress clutch pedal (if applicable). Using NGS tester, read IGN_GEM PID while rotating ignition switch through START,

RUN, OFF and ACC positions. If PID values match ignition switch positions, go to next step. If PID values do not agree with ignition switch positions, repair suspect open circuit between ignition switch and instrument panel fuse block. See appropriate wiring diagram in POWER DISTRIBUTION article in WIRING DIAGRAMS. Clear DTCs and retest system.

2) Disconnect instrument panel fuse/relay block Black connector C243. *See Fig. 3.* Measure voltage between ground and terminal No. 11 (Tan/Black wire) on connector C243. If voltage is more than 10 volts, go to next step. If voltage is 10 volts or less, repair open Tan/Black wire circuit. Clear DTCs and retest system.

3) Turn ignition off. Reconnect Black connector C243. Disconnect GEM 18-pin connector C267. GEM is mounted on back of instrument panel fuse/relay block. Turn ignition on. Measure voltage between ground and terminals No. 4 and 16 on component connector C267. *See Fig. 3.* If voltages are more than 10 volts, go to next step. If voltages are 10 volts or less, replace fuse/relay block. Clear DTCs and retest system.

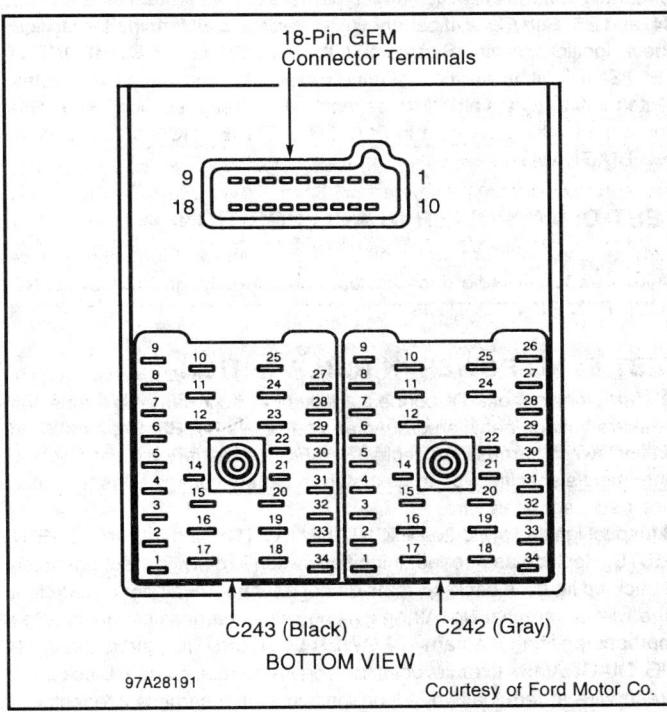

Fig. 3: Identifying Instrument Panel Fuse/Relay Block Terminals

4) Turn ignition off. Disconnect Gray GEM connector C239. Measure resistance between ground and terminal No. 26 (Black/Light Blue wire) on connector C239. *See Fig. 4.* If resistance is less than 5 ohms, go to next step. If resistance is 5 ohms or greater, repair open Black/Light Blue wire. Clear DTCs and retest system.

5) Measure resistance between ground and terminal No. 14 (Black/Light Blue wire) on connector C239. *See Fig. 4.* If resistance is less than 5 ohms, fault is in module communications network. See appropriate MODULE COMMUNICATIONS NETWORK article to continue diagnosis. If resistance is 5 ohms or greater, repair open in Black/Light Blue wire. Clear DTCs and retest system.

TEST B: UNABLE TO ENTER SELF-TEST

NOTE: Prior to replacement of GEM module, it is necessary to upload module configuration information using NGS tester. See COMPUTER RELEARN PROCEDURES article in GENERAL INFORMATION.

Connect New Generation Star (NGS) tester to Data Link Connector (DLC). Perform self-test diagnostics for GEM using NGS tester. If NGS tester communicates with GEM, replace GEM. If NGS tester does not communicate with GEM, go to TEST A: NO COMMUNICATION WITH GENERIC ELECTRONIC MODULE (GEM).

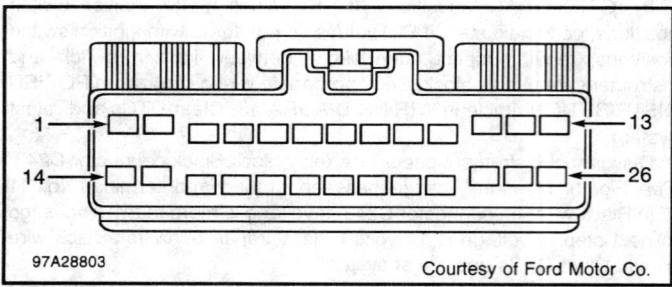

97A28803   Courtesy of Ford Motor Co.

Fig. 4: Identifying GEM 26-Pin (C239) Harness Connector Terminals

TEST C: IGNITION SWITCH INOPERATIVE

Turn ignition off. Disconnect ignition switch harness connector. Check for battery voltage at ignition switch harness connector terminals B1, B3, B4, and B5. *See Fig. 2*. If battery voltage exists at all terminals specified, check ignition switch. See IGNITION SWITCH under COMPONENT TESTS. If ignition switch is faulty, replace ignition switch and retest system. If battery voltage does not exist, repair suspect wire. See appropriate wiring diagram in POWER DISTRIBUTION article in WIRING DIAGRAMS.

TEST D: NO POWER IN ACC POSITION

Turn ignition on. Turn radio on. If radio operates correctly, replace ignition switch. If radio does not operate correctly, go to TEST E: NO POWER IN RUN POSITION.

TEST E: NO POWER IN RUN POSITION

1) Turn ignition off. Disconnect ignition switch harness connector. Measure voltage between ground and terminals B1, B3, B4, and B5 on ignition switch harness connector. *See Fig. 2*. If battery voltage exists at all terminals specified, go to next step. If battery voltage does not exist, repair suspect open wire.

2) Inspect ignition switch. See IGNITION SWITCH under COMPONENT TESTS. Replace as needed. If ignition switch is okay, inspect operation of back-up lights. If back-up lights do not operate, repair open Red/Light Blue wire at terminal No. A3 on ignition switch harness connector. See appropriate wiring diagram in POWER DISTRIBUTION article in WIRING DIAGRAMS. If radio does not operate, repair open Black/Light Green wire at terminal No. A1 on ignition switch harness connector. If instrument cluster does not operate, repair open Dark Blue/Light Green wire at terminal No. I1 on ignition switch harness connector. See appropriate wiring diagram in POWER DISTRIBUTION article in WIRING DIAGRAMS. If blower motor does not operate, repair open Gray/Yellow wire at terminal No. A4 on ignition switch harness connector.

TEST F: NO POWER IN START POSITION

1) Turn ignition off. Disconnect ignition switch harness connector. Measure voltage between ground and terminal B4 (Light Green/Violet wire) on ignition switch harness connector. *See Fig. 2*. If voltage is greater than 10 volts, go to next step. If voltage is 10 volts or less, repair open Light Green/Violet wire.

2) Inspect ignition switch. See IGNITION SWITCH under COMPONENT TESTS. If ignition switch is faulty, replace ignition switch and retest system. If ignition switch is okay, repair open Red/Light Blue wire on terminal STA on ignition switch harness connector. See appropriate wiring diagram in POWER DISTRIBUTION article in WIRING DIAGRAMS.

REMOVAL & INSTALLATION

WARNING: Deactivate air bag system before performing any service operation involving steering column components. See appropriate AIR BAG RESTRAINT SYSTEMS article. Do not apply electrical power to any component on steering column without first deactivating air bag system. Air bag may deploy.

CAUTION: When battery is disconnected, vehicle computer and memory system may lose memory data. Driveability problems may exist until computer systems have completed a relearn cycle. See COMPUTER RELEARN PROCEDURES article in GENERAL INFORMATION before disconnecting battery.

MULTIFUNCTION SWITCH

Removal & Installation – Disconnect negative battery cable. Remove lock cylinder. See LOCK CYLINDER. Remove upper and lower steering column shrouds. Remove retaining screws. Disconnect multifunction switch harness connectors. Remove switch. To install, reverse removal procedure.

IGNITION SWITCH

Removal & Installation – Disconnect negative battery cable. Remove steering column opening cover. Remove hood release handle and position aside. Remove parking brake release handle and set aside. Remove steering column opening cover reinforcement. Disconnect ignition switch harness connector. Remove 2 ignition switch screws and ignition switch. To install, reverse removal procedure.

LOCK CYLINDER

Removal & Installation (With Key) – Disconnect negative battery cable. Set ignition switch to RUN position. Insert a 1/8" drill bit or wire through access hole in trim steering column trim (below lock cylinder). Press retaining pin inward and pull out lock cylinder. To install, lubricate lock cylinder. Turn lock cylinder to RUN position. Press retaining pin inward and insert lock cylinder into housing. To install remaining components, reverse removal procedure.

Removal (Without Key) – **1)** Use this procedure to remove ignition lock cylinder if key is missing or cylinder is frozen. Disconnect negative battery cable. Remove steering wheel. Using pliers, twist cap until it separates from ignition switch lock cylinder.

2) Using a 3/8" drill bit, drill down middle of ignition lock key slot about 3/4-1" (19-25 mm) until ignition switch lock cylinder breaks loose from breakaway base of ignition switch lock cylinder. Remove ignition switch lock cylinder and drill shavings from lock cylinder housing.

3) Remove bearing retainer, bearing and gear. Thoroughly clean all metal shavings and other foreign material from housing. Carefully inspect housing for damage. If damage is apparent, replace housing.

Installation – **1)** Install gear, bearing, and retainer. Lubricate cylinder cavity. Rotate lock cylinder to RUN position. Press retaining pin inward and insert new lock cylinder into lock cylinder housing.

2) Before rotating key to OFF position, ensure cylinder is fully seated and aligned. Use key to rotate cylinder to ensure mechanical operation is okay in all positions.

WIRING DIAGRAMS

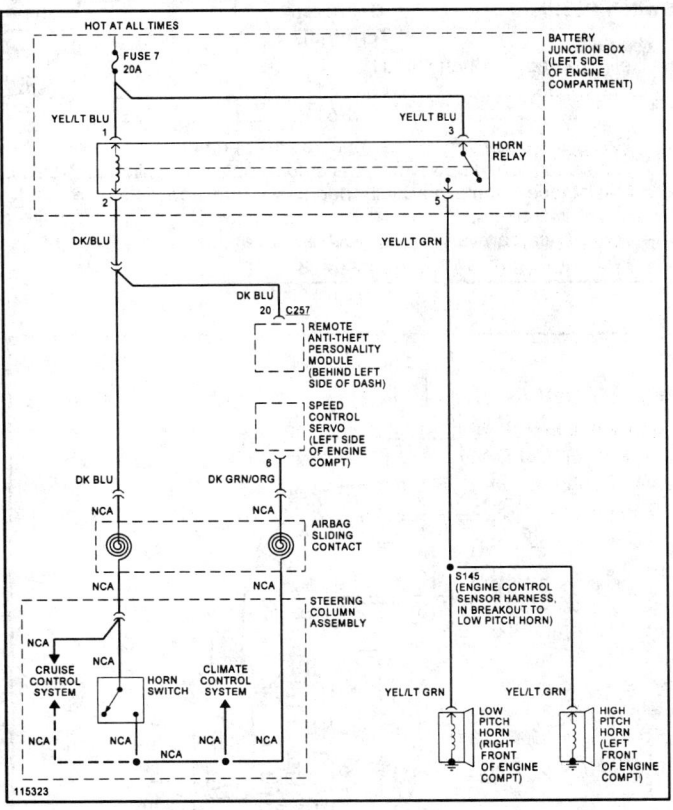

Fig. 5: Horn System Wiring Diagram (Expedition & Navigator)

DESCRIPTION & OPERATION

WARNING: Deactivate air bag system before performing any service operation involving steering column components. See appropriate AIR BAG RESTRAINT SYSTEMS article. Do not apply any electrical power to any component on steering column without first deactivating air bag system. Air bag may deploy.

The multifunction switch, located on the steering column, includes headlight dimmer, flash-to-pass and front windshield wiper/washer switches. The ignition switch and lock cylinder are also mounted on the steering column.

TROUBLE SHOOTING

Verify customers complaint by operating system in question. Inspect for obvious signs of mechanical and electrical damage. If problem exists, repair as necessary. If problem does not exist, perform self-diagnosis. See SELF-DIAGNOSTIC SYSTEM.

COMPONENT TESTS

CAUTION: When battery is disconnected, vehicle computer and memory system may lose memory data. Driveability problems may exist until computer systems have completed a relearn cycle. See COMPUTER RELEARN PROCEDURES article in GENERAL INFORMATION before disconnecting battery.

NOTE: Before performing following tests, ensure all multifunction switch grounds, wiring, and fuses are okay. Also, ensure all circuit connections are clean and tight. For ignition switch circuit identification, see appropriate wiring diagram in POWER DISTRIBUTION article in WIRING DIAGRAMS. For multifunction switch circuit identification, see appropriate wiring diagram in EXTERIOR LIGHTS article.

MULTIFUNCTION SWITCH

Remove and disconnect multifunction switch. See MULTIFUNCTION SWITCH under REMOVAL & INSTALLATION. Measure resistance between specified terminals while operating multifunction switch lever to positions as specified. See Fig. 1. See MULTIFUNCTION SWITCH TESTING table. If resistance is not as specified, replace multifunction switch.

MULTIFUNCTION SWITCH TESTING

Switch Position	Between Terminals	Ohms
Wiper Switch [1]		
Off	565 & 993	9550
Int	565 & 993	1910
Lo	565 & 993	401
Hi	565 & 993	0-4
Interval Time Adjust	590 & 993	[2]
Washer Switch		
Off	590 & 993	More Than 10,000
On	590 & 993	0-4
Hazard Switch		
On	2 & 385	0-4
On	3 & 385	0-4
On	385 & 511	More Than 10,000
Turn Signal Switch		
Left Turn Signal		
On	3 & 44	0-4
On	9 & 44	0-4
Right Turn Signal		
On	2 & 44	0-4
On	5 & 44	0-4
Dimmer Switch [3]		
High Beam On	12 & 196	0-4
Low Beam On	15 & 507	0-4

MULTIFUNCTION SWITCH TESTING (Cont.)

Switch Position	Between Terminals	Ohms
Brakelight Feed-Through Circuit		
[4]	5 & 511	0-4
[4]	9 & 511	0-4

[1] – Resistance can vary by as much as 10 percent.
[2] – Rotate control know from maximum delay to minimum delay. Resistance should gradually decrease from about 2670 ohms to about 249 ohms.
[3] – Resistance can vary by as much as 5 percent.
[4] – With turn signal switch in neutral position.

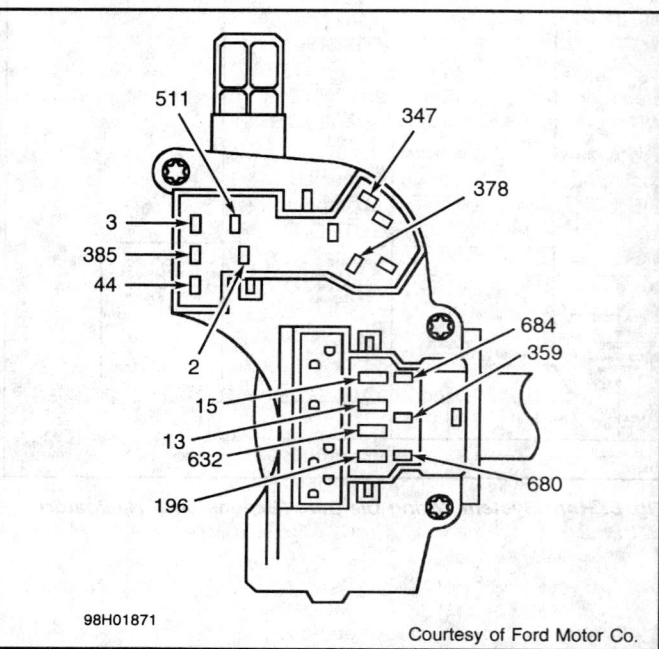

98H01871   Courtesy of Ford Motor Co.

Fig. 1: Identifying Multifunction Switch Terminals

IGNITION SWITCH

1) To inspect ignition switch for mechanical operation, rotate lock cylinder through all switch positions. Lock cylinder should not bind, and should return from START to RUN position without assistance.
2) To test electrical function of ignition switch, disconnect ignition switch connector. Check continuity between specified switch terminals using a self-powered test light or ohmmeter. See Fig. 2. See IGNITION SWITCH CONTINUITY table. If continuity is not as specified, replace ignition switch.

IGNITION SWITCH CONTINUITY TEST

Continuity Between Terminals	Switch Position
B4 & STA	Start
B4 & A4	Run
B2 & A2	Run
B5 & I1	Run
B1 & A1	Run
P1 & GND	Start

SELF-DIAGNOSTIC SYSTEM

Connect New Generation Star (NGS) tester to Data Link Connector (DLC), located beneath instrument panel. Using NGS tester, perform data link diagnostics test. See DATA LINK DIAGNOSTIC TEST under COMMUNICATION NETWORK DIAGNOSTICS in MODULE COMMUNICATIONS NETWORK – EXPLORER & MOUNTAINEER article. If NGS tester responds with CKT914, CKT915 or CKT70=ALL ECUS NO

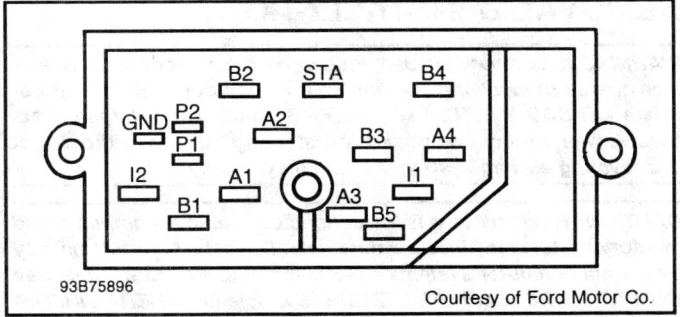

Fig. 2: Identifying Ignition Switch Terminals

RESP/NOT EQUIP, repair module communications concern. See MODULE COMMUNICATIONS NETWORK – EXPLORER & MOUNTAINEER article. If NGS tester displays NO RESP/NOT EQUIP for Generic Electronic Module (GEM), perform TEST A: NO COMMUNICATION WITH GEM/CTM under SYSTEM TESTS.

If NGS tester responds with SYSTEM PASSED, retrieve and record continuous DTCs. Erase continuous DTCs. Using NGS tester, perform GEM/CTM self-test. Perform appropriate test in accordance with DTC retrieved. See GENERIC ELECTRONIC MODULE/CENTRAL TIMER MODULE DTCS table. Codes listed in this table are only for testing covered in this article. For complete DTC listing, see MODULE COMMUNICATIONS NETWORK – EXPLORER & MOUNTAINEER article. If no DTCs are retrieved, repair by symptom. See SYMPTOM DIAGNOSIS table.

GENERIC ELECTRONIC MODULE/CENTRAL TIMING MODULE DTCS

DTC [1]	Description	Test
B1342	ECM/CTM Defective	[2]
B1355	Ignition RUN Circuit Failure	D
B1359	Ignition RUN/ACC Circuit Failure	C Or D

[1] – Codes listed in this table are only for testing covered in this article. For complete DTC listing, see MODULE COMMUNICATIONS NETWORK – EXPLORE & MOUNTAINEER article.

[2] – Using NGS tester, retrieve and document all continuous. Perform GEM/CTM self-test. If DTC B1342 is retrieved again, replace GEM/CTM.

SYMPTOM DIAGNOSIS

Symptom	Test
No Communication With GEM/CTM	A
Ignition Switch Inoperative	B
No Power In Acc Position	C
No Power In RUN Position	D
No Power In Start Position	E

SYSTEM TESTS

CAUTION: When battery is disconnected, vehicle computer and memory systems may lose memory data. Driveability problems may exist until computer systems have completed a relearn cycle. See COMPUTER RELEARN PROCEDURES article in GENERAL INFORMATION before disconnecting battery.

TEST A: NO COMMUNICATION WITH GEM/CTM MODULE

1) Check fuse No. 25 (7.5-amp) in instrument panel fuse block and maxi-fuse No. 1 (60-amp) in power distribution box. If fuses are okay, go to next step. If maxi-fuse No. 1 is blown, replace fuse and retest system. If fuse blows again, check for short to ground in Tan/Black wire. Repair as necessary. If fuse No. 25 is blown, replace fuse and retest system. If fuse blows again, check for short to ground in White/Yellow wire. Repair as necessary.

2) Using a voltmeter, measure voltage between ground and instrument panel fuse block fuse No. 25 (7.5-amp) terminal No. 2. *See Fig. 3*. If voltage is more than 10 volts, go to next step. If voltage is 10 volts or less, repair Tan/Black wire between power distribution center and instrument panel fuse block.

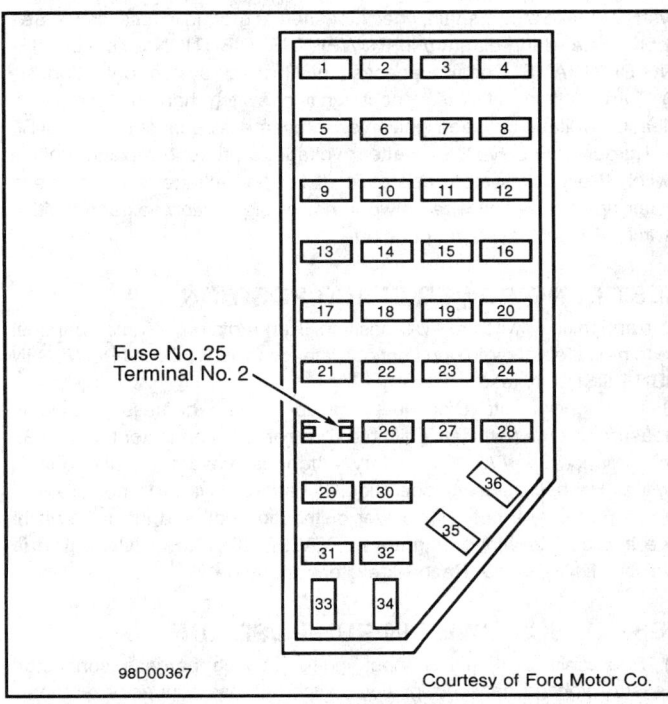

Fig. 3: Identifying Instrument Panel Fuse Block Fuse No. 25 Terminals

3) Disconnect GEM/CTM 18-pin connector, located behind center of instrument panel. Measure voltage between ground and terminal No. 11 (White/Yellow wire) at GEM/CTM 18-pin connector. *See Fig. 4*. If voltage is more than 10 volts, go to next step. If voltage is 10 volts or less, repair White/Yellow wire between GEM/CTM and instrument panel fuse block. Recheck system operation.

4) Disconnect GEM 26-pin connector. Measure resistance between ground and terminal No. 14 (Black/White wire) at GEM/CTM 26-pin connector. If resistance is less than 5 ohms, repair module communication concern. See MODULE COMMUNICATIONS NETWORK – EXPLORER & MOUNTAINEER article. If resistance is 5 ohms or more, repair open in Black/White wire(s). Recheck system operation.

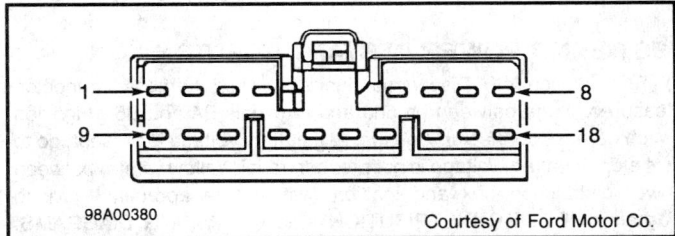

Fig. 4: Identifying GEM/CTM 18-Pin Connector Terminals

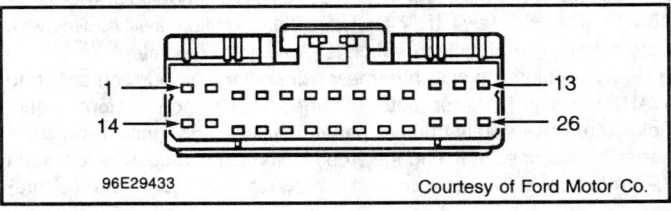

Fig. 5: Identifying GEM/CTM 26-Pin Connector Terminals

TEST B: IGNITION SWITCH INOPERATIVE

1) Check maxi-fuse No. 5 (50-amp) in power distribution box. If fuse is okay, go to next step. If fuse is blown, replace blown fuse and recheck system. If fuse blows again, check for short to ground in fuse circuit. See appropriate wiring diagram in POWER DISTRIBUTION article in WIRING DIAGRAMS. Repair as necessary. Recheck system operation.

2) Turn ignition off. Disconnect ignition switch harness connector. Measure voltage between ignition switch harness connector terminal B5 and ground. *See Fig. 2.* If battery voltage is present, replace ignition switch. Recheck system operation. If battery voltage is not present, repair open in Yellow wire between power distribution box and ignition switch. Recheck system operation.

TEST C: NO POWER IN ACC POSITION

1) Turn ignition switch to ACC position. Turn radio on. If radio operates, go to next step. If radio does not operate, go to TEST D: NO POWER IN RUN POSITION test.

2) Turn ignition off. Disconnect ignition switch harness connector. Measure voltage between ignition switch harness connector terminal B5 and ground. *See Fig. 2.* If battery voltage is present, replace ignition switch. Recheck system operation. If battery voltage is not present, repair Yellow wire between power distribution box and ignition switch. See appropriate wiring diagram in POWER DISTRIBUTION article in WIRING DIAGRAMS. Recheck system operation.

TEST D: NO POWER IN RUN POSITION

1) Turn ignition off. Disconnect ignition switch harness connector. Measure voltage between ignition switch harness connector terminals B1, B2, B4, B5 and ground. *See Fig. 2.* If battery voltage is present, go to next step. If battery voltage is not present, repair appropriate wire(s) between power distribution box and ignition switch. See appropriate wiring diagram in POWER DISTRIBUTION article in WIRING DIAGRAMS. Recheck system operation.

2) Check ignition switch. See IGNITION SWITCH under COMPONENT TESTS. If ignition switch is faulty, replace ignition switch. Recheck system operation. If ignition switch is okay, go to next step.

3) Reconnect ignition switch harness connector. Turn ignition on. Measure voltage between ground and load side (right side terminal) of fuse cavities No. 16 (30-amp), No. 10 (7.5-amp), No. 19 (24-amp) and No. 27 (15-amp). If battery voltage is present at all terminals, recheck system operation. If battery voltage is not present at any terminal, repair circuit in question. See appropriate wiring diagram in POWER DISTRIBUTION article in WIRING DIAGRAMS. Recheck system operation.

TEST E: NO POWER IN START POSITION

1) Turn ignition off. Disconnect ignition switch harness connector. Measure voltage between ground and terminals B4 and B5 at ignition switch harness connector. *See Fig. 2.* If battery voltage is present, go to next step. If battery voltage is not present, repair Yellow wire(s) between power distribution box and ignition switch. See appropriate wiring diagram in POWER DISTRIBUTION article in WIRING DIAGRAMS. Recheck system operation.

2) Check ignition switch. See IGNITION SWITCH under COMPONENT TESTS. If ignition switch is faulty, replace ignition switch. Recheck system operation. If ignition switch is okay, go to next step.

3) Reconnect ignition switch harness connector. Turn ignition switch to START position. If starter motor engages, repair short in Light Green/Violet wire between instrument panel fuse box and ignition switch. If starter motor does not engage, repair Red/Light Blue wire between instrument panel fuse box and ignition switch. Recheck system operation.

REMOVAL & INSTALLATION

WARNING: Deactivate air bag system before performing any service operation involving steering column components. See appropriate AIR BAG RESTRAINT SYSTEMS article. Do not apply electrical power to any component on steering column without first deactivating air bag system. Air bag may deploy.

CAUTION: When battery is disconnected, vehicle computer and memory system may lose memory data. Driveability problems may exist until computer systems have completed a relearn cycle. See COMPUTER RELEARN PROCEDURES article in GENERAL INFORMATION before disconnecting battery.

MULTIFUNCTION SWITCH

Removal & Installation – Disconnect negative battery cable. Remove lock cylinder. See LOCK CYLINDER. Twist tilt lever handle counter-clockwise and remove handle (if equipped). Remove upper and lower steering column covers. Remove multifunction switch retaining screws. Disconnect multifunction switch harness connectors and remove switch. To install, reverse removal procedure.

IGNITION SWITCH

Removal & Installation – Disconnect negative battery cable. Remove parking brake release handle. Remove hood release handle and position aside. Remove panel below steering column. Remove 5 bolts and steering column opening cover reinforcement. Disconnect ignition switch harness connector. Remove 2 ignition switch screws and ignition switch. To install, reverse removal procedure.

LOCK CYLINDER

Removal & Installation (With Key) – Disconnect negative battery cable. Set ignition switch to RUN position. Insert a 1/8" drill bit or wire through access hole in lower steering column cover (below lock cylinder). *See Fig. 6.* Press retaining pin inward and pull out lock cylinder. To install, lubricate lock cylinder. Turn lock cylinder to RUN position. Press retaining pin inward and insert lock cylinder into housing. To install remaining components, reverse removal procedure.

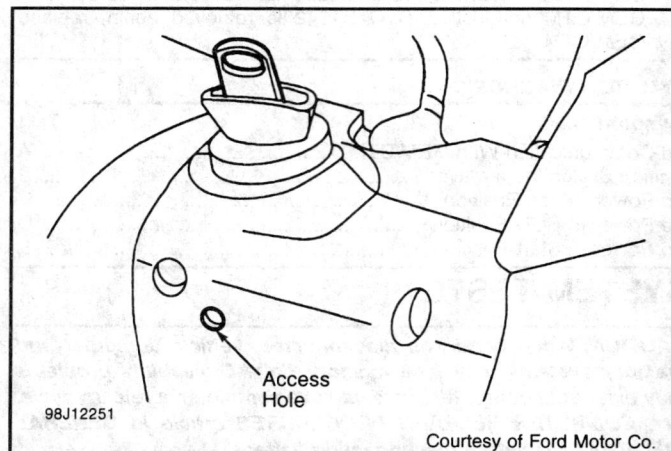

98J12251
Access Hole
Courtesy of Ford Motor Co.

Fig. 6: Identifying Lower Steering Column Cover Access Hole

Removal (Without Key) – 1) Use this procedure to remove ignition lock cylinder if key is missing or cylinder is frozen. Disconnect negative battery cable. Remove steering wheel. See STEERING WHEEL. Using pliers, twist cap until it separates from ignition switch lock cylinder.

2) Using a 1/8" drill bit, drill out lock cylinder retaining pin. Using a 3/8" drill bit, drill down middle of ignition lock key slot until ignition switch lock cylinder breaks loose. Remove ignition switch lock cylinder and drill shavings from lock cylinder housing.

3) Remove bearing retainer, bearing and gear. Thoroughly clean all metal shavings and other foreign material from housing. Carefully inspect housing for damage. If damage is apparent, replace housing.

STEERING WHEEL

WARNING: Deactivate air bag system before performing any service operation involving steering column components. See appropriate AIR BAG RESTRAINT SYSTEMS article. DO NOT apply electrical power to any component on steering column without first deactivating air bag system. Air bag may deploy.

Removal & Installation – 1) Ensure front wheels are in straight-ahead position. Disable air bag system. See appropriate AIR BAG RESTRAINT SYSTEMS article. Wait at least one minute for air bag back-up power supply to deplete. Remove air bag module retaining nuts/screws. Lift air bag module from steering wheel. Disconnect air bag wiring harness from module. Disconnect cruise control switch connector (if equipped).

2) Remove and discard steering wheel bolt. Remove steering wheel. While removing steering wheel, guide wiring harnesses through steering wheel. To install, reverse removal procedure. Install NEW steering wheel bolt and tighten to 25-34 ft. lbs. (34-46 N.m). Check AIR BAG light to verify proper system operation.

WIRING DIAGRAMS

NOTE: For ignition switch circuit identification, see appropriate wiring diagram in POWER DISTRIBUTION article in WIRING DIAGRAMS. For multifunction switch circuit identification, see appropriate wiring diagram in EXTERIOR LIGHTS article.

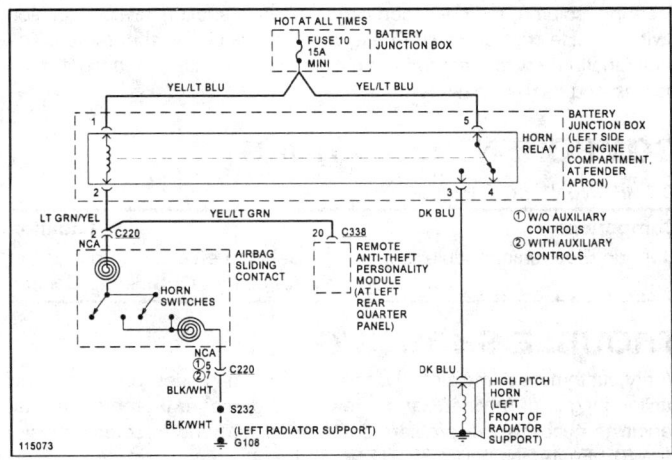

Fig. 7: Horn System Wiring Diagram (Explorer & Mountaineer)

DESCRIPTION

WARNING: Deactivate air bag system before performing any service operation involving steering column components. See appropriate AIR BAG RESTRAINT SYSTEMS article. DO NOT apply electrical power to any component on steering column without first deactivating air bag system. Air bag may deploy.

Steering column switches consist of a multifunction switch, ignition switch, cruise control switch (if equipped) and wiper/washer switch. The multifunction switch controls hazards, turn signals, headlight high beams and flash-to-pass feature.

COMPONENT LOCATIONS

COMPONENT LOCATIONS

Component	Location
Generic Electronic Module	Behind Left Side Of Instrument Panel, Left Of Steering Column

TROUBLE SHOOTING

Verify customers complaint by operating system in question. Inspect for obvious signs of mechanical and electrical damage. If problem exists, repair as necessary. If problem does not exist, perform self-diagnosis. See SELF-DIAGNOSTIC SYSTEM.

COMPONENT TESTS

CAUTION: When battery is disconnected, vehicle computer and memory system may lose memory data. Driveability problems may exist until computer systems have completed a relearn cycle. See COMPUTER RELEARN PROCEDURES article in GENERAL INFORMATION before disconnecting battery.

NOTE: Before performing following tests, ensure all multifunction switch grounds, wiring, and fuses are okay. Also, ensure all circuit connections are clean and tight. For ignition switch circuit identification, see appropriate wiring diagram in POWER DISTRIBUTION article in WIRING DIAGRAMS. For multifunction switch circuit identification, see appropriate wiring diagram in EXTERIOR LIGHTS article.

MULTIFUNCTION SWITCH

Disconnect multifunction switch harness connectors. Set hazard flasher switch to OFF position unless specified otherwise. Check resistance between appropriate terminals at multifunction switch with switch in appropriate position. See MULTIFUNCTION SWITCH CONTINUITY table. *See Fig. 1.* If continuity is not as specified or is poor in any switch position, replace multifunction switch.

MULTIFUNCTION SWITCH CONTINUITY

Switch Position	Between Circuits No.	Resistance (Ohms)
Left Turn [1]	2, 5 & 44	[2]
Right Turn [1]	2, 9 & 44	[2]
Brake Light Feed Through Circuit [1] [3]	5, 9 & 511	[2]
Hazard Switch On	2, 3, 5, 9 & 385	[2]
Flash-To-Pass On	12 & 196; 15 & 507	[2]
Headlight Dimmer		
On High Beam	12 & 15	[2]
On Low Beam	15 & 507	[2]
Washer		
Off	590 & 993	[4] 103,300
On	590 & 993	[2]
Wipers		
Off	685 & 993	[5] 47,600
Low	685 & 993	[5] 4080

MULTIFUNCTION SWITCH CONTINUITY (Cont.)

Switch Position	Between Circuits No.	Resistance (Ohms)
High	685 & 993	[2]
Intermittent	685 & 993	[5] [6] 11,330

[1] – Hazard switch MUST be off.
[2] – Resistance should be 5 ohms or less.
[3] – Turn signal switch MUST be in neutral position.
[4] – Resistance may as much as 10 percent.
[5] – Resistance may as much as 5 percent.
[6] – Also measure resistance between circuit No. 590 & 993. Resistance should increase smoothly from 3300 to 103,300 when rotating dial from min. to max. when wiper switch in intermittent position. Resistance should be 3300 ohms when wiper switch is in low or high position.

HEADLIGHT SWITCH

See appropriate INSTRUMENT PANELS article.

IGNITION SWITCH

Check continuity between specified terminals at ignition switch with switch in appropriate position. See IGNITION SWITCH CONTINUITY table. *See Fig. 2.* If continuity is not as specified, replace ignition switch.

IGNITION SWITCH CONTINUITY

Switch Position	Continuity Between Terminals
Accessory	A1 & B5
Run	A1 & B1; A2 & B2; A3 & B3; A4 & B4; B5 & I1
Start	B4 & STA; B5 & I1

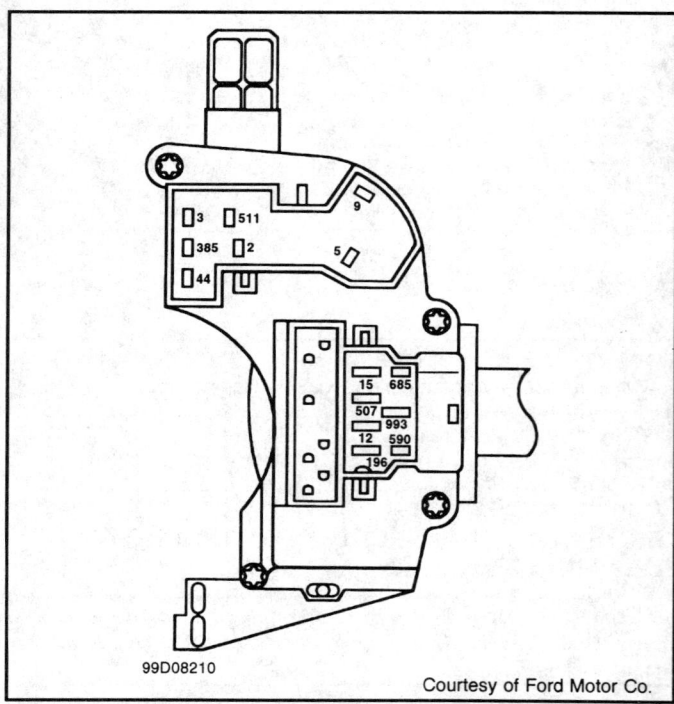

99D08210

Courtesy of Ford Motor Co.

Fig. 1: Identifying Multifunction Switch Circuit Terminals

SELF-DIAGNOSTIC SYSTEM

Connect New Generation Star (NGS) tester to Data Link Connector (DLC), located beneath instrument panel. Using NGS tester, perform data link diagnostics test. See DATA LINK DIAGNOSTIC TEST under COMMUNICATION NETWORK DIAGNOSTICS in MODULE COMMUNICATIONS NETWORK – MUSTANG article. If NGS tester responds

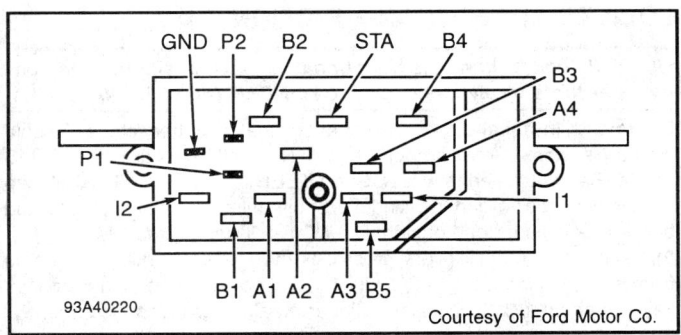

Fig. 2: Identifying Ignition Switch Terminals

with CKT914, CKT915 or CKT70=ALL ECUS NO RESP/NOT EQUIP, repair module communications concern. See MODULE COMMUNICATIONS NETWORK – MUSTANG article. If NGS tester displays NO RESP/NOT EQUIP for Generic Electronic Module (GEM), perform TEST A: NO COMMUNICATION WITH GENERIC ELECTRONIC MODULE under SYSTEM TESTS.

If NGS tester responds with SYSTEM PASSED, retrieve and record continuous DTCs. Erase continuous DTCs. Using NGS tester, perform GEM self-test. Perform appropriate test in accordance with DTC retrieved. See GENERIC ELECTRONIC MODULE DTC INDEX table. Codes listed in this table are only for testing covered in this article. For complete DTC listing, see MODULE COMMUNICATIONS NETWORK – MUSTANG article. If no DTCs are retrieved, repair by symptom. See SYMPTOM CHART table under SYSTEM TESTS.

GENERIC ELECTRONIC MODULE DTC INDEX

DTC [1]	Description	Test
B1342	ECU Defective	[2]
B1359	Ignition RUN/ACC Circuit Failure	E
B1555	Ignition RUN/START Circuit Failure	D

[1] – Codes listed in this table are only for testing covered in this article. For complete DTC listing, see MODULE COMMUNICATIONS NETWORK – MUSTANG article.

[2] – Using NGS tester, retrieve and document all continuous. Perform Generic Electronic Module (GEM) self-test. If DTC B1342 is retrieved again, replace GEM.

SYSTEM TEST

SYMPTOM CHART

Symptom	Test
No Communication With Generic Electronic Module	A
Ignition Switch Inoperative	B
No Power In ACC Position	C
No Power In RUN Position	D
No Power In START Position	E

TEST A: NO COMMUNICATION WITH GENERIC ELECTRONIC MODULE

NOTE: Before proceeding with this test ensure voltage exists at input side of fuse No. 39 (5-amp) in central junction box. Repair as necessary.

1) Turn ignition switch to LOCK position. Disconnect Generic Electronic Module (GEM) harness connector C291. Measure voltage at terminal No. 2 (White/Yellow wire) at GEM harness connector C291. *See Fig. 3.* If battery voltage exists, go to next step. If battery voltage does not exist, go to step **3)**.

2) Measure resistance between ground and terminal No. 4 (Black/White wire) at GEM harness connector C291. If resistance is 5 ohms or less, go to step **4)**. If resistance is greater than 5 ohms, repair open in Black/White wire.

3) Remove fuse No. 39 (5-amp) from central junction box. Measure resistance in White/Yellow wire between terminal No. 2 at GEM harness

connector C291 and output side of fuse No. 39. If resistance is 5 ohms or less, repair central junction box as necessary. If resistance is greater than 5 ohms, repair open in White/Yellow wire.

4) Measure voltage at terminal No. 4 (Black/White wire) at GEM harness connector C291. If any voltage exists, repair short to voltage in Black/White wire. If no voltage exists, repair module communication concern. See MODULE COMMUNICATIONS NETWORK – MUSTANG article.

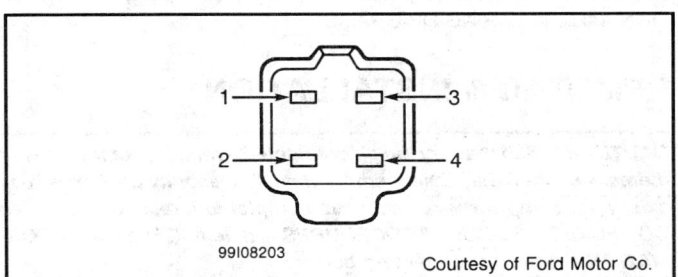

Fig. 3: Identifying GEM Harness Connector C291 Terminals

TEST B: IGNITION SWITCH INOPERATIVE

Test ignition switch. See IGNITION SWITCH under COMPONENT TESTS. If ignition switch is defective, replace ignition switch. If ignition switch is okay, repair power distribution circuit(s) as necessary. See appropriate wiring diagram in POWER DISTRIBUTION article in WIRING DIAGRAMS.

TEST C: NO POWER IN ACC POSITION

1) Turn ignition switch to ACC position. Check radio for proper operation. If radio operates, go to next step. If radio does not operate, perform TEST D: NO POWER IN RUN POSITION.

2) Turn ignition switch to LOCK position. Disconnect ignition switch harness connector C209. Measure voltage at terminal B5 at ignition switch harness connector C209. *See Fig. 4.* If battery voltage exists, replace ignition switch. If battery voltage does not exist, repair power distribution circuit.

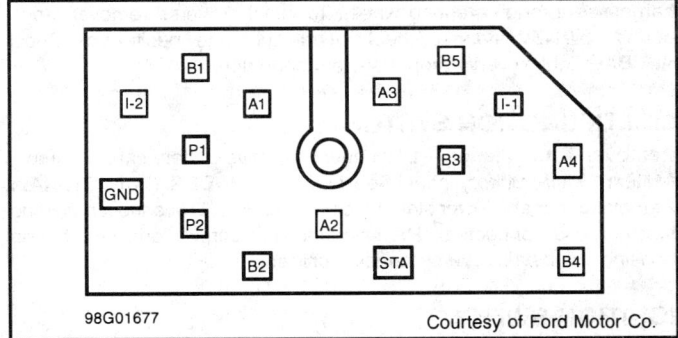

Fig. 4: Identifying Ignition Switch Harness Connector C209 Terminals

TEST D: NO POWER IN RUN POSITION

Test ignition switch. See IGNITION SWITCH under COMPONENT TESTS. If ignition switch is defective, replace ignition switch. If ignition switch is okay, repair power distribution circuit(s) as necessary. See appropriate wiring diagram in POWER DISTRIBUTION article in WIRING DIAGRAMS.

TEST E: NO POWER IN START POSITION

1) Turn ignition switch to LOCK position. Disconnect ignition switch harness connector C209. Measure voltage at terminals B4 (Light Green/Violet wire) and B5 (Light Green/Violet wire) at ignition switch harness connector C209. *See Fig. 4.* If battery voltage exists at both terminals, go to next step. If battery voltage does not exist at either terminal, repair appropriate power distribution circuit. See appropriate wiring diagram in POWER DISTRIBUTION article in WIRING DIAGRAMS.

2) Test ignition switch. See IGNITION SWITCH under COMPONENT TESTS. If ignition switch is okay, go to next step. If ignition switch is defective, replace ignition switch.

3) Connect ignition switch harness connector C209. Turn ignition switch to START position. If starter engages, repair open in Red/Light Blue wire. See appropriate wiring diagram in POWER DISTRIBUTION article in WIRING DIAGRAMS. If starter does not engage, repair open in White/Pink wire. See appropriate wiring diagram in POWER DISTRIBUTION article in WIRING DIAGRAMS.

REMOVAL & INSTALLATION

CAUTION: When battery is disconnected, vehicle computer and memory system may lose memory data. Driveability problems may exist until computer systems have completed a relearn cycle. See COMPUTER RELEARN PROCEDURES article in GENERAL INFORMATION before disconnecting battery.

STEERING WHEEL

WARNING: Deactivate air bag system before performing any service operation involving steering column components. See appropriate AIR BAG RESTRAINT SYSTEMS article. DO NOT apply electrical power to any component on steering column without first deactivating air bag system. Air bag may deploy.

Removal & Installation – 1) Ensure front wheels are in straight-ahead position. Disable air bag system. See appropriate AIR BAG RESTRAINT SYSTEMS article. Wait at least one minute for air bag back-up power supply to deplete.

2) Remove air bag module retaining nuts/screws. Lift air bag module from steering wheel. Disconnect air bag wiring harness from module. Disconnect cruise control switch connector (if equipped). Remove and discard steering wheel bolt.

3) Remove steering wheel. While removing steering wheel, guide wiring harnesses through steering wheel. To install, reverse removal procedure. Install NEW steering wheel bolt and tighten to specification. Check AIR BAG light to verify proper system operation.

MULTIFUNCTION SWITCH

Removal & Installation – Disconnect negative battery cable. Remove ignition switch lock cylinder. See LOCK CYLINDER (FUNCTIONAL). Remove upper and lower steering column covers. Disconnect multifunction harness connectors. Remove retaining screws and switch from housing. To install, reverse removal procedure.

IGNITION SWITCH

Removal & Installation – Disconnect negative battery cable. Remove driver's side instrument panel under cover. Remove instrument panel reinforcement. Disconnect ignition switch harness connector. Turn ignition switch to LOCK position. Remove mounting screws and ignition switch. To install, reverse removal procedure.

LOCK CYLINDER (FUNCTIONAL)

NOTE: See LOCK CYLINDER (NON-FUNCTIONAL) if lock cylinder is non-functional (lock cylinder cannot be rotated because of missing key or damaged lock cylinder).

Removal & Installation – Disconnect negative battery cable. Turn lock cylinder to RUN position. Locate hole in shroud under lock cylinder. Insert a 1/8" drill bit or punch into hole. Press lock cylinder retaining pin while pulling lock cylinder from housing. To install, turn lock cylinder to RUN position. Press retaining pin inward and insert lock cylinder into housing. Ensure lock cylinder is fully seated and aligned with interlocking washer.

LOCK CYLINDER (NON-FUNCTIONAL)

NOTE: If lock cylinder is functional (key is available and lock cylinder turns freely), see LOCK CYLINDER (FUNCTIONAL) .

Removal & Installation – 1) Disconnect negative battery cable. Disable air bag system. See appropriate AIR BAG RESTRAINT SYSTEMS article. Remove steering wheel. See STEERING WHEEL. Twist off cap from ignition lock cylinder. Using a 1/8" bit, drill out retaining pin located below lock cylinder on housing. DO NOT drill deeper than 1/2".

2) Using channel lock pliers, twist lock cylinder cap until it separates from lock cylinder. Using a 3/8" drill bit, drill down center of ignition lock key slot about 1 3/4" until lock cylinder breaks loose from its base.

3) Remove retainer, washer, and lock cylinder gear from housing. Remove metal shavings from lock cylinder bore. Replace housing if damaged. To install, reverse removal procedure. Connect negative battery cable. Check AIR BAG light for proper system operation.

TORQUE SPECIFICATIONS

TORQUE SPECIFICATIONS

Application	Ft. Lbs. (N.m)
Steering Wheel Bolt [1]	23-35
	(31-48)

[1] – Use NEW bolt when installing steering wheel.

WIRING DIAGRAMS

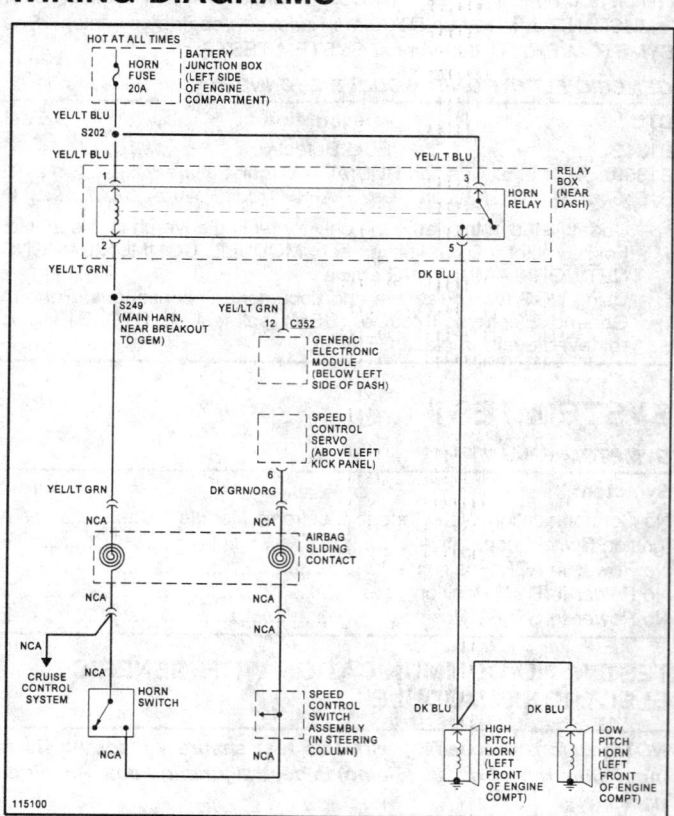

Fig. 5: Horn System Wiring Diagram (Mustang)

DESCRIPTION & OPERATION

The multifunction switch, located on the steering column, includes headlight dimmer, flash-to-pass and front windshield wiper/washer switches. The ignition switch and lock cylinder are also mounted on the steering column.

WARNING: Deactivate air bag system before performing any service operation involving steering column components. See appropriate AIR BAG RESTRAINT SYSTEMS article. Do not apply electrical power to any component on steering column without first deactivating air bag system. Air bag may deploy.

TROUBLE SHOOTING

Before performing individual component tests or system tests, inspect for the following possible causes of system malfunction. Correct any obvious defects before proceeding:

* Mechanical failure.
* Low battery charge.
* Faulty fuses.
* Loose or corroded connectors.
* Damaged wiring.

COMPONENT TESTS

CAUTION: When battery is disconnected, vehicle computer and memory system may lose memory data. Driveability problems may exist until computer systems have completed a relearn cycle. See COMPUTER RELEARN PROCEDURES article in GENERAL INFORMATION before disconnecting battery.

NOTE: Before performing following tests, ensure all multifunction switch grounds, wiring, and fuses are okay. Also, ensure all circuit connections are clean and tight. For ignition switch circuit identification, see appropriate wiring diagram in POWER DISTRIBUTION article in WIRING DIAGRAMS. For multifunction switch circuit identification, see appropriate wiring diagram in EXTERIOR LIGHTS article.

MULTIFUNCTION SWITCH

Remove and disconnect multifunction switch. See MULTIFUNCTION SWITCH under REMOVAL & INSTALLATION. Measure resistance between specified terminals while operating multifunction switch lever to positions as specified. *See Fig. 1.* See MULTIFUNCTION SWITCH TESTING table. If resistance is not as specified, replace multifunction switch.

MULTIFUNCTION SWITCH TESTING

Switch Position	Terminals	[1] Ohms
Wiper Switch		
OFF	5 & 6	47,600
INT	5 & 6	11,330
LO	5 & 6	4080
HI	5 & 6	0-4
Intermittent Wipers		
INT & OFF	6 & 7	[2]
LO & HI	6 & 7	3300
Washer Switch		
OFF	6 & 7	103,300
ON	6 & 7	0-4
Hazard Switch		
ON	B & I	0-4
ON	B & A	0-4
ON	B & G	0-4
ON	B & E	0-4
Left Turn Signal		
ON	C & A	0-4

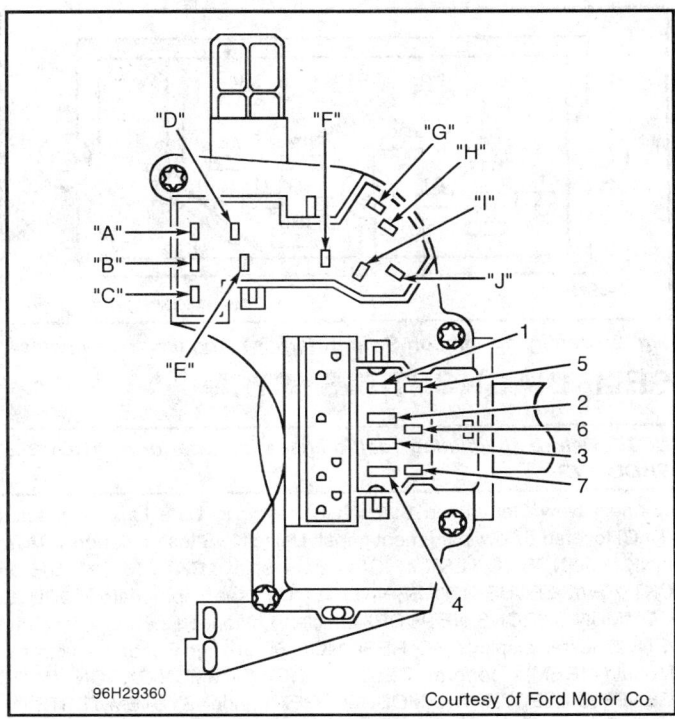

96H29360 — Courtesy of Ford Motor Co.

Fig. 1: Identifying Multifunction Switch Terminals

MULTIFUNCTION SWITCH TESTING (Cont.)

Switch Position	Terminals	[1] Ohms
ON	C & G	0-4
Right Turn Signal		
ON	C & I	0-4
ON	C & E	0-4
High Beam	1 & 3	0-4
Low Beam	1 & 2	0-4
Flash-To-Pass		
ON	4 & 3	0-4

[1] – Specification can vary by as much as 10 percent.
[2] – Rotate control from maximum delay to minimum delay. Resistance should gradually decrease from approximately 103,000 to 3300 ohms.

IGNITION SWITCH

1) To inspect ignition switch for mechanical operation, rotate lock cylinder through all switch positions. Lock cylinder should not bind, and should return from START to RUN position without assistance. Replace ignition switch as necessary.

2) To test electrical function of ignition switch, disconnect ignition switch connector. Check continuity between specified switch terminals using a self-powered test light or ohmmeter. *See Fig. 2.* See IGNITION SWITCH CONTINUITY table. If continuity is not as specified, replace ignition switch.

IGNITION SWITCH CONTINUITY

Switch Position	Continuity Between Terminals
Start	STA & B4
Run	B5 & I1; B1 & A1; B2 & A2; B3 & A3; B4 & A4
ACC	B5 & A1

FORD
4-1280

1999 ACCESSORIES & EQUIPMENT
Steering Column Switches
F150 & F250 Light-Duty Pickup (Cont.)

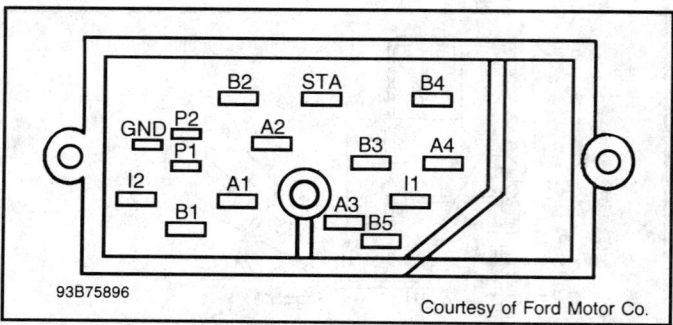

93B75896

Courtesy of Ford Motor Co.

Fig. 2: Identifying Ignition Switch Harness Connector Terminals

SELF-DIAGNOSTIC SYSTEM

NOTE: Before beginning self-diagnostics, perform TROUBLE SHOOTING.

Connect New Generation Star (NGS) tester to Data Link Connector (DLC) located below instrument panel. Using NGS tester, perform DATA LINK DIAGNOSTIC TEST. If NGS tester displays CKT 914, CKT 915 or CKT 70=ALL ECUS NO RESP/NOT EQUIP, see appropriate MODULE COMMUNICATIONS NETWORK article to diagnosis network concern. If NGS tester displays NO RESP/NOT EQUIP for Generic Electronic Module (GEM), perform TEST A: NO COMMUNICATION WITH GENERIC ELECTRONIC MODULE (GEM) under SYSTEM TESTS.

If NGS tester displays SYSTEM PASSED, retrieve and record continuous DTCs. Erase continuous DTCs. Perform self-test diagnostics for GEM using NGS tester. If GEM DTCs are retrieved, see GENERIC ELECTRONIC MODULE (GEM) DTC DEFINITIONS table to continue diagnosis. If no DTCs were retrieved, repair system by symptom. See SYMPTOM CHART table and perform appropriate test under SYSTEM TESTS.

GENERIC ELECTRONIC MODULE (GEM) DTC DEFINITIONS

DTC [1]	Description	Test
B1342	GEM Is Defective	[2]
B1355	Ignition Run Circuit Failure	E
B1359	Ignition RUN/ACC Circuit Failure	E
B1365	Ignition START Circuit Failure	F

[1] – Codes listed in this table are only for testing covered in this article. For complete DTC listing, see appropriate MODULE COMMUNICATIONS NETWORK article.

[2] – Clear DTCs. Retrieve DTCs. If DTC B1342 is retrieved, replace GEM and retest system operation.

SYMPTOM CHART

Symptom	Test
No Communication With Generic Electronic Module (GEM)	A
Unable To Enter Self-Test	B
Ignition Switch Inoperative	C
No Power In ACC Position	D
No Power In RUN Position	E
No Power In START Position	F

SYSTEM TESTS

CAUTION: When battery is disconnected, vehicle computer and memory system may lose memory data. Driveability problems may exist until computer systems have completed a relearn cycle. See COMPUTER RELEARN PROCEDURES article in GENERAL INFORMATION before disconnecting battery.

TEST A: NO COMMUNICATION WITH GENERIC ELECTRONIC MODULE (GEM)

1) Ensure ignition switch is off. Connect New Generation Star (NGS) tester to Data Link Connector (DLC). Depress clutch pedal (if applicable). Using NGS tester, read IGN_GEM PID while rotating ignition switch through START, RUN, OFF and ACC positions. If PID values match ignition switch positions, go to next step. If PID values do not agree with ignition switch positions, repair suspect open circuit between ignition switch and instrument panel fuse block. See appropriate wiring diagram in POWER DISTRIBUTION article in WIRING DIAGRAMS. Clear DTCs and retest system.

2) Disconnect instrument panel fuse/relay block Black connector C243. *See Fig. 3.* Measure voltage between ground and terminal No. 11 (Tan/Black wire) on connector C243. If voltage is more than 10 volts, go to next step. If voltage is 10 volts or less, repair open Tan/Black wire circuit. Clear DTCs and retest system.

3) Turn ignition switch to OFF position. Reconnect Black connector C243. Disconnect GEM 18-pin connector C267. GEM is mounted on back of instrument panel fuse/relay block. Turn ignition on. Measure voltage between ground and terminals No. 4 and 16 on GEM connector C267. *See Fig. 3.* If voltages are more than 10 volts, go to next step. If voltages are 10 volts or less, replace fuse/relay block. Clear DTCs and retest system.

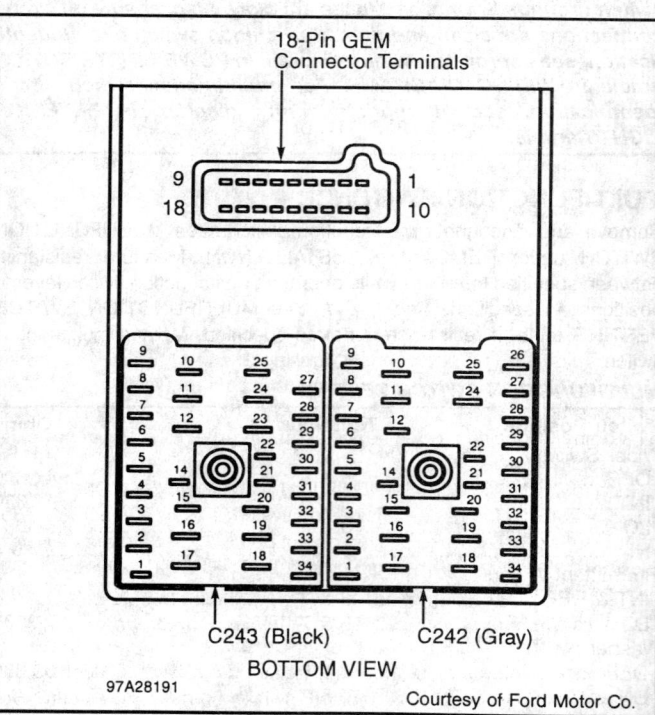

18-Pin GEM
Connector Terminals

C243 (Black)   C242 (Gray)

BOTTOM VIEW

97A28191

Courtesy of Ford Motor Co.

Fig. 3: Identifying Instrument Panel Fuse/Relay Block Terminals

4) Turn ignition off. Disconnect Gray GEM connector C239. Measure resistance between ground and terminal No. 26 (Black/Light Blue wire) on connector C239. *See Fig. 4.* If resistance is less than 5 ohms, go to next step. If resistance is 5 ohms or greater, repair open Black/Light Blue wire. Clear DTCs and retest system.

1999 ACCESSORIES & EQUIPMENT
Steering Column Switches
F150 & F250 Light-Duty Pickup (Cont.)

FORD
4-1281

5) Measure resistance between ground and terminal No. 14 (Black/Light Blue wire) on connector C239. *See Fig. 4.* If resistance is less than 5 ohms, fault is in module communications network. See appropriate MODULE COMMUNICATIONS NETWORK article to continue diagnosis. If resistance is 5 ohms or greater, repair open in Black/Light Blue wire circuit. Clear DTCs and retest system.

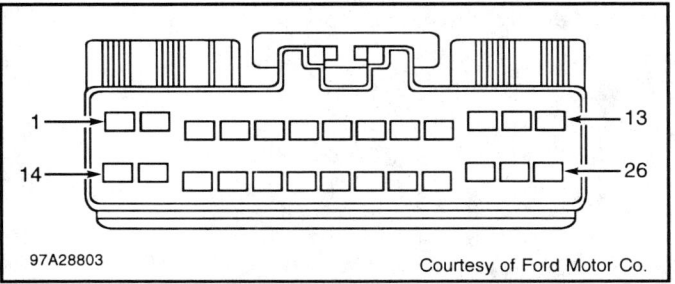

97A28803   Courtesy of Ford Motor Co.

Fig. 4: Identifying GEM C239 Connector Terminals

TEST B: UNABLE TO ENTER SELF-TEST

NOTE: Prior to replacement of GEM module, it is necessary to upload module configuration information using NGS tester. See COMPUTER RELEARN PROCEDURES article in GENERAL INFORMATION.

Connect New Generation Star (NGS) tester to Data Link Connector (DLC). Perform self-test diagnostics for GEM using NGS tester. If NGS tester communicates with GEM, replace GEM. If NGS tester does not communicate with GEM, go to TEST A: NO COMMUNICATION WITH GENERIC ELECTRONIC MODULE (GEM).

TEST C: IGNITION SWITCH INOPERATIVE

Turn ignition off. Disconnect ignition switch harness connector. Check for battery voltage between ground and terminals B1, B3, B4, and B5 on ignition switch harness connector. *See Fig. 2.* If battery voltage exists at all terminals specified, replace ignition switch and retest system. If battery voltage does not exist, repair suspect wire. See appropriate wiring diagram in POWER DISTRIBUTION article in WIRING DIAGRAMS.

TEST D: NO POWER IN ACC POSITION

Turn ignition on. Turn radio on. If radio operates correctly, replace ignition switch. If radio does not operate correctly, go to TEST E: NO POWER IN RUN POSITION.

TEST E: NO POWER IN RUN POSITION

1) Turn ignition off. Disconnect ignition switch harness connector. Measure voltage between ground and terminals B1, B3, B4, and B5 on ignition switch harness connector. *See Fig. 2.* If battery voltage exists at all terminals specified, go to next step. If battery voltage does not exist, repair suspect open wire.

2) Inspect ignition switch. See IGNITION SWITCH under COMPONENT TESTS. Replace as needed. If ignition switch is okay, inspect operation of back-up lights. If back-up lights do not operate, repair open Red/Light Blue wire at terminal No. A3 on ignition switch harness connector. See appropriate wiring diagram in POWER DISTRIBUTION article in WIRING DIAGRAMS. If radio does not operate, repair open Black/Light Green wire at terminal No. A1 on ignition switch harness connector. If instrument cluster does not operate, repair open Dark Blue/Light Green wire at terminal No. I1 on ignition switch harness connector. See appropriate wiring diagram in POWER DISTRIBUTION article in WIRING DIAGRAMS. If blower motor does not operate, repair open Gray/Yellow wire at terminal No. A4 on ignition switch harness connector.

TEST F: NO POWER IN START POSITION

1) Turn ignition off. Disconnect ignition switch harness connector. Measure voltage between ground and terminal B4 (Light Green/Violet wire) on ignition switch harness connector. *See Fig. 2.* If voltage is greater than 10 volts, go to next step. If voltage is 10 volts or less, repair open Light Green/Violet wire.

2) Inspect ignition switch. See IGNITION SWITCH under COMPONENT TESTS. If ignition switch is faulty, replace ignition switch and retest system. If ignition switch is okay, repair open Red/Light Blue wire on terminal STA on ignition switch harness connector. See appropriate wiring diagram in POWER DISTRIBUTION article in WIRING DIAGRAMS.

REMOVAL & INSTALLATION

WARNING: Deactivate air bag system before performing any service operation involving steering column components. See appropriate AIR BAG RESTRAINT SYSTEMS article. Do not apply electrical power to any component on steering column without first deactivating air bag system. Air bag may deploy.

CAUTION: When battery is disconnected, vehicle computer and memory system may lose memory data. Driveability problems may exist until computer systems have completed a relearn cycle. See COMPUTER RELEARN PROCEDURES article in GENERAL INFORMATION before disconnecting battery.

MULTIFUNCTION SWITCH

Removal & Installation – Disconnect negative battery cable. Remove lock cylinder. See LOCK CYLINDER. Remove upper and lower steering column shrouds. Remove retaining screws. Disconnect multifunction switch harness connectors. Remove switch. To install, reverse removal procedure.

IGNITION SWITCH

Removal & Installation – **1)** Disconnect negative battery cable. Remove steering column opening cover. Remove hood release handle and position aside. Remove parking brake release handle and set aside. **2)** Remove steering column opening cover reinforcement. Disconnect ignition switch harness connector. Remove 2 ignition switch screws and ignition switch. To install, reverse removal procedure.

LOCK CYLINDER

Removal & Installation (With Key) – Disconnect negative battery cable. Set ignition switch to RUN position. Insert a 1/8" drill bit or wire through access hole in steering column trim (below lock cylinder). Press retaining pin inward and pull out lock cylinder. To install, lubricate lock cylinder. Turn lock cylinder to RUN position. Press retaining pin inward and insert lock cylinder into housing. To install remaining components, reverse removal procedure.

Removal (Without Key) – **1)** Use this procedure to remove ignition lock cylinder if key is missing or cylinder is frozen. Disconnect negative battery cable. Remove steering wheel. Twist cap off ignition switch lock cylinder. Using 1/8" drill bit, drill out lock cylinder retaining pin.

2) Using a 3/8" drill bit, drill down middle of ignition lock key slot about 1 3/4" (44 mm) until ignition switch lock cylinder breaks loose from breakaway base of ignition switch lock cylinder. Remove ignition switch lock cylinder and drill shavings from lock cylinder housing.

3) Remove bearing retainer, bearing and gear. Thoroughly clean all metal shavings and other foreign material from housing. Carefully inspect housing for damage. If damage is apparent, replace housing.

Installation – **1)** Install gear, bearing, and retainer. Lubricate cylinder cavity. Rotate lock cylinder to RUN position. Press retaining pin inward and insert new lock cylinder into lock cylinder housing.

2) Before rotating key to OFF position, ensure cylinder is fully seated and aligned. Use key to rotate cylinder to ensure mechanical operation is okay in all positions. Install steering wheel.

FORD
4-1282

1999 ACCESSORIES & EQUIPMENT
Steering Column Switches
F150 & F250 Light-Duty Pickup (Cont.)

WIRING DIAGRAMS

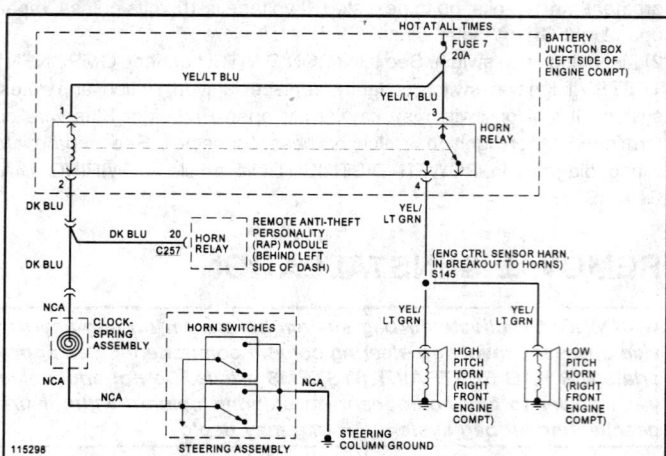

Fig. 5: Horn System Wiring Diagram
(F150 & F250 Light-Duty Pickup)

NOTE: This article includes Cab & Chassis.

DESCRIPTION

The multifunction switch, located on the steering column, includes headlight dimmer, flash-to-pass and front windshield wiper/washer switches. The ignition switch and lock cylinder are also mounted on the steering column.

WARNING: Deactivate air bag system before performing any service operation involving steering column components. See appropriate AIR BAG RESTRAINT SYSTEMS article. Do not apply electrical power to any component on steering column without first deactivating air bag system. Air bag may deploy.

TROUBLE SHOOTING

Verify customers complaint by operating multifunction switch or headlight switch. Check for obvious signs of mechanical or electrical damage. Check for blown fuse(s), loose or corroded connectors, or damaged wiring harness. Check for damaged ignition switch or ignition key. Repair or replace components as necessary. Before performing following tests, ensure all multifunction switch grounds, wiring, and fuses are okay.

Also, ensure all circuit connections are clean and tight. For ignition switch circuit identification, see appropriate wiring diagram in POWER DISTRIBUTION article in WIRING DIAGRAMS. For multifunction switch circuit identification, see appropriate wiring diagram in EXTERIOR LIGHTS article.

COMPONENT TESTS

CAUTION: When battery is disconnected, vehicle computer and memory system may lose memory data. Driveability problems may exist until computer systems have completed a relearn cycle. See COMPUTER RELEARN PROCEDURES article in GENERAL INFORMATION before disconnecting battery.

MULTIFUNCTION SWITCH

Remove and disconnect multifunction switch. See MULTIFUNCTION SWITCH under REMOVAL & INSTALLATION. Measure resistance between specified terminals while operating multifunction switch lever to positions as specified. *See Fig. 1.* See MULTIFUNCTION SWITCH TESTING table. If resistance is not as specified, replace multifunction switch.

MULTIFUNCTION SWITCH TESTING

Switch Position	Terminals	[1] Ohms
Wiper Switch		
OFF	5 & 6	47,600
INT	5 & 6	11,330
LO	5 & 6	4080
HI	5 & 6	0-4
Intermittent Wipers		
INT & OFF	6 & 7	[2]
LO & HI	6 & 7	3300
Washer Switch		
OFF	6 & 7	103,300
ON	6 & 7	0-4
Hazard Switch		
ON	B & I	0-4
ON	B & A	0-4
ON	B & G	0-4
ON	B & E	0-4
Left Turn Signal		
ON	C & A	0-4
ON	C & G	0-4

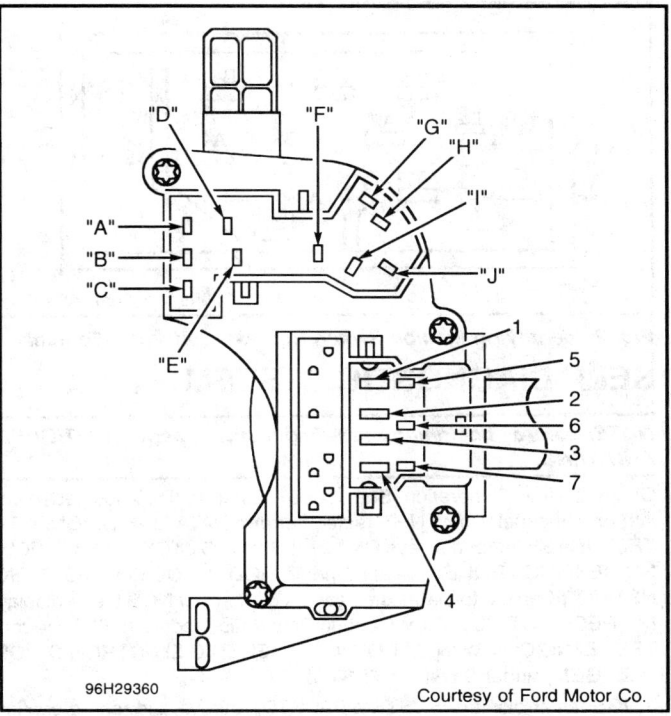

96H29360   Courtesy of Ford Motor Co.

Fig. 1: Identifying Multifunction Switch Terminals

MULTIFUNCTION SWITCH TESTING (Cont.)

Switch Position	Terminals	[1] Ohms
Right Turn Signal		
ON	C & I	0-4
ON	C & E	0-4
High Beam	1 & 3	0-4
Low Beam	1 & 2	0-4
Flash-To-Pass		
ON	4 & 3	0-4

[1] – Specification can vary by as much as 10 percent.
[2] – Rotate control from maximum delay to minimum delay. Resistance should gradually decrease from approximately 103,000 to 3300 ohms.

IGNITION SWITCH

1) To inspect ignition switch for mechanical operation, rotate lock cylinder through all switch positions. Lock cylinder should not bind, and should return from START to RUN position without assistance. Replace ignition switch as necessary.

2) To test electrical function of ignition switch, disconnect ignition switch connector. Check continuity between specified switch terminals using a self-powered test light or ohmmeter. *See Fig. 2.* See IGNITION SWITCH CONTINUITY table. If continuity is not as specified, replace ignition switch.

IGNITION SWITCH CONTINUITY

Switch Position	Continuity Between Terminals
Start	STA & B4
Run	B5 & I1; B1 & A1; B3 & A3; B4 & A4
ACC	B5 & A1

FORD
4-1284

1999 ACCESSORIES & EQUIPMENT
Steering Column Switches
F250 Super-Duty & F350 Pickup (Cont.)

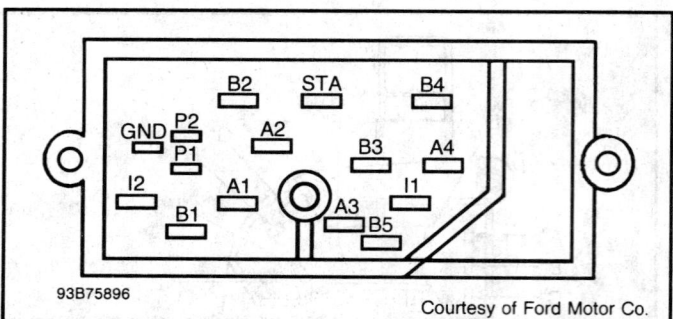

93B75896

Courtesy of Ford Motor Co.

Fig. 2: Identifying Ignition Switch Harness Connector Terminals

SELF-DIAGNOSTIC SYSTEM

NOTE: Before beginning self-diagnostics, perform TROUBLE SHOOTING.

Connect New Generation Star (NGS) tester to DLC located below instrument panel. Using NGS tester, perform DATA LINK DIAGNOSTIC TEST. If NGS tester displays CKT 914, CKT 915 or CKT 70=ALL ECUS NO RESP/NOT EQUIP, see appropriate MODULE COMMUNICATIONS NETWORK article to diagnosis network concern. If NGS tester displays NO RESP/NOT EQUIP for Generic Electronic Module (GEM), perform TEST E: NO COMMUNICATION WITH GENERIC ELECTRONIC MODULE (GEM) under SYSTEM TESTS.

If NGS tester displays SYSTEM PASSED, retrieve and record continuous DTCs. Erase continuous DTCs. Perform self-test diagnostics for GEM using NGS tester. If GEM DTCs are retrieved, see GENERIC ELECTRONIC MODULE (GEM) DTC DEFINITIONS table to continue diagnosis. If no DTCs were retrieved, repair system by symptom. See SYMPTOM CHART table and perform appropriate test under SYSTEM TESTS.

GENERIC ELECTRONIC MODULE (GEM) DTC DEFINITIONS

DTC	Description	Test
B1342	GEM Is Defective	1
B1355	Ignition Run Circuit Failure	C
B1359	Ignition RUN/ACC Circuit Failure	C
B1365	Ignition START Circuit Failure	D

[1] – Clear DTCs. Retrieve DTCs. If DTC B1342 is retrieved, replace GEM and retest system operation.

SYMPTOM CHART

Symptom	Test
Ignition Switch Inoperative	A
No Power In ACC Position	B
No Power In RUN Position	C
No Power In START Position	D
No Communication With Generic Electronic Module (GEM)	E

SYSTEM TESTS

CAUTION: When battery is disconnected, vehicle computer and memory system may lose memory data. Driveability problems may exist until computer systems have completed a relearn cycle. See COMPUTER RELEARN PROCEDURES article in GENERAL INFORMATION before disconnecting battery.

TEST A: IGNITION SWITCH INOPERATIVE

1) Check fuses No. 20 (50-amp) and 21 (50-amp) in power distribution box in engine compartment. If fuses are okay, go to next step. If either fuse is blown, replace blown fuse. If fuse repeatedly blows, repair suspect circuit between power distribution box and ignition switch for short to ground. See appropriate wiring diagram in POWER DISTRIBUTION article in WIRING DIAGRAMS.

2) Turn ignition off. Disconnect ignition switch harness connector. Measure voltage between ground and terminals B1, B3, B4, and B5 on ignition switch harness connector. *See Fig. 2.* If battery voltage exists at all specified terminals, check ignition switch. See IGNITION SWITCH under COMPONENT TESTS. If ignition switch is faulty, replace ignition switch and retest system. If battery voltage does not exist, repair suspect open circuit. See appropriate wiring diagram in POWER DISTRIBUTION article in WIRING DIAGRAMS.

TEST B: NO POWER IN ACC POSITION

Turn ignition on. Turn radio on. If radio operates correctly, replace ignition switch. If radio does not operate correctly, go to TEST C: NO POWER IN RUN POSITION.

TEST C: NO POWER IN RUN POSITION

1) Check fuses No. 20 (50-amp) and 21 (50-amp) in power distribution box in engine compartment. If fuses are okay, go to next step. If either fuse is blown, replace blown fuse. If fuse repeatedly blows, repair suspect circuit between power distribution box and ignition switch for short to ground. See appropriate wiring diagram in POWER DISTRIBUTION article in WIRING DIAGRAMS.

2) Turn ignition off. Disconnect ignition switch harness connector. Measure voltage between ground and terminals B1, B3, B4, and B5 on ignition switch harness connector. *See Fig. 2.* If battery voltage exists at all terminals specified, go to next step. If battery voltage does not exist, repair suspect open wire.

3) Inspect ignition switch. See IGNITION SWITCH under COMPONENT TESTS. Replace as needed. If ignition switch is okay, go to next step.

4) Turn ignition on. Measure voltage between ground and input terminals of fuses No. 8 (5-amp), 23 (10-amp) and 27 (10-amp) on interior fuse block. *See Fig. 3.* If voltage is greater than 10 volts on all circuits, system is currently functioning correctly. Retest system. If voltage is 10 volts or less on any circuit, repair open suspect circuit. See appropriate wiring diagram in POWER DISTRIBUTION article in WIRING DIAGRAMS.

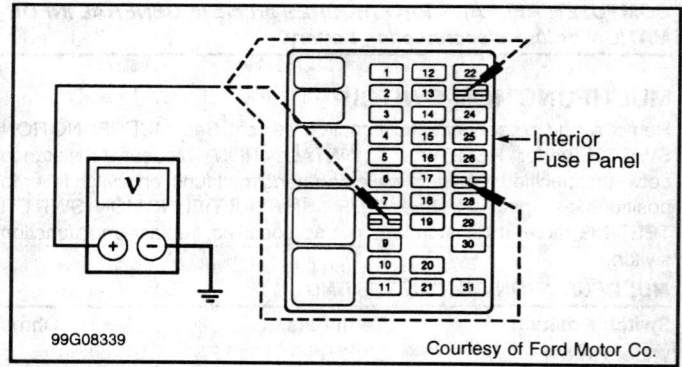

99G08339

Courtesy of Ford Motor Co.

Fig. 3: Checking Voltage Supply To Interior Fuse Panel

TEST D: NO POWER IN START POSITION

1) Check fuse No. 20 (50-amp) in power distribution box in engine compartment. If fuses are okay, go to next step. If fuse is blown, replace blown fuse. If fuse repeatedly blows, repair suspect circuit between power distribution box and ignition switch for short to ground. See appropriate wiring diagram in POWER DISTRIBUTION article in WIRING DIAGRAMS.

2) Turn ignition off. Disconnect ignition switch harness connector. Measure voltage between ground and terminal B4 and B5 (Light Green/Pink wires) on ignition switch harness connector. *See Fig. 2.* If voltage is greater than 10 volts, go to next step. If voltage is 10 volts or less, repair open Light Green/Pink wire(s).

3) Ensure ignition is off. Measure resistance of Red/Light Blue wire (circuit 32) between terminal STA on ignition switch harness connector and output terminal on interior fuse panel fuse No. 20. *See Figs. 2 and*

1999 ACCESSORIES & EQUIPMENT
Steering Column Switches
F250 Super-Duty & F350 Pickup (Cont.)

**FORD
4-1285**

4. Measure resistance of Red/Black wire (circuit 1050) between terminal I1 on ignition switch harness connector and output terminal on interior fuse panel fuse No. 29. If resistance is less than 5 ohms on both circuits, go to next step. If resistance is 5 ohms or greater for either circuit, repair suspect open circuit.

4) Inspect ignition switch. See IGNITION SWITCH under COMPONENT TESTS. If ignition switch is faulty, replace ignition switch and retest system. If ignition switch is okay, see appropriate starter article in STARTING & CHARGING SYSTEMS.

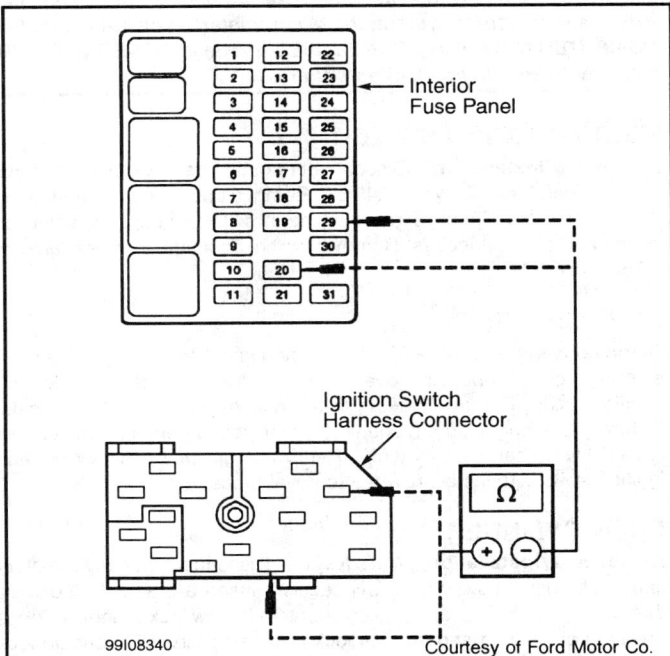

99I08340   Courtesy of Ford Motor Co.

Fig. 4: Checking Continuity Of Circuits 32 & 1050

TEST E: NO COMMUNICATION WITH GENERIC ELECTRONIC MODULE (GEM)

NOTE: If GEM replacement is necessary, it is necessary to upload module configuration information using NGS tester. See COMPUTER RELEARN PROCEDURES article in GENERAL INFORMATION.

1) Ensure ignition is off. Remove and inspect interior fuse block fuse No. 15 (5-amp). If fuse is okay, install fuse and go to next step. If fuse is blown, go to step **3)**.
2) Measure voltage between ground and input terminal on fuse No. 15 on interior fuse block socket. If voltage is greater than 10 volts, go to step **4)**. If voltage is 10 volts or less, go to step **5)**.
3) Remove fuse No. 15. Disconnect GEM from back of interior fuse block. Measure resistance between ground and terminals No. 4 and 16 on interior fuse block 18-pin connector. *See Fig. 5*. If resistance is greater than 10,000 ohms, go to step **16)**. If resistance is 10,000 ohms or less, replace interior fuse block.
4) Disconnect GEM 26-pin C239 connector. Measure resistance between ground and terminal No. 26 (Pink/Orange wire) on GEM 26-pin harness connector. *See Fig. 6*. If resistance is less than 5 ohms, go to step **7)**. If resistance is 5 ohms or greater, repair open Pink/Orange wire.
5) Ensure ignition is off. Remove and inspect power distribution box fuse No. 22 (50-amp). If fuse is okay, install fuse and go to next step. If fuse is blown, repair Tan/Black wire (circuit 1052) on fuse No. 22 for short to ground.
6) Measure voltage between ground and input terminal on power distribution box fuse No. 22 (50-amp) socket. If voltage is greater than

10 volts, repair open Tan/Black wire on fuse No. 22. If voltage is 10 volts or less, replace power distribution box.
7) Disconnect NGS tester from DLC. Measure resistance of Light Blue/White wire between terminal No. 25 on GEM 26-pin harness connector and terminal No. 7 on DLC. *See Figs. 6 and 7*. If resistance is less than 5 ohms, go to next step. If resistance is 5 ohms or greater, repair open Light Blue/White wire.
8) Measure voltage between ground and terminal No. 26 (Pink/Orange wire) on GEM 26-pin harness connector. If voltage is greater than 10 volts, repair Pink/Orange wire for short to voltage. If voltage is 10 volts or less and vehicle is equipped Electronic Shift On The Fly (ESOF), go to next step. If vehicle is not equipped with ESOF, go to step **11)**.
9) Turn ignition off. Disconnect GEM 22-pin C247 connector. Turn ignition on. Measure voltage between ground and terminal No. 3 (White/Light Blue wire) on GEM 22-pin harness connector. If voltage is greater than 10 volts, go to next step. If voltage is 10 volts or less, go to step **11)**.
10) Turn ignition off. Disconnect 4WD mode switch connector. Turn ignition on. Measure voltage between ground and terminal No. 3 (White/Light Blue wire) on GEM 22-pin harness connector. *See Fig. 8*. If voltage is greater than 10 volts, repair White/Light Blue wire for short to voltage. Replace GEM. If voltage is 10 volts or less, replace 4WD mode select switch. Replace GEM.
11) Measure voltage between ground and terminal No. 20 (Dark Blue wire) on GEM 26-pin harness connector. If voltage is greater than 10 volts, go to next step. If voltage is 10 volts or less, go to step **13)**.
12) Turn ignition off. Disconnect multifunction switch connector. Turn ignition on. Measure voltage between ground and terminal No. 20 (Dark Blue wire) on GEM 26-pin harness connector. *See Fig. 6*. If voltage is greater than 10 volts, repair Dark Blue wire for short to voltage. Replace GEM. If voltage is 10 volts or less, replace multifunction switch. Replace GEM.
13) Measure voltage between ground and terminal No. 23 (Pink/Yellow wire) on GEM 26-pin harness connector. If voltage is greater than 10 volts, go to next step. If voltage is 10 volts or less and vehicle is not equipped with ABS, go to step **15)**. If vehicle is equipped with ABS, replace GEM.
14) Turn ignition off. Disconnect multifunction switch connector. Turn ignition on. Measure voltage between ground and terminal No. 23 (Pink/Yellow wire) on GEM 26-pin harness connector. *See Fig. 6*. If voltage is greater than 10 volts, repair Pink/Yellow wire for short to voltage. Replace GEM. If voltage is 10 volts or less, replace multifunction switch. Replace GEM.
15) Turn ignition off. Disconnect rear differential speed sensor connector. Turn ignition on. Measure voltage between ground and terminal No. 9 (Light Green/Black wire) on GEM 26-pin harness connector. If voltage is greater than 10 volts, repair Light Green/Black wire for short to voltage. Replace GEM. If voltage is 10 volts or less, replace GEM.
16) Remove and test horn relay. See WIRING DIAGRAMS. Replace as needed. If horn relay is okay, go to next step.
17) Ensure ignition is off. Disconnect GEM from back of interior fuse block. Disconnect GEM 22-pin C247 connector. Disconnect Brake Pedal Position (BPP) switch connector. Measure resistance between ground and terminal No. 12 (Red/Light Green wire) on GEM 22-pin harness connector. If resistance is greater than 10,000 ohms, go to next step. If resistance is 10,000 ohms or less, repair Red/Light Green wire for short to ground.
18) Disconnect interior fuse block C243 connector. *See Fig. 5*. Measure resistance between terminal No. 3 (Light Blue/Black wire) on BPP switch harness connector. If resistance is greater than 10,000 ohms, replace BPP switch. If resistance is 10,000 ohms or less, repair Light Blue/Black wire for short to ground.

FORD
4-1286

1999 ACCESSORIES & EQUIPMENT
Steering Column Switches
F250 Super-Duty & F350 Pickup (Cont.)

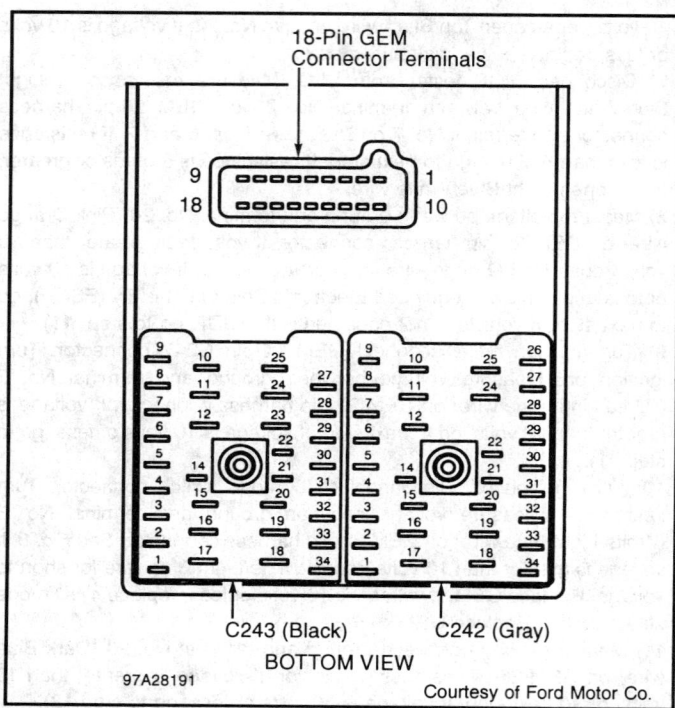

Fig. 5: Identifying Interior Fuse Block Connector Terminals

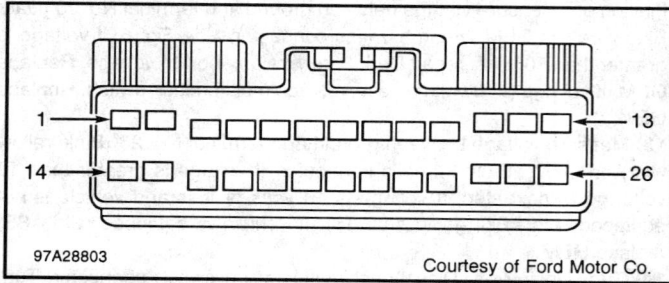

Fig. 6: Identifying GEM C239 26-Pin Connector Terminals

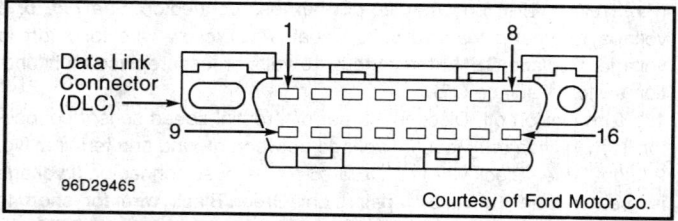

Fig. 7: Identifying DLC Harness Connector Terminals

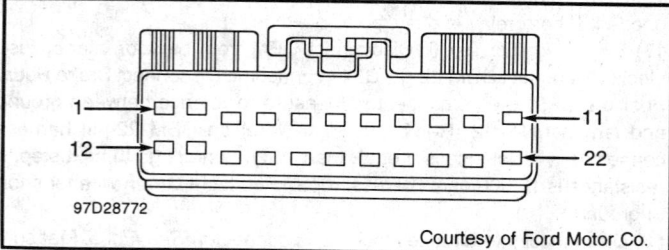

Fig. 8: Identifying GEM C239 22-Pin Connector Terminals

REMOVAL & INSTALLATION

WARNING: Deactivate air bag system before performing any service operation involving steering column components. See appropriate AIR BAG RESTRAINT SYSTEMS article. Do not apply electrical power to any component on steering column without first deactivating air bag system. Air bag may deploy.

CAUTION: When battery is disconnected, vehicle computer and memory system may lose memory data. Driveability problems may exist until computer systems have completed a relearn cycle. See COMPUTER RELEARN PROCEDURES article in GENERAL INFORMATION before disconnecting battery.

MULTIFUNCTION SWITCH

Removal & Installation – Disconnect negative battery cable. Remove lock cylinder. See LOCK CYLINDER. Remove upper and lower steering column shrouds. Remove retaining screws. Disconnect multifunction switch harness connectors. Remove switch. To install, reverse removal procedure.

IGNITION SWITCH

Removal & Installation – Disconnect negative battery cable. Remove steering column opening cover. Remove hood release handle and position aside. Remove parking brake release handle and set aside. Remove steering column opening cover reinforcement. Disconnect ignition switch harness connector. Remove 2 ignition switch screws and ignition switch. To install, reverse removal procedure.

LOCK CYLINDER

Removal & Installation (With Key) – Disconnect negative battery cable. Set ignition switch to RUN position. Insert a 1/8" drill bit or wire through access hole in steering column trim (below lock cylinder). Press retaining pin inward and pull out lock cylinder. To install, lubricate lock cylinder. Turn lock cylinder to RUN position. Press retaining pin inward and insert lock cylinder into housing. To install remaining components, reverse removal procedure.

Removal (Without Key) – 1) Use this procedure to remove ignition lock cylinder if key is missing or cylinder is frozen. Disconnect negative battery cable. Remove steering wheel. Twist cap off ignition switch lock cylinder. Using 1/8" drill bit, drill out lock cylinder retaining pin.

2) Using a 3/8" drill bit, drill down middle of ignition lock key slot about 1 3/4" (44 mm) until ignition switch lock cylinder breaks loose from breakaway base of ignition switch lock cylinder. Remove ignition switch lock cylinder and drill shavings from lock cylinder housing.

3) Remove bearing retainer, bearing and gear. Thoroughly clean all metal shavings and other foreign material from housing. Carefully inspect housing for damage. If damage is apparent, replace housing.

Installation – Install gear, bearing, and retainer. Lubricate cylinder cavity. Rotate lock cylinder to RUN position. Press retaining pin inward and insert new lock cylinder into lock cylinder housing. Before rotating key to OFF position, ensure cylinder is fully seated and aligned. Use key to rotate cylinder to ensure mechanical operation is okay in all positions. Install steering wheel.

WIRING DIAGRAMS

NOTE: For ignition switch circuit identification, see appropriate wiring diagram in POWER DISTRIBUTION article in WIRING DIAGRAMS. For multifunction switch circuit identification, see appropriate wiring diagram in EXTERIOR LIGHTS article.

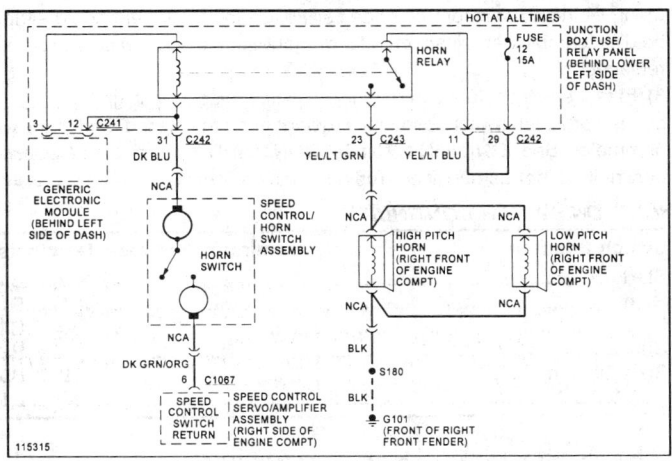

Fig. 9: Horn System Wiring Diagram
(F250 Super-Duty & F350 Pickup)

DESCRIPTION

The multifunction switch, located on the steering column, includes headlight dimmer, flash-to-pass and front windshield wiper/washer switches. *See Fig. 1*. The ignition switch and lock cylinder are also mounted on the steering column.

WARNING: Deactivate air bag system before performing any service operation involving steering column components. See appropriate AIR BAG RESTRAINT SYSTEMS article. DO NOT apply electrical power to any component on steering column without first deactivating air bag system. Air bag may deploy.

COMPONENT LOCATIONS

COMPONENT LOCATIONS

Component	Location
Air Bag Diagnostic Monitor [1]	Behind Right Kick Panel
Air Bag Sliding Contact	Base Of Steering Column
Central Junction Box	Behind Left Side Of Instrument Panel
Data Link Connector (DLC)	Below Driver's Side Of Instrument Panel, To Right Of Steering Column
Generic Electronic Module/Central Timer Module (GEM/CTM)	Behind Center Of Instrument Panel
Multifunction Switch	On Steering Column
Powertrain Control Module (PCM)	Mounted Through Firewall, On Passenger's Side
Speed Control Switches	In Steering Wheel
Transceiver Module	On Ignition Switch Lock Cylinder
Turn Signal/Hazard Flasher	Underdash Left Side Of Instrument Panel In Junction Box

[1] – Air bag diagnostic monitor may also be known as Electronic Crash Sensor (ECS) module.

ADJUSTMENTS

CAUTION: When battery is disconnected, vehicle computer and memory system may lose memory data. Driveability problems may exist until computer systems have completed a relearn cycle. See COMPUTER RELEARN PROCEDURES article in GENERAL INFORMATION before disconnecting battery.

IGNITION SWITCH

Disconnect negative battery cable. Set ignition switch to RUN position. Align switch pin with slot in lock/column assembly. Position slots in column/lock assembly with index mark on casing. Ignition switch is properly adjusted if:

- In ACCESSORY, accessory circuit is operative and steering wheel is locked. Automatic shift lever cannot be moved.
- In LOCK, all ignition switch electrical circuits are inoperative and steering wheel is locked. Automatic shift lever cannot be moved.
- In OFF, all ignition switch electrical circuits are inoperative and steering wheel is unlocked. Automatic shift lever can be moved.
- In ON (RUN), all ignition switch circuits or accessory circuits are operative except starter circuit and warning light check circuit. Steering wheel is unlocked and automatic shift lever can be moved.
- In START, only engine ignition, warning light check, and starter circuits are operative. Steering wheel is unlocked and automatic shifter can be moved.

TROUBLE SHOOTING

Before performing individual component tests, inspect for the following possible causes of system malfunction. Correct any obvious defects before proceeding.

- Mechanical Failure
- Low Battery Charge
- Faulty Fuses
- Damaged Multifunction Switch
- Damaged Ignition Switch
- Loose Or Corroded Connectors
- Damaged Wiring

COMPONENT TESTS

CAUTION: When battery is disconnected, vehicle computer and memory system may lose memory data. Driveability problems may exist until computer systems have completed a relearn cycle. See COMPUTER RELEARN PROCEDURES article in GENERAL INFORMATION before disconnecting battery.

NOTE: Before performing following tests, ensure all malfunction switch grounds, wiring, and fuses are okay. Also, ensure all circuit connections are clean and tight. For ignition switch circuit identification, see appropriate wiring diagram in POWER DISTRIBUTION article in WIRING DIAGRAMS. For multifunction switch circuit identification, see appropriate wiring diagram in EXTERIOR LIGHTS article.

DIMMER, FLASH-TO-PASS, TURN SIGNAL & HAZARD SWITCH

Remove and disconnect multifunction switch. See MULTIFUNCTION SWITCH under REMOVAL & INSTALLATION. Check continuity between specified terminals while operating multifunction switch lever to positions as specified. *See Fig. 1*. See DIMMER & TURN SIGNAL SWITCH TESTING table. If continuity is not as specified, replace multifunction switch.

DIMMER & TURN SIGNAL SWITCH TESTING

Switch Position	Check For Continuity Between Circuits No.
Left Turn Signal On	3 & 44
Right Turn Signal On	2 & 44
Hazard Switch On	2, 3 & 385
Flash To Pass On [1]	196 & 632
Headlight Dimmer	
On High Beam	15 & 632
On Low Beam	13 & 15

[1] – Lever pulled in halfway.

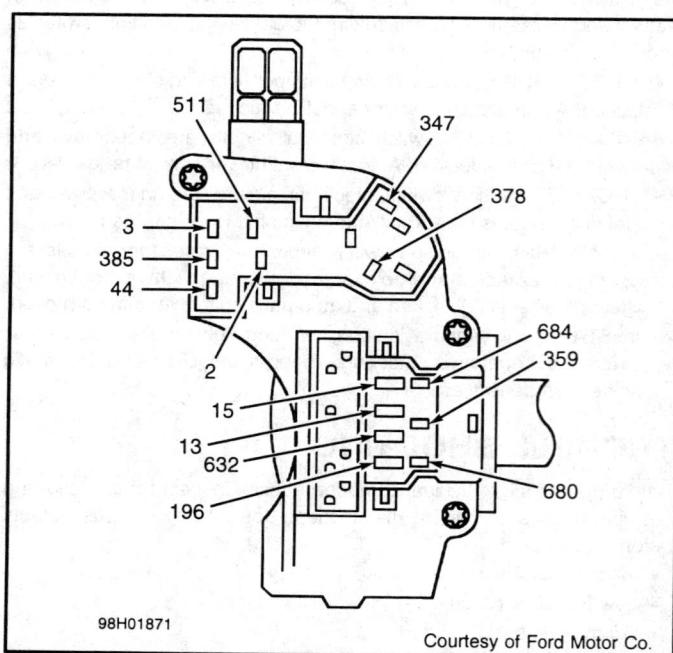

98H01871

Courtesy of Ford Motor Co.

Fig. 1: Identifying Multifunction Switch Circuit Terminals

WIPER/WASHER SWITCH

Remove and disconnect multifunction switch. See MULTIFUNCTION SWITCH under REMOVAL & INSTALLATION. Measure resistance between specified circuits while operating multifunction switch lever to positions as specified. See Fig. 1. See WIPER/WASHER SWITCH TESTING table. If resistance is not as specified, replace multifunction switch.

WIPER/WASHER SWITCH TESTING

Switch Position	Circuit No.	[1] Ohms
Wiper Switch		
Off	359 & 684	47,000
Int	359 & 684	11.000
Lo	359 & 684	4000
Hi	359 & 684	0-4
Washer Switch On	359 & 680	0-4
Wiper Intermittent	359 & 680	[2]

[1] – Specification can vary by as much as 10 percent.

[2] – Rotate control from maximum delay to minimum delay. Resistance should gradually decrease from approximately 224 k/ohms to 2.9 k/ohms.

IGNITION SWITCH

1) To inspect ignition switch for mechanical operation, rotate lock cylinder through all switch positions. Lock cylinder should not bind, and return from START to RUN position without assistance.

2) If binding or incorrect modes occur, ignition switch should be adjusted. See IGNITION SWITCH under ADJUSTMENTS. After adjust-

ment, if binding or incorrect modes still exist, lock cylinder should either be disassembled and inspected for damage, or ignition switch should be replaced.

3) To test electrical function of ignition switch, disconnect ignition switch connector. Test switch continuity using a self-powered test light or ohmmeter. See IGNITION SWITCH CONTINUITY table. See Fig. 2. If continuity is not as specified, replace ignition switch.

IGNITION SWITCH CONTINUITY

Switch Position	Continuity Between Terminals
Start	STA & B4
Start	GND & P1
Run	A4 & B4
Run	A2 & B2
Start Or Run	I1 & B5
Run & ACC	A1 & B1

SELF-DIAGNOSTIC SYSTEM

NOTE: Before beginning self-diagnostics, perform TROUBLE SHOOTING. A New Generation Star (NGS) tester is required to test system. If NGS tester does not communicate with vehicle, refer to NGS tester manual.

Verify customers complaint by operating ignition switch. Connect NGS tester to DLC located below instrument panel. Using NGS tester, perform DATA LINK DIAGNOSTIC TEST. If NGS tester displays CKT 914, CKT 915 or CKT 70=ALL ECUS NO RESP/NOT EQUIP, see appropriate MODULE COMMUNICATIONS NETWORK article to diagnosis network concern. If NGS tester displays NO RESP/NOT EQUIP for Generic Electronic Module (GEM), go to TEST E: NO COMMUNICATION WITH GEM/CTM MODULE under SYSTEM TESTS.

If NGS tester displays SYSTEM PASSED for GEM, retrieve and record continuous DTCs using NGS tester. Erase continuous DTCs. Perform GEM/CTM self-test diagnostics using NGS tester. If any DTCs are present, perform appropriate system test. See GENERIC ELECTRONIC MODULE/CENTRAL TIMER MODULE (GEM/CTM) DTC DEFINITIONS table. If no DTCs are retrieved, repair by symptom. See SYMPTOM CHART table under SYSTEM TESTS.

GENERIC ELECTRONIC MODULE/CENTRAL TIMER MODULE (GEM/CTM) DTC DEFINITIONS

DTC [1]	Description	Test
B1342	GEM/CTM Is Defective	[2]
B1355	Ignition RUN Circuit Failure	C
B1359	Ignition RUN/ACC Circuit Failure	B
B2141	NVM Configuration Failure	[3]

[1] – Codes listed in this table are for testing covered in this article. For complete DTC listing, see MODULE COMMUNICATIONS NETWORK – RANGER article.

[2] – Using NGS tester, clear DTCs. Retrieve DTCs. If DTC B1342 is retrieved, replace GEM/CTM and retest system operation.

[3] – Vehicle speed calibration data is not programmed into GEM/CTM. Use NGS tester configuration card help screen to program tire size and axle ratio. Retest system operation. If DTC B2141 is still present, replace GEM/CTM and retest system operation.

SYSTEM TESTS

CAUTION: When battery is disconnected or modules are replaced, vehicle computer and memory systems may lose memory data. Driveability problems may exist until computer systems have completed a relearn cycle. See COMPUTER RELEARN PROCEDURES article in GENERAL INFORMATION before disconnecting battery.

SYMPTOM CHART

Symptom	Test
Ignition Switch Inoperative	A
No Power In ACC Position	B
No Power In RUN Position	C
No Power In START Position	D
No Communication With GEM/CTM	E
Multifunction Switch Does Not Operate Properly	1

[1] – Perform appropriate test under COMPONENT TESTS.

TEST A: IGNITION SWITCH INOPERATIVE

NOTE: Testing is performed at ignition switch CONNECTOR terminals, illustration is a view of ignition switch. Ensure proper terminal on connector is being tested.

1) Check 50-amp fuse No. 14 located in power distribution center. Replace as necessary. If fuse is okay, go to next step. If fuse blows, check Yellow wire for short circuit to ground between ignition switch and battery junction box.
2) Turn ignition off. Disconnect ignition switch connector. Measure voltage between ignition switch connector terminal B5 (Yellow wire) and ground. *See Fig. 2.* If voltage is greater than 10 volts, replace ignition switch. See IGNITION SWITCH under REMOVAL & INSTALLATION. If voltage is 10 volts or less, repair open circuit in Yellow wire.

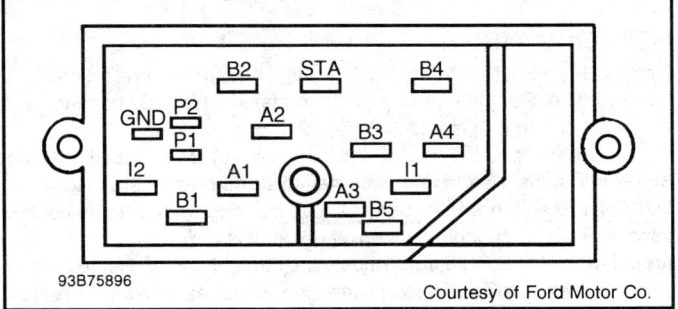

93B75896   Courtesy of Ford Motor Co.

Fig. 2: Identifying Ignition Switch Terminals

TEST B: NO POWER IN ACC

NOTE: Testing is performed at ignition switch CONNECTOR terminals, illustration is a view of ignition switch. Ensure proper terminal on connector is being tested.

1) Turn ignition on. Check wiper and radio operation. If wipers and radio operate, go to next step. If wipers and radio do not operate, go to TEST C: NO POWER IN RUN.
2) Disconnect ignition switch connector. Measure voltage between ignition switch connector terminal B5 (Yellow wire) and ground. *See Fig. 2.* If voltage is greater than 10 volts, replace ignition switch. See IGNITION SWITCH under REMOVAL & INSTALLATION. If voltage is 10 volts or less, repair open circuit in Yellow wire.

TEST C: NO POWER IN RUN

NOTE: Testing is performed at ignition switch CONNECTOR terminals, illustration is a view of ignition switch. Ensure proper terminal on connector is being tested.

1) Turn ignition off. Disconnect ignition switch connector. Measure voltage between ignition switch connector terminals B1, B2, B4 and B5 (Yellow wire) and ground. *See Fig. 2.* If voltages are greater than 10 volts, go to next step. If voltages are 10 volts or less, repair open circuit in Yellow wire.
2) Check ignition switch continuity. See IGNITION SWITCH under COMPONENT TESTS. If switch tests okay, go to next step. If ignition switch does not test okay, replace ignition switch. See IGNITION SWITCH under REMOVAL & INSTALLATION.
3) Reconnect ignition switch connector. Turn ignition on. Measure voltage between fuses No. 10 (Gray/White wire), No. 16 (Black/Light Green wire), No. 19 (Light Green/Purple wire), and No. 27 (Gray/Yellow wire) and ground. Fuses are located in central junction block behind left side of instrument panel. If voltages are greater than 10 volts, system is okay. If voltages are 10 volts or less, repair open circuit in wiring.

TEST D: NO POWER IN START

NOTE: Testing is performed at ignition switch CONNECTOR terminals, illustration is a view of ignition switch. Ensure proper terminal on connector is being tested.

1) Turn ignition off. Disconnect ignition switch connector. Measure voltage between ignition switch connector terminal B4 (Yellow wire) and ground, and between terminal B5 (Yellow wire) and ground. *See Fig. 2.* If voltages are greater than 10 volts, go to next step. If voltages are 10 volts or less, repair open circuit in Yellow wire.
2) Check ignition switch continuity. See IGNITION SWITCH under COMPONENT TESTS. If switch tests okay, go to next step. If ignition switch does not test okay, replace ignition switch. See IGNITION SWITCH under REMOVAL & INSTALLATION.
3) Reconnect ignition switch connector. Turn ignition switch to START position. If starter engages, repair open circuit in Light Green/Purple wire. If starter does not engage, repair open circuit in Red/Light Blue wire.

TEST E: NO COMMUNICATION WITH GEM/CTM MODULE

1) Check fuse No. 5 (50-amp) located in power distribution center. If fuse is okay, go to next step. If fuse is not okay, replace fuse. If fuse blows, check Tan/Black wire for a short circuit to ground.
2) Check fuse No. 25 (7.5-amp) located in central junction block behind left side of instrument panel. If fuse is okay, go to next step. If fuse is not okay, replace fuse. If fuse blows, check White/Yellow wire for a short circuit to ground.
3) Measure voltage between input side of fuse No. 25 (Tan/Black wire) and ground. If voltage is greater than 10 volts, go to next step. If voltage is 10 volts or less, repair open circuit in Tan/Black wire.
4) Turn ignition off. Disconnect GEM/CTM connectors. Measure voltage between GEM/CTM connector C224 terminal No. 11 (White/Yellow wire) and ground. *See Fig. 3.* If voltage is greater than 10 volts, go to next step. If voltage is 10 volts or less, repair open circuit in White/Yellow wire.
5) Ensure ignition is off. Measure resistance between GEM/CTM connector C221 terminal No. 14 (Black/White wire) and ground, and between GEM/CTM connector C221 terminal No. 26 (Black/White wire) and ground. If resistances are less than 5 ohms, go to next step. If resistances are 5 ohms or more, repair open Black/White wire.
6) Ensure ignition is off. Measure resistance between ground and GEM/CTM connector C224 terminal No. 18 (Light Green/Black wire (rear anti-lock brakes) or Black wire (4-wheel anti-lock brake system). If resistance is less than 5 ohms, replace GEM. If resistance is 5 ohms or more, repair open Light Green/Black or Black wire.

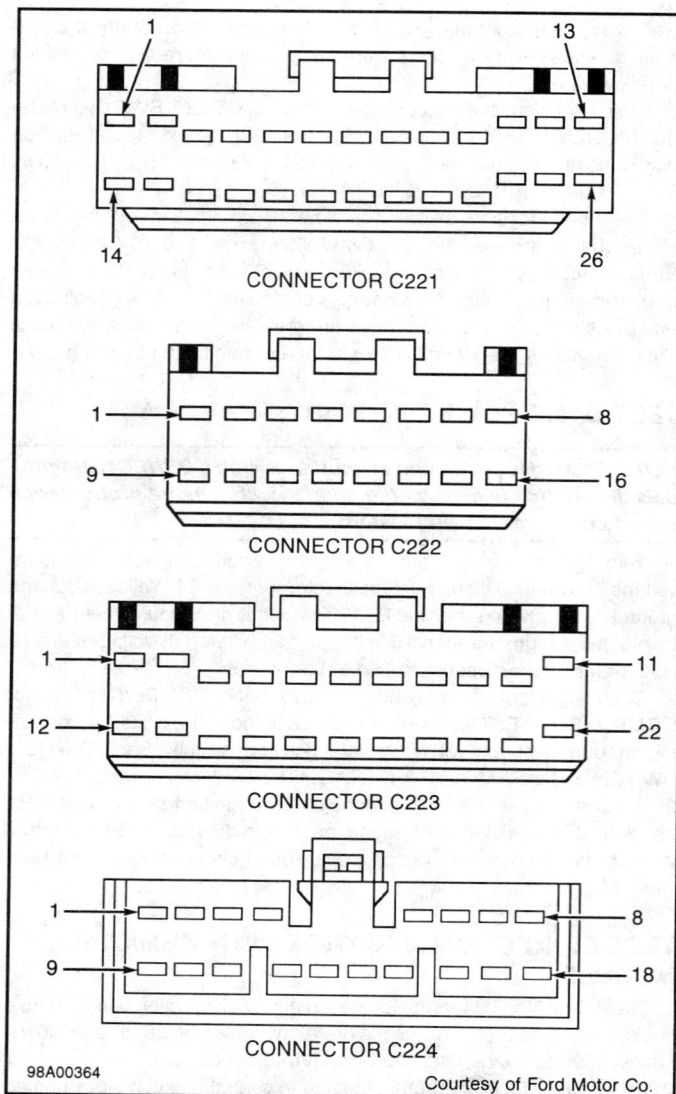

Fig. 3: Identifying GEM/CTM Connector Terminals

REMOVAL & INSTALLATION

> **WARNING:** *Deactivate air bag system before performing any service operation involving steering column components. See appropriate AIR BAG RESTRAINT SYSTEMS article. DO NOT apply electrical power to any component on steering column without first deactivating air bag system. Air bag may deploy.*

> **CAUTION:** *When battery is disconnected, vehicle computer and memory system may lose memory data. Driveability problems may exist until computer systems have completed a relearn cycle. See COMPUTER RELEARN PROCEDURES article in GENERAL INFORMATION before disconnecting battery.*

IGNITION SWITCH

Removal & Installation – 1) Disconnect negative battery cable. Remove parking brake release handle. Remove hood release handle and position aside. Remove steering column covers. Remove steering column opening cover reinforcement. Remove shift indicator retaining screw (A/T models).

2) Remove steering column-to-brake pedal retaining bolts. Lower steering column until steering column is resting on seat. Disconnect ignition switch harness connector. Remove 2 ignition switch screws and ignition switch. To install, reverse removal procedure.

MULTIFUNCTION SWITCH

Removal & Installation – Disconnect negative battery cable. Remove lock cylinder. See LOCK CYLINDER. Remove tilt lever handle (if equipped). Remove upper and lower steering column shrouds. Remove retaining screws. Disconnect multifunction switch harness connectors. Remove switch. To install, reverse removal procedure.

LOCK CYLINDER

Removal & Installation (With Key) – Disconnect negative battery cable. Turn ignition switch to RUN position. Insert an 1/8" drill bit or wire through access hole in trim steering column trim (below lock cylinder). Press retaining pin inward and pull out lock cylinder. To install, lubricate lock cylinder. Turn lock cylinder to RUN position. Press retaining pin inward and insert lock cylinder into housing. To complete installation, reverse removal procedure.

Removal (Without Key) – 1) Use this procedure to remove ignition lock cylinder if key is missing or cylinder is frozen. Disconnect negative battery cable. Remove steering wheel. See STEERING WHEEL. Using pliers, twist cap until it separates from ignition lock cylinder.

2) Using 1/8" drill bit, drill out lock cylinder retaining pin. Using a 3/8" drill bit, drill down the middle of the ignition lock cylinder key slot until ignition switch lock cylinder breaks loose.

3) Remove ignition lock cylinder and clean shavings from lock cylinder housing. Remove bearing retainer, bearing and gear. Carefully inspect housing for damage. Replace housing as necessary.

Installation (Without Key) – 1) Install gear, bearing and retainer. Lubricate cylinder cavity. Rotate lock cylinder to RUN position. Press retaining pin inward and insert new lock cylinder into lock cylinder housing.

2) Before rotating key to OFF position, ensure cylinder is fully seated and aligned. Use key to rotate cylinder to ensure mechanical operation is okay in all positions.

STEERING WHEEL

Removal – 1) Position front wheels straight ahead. Disconnect negative battery cable. Remove air bag module retaining nuts. Disconnect wire harness from air bag module. Remove air bag module.

2) Disconnect speed control wiring (if equipped). Mark steering wheel and shaft for installation reference. remove and discard steering wheel bolt. Using steering wheel puller, remove steering wheel. Route contact assembly wiring through steering wheel as it is removed.

Installation – 1) Ensure front wheels are straight ahead. Route contact assembly wire harness through steering wheel at 3 o'clock position. Position steering wheel onto steering shaft, ensuring marks are aligned. Check that air bag wiring is not pinched.

2) Install NEW steering wheel bolt and torque to specifications. See TORQUE SPECIFICATIONS. Connect speed control wiring (if equipped). Ensure wiring is not trapped between steering wheel and contact assembly. Connect air bag module and reattach air bag module to steering wheel.

TORQUE SPECIFICATIONS

TORQUE SPECIFICATIONS

Application	Ft. Lbs. (N.m)
Steering Wheel Bolt	25-34 (34-46)

WIRING DIAGRAMS

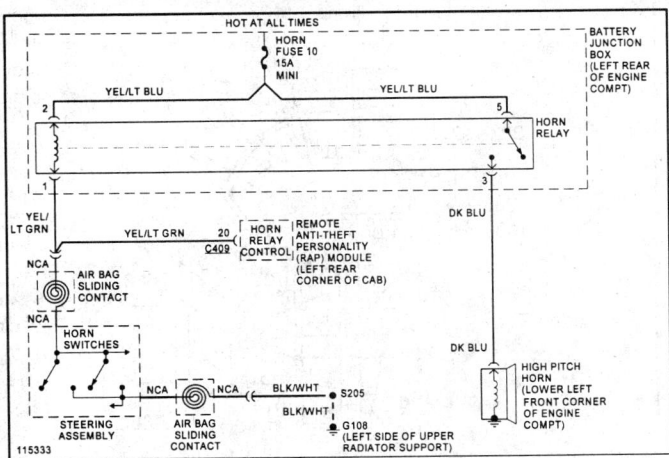

Fig. 4: Horn System Wiring Diagram (Ranger)

DESCRIPTION

WARNING: Deactivate air bag system before performing any service operation involving steering column components. See appropriate AIR BAG RESTRAINT SYSTEMS article. DO NOT apply electrical power to any component on steering column without first deactivating air bag system. Air bag may deploy.

Switches mounted on the steering column are the ignition switch, horn switch, multifunction switch and cruise control switches. Driver's side air bag is located on center of steering wheel.

COMPONENT LOCATIONS

COMPONENT LOCATIONS

Component	Location
Data Link Connector	Under Instrument Panel, Below Steering Column
Generic Electronic Module	Attached To Under Side Of Instrument Panel Fuse Box
Instrument Panel Fuse Box	Behind Left Side Of Instrument Panel
Powertrain Control Module	On Right Side Of Firewall In Engine Compartment

TROUBLE SHOOTING

Before performing individual component tests, system testing and/or individual diagnostic tests, inspect for the following possible causes of system malfunction. Correct any obvious defects before proceeding.
- Mechanical Failure
- Low Battery Charge
- Faulty Fuses
- Loose Or Corroded Connectors
- Damaged Wiring

COMPONENT TESTS

CAUTION: When battery is disconnected, vehicle computer and memory system may lose memory data. Driveability problems may exist until computer systems have completed a relearn cycle. See COMPUTER RELEARN PROCEDURES article in GENERAL INFORMATION before disconnecting battery.

NOTE: Before performing following tests, ensure all multifunction switch grounds, wiring, and fuses are okay. Also, ensure all circuit connections are clean and tight. For ignition switch circuit identification, see appropriate wiring diagram in POWER DISTRIBUTION article in WIRING DIAGRAMS. For multifunction switch circuit identification, see appropriate wiring diagram in EXTERIOR LIGHTS article.

MULTIFUNCTION SWITCH

Disconnect multifunction switch connectors. Set hazard flasher switch to OFF position unless specified otherwise. Check resistance between terminals with switch in specified position. See MULTIFUNCTION SWITCH CONTINUITY table. *See Fig. 1.* If resistance is not as specified, or is poor in any switch position, replace multifunction switch.

MULTIFUNCTION SWITCH CONTINUITY

Switch Position	Circuits No.	Ohms
Flash-To-Pass		
On	13 & 15; 12 & 196	1
Hazard Switch		
On	2, 3, 5, 9 & 44; 383 & 1039	1
Off	2, 3, 5, 9 & 44; 383 & 1039	2
Off	383 & 385	1

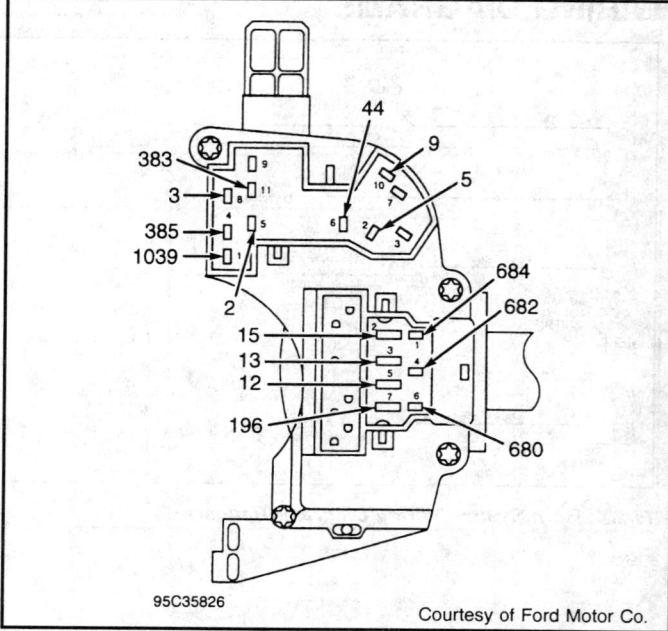

Fig. 1: Identifying Multifunction Switch Circuit Terminals

95C35826 — Courtesy of Ford Motor Co.

MULTIFUNCTION SWITCH CONTINUITY (Cont.)

Switch Position	Circuits No.	Ohms
Headlight Dimmer		
High Beam	12 & 15	1
Low Beam	13 & 15	1
Turn Signals [3]		
Left Turn	3, 9 & 44	1
Right Turn	2, 5 & 44	1
Washer		
On	680 & 682	1
Off	680 & 682	2
Wipers		
Off	682 & 684	47,600
Low Speed	682 & 684	4080
High Speed	682 & 684	1
Interval	682 & 684	11,330
Interval Delay		
Detent 1 (MAX)	608 & 682	[4] 103,000
Detent 2	608 & 682	[4] 82,300
Detent 3	608 & 682	[4] 68,300
Detent 4	608 & 682	[4] 51,300
Detent 5	608 & 682	[4] 36,300
Detent 6	608 & 682	[4] 20,300
Detent 7 (MIN)	608 & 682	[4] 3300

[1] – Resistance should be 5 ohms or less.
[2] – Resistance should be greater than 10 k/ohms.
[3] – Hazard switch MUST be off.
[4] – If wiper switch is in low or high position, resistance between circuits No. 608 and 682 should be within 10 percent of 3300 ohms.

HORN

Disconnect horn switch connector(s). Continuity should not exist between horn switch wires with horn button(s) released. Press horn button(s). Continuity should exist.

IGNITION SWITCH

Check for continuity between specified terminals with switch in each position. See IGNITION SWITCH CONTINUITY table. *See Fig. 2.* If continuity does not exist with switch in appropriate position, replace ignition switch.

IGNITION SWITCH CONTINUITY

Switch Position	Continuity Between Terminal
Accessory	A1 & B1
Run	A1 & B1; A3 & B3; A4 & B4; B5 & I1
Start	B5 & I1; P1 & GND; B4 & STA

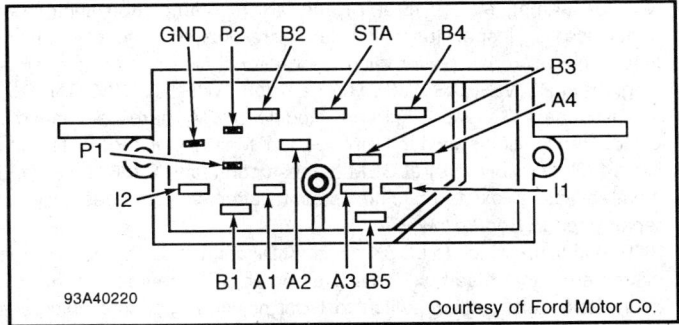

93A40220
Courtesy of Ford Motor Co.

Fig. 2: Identifying Ignition Switch Terminals

SELF-DIAGNOSTIC SYSTEM

NOTE: Before beginning self-diagnostics, perform TROUBLE SHOOTING.

NOTE: A New Generation Star (NGS) tester is required to test the system. All Diagnostic Trouble Code (DTC) tests are for use with NGS tester. If a generic scan tool is used, ensure scan tool is certified OBD-II standard.

Connect New Generation Star (NGS) tester to Data Link Connector (DLC), located beneath instrument panel. Using NGS tester, perform data link diagnostics test. See DATA LINK DIAGNOSTIC TEST under COMMUNICATION NETWORK DIAGNOSTICS in MODULE COMMUNICATIONS NETWORK – SABLE & TAURUS article. If NGS tester responds with CKT914, CKT915 or CKT70=ALL ECUS NO RESP/NOT EQUIP, repair module communications concern. See MODULE COMMUNICATIONS NETWORK – SABLE & TAURUS article. If NGS tester displays NO RESP/NOT EQUIP for Generic Electronic Module (GEM), perform TEST E: NO COMMUNICATION WITH GENERIC ELECTRONIC MODULE under SYSTEM TESTS.

If NGS tester responds with SYSTEM PASSED, retrieve and record continuous DTCs. Erase continuous DTCs. Using NGS tester, perform GEM self-test. Perform appropriate test in accordance with DTC retrieved. See GENERIC ELECTRONIC MODULE DTC INDEX table. Codes listed in this table are only for testing covered in this article. For complete DTC listing, see MODULE COMMUNICATIONS NETWORK – SABLE & TAURUS article. If no DTCs are retrieved, repair by symptom. See SYMPTOM CHART table under SYSTEM TESTS.

GENERIC ELECTRONIC MODULE DTC INDEX

DTC [1]	Description	Test
B1342	ECU Failure	[2]
B1359	Ignition RUN/ACC Circuit Failure	C
B1365	Ignition Start Circuit Short To Voltage	D
B1555	Ignition RUN/START Circuit Failure	C

[1] – Codes listed in this table are only for testing covered in this article. For complete DTC listing, see MODULE COMMUNICATIONS NETWORK – SABLE & TAURUS article.

[2] – Using NGS tester, retrieve and document all continuous DTCs. Perform Generic Electronic Module (GEM) self-test. If DTC B1342 is retrieved again, replace GEM.

SYSTEM TESTS

SYMPTOM CHART

Symptom	Test
Ignition Switch Inoperative	A
No Power In ACC Position	B
No Power In RUN Position	C
No Power In START Position	D
No Communication With Generic Electronic Module	E

TEST A: IGNITION SWITCH INOPERATIVE

1) Remove maxi fuses No. 3 (40-amp) and No. 5 (40-amp) from power distribution box. Inspect both fuses. If either fuse is blown, go to next step. If both fuses are okay, go to step **4)**.

2) Turn ignition switch to LOCK position. Disconnect ignition switch harness connector C299. Measure resistance between ground and output side of maxi fuses No. 3 and 5. If both resistance readings are greater than 10 k/ohms, go to next step. If either resistance reading is 10 k/ohms or less, repair short to ground in appropriate wire. See appropriate wiring diagram in POWER DISTRIBUTION article in WIRING DIAGRAMS.

3) Install maxi fuses No. 3 and 5. Measure voltage at terminals B1 (Yellow wire), B3 (Yellow wire), B4 (Light Green/Violet wire) and B5 (Light Green/Violet wire) at ignition switch harness connector C299. See Fig. 3. If battery voltage exists at all terminals, go to next step. If battery voltage does not exist at any terminals, repair open in appropriate wire.

4) Test ignition switch. See IGNITION SWITCH under COMPONENT TESTS. If ignition switch is okay, go to next step. If ignition switch is defective, replace ignition switch.

5) Ensure ignition switch harness connector is still disconnected. Remove fuses No. 5 (5-amp), No. 6 (15-amp), No. 7 (10-amp), No. 8 (5-amp), No. 9 (10-amp), No. 10 (20-amp), No. 11 (5-amp), No. 12 (5-amp), No. 13 (5-amp), No. 14 (5-amp), No. 15 (10-amp), No. 17 (30-amp), No. 18 (5-amp), No. 19 (15-amp) and No. 20 (5-amp) and from instrument panel fuse box. Measure resistance in wires between ignition switch harness connector C299 and input side of appropriate fuse. See CIRCUIT IDENTIFICATION table. If all resistance readings are 5 ohms or less, go to next step. If any resistance reading is greater than 5 ohms, repair open in appropriate wire.

CIRCUIT IDENTIFICATION

Switch Terminal	Wire Color	Fuse No.
A1	Black/Light Green	17, 18, 19 & 20
A3	Red/Light Blue	5 & 6
A4	Gray/Yellow	13, 14 & 15
I1	Red/Light Green	9, 10, 11 & 12
STA	Red/Light Blue	7 & 8

6) Measure resistance between ground and terminals at ignition switch harness connector C299. See CIRCUIT IDENTIFICATION table. If any resistance reading is 10 k/ohms or less, repair short to ground in appropriate wire. If all resistance readings are greater than 10 k/ohms, system is okay at this time. Check for poor connections and/or intermittent shorts/opens.

TEST B: NO POWER IN ACC POSITION

1) Test ignition switch. See IGNITION SWITCH under COMPONENT TESTS. If ignition switch is okay, go to next step. If ignition switch is defective, replace ignition switch.

2) Turn ignition switch to LOCK position. Connect ignition switch harness connector C299. Disconnect instrument panel fuse box harness connector C235. Turn ignition switch to ACC position. Measure voltage at terminal No. 7 (Black/Light Green wire) at instrument panel fuse box harness connector C235. See Fig. 4. If battery voltage exists, replace instrument panel fuse box. If battery voltage does not exist, repair open/short in Black/Light Green wire between ignition switch and instrument panel fuse box.

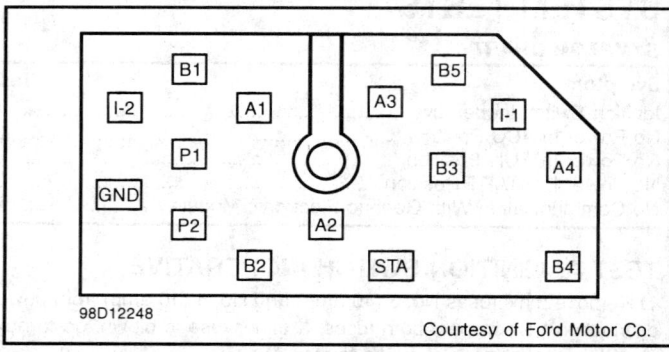

Fig. 3: Identifying Ignition Switch Harness Connector C299 Terminals

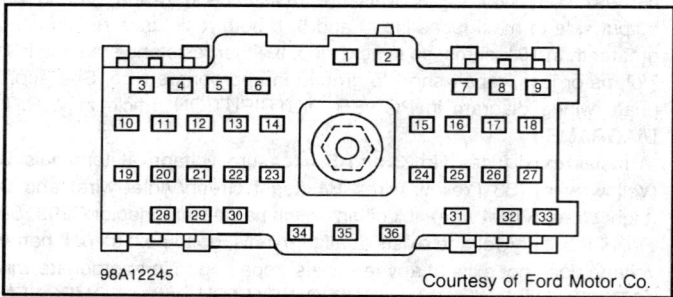

Fig. 4: Identifying Instrument Panel Fuse Box Harness Connector C235 Terminals

TEST C: NO POWER IN RUN POSITION

1) Remove maxi fuses No. 3 (40-amp) and No. 5 (40-amp) from power distribution box. Inspect both fuses. If either fuse is blown, go to next step. If both fuses are okay, go to step **4)**.

2) Turn ignition switch to LOCK position. Disconnect ignition switch harness connector C299. Measure resistance between ground and output side of maxi fuses No. 3 and 5. If both resistance readings are greater than 10 k/ohms, go to next step. If either resistance reading is 10 k/ohms or less, repair short to ground in appropriate wire. See appropriate wiring diagram in POWER DISTRIBUTION article in WIRING DIAGRAMS.

3) Install maxi fuses No. 3 and 5. Measure voltage at terminals B1 (Yellow wire), B3 (Yellow wire), B4 (Light Green/Violet wire) and B5 (Light Green/Violet wire) at ignition switch harness connector C299. *See Fig. 3*. If battery voltage exists at all terminals, go to next step. If battery voltage does not exist at any terminals, repair open in appropriate wire.

4) Test ignition switch. See IGNITION SWITCH under COMPONENT TESTS. If ignition switch is okay, go to next step. If ignition switch is defective, replace ignition switch.

5) Turn ignition switch to LOCK position. Connect ignition switch harness connector C299. Disconnect instrument panel fuse box harness connector C235. Turn ignition switch to RUN position. Measure voltage at terminals No. 1 (Gray/Yellow wire), No. 2 (Red/Light Green wire), No. 6 (Red/Light Blue wire) and No. 7 (Black/Light Green wire) at instrument panel fuse box harness connector C235. *See Fig. 4*. If battery voltage exists at all terminals, replace instrument panel fuse box. If battery voltage does not exists at any terminal, repair open in appropriate wire.

TEST D: NO POWER IN START POSITION

Test ignition switch. See IGNITION SWITCH under COMPONENT TESTS. If ignition switch is okay, repair open in Red/Light Blue wire. If ignition switch is defective, replace ignition switch.

TEST E: NO COMMUNICATION WITH GENERIC ELECTRONIC MODULE

NOTE: Manufacturer does not provide instrument panel fuse box connector illustration where Generic Electronic Module (GEM) connects (connector C201).

1) Turn ignition switch to LOCK position. Remove fuses No. 23 (5-amp), No. 20 (5-amp), No. 12 (5-amp) and No. 8 (5-amp) from instrument panel fuse box. Inspect fuses. If all fuses are okay, go to next step. If any fuse is blown, repair power distribution circuit. See appropriate wiring diagram in POWER DISTRIBUTION article in WIRING DIAGRAMS.

2) Disconnect Generic Electronic Module (GEM) harness connector C236. Turn ignition switch to RUN position. Measure voltage at terminal No. 14 (Red/Yellow wire) at GEM harness connector C236. *See Fig. 5*. If battery voltage exists, go to next step. If battery voltage does not exist, repair open in Red/Yellow wire.

3) Turn ignition switch to LOCK position. Disconnect GEM module from instrument panel fuse box, leaving all other GEM harness connectors connected. Turn ignition switch to RUN position. Measure voltage at terminals No. 5 and 10 at instrument panel where GEM was disconnected from. Battery voltage should exist. Measure voltage at terminal No. 14 at instrument panel where GEM was disconnected from while ignition switch is in START position. Battery voltage should exist. If voltage is as specified, go to next step. If voltage is not as specified, replace instrument panel fuse box.

4) Turn ignition switch to LOCK position. Disconnect GEM harness connector C248. Measure resistance between ground ant terminals No. 14 (Black wire) and No. 25 (Black wire) at GEM harness connector C248. *See Fig. 6*. If both resistance readings are 5 ohms or less, go to next step. If either resistance reading is greater than 5 ohms, repair open in Black wire.

5) Disconnect GEM harness connector C223. Measure resistance between ground and terminal No. 12 (Black/White wire) at GEM harness connector C223. *See Fig. 7*. If resistance is 5 ohms or less, go to next step. If resistance is greater than 5 ohms, repair open in Black/White wire.

6) Measure resistance between ground and terminal No. 22 (Black/Light Green wire) at GEM harness connector C223. If resistance is 5 ohms or less, repair module communications concern. See MODULE COMMUNICATIONS NETWORK – SABLE & TAURUS article. If resistance is greater than 5 ohms, repair open in Black/White wire.

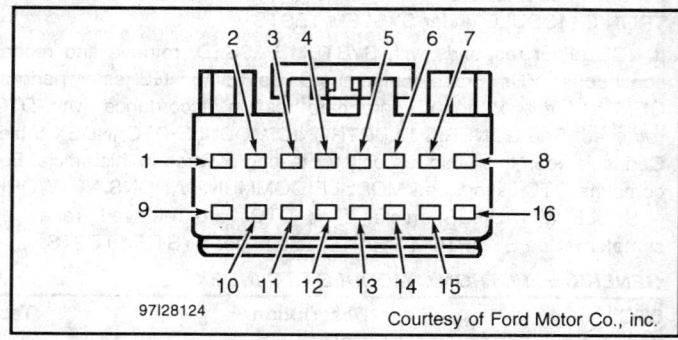

Fig. 5: Identifying GEM Harness Connector C236 Terminals

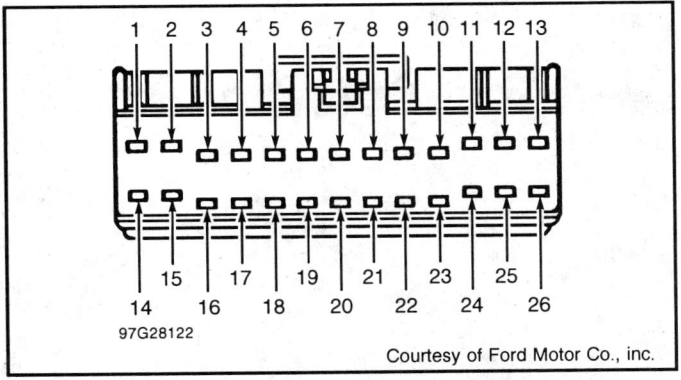

Fig. 6: Identifying GEM Harness Connector C248 Terminals

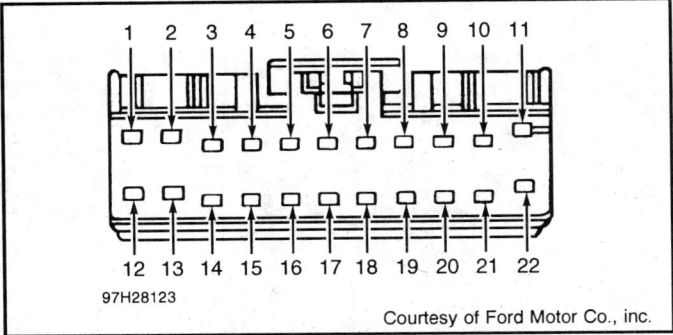

Fig. 7: Identifying GEM Harness Connector C223 Terminals

REMOVAL & INSTALLATION

CAUTION: When battery is disconnected, vehicle computer and memory system may lose memory data. Driveability problems may exist until computer systems have completed a relearn cycle. See COMPUTER RELEARN PROCEDURES article in GENERAL INFORMATION before disconnecting battery.

STEERING WHEEL

WARNING: Deactivate air bag system before performing any service operation involving steering column components. See appropriate AIR BAG RESTRAINT SYSTEMS article. DO NOT apply electrical power to any component on steering column without first deactivating air bag system. Air bag may deploy.

Removal & Installation – 1) Ensure front wheels are in straight-ahead position. Disable air bag system. See appropriate AIR BAG RESTRAINT SYSTEMS article. Wait at least one minute for air bag back-up power supply to deplete.
2) Remove air bag module retaining nuts/screws. Lift air bag module from steering wheel. Disconnect air bag wiring harness from module. Disconnect cruise control switch connector (if equipped). Remove and discard steering wheel bolt.
3) Remove steering wheel. While removing steering wheel, guide wiring harnesses through steering wheel. To install, reverse removal procedure. Install NEW steering wheel bolt and tighten to specification. Check AIR BAG light to verify proper system operation.

MULTIFUNCTION SWITCH

Removal & Installation – 1) Disconnect negative battery cable. On models with tilt wheel, adjust steering wheel to lowest position, then remove tilt lever. On all models, remove lock cylinder. See LOCK CYLINDER (FUNCTIONAL) or LOCK CYLINDER (NON-FUNCTIONAL).
2) Remove upper and lower steering column covers. On column shift models, disconnect transmission shift indicator column. On all models,

remove multifunction switch from housing. Remove wiring harness retainer. Disconnect multifunction switch connectors. To install, reverse removal procedure.

IGNITION SWITCH

Removal – Disconnect negative battery cable. Remove upper and lower steering column covers. Disconnect ignition switch connector. Turn ignition switch to RUN position. Remove retaining screws and ignition switch.
Installation – Set ignition switch to RUN position by turning ignition switch shaft to START position, then releasing shaft. Install ignition switch. It may be necessary to move ignition switch back and forth to align switch mounting holes with lock cylinder housing holes. Install and tighten switch retaining screws. To complete installation, reverse removal procedure.

LOCK CYLINDER (FUNCTIONAL)

NOTE: If lock cylinder is non-functional (lock cylinder cannot be rotated because of missing key or damaged lock cylinder), see LOCK CYLINDER (NON-FUNCTIONAL).

Removal – Disconnect negative battery cable. Turn lock cylinder to RUN position. Locate hole in shroud under lock cylinder. Insert a 1/8" drill bit or punch into hole. Press lock cylinder retaining pin while pulling lock cylinder from housing.
Installation – 1) Turn lock cylinder to RUN position. Press retaining pin inward and insert lock cylinder into housing. Ensure lock cylinder is fully seated and aligned with interlocking washer.
2) Rotate lock cylinder to OFF position. This allows retaining pin to extend into hole in housing. To install remaining components, reverse removal procedure.

LOCK CYLINDER (NON-FUNCTIONAL)

NOTE: If lock cylinder is functional (key is available and lock cylinder turns freely), see LOCK CYLINDER (FUNCTIONAL).

Removal & Installation – 1) Disconnect negative battery cable. Disable air bag system. See appropriate AIR BAG RESTRAINT SYSTEMS article. Remove steering wheel. See STEERING WHEEL. Using a 1/8" bit, drill out retaining pin located below lock cylinder on housing. DO NOT drill deeper than 1/2".
2) Using channel lock pliers, twist lock cylinder cap until it separates from lock cylinder. Using a 3/8" drill bit, drill down center of ignition lock key slot about 1 3/4" until lock cylinder breaks loose from its base.
3) Remove retainer, washer, and lock cylinder gear from housing. Remove metal shavings from lock cylinder bore. Replace housing if damaged. To install, reverse removal procedure. Connect negative battery cable. Check AIR BAG light for proper system operation.

TORQUE SPECIFICATIONS

TORQUE SPECIFICATIONS

Application	Ft. Lbs. (N.m)
Steering Wheel Bolt [1]	25-34 (34-46)

[1] – Use NEW bolt when installing steering wheel.

WIRING DIAGRAMS

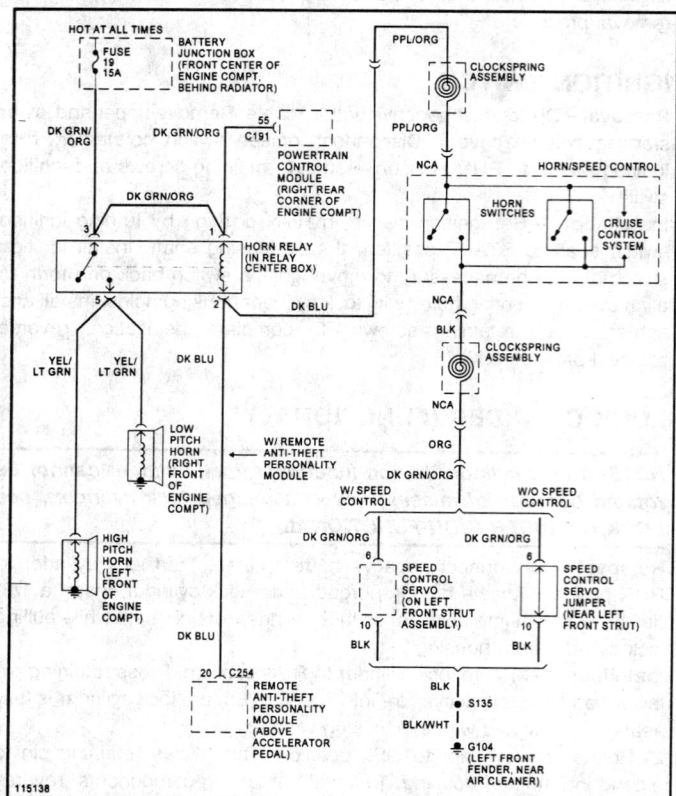

Fig. 8: Horn System Wiring Diagram (Sable & Taurus)

DESCRIPTION & OPERATION

WARNING: Deactivate air bag system before performing any service operation involving steering column components. See appropriate AIR BAG RESTRAINT SYSTEMS article. DO NOT apply electrical power to any component on steering column without first deactivating air bag system. Air bag may deploy.

Switches mounted on the steering column are the ignition switch, horn switch, multifunction switch and cruise control switches. Driver's side air bag is located on center of steering wheel.

TROUBLE SHOOTING

Verify customer complaint. Check for mechanical failure. Check for low battery charge. Check for faulty instrument panel box fuses No. 9, 14, 15, 17, 18, 21 or 22. Check for faulty power distribution box maxi fuses No. 1 and 2. Check for loose or corroded connectors. Check for damaged wiring.

COMPONENT TESTS

CAUTION: When battery is disconnected, vehicle computer and memory system may lose memory data. Driveability problems may exist until computer systems have completed a relearn cycle. See COMPUTER RELEARN PROCEDURES article in GENERAL INFORMATION before disconnecting battery.

NOTE: Before performing following tests, ensure all multifunction switch grounds, wiring, and fuses are okay. Also, ensure all circuit connections are clean and tight. For ignition switch circuit identification, see appropriate wiring diagram in POWER DISTRIBUTION article in WIRING DIAGRAMS. For multifunction switch circuit identification, see appropriate wiring diagram in EXTERIOR LIGHTS article.

MULTIFUNCTION SWITCH

Disconnect multifunction switch harness connectors. Set hazard flasher switch to OFF position unless specified otherwise. Resistance should be as specified between terminals with switch in specified position. See MULTIFUNCTION SWITCH RESISTANCE table. *See Fig. 1.* If resistance is not as specified, replace multifunction switch.

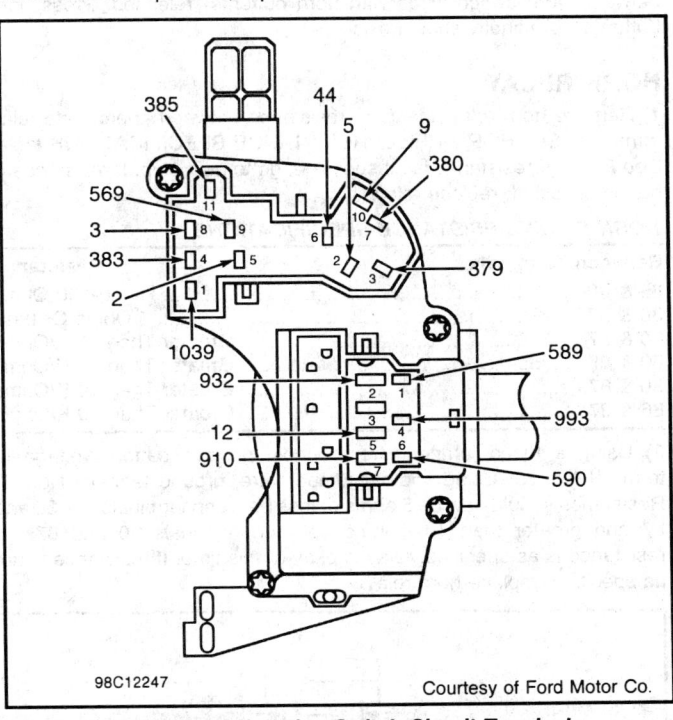

98C12247   Courtesy of Ford Motor Co.

Fig. 1: Identifying Multifunction Switch Circuit Terminals

MULTIFUNCTION SWITCH RESISTANCE

Switch Position	Circuits No.	Ohms
Brakelight Feed Through [1]	5, 9, & 569	[2]
Flash-To-Pass On	12 & 910	[2]
Hazard Switch On	2, 3, 5, 9 & 44	[2]
Headlight High Beam On	12 & 932	[2]
Turn Signals [3]		
Left Turn	3, 9 & 44; 380 & 932	[2]
Right Turn	2, 5 & 44; 379 & 932	[2]
Washer		
On	590 & 993	[2]
Off	590 & 993	[4] 103,300
Wipers		
Off	589 & 993	[5] 47,600
Low Speed	589 & 993	[5] 4080
High Speed	589 & 993	[2]
Interval	589 & 993	[5] 11,330
Interval Delay [6] [7]		
MAX	590 & 993	[4] 103,300
MIN	590 & 993	[4] 3300

[1] – Hazard switch off and turn signal switch in neutral position.
[2] – Resistance should be less than 5 ohms.
[3] – Hazard switch MUST be off.
[4] – Resistance may vary by as much as 10 percent.
[5] – Resistance may vary by as much as 15 percent.
[6] – Resistance should vary smoothly between specified limits as knob is rotated between MIN and MAX positions.
[7] – These values are with wiper switch in off position. If wiper switch is in low or high position, resistance between circuits No. 590 and 993 should be within 10 percent of 3300 ohms.

HEADLIGHT SWITCH

See INSTRUMENT PANELS – TOWN CAR article.

HORN SWITCH

Disconnect horn switch connector(s). Continuity should not exist between horn switch wires with horn button(s) released. Press horn button(s). Continuity should exist.

HORN RELAY

1) Remove horn relay. Measure resistance between appropriate relay terminals. See HORN RELAY RESISTANCE SPECIFICATIONS table. *See Fig. 2.* If resistance is as specified, go to next step. If resistance is not as specified, replace relay.

HORN RELAY RESISTANCE SPECIFICATIONS

Between Terminals	Resistance
85 & 86	50-100 Ohms
30 & 87a	5 Ohms Or Less
30 & 87	Greater Than 10 K/Ohms
30 & 86	Greater Than 10 K/Ohms
86 & 87a	Greater Than 10 K/Ohms
86 & 87	Greater Than 10 K/Ohms

2) Using a fused jumper wire, connect positive battery voltage to terminal No. 85. Using another jumper wire, ground terminal No. 86. Resistance should now be 5 ohms or less between terminals No. 30 and 87 and greater than 10 k/ohms between terminals 30 and 87a. If resistance is as specified, relay is okay at this time. If resistance is not as specified, replace horn relay.

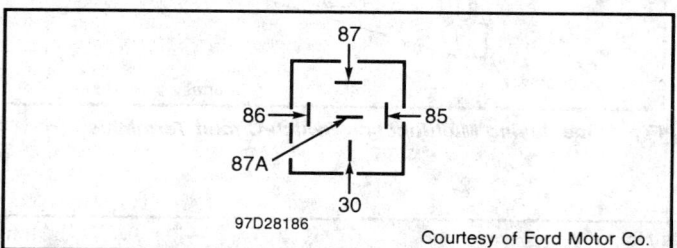

97D28186   Courtesy of Ford Motor Co.

Fig. 2: Identifying Horn Relay Terminals

IGNITION SWITCH

Disconnect ignition switch harness connector (remove switch if necessary). Continuity should exist between specified terminals with switch in specified position. See IGNITION SWITCH CONTINUITY table. *See Fig. 3.* Replace ignition switch if it does not test as specified.

IGNITION SWITCH CONTINUITY

Switch Position	Continuity Between Terminals
Accessory	A1 & B5
Run	A1 & B1; A2 & B2; A3 & B3; A4 & B4; B5 & I1; P1, P2 & GND
Start	B1 & I2; B5 & I1; B4 & STA

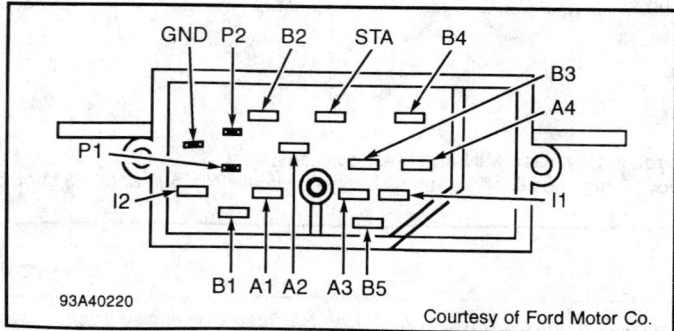

93A40220   Courtesy of Ford Motor Co.

Fig. 3: Identifying Ignition Switch Terminals

SELF-DIAGNOSTIC SYSTEM

NOTE: Perform trouble shooting procedure before proceeding with self-diagnostic system. See TROUBLE SHOOTING.

Verify customers complaint. Check for blown fuse(s), loose or corroded connectors, or damaged wiring harness. Repair or replace components as necessary. If all components are okay, connect NGS tester to Data Link Connector (DLC) located below instrument panel. Using NGS tester, perform DATA LINK DIAGNOSTIC TEST. If NGS tester displays CKT914, CKT915 or CKT70=ALL ECUS NO RESP/NOT EQUIP, repair communication concern. See MODULE COMMUNICATIONS NETWORK – TOWN CAR article. If NGS tester displays NO RESP/NOT EQUIP for Lighting Control Module (LCM), perform TEST A: NO COMMUNICATION WITH LIGHTING CONTROL MODULE under SYSTEM TESTS. If NGS tester displays SYSTEM PASSED, retrieve and record continuous DTCs. Erase continuous DTCs. Perform LCM self-test. Perform appropriate test in accordance with DTC retrieved. See LIGHTING CONTROL MODULE DTC INDEX table. Codes listed in this table are only for testing covered in this article. For complete DTC listing, see MODULE COMMUNICATIONS NETWORK – TOWN CAR article. If no DTCs are retrieved, repair by symptom. See SYMPTOM CHART table under SYSTEM TESTS.

LIGHTING CONTROL MODULE DTC INDEX

DTC	Description	Test
B1342	ECU Defective	1
B1359	Ignition RUN/ACC Input Circuit Failure	G
B1555	Ignition RUN/START Circuit Failure	H

[1] – Using NGS tester, retrieve and document all continuous. Perform Lighting Control Module (LCM) self-test. If DTC B1342 is retrieved again, replace LCM.

SYSTEM TESTS

CAUTION: When battery is disconnected or modules are replaced, vehicle computer and memory systems may lose memory data. Driveability problems may exist until computer systems have completed a relearn cycle. See COMPUTER RELEARN PROCEDURES article in GENERAL INFORMATION before disconnecting battery.

SYMPTOM CHART

Symptom	Test
No Communication With Lighting Control Module	A
Ignition Switch Inoperative	B
No Power In Acc Position	C
No Power In Start	D
Mutifunction Switch/Hazard Switch Does Not Operate Properly	E
Automatic Parking Brake Release Inoperative	F
Ignition Run/Acc Circuit Failure	G
Ignition Run/Start Circuit Failure	H

TEST A: NO COMMUNICATION WITH LIGHTING CONTROL MODULE

1) Turn ignition switch to LOCK position. Connect New Generation Star (NGS) tester to Data Link Connector (DLC). Turn ignition switch to RUN position. Monitor LCM PID IGN_LC. If UNABLE TO PERFORM TEST/ FUNCTION MODULE NOT RESPONDING:LCM CHECK IGNITION STATUS/VERIFY CABLE REQUIREMENTS CHECK CABLE CONNECTIONS? is not displayed, go to next step. If UNABLE TO PERFORM TEST/FUNCTION MODULE NOT RESPONDING:LCM CHECK IGNITION STATUS/VERIFY CABLE REQUIREMENTS CHECK CABLE CONNECTIONS? is displayed, go to step **8)**.

2) Monitor LCM PID IGN_LC on NGS tester while turn ignition switch to all positions except START. If OFF is not displayed in all positions, go to next step. If OFF is displayed in all positions, go to step **5)**.

3) Remove fuse No. 14 (7.5-amp) from instrument panel fuse box. Measure voltage at input side of fuse No. 14. If battery voltage exists, go to next step. If battery voltage does not exist, repair power distribution circuit. See appropriate wiring diagram in POWER DISTRIBUTION article in WIRING DIAGRAMS.

4) Inspect fuse No. 14. If fuse is blown, repair short to ground in Red/Yellow wire. If fuse is okay, repair open in Red/Yellow wire.

5) Remove fuse No. 18 (7.5-amp) from instrument panel fuse box. Turn ignition switch to RUN position. Measure voltage at input side of fuse No. 18. If battery voltage exists, go to next step. If battery voltage does not exist, repair power distribution circuit and/or replace ignition switch as necessary. See appropriate wiring diagram in POWER DISTRIBUTION article in WIRING DIAGRAMS.

6) Inspect fuse No. 18. If fuse is blown, repair short to ground in Dark Blue/Light Green wire. If fuse is okay, install fuse and go to next step.

7) Turn ignition switch to LOCK position. Disconnect LCM harness connector C220. Turn ignition switch to RUN position. Measure voltage at terminal No. 6 (Dark Blue/Light Green wire) at LCM harness connector C220. *See Fig. 4.* If battery voltage exists, replace LCM. If battery voltage does not exist, repair open in Dark Blue/Light Green wire.

8) Remove fuse No. 31 (7.5-amp) from instrument panel fuse box. Measure voltage at input side of fuse No. 31. If battery voltage exists, go to next step. If battery voltage does not exist, repair power distribution circuit. See appropriate wiring diagram in POWER DISTRIBUTION article in WIRING DIAGRAMS.

9) Inspect fuse No. 31. If fuse is blown, go to next step. If fuse is okay, repair open in Orange/White wire.

10) Ensure fuse No. 31 is still removed. Turn ignition switch to LOCK position. Disconnect headlight switch harness connector and LCM harness connector C221. Measure resistance between ground and terminal No. 25 (Orange/White wire) at LCM harness connector C221. *See Fig. 5.* If resistance is greater than 10 k/ohms, go to next step. If resistance is 10 k/ohms or less, repair short to ground in Orange/White wire.

11) Connect headlight switch harness connector. Measure resistance between ground and terminal No. 25 (Orange/White wire) at LCM harness connector C221. If resistance is greater than 10 k/ohms, go to next step. If resistance is 10 k/ohms or less, replace headlight switch.

12) Install fuse No. 31. Measure voltage at terminal No. 25 (Orange/White wire) at LCM harness connector C221. If battery voltage exists, go to next step. If battery voltage does not exist, repair open in Orange/White wire.

13) Disconnect LCM harness connector C222. Measure resistance between ground and terminal No. 23 (Pink/Orange wire) at LCM harness connector C221. Measure resistance between ground and terminal No. 13 (Pink/Orange wire) at LCM harness connector C222. *See Fig. 6.* If either resistance reading is greater than 5 ohms, repair open in Pink/Orange wire. If both resistance readings are 5 ohms or less, repair communication concern. See MODULE COMMUNICATIONS NETWORK – TOWN CAR article.

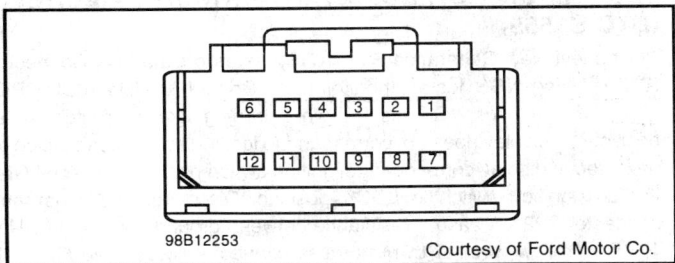

98B12253   Courtesy of Ford Motor Co.

Fig. 4: Identifying LCM Harness Connector C220 Terminals

TEST B: IGNITION SWITCH INOPERATIVE

1) Remove maxi fuses No. 1 (50-amp) and No. 2 (40-amp) from power distribution box. Inspect both fuses. If either fuse is blown, go to next step. If both fuses are okay, go to step **4)**.

2) Turn ignition switch to LOCK position. Ensure maxi fuses No. 1 and 2 are still removed. Disconnect ignition switch harness connector C292. Measure resistance between ground and output side of maxi fuses No. 1 and 2. If both resistance readings are greater than 10 k/ohms, go to

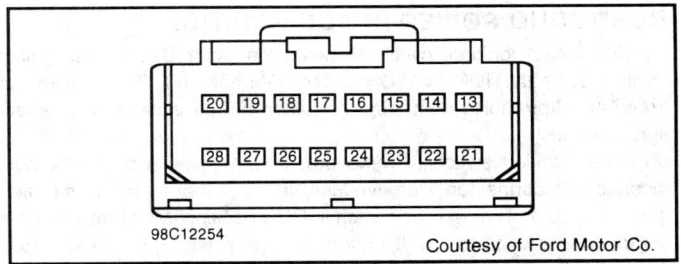

98C12254   Courtesy of Ford Motor Co.

Fig. 5: Identifying LCM Harness Connector C221 Terminals

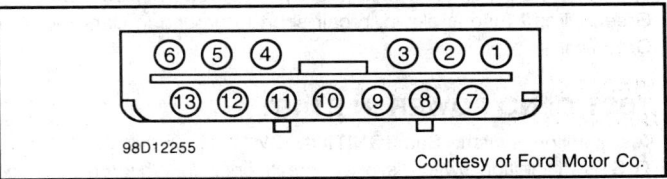

98D12255   Courtesy of Ford Motor Co.

Fig. 6: Identifying LCM Harness Connector C222 Terminals

next step. If either resistance reading is 10 k/ohms or less, repair short to ground in appropriate wire. See appropriate wiring diagram in POWER DISTRIBUTION article in WIRING DIAGRAMS.

3) Install maxi fuses No. 1 and 2. Measure voltage at terminals B1 (Light Green/Violet wire), B2 (Yellow wire), B3 (Yellow wire), B4 (Yellow wire) and B5 (Light Green/Violet wire) at ignition switch harness connector C292. *See Fig. 7.* If battery voltage exists at all terminals, go to next step. If battery voltage does not exist at any terminal, repair open in appropriate wire.

4) Disconnect ignition switch harness connector C292. Test ignition switch. See IGNITION SWITCH under COMPONENT TESTS. If ignition switch is okay, go to next step. If ignition switch is defective, replace ignition switch.

5) Ensure ignition switch harness connector is still disconnected. Remove fuses No. 12 (15-amp), No. 18 (7.5-amp) and No. 26 (5-amp) from instrument panel fuse box. Measure resistance in wires between ignition switch harness connector C292 and output side of appropriate fuse. See CIRCUIT IDENTIFICATION table. If all resistance readings are 5 ohms or less, go to next step. If any resistance reading is greater than 5 ohms, repair open in appropriate wire.

CIRCUIT IDENTIFICATION

Switch Terminal	Wire Color	Fuse No.
A1	Black/Light Green	18
I1	White/Yellow	12
STA	Red/Light Blue	26

6) Measure resistance between ground and terminals A1 (Black/Light Green), I1 (White/Yellow) and STA (Red/Light Blue) at ignition switch harness connector C292. If any resistance reading is 10 k/ohms or less, repair short to ground in appropriate wire. If all resistance readings are greater than 10 k/ohms, system is okay at this time. Check for poor connections and/or intermittent shorts/opens.

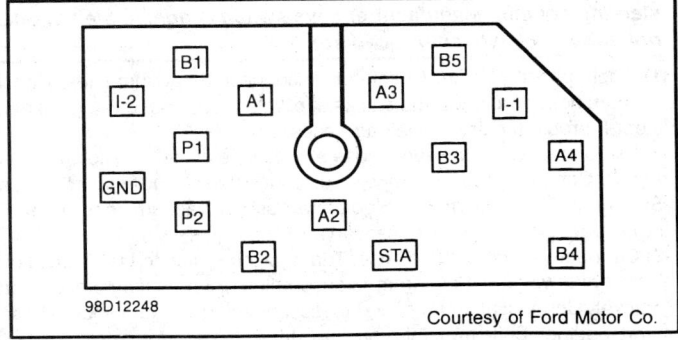

98D12248   Courtesy of Ford Motor Co.

Fig. 7: Identifying Ignition Switch Harness Connector C292 Terminals

TEST C: NO POWER IN ACC POSITION

1) Disconnect ignition switch harness connector C292. Test ignition switch. See IGNITION SWITCH under COMPONENT TESTS. If ignition switch is okay, go to next step. If ignition switch is defective, replace ignition switch.

2) Install ignition switch (if removed). Ensure ignition switch harness connector is connected. Remove fuse No. 18 (7.5-amp) from instrument panel fuse box. Turn ignition switch to RUN position. Measure voltage at input side of fuse No. 18. If battery voltage exists, go to next step. If battery voltage does not exist, repair open in Black/Light Green wire.

3) Inspect fuse No. 18. If fuse is okay, repair open in Dark Blue/Light Green wire. If fuse is blown, repair short to ground in Dark Blue/Light Green wire.

TEST D: NO POWER IN START

Test ignition switch. See IGNITION SWITCH under COMPONENT TESTS. If ignition switch is okay, repair open in White/Yellow and/or Red/Light Blue wires. See appropriate wiring diagram in POWER DISTRIBUTION article in WIRING DIAGRAMS. If ignition switch is defective, replace ignition switch.

TEST E: MULTIFUNCTION SWITCH/HAZARD SWITCH DOES NOT OPERATE PROPERLY

NOTE: This test is only checking the mechanical operation of the multifunction and hazard switches. If multifunction switch operates properly mechanically, test multifunction switch. See MULTIFUNCTION SWITCH under COMPONENT TESTS.

1) Ensure hazard switch is pushed all the way in. Turn ignition switch to RUN position. Check turn signal switch mechanical operation. If turn signal operates properly mechanically, go to next step. If turn signal does not operate properly mechanically, repair or replace components as necessary.

2) Check hazard switch mechanical operation. If hazard switch operates properly mechanically, go to next step. If hazard switch does not operate properly mechanically, repair or replace hazard switch as necessary.

3) Turn headlights on. Check high beam and flash-to-pass portion of multifunction switch mechanical operation. If multifunction switch operates properly mechanically, go to next step. If multifunction switch does not operate properly mechanically, repair or replace multifunction switch as necessary.

4) Check wiper portion of multifunction switch mechanical operation. If multifunction switch operates properly mechanically, multifunction switch mechanical operation is okay at this time. If multifunction switch does not operate properly mechanically, repair or replace multifunction switch as necessary.

TEST F: AUTOMATIC PARKING BRAKE RELEASE INOPERATIVE

NOTE: Parking brake release vacuum switch is attached to top of steering column. Manufacturer says switch is adjustable but does not supply adjustment procedures.

1) Apply parking brake. Check for disconnected vacuum lines. Check vacuum hoses for leaks and cracks. If problem does not exist, go to next step. If problem exists, repair as necessary.

2) Disconnect vacuum source hose at right side of steering column. *See Fig. 8.* Connect vacuum gauge to disconnected vacuum source hose. Start engine. If vacuum exists, go to next step. If vacuum does not exist, repair vacuum supply as necessary.

3) Connect vacuum source hose. Turn ignition switch to LOCK position. Disconnect vacuum hose from release actuator on parking brake pedal bracket. Connect vacuum gauge to disconnected vacuum source hose. Start engine. Shift transmission into drive. If vacuum exists, replace release actuator. If vacuum does not exist, adjust and/or replace parking brake release vacuum switch as necessary.

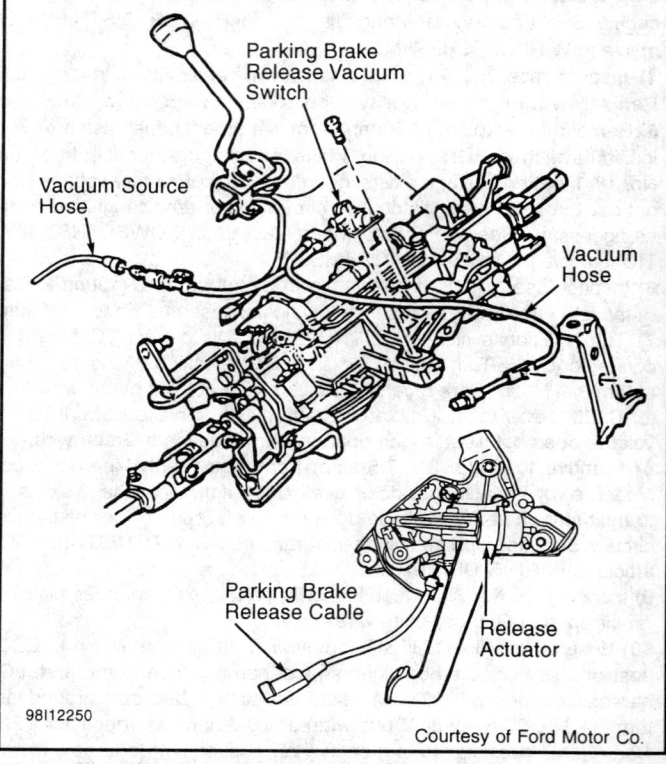

98I12250

Fig. 8: Identifying Automatic Parking Brake Release Components

Courtesy of Ford Motor Co.

TEST G: IGNITION RUN/ACC CIRCUIT FAILURE (DTC 1359)

1) Connect New Generation Star (NGS) tester to Data Link Connector (DLC). Using NGS tester, monitor Light Control Module (LCM) PID IGN_LCM. Monitor NGS display while turning ignition switch to all positions. If display does not correspond to ignition switch position, go to next step. If display correspond to ignition switch position, replace LCM.

2) Turn ignition switch to LOCK position. Disconnect LCM harness connector C220. Measure resistance between ground and terminal No. 6 (Dark Blue/Light Green wire) at LCM harness connector C220. *See Fig. 4.* If resistance is greater than 10 k/ohms, repair open in Dark Blue/Light Green wire. If resistance is 10 k/ohms or less, repair short to ground in Dark Blue/Light Green wire and replace fuse No. 18 (7.5-amp) in instrument panel fuse box.

TEST H: IGNITION RUN/START CIRCUIT FAILURE (DTC B1555)

1) Connect New Generation Star (NGS) tester to Data Link Connector (DLC). Using NGS tester, monitor Light Control Module (LCM) PID IGN_LCM. Monitor NGS display while turning ignition switch to all positions. If display does not correspond to ignition switch position, go to next step. If display correspond to ignition switch position, replace LCM.

2) Turn ignition switch to LOCK position. Disconnect LCM harness connector C221. Measure resistance between ground and terminal No. 17 (Red/Yellow wire) at LCM harness connector C221. *See Fig. 5.* If resistance is greater than 10 k/ohms, repair open in Red/Yellow wire. If resistance is 10 k/ohms or less, repair short to ground in Red/Yellow wire and replace fuse No. 14 (7.5–amp) in instrument panel fuse box.

REMOVAL & INSTALLATION

CAUTION: When battery is disconnected or modules are replaced, vehicle computer and memory systems may lose memory data. Driveability problems may exist until computer systems have completed a relearn cycle. See COMPUTER RELEARN PROCEDURES article in GENERAL INFORMATION before disconnecting battery.

STEERING WHEEL

WARNING: Deactivate air bag system before performing any service operation involving steering column components. See appropriate AIR BAG RESTRAINT SYSTEMS article. DO NOT apply electrical power to any component on steering column without first deactivating air bag system. Air bag may deploy.

Removal & Installation – 1) Ensure front wheels are in straight-ahead position. Disable air bag system. See appropriate AIR BAG RESTRAINT SYSTEMS article. Wait at least one minute for air bag back-up power supply to deplete.

2) Remove air bag module retaining nuts/screws. Lift air bag module from steering wheel. Disconnect air bag wiring harness from module. Disconnect cruise control switch connector (if equipped). Remove and discard steering wheel bolt.

3) Remove steering wheel. While removing steering wheel, guide wiring harnesses through steering wheel. To install, reverse removal procedure. Install NEW steering wheel bolt and tighten to specification. Check AIR BAG light to verify proper system operation.

MULTIFUNCTION SWITCH

Removal & Installation – 1) Disconnect negative battery cable. On models with tilt wheel, adjust steering wheel to lowest position, then remove tilt lever. On all models, turn ignition switch to RUN position. Using a punch, depress ignition switch lock cylinder release tab through access hole in lower steering column cover. *See Fig. 9.* Remove lock cylinder.

2) Remove upper and lower steering column covers. Remove multifunction switch from housing. Remove wiring harness retainer. Disconnect multifunction switch harness connectors. To install, reverse removal procedure.

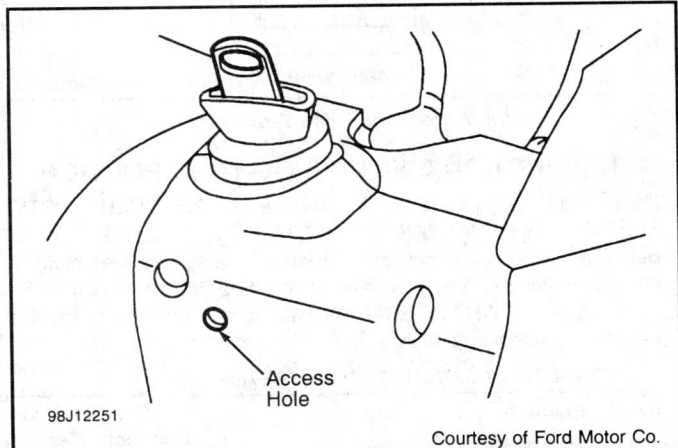

Fig. 9: Identifying Lower Steering Column Cover Access Hole

IGNITION SWITCH

Removal & Installation – Disconnect negative battery cable. Turn ignition switch to LOCK position. Remove instrument panel lower cover and insulator. Remove steering column opening cover and reinforcement. Remove upper and lower steering column covers. Disconnect ignition switch harness connector. Remove ignition switch retaining bolts and remove ignition switch. To install, reverse removal procedure.

IGNITION LOCK CYLINDER

Removal – Disconnect negative battery cable. Turn lock cylinder to RUN position. Locate access hole in lower steering column cover. *See Fig. 9.* Insert a 1/8" drill bit or punch into hole. Press lock cylinder retaining pin while pulling lock cylinder from housing.

Installation – 1) Turn lock cylinder to RUN position. Press retaining pin inward and insert lock cylinder into housing. Ensure lock cylinder is fully seated and aligned with interlocking washer.

2) Rotate lock cylinder to OFF position. This allows retaining pin to extend into hole in housing. To install remaining components, reverse removal procedure.

TORQUE SPECIFICATIONS

TORQUE SPECIFICATIONS

Application	Ft. Lbs. (N.m)
Steering Wheel Bolt [1]	23-33 (31-45)

[1] – Use NEW bolt when installing steering wheel.

WIRING DIAGRAMS

NOTE: For ignition switch circuit identification, see appropriate wiring diagram in POWER DISTRIBUTION article in WIRING DIAGRAMS. For multifunction switch circuit identification, see appropriate wiring diagram in EXTERIOR LIGHTS and HEADLIGHT SYSTEMS articles.

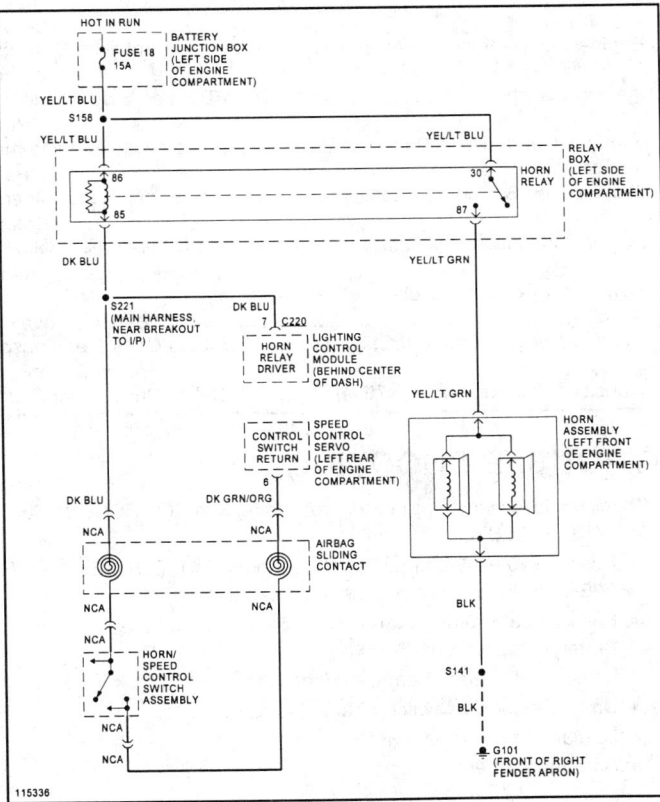

Fig. 10: Horn System Wiring Diagram (Town Car)

1999 ACCESSORIES & EQUIPMENT
Steering Column Switches – Villager

DESCRIPTION

The multifunction switch, located on the steering column, includes headlight dimmer, flash-to-pass and front windshield wiper/washer switches. The ignition switch and lock cylinder are also mounted on the steering column.

WARNING: Deactivate air bag system before performing any service operation involving steering column components. See AIR BAG RESTRAINT SYSTEMS – VILLAGER article. Do not apply electrical power to any component on steering column without first deactivating air bag system. Air bag may deploy.

CAUTION: When battery is disconnected, vehicle computer and memory system may lose memory data. Driveability problems may exist until computer systems have completed a relearn cycle. See COMPUTER RELEARN PROCEDURES article in GENERAL INFORMATION before disconnecting battery.

COMPONENT LOCATIONS

COMPONENT LOCATIONS

Component	Location
Battery Junction Box (BJB)	Left Front Side Of Engine Compartment
Data Link Connector (DLC)	Below Driver's Side Of Instrument Panel, To Right Of Steering Column
Engine Compartment Relay Box	Left Front Side Of Engine Compartment
Ignition Switch	On Top Left Side Of Steering Column
Interior Fuse Junction Panel	Below Left Side Of Instrument Panel
Multifunction Switch	Upper portion Of Steering Column
Power Distribution Box	In Engine Compartment, Next To Battery
Powertrain Control Module (PCM)	Behind Glove Box
Lighting Control Module (LCM)	Bottom Of Center Console, Below Dash Panel
Transaxle Control Module (TCM)	Behind Instrument Cluster

TROUBLE SHOOTING

Check the following items before proceeding with COMPONENT TESTS or SYSTEM TESTS:

- Fuses F36 (7.5-amp), F38 (7.5-amp), F40 (20-amp) and F42 (7.5-amp) in instrument panel fuse panel.
- Fuses F23 (30-amp) and F2 (15-amp) in engine compartment Battery Junction Box (BJB)
- Loose or damaged harness connectors.
- Damaged ignition switch or key.
- Damaged turn signal switch.
- Damaged wiper washer switch.

COMPONENT TESTS

CAUTION: When battery is disconnected, vehicle computer and memory system may lose memory data. Driveability problems may exist until computer systems have completed a relearn cycle. See COMPUTER RELEARN PROCEDURES article in GENERAL INFORMATION before disconnecting battery.

NOTE: Before performing following tests, ensure all multifunction switch grounds, wiring, and fuses are okay. Also, ensure all circuit connections are clean and tight. For ignition switch circuit identification, see appropriate wiring diagram in POWER DISTRIBUTION article in WIRING DIAGRAMS. For multifunction switch circuit identification, see appropriate wiring diagram in EXTERIOR LIGHTS article.

ACCESSORY RELAY

1) Remove accessory relay located in interior fuse junction panel. Using an ohmmeter, measure resistance between relay terminals No. 1 and 2. *See Fig. 1.* If resistance is 100-150 ohms, go to next step. If resistance is not 100-150 ohms, replace accessory relay.
2) Check continuity between all other terminals, except terminals No. 1 and 2. If continuity exists in any measurement, replace relay. If continuity does not exist in any measurement, go to next step.
3) Remove ohmmeter and apply battery voltage to relay terminals No. 1, 3 and 6. Apply ground to relay terminal No. 2. Check for voltage between relay terminals No. 2 and 7 and between No. 2 and 5. If battery voltage exists in both measurements, relay is okay. If battery voltage does not exist at either measurement, replace relay.

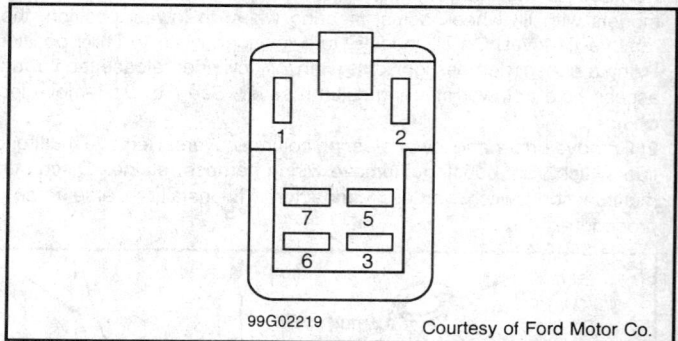

99G02219   Courtesy of Ford Motor Co.

Fig. 1: Identifying Accessory Relay Terminals

MULTIFUNCTION SWITCH – LIGHTING PORTION

Remove and disconnect multifunction switch. See MULTIFUNCTION SWITCH under REMOVAL & INSTALLATION. Check continuity between specified connectors and terminals while operating multifunction switch lever to positions as specified. *See Fig. 2.* See DIMMER & TURN SIGNAL SWITCH TESTING table. If continuity is not as specified, replace multifunction switch.

DIMMER & TURN SIGNAL SWITCH TESTING

Switch Position	Continuity Between Connector/Terminal
Left Turn Signal On	C224B/4 & C224B5
Right Turn Signal On	C224B/1 & C224B5
Flash-To-Pass On [1]	C224A/7 & C224A/8
Headlight Dimmer On High Beam	C224A/9 & C224A/10

[1] – Lever pulled in halfway.

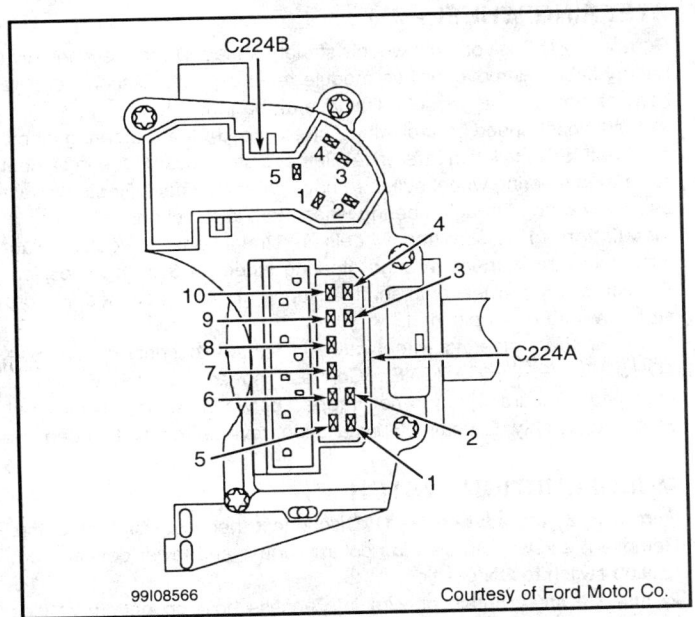

99I08566   Courtesy of Ford Motor Co.

Fig. 2: Identifying Multifunction Switch Circuit Terminals

WIPER/WASHER SWITCH

Remove and disconnect multifunction switch. See MULTIFUNCTION SWITCH under REMOVAL & INSTALLATION. Measure resistance between specified terminals of multifunction switch connector C224A while operating wiper/washer lever to positions as specified. *See Fig. 2.* See WIPER/WASHER SWITCH TESTING table. If resistance is not as specified, replace multifunction switch.

WIPER/WASHER SWITCH TESTING

Switch Position	Terminals	[1] Ohms
Wiper Switch		
Off	2 & 3	47,600
Int	2 & 3	11,330
Lo	2 & 3	4080
Hi	2 & 3	[2]
Washer Switch On	1 & 2	[2]
Wiper Intermittent	1 & 2	[3]

[1] – Specification can vary by as much as 10 percent.
[2] – Continuity should exist.
[3] – Rotate control from maximum delay to minimum delay. Resistance should gradually decrease from approximately 103 k/ohms to 3.3 k/ohms.

IGNITION SWITCH

1) To inspect ignition switch for mechanical operation, rotate lock cylinder through all switch positions. Lock cylinder should not bind, and should return from START to RUN position without assistance.
2) If binding or incorrect modes occur, lock cylinder should either be disassembled and inspected for damage, or ignition switch should be replaced.
3) To test electrical function of ignition switch, disconnect ignition switch harness connector. Check continuity between switch terminals. See IGNITION SWITCH CONTINUITY table. *See Fig. 4.* If continuity is not as specified, replace ignition switch.

IGNITION SWITCH CONTINUITY

Switch Position	Continuity Between Terminals
Start	1 & 3; 1 & 4
Start & Run	1 & 2
Start	1 & 4
Accessory & Run	1 & 5

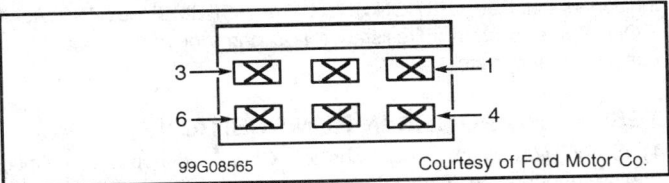

99G08565   Courtesy of Ford Motor Co.

Fig. 3: Identifying Ignition Switch Terminals

SYSTEM TESTS

CAUTION: When battery is disconnected, vehicle computer and memory system may lose memory data. Driveability problems may exist until computer systems have completed a relearn cycle. See COMPUTER RELEARN PROCEDURES article in GENERAL INFORMATION before disconnecting battery.

NOTE: Before performing following tests, ensure all multifunction switch grounds, wiring, and fuses are okay. Also, ensure all circuit connections are clean and tight. For ignition switch circuit identification, see appropriate wiring diagram in POWER DISTRIBUTION article in WIRING DIAGRAMS. For multifunction switch circuit identification, see appropriate wiring diagram in EXTERIOR LIGHTS article.

SYMPTOM CHART

Symptom	Test
Ignition Switch Inoperative	A
No Power In ACC Position	B
No Power In RUN Position	C
No Power In START Position	D
Multifunction Switch Does Not Operate Properly	[1]

[1] – Perform appropriate test under COMPONENT TESTS

TEST A: IGNITION SWITCH INOPERATIVE

Turn ignition off. Disconnect ignition switch harness connector. Measure voltage between ground and ignition switch harness connector C218 terminal No. 1 (White/Violet wire). *See Fig. 4.* If voltage is more than 10 volts, replace ignition switch. Retest system. If voltage is 10 volts or less, repair open White/Violet wire.

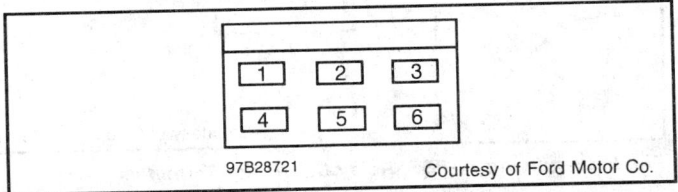

97B28721   Courtesy of Ford Motor Co.

Fig. 4: Identifying Ignition Switch Connector C218 & Interior Fuse Junction Panel Connector C204 Terminals

TEST B: NO POWER IN ACC POSITION

1) Turn ignition switch to ACC position. Check radio operation. If radio operates, go to next step. If radio does not operate, go to step **3)**.
2) Check accessory relay. See ACCESSORY RELAY under COMPONENT TESTS. If accessory relay is okay, replace fuse panel. Retest system. If accessory relay is bad, replace relay and retest system.
3) Turn ignition off. Disconnect interior fuse junction panel connector C204. C204 is located at center of fuse panel across from fuses. Turn ignition switch to ACC position. Measure voltage between ground interior fuse junction panel connector C204 terminal No. 1 (White/Green wire). *See Fig. 4.* If voltage is more than 10 volts, replace fuse panel. Retest system. If voltage is 10 volts or less, go to next step.
4) Turn ignition off. Disconnect ignition switch harness connector. Measure resistance of White/Green wire between ignition switch harness connector C218 terminal No. 5 and interior fuse junction panel connector C204 terminal No. 1. If resistance is less than 5 ohms, replace

ignition switch. See IGNITION SWITCH under REMOVAL & INSTALLATION. Retest system. If resistance is 5 ohms or more, replace fuse panel. Retest system.

TEST C: NO POWER IN RUN POSITION

1) Turn ignition switch to ACC position. Check radio operation. Check front wiper operation. If radio and front wiper operate properly, go to next step. If radio and front wiper do not operate properly, go to TEST B: NO POWER IN ACC POSITION.

2) Turn ignition off. Check ignition switch continuity. See IGNITION SWITCH under COMPONENT TESTS. If ignition switch tests okay, go to next step. If ignition switch does not test okay, replace ignition switch. See IGNITION SWITCH under REMOVAL & INSTALLATION.

3) Reconnect ignition switch connector. Disconnect interior fuse junction panel connector C204. C204 is located at center of fuse panel across from fuses. Turn ignition on. Measure voltage between ground and interior fuse junction panel connector C204 terminal No. 6 (Red/Green wire). *See Fig. 4.* If voltage is more than 10 volts, replace fuse panel. Retest system. If voltage is 10 volts or less, repair open Red/Green wire.

TEST D: NO POWER IN START POSITION

1) Turn ignition off. Check ignition switch continuity. See IGNITION SWITCH under COMPONENT TESTS. If ignition switch tests okay, go to next step. If ignition switch does not test okay, replace ignition switch. See IGNITION SWITCH under REMOVAL & INSTALLATION.

2) Reconnect ignition switch connector. Remove INHIBIT relay located in interior fuse junction panel. Check for continuity between interior fuse junction panel connector C204 terminal No. 5 (White/Blue wire) and INHIBIT relay socket connector terminal No. 7 (Red wire). *See Figs. 4 and 5.* If continuity exists, repair Blue/Black wire between PCM and fuse F38. Retest system. If continuity does not exist, repair open circuit. Retest system.

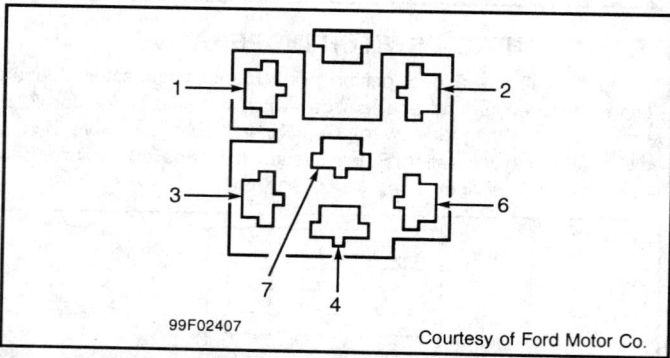

99F02407

Courtesy of Ford Motor Co.

Fig. 5: Identifying INHIBIT Relay Connector Terminals

REMOVAL & INSTALLATION

WARNING: Deactivate air bag system before performing any service operation involving steering column components. See AIR BAG RESTRAINT SYSTEMS – VILLAGER article. Do not apply electrical power to any component on steering column without first deactivating air bag system. Air bag may deploy.

CAUTION: When battery is disconnected, vehicle computer and memory system may lose memory data. Driveability problems may exist until computer systems have completed a relearn cycle. See COMPUTER RELEARN PROCEDURES article in GENERAL INFORMATION before disconnecting battery.

STEERING WHEEL

Removal – 1) Position front wheels straight ahead. Disconnect negative battery cable. Remove air bag module retaining nuts. Disconnect wire harness from air bag module. Remove air bag module.

2) Disconnect speed control wiring (if equipped). Mark steering wheel and shaft for installation reference. Remove and discard steering wheel nut. Using steering wheel puller, remove steering wheel. Route contact assembly wiring through steering wheel as it is removed.

Installation – 1) Ensure front wheels are straight ahead. Route contact assembly wire harness through steering wheel at 3 o'clock position. Position steering wheel onto shaft, ensuring marks are aligned. Ensure air bag wiring is not pinched.

2) Install NEW steering wheel nut and tighten to specification. See TORQUE SPECIFICATIONS. Connect speed control wiring (if equipped). Ensure wiring is not trapped between steering wheel and contact assembly. To complete installation, reverse removal procedure.

MULTIFUNCTION SWITCH

Removal & Installation – 1) Disconnect negative battery cable. Remove 2 screws and steering column upper and lower covers. Turn ignition switch to ON position.

2) Insert a small punch or wire into access hole on bottom of lock cylinder and pull lock cylinder out. Remove 2 multifunction switch screws and remove multifunction switch. Disconnect electrical connectors. To install, reverse removal procedure.

LOCK CYLINDER

Removal (With Key) – Disconnect negative battery cable. Turn ignition switch to RUN position. Remove upper and lower steering column covers. Using a 1/8" drill bit, press retaining pin inward and pull out lock cylinder.

NOTE: When removing lock cylinder, a small tension spring will pop out from under cylinder rod.

Installation – To install, lubricate lock cylinder. Turn lock cylinder to RUN position. Press retaining pin inward and insert lock cylinder into housing. To install remaining components, reverse removal procedure.

Removal (Without Key) – Use this procedure to remove ignition lock cylinder if key is missing or cylinder is frozen. Disconnect negative battery cable. Remove steering wheel. See STEERING WHEEL. Remove upper and lower steering column covers. Using a chisel, remove ignition lock bolts. Remove lock housing. Remove ignition switch lock cylinder from lock housing.

Installation – Position ignition switch lock cylinder in RUN position. Install lock cylinder into lock housing. Align upper and lower lock housing to accept ignition lock bolts. Tighten ignition lock bolts until bolt heads break off. To complete installation, reverse removal procedure.

TORQUE SPECIFICATIONS
TORQUE SPECIFICATIONS

Application	Ft. Lbs. (N.m)
Steering Wheel Nut	22-29 (30-39)

WIRING DIAGRAMS

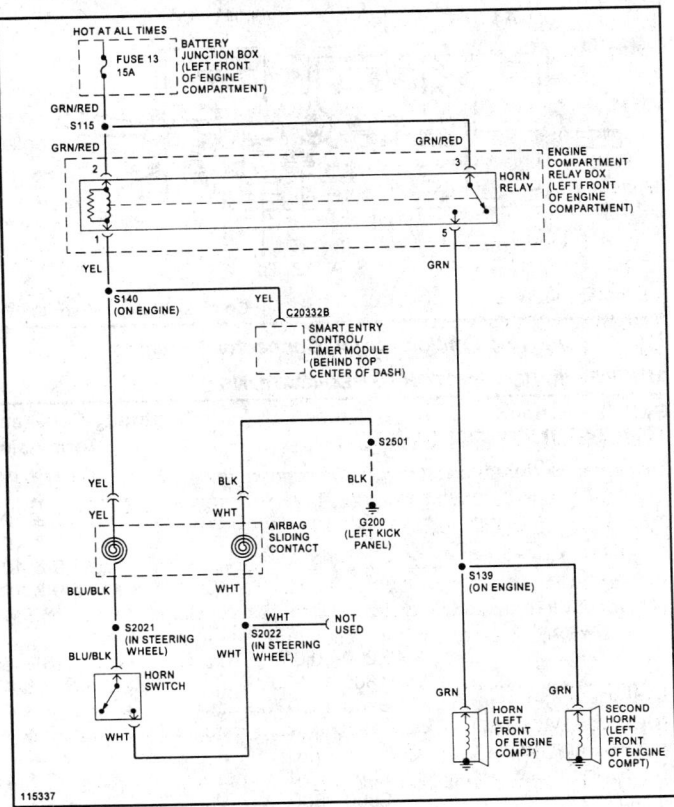

Fig. 6: Horn System Wiring Diagram (Villager)

1999 ACCESSORIES & EQUIPMENT
Steering Column Switches – Windstar

DESCRIPTION

The multifunction switch, located on the steering column, includes turn signal, headlight dimmer, flash-to-pass and front windshield wiper/washer switches. The ignition switch and lock cylinder are also mounted on the steering column.

WARNING: Deactivate air bag system before performing any service operation involving steering column components. See appropriate AIR BAG RESTRAINT SYSTEMS article. Do not apply electrical power to any component on steering column without first deactivating air bag system. Air bag may deploy.

CAUTION: When battery is disconnected, vehicle computer and memory system may lose memory data. Driveability problems may exist until computer systems have completed a relearn cycle. See COMPUTER RELEARN PROCEDURES article in GENERAL INFORMATION before disconnecting battery.

TROUBLE SHOOTING

Verify customers complaint by operating multifunction switch or headlight switch. Check for obvious signs of mechanical or electrical damage. Check for blown fuse(s), loose or corroded connectors, or damaged wiring harness. Check for damaged ignition switch or ignition key. Repair or replace components as necessary. For ignition switch circuit identification, see appropriate wiring diagram in POWER DISTRIBUTION article in WIRING DIAGRAMS. For multifunction switch circuit identification, see appropriate wiring diagram in EXTERIOR LIGHTS article.

COMPONENT TESTS

CAUTION: When battery is disconnected, vehicle computer and memory system may lose memory data. Driveability problems may exist until computer systems have completed a relearn cycle. See COMPUTER RELEARN PROCEDURES article in GENERAL INFORMATION before disconnecting battery.

IGNITION SWITCH CONTINUITY TEST

Disconnect ignition switch connector. Using ohmmeter, check continuity of ignition switch across specified terminals. *See Fig. 1.* See IGNITION SWITCH CONTINUITY TEST table. Continuity should not exist between ground terminal and any other terminal on ignition switch except P1 and P2 terminal with ignition switch in START position.

IGNITION SWITCH CONTINUITY TEST

Ignition Switch Position	Continuity Between Terminals
ACC	A1 & B5
LOCK	No Continuity
OFF	No Continuity
RUN	A1 & B1; A2 & B2; A3 & B3; A4 & B4; I1 & B5
START	I1 & B5; I2 & B1; STA & B4; P1 & GND; P2 & GND

MULTIFUNCTION SWITCH TEST

Disconnect multifunction switch connector. Using ohmmeter, check continuity or resistance of multifunction switch across specified terminals. See MULTIFUNCTION SWITCH SPECIFICATIONS table. *See Fig. 2.* If continuity or resistance is not as specified, replace switch as necessary.

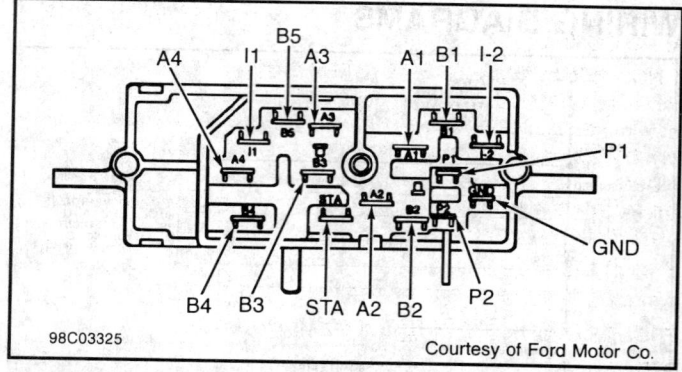

98C03325   Courtesy of Ford Motor Co.

Fig. 1: Identifying Ignition Switch Connector Terminals

MULTIFUNCTION SWITCH SPECIFICATIONS

Switch Position	Ohms	Continuity Between Terminals
Flash-To-Pass	1	6 & 10; 7 & 10
Low Beam	1	6 & 10
High Beam	1	7 & 10
Left Turn Signal	1	8 & 10
Right Turn Signal	1	9 & 10
Hazard Switch	1	8 & 10; 9 & 10
Washer Switch	1	3 & 4
Wiper Switch		
OFF	45,200-50,000	3 & 4
INT	10,800-11,900	3 & 4
LOW	3900-4300	3 & 4
HIGH	0	3 & 4
Interval Time Adjust		
INT & OFF	3300-103,300 [2]	3 & 4
LOW & HIGH	2900-3600	3 & 4
Rear Wiper/Washer Switch Circuit		
OFF	2900	1 & 5
INT 1	1000	1 & 2
INT 2	330	1 & 4
WASH	0	9 & 10

[1] – Continuity should exist between terminals.
[2] – Rotate control toward OFF position. Resistance should increase smoothly to maximum resistance.

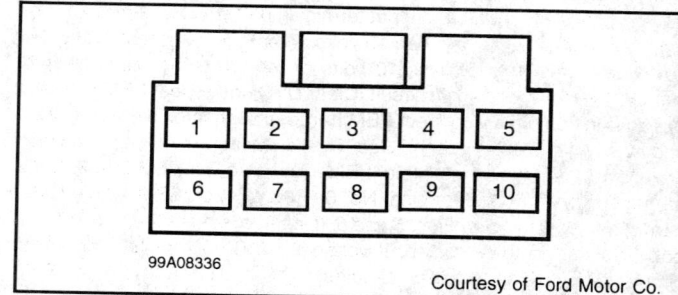

99A08336   Courtesy of Ford Motor Co.

Fig. 2: Identifying Multifunction Switch Connector Terminals

SELF-DIAGNOSTIC SYSTEM

NOTE: Before beginning self-diagnostics, perform TROUBLE SHOOTING.

Connect New Generation Star (NGS) tester to Data Link Connector (DLC), located beneath instrument panel. Using NGS tester, perform data link diagnostics test. See DATA LINK DIAGNOSTIC TEST under COMMUNICATION NETWORK DIAGNOSTICS in MODULE COMMUNICATIONS NETWORK – WINDSTAR article. If NGS tester responds with CKT914, CKT915 or CKT70=ALL ECUS NO RESP/NOT EQUIP, repair module communications concern. See MODULE COMMUNICATIONS NETWORK – WINDSTAR article. If NGS tester displays NO

RESP/NOT EQUIP for Front Electronics Module (FEM), perform TEST A: NO COMMUNICATION WITH FEM under SYSTEM TESTS.

If NGS tester responds with SYSTEM PASSED, retrieve and record continuous DTCs. Erase continuous DTCs. Using NGS tester, perform instrument cluster FEM self-test. Perform appropriate test in accordance with DTC retrieved. Go to FRONT ELECTRONIC MODULE (FEM) DTC INDEX. Codes listed in these tables are only for testing covered in this article. For complete DTC listing, see MODULE COMMUNICATIONS NETWORK – WINDSTAR article.

If no DTCs are retrieved though FEM self diagnostics, repair by symptom. See SYMPTOM CHART table.

FRONT ELECTRONIC MODULE (FEM) DTC INDEX

DTC [1]	Description	Test
B1342	ECU Defective	[2]
U1262	SCP Communication Bus Fault –	
	Carry out Network Communication Test	[3]

[1] – Codes listed in this table are only for testing covered in this article. For complete DTC listing, see MODULE COMMUNICATIONS NETWORK – WINDSTAR article.

[2] – Clear and document all DTCs. Perform FEM self-test. If DTC B1342 is retrieved again, replace Front Electronic Module (FEM). Prior to replacement of FEM module, it is necessary to upload module configuration information using NGS tester. See COMPUTER RELEARN PROCEDURES article in GENERAL INFORMATION.

[3] – Repair all DTCs related to fault first. If DTC U1262 is still recorded, see MODULE COMMUNICATIONS NETWORK – WINDSTAR article.

SYMPTOM CHART

Symptom	Test
No Communication With FEM Module	A
Ignition Switch Inoperative	B
No Power In ACC Position	C
No Power in RUN Position	D
No Power in START Position	E

SYSTEM TESTS

TEST A: NO COMMUNICATION WITH FEM

1) Turn ignition off. Remove Battery Junction Block (BJB) fuses No. 2 (5-amp) and 23 (15-amp). Turn ignition on. Using voltmeter, measure voltage between ground and input terminals on fuses No. 2 and 23. *See Fig. 3.* If voltage is greater than 10 volts on both fuses, install fuses and go to next step. If voltage is 10 volts or less on either circuit, repair suspect open power supply circuit. Clear DTC and repeat FEM self-test.

2) Turn ignition off. Disconnect FEM harness connector. FEM is located under driver's side of dash. *See Fig. 4.* Measure voltage between ground and terminals No. 1 (Light Blue/Red wire) on FEM 20-pin C346 harness connector and terminal No. 6 (Red wire) on FEM 12-pin C190 harness connector. *See Figs. 5 and 6.* If voltage is more than 10 volts for both circuits, go to next step. If voltages is 10 volts or less on either circuit, repair open suspect circuit(s). Clear DTC and repeat FEM self-test.

3) Turn ignition off. Check resistance between ground and terminal No. 12 (Black wire) on FEM 12-pin C190 harness connector and terminals No. 11, 13, 14 and 15 (Black wires) on FEM 17-pin C192 harness connector. *See Figs. 6 and 7.* If resistance is less than 5 ohms on all circuits, go to MODULE COMMUNICATIONS NETWORK – WINDSTAR article. If resistance is 5 ohms or more on any circuit, repair suspect open circuit(s). Repeat self-test and clear DTC.

TEST B: IGNITION SWITCH INOPERATIVE

Turn ignition off. Disconnect ignition switch connector. Using voltmeter, measure voltage between ground and terminals B1, B3, B4 and B5 on ignition switch harness connector. If voltage for all circuits is greater than 10 volts, install new ignition switch. If voltage is 10 volts or less on any circuit, repair suspect open circuit and retest system.

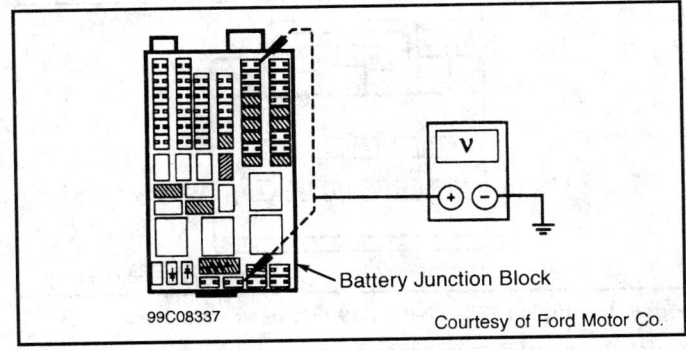

Fig. 3: Measuring Input Voltage On BJB Fuses No. 2 & 23

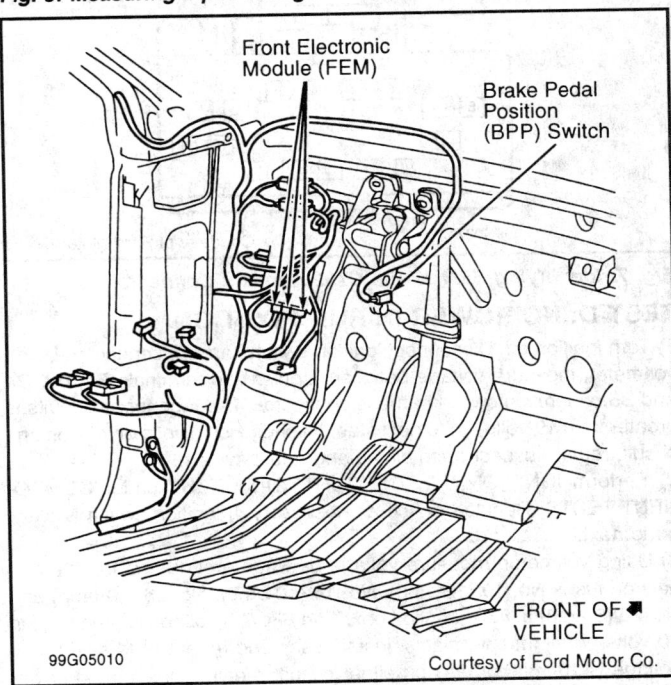

Fig. 4: Locating Front Electronics Module (FEM)

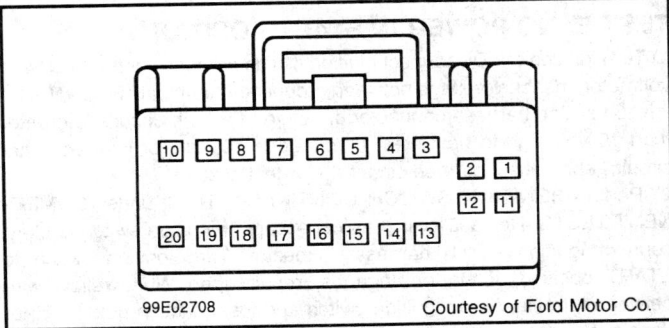

Fig. 5: Identifying FEM 20-Pin C346 Harness Connector

TEST C: NO POWER IN ACC POSITION

1) Turn ignition on. Turn radio on. If radio operates correctly, go to next step. If radio does not operate correctly, go to TEST D: NO POWER IN RUN POSITION.

2) Turn ignition off. Disconnect ignition switch connector. Using voltmeter, measure voltage between ground and terminal B5 (Light Green/Violet wire) on ignition switch harness connector. If voltage is greater than 10 volts, install new ignition switch. If voltage is 10 volts or less on any circuit, repair open Light Green/Violet wire and retest system.

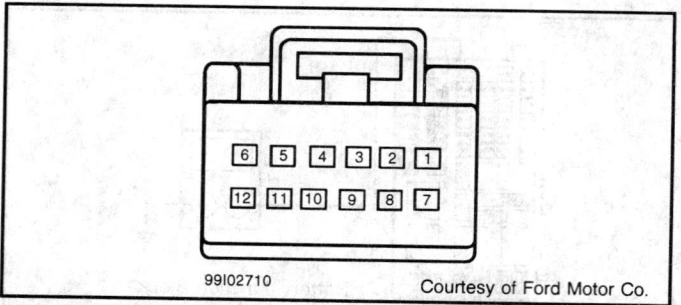

Fig. 6: Identifying FEM 12-Pin C190 Harness Connector

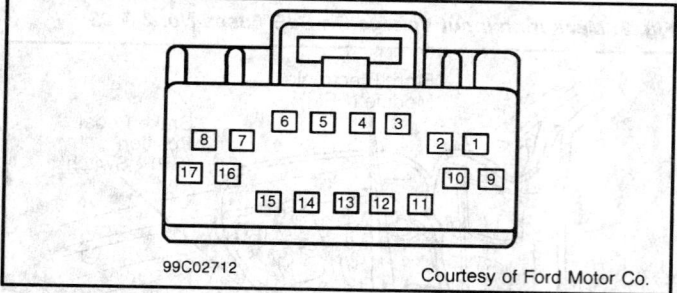

Fig. 7: Identifying FEM 17-Pin C192 Harness Connector

TEST D: NO POWER IN RUN POSITION

1) Turn ignition off. Disconnect ignition switch harness connector. Using voltmeter, measure voltage between ground and terminals B1, B3, B4 and B5 on ignition switch harness connector. If voltage for all circuits is greater than 10 volts, go to next step. If voltage is 10 volts or less on any circuit, repair suspect open circuit and retest system.

2) Perform IGNITION SWITCH CONTINUITY TEST under COMPONENT TESTS. Replace switch as necessary. If ignition switch is okay, go to next.

3) Using voltmeter, measure voltage between ground and input terminals on fuses No. 10 (10-amp), No. 14 (10-amp), No. 26 (10-amp) and No. 28 (5-amp) at fuse junction box. See Fig. 8. If voltage is greater than 10 volts on all fuse terminals, install fuses and repeat FEM self-test. If voltage is 10 volts or less on either circuit, repair suspect open power supply circuit. Clear DTC and repeat FEM self-test.

TEST E: NO POWER IN START POSITION

1) Turn ignition off. Disconnect ignition switch harness connector. Using voltmeter, measure voltage between ground and terminals B4 and B5 on ignition switch harness connector. If voltage for both circuits is greater than 10 volts, go to next step. If voltage is 10 volts or less on either circuit, repair suspect open circuit and retest system.

2) Perform IGNITION SWITCH CONTINUITY TEST under COMPONENT TESTS. Replace switch as necessary. If ignition switch is okay, connect ignition switch harness connector. Turn ignition switch to START position. If starter engages, repair open White/Yellow wire between terminal A1 on ignition switch and fuse junction box. If starter does not engage, repair open White/Light Blue wire.

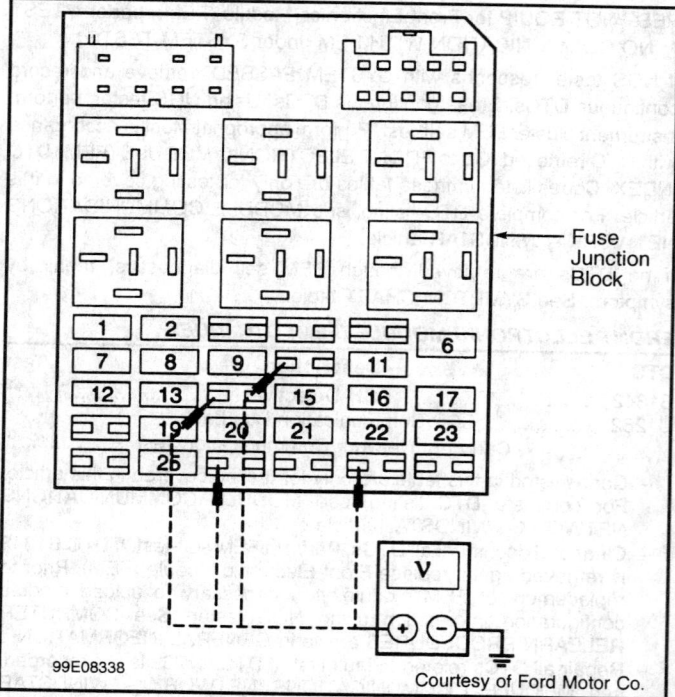

Fig. 8: Measuring Voltage Supply To Fuse Junction Box

REMOVAL & INSTALLATION

WARNING: *Deactivate air bag system before performing any service operation involving steering column components. See appropriate AIR BAG RESTRAINT SYSTEMS article. Do not apply electrical power to any component on steering column without first deactivating air bag system. Air bag may deploy.*

CAUTION: *When battery is disconnected, vehicle computer and memory system may lose memory data. Driveability problems may exist until computer systems have completed a relearn cycle. See COMPUTER RELEARN PROCEDURES article in GENERAL INFORMATION before disconnecting battery.*

IGNITION SWITCH

Removal & Installation – Disconnect negative battery cable. Wait at least 2 minutes for air bag back-up power supply to deplete. Remove key release lever, if equipped. Remove lower steering column shroud and reinforcement. Disconnect ignition switch harness connector. Turn ignition off. Remove 2 ignition switch screws and ignition switch. To install, reverse removal procedure.

MULTIFUNCTION SWITCH

Removal & Installation – Disconnect negative battery cable. Wait at least 2 minutes for air bag back-up power supply to deplete. Twist tilt wheel handle and shank counterclockwise and remove. Remove 3 screws and instrument panel steering column cover shroud. Remove 2 self-tapping screws and multifunction switch. Disconnect multifunction switch harness connectors. To install, reverse removal procedure.

TORQUE SPECIFICATIONS

TORQUE SPECIFICATIONS

Application	INCH Lbs. (N.m)
Ignition Switch Screws	60 (7)
Multifunction Switch-To-Steering Column Screws	27 (3)
Reinforcement Screws	106 (12)

WIRING DIAGRAMS

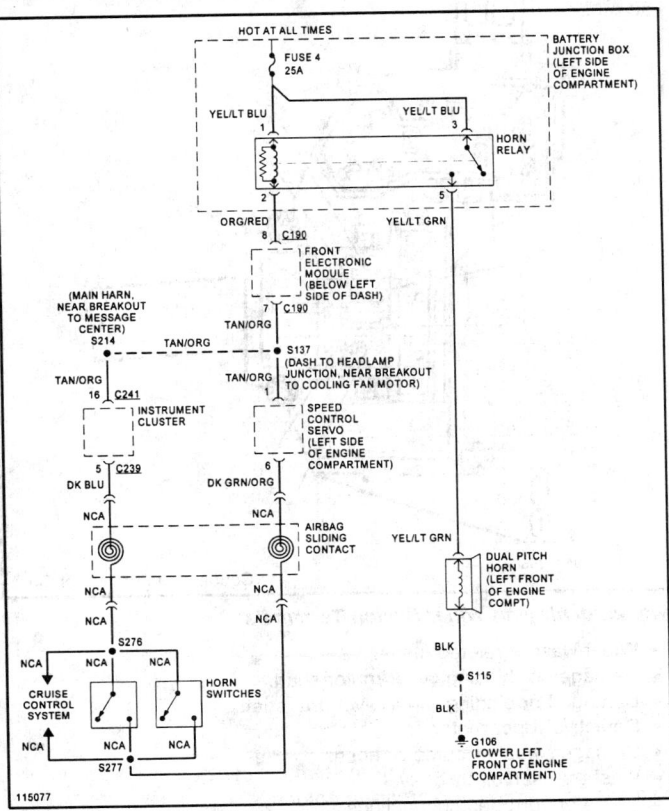

Fig. 9: Horn System Wiring Diagram (Windstar)

DESCRIPTION & OPERATION

All wiper/washer functions are controlled by the wiper switch and Wiper Control Module (WCM) located behind left side of instrument panel. When wiper switch is in INT (interval) position, wipe cycles are separated by adjustable intervals. Wiper arms have a separate PARK position when system is not in use.

ADJUSTMENTS

WIPER ARMS

Cycle wipers and turn wipers off. Allow wipers to return to park position. Wiper arms should park in rectangular alignment marks printed on glass. *See Fig. 1.* If alignment is off, remove wiper arms and reinstall to correct position.

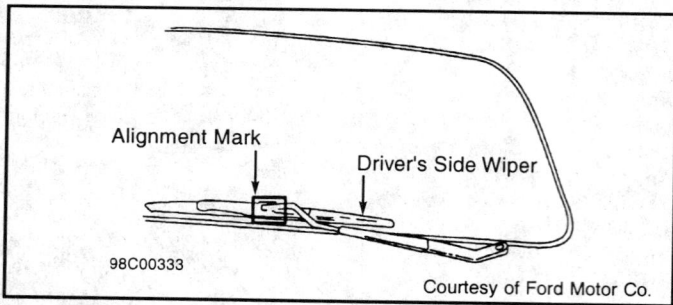

Fig. 1: Identifying Wiper Arm Alignment Marks

COMPONENT TESTS

WARNING: Vehicle is equipped with an air bag system. System MUST be disabled before working near steering column and instrument cluster to prevent air bag deployment. See appropriate AIR BAG RESTRAINT SYSTEMS article.

WIPER SWITCH

NOTE: Windshield wiper switch is an integral part of the multifunction switch located on steering column. Multifunction switch is serviced as an assembly.

Disconnect multifunction switch 7-pin connector located under steering column. Using a DVOM, test between specified terminals. See WIPER SWITCH CONTINUITY TEST table. *See Fig. 2.* Replace switch if readings are not as specified.

WIPER SWITCH CONTINUITY TEST

Switch Position	Terminals	[1] Resistance (k/ohms)
Wiper		
OFF	4 & 1	47.6
INT	4 & 1	10.9
Interval Adjust	4 & 6	[2]
LO	4 & 1	4.0
HI	4 & 1	Less Than 5 Ohms
Washer		
Pressed	4 & 6	Less Than 5 Ohms
Released	4 & 6	100
Mist		
Pressed	4 & 6	3.3
Released	4 & 6	100

[1] – Resistance values are approximate.
[2] – Rotate INT (interval) knob from minimum to maximum. Resistance should increase gradually from approximately 3.3 k/ohms (MIN) to approximately 100 k/ohms (MAX). All measurements should be within 10 percent of specification.

SYSTEM TESTS

Before performing any tests on wiper/washer system, check the following items to eliminate common problems:

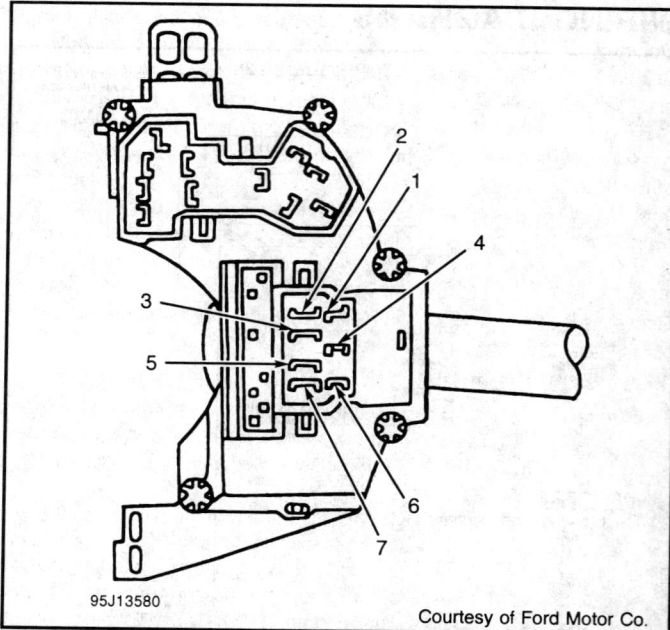

Fig. 2: Identifying Wiper Switch Terminals

- Wiper/washer related fuses.
- Damaged or binding wiper motor shaft.
- Damaged or binding wiper pivot arm shaft.
- Defective wiper motor.
- Damaged washer pump or hoses.
- Washer reservoir fluid level.
- Loose or corroded connections.
- Inoperative multifunction switch or circuit.

Refer to DIAGNOSTIC TEST INDEX table, then go to the appropriate test. For individual component testing, see COMPONENT TESTS.

DIAGNOSTIC TEST INDEX

Symptom	Test
Washers Inoperative	A
Wipers Inoperative	B
Low Speed Wipers Do Not Operate Properly	C
High Speed Wipers Do Not Operate Properly	D
Intermittent Wipers Do Not Operate Properly	E
Wipers Do Not Park Properly	F
Wipers Stay On Continuously	G
Headlights Inoperative When Wipers Are On	H

TEST A: WASHERS INOPERATIVE

1) Turn ignition on. Activate washer switch. If washer pump operates, go to next step. If washer pump does not operate, go to step **3)**.
2) If washer pump operates but fluid does not squirt from nozzles, inspect nozzles and hoses for blockage. Repair or replace as necessary and check system operation. If hoses and nozzles are okay, replace washer pump. See WASHER RESERVOIR & PUMP under REMOVAL & INSTALLATION.
3) Turn ignition off. Disconnect washer pump harness connector. Turn ignition on. Check for battery voltage on Black/White wire at washer pump harness connector while operating washer switch. If battery voltage exists, go to next step. If battery voltage does not exist, go to step **5)**.
4) Measure resistance of Black wire between washer pump harness connector and ground. If resistance is 5 ohms or less, replace washer pump. See WASHER RESERVOIR & PUMP under REMOVAL & INSTALLATION. If resistance is greater than 5 ohms, repair Black wire or ground connection. Restore electrical connections and check system operation.
5) Turn ignition off. Measure resistance between Black/White wire at washer motor harness connector and ground. If measured resistance is

greater than 10 k/ohms, go to next step. If resistance is less than 10 k/ohms, check for short to ground. If wire is okay, replace wiper switch. See WIPER SWITCH under REMOVAL & INSTALLATION. Restore electrical connections and check system operation.

6) Turn ignition off. Disconnect harness connector from wiper control module located under left side of instrument panel. Measure resistance of Black/White wire between wiper motor harness connector and wiper control module harness connector. If resistance is greater than 5 ohms, repair open Black/White wire and check system operation. If resistance is less than 5 ohms, replace wiper control module. See WIPER CONTROL MODULE (WCM) under REMOVAL & INSTALLATION. Restore electrical connections and check system operation.

TEST B: WIPERS INOPERATIVE

1) Turn ignition off. Check fuse No. 10 (30-amp) located in instrument panel fuse box. Replace fuse if necessary. If fuse blows again, check for short to ground and repair as necessary. See WIRING DIAGRAMS. If fuse is okay, go to next step.

2) Turn ignition off. Disconnect Wiper Control Module (WCM) connector. WCM is located under far left side of instrument panel. Turn ignition on. Measure voltage between ground and Wiper Control Module (WCM) harness connector terminals No. 2 and 11 (Dark Green wires). See Fig. 3. If battery voltage exists at both terminals, go to next step. If battery voltage does not exist at both terminals, repair open Dark Green wire to WCM. See WIRING DIAGRAMS. Restore electrical connections and check system operation.

3) Turn ignition off. Measure resistance between ground and WCM harness connector terminals No. 3 and 5. If resistance is less than 5 ohms, go to next step. If resistance is greater than 5 ohms, repair open Black wire or ground connection. See WIRING DIAGRAMS. Restore electrical connections and check system operation.

4) Test wiper switch. See WIPER SWITCH under COMPONENT TESTS. If wiper switch is okay, go to next step. Replace wiper switch if necessary. See WIPER SWITCH under REMOVAL & INSTALLATION. Restore electrical connections and check system operation.

5) Disconnect multifunction switch 7–pin connector. Measure resistance of Brown/White wire between multifunction switch 7–pin connector and WCM harness connector terminal No. 7. If resistance is less than 5 ohms, go to next step. If resistance is greater than 5 ohms, repair open Brown/White wire. Restore electrical connections and check system operation.

6) Measure resistance of Orange wire between multifunction switch 7-pin connector and WCM harness connector terminal No. 1. If resistance is less than 5 ohms, go to next step. If resistance is greater than 5 ohms, repair open Orange wire. Restore electrical connections and check system operation.

7) Reconnect WCM. Disconnect wiper motor harness connector. Turn ignition on. Turn multifunction switch to high speed position. Measure voltage between White wire and Yellow/Red wire at wiper motor harness connector. If battery voltage does not exist, go to next step. If battery voltage exists, replace wiper motor. See WIPER MOTOR & LINKAGE under REMOVAL & INSTALLATION. Restore electrical connections and check system operation.

8) Turn ignition off and disconnect WCM harness connector. Measure resistance of Yellow/Red wire between wiper motor harness connector terminal No. 3 and WCM harness connector terminal No. 10. See Fig. 3. If resistance is less than 5 ohms, replace WCM. See WIPER CONTROL MODULE (WCM) under REMOVAL & INSTALLATION. If resistance is greater than 5 ohms, repair open Yellow/Red wire. Restore electrical connections and check system operation.

TEST C: LOW SPEED WIPERS INOPERATIVE

1) Turn ignition off. Disconnect wiper motor harness connector. Turn ignition on. Set wiper switch for low speed operation. Measure voltage between Yellow/Red and Dark Blue/Orange wires at wiper motor harness connector. If battery voltage does not exist, go to next step. If battery voltage exists, replace wiper motor. See WIPER MOTOR & LINKAGE under REMOVAL & INSTALLATION. Restore electrical connections and check system operation.

2) Turn ignition off. Disconnect Wiper Control Module (WCM) harness connector. WCM is located below far left side of instrument panel. Measure resistance between Dark Blue/Orange wire at wiper motor harness connector and ground. If resistance is greater than 10 k/ohms, go to next step. If resistance is less than 10 k/ohms, repair short to ground in Dark Blue/Orange wire. Restore electrical connections and check system operation.

3) Measure resistance of Dark Blue/Orange wire between WCM harness connector terminal No. 8 and wiper motor harness connector. See Fig. 3. If resistance is less than 5 ohms, go to next step. If resistance is greater than 5 ohms, repair open Dark Blue/Orange wire. Restore electrical connections and check system operation.

4) Test wiper switch. See WIPER SWITCH under COMPONENT TESTS. Replace wiper switch if necessary. See WIPER SWITCH under REMOVAL & INSTALLATION. If wiper switch is okay, replace WCM. See WIPER CONTROL MODULE (WCM) under REMOVAL & INSTALLATION. Restore electrical connections and check system operation.

TEST D: HIGH SPEED WIPERS INOPERATIVE

1) Turn ignition off. Disconnect wiper motor harness connector. Turn ignition on. Set wiper switch for high speed operation. Measure voltage between Yellow/Red and White wires at wiper motor harness connector. If battery voltage does not exist, go to next step. If battery voltage exists, replace wiper motor. See WIPER MOTOR & LINKAGE under REMOVAL & INSTALLATION. Restore electrical connections and check system operation.

2) Turn ignition off. Disconnect Wiper Control Module (WCM) harness connector. Measure resistance between White wire at wiper motor harness connector and ground. If resistance is greater than 10 k/ohms, go to next step. If resistance is less than 10 k/ohms, repair short to ground in White wire. Restore electrical connections and check system operation.

3) Disconnect WCM harness connector. WCM is located below far left side of instrument panel. Measure resistance of White wire between WCM harness connector terminal No. 14 and wiper motor harness connector. See Fig. 3. If resistance is less than 5 ohms, go to next step. If resistance is greater than 5 ohms, repair open White wire. Restore electrical connections and check system operation.

4) Test wiper switch. See WIPER SWITCH under COMPONENT TESTS. Replace wiper switch if necessary. See WIPER SWITCH under REMOVAL & INSTALLATION. If wiper switch is okay, replace WCM. See WIPER CONTROL MODULE (WCM) under REMOVAL & INSTALLATION. Restore electrical connections and check system operation.

TEST E: INTERMITTENT WIPERS DO NOT OPERATE PROPERLY

1) Test wiper switch. See WIPER SWITCH under COMPONENT TESTS. Replace wiper switch if necessary. See WIPER SWITCH under REMOVAL & INSTALLATION. If wiper switch is okay, go to next step.

2) Disconnect Wiper Control Module (WCM) harness connector located below far left side of instrument panel. Measure resistance between ground and WCM harness connector terminal No. 9 (Dark Blue/White wire). If resistance is greater than 10 k/ohms, go to next step. If resistance is less than 10 k/ohms, repair Dark Blue/White wire for short to ground. Restore electrical connections and check system operation.

3) Disconnect 7-pin multifunction switch harness connector. Measure resistance of Dark Blue/White wire between 7-pin multifunction switch harness connector and WCM harness connector terminal No. 9. See Fig. 3. If resistance is less than 5 ohms, replace WCM. See WIPER CONTROL MODULE (WCM) under REMOVAL & INSTALLATION. If

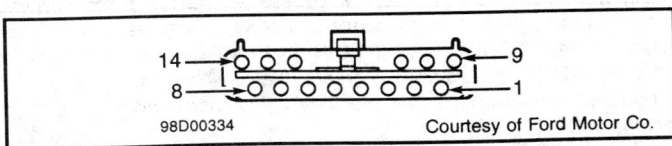

98D00334   Courtesy of Ford Motor Co.

Fig. 3: Identifying Wiper Control Module Harness Connector Terminals

resistance is greater than 5 ohms, repair open Dark Blue/White wire. Restore electrical connections and check system operation.

TEST F: WIPERS DO NOT PARK PROPERLY

1) Turn ignition off. Disconnect wiper motor connector. Turn ignition on. Measure voltage between Dark Green wire at wiper motor harness connector and ground. If battery voltage exists, go to next step. If battery voltage does not exist, repair open Dark Green wire. Restore electrical connections and check system operation.

2) Turn ignition off. Measure resistance between Black/Pink and Dark Blue/Orange wires at wiper motor harness connector. Also measure resistance between ground and Yellow/Red wire at wiper motor harness connector. If resistance is less than 5 ohms for both measurements, go to step **4)**. If resistance is not less than 5 ohms for both resistance measurements, go to next step.

3) Disconnect Wiper Control Module (WCM) harness connector. WCM is located under far left side of instrument panel. Measure resistance of Black/Pink, Yellow/Red and Dark Blue/Orange wires between wiper motor and WCM harness connectors. If resistance of all wires is less than 5 ohms, replace WCM. See WIPER CONTROL MODULE (WCM) under REMOVAL & INSTALLATION. If resistance of any wire is greater than 5 ohms, repair wire in question. See WIRING DIAGRAMS.

4) Check wiper linkage to ensure linkage is not bent, mispositioned or otherwise damaged. Repair or replace as necessary. If wiper linkage is okay, replace wiper motor. See WIPER MOTOR & LINKAGE under REMOVAL & INSTALLATION. Restore electrical connections and check system operation.

TEST G: WIPERS STAY ON CONTINUOUSLY

1) Test wiper switch. See WIPER SWITCH under COMPONENT TESTS. Replace wiper switch if necessary. See WIPER SWITCH under REMOVAL & INSTALLATION. If wiper switch is okay, go to next step.

2) Turn ignition off. Disconnect multifunction switch. Disconnect Wiper Control Module (WCM) located below far left side of instrument panel. Measure resistance between WCM harness connector terminal No. 1 (Orange wire) and ground. If resistance is greater than 10 k/ohms, go to next step. If resistance is less than 10 k/ohms, repair Orange wire for short to ground. Restore electrical connections and check system operation.

3) Measure resistance between WCM harness connector terminal No. 7 (Brown/White wire) and ground. *See Fig. 3.* If resistance is greater than 10 k/ohms, go to next step. If resistance is less than 10 k/ohms, repair Brown/White wire for short to ground. Restore electrical connections and check system operation.

4) Measure resistance between WCM harness connector terminal No. 9 (Dark Blue/White wire) and ground. If resistance is greater than 10 k/ohms, replace WCM. See WIPER CONTROL MODULE (WCM) under REMOVAL & INSTALLATION. If resistance is less than 10 k/ohms, repair Dark Blue/White wire for short to ground. Restore electrical connections and check system operation.

TEST H: HEADLIGHT INOPERATIVE WHEN WIPERS ARE ON

1) Turn headlight switch to ON position. If headlights operate, go to next step. If headlights do not operate, repair basic headlight system. See appropriate wiring diagram in HEADLIGHT SYSTEMS article.

NOTE: *Lamp Control Module (LCM) must be programmed using New Generation Star (NGS) tester if replaced during the following step:*

2) Turn ignition off. Disconnect Lighting Control Module (LCM) 22-pin harness connector and ground. LCM is located below left side of instrument panel. Turn wiper switch to low speed position. Turn ignition on. Wait at least 15 seconds. Measure voltage between LCM 22-pin harness connector terminal No. 15 (Black/Pink wire) and ground. If voltage varies between 0 and 10 volts, replace LCM. If voltage does not vary between 0 and 10 volts, repair open Black/Pink wire. Restore electrical connections and check system operation.

REMOVAL & INSTALLATION

WARNING: *Vehicle is equipped with an air bag system. System MUST be disabled before working near steering column and instrument cluster to prevent air bag deployment. See appropriate AIR BAG RESTRAINT SYSTEMS article.*

CAUTION: *When battery is disconnected, vehicle computer and memory systems may lose memory data. Driveability problems may exist until computer systems have completed a relearn cycle. See COMPUTER RELEARN PROCEDURES article in GENERAL INFORMATION before disconnecting battery.*

WIPER MOTOR & LINKAGE

Removal & Installation – 1) Disconnect battery ground cable. Remove wiper arms. Remove cowl top vent panels. Disconnect wiper motor harness connector. Remove mounting arm and pivot shaft assembly.
2) Remove nuts and wiper motor. Remove wiper motor crank arm bolt. Remove motor. To install, reverse removal procedure. See TORQUE SPECIFICATIONS.

WIPER SWITCH

NOTE: *Wiper switch is incorporated into multifunction switch on steering column. Wiper/washer portion of multifunction switch cannot be serviced separately.*

Removal & Installation – Disconnect battery ground cable. Turn ignition switch to RUN position, and press release tab by inserting punch through steering column access hole. Remove ignition switch lock cylinder. Unscrew tilt wheel lever. Remove instrument panel insulator below steering column. Separate and remove steering column cover halves. Disconnect harness connector and remove multifunction switch. To install, reverse removal procedure.

WIPER CONTROL MODULE (WCM)

Removal & Installation – Wiper Control Module (WCM) is mounted below left side of instrument panel. Disconnect negative battery cable. Remove insulator panel located below steering column. Remove instrument panel steering column cover. Remove hood release handle screws and position hood release handle aside. Remove parking brake lever bolts and move parking brake lever aside. Remove reinforcement panel below steering column. Disconnect and remove WCM. To install, reverse removal procedure.

WASHER RESERVOIR & PUMP

Removal & Installation – 1) Disconnect battery ground cable. Remove air compressor. Remove coolant reservoir bolts and position coolant reservoir aside. Remove upper and lower washer reservoir bolts.
2) Raise and support vehicle. Remove right front wheel. Remove screws, push pins and inner fender splash shield. Disconnect washer hoses and electrical connector. Pull pump from washer reservoir. To install, reverse removal procedure.

TORQUE SPECIFICATIONS
TORQUE SPECIFICATIONS

Application	Ft. Lbs. (N.m.)
Wiper Arm Nut	22-30 (30-40)
Wiper Motor-To-Mounting Arm Bolts	9-13 (13-17)
Wiper Motor-To-Crank Bolt	12-16 (17-23)

WIRING DIAGRAMS

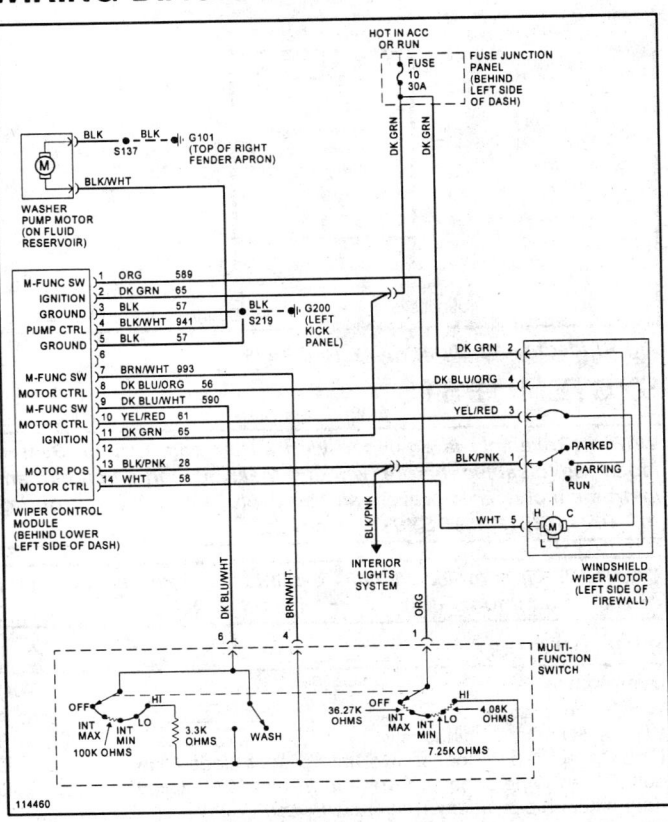

Fig. 4: Wiper/Washer System Wiring Diagram (Continental)

1999 ACCESSORIES & EQUIPMENT
Wiper/Washer Systems – Contour & Mystique

DESCRIPTION & OPERATION

Wiper/washer functions are controlled by the wiper/washer switch and Central Timer Module (CTM) located in the central junction box under left side of instrument panel. CTM controls wiper/washers, illuminated entry, rear window defogger, heated mirrors and warning chimes. Two models of Intermittent wipers are used, either with a fixed 9-second interval, or an adjustable interval.

COMPONENT LOCATIONS

COMPONENT LOCATIONS

Component	Location
Central Junction Box	Behind Left Side Of Instrument Panel
Central Timer Module	On Central Junction Box
Washer Reservoir & Motor	Under Right Front Fender
Wiper Relay	In Central Junction Box
Wiper/Washer Switch	Part Of Multifunction Switch

TROUBLE SHOOTING

Before performing any tests on wiper/washer system, check the following items to eliminate common problems:

- Fuse No. 20 (10-amp).
- Damaged wiper motor linkage.
- Damaged washer pump.
- Loose or corroded connections.
- Damaged wiring harness.
- Kinked or plugged washer hose.

COMPONENT TESTS

WIPER MOTOR

1) Turn ignition switch to LOCK position. Disconnect wiper motor harness connector. Using a jumper wire, ground terminal No. 4 (Black wire terminal) at wiper motor. Using a second jumper wire and in-line ammeter, connect battery voltage to terminal No. 5 (White/Black wire terminal) at wiper motor. Wiper motor should operate at high speed and should draw 4 amps or less. If wiper motor operation is as specified, go to next step. If wiper motor operation is not as specified, replace wiper motor.

2) Move battery voltage lead from terminal No. 5 at wiper motor to terminal No. 4 (White/Green wire terminal) at wiper motor. Wiper motor should operate at low speed and draw 2 amps or less. If wiper motor operation is as specified, disconnect jumper wires and go to next step. If wiper motor operation is not as specified, replace wiper motor.

3) Ensure wiper motor is not in park position. Measure resistance between terminals No. 1 (White/Blue wire terminal) and No. 2 (Violet wire terminal) at wiper motor. Resistance should be 5 ohms or less. If resistance is as specified, go to next step. If resistance is not as specified, replace wiper motor.

4) Measure resistance between terminals No. 2 (White/Blue wire terminal) and No. 3 (Black wire terminal) at wiper motor. Resistance should be 5 ohms or less. If resistance is not as specified, replace wiper motor. If resistance is as specified, wiper motor is okay at this time.

WIPER RELAY

1) Remove wiper relay. Measure resistance between terminal No. 1 and all other terminals on relay. See Fig. 1. All resistance readings should be greater than 5 ohms. If resistance is as specified, go to next step. If resistance is not as specified, replace wiper relay.

2) Using 2 fused jumper wires, apply battery voltage to terminals No. 2 and 3 of relay. Measure voltage at terminal No. 4 of relay. If battery voltage exists, go to next step. If battery voltage does not exist, replace wiper relay.

3) Using another jumper wire, ground terminal No. 1 at relay. Measure voltage at terminal No. 5 at relay. If battery voltage exists, relay is okay at this time. If battery voltage does not exist, replace wiper relay.

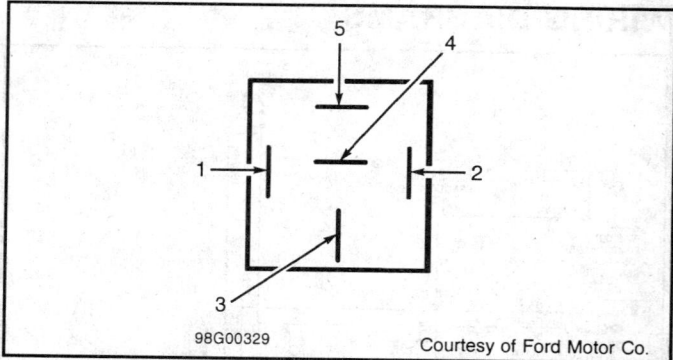

98G00329   Courtesy of Ford Motor Co.

Fig. 1: Identifying Wiper Relay Terminals

SYSTEM TESTS

WARNING: Vehicle is equipped with an air bag system. System MUST be disabled before working near steering column and instrument cluster to prevent air bag deployment. See appropriate AIR BAG RESTRAINT SYSTEMS article.

CAUTION: Wiper motor contains ceramic magnets that may crack or shatter if motor is dropped or handled roughly.

SYMPTOM CHART

Symptom	Test
Wipers Inoperative	A
Wipers Stay On Continuously	B
High Speed Wipers Inoperative (Intermittent Mode Okay)	C
Low Speed Wipers Inoperative (Intermittent Mode Okay)	D
Intermittent Mode Faulty (High/Low Speed Okay)	E
Wipers Do Not Park Properly	F
Washer Pump Inoperative	G

TEST A: WIPERS INOPERATIVE

1) Remove fuse No. 20 (10-amp) from central junction box. Check fuse. If fuse is okay, go to next step. If fuse is blown, replace fuse and check system operation. If fuse fails again, check system for short to ground. Repair as necessary.

2) Turn ignition switch to LOCK position. Disconnect wiper/washer switch harness connector C441. Turn ignition switch to RUN position. Measure voltage at terminal No. 8 (Violet/Orange wire) at wiper/washer switch harness connector C441. See Fig. 2. If battery voltage does not exist, go to next step. If battery voltage exists, go to step **4)**.

3) Turn ignition switch to LOCK position. Disconnect central junction box harness connector C372. Measure resistance in Violet/Orange wire between terminal No. 1 at central junction box harness connector C372 and terminal No. 14 at wiper/washer switch harness connector C441. See Figs. 2 and 3. If resistance is 5 ohms or less, repair/replace central junction box. If resistance is greater than 5 ohms, repair open in Violet/Orange wire.

4) Turn ignition switch to LOCK position. Using a fused jumper wire, connect terminals No. 1 (White/Green wire) and No. 8 (Violet/Orange wire) at wiper/washer switch harness connector C441. See Fig. 2. Turn ignition switch to RUN position. If wipers operate, replace wiper/washer switch. If wipers do not operate, replace wiper motor.

TEST B: WIPERS STAY ON CONTINUOUSLY

1) Turn wiper/washer switch to OFF position. Turn ignition switch to RUN position. If wipers operate in high speed, go to next step. If wipers operate at low speed, go to step **4)**.

2) Turn ignition switch to LOCK position. Disconnect wiper/washer switch harness connector C441. Turn ignition switch to RUN position. If wipers operate at high speed, go to next step. If wipers do not operate, replace wiper/washer switch.

3) Turn ignition switch to LOCK position. Disconnect wiper motor harness connector C848. Turn ignition switch to RUN position. Measure

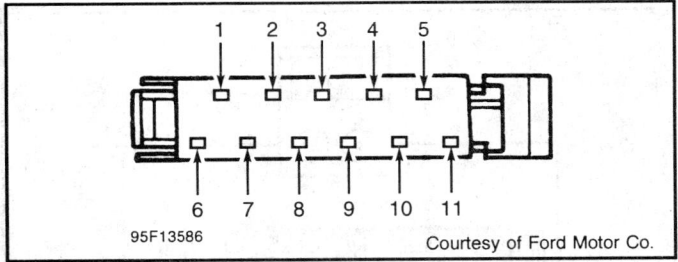

Fig. 2: Identifying Wiper/Washer Switch Harness Connector C441 Terminals

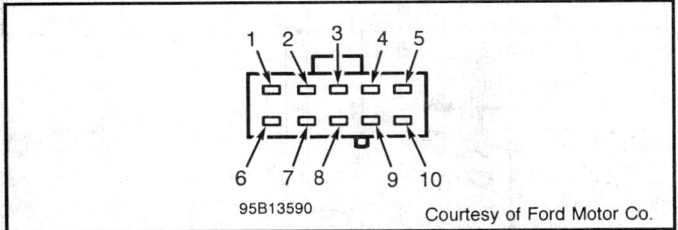

Fig. 3: Identifying Central Junction Box Harness Connector C372 Terminals

voltage at terminal No. 5 (White/Black wire) at wiper motor harness connector C848. *See Fig. 4.* If any voltage exists, repair short to voltage in White/Black wire. If no voltage exists, replace wiper motor.

4) Turn ignition switch to LOCK position. Remove wiper relay from central junction box. Turn ignition switch to RUN position. If wiper operates, go to next step. If wipers do not operate, go to step **9**).

5) Turn ignition switch to LOCK position. Disconnect wiper/washer switch harness connector C441. Turn ignition switch to RUN position. If wipers operate, go to next step. If wipers do not operate, go to step **7**).

6) Turn ignition switch to LOCK position. Disconnect wiper motor harness connector C848. Turn ignition switch to RUN position. Measure voltage at terminal No. 1 (White/Green wire) at wiper/washer switch harness connector C441. *See Fig. 2.* If any voltage exists, repair short to voltage in White/Green Wire. If no voltage exists, replace wiper motor.

7) Measure voltage at terminal No. 5 (White/Black wire) at wiper/washer switch harness connector C441. *See Fig. 2.* If any voltage exists, go to next step. If no voltage exists, replace wiper/washer switch.

8) Turn ignition switch to LOCK position. Disconnect central junction box harness connector C372. Turn ignition switch to RUN position. Measure voltage at terminal No. 4 (White/Black wire) at wiper/washer switch harness connector C441. If any voltage exists, repair short to voltage in White/Black wire. If no voltage exists, repair/replace central junction box.

9) Test wiper relay. See WIPER RELAY under COMPONENT TESTS. If relay is okay, go to next step. If relay is defective, replace relay.

10) Remove central timer module from back of central junction box. Measure resistance between ground and terminal No. 1 at wiper relay socket. *See Fig. 5.* If resistance is 10 k/ohms or less, replace central junction box. If resistance is greater than 10 k/ohms, replace central timer module.

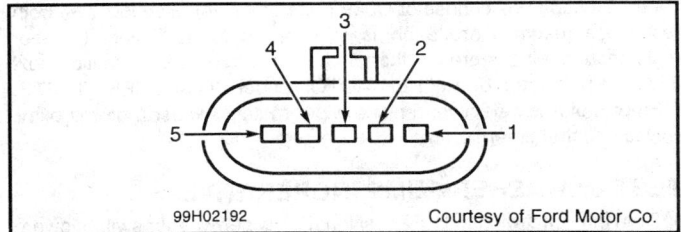

Fig. 4: Identifying Wiper Motor Harness Connector C848 Terminals

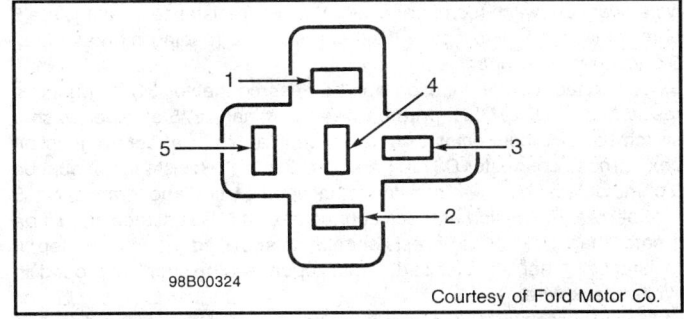

Fig. 5: Identifying Wiper Relay Socket Terminals

TEST C: HIGH SPEED WIPERS INOPERATIVE (INTERMITTENT MODE OKAY)

1) Turn ignition switch to LOCK position. Disconnect wiper/washer switch harness connector C441. Using a jumper wire, connect terminals No. 8 (Violet/Orange wire) and No. 2 (White/Black wire) at wiper/washer switch harness connector C441. *See Fig. 2.* Turn ignition switch to RUN position. If wipers do not operate, go to next step. If wipers operate at high speed, replace wiper/washer switch.

2) Turn ignition switch to LOCK position. Disconnect wiper motor harness connector C848. Measure resistance in White/Black wire between terminal No. 5 at wiper motor connector C848 and terminal No. 2 at wiper/washer switch harness connector C441. *See Figs. 2 and 4.* Resistance should be 5 ohms or less. Measure resistance between ground and terminal No. 5 (White/Black wire) at wiper motor harness connector C848. Resistance should be greater than 10 k/ohms. If resistance is as specified, replace wiper motor. If resistance is not as specified, repair open and/or short to ground in White/Black wire.

TEST D: LOW SPEED WIPERS INOPERATIVE (INTERMITTENT MODE OKAY)

1) Turn ignition switch to LOCK position. Disconnect wiper/washer switch harness connector C441. Using a fused jumper wire, connect terminals No. 8 (Violet/Orange wire) and No. 1 (White/Green wire) at wiper/washer switch harness connector C441. *See Fig. 2.* Turn ignition switch to RUN position. If wipers do not operate, go to next step. If wipers operate at low speed, replace wiper/washer switch.

2) Turn ignition switch to LOCK position. Disconnect wiper motor harness connector C848. Measure resistance in White/Green wire between terminal No. 4 at wiper motor connector C848 and terminal No. 1 at wiper/washer switch harness connector C441. *See Figs. 2 and 4.* Resistance should be 5 ohms or less. Measure resistance between ground and terminal No. 4 (White/Green wire) at wiper motor harness connector C848. Resistance should be greater than 10 k/ohms. If resistance is as specified, replace wiper motor. If resistance is not as specified, repair open and/or short to ground in White/Green wire.

TEST E: INTERMITTENT MODE FAULTY (HIGH/LOW SPEED OKAY)

1) Turn ignition switch to LOCK position. Remove wiper relay from central junction box. Turn ignition switch to RUN position. Measure voltage between terminals No. 2 and 5 at wiper relay socket. *See Fig. 5.* If battery voltage exists, go to next step. If battery voltage does not exist, replace central junction box.

2) Test wiper relay. See WIPER RELAY under COMPONENT TESTS. If relay is okay, go to next step. If relay is defective, replace relay.

3) Turn ignition switch to LOCK position. Remove central timer module from rear of central junction box. Measure resistance between terminal No. 1 at wiper relay socket and terminal No. 11 at central timer module connector. *See Figs. 5 and 6.* If resistance is 5 ohms or less, go to next step. If resistance is greater than 5 ohms, replace central junction box.

4) Disconnect wiper/washer switch harness connector C441. Turn wiper/washer switch to intermittent position. Measure resistance between terminals No. 1 and 4 at wiper/washer switch (component side). *See Fig. 2.* Measure resistance between terminals No. 5 and 8 at wiper/washer switch (component side). If both resistance readings are 5 ohms or less, go to next step. If either resistance reading is greater than 5 ohms, replace wiper/washer switch.

5) Disconnect central junction box harness connector C372. Measure resistance in White/Black wire between terminal No. 5 at wiper washer switch harness connector C441 and terminal No. 4 at central junction box harness connector C372. *See Figs. 2 and 3*. Resistance should be 5 ohms or less. Measure resistance between ground and terminal No. 5 at wiper/washer switch harness connector C441. Resistance should be greater than 10 k/ohms. If resistance is as specified, go to next step. If resistance is not as specified, repair open and/or short to ground in White/Black wire.

6) Measure resistance between terminal No. 5 at central junction box connector (fuse box side) and terminal No. 3 at wiper relay socket. *See Fig. 7*. Resistance should be 5 ohms or less. Measure resistance between ground and terminal No. 3 at wiper relay socket. *See Fig. 5*. Resistance should be greater than 10 k/ohms. If resistance is as specified, go to next step. If resistance is not as specified, replace central junction box.

7) Measure resistance in White/Black wire between terminal No. 4 at central junction box harness connector C372 and terminal No. 5 at wiper/washer switch harness connector C441. *See Figs. 2 and 3*. If resistance is 5 ohms or less, go to next step. If resistance is greater than 5 ohms, repair open in White/Black wire.

8) Connect central junction box harness connector C372. Measure resistance between terminal No. 5 (White/Black wire) at wiper washer switch harness connector C441 and terminal No. 14 at central timer module connector. *See Figs. 2 and 6*. If resistance is greater than 5 ohms, replace central junction box. If resistance is 5 ohms or less and vehicle is equipped with a variable intermittent wiper/washer switch, go to next step. If resistance is 5 ohms or less and vehicle is equipped with a fixed intermittent wiper/washer switch, replace central timer module.

9) Disconnect central junction box harness connector C372. Measure resistance in White wire between terminal No. 6 at wiper/washer switch harness connector C441 and terminal No. 3 at central junction box harness connector C372. *See Figs. 2 and 3*. If resistance is 5 ohms or less, go to next step. If resistance is greater than 5 ohms, repair open White wire.

10) Connect central junction box harness connector C372. Measure resistance between terminal No. 6 at wiper/washer switch harness connector C441 and terminal No. 17 at central timer module connector. *See Figs. 2 and 6*. If resistance is 5 ohms or less, replace central timer module. If resistance is greater than 5 ohms, replace central junction box.

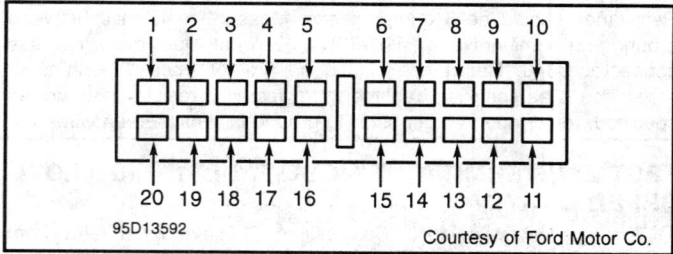

95D13592   Courtesy of Ford Motor Co.

Fig. 6: Identifying Central Timer Module Connector Terminals (On Junction Box)

TEST F: WIPERS DO NOT PARK PROPERLY

1) Turn ignition switch to LOCK position. Remove wiper relay from central junction box. Turn ignition switch to RUN position. Measure voltage at terminal No. 4 at wiper relay socket. *See Fig. 5*. If battery voltage exists, go to next step. If battery voltage does not exist, go to step 3).

2) Test wiper relay. See WIPER RELAY under COMPONENT TESTS. If relay is okay, replace wiper/washer switch. If wiper relay is defective, replace wiper relay.

3) Turn ignition switch to LOCK position. Disconnect wiper motor harness connector C848. Turn ignition switch to RUN position. Measure voltage at terminal No. 2 (Violet wire) at wiper motor harness connector

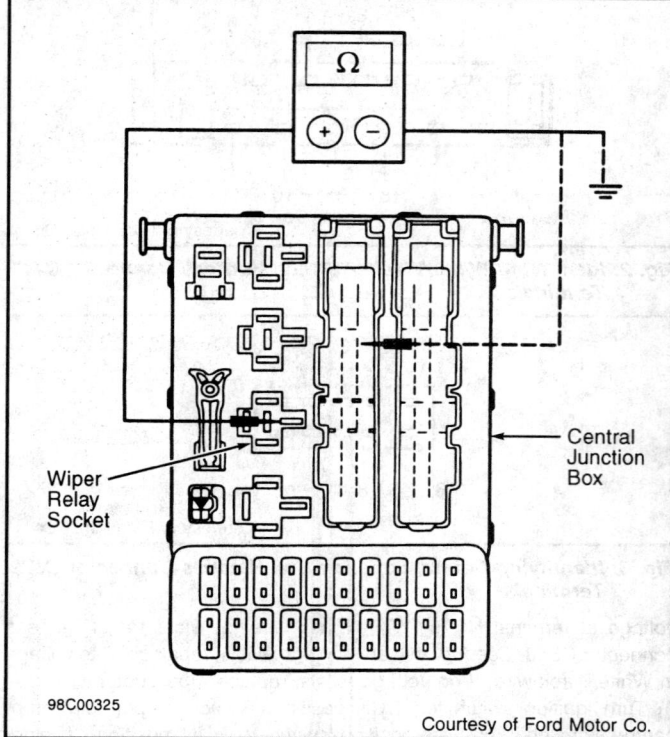

98C00325   Courtesy of Ford Motor Co.

Fig. 7: Testing Central Junction Box (Wiper Circuit)

C848. *See Fig. 4* . If battery voltage does not exist, go to next step. If battery voltage exists, go to step 5).

4) Turn ignition switch to LOCK position. Disconnect central junction box harness connector C369. Measure resistance in Violet wire between terminal No. 8 at central junction box harness connector C369 and terminal No. 2 at wiper motor harness connector C848. *See Figs. 4 and 8*. If resistance is 5 ohms or less, replace central junction box. If resistance is greater than 5 ohms, repair open in Violet wire.

5) Turn ignition switch to LOCK position. Disconnect central junction box harness connector C369. Measure resistance in White/Blue wire between terminal No. 4 at central junction box harness connector C369 and terminal No. 1 at wiper motor harness connector C848. *See Figs. 4 and 8*. Resistance should be 5 ohms or less. Measure resistance between ground and terminal No. 1 (White/Blue wire) at wiper motor harness connector C848. Resistance should be greater than 10 k/ohms. If resistance is as specified, go to next step. If resistance is not as specified, repair open and/or short to ground in White/Blue wire.

6) Turn ignition switch to LOCK position. Measure resistance between ground and terminal No. 3 (Black wire) at wiper motor harness connector C848. If resistance is 5 ohms or less, go to next step. If resistance is greater than 5 ohms, repair open Black wire.

7) Remove central timer module from rear of central junction box. Measure resistance between terminal No. 13 at central timer module connector and terminal No. 4 at wiper relay socket. Measure resistance between terminal No. 4 at wiper relay socket and terminal No. 4 at central junction box connector C369 (fuse box side). *See Fig. 9*. If both resistance readings are 5 ohms or less, go to next step. If either resistance reading is greater than 5 ohms, replace central junction box.

8) Test wiper motor. See WIPER MOTOR under COMPONENT TESTS. If wiper motor is defective, replace wiper motor. If wiper motor is okay, replace central timer module.

TEST G: WASHER PUMP INOPERATIVE

1) Turn ignition switch to RUN position. Pull wiper/washer switch toward steering wheel. If wipers cycle 3 times, go to next step. If wipers do not cycle 3 times, go to step 6).

2) Turn ignition switch to LOCK position. Disconnect washer pump motor harness connector C827. Measure resistance between ground

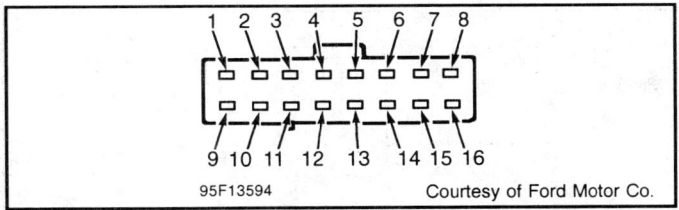

Fig. 8: Identifying Central Junction Box Connector C369 terminals

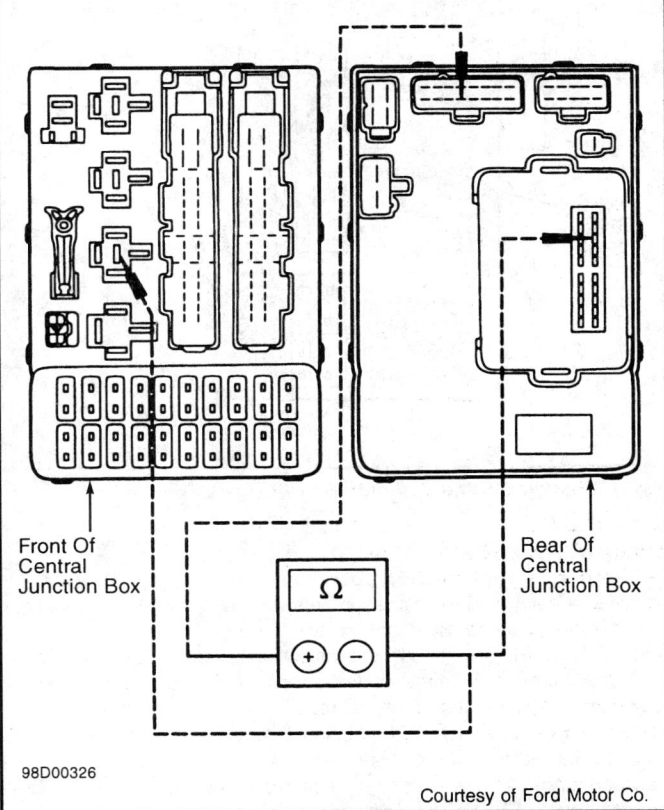

Fig. 9: Testing Central Junction Box (Interval Circuits)

and Black/White wire terminal at washer pump motor harness connector C827 while holding wiper/washer switch lever in WASH position. If resistance is greater than 5 ohms, go to next step. If resistance is 5 ohms or less, go to step **4).**

3) Disconnect central junction box harness connectors C369 and C372. Measure resistance between terminal No. 7 at central junction box connector C369 (fuse box side) and terminal No. 10 at central junction box connector C372 (fuse box side). See Fig. 10. If resistance is 5 ohms or less, repair open Black/White wire between central junction box and washer pump. If resistance is greater than 5 ohms, replace central junction box.

4) Disconnect wiper/washer switch harness connector C441. Measure resistance in Violet/White wire between terminal No. 11 at wiper/washer switch harness connector C441 and washer pump motor harness connector C827. If resistance is 5 ohms or less, go to next step. If resistance is greater than 5 ohms, repair open in Violet/White wire.

5) Measure resistance between terminals No. 8 and 11 at wiper/washer switch (component side). See Fig. 2. If resistance is 5 ohms or less, replace washer pump motor. If resistance is greater than 5 ohms, replace wiper/washer switch.

6) Turn ignition switch to LOCK position. Disconnect wiper/washer switch harness connector C441. Using a fused jumper wire, connect terminals No. 8 (Violet/Orange wire) and No. 11 (Violet/White wire) at wiper/washer switch harness connector C441. See Fig. 2. Using a

second jumper wire, connect terminals No. 9 (Yellow/Black wire) and No. 10 (Black wire) at wiper/washer switch harness connector C441. Turn ignition switch to RUN position. If wiper and washer do not operate, go to next step. If wiper and washer operates, replace wiper/washer switch.

7) Turn ignition switch to LOCK position. Disconnect central junction box harness connector C372. Measure resistance in Yellow/Black wire between terminal No. 9 at wiper/washer switch harness connector C441 and terminal No. 10 at central junction box harness connector C372. See Figs. 2 and 3. If resistance is 5 ohms or less, go to next step. If resistance is greater than 5 ohms, repair open Yellow/Black wire.

8) Disconnect central junction box harness connector C369. Measure resistance between terminal No. 7 at central junction box connector C369 (fuse box side) and terminal No. 10 at central junction box connector C372 (fuse box side). See Fig. 10. If resistance is 5 ohms or less, go to next step. If resistance is greater than 5 ohms, replace central junction box.

9) Measure resistance between ground and terminal No. 10 (Black wire) at wiper/washer switch harness connector C441. See Fig. 2. If resistance is greater than 5 ohms, repair open in Black wire. If resistance is 5 ohms or less, replace central timer module.

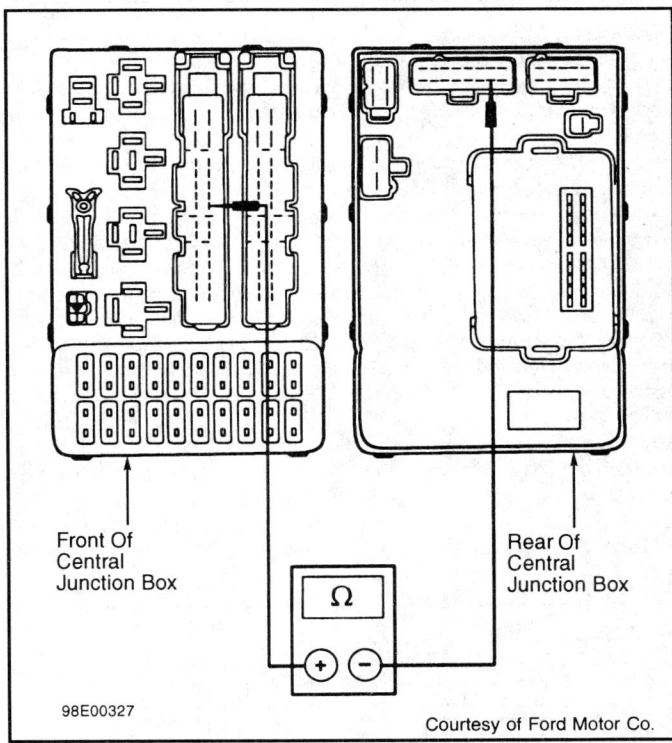

Fig. 10: Testing Central Junction Box (Wash Circuit)

REMOVAL & INSTALLATION

CAUTION: When battery is disconnected, vehicle computer and memory systems may lose memory data. Driveability problems may exist until computer systems have completed a relearn cycle. See COMPUTER RELEARN PROCEDURES article in GENERAL INFORMATION before disconnecting battery.

WINDSHIELD WIPER ARMS

NOTE: To prevent damage to glass or paint, DO NOT use a sharp or metal tool to pry windshield wiper pivot arms from windshield wiper pivot shafts.

Removal & Installation – 1) Lift caps on windshield wiper arms to expose attaching nuts. Remove nuts. Lift each wiper arm to service position and carefully rock wiper arms to loosen. Remove wiper arms.

2) To install, cycle wiper motor to park position. Position wiper arms on pivot shafts and align to park position. Install nuts on pivot shaft and tighten to 18 ft. lbs. (25 N.m). Replace nut caps.

WINDSHIELD WIPER MOTOR, PIVOT SHAFTS & LINKAGE

Removal & Installation – 1) Disconnect negative battery cable. Remove windshield wiper arms. See WINDSHIELD WIPER ARMS. Remove screws retaining cowl top vent panel.

2) Carefully remove cowl top vent panel. Disconnect windshield wiper motor harness. Remove wiper motor and linkage mounting bolts. Mark position of wiper motor arm in relation to motor mounting plate. Remove wiper motor and linkage assembly from vehicle.

3) To install, ensure wiper motor arm is aligned with removal mark. Install linkage retaining bolt on left side first. To complete installation, reverse removal procedure. Install wiper arms and tighten nuts to 18 ft. lbs. (25 N.m). See WINDSHIELD WIPER ARMS.

MULTIFUNCTION SWITCH

Removal & Installation – For multifunction switch removal and installation, see appropriate STEERING COLUMN SWITCHES article.

WIRING DIAGRAMS

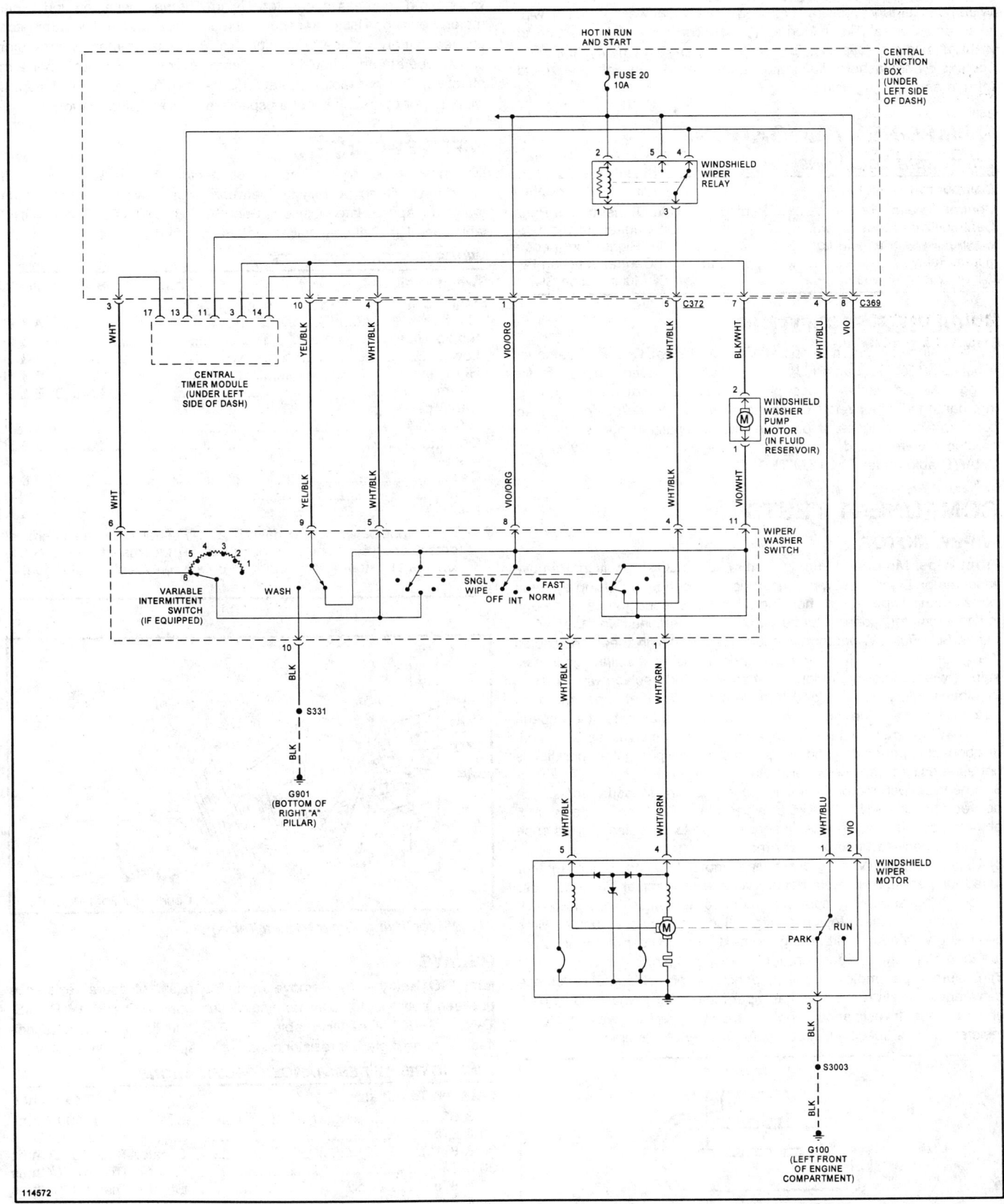

Fig. 11: Wiper/Washer System Wiring Diagram (Contour & Mystique)

114572

DESCRIPTION & OPERATION

Wiper/washer functions are controlled by the wiper/washer switch, wiper relay and Central Timer Module (CTM). The CTM is located on the instrument panel fuse box, under left side of instrument panel. CTM controls wiper/washers, illuminated entry, rear window defogger, heated mirrors and warning chimes.

COMPONENT LOCATIONS

COMPONENT LOCATIONS

Component	Location
Central Junction Box	Behind Left Side Of Instrument Panel
Central Timer Module	On Central Junction Box
Washer Reservoir & Motor	Under Right Front Fender
Wiper Relay	In Central Junction Box
Wiper/Washer Switch	Part Of Multifunction Switch

TROUBLE SHOOTING

Verify customer concern by operating wiper system. Check for damaged wiper pivot shaft, damaged wiper motor, damaged washer motor, plugged/kinked washer hoses, plugged washer nozzles, damaged wiring, damaged wiper relay, damaged switches, poor electrical connections and blown fuses. If problem exists, repair as necessary. If no problems were found, repair wipers by symptom. See SYMPTOM CHART table under SYSTEM TESTS.

COMPONENT TESTS

WIPER MOTOR

Front Wiper Motor – 1) Turn ignition switch to LOCK position. Remove wiper motor. Disconnect wiper motor harness connector. Using a jumper wire, ground wiper motor housing. Using a second jumper wire and in-line ammeter, connect battery voltage to terminal No. 1 at wiper motor. *See Fig. 1.* Wiper motor should operate at high speed and should draw 3 amps or less. If wiper motor operation is as specified, go to next step. If wiper motor operation is not as specified, replace wiper motor.
2) Move battery voltage lead from terminal No. 1 at wiper motor to terminal No. 2 at wiper motor. Wiper motor should operate at low speed and draw 2 amps or less. If wiper motor operation is as specified, disconnect jumper wires and go to next step. If wiper motor operation is not as specified, replace wiper motor.
3) Ensure wiper motor is not in park position. Measure resistance between terminals No. 4 and 5 at wiper motor. Resistance should be 5 ohms or less. If resistance is as specified, go to next step. If resistance is not as specified, replace wiper motor.
4) Using a jumper wire, ground wiper motor housing. Using another fused jumper wire, connect battery voltage to terminal No. 5 at wiper motor. Using another jumper wire, connect terminals No. 2 and 4. If wiper motor runs then stops in park position, disconnect all jumper wires beginning with power wire and go to next step. If wiper motor does not run then stops in park position, replace wiper motor.
5) Ensure wiper motor is still in park position. Measure resistance between terminals No. 3 and 4 at wiper motor. Resistance should be 5 ohms or less. If resistance is not as specified, replace wiper motor. If resistance is as specified, wiper motor is okay at this time.

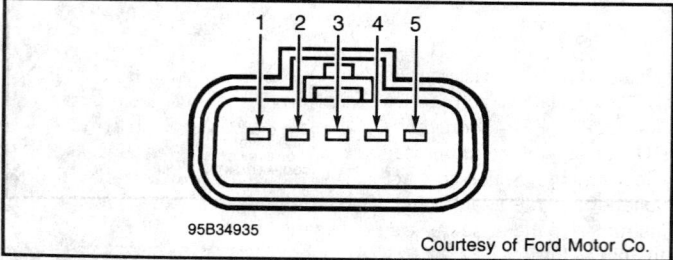

95B34935   Courtesy of Ford Motor Co.

Fig. 1: Identifying Front Wiper Motor Terminals

Rear Wiper Motor – Turn ignition switch to LOCK position. Disconnect wiper motor harness connector. Using a jumper wire, ground wiper motor housing. Using a second jumper wire and in-line ammeter, connect battery voltage to terminal No. 2 at wiper motor. Wiper motor should operate and should draw 2 amps or less (1 without wiper arm attached). If wiper motor operation is as specified, go to next step. If wiper motor operation is not as specified, replace wiper motor.

WIPER SWITCH

Disconnect wiper switch harness connector (remove wiper switch if necessary). Check continuity between wiper switch terminals with switch in appropriate position. See WIPER SWITCH CONTINUITY table. *See Fig. 2.* If continuity is not as specified, replace wiper switch.

WIPER SWITCH CONTINUITY

Switch Position	Continuity Between Terminals
Front Wiper	
Off	A & D
Single Wipe	A & H
Low	A & H
High	B & H
Intermittent	[1] A & D; E & H
Rear Wiper	
Off	G & I
On	G & H
Washer	
Off	H, I & K
Front	H & K; I & J
Rear	H & I; J & K

[1] – Resistance between terminals "E" and "F" should be one k/ohms at detent one, 10 k/ohms at detent 2, 20 k/ohms at detent 3, 30 k/ohms at detent 4, 40 k/ohms at detent 5, 47 k/ohms at detent 6.

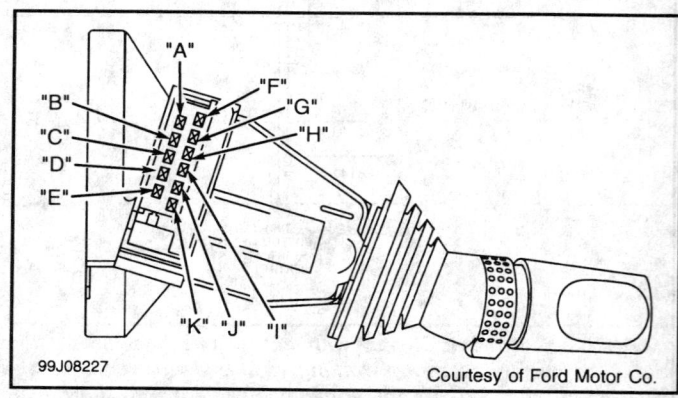

99J08227   Courtesy of Ford Motor Co.

Fig. 2: Identifying Wiper Switch Terminals

RELAYS

Mini ISO Relay – 1) Remove mini ISO relay. Measure resistance between appropriate relay terminals. See MINI ISO RELAY RESISTANCE SPECIFICATIONS table. *See Fig. 3.* If resistance is as specified, go to next step. If resistance is not as specified, replace relay.

MINI ISO RELAY RESISTANCE SPECIFICATIONS

Between Terminals	Resistance
85 & 86	50-100 Ohms
30 & 87a	5 Ohms Or Less
30 & 87	Greater Than 10 K/Ohms
30 & 86	Greater Than 10 K/Ohms
86 & 87a	Greater Than 10 K/Ohms
86 & 87	Greater Than 10 K/Ohms

2) Using a fused jumper wire, connect positive battery voltage to terminal No. 85. Using another jumper wire, ground terminal No. 86. Resistance should now be 5 ohms or less between terminals No. 30 and 87 and greater than 10 k/ohms between terminals No. 30 and 87a. If resistance is as specified, relay is okay at this time. If resistance is not as specified, replace relay.

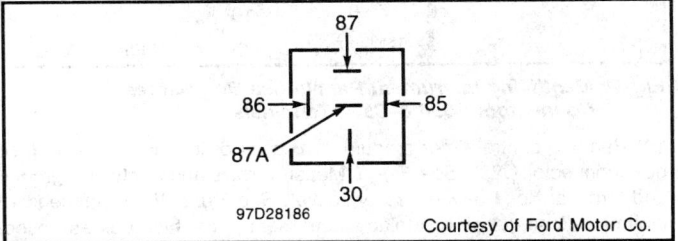

97D28186

Courtesy of Ford Motor Co.

Fig. 3: Identifying Mini ISO Relay Terminals

Micro ISO Relay – 1) Remove relay to be tested. Measure resistance between terminal No. 5 and all other terminals. *See Fig. 4.* If all resistance reading are greater than 5 ohms, go to next step. If any resistance reading is 5 ohms or less, replace relay.

2) Measure resistance between terminals No. 3 and 4. If resistance is 5 ohms or less, go to next step. If resistance is greater than 5 ohms, replace relay.

3) Apply battery voltage and ground between terminals No. 1 and 2. Measure resistance between terminals No. 3 and 5. Resistance should be 5 ohms or less. Measure resistance between terminals No. 3 and 4. Resistance should be greater than 10 k/ohms. If resistance is not as specified, replace relay. If resistance is as specified, relay is okay at this time.

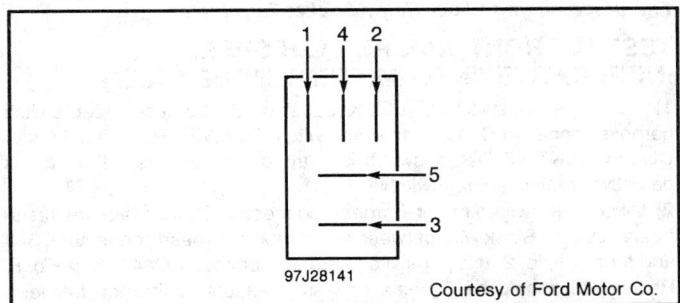

97J28141

Courtesy of Ford Motor Co.

Fig. 4: Identifying Micro ISO Relay Terminals

SYSTEM TESTS

WARNING: Vehicles equipped with an air bag system. System MUST be disabled before working near steering column and instrument cluster to prevent air bag deployment. See appropriate AIR BAG RESTRAINT SYSTEMS article.

CAUTION: Wiper motor contains ceramic magnets that may crack or shatter if motor is dropped or handled roughly.

SYMPTOM CHART

Symptom	Test
Front Wipers Inoperative	A
Front Wipers Stay On Continuously	B
Front Wipers High Speed Inoperative (Intermittent Mode Okay)	C
Front Wipers Low Speed Inoperative (Intermittent Mode Okay)	D
Front Wipers Intermittent Mode Faulty (High/Low Speed Okay)	E
Front Wiper Wash & Wipe Function Inoperative	F
Front Wiper Does Not Park Properly	G
Washer Pump Inoperative	H

SYMPTOM CHART (Cont.)

Symptom	Test
Rear Wiper Inoperative	I
Rear Wiper Stays On Continuously	J
Rear Wiper Does Not Park Properly	K

TEST A: FRONT WIPERS INOPERATIVE

1) Operate washers. If washers do not operate, go to next step. If washers operate, go to step **5**).

2) Remove fuse No. 20 (10-amp) from instrument panel fuse box. *See Fig. 5.* Inspect fuse. If fuse is okay, go to next step. If fuse is blown, replace fuse and check system operation. If fuse fails again, check system for short to ground in power distribution circuit. See appropriate wiring diagram in POWER DISTRIBUTION article in WIRING DIAGRAMS.

3) Turn ignition switch to LOCK position. Disconnect wiper switch harness connector C441. Turn ignition switch to RUN position. Measure voltage at terminal No. 8 (Violet/Orange wire) at wiper switch harness connector C441. *See Fig. 6.* If battery voltage does not exist, go to next step. If battery voltage exists, go to step **5**).

4) Turn ignition switch to LOCK position. Disconnect instrument panel fuse box harness connector C372. *See Fig. 5.* Measure resistance in Violet/Orange wire between terminal No. 1 at instrument panel fuse box harness connector C372 and terminal No. 8 at wiper switch harness connector C441. *See Figs. 6 and 7.* If resistance is 5 ohms or less, repair/replace instrument panel fuse box as necessary. If resistance is greater than 5 ohms, repair open in Violet/Orange wire.

5) Turn ignition switch to LOCK position. Test wiper switch. See WIPER SWITCH under COMPONENT TESTS. If switch is okay, go to next step. If switch is defective, replace wiper switch.

6) Measure resistance between ground and wiper motor housing. If resistance is 5 ohms or less, replace wiper motor. If resistance is greater than 5 ohms, repair ground connection as necessary.

TEST B: FRONT WIPERS STAY ON CONTINUOUSLY

1) Turn wiper switch off. Turn ignition switch to RUN position. If wipers operate in high speed, go to next step. If wipers operate at low speed, go to step **4**).

2) Turn ignition switch to LOCK position. Disconnect wiper switch harness connector C441. Turn ignition switch to RUN position. If wipers operate at high speed, go to next step. If wipers do not operate, replace wiper switch.

3) Turn ignition switch to LOCK position. Disconnect wiper motor harness connector C848. Turn ignition switch to RUN position. Measure voltage at White/Black wire terminal at wiper motor harness connector C848. If voltage exists, repair short to voltage in White/Black wire. If voltage does not exists, replace wiper motor.

4) Turn ignition switch to LOCK position. Remove wiper relay from instrument panel fuse box. Turn ignition switch to RUN position. If wiper operates, go to next step. If wipers do not operate, go to step **9**).

5) Turn ignition switch to LOCK position. Disconnect wiper switch harness connector C441. Turn ignition switch to RUN position. If wipers operate, go to next step. If wipers do not operate, go to step **7**).

6) Turn ignition switch to LOCK position. Disconnect wiper motor harness connector C848. Turn ignition switch to RUN position. Measure voltage at terminal No. 1 (White/Green wire) at wiper switch harness connector C441. *See Fig. 6.* If voltage exists, repair short to voltage in White/Green wire. If voltage does not exists, replace wiper motor.

7) Measure voltage at terminal No. 4 (White/Black wire) at wiper switch harness connector C441. *See Fig. 6.* If voltage exists, go to next step. If voltage does not exists, replace wiper switch.

8) Turn ignition switch to LOCK position. Disconnect instrument panel fuse box harness connector C372. *See Fig. 5.* Turn ignition switch to RUN position. Measure voltage at terminal No. 4 (White/Black wire) at wiper switch harness connector C441. If voltage exists, repair short to voltage in White/Black wire. If voltage does not exist, repair/replace instrument panel fuse box as necessary.

9) Test wiper relay. See RELAYS under COMPONENT TESTS. If relay is okay, go to next step. If relay is defective, replace relay.

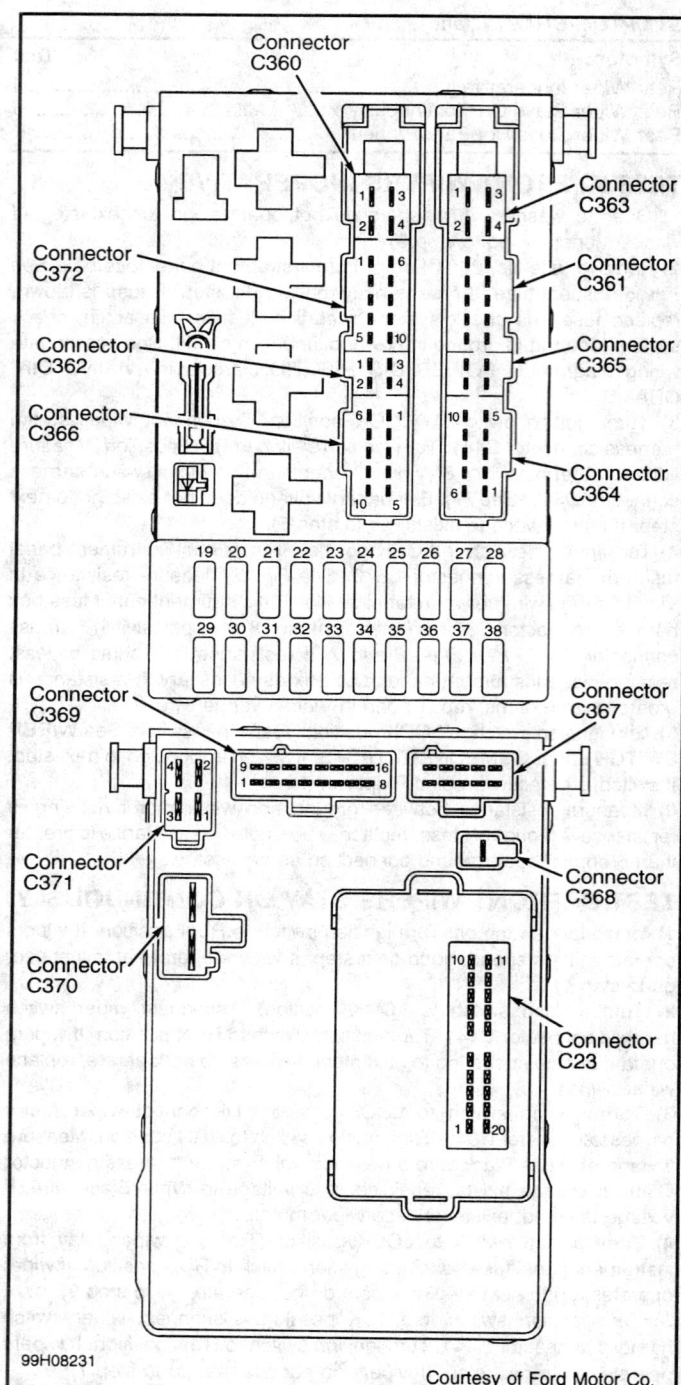

Fig. 5: Locating Instrument Panel Fuse Box Connectors

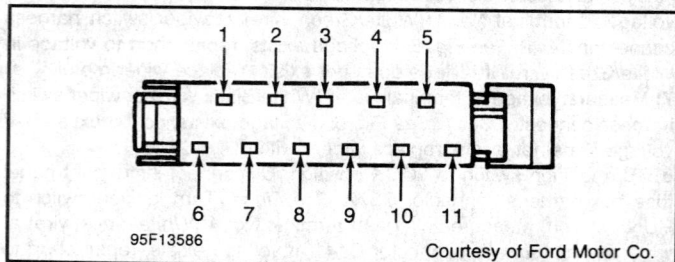

Fig. 6: Identifying Wiper Switch Harness Connector C441 Terminals

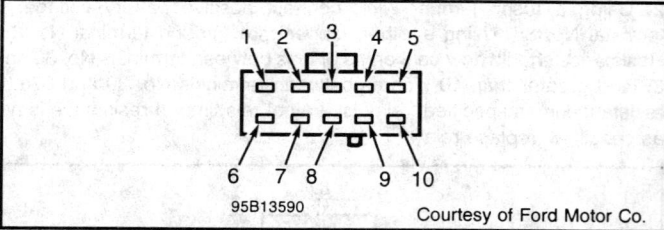

Fig. 7: Identifying Instrument Panel Fuse Box Harness Connectors C396 & C372 Terminals

10) Remove central timer module from back of instrument panel fuse box (connector C23). See Fig. 5. Measure resistance between ground and terminal No. 1 at wiper relay socket. See Fig. 8. If resistance is 10 k/ohms or less, repair or replace instrument panel fuse box as necessary. If resistance is greater than 10 k/ohms, replace central timer module.

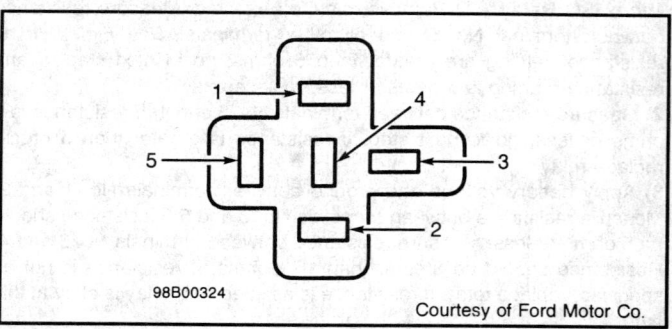

Fig. 8: Identifying Wiper Relay Socket Terminals

TEST C: FRONT WIPERS HIGH SPEED INOPERATIVE (INTERMITTENT MODE OKAY)

1) Turn ignition switch to LOCK position. Disconnect wiper switch harness connector C441. Test wiper switch. See WIPER SWITCH under COMPONENT TESTS. If switch is okay, go to next step. If switch is defective, replace wiper switch.

2) Disconnect wiper motor harness connector C848. Measure resistance in White/Black wire between wiper motor harness connector C848 and terminal No. 2 at wiper switch harness connector C441. See Fig. 6. Resistance should be 5 ohms or less. Measure resistance between ground and terminal No. 2 (White/Black wire) at wiper switch harness connector C441. Resistance should be greater than 10 k/ohms. If resistance is as specified, replace wiper motor. If resistance is not as specified, repair open and/or short to ground in White/Black wire.

TEST D: FRONT WIPERS LOW SPEED INOPERATIVE (INTERMITTENT MODE OKAY)

1) Turn ignition switch to LOCK position. Disconnect wiper switch harness connector C441. Test wiper switch. See WIPER SWITCH under COMPONENT TESTS. If switch is okay, go to next step. If switch is defective, replace wiper switch.

2) Turn ignition switch to LOCK position. Disconnect wiper motor harness connector C848. Measure resistance in White/Green wire between wiper motor harness connector C848 and terminal No. 1 at wiper switch harness connector C441. See Fig. 6. Resistance should be 5 ohms or less. Measure resistance between ground and terminal No. 1 (White/Green wire) at wiper switch harness connector C441. Resistance should be greater than 10 k/ohms. If resistance is as specified, replace wiper motor. If resistance is not as specified, repair open and/or short to ground in White/Green wire.

TEST E: FRONT WIPERS INTERMITTENT MODE FAULTY (HIGH/LOW SPEED OKAY)

1) Turn ignition switch to LOCK position. Remove wiper relay from instrument panel fuse box. Turn ignition switch to RUN position. Measure voltage at terminals No. 2 and 5 at wiper relay socket. See

Fig. 8. If battery voltage exists at both terminals, go to next step. If battery voltage does not exist at both terminals, repair or replace instrument panel fuse box as necessary.

2) Turn ignition switch to LOCK position. Test wiper relay. See RELAYS under COMPONENT TESTS. If relay is okay, go to next step. If relay is defective, replace relay.

3) Turn ignition switch to LOCK position. Remove central timer module from rear of instrument panel fuse box (connector C23). *See Fig. 5.* Measure resistance between terminal No. 1 at wiper relay socket and terminal No. 11 central timer module connector C23 (fuse box side). *See Figs. 5 and 8.* If resistance is 5 ohms or less, go to next step. If resistance is greater than 5 ohms, replace instrument panel fuse box.

4) Disconnect wiper switch harness connector C441. Test wiper switch. See WIPER SWITCH under COMPONENT TESTS. If switch is okay, go to next step. If switch is defective, replace wiper switch.

5) Disconnect instrument panel fuse box harness connector C372. *See Fig. 5.* Measure resistance in White/Black wire between terminal No. 4 at wiper washer switch harness connector C441 and terminal No. 5 at instrument panel fuse box harness connector C372. *See Figs. 6 and 7.* Resistance should be 5 ohms or less. Measure resistance between ground and terminal No. 4 (White/Black wire) at wiper switch harness connector C441. Resistance should be greater than 10 k/ohms. If resistance is as specified, go to next step. If resistance is not as specified, repair open and/or short to ground in White/Black wire.

6) Measure resistance between terminal No. 5 at instrument panel fuse box connector C372 (fuse box side) and terminals No. 3 at wiper relay socket. *See Figs. 5 and 8.* Resistance should be 5 ohms or less. Measure resistance between ground and terminal No. 3 at wiper relay socket. Resistance should be greater than 10 k/ohms. If resistance is as specified, go to next step. If resistance is not as specified, replace instrument panel fuse box.

7) Measure resistance in White/Black wire between terminal No. 5 at instrument panel fuse box harness connector C372 and terminal No. 4 at wiper switch harness connector C441. *See Figs. 6 and 7.* If resistance is 5 ohms or less, go to next step. If resistance is greater than 5 ohms, repair open in White/Black wire.

8) Connect instrument panel fuse box harness connector C372. Measure resistance wire between terminal No. 5 (White/Black) at wiper washer switch harness connector C441 and terminal No. 14 at central timer module connector C23 (fuse box side). *See Figs. 5 and 6.* If resistance is 5 ohms or less, go to next step. If resistance is greater than 5 ohms, replace instrument panel fuse box.

9) Disconnect instrument panel fuse box harness connector C372. *See Fig. 5.* Measure resistance in White wire between terminal No. 6 at wiper switch harness connector C441 and terminal No. 3 at instrument panel fuse box harness connector C372. *See Figs. 6 and 7.* If resistance is 5 ohms or less, go to next step. If resistance is greater than 5 ohms, repair open in White wire.

10) Connect instrument panel fuse box harness connector C372. Measure resistance between terminal No. 6 (White wire) at wiper switch harness connector C441 and terminal No. 17 at central timer module connector C23 (fuse box side). *See Figs. 5 and 6.* If resistance is 5 ohms or less, replace central timer module. If resistance is greater than 5 ohms, replace instrument panel fuse box.

TEST F: FRONT WIPER WASH & WIPE FUNCTION INOPERATIVE

1) Turn ignition switch to LOCK position. Disconnect wiper switch harness connector C441. Test wiper switch. See WIPER SWITCH under COMPONENT TESTS. If switch is okay, go to next step. If switch is defective, replace wiper switch.

2) Disconnect instrument panel fuse box harness connector C372. Remove central timer module from rear of instrument panel fuse box (connector C23). *See Fig. 5.* Measure resistance between terminal No. 10 at instrument panel fuse box connector C372 (fuse box side) and terminal No. 3 at central timer module connector (fuse box side). If resistance is 5 ohms or less, replace central timer module. If resistance is greater than 5 ohms, replace instrument panel fuse box.

TEST G: FRONT WIPER DOES NOT PARK PROPERLY

1) If wipers do not always park in same position, go to next step. If wipers always park in same position, adjust wipers as necessary.

2) Check intermittent wipers operation. If intermittent wipers operate, go to next step. If intermittent wipers do not operate, perform TEST E: FRONT WIPERS INTERMITTENT MODE FAULTY (HIGH/LOW SPEED OKAY).

3) Turn ignition switch to LOCK position. Remove wiper relay from instrument panel fuse box. Turn ignition switch to RUN position. Measure voltage at terminal No. 4 at wiper relay socket. *See Fig. 8.* If battery voltage does not exist, go to next step. If battery voltage exists, replace wiper switch.

4) Turn ignition switch to LOCK position. Disconnect wiper motor harness connector C848. Turn ignition switch to RUN position. Measure voltage at Violet wire terminal at wiper motor harness connector C848. If battery voltage does not exist, go to next step. If battery voltage exists, go to step **6)**.

5) Turn ignition switch to LOCK position. Disconnect instrument panel fuse box harness connector C369. *See Fig. 5.* Measure resistance in Violet wire between terminal No. 8 at instrument panel fuse box harness connector C369 and wiper motor harness connector C848. *See Fig. 9.* If resistance is 5 ohms or less, replace instrument panel fuse box. If resistance is greater than 5 ohms, repair open in Violet wire.

6) Turn ignition switch to LOCK position. Disconnect instrument panel fuse box harness connector C369. *See Fig. 5.* Measure resistance in White/Blue wire between terminal No. 4 at instrument panel fuse box harness connector C369 and wiper motor harness connector C848. *See Fig. 9.* Resistance should be 5 ohms or less. Measure resistance between ground and terminal No. 4 (White/Blue wire) at instrument panel fuse box harness connector C369. Resistance should be greater than 10 k/ohms. If resistance is as specified, go to next step. If resistance is not as specified, repair open and/or short to ground in White/Blue wire.

7) Measure resistance between ground and Black wire terminal at wiper motor harness connector C848. If resistance is 5 ohms or less, go to next step. If resistance is greater than 5 ohms, repair open in Black wire.

8) Remove central timer module from rear of instrument panel fuse box (connector C23). Measure resistance between terminal No. 13 at central timer module connector (fuse box side) and terminal No. 4 at wiper relay socket. Measure resistance between terminal No. 4 at wiper relay socket and terminal No. 4 instrument panel fuse box connector C369 (fuse box side). *See Figs. 5 and 8.* If both resistance readings are 5 ohms or less, go to next step. If either resistance reading is greater than 5 ohms, replace instrument panel fuse box.

9) Test wiper motor. See WIPER MOTOR under COMPONENT TESTS. If wiper motor is defective, replace wiper motor. If wiper motor is okay, replace central timer module.

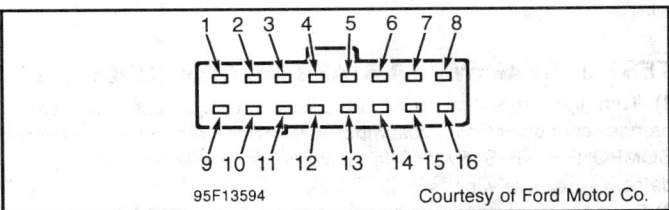

95F13594   Courtesy of Ford Motor Co.

Fig. 9: Identifying Instrument Panel Fuse Box Harness Connector C369 terminals

TEST H: WASHER PUMP INOPERATIVE

NOTE: Before performing this test, ensure washer hoses are not kinked, plugged, disconnected or split and washer nozzles are not plugged or damaged. Also, if vehicle is not equipped with rear wiper the rear washer circuits still exists.

1) Disconnect washer pump motor harness connector C828. Turn ignition switch to RUN position. Measure voltage between White/Black wire and Yellow/Black wire terminals at washer pump motor harness connector C828 while operating wiper switch to front and rear washer positions. If voltage does not exist in either position, go to next step. If voltage exists in only one position, replace wiper switch. If voltage exists in both positions, replace washer pump motor.

2) Turn ignition switch to LOCK position. Disconnect wiper switch harness connector C441. Test wiper switch. See WIPER SWITCH under COMPONENT TESTS. If switch is okay, go to next step. If switch is defective, replace wiper switch.

3) Measure resistance between ground and terminal No. 10 (Black wire) at wiper switch harness connector C441. See Fig. 6. If resistance is 5 ohms or less, go to next step. If resistance is greater than 5 ohms, repair open in Black wire.

4) Measure resistance in White/Black wire between washer pump motor harness connector C828 and terminal No. 11 at wiper switch harness connector C441. If resistance is 5 ohms or less, go to next step. If resistance is greater than 5 ohms, repair open in White/Black wire.

5) Disconnect instrument panel fuse box harness connector C372. See Fig. 5. Measure resistance in Yellow/Black wire between terminal No. 9 at wiper switch harness connector C441 and terminal No. 10 at instrument panel fuse box harness connector C372. See Figs. 6 and 7. If resistance is 5 ohms or less, go to next step. If resistance is greater than 5 ohms, repair open in Yellow/Black wire.

6) Disconnect instrument panel fuse box harness connector C369. Measure resistance between terminal No. 7 at instrument panel fuse box connector C369 (fuse box side) and terminal No. 10 at instrument panel fuse box connector C372 (fuse box side). See Fig. 5. If resistance is 5 ohms or less, repair open in Yellow/Black wire between instrument panel fuse box and washer pump. If resistance is greater than 5 ohms, replace instrument panel fuse box.

TEST I: REAR WIPER INOPERATIVE

1) Operate front wipers. If front wipers operate, go to next step. If front wipers do not operate, perform TEST A: FRONT WIPERS INOPERATIVE.

2) Turn ignition switch to LOCK position. Disconnect wiper switch harness connector C441. Test wiper switch. See WIPER SWITCH under COMPONENT TESTS. If switch is okay, go to next step. If switch is defective, replace wiper switch.

3) Measure resistance between ground and rear wiper motor housing ground. If resistance is 5 ohms or less, go to next step. If resistance is greater than 5 ohms, repair rear wiper motor housing ground.

4) Disconnect rear wiper motor harness connector C971. Measure resistance in White/Red wire between rear wiper motor harness connector C971 and terminal No. 7 at wiper switch harness connector C441. See Fig. 6. If resistance is 5 ohms or less, replace rear wiper motor. If resistance is greater than 5 ohms, repair open in White/Red wire.

TEST J: REAR WIPER STAYS ON CONTINUOUSLY

1) Turn ignition switch to LOCK position. Disconnect wiper switch harness connector C441. Test wiper switch. See WIPER SWITCH under COMPONENT TESTS. If switch is okay, go to next step. If switch is defective, replace wiper switch.

2) Disconnect rear wiper motor harness connector C971. Turn ignition switch to RUN position. Measure voltage at White/Red wire terminal at rear wiper motor harness connector C971. If voltage does not exist, replace rear wiper motor. If voltage exists, repair short to voltage in White/Red wire.

TEST K: REAR WIPER DOES NOT PARK PROPERLY

1) Turn ignition switch to LOCK position. Disconnect rear wiper motor harness connector C971. Turn ignition switch to RUN position. Measure voltage at Violet/Blue wire terminal at rear wiper motor harness connector C971. If voltage does not exist, go to next step. If voltage exists, replace rear wiper motor.

2) Turn ignition switch to LOCK position. Disconnect instrument panel fuse box harness connector C367. See Fig. 5. Measure resistance in Violet/Blue wire between rear wiper motor harness connector C971 and instrument panel fuse box harness connector C367. See Fig. 7. If resistance is 5 ohms or less, replace instrument panel fuse box. If resistance is greater than 5 ohms, repair open in Violet/Blue wire.

REMOVAL & INSTALLATION

CAUTION: When battery is disconnected, vehicle computer and memory systems may lose memory data. Driveability problems may exist until computer systems have completed a relearn cycle. See COMPUTER RELEARN PROCEDURES article in GENERAL INFORMATION before disconnecting battery.

WINDSHIELD WIPER ARMS

NOTE: To prevent damage to glass or paint, DO NOT use a sharp or metal tool to pry windshield wiper pivot arms from windshield wiper pivot shafts.

Removal & Installation – 1) Lift caps on windshield wiper arms to expose attaching nuts. Remove nuts. Lift each wiper arm to service position and carefully rock wiper arms to loosen. Remove wiper arms.

2) To install, cycle wiper motor to park position. Position wiper arms on pivot shafts and align to park position. Install nuts on pivot shaft and tighten to 18 ft. lbs. (25 N.m). Replace nut caps.

WINDSHIELD WIPER MOTOR, PIVOT SHAFTS & LINKAGE

Removal & Installation – 1) Disconnect negative battery cable. Remove windshield wiper arms. See WINDSHIELD WIPER ARMS. Remove screws retaining cowl top vent panel.

2) Carefully remove cowl top vent panel. Disconnect windshield wiper motor harness. Remove wiper motor and linkage mounting bolts. Mark position of wiper motor arm in relation to motor mounting plate. Remove wiper motor and linkage assembly from vehicle.

3) To install, ensure wiper motor arm is aligned with removal mark. Install linkage retaining bolt on left side first. To complete installation, reverse removal procedure. Install wiper arms and tighten nuts to 18 ft. lbs. (25 N.m). See WINDSHIELD WIPER ARMS.

WIPER SWITCH

Removal & Installation – Disconnect negative battery cable. Wait at least 2 minutes for air bag back-up power supply to deplete. Remove upper and lower steering column covers. Depress switch locking tab. Slide switch outward from steering column. Disconnect harness connector. Remove switch from housing. To install, reverse removal procedure.

WIRING DIAGRAMS

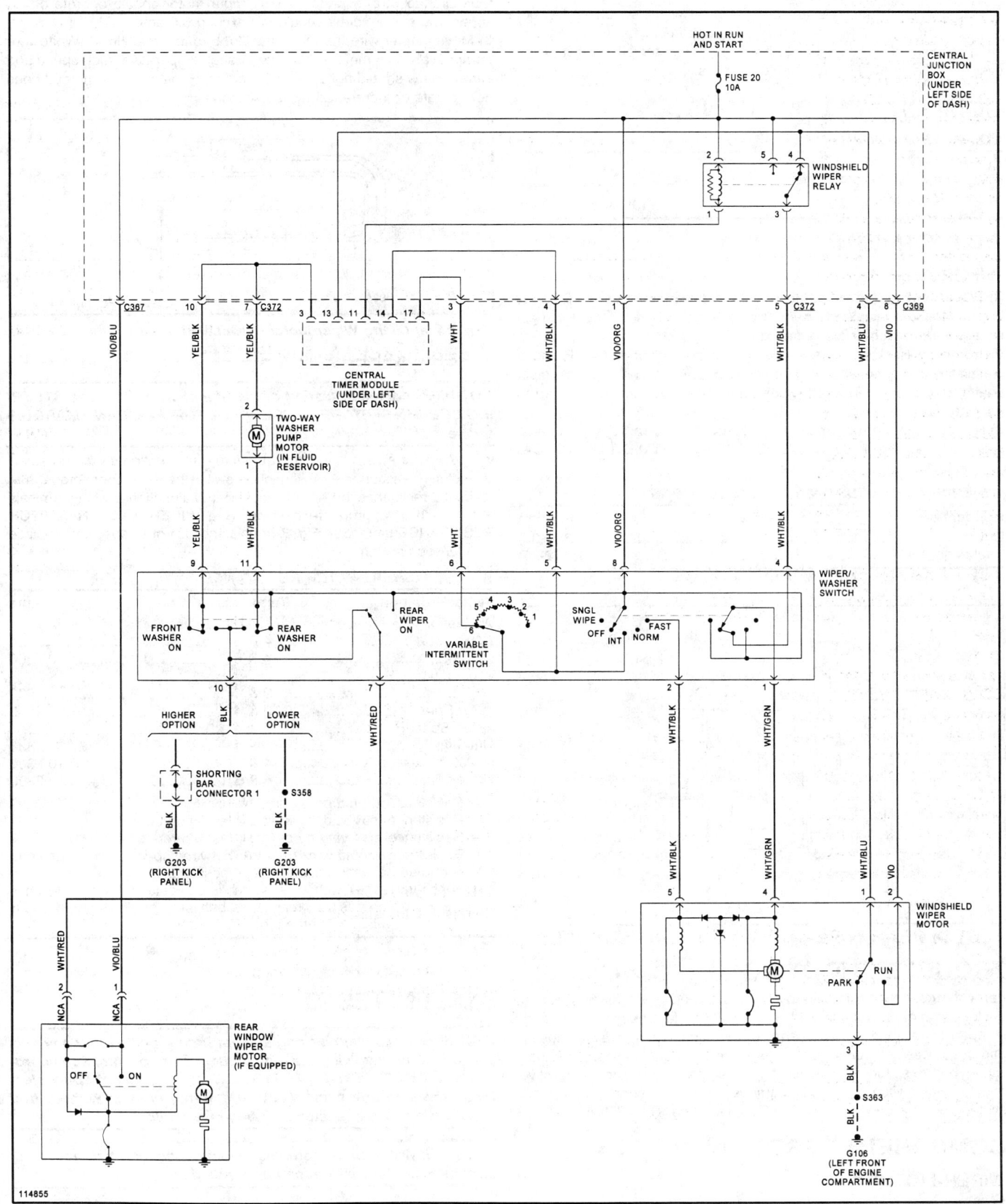

Fig. 10: Wiper/Washer System Wiring Diagram (Cougar)

DESCRIPTION & OPERATION

All wiper/washer functions are controlled by wiper switch and Wiper Control Module (WCM) located behind instrument panel, to right of steering column. When wiper switch is in INT (interval) position, wipe cycles are separated by adjustable intervals.

COMPONENT LOCATIONS

COMPONENT LOCATIONS

Component	Location
Wiper Control Module	Behind Instrument Panel, Right Of Steering Wheel

ADJUSTMENTS

WIPER ARM

1) Wiper arms are keyed to pivot shafts, adjustment of park position is not generally required. However, if park position is not correct inspect linkage for damage or disconnection.
2) If linkage is okay, remove wiper arms from pivot shafts. Remove plastic key from pivot shaft(s). Turn on wipers. Allow motor to cycle pivot shafts 2 or 3 times. Turn off wipers and allow pivot shafts to return to park position.
3) Reinstall wiper arms in proper positions. Dimension "X" should be as specified. See Fig. 1. See WIPER BLADE ADJUSTMENT SPECIFICATIONS table.

WIPER BLADE ADJUSTMENT SPECIFICATIONS

Application	In. (mm)
Driver Side	0.2-1.3 (5-33)
Passenger Side	0.1-1.0 (2-25)

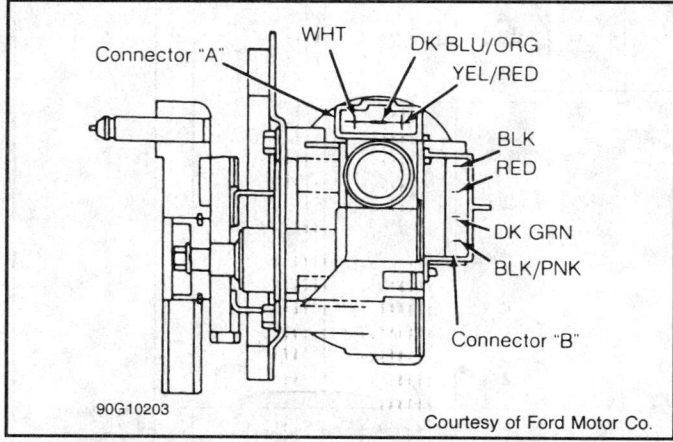

Fig. 1: Adjusting Wiper Arms

TROUBLE SHOOTING

Verify the customer complaint by operating wipers. Visually inspect for obvious sign of mechanical and electrical damage. Check for damaged/ stripped pivot shaft or wiper arm, blown wiper/washer related fuses, damaged washer pump, loose or corroded connections, damaged wiring harness, binding windshield wiper pivot arm and inoperative multifunction switch. If no visual damage is evident, perform appropriate system test. See SYMPTOM CHART table under SYSTEM TESTS.

COMPONENT TESTS

WIPER MOTOR

1) Disengage wiper linkage from wiper motor. Disconnect wiper motor harness connector C151. Using a fused jumper wire, connect ammeter between positive battery terminal and terminal No. 5 (Yellow/Red wire terminal) at wiper motor. See Fig. 2.

2) Using another fused jumper wire, ground terminal No. 6 (Dark Blue/Orange wire) at wiper motor. Wiper motor should operate at low speed and current draw should not exceed 3.5 amps.
3) Move jumper wire from terminal No. 6 to terminal No. 7 (White wire terminal) at wiper motor. Wiper motor should operate at high speed and current draw should not exceed 5.5 amps. Replace wiper motor it does not operate or if current draw is excessive.

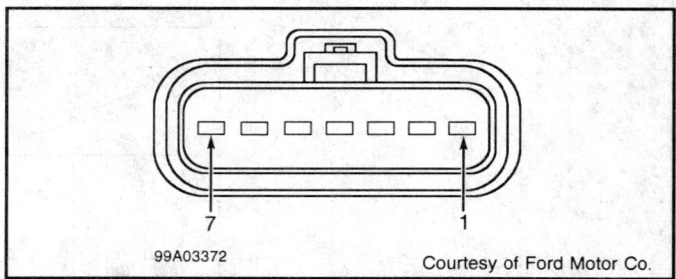

Fig. 2: Identifying Wiper Motor Terminals

WIPER/WASHER SWITCH

NOTE: For complete testing of multifunction switch, see STEERING COLUMN SWITCHES – CROWN VICTORIA & GRAND MARQUIS article.

Wiper/washer switch is incorporated into multifunction switch on steering column. Disconnect multifunction switch harness connector C269. Measure resistance between specified multifunction switch terminals with switch in appropriate position. See WIPER/WASHER SWITCH RESISTANCE table. See Fig. 3. If resistance is not as specified, replace multifunction switch.

WIPER/WASHER SWITCH RESISTANCE

Switch Position	Terminals	Ohms
Washer		
On	4 & 6	[1]
Off	4 & 6	[2] 103,300
Wipers		
Off	2 & 4	[3] 47,600
Low Speed	2 & 4	[3] 4080
High Speed	2 & 4	[1]
Interval	2 & 4	[3] 11,330
MAX	4 & 6	[3] [5] 103,300
MIN	4 & 6	[3] [5] 3300

[1] – Resistance should be 5 ohms or less.
[2] – Resistance may vary by as much as 10 percent.
[3] – Resistance may vary by as much as 5 percent.
[4] – Resistance should vary smoothly between specified limits as knob is rotated between MIN and MAX positions.
[5] – These values are with wiper switch in off position. If wiper switch is in low or high position, resistance between terminals No. 4 and 6 should be within 10 percent of 3300 ohms.

SYSTEM TESTS

WARNING: Deactivate air bag system before performing any service operation involving steering column components. See appropriate AIR BAG RESTRAINT SYSTEMS article. Do not apply electrical power to any component on steering column without first deactivating air bag system. Air bag may deploy.

CAUTION: Wiper motor contains ceramic magnets that may crack or shatter if motor is dropped or handled roughly.

SYMPTOM CHART

Symptom	Test
Washer Inoperative	A

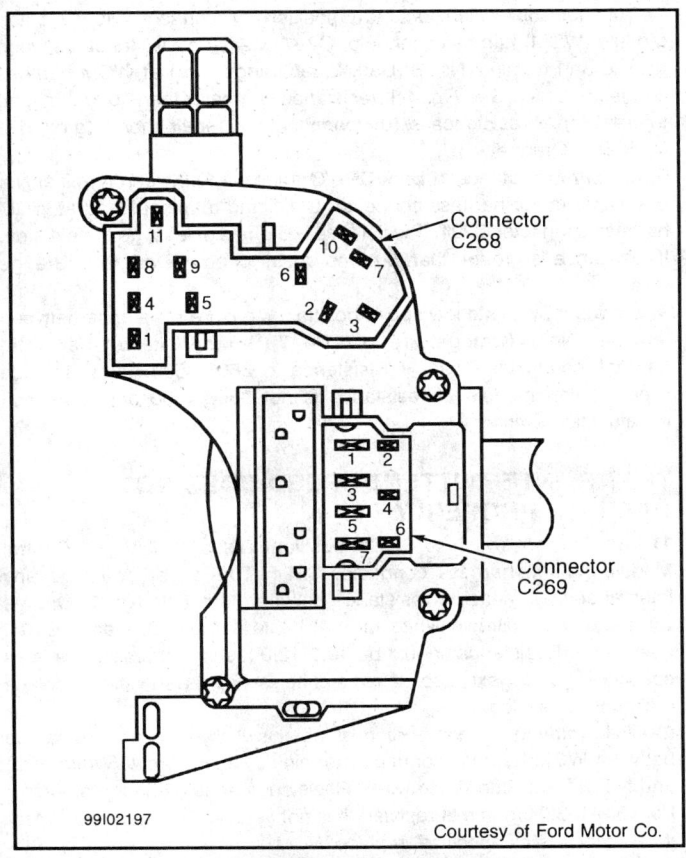

99I02197

Courtesy of Ford Motor Co.

Fig. 3: Identifying Multifunction Switch Terminals

SYMPTOM CHART (Cont.)

Symptom	Test
Washer Runs Continuously	B
Wipers Inoperative	C
Wipers Inoperative At High Speed	D
Wipers Inoperative At Low Speed	E
Intermittent Speed Does Not Operate Properly	F
Wipers Will Not Park Properly	G
Wipers Continue To Run When Switch Is Off	H

TEST A: WASHER INOPERATIVE

1) Turn ignition switch to RUN position. Operate wipers. If wipers operate, go to next step. If wipers do not operate, perform TEST C: WIPERS INOPERATIVE.

2) Operate washer switch. If washer pump operates, go to next step. If washer pump is inoperative, go to step **4)** .

3) Check for nozzles and hoses for blockage. If blockage exists, repair as necessary. If blockage does not exist, replace washer pump.

4) Turn ignition switch to LOCK position. Disconnect washer pump harness connector C1022. Turn ignition switch to RUN position. Measure voltage at Black/White terminal at washer pump harness connector C1022 while pressing washer switch. If battery voltage exists, go to next step. If battery voltage does not exist, go to step **6)**.

5) Turn ignition switch to LOCK position. Measure resistance between ground and Black wire terminal at washer pump harness connector C1022. If resistance is greater than 5 ohms, repair open in Black wire. If resistance is 5 ohms or less, replace washer pump.

6) Disconnect multifunction switch harness connectors. Test wiper/washer switch portion of multifunction switch. See WIPER/WASHER SWITCH under COMPONENT TESTS. If switch is okay, go to next step. If switch is defective, replace multifunction switch.

7) Disconnect Wiper Control Module (WCM) harness connector C294. Measure resistance in Black/White wire between washer pump harness connector C1022 and terminal No. 4 at WCM harness connector C294.

See Fig. 4. If resistance is 5 ohms or less, go to next step. If resistance is greater than 5 ohms, repair open in Black/White wire.

8) Measure resistance between ground and terminal No. 4 (Black/White wire) at WCM harness connector C294. If resistance is greater than 10 k/ohms, replace WCM. If resistance in 10 k/ohms or less, repair short to ground in Black/White wire.

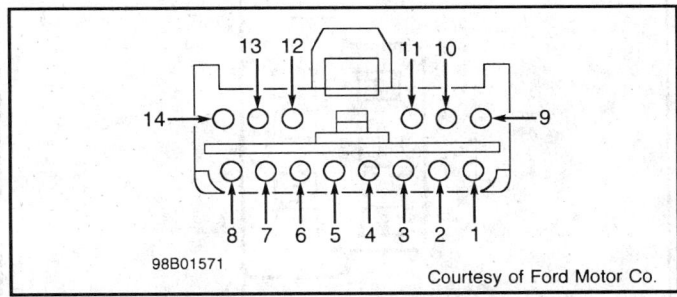

98B01571

Courtesy of Ford Motor Co.

Fig. 4: Identifying Wiper Control Module Harness Connector C294 Terminals

TEST B: WASHER RUNS CONTINUOUSLY

1) Turn ignition switch to LOCK position. Disconnect Wiper Control Module (WCM) harness connector C294. Turn ignition switch to RUN position. If washer does not run continuously, go to next step. If washer runs continuously, repair short to power in Black/White wire.

2) Turn ignition switch to LOCK position. Disconnect multifunction switch harness connector C269. Connect WCM harness connector C294. Turn ignition switch to RUN position. If washer does not run continuously, replace multifunction switch. If washer runs continuously, replace WCM.

TEST C: WIPERS INOPERATIVE

1) Turn ignition switch to LOCK position. Disconnect Wiper Control Module (WCM) harness connector C294. Turn ignition switch to RUN position. Measure voltage at terminal No. 2 (Dark Green wire) at WCM harness connector C294. *See Fig. 4.* If battery voltage exists, go to next step. If battery voltage does not exist, repair open or short to ground in Dark Green wire.

2) Turn ignition switch to LOCK position. Measure resistance between ground and terminals No. 3 and 5 (both Black wire) at WCM harness connector C294. If both resistance readings are 5 ohms or less, go to next step. If either resistance reading is greater than 5 ohms, repair open appropriate Black wire.

3) Turn ignition switch to LOCK position. Turn wiper switch to high speed setting. Measure resistance between terminals No. 1 (Orange wire) and No. 7 (Brown/White wire) at WCM harness connector C294. If resistance is greater than 5 ohms, go to next step. If resistance is 5 ohms or less, go to step **6)**.

4) Disconnect multifunction switch harness connector C269. Measure resistance in Brown/White wire between terminal No. 4 at multifunction switch harness connector C269 and terminal No. 7 at WCM harness connector C294. *See Figs. 4 and 5.* If resistance is 5 ohms or less, go to next step. If resistance is greater than 5 ohms, repair open in Brown/White wire.

5) Measure resistance in Orange wire between terminal No. 2 at multifunction switch harness connector C269 and terminal No. 1 at WCM harness connector C294. If resistance is 5 ohms or less, replace multifunction switch. If resistance is greater than 5 ohms, repair open Orange wire.

6) Connect WCM and multifunction switch harness connectors. Disconnect wiper motor harness connector C151. Set wiper switch to high speed position. Turn ignition switch to RUN position. Measure voltage between terminals No. 5 (Yellow/Red wire) and No. 7 (White wire) at wiper motor harness connector C151. *See Fig. 6.* If battery voltage does not exist, go to next step. If battery voltage exists, test wiper motor. See WIPER MOTOR under COMPONENT TESTS. If wiper motor is okay, repair wiper linkage as necessary.

7) Turn ignition switch to LOCK position. Disconnect WCM harness connector C294. Measure resistance in Yellow/Red wire between ter-

FORD
4-1328

1999 ACCESSORIES & EQUIPMENT
Wiper/Washer Systems – Crown Victoria & Grand Marquis (Cont.)

minal No. 12 at WCM harness connector C294 and terminal No. 5 at wiper motor harness connector C151. If resistance is 5 ohms or less, replace WCM. If resistance is greater than 5 ohms, repair open in Yellow/Red wire.

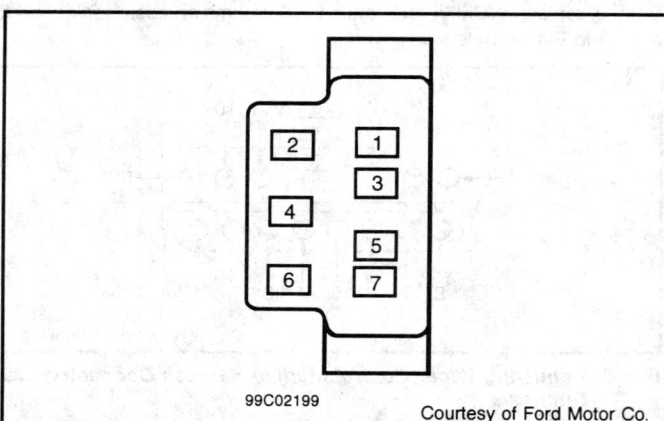

Fig. 5: Identifying Multifunction Switch Harness Connector C269 Terminals

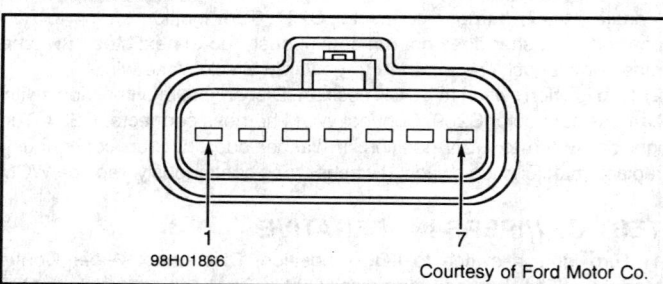

Fig. 6: Identifying Wiper Motor Harness Connector C151 Terminals

TEST D: WIPERS INOPERATIVE AT HIGH SPEED

1) Turn ignition switch to LOCK position. Disconnect wiper motor harness connector C151. Turn ignition switch to RUN position. Set wiper switch to high speed position. Measure voltage at terminal No. 7 (White wire) at wiper motor harness connector C151. *See Fig. 6.* If battery voltage does not exist, go to next step. If battery voltage exists, test wiper motor. See WIPER MOTOR under COMPONENT TESTS. If wiper motor is okay, repair wiper linkage as necessary.

2) Turn ignition switch to LOCK position. Disconnect Wiper Control Module (WCM) harness connector C294. Measure resistance in White wire between terminal No. 14 at WCM harness connector C294 and terminal No. 7 at wiper motor harness connector C151. *See Figs. 4 and 6.* If resistance is 5 ohms or less, go to next step. If resistance is greater than 5 ohms, repair open in White wire.

3) Measure resistance between ground and terminal No. 7 (White wire) at wiper motor harness connector C151. If resistance is greater than 10 k/ohms, go to next step. If resistance is 10 k/ohms or less, repair short to ground in White wire.

4) Set wiper switch to high speed position. Measure resistance between terminals No. 1 (Orange wire) and No. 7 (Brown/White wire) at WCM harness connector C294. If resistance is 5 ohms or less, replace WCM. If resistance is greater than 5 ohms, replace multifunction switch.

TEST E: WIPERS INOPERATIVE AT LOW SPEED

1) Turn ignition switch to LOCK position. Disconnect wiper motor harness connector C151. Turn ignition switch to RUN position. Set wiper switch for low speed operation. Measure voltage between terminals No. 6 (Dark Blue/Orange wire) and No. 5 (Yellow/Red wire) at wiper motor harness connector C151. *See Fig. 6.* If battery voltage does not exist, go to next step. If battery voltage exists, test wiper motor. See WIPER MOTOR under COMPONENT TESTS. If wiper motor is okay, repair wiper linkage as necessary.

2) Turn ignition switch to LOCK position. Disconnect Wiper Control Module (WCM) harness connector C294. Measure resistance between ground and terminal No. 8 (Dark Blue/Orange wire) at WCM harness connector C294. *See Fig. 4.* If resistance is greater than 10 k/ohms, go to next step. If resistance is 10 k/ohms or less, repair short to ground in Dark Blue/Orange wire.

3) Measure resistance in Dark Blue/Orange wire between terminal No. 6 at wiper motor harness connector C151 and terminal No. 8 at WCM harness connector C294. If resistance is 5 ohms or less, go to next step. If resistance is greater than 5 ohms, repair open in Dark Blue/Orange wire.

4) Set wiper switch to low speed position. Measure resistance between terminals No. 1 (Orange wire) and No. 7 (Brown/White wire) at WCM harness connector C294. If resistance is 3500-4500 ohms, replace wiper control module. If resistance is not 3500-4500 ohms, replace multifunction switch.

TEST F: INTERMITTENT SPEED DOES NOT OPERATE PROPERLY

1) Turn ignition switch to LOCK position. Disconnect Wiper Control Module (WCM) harness connector C294. Turn wiper switch to any interval setting. Measure resistance between terminals No. 1 (Orange wire) and No. 7 (Brown/White wire) at WCM harness connector C294. *See Fig. 4.* Resistance should be 10.5-12.0 k/ohms. If resistance is as specified, go to next step. If resistance is not as specified, replace multifunction switch.

2) While rotating interval portion of wiper switch, measure resistance between WCM harness connector terminals No. 7 (Brown/White wire) and No. 9 Dark Blue/White wire). Resistance should change smoothly from 3.3-103.0 k/ohms. If resistance is not as specified, go to next step. If resistance is as specified, replace WCM.

3) Disconnect multi function switch harness connector C269. Measure resistance between ground and terminal No. 9 (Dark Blue/White wire) at WCM harness connector C294. If resistance is greater than 10 k/ohms, go to next step. If resistance is 10 k/ohms or less, repair short to ground in Dark Blue/White wire.

4) Measure resistance in Dark Blue/White wire between terminal No. 9 at WCM harness connector C294 and terminal No. 6 at multifunction switch harness connector C269. *See Figs. 4 and 5.* If resistance is 5 ohms or less, replace multifunction switch. If resistance is 5 ohms or greater, repair open in Dark Blue/White wire.

TEST G: WIPERS WILL NOT PARK PROPERLY

1) Turn ignition switch to LOCK position. Disconnect wiper motor harness connector C151. Measure resistance between ground and terminal No. 4 (Black wire) at wiper motor harness connector C151. *See Fig. 6.* If resistance is 5 ohms or less, go to next step. If resistance is grater than 5 ohms, repair open in Black wire.

2) Turn ignition switch to RUN position. Measure voltage at terminal No. 1 (Dark Green wire) at wiper motor harness connector C151. If battery voltage exists, go to next step. If battery voltage does not exist, repair open in Dark Green wire.

3) Turn ignition switch to LOCK position. Disconnect Wiper Control Module (WCM) harness connector C294. Measure resistance in Red wire between terminal No. 13 at WCM harness connector C294 and terminal No. 3 at wiper motor harness connector C151. *See Figs. 4 and 6.* If resistance is 5 ohms or less, go to next step. If resistance is greater than 5 ohms, repair open in Red wire.

4) Measure resistance between ground and terminal No. 13 (Red wire) at WCM harness connector C294. If resistance is greater than 10 k/ohms, go to next step. If resistance is 10 k/ohs or less, repair short to ground in Red wire.

5) Measure resistance in Black/Pink wire between terminal No. 6 at WCM harness connector C294 and terminal No. 2 at wiper motor harness connector C151. If resistance is 5 ohms or less, go to next step. If resistance is greater than 5 ohms, repair open in Black/Pink wire.

1999 ACCESSORIES & EQUIPMENT
Wiper/Washer Systems – Crown Victoria & Grand Marquis (Cont.)

FORD
4-1329

6) Measure resistance between ground and terminal No. 6 (Black/Pink wire) at WCM harness connector C294. If resistance is greater than 10 k/ohms, replace WCM. If resistance is 10 k/ohms or less, repair short to ground in Black/Pink wire.

TEST H: WIPERS CONTINUE TO RUN WHEN SWITCH IS OFF

1) Turn ignition switch to LOCK position. Disconnect multifunction switch harness connector C269. Disconnect Wiper Control Module (WCM) harness connector C294. Measure resistance between ground and terminal No. 1 (Orange wire) at WCM harness connector C294. *See Fig. 4.* If resistance is greater than 10 k/ohms, go to next step. If resistance is 10 k/ohms or less, repair short to ground in Orange wire.

2) Measure resistance between ground and terminal No. 7 (Brown/White wire) at WCM harness connector C294. If resistance is greater than 10 k/ohms, go to next step. If resistance is 10 k/ohms or less, repair short to ground in Brown/White wire.

3) Connect multifunction switch harness connector C269. Set wiper switch to high speed setting. Measure resistance between ground and terminal No. 7 (Brown/White wire) at WCM harness connector C294. If resistance is 10 k/ohms or less, replace multifunction switch. If resistance is greater than 10 k/ohms, replace WCM.

REMOVAL & INSTALLATION

WARNING: Deactivate air bag system before performing any service operation involving steering column components. See appropriate AIR BAG RESTRAINT SYSTEMS article. Do not apply electrical power to any component on steering column without first deactivating air bag system. Air bag may deploy.

CAUTION: When battery is disconnected, vehicle computer and memory systems may lose memory data. Driveability problems may exist until computer systems have completed a relearn cycle. See COMPUTER RELEARN PROCEDURES article in GENERAL INFORMATION before disconnecting battery.

WIPER MOTOR

CAUTION: Wiper motor contains ceramic magnets that may crack or shatter if motor is dropped or handled roughly.

Removal & Installation – 1) Disconnect battery ground cable. Remove rear hood seal. Remove wiper arms. Remove cowl vent screens. Unplug harness connector from motor. Remove wiper motor.

2) Unsnap and remove wiper linkage cover. Lift locking tab, and pull clip away from shaft to disengage linkage from operating arm on motor. Remove motor. To install, reverse removal procedure.

MULTIFUNCTION SWITCH

Removal & Installation – Multifunction (wiper/washer) switch is part of multifunction switch on steering column. Disconnect battery ground cable. Separate and remove steering column cover halves. Disconnect multifunction switch harness connector. Remove 2 screws and multifunction switch. To install, reverse removal procedure.

WIRING DIAGRAMS

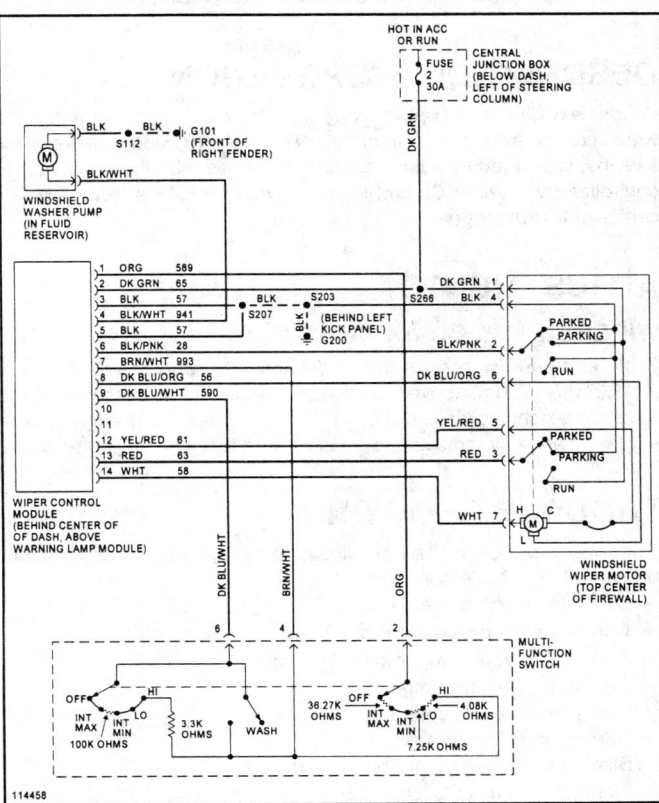

Fig. 7: Wiper/Washer System Wiring Diagram (Crown Victoria & Grand Marquis)

NOTE: This article includes Cutaway and RV Cutaway.

DESCRIPTION & OPERATION

Windshield wipers are operated by a permanent-magnet motor. When wiper control switch is in interval (INT) position, wipers make single sweeps, separated by adjustable-length pauses. All wiper functions are controlled by a Wiper Control Module (WCM). WCM is located behind center of instrument panel.

ADJUSTMENTS

WIPER ARM & BLADE ASSEMBLY

Cycle and park wipers. Center of driver's side wiper blade should be 2.1-3.0″ (53-77 mm) above top edge of cowl. Center of passenger's side wiper blade should be 2.6-3.6″ (67-91 mm) above top edge of cowl. Adjust distance by removing wiper blade and repositioning on pivot arm.

TROUBLE SHOOTING

Before performing any tests on wiper/washer system, check the following items to eliminate common problems:
- Central junction box fuse No. 9 (30-amp).
- Damaged/stripped wiper motor shaft.
- Damaged/stripped wiper pivot arm shaft.
- Damaged washer pump.
- Loose or corroded connections.
- Damaged wiring harness.
- Binding windshield wiper pivot arm.
- Inoperative multifunction switch.
- Wiper motor.

If problem is not found, identify wiper/washer symptom and perform appropriate symptom test. See TEST INDEX table. For individual component testing, see COMPONENT TESTS.

COMPONENT TESTS

WIPER MOTOR

Manufacturer did not provide test procedure.

WIPER/WASHER SWITCH

Wiper/washer switch is incorporated into multifunction switch on steering column. Wiper/washer portion of multifunction switch cannot be serviced separately. Replace entire multifunction switch if resistance is not as specified. See WIPER/WASHER SWITCH RESISTANCE TEST table. See Fig. 1.

WIPER/WASHER SWITCH RESISTANCE TEST

Switch Position	Switch Terminals	[1] k/ohms
OFF	589 & 993	47.6
LOW	589 & 993	4.08
HIGH	589 & 993	0
INT	589 & 993	11.33
WASH		
OFF	993 & 590	103.3
ON	993 & 590	0
INT Delay [2]		
MIN	993 & 590	3.3
MAX	993 & 590	103.3

[1] – Values are approximate.
[2] – Rotate (INT) interval knob from minimum to maximum. Resistance should gradually increase from 3.3 k/ohms (MIN) to 103.3 k/ohms (MAX).

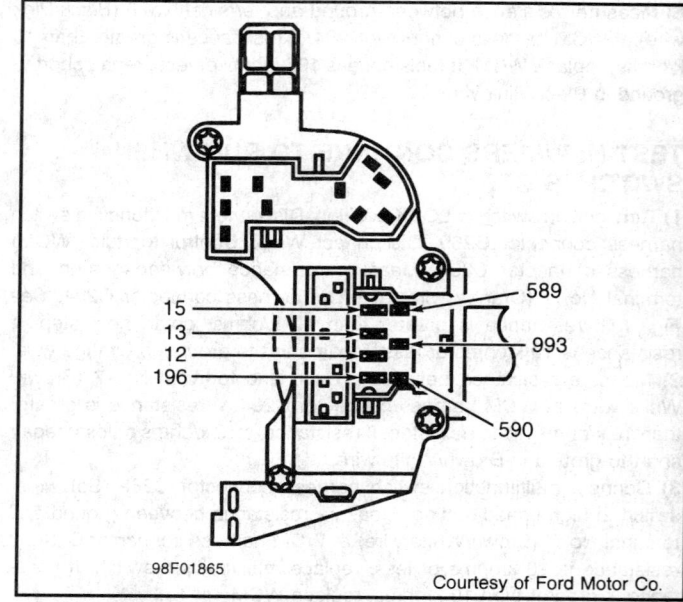

15
13
12
196

589
993
590

98F01865   Courtesy of Ford Motor Co.

Fig. 1: Identifying Multifunction Switch Terminals

SYSTEM TESTS

WARNING: Deactivate air bag system before performing any service operation involving steering column components. See appropriate AIR BAG RESTRAINT SYSTEMS article. Do not apply electrical power to any component on steering column without first deactivating air bag system. Air bag may deploy.

CAUTION: When battery is disconnected, vehicle computer and memory systems may lose memory data. Driveability problems may exist until computer systems have completed a relearn cycle. See COMPUTER RELEARN PROCEDURES article in GENERAL INFORMATION before disconnecting battery.

TEST INDEX

Symptom	Test
Washer Pump Inoperative	A
Wipers Inoperative	B
Low Speed Does Not Operate Properly	C
High Speed Does Not Operate Properly	D
Intermittent Speed Does Not Operate Properly	E
Wipers Will Not Park Properly	F
Wipers Continue To Run When Switch Is Off	G

TEST A: WASHER PUMP INOPERATIVE

NOTE: After repair, retest system operation.

1) Turn ignition on. Press washer button. If washer pump operates properly, go to next step. If washer pump does not operate properly, go to step 3).
2) Inspect washer system hoses, nozzles and pump for blockage or obstructions. Repair as necessary. If hoses, nozzles, etc. are okay, replace washer pump motor assembly.

3) Turn ignition off. Disconnect washer pump electrical connector. Connector is located in right front of engine compartment near grille. Turn ignition on. Depress and hold washer switch. Measure voltage between Black/White wire at washer pump connector and ground. If voltage is more than 10 volts, go to next step. If voltage is 10 volts or less, go to step **5**).

4) Turn ignition off. Measure resistance of Black wire between washer pump connector and ground. If resistance is less than 5 ohms, replace washer pump. See WASHER PUMP & RESERVOIR under REMOVAL & INSTALLATION. If resistance is 5 ohms or more, repair open in Black wire.

5) Turn ignition off. Disconnect Wiper Control Module (WCM) connector. To access, see WIPER CONTROL MODULE under REMOVAL & INSTALLATION. Measure resistance of Black/White wire between washer pump connector and ground. If resistance is more than 10 k/ohms, go to next step. If resistance is 10 k/ohms or less, repair Black/White wire short to ground.

6) Turn ignition off. Measure resistance of Black/White wire between washer pump connector and WCM connector terminal No. 4. *See Fig. 2.* If resistance is less than 5 ohms, go to next step. If resistance is 5 ohms or more, repair open in Black/White wire.

7) Disconnect multifunction switch 7-pin connector. Test wiper/washer switch. See WIPER/WASHER SWITCH under COMPONENT TESTS. If wiper/washer switch is faulty, replace multifunction switch. If wiper/washer switch is okay, replace WCM. See WIPER CONTROL MODULE under REMOVAL & INSTALLATION.

wire) and ground. If each resistance is less than 5 ohms, go to next step. If either resistance is 5 ohms or more, repair open in Black/Light Blue wire.

4) Turn ignition off. Turn wiper switch to high. Measure resistance between WCM connector terminals No. 1 (Orange wire) and No. 7 (Brown/White wire). *See Fig. 2.* If resistance is less than 5 ohms, go to step **7**). If resistance is 5 ohms or more, go to next step.

5) Disconnect multifunction switch 7-pin connector. Measure resistance of Brown/White wire between multifunction switch 7-pin connector and WCM connector terminal No. 7. *See Fig. 2.* If resistance is less than 5 ohms, go to next step. If resistance is 5 ohms or more, repair open in Brown/White wire.

6) Measure resistance of Orange wire between multifunction switch 7-pin connector and WCM connector terminal No. 1. *See Fig. 2.* If resistance is less than 5 ohms, replace multifunction switch. See MULTIFUNCTION SWITCH under REMOVAL & INSTALLATION. If resistance is 5 ohms or more, repair open in Orange wire.

7) Reconnect WCM connector. Disconnect wiper motor connector. Turn wiper switch to high. Turn ignition on. Measure voltage between wiper motor connector terminals No. 3 and 5. *See Fig. 3.* If voltage is 10 volts or less, go to next step. If voltage is more than 10 volts, replace wiper motor. See WIPER MOTOR under REMOVAL & INSTALLATION.

8) Turn ignition off. Disconnect WCM connector. Measure resistance of Yellow/Red wire between WCM connector terminal No. 10 and wiper motor connector terminal No. 3. *See Figs. 2 and 3.* If resistance is 5 ohms or more, repair open in Yellow/Red wire. If resistance is less than 5 ohms, replace WCM. See WIPER CONTROL MODULE under REMOVAL & INSTALLATION.

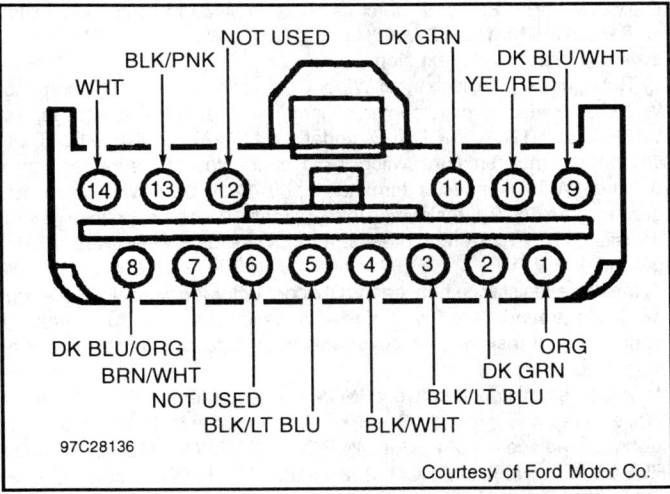

Fig. 2: Identifying Wiper Control Module (WCM) Terminals

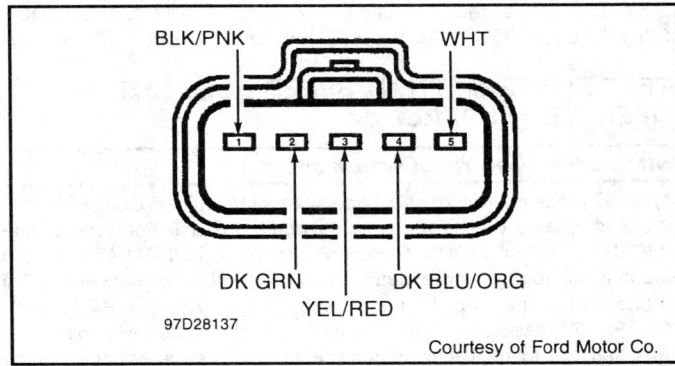

Fig. 3: Identifying Wiper Motor Connector Terminals

TEST C: LOW SPEED DOES NOT OPERATE PROPERLY

TEST B: WIPERS INOPERATIVE

NOTE: After repair, retest system operation.

1) Turn ignition off. Check central junction box fuse No. 9 (30-amp). Central junction box is located left and below steering column behind access panel. If fuse is okay, go to next step. If fuse is faulty, replace fuse and retest. If fuse fails again, check circuit for short to ground. See WIRING DIAGRAMS.

2) Disconnect Wiper Control Module (WCM) connector. WCM is located behind center of instrument panel. For access, see WIPER CONTROL MODULE under REMOVAL & INSTALLATION. Turn ignition on. Measure voltage between WCM connector terminal No. 2 (Dark Green wire) and ground. *See Fig. 2.* Measure voltage between WCM connector terminal No. 11 (Dark Green wire) and ground. If both voltage readings are more than 10 volts, go to next step. If either voltage readings is 10 volts or less, repair Dark Green wire(s) between central junction box and WCM.

3) Turn ignition off. Measure resistance between WCM connector terminal No. 3 (Black/Light Blue wire) and ground. *See Fig. 2.* Measure resistance between WCM connector terminal No. 5 (Black/Light Blue

NOTE: After repair, retest system operation.

1) Turn ignition off. Disconnect wiper motor connector. Turn ignition on. Set wiper switch to low. Measure voltage between wiper motor connector terminals No. 3 (Yellow/Red wire) and No. 4 (Dark Blue/Orange wire). *See Fig. 3.* If voltage is 10 volts or less, go to next step. If voltage is more than 10 volts, replace wiper motor. See WIPER MOTOR under REMOVAL & INSTALLATION.

2) Turn ignition off. Disconnect Wiper Control Module (WCM) connector. WCM is located behind center of instrument panel. For access, see WIPER CONTROL MODULE under REMOVAL & INSTALLATION. Measure resistance between wiper motor connector terminal No. 4 and ground. *See Fig. 3.* If resistance is more than 10 k/ohms, go to next step. If resistance is 10 k/ohms or less, repair Dark Blue/Orange wire short to ground.

3) Measure resistance between WCM connector terminal No. 8 (Dark Blue/Orange wire) and wiper motor connector terminal No. 4. *See Figs. 2 and 3.* If resistance is less than 5 ohms, go to next step. If resistance is 5 ohms or more, repair open in Dark Blue/Orange wire.

4) Measure resistance between WCM connector terminals No. 1 (Orange wire) and No. 7 (Brown/White wire). If resistance is 3500-4500 ohms, replace wiper control module. See WIPER CONTROL MODULE under REMOVAL & INSTALLATION. If resistance is not 3500-4500 ohms, replace multifunction switch. See MULTIFUNCTION SWITCH under REMOVAL & INSTALLATION.

TEST D: HIGH SPEED DOES NOT OPERATE PROPERLY

NOTE: After repair, retest system operation.

1) Turn ignition off. Disconnect wiper motor connector. Turn ignition on. Set wiper switch to high. Measure voltage between wiper motor connector terminals No. 3 (Yellow/Red wire) and No. 5 (White wire). *See Fig. 3.* If voltage is 10 volts or less than, go to next step. If voltage is more than 10 volts, replace wiper motor. See WIPER MOTOR under REMOVAL & INSTALLATION.

2) Disconnect Wiper Control Module (WCM) connector. WCM is located behind center of instrument panel. For access, see WIPER CONTROL MODULE under REMOVAL & INSTALLATION. Measure resistance between wiper motor connector terminal No. 5 (White wire) and ground. *See Fig. 3.* If resistance is more than 10 k/ohms, go to next step. If resistance is 10 k/ohms or less, repair White wire for short to ground.

3) Measure resistance of White wire between WCM connector terminal No. 14 and wiper motor connector terminal No. 5. *See Figs. 2 and 3.* If resistance is less than 5 ohms, go to next step. If resistance is 5 ohms or more, repair open in White wire.

4) Turn wiper switch to high. Measure resistance between WCM connector terminals No. 1 (Orange wire) and No. 7 (Brown/White wire). *See Fig. 2.* If resistance is less than 5 ohms, replace WCM. See WIPER CONTROL MODULE under REMOVAL & INSTALLATION. If resistance is 5 ohms or more, replace multifunction switch. See MULTIFUNCTION SWITCH under REMOVAL & INSTALLATION.

TEST E: INTERMITTENT SPEED DOES NOT OPERATE PROPERLY

NOTE: After repair, retest system operation.

1) Turn ignition off. Disconnect Wiper Control Module (WCM) connector. WCM is located behind center of instrument panel. For access, see WIPER CONTROL MODULE under REMOVAL & INSTALLATION. Turn wiper switch to any interval setting. Measure resistance between WCM connector terminals No. 1 (Orange wire) and No. 7 (Brown/White wire). *See Fig. 2.* Resistance should be 10.5-12.0 k/ohms. If resistance is as specified, go to next step. If resistance is not as specified, replace multifunction switch. See MULTIFUNCTION SWITCH under REMOVAL & INSTALLATION.

2) While rotating interval portion of wiper switch, measure resistance between WCM connector terminals No. 7 (Brown/White wire) and No. 9 (Dark Blue/White wire). *See Fig. 2.* Resistance should smoothly change from 3.3-103 k/ohms. If resistance is not as specified, go to next step. If resistance is as specified, replace WCM. See WIPER CONTROL MODULE under REMOVAL & INSTALLATION.

3) Measure resistance between WCM connector terminal No. 9 (Dark Blue/White wire) and ground. *See Fig. 2.* If resistance is more than 10 k/ohm, go to next step. If resistance is 10 k/ohms or less, repair Dark Blue/White wire short to ground. See WIRING DIAGRAMS.

4) Disconnect multifunction switch 7-pin connector. Measure resistance of Dark Blue/White wire between WCM connector terminal No. 9 and multifunction switch 7-pin connector. *See Fig. 2.* If resistance is less than 5 ohms, replace multifunction switch. See MULTIFUNCTION SWITCH under REMOVAL & INSTALLATION. If resistance is 5 ohms or more, repair open in Dark Blue/White wire.

TEST F: WIPERS WILL NOT PARK PROPERLY

NOTE: After repair, retest system operation.

1) Turn ignition off. Disconnect wiper motor connector. Turn ignition on. Measure voltage between wiper motor connector terminal No. 2 (Dark Green wire) and ground. *See Fig. 3.* If voltage is more than 10 volts, go to next step. If voltage is 10 volts or less, repair Dark Green wire.

2) Turn ignition off. Measure resistance between wiper motor connector terminals No. 1 (Black/Pink wire) and 4 (Dark Blue/Orange wire). *See Fig. 3.* Measure resistance between wiper motor connector terminal No. 3 (Yellow/Red wire) and ground. If each resistance is less than 5 ohms, go to step 4). If either resistance is 5 ohms or more, go to next step.

3) Disconnect Wiper Control Module (WCM) connector. WCM is located behind center of instrument panel. For access, see WIPER CONTROL MODULE under REMOVAL & INSTALLATION. Measure resistance of Black/Pink wire between wiper motor connector terminal No. 1 and WCM connector terminal No. 13. *See Figs. 2 and 3.* Measure resistance of Yellow/Red wire between wiper motor connector terminal No. 3 and WCM connector terminal No. 10. Measure resistance of Dark Blue/Orange wire between wiper motor connector terminal No. 4 and WCM connector terminal No. 8. If resistance of each wire is less than 5 ohms, replace WCM. See WIPER CONTROL MODULE under REMOVAL & INSTALLATION. If resistance of any wire is 5 ohms or more, repair open in appropriate wire(s).

4) Inspect wiper linkage for bends, cracks, etc. Repair linkage as necessary. If linkage is okay, replace wiper motor. See WIPER MOTOR under REMOVAL & INSTALLATION.

TEST G: WIPERS CONTINUE TO RUN WHEN SWITCH IS OFF

NOTE: After repair, retest system operation.

1) Disconnect multifunction 7-pin connector and test wiper/washer portion of multifunction switch. See WIPER/WASHER SWITCH under COMPONENT TESTS. If switch is faulty, replace multifunction switch. See MULTIFUNCTION SWITCH under REMOVAL & INSTALLATION. If switch is okay, go to next step.

2) Turn ignition off. Disconnect Wiper Control Module (WCM) connector. WCM is located behind center of instrument panel. For access, see WIPER CONTROL MODULE under REMOVAL & INSTALLATION. Disconnect multifunction switch 7-pin connector. Measure resistance between WCM connector terminal No. 9 (Dark Blue/White wire) and ground. *See Fig. 2.* If resistance is more than 10 k/ohms, go to next step. If resistance is 10 k/ohms or less, repair Dark Blue/White wire short to ground.

3) Measure resistance between WCM connector terminal No. 1 (Orange wire) and ground. *See Fig. 2.* If resistance is more than 10 k/ohms, go to next step. If resistance is 10 k/ohms or less, repair Orange wire short to ground.

4) Measure resistance between WCM connector terminal No. 7 (Brown/White wire) and ground. *See Fig. 2.* If resistance is more than 10 k/ohms, replace WCM. See WIPER CONTROL MODULE under REMOVAL & INSTALLATION. If resistance is 10 k/ohms or less, repair Brown/White wire short to ground.

REMOVAL & INSTALLATION

WARNING: Deactivate air bag system before performing any service operation involving steering column components. See appropriate AIR BAG RESTRAINT SYSTEMS article. Do not apply electrical power to any component on steering column without first deactivating air bag system. Air bag may deploy.

CAUTION: When battery is disconnected, vehicle computer and memory systems may lose memory data. Driveability problems may exist until computer systems have completed a relearn cycle. See COMPUTER RELEARN PROCEDURES article in GENERAL INFORMATION before disconnecting battery.

MULTIFUNCTION SWITCH

Removal & Installation – 1) Disconnect negative battery cable. Turn ignition switch to RUN position. Insert punch through hole in lower steering column shroud and push release tab while pulling out ignition switch lock cylinder.

2) If equipped, twist tilt wheel handle and remove. Remove steering column shrouds. Remove retaining screws, disconnect electrical connectors and remove multifunction switch. To install, reverse removal procedure.

WASHER PUMP & RESERVOIR

Removal & Installation – 1) Remove battery and battery tray. Remove reservoir retaining screws. Remove filler hose. Disconnect electrical connector and detach wiring harness locator.
2) Disconnect washer hose and drain reservoir. Remove pump from reservoir. To install, reverse removal procedure. Fill reservoir before making electrical connections.

WIPER CONTROL MODULE

Removal & Installation – Turn ignition off. Remove engine cover. Disconnect module connector. Push detent tabs on module through holes in mounting bracket and slide module off bracket. To install, reverse removal procedure.

WIPER MOTOR

Removal & Installation – 1) Disconnect negative battery cable. Remove wiper arms. Open hood. Remove cowl top vent panels. Remove access cover from dash panel, reach through access hole and remove motor drive arm retaining clip.
2) Disconnect wiper mounting arm and pivot shaft from wiper motor. Disconnect wiring from wiper motor. Remove motor. To install, reverse removal procedure. Tighten mounting bolts to 62-89 INCH lbs. (7-10 N.m).

WIRING DIAGRAMS

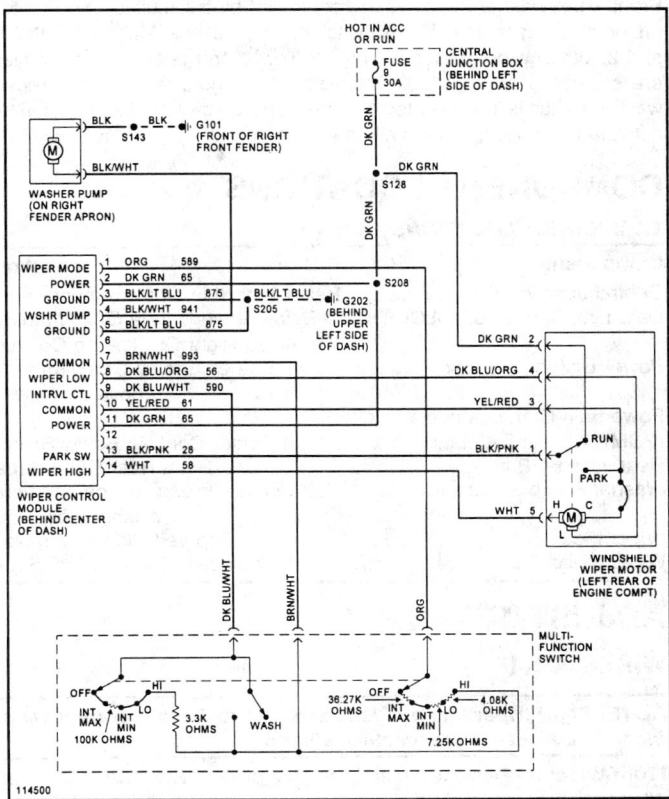

Fig. 4: Wiper/Washer System Wiring Diagram (Econoline)

1999 ACCESSORIES & EQUIPMENT
Wiper/Washer Systems – Escort & Tracer

DESCRIPTION & OPERATION

Front wiper/washer functions are controlled by the multifunction switch on the steering column. Wiper switch has 5 positions; MIST, OFF, INT, 1 and 2. When wiper switch is in INT (intermittent) position, wipe cycles are separated by adjustable intervals. On wagon, rear window wiper/washer switch is incorporated into multifunction switch. Washers can be activated by pulling wiper stalk toward driver.

COMPONENT LOCATIONS

COMPONENT LOCATIONS

Component	Location
Central Junction Box	Below Left Side Of Instrument Panel
Data Link Connector (DLC)	Below Driver's Side Of Instrument Panel, To Right Of Steering Column
Power Distribution Box	Left Side Of Engine Compartment, Above Wheelwell
Powertrain Control Module (PCM)	In Center Console Below Shifter
Rear Washer Pump	Right Rear Cargo Area
Washer Pump	Right Front Of Engine Compartment In Washer Reservoir
Wiper Motor	Top Left Side Of Firewall
Wiper Switch	Multifunction Switch Right Stalk

ADJUSTMENTS

WIPER ARM

NOTE: Right wiper blade is longer than left. Ensure correct wiper blade is installed on respective wiper arm.

Front Wipers – Remove wiper arms from pivot shafts. Turn wipers on. Allow motor to cycle pivot shafts 3 or 4 times. Turn switch off to park wipers. Install wiper arms with tips of wiper blades .8-1.1" (20-30 mm) from top of cowl grille.

Rear Wiper – Remove wiper arm from pivot shaft. Turn rear wiper on. Allow motor to operate through 3 or 4 cycles. Turn wiper off. Install wiper arm so clearance between tip of wiper blade and window molding is about 0.8-1.1" (20-30 mm). *See Fig. 1.*

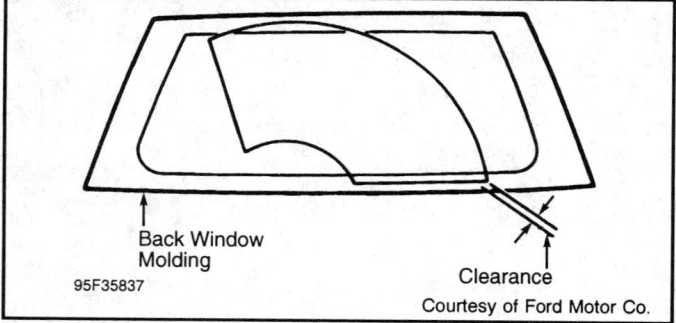

Back Window Molding

Clearance

95F35837

Courtesy of Ford Motor Co.

Fig. 1: Adjusting Rear Wiper Arm

TROUBLE SHOOTING

WARNING: Vehicle is equipped with an air bag system. System MUST be disabled before working near steering column and instrument cluster to prevent air bag deployment. See AIR BAG RESTRAINT SYSTEM – ESCORT & TRACER article.

CAUTION: Wiper motor contains ceramic magnets that may crack or shatter if motor is dropped or handled roughly.

Before performing any tests on wiper/washer system, check the following items to eliminate common problems:
Mechanical:
- Binding wiper pivot arms.
- Plugged or disconnected washer hoses or jets.
- Wiper mounting or linkage.

Electrical:
- Blown fuses.
- Damaged wiper motor.
- Damaged washer pump.
- Loose or corroded connections.
- Damaged wiring harness.
- Damaged multifunction switch.

COMPONENT TESTS

WIPER MOTOR

Front Motor – 1) Turn ignition off. Disengage wiper arm linkage and wiring harness from wiper motor. Connect Alternator, Regulator, Battery and Starter Tester (ARBST) Green test lead to negative battery terminal. Connect Red test lead to wiper motor terminal No. 3 (ground). Connect fused jumper wire between positive battery terminal and wiper motor terminal No. 4 (low speed), or terminal No. 5 (high speed). *See Fig. 2.* **2)** With jumper wire connected to terminal No. 4, motor should operate at low speed, drawing a maximum of 3.5 amps. With jumper wire connected to terminal No. 5, motor should operate at high speed, drawing a maximum of 5.5 amps. If motor does not operate or motor draw exceeds maximum specification, replace wiper motor.

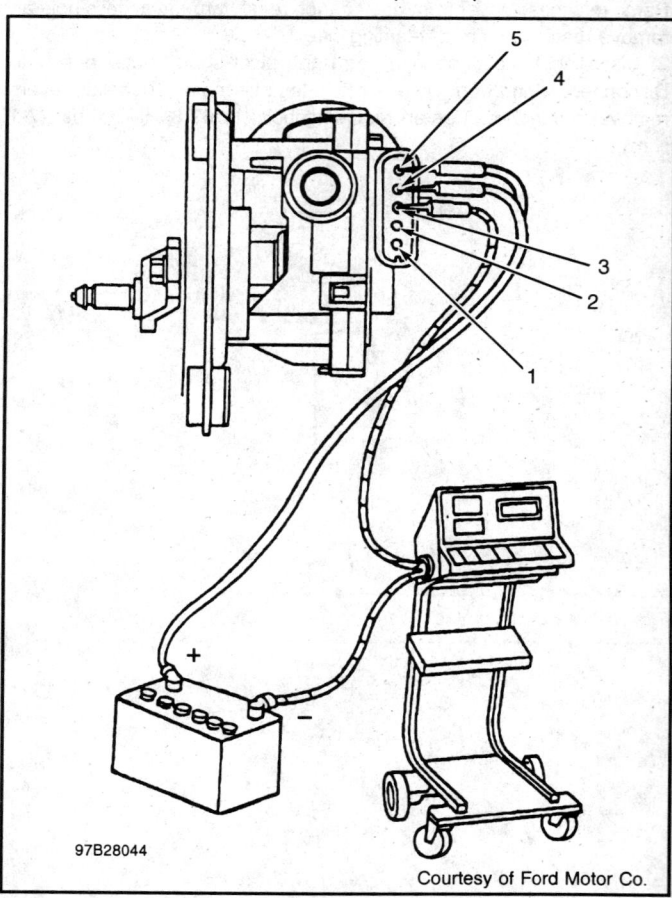

97B28044

Courtesy of Ford Motor Co.

Fig. 2: Testing Wiper Motor (Front)

Rear Motor – Turn ignition off. Disconnect rear wiper motor connector. Connect a fused jumper wire between positive battery terminal and Blue/Green wire terminal at wiper motor. Connect another jumper wire between ground and Blue/Black wire terminal at wiper motor. If wiper motor does not run, replace wiper motor.

WASHER PUMP

Front Pump – Disconnect front washer pump connector. Connect Black wire terminal of pump to ground. Connect Blue/Orange wire terminal to battery voltage. Replace washer pump if it does not run.

Rear Pump – Disconnect rear washer pump connector. Connect Orange wire terminal of pump to ground. Connect Blue/Pink wire terminal to battery voltage. Replace washer pump if it does not run.

WIPER/WASHER SWITCH

Disconnect appropriate wiper/washer switch connector. *See Figs. 3 and 4.* Resistance should be less than 5 ohms between specified switch terminals with switch in specified position. See WIPER/WASHER SWITCH TEST table. Replace switch if necessary.

WIPER/WASHER SWITCH TEST

Switch Position	Check Continuity Between Terminals
Front Wiper/Washer [1]	
1 (Low Speed)	3 & 6
2 (High Speed)	3 & 5
Mist	3 & 5
Wash (Pull)	2 & 3
Rear Wiper/Washer [2]	
On	1 & 3
Mist	2 & 3
Wash	1, 2 & 3

[1] – Measure resistance between terminals at multifunction switch 6-pin connector. *See Fig. 3.*

[2] – Measure resistance between terminals at multifunction switch 3-pin connector. *See Fig. 4.*

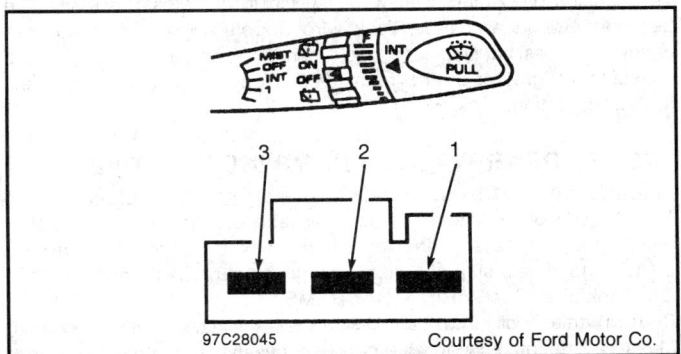

Fig. 3: Identifying Wiper/Washer Switch Terminals (Front)

97C28045   Courtesy of Ford Motor Co.

Fig. 4: Identifying Wiper/Washer Switch Terminals (Rear)

SYSTEM TESTING

WARNING: Deactivate air bag system before performing any service operation involving steering column components. See AIR BAG RESTRAINT SYSTEMS – ESCORT & TRACER article. Do not apply electrical power to any component on steering column without first deactivating air bag system. Air bag may deploy.

CAUTION: When battery is disconnected or modules are replaced, vehicle computer and memory systems may lose memory data. Driveability problems may exist until computer systems have completed a relearn cycle. See COMPUTER RELEARN PROCEDURES article in GENERAL INFORMATION before disconnecting battery.

NOTE: Before beginning system tests, perform TROUBLE SHOOTING.

Verify the customer complaint by operating power mirror. Visually inspect for obvious sign of mechanical and electrical damage. If no visual damage is evident, perform appropriate system test. See SYSTEM TEST INDEX table. A digital volt-ohmmeter is required to test the power mirror system. See WIRING DIAGRAMS for terminal numbers.

SYSTEM TEST INDEX

Symptom	Perform
Front Wipers Inoperative	TEST A
Front Wipers Stay On Constantly	TEST B
Front Wiper Inoperative At High Speed	TEST C
Front Wiper Inoperative At Low Speed	Replace Multifunction Switch
Front Wiper Intermittent Speed Inoperative	Replace Multifunction Switch
Front Wiper Will Not Park	TEST D
Front Washer Pump Inoperative	TEST E
Front Wash/Wipe Function Inoperative	[1] Replace Multifunction Switch
Front Mist Function Inoperative	Replace Multifunction Switch
Rear Wipers Inoperative	TEST F
Rear Washer Pump Inoperative	TEST G
Rear Wipers Stay On Constantly	TEST H
Rear Wiper Will Not Park	Replace Rear Wiper Motor

[1] – If washer pump is inoperative, replace multifunction switch. If washer pump operates, go to TEST E.

TEST A: FRONT WIPERS INOPERATIVE

1) Check WIPER fuse (20-amp) in central junction box. If fuse is okay, go to next step. If fuse is blown, inspect Blue wire between central junction box and wiper switch, and between central junction box and wiper motor, for short to ground. Repair Blue wire as necessary. If wire is okay, replace fuse and go to next step.

2) Turn ignition off. Measure resistance between ground and wiper motor harness connector terminal No. 3 (Black wire). *See Fig. 5.* If resistance is less than 5 ohms, go to next step. If resistance is greater than 5 ohms, repair Black wire between wiper motor harness connector and ground. See WIRING DIAGRAMS.

3) Disconnect wiper/washer switch 6-pin connector at multifunction switch. Turn ignition on. Measure voltage between ground and wiper/washer switch connector terminal No. 3 (Blue wire). *See Fig. 6.* If battery voltage is present, go to next step. If battery voltage is not present, repair Blue wire between wiper/washer switch connector and central junction box. See WIRING DIAGRAMS.

4) Measure resistance of Black wire between wiper washer switch 6-pin harness connector terminal No. 1 and ground. If resistance is less than

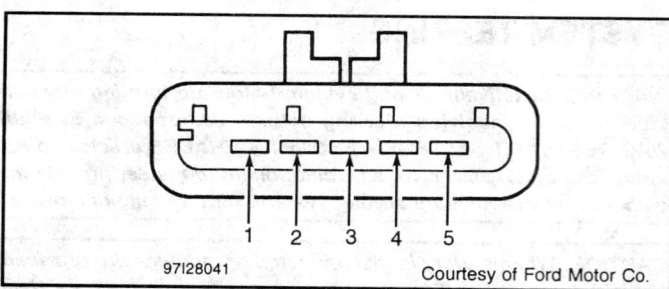

Fig. 5: Identifying Wiper Motor Harness Connector Terminals (Front)

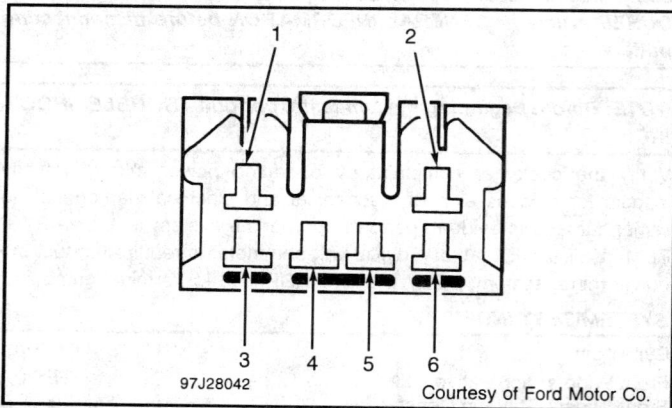

Fig. 6: Identifying Wiper/Washer Switch Harness Connector Terminals (Front)

5 ohms, go to next step. If resistance is greater than 5 ohms, repair open Black wire between wiper/washer switch harness connector and ground. See WIRING DIAGRAMS.

5) Perform wiper/washer switch test. See WIPER/WASHER SWITCH under COMPONENT TESTS. Replace switch as necessary. If switch is okay, test wiper motor. See WIPER MOTOR under COMPONENT TESTS. Replace wiper motor as necessary.

TEST B: FRONT WIPERS STAY ON CONSTANTLY

1) Turn ignition off. Disconnect wiper/washer switch 6-pin connector at multifunction switch. Turn ignition on. If wipers turn off, replace multifunction switch. If wipers do not turn off, go to next step.

2) Turn ignition off. Disconnect wiper motor. Turn ignition on. Measure voltage between ground and wiper/washer switch harness connector terminals No. 5 and 6. If any voltage is present, repair suspect circuit for short to power. If no voltage exists, replace wiper motor.

TEST C: FRONT WIPERS INOPERATIVE AT HIGH SPEED

1) Turn ignition off. Disconnect wiper motor connector. Turn ignition on. Set wiper switch for high speed operation (position 2). Measure voltage between ground and wiper motor harness connector terminal No. 5 (Red wire). *See Fig. 5.* If battery voltage is present, test front wiper motor. See WIPER MOTOR under COMPONENT TESTS. If battery voltage is not present, go to next step.

2) Perform wiper/washer switch test. See WIPER/WASHER SWITCH under COMPONENT TESTS. Replace switch if necessary. If switch is okay, repair open Red wire between switch and wiper motor harness connector.

TEST D: FRONT WIPERS WILL NOT PARK PROPERLY

1) Turn ignition off. Disconnect wiper motor connector. Turn ignition on. Measure voltage between ground and wiper motor harness connector terminal No. 2 (Blue wire). *See Fig. 5.* If battery voltage is present, go to next step. If battery voltage is not present, repair open Blue wire between wiper motor harness connector and central junction box. See WIRING DIAGRAMS.

2) Turn ignition off. Disconnect wiper/washer switch harness connector. Measure resistance of Blue/Yellow wire between wiper motor harness connector terminal No. 1 and wiper/washer switch harness connector terminal No. 4. *See Figs. 5 and 6.* If resistance is less than 5 ohms, go to next step. If resistance is 5 ohms or more, repair open in Blue/Yellow wire. See WIRING DIAGRAMS.

3) Measure resistance between wiper/washer switch harness connector terminal No. 4 (Blue/Yellow wire) and ground. If resistance is greater than 10 k/ohms, go to next step. If resistance is less than 10 k/ohms, repair open Blue/Yellow wire.

4) Perform wiper/washer switch test. See WIPER/WASHER SWITCH under COMPONENT TESTS. Replace switch as necessary. If switch is okay, repair Blue/Yellow wire. See WIRING DIAGRAMS.

TEST E: FRONT WASHER PUMP INOPERATIVE

1) Turn ignition off. Disconnect washer pump motor 2-pin connector. Turn ignition on. Measure voltage between ground and washer pump motor harness connector Blue/Orange wire while pulling wiper/washer switch toward steering wheel. If battery voltage is present, go to next step. If battery voltage is not present, go to step **3)**.

2) Turn ignition off. Measure resistance between ground and washer pump motor harness connector Black wire. If resistance is less than 5 ohms, check connections and replace washer pump motor. If resistance is greater than 5 ohms, repair open Black wire between washer pump motor harness connector and ground. See WIRING DIAGRAMS.

3) Perform wiper/washer switch test. See WIPER/WASHER SWITCH under COMPONENT TESTS. Replace switch if necessary. If switch is okay, repair Blue/Orange wire between switch and washer pump motor. See WIRING DIAGRAMS.

TEST F: REAR WIPER INOPERATIVE

1) Inspect RR WIPER fuse (10-amp) in central junction box. If fuse is okay, go to next step. If fuse is blown, check Blue/Pink wire for short to ground before replacing fuse. Repair wiring as necessary and retest system. See WIRING DIAGRAMS.

2) Turn ignition off. Disconnect 3-pin rear wiper/washer switch connector from multifunction switch assembly. Measure resistance between ground and Black wire at rear wiper/washer switch harness connector. If resistance is less than 5 ohms, go to next step. If resistance is 5 ohms or more, repair open in Black wire.

3) Disconnect rear wiper motor. Turn ignition on. Measure voltage between Blue/Pink wire at rear wiper motor harness connector and ground. If battery voltage is present, go to next step. If battery voltage is not present, repair open Blue/Pink wire. See WIRING DIAGRAMS.

4) Perform rear wiper switch test. See WIPER/WASHER SWITCH under COMPONENT TESTS. Replace switch if necessary. If switch is okay, go to next step.

5) Reconnect rear wiper switch harness connector (if disconnected). Turn ignition off. Rotate rear wiper switch to on. Measure resistance between ground and Blue/Black wire at rear wiper motor harness connector. If resistance is less than 5 ohms, replace rear wiper motor. If resistance is greater than 5 ohms, repair open Blue/Black wire. Test system operation.

TEST G: REAR WASHER PUMP INOPERATIVE

1) Turn ignition off. Disconnect rear washer pump motor 2-pin connector. Turn ignition on. Measure voltage between ground and rear washer pump motor harness connector Blue/Pink wire. If battery voltage is present, go to next step. If battery voltage is not present, repair open in Blue/Pink wire. See WIRING DIAGRAMS.

2) Turn ignition off. Turn rear wiper/washer switch to wash position. Measure resistance between ground and washer pump motor harness connector Orange wire. If resistance is less than 5 ohms, replace washer pump motor. If resistance is greater than 5 ohms, test wiper/washer switch. See WIPER/WASHER SWITCH under COMPONENT TESTS. Replace switch as necessary. If switch is okay, repair Orange wire between switch and washer pump motor. See WIRING DIAGRAMS.

TEST H: REAR WIPER WILL NOT TURN OFF

1) Turn ignition off. Disconnect rear wiper/washer switch 3-pin harness connector at multifunction switch. Turn ignition on. If rear wiper operation stops, replace rear wiper switch. If wiper continues to operate, go to next step.

2) Turn ignition off. Disconnect rear wiper motor connector. Measure resistance between Blue/Black wire at rear wiper motor harness connector and ground. If resistance is more than 10 k/ohms, replace wiper motor. If resistance is 10 k/ohms or less, repair short to ground in Blue/Black wire.

REMOVAL & INSTALLATION

WARNING: Deactivate air bag system before performing any service operation involving steering column components. See AIR BAG RESTRAINT SYSTEMS – ESCORT & TRACER article. Do not apply electrical power to any component on steering column without first deactivating air bag system. Air bag may deploy.

WASHER RESERVOIR & PUMP

Removal & Installation (Rear) – Washer reservoir/pump assembly is located behind right rear quarter trim panel. Disconnect negative battery cable. Remove right rear quarter trim panel. Remove reservoir mounting bolts. Pull reservoir straight up and remove. To install, reverse removal procedure.

WIPER MOTOR

Removal & Installation (Front) – 1) Park wipers. Disconnect negative battery cable. Remove wiper arm nut cover and nut. Remove wiper arm. Raise and support hood. Remove cowl top vent grille. Remove clip from wiper mounting arm and pivot shaft then slide mounting arm and pivot shaft off wiper motor. Disconnect wiper motor electrical connector. Remove wiper motor mounting bolts and motor.

2) To install, reverse removal procedure. Ensure wiper motor is in park position before connecting wiper mounting arm and pivot shaft.

Removal & Installation (Rear) – Disconnect negative battery cable. Remove wiper arm nut cover and nut. Remove wiper arm. Remove liftgate trim panel and watershield. Disconnect wiper motor electrical connector. Remove wiper motor mounting bolts and motor. To install, reverse removal procedure.

WIPER/WASHER SWITCH

Removal & Installation – Disconnect negative battery cable and wait one minute for air bag back-up power supply to be depleted. Remove upper and lower steering column shrouds. Remove 2 wiper/washer switch mounting screws. Disconnect switch electrical connectors and remove switch. To install, reverse removal procedure.

TORQUE SPECIFICATIONS

TORQUE SPECIFICATIONS

Application	Ft. Lbs. (N.m)
Wiper Pivot Arm Nut (Front)	12-14 (16–19)

	INCH Lbs. (N.m)
Wiper Pivot Arm Nut (Rear)	62-79 (6-9)
Wiper Motor Bolts	62-79 (6-9)
Washer Reservoir Bolts	62-79 (7-9)

WIRING DIAGRAMS

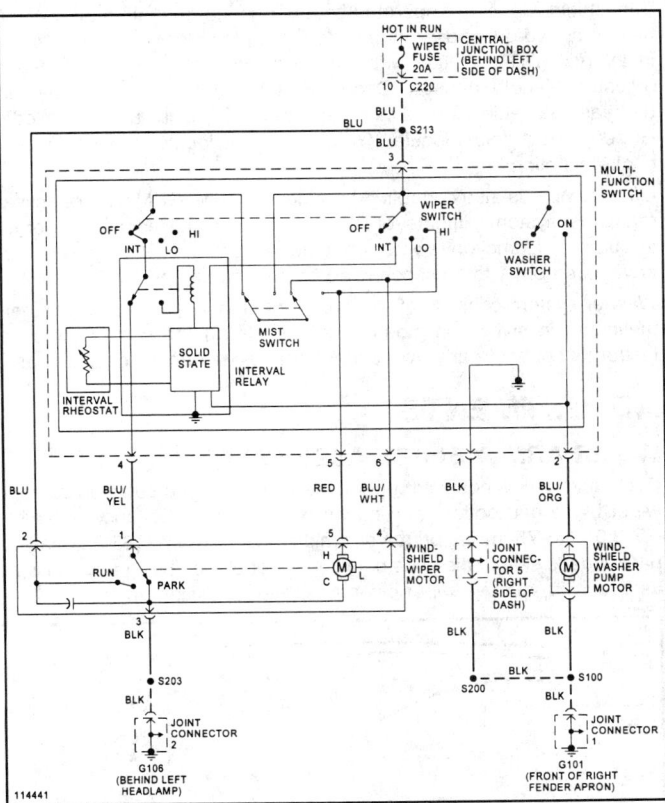

Fig. 7: Front Wiper/Washer System Wiring Diagram (Escort & Tracer)

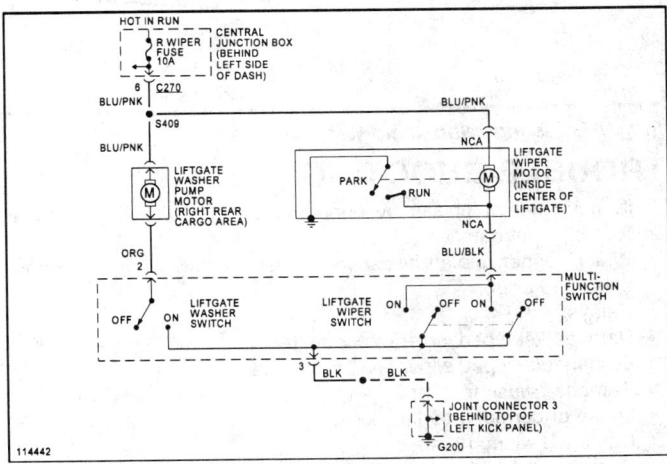

Fig. 8: Rear Wiper/Washer System Wiring Diagram (Escort & Tracer)

DESCRIPTION & OPERATION

Windshield wipers are operated by a permanent-magnet motor. Wipers have a speed dependent interval feature. When wiper control switch is in interval (INT) position, wipers make single sweeps, separated by adjustable-length pauses. Once set, interval time will automatically decrease as vehicle speed increases. Wiper functions are controlled by Generic Electronic Module (GEM). GEM is located on backside of central junction box.

Liftgate wiper is also controlled through the GEM. GEM will not activate rear wiper system if liftgate, or liftgate glass, is ajar. Rear wiper operates through multifunction switch on steering column. Wipers will cycle anywhere from 1 to 10 seconds apart, depending upon switch position.

Washer system consists of reservoir mounted in engine compartment, multifunction switch on steering column (front), or washer switch on instrument panel (rear), low washer fluid indicator and necessary hoses.

ADJUSTMENTS

WIPER ARM & BLADE ASSEMBLY

Cycle and park windshield wipers. Measure distance between center of wiper blade and bottom of windshield. See Fig. 1. Distance should be 1.7-3.0" (45-75 mm) for driver's side, and 2.6-3.7" (65-93 mm) for passenger's side. If distance between wiper blade and windshield is not as specified, remove wiper pivot arms and reposition arms.

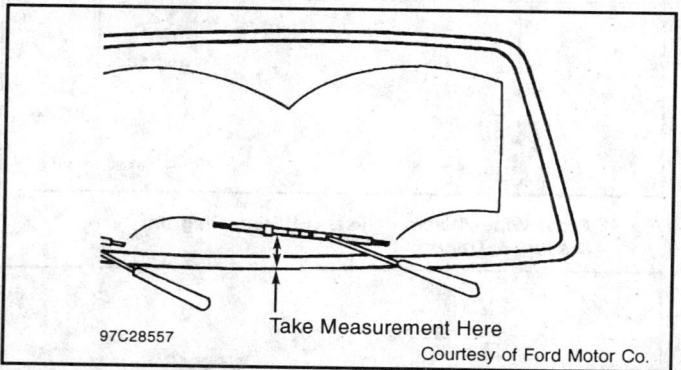

Take Measurement Here

97C28557

Courtesy of Ford Motor Co.

Fig. 1: Adjusting Windshield Wiper Blades

TROUBLE SHOOTING

Verify customer complaint by operating system. Visually inspect for obvious signs of damage:

- Wiper/washer related fuses No: 6 (5-amp), 8 (5-amp), 15 (5-amp), and 20 (5-amp).
- Relays.
- Damaged/stripped wiper motor shaft.
- Damaged/stripped wiper pivot arm shaft.
- Damaged washer pump.
- Loose or corroded connections.
- Damaged wiring harness.
- Binding windshield wiper pivot arm.
- Inoperative multifunction switch.

Correct any obvious problems before continuing testing. If problem still exists, go to SELF-DIAGNOSTICS.

COMPONENT TESTS

WIPER MOTOR

Disengage linkage from motor. Disconnect front wiper motor connector. Connect ammeter between battery negative terminal and wiper motor terminal No. 3 (Black wire). For mating connector view, see Fig. 2. Apply battery voltage to wiper motor terminal No. 4 (White wire) for low speed operation. For high speed operation apply battery voltage to wiper motor terminal No. 5 (Dark Blue/Orange wire). Current draw with wiper linkage disconnected should not exceed 3.5 amps at low speed and 5.5 amps at high speed.

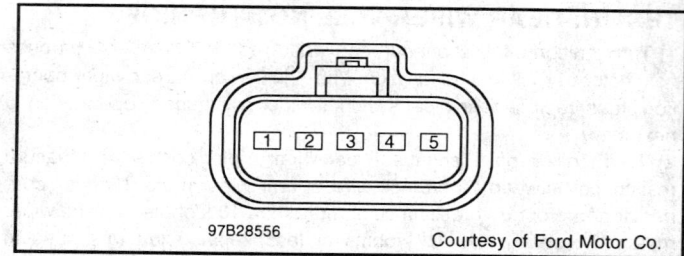

97B28556

Courtesy of Ford Motor Co.

Fig. 2: Identifying Front Wiper Motor Connector Terminals

WIPER SWITCH

Wiper switch is incorporated into multifunction switch on steering column and is not serviced separately. Replace multifunction switch if wiper switch resistance is not as specified. See WIPER SWITCH RESISTANCE TEST table. See Fig. 7.

WIPER SWITCH RESISTANCE TEST

Switch Position	Terminals	[1] k/ohms
Front Wiper		
Off	589 & 993	47.6
INT	589 & 993	11.33
Low	589 & 993	4.08
High	589 & 993	0
WASH		
On	590 & 993	0
Off	590 & 993	103.3
INT [2]		
MIN	590 & 993	3.3
MAX	590 & 993	103.3
Rear Wiper		
OFF	380 & 993	2.9
INT 1	380 & 993	1
INT 2	380 & 993	0.33
WASH	380 & 993	[3]

[1] – Values are approximate.
[2] – Rotate (INT) interval knob from minimum to maximum. Resistance should gradually increase from 3.3 k/ohms (MIN) to 103.3 k/ohms (MAX).
[3] – Less than 5 ohms.

WIPER RELAYS

Remove relay to be tested. Wiper relays are located in engine compartment battery junction box. Measure resistance between relay terminal No. 2 and all other terminals. See Fig. 3. If resistance is 5 ohms or less between relay terminal No. 2 and any other terminal, replace relay. If relay is okay, connect jumper wire between relay terminal No. 3 and battery positive terminal. Measure voltage between relay terminal No. 4 and ground. If battery voltage is not present, replace relay. If battery voltage is present, connect a second wire between relay terminal No. 1 and battery positive terminal. Connect a third jumper wire between relay terminal No. 2 and ground. Measure voltage between relay terminal No. 5 and ground. If battery voltage is not present, replace relay, If battery voltage is present, relay is okay.

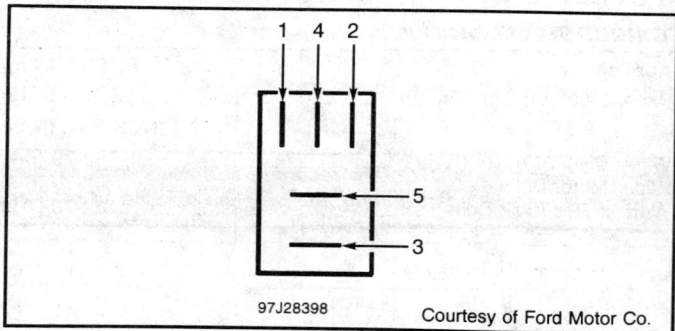

97J28398

Courtesy of Ford Motor Co.

Fig. 3: Identifying Relay Terminals

SELF-DIAGNOSTIC SYSTEM

NOTE: For further information on self-diagnostic system, see MODULE COMMUNICATIONS NETWORK – EXPEDITION & NAVIGATOR article.

The wiper/washers utilize a self-diagnostic system which may store a Diagnostic Trouble Code (DTC) if a problem exists in the system. DTCs may be retrieved using New Generation STAR (NGS) tester and Data Link Connector (DLC) for diagnosis of system. Before performing any testing, a preliminary procedure should be performed. See TROUBLE SHOOTING.

SELF-DIAGNOSTICS

1) If all components are okay, connect New Generation STAR (NGS) tester to DLC located below instrument panel. Using NGS tester, perform DATA LINK DIAGNOSTIC TEST. If NGS tester displays CKT914, CKT915 or CKT70 = ALL ECUS NO RESP/NOT EQUIP, see MODULE COMMUNICATIONS NETWORK – EXPEDITION & NAVIGATOR article to diagnosis network concern. If NGS tester displays NO RESPONSE/NOT EQUIPPED for Generic Electronic Module (GEM), perform TEST M: NO COMMUNICATION WITH MODULE under SYSTEM TESTS.

2) If NGS tester displays SYSTEM PASSED, retrieve and record continuous DTCs. Erase continuous DTCs. Perform self-test diagnostics for GEM using NGS tester. If GEM DTCs are retrieved, see GEM DTC TEST INDEX table to continue diagnosis. If no DTCs are retrieved, see SYMPTOM TEST INDEX under SYSTEM TESTS.

GEM DTC TEST INDEX

DTC [1]	Description	Test
B1240	Rear Washer Pump Relay Coil Circuit Failure	J
B1241	Rear Washer Pump Relay Coil Short To Power	J
B1342	GEM Is Defective	[2]
B1431	Front Wiper Brake/Run Relay Circuit Failure	A
B1432	Front Wiper Brake/Run Relay Short To Power	A
B1434	Front Wiper Hi/Low Speed Relay Circuit Failure	C
B1436	Front Wiper Hi/Low Speed Relay Circuit Short To Power	C
B1438	Front Wiper Mode Select Switch Circuit Failure	A
B1441	Front Wiper Mode Select Switch Input Short To Ground	A
B1446	Front Wiper Park Sense Circuit Failure	D
B1450	Front Wiper/Wash Interval Delay Switch Input Circuit Failure	A
B1453	Front Wiper/Wash Interval Delay Switch Input Short To Ground	A
B1454	Low Washer Fluid Indicator Circuit Failure	L
B1456	Low Washer Fluid Indicator Circuit Short To Power	L
B1458	Front Wiper/Washer Pump Motor Relay Circuit Failure	E
B1460	Front Wiper/Washer Pump Motor Relay Coil Short To Power	E
B1466	Front Wiper Hi/Low Speed Not Switching	C
B1473	Front Wiper Motor Low Speed Circuit Failure	C
B1476	Front Wiper Motor High Speed Circuit Failure	C
B1611	Rear Wiper Mode Select Switch Circuit Failure	G
B1614	Rear Wiper Mode Select Switch Circuit Short To Ground	K
B1814	Rear Wiper Motor Down Relay Circuit Failure	G
B1816	Rear Wiper Motor Down Relay Coil Circuit Short To Power	G
B1818	Rear Wiper Motor Up Relay Coil Circuit Failure	G
B1820	Rear Wiper Motor Up Relay Circuit Short To Power	G
B1839	Rear Wiper Motor Circuit Failure	H
B1840	Front Wiper Power Circuit Failure	A
B1894	Rear Wiper Motor Speed Sense Circuit Failure	G
P0500	Vehicle Speed Signal Circuit Failure	F

[1] – Codes listed in this table are only for testing covered in this article. For complete DTC listing, see MODULE COMMUNICATIONS NETWORK – EXPEDITION & NAVIGATOR article.

[2] – Using NGS tester clear DTCs. Retrieve DTCs. If DTC B1342 is retrieved, replace GEM. See GENERIC ELECTRONIC MODULE under REMOVAL & INSTALLATION.

SYSTEM TESTS

CAUTION: Disconnect the battery before disconnecting Generic Electronic Module (GEM) connectors. Failure to do so will result in GEM storing erroneous codes and may also result in erratic operation of GEM after reconnection.

NOTE: If continuous DTCs are recorded and the symptom is not present during pinpoint testing, the problem may be intermittent. Always check for loose connections and corroded terminals.

SYMPTOM TEST INDEX

Symptom	Test
Front Wipers Inoperative	A

SYMPTOM TEST INDEX (Cont.)

Symptom	Test
Front Wipers Stay On Continuously	B
Front Wipers Operate At Interval Setting, But Inoperative At High &/Or Low Speed	C
Front Wipers Inoperative At Interval Setting, But Operate At High & Low Speed	D
Front Washer Pump Inoperative	E
Front Wiper Speed Dependent Interval Mode Not Operating Properly	F
Rear Wipers Inoperative	G
Rear Wiper Will Not Park Properly	H
Rear Washer Pump Inoperative	J
Rear Wiper Stays On Continuously	K
Low Washer Fluid Indicator Does Not Operate Properly	L

SYMPTOM TEST INDEX (Cont.)

Symptom	Test
No Scan Tool Communication With GEM	M

TEST A: FRONT WIPERS INOPERATIVE

NOTE: After repair is completed, clear Diagnostic Trouble Codes (DTCs) and recheck system for proper operation.

1) Turn ignition on. Measure voltage at output side of fuse No. 15 (5-amp) at central junction box (interior fuse panel) . If voltage is 10 volts or more, go to next step. If voltage is less than 10 volts, replace fuse as necessary, or repair open to fuse input terminal. See WIRING DIAGRAMS. Recheck system operation. If fuse blows again, check for short to ground. Repair as necessary.
2) Turn ignition off. Using scan tool, access GEM PIDS IGN_A, IGN_R, IGN_S and IGN_O/L. Observe scan tool while turning ignition switch through all positions. If PID agrees with switch positions, go to next step. If PID does not agree with switch positions, repair circuit(s) between ignition switch and instrument panel fuse block. See appropriate wiring diagrams in POWER DISTRIBUTION article in WIRING DIAGRAMS.
3) Using scan tool retrieve and note any continuous DTCs for Generic Electronic Module (GEM). Clear continuous DTCs. Perform ON-DEMAND SELF-TEST. If no DTCs exist, go to step **5)**. If any DTCs exist, go to appropriate test step and continue diagnosis. See TEST A DTC INDEX table.

TEST A DTC INDEX

DTC	Step
B1342	[1]
B1431	12)
B1432	12)
B1438	5)
B1441	5)
B1450	5)
B1453	5)
B1840	4)

[1] – Replace GEM. See GENERIC ELECTRONIC MODULE under REMOVAL & INSTALLATION.

4) Turn ignition off. Remove wiper high/low relay and wiper run/park relay. Relays are in battery junction box located in engine compartment above left wheelwell. Turn ignition on. Measure voltage between each relay connector terminal No. 1 and ground. *See Fig. 4.* If voltage is more than 10 volts at each terminal, reinstall relays and go to next step. If voltage is 10 volts or less at either terminal, repair White/Black wire(s) as necessary. See WIRING DIAGRAMS.
5) Turn ignition on. Using scan tool, access GEM PID WPMODE. Observe scan tool while turning wiper switch through all positions. If PID agrees with all switch positions, go to step **12)**. If PID does not agree with all switch positions, go to next step.
6) Turn ignition off. Disconnect multifunction switch 7-pin connector C259. Check wiper switch portion of multifunction switch. See WIPER SWITCH under COMPONENT TESTS. Replace switch as necessary. If switch is okay, go to next step.
7) Disconnect GEM 26-pin connector C239. GEM is located on backside of central junction box (interior fuse panel). Disconnect multifunction switch 7-pin connector C259. Measure resistance between GEM connector C239 terminal No. 13 and multifunction switch connector C259 terminal No. 590. *See Figs. 5 and 6.* If resistance is less than 5 ohms, go to next step. If resistance is 5 ohms or more, repair open in Light Blue/Orange wire.
8) Measure resistance between GEM connector C239 terminal No. 21 and multifunction switch connector C259 terminal No. 993. *See Figs. 5 and 6.* If resistance is less than 5 ohms, go to next step. If resistance is 5 ohms or more, repair open in Dark Blue wire.
9) Measure resistance between GEM connector C239 terminal No. 22 and multifunction switch connector C259 terminal No. 685. *See Figs. 5 and 6.* If resistance is less than 5 ohms, go to next step. If resistance is 5 ohms or more, repair open in Pink/Yellow wire.

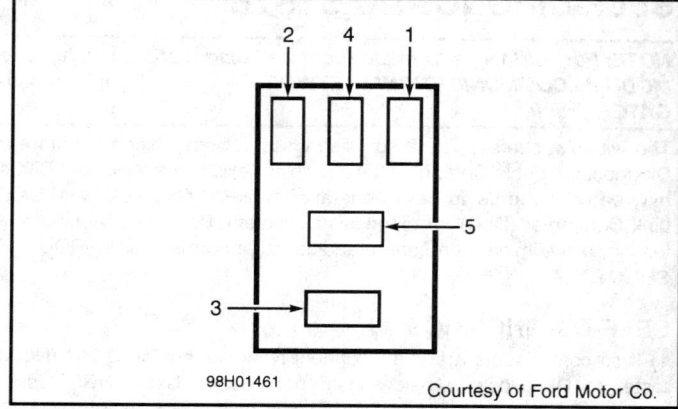

Fig. 4: Identifying Relay Connector Terminals

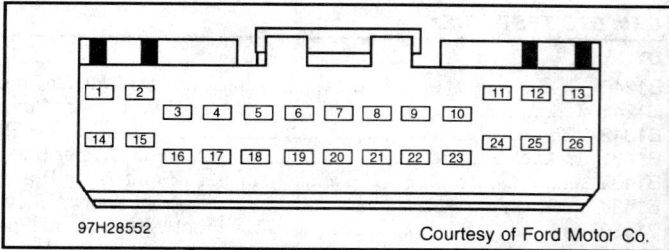

Fig. 5: Identifying GEM 26-Pin Connector C239 Terminals

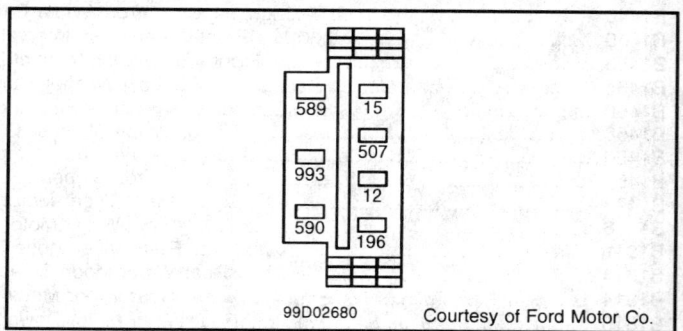

Fig. 6: Identifying Multifunction Switch 7-Pin Connector C259 Terminals

10) Turn ignition on. Measure voltage between GEM connector C239 terminal No. 13 and ground. *See Fig. 5.* If voltage is present, repair Light Blue/Orange wire short to voltage. If no voltage is present, go to next step.
11) Measure voltage between GEM connector C239 terminal No. 22 and ground. *See Fig. 5.* If voltage is present, repair Pink/Yellow wire short to voltage. If no voltage is present, replace the GEM. See GENERIC ELECTRONIC MODULE under REMOVAL & INSTALLATION.
12) Using scan tool, access GEM PID WPRUN. Observe scan tool while toggling active command mode WIPER RLY to ON and OFF. If WPRUN values agree with command mode and displays ON- - - and OFF- - -, go to step **18)**. If WPRUN values do not agree with command mode and displays OFFO-G, go to next step. If WPRUN values do not agree with command mode and displays ON-B-, go to step **16)**.
13) Turn ignition off. Remove wiper run/park relay. Relay is located in engine compartment battery junction box. Turn ignition on. Measure voltage between wiper run/park relay connector terminal No. 1 and ground. *See Fig. 4.* If voltage is more than 10 volts, go to next step. If voltage is 10 volts or less, repair White/Black wire.
14) Turn ignition off. Check wiper run/park relay. See WIPER RELAYS under COMPONENT TESTS. Replace relay as necessary. If relay is okay, go to next step.
15) Disconnect GEM 26-pin connector C239. Measure resistance between GEM connector C239 terminal No. 19 and wiper run/park relay

connector terminal No. 2. *See Figs. 4 and 5.* If resistance is less than 5 ohms, replace GEM. See GENERIC ELECTRONIC MODULE under REMOVAL & INSTALLATION. If resistance is 5 ohms or more, repair open in Yellow/White wire.

16) Turn ignition off. Check wiper run/park relay. See WIPER RELAYS under COMPONENT TESTS. Replace relay as necessary. If relay is okay, replace GEM. See GENERIC ELECTRONIC MODULE under REMOVAL & INSTALLATION.

17) Disconnect GEM 26-pin connector C239. Disconnect wiper run/park relay. Turn ignition on. Measure voltage between wiper run/park relay connector terminal No. 2 and ground. *See Fig. 4.* If any voltage is present, repair Yellow/White wire short to voltage. If no voltage is present, replace the wiper run/park relay.

18) Turn ignition off. Disconnect wiper high/low relay. Turn ignition on. Using scan tool, set active command mode WIPER RLY to ON. Measure voltage between high/low relay connector terminal No. 3 (Red wire) and ground. *See Fig. 4.* If voltage is 10 volts or less, go to next step. If voltage is more than 10 volts, go to step **21)**.

19) Turn ignition off. Disconnect wiper run/park relay. Measure resistance between wiper run/park relay connector terminal No. 3 and wiper high/low relay connector terminal No. 3. *See Fig. 4.* If resistance is less than 5 ohms, go to next step. If resistance is 5 ohms or more, repair open in Red wire.

20) Turn ignition on. Measure voltage between wiper run/park relay connector terminal No. 5 and ground. *See Fig. 4.* If voltage is more than 10 volts, replace wiper run/park relay. If voltage is 10 volts or less, repair White/Black wire.

21) Turn ignition on. Using scan tool, set active command WIPER RLY to ON. Connect a jumper wire between wiper high/low relay connector terminal No. 3 and terminal No. 5, or terminal No. 4. *See Fig. 4.* If wipers do not operate, go to next step. If wipers operate, replace high/low relay.

22) Turn ignition off. Disconnect wiper motor connector. Measure resistance between wiper motor connector terminal No. 3 and ground. *See Fig. 2.* If resistance is less than 5 ohms, go to next step. If resistance is 5 ohms or more, repair open in Black wire.

23) Remove wiper linkage from wiper motor. Check wiper linkage for free operation. If linkage is free of binding and operational resistance, check wiper motor. See WIPER MOTOR under COMPONENT TESTS. Replace wiper motor as necessary. If linkage does not operate freely, repair as necessary. Reconnect linkage.

TEST B: FRONT WIPERS STAY ON CONTINUOUSLY

NOTE: After repair is completed, clear Diagnostic Trouble Codes (DTCs) and recheck system for proper operation.

1) Turn ignition off. Observe scan tool GEM PIDS IGN_A, IGN_R, IGN_S and IGN_O/L while operating ignition switch through all positions. If PID values agree with switch positions, go to next step. If PID values do not agree with switch positions, repair circuit(s) between ignition switch and central junction box. See appropriate wiring diagrams in POWER DISTRIBUTION article in WIRING DIAGRAMS.

2) Using scan tool retrieve and note any continuous DTCs for Generic Electronic Module (GEM). Clear continuous DTCs. Perform ON-DEMAND SELF-TEST. If no DTCs exist, go to next step. If any DTCs exist, go to appropriate test step and continue diagnosis. See TEST B DTC INDEX table.

TEST B DTC INDEX

DTC	Step
B1342	1
B1431	7)
B1441	3)
B1453	3)

1 – Replace GEM. See GENERIC ELECTRONIC MODULE under REMOVAL & INSTALLATION.

3) Turn ignition on. Using scan tool, access GEM PID WPMODE. Observe scan tool while turning wiper switch through all positions. If PID values agree with all switch positions, go to step **7)**. If PID values do not agree with all switch positions, go to next step.

4) Turn ignition off. Disconnect multifunction switch 7-pin connector C259. Check wiper switch portion of multifunction switch. See WIPER SWITCH under COMPONENT TESTS. Replace switch as necessary. If switch is okay, go to next step.

5) Disconnect GEM 26-pin connector C239. GEM is located on backside of central junction box (interior fuse panel). Measure resistance between multifunction switch connector C259 terminal No. 590 and ground. *See Fig. 6.* If resistance is more than 10 k/ohms, go to next step. If resistance is 10 k/ohms or less, repair Light Blue/Orange wire short to ground.

6) Measure resistance between multifunction switch connector C259 terminal No. 589 and ground. *See Fig. 6.* If resistance is more than 10 k/ohms, replace GEM. See GENERIC ELECTRONIC MODULE under REMOVAL & INSTALLATION. If resistance is 10 k/ohms or less, repair Pink/Yellow wire short to ground.

7) Using scan tool, observe GEM PID WPRUN while toggling active command mode WIPER RLY to ON and OFF. If WPRUN values agree with command mode and displays ON- - - and OFF- - -, go to step **10)**. If WPRUN values do not agree with command mode and display OFFO-G, go to next step.

8) Turn ignition off. Remove wiper run/park relay. Relay is located in engine compartment battery junction box. Check wiper run/park relay. See WIPER RELAYS under COMPONENT TESTS. Replace relay as necessary. If relay is okay, go to next step.

9) Disconnect GEM 26-pin connector C239. Measure resistance between wiper run/park relay connector terminal No. 2 and ground. *See Fig. 4.* If resistance is more than 10 k/ohms, replace GEM. See GENERIC ELECTRONIC MODULE under REMOVAL & INSTALLATION. If resistance is 10 k/ohms or less, repair Yellow/White wire short to ground.

10) Turn ignition on. Remove wiper run/park relay. Relay is located in engine compartment battery junction box. If wipers stop, go to step **13)**. If wipers do not stop, reinstall wiper run/park relay and go to next step.

11) Turn ignition off. Disconnect wiper motor connector. Disconnect wiper high/low relay. Relay is located in engine compartment battery junction box. Turn ignition on. Measure voltage between wiper high/low relay connector terminal No. 5 and ground. *See Fig. 4.* If any voltage is present, repair Dark Blue/Orange wire short to voltage. If no voltage is present, go to next step.

12) Measure voltage between wiper high/low relay connector terminal No. 4 and ground. *See Fig. 4.* If any voltage is present, repair White wire short to voltage. If no voltage is present, replace wiper motor. See FRONT WIPER MOTOR under REMOVAL & INSTALLATION.

13) Turn ignition on. Turn front wiper/washer switch to OFF position. Measure voltage between wiper run/park relay connector terminal No. 4 and ground. *See Fig. 4.* If voltage is more than 10 volts, go to next step. If voltage is 10 volts or less, replace wiper run/park relay.

14) Turn ignition off. Disconnect wiper motor connector. Turn ignition on. Measure voltage between wiper run/park relay connector terminal No. 4 and ground. *See Fig. 4.* If any voltage is present, repair Light Blue wire short to power. If no voltage is present, replace wiper motor. See FRONT WIPER MOTOR under REMOVAL & INSTALLATION.

TEST C: FRONT WIPERS OPERATE AT INTERVAL SETTING, BUT INOPERATIVE AT HIGH &/OR LOW SPEED

NOTE: After repair is completed, clear Diagnostic Trouble Codes (DTCs) and recheck system for proper operation.

1) Connect scan tool. Turn ignition on. Using scan tool retrieve and note any continuous DTCs for GEM. Clear continuous DTCs. Perform ON-DEMAND SELF-TEST. Perform WIPER SELF-TEST. If no DTCs exist, go to next step. If any DTCs exist, go to appropriate test step and continue diagnosis. See TEST C DTC INDEX table.

TEST C DTC INDEX

DTC	Step
B1342	1
B1434	8)

TEST C DTC INDEX (Cont.)

DTC	Step
B1436	8)
B1438	2)
B1450	2)
B1466	2)
B1473	2)
B1476	2)

[1] – Replace GEM. See GENERIC ELECTRONIC MODULE under REMOVAL & INSTALLATION.

2) Turn ignition on. Using scan tool, observe GEM PID WPMODE while turning wiper switch through all positions. If PID values agree with all switch positions, go to step **8)**. If PID values do not agree with all switch positions, go to next step.

3) Turn ignition off. Disconnect multifunction switch 7-pin connector C259. Check wiper switch portion of multifunction switch. See WIPER SWITCH under COMPONENT TESTS. Replace switch as necessary. If switch is okay, go to next step.

4) Disconnect GEM 26-pin connector C239. GEM is located on backside of central junction box (interior fuse panel). Measure resistance between GEM connector C239 terminal No. 13 and multifunction switch connector C259 terminal No. 590. See Figs. 5 and 6. If resistance is less than 5 ohms, go to next step. If resistance is 5 ohms or more, repair open in Light Blue/Orange wire.

5) Measure resistance between GEM connector C239 terminal No. 22 and multifunction switch connector C259 terminal No. 589. See Figs. 5 and 6. If resistance is less than 5 ohms, go to next step. If resistance is more than 5 ohms, repair open in Pink/Yellow wire.

6) Turn ignition on. Measure voltage between multifunction switch connector C259 terminal No. 590 and ground. See Fig. 6. If no voltage is present, go to next step. If voltage is present, repair Light Blue/Orange wire short to voltage.

7) Measure voltage between multifunction switch connector C259 terminal No. 589 and ground. See Fig. 6. If no voltage is present, replace GEM. See GENERIC ELECTRONIC MODULE under REMOVAL & INSTALLATION. If voltage is present, repair Pink/Yellow wire short to voltage.

8) Using scan tool, observe GEM PID WPHISP while toggling active command mode SPEED RLY ON and OFF. If WPHISP values agree with command mode and displays ON- - - and OFF- - -, go to step **15)**. If WPHISP values do not agree with command mode and displays OFFO-G, go to step **11)**. If WPHISP values do not agree with command mode and displays ON-B-, go to next step.

9) Turn ignition off. Check wiper high/low relay. See WIPER RELAYS under COMPONENT TESTS. Replace relay as necessary. If relay is okay, go to next step.

10) Remove wiper high/low relay. Relay is located in engine compartment battery junction box. Disconnect GEM 26-pin connector C239. GEM is located on backside of central junction box (interior fuse panel). Turn ignition on. Measure voltage between high/low relay connector terminal No. 2 and ground. See Fig. 4. If any voltage is present, repair Gray/Light Blue wire short to voltage. If no voltage is present, replace the GEM. See GENERIC ELECTRONIC MODULE under REMOVAL & INSTALLATION.

11) Turn ignition off. Remove wiper high/low relay. Relay is located in engine compartment battery junction box. Check high/low relay. See WIPER RELAYS under COMPONENT TESTS. Replace relay as necessary. If relay is okay, go to next step.

12) Turn ignition on. Measure voltage between wiper high/low relay connector terminal No. 1 and ground. See Fig. 4. If voltage is more than 10 volts, go to next step. If voltage is 10 volts or less, repair White/Black wire between central junction box and high/low relay.

13) Disconnect GEM 26-pin connector C239. GEM is located on backside of central junction box (interior fuse panel). Measure resistance between wiper high/low relay connector terminal No. 2 and ground. See Fig. 4. If resistance is more than 10 k/ohms, go to next step. If resistance is 10 k/ohms or less, repair Gray/Light Blue wire short to ground.

14) Measure resistance between wiper high/low relay connector terminal No. 2 and GEM connector C239 terminal No. 18. See Figs. 4 and 5. If resistance is less than 5 ohms, replace GEM. See GENERIC ELECTRONIC MODULE under REMOVAL & INSTALLATION. If resistance is 5 ohms or more, repair open in Gray/Light Blue wire.

15) Turn ignition off. Disconnect wiper high/low relay. Relay is located in engine compartment battery junction box. Turn ignition on. Set wiper/washer switch to high speed wiper position. Connect a jumper wire between wiper high/low relay terminals No. 3 and 5. See Fig. 4. Wipers should operate at high speed. Remove jumper wire. Set wiper/washer switch to low speed position. Connect jumper wire between wiper high/low relay terminals No. 3 and 4. Wipers should operate at low speed. If wipers operate as specified, replace wiper high/low relay. If wipers do not operate as specified, remove jumper wire and go to next step.

16) Turn ignition off. Disconnect wiper motor connector. Measure resistance between wiper motor connector terminal No. 5 and wiper high/low relay connector terminal No. 5. See Figs. 4 and 2. If resistance is less than 5 ohms, go to next step. If resistance is 5 ohms or more, repair open in Dark Blue/Orange wire.

17) Measure resistance between wiper high/low relay connector terminal No. 4 and wiper motor connector terminal No. 4. See Figs. 4 and 2. If resistance is less than 5 ohms, check wiper motor. See WIPER MOTOR under COMPONENT TESTS. Replace wiper motor as necessary. If resistance is 5 ohms or more, repair open in White wire.

TEST D: FRONT WIPERS INOPERATIVE AT INTERVAL SETTING, BUT OPERATE AT HIGH & LOW SPEED

NOTE: After repair is completed, clear Diagnostic Trouble Codes (DTCs) and recheck system for proper operation.

1) Using scan tool retrieve and note any continuous DTCs for GEM. Clear continuous DTCs. Perform ON-DEMAND SELF-TEST. Perform WIPER SELF-TEST. If no DTCs exist, go to next step. If any DTCs exist, go to appropriate test step and continue diagnosis. See TEST D DTC INDEX table.

TEST D DTC INDEX

DTC	Step
B1342	[1]
B1438	2)
B1441	2)
B1446	8)
B1450	2)
B1453	2)

[1] – Replace GEM. See GENERIC ELECTRONIC MODULE under REMOVAL & INSTALLATION.

2) Turn ignition on. Using scan tool, observe GEM PID WPMODE while turning wiper switch through all positions. If PID values agree with all switch positions, go to step **8)**. If PID values do not agree with all switch positions, go to next step.

3) Turn ignition off. Disconnect multifunction switch 7-pin connector C259. Check wiper switch portion of multifunction switch. See WIPER SWITCH under COMPONENT TESTS. Replace switch as necessary. If switch is okay, go to next step.

4) Turn ignition off. Disconnect GEM 26-pin connector C239. GEM is located on backside of central junction box (interior fuse panel). Measure resistance between GEM connector C239 terminal No. 13 and multifunction switch connector C259 terminal No. 590. See Figs. 5 and 6. If resistance is less than 5 ohms, go to next step. If resistance is greater than 5 ohms, repair open in Light Blue/Orange wire.

5) Measure resistance between multifunction switch connector C259 terminal No. 589 and GEM connector C239 terminal No. 22. See Figs. 5 and 6. If resistance is less than 5 ohms, go to next step. If resistance is 5 ohms or more, repair open in Pink/Yellow wire.

6) Turn ignition on. Measure voltage between multifunction switch connector C259 terminal No. 590 and ground. *See Fig. 6.* If any voltage is present, repair Light Blue/Orange wire short to voltage. If no voltage is present, go to next step.

7) Measure voltage between multifunction switch connector C259 terminal No. 589 and ground. *See Fig. 6.* If no voltage is present, replace GEM. See GENERIC ELECTRONIC MODULE under REMOVAL & INSTALLATION. If voltage is present, repair Pink/Yellow wire short to voltage.

NOTE: Scan tool record function feature must be used in the following step.

8) Turn ignition on. Set wiper/washer switch to low speed position. Observe scan tool and record PID WPPRKSW while wipers are operating. Use scan tool view recorder areas to view stored WPPRKSW graph. If PID WPPRKSW indicates PARKED when wipers are at park position, and notPRK when wipers are out of park position, replace GEM. See GENERIC ELECTRONIC MODULE under REMOVAL & INSTALLATION. If PID WPPRKSW does not indicate PARKED when wipers are at park position, and notPRK when wipers are out of park position, go to next step.

9) Turn ignition off. Disconnect wiper motor connector. Turn ignition on. Measure voltage between wiper motor connector terminal No. 2 and ground. *See Fig. 2.* If voltage is more than 10 volts, go to next step. If voltage is 10 volts or less, repair White/Black wire.

10) Turn ignition off. Disconnect GEM 26-pin connector C239. GEM is located on backside of central junction box (interior fuse panel). Measure resistance between wiper motor connector terminal No. 1 and GEM connector C239 terminal No. 15. *See Figs. 5 and 2.* If resistance is less than 5 ohms, reconnect GEM connector C239 and go to next step. If resistance is 5 ohms or more, repair open in Light Blue wire.

11) Turn ignition on. Using scan tool, observe GEM PID WPPRKSW. Connect jumper wire between wiper motor connector terminal No. 1 and ground. *See Fig. 2.* Note PID values. Remove jumper wire. Reconnect jumper wire between wiper motor connector terminal No. 1 and positive battery terminal. Note PID values. If PID WPPRKSW indicates PARKED when wiper motor connector terminal No. 1 is grounded, and not PRK when battery voltage is applied, replace wiper motor. See FRONT WIPER MOTOR under REMOVAL & INSTALLATION. If PID WPPRKSW does not indicate PARKED when motor connector terminal No. 1 is grounded, and not PRK when battery voltage is applied, replace GEM. See GENERIC ELECTRONIC MODULE under REMOVAL & INSTALLATION.

TEST E: FRONT WASHER PUMP IS INOPERATIVE

NOTE: After repair is completed, clear Diagnostic Trouble Codes (DTCs) and recheck system for proper operation.

1) Using scan tool retrieve and note any continuous DTCs for GEM. Clear continuous DTCs. Perform ON-DEMAND SELF-TEST. Perform WIPER SELF-TEST. If no DTCs exist, go to step 12). If any DTCs exist, go to appropriate test step and continue diagnosis. See TEST E DTC INDEX table.

TEST E DTC INDEX

DTC	Step
B1342	1
B1450	2)
B1458	5)
B1460	5)

1 – Replace GEM. See GENERIC ELECTRONIC MODULE under REMOVAL & INSTALLATION.

2) Turn ignition on. Using scan tool, observe GEM PID WPMODE while turning wiper switch through all positions and depressing washer switch. If PID values agree with all switch positions, go to step 5). If PID values do not agree with all switch positions, go to next step.

3) Turn ignition off. Disconnect multifunction switch 7-pin connector C259. Measure resistance between multifunction switch terminals No.

590 and 993 while depressing washer switch. *See Fig. 7.* If resistance is less than 5 ohms with switch depressed, and more than 10 k/ohms with switch released, go to next step. If resistance is not as specified, replace multifunction switch. See MULTIFUNCTION SWITCH under REMOVAL & INSTALLATION.

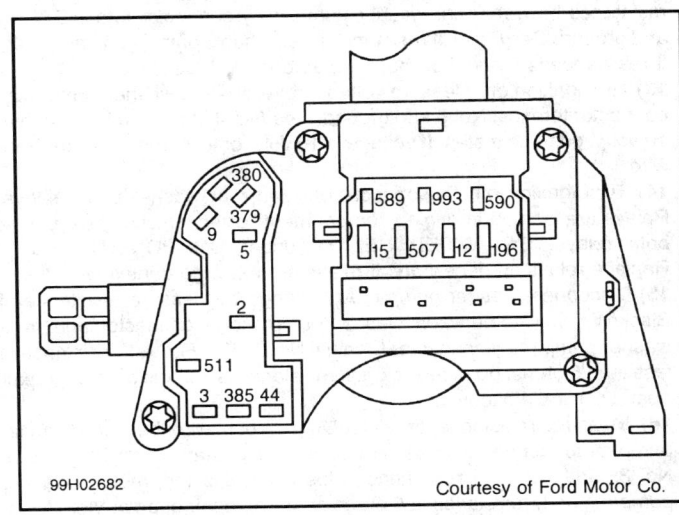

99H02682   Courtesy of Ford Motor Co.

Fig. 7: Identifying Multifunction Switch Terminals

4) Disconnect GEM 26-pin connector C239. GEM is located on backside of central junction box (interior fuse panel). Measure resistance between multifunction switch connector C259 terminal No. 590 and GEM connector C239 terminal No. 13. *See Figs. 5 and 6.* If resistance is less than 5 ohms, replace GEM. See GENERIC ELECTRONIC MODULE under REMOVAL & INSTALLATION. If resistance is 5 ohms or more, repair open in Light Blue/Orange wire.

5) Turn ignition on. Using scan tool, observe GEM PID WASHRLY while toggling active command mode WASHRLY to ON and OFF. If WASHRLY values agree with active command and displays ON- - - and OFF- - -, go to step 12). If WASHRLY values do not agree with active command and displays OFFO-G, go to next step. If WASHRLY values do not agree with active command and displays ON-B-, go to step 10).

6) Turn ignition off. Disconnect front washer pump relay. Relay is located in engine compartment power distribution center. Check relay. See COMPONENT TESTS. Replace relay as necessary. If relay is okay, go to next step.

7) Turn ignition on. Measure voltage between front washer pump relay connector terminal No. 1 and ground. *See Fig. 4.* If voltage is more than 10 volts, go to next step. If voltage is 10 volts or less, replace fuse No. 11 and/or repair White/Black wire between central junction box and front washer pump relay.

8) Turn ignition off. Disconnect GEM 26-pin connector C239. Measure resistance between GEM connector C239 terminal No. 24 and front washer pump relay connector terminal No. 2. *See Figs. 4 and 5.* If resistance is less than 5 ohms, go to next step. If resistance is 5 ohms or more, repair open in Tan/Red wire.

9) Measure resistance between front washer pump relay connector terminal No. 2 and ground. *See Fig. 4.* If resistance is more than 10 k/ohms, replace GEM. See GENERIC ELECTRONIC MODULE under REMOVAL & INSTALLATION. If resistance is 10 k/ohms or less, repair Tan/Red wire short to ground.

10) Turn ignition off. Disconnect front washer pump relay. Relay is located in engine compartment battery junction box. Check relay. See COMPONENT TESTS. Replace relay as necessary. If relay is okay, go to next step.

11) Disconnect GEM 26-pin connector C239. GEM is located on backside of central junction box (interior fuse panel). Turn ignition on. Measure voltage between front washer pump relay connector terminal No. 2 and ground. *See Fig. 4.* If any voltage is present, repair Tan/Red wire short to voltage. If no voltage is present, replace GEM. See GENERIC ELECTRONIC MODULE under REMOVAL & INSTALLATION.

12) Turn ignition off. Disconnect rear washer pump relay connector. Relay is located in engine compartment battery junction box. Measure resistance between rear washer pump relay connector terminal No. 4 and ground. *See Fig. 4.* If resistance is less than 5 ohms, go to next step. If resistance is 5 ohms or more, repair open in Black wire.

13) Turn ignition on. Measure voltage between front washer pump relay connector terminal No. 5 and ground. *See Fig. 4.* If voltage is more than 10 volts, go to next step. If voltage is 10 volts or less, repair White/Black wire.

14) Turn ignition off. Disconnect front and rear washer pump relays. Relays are located in engine compartment battery junction box. Check both relays. See WIPER RELAYS under COMPONENT TESTS. Replace relays as necessary. If relays are okay, go to next step.

15) Disconnect washer pump motor connector. Measure resistance of Black/White wire between washer pump motor connector and front washer pump relay connector terminal No. 3. *See Fig. 4.* If resistance is less than 5 ohms, go to next step. If resistance is 5 ohms or more, repair open in Black/White wire.

16) Measure resistance of Violet/Light Green wire between washer pump motor connector and rear washer pump relay connector terminal No. 3. *See Fig. 4.* If resistance is less than 5 ohms, replace washer pump motor. If resistance is 5 ohms or more, repair open in Violet/Light Green wire.

TEST F: FRONT WIPER SPEED DEPENDENT INTERVAL MODE INOPERATIVE

NOTE: After repair is completed, clear Diagnostic Trouble Codes (DTCs) and recheck system for proper operation.

1) Using scan tool perform WIPER SELF-TEST. Retrieve and note any continuous DTCs for GEM. Clear continuous DTCs. Perform ON-DEMAND SELF-TEST. If no DTCs exist, go to next step. If DTC P0500 exists, go to step **3)**. If DTC B1342 exists, replace GEM. See GENERIC ELECTRONIC MODULE under REMOVAL & INSTALLATION.

2) Turn ignition on. Using scan tool, observe GEM PID SPEEDWP. If SPEEDWP indicates ACTIVE, go to next step. If SPEEDWP does not indicate ACTIVE, set active command SPD WIPER to ON.

3) Using scan tool, observe GEM PID VSS while driving vehicle from 0 to 55 MPH. If GEM PID VSS agrees with speedometer, go to next step. If GEM PID VSS values do not agree with speedometer, go to step **5)**.

NOTE: For following test, vehicle doors must be closed and engine running to receive accurate data. Turning ignition off will end self-test.

4) Simultaneously start vehicle and press message center E/M and MODE buttons to enter MESSAGE CENTER SELF-TEST. Message center is located in overhead console. When MESSAGE CENTER SELF-TEST starts, release E/M and MODE buttons. Press MODE button 4 times advancing to SPEED INPUT TEST. Compass display will show SP. Numeric display will show vehicle speed. Drive vehicle. If message center displays vehicle speed, go to step **6)**. If message center does not display vehicle speed, go to next step.

5) Turn ignition off. Disconnect central junction box connector C243 and Powertrain Control Module (PCM) connector. Measure resistance between central junction block connector C243 terminal No. 21 to PCM connector terminal No. 68. *See Figs. 8 and 9.* If resistance is less than 5 ohms, see appropriate SELF-DIAGNOSTICS article in ENGINE PERFORMANCE in appropriate MITCHELL® manual. If resistance is 5 ohms or greater, repair open in Gray/Black wire.

6) Remove GEM. See GENERIC ELECTRONIC MODULE under REMOVAL & INSTALLATION. Measure internal resistance of central junction box between C267 terminal No. 18 and C243 terminal No. 21. *See Fig. 8.* If resistance is less than 5 ohms, replace GEM. See GENERIC ELECTRONIC MODULE under REMOVAL & INSTALLATION. If the resistance is 5 ohms or greater, replace central junction box.

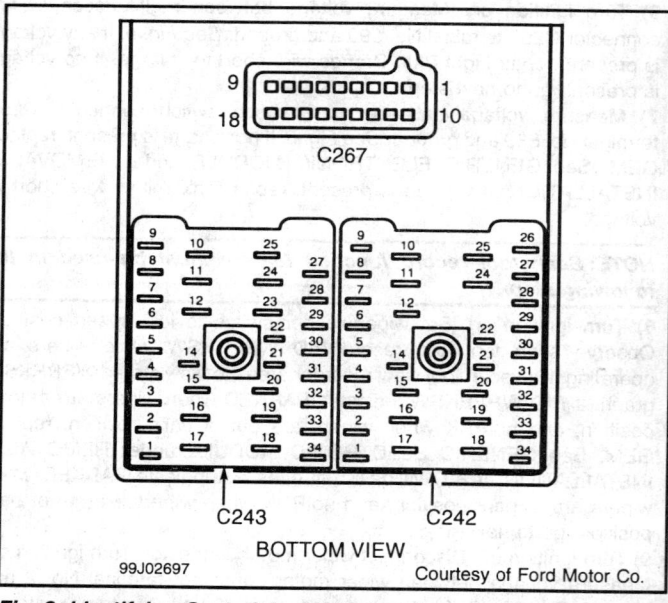

99J02697   Courtesy of Ford Motor Co.

Fig. 8: Identifying Central Junction Box Connectors & Terminals

TEST G: REAR WIPERS INOPERATIVE

NOTE: After repair is completed, clear Diagnostic Trouble Codes (DTCs) and recheck system for proper operation.

1) Turn ignition off. Measure voltage between output sides of fuse No. 103 (50-amp) in battery junction box in engine compartment, and fuse No. 15 (5-amp) in central junction box (interior fuse panel). If voltage is 10 volts or more, go to next step. If voltage is less than 10 volts, replace fuse as necessary, or repair open in Tan/Black wire between battery junction box and central junction box. See WIRING DIAGRAMS. Clear DTCs and test system for normal operation. If fuse blows again, check for short to ground. Repair as necessary.

2) Turn ignition off. Using scan tool, observe GEM PIDS IGN_A, IGN_R, IGN_S and IGN_O/L while operating ignition switch through all positions. If PID values agree with switch positions, go to next step. If PID values do not agree with switch positions, repair circuit(s) between ignition switch and central junction box. See appropriate wiring diagram in POWER DISTRIBUTION article in WIRING DIAGRAMS.

3) Using scan tool retrieve and note any continuous DTCs for GEM. Clear continuous DTCs. Perform ON-DEMAND SELF-TEST. Perform REAR WIPER SELF-TEST. If no DTCs exist, go to next step. If any DTCs exist, go to appropriate test step and continue diagnosis. See TEST G DTC INDEX table.

TEST G DTC INDEX

DTC	Step
B1334	1
B1342	2
B1611	4)
B1814	10)
B1816	10)
B1818	10)
B1820	10)

[1] – Problem is in interior lighting circuit. See appropriate wiring diagram in ILLUMINATION/INTERIOR LIGHTS article.

[2] – Replace GEM. See GENERIC ELECTRONIC MODULE under REMOVAL & INSTALLATION.

4) Using scan tool, observe PID R_WP_MD while turning rear wiper switch through all positions. If PID R_WP_MD values agree with all switch positions, go to step **10)**. If PID R_WP_MD values do not agree with all switch positions, go to next step.

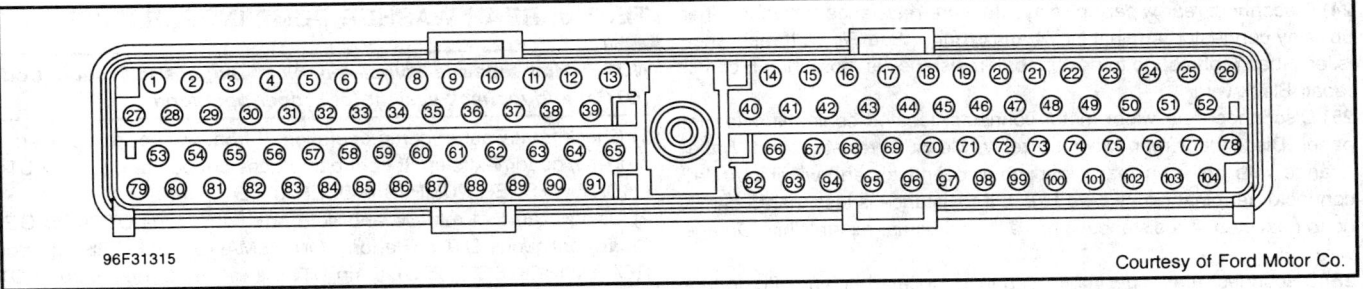

96F31315

Courtesy of Ford Motor Co.

Fig. 9: Identifying PCM Connector Terminals

5) Turn ignition off. Test wiper portion of multifunction switch. See WIPER SWITCH under COMPONENT TESTS. If switch is okay, go to next step. If resistances are not as specified, replace multifunction switch.

6) Disconnect GEM 16-pin connector C240. Disconnect multifunction switch 10-pin connector C258. Measure resistance between GEM connector C240 terminal No. 12 and multifunction switch connector C258 terminal No. 380. *See Figs. 10 and 11.* If resistance is less than 5 ohms, go to next step. If resistance is more than 5 ohms, repair Pink/Black wire.

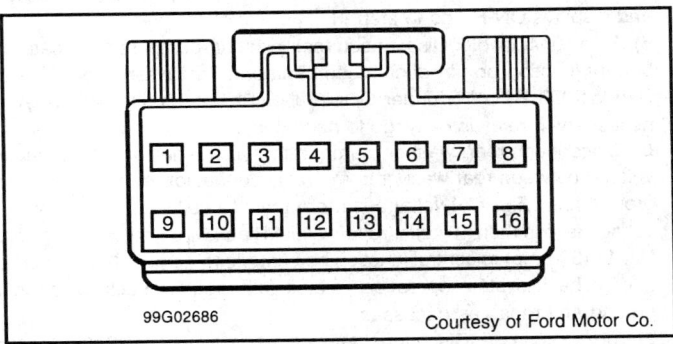

99G02686

Courtesy of Ford Motor Co.

Fig. 10: Identifying GEM 16-Pin Connector C240 Terminals

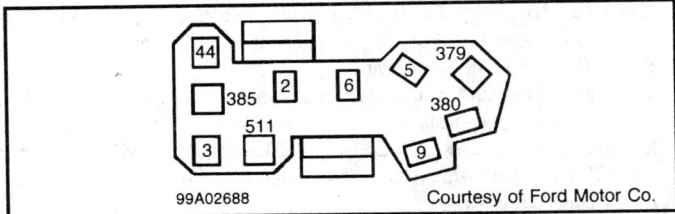

99A02688

Courtesy of Ford Motor Co.

Fig. 11: Identifying Multifunction Switch 10-Pin Connector C258 Terminals

7) Measure resistance between GEM connector C240 terminal No. 12 and ground. *See Fig. 10.* If resistance is more than 10 k/ohms, go to next step. If resistance is less than 10 k/ohms, repair Pink/Black wire.

8) Disconnect GEM 26-pin connector C239. Disconnect multifunction switch 7-pin connector C259. Measure resistance between GEM connector C239 terminal No. 21 and multifunction switch connector C259 terminal No. 993. *See Figs. 5 and 6.* If resistance is less than 5 ohms, go to next step. If resistance is more than 5 ohms, repair Dark Blue wire.

9) Turn ignition on. Disconnect GEM 16-pin connector C240. Measure voltage between GEM connector C240 terminal No. 12 and ground. *See Fig. 10.* If any voltage is indicated, repair Pink/Black wire. If no voltage is indicated, replace GEM. See GENERIC ELECTRONIC MODULE under REMOVAL & INSTALLATION.

10) Using scan tool, observe PIDS R_WP_UP and R_WP_DN while toggling active commands UP RELAY and DWN RELAY to ON and OFF. If PIDS agree with command mode, and display ON- - - and OFF- - -, go to step **20)**. If either, or both, PIDS do not agree with command mode and display ON-B-, go to step **17)**. If either, or both, PIDS do not agree with command mode and display OFF O-G, go to next step.

11) Turn ignition off. Disconnect rear wiper up and down relays located in battery junction box in engine compartment. Turn ignition on. Measure voltage between each relay connector terminal No. 1 and ground. *See Fig. 4.* If voltages are more than 10 volts, go to next step. If any voltage is less than 10 volts, repair appropriate Light Green/Orange wire.

12) Check rear wiper up and down relays. See WIPER RELAYS under COMPONENT TESTS. Replace relay(s) as necessary. If relays are okay, go to next step.

13) Turn ignition off. Disconnect GEM 16-pin connector C240. Disconnect wiper up relay. Measure resistance between GEM connector C240 terminal No. 8 and wiper up relay connector terminal No. 2. *See Figs. 4 and 10.* If resistance is less than 5 ohms, go to next step. If resistance is more than 5 ohms, repair Light Green wire.

14) Disconnect wiper down relay. Measure resistance between GEM connector C240 terminal No. 10 and wiper down relay connector terminal No. 2. *See Figs. 4 and 10.* If resistance is less than 5 ohms, go to next step. If resistance is more than 5 ohms, repair Tan wire.

15) Disconnect wiper up relay. Measure resistance between wiper up relay connector terminal No. 2 and ground. *See Fig. 4.* If resistance is more than 10 k/ohms, go to next step. If resistance is less than 10 k/ohms, repair Light Green wire.

16) Measure resistance between wiper down relay connector terminal No. 2 and ground. *See Fig. 4.* If resistance is more than 10 k/ohms, replace GEM. See GENERIC ELECTRONIC MODULE under REMOVAL & INSTALLATION. If resistance is less than 10 k/ohms, repair Tan wire.

17) Turn ignition off. Disconnect and check rear wiper up and down relays. See WIPER RELAYS under COMPONENT TESTS. Replace relay(s) as necessary. If relays are okay, go to next step.

18) Disconnect GEM 16-pin connector C240. Disconnect wiper up relay. Turn ignition on. Measure resistance between wiper up relay connector terminal No. 2 and ground. *See Fig. 4.* If any voltage is present, repair Light Green wire. If no voltage is present, go to next step.

19) Turn ignition off. Disconnect wiper down relay. Turn ignition on. Measure voltage between wiper down relay connector terminal No. 2 and ground. *See Fig. 4.* If any voltage is present, repair Tan wire. If no voltage is present, replace GEM. See GENERIC ELECTRONIC MODULE under REMOVAL & INSTALLATION.

20) Turn ignition off. Disconnect and check rear wiper up and down relays. See WIPER RELAYS under COMPONENT TESTS. Replace relay(s) as necessary. If relays are okay, go to next step.

21) Disconnect wiper down relay. Measure voltage between wiper down relay connector terminal No. 5 and ground. *See Fig. 4.* If voltage is more than 10 volts, go to next step. If voltage is less than 10 volts, repair Brown/White wire.

22) Disconnect rear wiper up relay. Measure voltage between wiper up relay connector terminal No. 5 and ground. *See Fig. 4.* If voltage is more than 10 volts, go to next step. If voltage is less than 10 volts, repair Brown/White wire.

23) Disconnect rear wiper down relay. Measure resistance between wiper down relay connector terminal No. 4 and ground. *See Fig. 4.* If resistance is less than 5 ohms, go to next step. If resistance is more than 5 ohms, repair Black wire.

24) Disconnect rear wiper up relay. Measure resistance between wiper up relay connector terminal No. 4 and ground. See Fig. 4. If resistance is less than 5 ohms, go to next step. If resistance is more than 5 ohms, repair Black wire.

25) Disconnect rear wiper motor connector located behind liftgate trim panel. Disconnect rear wiper up relay. Measure resistance of White/Orange wire between rear wiper motor connector and wiper up relay connector terminal No. 3. See Fig. 4. If resistance is less than 5 ohms, go to next step. If resistance is more than 5 ohms, repair White/Orange wire.

26) Disconnect rear wiper motor connector located behind liftgate trim panel. Disconnect rear wiper down relay. Measure resistance of Black/Light Blue wire between wiper motor connector and wiper down relay connector terminal No. 3. See Fig. 4. If resistance is less than 5 ohms, replace rear wiper motor. If resistance is more than 5 ohms, repair Black/Light Blue wire.

TEST H: REAR WIPERS WILL NOT PARK IN PROPER POSITION

NOTE: After repair is completed, clear Diagnostic Trouble Codes (DTCs) and recheck system for proper operation.

1) Using scan tool retrieve and note any continuous DTCs for GEM. Clear continuous DTCs. Perform ON-DEMAND SELF-TEST. Perform REAR WIPER SELF-TEST. If no DTCs, or DTC B1839 exist, go to next step. If DTC B1342 exists, replace GEM. See GENERIC ELECTRONIC MODULE under REMOVAL & INSTALLATION.

2) Using scan tool, observe PID R_WP_PK while rear wipers are moving. PID R_WP_PK should indicate PARKED when wiper is at high limit of travel and between low limit of travel and park. PID R_WP_PK should indicate notPARK when wiper is between high and low limit of travel. If PID agrees with wiper position, check wiper motor shaft for proper alignment. If PID does not agree with wiper position and always indicates PARKED, go to next step. If PID does not agree with wiper position and always indicates notPARK, go to step 5). If PID changes values, but does not agree with wiper position, check wiper arm for proper alignment with motor. If alignment is okay, replace rear wiper motor.

3) Turn ignition off. Disconnect rear wiper motor connector located behind liftgate trim panel. Using scan tool, observe PID R_WP_PK. If PID indicates PARKED, go to next step. If PID does not indicate PARKED, replace rear wiper motor.

4) Turn ignition off. Disconnect rear wiper motor connector. Disconnect GEM 16-pin connector C240. Measure resistance of Pink/Yellow wire between wiper motor connector and ground. If resistance is more than 10 k/ohms, replace GEM. See GENERIC ELECTRONIC MODULE under REMOVAL & INSTALLATION. If resistance is less than 10 k/ohms, repair Pink/Yellow wire.

5) Turn ignition off. Disconnect rear wiper motor connector. Measure resistance of Black wire between wiper motor connector and ground. If resistance is less than 5 ohms, go to next step. If resistance is more than 5 ohms, repair Black wire.

6) Turn ignition on. Connect jumper wire between Pink/Yellow and Black wire terminals at rear wiper motor connector. Using scan tool, observe PID R_WP_PK. If PID indicates PARKED, replace rear wiper motor. See REAR WIPER MOTOR under REMOVAL & INSTALLATION. If PID does not indicate PARKED, go to next step.

7) Turn ignition off. Disconnect rear wiper motor connector. Disconnect GEM 16-pin connector C240. Measure resistance of Pink/Yellow wire between wiper motor connector and GEM connector C240 terminal No. 7. See Fig. 10. If resistance is less than 5 ohms, replace GEM. See GENERIC ELECTRONIC MODULE under REMOVAL & INSTALLATION. If resistance is more than 5 ohms, repair Pink/Yellow wire.

TEST J: REAR WASHER PUMP INOPERATIVE

NOTE: After repair is completed, clear Diagnostic Trouble Codes (DTCs) and recheck system for proper operation.

1) Check front washer pump operation. If front washer pump operates properly, go to next step. If front pump does not operate go to TEST E FRONT WASHER PUMP IS INOPERATIVE.

2) Using scan tool retrieve and note any continuous DTCs for GEM. Clear continuous DTCs. Perform ON-DEMAND SELF-TEST. Perform REAR WIPER SELF-TEST. If no DTCs exist, go to next step. If DTC B1342 exists, replace GEM. See GENERIC ELECTRONIC MODULE under REMOVAL & INSTALLATION. Clear DTCs and recheck system operation. If DTCs B1240 or B1241 exist, go to step 4).

3) Using scan tool, observe PID R_WP_MD while activating rear washer switch. If PID R_WP_MD indicates WASH with switch activated, go to next step. If WASH is not indicated, replace multifunction switch. See MULTIFUNCTION SWITCH under REMOVAL & INSTALLATION.

4) Using scan tool, observe PID RWASHSW while toggling active command WASHRLY to ON and OFF. If PID RWASHSW agrees with command mode and displays ON--, OFFO-G, go to step 11). If PID RWASHSW does not agree with command mode and displays OFFO-G, go to next step. If PID RWASHSW does not agree with command mode and displays ON-B-, go to step 9).

5) Turn ignition off. Disconnect rear washer pump relay located in battery junction box in engine compartment. Test washer pump relay. See WIPER RELAYS under COMPONENT TESTS. Replace relay as necessary. If relay is okay, go to next step.

6) Disconnect rear washer pump relay. Turn ignition on. Measure voltage between rear washer pump relay connector terminal No. 1 and ground. See Fig. 4. If voltage is more than 10 volts, go to next step. If voltage is less than 10 volts, repair White/Black wire and/or replace fuse No. 11 (30-amp) in central junction box (interior fuse panel). Clear DTCs and recheck system operation. If fuse fails again, check for short to ground and repair as necessary.

7) Turn ignition off. Disconnect GEM 16-pin connector C240. Measure resistance between rear washer pump relay connector terminal No. 2 and GEM connector C240 terminal No. 15. See Figs. 4 and 10. If resistance is less than 5 ohms, go to next step. If resistance is more than 5 ohms, repair Dark Green wire.

8) Measure resistance between rear washer pump relay connector terminal No. 2 and ground. See Fig. 4. If resistance is more than 10 k/ohms, replace GEM. See GENERIC ELECTRONIC MODULE under REMOVAL & INSTALLATION. If resistance is less than 10 k/ohms, repair Dark Green wire.

9) Turn ignition off. Disconnect rear washer pump relay. Test washer pump relay. See WIPER RELAYS under COMPONENT TESTS. Replace relay as necessary. If relay is okay, go to next step.

10) Disconnect GEM 16-pin connector C240. Turn ignition on. Measure voltage between washer pump relay connector terminal No. 2 and ground. See Fig. 4. If any voltage is indicated, repair Dark Green wire. If no voltage is indicated, replace GEM. See GENERIC ELECTRONIC MODULE under REMOVAL & INSTALLATION.

11) Turn ignition off. Disconnect rear washer pump relay. Measure resistance between washer pump relay connector terminal No. 4 and ground. See Fig. 4. If resistance is less than 5 ohms, go to next step. If resistance is more than 5 ohms, repair Black wire.

12) Disconnect rear washer pump relay. Turn ignition on. Measure voltage between washer pump relay connector terminal No. 5 and ground. See Fig. 4. If voltage is more than 10 volts, go to next step. If voltage is less than 10 volts, repair White/Black wire.

13) Turn ignition off. Disconnect front and rear washer pump relays. Test washer pump relays. See WIPER RELAYS under COMPONENT TESTS. Replace relay(s) as necessary. If relays are okay, replace washer pump motor.

TEST K: REAR WIPERS REMAIN ON CONTINUOUSLY

NOTE: After repair is completed, clear Diagnostic Trouble Codes (DTCs) and recheck system for proper operation.

1) Turn ignition off. Place rear wiper switch in OFF position. Using scan tool retrieve and note any continuous DTCs for GEM. Clear continuous DTCs. Perform ON-DEMAND SELF-TEST. Perform REAR WIPER SELF-TEST. If no DTCs, or DTC B1614 exist, go to next step. If DTC B1342 exists, replace GEM. See GENERIC ELECTRONIC MODULE under REMOVAL & INSTALLATION.

2) Turn ignition off. Disconnect multifunction switch 7-pin connector C259 and 10-pin connector C258. Measure resistance between C259 connector terminal No. 993 and C258 connector terminal No. 380. *See Figs. 6 and 11.* If resistance is approximately 2900 ohms, go to next step. If resistance is not approximately 2900 ohms, replace multifunction switch. See MULTIFUNCTION SWITCH under REMOVAL & INSTALLATION.

3) Turn ignition off. Disconnect GEM 16-pin connector C240. Measure resistance between multifunction switch connector C258 terminal No. 380 and ground. *See Fig. 11.* If resistance is more than 10 k/ohms, replace GEM. See GENERIC ELECTRONIC MODULE under REMOVAL & INSTALLATION. If resistance is less than 10 k/ohms, repair Pink/Black wire.

TEST L: LOW WASHER FLUID INDICATOR DOES NOT OPERATE PROPERLY

NOTE: After repair is completed, clear Diagnostic Trouble Codes (DTCs) and recheck system for proper operation.

1) Using scan tool, observe PIDS IGN_A, IGN_R, IGN_S and IGN_O/L while turning ignition switch through all positions. If PID values agree with switch positions, go to next step. If PID values do not agree with switch positions, repair ignition circuit(s) as necessary. See appropriate wiring diagram in POWER DISTRIBUTION article in WIRING DIAGRAMS.

2) Turn ignition on. Using scan tool retrieve and note any continuous DTCs for GEM. Clear continuous DTCs. Perform WIPER CONTROL TEST. Perform WIPER SELF-TEST. If no DTCs exist, go to next step. If DTC B1342 exists, replace GEM. See GENERIC ELECTRONIC MODULE under REMOVAL & INSTALLATION. If DTCs B1454 or B1456 exist, problem is in instrument cluster. See ANALOG INSTRUMENT PANELS – EXPEDITION, F150 & F250 LIGHT-DUTY PICKUP, & NAVIGATOR article.

3) Turn ignition off. Disconnect washer fluid level switch 2-pin connector located on wiper/washer reservoir. Using scan tool, observe PID WFLUID. Connect and then remove jumper wire between fluid level switch connector terminals. If PID indicates LOW with jumper connected, and OK with jumper removed, replace fluid level switch. If PID did not indicate LOW and OK as described, go to next step.

4) Measure resistance of Black wire between fluid level switch connector and ground. If resistance is less than 5 ohms, go to next step. If resistance is more than 5 ohms, repair Black wire.

5) Turn ignition off. Disconnect GEM 16-pin connector C240. Measure resistance of Red/Light Green wire between fluid level switch connector and GEM connector C240 terminal No. 16. *See Fig. 10.* If resistance is less than 5 ohms, go to next step. If resistance is more than 5 ohms, repair Red/Light Green wire.

6) Measure resistance between GEM connector C240 terminal No. 16 and ground. *See Fig. 10.* If resistance is more than 10 k/ohms, replace GEM. See GENERIC ELECTRONIC MODULE under REMOVAL & INSTALLATION. If resistance is less than 10 k/ohms, repair Red/Light Green wire short to ground.

TEST M: NO COMMUNICATION WITH MODULE

NOTE: After repair is completed, clear Diagnostic Trouble Codes (DTCs) and recheck system for proper operation.

1) Using scan tool, observe PIDS IGN_A, IGN_R, IGN_S and IGN_O/L while turning ignition switch through all positions. If PID values agree with switch positions, go to next step. If PID values do not agree with switch positions, repair ignition circuit(s) as necessary. See appropriate wiring diagram in POWER DISTRIBUTION article in WIRING DIAGRAMS.

2) Turn ignition off. Disconnect central junction box 34-pin connector C243. *See Fig. 8.* Measure voltage between central junction box connector C243 terminal No. 11 and ground. If voltage is more than 10 volts, go to next step. If voltage is less than 10 volts, repair Tan/Black wire.

3) Turn ignition off. Remove GEM from central junction box. See GENERIC ELECTRONIC MODULE under REMOVAL & INSTALLATION. Reconnect central junction box connector C243. Measure voltage between central junction box connector C267 terminal No. 4 and ground. *See Fig. 8.* Measure voltage between central junction box connector C267 terminal No. 16 and ground. If voltages are more than 10 volts, go to next step. If voltages are less than 10 volts, replace central junction box.

4) Measure resistance between GEM connector C239 terminal No. 26 and ground. *See Fig. 5.* If resistance is less than 5 ohms, go to next step. If resistance is more than 5 ohms, repair Black/Light Blue wire.

5) Measure resistance between GEM connector 239 terminal No. 14 and ground. *See Fig. 5.* If resistance is less than 5 ohms, problem is in Module Communications Network. See MODULE COMMUNICATIONS NETWORK – EXPEDITION & NAVIGATOR article. If resistance is more than 5 ohms, repair Black/Light Blue wire.

REMOVAL & INSTALLATION

WARNING: Deactivate air bag system before performing any service operation involving steering column components. See appropriate AIR BAG RESTRAINT SYSTEMS article. Do not apply electrical power to any component on steering column without first deactivating air bag system. Air bag may deploy.

CAUTION: When battery is disconnected, vehicle computer and memory systems may lose memory data. Driveability problems may exist until computer systems have completed a relearn cycle. See COMPUTER RELEARN PROCEDURES article in GENERAL INFORMATION before disconnecting battery.

FRONT WIPER MOTOR

Removal & Installation – Remove wiper arms. Remove cowl top vent panels. Remove mounting arm and pivot shaft. Disconnect wiper motor connector. Remove wiper motor mounting nuts and motor. To install, reverse removal procedure.

GENERIC ELECTRONIC MODULE

CAUTION: If replacing the Generic Electronic Module (GEM) module, it is necessary to upload module configuration information to the New Generation STAR (NGS) tester. After installation, this information must be downloaded into the new GEM module.

CAUTION: Disconnect the battery before disconnecting GEM connectors. Failure to do so will result in GEM storing erroneous codes and may also result in erratic operation of GEM after reconnection.

Removal & Installation – Disconnect the battery ground cable. Remove the lower instrument panel steering column cover. Remove bulkhead electrical connectors (C243 and C242) from central junction box (interior fuse panel). Unbolt and remove central junction box.

Disconnect GEM electrical connectors. Remove screws and disconnect GEM from backside of central junction box. To install, reverse removal procedure.

MULTIFUNCTION SWITCH

Removal & Installation – 1) Disconnect battery ground cable. Turn ignition switch to RUN position. Insert punch through hole in lower steering column shroud and push ignition switch lock cylinder release tab while pulling out ignition switch lock cylinder. Twist tilt wheel handle and remove.

2) Set gear selector to lowest position. Remove steering column opening cover. Remove upper and lower steering column shrouds. Disconnect electrical connectors. Remove multifunction switch. To install, reverse removal procedure.

REAR WIPER MOTOR

Removal & Installation – Remove rear wiper arm. Remove upper liftgate trim panel. Remove liftgate assist strap. Remove lower liftgate trim panel and watershield. Disconnect motor electrical connector. Remove motor attaching screws and remove motor. To install, reverse removal procedure.

WIRING DIAGRAMS

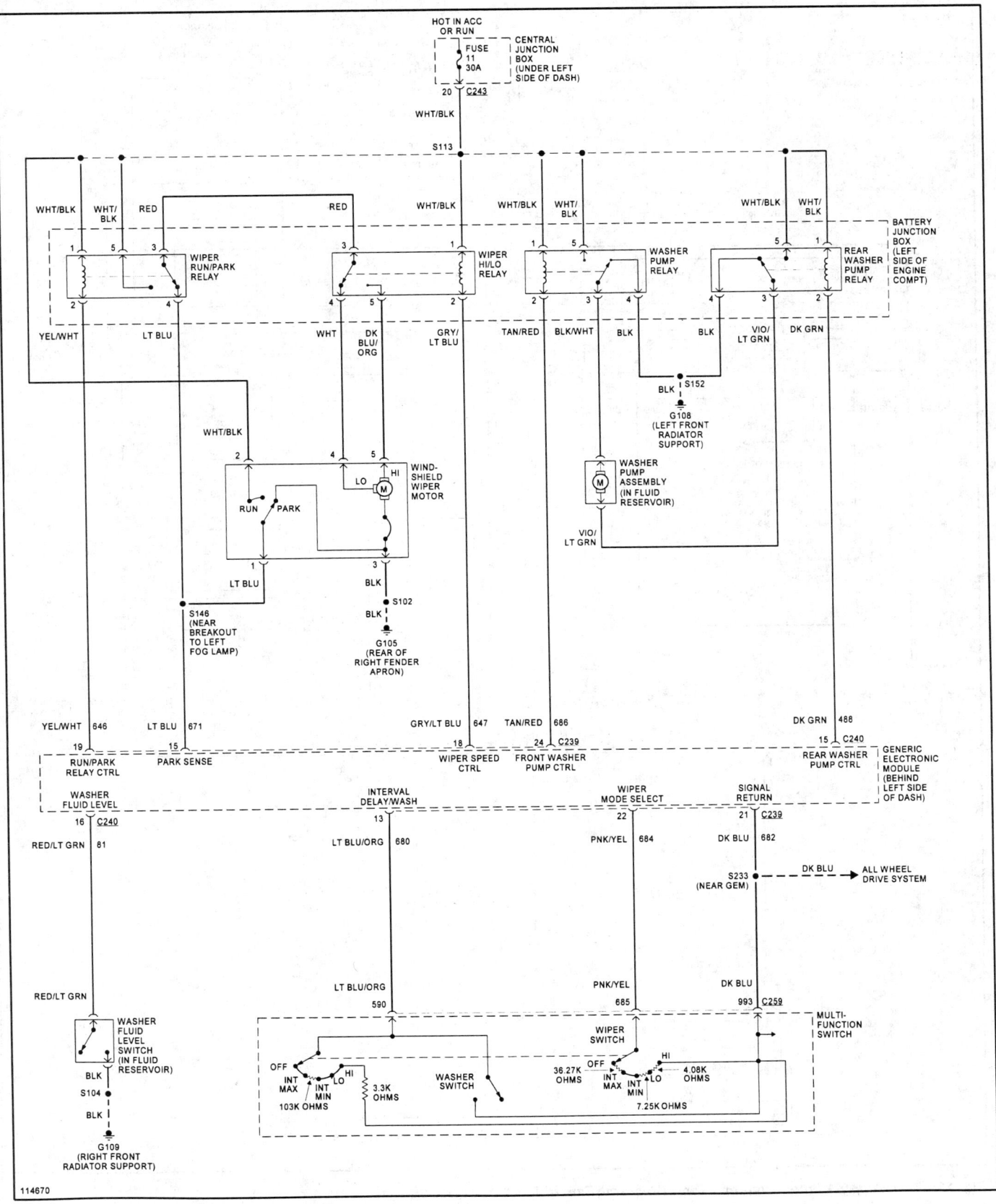

Fig. 12: Front Wiper/Washer System Wiring Diagram (Expedition & Navigator)

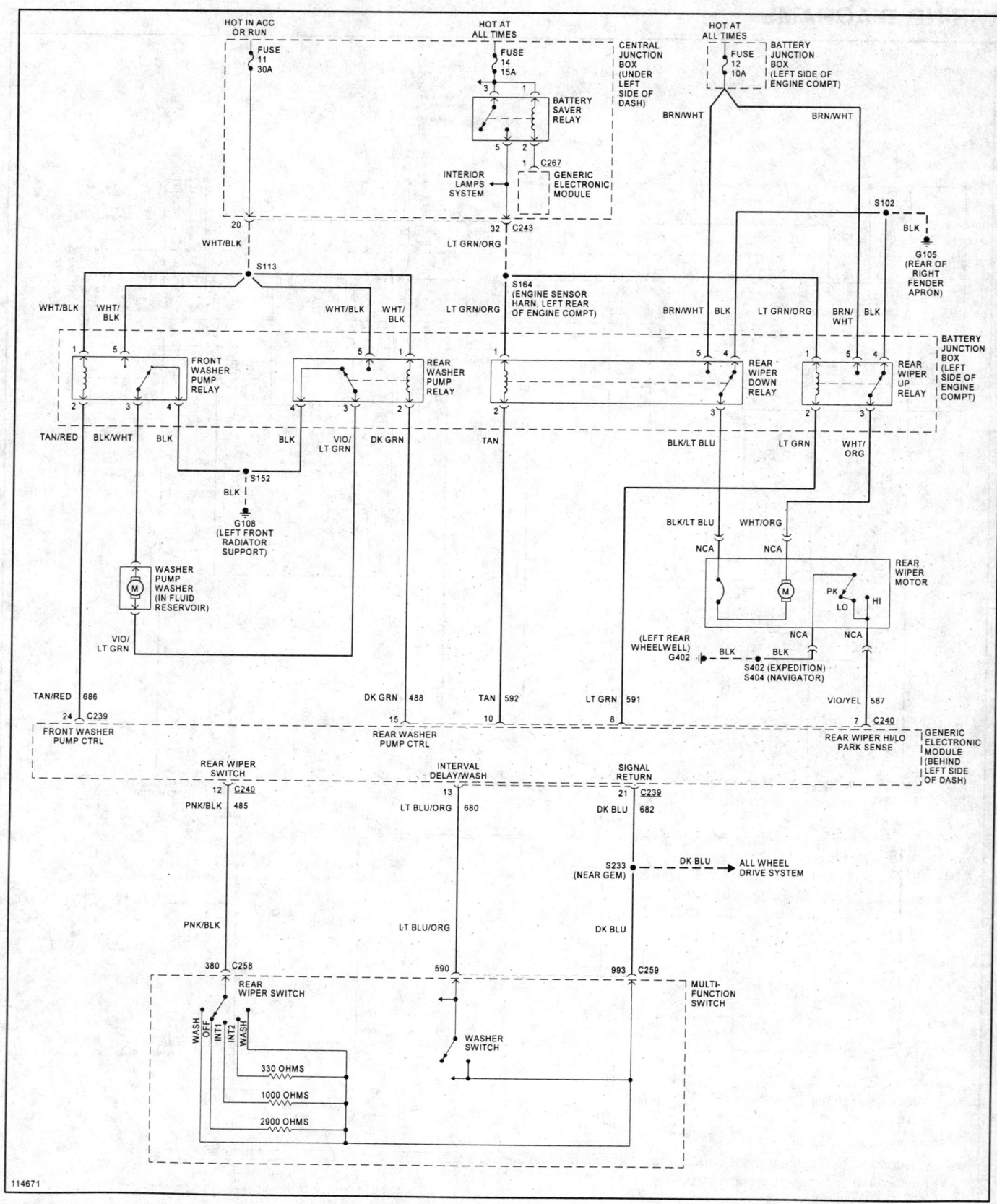

Fig. 13: Rear Wiper/Washer System Wiring Diagram (Expedition & Navigator)

114671

DESCRIPTION & OPERATION

Windshield wipers are operated by a permanent-magnet motor. When wiper control switch is in intermittent (INT) position, wipers make single sweeps, separated by adjustable-length pauses. On 2WD vehicles not equipped with power windows, all wiper functions are controlled by a Central Timer Module (CTM). On all other applications, wiper functions are controlled by Generic Electronic Module (GEM). CTM, or GEM, is located behind center instrument panel finish panel.

Vehicles with GEM may have speed dependent interval wipers. With this option, wiper speed interval automatically shortens as vehicle speed increases. Rear wipers are controlled by GEM. When liftgate or liftgate glass is ajar, rear wiper will be deactivated and return to park position. A check valve located in fluid line that passes through liftgate contains washer fluid in system between operations. Unintentional release of fluid is prevented by standpipe located along right rear pillar.

COMPONENT LOCATIONS

COMPONENT LOCATIONS

Component	Location
Auxiliary Relay Box #1	Right Side of Engine Compartment
Battery Junction Box	Engine Compartment Near Master Cylinder
Central Junction Box	Left Side of Instrument Panel Facing Driver Door
Central Timer Module	Behind Center Of Instrument Panel Finish Panel
Front Washer Pump Relay	Auxiliary Relay Box #1
Front Wiper High/Low Relay	Battery Junction Box
Front Wiper Run Relay	Battery Junction Box
Generic Electronic Module	Behind Center Of Instrument Panel Finish Panel
Rear Wiper Up & Down Relays	Battery Junction Box

ADJUSTMENTS

WIPER ARM & BLADE ASSEMBLY

Front – Information not available from manufacturer.

Rear – 1) Disconnect washer hose. Remove wiper arm nut cover. Remove nut and wiper arm. Turn ignition on and turn rear wiper on. Allow wiper motor to cycle then turn wiper off and allow wiper motor stop in park position.

2) Position wiper arm so wiper blade rests on outside of wiper arm stop. See Fig. 1. Place wiper arm/blade assembly on motor shaft. Tighten wiper arm nut to 9-13 ft. lbs. (12-18 N.m.). Reconnect washer hose. Operate rear wiper and check park operation.

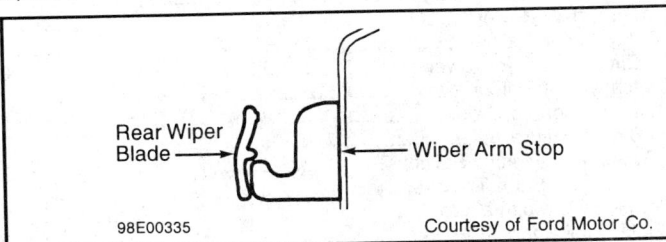

Rear Wiper Blade — Wiper Arm Stop

98E00335 — Courtesy of Ford Motor Co.

Fig. 1: Adjusting Rear Wiper Arm Park Position

TROUBLE SHOOTING

Before performing any system tests on wiper/washer system, check the following items to eliminate common problems:

- Check battery junction box fuses:
  - No. 1 (60-amp)
  - No. 8 (15-amp)
- Check central junction box (interior fuse panel) fuses:
  - No. 12 (7.5-amp)
  - No. 16 (30-amp)
  - No. 25 (7.5-amp)
- Damaged/stripped wiper motor shaft.
- Damaged/stripped wiper pivot arm shaft.
- Damaged washer pump.
- Loose or corroded connections.
- Damaged wiring harness.
- Binding windshield wiper pivot arm.

If problem is not found, check for Diagnostic Trouble Codes (DTCs). See SELF-DIAGNOSTICS under SELF-DIAGNOSTIC SYSTEM.

COMPONENT TESTS

REAR WIPER SWITCH

For rear wiper switch test procedure, see REAR WIPER SWITCH RESISTANCE TEST. Refer to TEST H: REAR WIPER STAYS ON CONTINUOUSLY under SYSTEM TESTS.

RELAYS

NOTE: Same test procedure may be used for all wiper/washer system relays.

1) Remove relay to be tested. Measure resistance between relay terminal No. 2 and all other terminals. See Fig. 2. If resistance is less than 5 ohms between relay terminal No. 2 and any other terminal, replace relay. If all resistances are 5 ohms or more, go to next step.

2) Connect a jumper wire between battery positive terminal and relay terminal No. 3. See Fig. 2. Measure voltage between relay terminal No. 4 and ground. If battery voltage is not present, replace relay. If battery voltage is present, go to next step.

3) Connect a second jumper wire from battery positive terminal to relay terminal No. 1. Connect a third jumper wire between relay terminal No. 2 and ground. Measure voltage between relay terminal No. 5 and ground. If battery voltage is not present, replace relay, If battery voltage is present, relay is okay.

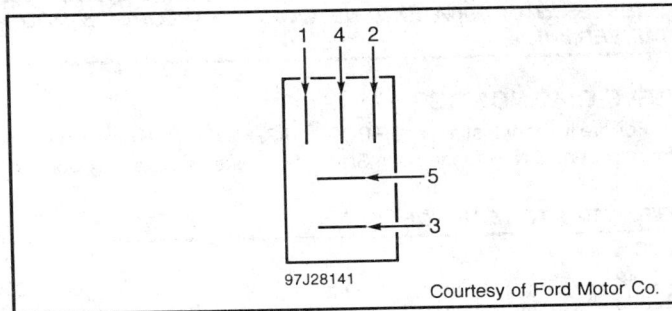

97J28141 — Courtesy of Ford Motor Co.

Fig. 2: Identifying Relay Terminals

WIPER MOTOR

Front Motor – 1) Disconnect negative battery cable. Disengage linkage from motor. Disconnect wiper connector. Connect Green lead from Starting And Charging System Tester (078-00005) to battery negative terminal.

2) Connect Red tester lead to wiper motor terminal No. 3. Connect a jumper wire between battery positive terminal and wiper motor terminal No. 4. For mating connector view, see Fig. 3. If current draw is 3.5 amps or less, remove jumper wire and go to next step. If current draw is more than 3.5 amps, replace wiper motor.

3) Connect a jumper wire between battery positive terminal and wiper motor terminal No. 5. For mating connector view, see Fig. 3. If current draw is more than 5.5 amps, replace wiper motor. If current draw is 5.5 amps or less, wiper motor is okay.

Rear Motor – Information not available from manufacturer.

WIPER SWITCH

Wiper switch is incorporated into multifunction switch on steering column. Disconnect wiper switch connector. Measure resistance between specified switch terminals with switch in specified position. See

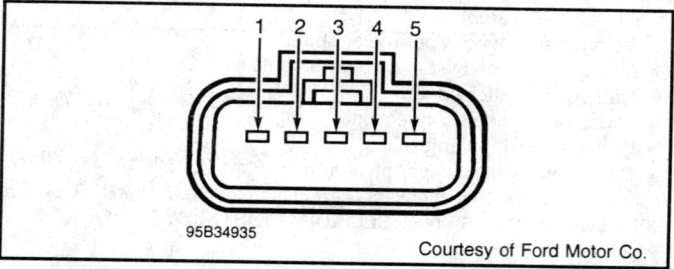

Fig. 3: Identifying Front Wiper Motor Connector Terminals

Fig. 4. See WIPER SWITCH TEST table. If resistance is not as specified, replace multifunction switch.

WIPER SWITCH TEST

Switch Position	Terminals	Resistance Ohms [1]
OFF	685 & 993	955
INT	685 & 993	1910
LOW	685 & 993	401
HIGH	685 & 993	0
INT [2]		
MIN	993 & 590	249
MAX	993 & 590	2670
WASH		
ON	993 & 590	0
OFF	993 & 590	2670

[1] – Values are approximate.
[2] – Rotate (INT) interval knob from minimum to maximum. Resistance should gradually increase from 249 ohms (MIN) to 12,670 ohms (MAX).

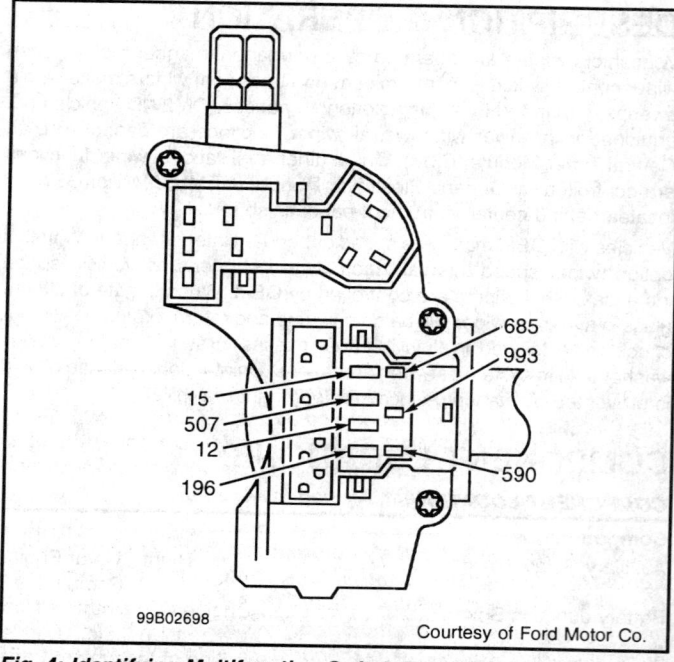

Fig. 4: Identifying Multifunction Switch Terminals

SELF-DIAGNOSTIC SYSTEM

NOTE: For further information on self-diagnostic system, see MODULE COMMUNICATIONS NETWORK – EXPLORER & MOUNTAINEER article.

SELF-DIAGNOSTICS

1) For preliminary testing, see TROUBLE SHOOTING. If problem is not found, connect New Generation Star (NGS) tester to Data Link Connector (DLC) located beneath left side of instrument panel. Using NGS tester, perform DATA LINK DIAGNOSTIC TEST. If NGS tester displays CKT914, CKT915 or CKT70 = ALL ECUS NO RESP/NOT EQUIP, see MODULE COMMUNICATIONS NETWORK – EXPLORER & MOUNTAINEER article to diagnose network concern. If NGS tester displays NO RESPONSE/NOT EQUIPPED for GEM/CTM, perform TEST M: NO COMMUNICATION WITH GEM/CTM under SYSTEM TESTS.

2) If NGS tester displays SYSTEM PASSED, retrieve and record continuous DTCs. Erase DTCs. Perform front and rear wiper self-test diagnostics for GEM/CTM using NGS tester. If GEM/CTM DTCs related to the concern are retrieved, see GEM/CTM DTC TEST INDEX table to continue diagnosis. If no DTCs related to the concern are retrieved, perform appropriate test based on symptom. See SYMPTOM TEST INDEX. For GEM/CTM DTCs not covered in this article, see MODULE COMMUNICATIONS NETWORK – EXPLORER & MOUNTAINEER.

GEM/CTM DTC TEST INDEX

DTC	Description	Test
B1342	GEM/CTM Is Defective	1
B1373	Interior Lamp Relay Coil Circuit Short To Power	B
B1431	Wiper Brake/Run Relay Circuit Failure	2
B1432	Wiper Brake/Run Relay Short To Power	A
B1434	Wiper Hi/Low Speed Relay Circuit Failure	2
B1436	Wiper Hi/Low Speed Relay Circuit Short To Power	C
B1438 [3]	Wiper Mode Select Switch Circuit Failure	2
B1441 [3]	Wiper Mode Select Switch Input Short To Ground	2
B1446 [3]	Wiper Park Sense Circuit Failure	D
B1450 [3]	Wiper/Washer Interval Delay Switch Input Circuit Failure	2
B1453 [3]	Wiper/Washer Interval Delay Switch Input Short To Ground	2
B1458	Wiper/Washer Pump Motor Relay Circuit Failure	E
B1460	Wiper/Washer Pump Motor Relay Coil Short To Power	E
B1466	Wiper Hi/Low Speed Not Switching	2
B1467	Wiper Motor Hi/Low Speed Circuit Short To Power	2
B1473	Wiper Motor Low Speed Circuit Failure	2
B1476	Wiper Motor High Speed Circuit Failure	2
B1611 [4]	Rear Wiper Mode Select Switch Circuit Failure	2
B1614 [4]	Rear Wiper Mode Select Switch Circuit Short To Ground	2
B1814 [4]	Rear Wiper Motor Down Relay Circuit Failure	K
B1816 [4]	Rear Wiper Motor Down Relay Coil Circuit Short To Power	K
B1818 [4]	Rear Wiper Motor Up Relay Coil Circuit Failure	K
B1820 [4]	Rear Wiper Motor Up Relay Circuit Short To Power	K
B1839 [4]	Rear Wiper Motor Circuit Failure	K

GEM/CTM DTC TEST INDEX (Cont.)

DTC	Description	Test
	Front Wiper Power Circuit Failure	A
B1840	Rear Wiper Motor Speed Sense Circuit Failure	K
B1894 [4]	Vehicle Speed Signal Circuit Failure	F
P0500 [4]		

[1] – Clear DTCs. Retrieve DTCs. If DTC B1342 is retrieved, replace GEM/CTM. See GENERIC ELECTRONIC MODULE/CENTRAL TIMER MODULE under REMOVAL & INSTALLATION. Clear DTCs and retest system.
[2] – See SYMPTOM TEST INDEX.
[3] – This DTC may also be present from GEM/CTM wiggle test.
[4] – GEM only code.

SYSTEM TESTS

WARNING: Deactivate air bag system before performing any service operation involving steering column components. See appropriate AIR BAG RESTRAINT SYSTEMS article. Do not apply electrical power to any component on steering column without first deactivating air bag system. Air bag may deploy.

CAUTION: Disconnect battery before disconnecting Generic Electronic Module (GEM) or Central Timer Module (CTM) connectors. Failure to do so will result in GEM/CTM storing erroneous codes and may also result in erratic operation of GEM/CTM after reconnection. When battery is disconnected, vehicle computer and memory systems may lose memory data. Driveability problems may exist until computer systems have completed a relearn cycle. See COMPUTER RELEARN PROCEDURES article in GENERAL INFORMATION before disconnecting battery.

SYMPTOM TEST INDEX

Symptom	Test
Wipers Inoperative	A
Wipers Stay On Continuously	B
High & Low Speeds Do Not Operate Properly	C
Intermittent Wipers Do Not Operate Properly	D
Front Washer Pump Inoperative	E
Speed Dependent Interval Does Not Operate Properly	F
Wipers Operate At High Speed Only	G
Rear Wiper Stays On Continuously	H
Rear Washer Pump Inoperative	J
Rear Wiper Inoperative	K
Rear Wiper Does Not Operate Properly	L
No Communication With GEM/CTM	M

TEST A: WIPERS INOPERATIVE

NOTE: After all repairs, clear DTCs and retest system.

1) Connect New Generation Star (NGS) Tester (007-00500) to Data Link Connector (DLC) located under left side of instrument panel. On manual transmission models, depress clutch pedal. Observe GEM/CTM PID IGN_GEM while turning ignition switch through all positions. If PID values agree with switch positions, go to next step. If PID values do NOT agree with switch positions, check ignition switch and ignition circuits. See STEERING COLUMN SWITCHES – EXPLORER & MOUNTAINEER article. Also see appropriate wiring diagram in POWER DISTRIBUTION article in WIRING DIAGRAMS.

2) Retrieve and note continuous DTCs stored in Generic Electronic Module/Central Timer Module (GEM/CTM). Clear continuous DTCs. Following NGS tester manufacturer's instructions, perform WIPER/WASHER SELF-TEST and note all DTCs. If any DTCs are retrieved, go to appropriate step. See TEST A DTC INDEX table. If no DTCs are retrieved, go to next step.

TEST A DTC INDEX

DTC	Step
B1342	1
B1431	4)

TEST A DTC INDEX (Cont.)

DTC	Step
B1432	4)
B1438	11)
B1450	11)
B1840	11)

[1] – Replace GEM/CTM. See GENERIC ELECTRONIC MODULE/CENTRAL TIMER MODULE under REMOVAL & INSTALLATION. Clear DTCs and retest system.

3) Check fuse No. 16 (30-amp) at central junction box (interior fuse panel). If fuse is okay, go to next step. If fuse is blown, check for short to ground. Repair wiring if necessary. See WIRING DIAGRAMS.

4) Turn ignition on. Using NGS tester, observe PID WPRUN while triggering active command WIPER RLY. If WPRUN PID agrees with command mode and displays ON- - - and OFF- - -, go to step 11). If WPRUN PID does not agree with command mode and displays OFFO-G, go to step 7). If WPRUN PID does not agree with command mode and displays ON-B-, go to next step.

5) Check wiper run relay. See RELAYS under COMPONENT TESTS. Replace relay if necessary. If relay is okay, go to next step.

6) Disconnect GEM/CTM 26-pin connector C280 and wiper run relay. Turn ignition on. Measure voltage between wiper run relay connector terminal No. 1 and ground. See Fig. 5. If there is voltage, repair Yellow/White wire short to power. See WIRING DIAGRAMS. If there is no voltage, replace GEM/CTM. See GENERIC ELECTRONIC MODULE/CENTRAL TIMER MODULE under REMOVAL & INSTALLATION.

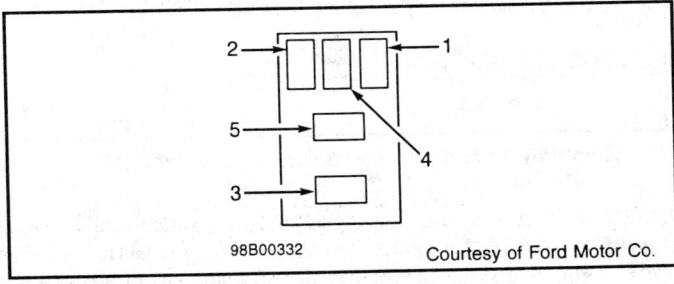

98B00332　　　Courtesy of Ford Motor Co.

Fig. 5: Identifying Relay Connector Terminals

7) Turn ignition off. Remove wiper run relay. Turn ignition on. Check for voltage between wiper run relay connector terminal No. 2 and ground. See Fig. 5. If voltage is more than 10 volts, reconnect wiper run relay and go to next step. If voltage is 10 volts or less, repair Red wire.

8) Turn ignition off. Disconnect GEM/CTM 26-pin connector C280. Measure resistance between wiper run relay connector terminal No. 1 and ground. See Fig. 5. If resistance is more than 10 k/ohms, go to next step. If resistance is 10 k/ohms or less, repair Yellow/White wire short to ground.

9) Check wiper run relay. See RELAYS under COMPONENT TESTS. Replace relay if necessary. If relay is okay, go to next step.

10) Disconnect GEM/CTM 26-pin connector C280. Measure resistance between GEM/CTM connector C280 terminal No. 19 and wiper run relay connector terminal No. 1. See Figs. 5 and 6. If resistance is less than 5 ohms, replace GEM/CTM. See GENERIC ELECTRONIC MODULE/

CENTRAL TIMER MODULE under REMOVAL & INSTALLATION. If resistance is 5 ohms or more, repair open in Yellow/White wire.

11) Using NGS tester, observe PID WPMODE while turning wiper switch through all positions. If PID values agree with switch positions, go to step 16). If PID values do not agree with switch positions, go to next step.

12) Turn ignition off. Disconnect multifunction switch 7-pin connector C210. Check wiper switch portion of multifunction switch. See WIPER SWITCH under COMPONENT TESTS. Replace switch as necessary. If switch is okay, go to next step.

13) Disconnect GEM/CTM 26-pin connector C280. Measure resistance between GEM/CTM connector C280 terminal No. 21 and multifunction switch connector C210 terminal No. 993. See Figs. 6 and 7. If resistance is less than 5 ohms, go to next step. If resistance is 5 ohms or more, repair Gray/Red wire.

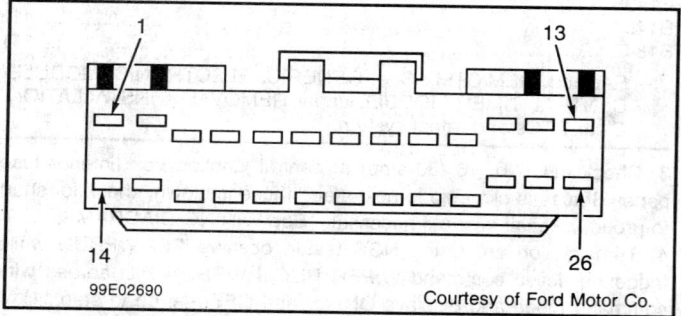

Fig. 6: Identifying GEM/CTM 26-Pin Connector C280 Terminals

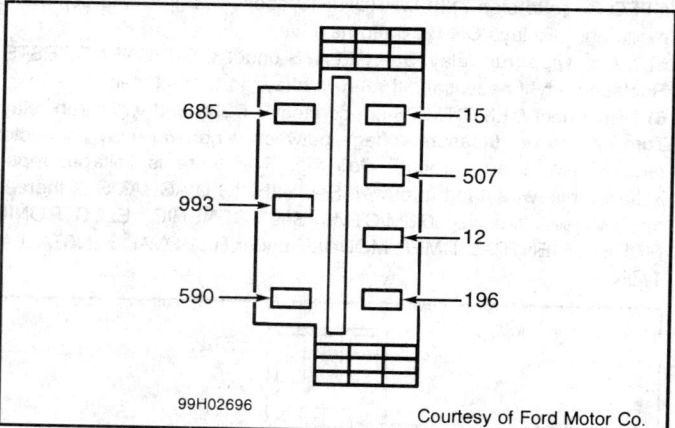

Fig. 7: Identifying Multifunction Switch Connector C210 Terminals

14) Measure resistance between GEM/CTM connector C280 terminal No. 13 and multifunction switch connector C210 terminal No. 590. See Figs. 6 and 7. If resistance is less than 5 ohms, go to next step. If resistance is 5 ohms or more, repair Light Blue/Orange wire.

15) Measure resistance between GEM/CTM connector C280 terminal No. 22 and multifunction switch connector C210 terminal No. 685. See Figs. 6 and 7. If resistance is less than 5 ohms, replace GEM/CTM. See GENERIC ELECTRONIC MODULE/CENTRAL TIMER MODULE under REMOVAL & INSTALLATION. If resistance is 5 ohms or more, repair Pink/Yellow wire.

16) Turn ignition off. Disconnect wiper run relay. Turn ignition on. Measure voltage between wiper run relay connector terminal No. 5 and ground. See Fig. 5. If voltage is more than 10 volts, reconnect wiper run relay and go to next step. If voltage is 10 volts or less, repair open in Red wire.

17) Turn ignition off. Disconnect wiper high/low relay. Turn ignition on. Connect a jumper wire between high/low relay connector terminals No. 3 and 4. See Fig. 5. Turn wiper switch through all positions. If wipers do not operate, go to next step. If wipers operate, replace high/low relay.

18) Turn ignition off. Disconnect wiper motor connector. Measure resistance between wiper motor connector terminal No. 3 and ground. See Fig. 3. If resistance is less than 5 ohms, go to next step. If resistance is 5 ohms or more, repair Black wire.

19) Turn ignition off. Disconnect wiper high/low relay. Turn ignition on. Using NGS tester, set active command WIPER RLY to ON. Measure voltage between high/low relay connector terminal No. 3 and ground. See Fig. 5. If voltage is more than 10 volts, go to next step. If voltage is 10 volts or less, repair Black/Pink wire. See WIRING DIAGRAMS.

20) Turn ignition off. Remove wiper linkage from wiper motor. Check wiper linkage for free operation. If linkage is free of binding and operational resistance, check wiper motor. See WIPER MOTOR under COMPONENT TESTS. Replace motor if necessary. If linkage does not operate freely, repair as necessary. Reconnect linkage.

TEST B: WIPERS STAY ON CONTINUOUSLY

NOTE: After all repairs, clear DTCs and retest system.

1) Connect New Generation Star (NGS) Tester (007-00500) to Data Link Connector (DLC) located under left side of instrument panel. On manual transmission models, depress clutch pedal. Observe GEM/CTM PID IGN_GEM while turning ignition switch through all positions. If PID values agree with switch positions, go to next step. If PID values do NOT agree with switch positions, check ignition switch and ignition circuits. See STEERING COLUMN SWITCHES – EXPLORER & MOUNTAINEER article. Also see appropriate wiring diagram in POWER DISTRIBUTION article in WIRING DIAGRAMS.

2) Retrieve and note continuous DTCs stored in GEM/CTM. Clear continuous DTCs. Perform WIPER/WASHER SELF-TEST and note all DTCs. If any DTCs are retrieved, go to appropriate step. See TEST B DTC INDEX table. If no DTCs are retrieved, go to next step.

TEST B DTC INDEX

DTC	Step
B1342	[1]
B1431	7)
B1441	3)
B1453	3)
B1473	10)
B1476	10)

[1] – Replace GEM/CTM. See GENERIC ELECTRONIC MODULE/CENTRAL TIMER MODULE under REMOVAL & INSTALLATION. Clear DTCs and retest system.

3) Turn ignition on. Using NGS tester, observe PID WPMODE while turning wiper switch through all positions. If PID values agree with switch positions, go to step 7). If PID values do not agree with switch positions, go to next step.

4) Turn ignition off. Disconnect multifunction switch 7-pin connector C210. Check wiper switch portion of multifunction switch. See WIPER SWITCH under COMPONENT TESTS. Replace switch as necessary. If switch is okay, go to next step.

5) Disconnect GEM/CTM 26-pin connector C280. Measure resistance between multifunction switch connector C210 terminal No. 590 and ground. See Fig. 7. If resistance is more than 10 k/ohms, go to next step. If resistance is 10 k/ohms or less, repair short to ground in Light Blue/Orange wire.

6) Measure resistance between multifunction switch connector C210 terminal No. 685 and ground. See Fig. 7. If resistance is more than 10 k/ohms, replace GEM/CTM. See GENERIC ELECTRONIC MODULE/CENTRAL TIMER MODULE under REMOVAL & INSTALLATION. If resistance is 10 k/ohms or less, repair short to ground in Pink/Yellow wire.

7) Turn ignition on. Using NGS tester, observe PID WPRUN while triggering active command WIPER RLY. If WPRUN PID does not agree with command mode and displays OFFO-G, go to next step. If WPRUN PID agrees with command mode and displays ON- - - and OFF- - -, go to step 10).

8) Turn ignition off. Remove and check wiper run relay. See RELAYS in COMPONENT TESTS. Replace relay as necessary. If relay is okay, go to next step.

9) Disconnect GEM/CTM 26-pin connector C280. Measure resistance between wiper run relay connector terminal No. 1 and ground. *See Fig. 5.* If resistance is more than 10 k/ohms, replace GEM/CTM. See GENERIC ELECTRONIC MODULE/CENTRAL TIMER MODULE under REMOVAL & INSTALLATION. If resistance is 10 k/ohms or less, repair Yellow/White wire.

10) Turn ignition on. Remove wiper run relay. If wipers stop operating, replace wiper run relay. If wipers continue to operate, go to next step.

11) Turn ignition off. Disconnect wiper motor connector and wiper high/low relay. Turn ignition on. Measure voltage between high/low relay connector terminal No. 5 and ground. *See Fig. 5.* If there is no voltage, go to next step. If there is voltage, repair Dark Blue/Orange wire.

12) Measure voltage between wiper high/low relay connector terminal No. 4 and ground. *See Fig. 5.* If there is no voltage, go to next step. If there is voltage, repair White wire short to power.

13) Measure voltage between wiper high/low relay connector terminal No. 3 and ground. *See Fig. 5.* If there is no voltage, replace wiper motor. If there is voltage, repair Black/Pink wire. See WIRING DIAGRAMS.

TEST C: HIGH & LOW SPEEDS DO NOT OPERATE PROPERLY

NOTE: After all repairs, clear DTCs and retest system.

1) Connect New Generation Star (NGS) Tester (007-00500) to Data Link Connector (DLC) located under left side of instrument panel. On manual transmission models, depress clutch pedal. Observe GEM/CTM PID IGN_GEM while turning ignition switch through all positions. If PID values agree with switch positions, go to next step. If PID values do NOT agree with switch positions, check ignition switch and ignition circuits. See STEERING COLUMN SWITCHES – EXPLORER & MOUNTAINEER article. Also see appropriate wiring diagram in POWER DISTRIBUTION article in WIRING DIAGRAMS.

2) Retrieve and note continuous DTCs stored in Generic Electronic Module/Central Timer Module (GEM/CTM). Clear continuous DTCs. Perform WIPER/WASHER SELF-TEST and note all DTCs. If any DTCs are retrieved, go to appropriate step. See TEST C DTC INDEX table. If no DTCs are retrieved, go to next step.

TEST C DTC INDEX

DTC	Step
B1342	1
B1434	9)
B1436	9)
B1438	3)
B1441	3)
B1450	3)
B1466	3)
B1473	3)
B1476	3)

[1] – Replace GEM/CTM. See GENERIC ELECTRONIC MODULE/CENTRAL TIMER MODULE under REMOVAL & INSTALLATION. Clear DTCs and retest system.

3) Turn ignition on. Using NGS tester, observe PID WPMODE while turning wiper switch through all positions. If PID values agree with switch positions, go to step **9)**. If PID values do not agree with switch positions, go to next step.

4) Turn ignition off. Disconnect multifunction switch 7-pin connector C210. Check wiper switch portion of multifunction switch. See WIPER SWITCH under COMPONENT TESTS. Replace as necessary. If switch is okay, go to next step.

5) Disconnect GEM/CTM 26-pin connector C280. Turn ignition on. Measure voltage between multifunction switch connector C210 terminal No. 590 and ground. *See Fig. 7.* If there is no voltage, go to next step. If there is voltage, repair Light Blue/Orange wire short to power.

6) Measure voltage between multifunction switch connector C210 terminal No. 685 and ground. *See Fig. 7.* If there is no voltage, go to next step. If there is voltage, repair Pink/Yellow wire short to power.

7) Turn ignition off. Measure resistance between GEM/CTM connector C280 terminal No. 13 and multifunction switch connector C210 terminal No. 590. *See Figs. 6 and 7.* If resistance is less than 5 ohms, go to next step. If resistance is 5 ohms or more, repair Light Blue/Orange wire.

8) Measure resistance between GEM/CTM connector C280 terminal No. 22 and multifunction switch connector C210 terminal No. 685. *See Figs. 6 and 7.* If resistance is less than 5 ohms, replace GEM. See GENERIC ELECTRONIC MODULE/CENTRAL TIMER MODULE under REMOVAL & INSTALLATION. If resistance is 5 ohms or more, repair Pink/Yellow wire.

9) Turn ignition on. Using NGS tester, observe PID WPHISP while triggering active command SPEED RLY. If PID WPHISP agrees with command mode and displays ON- - - and OFF- - -, go to step **16)**. If PID WPHISP does not agree with command mode and displays OFFO-G, go to step **12)**. If PID WPHISP does not agree with command mode and displays ON-B, go to next step.

10) Turn ignition off. Disconnect GEM/CTM 26-pin connector C280. Disconnect wiper high/low relay. Turn ignition on. Measure voltage between high/low relay connector terminal No. 1 and ground. *See Fig. 5.* If there is no voltage, go to next step. If there is voltage, repair Gray/Light Blue wire short to power.

11) Turn ignition off. Check wiper high/low relay. See RELAYS under COMPONENT TESTS. Replace relay as necessary. If relay is okay, replace GEM/CTM. See GENERIC ELECTRONIC MODULE/CENTRAL TIMER MODULE under REMOVAL & INSTALLATION.

12) Turn ignition off. Disconnect wiper high/low relay. Turn ignition on. Measure voltage between high/low relay connector terminal No. 2 and ground. *See Fig. 5.* If voltage is more than 10 volts, go to next step. If voltage is 10 volts or less, repair open in Red wire.

13) Turn ignition off. Remove wiper high/low relay. Check high/low relay. See RELAYS under COMPONENT TESTS. Replace relay as necessary. If relay is okay, go to next step.

14) Disconnect GEM/CTM 26-pin connector C280. Measure resistance between high/low relay connector terminal No. 1 and ground. *See Fig. 5.* If resistance is more than 10 k/ohms, go to next step. If resistance is 10 k/ohms or less, repair Gray/Light Blue wire short to ground.

15) Measure resistance between GEM/CTM connector C280 terminal No. 18 and high/low relay connector terminal No. 1. *See Figs. 5 and 6.* If resistance is less than 5 ohms, replace GEM/CTM. See GENERIC ELECTRONIC MODULE/CENTRAL TIMER MODULE under REMOVAL & INSTALLATION. If resistance is 5 ohms or more, repair open in Gray/Light Blue wire.

16) Turn ignition off. Disconnect wiper high/low relay. Connect a jumper wire between wiper high/low relay connector terminals No. 3 and 5. *See Fig. 5.* Turn ignition on. Set wiper switch on high speed. Observe wiper operation. Remove jumper wire and reconnect between wiper high/low relay connector terminals No. 3 and 4. Turn wiper switch to low speed. If wipers do not operate at correct speeds, remove jumper wire and go to next step. If wipers operate at correct speeds, replace wiper high/low relay.

17) Turn ignition off. Disconnect wiper motor connector. Measure resistance between wiper high/low relay connector terminal No. 5 and wiper motor connector terminal No. 5. *See Figs. 5 and 3.* If resistance is less than 5 ohms, go to next step. If resistance is 5 ohms or more, repair open in Dark Blue/Orange wire.

18) Measure resistance between wiper high/low relay connector terminal No. 4 and wiper motor connector terminal No. 4. *See Figs. 5 and 3.* If resistance is less than 5 ohms, check wiper motor. See WIPER MOTOR under COMPONENT TESTS. If resistance is 5 ohms or more, repair White wire.

TEST D: INTERMITTENT WIPERS DO NOT OPERATE PROPERLY

NOTE: *After all repairs, clear DTCs and retest system.*

1) Connect New Generation Star (NGS) Tester (007-00500) to Data Link Connector (DLC) located under left side of instrument panel. On manual transmission models, depress clutch pedal. Observe GEM/CTM PID IGN_GEM while turning ignition switch through all positions. If PID values agree with switch positions, go to next step. If PID values do NOT agree with switch positions, check ignition switch and ignition circuits. See STEERING COLUMN SWITCHES – EXPLORER & MOUNTAINEER article. Also see appropriate wiring diagram in POWER DISTRIBUTION article in WIRING DIAGRAMS.

2) Retrieve and note continuous DTCs stored in Generic Electronic Module/Central Timer Module (GEM/CTM). Clear continuous DTCs. Perform WIPER/WASHER SELF-TEST and note all DTCs. If any DTCs are retrieved, go to appropriate step. See TEST D DTC INDEX table. If no DTCs are retrieved, go to next step.

TEST D DTC INDEX

DTC	Step
B1342	[1]
B1438	3)
B1446	9)
B1450	3)
B1453	3)

[1] – Replace GEM/CTM. See GENERIC ELECTRONIC MODULE/CENTRAL TIMER MODULE under REMOVAL & INSTALLATION. Clear DTCs and retest system.

3) Turn ignition on. Observe GEM/CTM PID WPMODE while turning wiper switch through all positions. If PID values agree with switch positions, go to step 9). If PID values do not agree with switch positions, go to next step.

4) Turn ignition off. Disconnect multifunction switch 7-pin connector C210. Check wiper switch. See WIPER SWITCH under COMPONENT TESTS. Replace switch as necessary. If switch is okay, go to next step.

5) Disconnect GEM/CTM 26-pin connector C280. Turn ignition on. Measure voltage between multifunction switch connector C210 terminal No. 590 and ground. *See Fig. 7.* If there is no voltage, go to next step. If there is any voltage, repair Light Blue/Orange wire short to power.

6) Measure voltage between multifunction switch connector C210 terminal No. 685 and ground. *See Fig. 7.* If there is no voltage, go to next step. If there is any voltage, repair Pink/Yellow wire short to power.

7) Disconnect GEM/CTM 26-pin connector C280. Measure resistance between GEM/CTM connector C280 terminal No. 13 and multifunction switch connector C210 terminal No. 590. *See Figs. 6 and 7.* If resistance is less than 5 ohms, go to next step. If resistance is 5 ohms or more, repair Light Blue/Orange wire.

8) Measure resistance between GEM/CTM connector C280 terminal No. 22 and multifunction switch connector C210 terminal No. 685. *See Figs. 6 and 7.* If resistance is less than 5 ohms, replace GEM/CTM. See GENERIC ELECTRONIC MODULE/CENTRAL TIMER MODULE under REMOVAL & INSTALLATION. If resistance is 5 ohms or more, repair Pink/Yellow wire.

9) Turn ignition on. Using NGS tester, observe PID WPPRKSW while wipers are operating. If PID WPPRKSW agrees with status of wipers, replace GEM/CTM. See GENERIC ELECTRONIC MODULE/CENTRAL TIMER MODULE under REMOVAL & INSTALLATION. If WPPRKSW PID does not agree with status of wipers, go to next step.

10) Turn ignition off. Disconnect wiper motor connector. Turn ignition on. Measure voltage between wiper motor connector terminal No. 2 and ground. *See Fig. 3.* If voltage is more than 10 volts, go to next step. If voltage is 10 volts or less, repair Red wire.

11) Turn ignition off. Measure resistance between wiper motor connector terminal No. 3 and ground. *See Fig. 3.* If resistance is less than 5 ohms, go to next step. If resistance is 5 ohms or more, repair open in Black wire.

12) Turn ignition off. Disconnect GEM/CTM 26-pin connector C280 and wiper run relay. Measure resistance between GEM/CTM connector C280 terminal No. 15 and wiper motor connector terminal No. 1. *See Figs. 3 and 6.* If resistance is less than 5 ohms, go to next step. If resistance is 5 ohms or more, repair Black wire.

13) Measure resistance between wiper run relay connector terminal No. 4 and wiper motor connector terminal No. 1. *See Figs. 3 and 5.* If resistance is less than 5 ohms, go to next step. If resistance is 5 ohms or more, repair Black wire.

14) Measure resistance between wiper motor connector terminal No. 1 and ground. *See Fig. 3.* If resistance is 10 k/ohm or less, repair Black wire short to ground. If resistance is more than 10 k/ohms, reconnect GEM/CTM connector C280 and go to next step.

15) Connect a jumper wire between wiper motor connector terminal No. 1 and ground. *See Fig. 3.* Turn ignition on. Observe GEM/CTM PID WPPRKSW. If PID indicates PARKED, remove jumper wire and go to next step. If PID does not indicate PARKED, replace GEM/CTM. See GENERIC ELECTRONIC MODULE/CENTRAL TIMER MODULE under REMOVAL & INSTALLATION.

16) Turn ignition off. Observe PID WPPRKSW. Using a jumper wire, apply battery voltage to wiper motor connector terminal No. 1. *See Fig. 3.* If PID indicates notPRK, replace wiper motor. See FRONT WIPER MOTOR under REMOVAL & INSTALLATION. If PID does not indicate notPRK, replace GEM/CTM. See GENERIC ELECTRONIC MODULE/CENTRAL TIMER MODULE under REMOVAL & INSTALLATION.

TEST E: FRONT WASHER PUMP INOPERATIVE

NOTE: *After all repairs, clear DTCs and retest system.*

1) Connect New Generation Star (NGS) Tester (007-00500) to Data Link Connector (DLC) located under left side of instrument panel. On manual transmission models, depress clutch pedal. Observe GEM/CTM PID IGN_GEM while turning ignition switch through all positions. If PID values agree with switch positions, go to next step. If PID values do NOT agree with switch positions, check ignition switch and ignition circuits. See STEERING COLUMN SWITCHES – EXPLORER & MOUNTAINEER article. Also see appropriate wiring diagram in POWER DISTRIBUTION article in WIRING DIAGRAMS.

2) Retrieve and note continuous DTCs stored in Generic Electronic Module/Central Timer Module (GEM/CTM). Clear continuous DTCs. Perform WIPER/WASHER SELF-TEST and note all DTCs. If any DTCs are retrieved, go to appropriate step. See TEST E DTC INDEX table. If no DTCs are retrieved, go to next step.

TEST E DTC INDEX

DTC	Step
B1342	[1]
B1450	3)
B1453	3)
B1458	9)
B1460	9)

[1] – Replace GEM/CTM. See GENERIC ELECTRONIC MODULE/CENTRAL TIMER MODULE under REMOVAL & INSTALLATION. Clear DTCs and retest system.

3) Turn ignition on. Using NGS tester, observe PID WPMODE while turning wiper switch through all positions. If PID values agree with switch positions, go to next step. If PID values do not agree with switch positions, go to step 6).

4) Observe PID WASH_SW. Press washer switch. If PID WASH_SW indicates ON when switch is pressed and OFF when switch is released, go to step 9). If PID does not agree with switch position, go to next step.

5) Turn ignition off. Disconnect multifunction switch 7-pin connector C210. Measure resistance between multifunction switch terminals No. 590 and 993 while depressing and releasing washer switch. *See Fig. 4.* If resistance is less than 5 ohms with switch depressed and approximately 2670 ohms with switch released, go to next step. If resistance is not as specified, replace multifunction switch. See MULTIFUNCTION SWITCH under REMOVAL & INSTALLATION.

6) Disconnect GEM/CTM 26-pin connector C280. Turn ignition on. Measure voltage between multifunction switch connector C210 terminal No. 590 and ground. *See Fig. 7.* If there is voltage, repair Light Blue/Orange wire short to power. If there is no voltage, go to next step.

7) Turn ignition off. Measure resistance between multifunction switch connector C210 terminal No. 590 and ground. *See Fig. 7.* If resistance is more than 10 k/ohms, go to next step. If resistance is 10 k/ohms or less, repair Light Blue/Orange wire short to ground.

8) Disconnect GEM/CTM 26-pin connector C280. Measure resistance between multifunction switch connector C210 terminal No. 590 and GEM/CTM connector C280 terminal No. 13. *See Figs. 6 and 7.* If resistance is less than 5 ohms, replace GEM/CTM. See GENERIC ELECTRONIC MODULE/CENTRAL TIMER MODULE under REMOVAL & INSTALLATION. If resistance is 5 ohms or more, repair open in Light Blue/Orange wire.

9) Using NGS tester, observe PID WASHRLY while triggering active command WASHRLY ON and OFF. If PID WASHRLY agrees with command WASHRLY and displays ON- - - and OFF- - -, go to step 17). If WASHRLY does not agree with command WASHRLY and displays OFFO-G, go to next step. If WASHRLY does not agree with command WASHRLY and displays ON-B-, go to step 15).

10) Turn ignition off. Check fuse No. 12 (7.5-amp) located at central junction box (interior fuse panel). If fuse is okay, go to next step. If fuse is blown, replace fuse and retest system. If fuse blows again, repair short to ground. See WIRING DIAGRAMS.

11) Turn ignition on. Disconnect front washer pump relay. Measure voltage between washer pump relay connector terminal No. 1 and ground. Also measure voltage between washer pump relay terminal No. 5 and ground. *See Fig. 5.* If each voltage is more than 10 volts, go to next step. If either voltage is 10 volts or less, repair White/Black wire(s) as necessary.

12) Turn ignition off. Check washer pump relay. See RELAYS under COMPONENT TESTS. Replace relay as necessary. If relay is okay, go to next step.

13) Disconnect GEM/CTM 26-pin connector C280. Measure resistance between GEM/CTM connector C280 terminal No. 24 and front washer pump relay terminal No. 2. *See Figs. 5 and 6.* If resistance is less than 5 ohms, go to next step. If resistance is 5 ohms or more, repair open in Tan/Red wire.

14) Measure resistance between front washer pump relay connector terminal No. 2 and ground. *See Fig. 5.* If resistance is more than 10 k/ohms, replace GEM/CTM. See GENERIC ELECTRONIC MODULE/CENTRAL TIMER MODULE under REMOVAL & INSTALLATION. If resistance is 10 k/ohms or less, repair Tan/Red wire short to ground.

15) Turn ignition off. Check front washer pump relay. See RELAYS under COMPONENT TESTS. Replace relay as necessary. If relay is okay, go to next step.

16) Disconnect front washer pump relay and GEM/CTM 26-pin connector C280. Turn ignition on. Measure voltage between front washer pump relay connector terminal No. 2 and ground. *See Fig. 5.* If there is voltage, repair Tan/Red wire short to power. If there is no voltage, replace GEM/CTM. See GENERIC ELECTRONIC MODULE/CENTRAL TIMER MODULE under REMOVAL & INSTALLATION.

17) Turn ignition off. Disconnect front washer pump relay. Connect a jumper wire between front washer pump relay connector terminals No. 1 and 3. *See Fig. 5.* Turn ignition on. If washer pump motor does not operate, remove jumper wire and go to next step. If washer pump motor operates, replace front washer pump relay.

18) Turn ignition off. Disconnect washer pump connector. Measure resistance of Black/White wire between washer pump connector and washer pump relay connector terminal No. 3. *See Fig. 5.* If resistance is less than 5 ohms, go to next step. If resistance is 5 ohms or more, repair open in Black/White wire.

19) Measure resistance of Black/White wire between washer pump connector and ground. If resistance is less than 5 ohms, replace washer pump motor. If resistance is 5 ohms or more, go to next step.

20) Check rear washer relay. See RELAYS under COMPONENT TESTS. Replace relay as necessary.

21) Measure resistance between rear washer relay connector terminal No. 4 and ground. *See Fig. 5.* If resistance is less than 5 ohms, repair Dark Green wire between rear washer relay and rear washer pump. If resistance is 5 ohms or more, repair appropriate Black wire(s). See WIRING DIAGRAMS.

TEST F: SPEED DEPENDENT INTERVAL DOES NOT OPERATE PROPERLY

NOTE: After all repairs, clear DTCs and retest system.

1) Connect New Generation Star (NGS) Tester (007-00500) to Data Link Connector (DLC) located under left side of instrument panel. On manual transmission models, depress clutch pedal. Observe GEM/CTM PID IGN_GEM while turning ignition switch through all positions. If PID values agree with switch positions, go to next step. If PID values do NOT agree with switch positions, check ignition switch and ignition circuits. See STEERING COLUMN SWITCHES – EXPLORER & MOUNTAINEER article. Also see appropriate wiring diagram in POWER DISTRIBUTION article in WIRING DIAGRAMS.

2) Retrieve and note continuous DTCs stored in GEM/CTM. Clear continuous DTCs. Perform WIPER/WASHER SELF-TEST and note all DTCs. If no DTCs are retrieved, go to next step. If DTC P0500 is retrieved, go to next step. If DTC B1342 is retrieved, replace GEM/CTM. See GENERIC ELECTRONIC MODULE/CENTRAL TIMER MODULE under REMOVAL & INSTALLATION.

3) Using NGS tester, set GEM active command SPEED RLY to ON. Observe PID VSS_GEM while driving vehicle 0-55 MPH. If PID VSS_GEM agrees with speedometer, replace GEM. See GENERIC ELECTRONIC MODULE/CENTRAL TIMER MODULE under REMOVAL & INSTALLATION. If PID VSS_GEM does not agree with speedometer, go to next step.

4) Turn ignition off. Disconnect GEM/CTM 18-pin connector C283 and 4-wheel ABS control module connector. Measure resistance between 4-wheel ABS connector terminal No. 10 and GEM/CTM connector C283 terminal No. 9. *See Figs. 8 and 9.* If resistance is less than 5 ohms, problem exists in 4-wheel ABS system. See appropriate ANTI-LOCK article in BRAKES in appropriate MITCHELL® manual. If resistance is 5 ohms or more, repair open in Gray/Black wire.

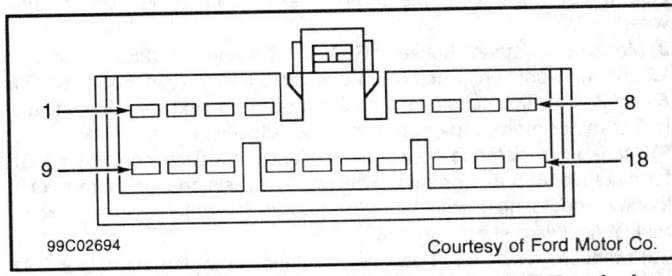

99C02694   Courtesy of Ford Motor Co.

Fig. 8: Identifying GEM/CTM 18-Pin Connector C283 Terminals

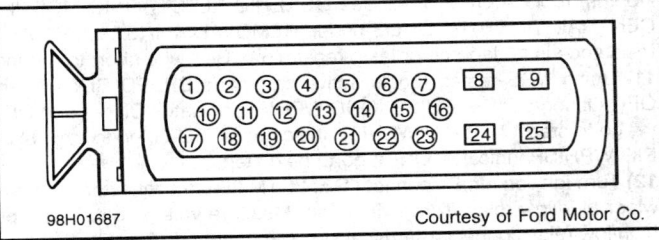

98H01687   Courtesy of Ford Motor Co.

Fig. 9: Identifying 4-Wheel ABS Connector Terminals

TEST G: WIPERS OPERATE AT HIGH SPEED ONLY

NOTE: After all repairs, clear DTCs and retest system.

1) Connect New Generation Star (NGS) Tester (007-00500) to Data Link Connector (DLC) located under left side of instrument panel. On manual transmission models, depress clutch pedal. Observe GEM/CTM PID IGN_GEM while turning ignition switch through all positions. If PID values agree with switch positions, go to next step. If PID values do NOT agree with switch positions, check ignition switch and ignition circuits. See STEERING COLUMN SWITCHES – EXPLORER & MOUNTAINEER article. Also see appropriate wiring diagram in POWER DISTRIBUTION article in WIRING DIAGRAMS.

2) Using NGS tester, retrieve and note continuous DTCs stored in Generic Electronic Module/Central Timer Module (GEM/CTM). If any DTCs are retrieved, go to appropriate step. See TEST G DTC INDEX table. If no DTCs are retrieved, go to next step.

TEST G DTC INDEX

DTC	Step
B1342	1
B1434	11)
B1436	11)
B1466	11)
B1467	11)
B1473	3)

[1] – Replace GEM/CTM. See GENERIC ELECTRONIC MODULE/ CENTRAL TIMER MODULE under REMOVAL & INSTALLATION. Clear DTCs and retest system.

3) Turn ignition on. Using NGS tester, observe GEM/CTM PID WPMODE while moving wiper switch through all positions. If PID WPMODE does not agree with all switch positions, go to next step. If PID WPMODE agrees with all switch positions, go to step **11)**.

4) Turn ignition off. Disconnect multifunction switch 7-pin connector C210. Check wiper switch. See WIPER SWITCH under COMPONENT TESTS. Replace switch as necessary. If switch is okay, go to next step.

5) Disconnect GEM/CTM 26-pin connector C280. Turn ignition on. Measure voltage between multifunction switch connector C210 terminal No. 590 and ground. See Fig. 7. If there is no voltage, go to next step. If there is voltage, repair Light Blue/Orange wire short to power.

6) Measure voltage between multifunction switch connector C210 terminal No. 685 and ground. See Fig. 7. If there is no voltage, go to next step. If there is voltage, repair Pink/Yellow wire short to power.

7) Turn ignition off. Measure resistance between GEM/CTM connector C280 terminal No. 13 and multifunction switch connector C210 terminal No. 590. See Figs. 6 and 7. If resistance is less than 5 ohms, go to next step. If resistance is 5 ohms or more, repair open in Light Blue/Orange wire.

8) Measure resistance between GEM/CTM connector C280 terminal No. 22 and multifunction switch connector C210 terminal No. 685. See Figs. 6 and 7. If resistance is less than 5 ohms, go to next step. If resistance is 5 ohms or more, repair open in Pink/Yellow wire.

9) Measure resistance between multifunction switch connector C210 terminal No. 685 and ground. See Fig. 7. If resistance is more than 10 k/ohms, go to next step. If resistance is 10 k/ohms or less, repair Pink/Yellow wire short to ground.

10) Measure resistance between multifunction switch connector C210 terminal No. 993 and ground. See Fig. 7. If resistance is more than 10 k/ohms, replace GEM/CTM. See GENERIC ELECTRONIC MODULE/ CENTRAL TIMER MODULE under REMOVAL & INSTALLATION. If resistance is 10 k/ohms or less, repair Gray/Red wire short to ground.

11) Using NGS tester, toggle active command SPEED RLY ON and OFF. Observe PID WPHISP. If PID WPHISP indicates ON- - - and OFF- - -, go to step **17)**. If PID WPHISP indicates OFFO-G, go to step **14)**. If PID WPHISP indicates ON-B, go to next step.

12) Turn ignition off. Disconnect GEM/CTM 26-pin connector C280 and wiper high/low relay. Turn ignition on. Measure voltage between wiper high/low relay connector terminal No. 1 and ground. See Fig. 5. If there is no voltage, go to next step. If there is voltage, repair Gray/Light Blue wire short to power.

13) Turn ignition off. Remove wiper high/low relay. Check wiper high/low relay. See RELAYS under COMPONENT TESTS. Replace relay as necessary. If relay is okay, replace GEM/CTM. See GENERIC ELECTRONIC MODULE/CENTRAL TIMER MODULE under REMOVAL & INSTALLATION.

14) Turn ignition off. Disconnect wiper high/low relay. Turn ignition on. Measure voltage between wiper high/low relay connector terminal No. 2

and ground. See Fig. 5. If voltage is more than 10 volts, go to next step. If voltage is 10 volts or less, repair Red wire.

15) Turn ignition off. Remove wiper high/low relay. Check wiper high/low relay. See RELAYS under COMPONENT TESTS. Replace relay as necessary. If relay is okay, go to next step.

16) Disconnect GEM/CTM 26-pin connector C280. Measure resistance between high/low relay connector terminal No. 1 and ground. See Fig. 5. If resistance is more than 10 k/ohms, replace GEM/CTM. See GENERIC ELECTRONIC MODULE/CENTRAL TIMER MODULE under REMOVAL & INSTALLATION. If resistance is 10 k/ohms or less, repair short to ground in Gray/Light Blue wire.

17) Turn ignition off. Remove wiper high/low relay. Connect jumper wire between high/low relay connector terminals No. 3 and 4. See Fig. 5. Set wiper switch to low speed. Turn ignition on. If wipers do not operate at low speed, remove jumper wire and go to next step. If wipers operate at low speed, replace wiper high/low relay.

18) Turn ignition off. Disconnect wiper motor connector. Measure resistance between wiper high/low relay connector terminal No. 4 and wiper motor connector terminal No. 4. See Figs. 3 and 5. If resistance is less than 5 ohms, check wiper motor. See WIPER MOTOR under COMPONENT TESTS. Replace wiper motor as necessary. If resistance is 5 ohms or more, repair open in White wire.

TEST H: REAR WIPER STAYS ON CONTINUOUSLY

NOTE: *After all repairs, clear DTCs and retest system.*

1) Connect New Generation Star (NGS) Tester (007-00500) to Data Link Connector (DLC) located under left side of instrument panel. On manual transmission models, depress clutch pedal. Observe GEM/CTM PID IGN_GEM while turning ignition switch through all positions. If PID values agree with switch positions, go to next step. If PID values do NOT agree with switch positions, check ignition switch and ignition circuits. See STEERING COLUMN SWITCHES – EXPLORER & MOUNTAINEER article. Also see appropriate wiring diagram in POWER DISTRIBUTION article in WIRING DIAGRAMS.

2) Retrieve and note continuous DTCs stored in GEM/CTM. Clear continuous DTCs. Following NGS tester manufacturer's instructions, perform WIPER/WASHER SELF-TEST and note all DTCs. If no DTCs are retrieved, or DTC B1614 is retrieved, go to next step. If DTC B1342 is retrieved, replace GEM/CTM. See GENERIC ELECTRONIC MODULE/CENTRAL TIMER MODULE under REMOVAL & INSTALLATION.

3) Turn ignition off. Disconnect rear wiper switch connector. Measure resistance between rear wiper switch terminals No. 2 and 5 while moving rear wiper switch through all positions. See mating connector view 10. See REAR WIPER SWITCH RESISTANCE TEST table. If resistance is as specified, go to next step. If resistance is not as specified, replace rear wiper switch. See REAR WIPER SWITCH under REMOVAL & INSTALLATION.

4) Disconnect GEM 16-pin connector C281. Measure resistance between GEM connector C281 terminal No. 12 and ground. See Fig. 11. If resistance is more than 10 k/ohms, replace GEM/CTM. See GENERIC ELECTRONIC MODULE/CENTRAL TIMER MODULE under REMOVAL & INSTALLATION. If resistance is 10 k/ohms or less, repair Pink/Black wire short to ground.

REAR WIPER SWITCH RESISTANCE TEST

Switch Position	Ohms
Off	4200-9100
First Interval Delay	1000-2420
Second Interval Delay	220-900
High	50-230

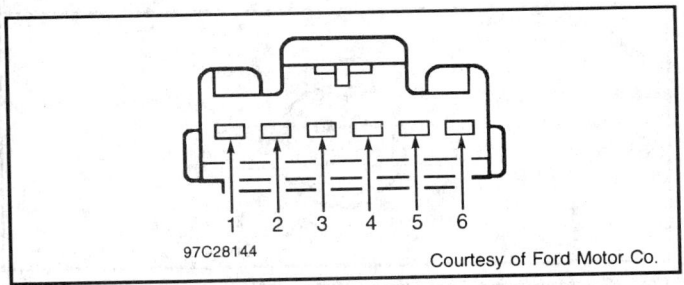

Fig. 10: Identifying Rear Wiper Switch Connector Terminals

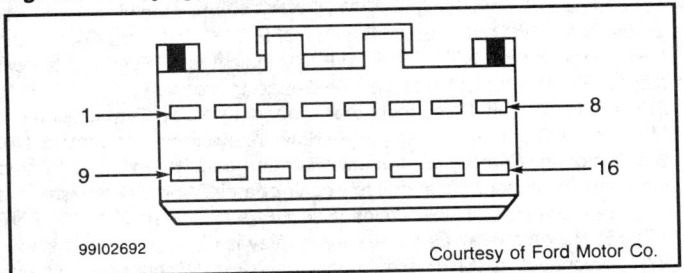

Fig. 11: Identifying GEM 16-In Connector C281 Terminals

TEST J: REAR WASHER PUMP INOPERATIVE

NOTE: After all repairs, clear DTCs and retest system.

1) Turn ignition on. Operate front washer switch. If front washers operate, go to next step. If front washers do not operate, go to TEST E: FRONT WASHER PUMP INOPERATIVE, step **18)**.

2) Turn ignition off. Connect New Generation Star (NGS) Tester (007-00500) to Data Link Connector (DLC). DLC is located under left side of instrument panel. Observe PID R_WP_MD while pressing rear washer switch. If PID does not indicate WASH, go to next step. If PID indicates WASH, go to step **4)**.

3) Turn ignition off. Disconnect rear wiper/washer switch connector. Measure resistance between rear wiper switch terminals No. 2 and 5 while pressing rear washer switch. See mating connector view 10. If resistance is less than 5 ohms, replace GEM/CTM. See GENERIC ELECTRONIC MODULE/CENTRAL TIMER MODULE under REMOVAL & INSTALLATION. If resistance is 5 ohms or more, replace rear wiper switch. See REAR WIPER SWITCH under REMOVAL & INSTALLATION.

4) Turn ignition off. Disconnect front washer pump relay. Measure resistance between front washer pump relay connector terminal No. 4 and ground. If resistance is less than 5 ohms, go to next step. If resistance is 5 ohms or more, repair Black wire.

5) Disconnect rear washer relay. Turn ignition on. While pressing rear washer switch measure voltage between rear washer relay connector terminal No. 5 and ground. *See Fig. 5.* Again, while pressing rear washer switch measure voltage between rear washer relay connector terminal No. 1 and ground. If either voltage is 10 volts or less, go to next step. If each voltage is more than 10 volts, go to step **8)**.

6) Turn ignition off. Disconnect rear wiper/washer switch connector. Turn ignition on. Measure voltage between rear wiper/washer switch connector terminal No. 4 and ground. *See Fig. 10.* If voltage is more than 10 volts, go to next step. If voltage is 10 volts or less, repair White/Black wire.

7) Turn ignition off. While pressing rear washer switch, measure resistance between rear wiper/washer switch terminals No. 1 and 4. For mating connector view, *see Fig. 10.* If resistance is 5 ohms or more, replace rear wiper switch. See REAR WIPER SWITCH under REMOVAL & INSTALLATION. If resistance is less than 5 ohms, repair open in Violet/Light Green wire.

8) Turn ignition off. Measure resistance between rear washer relay connector terminal No. 2 and ground. *See Fig. 5.* If resistance is less than 5 ohms, replace rear washer relay. If resistance is 5 ohms or more, repair open in Black ground wire.

TEST K: REAR WIPER INOPERATIVE

NOTE: After all repairs, clear DTCs and retest system.

1) Connect New Generation Star (NGS) Tester (007-00500) to Data Link Connector (DLC) located under left side of instrument panel. On manual transmission models, depress clutch pedal. Observe GEM/CTM PID IGN_GEM while turning ignition switch through all positions. If PID values agree with switch positions, go to next step. If PID values do NOT agree with switch positions, check ignition switch and ignition circuits. See STEERING COLUMN SWITCHES – EXPLORER & MOUNTAINEER article. Also see appropriate wiring diagram in POWER DISTRIBUTION article in WIRING DIAGRAMS.

2) Retrieve and note continuous DTCs stored in GEM/CTM. Clear continuous DTCs. Following NGS tester manufacturer's instructions, perform WIPER/WASHER SELF-TEST and REAR WIPER SELF-TEST and note all DTCs. If any DTCs are retrieved, go to appropriate test step. See TEST K DTC INDEX table. If no DTCs are retrieved, go to step **9)**.

TEST K DTC INDEX

DTC	Step [1]
B1342	3)
B1334	9)
B1611	24)
B1814	27)
B1816	16)
B1818	13)
B1820	8)
B1839	9)
B1894	9)

[1] – Replace GEM/CTM. See GENERIC ELECTRONIC MODULE/CENTRAL TIMER MODULE under REMOVAL & INSTALLATION. Clear DTCs and retest system.

3) Verify liftgate and liftgate glass are closed. Using NGS tester, observe PID LGATESW. If PID LGATESW indicates AJAR, go to next step. If PID LGATESW does not indicate AJAR, go to step **8)**.

4) Turn ignition off. Disconnect rear wiper disable switch. Switch is located in liftgate, under glass latch. Close liftgate and liftgate glass. Turn ignition on. Observe PID LGATESW. If PID LGATESW indicates AJAR, go to next step. If PID LGATESW does not indicate AJAR, replace liftgate wiper disable switch.

5) Turn ignition off. Disconnect right liftgate ajar switch. Switch is located in right side of liftgate, under trim panel. Turn ignition on. Observe PID LGATESW. If PID LGATESW indicates AJAR, go to next step. If PID LGATESW does not indicate AJAR, replace right liftgate ajar switch.

6) Reconnect right liftgate ajar switch. Turn ignition off. Disconnect left liftgate ajar switch. Switch is located in left side of liftgate, under trim panel. Close liftgate and liftgate glass. Turn ignition on. Observe PID LGATESW. If PID LGATESW indicates AJAR, go to next step. If PID LGATESW does not indicate AJAR, replace left liftgate ajar switch.

7) Turn ignition off. Disconnect GEM/CTM 26-pin connector C280. Measure resistance between GEM/CTM connector C280 terminal No. 4 and ground. *See Fig. 6.* If resistance is more than 10 k/ohms, replace GEM/CTM. See GENERIC ELECTRONIC MODULE/CENTRAL TIMER MODULE under REMOVAL & INSTALLATION. If resistance is 10 k/ohms or less, repair White/Violet wire short to ground.

8) Turn ignition off. Disconnect rear wiper down relay and rear wiper up relay. Measure resistance between each relay connector terminal No. 4 and ground. If either resistance is more than 5 ohms, repair open in Black wire. If each resistance is less than 5 ohms, reconnect relays and go to step **26)**.

NOTE: In next step, PID R_WP_MD should indicate LO when switch in high position.

9) Turn ignition on. Using NGS tester, observe PID R_WP_MD while turning rear wiper switch through all positions. If PID values do not agree with switch positions, go to next step. If PID values agree with switch positions, go to step **13)**.

10) Turn ignition off. Disconnect rear wiper switch connector. Measure resistance between rear wiper switch terminals No. 2 and 5 while moving rear wiper switch through all positions. See mating connector view 10. See REAR WIPER SWITCH RESISTANCE TEST table. If resistance is as specified, go to next step. If resistance is not as specified, replace rear wiper switch. See REAR WIPER SWITCH under REMOVAL & INSTALLATION.

REAR WIPER SWITCH RESISTANCE TEST

Switch Position	Ohms
Off	4200-9100
First Interval Delay	1000-2420
Second Interval Delay	220-950
High	50-230

11) Disconnect GEM/CTM 26-pin connector C280. Measure resistance between GEM/CTM connector C280 terminal No. 21 and rear wiper/washer switch connector terminal No. 5. See Figs. 6 and 10. If resistance is 5 ohms or less, go to next step. If resistance is 5 ohms or more, repair open in Gray/Red wire.

12) Disconnect GEM 16-pin connector C281. Measure resistance between GEM connector C281 terminal No. 12 and rear wiper switch connector terminal No. 2. See Figs. 10 and 11. If resistance is less than 5 ohms, replace GEM. See GENERIC ELECTRONIC MODULE/CENTRAL TIMER MODULE under REMOVAL & INSTALLATION. If resistance is 5 ohms or more, repair open in Pink/Black wire.

13) Using NGS tester, trigger GEM rear wiper active command UP RELAY ON and OFF. Observe PID R_WP_UP. If PID indicates ON- - - and OFF- - -, go to step 20). If PID R_WP_UP indicates OFFO-G, go to next step. If PID R_WP_UP indicates ON-B-, go to step 18).

14) Turn ignition off. Disconnect rear wiper up relay. Measure voltage between rear wiper up relay connector terminal No. 2. See Fig. 5. If voltage is more than 10 volts, go to next step. If voltage is 10 volts or less, repair open in White/Violet wire.

15) Check rear wiper up relay. See RELAYS under COMPONENT TESTS. Replace relay as necessary. If relay is okay, go to next step.

16) Disconnect GEM 16-pin connector C281. Measure resistance between rear wiper up relay connector terminal No. 1 and GEM connector C281 terminal No. 8. See Figs. 5 and 11. If resistance is less than 5 ohms, go to next step. If resistance is 5 ohms or more, repair open in Light Green wire.

17) Measure resistance between GEM connector C281 terminal No. 8 and ground. See Fig. 11. If resistance is more than 10 k/ohms, replace GEM. See GENERIC ELECTRONIC MODULE/CENTRAL TIMER MODULE under REMOVAL & INSTALLATION. If resistance is 10 k/ohms or less, repair Light Green wire short to ground.

18) Turn ignition off. Disconnect rear wiper up relay and GEM 16-pin connector C281. Turn ignition on. Measure voltage between rear wiper up relay connector terminal No. 1 and ground. If there is no voltage, go to next step. If there is voltage, repair Light Green wire short to power.

19) Check rear wiper up relay. See RELAYS under COMPONENT TESTS. Replace relay as necessary. If relay is okay, replace GEM. See GENERIC ELECTRONIC MODULE/CENTRAL TIMER MODULE under REMOVAL & INSTALLATION.

20) Turn ignition off. Check mini-fuse No. 8 (15-amp) located in battery junction box. If fuse is okay, go to next step. If faulty, replace fuse. If fuse fails again, repair White/Violet wire short to ground between mini-fuse No. 8 and rear wiper up relay. See WIRING DIAGRAMS.

21) Turn ignition off. Disconnect rear wiper motor connector. Turn ignition on. Using NGS tester, trigger GEM active command UP RELAY to ON. Measure voltage between rear wiper motor connector terminal No. 1 and ground. See Fig. 12. If voltage is 10 volts or less, go to next step. If voltage is more than 10 volts, go to step 24).

22) Measure resistance between rear wiper up relay connector terminal No. 3 and rear wiper motor connector terminal No. 1. See Figs. 5 and 12. If resistance is less than 5 ohms, go to next step. If resistance is 5 ohms or more, repair open in White/Orange wire.

23) Measure voltage between rear wiper up relay connector terminal No. 5 and ground. See Fig. 5. If voltage is more than 10 volts, replace rear wiper up relay. If voltage is 10 volts or less, repair White/Violet wire.

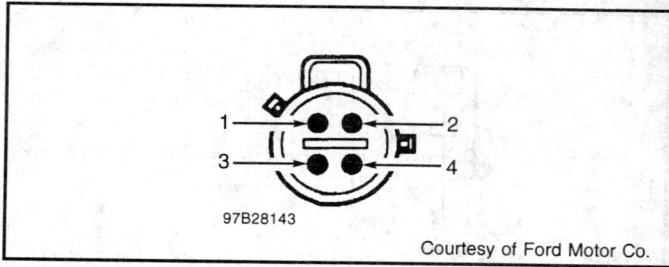

97B28143

Courtesy of Ford Motor Co.

Fig. 12: Identifying Rear Wiper Motor Connector Terminals

24) Using NGS tester, observe PID R_WP_DN while toggling rear wiper active command DWN RELAY ON and OFF. If PID indicates ON- - - and OFF- - -, go to step 30). If PID R_WP_DN indicates OFFO-G, go to next step. If PID R_WP_DN indicates ON-B-, go to step 28).

25) Turn ignition off. Disconnect rear wiper down relay. Turn ignition on. Measure voltage between rear wiper down relay connector terminal No. 2 and ground. See Fig. 5. If voltage is more than 10 volts, go to next step. If voltage is 10 volts or less, repair open in White/Violet wire.

26) Check rear wiper down relay. See RELAYS under COMPONENT TESTS. Replace relay as necessary. If relay is okay, go to next step.

27) Disconnect GEM 16-pin connector C281. Measure resistance between GEM connector C281 terminal No. 10 and rear wiper down relay connector terminal No. 1. See Figs. 5 and 11. If resistance is less than 5 ohms, replace GEM. See GENERIC ELECTRONIC MODULE/CENTRAL TIMER MODULE under REMOVAL & INSTALLATION. If resistance is 5 ohms or more, repair open in Tan wire.

28) Turn ignition off. Disconnect rear wiper down relay and GEM 16-pin connector C281. Turn ignition on. Measure voltage between rear wiper down relay connector terminal No. 1 and ground. See Fig. 5. If there is no voltage, go to next step. If there is voltage, repair Tan wire short to power.

29) Check rear wiper down relay. See RELAYS under COMPONENT TESTS. Replace relay as necessary. If relay is okay, replace GEM. See GENERIC ELECTRONIC MODULE/CENTRAL TIMER MODULE under REMOVAL & INSTALLATION.

30) Turn ignition off. Check mini-fuse No. 8 (15-amp) in battery junction box. If fuse is okay, go to next step. If faulty, replace fuse and retest system. If fuse fails again, repair short to ground. See WIRING DIAGRAMS.

31) Turn ignition off. Disconnect rear wiper motor connector. Turn ignition on. Using NGS tester, set rear wiper active command DWN RELAY to ON. Measure voltage between rear wiper motor connector terminal No. 2 and ground. See Fig. 12. If voltage is more than 10 volts, go to step 34). If voltage is 10 volts or less, go to next step.

32) Turn ignition off. Disconnect rear wiper down relay. Measure resistance between rear wiper down relay connector terminal No. 3 and rear wiper motor connector terminal No. 2. See Figs. 5 and 12. If resistance is less than 5 ohms, go to next step. If resistance is 5 ohms or more, repair open in Black/Light Blue wire.

33) Measure voltage between rear wiper down relay connector terminal No. 5 and ground. If voltage is more than 10 volts, replace rear wiper down relay. If voltage is 10 volts or less, repair open in White/Violet wire.

34) Turn ignition off. Disconnect rear wiper up and rear wiper down relays. Measure resistance between each relay connector terminal No. 4 and ground. See Fig. 5. If each resistance is less than 5 ohms, replace rear wiper motor. See REAR WIPER MOTOR under REMOVAL & INSTALLATION. If either resistance is 5 ohms or more, repair appropriate Black wire(s).

TEST L: REAR WIPER DOES NOT OPERATE PROPERLY

NOTE: After all repairs, clear DTCs and retest system.

1) Connect New Generation Star (NGS) Tester (007-00500) to Data Link Connector (DLC). DLC is located under left side of instrument panel. Retrieve and note continuous DTCs stored in Generic Electronic Module/Central Timer Module (GEM/CTM). Clear continuous DTCs.

Following NGS tester manufacturer's instructions, perform WIPER/WASHER SELF-TEST and REAR WIPER SELF-TEST. Note all DTCs. If DTCs are retrieved, go to appropriate test step. See TEST L DTC INDEX table. If no DTCs are retrieved, go to next step.

TEST L DTC INDEX

DTC	Step
B1342	1
B1611	2)
B1614	2)
B1839	6)
B1894	6)

1 – Replace GEM/CTM. See GENERIC ELECTRONIC MODULE/CENTRAL TIMER MODULE under REMOVAL & INSTALLATION. Clear DTCs and retest system.

2) Observe PID R_WP_MD while turning rear wiper switch through all positions. If PID values agree with switch positions, go to step **6)**. If PID values do not agree with switch positions, go to next step.

3) Turn ignition off. Disconnect rear wiper switch connector. Measure resistance between rear wiper switch terminals No. 2 and 5 while moving rear wiper switch through all positions. See mating connector view 10. See REAR WIPER SWITCH RESISTANCE TEST table. If resistances are as specified, go to next step. If resistances are not as specified, replace rear wiper switch.

REAR WIPER SWITCH RESISTANCE TEST

Switch Position	Ohms
Off	4200-9100
First Interval Delay	1000-2420
Second Interval Delay	220-950
High	50-230

4) Disconnect GEM 16-pin connector C281. Measure resistance between rear wiper switch connector terminal No. 2 and ground. See Fig. 10. If resistance is more than 10 k/ohms, go to next step. If resistance is 10 k/ohms or less, repair Pink/Black wire short to ground.

5) Measure resistance between rear wiper/washer switch connector terminal No. 5 and GEM/CTM connector C280 terminal No. 21. See Figs. 6 and 10. If resistance is more than 5 ohms, repair open in Gray/Red wire. If resistance is 5 ohms or less, replace GEM. See GENERIC ELECTRONIC MODULE/CENTRAL TIMER MODULE under REMOVAL & INSTALLATION.

6) Observe PID R_WP_PK. Move wiper arm to center of liftgate glass by triggering active commands REAR WIPER UP RELAY and REAR WIPER DOWN RELAY ON and OFF. GEM PID R_WP_PK should indicate PARKED when wiper arm is parked, and indicate notPARKED when arm is in center of glass. If PID value is as specified, replace rear wiper motor. See REAR WIPER MOTOR under REMOVAL & INSTALLATION. If PID value is not as specified, go to next step.

7) Turn ignition off. Disconnect rear wiper motor connector and GEM 16-pin connector C281. Measure resistance between GEM connector C281 terminal No. 4 and rear wiper motor connector terminal No. 3. See Figs. 11 and 12. If resistance is less than 5 ohms, go to next step. If resistance is 5 ohms or more, repair open in Violet/Yellow wire.

8) Measure resistance between GEM connector C281 terminal No. 4 and ground. If resistance is more than 10 k/ohms, go to next step. If resistance is 10 k/ohms or less, repair Violet/Yellow wire short to ground.

9) Measure resistance between rear wiper motor connector terminal No. 4 and ground. See Fig. 12. If resistance is less than 5 ohms, go to next step. If resistance is 5 ohms or more, repair open in Black wire.

10) Place wiper arm in PARKED position. Measure resistance between rear wiper motor terminals No. 3 and 4. See mating connector view, 12. If resistance is less than 5 ohms, go to next step. If resistance is 5 ohms or more, replace rear wiper motor. See REAR WIPER MOTOR under REMOVAL & INSTALLATION.

11) Place wiper arm in middle of glass. Measure resistance between rear wiper motor terminals No. 3 and 4. See mating connector view, 12. If resistance is more than 10 k/ohms, replace GEM. See GENERIC ELECTRONIC MODULE/CENTRAL TIMER MODULE under REMOVAL

& INSTALLATION. If resistance is 10 k/ohms or less, replace rear wiper motor. See REAR WIPER MOTOR under REMOVAL & INSTALLATION.

TEST M: NO COMMUNICATION WITH GEM/CTM

NOTE: After all repairs, clear DTCs and retest system.

1) Check maxi-fuse No. 1 (6-amp) in underhood battery junction box. If fuse is okay, go to next step. If fuse is blown, replace fuse. If fuse blows again, check Tan/Black wire for short to ground.

2) Check fuse No. 25 (7.5-amp) located in central junction box (interior fuse panel). If fuse is okay, go to next step. If fuse is blown, replace fuse. If fuse blows again, check White/Yellow wire for short to ground.

3) Measure voltage between supply side of central junction box fuse No. 25 (7.5-amp) and ground. If voltage is more than 10 volts, go to next step. If voltage is 10 volts or less, repair open in Tan/Black wire.

4) Turn ignition off. Disconnect GEM/CTM 18-pin connector C283. Measure voltage between GEM/CTM connector C283 terminal No. 11 and ground. See Fig. 8. If voltage is more than 10 volts, go to next step. If voltage is 10 volts or less, repair open in White/Yellow wire.

5) Disconnect GEM/CTM 26-pin connector C280. Measure resistance between GEM/CTM connector C280 terminal No. 14 and ground. See Fig. 6. Measure resistance between GEM/CTM connector C280 terminal No. 26 and ground. If each resistance is less than 5 ohms, go to next step. If either resistance is 5 ohms or more, repair open in Black/White wire.

6) Measure resistance between GEM/CTM connector C283 terminal No. 18 and ground. See Fig. 8. If resistance is 5 ohms or more, repair open in Black wire. If resistance is less than 5 ohms, problem exists in module communications system. See MODULE COMMUNICATIONS NETWORK – EXPLORER & MOUNTAINEER article.

REMOVAL & INSTALLATION

WARNING: Deactivate air bag system before performing any service operation involving steering column components. See appropriate AIR BAG RESTRAINT SYSTEMS article. Do not apply electrical power to any component on steering column without first deactivating air bag system. Air bag may deploy.

CAUTION: When battery is disconnected, vehicle computer and memory systems may lose memory data. Driveability problems may exist until computer systems have completed a relearn cycle. See COMPUTER RELEARN PROCEDURES article in GENERAL INFORMATION before disconnecting battery.

FRONT WIPER MOTOR

Removal & Installation – 1) Remove left wiper arm by pulling out tab at base of wiper arm. Remove left cowl vent panel screw and disconnect washer hose from left washer nozzle. Remove spring retainers and left cowl vent panel.

2) Reach through vent panel opening and unsnap wiper linkage clips. Disengage wiper linkage from motor crank pin. Unplug wiper motor connector. Remove wiper motor. To install, reverse removal procedure.

GENERIC ELECTRONIC MODULE/CENTRAL TIMER MODULE

CAUTION: Disconnect battery before disconnecting Generic Electronic Module (GEM) or Central Timer Module (CTM) connectors. Failure to do so will result in GEM/CTM storing erroneous codes and may also result in erratic operation of GEM/CTM after reconnection.

CAUTION: If replacing GEM/CTM, it is necessary to upload module configuration information to the New Generation STAR (NGS) tester. After installation this information needs to be downloaded into the new GEM/CTM module.

Removal & Installation – 1) Disconnect negative battery terminal. Insert radio removing tool (T87P-19061-A) into radio faceplate and remove radio chassis by pulling outward. Disconnect radio electrical connectors.
2) Remove center instrument panel finish panel. Disconnect electrical connectors.
3) Remove GEM/CTM retaining screw. Disconnect connectors and remove GEM/CTM. To install, reverse removal procedure.

MULTIFUNCTION SWITCH

NOTE: Windshield wiper switch is an integral part of multifunction switch and cannot be service separately. Multifunction switch is serviced as a complete assembly.

Removal & Installation – 1) Disconnect negative battery terminal. Turn ignition switch to RUN position. Insert punch through hole in steering column shroud and push ignition lock cylinder release tab while pulling out ignition switch lock cylinder. If equipped, twist and remove tilt wheel handle.
2) Remove steering column shrouds. Remove switch retaining screws. Unplug electrical connectors. To install, reverse removal procedure. Adjust PRNDL indicator after installation.

REAR WIPER MOTOR

Removal & Installation – 1) Disconnect negative battery terminal. Remove wiper arm and blade assembly. Remove liftgate trim panel.
2) Position watershield aside. Disconnect electrical connector. Remove retaining bolts. Remove motor. To install, reverse removal procedure.

REAR WIPER SWITCH

Removal & Installation – Remove 2 screws below radio. Remove center instrument panel trim panel. Disconnect electrical connectors. Remove the mounting bezel and release tabs retaining rear wiper/washer switch. Remove switch. To install, reverse removal procedure.

WIRING DIAGRAMS

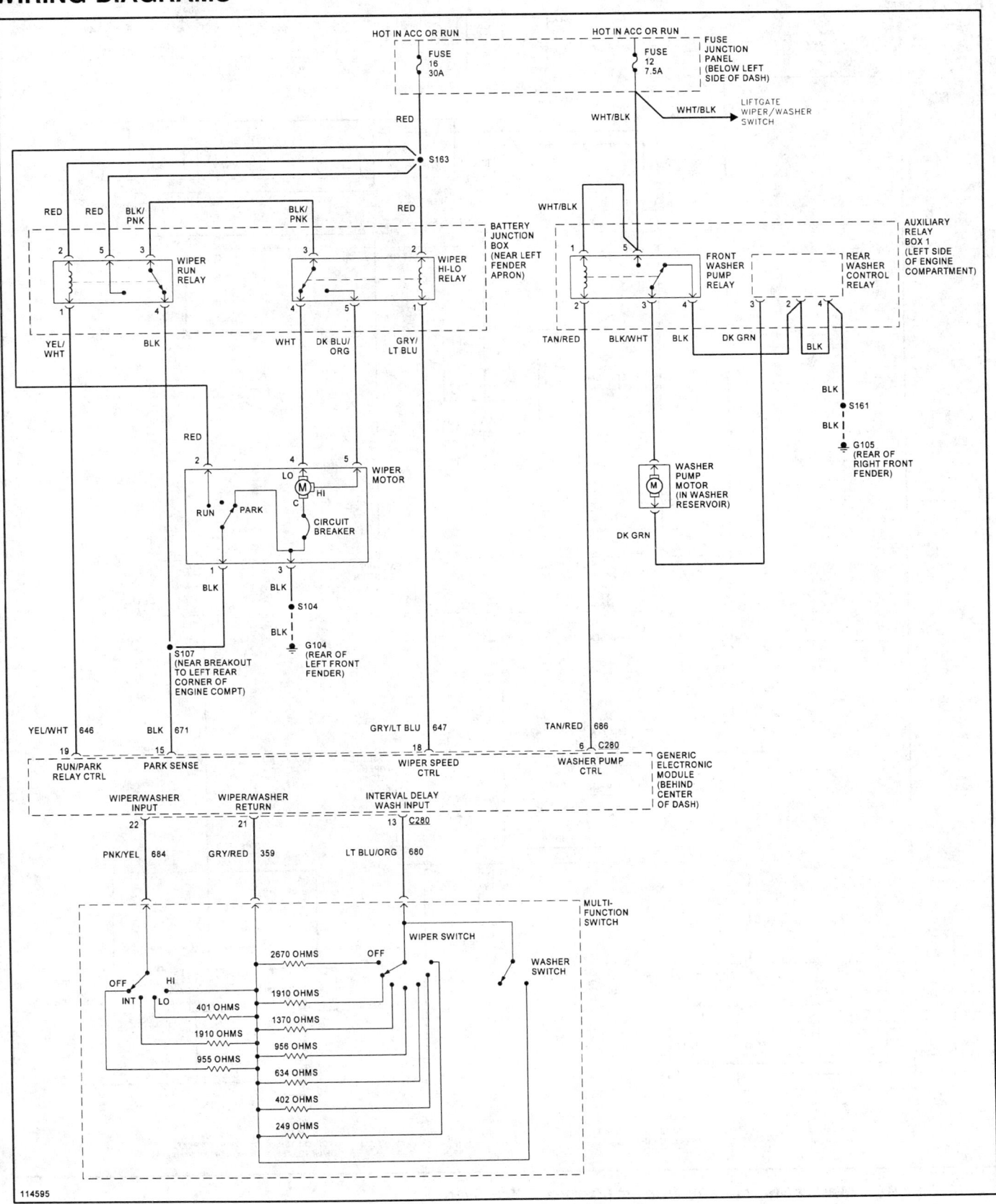

Fig. 13: Front Wiper/Washer System Wiring Diagram (Explorer & Mountaineer)

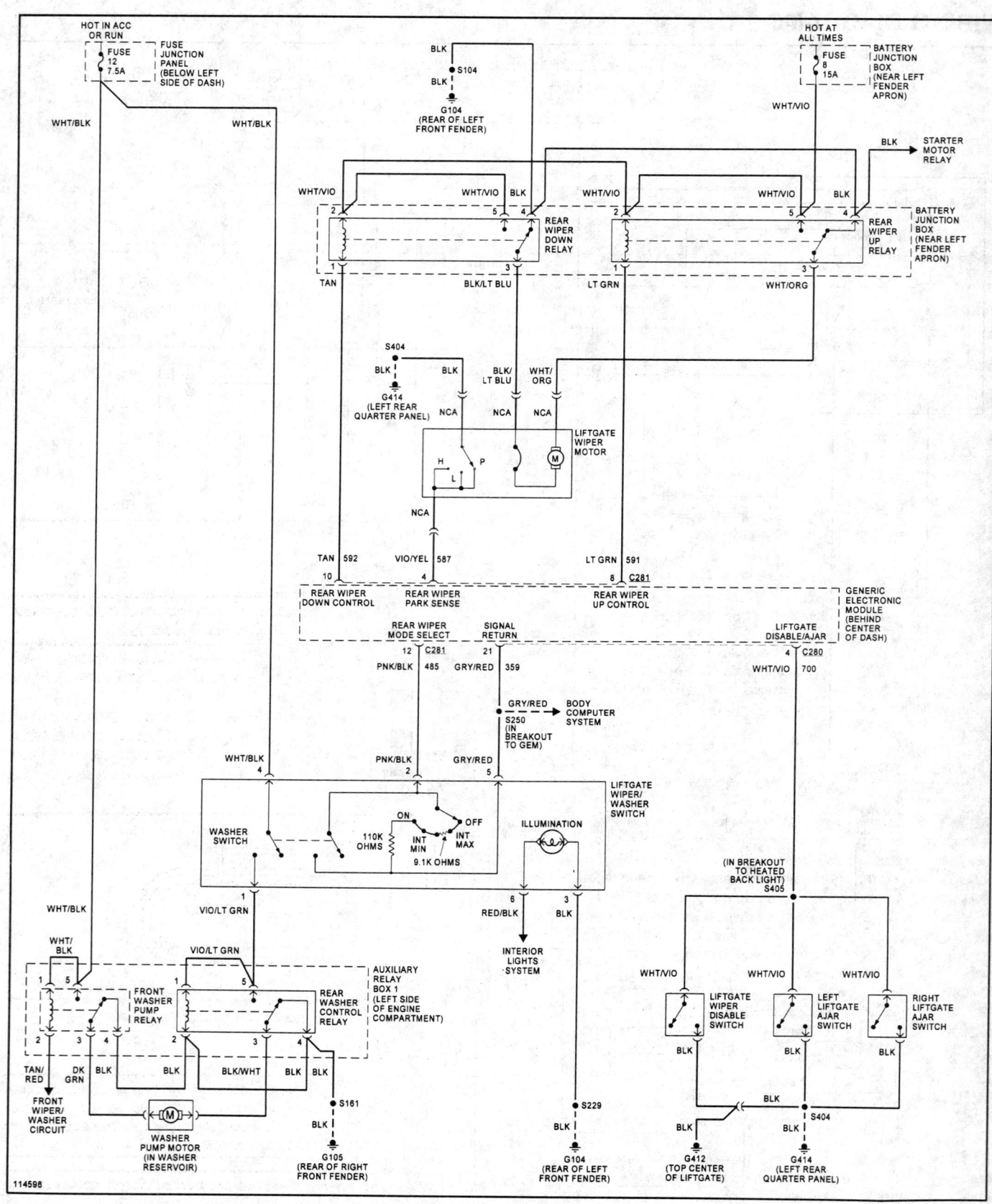

Fig. 14: Rear Wiper/Washer System Wiring Diagram (Explorer & Mountaineer)

DESCRIPTION & OPERATION

All wiper/washer functions are controlled by multifunction switch and Generic Electronic Module (GEM). GEM is located below left side of instrument panel. Wiper system has 2 speeds and 7 interval speeds. Interval delay times range 1.5-20 seconds.

COMPONENT LOCATIONS

COMPONENT LOCATIONS

Component	Location
Battery Junction Box	Left Side Engine Compartment Forward of Strut Tower
Central Junction Box	Below & Left of Steering Column
Generic Electronic Module	Below Left Side Instrument Panel
Relay Box	Near Instrument Panel
Washer Pump Relay	Relay Box
Wiper High/Low Relay	Battery Junction Box
Wiper On/Off (Int.) Relay	Battery Junction Box

ADJUSTMENTS

WIPER ARM

Cycle and park wipers. Distance between center of left hand blade and top edge of cowl top vent panel should be 2.20-3.14" (56-80 mm). Distance between center of right hand blade and top edge of cowl top vent panel should be 2.16-3.18" (55-88 mm). If distances are not as specified, remove wiper arms and reposition.

TROUBLE SHOOTING

Before performing any tests on wiper/washer system, verify customer complaint. Check for blown central junction box (interior fuse panel) fuses No. 26 (30-amp) and No. 39 (5-amp). Check for damaged wiring harness and loose or corroded connections. Check relays, wiper motor, multifunction switch, Generic Electronic Module (GEM), wiper linkage and washer pump hoses for damage. If all components are okay, retrieve Diagnostic Trouble Codes (DTCs) from GEM. See SELF-DIAGNOSTIC SYSTEM.

COMPONENT TESTS

MICRO RELAYS

1) Remove relay to be tested. Wiper on/off (Int.) relay is located in battery junction box. Washer pump relay is located in relay box. Measure resistance between relay terminal No. 2 and all other terminals. *See Fig. 1.* If any resistance is less than 5 ohms, replace relay. If all resistances are 5 ohms or greater, go to next step.

2) Attach jumper wire between battery positive and relay terminal No. 3. Measure voltage between relay terminal No. 4 and ground. If battery voltage is not present, replace relay. If battery voltage is present, go to next step.

3) Attach second jumper wire from battery positive to relay terminal No. 1. Attach third jumper wire between relay terminal No. 2 and ground. Measure voltage between relay terminal No. 5 and ground. If battery voltage is not present, replace relay. If battery voltage is present, relay is okay.

MINI RELAYS

1) Wiper high/low relay is located in battery junction box. Measure resistance between relay terminal No. 85 and all other terminals. *See Fig. 2.* If any resistance is less than 5 ohms, replace relay. If all resistances are 5 ohms or greater, go to next step.

2) Attach jumper wire between battery positive and relay terminal No. 30. Measure voltage between relay terminal No. 87A and ground. If battery voltage is not present, replace relay. If battery voltage is present, go to next step.

3) Attach second jumper wire from battery positive to relay terminal No. 86. Attach third jumper wire between relay terminal No. 85 and ground.

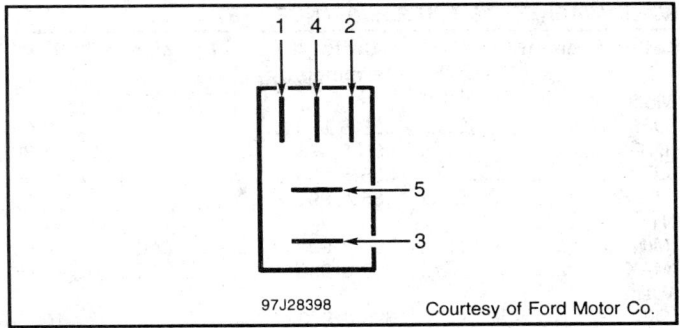

Fig. 1: Identifying Micro Relay Terminals

Measure voltage between relay terminal No. 87 and ground. If battery voltage is not present, replace relay. If battery voltage is present, relay is okay.

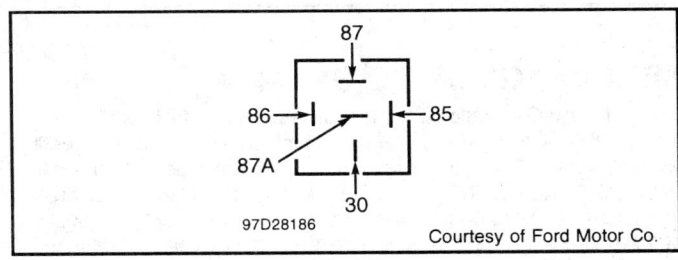

Fig. 2: Identifying Mini Relay Terminals

WIPER MOTOR

CAUTION: Wiper motor contains ceramic magnets that may crack or shatter if motor is dropped or handled roughly.

1) Disengage linkage from motor. Disconnect front wiper motor connector. Connect ammeter between battery ground and terminal No. 3 (Black wire) on motor. *See Fig. 3.*

2) Apply battery voltage to terminal No. 4 (Dark Blue/Orange wire) on motor for low speed operation. Apply battery voltage to terminal No. 5 (White wire) on motor for high speed operation. Current draw with wiper linkage disconnected should not exceed 3.5 amps at low speed and 5.5 amps at high speed.

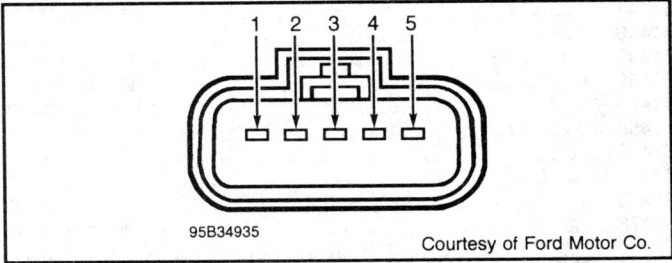

Fig. 3: Identifying Wiper Motor Connector Terminals

WIPER/WASHER SWITCH

WARNING: Vehicle is equipped with an air bag system. System MUST be disabled before working near steering column and instrument cluster to prevent air bag deployment. See appropriate AIR BAG RESTRAINT SYSTEMS article.

NOTE: Wiper and washer switches are part of multifunction switch assembly.

Disconnect wiper switch connector. Measure resistance between specified terminals with switch in appropriate position. See WIPER/WASHER SWITCH RESISTANCE TEST table. *See Fig. 4.* Replace switch if readings are not as specified.

WIPER/WASHER SWITCH RESISTANCE TEST

Switch Position	Switch Terminals	[1] Resistance (k/ohms)
Wiper		
OFF	685 & 993	47.6
INT	685 & 993	11.33
LOW	685 & 993	4.08
HIGH	685 & 993	Zero
INT [2]		
MIN	590 & 993	3.3
MAX	590 & 993	103.3
Washer		
OFF	590 & 993	103.3
ON	590 & 993	Zero

[1] – Values are approximate.

[2] – Rotate (INT) knob from minimum to maximum. Resistance should gradually increase from 3.3 k/ohms (MIN) to 103.3 k/ohms (MAX).

SELF-DIAGNOSTIC SYSTEM

Connect New Generation Star (NGS) tester to Data Link Connector (DLC). DLC is located behind instrument panel to right of steering column. Using NGS tester perform data link diagnostic test. See DATA LINK DIAGNOSTIC TEST under in MODULE COMMUNICATIONS NETWORK – MUSTANG article. If NGS tester displays CKT914, CKT915 or CKT70 = ECUS NO RESP/NOT EQUIP, repair module communication concern. See MODULE COMMUNICATIONS NETWORK – MUSTANG article. If NGS tester display NO RESPONSE/NOT EQUIPPED for GEM, perform TEST A: NO COMMUNICATION WITH GEM under SYSTEM TESTS.

If system passed, retrieve and record continuous DTCs. Erase DTCs. Perform GEM self-test. If GEM DTCs related to the concern are

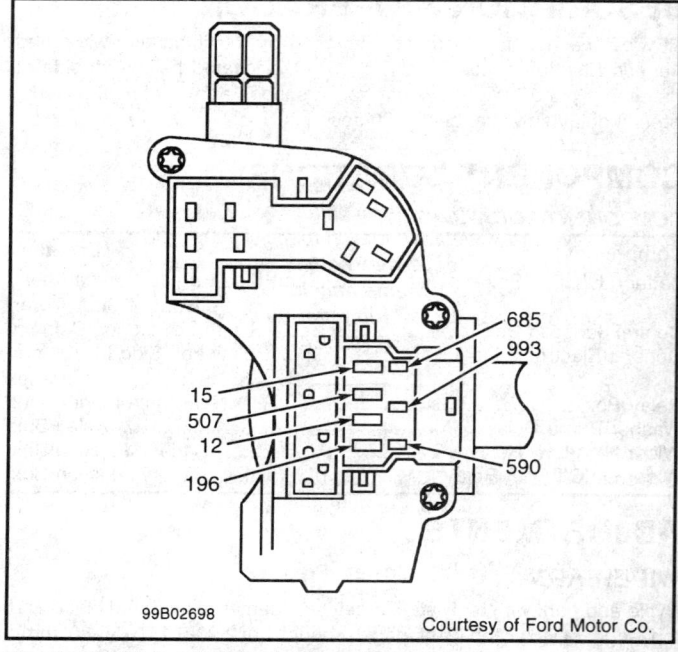

99B02698   Courtesy of Ford Motor Co.

Fig. 4: Identifying Multifunction Switch Terminals

retrieved, perform appropriate test. See GEM DTC TEST INDEX table. For GEM DTCs not covered in this article, see MODULE COMMUNICATIONS NETWORK – MUSTANG article. If no DTCs related to concern are retrieved, perform appropriate test based on symptom. See SYMPTOM TEST INDEX table under SYSTEM TESTS.

GEM DTC TEST INDEX

DTC [1]	Description	Test
B1342	GEM Defective	2
B1431	On/Off Relay Circuit Failure	B
B1432	On/Off Relay Circuit Short To Power	B
B1434	High/Low Relay Coil Circuit Failure	B
B1436	High/Low Relay Coil Circuit Short To Power	B
B1438	Wiper Switch Circuit Failure	B
B1441	Wiper Switch Circuit Short To Ground	B
B1446	Park Sense Circuit Failure	B
B1448	Park Sense Circuit Short To Power	B
B1450	Wash/Delay Switch Circuit Failure	C
B1453	Wash/Delay Switch Circuit Short To Ground	C
B1458	Washer Pump Relay Circuit Failure	C
B1460	Washer Pump Relay Coil Circuit Short To Power	C
B1466	High & Low Speeds Not Switching	B
B1473	Motor Low Speed Circuit Failure	B
B1476	Motor High Speed Circuit Failure	B

[1] – Codes listed in this table are only for testing covered in this article. For complete DTC listing, see MODULE COMMUNICATIONS NETWORK – MUSTANG article.

[2] – Clear DTCs. Retrieve DTCs. If B1342 is retrieved again, replace GEM. See GENERIC ELECTRONIC MODULE (GEM) under REMOVAL & INSTALLATION. Clear DTCs and retest.

SYSTEM TESTS

WARNING: Vehicle is equipped with an air bag system. System must be disabled before working near steering column and instrument cluster to prevent air bag deployment. See appropriate AIR BAG RESTRAINT SYSTEMS article.

CAUTION: Disconnect battery before disconnecting Generic Electronic Module (GEM) connectors. Failure to do so will result in GEM storing erroneous codes and may also result in erratic operation of GEM after reconnection. When battery is disconnected, vehicle computer and memory systems may lose memory data. Driveability problems may exist until computer systems have completed a relearn cycle. See COMPUTER RELEARN PROCEDURES article in GENERAL INFORMATION before disconnecting battery.

SYMPTOM TEST INDEX

Symptom	Test
No Communication With GEM	A
Wipers Inoperative	B
Wipers On Continuously	B
Low Speed Does Not Operated Properly	B
High & Low Speeds Do Not Operate Properly	B
Intermittent Does Not Operated Properly	B
Washer Pump Inoperative	C

TEST A: NO COMMUNICATION WITH GEM

NOTE: After repair, repeat GEM self-test and clear DTCs.

1) Turn ignition off. Disconnect Generic Electronic Module (GEM) 4-pin connector C291. Measure voltage between GEM connector C291 terminal No. 2 (White/Yellow wire) and ground. *See Fig. 5.* If voltage is greater than 10 volts, go to next step. If voltage is less than 10 volts, go to step **3)**.

2) Measure resistance between GEM connector C291 terminal No. 4 (Black/White wire) and ground. *See Fig. 5.* If resistance is less than 5 ohms, go to step **4)**. If resistance is 5 ohms or greater, repair open in Black/White wire.

3) Remove central junction box fuse No. 32 (15-amp). Central junction box is located below and left of steering column. Disconnect GEM 26-pin connector C352. Measure resistance IN Black/Pink wire between GEM connector C352 terminal No. 22 and fuse No. 32 (output side). *See Fig. 6.* If resistance is less than 5 ohms, go to next step. If resistance is 5 ohms or greater, repair open in Black/Pink wire.

4) Measure voltage between GEM connector C291 terminal No. 4 (Black/White wire) and ground. *See Fig. 5.* If voltage is greater than 10 volts, repair short to power in Black/White wire. If voltage is 10 volts or less, repair module communication concern. See MODULE COMMUNICATIONS NETWORK – MUSTANG article.

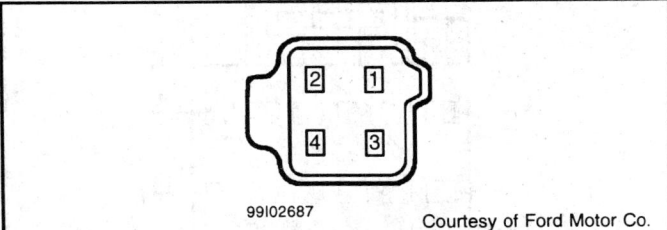

99I02687   Courtesy of Ford Motor Co.

Fig. 5: Identifying GEM 4-Pin Connector C291 Terminals

TEST B: WIPERS DO NOT OPERATE/OPERATE PROPERLY

NOTE: After repair, repeat GEM self-test and clear DTCs.

1) Turn ignition off. Connect New Generation Star (NGS) tester to Data Link Connector (DLC). DLC is located behind instrument panel to right of steering column. Depress clutch pedal (M/T). Observe GEM PIDs

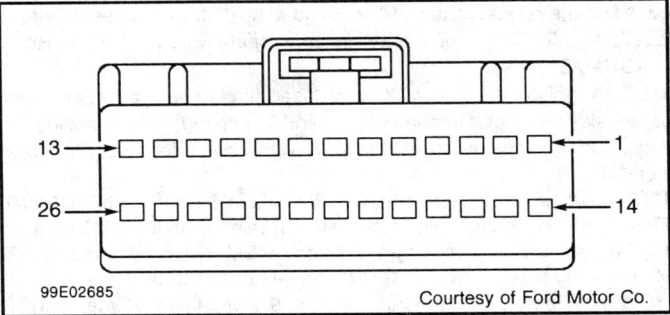

99E02685   Courtesy of Ford Motor Co.

Fig. 6: Identifying GEM 26-Pin Connector C352 Terminals

IGN_S, IGN_R, IGN_A and IGN_KEY while turning ignition switch through all positions. If PID values agree with switch positions, go to next step. If PID IGN_KEY values do not agree with switch positions, go to TEST D: KEY-IN-IGNITION CIRCUIT.

2) Turn ignition on. Observe PID WPMODE while turning wiper switch through all positions. If PID values agree with switch positions, go to next step. If PID values do not agree with switch positions, go to step **6)**.

3) Using NGS tester, trigger GEM active command WIPER RLY to ON and OFF. If the wipers turn on and off, go to next step. If wipers do not turn on and off, go to step **10)**.

4) Trigger GEM active command WIPER RLY to ON. Trigger GEM active command SPEED RLY to ON and OFF. If wiper speed changes on activation and deactivation of SPEED RLY, go to next step. If wiper speed does not change on activation and deactivation of SPEED RLY, go to step **16)**.

5) Observe GEM PID WPPRKSW while turning wipers on. If PID values agree with wiper position, replace GEM. See GENERIC ELECTRONIC MODULE (GEM) under REMOVAL & INSTALLATION. If PID values do not agree with wiper position, go to step **27)**.

6) Disconnect multifunction switch 7-pin connector C240. Test wiper portion of multifunction switch. See WIPER/WASHER SWITCH under COMPONENT TESTS. If switch is okay, go to next step. If switch is faulty, replace multifunction switch. See MULTIFUNCTION SWITCH under REMOVAL & INSTALLATION.

7) Disconnect GEM 26-pin connector C352. Turn ignition on. Measure voltage between GEM connector C352 terminal No. 5 (Dark Blue wire) and ground. *See Fig. 6.* Measure voltage between GEM connector C352 terminal No. 18 (Pink/Yellow wire) and ground. Measure voltage between GEM connector C352 terminal No. 19 (Light Blue/Orange wire) and ground. If any voltage is greater than 10 volts, repair short to power in appropriate wire(s). If each voltage is less than 10 volts, go to next step.

8) Turn ignition off. Measure resistance between GEM connector C352 terminal No. 5 (Dark Blue wire) and ground. *See Fig. 6.* Measure resistance between GEM connector C352 terminal No. 18 (Pink/Yellow wire) and ground. Measure resistance between GEM connector C352 terminal No. 19 (Light Blue/Orange wire) and ground. If any resistance is less than 10 k/ohms, repair short to ground in appropriate wire(s). See WIRING DIAGRAMS. If each resistance is 10 k/ohms or greater, go to next step.

9) Measure resistance in Dark Blue wire between GEM connector C352 terminal No. 5 and multifunction switch connector C240 terminal No. 685. *See Figs. 6 and 7.* Measure resistance in Pink/Yellow wire between GEM connector C352 terminal No. 18 and multifunction switch connector C240 terminal No. 590. Measure resistance in Light Blue/Orange wire between GEM connector C352 terminal No. 19 and multifunction switch connector C240 terminal No. 993. If any resistance is 5 ohms or greater, repair open in appropriate wire(s). If each resistance is less than 5 ohms, replace GEM. See GENERIC ELECTRONIC MODULE (GEM) under REMOVAL & INSTALLATION.

10) Remove wiper on/off relay from battery junction box. Measure voltage between wiper on/off relay connector terminal No. 5 (Dark Green wire) and ground. *See Fig. 8.* Measure voltage between wiper on/off relay connector terminal No. 2 (Dark Green wire) and ground. If each voltage is greater than 10 volts, go to next step. If either voltage is less than 10 volts, repair open in appropriate wire(s). See WIRING DIAGRAMS.

11) Turn ignition off. Attach 30-amp fused jumper wire between wiper on/off relay connector terminals No. 3 and 5. *See Fig. 8*. Turn ignition on. If wiper motor runs, go to next step. If wiper motor does not run, go to step **22)**.

12) Test wiper on/off relay. See MICRO RELAYS under COMPONENT TESTS. If relay is okay, go to next step. If relay is faulty, replace relay.

13) Remove wiper on/off relay. Disconnect GEM 12-pin connector C293. Measure voltage between GEM connector C293 terminal No. 12 (Yellow/White wire) and ground. *See Fig. 9*. If voltage is greater than 10 volts, repair short to power in Yellow/White wire. If voltage is less than 10 volts, go to next step.

14) Measure resistance between GEM connector C293 terminal No. 12 (Yellow/White wire) and ground. *See Fig. 9*. If resistance is greater than 10 k/ohms, go to next step. If resistance is 10 k/ohms or less, repair short to ground in Yellow/White wire.

15) Measure resistance in Yellow/White wire between GEM connector C293 terminal No. 12 and wiper on/off relay connector terminal No. 2. *See Figs. 8 and 9*. If resistance is less than 5 ohms, replace GEM. See GENERIC ELECTRONIC MODULE (GEM) under REMOVAL & INSTALLATION. If resistance is 5 ohms or greater, repair open in Yellow/White wire.

16) Remove wiper high/low relay. Using NGS tester, trigger GEM active command WIPER RLY to ON. Measure voltage between wiper high/low relay connector terminal No. 86 (Dark Green wire) and ground. *See Fig. 10*. Measure voltage between wiper high/low relay connector terminal No. 30 (Yellow/Red wire) and ground. If both voltages are greater than 10 volts, go to next step. If either voltage is less than 10 volts, repair open in appropriate wire(s). See WIRING DIAGRAMS.

17) Using NGS tester, trigger GEM active command WIPER RLY to ON. Attach 30-amp fused jumper wire between wiper high/low relay connector terminals No. 30 and 87A. *See Fig. 10*. Wipers should run at low speed. Disconnect jumper from high/low relay connector terminal No. 87A and attach to high/low relay connector terminal No. 87. Wipers should now run at high speed. If wipers operate as indicated, go to next step. If wipers do not operate as indicated, go to step **26)**.

18) Test wiper high/low relay. See MINI RELAYS under COMPONENT TESTS. If relay is okay, go to next step. If relay is faulty, replace relay.

19) Turn ignition off. Disconnect GEM 12-pin connector C293. Measure voltage between GEM connector C293 terminal No. 5 (Gray/Light Blue wire) and ground. *See Fig. 9*. If voltage is greater than 10 volts, repair short to power in Gray/Light Blue wire. If voltage is less than 10 volts, go to next step.

20) Measure resistance between GEM connector C293 terminal No. 5 (Gray/Light Blue wire) and ground. *See Fig. 9* . If resistance is greater than 10 k/ohms, go to next step. If resistance is 10 k/ohms or less repair short to ground in Gray/Light Blue wire.

21) Measure resistance in Gray/Light Blue wire between GEM connector C293 terminal No. 5 and high/low relay connector terminal No. 85. *See Figs. 9 and 10*. If resistance is less than 5 ohms, replace GEM. See GENERIC ELECTRONIC MODULE (GEM) under REMOVAL & INSTALLATION. If resistance is 5 ohms or greater, repair open in Gray/Light Blue wire.

22) Remove wiper high/low relay and on/off relay. Measure resistance in Yellow/Red wire between on/off relay connector terminal No. 3 and high/low relay connector terminal No. 30. *See Figs. 8 and 10*. If resistance is less than 5 ohms, go to next step. If resistance is 5 ohms or greater, repair open in Yellow/Red wire.

23) Test wiper high/low relay. See MINI RELAYS under COMPONENT TESTS. If relay is okay, go to next step. If relay is faulty, replace relay.

24) Disconnect wiper motor 5-pin connector. Measure resistance in Dark Blue/Orange wire between wiper high/low relay connector terminal No. 87A and wiper motor connector terminal No. 4. *See Figs. 3 and 10*. If resistance is less than 5 ohms, go to next step. If resistance is 5 ohms or greater, repair open in Dark Blue/Orange wire.

25) Measure resistance between wiper motor connector terminal No. 3 (Black wire) and ground. *See Fig. 3*. If resistance is less than 5 ohms,

test wiper motor. See WIPER MOTOR under COMPONENT TESTS. If resistance is 5 ohms or greater, repair open in Black ground wire.

26) Disconnect wiper motor 5-pin connector. Measure resistance in White wire between wiper motor connector terminal No. 5 and wiper high/low relay connector terminal No. 87. *See Figs. 10 and 3*. If resistance is less than 5 ohms, test wiper motor. See WIPER MOTOR under COMPONENT TESTS. If resistance is 5 ohms or greater, repair open in White wire.

27) Disconnect wiper motor 5-pin connector. Disconnect GEM 12-pin connector C293. Measure resistance in Black/Pink wire between wiper motor connector terminal No. 1 and GEM connector C293 terminal No. 1. *See Figs. 3 and 9*. If resistance is less than 5 ohms, replace wiper motor. See WIPER MOTOR under REMOVAL & INSTALLATION. If resistance is 5 ohms or greater, repair open in Black/Pink wire.

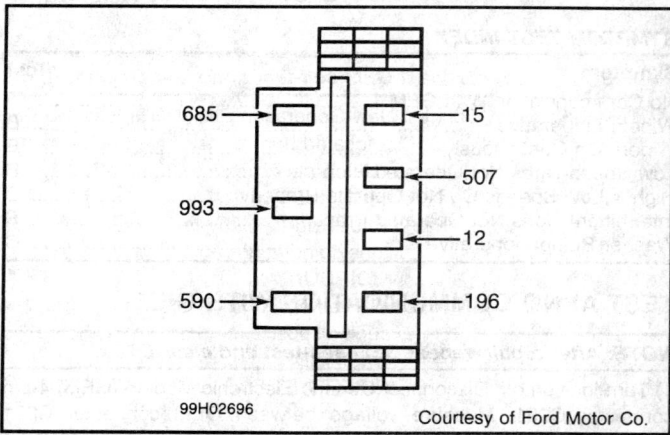

Fig. 7: Identifying Multifunction Switch 7-Pin Connector C240 Terminals

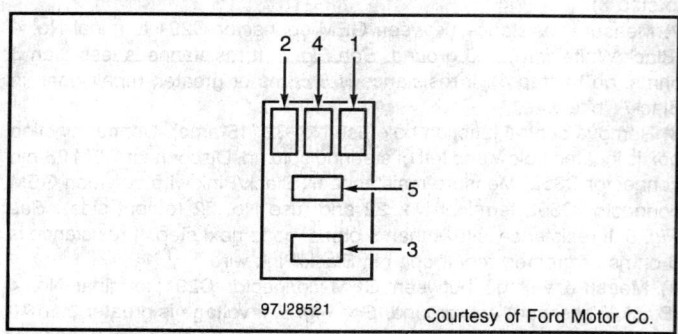

Fig. 8: Identifying Micro Relay Connector Terminals

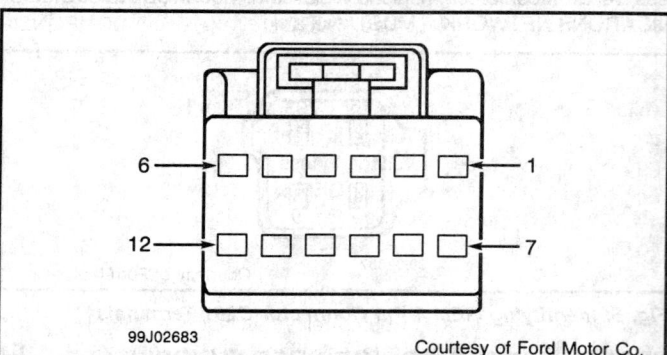

Fig. 9: Identifying GEM 12-Pin Connector C293 Terminals

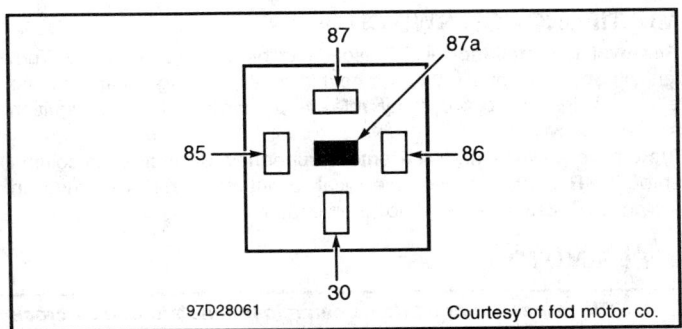

97D28061   Courtesy of fod motor co.

Fig. 10: Identifying Mini Relay Connector Terminals

TEST C: WASHERS DO NO OPERATE/OPERATE PROPERLY

NOTE: After repair, repeat GEM self-test and clear DTCs.

1) Turn ignition off. Connect New Generation Star (NGS) tester to Data Link Connector (DLC). DLC is located behind instrument panel to right of steering column. Depress clutch pedal (M/T). Observe GEM PIDs IGN_S, IGN_R, IGN_A and IGN_KEY while turning ignition switch through all positions. If PID values agree with switch positions, go to next step. If PID IGN_KEY values do not agree with switch positions, go to TEST D: KEY-IN-IGNITION CIRCUIT.

2) Turn ignition on. Using NGS tester, observe GEM PID WPMODE while turning wiper switch through all positions. If PID values agree with switch positions, go to next step. If PID values do not agree with switch positions, go to TEST B: WIPERS DO NOT OPERATE/OPERATE PROPERLY.

3) Using NGS tester, trigger GEM active command WASH RLY to ON and OFF. If wipers turn on and off, replace GEM. See GENERIC ELECTRONIC MODULE (GEM) under REMOVAL & INSTALLATION. If washers do not turn on and off, go to next step.

NOTE: Verify voltage at central junction box fuse No. 26 (30-amp) before performing next test.

4) Remove washer pump relay. Measure voltage between washer pump relay connector terminal No. 1 (Dark Green wire) and ground. *See Fig. 8.* Measure voltage between washer pump relay connector terminal No. 5 (Dark Green wire) and ground. If both voltages are greater than 10 volts, go to next step. If either voltage is less than 10 volts, repair open in Dark Green wire(s) between relay connector and central junction box.

5) Attach 30-amp fused jumper wire between washer pump relay connector terminals No. 3 and 5. *See Fig. 8.* If washer pump motor runs, go to next step. If washer pump motor does not run, go to step **10)**.

6) Test washer pump relay. See MICRO RELAYS under COMPONENT TESTS. If relay is okay, go to next step. If relay is faulty, replace relay.

7) Turn ignition off. Disconnect GEM 12-pin connector C293. Measure voltage between GEM connector C293 terminal No. 6 (Tan/Red wire) and ground. *See Fig. 9.* If voltage is greater than 10 volts, repair short to power in Tan/Red wire. If voltage is less than 10 volts, go to next step.

8) Measure resistance between GEM connector C293 terminal No. 6 (Tan/Red wire) and ground. *See Fig. 9.* If resistance is greater than 10 k/ohms, go to next step. If resistance is 10 k/ohms or less, repair short to ground Tan/Red wire.

9) Measure resistance in Tan/Red wirebetween GEM connector C293 terminal No. 6 and washer pump relay connector terminal No. 2. *See Figs. 8 and 9.* If resistance is less than 5 ohms, replace GEM. See GENERIC ELECTRONIC MODULE (GEM) under REMOVAL & INSTALLATION. If resistance is 5 ohms or greater, repair open in Tan/Red wire.

10) Disconnect washer pump motor 2-pin connector. Measure voltage between washer pump motor connector Black/White wire terminal and ground. If voltage is greater than 10 volts, repair short to power in Black/White wire. If voltage is less than 10 volts, go to next step.

11) Measure resistance of Black/White wire between washer pump motor connector and washer pump relay connector terminal No. 3. *See Fig. 8.* If resistance is less than 5 ohms, go to next step. If resistance is 5 ohms or greater, repair open in Black/White wire.

12) Measure resistance of Black wire between washer pump motor connector and ground. If resistance is less than 5 ohms, replace washer pump. If resistance is 5 ohms or greater, repair open in Black wire.

TEST D: KEY-IN-IGNITION CIRCUIT

NOTE: After repair, repeat GEM self-test and clear DTCs.

1) Remove central junction box fuse No. 28 (15-amp). Measure voltage between fuse No. 28 fuse holder (input side) and ground while turning ignition switch through all positions. If voltage is greater than 10 volts in RUN and START positions only, go to next step. If voltage is not greater than 10 volts in RUN and START positions only, repair central junction box. See appropriate wiring diagram in POWER DISTRIBUTION article in WIRING DIAGRAMS.

2) Remove central junction box fuse No. 32 (15-amp). Measure voltage between fuse No. 32 fuse holder (input side) and ground while turning ignition switch through all positions. If voltage is greater than 10 volts in RUN and ACC positions only, go to next step. If voltage is not greater than 10 volts in RUN and ACC positions only, repair central junction box. See appropriate wiring diagram in POWER DISTRIBUTION article in WIRING DIAGRAMS.

3) Disconnect GEM 26-pin connector C352. Insert ignition key. Measure resistance in White/Light Green wire between GEM connector C352 terminal No. 8 and fuse No. 28 fuse holder (output side). *See Fig. 6.* If resistance is less than 5 ohms, go to next step. If resistance is 5 ohms or greater, repair open in White/Light Green wire. See appropriate wiring diagram in POWER DISTRIBUTION article in WIRING DIAGRAMS.

4) Measure resistance in Black/Pink wire between GEM connector C352 terminal No. 22 and central junction box fuse No. 32 (15-amp) fuse holder (output side). *See Fig. 6.* If resistance is less than 5 ohms, go to next step. If resistance is 5 ohms or greater, repair open in Black/Pink wire. See appropriate wiring diagram in POWER DISTRIBUTION article in WIRING DIAGRAMS.

5) Measure resistance between GEM connector C352 terminal No. 9 (Black/Pink wire) and ground. *See Fig. 6.* If resistance is less than 5 ohms, go to next step. If resistance is 5 ohms or greater, repair open in Black/Pink wire and/or replace key-in-ignition warning switch.

6) Remove ignition key. Measure voltage between GEM connector C352 terminal No. 8 (White/Light Green wire) and ground. *See Fig. 6.* Measure voltage between GEM connector C352 terminal No. 22 (Black/Pink wire) and ground. If each voltage is less than 10 volts, go to next step. If either voltage is greater than 10 volts, repair short to power in appropriate wire(s).

7) Measure resistance between GEM connector C352 terminal No. 9 (Black/Pink wire) and ground. *See Fig. 6.* If resistance is greater than 10 k/ohms, replace GEM. See GENERIC ELECTRONIC MODULE (GEM) under REMOVAL & INSTALLATION. If resistance is 10 k/ohms or less, repair short to ground in Black/Pink wire.

REMOVAL & INSTALLATION

WARNING: Vehicle is equipped with an air bag system. System must be disabled before working near steering column and instrument cluster to prevent air bag deployment. See appropriate AIR BAG RESTRAINT SYSTEMS article.

CAUTION: When battery is disconnected, vehicle computer and memory systems may lose memory data. Driveability problems may exist until computer systems have completed a relearn cycle. See COMPUTER RELEARN PROCEDURES article in GENERAL INFORMATION before disconnecting battery.

GENERIC ELECTRONIC MODULE (GEM)

CAUTION: Disconnect battery before disconnecting Generic Electronic Module (GEM) connectors. Failure to do so will result in GEM storing erroneous codes and may also result in erratic operation of GEM after reconnection.

Removal & Installation – Generic Electronic Module (GEM) is located below left side of instrument panel. Disconnect battery ground cable. Remove 5 GEM electrical connectors. Release locking tab and slide GEM off bracket. To install, reverse removal procedure.

MULTIFUNCTION SWITCH

Removal & Installation – 1) Disconnect battery ground cable. Turn ignition on. Insert punch through hole in lower steering column shroud and push ignition lock cylinder release pin while pulling out ignition switch lock cylinder.

2) Remove tilt wheel handle. Remove upper and lower steering column shrouds. Remove screws, electrical connectors and multifunction switch. To install, reverse removal procedure.

WIPER MOTOR

CAUTION: Wiper motor contains ceramic magnets that may crack or shatter if motor is dropped or handled roughly.

Removal & Installation – 1) Park wiper blades in full upright position. Remove both wiper pivot arms. Remove screws and remove cowl top vent panels. Disconnect battery negative cable.

2) Remove clip and disconnect mounting arm and pivot shaft linkage from wiper motor. Disconnect wiper motor electrical connector. Remove bolts and wiper motor. To install, reverse removal procedure. Tighten wiper mounting bolts 11 ft. lbs. (15 N.m).

WIRING DIAGRAMS

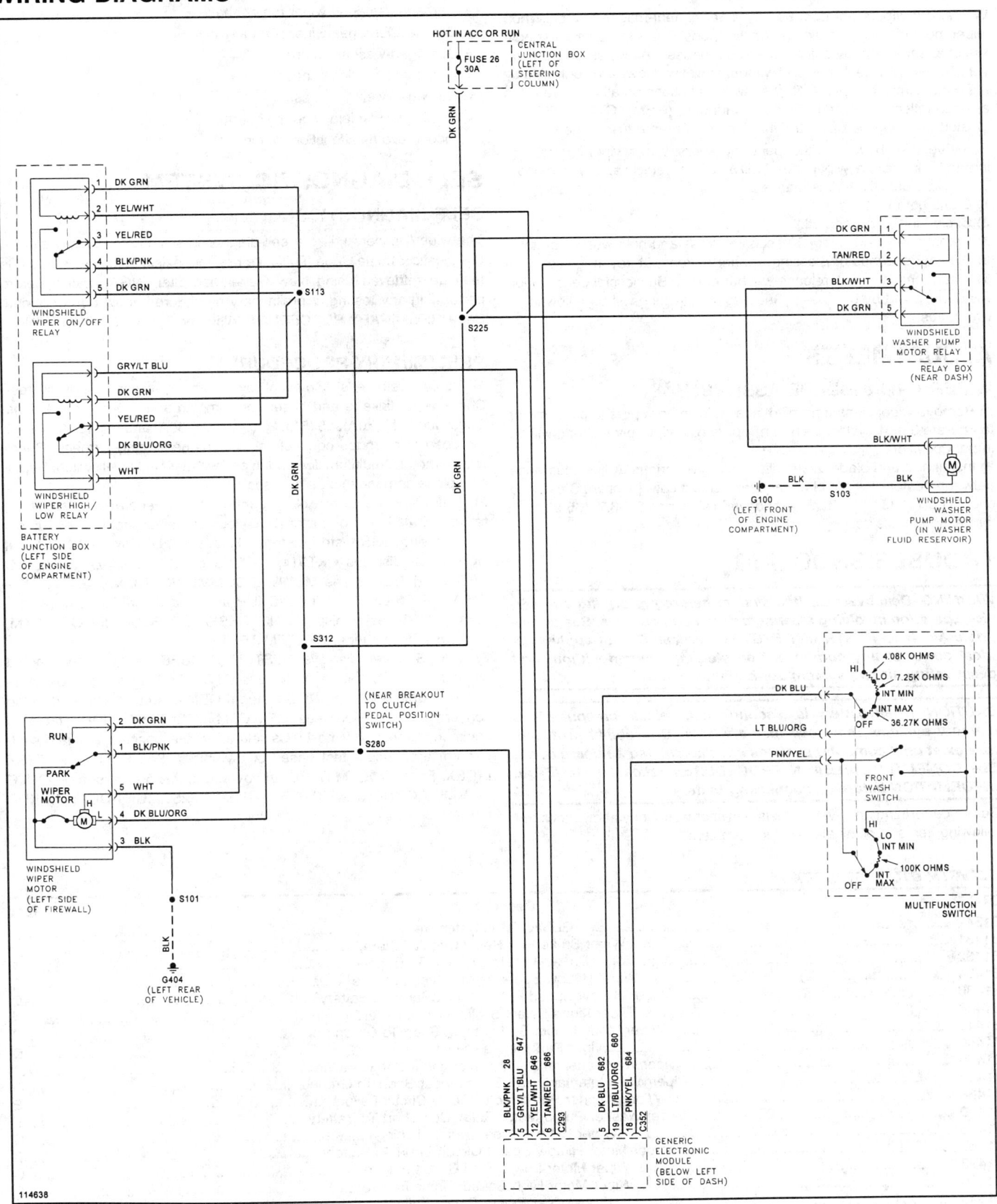

Fig. 11: Wiper/Washer System Wiring Diagram (Mustang)

114638

DESCRIPTION & OPERATION

Windshield wipers are operated by a permanent-magnet motor. When wiper control switch is in intermittent position, wipers make single sweeps, separated by adjustable-length pauses. All wiper functions on vehicles with 2-wheel drive and without power windows are controlled by a Central Timer Module (CTM). All wiper functions on all other vehicles are controlled by Generic Electronic Module (GEM). CTM or GEM is located on backside of central junction box (interior fuse panel).

Some vehicles have speed dependent wipers. When wiper control is in intermittent position, wiper speed will adjust as vehicle speed increases. To activate/deactivate this feature:
1) Close both front doors.
2) Cycle ignition on and off.
3) Remove key and within 30 seconds press and hold washer button.
4) Within 2 seconds of pressing washer button, put key in ignition.
5) When tone is heard, release washer button. Successful deactivation will be followed by one beep. Successful activation will be followed by two beeps.

ADJUSTMENTS

WIPER ARM & BLADE ASSEMBLY

1) Remove wiper arms from pivot shafts. Turn on wipers to allow motor to operate 3 or 4 cycles, then turn wipers off. Wiper pivot shafts will be in park position.
2) Install arm and blade assemblies onto pivot shafts. Adjust clearance between center of wiper blade and windshield/cowl junction. Clearance should be 1.7-3.0" (45-75 mm) for driver's side, and 2.6-3.7" (65-93 mm) for passenger's side.

TROUBLE SHOOTING

WARNING: Deactivate air bag system before performing any service operation involving steering column components. See appropriate AIR BAG RESTRAINT SYSTEMS article. Do not apply electrical power to any component on steering column without first deactivating air bag system. Air bag may deploy.

CAUTION: When battery is disconnected, vehicle computer and memory systems may lose memory data. Driveability problems may exist until computer systems have completed a relearn cycle. See COMPUTER RELEARN PROCEDURES article in GENERAL INFORMATION before disconnecting battery.

Before performing any system tests on wiper/washer system, check the following items to eliminate common problems:

- Wiper/washer related fuses.
- Damaged/stripped wiper motor shaft.
- Damaged/stripped wiper pivot arm shaft.
- Damaged washer pump.
- Loose or corroded connections.
- Damaged wiring harness.
- Binding windshield wiper pivot arm.
- Inoperative multifunction switch.

SELF-DIAGNOSTIC SYSTEM

SELF-DIAGNOSTICS

The wiper/washers utilize a self-diagnostic system which may store a Diagnostic Trouble Code (DTC) if a problem exists in the system. DTCs may be retrieved using New Generation Star (NGS) tester. Before performing any testing, a preliminary procedure should be performed. See PRELIMINARY PROCEDURE. Also see TROUBLE SHOOTING.

PRELIMINARY PROCEDURE

1) Verify customer's complaint by operating wiper/washer system. Check wiper linkage and hoses for crimping and proper connections. Check fuses 11 (30A), 15 (5A), 20 (50A), 21 (50A) and 103 (50A). Check for loose or corroded connectors, or damaged wiring harness. Check relays, motors, multifunction switch and washer fluid level switch. Repair or replace components as necessary.
2) If all components are okay, connect New Generation Star (NGS) tester to Data Link Connector (DLC) located below center of instrument panel. Using NGS tester, perform DATA LINK DIAGNOSTIC TEST. If NGS tester displays CKT914, CKT915 or CKT70 = ALL ECUS NO RESP/NOT EQUIP, see MODULE COMMUNICATIONS NETWORK – F150 & F250 LIGHT-DUTY PICKUP article to diagnose network concern. If NGS tester displays NO RESP/NOT EQUIP for GEM/CTM, perform TEST G under SYSTEM TESTS.
3) If NGS tester displays SYSTEM PASSED, retrieve and record continuous DTCs. Erase continuous DTCs. Perform self-test diagnostics for GEM/CTM using NGS tester. If GEM/CTM DTCs related to the concern are retrieved, see GEM/CTM DTC TEST INDEX table to continue diagnosis. If no DTCs related to the concern are retrieved, perform appropriate test based on symptom. See SYMPTOM TEST INDEX. For GEM/CTM DTCs not covered in this article, see MODULE COMMUNICATIONS NETWORK – F150 & F250 LIGHT-DUTY PICKUP article.

GEM/CTM DTC TEST INDEX [1] [2]

DTC	Description	Test
B1342	GEM/CTM Is Defective	3
B1431	Wiper Brake/Run Relay Circuit Failure	4
B1432	Wiper Brake/Run Relay Short To Battery	A
B1434	Wiper Hi/Low Speed Relay Circuit Failure	C
B1436	Wiper Hi/Low Speed Relay Circuit Short To Battery	C
B1438	Wiper Mode Select Switch Circuit Failure	4
B1441	Wiper Mode Select Switch Input Short To Ground	4
B1446	Wiper Park Sense Circuit Failure	D
B1450	Wiper/Wash Interval Delay Switch Input Circuit Failure	4
B1453	Wiper/Wash Interval Delay Switch Input Short To Ground	D
B1458	Wiper/Washer Pump Motor Relay Circuit Failure	E
B1460	Wiper/Washer Pump Motor Relay Coil Short To Battery	E
B1466 [5]	Wiper Hi/Low Speed Not Switching	C
B1467 [5]	Wiper Motor Hi/Low Speed Circuit Short To Battery	B
B1473	Wiper Motor Low Speed Circuit Failure	C
B1476	Wiper Motor High Speed Circuit Failure	C
B1840	Front Wiper Power Circuit Failure	A
P0500 [6]	Vehicle Speed Signal Circuit Failure	[7] F

[1] – All codes for both GEM and CTM systems except where noted.

1999 ACCESSORIES & EQUIPMENT
Wiper/Washer Systems – F150 & F250 Light-Duty Pickup (Cont.)

FORD
4-1373

GEM/CTM DTC TEST INDEX¹ ² (Cont.)

2 – Codes listed in this table are only for testing covered in this article. For complete DTC listing, see MODULE COMMUNICATIONS NETWORK – F150 & F250 LIGHT-DUTY PICKUP article.
3 – Using NGS tester clear DTCs. Retrieve DTCs. If DTC B1342 is retrieved, replace GEM or CTM and retest system.
4 – Refer to SYMPTOM TEST INDEX.
5 – CTM system only.
6 – GEM system only.
7 – If 4WD, also see BORG-WARNER 44–06 ELECTRONIC CONTROLS article.

SYSTEM TESTS

CAUTION: Disconnect battery before disconnecting Generic Electronic Module (GEM) or Central Timer Module (CTM) connectors. Failure to do so will result in GEM/CTM storing erroneous codes and may also result in erratic operation of GEM/CTM after reconnection.

NOTE: If continuous Diagnostic Trouble Codes (DTCs) are recorded and the symptom is not present during pinpoint testing, the problem may be intermittent. Always check for loose connections and corroded terminals.

NOTE: Complete entire pinpoint test related to the symptom before replacing GEM/CTM.

SYMPTOM TEST INDEX

Symptom	Test
Wipers Inoperative	A
Wipers Stay On Continuously	B
Wipers Operate At Interval Setting But Inoperative At High &/Or Low Speed	C
Wipers Inoperative At Interval Setting But Operate At High & Low Speed	D
Wash & Wipe Function Does Not Operate Properly	E
Speed Dependent Interval Mode Not Operating Properly – GEM	F
No Scan Tool Communication With GEM/CTM	G

TEST A: WIPERS INOPERATIVE

1) Turn ignition on. Measure voltage between output side of fuses No. 11 (30A) and No. 15 (5A) and ground. Fuses are located in central junction box (interior fuse panel). If reading is greater than 10 volts at each fuse, go to step **3)**. If reading is 10 volts or less at either fuse, go to next step.
2) Disconnect central junction box C242 and C243 connectors. Measure voltage between central junction box C243 connector terminal No. 11 and ground. *See Fig. 1.* If voltage is 10 volts or less, repair open in battery junction box fuse No. 103 (50A) or Tan/Black wire. See appropriate wiring diagram in POWER DISTRIBUTION article in WIRING DIAGRAMS. If voltage is greater than 10 volts, turn ignition on. Measure voltage between central junction box C242 connector terminal No. 16 and ground. If voltage is 10 volts or less, repair open in battery junction box fuse No. 113 (50A), Yellow wire between battery junction box and ignition switch, ignition switch or Black/Light Green wire between ignition switch and central junction box. See appropriate wiring diagram in POWER DISTRIBUTION article in WIRING DIAGRAMS. If both readings are greater than 10 volts, replace central junction box. Clear DTCs and retest system.
3) Turn ignition off. Connect New Generation Star (NGS) Tester (007-00500) to Data Link Connector (DLC) located below center of instrument panel. On manual transmission models, depress clutch pedal. Observe GEM/CTM PIDs IGN_A, IGN_S, IGN_OG/L and IGN_RD while turning the ignition switch through all positions. If PID values agree with switch positions, go to next step. If PID values do not agree with switch positions, repair appropriate ignition switch circuit(s). See appropriate wiring diagram in POWER DISTRIBUTION article in WIRING DIAGRAMS. Clear DTCs and retest system.
4) Retrieve continuous DTCs stored in GEM/CTM. Clear continuous DTCs. Perform ON-DEMAND SELF-TEST and note all DTCs. If any

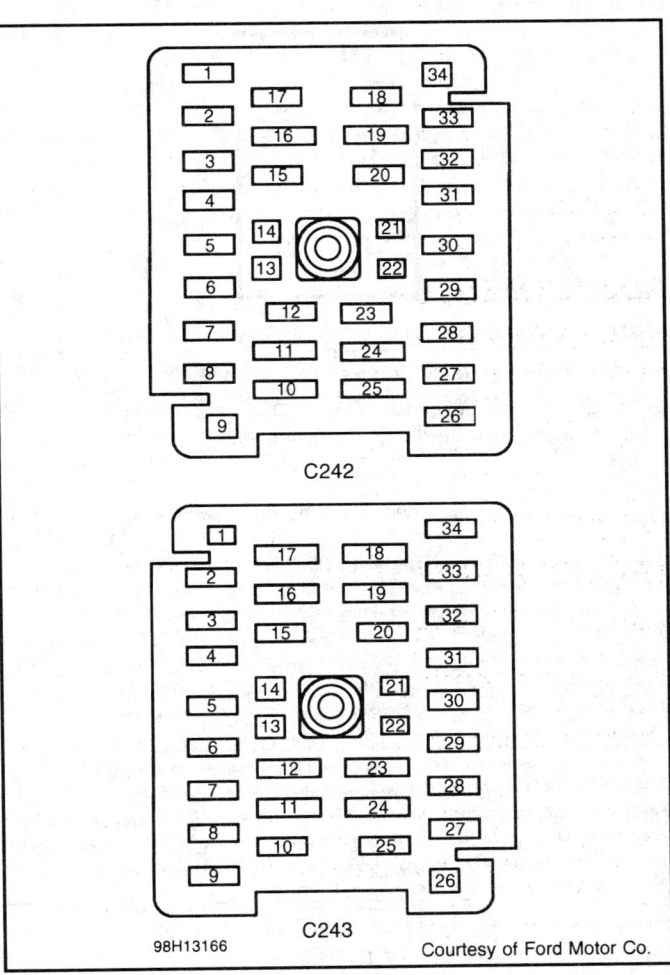

Fig. 1: Identifying Central Junction Box C242 & C243 Connector Terminals

DTCs exist, go to appropriate test step. See TEST A DTC INDEX table. If no DTCs exist, go to step **6)**.

TEST A DTC INDEX

DTC	Step
B1342	1
B1431	10
B1432	10
B1434	12
B1438	6
B1441	6
B1450	6
B1453	6
B1840	5

1 – Replace GEM/CTM, clear DTCs and retest system.

FORD
4-1374

1999 ACCESSORIES & EQUIPMENT
Wiper/Washer Systems – F150 & F250 Light-Duty Pickup (Cont.)

5) Turn ignition off. Remove wiper run/park relay. Turn ignition on. Check for voltage at run/park relay connector terminal No. 2 and ground. *See Fig. 2.* Check for voltage at wiper run/park relay connector terminal No. 5 and ground. If each is more than 10 volts, go to next step. If either reading is 10 volts or less, repair White/Black wires as necessary. Clear DTCs and retest system.

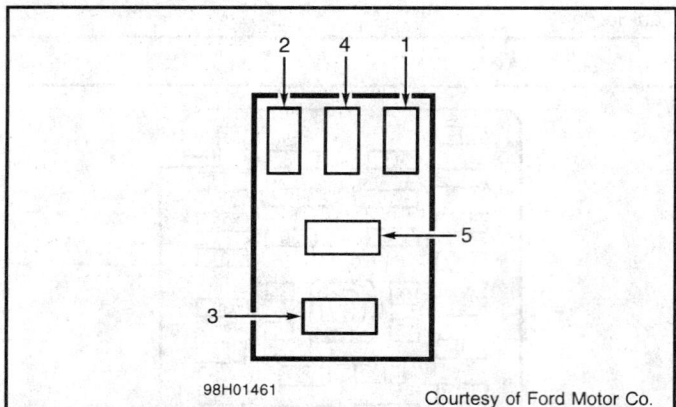

98H01461   Courtesy of Ford Motor Co.

Fig. 2: Identifying Relay Connector Terminals

6) Using NGS tester, observe PID WPMODE while turning wiper switch through all positions. If PID values agree with switch positions, go to step 10). If PID values do not agree with switch positions, go to next step.

7) Turn ignition off. Disconnect multifunction switch C259 7-pin connector. Check wiper switch portion of multifunction switch. See WIPER SWITCH under COMPONENT TESTS. If switch is good, go to next step. If switch is faulty, replace switch. See MULTIFUNCTION SWITCH under REMOVAL & INSTALLATION. Clear DTCs and retest system.

8) Disconnect GEM/CTM C239 26-pin connector. Measure resistance between GEM/CTM C239 connector terminal No. 13 and multifunction switch C259 connector terminal No. 590 (Light Blue/Orange wire). *See Figs. 3 and 4.* Measure resistance between GEM/CTM C239 connector terminal No. 21 and multifunction switch C259 connector terminal No. 993 (Dark Blue wire). Measure resistance between GEM/CTM C239 connector No. 22 and multifunction switch C259 connector terminal No. 685 (Pink/Yellow wire). If each circuit has resistance of less than 5 ohms, go to next step. If any resistance is 5 ohms or greater, repair appropriate wire. See WIRING DIAGRAMS. Clear DTCs and retest system.

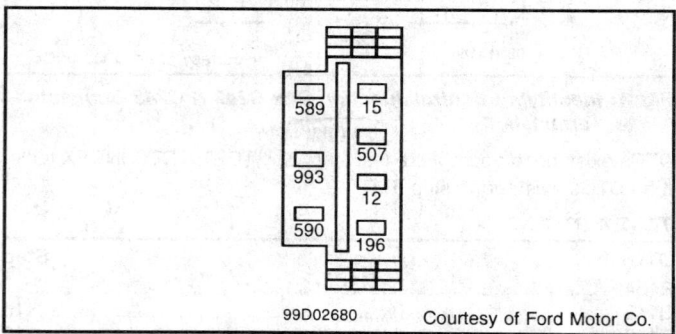

99D02680   Courtesy of Ford Motor Co.

Fig. 3: Identifying Multifunction Switch C259 7-Pin Connector Terminals

9) Turn ignition on. Measure voltage between GEM/CTM C239 connector terminal No. 13 and ground (Light Blue/Orange wire). *See Fig. 4.* Measure voltage between GEM/CTM C239 connector terminal No. 22 and ground (Pink/Yellow wire). If any voltage is present, repair wire(s) as necessary. See WIRING DIAGRAMS. Clear DTCs and retest system. If no voltage is present, replace GEM/CTM. See GEM/CTM under REMOVAL & INSTALLATION. Clear DTCs and retest system.

10) Using NGS tester, observe GEM/CTM PID WPRUN while triggering active command WIPER RLY. If PID WPRUN agrees with command mode, go to next step. If PID WPRUN does not agree with command

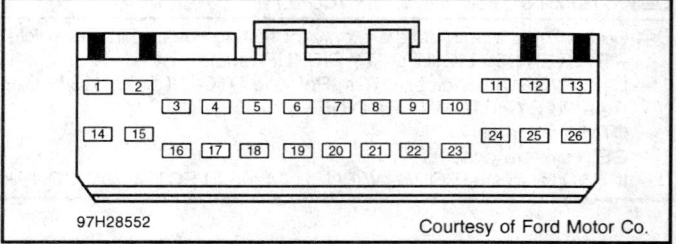

97H28552   Courtesy of Ford Motor Co.

Fig. 4: Identifying GEM/CTM C239 26-Pin Connector Terminals

mode replace GEM/CTM. See GEM/CTM under REMOVAL & INSTALLATION. Clear DTCs and retest system.

11) Turn ignition off. Remove wiper run/park relay. Turn ignition on. Measure voltage between wiper run/park relay connector terminal No. 2 and ground. *See Fig. 2.* If voltage is greater than 10 volts, go to next step. If voltage is 10 volts or less, repair White/Black wire. See WIRING DIAGRAMS. Clear DTCs and retest system.

12) Turn ignition off. Check wiper run/park relay. See RELAYS in COMPONENT TESTS. If relay is good, go to next step. If relay is faulty, replace relay. Clear DTCs and retest system.

13) Disconnect GEM/CTM C239 26-pin connector. Measure resistance between GEM/CTM C239 connector terminal No. 19 and wiper run/park relay connector terminal No. 1. *See Figs. 2 and 4.* If resistance is less than 5 ohms, go to next step. If resistance is 5 ohms or greater, repair Yellow/White wire. See WIRING DIAGRAMS. Clear DTCs and retest system.

14) Turn ignition off. Disconnect wiper run/park relay. Disconnect GEM/CTM C239 26-pin connector. Turn ignition on. Measure voltage between run/park relay connector terminal No. 1 and ground. *See Fig. 2.* If no voltage is present, go to next step. If any voltage is present, repair Yellow/White wire. See WIRING DIAGRAMS. Clear DTCs and retest system.

15) Turn ignition off. Disconnect wiper high/low relay. Turn ignition on. Using NGS tester, trigger the GEM/CTM active command WIPER RELAY ON. Measure the voltage between high/low relay connector terminal No. 3 and ground. *See Fig. 2.* If voltage is greater than 10 volts, go to step 18). If voltage is 10 volts or less, go to next step.

16) Turn ignition off. Disconnect wiper run/park relay. Measure resistance between high/low relay connector terminal No. 3 and run/park relay connector terminal No. 3. *See Fig. 2.* If resistance is less than 5 ohms, go to next step. If resistance is 5 ohms or greater, repair Red wire. See WIRING DIAGRAMS. Clear DTCs and retest system.

17) Turn ignition on. Measure voltage between wiper run/park relay connector terminal No. 5 and ground. *See Fig. 2.* If reading is greater than 10 volts, go to next step. If reading is 10 volts or less, repair White/Black wire. See WIRING DIAGRAMS. Clear DTCs and retest system.

18) Connect a jumper wire between wiper high/low relay connector terminal No. 3 and terminal No. 5 or terminal No. 4. *See Fig. 2.* Using NGS tester, trigger active command WIPER RELAY to ON. If wipers do not operate, go to next step. If wipers operate, replace high/low relay. Clear DTCs and retest system.

19) Turn ignition off. Disconnect wiper motor connector. Measure resistance between wiper motor connector terminal No. 3 and ground. *See Fig. 5.* If resistance is less than 5 ohms, go to next step. If resistance is 5 ohms or greater, repair Black wire. See WIRING DIAGRAMS. Clear DTCs and retest system.

20) Remove wiper linkage from wiper motor. Check wiper linkage for free operation. If linkage is free of binding and operational resistance, check wiper motor. See WIPER MOTOR under COMPONENT TESTS. If linkage does not operate freely, repair as necessary. Reconnect linkage, clear DTCs and retest system.

TEST B: WIPERS STAY ON CONTINUOUSLY

1) Turn ignition off. Connect New Generation Star (NGS) Tester (007-00500) to Data Link Connector (DLC). DLC is located below center of instrument panel. On manual transmission models, depress clutch pedal. Observe GEM/CTM PIDs IGN_A, IGN_S, IGN_OG/L and

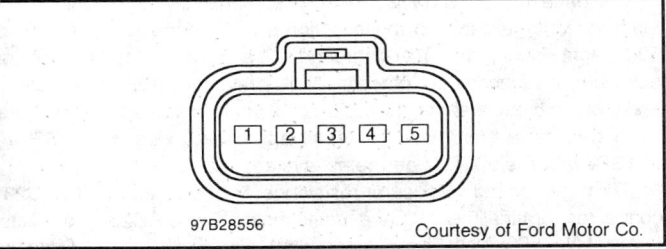

97B28556   Courtesy of Ford Motor Co.

Fig. 5: Identifying Wiper Motor Connector Terminals

IGN_RD while turning ignition switch through all positions. If PID values agree with switch positions, go to next step. If PID values do not agree with switch positions, repair appropriate ignition switch circuit(s). See appropriate wiring diagram in POWER DISTRIBUTION article in WIRING DIAGRAMS. Clear DTCs and retest system.

2) Using NGS tester retrieve continuous DTCs stored in GEM/CTM. Clear continuous DTCs. Perform ON-DEMAND SELF-TEST and note all DTCs. If DTCs exist, see TEST B DTC INDEX table. If no DTCs exist, go to next step.

TEST B DTC INDEX

DTC	Step
B1342	1
B1431	6
B1441	3
B1453	3

[1] – Replace GEM/CTM, clear DTCs and retest system.

3) Using NGS tester, observe PID WPMODE while turning wiper switch through all positions. If PID values agree with switch positions, go to step **6)**. If PID values do not agree with switch positions, go to next step.

4) Turn ignition off. Disconnect multifunction switch C259 7-pin connector. Check wiper switch portion of multifunction switch. See WIPER SWITCH under COMPONENT TESTS. If switch is good, go to next step. If switch is faulty, replace switch. Clear DTCs and retest system.

5) Disconnect GEM/CTM C239 26-pin connector. Measure resistance between multifunction switch C259 connector terminal No. 590 and ground (Light Blue/Orange wire). *See Fig. 3.* Measure resistance between multifunction switch C259 connector terminal No. 685 and ground (Pink/Yellow wire). If resistance in either wire is 10 k/ohms or less, repair short(s) to ground as necessary. See WIRING DIAGRAMS. If resistance in either wire is more than 10 k/ohms, replace GEM/CTM. See GEM/CTM under REMOVAL & INSTALLATION. Clear DTCs and retest system.

6) Using NGS tester, observe PID WPRUN while triggering active command mode WIPER RLY. If WPRUN PID agrees with command mode, go to next step. If WPRUN PID does not agree with command mode replace GEM/CTM. See GEM/CTM under REMOVAL & INSTALLATION. Clear DTCs and retest system.

7) Turn ignition off. Remove wiper run/park relay. Check run/park relay. See RELAYS under COMPONENT TESTS. If relay is good, go to next step. If relay is faulty, replace relay. Clear DTCs, and retest system.

8) Disconnect GEM/CTM C239 26-pin connector. Measure resistance between wiper run/park relay connector terminal No. 1 and ground. *See Fig. 2.* If resistance is greater than 10 k/ohms, go to next step. If resistance is 10 k/ohms or less, repair Yellow/White wire as necessary. See WIRING DIAGRAMS. Clear DTCs and retest system.

9) Turn ignition on. Turn wiper switch on. Remove wiper run/park relay. If wipers stop operating, go to step **11)** . If wipers continue to operate, reconnect relay and go to next step.

10) Turn ignition off. Disconnect wiper motor connector and wiper high/low relay. Turn ignition on. Measure voltage between high/low relay connector terminal No. 5 and ground (Dark Blue/Orange wire). *See Fig. 2.* Measure voltage between high/low relay connector terminal No. 4 and ground (White wire). If any reading is greater than 10 volts, repair appropriate wire(s). See WIRING DIAGRAMS. Clear DTCs and retest

system. If both readings are 10 volts or less, replace wiper motor. See WIPER MOTOR under REMOVAL & INSTALLATION. Clear DTCs and retest system.

11) Turn ignition off. Disconnect wiper motor connector. Turn ignition on. Measure voltage between wiper run/park relay connector terminal No. 4 and ground. *See Fig. 2.* If there is any voltage, repair Light Blue wire. See WIRING DIAGRAMS. If there is no voltage, replace wiper motor. See WIPER MOTOR under REMOVAL & INSTALLATION. Clear DTCs and retest system.

TEST C: WIPERS OPERATE AT INTERVAL SETTING BUT INOPERATIVE AT HIGH &/OR LOW SPEED

1) Turn ignition off. Connect New Generation Star (NGS) tester (007-00500) to Data Link Connector (DLC). DLC is located below center of instrument panel. On manual transmission models, depress clutch pedal. Observe GEM/CTM PIDs IGN_A, IGN_S, IGN_OG/L and IGN_RD while turning the ignition switch through all positions. If PID values agree with switch positions, go to next step. If PID values do not agree with switch positions, repair appropriate ignition switch circuit(s). See appropriate wiring diagram in POWER DISTRIBUTION article in WIRING DIAGRAMS. Clear DTCs and retest system.

2) Using NGS tester, retrieve DTCs stored in GEM/CTM. Clear DTCs. Perform ON-DEMAND SELF-TEST and note all DTCs. If any DTCs exist, go to appropriate test step. See TEST C DTC INDEX table. If no DTCs exist, go to next step.

TEST C DTC INDEX

DTC	Step
B1342	1
B1434	7
B1436	7
B1438	3
B1450	3
B1466	3

[1] – Replace GEM/CTM, clear DTCs and retest system.

3) Connect New Generation Star (NGS) Tester (007-00500) to Data Link Connector (DLC). DLC is located below center of instrument panel. Turn ignition on. Observe PID WPMODE while turning wiper switch through all positions. If PID values agree with switch positions, go to step **7)**. If PID values do not agree with switch positions, go to next step.

4) Turn ignition off. Disconnect multifunction switch 259 7-pin connector. Check wiper switch. See WIPER SWITCH under COMPONENT TESTS. If switch is good, go to next step. If switch is faulty, replace switch. Clear DTCs and retest system.

5) Disconnect GEM/CTM C239 26-pin connector. Turn ignition on. Measure voltage between multifunction switch C259 connector terminal No. 590 (Light Blue/Orange wire) and ground. *See Fig. 3.* Measure the voltage between multifunction switch C259 connector terminal No. 685 (Pink/Yellow wire) and ground. If there is no voltage, go to next step. If any voltage is indicated, repair appropriate wire(s). See WIRING DIAGRAMS. Clear DTCs and retest system.

6) Turn ignition off. Measure resistance between GEM/CTM C239 connector terminal No. 13 and multifunction switch C259 connector terminal No. 590 (Light Blue/Orange wire). *See Figs. 3 and 4.* Measure resistance between GEM/CTM C239 connector terminal No. 22 and multifunction switch C259 connector terminal No. 685 (Pink/Yellow wire). If each resistance is less than 5 ohms, replace GEM/CTM. See GEM/CTM under REMOVAL & INSTALLATION. Clear DTCs and retest system. If either resistance is 5 ohms or greater, repair appropriate wire(s). See WIRING DIAGRAMS. Clear DTCs and retest system.

7) Using NGS tester, observe PID WPHISP while triggering active command SPEED RELAY. If PID WPHISP agrees with command mode, go to next step. If PID WPHISP does not agree with command mode replace GEM/CTM. See GEM/CTM under REMOVAL & INSTALLATION. Clear DTCs and retest system.

8) Turn ignition off. Disconnect GEM/CTM C239 26-pin connector and wiper high/low relay. Turn ignition on. Measure voltage between high/low relay connector terminal No. 2 and ground. *See Fig. 2.* If reading is

FORD
4-1376

1999 ACCESSORIES & EQUIPMENT
Wiper/Washer Systems – F150 & F250 Light-Duty Pickup (Cont.)

10 volts or less, go to next step. If reading is greater than 10 volts, repair short to power in Gray/Light Blue wire. See WIRING DIAGRAMS. Clear DTCs and retest system.

9) Turn ignition off. Remove wiper high/low relay. Check high/low relay. See RELAYS under COMPONENT TESTS. If relay is good, go to next step. If relay is faulty, replace high/low relay. Clear DTCs and retest system.

10) Turn ignition on. Measure voltage between wiper high/low relay connector terminal No. 2 and ground. *See Fig. 2.* If reading is more than 10 volts, go to next step. If reading is 10 volts or less, repair short to power in White/Black wire. See WIRING DIAGRAMS. Clear DTCs and retest system.

11) Turn ignition off. Disconnect GEM C239 26-pin connector. Measure resistance between high/low relay connector terminal No. 1 and ground. *See Fig. 2.* If resistance is greater than 10 k/ohms, go to next step. If resistance is 10 k/ohms or less, repair short to ground in Gray/Light Blue wire. See WIRING DIAGRAMS. Clear DTCs and retest system.

12) Measure resistance between GEM/CTM C239 connector terminal No. 18 and high/low relay connector terminal No. 1. *See Figs. 2 and 4.* If resistance is less than 5 ohms, go to next step. If resistance is 5 ohms or more, repair open in Gray/Light Blue wire. See WIRING DIAGRAMS. Clear DTCs and retest system.

13) Turn ignition off. Disconnect wiper motor connector. Measure resistance between wiper high/low relay connector terminal No. 5 and wiper motor connector terminal No. 5 (Dark Blue/Orange wire). *See Figs. 2 and 5.* Measure resistance between high/low relay connector terminal No. 4 and wiper motor connector terminal No. 4 (White wire). Measure resistance between wiper motor connector terminal No. 3 (Black wire) and ground. If resistances are less than 5 ohms, check wiper motor current draw. See WIPER MOTOR under COMPONENT TESTS. If resistance of any circuit is 5 ohms or greater, repair appropriate wire(s) as necessary. See WIRING DIAGRAMS. Clear DTCs and retest system.

TEST D: WIPERS INOPERATIVE AT INTERVAL SETTING BUT OPERATE AT HIGH & LOW SPEED

1) Turn ignition off. Connect New Generation Star (NGS) Tester (007-00500) to Data Link Connector (DLC). DLC is located below center of instrument panel. On manual transmission models, depress clutch pedal. Observe GEM/CTM PIDs IGN_A, IGN_S, IGN_OG/L and IGN_RD while turning ignition switch through all positions. If PID values agree with switch positions, go to next step. If PID values do not agree with switch positions, repair appropriate ignition switch circuit(s). See appropriate wiring diagram in POWER DISTRIBUTION article in WIRING DIAGRAMS. Clear DTCs and retest system.

2) Using NGS Tester retrieve DTCs stored in GEM/CTM. Clear DTCs. Perform ON-DEMAND SELF-TEST and note all DTCs. If any DTCs exist, go to appropriate test step. See TEST D DTC INDEX table. If no DTCs exist, go to next step.

TEST D DTC INDEX

DTC	Step
B1342	1
B1431	7
B1438	3
B1441	3
B1446	7
B1450	3
B1453	3

[1] – Replace GEM/CTM, clear DTCs and retest system.

3) Turn ignition on. Using NGS tester observe PID WPMODE while turning wiper switch through all positions. If PID values agree with switch positions, go to step **7)**. If PID values do not agree with switch positions, go to next step.

4) Turn ignition off. Disconnect multifunction switch C259 7-pin connector. Check wiper switch. See WIPER SWITCH under COMPONENT TESTS. If switch is good, go to next step. If switch is faulty, replace switch. See MULTIFUNCTION SWITCH under REMOVAL & INSTALLATION. Clear DTCs and retest system.

5) Disconnect GEM/CTM C239 26-pin connector. Turn ignition on. Measure voltage between multifunction switch connector terminal No. 590 (Light Blue/Orange) and ground. *See Fig. 3.* Measure voltage between multifunction switch connector terminal No. 685 (Pink/Yellow) and ground. If each reading is less than 10 volts, go to next step. If either reading is more than 10 volts, repair appropriate wire. See WIRING DIAGRAMS. Clear DTCs and retest system.

6) Turn ignition off. Measure resistance between GEM/CTM C239 connector terminal No. 13 and multifunction switch C259 connector terminal No. 590 (Light Blue/Orange wire). *See Figs. 3 and 4.* Measure resistance between GEM/CTM C239 connector terminal No. 22 and multifunction switch C259 connector terminal No. 685 (Pink/Yellow wire). If resistances are less than 5 ohms, replace GEM/CTM. See GEM/CTM under REMOVAL & INSTALLATION. Clear DTCs and retest system. If either resistance is 5 ohms or greater, repair appropriate wire(s). See WIRING DIAGRAMS. Clear DTCs and retest system.

7) Turn ignition on. Using NGS tester, observe and record PID WPPRKSW while wipers are running on low speed. Using NGS view recorder areas, view WPPRKSW graph. If PID WPPRKSW indicates PARK when wipers are in park position and notPRK when wipers are in any other position, replace GEM/CTM. See GEM/CTM under REMOVAL & INSTALLATION. Clear DTCs and retest system. If PID WPPRKSW agrees with wiper position, go to next step.

8) Turn ignition off. Disconnect wiper motor connector. Turn ignition on. Measure voltage between wiper motor connector terminal No. 2 and ground. *See Fig. 5.* If reading is greater than 10 volts, go to next step. If reading 10 volts or less, repair White/Black wire. Clear DTCs and retest system.

9) Turn ignition off. Disconnect GEM/CTM C239 26-pin connector. Measure resistance between wiper motor connector terminal No. 1 and GEM/CTM C239 connector terminal No. 15. *See Figs. 4 and 5.* If resistance is less than 5 ohms, reconnect GEM/CTM and go to next step. If resistance is 5 ohms or greater, repair open in Light Blue wire. See WIRING DIAGRAMS. Clear DTCs and retest system.

10) Turn ignition on. Observe PID WPPRKSW. Attach 30-amp fused jumper wire between wiper motor connector terminal No. 1 and ground. *See Fig. 5.* Detach ground side of jumper wire and attach to battery positive. If PID WPPRKSW indicates PARKED when terminal No. 1 is grounded and notPRK when battery voltage is applied, replace wiper motor. See WIPER MOTOR under REMOVAL & INSTALLATION. Clear DTCs and retest system. If PID does not display as indicated, replace GEM/CTM. See GEM/CTM under REMOVAL & INSTALLATION. Clear DTCs and retest system.

TEST E: WASH & WIPE FUNCTION DOES NOT OPERATE PROPERLY

1) Turn ignition off. Connect New Generation Star (NGS) Tester (007-00500) to Data Link Connector (DLC). DLC is located below center of instrument panel. On manual transmission models, depress clutch pedal. Observe GEM/CTM PIDs IGN_A, IGN_S, IGN_OG/L and IGN_RD while turning ignition switch through all positions. If PID values agree with switch positions, go to next step. If PID values do not agree with switch positions, repair appropriate ignition switch circuit(s). See appropriate wiring diagram in POWER DISTRIBUTION article in WIRING DIAGRAMS. Clear DTCs and retest system.

2) Using NGS Tester retrieve continuous DTCs stored in GEM/CTM. Clear DTCs. Perform ON-DEMAND SELF-TEST and note all DTCs. If any DTCs exist, go to appropriate test step. See TEST E DTC INDEX table. If no DTCs exist, go to next step.

TEST E DTC INDEX

DTC	Step
B1342	1
B1450	3
B1453	3
B1458	7
B1460	7

[1] – Replace GEM/CTM, clear DTCs and retest system.

3) Using NGS tester, observe PID WPMODE while turning wiper switch through all positions. If PID values agree with switch positions, go to step **7)**. If PID values do not agree with switch positions, go to next step.

4) Turn ignition off. Disconnect multifunction switch C259 7-pin connector. Measure resistance between multifunction switch pins No. 993 and 590 while depressing and releasing washer switch. *See Fig. 6.* If resistance is less than 5 ohms with switch depressed and greater than 10 k/ohms with switch released, go to next step. If resistance is not as specified, replace multifunction switch. See MULTIFUNCTION SWITCH under REMOVAL & INSTALLATION. Clear DTCs and retest system.

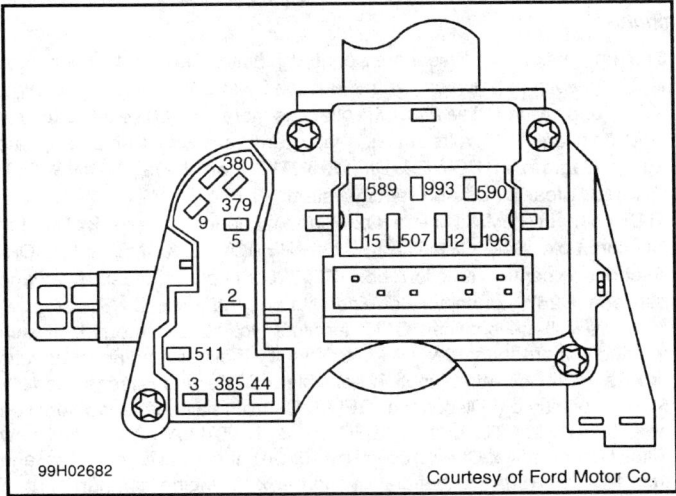

99H02682   Courtesy of Ford Motor Co.

Fig. 6: Identifying Multifunction Switch Terminals

5) Disconnect GEM/CTM 239 26-pin connector. Turn ignition on. Measure voltage between multifunction switch C259 connector terminal No. 590 and ground. If any voltage is indicated, repair Light Blue/Orange wire. Clear DTCs and retest system. If no voltage is indicated, go to next step.

6) Turn ignition off. Measure resistance between multifunction switch C259 connector terminal No. 590 and GEM/CTM C239 connector terminal No. 13. If resistance is less than 5 ohms, replace GEM/CTM. See GEM/CTM under REMOVAL & INSTALLATION. Clear DTCs and retest system. If resistance is 5 ohms or greater, repair open in Light Blue/Orange wire. Clear DTCs and retest system.

7) Turn ignition on. Using NGS tester, observe PID WASHRLY while triggering active command WASHRLY. If PID WASHRLY agrees with command mode, go to next step. If PID WASHRLY does not agree with command mode, replace GEM/CTM. See GEM/CTM under REMOVAL & INSTALLATION. Clear DTCs and retest system.

8) Turn ignition off. Disconnect washer pump relay. Turn ignition on. Measure voltage between washer pump relay connector terminal No. 3 and ground. *See Fig. 2.* If voltage is greater than 10 volts, go to next step. If voltage is 10 volts or less, repair White/Black wire. See WIRING DIAGRAMS. Clear DTCs and retest system.

9) Turn ignition off. Check washer pump relay. See RELAYS under COMPONENT TESTS. If relay is good, go to next step. If faulty, replace relay. Clear DTCs and retest system.

10) Disconnect GEM/CTM C239 26-pin connector. Measure resistance between GEM/CTM C239 connector terminal No. 24 and washer pump relay terminal No. 1. *See Figs. 2 and 4.* If resistance is less than 5 ohms, go to next step. If resistance is 5 ohms or greater, repair open in Tan/Red wire. See WIRING DIAGRAMS. Clear DTCs and retest system.

11) Disconnect GEM/CTM C239 26-pin connector. Turn ignition on. Measure voltage between washer pump relay connector terminal No. 1 and ground. *See Fig. 2.* If there is no voltage, go to next step. If there is any voltage, repair Tan/Red wire short to power. Clear DTCs and retest system.

12) Turn ignition off. Disconnect washer pump connector. Measure resistance of Black/White wire between washer pump connector and washer pump relay connector terminal No. 5. *See Fig. 2.* If resistance is less than 5 ohms, reconnect washer pump relay and go to next step. If resistance is 5 ohms or greater, repair Black/White wire. See WIRING DIAGRAMS. Clear DTCs and retest system.

13) Measure resistance of Black wire between washer pump connector and ground. If resistance is less than 5 ohms, replace washer pump. If resistance is 5 ohms or greater, repair Black wire and ground connection as necessary. Clear DTCs and retest system.

TEST F: SPEED DEPENDENT INTERVAL MODE NOT OPERATING PROPERLY – GEM

1) Turn ignition off. Connect New Generation Star (NGS) Tester (007-00500) to Data Link Connector (DLC). DLC is located below center of instrument panel. On manual transmission models, depress clutch pedal. Observe GEM PIDs IGN_A, IGN_S, IGN_OG/L and IGN_RD while turning ignition switch through all positions. If PID values agree with switch positions, go to next step. If PID values do not agree with switch positions, repair appropriate ignition switch circuit(s). See appropriate wiring diagram in POWER DISTRIBUTION article in WIRING DIAGRAMS. Clear DTCs and retest system.

2) Using NGS tester retrieve continuous DTCs stored in GEM. Clear continuous DTCs. Perform ON-DEMAND SELF-TEST and note all DTCs. If DTC P0500 exists, go to step **4)**. If DTC B1342 exists, replace GEM. See GEM/CTM under REMOVAL & INSTALLATION. Clear DTCs and retest system. If no DTCs exist, go to next step.

3) Using NGS tester, observe PID SPEEDWP. If PID SPEEDWP indicates ACTIVE go to next step. If PID SPEEDWP does not indicate ACTIVE, ENABLE the GEM SPEED DEPENDENT WIPER using the Service Bay Diagnostic System (SBDS) under module reprogramming. Clear DTCs and retest system.

4) Using NGS tester, observe GEM PID VSS while driving vehicle from 0 to 55 MPH. If GEM PID VSS values do not agree with speedometer, go to next step. If GEM PID VSS values agree with speedometer, replace GEM. See GEM/CTM under REMOVAL & INSTALLATION. Clear DTCs and retest system.

5) Turn ignition off. Disconnect central junction box C243 connector and Powertrain Control Module (PCM) connector. Measure resistance between central junction block C243 connector terminal No. 21 and PCM connector terminal No. 68. *See Figs. 1 and 7.* If resistance if 5 ohms or greater, repair open Gray/Black wire. See WIRING DIAGRAMS under ENGINE PERFORMANCE. If resistance is less than 5 ohms, see appropriate SELF-DIAGNOSTICS article under ENGINE PERFORMANCE. If Vehicle Speed Sensor (VSS) system tests okay, go to next step.

6) Remove GEM. See GEM/CTM under REMOVAL & INSTALLATION. Measure internal resistance of central junction box between C267 terminal No. 18 and C243 terminal No. 21. *See Fig. 8.* If resistance is less than 5 ohms, replace GEM. Clear the DTCs and retest system. If the resistance is 5 ohms or greater, replace the central junction box. Clear the DTCs and retest system.

FORD
4-1378

1999 ACCESSORIES & EQUIPMENT
Wiper/Washer Systems – F150 & F250 Light-Duty Pickup (Cont.)

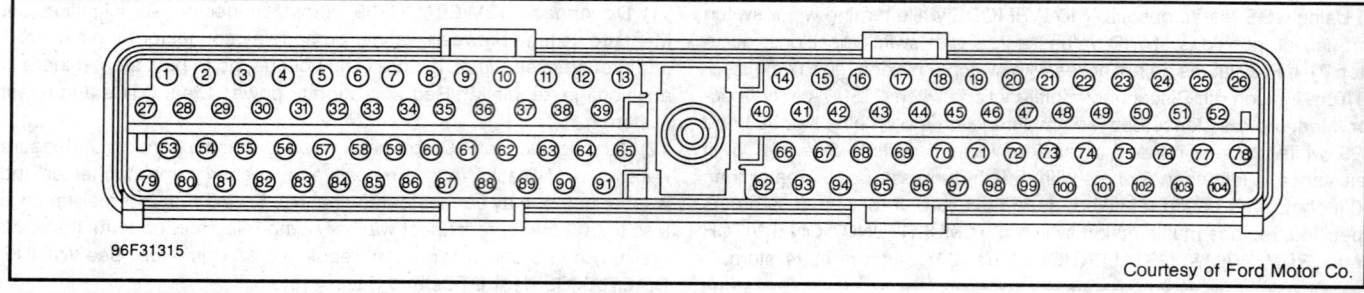

96F31315

Courtesy of Ford Motor Co.

Fig. 7: Identifying Powertrain Control Module (PCM) Connector Terminals

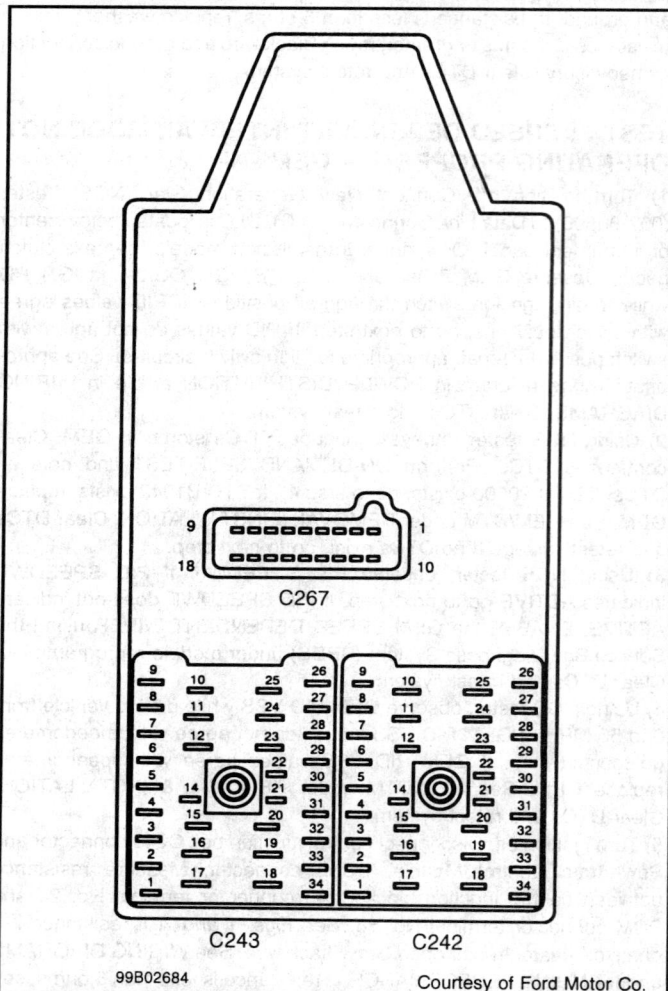

99B02684

Courtesy of Ford Motor Co.

Fig. 8: Identifying Central Junction Box Connector & Terminals

TEST G: NO SCAN TOOL COMMUNICATION WITH GEM/CTM

1) Turn ignition off. Connect New Generation Star (NGS) Tester (007-00500) to Data Link Connector (DLC). DLC is located below center of instrument panel. On manual transmission models, depress clutch pedal. Observe GEM PIDs IGN_A, IGN_S, IGN_OG/L and IGN_RD while turning ignition switch through all positions. If PID values agree with switch positions, go to next step. If PID values do not agree with switch positions, repair appropriate ignition switch circuit(s). See appropriate wiring diagram in POWER DISTRIBUTION article in WIRING DIAGRAMS. Clear DTCs and retest system.

2) Turn ignition off. Check fuses No. 15 (5A) at central junction box (interior fuse panel) and fuse No. 103 (50A) at battery junction box in engine compartment. If fuses are good, go to next step. If fuse(s) are blown, go to step **5)**.

3) Turn ignition off. Disconnect central junction box C243 connector. Measure voltage between central junction box C243 connector terminal No. 11 and ground. *See Fig. 1.* If voltage is more than 10 volts, go to next step. If voltage is 10 volts or less, repair Tan/Black wire. See appropriate wiring diagram in POWER DISTRIBUTION article in WIRING DIAGRAMS. Clear DTCs and retest system.

4) Disconnect GEM/CTM from C267 18-pin connector on back of central junction box. See GEM/CTM under REMOVAL & INSTALLATION. Reconnect central junction box C243 connector. Measure voltage between C267 connector terminal No. 4 and ground. *See Fig. 8.* Measure voltage between C267 terminal No. 16 and ground. If each reading is more than 10 volts, go to step **8)**. If either reading is 10 volts or less, replace central junction box. Clear DTCs and retest system.

5) Turn ignition off. Disconnect GEM/CTM from back of central junction box. See GEM/CTM under REMOVAL & INSTALLATION. Install new fuses if inoperative. Check fuses No. 15 (5A) at central junction box and fuse No. 103 (50A) at battery junction box in engine compartment. If both fuses are good, go to step **7)**. If fuse No. 103 is blown, go to next step. If fuse No. 15 is blown, go to step **10)**.

6) Disconnect central junction box C243 connector. Measure resistance between central junction box C243 connector terminal No. 11 and ground. If resistance is greater than 10 k/ohms, replace central junction box. Clear DTCs and retest system. If resistance is 10 k/ohms or less, repair Tan/Black wire. See appropriate wiring diagram in POWER DISTRIBUTION article in WIRING DIAGRAMS. Clear DTCs and retest system.

7) Disconnect central junction box C243 connector. Measure resistance between central junction box C243 connector terminal No. 11 and C267 connector terminal No. 4. *See Fig. 8.* Measure internal resistance between central junction box C243 connector terminal No. 11 and C267 connector terminal No. 16. If resistances are less than 5 ohms, go to next step. If any resistance is 5 ohms or more, replace central junction box. Clear DTCs and retest system.

8) Disconnect GEM/CTM C239 26-pin connector. Measure resistance between GEM/CTM C239 connector terminal No. 26 and ground. If resistance is less than 5 ohms, go to next step. If resistance is 5 ohms or more, repair open to ground in Black/Light Blue wire. Clear DTCs and retest system.

9) Measure resistance between GEM/CTM C239 connector terminal No. 14 and ground. If resistance is less than 5 ohms, problem is with Module Communications Network. See appropriate MODULE COMMUNICATIONS NETWORK article. If resistance is 5 ohms or more, repair open in Black/Light Blue wire. Clear DTCs and retest system.

10) Measure resistance between central junction box C267 terminal No. 4 and ground. *See Fig. 8.* If resistance is 10 k/ohms or less, replace central junction box. Clear DTCs and retest system. If resistance is more than 10 k/ohms, replace GEM/CTM. See GEM/CTM under REMOVAL & INSTALLATION. Clear DTCs and retest system.

COMPONENT TESTS

WIPER MOTOR

1) Disconnect negative battery cable. Disengage linkage from motor. Disconnect wiper connector. Connect Green lead from Starting And Charging System Tester (078-00005) to negative battery terminal.

1999 ACCESSORIES & EQUIPMENT
Wiper/Washer Systems – F150 & F250 Light-Duty Pickup (Cont.)

FORD
4-1379

2) Connect Red tester lead to wiper motor terminal No. 3 (Black wire on mating connector). Connect a jumper wire between positive battery terminal and wiper motor terminal No. 4 (White wire on mating connector). If current draw is 3.5 amps or less, remove jumper wire and go to next step. If current draw is more than 3.5 amps, replace wiper motor.
3) Connect a jumper wire between positive battery terminal and wiper motor terminal No. 5 (Dark Blue/Orange wire on mating connector). If current draw is more than 5.5 amps, replace wiper motor. If current draw is 5.5 amps or less, wiper motor is okay.

RELAYS

NOTE: Same test procedure may be used for all wiper/washer system relays.

1) Remove relay to be tested. Wiper relays are located in battery junction box in engine compartment. Measure resistance between relay terminal No. 2 and all other terminals. *See Fig. 9.* If resistance is less than 5 ohms between relay terminal No. 2 and any other terminal, replace relay. If all resistances are 5 ohms or greater, go to next step.
2) Connect a jumper between positive battery terminal and relay terminal No. 3. *See Fig. 9.* Measure voltage between ground and relay terminal No. 4. If battery voltage is not present, replace relay. If battery voltage is present, connect a second wire from positive battery terminal to relay terminal No. 1. Connect a third jumper wire between relay terminal No. 2 and ground. Measure voltage between ground and relay terminal No. 5. If battery voltage is not present, replace relay, If battery voltage is present, relay is okay.

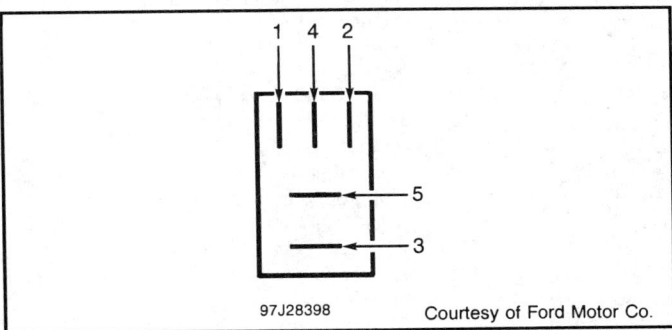

97J28398   Courtesy of Ford Motor Co.

Fig. 9: Identifying Relay Terminals

WIPER SWITCH

Wiper switch is incorporated into multifunction switch on steering column and is not serviced separately. Replace multifunction switch if resistance is not as specified. See WIPER SWITCH RESISTANCE TEST table. *See Fig. 6.*

WIPER SWITCH RESISTANCE TEST

Switch Position	Switch Terminals	[1] k/ohms
OFF	589 & 993	47.6
INT	589 & 993	11.3
LOW	589 & 993	4.08
HIGH	589 & 993	0
INT [2]		
MIN	590 & 993	3.3
MAX	590 & 993	103.3
WASH		
ON	590 & 993	0
OFF	590 & 993	103.3

[1] – Values are approximate.
[2] – Rotate (INT) interval knob from minimum to maximum. Resistance should gradually increase from 3.3 k/ohms (MIN) to 103.3 k/ohms (MAX).

REMOVAL & INSTALLATION

WARNING: Deactivate air bag system before performing any service operation involving steering column components. See appropriate AIR BAG RESTRAINT SYSTEMS article. Do not apply electrical power to any component on steering column without first deactivating air bag system. Air bag may deploy.

CAUTION: When battery is disconnected, vehicle computer and memory systems may lose memory data. Driveability problems may exist until computer systems have completed a relearn cycle. See COMPUTER RELEARN PROCEDURES article in GENERAL INFORMATION before disconnecting battery.

GEM/CTM

CAUTION: Disconnect battery before disconnecting Generic Electronic Module (GEM) or Central Timer Module (CTM) connectors. Failure to do so will result in GEM/CTM storing erroneous codes and may also result in erratic operation of GEM/CTM after reconnection.

CAUTION: If replacing GEM/CTM, it is necessary to upload module configuration information to the New Generation STAR (NGS) tester. After installation this information needs to be downloaded into the new GEM/CTM module.

Removal & Installation – Disconnect the battery ground cable. Remove the lower instrument panel steering column cover. Remove the bulkhead electrical connectors (C243 and C242) from the central junction box (interior fuse panel). Unbolt and remove the central junction box. Disconnect the GEM/CTM electrical connectors. Remove screws and disconnect the GEM/CTM from the backside of the central junction box. To install, reverse removal procedure.

MULTIFUNCTION SWITCH

Removal & Installation – Disconnect negative battery cable. Turn ignition switch to RUN. Insert punch through lower steering column shroud hole and push ignition lock cylinder release tab while pulling out ignition switch lock cylinder. Twist and remove tilt wheel handle. Move steering gear selector to lowest position. Release four clips and remove steering column opening cover. Remove steering column shrouds. Remove multifunction switch retaining screws. Disconnect electrical connector. Remove switch. To install, reverse removal procedure.

WASHER PUMP & RESERVOIR

Removal & Installation – Disconnect battery ground. Remove jack-handle from washer reservoir. Disconnect washer electrical connector. Remove reservoir retaining screws. Disconnect reservoir hose. Remove reservoir. Remove pump. To install, reverse removal procedure. Fill reservoir before making electrical connections.

WIPER MOTOR

Removal & Installation – Cycle wipers to high point of travel and turn ignition off. Remove wiper arms. Open hood. Remove cowl grille seal. Remove LH cowl grille first. Remove RH cowl grille. Disconnect wiper motor connector. Remove mounting arm and pivot shaft. Disconnect wiper linkage. Unbolt wiper motor. To install, reverse removal procedure.

FORD
4-1380

1999 ACCESSORIES & EQUIPMENT
Wiper/Washer Systems – F150 & F250 Light-Duty Pickup (Cont.)

WIRING DIAGRAMS

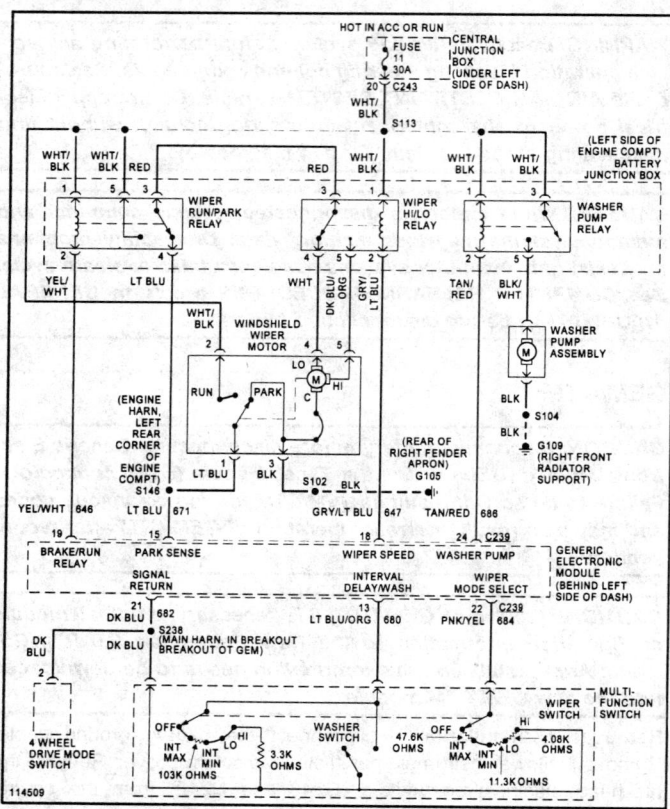

Fig. 10: Wiper/Washer System Wiring Diagram
(F150 & F250 Light-Duty Pickup)

NOTE: This article includes Cab & Chassis.

DESCRIPTION & OPERATION

Windshield wipers are operated by a permanent magnet motor. Wiper functions are controlled by the Generic Electronic Module (GEM). When wiper control switch is in interval (INT) position, wipers make single sweeps, separated by adjustable-length pauses. For all interval settings except INT 1, speed dependent interval feature will automatically shorten pauses as vehicle speed increases. GEM is located on the backside of the fuse junction panel located to the lower left of the steering wheel. Fuse junction panel is accessed by removing instrument panel steering column cover.

ADJUSTMENTS

WIPER ARM & BLADE ASSEMBLY

1) Remove wiper arms from pivot shafts. Turn on wipers to allow motor to operate 3 or 4 cycles, then turn wipers off. Wiper pivot shafts will be in park position.

2) Install arm and blade assemblies onto pivot shafts. Adjust clearance between center of wiper blade and windshield molding/cowl junction. Clearance should be 2.20" (56 mm) for driver's side, and 2.91" (74 mm) for passenger's side.

TROUBLE SHOOTING

Verify customer complaint by operating system. Visually inspect for obvious signs of damage:
- Power distribution box maxi-fuses:
  - No. 15 (30-amp)
  - No. 22 (50-amp)
- Fuse junction panel fuses:
  - No. 11 (10-amp)
  - No. 15 (5-amp)
- Damaged wiring harness.
- Loose or corroded connections.
- Open or shorted wiring.
- Washer pump hoses.
- Wiper/washer switch.
- Wiper linkage.
- Wiper motor.

If all components are okay, go to SELF-DIAGNOSTICS.

COMPONENT TESTS

HORN RELAY

1) Check resistance between relay terminal No. 85 and all other terminals. *See Fig. 1.* If resistance is 5 ohms or less between terminal No. 85 and any other terminal, replace relay. If resistance between relay terminal No. 85 and each terminal is more than 5 ohms, go to next step.

2) Attach 2 jumper wires from battery positive terminal to relay terminals No. 86 and 30. Measure voltage at terminal No. 87A. If battery voltage is NOT present, replace relay. If battery voltage is present, attach a third jumper wire between terminal No. 85 and ground. Measure voltage at terminal No. 87. If battery voltage is NOT present, replace relay. If battery voltage is present, relay is okay.

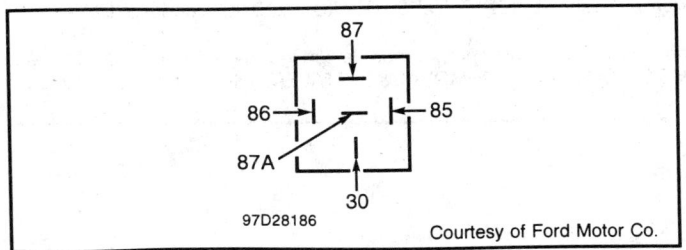

Fig. 1: Identifying Horn Relay Terminals

WIPER/WASHER SYSTEM RELAYS

1) Remove relay to be tested. Wiper relays are located in power distribution box in engine compartment near master cylinder. Measure resistance between relay terminal No. 2 and all other terminals. *See Fig. 2.* If resistance is less than 5 ohms between relay terminal No. 2 and any other terminal, replace relay. If all resistances are 5 ohms or more, go to next step.

2) Connect a jumper between positive battery terminal and relay terminal No. 3. *See Fig. 2.* Measure voltage between relay terminal No. 4 and ground. If battery voltage is NOT present, replace relay. If battery voltage is present, connect a second wire from positive battery terminal to relay terminal No. 1. Connect a third jumper wire between relay terminal No. 2 and ground. Measure voltage between ground and relay terminal No. 5. If battery voltage is NOT present, replace relay, If battery voltage is present, relay is okay.

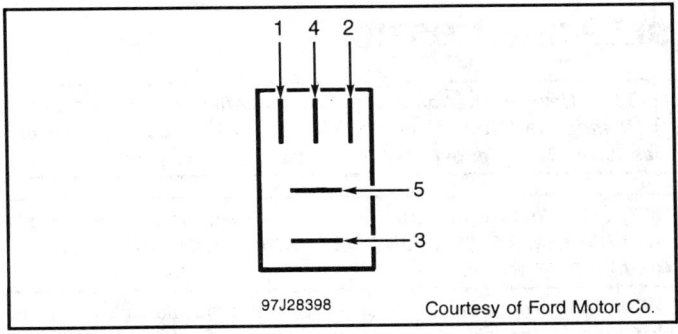

Fig. 2: Identifying Relay Terminals

WIPER MOTOR

1) Disconnect negative battery cable. Disengage linkage from motor. Disconnect wiper connector. Connect in-line ammeter between negative battery terminal and wiper motor terminal No. 3 (Black wire terminal). For mating connector view, *see Fig. 3.* Connect a jumper wire between positive battery terminal and wiper motor terminal No. 4 (White wire terminal).

2) Observe ammeter and note low speed current draw. If current draw is more than 3.5 amps, replace wiper motor. If current draw is 3.5 amps or less, disconnect jumper wire and go to next step.

3) Move jumper wire to wiper motor terminal No. 5 (Dark Blue/Orange wire terminal). Observe ammeter and note high speed current draw. If current draw is more than 5.5 amps, replace wiper motor.

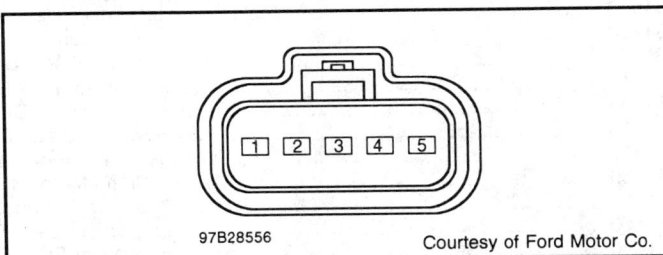

Fig. 3: Identifying Wiper Motor Connector Terminals

WIPER SWITCH

Wiper switch is incorporated into multifunction switch on steering column. Wiper/washer portion of multifunction switch cannot be serviced separately. Replace multifunction switch if resistance is not as specified. See WIPER SWITCH RESISTANCE TEST table. *See Fig. 4.*

WIPER SWITCH RESISTANCE TEST

Switch Position	Between Terminals	k/ohms
Wiper		
Off	589 & 993	47.6
Low	589 & 993	4.08
High	589 & 993	0

FORD
4-1382

1999 ACCESSORIES & EQUIPMENT
Wiper/Washer Systems – F250 Super-Duty & F350 Pickup (Cont.)

WIPER SWITCH RESISTANCE TEST (Cont.)

Switch Position	Between Terminals	k/ohms
INT	589 & 993	11.33
WASH		
On	590 & 993	0
Off	590 & 993	103.3
INT [1]		
MIN	590 & 993	3.3
MAX	590 & 993	103.3

[1] – Rotate (INT) interval knob from minimum to maximum. Resistance should gradually increase from 3.3 k/ohms (MIN) to 103.3 k/ohms (MAX).

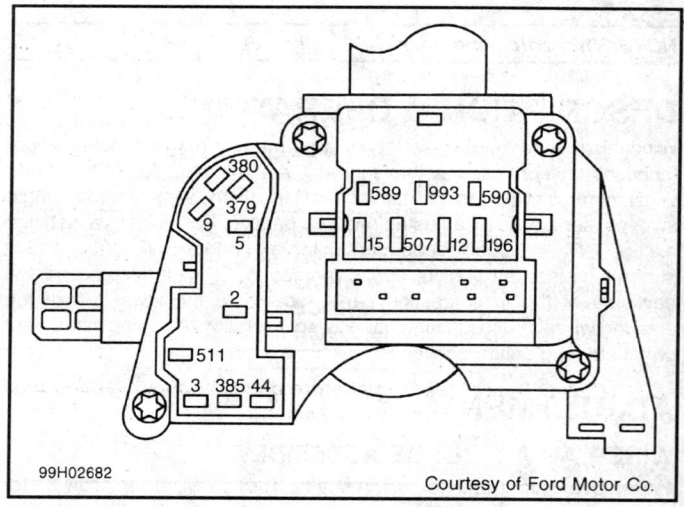

99H02682   Courtesy of Ford Motor Co.

Fig. 4: Identifying Multifunction Switch Terminals

SELF-DIAGNOSTICS

NOTE: A New Generation Star (NGS) tester (007–00500) is required for testing the Generic Electronic Module (GEM) controlled wiper/washer system. Follow NGS tester manufacturer's instructions.

NOTE: For further information on Self-Diagnostic System, see MODULE COMMUNICATIONS NETWORK – F250 SUPER-DUTY & F350 PICKUP article.

1) Connect New Generation Star (NGS) tester to Data Link Connector (DLC) located beneath center of instrument panel. Using NGS tester, perform DATA LINK DIAGNOSTIC TEST. If NGS tester displays CKT914, CKT915 or CKT70 = ALL ECUS NO RESP/NOT EQUIP, see MODULE COMMUNICATIONS NETWORK – F250 SUPER-DUTY & F350 PICKUP article to diagnose concern. If NGS tester displays NO RESP/NOT EQUIP for GEM, go to TEST A: NO SCAN TOOL COMMUNICATION WITH GEM under SYSTEM TESTS. If NGS tester displays SYSTEM PASSED, go to next step.

NOTE: When performing GEM self-test diagnostics, vehicles built prior to February 5, 1998 must have power windows completely up and headlamps and parking lamps off. Failure to do so will result in Diagnostic Trouble Codes (DTCs) B1577 and B2357 being set. Vehicles built after February 5, 1998 must have headlamps and parklamps on. Failure to do so will result in DTC B1575 being set.

2) Using NGS tester retrieve and note continuous Diagnostic Trouble Codes (DTCs). Perform GEM self-test diagnostics. If GEM DTCs related to the concern are retrieved, see GEM DTC TEST INDEX table to continue diagnosis. If no DTCs related to the concern are retrieved, perform appropriate test based on symptom. See SYMPTOM TEST INDEX under SYSTEM TESTS. For GEM DTCs not covered in this article, see MODULE COMMUNICATIONS NETWORK – F250 SUPER-DUTY & F350 PICKUP article.

GEM DTC TEST INDEX [1]

DTC	Description	Test
B1342	GEM Is Defective	[2]
B1431	Run/Park Relay Circuit Failure	B
B1432	Run/Park Circuit Short To Power	B
B1434	High/Low Relay Coil Circuit Failure	D
B1436	High/Low Relay Coil Circuit Short To Power	D
B1438	Wiper Mode Select Switch Circuit Failure	B
B1441	Wiper Mode Select Switch Circuit Short To Ground	C
B1446	Wiper Park Sense Circuit Failure	B
B1450	Wiper/Washer Delay Switch Circuit Failure	E
B1453	Wiper/Washer Delay Switch Circuit Short To Ground	C
B1458	Wiper/Washer Pump Motor Relay Coil Circuit Failure	F
B1460	Washer Pump Motor Relay Coil Circuit Short To Power	F
B1473	Low Speed Circuit Motor Failure	B
B1476	High Speed Circuit Motor Failure	B
B1840	Wiper Front Power Circuit Failure	B
B2141	NVM Configuration Failure	[3]
P0500	Vehicle Speed Signal Not Detected	G

[1] – Codes listed in this table are only for testing covered in this article. For complete GEM DTC listing, see MODULE COMMUNICATIONS NETWORK – F250 SUPER-DUTY & F350 PICKUP article.

[2] – Clear DTCs. Retrieve DTCs. If DTC B1342 is retrieved, replace GEM. See GENERIC ELECTRONIC MODULE under REMOVAL & INSTALLATION. Clear DTCs and retest system.

[3] – Check module configuration. Refer to NGS tester Ford Service Function (FSF) card to verify proper module configuration. Clear DTCs. Retrieve DTCs. If B2141 is retrieved, replace GEM. See GENERIC ELECTRONIC MODULE under REMOVAL & INSTALLATION. Clear DTCs and retest system.

1999 ACCESSORIES & EQUIPMENT
Wiper/Washer Systems – F250 Super-Duty & F350 Pickup (Cont.)

FORD
4-1383

SYSTEM TESTS

WARNING: Deactivate air bag system before performing any service operation involving steering column components. See appropriate AIR BAG RESTRAINT SYSTEMS article. Do not apply electrical power to any component on steering column without first deactivating air bag system. Air bag may deploy.

CAUTION: When battery is disconnected, vehicle computer and memory systems may lose memory data. Driveability problems may exist until computer systems have completed a relearn cycle. See COMPUTER RELEARN PROCEDURES article in GENERAL INFORMATION before disconnecting battery.

CAUTION: Disconnect battery before disconnecting Generic Electronic Module (GEM) connectors. Failure to do so will result in GEM storing erroneous codes and may also result in erratic operation of GEM after reconnection.

SYMPTOM TEST INDEX

Symptom	Test
No Scan Tool Communication With GEM	A
Wipers Inoperative	B
Wipers Stay On Continuously	C
High/Low Speeds Do Not Operate Properly	D
Interval Mode Does Not Operate Properly	E
Washer/Wiper Mode Does Not Operate Properly	F
Speed Dependent Interval Mode Does Not Operate Properly	G

TEST A: NO SCAN TOOL COMMUNICATION WITH GEM

NOTE: After all repairs, clear DTCs and retest system.

1) Turn ignition off. Check fuse No. 15 (5-amp) in fuse junction panel. Fuse junction panel is located lower left of steering column behind instrument panel steering column cover. If fuse is okay, reinstall fuse and go to next step. If fuse is bad, go to step **3)**.

2) Measure voltage between fuse junction panel fuse No. 15 (5-amp) and ground. If the voltage is 10 volts or less, go to step **5)**. If the voltage is more than 10 volts, go to next step.

3) Remove fuse No. 15 (5-amp) from fuse junction panel. Disconnect GEM from 18-pin connector C241 on back of fuse junction panel. Measure resistance between fuse junction panel connector C241 terminal No. 4 and ground. *See Fig. 5.* Measure resistance between fuse junction panel connector C241 terminal No. 16 and ground. If each resistance is more than 10 k/ohms, go to step **15)**. If either resistance is 10 k/ohms or less, replace the fuse junction panel.

4) Disconnect GEM 26-pin connector C239. Measure the resistance between GEM connector C239 terminal No. 26 and ground. *See Fig. 6.* If resistance is less than 5 ohms, go to step **7)**. If resistance is 5 ohms or more, repair open in Pink/Orange wire.

5) Check maxi-fuse No. 22 (50-amp) in power distribution box. Power distribution box is located under hood near master cylinder. If fuse is okay, reinstall fuse and go to next step. If fuse is bad, repair Tan/Black wire short to ground between power distribution box and fuse junction panel.

6) Measure voltage between power distribution box maxi-fuse No. 22 (50-amp) and ground. If voltage is more than 10 volts, repair open Tan/Black wire between power distribution box and fuse junction panel. If voltage if 10 volts or less, repair or replace power distribution box.

7) Disconnect GEM 26-pin connector C239. Make sure NGS tester is NOT hooked up. Measure resistance between GEM connector C239 terminal No. 25 and Data Link Connector (DLC) terminal No. 7. *See Figs. 6 and 7.* If resistance is less than 5 ohms, go to next step. If resistance is 5 ohms or more, repair open in Light Blue/White wire.

8) Measure voltage between GEM connector C239 terminal No. 26 and ground. *See Fig. 6.* If voltage is more than 10 volts, repair Pink/Orange wire short to power and replace GEM. See GENERIC ELECTRONIC

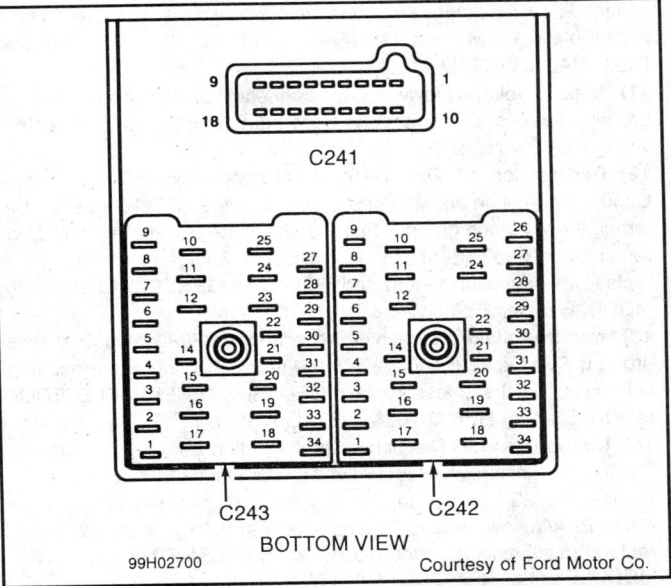

Fig. 5: Identifying Fuse Junction Panel Connectors & Terminals

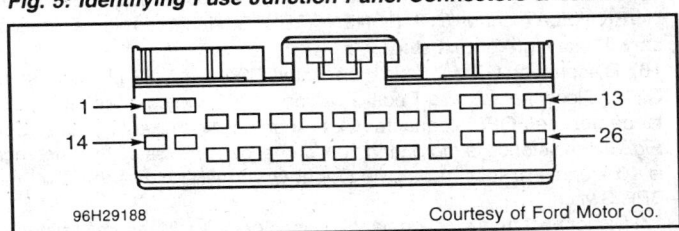

Fig. 6: Identifying GEM 26-Pin Connector C239 Terminals

MODULE under REMOVAL & INSTALLATION. If voltage is 10 volts or less, and vehicle has Electronic Shift On The Fly (ESOF), go to next step. If voltage is 10 volts or less, and vehicle does not have ESOF, go to step **11)**.

9) Turn ignition off. Disconnect GEM 22-pin connector C247. Turn ignition on. Measure voltage between GEM connector C247 terminal No. 3 and ground. *See Fig. 8.* If voltage is more than 10 volts, go to next step. If voltage is 10 volts or less, go to step **11)**.

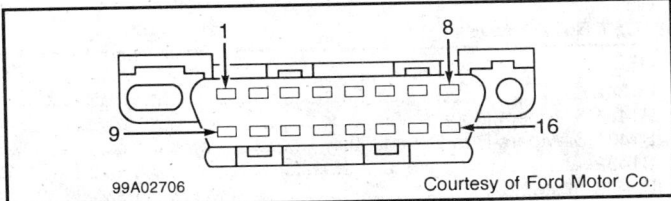

Fig. 7: Identifying Data Link Connector Terminals

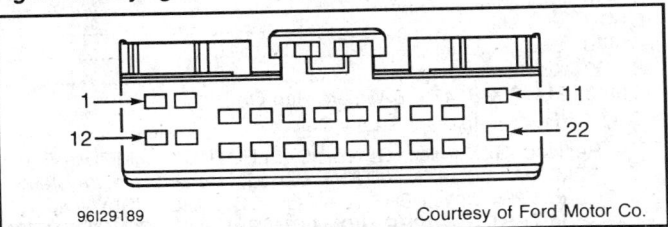

Fig. 8: Identifying GEM 22-Pin Connector C247 Terminals

10) Turn ignition off. Disconnect 4-wheel drive mode switch located at center of instrument panel. Turn ignition on. Measure voltage between GEM connector C247 terminal No. 3 and ground. *See Fig. 8.* If voltage is more than 10 volts, repair White/Light Blue wire and replace GEM. If

FORD
4-1384

1999 ACCESSORIES & EQUIPMENT
Wiper/Washer Systems – F250 Super-Duty & F350 Pickup (Cont.)

voltage is 10 volts or less, replace the 4-wheel drive mode select switch and replace GEM. See GENERIC ELECTRONIC MODULE under REMOVAL & INSTALLATION.

11) Measure voltage between GEM connector C239 terminal No. 20 and ground. *See Fig. 6.* If voltage is more than 10 volts, go to next step. If voltage is 10 volts or less, go to step **13).**

12) Turn ignition off. Disconnect multifunction switch 7-pin connector C230. Turn ignition on. Measure voltage between GEM connector C239 terminal No. 20 and ground. *See Fig. 6.* If voltage is more than 10 volts, repair Dark Blue wire and replace GEM. If voltage is 10 volts or less, replace multifunction switch and GEM. See GENERIC ELECTRONIC MODULE under REMOVAL & INSTALLATION.

13) Measure voltage between GEM connector C239 terminal No. 23 and ground. *See Fig. 6.* If voltage is more than 10 volts, go to next step. If voltage is 10 volts or less, replace GEM. See GENERIC ELECTRONIC MODULE under REMOVAL & INSTALLATION.

14) Turn ignition off. Disconnect multifunction switch 7-pin connector C230. Turn ignition on. Measure voltage between GEM connector C239 terminal No. 23 and ground. *See Fig. 6.* If voltage is more than 10 volts, repair Pink/Yellow wire and replace GEM. If voltage is 10 volts or less, replace multifunction switch and GEM. See GENERIC ELECTRONIC MODULE under REMOVAL & INSTALLATION.

15) Test the horn relay. Horn relay is located on fuse junction panel. See HORN RELAY under COMPONENT TESTS. Replace relay as necessary. If okay, go to next step.

16) Disconnect GEM 18-pin connector C241 and 22-pin connector C247. Disconnect Brake Pedal Position (BPP) Switch. Measure resistance between GEM connector C247 terminal No. 12 and ground. *See Fig. 8.* If resistance is more than 10 k/ohms, go to next step. If resistance is 10 k/ohms or less, repair Red/Light Green wire between GEM and BPP Switch.

17) Disconnect fuse junction panel connector C243. Measure resistance between center terminal of Brake Pedal Position (BPP) Switch and ground. If the resistance is more than 10 k/ohms, replace the BPP Switch. If resistance is 10 k/ohms or less, repair Light Blue/Black wire.

TEST B: WIPERS INOPERATIVE

NOTE: After all repairs, clear DTCs and retest system.

1) Turn ignition off. If any DTCs were noted from GEM self-test, go to appropriate test step. See TEST B INDEX table. If no DTCs exist, go to next step.

TEST B DTC INDEX

DTC	Step
B1342	1
B1431 & Wipers Inoperative	8)
B1431 & Wipers Run Continuously	2
B1432	12)
B1438	4)
B1446	2)
B1458	2)
B1473	2)
B1476	2)
B1480	2)
B1446, B1473 & B1476, & Wipers Run On High Only, Or Run On Interval & Low Only	3

1 – Replace GEM. See GENERIC ELECTRONIC MODULE under REMOVAL & INSTALLATION. Clear DTCs and retest system.
2 – Go to TEST C: WIPERS STAY ON CONTINUOUSLY, step **1).**
3 – Go to TEST D: WIPER HIGH/LOW SPEEDS DO NOT OPERATE PROPERLY, step **1).**

2) Turn ignition off. Check power distribution box maxi-fuse No. 15 (30-amp) and fuse junction panel fuse No. 11 (10-amp). Power distribution box is located near master cylinder. Fuse junction panel is located lower left of steering column behind instrument panel steering column cover. If both fuses are okay, go to next step. If maxi-fuse No. 15 (30-amp) is bad, go to step **21).** If fuse No. 11 (10-amp), go to step **27).**

3) Turn ignition on. Measure voltage between input terminal of power distribution box maxi-fuse No. 15 (30-amp) and ground. Also measure voltage between input terminal of fuse junction panel fuse No. 11 (10-amp) and ground. If voltages are more than 10 volts, and only DTCs B1446, B1473 and B1476 are present, and wipers do not operate, go to step **14).** If voltages are more than 10 volts, and only DTCs B1446, B1473 and B1476 are present, and only intermittent wipers do not operate, go to TEST E: INTERVAL MODE DOES NOT OPERATE PROPERLY. If voltages are more than 10 volts, and none of indicated DTCs are present, go to next step. If voltages are 10 volts or less, repair power input circuit to fuse in question.

4) Disconnect wiper run/park relay. Turn ignition on. Measure voltage between wiper run/park relay connector terminal No. 1 and ground. *See Fig. 9.* If voltage is more than 10 volts, go to next step. If voltage is 10 volts or less, repair Black/Light Green wire. See WIRING DIAGRAMS.

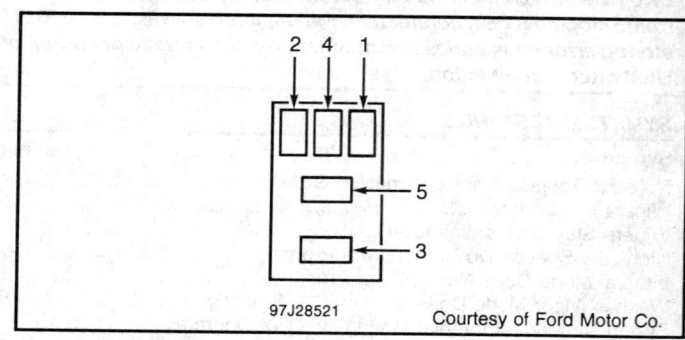

Fig. 9: Identifying Relay Connector Terminals

5) Using NGS tester observe GEM PID WPMODE while turning wiper switch through all positions. If the PID WPMODE values agree with wiper switch positions, go to step **8).** If PID WPMODE values do not agree with wiper switch positions, go to next step.

6) Turn ignition off. Disconnect multifunction switch 7-pin connector C230. Check wiper portion of multifunction switch. See WIPER SWITCH under COMPONENT TESTS. Replace switch as necessary. See MULTIFUNCTION SWITCH under REMOVAL & INSTALLATION. If switch is okay, go to next step.

7) Disconnect GEM 26-pin connector C239. Measure resistance between GEM connector C239 terminal No. 6 and multifunction switch connector C230 terminal No. 590 (Light Blue/Orange wire). *See Figs. 6 and 10.* Also measure resistance between GEM connector C239 terminal No. 20 and multifunction switch connector C230 terminal No. 993 (Dark Blue wire). And measure resistance between GEM connector C239 terminal No. 23 and multifunction switch connector C230 terminal No. 685 (Pink/Yellow wire). If resistances are less than 5 ohms, replace GEM. See GENERIC ELECTRONIC MODULE under REMOVAL & INSTALLATION. If any resistance is 5 ohms or more, repair open in appropriate wire(s). See WIRING DIAGRAMS.

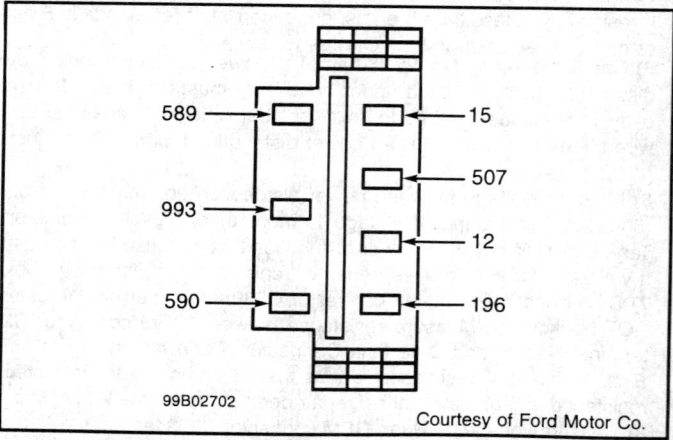

Fig. 10: Identifying Multifunction Switch 7-Pin Connector C230 Terminals

8) Turn ignition off. Disconnect wiper run/park relay. Turn ignition on. Measure voltage between wiper run/park relay connector terminal No. 1 and ground. *See Fig. 9.* If voltage is more than 10 volts, go to next step. If voltage is 10 volts or less, check fuse junction panel fuse No. 11 (10-amp) and/or repair White/Black wire. See WIRING DIAGRAMS.

9) Using NGS tester observe PID WPRUN while triggering GEM active command WIPER RLY. If wiper motor runs and PID WPRUN agrees with command mode and displays ON- - - and OFF- - -, replace GEM. See GENERIC ELECTRONIC MODULE under REMOVAL & INSTALLATION. If motor does not run and/or does not agree with command mode, go to next step.

10) Turn ignition off. Check wiper run/park relay. See WIPER/WASHER SYSTEM RELAYS under COMPONENT TESTS. Replace relay as necessary. If wiper run/park relay is okay, go to next step.

11) Disconnect GEM 26-pin connector C239. Measure resistance between GEM connector C239 terminal No. 3 and wiper run/park relay connector terminal No. 2. *See Figs. 6 and 9.* If resistance is less than 5 ohms, reconnect GEM and wiper run/park relay and go to step **14)**. If resistance is 5 ohms or more, repair open in Yellow/White wire.

12) Turn ignition off. Disconnect wiper run/park relay and GEM 26-pin connector C239. Turn ignition on. Measure voltage between wiper run/park relay connector terminal No. 2 and ground. *See Fig. 9.* If there is no voltage, go to next step. If there is any voltage, repair Yellow/White wire short to power. See WIRING DIAGRAMS.

13) Turn ignition off. Check wiper run/park relay. See WIPER/WASHER SYSTEM RELAYS under COMPONENT TESTS. Replace relay as necessary. If wiper run/park relay is okay, replace GEM. See GENERIC ELECTRONIC MODULE under REMOVAL & INSTALLATION.

14) Turn ignition off. Disconnect wiper high/low relay. Turn ignition on. Using NGS tester trigger active command WIPER RLY on. Measure voltage between wiper high/low relay connector terminal No. 3 and ground. *See Fig. 9.* If voltage is more than 10 volts, go to step **17)**. If voltage is 10 volts or less, go to next step.

15) Turn ignition off. Disconnect wiper run/park relay. Measure resistance between wiper high/low relay connector terminal No. 3 and wiper run/park relay connector terminal No. 3. *See Fig. 9.* If resistance is less than 5 ohms, go to next step. If resistance is 5 ohms or more, repair open in Red wire.

16) Turn ignition on. Measure voltage between wiper run/park relay connector terminal No. 5 and ground. *See Fig. 9.* If voltage is more than 10 volts, replace wiper run/park relay. If voltage is 10 volts or less, check power distribution box maxi-fuse No 15 (30-amp) and/or repair White/Black wire.

17) Turn ignition off. Turn wiper switch to low. Connect jumper wire between wiper high/low relay connector terminals No. 3 and 4, or 5. *See Fig. 9.* Turn ignition on. If wipers do not operate, go to next step. If wipers operate, replace wiper high/low relay.

18) Turn ignition off. Disconnect wiper motor connector. Measure resistance between wiper motor connector terminal No. 5 and wiper high/low relay connector terminal No. 5 (Dark Blue/Orange wire). *See Figs. 9 and 3.* Measure resistance between wiper motor connector terminal No. 4 and wiper high/low relay connector terminal No. 4 (White wire) . If resistances are less than 5 ohms, go to next step. If either resistance is 5 ohms or more, repair open in appropriate wire.

19) Turn ignition off. Disconnect wiper motor connector. Measure resistance between wiper motor connector terminal No. 3 and ground. *See Fig. 3.* If resistance is less than 5 ohms, go to next step. If resistance is 5 ohms or more, repair Black ground wire.

20) Remove linkage from wiper motor and check for binding. If wipers are free, go to step **26)**. If there is binding, repair linkage.

21) Turn ignition off. Remove power distribution box maxi-fuse No. 15 (30-amp) and wiper run/park relay. Disconnect wiper motor connector and GEM 26-pin connector C239. Measure resistance between wiper run/park relay connector terminal No. 5 and ground (White/Black wire). *See Fig. 3.* Measure resistance between wiper run/park relay connector terminal No. 4 and ground (Light Blue). If resistances are more than 10 k/ohms, go to next step. If either resistance is 10 k/ohms or less, repair appropriate wire(s) short to ground.

22) Check wiper run/park relay. See WIPER/WASHER SYSTEM RELAYS under COMPONENT TESTS. Replace relay as necessary. If the wiper run/park relay is okay, go to next step.

23) Disconnect wiper high/low relay. Measure resistance between wiper run/park relay connector terminal No. 3 and ground. *See Fig. 9.* If resistance is more than 10 k/ohms, go to next step. If resistance is 10 k/ohms or less, repair Red wire short to ground.

24) Check wiper high/low relay. See WIPER/WASHER SYSTEM RELAYS under COMPONENT TESTS. Replace relay as necessary. If relay is okay, go to next step.

25) Measure resistance between wiper motor connector terminal No. 5 and ground (Dark Blue/Orange wire). *See Fig. 3.* Measure resistance between wiper motor connector terminal No. 4 and ground (White wire). If resistances are more than 10 k/ohms, go to next step. If either resistance is 10 k/ohms or less, repair appropriate wire(s) short to ground.

26) Reconnect wiper run/park relay and GEM 26-pin connector C239. Turn ignition on. Using NGS tester observe PID WPPRKSW. Attach jumper wire between wiper motor connector terminal No. 1 and ground. *See Fig. 3.* Detach ground side of jumper wire and attach to battery positive terminal. If PID WPPRKSW displays PARKED when wiper motor is grounded and notPRK when battery voltage is applied, go to step **30)**. If PID does not display as indicated, replace GEM. See GENERIC ELECTRONIC MODULE under REMOVAL & INSTALLATION.

27) Turn ignition off. Disconnect wiper high/low, wiper run/park and washer pump relays. Disconnect fuse junction panel C243 connector. *See Fig. 5.* Measure resistance between fuse junction panel connector C243 terminal No. 19 and ground. *See Fig. 11.* If resistance is more than 10 k/ohms, go to next step. If resistance is 10 k/ohms or less, repair Black/Light Green wire short to ground.

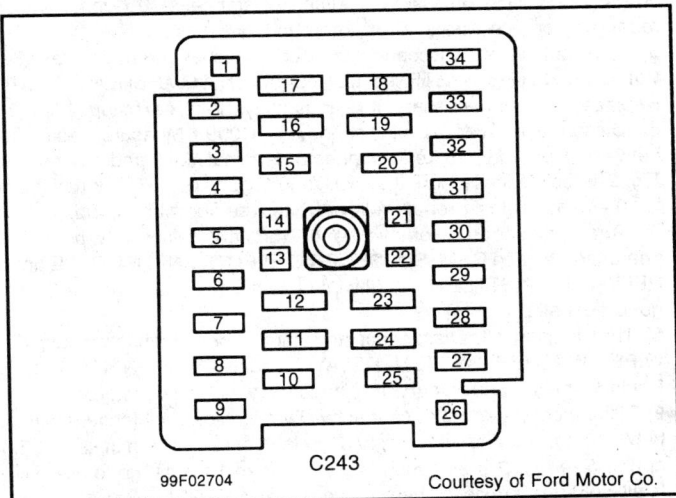

99F02704   C243   Courtesy of Ford Motor Co.

Fig. 11: Identifying Fuse Junction Panel Connector C243 Terminals

28) Check wiper high/low, wiper run/park and washer pump relays. See WIPER/WASHER SYSTEM RELAYS under COMPONENT TESTS. Replace relay(s) as necessary. If relays are okay, go to next step.

29) Disconnect washer pump motor connector. Measure resistance between washer pump relay connector terminal No. 5 and ground. *See Fig. 9.* If resistance is more than 10 k/ohms, replace washer pump motor. See WASHER PUMP & RESERVOIR under REMOVAL & INSTALLATION. If resistance is 10 k/ohms or less, repair Black/White wire short to ground.

30) Test wiper motor. See WIPER MOTOR under COMPONENT TESTS. Replace wiper motor as necessary. See WIPER MOTOR under REMOVAL & INSTALLATION. If motor is okay, replace GEM. See GENERIC ELECTRONIC MODULE under REMOVAL & INSTALLATION.

FORD
4-1386

1999 ACCESSORIES & EQUIPMENT
Wiper/Washer Systems – F250 Super-Duty & F350 Pickup (Cont.)

TEST C: WIPERS STAY ON CONTINUOUSLY

NOTE: After all repairs, clear DTCs and retest system.

1) Using NGS tester retrieve and note continuous DTCs stored in GEM. Clear DTCs. Perform GEM ON-DEMAND SELF-TEST. If any DTCs exist, go to appropriate test step. See TEST C DTC INDEX table. If no DTCs exist, go to next step.

TEST C DTC INDEX

DTC	Step
B1342	1
B1431	5)
B1441	3)
B1453	3)

1 – Replace GEM. See GENERIC ELECTRONIC MODULE under REMOVAL & INSTALLATION. Clear DTCs and retest system.

2) Observe PID WPMODE while turning wiper switch through all positions. If PID WPMODE display agrees with wiper switch positions, go to step **5)**. If PID WPMODE does not agree with wiper switch positions, go to next step.

3) Turn ignition off. Disconnect multifunction switch 7-pin connector C230. Check wiper/washer portion of multifunction switch. See WIPER SWITCH under COMPONENT TESTS. Replace switch as necessary. See MULTIFUNCTION SWITCH under REMOVAL & INSTALLATION. If switch tests okay, go to next step.

4) Disconnect GEM 26-pin connector C239. Measure resistance between multifunction switch connector C230 terminal No. 590 and ground (Light Blue/Orange wire). See Fig. 10. Measure resistance between multifunction switch connector C230 terminal No. 589 and ground (Pink/Yellow wire). If each resistance is more than 10 k/ohms, replace GEM. See GENERIC ELECTRONIC MODULE under REMOVAL & INSTALLATION. If either resistance is 10 k/ohms or less, repair appropriate wire(s) short to ground.

5) Turn ignition off. Disconnect and check wiper run/park relay. See WIPER/WASHER SYSTEM RELAYS under COMPONENT TESTS. Replace relay as necessary. If relay is okay, go to next step.

6) Disconnect GEM 26-pin connector C239. Measure resistance between wiper run/park relay connector terminal No. 2 and ground. See Fig. 9. If resistance is more than 10 k/ohms, go to next step. If resistance is 10 k/ohms or less, repair Yellow/White wire short to ground.

7) Turn ignition on. Remove wiper run/park relay. If wipers stop operating, replace GEM. See GENERIC ELECTRONIC MODULE under REMOVAL & INSTALLATION. If wipers do not stop, reconnect relay and go to next step.

8) Turn ignition off. Disconnect and check wiper high/low relay. See WIPER/WASHER SYSTEM RELAYS under COMPONENT TESTS. Replace relay as necessary. If relay is okay, go to next step.

9) Disconnect wiper motor connector. Turn ignition on. Measure voltage between ground and wiper high/low relay connector terminals No. 5, 4 and 3. See Fig. 9. If any voltage is more than 10 volts, go to next step. If all voltages are less than 10 volts, replace GEM. See GENERIC ELECTRONIC MODULE under REMOVAL & INSTALLATION.

10) Turn ignition off. Measure voltage between wiper high/low relay connector terminal No. 5 and ground (Dark Blue/Orange wire). See Fig. 9. Measure voltage between wiper high/low relay connector terminal No. 4 and ground (White wire). Measure voltage between wiper high/low relay connector terminal No. 3 and ground (Red wire). If any circuit shows voltage, repair appropriate wire(s) short to power. If each circuit reads no voltage, replace wiper motor. See WIPER MOTOR under REMOVAL & INSTALLATION.

TEST D: WIPER HIGH/LOW SPEEDS DO NOT OPERATE PROPERLY

NOTE: After all repairs, clear DTCs and retest system.

1) Using NGS tester retrieve and note continuous DTCs stored in GEM. Clear DTCs. Perform GEM ON-DEMAND SELF-TEST. If any DTCs exist, go to appropriate test step. See TEST D DTC INDEX table. If no DTCs exist, go to next step.

TEST D DTC INDEX

DTC	Step
B1342	
B1434	6
B1436	5
B1446	10
B1476	10
B1473	10

1 – Replace GEM. See GENERIC ELECTRONIC MODULE under REMOVAL & INSTALLATION. Clear DTCs and retest.

2) Observe PID WPMODE while turning wiper switch through all positions. If PID WPMODE display agrees with wiper switch positions, go to step **4)**. If PID WPMODE does not agree with wiper switch positions, go to next step.

3) Turn ignition switch off. Disconnect multifunction switch 7-pin connector C230. Check wiper/washer portion of multifunction switch. See WIPER SWITCH under COMPONENT TESTS. Replace switch as necessary. See MULTIFUNCTION SWITCH under REMOVAL & INSTALLATION. If switch tests okay, replace GEM. See GENERIC ELECTRONIC MODULE under REMOVAL & INSTALLATION.

4) Using NGS tester observe GEM PID WPHISP while triggering active command SPEED RLY. If PID WPHISP changes from OFF- - - to ON- - - then back to OFF- - -, then go to step **10)**. If PID WPHISP does not display as indicated, replace GEM. See GENERIC ELECTRONIC MODULE under REMOVAL & INSTALLATION.

5) Turn ignition off. Disconnect wiper high/low relay. Disconnect GEM 26-pin connector C239. Turn ignition on. Measure voltage between wiper high/low relay connector terminal No. 2 and ground. See Fig. 9. If voltage is 10 volts or less, go to step **9)**. If voltage is more than 10 volts, repair Gray/Light Blue wire short to power.

6) Turn ignition off. Disconnect GEM 26-pin connector C239. Disconnect wiper high/low relay. Measure resistance between wiper high/low relay connector terminal No. 2 and GEM connector C239 terminal No. 18. See Figs. 6 and 9. If resistance is less than 5 ohms, go to next step. If resistance is 5 ohms or more, repair open in Gray/Light Blue wire.

7) Measure resistance between wiper high/low relay connector terminal No. 2 and ground. See Fig. 9. If resistance is more than 10 k/ohms, to next step. If resistance is 10 k/ohms or less, repair Gray/Light Blue wire short to ground.

8) Turn ignition on. Measure voltage between wiper high/low relay connector terminal No. 1 and ground. See Fig. 9. If voltage is more than 10 volts, go to next step. If voltage is 10 volts or less, repair open in Black/Light Green wire.

9) Turn ignition off. Check wiper high/low relay. See WIPER/WASHER SYSTEM RELAYS under COMPONENT TESTS. Replace relay as necessary. If relay is okay, replace GEM. See GENERIC ELECTRONIC MODULE under REMOVAL & INSTALLATION.

10) Turn ignition off. Disconnect wiper high/low relay. Turn ignition on. Turn multifunction switch to high position. Attach jumper wire between wiper high/low relay connector terminals No. 3 and 5. See Fig. 9. Wipers should move at high speed. Detach jumper wire. Turn multifunction switch to low position. Attach jumper wire between wiper high/low relay connector terminals No. 3 and 4. Wipers should move at low speed. If wipers do not operate at correct speeds, detach jumper wire and go to next step. If wipers operate at correct speeds, replace wiper high/low relay.

11) Turn ignition off. Disconnect wiper motor connector. Measure resistance between wiper motor connector terminal No. 5 and wiper high/low relay connector terminal No. 5 (Dark Blue/Orange wire). See Figs. 3 and 9. Measure resistance between wiper motor connector terminal No. 4 and wiper high/low relay connector terminal No. 4 (White wire) . If each resistance is less than 5 ohms, check wiper motor. See WIPER MOTOR under COMPONENT TESTS. If either resistance is 5 ohms or more, repair appropriate wire(s).

1999 ACCESSORIES & EQUIPMENT
Wiper/Washer Systems – F250 Super-Duty & F350 Pickup (Cont.)

FORD
4-1387

TEST E: INTERVAL MODE DOES NOT OPERATE PROPERLY

NOTE: *After all repairs, clear DTCs and retest system.*

1) Using NGS tester retrieve and note continuous DTCs stored in GEM. Clear DTCs. Perform GEM ON-DEMAND SELF-TEST. If any DTCs exist, go to appropriate test step. See TEST E DTC INDEX table. If no DTCs exist, go to next step.

TEST E DTC INDEX [1]

DTC	Step
B1342	2
B1450	3
B1446	7
B1473	7
B1476	7

[1] – If any other DTCs are retrieved, diagnose them first.
[2] – Replace GEM. See GENERIC ELECTRONIC MODULE under REMOVAL & INSTALLATION. Clear DTCs and retest system.

2) Turn ignition switch on. Observe GEM PID WPMODE while turning wiper switch through all positions. If PID WPMODE values agree with all switch positions, go to step 6). If PID WPMODE values do not agree with switch positions, go to next step.

3) Turn ignition off. Disconnect multifunction switch 7-pin connector C230. Check wiper/washer portion of switch. See WIPER SWITCH under COMPONENT TESTS. Replace switch as necessary. See MULTIFUNCTION SWITCH under REMOVAL & INSTALLATION. If switch is okay, go to next step.

4) Disconnect GEM 26-pin connector C239. Turn ignition on. Measure voltage between multifunction switch connector C230 terminal No. 590 and ground. *See Fig. 10.* If there is no voltage, go to next step. If there is voltage, repair Light Blue/Orange wire short to power.

5) Turn ignition off. Measure resistance between GEM connector C239 terminal No. 6 and multifunction switch connector C230 terminal No 590. *See Figs. 6 and 10.* If resistance is less than 5 ohms, replace GEM. See GENERIC ELECTRONIC MODULE under REMOVAL & INSTALLATION. If resistance is 5 ohms or more, repair open in Light Blue/Orange wire.

6) Turn ignition on and set wiper switch to low speed. Observe and record GEM PID WPPRKSW while wipers are operating. Use NGS tester View Recorder Areas to view stored WPPRKSW graph. If GEM PID WPPRKSW displays PARK when wipers are in park position and notPRK when wipers are out of park position, replace GEM. See GENERIC ELECTRONIC MODULE under REMOVAL & INSTALLATION. If GEM PID WPPRKSW does not display as indicated, go to next step.

7) Turn ignition off. Disconnect GEM 26-pin connector C239. Remove wiper run/park relay. Measure resistance between wiper motor connector terminal No. 1 and GEM connector C239 terminal No. 14. *See Figs. 3 and 6.* Measure resistance between wiper motor connector terminal No. 1 and wiper run/park relay connector terminal No. 4. If resistances are less than 5 ohms, go to next step. If resistances are 5 ohms or more, repair open in Light Blue wire.

8) Turn ignition on. Measure resistance between wiper run/park relay connector terminal No. 5 and wiper motor connector terminal No. 2. *See Figs. 3 and 9.* If resistance is less than 5 ohms, go to next step. If resistance is 5 ohms or more, repair open in White/Black wire.

9) Turn ignition on. Attach jumper wire between wiper motor connector terminal No. 1 and ground. *See Fig. 3.* Observe GEM PID WPPRKSW. Detach ground wire. Observe PID WPPRKSW. If PID WPPRKSW displays PARKED when ground wire is attached and notPRK when ground is removed, replace wiper motor. See WIPER MOTOR under REMOVAL & INSTALLATION. If PID WPPRKSW does not display as indicated, replace GEM. See GENERIC ELECTRONIC MODULE under REMOVAL & INSTALLATION.

TEST F: WASHER/WIPER MODE DOES NOT OPERATE PROPERLY

NOTE: *After all repairs, clear DTCs and retest system.*

1) If any DTCs were noted from GEM self-test, go to appropriate test step. See TEST F DTC INDEX table. If no DTCs exist, go to next step.

TEST F DTC INDEX

DTC	Step
B1342	1
B1453	3
B1458	6)
B1458 & Wipers/Washer Inoperative	2
B1460	9

[1] – Replace GEM. See GENERIC ELECTRONIC MODULE under REMOVAL & INSTALLATION. Clear DTCs and retest system.
[2] – Go to TEST B: WIPERS INOPERATIVE.

2) Using NGS tester observe GEM PID WPMODE while turning wiper switch through all positions and depressing washer switch. If PID WPMODE agrees with all switch positions, go to step 5). If PID WPMODE does not agree with all switch positions, go to next step.

3) Turn ignition off. Disconnect multifunction 7-pin connector C230. Check wiper/washer portion of multifunction switch. See WIPER SWITCH under COMPONENT TESTS. Replace switch as necessary. See MULTIFUNCTION SWITCH under REMOVAL & INSTALLATION. If switch is okay, go to next step.

4) Disconnect GEM 26-pin connector C239. Measure resistance between multifunction switch connector terminal No. 590 and ground. If resistance is more than 10 k/ohms replace GEM. See GENERIC ELECTRONIC MODULE under REMOVAL & INSTALLATION. If resistance is 10 k/ohms or less, repair Light Blue/Orange wire short to ground.

5) Turn ignition on. Observe GEM PID WASH_SW while triggering active command WASHRRLY. If the washer pump runs and PID WASH_SW agrees with command mode, replace GEM. See GENERIC ELECTRONIC MODULE under REMOVAL & INSTALLATION. If DTCs were recorded in step 1, and washer pump does not run and/or PID WASH_SW does not agree with command mode, go to next step. If no DTCs were recorded in step 1, and washer pump does not run and/or PID WASH_SW does not agree with command mode, go to step 11).

6) Turn ignition off. Remove washer pump relay. Turn ignition on. Measure voltage between washer pump relay connector terminal No. 3 and ground. *See Fig. 9.* Measure voltage between washer pump relay connector terminal No. 1 and ground. If voltages are more than 10 volts, go to next step. If either voltage is 10 volts or less, repair fuse junction panel fuse No. 11 (10-amp) and/or Black/Light Green wire.

7) Disconnect GEM 26-pin connector C239. Measure resistance between washer pump relay connector terminal No. 2 and GEM connector C239 terminal No. 1. *See Figs. 6 and 9.* If resistance is less than 5 ohms, go to next step. If resistance is 5 ohms or more, repair open in Tan/Red wire.

8) Measure resistance between GEM connector C239 terminal No. 1 and ground. If resistance is more than 10 k/ohms, go to next step. If resistance is 10 k/ohms or less, repair Tan/Red wire short to ground.

9) Turn ignition on. Measure voltage between washer pump relay connector terminal No. 2 and ground. *See Fig. 9.* If there is any voltage, repair Tan/Red wire short to power. If there is no voltage, go to next step.

10) Turn ignition off. Check washer pump relay. See WIPER/WASHER SYSTEM RELAYS under COMPONENT TESTS. Replace relay as necessary. If washer pump relay is okay, replace GEM. See GENERIC ELECTRONIC MODULE under REMOVAL & INSTALLATION.

11) Turn ignition on. Measure voltage between washer pump relay connector terminal No. 3 and ground. *See Fig. 9.* Measure voltage between washer pump relay connector terminal No. 1 and ground. If each voltage is more than 10 volts, go to next step. If either voltage is 10 volts or less, repair appropriate Black/Light Green wire(s).

FORD
4-1388

1999 ACCESSORIES & EQUIPMENT
Wiper/Washer Systems – F250 Super-Duty & F350 Pickup (Cont.)

12) Turn ignition off. Check washer pump relay. See WIPER/WASHER SYSTEM RELAYS under COMPONENT TESTS. Replace relay as necessary. If washer pump relay is okay, go to next step.

13) Turn ignition off. Disconnect washer pump connector. Measure resistance of Black/White wire between washer pump connector and washer pump relay connector terminal No. 5. *See Fig. 9.* If resistance is less than 5 ohms, go to next step. If resistance is 5 ohms or more, repair Black/White wire.

14) Turn ignition off. Remove washer pump relay. Turn ignition on. Measure voltage between Black/White wire on washer pump motor connector and ground. If voltage is more than 10 volts, repair Black/White wire short to power. If voltage is 10 volts or less, go to next step.

15) Measure resistance between Black wire on washer pump motor connector and ground. If resistance is less than 5 ohms, reconnect washer pump and actuate the system. If pump does not operate properly, replace washer pump. See WASHER PUMP & RESERVOIR under REMOVAL & INSTALLATION. If resistance is 5 ohms or more, repair Black ground wire.

TEST G: SPEED DEPENDENT INTERVAL MODE DOES NOT OPERATE PROPERLY

NOTE: After all repairs, clear DTCs and retest system.

1) Use results from GEM self-test. If DTC P0500 retrieved, go to step **3)**. If DTC B1342 retrieved, replace GEM. See GENERIC ELECTRONIC MODULE under REMOVAL & INSTALLATION. If no DTCs exist, go to next step.

2) Verify GEM active command SPD WIPER is set to ACTIVE. If SPD WIPER is set to ACTIVE, go to next step. If SPD WIPER is not set to ACTIVE, ENABLE active command SPD WIPER.

3) Observe PID VSS_GEM while driving vehicle from 0 to 55 MPH. If PID VSS_GEM agrees with speedometer, replace GEM. See GENERIC ELECTRONIC MODULE under REMOVAL & INSTALLATION. If PID VSS_GEM does not agree with speedometer, go to next step.

4) Turn ignition off. Disconnect 4-Wheel Anti-Lock Brakes (4WABS) module 24-pin connector. Disconnect GEM from back of fuse junction panel. Measure resistance between 4WABS module connector terminal No. 16 and fuse junction panel connector C241 terminal No. 18. *See Figs. 5 and 12.* If resistance is less than 5 ohms, go to next step. If resistance is 5 ohms or more, repair open in Gray/Black wire. See appropriate wiring diagrams under ANTI-LOCK BRAKES.

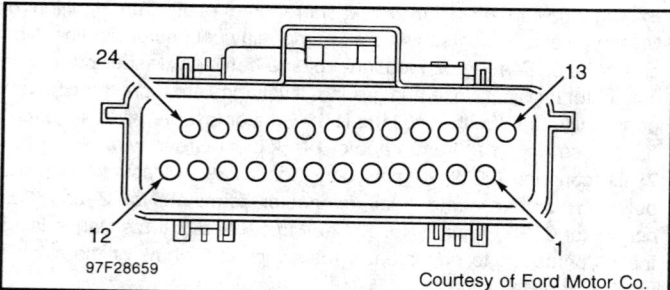

97F28659   Courtesy of Ford Motor Co.

Fig. 12: Identifying 4-Wheel Anti-Lock Brake Module Connector Terminals

5) Disconnect rear anti-lock brake sensor located on center of rear axle. Measure resistance between 4WABS module connector terminal No. 9 and ground (Red/Pink wire). *See Fig. 12.* Also measure resistance between 4WABS module connector terminal No. 21 and ground (Light Green/Black wire). If resistances are more than 10 k/ohms, go to next step. If either resistance is 10 k/ohms or less, repair short to ground on appropriate wire(s). See appropriate wiring diagrams under ANTI-LOCK BRAKES.

6) Measure resistance of Red/Pink wire between rear anti-lock brake sensor connector and 4WABS module connector terminal No. 9. *See Fig. 12.* Measure resistance of Light Green/Black wire between rear anti-lock brake sensor connector and 4WABS module connector terminal No. 21. If resistances are less than 5 ohms, go to next step. If either resistance is 5 ohms or more, repair open in appropriate wire(s). See appropriate wiring diagrams under ANTI-LOCK BRAKES. Test system for normal operation.

7) Measure voltage between 4WABS module connector terminal No. 9 and ground (Red/Pink wire). *See Fig. 12.* Measure voltage between 4WABS module connector terminal No. 21 and ground (Light Green/Black wire). If there is any voltage, repair appropriate wire(s) short to power. See appropriate wiring diagrams under ANTI-LOCK BRAKES. If there is no voltage, diagnose 4WABS system. See appropriate anti-lock article under BRAKES.

REMOVAL & INSTALLATION

WARNING: Deactivate air bag system before performing any service operation involving steering column components. See appropriate AIR BAG RESTRAINT SYSTEMS article. DO NOT apply electrical power to any component on steering column without first deactivating air bag system. Air bag may deploy.

CAUTION: When battery is disconnected, vehicle computer and memory systems may lose memory data. Driveability problems may exist until computer systems have completed a relearn cycle. See COMPUTER RELEARN PROCEDURES article in GENERAL INFORMATION before disconnecting battery.

GENERIC ELECTRONIC MODULE

CAUTION: Disconnect battery before disconnecting Generic Electronic Module (GEM) connectors. Failure to do so will result in GEM storing erroneous codes and may also result in erratic operation of GEM after reconnection.

NOTE: GEM must be reconfigured upon replacement. Refer to NGS tester help screen on Ford Service Function (FSF) card to program tire size and axle ratio.

Removal & Installation – Remove instrument panel steering column cover. Disconnect bulkhead connector from fuse junction panel. Remove fuse junction panel nuts and bolts and position aside. Disconnect GEM electrical connectors and screws. Remove GEM. To install, reverse removal procedure.

MULTIFUNCTION SWITCH

Removal & Installation – Disconnect negative battery cable. Turn ignition switch to RUN position. Insert punch through hole in lower steering column shroud and push ignition lock cylinder release pin while pulling out ignition switch lock cylinder. If equipped, twist and remove tilt wheel handle. Remove upper and lower steering column shrouds. Remove screws, electrical connectors and multifunction switch. To install, reverse removal procedure.

WASHER PUMP & RESERVOIR

Removal & Installation – Remove battery and battery tray. Unbolt washer reservoir. Disconnect electrical connector and washer hose. Remove pump from reservoir. To install, reverse removal procedure. Fill reservoir and check for leaks before connecting washer pump connector.

WIPER MOTOR

Removal & Installation – 1) Disconnect negative battery cable. Remove wiper arms and antenna. Remove cowl top vent panel retaining screws. Open hood. Disconnect washer hose. Remove cowl panel weatherstrip. Remove and discard cowl top vent panel push pins. Remove cowl top vent panel from center to avoid damaging locating pins.

2) Remove bolts, disconnect harness push pin and wiper motor electrical connector. Remove wiper mounting arm and pivot shaft. Remove wiper linkage and wiper motor. To install, reverse removal procedure.

Use new push pins. Tighten mounting bolts to 11 ft. lbs. (15 N.m).
Tighten linkage bolt to 13 ft. lbs. (17 N.m).

WIRING DIAGRAMS

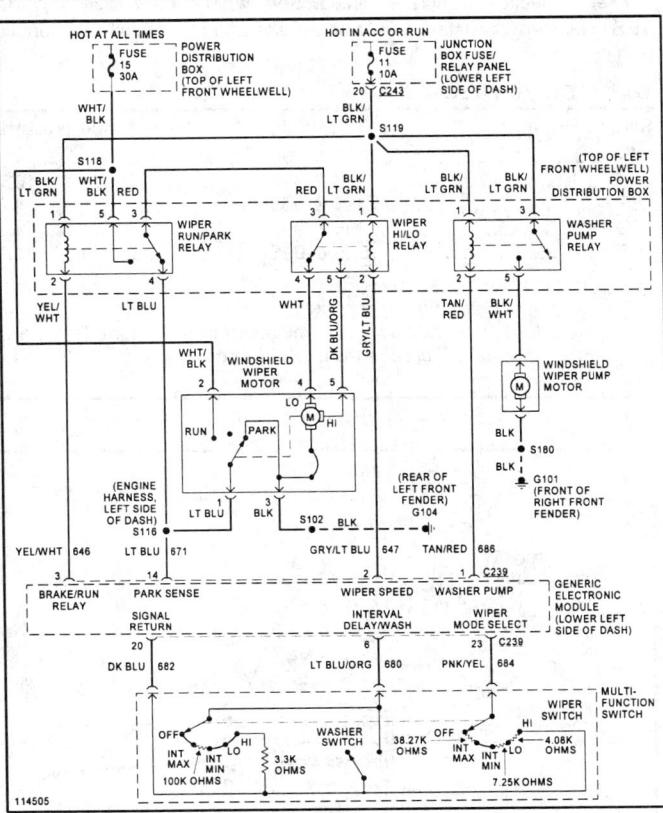

**Fig. 13: Wiper/Washer System Wiring Diagram
(F250 Super-Duty & F350 Pickup)**

DESCRIPTION & OPERATION

Wipers operate at high, low or variable intermittent speeds. When wipers are turned off, wipers will continue to run for a few sweeps until wiper motor parks. Intermittent speed interval decreases with increasing vehicle speed. Speed dependent interval is controlled by Generic Electronic Module (GEM) or Central Timer Module (CTM). Models equipped with 4-wheel drive or power windows are equipped with GEM, all other models are equipped with CTM. When wiper switch is activated, GEM/CTM receives a signal from wiper switch and activates wiper HI/LO relay, wiper run/park relay or washer pump relay.

COMPONENT LOCATIONS

COMPONENT LOCATIONS

Component	Location
Central Timer Module (CTM)/ Generic Electronic Module (GEM)	Behind Center Of Instrument Panel
Washer Relay	In Underhood Fuse/Relay Box
Wiper HI/LO Relay	In Underhood Fuse/Relay Box
Wiper Run/Park Relay	In Underhood Fuse/Relay Box

TROUBLE SHOOTING

WARNING: Vehicle is equipped with an air bag system. System MUST be disabled before working near steering column and instrument cluster to prevent air bag deployment. See AIR BAG RESTRAINT SYSTEMS – RANGER article.

CAUTION: Wiper motor contains ceramic magnets that may crack or shatter if motor is dropped or handled roughly.

Before performing any tests on wiper/washer system, check the following items to eliminate common problems:

- Blown fuses.
- Damaged wiper motor.
- Damaged washer pump.
- Loose or corroded connections.
- Damaged wiring harness.
- Inoperative multifunction switch.

If the preceding items appear okay, retrieve Diagnostic Trouble Codes (DTCs) from Generic Electronic Module (GEM). See SELF-DIAGNOSTIC SYSTEM. If no DTCs are retrieved, proceed with testing based on symptom. See SYSTEM TESTS.

COMPONENT TESTS

WIPER MOTOR

1) Turn ignition off. Disconnect wiper motor linkage from wiper motor. Disconnect wiper motor harness connector. Using a jumper wire, connect battery ground to wiper motor terminal No. 3 (Black wire terminal). Using a second jumper wire and in-line ammeter connect battery voltage to wiper motor terminal No. 5 (Dark Blue/Orange wire terminal). Wiper motor should operate at high speed and should draw 5.5 amps or less with wiper linkage disconnected. Replace wiper motor is operation is not as specified. If wiper operation is as specified, go to next step.

2) Move battery voltage lead from wiper motor terminal No. 5 to wiper motor terminal No. 4 (White wire terminal). Wiper motor should operate at low speed and draw 3.5 amps or less. Replace wiper motor if operation is not as specified.

WIPER SWITCH

Wiper switch is incorporated into multifunction switch on steering column. Disconnect wiper switch connector. Measure resistance between specified switch terminals. See Fig. 1. See WIPER SWITCH TEST table. If resistance is not as specified, replace multifunction switch.

WIPER SWITCH TEST

Switch Position	Terminals	Resistance (k/ohms)
OFF	685 & 590	47.6
OFF	590 & 993	103.3
LOW	685 & 993	4.0
HIGH	685 & 993	0
INT	685 & 993	11.3
INT	590 & 993	1
WASH	590 & 993	0

1 – Rotate (INT) interval knob from minimum to maximum. Resistance should gradually increase from 3.3 k/ohms (MIN) to 103.3 k/ohms (MAX).

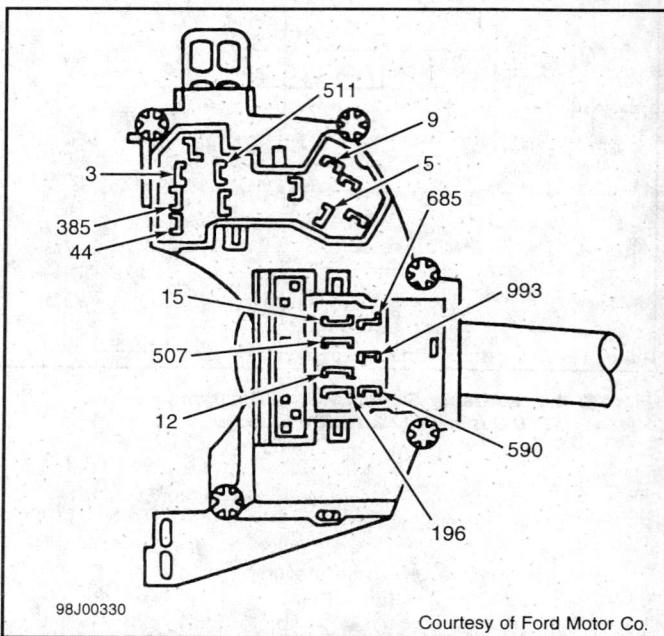

98J00330   Courtesy of Ford Motor Co.

Fig. 1: Identifying Multifunction Switch Terminals

WASHER PUMP

Connect ammeter in series with washer pump. Acceptable current draw is 1.7-4.0 amps while washer pump is running. If current draw is too high, inspect for plugged outlet lines or a dirty screen in reservoir. Repair as necessary. If outlet lines or a screen are okay, replace washer pump.

RELAYS

NOTE: Relays used in wiper/washer system are standardized ISO micro type relays and same test procedure is used for all relays of this type.

1) Remove relay. Measure resistance between relay terminal No. 2 and all other terminals. See Fig. 2. Resistance should be greater than 5 ohms between terminal No. 2 and all other terminals. Replace relay if resistance is not as specified. If resistance is as specified, go to next step.

2) Connect battery positive to relay terminals No. 1 and 3. Measure voltage between relay terminal No. 4 and battery negative. If battery voltage does not exist at relay terminal No. 4, replace relay. If battery voltage exists at relay terminal No. 4, go to next step.

3) With battery positive connected to terminals No. 1 and 3, connect battery negative to relay terminal No. 2. Measure voltage between relay terminal No. 5 and battery negative. Battery voltage should exist at relay terminal No. 5. Replace relay if voltage is not as specified.

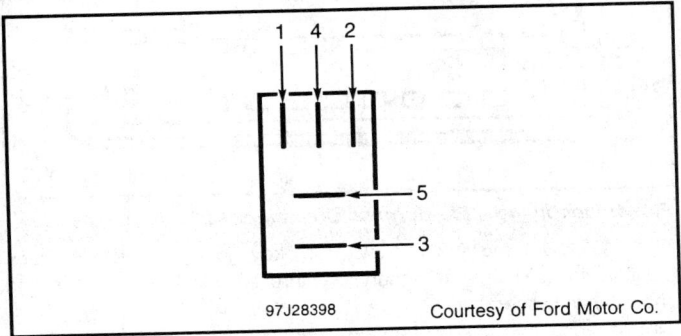

97J28398   Courtesy of Ford Motor Co.

Fig. 2: Identifying ISO Micro Relay Terminals

SELF-DIAGNOSTIC SYSTEM

Verify customers complaint by operating wipers and washers. Check for damaged multifunction switch, damaged mechanism or open fuses. Check for loose or corroded connectors or damaged wiring harness. Repair or replace components as necessary.

Connect New Generation Star (NGS) tester to Data Link Connector (DLC), located beneath instrument panel. Using NGS tester, preform data link diagnostics test. See DATA LINK DIAGNOSTIC TEST under COMMUNICATION NETWORK DIAGNOSTICS in MODULE COMMUNICATIONS NETWORK – RANGER article. If NGS tester responds with CKT914, CKT915 or CKT70=ALL ECUS NO RESP/NOT EQUIP, repair module communications concern. See MODULE COMMUNICATIONS NETWORK – RANGER article. If NGS tester displays NO RESP/NOT EQUIP for GEM/CTM, perform TEST H: NO COMMUNICATION WITH GEM/CTM under SYSTEM TESTS.

If NGS tester responds with SYSTEM PASSED, retrieve and record continuous DTCs. Erase continuous DTCs. Using NGS tester, perform wiper/washer self-test for GEM/CTM. Perform appropriate system test in accordance with DTC retrieved. See WIPER/WASHER SYSTEM MODULE DTC INDEX table. If no DTCs are retrieved, repair by symptom. See SYMPTOM INDEX table under SYSTEM TESTS.

WIPER/WASHER SYSTEM MODULE DTC INDEX

DTC [1]	Description	Test [2]
B1342	GEM/CTM Is Defective	A
B1431	Wiper Brake/Run Relay Circuit Failure	A
B1432	Wiper Brake/Run Relay Circuit Short To Battery	[3]
B1434	Wiper HI/LO Speed Relay Circuit Failure	C
B1436	Wiper HI/LO Speed Relay Circuit Short To Battery	[3]
B1438	[4] Wiper Mode Select Switch Circuit Failure	[3]
B1441	[4] Wiper Mode Select Switch Short To Ground	D
B1446	[4] Wiper Park Sense Circuit Failure	[3]
B1450	[4] Wiper/Wash Interval Delay Switch Input Failure	[3]
B1453	[4] Wiper/Wash Interval Delay Switch Input Short To Ground	E
B1458	Wiper/Washer Pump Motor Relay Circuit Failure	E
B1460	Wiper/Washer Pump Motor Relay Coil Short To Battery	C
B1466	Wiper HI/LO Speed Not Switching	[3]
B1467	Wiper Motor Hi/Low Speed Circuit Short To Battery	[3]
B1473	Wiper Motor Low Speed Circuit Failure	[3]
B1476	Wiper Motor High Speed Circuit Failure	A
B1840	Wiper Power Circuit Failure	F
P0500	Vehicle Speed Signal Circuit Failure	

[1] – Codes listed in this article are only for testing covered in this article. For complete listing of DTCs, see MODULE COMMUNICATIONS NETWORK – RANGER article.

[2] – Using NGS tester, clear DTCs. Retrieve DTCs. If DTC B1342 is retrieved, replace GEM/CTM and retest system operation.

[3] – Diagnose by symptom. See SYMPTOM INDEX table under SYSTEM TESTS.

[4] – This DTC may also be present from GEM/CTM wiggle test.

SYSTEM TESTS

Check items listed under TROUBLE SHOOTING before proceeding. If problem still exists after inspection, perform appropriate test according to symptom. See SYMPTOM INDEX table. Retrieve Diagnostic Trouble Codes (DTCs) from Generic Electronic Module/Central Timer Module (GEM/CTM) when instructed by specific tests.

SYMPTOM INDEX

Symptom	Test
Wipers Are Inoperative	A
Wipers Stay On Continuously	B
High & Low Wiper Speeds Do Not Operate Properly	C
Intermittent Wiper Speed Does Not Operate Properly	D
Washer Pump Inoperative	E
Speed Dependent Interval Inoperative	F
Low Speed Wiper Does Not Operate Properly	G
No Communication With GEM/CTM	H

TEST A: WIPERS ARE INOPERATIVE

1) Turn ignition off. Connect New Generation Star (NGS) tester to Data Link Connector (DLC). Access GEM/CTM. Monitor PID IGN_GEM while turning ignition switch through all positions. If PID values agree with actual ignition switch positions, go to next step. If PID values do not agree with actual ignition switch positions, check ignition switch power supply circuit. See appropriate wiring diagram in POWER DISTRIBUTION article in WIRING DIAGRAMS.

2) Using NGS tester, retrieve and record DTCs. Clear continuous DTCs and perform GEM/CTM wiper/washer self-test. If no DTCs are retrieved, go to next step. If any DTCs are retrieved, go to specified test step. See DTC TEST STEP DIRECTORY table.

DTC TEST STEP DIRECTORY

DTC Retrieved	Go To Test Step
B1342	4)
B1431	4)
B1432	11)
B1438	4)

DTC TEST STEP DIRECTORY (Cont.)

DTC Retrieved	Go To Test Step
B1450	11)
B1840	11)

1 – Replace GEM/CTM. Clear DTCs and retest.

3) Turn ignition off. Remove and check fuse No. 16 (30-amp). If fuse is okay, go to next step. If fuse is blown, replace fuse and retest system. If fuse blows repeatedly, check system for short to ground. See WIRING DIAGRAMS.

4) Turn ignition on. Check PID WPRUN while triggering active command WIPER RLY from GEM/CTM. If WPRUN PID values displayed are ON--- and OFF---, go to step 11). If PID displays OFFO-G, go to step 7). If PID displays ON-B-, go to next step.

5) Turn ignition off. Remove wiper run/park relay from underhood fuse/relay box. Test wiper run/park relay. See RELAYS under COMPONENT TESTS. Replace relay if necessary. If wiper relay is okay, go to next step.

6) Turn ignition off. Disconnect GEM/CTM harness connector C221 (26-pin). Turn ignition on. Measure voltage between wiper run/park relay socket terminal No. 2 and ground. See Fig. 3. If any voltage exists, repair short to power in Yellow/White wire. If voltage does not exist, replace GEM/CTM. Restore electrical connections and check system operation.

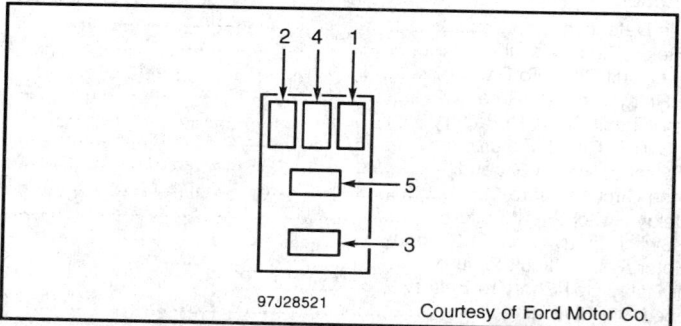

Fig. 3: Identifying Micro ISO Relay Socket Terminals

7) Turn ignition off. Remove wiper run/park relay from underhood fuse/relay box. Turn ignition on. Measure voltage between wiper run/ park relay socket terminal No. 1 (Red wire) and ground. If battery voltage exists, go to next step. If battery voltage does not exist, repair open Red wire between fuse panel and run/park relay connector. See WIRING DIAGRAMS.

8) Turn ignition off. Remove wiper run/park relay from underhood fuse/relay box. Test wiper run/park relay. See RELAYS under COMPONENT TESTS. Replace relay if necessary. Restore electrical connections and check system operation. If wiper relay is okay, go to next step.

9) Disconnect GEM/CTM harness connector C221 (26-pin). Measure resistance between wiper run/park relay socket terminal No. 2 and ground. See Fig. 3. If resistance is greater than 10 k/ohms, go to next step. If resistance is less than 10 k/ohms, repair short to ground in Yellow/White wire. Restore electrical connections and check system operation.

10) Measure resistance of Yellow/White wire between run/park relay socket terminal No. 2 and GEM/CTM harness connector C221 terminal No. 19. See Figs. 3 and 4. If resistance is less than 5 ohms, replace GEM/CTM. If resistance is greater than 5 ohms, repair open Yellow/ White wire. Restore electrical connections and check system operation.

11) Using NGS tester access GEM/CTM. Monitor WPMODE while turning wiper switch through all switch positions. If PID indicates correct wiper switch positions, go to step 16). If PID does not indicate correct wiper switch positions, go to next step.

12) Turn ignition off. Disconnect 7-pin wiper switch harness connector. Test wiper multifunction switch. See WIPER SWITCH under COMPO-

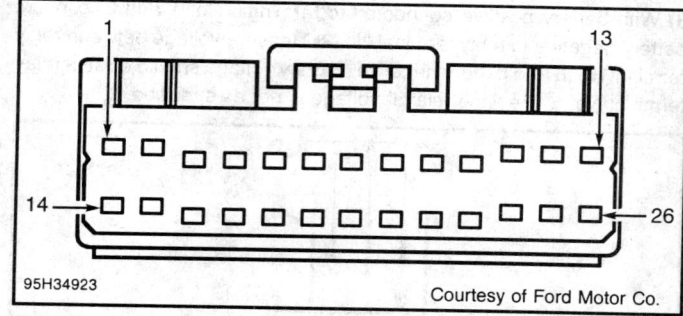

Fig. 4: Identifying GEM Harness Connector C221 Terminals

NENT TESTS. If multifunction switch is okay, go to next step. Replace multifunction switch if necessary. Restore electrical connections and check system operation.

13) Disconnect GEM/CTM harness connector C221. See Fig. 4. Measure resistance of Gray/Red wire between multifunction switch harness connector terminal No. 993 and GEM/CTM harness connector C221 terminal No. 21. If resistance is less than 5 ohms, go to next step. If resistance is greater than 5 ohms, repair open Gray/Red wire. Restore electrical connections and check system operation.

14) Measure resistance of Light Blue/Orange wire between multifunction switch harness connector terminal No. 590 and GEM/CTM harness connector C221 terminal No. 13. If resistance is less than 5 ohms, go to next step. If resistance is greater than 5 ohms, repair open Light Blue/Orange wire. Restore electrical connections and check system operation.

15) Measure resistance of Pink/Yellow wire between multifunction switch harness connector terminal No. 685 and GEM/CTM harness connector C221 terminal No. 22. If resistance is less than 5 ohms, replace GEM/CTM. If resistance is greater than 5 ohms, repair open Pink/Yellow wire. Restore electrical connections and check system operation.

16) Turn ignition off. Remove wiper run/park relay. Measure voltage between wiper run/park relay socket terminal No. 5. (Red wire) and ground. See Fig. 3. If battery voltage exists, install relay and go to next step. If battery voltage does not exist, repair open Red wire between fuse box and relay socket.

17) Turn ignition off. Remove wiper HI/LO relay. Turn ignition on. Connect a jumper wire between wiper HI/LO relay socket terminals No. 3 (Black/Pink wire) and No. 4 (White wire). See Fig. 3. If wipers do not operate, go to next step. If wipers operate, replace wiper HI/LO relay. Restore electrical connections and check system operation.

18) Turn ignition off. Disconnect wiper motor harness connector. Measure resistance of Black wire between wiper motor harness connector and ground. If resistance is less than 5 ohms, go to next step. If resistance is greater than 5 ohms, repair open Black wire.

19) Turn ignition on. Using NGS tester. Access GEM/CTM. Trigger active command WIPER RLY ON. Measure voltage between wiper HI/LO relay socket pin No. 3 (Black/Pink wire) and ground. If battery voltage exists, go to next step. If battery voltage does not exist, repair open Black/Pink wire. Restore electrical connections and check system operation.

20) Remove linkage from wiper motor. Move wipers by hand and ensure wiper linkage assembly moves freely. If wiper mechanism does not operate freely, repair as necessary. If wipers operate freely, test wiper motor. See WIPER MOTOR under COMPONENT TESTS.

TEST B: WIPERS STAY ON CONTINUOUSLY

1) Turn ignition off. Connect New Generation Star (NGS) tester to Data Link Connector (DLC). Access GEM/CTM. Monitor PID IGN_GEM while turning ignition switch through all positions. If PID values agree with actual switch positions, go to next step. If PID values do not agree with actual ignition switch positions, check ignition switch power supply circuit. See appropriate wiring diagram in POWER DISTRIBUTION article in WIRING DIAGRAMS.

2) Using NGS tester, retrieve and record DTCs. Clear continuous DTCs and perform GEM/CTM wiper/washer self-test. If no DTCs are retrieved, go to next step. If any DTCs are retrieved, go to specified test step. See DTC TEST STEP DIRECTORY table.

DTC TEST STEP DIRECTORY

DTC Retrieved	Go To Test Step[1]
B1342	7)
B1431	7)
B1432	3)
B1441	3)
B1453	3)
B1473	10)
B1476	10)

[1] – Replace GEM/CTM. Clear DTCs and retest.

3) Using NGS tester, access GEM/CTM. Monitor WPMODE while turning wiper switch through all switch positions. If PID indicates correct wiper switch positions, go to step **7)**. If PID does not indicate correct wiper positions, go to next step.

4) Turn ignition off. Disconnect 7-pin wiper switch harness connector. Test wiper multifunction switch. See WIPER SWITCH under COMPONENT TESTS. If multifunction switch is okay, go to next step. Replace multifunction switch if necessary. Restore electrical connections and check system operation.

5) Turn ignition off. Disconnect GEM/CTM harness connector C221. *See Fig. 4.* Measure resistance between multifunction switch harness connector terminal No. 590 (Light Blue/Orange wire) and ground. If resistance is greater than 10 k/ohms, go to next step. If resistance is less than 10 k/ohms, repair short to ground in Light Blue/Orange wire. Restore electrical connections and check system operation.

6) Measure resistance between multifunction switch harness connector terminal No. 685 (Pink/Yellow wire) and ground. If resistance is greater than 10 k/ohms, replace GEM/CTM. If resistance is less than 10 k/ohms, repair short to ground in Pink/Yellow wire. Restore electrical connections and check system operation.

7) Turn ignition on. Using NGS tester, access GEM/CTM. Monitor PID WPRUN while triggering active command WIPER RLY on and off. If PID displays, ON--- and OFF---, go to step **10)**. If PID displays, OFFO-G, go to next step.

8) Turn ignition off. Remove wiper run/park relay from underhood fuse/relay box. Test wiper run/park relay. See RELAYS under COMPONENT TESTS. If wiper relay is okay, go to next step. Replace relay if necessary. Restore electrical connections and check system operation.

9) Turn ignition off. Disconnect GEM/CTM harness connector C221 (26-pin). *See Fig. 4.* Measure resistance between wiper run/park relay socket terminal No. 2 and ground. *See Fig. 3.* If resistance is greater than 10 k/ohms, go to next step. If resistance is less than 10 k/ohms, repair short to ground in Yellow/White wire. Restore electrical connections and check system operation.

10) Turn ignition off. Remove wiper run/park relay from underhood fuse/relay box. Turn ignition on. Using NGS tester, access GEM/CTM active commands mode. Activate WIPER RLY ON. If wipers continue operating, go to next step. If wipers stop operating, replace wiper run/park relay. Restore electrical connections and check system operation.

11) Turn ignition on. Remove wiper HI/LO relay from underhood fuse/relay box. Disconnect wiper motor harness connector. Turn ignition on. Measure voltage between Dark/Blue Orange wire at wiper HI/LO relay socket terminal No. 5 and ground. *See Fig. 3.* If battery voltage does not exist, go to next step. If battery voltage exists, repair short to power in Dark Blue/Orange wire.

12) Measure voltage between wiper HI/LO relay socket terminal No. 4 (White wire) and ground. *See Fig. 3.* If voltage does not exist, go to next step. If any voltage exists, repair short to power in White wire. Restore electrical connections and check system operation.

13) Measure voltage between wiper HI/LO relay socket terminal No. 3 (Black/Pink wire) and ground. *See Fig. 3.* If voltage does not exist, replace wiper motor. If any voltage exists, repair short to power in White wire. Restore electrical connections and check system operation.

TEST C: HIGH & LOW WIPER SPEEDS DO NOT OPERATE PROPERLY

1) Turn ignition off. Connect New Generation Star (NGS) tester to Data Link Connector (DLC). Access GEM/CTM. Monitor PID IGN_GEM while turning ignition switch through all positions. If PID values agree with actual ignition switch positions, go to next step. If PID values do not agree with actual ignition switch positions, check ignition switch power supply circuit. See appropriate wiring diagram in POWER DISTRIBUTION article in WIRING DIAGRAMS.

2) Using NGS tester, retrieve and record DTCs. Clear continuous DTCs and perform GEM/CTM wiper/washer self-test. If no DTCs are retrieved, go to next step. If DTCs are retrieved, go to specified test step. See DTC TEST STEP DIRECTORY table.

DTC TEST STEP DIRECTORY

DTC Retrieved	Go To Test Step[1]
B1342	9)
B1434	9)
B1436	3)
B1438	3)
B1441	3)
B1450	3)
B1466	3)
B1476	3)

[1] – Replace GEM/CTM. Clear DTCs and retest.

3) Using NGS tester, access GEM/CTM. Monitor WPMODE while turning wiper switch through all switch positions. If PID indicates correct wiper switch positions, go to step **9)**. If PID does not indicate correct wiper positions, go to next step.

4) Turn ignition off. Disconnect 7-pin wiper switch harness connector. Test wiper portion of multifunction switch. See WIPER SWITCH under COMPONENT TESTS. If switch is okay, go to next step. Replace switch if necessary. Restore electrical connections and check system operation.

5) Turn ignition off. Disconnect GEM/CTM harness connector C221. *See Fig. 4.* Turn ignition on. Measure voltage between Light Blue/Orange wire at wiper switch harness connector and ground. If no voltage exists, go to next step. If any voltage exists, repair short to power in Light Blue/Orange wire. Restore electrical connections and check system operation.

6) Turn ignition off. Disconnect GEM/CTM harness connector C221. Turn ignition on. Measure voltage between Pink/Yellow wire at wiper switch harness connector and ground. If no voltage exists, go to next step. If any voltage exists, repair short to power in Pink/Yellow wire. Restore electrical connections and check system operation.

7) Measure resistance of Light Blue/Orange wire between multifunction switch harness connector terminal No. 590 and GEM/CTM harness connector C221 terminal No. 13. If resistance is less than 5 ohms, go to next step. If resistance is greater than 5 ohms, repair open Light Blue/Orange wire. Restore electrical connections and check system operation.

8) Measure resistance of Pink/Yellow wire between multifunction switch harness connector terminal No. 685 and GEM/CTM harness connector C221 terminal No. 22. If resistance is less than 5 ohms, replace GEM/CTM. If resistance is greater than 5 ohms, repair open Pink/Yellow wire. Restore electrical connections and check system operation.

9) Turn ignition on. Using NGS tester. Access GEM/CTM. Monitor PID WPHISP while triggering active command SPEED RLY. If PID displays, ON--- and OFF---, go to step **16)**. If PID displays, OFFO-G, go to step **12)**. If PID displays, ON-B, go to next step.

10) Turn ignition off. Remove wiper HI/LO relay from underhood fuse/relay box. Test wiper HI/LO relay. See RELAYS under COMPONENT TESTS. If wiper relay is okay, go to next step. Replace relay if necessary. Restore electrical connections and check system operation.

11) Disconnect GEM/CTM harness connector C221. *See Fig. 4.* Turn ignition on. Measure voltage between ground and wiper HI/LO relay socket terminal No. 2 (Gray/Light Blue wire). *See Fig. 3.* If any voltage exists, repair short to power in Gray/Light Blue wire. If no voltage exists, replace GEM/CTM. Restore electrical connections and check system operation.

12) Turn ignition off. Remove wiper HI/LO relay from underhood fuse/relay box. Turn ignition on. Measure voltage between ground and wiper HI/LO relay connector terminal No. 1 (Red wire). If battery voltage exists, go to next step. If battery voltage does not exist, repair open Red wire between instrument panel fuse box and underhood fuse/relay box.

13) Test wiper HI/LO relay. See RELAYS under COMPONENT TESTS. If wiper relay is okay, go to next step. Replace relay if necessary. Restore electrical connections and check system operation.

14) Disconnect GEM/CTM harness connector C221. See Fig. 4. Measure resistance between ground and wiper HI/LO relay socket terminal No. 2 (Gray/Light Blue wire). If resistance greater than 10 k/ohms, go to next step. If resistance is less than 10 k/ohms, repair short to ground in Gray/Light Blue wire.

15) Measure resistance of Gray/Light Blue wire between GEM/CTM connector C221 terminal No. 18 and wiper HI/LO relay socket terminal No. 2. See Figs. 3 and 4. If resistance is greater than 5 ohms, repair open Gray/Light Blue wire. If resistance is less than 5 ohms, replace GEM/CTM. Restore electrical connections and check system operation.

16) Turn ignition off. Remove wiper HI/LO relay from underhood fuse/relay box. Connect a jumper wire between wiper HI/LO relay socket terminals No. 3 and 5. See Fig. 3. Turn wiper switch to high position. Turn ignition on. Check wiper operation. Turn ignition off. Move jumper wire to connect HI/LO relay socket terminals No. 3 and 4. Turn wiper switch to low position. Turn ignition on. If wipers operate at correct speed, replace wiper HI/LO relay. If wipers do not operate at correct speeds, remove jumper wire and go to next step.

17) Turn ignition off. Disconnect wiper motor harness connector. Measure resistance of Dark Blue/Orange wire between wiper HI/LO relay socket terminal No. 5, and wiper motor harness connector. See Fig. 3. If resistance is less than 5 ohms, go to next step. If resistance is greater than 5 ohms, repair open Dark Blue/Orange wire. Restore electrical connections and check system operation.

18) Measure resistance of White wire between wiper HI/LO relay socket terminal No. 4, and wiper motor harness connector. See Fig. 3. If resistance is greater than 5 ohms, repair open White wire. Restore electrical connections and check system operation. If resistance is less than 5 ohms, test wiper motor. See WIPER MOTOR under COMPONENT TESTS. Replace motor if necessary.

TEST D: INTERMITTENT WIPER SPEED DOES NOT OPERATE PROPERLY

1) Turn ignition off. Connect New Generation Star (NGS) tester to Data Link Connector (DLC). Access GEM/CTM. Monitor PID IGN_GEM while turning ignition switch through all positions. If PID values agree with actual ignition switch positions, go to next step. If PID values do not agree with actual ignition switch positions, check ignition switch power supply circuit. See appropriate wiring diagram in POWER DISTRIBUTION article in WIRING DIAGRAMS.

2) Using NGS tester, retrieve and record DTCs. Clear continuous DTCs and perform GEM/CTM wiper/washer self-test. If no DTCs are retrieved, go to next step. If DTCs are retrieved, go to specified test step. See DTC TEST STEP DIRECTORY table.

DTC TEST STEP DIRECTORY

DTC Retrieved	Go To Test Step
B1342	1
B1438	3)
B1446	9)
B1450	3)
B1453	3)

[1] – Replace GEM/CTM. Clear DTCs and retest.

3) Using NGS tester access GEM/CTM. Monitor WPMODE while turning wiper switch through all switch positions. If PID indicates correct wiper switch positions, go to step **9)**. If PID does not indicate correct wiper positions, go to next step.

4) Turn ignition off. Disconnect 7-pin wiper switch harness connector. Test wiper portion of multifunction switch. See WIPER SWITCH under COMPONENT TESTS. If switch is okay, go to next step. Replace switch if necessary. Restore electrical connections and check system operation.

5) Turn ignition off. Disconnect GEM/CTM harness connector C221. See Fig. 4. Turn ignition on. Measure voltage between Light Blue/Orange wire at wiper switch harness connector and ground. If no voltage exists, go to next step. If any voltage exists, repair short to power in Light Blue/Orange wire. Restore electrical connections and check system operation.

6) Turn ignition off. Disconnect GEM/CTM harness connector C221. Turn ignition on. Measure voltage between Pink/Yellow wire at wiper switch harness connector and ground. If no voltage exists, go to next step. If any voltage exists, repair short to power in Pink/Yellow wire. Restore electrical connections and check system operation.

7) Measure resistance of Light Blue/Orange wire between multifunction switch harness connector terminal No. 590 and GEM/CTM harness connector C221 terminal No. 13. See Figs. 1 and 4. If resistance is less than 5 ohms, go to next step. If resistance is greater than 5 ohms, repair open Light Blue/Orange wire. Restore electrical connections and check system operation.

8) Measure resistance of Pink/Yellow wire between multifunction switch harness connector terminal No. 685 and GEM/CTM harness connector C221 terminal No. 22. If resistance is less than 5 ohms, replace GEM/CTM. If resistance is greater than 5 ohms, repair open Pink/Yellow wire. Restore electrical connections and check system operation.

9) Using NGS tester, access GEM/CTM. Monitor PID WPPRKSW while wipers are operating. If PID agrees with wiper status (PARKED or notPRK), replace GEM/CTM. Restore electrical connections and check system operation. If PID does not agree with wiper status (PARKED or notPRK), go to next step.

10) Turn ignition off. Disconnect wiper motor harness connector. Turn ignition on. Measure voltage between Red wire at wiper motor harness connector and ground. If battery voltage exists, go to next step. If battery voltage does not exist, repair open Red wire. Restore electrical connections and check system operation.

11) Measure resistance of Black (ground) wire between wiper motor harness connector and ground. If resistance is less than 5 ohms, go to next step. If resistance is greater than 5 ohms, repair open Black wire.

12) Disconnect GEM/CTM harness connector C221. Disconnect wiper run/park relay from underhood fuse/relay box. Measure resistance of Light Blue wire between wiper motor harness connector and GEM/CTM harness connector terminal No. 15. If resistance is less than 5 ohms, go to next step. If resistance is greater than 5 ohms, repair open Light Blue wire. Restore electrical connections and check system operation.

13) Measure resistance of Light Blue wire between wiper motor harness connector and wiper run/park relay socket terminal No. 4. See Fig. 3. If resistance is less than 5 ohms, go to next step. If resistance is greater than 5 ohms, repair open Light Blue wire.

14) Measure resistance between Light Blue wire at wiper motor harness connector and ground. If resistance is greater than 10 k/ohms, reconnect GEM/CTM and go to next step. If resistance is less than 10 k/ohms, repair short to ground in Light Blue wire. Restore electrical connections and check system operation.

15) Connect a jumper wire between Light Blue wire at wiper motor harness connector and ground. Turn ignition on. Using NGS tester, check GEM/CTM PID WPPRKSW. If PID indicates PARKED, remove jumper wire and go to next step. If PID does not indicate PARKED, replace GEM/CTM. Restore electrical connections and check system operation.

16) Turn ignition off. Connect a jumper wire between battery voltage and Light Blue wire at wiper motor harness connector. Check GEM/CTM PID WPPRKSW. If PID indicates notPRK, replace wiper motor. If PID does not indicate notPRK, replace GEM/CTM. Restore electrical connections and check system operation.

TEST E: WASHER PUMP INOPERATIVE

1) Turn ignition off. Connect New Generation Star (NGS) tester to Data Link Connector (DLC). Access GEM/CTM. Monitor PID IGN_GEM while turning ignition switch through all positions. If PID values agree with actual ignition switch positions, go to next step. If PID values do not agree with actual ignition switch positions, check ignition switch power supply circuit. See appropriate wiring diagram in POWER DISTRIBUTION article in WIRING DIAGRAMS.

2) Using NGS tester, retrieve and record DTCs. Clear continuous DTCs and perform GEM/CTM wiper/washer self-test. If no DTCs are retrieved, go to next step. If DTCs are retrieved, go to specified test step. See DTC TEST STEP DIRECTORY table.

DTC TEST STEP DIRECTORY

DTC Retrieved	Go To Test Step
B1342	1
B1450	3)
B1453	3)
B1458	9)
B1460	9)

¹ – Replace GEM/CTM. Clear DTCs and retest.

3) Using NGS tester access GEM/CTM. Monitor PID WPMODE while turning wiper switch through all wiper switch positions. If PID indicates all correct switch positions, go to next step. If PID does not indicate all correct switch positions, go to step **6)**.

4) Monitor PID WASH_SW while pressing washer switch. If PID indicates ON, go to step **9)**. If PID does not indicate ON, go to next step.

5) Turn ignition off. Disconnect 7-pin wiper/washer switch connector from multifunction switch. See Fig. 1. Measure between multifunction switch terminals No. 590 and 993 while pressing washer switch. If resistance is less than 5 ohms, go to next step. If resistance is greater than 5 ohms, replace multifunction switch.

6) Disconnect GEM/CTM harness connector C221. See Fig. 4. Turn ignition on. Measure voltage between connector C221 terminal No. 590 (Light Blue/Orange wire). If no voltage exists, go to next step. If any voltage exists, repair short to power in Light Blue/Orange wire.

7) Turn ignition off. Measure resistance between connector C221 terminal No. 590 (Light Blue/Orange wire) and ground. If resistance is greater than 10 k/ohms, go to next step. If resistance is less than 10 k/ohms, repair short to ground in Light Blue/Orange wire. Restore electrical connections and check system operation.

8) Measure resistance of Light Blue/Orange wire between multifunction switch harness connector terminal No. 590 and GEM/CTM harness connector C221 terminal No. 13. See Figs. 1 and 4. If resistance is less than 5 ohms, go to next step. If resistance is greater than 5 ohms, repair open Light Blue/Orange wire. Restore electrical connections and check system operation.

9) Using NGS tester, access GEM/CTM. Monitor PID WASHRLY while triggering active command WASH RLY on and off. If PID displays ON--- and OFF---, go to step **17)**. If PID displays OFFO-G, go to next step. If PID displays ON-B-, go to step **15)**.

10) Check fuse No. 16 (30-amp). Fuse No. 16 is located in central junction box under left side of instrument panel. If fuse is okay, go to next step. If fuse is blown, replace fuse. If fuse blows again, check circuit for short to ground. Restore electrical connections and check system operation.

11) Turn ignition off. Remove washer pump relay from underhood fuse/relay box. Turn ignition on. Measure voltage between ground and washer pump relay socket terminals No. 1 and 5 (White/Black wires). See Fig. 3. If battery voltage exists, go to next step. If battery voltage does not exist, repair open White/Black wire. Restore electrical connections and check system operation.

12) Test washer pump relay. See RELAYS under COMPONENT TESTS. If wiper relay is okay, go to next step. Replace relay if necessary. Restore electrical connections and check system operation.

13) Measure Tan/Red wire circuit resistance between washer pump relay socket terminal No. 2 and GEM/CTM harness connector C221 terminal No. 24. See Fig. 4. If resistance is less than 5 ohms, go to next

step. If resistance is greater than 5 ohms, repair open Tan/Red wire. Restore electrical connections and check system operation.

14) Measure resistance of Tan/Red wire between washer pump relay socket terminal No. 2 (Tan/Red wire) and ground. See Fig. 3. If resistance is greater than 10 k/ohms, replace GEM/CTM. If resistance is less than 10 k/ohms, repair short to ground in Tan/Red wire. Restore electrical connections and check system operation.

15) Test washer pump relay. See RELAYS under COMPONENT TESTS. If wiper relay is okay, go to next step. Replace relay if necessary. Restore electrical connections and check system operation.

16) Disconnect GEM/CTM harness connector C221. See Fig. 4. Turn ignition on. Measure voltage between washer relay socket terminal No. 2 (Tan/Red wire) and ground. See Fig. 3. If any voltage exists, repair short to power in Tan/Red wire. If no voltage exists, replace GEM/CTM. Restore electrical connections and check system operation.

17) Turn ignition off. Remove washer pump relay from underhood fuse/relay box. Connect a jumper wire between washer pump relay socket terminals No. 1 (White/Black wire) and No. 3 (Black/White wire). See Fig. 3. If washer does not operate, go to next step. If washer operates, replace washer pump relay. Restore electrical connections and check system operation.

18) Turn ignition off. Disconnect washer pump harness connector. Measure resistance of Black/White wire between washer pump harness connector and washer pump relay socket terminal No. 3. See Fig. 3. If resistance is less than 5 ohms, go to next step. If resistance is greater than 5 ohms, repair open Black/White wire. Restore electrical connections and check system operation.

19) Measure resistance of Black wire between washer pump harness connector and ground. If resistance is greater than 5 ohms, repair Black wire. If resistance is less than 5 ohms, replace washer pump motor. Restore electrical connections and check system operation.

TEST F: SPEED DEPENDENT INTERVAL INOPERATIVE

1) Turn ignition off. Connect New Generation Star (NGS) tester to Data Link Connector (DLC). Access GEM/CTM. Monitor PID IGN_GEM while turning ignition switch through all positions. If PID values agree with actual ignition switch positions, go to next step. If PID values do not agree with actual ignition switch positions, check ignition switch power supply circuit. See appropriate wiring diagram in POWER DISTRIBUTION article in WIRING DIAGRAMS.

2) Using NGS tester, retrieve and record DTCs. Clear continuous DTCs and perform GEM/CTM wiper/washer self-test. If no DTCs are retrieved, go to next step. If DTC P0500 is retrieved and vehicle is equipped with rear ABS, go to next step. If DTC P0500 is retrieved and vehicle is equipped with 4-wheel ABS, go to step **7)**. If DTC B1342 is retrieved, replace GEM/CTM. Clear DTCs and retest.

3) Turn ignition off. Disconnect GEM/CTM harness connector C224. See Fig. 5. Disconnect Rear Anti-lock Brake System (RABS) module harness connector and rear axle speed sensor harness connector. Measure resistance between GEM/CTM harness connector C224 terminal No. 9 (Red/Pink wire) and ground. Also measure resistance between GEM/CTM harness connector C224 terminal No. 18 (Light Green/Black wire) and ground. Both resistance measurements should be greater than 10 k/ohms. If resistance is as specified, go to next step. If resistance is not as specified, repair short to ground in suspect circuit. Restore electrical connections and check system operation.

4) Measure resistance or Red/Pink and Light Green/Black wires between rear axle speed sensor harness connector and GEM harness connector C224 terminals No. 9 (Red/Pink wire) and No. 18 (Light Green/Black wire). Both resistance measurements should be less than 5 ohms. If resistance is as specified, go to next step. If resistance is not as specified, repair open in suspect circuit. Restore electrical connections and check system operation.

5) Measure voltage between ground and GEM harness connector C214, terminals No. 9 (Red/Pink wire) and No. 18 (Light Green/Black wire). No voltage should exist on either wire. If no voltage exists, go to next step. If any voltage exists, repair short to power in suspect circuit. Restore electrical connections and check system operation.

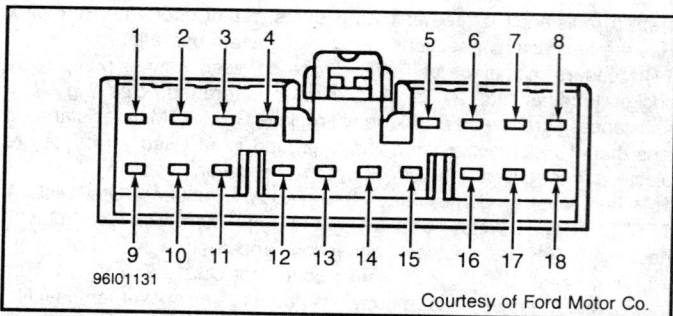

Fig. 5: Identifying GEM/CTM Harness Connector C224 Terminals

96I01131

Courtesy of Ford Motor Co.

6) Turn ignition off. Restore all electrical connections. Turn ignition on. Access GEM/CTM. Monitor PID VSS_GEM while driving vehicle. If PID value agrees with actual vehicle speed. Replace GEM/CTM. If PID value does not agree with actual vehicle speed, replace rear axle speed sensor. Restore electrical connections and check system operation. If problem still remains, replace GEM/CTM.

7) Turn ignition off. Disconnect GEM harness connector C224. *See Fig. 5*. Disconnect 4-Wheel Anti-lock Brake System (4WABS) module. Measure resistance of Gray/Black wire between GEM/CTM harness connector C224 terminal No. 4 and 4WABS module harness connector terminal No. 10. *See Fig. 6*. If resistance is greater than 5 ohms, repair open Gray/Black wire. Restore electrical connections and check system operation. If resistance is less than 5 ohms, problem exists in 4-WABS. See ANTI-LOCK – 4WAL – RANGER article in BRAKES in appropriate MITCHELL® manual.

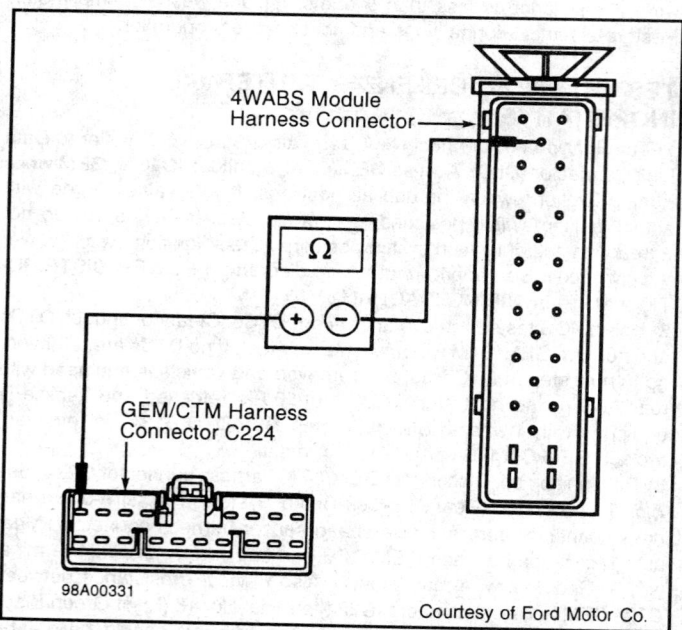

4WABS Module
Harness Connector

GEM/CTM Harness
Connector C224

98A00331

Courtesy of Ford Motor Co.

Fig. 6: Testing Gray/Black Wire

TEST G: LOW SPEED WIPER DOES NOT OPERATE PROPERLY

1) Turn ignition off. Connect New Generation Star (NGS) tester to Data Link Connector (DLC). Access GEM/CTM. Monitor PID IGN_GEM while turning ignition switch through all positions. If PID values agree with actual ignition switch positions, go to next step. If PID values do not agree with actual ignition switch positions, check ignition switch power supply circuit. See appropriate wiring diagram in POWER DISTRIBUTION article in WIRING DIAGRAMS.

2) Using NGS tester, retrieve and record DTCs. Clear continuous DTCs and perform GEM/CTM wiper/washer self-test. If no DTCs are retrieved, go to next step. If DTCs are retrieved, go to specified test step. See DTC TEST STEP DIRECTORY table.

DTC TEST STEP DIRECTORY

DTC Retrieved	Go To Test Step
B1342	1
B1434	11)
B1436	11)
B1466	11)
B1467	11)
B1473	3)

1 – Replace GEM/CTM. Clear DTCs and retest.

3) Using NGS tester, access GEM/CTM. Monitor WPMODE while turning wiper switch through all switch positions. If PID indicates correct wiper switch positions, go to step 11). If PID does not indicate correct wiper positions, go to next step.

4) Turn ignition off. Disconnect 7-pin multifunction (wiper) switch harness connector. Test wiper portion of multifunction switch. See WIPER SWITCH under COMPONENT TESTS. If multifunction switch is okay, go to next step. Replace multifunction switch if necessary. Restore electrical connections and check system operation.

5) Turn ignition off. Disconnect GEM/CTM harness connector C221. *See Fig. 4*. Measure resistance between Light Blue/Orange wire at multifunction switch harness connector and ground. If resistance is greater than 10 k/ohms, go to next step. If resistance is less than 10 k/ohms, repair short to ground in Light Blue/Orange wire. Restore electrical connections and check system operation.

6) Measure voltage between Pink/Yellow wire at multifunction switch harness connector and ground. If no voltage exists, go to next step. If any voltage exists, repair short to power in Pink/Yellow wire. Restore electrical connections and check system operation.

7) Measure resistance of Light Blue/Orange wire between multifunction switch harness connector terminal No. 590 and GEM/CTM harness connector C221 terminal No. 13. *See Figs. 1 and 4*. If resistance is less than 5 ohms, go to next step. If resistance is greater than 5 ohms, repair open Light Blue/Orange wire. Restore electrical connections and check system operation.

8) Measure resistance of Pink/Yellow wire between multifunction switch harness connector terminal No. 685 and GEM/CTM harness connector C221 terminal No. 22. If resistance is less than 5 ohms, go to next step. If resistance is greater than 5 ohms, repair open Pink/Yellow wire. Restore electrical connections and check system operation.

9) Measure resistance between multifunction switch harness connector terminal No. 685 (Pink/Yellow wire) and ground. If resistance is greater than 10 k/ohms, go to next step. If resistance is less than 10 k/ohms, repair Pink/Yellow wire for short to ground. Restore electrical connections and check system operation.

10) Measure resistance between multifunction switch harness connector terminal No. 993 (Gray/Red wire) and ground. If resistance is greater than 10 k/ohms, replace GEM/CTM. If resistance is less than 10 k/ohms, repair short to ground in Gray/Red wire. Restore electrical connections and check system operation.

11) Turn ignition on. Using NGS tester, access GEM/CTM. Monitor PID WPHISP while triggering active command SPEED RLY. If PID displays, ON--- and OFF---, go to step 17). If PID displays, OFFO-G, go to step 14). If PID displays, ON-B, go to next step.

12) Disconnect GEM/CTM harness connector C221. *See Fig. 4*. Remove wiper HI/LO relay from underhood fuse/relay box. Turn ignition on. Measure voltage between ground and wiper HI/LO relay socket terminal No. 2 (Gray/Light Blue wire). *See Fig. 3*. If no voltage exists, go to next step. If any voltage exists, repair short to ground in Gray/Light Blue wire. Restore electrical connections and check system operation.

13) Test wiper HI/LO relay. See RELAYS under COMPONENT TESTS. If wiper relay is okay, replace GEM/CTM. Replace relay if necessary. Restore electrical connections and check system operation.

14) Turn ignition off. Remove wiper HI/LO relay from underhood fuse/relay box. Turn ignition on. Measure voltage between ground and wiper HI/LO relay connector terminal No. 1 (Red wire). If battery voltage exists, go to next step. If battery voltage does not exist, repair open Red wire between instrument panel fuse box and underhood fuse/relay box.

15) Test wiper HI/LO relay. See RELAYS under COMPONENT TESTS. If wiper relay is okay, go to next step. Replace relay if necessary. Restore electrical connections and check system operation.

16) Disconnect GEM/CTM harness connector C221. Measure resistance between wiper HI/LO relay socket terminal No. 2 (Gray/Light Blue) and ground. If resistance is greater than 10 k/ohms, replace GEM/CTM. If resistance is less than 10 k/ohms, repair short to ground in Gray/Light Blue wire. Restore electrical connections and check system operation.

17) Turn ignition off. Disconnect wiper HI/LO relay. Connect a jumper wire between HI/LO relay socket terminals No. 3 (Black/Pink wire) and No. 4 (White wire). See Fig. 3. Turn wiper switch to low speed position. If wipers do not operate at low speed, remove jumper wire and go to next step. If wipers operate at low speed, replace wiper HI/LO relay. Clear and recheck DTCs. Restore electrical connections and check system operation.

18) Turn ignition off. Disconnect wiper motor harness connector. Measure resistance of White wire between wiper motor harness connector and wiper HI/LO relay socket terminal No. 4. If resistance is greater than 5 ohms, repair open White wire. If resistance is less than 5 ohms, replace wiper motor. Restore electrical connections and check system operation.

TEST H: NO COMMUNICATION WITH GEM/CTM

1) Using ohmmeter, check condition of maxi-fuse No. 1 (50-amp) in underhood fuse/relay box. If fuse is okay, go to next step. If fuse is not okay, replace fuse. Clear DTCs and retest system operation. If fuse fails again, check Tan/Black wire between underhood fuse/relay box and instrument panel fuse block for short to ground. Repair circuit as necessary.

2) Using ohmmeter, check condition of instrument panel fuse block fuse No. 25 (7.5-amp). If fuse is okay, go to next step. If fuse is not okay, replace fuse. Clear DTCs and retest system operation. If fuse fails again, check White/Yellow wire between instrument panel fuse block and GEM/CTM for short to ground. Repair circuit as necessary.

3) Measure voltage between ground and instrument panel fuse box fuse cavity No. 25, (Tan/Black wire). If voltage is more than 10 volts, go to next step. If voltage is 10 volts or less, repair Tan/Black wire. Clear DTCs and retest system operation.

4) Turn ignition off. Disconnect GEM/CTM 18-pin connector C224. See Fig. 5. GEM/CTM is located behind center of instrument panel. Measure voltage between ground and GEM/CTM 18-pin connector C224 terminal No. 11 (White/Yellow wire). See Fig. 2. If voltage is more than 10 volts, go to next step. If voltage is 10 volts or less, repair White/Yellow wire between instrument panel fuse box and GEM/CTM. Clear DTCs and retest system operation.

5) Disconnect GEM/CTM 26-pin connector C221. Measure resistance between ground and GEM/CTM 26-pin connector C221 terminal No. 14 (Black/White wire). See Fig. 4. Measure resistance between ground and GEM/CTM 26-pin connector C221 terminal No. 26 (Black/White wire). If resistance is less than 5 ohms in both checks, go to next step. If resistance is 5 ohms or more in either check, repair suspect circuit for open. Clear DTCs and retest system operation.

6) Measure resistance between ground and GEM/CTM 18-pin connector C224 terminal No. 18 (Light Green/Black or Black wire) . See Fig. 5. If resistance is less than 5 ohms, see MODULE COMMUNICATIONS NETWORK – RANGER article to continue diagnosis. If resistance is 5 ohms or more, repair open in suspect circuit. Clear DTCs and retest system operation.

REMOVAL & INSTALLATION

WARNING: Deactivate air bag system before performing any service operation involving steering column components. See AIR BAG RESTRAINT SYSTEMS – RANGER article. Do not apply electrical power to any component on steering column without first deactivating air bag system. Air bag may deploy.

CAUTION: When battery is disconnected, vehicle computer and memory systems may lose memory data. Driveability problems may exist until computer systems have completed a relearn cycle. See COMPUTER RELEARN PROCEDURES article in GENERAL INFORMATION before disconnecting battery.

GENERIC ELECTRONIC MODULE (GEM)/CENTRAL TIMER MODULE (CTM)

Removal & Installation – Disconnect negative battery terminal. Remove radio bezel finish panel screws. Remove radio bezel finish panel. Remove GEM/CTM retaining screw. Slide GEM/CTM from retainer tabs. Unplug connectors. To install, reverse removal procedure.

WINDSHIELD WIPER MOTOR

Removal & Installation – **1)** Turn ignition on. Turn wipers on. Use ignition switch to stop wipers when blades are vertical. Remove wiper arms. Disconnect negative battery terminal. Unplug wiper motor connector.

2) Remove right linkage access cover. Reach through access cover opening and unsnap wiper linkage clip from wiper motor shaft. Push clip away from linkage until it clears nib on crank pin. Disengage wiper linkage from motor crank pin. Remove nuts and wiper motor. To install, reverse removal procedure. Ensure linkage clip is securely seated.

WASHER PUMP & RESERVOIR

Removal & Installation – Drain washer fluid. Remove washer fluid hose and coolant overflow hose from reservoir. Position air filter housing aside. Remove reservoir mounting screws and reservoir. Remove pump washer retaining ring. Pull washer pump out. Remove seal. Clean reservoir. To install, reverse removal procedure.

WIRING DIAGRAMS

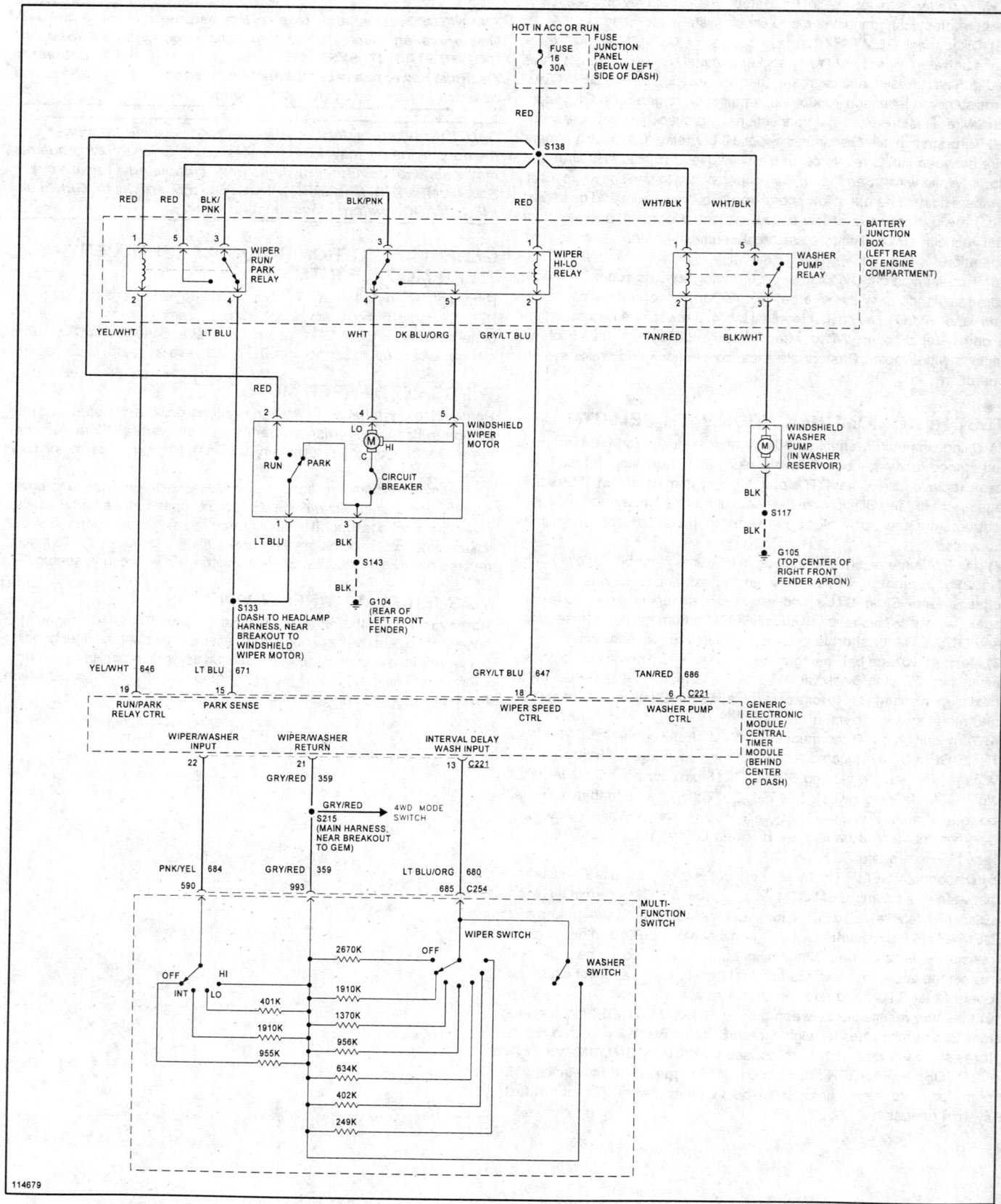

Fig. 7: Wiper/Washer System Wiring Diagram (Ranger)

DESCRIPTION & OPERATION

FRONT WIPERS

All wiper/washer functions are controlled by the multifunction switch and the Generic Electronic Module (GEM). GEM controls wiper/washer functions through 3 relays. Two relays control wipers and the third relay controls windshield washer. The wiper high/low relay switches between high and low speeds. The wiper run/park relay controls wiper park and interval functions. Interval delay is controlled by control knob on end of multifunction switch lever.

REAR WIPER

Rear wiper is controlled by rear wiper/washer switch. Rear wiper/washer switch has integral control module. Wiper/washer switch/control module is mounted on instrument panel. Rear wiper motor is mounted on rear glass.

COMPONENT LOCATIONS

COMPONENT LOCATIONS

Component	Location
Front Washer Pump & Reservoir	Between Right Hand Fender & Splash Shield
Fuse Junction Panel	Lower Left Of Steering Column
GEM	Underside Of Fuse Junction Panel
Rear Washer Pump & Reservoir	Right Rear Of Vehicle Below Cargo Floor
Rear Wiper/Washer Control	Lower Left Side Instrument Panel
Relay Center Box	Left of Battery Behind Headlamp
Washer Relay	Relay Center Box
Wiper High/Low Relay	Relay Center Box
Wiper Park Relay	Relay Center Box

ADJUSTMENTS

WIPER ARM ADJUSTMENT

Front Wipers – 1) A wiper alignment mark is printed on lower edge of windshield. Tips of wiper blades should rest in target areas when properly parked. *See Fig. 1.*

2) Run wipers. Turn off wipers and allow to self park. If wipers do not park in proper position, remove windshield wiper arms, cycle wiper motor several times and reinstall wiper arms. Tighten wiper arm to pivot shaft retaining nut 22-29 ft. lbs. (30-40 N.m).

Rear Wiper – Information is not available from manufacturer.

TROUBLE SHOOTING

Before performing any tests on wiper/washer system, verify customer complaint. Visually check following items for signs of mechanical and electrical damage:

- Check fuse junction panel fuses: No. 8 (5-amp), 12 (5-amp), 20 (5-amp), 23 (5-amp), 17 (30-amp) and 2 (5-amp) for windshield wipers and fuse No. 19 (15-amp) for rear wiper.
- Relays.
- Open thermal breaker internal to wiper motor.
- Inoperative switches.
- Loose, corroded or damaged connectors.
- Damaged wiring harness.
- Damaged wiper or pump motors.
- Binding wiper arms or linkage.
- Empty washer reservoir or kinked hoses.

If all components are okay, retrieve Diagnostic Trouble Codes (DTCs) from Generic Electronic Module (GEM). See SELF-DIAGNOSTICS.

SELF-DIAGNOSTICS

1) If concern remains after inspection, connect New Generation Star (NGS) tester (007-00500) or equivalent to DLC located below instrument panel. Perform Data Link Diagnostics Test. If NGS responds with

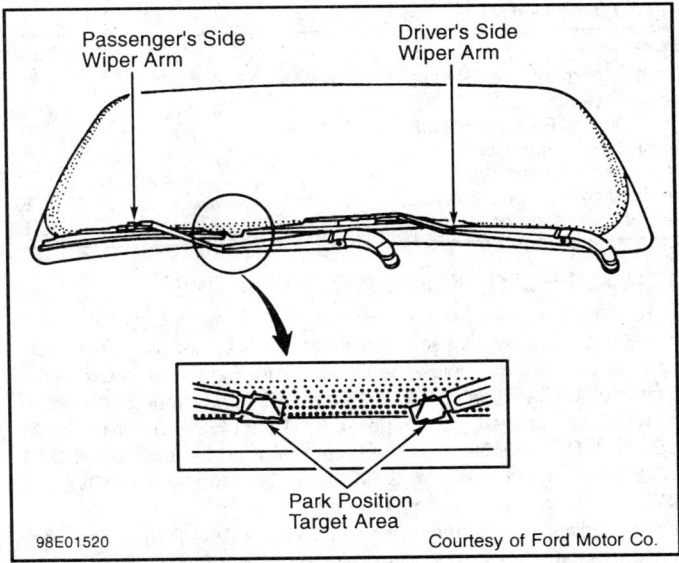

Park Position
Target Area

98E01520   Courtesy of Ford Motor Co.

Fig. 1: Identifying Wiper Park Position

NO RESPONSE/NOT EQUIPPED for Generic Electronic Module (GEM), go to TEST J. If GEM passes Diagnostic Data Link Test, retrieve continuous DTCs and perform self-test diagnostics for GEM.

2) If GEM DTCs related to the concern are retrieved, go to appropriate SYSTEM TEST. See GEM DTC TEST INDEX table. If no DTCs related to concern are retrieved, perform appropriate test based on symptom. See SYMPTOM TEST INDEX table under SYSTEM TESTS. For GEM DTCs not covered in this article, see MODULE COMMUNICATIONS NETWORK – SABLE & TAURUS.

GEM DTC TEST INDEX [1]

DTC	Description	Test
B1342	GEM Failure	[2]
B1432	Wiper Park Relay Circuit Short To Power	C
B1433	Wiper Park Relay Circuit Short To Ground	H
B1434	Wiper High/Low Speed Relay Circuit Failure	D
B1436	Wiper High/Low Speed Relay Short To Power	D
B1438	Wiper Mode Select Switch Circuit Failure	C
B1441	Wiper Mode Select Switch Short To Ground	C
B1446	Wiper Park Sense Circuit Failure	G
B1448	Wiper Park Sense Circuit Short To Power	H
B1450	Wiper/Washer Delay Switch Circuit Failure	C
B1453	Wiper/Washer Delay Switch Circuit Short To Ground	H
B1458	Wiper/Washer Pump Motor Relay Circuit Failure	A
B1460	Wiper Washer Pump Motor Relay Coil Short To Power	A
B1465	Wiper Park Relay Circuit Open	C
B1466	Wiper High/Low Speed Not Switching	C
B1840	Front Wiper Power Circuit Failure	C

[1] – Codes listed in this table are only for testing covered in this article. For complete DTC listing, see MODULE COMMUNICATIONS NETWORK – SABLE & TAURUS.

[2] – Replace GEM. See GEM under REMOVAL & INSTALLATION. Test system for normal operation.

SYSTEM TESTS

SYMPTOM TEST INDEX

Symptom	Test
Front Washer Inoperative	A
Front Washer Runs Continuously	B
Front Wipers Inoperative	C
Front Wipers High Speed Inoperative	D
Front Wipers Low Speed Inoperative	E

SYMPTOM TEST INDEX (Cont.)

TEST A: FRONT WASHER INOPERATIVE

1) Turn ignition off. Connect New Generation Star (NGS) tester (007-00500) or equivalent scan tool to Data Link Connector (DLC). DLC is on instrument panel below steering column. Retrieve and document continuous DTCs. Clear DTCs. Perform GEM On-Demand self-test. If no DTCs are retrieved, go to step **5)**. If DTC B1450 is retrieved, go to TEST C. If DTC B1458 or B1460 is retrieved, go to next step. If DTC B1342 is retrieved, replace GEM. See GEM under REMOVAL & INSTALLATION. Retest system operation.

2) Turn ignition off. Remove washer motor relay. Turn ignition on. Measure voltage between washer relay connector terminals No. 1 and ground. See Fig. 2. Measure voltage between washer relay connector terminal No. 3 and ground. If each reading is greater than 10 volts, go to next step. If either is 10 volts or less, repair appropriate White/Black wire(s). See WIRING DIAGRAMS. Retest system operation.

3) Turn ignition off. Disconnect GEM C223 (22-pin) connector . Measure resistance between GEM C223 connector terminal No. 6 and washer motor relay connector terminal No. 2. See Figs. 2 and 3. If resistance is 5 ohms or less, reconnect washer motor relay and go to next step. If resistance is greater than 5 ohms, repair open Tan/Red wire. Retest system operation.

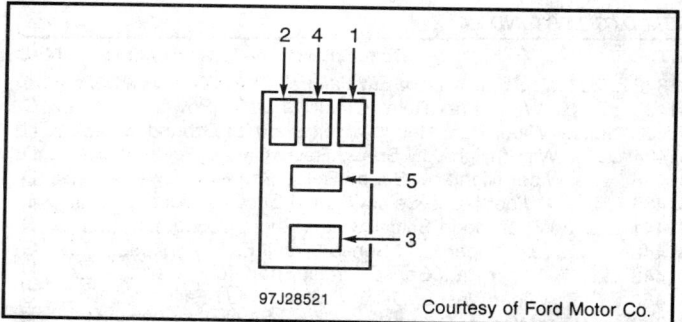

97J28521   Courtesy of Ford Motor Co.

Fig. 2: Identifying Relay Connector Terminals

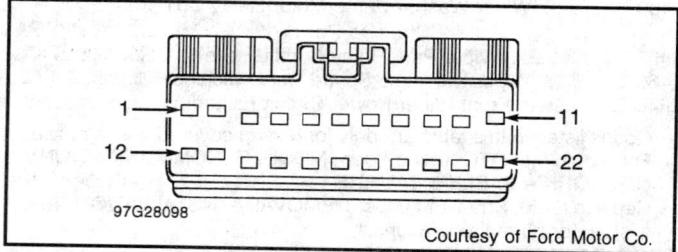

97G28098   Courtesy of Ford Motor Co.

Fig. 3: Identifying GEM C223 (22-Pin) Connector Terminals

4) Turn ignition on. Measure voltage between GEM C223 connector terminal No. 6 and ground. See Fig. 3. If voltage is 10 volts or less, replace washer motor relay. If voltage is greater than 10 volts, test washer motor relay. See RELAYS under COMPONENT TESTS. If relay is okay, replace GEM. See GEM under REMOVAL & INSTALLATION. After repair, retest system operation.

5) Turn ignition off. Disconnect multifunction switch (7-pin) connector. Test wiper/washer portion of multifunction switch. See WIPER/WASHER SWITCH under COMPONENT TESTS. If faulty, replace multifunction switch. Test system for normal operation. If multifunction switch is okay, reconnect multifunction switch and go to next step.

6) Turn ignition off. Disconnect washer pump motor connector. Measure resistance between washer pump motor connector Black wire and ground. If resistance is less than 5 ohms, go to next step. If resistance is 5 ohms or greater, repair open Black wire. Test system for normal operation.

7) Turn ignition on. While pressing wash switch, measure voltage between washer pump motor connector Black/White wire and ground. If voltage is 10 volts or less, go to next step. If voltage is greater than 10 volts, replace washer pump motor. See WASHER PUMP & RESERVOIR under REMOVAL & INSTALLATION. Retest system operation.

8) Remove washer pump motor relay. Measure resistance of Black/White wire between washer pump motor connector and washer motor relay connector terminal No. 5. See Fig. 2. Resistance should be less than 5 ohms. Measure resistance between washer motor relay connector terminal No. 5 and ground. Resistance should be greater than 10 k/ohms. If resistance measurements are as specified, replace washer motor relay. If resistance measurements are not as specified, repair Black/White wire as necessary. After repair, retest system operation.

TEST B: FRONT WASHER RUNS CONTINUOUSLY

1) Turn ignition off. Disconnect multifunction switch (7-pin) connector. Test wiper/washer portion of multifunction switch. See WIPER/WASHER SWITCH under COMPONENT TESTS. If faulty, replace multifunction switch. See MULTIFUNCTION SWITCH under REMOVAL & INSTALLATION. Test system for normal operation. If switch is okay, reconnect connector and go to next step.

2) Turn ignition off. Remove washer motor relay. Measure resistance between washer motor relay connector terminal No. 2 and ground. See Fig. 2. If resistance is 10 k/ohms or less, go to next step. If resistance is greater than 10 k/ohms, reconnect washer motor relay and go to step **4)**.

3) Disconnect GEM C223 (22-pin) connector. Measure resistance between washer motor relay connector terminal No. 2 and ground. See Fig. 2. If resistance is 10 k/ohms or less, repair short to ground in Tan/Red wire. See WIRING DIAGRAMS. If resistance is greater than 10 k/ohms, replace GEM. See GEM under REMOVAL & INSTALLATION. After repair, test system for normal operation.

4) Disconnect washer pump motor connector. Turn ignition on. Measure voltage between washer pump connector Black/White wire and ground. If any voltage exists, go to next step. If voltage does not exist, replace washer pump motor. See WASHER PUMP & RESERVOIR under REMOVAL & INSTALLATION. Test system for normal operation.

5) Turn ignition off. Remove washer motor relay. Turn ignition on. Measure voltage between washer pump motor connector Black/White wire and ground. If any voltage exists, repair short to power in Black/White wire. If no voltage exists, replace washer motor relay. After repair, test system for normal operation.

TEST C: FRONT WIPERS INOPERATIVE

1) Turn ignition off. Connect New Generation Star (NGS) scan tester to Data Link Connector (DLC). DLC is on instrument panel below steering column. Retrieve and record continuous DTCs. Clear DTCs. Perform On-Demand Self-Test. If no DTCs are retrieved, go to step **5)**. If the DTCs are retrieved, go to appropriate test step. See TEST C DTC INDEX table.

TEST C DTC INDEX

DTC Retrieved	Step
B1342	1
B1432	10
B1438	4
B1441	4
B1450	4
B1465	10
B1466	4
B1840	2

1 – Replace GEM. See GEM under REMOVAL & INSTALLATION. Retest system operation.

2) Turn ignition off. Remove wiper high/low relay. Turn ignition on. Measure voltage between wiper high/low relay connector terminal No. 2

and ground. *See Fig. 2*. If voltage is greater than 10 volts, go to next step. If voltage is 10 volts or less, check fuse No. 17 (30-amp). If fuse is okay, repair open White/Black wire. See WIRING DIAGRAMS. Retest system operation.

3) Turn ignition off. Disconnect wiper motor (5-pin) connector. Measure resistance between wiper motor connector terminal No. 3 and ground. *See Fig. 4*. If resistance is less than 5 ohms, go to next step. If resistance 5 ohms or greater, repair Black ground wire. Test system for normal operation.

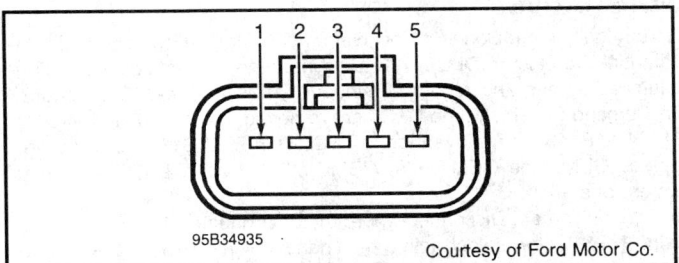

95B34935   Courtesy of Ford Motor Co.

Fig. 4: Identifying Wiper Motor Connector Terminals

4) Connect NGS tester and access GEM PID WPMODE. Observe PID WPMODE while turning wiper switch through all positions. If PID values agree with all wiper switch positions, go to step 10). If PID values do not agree with all wiper switch positions, go to next step.

5) Turn ignition off. Disconnect multifunction switch (7-pin) connector. Disconnect GEM C236 (16-pin) connector. Measure resistance between multifunction switch connector terminal No. 6 and GEM C236 connector terminal No. 3. *See Figs. 5 and 6*. If resistance is less than 5 ohms, next step. If resistance is 5 ohms or greater, repair open in Light Blue/Orange wire. Retest system operation.

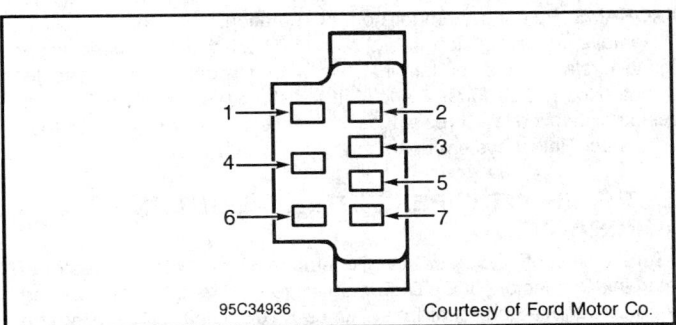

95C34936   Courtesy of Ford Motor Co.

Fig. 5: Identifying Multifunction Switch (7-Pin) Connector Terminals

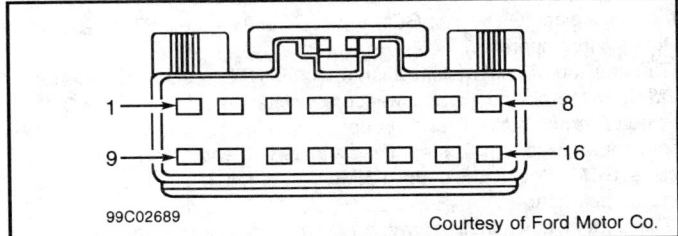

99C02689   Courtesy of Ford Motor Co.

Fig. 6: Identifying GEM C236 (16-Pin) Connector Terminals

6) Measure resistance between multifunction switch connector terminal No. 4 and GEM C236 connector terminal No. 16. *See Figs. 5 and 6*. If resistance is less than 5 ohms, go to next step. If resistance is 5 ohms or greater, repair open in Dark Blue wire. Retest system operation.

7) Measure resistance between multifunction switch connector terminal No. 1 and GEM C236 connector terminal No. 4. *See Figs. 5 and 6*. If resistance is less than 5 ohms, go to next step. If resistance is 5 ohms or greater, repair open in Pink/Yellow wire. Retest system operation.

8) Turn ignition on. Measure voltage between GEM C236 connector terminal No. 3 and ground. *See Fig. 6*. If no voltage exists, go to next step. If any voltage exists, repair short to power in Light Blue/Orange wire. Retest system operation.

9) Measure voltage between GEM C236 connector terminal No. 4 and ground. *See Fig. 6*. If no voltage exists, replace GEM. See GEM under REMOVAL & INSTALLATION. If any voltage exists, repair Pink/Yellow wire short to power. After repair, retest system operation.

10) Observe GEM PID WPRUN while toggling GEM active command WIPER RLY on and off. If PID values agree with command modes and scan tool displays ON--- and OFF---, go to step 17). If PID values do not agree with command modes and scan tool displays OFFO-G, go to next step. If PID values do not agree with command modes and scan tool displays ON-B-, go to step 15).

11) Turn ignition off. Remove wiper park relay. Turn ignition on. Measure voltage between wiper park relay connector terminal No. 2 and ground. *See Fig. 2*. If voltage is greater than 10 volts, go to next step. If voltage is less than 10 volts, repair White/Black wire. Retest system operation.

12) Turn ignition off. Remove wiper park relay. Observe GEM PID WPRUN. If scan tool displays SHORTVBAT, go to next step. If scan tester does not display SHORTVBAT, replace wiper park relay. Retest system operation.

13) Turn ignition off. Disconnect GEM C223 (22-pin) connector. Measure resistance between GEM C223 connector terminal No. 8 and wiper park relay connector terminal No. 1. *See Figs. 2 and 3*. If resistance is less than 5 ohms, go to next step. If resistance is 5 ohms or greater, repair open in Yellow/White wire. Retest system operation.

14) Turn ignition on. Measure voltage between GEM C223 connector terminal No. 8 and ground. *See Fig. 3*. If any voltage exists, repair Yellow/White wire short to power. If no voltage exists, replace GEM. See GEM under REMOVAL & INSTALLATION. After repair, retest system operation.

15) Turn ignition off. Remove wiper park relay. Observe GEM PID WPRUN. If PID WPRUN indicates SHORTVBAT, go to next step. If PID WPRUN does not indicate SHORTVBAT, replace wiper park relay. Retest system operation.

16) Disconnect GEM C223 (22-pin) connector. Measure resistance between GEM C223 connector terminal No. 8 and ground. *See Fig. 3*. If resistance is 10 k/ohms or less, repair Yellow/White wire short to ground. If resistance is greater than 10 k/ohms, replace GEM. See GEM under REMOVAL & INSTALLATION. After repair, retest system operation.

17) Turn ignition off. Remove wiper high/low relay. Turn ignition on. Set NGS tester active command mode WIPER RELY to ON. Measure voltage between wiper high/low relay connector terminal No. 3 and ground. *See Fig. 2*. If voltage is greater than 10 volts, go to step 20). If voltage is 10 volts or less, go to next step.

18) Turn ignition off. Remove wiper park relay. Measure resistance between wiper high/low relay connector terminal No. 3 and wiper park relay connector terminal No. 3. *See Fig. 2*. If resistance is less than 5 ohms, go to next step. If resistance is 5 ohms or greater, repair open in Yellow/Red wire. Retest system operation.

19) Turn ignition on. Measure voltage between wiper park relay connector terminal No. 5 and ground. *See Fig. 2*. If voltage is greater than 10 volts, replace wiper park relay. If voltage is 10 volts or less, repair White/Black wire. After repair, retest system operation.

20) Turn ignition on. Connect a jumper wire between high/low relay connector terminals No. 3 and 4. *See Fig. 2*. Using NGS tester, set active command WIPER RLY to ON. Wiper should operate at low speed. Disconnect jumper wire and reconnect it between high/low relay connector terminals No. 3 and 5. Using NGS tester, set active command WIPER RLY to ON. Wipers should operate at high speed. If wipers do not operate as specified, go to next step. If wipers operate as specified, replace wiper high/low relay. Retest system operation.

21) Turn ignition off. Disconnect wiper motor connector. Measure resistance between wiper motor connector terminal No. 3 and ground. *See Fig. 4*. If resistance is less than 5 ohms, go to next step. If resistance is greater than 5 ohms, repair Black ground wire. Retest system operation.

22) Measure resistance between wiper high/low relay connector terminal No. 5 and wiper motor connector terminal No. 5. *See Figs. 2 and 4.* If resistance is less than 5 ohms, go to next step. If resistance is greater than 5 ohms, repair open in Dark Blue/Orange wire. Retest system operation.

23) Measure resistance between wiper high/low relay connector terminal No. 4 and wiper motor connector terminal No. 4. *See Figs. 2 and 4.* If resistance is less than 5 ohms, go to next step. If resistance is 5 ohms or greater, repair open in White wire. Retest system operation.

24) Remove linkage from wiper motor. If wiper arms do not move freely, repair or replace wiper mechanism as necessary. If wiper arms move freely, test wiper motor. See WIPER MOTOR under COMPONENT TESTS. Replace wiper motor if necessary. After repair, retest system operation.

TEST D: FRONT WIPERS HIGH SPEED INOPERATIVE

1) Turn ignition off. Connect New Generation Star (NGS) scan tester to Data Link Connector (DLC). DLC is on instrument panel below steering column. Retrieve and record continuous DTCs. Clear DTCs. Perform On-Demand Self-Test. If DTCs B1434 or B1436 are retrieved, go to step **7)**. If B1342 is retrieved, replace GEM. See GEM under REMOVAL & INSTALLATION. Retest system. If no DTCs are retrieved, go to next step.

2) Turn ignition off. Disconnect wiper motor connector. Using NGS tester, select active commands WIPER RLY ON and SPEED RLY ON. Turn ignition on. Measure voltage between wiper motor connector terminal No. 5 and ground. *See Fig. 4.* If voltage is greater than 10 volts, go to next step. If voltage is 10 volts or less, select WIPER RLY OFF and go to step **4)**.

3) Turn ignition off. Test wiper motor. See WIPER MOTOR under COMPONENT TESTS. Replace wiper motor if necessary. Check system operation. If wiper motor is okay, go to next step.

4) Turn ignition off. Remove wiper high/low relay. Measure resistance between wiper high/low relay connector terminal No. 5 and ground. *See Fig. 2.* If resistance is greater than 10 k/ohms, go to next step. If resistance is 10 k/ohms or less, repair Dark Blue/Orange wire short to ground. See WIRING DIAGRAMS. Retest system operation.

5) Reconnect wiper high/low relay. Measure resistance between wiper motor connector terminal No. 5 and ground. *See Fig. 4* If resistance is greater than 10 k/ohms, go to next step. If resistance is 10 k/ohms or less, replace wiper high/low relay. Retest system operation.

6) Remove wiper high/low relay. Measure resistance between wiper motor connector terminal No. 5 and wiper motor high/low relay connector terminal No. 5. *See Figs. 2 and 4.* If resistance is less than 5 ohms, replace wiper high/low relay. If resistance is 5 ohms or greater, repair open in Dark Blue/Orange wire. Retest system operation.

7) Turn ignition off. Remove wiper high/low relay. Turn ignition on. Using NGS tester, observe GEM PID WPHISP. If PID reads SHORTVBAT, go to next step. If PID data does not read SHORTVBAT, go to step **9)**.

8) Turn ignition off. Disconnect GEM C223 (22-pin) connector. Measure resistance between wiper high/low relay connector terminal No. 1 and ground. *See Fig. 2.* If resistance is greater than 10 k/ohms, go to step **12)**. If resistance is 10 k/ohms or less, repair Gray/Light Blue wire short to ground. Retest system operation.

9) Turn ignition on. Measure voltage between wiper high/low relay connector terminal No. 2 and ground. *See Fig. 2.* If voltage is greater than 10 volts, go to next step. If voltage is 10 volts or less, repair open in White/Black wire. Retest system operation.

10) Turn ignition off. Reconnect wiper high/low relay. Disconnect GEM C223 (22-pin) connector. Turn ignition on. Measure voltage between GEM C223 connector terminal No. 7 and ground. *See Fig. 3.* If voltage is less than 10 volts, go to next step. If voltage is greater than 10 volts, replace GEM. See GEM under REMOVAL & INSTALLATION. Retest system operation.

11) Turn ignition off. Remove wiper high/low relay. Measure resistance between wiper high/low relay connector terminal No. 1 and GEM C223 connector terminal No. 7. *See Figs. 2 and 3.* If resistance is 5 ohms or greater, repair open in Gray/Light Blue wire. If resistance is less than 5 ohms, replace wiper high/low relay. After repair, retest system operation.

12) Turn ignition on. Measure voltage between GEM C223 connector terminal No. 7 and ground. *See Fig. 3.* If any voltage exists, repair Gray/Light Blue wire short to power. If no voltage exists, replace GEM. See GEM under REMOVAL & INSTALLATION. Retest system operation.

TEST E: FRONT WIPERS LOW SPEED INOPERATIVE

1) Turn ignition off. Connect New Generation Star (NGS) scan tester to Data Link Connector (DLC). DLC is on instrument panel below steering column. Retrieve and record continuous DTCs. Clear DTCs. Perform On-Demand Self-Test. If no DTCs are retrieved, go to next step. If DTC B1434 or B1436 is retrieved, go to TEST D. If DTC B1342 is retrieved, replace GEM. See GEM under REMOVAL & INSTALLATION. Retest system operation.

2) Turn ignition off. Disconnect wiper motor connector. Turn ignition on. Using NGS tester, select active command WIPER RLY ON. Measure voltage between wiper motor connector terminal No. 4 and ground. *See Fig. 4.* If voltage is greater than 10 volts, go to next step. If voltage is less than 10 volts, select WIPER RLY OFF and go to step 4.

3) Turn ignition off. Test wiper motor. See WIPER MOTOR under COMPONENT TESTS. Replace wiper motor if necessary. Check system operation. If wiper motor is okay, go to next step.

4) Turn ignition off. Measure resistance between wiper motor connector terminal No. 4 and ground. *See Fig. 4.* If resistance is greater than 10 k/ohms, go to step **6)**. If resistance is 10 k/ohms or less, go to next step.

5) Remove wiper high/low relay. Measure resistance between wiper motor connector terminal No. 4 and ground. *See Fig. 4.* If resistance is greater than 10 k/ohms, replace wiper high/low relay. If resistance is 10 k/ohms or less, repair White wire short to ground. See WIRING DIAGRAMS. Retest system for normal operation.

6) Remove wiper high/low relay. Measure resistance between wiper high/low relay connector terminal No. 4 and wiper motor connector terminal No. 4. *See Figs. 2 and 4.* If resistance is less than 5 ohms, replace high/low relay. If resistance is 5 ohms or greater, repair open in White wire. Retest system operation.

TEST F: FRONT WIPERS INTERVAL SETTING INOPERATIVE

1) Turn ignition off. Connect New Generation Star (NGS) scan tester to Data Link Connector (DLC). DLC is on instrument panel below steering column. Retrieve and record continuous DTCs. Clear DTCs. Perform On-Demand Self-Test. If no DTCs are retrieved, or if DTC B1453 is retrieved, go to next step. If DTC B1438, B1441 or B1450 is retrieved, go to TEST C. If DTC B1446 is retrieved, go to TEST G. If DTC B1342 is retrieved, replace GEM. See GEM under REMOVAL & INSTALLATION. Retest system operation.

2) Turn ignition off. Set multifunction switch in OFF position. Disconnect GEM C236 (16-pin) connector. Measure resistance between GEM C236 connector terminal No. 3 and ground. *See Fig. 6.* If resistance is 10 k/ohms or less, go to next step. If resistance is greater than 10 k/ohms, replace GEM. See GEM under REMOVAL & INSTALLATION. Retest system operation.

3) Disconnect multifunction switch (7-pin) connector. Measure resistance between GEM C236 connector terminal No. 3 and ground. *See Fig. 6.* If resistance is greater than 10 k/ohms, replace multifunction switch. See MULTIFUNCTION SWITCH under REMOVAL & INSTALLATION. If resistance is 10 k/ohms or less, repair Light Blue/Orange wire short to ground. See WIRING DIAGRAMS. After repair, retest system operation.

TEST G: FRONT WIPERS PARK IMPROPERLY

1) Ensure wiper arms are not bent or damaged. Replace if necessary. Check wiper arm adjustment and perform any necessary adjustments. See WIPER ARM under ADJUSTMENTS. Retest system operation. If okay, go to next step.

2) Turn ignition on. Connect New Generation Star (NGS) scan tester to Data Link Connector (DLC). DLC is on instrument panel below steering column. Retrieve and record continuous DTCs. Clear DTCs. Perform On-Demand self-test. If no DTCs are retrieved, go to next step. If the following DTCs are retrieved, go to specified step or test. See TEST G DIRECTORY table.

TEST G DIRECTORY

DTC Retrieved	Go To
B1342	1
B1438	TEST C
B1441	TEST C
B1446	Step 7)
B1448	Step 12)
B1450	TEST C
B1453	TEST F

1 – Replace GEM. See GEM under REMOVAL & INSTALLATION. Retest system operation.

3) Turn ignition off. Disconnect wiper motor connector. Connect jumper wire between wiper motor connector terminal No. 1 and ground. See Fig. 4. Using NGS tester observe GEM PID WPPRKSW. If PID indicates PARKED, go to next step. If PID does not indicate PARKED, go to step 6).

4) Turn ignition on. Measure voltage between wiper motor connector terminal No. 2 and ground. See Fig. 4. If voltage is greater than 10 volts, go to next step. If voltage is less than 10 volts, repair open White/Black wire. See WIRING DIAGRAMS. Retest system operation.

5) Turn ignition off. Connect a jumper wire between wiper motor connector terminals No. 1 and 3. See Fig. 4. Observe GEM PID WPPRKSW. If PID indicates PARKED, replace wiper motor. See FRONT WIPER MOTOR under REMOVAL & INSTALLATION. If PID does not indicate PARKED, repair open in Black ground wire. Ground connection point is on left inner fender near air cleaner. Retest system operation.

6) Turn ignition off. Disconnect GEM C223 (22-pin) connector. Measure resistance between GEM C223 connector terminal No. 11 and wiper motor connector terminal No. 1. See Figs. 3 and 4. If resistance is less than 5 ohms, replace GEM. See GEM under REMOVAL & INSTALLATION. If resistance is 5 ohms or greater, repair open in Dark Green wire. Retest system operation.

7) Turn ignition off. Disconnect wiper motor connector. Using NGS tester observe GEM PID WPPRKSW. If PID indicates PARKED, go to step 9). If PID does not indicate PARKED, go to next step.

8) Reconnect wiper motor connector. Turn ignition on. Turn multifunction switch to LO position. When wipers reach full up position, turn ignition off. Remove wiper park relay. Observe GEM PID WPPRKSW. If PID indicates PARKED, replace wiper motor. See FRONT WIPER MOTOR under REMOVAL & INSTALLATION. Retest system operation. If PID does not indicate PARKED, go to step 10).

9) Disconnect GEM C233 (22-pin) connector. Remove wiper park relay. Measure resistance between wiper motor connector terminal No. 1 and ground. See Fig. 4. If resistance is greater than 10 k/ohms, go to next step. If resistance is 10 k/ohms or less, repair Dark Green wire short to ground. Retest system operation.

10) Disconnect wiper motor connector. Measure resistance between wiper motor connector terminal No. 4 and ground. See Fig. 4. If resistance is greater than 10 k/ohms, go to next step. If resistance is 10 k/ohms or less, repair Yellow/Red wire or White wire short to ground. See WIRING DIAGRAMS. Retest system operation.

11) Reconnect wiper park relay. Measure resistance between wiper motor connector terminal No. 1 and ground. See Fig. 4. If resistance is greater than 10 k/ohms, replace GEM. See GEM under REMOVAL & INSTALLATION. If resistance is 10 k/ohms or less, replace wiper park relay. After repair, retest system.

12) Disconnect GEM C223 (22-pin) connector. Measure voltage between GEM C223 connector terminal No. 11 and ground. See Fig. 3. If voltage is greater than 10 volts, repair Dark Green wire short to power. Retest system operation. If voltage is less than 10 volts, go to next step.

13) Remove wiper park relay. Disconnect wiper motor connector. Measure resistance between GEM C223 connector terminal No. 11 and wiper motor connector terminal No. 1. See Figs. 3 and 4. Measure resistance between GEM C223 connector terminal No. 11 and wiper park relay connector terminal No. 4. If each resistance is less than 5 ohms, replace GEM. See GEM under REMOVAL & INSTALLATION. If either resistance is 5 ohms or greater, repair open in Dark Green wire. After repair, retest system operation.

TEST H: FRONT WIPERS RUN CONTINUOUSLY

1) Turn ignition off. Connect New Generation Star (NGS) scan tester to Data Link Connector (DLC). DLC is on instrument panel below steering column. Retrieve and record continuous DTCs. Clear DTCs. Perform On-Demand Self-Test. If no DTCs are retrieved, go to next step. If the following DTCs are retrieved, go to specified step or test. See TEST H DIRECTORY table.

TEST H DIRECTORY

DTC Retrieved	Go To
B1342	1
B1433	Step 6
B1441	TEST C
B1446	TEST G
B1448	Step 6
B1453	TEST F

1 – Replace GEM. See GEM under REMOVAL & INSTALLATION. Retest system operation.

2) Using NGS tester observe GEM PID WPMODE while turning wiper switch through all positions. If PID values agree with wiper switch positions, go to step 6). If PID values do not agree with wiper switch positions, go to next step.

3) Turn ignition off. Disconnect multifunction switch (7-pin) connector. Test wiper portion of multifunction switch. See WIPER/WASHER SWITCH under COMPONENT TESTS. If switch is okay, go to next step. If faulty, replace switch. See MULTIFUNCTION SWITCH under REMOVAL & INSTALLATION. Retest system operation.

4) Disconnect GEM C236 (16-pin) connector. Measure resistance between multifunction switch connector terminal No. 6 and ground. See Fig. 5. If resistance is greater than 10 k/ohms, go to next step. If resistance is 10 k/ohms or less, repair Light Blue/Orange wire short to ground. See WIRING DIAGRAMS. Retest system operation.

5) Measure resistance between multifunction switch connector terminal No. 1 and ground. See Fig. 5. If resistance is greater than 10 k/ohms, replace GEM. See GEM under REMOVAL & INSTALLATION. If resistance is 10 k/ohms or less, repair Pink/Yellow wire short to ground. After repair, retest system operation.

6) Using NGS tester observe GEM PID WPRUN while toggling GEM active command WIPER RLY on and off. If PID agrees with command mode and displays ON--- and OFF---, go to step 9). If PID does not agree with command mode and displays OFFO-G go to next step.

7) Turn ignition off. Remove fuse No. 17 (30-amp). Disconnect GEM C223 (22-pin) connector. Measure resistance between GEM C223 connector terminal No. 8 and ground. See Fig. 3. If resistance is 10 k/ohms or less, reinstall fuse and go to next step. If resistance is greater than 10 k/ohms, replace GEM. See GEM under REMOVAL & INSTALLATION. Retest system operation.

8) Remove wiper park relay. Measure resistance of between GEM C223 connector terminal No. 8 and ground. See Fig. 3. If resistance is greater than 10 k/ohms, replace wiper park relay. If resistance is 10 k/ohms or less, repair Yellow/White wire short to ground. After repair, retest system operation.

9) Turn ignition off. Remove wiper park relay. Turn ignition on. If wipers continue to operate, go to next step. If wipers stop operating, go to step 13).

10) Turn ignition off. Remove wiper high/low relay. Turn ignition on. Measure voltage between wiper park relay connector terminal No. 3 and ground. See Fig. 2. If no voltage is indicated, go to next step. If any voltage is indicated, repair Yellow/Red wire short to power. Retest system operation.

11) Measure voltage between wiper high/low relay connector terminal No. 5 and ground. *See Fig. 2.* If no voltage exists, go to next step. If any voltage exists, repair Dark Blue/Orange wire short to power. Retest system operation.

12) Measure voltage between wiper high/low relay connector terminal No. 4 and ground. *See Fig. 2.* If no voltage exists, replace wiper high/low relay. If any voltage exists, repair White wire short to power. Retest system operation.

13) Turn multifunction (wiper/washer) switch to OFF position. Measure voltage between wiper park relay connector terminal No. 4 and ground. *See Fig. 2.* If voltage is greater than 10 volts, go to next step. If is less than 10 volts, replace wiper park relay. Retest system operation.

14) Disconnect wiper motor connector. Turn ignition on. Measure voltage between wiper park relay connector terminal No. 4 and ground. *See Fig. 2.* If any voltage exists, go to next step. If no voltage exists, go to step **16)** .

15) Turn ignition off. Disconnect GEM C223 (22-pin) connector. Turn igniton on. Measure voltage between wiper park relay connector terminal No. 4 and ground. *See Fig. 2.* If any voltage exists, repair Dark Green wire short to power. If no voltage exists, replace GEM. See GEM under REMOVAL & INSTALLATION. Retest system operation.

16) Reconnect wiper motor. Measure voltage between wiper park relay connector terminal No. 4 and ground. *See Fig. 2.* If any voltage exists, replace wiper motor. See FRONT WIPER MOTOR under REMOVAL & INSTALLATION. If no voltage exists, repair Dark Green wire. After repair, test system operation.

TEST J: NO COMMUNICATION WITH GEM

1) Check the following fuse junction panel fuses:
- Fuse No. 23 (5-amp)
- Fuse No. 20 (5-amp)
- Fuse No. 12 (5-amp)
- Fuse No. 8 (5-amp).

Replace any blown fuses. If fuse blows again, check appropriate circuit for short to ground. If all fuses are okay, go to next step.

2) Turn ignition off. Disconnect GEM C236 (16-pin) connector. Turn ignition on. Measure voltage between GEM C236 connector terminal No. 14 and ground. *See Fig. 6.* If voltage is greater than 10 volts, go to next step. If voltage is less than 10 volts, repair Red/Yellow wire. Retest system operation.

3) Turn ignition off. Disconnect GEM from rear of fuse panel. Turn ignition on. Measure voltage between GEM/fuse junction panel connector terminal No. 5 and ground, and between terminal No. 15 and ground. Measure voltage between GEM/fuse panel connector terminal No. 14 and ground while holding key in start position. If each voltage is greater than 10 volts, go to next step. If any voltage is less than 10 volts, replace fuse junction panel. Retest system operation.

4) Turn ignition off. Disconnect GEM C248 (26-pin) connector. measure resistance between GEM C248 connector terminals No. 14 and 25. *See Fig. 7.* If resistance is less than 5 ohms, go to next step. If resistance is 5 ohms or greater, repair open Black wire. Circuit ground point is behind left kick panel. Retest system operation.

5) Disconnect GEM C223 (22-pin) connector. Measure resistance between GEM C223 connector terminal No. 12 and ground. *See Fig. 3.* If resistance is less than 5 ohms, go to next step. If resistance is 5 ohms or greater, repair open Black/White wire or ground at left front fender near air cleaner. Retest system operation.

6) Measure resistance between GEM C223 connector terminal No. 22 and ground. *See Fig. 3.* If resistance is 5 ohms or greater, repair open Black/Light Green wire. Black/Light Green wire changes to Black/White wire before grounding at left front fender near battery. Retest system operation. If resistance is less than 5 ohms, communication circuit is faulty. See appropriate MODULE COMMUNICATIONS NETWORK article.

TEST K: REAR WASHER INOPERATIVE

1) Turn ignition off. Disconnect rear washer pump motor connector. Turn ignition on. Measure voltage between rear washer pump motor connec-

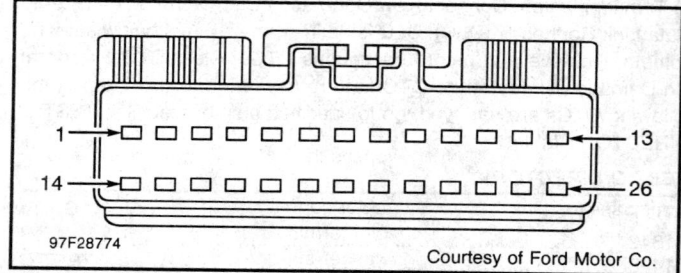

Fig. 7: Identifying GEM C248 (26-Pin) Harness Connector Terminals

tor Black/White wire and ground while activating rear washer switch. If voltage is greater than 10 volts, go to step 3). If voltage is less than 10 volts, go to next step.

2) Turn ignition off. Disconnect rear wiper/washer switch connector. Turn ignition on. Measure voltage between wiper/washer switch connector terminal No. 6 and ground. *See Fig. 8.* If voltage is greater than 10 volts, go to next step. If voltage is less than 10 volts, repair Brown/White wire. See WIRING DIAGRAMS. Retest system operation.

3) Measure voltage between rear washer pump motor connector Brown/White wire and ground. If voltage is greater than 10 volts, go to next step. If voltage is less than 10 volts, repair Brown/White wire. Retest system operation.

4) Measure resistance between rear washer pump connector Black/White wire and rear wiper/washer switch connector terminal No. 3. *See Fig. 8.* If resistance is less than 5 ohms, go to next step. If resistance is 5 ohms or greater, repair open Black/White wire. Retest system operation.

5) Measure resistance between rear washer pump motor connector Black/White wire and ground. If resistance is greater than 10 k/ohms, go to next step. If resistance is 10 k/ohms or less, repair Black/White wire short to ground. Retest system operation.

6) Measure resistance between rear wiper/washer switch connector terminal No. 2 and ground. *See Fig. 8.* If resistance is less than 5 ohms, replace rear wiper pump motor. If resistance is 5 ohms or greater, repair open Black wire or ground point at lower side of inner glove box frame. Retest system operation.

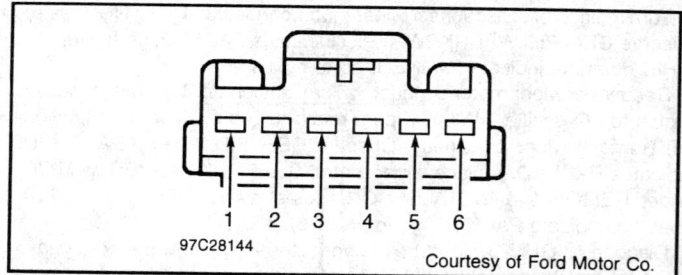

Fig. 8: Identifying Rear Wiper/Washer Switch Connector Terminals

TEST L: REAR WIPER INOPERATIVE

1) Turn ignition on. Press rear washer switch. If rear washer operates, go to step 5). If rear washer does not operate, go to next step.

2) Check fuse junction panel fuse No. 19 (15-amp). Replace fuse if necessary and retest system. If fuse blows again, check for short to ground and repair as necessary. If fuse is okay, go to next step.

3) Turn ignition off. Disconnect rear wiper/washer switch connector. Turn ignition on. Measure voltage between rear wiper/washer switch connector terminal No. 6 and ground. *See Fig. 8.* If voltage is greater than 10 volts, go to next step. If voltage is less than 10 volts, repair Brown/White wire. See WIRING DIAGRAMS. Retest system operation.

4) Turn ignition off. Measure resistance between rear wiper/washer switch connector terminal No. 2 and ground. *See Fig. 8.* If resistance is less than 5 ohms, replace rear wiper/washer switch. If resistance is 5 ohms or greater, repair Black ground wire. After repair, retest system operation.

5) Disconnect rear wiper motor connector. Turn ignition on. Measure voltage between rear wiper motor connector White/Orange wire and ground while pressing rear wiper switch. If voltage is greater than 10 volts, go to step **7)**. If voltage is less than 10 volts, go to next step.

6) Turn ignition off. Disconnect rear wiper/washer switch. Measure resistance between rear wiper motor connector White/Orange wire and rear wiper/washer switch connector terminal No. 4. *See Fig. 8*. Measure resistance between rear wiper/washer switch connector terminal No. 4 and ground. If resistance is less than 5 ohms between the two connectors and greater than 10 k/ohms between switch connector and ground, go to next step. If voltage and/or resistance are not as indicated, repair White/Orange wire. Retest system operation.

7) Measure resistance between rear wiper motor connector Black wire and ground. If resistance is less than 5 ohms, go to next step. If resistance is 5 ohms or greater, repair open in Black wire. Retest system operation.

8) Turn igniton on. Measure voltage between rear wiper motor connector Brown/White wire and ground. If voltage is greater than 10 volts, replace rear wiper motor. If voltage is less than 10 volts, repair Brown/White wire. After repair, retest system operation.

COMPONENT TESTS

WARNING: Vehicle is equipped with an air bag system. System MUST be disabled before working near steering column and instrument cluster to prevent air bag deployment. See appropriate AIR BAG RESTRAINT SYSTEMS article.

RELAYS

Measure resistance between relay terminal No. 2 and all other terminals. *See Fig. 9*. If resistance is less than 5 ohms between relay terminal No. 2 and any other terminal, replace relay. If all resistances are 5 ohms or greater, continue test. Attach jumper wire between battery positive and relay terminal No. 3. Measure voltage between relay terminal No. 4 and ground. If battery voltage is not present, replace relay. If battery voltage is present, attach second jumper wire from battery positive to relay terminal No. 1. Attach third jumper wire between relay terminal No. 2 and ground. Measure voltage between relay terminal No. 5 and ground. If battery voltage is not present, replace relay. If battery voltage is present, relay is okay.

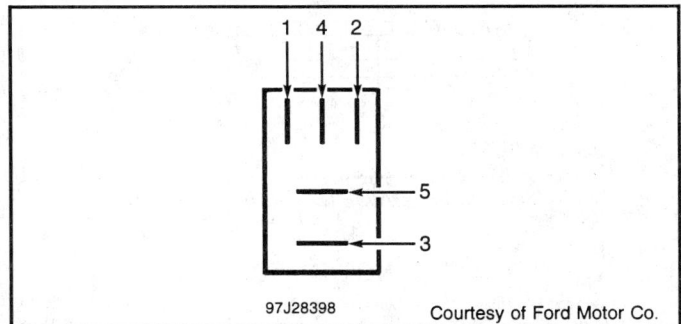

97J28398   Courtesy of Ford Motor Co.

Fig. 9: Identifying Relay Terminals

WIPER MOTOR

CAUTION: Wiper motor contains ceramic magnets that may crack or shatter if motor is dropped or handled roughly.

Disengage linkage from motor. Disconnect front wiper motor connector. Connect ammeter between battery ground and terminal No. 3 (Black wire) on motor. For mating connector view, *see Fig. 4*. Apply battery voltage to terminal No. 4 (White wire) on motor for low speed operation. For high speed apply battery voltage to terminal No. 5 (Dark

Blue/Orange wire) on motor. Current draw with wiper linkage disconnected should not exceed 3.5 amps at low speed and 5.5 amps at high speed.

WIPER/WASHER SWITCH

With multifunction switch in specified position, ensure indicated resistance exists between terminals listed. See WIPER/WASHER SWITCH TEST table. *See Fig. 10*. Replace multifunction switch if resistance is not within specification.

WIPER/WASHER SWITCH TEST

Switch Position	Switch Terminals	[1] k/ohms
Wiper		
OFF	1 & 4	47.6
INT	1 & 4	11.33
LOW	1 & 4	4.08
HIGH	1 & 4	0
Interval		
1 (MAX)	4 & 6	103
2	4 & 6	82.3
3	4 & 6	68.3
4	4 & 6	51.3
5	4 & 6	36.3
6	4 & 6	20.3
7	4 & 6	3.3
Washer		
OFF	4 & 6	Open Circuit
ON	4 & 6	0

[1] – Values are approximate.

95J13580   Courtesy of Ford Motor Co.

Fig. 10: Identifying Multifunction Switch Terminals

REMOVAL & INSTALLATION

CAUTION: When battery is disconnected, vehicle computer and memory systems may lose memory data. Driveability problems may exist until computer systems have completed a relearn cycle. See COMPUTER RELEARN PROCEDURES article in GENERAL INFORMATION before disconnecting battery.

GEM

Removal & Installation – Disconnect battery ground cable. Remove two nuts retaining fuse junction panel to dash panel. Pull upper ears of fuse junction panel down out of retaining bracket. Disengage locking tangs and disconnect GEM connectors. Turn fuse junction panel over, remove screw and disconnect GEM from fuse junction panel. To install, reverse removal procedure.

FRONT WASHER PUMP & RESERVOIR

Removal & Installation – 1) Drain radiator until coolant is out of radiator overflow bottle. Disconnect hoses at overflow bottle. Remove power steering oil reservoir retaining screws and position power steering oil reservoir out of the way. Remove overflow bottle return hose and clamp. Remove overflow bottle retainers and remove overflow bottle.

2) Disconnect windshield washer reservoir electrical connector. Remove two washer reservoir retaining nuts near suction accumulator/drier. Raise vehicle on hoist. Remove right front wheel. Remove front half of front fender splash shield. Remove screw retaining washer reservoir to inner fender. Disconnect washer hose and collect washer fluid. Remove washer reservoir. Using small bladed screwdriver pry out washer pump. To install, reverse removal procedure.

FRONT WIPER MOTOR

CAUTION: Wiper motor contains ceramic magnets that may crack or shatter if motor is dropped or handled roughly.

NOTE: Windshield wiper mounting arm and pivot shafts are connected with non-removable plastic ball joints. Assembly is non-repairable except for wiper motor.

Removal & Installation – Disconnect negative battery cable. Remove windshield wiper arms. Remove 8 plastic retainers attaching cowl vent screens to inner panels. Remove 6 clips retaining cowl vent screens to inner panels. Disconnect windshield wiper motor electrical connector. Remove screws retaining windshield wiper assembly to cowl. Remove windshield wiper assembly from vehicle. Remove 3 bolts retaining motor to windshield wiper assembly. To install, reverse removal procedure. Tighten wiper motor mounting bolts 10-12 ft. lbs. (13-17 N.m). Tighten wiper mounting arm and pivot shaft assembly mounting screws 89-124 INCH lbs. (89-124 N.m). Align wiper arms. See WIPER ARM ADJUSTMENT under ADJUSTMENTS.

MULTIFUNCTION SWITCH

Removal & Installation – Disconnect battery ground cable. Tilt column to lowest position. Remove tilt wheel handle. Turn ignition lock cylinder to RUN position. Insert punch through hole in lower steering column shroud. Use punch to press retaining pin while pulling out ignition switch lock cylinder. Remove upper and lower steering column shroud. Remove two screws retaining multifunction switch. Disconnect electrical connectors. Remove multifunction switch. To install, reverse removal procedure.

WIRING DIAGRAMS

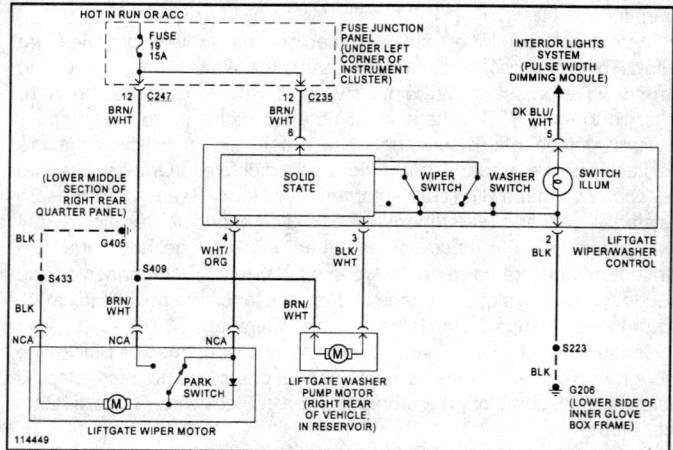

Fig. 11: Rear Wiper/Washer System Wiring Diagram (Sable & Taurus)

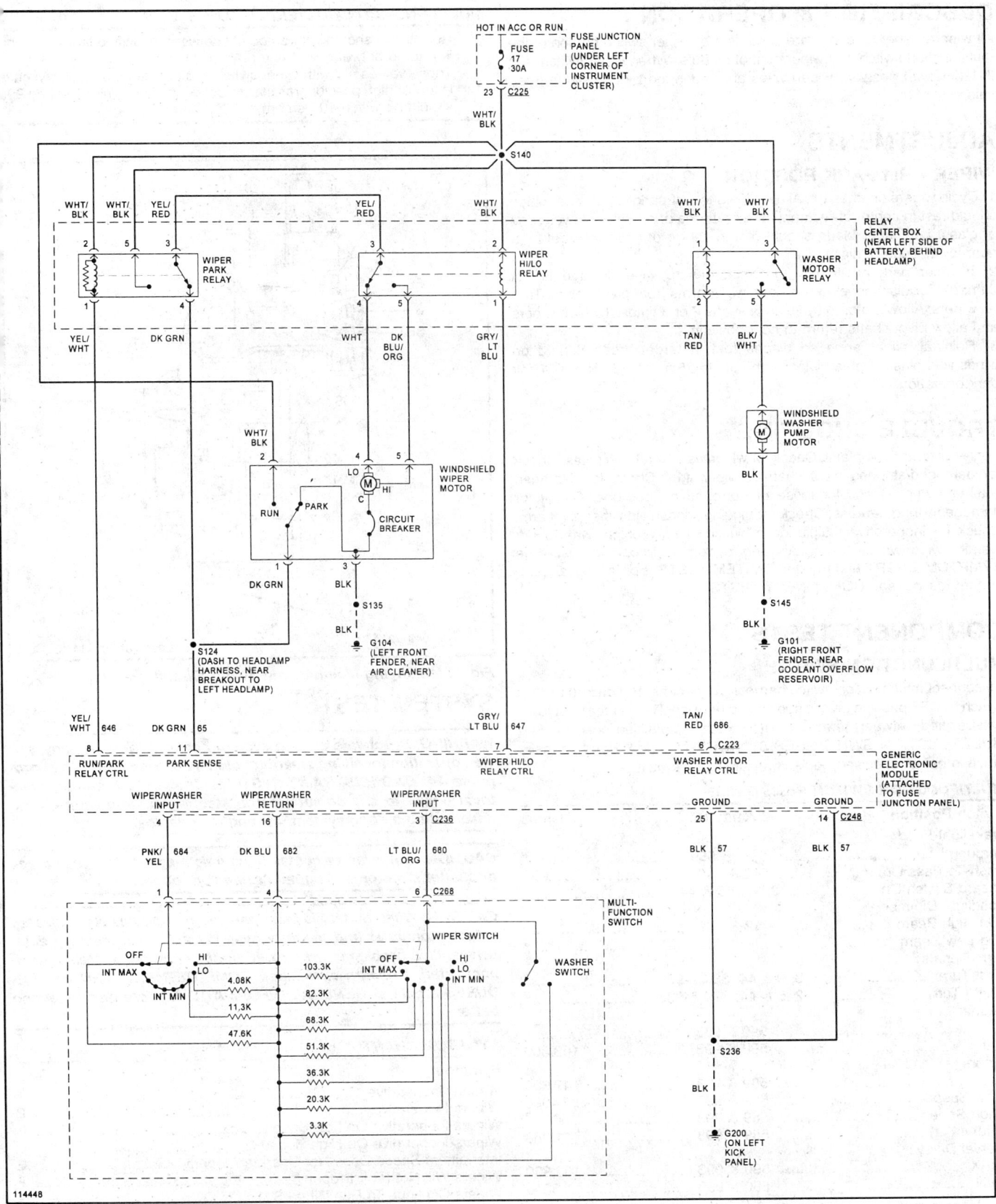

Fig. 12: *Front Wiper/Washer System Wiring Diagram (Sable & Taurus)*

114448

DESCRIPTION & OPERATION

All wiper/washer functions are controlled by wiper switch portion of the multifunction switch and wiper control module. When wiper switch is in INT (interval) position, wipe cycles are separated by adjustable intervals.

ADJUSTMENTS

WIPER ARM PARK POSITION

1) Cycle wipers on, then off. Allow wipers to self-park. Right wiper blade should rest in center of rectangular target area printed near lower edge of glass. Left wiper blade should rest in center of circular target area near lower edge of glass.

2) If wiper park position is incorrect, ensure wiper linkage is not damaged or disconnected. Remove wiper arms from pivot shafts. Turn on wipers. Allow motor to cycle pivot shafts 2 or 3 times. Turn off wipers and allow pivot shafts return to park position.

3) Reinstall wiper arms so blades rest in target areas printed on windshield glass. Tighten wiper arm nuts to 25 ft. lbs. (34 N.m.) Check park operation.

TROUBLE SHOOTING

Verify customer complaint. Check for wiper/washer related fuses. Check for damaged/stripped pivot shaft or wiper arm. Check for damaged washer pump. Check for loose or corroded connections. Check for damaged wiring harness. Check for binding windshield wiper pivot arm. Check for inoperative multifunction switch. If no problem was found, identify wiper/washer symptom and perform appropriate test. See SYMPTOM CHART table under SYSTEM TESTS. For individual component testing, see COMPONENT TESTS.

COMPONENT TESTS

MULTIFUNCTION SWITCH

Disconnect multifunction switch harness connectors. Set hazard flasher switch to OFF position unless specified otherwise. Resistance should be as specified between terminals with switch in specified position. See MULTIFUNCTION SWITCH RESISTANCE table. *See Fig. 1.* If resistance is not as specified, replace multifunction switch.

MULTIFUNCTION SWITCH RESISTANCE

Switch Position	Circuits No.	Ohms
Brakelight Feed		
Through [1]	5, 9, & 569	[2]
Flash-To-Pass On	12 & 910	[2]
Hazard Switch On	2, 3, 5, 9 & 44	[2]
Headlight Dimmer		
On High Beam	12 & 932	[2]
On Low Beam	13 & 932	[2]
Turn Signals [3]		
Left Turn	3, 9 & 44; 380 & 932	[2]
Right Turn	2, 5 & 44; 379 & 932	[2]
Washer		
On	590 & 993	[2]
Off	590 & 993	[4] 103,300
Wipers		
Off	589 & 993	[5] 47,600
Low Speed	589 & 993	[5] 4080
High Speed	589 & 993	[2]
Interval	589 & 993	[5] 11,330
Interval Delay [6] [7]		
MAX	590 & 993	[4] 103,300
MIN	590 & 993	[4] 3300

[1] – Hazard switch off and turn signal switch in neutral position.
[2] – Resistance should be less than 5 ohms.
[3] – Hazard switch MUST be off.
[4] – Resistance may vary by as much as 10 percent.
[5] – Resistance may vary by as much as 15 percent.

[6] – Resistance should vary smoothly between specified limits as knob is rotated between MIN and MAX positions.

[7] – These values are with wiper switch in off position. If wiper switch is in low or high position, resistance between circuits No. 590 and 993 should be within 10 percent of 3300 ohms.

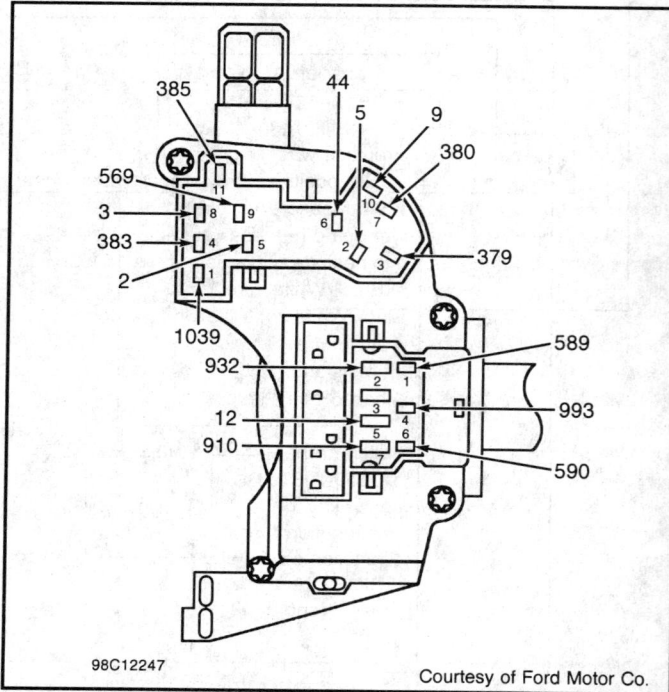

98C12247   Courtesy of Ford Motor Co.

Fig. 1: Identifying Multifunction Switch Circuit Terminals

SYSTEM TESTS

WARNING: Deactivate air bag system before performing any service operation involving steering column components. See appropriate AIR BAG RESTRAINT SYSTEMS article. Do not apply electrical power to any component on steering column without first deactivating air bag system. Air bag may deploy.

CAUTION: Wiper motor contains ceramic magnets that may crack or shatter if motor is dropped or handled roughly.

CAUTION: When battery is disconnected or modules are replaced, vehicle computer and memory systems may lose memory data. Driveability problems may exist until computer systems have completed a relearn cycle. See COMPUTER RELEARN PROCEDURES article in GENERAL INFORMATION before disconnecting battery.

SYMPTOM CHART

Symptom	Test
Washer Inoperative	A
Wipers Inoperative	B
Wipers Inoperative On Low Speed	C
Wipers Inoperative On High Speed	D
Intermittent Speed Does Not Operate Properly	E
Wipers Will Not Park Properly	F
Wipers Continue To Run When Switch Is Off	G

TEST A: WASHER INOPERATIVE

1) Turn ignition switch to RUN position. Press washer switch. If washer pump operates, go to next step. If washer pump does not operate, go to step **3)**.

2) Turn ignition switch to LOCK position. Inspect pump, nozzles, and hoses for obstructions or kinked hoses. If obstructions exist, repair as necessary. If no obstructions exist, replace washer pump.

3) Turn ignition switch to LOCK position. Disconnect washer pump harness connector C1022. Turn ignition switch to RUN position. Measure voltage at Black/White wire at washer pump harness connector while operating washer switch. Battery voltage should exist when washer switch is pressed and zero volts should exists when washer switch is not pressed. If voltage is as specified, go to next step. If voltage is not as specified, go to step **5)**.

4) Turn ignition switch to LOCK position. Measure resistance between ground and Black wire at washer pump harness connector C1022. If resistance is greater than 5 ohms, repair open in Black wire. If resistance is 5 ohms or less, replace washer pump.

5) Turn ignition switch to LOCK position. Disconnect wiper control module harness connector C294. Measure resistance between ground and Black/White wire at washer pump harness connector. If resistance is greater than 10 k/ohms, go to next step. If resistance is 10 k/ohms or less, repair short to ground in Black/White wire.

6) Measure resistance in Black/White wire between washer pump harness connector and terminal No. 4 at wiper control module harness connector C294. See Fig. 2. If resistance is 5 ohms or less, go to next step. If resistance is greater than 5 ohms, repair open in Black/White wire.

7) Disconnect multifunction switch harness connectors. Test multifunction switch. See MULTIFUNCTION SWITCH under COMPONENT TESTS. If wiper washer switch is okay, go to next step. If wiper/washer switch is defective, replace multifunction switch.

8) Check wiring between multifunction switch and wiper control module for open and/or shorts. See WIRING DIAGRAMS. If open or short exists, repair wiring as necessary. If open or short does not exist, replace wiper control module.

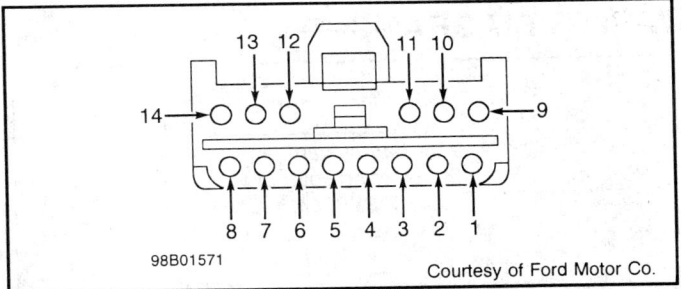

98B01571   Courtesy of Ford Motor Co.

Fig. 2: Identifying Wiper Control Module Harness Connector C294 Terminals

TEST B: WIPERS INOPERATIVE

1) Turn ignition switch to LOCK position. Check fuse No. 16 (30-amp) in instrument panel fuse box. If fuse is okay, go to next step. If fuse is blown, replace fuse. If fuse repeatedly fails, repair short to ground in Dark Green. See WIRING DIAGRAMS.

2) Turn ignition switch to LOCK position. Disconnect wiper control module harness connector C294. Measure voltage at terminals No. 2 and 11 (both Dark Green wires) at wiper control module harness connector C294. *See Fig. 2.* If battery voltage exists at both terminals, go to next step. If battery voltage does not exist at either terminal, repair open in Dark Green wire.

3) Turn ignition switch to LOCK position. Measure resistance between ground and terminals No. 3 and 5 (both Black wires) at wiper control module harness connector C294. If both resistance reading are 5 ohms or less, go to next step. If either resistance reading is greater than 5 ohms, repair open in Black wire.

4) Ensure ignition switch is in LOCK position. Disconnect multifunction switch harness connectors. Test multifunction switch. See MULTIFUNCTION SWITCH under COMPONENT TESTS. If multifunction switch is okay, go to next step. If multifunction switch is defective, replace multifunction switch.

5) Ensure multifunction switch harness connectors are still disconnected. Measure resistance in Brown/White wire between terminal No. 4 at multifunction switch harness connector C269 and terminal No. 7 at wiper control module harness connector C294. *See Figs. 2 and 3.* If resistance is 5 ohms or less, go to next step. If resistance is greater than 5 ohms, repair open Brown/White wire.

6) Measure resistance in Orange wire between terminal No. 1 at multifunction switch harness connector C269 and terminal No. 1 at wiper control module harness connector C294. If resistance is 5 ohms or less, go to next step. If resistance is greater than 5 ohms, repair open in Orange wire.

7) Connect wiper control module harness connector C294 and multifunction switch harness connectors. Disconnect wiper motor harness connector C152. Turn wiper switch to high speed position. Turn ignition switch to RUN position. Measure voltage between terminals No. 3 (Dark Blue/Orange wire) and No. 4 (Black wire) at wiper motor harness connector C152. *See Fig. 4.* If battery voltage does not exist, go to next step. If battery voltage exists, replace wiper motor.

8) Turn ignition switch to LOCK position. Measure resistance between ground and terminal No. 4 (Black wire) at wiper motor harness connector C152. If resistance is 5 ohms or less, replace wiper control module. If resistance is greater than 5 ohms, repair open in Black wire.

NOTE: For Figs. 3 and 4, see LATEST CHANGES & CORRECTIONS.

TEST C: WIPERS INOPERATIVE ON LOW SPEED

1) Turn ignition switch to LOCK position. Disconnect wiper motor harness connector C152. Turn ignition switch to RUN position. Turn wiper switch to low speed position. Measure voltage between terminal No. 1 (White wire) and No. 4 (Black wire) at wiper motor harness connector C152. *See Fig. 4.* If battery voltage does not exist, go to next step. If battery voltage exists, replace wiper motor.

2) Disconnect wiper control module harness connector C294. Measure resistance between ground and terminal No. 1 (White wire) at wiper motor harness connector C152. If resistance is greater than 10 k/ohms, go to next step. If resistance is 10 k/ohms or less, repair short to ground in White wire.

3) Measure resistance in White wire between terminal No. 1 at wiper motor harness connector C152 and terminal No. 8 at wiper control module harness connector C294. *See Figs. 2 and 4.* If resistance is 5 ohms or less, go to next step. If resistance is greater than 5 ohms, repair open in White wire.

4) Disconnect multifunction switch harness connectors. Test multifunction switch. See MULTIFUNCTION SWITCH under COMPONENT TESTS. If multifunction switch is defective, replace multifunction switch. If multifunction switch is okay, replace wiper control module.

TEST D: WIPERS INOPERATIVE ON HIGH SPEED

1) Turn ignition switch to LOCK position. Disconnect wiper motor harness connector C152. Turn wiper switch to high speed position. Measure voltage between terminals No. 3 (Dark Blue/Orange wire) and No. 4 (Black wire) at wiper motor harness connector C152. *See Fig. 4.* If battery voltage does not exist, go to next step. If battery voltage exists, replace wiper motor.

2) Turn ignition switch to LOCK position. Disconnect wiper control module harness connector C294. Measure resistance between ground and terminal No. 3 (Dark Blue/Orange wire) at wiper motor harness connector C152. If resistance is greater than 10 k/ohms, go to next step. If resistance is 10 k/ohms or less, repair short to ground in Dark Blue/Orange wire.

3) Measure resistance in Dark Blue/Orange wire between terminal No. 3 at wiper motor harness connector C152 and terminal No. 14 at wiper control module harness connector C294. *See Figs. 2 and 4.* If resistance is 5 ohms or less, go to next step. If resistance is greater than 5 ohms, repair in open Dark Blue/Orange wire.

4) Disconnect multifunction switch harness connectors. Test multifunction switch. See MULTIFUNCTION SWITCH under COMPONENT TESTS. If multifunction switch is defective, replace multifunction switch. If multifunction switch is okay, replace wiper control module.

TEST E: INTERMITTENT SPEED DOES NOT OPERATE PROPERLY

1) Disconnect multifunction switch harness connectors. Test multifunction switch. See MULTIFUNCTION SWITCH under COMPONENT TESTS. If multifunction switch is okay, go to next step. If multifunction switch is defective, replace multifunction switch.

2) Disconnect wiper control module harness connector C294. Measure resistance between ground and terminal No. 9 (Dark Blue/White wire) at wiper control module harness connector C294. *See Fig. 2.* If resistance is greater than 10 k/ohms, go to next step. If resistance is 10 k/ohms or less, repair short to ground in Dark Blue/White wire.

3) Measure resistance in Dark Blue/White wire between terminal No. 6 at multifunction switch harness connector C269 and terminal No. 9 at wiper control module harness connector C294. *See Figs. 2 and 3.* If resistance is 5 ohms or less, replace wiper control module. If resistance is greater than 5 ohms, repair open in Dark Blue/White wire.

TEST F: WIPERS WILL NOT PARK PROPERLY

1) Turn ignition switch to LOCK position. Disconnect wiper motor harness connector C152. Turn ignition switch to RUN position. Measure voltage at terminal No. 8 (Dark Green wire) at wiper motor harness connector C152. *See Fig. 4.* If battery voltage exists, go to next step. If battery voltage does not exist, repair open in Dark Green wire.

2) Turn ignition switch to LOCK position. Measure resistance between terminal No. 7 (Black/Pink wire) and terminal No. 1 (White wire) at wiper motor harness connector C152. If resistance is greater than 5 ohms, go to next step. If resistance is 5 ohms or less, go to step **4)**.

3) Measure resistance in White wire between terminal No. 1 at wiper motor harness connector C152 and terminal No. 8 at wiper control module harness connector C294. Also measure resistance in Black/Pink wire between terminal No. 7 at wiper motor harness connector C152 and terminal No. 13 at wiper control module harness connector C294. *See Figs. 2 and 4.* If both resistance readings are 5 ohms or less, replace wiper control module. If either resistance reading is greater than 5 ohms, repair open in appropriate circuit.

4) Inspect wiper linkage. Ensure linkage is not bent, cracked or disconnected. If problem exists, repair or replace if necessary. If problem does not exist, replace wiper motor.

TEST G: WIPERS CONTINUE TO RUN WHEN SWITCH IS OFF

1) Disconnect multifunction switch harness connectors. Test multifunction switch. See MULTIFUNCTION SWITCH under COMPONENT TESTS. If multifunction switch is okay, go to next step. If multifunction switch is defective, replace multifunction switch.

2) Disconnect wiper control module harness connector C294. Measure resistance between ground and terminal No. 1 (Orange wire) at wiper control module harness connector C294. *See Fig. 2.* If resistance is greater than 10 k/ohms, go to next step. If resistance is 10 k/ohms or less, repair open/short in Orange wire.

3) Measure resistance between ground and terminal No. 7 (Brown/White wire) at wiper control module harness connector C294. If resistance is greater than 10 k/ohms, go to next step. If resistance is 10 k/ohms or less, repair open/short in Brown/White wire.

4) Measure resistance between ground and terminal No. 9 (Dark Blue/White wire) at wiper control module harness connector C294. If resistance is greater than 10 k/ohms, replace wiper control module. If resistance is 10 k/ohms or less, repair open/short in Brown/White wire.

REMOVAL & INSTALLATION

WARNING: Deactivate air bag system before performing any service operation involving steering column components. See appropriate AIR BAG RESTRAINT SYSTEMS article. Do not apply electrical power to any component on steering column without first deactivating air bag system. Air bag may deploy.

CAUTION: When battery is disconnected or modules are replaced, vehicle computer and memory systems may lose memory data. Driveability problems may exist until computer systems have completed a relearn cycle. See COMPUTER RELEARN PROCEDURES article in GENERAL INFORMATION before disconnecting battery.

WIPER MOTOR

CAUTION: Wiper motor contains ceramic magnets that may crack or shatter if motor is dropped or handled roughly.

Removal & Installation – 1) Disconnect battery ground cable. Remove rear hood seal. Remove wiper arms. Remove cowl vent screens. Unplug harness connector from motor. Remove wiper motor.

2) Unsnap and remove wiper linkage cover. Lift locking tab, and pull clip away from shaft to disengage linkage from operating arm on motor. Remove motor. To install, reverse removal procedure.

MULTIFUNCTION SWITCH

Removal & Installation – Wiper/washer switch is incorporated into multifunction switch on steering column. Disconnect battery ground cable. Separate and remove steering column cover halves. Disconnect multifunction switch harness connectors. Remove multifunction switch. To install, reverse removal procedure.

WIRING DIAGRAMS

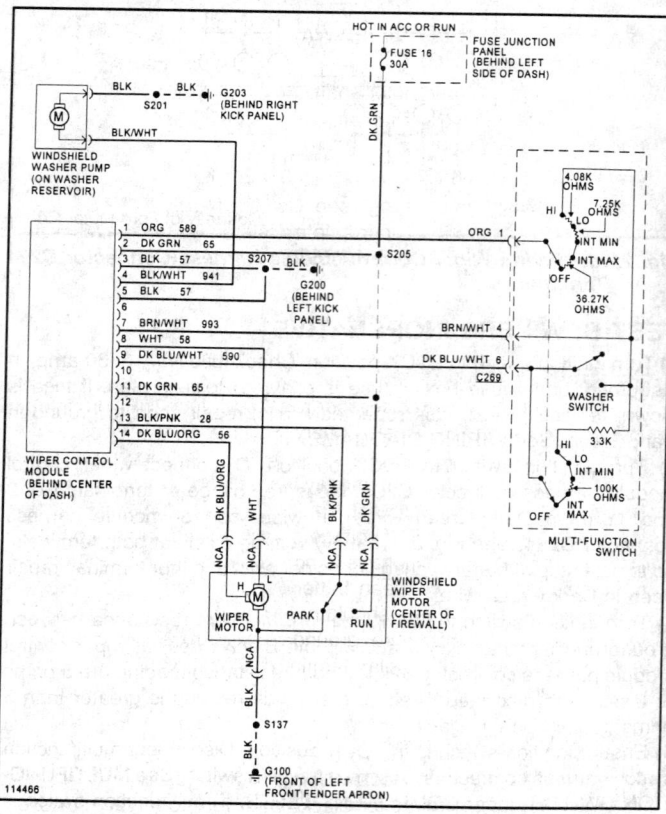

Fig. 3: Wiper/Washer System Wiring Diagram (Town Car)

DESCRIPTION & OPERATION

Front wiper/washer functions are controlled by the multifunction switch and Front Wiper/Washer Amplifier (FWWA). FWWA is located on front of left front strut tower. Wiper/washer switch is incorporated into multifunction switch on steering column. When wiper/washer switch is in INT (interval) position, wipe cycles are separated by adjustable intervals. FWWA sends constant voltage to multifunction switch and grounds appropriate circuit based on returned voltage value.

Rear wiper/washer switch is located to right of instrument cluster. Vehicles with movable liftgate glass have liftgate glass ajar switch. Liftgate ajar switch prevents rear wiper operation when liftgate glass is open. Same switch causes rear wiper to drop about 3" (76 mm) when liftgate latch is released.

ADJUSTMENTS

WIPER ARM

Front wiper arms are not adjustable. To adjust rear wiper arm, remove rear wiper pivot arm and wiper blade. Turn ignition on. Depress rear window wiper/washer switch and allow rear wiper motor to cycle 3-4 times. Turn ignition off. Adjust rear wiper arm so outer tip of blade is about 1.2" (30 mm) from bottom of window.

TROUBLE SHOOTING

Before performing any tests on wiper/washer system, verify customer complaint. Visually check following for obvious signs of electrical and mechanical damage:

- Fuse junction panel fuses: F44 (10-amp), F46 (20-amp) and F58 (10-amp).
- Loose or corroded connectors.
- Damaged wiring harness.
- Wiper motor.
- Washer pump motor.
- Front Wiper/Washer Amplifier (FWWA) assembly.
- Multifunction Switch.
- Damaged/stripped wiper motor shaft.
- Damaged/stripped pivot arm shaft.
- Empty washer reservoir.
- Washer hoses and nozzles.

For individual component testing, see COMPONENT TESTS. If all components are okay, perform appropriate system test. See SYMPTOM TEST INDEX table under SYSTEM TESTS.

COMPONENT TESTS

ACCESSORY RELAY

1) Turn ignition off. Remove accessory relay from fuse junction panel. Connect a jumper wire between battery positive terminal and relay terminals No. 1 and 5. *See Fig. 1.*
2) Voltage should not be present at relay terminal No. 3. Using another jumper wire, ground relay terminal No. 2. Battery voltage should be present at relay terminal No. 3. If voltage is as specified, remove jumper wires and go to next step. If voltage is not as specified, replace relay.
3) Connect jumper wires between battery positive terminal and relay terminals No. 1 and 7. Voltage should not be present at relay terminal No. 6. Using another jumper wire, ground relay terminal No. 2. Battery voltage should be present at relay terminal No. 6. If voltage is not as specified, replace relay.

FRONT WASHER PUMP

Disconnect washer pump connector. Using 10-amp fused jumper wire, connect washer pump terminal for Black/White wire to battery positive terminal. Connect pump terminal for Yellow/Red wire to ground. Replace pump if it does not operate.

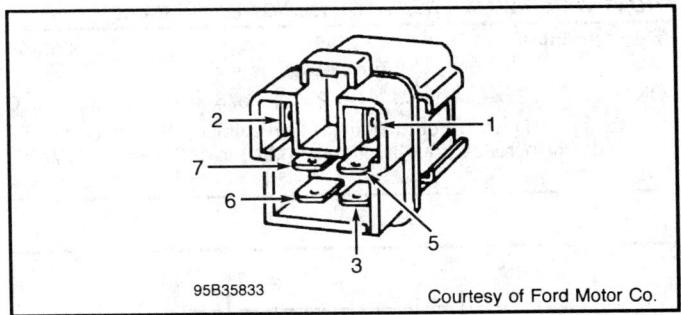

95B35833   Courtesy of Ford Motor Co.

Fig. 1: Identifying Accessory Relay Terminals

FRONT WIPER MOTOR

1) Disengage wiper arm linkage from wiper motor. Disconnect wiper motor 6-pin connector. Using 20-amp fused jumper wire, connect battery positive terminal to wiper motor terminal No. 6. *See Fig. 2.*
2) Using second jumper wire, ground wiper motor terminal No. 2. Motor should run at low speed. Disconnect jumper wire from terminal No. 2 and connect it to wiper motor terminal No. 1. Motor should run at high speed. If wiper motor operates as specified, go to next step. If wiper motor does not operate as specified, replace wiper motor.
3) Reconnect wiper motor 6-pin connector. Turn ignition on. Cycle wipers until they reach fully parked position. Turn ignition off. Disconnect wiper motor 6-pin connector. Measure resistances between wiper motor terminals as indicated. See FRONT WIPER MOTOR RESISTANCES table. *See Fig. 2.* If resistances are as indicated, wiper motor is okay. If resistances are not as specified, replace wiper motor. See WIPER MOTOR under REMOVAL & INSTALLATION.

FRONT WIPER MOTOR RESISTANCES

Front Wiper Position	Terminals 5 & 6	Terminals 4 & 5
Park	Less Than 5 Ohms	Greater Than 10 k/ohms
Run	Greater Than 10 k/ohms	Less Than 5 Ohms

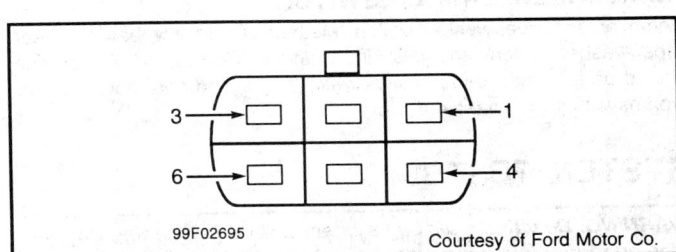

99F02695   Courtesy of Ford Motor Co.

Fig. 2: Identifying Front Wiper Motor Terminals

FRONT WIPER/WASHER SWITCH

Wiper/washer switch is incorporated into multifunction switch on steering column. Disconnect multifunction switch 10-pin connector. Measure resistance between specified terminals. See FRONT WIPER/WASHER SWITCH RESISTANCES table. *See Fig. 3.* If resistances are not as specified, replace multifunction switch. See WIPER/WASHER SWITCH under REMOVAL & INSTALLATION.

FRONT WIPER/WASHER SWITCH RESISTANCES

Switch Position	Switch Terminals	k/ohms
OFF	2 & 3	47.60
FAST	2 & 3	11.33
LOW	2 & 3	4.08
HIGH	2 & 3	0
INT Delay [1]		
MIN	1 & 2	3.30
MAX	1 & 2	103.30
WASH		
OFF	1 & 2	103,300

FRONT WIPER/WASHER SWITCH RESISTANCES (Cont.)

Switch Position	Switch Terminals	k/ohms
ON	1 & 2	0

[1] – Rotate (INT) knob from minimum to maximum. Reistance should gradually increase from 3.3 k/ohms (MIN) to 103.3 k/ohms (MAX).

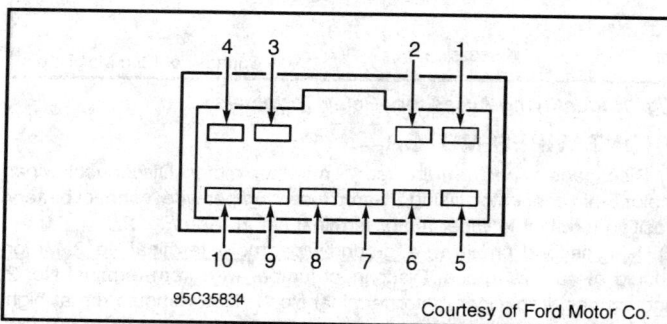

95C35834

Courtesy of Ford Motor Co.

Fig. 3: Identifying Front Wiper/Washer Switch Terminals

REAR WASHER PUMP

Disconnect washer pump connector. Using 10-amp fused jumper wire, connect washer pump terminal for Yellow/Black wire to battery positive terminal. Connect pump terminal for Blue wire to ground. Replace pump if it does not operate.

REAR WIPER MOTOR

For diagnosis of rear wiper motor with fixed rear window, see TEST I: REAR WIPER INOPERATIVE (FIXED REAR WINDOW) under SYSTEM TESTS. For diagnosis of rear wiper motor with movable rear window, see TEST J: REAR WIPER INOPERATIVE (MOVABLE REAR WINDOW) under SYSTEM TESTS.

REAR WIPER/WASHER SWITCH

Remove rear wiper/washer switch. Measure resistance between rear wiper/washer switch terminals No. 2 and 6. See Fig. 4. Resistance should be less than 5 ohms with switch depressed and more than 10 k/ohms with switch released.

SYSTEM TESTS

WARNING: Deactivate air bag system before performing any service operation involving steering column components. See appropriate AIR BAG RESTRAINT SYSTEMS article. Do not apply electrical power to any component on steering column without first deactivating air bag system. Air bag may deploy.

CAUTION: When battery is disconnected, vehicle computer and memory systems may lose memory data. Driveability problems may exist until computer systems have completed a relearn cycle. See COMPUTER RELEARN PROCEDURES article in GENERAL INFORMATION before disconnecting battery.

SYMPTOM TEST INDEX

Symptom	Test
Front Washer Inoperative	A
Front Wipers Inoperative	B
Front Wipers Inoperative At High Speed	C
Front Wipers Inoperative At Low Speed	D
Front Wipers Inoperative At Interval Setting	E
Front Wipers Will Not Park Properly	F
Front Wipers Continue To Run When Switch Is Off	G
Rear Washer Inoperative	H
Rear Wiper Inoperative	

SYMPTOM TEST INDEX (Cont.)

Symptom	Tes
Fixed Rear Window	
Movable Rear Window	
Rear Wiper Will Not Park Properly	
Fixed Rear Window	K
Movable Rear Window	
Rear Wiper Will Not Turn Off	L
Rear Wiper Will Not Move To Liftgate Window Open Position	M

[1] – Replace rear wiper motor.

TEST A: FRONT WASHER INOPERATIVE

NOTE: After repairs, retest system for normal operation.

1) Disconnect front washer pump 2-pin connector. Connector is located near right headlight. Turn ignition on. Measure voltage between front washer pump connector Black/White wire terminal and ground. If battery voltage exists, go to next step. If battery voltage does not exist, repair Black/White wire between washer pump connector and fuse F46 (20-amp).

2) Turn ignition off. Connect 10-amp fused jumper wire between front washer pump terminal for Black/White wire and battery positive terminal. Ground front washer pump motor terminal for Yellow/Red wire. If front washer pump is inoperative, replace pump. See WASHER PUMP & RESERVOIR under REMOVAL & INSTALLATION. If washer pump operates, go to next step.

3) Disconnect Front Wiper/Washer Amplifier (FWWA) 6-pin connector. FWWA is located on front of left front strut tower. Measure resistance of Yellow/Red wire between front washer pump connector and FWWA 6-pin connector. If resistance is less than 5 ohms, go to next step. If resistance is 5 ohms or more, repair open in Yellow/Red wire.

4) Test front wiper/washer switch. See FRONT WIPER/WASHER SWITCH under COMPONENT TESTS. If switch is faulty, replace multifunction switch. See WIPER/WASHER SWITCH under REMOVAL & INSTALLATION. If switch is okay, go to next step.

5) Turn ignition off. Disconnect FWWA 4-pin connector. Disconnect multifunction switch 10-pin connector. Measure resistance of Pink wire between FWWA 4-pin connector and multifunction switch 10-pin connector. Also measure resistance of Pink wire between multifunction switch 10-pin connector and ground. If resistance is less than 5 ohms between FWWA connector and multifunction switch connector, and more than 10 k/ohms between multifunction switch connector and ground, go to next step. If resistances are not as indicated, repair open or short to ground in Pink wire.

6) Measure resistance of Green wire between multifunction switch 10-pin connector and FWWA 4-pin connector. Also measure resistance of Green wire between multifunction switch 10-pin connector and ground. If resistance is less than 5 ohms between multifunction switch connector and FWWA connector, and more than 10 k/ohms between multifunction switch connector and ground, go to next step. If resistances are not as indicated, repair open or short to ground in Green wire.

7) Turn ignition off. Measure resistance of Black wire between FWWA 6-pin connector and ground. Also measure resistance of Black wire between FWWA 4-pin connector and ground. If resistances are less than 5 ohms, replace FWWA. If either resistance is 5 ohms or more, repair open in Black wire. Grounds points are located at FWWA and left front strut tower.

TEST B: FRONT WIPERS INOPERATIVE

NOTE: After repairs, retest system for normal operation.

1) Disconnect front wiper motor 6-pin connector. Turn ignition on. Measure voltage between wiper motor 6-pin connector Black/White wire and ground. If battery voltage exists, go to next step. If battery voltage does not exist, repair Black/White wire.

2) Test accessory relay. See ACCESSORY RELAY under COMPONENT TESTS. If relay is okay, go to next step. If relay is faulty, replace relay.

3) Test front wiper/washer switch. See FRONT WIPER/WASHER SWITCH under COMPONENT TESTS. If switch is okay, go to next step. If switch is faulty, replace multifunction switch. See WIPER/WASHER SWITCH under REMOVAL & INSTALLATION.

4) Test front wiper motor. See FRONT WIPER MOTOR under COMPONENT TESTS. If wiper motor is faulty, replace wiper motor. See WIPER MOTOR under REMOVAL & INSTALLATION. If wiper motor is okay, go to next step.

5) Disconnect Front Wiper/Washer Amplifier (FWWA) assembly 4-pin and 6-pin connectors. Measure resistances of Black wires between FWWA 4-pin and 6-pin connectors and ground. Also measure resistance of Black wire between front wiper motor 6-pin connector and ground. If each resistance is less than 5 ohms, go to next step. If any resistance is 5 ohms or more, repair Black wire(s). Ground points are located at FWWA and left front strut tower. See WIRING DIAGRAMS.

6) Disconnect multifunction switch 10-pin connector. Measure resistance of White wire between multifunction switch 10-pin connector and FWWA 4-pin connector. Also measure resistance of White wire between multifunction switch 10-pin connector and ground. If resistance is less than 5 ohms between multifunction switch connector and FWWA connector, and more than 10 k/ohms between multifunction switch connector and ground, go to next step. If resistances are not as indicated, repair open or short to ground in White wire.

7) Measure resistance of Pink wire between multifunction switch 10-pin connector and FWWA 4-pin connector. Also measure resistance of Pink wire between multifunction switch 10-pin connector and ground. If resistance is less than 5 ohms between multifunction switch connector and FWWA connector, and more than 10 k/ohms between multifunction switch connector and ground, go to next step. If resistances are not as indicated, repair open or short to ground in Pink wire.

8) Measure resistance of Green wire between multifunction switch 10-pin connector and FWWA 4-pin connector. Also measure resistance of Green wire between multifunction switch 10-pin connector and ground. If resistance is less than 5 ohms between multifunction switch connector and FWWA connector, and more than 10 k/ohms between multifunction switch connector and ground, replace FWWA. If resistances are not as indicated, repair open or short to ground in Green wire.

TEST C: FRONT WIPERS INOPERATIVE AT HIGH SPEED

NOTE: After repairs, retest system for normal operation.

1) Disconnect front wiper motor 6-pin connector. Measure resistance of Blue/Orange wire between front wiper motor 6-pin connector and Front Wiper/Washer Amplifier (FWWA) 6-pin connector. Also measure resistance of Blue/Orange wire between front wiper motor 6-pin connector and ground. If resistance is less than 5 ohms between front wiper motor connector and FWWA connector, and more than 10 k/ohms between front wiper motor connector and ground, go to next step. If resistances are not as indicated, repair open or short to ground in Blue/Orange wire.

2) Test front wiper motor. See FRONT WIPER MOTOR under COMPONENT TESTS. If wiper motor is faulty, replace motor. See WIPER MOTOR under REMOVAL & INSTALLATION. If wiper motor is okay, go to next step.

3) Test front wiper/washer switch. See FRONT WIPER/WASHER SWITCH under COMPONENT TESTS. If switch is faulty, replace multifunction switch. See WIPER/WASHER SWITCH under REMOVAL & INSTALLATION. If switch is okay, replace FWWA. FWWA is located on front of left front strut tower.

TEST D: FRONT WIPERS INOPERATIVE AT LOW SPEED

NOTE: After repairs, retest system for normal operation.

1) Turn ignition off. Disconnect front wiper motor 6-pin connector. Disconnect Front Wiper/Washer Amplifier (FWWA) 6-pin connector. FWWA is located on front of left front strut tower. Measure resistance of Brown/White wire between wiper motor 6-pin connector and FWWA

6-pin connector. Also measure resistance of Brown/White wire between wiper motor 6-pin connector and ground. If resistance is less than 5 ohms between wiper motor connector and FWWA connector, and more than 10 k/ohms between wiper motor connector and ground, go to next step. If resistances are not as indicated, repair open or short to ground in Brown/White wire.

2) Test front wiper motor. See FRONT WIPER MOTOR under COMPONENT TESTS. If wiper motor is okay, go to next step. If wiper motor is faulty, replace wiper motor. See WIPER MOTOR under REMOVAL & INSTALLATION.

3) Test front wiper/washer switch. See FRONT WIPER/WASHER SWITCH under COMPONENT TESTS. If switch is okay, replace FWWA. If switch is faulty, replace multifunction switch. See WIPER/WASHER SWITCH under REMOVAL & INSTALLATION.

TEST E: FRONT WIPERS INOPERATIVE AT INTERVAL SETTING

NOTE: After repairs, retest system for normal operation.

Test front wiper/washer switch. See FRONT WIPER/WASHER SWITCH under COMPONENT TESTS. If switch is okay, replace Front Wiper Washer Amplifier (FWWA). FWWA is located on front of front left strut tower. If switch is faulty, replace multifunction switch. See WIPER/WASHER SWITCH under REMOVAL & INSTALLATION.

TEST F: FRONT WIPERS DO NOT PARK PROPERLY

NOTE: After repairs, retest system for normal operation.

1) Test front wiper motor. See FRONT WIPER MOTOR under COMPONENT TESTS. If wiper motor is okay, go to next step. If wiper motor is faulty, replace motor. See WIPER MOTOR under REMOVAL & INSTALLATION.

2) Disconnect Front Wiper/Washer Amplifier (FWWA) 6-pin connector and front wiper motor 6-pin connector. Measure resistance of Red wire between FWWA 6-pin connector and wiper motor 6-pin connector. If resistance is less than 5 ohms, go to next step. If resistance is 5 ohms or more, repair open in Red wire.

3) Measure resistance of Brown/White wire between wiper motor 6-pin connector and FWWA 6-pin connector. If resistance is less than 5 ohms, replace FWWA. FWWA is located on front of left front strut tower. If resistance is 5 ohms or more, repair open in Brown/White wire.

TEST G: FRONT WIPERS RUN WITH SWITCH OFF

NOTE: After repairs, retest system for normal operation.

1) Test front wiper/washer switch. See FRONT WIPER/WASHER SWITCH under COMPONENT TESTS. If switch is okay, go to next step. If switch is faulty, replace switch. See WIPER/WASHER SWITCH under REMOVAL & INSTALLATION.

2) Turn ignition off. Disconnect wiper motor 6-pin connector and Front Wiper/Washer Amplifier (FWWA) 6-pin connector. FWWA is located on front of left front strut tower. Measure resistance of Blue/Orange wire between FWWA 6-pin connector and ground. If resistance is more than 10 k/ohms, go to next step. If resistance is 10 k/ohms or less, repair Blue/Orange wire short to ground.

3) Measure resistance of Brown/White wire between FWWA 6-pin connector and ground. If resistance is more than 10 k/ohms, go to next step. If resistance is 10 k/ohms or less, repair Brown/White wire short to ground.

4) Measure resistance of Red wire between FWWA 6-pin connector and front wiper motor 6-pin connector. Also measure resistance of Red wire between FWWA 6-pin connector and ground. If resistances are less than 5 ohms between FWWA connector and front wiper motor connector, and more than 10 k/ohms between FWWA connector and ground, replace FWWA. If resistances are not as indicated, repair open or short to ground in Red wire.

TEST H: REAR WASHER INOPERATIVE

NOTE: After repairs, retest system for normal operation.

1) Turn ignition off. Disconnect rear window washer pump 2-pin connector. Connector is located near right headlight. Connect 10-amp fused jumper wire between battery positive terminal and washer pump motor terminal for Yellow/Black wire. Ground washer pump motor terminal for Blue wire. If washer pump operates, go to next step. If washer pump does not operate, replace pump.

2) Turn ignition on. Measure voltage between washer motor 2-pin connector Yellow/Black wire terminal and ground. If battery voltage exists, go to next step. If battery voltage does not exist, repair Yellow/Black wire.

3) Remove rear wiper/washer switch. Measure resistance between rear wiper/washer switch terminals No. 1 and 2. *See Fig. 4.* If resistance is less than 5 ohms with switch depressed, and more than 10 k/ohms with switch released, repair Blue wire. See WIRING DIAGRAMS. If resistances are not as indicated, replace switch.

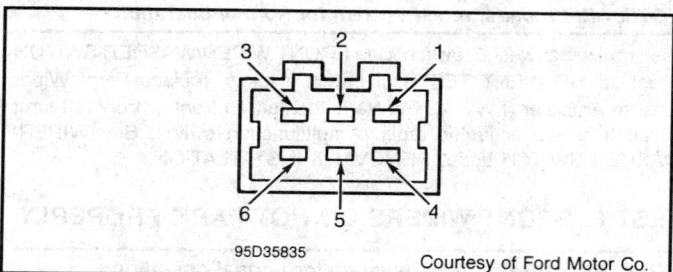

Fig. 4: Identifying Rear Wiper/Washer Switch Terminals

TEST I: REAR WIPER INOPERATIVE (FIXED REAR WINDOW)

NOTE: After repairs, retest system for normal operation.

1) Remove rear wiper/washer switch. Measure resistance between rear wiper/washer switch terminals No. 6 and 2. *See Fig. 4.* If resistance is less than 5 ohms with switch depressed, and more than 10 k/ohms with switch released, go to next step. If resistances are not as indicated, replace rear wiper/washer switch.

2) Turn ignition off. Disconnect rear wiper motor 4-pin connector. Connect 10-amp fused jumper wire between battery positive terminal and rear wiper motor terminal No. 1. Ground rear wiper motor terminal No. 3. *See Fig. 5.* If wiper motor runs, go to next step. If wiper motor does not run, replace rear wiper motor. See WIPER MOTOR under REMOVAL & INSTALLATION.

3) Turn ignition on. Measure voltage between rear wiper motor 4-pin connector Yellow/Black wire and ground. If battery voltage exists, go to next step. If battery voltage does not exist, repair Yellow/Black wire. See WIRING DIAGRAMS.

4) Turn ignition off. Disconnect rear wiper/washer switch 6-pin connector. Measure resistance of Black wire between rear wiper/washer switch 6-pin connector terminal and ground. Also measure resistance of Black wire between rear wiper motor 4-pin connector and ground. If each resistance is less than 5 ohms, go to next step. If any resistance is 5 ohms or more, repair open in appropriate Black wire(s). Ground points are located on lower and center left D-pillar.

5) Measure resistance of Blue/Yellow wire between rear wiper motor 4-pin connector and rear wiper/washer switch 6-pin connector. Also measure resistance of Blue/Yellow wire between rear wiper motor 4-pin connector and ground. If resistance is less than 5 ohms between rear wiper motor connector and rear wiper/washer switch connector, and more than 10 k/ohms between rear wiper motor connector and ground, repair Blue wire. See WIRING DIAGRAMS. If resistances are not as indicated, repair open or short to ground in Blue/Yellow wire.

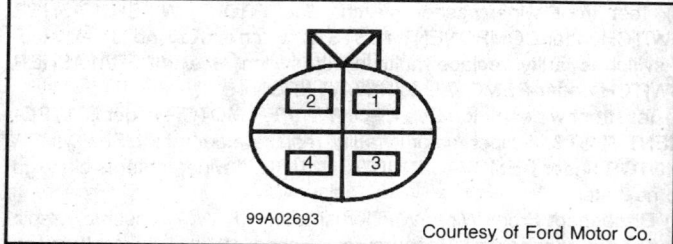

99A02693
Courtesy of Ford Motor Co.

Fig. 5: Identifying Rear Wiper Motor Terminals – Fixed Rear Window

TEST J: REAR WIPER INOPERATIVE (MOVABLE REAR WINDOW)

NOTE: After repairs, retest system for normal operation.

1) Remove rear wiper/washer switch. Measure resistance between rear wiper/washer switch terminals No. 6 and 2. *See Fig. 4.* If resistance is less than 5 ohms with switch depressed, and more than 10 k/ohms with switch released, go to next step. If resistances are not as indicated, replace rear wiper/washer switch.

2) Turn ignition off. Disconnect rear wiper motor 6-pin connector. Connect 2 10-amp fused jumper wires between battery positive and rear wiper motor terminals for Purple and Yellow/Black wires. Using 2 jumper wires, ground rear wiper motor terminals for Black wire and Black/Yellow wire. If rear wiper motor runs, go to next step. If rear wiper motor does not run, replace wiper motor. See WIPER MOTOR under REMOVAL & INSTALLATION.

3) Turn ignition off. Disconnect liftgate glass switch 2-pin connector. Measure resistance across liftgate glass switch terminals. If resistance is more than 10 k/ohms with switch in CLOSED position, and less than 5 ohms with switch in OPEN position, go to next step. If resistances are not as indicated, replace liftgate glass switch.

4) Measure resistance of Black/Yellow wire between liftgate glass switch 2-pin connector and ground. If resistance is more than 10 k/ohms, go to next step. If resistance is 10 k/ohms or less, repair Black/Yellow wire short to ground.

5) Measure resistance of Black/Yellow wire between liftgate glass switch 2-pin connector and rear wiper motor 6-pin connector. If resistance is less than 5 ohms, go to next step. If resistance is 5 ohms or more, repair open in Black/Yellow wire.

6) Measure resistance of Black wire between liftgate glass switch 2-pin connector and ground. If resistance is less than 5 ohms, go to next step. If resistance is 5 ohms or more, repair open in Black wire. Ground is at left D-pillar.

7) Turn ignition on. Measure voltage between rear wiper motor 6-pin connector Yellow/Black wire terminal and ground. Also measure voltage between rear wiper motor 6-pin connector Violet wire and ground. If battery voltage exists at both wires, go to next step. If battery voltage does not exist, repair appropriate wire(s).

8) Turn ignition off. Measure resistance of Black wire between rear wiper/washer switch 6-pin connector and ground. Measure resistance of Black wire between rear wiper motor 6-pin connector and ground. If each resistance is less than 5 ohms, go to next step. If any resistance is 5 ohms or more, repair open in appropriate Black wire(s). Both ground points are at lower and center left D-pillar.

9) Measure resistance of Blue/Yellow wire between rear wiper motor 6-pin connector and rear wiper/washer switch 6-pin connector. If resistance is less than 5 ohms, repair Blue wire between rear wiper motor and rear wiper/washer switch. If resistance is 5 ohms or more, repair open in Blue/Yellow wire.

TEST K: REAR WINDOW WIPER WILL NOT PARK PROPERLY (FIXED REAR WINDOW)

NOTE: After repairs, retest system for normal operation.

1) Turn ignition on. Cycle rear wiper until it reaches fully parked position. If necessary, use 10-amp fused jumper to apply battery voltage to rear wiper motor terminal No. 1. Using 2 jumpers, ground rear wiper motor terminals No. 2 and 3. *See Fig. 5.* Run until wiper arm reaches parked position. Turn ignition off. Disconnect rear wiper motor 4-pin connector. Measure resistance between rear wiper motor terminals as indicated. See REAR WIPER MOTOR RESISTANCES table. *See Fig. 5.* If rear wiper motor cycles to park position and shows specified resistance values, go to next step. If rear wiper motor does not cycle to park or resistance is not as specified, replace motor. See WIPER MOTOR under REMOVAL & INSTALLATION.

REAR WIPER MOTOR RESISTANCES

Front Wiper Position	Terminals 1 & 4	Terminals 1 & 2
Park	Less Than 5 Ohms	Greater Than 10 k/ohms
Run	Greater Than 10 k/ohms	Less Than 5 Ohms

2) Measure resistance of Black wire between rear wiper motor 4-pin connector and ground. If resistance is less than 5 ohms, replace rear wiper motor. See WIPER MOTOR under REMOVAL & INSTALLATION. If resistance is 5 ohms or more, repair open in Black wire. Ground point is at left D-pillar.

TEST L: REAR WIPER WILL NOT TURN OFF

NOTE: After repairs, retest system for normal operation.

1) Turn ignition off. Remove rear wiper/washer switch. Measure resistance between rear wiper/washer switch terminals No. 6 and 2. *See Fig. 4.* If resistance is less than 5 ohms with switch depressed, and more than 10 k/ohms with switch released, go to next step. If resistances are not as indicated, replace switch.

2) Measure resistance of Blue/Yellow wire between rear wiper/washer switch 6-pin connector and ground. If resistance is more than 10 k/ohms, replace rear wiper/washer switch. If resistance is 10 k/ohms or less, repair Blue/Yellow wire short to ground.

TEST M: REAR WIPER WILL NOT MOVE TO LIFTGATE WINDOW OPEN POSITION

NOTE: After repairs, retest system for normal operation.

1) Turn ignition off. Disconnect liftgate glass switch 2-pin connector. Make sure liftgate glass is securely closed. Measure resistance across liftgate glass switch terminals. If resistance is more than 10 k/ohms, go to next step. If resistance is 10 k/ohms or less, replace liftgate glass switch.

2) Disconnect rear wiper motor 6-pin connector. Measure resistance of Black/Yellow wire between rear wiper motor 6-pin connector and liftgate glass switch 2-pin connector. If resistance is less than 5 ohms, go to next step. If resistance is 5 ohms or more, repair Black/Yellow wire short to ground.

3) Measure resistance of Black wire between liftgate glass switch 2-pin connector and ground. If resistance is less than 5 ohms, replace rear wiper motor. See WIPER MOTOR under REMOVAL & INSTALLATION. If resistance is 5 ohms or more, repair open in Black wire. Ground point is at left D-pillar.

REMOVAL & INSTALLATION

WARNING: Deactivate air bag system before performing any service operation involving steering column components. See appropriate AIR BAG RESTRAINT SYSTEMS article. Do not apply electrical power to any component on steering column without first deactivating air bag system. Air bag may deploy.

CAUTION: When battery is disconnected, vehicle computer and memory systems may lose memory data. Driveability problems may exist until computer systems have completed a relearn cycle. See COMPUTER RELEARN PROCEDURES article in GENERAL INFORMATION before disconnecting battery.

WASHER PUMP & RESERVOIR

CAUTION: Fill reservoir before operating pump.

NOTE: Front and rear washer pumps are mounted to same reservoir.

Removal & Installation – Remove right front wheel. Remove screws, pin-type retainers and position right hand splash shield aside. Disconnect electrical connector. Disconnect washer hoses and drain fluid from reservoir. Remove reservoir. Remove washer pump(s). To install, reverse removal procedure.

WIPER MOTOR

Removal & Installation (Front) – Disconnect negative battery cable. Remove wiper arms. Remove cowl top vent panel, raising and lowering hood as necessary. Disconnect wiper motor linkage. Disconnect harness connector from motor. Remove wiper motor. To install, reverse removal procedure.

Removal & Installation (Rear) – Disconnect negative battery cable. Disconnect washer hose. Depress locking clip and remove wiper arm. Remove motor shaft nut. Remove outer collar and seal from liftgate. Remove liftgate door trim panel. Remove rear wiper motor and bracket. Remove motor from bracket. To install, reverse removal procedure.

WIPER/WASHER SWITCH

Removal & Installation (Front) – Disconnect negative battery cable. Unscrew tilt wheel handle (if necessary). Remove upper and lower steering column covers. Disconnect multifunction harness connectors. Remove multifunction switch. To install, reverse removal procedure.

Removal & Installation (Rear) – Disconnect negative battery cable. Carefully pull rear wiper/washer switch from instrument panel. Disconnect switch connector. To install, reverse removal procedure.

WIRING DIAGRAMS

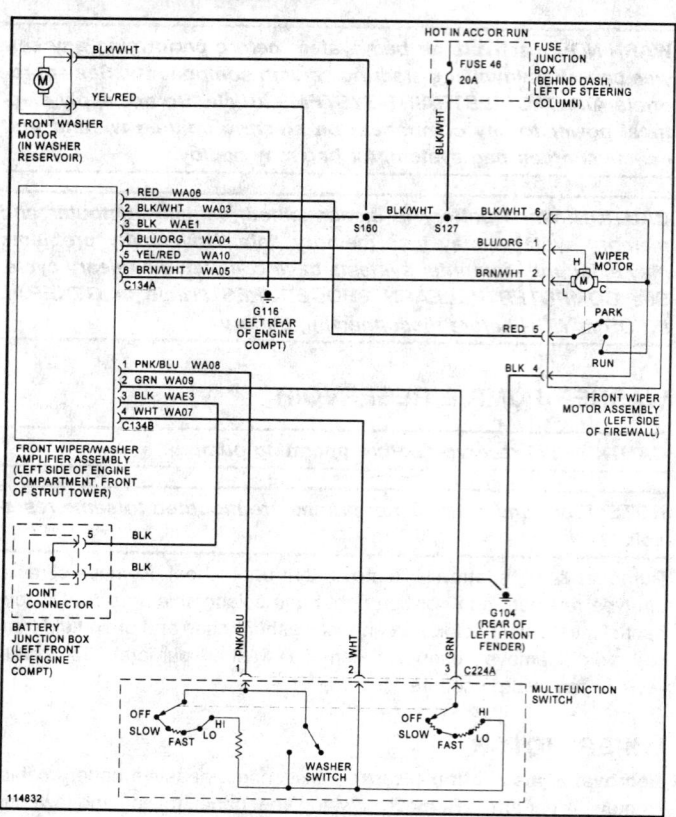

Fig. 6: Front Wiper/Washer System Wiring Diagram (Villager)

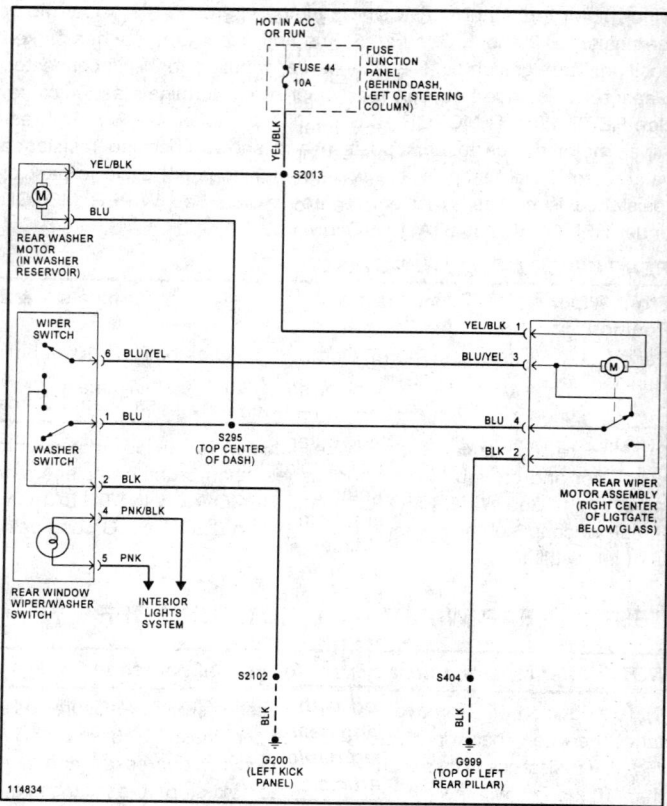

Fig. 8: Rear Wiper/Washer System Wiring Diagram (Villager – Without Movable Liftgate Glass)

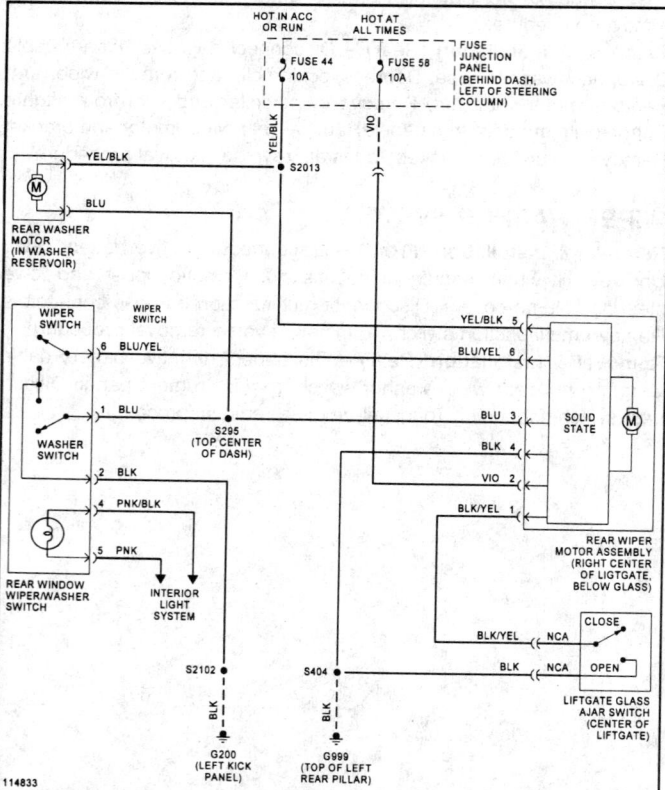

Fig. 7: Rear Wiper/Washer System Wiring Diagram (Villager – With Movable Liftgate Glass)

DESCRIPTION & OPERATION

All wiper/washer functions are controlled by the multifunction switch and Front Electronic Module (FEM). FEM is located behind left side of instrument panel. FEM controls wiper/washer functions through 3 relays located in the battery junction box. Interval wiper delay can vary with vehicle speed. Using vehicle speed inputs from PCM and anti-lock control module, FEM will decrease interval delay time when vehicle is above 10 MPH. FEM fault management logic provides limited front wiper functionality in event of multifunction switch or ignition switch failure.

ADJUSTMENTS

WIPER ARM

Front – 1) Remove nut and windshield wiper arm from pivot shaft. Turn windshield wipers on and allow pivot shafts to cycle 3-4 times. Turn windshield wipers off and allow to return to PARK position.

2) Position driver's side wiper blade outer tip 2.6" (65 mm) from edge of cowl. Position passenger's side wiper blade outer tip 3" (75 mm) from edge of cowl. Tighten pivot arm nuts 26 ft. lbs. (35 N.m).

Rear – Remove nut and wiper arm from pivot shaft. Turn rear wiper on and allow pivot shaft to cycle 3-4 times. Position rear blade so outer tip rests on right lower portion of glass in area of bottom two defroster lines. Tighten pivot arm nut to 11 ft. lbs. (15 N.m).

TROUBLE SHOOTING

WARNING: Vehicle is equipped with an air bag system. System must be disabled before working near steering column and instrument cluster to prevent air bag deployment. See appropriate AIR BAG RESTRAINT SYSTEMS article.

Before performing any tests on wiper/washer system, verify customer complaint. Check battery junction box fuses No. 2 (10-amp), No. 23 (15-amp), No. 5 (30-amp) and No. 8 (25-amp). Check for loose or corroded connections. Check for damaged wiring harness, wiper motor and washer pump. Ensure washer reservoir is full. Check multifunction switch. Check for kinked or broken washer hoses. If all components are okay, retrieve Diagnostic Trouble Codes (DTCs) from Front Electronic Module (FEM). See SELF-DIAGNOSTIC SYSTEM.

COMPONENT TESTS

FRONT WIPER MOTOR

Disengage linkage from motor. Disconnect front wiper motor connector. Ground terminal No. 3 (Black wire) on motor. *See Fig. 1.* Apply battery voltage to terminal No. 4 (Black/Pink wire) on motor for low speed operation. For high speed operation apply battery voltage to terminal No. 5 (Dark Blue/Orange wire) on motor. Current draw with wiper linkage disconnected should not exceed 3.5 amps at low speed and 5.5 amps at high speed.

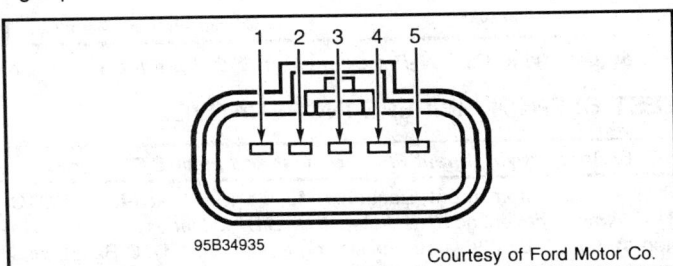

95B34935   Courtesy of Ford Motor Co.

Fig. 1: Identifying Front Wiper Motor Connector Terminals

WIPER & WASHER RELAYS

1) Remove relay to be tested. Wiper relays are located in power distribution box near battery. Measure resistance between relay terminal No. 2 and all other terminals. *See Fig. 2.* If any resistance is less than 5 ohms, replace relay. If all resistances are 5 ohms or more, go to next step.

2) Connect a jumper between battery positive terminal and relay terminal No. 3. Measure voltage between ground and relay terminal No. 4. If battery voltage is not present, replace relay. If battery voltage is present, go to next step.

3) Connect a second wire from battery positive terminal to relay terminal No. 1. Connect a third jumper wire between relay terminal No. 2 and ground. Measure voltage between ground and relay terminal No. 5. If battery voltage is not present, replace relay, If battery voltage is present, relay is okay.

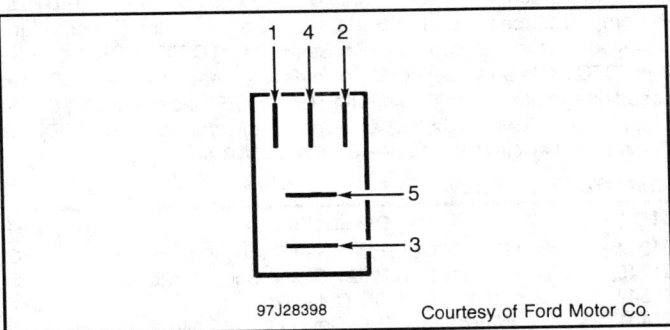

97J28398   Courtesy of Ford Motor Co.

Fig. 2: Identifying Relay Terminals

WIPER/WASHER SWITCH

Disconnect multifunction switch. Check continuity between appropriate multifunction switch terminals with switch in appropriate position. See WIPER/WASHER SWITCH CONTINUITY TEST table. *See Fig. 3.* If resistance is not as specified, replace multifunction switch.

WIPER/WASHER SWITCH CONTINUITY TEST

Switch Position	Terminals	[1] Resistance (Ohms)
Front Wiper		
OFF	3 & 5	47,600
INT	3 & 5	11,330
LOW	3 & 5	4,080
HIGH	3 & 5	0
INT [2]		
MIN	3 & 4	3,300
MAX	3 & 4	103,300
Front Washer		
OFF	3 & 4	103,300
ON	3 & 4	0
Rear Wiper/Washer		
OFF	3 & 2	2.9
INT 1	3 & 2	1
INT 2	3 & 2	330
WASH	3 & 2	0

[1] – Values are approximate.
[2] – Rotate (INT) interval knob from minimum to maximum. Resistance should gradually increase from 3.3 k/ohms (MIN) to 103.3 k/ohms (MAX).

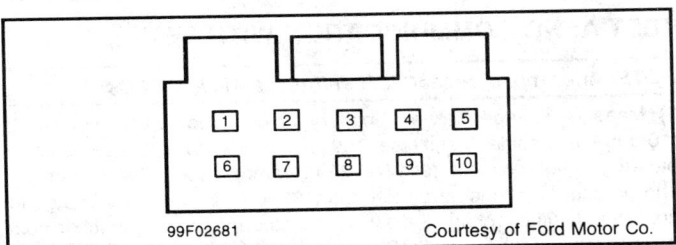

99F02681   Courtesy of Ford Motor Co.

Fig. 3: Identifying Multifunction Switch Terminals

SELF-DIAGNOSTIC SYSTEM

Connect New Generation Star (NGS) tester to Data Link Connector (DLC) located below instrument panel to right of steering column. Using NGS tester, perform data link diagnostic test. See DATA LINK DIAG-

NOSTIC TEST under COMMUNICATION NETWORK DIAGNOSTICS in MODULE COMMUNICATIONS NETWORK – WINDSTAR article. If NGS tester displays CKT914, CKT915 or CKT70 = ECUS NO RESP/NOT EQUIP, repair module communications concern. See MODULE COMMUNICATIONS NETWORK – WINDSTAR article. If NGS tester displays NO RESP/NOT EQUIP for Front Electronic Module (FEM), perform TEST A: NO COMMUNICATION WITH FEM under SYSTEM TESTS.

If system passed, retrieve and record continuous DTCs. Erase DTCs. Perform FEM self-test. If FEM DTCs related to the concern are retrieved, perform appropriate test. See FEM DTC TEST INDEX table. If no DTCs related to concern are retrieved, perform appropriate test based on symptom. See SYMPTOM TEST INDEX table under SYSTEM TESTS. For FEM DTCs not covered in this article, see MODULE COMMUNICATIONS NETWORK – WINDSTAR article.

FEM DTC TEST INDEX

DTC [1]	Description	Test
B1244	Rear Wiper Run Relay Circuit Failure	C
B1245	Rear Wiper Run Relay Circuit Short To Power	C
B1342	ECU Defective	[2]
B1431	Wiper Brake/Run Relay Circuit Failure	B
B1432	Wiper Brake/Run Relay Circuit Short To Power	B
B1436	Wiper High/Low Relay Coil Circuit Short To Power	H
B1438	Wiper Switch Circuit Failure	B
B1446	Front Wiper Park Sense Circuit Failure	E
B1448	Wiper Park Sense Circuit Short To Power	E
B1450	Wiper Wash/Delay Switch Circuit Failure	B
B1611	Rear Wiper Switch Circuit Failure	C

[1] – Codes listed in this table are only for testing covered in this article. For complete DTC listing, see MODULE COMMUNICATIONS NETWORK – WINDSTAR article.

[2] – Replace FEM. See FRONT ELECTRONIC MODULE (FEM) under REMOVAL & INSTALLATION. Clear DTCs and retest.

SYSTEM TESTS

WARNING: Vehicle is equipped with an air bag system. System MUST be disabled before working near steering column and instrument cluster to prevent air bag deployment. See appropriate AIR BAG RESTRAINT SYSTEMS article.

SYMPTOM TEST INDEX

Symptom	Test
No Communication With FEM	A
Front Wipers Inoperative	B
Rear Wipers Inoperative	C
Front Or Rear Wipers On Continuously	D
Intermittent Does Not Operate Properly	E
Front Or Rear Washer Pump Inoperative	F
Front Or Rear Washer Stays On Continuously	G
Wiper High/Low Speeds Do Not Operate Properly	H

TEST A: NO COMMUNICATION WITH FEM

NOTE: After repair, repeat FEM self-test and clear DTCs.

1) Measure voltage between battery junction box mini-fuse No. 2 (10-amp) fuse holder (input side) and ground. Measure voltage between battery junction box mini-fuse No. 23 (15-amp) fuse holder (input side) and ground. If voltages are more than 10 volts, install fuses and go to next step. If either voltage is 10 volts or less, repair battery junction box.
2) Turn ignition switch to LOCK position. Disconnect Front Electronic Module (FEM) 20-pin connector C346, 12-pin connector C190 and 17-pin connector C192. See FRONT ELECTRONIC MODULE (FEM) under REMOVAL & INSTALLATION. Turn ignition switch to RUN position. Measure voltage between GEM connector C346 terminal No. 1 (Light Blue/Red wire) and ground. See Fig. 4. Measure voltage between FEM connector C190 terminal No. 6 (Red wire) and ground. See Fig. 5. If voltages are more than 10 volts, go to next step. If either voltage is 10

volts or less, repair appropriate wire(s). See appropriate wiring diagram in POWER DISTRIBUTION article in WIRING DIAGRAMS.
3) Turn ignition switch to LOCK position. Disconnect FEM 4-pin connector C348. Measure resistance between FEM connector C190 terminal No. 12 (Black wire) and ground. See Fig. 5. Measure resistances between FEM connector C192 terminals No. 11, 13, 14, 15 (all Black wires) and ground. See Fig. 6. If all resistance is less than 5 ohms, repair module communication concern. See MODULE COMMUNICATIONS NETWORK – WINDSTAR article. If still unable to communicate with FEM, replace FEM. See FRONT ELECTRONIC MODULE (FEM) under REMOVAL & INSTALLATION. If any resistance is 5 ohms or more, repair open in appropriate Black wire.

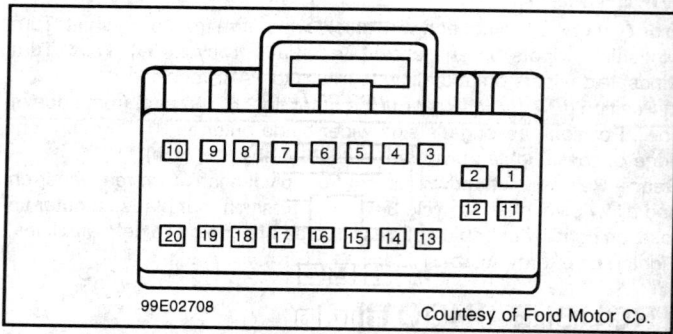

99E02708   Courtesy of Ford Motor Co.

Fig. 4: Identifying FEM 20-Pin Connector C346 Terminals

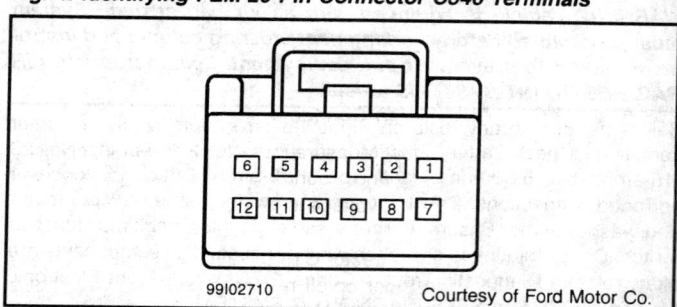

99I02710   Courtesy of Ford Motor Co.

Fig. 5: Identifying FEM 12-Pin Connector C190 Terminals

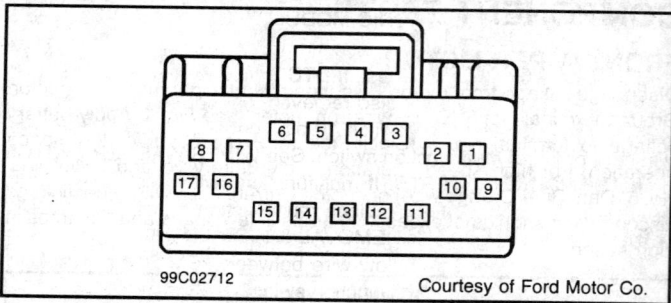

99C02712   Courtesy of Ford Motor Co.

Fig. 6: Identifying FEM 17-Pin Connector C192 Terminals

TEST B: FRONT WIPERS INOPERATIVE

NOTE: After repair, repeat FEM self-test and clear DTCs.

1) Use results from Front Electronic Module (FEM) self-test. If DTC B1431 was retrieved, go to next step. If DTC B1432 was retrieved, go to step 4). If DTC B1438 was retrieved, go to step 6). If DTC B1450 was retrieved, go to step 9). If no DTCs were retrieved, go to step 12).
2) Remove wiper on/off relay. Using NGS tester, access FEM active command WIPER RLY. Trigger WIPER RLY on. Measure resistance between wiper on/off relay connector terminal No. 2 (Dark Green/White wire) and ground. See Fig. 7. If resistance is 5 ohms or more, go to next step. If resistance is less than 5 ohms, replace wiper on/off relay.
3) Disconnect FEM 22-pin connector C191. Measure resistance in Dark Green/White wire between FEM connector C191 terminal No. 1 and wiper on/off relay connector terminal No. 2. See Figs. 7 and 8. If

resistance is less than 5 ohms, replace FEM. See FRONT ELEC-TRONIC MODULE (FEM) under REMOVAL & INSTALLATION. If resistance is 5 ohms or more, repair open in Dark Green/White wire.

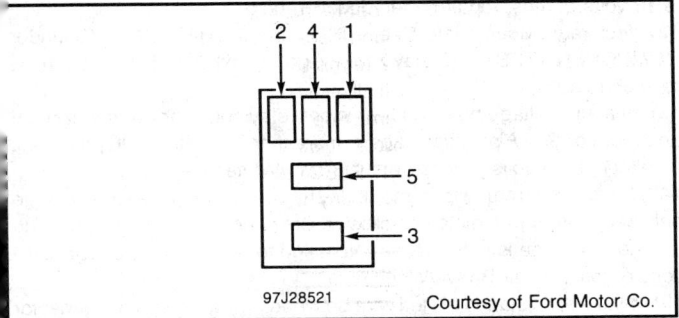

Fig. 7: Identifying Relay Connector Terminals

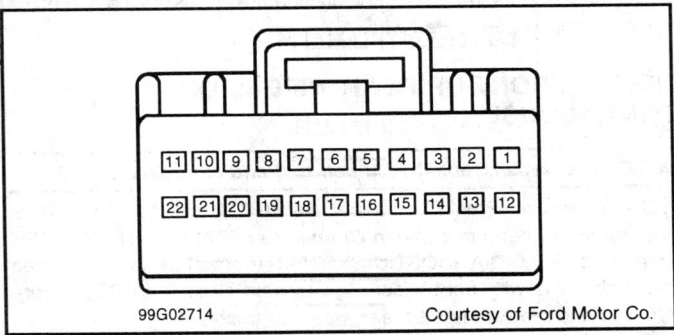

Fig. 8: Identifying FEM 22-Pin Connector C191 Terminals

4) Remove wiper on/off relay. Measure voltage between wiper on/off relay connector terminal No. 2 and ground. *See Fig. 7.* If voltage is more than 10 volts, go to next step. If voltage is 10 volts or less, replace wiper on/off relay.

5) Disconnect FEM 22-pin connector C191. Remove wiper on/off relay. Measure voltage between wiper on/off relay connector terminal No. 2 and ground. *See Fig. 7.* If voltage is more than 10 volts, repair short to power in Dark Green/White wire. If voltage is 10 volts or less, replace FEM. See FRONT ELECTRONIC MODULE (FEM) under REMOVAL & INSTALLATION.

6) Use results from FEM self-test. If DTC B1450 is also retrieved, go to step 9). If DTC B1450 is not also retrieved, go to next step.

7) Disconnect multifunction switch 10-pin connector C263. Test wiper/washer portion of multifunction switch. See WIPER/WASHER SWITCH under COMPONENT TESTS. If multifunction switch tests okay, go to next step. If switch is faulty, replace multifunction switch. See MULTI-FUNCTION SWITCH under REMOVAL & INSTALLATION.

8) Measure resistance in Yellow wire between FEM 20-pin connector C346 terminal No. 2 and multifunction switch C263 terminal No. 5. *See Figs. 4 and 9.* If resistance is less than 5 ohms, replace FEM. See FRONT ELECTRONIC MODULE (FEM) under REMOVAL & INSTAL-LATION. If resistance is 5 ohms or more, repair open in Yellow wire.

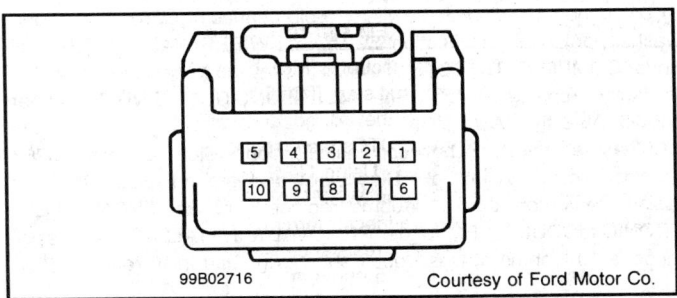

Fig. 9: Identifying Multifunction Switch 10-Pin Connector C263 Terminals

9) Disconnect multifunction switch 10-pin connector. Test wiper/washer portion of multifunction switch. See WIPER/WASHER SWITCH under COMPONENT TESTS. If switch is okay, go to next step. If switch is faulty, replace multifunction switch. See MULTIFUNCTION SWITCH under REMOVAL & INSTALLATION.

10) Disconnect FEM 20-pin connector C346. Measure resistance in White/Light Green wire between FEM connector C346 terminal No. 14 and multifunction switch connector C263 terminal No. 3. *See Figs. 4 and 9.* If resistance is less than 5 ohms, go to next step. If resistance is 5 ohms or more, repair open in White/Light Green wire.

11) Measure resistance in Pink wire between FEM connector C346 terminal No. 13 and multifunction switch connector C263 terminal No. 4. *See Figs. 4 and 9.* If resistance is less than 5 ohms, replace multifunction switch. See MULTIFUNCTION SWITCH under REMOVAL & INSTALLATION. If resistance is 5 ohms or more, repair open in Pink wire.

12) Turn ignition switch to LOCK position. Connect NGS tester to Data Link Connector (DLC). DLC is located below instrument panel to right of steering wheel. Turn ignition switch to RUN position. Observe FEM PID WPMODE while turning wiper switch through all positions. If PID values agree with switch positions, go to step 16). If PID values do not agree with switch positions, go to next step.

13) Disconnect multifunction switch 10-pin connector C263. Test wiper/washer portion of multifunction switch. See WIPER/WASHER SWITCH under COMPONENT TESTS. If switch is okay, go to next step. If switch is faulty, replace multifunction switch. See MULTIFUNCTION SWITCH under REMOVAL & INSTALLATION.

14) Disconnect FEM 22-pin connector C191. Measure resistance in Violet wire between FEM 20-pin connector C346 terminal No. 13 and multifunction switch terminal No. 4. *See Figs. 4 and 9.* Measure resistance in Yellow wire between FEM connector C346 terminal No. 2 and multifunction switch connector C263 terminal No. 5. Measure resistance in White/Light Green wire between FEM connector C346 terminal No. 14 and multifunction switch connector C263 terminal No. 3. If all resistances are less than 5 ohms, go to next step. If any resistance is 5 ohms or more, repair open in appropriate wire(s).

15) Measure voltage between FEM connector C346 terminal No. 13 (Violet wire) and ground. *See Fig. 4.* Measure voltage between FEM connector C346 terminal No. 2 (Yellow wire) and ground. Measure voltage between FEM connector C346 terminal No. 14 (White/Light Green wire) and ground. If any reading indicates voltage, repair short to power in appropriate wire(s). If no reading indicates voltage, replace FEM. See FRONT ELECTRONIC MODULE (FEM) under REMOVAL & INSTALLATION.

16) Using NGS tester, trigger FEM active command WIPER RLY on. If wipers operate, replace FEM. See FRONT ELECTRONIC MODULE (FEM) under REMOVAL & INSTALLATION. If wipers do not operate, go to next step.

17) Remove battery junction box mini-fuse No. 6 (30-amp). Measure voltage between mini-fuse No. 6 fuse holder (input side) and ground. If voltage is more than 10 volts, install fuse and go to next step. If voltage is 10 volts or less, repair battery junction box.

18) Remove and test wiper on/off relay. See WIPER & WASHER RELAYS under COMPONENT TESTS. If relay is okay, go to next step. If relay is faulty, replace relay.

19) Measure voltage between wiper on/off relay connector terminal No. 1 and ground. *See Fig. 7.* If voltage is more than 10 volts, go to next step. If voltage is 10 volts or less, repair Dark Green wire.

20) Disconnect front wiper motor connector. Measure resistance in Dark Green wire between wiper on/off relay connector terminal No. 5 and wiper motor connector terminal No. 2. *See Figs. 1 and 7.* If resistance is less than 5 ohms, go to next step. If resistance is 5 ohms or more, repair open in Dark Green wire.

21) Measure voltage between wiper on/off relay connector terminal No. 4 and ground. See. 7. If voltage is more than 10 volts, repair short to power in Black/Pink wire. If voltage is 10 volts or less, go to next step.

22) Measure resistance between front wiper motor connector terminal No. 3 and ground. *See Fig. 1.* If resistance is less than 5 ohms, go to next step. If resistance is 5 ohms or more, repair open in Black wire.

23) Disconnect FEM 20-pin connector C346. Measure voltage between FEM connector C346 terminal No. 3 (Red/Yellow wire) and ground. *See Fig. 4*. If any reading indicates voltage, repair short to power in Red/Yellow wire. If no reading indicates voltage, replace front wiper motor. See FRONT WIPER MOTOR under REMOVAL & INSTALLATION.

TEST C: REAR WIPERS INOPERATIVE

NOTE: After repair, repeat FEM self-test and clear DTCs.

1) Use results from Front Electronic Module (FEM) self-test. If DTC B1244 was retrieved, go to next step. If DTC B1245 was retrieved, go to step 5). If DTC B1611 was retrieved, go to step 7). If no DTCs were retrieved, go to step 9).

2) Remove and test rear wiper relay. See WIPER & WASHER RELAYS under COMPONENT TESTS. If relay is okay, go to next step. If relay is faulty, replace relay.

3) Make sure rear wiper switch is turned off. Measure resistance between rear wiper relay connector terminal No. 2 and ground. *See Fig. 7*. If resistance is more than 10 k/ohms, go to next step. If resistance is 10 k/ohms or less, repair short to ground in Dark Green/Violet wire.

4) Disconnect FEM 12-pin connector C190. Measure resistance in Dark Green/Violet wire between FEM connector C190 terminal No. 4 and rear wiper relay connector terminal No. 2. *See Figs. 5 and 7*. If resistance is less than 5 ohms, replace FEM. See FRONT ELECTRONIC MODULE (FEM) under REMOVAL & INSTALLATION. If resistance is 5 ohms or more, repair open in Dark Green/Violet wire.

5) Test rear wiper relay. See WIPER & WASHER RELAYS under COMPONENT TESTS. If relay is okay, go to next step. If relay is faulty, replace relay.

6) Measure voltage between FEM connector C190 terminal No. 4 (Dark Green/Violet wire) and ground. *See Fig. 5*. If voltage is more than 10 volts, repair short to power in Dark Green/Violet wire. If voltage is 10 volts or less, replace FEM. See FRONT ELECTRONIC MODULE (FEM) under REMOVAL & INSTALLATION.

7) Disconnect multifunction 10-pin connector C263. Check wiper/washer portion of multifunction switch. See WIPER/WASHER SWITCH under COMPONENT TESTS. If switch is okay, go to next step. If switch is faulty, replace multifunction switch. See MULTIFUNCTION SWITCH under REMOVAL & INSTALLATION.

8) Disconnect FEM 26-pin connector C347. Measure resistance between FEM connector C347 terminal No. 5 and multifunction switch connector C263 terminal No. 2. *See Figs. 9 and 10*. If resistance is less than 5 ohms, replace FEM. See FRONT ELECTRONIC MODULE (FEM) under REMOVAL & INSTALLATION. If resistance is 5 ohms or more, repair open in Violet/Light Blue wire.

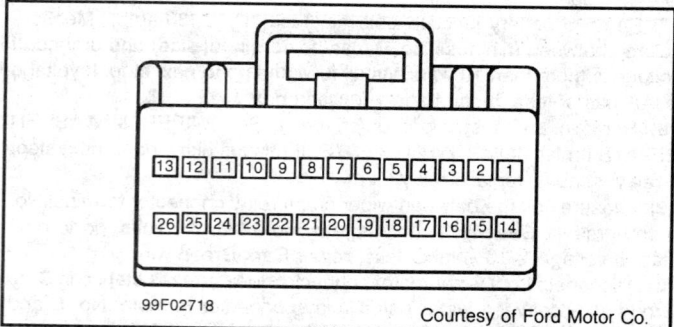

99F02718   Courtesy of Ford Motor Co.

Fig. 10: Identifying FEM 26-Pin Connector C347 Terminals

9) Using NGS tester, observe FEM PID R_WPRUN. If PID displays ON, repair Violet/Light Blue wire between FEM and multifunction switch. If PID does not display ON, go to next step.

10) Using NGS tester, access FEM active command WIPER RLY, activate and deactivate rear wiper. If wiper operates correctly, replace FEM. See FRONT ELECTRONIC MODULE (FEM) under REMOVAL & INSTALLATION. If wiper does not operate correctly, go to next step.

11) Remove battery junction box mini-fuse No. 7 (25-amp). Measure voltage between mini-fuse No. 7 fuse holder (input side) and ground. If voltage is more than 10 volts, install fuse and go to next step. If voltage is 10 volts or less, repair battery junction box.

12) Test rear wiper relay. See WIPER & WASHER RELAYS under COMPONENT TESTS. If relay is okay, go to next step. If relay is faulty, replace relay.

13) Measure voltage between rear wiper relay connector terminal No. 5 and ground. *See Fig. 7*. If voltage is more than 10 volts, go to next step. If voltage is 10 volts or less, repair Brown/White wire.

14) Disconnect rear wiper motor 3-pin connector. Measure voltage between rear wiper motor connector Brown/White wire terminal and ground. If voltage is more than 10 volts, go to next step. If voltage is 10 volts or less, repair Brown/White wire.

15) Measure resistance of Red wire between rear wiper motor connector and rear wiper relay connector terminal No. 3. *See Fig. 7*. If resistance is less than 5 ohms, repair battery junction box. If resistance is 5 ohms or more, repair open in Red wire.

TEST D: FRONT OR REAR WIPERS ON CONTINUOUSLY

NOTE: After repair, repeat FEM self-test and clear DTCs.

1) Use results from Front Electronic Module (FEM) self-test. If any DTCs were retrieved, perform appropriate test. See FEM DTC TEST INDEX table under SELF-DIAGNOSTIC SYSTEM. If no DTCs were retrieved and problem is with front wipers, go to next step. If no DTCs were retrieved and problem is with rear wiper, go to step 6).

2) Test wiper on/off relay. See WIPER & WASHER RELAYS under COMPONENT TESTS. If relay is okay, go to next step. If relay is faulty, replace relay.

3) Make sure front wiper switch is off. Measure resistance between wiper on/off relay connector terminal No. 2 and ground. *See Fig. 7*. If resistance is more than 10 k/ohms, go to next step. If resistance is 10 k/ohms or less, repair short to ground in Dark Green/White wire.

4) Disconnect multifunction switch 10-pin connector C263. Test wiper/washer portion of multifunction switch. See WIPER/WASHER SWITCH under COMPONENT TESTS. If switch is okay, go to next step. If switch is faulty, replace multifunction switch. See MULTIFUNCTION SWITCH under REMOVAL & INSTALLATION.

5) Measure resistance between multifunction switch connector C263 terminal No. 5 (Yellow wire) and ground. *See Fig. 9*. If resistance is more than 10 k/ohms, replace FEM. See FRONT ELECTRONIC MODULE (FEM) under REMOVAL & INSTALLATION. If resistance is 10 k/ohms or less, repair short to ground in Yellow wire.

6) Test rear wiper relay. See WIPER & WASHER RELAYS under COMPONENT TESTS. If relay is okay, go to next step. If relay is faulty, replace relay.

7) Make sure rear wiper switch is off. Measure resistance between rear wiper relay connector terminal No. 2 and ground. *See Fig. 7*. If resistance is more than 10 k/ohms, go to next step. If resistance is 10 k/ohms or less, repair short to ground in Dark Green/Violet wire.

8) Disconnect multifunction switch 10-pin connector C263. Test wiper/washer portion of multifunction switch. See WIPER/WASHER SWITCH under COMPONENT TESTS. If switch is okay, go to next step. If switch is faulty, replace switch. See MULTIFUNCTION SWITCH under REMOVAL & INSTALLATION.

9) Measure resistance between multifunction switch connector C263 terminal No. 2 (Violet/Light Blue wire) and ground. *See Fig. 9*. If resistance is more than 10 k/ohms, replace FEM. See FRONT ELECTRONIC MODULE (FEM) under REMOVAL & INSTALLATION. If resistance is 10 k/ohms or less, repair short to ground in Violet/Light Blue wire.

TEST E: INTERMITTENT DOES NOT OPERATE PROPERLY

NOTE: *After repair, repeat FEM self-test and clear DTCs.*

1) Use results from Front Electronic Module (FEM) self-test. If DTC B1446 was retrieved, go to next step. If DTC B1448 was retrieved, go to step 4). If no DTCs were retrieved, go to step 6).

2) Test wiper on/off relay. See WIPER & WASHER RELAYS under COMPONENT TESTS. If wiper on/off relay is okay, go to next step. If relay is faulty, replace relay.

3) Disconnect FEM 22-pin connector C191. Measure resistance in Black/Pink wire between FEM connector C191 terminal No. 13 and wiper on/off relay connector terminal No. 4. *See Figs. 7 and 8.* If resistance is less than 5 ohms, replace FEM. See FRONT ELECTRONIC MODULE (FEM) under REMOVAL & INSTALLATION. If resistance is 5 ohms or more, repair open in Black/Pink wire.

4) Test wiper on/off relay. See WIPER & WASHER RELAYS under COMPONENT TESTS. If relay is okay, go to next step. If relay is faulty, replace relay.

5) Disconnect FEM 22-pin connector C191. Measure voltage between wiper on/off relay connector terminal No. 4 (Black/Pink wire) and ground. *See Fig. 7.* If any reading indicates voltage, repair short to power in Black/Pink wire. If no reading indicates voltage, replace FEM. See FRONT ELECTRONIC MODULE (FEM) under REMOVAL & INSTALLATION.

6) Disconnect multifunction switch 10-pin connector C263. Test wiper/washer portion of multifunction switch. See WIPER/WASHER SWITCH under COMPONENT TESTS. If switch is okay, go to next step. If switch is faulty, replace multifunction switch. See MULTIFUNCTION SWITCH under REMOVAL & INSTALLATION.

7) Disconnect FEM 20-pin connector C346. Measure voltage between FEM connector C346 terminal No. 3 (Red/Yellow wire) and ground. *See Fig. 4.* If any reading indicates voltage, repair short to power in Red/Yellow wire. If no reading indicates voltage, replace FEM. See FRONT ELECTRONIC MODULE (FEM) under REMOVAL & INSTALLATION.

TEST F: FRONT OR REAR WASHER PUMP INOPERATIVE

NOTE: *After repair, repeat FEM self-test and clear DTCs.*

1) If front washer is inoperative, go to next step. If rear washer is inoperative, go to step 5).

2) Disconnect multifunction switch 10-pin connector C263. Test wiper/washer portion of multifunction switch. See WIPER/WASHER SWITCH under COMPONENT TESTS. If switch is okay, go to next step. If switch is faulty, replace multifunction switch. See MULTIFUNCTION SWITCH under REMOVAL & INSTALLATION.

3) Disconnect Front Electronic Module (FEM) 22-pin connector C191. Disconnect front washer pump motor 2-pin connector. Measure resistance in Tan/Black wire between front washer pump connector and FEM connector C191 terminal No. 14. *See Fig. 8.* If resistance is less than 5 ohms, go to next step. If resistance is 5 ohms or more, repair open in Tan/Black wire. Repeat FEM self-test and clear DTCs.

4) Connect front washer pump connector. Connect a 10-amp fused jumper wire between FEM connector C191 terminal No. 14 (Tan/Black wire) and ground. *See Fig. 8.* If front washer pump operates, replace FEM. See FRONT ELECTRONIC MODULE (FEM) under REMOVAL & INSTALLATION. If front washer pump does not operate, replace washer pump. See WASHER PUMP & RESERVOIR under REMOVAL & INSTALLATION.

5) Remove battery junction box mini-fuse No. 7 (25-amp). Measure voltage between mini-fuse No. 7 fuse holder (input side) and ground. If voltage is more than 10 volts, install fuse and go to next step. If voltage is 10 volts or less, repair battery junction box.

6) Disconnect rear washer pump 2-pin connector. Measure voltage between rear washer pump connector Brown/White wire terminal and ground. If voltage is more than 10 volts, go to next step. If voltage is 10 volts or less, repair Brown/White wire.

7) Connect rear washer pump connector. Connect a 10-amp fused jumper wire between FEM connector C191 terminal No. 5 (Light Blue/White wire) and ground. *See Fig. 8.* If the rear washer pump operates, go to next step. If rear washer pump does not operate, replace rear washer pump. See WASHER PUMP & RESERVOIR under REMOVAL & INSTALLATION.

8) Measure resistance in Light Blue/White wire between rear washer pump connector and FEM connector C191 terminal No. 5. *See Fig. 8.* If resistance is less than 5 ohms, go to next step. If resistance is 5 ohms or more, repair open in Light Blue/White wire.

9) Disconnect multifunction switch 10-pin connector C263. Test wiper/washer portion of multifunction switch. See WIPER/WASHER SWITCH under COMPONENT TESTS. If switch is okay, repair Light Blue/White wire. If switch is faulty, replace switch. See MULTIFUNCTION SWITCH under REMOVAL & INSTALLATION.

TEST G: FRONT OR REAR WASHER STAYS ON CONTINUOUSLY

NOTE: *After repair, repeat FEM self-test and clear DTCs.*

1) Use results from Front Electronic Module (FEM) self-test. If any DTCs were retrieved, perform appropriate test. See FEM DTC TEST INDEX table under SELF-DIAGNOSTIC SYSTEM. If no DTCs are retrieved, go to next step.

2) Disconnect multifunction switch 10-pin connector C263. Test wiper/washer portion of multifunction switch. See WIPER/WASHER SWITCH under COMPONENT TESTS. If switch is okay and front washer pump runs continuously, go to next step. If switch is okay and rear pump runs continuously, go to step 4). If switch is faulty, replace switch. See MULTIFUNCTION SWITCH under REMOVAL & INSTALLATION.

3) Disconnect front washer pump motor 2-pin connector. Disconnect FEM 22-pin connector C191. Measure resistance between FEM connector C191 terminal No. 14 (Tan/Black wire) and ground. *See Fig. 8.* If resistance is more than 10 k/ohms, replace FEM. See FRONT ELECTRONIC MODULE (FEM) under REMOVAL & INSTALLATION. If resistance is 10 k/ohms or less, repair short to ground in Tan/Black wire.

4) Disconnect rear washer pump motor 2-pin connector. Disconnect FEM 22-pin connector C191. Measure resistance between FEM connector C191 terminal No. 5 (Light Blue/White wire) and ground. *See Fig. 8.* If resistance is more than 10 k/ohms, replace FEM. See FRONT ELECTRONIC MODULE (FEM) under REMOVAL & INSTALLATION. If resistance is 10 k/ohms or less, repair short to ground in Light Blue/White wire.

TEST H: WIPER HIGH/LOW SPEEDS DO NOT OPERATE PROPERLY

NOTE: *After repair, repeat FEM self-test and clear DTCs.*

1) Use results from Front Electronic Module (FEM) self-test. If DTC B1436 was retrieved, go to next step. If DTC B1436 was not retrieved, go to step 4).

2) Test wiper high/low relay. See WIPER & WASHER RELAYS under COMPONENT TESTS. If relay is okay, go to next step. If relay is faulty, replace relay.

3) Disconnect FEM 22-pin connector C191. Measure voltage between FEM connector C191 terminal No. 3 (Violet/White wire) and ground. *See Fig. 8.* If voltage is more than 10 volts, repair short to power in Violet/White wire. If voltage is 10 volts or less, replace FEM. See FRONT ELECTRONIC MODULE (FEM) under REMOVAL & INSTALLATION.

4) Using NGS tester, trigger FEM active command SPEED RLY on. If high/low relay energizes, go to next step. If high/low relay does not energize, replace FEM. See FRONT ELECTRONIC MODULE (FEM) under REMOVAL & INSTALLATION.

5) Test high/low relay. See WIPER & WASHER RELAYS under COMPONENT TESTS. If relay is okay, go to next step. If relay is faulty, replace relay.

6) Disconnect FEM 22-pin connector C191. Measure resistance between FEM connector C191 terminal No. 3 (Violet/White wire) and ground. *See Fig. 8.* If resistance is more than 10 k/ohms go to next step. If resistance is 10 k/ohms or less, repair short to ground in Violet/White wire.

7) Measure resistance in Violet/White wire between FEM connector C191 terminal No. 3 and wiper high/low relay connector terminal No. 2. *See Figs. 7 and 8.* If resistance is less than 5 ohms, go to next step. If resistance is 5 ohms or more, repair open in Violet/White wire.

8) Connect FEM 22-pin connector C191. Remove wiper high/low relay. Measure voltage between wiper high/low relay connector terminal No. 1 and ground. *See Fig. 7.* If voltage is more than 10 volts, go to next step. If voltage is 10 volts or less, repair open in Dark Green wire.

9) Remove wiper on/off relay. Measure resistance in Orange wire between wiper high/low relay connector terminal No. 3 and wiper on/off relay connector terminal No. 3. *See Fig. 7.* If resistance is less than 5 ohms, install on/off relay and go to next step. If resistance is 5 ohms or more, repair open in Orange wire.

10) Disconnect front wiper motor connector. Measure resistance between wiper high/low relay connector terminal No. 5 (Dark Blue/Orange wire) and ground. *See Fig. 7.* Measure resistance between wiper high/low relay connector terminal No. 4 (Black/Pink wire) and ground. If all resistances are more than 10 k/ohms, go to next step. If any resistance is 10 k/ohms or less, repair short to ground in appropriate wire(s).

11) Measure resistance in Dark Blue/Orange wire between wiper high/low relay connector terminal No. 5 and front wiper motor connector terminal No. 5. *See Figs. 1 and 7.* Measure resistance in Black/Pink wire between wiper high/low relay connector terminal No. 4 and front wiper motor connector terminal No. 4. If all resistances are less than 5 ohms, go to next step. If any resistance is 5 ohms or more, repair open in appropriate wire(s).

12) Measure voltage between wiper high/low relay connector terminal No. 5 (Dark Blue/Orange wire) and ground. *See Fig. 7.* Measure voltage between wiper high/low relay connector terminal No. 4 (Dark Black/Pink wire) and ground. If any reading indicates voltage, repair short to power in appropriate wire(s). If no reading indicates voltage, replace front wiper motor. See FRONT WIPER MOTOR under REMOVAL & INSTALLATION.

REMOVAL & INSTALLATION

CAUTION: When battery is disconnected, vehicle computer and memory systems may lose memory data. Driveability problems may exist until computer systems have completed a relearn cycle. See COMPUTER RELEARN PROCEDURES article in GENERAL INFORMATION before disconnecting battery.

FRONT ELECTRONIC MODULE (FEM)

CAUTION: If replacing Front Electronic Module (FEM), it is necessary to upload module configuration information using the Ford Service Function (FSF) card and the New Generation Star (NGS) tester. After installation, this information needs to be downloaded into new FEM. NGS tester will not hold downloaded information for more than 24 hours.

Removal & Installation – Disconnect battery ground cable. Remove instrument panel lower steering column opening cover. Remove instrument panel opening cover reinforcement. Remove FEM five electrical connectors. Remove bolts and FEM. To install, reverse removal procedure.

FRONT WIPER MOTOR

CAUTION: Wiper motor contains ceramic magnets that may crack or shatter if motor is dropped or handled roughly.

Removal & Installation – 1) Disconnect negative battery cable. Remove wiper arms. Remove screws and clips retaining cowl top vent panel. Disconnect windshield washer hose. Remove cowl top vent panel.

2) Disconnect two electrical connectors. Unbolt and remove lower cowl top vent panel assembly. Remove mounting arm and pivot shaft. Remove wiper motor linkage from motor. Remove wiper motor.

3) To install, reverse removal procedure. Tighten wiper motor mounting bolts 11 ft. lbs. (15 N.m). Tighten linkage to wiper motor bolt 13 ft. lbs. (17 N.m). Adjust windshield wiper arms. See WIPER ARM under ADJUSTMENTS.

MULTIFUNCTION SWITCH

Removal & Installation – Disconnect battery ground cable. Twist tilt wheel handle counterclockwise and remove. Remove upper and lower steering column shrouds. Remove switch screws. Disconnect electrical connectors. Remove switch. To install, reverse removal procedure.

REAR WIPER MOTOR

CAUTION: Wiper motor contains ceramic magnets that may crack or shatter if motor is dropped or handled roughly.

Removal & Installation – Remove rear pivot arm. Remove liftgate upper trim panel and garnish molding. Remove liftgate interior pull handle screw covers and screws. Remove liftgate inside trim panel screw. Remove liftgate inside trim panel. Disconnect rear wiper electrical connector. Remove wiper motor. To install, reverse procedure. Adjust windshield wiper arms. See WIPER ARM under ADJUSTMENTS. Tighten wiper mounting bolts 97 INCH lbs. (11 N.m).

WASHER PUMP & RESERVOIR

Removal & Installation – Remove upper washer reservoir bolts. Remove right front wheel and right front splash shield. Remove screws and position cornering lamp aside. Remove lower reservoir bolt. Disconnect electrical connectors. Disconnect washer hoses and collect fluid. Remove reservoir. Remove washer pumps from reservoir. To install, reverse removal procedure.

WIRING DIAGRAMS

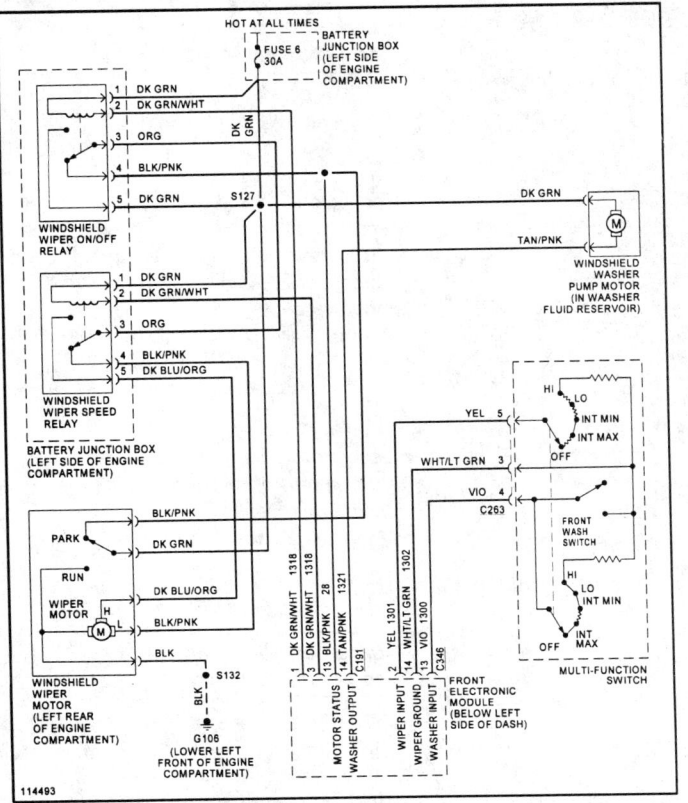

Fig. 11: Front Wiper/Washer System Wiring Diagram (Windstar)

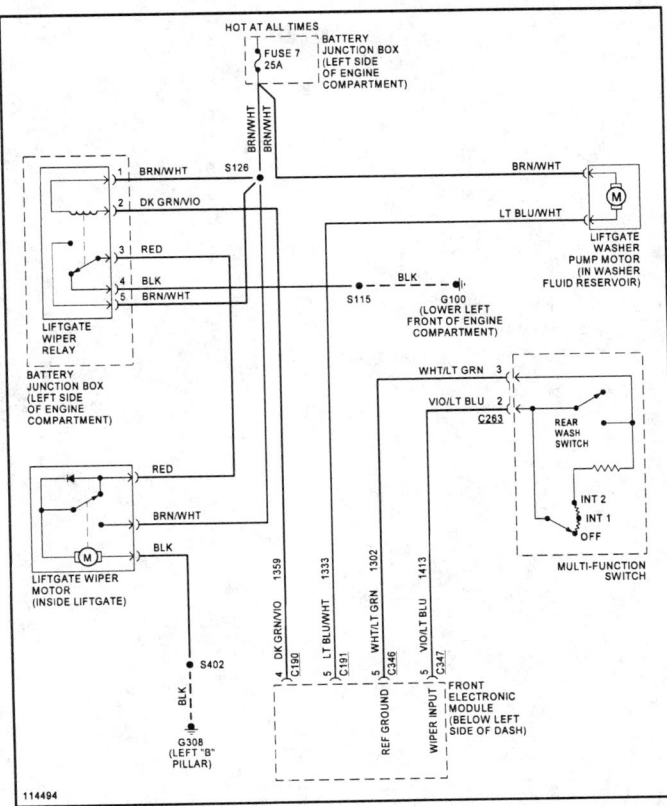

Fig. 12: Rear Wiper/Washer System Wiring Diagram (Windstar)

NOTE: LATEST CHANGES & CORRECTIONS represents a collection of last minute information and relevant technical service bulletins. Read this section and make notations in appropriate manuals for easy reference later.

FORD MOTOR CO.

ACCESSORIES & EQUIPMENT

➤ *1998 AUTOLAMPS – EXPLORER & MOUNTAINEER: TEST REVISION –* Please note that step **8)** under TEST A: AUTOLAMPS INOPERATIVE has been revised as follows:

8) Measure voltage between ground and terminal No. 1 (Tan/White wire) at headlight relay wiring harness connector. If battery voltage is present, install relay and go to next step. If battery voltage is not present, repair Tan/White wire between relay and fuse No. 11 in power distribution center. Recheck system operation.

This revision applies to the following publication:
ELECTRICAL SERVICE & REPAIR manual for DOMESTIC CARS, LIGHT TRUCKS & VANS.
- **1998** – Page FORD 4-445.

➤ *1998 STEERING COLUMN SWITCHES – EXPLORER & MOUNTAINEER: IGNITION SWITCH CONTINUITY TEST REVISION –* Please note the IGNITION SWITCH CONTINUITY table has been revised as follows:

IGNITION SWITCH CONTINUITY TEST

Continuity Between Terminals	Switch Position
B4 & STA	Start
B4 & A4	Run
B2 & A2	Run
B5 & I1	Run
B1 & A1	Run
P1 & GND	Start

This revision applies to the following publication:
ELECTRICAL SERVICE & REPAIR manual for DOMESTIC LIGHT TRUCKS & VANS.
- **1998** – Page FORD 4-1327.

➤ *1998 STEERING COLUMN SWITCHES – WINDSTAR: IGNITION SWITCH CONTINUITY TEST REVISION –* Please note that the IGNITION SWITCH CONTINUITY table has been revised as follows:

IGNITION SWITCH CONTINUITY TEST

Ignition Switch Position	Continuity Between Terminals
ACC	A1 & B5
LOCK	No Continuity
OFF	No Continuity
RUN	A1 & B1; A2 & B2; A3 & B3; A4 & B4; I1 & B5
START	I1 & B5; I2 & B1; STA & B4; P1 & GND; P2 & GND

This revision applies to the following publication:
ELECTRICAL SERVICE & REPAIR manual for DOMESTIC CARS, LIGHT TRUCKS & VANS.
- **1998** – Page FORD 4-1379.

➤ *1999 WIPER/WASHER SYSTEMS – TOWN CAR REVISION –* Please note that Figs. 3 and 4 are now available.

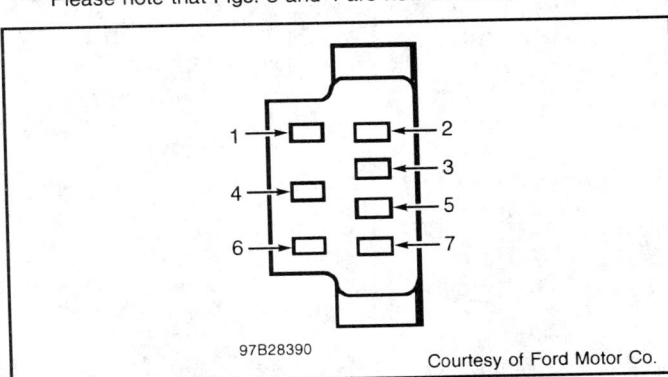

97B28390   Courtesy of Ford Motor Co.

Fig. 3: Identifying Multifunction Switch Harness Connector C269 Terminals

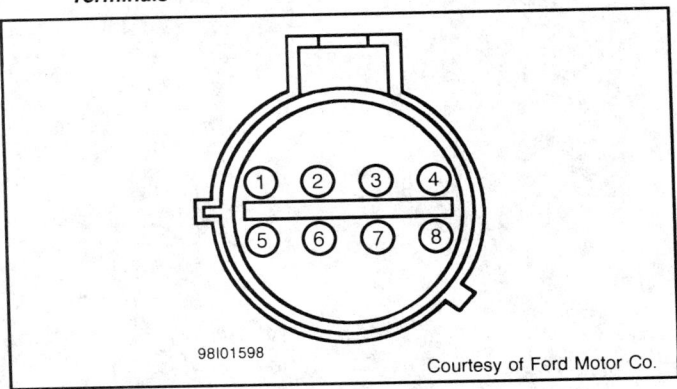

98I01598   Courtesy of Ford Motor Co.

Fig. 4: Identifying Wiper Motor Harness Connector C152 Terminals

This revision applies to the following publication:
ELECTRICAL SERVICE & REPAIR manual for DOMESTIC CARS, LIGHT TRUCKS & VANS.
- **1999** – Page FORD 4-1408.

NOTES

NOTES

NOTES

NOTES

NOTES

NOTES

NOTES

NOTES

NOTES

NOTES

NOTES

NOTES